KJV • NKJV PARALLEL REFERENCE™ BIBLE

King James Version
New King James Version

A Dual-Translation Center-Column Reference Bible

THOMAS NELSON PUBLISHERS
Nashville

Printed in the United States of America

1 2 3 4 5 6 7 8 9 10—94 93 92 91

Contents

The Old Testament

The New Testament

Special Abbreviations

Arab.	Arabic
Aram.	Aramaic
Bg.	the 1524–25 edition of the Hebrew Old Testament published by Daniel Bomberg (see Preface, "The Old Testament Text")
cf.	compare
ch., chs.	chapter, chapters
DSS	Dead Sea Scrolls
fem.	feminine
f., ff.	following verse, following verses
Gr.	Greek
Heb.	Hebrew
i.e.	that is
Kt.	Kethib (literally, in Aramaic, "written")—the written words of the Hebrew Old Testament preserved by the Masoretes (see "Qr.")
Lat.	Latin
lit.	literally
LXX	Septuagint—an ancient translation of the Old Testament into Greek
M	Majority Text (see Preface, "The New Testament Text")
ms., mss.	manuscript, manuscripts
masc.	masculine
MT	Masoretic Text—the traditional Hebrew Old Testament (see Preface, "The Old Testament Text")
NU	the most prominent modern Critical Text of the Greek New Testament, published in the twenty-sixth edition of the Nestle-Aland Greek New Testament and in the third edition of the United Bible Societies' Greek New Testament (see Preface, "The New Testament Text")
pl.	plural
Qr.	Qere (literally, in Aramaic, "read")—certain words read aloud, differing from the written words, in the Masoretic tradition of the Hebrew Old Testament (see "Kt.")
Sam.	Samaritan Pentateuch—a variant Hebrew edition of the books of Moses, used by the Samaritan community
sing.	singular
Syr.	Syriac
Tg.	Targum—an Aramaic paraphrase of the Old Testament
TR	Textus Receptus or Received Text (see Preface, "The New Testament Text")
v., vv.	verse, verses
vss.	versions—ancient translations of the Bible
Vg.	Vulgate—an ancient translation of the Bible into Latin, translated and edited by Jerome

Introduction

England in the early 1600s was the setting for the most influential English Bible translation of all time. Queen Elizabeth I, the so-called "Virgin Queen," was ending her long and dazzling reign (1558–1603), and England had become an established Protestant realm in which Bible reading was not only no longer dangerous but even encouraged by monarch and clergy.

Upon her death, Elizabeth's cousin, King James VI of Scotland, became King James I of England. James was unimpressive physically and personally, but he was a scholar. One of the first and also most significant events of James I's reign was the conference at Hampton Court held in January of 1604. The Puritans had petitioned the new king for improved conditions in the church. Dr. John Reynolds, president of Corpus Christi College, Oxford, and spokesman for the moderate Puritans, recommended that the king authorize a revision of the Bishops' Bible. The king was receptive to the idea, and a letter was soon written to initiate the work. The result would be the first edition of the Authorized Version, or as North Americans refer to it, the "King James" Version.

Even with the accumulated changes in the English language through the nearly four centuries since that time, people are still being transformed by the spiritual message of the Scriptures in the King James Version. However, its now archaic and sometimes obsolete vocabulary and phraseology led Thomas Nelson Publishers in 1975 to consult with informed representatives of the Bible-reading public on the need for a revision of the King James Version. Christian leaders, both men and women, both clergy and laity, were invited to meetings in Chicago, Illinois; Nashville, Tennessee; and London, England. Over one hundred church leaders representing a broad spectrum of biblically oriented Christianity attended the three conferences. The consensus of these leaders was that a careful revision of the King James Bible should be made, one that would retain as much as possible of the text and language of that historic version. The result would be the New King James Version—a translation of the biblical texts that represents the fifth *major* revision of the Authorized Version.

The KJV • NKJV Parallel Reference Bible

The beauty, accuracy, and majesty of a classic translation—the King James Version—can now be studied alongside the beauty, accuracy, and completeness of a modern translation—the New King James Version. Bible students can benefit by comparing the work of the 54 prominent Greek and Hebrew scholars of the Church of England who labored at Oxford, Cambridge, and Westminster to translate the King James Version, with the insights of the over 130 scholars, editors, church leaders, and Christian laity who were commissioned to work on the New King James Version.

In bringing these two great versions together in one volume, each has been allowed to retain its own character, while also relating the two to each other for easy, comparative study. The versions share certain common features:

1. Parallel Columns—The Bible texts of the KJV and NKJV appear side by side. For every verse of Scripture the KJV and NKJV are conveniently located on the same page.
2. Subject Headings—Identical subject headings have been used in both versions. The headings not only summarize the essential content and significance of the major sections of Scripture, but also make it easier to locate the beginnings of those sections in both the KJV and NKJV. Cross references to nearly identical or similar passages elsewhere in Scripture are given below many of the headings.
3. Center-Column References—The more than 60,000 center-column cross references work interchangeably with both versions. Identical superior letters in the two Bible texts make it possible to locate the corresponding words or phrases of both the KJV and NKJV for any particular cross reference.

In addition to the parallel columns, subject headings, and center-column references which the two versions hold in common, there are other features which are unique to either the KJV or NKJV.

The New King James Version brings to the Parallel Reference Bible the format of a modern translation, structuring poetry in contemporary verse. The work of scholars over the past 150 years in studying important textual variants in the Old and New Testaments is reflected in the textual notes to the NKJV. An asterisk (*) in the NKJV Bible text tells you to look to the bottom of the center reference column for this textual information.

The King James Version preserves for the Parallel Reference Bible the majestic language of the great literary craftsmen of the Elizabethan era. The use of singular and plural in second person pronouns, as in the original Hebrew and Greek, is a distinguishing mark of the KJV which uses "thou/thee" for singular and "ye/you" for plural.

A Close Relationship Between Two Great Translations

It is entirely fitting that the King James Version and New King James Version should appear together in a Parallel Bible. The New King James as a modern translation continues the great tradition of the King James. Included in the Statement of Purpose of the New King James translators were these goals:

To preserve the original intended purity of the King James Version in its communication of God's Word to man;

To clarify the King James Version by the use of current words, grammar, and sentence structure so that the New King James would speak to the individual reader in the twentieth century in as clear, simple, and accurate a manner as the original translators of the King James Version in 1611 endeavored to speak to their readers;

To neither add to, take away from, nor alter the communication that was the intent of the King James translators but to transfer the Elizabethan word forms into twentieth-century English.

Specific guidelines were followed to accomplish these goals:

1. Retain all doctrinal and theological words unless the Greek or Hebrew clearly indicates otherwise.
2. Retain words for items no longer in current use (e.g., *chariot* or *phylacteries*).
3. Replace words that have changed meaning since 1611 with their modern equivalents.
4. Replace archaic idioms with their modern equivalents.
5. Replace words and expressions that have become vulgar or indelicate in current English usage with their proper equivalents.
6. Alter punctuation to conform with that currently used.
7. Change all Elizabethan pronouns, verb forms, and words having archaic endings to their current equivalents.
8. Attempt to keep King James word order. However, when comprehension or readability is affected, transpose or revise sentence structure.
9. Eliminate the inordinate usage of the auxiliary verb "shall." Follow current grammatical style for these changes.
10. Attempt to keep sentences reasonably short without affecting text or meaning.
11. Attempt to use words that avoid misunderstanding.
12. When making corrections, use other words already represented by the same Greek or Hebrew word in the King James if possible.
13. Capitalize all personal pronouns referring to deity.
14. Make New Testament proper names agree with Old Testament spellings (e.g., *Isaiah*, not *Esaias; Elijah*, not *Elias*).
15. Replace all obsolete and archaic words as defined by one or more recognized dictionaries with their current equivalents. This applies to phrases and idioms as well.

The close relationship between the New King James and King James means that comparative study using these two translations will be most fruitful. For that reason *The KJV • NKJV Parallel Reference*™ Bible is offered as a dual-translation reference Bible, joining the classic King James Version and the modern New King James Version into a single-volume resource for effective Bible study.

Arthur L. Farstad
Executive Editor, New King James Version

Those with further interest in the history of the King James Version and/or New King James Version should consult the following:

The Holy Bible, 1611 Edition, King James Version

"The Translators to the Reader," p. ix
(The Preface of the translators of the 1611 King James Version, updated to modern English.)

The New King James Version in the Great Tradition by Arthur L. Farstad

The
Holy Bible

CONTAINING THE OLD AND NEW TESTAMENTS

Authorized King James Version

TRANSLATED OUT OF THE ORIGINAL TONGUES AND WITH THE FORMER TRANSLATIONS DILIGENTLY COMPARED AND REVISED BY HIS MAJESTY'S SPECIAL COMMAND

Appointed to be read in Churches

The Translators
to the Reader

The Best Things Have Been Calumniated

Zeal to promote the common good, whether it be by devising anything ourselves, or revising that which has been done by others, certainly deserves much respect and esteem, but yet it finds but cold entertainment in the world. It is welcomed with suspicion instead of love, and with jealousy instead of thanks: and if there is any room left for criticism to enter (and criticism, if it does not find room, will make it), it is sure to be misconstrued, and is in danger of being condemned. This will easily be granted by as many as know history or have any experience. For was there ever anything proposed that favored newness or renewing it anyway, but the same endured many storms of gainsaying or opposition? A man would think that courtesy, wholesome laws, learning and eloquence, synods, and Church support (that we speak of no more things of this kind) should be as safe as a sanctuary, and out of shot, as they say, that no man would lift up the heel, no, nor move his tongue against anyone proposing them. For by the first, we are distinguished from brute beasts led with sensuality. By the second, we are bridled and restrained from outrageous behavior, and from doing injuries whether by fraud or by violence. By the third, we are enabled to inform and reform others, by the light and feeling that we have attained unto ourselves. Briefly, by the fourth, being brought together to a parley face to face, we more quickly resolve our differences than by writings, which are endless. And lastly, that the Church be sufficiently provided for is so agreeable to good reason and conscience, that those mothers are held to be less cruel that kill their children as soon as they are born, than those nursing fathers and mothers (wherever they be) that withdraw from those who hang upon their breasts (and upon whose breasts again they themselves hang to receive the spiritual and sincere milk of the Word) livelihood and support fit for their estates. Thus it is apparent that these things of which we speak are of most necessary use, and therefore, that none, either without absurdity can speak against them, or without note of wickedness can kick against them.

Yet for all that, the learned know that certain worthy men have been brought to an untimely death for no other fault than for seeking to reduce their countrymen to good order and discipline: and that in some commonwealths it was made a capital crime, once to propose making a new law for the abrogation of an old one, though the same was most pernicious. And that certain ones, who would be counted pillars of the state and patterns of virtue and prudence, could not be brought for a long time to give way to good letters and refined speech, but bore themselves as being averse to them, as from rocks or boxes of poison. And fourthly, that he was no babe, but a great scholar, who stated (and in writing to remain for posterity), in passion perhaps, but yet he stated that he had seen no profit come by any synod or meeting of the clergy, but rather the contrary. And lastly, against Church support and allowance, in such sort, as the ambassadors and messengers of the great King of Kings should be furnished, it is not unknown what fiction or fable (so it is esteemed, and for no better by the reporter himself, though superstitious) was devised, namely, that at such time as the professors and teachers of Christianity in the Church of Rome, then a true Church, were liberally endowed, a voice indeed was heard from heaven, saying, "Now is poison poured down into the Church." Thus not only as often as we speak, as one said, but also as often as we do anything of note or consequence, we subject ourselves to everyone's censure. And happy is he who is left tossed upon tongues; for utterly to escape their grasp is impossible. If any man imagine that this is the lot and portion of the meaner sort only, and that princes are privileged by their high estate, he is deceived. As "the sword devours as well one as the other," as it is in 2 Samuel 11:25, may as the great commander charged his soldiers in a certain battle to strike at no part of the enemy but the face, and as the king of Syria commanded his chief captains "to fight neither with small nor great, save only against the king of Israel," so it is also true, that envy strikes most spitefully at the fairest, and at the chiefest. David was a worthy prince, and no man is to be compared to him for his first deeds, and yet for as worthy an act as ever he did (even for bringing back the ark of God in solemnity) he was scorned and scoffed at by his own wife. Solomon was greater than David, though not in virtue, yet in power. And by his power and wisdom he built a Temple to the LORD, such as was the glory of the land of Israel and the wonder of the whole world. But was that magnificence of his liked by all? We doubt it. Otherwise, why do they lay it in his son's dish and call on him to ease the burden. "Make," say they, "the grievous servitude of your father, and his sore yoke, lighter." Probably he had charged them with some levies, and troubled them with some burdens. On this they raised up a tragedy, and wished in their hearts that the Temple had never been built. So hard it is to please all, even when we please God best, and seek to approve ourselves to everyone's conscience.

The Highest Personages Have Been Calumniated

If we will descend to later times, we shall find many like examples of this kind, or rather unkind acceptance. The first Roman Emperor never did a more pleasing deed to the learned, nor more profitable to posterity, for conserving the record of times in true reckoning, than when he corrected the calendar, and ordered the year according to the course of the sun; and yet this was imputed to him for novelty, and arrogance, and procured him great abuse. So the first christened Emperor (at least wise who openly professed the faith himself, and allowed others to do the same) for strengthening the Empire at his great expense, and providing for the Church, as he did, got for his labor the name *Pupillus*, as one would say, a wasteful prince, who had need of a guardian or overseer. So the best christened Emperor, for the love that he bore for peace, thereby to enrich both himself and his subjects, and because he did not seek war but found it, was judged to be no man-at-arms (though in deed he excelled in feats of chivalry, and showed so much when he was provoked), and was condemned for giving himself to his ease and to his pleasure. To be short, the most learned emperor of former times (at least, the greatest politician), what thanks had he for cutting off the superfluities of the laws, and digesting them into some order and method? This: that he has been criticized by some to be an epitomist, that is, one that extinguished worthy whole volumes, to bring his abridgements into request. This is the measure that has been rendered to excellent princes in former times, even, *Cum bene facerent, male audire,* "For their good deeds to be evil spoken of." Neither is there any likelihood that envy and malignity died, and were buried with the ancients. No, no, the reproof of Moses takes hold of most ages; "You are risen up in your fathers stead, an increase of sinful men." "What is that that has been done? That which shall be done: and there is no new thing under the sun," says the wiseman; and St. Steven, "As your fathers did, so do you." This, and more to this purpose, His Majesty that now reigns (and long may he reign, and his offspring forever, "Himself and children and children's children always") knew full well, according to the singular wisdom given unto him by God, and the rare learning and experience to which he has attained, namely that whoever attempts anything for the public (specially if it pertains to religion, and to the opening and clarifying of the Word of God) the same sets himself upon a stage to be frowned at by every evil eye, yea, he casts himself headlong upon pikes, to be gored by every sharp tongue. For he that meddles with men's religion in any part, meddles with their custom, indeed, with their freehold; and though they find no contentment in that which they have, yet they cannot bear to hear of altering it. Notwithstanding his royal heart was not daunted or discouraged for this or that opinion, but he stood resolute, "as a statue immovable, and an anvil not easy to be beaten into pieces," as one said; he knew who had chosen him to be a soldier, or rather a captain, and being assured that the course which he intended made much of the glory of God and the building up of his Church, he would not suffer it to be broken off for whatever speeches or practices. It does certainly belong unto kings, yea, it does specially belong unto them, to have care of religion, yea, to know it aright, yea, to profess it zealously, yea, to promote it to the uttermost of their power. This is their glory before all nations which mean well, and this will bring unto them a far more excellent weight of glory in the day of the Lord Jesus. For the Scripture says not in vain, "Them that honor me, I will honor," neither was it a vain word that Eusebius delivered long ago, that piety towards God was the weapon, and the only weapon that both preserved Constantine's person, and avenged him of his enemies.

The Praise of the Holy Scriptures

But now what is piety without truth? What truth (what saving truth) without the Word of God? What is the Word of God (whereof we may be sure) without the Scripture? We are commanded to search the Scriptures (John 5:39; Isa. 8:20). They are commended who have searched and studied them (Acts 17:11 and 8:28, 29). They are reproved that were unskillful in them, or slow to believe them (Matt. 22:29; Luke 24:25). They can make us wise unto salvation (2 Tim. 3:15). If we are ignorant, they will instruct us; if out of the way, they will bring us home; if out of order, they will reform us, if in heaviness, comfort us; if dull, quicken us; if cold, inflame us. *Tolle, lege; Tolle, lege,* "Take up and read, take up and read" the Scriptures (for unto them was the direction), it was said unto St. Augustine by a supernatural voice. "Whatever is in the Scriptures, believe me," said the same St. Augustine, "is high and divine; there is verily truth, and a doctrine most fit for the refreshing and renewing of men's minds, and truly so tempered, that every one may draw from there that which is sufficient for him, if he comes to draw with a devout and pious mind, as true religion requires." Thus St. Augustine, and St. Jerome: *Ama Scripturas, Et amabitte Sapientia, etc.* "Love the Scriptures and wisdom will love you." And St. Cyril against Julian, "Even boys that are bred up in the Scriptures, become most religious, etc." But what mention we three or four uses of the Scripture, whereas whatever is to be believed or practiced, or hoped for, is contained in them? Or three or four sentences of the Fathers, since whoever is worthy of the name of a Father, from Christ's time downward, has likewise written not only of the riches, but also of the perfection of the Scripture? "I adore the fulness of the Scripture," said Tertullian against Hermogenes. And again to Apelles a heretic of the like stamp, he said, "I do not admit that which you bring in (or conclude) of your own (head or store, *de tuo*)" without Scripture. So Saint Justin Martyr before him, "We must know by all means," said he, "that it is not lawful (or possible) to learn (anything) of God or of right piety, except only from out of the Prophets, who teach us by divine inspiration." So Saint Basill after Tertullian, "It is a manifest falling away from the faith, and a fault of presumption, either to reject any of those things that are written, or to bring in (upon the head of them) any of those things" that are not written. We omit to cite to the same effect, St. Cyril B. of Jerusalem in his fourth *Cataches*, Saint Jerome against Helvidius, Saint Augustine in his third book against the letters of Petilian, and in very many other places of his works. Also we forbear to descend to later Fathers, because we will not weary the reader. The Scriptures then being acknowledged to be so full and so perfect, how can we excuse ourselves of negligence, if we do not study them, of curiosity, if we are not content with them? Men talk much of *Eiresiōnē**, how many sweet and goodly things it had hanging on it; of the Philosopher's stone, that it turns copper into gold; of *Cournu copia,* that it had all things for food in it, of *Panaces* the herb, that it was good for all diseases; of *Catholicon* the drug, that it is instead of all purges; of Vulcan's armor, that it was impenetrable against all thrusts, and all blows, etc. Well, that which they falsely or vainly attributed to these things for bodily good, we may justly and with full measure ascribe unto the Scripture, for spiritual good. It is not only armor but also a whole armory of weapons, both offensive and defensive, whereby we may save ourselves and put the enemy to flight. It is not an herb, but a tree, or rather a whole paradise of trees of life, which bring forth fruit every month, and its fruit is for food and the leaves for medicine. It is not a pot of Manna, or a cruse of oil, which we were for memory only, or for a meal or two, but as it were a shower of heavenly bread sufficient for a whole army, be it ever so great, and as it were a whole cellar full of oil vessels whereby all our necessities may be provided and our debts discharged. In a word, it is a storehouse of wholesome food against famishing traditions, a physician's shop (Saint Basill called it) of preservatives against poisoned heresies, a complete treatise of profitable laws against rebellious spirits, a treasury of most costly jewels against beggarly rudiments; finally, a fountain of most pure water springing up unto everlasting life. And what marvel? The original of it is from heaven not from earth, the author is God not man, the editor is the Holy Spirit not the wit of the Apostles or Prophets, the pen men were such as were sanctified from the womb and endowed with a principal portion of God's Spirit, the matter is verity, piety, purity, uprightness, the form is God's word, God's testimony, God's oracles, the word of truth, the word of salvation, etc., the effects are light of understanding, stableness of persuasion, repentance from dead words, newness of life, holiness, peace, joy in the Holy Ghost; lastly, the end and reward of the studies of it are fellowship with the saints, participation of the heavenly nature, fruition of an inheritance immortal, undefiled, and that never shall fade away. Happy is the man that delights in the Scripture, and thrice happy is he who meditates in it day and night.

Translation Necessary

But how shall men meditate in that which they cannot understand? How shall they understand that which is kept closed in an unknown tongue? As it is written, "Except I know the power of the voice I shall be to him that speaks a barbarian, and he that speaks shall be a barbarian to me." The Apostle excepted no tongue: not Hebrew the most ancient, not Greek the most copious, not Latin the finest. Nature taught a natural man to confess that all of us in those tongues which we do not understand are plainly deaf, we may turn the deaf ear unto them. The Scythian counted the Athenian, whom he did not understand, barbarous; so the Roman did the Syrian and the Jew (even St. Jerome himself called the Hebrew tongue barbarous, probably because it was strange to so many); so the Emperor of Constantinople called the Latin tongue barbarous, though Pope Nicolas objected to it; so the Jews long before Christ called all other nations *Lognazim,* which is little better than barbarous. Therefore, as one complained that always in the Senate of Rome there was one or another that called for an interpreter, so lest the Church be driven to like exigency, it is necessary to have translations in a readiness. Translation is what opens the window to let in the light, that breaks the shell that we may eat the kernel, that pulls aside the curtain that we may look into the most Holy place, that removes the cover of the well that we may obtain the water, even as Jacob rolled away the stone from the mouth of the well, by means of which the flocks of Laban were watered. Indeed without translation into the common language, the unlearned are but like children at Jacob's well (which was deep) without a bucket or something with which to draw, or as that person mentioned by Isaiah to whom, when a sealed book was delivered with this instruction, "Read this, I pray thee," he was forced to make this answer, "I cannot for it is sealed."

The Translation of the Old Testament Out of the Hebrew into Greek

While God would be known only in Jacob, and have his Name great only in Israel and in no other place, while the dew lay on Gideon's fleece only and all the earth besides was dry, then, for one and the same people which all spoke the language of Canaan, that is Hebrew, one and the same original in Hebrew was sufficient. But when the fulness of time drew near that the Sun of righteousness, the Son of God, should come into the world, whom God ordained to be a reconciliation through faith in his blood, not of the Jew only, but also of the Greek, yea, of all them that were scattered abroad, then behold, it pleased the Lord to stir up the spirit of a Greek prince (Greek for descent and language) even of Ptolemy Philadelphus, king of Egypt, to procure the translating of the Book of God out of Hebrew into Greek. This is the translation of the Seventy Interpreters*, commonly so called, which prepared the way for our Savior among the Gentiles by written preaching, as Saint John the Baptist did among the Jews vocally. For the Grecians, being desirous of learning, would not let books of worth lie molding in kings' libraries, but had many of their servants, ready scribes, to copy them out, and so they were dispersed and made common. Again, the Greek tongue was well known and made familiar to most inhabitants of Asia, by reason of the conquest that the Grecians had made there, as also by the colonies which they had sent there. For the same cause also it was well understood in many places of Europe, yea, and of Africa too. Therefore the Word of God, because it was set forth in Greek, became like a candle set upon a candlestick, which gives light to all who are in the house, or like a proclamation sounded forth in the market place, which most men presently take knowledge of; and

* An olive branch wrapped about with wool, upon which hung figs, bread, a pot of honey, and oil.

* Now called the Septuagint, abbreviated LXX.

therefore that language was most fit to contain the Scriptures, both for the first preachers of the Gospel to appeal to for witness, and for the learners also of those times to make search and trial. It is certain that the translation was not so sound and so perfect, but that it needed in many places correction; and who had been so sufficient for this work as the Apostles or apostolic men? Yet it seemed good to the Holy Ghost and to them, to take that which they found (the same being for the greatest part true and sufficient) rather than by making a new translation, in that new world and green age of the Church, to expose themselves to many exceptions and criticisms, as though they made a translation to serve their own interests, and therefore, bearing witness to themselves, their witness would not be regarded. This may be supposed to be the reason why the translation of the Seventy was allowed to be in common use. Notwithstanding, though it was commended generally, yet it did not fully satisfy the learned, no, not those of the Jews. For not long after Christ, Aquila undertook a new translation, and after him Theodotion, and after him Symmachus; indeed there was a fifth and a sixth edition, whose authors were not known. These, with the Seventy, made up the *Hexapla*, and were worthily and to great purpose compiled together by Origen. However the edition of the Seventy was most widely accepted, and therefore not only was placed in the midst by Origen (for its worth and excellence above the rest, as Epiphanius gathered) but also was used by the Greek fathers for the ground and foundation of their commentaries. Indeed, Epiphanius above named attributed so much unto it, that he held its authors not only to be interpreters, but also to be prophets in some respect. And Justinian the Emperor when enjoining his subjects the Jews to specially use the translation of the Seventy, gave this reason for it: because they were as it were enlightened with prophetical grace. Yet for all that, as the Egyptians are said by the prophet to be men and not God, and their horses flesh and not spirit, so it is evident (and Saint Jerome affirmed as much) that the Seventy were interpreters, they were not prophets; they did many things well, as learned men; but yet as men they stumbled and fell, sometimes through oversight, other times through ignorance, indeed, sometimes they may be observed to add to the original Hebrew, and sometimes to take from it. This made the Apostles leave them many times, when they left the Hebrew, and deliver its sense according to the truth of the word, as the spirit gave them utterance. This may be enough about the Greek translations of the Old Testament.

Translation Out of Hebrew and Greek into Latin

There were also within a few hundred years after Christ, many translations into the Latin tongue: for this tongue also was very fit to convey the Law and the Gospel, because in those times very many countries of the West, of the South, East and North, spoke or understood Latin, being made provinces of the Romans. But now the Latin translations were too many to be all good, for they were infinite (*Latini Interpretes nullo modo numerari possunt,* said St. Augustine). Again they were not out of the Hebrew fountain (we speak of the Latin translations of the Old Testament) but out of the Greek stream. Therefore, since the Greek was not altogether clear, the Latin which was derived from it must needs be muddy. This moved St. Jerome, a most learned Father and without controversy the best linguist of his age, or of any that went before him, to undertake the translating of the Old Testament out of the very fountains themselves, which he performed with such evidence of great learning, judgment, industry and faithfulness, that he has forever bound the Church to him in a debt of special remembrance and thankfulness.

The Translation of the Scriptures into the Common Languages

Now though the Church was thus furnished with Greek and Latin translations, even before the faith of Christ was generally embraced in the Empire (for the learned know that even in St. Jerome's time, the Consul of Rome and his wife were both pagans, and about the same time the greatest part of the Senate also), yet for all that, the godly learned were not content to have the Scriptures in the language which they themselves understood, Greek and Latin (as the good lepers were not content to fare well themselves, but acquainted their neighbors with the store that God had sent, that they also might provide for themselves) but also for the benefit and edifying of the unlearned who hungered and thirsted after righteousness, and had souls to be saved as well as they, they provided translations into the common languages for their countrymen; insomuch that most nations under heaven, shortly after their conversion, heard Christ speaking unto them in their mother tongue, not by the voice of their minister only, but also by the written Word translated. If anyone doubts this, he may be satisfied by some examples if a few will serve the need. First St. Jerome said, *Multarum gentiu linguis Scriptura ante translata docet falsa esse quae addita sunt, etc.* "The Scripture being translated before in the languages of many nations, does show that those things that were added (by Lucian or Hesychius) are false," so St. Jerome in that place. The same Jerome elsewhere affirmed that he, in his time, had set forth the translation of the Seventy, *suae linguae hominibus, i,* for his countrymen of Dalmatia. These words not only Erasmus understood to mean, that St. Jerome translated the Scripture into the Dalmatian tongue, but also Sixtus Senensis and Alphonsus d Castro (that we speak of no more), men not to be contradicted by them of Rome, have ingeniously confessed as much. So, St. Chrysostome who lived in St. Jerome's time, gave evidence with him: "The doctrine of St. John (says he) did not in such sort (as the philosophers did) vanish away, but the Syrians, Egyptians, Indians, Persians, Ethiopians, and infinite other nations being barbarous people, translated it into their mother tongue, and have learned to be true philosophers," he meant Christians. To this may be added Theodoret, as next unto him, both for antiquity and for learning. His words are these, "Every country that is under the sun, is full of these words (of the Apostles and Prophets) and the Hebrew tongue (he meant the Scriptures in the Hebrew tongue) is turned not only into the language of the Grecians, but also of the Romans, and Egyptians, and Persians, and Indians, and Armenians and Scythians, and Sauromatians, and briefly unto all the languages that any nation uses." In like manner, Ulphilas is reported by Paulus Diaconus and Isidor (and before them by Sozomen) to have translated the Scriptures into the Gothic tongue; John, Bishop of Sivil by Vasseus, to have turned them into Arabic, about the year of our Lord 717; Beda by Cistertiensis, to have turned a great part of them into Saxon; Esnard by Trithemius, to have abridged the French Psalter, as Beda had done the Hebrew, about the year 800; King Alfred by the said Cistertiensis, to have turned the Psalter into Saxon; Methodius by Aventinus (printed at Ingolstad) to have turned the Scriptures into Sclavonian; Valdo, Bishop of Frising by Beatus Rhenanus, to have caused about that time, the Gospels to be translated into Dutch-rhythm, yet extant in the Library of Corbinian; Valdius, by various ones to have turned them himself, or to have gotten them turned into French, about the year 1160; Charles the Fifth with that name, surnamed The Wise, to have caused them to be turned into French, about 200 years after Valdius time, of which translation there be many copies yet extant, as witnessed Beroaldus. Much about that time, even in the days of our King Richard the Second, John Trevisa translated them into English, and many English Bibles in written hand are yet to be seen with various ones translated as it is very probable, in that age. So the Syrian translation of the New Testament is in most learned men's libraries, as Widminstadius sets forth, and the Psalter in Arabic is with many, as Augustinus Nebiensis sets forth. So Postel affirmed, that in his travel he saw the Gospels in the Ethiopian tongue. And Ambrose Thesius alleged the Psalter of the Indians, which he testified to have been set forth by Potken in Syrian characters. So that, to have the Scriptures in the mother tongue is not a quaint idea lately taken up, either by the Lord Cromwell in England, or by the Lord Radevil in Polony, or by the Lord Ungnadius in the Emperor's dominion, but has been thought upon, and put in practice of old, even from the first times of the conversion of any nation, no doubt because it was esteemed most profitable to cause faith to grow in men's hearts the sooner and to make them able to say with the words of the Psalm, "As we have heard, so we have seen . . ."*

The Unwillingness of Our Chief Adversaries that the Scriptures Should Be Divulged in the Mother Tongue

Now the Church of Rome would seem at length to bear a motherly affection towards her children, and to allow them to have the Scriptures in their mother tongue. But indeed it is a gift, not deserving to be called a gift, an unprofitable gift. They must first get a license in writing before they may use them, and to get that, they must approve themselves to their confessor, that is, to be such as are, if not frozen in the dregs, yet soured with the leaven of their superstition. However, it seemed too much to Clement the Eighth that there should be any license granted to have them in the Common language, and therefore he overruled and frustrated the grant of Pius the Fourth. So much are they afraid of the light of the Scripture (*Lucisugae Scripturarum,* as Tertullian spoke) that they will not trust the people with it, no not as it is set forth by their own sworn men, no not with the license of their own bishops and inquisitors. Indeed, so unwilling are they to communicate the Scriptures to the people's understanding in any sort, that they are not ashamed to confess that we have forced them to translate it into English against their wills. This seems to argue a bad cause, or a bad conscience, or both. We are sure that it is not he who has good gold who is afraid to bring it to the touch stone, but he who has the counterfeit; neither is it the true man who shuns the light, but the malefactor, lest his deeds should be reproved; neither is it the honest merchant who is unwilling to have the weights or the meteryard brought in place, but he who uses deceit. But we will let them alone for this fault, and return to translation.

Many men's mouths have been open a good while (and still are not stopped) with speeches about the translation, so long in hand, or rather perusals or translations made before. And they ask what may be the reason, what the necessity of the present undertaking. Has the Church been deceived, say they, all this while? Has her sweet bread been mingled with leaven, her silver with dross, her wine with water, her milk with lime? (*Lacte gypsum male miscetur,* said St. Irenaeus). We hoped that we had been in the right way, that we had possessed the Oracles of God delivered unto us, and that though all the world had cause to be offended and to complain, yet that we had none. Has the nurse held out the breast with nothing but wind in it? Has the bread been delivered by the fathers of the Church, and the same proved to be *lapidosus,* as Seneca spoke? What is it to handle the word of God deceitfully, if this is not it? Thus say certain brethren. Also the adversaries of Judah and Jerusalem, like Sanballat in Nehemiah, mock as we hear, both at the work and workman saying: "What do these weak Jews, etc., will they make the stones whole again out of the heaps of dust which are burnt? Although they build, yet if a fox go up, he shall even break down their stony wall." Was their translation good before? Why do they now mend it? Was it not good? Why then was it presented to the people? Indeed, why did the Catholics (meaning Popish Romanists) always go in jeopardy, for refusing to go to hear it? Nay, if it must be translated into English, Catholics are the most fit to do it. They have learning, and they know when a thing is well, they can *manum de tabula.* We will briefly answer them both: and the former, being brethren, thus, with St. Jerome: *Damnamus veteres? Minime, sed post priorum studia in domo Domini quod possumus laboramus.* That is, "Do we condemn the ancients: Not at all; but after the endeavors of them that were before us, we take the best pains we can in the house of God." As if he said, being provoked by the example of the learned that lived before my time, I have thought it my duty to determine whether my talent in the knowledge of the languages may be

* Ps. 48:8

profitable in any measure to God's Church, lest I should seem to have labored in them in vain, and lest I should be thought to glory in men (although ancient) above that which was in them. Thus St. Jerome may be thought to speak.

And to the same effect we say, that we are so far off from condemning any of their labors that traveled before us in this manner, either in this land or beyond the sea, either in King Henry's time, or King Edward's (if there were any translation or correction of a translation in his time) or Queen Elizabeth's of ever-renowned memory, that we acknowledge them to have been raised up of God, for the building and furnishing of his Church, and that they deserve to be held by us and posterity in everlasting remembrance. The judgment of Aristotle is worthy and well known: "If Timotheus had not been, we would not have much sweet music; but if Phrynis (Timotheus' master) had not been, we would not have Timotheus. Therefore blessed be they, and most honored be their name, who break the ice, and give start to that which helps forward the saving of souls. Now what can be more available for that, than to deliver God's book to God's people in a tongue which they understand? Since a hidden treasure and a sealed fountain are of no profit, as Ptolemy Philadelphus wrote to the Rabbins or masters of the Jews, as Epiphanius witnessed. And as St. Augustine said, "A man had rather be with his dog than with a stranger (whose tongue is strange unto him)." Yet for all that, since nothing is begun and completed at the same time, and since the later thoughts are thought to be the wiser, so if we, building upon their foundation who went before us, and being held by their labors, endeavor to make better what they left so good, no man, we are sure, has cause to dislike us. We persuade ourselves that if they were alive, they would thank us. The vintage of Abiezer was what struck the stroke, yet the gleaning of the grapes of Ephraim was not to be despised. (See Judges 8, verse 2). Joash the king of Israel did not satisfy himself till he had smitten the ground three times, and yet he offended the Prophet for stopping then. Aquila, of whom we spoke before, translated the Bible as carefully and skillfully as he could, and yet he thought it good to go over it again, and then it got the credit with the Jews to be called . . . accurately done, as Saint Jerome witnessed. How many books of profane learning have been gone over again and again, by the same translators, or by others? Of one and the same book of Aristotle's *Ethics*, there are extant not so few as six or seven different translations. Now, if this cost may be bestowed upon the gourd, which affords us a little shade, and which today flourishes but tomorrow is cut down, what may we bestow, indeed what ought we not to bestow upon the vine whose fruit makes glad the conscience of man, and whose stem abides forever? And this is the Word of God, which we translate. "What is the chaff to the wheat, saith the Lord?" *Tanti vitreum, quanti verum margaritum,* said Tertullian: "if a toy of glass be of that esteem to us, how ought we to value the true pearl?" Therefore let no man's eye be evil because his Majesty's is good; neither let any be grieved that we have a prince who seeks the increase of the spiritual wealth of Israel (let Sanballats and Tobiahs do so who therefore do bear their just reproof), but let us rather bless God from the bottom of our heart, for working this religious care in him, to have the translations of the Bible maturely considered and examined. For by this means it comes to pass, that whatever is sound already (and all is sound of substance, in one or the other of our editions, and the worst of ours is far better than their authentic common language translation), the same will shine as gold more brightly, being rubbed and polished; also, if anything be halting, or superfluous, or not so agreeable to the original, the same will be corrected, and the truth set in place. And what can the King command to be done that will bring him more true honor than this? And in what could they who have been put to work approve their duty to the King, indeed their obedience to God and love to his saints more, than by yielding their service and all that is within them, for the performing of the work? But besides all this, they were the principal motives for it, and therefore ought least to argue against it; for the very historical truth is, that upon the urgent petitions of the Puritans when his Majesty came to this Crown, the Conference at Hampton Court was appointed to hear their complaints. And when by force of reason they were put down on all other grounds, they had recourse at last to this point: that they could not with good conscience subscribe to the communion book, since it maintained the Bible as it was there translated, which was, as they said, a most corrupted translation. And although this was judged to be but a very poor and empty point, yet even because of it his Majesty began to think about the good that might ensue by a new translation, and soon afterward he gave order for this translation which is now presented unto you. Thus much to satisfy our scrupulous brethren.

An Answer to the Imputation of Our Adversaries

Now to the latter we answer that we do not deny, indeed we affirm and avow, that the very meanest translation of the Bible in English, set forth by men of our profession (for we have seen none of theirs of the whole Bible as yet) contains the Word of God, indeed is the Word of God. As the King's speech which he uttered in Parliament, being translated into French, Dutch, Italian and Latin, is still the King's speech, though it is not interpreted by every translator with like grace, nor perhaps so fitly for phrase, nor so expressly for sense, everywhere. For it is confessed, that things are to take their denomination of the greater part; and a natural man could say, *Verum ubi multa nitent in carmine, non ego paucis offendor maculis, etc.* "A man may be counted a virtuous man, though he has made many slips in his life" (else there were none virtuous, for "in many things we offend all"), also a handsome man may be counted good looking, though he has some warts upon his hand, yea, not only freckles upon his face, but also scars. There is no reason therefore why the translated Word should be denied to be the Word, or forbidden to be in common use, notwithstanding that some imperfections and blemishes may be noted in setting it forth. For whatever was perfect under the sun, where

Apostles or apostolic men, that is, men indued with an extraordinary measure of God's spirit, and privileged with the privilege of infallibility, had not their hand? The Romanists therefore in refusing to hear, and daring to burn the translated Word, did no less than despite the Spirit of grace, from whom originally it proceeded, and whose sense and meaning, as well as man's weakness would enable, it did express. Judge by an example or two. Plutarch writes, that after Rome had been burnt by the Galls, they fell soon to build it again, but doing it in haste, they did not cast the streets, nor proportion the houses in such comely fashion, as had been most sightly and convenient. Was Catiline therefore an honest man, or a good patriot, who sought to bring it to combustion? Or Nero a good prince, who did indeed set it on fire? So, by the story of Ezra and the prophecy of Haggai, it may be gathered that the Temple built by Zerubbabel after the return from Babylon was by no means to be compared to the former built by Solomon (for they who remembered the former wept when they considered the latter). Notwithstanding, might this latter either have been abhorred and forsaken by the Jews, or profaned by the Greeks? We are to think the same of translations. The translation of the Seventy differs from the original in many places, neither does it come near it, for perspicuity, gravity, majesty; yet which of the Apostles condemned it? Condemn it? Nay, they used it (as it is apparent, and as Saint Jerome and most learned men confess), which they would not have done, nor by their example of using it, so grace and commend it to the Church, if it had been unworthy of the appellation and name of the Word of God. And whereas they urge for their second defense of their vilifying and abusing of the English Bibles, or some pieces of them which they meet up with, that heretics (indeed) were the authors of the translations (heretics they call us by the same right that they call themselves catholics, both being wrong); we wonder what divinity taught them so. We are sure Tertullian was of another mind: *Ex perfonis probamus fidem, an ex fide personas?* "Do we try men's faith by their persons? We should try their persons by their faith." Also St. Augustine was of another mind; for when he came upon certain rules made by Tychonius a Donatist, for the better understanding of the word, he was not ashamed to make use of them, indeed to insert them into his own book, with commendation for them so far as they were worthy to be commended, as may be seen in St. Augustine's third book *De doctrina Christiana.* To be short, Origen and the whole Church of God for several hundred years were of another mind, for they were so far from treading under foot (much more from burning) the translation of Aquila a proselyte (that is, one that had turned Jew), of Symmachus, and Theodotion, both Ebionites (that is, most vile heretics), that they joined them together with the Hebrew original, and the translation of the Seventy (as has been before signified out of Epiphanius) and set forth openly to be considered of and read by all. But we weary the unlearned, who need not know so much, and trouble the learned, who know it already.

Yet before we end, we must answer a third criticism and objection of theirs against us, for altering and amending our translations so often, wherein truly they deal hardly, and strangely with us. For to whomever was it imputed for a fault (by such as were wise) to go over that which he had done, and to amend it where he saw cause? Saint Augustine was not afraid to exhort St. Jerome to make a retraction or recantation; the same St. Augustine was not ashamed to retract, we might say revoke, many things that had passed him, and he even gloried that he saw his infirmities. If we will be sons of the truth, we must consider what it speaks, and trample upon our own credit, indeed and upon other men's too, if either be in anyway a hinderance to it.

This concludes our answer to the cause; now to the persons we say, that of all men they ought to be most silent in this case. For what varieties and what alterations have they made, not only of their service books, portesses and breviaries,* but also of their Latin translation? The service book supposed to have been made by St. Ambrose (*Officium Abrosianum*) was a great while in special use and request, but Pope Hadrian, calling a council with the aid of Charles the Emperor, abolished it, indeed, burned it, and commanded the service book of Saint Gregory universally to be used. Well, *Officium Gregorianun* got by this means to be in credit, but did it continue without change or altering? No, the very Roman service was of two fashions, the New fashion and the Old (the one used in one Church, the other in another), as is seen in Pamelius, a Romanist, in his preface before *Micrologus.* The same Pamelius reported out of *Radulphus de Riuo,* that about the year of our Lord 1277, Pope Nicolas the Third removed out of the Churches of Rome, the more ancient service books and brought into use the Missals of the Frier's Minorities, and commanded them to be observed there; insomuch that about a hundred years afterward, when the above named Radulphus happened to be at Rome, he found all the books to be new (of the new stamp). Neither was this chopping and changing in the more ancient times only, but also of late. Pius Quintus himself confessed that almost every bishopric had a peculiar kind of service, most unlike that which others had. This moved him to abolish all other service books, no matter how ancient and privileged and published by bishops in their dioceses, and to establish and ratify only that which was of his own setting forth in the year 1568. Now, when the father of their Church, who gladly would heal the sore of the daughter of his people softly and slightly, and make the best of it, found so great fault with them for their conflicts and disagreements, we hope the children have no great cause to boast of their uniformity. But the difference that appears between our translations, and our often correcting of them, is the thing that we are specially charged with. Let us see therefore whether they themselves be without fault in this way (if it may be counted a fault to be correct) and whether they befit men to throw stones at us: *O tandem major parcas insane minori:* "they that are less sound themselves, ought not to object to infirmities in

* Medieval prayer books

others." If we should tell them that Valla, Stapulensis, Erasmus, and Vines found fault with their Vulgate translation, and consequently wished the same to be mended, or a new one to be made, perhaps they would answer that we have produced their enemies for witness against them; however, they were in no other manner enemies than was St. Paul to the Galatians for telling them the truth. And it may be wished that they had dared to tell it to them more plainly and more often. But what will they say to this, that Pope Leo the Tenth allowed Erasmus' translation of the New Testament, so much different from the Vulgate, by his Apostolic Letter and Bull, that the same Leo exhorted Pagnin to translate the whole Bible, and bare whatever charges were necessary for the work? Surely, as the Apostle reasoned to the Hebrews, that "if the former Law and Testament had been sufficient, there had been no need of the latter." So we may say, that if the old Vulgate had been in all points allowable, there was small reason for labor and charges to be undergone for framing a new one. If they say, "it was one Pope's private opinion, and he consulted only himself," then we are able to go further with them and say that more of their chief men of all sorts, even their own Trent champions Paiua and Vega, and their own inquisitors, Hieronymus ab Oleastro, and their own Bishop Sidorus Clarius, and their own Cardinal Thomas d Vio Caietan, have either made new translations themselves, or follow new ones of other men's making, or made note of the Vulgate interpreter's defects. None of them fear to dissent from him, nor yet to take exception with him. And do they call this a uniform tenor of text and judgment about the text, with so many of their worthies disclaiming the now received opinion? Indeed, yet we will come nearer the quick: does not their Paris edition differ from the Lovaine, and Hentenius' edition from them both? And yet are not all of them allowed by authority? Indeed, does not Sixtus Quintus confess that certain Catholics (meaning certain of his own side) were in such a humor of translating the Scriptures into Latin, that Satan taking occasion by them, though they thought of no such matter, did the best he could, out of so uncertain and manifold a variety of translations, so to mingle all things that nothing might seem to be left certain and firm in them? Indeed further, did not the same Sixtus ordain by an inviolable decree, and that with the counsel and consent of his cardinals, that the Latin edition of the Old and New Testament, which the Council of Trent would have to be authentic, was the same without controversy which he then set forth, being diligently corrected and printed in the printing house of the Vatican? Thus Sixtus wrote in the preface to his Bible. And yet Clement the Eighth, his immediate successor, published another edition of the Bible, containing in it infinite differences from that of Sixtus (and many of them weighty and material), and yet this must be authentic by all means. What is it to have the faith of our glorious Lord Jesus Christ with both yea and nay, if this is not it? Again, what is sweet harmony and consent, if this is it? Therefore, as Demaratus of Corinth advised a great King, that before he talked of the dissensions among the Grecians, he ought to calm his own domestic problems (for at that time his Queen and his son and heir were at deadly feud with him), so all the time that our adversaries make so many and so various editions themselves, and err so much about the worth and authority of them, they can with no show of equity challenge us for changing and correcting.

The Purpose of the Translators, with Their Number, Furniture, Care

But it is high time to leave them, and to show in brief what we proposed to ourselves, and what course we held in this our perusal and survey of the Bible. Truly, good Christian reader, we never thought from the beginning, that we should need to make a new translation, nor yet to make of a bad one a good one (for then the imputation of Sixtus had been true in some sort, that our people had been fed with the gall of dragons instead of wine, with whey instead of milk), but to make a good one better, or out of many good ones, one principal good one, against which none could justly take exception; that has been our endeavor, that our mark. To that purpose there were many chosen who were greater in other men's eyes than in their own, and who sought the truth rather than their own praise. Again, they came or were thought to come to the work, not *exercendi causa*, as one said, but *exercitati*, that is, learned, not to learn. For the chief overseer . . . under his Majesty, to whom not only we, but also our whole Church was much bound, knew by his wisdom, that which also Nazianzen taught so long ago, that it is a preposterous order to teach first and to learn afterward; indeed . . . to learn and practice together is neither commendable for the workman, nor safe for the work. Therefore such were considered who could say modestly with Saint Jerome, *Et Hebraeum Sermonem ex parte didicimus in Latino penè ab ipsis incunabulis*, etc., *detriti sumus:* "Both we have learned the Hebrew tongue in part, and in the Latin we have been exercised almost from our very cradle." St. Jerome made no mention of the Greek tongue, in which he also excelled, because he did not translate the Old Testament out of Greek, but out of Hebrew. And in what manner did these men assemble? In the trust of their own knowledge, or of their sharpness of wit, or deepness of judgment, as it were in an arm of flesh? Not at all. They trusted in him who has the key of David, opening and no man shutting; they prayed to the Lord, the Father of our Lord, to the effect that St. Augustine did: "O let thy Scriptures be my pure delight, let me not be deceived in them, neither let me deceive by them." In this confidence, and with this devotion they assembled together; not too many, lest one should trouble another; and yet many, lest perhaps many things might escape them. If you ask what they had before them, truly it was the Hebrew text of the Old Testament and the Greek of the New. These are the two golden pipes, or rather conduits, through which the olive branches empty themselves into the golden bowl. Saint Augustine called them precedent, or original tongues; Saint Jerome, fountains. The same Saint Jerome affirmed, and Gratian has not spared to put it into his decree, that "as the credit of the old Books (he means of the Old Testament) is to be tried by the Hebrew volumes, so of the New by the Greek tongue," he means by the original Greek. If truth is to be tried by these tongues, then whence should a translation be made but out of them? These tongues therefore, we should say the Scriptures in those tongues, we set before us to translate, being the tongues in which God was pleased to speak to his Church by his Prophets and Apostles. Neither did we run over the work with that posthaste that the Septuagint did, if that is true which is reported of them, that they finished it in 72 days; neither were we barred or hindered from going over it again, having once done it, like St. Jerome, if that is true which he himself reported, that he could no sooner write anything, but it was presently taken from him and published, and he could not have permission to mend it. Neither, to be short, were we the first who took in hand to translate the Scripture into English, and consequently destitute of former helps, as it is written of Origen, that he was the first in a manner, who put his hand to write commentaries upon the Scriptures, and therefore no marvel, if he overshot himself many times. There were of these things. The work has not been thrown together in 72 days, but has cost the workmen, as light as it seems, the pains of twice seven times seventy-two days and more. Matters of such weight and consequence are to be speeded with maturity; for in important business a man does not fear the blame of convenient slackness. Neither did we think lightly of consulting the translators or commentators, Chaldee, Hebrew, Syrian, Greek, or Latin, no nor the Spanish, French, Italian, or Dutch; neither did we disdain to revise that which we had done, and to bring back to the anvil that which we had hammered. But having and using helps as great as were needful, and fearing no reproach for slowness, nor coveting praise for expedition, we have at the length, through the good hand of the Lord upon us, brought the work to pass that you now see.

Reasons Moving Us to Set Diverse Senses in the Margin

Some perhaps would have no variety of senses to be set in the margin, lest the authority of the Scriptures for deciding controversies, by that show of uncertainty, should somewhat be shaken. But we do not hold their judgment to be so sound in this point. For though, "whatever things are necessary are manifest," as St. Chrysostome said, and as St. Augustine said, "In those things that are plainly set down in the Scriptures all such matters are found that concern faith, hope, and charity." Yet for all that it cannot be ignored, that partly to exercise and whet our wits, partly to wean the curious from loathing of them for their uniform plainness, partly also to stir up our devotion to crave the assistance of God's spirit by prayer, and lastly, that we might be forward to seek aid of our brethren by conference, and never scorn those that are not in all respects so complete as they should be, being for us to seek out many things ourselves, it has pleased God in his divine providence, here and there to scatter words and sentences of that difficulty and doubtfulness, not in doctrinal points that concern salvation (for in such it has been vouched that the Scriptures are plain), but in matters of less importance, that fearfulness would better become us than confidence, and if we will resolve, to resolve upon modesty with St. Augustine (though not in this same case altogether, yet upon the same ground) *Melius est dubitare de occultis, quam litigare de incertis,* "it is better to make doubt of those things which are secret, than to strive about those things that are uncertain." There are many words in the Scriptures which are never found there but once (having neither brother nor neighbor, as the Hebrews speak) so that we cannot be held by comparing parallel passages. Again, there are many rare names of certain birds, beasts and precious stones, etc., concerning which the Hebrews themselves are so divided among themselves for judgment, that they may seem to have defined this or that, rather because they would say something, than because they were sure of that which they said, as St. Jerome somewhere said of the Septuagint. Now in such a case, does not a margin do well to admonish the reader to seek further, and not to conclude or dogmatize upon this or that without investigation? For as it is a fault of incredulity to doubt those things that are evident, so to determine such things as the Spirit of God hath left questionable (even in the judgment of the judicious), can be no less than presumption. Therefore as St. Augustine said that "variety of translations is profitable for the finding out of the sense of the Scriptures," so diversity of signification and sense in the margin, where the text is not so clear, must needs do good, indeed, it is necessary, as we are persuaded. We know that Sixtus Quintus expressly forbid that any variety of readings of their Vulgate edition should be put in the margin (which though it is not altogether the same thing to what we have in hand, yet it looks that way), but we think he does not have all of his own side in his favor for this idea. They that are wise had rather have their judgments at liberty in differences of readings, than to be captivated to one, when it may be the other. If they were sure that their high Priest had all laws shut up in his breast, as Paul the Second bragged, and that he were as free from error by special privilege as the dictators of Rome were made by law inviolable, it would be another matter; then his word would be an oracle, his opinion a decision. But the eyes of the world are now open, God be thanked, and have been a great while; they find that he is subject to the same affections and infirmities that others are, that his skin is penetrable, and therefore as much as he proves, not as much as he claims, they grant and embrace.

Reasons Inducing Us Not To Stand Curiously upon an Identify of Phrasing

Another thing we thought good to advise you of, gentle reader, that we have not tied ourselves to uniformity of phrasing, or to an identity of words, as some perhaps would wish that we had done, because they observe that some learned men somewhere have been as exact as they could that way. Truly, that we might not vary from the sense of that which we had translated before, if the word signified the same thing in both places (for there are some words that are not of the same sense everywhere) we were especially careful, and were conscientious, according to our duty.

But, that we should express that same notion in the same particular words, as for example, if we translate the Hebrew or Greek word once by *purpose,* never to call it *intent;* if in one place *journeying,* never *traveling;* if in one place *think,* never *suppose;* if in one place *pain,* never *ache;* if in one place *joy,* never *gladness,* etc. Thus to mince the matter, we thought to favor more curiosity than wisdom, and that rather it would breed scorn in the atheist, than bring profit to the godly reader. For is the kingdom of God become words or syllables? Why should we be in bondage to them if we may be free? Why use one precisely when we may use another no less fit, as commodiously? A godly father in primitive time showed himself greatly moved, that one who was fond of novelty called *Krabbaton skimpous,* though the difference is little or none; and another reported that he was much abused for changing *Cucurbita* (to which reading the people had been accustomed) to *Hedera.* Now if this happen in better times, and upon so small occasions, we might justly fear hard censure, if generally we should make verbal and unnecessary charges. We might also be charged (by scoffers) with some unequal dealing towards a great number of good English words. For as it is written of a certain great philosopher, that he should say, that "those logs were happy that were made images to be worshiped; for their fellows, as good as they, lay for blocks behind the fire." So if we should say, as it were, unto certain words, "Stand up higher, have a place in the Bible always, and to others of like quality, "Get ye hence, be banished forever," we might be taxed perhaps with St. James' words, namely, "To be partial in ourselves and judges of evil thoughts." Add to this, that niceness in words was always counted the next step to trifling, and so was it to be curious about names too. Also that we cannot follow a better pattern for elocution than God himself; therefore, he using different words in his Holy Writ, and indifferently for one thing in nature, we, if we will not be superstitious, may use the same liberty in our English versions out of Hebrew and Greek, for that copy or story that he has given us. Lastly, we have on the one side avoided the scrupulosity of the Puritans, who forsake the old ecclesiastical words, and make use of others, as when they put *washing* for *baptism,* and *congregation* instead of *church.* Also on the other side we have shunned the obscurity of the Papists, in their *azimes, tunike, rational, holocausts, prapuce, pasche,* and a number of such like, of which their recent translation is full, and that on purpose to darken the sense, that since they must needs translate the Bible, yet by its language, it may be kept from being understood. But we desire that the Scripture may speak like itself, as in the language of Canaan, that it may be understood even of the very common people.

Many other things we might give you warning of, gentle reader, if we had not exceeded the measure of a preface already. It remains that we commend you to God, and to the Spirit of his grace, who is able to build further than we can ask or think. He removes the scales from our eyes, the veil from our hearts, opening our wits that we may understand his Word, enlarging our hearts, indeed correcting our affections, that we may love it above gold and silver, indeed that we may love it to the end. You are brought unto fountains of living water which you digged not; do not cast earth into them with the Philistines, neither prefer broken pits before them with the wicked Jews. Others have labored, and you may enter into their labors; O receive not so great things in vain, O despise not so great salvation! Be not like swine to tread under foot so precious things, neither yet like dogs to tear and abuse holy things. Say no to our Savior with the Gergesites, "Depart out of our coasts"; neither yet with Esau sell your birthright for a mess of pottage. If light be come into the world, love not darkness more than light; if food, if clothing be offered, go not naked, starve not yourselves. Remember the advice of Nazianzene, "It is a grievous thing (or dangerous) to neglect a great fair, and to seek to make markets afterwards"; also the encouragement of St. Chrysostome, "It is altogether impossible, that he that is sober (and watchful) should any time be neglected." Lastly, the admonition and warning of St. Augustine, "They that despise God's will inviting them shall feel God's will taking vengeance of them." It is a fearful thing to fall into the hands of the living God; but a blessed thing it is, and it will bring us to everlasting blessedness in the end, when God speaks unto us, to hearken; when he sets his Word before us to read it; when he stretches out his hand and calls, to answer, "Here am I, here we are to do thy will, O God." The Lord work a care and conscience in us to know him and serve him, that we may be acknowledged of him at the appearing of our Lord Jesus Christ, to whom with the Holy Ghost, be all praise and thanksgiving. Amen.

The

Holy Bible

New King James Version

Logo: The triquetra (from a Latin word meaning "three-cornered") is an ancient symbol for the Trinity. It comprises three interwoven arcs, distinct yet equal and inseparable, symbolizing that the Father, Son, and Holy Spirit are three distinct yet equal Persons and indivisibly One God.

Preface
to the New King James Version

Purpose

In the preface to the 1611 edition, the translators of the Authorized Version, known popularly as the King James Bible, state that it was not their purpose "to make a new translation . . . but to make a good one better." Indebted to the earlier work of William Tyndale and others, they saw their best contribution to consist in revising and enhancing the excellence of the English versions which had sprung from the Reformation of the sixteenth century. In harmony with the purpose of the King James scholars, the translators and editors of the present work have not pursued a goal of innovation. They have perceived the Holy Bible, New King James Version, as a continuation of the labors of the earlier translators, thus unlocking for today's readers the spiritual treasures found especially in the Authorized Version of the Holy Scriptures.

A Living Legacy

For nearly four hundred years, and throughout several revisions of its English form, the King James Bible has been deeply revered among the English-speaking peoples of the world. The precision of translation for which it is historically renowned, and its majesty of style, have enabled that monumental version of the word of God to become the mainspring of the religion, language, and legal foundations of our civilization.

Although the Elizabethan period and our own era share in zeal for technical advance, the former period was more aggressively devoted to classical learning. Along with this awakened concern for the classics came a flourishing companion interest in the Scriptures, an interest that was enlivened by the conviction that the manuscripts were providentially handed down and were a trustworthy record of the inspired Word of God. The King James translators were committed to producing an English Bible that would be a precise translation, and by no means a paraphrase or a broadly approximate rendering. On the one hand, the scholars were almost as familiar with the original languages of the Bible as with their native English. On the other hand, their reverence for the divine Author and His Word assured a translation of the Scriptures in which only a principle of utmost accuracy could be accepted.

In 1786 Catholic scholar Alexander Geddes said of the King James Bible, "If accuracy and strictest attention to the letter of the text be supposed to constitute an excellent version, this is of all versions the most excellent." George Bernard Shaw became a literary legend in our century because of his severe and often humorous criticisms of our most cherished values. Surprisingly, however, Shaw pays the following tribute to the scholars commissioned by King James: "The translation was extraordinarily well done because to the translators what they were translating was not merely a curious collection of ancient books written by different authors in different stages of culture, but the Word of God divinely revealed through His chosen and expressly inspired scribes. In this conviction they carried out their work with boundless reverence and care and achieved a beautifully artistic result." History agrees with these estimates. Therefore, while seeking to unveil the excellent *form* of the traditional English Bible, special care has also been taken in the present edition to preserve the work of *precision* which is the legacy of the 1611 translators.

Complete Equivalence in Translation

Where new translation has been necessary in the New King James Version, the most complete representation of the original has been rendered by considering the history of usage and etymology of words in their contexts. This principle of complete equivalence seeks to preserve *all* of the information in the text, while presenting it in good literary form. Dynamic equivalence, a recent procedure in Bible translation, commonly results in paraphrasing where a more literal rendering is needed to reflect a specific and vital sense. For example, complete equivalence truly renders the original text in expressions such as "lifted her voice and wept" (Gen. 21:16); "I gave you cleanness of teeth" (Amos 4:6); "Jesus met them, saying, 'Rejoice!' " (Matt. 28:9); and " 'Woman, what does your concern have to do with Me?' " (John 2:4). Complete equivalence translates fully, in order to provide an English text that is both accurate and readable.

In keeping with the principle of complete equivalence, it is the policy to translate interjections which are commonly omitted in modern language renderings of the Bible. As an example, the interjection *behold,* in the older King James editions, continues to have a place in English usage, especially in dramatically calling attention to a spectacular scene, or an event of profound importance such as the Immanuel prophecy of Isaiah 7:14. Consequently, *behold* is retained for these occasions in the present edition. However, the Hebrew and Greek originals for this word can be translated variously, depending on the circumstances in the passage. Therefore, in addition to *behold,* words such as *indeed, look, see,* and *surely* are also rendered to convey the appropriate sense suggested by the context in each case.

In faithfulness to God and to our readers, it was deemed appropriate that all participating scholars sign a statement affirming their belief in the verbal and plenary inspiration of Scripture, and in the inerrancy of the original autographs.

Devotional Quality

The King James scholars readily appreciated the intrinsic beauty of divine revelation. They accordingly disciplined their talents to render well-chosen English words of their time, as well as a graceful, often musical arrangement of language, which has stirred the hearts of Bible readers through the years. The translators, the committees, and the editors of the present edition, while sensitive to the late-twentieth-century English idiom, and while adhering faithfully to the Hebrew, Aramaic, and Greek texts, have sought to maintain those lyrical and devotional qualities that are so highly regarded in the Authorized Version. This devotional quality is especially apparent in the poetic and prophetic books, although even the relatively plain style of the Gospels and Epistles cannot strictly be likened, as sometimes suggested, to modern newspaper style. The Koine Greek of the New Testament is influenced by the Hebrew background of the writers, for whom even the gospel narratives were not merely flat utterance, but often song in various degrees of rhythm.

The Style

Students of the Bible applaud the timeless devotional character of our historic Bible. Yet it is also universally understood that our language, like all living languages, has undergone profound change since 1611. Subsequent revisions of the King James Bible have sought to keep abreast of changes in English speech. The present work is a further step toward this objective. Where obsolescence and other reading difficulties exist, present-day vocabulary, punctuation, and grammar have been carefully integrated. Words representing ancient objects, such as *chariot* and *phylactery*, have no modern substitutes and are therefore retained.

A special feature of the New King James Version is its conformity to the thought flow of the 1611 Bible. The reader discovers that the sequence and selection of words, phrases, and clauses of the new edition, while much clearer, are so close to the traditional that there is remarkable ease in listening to the reading of either edition while following with the other.

In the discipline of translating biblical and other ancient languages, a standard method of transliteration, that is, the English spelling of untranslated words, such as names of persons and places, has never been commonly adopted. In keeping with the design of the present work, the King James spelling of untranslated words is retained, although made uniform throughout. For example, instead of the spellings *Isaiah* and *Elijah* in the Old Testament, and *Esaias* and *Elias* in the New Testament, *Isaiah* and *Elijah* now appear in both Testaments.

King James doctrinal and theological terms, for example, *propitiation, justification,* and *sanctification,* are generally familiar to English-speaking peoples. Such terms have been retained except where the original language indicates need for a more precise translation.

Readers of the Authorized Version will immediately be struck by the absence of several pronouns: *thee, thou,* and *ye* are replaced by the simple *you,* while *your* and *yours* are substituted for *thy* and *thine* as applicable. *Thee, thou, thy* and *thine* were once forms of address to express a special relationship to human as well as divine persons. These pronouns are no longer part of our language. However, reverence for God in the present work is preserved by capitalizing pronouns, including *You, Your,* and *Yours,* which refer to Him. Additionally, capitalization of these pronouns benefits the reader by clearly distinguishing divine and human persons referred to in a passage. Without such capitalization the distinction is often obscure, because the antecedent of a pronoun is not always clear in the English translation.

In addition to the pronoun usages of the seventeenth century, the *-eth* and *-est* verb endings, so familiar in the earlier King James editions, are now obsolete. Unless a speaker is schooled in these verb endings, there is common difficulty in selecting the correct form to be used with a given subject of the verb in vocal prayer. That is, should we use *love, loveth,* or *lovest? do, doeth, doest,* or *dost? have, hath,* or *hast?* Because these forms are obsolete, contemporary English usage has been substituted for the previous verb endings.

In older editions of the King James Version, the frequency of the connective *and* far exceeded the limits of present English usage. Also, biblical linguists agree that the Hebrew and Greek original words for this conjunction may commonly be translated otherwise, depending on the immediate context. Therefore, instead of *and,* alternatives such as *also, but, however, now, so, then,* and *thus* are accordingly rendered in the present edition, when the original language permits.

The real character of the Authorized Version does not reside in its archaic pronouns or verbs or other grammatical forms of the seventeenth century, but rather in the care taken by its scholars to impart the letter and spirit of the original text in a majestic and reverent style.

The Format

The format of the New King James Version is designed to enhance the vividness and devotional quality of the Holy Scriptures:

—Subject headings assist the reader to identify topics and transitions in the biblical content.

—Words or phrases in *italics* indicate expressions in the original language which require clarification by additional English words, as also done throughout the history of the King James Bible.

—*Oblique type* in the New Testament indicates a quotation from the Old Testament.

—Verse numbers in **bold type** indicate the beginning of a paragraph.

—Poetry is structured as contemporary verse to reflect the poetic form and beauty of the passage in the original language.

—The covenant name of God was usually translated from the Hebrew as "LORD" or "GOD" (using capital letters as shown) in the King James Old Testament. This tradition is maintained. In the present edition the name is so capitalized whenever the covenant name is quoted in the New Testament from a passage in the Old Testament.

The Old Testament Text

The Hebrew Bible has come down to us through the scrupulous care of ancient scribes who copied the original text in successive generations. By the sixth century A.D. the scribes were succeeded by a group known as the Masoretes, who continued to preserve the sacred Scriptures for another five hundred years in a form known as the Masoretic Text. Babylonia, Palestine, and Tiberias were the main centers of Masoretic activity; but by the tenth century A.D. the Masoretes of Tiberias, led by the family of ben Asher, gained the ascendancy. Through subsequent editions, the ben Asher text became in the twelfth century the only recognized form of the Hebrew Scriptures.

Daniel Bomberg printed the first Rabbinic Bible in 1516–17; that work was followed in 1524–25 by a second edition prepared by Jacob ben Chayyim and also published by Bomberg. The text of ben Chayyim was adopted in most subsequent Hebrew Bibles, including those used by the King James translators. The ben Chayyim text was also used for the first two editions of Rudolph Kittel's *Biblia Hebraica* of 1906 and 1912. In 1937 Paul Kahle published a third edition of *Biblia Hebraica*. This edition was based on the oldest dated manuscript of the ben Asher text, the Leningrad Manuscript B19a (A.D. 1008), which Kahle regarded as superior to that used by ben Chayyim.

For the New King James Version the text used was the 1967/1977 Stuttgart edition of the *Biblia Hebraica*, with frequent comparisons being made with the Bomberg edition of 1524–25. The Septuagint (Greek) Version of the Old Testament and the Latin Vulgate also were consulted. In addition to referring to a variety of ancient versions of the Hebrew Scriptures, the New King James Version draws on the resources of relevant manuscripts from the Dead Sea caves. In the few places where the Hebrew was so obscure that the 1611 King James was compelled to follow one of the versions, but where information is now available to resolve the problems, the New King James Version follows the Hebrew text. Significant variations are recorded in the textual footnotes.

The New Testament Text

There is more manuscript support for the New Testament than for any other body of ancient literature. Over five thousand Greek, eight thousand Latin, and many more manuscripts in other languages attest the integrity of the New Testament. There is only one basic New Testament used by Protestants, Roman Catholics, and Orthodox, by conservatives and liberals. Minor variations in hand copying have appeared through the centuries, before mechanical printing began about A.D. 1450.

Some variations exist in the spelling of Greek words, in word order, and in similar details. These ordinarily do not show up in translation and do not affect the sense of the text in any way.

Other manuscript differences such as omission or inclusion of a word or a clause, and two paragraphs in the Gospels, should not overshadow the overwhelming degree of *agreement* which exists among the ancient records. Bible readers may be assured that the most important differences in English New Testaments of today are due, not to manuscript divergence, but to the way in which translators view the task of translation: How literally should the text be rendered? How does the translator view the matter of biblical inspiration? Does the translator adopt a paraphrase when a literal rendering would be quite clear and more to the point? The New King James Version follows the historic precedent of the Authorized Version in maintaining a literal approach to translation, except where the idiom of the original language cannot be translated directly into our tongue.

The King James New Testament was based on the traditional text of the Greek-speaking churches, first published in 1516, and later called the Textus Receptus or Received Text. Although based on the relatively few available manuscripts, these were representative of many more which existed at the time but only became known later. In the late nineteenth century, B. Wescott and F. Hort taught that this text had been officially edited by the fourth-century church, but a total lack of historical evidence for this event has forced a revision of the theory. It is now widely held that the Byzantine Text that largely supports the Textus Receptus has as much right as the Alexandrian or any other tradition to be weighed in determining the text of the New Testament. Those readings in the Textus Receptus which have weak support are indicated in the textual footnotes as being opposed by both Critical and Majority Texts (see "Textual Footnotes").

Since the 1880s most contemporary translations of the New Testament have relied upon a relatively few manuscripts discovered chiefly in the late nineteenth and early twentieth centuries. Such translations depend primarily on two manuscripts, Codex Vaticanus and Codex Sinaiticus, because of their greater age. The Greek text obtained by using these sources and the related papyri (our most ancient manuscripts) is known as the Alexandrian Text. However, some scholars have grounds for doubting the faithfulness of Vaticanus and Sinaiticus, since they often disagree with one another, and Sinaiticus exhibits excessive omission.

A third viewpoint of New Testament scholarship holds that the best text is based on the consensus of the majority of existing Greek manuscripts. This text is called the Majority Text. Most of these manuscripts are in substantial agreement. Even though many are late, and none is earlier than the fifth century, usually their readings are verified by papyri, ancient versions, quotations from the early church fathers, or a combination of these. The Majority Text is similar to the Textus Receptus, but it corrects those readings which have little or no support in the Greek manuscript tradition.

Today, scholars agree that the science of New Testament textual criticism is in a state of flux. Very few scholars still favor the Textus Receptus as such, and then often for its historical prestige as the text of Luther, Calvin, Tyndale, and the King James Version. For about a century most have followed a Critical Text (so called because it is edited according to specific principles of textual criticism) which depends heavily upon the Alexandrian type of text. More recently many have abandoned this Critical Text (which is quite similar to the one edited by Westcott and Hort) for one that is more eclectic. Finally, a small but growing number of scholars prefer the Majority Text, which is close to the traditional text except in the Revelation.

In light of these facts, and also because the New King James Version is the fifth revision of a historic document translated from specific Greek texts, the editors decided to retain the traditional text in the body of the New Testament and to indicate major Critical and Majority Text variant readings in the textual footnotes. Although these variations are duly indicated in the footnotes of the present edition, it is most important to emphasize that fully eighty-five percent of the New Testament text is the same in the Textus Receptus, the Alexandrian Text, and the Majority Text.

Textual Footnotes

Significant explanatory notes, alternate translations, literal translations, and language notes are supplied in the footnotes.

Important textual variants in the Old Testament are identified in a standard form.

The textual notes in the present edition of the New Testament make no evaluation of readings, but do clearly indicate the manuscript sources of readings. They objectively present the facts without such tendentious remarks as "the best manuscripts omit" or "the most reliable manuscripts read." Such notes are value judgments that differ according to varying viewpoints on the text. By giving a clearly defined set of variants the New King James Version benefits readers of all textual persuasions.

Where significant variations occur in the New Testament Greek manuscripts, textual notes are classified as follows:

1. NU-Text
   These variations from the traditional text generally represent the Alexandrian or Egyptian type of text described previously in "The New Testament Text." They are found in the Critical Text published in the twenty-sixth edition of the Nestle-Aland Greek New Testament (N) and in the United Bible Societies' third edition (U), hence the acronym, "NU-Text."
2. M-Text
   This symbol indicates points of variation in the Majority Text from the traditional text, as also previously discussed in "The New Testament Text." It should be noted that M stands for whatever reading is printed in the published *Greek New Testament According to the Majority Text*, whether supported by overwhelming, strong, or only a divided majority textual tradition.

The textual notes reflect the scholarship of the past 150 years and will assist the reader to observe the variations between the different manuscript traditions of the New Testament. Such information is generally not available in English translations of the New Testament.

The
Old Testament

KJV

THE FIRST BOOK OF MOSES CALLED

GENESIS

The History of Creation
(Gen. 2:4–9; Job 38:4–11; John 1:1–5)

1 In the [a]beginning [b]God created the heaven and the earth.

2 And the earth was [a]without form, and void; and darkness *was* upon the face of the deep. [b]And the Spirit of God moved upon the face of the waters.

3 [a]And God said, [b]Let there be [c]light: and there was light.

4 And God saw the light, that *it was* good: and God divided the light from the darkness.

5 And God called the light Day, and the [a]darkness he called Night. And the evening and the morning were the first day.

6 And God said, [a]Let there be a firmament in the midst of the waters, and let it divide the waters from the waters.

7 And God made the firmament, [a]and divided the waters which *were* under the firmament from the waters which *were* [b]above the firmament: and it was so.

8 And God called the firmament Heaven. And the evening and the morning were the second day.

9 And God said, [a]Let the waters under the heaven be gathered together unto one place, and [b]let the dry *land* appear: and it was so.

10 And God called the dry *land* Earth; and the gathering together of the waters called he Seas: and God saw that *it was* good.

11 And God said, Let the earth [a]bring forth grass, the herb yielding seed, *and* the [b]fruit tree yielding fruit after his kind, whose seed *is* in itself, upon the earth: and it was so.

12 And the earth brought forth grass, *and* herb yielding seed after his kind, and the tree yielding fruit, whose seed *was* in itself, after his kind: and God saw that *it was* good.

13 And the evening and the morning were the third day.

14 And God said, Let there be [a]lights in the firmament of the heaven to divide the day from the night; and let them be for signs, and for [b]seasons, and for days, and years:

15 And let them be for lights in the firmament of the heaven to give light upon the earth: and it was so.

16 And God made two great lights; the [a]greater light to rule the day, and the [b]lesser light to rule the night: *he made* [c]the stars also.

17 And God set them in the firmament of the [a]heaven to give light upon the earth,

18 And to [a]rule over the day and over the night, and to divide the light from the darkness: and God saw that *it was* good.

19 And the evening and the morning were the fourth day.

20 And God said, Let the waters bring forth abundantly the moving creature that hath life, and fowl *that* may fly above the earth in the open firmament of heaven.

21 And [a]God created great whales, and every living creature that moveth, which the waters brought forth abundantly, after their kind, and

CHAPTER 1

1 [a]Ps. 102:25; Is. 40:21; [John 1:1–3; Heb. 1:10] [b]Gen. 2:4; [Ps. 8:3; 89:11; 90:2]; Is. 44:24; Acts 17:24; Rom. 1:20; [Heb. 1:2; 11:3]; Rev. 4:11
2 [a]Jer. 4:23 [b][Gen. 6:3]; Job 26:13; Ps. 33:6; 104:30; Is. 40:13, 14
3 [a]Ps. 33:6, 9 [b]2 Cor. 4:6 [c][Heb. 11:3]
5 [a]Job 37:18; Ps. 19:2; 33:6; 74:16; 104:20; 136:5; Jer. 10:12
6 [a]Job 37:18; Jer. 10:12; 2 Pet. 3:5
7 [a]Job 38:8–11; Prov. 8:27–29 [b]Ps. 148:4
9 [a]Job 26:10; Ps. 104:6–9; Prov. 8:29; Jer. 5:22; 2 Pet. 3:5 [b]Ps. 24:1, 2; 33:7; 95:5
11 [a]Ps. 65:9–13; 104:14; Heb. 6:7 [b]2 Sam. 16:1; Luke 6:44
14 [a]Deut. 4:19; Ps. 74:16; 136:5–9 [b]Ps. 104:19
16 [a]Ps. 136:8 [b]Deut. 17:3; Ps. 8:3 [c]Deut. 4:19; Job 38:7; Is. 40:26
17 [a]Gen. 15:5; Jer. 33:20, 25
18 [a]Jer. 31:35
21 [a]Ps. 104:25–28

*

1:2 Words in italic type have been added for clarity. They are not found in the original Hebrew or Aramaic.

NKJV

THE FIRST BOOK OF MOSES CALLED

GENESIS

The History of Creation
(Gen. 2:4–9; Job 38:4–11; John 1:1–5)

1 In the [a]beginning [b]God created the heavens and the earth.

2 The earth was [a]without form, and void; and darkness **was* on the face of the deep. [b]And the Spirit of God was hovering over the face of the waters.

3 [a]Then God said, [b]"Let there be [c]light"; and there was light.

4 And God saw the light, that *it was* good; and God divided the light from the darkness.

5 God called the light Day, and the [a]darkness He called Night. So the evening and the morning were the first day.

6 Then God said, [a]"Let there be a firmament in the midst of the waters, and let it divide the waters from the waters."

7 Thus God made the firmament, [a]and divided the waters which *were* under the firmament from the waters which *were* [b]above the firmament; and it was so.

8 And God called the firmament Heaven. So the evening and the morning were the second day.

9 Then God said, [a]"Let the waters under the heavens be gathered together into one place, and [b]let the dry *land* appear"; and it was so.

10 And God called the dry *land* Earth, and the gathering together of the waters He called Seas. And God saw that *it was* good.

11 Then God said, "Let the earth [a]bring forth grass, the herb *that* yields seed, *and* the [b]fruit tree *that* yields fruit according to its kind, whose seed *is* in itself, on the earth"; and it was so.

12 And the earth brought forth grass, the herb *that* yields seed according to its kind, and the tree *that* yields fruit, whose seed *is* in itself according to its kind. And God saw that *it was* good.

13 So the evening and the morning were the third day.

14 Then God said, "Let there be [a]lights in the firmament of the heavens to divide the day from the night; and let them be for signs and [b]seasons, and for days and years;

15 "and let them be for lights in the firmament of the heavens to give light on the earth"; and it was so.

16 Then God made two great lights: the [a]greater light to rule the day, and the [b]lesser light to rule the night. *He made* [c]the stars also.

17 God set them in the firmament of the [a]heavens to give light on the earth,

18 and to [a]rule over the day and over the night, and to divide the light from the darkness. And God saw that *it was* good.

19 So the evening and the morning were the fourth day.

20 Then God said, "Let the waters abound with an abundance of living creatures, and let birds fly above the earth across the face of the firmament of the heavens."

21 So [a]God created great sea creatures and every living thing that moves, with which the waters abounded, according to their kind, and every

KJV

every winged fowl after his kind: and God saw that *it was* good.

22 And God blessed them, saying, [a]Be fruitful, and multiply, and fill the waters in the seas, and let fowl multiply in the earth.

23 And the evening and the morning were the fifth day.

24 And God said, Let the earth bring forth the living creature after his kind, cattle, and creeping thing, and beast of the earth after his kind: and it was so.

25 And God made the beast of the earth after his kind, and cattle after their kind, and every thing that creepeth upon the earth after his kind: and God saw that *it was* good.

26 And God said, [a]Let us make man in our image, after our likeness: and [b]let them have dominion over the fish of the sea, and over the fowl of the air, and over the cattle, and over all the earth, and over every creeping thing that creepeth upon the earth.

27 So God created man [a]in his *own* image, in the image of God created he him; [b]male and female created he them.

28 And God blessed them, and God said unto them, [a]Be fruitful, and multiply, and replenish the earth, and [b]subdue it: and have dominion over the fish of the sea, and over the fowl of the air, and over every living thing that moveth upon the earth.

29 And God said, Behold, I have given you every herb bearing seed, which *is* upon the face of all the earth, and every tree, in the which *is* the fruit of a tree yielding seed; [a]to you it shall be for meat.

30 And to [a]every beast of the earth, and to every [b]fowl of the air, and to every thing that creepeth upon the earth, wherein *there is* life, *I have given* every green herb for meat: and it was so.

31 And [a]God saw every thing that he had made, and, behold, *it was* very good. And the evening and the morning were the sixth day.

2 Thus the heavens and the earth were finished, and [a]all the host of them.

2 [a]And on the seventh day God ended his work which he had made; and he rested on the seventh day from all his work which he had made.

3 And God [a]blessed the seventh day, and sanctified it: because that in it he had rested from all his work which God created and made.

4 [a]These *are* the generations of the heavens and of the earth when they were created, in the day that the LORD God made the earth and the heavens,

5 And every [a]plant of the field before it was in the earth, and every herb of the field before it grew: for the LORD God had not [b]caused it to rain upon the earth, and *there was* not a man [c]to till the ground.

6 But there went up a mist from the earth, and watered the whole face of the ground.

7 And the LORD God formed man *of* the [a]dust of the ground, and [b]breathed into his [c]nostrils the breath of life; and [d]man became a living soul.

Life in God's Garden

8 And the LORD God planted [a]a garden [b]eastward in [c]Eden; and there he put the man whom he had formed.

9 And out of the ground made the LORD God to grow [a]every tree that is pleasant to the sight, and good for food; [b]the tree of life also in the midst of the garden, and the tree of knowledge of good and [c]evil.

10 And a river went out of Eden to water the garden; and from thence it was parted, and became into four heads.

11 The name of the first *is* Pison: that *is* it which compasseth [a]the whole land of Havilah, where *there is* gold;

22 [a]Gen. 8:17
26 [a]Gen. 9:6; Ps. 100:3; Eccl. 7:29; [Eph. 4:24]; James 3:9 [b]Gen. 9:2; Ps. 8:6–8
27 [a]Gen. 5:2; 1 Cor. 11:7 [b]Matt. 19:4; [Mark 10:6–8]
28 [a]Gen. 9:1, 7; Lev. 26:9 [b]1 Cor. 9:27
29 [a]Gen. 9:3; Ps. 104:14, 15
30 [a]Ps. 145:15 [b]Job 38:41
31 [a][Ps. 104:24; 1 Tim. 4:4]

CHAPTER 2
1 [a]Ps. 33:6
2 [a]Ex. 20:9–11; 31:17; Heb. 4:4, 10
3 [a][Is. 58:13]
4 [a]Gen. 1:1; Ps. 90:1, 2
5 [a]Gen. 1:11, 12 [b]Gen. 7:4; Job 5:10; 38:26–28 [c]Gen. 3:23
7 [a]Gen. 3:19, 23; Ps. 103:14 [b]Job 33:4 [c]Gen. 7:22 [d]1 Cor. 15:45
8 [a]Is. 51:3 [b]Gen. 3:23, 24 [c]Gen. 4:16
9 [a]Ezek. 31:8 [b][Gen. 3:22; Rev. 2:7; 22:2, 14] [c][Deut. 1:39]
11 [a]Gen. 25:18

*

1:26 Syr. *all the wild animals of*
2:4 Heb. *toledoth*, lit. *generations*

NKJV

winged bird according to its kind. And God saw that *it was* good.

22 And God blessed them, saying, [a]"Be fruitful and multiply, and fill the waters in the seas, and let birds multiply on the earth."

23 So the evening and the morning were the fifth day.

24 Then God said, "Let the earth bring forth the living creature according to its kind: cattle and creeping thing and beast of the earth, *each* according to its kind"; and it was so.

25 And God made the beast of the earth according to its kind, cattle according to its kind, and everything that creeps on the earth according to its kind. And God saw that *it was* good.

26 Then God said, [a]"Let Us make man in Our image, according to Our likeness; [b]let them have dominion over the fish of the sea, over the birds of the air, and over the cattle, over *all the earth and over every creeping thing that creeps on the earth."

27 So God created man [a]in His *own* image; in the image of God He created him; [b]male and female He created them.

28 Then God blessed them, and God said to them, [a]"Be fruitful and multiply; fill the earth and [b]subdue it; have dominion over the fish of the sea, over the birds of the air, and over every living thing that moves on the earth."

29 And God said, "See, I have given you every herb *that* yields seed which *is* on the face of all the earth, and every tree whose fruit yields seed; [a]to you it shall be for food.

30 "Also, to [a]every beast of the earth, to every [b]bird of the air, and to everything that creeps on the earth, in which *there is* life, *I have given* every green herb for food"; and it was so.

31 Then [a]God saw everything that He had made, and indeed *it was* very good. So the evening and the morning were the sixth day.

2 Thus the heavens and the earth, and [a]all the host of them, were finished.

2 [a]And on the seventh day God ended His work which He had done, and He rested on the seventh day from all His work which He had done.

3 Then God [a]blessed the seventh day and sanctified it, because in it He rested from all His work which God had created and made.

4 [a]This *is* the *history of the heavens and the earth when they were created, in the day that the LORD God made the earth and the heavens,

5 before any [a]plant of the field was in the earth and before any herb of the field had grown. For the LORD God had not [b]caused it to rain on the earth, and *there was* no man [c]to till the ground;

6 but a mist went up from the earth and watered the whole face of the ground.

7 And the LORD God formed man *of* the [a]dust of the ground, and [b]breathed into his [c]nostrils the breath of life; and [d]man became a living being.

Life in God's Garden

8 The LORD God planted [a]a garden [b]eastward in [c]Eden, and there He put the man whom He had formed.

9 And out of the ground the LORD God made [a]every tree grow that is pleasant to the sight and good for food. [b]The tree of life *was* also in the midst of the garden, and the tree of the knowledge of good and [c]evil.

10 Now a river went out of Eden to water the garden, and from there it parted and became four riverheads.

11 The name of the first *is* Pishon; it *is* the one which skirts [a]the whole land of Havilah, where *there is* gold.

KJV

12 And the gold of that land *is* good: [a]there *is* bdellium and the onyx stone.

13 And the name of the second river *is* Gihon: the same *is* it that compasseth the whole land of Ethiopia.

14 And the name of the third river *is* [a]Hiddekel: that *is* it which goeth toward the east of Assyria. And the fourth river *is* Euphrates.

15 And the LORD God took the man, and put him into the garden of Eden to dress it and to keep it.

16 And the LORD God commanded the man, saying, Of every tree of the garden thou mayest freely eat:

17 But of the tree of the knowledge of good and evil, [a]thou shalt not eat of it: for in the day that thou eatest thereof [b]thou shalt surely [c]die.

18 And the LORD God said, *It is* not good that the man should be alone; [a]I will make him an help meet for him.

19 [a]And out of the ground the LORD God formed every beast of the field, and every fowl of the air; and [b]brought *them* unto Adam to see what he would call them: and whatsoever Adam called every living creature, that *was* the name thereof.

20 And Adam gave names to all cattle, and to the fowl of the air, and to every beast of the field; but for Adam there was not found an help meet for him.

21 And the LORD God caused a [a]deep sleep to fall upon Adam, and he slept: and he took one of his ribs, and closed up the flesh instead thereof;

22 And the rib, which the LORD God had taken from man, made he a woman, [a]and [b]brought her unto the man.

23 And Adam said, This *is* now [a]bone of my bones, and flesh of my flesh: she shall be called Woman, because she was [b]taken out of Man.

24 [a]Therefore shall a man leave his father and his mother, and shall [b]cleave unto his wife: and they shall be one flesh.

25 [a]And they were both naked, the man and his wife, and were not [b]ashamed.

The Temptation and Fall of Man
(Rom. 5:12–21)

3 Now [a]the serpent was [b]more subtil than any beast of the field which the LORD God had made. And he said unto the woman, Yea, hath God said, Ye shall not eat of every tree of the garden?

2 And the woman said unto the serpent, We may eat of the [a]fruit of the trees of the garden:

3 But of the fruit of the tree which *is* in the midst of the garden, God hath said, Ye shall not eat of it, neither shall ye [a]touch it, lest ye die.

4 [a]And the serpent said unto the woman, Ye shall not surely die:

5 For God doth know that in the day ye eat thereof, then your eyes shall be opened, and ye shall be as gods, knowing good and evil.

6 And when the woman [a]saw that the tree *was* good for food, and that it *was* pleasant to the eyes, and a tree to be desired to make *one* wise, she took of the fruit thereof, [b]and did eat, and gave also unto her husband with her; and he did eat.

7 And the eyes of them both were opened, [a]and they knew that they *were* naked; and they sewed fig leaves together, and made themselves aprons.

8 And they heard [a]the voice of the LORD God walking in the garden in the cool of the day: and Adam and his wife [b]hid themselves from the presence of the LORD God amongst the trees of the garden.

9 And the LORD God called unto Adam, and said unto him, Where *art* thou?

12 [a]Num. 11:7 **14** [a]Dan. 10:4 **17** [a]Gen. 3:1, 3, 11, 17 [b]Gen. 3:3, 19; [Rom. 6:23] [c]Rom. 5:12; 1 Cor. 15:21, 22 **18** [a]1 Cor. 11:8, 9; 1 Tim. 2:13 **19** [a]Gen. 1:20, 24 [b]Ps. 8:6 **21** [a]Gen. 15:12; 1 Sam. 26:12 **22** [a]Gen. 3:20; 1 Tim. 2:13 [b]Heb. 13:4 **23** [a]Gen. 29:14; Eph. 5:28–30 [b]1 Cor. 11:8, 9 **24** [a]Matt. 19:5; Eph. 5:31 [b]Mark 10:6–8; 1 Cor. 6:16 **25** [a]Gen. 3:7, 10 [b]Is. 47:3

CHAPTER 3

1 [a]1 Chr. 21:1; [Rev. 12:9; 20:2, 10] [b]2 Cor. 11:3 **2** [a]Gen. 2:16, 17 **3** [a]Ex. 19:12, 13; Rev. 22:14 **4** [a]John 8:44; [2 Cor. 11:3; 1 Tim. 2:14] **6** [a]1 John 2:16 [b]1 Tim. 2:14 **7** [a]Gen. 2:25 **8** [a]Job 38:1 [b]Job 31:33; Jer. 23:24

NKJV

12 And the gold of that land *is* good. [a]Bdellium and the onyx stone *are* there.

13 The name of the second river *is* Gihon; it *is* the one which goes around the whole land of Cush.

14 The name of the third river *is* [a]Hiddekel;* it *is* the one which goes toward the east of Assyria. The fourth river *is* the Euphrates.

15 Then the LORD God took the man and put him in the garden of Eden to tend and keep it.

16 And the LORD God commanded the man, saying, "Of every tree of the garden you may freely eat;

17 "but of the tree of the knowledge of good and evil [a]you shall not eat, for in the day that you eat of it [b]you shall surely [c]die."

18 And the LORD God said, "*It is* not good that man should be alone; [a]I will make him a helper comparable to him."

19 [a]Out of the ground the LORD God formed every beast of the field and every bird of the air, and [b]brought *them* to Adam to see what he would call them. And whatever Adam called each living creature, that *was* its name.

20 So Adam gave names to all cattle, to the birds of the air, and to every beast of the field. But for Adam there was not found a helper comparable to him.

21 And the LORD God caused a [a]deep sleep to fall on Adam, and he slept; and He took one of his ribs, and closed up the flesh in its place.

22 Then the rib which the LORD God had taken from man He made into a woman, [a]and He [b]brought her to the man.

23 And Adam said:

"This *is* now [a]bone of my bones
And flesh of my flesh;
She shall be called Woman,
Because she was [b]taken out of Man."

24 [a]Therefore a man shall leave his father and mother and [b]be joined to his wife, and they shall become one flesh.

25 [a]And they were both naked, the man and his wife, and were not [b]ashamed.

The Temptation and Fall of Man
(Rom. 5:12–21)

3 Now [a]the serpent was [b]more cunning than any beast of the field which the LORD God had made. And he said to the woman, "Has God indeed said, 'You shall not eat of every tree of the garden'?"

2 And the woman said to the serpent, "We may eat the [a]fruit of the trees of the garden;

3 "but of the fruit of the tree which *is* in the midst of the garden, God has said, 'You shall not eat it, nor shall you [a]touch it, lest you die.' "

4 [a]Then the serpent said to the woman, "You will not surely die.

5 "For God knows that in the day you eat of it your eyes will be opened, and you will be like God, knowing good and evil."

6 So when the woman [a]saw that the tree *was* good for food, that it *was* pleasant to the eyes, and a tree desirable to make *one* wise, she took of its fruit [b]and ate. She also gave to her husband with her, and he ate.

7 Then the eyes of both of them were opened, [a]and they knew that they *were* naked; and they sewed fig leaves together and made themselves coverings.

8 And they heard [a]the sound of the LORD God walking in the garden in the cool of the day, and Adam and his wife [b]hid themselves from the presence of the LORD God among the trees of the garden.

9 Then the LORD God called to Adam and said to him, "Where *are* you?"

***2:14** Or *Tigris*

KJV

10 And he said, I heard thy voice in the garden, [a]and I was afraid, because I *was* naked; and I hid myself.

11 And he said, Who told thee that thou *wast* naked? Hast thou eaten of the tree, whereof I commanded thee that thou shouldest not eat?

12 And the man said, [a]The woman whom thou gavest *to be* with me, she gave me of the tree, and I did eat.

13 And the LORD God said unto the woman, What *is* this *that* thou hast done? And the woman said, [a]The serpent beguiled me, and I did eat.

14 And the LORD God said unto the serpent, Because thou hast done this, thou *art* cursed above all cattle, and above every beast of the field; upon thy belly shalt thou go, and [a]dust shalt thou eat all the days of thy life:

15 And I will put enmity between thee and the woman, and between [a]thy seed and [b]her seed; [c]it shall bruise thy head, and thou shalt bruise his heel.

16 Unto the woman he said, I will greatly multiply thy sorrow and thy conception; [a]in sorrow thou shalt bring forth children; [b]and thy desire *shall be* to thy husband, and he shall [c]rule over thee.

17 And unto Adam he said, [a]Because thou hast hearkened unto the voice of thy wife, and hast eaten of the tree, [b]of which I commanded thee, saying, Thou shalt not eat of it: [c]cursed *is* the ground for thy sake; [d]in sorrow shalt thou eat *of* it all the days of thy life;

18 Thorns also and thistles shall it bring forth to thee; and [a]thou shalt eat the herb of the field;

19 [a]In the sweat of thy face shalt thou eat bread, till thou return unto the ground; for out of it wast thou taken: [b]for dust thou *art*, and [c]unto dust shalt thou return.

20 And Adam called his wife's name [a]Eve; because she was the mother of all living.

21 Unto Adam also and to his wife did the LORD God make coats of skins, and clothed them.

22 And the LORD God said, Behold, the man is become as one of us, to know good and evil: and now, lest he put forth his hand, and take also of the tree of life, and eat, and live for ever:

23 Therefore the LORD God sent him forth from the garden of Eden, [a]to till the ground from whence he was taken.

24 So [a]he drove out the man; and he placed [c]at the east of the garden of Eden [b]Cherubims, and a flaming sword which turned every way, to keep the way of the tree of [d]life.

10 [a]Gen. 2:25; Ex. 3:6; Deut. 9:19; 1 John 3:20
12 [a][Prov. 28:13]
13 [a]Gen. 3:4; 2 Cor. 11:3; 1 Tim. 2:14
14 [a]Deut. 28:15–20; Is. 65:25; Mic. 7:17
15 [a]John 8:44; Acts 13:10; 1 John 3:8 [b]Is. 7:14; Luke 1:31, 34, 35; Gal. 4:4 [c]Rom. 16:20; [Rev. 12:7, 17]
16 [a]Is. 13:8; John 16:21 [b]Gen. 4:7 [c]1 Cor. 11:3; Eph. 5:22; 1 Tim. 2:12, 15
17 [a]1 Sam. 15:23 [b]Gen. 2:17 [c]Gen. 5:29; Rom. 8:20–22; Heb. 6:8 [d]Job 5:7; 14:1; Eccl. 2:23
18 [a]Ps. 104:14
19 [a]2 Thess. 3:10 [b]Gen. 2:7; 5:5 [c]Job 21:26; Eccl. 3:20
20 [a]2 Cor. 11:3; 1 Tim. 2:13
23 [a]Gen. 4:2; 9:20
24 [a]Ezek. 31:3, 11 [b]Ex. 25:18–22; Ps. 104:4; Ezek. 10:1–20; Heb. 1:7 [c]Gen. 2:8 [d]Gen. 2:9; [Rev. 22:2]

NKJV

10 So he said, "I heard Your voice in the garden, [a]and I was afraid because I was naked; and I hid myself."

11 And He said, "Who told you that you *were* naked? Have you eaten from the tree of which I commanded you that you should not eat?"

12 Then the man said, [a]"The woman whom You gave *to be* with me, she gave me of the tree, and I ate."

13 And the LORD God said to the woman, "What *is* this you have done?" The woman said, [a]"The serpent deceived me, and I ate."

14 So the LORD God said to the serpent:

"Because you have done this,
You *are* cursed more than all cattle,
And more than every beast of the field;
On your belly you shall go,
And [a]you shall eat dust
All the days of your life.
15 And I will put enmity
Between you and the woman,
And between [a]your seed and [b]her Seed;
[c]He shall bruise your head,
And you shall bruise His heel."

16 To the woman He said:

"I will greatly multiply your sorrow and your conception;
[a]In pain you shall bring forth children;
[b]Your desire *shall be* for your husband,
And he shall [c]rule over you."

17 Then to Adam He said, [a]"Because you have heeded the voice of your wife, and have eaten from the tree [b]of which I commanded you, saying, 'You shall not eat of it':

[c]"Cursed *is* the ground for your sake;
[d]In toil you shall eat *of* it
All the days of your life.
18 Both thorns and thistles it shall bring forth for you,
And [a]you shall eat the herb of the field.
19 [a]In the sweat of your face you shall eat bread
Till you return to the ground,
For out of it you were taken;
[b]For dust you *are*,
And [c]to dust you shall return."

20 And Adam called his wife's name [a]Eve, because she was the mother of all living.

21 Also for Adam and his wife the LORD God made tunics of skin, and clothed them.

22 Then the LORD God said, "Behold, the man has become like one of Us, to know good and evil. And now, lest he put out his hand and take also of the tree of life, and eat, and live forever"—

23 therefore the LORD God sent him out of the garden of Eden [a]to till the ground from which he was taken.

24 So [a]He drove out the man; and He placed [b]cherubim [c]at the east of the garden of Eden, and a flaming sword which turned every way, to guard the way to the tree of [d]life.

Cain Murders Abel
(Luke 11:51; Heb. 11:4; 12:24)

4 And Adam knew Eve his wife; and she conceived, and bare Cain, and said, I have gotten a man from the LORD.

2 And she again bare his brother Abel. And [a]Abel was a keeper of sheep, but Cain was a tiller of the ground.

3 And in process of time it came to pass, that Cain brought of the fruit [a]of the ground an offering unto the LORD.

4 And Abel, he also brought of [a]the firstlings of his flock and of [b]the fat thereof. And the LORD had [c]respect unto Abel and to his offering:

CHAPTER 4

2 [a]Luke 11:50, 51
3 [a]Num. 18:12
4 [a]Num. 18:17 [b]Lev. 3:16 [c]Heb. 11:4

Cain Murders Abel
(Luke 11:51; Heb. 11:4; 12:24)

4 Now Adam knew Eve his wife, and she conceived and bore Cain, and said, "I have acquired a man from the LORD."

2 Then she bore again, this time his brother Abel. Now [a]Abel was a keeper of sheep, but Cain was a tiller of the ground.

3 And in the process of time it came to pass that Cain brought an offering of the fruit [a]of the ground to the LORD.

4 Abel also brought of [a]the firstborn of his flock and of [b]their fat. And the LORD [c]respected Abel and his offering,

KJV

5 But unto Cain and to his offering he had
not respect. And Cain was very wroth, and his
countenance fell.
6 And the LORD said unto Cain, Why art
thou wroth? and why is thy countenance fallen?
7 If thou doest well, shalt thou not be accepted? and if thou doest not well, sin lieth at the
door. And unto thee *shall be* his desire, and thou
shalt rule over him.
8 And Cain talked with Abel his brother:
and it came to pass, when they were in the field,
that Cain rose up against Abel his brother, and
[a]slew him.
9 And the LORD said unto Cain, Where *is*
Abel thy brother? And he said, [a]I know not: *Am*
I [b]my brother's keeper?
10 And he said, What hast thou done? the
voice of thy brother's blood [a]crieth unto me from
the ground.
11 And now *art* [a]thou cursed from the earth,
which hath opened her mouth to receive thy
brother's blood from thy hand;
12 When thou tillest the ground, it shall not
henceforth yield unto thee her strength; a fugitive
and a vagabond shalt thou be in the earth.
13 And Cain said unto the LORD, My punishment *is* greater than I can bear.
14 Behold, thou hast driven me out this day
from the face of the earth; and [a]from thy face
shall I be [b]hid; and I shall be a fugitive and a
vagabond in the earth; and it shall come to pass,
[c]*that* every one that findeth me shall slay me.
15 And the LORD said unto him, Therefore
whosoever slayeth Cain, vengeance shall be taken
on him [a]sevenfold. And the LORD set a [b]mark
upon Cain, lest any finding him should kill him.

The Family of Cain

16 And Cain [a]went out from the [b]presence
of the LORD, and dwelt in the land of Nod, on the
east of Eden.
17 And Cain knew his wife; and she conceived, and bare Enoch: and he builded a city,
[a]and called the name of the city, after the name
of his son, Enoch.
18 And unto Enoch was born Irad: and Irad
begat Mehujael: and Mehujael begat Methusael:
and Methusael begat Lamech.
19 And Lamech took unto him [a]two wives:
the name of the one *was* Adah, and the name of
the other Zillah.
20 And Adah bare Jabal: he was the father
of such as dwell in tents, and *of such as have*
cattle.
21 And his brother's name *was* Jubal: he was
the father of all such as handle the harp and
organ.
22 And Zillah, she also bare Tubal–cain, an
instructer of every artificer in brass and iron: and
the sister of Tubal–cain *was* Naamah.
23 And Lamech said unto his wives, Adah
and Zillah, Hear my voice; ye wives of Lamech,
hearken unto my speech: for I have slain a man
to my wounding, and a young man to my hurt.
24 [a]If Cain shall be avenged sevenfold, truly
Lamech seventy and sevenfold.

A New Son

25 And Adam knew his wife again; and she
bare a son, and [a]called his name Seth: For God,
said she, hath appointed me another seed instead
of Abel, whom Cain slew.
26 And to Seth, [a]to him also there was born
a son; and he called his name Enos: then began
men [b]to call upon the name of the LORD.

The Family of Adam
(1 Chr. 1:1–4; Luke 3:36–38)

5 This *is* the book of the [a]generations of Adam.
In the day that God created man, in [b]the likeness of God made he him;
2 [a]Male and female created he them; and

8 [a]Matt. 23:35; Luke 11:51; [1 John 3:12–15]; Jude 11
9 [a]John 8:44 [b]1 Cor. 8:11–13
10 [a]Num. 35:33; Deut. 21:1–9; Heb. 12:24; Rev. 6:9, 10
11 [a]Gen. 3:14; Deut. 11:28; 28:15–20; Gal. 3:10
14 [a]Ps. 51:11 [b]Deut. 31:18; Is. 1:15 [c]Gen. 9:6; Num. 35:19, 21, 27
15 [a]Gen. 4:24; Ps. 79:12 [b]Gen. 9:6; Ezek. 9:4, 6
16 [a]2 Kin. 13:23; 24:20; Jer. 23:39; 52:3 [b]Jon. 1:3
17 [a]Ps. 49:11
19 [a]Gen. 2:24; 16:3; 1 Tim. 3:2
24 [a]Gen. 4:15
25 [a]Gen. 5:3
26 [a]Gen. 5:6 [b]Gen. 12:8; 26:25; 1 Kin. 18:24; Ps. 116:17; Joel 2:32; Zeph. 3:9; 1 Cor. 1:2

CHAPTER 5

1 [a]Gen. 2:4; 6:9; 1 Chr. 1:1; Matt. 1:1 [b]Gen. 1:26; 9:6; [Eph. 4:24; Col. 3:10]
2 [a]Gen. 1:27; Deut. 4:32; Matt. 19:4; Mark 10:6

*

4:8 Sam., LXX, Syr., Vg. add *"Let us go out to the field."*
4:15 So with MT, Tg.; LXX, Syr., Vg. *Not so;*
4:26 Gr. *Enos,* Luke 3:38

NKJV

5 but He did not respect Cain and his offering. And Cain was very angry, and his countenance fell.
6 So the LORD said to Cain, "Why are you
angry? And why has your countenance fallen?
7 "If you do well, will you not be accepted?
And if you do not do well, sin lies at the door.
And its desire *is* for you, but you should rule over
it."
8 Now Cain talked with Abel his *brother;
and it came to pass, when they were in the field,
that Cain rose up against Abel his brother and
[a]killed him.
9 Then the LORD said to Cain, "Where *is*
Abel your brother?" He said, [a]"I do not know.
Am I [b]my brother's keeper?"
10 And He said, "What have you done? The
voice of your brother's blood [a]cries out to Me from
the ground.
11 "So now [a]you *are* cursed from the earth,
which has opened its mouth to receive your
brother's blood from your hand.
12 "When you till the ground, it shall no
longer yield its strength to you. A fugitive and a
vagabond you shall be on the earth."
13 And Cain said to the LORD, "My punishment *is* greater than I can bear!
14 "Surely You have driven me out this day
from the face of the ground; [a]I shall be [b]hidden
from Your face; I shall be a fugitive and a vagabond on the earth, and it will happen *that* [c]anyone
who finds me will kill me."
15 And the LORD said to him, *"Therefore,
whoever kills Cain, vengeance shall be taken on
him [a]sevenfold." And the LORD set a [b]mark on
Cain, lest anyone finding him should kill him.

The Family of Cain

16 Then Cain [a]went out from the [b]presence
of the LORD and dwelt in the land of Nod on the
east of Eden.
17 And Cain knew his wife, and she conceived and bore Enoch. And he built a city, [a]and
called the name of the city after the name of his
son—Enoch.
18 To Enoch was born Irad; and Irad begot
Mehujael, and Mehujael begot Methushael, and
Methushael begot Lamech.
19 Then Lamech took for himself [a]two wives:
the name of one *was* Adah, and the name of the
second *was* Zillah.
20 And Adah bore Jabal. He was the father
of those who dwell in tents and have livestock.
21 His brother's name *was* Jubal. He was the
father of all those who play the harp and flute.
22 And as for Zillah, she also bore Tubal-
Cain, an instructor of every craftsman in bronze
and iron. And the sister of Tubal-Cain *was*
Naamah.
23 Then Lamech said to his wives:

"Adah and Zillah, hear my voice;
Wives of Lamech, listen to my speech!
For I have killed a man for wounding me,
Even a young man for hurting me.
24 [a]If Cain shall be avenged sevenfold,
Then Lamech seventy-sevenfold."

A New Son

25 And Adam knew his wife again, and she
bore a son and [a]named him Seth, "For God has
appointed another seed for me instead of Abel,
whom Cain killed."
26 And as for Seth, [a]to him also a son was
born; and he named him *Enosh. Then *men* began
[b]to call on the name of the LORD.

The Family of Adam
(1 Chr. 1:1–4; Luke 3:36–38)

5 This is the book of the [a]genealogy of Adam.
In the day that God created man, He made
him in [b]the likeness of God.
2 He created them [a]male and female, and

KJV

[b]blessed them, and called their name Adam, in the day when they were created.

3 And Adam lived an hundred and thirty years, and begat *a son* [a]in his own likeness, after his image; and [b]called his name Seth:

4 [a]And the days of Adam after he had begotten Seth were eight hundred years: [b]and he begat sons and daughters:

5 And all the days that Adam lived were nine hundred and thirty years: [a]and he died.

6 And Seth lived an hundred and five years, and begat [a]Enos:

7 And Seth lived after he begat Enos eight hundred and seven years, and begat sons and daughters:

8 And all the days of Seth were nine hundred and twelve years: and he died.

9 And Enos lived ninety years, and begat Cainan:

10 And Enos lived after he begat Cainan eight hundred and fifteen years, and begat sons and daughters:

11 And all the days of Enos were nine hundred and five years: and he died.

12 And Cainan lived seventy years, and begat Mahalaleel:

13 And Cainan lived after he begat Mahalaleel eight hundred and forty years, and begat sons and daughters:

14 And all the days of Cainan were nine hundred and ten years: and he died.

15 And Mahalaleel lived sixty and five years, and begat Jared:

16 And Mahalaleel lived after he begat Jared eight hundred and thirty years, and begat sons and daughters:

17 And all the days of Mahalaleel were eight hundred ninety and five years: and he died.

18 And Jared lived an hundred sixty and two years, and he begat [a]Enoch:

19 And Jared lived after he begat Enoch eight hundred years, and begat sons and daughters:

20 And all the days of Jared were nine hundred sixty and two years: and he died.

21 And Enoch lived sixty and five years, and begat Methuselah:

22 And Enoch [a]walked with God after he begat Methuselah three hundred years, and begat sons and daughters:

23 And all the days of Enoch were three hundred sixty and five years:

24 And [a]Enoch walked with God: and he *was* not; for God [b]took him.

25 And Methuselah lived an hundred eighty and seven years, and begat Lamech:

26 And Methuselah lived after he begat Lamech seven hundred eighty and two years, and begat sons and daughters:

27 And all the days of Methuselah were nine hundred sixty and nine years: and he died.

28 And Lamech lived an hundred eighty and two years, and begat a son:

29 And he called his name [a]Noah, saying, This *same* shall comfort us concerning our work and toil of our hands, because of the ground [b]which the LORD hath cursed.

30 And Lamech lived after he begat Noah five hundred ninety and five years, and begat sons and daughters:

31 And all the days of Lamech were seven hundred seventy and seven years: and he died.

32 And Noah was five hundred years old: and Noah begat [a]Shem, Ham, [b]and Japheth.

The Wickedness and Judgment of Man

6 And it came to pass, [a]when men began to multiply on the face of the earth, and daughters were born unto them,

2 That the sons of God saw the daughters of men that they *were* fair; and they [a]took them wives of all which they chose.

3 And the LORD said, [a]My spirit shall not

2 [b]Gen. 1:28; 9:1
3 [a]1 Cor. 15:48, 49 [b]Gen. 4:25
4 [a]1 Chr. 1:1–4; Luke 3:36–38 [b]Gen. 1:28; 4:25
5 [a]Gen. 2:17; 3:19; 6:17; [Heb. 9:27]
6 [a]Gen. 4:26
18 [a]Jude 14, 15
22 [a]Gen. 6:9; 17:1; 24:40; 48:15; 2 Kin. 20:3; Ps. 16:8; [Mic. 6:8]; Mal. 2:6; 1 Thess. 2:12; [Heb. 11:39]
24 [a]2 Kin. 2:11; Jude 14 [b]2 Kin. 2:10; Ps. 49:15; 73:24; Heb. 11:5
29 [a]Luke 3:36; Heb. 11:7; 1 Pet. 3:20 [b]Gen. 3:17–19; 4:11
32 [a]Gen. 6:10; 7:13 [b]Gen. 10:21

CHAPTER 6
1 [a]Gen. 1:28
2 [a]Deut. 7:3, 4
3 [a]Gen. 41:38; [Gal. 5:16, 17]; 1 Pet. 3:19, 20

*5:9 Heb. *Qenan*

NKJV

[b]blessed them and called them Mankind in the day they were created.

3 And Adam lived one hundred and thirty years, and begot *a son* [a]in his own likeness, after his image, and [b]named him Seth.

4 After he begot Seth, [a]the days of Adam were eight hundred years; [b]and he had sons and daughters.

5 So all the days that Adam lived were nine hundred and thirty years; [a]and he died.

6 Seth lived one hundred and five years, and begot [a]Enosh.

7 After he begot Enosh, Seth lived eight hundred and seven years, and had sons and daughters.

8 So all the days of Seth were nine hundred and twelve years; and he died.

9 Enosh lived ninety years, and begot *Cainan.

10 After he begot Cainan, Enosh lived eight hundred and fifteen years, and had sons and daughters.

11 So all the days of Enosh were nine hundred and five years; and he died.

12 Cainan lived seventy years, and begot Mahalalel.

13 After he begot Mahalalel, Cainan lived eight hundred and forty years, and had sons and daughters.

14 So all the days of Cainan were nine hundred and ten years; and he died.

15 Mahalalel lived sixty-five years, and begot Jared.

16 After he begot Jared, Mahalalel lived eight hundred and thirty years, and had sons and daughters.

17 So all the days of Mahalalel were eight hundred and ninety-five years; and he died.

18 Jared lived one hundred and sixty-two years, and begot [a]Enoch.

19 After he begot Enoch, Jared lived eight hundred years, and had sons and daughters.

20 So all the days of Jared were nine hundred and sixty-two years; and he died.

21 Enoch lived sixty-five years, and begot Methuselah.

22 After he begot Methuselah, Enoch [a]walked with God three hundred years, and had sons and daughters.

23 So all the days of Enoch were three hundred and sixty-five years.

24 And [a]Enoch walked with God; and he *was* not, for God [b]took him.

25 Methuselah lived one hundred and eighty-seven years, and begot Lamech.

26 After he begot Lamech, Methuselah lived seven hundred and eighty-two years, and had sons and daughters.

27 So all the days of Methuselah were nine hundred and sixty-nine years; and he died.

28 Lamech lived one hundred and eighty-two years, and had a son.

29 And he called his name [a]Noah, saying, "This *one* will comfort us concerning our work and the toil of our hands, because of the ground [b]which the LORD has cursed."

30 After he begot Noah, Lamech lived five hundred and ninety-five years, and had sons and daughters.

31 So all the days of Lamech were seven hundred and seventy-seven years; and he died.

32 And Noah was five hundred years old, and Noah begot [a]Shem, Ham, [b]and Japheth.

The Wickedness and Judgment of Man

6 Now it came to pass, [a]when men began to multiply on the face of the earth, and daughters were born to them,

2 that the sons of God saw the daughters of men, that they *were* beautiful; and they [a]took wives for themselves of all whom they chose.

3 And the LORD said, [a]"My Spirit shall not

KJV

always [b]strive with man, [c]for that he also *is* flesh: yet his days shall be an hundred and twenty years.

4 There were giants in the earth in those [a]days; and also after that, when the sons of God came in unto the daughters of men, and they bare *children* to them, the same *became* mighty men which *were* of old, men of renown.

5 And GOD saw that the wickedness of man *was* great in the earth, and *that* every [a]imagination of the thoughts of his heart *was* only evil continually.

6 And [a]it repented the LORD that he had made man on the earth, and it [b]grieved him at his [c]heart.

7 And the LORD said, I will [a]destroy man whom I have created from the face of the earth; both man, and beast, and the creeping thing, and the fowls of the air; for it repenteth me that I have made them.

8 But Noah [a]found grace in the eyes of the LORD.

Noah Pleases God

9 These *are* the generations of Noah: [a]Noah was a just man *and* perfect in his generations, *and* Noah [b]walked with God.

10 And Noah begat three sons, [a]Shem, Ham, and Japheth.

11 The earth also was corrupt [a]before God, and the earth was [b]filled with violence.

12 And God [a]looked upon the earth, and, behold, it was corrupt; for [b]all flesh had corrupted his way upon the earth.

The Ark Prepared
(Heb. 11:7; 1 Pet. 3:20)

13 And God said unto Noah, [a]The end of all flesh is come before me; for the earth is filled with violence through them; [b]and, behold, [c]I will destroy them with the earth.

14 Make thee an ark of gopher wood; rooms shalt thou make in the ark, and shalt pitch it within and without with pitch.

15 And this *is the fashion* which thou shalt make it *of:* The length of the ark *shall be* three hundred cubits, the breadth of it fifty cubits, and the height of it thirty cubits.

16 A window shalt thou make to the ark, and in a cubit shalt thou finish it above; and the door of the ark shalt thou set in the side thereof; *with* lower, second, and third *stories* shalt thou make it.

17 [a]And, behold, I, even I, do bring a [b]flood of waters upon the earth, to destroy all flesh, wherein *is* the breath of life, from under heaven; *and* every thing that *is* in the earth shall [c]die.

18 But with thee will I establish my [a]covenant; and [b]thou shalt come into the ark, thou, and thy sons, and thy wife, and thy sons' wives with thee.

19 And of every living thing of all flesh, [a]two of every *sort* shalt thou bring into the ark, to keep *them* alive with thee; they shall be male and female.

20 Of fowls after their kind, and of cattle after their kind, of every creeping thing of the earth after his kind, two of every *sort* [a]shall come unto thee, to keep *them* alive.

21 And take thou unto thee of all food that is eaten, and thou shalt gather *it* to thee; and it shall be for food for thee, and for them.

22 [a]Thus did Noah; [b]according to all that [c]God commanded him, so did he.

The Great Flood
(Luke 17:26, 27)

7 And the [a]LORD said unto Noah, [b]Come thou and all thy house into the ark; for [c]thee have I seen righteous before me in this generation.

---

3 [b]2 Thess. 2:7 [c]Ps. 78:39
4 [a]Num. 13:32, 33; Luke 17:27
5 [a]Gen. 8:21; Ps. 14:1–3; Prov. 6:18; Matt. 15:19; Rom. 1:28–32
6 [a]Gen. 6:7; 1 Sam. 15:11, 29; 2 Sam. 24:16; Jer. 18:7–10; Zech. 8:14 [b]Ps. 78:40; Is. 63:10; Eph. 4:30 [c]Mark 3:5
7 [a]Gen. 7:4, 23; Deut. 28:63; 29:20; Ps. 7:11
8 [a]Gen. 19:19; Ex. 33:12, 17; Luke 1:30; Acts 7:46
9 [a]Gen. 7:1; Ezek. 14:14, 20; Heb. 11:7; 2 Pet. 2:5 [b]Gen. 5:22, 24; 2 Kin. 23:3
10 [a]Gen. 5:32; 7:13
11 [a]Deut. 31:29; Judg. 2:19; Rom. 2:13 [b]Ezek. 8:17
12 [a]Ps. 14:2; 53:2, 3 [b]Ps. 14:1–3; Is. 28:8
13 [a]Is. 34:1–4; Jer. 51:13; Ezek. 7:2, 3; Amos 8:2; 1 Pet. 4:7 [b]Gen. 6:17 [c]2 Pet. 2:4–10
17 [a]Gen. 7:4, 21–23; 2 Pet. 2:5 [b]2 Pet. 3:6 [c]Luke 16:22
18 [a]Gen. 8:20—9:17; 17:7 [b]Gen. 7:1, 7, 13; 1 Pet. 3:20; 2 Pet. 2:5
19 [a]Gen. 7:2, 8, 9, 14–16
20 [a]Gen. 7:9, 15
22 [a]Gen. 7:5; 12:4, 5; Heb. 11:7 [b]Gen. 7:5, 9, 16 [c][1 John 5:3]

CHAPTER 7

1 [a]Matt. 11:28 [b]Matt. 24:38; Luke 17:26; Heb. 11:7; 1 Pet. 3:20; 2 Pet. 2:5 [c]Gen. 6:9; Ps. 33:18; Prov. 10:9; 2 Pet. 2:9

*

6:3 LXX, Syr., Tg., Vg. *abide*
6:5 So with MT, Tg.; Vg. *God;* LXX LORD *God*

NKJV

[b]strive* with man forever, [c]for he *is* indeed flesh; yet his days shall be one hundred and twenty years."

4 There were giants on the earth in those [a]days, and also afterward, when the sons of God came in to the daughters of men and they bore *children* to them. Those *were* the mighty men who *were* of old, men of renown.

5 Then *the LORD saw that the wickedness of man *was* great in the earth, and *that* every [a]intent of the thoughts of his heart *was* only evil continually.

6 And [a]the LORD was sorry that He had made man on the earth, and [b]He was grieved in His [c]heart.

7 So the LORD said, "I will [a]destroy man whom I have created from the face of the earth, both man and beast, creeping thing and birds of the air, for I am sorry that I have made them."

8 But Noah [a]found grace in the eyes of the LORD.

Noah Pleases God

9 This is the genealogy of Noah. [a]Noah was a just man, perfect in his generations. Noah [b]walked with God.

10 And Noah begot three sons: [a]Shem, Ham, and Japheth.

11 The earth also was corrupt [a]before God, and the earth was [b]filled with violence.

12 So God [a]looked upon the earth, and indeed it was corrupt; for [b]all flesh had corrupted their way on the earth.

The Ark Prepared
(Heb. 11:7; 1 Pet. 3:20)

13 And God said to Noah, [a]"The end of all flesh has come before Me, for the earth is filled with violence through them; [b]and behold, [c]I will destroy them with the earth.

14 "Make yourself an ark of gopherwood; make rooms in the ark, and cover it inside and outside with pitch.

15 "And this is how you shall make it: The length of the ark *shall be* three hundred cubits, its width fifty cubits, and its height thirty cubits.

16 "You shall make a window for the ark, and you shall finish it to a cubit from above; and set the door of the ark in its side. You shall make it *with* lower, second, and third *decks.*

17 [a]"And behold, I Myself am bringing [b]floodwaters on the earth, to destroy from under heaven all flesh in which *is* the breath of life; everything that *is* on the earth shall [c]die.

18 "But I will establish My [a]covenant with you; and [b]you shall go into the ark—you, your sons, your wife, and your sons' wives with you.

19 "And of every living thing of all flesh you shall bring [a]two of every *sort* into the ark, to keep *them* alive with you; they shall be male and female.

20 "Of the birds after their kind, of animals after their kind, and of every creeping thing of the earth after its kind, two of every *kind* [a]will come to you to keep *them* alive.

21 "And you shall take for yourself of all food that is eaten, and you shall gather *it* to yourself; and it shall be food for you and for them."

22 [a]Thus Noah did; [b]according to all that [c]God commanded him, so he did.

The Great Flood
(Luke 17:26, 27)

7 Then the [a]LORD said to Noah, [b]"Come into the ark, you and all your household, because I have seen *that* [c]you *are* righteous before Me in this generation.

KJV

2 Of every [a]clean beast thou shalt take to thee by sevens, the male and his female: [b]and of beasts that *are* not clean by two, the male and his female.

3 Of fowls also of the air by sevens, the male and the female; to keep seed alive upon the face of all the earth.

4 For yet [a]seven days, and I will cause it to rain upon the earth [b]forty days and forty nights; and every living substance that I have made will I destroy from off the face of the earth.

5 [a]And Noah did according unto all that the LORD commanded him.

6 And Noah *was* [a]six hundred years old when the flood of waters was upon the earth.

7 [a]And Noah went in, and his sons, and his wife, and his sons' wives with him, into the ark, because of the waters of the flood.

8 Of clean beasts, and of beasts that *are* not clean, and of fowls, and of every thing that creepeth upon the earth,

9 There went in two and two unto Noah into the ark, the male and the female, as God had commanded Noah.

10 And it came to pass after seven days, that the waters of the flood were upon the earth.

11 In the six hundredth year of Noah's life, in the second month, the seventeenth day of the month, the [a]same day were all [b]the fountains of the great deep broken up, and the [c]windows of heaven were opened.

12 [a]And the rain was upon the earth forty days and forty nights.

13 In the selfsame day entered Noah, and Shem, and Ham, and Japheth, the sons of Noah, and Noah's wife, and the three wives of his sons with them, into the ark;

14 [a]They, and every beast after his kind, and all the cattle after their kind, and every creeping thing that creepeth upon the earth after his kind, and every fowl after his kind, every bird of every [b]sort.

15 And they [a]went in unto Noah into the ark, two and two of all flesh, wherein *is* the breath of life.

16 And they that went in, went in male and female of all flesh, [a]as God had commanded him: and the LORD shut him in.

17 [a]And the flood was forty days upon the earth; and the waters increased, and bare up the ark, and it was lift up above the earth.

18 And the waters prevailed, and were increased greatly upon the earth; [a]and the ark went upon the face of the waters.

19 And the waters prevailed exceedingly upon the earth; and all the high hills, that *were* under the whole heaven, were covered.

20 Fifteen cubits upward did the waters prevail; and the mountains were covered.

21 [a]And all flesh died that moved upon the earth, both of fowl, and of cattle, and of beast, and of every creeping thing that creepeth upon the earth, and every man:

22 All in [a]whose nostrils *was* the breath of life, of all that *was* in the dry *land,* died.

23 And every living substance was destroyed which was upon the face of the ground, both man, and cattle, and the creeping things, and the fowl of the heaven; and they were destroyed from the earth: and [a]Noah only remained *alive,* and they that *were* with him in the ark.

24 [a]And the waters prevailed upon the earth an hundred and fifty days.

Noah's Deliverance

8 And God [a]remembered Noah, and every living thing, and all the cattle that *was* with him in the ark: [b]and God made a wind to pass over the earth, and the waters asswaged;

2 [a]The fountains also of the deep and the windows of heaven were [b]stopped, and [c]the rain from heaven was restrained;

2 [a]Lev. 11; Deut. 14:3–20 [b]Lev. 10:10; Ezek. 44:23
4 [a]Gen. 7:10; Ex. 7:25 [b]Gen. 7:12, 17
5 [a]Gen. 6:22
6 [a]Gen. 5:4, 32
7 [a]Gen. 6:18; 7:1, 13; Matt. 24:38; Luke 17:27
11 [a]Matt. 24:39; Luke 17:27; 2 Pet. 2:5; 3:6 [b]Gen. 8:2; Prov. 8:28; Is. 51:10; Ezek. 26:19 [c]Gen. 8:2; Ps. 78:23
12 [a]Gen. 7:4, 17; 1 Sam. 12:18
14 [a]Gen. 6:19 [b]Gen. 1:21
15 [a]Gen. 6:19, 20; 7:9
16 [a]Gen. 7:2, 3
17 [a]Gen. 7:4, 12; 8:6
18 [a]Ps. 104:26
21 [a]Gen. 6:7, 13, 17; 7:4
22 [a]Gen. 2:7
23 [a]Matt. 24:38, 39; Luke 17:26, 27; Heb. 11:7; 1 Pet. 3:20; 2 Pet. 2:5
24 [a]Gen. 8:3, 4

CHAPTER 8

1 [a]Gen. 19:29; Ex. 2:24; 1 Sam. 1:19; Ps. 105:42; 106:4 [b]Ex. 14:21; 15:10; Job 12:15; Ps. 29:10; Is. 44:27; Nah. 1:4
2 [a]Gen. 7:11 [b]Deut. 11:17 [c]Gen. 7:4, 12; Job 38:37

*

7:22 LXX, Vg. omit *of the spirit*

NKJV

2 "You shall take with you seven each of every [a]clean animal, a male and his female; [b]two each of animals that *are* unclean, a male and his female;

3 "also seven each of birds of the air, male and female, to keep the species alive on the face of all the earth.

4 "For after [a]seven more days I will cause it to rain on the earth [b]forty days and forty nights, and I will destroy from the face of the earth all living things that I have made."

5 [a]And Noah did according to all that the LORD commanded him.

6 Noah *was* [a]six hundred years old when the floodwaters were on the earth.

7 [a]So Noah, with his sons, his wife, and his sons' wives, went into the ark because of the waters of the flood.

8 Of clean animals, of animals that *are* unclean, of birds, and of everything that creeps on the earth,

9 two by two they went into the ark to Noah, male and female, as God had commanded Noah.

10 And it came to pass after seven days that the waters of the flood were on the earth.

11 In the six hundredth year of Noah's life, in the second month, the seventeenth day of the month, on [a]that day all [b]the fountains of the great deep were broken up, and the [c]windows of heaven were opened.

12 [a]And the rain was on the earth forty days and forty nights.

13 On the very same day Noah and Noah's sons, Shem, Ham, and Japheth, and Noah's wife and the three wives of his sons with them, entered the ark—

14 [a]they and every beast after its kind, all cattle after their kind, every creeping thing that creeps on the earth after its kind, and every bird after its kind, every bird of every [b]sort.

15 And they [a]went into the ark to Noah, two by two, of all flesh in which *is* the breath of life.

16 So those that entered, male and female of all flesh, went in [a]as God had commanded him; and the LORD shut him in.

17 [a]Now the flood was on the earth forty days. The waters increased and lifted up the ark, and it rose high above the earth.

18 The waters prevailed and greatly increased on the earth, [a]and the ark moved about on the surface of the waters.

19 And the waters prevailed exceedingly on the earth, and all the high hills under the whole heaven were covered.

20 The waters prevailed fifteen cubits upward, and the mountains were covered.

21 [a]And all flesh died that moved on the earth: birds and cattle and beasts and every creeping thing that creeps on the earth, and every man.

22 All in [a]whose nostrils *was* the breath *of the spirit of life, all that *was* on the dry *land,* died.

23 So He destroyed all living things which were on the face of the ground: both man and cattle, creeping thing and bird of the air. They were destroyed from the earth. Only [a]Noah and those who *were* with him in the ark remained *alive.*

24 [a]And the waters prevailed on the earth one hundred and fifty days.

Noah's Deliverance

8 Then God [a]remembered Noah, and every living thing, and all the animals that *were* with him in the ark. [b]And God made a wind to pass over the earth, and the waters subsided.

2 [a]The fountains of the deep and the windows of heaven were also [b]stopped, and [c]the rain from heaven was restrained.

KJV

3 And the waters returned from off the earth continually: and after the end [a]of the hundred and fifty days the waters were abated.
4 And the ark rested in the seventh month, on the seventeenth day of the month, upon the mountains of Ararat.
5 And the waters decreased continually until the tenth month: in the tenth *month,* on the first *day* of the month, were the tops of the mountains seen.
6 And it came to pass at the end of forty days, that Noah opened [a]the window of the ark which he had made:
7 And he sent forth a raven, which went forth to and fro, until the waters were dried up from off the earth.
8 Also he sent forth a dove from him, to see if the waters were abated from off the face of the ground;
9 But the dove found no rest for the sole of her foot, and she returned unto him into the ark, for the waters *were* on the face of the whole earth: then he put forth his hand, and took her, and pulled her in unto him into the ark.
10 And he stayed yet other seven days; and again he sent forth the dove out of the ark;
11 And the dove came in to him in the evening; and, lo, in her mouth *was* an olive leaf pluckt off: so Noah knew that the waters were abated from off the earth.
12 And he stayed yet other seven days; and sent forth the dove; which returned not again unto him any more.
13 And it came to pass in the six hundredth and first year, in the first *month,* the first *day* of the month, the waters were dried up from off the earth: and Noah removed the covering of the ark, and looked, and, behold, the face of the ground was dry.
14 And in the second month, on the seven and twentieth day of the month, was the earth dried.
15 And God spake unto Noah, saying,
16 Go forth of the ark, [a]thou, and thy wife, and thy sons, and thy sons' wives with thee.
17 Bring forth with thee every living thing that *is* with thee, of all flesh, *both* of fowl, and of cattle, and of every creeping thing that creepeth upon the earth; that they may breed abundantly in the earth, and [a]be fruitful, and multiply upon the earth.
18 And Noah went forth, and his sons, and his wife, and his sons' wives with him:
19 Every beast, every creeping thing, and every fowl, *and* whatsoever creepeth upon the earth, after their kinds, went forth out of the ark.

God's Covenant with Creation

20 And Noah builded an [a]altar unto the LORD; and took of [b]every clean beast, and of every clean fowl, and offered [c]burnt offerings on the altar.
21 And the LORD smelled [a]a sweet savour; and the LORD said in his heart, I will not again [b]curse the ground any more for man's sake; for the [c]imagination of man's heart *is* evil from his youth; [d]neither will I again smite any more every thing living, as I have done.
22 [a]While the earth remaineth, seedtime and harvest, and cold and heat, and summer and winter, and [b]day and night shall not cease.

9 And God blessed Noah and his sons, and said unto them, [a]Be fruitful, and multiply, and replenish the earth.
2 [a]And the fear of you and the dread of you shall be upon every beast of the earth, and upon every fowl of the air, upon all that moveth *upon*

3 [a]Gen. 7:24 **6** [a]Gen. 6:16 **16** [a]Gen. 7:13 **17** [a]Gen. 1:22, 28; 9:1, 7 **20** [a]Gen. 12:7; Ex. 29:18, 25 [b]Gen. 7:2; Lev. 11 [c]Gen. 22:2; Ex. 10:25 **21** [a]Ex. 29:18, 25; Lev. 1:9; Ezek. 20:41; 2 Cor. 2:15; Eph. 5:2 [b]Gen. 3:17; 6:7, 13, 17; Is. 54:9 [c]Gen. 6:5; 11:6; Job 14:4; Ps. 51:5; Jer. 17:9; Rom. 1:21; 3:23; Eph. 2:1–3 [d]Gen. 9:11, 15 **22** [a]Is. 54:9 [b]Ps. 74:16; Jer. 33:20, 25

CHAPTER 9

1 [a]Gen. 1:28, 29; 8:17; 9:7, 19; 10:32 **2** [a]Gen. 1:26, 28; Ps. 8:6

NKJV

3 And the waters receded continually from the earth. At the end [a]of the hundred and fifty days the waters decreased.
4 Then the ark rested in the seventh month, the seventeenth day of the month, on the mountains of Ararat.
5 And the waters decreased continually until the tenth month. In the tenth *month,* on the first *day* of the month, the tops of the mountains were seen.
6 So it came to pass, at the end of forty days, that Noah opened [a]the window of the ark which he had made.
7 Then he sent out a raven, which kept going to and fro until the waters had dried up from the earth.
8 He also sent out from himself a dove, to see if the waters had receded from the face of the ground.
9 But the dove found no resting place for the sole of her foot, and she returned into the ark to him, for the waters *were* on the face of the whole earth. So he put out his hand and took her, and drew her into the ark to himself.
10 And he waited yet another seven days, and again he sent the dove out from the ark.
11 Then the dove came to him in the evening, and behold, a freshly plucked olive leaf *was* in her mouth; and Noah knew that the waters had receded from the earth.
12 So he waited yet another seven days and sent out the dove, which did not return again to him anymore.
13 And it came to pass in the six hundred and first year, in the first *month,* the first *day* of the month, that the waters were dried up from the earth; and Noah removed the covering of the ark and looked, and indeed the surface of the ground was dry.
14 And in the second month, on the twenty-seventh day of the month, the earth was dried.
15 Then God spoke to Noah, saying,
16 "Go out of the ark, [a]you and your wife, and your sons and your sons' wives with you.
17 "Bring out with you every living thing of all flesh that *is* with you: birds and cattle and every creeping thing that creeps on the earth, so that they may abound on the earth, and [a]be fruitful and multiply on the earth."
18 So Noah went out, and his sons and his wife and his sons' wives with him.
19 Every animal, every creeping thing, every bird, *and* whatever creeps on the earth, according to their families, went out of the ark.

God's Covenant with Creation

20 Then Noah built an [a]altar to the LORD, and took of [b]every clean animal and of every clean bird, and offered [c]burnt offerings on the altar.
21 And the LORD smelled [a]a soothing aroma. Then the LORD said in His heart, "I will never again [b]curse the ground for man's sake, although the [c]imagination of man's heart *is* evil from his youth; [d]nor will I again destroy every living thing as I have done.

22 "While the earth [a]remains,
Seedtime and harvest,
Cold and heat,
Winter and summer,
And [b]day and night
Shall not cease."

9 So God blessed Noah and his sons, and said to them: [a]"Be fruitful and multiply, and fill the earth.
2 [a]"And the fear of you and the dread of you shall be on every beast of the earth, on every bird of the air, on all that move *on* the earth, and

KJV

the earth, and upon all the fishes of the sea; into your hand are they delivered.

3 [a]Every moving thing that liveth shall be meat for you; even as the [c]green herb have I given you [b]all things.

4 [a]But flesh with the life thereof, *which is* the blood thereof, shall ye not eat.

5 And surely your blood of your lives will I require; [a]at the hand of every beast will I require it, and [b]at the hand of man; at the hand of every [c]man's brother will I require the life of man.

6 [a]Whoso sheddeth man's blood, by man shall his blood be shed: [b]for in the image of God made he man.

7 And you, [a]be ye fruitful, and multiply; bring forth abundantly in the earth, and multiply therein.

8 And God spake unto Noah, and to his sons with him, saying,

9 And I, [a]behold, I establish [b]my covenant with you, and with your seed after you;

10 [a]And with every living creature that *is* with you, of the fowl, of the cattle, and of every beast of the earth with you; from all that go out of the ark, to every beast of the earth.

11 And [a]I will establish my covenant with you; neither shall all flesh be cut off any more by the waters of a flood; neither shall there any more be a flood to destroy the earth.

12 And God said, [a]This *is* the token of the covenant which I make between me and you and every living creature that *is* with you, for perpetual generations:

13 I do set [a]my bow in the cloud, and it shall be for a token of a covenant between me and the earth.

14 And it shall come to pass, when I bring a cloud over the earth, that the bow shall be seen in the cloud:

15 And [a]I will remember my covenant, which *is* between me and you and every living creature of all flesh; and the waters shall no more become a flood to destroy all flesh.

16 And the bow shall be in the cloud; and I will look upon it, that I may remember [a]the everlasting covenant between God and every living creature of all flesh that *is* upon the earth.

17 And God said unto Noah, This *is* the token of the covenant, which I have established between me and all flesh that *is* upon the earth.

Noah and His Sons

18 And the sons of Noah, that went forth of the ark, were Shem, and Ham, and Japheth: [a]and Ham *is* the father of Canaan.

19 [a]These *are* the three sons of Noah: [b]and of them was the whole earth overspread.

20 And Noah began *to be* [a]an husbandman, and he planted a vineyard:

21 And he drank of the wine, [a]and was drunken; and he was uncovered within his tent.

22 And Ham, the father of Canaan, saw the nakedness of his father, and told his two brethren without.

23 [a]And Shem and Japheth took a garment, and laid *it* upon both their shoulders, and went backward, and covered the nakedness of their father; and their faces *were* backward, and they saw not their father's nakedness.

24 And Noah awoke from his wine, and knew what his younger son had done unto him.

25 And he said, [a]Cursed *be* Canaan; a [b]servant of servants shall he be unto his brethren.

NKJV

on all the fish of the sea. They are given into your hand.

3 [a]"Every moving thing that lives shall be food for you. I have given you [b]all things, even as the [c]green herbs.

4 [a]"But you shall not eat flesh with its life, *that is,* its blood.

5 "Surely for your lifeblood I will demand *a reckoning;* [a]from the hand of every beast I will require it, and [b]from the hand of man. From the hand of every [c]man's brother I will require the life of man.

6 "Whoever [a]sheds man's blood,
By man his blood shall be shed;
[b]For in the image of God
He made man.
7 And as for you, [a]be fruitful and multiply;
Bring forth abundantly in the earth
And multiply in it."

8 Then God spoke to Noah and to his sons with him, saying:

9 "And as for Me, [a]behold, I establish [b]My covenant with you and with your *descendants after you,

10 [a]"and with every living creature that *is* with you: the birds, the cattle, and every beast of the earth with you, of all that go out of the ark, every beast of the earth.

11 "Thus [a]I establish My covenant with you: Never again shall all flesh be cut off by the waters of the flood; never again shall there be a flood to destroy the earth."

12 And God said: [a]"This *is* the sign of the covenant which I make between Me and you, and every living creature that *is* with you, for perpetual generations:

13 "I set [a]My rainbow in the cloud, and it shall be for the sign of the covenant between Me and the earth.

14 "It shall be, when I bring a cloud over the earth, that the rainbow shall be seen in the cloud;

15 "and [a]I will remember My covenant which *is* between Me and you and every living creature of all flesh; the waters shall never again become a flood to destroy all flesh.

16 "The rainbow shall be in the cloud, and I will look on it to remember [a]the everlasting covenant between God and every living creature of all flesh that *is* on the earth."

17 And God said to Noah, "This *is* the sign of the covenant which I have established between Me and all flesh that *is* on the earth."

Noah and His Sons

18 Now the sons of Noah who went out of the ark were Shem, Ham, and Japheth. [a]And Ham *was* the father of Canaan.

19 [a]These three *were* the sons of Noah, [b]and from these the whole earth was populated.

20 And Noah began *to be* [a]a farmer, and he planted a vineyard.

21 Then he drank of the wine [a]and was drunk, and became uncovered in his tent.

22 And Ham, the father of Canaan, saw the nakedness of his father, and told his two brothers outside.

23 [a]But Shem and Japheth took a garment, laid *it* on both their shoulders, and went backward and covered the nakedness of their father. Their faces *were* turned away, and they did not see their father's nakedness.

24 So Noah awoke from his wine, and knew what his younger son had done to him.

25 Then he said:

[a]"Cursed *be* Canaan;
A [b]servant of servants
He shall be to his brethren."

---

3 [a]Deut. 12:15; 14:3, 9, 11; Acts 10:12, 13 [b]Rom. 14:14, 20; 1 Cor. 10:23, 26; Col. 2:16; [1 Tim. 4:3, 4] [c]Gen. 1:29
4 [a]Lev. 7:26; 17:10–16; 19:26; Deut. 12:16, 23; 15:23; 1 Sam. 14:33, 34; Acts 15:20, 29
5 [a]Ex. 21:28 [b]Gen. 4:9, 10; Ps. 9:12 [c]Acts 17:26
6 [a]Ex. 21:12–14; Lev. 24:17; Num. 35:33; Matt. 26:52 [b]Gen. 1:26, 27
7 [a]Gen. 9:1, 19
9 [a]Gen. 6:18 [b]Is. 54:9
10 [a]Ps. 145:9
11 [a]Gen. 8:21; Is. 54:9
12 [a]Gen. 9:13, 17; 17:11
13 [a]Ezek. 1:28; Rev. 4:3
15 [a]Lev. 26:42, 45; Deut. 7:9; Ezek. 16:60
16 [a]Gen. 17:13, 19; 2 Sam. 23:5; Is. 55:3; Jer. 32:40; Heb. 13:20
18 [a]Gen. 9:25–27; 10:6
19 [a]Gen. 5:32 [b]Gen. 9:1, 7; 10:32; 1 Chr. 1:4
20 [a]Gen. 3:19, 23; 4:2; Prov. 12:11; Jer. 31:24
21 [a]Prov. 20:1; Eph. 5:18
23 [a]Ex. 20:12; Gal. 6:1
25 [a]Deut. 27:16; Josh. 9:23, 27 [b]Josh. 9:23; 1 Kin. 9:20, 21

*______

9:9 Lit. *seed*

KJV

26 And he said, [a]Blessed *be* the LORD God
of Shem; and Canaan shall be his servant.
27 God shall [a]enlarge Japheth, [b]and he shall
dwell in the tents of Shem; and Canaan shall be
his servant.
28 And Noah lived after the flood three hundred and fifty years.
29 And all the days of Noah were nine hundred and fifty years: and he died.

Nations Descended from Noah
(1 Chr. 1:5–27)

10 Now these *are* the generations of the sons
of Noah, Shem, Ham, and Japheth: [a]and
unto them were sons born after the flood.
2 [a]The sons of Japheth; Gomer, and Magog,
and Madai, and Javan, and Tubal, and Meshech,
and Tiras.
3 And the sons of Gomer; Ashkenaz, and
Riphath, and Togarmah.
4 And the sons of Javan; Elishah, and
Tarshish, Kittim, and Dodanim.
5 By these were [a]the isles of the Gentiles
divided in their lands; every one after his tongue,
after their families, in their nations.
6 [a]And the sons of Ham; Cush, and
Mizraim, and Phut, and Canaan.
7 And the sons of Cush; Seba, and Havilah,
and Sabtah, and Raamah, and Sabtechah: and the
sons of Raamah; Sheba, and Dedan.
8 And Cush begat [a]Nimrod: he began to be
a mighty one in the earth.
9 He was a mighty [a]hunter [b]before the
LORD: wherefore it is said, Even as Nimrod the
mighty hunter before the LORD.
10 [a]And the beginning of his kingdom was
[b]Babel, and Erech, and Accad, and Calneh, in the
land of Shinar.
11 Out of that land went [a]forth Asshur, and
builded Nineveh, and the city Rehoboth, and
Calah,
12 And Resen between Nineveh and Calah:
the same *is* a great city.
13 And Mizraim begat Ludim, and Anamim,
and Lehabim, and Naphtuhim,
14 And Pathrusim, and Casluhim, ([a]out of
whom came Philistim,) and Caphtorim.
15 And Canaan begat Sidon his firstborn,
and [a]Heth,
16 [a]And the Jebusite, and the Amorite, and
the Girgasite,
17 And the Hivite, and the Arkite, and the
Sinite,
18 And the Arvadite, and the Zemarite, and
the Hamathite: and afterward were the families
of the Canaanites spread abroad.
19 [a]And the border of the Canaanites was
from Sidon, as thou comest to Gerar, unto Gaza;
as thou goest, unto Sodom, and Gomorrah, and
Admah, and Zeboim, even unto Lasha.
20 These *are* the sons of Ham, after their families, after their tongues, in their countries, *and*
in their nations.
21 Unto Shem also, the father of all the children of Eber, the brother of Japheth the elder,
even to him were *children* born.
22 The [a]children of Shem; Elam, and Asshur,
and [b]Arphaxad, and Lud, and Aram.
23 And the children of Aram; Uz, and Hul,
and Gether, and Mash.
24 And Arphaxad begat [a]Salah; and Salah
begat Eber.
25 [a]And unto Eber were born two sons: the
name of one *was* Peleg; for in his days was the
earth divided; and his brother's name *was* Joktan.
26 And Joktan begat Almodad, and Sheleph,
and Hazar–maveth, and Jerah,
27 And Hadoram, and Uzal, and Diklah,

26 [a]Gen. 14:20; 24:27; Ps. 144:15; Heb. 11:16
27 [a]Gen. 10:2–5; 39:3; Is. 66:19 [b]Luke 3:36; John 1:14; Eph. 2:13, 14; 3:6

CHAPTER 10

1 [a]Gen. 9:1, 7, 19
2 [a]1 Chr. 1:5–7
5 [a]Gen. 11:8; Ps. 72:10; Jer. 2:10; 25:22
6 [a]1 Chr. 1:8–16
8 [a]Mic. 5:6
9 [a]Jer. 16:16; Mic. 7:2 [b]Gen. 21:20
10 [a]Mic. 5:6 [b]Gen. 11:9
11 [a]Gen. 25:18; 2 Kin. 19:36; Mic. 5:6
14 [a]1 Chr. 1:12
15 [a]Gen. 23:3
16 [a]Gen. 14:7; 15:19–21; Deut. 7:1; Neh. 9:8
19 [a]Gen. 13:12, 14, 15, 17; 15:18–21; Num. 34:2–12
22 [a]Gen. 11:10–26; 1 Chr. 1:17–28 [b]Gen. 10:24; 11:10; Luke 3:36
24 [a]Gen. 11:12; Luke 3:35
25 [a]1 Chr. 1:19

*

10:3 *Diphath,* 1 Chr. 1:6
10:4 Sam. *Rodanim* and 1 Chr. 1:7
10:6 Or *Phut*
10:23 LXX *Meshech* and 1 Chr. 1:17
10:24 So with MT, Vg., Tg.; LXX *Arphaxad begot Cainan, and Cainan begot Salah* (cf. Luke 3:35, 36)

NKJV

26 And he said:

[a]"Blessed *be* the LORD,
The God of Shem,
And may Canaan be his servant.
27 May God [a]enlarge Japheth,
[b]And may he dwell in the tents of Shem;
And may Canaan be his servant."

28 And Noah lived after the flood three hundred and fifty years.
29 So all the days of Noah were nine hundred
and fifty years; and he died.

Nations Descended from Noah
(1 Chr. 1:5–27)

10 Now this *is* the genealogy of the sons of
Noah: Shem, Ham, and Japheth. [a]And sons
were born to them after the flood.
2 [a]The sons of Japheth *were* Gomer, Magog,
Madai, Javan, Tubal, Meshech, and Tiras.
3 The sons of Gomer *were* Ashkenaz, *Riphath, and Togarmah.
4 The sons of Javan *were* Elishah, Tarshish,
Kittim, and *Dodanim.
5 From these [a]the coastland *peoples* of the
Gentiles were separated into their lands, everyone
according to his language, according to their families, into their nations.
6 [a]The sons of Ham *were* Cush, Mizraim,
*Put, and Canaan.
7 The sons of Cush *were* Seba, Havilah,
Sabtah, Raamah, and Sabtechah; and the sons of
Raamah *were* Sheba and Dedan.
8 Cush begot [a]Nimrod; he began to be a
mighty one on the earth.
9 He was a mighty [a]hunter [b]before the
LORD; therefore it is said, "Like Nimrod the
mighty hunter before the LORD."
10 [a]And the beginning of his kingdom was
[b]Babel, Erech, Accad, and Calneh, in the land of
Shinar.
11 From that land he went [a]to Assyria and
built Nineveh, Rehoboth Ir, Calah,
12 and Resen between Nineveh and Calah
(that *is* the principal city).
13 Mizraim begot Ludim, Anamim, Lehabim,
Naphtuhim,
14 Pathrusim, and Casluhim [a](from whom
came the Philistines and Caphtorim).
15 Canaan begot Sidon his firstborn, and
[a]Heth;
16 [a]the Jebusite, the Amorite, and the Girgashite;
17 the Hivite, the Arkite, and the Sinite;
18 the Arvadite, the Zemarite, and the Hamathite. Afterward the families of the Canaanites
were dispersed.
19 [a]And the border of the Canaanites was
from Sidon as you go toward Gerar, as far as
Gaza; then as you go toward Sodom, Gomorrah,
Admah, and Zeboiim, as far as Lasha.
20 These *were* the sons of Ham, according
to their families, according to their languages, in
their lands *and* in their nations.
21 And *children* were born also to Shem, the
father of all the children of Eber, the brother of
Japheth the elder.
22 The [a]sons of Shem *were* Elam, Asshur,
[b]Arphaxad, Lud, and Aram.
23 The sons of Aram *were* Uz, Hul, Gether,
and *Mash.
24 *Arphaxad begot [a]Salah, and Salah begot
Eber.
25 [a]To Eber were born two sons: the name
of one *was* Peleg, for in his days the earth was
divided; and his brother's name *was* Joktan.
26 Joktan begot Almodad, Sheleph, Hazar-
maveth, Jerah,
27 Hadoram, Uzal, Diklah,

KJV

28 And Obal, and Abimael, and Sheba,
29 And Ophir, and Havilah, and Jobab: all
these *were* the sons of Joktan.
30 And their dwelling was from Mesha, as
thou goest unto Sephar a mount of the east.
31 These *are* the sons of Shem, after their
families, after their tongues, in their lands, after
their nations.
32 [a]These *are* the families of the sons of
Noah, after their generations, in their nations:
[b]and by these were the nations divided in the
earth after the flood.

The Tower of Babel

11 And the whole earth was of one language,
and of one speech.
2 And it came to pass, as they journeyed
from the east, that they found a plain in the land
[a]of Shinar; and they dwelt there.
3 And they said one to another, Go to, let
us make brick, and burn them throughly. And
they had brick for stone, and slime had they for
morter.
4 And they said, Go to, let us build us a city
and a tower, [a]whose top *may reach* unto heaven;
and let us make us a [b]name, lest we [c]be scattered
abroad upon the face of the whole earth.
5 [a]And the LORD came down to see the
city and the tower, which the children of men
builded.
6 And the LORD said, Behold, [a]the people
is one, and they have all [b]one language; and this
they begin to do: and now nothing will be restrained from them, which they have [c]imagined
to do.
7 Go to, [a]let us go down, and there [b]con-
found their language, that they may not understand one another's speech.
8 So [a]the LORD scattered them abroad from
thence [b]upon the face of all the earth: and they
left off to build the city.
9 Therefore is the name of it called Babel;
[a]because the LORD did there confound the language of all the earth: and from thence did the
LORD scatter them abroad upon the face of all the
earth.

Shem's Descendants
(1 Chr. 1:17–27; Luke 3:34–36)

10 [a]These *are* the generations of Shem: Shem
was an hundred years old, and begat Arphaxad
two years after the flood:
11 And Shem lived after he begat Arphaxad
five hundred years, and begat sons and daughters.
12 And Arphaxad lived five and thirty years,
[a]and begat Salah:
13 And Arphaxad lived after he begat Salah
four hundred and three years, and begat sons and
daughters.
14 And Salah lived thirty years, and begat
Eber:
15 And Salah lived after he begat Eber four
hundred and three years, and begat sons and
daughters.
16 [a]And Eber lived four and thirty years, and
begat [b]Peleg:
17 And Eber lived after he begat Peleg four
hundred and thirty years, and begat sons and
daughters.
18 And Peleg lived thirty years, and begat
Reu:
19 And Peleg lived after he begat Reu two
hundred and nine years, and begat sons and
daughters.
20 And Reu lived two and thirty years, and
begat [a]Serug:
21 And Reu lived after he begat Serug two
hundred and seven years, and begat sons and
daughters.
22 And Serug lived thirty years, and begat
Nahor:

32 [a]Gen. 10:1 [b]Gen. 9:19; 11:8

CHAPTER 11

2 [a]Gen. 10:10; 14:1; Dan. 1:2
4 [a]Deut. 1:28; 9:1; Ps. 107:26 [b]Gen. 6:4; 2 Sam. 8:13 [c]Deut. 4:27
5 [a]Gen. 18:21; Ex. 3:8; 19:11, 18, 20
6 [a]Gen. 9:19; Acts 17:26 [b]Gen. 11:1 [c]Deut. 31:21; Ps. 2:1
7 [a]Gen. 1:26 [b]Gen. 42:23; Ex. 4:11; Deut. 28:49; Is. 33:19; Jer. 5:15
8 [a]Gen. 11:4; Deut. 32:8; Ps. 92:9; [Luke 1:51] [b]Gen. 10:25, 32
9 [a]1 Cor. 14:23
10 [a]Gen. 10:22–25; 1 Chr. 1:17
12 [a]Luke 3:35
16 [a]1 Chr. 1:19 [b]Luke 3:35
20 [a]Luke 3:35

NKJV

28 *Obal, Abimael, Sheba,
29 Ophir, Havilah, and Jobab. All these *were*
the sons of Joktan.
30 And their dwelling place was from Mesha
as you go toward Sephar, the mountain of the
east.
31 These *were* the sons of Shem, according
to their families, according to their languages, in
their lands, according to their nations.
32 [a]These *were* the families of the sons of
Noah, according to their generations, in their nations; [b]and from these the nations were divided
on the earth after the flood.

The Tower of Babel

11 Now the whole earth had one language and
one speech.
2 And it came to pass, as they journeyed
from the east, that they found a plain in the land
[a]of Shinar, and they dwelt there.
3 Then they said to one another, "Come, let
us make bricks and bake *them* thoroughly." They
had brick for stone, and they had asphalt for
mortar.
4 And they said, "Come, let us build ourselves a city, and a tower [a]whose top *is* in the
heavens; let us make a [b]name for ourselves, lest
we [c]be scattered abroad over the face of the whole
earth."
5 [a]But the LORD came down to see the city
and the tower which the sons of men had built.
6 And the LORD said, "Indeed [a]the people
are one and they all have [b]one language, and this
is what they begin to do; now nothing that they
[c]propose to do will be withheld from them.
7 "Come, [a]let Us go down and there [b]con-
fuse their language, that they may not understand
one another's speech."
8 So [a]the LORD scattered them abroad from
there [b]over the face of all the earth, and they
ceased building the city.
9 Therefore its name is called Babel, [a]be-
cause there the LORD confused the language of
all the earth; and from there the LORD scattered
them abroad over the face of all the earth.

Shem's Descendants
(1 Chr. 1:17–27; Luke 3:34–36)

10 [a]This *is* the genealogy of Shem: Shem *was*
one hundred years old, and begot Arphaxad two
years after the flood.
11 After he begot Arphaxad, Shem lived five
hundred years, and begot sons and daughters.
12 Arphaxad lived thirty-five years, [a]and begot Salah.
13 After he begot Salah, Arphaxad lived four
hundred and three years, and begot sons and
daughters.
14 Salah lived thirty years, and begot Eber.
15 After he begot Eber, Salah lived four hundred and three years, and begot sons and
daughters.
16 [a]Eber lived thirty-four years, and begot
[b]Peleg.
17 After he begot Peleg, Eber lived four hundred and thirty years, and begot sons and
daughters.
18 Peleg lived thirty years, and begot Reu.
19 After he begot Reu, Peleg lived two hundred and nine years, and begot sons and
daughters.
20 Reu lived thirty-two years, and begot
[a]Serug.
21 After he begot Serug, Reu lived two hundred and seven years, and begot sons and
daughters.
22 Serug lived thirty years, and begot
Nahor.

*
10:28 *Ebal,* 1 Chr. 1:22

KJV

23 And Serug lived after he begat Nahor two hundred years, and begat sons and daughters.

24 And Nahor lived nine and twenty years, and begat [a]Terah:

25 And Nahor lived after he begat Terah an hundred and nineteen years, and begat sons and daughters.

26 And Terah lived seventy years, and [a]begat Abram, Nahor, and Haran.

Terah's Descendants

27 Now these *are* the generations of Terah: Terah begat [a]Abram, Nahor, and Haran; and Haran begat Lot.

28 And Haran died before his father Terah in the land of his nativity, in Ur of the Chaldees.

29 And Abram and Nahor took them wives: the name of Abram's wife *was* [a]Sarai; and the name of Nahor's wife, [b]Milcah, the daughter of Haran, the father of Milcah, and the father of Iscah.

30 But [a]Sarai was barren; she *had* no child.

31 And Terah [a]took Abram his son, and Lot the son of Haran his son's son, and Sarai his daughter in law, his son Abram's wife; and they went forth with them from [b]Ur of the Chaldees, to go into [c]the land of Canaan; and they came unto Haran, and dwelt there.

32 And the days of Terah were two hundred and five years: and Terah died in Haran.

Promises to Abram
(Acts 7:2–5)

12 Now the [a]LORD had said unto Abram, Get thee [b]out of thy country, and from thy kindred, and from thy father's house, unto a land that I will shew thee:

2 [a]And I will make of thee a great nation, [b]and I will bless thee, and make thy name great; [c]and thou shalt be a blessing:

3 [a]And I will bless them that bless thee, and curse him that curseth thee: and in [b]thee shall all families of the earth be [c]blessed.

4 So Abram departed, as the LORD had spoken unto him; and Lot went with him: and Abram *was* seventy and five years old when he departed out of Haran.

5 And Abram took Sarai his wife, and Lot his brother's son, and all their substance that they had gathered, and [a]the souls that they had gotten [b]in Haran; and they [c]went forth to go into the land of Canaan; and into the land of Canaan they came.

6 And Abram [a]passed through the land unto the place of Sichem, [b]unto the plain of Moreh. [c]And the Canaanite *was* then in the land.

7 [a]And the LORD appeared unto Abram, and said, [b]Unto thy seed will I give this land: and there builded he an [c]altar unto the LORD, who appeared unto him.

8 And he removed from thence unto a mountain on the east of Beth–el, and pitched his tent, *having* Beth–el on the west, and Hai on the east: and there he builded an altar unto the LORD, and [a]called upon the name of the LORD.

9 And Abram journeyed, [a]going on still toward the south.

Abram in Egypt

10 And there was [a]a famine in the land: and Abram [b]went down into Egypt to sojourn there; for the famine *was* [c]grievous in the land.

11 And it came to pass, when he was come near to enter into Egypt, that he said unto Sarai

24 [a]Gen. 11:31; Josh. 24:2; Luke 3:34
26 [a]Josh. 24:2; 1 Chr. 1:26
27 [a]Gen. 11:31; 17:5
29 [a]Gen. 17:15; 20:12 [b]Gen. 22:20, 23; 24:15
30 [a]Gen. 16:1, 2; Luke 1:36
31 [a]Gen. 12:1 [b]Gen. 15:7; Neh. 9:7; Acts 7:4 [c]Gen. 10:19

CHAPTER 12

1 [a]Gen. 15:7; Acts 7:2, 3; [Heb. 11:8] [b]Gen. 13:9
2 [a][Gen. 17:4–6]; 18:18; 46:3; Deut. 26:5; 1 Kin. 3:8 [b]Gen. 22:17; 24:35 [c]Gen. 28:4; Zech. 8:13; Gal. 3:14
3 [a]Gen. 24:35; 27:29; Ex. 23:22; Num. 24:9 [b]Gen. 18:18; 22:18; 26:4; 28:14; Ps. 72:17; Matt. 1:1; Luke 3:34; Acts 3:25; [Gal. 3:8] [c]Is. 41:27
5 [a]Gen. 14:14 [b]Gen. 11:31 [c]Gen. 13:18
6 [a]Heb. 11:9 [b]Deut. 11:30; Judg. 7:1 [c]Gen. 10:18, 19
7 [a]Gen. 17:1; 18:1 [b]Gen. 13:15; 15:18; 17:8; Deut. 34:4; Ps. 105:9–12; Acts 7:5; Gal. 3:16 [c]Gen. 13:4, 18; 22:9
8 [a]Gen. 4:26; 13:4; 21:33
9 [a]Gen. 13:1, 3; 20:1; 24:62
10 [a]Gen. 26:1 [b]Ps. 105:13 [c]Gen. 43:1

*

12:6 Heb. *Alon Moreh*
12:9 Heb. *Negev*

NKJV

23 After he begot Nahor, Serug lived two hundred years, and begot sons and daughters.

24 Nahor lived twenty-nine years, and begot [a]Terah.

25 After he begot Terah, Nahor lived one hundred and nineteen years, and begot sons and daughters.

26 Now Terah lived seventy years, and [a]begot Abram, Nahor, and Haran.

Terah's Descendants

27 This *is* the genealogy of Terah: Terah begot [a]Abram, Nahor, and Haran. Haran begot Lot.

28 And Haran died before his father Terah in his native land, in Ur of the Chaldeans.

29 Then Abram and Nahor took wives: the name of Abram's wife *was* [a]Sarai, and the name of Nahor's wife, [b]Milcah, the daughter of Haran the father of Milcah and the father of Iscah.

30 But [a]Sarai was barren; she had no child.

31 And Terah [a]took his son Abram and his grandson Lot, the son of Haran, and his daughter-in-law Sarai, his son Abram's wife, and they went out with them from [b]Ur of the Chaldeans to go to [c]the land of Canaan; and they came to Haran and dwelt there.

32 So the days of Terah were two hundred and five years, and Terah died in Haran.

Promises to Abram
(Acts 7:2–5)

12 Now the [a]LORD had said to Abram:

"Get [b]out of your country,
From your family
And from your father's house,
To a land that I will show you.
2 [a]I will make you a great nation;
[b]I will bless you
And make your name great;
[c]And you shall be a blessing.
3 [a]I will bless those who bless you,
And I will curse him who curses you;
And in [b]you all the families of the earth
shall be [c]blessed."

4 So Abram departed as the LORD had spoken to him, and Lot went with him. And Abram *was* seventy-five years old when he departed from Haran.

5 Then Abram took Sarai his wife and Lot his brother's son, and all their possessions that they had gathered, and [a]the people whom they had acquired [b]in Haran, and they [c]departed to go to the land of Canaan. So they came to the land of Canaan.

6 Abram [a]passed through the land to the place of Shechem, [b]as far as *the terebinth tree of Moreh. [c]And the Canaanites *were* then in the land.

7 [a]Then the LORD appeared to Abram and said, [b]"To your descendants I will give this land." And there he built an [c]altar to the LORD, who had appeared to him.

8 And he moved from there to the mountain east of Bethel, and he pitched his tent *with* Bethel on the west and Ai on the east; there he built an altar to the LORD and [a]called on the name of the LORD.

9 So Abram journeyed, [a]going on still toward the *South.

Abram in Egypt

10 Now there was [a]a famine in the land, and Abram [b]went down to Egypt to dwell there, for the famine *was* [c]severe in the land.

11 And it came to pass, when he was close to entering Egypt, that he said to Sarai his wife,

KJV

his wife, Behold now, I know that thou *art* [a]a fair woman to look upon:

12 Therefore it shall come to pass, when the Egyptians shall see thee, that they shall say, This *is* his wife: and they [a]will kill me, but they will save thee alive.

13 [a]Say, I pray thee, thou *art* my [b]sister: that it may be well with me for thy sake; and my soul shall live because of thee.

14 And it came to pass, that, when Abram was come into Egypt, the Egyptians beheld the woman that she *was* very fair.

15 The princes also of Pharaoh saw her, and commended her before Pharaoh: and the woman was taken into Pharaoh's house.

16 And he [a]entreated Abram well for her sake: and he [b]had sheep, and oxen, and he asses, and menservants, and maidservants, and she asses, and camels.

17 And the LORD [a]plagued Pharaoh and his house with great plagues because of Sarai Abram's wife.

18 And Pharaoh called Abram, and said, [a]What *is* this *that* thou hast done unto me? why didst thou not tell me that she *was* thy wife?

19 Why saidst thou, She *is* my sister? so I might have taken her to me to wife: now therefore behold thy wife, take *her*, and go thy way.

20 [a]And Pharaoh commanded *his* men concerning him: and they sent him away, and his wife, and all that he had.

Abram Inherits Canaan

13 And Abram went up out of Egypt, he, and his wife, and all that he had, and [a]Lot with him, [b]into the south.

2 [a]And Abram *was* very rich in cattle, in silver, and in gold.

3 And he went on his journeys [a]from the south even to Beth–el, unto the place where his tent had been at the beginning, between Beth–el and Hai;

4 Unto the [a]place of the altar, which he had made there at the first: and there Abram [b]called on the name of the LORD.

5 And Lot also, which went with Abram, had flocks, and herds, and tents.

6 And [a]the land was not able to bear them, that they might dwell together: for their substance was great, so that they could not dwell together.

7 And there was [a]a strife between the herdmen of Abram's cattle and the herdmen of Lot's cattle: [b]and the Canaanite and the Perizzite dwelled then in the land.

8 And Abram said unto Lot, [a]Let there be no strife, I pray thee, between me and thee, and between my herdmen and thy herdmen; for we *be* brethren.

9 [a]*Is* not the whole land before thee? [b]separate thyself, I pray thee, from me: [c]if *thou wilt take* the left hand, then I will go to the right; or if *thou depart* to the right hand, then I will go to the left.

10 And Lot lifted up his eyes, and beheld all [a]the plain of Jordan, that it *was* well watered every where, before the LORD [b]destroyed Sodom and Gomorrah, [c]*even* as the garden of the LORD, like the land of Egypt, as thou comest unto [d]Zoar.

11 Then Lot chose him all the plain of Jordan; and Lot journeyed east: and they separated themselves the one from the other.

12 Abram dwelled in the land of Canaan, and Lot [a]dwelled in the cities of the plain, and [b]pitched *his* tent toward Sodom.

13 But the men of Sodom [a]*were* wicked and [b]sinners before the LORD exceedingly.

14 And the LORD said unto Abram, after that Lot [a]was separated from him, Lift up now thine eyes, and look from the place where thou art [b]northward, and southward, and eastward, and westward:

---

11 [a]Gen. 12:14; 26:7; 29:17
12 [a]Gen. 20:11; 26:7
13 [a]Gen. 20:1–18; 26:6–11 [b]Gen. 20:12
16 [a]Gen. 20:14 [b]Gen. 13:2
17 [a]Gen. 20:18; 1 Chr. 16:21; [Ps. 105:14]
18 [a]Gen. 20:9, 10; 26:10
20 [a][Prov. 21:1]

CHAPTER 13

1 [a]Gen. 12:4; 14:12, 16 [b]Gen. 12:9
2 [a]Gen. 24:35; 26:14; Ps. 112:3; Prov. 10:22
3 [a]Gen. 12:8, 9
4 [a]Gen. 12:7, 8; 21:33 [b]Ps. 116:17
6 [a]Gen. 36:7
7 [a]Gen. 26:20 [b]Gen. 12:6; 15:20, 21
8 [a]1 Cor. 6:7; [Phil. 2:14, 15]
9 [a]Gen. 20:15; 34:10 [b]Gen. 13:11, 14 [c][Rom. 12:18]
10 [a]Gen. 19:17–29; Deut. 34:3 [b]Gen. 19:24 [c]Gen. 2:8, 10; Is. 51:3 [d]Gen. 14:2, 8; 19:22; Deut. 34:3
12 [a]Gen. 19:24, 25, 29 [b]Gen. 14:12, 19
13 [a]Gen. 18:20, 21; Ezek. 16:49; 2 Pet. 2:7, 8 [b]Gen. 6:11; 39:9; Num. 32:23
14 [a]Gen. 13:11 [b]Gen. 28:14

*

12:13 Lit. *my soul*
13:1 Heb. *Negev*

NKJV

"Indeed I know that you *are* [a]a woman of beautiful countenance.

12 "Therefore it will happen, when the Egyptians see you, that they will say, 'This *is* his wife'; and they [a]will kill me, but they will let you live.

13 [a]"Please say you *are* my [b]sister, that it may be well with me for your sake, and that *I may live because of you."

14 So it was, when Abram came into Egypt, that the Egyptians saw the woman, that she *was* very beautiful.

15 The princes of Pharaoh also saw her and commended her to Pharaoh. And the woman was taken to Pharaoh's house.

16 He [a]treated Abram well for her sake. He [b]had sheep, oxen, male donkeys, male and female servants, female donkeys, and camels.

17 But the LORD [a]plagued Pharaoh and his house with great plagues because of Sarai, Abram's wife.

18 And Pharaoh called Abram and said, [a]"What *is* this you have done to me? Why did you not tell me that she *was* your wife?

19 "Why did you say, 'She *is* my sister'? I might have taken her as my wife. Now therefore, here is your wife; take *her* and go your way."

20 [a]So Pharaoh commanded *his* men concerning him; and they sent him away, with his wife and all that he had.

Abram Inherits Canaan

13 Then Abram went up from Egypt, he and his wife and all that he had, and [a]Lot with him, [b]to the *South.

2 [a]Abram *was* very rich in livestock, in silver, and in gold.

3 And he went on his journey [a]from the South as far as Bethel, to the place where his tent had been at the beginning, between Bethel and Ai,

4 to the [a]place of the altar which he had made there at first. And there Abram [b]called on the name of the LORD.

5 Lot also, who went with Abram, had flocks and herds and tents.

6 Now [a]the land was not able to support them, that they might dwell together, for their possessions were so great that they could not dwell together.

7 And there was [a]strife between the herdsmen of Abram's livestock and the herdsmen of Lot's livestock. [b]The Canaanites and the Perizzites then dwelt in the land.

8 So Abram said to Lot, [a]"Please let there be no strife between you and me, and between my herdsmen and your herdsmen; for we *are* brethren.

9 [a]"*Is* not the whole land before you? Please [b]separate from me. [c]If *you take* the left, then I will go to the right; or, if *you go* to the right, then I will go to the left."

10 And Lot lifted his eyes and saw all [a]the plain of Jordan, that it *was* well watered everywhere (before the LORD [b]destroyed Sodom and Gomorrah) [c]like the garden of the LORD, like the land of Egypt as you go toward [d]Zoar.

11 Then Lot chose for himself all the plain of Jordan, and Lot journeyed east. And they separated from each other.

12 Abram dwelt in the land of Canaan, and Lot [a]dwelt in the cities of the plain and [b]pitched *his* tent even as far as Sodom.

13 But the men of Sodom [a]*were* exceedingly wicked and [b]sinful against the LORD.

14 And the LORD said to Abram, after Lot [a]had separated from him: "Lift your eyes now and look from the place where you are—[b]northward, southward, eastward, and westward;

KJV

15 For all the land which thou seest, [a]to thee
will I give it, and [b]to thy seed for ever.
16 And [a]I will make thy seed as the dust of
the earth: so that if a man can number the dust
of the earth, *then* shall thy seed also be numbered.
17 Arise, walk through the land in the length
of it and in the breadth of it; for I will give it
unto thee.
18 [a]Then Abram removed *his* tent, and came
and [b]dwelt in the plain of Mamre, [c]which *is* in
Hebron, and built there an [d]altar unto the LORD.

Lot's Captivity and Rescue

14 And it came to pass in the days of Amraphel king [a]of Shinar, Arioch king of Ellasar, Chedorlaomer king of [b]Elam, and Tidal king
of nations;
2 *That these* made war with Bera king of
Sodom, and with Birsha king of Gomorrah, Shinab king of [a]Admah, and Shemeber king of Zeboiim, and the king of Bela, which is [b]Zoar.
3 All these were joined together in the vale
of Siddim, [a]which is the salt sea.
4 Twelve years [a]they served Chedorlaomer,
and in the thirteenth year they rebelled.
5 And in the fourteenth year came Chedorlaomer, and the kings that *were* with him, and
smote [a]the Rephaims in Ashteroth Karnaim, and
[b]the Zuzims in Ham, [c]and the Emims in Shaveh
Kiriathaim,
6 [a]And the Horites in their mount Seir, unto
El–paran, which *is* by the wilderness.
7 And they returned, and came to En–mishpat, which *is* Kadesh, and smote all the country
of the Amalekites, and also the Amorites, that
dwelt [a]in Hazezon–tamar.
8 And there went out the king of Sodom,
and the king of Gomorrah, and the king of Admah, and the king of Zeboiim, and the king of
Bela (the same *is* Zoar;) and they joined battle
with them in the vale of Siddim;
9 With Chedorlaomer the king of Elam, and
with Tidal king of nations, and Amraphel king
of Shinar, and Arioch king of Ellasar; four kings
with five.
10 And the vale of Siddim *was full of* [a]slime-
pits; and the kings of Sodom and Gomorrah fled,
and fell there; and they that remained fled [b]to
the mountain.
11 And they took [a]all the goods of Sodom
and Gomorrah, and all their victuals, and went
their way.
12 And they took Lot, Abram's [a]brother's
son, [b]who dwelt in Sodom, and his goods, and
departed.
13 And there came one that had escaped, and
told Abram the [a]Hebrew; for [b]he dwelt in the
plain of Mamre the Amorite, brother of Eshcol,
and brother of Aner: [c]and these *were* confederate
with Abram.
14 And [a]when Abram heard that [b]his brother
was taken captive, he armed his trained *servants*,
[c]born in his own house, three hundred and eighteen, and pursued *them* [d]unto Dan.
15 And he divided himself against them, he
and his servants, by night, and [a]smote them, and
pursued them unto Hobah, which *is* on the left
hand of Damascus.
16 And he [a]brought back all the goods, and
also brought again his brother Lot, and his goods,
and the women also, and the people.
17 And the king of Sodom [a]went out to meet
him [c]after his return from the slaughter of Chedorlaomer, and of the kings that *were* with him, at
the valley of Shaveh, which *is* the [b]king's dale.

Abram and Melchizedek
(Heb. 7:1, 2)

18 And [a]Melchizedek king of Salem brought
forth [b]bread and wine: and he *was* [c]the priest of
[d]the most high God.

15 [a]Gen. 12:7; 13:17; 15:7, 18; 17:8; Deut. 34:4; Acts 7:5 [b]2 Chr. 20:7; Ps. 37:22
16 [a]Gen. 22:17; Ex. 32:13; Num. 23:10
18 [a]Gen. 26:17 [b]Gen. 14:13 [c]Gen. 23:2; 35:27 [d]Gen. 8:20; 22:8, 9

CHAPTER 14

1 [a]Gen. 10:10; 11:2 [b]Is. 11:11; 21:2; Dan. 8:2
2 [a]Gen. 10:19; Deut. 29:23 [b]Gen. 13:10; 19:22
3 [a]Num. 34:12; Deut. 3:17; Josh. 3:16
4 [a]Gen. 9:26
5 [a]Gen. 15:20 [b]Deut. 2:20 [c]Num. 32:37; Deut. 2:10
6 [a]Gen. 36:20; Deut. 2:12, 22
7 [a]2 Chr. 20:2
10 [a]Gen. 11:3 [b]Gen. 19:17, 30
11 [a]Gen. 14:16, 21
12 [a]Gen. 11:27; 12:5 [b]Gen. 13:12
13 [a]Gen. 39:14; 40:15 [b]Gen. 13:18 [c]Gen. 14:24; 21:27, 32
14 [a]Gen. 19:29 [b]Gen. 13:8; 14:12 [c]Gen. 12:5; 15:3; 17:27; Eccl. 2:7 [d]Deut. 34:1; Judg. 18:29; 1 Kin. 15:20
15 [a]Is. 41:2, 3
16 [a]Gen. 31:18; 1 Sam. 30:8, 18, 19
17 [a]1 Sam. 18:6 [b]2 Sam. 18:18 [c]Heb. 7:1
18 [a]Ps. 110:4; Heb. 7:1–10 [b]Gen. 18:5; Ex. 29:40; Ps. 104:15 [c]Ps. 110:4; Heb. 5:6 [d]Acts 16:17

*

13:15 Lit. *seed*
13:18 Heb. *Alon Mamre*
14:1 Heb. *goyim*
14:9 Heb. *goyim*
14:13 Heb. *Alon Mamre*

NKJV

15 "for all the land which you see [a]I give to
you and [b]your *descendants forever.
16 "And [a]I will make your descendants as
the dust of the earth; so that if a man could number the dust of the earth, *then* your descendants
also could be numbered.
17 "Arise, walk in the land through its length
and its width, for I give it to you."
18 [a]Then Abram moved *his* tent, and went
and [b]dwelt by *the terebinth trees of Mamre,
[c]which *are* in Hebron, and built an [d]altar there
to the LORD.

Lot's Captivity and Rescue

14 And it came to pass in the days of Amraphel king [a]of Shinar, Arioch king of Ellasar, Chedorlaomer king of [b]Elam, and Tidal king
of *nations,
2 *that* they made war with Bera king of
Sodom, Birsha king of Gomorrah, Shinab king
of [a]Admah, Shemeber king of Zeboiim, and the
king of Bela (that is, [b]Zoar).
3 All these joined together in the Valley of
Siddim [a](that is, the Salt Sea).
4 Twelve years [a]they served Chedorlaomer,
and in the thirteenth year they rebelled.
5 In the fourteenth year Chedorlaomer and
the kings that *were* with him came and attacked
[a]the Rephaim in Ashteroth Karnaim, [b]the Zuzim
in Ham, [c]the Emim in Shaveh Kiriathaim,
6 [a]and the Horites in their mountain of Seir,
as far as El Paran, which *is* by the wilderness.
7 Then they turned back and came to En
Mishpat (that *is*, Kadesh), and attacked all the
country of the Amalekites, and also the Amorites
who dwelt [a]in Hazezon Tamar.
8 And the king of Sodom, the king of Gomorrah, the king of Admah, the king of Zeboiim,
and the king of Bela (that *is*, Zoar) went out and
joined together in battle in the Valley of Siddim
9 against Chedorlaomer king of Elam, Tidal
king of *nations, Amraphel king of Shinar,
and Arioch king of Ellasar—four kings against
five.
10 Now the Valley of Siddim *was full of* [a]as-
phalt pits; and the kings of Sodom and Gomorrah
fled; *some* fell there, and the remainder fled [b]to
the mountains.
11 Then they took [a]all the goods of Sodom
and Gomorrah, and all their provisions, and went
their way.
12 They also took Lot, Abram's [a]brother's
son [b]who dwelt in Sodom, and his goods, and
departed.
13 Then one who had escaped came and told
Abram the [a]Hebrew, for [b]he dwelt by *the terebinth trees of Mamre the Amorite, brother of Eshcol and brother of Aner; [c]and they *were* allies with
Abram.
14 Now [a]when Abram heard that [b]his
brother was taken captive, he armed his three
hundred and eighteen trained *servants* who were
[c]born in his own house, and went in pursuit [d]as
far as Dan.
15 He divided his forces against them by
night, and he and his servants [a]attacked them and
pursued them as far as Hobah, which *is* north of
Damascus.
16 So he [a]brought back all the goods, and
also brought back his brother Lot and his goods,
as well as the women and the people.
17 And the king of Sodom [a]went out to meet
him at the Valley of Shaveh (that *is*, the [b]King's
Valley), [c]after his return from the defeat of Chedorlaomer and the kings who *were* with him.

Abram and Melchizedek
(Heb. 7:1, 2)

18 Then [a]Melchizedek king of Salem brought
out [b]bread and wine; he *was* [c]the priest of [d]God
Most High.

KJV

19 And he blessed him, and said, [a]Blessed *be* Abram of the most high God, [b]possessor of heaven and earth:

20 And [a]blessed be the most high God, which hath delivered thine enemies into thy hand. And he [b]gave him tithes of all.

21 And the king of Sodom said unto Abram, Give me the persons, and take the goods to thyself.

22 And Abram [a]said to the king of Sodom, I [b]have lift up mine hand unto the LORD, the most high God, [c]the possessor of heaven and earth,

23 That [a]I will not *take* from a thread even to a shoelatchet, and that I will not take any thing that *is* thine, lest thou shouldest say, I have made Abram rich:

24 Save only that which the young men have eaten, and the portion of the men which went with me, Aner, Eshcol, and Mamre; let them take their portion.

God's Covenant with Abram
(Heb. 11:8–10)

15 After these things the word of the LORD came unto Abram [a]in a vision, saying, [b]Fear not, Abram: I *am* thy [c]shield, *and* thy exceeding [d]great reward.

2 [a]And Abram said, Lord GOD, what wilt thou give me, [b]seeing I go childless, and the steward of my house *is* this Eliezer of Damascus?

3 And Abram said, Behold, to me thou hast given no seed: and, lo, [a]one born in my house is mine heir.

4 And, behold, the word of the LORD *came* unto him, saying, This shall not be thine heir; but he that [a]shall come forth out of thine own bowels shall be thine heir.

5 And he brought him forth abroad, and said, Look now toward heaven, and [a]tell [b]the stars, if thou be able to number them: and he said unto him, [c]So shall thy [d]seed be.

6 And he [a]believed in the LORD; and he [b]counted it to him for righteousness.

7 And he said unto him, I *am* the LORD that [a]brought thee out of [b]Ur of the Chaldees, [c]to give thee this land to inherit it.

8 And he said, Lord GOD, [a]whereby shall I know that I shall inherit it?

9 And he said unto him, Take me an heifer of three years old, and a she goat of three years old, and a ram of three years old, and a turtledove, and a young pigeon.

10 And he took unto him all these, and [a]divided them in the midst, and laid each piece one against another: but [b]the birds divided he not.

11 And when the fowls came down upon the carcases, Abram drove them away.

12 And when the sun was going down, [a]a deep sleep fell upon Abram; and, lo, an horror of great darkness fell upon him.

13 And he said unto Abram, Know of a surety [a]that thy seed shall be a stranger in a land *that is* not their's, and shall serve them; and [b]they shall afflict them four hundred years;

14 And also that nation, whom they shall serve, [a]will I judge: and afterward [b]shall they come out with great substance.

15 And [a]thou shalt go [b]to thy fathers in peace; [c]thou shalt be buried in a good old age.

16 But [a]in the fourth generation they shall come hither again: for the iniquity [b]of the Amorites [c]*is* not yet full.

17 And it came to pass, that, when the sun went down, and it was dark, behold a smoking furnace, and a burning lamp that [a]passed between those pieces.

19 [a]Ruth 3:10 [b]Gen. 14:22; Matt. 11:25
20 [a]Gen. 24:27 [b]Gen. 28:22; Heb. 7:4
22 [a]Gen. 14:2, 8, 10 [b]Dan. 12:7 [c]Gen. 14:19
23 [a]2 Kin. 5:16; Esth. 9:15, 16

CHAPTER 15

1 [a]Gen. 15:4; 46:2; 1 Sam. 15:10; Dan. 10:1 [b]Gen. 21:17; 26:24; Is. 41:10; Dan. 10:12 [c]Deut. 33:29; Ps. 3:3; 84:11; 91:4 [d]Num. 18:20; Ps. 58:11; Prov. 11:18
2 [a]Gen. 17:18 [b]Acts 7:5
3 [a]Gen. 14:14
4 [a]2 Sam. 7:12; Gal. 4:28
5 [a]Gen. 22:17; 26:4; Deut. 1:10; Ps. 147:4 [b]Jer. 33:22 [c]Ex. 32:13; Rom. 4:18; Heb. 11:12 [d]Gen. 17:19
6 [a]Gen. 21:1; Rom. 4:3, 9, 22; Gal. 3:6; James 2:23 [b]Ps. 32:2; 106:31
7 [a]Gen. 12:1 [b]Gen. 11:28, 31 [c]Gen. 13:15, 17; Ps. 105:42, 44
8 [a]Gen. 24:13, 14; Judg. 6:36–40; 1 Sam. 14:9, 10; Luke 1:18
10 [a]Gen. 15:17; Jer. 34:18 [b]Lev. 1:17
12 [a]Gen. 2:21; 28:11; Job 33:15
13 [a]Ex. 1:11; Acts 7:6 [b]Ex. 12:40
14 [a]Ex. 6:6 [b]Ex. 12:36
15 [a]Job 5:26 [b]Gen. 25:8; 47:30 [c]Gen. 25:8
16 [a]Gen. 15:13; Ex. 12:41 [b]Gen. 48:22; Lev. 18:24–28; 1 Kin. 21:26 [c]1 Kin. 11:12; Matt. 23:32
17 [a]Jer. 34:18, 19

NKJV

19 And he blessed him and said:

[a]"Blessed be Abram of God Most High,
[b]Possessor of heaven and earth;
20 And [a]blessed be God Most High,
Who has delivered your enemies into your hand."

And he [b]gave him a tithe of all.

21 Now the king of Sodom said to Abram, "Give me the persons, and take the goods for yourself."

22 But Abram [a]said to the king of Sodom, "I [b]have raised my hand to the LORD, God Most High, [c]the Possessor of heaven and earth,

23 "that [a]I *will take* nothing, from a thread to a sandal strap, and that I will not take anything that *is* yours, lest you should say, 'I have made Abram rich'—

24 "except only what the young men have eaten, and the portion of the men who went with me: Aner, Eshcol, and Mamre; let them take their portion."

God's Covenant with Abram
(Heb. 11:8–10)

15 After these things the word of the LORD came to Abram [a]in a vision, saying, [b]"Do not be afraid, Abram. I *am* your [c]shield, your exceedingly [d]great reward."

2 [a]But Abram said, "Lord GOD, what will You give me, [b]seeing I go childless, and the heir of my house *is* Eliezer of Damascus?"

3 Then Abram said, "Look, You have given me no offspring; indeed [a]one born in my house is my heir!"

4 And behold, the word of the LORD *came* to him, saying, "This one shall not be your heir, but one who [a]will come from your own body shall be your heir."

5 Then He brought him outside and said, "Look now toward heaven, and [a]count the [b]stars if you are able to number them." And He said to him, [c]"So shall your [d]descendants be."

6 And he [a]believed in the LORD, and He [b]accounted it to him for righteousness.

7 Then He said to him, "I *am* the LORD, who [a]brought you out of [b]Ur of the Chaldeans, [c]to give you this land to inherit it."

8 And he said, "Lord GOD, [a]how shall I know that I will inherit it?"

9 So He said to him, "Bring Me a three-year-old heifer, a three-year-old female goat, a three-year-old ram, a turtledove, and a young pigeon."

10 Then he brought all these to Him and [a]cut them in two, down the middle, and placed each piece opposite the other; but he did not cut [b]the birds in two.

11 And when the vultures came down on the carcasses, Abram drove them away.

12 Now when the sun was going down, [a]a deep sleep fell upon Abram; and behold, horror *and* great darkness fell upon him.

13 Then He said to Abram: "Know certainly [a]that your descendants will be strangers in a land *that is* not theirs, and will serve them, and [b]they will afflict them four hundred years.

14 "And also the nation whom they serve [a]I will judge; afterward [b]they shall come out with great possessions.

15 "Now as for you, [a]you shall go [b]to your fathers in peace; [c]you shall be buried at a good old age.

16 "But [a]in the fourth generation they shall return here, for the iniquity [b]of the Amorites [c]*is* not yet complete."

17 And it came to pass, when the sun went down and it was dark, that behold, there appeared a smoking oven and a burning torch that [a]passed between those pieces.

KJV

18 In the same day the LORD [a]made a covenant with Abram, saying, [b]Unto thy seed have I
given this land, from the river of Egypt unto the
great river, the river Euphrates:
19 The Kenites, and the Kenizzites, and the
Kadmonites,
20 And the Hittites, and the Perizzites, and
the Rephaims,
21 And the Amorites, and the Canaanites,
and the Girgashites, and the Jebusites.

Hagar and Ishmael

16 Now Sarai Abram's wife [a]bare him no children: and she had an handmaid, [b]an Egyptian, whose name *was* [c]Hagar.
2 [a]And Sarai said unto Abram, Behold now,
the LORD [b]hath restrained me from bearing: I pray
thee, [c]go in unto my maid; it may be that I may
obtain children by her. And Abram [d]hearkened
to the voice of Sarai.
3 And Sarai Abram's wife took Hagar her
maid the Egyptian, after Abram [a]had dwelt ten
years in the land of Canaan, and gave her to her
husband Abram to be his wife.
4 And he went in unto Hagar, and she conceived: and when she saw that she had conceived,
her mistress was [a]despised in her eyes.
5 And Sarai said unto Abram, My wrong
be upon thee: I have given my maid into thy bosom; and when she saw that she had conceived,
I was despised in her eyes: [a]the LORD judge between me and thee.
6 [a]But Abram said unto Sarai, Behold, thy
maid *is* in thy hand; do to her as it pleaseth thee.
And when Sarai dealt hardly with her, [b]she fled
from her face.
7 And the [a]angel of the LORD found her by
a fountain of water in the wilderness, [b]by the
fountain in the way to [c]Shur.
8 And he said, Hagar, Sarai's maid, whence
camest thou? and whither wilt thou go? And she
said, I flee from the face of my mistress Sarai.
9 And the angel of the LORD said unto her,
Return to thy mistress, and [a]submit thyself under
her hands.
10 And the angel of the LORD said unto her,
[a]I will multiply thy seed exceedingly, that it shall
not be numbered for multitude.
11 And the angel of the LORD said unto her,
Behold, thou *art* with child, [a]and shalt bear a son,
and shalt call his name Ishmael; because the LORD
hath heard thy affliction.
12 [a]And he will be a wild man; his hand *will*
be against every man, and every man's hand
against him; [b]and he shall dwell in the presence
of all his brethren.
13 And she called the name of the LORD that
spake unto her, Thou God seest me: for she said,
Have I also here looked after him [a]that seeth me?
14 Wherefore the well was called [a]Beer-
lahai-roi; behold, *it is* [b]between Kadesh and
Bered.
15 And [a]Hagar bare Abram a son: and
Abram called his son's name, which Hagar bare,
Ishmael.
16 And Abram *was* fourscore and six years
old, when Hagar bare Ishmael to Abram.

The Sign of the Covenant
(Ex. 12:43—13:2)

17 And when Abram was ninety years old and
nine, the LORD [a]appeared to Abram, and
said unto him, [b]I *am* the Almighty God; [c]walk
before me, and be thou [d]perfect.
2 And I will make my [a]covenant between
me and thee, and [b]will multiply thee exceedingly.

---

18 [a]Gen. 24:7 [b]Gen. 12:7; 17:8; Ex. 23:31; Num. 34:3; Deut. 11:24; Josh. 1:4; 21:43; Acts 7:5

CHAPTER 16

1 [a]Gen. 11:30; 15:2, 3 [b]Gen. 12:16; 21:9 [c]Gal. 4:24
2 [a]Gen. 30:3 [b]Gen. 20:18 [c]Gen. 30:3, 9 [d]Gen. 3:17
3 [a]Gen. 12:4, 5
4 [a]1 Sam. 1:6, 7; [Prov. 30:21, 23]
5 [a]Gen. 31:53; Ex. 5:21
6 [a]1 Pet. 3:7 [b]Gen. 16:9; Ex. 2:15
7 [a]Gen. 21:17, 18; 22:11, 15; 31:11 [b]Gen. 20:1; 25:18 [c]Ex. 15:22
9 [a][Titus 2:9]
10 [a]Gen. 17:20
11 [a]Luke 1:13, 31
12 [a]Gen. 21:20; Job 24:5; 39:5–8 [b]Gen. 25:18
13 [a]Gen. 31:42
14 [a]Gen. 24:62 [b]Gen. 14:7; Num. 13:26
15 [a]Gal. 4:22

CHAPTER 17

1 [a]Gen. 12:7; 18:1 [b]Gen. 28:3; 35:11; Ex. 6:3; Job 42:2 [c]2 Kin. 20:3 [d]Gen. 6:9; Deut. 18:13
2 [a]Gen. 15:18; Ex. 6:4; [Gal. 3:19] [b]Gen. 12:2; 13:16; 15:5; 18:18

*———

16:14 Lit. *Well of the One Who Lives and Sees Me*

NKJV

18 On the same day the LORD [a]made a covenant with Abram, saying:
[a]"To your descendants I have given this
land, from the river of Egypt to the great river,
the River Euphrates—
19 "the Kenites, the Kenezzites, the Kadmonites,
20 "the Hittites, the Perizzites, the Rephaim,
21 "the Amorites, the Canaanites, the Girgashites, and the Jebusites."

Hagar and Ishmael

16 Now Sarai, Abram's wife, [a]had borne him
no *children.* And she had [b]an Egyptian
maidservant whose name was [c]Hagar.
2 [a]So Sarai said to Abram, "See now, the
LORD [b]has restrained me from bearing *children.*
Please, [c]go in to my maid; perhaps I shall obtain
children by her." And Abram [d]heeded the voice
of Sarai.
3 Then Sarai, Abram's wife, took Hagar her
maid, the Egyptian, and gave her to her husband
Abram to be his wife, after Abram [a]had dwelt
ten years in the land of Canaan.
4 So he went in to Hagar, and she conceived. And when she saw that she had conceived,
her mistress became [a]despised in her eyes.
5 Then Sarai said to Abram, "My wrong *be*
upon you! I gave my maid into your embrace; and
when she saw that she had conceived, I became
despised in her eyes. [a]The LORD judge between
you and me."
6 [a]So Abram said to Sarai, "Indeed your
maid *is* in your hand; do to her as you please."
And when Sarai dealt harshly with her, [b]she fled
from her presence.
7 Now the [a]Angel of the LORD found her by
a spring of water in the wilderness, [b]by the spring
on the way to [c]Shur.
8 And He said, "Hagar, Sarai's maid, where
have you come from, and where are you going?"
She said, "I am fleeing from the presence of my
mistress Sarai."
9 The Angel of the LORD said to her, "Return
to your mistress, and [a]submit yourself under her
hand."
10 Then the Angel of the LORD said to her,
[a]"I will multiply your descendants exceedingly,
so that they shall not be counted for multitude."
11 And the Angel of the LORD said to her:

"Behold, you *are* with child,
[a]And you shall bear a son.
You shall call his name Ishmael,
Because the LORD has heard your
affliction.
12 [a]He shall be a wild man;
His hand *shall be* against every man,
And every man's hand against him.
[b]And he shall dwell in the presence of all
his brethren."

13 Then she called the name of the LORD who
spoke to her, You-Are-the-God-Who-Sees; for
she said, "Have I also here seen Him [a]who sees
me?"
14 Therefore the well was called [a]Beer Lahai
Roi;* observe, *it is* [b]between Kadesh and Bered.
15 So [a]Hagar bore Abram a son; and Abram
named his son, whom Hagar bore, Ishmael.
16 Abram *was* eighty-six years old when Hagar bore Ishmael to Abram.

The Sign of the Covenant
(Ex. 12:43—13:2)

17 When Abram was ninety-nine years old,
the LORD [a]appeared to Abram and said to
him, [b]"I *am* Almighty God; [c]walk before Me and
be [d]blameless.
2 "And I will make My [a]covenant between
Me and you, and [b]will multiply you exceedingly."

KJV

3 And Abram fell on his face: and God talked with him, saying,

4 As for me, behold, my covenant *is* with thee, and thou shalt be [a]a father of many nations.

5 Neither shall thy name any more be called Abram, but [a]thy name shall be Abraham; [b]for a father of many nations have I made thee.

6 And I will make thee exceeding fruitful, and I will make [a]nations of thee, and [b]kings shall come out of thee.

7 And I will [a]establish my covenant between me and thee and thy seed after thee in their generations for an everlasting covenant, [b]to be a God unto thee, and to [c]thy seed after thee.

8 And [a]I will give unto thee, and to thy seed after thee, the land [b]wherein thou art a stranger, all the land of Canaan, for an everlasting possession; and [c]I will be their God.

9 And God said unto Abraham, [a]Thou shalt keep my covenant therefore, thou, and thy seed after thee in their generations.

10 This *is* my covenant, which ye shall keep, between me and you and thy seed after thee; [a]Every man child among you shall be circumcised.

11 And ye shall circumcise the flesh of your foreskin; and it shall be [a]a token of the covenant betwixt me and you.

12 And he that is eight days old [a]shall be circumcised among you, every man child in your generations, he that is born in the house, or bought with money of any stranger, which *is* not of thy seed.

13 He that is born in thy house, and he that is bought with thy money, must needs be circumcised: and my covenant shall be in your flesh for an everlasting covenant.

14 And the uncircumcised man child whose flesh of his foreskin is not circumcised, that soul [a]shall be cut off from his people; he hath broken my covenant.

15 And God said unto Abraham, As for Sarai thy wife, thou shalt not call her name Sarai, but Sarah *shall* her name *be*.

16 And I will bless her, [a]and give thee a son also of her: yea, I will bless her, and she shall be *a mother* [b]of nations; [c]kings of people shall be of her.

17 Then Abraham fell upon his face, [a]and laughed, and said in his heart, Shall *a child* be born unto him that is an hundred years old? and shall Sarah, that is ninety years old, bear?

18 And Abraham [a]said unto God, O that Ishmael might live before thee!

19 And God said, [a]Sarah thy wife shall bear thee a son indeed; and thou shalt call his name Isaac: and I will establish my [b]covenant with him for an everlasting covenant, *and* with his seed after him.

20 And as for Ishmael, I have heard thee: Behold, I have blessed him, and will make him fruitful, and [a]will multiply him exceedingly; [b]twelve princes shall he beget, [c]and I will make him a great nation.

21 But my [a]covenant will I establish with Isaac, [b]which Sarah shall bear unto thee at this [c]set time in the next year.

22 And he left off talking with him, and God went up from Abraham.

23 And Abraham took Ishmael his son, and all that were born in his house, and all that were bought with his money, every male among the men of Abraham's house; and circumcised the flesh of their foreskin in the selfsame day, as God had said unto him.

24 And Abraham *was* ninety years old and nine, when he was circumcised in the flesh of his foreskin.

25 And Ishmael his son *was* thirteen years

4 [a][Rom. 4:11, 12, 16]
5 [a]Neh. 9:7 [b]Rom. 4:17
6 [a]Gen. 17:16; 35:11 [b]Matt. 1:6
7 [a][Gal. 3:17] [b]Gen. 26:24; 28:13; Lev. 11:45; 26:12, 45; Heb. 11:16 [c]Rom. 9:8; Gal. 3:16
8 [a]Gen. 12:7; 13:15, 17; Acts 7:5 [b]Gen. 23:4; 28:4 [c]Ex. 6:7; 29:45; Lev. 26:12; Deut. 29:13; Rev. 21:7
9 [a]Ex. 19:5
10 [a]John 7:22; Acts 7:8
11 [a]Ex. 12:13, 48; [Rom. 4:11]
12 [a]Lev. 12:3
14 [a]Ex. 4:24–26
16 [a]Gen. 18:10 [b]Gen. 35:11; Gal. 4:31; 1 Pet. 3:6 [c]Gen. 17:6; 36:31; 1 Sam. 8:22
17 [a]Gen. 17:3; 18:12; 21:6
18 [a]Gen. 18:23
19 [a]Gen. 18:10; 21:2; [Gal. 4:28] [b]Gen. 22:16; Matt. 1:2; Luke 3:34
20 [a]Gen. 16:10 [b]Gen. 25:12–16 [c]Gen. 21:13, 18
21 [a]Gen. 26:2–5 [b]Gen. 21:2 [c]Gen. 18:14

NKJV

3 Then Abram fell on his face, and God talked with him, saying:

4 "As for Me, behold, My covenant is with you, and you shall be [a]a father of many nations.

5 "No longer shall [a]your name be called Abram, but your name shall be Abraham; [b]for I have made you a father of many nations.

6 "I will make you exceedingly fruitful; and I will make [a]nations of you, and [b]kings shall come from you.

7 "And I will [a]establish My covenant between Me and you and your descendants after you in their generations, for an everlasting covenant, [b]to be God to you and [c]your descendants after you.

8 "Also [a]I give to you and your descendants after you the land [b]in which you are a stranger, all the land of Canaan, as an everlasting possession; and [c]I will be their God."

9 And God said to Abraham: "As for you, [a]you shall keep My covenant, you and your descendants after you throughout their generations.

10 "This *is* My covenant which you shall keep, between Me and you and your descendants after you: [a]Every male child among you shall be circumcised;

11 "and you shall be circumcised in the flesh of your foreskins, and it shall be [a]a sign of the covenant between Me and you.

12 "He who is eight days old among you [a]shall be circumcised, every male child in your generations, he who is born in your house or bought with money from any foreigner who is not your descendant.

13 "He who is born in your house and he who is bought with your money must be circumcised, and My covenant shall be in your flesh for an everlasting covenant.

14 "And the uncircumcised male child, who is not circumcised in the flesh of his foreskin, that person [a]shall be cut off from his people; he has broken My covenant."

15 Then God said to Abraham, "As for Sarai your wife, you shall not call her name Sarai, but Sarah *shall be* her name.

16 "And I will bless her [a]and also give you a son by her; then I will bless her, and she shall be *a mother* [b]*of* nations; [c]kings of peoples shall be from her."

17 Then Abraham fell on his face [a]and laughed, and said in his heart, "Shall *a child* be born to a man who is one hundred years old? And shall Sarah, who is ninety years old, bear *a child?*"

18 And Abraham [a]said to God, "Oh, that Ishmael might live before You!"

19 Then God said: "No, [a]Sarah your wife shall bear you a son, and you shall call his name Isaac; I will establish My [b]covenant with him for an everlasting covenant, *and* with his descendants after him.

20 "And as for Ishmael, I have heard you. Behold, I have blessed him, and will make him fruitful, and [a]will multiply him exceedingly. He shall beget [b]twelve princes, [c]and I will make him a great nation.

21 "But My [a]covenant I will establish with Isaac, [b]whom Sarah shall bear to you at this [c]set time next year."

22 Then He finished talking with him, and God went up from Abraham.

23 So Abraham took Ishmael his son, all who were born in his house and all who were bought with his money, every male among the men of Abraham's house, and circumcised the flesh of their foreskins that very same day, as God had said to him.

24 Abraham *was* ninety-nine years old when he was circumcised in the flesh of his foreskin.

25 And Ishmael his son *was* thirteen years

KJV

old, when he was circumcised in the flesh of his foreskin.
26 In the selfsame day was Abraham circumcised, and Ishmael his son.
27 And [a]all the men of his house, born in the house, and bought with money of the stranger, were circumcised with him.

The Son of Promise
(Heb. 13:2)

18 And the LORD appeared unto him in the [a]plains of Mamre: and he sat in the tent door in the heat of the day;
2 [a]And he lift up his eyes and looked, and, lo, three men stood by him: [b]and when he saw *them,* he ran to meet them from the tent door, and bowed himself toward the ground,
3 And said, My Lord, if now I have found favour in thy sight, pass not away, I pray thee, from thy servant:
4 Let [a]a little water, I pray you, be fetched, and wash your feet, and rest yourselves under the tree:
5 And [a]I will fetch a morsel of bread, and [b]comfort ye your hearts; after that ye shall pass on: [c]for therefore are ye come to your servant. And they said, So do, as thou hast said.
6 And Abraham hastened into the tent unto Sarah, and said, Make ready quickly three measures of fine meal, knead *it,* and make cakes upon the hearth.
7 And Abraham ran unto the herd, and fetcht a calf tender and good, and gave *it* unto a young man; and he hasted to dress it.
8 And [a]he took butter, and milk, and the calf which he had dressed, and set *it* before them; and he stood by them under the tree, and they did eat.
9 And they said unto him, Where *is* Sarah thy wife? And he said, Behold, [a]in the tent.
10 And he said, I will certainly return unto thee [a]according to the time of life; and, lo, [b]Sarah thy wife shall have a son. And Sarah heard *it* in the tent door, which *was* behind him.
11 Now [a]Abraham and Sarah *were* old *and* well stricken in age; *and* it ceased to be with Sarah [b]after the manner of women.
12 Therefore Sarah [a]laughed within herself, saying, [b]After I am waxed old shall I have pleasure, my [c]lord being old also?
13 And the LORD said unto Abraham, Wherefore did Sarah laugh, saying, Shall I of a surety bear a child, which am old?
14 [a]Is any thing too hard for the LORD? [b]At the time appointed I will return unto thee, according to the time of life, and Sarah shall have a son.
15 Then Sarah denied, saying, I laughed not; for she was afraid. And he said, Nay; but thou didst laugh.

Abraham Intercedes for Sodom

16 And the men rose up from thence, and looked toward Sodom: and Abraham went with them [a]to bring them on the way.
17 And the LORD said, [a]Shall I hide from Abraham that thing which I do;
18 Seeing that Abraham shall surely become a great and mighty nation, and all the nations of the earth shall be [a]blessed in him?
19 For I know him, [a]that he will command his children and his household after him, and they shall keep the way of the LORD, to do justice and judgment; that the LORD may bring upon Abraham that which he hath spoken of him.
20 And the LORD said, Because [a]the cry of Sodom and Gomorrah is great, and because their [b]sin is very grievous;
21 [a]I will go down now, and see whether they have done altogether according to the cry of it, which is come unto me; and if not, [b]I will know.
22 And the men turned their faces from

27 [a]Gen. 18:19

CHAPTER 18

1 [a]Gen. 13:18; 14:13
2 [a]Gen. 18:16, 22; 32:24; Josh. 5:13; Judg. 13:6–11; Heb. 13:2 [b]Gen. 19:1; 1 Pet. 4:9
4 [a]Gen. 19:2; 24:32; 43:24
5 [a]Judg. 6:18, 19; 13:15, 16 [b]Judg. 19:5; Ps. 104:15 [c]Gen. 19:8; 33:10
8 [a]Gen. 19:3
9 [a]Gen. 24:67
10 [a]2 Kin. 4:16 [b]Gen. 17:19, 21; 21:2; Rom. 9:9
11 [a]Gen. 17:17; Luke 1:18; Rom. 4:19; Heb. 11:11, 12, 19 [b]Gen. 31:35
12 [a]Gen. 17:17 [b]Luke 1:18 [c]1 Pet. 3:6
14 [a]Num. 11:23; Jer. 32:17; Zech. 8:6; Matt. 3:9; 19:26; Luke 1:37; Rom. 4:21 [b]Gen. 17:21; 18:10; 2 Kin. 4:16
16 [a]Acts 15:3; Rom. 15:24
17 [a]Gen. 18:22, 26, 33; Ps. 25:14; Amos 3:7; [John 15:15]
18 [a][Gen. 12:3; 22:18]; Matt. 1:1; Luke 3:34; [Acts 3:25, 26; Gal. 3:8]
19 [a][Deut. 4:9, 10; 6:6, 7]
20 [a]Gen. 4:10; 19:13; Ezek. 16:49, 50 [b]Gen. 13:13
21 [a]Gen. 11:5; Ex. 3:8; Ps. 14:2 [b]Deut. 8:2; 13:3; Josh. 22:22; Luke 16:15; 2 Cor. 11:11

*

18:1 Heb. *Alon Mamre*
18:11 Lit. *the manner of women had ceased to be with Sarah*

NKJV

old when he was circumcised in the flesh of his foreskin.
26 That very same day Abraham was circumcised, and his son Ishmael;
27 and [a]all the men of his house, born in the house or bought with money from a foreigner, were circumcised with him.

The Son of Promise
(Heb. 13:2)

18 Then the LORD appeared to him by *the [a]terebinth trees of Mamre, as he was sitting in the tent door in the heat of the day.
2 [a]So he lifted his eyes and looked, and behold, three men were standing by him; [b]and when he saw *them,* he ran from the tent door to meet them, and bowed himself to the ground,
3 and said, "My Lord, if I have now found favor in Your sight, do not pass on by Your servant.
4 "Please let [a]a little water be brought, and wash your feet, and rest yourselves under the tree.
5 "And [a]I will bring a morsel of bread, that [b]you may refresh your hearts. After that you may pass by, [c]inasmuch as you have come to your servant." They said, "Do as you have said."
6 So Abraham hurried into the tent to Sarah and said, "Quickly, make ready three measures of fine meal; knead *it* and make cakes."
7 And Abraham ran to the herd, took a tender and good calf, gave *it* to a young man, and he hastened to prepare it.
8 So [a]he took butter and milk and the calf which he had prepared, and set *it* before them; and he stood by them under the tree as they ate.
9 Then they said to him, "Where *is* Sarah your wife?" So he said, "Here, [a]in the tent."
10 And He said, "I will certainly return to you [a]according to the time of life, and behold, [b]Sarah your wife shall have a son." (Sarah was listening in the tent door which *was* behind him.)
11 Now [a]Abraham and Sarah were old, well advanced in age; *and* *Sarah [b]had passed the age of childbearing.
12 Therefore Sarah [a]laughed within herself, saying, [b]"After I have grown old, shall I have pleasure, my [c]lord being old also?"
13 And the LORD said to Abraham, "Why did Sarah laugh, saying, 'Shall I surely bear *a child,* since I am old?'
14 [a]"Is anything too hard for the LORD? [b]At the appointed time I will return to you, according to the time of life, and Sarah shall have a son."
15 But Sarah denied *it,* saying, "I did not laugh," for she was afraid. And He said, "No, but you did laugh!"

Abraham Intercedes for Sodom

16 Then the men rose from there and looked toward Sodom, and Abraham went with them [a]to send them on the way.
17 And the LORD said, [a]"Shall I hide from Abraham what I am doing,
18 "since Abraham shall surely become a great and mighty nation, and all the nations of the earth shall be [a]blessed in him?
19 "For I have known him, in order [a]that he may command his children and his household after him, that they keep the way of the LORD, to do righteousness and justice, that the LORD may bring to Abraham what He has spoken to him."
20 And the LORD said, "Because [a]the outcry against Sodom and Gomorrah is great, and because their [b]sin is very grave,
21 [a]"I will go down now and see whether they have done altogether according to the outcry against it that has come to Me; and if not, [b]I will know."
22 Then the men turned away from there

KJV

thence, [a]and went toward Sodom: but Abraham
stood yet before the LORD.
23 And Abraham [a]drew near, and said, [b]Wilt
thou also [c]destroy the [d]righteous with the wicked?
24 Peradventure there be fifty righteous
within the city: wilt thou also destroy and not
spare the place for the fifty righteous that *are*
therein?
25 That be far from thee to do after this manner, to slay the righteous with the wicked: and
[a]that the righteous should be as the wicked, that
be far from thee: [b]Shall not the Judge of all the
earth do right?
26 And the LORD said, [a]If I find in Sodom
fifty righteous within the city, then I will spare
all the place for their sakes.
27 And Abraham answered and said, Behold
now, I have taken upon me to speak unto the Lord,
which *am* [a]*but* dust and ashes:
28 Peradventure there shall lack five of the
fifty righteous: wilt thou destroy all the city for
lack of five? And he said, If I find there forty and
five, I will not destroy *it*.
29 And he spake unto him yet again, and
said, Peradventure there shall be forty found
there. And he said, I will not do *it* for forty's sake.
30 And he said *unto him,* Oh let not the Lord
be angry, and I will speak: Peradventure there
shall thirty be found there. And he said, I will
not do *it,* if I find thirty there.
31 And he said, Behold now, I have taken
upon me to speak unto the Lord: Peradventure
there shall be twenty found there. And he said, I
will not destroy *it* for twenty's sake.
32 And he said, [a]Oh let not the Lord be angry, and I will speak yet but this once: Peradventure ten shall be found there. [b]And he said, I will
not destroy *it* for ten's sake.
33 And the LORD went his way, as soon as
he had left communing with Abraham: and Abraham returned unto his place.

Sodom's Depravity

19 And there [a]came two angels to Sodom at
even; and [b]Lot sat in the gate of Sodom:
and Lot seeing *them* rose up to meet them; and
he bowed himself with his face toward the
ground;
2 And he said, Behold now, my lords, [a]turn
in, I pray you, into your servant's house, and tarry
all night, and [b]wash your feet, and ye shall rise
up early, and go on your ways. And they said,
[c]Nay; but we will abide in the street all night.
3 And he pressed upon them greatly; and
they turned in unto him, and entered into his
house; [a]and he made them a feast, and did bake
[b]unleavened bread, and they did eat.
4 But before they lay down, the men of the
city, *even* the men of Sodom, compassed the
house round, both old and young, all the people
from every quarter:
5 [a]And they called unto Lot, and said unto
him, Where *are* the men which came in to thee
this night? [b]bring them out unto us, that we [c]may
know them.
6 And [a]Lot went out at the door unto them,
and shut the door after him,
7 And said, I pray you, brethren, do not so
wickedly.
8 [a]Behold now, I have two daughters which
have not known man; let me, I pray you, bring
them out unto you, and do ye to them as *is* good
in your eyes: only unto these men do nothing;
[b]for therefore came they under the shadow of my
roof.
9 And they said, Stand back. And they said
again, This one *fellow* [a]came in to sojourn, [b]and
he will needs be a judge: now will we deal worse
with thee, than with them. And they pressed sore
upon the man, *even* Lot, and came near to break
the door.

22 [a]Gen. 18:16; 19:1
23 [a][Heb. 10:22] [b]Ex. 23:7; Num. 16:22; 2 Sam. 24:17; Ps. 11:4–7 [c]Job 9:22 [d]Gen. 20:4
25 [a]Job 8:20; Is. 3:10, 11 [b]Deut. 1:16, 17; 32:4; Job 8:3, 20; 34:17; Ps. 58:11; 94:2; Is. 3:10, 11; Rom. 3:5, 6
26 [a]Jer. 5:1; Ezek. 22:30
27 [a][Gen. 3:19]; Job 4:19; 30:19; 42:6; [1 Cor. 15:47, 48]
32 [a]Judg. 6:39 [b]James 5:16

CHAPTER 19
1 [a]Gen. 18:2, 16, 22 [b]Gen. 18:1–5
2 [a]Gen. 24:31; [Heb. 13:2] [b]Gen. 18:4; 24:32 [c]Luke 24:28
3 [a]Gen. 18:6–8; Ex. 23:15; Num. 9:11; 28:17 [b]Ex. 12:8
5 [a]Is. 3:9 [b]Judg. 19:22 [c]Gen. 4:1; Rom. 1:24, 27; Jude 7
6 [a]Judg. 19:23
8 [a]Judg. 19:24 [b]Gen. 18:5
9 [a]2 Pet. 2:7, 8 [b]Ex. 2:14

NKJV

[a]and went toward Sodom, but Abraham still stood
before the LORD.
23 And Abraham [a]came near and said,
[b]"Would You also [c]destroy the [d]righteous with
the wicked?
24 "Suppose there were fifty righteous within
the city; would You also destroy the place and
not spare *it* for the fifty righteous that were in
it?
25 "Far be it from You to do such a thing as
this, to slay the righteous with the wicked, so [a]that
the righteous should be as the wicked; far be it
from You! [b]Shall not the Judge of all the earth
do right?"
26 So the LORD said, [a]"If I find in Sodom fifty
righteous within the city, then I will spare all the
place for their sakes."
27 Then Abraham answered and said, "Indeed now, I who *am* [a]*but* dust and ashes have
taken it upon myself to speak to the Lord:
28 "Suppose there were five less than the
fifty righteous; would You destroy all of the city
for *lack of* five?" So He said, "If I find there forty-
five, I will not destroy *it*."
29 And he spoke to Him yet again and said,
"Suppose there should be forty found there?" So
He said, "I will not do *it* for the sake of forty."
30 Then he said, "Let not the Lord be angry,
and I will speak: Suppose thirty should be found
there?" So He said, "I will not do *it* if I find thirty
there."
31 And he said, "Indeed now, I have taken
it upon myself to speak to the Lord: Suppose
twenty should be found there?" So He said, "I
will not destroy *it* for the sake of twenty."
32 Then he said, [a]"Let not the Lord be angry,
and I will speak but once more: Suppose ten
should be found there?" [b]And He said, "I will not
destroy *it* for the sake of ten."
33 So the LORD went His way as soon as He
had finished speaking with Abraham; and Abraham returned to his place.

Sodom's Depravity

19 Now [a]the two angels came to Sodom in the
evening, and [b]Lot was sitting in the gate
of Sodom. When Lot saw *them,* he rose to meet
them, and he bowed himself with his face toward
the ground.
2 And he said, "Here now, my lords, please
[a]turn in to your servant's house and spend the
night, and [b]wash your feet; then you may rise
early and go on your way." And they said, [c]"No,
but we will spend the night in the open square."
3 But he insisted strongly; so they turned
in to him and entered his house. [a]Then he made
them a feast, and baked [b]unleavened bread, and
they ate.
4 Now before they lay down, the men of the
city, the men of Sodom, both old and young, all
the people from every quarter, surrounded the
house.
5 [a]And they called to Lot and said to him,
"Where are the men who came to you tonight?
[b]Bring them out to us that we [c]may know them
carnally."
6 So [a]Lot went out to them through the
doorway, shut the door behind him,
7 and said, "Please, my brethren, do not do
so wickedly!
8 [a]"See now, I have two daughters who
have not known a man; please, let me bring them
out to you, and you may do to them as you wish;
only do nothing to these men, [b]since this is the
reason they have come under the shadow of my
roof."
9 And they said, "Stand back!" Then they
said, "This one [a]came in to stay *here,* [b]and he
keeps acting as a judge; now we will deal worse
with you than with them." So they pressed hard
against the man Lot, and came near to break
down the door.

KJV

10 But the men put forth their hand, and pulled Lot into the house to them, and shut to the door.

11 And they [a]smote the men that *were* at the door of the house with blindness, both small and great: so that they wearied themselves to find the door.

Sodom and Gomorrah Destroyed
(Matt. 11:23, 24; Luke 17:28–32)

12 And the men said unto Lot, Hast thou here any besides? son in law, and thy sons, and thy daughters, and whatsoever thou hast in the city, [a]bring *them* out of this place:

13 For we will destroy this place, because the [a]cry of them is waxen great before the face of the LORD; and [b]the LORD hath sent us to destroy it.

14 And Lot went out, and spake unto his sons in law, [a]which married his daughters, and said, [b]Up, get you out of this place; for the LORD will destroy this city. [c]But he seemed as one that mocked unto his sons in law.

15 And when the morning arose, then the angels hastened Lot, saying, [a]Arise, take thy wife, and thy two daughters, which are here; lest thou be consumed in the iniquity of the city.

16 And while he lingered, the men [a]laid hold upon his hand, and upon the hand of his wife, and upon the hand of his two daughters; the [b]LORD being merciful unto him: [c]and they brought him forth, and set him without the city.

17 And it came to pass, when they had brought them forth abroad, that he said, [a]Escape for thy life; [b]look not behind thee, neither stay thou in all the plain; escape [c]to the mountain, lest thou be consumed.

18 And Lot said unto them, Oh, [a]not so, my Lord:

19 Behold now, thy servant hath found grace in thy sight, and thou hast magnified thy mercy, which thou hast shewed unto me in saving my life; and I cannot escape to the mountain, lest some evil take me, and I die:

20 Behold now, this city *is* near to flee unto, and it *is* a little one: Oh, let me escape thither, (*is* it not a little one?) and my soul shall live.

21 And he said unto him, See, [a]I have accepted thee concerning this thing also, that I will not overthrow this city, for the which thou hast spoken.

22 Haste thee, escape thither; for [a]I cannot do any thing till thou be come thither. Therefore [b]the name of the city was called Zoar.

23 The sun was risen upon the earth when Lot entered into Zoar.

24 Then the LORD rained upon [a]Sodom and upon Gomorrah brimstone and [b]fire from the LORD out of heaven;

25 And he overthrew those cities, and all the plain, and all the inhabitants of the cities, and [a]that which grew upon the ground.

26 But his wife looked back from behind him, and she became [a]a pillar of salt.

27 And Abraham gat up early in the morning to the place where [a]he stood before the LORD:

28 And he looked toward Sodom and Gomorrah, and toward all the land of the plain, and beheld, and, lo, [a]the smoke of the country went up as the smoke of a furnace.

29 And it came to pass, when God destroyed the cities of the plain, that God [a]remembered Abraham, and sent Lot out of the midst of the overthrow, when he overthrew the cities in the which Lot dwelt.

The Descendants of Lot

30 And Lot went up out of Zoar, and [a]dwelt in the mountain, and his two daughters with him; for he feared to dwell in Zoar: and he dwelt in a cave, he and his two daughters.

31 And the firstborn said unto the younger,

11 [a]Gen. 20:17
12 [a]Gen. 7:1; 2 Pet. 2:7, 9
13 [a]Gen. 18:20 [b]Lev. 26:30–33; Deut. 4:26; 28:45; 1 Chr. 21:15
14 [a]Matt. 1:18 [b]Num. 16:21, 24, 26, 45; Rev. 18:4 [c]Ex. 9:21; Jer. 43:1, 2; Luke 17:28; 24:11
15 [a]Ps. 37:2; Rev. 18:4
16 [a]Deut. 5:15; 6:21; 7:8; 2 Pet. 2:7 [b]Ex. 34:7; Ps. 32:10; 33:18, 19; Luke 18:13 [c]Ps. 34:22
17 [a]1 Kin. 19:3; Jer. 48:6 [b]Gen. 19:26; Matt. 24:16–18; Luke 9:62; Phil. 3:13, 14 [c]Gen. 14:10
18 [a]Acts 10:14
21 [a]Job 42:8, 9; Ps. 145:19
22 [a]Ex. 32:10; Deut. 9:14 [b]Gen. 13:10; 14:2
24 [a]Deut. 29:23; Ps. 11:6; Is. 13:19; Jer. 20:16; 23:14; 49:18; 50:40; Ezek. 16:49, 50; Hos. 11:8; Amos 4:11; Zeph. 2:9; Matt. 10:15; Mark 6:11; Luke 17:29; Rom. 9:29; 2 Pet. 2:6; Jude 7; Rev. 11:8 [b]Lev. 10:2
25 [a]Ps. 107:34
26 [a]Gen. 19:17; Luke 17:32
27 [a]Gen. 18:22
28 [a]Rev. 9:2; 18:9
29 [a]Gen. 8:1; 18:23; Deut. 7:8; 9:5, 27
30 [a]Gen. 19:17, 19

NKJV

10 But the men reached out their hands and pulled Lot into the house with them, and shut the door.

11 And they [a]struck the men who *were* at the doorway of the house with blindness, both small and great, so that they became weary *trying* to find the door.

Sodom and Gomorrah Destroyed
(Matt. 11:23, 24; Luke 17:28–32)

12 Then the men said to Lot, "Have you anyone else here? Son-in-law, your sons, your daughters, and whomever you have in the city—[a]take *them* out of this place!

13 "For we will destroy this place, because the [a]outcry against them has grown great before the face of the LORD, and [b]the LORD has sent us to destroy it."

14 So Lot went out and spoke to his sons-in-law, [a]who had married his daughters, and said, [b]"Get up, get out of this place; for the LORD will destroy this city!" [c]But to his sons-in-law he seemed to be joking.

15 When the morning dawned, the angels urged Lot to hurry, saying, [a]"Arise, take your wife and your two daughters who are here, lest you be consumed in the punishment of the city."

16 And while he lingered, the men [a]took hold of his hand, his wife's hand, and the hands of his two daughters, the [b]LORD being merciful to him, [c]and they brought him out and set him outside the city.

17 So it came to pass, when they had brought them outside, that *he said, [a]"Escape for your life! [b]Do not look behind you nor stay anywhere in the plain. Escape [c]to the mountains, lest you be destroyed."

18 Then Lot said to them, "Please, [a]no, my lords!

19 "Indeed now, your servant has found favor in your sight, and you have increased your mercy which you have shown me by saving my life; but I cannot escape to the mountains, lest some evil overtake me and I die.

20 "See now, this city *is* near *enough* to flee to, and it *is* a little one; please let me escape there (*is* it not a little one?) and my soul shall live."

21 And he said to him, "See, [a]I have favored you concerning this thing also, in that I will not overthrow this city for which you have spoken.

22 "Hurry, escape there. For [a]I cannot do anything until you arrive there." Therefore [b]the name of the city was called Zoar.

23 The sun had risen upon the earth when Lot entered Zoar.

24 Then the LORD rained [a]brimstone and [b]fire on Sodom and Gomorrah, from the LORD out of the heavens.

25 So He overthrew those cities, all the plain, all the inhabitants of the cities, and [a]what grew on the ground.

26 But his wife looked back behind him, and she became [a]a pillar of salt.

27 And Abraham went early in the morning to the place where [a]he had stood before the LORD.

28 Then he looked toward Sodom and Gomorrah, and toward all the land of the plain; and he saw, and behold, [a]the smoke of the land which went up like the smoke of a furnace.

29 And it came to pass, when God destroyed the cities of the plain, that God [a]remembered Abraham, and sent Lot out of the midst of the overthrow, when He overthrew the cities in which Lot had dwelt.

The Descendants of Lot

30 Then Lot went up out of Zoar and [a]dwelt in the mountains, and his two daughters were with him; for he was afraid to dwell in Zoar. And he and his two daughters dwelt in a cave.

31 Now the firstborn said to the younger,

*19:17 LXX, Syr., Vg. *they*

KJV

Our father *is* old, and *there is* not a man in the earth [a]to come in unto us after the manner of all the earth:

32 Come, let us make our father drink wine, and we will lie with him, that we [a]may preserve seed of our father.

33 And they made their father drink wine that night: and the firstborn went in, and lay with her father; and he perceived not when she lay down, nor when she arose.

34 And it came to pass on the morrow, that the firstborn said unto the younger, Behold, I lay yesternight with my father: let us make him drink wine this night also; and go thou in, *and* lie with him, that we may preserve seed of our father.

35 And they made their father drink wine that night also: and the younger arose, and lay with him; and he perceived not when she lay down, nor when she arose.

36 Thus were both the daughters of Lot with child by their father.

37 And the firstborn bare a son, and called his name Moab: [a]the same *is* the father of the Moabites unto this day.

38 And the younger, she also bare a son, and called his name Ben–ammi: [a]the same *is* the father of the children of Ammon unto this day.

Abraham and Abimelech

20 And Abraham journeyed from [a]thence toward the south country, and dwelled between [b]Kadesh and Shur, and [c]sojourned in Gerar.

2 And Abraham said of Sarah his wife, [a]She *is* my sister: and Abimelech king of Gerar sent, and [b]took Sarah.

3 But [a]God came to Abimelech [b]in a dream by night, and said to him, [c]Behold, thou *art but* a dead man, for the woman which thou hast taken; for she *is* a man's wife.

4 But Abimelech had not come near her: and he said, Lord, [a]wilt thou slay also a righteous nation?

5 Said he not unto me, She *is* my sister? and she, even she herself said, He *is* my brother: [a]in the integrity of my heart and innocency of my hands have I done this.

6 And God said unto him in a dream, Yea, I know that thou didst this in the integrity of thy heart; for [a]I also withheld thee from sinning [b]against me: therefore suffered I thee not to touch her.

7 Now therefore restore the man *his* wife; [a]for he *is* a prophet, and he shall pray for thee, and thou shalt live: and if thou restore *her* not, [b]know thou that thou shalt surely die, thou, [c]and all that *are* thine.

8 Therefore Abimelech rose early in the morning, and called all his servants, and told all these things in their ears: and the men were sore afraid.

9 Then Abimelech called Abraham, and said unto him, What hast thou done unto us? and what have I offended thee, [a]that thou hast brought on me and on my kingdom a great sin? thou hast done deeds unto me [b]that ought not to be done.

10 And Abimelech said unto Abraham, What sawest thou, that thou hast done this thing?

11 And Abraham said, Because I thought, Surely [a]the fear of God *is* not in this place; and [b]they will slay me for my wife's sake.

12 And yet indeed [a]*she is* my sister; she *is* the daughter of my father, but not the daughter of my mother; and she became my wife.

13 And it came to pass, when [a]God caused me to wander from my father's house, that I said unto her, This *is* thy kindness which thou shalt shew unto me; at every place whither we shall come, [b]say of me, He *is* my brother.

14 And Abimelech [a]took sheep, and oxen,

31 [a]Gen. 16:2, 4; 38:8, 9; Deut. 25:5
32 [a][Mark 12:19]
37 [a]Num. 25:1; Deut. 2:9
38 [a]Num. 21:24; Deut. 2:19

CHAPTER 20

1 [a]Gen. 18:1 [b]Gen. 12:9; 16:7, 14 [c]Gen. 26:1, 6
2 [a]Gen. 12:11–13; 26:7 [b]Gen. 12:15
3 [a]Ps. 105:14 [b]Job 33:15 [c]Gen. 20:7
4 [a]Gen. 18:23–25; Num. 16:22
5 [a]1 Kin. 9:4; 2 Kin. 20:3; Ps. 7:8; 26:6
6 [a]Gen. 31:7; 35:5; Ex. 34:24; 1 Sam. 25:26, 34 [b]Gen. 39:9; 2 Sam. 12:13
7 [a]1 Sam. 7:5; 2 Kin. 5:11; Job 42:8; James 5:14, 15 [b]Gen. 2:17 [c]Num. 16:32, 33
9 [a]Gen. 26:10; 39:9; Ex. 32:21; Josh. 7:25 [b]Gen. 34:7
11 [a]Gen. 42:18; Neh. 5:15; Ps. 36:1; Prov. 16:6 [b]Gen. 12:12; 26:7
12 [a]Gen. 11:29
13 [a]Gen. 12:1–9, 11; [Heb. 11:8] [b]Gen. 12:13; 20:5
14 [a]Gen. 12:16

NKJV

"Our father *is* old, and *there is* no man on the earth [a]to come in to us as is the custom of all the earth.

32 "Come, let us make our father drink wine, and we will lie with him, that we [a]may preserve the lineage of our father."

33 So they made their father drink wine that night. And the firstborn went in and lay with her father, and he did not know when she lay down or when she arose.

34 It happened on the next day that the firstborn said to the younger, "Indeed I lay with my father last night; let us make him drink wine tonight also, and you go in *and* lie with him, that we may preserve the lineage of our father."

35 Then they made their father drink wine that night also. And the younger arose and lay with him, and he did not know when she lay down or when she arose.

36 Thus both the daughters of Lot were with child by their father.

37 The firstborn bore a son and called his name Moab; [a]he *is* the father of the Moabites to this day.

38 And the younger, she also bore a son and called his name Ben-Ammi; [a]he *is* the father of the people of Ammon to this day.

Abraham and Abimelech

20 And Abraham journeyed from [a]there to the South, and dwelt between [b]Kadesh and Shur, and [c]stayed in Gerar.

2 Now Abraham said of Sarah his wife, [a]"She *is* my sister." And Abimelech king of Gerar sent and [b]took Sarah.

3 But [a]God came to Abimelech [b]in a dream by night, and said to him, [c]"Indeed you *are* a dead man because of the woman whom you have taken, for she *is* a man's wife."

4 But Abimelech had not come near her; and he said, "Lord, [a]will You slay a righteous nation also?

5 "Did he not say to me, 'She *is* my sister'? And she, even she herself said, 'He *is* my brother.' [a]In the integrity of my heart and innocence of my hands I have done this."

6 And God said to him in a dream, "Yes, I know that you did this in the integrity of your heart. For [a]I also withheld you from sinning [b]against Me; therefore I did not let you touch her.

7 "Now therefore, restore the man's wife; [a]for he *is* a prophet, and he will pray for you and you shall live. But if you do not restore *her,* [b]know that you shall surely die, you [c]and all who *are* yours."

8 So Abimelech rose early in the morning, called all his servants, and told all these things in their hearing; and the men were very much afraid.

9 And Abimelech called Abraham and said to him, "What have you done to us? How have I offended you, [a]that you have brought on me and on my kingdom a great sin? You have done deeds to me [b]that ought not to be done."

10 Then Abimelech said to Abraham, "What did you have in view, that you have done this thing?"

11 And Abraham said, "Because I thought, surely [a]the fear of God *is* not in this place; and [b]they will kill me on account of my wife.

12 "But indeed [a]*she is* truly my sister. She *is* the daughter of my father, but not the daughter of my mother; and she became my wife.

13 "And it came to pass, when [a]God caused me to wander from my father's house, that I said to her, 'This *is* your kindness that you should do for me: in every place, wherever we go, [b]say of me, "He *is* my brother." ' "

14 Then Abimelech [a]took sheep, oxen, and

KJV

and menservants, and womenservants, and gave
them unto Abraham, and restored him Sarah his
wife.
15 And Abimelech said, Behold, [a]my land *is*
before thee: dwell where it pleaseth thee.
16 And unto Sarah he said, Behold, I have
given thy brother a thousand *pieces* of silver: [a]be-
hold, he *is* to thee [b]a covering of the eyes, unto
all that *are* with thee, and with all *other*: thus she
was reproved.
17 So Abraham [a]prayed unto God: and God
[b]healed Abimelech, and his wife, and his maidservants; and they bare *children*.
18 For the LORD [a]had fast closed up all the
wombs of the house of Abimelech, because of
Sarah Abraham's wife.

Isaac Is Born
(Heb. 11:11)

21 And the LORD [a]visited Sarah as he had said,
and the LORD did unto Sarah [b]as he had
spoken.
2 For Sarah [a]conceived, and bare Abraham
a son in his old age, [b]at the set time of which
God had spoken to him.
3 And Abraham called the name of his son
that was born unto him, whom Sarah bare to him,
[a]Isaac.
4 And Abraham [a]circumcised his son Isaac
being eight days old, [b]as God had commanded
him.
5 And [a]Abraham was an hundred years old,
when his son Isaac was born unto him.
6 And Sarah said, [a]God hath made me to
laugh, *so that* all that hear [b]will laugh with
me.
7 And she said, Who would have said unto
Abraham, that Sarah should have given children
suck? [a]for I have born *him* a son in his old age.

Hagar and Ishmael Depart
(Gal. 4:21–30)

8 And the child grew, and was weaned: and
Abraham made a great feast the *same* day that
Isaac was weaned.
9 And Sarah saw the son of Hagar [a]the
Egyptian, which she had born unto Abraham,
[b]mocking.
10 Wherefore she said unto Abraham, [a]Cast
out this bondwoman and her son: for the son of
this bondwoman shall not be heir with my son,
even with Isaac.
11 And the thing was very grievous in Abraham's sight [a]because of his son.
12 And God said unto Abraham, Let it not
be grievous in thy sight because of the lad, and
because of thy bondwoman; in all that Sarah hath
said unto thee, hearken unto her voice; for [a]in
Isaac shall thy seed be called.
13 And also of the son of the bondwoman
will I make [a]a nation, because he *is* thy seed.
14 And Abraham rose up early in the morning, and took bread, and a bottle of water, and
gave *it* unto Hagar, putting *it* on her shoulder,
and the child, and [a]sent her away: and she departed, and wandered in the wilderness of Beersheba.
15 And the water was spent in the bottle, and
she cast the child under one of the shrubs.
16 And she went, and sat her down over
against *him* a good way off, as it were a bowshot:
for she said, Let me not see the death of the child.
And she sat over against *him*, and lift up her voice,
and wept.
17 And [a]God heard the voice of the lad; and
the [b]angel of God called to Hagar out of heaven,
and said unto her, What aileth thee, Hagar? fear
not; for God hath heard the voice of the lad where
he *is*.
18 Arise, lift up the lad, and hold him in thine
hand; for [a]I will make him a great nation.
19 And [a]God opened her eyes, and she saw

15 [a]Gen. 13:9; 34:10; 47:6
16 [a]Gen. 26:11 [b]Gen. 24:65
17 [a]Num. 12:13; 21:7; Job 42:9; [James 5:16] [b]Gen. 21:2
18 [a]Gen. 12:17

CHAPTER 21

1 [a]1 Sam. 2:21 [b]Gen. 17:16, 19, 21; 18:10, 14; [Gal. 4:23, 28]
2 [a]Acts 7:8; Gal. 4:22; Heb. 11:11, 12 [b]Gen. 17:21; 18:10, 14; Gal. 4:4
3 [a]Gen. 17:19, 21
4 [a]Acts 7:8 [b]Gen. 17:10, 12; Lev. 12:3
5 [a]Gen. 17:1, 17
6 [a]Gen. 18:13; Ps. 126:2; Is. 54:1 [b]Luke 1:58
7 [a]Gen. 18:11, 12
9 [a]Gen. 16:1, 4, 15 [b][Gal. 4:29]
10 [a]Gen. 25:6; 36:6, 7; Gal. 3:18; 4:30
11 [a]Gen. 17:18
12 [a]Matt. 1:2; Luke 3:34; [Rom. 9:7, 8]; Heb. 11:18
13 [a]Gen. 16:10; 17:20; 21:18; 25:12–18
14 [a]John 8:35
17 [a]Ex. 3:7; Deut. 26:7; Ps. 6:8 [b]Gen. 22:11
18 [a]Gen. 16:10; 21:13; 25:12–16
19 [a]Gen. 3:7; Num. 22:31; 2 Kin. 6:17; Luke 24:31

NKJV

male and female servants, and gave *them* to Abraham; and he restored Sarah his wife to him.
15 And Abimelech said, "See, [a]my land *is* before you; dwell where it pleases you."
16 Then to Sarah he said, "Behold, I have
given your brother a thousand *pieces* of silver;
[a]indeed this *vindicates you [b]before all who *are*
with you and before everybody." Thus she was
rebuked.
17 So Abraham [a]prayed to God; and God
[b]healed Abimelech, his wife, and his female servants. Then they bore *children;*
18 for the LORD [a]had closed up all the wombs
of the house of Abimelech because of Sarah,
Abraham's wife.

Isaac Is Born
(Heb. 11:11)

21 And the LORD [a]visited Sarah as He had
said, and the LORD did for Sarah [b]as He
had spoken.
2 For Sarah [a]conceived and bore Abraham
a son in his old age, [b]at the set time of which
God had spoken to him.
3 And Abraham called the name of his son
who was born to him—whom Sarah bore to him—
[a]Isaac.
4 Then Abraham [a]circumcised his son Isaac
when he was eight days old, [b]as God had commanded him.
5 Now [a]Abraham was one hundred years
old when his son Isaac was born to him.
6 And Sarah said, [a]"God has made me
laugh, *and* all who hear [b]will laugh with me."
7 She also said, "Who would have said to
Abraham that Sarah would nurse children? [a]For
I have borne *him* a son in his old age."

Hagar and Ishmael Depart
(Gal. 4:21–30)

8 So the child grew and was weaned. And
Abraham made a great feast on the same day that
Isaac was weaned.
9 And Sarah saw the son of Hagar [a]the
Egyptian, whom she had borne to Abraham,
[b]scoffing.
10 Therefore she said to Abraham, [a]"Cast
out this bondwoman and her son; for the son of
this bondwoman shall not be heir with my son,
namely with Isaac."
11 And the matter was very displeasing in
Abraham's sight [a]because of his son.
12 But God said to Abraham, "Do not let it
be displeasing in your sight because of the lad
or because of your bondwoman. Whatever Sarah
has said to you, listen to her voice; for [a]in Isaac
your seed shall be called.
13 "Yet I will also make [a]a nation of the son
of the bondwoman, because he *is* your seed."
14 So Abraham rose early in the morning,
and took bread and a skin of water; and putting
it on her shoulder, he gave *it* and the boy to Hagar, and [a]sent her away. Then she departed and
wandered in the Wilderness of Beersheba.
15 And the water in the skin was used up,
and she placed the boy under one of the shrubs.
16 Then she went and sat down across from
him at a distance of about a bowshot; for she said
to herself, "Let me not see the death of the boy."
So she sat opposite *him*, and lifted her voice and
wept.
17 And [a]God heard the voice of the lad. Then
the [b]angel of God called to Hagar out of heaven,
and said to her, "What ails you, Hagar? Fear not,
for God has heard the voice of the lad where he
is.
18 "Arise, lift up the lad and hold him with
your hand, for [a]I will make him a great nation."
19 Then [a]God opened her eyes, and she saw

*———

20:16 Lit. *is a covering of the eyes for you to all*

KJV

a well of water; and she went, and filled the bottle
with water, and gave the lad drink.
20 And God [a]was with the lad; and he grew,
and dwelt in the wilderness, [b]and became an
archer.
21 And he dwelt in the wilderness of Paran:
and his mother [a]took him a wife out of the land
of Egypt.

A Covenant with Abimelech

22 And it came to pass at that time, that
[a]Abimelech and Phichol the chief captain of his
host spake unto Abraham, saying, [b]God *is* with
thee in all that thou doest:
23 Now therefore [a]swear unto me here by
God that thou wilt not deal falsely with me, nor
with my son, nor with my son's son: *but* according
to the kindness that I have done unto thee, thou
shalt do unto me, and to the land wherein thou
hast sojourned.
24 And Abraham said, I will swear.
25 And Abraham reproved Abimelech because of a well of water, which Abimelech's servants [a]had violently taken away.
26 And Abimelech said, I wot not who hath
done this thing: neither didst thou tell me, neither
yet heard I *of it*, but to day.
27 And Abraham took sheep and oxen, and
gave them unto Abimelech; and both of them
[a]made a covenant.
28 And Abraham set seven ewe lambs of the
flock by themselves.
29 And Abimelech said unto Abraham,
[a]What *mean* these seven ewe lambs which thou
hast set by themselves?
30 And he said, For *these* seven ewe lambs
shalt thou take of my hand, that [a]they may be a
witness unto me, that I have digged this well.
31 Wherefore he [a]called that place Beer–
sheba; because there they sware both of them.
32 Thus they made a covenant at Beer–
sheba: then Abimelech rose up, and Phichol the
chief captain of his host, and they returned into
the land of the Philistines.
33 And *Abraham* planted a grove in Beer–
sheba, and [a]called there on the name of the LORD,
[b]the everlasting God.
34 And Abraham sojourned in the Philistines' land many days.

Abraham's Faith Confirmed
(Heb. 11:17–19)

22 And it came to pass after these things, that
[a]God did tempt Abraham, and said unto
him, Abraham: and he said, Behold, *here* I *am*.
2 And he said, Take now thy son, [a]thine
only *son* Isaac, whom thou [b]lovest, and get thee
[c]into the land of Moriah; and offer him there for
a [d]burnt offering upon one of the mountains
which I will tell thee of.
3 And Abraham rose up early in the morning, and saddled his ass, and took two of his
young men with him, and Isaac his son, and clave
the wood for the burnt offering, and rose up, and
went unto the place of which God had told him.
4 Then on the third day Abraham lifted up
his eyes, and saw the place afar off.
5 And Abraham said unto his young men,
Abide ye here with the ass; and I and the lad will
go yonder and worship, and [a]come again to you.
6 And Abraham took the wood of the burnt
offering, and [a]laid *it* upon Isaac his son; and he
took the fire in his hand, and a knife; and they
went both of them together.
7 And Isaac spake unto Abraham his father,
and said, My father: and he said, Here *am* I, my
son. And he said, Behold the fire and the wood:
but where *is* the lamb for a burnt offering?
8 And Abraham said, My son, God will provide himself a [a]lamb for a [b]burnt offering: so they
went both of them together.

20 [a]Gen. 28:15; 39:2, 3, 21 [b]Gen. 16:12
21 [a]Gen. 24:4
22 [a]Gen. 20:2, 14; 26:26 [b]Gen. 26:28; Is. 8:10
23 [a]Josh. 2:12; 1 Sam. 24:21
25 [a]Gen. 26:15, 18, 20–22
27 [a]Gen. 26:31; 31:44; 1 Sam. 18:3
29 [a]Gen. 33:8
30 [a]Gen. 31:48, 52
31 [a]Gen. 21:14; 26:33
33 [a]Gen. 4:26; 12:8; 13:4; 26:25 [b]Gen. 35:11; Ex. 15:18; Deut. 32:40; 33:27; Ps. 90:2; 93:2; Is. 40:28; Jer. 10:10; Hab. 1:12; Heb. 13:8

CHAPTER 22

1 [a]Deut. 8:2, 16; 1 Cor. 10:13; Heb. 11:17; [James 1:12–14; 1 Pet. 1:7]
2 [a]Gen. 22:12, 16; John 3:16; Heb. 11:17; 1 John 4:9 [b]John 5:20 [c]2 Chr. 3:1 [d]Gen. 8:20; 31:54
5 [a][Heb. 11:19]
6 [a]John 19:17
8 [a]John 1:29, 36 [b]Ex. 12:3–6

*

21:31 Lit. *Well of the Oath* or *Well of the Seven*
22:5 Or *young man*

NKJV

a well of water. And she went and filled the skin
with water, and gave the lad a drink.
20 So God [a]was with the lad; and he grew
and dwelt in the wilderness, [b]and became an
archer.
21 He dwelt in the Wilderness of Paran; and
his mother [a]took a wife for him from the land of
Egypt.

A Covenant with Abimelech

22 And it came to pass at that time that
[a]Abimelech and Phichol, the commander of his
army, spoke to Abraham, saying, [b]"God *is* with
you in all that you do.
23 "Now therefore, [a]swear to me by God that
you will not deal falsely with me, with my offspring, or with my posterity; but that according
to the kindness that I have done to you, you will
do to me and to the land in which you have dwelt."
24 And Abraham said, "I will swear."
25 Then Abraham rebuked Abimelech because of a well of water which Abimelech's servants [a]had seized.
26 And Abimelech said, "I do not know who
has done this thing; you did not tell me, nor had
I heard *of it* until today."
27 So Abraham took sheep and oxen and
gave them to Abimelech, and the two of them
[a]made a covenant.
28 And Abraham set seven ewe lambs of the
flock by themselves.
29 Then Abimelech asked Abraham, [a]"What
is the meaning of these seven ewe lambs which
you have set by themselves?"
30 And he said, "You will take *these* seven
ewe lambs from my hand, that [a]they may be my
witness that I have dug this well."
31 Therefore he [a]called that place *Beersheba, because the two of them swore an oath
there.
32 Thus they made a covenant at Beersheba.
So Abimelech rose with Phichol, the commander
of his army, and they returned to the land of the
Philistines.
33 Then *Abraham* planted a tamarisk tree in
Beersheba, and [a]there called on the name of the
LORD, [b]the Everlasting God.
34 And Abraham stayed in the land of the
Philistines many days.

Abraham's Faith Confirmed
(Heb. 11:17–19)

22 Now it came to pass after these things that
[a]God tested Abraham, and said to him,
"Abraham!" And he said, "Here I am."
2 Then He said, "Take now your son, [a]your
only *son* Isaac, whom you [b]love, and go [c]to the
land of Moriah, and offer him there as a [d]burnt
offering on one of the mountains of which I shall
tell you."
3 So Abraham rose early in the morning
and saddled his donkey, and took two of his
young men with him, and Isaac his son; and he
split the wood for the burnt offering, and arose
and went to the place of which God had told him.
4 Then on the third day Abraham lifted his
eyes and saw the place afar off.
5 And Abraham said to his young men,
"Stay here with the donkey; the *lad and I will
go yonder and worship, and we will [a]come back
to you."
6 So Abraham took the wood of the burnt
offering and [a]laid *it* on Isaac his son; and he took
the fire in his hand, and a knife, and the two of
them went together.
7 But Isaac spoke to Abraham his father and
said, "My father!" And he said, "Here I am, my
son." Then he said, "Look, the fire and the wood,
but where *is* the lamb for a burnt offering?"
8 And Abraham said, "My son, God will
provide for Himself the [a]lamb for a [b]burnt offering." So the two of them went together.

KJV

9 And they came to the place which God
had told him of; and Abraham built an altar there,
and laid the wood in order, and bound Isaac his
son, and [a]laid him on the altar upon the wood.
10 And Abraham stretched forth his hand,
and took the knife to slay his son.
11 And the [a]angel of the LORD called unto
him out of heaven, and said, Abraham, Abraham:
and he said, Here *am* I.
12 And he said, [a]Lay not thine hand upon
the lad, neither do thou any thing unto him: for
[b]now I know that thou fearest God, seeing thou
hast not [c]withheld thy son, thine only *son* from
me.
13 And Abraham lifted up his eyes, and
looked, and behold behind *him* a ram caught in
a thicket by his horns: and Abraham went and
took the ram, and offered him up for a burnt offering in the stead of his son.
14 And Abraham called the name of that
place Jehovah–jireh: as it is said *to* this day, In
the mount of the LORD it shall be seen.
15 And the angel of the LORD called unto
Abraham out of heaven the second time,
16 And said, [a]By myself have I sworn, saith
the LORD, for because thou hast done this thing,
and hast not withheld thy son, thine only *son:*
17 That in blessing I will [a]bless thee, and in
multiplying I will multiply thy seed [b]as the stars
of the heaven, [c]and as the sand which *is* upon
the sea shore; and [d]thy seed shall possess the gate
of his enemies;
18 [a]And in thy seed shall all the nations of
the earth be blessed; [b]because thou hast obeyed
my voice.
19 So Abraham returned unto his young
men, and they rose up and went together to
[a]Beer–sheba; and Abraham dwelt at Beer–sheba.

The Family of Nahor

20 And it came to pass after these things, that
it was told Abraham, saying, Behold, [a]Milcah,
she hath also born children unto thy brother
Nahor;
21 [a]Huz his firstborn, and Buz his brother,
and Kemuel the father [b]of Aram,
22 And Chesed, and Hazo, and Pildash, and
Jidlaph, and Bethuel.
23 And [a]Bethuel begat Rebekah: these eight
Milcah did bear to Nahor, Abraham's brother.
24 And his concubine, whose name *was* Reumah, she bare also Tebah, and Gaham, and Thahash, and Maachah.

Sarah's Death and Burial

23 And Sarah was an hundred and seven and
twenty years old: *these were* the years of
the life of Sarah.
2 And Sarah died in [a]Kirjath–arba; the
same *is* [b]Hebron in the land of Canaan: and Abraham came to mourn for Sarah, and to weep for
her.
3 And Abraham stood up from before his
dead, and spake unto the sons of [a]Heth, saying,
4 [a]I *am* a stranger and a sojourner with you:
[b]give me a possession of a buryingplace with you,
that I may bury my dead out of my sight.
5 And the children of Heth answered Abraham, saying unto him,
6 Hear us, my lord: thou *art* [a]a mighty
prince among us: in the choice of our sepulchres
bury thy dead; none of us shall withhold from
thee his sepulchre, but that thou mayest bury thy
dead.
7 And Abraham stood up, and bowed him-
self to the people of the land, *even* to the children
of Heth.
8 And he communed with them, saying, If
it be your mind that I should bury my dead out
of my sight; hear me, and intreat for me to Ephron
the son of Zohar,

9 [a][Heb. 11:17–19; James 2:21]
11 [a]Gen. 16:7–11; 21:17, 18; 31:11
12 [a]1 Sam. 15:22 [b]Gen. 26:5; James 2:21, 22 [c]Gen. 22:2, 16; John 3:16
16 [a]Ps. 105:9; Luke 1:73; [Heb. 6:13, 14]
17 [a]Gen. 17:16; 26:3, 24 [b]Gen. 15:5; 26:4; Deut. 1:10; Jer. 33:22; Heb. 11:12 [c]Gen. 13:16; 32:12; 1 Kin. 4:20 [d]Gen. 24:60
18 [a]Gen. 12:3; 18:18; 26:4; Matt. 1:1; Luke 3:34; [Acts 3:25, 26]; Gal. 3:8, 9, 16, 18 [b]Gen. 18:19; 22:3, 10; 26:5
19 [a]Gen. 21:31
20 [a]Gen. 11:29; 24:15
21 [a]Job 1:1 [b]Job 32:2
23 [a]Gen. 24:15

CHAPTER 23

2 [a]Gen. 35:27; Josh. 14:15; 15:13; 21:11 [b]Gen. 13:18; 23:19
3 [a]Gen. 10:15; 15:20; 2 Kin. 7:6
4 [a][Gen. 17:8]; Lev. 25:23; 1 Chr. 29:15; Ps. 39:12; 105:12; 119:19; [Heb. 11:9, 13] [b]Acts 7:5, 16
6 [a]Gen. 13:2; 14:14; 24:35

*

22:14 Heb. *YHWH Yireh*
22:23 *Rebecca,* Rom. 9:10

NKJV

9 Then they came to the place of which God
had told him. And Abraham built an altar there
and placed the wood in order; and he bound Isaac
his son and [a]laid him on the altar, upon the wood.
10 And Abraham stretched out his hand and
took the knife to slay his son.
11 But the [a]Angel of the LORD called to him
from heaven and said, "Abraham, Abraham!" So
he said, "Here I am."
12 And He said, [a]"Do not lay your hand on
the lad, or do anything to him; for [b]now I know
that you fear God, since you have not [c]withheld
your son, your only *son,* from Me."
13 Then Abraham lifted his eyes and looked,
and there behind *him was* a ram caught in a
thicket by its horns. So Abraham went and took
the ram, and offered it up for a burnt offering instead of his son.
14 And Abraham called the name of the
place, *The-LORD-Will-Provide; as it is said *to* this
day, "In the Mount of the LORD it shall be
provided."
15 Then the Angel of the LORD called to Abraham a second time out of heaven,
16 and said: [a]"By Myself I have sworn, says
the LORD, because you have done this thing, and
have not withheld your son, your only *son*—
17 "blessing I will [a]bless you, and multiplying I will multiply your descendants [b]as the stars
of the heaven [c]and as the sand which *is* on the
seashore; and [d]your descendants shall possess the
gate of their enemies.
18 [a]"In your seed all the nations of the earth
shall be blessed, [b]because you have obeyed My
voice."
19 So Abraham returned to his young men,
and they rose and went together to [a]Beersheba;
and Abraham dwelt at Beersheba.

The Family of Nahor

20 Now it came to pass after these things that
it was told Abraham, saying, "Indeed [a]Milcah also
has borne children to your brother Nahor:
21 [a]"Huz his firstborn, Buz his brother, Kemuel the father [b]of Aram,
22 "Chesed, Hazo, Pildash, Jidlaph, and
Bethuel."
23 And [a]Bethuel begot *Rebekah. These
eight Milcah bore to Nahor, Abraham's brother.
24 His concubine, whose name was Reumah,
also bore Tebah, Gaham, Thahash, and Maachah.

Sarah's Death and Burial

23 Sarah lived one hundred and twenty-seven
years; *these were* the years of the life of
Sarah.
2 So Sarah died in [a]Kirjath Arba (that *is,*
[b]Hebron) in the land of Canaan, and Abraham
came to mourn for Sarah and to weep for her.
3 Then Abraham stood up from before his
dead, and spoke to the sons of [a]Heth, saying,
4 [a]"I *am* a foreigner and a visitor among
you. [b]Give me property for a burial place among
you, that I may bury my dead out of my sight."
5 And the sons of Heth answered Abraham,
saying to him,
6 "Hear us, my lord: You *are* [a]a mighty
prince among us; bury your dead in the choicest
of our burial places. None of us will withhold from
you his burial place, that you may bury your
dead."
7 Then Abraham stood up and bowed himself to the people of the land, the sons of Heth.
8 And he spoke with them, saying, "If it is
your wish that I bury my dead out of my sight,
hear me, and meet with Ephron the son of Zohar
for me,

KJV

9 That he may give me the cave of [a]Machpelah, which he hath, which *is* in the end of his field; for as much money as it is worth he shall give it me for a possession of a buryingplace amongst you.

10 And Ephron dwelt among the children of Heth: and Ephron the Hittite answered Abraham in the audience of the children of Heth, *even* of all that [a]went in at the gate of his city, saying,

11 [a]Nay, my lord, hear me: the field give I thee, and the cave that *is* therein, I give it thee; in the presence of the sons of my people give I it thee: bury thy dead.

12 And Abraham bowed down himself before the people of the land.

13 And he spake unto Ephron in the audience of the people of the land, saying, But if thou *wilt give it*, I pray thee, hear me: I will give thee money for the field; take *it* of me, and I will bury my dead there.

14 And Ephron answered Abraham, saying unto him,

15 My lord, hearken unto me: the land *is worth* four hundred [a]shekels of silver; what *is* that betwixt me and thee? bury therefore thy dead.

16 And Abraham hearkened unto Ephron; and Abraham [a]weighed to Ephron the silver, which he had named in the audience of the sons of Heth, four hundred shekels of silver, current *money* with the merchant.

17 And [a]the field of Ephron, which *was* in Machpelah, which *was* before Mamre, the field, and the cave which *was* therein, and all the trees that *were* in the field, that *were* in all the borders round about, were made sure

18 Unto Abraham for a possession in the presence of the children of Heth, before all that went in at the gate of his city.

19 And after this, Abraham buried Sarah his wife in the cave of the field of Machpelah before Mamre: the same *is* Hebron in the land of Canaan.

20 And the field, and the cave that *is* therein, [a]were made sure unto Abraham for a possession of a buryingplace by the sons of Heth.

A Bride for Isaac

24 And Abraham [a]was old, *and* well stricken in age: and the LORD [b]had blessed Abraham in all things.

2 And Abraham said [a]unto his eldest servant of his house, that [b]ruled over all that he had, [c]Put, I pray thee, thy hand under my thigh:

3 And I will make thee [a]swear by the LORD, the God of heaven, and the God of the earth, that [b]thou shalt not take a wife unto my son of the daughters of the Canaanites, among whom I dwell:

4 [a]But thou shalt go [b]unto my country, and to my kindred, and take a wife unto my son Isaac.

5 And the servant said unto him, Peradventure the woman will not be willing to follow me unto this land: must I needs bring thy son again unto the land from whence thou camest?

6 And Abraham said unto him, Beware thou that thou bring not my son thither again.

7 The LORD God of heaven, which [a]took me from my father's house, and from the land of my kindred, and which spake unto me, and that sware unto me, saying, [b]Unto thy seed will I give this land; [c]he shall send his angel before thee, and thou shalt take a wife unto my son from thence.

8 And if the woman will not be willing to follow thee, then [a]thou shalt be clear from this my oath: only bring not my son thither again.

9 And the servant put his hand under the thigh of Abraham his master, and sware to him concerning that matter.

10 And the servant took ten camels of the camels of his master, and departed; [a]for all the goods of his master *were* in his hand: and he arose, and went to Mesopotamia, unto [b]the city of Nahor.

9 [a]Gen. 25:9
10 [a]Gen. 23:18; 34:20, 24; Ruth 4:1, 4, 11
11 [a]2 Sam. 24:21–24
15 [a]Ex. 30:13; Ezek. 45:12
16 [a]2 Sam. 14:26; Jer. 32:9, 10; Zech. 11:12
17 [a]Gen. 25:9; 49:29–32; 50:13; Acts 7:16
20 [a]Jer. 32:10, 11

CHAPTER 24

1 [a]Gen. 18:11; 21:5 [b]Gen. 12:2; 13:2; 24:35; Ps. 112:3; Prov. 10:22; [Gal. 3:9]
2 [a]Gen. 15:2 [b]Gen. 24:10; 39:4–6 [c]Gen. 47:29; 1 Chr. 29:24
3 [a]Gen. 14:19, 22 [b]Gen. 26:35; 28:2; Ex. 34:16; Deut. 7:3; 2 Cor. 6:14–17
4 [a]Gen. 28:2 [b]Gen. 12:1; Heb. 11:15
7 [a]Gen. 12:1; 24:3 [b]Gen. 12:7; 13:15; 15:18; 17:8; Ex. 32:13; Deut. 1:8; 34:4; Acts 7:5 [c]Gen. 16:7; 21:17; 22:11; Ex. 23:20, 23; 33:2; Heb. 1:4, 14
8 [a]Josh. 2:17–20
10 [a]Gen. 24:2, 22 [b]Gen. 11:31, 32; 22:20; 27:43; 29:5

*———

24:7 Lit. *seed*

NKJV

9 "that he may give me the cave of [a]Machpelah which he has, which *is* at the end of his field. Let him give it to me at the full price, as property for a burial place among you."

10 Now Ephron dwelt among the sons of Heth; and Ephron the Hittite answered Abraham in the presence of the sons of Heth, all who [a]entered at the gate of his city, saying,

11 [a]"No, my lord, hear me: I give you the field and the cave that *is* in it; I give it to you in the presence of the sons of my people. I give it to you. Bury your dead!"

12 Then Abraham bowed himself down before the people of the land;

13 and he spoke to Ephron in the hearing of the people of the land, saying, "If you *will give it*, please hear me. I will give you money for the field; take *it* from me and I will bury my dead there."

14 And Ephron answered Abraham, saying to him,

15 "My lord, listen to me; the land *is worth* four hundred [a]shekels of silver. What *is* that between you and me? So bury your dead."

16 And Abraham listened to Ephron; and Abraham [a]weighed out the silver for Ephron which he had named in the hearing of the sons of Heth, four hundred shekels of silver, currency of the merchants.

17 So [a]the field of Ephron which *was* in Machpelah, which *was* before Mamre, the field and the cave which *was* in it, and all the trees that *were* in the field, which *were* within all the surrounding borders, were deeded

18 to Abraham as a possession in the presence of the sons of Heth, before all who went in at the gate of his city.

19 And after this, Abraham buried Sarah his wife in the cave of the field of Machpelah, before Mamre (that *is*, Hebron) in the land of Canaan.

20 So the field and the cave that *is* in it [a]were deeded to Abraham by the sons of Heth as property for a burial place.

A Bride for Isaac

24 Now Abraham [a]was old, well advanced in age; and the LORD [b]had blessed Abraham in all things.

2 So Abraham said [a]to the oldest servant of his house, who [b]ruled over all that he had, "Please, [c]put your hand under my thigh,

3 "and I will make you [a]swear by the LORD, the God of heaven and the God of the earth, that [b]you will not take a wife for my son from the daughters of the Canaanites, among whom I dwell;

4 [a]"but you shall go [b]to my country and to my family, and take a wife for my son Isaac."

5 And the servant said to him, "Perhaps the woman will not be willing to follow me to this land. Must I take your son back to the land from which you came?"

6 But Abraham said to him, "Beware that you do not take my son back there.

7 "The LORD God of heaven, who [a]took me from my father's house and from the land of my family, and who spoke to me and swore to me, saying, [b]'To your *descendants I give this land,' [c]He will send His angel before you, and you shall take a wife for my son from there.

8 "And if the woman is not willing to follow you, then [a]you will be released from this oath; only do not take my son back there."

9 So the servant put his hand under the thigh of Abraham his master, and swore to him concerning this matter.

10 Then the servant took ten of his master's camels and departed, [a]for all his master's goods *were in* his hand. And he arose and went to Mesopotamia, to [b]the city of Nahor.

KJV

11 And he made his camels to kneel down
without the city by a well of water at the time of
the evening, *even* the time [a]that women go out
to draw *water.*
12 And he [a]said, O LORD God of my master
Abraham, I pray thee, [b]send me good speed this
day, and shew kindness unto my master
Abraham.
13 Behold, [a]I stand *here* by the well of water;
and [b]the daughters of the men of the city come
out to draw water:
14 And let it come to pass, that the damsel
to whom I shall say, Let down thy pitcher, I pray
thee, that I may drink; and she shall say, Drink,
and I will give thy camels drink also: *let the same
be* she *that* thou hast appointed for thy servant
Isaac; and [a]thereby shall I know that thou hast
shewed kindness unto my master.
15 And it came to pass, [a]before he had done
speaking, that, behold, [b]Rebekah came out, who
was born to Bethuel, son of [c]Milcah, the wife of
Nahor, Abraham's brother, with her pitcher upon
her shoulder.
16 And the damsel [a]*was* very fair to look
upon, a virgin, neither had any man known her:
and she went down to the well, and filled her
pitcher, and came up.
17 And the servant ran to meet her, and said,
Let me, I pray thee, drink a little water of thy
pitcher.
18 [a]And she said, Drink, my lord: and she
hasted, and let down her pitcher upon her hand,
and gave him drink.
19 And when she had done giving him drink,
she said, I will draw *water* for thy camels also,
until they have done drinking.
20 And she hasted, and emptied her pitcher
into the trough, and ran again unto the well to
draw *water,* and drew for all his camels.
21 And the man wondering at her held his
peace, to wit whether [a]the LORD had made his
journey prosperous or not.
22 And it came to pass, as the camels had
done drinking, that the man took a golden
[a]earring of half a shekel weight, and two
bracelets for her hands of ten *shekels* weight of
gold;
23 And said, Whose daughter *art* thou? tell
me, I pray thee: is there room *in* thy father's house
for us to lodge in?
24 And she said unto him, [a]I *am* the daughter
of Bethuel the son of Milcah, which she bare unto
Nahor.
25 She said moreover unto him, We have
both straw and provender enough, and room to
lodge in.
26 And the man [a]bowed down his head, and
worshipped the LORD.
27 And he said, [a]Blessed *be* the LORD God
of my master Abraham, who hath not left destitute
my master of [b]his mercy and his truth: I *being* in
the way, the LORD [c]led me to the house of my
master's brethren.
28 And the damsel ran, and told *them of* her
mother's house these things.
29 And Rebekah had a brother, and his name
was [a]Laban: and Laban ran out unto the man,
unto the well.
30 And it came to pass, when he saw the earring and bracelets upon his sister's hands, and
when he heard the words of Rebekah his sister,
saying, Thus spake the man unto me; that he came
unto the man; and, behold, he stood by the camels
at the well.
31 And he said, Come in, [a]thou blessed of
the LORD; wherefore standest thou without? for I
have prepared the house, and room for the
camels.
32 And the man came into the house: and
he ungirded his camels, and [a]gave straw and provender for the camels, and water to [b]wash his
feet, and the men's feet that *were* with him.

11 [a]Ex. 2:16; 1 Sam. 9:11
12 [a]Gen. 24:27, 42, 48; 26:24; 32:9; Ex. 3:6, 15 [b]Gen. 27:20; Neh. 1:11; Ps. 37:5
13 [a]Gen. 24:43 [b]Ex. 2:16
14 [a]Judg. 6:17, 37; 1 Sam. 14:10; 16:7; 20:7; 2 Kin. 20:9; Prov. 16:33; Acts 1:26
15 [a]Is. 65:24 [b]Gen. 24:45; 25:20 [c]Gen. 22:20, 23
16 [a]Gen. 12:11; 26:7; 29:17
18 [a]Gen. 24:14, 46; [1 Pet. 3:8, 9]
21 [a]Gen. 24:12–14, 27, 52
22 [a]Gen. 24:47; Ex. 32:2, 3; Is. 3:19–21
24 [a]Gen. 22:23; 24:15
26 [a]Gen. 24:48, 52; Ex. 4:31
27 [a]Gen. 24:12, 42, 48; Ex. 18:10; Ruth 4:14; 1 Sam. 25:32, 39; 2 Sam. 18:28; Luke 1:68 [b]Gen. 32:10; Ps. 98:3 [c]Gen. 24:21, 48
29 [a]Gen. 29:5, 13
31 [a]Gen. 26:29; Judg. 17:2; Ruth 3:10; Ps. 115:15
32 [a]Gen. 43:24; Judg. 19:21 [b]Gen. 19:2; John 13:5, 13–15

NKJV

11 And he made his camels kneel down outside the city by a well of water at evening time,
the time [a]when women go out to draw *water.*
12 Then he [a]said, "O LORD God of my master
Abraham, please [b]give me success this day, and
show kindness to my master Abraham.
13 "Behold, *here* [a]I stand by the well of water, and [b]the daughters of the men of the city are
coming out to draw water.
14 "Now let it be that the young woman to
whom I say, 'Please let down your pitcher that I
may drink,' and she says, 'Drink, and I will also
give your camels a drink'—*let* her *be the one* You
have appointed for Your servant Isaac. And [a]by
this I will know that You have shown kindness
to my master."
15 And it happened, [a]before he had finished
speaking, that behold, [b]Rebekah, who was born
to Bethuel, son of [c]Milcah, the wife of Nahor,
Abraham's brother, came out with her pitcher on
her shoulder.
16 Now the young woman [a]*was* very beautiful to behold, a virgin; no man had known her.
And she went down to the well, filled her pitcher,
and came up.
17 And the servant ran to meet her and said,
"Please let me drink a little water from your
pitcher."
18 [a]So she said, "Drink, my lord." Then she
quickly let her pitcher down to her hand, and gave
him a drink.
19 And when she had finished giving him a
drink, she said, "I will draw *water* for your camels
also, until they have finished drinking."
20 Then she quickly emptied her pitcher into
the trough, ran back to the well to draw *water,*
and drew for all his camels.
21 And the man, wondering at her, remained
silent so as to know whether [a]the LORD had made
his journey prosperous or not.
22 So it was, when the camels had finished
drinking, that the man took a golden [a]nose ring
weighing half a shekel, and two bracelets for her
wrists weighing ten *shekels* of gold,
23 and said, "Whose daughter *are* you? Tell
me, please, is there room *in* your father's house
for us to lodge?"
24 So she said to him, [a]"I *am* the daughter
of Bethuel, Milcah's son, whom she bore to
Nahor."
25 Moreover she said to him, "We have both
straw and feed enough, and room to lodge."
26 Then the man [a]bowed down his head and
worshiped the LORD.
27 And he said, [a]"Blessed *be* the LORD God
of my master Abraham, who has not forsaken
[b]His mercy and His truth toward my master. As
for me, being on the way, the LORD [c]led me to
the house of my master's brethren."
28 So the young woman ran and told her
mother's household these things.
29 Now Rebekah had a brother whose name
was [a]Laban, and Laban ran out to the man by
the well.
30 So it came to pass, when he saw the nose
ring, and the bracelets on his sister's wrists, and
when he heard the words of his sister Rebekah,
saying, "Thus the man spoke to me," that he went
to the man. And there he stood by the camels at
the well.
31 And he said, "Come in, [a]O blessed of the
LORD! Why do you stand outside? For I have prepared the house, and a place for the camels."
32 Then the man came to the house. And he
unloaded the camels, and [a]provided straw and
feed for the camels, and water to [b]wash his feet
and the feet of the men who *were* with him.

KJV

33 And there was set *meat* before him to eat: but he said, [a]I will not eat, until I have told mine errand. And he said, Speak on.

34 And he said, I *am* Abraham's servant.

35 And the LORD [a]hath blessed my master greatly; and he is become great: and he hath given him flocks, and herds, and silver, and gold, and menservants, and maidservants, and camels, and asses.

36 And Sarah my master's wife [a]bare a son to my master when she was old: and [b]unto him hath he given all that he hath.

37 And my master [a]made me swear, saying, Thou shalt not take a wife to my son of the daughters of the Canaanites, in whose land I dwell:

38 [a]But thou shalt go unto my father's house, and to my kindred, and take a wife unto my son.

39 [a]And I said unto my master, Peradventure the woman will not follow me.

40 [a]And he said unto me, The LORD, [b]before whom I walk, will send his angel with thee, and prosper thy way; and thou shalt take a wife for my son of my kindred, and of my father's house:

41 [a]Then shalt thou be clear from *this* my oath, when thou comest to my kindred; and if they give not thee *one,* thou shalt be clear from my oath.

42 And I came this day unto the well, and said, [a]O LORD God of my master Abraham, if now thou do prosper my way which I go:

43 [a]Behold, I stand by the well of water; and it shall come to pass, that when the virgin cometh forth to draw *water,* and I say to her, Give me, I pray thee, a little water of thy pitcher to drink;

44 And she say to me, Both drink thou, and I will also draw for thy camels: *let* the same *be* the woman whom the LORD hath appointed out for my master's son.

45 [a]And before I had done [b]speaking in mine heart, behold, Rebekah came forth with her pitcher on her shoulder; and she went down unto the well, and drew *water:* and I said unto her, Let me drink, I pray thee.

46 And she made haste, and let down her pitcher from her *shoulder,* and said, Drink, and I will give thy camels drink also: so I drank, and she made the camels drink also.

47 And I asked her, and said, Whose daughter *art* thou? And she said, The daughter of Bethuel, Nahor's son, whom Milcah bare unto him: and I put the earring upon her face, and the bracelets upon her hands.

48 [a]And I bowed down my head, and worshipped the LORD, and blessed the LORD God of my master Abraham, which had led me in the right way to [b]take my master's brother's daughter unto his son.

49 And now if ye will [a]deal kindly and truly with my master, tell me: and if not, tell me; that I may turn to the right hand, or to the left.

50 Then Laban and Bethuel answered and said, [a]The thing proceedeth from the LORD: we cannot [b]speak unto thee bad or good.

51 Behold, Rebekah [a]*is* before thee, take *her,* and go, and let her be thy master's son's wife, as the LORD hath spoken.

52 And it came to pass, that, when Abraham's servant heard their words, [a]he worshipped the LORD, *bowing himself* to the earth.

53 And the servant brought forth [a]jewels of silver, and jewels of gold, and raiment, and gave *them* to Rebekah: he gave also to her brother and to her mother [b]precious things.

54 And they did eat and drink, he and the men that *were* with him, and tarried all night; and they rose up in the morning, and he said, [a]Send me away unto my master.

55 And her brother and her mother said, Let the damsel abide with us *a few* days, at the least ten; after that she shall go.

56 And he said unto them, Hinder me not,

33 [a]Job 23:12; John 4:34; Eph. 6:5–7
35 [a]Gen. 13:2; 24:1
36 [a]Gen. 21:1–7 [b]Gen. 21:10; 25:5
37 [a]Gen. 24:2–4
38 [a]Gen. 24:4
39 [a]Gen. 24:5
40 [a]Gen. 24:7 [b]Gen. 5:22, 24; 17:1; 1 Kin. 8:23
41 [a]Gen. 24:8
42 [a]Gen. 24:12
43 [a]Gen. 24:13
45 [a]Gen. 24:15 [b]1 Sam. 1:13
48 [a]Gen. 24:26, 52 [b]Gen. 22:23; 24:27; Ps. 32:8; 48:14; Is. 48:17
49 [a]Gen. 47:29; Josh. 2:14
50 [a]Ps. 118:23; Matt. 21:42; Mark 12:11 [b]Gen. 31:24, 29
51 [a]Gen. 20:15
52 [a]Gen. 24:26, 48
53 [a]Gen. 24:10, 22; Ex. 3:22; 11:2; 12:35 [b]2 Chr. 21:3; Ezra 1:6
54 [a]Gen. 24:56, 59; 30:25

NKJV

33 *Food* was set before him to eat, but he said, [a]"I will not eat until I have told about my errand." And he said, "Speak on."

34 So he said, "I *am* Abraham's servant.

35 "The LORD [a]has blessed my master greatly, and he has become great; and He has given him flocks and herds, silver and gold, male and female servants, and camels and donkeys.

36 "And Sarah my master's wife [a]bore a son to my master when she was old; and [b]to him he has given all that he has.

37 "Now my master [a]made me swear, saying, 'You shall not take a wife for my son from the daughters of the Canaanites, in whose land I dwell;

38 [a]'but you shall go to my father's house and to my family, and take a wife for my son.'

39 [a]"And I said to my master, 'Perhaps the woman will not follow me.'

40 [a]"But he said to me, 'The LORD, [b]before whom I walk, will send His angel with you and prosper your way; and you shall take a wife for my son from my family and from my father's house.

41 [a]'You will be clear from this oath when you arrive among my family; for if they will not give *her* to you, then you will be released from my oath.'

42 "And this day I came to the well and said, [a]'O LORD God of my master Abraham, if You will now prosper the way in which I go,

43 [a]'behold, I stand by the well of water; and it shall come to pass that when the virgin comes out to draw *water,* and I say to her, "Please give me a little water from your pitcher to drink,"

44 'and she says to me, "Drink, and I will draw for your camels also,"—*let* her *be* the woman whom the LORD has appointed for my master's son.'

45 [a]"But before I had finished [b]speaking in my heart, there was Rebekah, coming out with her pitcher on her shoulder; and she went down to the well and drew *water.* And I said to her, 'Please let me drink.'

46 "And she made haste and let her pitcher down from her *shoulder,* and said, 'Drink, and I will give your camels a drink also.' So I drank, and she gave the camels a drink also.

47 "Then I asked her, and said, 'Whose daughter *are* you?' And she said, 'The daughter of Bethuel, Nahor's son, whom Milcah bore to him.' So I put the nose ring on her nose and the bracelets on her wrists.

48 [a]"And I bowed my head and worshiped the LORD, and blessed the LORD God of my master Abraham, who had led me in the way of truth to [b]take the daughter of my master's brother for his son.

49 "Now if you will [a]deal kindly and truly with my master, tell me. And if not, tell me, that I may turn to the right hand or to the left."

50 Then Laban and Bethuel answered and said, [a]"The thing comes from the LORD; we cannot [b]speak to you either bad or good.

51 [a]"Here *is* Rebekah before you; take *her* and go, and let her be your master's son's wife, as the LORD has spoken."

52 And it came to pass, when Abraham's servant heard their words, that [a]he worshiped the LORD, *bowing himself* to the earth.

53 Then the servant brought out [a]jewelry of silver, jewelry of gold, and clothing, and gave *them* to Rebekah. He also gave [b]precious things to her brother and to her mother.

54 And he and the men who *were* with him ate and drank and stayed all night. Then they arose in the morning, and he said, [a]"Send me away to my master."

55 But her brother and her mother said, "Let the young woman stay with us *a few* days, at least ten; after that she may go."

56 And he said to them, "Do not hinder me,

Adam / Eve
Cain
Noah
Abraham
Abimelech, King of (philistines) Gerar
Lot
Hagar

KJV

seeing the LORD hath prospered my way; send me away that I may go to my master.

57 And they said, We will call the damsel, and enquire at her mouth.

58 And they called Rebekah, and said unto her, Wilt thou go with this man? And she said, I will go.

59 And they sent away Rebekah their sister, [a]and her nurse, and Abraham's servant, and his men.

60 And they blessed Rebekah, and said unto her, Thou *art* our sister, be thou [a]*the mother* of thousands of millions, and [b]let thy seed possess the gate of those which hate them.

61 And Rebekah arose, and her damsels, and they rode upon the camels, and followed the man: and the servant took Rebekah, and went his way.

62 And Isaac came from the way of the [a]well Lahai–roi; for he dwelt in the south country.

63 And Isaac went out [a]to meditate in the field at the eventide: and he lifted up his eyes, and saw, and, behold, the camels *were* coming.

64 And Rebekah lifted up her eyes, and when she saw Isaac, [a]she lighted off the camel.

65 For she *had* said unto the servant, What man *is* this that walketh in the field to meet us? And the servant *had* said, It *is* my master: therefore she took a vail, and covered herself.

66 And the servant told Isaac all things that he had done.

67 And Isaac brought her into his mother Sarah's tent, and [a]took Rebekah, and she became his wife; and he loved her: and Isaac [b]was comforted after his mother's *death.*

Abraham and Keturah
(*1 Chr. 1:32, 33*)

25 Then again Abraham took a wife, and her name *was* [a]Keturah.

2 And [a]she bare him Zimran, and Jokshan, and Medan, and Midian, and Ishbak, and Shuah.

3 And Jokshan begat Sheba, and Dedan. And the sons of Dedan were Asshurim, and Letushim, and Leummim.

4 And the sons of Midian; Ephah, and Epher, and Hanoch, and Abidah, and Eldaah. All these *were* the children of Keturah.

5 And [a]Abraham gave all that he had unto Isaac.

6 But unto the sons of the concubines, which Abraham had, Abraham gave gifts, and [a]sent them away from Isaac his son, while he yet lived, eastward, unto [b]the east country.

Abraham's Death and Burial

7 And these *are* the days of the years of Abraham's life which he lived, an hundred threescore and fifteen years.

8 Then Abraham gave up the ghost, and [a]died in a good old age, an old man, and full *of years;* and [b]was gathered to his people.

9 And [a]his sons Isaac and Ishmael buried him in the cave of [b]Machpelah, in the field of Ephron the son of Zohar the Hittite, which *is* before Mamre;

10 [a]The field which Abraham purchased of the sons of Heth: [b]there was Abraham buried, and Sarah his wife.

11 And it came to pass after the death of Abraham, that God blessed his son Isaac; and Isaac dwelt by the [a]well Lahai–roi.

The Families of Ishmael and Isaac
(*1 Chr. 1:29–31*)

12 Now these *are* the [a]generations of Ishmael, Abraham's son, whom Hagar the Egyptian, Sarah's handmaid, bare unto Abraham:

13 And [a]these *are* the names of the sons of

---

59 [a]Gen. 35:8
60 [a]Gen. 17:16 [b]Gen. 22:17; 28:14
62 [a]Gen. 16:14; 25:11
63 [a]Josh. 1:8; Ps. 1:2; 77:12; 119:15, 27, 48; 143:5; 145:5
64 [a]Josh. 15:18
67 [a]Gen. 25:20; 29:20; Prov. 18:22 [b]Gen. 23:1, 2; 38:12

CHAPTER 25

1 [a]1 Chr. 1:32, 33
2 [a]1 Chr. 1:32, 33
5 [a]Gen. 24:35, 36
6 [a]Gen. 21:14 [b]Judg. 6:3
8 [a]Gen. 15:15; 47:8, 9 [b]Gen. 25:17; 35:29; 49:29, 33
9 [a]Gen. 35:29; 50:13 [b]Gen. 23:9, 17; 49:30
10 [a]Gen. 23:3–16 [b]Gen. 49:31
11 [a]Gen. 16:14
12 [a]Gen. 11:10, 27; 16:15
13 [a]1 Chr. 1:29–31

NKJV

since the LORD has prospered my way; send me away so that I may go to my master."

57 So they said, "We will call the young woman and ask her personally."

58 Then they called Rebekah and said to her, "Will you go with this man?" And she said, "I will go."

59 So they sent away Rebekah their sister [a]and her nurse, and Abraham's servant and his men.

60 And they blessed Rebekah and said to her:

"Our sister, *may* you *become*
[a]*The mother of* thousands of ten
thousands;
[b]And may your descendants possess
The gates of those who hate them."

61 Then Rebekah and her maids arose, and they rode on the camels and followed the man. So the servant took Rebekah and departed.

62 Now Isaac came from the way of [a]Beer Lahai Roi, for he dwelt in the South.

63 And Isaac went out [a]to meditate in the field in the evening; and he lifted his eyes and looked, and there, the camels *were* coming.

64 Then Rebekah lifted her eyes, and when she saw Isaac [a]she dismounted from her camel;

65 for she had said to the servant, "Who *is* this man walking in the field to meet us?" The servant said, "It *is* my master." So she took a veil and covered herself.

66 And the servant told Isaac all the things that he had done.

67 Then Isaac brought her into his mother Sarah's tent; and he [a]took Rebekah and she became his wife, and he loved her. So Isaac [b]was comforted after his mother's *death.*

Abraham and Keturah
(*1 Chr. 1:32, 33*)

25 Abraham again took a wife, and her name *was* [a]Keturah.

2 And [a]she bore him Zimran, Jokshan, Medan, Midian, Ishbak, and Shuah.

3 Jokshan begot Sheba and Dedan. And the sons of Dedan were Asshurim, Letushim, and Leummim.

4 And the sons of Midian *were* Ephah, Epher, Hanoch, Abidah, and Eldaah. All these *were* the children of Keturah.

5 And [a]Abraham gave all that he had to Isaac.

6 But Abraham gave gifts to the sons of the concubines which Abraham had; and while he was still living he [a]sent them eastward, away from Isaac his son, to [b]the country of the east.

Abraham's Death and Burial

7 This *is* the sum of the years of Abraham's life which he lived: one hundred and seventy-five years.

8 Then Abraham breathed his last and [a]died in a good old age, an old man and full *of years,* and [b]was gathered to his people.

9 And [a]his sons Isaac and Ishmael buried him in the cave of [b]Machpelah, which *is* before Mamre, in the field of Ephron the son of Zohar the Hittite,

10 [a]the field which Abraham purchased from the sons of Heth. [b]There Abraham was buried, and Sarah his wife.

11 And it came to pass, after the death of Abraham, that God blessed his son Isaac. And Isaac dwelt at [a]Beer Lahai Roi.

The Families of Ishmael and Isaac
(*1 Chr. 1:29–31*)

12 Now this *is* the [a]genealogy of Ishmael, Abraham's son, whom Hagar the Egyptian, Sarah's maidservant, bore to Abraham.

13 And [a]these *were* the names of the sons

KJV

Ishmael, by their names, according to their generations: the firstborn of Ishmael, Nebajoth; and Kedar, and Adbeel, and Mibsam,
14 And Mishma, and Dumah, and Massa,
15 Hadar, and Tema, Jetur, Naphish, and
Kedemah:
16 These *are* the sons of Ishmael, and these
are their names, by their towns, and by their castles; [a]twelve princes according to their nations.
17 And these *are* the years of the life of Ishmael, an hundred and thirty and seven years: and
[a]he gave up the ghost and died; and was gathered
unto his people.
18 [a]And they dwelt from Havilah unto Shur,
that *is* before Egypt, as thou goest toward Assyria:
and he died [b]in the presence of all his brethren.
19 And these *are* the [a]generations of Isaac,
Abraham's son: [b]Abraham begat Isaac:
20 And Isaac was forty years old when he
took Rebekah to wife, [a]the daughter of Bethuel
the Syrian of Padan–aram, [b]the sister to Laban
the Syrian.
21 And Isaac intreated the LORD for his wife,
because she *was* barren: [a]and the LORD was intreated of him, and [b]Rebekah his wife conceived.
22 And the children struggled together
within her; and she said, If *it be* so, why *am* I
thus? [a]And she went to enquire of the LORD.
23 And the LORD said unto her, [a]Two nations
are in thy womb, and two manner of people shall
be separated from thy bowels; and [b]*the one* people shall be stronger than *the other* people; and
[c]the elder shall serve the younger.
24 And when her days to be delivered were
fulfilled, behold, *there were* twins in her womb.
25 And the first came out red, [a]all over like
an hairy garment; and they called his name Esau.
26 And after that came his brother out, and
[a]his hand took hold on Esau's heel; and [b]his name
was called Jacob: and Isaac *was* threescore years
old when she bare them.
27 And the boys grew: and Esau was [a]a cunning hunter, a man of the field; and Jacob *was*
[b]a plain man, [c]dwelling in tents.
28 And Isaac loved Esau, because he did [a]eat
of *his* venison: [b]but Rebekah loved Jacob.

Esau Sells His Birthright
(*Heb. 12:16*)

29 And Jacob sod pottage: and Esau came
from the field, and he *was* faint:
30 And Esau said to Jacob, Feed me, I pray
thee, with that same red *pottage;* for I *am* faint:
therefore was his name called Edom.
31 And Jacob said, Sell me this day thy
birthright.
32 And Esau said, Behold, I *am* at the point
to die: and [a]what profit shall this birthright do
to me?
33 And Jacob said, Swear to me this day; and
he sware unto him: and [a]he sold his birthright
unto Jacob.
34 Then Jacob gave Esau bread and pottage
of lentiles; and [a]he did eat and drink, and rose
up, and went his way: thus Esau [b]despised *his*
birthright.

Isaac and Abimelech

26 And there was a famine in the land, beside
[a]the first famine that was in the days of
Abraham. And Isaac went unto [b]Abimelech king
of the Philistines unto Gerar.
2 And the LORD appeared unto him, and
said, [a]Go not down into Egypt; dwell in [b]the land
which I shall tell thee of:
3 [a]Sojourn in this land, and [b]I will be with

16 [a]Gen. 17:20
17 [a]Gen. 25:8; 49:33
18 [a]Gen. 20:1; 1 Sam. 15:7 [b]Gen. 16:12
19 [a]Gen. 36:1, 9 [b]Matt. 1:2
20 [a]Gen. 22:23; 24:15, 29, 67 [b]Gen. 24:29
21 [a]1 Sam. 1:17; 1 Chr. 5:20; 2 Chr. 33:13; Ezra 8:23; Ps. 127:3 [b]Rom. 9:10–13
22 [a]1 Sam. 1:15; 9:9; 10:22
23 [a]Gen. 17:4–6, 16; 24:60; Num. 20:14; Deut. 2:4–8 [b]2 Sam. 8:14 [c]Gen. 27:29, 40; Mal. 1:2, 3; Rom. 9:12
25 [a]Gen. 27:11, 16, 23
26 [a]Hos. 12:3 [b]Gen. 27:36
27 [a]Gen. 27:3, 5 [b]Job 1:1, 8 [c]Heb. 11:9
28 [a]Gen. 27:4, 19, 25, 31 [b]Gen. 27:6–10
32 [a]Matt. 16:26; Mark 8:36, 37
33 [a]Heb. 12:16
34 [a]Eccl. 8:15; Is. 22:13; 1 Cor. 15:32 [b]Heb. 12:16, 17

CHAPTER 26

1 [a]Gen. 12:10 [b]Gen. 20:1, 2
2 [a]Gen. 12:7; 17:1; 18:1; 35:9 [b]Gen. 12:1
3 [a]Gen. 20:1; Ps. 39:12; Heb. 11:9 [b]Gen. 28:13, 15

*

25:15 MT *Hadad*
25:25 Lit. *Hairy*
25:26 *Supplanter* or *Deceitful,* lit. *One Who Takes the Heel*
25:30 Lit. *Red*

NKJV

of Ishmael, by their names, according to their generations: The firstborn of Ishmael, Nebajoth; then
Kedar, Adbeel, Mibsam,
14 Mishma, Dumah, Massa,
15 *Hadar, Tema, Jetur, Naphish, and
Kedemah.
16 These *were* the sons of Ishmael and these
were their names, by their towns and their settlements, [a]twelve princes according to their nations.
17 These *were* the years of the life of Ishmael:
one hundred and thirty-seven years; and [a]he
breathed his last and died, and was gathered to
his people.
18 [a](They dwelt from Havilah as far as Shur,
which *is* east of Egypt as you go toward Assyria.)
He died [b]in the presence of all his brethren.
19 This *is* the [a]genealogy of Isaac, Abraham's son. [b]Abraham begot Isaac.
20 Isaac was forty years old when he took
Rebekah as wife, [a]the daughter of Bethuel the
Syrian of Padan Aram, [b]the sister of Laban the
Syrian.
21 Now Isaac pleaded with the LORD for his
wife, because she *was* barren; [a]and the LORD
granted his plea, [b]and Rebekah his wife conceived.
22 But the children struggled together within
her; and she said, "If *all is* well, why *am I like*
this?" [a]So she went to inquire of the LORD.
23 And the LORD said to her:

[a]"Two nations *are* in your womb,
Two peoples shall be separated from your
body;
One people shall be stronger than [b]the
other,
[c]And the older shall serve the younger."

24 So when her days were fulfilled *for her*
to give birth, indeed *there were* twins in her
womb.
25 And the first came out red. *He was* [a]like
a hairy garment all over; so they called his name
*Esau.
26 Afterward his brother came out, and [a]his
hand took hold of Esau's heel; so [b]his name was
called *Jacob. Isaac *was* sixty years old when she
bore them.
27 So the boys grew. And Esau was [a]a skillful hunter, a man of the field; but Jacob was [b]a
mild man, [c]dwelling in tents.
28 And Isaac loved Esau because he [a]ate *of*
his game, [b]but Rebekah loved Jacob.

Esau Sells His Birthright
(*Heb. 12:16*)

29 Now Jacob cooked a stew; and Esau came
in from the field, and he *was* weary.
30 And Esau said to Jacob, "Please feed me
with that same red *stew,* for I *am* weary." Therefore his name was called *Edom.
31 But Jacob said, "Sell me your birthright
as of this day."
32 And Esau said, "Look, I *am* about to die;
so [a]what *is* this birthright to me?"
33 Then Jacob said, "Swear to me as of this
day." So he swore to him, and [a]sold his birthright
to Jacob.
34 And Jacob gave Esau bread and stew of
lentils; then [a]he ate and drank, arose, and went
his way. Thus Esau [b]despised *his* birthright.

Isaac and Abimelech

26 There was a famine in the land, besides
[a]the first famine that was in the days of
Abraham. And Isaac went to [b]Abimelech king of
the Philistines, in Gerar.
2 Then the LORD appeared to him and said:
[a]"Do not go down to Egypt; live in [b]the land of
which I shall tell you.
3 [a]"Dwell in this land, and [b]I will be with

KJV

thee, and [c]will bless thee; for unto thee, and unto thy seed, [d]I will give all these countries, and I will perform [e]the oath which I sware unto Abraham thy father;

4 And [a]I will make thy seed to multiply as the stars of heaven, and will give unto thy seed all these countries; [b]and in thy seed shall all the nations of the earth be blessed;

5 [a]Because that Abraham obeyed my voice, and kept my charge, my commandments, my statutes, and my laws.

6 And Isaac dwelt in Gerar:

7 And the men of the place asked *him* of his wife; and [a]he said, She *is* my sister: for [b]he feared to say, *She is* my wife; lest, *said he,* the men of the place should kill me for Rebekah; because she [c]*was* fair to look upon.

8 And it came to pass, when he had been there a long time, that Abimelech king of the Philistines looked out at a window, and saw, and, behold, Isaac *was* sporting with Rebekah his wife.

9 And Abimelech called Isaac, and said, Behold, of a surety she *is* thy wife: and how saidst thou, She *is* my sister? And Isaac said unto him, Because I said, Lest I die for her.

10 And Abimelech said, What *is* this thou hast done unto us? one of the people might lightly have lien with thy wife, and [a]thou shouldest have brought guiltiness upon us.

11 And Abimelech charged all *his* people, saying, He that [a]toucheth this man or his wife shall surely be put to death.

12 Then Isaac sowed in that land, and received in the same year [a]an hundredfold: and the LORD [b]blessed him.

13 And the man [a]waxed great, and went forward, and grew until he became very great:

14 For he had possession of flocks, and possession of herds, and great store of servants: and the Philistines [a]envied him.

15 For all the wells [a]which his father's servants had digged in the days of Abraham his father, the Philistines had stopped them, and filled them with earth.

16 And Abimelech said unto Isaac, Go from us; for [a]thou art much mightier than we.

17 And Isaac departed thence, and pitched his tent in the valley of Gerar, and dwelt there.

18 And Isaac digged again the wells of water, which they had digged in the days of Abraham his father; for the Philistines had stopped them after the death of Abraham: [a]and he called their names after the names by which his father had called them.

19 And Isaac's servants digged in the valley, and found there a well of springing water.

20 And the herdmen of Gerar [a]did strive with Isaac's herdmen, saying, The water *is* our's: and he called the name of the well Esek; because they strove with him.

21 And they digged another well, and strove for that also: and he called the name of it Sitnah.

22 And he removed from thence, and digged another well; and for that they strove not: and he called the name of it Rehoboth; and he said, For now the LORD hath made room for us, and we shall [a]be fruitful in the land.

23 And he went up from thence to Beersheba.

24 And the LORD [a]appeared unto him the same night, and said, [b]I *am* the God of Abraham thy father: [c]fear not, for [d]I *am* with thee, and will bless thee, and multiply thy seed for my servant Abraham's sake.

25 And he [a]builded an altar there, and [b]called upon the name of the LORD, and pitched his tent there: and there Isaac's servants digged a well.

26 Then Abimelech went to him from Gerar, and Ahuzzath one of his friends, [a]and Phichol the chief captain of his army.

27 And Isaac said unto them, Wherefore

NKJV

you and [c]bless you; for to you and your descendants [d]I give all these lands, and I will perform [e]the oath which I swore to Abraham your father.

4 "And [a]I will make your descendants multiply as the stars of heaven; I will give to your descendants all these lands; [b]and in your seed all the nations of the earth shall be blessed;

5 [a]"because Abraham obeyed My voice and kept My charge, My commandments, My statutes, and My laws."

6 So Isaac dwelt in Gerar.

7 And the men of the place asked about his wife. And [a]he said, "She *is* my sister"; for [b]he was afraid to say, "*She is* my wife," *because he thought,* "lest the men of the place kill me for Rebekah, because she *is* [c]beautiful to behold."

8 Now it came to pass, when he had been there a long time, that Abimelech king of the Philistines looked through a window, and saw, and there was Isaac, showing endearment to Rebekah his wife.

9 Then Abimelech called Isaac and said, "Quite obviously she *is* your wife; so how could you say, 'She *is* my sister'?" Isaac said to him, "Because I said, 'Lest I die on account of her.' "

10 And Abimelech said, "What *is* this you have done to us? One of the people might soon have lain with your wife, and [a]you would have brought guilt on us."

11 So Abimelech charged all *his* people, saying, "He who [a]touches this man or his wife shall surely be put to death."

12 Then Isaac sowed in that land, and reaped in the same year [a]a hundredfold; and the LORD [b]blessed him.

13 The man [a]began to prosper, and continued prospering until he became very prosperous;

14 for he had possessions of flocks and possessions of herds and a great number of servants. So the Philistines [a]envied him.

15 Now the Philistines had stopped up all the wells [a]which his father's servants had dug in the days of Abraham his father, and they had filled them with earth.

16 And Abimelech said to Isaac, "Go away from us, for [a]you are much mightier than we."

17 Then Isaac departed from there and pitched his tent in the Valley of Gerar, and dwelt there.

18 And Isaac dug again the wells of water which they had dug in the days of Abraham his father, for the Philistines had stopped them up after the death of Abraham. [a]He called them by the names which his father had called them.

19 Also Isaac's servants dug in the valley, and found a well of running water there.

20 But the herdsmen of Gerar [a]quarreled with Isaac's herdsmen, saying, "The water *is* ours." So he called the name of the well *Esek, because they quarreled with him.

21 Then they dug another well, and they quarreled over that *one* also. So he called its name *Sitnah.

22 And he moved from there and dug another well, and they did not quarrel over it. So he called its name *Rehoboth, because he said, "For now the LORD has made room for us, and we shall [a]be fruitful in the land."

23 Then he went up from there to Beersheba.

24 And the LORD [a]appeared to him the same night and said, [b]"I *am* the God of your father Abraham; [c]do not fear, for [d]I *am* with you. I will bless you and multiply your descendants for My servant Abraham's sake."

25 So he [a]built an altar there and [b]called on the name of the LORD, and he pitched his tent there; and there Isaac's servants dug a well.

26 Then Abimelech came to him from Gerar with Ahuzzath, one of his friends, [a]and Phichol the commander of his army.

27 And Isaac said to them, "Why have you

---

3 [c]Gen. 12:2 [d]Gen. 12:7; 13:15; 15:18 [e]Gen. 22:16; Ps. 105:9
4 [a]Gen. 15:5; 22:17; Ex. 32:13 [b]Gen. 12:3; 22:18; Gal. 3:8
5 [a]Gen. 22:16, 18
7 [a]Gen. 12:13; 20:2, 12, 13 [b]Prov. 29:25 [c]Gen. 12:11; 24:16; 29:17
10 [a]Gen. 20:9
11 [a]Ps. 105:15
12 [a]Matt. 13:8, 23; Mark 4:8 [b]Gen. 24:1; 25:3, 11; 26:3; Job 42:12; Prov. 10:22
13 [a]Gen. 24:35; [Prov. 10:22]
14 [a]Gen. 37:11; Eccl. 4:4
15 [a]Gen. 21:25, 30
16 [a]Ex. 1:9
18 [a]Gen. 21:31
20 [a]Gen. 21:25
22 [a]Gen. 17:6; 28:3; 41:52; Ex. 1:7
24 [a]Gen. 26:2 [b]Gen. 17:7, 8; 24:12; Ex. 3:6; Acts 7:32 [c]Gen. 15:1 [d]Gen. 26:3, 4
25 [a]Gen. 12:7, 8; 13:4, 18; 22:9; 33:20 [b]Gen. 21:33; Ps. 116:17
26 [a]Gen. 21:22

*
26:20 Lit. *Quarrel*
26:21 Lit. *Enmity*
26:22 Lit. *Spaciousness*

KJV

come ye to me, [a]seeing ye hate me, and have [b]sent
me away from you?
28 And they said, We saw certainly that the
LORD [a]was with thee: and we said, Let there be
now an oath betwixt us, *even* betwixt us and thee,
and let us make a covenant with thee;
29 That thou wilt do us no hurt, as we have
not touched thee, and as we have done unto thee
nothing but good, and have sent thee away in
peace: [a]thou *art* now the blessed of the LORD.
30 [a]And he made them a feast, and they did
eat and drink.
31 And they rose up betimes in the morning,
and [a]sware one to another: and Isaac sent them
away, and they departed from him in peace.
32 And it came to pass the same day, that
Isaac's servants came, and told him concerning
the well which they had digged, and said unto
him, We have found water.
33 And he called it Shebah: [a]therefore the
name of the city *is* Beer–sheba unto this day.
34 [a]And Esau was forty years old when he
took to wife Judith the daughter of Beeri the Hittite, and Bashemath the daughter of Elon the
Hittite:
35 Which [a]were a grief of mind unto Isaac
and to Rebekah.

Isaac Blesses Jacob

27 And it came to pass, that when Isaac was
[a]old, and [b]his eyes were dim, so that he
could not see, he called Esau his eldest son, and
said unto him, My son: and he said unto him, Behold, *here am* I.
2 And he said, Behold now, I am old, I
[a]know not the day of my death:
3 [a]Now therefore take, I pray thee, thy
weapons, thy quiver and thy bow, and go out to
the field, and take me *some* venison;
4 And make me savoury meat, such as I
love, and bring *it* to me, that I may eat; that my
soul [a]may bless thee before I die.
5 And Rebekah heard when Isaac spake to
Esau his son. And Esau went to the field to hunt
for venison, *and* to bring *it*.
6 And Rebekah spake unto Jacob her son,
saying, Behold, I heard thy father speak unto Esau
thy brother, saying,
7 Bring me venison, and make me savoury
meat, that I may eat, and bless thee before the
LORD before my death.
8 Now therefore, my son, [a]obey my voice
according to that which I command thee.
9 Go now to the flock, and fetch me from
thence two good kids of the goats; and I will make
them [a]savoury meat for thy father, such as he
loveth:
10 And thou shalt bring *it* to thy father, that
he may eat, and that he [a]may bless thee before
his death.
11 And Jacob said to Rebekah his mother,
Behold, [a]Esau my brother *is* a hairy man, and I
am a smooth man:
12 My father peradventure will [a]feel me, and
I shall seem to him as a deceiver; and I shall bring
[b]a curse upon me, and not a blessing.
13 And his mother said unto him, [a]Upon me
be thy curse, my son: only obey my voice, and
go fetch me *them*.
14 And he went, and fetched, and brought
them to his mother: and his mother [a]made savoury meat, such as his father loved.
15 And Rebekah took [a]goodly raiment of her
eldest son Esau, which *were* with her in the house,
and put them upon Jacob her younger son:
16 And she put the skins of the kids of the
goats upon his hands, and upon the smooth of
his neck:
17 And she gave the savoury meat and the
bread, which she had prepared, into the hand of
her son Jacob.

27 [a]Judg. 11:7 [b]Gen. 26:16
28 [a]Gen. 21:22, 23
29 [a]Gen. 24:31; Ps. 115:15
30 [a]Gen. 19:3
31 [a]Gen. 21:31
33 [a]Gen. 21:31; 28:10
34 [a]Gen. 28:8; 36:2
35 [a]Gen. 27:46; 28:1, 8

CHAPTER 27

1 [a]Gen. 35:28 [b]Gen. 48:10; 1 Sam. 3:2
2 [a][Prov. 27:1; James 4:14]
3 [a]Gen. 25:27, 28
4 [a]Gen. 27:19, 25, 27, 31; 48:9, 15, 16; 49:28; Deut. 33:1; Heb. 11:20
8 [a]Gen. 27:13, 43
9 [a]Gen. 27:4
10 [a]Gen. 27:4; 48:16
11 [a]Gen. 25:25
12 [a]Gen. 27:21, 22 [b]Gen. 9:25; Deut. 27:18
13 [a]Gen. 43:9; 1 Sam. 25:24; 2 Sam. 14:9; Matt. 27:25
14 [a]Prov. 23:3; Luke 21:34
15 [a]Gen. 27:27

NKJV

come to me, [a]since you hate me and have [b]sent
me away from you?"
28 But they said, "We have certainly seen
that the LORD [a]is with you. So we said, 'Let there
now be an oath between us, between you and us;
and let us make a covenant with you,
29 'that you will do us no harm, since we
have not touched you, and since we have done
nothing to you but good and have sent you away
in peace. [a]You *are* now the blessed of the LORD.' "
30 [a]So he made them a feast, and they ate
and drank.
31 Then they arose early in the morning and
[a]swore an oath with one another; and Isaac sent
them away, and they departed from him in peace.
32 It came to pass the same day that Isaac's
servants came and told him about the well which
they had dug, and said to him, "We have found
water."
33 So he called it *Shebah. [a]Therefore the
name of the city *is* *Beersheba to this day.
34 [a]When Esau was forty years old, he took
as wives Judith the daughter of Beeri the Hittite,
and Basemath the daughter of Elon the Hittite.
35 And [a]they were a grief of mind to Isaac
and Rebekah.

Isaac Blesses Jacob

27 Now it came to pass, when Isaac was [a]old
and [b]his eyes were so dim that he could
not see, that he called Esau his older son and said
to him, "My son." And he answered him, "Here
I am."
2 Then he said, "Behold now, I am old. I
[a]do not know the day of my death.
3 [a]"Now therefore, please take your weapons, your quiver and your bow, and go out to the
field and hunt game for me.
4 "And make me savory food, such as I love,
and bring *it* to me that I may eat, that my soul
[a]may bless you before I die."
5 Now Rebekah was listening when Isaac
spoke to Esau his son. And Esau went to the field
to hunt game and to bring *it*.
6 So Rebekah spoke to Jacob her son, saying, "Indeed I heard your father speak to Esau
your brother, saying,
7 'Bring me game and make savory food for
me, that I may eat it and bless you in the presence
of the LORD before my death.'
8 "Now therefore, my son, [a]obey my voice
according to what I command you.
9 "Go now to the flock and bring me from
there two choice kids of the goats, and I will make
[a]savory food from them for your father, such as
he loves.
10 "Then you shall take *it* to your father, that
he may eat *it*, and that he [a]may bless you before
his death."
11 And Jacob said to Rebekah his mother,
"Look, [a]Esau my brother *is* a hairy man, and I
am a smooth-*skinned* man.
12 "Perhaps my father will [a]feel me, and I
shall seem to be a deceiver to him; and I shall
bring [b]a curse on myself and not a blessing."
13 But his mother said to him, [a]"*Let* your
curse *be* on me, my son; only obey my voice, and
go, get *them* for me."
14 And he went and got *them* and brought
them to his mother, and his mother [a]made savory
food, such as his father loved.
15 Then Rebekah took [a]the choice clothes of
her elder son Esau, which *were* with her in the
house, and put them on Jacob her younger
son.
16 And she put the skins of the kids of the
goats on his hands and on the smooth part of his
neck.
17 Then she gave the savory food and the
bread, which she had prepared, into the hand of
her son Jacob.

26:33 Lit. *Oath* or *Seven* • Lit. *Well of the Oath* or *Well of the Seven*

KJV

18 And he came unto his father, and said, My father: and he said, Here *am* I; who *art* thou, my son?

19 And Jacob said unto his father, I *am* Esau thy firstborn; I have done according as thou badest me: arise, I pray thee, sit and eat of my venison, [a]that thy soul may bless me.

20 And Isaac said unto his son, How *is it* that thou hast found *it* so quickly, my son? And he said, Because the LORD thy God brought *it* to me.

21 And Isaac said unto Jacob, Come near, I pray thee, that I [a]may feel thee, my son, whether thou *be* my very son Esau or not.

22 And Jacob went near unto Isaac his father; and he felt him, and said, The voice *is* Jacob's voice, but the hands *are* the hands of Esau.

23 And he discerned him not, because [a]his hands were hairy, as his brother Esau's hands: so he blessed him.

24 And he said, *Art* thou my very son Esau? And he said, I *am*.

25 And he said, Bring *it* near to me, and I will eat of my son's venison, [a]that my soul may bless thee. And he brought *it* near to him, and he did eat: and he brought him wine, and he drank.

26 And his father Isaac said unto him, Come near now, and kiss me, my son.

27 And he came near, and [a]kissed him: and he smelled the smell of his raiment, and blessed him, and said, See, [b]the smell of my son *is* as the smell of a field which the LORD hath blessed:

28 Therefore [a]God give thee of [b]the dew of heaven, and [c]the fatness of the earth, and [d]plenty of corn and wine:

29 [a]Let people serve thee, and nations bow down to thee: be lord over thy brethren, and [b]let thy mother's sons bow down to thee: [c]cursed *be* every one that curseth thee, and blessed *be* he that blesseth thee.

Esau's Lost Hope
(*Heb. 12:17*)

30 And it came to pass, as soon as Isaac had made an end of blessing Jacob, and Jacob was yet scarce gone out from the presence of Isaac his father, that Esau his brother came in from his hunting.

31 And he also had made savoury meat, and brought it unto his father, and said unto his father, Let my father arise, and [a]eat of his son's venison, that thy soul may bless me.

32 And Isaac his father said unto him, Who *art* thou? And he said, I *am* thy son, thy firstborn Esau.

33 And Isaac trembled very exceedingly, and said, Who? where *is* he that hath taken venison, and brought *it* me, and I have eaten of all before thou camest, and have blessed him? yea, [a]*and* he shall be blessed.

34 And when Esau heard the words of his father, [a]he cried with a great and exceeding bitter cry, and said unto his father, Bless me, *even* me also, O my father.

35 And he said, Thy brother came with subtilty, and hath taken away thy blessing.

36 And he said, [a]Is not he rightly named Jacob? for he hath supplanted me these two times: he took away my birthright; and, behold, now he hath taken away my blessing. And he said, Hast thou not reserved a blessing for me?

37 And Isaac answered and said unto Esau, [a]Behold, I have made him thy lord, and all his brethren have I given to him for servants; and [b]with corn and wine have I sustained him: and what shall I do now unto thee, my son?

38 And Esau said unto his father, Hast thou

19 [a]Gen. 27:4
21 [a]Gen. 27:12
23 [a]Gen. 27:16
25 [a]Gen. 27:4, 10, 19, 31
27 [a]Gen. 29:13 [b]Song 4:11; Hos. 14:6
28 [a]Heb. 11:20 [b]Gen. 27:39; Deut. 33:13, 28; 2 Sam. 1:21; Ps. 133:3; Prov. 3:20; Mic. 5:7; Zech. 8:12 [c]Gen. 45:18; Num. 18:12 [d]Deut. 7:13; 33:28
29 [a]Gen. 9:25; 25:23; Is. 45:14; 49:7; 60:12, 14 [b]Gen. 37:7, 10; 49:8 [c]Gen. 12:2, 3; Zeph. 2:8, 9
31 [a]Gen. 27:4
33 [a]Gen. 25:23; 28:3, 4; Num. 23:20; Rom. 11:29
34 [a][Heb. 12:17]
36 [a]Gen. 25:26, 32–34
37 [a]2 Sam. 8:14 [b]Gen. 27:28, 29

NKJV

18 So he went to his father and said, "My father." And he said, "Here I am. Who *are* you, my son?"

19 Jacob said to his father, "I *am* Esau your firstborn; I have done just as you told me; please arise, sit and eat of my game, [a]that your soul may bless me."

20 But Isaac said to his son, "How *is it* that you have found *it* so quickly, my son?" And he said, "Because the LORD your God brought *it* to me."

21 Then Isaac said to Jacob, "Please come near, that I [a]may feel you, my son, whether you *are* really my son Esau or not."

22 So Jacob went near to Isaac his father, and he felt him and said, "The voice *is* Jacob's voice, but the hands *are* the hands of Esau."

23 And he did not recognize him, because [a]his hands were hairy like his brother Esau's hands; so he blessed him.

24 Then he said, "*Are* you really my son Esau?" He said, "I *am*."

25 He said, "Bring *it* near to me, and I will eat of my son's game, so [a]that my soul may bless you." So he brought *it* near to him, and he ate; and he brought him wine, and he drank.

26 Then his father Isaac said to him, "Come near now and kiss me, my son."

27 And he came near and [a]kissed him; and he smelled the smell of his clothing, and blessed him and said:

"Surely, [b]the smell of my son
Is like the smell of a field
Which the LORD has blessed.

28 Therefore may [a]God give you
Of [b]the dew of heaven,
Of [c]the fatness of the earth,
And [d]plenty of grain and wine.

29 [a]Let peoples serve you,
And nations bow down to you.
Be master over your brethren,
And [b]let your mother's sons bow down
to you.
[c]Cursed *be* everyone who curses you,
And blessed *be* those who bless you!"

Esau's Lost Hope
(*Heb. 12:17*)

30 Now it happened, as soon as Isaac had finished blessing Jacob, and Jacob had scarcely gone out from the presence of Isaac his father, that Esau his brother came in from his hunting.

31 He also had made savory food, and brought it to his father, and said to his father, "Let my father arise and [a]eat of his son's game, that your soul may bless me."

32 And his father Isaac said to him, "Who *are* you?" So he said, "I *am* your son, your firstborn, Esau."

33 Then Isaac trembled exceedingly, and said, "Who? Where *is* the one who hunted game and brought *it* to me? I ate all *of it* before you came, and I have blessed him—[a]*and* indeed he shall be blessed."

34 When Esau heard the words of his father, [a]he cried with an exceedingly great and bitter cry, and said to his father, "Bless me—me also, O my father!"

35 But he said, "Your brother came with deceit and has taken away your blessing."

36 And *Esau* said, [a]"Is he not rightly named Jacob? For he has supplanted me these two times. He took away my birthright, and now look, he has taken away my blessing!" And he said, "Have you not reserved a blessing for me?"

37 Then Isaac answered and said to Esau, [a]"Indeed I have made him your master, and all his brethren I have given to him as servants; with [b]grain and wine I have sustained him. What shall I do now for you, my son?"

38 And Esau said to his father, "Have you

KJV

but one blessing, my father? bless me, *even* me
also, O my father. And Esau lifted up his voice,
[a]and wept.
39 And Isaac his father answered and said
unto him, Behold, [a]thy dwelling shall be the fatness of the earth, and of the dew of heaven from
above;
40 And by thy sword shalt thou live, and
[a]shalt serve thy brother; and [b]it shall come to pass
when thou shalt have the dominion, that thou
shalt break his yoke from off thy neck.

Jacob Escapes from Esau

41 And Esau [a]hated Jacob because of the
blessing wherewith his father blessed him: and
Esau said in his heart, [b]The days of mourning
for my father are at hand; [c]then will I slay my
brother Jacob.
42 And these words of Esau her elder son
were told to Rebekah: and she sent and called
Jacob her younger son, and said unto him, Behold,
thy brother Esau, as touching thee, doth [a]comfort
himself, *purposing* to kill thee.
43 Now therefore, my son, obey my voice;
and arise, flee thou to Laban my brother [a]to
Haran;
44 And tarry with him a [a]few days, until thy
brother's fury turn away;
45 Until thy brother's anger turn away from
thee, and he forget *that* which thou hast done to
him: then I will send, and fetch thee from thence:
why should I be deprived also of you both in one
day?
46 And Rebekah said to Isaac, [a]I am weary
of my life because of the daughters of Heth: [b]if
Jacob take a wife of the daughters of Heth, such
as these *which are* of the daughters of the land,
what good shall my life do me?

28 And Isaac called Jacob, and [a]blessed him,
and charged him, and said unto him, [b]Thou
shalt not take a wife of the daughters of Canaan.
2 [a]Arise, go to [b]Padan–aram, to the house
of [c]Bethuel thy mother's father; and take thee a
wife from thence of the daughters of [d]Laban thy
mother's brother.
3 [a]And God Almighty bless thee, and make
thee [b]fruitful, and multiply thee, that thou mayest
be a multitude of people;
4 And give thee [a]the blessing of Abraham,
to thee, and to thy seed with thee; that thou mayest inherit the land [b]wherein thou art a stranger,
which God gave unto Abraham.
5 And Isaac sent away Jacob: and he went
to Padan–aram unto Laban, son of Bethuel the
Syrian, the brother of Rebekah, Jacob's and
Esau's mother.

Esau Marries Mahalath

6 When Esau saw that Isaac had blessed Jacob, and sent him away to Padan–aram, to take
him a wife from thence; and that as he blessed
him he gave him a charge, saying, Thou shalt not
take a wife of the daughters of Canaan;
7 And that Jacob obeyed his father and his
mother, and was gone to Padan–aram;
8 And Esau seeing [a]that the daughters of
Canaan pleased not Isaac his father;
9 Then went Esau unto Ishmael, and [a]took
unto the wives which he had [b]Mahalath the
daughter of Ishmael Abraham's son, [c]the sister
of Nebajoth, to be his wife.

Jacob's Vow at Bethel

10 And Jacob [a]went out from Beer–sheba,
and went toward [b]Haran.

38 [a]Heb. 12:17
39 [a]Gen. 27:28; Heb. 11:20
40 [a]Gen. 25:23; 27:29; 2 Sam. 8:14; [Obad. 18–20] [b]2 Kin. 8:20–22
41 [a]Gen. 26:27; 32:3–11; 37:4, 5, 8 [b]Gen. 50:2–4, 10 [c]Obad. 10
42 [a]Ps. 64:5
43 [a]Gen. 11:31; 25:20; 28:2, 5
44 [a]Gen. 31:41
46 [a]Gen. 26:34, 35; 28:8 [b]Gen. 24:3

CHAPTER 28

1 [a]Gen. 27:33 [b]Gen. 24:3
2 [a]Hos. 12:12 [b]Gen. 25:20 [c]Gen. 22:23 [d]Gen. 24:29; 27:43; 29:5
3 [a]Gen. 17:16; 35:11; 48:3 [b]Gen. 26:4, 24
4 [a]Gen. 12:2, 3; 22:17; Gal. 3:8 [b]Gen. 17:8; 23:4; 36:7; 1 Chr. 29:15; Ps. 39:12
8 [a]Gen. 24:3; 26:34, 35; 27:46
9 [a]Gen. 26:34, 35 [b]Gen. 36:2, 3 [c]Gen. 25:13
10 [a]Gen. 26:23; 46:1; Hos. 12:12 [b]Gen. 12:4, 5; 27:43; 29:4; 2 Kin. 19:12; Acts 7:2

NKJV

only one blessing, my father? Bless me—me also,
O my father!" And Esau lifted up his voice [a]and
wept.
39 Then Isaac his father answered and said
to him:

"Behold, [a]your dwelling shall be of the
fatness of the earth,
And of the dew of heaven from above.
40 By your sword you shall live,
And [a]you shall serve your brother;
And [b]it shall come to pass, when you
become restless,
That you shall break his yoke from your
neck."

Jacob Escapes from Esau

41 So Esau [a]hated Jacob because of the
blessing with which his father blessed him, and
Esau said in his heart, [b]"The days of mourning
for my father are at hand; [c]then I will kill my
brother Jacob."
42 And the words of Esau her older son were
told to Rebekah. So she sent and called Jacob her
younger son, and said to him, "Surely your
brother Esau [a]comforts himself concerning you
by intending to kill you.
43 "Now therefore, my son, obey my voice:
arise, flee to my brother Laban [a]in Haran.
44 "And stay with him a [a]few days, until your
brother's fury turns away,
45 "until your brother's anger turns away
from you, and he forgets what you have done to
him; then I will send and bring you from there.
Why should I be bereaved also of you both in
one day?"
46 And Rebekah said to Isaac, [a]"I am weary
of my life because of the daughters of Heth; [b]if
Jacob takes a wife of the daughters of Heth, like
these *who are* the daughters of the land, what
good will my life be to me?"

28 Then Isaac called Jacob and [a]blessed him,
and charged him, and said to him: [b]"You
shall not take a wife from the daughters of
Canaan.
2 [a]"Arise, go to [b]Padan Aram, to the house
of [c]Bethuel your mother's father; and take yourself a wife from there of the daughters of [d]Laban
your mother's brother.

3 "May [a]God Almighty bless you,
And make you [b]fruitful and multiply you,
That you may be an assembly of peoples;
4 And give you [a]the blessing of Abraham,
To you and your descendants with you,
That you may inherit the land
[b]In which you are a stranger,
Which God gave to Abraham."

5 So Isaac sent Jacob away, and he went
to Padan Aram, to Laban the son of Bethuel the
Syrian, the brother of Rebekah, the mother of Jacob and Esau.

Esau Marries Mahalath

6 Esau saw that Isaac had blessed Jacob and
sent him away to Padan Aram to take himself a
wife from there, *and that* as he blessed him he
gave him a charge, saying, "You shall not take a
wife from the daughters of Canaan,"
7 and that Jacob had obeyed his father and
his mother and had gone to Padan Aram.
8 Also Esau saw [a]that the daughters of Canaan did not please his father Isaac.
9 So Esau went to Ishmael and [a]took [b]Ma-
halath the daughter of Ishmael, Abraham's son,
[c]the sister of Nebajoth, to be his wife in addition
to the wives he had.

Jacob's Vow at Bethel

10 Now Jacob [a]went out from Beersheba and
went toward [b]Haran.

KJV

11 And he lighted upon a certain place, and tarried there all night, because the sun was set; and he took of the stones of that place, and put *them for* his pillows, and lay down in that place to sleep.

12 And he [a]dreamed, and behold a ladder set up on the earth, and the top of it reached to heaven: and behold [b]the angels of God ascending and descending on it.

13 [a]And, behold, the LORD stood above it, and said, [b]I *am* the LORD God of Abraham thy father, and the God of Isaac: [c]the land whereon thou liest, to thee will I give it, and to thy seed;

14 And thy [a]seed shall be as the dust of the earth, and thou shalt spread abroad [b]to the west, and to the east, and to the north, and to the south: and in thee and [c]in thy seed shall all the families of the earth be blessed.

15 And, behold, [a]I *am* with thee, and will [b]keep thee in all *places* whither thou goest, and will [c]bring thee again into this land; for [d]I will not leave thee, [e]until I have done *that* which I have spoken to thee of.

16 And Jacob awaked out of his sleep, and he said, Surely the LORD is in [a]this place; and I knew *it* not.

17 And he was afraid, and said, How dreadful *is* this place! this *is* none other but the house of God, and this *is* the gate of heaven.

18 And Jacob rose up early in the morning, and took the stone that he had put *for* his pillows, and [a]set it up *for* a pillar, [b]and poured oil upon the top of it.

19 And he called the name of [a]that place Beth–el: but the name of that city *was called* Luz at the first.

20 [a]And Jacob vowed a vow, saying, If [b]God will be with me, and will keep me in this way that I go, and will give me [c]bread to eat, and raiment to put on,

21 So that [a]I come again to my father's house in peace; [b]then shall the LORD be my God:

22 And this stone, which I have set *for* a pillar, [a]shall be God's house: [b]and of all that thou shalt give me I will surely give the tenth unto thee.

Jacob Meets Rachel

29 Then Jacob went on his journey, [a]and came into the land of the people of the east.

2 And he looked, and behold a [a]well in the field, and, lo, there *were* three flocks of sheep lying by it; for out of that well they watered the flocks: and a great stone *was* upon the well's mouth.

3 And thither were all the flocks gathered: and they rolled the stone from the well's mouth, and watered the sheep, and put the stone again upon the well's mouth in his place.

4 And Jacob said unto them, My brethren, whence *be* ye? And they said, Of [a]Haran *are* we.

5 And he said unto them, Know ye [a]Laban the son of Nahor? And they said, We know *him.*

6 And he said unto them, [a]*Is* he well? And they said, *He is* well: and, behold, Rachel his daughter [b]cometh with the sheep.

7 And he said, Lo, *it is* yet high day, neither *is it* time that the cattle should be gathered together: water ye the sheep, and go *and* feed *them.*

8 And they said, We cannot, until all the flocks be gathered together, and *till* they roll the stone from the well's mouth; then we water the sheep.

9 And while he yet spake with them, [a]Rachel came with her father's sheep: for she kept them.

10 And it came to pass, when Jacob saw Rachel the daughter of Laban his mother's brother, and the sheep of Laban his mother's brother, that Jacob went near, and [a]rolled the stone from the

---

12 [a]Gen. 31:10; 41:1; Num. 12:6 [b]John 1:51; Heb. 1:4, 14
13 [a]Gen. 35:1; 48:3; Amos 7:7 [b]Gen. 26:24 [c]Gen. 13:15, 17; 26:3; 35:12
14 [a]Gen. 13:16; 22:17 [b]Gen. 13:14, 15; Deut. 12:20 [c]Gen. 12:3; 18:18; 22:18; 26:4; Matt. 1:2; Luke 3:34; Gal. 3:8
15 [a]Gen. 26:3, 24; 31:3 [b]Gen. 48:16; Num. 6:24; Ps. 121:5, 7, 8 [c]Gen. 35:6; 48:21; Deut. 30:3 [d]Lev. 26:44; Deut. 7:9; 31:6, 8; Josh. 1:5; 1 Kin. 8:57; Heb. 13:5 [e]Num. 23:19
16 [a]Ex. 3:5; Josh. 5:15; Ps. 139:7–12
18 [a]Gen. 31:13, 45 [b]Lev. 8:10–12
19 [a]Judg. 1:23, 26
20 [a]Gen. 31:13; Judg. 11:30; 2 Sam. 15:8 [b]Gen. 28:15 [c]1 Tim. 6:8
21 [a]Judg. 11:31; 2 Sam. 19:24, 30 [b]Deut. 26:17; 2 Sam. 15:8
22 [a]Gen. 35:7, 14 [b]Gen. 14:20; [Lev. 27:30]; Deut. 14:22

CHAPTER 29

1 [a]Gen. 25:6; Num. 23:7; Judg. 6:3, 33; Hos. 12:12
2 [a]Gen. 24:10, 11; Ex. 2:15, 16
4 [a]Gen. 11:31; 28:10
5 [a]Gen. 24:24, 29; 28:2
6 [a]Gen. 43:27 [b]Gen. 24:11; Ex. 2:16, 17
9 [a]Ex. 2:16
10 [a]Ex. 2:17

*———

28:19 Lit. *House of God*

NKJV

11 So he came to a certain place and stayed there all night, because the sun had set. And he took one of the stones of that place and put it at his head, and he lay down in that place to sleep.

12 Then he [a]dreamed, and behold, a ladder *was* set up on the earth, and its top reached to heaven; and there [b]the angels of God were ascending and descending on it.

13 [a]And behold, the LORD stood above it and said: [b]"I *am* the LORD God of Abraham your father and the God of Isaac; [c]the land on which you lie I will give to you and your descendants.

14 "Also your [a]descendants shall be as the dust of the earth; you shall spread abroad [b]to the west and the east, to the north and the south; and in you and [c]in your seed all the families of the earth shall be blessed.

15 "Behold, [a]I *am* with you and will [b]keep you wherever you go, and will [c]bring you back to this land; for [d]I will not leave you [e]until I have done what I have spoken to you."

16 Then Jacob awoke from his sleep and said, "Surely the LORD is in [a]this place, and I did not know *it.*"

17 And he was afraid and said, "How awesome *is* this place! This *is* none other than the house of God, and this *is* the gate of heaven!"

18 Then Jacob rose early in the morning, and took the stone that he had put at his head, [a]set it up as a pillar, [b]and poured oil on top of it.

19 And he called the name of [a]that place *Bethel; but the name of that city had been Luz previously.

20 [a]Then Jacob made a vow, saying, "If [b]God will be with me, and keep me in this way that I am going, and give me [c]bread to eat and clothing to put on,

21 "so that [a]I come back to my father's house in peace, [b]then the LORD shall be my God.

22 "And this stone which I have set as a pillar [a]shall be God's house, [b]and of all that You give me I will surely give a tenth to You."

Jacob Meets Rachel

29 So Jacob went on his journey [a]and came to the land of the people of the East.

2 And he looked, and saw a [a]well in the field; and behold, there *were* three flocks of sheep lying by it; for out of that well they watered the flocks. A large stone *was* on the well's mouth.

3 Now all the flocks would be gathered there; and they would roll the stone from the well's mouth, water the sheep, and put the stone back in its place on the well's mouth.

4 And Jacob said to them, "My brethren, where *are* you from?" And they said, "We *are* from [a]Haran."

5 Then he said to them, "Do you know [a]Laban the son of Nahor?" And they said, "We know him."

6 So he said to them, [a]"Is he well?" And they said, "*He is* well. And look, his daughter Rachel [b]is coming with the sheep."

7 Then he said, "Look, *it is* still high day; *it is* not time for the cattle to be gathered together. Water the sheep, and go and feed *them.*"

8 But they said, "We cannot until all the flocks are gathered together, and they have rolled the stone from the well's mouth; then we water the sheep."

9 Now while he was still speaking with them, [a]Rachel came with her father's sheep, for she was a shepherdess.

10 And it came to pass, when Jacob saw Rachel the daughter of Laban his mother's brother, and the sheep of Laban his mother's brother, that Jacob went near and [a]rolled the stone from the

KJV

well's mouth, and watered the flock of Laban his
mother's brother.
11 And Jacob [a]kissed Rachel, and lifted up
his voice, and wept.
12 And Jacob told Rachel that he *was* [a]her
father's brother, and that he *was* Rebekah's son:
[b]and she ran and told her father.
13 And it came to pass, when Laban heard
the tidings of Jacob his sister's son, that [a]he ran
to meet him, and embraced him, and kissed him,
and brought him to his house. And he told Laban
all these things.
14 And Laban said to him, [a]Surely thou *art*
my bone and my flesh. And he abode with him
the space of a month.

Jacob Marries Leah and Rachel

15 And Laban said unto Jacob, Because thou
art my brother, shouldest thou therefore serve me
for nought? tell me, [a]what *shall* thy wages *be*?
16 And Laban had two daughters: the name
of the elder *was* Leah, and the name of the younger *was* Rachel.
17 Leah *was* tender eyed; but Rachel was
[a]beautiful and well favoured.
18 And Jacob loved Rachel; and said, [a]I will
serve thee seven years for Rachel thy younger
daughter.
19 And Laban said, *It is* better that I give her
to thee, than that I should give her to another man:
abide with me.
20 And Jacob [a]served seven years for Rachel; and they seemed unto him *but* a few days,
for the love he had to her.
21 And Jacob said unto Laban, Give *me* my
wife, for my days are fulfilled, that I may [a]go in
unto her.
22 And Laban gathered together all the men
of the place, and [a]made a feast.
23 And it came to pass in the evening, that
he took Leah his daughter, and brought her to
him; and he went in unto her.
24 And Laban gave unto his daughter Leah
[a]Zilpah his maid *for* an handmaid.
25 And it came to pass, that in the morning,
behold, it *was* Leah: and he said to Laban, What
is this thou hast done unto me? did not I serve
with thee for Rachel? wherefore then hast thou
[a]beguiled me?
26 And Laban said, It must not be so done
in our country, to give the younger before the
firstborn.
27 [a]Fulfil her week, and we will give thee this
also for the service which thou shalt serve with
me yet seven other years.
28 And Jacob did so, and fulfilled her week:
and he gave him Rachel his daughter to wife
also.
29 And Laban gave to Rachel his daughter
[a]Bilhah his handmaid to be her maid.
30 And he went in also unto Rachel, and he
[a]loved also Rachel more than Leah, and served
with him [b]yet seven other years.

The Children of Jacob

31 And when the LORD [a]saw that Leah *was*
hated, he [b]opened her womb: but Rachel *was*
barren.
32 And Leah conceived, and bare a son, and
she called his name Reuben: for she said, Surely
the LORD hath [a]looked upon my affliction; now
therefore my husband will love me.
33 And she conceived again, and bare a son;
and said, Because the LORD hath heard that I *was*
hated, he hath therefore given me this *son* also:
and she called his name Simeon.
34 And she conceived again, and bare a son;
and said, Now this time will my husband be joined
unto me, because I have born him three sons:
therefore was his name called Levi.
35 And she conceived again, and bare a son:

11 [a]Gen. 33:4; 45:14, 15
12 [a]Gen. 13:8; 14:14, 16; 28:5 [b]Gen. 24:28
13 [a]Gen. 24:29–31; Luke 15:20
14 [a]Gen. 2:23; 37:27; Judg. 9:2; 2 Sam. 5:1; 19:12, 13
15 [a]Gen. 30:28; 31:41
17 [a]Gen. 12:11, 14; 26:7
18 [a]Gen. 31:41; 2 Sam. 3:14; Hos. 12:12
20 [a]Gen. 30:26; Hos. 12:12
21 [a]Judg. 15:1
22 [a]Judg. 14:10; John 2:1, 2
24 [a]Gen. 30:9, 10
25 [a]Gen. 27:35; 31:7; 1 Sam. 28:12
27 [a]Gen. 31:41; Judg. 14:2
29 [a]Gen. 30:3–5
30 [a]Gen. 29:17–20; Deut. 21:15–17 [b]Gen. 30:26; 31:41; Hos. 12:12
31 [a]Ps. 127:3 [b]Gen. 30:1
32 [a]Gen. 16:11; 31:42; Ex. 3:7; 4:31; Deut. 26:7; Ps. 25:18

NKJV

well's mouth, and watered the flock of Laban his
mother's brother.
11 Then Jacob [a]kissed Rachel, and lifted up
his voice and wept.
12 And Jacob told Rachel that he *was* [a]her
father's relative and that he *was* Rebekah's son.
[b]So she ran and told her father.
13 Then it came to pass, when Laban heard
the report about Jacob his sister's son, that [a]he
ran to meet him, and embraced him and kissed
him, and brought him to his house. So he told
Laban all these things.
14 And Laban said to him, [a]"Surely you *are*
my bone and my flesh." And he stayed with him
for a month.

Jacob Marries Leah and Rachel

15 Then Laban said to Jacob, "Because you
are my relative, should you therefore serve me
for nothing? Tell me, [a]what *should* your wages
be?"
16 Now Laban had two daughters: the name
of the elder *was* Leah, and the name of the younger *was* Rachel.
17 Leah's eyes *were* delicate, but Rachel was
[a]beautiful of form and appearance.
18 Now Jacob loved Rachel; so he said, [a]"I
will serve you seven years for Rachel your younger daughter."
19 And Laban said, "*It is* better that I give
her to you than that I should give her to another
man. Stay with me."
20 So Jacob [a]served seven years for Rachel,
and they seemed *only* a few days to him because
of the love he had for her.
21 Then Jacob said to Laban, "Give *me* my
wife, for my days are fulfilled, that I may [a]go in
to her."
22 And Laban gathered together all the men
of the place and [a]made a feast.
23 Now it came to pass in the evening, that
he took Leah his daughter and brought her to Jacob; and he went in to her.
24 And Laban gave his maid [a]Zilpah to his
daughter Leah *as* a maid.
25 So it came to pass in the morning, that
behold, it *was* Leah. And he said to Laban, "What
is this you have done to me? Was it not for Rachel
that I served you? Why then have you [a]deceived
me?"
26 And Laban said, "It must not be done so
in our country, to give the younger before the
firstborn.
27 [a]"Fulfill her week, and we will give you
this one also for the service which you will serve
with me still another seven years."
28 Then Jacob did so and fulfilled her week.
So he gave him his daughter Rachel as wife
also.
29 And Laban gave his maid [a]Bilhah to his
daughter Rachel as a maid.
30 Then *Jacob* also went in to Rachel, and
he also [a]loved Rachel more than Leah. And he
served with Laban [b]still another seven years.

The Children of Jacob

31 When the LORD [a]saw that Leah *was* unloved, He [b]opened her womb; but Rachel *was*
barren.
32 So Leah conceived and bore a son, and
she called his name *Reuben; for she said, "The
LORD has surely [a]looked on my affliction. Now
therefore, my husband will love me."
33 Then she conceived again and bore a son,
and said, "Because the LORD has heard that I *am*
unloved, He has therefore given me this *son* also."
And she called his name *Simeon.
34 She conceived again and bore a son, and
said, "Now this time my husband will become attached to me, because I have borne him three
sons." Therefore his name was called *Levi.
35 And she conceived again and bore a son,

*

29:32 Lit. *See, a Son*
29:33 Lit. *Heard*
29:34 Lit. *Attached*

KJV

and she said, Now will I praise the LORD: therefore she called his name [a]Judah; and left bearing.

30

30 And when Rachel saw that [a]she bare Jacob no children, Rachel [b]envied her sister; and said unto Jacob, Give me children, [c]or else I die.

2 And Jacob's anger was kindled against Rachel: and he said, [a]*Am* I in God's stead, who hath withheld from thee the fruit of the womb?

3 And she said, Behold [a]my maid Bilhah, go in unto her; [b]and she shall bear upon my knees, [c]that I may also have children by her.

4 And she gave him Bilhah her handmaid [a]to wife: and Jacob went in unto her.

5 And Bilhah conceived, and bare Jacob a son.

6 And Rachel said, God hath [a]judged me, and hath also heard my voice, and hath given me a son: therefore called she his name Dan.

7 And Bilhah Rachel's maid conceived again, and bare Jacob a second son.

8 And Rachel said, With great wrestlings have I wrestled with my sister, and I have prevailed: and she called his name Naphtali.

9 When Leah saw that she had left bearing, she took Zilpah her maid, and [a]gave her Jacob to wife.

10 And Zilpah Leah's maid bare Jacob a son.

11 And Leah said, A troop cometh: and she called his name Gad.

12 And Zilpah Leah's maid bare Jacob a second son.

13 And Leah said, Happy am I, for the daughters [a]will call me blessed: and she called his name Asher.

14 And Reuben went in the days of wheat harvest, and found mandrakes in the field, and brought them unto his mother Leah. Then Rachel said to Leah, [a]Give me, I pray thee, of thy son's mandrakes.

15 And she said unto her, [a]*Is it* a small matter that thou hast taken my husband? and wouldest thou take away my son's mandrakes also? And Rachel said, Therefore he shall lie with thee to night for thy son's mandrakes.

16 And Jacob came out of the field in the evening, and Leah went out to meet him, and said, Thou must come in unto me; for surely I have hired thee with my son's mandrakes. And he lay with her that night.

17 And God hearkened unto Leah, and she conceived, and bare Jacob the fifth son.

18 And Leah said, God hath given me my hire, because I have given my maiden to my husband: and she called his name Issachar.

19 And Leah conceived again, and bare Jacob the sixth son.

20 And Leah said, God hath endued me *with* a good dowry; now will my husband dwell with me, because I have born him six sons: and she called his name Zebulun.

21 And afterwards she bare a [a]daughter, and called her name Dinah.

22 And God [a]remembered Rachel, and God hearkened to her, and [b]opened her womb.

23 And she conceived, and bare a son; and said, God hath taken away [a]my reproach:

24 And she called his name Joseph; and said, [a]The LORD shall add to me another son.

Jacob's Agreement with Laban

25 And it came to pass, when Rachel had born Joseph, that Jacob said unto Laban, [a]Send me away, that I may go unto [b]mine own place, and to my country.

26 Give *me* my wives and my children, [a]for whom I have served thee, and let me go: for thou knowest my service which I have done thee.

27 And Laban said unto him, I pray thee, if I have found favour in thine eyes, *tarry: for* [a]I

---

35 [a]Gen. 49:8; Matt. 1:2

CHAPTER 30

1 [a]Gen. 16:1, 2; 29:31 [b]Gen. 37:11 [c]1 Sam. 1:5, 6; [Job 5:2]
2 [a]Gen. 16:2; 1 Sam. 1:5
3 [a]Gen. 16:2 [b]Gen. 50:23; Job 3:12 [c]Gen. 16:2, 3
4 [a]Gen. 16:3, 4
6 [a]Gen. 18:25; Ps. 35:24; 43:1; Lam. 3:59
9 [a]Gen. 30:4
13 [a]Prov. 31:28; Luke 1:48
14 [a]Gen. 25:30
15 [a][Num. 16:9, 13]
21 [a]Gen. 34:1
22 [a]Gen. 19:29; 1 Sam. 1:19, 20 [b]Gen. 29:31
23 [a]1 Sam. 1:6; Is. 4:1; Luke 1:25
24 [a]Gen. 35:16–18
25 [a]Gen. 24:54, 56 [b]Gen. 18:33
26 [a]Gen. 29:18–20, 27, 30; Hos. 12:12
27 [a]Gen. 26:24; 39:3; Is. 61:9

*

29:35 Lit. *Praise*
30:6 Lit. *Judge*
30:8 Lit. *My Wrestling*
30:11 So with Qr., Syr., Tg.; Kt., LXX, Vg. *in fortune* • Lit. *Troop* or *Fortune*
30:13 Lit. *Happy*
30:18 Lit. *Wages*
30:20 Lit. *Dwelling*
30:24 Lit. *He Will Add*

NKJV

and said, "Now I will praise the LORD." Therefore she called his name [a]Judah.* Then she stopped bearing.

30

30 Now when Rachel saw that [a]she bore Jacob no children, Rachel [b]envied her sister, and said to Jacob, "Give me children, [c]or else I die!"

2 And Jacob's anger was aroused against Rachel, and he said, [a]"*Am* I in the place of God, who has withheld from you the fruit of the womb?"

3 So she said, "Here is [a]my maid Bilhah; go in to her, [b]and she will bear *a child* on my knees, [c]that I also may have children by her."

4 Then she gave him Bilhah her maid [a]as wife, and Jacob went in to her.

5 And Bilhah conceived and bore Jacob a son.

6 Then Rachel said, "God has [a]judged my case; and He has also heard my voice and given me a son." Therefore she called his name *Dan.

7 And Rachel's maid Bilhah conceived again and bore Jacob a second son.

8 Then Rachel said, "With great wrestlings I have wrestled with my sister, *and* indeed I have prevailed." So she called his name *Naphtali.

9 When Leah saw that she had stopped bearing, she took Zilpah her maid and [a]gave her to Jacob as wife.

10 And Leah's maid Zilpah bore Jacob a son.

11 Then Leah said, *"A troop comes!" So she called his name *Gad.

12 And Leah's maid Zilpah bore Jacob a second son.

13 Then Leah said, "I am happy, for the daughters [a]will call me blessed." So she called his name *Asher.

14 Now Reuben went in the days of wheat harvest and found mandrakes in the field, and brought them to his mother Leah. Then Rachel said to Leah, [a]"Please give me *some* of your son's mandrakes."

15 But she said to her, [a]"*Is it* a small matter that you have taken away my husband? Would you take away my son's mandrakes also?" And Rachel said, "Therefore he will lie with you tonight for your son's mandrakes."

16 When Jacob came out of the field in the evening, Leah went out to meet him and said, "You must come in to me, for I have surely hired you with my son's mandrakes." And he lay with her that night.

17 And God listened to Leah, and she conceived and bore Jacob a fifth son.

18 Leah said, "God has given me my wages, because I have given my maid to my husband." So she called his name *Issachar.

19 Then Leah conceived again and bore Jacob a sixth son.

20 And Leah said, "God has endowed me *with* a good endowment; now my husband will dwell with me, because I have borne him six sons." So she called his name *Zebulun.

21 Afterward she bore a [a]daughter, and called her name Dinah.

22 Then God [a]remembered Rachel, and God listened to her and [b]opened her womb.

23 And she conceived and bore a son, and said, "God has taken away [a]my reproach."

24 So she called his name *Joseph, and said, [a]"The LORD shall add to me another son."

Jacob's Agreement with Laban

25 And it came to pass, when Rachel had borne Joseph, that Jacob said to Laban, [a]"Send me away, that I may go to [b]my own place and to my country.

26 "Give *me* my wives and my children [a]for whom I have served you, and let me go; for you know my service which I have done for you."

27 And Laban said to him, "Please *stay,* if I have found favor in your eyes, *for* [a]I have learned

KJV

have learned by experience that the LORD hath blessed me for thy sake.

28 And he said, [a]Appoint me thy wages, and I will give *it*.

29 And he said unto him, [a]Thou knowest how I have served thee, and how thy cattle was with me.

30 For *it was* little which thou hadst before I *came*, and it is *now* increased unto a multitude; and the LORD hath blessed thee since my coming: and now when shall I [a]provide for mine own house also?

31 And he said, What shall I give thee? And Jacob said, Thou shalt not give me any thing: if thou wilt do this thing for me, I will again feed *and* keep thy flock.

32 I will pass through all thy flock to day, removing from thence all the speckled and spotted cattle, and all the brown cattle among the sheep, and the spotted and speckled among the goats: and [a]*of such* shall be my hire.

33 So shall my [a]righteousness answer for me in time to come, when it shall come for my hire before thy face: every one that *is* not speckled and spotted among the goats, and brown among the sheep, that shall be counted stolen with me.

34 And Laban said, Behold, I would it might be according to thy word.

35 And he removed that day the he goats that were [a]ringstraked and spotted, and all the she goats that were speckled and spotted, *and* every one that had *some* white in it, and all the brown among the sheep, and gave *them* into the hand of his sons.

36 And he set three days' journey betwixt himself and Jacob: and Jacob fed the rest of Laban's flocks.

37 And [a]Jacob took him rods of green poplar, and of the hazel and chesnut tree; and pilled white strakes in them, and made the white appear which *was* in the rods.

38 And he set the rods which he had pilled before the flocks in the gutters in the watering troughs when the flocks came to drink, that they should conceive when they came to drink.

39 And the flocks conceived before the rods, and brought forth cattle ringstraked, speckled, and spotted.

40 And Jacob did separate the lambs, and set the faces of the flocks toward the ringstraked, and all the brown in the flock of Laban; and he put his own flocks by themselves, and put them not unto Laban's cattle.

41 And it came to pass, whensoever the stronger cattle did conceive, that Jacob laid the rods before the eyes of the cattle in the gutters, that they might conceive among the rods.

42 But when the cattle were feeble, he put *them* not in: so the feebler were Laban's, and the stronger Jacob's.

43 And the man [a]increased exceedingly, and [b]had much cattle, and maidservants, and menservants, and camels, and asses.

Jacob Flees from Laban

31 And he heard the words of Laban's sons, saying, Jacob hath taken away all that *was* our father's; and of *that* which *was* our father's hath he gotten all this [a]glory.

2 And Jacob beheld the [a]countenance of Laban, and, behold, it *was* not [b]toward him as before.

3 And the LORD said unto Jacob, [a]Return unto the land of thy fathers, and to thy kindred; and I will [b]be with thee.

4 And Jacob sent and called Rachel and Leah to the field unto his flock,

5 And said unto them, [a]I see your father's countenance, that it *is* not toward me as before; but the God of my father [b]hath been with me.

28 [a]Gen. 29:15; 31:7, 41 **29** [a]Gen. 31:6, 38–40; Matt. 24:45; Titus 2:10 **30** [a][1 Tim. 5:8] **32** [a]Gen. 31:8 **33** [a]Ps. 37:6 **35** [a]Gen. 31:9–12 **37** [a]Gen. 31:9–12 **43** [a]Gen. 12:16; 30:30 [b]Gen. 13:2; 24:35; 26:13, 14

CHAPTER 31

1 [a]Ps. 49:16 **2** [a]Gen. 4:5 [b]Deut. 28:54 **3** [a]Gen. 28:15, 20, 21; 32:9 [b]Gen. 46:4 **5** [a]Gen. 31:2, 3 [b]Gen. 21:22; 28:13, 15; 31:29, 42, 53; Is. 41:10; Heb. 13:5

NKJV

by experience that the LORD has blessed me for your sake."

28 Then he said, [a]"Name me your wages, and I will give *it*."

29 So *Jacob* said to him, [a]"You know how I have served you and how your livestock has been with me.

30 "For what you had before I *came was* little, and it has increased to a great amount; the LORD has blessed you since my coming. And now, when shall I also [a]provide for my own house?"

31 So he said, "What shall I give you?" And Jacob said, "You shall not give me anything. If you will do this thing for me, I will again feed and keep your flocks:

32 "Let me pass through all your flock today, removing from there all the speckled and spotted sheep, and all the brown ones among the lambs, and the spotted and speckled among the goats; and [a]*these* shall be my wages.

33 "So my [a]righteousness will answer for me in time to come, when the subject of my wages comes before you: every one that *is* not speckled and spotted among the goats, and brown among the lambs, will be considered stolen, if *it is* with me."

34 And Laban said, "Oh, that it were according to your word!"

35 So he removed that day the male goats that were [a]speckled and spotted, all the female goats that were speckled and spotted, every one that had *some* white in it, and all the brown ones among the lambs, and gave *them* into the hand of his sons.

36 Then he put three days' journey between himself and Jacob, and Jacob fed the rest of Laban's flocks.

37 Now [a]Jacob took for himself rods of green poplar and of the almond and chestnut trees, peeled white strips in them, and exposed the white which *was* in the rods.

38 And the rods which he had peeled, he set before the flocks in the gutters, in the watering troughs where the flocks came to drink, so that they should conceive when they came to drink.

39 So the flocks conceived before the rods, and the flocks brought forth streaked, speckled, and spotted.

40 Then Jacob separated the lambs, and made the flocks face toward the streaked and all the brown in the flock of Laban; but he put his own flocks by themselves and did not put them with Laban's flock.

41 And it came to pass, whenever the stronger livestock conceived, that Jacob placed the rods before the eyes of the livestock in the gutters, that they might conceive among the rods.

42 But when the flocks were feeble, he did not put *them* in; so the feebler were Laban's and the stronger Jacob's.

43 Thus the man [a]became exceedingly prosperous, and [b]had large flocks, female and male servants, and camels and donkeys.

Jacob Flees from Laban

31 Now *Jacob* heard the words of Laban's sons, saying, "Jacob has taken away all that was our father's, and from what was our father's he has acquired all this [a]wealth."

2 And Jacob saw the [a]countenance of Laban, and indeed it *was* not [b]*favorable* toward him as before.

3 Then the LORD said to Jacob, [a]"Return to the land of your fathers and to your family, and I will [b]be with you."

4 So Jacob sent and called Rachel and Leah to the field, to his flock,

5 and said to them, [a]"I see your father's countenance, that it *is* not *favorable* toward me as before; but the God of my father [b]has been with me.

KJV

6 And [a]ye know that with all my power I have served your father.

7 And your father hath deceived me, and [a]changed my wages [b]ten times; but God [c]suffered him not to hurt me.

8 If he said thus, [a]The speckled shall be thy wages; then all the cattle bare speckled: and if he said thus, The ringstraked shall be thy hire; then bare all the cattle ringstraked.

9 Thus God hath [a]taken away the cattle of your father, and given *them* to me.

10 And it came to pass at the time that the cattle conceived, that I lifted up mine eyes, and saw in a dream, and, behold, the rams which leaped upon the cattle *were* ringstraked, speckled, and grisled.

11 And [a]the angel of God spake unto me in a dream, *saying*, Jacob: And I said, Here *am* I.

12 And he said, Lift up now thine eyes, and see, all the rams which leap upon the cattle *are* ringstraked, speckled, and grisled: for [a]I have seen all that Laban doeth unto thee.

13 I *am* the God of Beth–el, [a]where thou anointedst the pillar, *and* where thou vowedst a vow unto me: now [b]arise, get thee out from this land, and return unto the land of thy kindred.

14 And Rachel and Leah answered and said unto him, [a]*Is there* yet any portion or inheritance for us in our father's house?

15 Are we not counted of him strangers? for [a]he hath sold us, and hath quite devoured also our money.

16 For all the riches which God hath taken from our father, that *is* our's, and our children's: now then, whatsoever God hath said unto thee, do.

17 Then Jacob rose up, and set his sons and his wives upon camels;

18 And he carried away all his cattle, and all his goods which he had gotten, the cattle of his getting, which he had gotten in Padan–aram, for to go to Isaac his father in the land of [a]Canaan.

19 And Laban went to shear his sheep: and Rachel had stolen the [a]images that *were* her father's.

20 And Jacob stole away unawares to Laban the Syrian, in that he told him not that he fled.

21 So he fled with all that he had; and he rose up, and passed over the river, and [a]set his face *toward* the mount Gilead.

Laban Pursues Jacob

22 And it was told Laban on the third day that Jacob was fled.

23 And he took [a]his brethren with him, and pursued after him seven days' journey; and they overtook him in the mount Gilead.

24 And God [a]came to Laban the Syrian in a dream by night, and said unto him, Take heed that thou [b]speak not to Jacob either good or bad.

25 Then Laban overtook Jacob. Now Jacob had pitched his tent in the mount: and Laban with his brethren pitched in the mount of Gilead.

26 And Laban said to Jacob, What hast thou done, that thou hast stolen away unawares to me, and [a]carried away my daughters, as captives *taken* with the sword?

27 Wherefore didst thou flee away secretly, and steal away from me; and didst not tell me, that I might have sent thee away with mirth, and with songs, with tabret, and with harp?

28 And hast not suffered me [a]to kiss my sons and my daughters? [b]thou hast now done foolishly in *so* doing.

29 It is in the power of my hand to do you hurt: but the [a]God of your father spake unto me [b]yesternight, saying, Take thou heed that thou speak not to Jacob either good or bad.

30 And now, *though* thou wouldest needs be

6 [a]Gen. 30:29; 31:38–41
7 [a]Gen. 29:25; 31:41 [b]Num. 14:22; Neh. 4:12; Job 19:3; Zech. 8:23 [c]Gen. 15:1; 20:6; 31:29; Job 1:10; Ps. 37:28; 105:14
8 [a]Gen. 30:32
9 [a]Gen. 31:1, 16
11 [a]Gen. 16:7–11; 22:11, 15; 31:13; 48:16
12 [a]Gen. 31:42; Ex. 3:7; Ps. 139:3; Eccl. 5:8
13 [a]Gen. 28:16–22; 35:1, 6, 15 [b]Gen. 31:3; 32:9
14 [a]Gen. 2:24
15 [a]Gen. 29:15, 20, 23, 27; Neh. 5:8
18 [a]Gen. 17:8; 33:18; 35:27
19 [a]Gen. 31:30, 34; 35:2; Judg. 17:5; 1 Sam. 19:13; Hos. 3:4
21 [a]Gen. 46:28; 2 Kin. 12:17; Luke 9:51, 53
23 [a]Gen. 13:8
24 [a]Gen. 20:3; 31:29; 46:2–4; Job 33:15; Matt. 1:20 [b]Gen. 24:50; 31:7, 29
26 [a]1 Sam. 30:2
28 [a]Gen. 31:55; Ruth 1:9, 14; 1 Kin. 19:20; Acts 20:37 [b]1 Sam. 13:13
29 [a]Gen. 28:13; 31:5, 24, 42, 53 [b]Gen. 31:24

NKJV

6 "And [a]you know that with all my might I have served your father.

7 "Yet your father has deceived me and [a]changed my wages [b]ten times, but God [c]did not allow him to hurt me.

8 "If he said thus: [a]'The speckled shall be your wages,' then all the flocks bore speckled. And if he said thus: 'The streaked shall be your wages,' then all the flocks bore streaked.

9 "So God has [a]taken away the livestock of your father and given *them* to me.

10 "And it happened, at the time when the flocks conceived, that I lifted my eyes and saw in a dream, and behold, the rams which leaped upon the flocks *were* streaked, speckled, and gray-spotted.

11 "Then [a]the Angel of God spoke to me in a dream, saying, 'Jacob.' And I said, 'Here I am.'

12 "And He said, 'Lift your eyes now and see, all the rams which leap on the flocks *are* streaked, speckled, and gray-spotted; for [a]I have seen all that Laban is doing to you.

13 'I *am* the God of Bethel, [a]where you anointed the pillar *and* where you made a vow to Me. Now [b]arise, get out of this land, and return to the land of your family.' "

14 Then Rachel and Leah answered and said to him, [a]"Is there still any portion or inheritance for us in our father's house?

15 "Are we not considered strangers by him? For [a]he has sold us, and also completely consumed our money.

16 "For all these riches which God has taken from our father are *really* ours and our children's; now then, whatever God has said to you, do it."

17 Then Jacob rose and set his sons and his wives on camels.

18 And he carried away all his livestock and all his possessions which he had gained, his acquired livestock which he had gained in Padan Aram, to go to his father Isaac in the land of [a]Canaan.

19 Now Laban had gone to shear his sheep, and Rachel had stolen the [a]household idols that were her father's.

20 And Jacob stole away, unknown to Laban the Syrian, in that he did not tell him that he intended to flee.

21 So he fled with all that he had. He arose and crossed the river, and [a]headed toward the mountains of Gilead.

Laban Pursues Jacob

22 And Laban was told on the third day that Jacob had fled.

23 Then he took [a]his brethren with him and pursued him for seven days' journey, and he overtook him in the mountains of Gilead.

24 But God [a]had come to Laban the Syrian in a dream by night, and said to him, "Be careful that you [b]speak to Jacob neither good nor bad."

25 So Laban overtook Jacob. Now Jacob had pitched his tent in the mountains, and Laban with his brethren pitched in the mountains of Gilead.

26 And Laban said to Jacob: "What have you done, that you have stolen away unknown to me, and [a]carried away my daughters like captives *taken* with the sword?

27 "Why did you flee away secretly, and steal away from me, and not tell me; for I might have sent you away with joy and songs, with timbrel and harp?

28 "And you did not allow me [a]to kiss my sons and my daughters. Now [b]you have done foolishly in *so* doing.

29 "It is in my power to do you harm, but the [a]God of your father spoke to me [b]last night, saying, 'Be careful that you speak to Jacob neither good nor bad.'

30 "And now you have surely gone because

KJV

gone, because thou sore longedst after thy father's house, *yet* wherefore hast thou [a]stolen my gods?

31 And Jacob answered and said to Laban, Because I was [a]afraid: for I said, Peradventure thou wouldest take by force thy daughters from me.

32 With whomsoever thou findest thy gods, [a]let him not live: before our brethren discern thou what *is* thine with me, and take *it* to thee. For Jacob knew not that Rachel had stolen them.

33 And Laban went into Jacob's tent, and into Leah's tent, and into the two maidservants' tents; but he found *them* not. Then went he out of Leah's tent, and entered into Rachel's tent.

34 Now Rachel had taken the images, and put them in the camel's furniture, and sat upon them. And Laban searched all the tent, but found *them* not.

35 And she said to her father, Let it not displease my lord that I cannot [a]rise up before thee; for the custom of women *is* upon me. And he searched, but found not the images.

36 And Jacob was wroth, and chode with Laban: and Jacob answered and said to Laban, What *is* my trespass? what *is* my sin, that thou hast so hotly pursued after me?

37 Whereas thou hast searched all my stuff, what hast thou found of all thy household stuff? set *it* here before my brethren and thy brethren, that they may judge betwixt us both.

38 This twenty years *have* I *been* with thee; thy ewes and thy she goats have not cast their young, and the rams of thy flock have I not eaten.

39 [a]That which was torn *of beasts* I brought not unto thee; I bare the loss of it; of [b]my hand didst thou require it, *whether* stolen by day, or stolen by night.

40 *Thus* I was; in the day the drought consumed me, and the frost by night; and my sleep departed from mine eyes.

41 Thus have I been twenty years in thy house; I [a]served thee fourteen years for thy two daughters, and six years for thy cattle: and [b]thou hast changed my wages ten times.

42 [a]Except the God of my father, the God of Abraham, and [b]the fear of Isaac, had been with me, surely thou hadst sent me away now empty. [c]God hath seen mine affliction and the labour of my hands, and [d]rebuked *thee* yesternight.

Laban's Covenant with Jacob

43 And Laban answered and said unto Jacob, *These* daughters *are* my daughters, and *these* children *are* my children, and *these* cattle *are* my cattle, and all that thou seest *is* mine: and what can I do this day unto these my daughters, or unto their children which they have born?

44 Now therefore come thou, [a]let us make a covenant, I [b]and thou; and let it be for a witness between me and thee.

45 And Jacob [a]took a stone, and set it up *for* a pillar.

46 And Jacob said unto his brethren, Gather stones; and they took stones, and made an heap: and they did eat there upon the heap.

47 And Laban called it Jegar–sahadutha: but Jacob called it Galeed.

48 And Laban said, [a]This heap *is* a witness between me and thee this day. Therefore was the name of it called Galeed;

49 And [a]Mizpah; for he said, The LORD watch between me and thee, when we are absent one from another.

50 If thou shalt afflict my daughters, or if thou shalt take *other* wives beside my daughters, no man *is* with us; see, God *is* witness betwixt me and thee.

51 And Laban said to Jacob, Behold this

---

30 [a]Gen. 31:19; Josh. 24:2; Judg. 17:5; 18:24
31 [a]Gen. 26:7; 32:7, 11
32 [a]Gen. 44:9
35 [a]Ex. 20:12; Lev. 19:32
39 [a]Ex. 22:10 [b]Ex. 22:10–13
41 [a]Gen. 29:20, 27–30 [b]Gen. 31:7
42 [a]Gen. 31:5, 29, 53; Ps. 124:1, 2 [b]Gen. 31:53; Is. 8:13 [c]Gen. 29:32; Ex. 3:7 [d]Gen. 31:24, 29; 1 Chr. 12:17
44 [a]Gen. 21:27, 32; 26:28 [b]Josh. 24:27
45 [a]Gen. 28:18; 35:14; Josh. 24:26, 27
48 [a]Josh. 24:27
49 [a]Judg. 10:17; 11:29; 1 Sam. 7:5, 6

NKJV

you greatly long for your father's house, *but* why did you [a]steal my gods?"

31 Then Jacob answered and said to Laban, "Because I was [a]afraid, for I said, 'Perhaps you would take your daughters from me by force.'

32 "With whomever you find your gods, [a]do not let him live. In the presence of our brethren, identify what I have of yours and take *it* with you." For Jacob did not know that Rachel had stolen them.

33 And Laban went into Jacob's tent, into Leah's tent, and into the two maids' tents, but he did not find *them.* Then he went out of Leah's tent and entered Rachel's tent.

34 Now Rachel had taken the household idols, put them in the camel's saddle, and sat on them. And Laban searched all about the tent but did not find *them.*

35 And she said to her father, "Let it not displease my lord that I cannot [a]rise before you, for the manner of women *is* with me." And he searched but did not find the household idols.

36 Then Jacob was angry and rebuked Laban, and Jacob answered and said to Laban: "What *is* my trespass? What *is* my sin, that you have so hotly pursued me?

37 "Although you have searched all my things, what part of your household things have you found? Set *it* here before my brethren and your brethren, that they may judge between us both!

38 "These twenty years I *have been* with you; your ewes and your female goats have not miscarried their young, and I have not eaten the rams of your flock.

39 [a]"That which was torn *by beasts* I did not bring to you; I bore the loss of it. [b]You required it from my hand, *whether* stolen by day or stolen by night.

40 "*There* I was! In the day the drought consumed me, and the frost by night, and my sleep departed from my eyes.

41 "Thus I have been in your house twenty years; I [a]served you fourteen years for your two daughters, and six years for your flock, and [b]you have changed my wages ten times.

42 [a]"Unless the God of my father, the God of Abraham and [b]the Fear of Isaac, had been with me, surely now you would have sent me away empty-handed. [c]God has seen my affliction and the labor of my hands, and [d]rebuked *you* last night."

Laban's Covenant with Jacob

43 And Laban answered and said to Jacob, "*These* daughters *are* my daughters, and *these* children *are* my children, and *this* flock *is* my flock; all that you see *is* mine. But what can I do this day to these my daughters or to their children whom they have borne?

44 "Now therefore, come, [a]let us make a covenant, [b]you and I, and let it be a witness between you and me."

45 So Jacob [a]took a stone and set it up *as* a pillar.

46 Then Jacob said to his brethren, "Gather stones." And they took stones and made a heap, and they ate there on the heap.

47 Laban called it *Jegar Sahadutha, but Jacob called it *Galeed.

48 And Laban said, [a]"This heap *is* a witness between you and me this day." Therefore its name was called Galeed,

49 also [a]Mizpah,* because he said, "May the LORD watch between you and me when we are absent one from another.

50 "If you afflict my daughters, or if you take *other* wives besides my daughters, *although* no man *is* with us—see, God *is* witness between you and me!"

51 Then Laban said to Jacob, "Here is this

---

*

31:47 Lit., in Aram., *Heap of Witness* • Lit., in Heb., *Heap of Witness*
31:49 Lit. *Watch*

KJV

heap, and behold *this* pillar, which I have cast betwixt me and thee;

52 This heap *be* witness, and *this* pillar *be* witness, that I will not pass over this heap to thee, and that thou shalt not pass over this heap and this pillar unto me, for harm.

53 The God of Abraham, and the God of Nahor, the God of their father, [a]judge betwixt us. And Jacob [b]sware by [c]the fear of his father Isaac.

54 Then Jacob offered sacrifice upon the mount, and called his brethren to eat bread: and they did eat bread, and tarried all night in the mount.

55 And early in the morning Laban rose up, and [a]kissed his sons and his daughters, and [b]blessed them: and Laban departed, and [c]returned unto his place.

Esau Comes to Meet Jacob

32 And Jacob went on his way, and [a]the angels of God met him.

2 And when Jacob saw them, he said, This *is* God's [a]host: and he called the name of that place Mahanaim.

3 And Jacob sent messengers before him to Esau his brother [a]unto the land of Seir, [b]the country of Edom.

4 And he commanded them, saying, [a]Thus shall ye speak unto my lord Esau; Thy servant Jacob saith thus, I have sojourned with Laban, and stayed there until now:

5 And [a]I have oxen, and asses, flocks, and menservants, and womenservants: and I have sent to tell my lord, that [b]I may find grace in thy sight.

6 And the messengers returned to Jacob, saying, We came to thy brother Esau, and also [a]he cometh to meet thee, and four hundred men with him.

7 Then Jacob was greatly afraid and [a]distressed: and he divided the people that *was* with him, and the flocks, and herds, and the camels, into two bands;

8 And said, If Esau come to the one company, and smite it, then the other company which is left shall escape.

9 [a]And Jacob said, [b]O God of my father Abraham, and God of my father Isaac, the LORD [c]which saidst unto me, Return unto thy country, and to thy kindred, and I will deal well with thee:

10 I am not worthy of the least of all the [a]mercies, and of all the truth, which thou hast shewed unto thy servant; for with [b]my staff I passed over this Jordan; and now I am become two bands.

11 [a]Deliver me, I pray thee, from the hand of my brother, from the hand of Esau: for I fear him, lest he will come and smite me, *and* [b]the mother with the children.

12 And [a]thou saidst, I will surely do thee good, and make thy seed as the [b]sand of the sea, which cannot be numbered for multitude.

13 And he lodged there that same night; and took of that which came to his hand [a]a present for Esau his brother;

14 Two hundred she goats, and twenty he goats, two hundred ewes, and twenty rams,

15 Thirty milch camels with their colts, forty kine, and ten bulls, twenty she asses, and ten foals.

16 And he delivered *them* into the hand of his servants, every drove by themselves; and said unto his servants, Pass over before me, and put a space betwixt drove and drove.

17 And he commanded the foremost, saying, When Esau my brother meeteth thee, and asketh thee, saying, Whose *art* thou? and whither goest thou? and whose *are* these before thee?

18 Then thou shalt say, *They be* thy servant

53 [a]Gen. 16:5 [b]Gen. 21:23 [c]Gen. 31:42
55 [a]Gen. 29:11, 13; 31:28, 43 [b]Gen. 28:1 [c]Gen. 18:33; 30:25; Num. 24:25

CHAPTER 32

1 [a]Num. 22:31; 2 Kin. 6:16, 17; [Ps. 34:7; 91:1; Heb. 1:14]
2 [a]Josh. 5:14; Ps. 103:21; 148:2; Luke 2:13
3 [a]Gen. 14:6; 33:14, 16 [b]Gen. 25:30; 36:6–9; Deut. 2:5; Josh. 24:4
4 [a]Prov. 15:1
5 [a]Gen. 30:43 [b]Gen. 33:8, 15
6 [a]Gen. 33:1
7 [a]Gen. 32:11; 35:3
9 [a][Ps. 50:15] [b]Gen. 28:13; 31:42 [c]Gen. 31:3, 13
10 [a]Gen. 24:27 [b]Job 8:7
11 [a]Ps. 59:1, 2 [b]Hos. 10:14
12 [a]Gen. 28:13–15 [b]Gen. 22:17
13 [a]Gen. 43:11

NKJV

heap and here is *this* pillar, which I have placed between you and me.

52 "This heap *is* a witness, and *this* pillar *is* a witness, that I will not pass beyond this heap to you, and you will not pass beyond this heap and this pillar to me, for harm.

53 "The God of Abraham, the God of Nahor, and the God of their father [a]judge between us." And Jacob [b]swore by [c]the Fear of his father Isaac.

54 Then Jacob offered a sacrifice on the mountain, and called his brethren to eat bread. And they ate bread and stayed all night on the mountain.

55 And early in the morning Laban arose, and [a]kissed his sons and daughters and [b]blessed them. Then Laban departed and [c]returned to his place.

Esau Comes to Meet Jacob

32 So Jacob went on his way, and [a]the angels of God met him.

2 When Jacob saw them, he said, "This *is* God's [a]camp." And he called the name of that place *Mahanaim.

3 Then Jacob sent messengers before him to Esau his brother [a]in the land of Seir, [b]the country of Edom.

4 And he commanded them, saying, [a]"Speak thus to my lord Esau, 'Thus your servant Jacob says: "I have dwelt with Laban and stayed there until now.

5 [a]"I have oxen, donkeys, flocks, and male and female servants; and I have sent to tell my lord, that [b]I may find favor in your sight." ' "

6 Then the messengers returned to Jacob, saying, "We came to your brother Esau, and [a]he also is coming to meet you, and four hundred men *are* with him."

7 So Jacob was greatly afraid and [a]distressed; and he divided the people that *were* with him, and the flocks and herds and camels, into two companies.

8 And he said, "If Esau comes to the one company and attacks it, then the other company which is left will escape."

9 [a]Then Jacob said, [b]"O God of my father Abraham and God of my father Isaac, the LORD [c]who said to me, 'Return to your country and to your family, and I will deal well with you':

10 "I am not worthy of the least of all the [a]mercies and of all the truth which You have shown Your servant; for I crossed over this Jordan with [b]my staff, and now I have become two companies.

11 [a]"Deliver me, I pray, from the hand of my brother, from the hand of Esau; for I fear him, lest he come and attack me *and* [b]the mother with the children.

12 "For [a]You said, 'I will surely treat you well, and make your descendants as the [b]sand of the sea, which cannot be numbered for multitude.' "

13 So he lodged there that same night, and took what came to his hand as [a]a present for Esau his brother:

14 two hundred female goats and twenty male goats, two hundred ewes and twenty rams,

15 thirty milk camels with their colts, forty cows and ten bulls, twenty female donkeys and ten foals.

16 Then he delivered *them* to the hand of his servants, every drove by itself, and said to his servants, "Pass over before me, and put some distance between successive droves."

17 And he commanded the first one, saying, "When Esau my brother meets you and asks you, saying, 'To whom do you belong, and where are you going? Whose *are* these in front of you?'

18 "then you shall say, 'They *are* your ser-

32:2 Lit. *Double Camp*

KJV

Jacob's; it *is* a present sent unto my lord Esau: and, behold, also he *is* behind us.

19 And so commanded he the second, and the third, and all that followed the droves, saying, On this manner shall ye speak unto Esau, when ye find him.

20 And say ye moreover, Behold, thy servant Jacob *is* behind us. For he said, I will [a]appease him with the present that goeth before me, and afterward I will see his face; peradventure he will accept of me.

21 So went the present over before him: and himself lodged that night in the company.

Wrestling with God

22 And he rose up that night, and took his two wives, and his two womenservants, and his eleven sons, [a]and passed over the ford Jabbok.

23 And he took them, and sent them over the brook, and sent over that he had.

24 And Jacob was left alone; and there [a]wrestled a man with him until the breaking of the day.

25 And when he saw that he prevailed not against him, he touched the hollow of his thigh; and [a]the hollow of Jacob's thigh was out of joint, as he wrestled with him.

26 And [a]he said, Let me go, for the day breaketh. And he said, [b]I will not let thee go, except thou bless me.

27 And he said unto him, What *is* thy name? And he said, Jacob.

28 And he said, [a]Thy name shall be called no more Jacob, but Israel: for as a prince hast thou [b]power with God and [c]with men, and hast prevailed.

29 And Jacob asked *him*, and said, Tell *me*, I pray thee, thy name. And he said, [a]Wherefore *is* it *that* thou dost ask after my name? And he [b]blessed him there.

30 And Jacob called the name of the place Peniel: for [a]I have seen God face to face, and my life is preserved.

31 And as he passed over Penuel the sun rose upon him, and he halted upon his thigh.

32 Therefore the children of Israel eat not *of* the sinew which shrank, which *is* upon the hollow of the thigh, unto this day: because he touched the hollow of Jacob's thigh in the sinew that shrank.

Jacob and Esau Meet

33 And Jacob lifted up his eyes, and looked, and, behold, [a]Esau came, and with him four hundred men. And he divided the children unto Leah, and unto Rachel, and unto the two handmaids.

2 And he put the handmaids and their children foremost, and Leah and her children after, and Rachel and Joseph hindermost.

3 And he passed over before them, and [a]bowed himself to the ground seven times, until he came near to his brother.

4 [a]And Esau ran to meet him, and embraced him, [b]and fell on his neck, and kissed him: and they wept.

5 And he lifted up his eyes, and saw the women and the children; and said, Who *are* those with thee? And he said, The children [a]which God hath graciously given thy servant.

6 Then the handmaidens came near, they and their children, and they bowed themselves.

7 And Leah also with her children came near, and bowed themselves: and after came Joseph near and Rachel, and they bowed themselves.

8 And he said, What *meanest* thou by [a]all this drove which I met? And he said, *These are* [b]to find grace in the sight of my lord.

9 And Esau said, I have enough, my brother; keep that thou hast unto thyself.

10 And Jacob said, Nay, I pray thee, if now I have found grace in thy sight, then receive my

20 [a][Prov. 21:14]
22 [a]Num. 21:24; Deut. 3:16; Josh. 12:2
24 [a]Josh. 5:13–15; Hos. 12:2–4
25 [a]Matt. 26:41; 2 Cor. 12:7
26 [a]Luke 24:28 [b]Hos. 12:4
28 [a]Gen. 35:10; 1 Kin. 18:31; 2 Kin. 17:34 [b]Hos. 12:3, 4 [c]Gen. 25:31; 27:33
29 [a]Judg. 13:17, 18 [b]Gen. 35:9
30 [a]Gen. 16:13; Ex. 24:10, 11; 33:20; Num. 12:8; Deut. 5:24; Judg. 6:22; Is. 6:5; [Matt. 5:8; 1 Cor. 13:12]

CHAPTER 33

1 [a]Gen. 32:6
3 [a]Gen. 18:2; 42:6
4 [a]Gen. 32:28 [b]Gen. 45:14, 15
5 [a]Gen. 48:9; [Ps. 127:3]; Is. 8:18
8 [a]Gen. 32:13–16 [b]Gen. 32:5

NKJV

vant Jacob's. It *is* a present sent to my lord Esau; and behold, he also *is* behind us.' "

19 So he commanded the second, the third, and all who followed the droves, saying, "In this manner you shall speak to Esau when you find him;

20 "and also say, 'Behold, your servant Jacob *is* behind us.' " For he said, "I will [a]appease him with the present that goes before me, and afterward I will see his face; perhaps he will accept me."

21 So the present went on over before him, but he himself lodged that night in the camp.

Wrestling with God

22 And he arose that night and took his two wives, his two female servants, and his eleven sons, [a]and crossed over the ford of Jabbok.

23 He took them, sent them over the brook, and sent over what he had.

24 Then Jacob was left alone; and [a]a Man wrestled with him until the breaking of day.

25 Now when He saw that He did not prevail against him, He touched the socket of his hip; and [a]the socket of Jacob's hip was out of joint as He wrestled with him.

26 And [a]He said, "Let Me go, for the day breaks." But he said, [b]"I will not let You go unless You bless me!"

27 So He said to him, "What *is* your name?" He said, "Jacob."

28 And He said, [a]"Your name shall no longer be called Jacob, but *Israel; for you have [b]struggled with God and [c]with men, and have prevailed."

29 Then Jacob asked, saying, "Tell *me* Your name, I pray." And He said, [a]"Why *is* it *that* you ask about My name?" And He [b]blessed him there.

30 So Jacob called the name of the place *Peniel: "For [a]I have seen God face to face, and my life is preserved."

31 Just as he crossed over *Penuel the sun rose on him, and he limped on his hip.

32 Therefore to this day the children of Israel do not eat the muscle that shrank, which *is* on the hip socket, because He touched the socket of Jacob's hip in the muscle that shrank.

Jacob and Esau Meet

33 Now Jacob lifted his eyes and looked, and there, [a]Esau was coming, and with him were four hundred men. So he divided the children among Leah, Rachel, and the two maidservants.

2 And he put the maidservants and their children in front, Leah and her children behind, and Rachel and Joseph last.

3 Then he crossed over before them and [a]bowed himself to the ground seven times, until he came near to his brother.

4 [a]But Esau ran to meet him, and embraced him, [b]and fell on his neck and kissed him, and they wept.

5 And he lifted his eyes and saw the women and children, and said, "Who *are* these with you?" So he said, "The children [a]whom God has graciously given your servant."

6 Then the maidservants came near, they and their children, and bowed down.

7 And Leah also came near with her children, and they bowed down. Afterward Joseph and Rachel came near, and they bowed down.

8 Then Esau said, "What *do* you *mean by* [a]all this company which I met?" And he said, "*These are* [b]to find favor in the sight of my lord."

9 But Esau said, "I have enough, my brother; keep what you have for yourself."

10 And Jacob said, "No, please, if I have now found favor in your sight, then receive my present

*

32:28 Lit. *Prince with God*
32:30 Lit. *Face of God*
32:31 Lit. *Face of God;* same as *Peniel,* v. 30

KJV

present at my hand: for therefore I [a]have seen thy face, as though I had seen the face of God, and thou wast pleased with me.

11 Take, I pray thee, [a]my blessing that is brought to thee; because God hath dealt [b]graciously with me, and because I have enough. [c]And he urged him, and he took *it*.

12 And he said, Let us take our journey, and let us go, and I will go before thee.

13 And he said unto him, My lord knoweth that the children *are* tender, and the flocks and herds with young *are* with me: and if men should overdrive them one day, all the flock will die.

14 Let my lord, I pray thee, pass over before his servant: and I will lead on softly, according as the cattle that goeth before me and the children be able to endure, until I come unto my lord [a]unto Seir.

15 And Esau said, Let me now leave with thee *some* of the folk that *are* with me. And he said, What needeth it? [a]let me find grace in the sight of my lord.

16 So Esau returned that day on his way unto Seir.

17 And Jacob journeyed to [a]Succoth, and built him an house, and made booths for his cattle: therefore the name of the place is called Succoth.

Jacob Comes to Canaan

18 And Jacob came to [a]Shalem, a city of [b]Shechem, which *is* in the land of Canaan, when he came from Padan–aram; and pitched his tent before the city.

19 And [a]he bought a parcel of a field, where he had spread his tent, at the hand of the children of Hamor, Shechem's father, for an hundred pieces of money.

20 And he erected there an altar, and [a]called it El–elohe–Israel.

The Dinah Incident

34 And [a]Dinah the daughter of Leah, which she bare unto Jacob, went out to see the daughters of the land.

2 And when Shechem the son of Hamor the Hivite, prince of the country, saw her, he [a]took her, and lay with her, and defiled her.

3 And his soul clave unto Dinah the daughter of Jacob, and he loved the damsel, and spake kindly unto the damsel.

4 And Shechem [a]spake unto his father Hamor, saying, Get me this damsel to wife.

5 And Jacob heard that he had defiled Dinah his daughter: now his sons were with his cattle in the field: and Jacob [a]held his peace until they were come.

6 And Hamor the father of Shechem went out unto Jacob to commune with him.

7 And the sons of Jacob came out of the field when they heard *it:* and the men were grieved, and they were very wroth, because he [a]had wrought folly in Israel in lying with Jacob's daughter; [b]which thing ought not to be done.

8 And Hamor communed with them, saying, The soul of my son Shechem longeth for your daughter: I pray you give her him to wife.

9 And make ye marriages with us, *and* give your daughters unto us, and take our daughters unto you.

10 And ye shall dwell with us: and the land shall be before you; dwell and trade ye therein, and get you possessions therein.

11 And Shechem said unto her father and unto her brethren, Let me find grace in your eyes, and what ye shall say unto me I will give.

12 Ask me never so much [a]dowry and gift, and I will give according as ye shall say unto me: but give me the damsel to wife.

13 And the sons of Jacob answered Shechem

10 [a]Gen. 43:3; 2 Sam. 3:13; 14:24, 28, 32
11 [a]Judg. 1:15; 1 Sam. 25:27; 30:26 [b]Gen. 30:43; Ex. 33:19 [c]2 Kin. 5:23
14 [a]Gen. 32:3; 36:8
15 [a]Gen. 34:11; 47:25; Ruth 2:13
17 [a]Josh. 13:27; Judg. 8:5; Ps. 60:6
18 [a]John 3:23 [b]Gen. 12:6; 35:4; Josh. 24:1; Judg. 9:1; Ps. 60:6
19 [a]Josh. 24:32; John 4:5
20 [a]Gen. 35:7

CHAPTER 34

1 [a]Gen. 30:21
2 [a]Gen. 20:2
4 [a]Judg. 14:2
5 [a]2 Sam. 13:22
7 [a]Deut. 22:20–30; Josh. 7:15; Judg. 20:6 [b]Deut. 23:17; 2 Sam. 13:12
12 [a]Ex. 22:16, 17; Deut. 22:29

*

33:17 Lit. *Booths*
33:20 Lit. *God, the God of Israel*

NKJV

from my hand, inasmuch as I [a]have seen your face as though I had seen the face of God, and you were pleased with me.

11 "Please, take [a]my blessing that is brought to you, because God has dealt [b]graciously with me, and because I have enough." [c]So he urged him, and he took *it*.

12 Then Esau said, "Let us take our journey; let us go, and I will go before you."

13 But Jacob said to him, "My lord knows that the children *are* weak, and the flocks and herds which are nursing *are* with me. And if the men should drive them hard one day, all the flock will die.

14 "Please let my lord go on ahead before his servant. I will lead on slowly at a pace which the livestock that go before me, and the children, are able to endure, until I come to my lord [a]in Seir."

15 And Esau said, "Now let me leave with you *some* of the people who *are* with me." But he said, "What need is there? [a]Let me find favor in the sight of my lord."

16 So Esau returned that day on his way to Seir.

17 And Jacob journeyed to [a]Succoth, built himself a house, and made booths for his livestock. Therefore the name of the place is called *Succoth.

Jacob Comes to Canaan

18 Then Jacob came safely to [a]the city of [b]Shechem, which *is* in the land of Canaan, when he came from Padan Aram; and he pitched his tent before the city.

19 And [a]he bought the parcel of land, where he had pitched his tent, from the children of Hamor, Shechem's father, for one hundred pieces of money.

20 Then he erected an altar there and called it [a]El* Elohe Israel.

The Dinah Incident

34 Now [a]Dinah the daughter of Leah, whom she had borne to Jacob, went out to see the daughters of the land.

2 And when Shechem the son of Hamor the Hivite, prince of the country, saw her, he [a]took her and lay with her, and violated her.

3 His soul was strongly attracted to Dinah the daughter of Jacob, and he loved the young woman and spoke kindly to the young woman.

4 So Shechem [a]spoke to his father Hamor, saying, "Get me this young woman as a wife."

5 And Jacob heard that he had defiled Dinah his daughter. Now his sons were with his livestock in the field; so Jacob [a]held his peace until they came.

6 Then Hamor the father of Shechem went out to Jacob to speak with him.

7 And the sons of Jacob came in from the field when they heard *it;* and the men were grieved and very angry, because he [a]had done a disgraceful thing in Israel by lying with Jacob's daughter, [b]a thing which ought not to be done.

8 But Hamor spoke with them, saying, "The soul of my son Shechem longs for your daughter. Please give her to him as a wife.

9 "And make marriages with us; give your daughters to us, and take our daughters to yourselves.

10 "So you shall dwell with us, and the land shall be before you. Dwell and trade in it, and acquire possessions for yourselves in it."

11 Then Shechem said to her father and her brothers, "Let me find favor in your eyes, and whatever you say to me I will give.

12 "Ask me ever so much [a]dowry and gift, and I will give according to what you say to me; but give me the young woman as a wife."

13 But the sons of Jacob answered Shechem

KJV

and Hamor his father [a]deceitfully, and said, because he had defiled Dinah their sister:

14 And they said unto them, We cannot do this thing, to give our sister to one that is [a]uncircumcised; for [b]that *were* a reproach unto us:

15 But in this will we consent unto you: If ye will be as we *be*, that every male of you be circumcised;

16 Then will we give our daughters unto you, and we will take your daughters to us, and we will dwell with you, and we will become one people.

17 But if ye will not hearken unto us, to be circumcised; then will we take our daughter, and we will be gone.

18 And their words pleased Hamor, and Shechem Hamor's son.

19 And the young man deferred not to do the thing, because he had delight in Jacob's daughter: and he *was* [a]more honourable than all the house of his father.

20 And Hamor and Shechem his son came unto the [a]gate of their city, and communed with the men of their city, saying,

21 These men *are* peaceable with us; therefore let them dwell in the land, and trade therein; for the land, behold, *it is* large enough for them; let us take their daughters to us for wives, and let us give them our daughters.

22 Only herein will the men consent unto us for to dwell with us, to be one people, if every male among us be circumcised, as they *are* circumcised.

23 *Shall* not their cattle and their substance and every beast of their's *be* our's? only let us consent unto them, and they will dwell with us.

24 And unto Hamor and unto Shechem his son hearkened all that [a]went out of the gate of his city; and every male was circumcised, all that went out of the gate of his city.

25 And it came to pass on the third day, when they were sore, that two of the sons of Jacob, [a]Simeon and Levi, Dinah's brethren, took each man his sword, and came upon the city boldly, and slew all the males.

26 And they [a]slew Hamor and Shechem his son with the edge of the sword, and took Dinah out of Shechem's house, and went out.

27 The sons of Jacob came upon the slain, and spoiled the city, because they had defiled their sister.

28 They took their sheep, and their oxen, and their asses, and that which *was* in the city, and that which *was* in the field,

29 And all their wealth, and all their little ones, and their wives took they captive, and spoiled even all that *was* in the house.

30 And Jacob said to Simeon and Levi, [a]Ye have [b]troubled me [c]to make me to stink among the inhabitants of the land, among the Canaanites and the Perizzites: [d]and I *being* few in number, they shall gather themselves together against me, and slay me; and I shall be destroyed, I and my house.

31 And they said, Should he deal with our sister as with an harlot?

Jacob's Return to Bethel

35 And God said unto Jacob, Arise, go up to [a]Beth–el, and dwell there: and make there an altar unto God, [b]that appeared unto thee [c]when thou fleddest from the face of Esau thy brother.

2 Then Jacob said unto his [a]household, and to all that *were* with him, Put away [b]the strange gods that *are* among you, and [c]be clean, and change your garments:

3 And let us arise, and go up to Beth–el; and I will make there an altar unto God, [a]who answered me in the day of my distress, [b]and was with me in the way which I went.

4 And they gave unto Jacob all the strange

13 [a]Gen. 31:7; Ex. 8:29
14 [a]Ex. 12:48 [b]Josh. 5:2–9
19 [a]1 Chr. 4:9
20 [a]Gen. 19:1; 23:10; Ruth 4:1, 11; 2 Sam. 15:2
24 [a]Gen. 23:10, 18
25 [a]Gen. 29:33, 34; 42:24; 49:5–7
26 [a]Gen. 49:5, 6
30 [a]Gen. 49:6 [b]Josh. 7:25 [c]Ex. 5:21; 1 Sam. 13:4; 2 Sam. 10:6 [d]Gen. 46:26, 27; Deut. 4:27; 1 Chr. 16:19; Ps. 105:12

CHAPTER 35

1 [a]Gen. 28:19; 31:13 [b]Gen. 28:13 [c]Gen. 27:43
2 [a]Gen. 18:19; Josh. 24:15 [b]Gen. 31:19, 30, 34; Josh. 24:2, 14, 23 [c]Ex. 19:10, 14; Lev. 13:6
3 [a]Gen. 32:7, 24; Ps. 107:6 [b]Gen. 28:15, 20; 31:3, 42

NKJV

and Hamor his father, and spoke [a]deceitfully, because he had defiled Dinah their sister.

14 And they said to them, "We cannot do this thing, to give our sister to one who is [a]uncircumcised, for [b]that *would be* a reproach to us.

15 "But on this *condition* we will consent to you: If you will become as we *are*, if every male of you is circumcised,

16 "then we will give our daughters to you, and we will take your daughters to us; and we will dwell with you, and we will become one people.

17 "But if you will not heed us and be circumcised, then we will take our daughter and be gone."

18 And their words pleased Hamor and Shechem, Hamor's son.

19 So the young man did not delay to do the thing, because he delighted in Jacob's daughter. He *was* [a]more honorable than all the household of his father.

20 And Hamor and Shechem his son came to the [a]gate of their city, and spoke with the men of their city, saying:

21 "These men *are* at peace with us. Therefore let them dwell in the land and trade in it. For indeed the land *is* large enough for them. Let us take their daughters to us as wives, and let us give them our daughters.

22 "Only on this *condition* will the men consent to dwell with us, to be one people: if every male among us is circumcised as they *are* circumcised.

23 "*Will* not their livestock, their property, and every animal of theirs *be* ours? Only let us consent to them, and they will dwell with us."

24 And all who went out of the gate of his city heeded Hamor and Shechem his son; every male was circumcised, all who [a]went out of the gate of his city.

25 Now it came to pass on the third day, when they were in pain, that two of the sons of Jacob, [a]Simeon and Levi, Dinah's brothers, each took his sword and came boldly upon the city and killed all the males.

26 And they [a]killed Hamor and Shechem his son with the edge of the sword, and took Dinah from Shechem's house, and went out.

27 The sons of Jacob came upon the slain, and plundered the city, because their sister had been defiled.

28 They took their sheep, their oxen, and their donkeys, what *was* in the city and what *was* in the field,

29 and all their wealth. All their little ones and their wives they took captive; and they plundered even all that *was* in the houses.

30 Then Jacob said to Simeon and Levi, [a]"You have [b]troubled me [c]by making me obnoxious among the inhabitants of the land, among the Canaanites and the Perizzites; [d]and since I *am* few in number, they will gather themselves together against me and kill me. I shall be destroyed, my household and I."

31 But they said, "Should he treat our sister like a harlot?"

Jacob's Return to Bethel

35 Then God said to Jacob, "Arise, go up to [a]Bethel and dwell there; and make an altar there to God, [b]who appeared to you [c]when you fled from the face of Esau your brother."

2 And Jacob said to his [a]household and to all who *were* with him, "Put away [b]the foreign gods that *are* among you, [c]purify yourselves, and change your garments.

3 "Then let us arise and go up to Bethel; and I will make an altar there to God, [a]who answered me in the day of my distress [b]and has been with me in the way which I have gone."

4 So they gave Jacob all the foreign gods

KJV

gods which *were* in their hand, and *all their* [a]ear-
rings which *were* in their ears; and Jacob hid them
under [b]the oak which *was* by Shechem.
5 And they journeyed: and [a]the terror of
God was upon the cities that *were* round about
them, and they did not pursue after the sons of
Jacob.
6 So Jacob came to [a]Luz, which *is* in the
land of Canaan, that *is*, Beth–el, he and all the
people that *were* with him.
7 And he [a]built there an altar, and called
the place El–beth–el: because [b]there God appeared unto him, when he fled from the face of
his brother.
8 But [a]Deborah Rebekah's nurse died, and
she was buried beneath Beth–el under an oak:
and the name of it was called Allon–bachuth.
9 And [a]God appeared unto Jacob again,
when he came out of Padan–aram, and [b]blessed
him.
10 And God said unto him, Thy name *is* Jacob: [a]thy name shall not be called any more
Jacob, [b]but Israel shall be thy name: and he called
his name Israel.
11 And God said unto him, [a]I *am* God Almighty: [b]be fruitful and multiply; [c]a nation and
a company of nations shall be of thee, and kings
shall come out of thy loins;
12 And the [a]land which I gave Abraham and
Isaac, to thee I will give it, and to thy seed after
thee will I give the land.
13 And God [a]went up from him in the place
where he talked with him.
14 And Jacob [a]set up a pillar in the place
where he talked with him, *even* a pillar of stone:
and he poured a drink offering thereon, and he
poured oil thereon.
15 And Jacob called the name of the place
where God spake with him, [a]Beth–el.

Death of Rachel

16 And they journeyed from Beth–el; and
there was but a little way to come to Ephrath:
and Rachel travailed, and she had hard labour.
17 And it came to pass, when she was in hard
labour, that the midwife said unto her, Fear not;
[a]thou shalt have this son also.
18 And it came to pass, as her soul was
in departing, (for she died) that she called his
name Ben–oni: but his father called him Benjamin.
19 And [a]Rachel died, and was buried in the
way to [b]Ephrath, which *is* Beth–lehem.
20 And Jacob set a pillar upon her grave: that
is the pillar of Rachel's grave [a]unto this day.
21 And Israel journeyed, and spread his tent
beyond [a]the tower of Edar.
22 And it came to pass, when Israel dwelt
in that land, that Reuben went and [a]lay with
Bilhah his father's concubine: and Israel heard
it.

Jacob's Twelve Sons

Now the sons of Jacob were twelve:
23 The sons of Leah; [a]Reuben, Jacob's firstborn, and Simeon, and Levi, and Judah, and Issachar, and Zebulun:
24 The sons of Rachel; Joseph, and Benjamin:
25 And the sons of Bilhah, Rachel's handmaid; Dan, and Naphtali:
26 And the sons of Zilpah, Leah's handmaid;
Gad, and Asher: these *are* the sons of Jacob,
which were born to him in Padan–aram.

Death of Isaac

27 And Jacob came unto Isaac his father unto
[a]Mamre, unto the [b]city of Arbah, which *is* Hebron,
where Abraham and Isaac sojourned.
28 And the days of Isaac were an hundred
and fourscore years.
29 And Isaac gave up the ghost, and died,

4 [a]Hos. 2:13 [b]Josh. 24:26; Judg. 9:6
5 [a]Ex. 15:16; 23:27; [Deut. 2:25; 11:25]; Josh. 2:9; 1 Sam. 14:15
6 [a]Gen. 28:19, 22; 48:3
7 [a]Gen. 33:20; 35:3; Eccl. 5:4 [b]Gen. 28:13
8 [a]Gen. 24:59
9 [a]Josh. 5:13; Dan. 10:5 [b]Gen. 32:29; Hos. 12:4
10 [a]Gen. 17:5 [b]Gen. 32:28
11 [a]Gen. 17:1; 28:3; 48:3, 4; Ex. 6:3 [b]Gen. 9:1, 7 [c]Gen. 17:5, 6, 16; 28:3; 48:4
12 [a]Gen. 12:7; 13:15; 26:3, 4; 28:13; 48:4; Ex. 32:13
13 [a]Gen. 17:22; 18:33
14 [a]Gen. 28:18, 19; 31:45
15 [a]Gen. 28:19
17 [a]Gen. 30:24; 1 Sam. 4:20
19 [a]Gen. 48:7 [b]Ruth 1:2; 4:11; Mic. 5:2; Matt. 2:6
20 [a]1 Sam. 10:2
21 [a]Mic. 4:8
22 [a]Gen. 49:4; 1 Chr. 5:1
23 [a]Gen. 29:31–35; 30:18–20; 46:8; Ex. 1:1–4
27 [a]Gen. 13:18; 18:1; 23:19 [b]Josh. 14:15

*

35:7 Lit. *God of the House of God*
35:8 Lit. *Terebinth of Weeping*
35:18 Lit. *Son of My Sorrow* • Lit. *Son of the Right Hand*
35:27 Lit. *Town* or *City of Arba*

NKJV

which *were* in their hands, and the [a]earrings
which *were* in their ears; and Jacob hid them under [b]the terebinth tree which *was* by Shechem.
5 And they journeyed, and [a]the terror of
God was upon the cities that *were* all around
them, and they did not pursue the sons of Jacob.
6 So Jacob came to [a]Luz (that *is*, Bethel),
which *is* in the land of Canaan, he and all the
people who *were* with him.
7 And he [a]built an altar there and called the
place *El Bethel, because [b]there God appeared to
him when he fled from the face of his brother.
8 Now [a]Deborah, Rebekah's nurse, died,
and she was buried below Bethel under the terebinth tree. So the name of it was called *Allon
Bachuth.
9 Then [a]God appeared to Jacob again, when
he came from Padan Aram, and [b]blessed him.
10 And God said to him, "Your name *is* Jacob; [a]your name shall not be called Jacob anymore, [b]but Israel shall be your name." So He
called his name Israel.
11 Also God said to him: [a]"I *am* God Almighty. [b]Be fruitful and multiply; [c]a nation and
a company of nations shall proceed from you, and
kings shall come from your body.
12 "The [a]land which I gave Abraham and
Isaac I give to you; and to your descendants after
you I give this land."
13 Then God [a]went up from him in the place
where He talked with him.
14 So Jacob [a]set up a pillar in the place
where He talked with him, a pillar of stone; and
he poured a drink offering on it, and he poured
oil on it.
15 And Jacob called the name of the place
where God spoke with him, [a]Bethel.

Death of Rachel

16 Then they journeyed from Bethel. And
when there was but a little distance to go to
Ephrath, Rachel labored *in childbirth*, and she had
hard labor.
17 Now it came to pass, when she was in hard
labor, that the midwife said to her, "Do not fear;
[a]you will have this son also."
18 And so it was, as her soul was departing
(for she died), that she called his name *Ben-Oni;
but his father called him *Benjamin.
19 So [a]Rachel died and was buried on the
way to [b]Ephrath (that *is*, Bethlehem).
20 And Jacob set a pillar on her grave, which
is the pillar of Rachel's grave [a]to this day.
21 Then Israel journeyed and pitched his tent
beyond [a]the tower of Eder.
22 And it happened, when Israel dwelt in that
land, that Reuben went and [a]lay with Bilhah his
father's concubine; and Israel heard *about it*.

Jacob's Twelve Sons

Now the sons of Jacob were twelve:
23 the sons of Leah *were* [a]Reuben, Jacob's
firstborn, and Simeon, Levi, Judah, Issachar, and
Zebulun;
24 the sons of Rachel *were* Joseph and
Benjamin;
25 the sons of Bilhah, Rachel's maidservant,
were Dan and Naphtali;
26 and the sons of Zilpah, Leah's maidservant, *were* Gad and Asher. These *were* the sons
of Jacob who were born to him in Padan Aram.

Death of Isaac

27 Then Jacob came to his father Isaac at
[a]Mamre, or [b]Kirjath Arba* (that *is*, Hebron),
where Abraham and Isaac had dwelt.
28 Now the days of Isaac were one hundred
and eighty years.
29 So Isaac breathed his last and died, and

KJV

and [a]was gathered unto his people, *being* old and full of days: and [b]his sons Esau and Jacob buried him.

The Family of Esau
(1 Chr. 1:35–42)

36 Now these *are* the generations of Esau, [a]who *is* Edom.

2 [a]Esau took his wives of the daughters of Canaan; Adah the daughter of Elon the [b]Hittite, and [c]Aholibamah the daughter of Anah the daughter of Zibeon the Hivite;

3 And [a]Bashemath Ishmael's daughter, sister of Nebajoth.

4 And [a]Adah bare to Esau Eliphaz; and Bashemath bare Reuel;

5 And Aholibamah bare Jeush, and Jaalam, and Korah: these *are* the sons of Esau, which were born unto him in the land of Canaan.

6 And Esau took his wives, and his sons, and his daughters, and all the persons of his house, and his cattle, and all his beasts, and all his substance, which he had got in the land of Canaan; and went into the country from the face of his brother Jacob.

7 [a]For their riches were more than that they might dwell together; and [b]the land wherein they were strangers could not bear them because of their cattle.

8 Thus dwelt Esau in [a]mount Seir: [b]Esau *is* Edom.

9 And these *are* the generations of Esau the father of the Edomites in mount Seir:

10 These *are* the names of Esau's sons; [a]Eliphaz the son of Adah the wife of Esau, Reuel the son of Bashemath the wife of Esau.

11 And the sons of Eliphaz were Teman, Omar, Zepho, and Gatam, and Kenaz.

12 And Timna was concubine to Eliphaz Esau's son; and she bare to Eliphaz [a]Amalek: these *were* the sons of Adah Esau's wife.

13 And these *are* the sons of Reuel; Nahath, and Zerah, Shammah, and Mizzah: these were the sons of Bashemath Esau's wife.

14 And these were the sons of Aholibamah, the daughter of Anah the daughter of Zibeon, Esau's wife: and she bare to Esau Jeush, and Jaalam, and Korah.

The Chiefs of Edom

15 These *were* dukes of the sons of Esau: the sons of Eliphaz the firstborn *son* of Esau; duke Teman, duke Omar, duke Zepho, duke Kenaz,

16 Duke Korah, duke Gatam, *and* duke Amalek: these *are* the dukes *that came* of Eliphaz in the land of Edom; these *were* the sons of Adah.

17 And these *are* the sons of Reuel Esau's son; duke Nahath, duke Zerah, duke Shammah, duke Mizzah: these *are* the dukes *that came* of Reuel in the land of Edom; these *are* the sons of Bashemath Esau's wife.

18 And these *are* the sons of Aholibamah Esau's wife; duke Jeush, duke Jaalam, duke Korah: these *were* the dukes *that came* of Aholibamah the daughter of Anah, Esau's wife.

19 These *are* the sons of Esau, who *is* Edom, and these *are* their dukes.

The Sons of Seir

20 [a]These *are* the sons of Seir [b]the Horite, who inhabited the land; Lotan, and Shobal, and Zibeon, and Anah,

21 And Dishon, and Ezer, and Dishan: these *are* the dukes of the Horites, the children of Seir in the land of Edom.

22 And the children of Lotan were Hori and Hemam; and Lotan's sister *was* Timna.

23 And the children of Shobal *were* these; Alvan, and Manahath, and Ebal, Shepho, and Onam.

24 And these *are* the children of Zibeon; both

29 [a]Gen. 15:15; 25:8; 49:33 [b]Gen. 25:9; 49:31

CHAPTER 36

1 [a]Gen. 25:30
2 [a]Gen. 26:34; 28:9 [b]2 Kin. 7:6 [c]Gen. 36:25
3 [a]Gen. 28:9
4 [a]1 Chr. 1:35
7 [a]Gen. 13:6, 11 [b]Gen. 17:8; 28:4; Heb. 11:9
8 [a]Gen. 32:3; Deut. 2:5; Josh. 24:4 [b]Gen. 36:1, 19
10 [a]1 Chr. 1:35
12 [a]Ex. 17:8–16; Num. 24:20; Deut. 25:17–19; 1 Sam. 15:2, 3
20 [a]1 Chr. 1:38–42 [b]Gen. 14:6; Deut. 2:12, 22

NKJV

[a]was gathered to his people, *being* old and full of days. And [b]his sons Esau and Jacob buried him.

The Family of Esau
(1 Chr. 1:35–42)

36 Now this *is* the genealogy of Esau, [a]who is Edom.

2 [a]Esau took his wives from the daughters of Canaan: Adah the daughter of Elon the [b]Hittite; [c]Aholibamah the daughter of Anah, the daughter of Zibeon the Hivite;

3 and [a]Basemath, Ishmael's daughter, sister of Nebajoth.

4 Now [a]Adah bore Eliphaz to Esau, and Basemath bore Reuel.

5 And Aholibamah bore Jeush, Jaalam, and Korah. These *were* the sons of Esau who were born to him in the land of Canaan.

6 Then Esau took his wives, his sons, his daughters, and all the persons of his household, his cattle and all his animals, and all his goods which he had gained in the land of Canaan, and went to a country away from the presence of his brother Jacob.

7 [a]For their possessions were too great for them to dwell together, and [b]the land where they were strangers could not support them because of their livestock.

8 So Esau dwelt in [a]Mount Seir. [b]Esau *is* Edom.

9 And this *is* the genealogy of Esau the father of the Edomites in Mount Seir.

10 These *were* the names of Esau's sons: [a]Eliphaz the son of Adah the wife of Esau, and Reuel the son of Basemath the wife of Esau.

11 And the sons of Eliphaz were Teman, Omar, *Zepho, Gatam, and Kenaz.

12 Now Timna was the concubine of Eliphaz, Esau's son, and she bore [a]Amalek to Eliphaz. These *were* the sons of Adah, Esau's wife.

13 These *were* the sons of Reuel: Nahath, Zerah, Shammah, and Mizzah. These were the sons of Basemath, Esau's wife.

14 These were the sons of Aholibamah, Esau's wife, the daughter of Anah, the daughter of Zibeon. And she bore to Esau: Jeush, Jaalam, and Korah.

The Chiefs of Edom

15 These *were* the chiefs of the sons of Esau. The sons of Eliphaz, the firstborn *son* of Esau, were Chief Teman, Chief Omar, Chief Zepho, Chief Kenaz,

16 *Chief Korah, Chief Gatam, *and* Chief Amalek. These *were* the chiefs of Eliphaz in the land of Edom. They *were* the sons of Adah.

17 These *were* the sons of Reuel, Esau's son: Chief Nahath, Chief Zerah, Chief Shammah, and Chief Mizzah. These *were* the chiefs of Reuel in the land of Edom. These *were* the sons of Basemath, Esau's wife.

18 And these *were* the sons of Aholibamah, Esau's wife: Chief Jeush, Chief Jaalam, and Chief Korah. These *were* the chiefs *who descended* from Aholibamah, Esau's wife, the daughter of Anah.

19 These *were* the sons of Esau, who is Edom, and these *were* their chiefs.

The Sons of Seir

20 [a]These *were* the sons of Seir [b]the Horite who inhabited the land: Lotan, Shobal, Zibeon, Anah,

21 Dishon, Ezer, and Dishan. These *were* the chiefs of the Horites, the sons of Seir, in the land of Edom.

22 And the sons of Lotan were Hori and *Hemam. Lotan's sister *was* Timna.

23 These *were* the sons of Shobal: *Alvan, Manahath, Ebal, *Shepho, and Onam.

24 These *were* the sons of Zibeon: both Ajah

*

36:11 *Zephi,* 1 Chr. 1:36
36:16 Sam. omits *Chief Korah*
36:22 *Homam,* 1 Chr. 1:39
36:23 *Alian,* 1 Chr. 1:40 • *Shephi,* 1 Chr. 1:40

KJV

Ajah, and Anah: this *was that* Anah that found
[a]the mules in the wilderness, as he fed the asses
of Zibeon his father.
25 And the children of Anah *were* these; Dishon, and Aholibamah the daughter of Anah.
26 And these *are* the children of Dishon;
Hemdan, and Eshban, and Ithran, and Cheran.
27 The children of Ezer *are* these; Bilhan, and
Zaavan, and Akan.
28 The children of Dishan *are* these; [a]Uz, and
Aran.
29 These *are* the dukes *that came* of the Horites; duke Lotan, duke Shobal, duke Zibeon,
duke Anah,
30 Duke Dishon, duke Ezer, duke Dishan:
these *are* the dukes *that came* of Hori, among
their dukes in the land of Seir.

The Kings of Edom

31 And [a]these *are* the kings that reigned in
the land of Edom, before there reigned any king
over the children of Israel.
32 And Bela the son of Beor reigned in Edom:
and the name of his city *was* Dinhabah.
33 And Bela died, and Jobab the son of Zerah
of Bozrah reigned in his stead.
34 And Jobab died, and Husham of the land
of Temani reigned in his stead.
35 And Husham died, and Hadad the son of
Bedad, who smote Midian in the field of Moab,
reigned in his stead: and the name of his city *was*
Avith.
36 And Hadad died, and Samlah of Masrekah
reigned in his stead.
37 And Samlah died, and Saul of [a]Rehoboth
by the river reigned in his stead.
38 And Saul died, and Baal-hanan the son
of Achbor reigned in his stead.
39 And Baal-hanan the son of Achbor died,
and Hadar reigned in his stead: and the name of
his city *was* Pau; and his wife's name *was* Mehetabel, the daughter of Matred, the daughter of Mezahab.

The Chiefs of Esau

40 And these *are* the names of the dukes *that*
came of Esau, according to their families, after
their places, by their names; duke Timnah, duke
Alvah, duke Jetheth,
41 Duke Aholibamah, duke Elah, duke
Pinon,
42 Duke Kenaz, duke Teman, duke Mibzar,
43 Duke Magdiel, duke Iram: these *be* the
dukes of Edom, according to their habitations in
the land of their possession: he *is* Esau the father
of the Edomites.

Joseph Dreams of Greatness

37 And Jacob dwelt in the land [a]wherein his
father was a stranger, in the land of
Canaan.
2 These *are* the generations of Jacob. Joseph, *being* seventeen years old, was feeding the
flock with his brethren; and the lad *was* with the
sons of Bilhah, and with the sons of Zilpah, his
father's wives: and Joseph brought unto his father
[a]their evil report.
3 Now Israel loved Joseph more than all his
children, because he *was* [a]the son of his old age:
and he [b]made him a coat of *many* colours.
4 And when his brethren saw that their father loved him more than all his brethren, they
[a]hated him, and could not speak peaceably unto
him.
5 And Joseph dreamed a dream, and he told
it his brethren: and they hated him yet the more.
6 And he said unto them, Hear, I pray you,
this dream which I have dreamed:
7 For, [a]behold, we *were* binding sheaves in
the field, and, lo, my sheaf arose, and also stood
upright; and, behold, your sheaves stood round
about, and made obeisance to my sheaf.

24 [a]Lev. 19:19
28 [a]Job 1:1
31 [a]Gen. 17:6, 16; 35:11; 1 Chr. 1:43
37 [a]Gen. 10:11

CHAPTER 37

1 [a]Gen. 17:8; 23:4; 28:4; 36:7; Heb. 11:9
2 [a]Gen. 35:25, 26; 1 Sam. 2:22–24
3 [a]Gen. 44:20 [b]Gen. 37:23, 32; Judg. 5:30; 1 Sam. 2:19
4 [a]Gen. 27:41; 49:23; 1 Sam. 17:28; John 15:18–20
7 [a]Gen. 42:6, 9; 43:26; 44:14

*

36:24 So with MT, Vg. (*hot springs*); LXX *Jamin;* Tg. *mighty men;* Talmud *mules*
36:26 Heb. *Dishan* • *Hamran,* 1 Chr. 1:41
36:27 *Jaakan,* 1 Chr. 1:42
36:39 Sam., Syr. *Hadad* and 1 Chr. 1:50 • *Pai,* 1 Chr. 1:50
36:40 *Aliah,* 1 Chr. 1:51

NKJV

and Anah. This *was the* Anah who found the *water in the wilderness as he pastured [a]the donkeys
of his father Zibeon.
25 These *were* the children of Anah: Dishon
and Aholibamah the daughter of Anah.
26 These *were* the sons of *Dishon: *Hemdan, Eshban, Ithran, and Cheran.
27 These *were* the sons of Ezer: Bilhan, Zaavan, and *Akan.
28 These *were* the sons of Dishan: [a]Uz and
Aran.
29 These *were* the chiefs of the Horites: Chief
Lotan, Chief Shobal, Chief Zibeon, Chief Anah,
30 Chief Dishon, Chief Ezer, and Chief
Dishan. These *were* the chiefs of the Horites, according to their chiefs in the land of Seir.

The Kings of Edom

31 [a]Now these *were* the kings who reigned
in the land of Edom before any king reigned over
the children of Israel:
32 Bela the son of Beor reigned in Edom, and
the name of his city *was* Dinhabah.
33 And when Bela died, Jobab the son of
Zerah of Bozrah reigned in his place.
34 When Jobab died, Husham of the land of
the Temanites reigned in his place.
35 And when Husham died, Hadad the son
of Bedad, who attacked Midian in the field of
Moab, reigned in his place. And the name of his
city *was* Avith.
36 When Hadad died, Samlah of Masrekah
reigned in his place.
37 And when Samlah died, Saul of [a]Reho-
both-*by*-the-River reigned in his place.
38 When Saul died, Baal-Hanan the son of
Achbor reigned in his place.
39 And when Baal-Hanan the son of Achbor
died, *Hadar reigned in his place; and the name
of his city *was* *Pau. His wife's name *was* Mehetabel, the daughter of Matred, the daughter of Mezahab.

The Chiefs of Esau

40 And these *were* the names of the chiefs
of Esau, according to their families and their
places, by their names: Chief Timnah, Chief *Alvah, Chief Jetheth,
41 Chief Aholibamah, Chief Elah, Chief
Pinon,
42 Chief Kenaz, Chief Teman, Chief Mibzar,
43 Chief Magdiel, and Chief Iram. These
were the chiefs of Edom, according to their dwelling places in the land of their possession. Esau
was the father of the Edomites.

Joseph Dreams of Greatness

37 Now Jacob dwelt in the land [a]where his
father was a stranger, in the land of
Canaan.
2 This *is* the history of Jacob. Joseph, *being*
seventeen years old, was feeding the flock with
his brothers. And the lad *was* with the sons of
Bilhah and the sons of Zilpah, his father's wives;
and Joseph brought [a]a bad report of them to his
father.
3 Now Israel loved Joseph more than all his
children, because he *was* [a]the son of his old age.
Also he [b]made him a tunic of *many* colors.
4 But when his brothers saw that their father loved him more than all his brothers, they
[a]hated him and could not speak peaceably to him.
5 Now Joseph had a dream, and he told *it*
to his brothers; and they hated him even more.
6 So he said to them, "Please hear this
dream which I have dreamed:
7 [a]"There we were, binding sheaves in the
field. Then behold, my sheaf arose and also stood
upright; and indeed your sheaves stood all around
and bowed down to my sheaf."

KJV

8 And his brethren said to him, Shalt thou indeed reign over us? or shalt thou indeed have dominion over us? And they hated him yet the more for his dreams, and for his words.

9 And he dreamed yet another dream, and told it his brethren, and said, Behold, I have dreamed a dream more; and, behold, [a]the sun and the moon and the eleven stars made obeisance to me.

10 And he told *it* to his father, and to his brethren: and his father rebuked him, and said unto him, What *is* this dream that thou hast dreamed? Shall I and thy mother and [a]thy brethren indeed come to bow down ourselves to thee to the earth?

11 And [a]his brethren envied him; but his father [b]observed the saying.

Joseph Sold by His Brothers

12 And his brethren went to feed their father's flock in [a]Shechem.

13 And Israel said unto Joseph, Do not thy brethren feed *the flock* in Shechem? come, and I will send thee unto them. And he said to him, Here *am I.*

14 And he said to him, Go, I pray thee, see whether it be well with thy brethren, and well with the flocks; and bring me word again. So he sent him out of the vale of [a]Hebron, and he came to Shechem.

15 And a certain man found him, and, behold, *he was* wandering in the field: and the man asked him, saying, What seekest thou?

16 And he said, I seek my brethren: [a]tell me, I pray thee, where they feed *their flocks.*

17 And the man said, They are departed hence; for I heard them say, Let us go to Dothan. And Joseph went after his brethren, and found them in [a]Dothan.

18 And when they saw him afar off, even before he came near unto them, [a]they conspired against him to slay him.

19 And they said one to another, Behold, this dreamer cometh.

20 [a]Come now therefore, and let us slay him, and cast him into some pit, and we will say, Some evil beast hath devoured him: and we shall see what will become of his dreams.

21 And [a]Reuben heard *it,* and he delivered him out of their hands; and said, Let us not kill him.

22 And Reuben said unto them, Shed no blood, *but* cast him into this pit that *is* in the wilderness, and lay no hand upon him; that he might rid him out of their hands, to deliver him to his father again.

23 And it came to pass, when Joseph was come unto his brethren, that they [a]stript Joseph out of his coat, *his* coat of *many* colours that *was* on him;

24 And they took him, and cast him into a pit: and the pit *was* empty, *there was* no water in it.

25 [a]And they sat down to eat bread: and they lifted up their eyes and looked, and, behold, a company of [b]Ishmeelites came from Gilead with their camels bearing spicery and [c]balm and myrrh, going to carry *it* down to Egypt.

26 And Judah said unto his brethren, What profit *is it* if we slay our brother, and [a]conceal his blood?

27 Come, and let us sell him to the Ishmeelites, and [a]let not our hand be upon him; for he *is* [b]our brother *and* [c]our flesh. And his brethren were content.

28 Then there passed by [a]Midianites merchantmen; and they drew and lifted up Joseph out of the pit, [b]and sold Joseph to the Ishmeelites for [c]twenty *pieces* of silver: and they brought Joseph into Egypt.

29 And Reuben returned unto the pit; and,

9 [a]Gen. 46:29; 47:25
10 [a]Gen. 27:29
11 [a]Matt. 27:17, 18; Acts 7:9 [b]Dan. 7:28; Luke 2:19, 51
12 [a]Gen. 33:18–20
14 [a]Gen. 13:18; 23:2, 19; 35:27; Josh. 14:14, 15; Judg. 1:10
16 [a]Song 1:7
17 [a]2 Kin. 6:13
18 [a]1 Sam. 19:1; Ps. 31:13; 37:12, 32; Matt. 21:38; 26:3, 4; 27:1; Mark 14:1; John 11:53; Acts 23:12
20 [a]Gen. 37:22; Prov. 1:11
21 [a]Gen. 42:22
23 [a]Matt. 27:28
25 [a]Prov. 30:20 [b]Gen. 16:11, 12; 37:28, 36; 39:1 [c]Jer. 8:22
26 [a]Gen. 37:20
27 [a]1 Sam. 18:17 [b]Gen. 42:21 [c]Gen. 29:14
28 [a]Gen. 37:25; Judg. 6:1–3; 8:22, 24 [b]Gen. 45:4, 5; Ps. 105:17; Acts 7:9 [c]Matt. 27:9

NKJV

8 And his brothers said to him, "Shall you indeed reign over us? Or shall you indeed have dominion over us?" So they hated him even more for his dreams and for his words.

9 Then he dreamed still another dream and told it to his brothers, and said, "Look, I have dreamed another dream. And this time, [a]the sun, the moon, and the eleven stars bowed down to me."

10 So he told *it* to his father and his brothers; and his father rebuked him and said to him, "What *is* this dream that you have dreamed? Shall your mother and I and [a]your brothers indeed come to bow down to the earth before you?"

11 And [a]his brothers envied him, but his father [b]kept the matter *in mind.*

Joseph Sold by His Brothers

12 Then his brothers went to feed their father's flock in [a]Shechem.

13 And Israel said to Joseph, "Are not your brothers feeding *the flock* in Shechem? Come, I will send you to them." So he said to him, "Here I am."

14 Then he said to him, "Please go and see if it is well with your brothers and well with the flocks, and bring back word to me." So he sent him out of the Valley of [a]Hebron, and he went to Shechem.

15 Now a certain man found him, and there he was, wandering in the field. And the man asked him, saying, "What are you seeking?"

16 So he said, "I am seeking my brothers. [a]Please tell me where they are feeding *their flocks.*"

17 And the man said, "They have departed from here, for I heard them say, 'Let us go to Dothan.' " So Joseph went after his brothers and found them in [a]Dothan.

18 Now when they saw him afar off, even before he came near them, [a]they conspired against him to kill him.

19 Then they said to one another, "Look, this dreamer is coming!

20 [a]"Come therefore, let us now kill him and cast him into some pit; and we shall say, 'Some wild beast has devoured him.' We shall see what will become of his dreams!"

21 But [a]Reuben heard *it,* and he delivered him out of their hands, and said, "Let us not kill him."

22 And Reuben said to them, "Shed no blood, *but* cast him into this pit which *is* in the wilderness, and do not lay a hand on him"—that he might deliver him out of their hands, and bring him back to his father.

23 So it came to pass, when Joseph had come to his brothers, that they [a]stripped Joseph *of* his tunic, the tunic of *many* colors that *was* on him.

24 Then they took him and cast him into a pit. And the pit *was* empty; *there was* no water in it.

25 [a]And they sat down to eat a meal. Then they lifted their eyes and looked, and there was a company of [b]Ishmaelites, coming from Gilead with their camels, bearing spices, [c]balm, and myrrh, on their way to carry *them* down to Egypt.

26 So Judah said to his brothers, "What profit *is there* if we kill our brother and [a]conceal his blood?

27 "Come and let us sell him to the Ishmaelites, and [a]let not our hand be upon him, for he *is* [b]our brother *and* [c]our flesh." And his brothers listened.

28 Then [a]Midianite traders passed by; so *the brothers* pulled Joseph up and lifted him out of the pit, [b]and sold him to the Ishmaelites for [c]twenty *shekels* of silver. And they took Joseph to Egypt.

29 Then Reuben returned to the pit, and in-

KJV

behold, Joseph *was* not in the pit; and he [a]rent
his clothes.
30 And he returned unto his brethren, and
said, The child [a]*is* not; and I, whither shall I go?
31 And they took [a]Joseph's coat, and killed
a kid of the goats, and dipped the coat in the
blood;
32 And they sent the coat of *many* colours,
and they brought *it* to their father; and said, This
have we found: know now whether it *be* thy son's
coat or no.
33 And he knew it, and said, *It is* my son's
coat; an [a]evil beast hath devoured him; Joseph
is without doubt rent in pieces.
34 And Jacob [a]rent his clothes, and put sackcloth upon his loins, and [b]mourned for his son
many days.
35 And all his sons and all his daughters
[a]rose up to comfort him; but he refused to be comforted; and he said, For [b]I will go down into the
grave unto my son mourning. Thus his father
wept for him.
36 And [a]the Midianites sold him into Egypt
unto Potiphar, an officer of Pharaoh's, *and* captain
of the guard.

Judah and Tamar

38 And it came to pass at that time, that Judah
went down from his brethren, and [a]turned
in to a certain Adullamite, whose name *was*
Hirah.
2 And Judah [a]saw there a daughter of a certain Canaanite, whose name *was* [b]Shuah; and he
took her, and went in unto her.
3 And she conceived, and bare a son; and
he called his name [a]Er.
4 And she conceived again, and bare a son;
and she called his name [a]Onan.
5 And she yet again conceived, and bare a
son; and called his name [a]Shelah: and he was at
Chezib, when she bare him.
6 And Judah [a]took a wife for Er his firstborn, whose name *was* [b]Tamar.
7 And [a]Er, Judah's firstborn, was wicked
in the sight of the LORD; [b]and the LORD slew
him.
8 And Judah said unto Onan, Go in unto
[a]thy brother's wife, and marry her, and raise up
seed to thy brother.
9 And Onan knew that the seed should not
be [a]his; and it came to pass, when he went in
unto his brother's wife, that he spilled *it* on the
ground, lest that he should give seed to his
brother.
10 And the thing which he did displeased the
LORD: wherefore he slew [a]him also.
11 Then said Judah to Tamar his daughter
in law, [a]Remain a widow at thy father's house,
till Shelah my son be grown: for he said, Lest
peradventure he die also, as his brethren *did*. And
Tamar went and dwelt [b]in her father's house.
12 And in process of time the daughter of
Shuah Judah's wife died; and Judah [a]was comforted, and went up unto his sheepshearers to
Timnath, he and his friend Hirah the Adullamite.
13 And it was told Tamar, saying, Behold thy
father in law goeth up [a]to Timnath to shear his
sheep.
14 And she put her widow's garments off
from her, and covered her with a vail, and
wrapped herself, and [a]sat in an open place, which
is by the way to Timnath; for she saw [b]that Shelah
was grown, and she was not given unto him to
wife.
15 When Judah saw her, he thought her *to
be* an harlot; because she had covered her face.
16 And he turned unto her by the way, and
said, Go to, I pray thee, let me come in unto thee;
(for he knew not that she *was* his daughter in
law.) And she said, What wilt thou give me, that
thou mayest come in unto me?
17 And he said, [a]I will send *thee* a kid from

29 [a]Gen. 37:34; 44:13; Job 1:20
30 [a]Gen. 42:13, 36
31 [a]Gen. 37:3, 23
33 [a]Gen. 37:20
34 [a]Gen. 37:29; 2 Sam. 3:31 [b]Gen. 50:10
35 [a]2 Sam. 12:17 [b]Gen. 25:8; 35:29; 42:38; 44:29, 31
36 [a]Gen. 39:1

CHAPTER 38

1 [a]2 Kin. 4:8
2 [a]Gen. 34:2 [b]1 Chr. 2:3
3 [a]Gen. 46:12; Num. 26:19
4 [a]Gen. 46:12; Num. 26:19
5 [a]Num. 26:20
6 [a]Gen. 21:21 [b]Ruth 4:12
7 [a]Gen. 46:12; Num. 26:19 [b]1 Chr. 2:3
8 [a]Deut. 25:5, 6; Matt. 22:24
9 [a]Deut. 25:6
10 [a]Gen. 46:12; Num. 26:19
11 [a]Ruth 1:12, 13 [b]Lev. 22:13
12 [a]2 Sam. 13:39
13 [a]Josh. 15:10, 57; Judg. 14:1
14 [a]Prov. 7:12 [b]Gen. 38:11, 26
17 [a]Judg. 15:1; Ezek. 16:33

*

37:36 MT *Medanites*

NKJV

deed Joseph *was* not in the pit; and he [a]tore his
clothes.
30 And he returned to his brothers and said,
"The lad [a]*is* no *more;* and I, where shall I go?"
31 So they took [a]Joseph's tunic, killed a kid
of the goats, and dipped the tunic in the blood.
32 Then they sent the tunic of *many* colors,
and they brought *it* to their father and said, "We
have found this. Do you know whether it *is* your
son's tunic or not?"
33 And he recognized it and said, "*It is* my
son's tunic. A [a]wild beast has devoured him. Without doubt Joseph is torn to pieces."
34 Then Jacob [a]tore his clothes, put sackcloth on his waist, and [b]mourned for his son many
days.
35 And all his sons and all his daughters
[a]arose to comfort him; but he refused to be comforted, and he said, "For [b]I shall go down into
the grave to my son in mourning." Thus his father
wept for him.
36 Now [a]the *Midianites had sold him in
Egypt to Potiphar, an officer of Pharaoh *and* captain of the guard.

Judah and Tamar

38 It came to pass at that time that Judah departed from his brothers, and [a]visited a certain Adullamite whose name *was* Hirah.
2 And Judah [a]saw there a daughter of a certain Canaanite whose name *was* [b]Shua, and he
married her and went in to her.
3 So she conceived and bore a son, and he
called his name [a]Er.
4 She conceived again and bore a son, and
she called his name [a]Onan.
5 And she conceived yet again and bore a
son, and called his name [a]Shelah. He was at
Chezib when she bore him.
6 Then Judah [a]took a wife for Er his firstborn, and her name *was* [b]Tamar.
7 But [a]Er, Judah's firstborn, was wicked in
the sight of the LORD, [b]and the LORD killed him.
8 And Judah said to Onan, "Go in to [a]your
brother's wife and marry her, and raise up an heir
to your brother."
9 But Onan knew that the heir would not
be [a]his; and it came to pass, when he went in to
his brother's wife, that he emitted on the ground,
lest he should give an heir to his brother.
10 And the thing which he did displeased the
LORD; therefore He killed [a]him also.
11 Then Judah said to Tamar his daughter-
in-law, [a]"Remain a widow in your father's house
till my son Shelah is grown." For he said, "Lest
he also die like his brothers." And Tamar went
and dwelt [b]in her father's house.
12 Now in the process of time the daughter
of Shua, Judah's wife, died; and Judah [a]was comforted, and went up to his sheepshearers at Timnah, he and his friend Hirah the Adullamite.
13 And it was told Tamar, saying, "Look,
your father-in-law is going up [a]to Timnah to shear
his sheep."
14 So she took off her widow's garments,
covered *herself* with a veil and wrapped herself,
and [a]sat in an open place which *was* on the way
to Timnah; for she saw [b]that Shelah was grown,
and she was not given to him as a wife.
15 When Judah saw her, he thought she *was*
a harlot, because she had covered her face.
16 Then he turned to her by the way, and
said, "Please let me come in to you"; for he did
not know that she *was* his daughter-in-law. So
she said, "What will you give me, that you may
come in to me?"
17 And he said, [a]"I will send a young goat

KJV

the flock. And she said, [b]Wilt thou give *me* a
pledge, till thou send *it?*
18 And he said, What pledge shall I give
thee? And she said, [a]Thy signet, and thy bracelets,
and thy staff that *is* in thine hand. And he gave
it her, and came in unto her, and she conceived
by him.
19 And she arose, and went away, and [a]laid
by her vail from her, and put on the garments of
her widowhood.
20 And Judah sent the kid by the hand of
his friend the Adullamite, to receive *his* pledge
from the woman's hand: but he found her not.
21 Then he asked the men of that place, saying, Where *is* the harlot, that *was* openly by the
way side? And they said, There was no harlot in
this *place*.
22 And he returned to Judah, and said, I cannot find her; and also the men of the place said,
that there was no harlot in this *place*.
23 And Judah said, Let her take *it* to her, lest
we be shamed: behold, I sent this kid, and thou
hast not found her.
24 And it came to pass about three months
after, that it was told Judah, saying, Tamar thy
daughter in law hath [a]played the harlot; and also,
behold, she *is* with child by whoredom. And Judah
said, Bring her forth, [b]and let her be burnt.
25 When she *was* brought forth, she sent to
her father in law, saying, By the man, whose these
are, *am* I with child: and she said, [a]Discern, I pray
thee, whose *are* these, the signet, and bracelets,
and staff.
26 And Judah [a]acknowledged *them*, and
said, [b]She hath been more righteous than I; because that [c]I gave her not to Shelah my son. And
he knew her again [d]no more.
27 And it came to pass in the time of her travail, that, behold, twins *were* in her womb.
28 And it came to pass, when she travailed,
that *the one* put out *his* hand: and the midwife
took and bound upon his hand a scarlet thread,
saying, This came out first.
29 And it came to pass, as he drew back his
hand, that, behold, his brother came out: and she
said, How hast thou broken forth? *this* breach *be*
upon thee: therefore his name was called [a]Pharez.
30 And afterward came out his brother, that
had the scarlet thread upon his hand: and his
name was called [a]Zarah.

Joseph a Slave in Egypt

39 And Joseph was brought [a]down to Egypt;
and [b]Potiphar, an officer of Pharaoh, captain of the guard, an Egyptian, [c]bought him of
the hands of the Ishmeelites, which had brought
him down thither.
2 And [a]the LORD was with Joseph, and he
was a prosperous man; and he was in the house
of his master the Egyptian.
3 And his master saw that the LORD *was*
with him, and that the LORD [a]made all that he
did to prosper in his hand.
4 And Joseph [a]found grace in his sight, and
he served him: and he made him [b]overseer over
his house, and all *that* he had he put into his hand.
5 And it came to pass from the time *that*
he had made him overseer in his house, and over
all that he had, that [a]the LORD blessed the Egyptian's house for Joseph's sake; and the blessing
of the LORD was upon all that he had in the house,
and in the field.
6 And he left all that he had in Joseph's
hand; and he knew not ought he had, save the
bread which he did eat. And Joseph [a]was *a* goodly
person, and well favoured.
7 And it came to pass after these things, that
his master's wife cast her eyes upon Joseph; and
she said, [a]Lie with me.
8 But he refused, and said unto his master's

17 [b]Gen. 38:20
18 [a]Gen. 38:25; 41:42
19 [a]Gen. 38:14
24 [a]Judg. 19:2 [b]Lev. 20:14; 21:9; Deut. 22:21
25 [a]Gen. 37:32; 38:18
26 [a]Gen. 37:33 [b]1 Sam. 24:17 [c]Gen. 38:14 [d]Job 34:31, 32
29 [a]Gen. 46:12; Num. 26:20; Ruth 4:12; 1 Chr. 2:4; Matt. 1:3
30 [a]Gen. 46:12; 1 Chr. 2:4; Matt. 1:3

CHAPTER 39

1 [a]Gen. 12:10; 43:15 [b]Gen. 37:36; Ps. 105:17 [c]Gen. 37:28; 45:4
2 [a]Gen. 26:24, 28; 28:15; 35:3; 39:3, 21, 23; 1 Sam. 16:18; 18:14, 28; Acts 7:9
3 [a]Ps. 1:3
4 [a]Gen. 18:3; 19:19; 39:21 [b]Gen. 24:2, 10; 39:8, 22; 41:40
5 [a]Gen. 18:26; 30:27; 2 Sam. 6:11
6 [a]Gen. 29:17; 1 Sam. 16:12
7 [a]2 Sam. 13:11

**38:29* Lit. *Breach* or *Breakthrough*

NKJV

from the flock." So she said, [b]"Will you give *me*
a pledge till you send *it?*"
18 Then he said, "What pledge shall I give
you?" So she said, [a]"Your signet and cord, and
your staff that *is* in your hand." Then he gave
them to her, and went in to her, and she conceived
by him.
19 So she arose and went away, and [a]laid
aside her veil and put on the garments of her
widowhood.
20 And Judah sent the young goat by the
hand of his friend the Adullamite, to receive *his*
pledge from the woman's hand, but he did not
find her.
21 Then he asked the men of that place, saying, "Where is the harlot who *was* openly by the
roadside?" And they said, "There was no harlot
in this *place*."
22 So he returned to Judah and said, "I cannot find her. Also, the men of the place said there
was no harlot in this *place*."
23 Then Judah said, "Let her take *them* for
herself, lest we be shamed; for I sent this young
goat and you have not found her."
24 And it came to pass, about three months
after, that Judah was told, saying, "Tamar your
daughter-in-law has [a]played the harlot; furthermore she *is* with child by harlotry." So Judah said,
"Bring her out [b]and let her be burned!"
25 When she *was* brought out, she sent to
her father-in-law, saying, "By the man to whom
these belong, I *am* with child." And she said,
[a]"Please determine whose these *are*—the signet
and cord, and staff."
26 So Judah [a]acknowledged *them* and said,
[b]"She has been more righteous than I, because
[c]I did not give her to Shelah my son." And he
[d]never knew her again.
27 Now it came to pass, at the time for giving
birth, that behold, twins *were* in her womb.
28 And so it was, when she was giving birth,
that *the one* put out *his* hand; and the midwife
took a scarlet *thread* and bound it on his hand,
saying, "This one came out first."
29 Then it happened, as he drew back his
hand, that his brother came out unexpectedly; and
she said, "How did you break through? *This*
breach *be* upon you!" Therefore his name was
called [a]Perez.*
30 Afterward his brother came out who had
the scarlet *thread* on his hand. And his name was
called [a]Zerah.

Joseph a Slave in Egypt

39 Now Joseph had been taken [a]down to
Egypt. And [b]Potiphar, an officer of Pharaoh, captain of the guard, an Egyptian, [c]bought
him from the Ishmaelites who had taken him
down there.
2 [a]The LORD was with Joseph, and he was
a successful man; and he was in the house of his
master the Egyptian.
3 And his master saw that the LORD *was*
with him and that the LORD [a]made all he did to
prosper in his hand.
4 So Joseph [a]found favor in his sight, and
served him. Then he made him [b]overseer of his
house, and all *that* he had he put under his
authority.
5 So it was, from the time *that* he had made
him overseer of his house and all that he had,
that [a]the LORD blessed the Egyptian's house for
Joseph's sake; and the blessing of the LORD was
on all that he had in the house and in the field.
6 Thus he left all that he had in Joseph's
hand, and he did not know what he had except
for the bread which he ate. Now Joseph [a]was
handsome in form and appearance.
7 And it came to pass after these things that
his master's wife cast longing eyes on Joseph, and
she said, [a]"Lie with me."
8 But he refused and said to his master's

KJV

wife, Behold, my master wotteth not what *is* with
me in the house, and he hath committed all that
he hath to my hand;
9 *There is* none greater in this house than
I; neither hath he kept back any thing from me
but thee, because thou *art* his wife: [a]how then
can I do this great wickedness, and [b]sin against
God?
10 And it came to pass, as she spake to Joseph day by day, that he hearkened [a]not unto her,
to lie by her, *or* to be with her.
11 And it came to pass about this time, that
Joseph went into the house to do his business;
and *there was* none of the men of the house there
within.
12 And she [a]caught him by his garment, saying, Lie with me: and he left his garment in her
hand, and fled, and got him out.
13 And it came to pass, when she saw that
he had left his garment in her hand, and was fled
forth,
14 That she called unto the men of her house,
and spake unto them, saying, See, he hath brought
in an [a]Hebrew unto us to mock us; he came in
unto me to lie with me, and I cried with a loud
voice:
15 And it came to pass, when he heard that
I lifted up my voice and cried, that he left his garment with me, and fled, and got him out.
16 And she laid up his garment by her, until
his lord came home.
17 And she [a]spake unto him according to
these words, saying, The Hebrew servant, which
thou hast brought unto us, came in unto me to
mock me:
18 And it came to pass, as I lifted up my voice
and cried, that he left his garment with me, and
fled out.
19 And it came to pass, when his master
heard the words of his wife, which she spake unto
him, saying, After this manner did thy servant to
me; that his [a]wrath was kindled.
20 And Joseph's master took him, and [a]put
him into the [b]prison, a place where the king's
prisoners *were* bound: and he was there in the
prison.
21 But the LORD was with Joseph, and
shewed him mercy, and [a]gave him favour in the
sight of the keeper of the prison.
22 And the keeper of the prison [a]committed
to Joseph's hand all the prisoners that *were* in
the prison; and whatsoever they did there, he was
the doer *of it*.
23 The keeper of the prison looked not to any
thing *that was* under his hand; because [a]the LORD
was with him, and *that* which he did, the LORD
made *it* to prosper.

The Prisoners' Dreams

40 And it came to pass after these things, *that*
the [a]butler of the king of Egypt and *his*
baker had offended their lord the king of Egypt.
2 And Pharaoh was [a]wroth against two *of*
his officers, against the chief of the butlers, and
against the chief of the bakers.
3 [a]And he put them in ward in the house
of the captain of the guard, into the prison, the
place where Joseph *was* bound.
4 And the captain of the guard charged Joseph with them, and he served them: and they
continued a season in ward.
5 And they [a]dreamed a dream both of them,
each man his dream in one night, each man according to the interpretation of his dream, the butler and the baker of the king of Egypt, which *were*
bound in the prison.
6 And Joseph came in unto them in the
morning, and looked upon them, and, behold, they
were sad.
7 And he asked Pharaoh's officers that *were*
with him in the ward of his lord's house, saying,
[a]Wherefore look ye *so* sadly to day?

9 [a]Lev. 20:10; Prov. 6:29, 32 [b]Gen. 20:6; 42:18; 2 Sam. 12:13; Ps. 51:4
10 [a]Prov. 1:10
12 [a]Prov. 7:13
14 [a]Gen. 14:13; 41:12
17 [a]Ex. 23:1; Ps. 120:3; Prov. 26:28
19 [a]Prov. 6:34, 35
20 [a]Ps. 105:18; [1 Pet. 2:19] [b]Gen. 40:3, 15; 41:14
21 [a]Gen. 39:2; Ex. 3:21; Ps. 105:19; [Prov. 16:7]; Dan. 1:9; Acts 7:9, 10
22 [a]Gen. 39:4; 40:3, 4
23 [a]Gen. 39:2, 3

CHAPTER 40

1 [a]Gen. 40:11, 13; Neh. 1:11
2 [a]Prov. 16:14
3 [a]Gen. 39:1, 20, 23; 41:10
5 [a]Gen. 37:5; 41:1
7 [a]Neh. 2:2

*

39:23 Lit. *his hand*

NKJV

wife, "Look, my master does not know what *is*
with me in the house, and he has committed all
that he has to my hand.
9 "*There is* no one greater in this house than
I, nor has he kept back anything from me but you,
because you *are* his wife. [a]How then can I do this
great wickedness, and [b]sin against God?"
10 So it was, as she spoke to Joseph day by
day, that he [a]did not heed her, to lie with her *or*
to be with her.
11 But it happened about this time, when Joseph went into the house to do his work, and none
of the men of the house *was* inside,
12 that she [a]caught him by his garment, saying, "Lie with me." But he left his garment in her
hand, and fled and ran outside.
13 And so it was, when she saw that he had
left his garment in her hand and fled outside,
14 that she called to the men of her house
and spoke to them, saying, "See, he has brought
in to us a [a]Hebrew to mock us. He came in to
me to lie with me, and I cried out with a loud
voice.
15 "And it happened, when he heard that I
lifted my voice and cried out, that he left his garment with me, and fled and went outside."
16 So she kept his garment with her until his
master came home.
17 Then she [a]spoke to him with words like
these, saying, "The Hebrew servant whom you
brought to us came in to me to mock me;
18 "so it happened, as I lifted my voice and
cried out, that he left his garment with me and
fled outside."
19 So it was, when his master heard the
words which his wife spoke to him, saying, "Your
servant did to me after this manner," that his [a]an-
ger was aroused.
20 Then Joseph's master took him and [a]put
him into the [b]prison, a place where the king's prisoners *were* confined. And he was there in the
prison.
21 But the LORD was with Joseph and showed
him mercy, and He [a]gave him favor in the sight
of the keeper of the prison.
22 And the keeper of the prison [a]committed
to Joseph's hand all the prisoners who *were* in
the prison; whatever they did there, it was his
doing.
23 The keeper of the prison did not look into
anything *that was* under **Joseph's* authority, because [a]the LORD was with him; and whatever he
did, the LORD made *it* prosper.

The Prisoners' Dreams

40 It came to pass after these things *that* the
[a]butler and the baker of the king of Egypt
offended their lord, the king of Egypt.
2 And Pharaoh was [a]angry with his two officers, the chief butler and the chief baker.
3 [a]So he put them in custody in the house
of the captain of the guard, in the prison, the place
where Joseph *was* confined.
4 And the captain of the guard charged Joseph with them, and he served them; so they were
in custody for a while.
5 Then the butler and the baker of the king
of Egypt, who *were* confined in the prison, [a]had
a dream, both of them, each man's dream in one
night *and* each man's dream with its *own*
interpretation.
6 And Joseph came in to them in the morning and looked at them, and saw that they *were*
sad.
7 So he asked Pharaoh's officers who *were*
with him in the custody of his lord's house, saying,
[a]"Why do you look *so* sad today?"

KJV

8 And they said unto him, [a]We have dreamed a dream, and *there is* no interpreter of it. And Joseph said unto them, [b]*Do* not interpretations *belong* to God? tell me *them*, I pray you.

9 And the chief butler told his dream to Joseph, and said to him, In my dream, behold, a vine *was* before me;

10 And in the vine *were* three branches: and it *was* as though it budded, *and* her blossoms shot forth; and the clusters thereof brought forth ripe grapes:

11 And Pharaoh's cup *was* in my hand: and I took the grapes, and pressed them into Pharaoh's cup, and I gave the cup into Pharaoh's hand.

12 And Joseph said unto him, [a]This *is* the interpretation of it: The three branches [b]*are* three days:

13 Yet within three days shall Pharaoh [a]lift up thine head, and restore thee unto thy place: and thou shalt deliver Pharaoh's cup into his hand, after the former manner when thou wast his butler.

14 But [a]think on me when it shall be well with thee, and [b]shew kindness, I pray thee, unto me, and make mention of me unto Pharaoh, and bring me out of this house:

15 For indeed I was [a]stolen away out of the land of the Hebrews: [b]and here also have I done nothing that they should put me into the dungeon.

16 When the chief baker saw that the interpretation was good, he said unto Joseph, I also *was* in my dream, and, behold, *I had* three white baskets on my head:

17 And in the uppermost basket *there was* of all manner of bakemeats for Pharaoh; and the birds did eat them out of the basket upon my head.

18 And Joseph answered and said, [a]This *is* the interpretation thereof: The three baskets *are* three days:

19 [a]Yet within three days shall Pharaoh lift up thy head from off thee, and shall [b]hang thee on a tree; and the birds shall eat thy flesh from off thee.

20 And it came to pass the third day, *which was* Pharaoh's [a]birthday, that he [b]made a feast unto all his servants: and he [c]lifted up the head of the chief butler and of the chief baker among his servants.

21 And he [a]restored the chief butler unto his butlership again; and [b]he gave the cup into Pharaoh's hand:

22 But he [a]hanged the chief baker: as Joseph had interpreted to them.

23 Yet did not the chief butler remember Joseph, but [a]forgat him.

Pharaoh's Dreams

41 And it came to pass at the end of two full years, that [a]Pharaoh dreamed: and, behold, he stood by the river.

2 And, behold, there came up out of the river seven well favoured kine and fatfleshed; and they fed in a meadow.

3 And, behold, seven other kine came up after them out of the river, ill favoured and leanfleshed; and stood by the *other* kine upon the brink of the river.

4 And the ill favoured and leanfleshed kine did eat up the seven well favoured and fat kine. So Pharaoh awoke.

5 And he slept and dreamed the second time: and, behold, seven ears of corn came up upon one stalk, rank and good.

6 And, behold, seven thin ears and blasted with the [a]east wind sprung up after them.

7 And the seven thin ears devoured the seven rank and full ears. And Pharaoh awoke, and, behold, *it was* a dream.

8 And it came to pass in the morning [a]that his spirit was troubled; and he sent and called for all [b]the magicians of Egypt, and all the [c]wise men thereof: and Pharaoh told them his dream;

8 [a]Gen. 41:15 [b][Gen. 41:16; Dan. 2:11, 20–22, 27, 28, 47]
12 [a]Gen. 40:18; 41:12, 25; Judg. 7:14; Dan. 2:36; 4:18, 19 [b]Gen. 40:18; 42:17
13 [a]2 Kin. 25:27; Ps. 3:3; Jer. 52:31
14 [a]1 Sam. 25:31; Luke 23:42 [b]Gen. 24:49; 47:29; Josh. 2:12; 1 Sam. 20:14, 15; 2 Sam. 9:1; 1 Kin. 2:7
15 [a]Gen. 37:26–28 [b]Gen. 39:20
18 [a]Gen. 40:12
19 [a]Gen. 40:13 [b]Deut. 21:22
20 [a]Matt. 14:6–10 [b]Mark 6:21 [c]Gen. 40:13, 19; 2 Kin. 25:27; Jer. 52:31; Matt. 25:19
21 [a]Gen. 40:13 [b]Neh. 2:1
22 [a]Gen. 40:19; Deut. 21:23; Esth. 7:10
23 [a]Job 19:14; Ps. 31:12; Eccl. 9:15, 16; Is. 49:15; Amos 6:6

CHAPTER 41
1 [a]Gen. 40:5; Judg. 7:13
6 [a]Ex. 10:13; Ezek. 17:10
8 [a]Dan. 2:1, 3; 4:5, 19 [b]Ex. 7:11, 22; Is. 29:14; Dan. 1:20; 2:2; 4:7 [c]Matt. 2:1

NKJV

8 And they said to him, [a]"We each have had a dream, and *there is* no interpreter of it." So Joseph said to them, [b]"Do not interpretations belong to God? Tell *them* to me, please."

9 Then the chief butler told his dream to Joseph, and said to him, "Behold, in my dream a vine *was* before me,

10 "and in the vine *were* three branches; it *was* as though it budded, its blossoms shot forth, and its clusters brought forth ripe grapes.

11 "Then Pharaoh's cup *was* in my hand; and I took the grapes and pressed them into Pharaoh's cup, and placed the cup in Pharaoh's hand."

12 And Joseph said to him, [a]"This *is* the interpretation of it: The three branches [b]*are* three days.

13 "Now within three days Pharaoh will [a]lift up your head and restore you to your place, and you will put Pharaoh's cup in his hand according to the former manner, when you were his butler.

14 "But [a]remember me when it is well with you, and [b]please show kindness to me; make mention of me to Pharaoh, and get me out of this house.

15 "For indeed I was [a]stolen away from the land of the Hebrews; [b]and also I have done nothing here that they should put me into the dungeon."

16 When the chief baker saw that the interpretation was good, he said to Joseph, "I also *was* in my dream, and there *were* three white baskets on my head.

17 "In the uppermost basket *were* all kinds of baked goods for Pharaoh, and the birds ate them out of the basket on my head."

18 So Joseph answered and said, [a]"This *is* the interpretation of it: The three baskets *are* three days.

19 [a]"Within three days Pharaoh will lift off your head from you and [b]hang you on a tree; and the birds will eat your flesh from you."

20 Now it came to pass on the third day, *which was* Pharaoh's [a]birthday, that he [b]made a feast for all his servants; and he [c]lifted up the head of the chief butler and of the chief baker among his servants.

21 Then he [a]restored the chief butler to his butlership again, and [b]he placed the cup in Pharaoh's hand.

22 But he [a]hanged the chief baker, as Joseph had interpreted to them.

23 Yet the chief butler did not remember Joseph, but [a]forgot him.

Pharaoh's Dreams

41 Then it came to pass, at the end of two full years, that [a]Pharaoh had a dream; and behold, he stood by the river.

2 Suddenly there came up out of the river seven cows, fine looking and fat; and they fed in the meadow.

3 Then behold, seven other cows came up after them out of the river, ugly and gaunt, and stood by the *other* cows on the bank of the river.

4 And the ugly and gaunt cows ate up the seven fine looking and fat cows. So Pharaoh awoke.

5 He slept and dreamed a second time; and suddenly seven heads of grain came up on one stalk, plump and good.

6 Then behold, seven thin heads, blighted by the [a]east wind, sprang up after them.

7 And the seven thin heads devoured the seven plump and full heads. So Pharaoh awoke, and indeed, *it was* a dream.

8 Now it came to pass in the morning [a]that his spirit was troubled, and he sent and called for all [b]the magicians of Egypt and all its [c]wise men. And Pharaoh told them his dreams, but

KJV

but *there was* none that could interpret them unto Pharaoh.

9 Then spake the [a]chief butler unto Pharaoh, saying, I do remember my faults this day:

10 Pharaoh was [a]wroth with his servants, [b]and put me in ward in the captain of the guard's house, *both* me and the chief baker:

11 And [a]we dreamed a dream in one night, I and he; we dreamed each man according to the interpretation of his dream.

12 And *there was* there with us a young man, [a]an Hebrew, [b]servant to the captain of the guard; and we told him, and he [c]interpreted to us our dreams; to each man according to his dream he did interpret.

13 And it came to pass, [a]as he interpreted to us, so it was; me he restored unto mine office, and him he hanged.

14 [a]Then Pharaoh sent and called Joseph, and they [b]brought him hastily [c]out of the dungeon: and he shaved *himself*, and [d]changed his raiment, and came in unto Pharaoh.

15 And Pharaoh said unto Joseph, I have dreamed a dream, and *there is* none that can interpret it: [a]and I have heard say of thee, *that* thou canst understand a dream to interpret it.

16 And Joseph answered Pharaoh, saying, [a]*It is* not in me: [b]God shall give Pharaoh an answer of peace.

17 And Pharaoh said unto Joseph, [a]In my dream, behold, I stood upon the bank of the river:

18 And, behold, there came up out of the river seven kine, fatfleshed and well favoured; and they fed in a meadow:

19 And, behold, seven other kine came up after them, poor and very ill favoured and leanfleshed, such as I never saw in all the land of Egypt for badness:

20 And the lean and the ill favoured kine did eat up the first seven fat kine:

21 And when they had eaten them up, it could not be known that they had eaten them; but they *were* still ill favoured, as at the beginning. So I awoke.

22 And I saw in my dream, and, behold, seven ears came up in one stalk, full and good:

23 And, behold, seven ears, withered, thin, *and* blasted with the east wind, sprung up after them:

24 And the thin ears devoured the seven good ears: and [a]I told *this* unto the magicians; but *there was* none that could declare *it* to me.

25 And Joseph said unto Pharaoh, The dream of Pharaoh *is* one: [a]God hath shewed Pharaoh what he *is* about to do.

26 The seven good kine *are* seven years; and the seven good ears *are* seven years: the dream *is* one.

27 And the seven thin and ill favoured kine that came up after them *are* seven years; and the seven empty ears blasted with the east wind shall be [a]seven years of famine.

28 [a]This *is* the thing which I have spoken unto Pharaoh: What God *is* about to do he sheweth unto Pharaoh.

29 Behold, there come [a]seven years of great plenty throughout all the land of Egypt:

30 And there shall [a]arise after them seven years of famine; and all the plenty shall be forgotten in the land of Egypt; and the famine [b]shall consume the land;

31 And the plenty shall not be known in the land by reason of that famine following; for it *shall be* very grievous.

32 And for that the dream was doubled unto Pharaoh twice; *it is* because the [a]thing *is* established by God, and God will shortly bring it to pass.

33 Now therefore let Pharaoh look out a man

9 [a]Gen. 40:1, 14, 23
10 [a]Gen. 40:2, 3 [b]Gen. 39:20
11 [a]Gen. 40:5; Judg. 7:15
12 [a]Gen. 39:14; 43:32 [b]Gen. 37:36 [c]Gen. 40:12
13 [a]Gen. 40:21, 22
14 [a]Ps. 105:20 [b]Dan. 2:25 [c][1 Sam. 2:8] [d]2 Kin. 25:27–29
15 [a]Gen. 41:8, 12; Dan. 5:16
16 [a]Dan. 2:30; Acts 3:12; [2 Cor. 3:5] [b]Gen. 40:8; 41:25, 28, 32; Deut. 29:29; Dan. 2:22, 28, 47
17 [a]Gen. 41:1
24 [a]Gen. 41:8; Ex. 7:11; Is. 8:19; Dan. 4:7
25 [a]Gen. 41:28, 32; Dan. 2:28, 29, 45; Rev. 4:1
27 [a]2 Kin. 8:1
28 [a][Gen. 41:25, 32; Dan. 2:28]
29 [a]Gen. 41:47
30 [a]Gen. 41:54, 56 [b]Gen. 47:13; Ps. 105:16
32 [a]Gen. 41:25, 28; Num. 23:19; Is. 46:10, 11

NKJV

there was no one who could interpret them for Pharaoh.

9 Then the [a]chief butler spoke to Pharaoh, saying: "I remember my faults this day.

10 "When Pharaoh was [a]angry with his servants, [b]and put me in custody in the house of the captain of the guard, *both* me and the chief baker,

11 [a]"we each had a dream in one night, he and I. Each of us dreamed according to the interpretation of his *own* dream.

12 "Now there *was* a young [a]Hebrew man with us there, a [b]servant of the captain of the guard. And we told him, and he [c]interpreted our dreams for us; to each man he interpreted according to his *own* dream.

13 "And it came to pass, just [a]as he interpreted for us, so it happened. He restored me to my office, and he hanged him."

14 [a]Then Pharaoh sent and called Joseph, and they [b]brought him quickly [c]out of the dungeon; and he shaved, [d]changed his clothing, and came to Pharaoh.

15 And Pharaoh said to Joseph, "I have had a dream, and *there is* no one who can interpret it. [a]But I have heard it said of you *that* you can understand a dream, to interpret it."

16 So Joseph answered Pharaoh, saying, [a]"*It is* not in me; [b]God will give Pharaoh an answer of peace."

17 Then Pharaoh said to Joseph: "Behold, [a]in my dream I stood on the bank of the river.

18 "Suddenly seven cows came up out of the river, fine looking and fat; and they fed in the meadow.

19 "Then behold, seven other cows came up after them, poor and very ugly and gaunt, such ugliness as I have never seen in all the land of Egypt.

20 "And the gaunt and ugly cows ate up the first seven, the fat cows.

21 "When they had eaten them up, no one would have known that they had eaten them, for they *were* just as ugly as at the beginning. So I awoke.

22 "Also I saw in my dream, and suddenly seven heads came up on one stalk, full and good.

23 "Then behold, seven heads, withered, thin, *and* blighted by the east wind, sprang up after them.

24 "And the thin heads devoured the seven good heads. So [a]I told *this* to the magicians, but *there was* no one who could explain *it* to me."

25 Then Joseph said to Pharaoh, "The dreams of Pharaoh *are* one; [a]God has shown Pharaoh what He *is* about to do:

26 "The seven good cows *are* seven years, and the seven good heads *are* seven years; the dreams *are* one.

27 "And the seven thin and ugly cows which came up after them *are* seven years, and the seven empty heads blighted by the east wind are [a]seven years of famine.

28 [a]"This *is* the thing which I have spoken to Pharaoh. God has shown Pharaoh what He *is* about to do.

29 "Indeed [a]seven years of great plenty will come throughout all the land of Egypt;

30 "but after them seven years of famine will [a]arise, and all the plenty will be forgotten in the land of Egypt; and the famine [b]will deplete the land.

31 "So the plenty will not be known in the land because of the famine following, for it *will be* very severe.

32 "And the dream was repeated to Pharaoh twice because the [a]thing *is* established by God, and God will shortly bring it to pass.

33 "Now therefore, let Pharaoh select a dis-

KJV

discreet and wise, and set him over the land of Egypt.

34 Let Pharaoh do *this,* and let him appoint officers over the land, and [a]take up the fifth part of the land of Egypt in the seven plenteous years.

35 And [a]let them gather all the food of those good years that come, and lay up corn under the hand of Pharaoh, and let them keep food in the cities.

36 And that food shall be for store to the land against the seven years of famine, which shall be in the land of Egypt; that the land [a]perish not through the famine.

Joseph's Rise to Power

37 And [a]the thing was good in the eyes of Pharaoh, and in the eyes of all his servants.

38 And Pharaoh said unto his servants, Can we find *such a one* as this *is,* a man [a]in whom the Spirit of God *is?*

39 And Pharaoh said unto Joseph, Forasmuch as God hath shewed thee all this, *there is* none so discreet and wise as thou *art:*

40 [a]Thou shalt be over my house, and according unto thy word shall all my people be ruled: only in the throne will I be greater than thou.

41 And Pharaoh said unto Joseph, See, I have [a]set thee over all the land of Egypt.

42 And Pharaoh [a]took off his ring from his hand, and put it upon Joseph's hand, and [b]arrayed him in vestures of fine linen, [c]and put a gold chain about his neck;

43 And he made him to ride in the second [a]chariot which he had; [b]and they cried before him, Bow the knee: and he made him *ruler* [c]over all the land of Egypt.

44 And Pharaoh said unto Joseph, I *am* Pharaoh, and without thee shall no man lift up his hand or foot in all the land of Egypt.

45 And Pharaoh called Joseph's name Zaphnath–paaneah; and he gave him to wife [a]Asenath the daughter of Potipherah priest of On. And Joseph went out over *all* the land of Egypt.

46 And Joseph *was* thirty years old when he [a]stood before Pharaoh king of Egypt. And Joseph went out from the presence of Pharaoh, and went throughout all the land of Egypt.

47 And in the seven plenteous years the earth brought forth by handfuls.

48 And he gathered up all the food of the seven years, which were in the land of Egypt, and laid up the food in the cities: the food of the field, which *was* round about every city, laid he up in the same.

49 And Joseph gathered corn [a]as the sand of the sea, very much, until he left numbering; for *it was* without number.

50 [a]And unto Joseph were born two sons before the years of famine came, which Asenath the daughter of Potipherah priest of On bare unto him.

51 And Joseph called the name of the firstborn Manasseh: For God, *said he,* hath made me forget all my toil, and all my [a]father's house.

52 And the name of the second called he Ephraim: For God hath caused me to be [a]fruitful in the land of my affliction.

53 And the seven years of plenteousness, that was in the land of Egypt, were ended.

54 [a]And the seven years of dearth began to come, [b]according as Joseph had said: and the dearth was in all lands; but in all the land of Egypt there was bread.

55 And when all the land of Egypt was famished, the people cried to Pharaoh for bread: and Pharaoh said unto all the Egyptians, Go unto Joseph; [a]what he saith to you, do.

56 And the famine was over all the face of the earth: And Joseph opened all the storehouses,

34 [a][Prov. 6:6–8]
35 [a]Gen. 41:48
36 [a]Gen. 47:15, 19
37 [a]Ps. 105:19; Acts 7:10
38 [a]Num. 27:18; [Job 32:8; Prov. 2:6]; Dan. 4:8, 9, 18; 5:11, 14; 6:3
40 [a]Ps. 105:21; Acts 7:10
41 [a]Gen. 42:6; Ps. 105:21; Dan. 6:3; Acts 7:10
42 [a]Esth. 3:10 [b]Esth. 8:2, 15 [c]Dan. 5:7, 16, 29
43 [a]Gen. 46:29 [b]Esth. 6:9 [c]Gen. 42:6
45 [a]Gen. 46:20
46 [a]1 Sam. 16:21; 1 Kin. 12:6, 8; Dan. 1:19
49 [a]Gen. 22:17; Judg. 7:12; 1 Sam. 13:5
50 [a]Gen. 46:20; 48:5
51 [a]Ps. 45:10
52 [a]Gen. 17:6; 28:3; 49:22
54 [a]Ps. 105:16; Acts 7:11 [b]Gen. 41:30
55 [a]John 2:5

NKJV

cerning and wise man, and set him over the land of Egypt.

34 "Let Pharaoh do *this,* and let him appoint officers over the land, [a]to collect one-fifth *of the produce* of the land of Egypt in the seven plentiful years.

35 "And [a]let them gather all the food of those good years that are coming, and store up grain under the authority of Pharaoh, and let them keep food in the cities.

36 "Then that food shall be as a reserve for the land for the seven years of famine which shall be in the land of Egypt, that the land [a]may not perish during the famine."

Joseph's Rise to Power

37 So [a]the advice was good in the eyes of Pharaoh and in the eyes of all his servants.

38 And Pharaoh said to his servants, "Can we find *such a one* as this, a man [a]in whom *is* the Spirit of God?"

39 Then Pharaoh said to Joseph, "Inasmuch as God has shown you all this, *there is* no one as discerning and wise as you.

40 [a]"You shall be over my house, and all my people shall be ruled according to your word; only in regard to the throne will I be greater than you."

41 And Pharaoh said to Joseph, "See, I have [a]set you over all the land of Egypt."

42 Then Pharaoh [a]took his signet ring off his hand and put it on Joseph's hand; and he [b]clothed him in garments of fine linen [c]and put a gold chain around his neck.

43 And he had him ride in the second [a]chariot which he had; [b]and they cried out before him, "Bow the knee!" So he set him [c]over all the land of Egypt.

44 Pharaoh also said to Joseph, "I *am* Pharaoh, and without your consent no man may lift his hand or foot in all the land of Egypt."

45 And Pharaoh called Joseph's name Zaphnath-Paaneah. And he gave him as a wife [a]Asenath, the daughter of Poti-Pherah priest of On. So Joseph went out over *all* the land of Egypt.

46 Joseph was thirty years old when he [a]stood before Pharaoh king of Egypt. And Joseph went out from the presence of Pharaoh, and went throughout all the land of Egypt.

47 Now in the seven plentiful years the ground brought forth abundantly.

48 So he gathered up all the food of the seven years which were in the land of Egypt, and laid up the food in the cities; he laid up in every city the food of the fields which surrounded them.

49 Joseph gathered very much grain, [a]as the sand of the sea, until he stopped counting, for *it was* immeasurable.

50 [a]And to Joseph were born two sons before the years of famine came, whom Asenath, the daughter of Poti-Pherah priest of On, bore to him.

51 Joseph called the name of the firstborn *Manasseh: "For God has made me forget all my toil and all my [a]father's house."

52 And the name of the second he called *Ephraim: "For God has caused me to be [a]fruitful in the land of my affliction."

53 Then the seven years of plenty which were in the land of Egypt ended,

54 [a]and the seven years of famine began to come, [b]as Joseph had said. The famine was in all lands, but in all the land of Egypt there was bread.

55 So when all the land of Egypt was famished, the people cried to Pharaoh for bread. Then Pharaoh said to all the Egyptians, "Go to Joseph; [a]whatever he says to you, do."

56 The famine was over all the face of the earth, and Joseph opened *all the storehouses and

*———

41:51 Lit. *Making Forgetful*
41:52 Lit. *Fruitfulness*
41:56 Lit. *all that was in them*

KJV

and [a]sold unto the Egyptians; and the famine waxed sore in the land of Egypt.

57 [a]And all countries came into Egypt to Joseph for to [b]buy *corn;* because that the famine was *so* sore in all lands.

Joseph's Brothers Go to Egypt

42 Now when [a]Jacob saw that there was corn in Egypt, Jacob said unto his sons, Why do ye look one upon another?

2 And he said, Behold, I have heard that there is corn in Egypt: get you down thither, and buy for us from thence; that we may [a]live, and not die.

3 And Joseph's ten brethren went down to buy corn in Egypt.

4 But Benjamin, Joseph's brother, Jacob sent not with his brethren; for he said, [a]Lest peradventure mischief befall him.

5 And the sons of Israel came to buy *corn* among those that came: for the famine was [a]in the land of Canaan.

6 And Joseph *was* the governor [a]over the land, *and* he *it was* that sold to all the people of the land: and Joseph's brethren came, and [b]bowed down themselves before him *with* their faces to the earth.

7 And Joseph saw his brethren, and he knew them, but made himself [a]strange unto them, and spake roughly unto them; and he said unto them, Whence come ye? And they said, From the land of Canaan to buy food.

8 And Joseph knew his brethren, but they knew not him.

9 And Joseph [a]remembered the dreams which he dreamed of them, and said unto them, Ye *are* spies; to see the nakedness of the land ye are come.

10 And they said unto him, Nay, my lord, but to buy food are thy servants come.

11 We *are* all one man's sons; we *are* true *men,* thy servants are no spies.

12 And he said unto them, Nay, but to see the nakedness of the land ye are come.

13 And they said, Thy servants *are* twelve brethren, the sons of one man in the land of Canaan; and, behold, the youngest *is* this day with our father, and one [a]*is* not.

14 And Joseph said unto them, That *is it* that I spake unto you, saying, Ye *are* spies:

15 Hereby ye shall be proved: [a]By the life of Pharaoh ye shall not go forth hence, except your youngest brother come hither.

16 Send one of you, and let him fetch your brother, and ye shall be kept in prison, that your words may be proved, whether *there be any* truth in you: or else by the life of Pharaoh surely ye *are* spies.

17 And he put them all together into ward [a]three days.

18 And Joseph said unto them the third day, This do, and live; [a]*for* I fear God:

19 If ye *be* true *men,* let one of your brethren be bound in the house of your prison: go ye, carry corn for the famine of your houses:

20 But [a]bring your youngest brother unto me; so shall your words be verified, and ye shall not die. And they did so.

21 And they said one to another, [a]We *are* verily guilty concerning our brother, in that we saw the anguish of his soul, when he besought us, and we would not hear; [b]therefore is this distress come upon us.

22 And Reuben answered them, saying, [a]Spake I not unto you, saying, Do not sin against the child; and ye would not hear? therefore, behold, also his blood is [b]required.

23 And they knew not that Joseph understood *them;* for he spake unto them by an interpreter.

24 And he turned himself about from them, and [a]wept; and returned to them again, and

---

56 [a]Gen. 42:6
57 [a]Ezek. 29:12 [b]Gen. 27:28, 37; 42:3

CHAPTER 42

1 [a]Acts 7:12
2 [a]Gen. 43:8; Ps. 33:18, 19; Is. 38:1
4 [a]Gen. 42:38
5 [a]Gen. 12:10; 26:1; 41:57; Acts 7:11
6 [a]Gen. 41:41, 55 [b]Gen. 37:7–10; 41:43; Is. 60:14
7 [a]Gen. 45:1, 2
9 [a]Gen. 37:5–9
13 [a]Gen. 37:30; 42:32; 44:20; Lam. 5:7
15 [a]1 Sam. 1:26; 17:55
17 [a]Gen. 40:4, 7, 12
18 [a]Gen. 22:12; 39:9; Ex. 1:17; Lev. 25:43; Neh. 5:15; Prov. 1:7; 9:10
20 [a]Gen. 42:34; 43:5; 44:23
21 [a]Gen. 37:26–28; 44:16; 45:3; Job 36:8, 9; Hos. 5:15 [b]Prov. 21:13; Matt. 7:2
22 [a]Gen. 37:21, 22, 29 [b]Gen. 9:5, 6; 1 Kin. 2:32; 2 Chr. 24:22; Ps. 9:12; Luke 11:50, 51
24 [a]Gen. 43:30; 45:14, 15

NKJV

[a]sold to the Egyptians. And the famine became severe in the land of Egypt.

57 [a]So all countries came to Joseph in Egypt to [b]buy *grain,* because the famine was severe in all lands.

Joseph's Brothers Go to Egypt

42 When [a]Jacob saw that there was grain in Egypt, Jacob said to his sons, "Why do you look at one another?"

2 And he said, "Indeed I have heard that there is grain in Egypt; go down to that place and buy for us there, that we may [a]live and not die."

3 So Joseph's ten brothers went down to buy grain in Egypt.

4 But Jacob did not send Joseph's brother Benjamin with his brothers, for he said, [a]"Lest some calamity befall him."

5 And the sons of Israel went to buy *grain* among those who journeyed, for the famine was [a]in the land of Canaan.

6 Now Joseph *was* governor [a]over the land; and it was he who sold to all the people of the land. And Joseph's brothers came and [b]bowed down before him with *their* faces to the earth.

7 Joseph saw his brothers and recognized them, but he acted as [a]a stranger to them and spoke roughly to them. Then he said to them, "Where do you come from?" And they said, "From the land of Canaan to buy food."

8 So Joseph recognized his brothers, but they did not recognize him.

9 Then Joseph [a]remembered the dreams which he had dreamed about them, and said to them, "You *are* spies! You have come to see the nakedness of the land!"

10 And they said to him, "No, my lord, but your servants have come to buy food.

11 "We *are* all one man's sons; we *are* honest *men;* your servants are not spies."

12 But he said to them, "No, but you have come to see the nakedness of the land."

13 And they said, "Your servants *are* twelve brothers, the sons of one man in the land of Canaan; and in fact, the youngest *is* with our father today, and one [a]*is* no more."

14 But Joseph said to them, "It *is* as I spoke to you, saying, 'You *are* spies!'

15 "In this *manner* you shall be tested: [a]By the life of Pharaoh, you shall not leave this place unless your youngest brother comes here.

16 "Send one of you, and let him bring your brother; and you shall be kept in prison, that your words may be tested to see whether *there is* any truth in you; or else, by the life of Pharaoh, surely you *are* spies!"

17 So he put them all together in prison [a]three days.

18 Then Joseph said to them the third day, "Do this and live, [a]*for* I fear God:

19 "If you *are* honest *men,* let one of your brothers be confined to your prison house; but you, go and carry grain for the famine of your houses.

20 "And [a]bring your youngest brother to me; so your words will be verified, and you shall not die." And they did so.

21 Then they said to one another, [a]"We *are* truly guilty concerning our brother, for we saw the anguish of his soul when he pleaded with us, and we would not hear; [b]therefore this distress has come upon us."

22 And Reuben answered them, saying, [a]"Did I not speak to you, saying, 'Do not sin against the boy'; and you would not listen? Therefore behold, his blood is now [b]required of us."

23 But they did not know that Joseph understood *them,* for he spoke to them through an interpreter.

24 And he turned himself away from them and [a]wept. Then he returned to them again, and

KJV

communed with them, and took from them [b]Simeon, and bound him before their eyes.

The Brothers Return to Canaan

25 Then Joseph [a]commanded to fill their sacks with corn, and to [b]restore every man's money into his sack, and to give them provision for the way: and [c]thus did he unto them.

26 And they laded their asses with the corn, and departed thence.

27 And as [a]one of them opened his sack to give his ass provender in the inn, he espied his money; for, behold, it *was* in his sack's mouth.

28 And he said unto his brethren, My money is restored; and, lo, *it is* even in my sack: and their heart failed *them,* and they were afraid, saying one to another, What *is* this *that* God hath done unto us?

29 And they came unto Jacob their father unto the land of Canaan, and told him all that befell unto them; saying,

30 The man, *who is* the lord of the land, [a]spake roughly to us, and took us for spies of the country.

31 And we said unto him, We *are* true *men;* we are no spies:

32 We *be* twelve brethren, sons of our father; one *is* not, and the youngest *is* this day with our father in the land of Canaan.

33 And the man, the lord of the country, said unto us, [a]Hereby shall I know that ye *are* true *men;* leave one of your brethren *here* with me, and take *food for* the famine of your households, and be gone:

34 And bring your [a]youngest brother unto me: then shall I know that ye *are* no spies, but *that* ye *are* true *men: so* will I deliver you your brother, and ye shall [b]traffick in the land.

35 And it came to pass as they emptied their sacks, that, behold, [a]every man's bundle of money *was* in his sack: and when *both* they and their father saw the bundles of money, they were afraid.

36 And Jacob their father said unto them, Me have ye [a]bereaved *of my children:* Joseph *is* not, and Simeon *is* not, and ye will take [b]Benjamin *away:* all these things are against me.

37 And Reuben spake unto his father, saying, Slay my two sons, if I bring him not to thee: deliver him into my hand, and I will bring him to thee again.

38 And he said, My son shall not go down with you; for [a]his brother is dead, and he is left alone: [b]if mischief befall him by the way in the which ye go, then shall ye [c]bring down my gray hairs with sorrow to the grave.

Joseph's Brothers Return with Benjamin

43 And the famine *was* [a]sore in the land.

2 And it came to pass, when they had eaten up the corn which they had brought out of Egypt, their father said unto them, Go [a]again, buy us a little food.

3 And Judah spake unto him, saying, The man did solemnly protest unto us, saying, Ye shall not see my face, except your [a]brother *be* with you.

4 If thou wilt send our brother with us, we will go down and buy thee food:

5 But if thou wilt not send *him,* we will not go down: for the man said unto us, Ye shall not see my face, except your brother *be* with you.

6 And Israel said, Wherefore dealt ye *so* ill with me, *as* to tell the man whether ye had yet a brother?

7 And they said, The man asked us straitly of our state, and of our kindred, saying, *Is* your father yet alive? have ye *another* brother? and we told him according to the tenor of these words: could we certainly know that he would say, Bring your brother down?

---

24 [b]Gen. 34:25, 30; 43:14, 23
25 [a]Gen. 44:1 [b]Gen. 43:12 [c][Matt. 5:44; Rom. 12:17, 20, 21; 1 Pet. 3:9]
27 [a]Gen. 43:21, 22
30 [a]Gen. 42:7
33 [a]Gen. 42:15, 19, 20
34 [a]Gen. 42:20; 43:3, 5 [b]Gen. 34:10
35 [a]Gen. 43:12, 15, 21
36 [a]Gen. 43:14 [b]Gen. 35:18; [Rom. 8:28, 31]
38 [a]Gen. 37:22; 42:13; 44:20, 28 [b]Gen. 42:4; 44:29 [c]Gen. 37:35; 44:31

CHAPTER 43

1 [a]Gen. 41:54, 57; 42:5; 45:6, 11
2 [a]Gen. 42:2; 44:25
3 [a]Gen. 42:20; 43:5; 44:23

NKJV

talked with them. And he took [b]Simeon from them and bound him before their eyes.

The Brothers Return to Canaan

25 Then Joseph [a]gave a command to fill their sacks with grain, to [b]restore every man's money to his sack, and to give them provisions for the journey. [c]Thus he did for them.

26 So they loaded their donkeys with the grain and departed from there.

27 But as [a]one *of them* opened his sack to give his donkey feed at the encampment, he saw his money; and there it was, in the mouth of his sack.

28 So he said to his brothers, "My money has been restored, and there it is, in my sack!" Then their hearts failed *them* and they were afraid, saying to one another, "What *is* this *that* God has done to us?"

29 Then they went to Jacob their father in the land of Canaan and told him all that had happened to them, saying:

30 "The man *who is* lord of the land [a]spoke roughly to us, and took us for spies of the country.

31 "But we said to him, 'We *are* honest *men;* we are not spies.

32 'We *are* twelve brothers, sons of our father; one *is* no *more,* and the youngest *is* with our father this day in the land of Canaan.'

33 "Then the man, the lord of the country, said to us, [a]'By this I will know that you *are* honest *men:* Leave one of your brothers *here* with me, take *food for* the famine of your households, and be gone.

34 'And bring your [a]youngest brother to me; so I shall know that you *are* not spies, but *that* you *are* honest *men.* I will grant your brother to you, and you may [b]trade in the land.' "

35 Then it happened as they emptied their sacks, that surprisingly [a]each man's bundle of money *was* in his sack; and when they and their father saw the bundles of money, they were afraid.

36 And Jacob their father said to them, "You have [a]bereaved me: Joseph is no *more,* Simeon is no *more,* and you want to take [b]Benjamin. All these things are against me."

37 Then Reuben spoke to his father, saying, "Kill my two sons if I do not bring him *back* to you; put him in my hands, and I will bring him back to you."

38 But he said, "My son shall not go down with you, for [a]his brother is dead, and he is left alone. [b]If any calamity should befall him along the way in which you go, then you would [c]bring down my gray hair with sorrow to the grave."

Joseph's Brothers Return with Benjamin

43 Now the famine *was* [a]severe in the land.

2 And it came to pass, when they had eaten up the grain which they had brought from Egypt, that their father said to them, "Go [a]back, buy us a little food."

3 But Judah spoke to him, saying, "The man solemnly warned us, saying, 'You shall not see my face unless your [a]brother *is* with you.'

4 "If you send our brother with us, we will go down and buy you food.

5 "But if you will not send *him,* we will not go down; for the man said to us, 'You shall not see my face unless your brother *is* with you.' "

6 And Israel said, "Why did you deal *so* wrongfully with me *as* to tell the man whether you had still *another* brother?"

7 But they said, "The man asked us pointedly about ourselves and our family, saying, '*Is* your father still alive? Have you *another* brother?' And we told him according to these words. Could we possibly have known that he would say, 'Bring your brother down'?"

KJV

8 And Judah said unto Israel his father, Send the lad with me, and we will arise and go; that we may [a]live, and not die, both we, and thou, *and* also our little ones.

9 I will be surety for him; of my hand shalt thou require him: [a]if I bring him not unto thee, and set him before thee, then let me bear the blame for ever:

10 For except we had lingered, surely now we had returned this second time.

11 And their father Israel said unto them, If *it must be* so now, do this; take of the best fruits in the land in your vessels, and [a]carry down the man a present, a little [b]balm, and a little honey, spices, and myrrh, nuts, and almonds:

12 And take double money in your hand; and the money [a]that was brought again in the mouth of your sacks, carry *it* again in your hand; peradventure it *was* an oversight:

13 Take also your brother, and arise, go again unto the man:

14 And God [a]Almighty [b]give you mercy before the man, that he may send away your other brother, and Benjamin. [c]If I be bereaved *of my children,* I am bereaved.

15 And the men took that present, and they took double money in their hand, and Benjamin; and rose up, and went [a]down to Egypt, and stood before Joseph.

16 And when Joseph saw Benjamin with them, he said to the [a]ruler of his house, Bring *these* men home, and slay, and make ready; for *these* men shall dine with me at noon.

17 And the man did as Joseph bade; and the man brought the men into Joseph's house.

18 And the men were [a]afraid, because they were brought into Joseph's house; and they said, Because of the money that was returned in our sacks at the first time are we brought in; that he may seek occasion against us, and fall upon us, and take us for bondmen, and our asses.

19 And they came near to the steward of Joseph's house, and they communed with him at the door of the house,

20 And said, O sir, [a]we came indeed down at the first time to buy food:

21 And [a]it came to pass, when we came to the inn, that we opened our sacks, and, behold, *every* man's money *was* in the mouth of his sack, our money in full weight: and we have brought it again in our hand.

22 And other money have we brought down in our hands to buy food: we cannot tell who put our money in our sacks.

23 And he said, Peace *be* to you, fear not: your God, and the God of your father, hath given you treasure in your sacks: I had your money. And he brought [a]Simeon out unto them.

24 And the man brought the men into Joseph's house, and [a]gave *them* water, and they washed their feet; and he gave their asses provender.

25 And they made ready the present against Joseph came at noon: for they heard that they should eat bread there.

26 And when Joseph came home, they brought him the present which *was* in their hand into the house, and [a]bowed themselves to him to the earth.

27 And he asked them of *their* welfare, and said, *Is* your father well, the old man [a]of whom ye spake? *Is* he yet alive?

28 And they answered, Thy servant our father *is* in good health, he *is* yet alive. [a]And they bowed down their heads, and made obeisance.

29 And he lifted up his eyes, and saw his brother Benjamin, [a]his mother's son, and said, *Is* this your younger brother, [b]of whom ye spake

8 [a]Gen. 42:2; 47:19
9 [a]Gen. 42:37; 44:32; Philem. 18, 19
11 [a]Gen. 32:20; 33:10; 43:25, 26; [Prov. 18:16] [b]Gen. 37:25; Jer. 8:22; Ezek. 27:17
12 [a]Gen. 42:25, 35; 43:21, 22
14 [a]Gen. 17:1; 28:3; 35:11; 48:3 [b]Gen. 39:21; Ps. 106:46 [c]Gen. 42:36; Esth. 4:16
15 [a]Gen. 39:1; 46:3, 6
16 [a]Gen. 24:2; 39:4; 44:1
18 [a]Gen. 42:28
20 [a]Gen. 42:3, 10
21 [a]Gen. 42:27, 35
23 [a]Gen. 42:24
24 [a]Gen. 18:4; 19:2; 24:32
26 [a]Gen. 37:7, 10; 42:6; 44:14
27 [a]Gen. 29:6; 42:11, 13; 43:7; 45:3; 2 Kin. 4:26
28 [a]Gen. 37:7, 10
29 [a]Gen. 35:17, 18 [b]Gen. 42:13

NKJV

8 Then Judah said to Israel his father, "Send the lad with me, and we will arise and go, that we may [a]live and not die, both we and you *and* also our little ones.

9 "I myself will be surety for him; from my hand you shall require him. [a]If I do not bring him *back* to you and set him before you, then let me bear the blame forever.

10 "For if we had not lingered, surely by now we would have returned this second time."

11 And their father Israel said to them, "If *it must be* so, then do this: Take some of the best fruits of the land in your vessels and [a]carry down a present for the man—a little [b]balm and a little honey, spices and myrrh, pistachio nuts and almonds.

12 "Take double money in your hand, and take back in your hand the money [a]that was returned in the mouth of your sacks; perhaps it was an oversight.

13 "Take your brother also, and arise, go back to the man.

14 "And may God [a]Almighty [b]give you mercy before the man, that he may release your other brother and Benjamin. [c]If I am bereaved, I am bereaved!"

15 So the men took that present and Benjamin, and they took double money in their hand, and arose and went [a]down to Egypt; and they stood before Joseph.

16 When Joseph saw Benjamin with them, he said to the [a]steward of his house, "Take *these* men to my home, and slaughter an animal and make ready; for *these* men will dine with me at noon."

17 Then the man did as Joseph ordered, and the man brought the men into Joseph's house.

18 Now the men were [a]afraid because they were brought into Joseph's house; and they said, "*It is* because of the money, which was returned in our sacks the first time, that we are brought in, so that he may make a case against us and seize us, to take us as slaves with our donkeys."

19 When they drew near to the steward of Joseph's house, they talked with him at the door of the house,

20 and said, "O sir, [a]we indeed came down the first time to buy food;

21 "but [a]it happened, when we came to the encampment, that we opened our sacks, and there, *each* man's money *was* in the mouth of his sack, our money in full weight; so we have brought it back in our hand.

22 "And we have brought down other money in our hands to buy food. We do not know who put our money in our sacks."

23 But he said, "Peace *be* with you, do not be afraid. Your God and the God of your father has given you treasure in your sacks; I had your money." Then he brought [a]Simeon out to them.

24 So the man brought the men into Joseph's house and [a]gave *them* water, and they washed their feet; and he gave their donkeys feed.

25 Then they made the present ready for Joseph's coming at noon, for they heard that they would eat bread there.

26 And when Joseph came home, they brought him the present which *was* in their hand into the house, and [a]bowed down before him to the earth.

27 Then he asked them about *their* well-being, and said, "*Is* your father well, the old man [a]of whom you spoke? *Is* he still alive?"

28 And they answered, "Your servant our father *is* in good health; he *is* still alive." [a]And they bowed their heads down and prostrated themselves.

29 Then he lifted his eyes and saw his brother Benjamin, [a]his mother's son, and said, "*Is* this your younger brother [b]of whom you spoke to

KJV

unto me? And he said, God be gracious unto thee, my son.

30 And Joseph made haste; for [a]his bowels did yearn upon his brother: and he sought *where* to weep; and he entered into *his* chamber, and [b]wept there.

31 And he washed his face, and went out, and refrained himself, and said, Set on [a]bread.

32 And they set on for him by himself, and for them by themselves, and for the Egyptians, which did eat with him, by themselves: because the Egyptians might not eat bread with the [a]Hebrews; for that *is* [b]an abomination unto the Egyptians.

33 And they sat before him, the firstborn according to his [a]birthright, and the youngest according to his youth: and the men marvelled one at another.

34 And he took *and sent* messes unto them from before him: but Benjamin's mess was [a]five times so much as any of their's. And they drank, and were merry with him.

Joseph's Cup

44 And he commanded the [a]steward of his house, saying, [b]Fill the men's sacks *with* food, as much as they can carry, and put every man's money in his sack's mouth.

2 And put my cup, the silver cup, in the sack's mouth of the youngest, and his corn money. And he did according to the word that Joseph had spoken.

3 As soon as the morning was light, the men were sent away, they and their asses.

4 *And* when they were gone out of the city, *and* not *yet* far off, Joseph said unto his steward, Up, follow after the men; and when thou dost overtake them, say unto them, Wherefore have ye [a]rewarded evil for good?

5 *Is* not this *it* in which my lord drinketh, and whereby indeed he divineth? ye have done evil in so doing.

6 And he overtook them, and he spake unto them these same words.

7 And they said unto him, Wherefore saith my lord these words? God forbid that thy servants should do according to this thing:

8 Behold, [a]the money, which we found in our sacks' mouths, we brought again unto thee out of the land of Canaan: how then should we steal out of thy lord's house silver or gold?

9 With whomsoever of thy servants it be found, [a]both let him die, and we also will be my lord's bondmen.

10 And he said, Now also *let* it *be* according unto your words: he with whom it is found shall be my servant; and ye shall be blameless.

11 Then they speedily took down every man his sack to the ground, and opened every man his sack.

12 And he searched, *and* began at the eldest, and left at the youngest: and the cup was found in Benjamin's sack.

13 Then they [a]rent their clothes, and laded every man his ass, and returned to the city.

14 And Judah and his brethren came to Joseph's house; for he *was* yet there: and they [a]fell before him on the ground.

15 And Joseph said unto them, What deed *is* this that ye have done? wot ye not that such a man as I can certainly divine?

16 And Judah said, What shall we say unto my lord? what shall we speak? or how shall we clear ourselves? God hath [a]found out the iniquity of thy servants: behold, [b]we *are* my lord's servants, both we, and *he* also with whom the cup is found.

17 And he said, [a]God forbid that I should do so: *but* the man in whose hand the cup is found, he shall be my servant; and as for you, get you up in peace unto your father.

30 [a]1 Kin. 3:26 [b]Gen. 42:24; 45:2, 14, 15; 46:29
31 [a]Gen. 43:25
32 [a]Gen. 41:12; Ex. 1:15 [b]Gen. 46:34; Ex. 8:26
33 [a]Gen. 27:36; 42:7; Deut. 21:16, 17
34 [a]Gen. 35:24; 45:22

CHAPTER 44

1 [a]Gen. 43:16 [b]Gen. 42:25
4 [a]1 Sam. 25:21
8 [a]Gen. 43:21
9 [a]Gen. 31:32
13 [a]Gen. 37:29, 34; Num. 14:6; 2 Sam. 1:11
14 [a]Gen. 37:7, 10
16 [a][Num. 32:23] [b]Gen. 44:9
17 [a]Prov. 17:15

NKJV

me?" And he said, "God be gracious to you, my son."

30 Now [a]his heart yearned for his brother; so Joseph made haste and sought *somewhere* to weep. And he went into *his* chamber and [b]wept there.

31 Then he washed his face and came out; and he restrained himself, and said, "Serve the [a]bread."

32 So they set him a place by himself, and them by themselves, and the Egyptians who ate with him by themselves; because the Egyptians could not eat food with the [a]Hebrews, for that *is* [b]an abomination to the Egyptians.

33 And they sat before him, the firstborn according to his [a]birthright and the youngest according to his youth; and the men looked in astonishment at one another.

34 Then he took servings to them from before him, but Benjamin's serving was [a]five times as much as any of theirs. So they drank and were merry with him.

Joseph's Cup

44 And he commanded the [a]steward of his house, saying, [b]"Fill the men's sacks with food, as much as they can carry, and put each man's money in the mouth of his sack.

2 "Also put my cup, the silver cup, in the mouth of the sack of the youngest, and his grain money." So he did according to the word that Joseph had spoken.

3 As soon as the morning dawned, the men were sent away, they and their donkeys.

4 When they had gone out of the city, *and* were not *yet* far off, Joseph said to his steward, "Get up, follow the men; and when you overtake them, say to them, 'Why have you [a]repaid evil for good?

5 '*Is* not this *the one* from which my lord drinks, and with which he indeed practices divination? You have done evil in so doing.' "

6 So he overtook them, and he spoke to them these same words.

7 And they said to him, "Why does my lord say these words? Far be it from us that your servants should do such a thing.

8 "Look, we brought back to you from the land of Canaan [a]the money which we found in the mouth of our sacks. How then could we steal silver or gold from your lord's house?

9 "With whomever of your servants it is found, [a]let him die, and we also will be my lord's slaves."

10 And he said, "Now also *let* it *be* according to your words; he with whom it is found shall be my slave, and you shall be blameless."

11 Then each man speedily let down his sack to the ground, and each opened his sack.

12 So he searched. He began with the oldest and left off with the youngest; and the cup was found in Benjamin's sack.

13 Then they [a]tore their clothes, and each man loaded his donkey and returned to the city.

14 So Judah and his brothers came to Joseph's house, and he *was* still there; and they [a]fell before him on the ground.

15 And Joseph said to them, "What deed *is* this you have done? Did you not know that such a man as I can certainly practice divination?"

16 Then Judah said, "What shall we say to my lord? What shall we speak? Or how shall we clear ourselves? God has [a]found out the iniquity of your servants; here [b]we are, my lord's slaves, both we and *he* also with whom the cup was found."

17 But he said, [a]"Far be it from me that I should do so; the man in whose hand the cup was found, he shall be my slave. And as for you, go up in peace to your father."

KJV

Judah Intercedes for Benjamin

18 Then Judah came near unto him, and said,
Oh my lord, let thy servant, I pray thee, speak a
word in my lord's ears, and [a]let not thine anger
burn against thy servant: for thou *art* even as
Pharaoh.
19 My lord asked his servants, saying, Have
ye a father, or a brother?
20 And we said unto my lord, We have a father, an old man, and [a]a child of his old age, a
little one; and his brother is [b]dead, and he [c]alone
is left of his mother, and his [d]father loveth him.
21 And thou saidst unto thy servants, [a]Bring
him down unto me, that I may set mine eyes upon
him.
22 And we said unto my lord, The lad cannot
leave his father: for *if* he should leave his father,
his father would die.
23 And thou saidst unto thy servants, [a]Ex-
cept your youngest brother come down with you,
ye shall see my face no more.
24 And it came to pass when we came up
unto thy servant my father, we told him the words
of my lord.
25 And [a]our father said, Go again, *and* buy
us a little food.
26 And we said, We cannot go down: if our
youngest brother be with us, then will we go
down: for we may not see the man's face, except
our youngest brother *be* with us.
27 And thy servant my father said unto us,
Ye know that [a]my wife bare me two *sons:*
28 And the one went out from me, and I said,
[a]Surely he is torn in pieces; and I saw him not
since:
29 And if ye [a]take this also from me, and mischief befall him, ye shall bring down my gray
hairs with sorrow to the grave.
30 Now therefore when I come to thy servant
my father, and the lad *be* not with us; seeing that
[a]his life is bound up in the lad's life;
31 It shall come to pass, when he seeth that
the lad *is* not *with us,* that he will die: and thy
servants shall bring down the gray hairs of thy
servant our father with sorrow to the grave.
32 For thy servant became surety for the lad
unto my father, saying, [a]If I bring him not unto
thee, then I shall bear the blame to my father for
ever.
33 Now therefore, I pray thee, [a]let thy servant abide instead of the lad a bondman to my
lord; and let the lad go up with his brethren.
34 For how shall I go up to my father, and
the lad *be* not with me? lest peradventure I see
the evil that shall come on my father.

Joseph Revealed to His Brothers

45 Then Joseph could not refrain himself before all them that stood by him; and he
cried, Cause every man to go out from me. And
there stood no man with him, [a]while Joseph made
himself known unto his brethren.
2 And he [a]wept aloud: and the Egyptians
and the house of Pharaoh heard.
3 And Joseph said unto his brethren, [a]I *am*
Joseph; doth my father yet live? And his brethren
could not answer him; for they were troubled at
his presence.
4 And Joseph said unto his brethren, Come
near to me, I pray you. And they came near. And
he said, I *am* Joseph your brother, [a]whom ye sold
into Egypt.
5 Now therefore be not grieved, nor angry
with yourselves, that ye sold me hither: [a]for God
did send me before you to preserve life.
6 For these two years *hath* the [a]famine *been*
in the land: and yet *there are* five years, in the
which *there shall* neither *be* earing nor harvest.
7 And God [a]sent me before you to preserve
you a posterity in the earth, and to save your lives
by a great deliverance.

18 [a]Gen. 18:30, 32; Ex. 32:22
20 [a]Gen. 37:3; 43:8; 44:30 [b]Gen. 42:38 [c]Gen. 46:19 [d]Gen. 42:4
21 [a]Gen. 42:15, 20
23 [a]Gen. 43:3, 5
25 [a]Gen. 43:2
27 [a]Gen. 30:22–24; 35:16–18; 46:19
28 [a]Gen. 37:31–35
29 [a]Gen. 42:36, 38; 44:31
30 [a][1 Sam. 18:1; 25:29]
32 [a]Gen. 43:9
33 [a]Ex. 32:32

CHAPTER 45

1 [a]Acts 7:13
2 [a]Gen. 43:30; 46:29
3 [a]Gen. 43:27; Acts 7:13
4 [a]Gen. 37:28; 39:1; Ps. 105:17
5 [a]Gen. 45:7, 8; 50:20; Ps. 105:16, 17
6 [a]Gen. 43:1; 47:4, 13
7 [a]Gen. 45:5; 50:20

NKJV

Judah Intercedes for Benjamin

18 Then Judah came near to him and said:
"O my lord, please let your servant speak a word
in my lord's hearing, and [a]do not let your anger
burn against your servant; for you *are* even like
Pharaoh.
19 "My lord asked his servants, saying,
'Have you a father or a brother?'
20 "And we said to my lord, 'We have a father, an old man, and [a]a child of *his* old age, *who*
is young; his brother is [b]dead, and he [c]alone is
left of his mother's children, and his [d]father loves
him.'
21 "Then you said to your servants, [a]'Bring
him down to me, that I may set my eyes on him.'
22 "And we said to my lord, 'The lad cannot
leave his father, for *if* he should leave his father,
his father would die.'
23 "But you said to your servants, [a]'Unless
your youngest brother comes down with you, you
shall see my face no more.'
24 "So it was, when we went up to your servant my father, that we told him the words of
my lord.
25 "And [a]our father said, 'Go back *and* buy
us a little food.'
26 "But we said, 'We cannot go down; if our
youngest brother is with us, then we will go down;
for we may not see the man's face unless our
youngest brother *is* with us.'
27 "Then your servant my father said to us,
'You know that [a]my wife bore me two sons;
28 'and the one went out from me, and I said,
[a]"Surely he is torn to pieces"; and I have not seen
him since.
29 'But if you [a]take this one also from me,
and calamity befalls him, you shall bring down
my gray hair with sorrow to the grave.'
30 "Now therefore, when I come to your servant my father, and the lad *is* not with us, since
[a]his life is bound up in the lad's life,
31 "it will happen, when he sees that the lad
is not *with us,* that he will die. So your servants
will bring down the gray hair of your servant our
father with sorrow to the grave.
32 "For your servant became surety for the
lad to my father, saying, [a]'If I do not bring him
back to you, then I shall bear the blame before
my father forever.'
33 "Now therefore, please [a]let your servant
remain instead of the lad as a slave to my lord,
and let the lad go up with his brothers.
34 "For how shall I go up to my father if the
lad *is* not with me, lest perhaps I see the evil that
would come upon my father?"

Joseph Revealed to His Brothers

45 Then Joseph could not restrain himself before all those who stood by him, and he
cried out, "Make everyone go out from me!" So
no one stood with him [a]while Joseph made himself known to his brothers.
2 And he [a]wept aloud, and the Egyptians
and the house of Pharaoh heard *it.*
3 Then Joseph said to his brothers, [a]"I *am*
Joseph; does my father still live?" But his brothers
could not answer him, for they were dismayed
in his presence.
4 And Joseph said to his brothers, "Please
come near to me." So they came near. Then he
said: "I *am* Joseph your brother, [a]whom you sold
into Egypt.
5 "But now, do not therefore be grieved or
angry with yourselves because you sold me here;
[a]for God sent me before you to preserve life.
6 "For these two years the [a]famine *has been*
in the land, and *there are* still five years in which
there will be neither plowing nor harvesting.
7 "And God [a]sent me before you to preserve
a posterity for you in the earth, and to save your
lives by a great deliverance.

KJV

8 So now *it was* not you *that* sent me hither, but [a]God: and he hath made me [b]a father to Pharaoh, and lord of all his house, and a [c]ruler throughout all the land of Egypt.

9 Haste ye, and go up to my father, and say unto him, Thus saith thy son Joseph, God hath made me lord of all Egypt: come down unto me, tarry not:

10 And [a]thou shalt dwell in the land of Goshen, and thou shalt be near unto me, thou, and thy children, and thy children's children, and thy flocks, and thy herds, and all that thou hast:

11 And there will I [a]nourish thee; for yet *there are* five years of famine; lest thou, and thy household, and all that thou hast, come to poverty.

12 And, behold, your eyes see, and the eyes of my brother Benjamin, that *it is* [a]my mouth that speaketh unto you.

13 And ye shall tell my father of all my glory in Egypt, and of all that ye have seen; and ye shall haste and [a]bring down my father hither.

14 And he fell upon his brother Benjamin's neck, and wept; and Benjamin wept upon his neck.

15 Moreover he [a]kissed all his brethren, and wept upon them: and after that his brethren talked with him.

16 And the fame thereof was heard in Pharaoh's house, saying, Joseph's brethren are come: and it pleased Pharaoh well, and his servants.

17 And Pharaoh said unto Joseph, Say unto thy brethren, This do ye; lade your beasts, and go, get you unto the land of Canaan;

18 And take your father and your households, and come unto me: and I will give you the good of the land of Egypt, and ye shall eat [a]the fat of the land.

19 Now thou art commanded, this do ye; take you wagons out of the land of Egypt for your little ones, and for your wives, and bring your father, and come.

20 Also regard not your stuff; for the good of all the land of Egypt *is* your's.

21 And the children of Israel did so: and Joseph gave them [a]wagons, according to the commandment of Pharaoh, and gave them provision for the way.

22 To all of them he gave each man [a]changes of raiment; but to Benjamin he gave three hundred *pieces* of silver, and [b]five changes of raiment.

23 And to his father he sent after this *manner;* ten asses laden with the good things of Egypt, and ten she asses laden with corn and bread and meat for his father by the way.

24 So he sent his brethren away, and they departed: and he said unto them, See that ye fall not out by the way.

25 And they went up out of Egypt, and came into the land of Canaan unto Jacob their father,

26 And told him, saying, Joseph *is* yet alive, and he *is* governor over all the land of Egypt. [a]And Jacob's heart fainted, for he believed them not.

27 And they told him all the words of Joseph, which he had said unto them: and when he saw the wagons which Joseph had sent to carry him, the spirit [a]of Jacob their father revived:

28 And Israel said, *It is* enough; Joseph my son *is* yet alive: I will go and see him before I die.

Jacob's Journey to Egypt
(Ex. 6:14–25)

46 And Israel took his journey with all that he had, and came to [a]Beer–sheba, and offered sacrifices [b]unto the God of his father Isaac.

2 And God spake unto Israel [a]in the visions of the night, and said, Jacob, Jacob. And he said, Here *am* I.

3 And he said, I *am* God, [a]the God of thy

---

8 [a][Rom. 8:28] [b]Judg. 17:10; Is. 22:21 [c]Gen. 41:43; 42:6
10 [a]Gen. 46:28, 34; 47:1, 6; Ex. 9:26
11 [a]Gen. 47:12
12 [a]Gen. 42:23
13 [a]Gen. 46:6–28; Acts 7:14
15 [a]Gen. 48:10
18 [a]Gen. 27:28; 47:6; Deut. 32:9–14
21 [a]Gen. 45:19; 46:5
22 [a]2 Kin. 5:5 [b]Gen. 43:34
26 [a]Job 29:24; Ps. 126:1; Luke 24:11, 41
27 [a]Judg. 15:19; Is. 40:29

CHAPTER 46

1 [a]Gen. 21:31, 33; 26:32, 33; 28:10 [b]Gen. 26:24, 25; 28:13; 31:42; 32:9
2 [a]Gen. 15:1; 22:11; 31:11; Num. 12:6; Job 33:14, 15
3 [a]Gen. 17:1; 28:13

NKJV

8 "So now *it was* not you *who* sent me here, but [a]God; and He has made me [b]a father to Pharaoh, and lord of all his house, and a [c]ruler throughout all the land of Egypt.

9 "Hurry and go up to my father, and say to him, 'Thus says your son Joseph: "God has made me lord of all Egypt; come down to me, do not tarry.

10 [a]"You shall dwell in the land of Goshen, and you shall be near to me, you and your children, your children's children, your flocks and your herds, and all that you have.

11 "There I will [a]provide for you, lest you and your household, and all that you have, come to poverty; for *there are* still five years of famine." '

12 "And behold, your eyes and the eyes of my brother Benjamin see that *it is* [a]my mouth that speaks to you.

13 "So you shall tell my father of all my glory in Egypt, and of all that you have seen; and you shall hurry and [a]bring my father down here."

14 Then he fell on his brother Benjamin's neck and wept, and Benjamin wept on his neck.

15 Moreover he [a]kissed all his brothers and wept over them, and after that his brothers talked with him.

16 Now the report of it was heard in Pharaoh's house, saying, "Joseph's brothers have come." So it pleased Pharaoh and his servants well.

17 And Pharaoh said to Joseph, "Say to your brothers, 'Do this: Load your animals and depart; go to the land of Canaan.

18 'Bring your father and your households and come to me; I will give you the best of the land of Egypt, and you will eat [a]the fat of the land.

19 'Now you are commanded—do this: Take carts out of the land of Egypt for your little ones and your wives; bring your father and come.

20 'Also do not be concerned about your goods, for the best of all the land of Egypt *is* yours.' "

21 Then the sons of Israel did so; and Joseph gave them [a]carts, according to the command of Pharaoh, and he gave them provisions for the journey.

22 He gave to all of them, to each man, [a]changes of garments; but to Benjamin he gave three hundred *pieces* of silver and [b]five changes of garments.

23 And he sent to his father these *things:* ten donkeys loaded with the good things of Egypt, and ten female donkeys loaded with grain, bread, and food for his father for the journey.

24 So he sent his brothers away, and they departed; and he said to them, "See that you do not become troubled along the way."

25 Then they went up out of Egypt, and came to the land of Canaan to Jacob their father.

26 And they told him, saying, "Joseph *is* still alive, and he *is* governor over all the land of Egypt." [a]And Jacob's heart stood still, because he did not believe them.

27 But when they told him all the words which Joseph had said to them, and when he saw the carts which Joseph had sent to carry him, the spirit [a]of Jacob their father revived.

28 Then Israel said, "*It is* enough. Joseph my son *is* still alive. I will go and see him before I die."

Jacob's Journey to Egypt
(Ex. 6:14–25)

46 So Israel took his journey with all that he had, and came to [a]Beersheba, and offered sacrifices [b]to the God of his father Isaac.

2 Then God spoke to Israel [a]in the visions of the night, and said, "Jacob, Jacob!" And he said, "Here I am."

3 So He said, "I *am* God, [a]the God of your

KJV

father: fear not to go down into Egypt; for I will
there [b]make of thee a great nation:
4 [a]I will go down with thee into Egypt; and
I will also surely [b]bring thee up *again:* and [c]Jo-
seph shall put his hand upon thine eyes.
5 And [a]Jacob rose up from Beer–sheba: and
the sons of Israel carried Jacob their father, and
their little ones, and their wives, in the wagons
[b]which Pharaoh had sent to carry him.
6 And they took their cattle, and their
goods, which they had gotten in the land of Canaan, and came into Egypt, [a]Jacob, and all his
seed with him:
7 His sons, and his sons' sons with him, his
daughters, and his sons' daughters, and all his
seed brought he with him into Egypt.
8 And [a]these *are* the names of the children
of Israel, which came into Egypt, Jacob and his
sons: [b]Reuben, Jacob's firstborn.
9 And the [a]sons of Reuben; Hanoch, and
Phallu, and Hezron, and Carmi.
10 And [a]the sons of Simeon; Jemuel, and Jamin, and Ohad, and Jachin, and Zohar, and Shaul
the son of a Canaanitish woman.
11 And the sons of [a]Levi; Gershon, Kohath,
and Merari.
12 And the sons of [a]Judah; [b]Er, and Onan,
and Shelah, and Pharez, and Zarah: but Er and
Onan died in the land of Canaan. And [c]the sons
of Pharez were Hezron and Hamul.
13 And the sons of Issachar; Tola, and Phu-
vah, and Job, and Shimron.
14 And the [a]sons of Zebulun; Sered, and
Elon, and Jahleel.
15 These *be* the [a]sons of Leah, which she
bare unto Jacob in Padan–aram, with his daughter
Dinah: all the souls of his sons and his daughters
were thirty and three.
16 And the sons of Gad; Ziphion, and Haggi,
Shuni, and Ezbon, Eri, and Arodi, and Areli.
17 [a]And the sons of Asher; Jimnah, and Ishuah, and Isui, and Beriah, and Serah their sister:
and the sons of Beriah; Heber, and Malchiel.
18 [a]These *are* the sons of Zilpah, [b]whom Laban gave to Leah his daughter, and these she bare
unto Jacob, *even* sixteen souls.
19 The [a]sons of Rachel [b]Jacob's wife; Joseph, and Benjamin.
20 [a]And unto Joseph in the land of Egypt
were born Manasseh and Ephraim, which Asenath the daughter of Poti–pherah priest of On bare
unto him.
21 [a]And the sons of Benjamin *were* Belah,
and Becher, and Ashbel, Gera, and Naaman, [b]Ehi,
and Rosh, [c]Muppim, and Huppim, and Ard.
22 These *are* the sons of Rachel, which were
born to Jacob: all the souls *were* fourteen.
23 And the sons of Dan; Hushim.
24 [a]And the sons of Naphtali; Jahzeel, and
Guni, and Jezer, and Shillem.
25 [a]These *are* the sons of Bilhah, [b]which Laban gave unto Rachel his daughter, and she bare
these unto Jacob: all the souls *were* seven.
26 [a]All the souls that came with Jacob into
Egypt, which came out of his loins, [b]besides Jacob's sons' wives, all the souls *were* threescore
and six;
27 And the sons of Joseph, which were born
him in Egypt, *were* two souls: [a]all the souls of
the house of Jacob, which came into Egypt, *were*
threescore and ten.

Jacob Settles in Goshen

28 And he sent Judah before him unto Joseph, [a]to direct his face unto Goshen; and they
came [b]into the land of Goshen.
29 And Joseph made ready his [a]chariot, and
went up to meet Israel his father, to Goshen, and
presented himself unto him; and he [b]fell on his
neck, and wept on his neck a good while.
30 And Israel said unto Joseph, [a]Now let me

3 [a]Deut. 26:5
4 [a]Gen. 28:15; 31:3; 48:21 [b]Gen. 15:16; 50:12, 24, 25 [c]Gen. 50:1
5 [a]Acts 7:15 [b]Gen. 45:19–21
6 [a]Deut. 26:5
8 [a]Ex. 1:1–4 [b]Num. 26:4, 5
9 [a]Ex. 6:14
10 [a]Ex. 6:15
11 [a]1 Chr. 6:1, 16
12 [a]1 Chr. 2:3; 4:21 [b]Gen. 38:3, 7, 10 [c]Gen. 38:29
14 [a]Num. 26:26
15 [a]Gen. 35:23; 49:31
17 [a]1 Chr. 7:30
18 [a]Gen. 30:10; 37:2 [b]Gen. 29:24
19 [a]Gen. 35:24 [b]Gen. 44:27
20 [a]Gen. 41:45, 50–52; 48:1
21 [a]1 Chr. 7:6; 8:1 [b]Num. 26:38 [c]Num. 26:39
24 [a]Num. 26:48
25 [a]Gen. 30:5, 7 [b]Gen. 29:29
26 [a]Ex. 1:5 [b]Gen. 35:11
27 [a]Deut. 10:22
28 [a]Gen. 31:21 [b]Gen. 47:1
29 [a]Gen. 41:43 [b]Gen. 45:14, 15
30 [a]Luke 2:29, 30

*———

46:10 *Nemuel,* 1 Chr. 4:24 • *Jarib,* 1 Chr. 4:24 • *Zerah,* 1 Chr. 4:24
46:13 *Puah,* Num. 26:23; 1 Chr. 7:1 • *Jashub,* Num. 26:24; 1 Chr. 7:1
46:16 Sam., LXX *Zephon* and Num. 26:15 • *Ozni,* Num. 26:16 • *Arod,* Num. 26:17
46:21 *Hupham,* Num. 26:39
46:23 *Shuham,* Num. 26:42
46:24 *Jahziel,* 1 Chr. 7:13 • *Shallum,* 1 Chr. 7:13

NKJV

father; do not fear to go down to Egypt, for I will
[b]make of you a great nation there.
4 [a]"I will go down with you to Egypt, and
I will also surely [b]bring you up *again;* and [c]Joseph
will put his hand on your eyes."
5 Then [a]Jacob arose from Beersheba; and
the sons of Israel carried their father Jacob, their
little ones, and their wives, in the carts [b]which
Pharaoh had sent to carry him.
6 So they took their livestock and their
goods, which they had acquired in the land of Canaan, and went to Egypt, [a]Jacob and all his descendants with him.
7 His sons and his sons' sons, his daughters
and his sons' daughters, and all his descendants
he brought with him to Egypt.
8 Now [a]these *were* the names of the children of Israel, Jacob and his sons, who went to
Egypt: [b]Reuben *was* Jacob's firstborn.
9 The [a]sons of Reuben *were* Hanoch, Pallu,
Hezron, and Carmi.
10 [a]The sons of Simeon *were* *Jemuel, Jamin,
Ohad, *Jachin, *Zohar, and Shaul, the son of a
Canaanite woman.
11 The sons of [a]Levi *were* Gershon, Kohath,
and Merari.
12 The sons of [a]Judah *were* [b]Er, Onan, Shelah, Perez, and Zerah (but Er and Onan died in
the land of Canaan). [c]The sons of Perez were
Hezron and Hamul.
13 The sons of Issachar *were* Tola, *Puvah,
*Job, and Shimron.
14 The [a]sons of Zebulun *were* Sered, Elon,
and Jahleel.
15 These *were* the [a]sons of Leah, whom she
bore to Jacob in Padan Aram, with his daughter
Dinah. All the persons, his sons and his daughters, *were* thirty-three.
16 The sons of Gad *were* *Ziphion, Haggi,
Shuni, *Ezbon, Eri, *Arodi, and Areli.
17 [a]The sons of Asher *were* Jimnah, Ishuah,
Isui, Beriah, and Serah, their sister. And the sons
of Beriah *were* Heber and Malchiel.
18 [a]These *were* the sons of Zilpah, [b]whom
Laban gave to Leah his daughter; and these she
bore to Jacob: sixteen persons.
19 The [a]sons of Rachel, [b]Jacob's wife, *were*
Joseph and Benjamin.
20 [a]And to Joseph in the land of Egypt were
born Manasseh and Ephraim, whom Asenath, the
daughter of Poti-Pherah priest of On, bore to him.
21 [a]The sons of Benjamin *were* Belah,
Becher, Ashbel, Gera, Naaman, [b]Ehi, Rosh,
[c]Muppim, *Huppim, and Ard.
22 These *were* the sons of Rachel, who were
born to Jacob: fourteen persons in all.
23 The son of Dan *was* *Hushim.
24 [a]The sons of Naphtali *were* *Jahzeel,
Guni, Jezer, and *Shillem.
25 [a]These *were* the sons of Bilhah, [b]whom
Laban gave to Rachel his daughter, and she bore
these to Jacob: seven persons in all.
26 [a]All the persons who went with Jacob to
Egypt, who came from his body, [b]besides Jacob's
sons' wives, *were* sixty-six persons in all.
27 And the sons of Joseph who were born
to him in Egypt *were* two persons. [a]All the persons of the house of Jacob who went to Egypt
were seventy.

Jacob Settles in Goshen

28 Then he sent Judah before him to Joseph,
[a]to point out before him *the way* to Goshen. And
they came [b]to the land of Goshen.
29 So Joseph made ready his [a]chariot and
went up to Goshen to meet his father Israel; and
he presented himself to him, and [b]fell on his neck
and wept on his neck a good while.
30 And Israel said to Joseph, [a]"Now let me

KJV

die, since I have seen thy face, because thou *art* yet alive.

31 And Joseph said unto his brethren, and unto his father's house, [a]I will go up, and shew Pharaoh, and say unto him, My brethren, and my father's house, which *were* in the land of Canaan, are come unto me;

32 And the men *are* [a]shepherds, for their trade hath been to feed cattle; and they have brought their flocks, and their herds, and all that they have.

33 And it shall come to pass, when Pharaoh shall call you, and shall say, [a]What *is* your occupation?

34 That ye shall say, Thy servants' [a]trade hath been about cattle [b]from our youth even until now, both we, *and* also our fathers: that ye may dwell in the land of Goshen; for every shepherd *is* [c]an abomination unto the Egyptians.

47 Then Joseph [a]came and told Pharaoh, and said, My father and my brethren, and their flocks, and their herds, and all that they have, are come out of the land of Canaan; and, behold, they *are* in [b]the land of Goshen.

2 And he took some of his brethren, *even* five men, and [a]presented them unto Pharaoh.

3 And Pharaoh said unto his brethren, [a]What *is* your occupation? And they said unto Pharaoh, [b]Thy servants *are* shepherds, both we, *and* also our fathers.

4 They said moreover unto Pharaoh, [a]For to sojourn in the land are we come; for thy servants have no pasture for their flocks; [b]for the famine *is* sore in the land of Canaan: now therefore, we pray thee, let thy servants [c]dwell in the land of Goshen.

5 And Pharaoh spake unto Joseph, saying, Thy father and thy brethren are come unto thee:

6 [a]The land of Egypt *is* before thee; in the best of the land make thy father and brethren to dwell; [b]in the land of Goshen let them dwell: and if thou knowest *any* men of activity among them, then make them rulers over my cattle.

7 And Joseph brought in Jacob his father, and set him before Pharaoh: and Jacob [a]blessed Pharaoh.

8 And Pharaoh said unto Jacob, How old *art* thou?

9 And Jacob said unto Pharaoh, [a]The days of the years of my pilgrimage *are* an [b]hundred and thirty years: [c]few and evil have the days of the years of my life been, and [d]have not attained unto the days of the years of the life of my fathers in the days of their pilgrimage.

10 And Jacob [a]blessed Pharaoh, and went out from before Pharaoh.

11 And Joseph placed his father and his brethren, and gave them a possession in the land of Egypt, in the best of the land, in the land of [a]Rameses, [b]as Pharaoh had commanded.

12 And Joseph nourished [a]his father, and his brethren, and all his father's household, with bread, according to *their* families.

Joseph Deals with the Famine

13 And *there was* no bread in all the land; for the famine *was* very sore, [a]so that the land of Egypt and *all* the land of Canaan fainted by reason of the famine.

14 [a]And Joseph gathered up all the money that was found in the land of Egypt, and in the land of Canaan, for the corn which they bought: and Joseph brought the money into Pharaoh's house.

15 And when money failed in the land of Egypt, and in the land of Canaan, all the Egyptians came unto Joseph, and said, Give us bread: for [a]why should we die in thy presence? for the money faileth.

31 [a]Gen. 47:1
32 [a]Gen. 47:3
33 [a]Gen. 47:2, 3
34 [a]Gen. 47:3 [b]Gen. 30:35; 34:5; 37:17 [c]Gen. 43:32; Ex. 8:26

CHAPTER 47

1 [a]Gen. 46:31 [b]Gen. 45:10; 46:28; 50:8
2 [a]Acts 7:13
3 [a]Gen. 46:33; Jon. 1:8 [b]Gen. 46:32, 34; Ex. 2:17, 19
4 [a]Gen. 15:13; Deut. 26:5; Ps. 105:23 [b]Gen. 43:1; Acts 7:11 [c]Gen. 46:34
6 [a]Gen. 20:15; 45:10, 18; 47:11 [b]Gen. 47:4
7 [a]Gen. 47:10; 48:15, 20; 2 Sam. 14:22; 1 Kin. 8:66; Heb. 7:7
9 [a]Ps. 39:12; [Heb. 11:9, 13] [b]Gen. 47:28 [c][Job 14:1] [d]Gen. 5:5; 11:10, 11; 25:7, 8; 35:28
10 [a]Gen. 47:7
11 [a]Ex. 1:11; 12:37 [b]Gen. 47:6, 27
12 [a]Gen. 45:11; 50:21
13 [a]Gen. 41:30; Acts 7:11
14 [a]Gen. 41:56; 42:6
15 [a]Gen. 47:19

NKJV

die, since I have seen your face, because you *are* still alive."

31 Then Joseph said to his brothers and to his father's household, [a]"I will go up and tell Pharaoh, and say to him, 'My brothers and those of my father's house, who *were* in the land of Canaan, have come to me.

32 'And the men *are* [a]shepherds, for their occupation has been to feed livestock; and they have brought their flocks, their herds, and all that they have.'

33 "So it shall be, when Pharaoh calls you and says, [a]'What is your occupation?'

34 "that you shall say, 'Your servants' [a]occupation has been with livestock [b]from our youth even till now, both we *and* also our fathers,' that you may dwell in the land of Goshen; for every shepherd *is* [c]an abomination to the Egyptians."

47 Then Joseph [a]went and told Pharaoh, and said, "My father and my brothers, their flocks and their herds and all that they possess, have come from the land of Canaan; and indeed they *are* in [b]the land of Goshen."

2 And he took five men from among his brothers and [a]presented them to Pharaoh.

3 Then Pharaoh said to his brothers, [a]"What *is* your occupation?" And they said to Pharaoh, [b]"Your servants *are* shepherds, both we *and* also our fathers."

4 And they said to Pharaoh, [a]"We have come to dwell in the land, because your servants have no pasture for their flocks, [b]for the famine *is* severe in the land of Canaan. Now therefore, please let your servants [c]dwell in the land of Goshen."

5 Then Pharaoh spoke to Joseph, saying, "Your father and your brothers have come to you.

6 [a]"The land of Egypt *is* before you. Have your father and brothers dwell in the best of the land; let them dwell [b]in the land of Goshen. And if you know *any* competent men among them, then make them chief herdsmen over my livestock."

7 Then Joseph brought in his father Jacob and set him before Pharaoh; and Jacob [a]blessed Pharaoh.

8 Pharaoh said to Jacob, "How old *are* you?"

9 And Jacob said to Pharaoh, [a]"The days of the years of my pilgrimage *are* [b]one hundred and thirty years; [c]few and evil have been the days of the years of my life, and [d]they have not attained to the days of the years of the life of my fathers in the days of their pilgrimage."

10 So Jacob [a]blessed Pharaoh, and went out from before Pharaoh.

11 And Joseph situated his father and his brothers, and gave them a possession in the land of Egypt, in the best of the land, in the land of [a]Rameses, [b]as Pharaoh had commanded.

12 Then Joseph provided [a]his father, his brothers, and all his father's household with bread, according to the number in *their* families.

Joseph Deals with the Famine

13 Now *there was* no bread in all the land; for the famine *was* very severe, [a]so that the land of Egypt and the land of Canaan languished because of the famine.

14 [a]And Joseph gathered up all the money that was found in the land of Egypt and in the land of Canaan, for the grain which they bought; and Joseph brought the money into Pharaoh's house.

15 So when the money failed in the land of Egypt and in the land of Canaan, all the Egyptians came to Joseph and said, "Give us bread, for [a]why should we die in your presence? For the money has failed."

KJV

16 And Joseph said, Give your cattle; and I will give you for your cattle, if money fail.

17 And they brought their cattle unto Joseph: and Joseph gave them bread *in exchange* for horses, and for the flocks, and for the cattle of the herds, and for the asses: and he fed them with bread for all their cattle for that year.

18 When that year was ended, they came unto him the second year, and said unto him, We will not hide *it* from my lord, how that our money is spent; my lord also hath our herds of cattle; there is not ought left in the sight of my lord, but our bodies, and our lands:

19 Wherefore shall we die before thine eyes, both we and our land? buy us and our land for bread, and we and our land will be servants unto Pharaoh: and give *us* seed, that we may [a]live, and not die, that the land be not desolate.

20 And Joseph [a]bought all the land of Egypt for Pharaoh; for the Egyptians sold every man his field, because the famine prevailed over them: so the land became Pharaoh's.

21 And as for the people, he removed them to cities from *one* end of the borders of Egypt even to the *other* end thereof.

22 [a]Only the land of the [b]priests bought he not; for the priests had a portion *assigned them* of Pharaoh, and did eat their portion which Pharaoh gave them: wherefore they sold not their lands.

23 Then Joseph said unto the people, Behold, I have bought you this day and your land for Pharaoh: lo, *here is* seed for you, and ye shall sow the land.

24 And it shall come to pass in the increase, that ye shall give the fifth *part* unto Pharaoh, and four parts shall be your own, for seed of the field, and for your food, and for them of your households, and for food for your little ones.

25 And they said, Thou hast saved [a]our lives: let us find grace in the sight of my lord, and we will be Pharaoh's servants.

26 And Joseph made it a law over the land of Egypt unto this day, *that* Pharaoh should have the fifth *part;* [a]except the land of the priests only, *which* became not Pharaoh's.

Joseph's Vow to Jacob

27 And Israel [a]dwelt in the land of Egypt, in the country of Goshen; and they had possessions therein, and [b]grew, and multiplied exceedingly.

28 And Jacob lived in the land of Egypt seventeen years: so the whole age of Jacob was an hundred forty and seven years.

29 And the time [a]drew nigh that Israel must die: and he called his son Joseph, and said unto him, If now I have found grace in thy sight, [b]put, I pray thee, thy hand under my thigh, and [c]deal kindly and truly with me; [d]bury me not, I pray thee, in Egypt:

30 But [a]I will lie with my fathers, and thou shalt carry me out of Egypt, and [b]bury me in their buryingplace. And he said, I will do as thou hast said.

31 And he said, Swear unto me. And he sware unto him. And [a]Israel bowed himself upon the bed's head.

Jacob Blesses Joseph's Sons
(Heb. 11:21)

48 And it came to pass after these things, that *one* told Joseph, Behold, thy father *is* sick: and he took with him his two sons, [a]Manasseh and Ephraim.

2 And *one* told Jacob, and said, Behold, thy son Joseph cometh unto thee: and Israel strengthened himself, and sat upon the bed.

3 And Jacob said unto Joseph, God [a]Almighty appeared unto me at [b]Luz in the land of Canaan, and blessed me,

19 [a]Gen. 43:8
20 [a]Jer. 32:43
22 [a]Lev. 25:34; Ezra 7:24 [b]Gen. 41:45
25 [a]Gen. 33:15
26 [a]Gen. 47:22
27 [a]Gen. 47:11 [b]Gen. 17:6; 26:4; 35:11; 46:3; Ex. 1:7; Deut. 26:5; Acts 7:17
29 [a]Deut. 31:14; 1 Kin. 2:1 [b]Gen. 24:2–4 [c]Gen. 24:49; Josh. 2:14 [d]Gen. 50:25
30 [a]2 Sam. 19:37 [b]Gen. 49:29; 50:5–13; Heb. 11:21
31 [a]Gen. 48:2; 1 Kin. 1:47; Heb. 11:21

CHAPTER 48

1 [a]Gen. 41:51, 56; 46:20; 50:23; Josh. 14:4
3 [a]Gen. 43:14; 49:25 [b]Gen. 28:13, 19; 35:6, 9

*

47:21 So with MT, Tg.; Sam., LXX, Vg. *made the people virtual slaves*

NKJV

16 Then Joseph said, "Give your livestock, and I will give you *bread* for your livestock, if the money is gone."

17 So they brought their livestock to Joseph, and Joseph gave them bread *in exchange* for the horses, the flocks, the cattle of the herds, and for the donkeys. Thus he fed them with bread *in exchange* for all their livestock that year.

18 When that year had ended, they came to him the next year and said to him, "We will not hide from my lord that our money is gone; my lord also has our herds of livestock. There is nothing left in the sight of my lord but our bodies and our lands.

19 "Why should we die before your eyes, both we and our land? Buy us and our land for bread, and we and our land will be servants of Pharaoh; give *us* seed, that we may [a]live and not die, that the land may not be desolate."

20 Then Joseph [a]bought all the land of Egypt for Pharaoh; for every man of the Egyptians sold his field, because the famine was severe upon them. So the land became Pharaoh's.

21 And as for the people, he *moved them into the cities, from *one* end of the borders of Egypt to the *other* end.

22 [a]Only the land of the [b]priests he did not buy; for the priests had rations *allotted to them* by Pharaoh, and they ate their rations which Pharaoh gave them; therefore they did not sell their lands.

23 Then Joseph said to the people, "Indeed I have bought you and your land this day for Pharaoh. Look, *here is* seed for you, and you shall sow the land.

24 "And it shall come to pass in the harvest that you shall give one-fifth to Pharaoh. Four-fifths shall be your own, as seed for the field and for your food, for those of your households and as food for your little ones."

25 So they said, "You have saved [a]our lives; let us find favor in the sight of my lord, and we will be Pharaoh's servants."

26 And Joseph made it a law over the land of Egypt to this day, *that* Pharaoh should have one-fifth, [a]except for the land of the priests only, *which* did not become Pharaoh's.

Joseph's Vow to Jacob

27 So Israel [a]dwelt in the land of Egypt, in the country of Goshen; and they had possessions there and [b]grew and multiplied exceedingly.

28 And Jacob lived in the land of Egypt seventeen years. So the length of Jacob's life was one hundred and forty-seven years.

29 When the time [a]drew near that Israel must die, he called his son Joseph and said to him, "Now if I have found favor in your sight, please [b]put your hand under my thigh, and [c]deal kindly and truly with me. [d]Please do not bury me in Egypt,

30 "but [a]let me lie with my fathers; you shall carry me out of Egypt and [b]bury me in their burial place." And he said, "I will do as you have said."

31 Then he said, "Swear to me." And he swore to him. So [a]Israel bowed himself on the head of the bed.

Jacob Blesses Joseph's Sons
(Heb. 11:21)

48 Now it came to pass after these things that Joseph was told, "Indeed your father *is* sick"; and he took with him his two sons, [a]Manasseh and Ephraim.

2 And Jacob was told, "Look, your son Joseph is coming to you"; and Israel strengthened himself and sat up on the bed.

3 Then Jacob said to Joseph: "God [a]Almighty appeared to me at [b]Luz in the land of Canaan and blessed me,

KJV

4 And said unto me, Behold, I will [a]make thee fruitful, and multiply thee, and I will make of thee a multitude of people; and will [b]give this land to thy seed after thee [c]*for* an everlasting possession.

5 And now thy [a]two sons, Ephraim and Manasseh, which were born unto thee in the land of Egypt before I came unto thee into Egypt, *are* mine; as Reuben and Simeon, they shall be mine.

6 And thy issue, which thou begettest after them, shall be thine, *and* shall be called after the name of their brethren in their inheritance.

7 And as for me, when I came from Padan, [a]Rachel died by me in the land of Canaan in the way, when yet *there was* but a little way to come unto Ephrath: and I buried her there in the way of Ephrath; the same *is* Beth–lehem.

8 And Israel beheld Joseph's sons, and said, Who *are* these?

9 And Joseph said unto his father, They *are* my sons, whom God hath given me in this *place*. And he said, Bring them, I pray thee, unto me, and [a]I will bless them.

10 Now [a]the eyes of Israel were dim for age, *so that* he could not see. And he brought them near unto him; and he [b]kissed them, and embraced them.

11 And Israel said unto Joseph, [a]I had not thought to see thy face: and, lo, God hath shewed me also thy seed.

12 And Joseph brought them out from between his knees, and he bowed himself with his face to the earth.

13 And Joseph took them both, Ephraim in his right hand toward Israel's left hand, and Manasseh in his left hand toward Israel's right hand, and brought *them* near unto him.

14 And Israel stretched out his right hand, and [a]laid *it* upon Ephraim's head, who *was* the younger, and his left hand upon Manasseh's head, [b]guiding his hands wittingly; for Manasseh *was* the [c]firstborn.

15 And [a]he blessed Joseph, and said, God, [b]before whom my fathers Abraham and Isaac did walk, the God which fed me all my life long unto this day,

16 The Angel [a]which redeemed me from all evil, bless the lads; and let [b]my name be named on them, and the name of my fathers Abraham and Isaac; and let them [c]grow into a multitude in the midst of the earth.

17 And when Joseph saw that his father [a]laid his right hand upon the head of Ephraim, it displeased him: and he held up his father's hand, to remove it from Ephraim's head unto Manasseh's head.

18 And Joseph said unto his father, Not so, my father: for this *is* the firstborn; put thy right hand upon his head.

19 And his father refused, and said, [a]I know *it*, my son, I know *it:* he also shall become a people, and he also shall be great: but truly [b]his younger brother shall be greater than he, and his seed shall become a multitude of nations.

20 And he blessed them that day, saying, [a]In thee shall Israel bless, saying, God make thee as Ephraim and as Manasseh: and he set Ephraim before Manasseh.

21 And Israel said unto Joseph, Behold, I die: but [a]God shall be with you, and bring you again unto the land of your fathers.

22 Moreover [a]I have given to thee one portion above thy brethren, which I took out of the hand [b]of the Amorite with my sword and with my bow.

4 [a]Gen. 46:3 [b]Gen. 35:12; Ex. 6:8 [c]Gen. 17:8
5 [a]Gen. 41:50; 46:20; 48:8; Josh. 13:7; 14:4
7 [a]Gen. 35:9, 16, 19, 20
9 [a]Gen. 27:4; 47:15
10 [a]Gen. 27:1; 1 Sam. 3:2 [b]Gen. 27:27; 45:15; 50:1
11 [a]Gen. 45:26
14 [a]Matt. 19:15; Mark 10:16 [b]Gen. 48:19 [c]Gen. 41:51, 52; Josh. 17:1
15 [a]Gen. 47:7, 10; 49:24; [Heb. 11:21] [b]Gen. 17:1; 24:40; 2 Kin. 20:3
16 [a]Gen. 22:11, 15–18; 28:13–15; 31:11; [Ps. 34:22; 121:7] [b]Amos 9:12; Acts 15:17 [c]Num. 26:34, 37
17 [a]Gen. 48:14
19 [a]Gen. 48:14 [b]Num. 1:33, 35; Deut. 33:17
20 [a]Ruth 4:11, 12
21 [a]Gen. 28:15; 46:4; 50:24
22 [a]Gen. 14:7; Josh. 24:32; John 4:5 [b]Gen. 34:28

NKJV

4 "and said to me, 'Behold, I will [a]make you fruitful and multiply you, and I will make of you a multitude of people, and [b]give this land to your descendants after you [c]*as* an everlasting possession.'

5 "And now your [a]two sons, Ephraim and Manasseh, who were born to you in the land of Egypt before I came to you in Egypt, *are* mine; as Reuben and Simeon, they shall be mine.

6 "Your offspring whom you beget after them shall be yours; they will be called by the name of their brothers in their inheritance.

7 "But as for me, when I came from Padan, [a]Rachel died beside me in the land of Canaan on the way, when *there was* but a little distance to go to Ephrath; and I buried her there on the way to Ephrath (that is, Bethlehem)."

8 Then Israel saw Joseph's sons, and said, "Who *are* these?"

9 And Joseph said to his father, "They *are* my sons, whom God has given me in this *place*." And he said, "Please bring them to me, and [a]I will bless them."

10 Now [a]the eyes of Israel were dim with age, *so that* he could not see. Then Joseph brought them near him, and he [b]kissed them and embraced them.

11 And Israel said to Joseph, [a]"I had not thought to see your face; but in fact, God has also shown me your offspring!"

12 So Joseph brought them from beside his knees, and he bowed down with his face to the earth.

13 And Joseph took them both, Ephraim with his right hand toward Israel's left hand, and Manasseh with his left hand toward Israel's right hand, and brought *them* near him.

14 Then Israel stretched out his right hand and [a]laid *it* on Ephraim's head, who *was* the younger, and his left hand on Manasseh's head, [b]guiding his hands knowingly, for Manasseh *was* the [c]firstborn.

15 And [a]he blessed Joseph, and said:

"God, [b]before whom my fathers Abraham
and Isaac walked,
The God who has fed me all my life long
to this day,

16 The Angel [a]who has redeemed me from
all evil,
Bless the lads;
Let [b]my name be named upon them,
And the name of my fathers Abraham and
Isaac;
And let them [c]grow into a multitude in
the midst of the earth."

17 Now when Joseph saw that his father [a]laid his right hand on the head of Ephraim, it displeased him; so he took hold of his father's hand to remove it from Ephraim's head to Manasseh's head.

18 And Joseph said to his father, "Not so, my father, for this *one is* the firstborn; put your right hand on his head."

19 But his father refused and said, [a]"I know, my son, I know. He also shall become a people, and he also shall be great; but truly [b]his younger brother shall be greater than he, and his descendants shall become a multitude of nations."

20 So he blessed them that day, saying, [a]"By you Israel will bless, saying, 'May God make you as Ephraim and as Manasseh!' " And thus he set Ephraim before Manasseh.

21 Then Israel said to Joseph, "Behold, I am dying, but [a]God will be with you and bring you back to the land of your fathers.

22 "Moreover [a]I have given to you one portion above your brothers, which I took from the hand [b]of the Amorite with my sword and my bow."

KJV

Jacob's Last Words to His Sons

49 And Jacob called unto his sons, and said, Gather yourselves together, that I may [a]tell you *that* which shall befall you [b]in the last days.

2 Gather yourselves together, and hear, ye sons of Jacob; and hearken unto Israel your father.

3 Reuben, thou *art* [a]my firstborn, my might, and the beginning of my strength, the excellency of dignity, and the excellency of power:

4 Unstable as water, thou shalt not excel; because thou [a]wentest up to thy father's bed; then defiledst thou *it:* he went up to my couch.

5 Simeon and Levi *are* brethren; instruments of cruelty *are in* their habitations.

6 O my soul, [a]come not thou into their secret; [b]unto their assembly, mine honour, be not thou united: [c]for in their anger they slew a man, and in their selfwill they digged down a wall.

7 Cursed *be* their anger, for *it was* fierce; and their wrath, for it was cruel: [a]I will divide them in Jacob, and scatter them in Israel.

8 [a]Judah, thou *art he* whom thy brethren shall praise: [b]thy hand *shall be* in the neck of thine enemies; [c]thy father's children shall bow down before thee.

9 Judah *is* [a]a lion's whelp: from the prey, my son, thou art gone up: [b]he stooped down, he couched as a lion, and as an old lion; who shall rouse him up?

10 [a]The sceptre shall not depart from Judah, nor [b]a lawgiver from between his feet, [c]until Shiloh come; [d]and unto him *shall* the gathering of the people *be.*

11 Binding his foal unto the vine, and his ass's colt unto the choice vine; he washed his garments in wine, and his clothes in the blood of grapes:

12 His eyes *shall be* red with wine, and his teeth white with milk.

13 [a]Zebulun shall dwell at the haven of the sea; and he *shall be* for an haven of ships; and his border *shall be* unto [b]Zidon.

14 [a]Issachar *is* a strong ass couching down between two burdens:

15 And he saw that rest *was* good, and the land that *it was* pleasant; and bowed [a]his shoulder to bear, and became a servant unto tribute.

16 [a]Dan shall judge his people, as one of the tribes of Israel.

17 [a]Dan shall be a serpent by the way, an adder in the path, that biteth the horse heels, so that his rider shall fall backward.

18 [a]I have waited for thy salvation, O LORD.

19 [a]Gad, a troop shall overcome him: but he shall overcome at the last.

20 [a]Out of Asher his bread *shall be* fat, and he shall yield royal dainties.

21 [a]Naphtali *is* a hind let loose: he giveth goodly words.

CHAPTER 49

1 [a]Deut. 33:1, 6–25; [Amos 3:7] [b]Num. 24:14; [Deut. 4:30]; Is. 2:2; 39:6; Jer. 23:20; Heb. 1:2
3 [a]Gen. 29:32
4 [a]Gen. 35:22; Deut. 27:20; 1 Chr. 5:1
6 [a]Ps. 64:2; Prov. 1:15, 16 [b]Ps. 26:9; Eph. 5:11 [c]Gen. 34:26
7 [a]Num. 18:24; Josh. 19:1, 9; 21:1–42; 1 Chr. 4:24–27
8 [a]Deut. 33:7; Rev. 5:5 [b]Ps. 18:40 [c]Gen. 27:29; 1 Chr. 5:2
9 [a]Deut. 33:22; Ezek. 19:5–7; Mic. 5:8; [Rev. 5:5] [b]Num. 23:24; 24:9
10 [a]Num. 24:17; Jer. 30:21; Matt. 1:3; 2:6; Luke 3:33; Rev. 5:5 [b]Ps. 60:7 [c]Is. 11:1; [Matt. 21:9] [d]Deut. 18:15; Ps. 2:6–9; 72:8–11; Is. 42:1, 4; 49:6; 60:1–5; [Luke 2:30–32]
13 [a]Deut. 33:18, 19; Josh. 19:10, 11 [b]Gen. 10:19; Josh. 11:8
14 [a]1 Chr. 12:32
15 [a]1 Sam. 10:9
16 [a]Gen. 30:6; Deut. 33:22; Judg. 18:26, 27
17 [a]Judg. 18:27
18 [a]Ex. 15:2; Ps. 25:5; 40:1–3; 119:166, 174; Is. 25:9; Mic. 7:7
19 [a]Gen. 30:11; Deut. 33:20; 1 Chr. 5:18
20 [a]Deut. 33:24; Josh. 19:24–31
21 [a]Deut. 33:23

NKJV

Jacob's Last Words to His Sons

49 And Jacob called his sons and said, "Gather together, that I may [a]tell you what shall befall you [b]in the last days:

2 "Gather together and hear, you sons of Jacob,
And listen to Israel your father.

3 "Reuben, you are [a]my firstborn,
My might and the beginning of my strength,
The excellency of dignity and the excellency of power.
4 Unstable as water, you shall not excel,
Because you [a]went up to your father's bed;
Then you defiled *it*—
He went up to my couch.

5 "Simeon and Levi *are* brothers;
Instruments of cruelty *are in* their dwelling place.
6 [a]Let not my soul enter their council;
Let not my honor be united [b]to their assembly;
[c]For in their anger they slew a man,
And in their self-will they hamstrung an ox.
7 Cursed *be* their anger, for *it is* fierce;
And their wrath, for it is cruel!
[a]I will divide them in Jacob
And scatter them in Israel.

8 "Judah,[a] you *are he* whom your brothers shall praise;
[b]Your hand *shall be* on the neck of your enemies;
[c]Your father's children shall bow down before you.
9 Judah *is* [a]a lion's whelp;
From the prey, my son, you have gone up.
[b]He bows down, he lies down as a lion;
And as a lion, who shall rouse him?
10 [a]The scepter shall not depart from Judah,
Nor [b]a lawgiver from between his feet,
[c]Until Shiloh comes;
[d]And to Him *shall be* the obedience of the people.
11 Binding his donkey to the vine,
And his donkey's colt to the choice vine,
He washed his garments in wine,
And his clothes in the blood of grapes.
12 His eyes *are* darker than wine,
And his teeth whiter than milk.

13 "Zebulun[a] shall dwell by the haven of the sea;
He *shall become* a haven for ships,
And his border shall [b]adjoin Sidon.

14 "Issachar[a] is a strong donkey,
Lying down between two burdens;
15 He saw that rest *was* good,
And that the land *was* pleasant;
He bowed [a]his shoulder to bear *a burden,*
And became a band of slaves.

16 "Dan[a] shall judge his people
As one of the tribes of Israel.
17 [a]Dan shall be a serpent by the way,
A viper by the path,
That bites the horse's heels
So that its rider shall fall backward.
18 [a]I have waited for your salvation, O LORD!

19 "Gad,[a] a troop shall tramp upon him,
But he shall triumph at last.

20 "Bread from [a]Asher *shall be* rich,
And he shall yield royal dainties.

21 "Naphtali[a] *is* a deer let loose;
He uses beautiful words.

KJV

22 Joseph *is* a fruitful bough, *even* a fruitful
bough by a well; *whose* branches run over the
wall:
23 The archers have [a]sorely grieved him, and
shot *at him,* and hated him:
24 But his [a]bow abode in strength, and the
arms of his hands were made strong by the hands
of [b]the mighty *God* of Jacob; [c](from thence [d]*is*
the shepherd, [e]the stone of Israel:)
25 [a]*Even* by the God of thy father, who shall
help thee; [b]and by the Almighty, [c]who shall bless
thee with blessings of heaven above, blessings of
the deep that lieth under, blessings of the breasts,
and of the womb:
26 The blessings of thy father have prevailed
above the blessings of my progenitors [a]unto the
utmost bound of the everlasting hills: [b]they shall
be on the head of Joseph, and on the crown of
the head of him that was separate from his
brethren.
27 Benjamin shall [a]ravin *as* a wolf: in the
morning he shall devour the prey, [b]and at night
he shall divide the spoil.
28 All these *are* the twelve tribes of Israel:
and this *is it* that their father spake unto them,
and blessed them; every one according to his
blessing he blessed them.

Jacob's Death and Burial

29 And he charged them, and said unto them,
I [a]am to be gathered unto my people: [b]bury me
with my fathers [c]in the cave that *is* in the field
of Ephron the Hittite,
30 In the cave that *is* in the field of Machpelah, which *is* before Mamre, in the land of Canaan,
[a]which Abraham bought with the field of Ephron
the Hittite for a possession of a buryingplace.
31 [a]There they buried Abraham and Sarah
his wife; [b]there they buried Isaac and Rebekah
his wife; and there I buried Leah.
32 The purchase of the field and of the cave
that *is* therein *was* from the children of Heth.
33 And when Jacob had made an end of commanding his sons, he gathered up his feet into
the bed, and yielded up the ghost, and was gathered unto his people.

50 And Joseph [a]fell upon his father's face, and
[b]wept upon him, and kissed him.
2 And Joseph commanded his servants the
physicians to [a]embalm his father: and the physicians embalmed Israel.
3 And forty days were fulfilled for him; for
so are fulfilled the days of those which are embalmed: and the Egyptians [a]mourned for him
threescore and ten days.
4 And when the days of his mourning were
past, Joseph spake unto [a]the house of Pharaoh,
saying, If now I have found grace in your eyes,
speak, I pray you, in the ears of Pharaoh, saying,
5 [a]My father made me swear, saying, Lo, I
die: in my grave [b]which I have digged for me in
the land of Canaan, there shalt thou bury me. Now
therefore let me go up, I pray thee, and bury my
father, and I will come again.
6 And Pharaoh said, Go up, and bury thy
father, according as he made thee swear.
7 And Joseph went up to bury his father:
and with him went up all the servants of Pharaoh,
the elders of his house, and all the elders of the
land of Egypt,
8 And all the house of Joseph, and his brethren, and his father's house: only their little ones,

23 [a]Gen. 37:4, 24; Ps. 118:13
24 [a]Job 29:20; Ps. 37:15 [b]Ps. 132:2, 5; Is. 1:24; 49:26 [c]Gen. 45:11; 47:12 [d][Ps. 23:1; 80:1] [e][Ps. 118:22]; Is. 28:16; [1 Pet. 2:6–8]
25 [a]Gen. 28:13; 32:9; 35:3; 43:23; 50:17 [b]Gen. 17:1; 35:11 [c]Deut. 33:13
26 [a]Deut. 33:15; Hab. 3:6 [b]Deut. 33:16
27 [a]Judg. 20:21, 25 [b]Num. 23:24; Esth. 8:11; Ezek. 39:10; Zech. 14:1
29 [a]Gen. 15:15; 25:8; 35:29 [b]Gen. 47:30; 2 Sam. 19:37 [c]Gen. 23:16–20; 50:13
30 [a]Gen. 23:3–20
31 [a]Gen. 23:19, 20; 25:9 [b]Gen. 35:29; 50:13

CHAPTER 50

1 [a]Gen. 46:4, 29 [b]2 Kin. 13:14
2 [a]Gen. 50:26; 2 Chr. 16:14; Matt. 26:12; Mark 16:1; Luke 24:1; John 19:39, 40
3 [a]Gen. 37:34; Num. 20:29; Deut. 34:8
4 [a]Esth. 4:2
5 [a]Gen. 47:29–31 [b]2 Chr. 16:14; Is. 22:16; Matt. 27:60

NKJV

22 "Joseph *is* a fruitful bough,
A fruitful bough by a well;
His branches run over the wall.
23 The archers have [a]bitterly grieved him,
Shot *at him* and hated him.
24 But his [a]bow remained in strength,
And the arms of his hands were made
strong
By the hands of [b]the Mighty *God* of Jacob
[c](From there [d]*is* the Shepherd, [e]the Stone
of Israel),
25 [a]By the God of your father who will help
you,
[b]And by the Almighty [c]who will bless you
With blessings of heaven above,
Blessings of the deep that lies beneath,
Blessings of the breasts and of the womb.
26 The blessings of your father
Have excelled the blessings of my
ancestors,
[a]Up to the utmost bound of the everlasting
hills.
[b]They shall be on the head of Joseph,
And on the crown of the head of him who
was separate from his brothers.

27 "Benjamin is a [a]ravenous wolf;
In the morning he shall devour the prey,
[b]And at night he shall divide the spoil."

28 All these *are* the twelve tribes of Israel,
and this *is* what their father spoke to them. And
he blessed them; he blessed each one according
to his own blessing.

Jacob's Death and Burial

29 Then he charged them and said to them:
"I [a]am to be gathered to my people; [b]bury me
with my fathers [c]in the cave that *is* in the field
of Ephron the Hittite,
30 "in the cave that *is* in the field of Machpelah, which *is* before Mamre in the land of Canaan,
[a]which Abraham bought with the field of Ephron
the Hittite as a possession for a burial place.
31 [a]"There they buried Abraham and Sarah
his wife, [b]there they buried Isaac and Rebekah
his wife, and there I buried Leah.
32 "The field and the cave that *is* there *were*
purchased from the sons of Heth."
33 And when Jacob had finished commanding his sons, he drew his feet up into the bed
and breathed his last, and was gathered to his
people.

50 Then Joseph [a]fell on his father's face, and
[b]wept over him, and kissed him.
2 And Joseph commanded his servants the
physicians to [a]embalm his father. So the physicians embalmed Israel.
3 Forty days were required for him, for such
are the days required for those who are embalmed; and the Egyptians [a]mourned for him seventy days.
4 Now when the days of his mourning were
past, Joseph spoke to [a]the household of Pharaoh, saying, "If now I have found favor in your
eyes, please speak in the hearing of Pharaoh,
saying,
5 [a]'My father made me swear, saying, "Behold, I am dying; in my grave [b]which I dug for
myself in the land of Canaan, there you shall bury
me." Now therefore, please let me go up and bury
my father, and I will come back.' "
6 And Pharaoh said, "Go up and bury your
father, as he made you swear."
7 So Joseph went up to bury his father; and
with him went up all the servants of Pharaoh, the
elders of his house, and all the elders of the land
of Egypt,
8 as well as all the house of Joseph, his
brothers, and his father's house. Only their little

KJV

and their flocks, and their herds, they left in the land of Goshen.

9 And there went up with him both chariots and horsemen: and it was a very great company.

10 And they came to the threshingfloor of Atad, which *is* beyond Jordan, and there they [a]mourned with a great and very sore lamentation: [b]and he made a mourning for his father seven days.

11 And when the inhabitants of the land, the Canaanites, saw the mourning in the floor of Atad, they said, This *is* a grievous mourning to the Egyptians: wherefore the name of it was called Abel–mizraim, which *is* beyond Jordan.

12 And his sons did unto him according as he commanded them:

13 For [a]his sons carried him into the land of Canaan, and buried him in the cave of the field of Machpelah, which Abraham [b]bought with the field for a possession of a buryingplace of Ephron the Hittite, before Mamre.

14 And Joseph returned into Egypt, he, and his brethren, and all that went up with him to bury his father, after he had buried his father.

Joseph Reassures His Brothers

15 And when Joseph's brethren saw that their father was dead, [a]they said, Joseph will peradventure hate us, and will certainly requite us all the evil which we did unto him.

16 And they sent a messenger unto Joseph, saying, Thy father did command before he died, saying,

17 So shall ye say unto Joseph, Forgive, I pray thee now, the trespass of thy brethren, and their sin; [a]for they did unto thee evil: and now, we pray thee, forgive the trespass of the servants of [b]the God of thy father. And Joseph wept when they spake unto him.

18 And his brethren also went and [a]fell down before his face; and they said, Behold, we *be* thy servants.

19 And Joseph said unto them, [a]Fear not: [b]for *am* I in the place of God?

20 [a]But as for you, ye thought evil against me; *but* [b]God meant it unto good, to bring to pass, as *it is* this day, to save much people alive.

21 Now therefore fear ye not: [a]I will nourish you, and your little ones. And he comforted them, and spake kindly unto them.

Death of Joseph
(Heb. 11:22)

22 And Joseph dwelt in Egypt, he, and his father's house: and Joseph lived an hundred and ten years.

23 And Joseph saw Ephraim's children [a]of the third *generation:* [b]the children also of Machir the son of Manasseh [c]were brought up upon Joseph's knees.

24 And Joseph said unto his brethren, I die: and [a]God will surely visit you, and bring you out of this land unto the land [b]which he sware to Abraham, to Isaac, and to Jacob.

25 And [a]Joseph took an oath of the children of Israel, saying, God will surely visit you, and [b]ye shall carry up my [c]bones from hence.

26 So Joseph died, *being* an hundred and ten years old: and they embalmed him, and he was put in a coffin in Egypt.

NKJV

ones, their flocks, and their herds they left in the land of Goshen.

9 And there went up with him both chariots and horsemen, and it was a very great gathering.

10 Then they came to the threshing floor of Atad, which *is* beyond the Jordan, and they [a]mourned there with a great and very solemn lamentation. [b]He observed seven days of mourning for his father.

11 And when the inhabitants of the land, the Canaanites, saw the mourning at the threshing floor of Atad, they said, "This *is* a deep mourning of the Egyptians." Therefore its name was called *Abel Mizraim, which *is* beyond the Jordan.

12 So his sons did for him just as he had commanded them.

13 For [a]his sons carried him to the land of Canaan, and buried him in the cave of the field of Machpelah, before Mamre, which Abraham [b]bought with the field from Ephron the Hittite as property for a burial place.

14 And after he had buried his father, Joseph returned to Egypt, he and his brothers and all who went up with him to bury his father.

Joseph Reassures His Brothers

15 When Joseph's brothers saw that their father was dead, [a]they said, "Perhaps Joseph will hate us, and may actually repay us for all the evil which we did to him."

16 So they sent *messengers* to Joseph, saying, "Before your father died he commanded, saying,

17 'Thus you shall say to Joseph: "I beg you, please forgive the trespass of your brothers and their sin; [a]for they did evil to you." ' Now, please, forgive the trespass of the servants of [b]the God of your father." And Joseph wept when they spoke to him.

18 Then his brothers also went and [a]fell down before his face, and they said, "Behold, we *are* your servants."

19 Joseph said to them, [a]"Do not be afraid, [b]for *am* I in the place of God?

20 [a]"But as for you, you meant evil against me; *but* [b]God meant it for good, in order to bring it about as *it is* this day, to save many people alive.

21 "Now therefore, do not be afraid; [a]I will provide for you and your little ones." And he comforted them and spoke kindly to them.

Death of Joseph
(Heb. 11:22)

22 So Joseph dwelt in Egypt, he and his father's household. And Joseph lived one hundred and ten years.

23 Joseph saw Ephraim's children [a]to the third *generation.* [b]The children of Machir, the son of Manasseh, [c]were also brought up on Joseph's knees.

24 And Joseph said to his brethren, "I am dying; but [a]God will surely visit you, and bring you out of this land to the land [b]of which He swore to Abraham, to Isaac, and to Jacob."

25 Then [a]Joseph took an oath from the children of Israel, saying, "God will surely visit you, and [b]you shall carry up my [c]bones from here."

26 So Joseph died, *being* one hundred and ten years old; and they embalmed him, and he was put in a coffin in Egypt.

---

10 [a]Acts 8:2 [b]1 Sam. 31:13; Job 2:13
13 [a]Gen. 49:29–31; Acts 7:16 [b]Gen. 23:16–20
15 [a][Job 15:21]
17 [a][Prov. 28:13] [b]Gen. 49:25
18 [a]Gen. 37:7–10; 41:43; 44:14
19 [a]Gen. 45:5 [b]Gen. 30:2; 2 Kin. 5:7
20 [a]Gen. 45:5, 7; Ps. 56:5 [b][Acts 3:13–15]
21 [a][Matt. 5:44]
23 [a]Gen. 48:1; Job 42:16 [b]Num. 26:29; 32:39 [c]Gen. 30:3
24 [a]Gen. 15:14; 46:4; 48:21; Ex. 3:16, 17; Josh. 3:17; Heb. 11:22 [b]Gen. 26:3; 35:12; 46:4; Ex. 6:8
25 [a]Gen. 47:29, 30; Ex. 13:19; Josh. 24:32; Acts 7:15, 16; Heb. 11:22 [b]Gen. 17:8; 28:13; 35:12; Deut. 1:8; 30:1–8 [c]Ex. 13:19

*
50:11 Lit. *Mourning of Egypt*

KJV

THE SECOND BOOK OF MOSES CALLED

EXODUS

Israel's Suffering in Egypt

1 Now [a]these *are* the names of the children of Israel, which came into Egypt; every man and his household came with Jacob.

2 Reuben, Simeon, Levi, and Judah,

3 Issachar, Zebulun, and Benjamin,

4 Dan, and Naphtali, Gad, and Asher.

5 And all the souls that came out of the loins of Jacob were [a]seventy souls: for Joseph was in Egypt *already*.

6 And [a]Joseph died, and all his brethren, and all that generation.

7 [a]And the children of Israel were fruitful, and increased abundantly, and multiplied, and waxed exceeding mighty; and the land was filled with them.

8 Now there arose up a new king over Egypt, [a]which knew not Joseph.

9 And he said unto his people, Behold, the people of the children of Israel *are* more and [a]mightier than we:

10 [a]Come on, let us [b]deal wisely with them; lest they multiply, and it come to pass, that, when there falleth out any war, they join also unto our enemies, and fight against us, and *so* get them up out of the land.

11 Therefore they did set over them taskmasters [a]to afflict them with their [b]burdens. And they built for Pharaoh [c]treasure cities, Pithom [d]and Raamses.

12 But the more they afflicted them, the more they multiplied and grew. And they were grieved because of the children of Israel.

13 And the Egyptians made the children of Israel to [a]serve with rigour:

14 And they [a]made their lives bitter with hard bondage, [b]in morter, and in brick, and in all manner of service in the field: all their service, wherein they made them serve, *was* with rigour.

15 And the king of Egypt spake to the [a]Hebrew midwives, of which the name of the one *was* Shiphrah, and the name of the other Puah:

16 And he said, When ye do the office of a midwife to the Hebrew women, and see *them* upon the stools; if it *be* a [a]son, then ye shall kill him: but if it *be* a daughter, then she shall live.

17 But the midwives [a]feared God, and did not [b]as the king of Egypt commanded them, but saved the men children alive.

18 And the king of Egypt called for the midwives, and said unto them, Why have ye done this thing, and have saved the men children alive?

19 And [a]the midwives said unto Pharaoh, Because the Hebrew women *are* not as the Egyptian women; for they *are* lively, and are delivered ere the midwives come in unto them.

20 [a]Therefore God dealt well with the midwives: and the people multiplied, and waxed very mighty.

21 And it came to pass, because the midwives feared God, [a]that he made them houses.

22 And Pharaoh charged all his people, saying, [a]Every son that is born ye shall cast into the river, and every daughter ye shall save alive.

CHAPTER 1

1 [a]Gen. 46:8–27
5 [a]Gen. 46:26, 27
6 [a]Gen. 50:26
7 [a]Acts 7:17
8 [a]Acts 7:18, 19
9 [a]Gen. 26:16
10 [a]Ps. 83:3, 4 [b]Acts 7:19
11 [a]Ex. 3:7; 5:6 [b]Ex. 1:14; 2:11; 5:4–9; 6:6 [c]1 Kin. 9:19 [d]Gen. 47:11
13 [a]Gen. 15:13
14 [a]Num. 20:15 [b]Ps. 81:6
15 [a]Ex. 2:6
16 [a]Acts 7:19
17 [a]Prov. 16:6 [b]Dan. 3:16, 18
19 [a]Josh. 2:4
20 [a][Prov. 11:18]
21 [a]1 Sam. 2:35
22 [a]Acts 7:19

*

1:5 Lit. *who came from the loins of* • DSS, LXX *seventy-five;* cf. Acts 7:14
1:22 Sam., LXX, Tg. add *to the Hebrews*

NKJV

THE SECOND BOOK OF MOSES CALLED

EXODUS

Israel's Suffering in Egypt

1 Now [a]these *are* the names of the children of Israel who came to Egypt; each man and his household came with Jacob:

2 Reuben, Simeon, Levi, and Judah;

3 Issachar, Zebulun, and Benjamin;

4 Dan, Naphtali, Gad, and Asher.

5 All those *who were descendants of Jacob were [a]seventy* persons (for Joseph was in Egypt *already*).

6 And [a]Joseph died, all his brothers, and all that generation.

7 [a]But the children of Israel were fruitful and increased abundantly, multiplied and grew exceedingly mighty; and the land was filled with them.

8 Now there arose a new king over Egypt, [a]who did not know Joseph.

9 And he said to his people, "Look, the people of the children of Israel *are* more and [a]mightier than we;

10 [a]"come, let us [b]deal shrewdly with them, lest they multiply, and it happen, in the event of war, that they also join our enemies and fight against us, and *so* go up out of the land."

11 Therefore they set taskmasters over them [a]to afflict them with their [b]burdens. And they built for Pharaoh [c]supply cities, Pithom [d]and Raamses.

12 But the more they afflicted them, the more they multiplied and grew. And they were in dread of the children of Israel.

13 So the Egyptians made the children of Israel [a]serve with rigor.

14 And they [a]made their lives bitter with hard bondage—[b]in mortar, in brick, and in all manner of service in the field. All their service in which they made them serve *was* with rigor.

15 Then the king of Egypt spoke to the [a]Hebrew midwives, of whom the name of one *was* Shiphrah and the name of the other Puah;

16 and he said, "When you do the duties of a midwife for the Hebrew women, and see *them* on the birthstools, if it *is* a [a]son, then you shall kill him; but if it *is* a daughter, then she shall live."

17 But the midwives [a]feared God, and did not do [b]as the king of Egypt commanded them, but saved the male children alive.

18 So the king of Egypt called for the midwives and said to them, "Why have you done this thing, and saved the male children alive?"

19 And [a]the midwives said to Pharaoh, "Because the Hebrew women *are* not like the Egyptian women; for they *are* lively and give birth before the midwives come to them."

20 [a]Therefore God dealt well with the midwives, and the people multiplied and grew very mighty.

21 And so it was, because the midwives feared God, [a]that He provided households for them.

22 So Pharaoh commanded all his people, saying, [a]"Every son who is *born you shall cast into the river, and every daughter you shall save alive."

KJV

Moses Is Born
(Heb. 11:23)

2 And there went [a]a man of the house of Levi,
and took *to wife* a daughter of Levi.
2 And the woman conceived, and bare a
son: and [a]when she saw him that he *was a* goodly
child, she hid him three months.
3 And when she could not longer hide him,
she took for him an ark of [a]bulrushes, and daubed
it with [b]slime and with [c]pitch, and put the child
therein; and she laid *it* in the flags [d]by the river's
brink.
4 [a]And his sister stood afar off, to wit what
would be done to him.
5 And the [a]daughter of Pharaoh came down
to wash *herself* at the river; and her maidens
walked along by the river's side; and when she
saw the ark among the flags, she sent her maid
to fetch it.
6 And when she had opened *it,* she saw the
child: and, behold, the babe wept. And she had
compassion on him, and said, This *is one* of the
Hebrews' children.
7 Then said his sister to Pharaoh's daughter,
Shall I go and call to thee a nurse of the Hebrew
women, that she may nurse the child for thee?
8 And Pharaoh's daughter said to her, Go.
And the maid went and called the child's mother.
9 And Pharaoh's daughter said unto her,
Take this child away, and nurse it for me, and I
will give *thee* thy wages. And the woman took
the child, and nursed it.
10 And the child grew, and she brought him
unto Pharaoh's daughter, and he became [a]her
son. And she called his name Moses: and she said,
Because I drew him out of the water.

Moses Flees to Midian
(Heb. 11:24, 25)

11 And it came to pass in those days, [a]when
Moses was grown, that he went out unto his brethren, and looked on their burdens: and he spied
an Egyptian smiting an Hebrew, one of his
brethren.
12 And he looked this way and that way, and
when he saw that *there was* no man, he [a]slew
the Egyptian, and hid him in the sand.
13 And [a]when he went out the second day,
behold, two men of the Hebrews [b]strove together:
and he said to him that did the wrong, Wherefore
smitest thou thy fellow?
14 And he said, [a]Who made thee a prince
and a judge over us? intendest thou to kill me,
as thou killedst the Egyptian? And Moses [b]feared,
and said, Surely this thing is known.
15 Now when Pharaoh heard this thing, he
sought to slay Moses. But [a]Moses fled from the
face of Pharaoh, and dwelt in the land of [b]Midian:
and he sat down by [c]a well.
16 [a]Now the priest of Midian had seven
daughters: [b]and they came and drew *water,* and
filled the [c]troughs to water their father's flock.
17 And the [a]shepherds came and [b]drove
them away: but Moses stood up and helped them,
and [c]watered their flock.
18 And when they came to [a]Reuel their father, [b]he said, How *is it that* ye are come so soon
to day?
19 And they said, An Egyptian delivered us
out of the hand of the shepherds, and also drew
water enough for us, and watered the flock.
20 And he said unto his daughters, And
where *is* he? why *is* it *that* ye have left the man?
call him, that he may [a]eat bread.
21 And Moses was content to dwell with the
man: and he gave Moses [a]Zipporah his daughter.
22 And she bare *him* a son, and he called his
name [a]Gershom: for he said, I have been [b]a
stranger in a strange land.
23 And it came to pass [a]in process of time,
that the king of Egypt died: and the children of

NKJV

Moses Is Born
(Heb. 11:23)

2 And [a]a man of the house of Levi went and
took *as wife* a daughter of Levi.
2 So the woman conceived and bore a son.
And [a]when she saw that he *was* a beautiful *child,*
she hid him three months.
3 But when she could no longer hide him,
she took an ark of [a]bulrushes for him, daubed it
with [b]asphalt and [c]pitch, put the child in it, and
laid *it* in the reeds [d]by the river's bank.
4 [a]And his sister stood afar off, to know
what would be done to him.
5 Then the [a]daughter of Pharaoh came
down to bathe at the river. And her maidens
walked along the riverside; and when she saw
the ark among the reeds, she sent her maid to
get it.
6 And when she opened *it,* she saw the
child, and behold, the baby wept. So she had compassion on him, and said, "This is one of the Hebrews' children."
7 Then his sister said to Pharaoh's daughter,
"Shall I go and call a nurse for you from the Hebrew women, that she may nurse the child for
you?"
8 And Pharaoh's daughter said to her, "Go."
So the maiden went and called the child's mother.
9 Then Pharaoh's daughter said to her,
"Take this child away and nurse him for me, and
I will give *you* your wages." So the woman took
the child and nursed him.
10 And the child grew, and she brought him
to Pharaoh's daughter, and he became [a]her son.
So she called his name *Moses, saying, "Because
I drew him out of the water."

Moses Flees to Midian
(Heb. 11:24, 25)

11 Now it came to pass in those days, [a]when
Moses was grown, that he went out to his brethren
and looked at their burdens. And he saw an Egyptian beating a Hebrew, one of his brethren.
12 So he looked this way and that way, and
when he saw no one, he [a]killed the Egyptian and
hid him in the sand.
13 And [a]when he went out the second day,
behold, two Hebrew men [b]were fighting, and he
said to the one who did the wrong, "Why are you
striking your companion?"
14 Then he said, [a]"Who made you a prince
and a judge over us? Do you intend to kill me as
you killed the Egyptian?" So Moses [b]feared and
said, "Surely this thing is known!"
15 When Pharaoh heard of this matter, he
sought to kill Moses. But [a]Moses fled from the
face of Pharaoh and dwelt in the land of [b]Midian;
and he sat down by [c]a well.
16 [a]Now the priest of Midian had seven
daughters. [b]And they came and drew water, and
they filled the [c]troughs to water their father's
flock.
17 Then the [a]shepherds came and [b]drove
them away; but Moses stood up and helped them,
and [c]watered their flock.
18 When they came to [a]Reuel their father,
[b]he said, "How *is it that* you have come so soon
today?"
19 And they said, "An Egyptian delivered us
from the hand of the shepherds, and he also drew
enough water for us and watered the flock."
20 So he said to his daughters, "And where
is he? Why *is it that* you have left the man? Call
him, that he may [a]eat bread."
21 Then Moses was content to live with the
man, and he gave [a]Zipporah his daughter to
Moses.
22 And she bore *him* a son. He called his
name [a]Gershom,* for he said, "I have been [b]a
stranger in a foreign land."
23 Now it happened [a]in the process of time

CHAPTER 2
1 [a]Ex. 6:16–20; Num. 26:59; 1 Chr. 23:14
2 [a]Acts 7:20; Heb. 11:23
3 [a]Is. 18:2 [b]Gen. 14:10 [c]Gen. 6:14; Is. 34:9 [d]Is. 19:6
4 [a]Ex. 15:20; Num. 26:59
5 [a]Ex. 7:15; Acts 7:21
10 [a]Acts 7:21
11 [a]Acts 7:23, 24; Heb. 11:24–26
12 [a]Acts 7:24, 25
13 [a]Acts 7:26–28 [b]Prov. 25:8
14 [a]Gen. 19:9; Acts 7:27, 28 [b]Judg. 6:27; Heb. 11:27
15 [a]Acts 7:29; Heb. 11:27 [b]Ex. 3:1 [c]Gen. 24:11; 29:2; Ex. 15:27
16 [a]Ex. 3:1; 4:18; 18:12 [b]Gen. 24:11, 13, 19; 29:6–10; 1 Sam. 9:11 [c]Gen. 30:38
17 [a]Gen. 47:3; 1 Sam. 25:7 [b]Gen. 26:19–21 [c]Gen. 29:3, 10
18 [a]Num. 10:29 [b]Ex. 3:1; 4:18
20 [a]Gen. 31:54; 43:25
21 [a]Ex. 4:25; 18:2
22 [a]Ex. 4:20; 18:3, 4 [b]Gen. 23:4; Lev. 25:23; Acts 7:29; Heb. 11:13, 14
23 [a]Acts 7:34

*

2:10 Heb. *Mosheh,* lit. *Drawn Out*
2:22 Lit. *Stranger There*

KJV

Israel [b]sighed by reason of the bondage, and they
cried, and [c]their cry came up unto God by reason
of the bondage.
24 And God [a]heard their groaning, and God
[b]remembered his [c]covenant with Abraham, with
Isaac, and with Jacob.
25 And God [a]looked upon the children of Israel, and God [b]had respect unto *them*.

Moses at the Burning Bush
(*Ex. 6:2—7:7; 11:1–4; 12:35, 36*)

3 Now Moses kept the flock of [a]Jethro his father
in law, [b]the priest of Midian: and he led the
flock to the backside of the desert, and came [d]to
the mountain of God, *even* to [c]Horeb.
2 And [a]the angel of the LORD appeared unto
him in a flame of fire out of the midst of a bush:
and he looked, and, behold, the bush burned with
fire, and the bush *was* not consumed.
3 And Moses said, I will now turn aside, and
see this [a]great sight, why the bush is not burnt.
4 And when the LORD saw that he turned
aside to see, God called [a]unto him out of the midst
of the bush, and said, Moses, Moses. And he said,
Here *am* I.
5 And he said, Draw not nigh hither: [a]put
off thy shoes from off thy feet, for the place
whereon thou standest *is* holy ground.
6 Moreover he said, [a]I *am* the God of thy
father, the God of Abraham, the God of Isaac,
and the God of Jacob. And Moses hid his face;
for [b]he was afraid to look upon God.
7 And the LORD said, [a]I have surely seen
the affliction of my people which *are* in Egypt,
and have heard their cry [b]by reason of their taskmasters; [c]for I know their sorrows;
8 And [a]I am come down to [b]deliver them
out of the hand of the Egyptians, and to bring
them up out of that land [c]unto a good land and
a large, unto a land [d]flowing with milk and honey;
unto the place of [e]the Canaanites, and the Hittites,
and the Amorites, and the Perizzites, and the Hivites, and the Jebusites.
9 Now therefore, behold, [a]the cry of the
children of Israel is come unto me: and I have
also seen the [b]oppression wherewith the Egyptians oppress them.
10 [a]Come now therefore, and I will send thee
unto Pharaoh, that thou mayest bring forth my
people the children of Israel out of Egypt.
11 And Moses said unto God, [a]Who *am* I, that
I should go unto Pharaoh, and that I should bring
forth the children of Israel out of Egypt?
12 And he said, [a]Certainly I will be with thee;
and this *shall be* a [b]token unto thee, that I have
sent thee: When thou hast brought forth the people out of Egypt, ye shall serve God upon this
mountain.
13 And Moses said unto God, Behold, *when*
I come unto the children of Israel, and shall say
unto them, The God of your fathers hath sent me
unto you; and they shall say to me, What *is* his
name? what shall I say unto them?
14 And God said unto Moses, I AM THAT I
AM: and he said, Thus shalt thou say unto the
children of Israel, [a]I AM hath sent me unto you.
15 And God said moreover unto Moses, Thus
shalt thou say unto the children of Israel, The
LORD God of your fathers, the God of Abraham,
the God of Isaac, and the God of Jacob, hath sent
me unto you: this *is* [a]my name for ever, and this
is my memorial unto all generations.
16 Go, and [a]gather the elders of Israel together, and say unto them, The LORD God of your
fathers, the God of Abraham, of Isaac, and of Jacob, appeared unto me, saying, [b]I have surely visited you, and *seen* that which is done to you in
Egypt:
17 And I have said, [a]I will bring you up out
of the affliction of Egypt unto the land of the Canaanites, and the Hittites, and the Amorites, and

23 [b]Deut. 26:7 [c]James 5:4
24 [a]Ex. 6:5 [b]Gen. 15:13; 22:16–18; 26:2–5; 28:13–15 [c]Gen. 12:1–3; 15:14; 17:1–14
25 [a]Ex. 4:31 [b]Ex. 3:7

CHAPTER 3

1 [a]Ex. 4:18 [b]Ex. 2:16 [c]Ex. 18:5 [d]Ex. 17:6
2 [a]Deut. 33:16
3 [a]Acts 7:31
4 [a]Deut. 33:16
5 [a]Josh. 5:15
6 [a][Matt. 22:32] [b]1 Kin. 19:13
7 [a]Ex. 2:23–25 [b]Ex. 1:11 [c]Ex. 2:25
8 [a]Gen. 15:13–16; 46:4; 50:24, 25 [b]Ex. 6:6–8; 12:51 [c]Deut. 1:25; 8:7–9 [d]Jer. 11:5 [e]Gen. 15:19–21
9 [a]Ex. 2:23 [b]Ex. 1:11, 13, 14
10 [a][Mic. 6:4]
11 [a]Ex. 4:10; 6:12
12 [a]Gen. 31:3 [b]Ex. 4:8; 19:3
14 [a][John 8:24, 28, 58]
15 [a]Ps. 30:4; 97:12; 102:12; 135:13
16 [a]Ex. 4:29 [b]Ex. 2:25; 4:31
17 [a]Gen. 15:13–21; 46:4; 50:24, 25

NKJV

that the king of Egypt died. Then the children of
Israel [b]groaned because of the bondage, and they
cried out; and [c]their cry came up to God because
of the bondage.
24 So God [a]heard their groaning, and God
[b]remembered His [c]covenant with Abraham, with
Isaac, and with Jacob.
25 And God [a]looked upon the children of Israel, and God [b]acknowledged *them*.

Moses at the Burning Bush
(*Ex. 6:2—7:7; 11:1–4; 12:35, 36*)

3 Now Moses was tending the flock of [a]Jethro
his father-in-law, [b]the priest of Midian. And
he led the flock to the back of the desert, and
came to [c]Horeb, [d]the mountain of God.
2 And [a]the Angel of the LORD appeared to
him in a flame of fire from the midst of a bush.
So he looked, and behold, the bush was burning
with fire, but the bush *was* not consumed.
3 Then Moses said, "I will now turn aside
and see this [a]great sight, why the bush does not
burn."
4 So when the LORD saw that he turned
aside to look, God called [a]to him from the midst
of the bush and said, "Moses, Moses!" And he
said, "Here I am."
5 Then He said, "Do not draw near this
place. [a]Take your sandals off your feet, for the
place where you stand *is* holy ground."
6 Moreover He said, [a]"I *am* the God of your
father—the God of Abraham, the God of Isaac,
and the God of Jacob." And Moses hid his face,
for [b]he was afraid to look upon God.
7 And the LORD said: [a]"I have surely seen
the oppression of My people who *are* in Egypt,
and have heard their cry [b]because of their taskmasters, [c]for I know their sorrows.
8 "So [a]I have come down to [b]deliver them
out of the hand of the Egyptians, and to bring
them up from that land [c]to a good and large land,
to a land [d]flowing with milk and honey, to the
place of [e]the Canaanites and the Hittites and the
Amorites and the Perizzites and the Hivites and
the Jebusites.
9 "Now therefore, behold, [a]the cry of the
children of Israel has come to Me, and I have also
seen the [b]oppression with which the Egyptians
oppress them.
10 [a]"Come now, therefore, and I will send
you to Pharaoh that you may bring My people,
the children of Israel, out of Egypt."
11 But Moses said to God, [a]"Who *am* I that
I should go to Pharaoh, and that I should bring
the children of Israel out of Egypt?"
12 So He said, [a]"I will certainly be with you.
And this *shall be* a [b]sign to you that I have sent
you: When you have brought the people out of
Egypt, you shall serve God on this mountain."
13 Then Moses said to God, "Indeed, *when* I
come to the children of Israel and say to them,
'The God of your fathers has sent me to you,' and
they say to me, 'What *is* His name?' what shall I
say to them?"
14 And God said to Moses, "I AM WHO I
AM." And He said, "Thus you shall say to the
children of Israel, [a]'I AM has sent me to you.'"
15 Moreover God said to Moses, "Thus you
shall say to the children of Israel: 'The LORD God
of your fathers, the God of Abraham, the God of
Isaac, and the God of Jacob, has sent me to you.
This *is* [a]My name forever, and this *is* My memorial
to all generations.'
16 "Go and [a]gather the elders of Israel together, and say to them, 'The LORD God of your
fathers, the God of Abraham, of Isaac, and of Jacob, appeared to me, saying, [b]"I have surely visited you and *seen* what is done to you in Egypt;
17 "and I have said [a]I will bring you up out
of the affliction of Egypt to the land of the Canaanites and the Hittites and the Amorites and the Per-

KJV

the Perizzites, and the Hivites, and the Jebusites, unto a land flowing with milk and honey.

18 And [a]they shall hearken to thy voice: and [b]thou shalt come, thou and the elders of Israel, unto the king of Egypt, and ye shall say unto him, The LORD God of the Hebrews hath [c]met with us: and now let us go, we beseech thee, three days' journey into the wilderness, that we may sacrifice to the LORD our God.

19 And I am sure that the king of Egypt [a]will not let you go, no, not by a mighty hand.

20 And I will [a]stretch out my hand, and smite Egypt with [b]all my wonders which I will do in the midst thereof: and [c]after that he will let you go.

21 And [a]I will give this people favour in the sight of the Egyptians: and it shall come to pass, that, when ye go, ye shall not go empty:

22 [a]But every woman shall borrow of her neighbour, and of her that sojourneth in her house, [b]jewels of silver, and jewels of gold, and raiment: and ye shall put *them* upon your sons, and upon your daughters; and [c]ye shall spoil the Egyptians.

Miraculous Signs for Pharaoh

4 And Moses answered and said, But, behold, they will not believe me, nor hearken unto my voice: for they will say, The LORD hath not appeared unto thee.

2 And the LORD said unto him, What *is* that in thine hand? And he said, A rod.

3 And he said, Cast it on the ground. And he cast it on the ground, and it became a serpent; and Moses fled from before it.

4 And the LORD said unto Moses, Put forth thine hand, and take it by the tail. And he put forth his hand, and caught it, and it became a rod in his hand:

5 That they may [a]believe that the [b]LORD God of their fathers, the God of Abraham, the God of Isaac, and the God of Jacob, hath appeared unto thee.

6 And the LORD said furthermore unto him, Put now thine hand into thy bosom. And he put his hand into his bosom: and when he took it out, behold, his hand *was* leprous [a]as snow.

7 And he said, Put thine hand into thy bosom again. And he put his hand into his bosom again; and plucked it out of his bosom, and, behold, [a]it was turned again as his *other* flesh.

8 And it shall come to pass, if they will not believe thee, neither hearken to the voice of the [a]first sign, that they will believe the voice of the latter sign.

9 And it shall come to pass, if they will not believe also these two signs, neither hearken unto thy voice, that thou shalt take of the water of the river, and pour *it* upon the dry *land:* and [a]the water which thou takest out of the river shall become blood upon the dry *land.*

10 And Moses said unto the LORD, O my Lord, I *am* not eloquent, neither heretofore, nor since thou hast spoken unto thy servant: but [a]I *am* slow of speech, and of a slow tongue.

11 And the LORD said unto him, [a]Who hath made man's mouth? or who maketh the dumb, or deaf, or the seeing, or the blind? have not I the LORD?

12 Now therefore go, and I will be [a]with thy mouth, and teach thee what thou shalt say.

13 And he said, O my LORD, [a]send, I pray thee, by the hand *of him whom* thou wilt send.

14 And [a]the anger of the LORD was kindled against Moses, and he said, *Is* not Aaron the Levite thy [b]brother? I know that he can speak well. And also, behold, [c]he cometh forth to meet thee: and when he seeth thee, he will be glad in his heart.

15 And [a]thou shalt speak unto him, and [b]put words in his mouth: and I will be with thy mouth,

18 [a]Ex. 4:31 [b]Ex. 5:1, 3 [c]Num. 23:3, 4, 15, 16
19 [a]Ex. 5:2
20 [a]Ex. 6:6; 9:15 [b]Deut. 6:22; Neh. 9:10; Ps. 105:27; 135:9; Jer. 32:20; Acts 7:36 [c]Ex. 11:1; 12:31–37
21 [a]Ex. 11:3; 12:36; 1 Kin. 8:50; Ps. 105:37; 106:46; [Prov. 16:7]
22 [a]Ex. 11:2 [b]Ex. 33:6 [c]Job 27:17; Prov. 13:22; [Ezek. 39:10]

CHAPTER 4
5 [a]Ex. 4:31; 19:9 [b]Gen. 28:13; 48:15; Ex. 3:6, 15
6 [a]Num. 12:10; 2 Kin. 5:27
7 [a]Num. 12:13–15; Deut. 32:39
8 [a]Ex. 7:6–13
9 [a]Ex. 7:19, 20
10 [a]Ex. 3:11; 4:1; 6:12; Jer. 1:6
11 [a]Ps. 94:9; 146:8; Matt. 11:5; Luke 1:20, 64
12 [a]Ex. 4:15, 16; Deut. 18:18; Is. 50:4; Jer. 1:9; [Matt. 10:19; Mark 13:11; Luke 12:11, 12; 21:14, 15]
13 [a]Jon. 1:3
14 [a]Num. 11:1, 33 [b]Num. 26:59 [c]Ex. 4:27; 1 Sam. 10:2, 3, 5
15 [a]Ex. 4:12, 30; 7:1, 2 [b]Num. 23:5, 12; Deut. 18:18; 2 Sam. 14:3, 19; Is. 51:16; 59:21; Jer. 1:9

*________
4:9 The Nile

NKJV

izzites and the Hivites and the Jebusites, to a land flowing with milk and honey." '

18 "Then [a]they will heed your voice; and [b]you shall come, you and the elders of Israel, to the king of Egypt; and you shall say to him, 'The LORD God of the Hebrews has [c]met with us; and now, please, let us go three days' journey into the wilderness, that we may sacrifice to the LORD our God.'

19 "But I am sure that the king of Egypt [a]will not let you go, not even by a mighty hand.

20 "So I will [a]stretch out My hand and strike Egypt with [b]all My wonders which I will do in its midst; and [c]after that he will let you go.

21 "And [a]I will give this people favor in the sight of the Egyptians; and it shall be, when you go, that you shall not go empty-handed.

22 [a]"But every woman shall ask of her neighbor, namely, of her who dwells near her house, [b]articles of silver, articles of gold, and clothing; and you shall put *them* on your sons and on your daughters. So [c]you shall plunder the Egyptians."

Miraculous Signs for Pharaoh

4 Then Moses answered and said, "But suppose they will not believe me or listen to my voice; suppose they say, 'The LORD has not appeared to you.' "

2 So the LORD said to him, "What *is* that in your hand?" He said, "A rod."

3 And He said, "Cast it on the ground." So he cast it on the ground, and it became a serpent; and Moses fled from it.

4 Then the LORD said to Moses, "Reach out your hand and take *it* by the tail" (and he reached out his hand and caught it, and it became a rod in his hand),

5 "that they may [a]believe that the [b]LORD God of their fathers, the God of Abraham, the God of Isaac, and the God of Jacob, has appeared to you."

6 Furthermore the LORD said to him, "Now put your hand in your bosom." And he put his hand in his bosom, and when he took it out, behold, his hand *was* leprous, [a]like snow.

7 And He said, "Put your hand in your bosom again." So he put his hand in his bosom again, and drew it out of his bosom, and behold, [a]it was restored like his *other* flesh.

8 "Then it will be, if they do not believe you, nor heed the message of the [a]first sign, that they may believe the message of the latter sign.

9 "And it shall be, if they do not believe even these two signs, or listen to your voice, that you shall take water from *the river and pour *it* on the dry *land.* [a]The water which you take from the river will become blood on the dry *land.*"

10 Then Moses said to the LORD, "O my Lord, I *am* not eloquent, neither before nor since You have spoken to Your servant; but [a]I *am* slow of speech and slow of tongue."

11 So the LORD said to him, [a]"Who has made man's mouth? Or who makes the mute, the deaf, the seeing, or the blind? *Have* not I, the LORD?

12 "Now therefore, go, and I will be [a]with your mouth and teach you what you shall say."

13 But he said, "O my Lord, [a]please send by the hand of whomever *else* You may send."

14 So [a]the anger of the LORD was kindled against Moses, and He said: "Is not Aaron the Levite your [b]brother? I know that he can speak well. And look, [c]he is also coming out to meet you. When he sees you, he will be glad in his heart.

15 "Now [a]you shall speak to him and [b]put the words in his mouth. And I will be with your

KJV

and with his mouth, and [c]will teach you what ye shall do.

16 And he shall be thy spokesman unto the people: and he shall be, *even* he shall be to thee instead of a mouth, and [a]thou shalt be to him instead of God.

17 And thou shalt take this rod in thine hand, wherewith thou shalt do signs.

Moses Goes to Egypt

18 And Moses went and returned to [a]Jethro his father in law, and said unto him, Let me go, I pray thee, and return unto my brethren which *are* in Egypt, and see whether they be yet alive. And Jethro said to Moses, [b]Go in peace.

19 And the LORD said unto Moses in [a]Midian, Go, return into [b]Egypt: for [c]all the men are dead which sought thy life.

20 And Moses [a]took his wife and his sons, and set them upon an ass, and he returned to the land of Egypt: and Moses took [b]the rod of God in his hand.

21 And the LORD said unto Moses, When thou goest to return into Egypt, see that thou do all those [a]wonders before Pharaoh, which I have put in thine hand: but [b]I will harden his heart, that he shall not let the people go.

22 And thou shalt [a]say unto Pharaoh, Thus saith the LORD, [b]Israel *is* my son, [c]*even* my firstborn:

23 And I say unto thee, Let my son go, that he may serve me: and if thou refuse to let him go, behold, [a]I will slay thy son, *even* thy firstborn.

24 And it came to pass by the way in the [a]inn, that the LORD [b]met him, and sought to [c]kill him.

25 Then [a]Zipporah took [b]a sharp stone, and cut off the foreskin of her son, and cast *it* at his feet, and said, Surely a bloody husband *art* thou to me.

26 So he let him go: then she said, A bloody husband *thou art*, because of the circumcision.

27 And the LORD said to Aaron, Go into the wilderness [a]to meet Moses. And he went, and met him in [b]the mount of God, and kissed him.

28 And Moses [a]told Aaron all the words of the LORD who had sent him, and all the [b]signs which he had commanded him.

29 And Moses and Aaron [a]went and gathered together all the elders of the children of Israel:

30 [a]And Aaron spake all the words which the LORD had spoken unto Moses, and did the signs in the sight of the people.

31 And the people [a]believed: and when they heard that the LORD had [b]visited the children of Israel, and that he [c]had looked upon their affliction, then [d]they bowed their heads and worshipped.

First Encounter with Pharaoh

5 And afterward Moses and Aaron went in, and told Pharaoh, Thus saith the LORD God of Israel, Let my people go, that they may hold [a]a feast unto me in the wilderness.

2 And Pharaoh said, [a]Who *is* the LORD, that I should obey his voice to let Israel go? I know not the LORD, [b]neither will I let Israel go.

3 And they said, [a]The God of the Hebrews hath [b]met with us: let us go, we pray thee, three days' journey into the desert, and sacrifice unto the LORD our God; lest he fall upon us with [c]pestilence, or with the sword.

4 And the king of Egypt said unto them, Wherefore do ye, Moses and Aaron, let the people from their works? get you unto your [a]burdens.

5 And Pharaoh said, Behold, the people of the land now *are* [a]many, and ye make them rest from their burdens.

6 And Pharaoh commanded the same day the [a]taskmasters of the people, and their officers, saying,

7 Ye shall no more give the people straw

---

15 [c]Deut. 5:31
16 [a]Ex. 7:1, 2
18 [a]Ex. 2:21; 3:1; 4:18 [b]Gen. 43:23; Judg. 18:6
19 [a]Ex. 3:1; 18:1 [b]Gen. 46:3, 6 [c]Ex. 2:15, 23; Matt. 2:20
20 [a]Ex. 18:2–5; Acts 7:29 [b]Ex. 4:17; 17:9; Num. 20:8, 9, 11
21 [a]Ex. 3:20; 11:9, 10 [b]Ex. 7:3, 13; 9:12, 35; 10:1, 20, 27; 14:4, 8; Deut. 2:30; Josh. 11:20; 1 Sam. 6:6; Is. 63:17; John 12:40; Rom. 9:18
22 [a]Ex. 5:1 [b]Is. 63:16; 64:8; Hos. 11:1; [Rom. 9:4; 2 Cor. 6:16, 18] [c]Jer. 31:9; [James 1:18]
23 [a]Ex. 11:5; 12:29; Ps. 105:36; 135:8; 136:10
24 [a]Gen. 42:27 [b]Ex. 3:18; 5:3; Num. 22:22 [c]Gen. 17:14
25 [a]Ex. 2:21; 18:2 [b]Gen. 17:14; Josh. 5:2, 3
27 [a]Ex. 4:14 [b]Ex. 3:1; 18:5; 24:13
28 [a]Ex. 4:15, 16 [b]Ex. 4:8, 9
29 [a]Ex. 3:16; 12:21
30 [a]Ex. 4:15, 16
31 [a]Ex. 3:18; 4:8, 9; 19:9 [b]Gen. 50:24; Ex. 3:16 [c]Ex. 2:25; 3:7 [d]Gen. 24:26; Ex. 12:27; 1 Chr. 29:20

CHAPTER 5

1 [a]Ex. 3:18; 7:16; 10:9
2 [a]2 Kin. 18:35; 2 Chr. 32:14; Job 21:15 [b]Ex. 3:19; 7:14
3 [a]Ex. 3:18; 7:16 [b]Ex. 4:24; Num. 23:3 [c]Ex. 9:15
4 [a]Ex. 1:11; 2:11; 6:6
5 [a]Ex. 1:7, 9
6 [a]Ex. 1:11; 3:7; 5:10, 13, 14

*

4:25 Lit. *his*

NKJV

mouth and with his mouth, and [c]I will teach you what you shall do.

16 "So he shall be your spokesman to the people. And he himself shall be as a mouth for you, and [a]you shall be to him as God.

17 "And you shall take this rod in your hand, with which you shall do the signs."

Moses Goes to Egypt

18 So Moses went and returned to [a]Jethro his father-in-law, and said to him, "Please let me go and return to my brethren who *are* in Egypt, and see whether they are still alive." And Jethro said to Moses, [b]"Go in peace."

19 Now the LORD said to Moses in [a]Midian, "Go, return to [b]Egypt; for [c]all the men who sought your life are dead."

20 Then Moses [a]took his wife and his sons and set them on a donkey, and he returned to the land of Egypt. And Moses took [b]the rod of God in his hand.

21 And the LORD said to Moses, "When you go back to Egypt, see that you do all those [a]wonders before Pharaoh which I have put in your hand. But [b]I will harden his heart, so that he will not let the people go.

22 "Then you shall [a]say to Pharaoh, 'Thus says the LORD: [b]"Israel *is* My son, [c]My firstborn.

23 "So I say to you, let My son go that he may serve Me. But if you refuse to let him go, indeed [a]I will kill your son, your firstborn." ' "

24 And it came to pass on the way, at the [a]encampment, that the LORD [b]met him and sought to [c]kill him.

25 Then [a]Zipporah took [b]a sharp stone and cut off the foreskin of her son and cast *it* at **Moses'* feet, and said, "Surely you *are* a husband of blood to me!"

26 So He let him go. Then she said, "*You are* a husband of blood!"—because of the circumcision.

27 And the LORD said to Aaron, "Go into the wilderness [a]to meet Moses." So he went and met him on [b]the mountain of God, and kissed him.

28 So Moses [a]told Aaron all the words of the LORD who had sent him, and all the [b]signs which He had commanded him.

29 Then Moses and Aaron [a]went and gathered together all the elders of the children of Israel.

30 [a]And Aaron spoke all the words which the LORD had spoken to Moses. Then he did the signs in the sight of the people.

31 So the people [a]believed; and when they heard that the LORD had [b]visited the children of Israel and that He [c]had looked on their affliction, then [d]they bowed their heads and worshiped.

First Encounter with Pharaoh

5 Afterward Moses and Aaron went in and told Pharaoh, "Thus says the LORD God of Israel: 'Let My people go, that they may hold [a]a feast to Me in the wilderness.' "

2 And Pharaoh said, [a]"Who *is* the LORD, that I should obey His voice to let Israel go? I do not know the LORD, [b]nor will I let Israel go."

3 So they said, [a]"The God of the Hebrews has [b]met with us. Please, let us go three days' journey into the desert and sacrifice to the LORD our God, lest He fall upon us with [c]pestilence or with the sword."

4 Then the king of Egypt said to them, "Moses and Aaron, why do you take the people from their work? Get *back* to your [a]labor."

5 And Pharaoh said, "Look, the people of the land *are* [a]many now, and you make them rest from their labor!"

6 So the same day Pharaoh commanded the [a]taskmasters of the people and their officers, saying,

7 "You shall no longer give the people straw

KJV

to make [a]brick, as heretofore: let them go and
gather straw for themselves.
8 And the tale of the bricks, which they did
make heretofore, ye shall lay upon them; ye shall
not diminish *ought* thereof: for they *be* idle; therefore they cry, saying, Let us go *and* sacrifice to
our God.
9 Let there more work be laid upon the men,
that they may labour therein; and let them not
regard vain words.
10 And the taskmasters of the people went
out, and their officers, and they spake to the people, saying, Thus saith Pharaoh, I will not give
you straw.
11 Go ye, get you straw where ye can find
it: yet not ought of your work shall be diminished.
12 So the people were scattered abroad
throughout all the land of Egypt to gather stubble
instead of straw.
13 And the taskmasters hasted *them*, saying,
Fulfil your works, *your* daily tasks, as when there
was straw.
14 And the [a]officers of the children of Israel,
which Pharaoh's taskmasters had set over them,
were [b]beaten, *and* demanded, Wherefore have ye
not fulfilled your task in making brick both yesterday and to day, as heretofore?
15 Then the officers of the children of Israel
came and cried unto Pharaoh, saying, Wherefore
dealest thou thus with thy servants?
16 There is no straw given unto thy servants,
and they say to us, Make brick: and, behold, thy
servants *are* beaten; but the fault *is* in thine own
people.
17 But he said, Ye *are* idle, *ye are* idle: therefore ye say, Let us go *and* do sacrifice to the LORD.
18 Go therefore now, *and* work; for there
shall no straw be given you, yet shall ye deliver
the tale of bricks.
19 And the officers of the children of Israel
did see *that* they *were* in evil *case*, after it was
said, Ye shall not minish *ought* from your bricks
of your daily task.
20 And they met Moses and Aaron, who
stood in the way, as they came forth from
Pharaoh:
21 [a]And they said unto them, The LORD look
upon you, and judge; because ye have made our
savour to be abhorred in the eyes of Pharaoh, and
in the eyes of his servants, to put a sword in their
hand to slay us.

Israel's Deliverance Assured
(Ex. 3:1—4:17)

22 And Moses returned unto the LORD, and
said, Lord, wherefore hast thou *so* evil entreated
this people? why *is* it *that* thou hast sent me?
23 For since I came to Pharaoh to speak in
thy name, he hath done evil to this people; neither
hast thou delivered thy people at all.

6 Then the LORD said unto Moses, Now shalt
thou see what I will do to Pharaoh: for [a]with
a strong hand shall he let them go, and with a
strong hand [b]shall he drive them out of his land.
2 And God spake unto Moses, and said unto
him, I *am* the LORD:
3 And I [a]appeared unto Abraham, unto
Isaac, and unto Jacob, by *the name of* [b]God Almighty, but by my name [c]JEHOVAH was I not
known to them.
4 [a]And I have also established my covenant
with them, [b]to give them the land of Canaan, the
land of their pilgrimage, [c]wherein they were
strangers.
5 And [a]I have also heard the groaning of
the children of Israel, whom the Egyptians keep
in bondage; and I have remembered my covenant.
6 Wherefore say unto the children of Israel,
[a]I *am* the LORD, and [b]I will bring you out from
under the burdens of the Egyptians, and I will
rid you out of their bondage, and I will [c]redeem

7 [a]Ex. 1:14
14 [a]Ex. 5:6
[b]Is. 10:24
21 [a]Ex. 6:9;
14:11; 15:24;
16:2

CHAPTER 6

1 [a]Ex. 3:19
[b]Ex. 12:31,
33, 39
3 [a]Gen. 17:1;
35:9; 48:3
[b]Gen. 28:3;
35:11 [c]Ex.
3:14, 15; 15:3;
Ps. 68:4;
83:18; Is. 52:6;
Jer. 16:21;
Ezek. 37:6, 13;
John 8:58
4 [a]Gen. 12:7;
15:18; 17:4, 7,
8; 26:3; 28:4,
13 [b]Gen. 47:9;
Lev. 25:23
[c]Gen. 28:4
5 [a]Ex. 2:24;
[Job 34:28];
Acts 7:34
6 [a]Ex. 13:3,
14; 20:2; Deut.
6:12 [b]Ex. 3:17;
7:4; 12:51;
16:6; 18:1;
Deut. 26:8; Ps.
136:11 [c]Ex.
15:13; Deut.
7:8; 1 Chr.
17:21; Neh.
1:10

*———
6:3 Heb. *YHWH*, traditionally *Jehovah*

NKJV

to make [a]brick as before. Let them go and gather
straw for themselves.
8 "And you shall lay on them the quota of
bricks which they made before. You shall not reduce it. For they are idle; therefore they cry out,
saying, 'Let us go *and* sacrifice to our God.'
9 "Let more work be laid on the men, that
they may labor in it, and let them not regard false
words."
10 And the taskmasters of the people and
their officers went out and spoke to the people,
saying, "Thus says Pharaoh: 'I will not give you
straw.
11 'Go, get yourselves straw where you can
find it; yet none of your work will be reduced.' "
12 So the people were scattered abroad
throughout all the land of Egypt to gather stubble
instead of straw.
13 And the taskmasters forced *them* to hurry,
saying, "Fulfill your work, *your* daily quota, as
when there was straw."
14 Also the [a]officers of the children of Israel,
whom Pharaoh's taskmasters had set over them,
were [b]beaten *and* were asked, "Why have you
not fulfilled your task in making brick both yesterday and today, as before?"
15 Then the officers of the children of Israel
came and cried out to Pharaoh, saying, "Why are
you dealing thus with your servants?
16 "There is no straw given to your servants,
and they say to us, 'Make brick!' And indeed your
servants *are* beaten, but the fault *is* in your *own*
people."
17 But he said, "You *are* idle! Idle! Therefore
you say, 'Let us go *and* sacrifice to the LORD.'
18 "Therefore go now *and* work; for no straw
shall be given you, yet you shall deliver the quota
of bricks."
19 And the officers of the children of Israel
saw *that* they *were* in trouble after it was said,
"You shall not reduce *any* bricks from your daily
quota."
20 Then, as they came out from Pharaoh,
they met Moses and Aaron who stood there to
meet them.
21 [a]And they said to them, "Let the LORD
look on you and judge, because you have made
us abhorrent in the sight of Pharaoh and in the
sight of his servants, to put a sword in their hand
to kill us."

Israel's Deliverance Assured
(Ex. 3:1—4:17)

22 So Moses returned to the LORD and said,
"Lord, why have You brought trouble on this people? Why *is* it You have sent me?
23 "For since I came to Pharaoh to speak in
Your name, he has done evil to this people; neither have You delivered Your people at all."

6 Then the LORD said to Moses, "Now you shall
see what I will do to Pharaoh. For [a]with a
strong hand he will let them go, and with a strong
hand [b]he will drive them out of his land."
2 And God spoke to Moses and said to him:
"I *am* the LORD.
3 [a]"I appeared to Abraham, to Isaac, and
to Jacob, as [b]God Almighty, but *by* My name
[c]LORD* I was not known to them.
4 [a]"I have also established My covenant
with them, [b]to give them the land of Canaan, the
land of their pilgrimage, [c]in which they were
strangers.
5 "And [a]I have also heard the groaning of
the children of Israel whom the Egyptians keep
in bondage, and I have remembered My covenant.
6 "Therefore say to the children of Israel:
[a]'I *am* the LORD; [b]I will bring you out from under
the burdens of the Egyptians, I will [c]rescue you

KJV

you with a stretched out arm, and with great judgments:

7 And I will [a]take you to me for a people, and [b]I will be to you a God: and ye shall know that I *am* the LORD your God, which bringeth you out [c]from under the burdens of the Egyptians.

8 And I will bring you in unto the land, concerning the which I did [a]swear to give it to Abraham, to Isaac, and to Jacob; and I will give it you for an heritage: I *am* the LORD.

9 And Moses spake so unto the children of Israel: [a]but they hearkened not unto Moses for [b]anguish of spirit, and for cruel bondage.

10 And the LORD spake unto Moses, saying,

11 Go in, speak unto Pharaoh king of Egypt, that he let the children of Israel go out of his land.

12 And Moses spake before the LORD, saying, Behold, the children of Israel have not hearkened unto me; how then shall Pharaoh hear me, [a]who *am* of uncircumcised lips?

13 And the LORD spake unto Moses and unto Aaron, and gave them a [a]charge unto the children of Israel, and unto Pharaoh king of Egypt, to bring the children of Israel out of the land of Egypt.

The Family of Moses and Aaron (Gen. 46:8–27)

14 These *be* the heads of their fathers' houses: [a]The sons of Reuben the firstborn of Israel; Hanoch, and Pallu, Hezron, and Carmi: these *be* the families of Reuben.

15 [a]And the sons of Simeon; Jemuel, and Jamin, and Ohad, and Jachin, and Zohar, and Shaul the son of a Canaanitish woman: these *are* the families of Simeon.

16 And these *are* the names of [a]the sons of Levi according to their generations; Gershon, and Kohath, and Merari: and the years of the life of Levi *were* an hundred thirty and seven years.

17 [a]The sons of Gershon; Libni, and Shimi, according to their families.

18 And [a]the sons of Kohath; Amram, and Izhar, and Hebron, and Uzziel: and the years of the life of Kohath *were* an hundred thirty and three years.

19 And [a]the sons of Merari; Mahali and Mushi: these *are* the families of Levi according to their generations.

20 And [a]Amram took him [b]Jochebed his father's sister to wife; and she bare him [c]Aaron and Moses: and the years of the life of Amram *were* an hundred and thirty and seven years.

21 And [a]the sons of Izhar; Korah, and Nepheg, and Zichri.

22 And [a]the sons of Uzziel; Mishael, and Elzaphan, and Zithri.

23 And Aaron took him Elisheba, daughter of [a]Amminadab, sister of Naashon, to wife; and she bare him [b]Nadab, and Abihu, [c]Eleazar, and Ithamar.

24 And [a]the sons of Korah; Assir, and Elkanah, and Abiasaph: these *are* the families of the Korhites.

25 And Eleazar Aaron's son took him *one* of the daughters of Putiel to wife; and [a]she bare him Phinehas: these *are* the heads of the fathers of the Levites according to their families.

26 These *are* that Aaron and Moses, to whom the LORD said, Bring out the children of Israel from the land of Egypt according to their [a]armies.

27 These *are* they which spake to Pharaoh king of Egypt, [a]to bring out the children of Israel from Egypt: these *are* that Moses and Aaron.

Aaron Is Moses' Spokesman

28 And it came to pass on the day *when* the LORD spake unto Moses in the land of Egypt,

29 That the LORD spake unto Moses, saying, I *am* the LORD: [a]speak thou unto Pharaoh king of Egypt all that I say unto thee.

30 And Moses said before the LORD, Behold,

7 [a]Ex. 19:5; Deut. 4:20; 7:6; 2 Sam. 7:24 [b]Gen. 17:7; Ex. 29:45, 46; Lev. 26:12, 13, 45; Deut. 29:13; Rev. 21:7 [c]Ex. 5:4, 5
8 [a]Gen. 15:18; 26:3; Num. 14:30; Neh. 9:15; Ezek. 20:5, 6
9 [a]Ex. 5:21 [b]Ex. 2:23; Num. 21:4
12 [a]Ex. 4:10; 6:30; Jer. 1:6
13 [a]Num. 27:19, 23; Deut. 31:14
14 [a]Gen. 46:9; Num. 26:5–11; 1 Chr. 5:3
15 [a]Gen. 46:10; Num. 26:12–14; 1 Chr. 4:24
16 [a]Gen. 46:11; Num. 3:17; 1 Chr. 6:16–30
17 [a]1 Chr. 6:17
18 [a]1 Chr. 6:2, 18
19 [a]1 Chr. 6:19; 23:21
20 [a]Ex. 2:1, 2; Num. 3:19 [b]Num. 26:59 [c]Num. 26:59
21 [a]Num. 16:1; 1 Chr. 6:37, 38
22 [a]Lev. 10:4
23 [a]Ruth 4:19, 20; 1 Chr. 2:10; Matt. 1:4 [b]Lev. 10:1; Num. 3:2; 26:60 [c]Ex. 28:1
24 [a]Num. 26:11
25 [a]Num. 25:7, 11; Josh. 24:33
26 [a]Ex. 7:4; 12:17, 51; Num. 33:1
27 [a]Ex. 6:13; 32:7; 33:1; Ps. 77:20
29 [a]Ex. 6:11; 7:2

NKJV

from their bondage, and I will redeem you with an outstretched arm and with great judgments.

7 'I will [a]take you as My people, and [b]I will be your God. Then you shall know that I *am* the LORD your God who brings you out [c]from under the burdens of the Egyptians.

8 'And I will bring you into the land which I [a]swore to give to Abraham, Isaac, and Jacob; and I will give it to you *as* a heritage: I *am* the LORD.' "

9 So Moses spoke thus to the children of Israel; [a]but they did not heed Moses, because of [b]anguish of spirit and cruel bondage.

10 And the LORD spoke to Moses, saying,

11 "Go in, tell Pharaoh king of Egypt to let the children of Israel go out of his land."

12 And Moses spoke before the LORD, saying, "The children of Israel have not heeded me. How then shall Pharaoh heed me, for [a]I *am* of uncircumcised lips?"

13 Then the LORD spoke to Moses and Aaron, and gave them a [a]command for the children of Israel and for Pharaoh king of Egypt, to bring the children of Israel out of the land of Egypt.

The Family of Moses and Aaron (Gen. 46:8–27)

14 These *are* the heads of their fathers' houses: [a]The sons of Reuben, the firstborn of Israel, *were* Hanoch, Pallu, Hezron, and Carmi. These are the families of Reuben.

15 [a]And the sons of Simeon *were* *Jemuel, Jamin, Ohad, Jachin, Zohar, and Shaul the son of a Canaanite woman. These *are* the families of Simeon.

16 These *are* the names of [a]the sons of Levi according to their generations: Gershon, Kohath, and Merari. And the years of the life of Levi *were* one hundred and thirty-seven.

17 [a]The sons of Gershon *were* Libni and Shimi according to their families.

18 And [a]the sons of Kohath *were* Amram, Izhar, Hebron, and Uzziel. And the years of the life of Kohath *were* one hundred and thirty-three.

19 [a]The sons of Merari *were* Mahli and Mushi. These *are* the families of Levi according to their generations.

20 Now [a]Amram took for himself [b]Jochebed, his father's sister, as wife; and she bore him [c]Aaron and Moses. And the years of the life of Amram *were* one hundred and thirty-seven.

21 [a]The sons of Izhar *were* Korah, Nepheg, and Zichri.

22 And [a]the sons of Uzziel *were* Mishael, Elzaphan, and Zithri.

23 Aaron took to himself Elisheba, daughter of [a]Amminadab, sister of Nahshon, as wife; and she bore him [b]Nadab, Abihu, [c]Eleazar, and Ithamar.

24 And [a]the sons of Korah *were* Assir, Elkanah, and Abiasaph. These are the families of the Korahites.

25 Eleazar, Aaron's son, took for himself one of the daughters of Putiel as wife; and [a]she bore him Phinehas. These *are* the heads of the fathers' houses of the Levites according to their families.

26 These *are the same* Aaron and Moses to whom the LORD said, "Bring out the children of Israel from the land of Egypt according to their [a]armies."

27 These *are* the ones who spoke to Pharaoh king of Egypt, [a]to bring out the children of Israel from Egypt. These *are the same* Moses and Aaron.

Aaron Is Moses' Spokesman

28 And it came to pass, on the day the LORD spoke to Moses in the land of Egypt,

29 that the LORD spoke to Moses, saying, "I *am* the LORD. [a]Speak to Pharaoh king of Egypt all that I say to you."

30 But Moses said before the LORD, "Behold,

*———
6:15 *Nemuel,* Num. 26:12

KJV

[a]I *am* of uncircumcised lips, and how shall Pharaoh hearken unto me?

7 And the LORD said unto Moses, See, I have made thee [a]a god to Pharaoh: and Aaron thy brother shall be [b]thy prophet.

2 Thou [a]shalt speak all that I command thee: and Aaron thy brother shall speak unto Pharaoh, that he send the children of Israel out of his land.

3 And [a]I will harden Pharaoh's heart, and [b]multiply my [c]signs and my wonders in the land of Egypt.

4 But [a]Pharaoh shall not hearken unto you, [b]that I may lay my hand upon Egypt, and bring forth mine armies, *and* my people the children of Israel, out of the land of Egypt [c]by great judgments.

5 And the Egyptians [a]shall know that I *am* the LORD, when I [b]stretch forth mine hand upon Egypt, and [c]bring out the children of Israel from among them.

6 And Moses and Aaron [a]did as the LORD commanded them, so did they.

7 And Moses *was* [a]fourscore years old, and [b]Aaron fourscore and three years old, when they spake unto Pharaoh.

Aaron's Miraculous Rod
(Ex. 4:1–5)

8 And the LORD spake unto Moses and unto Aaron, saying,

9 When Pharaoh shall speak unto you, saying, [a]Shew a miracle for you: then thou shalt say unto Aaron, [b]Take thy rod, and cast *it* before Pharaoh, *and* it shall become a serpent.

10 And Moses and Aaron went in unto Pharaoh, and they did so [a]as the LORD had commanded: and Aaron cast down his rod before Pharaoh, and before his servants, and it [b]became a serpent.

11 Then Pharaoh also [a]called the wise men and [b]the sorcerers: now the magicians of Egypt, they also [c]did in like manner with their enchantments.

12 For they cast down every man his rod, and they became serpents: but Aaron's rod swallowed up their rods.

13 And he hardened Pharaoh's heart, that he hearkened not unto them; as the LORD had said.

The First Plague: Waters Become Blood

14 And the LORD said unto Moses, [a]Pharaoh's heart *is* hardened, he refuseth to let the people go.

15 Get thee unto Pharaoh in the morning; lo, he goeth out unto the [a]water; and thou shalt stand by the river's brink against he come; and [b]the rod which was turned to a serpent shalt thou take in thine hand.

16 And thou shalt say unto him, [a]The LORD God of the Hebrews hath sent me unto thee, saying, Let my people go, [b]that they may serve me in the wilderness: and, behold, hitherto thou wouldest not hear.

17 Thus saith the LORD, In this [a]thou shalt know that I *am* the LORD: behold, I will smite with the rod that *is* in mine hand upon the waters which *are* in the river, and [b]they shall be turned [c]to blood.

18 And the fish that *is* in the river shall die, and the river shall stink; and the Egyptians shall [a]lothe to drink of the water of the river.

19 And the LORD spake unto Moses, Say unto Aaron, Take thy rod, and [a]stretch out thine hand upon the waters of Egypt, upon their streams, upon their rivers, and upon their ponds, and upon all their pools of water, that they may become blood; and *that* there may be blood throughout all the land of Egypt, both in *vessels of* wood, and in *vessels of* stone.

20 And Moses and Aaron did so, as the LORD

30 [a]Ex. 4:10; 6:12; Jer. 1:6

CHAPTER 7

1 [a]Ex. 4:16; Jer. 1:10 [b]Ex. 4:15, 16
2 [a]Ex. 4:15; Deut. 18:18
3 [a]Ex. 4:21; 9:12 [b]Ex. 11:9; Acts 7:36 [c]Ex. 4:7; Deut. 4:34
4 [a]Ex. 3:19, 20; 10:1; 11:9 [b]Ex. 9:14 [c]Ex. 6:6; 12:12
5 [a]Ex. 7:17; 8:22; 14:4, 18; Ps. 9:16 [b]Ex. 9:15 [c]Ex. 3:20; 6:6; 12:51
6 [a]Ex. 7:2
7 [a]Deut. 29:5; 31:2; 34:7; Acts 7:23, 30 [b]Num. 33:39
9 [a]Ex. 10:1; Is. 7:11; John 2:18; 6:30 [b]Ex. 4:2, 3, 17
10 [a]Ex. 7:9 [b]Ex. 4:3
11 [a]Gen. 41:8 [b]Dan. 2:2; 2 Tim. 3:8 [c]Ex. 7:22; 8:7, 18; 2 Tim. 3:9; Rev. 13:13, 14
14 [a]Ex. 8:15; 10:1, 20, 27
15 [a]Ex. 2:5; 8:20 [b]Ex. 4:2, 3; 7:10
16 [a]Ex. 3:13, 18; 4:22 [b]Ex. 3:12, 18; 4:23; 5:1, 3; 8:1
17 [a]Ex. 5:2; 7:5; 10:2; Ps. 9:16; Ezek. 25:17 [b]Ex. 4:9; 7:20 [c]Rev. 11:6; 16:4, 6
18 [a]Ex. 7:24
19 [a]Ex. 8:5, 6, 16; 9:22; 10:12, 21; 14:21, 26

NKJV

[a]I *am* of uncircumcised lips, and how shall Pharaoh heed me?"

7 So the LORD said to Moses: "See, I have made you [a]*as* God to Pharaoh, and Aaron your brother shall be [b]your prophet.

2 "You [a]shall speak all that I command you. And Aaron your brother shall tell Pharaoh to send the children of Israel out of his land.

3 "And [a]I will harden Pharaoh's heart, and [b]multiply My [c]signs and My wonders in the land of Egypt.

4 "But [a]Pharaoh will not heed you, so [b]that I may lay My hand on Egypt and bring My armies *and* My people, the children of Israel, out of the land of Egypt [c]by great judgments.

5 "And the Egyptians [a]shall know that I *am* the LORD, when I [b]stretch out My hand on Egypt and [c]bring out the children of Israel from among them."

6 Then Moses and Aaron [a]did *so;* just as the LORD commanded them, so they did.

7 And Moses *was* [a]eighty years old and [b]Aaron eighty-three years old when they spoke to Pharaoh.

Aaron's Miraculous Rod
(Ex. 4:1–5)

8 Then the LORD spoke to Moses and Aaron, saying,

9 "When Pharaoh speaks to you, saying, [a]'Show a miracle for yourselves,' then you shall say to Aaron, [b]'Take your rod and cast *it* before Pharaoh, *and* let it become a serpent.' "

10 So Moses and Aaron went in to Pharaoh, and they did so, just [a]as the LORD commanded. And Aaron cast down his rod before Pharaoh and before his servants, and it [b]became a serpent.

11 But Pharaoh also [a]called the wise men and [b]the sorcerers; so the magicians of Egypt, they also [c]did in like manner with their enchantments.

12 For every man threw down his rod, and they became serpents. But Aaron's rod swallowed up their rods.

13 And Pharaoh's heart grew hard, and he did not heed them, as the LORD had said.

The First Plague: Waters Become Blood

14 So the LORD said to Moses: [a]"Pharaoh's heart *is* hard; he refuses to let the people go.

15 "Go to Pharaoh in the morning, when he goes out to the [a]water, and you shall stand by the river's bank to meet him; and [b]the rod which was turned to a serpent you shall take in your hand.

16 "And you shall say to him, [a]'The LORD God of the Hebrews has sent me to you, saying, "Let My people go, [b]that they may serve Me in the wilderness"; but indeed, until now you would not hear!

17 'Thus says the LORD: "By this [a]you shall know that I *am* the LORD. Behold, I will strike the waters which *are* in the river with the rod that *is* in my hand, and [b]they shall be turned [c]to blood.

18 "And the fish that *are* in the river shall die, the river shall stink, and the Egyptians will [a]loathe to drink the water of the river." ' "

19 Then the LORD spoke to Moses, "Say to Aaron, 'Take your rod and [a]stretch out your hand over the waters of Egypt, over their streams, over their rivers, over their ponds, and over all their pools of water, that they may become blood. And there shall be blood throughout all the land of Egypt, both in *buckets of* wood and *pitchers of* stone.' "

20 And Moses and Aaron did so, just as the

KJV

commanded; and he [a]lifted up the rod, and smote the waters that *were* in the river, in the sight of Pharaoh, and in the sight of his servants; and all the [b]waters that *were* in the river were turned to blood.

21 And the fish that *was* in the river died; and the river stank, and the Egyptians [a]could not drink of the water of the river; and there was blood throughout all the land of Egypt.

22 [a]And the magicians of Egypt did [b]so with their enchantments: and Pharaoh's heart was hardened, neither did he hearken unto them; [c]as the LORD had said.

23 And Pharaoh turned and went into his house, neither did he set his heart to this also.

24 And all the Egyptians digged round about the river for water to drink; for they could not drink of the water of the river.

25 And seven days were fulfilled, after that the LORD had smitten the river.

The Second Plague: Frogs

8 And the LORD spake unto Moses, Go unto Pharaoh, and say unto him, Thus saith the LORD, Let my people go, [a]that they may serve me.

2 And if thou [a]refuse to let *them* go, behold, I will smite all thy borders with [b]frogs:

3 And the river shall bring forth frogs abundantly, which shall go up and come into thine house, and into thy [a]bedchamber, and upon thy bed, and into the house of thy servants, and upon thy people, and into thine ovens, and into thy kneadingtroughs:

4 And the frogs shall come up both on thee, and upon thy people, and upon all thy servants.

5 And the LORD spake unto Moses, Say unto Aaron, [a]Stretch forth thine hand with thy rod over the streams, over the rivers, and over the ponds, and cause frogs to come up upon the land of Egypt.

6 And Aaron stretched out his hand over the waters of Egypt; and [a]the frogs came up, and covered the land of Egypt.

7 [a]And the magicians did so with their enchantments, and brought up frogs upon the land of Egypt.

8 Then Pharaoh called for Moses and Aaron, and said, [a]Intreat the LORD, that he may take away the frogs from me, and from my people; and I will let the people [b]go, that they may do sacrifice unto the LORD.

9 And Moses said unto Pharaoh, Glory over me: when shall I intreat for thee, and for thy servants, and for thy people, to destroy the frogs from thee and thy houses, *that* they may remain in the river only?

10 And he said, To morrow. And he said, *Be it* according to thy word: that thou mayest know that [a]*there is* none like unto the LORD our God.

11 And the frogs shall depart from thee, and from thy houses, and from thy servants, and from thy people; they shall remain in the river only.

12 And Moses and Aaron went out from Pharaoh: and Moses [a]cried unto the LORD because of the frogs which he had brought against Pharaoh.

13 And the LORD did according to the word of Moses; and the frogs died out of the houses, out of the villages, and out of the fields.

14 And they gathered them together upon heaps: and the land stank.

15 But when Pharaoh saw that there was [a]respite, [b]he hardened his heart, and hearkened not unto them; as the LORD had said.

The Third Plague: Lice

16 And the LORD said unto Moses, Say unto Aaron, Stretch out thy rod, and smite the dust of the land, that it may become lice throughout all the land of Egypt.

17 And they did so; for Aaron stretched out his hand with his rod, and smote the dust of the

20 [a]Ex. 17:5 [b]Ps. 78:44; 105:29, 30
21 [a]Ex. 7:18
22 [a]Ex. 7:11 [b]Ex. 8:7 [c]Ex. 3:19; 7:3

CHAPTER 8

1 [a]Ex. 3:12, 18; 4:23; 5:1, 3
2 [a]Ex. 7:14; 9:2 [b]Rev. 16:13
3 [a]Ps. 105:30
5 [a]Ex. 7:19
6 [a]Ps. 78:45; 105:30
7 [a]Ex. 7:11, 22
8 [a]Ex. 8:28; 9:28; 10:17; Num. 21:7; 1 Kin. 13:6 [b]Ex. 10:8, 24
10 [a]Ex. 9:14; 15:11; Deut. 4:35, 39; 33:26; 2 Sam. 7:22; 1 Chr. 17:20; Ps. 86:8; Is. 46:9; [Jer. 10:6, 7]
12 [a]Ex. 8:30; 9:33; 10:18; 32:11; [James 5:16–18]
15 [a]Eccl. 8:11 [b]Ex. 7:14, 22; 9:34; 1 Sam. 6:6

NKJV

LORD commanded. So he [a]lifted up the rod and struck the waters that *were* in the river, in the sight of Pharaoh and in the sight of his servants. And all the [b]waters that *were* in the river were turned to blood.

21 The fish that *were* in the river died, the river stank, and the Egyptians [a]could not drink the water of the river. So there was blood throughout all the land of Egypt.

22 [a]Then the magicians of Egypt did [b]so with their enchantments; and Pharaoh's heart grew hard, and he did not heed them, [c]as the LORD had said.

23 And Pharaoh turned and went into his house. Neither was his heart moved by this.

24 So all the Egyptians dug all around the river for water to drink, because they could not drink the water of the river.

25 And seven days passed after the LORD had struck the river.

The Second Plague: Frogs

8 And the LORD spoke to Moses, "Go to Pharaoh and say to him, 'Thus says the LORD: "Let My people go, [a]that they may serve Me.

2 "But if you [a]refuse to let *them* go, behold, I will smite all your territory with [b]frogs.

3 "So the river shall bring forth frogs abundantly, which shall go up and come into your house, into your [a]bedroom, on your bed, into the houses of your servants, on your people, into your ovens, and into your kneading bowls.

4 "And the frogs shall come up on you, on your people, and on all your servants." ' "

5 Then the LORD spoke to Moses, "Say to Aaron, [a]'Stretch out your hand with your rod over the streams, over the rivers, and over the ponds, and cause frogs to come up on the land of Egypt.' "

6 So Aaron stretched out his hand over the waters of Egypt, and [a]the frogs came up and covered the land of Egypt.

7 [a]And the magicians did so with their enchantments, and brought up frogs on the land of Egypt.

8 Then Pharaoh called for Moses and Aaron, and said, [a]"Entreat the LORD that He may take away the frogs from me and from my people; and I will let the people [b]go, that they may sacrifice to the LORD."

9 And Moses said to Pharaoh, "Accept the honor of saying when I shall intercede for you, for your servants, and for your people, to destroy the frogs from you and your houses, *that* they may remain in the river only."

10 So he said, "Tomorrow." And he said, "*Let it be* according to your word, that you may know that [a]*there is* no one like the LORD our God.

11 "And the frogs shall depart from you, from your houses, from your servants, and from your people. They shall remain in the river only."

12 Then Moses and Aaron went out from Pharaoh. And Moses [a]cried out to the LORD concerning the frogs which He had brought against Pharaoh.

13 So the LORD did according to the word of Moses. And the frogs died out of the houses, out of the courtyards, and out of the fields.

14 They gathered them together in heaps, and the land stank.

15 But when Pharaoh saw that there was [a]relief, [b]he hardened his heart and did not heed them, as the LORD had said.

The Third Plague: Lice

16 So the LORD said to Moses, "Say to Aaron, 'Stretch out your rod, and strike the dust of the land, so that it may become lice throughout all the land of Egypt.' "

17 And they did so. For Aaron stretched out his hand with his rod and struck the dust of the

KJV

earth, and [a]it became lice in man, and in beast; all the dust of the land became lice throughout all the land of Egypt.

18 And [a]the magicians did so with their enchantments to bring forth lice, but they [b]could not: so there were lice upon man, and upon beast.

19 Then the magicians said unto Pharaoh, This *is* [a]the finger of God: and Pharaoh's [b]heart was hardened, and he hearkened not unto them; as the LORD had said.

The Fourth Plague: Flies

20 And the LORD said unto Moses, [a]Rise up early in the morning, and stand before Pharaoh; lo, he cometh forth to the water; and say unto him, Thus saith the LORD, [b]Let my people go, that they may serve me.

21 Else, if thou wilt not let my people go, behold, I will send swarms *of flies* upon thee, and upon thy servants, and upon thy people, and into thy houses: and the houses of the Egyptians shall be full of swarms *of flies,* and also the ground whereon they *are.*

22 And [a]I will sever in that day the land of [b]Goshen, in which my people dwell, that no swarms *of flies* shall be there; to the end thou mayest [c]know that I *am* the LORD in the midst of the [d]earth.

23 And I will put a division between my people and thy people: to morrow shall this [a]sign be.

24 And the LORD did so; and [a]there came a grievous swarm *of flies* into the house of Pharaoh, and *into* his servants' houses, and into all the land of Egypt: the land was corrupted by reason of the swarm *of flies.*

25 And Pharaoh called for Moses and for Aaron, and said, Go ye, sacrifice to your God in the land.

26 And Moses said, It is not meet so to do; for we shall sacrifice [a]the abomination of the Egyptians to the LORD our God: lo, shall we sacrifice the abomination of the Egyptians before their eyes, and will they not stone us?

27 We will go [a]three days' journey into the wilderness, and sacrifice to the LORD our God, as [b]he shall command us.

28 And Pharaoh said, I will let you go, that ye may sacrifice to the LORD your God in the wilderness; only ye shall not go very far away: [a]intreat for me.

29 And Moses said, Behold, I go out from thee, and I will intreat the LORD that the swarms *of flies* may depart from Pharaoh, from his servants, and from his people, to morrow: but let not Pharaoh [a]deal deceitfully any more in not letting the people go to sacrifice to the LORD.

30 And Moses went out from Pharaoh, and [a]intreated the LORD.

31 And the LORD did according to the word of Moses; and he removed the swarms *of flies* from Pharaoh, from his servants, and from his people; there remained not one.

32 And Pharaoh [a]hardened his heart at this time also, neither would he let the people go.

The Fifth Plague: Livestock Diseased

9 Then the LORD said unto Moses, [a]Go in unto Pharaoh, and tell him, Thus saith the LORD God of the Hebrews, Let my people go, that they may [b]serve me.

2 For if thou [a]refuse to let *them* go, and wilt hold them still,

3 Behold, the [a]hand of the LORD is upon thy cattle which *is* in the field, upon the horses, upon the asses, upon the camels, upon the oxen, and upon the sheep: *there shall be* a very grievous murrain.

4 And [a]the LORD shall sever between the cattle of Israel and the cattle of Egypt: and there shall nothing die of all *that is* the children's of Israel.

5 And the LORD appointed a set time, saying,

17 [a]Ps. 105:31
18 [a]Ex. 7:11, 12; 8:7 [b]Dan. 5:8; 2 Tim. 3:8, 9
19 [a]Ex. 7:5; 10:7; 1 Sam. 6:3, 9; Ps. 8:3; Luke 11:20 [b]Ex. 8:15
20 [a]Ex. 7:15; 9:13 [b]Ex. 3:18; 4:23; 5:1, 3; 8:1
22 [a]Ex. 9:4, 6, 26; 10:23; 11:6, 7; 12:13 [b]Gen. 50:8 [c]Ex. 7:5, 17; 10:2; 14:4 [d]Ex. 9:29
23 [a]Ex. 4:8
24 [a]Ps. 78:45; 105:31
26 [a]Gen. 43:32; 46:34; [Deut. 7:25, 26; 12:31]
27 [a]Ex. 3:18; 5:3 [b]Ex. 3:12
28 [a]Ex. 8:8, 15, 29, 32; 9:28; 1 Kin. 13:6
29 [a]Ex. 8:8, 15
30 [a]Ex. 8:12
32 [a]Ex. 4:21; 8:8, 15; Ps. 52:2

CHAPTER 9

1 [a]Ex. 4:23; 8:1 [b]Ex. 7:16
2 [a]Ex. 8:2
3 [a]Ex. 7:4; 1 Sam. 5:6; Ps. 39:10; Acts 13:11
4 [a]Ex. 8:22

*8:23 Lit. *set a ransom,* Ex. 9:4; 11:7

NKJV

earth, and [a]it became lice on man and beast. All the dust of the land became lice throughout all the land of Egypt.

18 Now [a]the magicians so worked with their enchantments to bring forth lice, but they [b]could not. So there were lice on man and beast.

19 Then the magicians said to Pharaoh, "This *is* [a]the finger of God." But Pharaoh's [b]heart grew hard, and he did not heed them, just as the LORD had said.

The Fourth Plague: Flies

20 And the LORD said to Moses, [a]"Rise early in the morning and stand before Pharaoh as he comes out to the water. Then say to him, 'Thus says the LORD: [b]"Let My people go, that they may serve Me.

21 "Or else, if you will not let My people go, behold, I will send swarms *of flies* on you and your servants, on your people and into your houses. The houses of the Egyptians shall be full of swarms *of flies,* and also the ground on which they *stand.*

22 "And in that day [a]I will set apart the land of [b]Goshen, in which My people dwell, that no swarms *of flies* shall be there, in order that you may [c]know that I *am* the LORD in the midst of the [d]land.

23 "I will *make a difference between My people and your people. Tomorrow this [a]sign shall be." ' "

24 And the LORD did so. [a]Thick swarms *of flies* came into the house of Pharaoh, *into* his servants' houses, and into all the land of Egypt. The land was corrupted because of the swarms *of flies.*

25 Then Pharaoh called for Moses and Aaron, and said, "Go, sacrifice to your God in the land."

26 And Moses said, "It is not right to do so, for we would be sacrificing [a]the abomination of the Egyptians to the LORD our God. If we sacrifice the abomination of the Egyptians before their eyes, then will they not stone us?

27 "We will go [a]three days' journey into the wilderness and sacrifice to the LORD our God as [b]He will command us."

28 So Pharaoh said, "I will let you go, that you may sacrifice to the LORD your God in the wilderness; only you shall not go very far away. [a]Intercede for me."

29 Then Moses said, "Indeed I am going out from you, and I will entreat the LORD, that the swarms *of flies* may depart tomorrow from Pharaoh, from his servants, and from his people. But let Pharaoh not [a]deal deceitfully anymore in not letting the people go to sacrifice to the LORD."

30 So Moses went out from Pharaoh and [a]entreated the LORD.

31 And the LORD did according to the word of Moses; He removed the swarms *of flies* from Pharaoh, from his servants, and from his people. Not one remained.

32 But Pharaoh [a]hardened his heart at this time also; neither would he let the people go.

The Fifth Plague: Livestock Diseased

9 Then the LORD said to Moses, [a]"Go in to Pharaoh and tell him, 'Thus says the LORD God of the Hebrews: "Let My people go, that they may [b]serve Me.

2 "For if you [a]refuse to let *them* go, and still hold them,

3 "behold, the [a]hand of the LORD will be on your cattle in the field, on the horses, on the donkeys, on the camels, on the oxen, and on the sheep—a very severe pestilence.

4 "And [a]the LORD will make a difference between the livestock of Israel and the livestock of Egypt. So nothing shall die of all *that* belongs to the children of Israel." ' "

5 Then the LORD appointed a set time, say-

KJV

To morrow the LORD shall do this thing in the
land.
6 And the LORD did that thing on the morrow, and [a]all the cattle of Egypt died: but of the
cattle of the children of Israel died not one.
7 And Pharaoh sent, and, behold, there was
not one of the cattle of the Israelites dead. And
the [a]heart of Pharaoh was hardened, and he did
not let the people go.

The Sixth Plague: Boils
(Deut. 28:27)

8 And the LORD said unto Moses and unto
Aaron, Take to you handfuls of ashes of the furnace, and let Moses sprinkle it toward the heaven
in the sight of Pharaoh.
9 And it shall become small dust in all the
land of Egypt, and shall be [a]a boil breaking forth
with blains upon man, and upon beast, throughout all the land of Egypt.
10 And they took ashes of the furnace, and
stood before Pharaoh; and Moses sprinkled it up
toward heaven; and it became [a]a boil breaking
forth *with* blains upon man, and upon beast.
11 And the [a]magicians could not stand
before Moses because of the [b]boils; for the boil
was upon the magicians, and upon all the
Egyptians.
12 And the LORD hardened the heart of Pharaoh, and he [a]hearkened not unto them; [b]as the
LORD had spoken unto Moses.

The Seventh Plague: Hail

13 And the LORD said unto Moses, [a]Rise up
early in the morning, and stand before Pharaoh,
and say unto him, Thus saith the LORD God of
the Hebrews, Let my people go, that they may
[b]serve me.
14 For I will at this time send all my plagues
upon thine heart, and upon thy servants, and upon
thy people; [a]that thou mayest know that *there is*
none like me in all the earth.
15 For now I will [a]stretch out my hand, that
I may smite thee and thy people with [b]pestilence;
and thou shalt be cut off from the earth.
16 And in very deed for [a]this *cause* have I
raised thee up, for to [b]shew *in* thee my power;
and that my [c]name may be declared throughout
all the earth.
17 As yet exaltest thou thyself against my
people, that thou wilt not let them go?
18 Behold, to morrow about this time I will
cause it to rain a very grievous hail, such as hath
not been in Egypt since the foundation thereof
even until now.
19 Send therefore now, *and* gather thy cattle,
and all that thou hast in the field; *for upon* every
man and beast which shall be found in the field,
and shall not be brought home, the hail shall come
down upon them, and they shall die.
20 He that [a]feared the word of the LORD
among the [b]servants of Pharaoh made his servants and his cattle flee into the houses:
21 And he that regarded not the word of the
LORD left his servants and his cattle in the field.
22 And the LORD said unto Moses, Stretch
forth thine hand toward heaven, that there may
be [a]hail in all the land of Egypt, upon man, and
upon beast, and upon every herb of the field,
throughout the land of Egypt.
23 And Moses stretched forth his rod toward
heaven: and [a]the LORD sent thunder and hail, and
the fire ran along upon the ground; and the LORD
rained hail upon the land of Egypt.
24 So there was hail, and fire mingled with
the hail, very grievous, such as there was none
like it in all the land of Egypt since it became a
nation.
25 And the [a]hail smote throughout all the
land of Egypt all that *was* in the field, both man
and beast; and the hail smote every herb of the
field, and brake every tree of the field.

6 [a]Ex. 9:19, 20, 25; Ps. 78:48, 50
7 [a]Ex. 7:14; 8:32
9 [a]Deut. 28:27; Rev. 16:2
10 [a]Deut. 28:27
11 [a][Ex. 8:18, 19; 2 Tim. 3:9] [b]Deut. 28:27; Job 2:7; Rev. 16:1, 2
12 [a]Ex. 7:13 [b]Ex. 4:21
13 [a]Ex. 8:20 [b]Ex. 9:1
14 [a]Ex. 8:10; Deut. 3:24; 2 Sam. 7:22; 1 Chr. 17:20; Ps. 86:8; Is. 45:5–8; 46:9; Jer. 10:6, 7
15 [a]Ex. 3:20; 7:5 [b]Ex. 5:3
16 [a]Ex. 14:17; Prov. 16:4; [Rom. 9:17, 18; 1 Pet. 2:8, 9] [b]Ex. 7:4, 5; 10:1; 11:9; 14:17 [c]1 Kin. 8:43
20 [a]Ex. 1:17; 14:31; [Prov. 13:13] [b]Ex. 8:19; 10:7
22 [a]Rev. 16:21
23 [a]Gen. 19:24; Josh. 10:11; Ps. 18:13; 78:47; 105:32; 148:8; Is. 30:30; Ezek. 38:22; Rev. 8:7
25 [a]Ex. 9:19; Ps. 78:47, 48; 105:32, 33

NKJV

ing, "Tomorrow the LORD will do this thing in the
land."
6 So the LORD did this thing on the next day,
and [a]all the livestock of Egypt died; but of the
livestock of the children of Israel, not one died.
7 Then Pharaoh sent, and indeed, not even
one of the livestock of the Israelites was dead.
But the [a]heart of Pharaoh became hard, and he
did not let the people go.

The Sixth Plague: Boils
(Deut. 28:27)

8 So the LORD said to Moses and Aaron,
"Take for yourselves handfuls of ashes from a
furnace, and let Moses scatter it toward the heavens in the sight of Pharaoh.
9 "And it will become fine dust in all the
land of Egypt, and it will cause [a]boils that break
out in sores on man and beast throughout all the
land of Egypt."
10 Then they took ashes from the furnace
and stood before Pharaoh, and Moses scattered
them toward heaven. And *they* caused [a]boils that
break out in sores on man and beast.
11 And the [a]magicians could not stand before Moses because of the [b]boils, for the boils
were on the magicians and on all the Egyptians.
12 But the LORD hardened the heart of Pharaoh; and he [a]did not heed them, just [b]as the LORD
had spoken to Moses.

The Seventh Plague: Hail

13 Then the LORD said to Moses, [a]"Rise early
in the morning and stand before Pharaoh, and
say to him, 'Thus says the LORD God of the Hebrews: "Let My people go, that they may [b]serve
Me,
14 "for at this time I will send all My plagues
to your very heart, and on your servants and on
your people, [a]that you may know that *there is*
none like Me in all the earth.
15 "Now if I had [a]stretched out My hand and
struck you and your people with [b]pestilence, then
you would have been cut off from the earth.
16 "But indeed for [a]this *purpose* I have raised
you up, that I may [b]show My power *in* you, and
that My [c]name may be declared in all the earth.
17 "As yet you exalt yourself against My people in that you will not let them go.
18 "Behold, tomorrow about this time I will
cause very heavy hail to rain down, such as has
not been in Egypt since its founding until now.
19 "Therefore send now *and* gather your livestock and all that you have in the field, for the
hail shall come down on every man and every
animal which is found in the field and is not
brought home; and they shall die."'"
20 He who [a]feared the word of the LORD
among the [b]servants of Pharaoh made his servants and his livestock flee to the houses.
21 But he who did not regard the word of
the LORD left his servants and his livestock in the
field.
22 Then the LORD said to Moses, "Stretch out
your hand toward heaven, that there may be [a]hail
in all the land of Egypt—on man, on beast, and
on every herb of the field, throughout the land
of Egypt."
23 And Moses stretched out his rod toward
heaven; and [a]the LORD sent thunder and hail, and
fire darted to the ground. And the LORD rained
hail on the land of Egypt.
24 So there was hail, and fire mingled with
the hail, so very heavy that there was none like
it in all the land of Egypt since it became a nation.
25 And the [a]hail struck throughout the whole
land of Egypt, all that *was* in the field, both man
and beast; and the hail struck every herb of the
field and broke every tree of the field.

KJV

26 [a]Only in the land of Goshen, where the children of Israel *were,* was there no hail.

27 And Pharaoh sent, and [a]called for Moses and Aaron, and said unto them, [b]I have sinned this time: [c]the LORD *is* righteous, and I and my people *are* wicked.

28 [a]Intreat the LORD (for *it is* enough) that there be no *more* mighty thunderings and hail; and I will let you [b]go, and ye shall stay no longer.

29 And Moses said unto him, As soon as I am gone out of the city, I will [a]spread abroad my hands unto the LORD; *and* the thunder shall cease, neither shall there be any more hail; that thou mayest know how that the [b]earth *is* the LORD'S.

30 But as for thee and thy servants, [a]I know that ye will not yet fear the LORD God.

31 And the flax and the barley was smitten: [a]for the barley *was* in the ear, and the flax *was* bolled.

32 But the wheat and the rie were not smitten: for they *were* not grown up.

33 And Moses went out of the city from Pharaoh, and [a]spread abroad his hands unto the LORD: and the thunders and hail ceased, and the rain was not poured upon the earth.

34 And when Pharaoh saw that the rain and the hail and the thunders were ceased, he sinned yet more, and hardened his heart, he and his servants.

35 And [a]the heart of Pharaoh was hardened, neither would he let the children of Israel go; as the LORD had spoken by Moses.

The Eighth Plague: Locusts
(Joel 1:2–4)

10 And the LORD said unto Moses, Go in unto Pharaoh: [a]for I have hardened his heart, and the heart of his servants, [b]that I might shew these my signs before him:

2 And that [a]thou mayest tell in the ears of thy son, and of thy son's son, what things I have wrought in Egypt, and my signs which I have done among them; that ye may [b]know how that I *am* the LORD.

3 And Moses and Aaron came in unto Pharaoh, and said unto him, Thus saith the LORD God of the Hebrews, How long wilt thou refuse to [a]humble thyself before me? let my people go, that they may [b]serve me.

4 Else, if thou refuse to let my people go, behold, to morrow will I bring the [a]locusts into thy coast:

5 And they shall cover the face of the earth, that one cannot be able to see the earth: and [a]they shall eat the residue of that which is escaped, which remaineth unto you from the hail, and shall eat every tree which groweth for you out of the field:

6 And they shall [a]fill thy houses, and the houses of all thy servants, and the houses of all the Egyptians; which neither thy fathers, nor thy fathers' fathers have seen, since the day that they were upon the earth unto this day. And he turned himself, and went out from Pharaoh.

7 And Pharaoh's [a]servants said unto him, How long shall this man be [b]a snare unto us? let the men go, that they may serve the LORD their God: knowest thou not yet that Egypt is destroyed?

8 And Moses and Aaron were brought again unto Pharaoh: and he said unto them, Go, serve the LORD your God: *but* who *are* they that shall go?

9 And Moses said, We will go with our young and with our old, with our sons and with our daughters, with our flocks and with our herds will we go; for [a]we *must hold* a feast unto the LORD.

10 And he said unto them, Let the LORD be so with you, as I will let you go, and your little ones: look *to it;* for evil *is* before you.

11 Not so: go now ye *that are* men, and serve

26 [a]Ex. 8:22, 23; 9:4, 6; 10:23; 11:7; 12:13; Is. 32:18, 19
27 [a]Ex. 8:8 [b]Ex. 9:34; 10:16, 17 [c]2 Chr. 12:6; Ps. 129:4; 145:17; Lam. 1:18
28 [a]Ex. 8:8, 28; 10:17; Acts 8:24 [b]Ex. 8:25; 10:8, 24
29 [a]1 Kin. 8:22, 38; Ps. 143:6; Is. 1:15 [b]Ex. 8:22; 19:5; 20:11; Ps. 24:1; 1 Cor. 10:26, 28
30 [a]Ex. 8:29; [Is. 26:10]
31 [a]Ruth 1:22; 2:23
33 [a]Ex. 8:12; 9:29
35 [a]Ex. 4:21

CHAPTER 10

1 [a]Ex. 4:21; 7:14; 9:12; 10:27; 11:10; 14:4; Josh. 11:20; John 12:40; Rom. 9:18 [b]Ex. 7:4; 9:16
2 [a]Ex. 12:26; 13:8, 14; Deut. 4:9; 6:7; 11:19; Ps. 44:1; 78:5; Joel 1:3 [b]Ex. 7:5, 17; 8:22
3 [a][1 Kin. 21:29; 2 Chr. 34:27]; Job 42:6; [James 4:10; 1 Pet. 5:6] [b]Ex. 4:23; 8:1; 9:1
4 [a]Prov. 30:27; Rev. 9:3
5 [a]Ex. 9:32; Joel 1:4; 2:25
6 [a]Ex. 8:3, 21
7 [a]Ex. 7:5; 8:19; 9:20; 12:33 [b]Ex. 23:33; Josh. 23:13; 1 Sam. 18:21; Eccl. 7:26; 1 Cor. 7:35
9 [a]Ex. 5:1; 7:16

NKJV

26 [a]Only in the land of Goshen, where the children of Israel *were,* there was no hail.

27 And Pharaoh sent and [a]called for Moses and Aaron, and said to them, [b]"I have sinned this time. [c]The LORD *is* righteous, and my people and I *are* wicked.

28 [a]"Entreat the LORD, that there may be no *more* mighty thundering and hail, for *it is* enough. I will let you [b]go, and you shall stay no longer."

29 So Moses said to him, "As soon as I have gone out of the city, I will [a]spread out my hands to the LORD; the thunder will cease, and there will be no more hail, that you may know that the [b]earth *is* the LORD'S.

30 "But as for you and your servants, [a]I know that you will not yet fear the LORD God."

31 Now the flax and the barley were struck, [a]for the barley *was* in the head and the flax *was* in bud.

32 But the wheat and the spelt were not struck, for they *are* late crops.

33 So Moses went out of the city from Pharaoh and [a]spread out his hands to the LORD; then the thunder and the hail ceased, and the rain was not poured on the earth.

34 And when Pharaoh saw that the rain, the hail, and the thunder had ceased, he sinned yet more; and he hardened his heart, he and his servants.

35 So [a]the heart of Pharaoh was hard; neither would he let the children of Israel go, as the LORD had spoken by Moses.

The Eighth Plague: Locusts
(Joel 1:2–4)

10 Now the LORD said to Moses, "Go in to Pharaoh; [a]for I have hardened his heart and the hearts of his servants, [b]that I may show these signs of Mine before him,

2 "and that [a]you may tell in the hearing of your son and your son's son the mighty things I have done in Egypt, and My signs which I have done among them, that you may [b]know that I *am* the LORD."

3 So Moses and Aaron came in to Pharaoh and said to him, "Thus says the LORD God of the Hebrews: 'How long will you refuse to [a]humble yourself before Me? Let My people go, that they may [b]serve Me.

4 'Or else, if you refuse to let My people go, behold, tomorrow I will bring [a]locusts into your territory.

5 'And they shall cover the face of the earth, so that no one will be able to see the earth; and [a]they shall eat the residue of what is left, which remains to you from the hail, and they shall eat every tree which grows up for you out of the field.

6 'They shall [a]fill your houses, the houses of all your servants, and the houses of all the Egyptians—which neither your fathers nor your fathers' fathers have seen, since the day that they were on the earth to this day.'" And he turned and went out from Pharaoh.

7 Then Pharaoh's [a]servants said to him, "How long shall this man be [b]a snare to us? Let the men go, that they may serve the LORD their God. Do you not yet know that Egypt is destroyed?"

8 So Moses and Aaron were brought again to Pharaoh, and he said to them, "Go, serve the LORD your God. Who *are* the ones that are going?"

9 And Moses said, "We will go with our young and our old; with our sons and our daughters, with our flocks and our herds we will go, for [a]we must hold a feast to the LORD."

10 Then he said to them, "The LORD had better be with you when I let you and your little ones go! Beware, for evil is ahead of you.

11 "Not so! Go now, you *who are* men, and

KJV

the LORD; for that ye did desire. And they were driven [a]out from Pharaoh's presence.

12 And the LORD said unto Moses, [a]Stretch out thine hand over the land of Egypt for the locusts, that they may come up upon the land of Egypt, and [b]eat every herb of the land, *even* all that the hail hath left.

13 And Moses stretched forth his rod over the land of Egypt, and the LORD brought an east wind upon the land all that day, and all *that* night; *and* when it was morning, the east wind brought the locusts.

14 And [a]the locusts went up over all the land of Egypt, and rested in all the coasts of Egypt: very grievous *were they;* [b]before them there were no such locusts as they, neither after them shall be such.

15 For they [a]covered the face of the whole earth, so that the land was darkened; and they [b]did eat every herb of the land, and all the fruit of the trees which the hail had left: and there remained not any green thing in the trees, or in the herbs of the field, through all the land of Egypt.

16 Then Pharaoh called [a]for Moses and Aaron in haste; and he said, [b]I have sinned against the LORD your God, and against you.

17 Now therefore forgive, I pray thee, my sin only this once, and [a]intreat the LORD your God, that he may take away from me this death only.

18 And he [a]went out from Pharaoh, and intreated the LORD.

19 And the LORD turned a mighty strong west wind, which took away the locusts, and cast them [a]into the Red sea; there remained not one locust in all the coasts of Egypt.

20 But the LORD [a]hardened Pharaoh's heart, so that he would not let the children of Israel go.

The Ninth Plague: Darkness

21 And the LORD said unto Moses, [a]Stretch out thine hand toward heaven, that there may be darkness over the land of Egypt, even darkness *which* may be felt.

22 And Moses stretched forth his hand toward heaven; and there was a [a]thick darkness in all the land of Egypt [b]three days:

23 They saw not one another, neither rose any from his place for three days: [a]but all the children of Israel had light in their dwellings.

24 And Pharaoh called unto Moses, and [a]said, Go ye, serve the LORD; only let your flocks and your herds be stayed: let your [b]little ones also go with you.

25 And Moses said, Thou must give us also sacrifices and burnt offerings, that we may sacrifice unto the LORD our God.

26 Our [a]cattle also shall go with us; there shall not an hoof be left behind; for thereof must we take to serve the LORD our God; and we know not with what we must serve the LORD, until we come thither.

27 But the LORD [a]hardened Pharaoh's heart, and he would not let them go.

28 And Pharaoh said unto him, [a]Get thee from me, take heed to thyself, see my face no more; for in *that* day thou seest my face thou shalt die.

29 And Moses said, Thou hast spoken well, [a]I will see thy face again no more.

Death of the Firstborn Announced
(Ex. 3:21, 22; 12:35, 36)

11 And the LORD said unto Moses, Yet will I bring one plague *more* upon Pharaoh, and upon Egypt; [a]afterwards he will let you go hence: [b]when he shall let *you* go, he shall surely thrust you out hence altogether.

2 Speak now in the ears of the people, and let every man borrow of his neighbour, and every woman of her neighbour, [a]jewels of silver, and jewels of gold.

3 [a]And the LORD gave the people favour in

---

11 [a]Ex. 10:28
12 [a]Ex. 7:19 [b]Ex. 10:5, 15
14 [a]Deut. 28:38; Ps. 78:46; 105:34 [b]Joel 1:4, 7; 2:1–11; Rev. 9:3
15 [a]Ex. 10:5 [b]Ps. 105:35
16 [a]Ex. 8:8 [b]Ex. 9:27
17 [a]Ex. 8:8, 28; 9:28; 1 Kin. 13:6
18 [a]Ex. 8:30
19 [a]Joel 2:20
20 [a]Ex. 4:21; 10:1; 11:10
21 [a]Ex. 9:22
22 [a]Ps. 105:28; Rev. 16:10 [b]Ex. 3:18
23 [a]Ex. 8:22, 23
24 [a]Ex. 8:8, 25; 10:8 [b]Ex. 10:10
26 [a]Ex. 10:9
27 [a]Ex. 4:21; 10:1, 20; 14:4, 8
28 [a]Ex. 10:11
29 [a]Ex. 11:8; Heb. 11:27

CHAPTER 11

1 [a]Ex. 12:31, 33, 39 [b]Ex. 6:1; 12:39
2 [a]Ex. 3:22; 12:35, 36
3 [a]Ex. 3:21; 12:36; Ps. 106:46

NKJV

serve the LORD, for that is what you desired." And they were driven [a]out from Pharaoh's presence.

12 Then the LORD said to Moses, [a]"Stretch out your hand over the land of Egypt for the locusts, that they may come upon the land of Egypt, and [b]eat every herb of the land—all that the hail has left."

13 So Moses stretched out his rod over the land of Egypt, and the LORD brought an east wind on the land all that day and all *that* night. When it was morning, the east wind brought the locusts.

14 And [a]the locusts went up over all the land of Egypt and rested on all the territory of Egypt. *They were* very severe; [b]previously there had been no such locusts as they, nor shall there be such after them.

15 For they [a]covered the face of the whole earth, so that the land was darkened; and they [b]ate every herb of the land and all the fruit of the trees which the hail had left. So there remained nothing green on the trees or on the plants of the field throughout all the land of Egypt.

16 Then Pharaoh called [a]for Moses and Aaron in haste, and said, [b]"I have sinned against the LORD your God and against you.

17 "Now therefore, please forgive my sin only this once, and [a]entreat the LORD your God, that He may take away from me this death only."

18 So he [a]went out from Pharaoh and entreated the LORD.

19 And the LORD turned a very strong west wind, which took the locusts away and blew them [a]into the Red Sea. There remained not one locust in all the territory of Egypt.

20 But the LORD [a]hardened Pharaoh's heart, and he did not let the children of Israel go.

The Ninth Plague: Darkness

21 Then the LORD said to Moses, [a]"Stretch out your hand toward heaven, that there may be darkness over the land of Egypt, darkness *which* may even be felt."

22 So Moses stretched out his hand toward heaven, and there was [a]thick darkness in all the land of Egypt [b]three days.

23 They did not see one another; nor did anyone rise from his place for three days. [a]But all the children of Israel had light in their dwellings.

24 Then Pharaoh called to Moses and [a]said, "Go, serve the LORD; only let your flocks and your herds be kept back. Let your [b]little ones also go with you."

25 But Moses said, "You must also give us sacrifices and burnt offerings, that we may sacrifice to the LORD our God.

26 "Our [a]livestock also shall go with us; not a hoof shall be left behind. For we must take some of them to serve the LORD our God, and even we do not know with what we must serve the LORD until we arrive there."

27 But the LORD [a]hardened Pharaoh's heart, and he would not let them go.

28 Then Pharaoh said to him, [a]"Get away from me! Take heed to yourself and see my face no more! For in the day you see my face you shall die!"

29 So Moses said, "You have spoken well. [a]I will never see your face again."

Death of the Firstborn Announced
(Ex. 3:21, 22; 12:35, 36)

11 And the LORD said to Moses, "I will bring one more plague on Pharaoh and on Egypt. [a]Afterward he will let you go from here. [b]When he lets *you* go, he will surely drive you out of here altogether.

2 "Speak now in the hearing of the people, and let every man ask from his neighbor and every woman from her neighbor, [a]articles of silver and articles of gold."

3 [a]And the LORD gave the people favor in

KJV

the sight of the Egyptians. Moreover the man [b]Moses *was* very great in the land of Egypt, in the sight of Pharaoh's servants, and in the sight of the people.

4 And Moses said, Thus saith the LORD, [a]About midnight will I go out into the midst of Egypt:

5 And [a]all the firstborn in the land of Egypt shall die, from the firstborn of Pharaoh that sitteth upon his throne, even unto the firstborn of the maidservant that *is* behind the mill; and all the firstborn of beasts.

6 [a]And there shall be a great cry throughout all the land of Egypt, [b]such as there was none like it, nor shall be like it any more.

7 [a]But against any of the children of Israel [b]shall not a dog move his tongue, against man or beast: that ye may know how that the LORD doth put a difference between the Egyptians and Israel.

8 And [a]all these thy servants shall come down unto me, and bow down themselves unto me, saying, Get thee out, and all the people that follow thee: and after that I will go out. [b]And he went out from Pharaoh in a great anger.

9 And the LORD said unto Moses, [a]Pharaoh shall not hearken unto you; that [b]my wonders may be multiplied in the land of Egypt.

10 And Moses and Aaron did all these wonders before Pharaoh: [a]and the LORD hardened Pharaoh's heart, so that he would not let the children of Israel go out of his land.

The Passover Instituted
(Num. 9:1–14; Deut. 16:1–8; Ezek. 45:21–25)

12 And the LORD spake unto Moses and Aaron in the land of Egypt, saying,

2 [a]This month *shall be* unto you the beginning of months: it *shall be* the first month of the year to you.

3 Speak ye unto all the congregation of Israel, saying, In the [a]tenth *day* of this month they shall take to them every man a lamb, according to the house of *their* fathers, a lamb for an house:

4 And if the household be too little for the lamb, let him and his neighbour next unto his house take *it* according to the number of the souls; every man according to his eating shall make your count for the lamb.

5 Your lamb shall be [a]without blemish, a male of the first year: ye shall take *it* out from the sheep, or from the goats:

6 And ye shall keep it up until the [a]fourteenth day of the same month: and the whole assembly of the congregation of Israel shall kill it in the evening.

7 And they shall take of the blood, and strike *it* on the two side posts and on the upper door post of the houses, wherein they shall eat it.

8 And they shall eat the flesh in that [a]night, [b]roast with fire, and [c]unleavened bread; *and* with bitter *herbs* they shall eat it.

9 Eat not of it raw, nor sodden at all with water, but [a]roast *with* fire; his head with his legs, and with the purtenance thereof.

10 [a]And ye shall let nothing of it remain until the morning; and that which remaineth of it until the morning ye shall burn with fire.

11 And thus shall ye eat it; *with* your loins girded, your shoes on your feet, and your staff in your hand; and ye shall eat it in haste: [a]it *is* the LORD's passover.

12 For I [a]will pass through the land of Egypt this night, and will smite all the firstborn in the land of Egypt, both man and beast; and [b]against all the gods of Egypt I will execute judgment: [c]I *am* the LORD.

13 And the blood shall be to you for a token upon the houses where ye *are:* and when I see the blood, I will pass over you, and the plague

---

3 [b]Deut. 34:10–12; 2 Sam. 7:9; Esth. 9:4
4 [a]Ex. 12:12, 23, 29
5 [a]Ex. 4:23; 12:12, 29; Ps. 78:51; 105:36; 135:8; 136:10; Amos 4:10
6 [a]Ex. 12:30; Amos 5:17 [b]Ex. 10:14
7 [a]Ex. 8:22 [b]Josh. 10:21
8 [a]Ex. 12:31–33 [b]Ex. 10:29; Heb. 11:27
9 [a]Ex. 3:19; 7:4; 10:1 [b]Ex. 7:3; 9:16
10 [a]Ex. 7:3; 9:12; 10:1, 20, 27; Josh. 11:20; Is. 63:17; John 12:40; Rom. 2:5

CHAPTER 12

2 [a]Ex. 13:4; 23:15; 34:18; Deut. 16:1
3 [a]Josh. 4:19
5 [a]Lev. 22:18–21; 23:12; Mal. 1:8, 14; [Heb. 9:14; 1 Pet. 1:19]
6 [a]Ex. 12:14, 17; Lev. 23:5; Num. 9:1–3, 11; 28:16; Deut. 16:1, 4, 6
8 [a]Ex. 34:25; Num. 9:12 [b]Deut. 16:7 [c]Deut. 16:3, 4; 1 Cor. 5:8
9 [a]Deut. 16:7
10 [a]Ex. 16:19; 23:18; 34:25
11 [a]Ex. 12:13, 21, 27, 43
12 [a]Ex. 11:4, 5 [b]Num. 33:4 [c]Ex. 6:2

NKJV

the sight of the Egyptians. Moreover the man [b]Moses *was* very great in the land of Egypt, in the sight of Pharaoh's servants and in the sight of the people.

4 Then Moses said, "Thus says the LORD: [a]'About midnight I will go out into the midst of Egypt;

5 'and [a]all the firstborn in the land of Egypt shall die, from the firstborn of Pharaoh who sits on his throne, even to the firstborn of the female servant who *is* behind the handmill, and all the firstborn of the animals.

6 [a]'Then there shall be a great cry throughout all the land of Egypt, [b]such as was not like it *before,* nor shall be like it again.

7 [a]'But against none of the children of Israel [b]shall a dog move its tongue, against man or beast, that you may know that the LORD does make a difference between the Egyptians and Israel.'

8 "And [a]all these your servants shall come down to me and bow down to me, saying, 'Get out, and all the people who follow you!' After that I will go out." [b]Then he went out from Pharaoh in great anger.

9 But the LORD said to Moses, [a]"Pharaoh will not heed you, so that [b]My wonders may be multiplied in the land of Egypt."

10 So Moses and Aaron did all these wonders before Pharaoh; [a]and the LORD hardened Pharaoh's heart, and he did not let the children of Israel go out of his land.

The Passover Instituted
(Num. 9:1–14; Deut. 16:1–8; Ezek. 45:21–25)

12 Now the LORD spoke to Moses and Aaron in the land of Egypt, saying,

2 [a]"This month *shall be* your beginning of months; it *shall be* the first month of the year to you.

3 "Speak to all the congregation of Israel, saying: 'On the [a]tenth of this month every man shall take for himself a lamb, according to the house of *his* father, a lamb for a household.

4 'And if the household is too small for the lamb, let him and his neighbor next to his house take *it* according to the number of the persons; according to each man's need you shall make your count for the lamb.

5 'Your lamb shall be [a]without blemish, a male of the first year. You may take *it* from the sheep or from the goats.

6 'Now you shall keep it until the [a]fourteenth day of the same month. Then the whole assembly of the congregation of Israel shall kill it at twilight.

7 'And they shall take *some* of the blood and put *it* on the two doorposts and on the lintel of the houses where they eat it.

8 'Then they shall eat the flesh on that [a]night; [b]roasted in fire, with [c]unleavened bread *and* with bitter *herbs* they shall eat it.

9 'Do not eat it raw, nor boiled at all with water, but [a]roasted in fire—its head with its legs and its entrails.

10 [a]'You shall let none of it remain until morning, and what remains of it until morning you shall burn with fire.

11 'And thus you shall eat it: *with* a belt on your waist, your sandals on your feet, and your staff in your hand. So you shall eat it in haste. [a]It *is* the LORD's Passover.

12 'For I [a]will pass through the land of Egypt on that night, and will strike all the firstborn in the land of Egypt, both man and beast; and [b]against all the gods of Egypt I will execute judgment: [c]I *am* the LORD.

13 'Now the blood shall be a sign for you on the houses where you *are.* And when I see the blood, I will pass over you; and the plague shall

KJV

shall not be upon you to destroy *you,* when I smite
the land of Egypt.
14 And this day shall be unto you [a]for a memorial; and ye shall keep it a [b]feast to the LORD
throughout your generations; ye shall keep it a
feast [c]by an ordinance for ever.
15 [a]Seven days shall ye eat unleavened
bread; even the first day ye shall put away leaven
out of your houses: for whosoever eateth leavened
bread from the first day until the seventh day,
[b]that soul shall be cut off from Israel.
16 And in the first day *there shall be* [a]an holy
convocation, and in the seventh day there shall
be an holy convocation to you; no manner of work
shall be done in them, save *that* which every man
must eat, that only may be done of you.
17 And ye shall observe *the feast of* unleavened bread; for [a]in this selfsame day have I
brought your armies [b]out of the land of Egypt:
therefore shall ye observe this day in your generations by an ordinance for ever.
18 [a]In the first *month,* on the fourteenth day
of the month at even, ye shall eat unleavened
bread, until the one and twentieth day of the
month at even.
19 [a]Seven days shall there be no leaven
found in your houses: for whosoever eateth that
which is leavened, even that soul shall be cut off
from the congregation of Israel, whether he be a
stranger, or born in the land.
20 Ye shall eat nothing leavened; in all your
habitations shall ye eat unleavened bread.
21 Then [a]Moses called for all the [b]elders of
Israel, and said unto them, [c]Draw out and take
you a lamb according to your families, and kill
the passover.
22 [a]And ye shall take a bunch of hyssop, and
dip *it* in the blood that *is* in the bason, and [b]strike
the lintel and the two side posts with the blood
that *is* in the bason; and none of you shall go out
at the door of his house until the morning.
23 [a]For the LORD will pass through to smite
the Egyptians; and when he seeth the [b]blood upon
the lintel, and on the two side posts, the LORD
will pass over the door, and [c]will not suffer [d]the
destroyer to come in unto your houses to smite
you.
24 And ye shall [a]observe this thing for an
ordinance to thee and to thy sons for ever.
25 And it shall come to pass, when ye be
come to the land which the LORD will give you,
[a]according as he hath promised, that ye shall keep
this service.
26 [a]And it shall come to pass, when your children shall say unto you, What mean ye by this
service?
27 That ye shall say, [a]It *is* the sacrifice of
the LORD's passover, who passed over the houses
of the children of Israel in Egypt, when he smote
the Egyptians, and delivered our houses. And the
people [b]bowed the head and worshipped.
28 And the children of Israel went away, and
[a]did as the LORD had commanded Moses and
Aaron, so did they.

The Tenth Plague: Death of the Firstborn
(Ex. 11:1–10)

29 [a]And it came to pass, that at midnight [b]the
LORD smote all the firstborn in the land of Egypt,
from the firstborn of Pharaoh that sat on his
throne unto the firstborn of the captive that *was*
in the dungeon; and all the firstborn of [c]cattle.
30 And Pharaoh rose up in the night, he, and
all his servants, and all the Egyptians; and there
was a great cry in Egypt; for *there was* not a house
where *there was* not one dead.

The Exodus

31 And he [a]called for Moses and Aaron by
night, and said, Rise up, *and* get you forth from
among my people, [b]both ye and the children of
Israel; and go, serve the LORD, as ye have [c]said.

14 [a]Ex. 13:9 [b]Lev. 23:4, 5; 2 Kin. 23:21 [c]Ex. 12:17, 24; 13:10
15 [a]Ex. 13:6, 7; 23:15; 34:18; Lev. 23:6; Num. 28:17; Deut. 16:3, 8 [b]Gen. 17:14; Ex. 12:19; Num. 9:13
16 [a]Lev. 23:2, 7, 8; Num. 28:18, 25
17 [a]Ex. 12:14; 13:3, 10 [b]Num. 33:1
18 [a]Ex. 12:2; Lev. 23:5–8; Num. 28:16–25
19 [a]Ex. 12:15; 23:15; 34:18
21 [a][Heb. 11:28] [b]Ex. 3:16 [c]Ex. 12:3; Num. 9:4; Josh. 5:10; 2 Kin. 23:21; Ezra 6:20; Mark 14:12–16
22 [a]Heb. 11:28 [b]Ex. 12:7
23 [a]Ex. 11:4; 12:12, 13 [b]Ex. 24:8 [c]Ezek. 9:6; Rev. 7:3; 9:4 [d]1 Cor. 10:10; Heb. 11:28
24 [a]Ex. 12:14, 17; 13:5, 10
25 [a]Ex. 3:8, 17
26 [a]Ex. 10:2; 13:8, 14, 15; Deut. 32:7; Josh. 4:6; Ps. 78:6
27 [a]Ex. 12:11 [b]Ex. 4:31
28 [a][Heb. 11:28]
29 [a]Ex. 11:4, 5 [b]Num. 8:17; 33:4; Ps. 135:8; 136:10 [c]Ex. 9:6
31 [a]Ex. 10:28, 29 [b]Ex. 8:25; 11:1 [c]Ex. 10:9

NKJV

not be on you to destroy *you* when I strike the
land of Egypt.
14 'So this day shall be to you [a]a memorial;
and you shall keep it as a [b]feast to the LORD
throughout your generations. You shall keep it
as a feast [c]by an everlasting ordinance.
15 [a]'Seven days you shall eat unleavened
bread. On the first day you shall remove leaven
from your houses. For whoever eats leavened
bread from the first day until the seventh day,
[b]that person shall be cut off from Israel.
16 'On the first day *there shall be* [a]a holy
convocation, and on the seventh day there shall
be a holy convocation for you. No manner of work
shall be done on them; but *that* which everyone
must eat—that only may be prepared by you.
17 'So you shall observe *the Feast of* Unleavened Bread, for [a]on this same day I will have
brought your armies [b]out of the land of Egypt.
Therefore you shall observe this day throughout
your generations as an everlasting ordinance.
18 [a]'In the first *month,* on the fourteenth day
of the month at evening, you shall eat unleavened
bread, until the twenty-first day of the month at
evening.
19 'For [a]seven days no leaven shall be found
in your houses, since whoever eats what is leavened, that same person shall be cut off from the
congregation of Israel, whether *he is* a stranger
or a native of the land.
20 'You shall eat nothing leavened; in all
your dwellings you shall eat unleavened bread.' "
21 Then [a]Moses called for all the [b]elders of
Israel and said to them, [c]"Pick out and take lambs
for yourselves according to your families, and kill
the Passover *lamb.*
22 [a]"And you shall take a bunch of hyssop,
dip *it* in the blood that *is* in the basin, and [b]strike
the lintel and the two doorposts with the blood
that *is* in the basin. And none of you shall go out
of the door of his house until morning.
23 [a]"For the LORD will pass through to strike
the Egyptians; and when He sees the [b]blood on
the lintel and on the two doorposts, the LORD will
pass over the door and [c]not allow [d]the destroyer
to come into your houses to strike *you.*
24 "And you shall [a]observe this thing as an
ordinance for you and your sons forever.
25 "It will come to pass when you come to
the land which the LORD will give you, [a]just as
He promised, that you shall keep this service.
26 [a]"And it shall be, when your children say
to you, 'What do you mean by this service?'
27 "that you shall say, [a]'It *is* the Passover
sacrifice of the LORD, who passed over the houses
of the children of Israel in Egypt when He struck
the Egyptians and delivered our households.' " So
the people [b]bowed their heads and worshiped.
28 Then the children of Israel went away and
[a]did *so;* just as the LORD had commanded Moses
and Aaron, so they did.

The Tenth Plague: Death of the Firstborn
(Ex. 11:1–10)

29 [a]And it came to pass at midnight that [b]the
LORD struck all the firstborn in the land of Egypt,
from the firstborn of Pharaoh who sat on his
throne to the firstborn of the captive who *was* in
the dungeon, and all the firstborn of [c]livestock.
30 So Pharaoh rose in the night, he, all his
servants, and all the Egyptians; and there was a
great cry in Egypt, for *there was* not a house
where *there was* not one dead.

The Exodus

31 Then he [a]called for Moses and Aaron by
night, and said, "Rise, go out from among my people, [b]both you and the children of Israel. And go,
serve the LORD as you have [c]said.

KJV

32 [a]Also take your flocks and your herds, as ye have said, and be gone; and bless me also.

33 [a]And the Egyptians were [b]urgent upon the people, that they might send them out of the land in haste; for they said, We *be* all dead *men*.

34 And the people took their dough before it was leavened, their kneadingtroughs being bound up in their clothes upon their shoulders.

35 And the children of Israel did according to the word of Moses; and they borrowed of the Egyptians [a]jewels of silver, and jewels of gold, and raiment:

36 [a]And the LORD gave the people favour in the sight of the Egyptians, so that they lent unto them *such things as they required.* And [b]they spoiled the Egyptians.

37 And [a]the children of Israel journeyed from [b]Rameses to Succoth, about [c]six hundred thousand on foot *that were* men, beside children.

38 And a [a]mixed multitude went up also with them; and flocks, and herds, *even* very much [b]cattle.

39 And they baked unleavened cakes of the dough which they brought forth out of Egypt, for it was not leavened; because [a]they were thrust out of Egypt, and could not tarry, neither had they prepared for themselves any victual.

40 Now the sojourning of the children of Israel, who dwelt in Egypt, *was* [a]four hundred and thirty years.

41 And it came to pass at the end of the four hundred and thirty years, even the selfsame day it came to pass, that [a]all the hosts of the LORD went out from the land of Egypt.

42 It *is* [a]a night to be much observed unto the LORD for bringing them out from the land of Egypt: this *is* that night of the LORD to be observed of all the children of Israel in their generations.

Passover Regulations
(Gen. 17:9–14; Ex. 12:1–13)

43 And the LORD said unto Moses and Aaron, This *is* [a]the ordinance of the passover: There shall no stranger eat thereof:

44 But every man's servant that is bought for money, when thou hast [a]circumcised him, then shall he eat thereof.

45 [a]A foreigner and an hired servant shall not eat thereof.

46 In one house shall it be eaten; thou shalt not carry forth ought of the flesh abroad out of the house; [a]neither shall ye break a bone thereof.

47 [a]All the congregation of Israel shall keep it.

48 And [a]when a stranger shall sojourn with thee, and will keep the passover to the LORD, let all his males be circumcised, and then let him come near and keep it; and he shall be as one that is born in the land: for no uncircumcised person shall eat thereof.

49 [a]One law shall be to him that is homeborn, and unto the stranger that sojourneth among you.

50 Thus did all the children of Israel; as the LORD commanded Moses and Aaron, so did they.

51 [a]And it came to pass the selfsame day, *that* the LORD did bring the children of Israel out of the land of Egypt [b]by their armies.

The Firstborn Consecrated

13 And the LORD spake unto Moses, saying,
2 [a]Sanctify unto me all the firstborn, whatsoever openeth the womb among the children of Israel, *both* of man and of beast: it *is* mine.

The Feast of Unleavened Bread
(Ex. 12:14–20)

3 And Moses said unto the people, [a]Remember this day, in which ye came out from Egypt, out of the house of bondage; for [b]by strength of

32 [a]Ex. 10:9, 26
33 [a]Ex. 10:7 [b]Ex. 11:8; Ps. 105:38
35 [a]Ex. 3:21, 22; 11:2, 3; Ps. 105:37
36 [a]Ex. 3:21 [b]Gen. 15:14
37 [a]Num. 33:3, 5 [b]Gen. 47:11; Ex. 1:11; Num. 33:3, 4 [c]Gen. 12:2; Ex. 38:26; Num. 1:46; 2:32; 11:21; 26:51
38 [a]Num. 11:4 [b]Ex. 17:3; Num. 20:19; 32:1; Deut. 3:19
39 [a]Ex. 6:1; 11:1; 12:31–33
40 [a]Gen. 15:13, 16; Acts 7:6; Gal. 3:17
41 [a]Ex. 3:8, 10; 6:6; 7:4
42 [a]Ex. 13:10; 34:18; Deut. 16:1, 6
43 [a]Ex. 12:11; Num. 9:14
44 [a]Gen. 17:12, 13; Lev. 22:11
45 [a]Lev. 22:10
46 [a]Num. 9:12; Ps. 34:20; [John 19:33, 36]
47 [a]Ex. 12:6; Num. 9:13, 14
48 [a]Num. 9:14
49 [a]Lev. 24:22; Num. 15:15, 16; [Gal. 3:28]
51 [a]Ex. 12:41; 20:2 [b]Ex. 6:26

CHAPTER 13

2 [a]Ex. 13:12, 13, 15; 22:29; Lev. 27:26; Num. 3:13; 8:16; 18:15; Deut. 15:19; Luke 2:23
3 [a]Ex. 12:42; Deut. 16:3 [b]Ex. 3:20; 6:1

*

12:40 Sam., LXX *Egypt and Canaan*

NKJV

32 [a]"Also take your flocks and your herds, as you have said, and be gone; and bless me also."

33 [a]And the Egyptians [b]urged the people, that they might send them out of the land in haste. For they said, "We *shall* all *be* dead."

34 So the people took their dough before it was leavened, having their kneading bowls bound up in their clothes on their shoulders.

35 Now the children of Israel had done according to the word of Moses, and they had asked from the Egyptians [a]articles of silver, articles of gold, and clothing.

36 [a]And the LORD had given the people favor in the sight of the Egyptians, so that they granted them *what they requested.* Thus [b]they plundered the Egyptians.

37 Then [a]the children of Israel journeyed from [b]Rameses to Succoth, about [c]six hundred thousand men on foot, besides children.

38 A [a]mixed multitude went up with them also, and flocks and herds—a great deal of [b]livestock.

39 And they baked unleavened cakes of the dough which they had brought out of Egypt; for it was not leavened, because [a]they were driven out of Egypt and could not wait, nor had they prepared provisions for themselves.

40 Now the sojourn of the children of Israel who lived in *Egypt *was* [a]four hundred and thirty years.

41 And it came to pass at the end of the four hundred and thirty years—on that very same day—it came to pass that [a]all the armies of the LORD went out from the land of Egypt.

42 It *is* [a]a night of solemn observance to the LORD for bringing them out of the land of Egypt. This *is* that night of the LORD, a solemn observance for all the children of Israel throughout their generations.

Passover Regulations
(Gen. 17:9–14; Ex. 12:1–13)

43 And the LORD said to Moses and Aaron, "This *is* [a]the ordinance of the Passover: No foreigner shall eat it.

44 "But every man's servant who is bought for money, when you have [a]circumcised him, then he may eat it.

45 [a]"A sojourner and a hired servant shall not eat it.

46 "In one house it shall be eaten; you shall not carry any of the flesh outside the house, [a]nor shall you break one of its bones.

47 [a]"All the congregation of Israel shall keep it.

48 "And [a]when a stranger dwells with you *and wants* to keep the Passover to the LORD, let all his males be circumcised, and then let him come near and keep it; and he shall be as a native of the land. For no uncircumcised person shall eat it.

49 [a]"One law shall be for the native-born and for the stranger who dwells among you."

50 Thus all the children of Israel did; as the LORD commanded Moses and Aaron, so they did.

51 [a]And it came to pass, on that very same day, that the LORD brought the children of Israel out of the land of Egypt [b]according to their armies.

The Firstborn Consecrated

13 Then the LORD spoke to Moses, saying,
2 [a]"Consecrate to Me all the firstborn, whatever opens the womb among the children of Israel, *both* of man and beast; it is Mine."

The Feast of Unleavened Bread
(Ex. 12:14–20)

3 And Moses said to the people: [a]"Remember this day in which you went out of Egypt, out of the house of bondage; for [b]by strength of hand

KJV

hand the LORD brought you out from this *place:* [c]there shall no leavened bread be eaten.

4 [a]This day came ye out in the month Abib.

5 And it shall be when the LORD shall [a]bring thee into the [b]land of the Canaanites, and the Hittites, and the Amorites, and the Hivites, and the Jebusites, which he [c]sware unto thy fathers to give thee, a land flowing with milk and honey, [d]that thou shalt keep this service in this month.

6 [a]Seven days thou shalt eat unleavened bread, and in the seventh day *shall be* a feast to the LORD.

7 Unleavened bread shall be eaten seven days; and there shall [a]no leavened bread be seen with thee, neither shall there be leaven seen with thee in all thy quarters.

8 And thou shalt [a]shew thy son in that day, saying, *This is done* because of that *which* the LORD did unto me when I came forth out of Egypt.

9 And it shall be for [a]a sign unto thee upon thine hand, and for a memorial between thine eyes, that the LORD'S law may be in thy mouth: for with a strong hand hath the LORD brought thee out of Egypt.

10 [a]Thou shalt therefore keep this ordinance in his season from year to year.

The Law of the Firstborn

11 And it shall be when the LORD shall [a]bring thee into the land of the [b]Canaanites, as he sware unto thee and to thy fathers, and shall give it thee,

12 [a]That thou shalt set apart unto the LORD all that openeth the matrix, and every firstling that cometh of a beast which thou hast; the males *shall be* the LORD'S.

13 And [a]every firstling of an ass thou shalt redeem with a lamb; and if thou wilt not redeem it, then thou shalt break his neck: and all the firstborn of man among thy children [b]shalt thou redeem.

14 [a]And it shall be when thy son asketh thee in time to come, saying, What *is* this? that thou shalt say unto him, [b]By strength of hand the LORD brought us out from Egypt, from the house of bondage:

15 And it came to pass, when Pharaoh would hardly let us go, that [a]the LORD slew all the firstborn in the land of Egypt, both the firstborn of man, and the firstborn of beast: therefore I sacrifice to the LORD all that openeth the matrix, being males; but all the firstborn of my children I redeem.

16 And it shall be for [a]a token upon thine hand, and for frontlets between thine eyes: for by strength of hand the LORD brought us forth out of Egypt.

The Wilderness Way
(Ex. 40:34–38; Num. 9:15–23; 1 Kin. 8:10, 11)

17 And it came to pass, when Pharaoh had let the people go, that God led them not *through* the way of the land of the Philistines, although that *was* near; for God said, Lest peradventure the people [a]repent when they see war, and [b]they return to Egypt:

18 But God [a]led the people about, *through* the way of the wilderness of the Red sea: and the children of Israel went up harnessed out of the land of Egypt.

19 And Moses took the [a]bones of [b]Joseph with him: for he had straitly sworn the children of Israel, saying, [c]God will surely visit you; and ye shall carry up my bones away hence with you.

20 And [a]they took their journey from [b]Succoth, and encamped in Etham, in the edge of the wilderness.

21 And [a]the LORD went before them by day in a pillar of a cloud, to lead them the way; and by night in a pillar of fire, to give them light; to go by day and night:

22 He took not away the pillar of the cloud

---

3 [c]Ex. 12:8, 19 **4** [a]Ex. 12:2; 23:15; 34:18; Deut. 16:1 **5** [a]Ex. 3:8, 17; Josh. 24:11 [b]Gen. 17:8; Deut. 30:5 [c]Ex. 6:8 [d]Ex. 12:25, 26 **6** [a]Ex. 12:15–20 **7** [a]Ex. 12:19 **8** [a]Ex. 10:2; 12:26; 13:14; Ps. 44:1 **9** [a]Ex. 12:14; 13:16; 31:13; Deut. 6:8; 11:18; Matt. 23:5 **10** [a]Ex. 12:14, 24 **11** [a]Ex. 13:5 [b]Num. 21:3 **12** [a]Ex. 13:1, 2; 22:29; 34:19; Lev. 27:26; Num. 18:15; Ezek. 44:30; Luke 2:23 **13** [a]Ex. 34:20; Num. 18:15 [b]Num. 3:46, 47; 18:15, 16 **14** [a]Ex. 10:2; 12:26, 27; 13:8; Deut. 6:20; Josh. 4:6, 21 [b]Ex. 13:3, 9 **15** [a]Ex. 12:29 **16** [a]Ex. 13:9; Deut. 6:8 **17** [a]Ex. 14:11; Num. 14:1–4 [b]Deut. 17:16 **18** [a]Ex. 14:2; Num. 33:6 **19** [a]Gen. 50:24, 25; Josh. 24:32 [b]Ex. 1:6; Deut. 33:13–17 [c]Ex. 4:31 **20** [a]Num. 33:6–8 [b]Ex. 12:37 **21** [a]Ex. 14:19, 24; 33:9, 10; Num. 9:15; 14:14; Deut. 1:33; Neh. 9:12; Ps. 78:14; 99:7; 105:39; [Is. 4:5]; 1 Cor. 10:1

NKJV

the LORD brought you out of this *place.* [c]No leavened bread shall be eaten.

4 [a]"On this day you are going out, in the month Abib.

5 "And it shall be, when the LORD [a]brings you into the [b]land of the Canaanites and the Hittites and the Amorites and the Hivites and the Jebusites, which He [c]swore to your fathers to give you, a land flowing with milk and honey, [d]that you shall keep this service in this month.

6 [a]"Seven days you shall eat unleavened bread, and on the seventh day *there shall be* a feast to the LORD.

7 "Unleavened bread shall be eaten seven days. And [a]no leavened bread shall be seen among you, nor shall leaven be seen among you in all your quarters.

8 "And you shall [a]tell your son in that day, saying, '*This is done* because of what the LORD did for me when I came up from Egypt.'

9 "It shall be as [a]a sign to you on your hand and as a memorial between your eyes, that the LORD'S law may be in your mouth; for with a strong hand the LORD has brought you out of Egypt.

10 [a]"You shall therefore keep this ordinance in its season from year to year.

The Law of the Firstborn

11 "And it shall be, when the LORD [a]brings you into the land of the [b]Canaanites, as He swore to you and your fathers, and gives it to you,

12 [a]"that you shall set apart to the LORD all that open the womb, that is, every firstborn that comes from an animal which you have; the males *shall be* the LORD'S.

13 "But [a]every firstborn of a donkey you shall redeem with a lamb; and if you will not redeem *it,* then you shall break its neck. And all the firstborn of man among your sons [b]you shall redeem.

14 [a]"So it shall be, when your son asks you in time to come, saying, 'What *is* this?' that you shall say to him, [b]'By strength of hand the LORD brought us out of Egypt, out of the house of bondage.

15 'And it came to pass, when Pharaoh was stubborn about letting us go, that [a]the LORD killed all the firstborn in the land of Egypt, both the firstborn of man and the firstborn of beast. Therefore I sacrifice to the LORD all males that open the womb, but all the firstborn of my sons I redeem.'

16 "It shall be as [a]a sign on your hand and as frontlets between your eyes, for by strength of hand the LORD brought us out of Egypt."

The Wilderness Way
(Ex. 40:34–38; Num. 9:15–23; 1 Kin. 8:10, 11)

17 Then it came to pass, when Pharaoh had let the people go, that God did not lead them *by* way of the land of the Philistines, although that *was* near; for God said, "Lest perhaps the people [a]change their minds when they see war, and [b]return to Egypt."

18 So God [a]led the people around *by* way of the wilderness of the Red Sea. And the children of Israel went up in orderly ranks out of the land of Egypt.

19 And Moses took the [a]bones of [b]Joseph with him, for he had placed the children of Israel under solemn oath, saying, [c]"God will surely visit you, and you shall carry up my bones from here with you."

20 So [a]they took their journey from [b]Succoth and camped in Etham at the edge of the wilderness.

21 And [a]the LORD went before them by day in a pillar of cloud to lead the way, and by night in a pillar of fire to give them light, so as to go by day and night.

22 He did not take away the pillar of cloud

KJV

by day, nor the pillar of fire by night, *from* before the people.

The Red Sea Crossing

14 And the LORD spake unto Moses, saying,
2 Speak unto the children of Israel, [a]that they turn and encamp before [b]Pi–hahiroth, between [c]Migdol and the sea, over against Baal–zephon: before it shall ye encamp by the sea.

3 For Pharaoh will say of the children of Israel, [a]They *are* entangled in the land, the wilderness hath shut them in.

4 And [a]I will harden Pharaoh's heart, that he shall follow after them; and I [b]will be honoured upon Pharaoh, and upon all his host; [c]that the Egyptians may know that I *am* the LORD. And they did so.

5 And it was told the king of Egypt that the people fled: and [a]the heart of Pharaoh and of his servants was turned against the people, and they said, Why have we done this, that we have let Israel go from serving us?

6 And he made ready his chariot, and took his people with him:

7 And he took [a]six hundred chosen chariots, and all the chariots of Egypt, and captains over every one of them.

8 And the LORD [a]hardened the heart of Pharaoh king of Egypt, and he pursued after the children of Israel: and [b]the children of Israel went out with an high hand.

9 But the [a]Egyptians pursued after them, all the horses *and* chariots of Pharaoh, and his horsemen, and his army, and overtook them encamping by the sea, beside Pi–hahiroth, before Baal–zephon.

10 And when Pharaoh drew nigh, the children of Israel lifted up their eyes, and, behold, the Egyptians marched after them; and they were sore afraid: and the children of Israel [a]cried out unto the LORD.

11 [a]And they said unto Moses, Because *there were* no graves in Egypt, hast thou taken us away to die in the wilderness? wherefore hast thou dealt thus with us, to carry us forth out of Egypt?

12 [a]*Is* not this the word that we did tell thee in Egypt, saying, Let us alone, that we may serve the Egyptians? For *it had been* better for us to serve the Egyptians, than that we should die in the wilderness.

13 And Moses said unto the people, [a]Fear ye not, [b]stand still, and see the [c]salvation of the LORD, which he will shew to you to day: for the Egyptians whom ye have seen to day, ye shall [d]see them again no more for ever.

14 [a]The LORD shall fight for you, and ye shall [b]hold your peace.

15 And the LORD said unto Moses, Wherefore criest thou unto me? speak unto the children of Israel, that they go forward:

16 But [a]lift thou up thy rod, and stretch out thine hand over the sea, and divide it: and the children of Israel shall go on dry *ground* through the midst of the sea.

17 And I, behold, I will [a]harden the hearts of the Egyptians, and they shall follow them: and I will [b]get me honour upon Pharaoh, and upon all his host, upon his chariots, and upon his horsemen.

18 And the Egyptians shall know that I *am* the LORD, when I have gotten me honour upon Pharaoh, upon his chariots, and upon his horsemen.

19 And the angel of God, [a]which went before the camp of Israel, removed and went behind them; and the pillar of the cloud went from before their face, and stood behind them:

20 And it came between the camp of the Egyptians and the camp of Israel; and it was a cloud and darkness *to them,* but it gave light by night *to these:* so that the one came not near the other all the night.

CHAPTER 14

2 [a]Ex. 13:18 [b]Num. 33:7 [c]Jer. 44:1
3 [a]Ps. 71:11
4 [a]Ex. 4:21; 7:3; 14:17 [b]Ex. 9:16; 14:17, 18, 23; Rom. 9:17, 22, 23 [c]Ex. 7:5; 14:25
5 [a]Ps. 105:25
7 [a]Ex. 15:4
8 [a]Ex. 14:4 [b]Ex. 6:1; 13:9; Num. 33:3; Acts 13:17
9 [a]Ex. 15:9; Josh. 24:6
10 [a]Josh. 24:7; Neh. 9:9; Ps. 34:17; 107:6
11 [a]Ex. 5:21; 15:24; 16:2; 17:3; Num. 14:2, 3; 20:3; Ps. 106:7, 8
12 [a]Ex. 5:21; 6:9
13 [a]Gen. 15:1; 46:3; Ex. 20:20; 2 Chr. 20:15, 17; Is. 41:10, 13, 14 [b]Ps. 46:10, 11 [c]Ex. 14:30; 15:2 [d]Deut. 28:68
14 [a]Ex. 14:25; 15:3; Deut. 1:30; 3:22; Josh. 10:14, 42; 23:2; 2 Chr. 20:29; Neh. 4:20; Is. 31:4 [b][Is. 30:15]
16 [a]Ex. 4:17, 20; 7:19; 14:21, 26; 17:5, 6, 9; Num. 20:8, 9, 11; Is. 10:26
17 [a]Ex. 14:8 [b]Ex. 14:4
19 [a]Ex. 13:21, 22; [Is. 63:9]

NKJV

by day or the pillar of fire by night *from* before the people.

The Red Sea Crossing

14 Now the LORD spoke to Moses, saying:
2 "Speak to the children of Israel, [a]that they turn and camp before [b]Pi Hahiroth, between [c]Migdol and the sea, opposite Baal Zephon; you shall camp before it by the sea.

3 "For Pharaoh will say of the children of Israel, [a]'They *are* bewildered by the land; the wilderness has closed them in.'

4 "Then [a]I will harden Pharaoh's heart, so that he will pursue them; and I [b]will gain honor over Pharaoh and over all his army, [c]that the Egyptians may know that I *am* the LORD." And they did so.

5 Now it was told the king of Egypt that the people had fled, and [a]the heart of Pharaoh and his servants was turned against the people; and they said, "Why have we done this, that we have let Israel go from serving us?"

6 So he made ready his chariot and took his people with him.

7 Also, he took [a]six hundred choice chariots, and all the chariots of Egypt with captains over every one of them.

8 And the LORD [a]hardened the heart of Pharaoh king of Egypt, and he pursued the children of Israel; and [b]the children of Israel went out with boldness.

9 So the [a]Egyptians pursued them, all the horses *and* chariots of Pharaoh, his horsemen and his army, and overtook them camping by the sea beside Pi Hahiroth, before Baal Zephon.

10 And when Pharaoh drew near, the children of Israel lifted their eyes, and behold, the Egyptians marched after them. So they were very afraid, and the children of Israel [a]cried out to the LORD.

11 [a]Then they said to Moses, "Because *there were* no graves in Egypt, have you taken us away to die in the wilderness? Why have you so dealt with us, to bring us up out of Egypt?

12 [a]"*Is* this not the word that we told you in Egypt, saying, 'Let us alone that we may serve the Egyptians'? For *it would have been* better for us to serve the Egyptians than that we should die in the wilderness."

13 And Moses said to the people, [a]"Do not be afraid. [b]Stand still, and see the [c]salvation of the LORD, which He will accomplish for you today. For the Egyptians whom you see today, you shall [d]see again no more forever.

14 [a]"The LORD will fight for you, and you shall [b]hold your peace."

15 And the LORD said to Moses, "Why do you cry to Me? Tell the children of Israel to go forward.

16 "But [a]lift up your rod, and stretch out your hand over the sea and divide it. And the children of Israel shall go on dry *ground* through the midst of the sea.

17 "And I indeed will [a]harden the hearts of the Egyptians, and they shall follow them. So I will [b]gain honor over Pharaoh and over all his army, his chariots, and his horsemen.

18 "Then the Egyptians shall know that I *am* the LORD, when I have gained honor for Myself over Pharaoh, his chariots, and his horsemen."

19 And the Angel of God, [a]who went before the camp of Israel, moved and went behind them; and the pillar of cloud went from before them and stood behind them.

20 So it came between the camp of the Egyptians and the camp of Israel. Thus it was a cloud and darkness *to the one,* and it gave light by night *to the other,* so that the one did not come near the other all that night.

KJV

21 And Moses stretched out his hand over
the sea; and the LORD caused the sea to go *back*
by a strong east wind all that night, and [a]made
the sea dry *land*, and the waters were [b]divided.
22 And [a]the children of Israel went into the
midst of the sea upon the dry *ground*: and the
waters *were* [b]a wall unto them on their right hand,
and on their left.
23 And the Egyptians pursued, and went in
after them to the midst of the sea, *even* all Pharaoh's horses, his chariots, and his horsemen.
24 And it came to pass, that in the morning
[a]watch [b]the LORD looked unto the host of the
Egyptians through the pillar of fire and of the
cloud, and troubled the host of the Egyptians,
25 And took off their chariot wheels, that
they drave them heavily: so that the Egyptians
said, Let us flee from the face of Israel; for the
LORD [a]fighteth for them against the Egyptians.
26 And the LORD said unto Moses, Stretch out
thine hand over the sea, that the waters may come
again upon the Egyptians, upon their chariots,
and upon their horsemen.
27 And Moses stretched forth his hand over
the sea, and the sea [a]returned to his strength
when the morning appeared; and the Egyptians
fled against it; and the LORD [b]overthrew the Egyptians in the midst of the sea.
28 And the waters returned, and [a]covered the
chariots, and the horsemen, *and* all the host of
Pharaoh that came into the sea after them; there
remained not so much as one of them.
29 But [a]the children of Israel walked upon
dry *land* in the midst of the sea; and the waters
were a wall unto them on their right hand, and
on their left.
30 Thus the LORD [a]saved Israel that day out
of the hand of the Egyptians; and Israel [b]saw the
Egyptians dead upon the sea shore.
31 And Israel saw that great work which the
LORD did upon the Egyptians: and the people
feared the LORD, and [a]believed the LORD, and his
servant Moses.

The Song of Moses
(Ex. 14:13, 14; Ps. 78:12–14)

15 Then sang [a]Moses and the children of Israel this song unto the LORD, and spake,
saying, I will [b]sing unto the LORD, for he hath
triumphed gloriously: the horse and his rider hath
he thrown into the sea.
2 The LORD *is* my strength and [a]song, and
he is become my salvation: he *is* my God, and I
will [b]prepare him an habitation; my [c]father's God,
and I [d]will exalt him.
3 The LORD *is* a man of [a]war: the LORD *is*
his [b]name.
4 [a]Pharaoh's chariots and his host hath he
cast into the sea: [b]his chosen captains also are
drowned in the Red sea.
5 The depths have covered them: [a]they sank
into the bottom as a stone.
6 [a]Thy right hand, O LORD, is become glorious in power: thy right hand, O LORD, hath dashed
in pieces the enemy.
7 And in the greatness of thine [a]excellency
thou hast overthrown them that rose up against
thee: thou sentest forth thy [b]wrath, *which* [c]con-
sumed them [d]as stubble.
8 And [a]with the blast of thy nostrils the waters were gathered together, [b]the floods stood up-

21 [a]Ps. 66:6; 106:9; 136:13, 14 [b]Ex. 15:8; Josh. 3:16; 4:23; Neh. 9:11; Ps. 74:13; 78:13; 114:3, 5; Is. 63:12, 13
22 [a]Ex. 15:19; Josh. 3:17; 4:22; Neh. 9:11; Ps. 66:6; 78:13; Is. 63:13; 1 Cor. 10:1; Heb. 11:29 [b]Ex. 14:29; 15:8; Hab. 3:10
24 [a]Judg. 7:19 [b]Ex. 13:21
25 [a]Ex. 7:5; 14:4, 14, 18
27 [a]Josh. 4:18 [b]Ex. 15:1, 7; Deut. 11:4; Neh. 9:11; Ps. 78:53; Heb. 11:29
28 [a]Ps. 78:53; 106:11
29 [a]Ex. 14:22; Ps. 66:6; 78:52, 53; Is. 11:15
30 [a]Ex. 14:13; Ps. 106:8, 10; Is. 63:8, 11 [b]Ps. 58:10; 59:10
31 [a]Ex. 4:31; 19:9; Ps. 106:12; John 2:11; 11:45

CHAPTER 15

1 [a]Ps. 106:12; Rev. 15:3 [b]Is. 12:1–6
2 [a]Ps. 18:1, 2; Is. 12:2; Hab. 3:18, 19 [b]Gen. 28:21, 22 [c]Ex. 3:6, 15, 16 [d]2 Sam. 22:47; Ps. 99:5; Is. 25:1
3 [a]Ex. 14:14; Rev. 19:11 [b]Ex. 3:15; 6:2, 3, 7, 8; Ps. 24:8; 83:18
4 [a]Ex. 14:28 [b]Ex. 14:7
5 [a]Ex. 15:10; Neh. 9:11
6 [a]Ex. 3:20; Ps. 17:7; 118:15
7 [a]Deut. 33:26 [b]Ps. 78:49, 50 [c]Ps. 59:13 [d]Deut. 4:24; Is. 5:24; Heb. 12:29
8 [a]Ex. 14:21, 22, 29 [b]Ps. 78:13

*———

14:25 Sam., LXX, Syr. *bound*

NKJV

21 Then Moses stretched out his hand over
the sea; and the LORD caused the sea to go *back*
by a strong east wind all that night, and [a]made
the sea into dry *land*, and the waters were
[b]divided.
22 So [a]the children of Israel went into the
midst of the sea on the dry *ground*, and the waters
were [b]a wall to them on their right hand and on
their left.
23 And the Egyptians pursued and went after
them into the midst of the sea, all Pharaoh's
horses, his chariots, and his horsemen.
24 Now it came to pass, in the morning
[a]watch, that [b]the LORD looked down upon the
army of the Egyptians through the pillar of fire
and cloud, and He troubled the army of the
Egyptians.
25 And He *took off their chariot wheels, so
that they drove them with difficulty; and the Egyptians said, "Let us flee from the face of Israel,
for the LORD [a]fights for them against the
Egyptians."
26 Then the LORD said to Moses, "Stretch out
your hand over the sea, that the waters may come
back upon the Egyptians, on their chariots, and
on their horsemen."
27 And Moses stretched out his hand over
the sea; and when the morning appeared, the sea
[a]returned to its full depth, while the Egyptians
were fleeing into it. So the LORD [b]overthrew the
Egyptians in the midst of the sea.
28 Then [a]the waters returned and covered
the chariots, the horsemen, *and* all the army of
Pharaoh that came into the sea after them. Not
so much as one of them remained.
29 But [a]the children of Israel had walked on
dry *land* in the midst of the sea, and the waters
were a wall to them on their right hand and on
their left.
30 So the LORD [a]saved Israel that day out of
the hand of the Egyptians, and Israel [b]saw the
Egyptians dead on the seashore.
31 Thus Israel saw the great work which the
LORD had done in Egypt; so the people feared the
LORD, and [a]believed the LORD and His servant Moses.

The Song of Moses
(Ex. 14:13, 14; Ps. 78:12–14)

15 Then [a]Moses and the children of Israel
sang this song to the LORD, and spoke,
saying:

"I will [b]sing to the LORD,
For He has triumphed gloriously!
The horse and its rider
He has thrown into the sea!
2 The LORD *is* my strength and [a]song,
And He has become my salvation;
He *is* my God, and [b]I will praise Him;
My [c]father's God, and I [d]will exalt Him.
3 The LORD *is* a man of [a]war;
The LORD *is* His [b]name.
4 [a]Pharaoh's chariots and his army He has
cast into the sea;
[b]His chosen captains also are drowned in
the Red Sea.
5 The depths have covered them;
[a]They sank to the bottom like a stone.

6 "Your [a]right hand, O LORD, has become
glorious in power;
Your right hand, O LORD, has dashed the
enemy in pieces.
7 And in the greatness of Your [a]excellence
You have overthrown those who rose
against You;
You sent forth [b]Your wrath;
It [c]consumed them [d]like stubble.
8 And [a]with the blast of Your nostrils
The waters were gathered together;
[b]The floods stood upright like a heap;

KJV

right as an heap, *and* the depths were congealed in the heart of the sea.

9 [a]The enemy said, I will pursue, I will overtake, I will [b]divide the spoil; my lust shall be satisfied upon them; I will draw my sword, my hand shall destroy them.

10 Thou didst blow with thy wind, the sea covered them: they sank as lead in the mighty waters.

11 [a]Who *is* like unto thee, O LORD, among the gods? who *is* like thee, [b]glorious in holiness, fearful *in* [c]praises, [d]doing wonders?

12 Thou stretchedst out thy right hand, the earth swallowed them.

13 Thou in thy mercy hast [a]led forth the people *which* thou hast redeemed: thou hast guided *them* in thy strength unto [b]thy holy habitation.

14 [a]The people shall hear, *and* be afraid: [b]sorrow shall take hold on the inhabitants of Palestina.

15 [a]Then [b]the dukes of Edom shall be amazed; [c]the mighty men of Moab, trembling shall take hold upon them; [d]all the inhabitants of Canaan shall [e]melt away.

16 [a]Fear and dread shall fall upon them; by the greatness of thine arm they shall be [b]*as* still as a stone; till thy people pass over, O LORD, till the people pass over, [c]*which* thou hast purchased.

17 Thou shalt bring them in, and [a]plant them in the [b]mountain of thine inheritance, *in* the place, O LORD, *which* thou hast made for thee to dwell in, *in* the [c]Sanctuary, O Lord, *which* thy hands have established.

18 [a]The LORD shall reign for ever and ever.

19 For the [a]horse of Pharaoh went in with his chariots and with his horsemen into the sea, and [b]the LORD brought again the waters of the sea upon them; but the children of Israel went on dry *land* in the midst of the sea.

The Song of Miriam
(*Num. 26:59*)

20 And Miriam [a]the prophetess, [b]the sister of Aaron, [c]took a timbrel in her hand; and all the women went out after her [d]with timbrels and with dances.

21 And Miriam [a]answered them, [b]Sing ye to the LORD, for he hath triumphed gloriously; the horse and his rider hath he thrown into the sea.

Bitter Waters Made Sweet

22 So Moses brought Israel from the Red sea, and they went out into the wilderness of [a]Shur; and they went three days in the wilderness, and found no [b]water.

23 And when they came to [a]Marah, they could not drink of the waters of Marah, for they *were* bitter: therefore the name of it was called Marah.

24 And the people [a]murmured against Moses, saying, What shall we drink?

25 And he cried unto the LORD; and the LORD shewed him a tree, [a]*which* when he had cast into the waters, the waters were made sweet: there he [b]made for them a statute and an ordinance, and there [c]he proved them,

9 [a]Judg. 5:30 [b]Is. 53:12
11 [a]Ex. 8:10; 9:14; Deut. 3:24; 2 Sam. 7:22; 1 Kin. 8:23; Ps. 71:19; 86:8; Mic. 7:18 [b]Ps. 68:35; Is. 6:3; Rev. 4:8 [c]1 Chr. 16:25 [d]Ex. 3:20; Ps. 77:11, 14
13 [a]Neh. 9:12; [Ps. 77:20] [b]Ex. 15:17; Deut. 12:5; Ps. 78:54
14 [a]Josh. 2:9 [b]Ps. 48:6
15 [a]Gen. 36:15, 40 [b]Deut. 2:4 [c]Num. 22:3, 4 [d]Josh. 5:1 [e]Josh. 2:9–11, 24
16 [a]Ex. 23:27; Deut. 2:25; Josh. 2:9 [b]1 Sam. 25:37 [c]Ex. 15:13; Ps. 74:2; Is. 43:1; Jer. 31:11; [Titus 2:14]; 2 Pet. 2:1
17 [a]Ps. 44:2; 80:8, 15 [b]Ps. 2:6; 78:54, 68 [c]Ps. 68:16; 76:2; 132:13, 14
18 [a]2 Sam. 7:16; Ps. 10:16; 29:10; Is. 57:15
19 [a]Ex. 14:23 [b]Ex. 14:28
20 [a]Judg. 4:4 [b]Ex. 2:4; Num. 26:59; 1 Chr. 6:3; Mic. 6:4 [c]1 Sam. 18:6; 1 Chr. 15:16; Ps. 68:25; 81:2; 149:3; Jer. 31:4 [d]Judg. 11:34; 21:21; 2 Sam. 6:16; Ps. 30:11; 150:4
21 [a]1 Sam. 18:7 [b]Ex. 15:1
22 [a]Gen. 16:7; 20:1; 25:18; Num. 33:8 [b]Ex. 17:1; Num. 20:2
23 [a]Num. 33:8; Ruth 1:20
24 [a]Ex. 14:11; 16:2; Ps. 106:13
25 [a]2 Kin. 2:21 [b]Josh. 24:25 [c]Ex. 16:4; Deut. 8:2, 16; Judg. 2:22; 3:1, 4; Ps. 66:10

*

15:23 Lit. *Bitter*

NKJV

The depths congealed in the heart of the sea.

9 [a]The enemy said, 'I will pursue,
I will overtake,
I will [b]divide the spoil;
My desire shall be satisfied on them.
I will draw my sword,
My hand shall destroy them.'

10 You blew with Your wind,
The sea covered them;
They sank like lead in the mighty waters.

11 "Who[a] *is* like You, O LORD, among the gods?
Who *is* like You, [b]glorious in holiness,
Fearful in [c]praises, [d]doing wonders?

12 You stretched out Your right hand;
The earth swallowed them.

13 You in Your mercy have [a]led forth
The people whom You have redeemed;
You have guided *them* in Your strength
To [b]Your holy habitation.

14 "The [a]people will hear *and* be afraid;
[b]Sorrow will take hold of the inhabitants of Philistia.

15 [a]Then [b]the chiefs of Edom will be dismayed;
[c]The mighty men of Moab,
Trembling will take hold of them;
[d]All the inhabitants of Canaan will [e]melt away.

16 [a]Fear and dread will fall on them;
By the greatness of Your arm
They will be [b]*as* still as a stone,
Till Your people pass over, O LORD,
Till the people pass over
[c]Whom You have purchased.

17 You will bring them in and [a]plant them
In the [b]mountain of Your inheritance,
In the place, O LORD, *which* You have made
For Your own dwelling,
The [c]sanctuary, O LORD, *which* Your hands have established.

18 "The[a] LORD shall reign forever and ever."

19 For the [a]horses of Pharaoh went with his chariots and his horsemen into the sea, and [b]the LORD brought back the waters of the sea upon them. But the children of Israel went on dry *land* in the midst of the sea.

The Song of Miriam
(*Num. 26:59*)

20 Then Miriam [a]the prophetess, [b]the sister of Aaron, [c]took the timbrel in her hand; and all the women went out after her [d]with timbrels and with dances.

21 And Miriam [a]answered them:

[b]"Sing to the LORD,
For He has triumphed gloriously!
The horse and its rider
He has thrown into the sea!"

Bitter Waters Made Sweet

22 So Moses brought Israel from the Red Sea; then they went out into the Wilderness of [a]Shur. And they went three days in the wilderness and found no [b]water.

23 Now when they came to [a]Marah, they could not drink the waters of Marah, for they *were* bitter. Therefore the name of it was called *Marah.

24 And the people [a]complained against Moses, saying, "What shall we drink?"

25 So he cried out to the LORD, and the LORD showed him a tree. [a]When he cast *it* into the waters, the waters were made sweet. There He [b]made a statute and an ordinance for them, and there [c]He tested them,

KJV

26 And said, [a]If thou wilt diligently hearken to the voice of the LORD thy God, and wilt do that which is right in his sight, and wilt give ear to his commandments, and keep all his statutes, I will put none of these [b]diseases upon thee, which I have brought upon the Egyptians: for I *am* the LORD [c]that healeth thee.

27 [a]And they came to Elim, where *were* twelve wells of water, and threescore and ten palm trees: and they encamped there by the waters.

Bread from Heaven

16 And they [a]took their journey from Elim, and all the congregation of the children of Israel came unto the wilderness of Sin, which *is* between Elim and [b]Sinai, on the fifteenth day of the second month after their departing out of the land of Egypt.

2 And the whole congregation of the children of Israel [a]murmured against Moses and Aaron in the wilderness:

3 And the children of Israel said unto them, [a]Would to God we had died by the hand of the LORD in the land of Egypt, [b]when we sat by the flesh pots, *and* when we did eat bread to the full; for ye have brought us forth into this wilderness, to kill this whole assembly with hunger.

4 Then said the LORD unto Moses, Behold, I will rain [a]bread from heaven for you; and the people shall go out and gather a certain rate every day, that I may [b]prove them, whether they will [c]walk in my law, or no.

5 And it shall come to pass, that on the sixth day they shall prepare *that* which they bring in; and [a]it shall be twice as much as they gather daily.

6 And Moses and Aaron said unto all the children of Israel, [a]At even, then ye shall know that the LORD hath brought you out from the land of Egypt:

7 And in the morning, then ye shall see [a]the glory of the LORD; for that he [b]heareth your murmurings against the LORD: and [c]what *are* we, that ye murmur against us?

8 And Moses said, *This shall be,* when the LORD shall give you in the evening flesh to eat, and in the morning bread to the full; for that the LORD heareth your murmurings which ye murmur against him: and what *are* we? your murmurings *are* not against us, but [a]against the LORD.

9 And Moses spake unto Aaron, Say unto all the congregation of the children of Israel, [a]Come near before the LORD: for he hath heard your murmurings.

10 And it came to pass, as Aaron spake unto the whole congregation of the children of Israel, that they looked toward the wilderness, and, behold, the glory of the LORD [a]appeared in the cloud.

11 And the LORD spake unto Moses, saying,

12 [a]I have heard the murmurings of the children of Israel: speak unto them, saying, [b]At even ye shall eat flesh, and [c]in the morning ye shall be filled with bread; and ye shall know that I *am* the LORD your God.

13 And it came to pass, that at even [a]the quails came up, and covered the camp: and in the morning [b]the dew lay round about the host.

14 And when the dew that lay was gone up, behold, upon the face of the wilderness *there lay* a small round [a]thing, *as* small as the [b]hoar frost on the ground.

15 And when the children of Israel saw *it,* they said one to another, It *is* manna: for they wist not what it *was.* And Moses said unto them, [a]This *is* the bread which the LORD hath given you to eat.

16 This *is* the thing which the LORD hath commanded, Gather of it every man [a]according to his eating, an [b]omer for every man, *according to* the number of your persons; take ye every man for *them* which *are* in his tents.

26 [a]Ex. 19:5, 6; Deut. 7:12, 15 [b]Deut. 28:27, 58, 60 [c]Ex. 23:25; Deut. 32:39; Ps. 41:3, 4; 103:3; 147:3
27 [a]Num. 33:9

CHAPTER 16

1 [a]Num. 33:10, 11; Ezek. 30:15 [b]Ex. 12:6, 51; 19:1
2 [a]Ex. 14:11; 15:24; Ps. 106:25; 1 Cor. 10:10
3 [a]Ex. 17:3; Num. 14:2, 3; 20:3; Lam. 4:9 [b]Num. 11:4, 5
4 [a]Neh. 9:15; Ps. 78:23–25; 105:40; [John 6:31–35]; 1 Cor. 10:3 [b]Ex. 15:25; Deut. 8:2, 16 [c]Judg. 2:22
5 [a]Ex. 16:22, 29; Lev. 25:21
6 [a]Ex. 6:7
7 [a]Ex. 16:10, 12; Is. 35:2; 40:5; John 11:4, 40 [b]Num. 14:27; 17:5 [c]Num. 16:11
8 [a]1 Sam. 8:7; Luke 10:16; [Rom. 13:2]; 1 Thess. 4:8
9 [a]Num. 16:16
10 [a]Ex. 13:21; 16:7; Num. 16:19; 1 Kin. 8:10
12 [a]Ex. 16:8; Num. 14:27 [b]Ex. 16:6 [c]Ex. 16:7; 1 Kin. 20:28; Joel 3:17
13 [a]Num. 11:31; Ps. 78:27–29; 105:40 [b]Num. 11:9
14 [a]Ex. 16:31; Num. 11:7, 8; Deut. 8:3; Neh. 9:15; Ps. 78:24; 105:40 [b]Ps. 147:16
15 [a]Ex. 16:4; Neh. 9:15; Ps. 78:24; [John 6:31, 49, 58]; 1 Cor. 10:3
16 [a]Ex. 12:4 [b]Ex. 16:32, 36

NKJV

26 and said, [a]"If you diligently heed the voice of the LORD your God and do what is right in His sight, give ear to His commandments and keep all His statutes, I will put none of the [b]diseases on you which I have brought on the Egyptians. For I *am* the LORD [c]who heals you."

27 [a]Then they came to Elim, where there *were* twelve wells of water and seventy palm trees; so they camped there by the waters.

Bread from Heaven

16 And they [a]journeyed from Elim, and all the congregation of the children of Israel came to the Wilderness of Sin, which is between Elim and [b]Sinai, on the fifteenth day of the second month after they departed from the land of Egypt.

2 Then the whole congregation of the children of Israel [a]complained against Moses and Aaron in the wilderness.

3 And the children of Israel said to them, [a]"Oh, that we had died by the hand of the LORD in the land of Egypt, [b]when we sat by the pots of meat *and* when we ate bread to the full! For you have brought us out into this wilderness to kill this whole assembly with hunger."

4 Then the LORD said to Moses, "Behold, I will rain [a]bread from heaven for you. And the people shall go out and gather a certain quota every day, that I may [b]test them, whether they will [c]walk in My law or not.

5 "And it shall be on the sixth day that they shall prepare what they bring in, and [a]it shall be twice as much as they gather daily."

6 Then Moses and Aaron said to all the children of Israel, [a]"At evening you shall know that the LORD has brought you out of the land of Egypt.

7 "And in the morning you shall see [a]the glory of the LORD; for He [b]hears your complaints against the LORD. But [c]what *are* we, that you complain against us?"

8 Also Moses said, "*This shall be seen* when the LORD gives you meat to eat in the evening, and in the morning bread to the full; for the LORD hears your complaints which you make against Him. And what *are* we? Your complaints *are* not against us but [a]against the LORD."

9 Then Moses spoke to Aaron, "Say to all the congregation of the children of Israel, [a]'Come near before the LORD, for He has heard your complaints.' "

10 Now it came to pass, as Aaron spoke to the whole congregation of the children of Israel, that they looked toward the wilderness, and behold, the glory of the LORD [a]appeared in the cloud.

11 And the LORD spoke to Moses, saying,

12 [a]"I have heard the complaints of the children of Israel. Speak to them, saying, [b]'At twilight you shall eat meat, and [c]in the morning you shall be filled with bread. And you shall know that I *am* the LORD your God.' "

13 So it was that [a]quails came up at evening and covered the camp, and in the morning [b]the dew lay all around the camp.

14 And when the layer of dew lifted, there, on the surface of the wilderness, was [a]a small round [b]substance, *as* fine as frost on the ground.

15 So when the children of Israel saw *it,* they said to one another, "What is it?" For they did not know what it *was.* And Moses said to them, [a]"This *is* the bread which the LORD has given you to eat.

16 "This is the thing which the LORD has commanded: 'Let every man gather it [a]according to each one's need, one [b]omer for each person, *according to the* number of persons; let every man take for *those* who *are* in his tent.' "

KJV

17 And the children of Israel did so, and gathered, some more, some less.

18 And when they did mete *it* with an omer, [a]he that gathered much had nothing over, and he that gathered little had no lack; they gathered every man according to his eating.

19 And Moses said, Let no man [a]leave of it till the morning.

20 Notwithstanding they hearkened not unto Moses; but some of them left of it until the morning, and it bred worms, and stank: and Moses was wroth with them.

21 And they gathered it every morning, every man according to his eating: and when the sun waxed hot, it melted.

22 And it came to pass, *that* on the sixth day they gathered twice as much bread, two omers for one *man:* and all the rulers of the congregation came and told Moses.

23 And he said unto them, This *is that* which the LORD hath said, To morrow *is* [a]the rest of the holy sabbath unto the LORD: bake *that* which ye will bake *to day,* and seethe that ye will seethe; and that which remaineth over lay up for you to be kept until the morning.

24 And they laid it up till the morning, as Moses bade: and it did not [a]stink, neither was there any worm therein.

25 And Moses said, Eat that to day; for to day *is* a sabbath unto the LORD: to day ye shall not find it in the field.

26 [a]Six days ye shall gather it; but on the seventh day, *which is* the sabbath, in it there shall be none.

27 And it came to pass, *that* there went out *some* of the people on the seventh day for to gather, and they found none.

28 And the LORD said unto Moses, How long [a]refuse ye to keep my commandments and my laws?

29 See, for that the LORD hath given you the sabbath, therefore he giveth you on the sixth day the bread of two days; abide ye every man in his place, let no man go out of his place on the seventh day.

30 So the people rested on the seventh day.

31 And the house of Israel called the name thereof Manna: and [a]it *was* like coriander seed, white; and the taste of it *was* like wafers *made* with honey.

32 And Moses said, This *is* the thing which the LORD commandeth, Fill an omer of it to be kept for your generations; that they may see the bread wherewith I have fed you in the wilderness, when I brought you forth from the land of Egypt.

33 And Moses said unto Aaron, [a]Take a pot, and put an omer full of manna therein, and lay it up before the LORD, to be kept for your generations.

34 As the LORD commanded Moses, so Aaron laid it up [a]before the Testimony, to be kept.

35 And the children of Israel did [a]eat manna [b]forty years, [c]until they came to a land inhabited; they did eat manna, until they came unto the borders of the land of Canaan.

36 Now an omer *is* the tenth *part* of an ephah.

Water from the Rock
(*Num. 20:1–13*)

17 And [a]all the congregation of the children of Israel journeyed from the wilderness of [b]Sin, after their journeys, according to the commandment of the LORD, and pitched in Rephidim: and *there was* no water for the people to [c]drink.

2 [a]Wherefore the people did chide with Moses, and said, Give us water that we may drink. And Moses said unto them, Why chide ye with me? wherefore do ye [b]tempt the LORD?

3 And the people thirsted there for water; and the people [a]murmured against Moses, and said, Wherefore *is* this *that* thou hast brought us

18 [a]2 Cor. 8:15
19 [a]Ex. 12:10; 16:23; 23:18
23 [a]Gen. 2:3; Ex. 20:8–11; 23:12; 31:15; 35:2; Lev. 23:3; Neh. 9:13, 14
24 [a]Ex. 16:20
26 [a]Ex. 20:9, 10
28 [a]2 Kin. 17:14; Ps. 78:10; 106:13
31 [a]Num. 11:7–9; Deut. 8:3, 16
33 [a]Heb. 9:4; Rev. 2:17
34 [a]Ex. 25:16, 21; 27:21; 40:20; Num. 17:10
35 [a]Deut. 8:3, 16 [b]Num. 33:38; John 6:31, 49 [c]Josh. 5:12; Neh. 9:20, 21

CHAPTER 17
1 [a]Ex. 16:1 [b]Num. 33:11–15 [c]Ex. 15:22; Num. 20:2
2 [a]Ex. 14:11; Num. 20:2, 3, 13 [b][Deut. 6:16]; Ps. 78:18, 41; [Matt. 4:7]; 1 Cor. 10:9
3 [a]Ex. 16:2, 3

*16:31 Lit. *What?* Ex. 16:15

NKJV

17 Then the children of Israel did so and gathered, some more, some less.

18 So when they measured *it* by omers, [a]he who gathered much had nothing left over, and he who gathered little had no lack. Every man had gathered according to each one's need.

19 And Moses said, "Let no one [a]leave any of it till morning."

20 Notwithstanding they did not heed Moses. But some of them left part of it until morning, and it bred worms and stank. And Moses was angry with them.

21 So they gathered it every morning, every man according to his need. And when the sun became hot, it melted.

22 And so it was, on the sixth day, *that* they gathered twice as much bread, two omers for each one. And all the rulers of the congregation came and told Moses.

23 Then he said to them, "This *is what* the LORD has said: 'Tomorrow *is* [a]a Sabbath rest, a holy Sabbath to the LORD. Bake what you will bake *today,* and boil what you will boil; and lay up for yourselves all that remains, to be kept until morning.' "

24 So they laid it up till morning, as Moses commanded; and it did not [a]stink, nor were there any worms in it.

25 Then Moses said, "Eat that today, for today *is* a Sabbath to the LORD; today you will not find it in the field.

26 [a]"Six days you shall gather it, but on the seventh day, the Sabbath, there will be none."

27 Now it happened *that some* of the people went out on the seventh day to gather, but they found none.

28 And the LORD said to Moses, "How long [a]do you refuse to keep My commandments and My laws?

29 "See! For the LORD has given you the Sabbath; therefore He gives you on the sixth day bread for two days. Let every man remain in his place; let no man go out of his place on the seventh day."

30 So the people rested on the seventh day.

31 And the house of Israel called its name *Manna. And [a]it *was* like white coriander seed, and the taste of it *was* like wafers *made* with honey.

32 Then Moses said, "This *is* the thing which the LORD has commanded: 'Fill an omer with it, to be kept for your generations, that they may see the bread with which I fed you in the wilderness, when I brought you out of the land of Egypt.' "

33 And Moses said to Aaron, [a]"Take a pot and put an omer of manna in it, and lay it up before the LORD, to be kept for your generations."

34 As the LORD commanded Moses, so Aaron laid it up [a]before the Testimony, to be kept.

35 And the children of Israel [a]ate manna [b]forty years, [c]until they came to an inhabited land; they ate manna until they came to the border of the land of Canaan.

36 Now an omer *is* one-tenth of an ephah.

Water from the Rock
(*Num. 20:1–13*)

17 Then [a]all the congregation of the children of Israel set out on their journey from the Wilderness of [b]Sin, according to the commandment of the LORD, and camped in Rephidim; but *there was* no water for the people to [c]drink.

2 [a]Therefore the people contended with Moses, and said, "Give us water, that we may drink." So Moses said to them, "Why do you contend with me? Why do you [b]tempt the LORD?"

3 And the people thirsted there for water, and the people [a]complained against Moses, and said, "Why *is* it you have brought us up out of

KJV

up out of Egypt, to kill us and our children and
our [b]cattle with thirst?
4 And Moses [a]cried unto the LORD, saying,
What shall I do unto this people? they be almost
ready to [b]stone me.
5 And the LORD said unto Moses, [a]Go on
before the people, and take with thee of the elders
of Israel; and thy rod, wherewith [b]thou smotest
the river, take in thine hand, and go.
6 [a]Behold, I will stand before thee there
upon the rock in Horeb; and thou shalt smite the
rock, and there shall come water out of it, that
the people may drink. And Moses did so in the
sight of the elders of Israel.
7 And he called the name of the place [a]Mas-
sah, and Meribah, because of the chiding of the
children of Israel, and because they tempted the
LORD, saying, Is the LORD among us, or not?

Victory over the Amalekites
(Gen. 14:7; Num. 13:29; 14:25)

8 [a]Then came Amalek, and fought with Israel in Rephidim.
9 And Moses said unto Joshua, Choose us
out men, and go out, fight with Amalek: to morrow I will stand on the top of the hill with [a]the
rod of God in mine hand.
10 So Joshua did as Moses had said to him,
and fought with Amalek: and Moses, Aaron, and
Hur went up to the top of the hill.
11 And it came to pass, when Moses [a]held
up his hand, that Israel prevailed: and when he
let down his hand, Amalek prevailed.
12 But Moses' hands *were* heavy; and they
took a stone, and put *it* under him, and he sat
thereon; and Aaron and Hur stayed up his hands,
the one on the one side, and the other on the other
side; and his hands were steady until the going
down of the sun.
13 And Joshua discomfited Amalek and his
people with the edge of the sword.
14 And the LORD said unto Moses, [a]Write this
for a memorial in a book, and rehearse *it* in the
ears of Joshua: for [b]I will utterly put out the remembrance of Amalek from under heaven.
15 And Moses built an altar, and called the
name of it Jehovah–nissi:
16 For he said, Because the LORD hath [a]sworn
that the LORD *will have* war with Amalek from
generation to generation.

Jethro's Advice
(Deut. 1:9–18)

18 When [a]Jethro, the priest of Midian, Moses'
father in law, heard of all that [b]God had
done for Moses, and for Israel his people, *and* that
the LORD had brought Israel out of Egypt;
2 Then Jethro, Moses' father in law, took
[a]Zipporah, Moses' wife, after he had sent her
back,
3 And her [a]two sons; of which the [b]name
of the one *was* Gershom; for he said, I have been
an alien in a strange land:
4 And the name of the other *was* Eliezer;
for the God of my father, *said he, was* mine [a]help,
and delivered me from the sword of Pharaoh:
5 And Jethro, Moses' father in law, came
with his sons and his wife unto Moses into the
wilderness, where he encamped at [a]the mount of
God:
6 And he said unto Moses, I thy father in
law Jethro am come unto thee, and thy wife, and
her two sons with her.
7 And Moses [a]went out to meet his father
in law, and did obeisance, and [b]kissed him; and
they asked each other of *their* welfare; and they
came into the tent.
8 And Moses told his father in law all that
the LORD had done unto Pharaoh and to the Egyptians for Israel's sake, *and* all the travail that had
come upon them by the way, and *how* the LORD
[a]delivered them.

3 [b]Ex. 12:38
4 [a]Ex. 14:15 [b]John 8:59; 10:31
5 [a]Ezek. 2:6 [b]Num. 20:8
6 [a]Num. 20:10, 11; Deut. 8:15; Neh. 9:15; Ps. 78:15; 105:41; 114:8; [1 Cor. 10:4]
7 [a]Num. 20:13, 24; 27:14; Ps. 81:7
8 [a]Gen. 36:12; Num. 24:20; Deut. 25:17–19; 1 Sam. 15:2
9 [a]Ex. 4:20
11 [a][James 5:16]
14 [a]Ex. 24:4; 34:27; Num. 33:2 [b]Deut. 25:19; 1 Sam. 15:3; 2 Sam. 1:1; 1 Chr. 4:43
16 [a]Gen. 22:14–16

CHAPTER 18

1 [a]Ex. 2:16, 18; 3:1 [b][Ps. 106:2, 8]
2 [a]Ex. 2:21; 4:20–26
3 [a]Ex. 2:20; 4:20; Acts 7:29 [b]Ex. 2:22
4 [a]Gen. 49:25
5 [a]Ex. 3:1, 12; 4:27; 24:13
7 [a]Gen. 18:2 [b]Gen. 29:13; Ex. 4:27
8 [a]Ex. 15:6, 16; Ps. 81:7

*

17:7 Lit. *Tempted* • Lit. *Contention*
17:15 Heb. *YHWH Nissi*
18:4 Lit. *My God Is Help*

NKJV

Egypt, to kill us and our children and our [b]live-
stock with thirst?"
4 So Moses [a]cried out to the LORD, saying,
"What shall I do with this people? They are almost
ready to [b]stone me!"
5 And the LORD said to Moses, [a]"Go on before the people, and take with you some of the
elders of Israel. Also take in your hand your rod
with which [b]you struck the river, and go.
6 [a]"Behold, I will stand before you there on
the rock in Horeb; and you shall strike the rock,
and water will come out of it, that the people may
drink." And Moses did so in the sight of the elders
of Israel.
7 So he called the name of the place [a]Mas-
sah* and *Meribah, because of the contention of
the children of Israel, and because they tempted
the LORD, saying, "Is the LORD among us or not?"

Victory over the Amalekites
(Gen. 14:7; Num. 13:29; 14:25)

8 [a]Now Amalek came and fought with Israel in Rephidim.
9 And Moses said to Joshua, "Choose us
some men and go out, fight with Amalek. Tomorrow I will stand on the top of the hill with [a]the
rod of God in my hand."
10 So Joshua did as Moses said to him, and
fought with Amalek. And Moses, Aaron, and Hur
went up to the top of the hill.
11 And so it was, when Moses [a]held up his
hand, that Israel prevailed; and when he let down
his hand, Amalek prevailed.
12 But Moses' hands *became* heavy; so they
took a stone and put *it* under him, and he sat on
it. And Aaron and Hur supported his hands, one
on one side, and the other on the other side; and
his hands were steady until the going down of
the sun.
13 So Joshua defeated Amalek and his people with the edge of the sword.
14 Then the LORD said to Moses, [a]"Write this
for a memorial in the book and recount *it* in the
hearing of Joshua, that [b]I will utterly blot out the
remembrance of Amalek from under heaven."
15 And Moses built an altar and called its
name, *The-LORD-Is-My-Banner;
16 for he said, "Because the LORD has
[a]sworn: the LORD *will have* war with Amalek from
generation to generation."

Jethro's Advice
(Deut. 1:9–18)

18 And [a]Jethro, the priest of Midian, Moses'
father-in-law, heard of all that [b]God had
done for Moses and for Israel His people—that
the LORD had brought Israel out of Egypt.
2 Then Jethro, Moses' father-in-law, took
[a]Zipporah, Moses' wife, after he had sent her
back,
3 with her [a]two sons, of whom the name
of one *was* Gershom (for he said, [b]"I have been
a stranger in a foreign land")
4 and the name of the other *was* *Eliezer
(for *he said,* "The God of my father *was* my [a]help,
and delivered me from the sword of Pharaoh");
5 and Jethro, Moses' father-in-law, came
with his sons and his wife to Moses in the wilderness, where he was encamped at [a]the mountain
of God.
6 Now he had said to Moses, "I, your father-
in-law Jethro, am coming to you with your wife
and her two sons with her."
7 So Moses [a]went out to meet his father-in-
law, bowed down, and [b]kissed him. And they
asked each other about *their* well-being, and they
went into the tent.
8 And Moses told his father-in-law all that
the LORD had done to Pharaoh and to the Egyptians for Israel's sake, all the hardship that had
come upon them on the way, and *how* the LORD
had [a]delivered them.

KJV

9 And Jethro rejoiced for all the [a]goodness which the LORD had done to Israel, whom he had delivered out of the hand of the Egyptians.

10 And Jethro said, [a]Blessed *be* the LORD, who hath delivered you out of the hand of the Egyptians, and out of the hand of Pharaoh, who hath delivered the people from under the hand of the Egyptians.

11 Now I know that the LORD *is* [a]greater than all gods: [b]for in the thing wherein they dealt [c]proudly *he was* above them.

12 And Jethro, Moses' father in law, took a burnt [a]offering and sacrifices for God: and Aaron came, and all the elders of Israel, [b]to eat bread with Moses' father in law before God.

13 And it came to pass on the morrow, that Moses [a]sat to judge the people: and the people stood by Moses from the morning unto the evening.

14 And when Moses' father in law saw all that he did to the people, he said, What *is* this thing that thou doest to the people? why sittest thou thyself alone, and all the people stand by thee from morning unto even?

15 And Moses said unto his father in law, Because [a]the people come unto me to enquire of God:

16 When they have [a]a matter, they come unto me; and I judge between one and another, and I do make *them* know the statutes of God, and his laws.

17 And Moses' father in law said unto him, The thing that thou doest *is* not good.

18 Thou wilt surely wear away, both thou, and this people that *is* with thee: for this thing *is* too heavy for thee; [a]thou art not able to perform it thyself alone.

19 Hearken now unto my voice, I will give thee counsel, and God shall be with thee: Be thou for the people to [a]God-ward, that thou mayest [b]bring the causes unto God:

20 And thou shalt [a]teach them ordinances and laws, and shalt shew them the way wherein they must walk, and [b]the work that they must do.

21 Moreover thou shalt provide out of all the people [a]able men, such as [b]fear God, [c]men of truth, [d]hating covetousness; and place *such* over them, *to be* rulers of thousands, *and* rulers of hundreds, rulers of fifties, and rulers of tens:

22 And let them judge the people at all seasons: [a]and it shall be, *that* every great matter they shall bring unto thee, but every small matter they shall judge: so shall it be easier for thyself, and [b]they shall bear *the burden* with thee.

23 If thou shalt do this thing, and God command thee *so*, then thou shalt be able to endure, and all this people shall also go to their [a]place in peace.

24 So Moses hearkened to the voice of his father in law, and did all that he had said.

25 And [a]Moses chose able men out of all Israel, and made them heads over the people, rulers of thousands, rulers of hundreds, rulers of fifties, and rulers of tens.

26 And they judged the people at all seasons: the [a]hard causes they brought unto Moses, but every small matter they judged themselves.

27 And Moses let his father in law depart; and [a]he went his way into his own land.

Israel at Mount Sinai

19 In the third month, when the children of Israel were gone forth out of the land of Egypt, the same day [a]came they *into* the wilderness of Sinai.

2 For they were departed from [a]Rephidim, and were come *to* the desert of Sinai, and had pitched in the wilderness; and there Israel camped before [b]the mount.

3 And [a]Moses went up unto God, and the LORD [b]called unto him out of the mountain, say-

9 [a][Is. 63:7–14] **10** [a]Gen. 14:20; 2 Sam. 18:28; 1 Kin. 8:56; Ps. 68:19, 20 **11** [a]Ex. 12:12; 15:11; 2 Chr. 2:5; Ps. 95:3; 97:9; 135:5 [b]Ex. 1:10, 16, 22; 5:2, 7 [c]Luke 1:51 **12** [a]Ex. 24:5 [b]Gen. 31:54; Deut. 12:7 **13** [a]Deut. 33:4, 5; Matt. 23:2 **15** [a]Lev. 24:12; Num. 9:6, 8; 27:5; Deut. 17:8–13 **16** [a]Ex. 24:14; Deut. 19:17 **18** [a]Num. 11:14, 17; Deut. 1:12 **19** [a]Ex. 4:16; 20:19 [b]Num. 9:8; 27:5 **20** [a]Deut. 5:1 [b]Deut. 1:18 **21** [a]Ex. 18:24, 25; Deut. 1:13, 15; 2 Chr. 19:5–10; Ps. 15:1–5; Acts 6:3 [b]Gen. 42:18; 2 Sam. 23:3 [c]Ezek. 18:8 [d]Deut. 16:19 **22** [a]Lev. 24:11; Deut. 1:17 [b]Num. 11:17 **23** [a]Ex. 16:29 **25** [a]Ex. 18:21; Deut. 1:15 **26** [a]Job 29:16 **27** [a]Num. 10:29, 30

CHAPTER 19

1 [a]Num. 33:15 **2** [a]Ex. 17:1 [b]Ex. 3:1, 12; 18:5 **3** [a]Acts 7:38 [b]Ex. 3:4

*

18:12 So with MT, LXX; Syr., Tg., Vg. *offered*

NKJV

9 Then Jethro rejoiced for all the [a]good which the LORD had done for Israel, whom He had delivered out of the hand of the Egyptians.

10 And Jethro said, [a]"Blessed *be* the LORD, who has delivered you out of the hand of the Egyptians and out of the hand of Pharaoh, *and* who has delivered the people from under the hand of the Egyptians.

11 "Now I know that the LORD *is* [a]greater than all the gods; [b]for in the very thing in which they behaved [c]proudly, *He was* above them."

12 Then Jethro, Moses' father-in-law, *took a burnt [a]offering and *other* sacrifices *to offer* to God. And Aaron came with all the elders of Israel [b]to eat bread with Moses' father-in-law before God.

13 And so it was, on the next day, that Moses [a]sat to judge the people; and the people stood before Moses from morning until evening.

14 So when Moses' father-in-law saw all that he did for the people, he said, "What *is* this thing that you are doing for the people? Why do you alone sit, and all the people stand before you from morning until evening?"

15 And Moses said to his father-in-law, "Because [a]the people come to me to inquire of God.

16 "When they have [a]a difficulty, they come to me, and I judge between one and another; and I make known the statutes of God and His laws."

17 So Moses' father-in-law said to him, "The thing that you do *is* not good.

18 "Both you and these people who *are* with you will surely wear yourselves out. For this thing *is* too much for you; [a]you are not able to perform it by yourself.

19 "Listen now to my voice; I will give you counsel, and God will be with you: Stand [a]before God for the people, so that you may [b]bring the difficulties to God.

20 "And you shall [a]teach them the statutes and the laws, and show them the way in which they must walk and [b]the work they must do.

21 "Moreover you shall select from all the people [a]able men, such as [b]fear God, [c]men of truth, [d]hating covetousness; and place *such* over them *to be* rulers of thousands, rulers of hundreds, rulers of fifties, and rulers of tens.

22 "And let them judge the people at all times. [a]Then it will be *that* every great matter they shall bring to you, but every small matter they themselves shall judge. So it will be easier for you, for [b]they will bear *the burden* with you.

23 "If you do this thing, and God *so* commands you, then you will be able to endure, and all this people will also go to their [a]place in peace."

24 So Moses heeded the voice of his father-in-law and did all that he had said.

25 And [a]Moses chose able men out of all Israel, and made them heads over the people: rulers of thousands, rulers of hundreds, rulers of fifties, and rulers of tens.

26 So they judged the people at all times; the [a]hard cases they brought to Moses, but they judged every small case themselves.

27 Then Moses let his father-in-law depart, and [a]he went his way to his own land.

Israel at Mount Sinai

19 In the third month after the children of Israel had gone out of the land of Egypt, on the same day, [a]they came *to* the Wilderness of Sinai.

2 For they had departed from [a]Rephidim, had come *to* the Wilderness of Sinai, and camped in the wilderness. So Israel camped there before [b]the mountain.

3 And [a]Moses went up to God, and the LORD [b]called to him from the mountain, saying, "Thus

KJV

ing, Thus shalt thou say to the house of Jacob, and tell the children of Israel;

4 [a]Ye have seen what I did unto the Egyptians, and *how* [b]I bare you on eagles' wings, and brought you unto myself.

5 Now [a]therefore, if ye will obey my voice indeed, and [b]keep my covenant, then [c]ye shall be a peculiar treasure unto me above all people: for all the earth *is* [d]mine:

6 And ye shall be unto me a [a]kingdom of priests, and an [b]holy nation. These *are* the words which thou shalt speak unto the children of Israel.

7 And Moses came and called for the [a]elders of the people, and laid before their faces all these words which the LORD commanded him.

8 And [a]all the people answered together, and said, All that the LORD hath spoken we will do. And Moses returned the words of the people unto the LORD.

9 And the LORD said unto Moses, Lo, I come unto thee [a]in a thick cloud, [b]that the people may hear when I speak with thee, and believe thee for ever. And Moses told the words of the people unto the LORD.

10 And the LORD said unto Moses, Go unto the people, and [a]sanctify them to day and to morrow, and let them wash their clothes,

11 And be ready against the third day: for the third day the LORD will come down in the sight of all the people upon mount Sinai.

12 And thou shalt set bounds unto the people round about, saying, Take heed to yourselves, *that ye* go *not* up into the mount, or touch the border of it: [a]whosoever toucheth the mount shall be surely put to death:

13 There shall not an hand touch it, but he shall surely be stoned, or shot through; whether *it be* beast or man, it shall not live: when the trumpet soundeth long, they shall come up to the mount.

14 And Moses went down from the mount unto the people, and sanctified the people; and they washed their clothes.

15 And he said unto the people, Be ready against the third day: [a]come not at *your* wives.

16 And it came to pass on the third day in the morning, that there were [a]thunders and lightnings, and a thick cloud upon the mount, and the voice of the trumpet exceeding loud; so that all the people that *was* in the camp [b]trembled.

17 And [a]Moses brought forth the people out of the camp to meet with God; and they stood at the nether part of the mount.

18 And [a]mount Sinai was altogether on a smoke, because the LORD descended upon [b]it in fire: [c]and the smoke thereof ascended as the smoke of a furnace, and the [d]whole mount quaked greatly.

19 And when the voice of the trumpet sounded long, and waxed louder and louder, [a]Moses spake, and [b]God answered him by a voice.

20 And the LORD came down upon mount Sinai, on the top of the mount: and the LORD called Moses *up* to the top of the mount; and Moses went up.

21 And the LORD said unto Moses, Go down, charge the people, lest they break through unto the LORD [a]to gaze, and many of them perish.

22 And let the [a]priests also, which come near to the LORD, [b]sanctify themselves, lest the LORD [c]break forth upon them.

23 And Moses said unto the LORD, The people cannot come up to mount Sinai: for thou chargedst us, saying, [a]Set bounds about the mount, and sanctify it.

24 And the LORD said unto him, Away, get thee down, and thou shalt come up, thou, and Aaron with thee: but let not the priests and the people break through to come up unto the LORD, lest he break forth upon them.

25 So Moses went down unto the people, and spake unto them.

4 [a]Deut. 29:2 [b]Deut. 32:11; Is. 63:9; Rev. 12:14
5 [a]Ex. 15:26; 23:22 [b]Deut. 5:2; Ps. 78:10 [c]Deut. 4:20; 7:6; 14:2; 26:18; 1 Kin. 8:53; Ps. 135:4; Titus 2:14; 1 Pet. 2:9 [d]Ex. 9:29; Deut. 10:14; Job 41:11; Ps. 50:12; 1 Cor. 10:26
6 [a]Deut. 33:2–4; [1 Pet. 2:5, 9; Rev. 1:6; 5:10] [b]Deut. 7:6; 14:21; 26:19; Is. 62:12; [1 Cor. 3:17]
7 [a]Ex. 4:29, 30
8 [a]Ex. 4:31; 24:3, 7; Deut. 5:27; 26:17
9 [a]Ex. 19:16; 20:21; 24:15; Deut. 4:11; Ps. 99:7; Matt. 17:5 [b]Deut. 4:12, 36; John 12:29, 30
10 [a]Lev. 11:44, 45; [Heb. 10:22]
12 [a]Ex. 34:3; Heb. 12:20
15 [a][1 Cor. 7:5]
16 [a]Heb. 12:18, 19 [b]Heb. 12:21
17 [a]Deut. 4:10
18 [a]Deut. 4:11; Judg. 5:5; Ps. 104:32; 144:5 [b]Ex. 3:2; 24:17; Deut. 5:4; 2 Chr. 7:1–3; Heb. 12:18 [c]Gen. 15:17; 19:28; Rev. 15:8 [d]Ps. 68:8; 1 Kin. 19:12; Jer. 4:24; [Heb. 12:26]
19 [a]Heb. 12:21 [b]Neh. 9:13; Ps. 81:7
21 [a]1 Sam. 6:19
22 [a]Ex. 19:24; 24:5 [b]Lev. 10:3; 21:6–8 [c]2 Sam. 6:7, 8
23 [a]Ex. 19:12

NKJV

you shall say to the house of Jacob, and tell the children of Israel:

4 [a]'You have seen what I did to the Egyptians, and *how* [b]I bore you on eagles' wings and brought you to Myself.

5 'Now [a]therefore, if you will indeed obey My voice and [b]keep My covenant, then [c]you shall be a special treasure to Me above all people; for all the earth *is* [d]Mine.

6 'And you shall be to Me a [a]kingdom of priests and a [b]holy nation.' These *are* the words which you shall speak to the children of Israel."

7 So Moses came and called for the [a]elders of the people, and laid before them all these words which the LORD commanded him.

8 Then [a]all the people answered together and said, "All that the LORD has spoken we will do." So Moses brought back the words of the people to the LORD.

9 And the LORD said to Moses, "Behold, I come to you [a]in the thick cloud, [b]that the people may hear when I speak with you, and believe you forever." So Moses told the words of the people to the LORD.

10 Then the LORD said to Moses, "Go to the people and [a]consecrate them today and tomorrow, and let them wash their clothes.

11 "And let them be ready for the third day. For on the third day the LORD will come down upon Mount Sinai in the sight of all the people.

12 "You shall set bounds for the people all around, saying, 'Take heed to yourselves *that* you do *not* go up to the mountain or touch its base. [a]Whoever touches the mountain shall surely be put to death.

13 'Not a hand shall touch him, but he shall surely be stoned or shot *with an arrow;* whether man or beast, he shall not live.' When the trumpet sounds long, they shall come near the mountain."

14 So Moses went down from the mountain to the people and sanctified the people, and they washed their clothes.

15 And he said to the people, "Be ready for the third day; [a]do not come near *your* wives."

16 Then it came to pass on the third day, in the morning, that there were [a]thunderings and lightnings, and a thick cloud on the mountain; and the sound of the trumpet was very loud, so that all the people who *were* in the camp [b]trembled.

17 And [a]Moses brought the people out of the camp to meet with God, and they stood at the foot of the mountain.

18 Now [a]Mount Sinai *was* completely in smoke, because the LORD descended upon [b]it in fire. [c]Its smoke ascended like the smoke of a furnace, and *the [d]whole mountain quaked greatly.

19 And when the blast of the trumpet sounded long and became louder and louder, [a]Moses spoke, and [b]God answered him by voice.

20 Then the LORD came down upon Mount Sinai, on the top of the mountain. And the LORD called Moses to the top of the mountain, and Moses went up.

21 And the LORD said to Moses, "Go down and warn the people, lest they break through [a]to gaze at the LORD, and many of them perish.

22 "Also let the [a]priests who come near the LORD [b]consecrate themselves, lest the LORD [c]break out against them."

23 But Moses said to the LORD, "The people cannot come up to Mount Sinai; for You warned us, saying, [a]'Set bounds around the mountain and consecrate it.' "

24 Then the LORD said to him, "Away! Get down and then come up, you and Aaron with you. But do not let the priests and the people break through to come up to the LORD, lest He break out against them."

25 So Moses went down to the people and spoke to them.

*
19:18 LXX *all the people*

KJV

The Ten Commandments
(Deut. 5:1–22)

20 And God spake [a]all these words, saying,
2 [a]I *am* the LORD thy God, which have brought thee out of the land of Egypt, [b]out of the house of bondage.
3 [a]Thou shalt have no other gods before me.
4 [a]Thou shalt not make unto thee any graven image, or any likeness *of any thing* that *is* in heaven above, or that *is* in the earth beneath, or that *is* in the water under the earth:
5 [a]Thou shalt not bow down thyself to them, nor serve them: [b]for I the LORD thy God *am* a jealous God, [c]visiting the iniquity of the fathers upon the children unto the third and fourth *generation* of them that hate me;
6 And [a]shewing mercy unto thousands of them that love me, and keep my commandments.
7 [a]Thou shalt not take the name of the LORD thy God in vain; for the LORD [b]will not hold him guiltless that taketh his name in vain.
8 [a]Remember the sabbath day, to keep it holy.
9 [a]Six days shalt thou labour, and do all thy work:
10 But the [a]seventh day *is* the sabbath of the LORD thy God: *in it* thou shalt not do any work, thou, nor thy son, nor thy daughter, thy manservant, nor thy maidservant, nor thy cattle, [b]nor thy stranger that *is* within thy gates:
11 For [a]*in* six days the LORD made heaven and earth, the sea, and all that in them *is*, and rested the seventh day: wherefore the LORD blessed the sabbath day, and hallowed it.
12 [a]Honour thy father and thy mother: that thy days may be [b]long upon the land which the LORD thy God giveth thee.
13 [a]Thou shalt not kill.
14 [a]Thou shalt not commit [b]adultery.
15 [a]Thou shalt not steal.
16 [a]Thou shalt not bear false witness against thy neighbour.
17 [a]Thou shalt not covet thy neighbour's house, [b]thou shalt not covet thy neighbour's wife, nor his manservant, nor his maidservant, nor his ox, nor his ass, nor any thing that *is* thy neighbour's.

The People Afraid of God's Presence

18 And [a]all the people [b]saw the thunderings, and the lightnings, and the noise of the trumpet, and the mountain [c]smoking: and when the people saw *it*, they removed, and stood afar off.
19 And they said unto Moses, [a]Speak thou with us, and we will hear: but [b]let not God speak with us, lest we die.
20 And Moses said unto the people, [a]Fear not: [b]for God is come to prove you, and [c]that his fear may be before your faces, that ye sin not.
21 And the people stood afar off, and Moses drew near unto [a]the thick darkness where God *was*.

The Law of the Altar

22 And the LORD said unto Moses, Thus thou shalt say unto the children of Israel, Ye have seen that I have talked with you [a]from heaven.
23 Ye shall not make [a]with me gods of silver, neither shall ye make unto you gods of gold.
24 An altar of [a]earth thou shalt make unto

CHAPTER 20
1 [a]Deut. 5:22
2 [a]Hos. 13:4 [b]Ex. 13:3
3 [a]Jer. 25:6; 35:15
4 [a]Deut. 4:15–19; 27:15
5 [a]Is. 44:15, 19 [b]Deut. 4:24 [c]Num. 14:18, 33
6 [a]Deut. 7:9
7 [a]Lev. 19:12 [b]Mic. 6:11
8 [a]Lev. 26:2
9 [a]Luke 13:14
10 [a]Gen. 2:2, 3 [b]Neh. 13:16–19
11 [a]Ex. 31:17
12 [a]Lev. 19:3 [b]Deut. 5:16, 33; 6:2; 11:8, 9
13 [a]Rom. 13:9
14 [a]Matt. 5:27 [b]Deut. 5:18
15 [a]Lev. 19:11, 13
16 [a]Deut. 5:20
17 [a][Eph. 5:3, 5] [b][Matt. 5:28]
18 [a]Heb. 12:18, 19 [b]Rev. 1:10, 12 [c]Ex. 19:16, 18
19 [a]Heb. 12:19 [b]Deut. 5:5, 23–27
20 [a][Is. 41:10, 13] [b][Deut. 13:3] [c]Is. 8:13
21 [a]Ex. 19:16
22 [a]Deut. 4:36; 5:24, 26
23 [a]Ex. 32:1, 2, 4
24 [a]Ex. 20:25; 27:1–8

NKJV

The Ten Commandments
(Deut. 5:1–22)

20 And God spoke [a]all these words, saying:
2 [a]"I *am* the LORD your God, who brought you out of the land of Egypt, [b]out of the house of bondage.
3 [a]"You shall have no other gods before Me.
4 [a]"You shall not make for yourself a carved image—any likeness *of anything* that *is* in heaven above, or that *is* in the earth beneath, or that *is* in the water under the earth;
5 [a]you shall not bow down to them nor serve them. [b]For I, the LORD your God, *am* a jealous God, [c]visiting the iniquity of the fathers upon the children to the third and fourth *generations* of those who hate Me,
6 but [a]showing mercy to thousands, to those who love Me and keep My commandments.
7 [a]"You shall not take the name of the LORD your God in vain, for the LORD [b]will not hold *him* guiltless who takes His name in vain.
8 [a]"Remember the Sabbath day, to keep it holy.
9 [a]Six days you shall labor and do all your work,
10 but the [a]seventh day *is* the Sabbath of the LORD your God. *In it* you shall do no work: you, nor your son, nor your daughter, nor your male servant, nor your female servant, nor your cattle, [b]nor your stranger who *is* within your gates.
11 For [a]*in* six days the LORD made the heavens and the earth, the sea, and all that *is* in them, and rested the seventh day. Therefore the LORD blessed the Sabbath day and hallowed it.
12 [a]"Honor your father and your mother, that your days may be [b]long upon the land which the LORD your God is giving you.
13 [a]"You shall not murder.
14 [a]"You shall not commit [b]adultery.
15 [a]"You shall not steal.
16 [a]"You shall not bear false witness against your neighbor.
17 [a]"You shall not covet your neighbor's house; [b]you shall not covet your neighbor's wife, nor his male servant, nor his female servant, nor his ox, nor his donkey, nor anything that *is* your neighbor's."

The People Afraid of God's Presence

18 Now [a]all the people [b]witnessed the thunderings, the lightning flashes, the sound of the trumpet, and the mountain [c]smoking; and when the people saw *it*, they trembled and stood afar off.
19 Then they said to Moses, [a]"You speak with us, and we will hear; but [b]let not God speak with us, lest we die."
20 And Moses said to the people, [a]"Do not fear; [b]for God has come to test you, and [c]that His fear may be before you, so that you may not sin."
21 So the people stood afar off, but Moses drew near [a]the thick darkness where God *was*.

The Law of the Altar

22 Then the LORD said to Moses, "Thus you shall say to the children of Israel: 'You have seen that I have talked with you [a]from heaven.
23 'You shall not make *anything to be* [a]with Me—gods of silver or gods of gold you shall not make for yourselves.
24 'An altar of [a]earth you shall make for Me,

KJV

me, and shalt sacrifice thereon thy burnt offerings, and thy peace offerings, [b]thy sheep, and
thine oxen: in all [c]places where I record my name
I will come unto thee, and I will [d]bless thee.
25 And [a]if thou wilt make me an altar of
stone, thou shalt not build it of hewn stone: for
if thou [b]lift up thy tool upon it, thou hast polluted
it.
26 Neither shalt thou go up by steps unto
mine altar, that thy [a]nakedness be not discovered
thereon.

The Law Concerning Servants
(Deut. 15:12–18)

21 Now these *are* the judgments which thou
shalt [a]set before them.
2 [a]If thou buy an Hebrew servant, six years
he shall serve: and in the seventh he shall go out
free for nothing.
3 If he came in by himself, he shall go out
by himself: if he were married, then his wife shall
go out with him.
4 If his master have given him a wife, and
she have born him sons or daughters; the wife
and her children shall be her master's, and he
shall go out by himself.
5 [a]And if the servant shall plainly say, I love
my master, my wife, and my children; I will not
go out free:
6 Then his master shall bring him unto the
[a]judges; he shall also bring him to the door, or
unto the door post; and his master shall bore his
ear through with an aul; and he shall serve him
for ever.
7 And if a man [a]sell his daughter to be a
maidservant, she shall not go out as the menservants do.
8 If she please not her master, who hath betrothed her to himself, then shall he let her be
redeemed: to sell her unto a strange nation he
shall have no power, seeing he hath dealt deceitfully with her.
9 And if he have betrothed her unto his son,
he shall deal with her after the manner of
daughters.
10 If he take him another *wife;* her food, her
raiment, [a]and her duty of marriage, shall he not
diminish.
11 And if he do not these three unto her, then
shall she go out free without money.

The Law Concerning Violence

12 [a]He that smiteth a man, so that he die,
shall be surely put to death.
13 And [a]if a man lie not in wait, but God [b]de-
liver *him* into his hand; then [c]I will appoint thee
a place whither he shall flee.
14 But if a man come [a]presumptuously upon
his neighbour, to slay him with guile; [b]thou shalt
take him from mine altar, that he may die.
15 And he that smiteth his father, or his
mother, shall be surely put to death.
16 And [a]he that stealeth a man, and [b]selleth
him, or if he be [c]found in his hand, he shall surely
be put to death.
17 And [a]he that curseth his father, or his
mother, shall surely be put to death.
18 And if men strive together, and one smite
another with a stone, or with *his* fist, and he die
not, but keepeth *his* bed:
19 If he rise again, and walk abroad [a]upon
his staff, then shall he that smote *him* be quit:
only he shall pay *for* the loss of his time, and shall
cause *him* to be thoroughly healed.
20 And if a man smite his servant, or his
maid, with a rod, and he die under his hand; he
shall be surely punished.
21 Notwithstanding, if he continue a day or
two, he shall not be punished: for he *is* his
[a]money.
22 If men strive, and hurt a woman with

---

24 [b]Ex. 24:5;
Lev. 1:2
[c]Deut. 12:5;
16:6, 11; 1 Kin.
9:3; 2 Chr. 6:6
[d]Gen. 12:2
25 [a]Deut. 27:5
[b]Josh. 8:30, 31
26 [a]Ex. 28:42,
43

CHAPTER 21

1 [a]Ex. 24:3, 4;
Deut. 4:14; 6:1
2 [a]Lev. 25:39–
43; Deut.
15:12–18; Jer.
34:14
5 [a]Deut.
15:16, 17
6 [a]Ex. 12:12;
22:8, 9
7 [a]Neh. 5:5
10 [a][1 Cor.
7:3, 5]
12 [a]Gen. 9:6;
Lev. 24:17;
Num. 35:30;
[Matt. 26:52]
13 [a]Deut.
19:4, 5
[b]1 Sam. 24:4,
10, 18 [c]Num.
35:11; Deut.
19:3; Josh.
20:2
14 [a]Deut.
19:11, 12;
[Heb. 10:26]
[b]1 Kin. 2:28–
34
16 [a]Deut. 24:7
[b]Gen. 37:28
[c]Ex. 22:4
17 [a]Lev. 20:9;
Prov. 20:20;
Matt. 15:4;
Mark 7:10
19 [a]2 Sam.
3:29
21 [a]Lev.
25:44–46

NKJV

and you shall sacrifice on it your burnt offerings
and your peace offerings, [b]your sheep and your
oxen. In every [c]place where I record My name I
will come to you, and I will [d]bless you.
25 'And [a]if you make Me an altar of stone,
you shall not build it of hewn stone; for if you
[b]use your tool on it, you have profaned it.
26 'Nor shall you go up by steps to My altar,
that your [a]nakedness may not be exposed on it.'

The Law Concerning Servants
(Deut. 15:12–18)

21 "Now these *are* the judgments which you
shall [a]set before them:
2 [a]"If you buy a Hebrew servant, he shall
serve six years; and in the seventh he shall go
out free and pay nothing.
3 "If he comes in by himself, he shall go
out by himself; if he *comes in* married, then his
wife shall go out with him.
4 "If his master has given him a wife, and
she has borne him sons or daughters, the wife
and her children shall be her master's, and he
shall go out by himself.
5 [a]"But if the servant plainly says, 'I love
my master, my wife, and my children; I will not
go out free,'
6 "then his master shall bring him to the
[a]judges. He shall also bring him to the door, or
to the doorpost, and his master shall pierce his
ear with an awl; and he shall serve him forever.
7 "And if a man [a]sells his daughter to be a
female slave, she shall not go out as the male
slaves do.
8 "If she does not please her master, who
has betrothed her to himself, then he shall let her
be redeemed. He shall have no right to sell her
to a foreign people, since he has dealt deceitfully
with her.
9 "And if he has betrothed her to his son,
he shall deal with her according to the custom of
daughters.
10 "If he takes another *wife,* he shall not diminish her food, her clothing, [a]and her marriage
rights.
11 "And if he does not do these three for her,
then she shall go out free, without *paying* money.

The Law Concerning Violence

12 [a]"He who strikes a man so that he dies
shall surely be put to death.
13 "However, [a]if he did not lie in wait, but
God [b]delivered *him* into his hand, then [c]I will appoint for you a place where he may flee.
14 "But if a man acts with [a]premeditation
against his neighbor, to kill him by treachery,
[b]you shall take him from My altar, that he may
die.
15 "And he who strikes his father or his
mother shall surely be put to death.
16 [a]"He who kidnaps a man and [b]sells him,
or if he is [c]found in his hand, shall surely be put
to death.
17 "And [a]he who curses his father or his
mother shall surely be put to death.
18 "If men contend with each other, and one
strikes the other with a stone or with *his* fist, and
he does not die but is confined to *his* bed,
19 "if he rises again and walks about outside
[a]with his staff, then he who struck *him* shall be
acquitted. He shall only pay *for* the loss of his
time, and shall provide *for him* to be thoroughly
healed.
20 "And if a man beats his male or female
servant with a rod, so that he dies under his hand,
he shall surely be punished.
21 "Notwithstanding, if he remains alive a
day or two, he shall not be punished; for he *is*
his [a]property.
22 "If men fight, and hurt a woman with

KJV

child, so that her fruit depart *from her,* and yet no mischief follow: he shall be surely punished, according as the woman's husband will lay upon him; and he shall [a]pay as the judges *determine.*

23 And if *any* mischief follow, then thou shalt give life for life,

24 [a]Eye for eye, tooth for tooth, hand for hand, foot for foot,

25 Burning for burning, wound for wound, stripe for stripe.

26 And if a man smite the eye of his servant, or the eye of his maid, that it perish; he shall let him go free for his eye's sake.

27 And if he smite out his manservant's tooth, or his maidservant's tooth; he shall let him go free for his tooth's sake.

Animal Control Laws

28 If an ox gore a man or a woman, that they die: then [a]the ox shall be surely stoned, and his flesh shall not be eaten; but the owner of the ox *shall be* quit.

29 But if the ox were wont to push with his horn in time past, and it hath been testified to his owner, and he hath not kept him in, but that he hath killed a man or a woman; the ox shall be stoned, and his owner also shall be put to death.

30 If there be laid on him a sum of money, then he shall give for [a]the ransom of his life whatsoever is laid upon him.

31 Whether he have gored a son, or have gored a daughter, according to this judgment shall it be done unto him.

32 If the ox shall push a manservant or a maidservant; he shall give unto their master [a]thirty shekels of silver, and the [b]ox shall be stoned.

33 And if a man shall open a pit, or if a man shall dig a pit, and not cover it, and an ox or an ass fall therein;

34 The owner of the pit shall make *it* good, *and* give money unto the owner of them; and the dead *beast* shall be his.

35 And if one man's ox hurt another's, that he die; then they shall sell the live ox, and divide the money of it; and the dead *ox* also they shall divide.

36 Or if it be known that the ox hath used to push in time past, and his owner hath not kept him in; he shall surely pay ox for ox; and the dead shall be his own.

Responsibility for Property

22 If a man shall steal an ox, or a sheep, and kill it, or sell it; he shall [a]restore five oxen for an ox, and four sheep for a sheep.

2 If a thief be found [a]breaking up, and be smitten that he die, *there shall* [b]no blood *be shed* for him.

3 If the sun be risen upon him, *there shall be* blood *shed* for him; *for* he should make full restitution; if he have nothing, then he shall be [a]sold for his theft.

4 If the theft be certainly [a]found in his hand alive, whether it be ox, or ass, or sheep; he shall [b]restore double.

5 If a man shall cause a field or vineyard to be eaten, and shall put in his beast, and shall feed in another man's field; of the best of his own field, and of the best of his own vineyard, shall he make restitution.

6 If fire break out, and catch in thorns, so that the stacks of corn, or the standing corn, or the field, be consumed *therewith;* he that kindled the fire shall surely make restitution.

7 If a man shall [a]deliver unto his neighbour money or stuff to keep, and it be stolen out of the man's house; [b]if the thief be found, let him pay double.

8 If the thief be not found, then the master of the house shall be brought unto the [a]judges,

22 [a]Ex. 18:21, 22; 21:30; Deut. 22:18
24 [a]Lev. 24:20; Deut. 19:21; [Matt. 5:38–44; 1 Pet. 2:19–21]
28 [a]Gen. 9:5
30 [a]Ex. 21:22; Num. 35:31
32 [a]Zech. 11:12, 13; Matt. 26:15; 27:3, 9 [b]Ex. 21:28

CHAPTER 22

1 [a]2 Sam. 12:6; Prov. 6:31; Luke 19:8
2 [a]Job 24:16; Matt. 6:19; 24:43; 1 Pet. 4:15 [b]Num. 35:27
3 [a]Ex. 21:2; Matt. 18:25
4 [a]Ex. 21:16 [b]Prov. 6:31
7 [a]Lev. 6:1–7 [b]Ex. 22:4
8 [a]Ex. 21:6, 22; 22:28; Deut. 17:8, 9; 19:17

NKJV

child, so that she gives birth prematurely, yet no harm follows, he shall surely be punished accordingly as the woman's husband imposes on him; and he shall [a]pay as the judges *determine.*

23 "But if *any* harm follows, then you shall give life for life,

24 [a]"eye for eye, tooth for tooth, hand for hand, foot for foot,

25 "burn for burn, wound for wound, stripe for stripe.

26 "If a man strikes the eye of his male or female servant, and destroys it, he shall let him go free for the sake of his eye.

27 "And if he knocks out the tooth of his male or female servant, he shall let him go free for the sake of his tooth.

Animal Control Laws

28 "If an ox gores a man or a woman to death, then [a]the ox shall surely be stoned, and its flesh shall not be eaten; but the owner of the ox *shall be* acquitted.

29 "But if the ox tended to thrust with its horn in times past, and it has been made known to his owner, and he has not kept it confined, so that it has killed a man or a woman, the ox shall be stoned and its owner also shall be put to death.

30 "If there is imposed on him a sum of money, then he shall pay [a]to redeem his life, whatever is imposed on him.

31 "Whether it has gored a son or gored a daughter, according to this judgment it shall be done to him.

32 "If the ox gores a male or female servant, he shall give to their master [a]thirty shekels of silver, and the [b]ox shall be stoned.

33 "And if a man opens a pit, or if a man digs a pit and does not cover it, and an ox or a donkey falls in it,

34 "the owner of the pit shall make *it* good; he shall give money to their owner, but the dead *animal* shall be his.

35 "If one man's ox hurts another's, so that it dies, then they shall sell the live ox and divide the money from it; and the dead *ox* they shall also divide.

36 "Or if it was known that the ox tended to thrust in time past, and its owner has not kept it confined, he shall surely pay ox for ox, and the dead animal shall be his own.

Responsibility for Property

22 "If a man steals an ox or a sheep, and slaughters it or sells it, he shall [a]restore five oxen for an ox and four sheep for a sheep.

2 "If the thief is found [a]breaking in, and he is struck so that he dies, *there shall be* [b]no guilt for his bloodshed.

3 "If the sun has risen on him, *there shall be* guilt for his bloodshed. He should make full restitution; if he has nothing, then he shall be [a]sold for his theft.

4 "If the theft is certainly [a]found alive in his hand, whether it is an ox or donkey or sheep, he shall [b]restore double.

5 "If a man causes a field or vineyard to be grazed, and lets loose his animal, and it feeds in another man's field, he shall make restitution from the best of his own field and the best of his own vineyard.

6 "If fire breaks out and catches in thorns, so that stacked grain, standing grain, or the field is consumed, he who kindled the fire shall surely make restitution.

7 "If a man [a]delivers to his neighbor money or articles to keep, and it is stolen out of the man's house, [b]if the thief is found, he shall pay double.

8 "If the thief is not found, then the master of the house shall be brought to the [a]judges *to*

KJV

to see whether he have put his hand unto his neighbour's goods.

9 For all manner of trespass, *whether it be* for ox, for ass, for sheep, for raiment, *or* for any manner of lost thing, which *another* challengeth to be his, the [a]cause of both parties shall come before the judges; *and* whom the judges shall condemn, he shall pay double unto his neighbour.

10 If a man deliver unto his neighbour an ass, or an ox, or a sheep, or any beast, to keep; and it die, or be hurt, or driven away, no man seeing *it:*

11 *Then* shall an [a]oath of the LORD be between them both, that he hath not put his hand unto his neighbour's goods; and the owner of it shall accept *thereof,* and he shall not make *it* good.

12 And [a]if it be stolen from him, he shall make restitution unto the owner thereof.

13 If it be [a]torn in pieces, *then* let him bring it *for* witness, *and* he shall not make good that which was torn.

14 And if a man borrow *ought* of his neighbour, and it be hurt, or die, the owner thereof *being* not with it, he shall surely make *it* good.

15 *But* if the owner thereof *be* with it, he shall not make *it* good: if it *be* an hired *thing,* it came for his hire.

Moral and Ceremonial Principles

16 And [a]if a man entice a maid that is not betrothed, and lie with her, he shall surely endow her to be his wife.

17 If her father utterly refuse to give her unto him, he shall pay money according to the [a]dowry of virgins.

18 [a]Thou shalt not suffer a witch to live.

19 [a]Whosoever lieth with a beast shall surely be put to death.

20 [a]He that sacrificeth unto *any* god, save unto the LORD only, he shall be utterly destroyed.

21 [a]Thou shalt neither vex a stranger, nor oppress him: for ye were strangers in the land of Egypt.

22 [a]Ye shall not afflict any widow, or fatherless child.

23 If thou afflict them in any wise, and they [a]cry at all unto me, I will surely [b]hear their cry;

24 And my [a]wrath shall wax hot, and I will kill you with the sword; and [b]your wives shall be widows, and your children fatherless.

25 [a]If thou lend money to *any of* my people *that is* poor by thee, thou shalt not be to him as an usurer, neither shalt thou lay upon him [b]usury.

26 [a]If thou at all take thy neighbour's raiment to pledge, thou shalt deliver it unto him by that the sun goeth down:

27 For that *is* his covering only, it *is* his raiment for his skin: wherein shall he sleep? and it shall come to pass, when he crieth unto me, that I will hear; for I *am* [a]gracious.

28 [a]Thou shalt not revile the gods, nor curse the [b]ruler of thy people.

29 Thou shalt not delay *to offer* [a]the first of thy ripe fruits, and of thy liquors: [b]the firstborn of thy sons shalt thou give unto me.

30 [a]Likewise shalt thou do with thine oxen, *and* with thy sheep: [b]seven days it shall be with his dam; on the eighth day thou shalt give it me.

31 And ye shall be [a]holy men unto me: [b]neither shall ye eat *any* flesh *that is* torn of beasts in the field; ye shall cast it to the dogs.

Justice for All

23 Thou [a]shalt not raise a false report: put not thine hand with the wicked to be an [b]unrighteous witness.

2 [a]Thou shalt not follow a multitude to *do* evil; [b]neither shalt thou speak in a cause to decline after many to wrest *judgment:*

3 Neither shalt thou countenance a [a]poor man in his cause.

---

9 [a]Deut. 25:1; 2 Chr. 19:10
11 [a]Heb. 6:16
12 [a]Gen. 31:39
13 [a]Gen. 31:39
16 [a]Deut. 22:28, 29
17 [a]Gen. 34:12; 1 Sam. 18:25
18 [a]Lev. 19:31; 20:6, 27; Deut. 18:10, 11; 1 Sam. 28:3–10; Jer. 27:9, 10
19 [a]Lev. 18:23; 20:15, 16; Deut. 27:21
20 [a]Ex. 32:8; 34:15; Lev. 17:7; Num. 25:2; Deut. 17:2, 3, 5; 1 Kin. 18:40; 2 Kin. 10:25
21 [a]Ex. 23:9; Deut. 10:19; Zech. 7:10
22 [a]Deut. 24:17, 18; Prov. 23:10, 11; Jer. 7:6, 7; [James 1:27]
23 [a][Luke 18:7] [b]Deut. 10:17, 18; Ps. 18:6
24 [a]Ps. 69:24 [b]Ps. 109:9
25 [a]Lev. 25:35–37 [b]Deut. 23:19, 20; Neh. 5:1–13; Ps. 15:5; Ezek. 18:8
26 [a]Deut. 24:6, 10–13; Job 24:3; Prov. 20:16; Amos 2:8
27 [a]Ex. 34:6, 7
28 [a]Eccl. 10:20 [b]Acts 23:5
29 [a]Ex. 23:16, 19; Deut. 26:2–11; Prov. 3:9 [b]Ex. 13:2, 12, 15
30 [a]Deut. 15:19 [b]Lev. 22:27
31 [a]Ex. 19:6; Lev. 11:44; 19:2 [b]Lev. 7:24; 17:15; Ezek. 4:14

CHAPTER 23

1 [a]Ex. 20:16; Lev. 19:11; Deut. 5:20; Ps. 101:5; [Prov. 10:18] [b]Deut. 19:16–21; Ps. 35:11; [Prov. 19:5]; Acts 6:11
2 [a]Gen. 7:1 [b]Lev. 19:5
3 [a]Ex. 23:6; Lev. 19:15; Deut. 1:17; 16:19

NKJV

see whether he has put his hand into his neighbor's goods.

9 "For any kind of trespass, *whether it concerns* an ox, a donkey, a sheep, or clothing, *or* for any kind of lost thing which *another* claims to be his, the [a]cause of both parties shall come before the judges; *and* whomever the judges condemn shall pay double to his neighbor.

10 "If a man delivers to his neighbor a donkey, an ox, a sheep, or any animal to keep, and it dies, is hurt, or driven away, no one seeing *it,*

11 "*then* an [a]oath of the LORD shall be between them both, that he has not put his hand into his neighbor's goods; and the owner of it shall accept *that,* and he shall not make *it* good.

12 "But [a]if, in fact, it is stolen from him, he shall make restitution to the owner of it.

13 "If it is [a]torn to pieces *by a beast, then* he shall bring it as evidence, *and* he shall not make good what was torn.

14 "And if a man borrows *anything* from his neighbor, and it becomes injured or dies, the owner of it not *being* with it, he shall surely make *it* good.

15 "If its owner *was* with it, he shall not make *it* good; if it *was* hired, it came for its hire.

Moral and Ceremonial Principles

16 [a]"If a man entices a virgin who is not betrothed, and lies with her, he shall surely pay the bride-price for her *to be* his wife.

17 "If her father utterly refuses to give her to him, he shall pay money according to the [a]bride-price of virgins.

18 [a]"You shall not permit a sorceress to live.

19 [a]"Whoever lies with an animal shall surely be put to death.

20 [a]"He who sacrifices to *any* god, except to the LORD only, he shall be utterly destroyed.

21 [a]"You shall neither mistreat a stranger nor oppress him, for you were strangers in the land of Egypt.

22 [a]"You shall not afflict any widow or fatherless child.

23 "If you afflict them in any way, *and* they [a]cry at all to Me, I will surely [b]hear their cry;

24 "and My [a]wrath will become hot, and I will kill you with the sword; [b]your wives shall be widows, and your children fatherless.

25 [a]"If you lend money to *any of* My people *who are* poor among you, you shall not be like a moneylender to him; you shall not charge him [b]interest.

26 [a]"If you ever take your neighbor's garment as a pledge, you shall return it to him before the sun goes down.

27 "For that *is* his only covering, it *is* his garment for his skin. What will he sleep in? And it will be that when he cries to Me, I will hear, for I *am* [a]gracious.

28 [a]"You shall not revile God, nor curse a [b]ruler of your people.

29 "You shall not delay *to offer* [a]the first of your ripe produce and your juices. [b]The firstborn of your sons you shall give to Me.

30 [a]"Likewise you shall do with your oxen *and* your sheep. It shall be with its mother [b]seven days; on the eighth day you shall give it to Me.

31 "And you shall be [a]holy men to Me: [b]you shall not eat meat torn *by beasts* in the field; you shall throw it to the dogs.

Justice for All

23 "You [a]shall not circulate a false report. Do not put your hand with the wicked to be an [b]unrighteous witness.

2 [a]"You shall not follow a crowd to do evil; [b]nor shall you testify in a dispute so as to turn aside after many to pervert *justice.*

3 "You shall not show partiality to a [a]poor man in his dispute.

KJV

4 [a]If thou meet thine enemy's ox or his ass
going astray, thou shalt surely bring it back to
him again.
5 [a]If thou see the ass of him that hateth thee
lying under his burden, and wouldest forbear to
help him, thou shalt surely help with him.
6 [a]Thou shalt not wrest the judgment of thy
poor in his cause.
7 [a]Keep thee far from a false matter; [b]and
the innocent and righteous slay thou not: for [c]I
will not justify the wicked.
8 And [a]thou shalt take no gift: for the gift
blindeth the wise, and perverteth the words of the
righteous.
9 Also [a]thou shalt not oppress a stranger:
for ye know the heart of a stranger, seeing ye
were strangers in the land of Egypt.

The Law of Sabbaths

10 And [a]six years thou shalt sow thy land,
and shalt gather in the fruits thereof:
11 But the seventh *year* thou shalt let it rest
and lie still; that the poor of thy people may eat:
and what they leave the beasts of the field shall
eat. In like manner thou shalt deal with thy vineyard, *and* with thy oliveyard.
12 [a]Six days thou shalt do thy work, and on
the seventh day thou shalt rest: that thine ox and
thine ass may rest, and the son of thy handmaid,
and the stranger, may be refreshed.
13 And in all *things* that I have said unto you
[a]be circumspect: and [b]make no mention of the
name of other gods, neither let it be heard out of
thy mouth.

Three Annual Feasts
(Ex. 34:18–26; Deut. 16:1–17)

14 [a]Three times thou shalt keep a feast unto
me in the year.
15 [a]Thou shalt keep the feast of unleavened
bread: (thou shalt eat unleavened bread seven
days, as I commanded thee, in the time appointed
of the month Abib; for in it thou camest out from
Egypt: [b]and none shall appear before me empty:)
16 [a]And the feast of harvest, the firstfruits
of thy labours, which thou hast sown in the field:
and [b]the feast of ingathering, *which is* in the end
of the year, when thou hast gathered in thy labours out of the field.
17 [a]Three times in the year all thy males shall
appear before the Lord GOD.
18 [a]Thou shalt not offer the blood of my sacrifice with leavened [b]bread; neither shall the fat
of my sacrifice remain until the morning.
19 [a]The first of the firstfruits of thy land thou
shalt bring into the house of the LORD thy God.
[b]Thou shalt not seethe a kid in his mother's milk.

The Angel and the Promises

20 [a]Behold, I send an Angel before thee, to
keep thee in the way, and to bring thee into the
place which I have prepared.
21 Beware of him, and obey his voice, [a]pro-
voke him not; for he will [b]not pardon your transgressions: for [c]my name *is* in him.
22 But if thou shalt indeed obey his voice,
and do all that I speak; then [a]I will be an enemy
unto thine enemies, and an adversary unto thine
adversaries.
23 [a]For mine Angel shall go before thee, and
[b]bring thee in unto the Amorites, and the Hittites,
and the Perizzites, and the Canaanites, the Hivites, and the Jebusites: and I will cut them off.
24 Thou shalt not [a]bow down to their gods,
nor serve them, [b]nor do after their works: [c]but
thou shalt utterly overthrow them, and quite
break down their images.
25 And ye shall [a]serve the LORD your God,
and [b]he shall bless thy bread, and thy water; and
[c]I will take sickness away from the midst of thee.
26 [a]There shall nothing cast their young, nor

4 [a][Rom. 12:20]
5 [a]Deut. 22:4
6 [a]Eccl. 5:8
7 [a]Eph. 4:25 [b]Matt. 27:4 [c]Rom. 1:18
8 [a]Prov. 15:27; 17:8, 23
9 [a]Ex. 22:21
10 [a]Lev. 25:1–7
12 [a]Luke 13:14
13 [a]1 Tim. 4:16 [b]Josh. 23:7
14 [a]Ex. 23:17; 34:22–24
15 [a]Ex. 12:14–20 [b]Ex. 22:29; 34:20
16 [a]Ex. 34:22 [b]Deut. 16:13
17 [a]Deut. 16:16
18 [a]Ex. 34:25 [b]Deut. 16:4
19 [a]Deut. 26:2, 10 [b]Deut. 14:21
20 [a]Ex. 3:2; 13:15; 14:19
21 [a]Ps. 78:40, 56 [b]Deut. 18:19 [c]Is. 9:6
22 [a]Deut. 30:7
23 [a]Ex. 23:20 [b]Josh. 24:8, 11
24 [a]Ex. 20:5; 23:13, 33 [b]Deut. 12:30, 31 [c]Num. 33:52
25 [a]Deut. 6:13 [b]Deut. 28:5 [c]Ex. 15:26
26 [a]Deut. 7:14; 28:4

*

23:17 Heb. *YHWH*, usually translated LORD

NKJV

4 [a]"If you meet your enemy's ox or his donkey going astray, you shall surely bring it back
to him again.
5 [a]"If you see the donkey of one who hates
you lying under its burden, and you would refrain
from helping it, you shall surely help him with
it.
6 [a]"You shall not pervert the judgment of
your poor in his dispute.
7 [a]"Keep yourself far from a false matter;
[b]do not kill the innocent and righteous. For [c]I will
not justify the wicked.
8 "And [a]you shall take no bribe, for a bribe
blinds the discerning and perverts the words of
the righteous.
9 "Also [a]you shall not oppress a stranger,
for you know the heart of a stranger, because you
were strangers in the land of Egypt.

The Law of Sabbaths

10 [a]"Six years you shall sow your land and
gather in its produce,
11 "but the seventh *year* you shall let it rest
and lie fallow, that the poor of your people may
eat; and what they leave, the beasts of the field
may eat. In like manner you shall do with your
vineyard *and* your olive grove.
12 [a]"Six days you shall do your work, and
on the seventh day you shall rest, that your ox
and your donkey may rest, and the son of your
female servant and the stranger may be refreshed.
13 "And in all that I have said to you, [a]be
circumspect and [b]make no mention of the name
of other gods, nor let it be heard from your mouth.

Three Annual Feasts
(Ex. 34:18–26; Deut. 16:1–17)

14 [a]"Three times you shall keep a feast to
Me in the year:
15 [a]"You shall keep the Feast of Unleavened
Bread (you shall eat unleavened bread seven days,
as I commanded you, at the time appointed in the
month of Abib, for in it you came out of Egypt;
[b]none shall appear before Me empty);
16 [a]"and the Feast of Harvest, the firstfruits
of your labors which you have sown in the field;
and [b]the Feast of Ingathering at the end of the
year, when you have gathered in *the fruit of* your
labors from the field.
17 [a]"Three times in the year all your males
shall appear before the Lord *GOD.
18 [a]"You shall not offer the blood of My sacrifice with leavened [b]bread; nor shall the fat of
My sacrifice remain until morning.
19 [a]"The first of the firstfruits of your land
you shall bring into the house of the LORD your
God. [b]You shall not boil a young goat in its
mother's milk.

The Angel and the Promises

20 [a]"Behold, I send an Angel before you to
keep you in the way and to bring you into the
place which I have prepared.
21 "Beware of Him and obey His voice; [a]do
not provoke Him, for He will [b]not pardon your
transgressions; for [c]My name *is* in Him.
22 "But if you indeed obey His voice and do
all that I speak, then [a]I will be an enemy to your
enemies and an adversary to your adversaries.
23 [a]"For My Angel will go before you and
[b]bring you in to the Amorites and the Hittites and
the Perizzites and the Canaanites and the Hivites
and the Jebusites; and I will cut them off.
24 "You shall not [a]bow down to their gods,
nor serve them, [b]nor do according to their works;
[c]but you shall utterly overthrow them and completely break down their *sacred* pillars.
25 "So you shall [a]serve the LORD your God,
and [b]He will bless your bread and your water.
And [c]I will take sickness away from the midst of
you.
26 [a]"No one shall suffer miscarriage or be

KJV

be barren, in thy land: the number of thy days I
will [b]fulfil.
27 I will send [a]my fear before thee, and will
[b]destroy all the people to whom thou shalt come,
and I will make all thine enemies turn their backs
unto thee.
28 And [a]I will send hornets before thee,
which shall drive out the Hivite, the Canaanite,
and the Hittite, from before thee.
29 [a]I will not drive them out from before thee
in one year; lest the land become desolate, and
the beast of the field multiply against thee.
30 By little and little I will drive them out
from before thee, until thou be increased, and inherit the land.
31 And [a]I will set thy bounds from the Red
sea even unto the sea of the Philistines, and from
the desert unto the river: for I will [b]deliver the
inhabitants of the land into your hand; and thou
shalt drive them out before thee.
32 [a]Thou shalt make no covenant with them,
nor with their gods.
33 They shall not dwell in thy land, lest they
make thee sin against me: for if thou serve their
gods, [a]it will surely be a snare unto thee.

Israel Affirms the Covenant

24 And he said unto Moses, Come up unto the
LORD, thou, and Aaron, [a]Nadab, and Abihu,
[b]and seventy of the elders of Israel; and worship
ye afar off.
2 And Moses alone shall come near the
LORD: but they shall not come nigh; neither shall
the people go up with him.
3 And Moses came and told the people all
the words of the LORD, and all the judgments: and
all the people answered with one voice, and said,
[a]All the words which the LORD hath said will we
do.
4 And Moses [a]wrote all the words of the
LORD, and rose up early in the morning, and
builded an altar under the hill, and twelve [b]pillars,
according to the twelve tribes of Israel.
5 And he sent young men of the children
of Israel, which offered [a]burnt offerings, and sacrificed peace offerings of oxen unto the LORD.
6 And Moses [a]took half of the blood, and
put *it* in basons; and half of the blood he sprinkled
on the altar.
7 And he [a]took the book of the covenant,
and read in the audience of the people: and they
said, All that the LORD hath said will we do, and
be obedient.
8 And Moses took the blood, and sprinkled
it on the people, and said, Behold [a]the blood of
the covenant, which the LORD hath made with you
concerning all these words.

On the Mountain with God

9 Then went up Moses, and Aaron, Nadab,
and Abihu, and seventy of the elders of Israel:
10 And they [a]saw the God of Israel: and *there*
was under his feet as it were a paved work of a
[b]sapphire stone, and as it were the [c]body of
heaven in *his* clearness.
11 And upon the nobles of the children of
Israel he [a]laid not his hand: also [b]they saw God,
and did [c]eat and drink.
12 And the LORD said unto Moses, [a]Come up
to me into the mount, and be there: and I will
give thee [b]tables of stone, and a law, and commandments which I have written; that thou mayest teach them.
13 And Moses rose up, and [a]his minister
Joshua: and Moses went up into the mount of God.
14 And he said unto the elders, Tarry ye here
for us, until we come again unto you: and, behold,
Aaron and [a]Hur *are* with you: if any man have
any matters to do, let him come unto them.

26 [b]1 Chr. 23:1
27 [a]Ex. 15:16 [b]Deut. 7:23
28 [a]Josh. 24:12
29 [a]Deut. 7:22
31 [a]Gen. 15:18 [b]Josh. 21:44
32 [a]Ex. 34:12, 15
33 [a]Ps. 106:36

CHAPTER 24

1 [a]Lev. 10:1, 2 [b]Num. 11:16
3 [a]Ex. 19:8; 24:7
4 [a]Deut. 31:9 [b]Gen. 28:18
5 [a]Ex. 18:12; 20:24
6 [a]Heb. 9:18
7 [a]Heb. 9:19
8 [a][Luke 22:20]
10 [a][John 1:18; 6:46] [b]Ezek. 1:26 [c]Matt. 17:2
11 [a]Ex. 19:21 [b]Gen. 32:30 [c]1 Cor. 10:18
12 [a]Ex. 24:2, 15 [b]Ex. 31:18; 32:15
13 [a]Ex. 32:17
14 [a]Ex. 17:10, 12

*23:31 Heb. *Nahar*, the Euphrates

NKJV

barren in your land; I will [b]fulfill the number of
your days.
27 "I will send [a]My fear before you, I will
[b]cause confusion among all the people to whom
you come, and will make all your enemies turn
their backs to you.
28 "And [a]I will send hornets before you,
which shall drive out the Hivite, the Canaanite,
and the Hittite from before you.
29 [a]"I will not drive them out from before
you in one year, lest the land become desolate
and the beasts of the field become too numerous
for you.
30 "Little by little I will drive them out from
before you, until you have increased, and you inherit the land.
31 "And [a]I will set your bounds from the Red
Sea to the sea, Philistia, and from the desert to
the *River. For I will [b]deliver the inhabitants of
the land into your hand, and you shall drive them
out before you.
32 [a]"You shall make no covenant with them,
nor with their gods.
33 "They shall not dwell in your land, lest
they make you sin against Me. For *if* you serve
their gods, [a]it will surely be a snare to you."

Israel Affirms the Covenant

24 Now He said to Moses, "Come up to the
LORD, you and Aaron, [a]Nadab and Abihu,
[b]and seventy of the elders of Israel, and worship
from afar.
2 "And Moses alone shall come near the
LORD, but they shall not come near; nor shall the
people go up with him."
3 So Moses came and told the people all the
words of the LORD and all the judgments. And
all the people answered with one voice and said,
[a]"All the words which the LORD has said we will
do."
4 And Moses [a]wrote all the words of the
LORD. And he rose early in the morning, and built
an altar at the foot of the mountain, and twelve
[b]pillars according to the twelve tribes of Israel.
5 Then he sent young men of the children
of Israel, who offered [a]burnt offerings and sacrificed peace offerings of oxen to the LORD.
6 And Moses [a]took half the blood and put
it in basins, and half the blood he sprinkled on
the altar.
7 Then he [a]took the Book of the Covenant
and read in the hearing of the people. And they
said, "All that the LORD has said we will do, and
be obedient."
8 And Moses took the blood, sprinkled *it*
on the people, and said, "This is [a]the blood of
the covenant which the LORD has made with you
according to all these words."

On the Mountain with God

9 Then Moses went up, also Aaron, Nadab,
and Abihu, and seventy of the elders of Israel,
10 and they [a]saw the God of Israel. And *there*
was under His feet as it were a paved work of
[b]sapphire stone, and it was like the [c]very heavens
in *its* clarity.
11 But on the nobles of the children of Israel
He [a]did not lay His hand. So [b]they saw God, and
they [c]ate and drank.
12 Then the LORD said to Moses, [a]"Come up
to Me on the mountain and be there; and I will
give you [b]tablets of stone, and the law and commandments which I have written, that you may
teach them."
13 So Moses arose with [a]his assistant
Joshua, and Moses went up to the mountain of
God.
14 And he said to the elders, "Wait here for
us until we come back to you. Indeed, Aaron and
[a]Hur *are* with you. If any man has a difficulty,
let him go to them."

KJV

15 And Moses went up into the mount, and [a]a cloud covered the mount.

16 And [a]the glory of the LORD abode upon mount Sinai, and the cloud covered it six days: and the seventh day he called unto Moses out of the midst of the cloud.

17 And the sight of the glory of the LORD *was* like [a]devouring fire on the top of the mount in the eyes of the children of Israel.

18 And Moses went into the midst of the cloud, and gat him up into the mount: and [a]Moses was in the mount forty days and forty nights.

Offerings for the Sanctuary
(Ex. 35:4–9)

25 And the LORD spake unto Moses, saying,
2 Speak unto the children of Israel, that they bring me an offering: [a]of every man that giveth it willingly with his heart ye shall take my offering.

3 And this *is* the offering which ye shall take of them; gold, and silver, and brass,

4 And blue, and purple, and scarlet, and fine linen, and goats' *hair,*

5 And rams' skins dyed red, and badgers' skins, and shittim wood,

6 [a]Oil for the light, [b]spices for anointing oil, and for sweet incense,

7 Onyx stones, and stones to be set in the [a]ephod, and in the breastplate.

8 And let them make me a [a]sanctuary; that [b]I may dwell among them.

9 According to all that I shew thee, *after* the pattern of the tabernacle, and the pattern of all the instruments thereof, even so shall ye make *it.*

The Ark of the Testimony
(Ex. 37:1–9)

10 [a]And they shall make an ark *of* shittim wood: two cubits and a half *shall be* the length thereof, and a cubit and a half the breadth thereof, and a cubit and a half the height thereof.

11 And thou shalt overlay it with pure gold, within and without shalt thou overlay it, and shalt make upon it a crown of [a]gold round about.

12 And thou shalt cast four rings of gold for it, and put *them* in the four corners thereof; and two rings *shall be* in the one side of it, and two rings in the other side of it.

13 And thou shalt make staves *of* shittim wood, and overlay them with gold.

14 And thou shalt put the staves into the rings by the sides of the ark, that the ark may be borne with them.

15 [a]The staves shall be in the rings of the ark: they shall not be taken from it.

16 And thou shalt put into the ark [a]the testimony which I shall give thee.

17 And [a]thou shalt make a mercy seat *of* pure gold: two cubits and a half *shall be* the length thereof, and a cubit and a half the breadth thereof.

18 And thou shalt make two cherubims *of* gold, *of* beaten work shalt thou make them, in the two ends of the mercy seat.

19 And make one cherub on the one end, and the other cherub on the other end: *even* of the mercy seat shall ye make the cherubims on the two ends thereof.

20 And [a]the cherubims shall stretch forth *their* wings on high, covering the mercy seat with their wings, and their faces *shall look* one to another; toward the mercy seat shall the faces of the cherubims be.

21 [a]And thou shalt put the mercy seat above upon the ark; and [b]in the ark thou shalt put the testimony that I shall give thee.

22 And [a]there I will meet with thee, and I will commune with thee from above the mercy seat, from [b]between the two cherubims which *are* upon the ark of the testimony, of all *things* which

15 [a]Ex. 19:9; Matt. 17:5
16 [a]Ex. 16:10; 33:18; Num. 14:10
17 [a]Ex. 3:2; Deut. 4:26, 36; 9:3; Heb. 12:18, 29
18 [a]Ex. 34:28; Deut. 9:9; 10:10

CHAPTER 25

2 [a]Ex. 35:4–9, 21; 1 Chr. 29:3, 5, 9; Ezra 2:68; Neh. 11:2; [2 Cor. 8:11–13; 9:7]
6 [a]Ex. 27:20 [b]Ex. 30:23
7 [a]Ex. 28:4, 6–14
8 [a]Ex. 36:1, 3, 4; Lev. 4:6; 10:4; 21:12; Heb. 9:1, 2 [b]Ex. 29:45; 1 Kin. 6:13; [2 Cor. 6:16; Heb. 3:6; Rev. 2:13]
10 [a]Ex. 37:1–9; Deut. 10:3; Heb. 9:4
11 [a]Ex. 37:2; Heb. 9:4
15 [a]Num. 4:6; 1 Kin. 8:8
16 [a]Ex. 16:34; 31:18; Deut. 10:2; 31:26; 1 Kin. 8:9; Heb. 9:4
17 [a]Ex. 37:6; Heb. 9:5
20 [a]1 Kin. 8:7; 1 Chr. 28:18; Heb. 9:5
21 [a]Ex. 26:34; 40:20 [b]Ex. 25:16
22 [a]Ex. 29:42, 43; 30:6, 36; Lev. 16:2; Num. 17:4 [b]Num. 7:89; 1 Sam. 4:4; 2 Sam. 6:2; 2 Kin. 19:15; Ps. 80:1; Is. 37:16

NKJV

15 Then Moses went up into the mountain, and [a]a cloud covered the mountain.

16 Now [a]the glory of the LORD rested on Mount Sinai, and the cloud covered it six days. And on the seventh day He called to Moses out of the midst of the cloud.

17 The sight of the glory of the LORD *was* like [a]a consuming fire on the top of the mountain in the eyes of the children of Israel.

18 So Moses went into the midst of the cloud and went up into the mountain. And [a]Moses was on the mountain forty days and forty nights.

Offerings for the Sanctuary
(Ex. 35:4–9)

25 Then the LORD spoke to Moses, saying:
2 "Speak to the children of Israel, that they bring Me an offering. [a]From everyone who gives it willingly with his heart you shall take My offering.

3 "And this *is* the offering which you shall take from them: gold, silver, and bronze;

4 "blue, purple, and scarlet *thread,* fine linen, and goats' *hair;*

5 "ram skins dyed red, badger skins, and acacia wood;

6 [a]"oil for the light, and [b]spices for the anointing oil and for the sweet incense;

7 "onyx stones, and stones to be set in the [a]ephod and in the breastplate.

8 "And let them make Me a [a]sanctuary, that [b]I may dwell among them.

9 "According to all that I show you, *that is,* the pattern of the tabernacle and the pattern of all its furnishings, just so you shall make *it.*

The Ark of the Testimony
(Ex. 37:1–9)

10 [a]"And they shall make an ark of acacia wood; two and a half cubits *shall be* its length, a cubit and a half its width, and a cubit and a half its height.

11 "And you shall overlay it with pure gold, inside and out you shall overlay it, and shall make on it a molding of [a]gold all around.

12 "You shall cast four rings of gold for it, and put *them* in its four corners; two rings *shall be* on one side, and two rings on the other side.

13 "And you shall make poles *of* acacia wood, and overlay them with gold.

14 "You shall put the poles into the rings on the sides of the ark, that the ark may be carried by them.

15 [a]"The poles shall be in the rings of the ark; they shall not be taken from it.

16 "And you shall put into the ark [a]the Testimony which I will give you.

17 [a]"You shall make a mercy seat of pure gold; two and a half cubits *shall be* its length and a cubit and a half its width.

18 "And you shall make two cherubim of gold; of hammered work you shall make them at the two ends of the mercy seat.

19 "Make one cherub at one end, and the other cherub at the other end; you shall make the cherubim at the two ends of it *of one piece* with the mercy seat.

20 "And [a]the cherubim shall stretch out *their* wings above, covering the mercy seat with their wings, and they shall face one another; the faces of the cherubim *shall be* toward the mercy seat.

21 [a]"You shall put the mercy seat on top of the ark, and [b]in the ark you shall put the Testimony that I will give you.

22 "And [a]there I will meet with you, and I will speak with you from above the mercy seat, from [b]between the two cherubim which *are* on the ark of the Testimony, about everything which

KJV

I will give thee in commandment unto the children of Israel.

The Table for the Showbread
(*Ex. 37:10–16*)

23 [a]Thou shalt also make a table *of* shittim wood: two cubits *shall be* the length thereof, and a cubit the breadth thereof, and a cubit and a half the height thereof.

24 And thou shalt overlay it with pure gold, and make thereto a crown of gold round about.

25 And thou shalt make unto it a border of an hand breadth round about, and thou shalt make a golden crown to the border thereof round about.

26 And thou shalt make for it four rings of gold, and put the rings in the four corners that *are* on the four feet thereof.

27 Over against the border shall the rings be for places of the staves to bear the table.

28 And thou shalt make the staves *of* shittim wood, and overlay them with gold, that the table may be borne with them.

29 And thou shalt make [a]the dishes thereof, and spoons thereof, and covers thereof, and bowls thereof, to cover withal: *of* pure gold shalt thou make them.

30 And thou shalt set upon the table [a]shewbread before me alway.

The Gold Lampstand
(*Ex. 37:17–24*)

31 [a]And thou shalt make a candlestick *of* pure gold: *of* beaten work shall the candlestick be made: his shaft, and his branches, his bowls, his knops, and his flowers, shall be of the same.

32 And six branches shall come out of the sides of it; three branches of the candlestick out of the one side, and three branches of the candlestick out of the other side:

33 [a]Three bowls made like unto almonds, *with* a knop and a flower in one branch; and three bowls made like almonds in the other branch, *with* a knop and a flower: so in the six branches that come out of the candlestick.

34 And [a]in the candlestick *shall be* four bowls made like unto almonds, *with* their knops and their flowers.

35 And *there shall be* a knop under two branches of the same, and a knop under two branches of the same, and a knop under two branches of the same, according to the six branches that proceed out of the candlestick.

36 Their knops and their branches shall be of the same: all it *shall be* one beaten work *of* pure gold.

37 And thou shalt make the seven lamps thereof: and [a]they shall light the lamps thereof, that they may [b]give light over against it.

38 And the tongs thereof, and the snuffdishes thereof, *shall be of* pure gold.

39 *Of* a talent of pure gold shall he make it, with all these vessels.

40 And [a]look that thou make *them* after their pattern, which was shewed thee in the mount.

The Tabernacle
(*Ex. 36:8–38*)

26 Moreover [a]thou shalt make the tabernacle *with* ten curtains *of* fine twined linen, and blue, and purple, and scarlet: *with* cherubims of cunning work shalt thou make them.

2 The length of one curtain *shall be* eight and twenty cubits, and the breadth of one curtain four cubits: and every one of the curtains shall have one measure.

3 The five curtains shall be coupled together one to another; and *other* five curtains *shall be* coupled one to another.

4 And thou shalt make loops of blue upon the edge of the one curtain from the selvedge in

---

23 [a]Ex. 37:10–16; 1 Kin. 7:48; 2 Chr. 4:8; Heb. 9:2
29 [a]Ex. 37:16; Num. 4:7
30 [a]Ex. 39:36; 40:23; Lev. 24:5–9
31 [a]Ex. 37:17–24; 1 Kin. 7:49; Zech. 4:2; Heb. 9:2; Rev. 1:12
33 [a]Ex. 37:19
34 [a]Ex. 37:20–22
37 [a]Ex. 27:21; 30:8; Lev. 24:3, 4; 2 Chr. 13:11 [b]Num. 8:2
40 [a]Ex. 25:9; 26:30; Num. 8:4; 1 Chr. 28:11, 19; Acts 7:44; [Heb. 8:5]

CHAPTER 26

1 [a]Ex. 36:8–19

NKJV

I will give you in commandment to the children of Israel.

The Table for the Showbread
(*Ex. 37:10–16*)

23 [a]"You shall also make a table of acacia wood; two cubits *shall be* its length, a cubit its width, and a cubit and a half its height.

24 "And you shall overlay it with pure gold, and make a molding of gold all around.

25 "You shall make for it a frame of a handbreadth all around, and you shall make a gold molding for the frame all around.

26 "And you shall make for it four rings of gold, and put the rings on the four corners that *are* at its four legs.

27 "The rings shall be close to the frame, as holders for the poles to bear the table.

28 "And you shall make the poles of acacia wood, and overlay them with gold, that the table may be carried with them.

29 "You shall make [a]its dishes, its pans, its pitchers, and its bowls for pouring. You shall make them of pure gold.

30 "And you shall set the [a]showbread on the table before Me always.

The Gold Lampstand
(*Ex. 37:17–24*)

31 [a]"You shall also make a lampstand of pure gold; the lampstand shall be of hammered work. Its shaft, its branches, its bowls, its *ornamental* knobs, and flowers shall be *of one piece.*

32 "And six branches shall come out of its sides: three branches of the lampstand out of one side, and three branches of the lampstand out of the other side.

33 [a]"Three bowls *shall be* made like almond *blossoms* on one branch, *with* an *ornamental* knob and a flower, and three bowls made like almond *blossoms* on the other branch, *with* an *ornamental* knob and a flower—and so for the six branches that come out of the lampstand.

34 [a]"On the lampstand itself four bowls *shall be* made like almond *blossoms, each with* its *ornamental* knob and flower.

35 "And *there shall be* a knob under the *first* two branches of the same, a knob under the *second* two branches of the same, and a knob under the *third* two branches of the same, according to the six branches that extend from the lampstand.

36 "Their knobs and their branches *shall be of one piece;* all of it *shall be* one hammered piece of pure gold.

37 "You shall make seven lamps for it, and [a]they shall arrange its lamps so that they [b]give light in front of it.

38 "And its wick-trimmers and their trays *shall be* of pure gold.

39 "It shall be made of a talent of pure gold, with all these utensils.

40 "And [a]see to it that you make *them* according to the pattern which was shown you on the mountain.

The Tabernacle
(*Ex. 36:8–38*)

26 "Moreover [a]you shall make the tabernacle *with* ten curtains *of* fine woven linen, and blue, purple, and scarlet *thread;* with artistic designs of cherubim you shall weave them.

2 "The length of each curtain *shall be* twenty-eight cubits, and the width of each curtain four cubits. And every one of the curtains shall have the same measurements.

3 "Five curtains shall be coupled to one another, and *the other* five curtains *shall be* coupled to one another.

4 "And you shall make loops of blue *yarn* on the edge of the curtain on the selvedge of *one*

KJV

the coupling; and likewise shalt thou make in the uttermost edge of *another* curtain, in the coupling of the second.

5 Fifty loops shalt thou make in the one curtain, and fifty loops shalt thou make in the edge of the curtain that *is* in the coupling of the second; that the loops may take hold one of another.

6 And thou shalt make fifty taches of gold, and couple the curtains together with the taches: and it shall be one tabernacle.

7 And [a]thou shalt make curtains *of* goats' *hair* to be a covering upon the tabernacle: eleven curtains shalt thou make.

8 The length of one curtain *shall be* thirty cubits, and the breadth of one curtain four cubits: and the eleven curtains *shall be all* of one measure.

9 And thou shalt couple five curtains by themselves, and six curtains by themselves, and shalt double the sixth curtain in the forefront of the tabernacle.

10 And thou shalt make fifty loops on the edge of the one curtain *that is* outmost in the coupling, and fifty loops in the edge of the curtain which coupleth the second.

11 And thou shalt make fifty taches of brass, and put the taches into the loops, and couple the tent together, that it may be one.

12 And the remnant that remaineth of the curtains of the tent, the half curtain that remaineth, shall hang over the backside of the tabernacle.

13 And a cubit on the one side, and a cubit on the other side of that which remaineth in the length of the curtains of the tent, it shall hang over the sides of the tabernacle on this side and on that side, to cover it.

14 And [a]thou shalt make a covering for the tent *of* rams' skins dyed red, and a covering above *of* badgers' skins.

15 And thou shalt [a]make boards for the tabernacle *of* shittim wood standing up.

16 Ten cubits *shall be* the length of a board, and a cubit and a half *shall be* the breadth of one board.

17 Two tenons *shall there be* in one board, set in order one against another: thus shalt thou make for all the boards of the tabernacle.

18 And thou shalt make the boards for the tabernacle, twenty boards on the south side southward.

19 And thou shalt make forty sockets of silver under the twenty boards; two sockets under one board for his two tenons, and two sockets under another board for his two tenons.

20 And for the second side of the tabernacle on the north side *there shall be* twenty boards:

21 And their forty sockets *of* silver; two sockets under one board, and two sockets under another board.

22 And for the sides of the tabernacle westward thou shalt make six boards.

23 And two boards shalt thou make for the corners of the tabernacle in the two sides.

24 And they shall be coupled together beneath, and they shall be coupled together above the head of it unto one ring: thus shall it be for them both; they shall be for the two corners.

25 And they shall be eight boards, and their sockets *of* silver, sixteen sockets; two sockets under one board, and two sockets under another board.

26 And thou shalt make bars *of* shittim wood; five for the boards of the one side of the tabernacle,

27 And five bars for the boards of the other side of the tabernacle, and five bars for the boards of the side of the tabernacle, for the two sides westward.

28 And the [a]middle bar in the midst of the boards shall reach from end to end.

29 And thou shalt overlay the boards with

7 [a]Ex. 36:14
14 [a]Ex. 35:7, 23; 36:19
15 [a]Ex. 36:20–34
28 [a]Ex. 36:33

NKJV

set, and likewise you shall do on the outer edge of *the other* curtain of the second set.

5 "Fifty loops you shall make in the one curtain, and fifty loops you shall make on the edge of the curtain that *is* on the end of the second set, that the loops may be clasped to one another.

6 "And you shall make fifty clasps of gold, and couple the curtains together with the clasps, so that it may be one tabernacle.

7 [a]"You shall also make curtains of goats' *hair,* to be a tent over the tabernacle. You shall make eleven curtains.

8 "The length of each curtain *shall be* thirty cubits, and the width of each curtain four cubits; and the eleven curtains shall all have the same measurements.

9 "And you shall couple five curtains by themselves and six curtains by themselves, and you shall double over the sixth curtain at the forefront of the tent.

10 "You shall make fifty loops on the edge of the curtain that is outermost in *one* set, and fifty loops on the edge of the curtain of the second set.

11 "And you shall make fifty bronze clasps, put the clasps into the loops, and couple the tent together, that it may be one.

12 "The remnant that remains of the curtains of the tent, the half curtain that remains, shall hang over the back of the tabernacle.

13 "And a cubit on one side and a cubit on the other side, of what remains of the length of the curtains of the tent, shall hang over the sides of the tabernacle, on this side and on that side, to cover it.

14 [a]"You shall also make a covering of ram skins dyed red for the tent, and a covering of badger skins above that.

15 "And for the tabernacle you shall [a]make the boards of acacia wood, standing upright.

16 "Ten cubits *shall be* the length of a board, and a cubit and a half *shall be* the width of each board.

17 "Two tenons *shall be* in each board for binding one to another. Thus you shall make for all the boards of the tabernacle.

18 "And you shall make the boards for the tabernacle, twenty boards for the south side.

19 "You shall make forty sockets of silver under the twenty boards: two sockets under each of the boards for its two tenons.

20 "And for the second side of the tabernacle, the north side, *there shall be* twenty boards

21 "and their forty sockets of silver: two sockets under each of the boards.

22 "For the far side of the tabernacle, westward, you shall make six boards.

23 "And you shall also make two boards for the two back corners of the tabernacle.

24 "They shall be coupled together at the bottom and they shall be coupled together at the top by one ring. Thus it shall be for both of them. They shall be for the two corners.

25 "So there shall be eight boards with their sockets of silver—sixteen sockets—two sockets under each of the boards.

26 "And you shall make bars of acacia wood: five for the boards on one side of the tabernacle,

27 "five bars for the boards on the other side of the tabernacle, and five bars for the boards of the side of the tabernacle, for the far side westward.

28 "The [a]middle bar shall pass through the midst of the boards from end to end.

29 "You shall overlay the boards with gold,

KJV

gold, and make their rings *of* gold *for* places for the bars: and thou shalt overlay the bars with gold.

30 And thou shalt rear up the tabernacle [a]according to the fashion thereof which was shewed thee in the mount.

31 And [a]thou shalt make a vail *of* blue, and purple, and scarlet, and fine twined linen of cunning work: with cherubims shall it be made:

32 And thou shalt hang it upon four pillars of shittim *wood* overlaid with gold: their hooks *shall be of* gold, upon the four sockets of silver.

33 And thou shalt hang up the vail under the taches, that thou mayest bring in thither within the vail [a]the ark of the testimony: and the vail shall divide unto you between [b]the holy *place* and the most holy.

34 And [a]thou shalt put the mercy seat upon the ark of the testimony in the most holy *place*.

35 And [a]thou shalt set the table without the vail, and [b]the candlestick over against the table on the side of the tabernacle toward the south: and thou shalt put the table on the north side.

36 And [a]thou shalt make an hanging for the door of the tent, *of* blue, and purple, and scarlet, and fine twined linen, wrought with needlework.

37 And thou shalt make for the hanging [a]five pillars *of* shittim *wood,* and overlay them with gold, *and* their hooks *shall be of* gold: and thou shalt cast five sockets of brass for them.

The Altar of Burnt Offering
(Ex. 38:1–7)

27 And thou shalt make [a]an altar *of* shittim wood, five cubits long, and five cubits broad; the altar shall be foursquare: and the height thereof *shall be* three cubits.

2 And thou shalt make the horns of it upon the four corners thereof: his horns shall be of the same: and thou shalt overlay it with brass.

3 And thou shalt make his pans to receive his ashes, and his shovels, and his basons, and his fleshhooks, and his firepans: all the vessels thereof thou shalt make *of* brass.

4 And thou shalt make for it a grate of network *of* brass; and upon the net shalt thou make four brasen rings in the four corners thereof.

5 And thou shalt put it under the compass of the altar beneath, that the net may be even to the midst of the altar.

6 And thou shalt make staves for the altar, staves *of* shittim wood, and overlay them with brass.

7 And the staves shall be put into the rings, and the staves shall be upon the two sides of the altar, to bear it.

8 Hollow with boards shalt thou make it: [a]as it was shewed thee in the mount, so shall they make *it.*

The Court of the Tabernacle
(Ex. 38:9–20)

9 And [a]thou shalt make the court of the tabernacle: for the south side southward *there shall be* hangings for the court *of* fine twined linen of an hundred cubits long for one side:

10 And the twenty pillars thereof and their twenty sockets *shall be of* brass; the hooks of the pillars and their fillets *shall be of* silver.

11 And likewise for the north side in length *there shall be* hangings of an hundred *cubits* long, and his twenty pillars and their twenty sockets *of* brass; the hooks of the pillars and their fillets *of* silver.

12 And *for* the breadth of the court on the west side *shall be* hangings of fifty cubits: their pillars ten, and their sockets ten.

13 And the breadth of the court on the east side eastward *shall be* fifty cubits.

14 The hangings of one side *of the gate shall*

30 [a]Ex. 25:9, 40; 27:8; 39:32; Num. 8:4; Acts 7:44; [Heb. 8:2, 5]
31 [a]Ex. 27:21; 36:35–38; Lev. 16:2; 2 Chr. 3:14; Matt. 27:51; Heb. 9:3; 10:20
33 [a]Ex. 25:10–16; 40:21 [b]Lev. 16:2; Heb. 9:2, 3
34 [a]Ex. 25:17–22; 40:20; Heb. 9:5
35 [a]Ex. 40:22; Heb. 9:2 [b]Ex. 40:24
36 [a]Ex. 36:37
37 [a]Ex. 36:38

CHAPTER 27
1 [a]Ex. 38:1; Ezek. 43:13
8 [a]Ex. 25:40; 26:30; Acts 7:44; [Heb. 8:5]
9 [a]Ex. 38:9–20

NKJV

make their rings of gold *as* holders for the bars, and overlay the bars with gold.

30 "And you shall raise up the tabernacle [a]according to its pattern which you were shown on the mountain.

31 [a]"You shall make a veil woven of blue, purple, and scarlet *thread,* and fine woven linen. It shall be woven with an artistic design of cherubim.

32 "You shall hang it upon the four pillars of acacia *wood* overlaid with gold. Their hooks *shall be* gold, upon four sockets of silver.

33 "And you shall hang the veil from the clasps. Then you shall bring [a]the ark of the Testimony in there, behind the veil. The veil shall be a divider for you between [b]the holy *place* and the Most Holy.

34 [a]"You shall put the mercy seat upon the ark of the Testimony in the Most Holy.

35 [a]"You shall set the table outside the veil, and [b]the lampstand across from the table on the side of the tabernacle toward the south; and you shall put the table on the north side.

36 [a]"You shall make a screen for the door of the tabernacle, *woven of* blue, purple, and scarlet *thread,* and fine woven linen, made by a weaver.

37 "And you shall make for the screen [a]five pillars of acacia *wood,* and overlay them with gold; their hooks *shall be* gold, and you shall cast five sockets of bronze for them.

The Altar of Burnt Offering
(Ex. 38:1–7)

27 "You shall make [a]an altar of acacia wood, five cubits long and five cubits wide—the altar shall be square—and its height *shall be* three cubits.

2 "You shall make its horns on its four corners; its horns shall be of one piece with it. And you shall overlay it with bronze.

3 "Also you shall make its pans to receive its ashes, and its shovels and its basins and its forks and its firepans; you shall make all its utensils of bronze.

4 "You shall make a grate for it, a network of bronze; and on the network you shall make four bronze rings at its four corners.

5 "You shall put it under the rim of the altar beneath, that the network may be midway up the altar.

6 "And you shall make poles for the altar, poles of acacia wood, and overlay them with bronze.

7 "The poles shall be put in the rings, and the poles shall be on the two sides of the altar to bear it.

8 "You shall make it hollow with boards; [a]as it was shown you on the mountain, so shall they make *it.*

The Court of the Tabernacle
(Ex. 38:9–20)

9 [a]"You shall also make the court of the tabernacle. For the south side *there shall be* hangings for the court *made of* fine woven linen, one hundred cubits long for one side.

10 "And its twenty pillars and their twenty sockets *shall be* bronze. The hooks of the pillars and their bands *shall be* silver.

11 "Likewise along the length of the north side *there shall be* hangings one hundred *cubits* long, with its twenty pillars and their twenty sockets of bronze, and the hooks of the pillars and their bands of silver.

12 "And along the width of the court on the west side *shall be* hangings of fifty cubits, with their ten pillars and their ten sockets.

13 "The width of the court on the east side *shall be* fifty cubits.

14 "The hangings on *one* side *of the gate*

KJV

be fifteen cubits: their pillars three, and their sockets three.

15 And on the other side *shall be* hangings fifteen *cubits:* their pillars three, and their sockets three.

16 And for the gate of the court *shall be* an hanging of twenty cubits, *of* blue, and purple, and scarlet, and fine twined linen, wrought with needlework: *and* their pillars *shall be* four, and their sockets four.

17 All the pillars round about the court *shall be* filleted with silver; their [a]hooks *shall be of* silver, and their sockets *of* brass.

18 The length of the court *shall be* an hundred cubits, and the breadth fifty every where, and the height five cubits *of* fine twined linen, and their sockets *of* brass.

19 All the vessels of the tabernacle in all the service thereof, and all the pins thereof, and all the pins of the court, *shall be of* brass.

The Care of the Lampstand
(Lev. 24:1–4)

20 And [a]thou shalt command the children of Israel, that they bring thee pure oil olive beaten for the light, to cause the lamp to burn always.

21 In the tabernacle of the congregation [a]without the vail, which *is* before the testimony, [b]Aaron and his sons shall order it from evening to morning before the LORD: [c]*it shall be* a statute for ever unto their generations on the behalf of the children of Israel.

Garments for the Priesthood
(Ex. 39:1–7)

28 And take thou unto thee [a]Aaron thy brother, and his sons with him, from among the children of Israel, that he may minister unto me in the priest's [b]office, *even* Aaron, [c]Nadab and Abihu, [d]Eleazar and Ithamar, Aaron's sons.

2 And [a]thou shalt make holy garments for Aaron thy brother for glory and for beauty.

3 And [a]thou shalt speak unto all *that are* wise hearted, [b]whom I have filled with the spirit of wisdom, that they may make Aaron's garments to consecrate him, that he may minister unto me in the priest's office.

4 And these *are* the garments which they shall make; [a]a breastplate, and [b]an ephod, and [c]a robe, and [d]a broidered coat, a mitre, and [e]a girdle: and they shall make holy garments for Aaron thy brother, and his sons, that he may minister unto me in the priest's office.

The Ephod

5 And they shall take gold, and blue, and purple, and scarlet, and fine linen.

6 [a]And they shall make the ephod *of* gold, *of* blue, and *of* purple, *of* scarlet, and fine twined linen, with cunning work.

7 It shall have the two shoulderpieces thereof joined at the two edges thereof; and *so* it shall be joined together.

8 And the curious girdle of the ephod, which *is* upon it, shall be of the same, according to the work thereof; *even of* gold, *of* blue, and purple, and scarlet, and fine twined linen.

9 And thou shalt take two onyx [a]stones, and grave on them the names of the children of Israel:

10 Six of their names on one stone, and *the other* six names of the rest on the other stone, according to their [a]birth.

11 With the work of an [a]engraver in stone, *like* the engravings of a signet, shalt thou engrave the two stones with the names of the children of Israel: thou shalt make them to be set in ouches of gold.

12 And thou shalt put the two stones upon the shoulders of the ephod *for* stones of memorial unto the children of Israel: and [a]Aaron shall bear

---

17 [a]Ex. 38:19
20 [a]Ex. 35:8, 28; Lev. 24:1–4
21 [a]Ex. 26:31, 33 [b]Ex. 30:8; 1 Sam. 3:3; 2 Chr. 13:11 [c]Ex. 28:43; 29:9; Lev. 3:17; 16:34; Num. 18:23; 19:21; 1 Sam. 30:25

CHAPTER 28

1 [a]Num. 3:10; 18:7 [b]Ps. 99:6; Heb. 5:4 [c]Ex. 24:1, 9; Lev. 10:1 [d]Ex. 6:23; Lev. 10:6, 16
2 [a]Ex. 29:5, 29; 31:10; 39:1–31; Lev. 8:7–9, 30
3 [a]Ex. 31:6; 36:1 [b]Ex. 31:3; 35:30, 31; Is. 11:2; Eph. 1:17
4 [a]Ex. 28:15 [b]Ex. 28:6 [c]Ex. 28:31 [d]Ex. 28:39 [e]Lev. 8:7
6 [a]Ex. 39:2–7; Lev. 8:7
9 [a]Ex. 35:27
10 [a]Gen. 29:31—30:24; 35:16–18
11 [a]Ex. 35:35
12 [a]Ex. 28:29, 30; 39:6, 7

*

28:4 Ornamented vest

NKJV

shall be fifteen cubits, *with* their three pillars and their three sockets.

15 "And on the other side *shall be* hangings of fifteen *cubits, with* their three pillars and their three sockets.

16 "For the gate of the court *there shall be* a screen twenty cubits long, *woven of* blue, purple, and scarlet *thread,* and fine woven linen, made by a weaver. It *shall have* four pillars and four sockets.

17 "All the pillars around the court shall have bands of silver; their [a]hooks *shall be* of silver and their sockets of bronze.

18 "The length of the court *shall be* one hundred cubits, the width fifty throughout, and the height five cubits, *made of* fine woven linen, and its sockets of bronze.

19 "All the utensils of the tabernacle for all its service, all its pegs, and all the pegs of the court, *shall be* of bronze.

The Care of the Lampstand
(Lev. 24:1–4)

20 "And [a]you shall command the children of Israel that they bring you pure oil of pressed olives for the light, to cause the lamp to burn continually.

21 "In the tabernacle of meeting, [a]outside the veil which *is* before the Testimony, [b]Aaron and his sons shall tend it from evening until morning before the LORD. [c]*It shall be* a statute forever to their generations on behalf of the children of Israel.

Garments for the Priesthood
(Ex. 39:1–7)

28 "Now take [a]Aaron your brother, and his sons with him, from among the children of Israel, that he may minister to Me as [b]priest, Aaron *and* Aaron's sons: [c]Nadab, Abihu, [d]Eleazar, and Ithamar.

2 "And [a]you shall make holy garments for Aaron your brother, for glory and for beauty.

3 "So [a]you shall speak to all *who are* gifted artisans, [b]whom I have filled with the spirit of wisdom, that they may make Aaron's garments, to consecrate him, that he may minister to Me as priest.

4 "And these *are* the garments which they shall make: [a]a breastplate, [b]an *ephod, [c]a robe, [d]a skillfully woven tunic, a turban, and [e]a sash. So they shall make holy garments for Aaron your brother and his sons, that he may minister to Me as priest.

The Ephod

5 "They shall take the gold, blue, purple, and scarlet *thread,* and the fine linen,

6 [a]"and they shall make the ephod of gold, blue, purple, *and* scarlet *thread,* and fine woven linen, artistically worked.

7 "It shall have two shoulder straps joined at its two edges, and *so* it shall be joined together.

8 "And the intricately woven band of the ephod, which *is* on it, shall be of the same workmanship, *made of* gold, blue, purple, and scarlet *thread,* and fine woven linen.

9 "Then you shall take two onyx [a]stones and engrave on them the names of the sons of Israel:

10 "six of their names on one stone and six names on the other stone, in order of their [a]birth.

11 "With the work of an [a]engraver in stone, *like* the engravings of a signet, you shall engrave the two stones with the names of the sons of Israel. You shall set them in settings of gold.

12 "And you shall put the two stones on the shoulders of the ephod *as* memorial stones for the sons of Israel. So [a]Aaron shall bear their

KJV

their names before the LORD upon his two shoulders [b]for a memorial.

13 And thou shalt make ouches *of* gold;

14 And two chains *of* pure gold at the ends; *of* wreathen work shalt thou make them, and fasten the wreathen chains to the ouches.

The Breastplate
(Ex. 39:8–21)

15 And [a]thou shalt make the breastplate of judgment with cunning work; after the work of the ephod thou shalt make it; *of* gold, *of* blue, and *of* purple, and *of* scarlet, and *of* fine twined linen, shalt thou make it.

16 Foursquare it shall be *being* doubled; a span *shall be* the length thereof, and a span *shall be* the breadth thereof.

17 [a]And thou shalt set in it settings of stones, *even* four rows of stones: *the first* row *shall be* a sardius, a topaz, and a carbuncle: *this shall be* the first row.

18 And the second row *shall be* an emerald, a sapphire, and a diamond.

19 And the third row a ligure, an agate, and an amethyst.

20 And the fourth row a beryl, and an onyx, and a jasper: they shall be set in gold in their inclosings.

21 And the stones shall be with the names of the children of Israel, twelve, according to their names, *like* the engravings of a signet; every one with his name shall they be according to the twelve tribes.

22 And thou shalt make upon the breastplate chains at the ends *of* wreathen work *of* pure gold.

23 And thou shalt make upon the breastplate two rings of gold, and shalt put the two rings on the two ends of the breastplate.

24 And thou shalt put the two wreathen *chains* of gold in the two rings *which are* on the ends of the breastplate.

25 And *the other* two ends of the two wreathen *chains* thou shalt fasten in the two ouches, and put *them* on the shoulderpieces of the ephod before it.

26 And thou shalt make two rings of gold, and thou shalt put them upon the two ends of the breastplate in the border thereof, which *is* in the side of the ephod inward.

27 And two *other* rings of gold thou shalt make, and shalt put them on the two sides of the ephod underneath, toward the forepart thereof, over against the *other* coupling thereof, above the curious girdle of the ephod.

28 And they shall bind the breastplate by the rings thereof unto the rings of the ephod with a lace of blue, that *it* may be above the curious girdle of the ephod, and that the breastplate be not loosed from the ephod.

29 And Aaron shall [a]bear the names of the children of Israel in the breastplate of judgment upon his heart, when he goeth in unto the holy *place*, for a memorial before the LORD continually.

30 And [a]thou shalt put in the breastplate of judgment the Urim and the Thummim; and they shall be upon Aaron's heart, when he goeth in before the LORD: and Aaron shall bear the judgment of the children of Israel upon his heart before the LORD continually.

Other Priestly Garments
(Ex. 39:22–31)

31 And [a]thou shalt make the robe of the ephod all *of* blue.

32 And there shall be an hole in the top of it, in the midst thereof: it shall have a binding of woven work round about the hole of it, as it were the hole of an habergeon, that it be not rent.

33 And *beneath* upon the hem of it thou shalt make pomegranates *of* blue, and *of* purple, and *of* scarlet, round about the hem thereof; and bells of gold between them round about:

12 [b]Lev. 24:7; Num. 31:54; Josh. 4:7; Zech. 6:14; 1 Cor. 11:24
15 [a]Ex. 39:8–21
17 [a]Ex. 39:10
29 [a]Ex. 28:12
30 [a]Lev. 8:8; Num. 27:21; Deut. 33:8; 1 Sam. 28:6; Ezra 2:63; Neh. 7:65
31 [a]Ex. 39:22–26

NKJV

names before the LORD on his two shoulders [b]as a memorial.

13 "You shall also make settings of gold,

14 "and you shall make two chains of pure gold like braided cords, and fasten the braided chains to the settings.

The Breastplate
(Ex. 39:8–21)

15 [a]"You shall make the breastplate of judgment. Artistically woven according to the workmanship of the ephod you shall make it: of gold, blue, purple, and scarlet *thread,* and fine woven linen, you shall make it.

16 "It shall be doubled into a square: a span *shall be* its length, and a span *shall be* its width.

17 [a]"And you shall put settings of stones in it, four rows of stones: *The first* row *shall be* a sardius, a topaz, and an emerald; *this shall be* the first row;

18 "the second row *shall be* a turquoise, a sapphire, and a diamond;

19 "the third row, a jacinth, an agate, and an amethyst;

20 "and the fourth row, a beryl, an onyx, and a jasper. They shall be set in gold settings.

21 "And the stones shall have the names of the sons of Israel, twelve according to their names, *like* the engravings of a signet, each one with its own name; they shall be according to the twelve tribes.

22 "You shall make chains for the breastplate at the end, like braided cords of pure gold.

23 "And you shall make two rings of gold for the breastplate, and put the two rings on the two ends of the breastplate.

24 "Then you shall put the two braided *chains* of gold in the two rings which are on the ends of the breastplate;

25 "and the *other* two ends of the two braided *chains* you shall fasten to the two settings, and put them on the shoulder straps of the ephod in the front.

26 "You shall make two rings of gold, and put them on the two ends of the breastplate, on the edge of it, which is on the inner side of the ephod.

27 "And two *other* rings of gold you shall make, and put them on the two shoulder straps, underneath the ephod toward its front, right at the seam above the intricately woven band of the ephod.

28 "They shall bind the breastplate by means of its rings to the rings of the ephod, using a blue cord, so that it is above the intricately woven band of the ephod, and so that the breastplate does not come loose from the ephod.

29 "So Aaron shall [a]bear the names of the sons of Israel on the breastplate of judgment over his heart, when he goes into the holy *place,* as a memorial before the LORD continually.

30 "And [a]you shall put in the breastplate of judgment the *Urim and the Thummim, and they shall be over Aaron's heart when he goes in before the LORD. So Aaron shall bear the judgment of the children of Israel over his heart before the LORD continually.

Other Priestly Garments
(Ex. 39:22–31)

31 [a]"You shall make the robe of the ephod all of blue.

32 "There shall be an opening for his head in the middle of it; it shall have a woven binding all around its opening, like the opening in a coat of mail, so that it does not tear.

33 "And upon its hem you shall make pomegranates of blue, purple, and scarlet, all around its hem, and bells of gold between them all around:

*———
28:30 Lit. *Lights and the Perfections*

KJV

34 A golden bell and a pomegranate, a golden bell and a pomegranate, upon the hem of the robe round about.

35 And it shall be upon Aaron to minister: and his sound shall be heard when he goeth in unto the holy *place* before the LORD, and when he cometh out, that he die not.

36 And [a]thou shalt make a plate *of* pure gold, and grave upon it, *like* the engravings of a signet, HOLINESS TO THE LORD.

37 And thou shalt put it on a blue lace, that it may be upon the mitre; upon the forefront of the mitre it shall be.

38 And it shall be upon Aaron's forehead, that Aaron may [a]bear the iniquity of the holy things, which the children of Israel shall hallow in all their holy gifts; and it shall be always upon his forehead, that they may be [b]accepted before the LORD.

39 And thou shalt [a]embroider the coat of fine linen, and thou shalt make the mitre *of* fine linen, and thou shalt make the girdle *of* needlework.

40 [a]And for Aaron's sons thou shalt make coats, and thou shalt make for them girdles, and bonnets shalt thou make for them, for glory and for [b]beauty.

41 And thou shalt put them upon Aaron thy brother, and his sons with him; and shalt [a]anoint them, and [b]consecrate them, and sanctify them, that they may minister unto me in the priest's office.

42 And thou shalt make them [a]linen breeches to cover their nakedness; from the loins even unto the thighs they shall reach:

43 And they shall be upon Aaron, and upon his sons, when they come in unto the tabernacle of the congregation, or when they come near [a]unto the altar to minister in the holy *place;* that they [b]bear not iniquity, and die: [c]*it shall be* a statute for ever unto him and his seed after him.

Aaron and His Sons Consecrated
(Lev. 8:1–36)

29 And this *is* the thing that thou shalt do unto them to hallow them, to minister unto me in the priest's office: [a]Take one young bullock, and two rams without blemish,

2 And [a]unleavened bread, and cakes unleavened tempered with oil, and wafers unleavened anointed with oil: *of* wheaten flour shalt thou make them.

3 And thou shalt put them into one basket, and bring them in the basket, with the bullock and the two rams.

4 And Aaron and his sons thou shalt bring unto the door of the tabernacle of the congregation, [a]and shalt wash them with water.

5 [a]And thou shalt take the garments, and put upon Aaron the coat, and the robe of the ephod, and the ephod, and the breastplate, and gird him with [b]the curious girdle of the ephod:

6 [a]And thou shalt put the mitre upon his head, and put the holy crown upon the mitre.

7 Then shalt thou take the anointing [a]oil, and pour *it* upon his head, and anoint him.

8 And [a]thou shalt bring his sons, and put coats upon them.

9 And thou shalt gird them with girdles, Aaron and his sons, and put the bonnets on them: and [a]the priest's office shall be their's for a perpetual statute: and thou shalt [b]consecrate Aaron and his sons.

10 And thou shalt cause a bullock to be brought before the tabernacle of the congregation: and [a]Aaron and his sons shall put their hands upon the head of the bullock.

11 And thou shalt kill the bullock before the LORD, *by* the door of the tabernacle of the congregation.

12 And thou shalt take of the blood of the bullock, and put *it* upon [a]the horns of the altar

---

36 [a]Ex. 39:30, 31; Lev. 8:9; Zech. 14:20
38 [a]Ex. 28:43; Lev. 10:17; 22:9, 16; Num. 18:1; [Is. 53:11]; Ezek. 4:4–6; [John 1:29; Heb. 9:28; 1 Pet. 2:24] [b]Lev. 1:4; 22:27; 23:11; Is. 56:7
39 [a]Ex. 35:35; 39:27–29
40 [a]Ex. 28:4; 39:27–29, 41; Ezek. 44:17, 18 [b]Ex. 28:2
41 [a]Ex. 29:7–9; 30:30; 40:15; Lev. 10:7 [b]Ex. 29:9; Lev. 8; Heb. 7:28
42 [a]Ex. 39:28; Lev. 6:10; 16:4; Ezek. 44:18
43 [a]Ex. 20:26 [b]Lev. 5:1, 17; 20:19, 20; 22:9; Num. 9:13; 18:22 [c]Ex. 27:21; Lev. 17:7

CHAPTER 29

1 [a]Lev. 8; [Heb. 7:26–28]
2 [a]Lev. 2:4; 6:19–23
4 [a]Ex. 40:12; Lev. 8:6; [Heb. 10:22]
5 [a]Ex. 28:2; Lev. 8:7 [b]Ex. 28:8
6 [a]Ex. 28:36, 37; Lev. 8:9
7 [a]Ex. 25:6; 30:25–31; Lev. 8:12; 10:7; 21:10; Num. 35:25; Ps. 133:2
8 [a]Ex. 28:39, 40; Lev. 8:13
9 [a]Ex. 40:15; Num. 3:10; 18:7; 25:13; Deut. 18:5 [b]Ex. 28:41; Lev. 8
10 [a]Lev. 1:4; 8:14
12 [a]Lev. 8:15

NKJV

34 "a golden bell and a pomegranate, a golden bell and a pomegranate, upon the hem of the robe all around.

35 "And it shall be upon Aaron when he ministers, and its sound will be heard when he goes into the holy *place* before the LORD and when he comes out, that he may not die.

36 [a]"You shall also make a plate of pure gold and engrave on it, *like* the engraving of a signet:

HOLINESS TO THE LORD.

37 "And you shall put it on a blue cord, that it may be on the turban; it shall be on the front of the turban.

38 "So it shall be on Aaron's forehead, that Aaron may [a]bear the iniquity of the holy things which the children of Israel hallow in all their holy gifts; and it shall always be on his forehead, that they may be [b]accepted before the LORD.

39 "You shall [a]skillfully weave the tunic of fine linen *thread,* you shall make the turban of fine linen, and you shall make the sash of woven work.

40 [a]"For Aaron's sons you shall make tunics, and you shall make sashes for them. And you shall make hats for them, for glory and [b]beauty.

41 "So you shall put them on Aaron your brother and on his sons with him. You shall [a]anoint them, [b]consecrate them, and sanctify them, that they may minister to Me as priests.

42 "And you shall make [a]for them linen trousers to cover their nakedness; they shall reach from the waist to the thighs.

43 "They shall be on Aaron and on his sons when they come into the tabernacle of meeting, or when they come near [a]the altar to minister in the holy *place,* that they [b]do not incur iniquity and die. [c]*It shall be* a statute forever to him and his descendants after him.

Aaron and His Sons Consecrated
(Lev. 8:1–36)

29 "And this is what you shall do to them to hallow them for ministering to Me as priests: [a]Take one young bull and two rams without blemish,

2 "and [a]unleavened bread, unleavened cakes mixed with oil, and unleavened wafers anointed with oil (you shall make them of wheat flour).

3 "You shall put them in one basket and bring them in the basket, with the bull and the two rams.

4 "And Aaron and his sons you shall bring to the door of the tabernacle of meeting, [a]and you shall wash them with water.

5 [a]"Then you shall take the garments, put the tunic on Aaron, and the robe of the ephod, the ephod, and the breastplate, and gird him with [b]the intricately woven band of the ephod.

6 [a]"You shall put the turban on his head, and put the holy crown on the turban.

7 "And you shall take the anointing [a]oil, pour *it* on his head, and anoint him.

8 "Then [a]you shall bring his sons and put tunics on them.

9 "And you shall gird them with sashes, Aaron and his sons, and put the hats on them. [a]The priesthood shall be theirs for a perpetual statute. So you shall [b]consecrate Aaron and his sons.

10 "You shall also have the bull brought before the tabernacle of meeting, and [a]Aaron and his sons shall put their hands on the head of the bull.

11 "Then you shall kill the bull before the LORD, *by* the door of the tabernacle of meeting.

12 "You shall take *some* of the blood of the bull and put *it* on [a]the horns of the altar with

KJV

with thy finger, and [b]pour all the blood beside the bottom of the altar.

13 And [a]thou shalt take all the fat that covereth the inwards, and the caul *that is* above the liver, and the two kidneys, and the fat that *is* upon them, and burn *them* upon the altar.

14 But [a]the flesh of the bullock, and his skin, and his dung, shalt thou burn with fire without the camp: it *is* a sin offering.

15 [a]Thou shalt also take one ram; and Aaron and his sons shall [b]put their hands upon the head of the ram.

16 And thou shalt slay the ram, and thou shalt take his blood, and [a]sprinkle *it* round about upon the altar.

17 And thou shalt cut the ram in pieces, and wash the inwards of him, and his legs, and put *them* unto his pieces, and unto his head.

18 And thou shalt burn the whole ram upon the altar: it *is* a [a]burnt offering unto the LORD: it *is* a sweet savour, an offering made by fire unto the LORD.

19 [a]And thou shalt take the other ram; and Aaron and his sons shall put their hands upon the head of the ram.

20 Then shalt thou kill the ram, and take of his blood, and put *it* upon the tip of the right ear of Aaron, and upon the tip of the right ear of his sons, and upon the thumb of their right hand, and upon the great toe of their right foot, and sprinkle the blood upon the altar round about.

21 And thou shalt take of the blood that *is* upon the altar, and of [a]the anointing oil, and sprinkle *it* upon Aaron, and upon his garments, and upon his sons, and upon the garments of his sons with him: and [b]he shall be hallowed, and his garments, and his sons, and his sons' garments with him.

22 Also thou shalt take of the ram the fat and the rump, and the fat that covereth the inwards, and the caul *above* the liver, and the two kidneys, and the fat that *is* upon them, and the right shoulder; for it *is* a ram of consecration:

23 [a]And one loaf of bread, and one cake of oiled bread, and one wafer out of the basket of the unleavened bread that *is* before the LORD:

24 And thou shalt put all in the hands of Aaron, and in the hands of his sons; and shalt [a]wave them *for* a wave offering before the LORD.

25 [a]And thou shalt receive them of their hands, and burn *them* upon the altar for a burnt offering, for a sweet savour before the LORD: it *is* an offering made by fire unto the LORD.

26 And thou shalt take [a]the breast of the ram of Aaron's consecration, and wave it *for* a wave offering before the LORD: and it shall be thy part.

27 And thou shalt sanctify [a]the breast of the wave offering, and the shoulder of the heave offering, which is waved, and which is heaved up, of the ram of the consecration, *even* of *that* which *is* for Aaron, and of *that* which is for his sons:

28 And it shall be Aaron's and his sons' [a]by a statute for ever from the children of Israel: for it *is* an heave offering: and [b]it shall be an heave offering from the children of Israel of the sacrifice of their peace offerings, *even* their heave offering unto the LORD.

29 And the [a]holy garments of Aaron [b]shall be his sons' after him, [c]to be anointed therein, and to be consecrated in them.

30 *And* [a]that son that is priest in his stead shall put them on [b]seven days, when he cometh into the tabernacle of the congregation to minister in the holy *place*.

31 And thou shalt take the ram of the consecration, and [a]seethe his flesh in the holy place.

32 And Aaron and his sons shall eat the flesh of the ram, and the [a]bread that *is* in the basket, *by* the door of the tabernacle of the congregation.

33 And [a]they shall eat those things wherewith the atonement was made, to consecrate *and*

12 [b]Ex. 27:2; 30:2; Lev. 4:7
13 [a]Lev. 1:8; 3:3, 4
14 [a]Lev. 4:11, 12, 21; Heb. 13:11
15 [a]Lev. 8:18 [b]Lev. 1:4–9
16 [a]Ex. 24:6; Lev. 1:5, 11
18 [a]Ex. 20:24
19 [a]Lev. 8:22
21 [a]Ex. 30:25, 31; Lev. 8:30 [b]Ex. 28:41; 29:1; [Heb. 9:22]
23 [a]Lev. 8:26
24 [a]Lev. 7:30; 10:14
25 [a]Lev. 8:28
26 [a]Lev. 7:31, 34; 8:29
27 [a]Lev. 7:31, 34; Num. 18:11, 18; Deut. 18:3
28 [a]Lev. 10:15 [b]Lev. 3:1; 7:34
29 [a]Ex. 28:2 [b]Num. 20:26, 28 [c]Ex. 28:41; 30:30; Num. 18:8
30 [a]Num. 20:28 [b]Lev. 8:35
31 [a]Lev. 8:31
32 [a]Matt. 12:4
33 [a]Lev. 10:14, 15, 17

NKJV

your finger, and [b]pour all the blood beside the base of the altar.

13 "And [a]you shall take all the fat that covers the entrails, the fatty lobe *attached* to the liver, and the two kidneys and the fat that *is* on them, and burn *them* on the altar.

14 "But [a]the flesh of the bull, with its skin and its offal, you shall burn with fire outside the camp. It *is* a sin offering.

15 [a]"You shall also take one ram, and Aaron and his sons shall [b]put their hands on the head of the ram;

16 "and you shall kill the ram, and you shall take its blood and [a]sprinkle *it* all around on the altar.

17 "Then you shall cut the ram in pieces, wash its entrails and its legs, and put *them* with its pieces and with its head.

18 "And you shall burn the whole ram on the altar. It *is* a [a]burnt offering to the LORD; it *is* a sweet aroma, an offering made by fire to the LORD.

19 [a]"You shall also take the other ram, and Aaron and his sons shall put their hands on the head of the ram.

20 "Then you shall kill the ram, and take some of its blood and put *it* on the tip of the right ear of Aaron and on the tip of the right ear of his sons, on the thumb of their right hand and on the big toe of their right foot, and sprinkle the blood all around on the altar.

21 "And you shall take some of the blood that is on the altar, and some of [a]the anointing oil, and sprinkle *it* on Aaron and on his garments, on his sons and on the garments of his sons with him; and [b]he and his garments shall be hallowed, and his sons and his sons' garments with him.

22 "Also you shall take the fat of the ram, the fat tail, the fat that covers the entrails, the fatty lobe *attached to* the liver, the two kidneys and the fat on them, the right thigh (for it *is* a ram of consecration),

23 [a]"one loaf of bread, one cake *made with* oil, and one wafer from the basket of the unleavened bread that *is* before the LORD;

24 "and you shall put all these in the hands of Aaron and in the hands of his sons, and you shall [a]wave them *as* a wave offering before the LORD.

25 [a]"You shall receive them back from their hands and burn *them* on the altar as a burnt offering, as a sweet aroma before the LORD. It *is* an offering made by fire to the LORD.

26 "Then you shall take [a]the breast of the ram of Aaron's consecration and wave it *as* a wave offering before the LORD; and it shall be your portion.

27 "And from the ram of the consecration you shall consecrate [a]the breast of the wave offering which is waved, and the thigh of the heave offering which is raised, of *that* which *is* for Aaron and of *that* which is for his sons.

28 "It shall be from the children of Israel *for* Aaron and his sons [a]by a statute forever. For it is a heave offering; [b]it shall be a heave offering from the children of Israel from the sacrifices of their peace offerings, *that is,* their heave offering to the LORD.

29 "And the [a]holy garments of Aaron [b]shall be his sons' after him, [c]to be anointed in them and to be consecrated in them.

30 [a]"That son who becomes priest in his place shall put them on for [b]seven days, when he enters the tabernacle of meeting to minister in the holy *place*.

31 "And you shall take the ram of the consecration and [a]boil its flesh in the holy place.

32 "Then Aaron and his sons shall eat the flesh of the ram, and the [a]bread that *is* in the basket, *by* the door of the tabernacle of meeting.

33 [a]"They shall eat those things with which the atonement was made, to consecrate *and* to

KJV

to sanctify them: [b]but a stranger shall not eat
thereof, because they *are* holy.
34 And if ought of the flesh of the consecrations, or of the bread, remain unto the morning,
then [a]thou shalt burn the remainder with fire: it
shall not be eaten, because it *is* holy.
35 And thus shalt thou do unto Aaron, and
to his sons, according to all *things* which I have
commanded thee: [a]seven days shalt thou consecrate them.
36 And thou [a]shalt offer every day a bullock
for a sin offering for atonement: and thou shalt
cleanse the altar, when thou hast made an atonement for it, [b]and thou shalt anoint it, to sanctify
it.
37 Seven days thou shalt make an atonement
for the altar, and sanctify it; and it shall be an
altar most holy: [a]whatsoever toucheth the altar
shall be holy.

The Daily Offerings
(Num. 28:1–8)

38 Now this *is that* which thou shalt offer
upon the altar; [a]two lambs of the first year [b]day
by day continually.
39 The one lamb thou shalt offer [a]in the
morning; and the other lamb thou shalt offer at
even:
40 And with the one lamb a tenth deal of
flour mingled with the fourth part of an hin of
beaten oil; and the fourth part of an hin of wine
for a drink offering.
41 And the other lamb thou shalt [a]offer at
even, and shalt do thereto according to the meat
offering of the morning, and according to the
drink offering thereof, for a sweet savour, an offering made by fire unto the LORD.
42 *This shall be* [a]a continual burnt offering
throughout your generations *at* the door of the
tabernacle of the congregation before the LORD:
[b]where I will meet you, to speak there unto thee.
43 And there I will meet with the children
of Israel, and *the tabernacle* [a]shall be sanctified
by my glory.
44 And I will sanctify the tabernacle of the
congregation, and the altar: I will [a]sanctify also
both Aaron and his sons, to minister to me in the
priest's office.
45 And [a]I will dwell among the children of
Israel, and will [b]be their God.
46 And they shall know that [a]I *am* the LORD
their God, that [b]brought them forth out of the land
of Egypt, that I may dwell among them: I *am* the
LORD their God.

The Altar of Incense
(Ex. 37:25–28)

30 And thou shalt make [a]an altar to burn incense upon: *of* shittim wood shalt thou
make it.
2 A cubit *shall be* the length thereof, and a
cubit the breadth thereof; foursquare shall it be:
and two cubits *shall be* the height thereof: the
horns thereof *shall be* of the same.
3 And thou shalt overlay it with pure gold,
the top thereof, and the sides thereof round about,
and the horns thereof; and thou shalt make unto
it a crown of gold round about.
4 And two golden rings shalt thou make to
it under the crown of it, by the two corners
thereof, upon the two sides of it shalt thou make
it; and they shall be for places for the staves to
bear it withal.
5 And thou shalt make the staves *of* shittim
wood, and overlay them with gold.
6 And thou shalt put it before the [a]vail that
is by the ark of the testimony, before the [b]mercy
seat that *is* over the testimony, where I will meet
with thee.
7 And Aaron shall burn thereon [a]sweet incense every morning: when [b]he dresseth the
lamps, he shall burn incense upon it.

33 [b]Ex. 12:43; Lev. 22:10
34 [a]Ex. 12:10; 23:18; 34:25; Lev. 7:18; 8:32
35 [a]Lev. 8:33–35
36 [a]Heb. 10:11 [b]Ex. 30:26–29; 40:10, 11
37 [a]Num. 4:15; Hag. 2:11–13; Matt. 23:19
38 [a]Num. 28:3–31; 29:6–38; 1 Chr. 16:40; Ezra 3:3 [b]Dan. 12:11
39 [a]Ezek. 46:13–15
41 [a]1 Kin. 18:29, 36; 2 Kin. 16:15; Ezra 9:4, 5; Ps. 141:2
42 [a]Ex. 30:8 [b]Ex. 25:22; 33:7, 9; Num. 17:4
43 [a]Ex. 40:34; 1 Kin. 8:11; 2 Chr. 5:14; Ezek. 43:5; Hag. 2:7, 9
44 [a]Lev. 21:15
45 [a]Ex. 25:8; Lev. 26:12; Num. 5:3; Deut. 12:11; Zech. 2:10; [John 14:17, 23; Rev. 21:3] [b]Gen. 17:8; Lev. 11:45
46 [a]Ex. 16:12; 20:2; Deut. 4:35 [b]Lev. 11:45

CHAPTER 30
1 [a]Ex. 37:25–29
6 [a]Ex. 26:31–35 [b]Ex. 25:21, 22
7 [a]Ex. 30:34; 1 Sam. 2:28; 1 Chr. 23:13; Luke 1:9 [b]Ex. 27:20, 21

NKJV

sanctify them; [b]but an outsider shall not eat *them,*
because they *are* holy.
34 "And if any of the flesh of the consecration offerings, or of the bread, remains until the
morning, then [a]you shall burn the remainder with
fire. It shall not be eaten, because it *is* holy.
35 "Thus you shall do to Aaron and his sons,
according to all that I have commanded you.
[a]Seven days you shall consecrate them.
36 "And you [a]shall offer a bull every day *as*
a sin offering for atonement. [b]You shall cleanse
the altar when you make atonement for it, and
you shall anoint it to sanctify it.
37 "Seven days you shall make atonement
for the altar and sanctify it. And the altar shall
be most holy. [a]Whatever touches the altar must
be holy.

The Daily Offerings
(Num. 28:1–8)

38 "Now this *is* what you shall offer on the
altar: [a]two lambs of the first year, [b]day by day
continually.
39 "One lamb you shall offer [a]in the morning,
and the other lamb you shall offer at twilight.
40 "With the one lamb shall be one-tenth *of*
an ephah of flour mixed with one-fourth of a hin
of pressed oil, and one-fourth of a hin of wine *as*
a drink offering.
41 "And the other lamb you shall [a]offer at
twilight; and you shall offer with it the grain offering and the drink offering, as in the morning, for
a sweet aroma, an offering made by fire to the
LORD.
42 "*This shall be* [a]a continual burnt offering
throughout your generations *at* the door of the
tabernacle of meeting before the LORD, [b]where I
will meet you to speak with you.
43 "And there I will meet with the children
of Israel, and *the tabernacle* [a]shall be sanctified
by My glory.
44 "So I will consecrate the tabernacle of
meeting and the altar. I will also [a]consecrate both
Aaron and his sons to minister to Me as priests.
45 [a]"I will dwell among the children of Israel
and will [b]be their God.
46 "And they shall know that [a]I *am* the LORD
their God, who [b]brought them up out of the land
of Egypt, that I may dwell among them. I *am* the
LORD their God.

The Altar of Incense
(Ex. 37:25–28)

30 "You shall make [a]an altar to burn incense
on; you shall make it of acacia wood.
2 "A cubit *shall be* its length and a cubit
its width—it shall be square—and two cubits *shall*
be its height. Its horns *shall be* of one piece with
it.
3 "And you shall overlay its top, its sides
all around, and its horns with pure gold; and you
shall make for it a molding of gold all around.
4 "Two gold rings you shall make for it, under the molding on both its sides. You shall place
them on its two sides, and they will be holders
for the poles with which to bear it.
5 "You shall make the poles of acacia wood,
and overlay them with gold.
6 "And you shall put it before the [a]veil that
is before the ark of the Testimony, before the
[b]mercy seat that *is* over the Testimony, where I
will meet with you.
7 "Aaron shall burn on it [a]sweet incense
every morning; when [b]he tends the lamps, he
shall burn incense on it.

KJV

8 And when Aaron lighteth the lamps at even, he shall burn incense upon it, a perpetual incense before the LORD throughout your generations.

9 Ye shall offer no [a]strange incense thereon, nor burnt sacrifice, nor meat offering; neither shall ye pour drink offering thereon.

10 And [a]Aaron shall make an atonement upon the horns of it once in a year with the blood of the sin offering of atonements: once in the year shall he make atonement upon it throughout your generations: it *is* most holy unto the LORD.

The Ransom Money

11 And the LORD spake unto Moses, saying,

12 [a]When thou takest the sum of the children of Israel after their number, then shall they give every man [b]a ransom for his soul unto the LORD, when thou numberest them; that there be no [c]plague among them, when *thou* numberest them.

13 [a]This they shall give, every one that passeth among them that are numbered, half a shekel after the shekel of the sanctuary: [b](a shekel *is* twenty gerahs:) [c]an half shekel *shall be* the offering of the LORD.

14 Every one that passeth among them that are numbered, from twenty years old and above, shall give an offering unto the LORD.

15 The [a]rich shall not give more, and the poor shall not give less than half a shekel, when *they* give an offering unto the LORD, to make an atonement for your souls.

16 And thou shalt take the atonement money of the children of Israel, and [a]shalt appoint it for the service of the tabernacle of the congregation; that it may be [b]a memorial unto the children of Israel before the LORD, to make an atonement for your souls.

The Bronze Laver

17 And the LORD spake unto Moses, saying,

18 [a]Thou shalt also make a laver *of* brass, and his foot *also of* brass, to wash *withal:* and thou shalt [b]put it between the tabernacle of the congregation and the altar, and thou shalt put water therein.

19 For Aaron and his sons [a]shall wash their hands and their feet thereat:

20 When they go into the tabernacle of the congregation, they shall wash with water, that they die not; or when they come near to the altar to minister, to burn offering made by fire unto the LORD:

21 So they shall wash their hands and their feet, that they die not: and [a]it shall be a statute for ever to them, *even* to him and to his seed throughout their generations.

The Holy Anointing Oil
(Ex. 37:29)

22 Moreover the LORD spake unto Moses, saying,

23 Take thou also unto thee [a]principal spices, of pure [b]myrrh five hundred *shekels,* and of sweet cinnamon half so much, *even* two hundred and fifty *shekels,* and of sweet [c]calamus two hundred and fifty *shekels,*

24 And of [a]cassia five hundred *shekels,* after the shekel of the sanctuary, and of oil olive an [b]hin:

25 And thou shalt make it an oil of holy ointment, an ointment compound after the art of the apothecary: it shall be [a]an holy anointing oil.

26 [a]And thou shalt anoint the tabernacle of the congregation therewith, and the ark of the testimony,

27 And the table and all his vessels, and the candlestick and his vessels, and the altar of incense,

28 And the altar of burnt offering with all his vessels, and the laver and his foot.

29 And thou shalt sanctify them, that they

---

9 [a]Lev. 10:1
10 [a]Lev. 16:3–34
12 [a]Ex. 38:25, 26; Num. 1:2; 26:2; 2 Sam. 24:2 [b]Num. 31:50; [Matt. 20:28; 1 Pet. 1:18, 19] [c]2 Sam. 24:15
13 [a]Matt. 17:24 [b]Lev. 27:25; Num. 3:47; Ezek. 45:12 [c]Ex. 38:26
15 [a]Job 34:19; Prov. 22:2; [Eph. 6:9]
16 [a]Ex. 38:25–31 [b]Num. 16:40
18 [a]Ex. 38:8; 1 Kin. 7:38 [b]Ex. 40:30
19 [a]Ex. 40:31, 32; Ps. 26:6; Is. 52:11; John 13:8, 10; Heb. 10:22
21 [a]Ex. 28:43
23 [a]Song 4:14; Ezek. 27:22 [b]Ps. 45:8; Prov. 7:17 [c]Song 4:14; Jer. 6:20
24 [a]Ps. 45:8 [b]Ex. 29:40
25 [a]Ex. 37:29; 40:9; Lev. 8:10; Num. 35:25; Ps. 89:20; 133:2
26 [a]Ex. 40:9; Lev. 8:10; Num. 7:1

NKJV

8 "And when Aaron lights the lamps at twilight, he shall burn incense on it, a perpetual incense before the LORD throughout your generations.

9 "You shall not offer [a]strange incense on it, or a burnt offering, or a grain offering; nor shall you pour a drink offering on it.

10 "And [a]Aaron shall make atonement upon its horns once a year with the blood of the sin offering of atonement; once a year he shall make atonement upon it throughout your generations. It *is* most holy to the LORD."

The Ransom Money

11 Then the LORD spoke to Moses, saying:

12 [a]"When you take the census of the children of Israel for their number, then every man shall give [b]a ransom for himself to the LORD, when you number them, that there may be no [c]plague among them when *you* number them.

13 [a]"This is what everyone among those who are numbered shall give: half a shekel according to the shekel of the sanctuary [b](a shekel *is* twenty gerahs). [c]The half-shekel *shall be* an offering to the LORD.

14 "Everyone included among those who are numbered, from twenty years old and above, shall give an offering to the LORD.

15 "The [a]rich shall not give more and the poor shall not give less than half a shekel, when *you* give an offering to the LORD, to make atonement for yourselves.

16 "And you shall take the atonement money of the children of Israel, and [a]shall appoint it for the service of the tabernacle of meeting, that it may be [b]a memorial for the children of Israel before the LORD, to make atonement for yourselves."

The Bronze Laver

17 Then the LORD spoke to Moses, saying:

18 [a]"You shall also make a laver of bronze, with its base also of bronze, for washing. You shall [b]put it between the tabernacle of meeting and the altar. And you shall put water in it,

19 "for Aaron and his sons [a]shall wash their hands and their feet in water from it.

20 "When they go into the tabernacle of meeting, or when they come near the altar to minister, to burn an offering made by fire to the LORD, they shall wash with water, lest they die.

21 "So they shall wash their hands and their feet, lest they die. And [a]it shall be a statute forever to them—to him and his descendants throughout their generations."

The Holy Anointing Oil
(Ex. 37:29)

22 Moreover the LORD spoke to Moses, saying:

23 "Also take for yourself [a]quality spices—five hundred *shekels* of liquid [b]myrrh, half as much sweet-smelling cinnamon (two hundred and fifty *shekels*), two hundred and fifty *shekels* of sweet-smelling [c]cane,

24 "five hundred *shekels* of [a]cassia, according to the shekel of the sanctuary, and a [b]hin of olive oil.

25 "And you shall make from these a holy anointing oil, an ointment compounded according to the art of the perfumer. It shall be [a]a holy anointing oil.

26 [a]"With it you shall anoint the tabernacle of meeting and the ark of the Testimony;

27 "the table and all its utensils, the lampstand and its utensils, and the altar of incense;

28 "the altar of burnt offering with all its utensils, and the laver and its base.

29 "You shall consecrate them, that they may

KJV

may be most holy: [a]whatsoever toucheth them shall be holy.

30 [a]And thou shalt anoint Aaron and his sons, and consecrate them, that *they* may minister unto me in the priest's office.

31 And thou shalt speak unto the children of Israel, saying, This shall be an holy anointing oil unto me throughout your generations.

32 Upon man's flesh shall it not be poured, neither shall ye make *any other* like it, after the composition of it: [a]it *is* holy, *and* it shall be holy unto you.

33 [a]Whosoever compoundeth *any* like it, or whosoever putteth *any* of it upon a stranger, [b]shall even be cut off from his people.

The Incense
(Ex. 37:29)

34 And the LORD said unto Moses, [a]Take unto thee sweet spices, stacte, and onycha, and galbanum; *these* sweet spices with pure frankincense: of each shall there be a like *weight:*

35 And thou shalt make it a perfume, a confection [a]after the art of the apothecary, tempered together, pure *and* holy:

36 And thou shalt beat *some* of it very small, and put of it before the testimony in the tabernacle of the congregation, [a]where I will meet with thee: [b]it shall be unto you most holy.

37 And *as for* the perfume which thou shalt make, [a]ye shall not make to yourselves according to the composition thereof: it shall be unto thee holy for the LORD.

38 [a]Whosoever shall make like unto that, to smell thereto, shall even be cut off from his people.

Artisans for Building the Tabernacle
(Ex. 35:30—36:1)

31 And the LORD spake unto Moses, saying,
2 [a]See, I have called by name Bezaleel the [b]son of Uri, the son of Hur, of the tribe of Judah:

3 And I have [a]filled him with the spirit of God, in wisdom, and in understanding, and in knowledge, and in all manner of workmanship,

4 To devise cunning works, to work in gold, and in silver, and in brass,

5 And in cutting of stones, to set *them,* and in carving of timber, to work in all manner of workmanship.

6 And I, behold, I have given with him [a]Aholiab, the son of Ahisamach, of the tribe of Dan: and in the hearts of all that are [b]wise hearted I have put wisdom, that they may make all that I have commanded thee;

7 [a]The tabernacle of the congregation, and [b]the ark of the testimony, and [c]the mercy seat that *is* thereupon, and all the furniture of the tabernacle,

8 And [a]the table and his furniture, and [b]the pure candlestick with all his furniture, and the altar of incense,

9 And [a]the altar of burnt offering with all his furniture, and [b]the laver and his foot,

10 And [a]the cloths of service, and the holy garments for Aaron the priest, and the garments of his sons, to minister in the priest's office,

11 [a]And the anointing oil, and [b]sweet incense for the holy *place:* according to all that I have commanded thee shall they do.

The Sabbath Law

12 And the LORD spake unto Moses, saying,

13 Speak thou also unto the children of Israel, saying, [a]Verily my sabbaths ye shall keep: for it *is* a sign between me and you throughout your generations; that *ye* may know that I *am* the LORD that doth [b]sanctify you.

14 [a]Ye shall keep the sabbath therefore; for it *is* holy unto you: every one that defileth it shall surely be put to death: for [b]whosoever doeth *any*

29 [a]Ex. 29:37; Num. 4:15; Hag. 2:11–13
30 [a]Ex. 29:7; Lev. 8:12
32 [a]Ex. 30:25, 37
33 [a]Ex. 30:38 [b]Gen. 17:14; Ex. 12:15; Lev. 7:20, 21
34 [a]Ex. 25:6; 37:29
35 [a]Ex. 30:25
36 [a]Ex. 29:42; Lev. 16:2 [b][Ex. 29:37; 30:32]; Lev. 2:3
37 [a]Ex. 30:32
38 [a]Ex. 30:33

CHAPTER 31
2 [a]Ex. 35:30—36:1 [b]1 Chr. 2:20
3 [a]Ex. 28:3; 35:31; 1 Kin. 7:14; Eph. 1:17
6 [a]Ex. 35:34 [b]Ex. 28:3; 35:10, 35; 36:1
7 [a]Ex. 36:8 [b]Ex. 37:1–5 [c]Ex. 37:6–9
8 [a]Ex. 37:10–16 [b]Ex. 37:17–24; Lev. 24:4
9 [a]Ex. 38:1–7 [b]Ex. 38:8
10 [a]Ex. 39:1, 41
11 [a]Ex. 30:23–33 [b]Ex. 30:34–38
13 [a]Ex. 31:17; Lev. 19:3, 30; 26:2; Ezek. 20:12, 20 [b]Lev. 20:8
14 [a]Ex. 20:8; Deut. 5:12 [b]Ex. 31:15; 35:2; Num. 15:32–36; John 7:23

*———
31:10 Or *woven garments*

NKJV

be most holy; [a]whatever touches them must be holy.

30 [a]"And you shall anoint Aaron and his sons, and consecrate them, that *they* may minister to Me as priests.

31 "And you shall speak to the children of Israel, saying: 'This shall be a holy anointing oil to Me throughout your generations.

32 'It shall not be poured on man's flesh; nor shall you make *any other* like it, according to its composition. [a]It *is* holy, *and* it shall be holy to you.

33 [a]'Whoever compounds *any* like it, or whoever puts *any* of it on an outsider, [b]shall be cut off from his people.' "

The Incense
(Ex. 37:29)

34 And the LORD said to Moses: [a]"Take sweet spices, stacte and onycha and galbanum, and pure frankincense with *these* sweet spices; there shall be equal amounts of each.

35 "You shall make of these an incense, a compound [a]according to the art of the perfumer, salted, pure, *and* holy.

36 "And you shall beat *some* of it very fine, and put some of it before the Testimony in the tabernacle of meeting [a]where I will meet with you. [b]It shall be most holy to you.

37 "But *as for* the incense which you shall make, [a]you shall not make any for yourselves, according to its composition. It shall be to you holy for the LORD.

38 [a]"Whoever makes *any* like it, to smell it, he shall be cut off from his people."

Artisans for Building the Tabernacle
(Ex. 35:30—36:1)

31 Then the LORD spoke to Moses, saying:
2 [a]"See, I have called by name Bezalel the [b]son of Uri, the son of Hur, of the tribe of Judah.

3 "And I have [a]filled him with the Spirit of God, in wisdom, in understanding, in knowledge, and in all *manner of* workmanship,

4 "to design artistic works, to work in gold, in silver, in bronze,

5 "in cutting jewels for setting, in carving wood, and to work in all *manner of* workmanship.

6 "And I, indeed I, have appointed with him [a]Aholiab the son of Ahisamach, of the tribe of Dan; and I have put wisdom in the hearts of all the [b]gifted artisans, that they may make all that I have commanded you:

7 [a]"the tabernacle of meeting, [b]the ark of the Testimony and [c]the mercy seat that *is* on it, and all the furniture of the tabernacle—

8 [a]"the table and its utensils, [b]the pure *gold* lampstand with all its utensils, the altar of incense,

9 [a]"the altar of burnt offering with all its utensils, and [b]the laver and its base—

10 [a]"the *garments of ministry, the holy garments for Aaron the priest and the garments of his sons, to minister as priests,

11 [a]"and the anointing oil and [b]sweet incense for the holy *place.* According to all that I have commanded you they shall do."

The Sabbath Law

12 And the LORD spoke to Moses, saying,

13 "Speak also to the children of Israel, saying: [a]'Surely My Sabbaths you shall keep, for it *is* a sign between Me and you throughout your generations, that *you* may know that I *am* the LORD who [b]sanctifies you.

14 [a]'You shall keep the Sabbath, therefore, for *it is* holy to you. Everyone who profanes it shall surely be put to death; for [b]whoever does

KJV

work therein, that soul shall be cut off from
among his people.
15 [a]Six days may work be done; but in the
[b]seventh *is* the sabbath of rest, holy to the LORD:
whosoever doeth *any* work in the sabbath day,
he shall surely be put to death.
16 Wherefore the children of Israel shall
keep the sabbath, to observe the sabbath throughout their generations, *for* a perpetual covenant.
17 It *is* [a]a sign between me and the children
of Israel for ever: for [b]*in* six days the LORD made
heaven and earth, and on the seventh day he
rested, and was refreshed.
18 And he gave unto Moses, when he had
made an end of communing with him upon mount
Sinai, [a]two tables of testimony, tables of stone,
written with the finger of God.

The Gold Calf
(Deut. 9:6–29)

32 And when the people saw that Moses [a]de-
layed to come down out of the mount, the
people [b]gathered themselves together unto
Aaron, and said unto him, [c]Up, make us gods,
which shall [d]go before us; for *as for* this Moses,
the man that [e]brought us up out of the land of
Egypt, we wot not what is become of him.
2 And Aaron said unto them, Break off the
[a]golden earrings, which *are* in the ears of your
wives, of your sons, and of your daughters, and
bring *them* unto me.
3 And all the people brake off the golden
earrings which *were* in their ears, and brought
them unto Aaron.
4 [a]And he received *them* at their hand, and
fashioned it with a graving tool, after he had made
it a molten calf: and they said, These *be* thy gods,
O Israel, which [b]brought thee up out of the land
of Egypt.
5 And when Aaron saw *it,* he built an altar
before it; and Aaron made [a]proclamation, and
said, To morrow *is* a feast to the LORD.
6 And they rose up early on the morrow,
and offered burnt offerings, and brought peace
offerings; and the people [a]sat down to eat and to
drink, and rose up to play.
7 And the LORD said unto Moses, [a]Go, get
thee down; for thy people, which thou broughtest
out of the land of Egypt, [b]have corrupted
themselves:
8 They have turned aside quickly out of the
way which [a]I commanded them: they have made
them a molten calf, and have worshipped it, and
have sacrificed thereunto, and said, [b]These *be* thy
gods, O Israel, which have brought thee up out
of the land of Egypt.
9 And the LORD said unto Moses, [a]I have
seen this people, and, behold, it *is* a stiffnecked
people:
10 Now therefore [a]let me alone, that [b]my
wrath may wax hot against them, and that I may
consume them: and [c]I will make of thee a great
nation.
11 [a]And Moses besought the LORD his God,
and said, LORD, why doth thy wrath wax hot
against thy people, which thou hast brought forth
out of the land of Egypt with great power, and
with a mighty hand?
12 [a]Wherefore should the Egyptians speak,
and say, For mischief did he bring them out, to
slay them in the mountains, and to consume them
from the face of the earth? Turn from thy fierce
wrath, and [b]repent of this evil against thy people.
13 Remember Abraham, Isaac, and Israel,
thy servants, to whom thou [a]swarest by thine own
self, and saidst unto them, [b]I will multiply your
seed as the stars of heaven, and all this land that
I have spoken of will I give unto your seed, and
they shall inherit *it* for ever.
14 And the LORD [a]repented of the evil which
he thought to do unto his people.
15 And [a]Moses turned, and went down from

15 [a]Ex. 20:9–11; Lev. 23:3; Deut. 5:12–14 [b]Gen. 2:2; Ex. 16:23; 20:8; 35:2
17 [a]Ex. 31:13; Ezek. 20:12 [b]Gen. 1:31; 2:2, 3; Ex. 20:11
18 [a][Ex. 24:12; 32:15, 16; Deut. 4:13; 5:22; 2 Cor. 3:3]

CHAPTER 32

1 [a]Ex. 24:18; Deut. 9:9–12 [b]Ex. 17:1–3 [c]Acts 7:40 [d]Ex. 13:21 [e]Ex. 32:8
2 [a]Ex. 11:2; 35:22; Judg. 8:24–27
4 [a]Ex. 20:3, 4, 23; Deut. 9:16; Judg. 17:3, 4; 1 Kin. 12:28; Neh. 9:18; Ps. 106:19; Acts 7:41 [b]Ex. 29:45, 46
5 [a]Lev. 23:2, 4, 21, 37; 2 Kin. 10:20; 2 Chr. 30:5
6 [a]Ex. 32:17–19; Num. 25:2; 1 Cor. 10:7
7 [a]Deut. 9:8–21; Dan. 9:14 [b]Gen. 6:11, 12
8 [a]Ex. 20:3, 4, 23; Deut. 32:17 [b]1 Kin. 12:28
9 [a]Ex. 33:3, 5; 34:9; Deut. 9:6; 2 Chr. 30:8; Is. 48:4; [Acts 7:51]
10 [a]Deut. 9:14, 19 [b]Ex. 22:24 [c]Num. 14:12
11 [a]Deut. 9:18, 26–29
12 [a]Num. 14:13–19; Deut. 9:28; Josh. 7:9 [b]Ex. 32:14
13 [a]Gen. 22:16–18; [Heb. 6:13] [b]Gen. 12:7; 13:15; 15:7, 18; 22:17; 26:4; 35:11, 12; Ex. 13:5, 11; 33:1
14 [a]2 Sam. 24:16
15 [a]Deut. 9:15

NKJV

any work on it, that person shall be cut off from
among his people.
15 'Work shall be done for [a]six days, but the
[b]seventh *is* the Sabbath of rest, holy to the LORD.
Whoever does *any* work on the Sabbath day, he
shall surely be put to death.
16 'Therefore the children of Israel shall keep
the Sabbath, to observe the Sabbath throughout
their generations *as* a perpetual covenant.
17 'It *is* [a]a sign between Me and the children
of Israel forever; for [b]*in* six days the LORD made
the heavens and the earth, and on the seventh
day He rested and was refreshed.' "
18 And when He had made an end of speaking with him on Mount Sinai, He gave Moses [a]two
tablets of the Testimony, tablets of stone, written
with the finger of God.

The Gold Calf
(Deut. 9:6–29)

32 Now when the people saw that Moses [a]de-
layed coming down from the mountain, the
people [b]gathered together to Aaron, and said to
him, [c]"Come, make us gods that shall [d]go before
us; for *as for* this Moses, the man who [e]brought
us up out of the land of Egypt, we do not know
what has become of him."
2 And Aaron said to them, "Break off the
[a]golden earrings which *are* in the ears of your
wives, your sons, and your daughters, and bring
them to me."
3 So all the people broke off the golden earrings which *were* in their ears, and brought *them*
to Aaron.
4 [a]And he received *the gold* from their
hand, and he fashioned it with an engraving tool,
and made a molded calf. Then they said, "This *is*
your god, O Israel, that [b]brought you out of the
land of Egypt!"
5 So when Aaron saw *it,* he built an altar
before it. And Aaron made a [a]proclamation and
said, "Tomorrow *is* a feast to the LORD."
6 Then they rose early on the next day, offered burnt offerings, and brought peace offerings; and the people [a]sat down to eat and drink,
and rose up to play.
7 And the LORD said to Moses, [a]"Go, get
down! For your people whom you brought out of
the land of Egypt [b]have corrupted *themselves.*
8 "They have turned aside quickly out of
the way which [a]I commanded them. They have
made themselves a molded calf, and worshiped
it and sacrificed to it, and said, [b]'This *is* your god,
O Israel, that brought you out of the land of
Egypt!' "
9 And the LORD said to Moses, [a]"I have seen
this people, and indeed it *is* a stiff-necked people!
10 "Now therefore, [a]let Me alone, that [b]My
wrath may burn hot against them and I may consume them. And [c]I will make of you a great
nation."
11 [a]Then Moses pleaded with the LORD his
God, and said: "LORD, why does Your wrath burn
hot against Your people whom You have brought
out of the land of Egypt with great power and
with a mighty hand?
12 [a]"Why should the Egyptians speak, and
say, 'He brought them out to harm them, to kill
them in the mountains, and to consume them from
the face of the earth'? Turn from Your fierce
wrath, and [b]relent from this harm to Your people.
13 "Remember Abraham, Isaac, and Israel,
Your servants, to whom You [a]swore by Your own
self, and said to them, [b]'I will multiply your descendants as the stars of heaven; and all this land
that I have spoken of I give to your descendants,
and they shall inherit *it* forever.' "
14 So the LORD [a]relented from the harm
which He said He would do to His people.
15 And [a]Moses turned and went down from

KJV

the mount, and the two tables of the testimony *were* in his hand: the tables *were* written on both their sides; on the one side and on the other *were* they written.

16 And the [a]tables *were* the work of God, and the writing *was* the writing of God, graven upon the tables.

17 And when Joshua heard the noise of the people as they shouted, he said unto Moses, *There is* a noise of war in the camp.

18 And he said, *It is* not the voice of *them that* shout for mastery, neither *is it* the voice of *them that* cry for being overcome: *but* the noise of *them that* sing do I hear.

19 And it came to pass, as soon as he came nigh unto the camp, that [a]he saw the calf, and the dancing: and Moses' anger waxed hot, and he cast the tables out of his hands, and brake them beneath the mount.

20 [a]And he took the calf which they had made, and burnt *it* in the fire, and ground *it* to powder, and strawed *it* upon the water, and made the children of Israel drink *of it*.

21 And Moses said unto Aaron, [a]What did this people unto thee, that thou hast brought so great a sin upon them?

22 And Aaron said, Let not the anger of my lord wax hot: [a]thou knowest the people, that they *are set* on mischief.

23 For they said unto me, Make us gods, which shall go before us: for *as for* this Moses, the man that brought us up out of the land of Egypt, we wot not what is become of him.

24 And I said unto them, Whosoever hath any gold, let them break *it* off. So they gave *it* me: then I cast it into the fire, and there came out this calf.

25 And when Moses saw that the people *were* [a]naked; (for Aaron [b]had made them naked unto *their* shame among their enemies:)

26 Then Moses stood in the gate of the camp, and said, Who *is* on the LORD's side? *let him come* unto me. And all the sons of Levi gathered themselves together unto him.

27 And he said unto them, Thus saith the LORD God of Israel, Put every man his sword by his side, *and* go in and out from gate to gate throughout the camp, and [a]slay every man his brother, and every man his companion, and every man his neighbour.

28 And the children of Levi did according to the word of Moses: and there fell of the people that day about three thousand men.

29 [a]For Moses had said, Consecrate yourselves to day to the LORD, even every man upon his son, and upon his brother; that he may bestow upon you a blessing this day.

30 And it came to pass on the morrow, that Moses said unto the people, [a]Ye have sinned a great sin: and now I will go up unto the LORD; [b]peradventure I shall [c]make an atonement for your sin.

31 And Moses [a]returned unto the LORD, and said, Oh, this people have sinned a great sin, and have [b]made them gods of gold.

32 Yet now, if thou wilt forgive their sin—; and if not, [a]blot me, I pray thee, [b]out of thy book which thou hast written.

33 And the LORD said unto Moses, [a]Whosoever hath sinned against me, him will I [b]blot out of my book.

34 Therefore now go, lead the people unto *the place* of which I have [a]spoken unto thee: [b]behold, mine Angel shall go before thee: nevertheless [c]in the day when I [d]visit I will visit their sin upon them.

35 And the LORD plagued the people, because [a]they made the calf, which Aaron made.

The Command to Leave Sinai

33 And the LORD said unto Moses, Depart, *and* go up hence, thou [a]and the people which

---

16 [a]Ex. 31:18
19 [a]Deut. 9:16, 17
20 [a]Num. 5:17, 24; Deut. 9:21
21 [a]Gen. 26:10
22 [a]Ex. 14:11; Deut. 9:24
25 [a]Ex. 33:4, 5 [b]2 Chr. 28:19
27 [a]Num. 25:5–13
29 [a]Ex. 28:41; 1 Sam. 15:18, 22; Prov. 21:3; Zech. 13:3
30 [a]1 Sam. 12:20, 23 [b]2 Sam. 16:12 [c]Num. 25:13
31 [a]Deut. 9:18 [b]Ex. 20:23
32 [a]Ps. 69:28; Is. 4:3; Mal. 3:16; Rom. 9:3 [b]Dan. 12:1; Phil. 4:3; Rev. 3:5; 21:27
33 [a]Lev. 23:30; [Ezek. 18:4; 33:2, 14, 15] [b]Ex. 17:14; Deut. 29:20; Ps. 9:5; Rev. 3:5; 21:27
34 [a]Ex. 3:17 [b]Ex. 23:20; Josh. 5:14 [c]Deut. 32:35; Rom. 2:5, 6 [d]Ps. 89:32
35 [a]Neh. 9:18

CHAPTER 33
1 [a]Ex. 32:1, 7, 13; Josh. 3:17

NKJV

the mountain, and the two tablets of the Testimony *were* in his hand. The tablets *were* written on both sides; on the one *side* and on the other they were written.

16 Now the [a]tablets *were* the work of God, and the writing *was* the writing of God engraved on the tablets.

17 And when Joshua heard the noise of the people as they shouted, he said to Moses, "*There is* a noise of war in the camp."

18 But he said:

"*It is* not the noise of the shout of victory,
Nor the noise of the cry of defeat,
But the sound of singing I hear."

19 So it was, as soon as he came near the camp, that [a]he saw the calf *and* the dancing. So Moses' anger became hot, and he cast the tablets out of his hands and broke them at the foot of the mountain.

20 [a]Then he took the calf which they had made, burned *it* in the fire, and ground *it* to powder; and he scattered *it* on the water and made the children of Israel drink *it*.

21 And Moses said to Aaron, [a]"What did this people do to you that you have brought *so* great a sin upon them?"

22 So Aaron said, "Do not let the anger of my lord become hot. [a]You know the people, that they *are set* on evil.

23 "For they said to me, 'Make us gods that shall go before us; *as for* this Moses, the man who brought us out of the land of Egypt, we do not know what has become of him.'

24 "And I said to them, 'Whoever has any gold, let them break *it* off.' So they gave *it* to me, and I cast it into the fire, and this calf came out."

25 Now when Moses saw that the people *were* [a]unrestrained (for Aaron [b]had not restrained them, to *their* shame among their enemies),

26 then Moses stood in the entrance of the camp, and said, "Whoever *is* on the LORD's side—*come* to me!" And all the sons of Levi gathered themselves together to him.

27 And he said to them, "Thus says the LORD God of Israel: 'Let every man put his sword on his side, and go in and out from entrance to entrance throughout the camp, and [a]let every man kill his brother, every man his companion, and every man his neighbor.' "

28 So the sons of Levi did according to the word of Moses. And about three thousand men of the people fell that day.

29 [a]Then Moses said, "Consecrate yourselves today to the LORD, that He may bestow on you a blessing this day, for every man has opposed his son and his brother."

30 Now it came to pass on the next day that Moses said to the people, [a]"You have committed a great sin. So now I will go up to the LORD; [b]perhaps I can [c]make atonement for your sin."

31 Then Moses [a]returned to the LORD and said, "Oh, these people have committed a great sin, and have [b]made for themselves a god of gold!

32 "Yet now, if You will forgive their sin—but if not, I pray, [a]blot me [b]out of Your book which You have written."

33 And the LORD said to Moses, [a]"Whoever has sinned against Me, I will [b]blot him out of My book.

34 "Now therefore, go, lead the people to *the place* of which I have [a]spoken to you. [b]Behold, My Angel shall go before you. Nevertheless, [c]in the day when I [d]visit for punishment, I will visit punishment upon them for their sin."

35 So the LORD plagued the people because of [a]what they did with the calf which Aaron made.

The Command to Leave Sinai

33 Then the LORD said to Moses, "Depart *and* go up from here, you [a]and the people whom

KJV

thou hast brought up out of the land of Egypt, unto the land which I sware unto Abraham, to Isaac, and to Jacob, saying, [b]Unto thy seed will I give it:

2 [a]And I will send an angel before thee; [b]and I will drive out the Canaanite, the Amorite, and the Hittite, and the Perizzite, the Hivite, and the Jebusite:

3 [a]Unto a land flowing with milk and honey: for I will not go up in the midst of thee; for thou *art* a [c]stiffnecked people: lest [b]I consume thee in the way.

4 And when the people heard these evil tidings, [a]they mourned: [b]and no man did put on him his ornaments.

5 For the LORD had said unto Moses, Say unto the children of Israel, Ye *are* a stiffnecked people: I will come up into the midst of thee in a moment, and consume thee: therefore now put off thy ornaments from thee, that I may [a]know what to do unto thee.

6 And the children of Israel stripped themselves of their ornaments by the mount Horeb.

Moses Meets with the LORD

7 And Moses took the tabernacle, and pitched it without the camp, afar off from the camp, and [a]called it the Tabernacle of the congregation. And it came to pass, *that* every one which [b]sought the LORD went out unto the tabernacle of the congregation, which *was* without the camp.

8 And it came to pass, when Moses went out unto the tabernacle, *that* all the people rose up, and stood every man [a]*at* his tent door, and looked after Moses, until he was gone into the tabernacle.

9 And it came to pass, as Moses entered into the tabernacle, the cloudy pillar descended, and stood *at* the door of the tabernacle, and *the LORD* [a]talked with Moses.

10 And all the people saw the cloudy pillar stand *at* the tabernacle door: and all the people rose up and [a]worshipped, every man *in* his tent door.

11 And [a]the LORD spake unto Moses face to face, as a man speaketh unto his friend. And he turned again into the camp: but [b]his servant Joshua, the son of Nun, a young man, departed not out of the tabernacle.

The Promise of God's Presence

12 And Moses said unto the LORD, See, [a]thou sayest unto me, Bring up this people: and thou hast not let me know whom thou wilt send with me. Yet thou hast said, [b]I know thee by name, and thou hast also found grace in my sight.

13 Now therefore, I pray thee, [a]if I have found grace in thy sight, [b]shew me now thy way, that I may know thee, that I may find grace in thy sight: and consider that this nation *is* [c]thy people.

14 And he said, [a]My presence shall go *with thee*, and I will give thee [b]rest.

15 And he said unto him, [a]If thy presence go not *with me*, carry us not up hence.

16 For wherein shall it be known here that I and thy people have found grace in thy sight? [a]*is it* not in that thou goest with us? so [b]shall we be separated, I and thy people, from all the people that *are* upon the face of the earth.

17 And the LORD said unto Moses, [a]I will do this thing also that thou hast spoken: for thou hast found grace in my sight, and I know thee by name.

18 And he said, I beseech thee, shew me [a]thy glory.

19 And he said, I will make all my [a]goodness pass before thee, and I will proclaim the name of the LORD before thee; [b]and will be gracious to whom I will be [c]gracious, and will shew mercy on whom I will shew mercy.

20 And he said, Thou canst not see my face: for [a]there shall no man see me, and live.

---

1 [b]Gen. 12:7
2 [a]Ex. 32:34; Josh. 5:14 [b]Ex. 23:27–31; Josh. 24:11
3 [a]Ex. 3:8 [b]Num. 16:21, 45 [c]Ex. 32:9; 33:5
4 [a]Num. 14:1, 39 [b]Ezra 9:3; Esth. 4:1, 4; Ezek. 24:17, 23
5 [a][Ps. 139:23]
7 [a]Ex. 29:42, 43 [b]Deut. 4:29
8 [a]Num. 16:27
9 [a]Ex. 25:22; 31:18; Ps. 99:7
10 [a]Ex. 4:31
11 [a]Num. 12:8; Deut. 34:10 [b]Ex. 24:13
12 [a]Ex. 3:10; 32:34 [b]Ex. 33:17; John 10:14, 15; 2 Tim. 2:19
13 [a]Ex. 34:9 [b]Ps. 25:4; 27:11; 86:11; 119:33 [c]Ex. 3:7, 10; 5:1; 32:12, 14; Deut. 9:26, 29
14 [a]Ex. 3:12; Deut. 4:37; Is. 63:9 [b]Deut. 12:10; 25:19; Josh. 21:44; 22:4
15 [a]Ex. 33:3
16 [a]Num. 14:14 [b]Ex. 34:10; Deut. 4:7, 34
17 [a][James 5:16]
18 [a]Ex. 24:16, 17; [1 Tim. 6:16]
19 [a]Ex. 34:6, 7 [b][Rom. 9:15, 16, 18] [c][Rom. 4:4, 16]
20 [a][Gen. 32:30]

NKJV

you have brought out of the land of Egypt, to the land of which I swore to Abraham, Isaac, and Jacob, saying, [b]'To your descendants I will give it.'

2 [a]"And I will send *My* Angel before you, [b]and I will drive out the Canaanite and the Amorite and the Hittite and the Perizzite and the Hivite and the Jebusite.

3 "*Go up* [a]to a land flowing with milk and honey; for I will not go up in your midst, lest [b]I consume you on the way, for you *are* a [c]stiff-necked people."

4 And when the people heard this bad news, [a]they mourned, [b]and no one put on his ornaments.

5 For the LORD had said to Moses, "Say to the children of Israel, 'You *are* a stiff-necked people. I could come up into your midst in one moment and consume you. Now therefore, take off your ornaments, that I may [a]know what to do to you.' "

6 So the children of Israel stripped themselves of their ornaments by Mount Horeb.

Moses Meets with the LORD

7 Moses took his tent and pitched it outside the camp, far from the camp, and [a]called it the tabernacle of meeting. And it came to pass *that* everyone who [b]sought the LORD went out to the tabernacle of meeting which *was* outside the camp.

8 So it was, whenever Moses went out to the tabernacle, *that* all the people rose, and each man stood [a]*at* his tent door and watched Moses until he had gone into the tabernacle.

9 And it came to pass, when Moses entered the tabernacle, that the pillar of cloud descended and stood *at* the door of the tabernacle, and *the LORD* [a]talked with Moses.

10 All the people saw the pillar of cloud standing *at* the tabernacle door, and all the people rose and [a]worshiped, each man *in* his tent door.

11 So [a]the LORD spoke to Moses face to face, as a man speaks to his friend. And he would return to the camp, but [b]his servant Joshua the son of Nun, a young man, did not depart from the tabernacle.

The Promise of God's Presence

12 Then Moses said to the LORD, "See, [a]You say to me, 'Bring up this people.' But You have not let me know whom You will send with me. Yet You have said, [b]'I know you by name, and you have also found grace in My sight.'

13 "Now therefore, I pray, [a]if I have found grace in Your sight, [b]show me now Your way, that I may know You and that I may find grace in Your sight. And consider that this nation *is* [c]Your people."

14 And He said, [a]"My Presence will go *with you*, and I will give you [b]rest."

15 Then he said to Him, [a]"If Your Presence does not go *with us*, do not bring us up from here.

16 "For how then will it be known that Your people and I have found grace in Your sight, [a]except You go with us? So we [b]shall be separate, Your people and I, from all the people who *are* upon the face of the earth."

17 So the LORD said to Moses, [a]"I will also do this thing that you have spoken; for you have found grace in My sight, and I know you by name."

18 And he said, "Please, show me [a]Your glory."

19 Then He said, "I will make all My [a]goodness pass before you, and I will proclaim the name of the LORD before you. [b]I will be gracious to whom I will be [c]gracious, and I will have compassion on whom I will have compassion."

20 But He said, "You cannot see My face; for [a]no man shall see Me, and live."

KJV

21 And the LORD said, Behold, *there is* a place
by me, and thou shalt stand upon a rock:
22 And it shall come to pass, while my glory
passeth by, that I will put thee [a]in a clift of the
rock, and will [b]cover thee with my hand while I
pass by:
23 And I will take away mine hand, and thou
shalt see my back parts: but my face shall [a]not
be seen.

Moses Makes New Tablets
(Deut. 10:1–5)

34 And the LORD said unto Moses, [a]Hew thee
two tables of stone like unto the first: and
[b]I will write upon *these* tables the words that were
in the first tables, which thou brakest.
2 And be ready in the morning, and come
up in the morning unto mount Sinai, and present
thyself there to me [a]in the top of the mount.
3 And no man shall [a]come up with thee, neither let any man be seen throughout all the mount;
neither let the flocks nor herds feed before that
mount.
4 And he hewed two tables of stone like
unto the first; and Moses rose up early in the
morning, and went up unto mount Sinai, as the
LORD had commanded him, and took in his hand
the two tables of stone.
5 And the LORD descended in the [a]cloud,
and stood with him there, and [b]proclaimed the
name of the LORD.
6 And the LORD passed by before him, and
proclaimed, The LORD, The LORD [a]God, merciful
and gracious, longsuffering, and abundant in
[b]goodness and [c]truth,
7 [a]Keeping mercy for thousands, [b]forgiving
iniquity and transgression and sin, and [c]that will
by no means clear *the guilty;* visiting the iniquity
of the fathers upon the children, and upon the
children's children, unto the third and to the
fourth *generation.*
8 And Moses made haste, and [a]bowed his
head toward the earth, and worshipped.
9 And he said, If now I have found grace
in thy sight, O Lord, [a]let my Lord, I pray thee,
go among us; for it *is* a [b]stiffnecked people; and
pardon our iniquity and our sin, and take us for
[c]thine inheritance.

The Covenant Renewed
(Ex. 23:14–19; Deut. 7:1–6; 16:1–17)

10 And he said, Behold, [a]I make a covenant:
before all thy people I will [b]do marvels, such as
have not been done in all the earth, nor in any
nation: and all the people among which thou *art*
shall see the work of the LORD: for it *is* [c]a terrible
thing that I will do with thee.
11 [a]Observe thou that which I command thee
this day: behold, [b]I drive out before thee the Amorite, and the Canaanite, and the Hittite, and the
Perizzite, and the Hivite, and the Jebusite.
12 [a]Take heed to thyself, lest thou make a
covenant with the inhabitants of the land whither
thou goest, lest it be for a snare in the midst of
thee:
13 But ye shall [a]destroy their altars, break
their images, and [b]cut down their groves:
14 For thou shalt worship [a]no other god: for
the LORD, whose [b]name *is* Jealous, *is* a [c]jealous
God:
15 Lest thou make a covenant with the inhabitants of the land, and they [a]go a whoring after
their gods, and do sacrifice unto their gods, and
one [b]call thee, and thou [c]eat of his sacrifice;
16 And thou take of [a]their daughters unto thy
sons, and their daughters [b]go a whoring after
their gods, and make thy sons go a whoring after
their gods.
17 [a]Thou shalt make thee no molten gods.
18 The feast of [a]unleavened bread shalt thou
keep. Seven days thou shalt eat unleavened bread,

22 [a]Song 2:14; Is. 2:21 [b]Ps. 91:1, 4; Is. 49:2; 51:16
23 [a]Ex. 33:20; [John 1:18]

CHAPTER 34

1 [a][Ex. 24:12; 31:18; 32:15, 16, 19; Deut. 4:13] [b]Deut. 10:2, 4
2 [a]Ex. 19:11, 18, 20
3 [a]Ex. 19:12, 13; 24:9–11
5 [a]Ex. 19:9 [b]Ex. 33:19
6 [a]Num. 14:18; Deut. 4:31; Neh. 9:17; Joel 2:13 [b]Rom. 2:4 [c]Ps. 108:4
7 [a]Ex. 20:6 [b]Ps. 103:3, 4; Dan. 9:9; Eph. 4:32; 1 John 1:9 [c]Josh. 24:19; Job 10:14; Mic. 6:11; Nah. 1:3
8 [a]Ex. 4:31
9 [a]Ex. 33:12–16 [b]Ex. 33:3 [c]Ps. 33:12; 94:14
10 [a]Ex. 34:27, 28; Deut. 5:2 [b]Deut. 4:32; Ps. 77:14 [c]Ps. 145:6
11 [a]Deut. 6:25 [b]Ex. 23:20–33; 33:2; Josh. 11:23
12 [a]Ex. 23:32, 33
13 [a]Ex. 23:24; Deut. 12:3 [b]Deut. 16:21; Judg. 6:25, 26; 2 Kin. 18:4; 2 Chr. 34:3, 4
14 [a][Ex. 20:3–5] [b][Is. 9:6; 57:15] [c][Ex. 20:5; Deut. 4:24]
15 [a]Judg. 2:17 [b]Num. 25:1, 2; Deut. 32:37, 38 [c]1 Cor. 8:4, 7, 10
16 [a]Gen. 28:1; Deut. 7:3; Josh. 23:12, 13; 1 Kin. 11:2; Ezra 9:2; Neh. 13:25 [b]Num. 25:1, 2; 1 Kin. 11:4
17 [a]Ex. 20:4, 23; 32:8; Lev. 19:4; Deut. 5:8
18 [a]Ex. 12:15, 16

NKJV

21 And the LORD said, "Here is a place by
Me, and you shall stand on the rock.
22 "So it shall be, while My glory passes by,
that I will put you [a]in the cleft of the rock, and
will [b]cover you with My hand while I pass by.
23 "Then I will take away My hand, and you
shall see My back; but My face shall [a]not be
seen."

Moses Makes New Tablets
(Deut. 10:1–5)

34 And the LORD said to Moses, [a]"Cut two
tablets of stone like the first *ones,* and [b]I
will write on *these* tablets the words that were
on the first tablets which you broke.
2 "So be ready in the morning, and come
up in the morning to Mount Sinai, and present
yourself to Me there [a]on the top of the mountain.
3 "And no man shall [a]come up with you,
and let no man be seen throughout all the mountain; let neither flocks nor herds feed before that
mountain."
4 So he cut two tablets of stone like the first
ones. Then Moses rose early in the morning and
went up Mount Sinai, as the LORD had commanded him; and he took in his hand the two
tablets of stone.
5 Now the LORD descended in the [a]cloud
and stood with him there, and [b]proclaimed the
name of the LORD.
6 And the LORD passed before him and proclaimed, "The LORD, the LORD [a]God, merciful and
gracious, longsuffering, and abounding in [b]good-
ness and [c]truth,
7 [a]"keeping mercy for thousands, [b]forgiv-
ing iniquity and transgression and sin, [c]by no
means clearing *the guilty,* visiting the iniquity of
the fathers upon the children and the children's
children to the third and the fourth generation."
8 So Moses made haste and [a]bowed his
head toward the earth, and worshiped.
9 Then he said, "If now I have found grace
in Your sight, O Lord, [a]let my Lord, I pray, go
among us, even though we *are* a [b]stiff-necked people; and pardon our iniquity and our sin, and take
us as [c]Your inheritance."

The Covenant Renewed
(Ex. 23:14–19; Deut. 7:1–6; 16:1–17)

10 And He said: "Behold, [a]I make a covenant. Before all your people I will [b]do marvels
such as have not been done in all the earth, nor
in any nation; and all the people among whom
you *are* shall see the work of the LORD. For it *is*
[c]an awesome thing that I will do with you.
11 [a]"Observe what I command you this day.
Behold, [b]I am driving out from before you the
Amorite and the Canaanite and the Hittite and
the Perizzite and the Hivite and the Jebusite.
12 [a]"Take heed to yourself, lest you make a
covenant with the inhabitants of the land where
you are going, lest it be a snare in your midst.
13 "But you shall [a]destroy their altars, break
their *sacred* pillars, and [b]cut down their wooden
images
14 "(for you shall worship [a]no other god, for
the LORD, whose [b]name *is* Jealous, *is* a [c]jealous
God),
15 "lest you make a covenant with the inhabitants of the land, and they [a]play the harlot with
their gods and make sacrifice to their gods, and
one of them [b]invites you and you [c]eat of his
sacrifice,
16 "and you take of [a]his daughters for your
sons, and his daughters [b]play the harlot with their
gods and make your sons play the harlot with
their gods.
17 [a]"You shall make no molded gods for
yourselves.
18 "The Feast of [a]Unleavened Bread you
shall keep. Seven days you shall eat unleavened

KJV

as I commanded thee, in the time of the [b]month Abib: for in the month Abib thou camest out from Egypt.

19 [a]All that openeth the matrix *is* mine; and every firstling among thy cattle, *whether* ox or sheep, *that is male*.

20 But [a]the firstling of an ass thou shalt redeem with a lamb: and if thou redeem *him* not, then shalt thou break his neck. All the firstborn of thy sons thou shalt redeem. And none shall appear before me [b]empty.

21 [a]Six days thou shalt work, but on the seventh day thou shalt rest: in earing time and in harvest thou shalt rest.

22 And thou shalt observe the feast of weeks, of the firstfruits of wheat harvest, and the feast of ingathering at the year's end.

23 [a]Thrice in the year shall all your men children appear before the Lord GOD, the God of Israel.

24 For I will [a]cast out the nations before thee, and enlarge thy borders: neither shall any man desire thy land, when thou shalt go up to appear before the LORD thy God thrice in the year.

25 Thou shalt not offer the blood of my sacrifice with leaven; [a]neither shall the sacrifice of the feast of the passover be left unto the morning.

26 [a]The first of the firstfruits of thy land thou shalt bring unto the house of the LORD thy God. Thou shalt not seethe a kid in his mother's milk.

27 And the LORD said unto Moses, Write thou [a]these words: for after the tenor of these words I have made a covenant with thee and with Israel.

28 [a]And he was there with the LORD forty days and forty nights; he did neither eat bread, nor drink water. And [b]he wrote upon the tables the words of the covenant, the ten commandments.

The Shining Face of Moses

29 And it came to pass, when Moses came down from mount Sinai with the [a]two tables of testimony in Moses' hand, when he came down from the mount, that Moses wist not that [b]the skin of his face shone while he talked with him.

30 And when Aaron and all the children of Israel saw Moses, behold, the skin of his face shone; and they were afraid to come nigh him.

31 And Moses called unto them; and Aaron and all the rulers of the congregation returned unto him: and Moses talked with them.

32 And afterward all the children of Israel came nigh: [a]and he gave them in commandment all that the LORD had spoken with him in mount Sinai.

33 And *till* Moses had done speaking with them, he put [a]a vail on his face.

34 But [a]when Moses went in before the LORD to speak with him, he took the vail off, until he came out. And he came out, and spake unto the children of Israel *that* which he was commanded.

35 And the children of Israel saw the face of Moses, that the skin of Moses' face shone: and Moses put the vail upon his face again, until he went in to speak with him.

Sabbath Regulations

35 And Moses gathered all the congregation of the children of Israel together, and said unto them, [a]These *are* the words which the LORD hath commanded, that *ye* should do them.

2 [a]Six days shall work be done, but on the seventh day there shall be to you an holy day, a sabbath of rest to the LORD: whosoever doeth work therein shall be put to [b]death.

3 [a]Ye shall kindle no fire throughout your habitations upon the sabbath day.

---

18 [b]Ex. 12:2; 13:4
19 [a]Ex. 13:2; 22:29
20 [a]Ex. 13:13 [b]Ex. 22:29; 23:15; Deut. 16:16
21 [a]Ex. 20:9; 23:12; 31:15; 35:2; Lev. 23:3; Deut. 5:13
23 [a]Ex. 23:14–17
24 [a][Ex. 33:2]; Josh. 11:23; 1 Kin. 4:21; 2 Chr. 36:14–16; Ps. 78:55
25 [a]Ex. 12:10
26 [a]Ex. 23:19; Deut. 26:2
27 [a]Ex. 17:14; 24:4; Deut. 31:9
28 [a]Ex. 24:18 [b]Ex. 34:1, 4; Deut. 4:31; 10:2, 4
29 [a]Ex. 32:15 [b]Matt. 17:2; 2 Cor. 3:7
32 [a]Ex. 24:3
33 [a][2 Cor. 3:13, 14]
34 [a][2 Cor. 3:13–16]

CHAPTER 35

1 [a]Ex. 34:32
2 [a]Ex. 20:9, 10; Lev. 23:3; Deut. 5:13 [b]Num. 15:32–36
3 [a]Ex. 12:16; 16:23

*

34:28 Lit. *Ten Words*

NKJV

bread, as I commanded you, in the appointed time of the month of Abib; for in the [b]month of Abib you came out from Egypt.

19 [a]"All that open the womb *are* Mine, and every male firstborn among your livestock, *whether* ox or sheep.

20 "But [a]the firstborn of a donkey you shall redeem with a lamb. And if you will not redeem *him,* then you shall break his neck. All the firstborn of your sons you shall redeem. And none shall appear before Me [b]empty-handed.

21 [a]"Six days you shall work, but on the seventh day you shall rest; in plowing time and in harvest you shall rest.

22 "And you shall observe the Feast of Weeks, of the firstfruits of wheat harvest, and the Feast of Ingathering at the year's end.

23 [a]"Three times in the year all your men shall appear before the Lord, the LORD God of Israel.

24 "For I will [a]cast out the nations before you and enlarge your borders; neither will any man covet your land when you go up to appear before the LORD your God three times in the year.

25 "You shall not offer the blood of My sacrifice with leaven, [a]nor shall the sacrifice of the Feast of the Passover be left until morning.

26 [a]"The first of the firstfruits of your land you shall bring to the house of the LORD your God. You shall not boil a young goat in its mother's milk."

27 Then the LORD said to Moses, "Write [a]these words, for according to the tenor of these words I have made a covenant with you and with Israel."

28 [a]So he was there with the LORD forty days and forty nights; he neither ate bread nor drank water. And [b]He wrote on the tablets the words of the covenant, the *Ten Commandments.

The Shining Face of Moses

29 Now it was so, when Moses came down from Mount Sinai (and the [a]two tablets of the Testimony *were* in Moses' hand when he came down from the mountain), that Moses did not know that [b]the skin of his face shone while he talked with Him.

30 So when Aaron and all the children of Israel saw Moses, behold, the skin of his face shone, and they were afraid to come near him.

31 Then Moses called to them, and Aaron and all the rulers of the congregation returned to him; and Moses talked with them.

32 Afterward all the children of Israel came near, [a]and he gave them as commandments all that the LORD had spoken with him on Mount Sinai.

33 And when Moses had finished speaking with them, he put [a]a veil on his face.

34 But [a]whenever Moses went in before the LORD to speak with Him, he would take the veil off until he came out; and he would come out and speak to the children of Israel whatever he had been commanded.

35 And whenever the children of Israel saw the face of Moses, that the skin of Moses' face shone, then Moses would put the veil on his face again, until he went in to speak with Him.

Sabbath Regulations

35 Then Moses gathered all the congregation of the children of Israel together, and said to them, [a]"These *are* the words which the LORD has commanded *you* to do:

2 "Work shall be done for [a]six days, but the seventh day shall be a holy day for you, a Sabbath of rest to the LORD. Whoever does any work on it shall be put to [b]death.

3 [a]"You shall kindle no fire throughout your dwellings on the Sabbath day."

KJV

Offerings for the Tabernacle
(Ex. 25:1–9; 39:32–43)

4 And Moses spake unto all the congregation of the children of Israel, saying, [a]This *is* the thing which the LORD commanded, saying,

5 Take ye from among you an offering unto the LORD: [a]whosoever *is* of a willing heart, let him bring it, an offering of the LORD; [b]gold, and silver, and brass,

6 And [a]blue, and purple, and scarlet, and fine linen, and [b]goats' *hair,*

7 And rams' skins dyed red, and badgers' skins, and shittim wood,

8 And oil for the light, [a]and spices for anointing oil, and for the sweet incense,

9 And onyx stones, and stones to be set for the ephod, and for the breastplate.

Articles of the Tabernacle

10 And [a]every wise hearted among you shall come, and make all that the LORD hath commanded;

11 [a]The tabernacle, his tent, and his covering, his taches, and his boards, his bars, his pillars, and his sockets,

12 [a]The ark, and the staves thereof, *with* the mercy seat, and the vail of the covering,

13 The [a]table, and his staves, and all his vessels, [b]and the shewbread,

14 [a]The candlestick also for the light, and his furniture, and his lamps, with the oil for the light,

15 [a]And the incense altar, and his staves, [b]and the anointing oil, and [c]the sweet incense, and the hanging for the door at the entering in of the tabernacle,

16 [a]The altar of burnt offering, with his brasen grate, his staves, and all his vessels, the laver and his foot,

17 [a]The hangings of the court, his pillars, and their sockets, and the hanging for the door of the court,

18 The pins of the tabernacle, and the pins of the court, and their cords,

19 [a]The cloths of service, to do service in the holy *place,* the holy garments for Aaron the priest, and the garments of his sons, to minister in the priest's office.

The Tabernacle Offerings Presented

20 And all the congregation of the children of Israel departed from the presence of Moses.

21 And they came, every one [a]whose heart stirred him up, and every one whom his spirit made willing, *and* they [b]brought the LORD's offering to the work of the tabernacle of the congregation, and for all his service, and for the holy garments.

22 And they came, both men and women, as many as were willing hearted, *and* brought bracelets, and [a]earrings, and rings, and tablets, all [b]jewels of gold: and every man that offered *offered* an offering of gold unto the LORD.

23 And [a]every man, with whom was found blue, and purple, and scarlet, and fine linen, and goats' *hair,* and red skins of rams, and badgers' skins, brought *them.*

24 Every one that did offer an offering of silver and brass brought the LORD's offering: and every man, with whom was found shittim wood for any work of the service, brought *it.*

25 And all the women that were [a]wise hearted did spin with their hands, and brought that which they had spun, *both* of blue, and of purple, *and* of scarlet, and of fine linen.

26 And all the women whose heart stirred them up in wisdom spun goats' *hair.*

27 And [a]the rulers brought onyx stones, and stones to be set, for the ephod, and for the breastplate;

28 And [a]spice, and oil for the light, and for the anointing oil, and for the sweet incense.

4 [a]Ex. 25:1, 2
5 [a]Ex. 25:2; 1 Chr. 29:14; Mark 12:41–44; 2 Cor. 8:10–12; 9:7 [b]Ex. 38:24
6 [a]Ex. 36:8 [b]Ex. 36:14
8 [a]Ex. 25:6; 30:23–25
10 [a]Ex. 31:2–6; 36:1, 2
11 [a]Ex. 26:1, 2; 36:14
12 [a]Ex. 25:10–22
13 [a]Ex. 25:23 [b]Ex. 25:30; Lev. 24:5, 6
14 [a]Ex. 25:31
15 [a]Ex. 30:1 [b]Ex. 30:25 [c]Ex. 30:34–38
16 [a]Ex. 27:1–8
17 [a]Ex. 27:9–18
19 [a]Ex. 31:10; 39:1, 41
21 [a]Ex. 25:2; 35:5, 22, 26, 29; 36:2 [b]Ex. 35:24
22 [a]Ex. 32:2, 3 [b]Ex. 11:2
23 [a]1 Chr. 29:8
25 [a]Ex. 28:3; 31:6; 36:1
27 [a]1 Chr. 29:6; Ezra 2:68
28 [a]Ex. 30:23

NKJV

Offerings for the Tabernacle
(Ex. 25:1–9; 39:32–43)

4 And Moses spoke to all the congregation of the children of Israel, saying, [a]"This *is* the thing which the LORD commanded, saying:

5 'Take from among you an offering to the LORD. [a]Whoever *is* of a willing heart, let him bring it as an offering to the LORD: [b]gold, silver, and bronze;

6 [a]'blue, purple, and scarlet *thread,* fine linen, and [b]goats' *hair;*

7 'ram skins dyed red, badger skins, and acacia wood;

8 'oil for the light, [a]and spices for the anointing oil and for the sweet incense;

9 'onyx stones, and stones to be set in the ephod and in the breastplate.

Articles of the Tabernacle

10 [a]'All *who are* gifted artisans among you shall come and make all that the LORD has commanded:

11 [a]'the tabernacle, its tent, its covering, its clasps, its boards, its bars, its pillars, and its sockets;

12 [a]'the ark and its poles, *with* the mercy seat, and the veil of the covering;

13 'the [a]table and its poles, all its utensils, [b]and the showbread;

14 'also [a]the lampstand for the light, its utensils, its lamps, and the oil for the light;

15 [a]'the incense altar, its poles, [b]the anointing oil, [c]the sweet incense, and the screen for the door at the entrance of the tabernacle;

16 [a]'the altar of burnt offering with its bronze grating, its poles, all its utensils, *and* the laver and its base;

17 [a]'the hangings of the court, its pillars, their sockets, and the screen for the gate of the court;

18 'the pegs of the tabernacle, the pegs of the court, and their cords;

19 [a]'the *garments of ministry, for ministering in the holy *place*—the holy garments for Aaron the priest and the garments of his sons, to minister as priests.' "

The Tabernacle Offerings Presented

20 And all the congregation of the children of Israel departed from the presence of Moses.

21 Then everyone came [a]whose heart was stirred, and everyone whose spirit was willing, *and* they [b]brought the LORD's offering for the work of the tabernacle of meeting, for all its service, and for the holy garments.

22 They came, both men and women, as many as had a willing heart, *and* brought [a]earrings and nose rings, rings and necklaces, all [b]jewelry of gold, that is, every man who *made* an offering of gold to the LORD.

23 And [a]every man, with whom was found blue, purple, and scarlet *thread,* fine linen, and goats' *hair,* red skins of rams, and badger skins, brought *them.*

24 Everyone who offered an offering of silver or bronze brought the LORD's offering. And everyone with whom was found acacia wood for any work of the service, brought *it.*

25 All the women *who were* [a]gifted artisans spun yarn with their hands, and brought what they had spun, of blue, purple, *and* scarlet, and fine linen.

26 And all the women whose hearts stirred with wisdom spun yarn of goats' *hair.*

27 [a]The rulers brought onyx stones, and the stones to be set in the ephod and in the breastplate,

28 and [a]spices and oil for the light, for the anointing oil, and for the sweet incense.

*———
35:19 Or *woven garments*

KJV

29 The children of Israel brought a [a]willing offering unto the LORD, every man and woman, whose heart made them willing to bring for all manner of work, which the LORD had commanded to be made by the hand of Moses.

The Artisans Called by God
(*Ex. 31:1–11*)

30 And Moses said unto the children of Israel, See, [a]the LORD hath called by name Bezaleel the son of Uri, the son of Hur, of the tribe of Judah;

31 And he hath filled him with the spirit of God, in wisdom, in understanding, and in knowledge, and in all manner of workmanship;

32 And to devise curious works, to work in gold, and in silver, and in brass,

33 And in the cutting of stones, to set *them*, and in carving of wood, to make any manner of cunning work.

34 And he hath put in his heart that he may teach, *both* he, and [a]Aholiab, the son of Ahisamach, of the tribe of Dan.

35 Them hath he [a]filled with wisdom of heart, to work all manner of work, of the engraver, and of the cunning workman, and of the embroiderer, in blue, and in purple, in scarlet, and in fine linen, and of the weaver, *even* of them that do any work, and of those that devise cunning work.

36 Then wrought Bezaleel and Aholiab, and every [a]wise hearted man, in whom the LORD put wisdom and understanding to know how to work all manner of work for the service of the [b]sanctuary, according to all that the LORD had commanded.

The People Give More than Enough

2 And Moses called Bezaleel and Aholiab, and every wise hearted man, in whose heart the LORD had put wisdom, *even* every one [a]whose heart stirred him up to come unto the work to do it:

3 And they received of Moses all the [a]offering, which the children of Israel [b]had brought for the work of the service of the sanctuary, to make it *withal*. And they brought yet unto him free offerings every morning.

4 And all the wise men, that wrought all the work of the sanctuary, came every man from his work which they made;

5 And they spake unto Moses, saying, [a]The people bring much more than enough for the service of the work, which the LORD commanded to make.

6 And Moses gave commandment, and they caused it to be proclaimed throughout the camp, saying, Let neither man nor woman make any more work for the offering of the sanctuary. So the people were restrained from bringing.

7 For the stuff they had was sufficient for all the work to make it, and too [a]much.

Building the Tabernacle
(*Ex. 26:1–37*)

8 [a]And every wise hearted man among them that wrought the work of the tabernacle made ten curtains *of* fine twined linen, and blue, and purple, and scarlet: *with* cherubims of cunning work made he them.

9 The length of one curtain *was* twenty and eight cubits, and the breadth of one curtain four cubits: the curtains *were* all of one size.

10 And he coupled the five curtains one unto another: and *the other* five curtains he coupled one unto another.

11 And he made loops of blue on the edge of one curtain from the selvedge in the coupling: likewise he made in the uttermost side of *another* curtain, in the coupling of the second.

12 [a]Fifty loops made he in one curtain, and

---

29 [a]Ex. 35:5, 21; 36:3; 1 Chr. 29:9
30 [a]Ex. 31:1–6
34 [a]Ex. 31:6
35 [a]Ex. 31:3, 6; 35:31; 1 Kin. 7:14; 2 Chr. 2:14; Is. 28:26

CHAPTER 36

1 [a]Ex. 28:3; 31:6; 35:10, 35 [b]Ex. 25:8
2 [a]Ex. 35:21, 26; 1 Chr. 29:5, 9, 17
3 [a]Ex. 35:5 [b]Ex. 35:27
5 [a]2 Chr. 24:14; 31:6–10; [2 Cor. 8:2, 3]
7 [a]1 Kin. 8:64
8 [a]Ex. 26:1–14
12 [a]Ex. 26:5

NKJV

29 The children of Israel brought a [a]freewill offering to the LORD, all the men and women whose hearts were willing to bring *material* for all kinds of work which the LORD, by the hand of Moses, had commanded to be done.

The Artisans Called by God
(*Ex. 31:1–11*)

30 And Moses said to the children of Israel, "See, [a]the LORD has called by name Bezalel the son of Uri, the son of Hur, of the tribe of Judah;

31 "and He has filled him with the Spirit of God, in wisdom and understanding, in knowledge and all manner of workmanship,

32 "to design artistic works, to work in gold and silver and bronze,

33 "in cutting jewels for setting, in carving wood, and to work in all manner of artistic workmanship.

34 "And He has put in his heart the ability to teach, *in* him and [a]Aholiab the son of Ahisamach, of the tribe of Dan.

35 "He has [a]filled them with skill to do all manner of work of the engraver and the designer and the tapestry maker, in blue, purple, and scarlet *thread*, and fine linen, and of the weaver—those who do every work and those who design artistic works.

36 "And Bezalel and Aholiab, and every [a]gifted artisan in whom the LORD has put wisdom and understanding, to know how to do all manner of work for the service of the [b]sanctuary, shall do according to all that the LORD has commanded."

The People Give More than Enough

2 Then Moses called Bezalel and Aholiab, and every gifted artisan in whose heart the LORD had put wisdom, everyone [a]whose heart was stirred, to come and do the work.

3 And they received from Moses all the [a]offering which the children of Israel [b]had brought for the work of the service of making the sanctuary. So they continued bringing to him freewill offerings every morning.

4 Then all the craftsmen who were doing all the work of the sanctuary came, each from the work he was doing,

5 and they spoke to Moses, saying, [a]"The people bring much more than enough for the service of the work which the LORD commanded *us* to do."

6 So Moses gave a commandment, and they caused it to be proclaimed throughout the camp, saying, "Let neither man nor woman do any more work for the offering of the sanctuary." And the people were restrained from bringing,

7 for the material they had was sufficient for all the work to be done—indeed too [a]much.

Building the Tabernacle
(*Ex. 26:1–37*)

8 [a]Then all the gifted artisans among them who worked on the tabernacle made ten curtains woven of fine linen, and of blue, purple, and scarlet *thread; with* artistic designs of cherubim they made them.

9 The length of each curtain *was* twenty-eight cubits, and the width of each curtain four cubits; the curtains *were* all the same size.

10 And he coupled five curtains to one another, and *the other* five curtains he coupled to one another.

11 He made loops of blue *yarn* on the edge of the curtain on the selvedge of one set; likewise he did on the outer edge of *the other* curtain of the second set.

12 [a]Fifty loops he made on one curtain, and

KJV

fifty loops made he in the edge of the curtain which *was* in the coupling of the second: the loops held one *curtain* to another.

13 And he made fifty taches of gold, and coupled the curtains one unto another with the taches: so it became one tabernacle.

14 [a]And he made curtains *of* goats' *hair* for the tent over the tabernacle: eleven curtains he made them.

15 The length of one curtain *was* thirty cubits, and four cubits *was* the breadth of one curtain: the eleven curtains *were* of one size.

16 And he coupled five curtains by themselves, and six curtains by themselves.

17 And he made fifty loops upon the uttermost edge of the curtain in the coupling, and fifty loops made he upon the edge of the curtain which coupleth the second.

18 And he made fifty taches *of* brass to couple the tent together, that it might be one.

19 [a]And he made a covering for the tent *of* rams' skins dyed red, and a covering *of* badgers' skins above *that*.

20 [a]And he made boards for the tabernacle *of* shittim wood, standing up.

21 The length of a board *was* ten cubits, and the breadth of a board one cubit and a half.

22 One board had two tenons, [a]equally distant one from another: thus did he make for all the boards of the tabernacle.

23 And he made boards for the tabernacle; twenty boards for the south side southward:

24 And forty sockets of silver he made under the twenty boards; two sockets under one board for his two tenons, and two sockets under another board for his two tenons.

25 And for the other side of the tabernacle, *which is* toward the north corner, he made twenty boards,

26 And their forty sockets of silver; two sockets under one board, and two sockets under another board.

27 And for the sides of the tabernacle westward he made six boards.

28 And two boards made he for the corners of the tabernacle in the two sides.

29 And they were coupled beneath, and coupled together at the head thereof, to one ring: thus he did to both of them in both the corners.

30 And there were eight boards; and their sockets *were* sixteen sockets of silver, under every board two sockets.

31 And he made [a]bars of shittim wood; five for the boards of the one side of the tabernacle,

32 And five bars for the boards of the other side of the tabernacle, and five bars for the boards of the tabernacle for the sides westward.

33 And he made the middle bar to shoot through the boards from the one end to the other.

34 And he overlaid the boards with gold, and made their rings *of* gold *to be* places for the bars, and overlaid the bars with gold.

35 And he made [a]a vail *of* blue, and purple, and scarlet, and fine twined linen: *with* cherubims made he it of cunning work.

36 And he made thereunto four pillars *of* shittim *wood*, and overlaid them with gold: their hooks *were of* gold; and he cast for them four sockets of silver.

37 And he made an [a]hanging for the tabernacle door *of* blue, and purple, and scarlet, and fine twined linen, of needlework;

38 And the five pillars of it with their hooks: and he overlaid their chapiters and their fillets with gold: but their five sockets *were of* brass.

Making the Ark of the Testimony
(Ex. 25:10–22)

37 And [a]Bezaleel made [b]the ark *of* shittim wood: two cubits and a half *was* the length of it, and a cubit and a half the breadth of it, and a cubit and a half the height of it:

14 [a]Ex. 26:7
19 [a]Ex. 26:14
20 [a]Ex. 26:15–29
22 [a]Ex. 26:17
31 [a]Ex. 26:26–29
35 [a]Ex. 26:31–37
37 [a]Ex. 26:36

CHAPTER 37
1 [a]Ex. 35:30; 36:1 [b]Ex. 25:10–20

NKJV

fifty loops he made on the edge of the curtain on the end of the second set; the loops held one *curtain* to another.

13 And he made fifty clasps of gold, and coupled the curtains to one another with the clasps, that it might be one tabernacle.

14 [a]He made curtains of goats' *hair* for the tent over the tabernacle; he made eleven curtains.

15 The length of each curtain *was* thirty cubits, and the width of each curtain four cubits; the eleven curtains *were* the same size.

16 He coupled five curtains by themselves and six curtains by themselves.

17 And he made fifty loops on the edge of the curtain that is outermost in one set, and fifty loops he made on the edge of the curtain of the second set.

18 He also made fifty bronze clasps to couple the tent together, that it might be one.

19 [a]Then he made a covering for the tent of ram skins dyed red, and a covering of badger skins above *that*.

20 For the tabernacle [a]he made boards of acacia wood, standing upright.

21 The length of each board *was* ten cubits, and the width of each board a cubit and a half.

22 Each board had two tenons [a]for binding one to another. Thus he made for all the boards of the tabernacle.

23 And he made boards for the tabernacle, twenty boards for the south side.

24 Forty sockets of silver he made to go under the twenty boards: two sockets under each of the boards for its two tenons.

25 And for the other side of the tabernacle, the north side, he made twenty boards

26 and their forty sockets of silver: two sockets under each of the boards.

27 For the west side of the tabernacle he made six boards.

28 He also made two boards for the two back corners of the tabernacle.

29 And they were coupled at the bottom and coupled together at the top by one ring. Thus he made both of them for the two corners.

30 So there were eight boards and their sockets—sixteen sockets of silver—two sockets under each of the boards.

31 And he made [a]bars of acacia wood: five for the boards on one side of the tabernacle,

32 five bars for the boards on the other side of the tabernacle, and five bars for the boards of the tabernacle on the far side westward.

33 And he made the middle bar to pass through the boards from one end to the other.

34 He overlaid the boards with gold, made their rings of gold *to be* holders for the bars, and overlaid the bars with gold.

35 And he made [a]a veil of blue, purple, and scarlet *thread,* and fine woven linen; it was worked *with* an artistic design of cherubim.

36 He made for it four pillars of acacia *wood,* and overlaid them with gold, with their hooks of gold; and he cast four sockets of silver for them.

37 He also made a [a]screen for the tabernacle door, of blue, purple, and scarlet *thread,* and fine woven linen, made by a weaver,

38 and its five pillars with their hooks. And he overlaid their capitals and their rings with gold, but their five sockets *were* bronze.

Making the Ark of the Testimony
(Ex. 25:10–22)

37 Then [a]Bezalel made [b]the ark of acacia wood; two and a half cubits *was* its length, a cubit and a half its width, and a cubit and a half its height.

KJV

2 And he overlaid it with pure gold within and without, and made a crown of gold to it round about.

3 And he cast for it four rings of gold, *to be set* by the four corners of it; even two rings upon the one side of it, and two rings upon the other side of it.

4 And he made staves *of* shittim wood, and overlaid them with gold.

5 And he put the staves into the rings by the sides of the ark, to bear the ark.

6 And he made the [a]mercy seat *of* pure gold: two cubits and a half *was* the length thereof, and one cubit and a half the breadth thereof.

7 And he made two cherubims *of* gold, beaten out of one piece made he them, on the two ends of the mercy seat;

8 One cherub on the end on this side, and another cherub on the *other* end on that side: out of the mercy seat made he the cherubims on the two ends thereof.

9 [a]And the cherubims spread out *their* wings on high, *and* covered with their wings over the mercy seat, with their faces one to another; *even* to the mercy seatward were the faces of the cherubims.

Making the Table for the Showbread
(Ex. 25:23–30)

10 And he made [a]the table *of* shittim wood: two cubits *was* the length thereof, and a cubit the breadth thereof, and a cubit and a half the height thereof:

11 And he overlaid it with pure gold, and made thereunto a crown of gold round about.

12 Also he made thereunto a border of an handbreadth round about; and made a crown of gold for the border thereof round about.

13 And he cast for it four rings of gold, and put the rings upon the four corners that *were* in the four feet thereof.

14 Over against the border were the rings, the places for the staves to bear the table.

15 And he made the staves *of* shittim wood, and overlaid them with gold, to bear the table.

16 And he made the vessels which *were* upon the table, his [a]dishes, and his spoons, and his bowls, and his covers to cover withal, *of* pure gold.

Making the Gold Lampstand
(Ex. 25:31–40)

17 And he made the [a]candlestick *of* pure gold: *of* beaten work made he the candlestick; his shaft, and his branch, his bowls, his knops, and his flowers, were of the same:

18 And six branches going out of the sides thereof; three branches of the candlestick out of the one side thereof, and three branches of the candlestick out of the other side thereof:

19 Three bowls made after the fashion of almonds in one branch, a knop and a flower; and three bowls made like almonds in another branch, a knop and a flower: so throughout the six branches going out of the candlestick.

20 And in the candlestick *were* four bowls made like almonds, his knops, and his flowers:

21 And a knop under two branches of the same, and a knop under two branches of the same, and a knop under two branches of the same, according to the six branches going out of it.

22 Their knops and their branches were of the same: all of it *was* one beaten work *of* pure gold.

23 And he made his seven lamps, and his [a]snuffers, and his snuffdishes, *of* pure gold.

24 *Of* a talent of pure gold made he it, and all the vessels thereof.

Making the Altar of Incense
(Ex. 30:1–5)

25 [a]And he made the incense altar *of* shittim wood: the length of it *was* a cubit, and the breadth

6 [a]Ex. 25:17
9 [a]Ex. 25:20
10 [a]Ex. 25:23–29
16 [a]Ex. 25:29
17 [a]Ex. 25:31–39
23 [a]Num. 4:9
25 [a]Ex. 30:1–5

NKJV

2 He overlaid it with pure gold inside and outside, and made a molding of gold all around it.

3 And he cast for it four rings of gold *to be set* in its four corners: two rings on one side, and two rings on the other side of it.

4 He made poles of acacia wood, and overlaid them with gold.

5 And he put the poles into the rings at the sides of the ark, to bear the ark.

6 He also made the [a]mercy seat of pure gold; two and a half cubits *was* its length and a cubit and a half its width.

7 He made two cherubim of beaten gold; he made them of one piece at the two ends of the mercy seat:

8 one cherub at one end on this side, and the other cherub at the *other* end on that side. He made the cherubim at the two ends *of one piece* with the mercy seat.

9 The cherubim spread out *their* wings above, *and* covered the [a]mercy seat with their wings. They faced one another; the faces of the cherubim were toward the mercy seat.

Making the Table for the Showbread
(Ex. 25:23–30)

10 He made [a]the table of acacia wood; two cubits *was* its length, a cubit its width, and a cubit and a half its height.

11 And he overlaid it with pure gold, and made a molding of gold all around it.

12 Also he made a frame of a handbreadth all around it, and made a molding of gold for the frame all around it.

13 And he cast for it four rings of gold, and put the rings on the four corners that *were* at its four legs.

14 The rings were close to the frame, as holders for the poles to bear the table.

15 And he made the poles of acacia wood to bear the table, and overlaid them with gold.

16 He made of pure gold the utensils which were on the table: its [a]dishes, its cups, its bowls, and its pitchers for pouring.

Making the Gold Lampstand
(Ex. 25:31–40)

17 He also made the [a]lampstand of pure gold; of hammered work he made the lampstand. Its shaft, its branches, its bowls, its *ornamental* knobs, and its flowers were of the same piece.

18 And six branches came out of its sides: three branches of the lampstand out of one side, and three branches of the lampstand out of the other side.

19 There were three bowls made like almond *blossoms* on one branch, with an *ornamental* knob and a flower, and three bowls made like almond *blossoms* on the other branch, with an *ornamental* knob and a flower—and so for the six branches coming out of the lampstand.

20 And on the lampstand itself *were* four bowls made like almond *blossoms, each with* its *ornamental* knob and flower.

21 *There was* a knob under the *first* two branches of the same, a knob under the *second* two branches of the same, and a knob under the *third* two branches of the same, according to the six branches extending from it.

22 Their knobs and their branches were of one piece; all of it *was* one hammered piece of pure gold.

23 And he made its seven lamps, its [a]wick-trimmers, and its trays of pure gold.

24 Of a talent of pure gold he made it, with all its utensils.

Making the Altar of Incense
(Ex. 30:1–5)

25 [a]He made the incense altar of acacia wood. Its length *was* a cubit and its width a cu-

KJV

of it a cubit; *it was* foursquare; and two cubits *was* the height of it; the horns thereof were of the same.
26 And he overlaid it with pure gold, *both* the top of it, and the sides thereof round about, and the horns of it: also he made unto it a crown of gold round about.
27 And he made two rings of gold for it under the crown thereof, by the two corners of it, upon the two sides thereof, to be places for the staves to bear it withal.
28 And he [a]made the staves *of* shittim wood, and overlaid them with gold.

Making the Anointing Oil and the Incense
(Ex. 30:22–38)

29 And he made [a]the holy anointing oil, and the pure incense of sweet spices, according to the work of the apothecary.

Making the Altar of Burnt Offering
(Ex. 27:1–8)

38 And [a]he made the altar of burnt offering *of* shittim wood: five cubits *was* the length thereof, and five cubits the breadth thereof; *it was* foursquare; and three cubits the height thereof.
2 And he made the horns thereof on the four corners of it; the horns thereof were of the same: and he overlaid it with brass.
3 And he made all the vessels of the altar, the pots, and the shovels, and the basons, *and* the fleshhooks, and the firepans: all the vessels thereof made he *of* brass.
4 And he made for the altar a brasen grate of network under the compass thereof beneath unto the midst of it.
5 And he cast four rings for the four ends of the grate of brass, *to be* places for the staves.
6 And he made the staves *of* shittim wood, and overlaid them with brass.
7 And he put the staves into the rings on the sides of the altar, to bear it withal; he made the altar hollow with boards.

Making the Bronze Laver

8 And he made [a]the laver *of* brass, and the foot of it *of* brass, of the lookingglasses of *the women* assembling, which assembled *at* the door of the tabernacle of the congregation.

Making the Court of the Tabernacle
(Ex. 27:9–19)

9 And he made [a]the court: on the south side southward the hangings of the court *were of* fine twined linen, an hundred cubits:
10 Their pillars *were* twenty, and their brasen sockets twenty; the hooks of the pillars and their fillets *were of* silver.
11 And for the north side *the hangings were* an hundred cubits, their pillars *were* twenty, and their sockets of brass twenty; the hooks of the pillars and their fillets *of* silver.
12 And for the west side *were* hangings of fifty cubits, their pillars ten, and their sockets ten; the hooks of the pillars and their fillets *of* silver.
13 And for the east side eastward fifty cubits.
14 The hangings of the one side *of the gate were* fifteen cubits; their pillars three, and their sockets three.
15 And for the other side of the court gate, on this hand and that hand, *were* hangings of fifteen cubits; their pillars three, and their sockets three.
16 All the hangings of the court round about *were* of fine twined linen.
17 And the sockets for the pillars *were of* brass; the hooks of the pillars and their fillets *of* silver; and the overlaying of their chapiters *of* silver; and all the pillars of the court *were* filleted with silver.
18 And the hanging for the gate of the court *was* needlework, *of* blue, and purple, and scarlet,

28 [a]Ex. 30:5
29 [a]Ex. 30:23–25

CHAPTER 38
1 [a]Ex. 27:1–8
8 [a]Ex. 30:18
9 [a]Ex. 27:9–19

NKJV

bit—*it was* square—and two cubits *was* its height. Its horns were *of one piece* with it.
26 And he overlaid it with pure gold: its top, its sides all around, and its horns. He also made for it a molding of gold all around it.
27 He made two rings of gold for it under its molding, by its two corners on both sides, as holders for the poles with which to bear it.
28 And he [a]made the poles of acacia wood, and overlaid them with gold.

Making the Anointing Oil and the Incense
(Ex. 30:22–38)

29 He also made [a]the holy anointing oil and the pure incense of sweet spices, according to the work of the perfumer.

Making the Altar of Burnt Offering
(Ex. 27:1–8)

38 He made [a]the altar of burnt offering of acacia wood; five cubits *was* its length and five cubits its width—*it was* square—and its height *was* three cubits.
2 He made its horns on its four corners; the horns were *of one piece* with it. And he overlaid it with bronze.
3 He made all the utensils for the altar: the pans, the shovels, the basins, the forks, and the firepans; all its utensils he made of bronze.
4 And he made a grate of bronze network for the altar, under its rim, midway from the bottom.
5 He cast four rings for the four corners of the bronze grating, *as* holders for the poles.
6 And he made the poles of acacia wood, and overlaid them with bronze.
7 Then he put the poles into the rings on the sides of the altar, with which to bear it. He made the altar hollow with boards.

Making the Bronze Laver

8 He made [a]the laver of bronze and its base of bronze, from the bronze mirrors of the serving women who assembled at the door of the tabernacle of meeting.

Making the Court of the Tabernacle
(Ex. 27:9–19)

9 Then he made [a]the court on the south side; the hangings of the court *were of* fine woven linen, one hundred cubits long.
10 There *were* twenty pillars for them, with twenty bronze sockets. The hooks of the pillars and their bands *were* silver.
11 On the north side *the hangings were* one hundred cubits *long*, with twenty pillars and their twenty bronze sockets. The hooks of the pillars and their bands *were* silver.
12 And on the west side *there were* hangings of fifty cubits, with ten pillars and their ten sockets. The hooks of the pillars and their bands *were* silver.
13 For the east side *the hangings were* fifty cubits.
14 The hangings of one side *of the gate were* fifteen cubits *long, with* their three pillars and their three sockets,
15 and the same for the other side of the court gate; on this side and that *were* hangings of fifteen cubits, *with* their three pillars and their three sockets.
16 All the hangings of the court all around *were of* fine woven linen.
17 The sockets for the pillars *were* bronze, the hooks of the pillars and their bands *were* silver, and the overlay of their capitals *was* silver; and all the pillars of the court had bands of silver.
18 The screen for the gate of the court *was* woven of blue, purple, and scarlet *thread*, and of

KJV

and fine twined linen: and twenty cubits *was* the length, and the height in the breadth *was* five cubits, answerable to the hangings of the court.

19 And their pillars *were* four, and their sockets *of* brass four; their hooks *of* silver, and the overlaying of their chapiters and their fillets *of* silver.

20 And all the [a]pins of the tabernacle, and of the court round about, *were of* brass.

Materials of the Tabernacle

21 This is the sum of the tabernacle, *even* of [a]the tabernacle of testimony, as it was counted, according to the commandment of Moses, *for* the service of the Levites, [b]by the hand of [c]Ithamar, son to Aaron the priest.

22 And [a]Bezaleel the son of Uri, the son of Hur, of the tribe of Judah, made all that the LORD commanded Moses.

23 And with him *was* [a]Aholiab, son of Ahisamach, of the tribe of Dan, an engraver, and a cunning workman, and an embroiderer in blue, and in purple, and in scarlet, and fine linen.

24 All the gold that was occupied for the work in all the work of the holy *place,* even the gold of the [a]offering, was twenty and nine talents, and seven hundred and thirty shekels, after [b]the shekel of the sanctuary.

25 And the silver of them that were [a]numbered of the congregation *was* an hundred talents, and a thousand seven hundred and threescore and fifteen shekels, after the shekel of the sanctuary:

26 [a]A bekah for every man, *that is,* half a shekel, after the shekel of the sanctuary, for every one that went to be numbered, from twenty years old and upward, for [b]six hundred thousand and three thousand and five hundred and fifty *men.*

27 And of the hundred talents of silver were cast [a]the sockets of the sanctuary, and the sockets of the vail; an hundred sockets of the hundred talents, a talent for a socket.

28 And of the thousand seven hundred seventy and five *shekels* he made hooks for the pillars, and overlaid their chapiters, and [a]filleted them.

29 And the brass of the offering *was* seventy talents, and two thousand and four hundred shekels.

30 And therewith he made the sockets to the door of the tabernacle of the congregation, and the brasen altar, and the brasen grate for it, and all the vessels of the altar,

31 And the sockets of the court round about, and the sockets of the court gate, and all the pins of the tabernacle, and all the pins of the court round about.

Making the Garments of the Priesthood
(*Ex. 28:1–43*)

39 And of the [a]blue, and purple, and scarlet, they made [b]cloths of service, to do service in the holy *place,* and made the holy garments for Aaron; [c]as the LORD commanded Moses.

Making the Ephod

2 [a]And he made the [b]ephod *of* gold, blue, and purple, and scarlet, and fine twined linen.

3 And they did beat the gold into thin plates, and cut *it into* wires, to work *it* in the blue, and in the purple, and in the scarlet, and in the fine linen, *with* cunning work.

4 They made shoulderpieces for it, to couple *it* together: by the two edges was it coupled together.

5 And the curious girdle of his ephod, that *was* upon it, *was* of the same, according to the work thereof; *of* gold, blue, and purple, and scarlet, and fine twined linen; as the LORD commanded Moses.

6 [a]And they wrought onyx stones inclosed

20 [a]Ex. 27:19 **21** [a]Num. 1:50, 53; 9:15; 10:11; 17:7, 8; 2 Chr. 24:6; Acts 7:44 [b]Num. 4:28, 33 [c]Ex. 28:1; Lev. 10:6, 16 **22** [a]Ex. 31:2, 6; 1 Chr. 2:18–20 **23** [a]Ex. 31:6; 36:1 **24** [a]Ex. 35:5, 22 [b]Ex. 30:13, 24; Lev. 5:15; 27:3, 25; Num. 3:47; 18:16 **25** [a]Ex. 30:11–16; Num. 1:2 **26** [a]Ex. 30:13, 15 [b]Ex. 12:37; Num. 1:46; 26:51 **27** [a]Ex. 26:19, 21, 25, 32 **28** [a]Ex. 27:17

CHAPTER 39

1 [a]Ex. 25:4; 35:23 [b]Ex. 31:10; 35:19 [c]Ex. 28:4 **2** [a]Ex. 28:6–14 [b]Lev. 8:7 **6** [a]Ex. 28:9–11

NKJV

fine woven linen. The length *was* twenty cubits, and the height along its width *was* five cubits, corresponding to the hangings of the court.

19 And *there were* four pillars *with* their four sockets of bronze; their hooks *were* silver, and the overlay of their capitals and their bands *was* silver.

20 All the [a]pegs of the tabernacle, and of the court all around, *were* bronze.

Materials of the Tabernacle

21 This is the inventory of the tabernacle, [a]the tabernacle of the Testimony, which was counted according to the commandment of Moses, for the service of the Levites, [b]by the hand of [c]Ithamar, son of Aaron the priest.

22 [a]Bezalel the son of Uri, the son of Hur, of the tribe of Judah, made all that the LORD had commanded Moses.

23 And with him *was* [a]Aholiab the son of Ahisamach, of the tribe of Dan, an engraver and designer, a weaver of blue, purple, and scarlet *thread,* and of fine linen.

24 All the gold that was used in all the work of the holy *place,* that is, the gold of the [a]offering, was twenty-nine talents and seven hundred and thirty shekels, according to [b]the shekel of the sanctuary.

25 And the silver from those who were [a]numbered of the congregation *was* one hundred talents and one thousand seven hundred and seventy-five shekels, according to the shekel of the sanctuary:

26 [a]a bekah for each man (*that is,* half a shekel, according to the shekel of the sanctuary), for everyone included in the numbering from twenty years old and above, for [b]six hundred and three thousand, five hundred and fifty *men.*

27 And from the hundred talents of silver were cast [a]the sockets of the sanctuary and the bases of the veil: one hundred sockets from the hundred talents, one talent for each socket.

28 Then from the one thousand seven hundred and seventy-five *shekels* he made hooks for the pillars, overlaid their capitals, and [a]made bands for them.

29 The offering of bronze *was* seventy talents and two thousand four hundred shekels.

30 And with it he made the sockets for the door of the tabernacle of meeting, the bronze altar, the bronze grating for it, and all the utensils for the altar,

31 the sockets for the court all around, the bases for the court gate, all the pegs for the tabernacle, and all the pegs for the court all around.

Making the Garments of the Priesthood
(*Ex. 28:1–43*)

39 Of the [a]blue, purple, and scarlet *thread* they made [b]garments* of ministry, for ministering in the holy *place,* and made the holy garments for Aaron, [c]as the LORD had commanded Moses.

Making the Ephod

2 [a]He made the [b]ephod of gold, blue, purple, and scarlet *thread,* and of fine woven linen.

3 And they beat the gold into thin sheets and cut *it into* threads, to work *it* in *with* the blue, purple, and scarlet *thread,* and the fine linen, *into* artistic designs.

4 They made shoulder straps for it to couple *it* together; it was coupled together at its two edges.

5 And the intricately woven band of his ephod that *was* on it *was* of the same workmanship, *woven of* gold, blue, purple, and scarlet *thread,* and *of* fine woven linen, as the LORD had commanded Moses.

6 [a]And they set onyx stones, enclosed in set-

*39:1 Or *woven garments*

KJV

in ouches of gold, graven, as signets are graven, with the names of the children of Israel.

7 And he put them on the shoulders of the ephod, *that they should be* stones for a [a]memorial to the children of Israel; as the LORD commanded Moses.

Making the Breastplate

8 [a]And he made the breastplate *of* cunning work, like the work of the ephod; *of* gold, blue, and purple, and scarlet, and fine twined linen.

9 It was foursquare; they made the breastplate double: a span *was* the length thereof, and a span the breadth thereof, *being* doubled.

10 [a]And they set in it four rows of stones: *the first* row *was* a sardius, a topaz, and a carbuncle: this *was* the first row.

11 And the second row, an emerald, a sapphire, and a diamond.

12 And the third row, a ligure, an agate, and an amethyst.

13 And the fourth row, a beryl, an onyx, and a jasper: *they were* inclosed in ouches of gold in their inclosings.

14 And the stones *were* according to the names of the children of Israel, [a]twelve, according to their names, *like* the engravings of a signet, every one with his name, according to the twelve tribes.

15 And they made upon the breastplate chains at the ends, *of* wreathen work *of* pure gold.

16 And they made two ouches *of* gold, and two gold rings; and put the two rings in the two ends of the breastplate.

17 And they put the two wreathen chains of gold in the two rings on the ends of the breastplate.

18 And the two ends of the two wreathen chains they fastened in the two ouches, and put them on the shoulderpieces of the ephod, before it.

19 And they made two rings of gold, and put *them* on the two ends of the breastplate, upon the border of it, which *was* on the side of the ephod inward.

20 And they made two *other* golden rings, and put them on the two sides of the ephod underneath, toward the forepart of it, over against the *other* coupling thereof, above the curious girdle of the ephod.

21 And they did bind the breastplate by his rings unto the rings of the ephod with a lace of blue, that it might be above the curious girdle of the ephod, and that the breastplate might not be loosed from the ephod; as the LORD commanded Moses.

Making the Other Priestly Garments

22 [a]And he made the [b]robe of the ephod *of* woven work, all *of* blue.

23 And *there was* an hole in the midst of the robe, as the hole of an habergeon, *with* a band round about the hole, that it should not rend.

24 And they made upon the hems of the robe pomegranates *of* blue, and purple, and scarlet, *and* twined *linen.*

25 And they made [a]bells *of* pure gold, and put the bells between the pomegranates upon the hem of the robe, round about between the pomegranates;

26 A bell and a pomegranate, a bell and a pomegranate, round about the hem of the robe to minister *in;* as the LORD commanded Moses.

27 [a]And they made coats *of* fine linen *of* woven work for Aaron, and for his sons,

28 [a]And a mitre *of* fine linen, and goodly bonnets *of* fine linen, and [b]linen breeches *of* fine twined linen,

29 [a]And a girdle *of* fine twined linen, and blue, and purple, and scarlet, *of* needlework; as the LORD commanded Moses.

30 [a]And they made the plate of the holy

7 [a]Ex. 28:12, 29; Josh. 4:7 **8** [a]Ex. 28:15–30 **10** [a]Ex. 28:17 **14** [a]Rev. 21:12 **22** [a]Ex. 28:31–35 [b]Ex. 29:5; Lev. 8:7 **25** [a]Ex. 28:33 **27** [a]Ex. 28:39, 40 **28** [a]Ex. 28:4, 39; Lev. 8:9; Ezek. 44:18 [b]Ex. 28:42; Lev. 6:10 **29** [a]Ex. 28:39 **30** [a]Ex. 28:36, 37

NKJV

tings of gold; they were engraved, as signets are engraved, with the names of the sons of Israel.

7 He put them on the shoulders of the ephod *as* [a]memorial stones for the sons of Israel, as the LORD had commanded Moses.

Making the Breastplate

8 [a]And he made the breastplate, artistically woven like the workmanship of the ephod, of gold, blue, purple, and scarlet *thread,* and of fine woven linen.

9 They made the breastplate square by doubling it; a span *was* its length and a span its width when doubled.

10 [a]And they set in it four rows of stones: a row with a sardius, a topaz, and an emerald was the first row;

11 the second row, a turquoise, a sapphire, and a diamond;

12 the third row, a jacinth, an agate, and an amethyst;

13 the fourth row, a beryl, an onyx, and a jasper. *They were* enclosed in settings of gold in their mountings.

14 *There were* [a]twelve stones according to the names of the sons of Israel: according to their names, *engraved like* a signet, each one with its own name according to the twelve tribes.

15 And they made chains for the breastplate at the ends, like braided cords of pure gold.

16 They also made two settings of gold and two gold rings, and put the two rings on the two ends of the breastplate.

17 And they put the two braided *chains* of gold in the two rings on the ends of the breastplate.

18 The two ends of the two braided *chains* they fastened in the two settings, and put them on the shoulder straps of the ephod in the front.

19 And they made two rings of gold and put *them* on the two ends of the breastplate, on the edge of it, which *was* on the inward side of the ephod.

20 They made two *other* gold rings and put them on the two shoulder straps, underneath the ephod toward its front, right at the seam above the intricately woven band of the ephod.

21 And they bound the breastplate by means of its rings to the rings of the ephod with a blue cord, so that it would be above the intricately woven band of the ephod, and that the breastplate would not come loose from the ephod, as the LORD had commanded Moses.

Making the Other Priestly Garments

22 [a]He made the [b]robe of the ephod of woven work, all of blue.

23 And *there was* an opening in the middle of the robe, like the opening in a coat of mail, *with* a woven binding all around the opening, so that it would not tear.

24 They made on the hem of the robe pomegranates of blue, purple, and scarlet, and of fine woven *linen.*

25 And they made [a]bells of pure gold, and put the bells between the pomegranates on the hem of the robe all around between the pomegranates:

26 a bell and a pomegranate, a bell and a pomegranate, all around the hem of the robe to minister in, as the LORD had commanded Moses.

27 [a]They made tunics, artistically woven of fine linen, for Aaron and his sons,

28 [a]a turban of fine linen, exquisite hats of fine linen, [b]short trousers of fine woven linen,

29 [a]and a sash of fine woven linen with blue, purple, and scarlet *thread,* made by a weaver, as the LORD had commanded Moses.

30 [a]Then they made the plate of the holy

KJV

crown *of* pure gold, and wrote upon it a writing,
like to the engravings of a signet, [b]HOLINESS
TO THE LORD.
31 And they tied unto it a lace of blue, to fasten *it* on high upon the mitre; as the LORD commanded Moses.

The Work Completed
(Ex. 35:10–19)

32 Thus was all the work of the tabernacle
of the tent of the congregation [a]finished: and the
children of Israel did [b]according to all that the
LORD commanded Moses, so did they.
33 And they brought the tabernacle unto Moses, the tent, and all his furniture, his taches, his
boards, his bars, and his pillars, and his sockets,
34 And the covering of rams' skins dyed red,
and the covering of badgers' skins, and the vail
of the covering,
35 The ark of the testimony, and the staves
thereof, and the mercy seat,
36 The table, *and* all the vessels thereof, and
the [a]shewbread,
37 The pure candlestick, *with* the lamps
thereof, *even with* the lamps to be set in order,
and all the vessels thereof, and the oil for
light,
38 And the golden altar, and the anointing
oil, and the sweet incense, and the hanging for
the tabernacle door,
39 The brasen altar, and his grate of brass,
his staves, and all his vessels, the laver and his
foot,
40 The hangings of the court, his pillars, and
his sockets, and the hanging for the court gate,
his cords, and his pins, and all the vessels of the
service of the tabernacle, for the tent of the
congregation,
41 The cloths of service to do service in the
holy *place*, and the holy garments for Aaron the
priest, and his sons' garments, to minister in
the priest's office.
42 According to all that the LORD commanded Moses, so the children of Israel [a]made
all the work.
43 And Moses did look upon all the work,
and, behold, they had done it as the LORD had
commanded, even so had they done it: and Moses
[a]blessed them.

The Tabernacle Erected and Arranged

40 And the LORD [a]spake unto Moses, saying,
2 On the first day of the [a]first month
shalt thou set up [b]the tabernacle of the tent of
the congregation.
3 And [a]thou shalt put therein the ark of the
testimony, and cover the ark with the vail.
4 And [a]thou shalt bring in the table, and
[b]set in order the things that are to be set in order
upon it; [c]and thou shalt bring in the candlestick,
and light the lamps thereof.
5 [a]And thou shalt set the altar of gold for
the incense before the ark of the testimony, and
put the hanging of the door to the tabernacle.
6 And thou shalt set the [a]altar of the burnt
offering before the door of the tabernacle of the
tent of the congregation.
7 And [a]thou shalt set the laver between the
tent of the congregation and the altar, and shalt
put water therein.
8 And thou shalt set up the court round
about, and hang up the hanging at the court
gate.
9 And thou shalt take the anointing oil, and
[a]anoint the tabernacle, and all that *is* therein, and
shalt hallow it, and all the vessels thereof: and it
shall be holy.
10 And thou shalt [a]anoint the altar of the
burnt offering, and all his vessels, and sanctify
the altar: and [b]it shall be an altar most holy.
11 And thou shalt anoint the laver and his
foot, and sanctify it.

30 [b]Zech. 14:20
32 [a]Ex. 40:17 [b]Ex. 25:40; 39:42, 43
36 [a]Ex. 25:23–30
42 [a]Ex. 35:10
43 [a]Lev. 9:22, 23; Num. 6:23–26; Josh. 22:6; 2 Sam. 6:18; 1 Kin. 8:14; 2 Chr. 30:27

CHAPTER 40

1 [a]Ex. 25:1—31:18
2 [a]Ex. 12:2; 13:4 [b]Ex. 26:1, 30; 40:17
3 [a]Ex. 26:33; 40:21; Lev. 16:2; Num. 4:5
4 [a]Ex. 26:35; 40:22 [b]Ex. 25:30; 40:23 [c]Ex. 40:24, 25
5 [a]Ex. 40:26
6 [a]Ex. 39:39
7 [a]Ex. 30:18; 40:30
9 [a]Ex. 30:26; Lev. 8:10
10 [a]Ex. 30:26–30 [b]Ex. 29:36, 37

*39:41 Or *woven garments*

NKJV

crown of pure gold, and wrote on it an inscription
like the engraving of a signet:

[b]HOLINESS TO THE LORD.

31 And they tied to it a blue cord, to fasten
it above on the turban, as the LORD had commanded Moses.

The Work Completed
(Ex. 35:10–19)

32 Thus all the work of the tabernacle of the
tent of meeting was [a]finished. And the children
of Israel did [b]according to all that the LORD had
commanded Moses; so they did.
33 And they brought the tabernacle to Moses,
the tent and all its furnishings: its clasps, its
boards, its bars, its pillars, and its sockets;
34 the covering of ram skins dyed red, the
covering of badger skins, and the veil of the
covering;
35 the ark of the Testimony with its poles,
and the mercy seat;
36 the table, all its utensils, and the [a]show-
bread;
37 the pure *gold* lampstand with its lamps
(the lamps set in order), all its utensils, and the
oil for light;
38 the gold altar, the anointing oil, and the
sweet incense; the screen for the tabernacle door;
39 the bronze altar, its grate of bronze, its
poles, and all its utensils; the laver with its base;
40 the hangings of the court, its pillars and
its sockets, the screen for the court gate, its cords,
and its pegs; all the utensils for the service of the
tabernacle, for the tent of meeting;
41 and the *garments of ministry, to minister
in the holy *place:* the holy garments for Aaron
the priest, and his sons' garments, to minister as
priests.
42 According to all that the LORD had commanded Moses, so the children of Israel [a]did all
the work.
43 Then Moses looked over all the work, and
indeed they had done it; as the LORD had commanded, just so they had done it. And Moses
[a]blessed them.

The Tabernacle Erected and Arranged

40 Then the LORD [a]spoke to Moses, saying:
2 "On the first day of the [a]first month
you shall set up [b]the tabernacle of the tent of
meeting.
3 [a]"You shall put in it the ark of the Testimony, and partition off the ark with the veil.
4 [a]"You shall bring in the table and [b]ar-
range the things that are to be set in order on it;
[c]and you shall bring in the lampstand and light
its lamps.
5 [a]"You shall also set the altar of gold for
the incense before the ark of the Testimony, and
put up the screen for the door of the tabernacle.
6 "Then you shall set the [a]altar of the burnt
offering before the door of the tabernacle of the
tent of meeting.
7 "And [a]you shall set the laver between the
tabernacle of meeting and the altar, and put water
in it.
8 "You shall set up the court all around, and
hang up the screen at the court gate.
9 "And you shall take the anointing oil, and
[a]anoint the tabernacle and all that *is* in it; and
you shall hallow it and all its utensils, and it shall
be holy.
10 "You shall [a]anoint the altar of the burnt
offering and all its utensils, and consecrate the
altar. [b]The altar shall be most holy.
11 "And you shall anoint the laver and its
base, and consecrate it.

KJV

12 [a]And thou shalt bring Aaron and his sons unto the door of the tabernacle of the congregation, and wash them with water.

13 And thou shalt put upon Aaron the holy [a]garments, [b]and anoint him, and sanctify him; that he may minister unto me in the priest's office.

14 And thou shalt bring his sons, and clothe them with coats:

15 And thou shalt anoint them, as thou didst anoint their father, that they may minister unto me in the priest's office: for their anointing shall surely be [a]an everlasting priesthood throughout their generations.

16 Thus did Moses: according to all that the LORD commanded him, so did he.

17 And it came to pass in the first month in the second year, on the first *day* of the month, *that* the [a]tabernacle was reared up.

18 And Moses reared up the tabernacle, and fastened his sockets, and set up the boards thereof, and put in the bars thereof, and reared up his pillars.

19 And he spread abroad the tent over the tabernacle, and put the covering of the tent above upon it; as the LORD commanded Moses.

20 And he took and put [a]the testimony into the ark, and set the staves on the ark, and put the mercy seat above upon the ark:

21 And he brought the ark into the tabernacle, and [a]set up the vail of the covering, and covered the ark of the testimony; as the LORD commanded Moses.

22 [a]And he put the table in the tent of the congregation, upon the side of the tabernacle northward, without the vail.

23 [a]And he set the bread in order upon it before the LORD; as the LORD had commanded Moses.

24 [a]And he put the candlestick in the tent of the congregation, over against the table, on the side of the tabernacle southward.

25 And [a]he lighted the lamps before the LORD; as the LORD commanded Moses.

26 [a]And he put the golden altar in the tent of the congregation before the vail:

27 [a]And he burnt sweet incense thereon; as the LORD commanded Moses.

28 [a]And he set up the hanging *at* the door of the tabernacle.

29 [a]And he put the altar of burnt offering *by* the door of the tabernacle of the tent of the congregation, and [b]offered upon it the burnt offering and the meat offering; as the LORD commanded Moses.

30 [a]And he set the laver between the tent of the congregation and the altar, and put water there, to wash *withal.*

31 And Moses and Aaron and his sons [a]washed their hands and their feet thereat:

32 When they went into the tent of the congregation, and when they came near unto the altar, they washed; [a]as the LORD commanded Moses.

33 [a]And he reared up the court round about the tabernacle and the altar, and set up the hanging of the court gate. So Moses [b]finished the work.

The Cloud and the Glory
(Ex. 13:21, 22; Num. 9:15–23)

34 [a]Then a [b]cloud covered the tent of the congregation, and the [c]glory of the LORD filled the tabernacle.

35 And Moses [a]was not able to enter into the tent of the congregation, because the cloud abode thereon, and the glory of the LORD filled the tabernacle.

36 [a]And when the cloud was taken up from over the tabernacle, the children of Israel went onward in all their journeys:

37 But [a]if the cloud were not taken up, then

12 [a]Ex. 29:4–9; Lev. 8:1–13
13 [a]Ex. 29:5; 39:1, 41 [b][Ex. 28:41]; Lev. 8:12
15 [a]Ex. 29:9; Num. 25:13
17 [a]Ex. 40:2; Num. 7:1
20 [a]Ex. 25:16; Deut. 10:5; 1 Kin. 8:9; 2 Chr. 5:10; Heb. 9:4
21 [a]Ex. 26:33
22 [a]Ex. 26:35
23 [a]Ex. 40:4; Lev. 24:5, 6
24 [a]Ex. 26:35
25 [a]Ex. 25:37; 30:7, 8; 40:4; Lev. 24:3, 4
26 [a]Ex. 30:1, 6; 40:5
27 [a]Ex. 30:7
28 [a]Ex. 26:36; 40:5
29 [a]Ex. 40:6 [b]Ex. 29:38–42
30 [a]Ex. 30:18; 40:7
31 [a]Ex. 30:19, 20; John 13:8
32 [a]Ex. 30:19
33 [a]Ex. 27:9–18; 40:8 [b][Heb. 3:2–5]
34 [a]Ex. 29:43; Lev. 16:2; Num. 9:15; 2 Chr. 5:13; Is. 6:4 [b]1 Kin. 8:10, 11 [c]Lev. 9:6, 23
35 [a][Lev. 16:2]; 1 Kin. 8:11; 2 Chr. 5:13, 14
36 [a]Ex. 13:21, 22; Num. 9:17; Neh. 9:19
37 [a]Num. 9:19–22

NKJV

12 [a]"Then you shall bring Aaron and his sons to the door of the tabernacle of meeting and wash them with water.

13 "You shall put the holy [a]garments on Aaron, [b]and anoint him and consecrate him, that he may minister to Me as priest.

14 "And you shall bring his sons and clothe them with tunics.

15 "You shall anoint them, as you anointed their father, that they may minister to Me as priests; for their anointing shall surely be [a]an everlasting priesthood throughout their generations."

16 Thus Moses did; according to all that the LORD had commanded him, so he did.

17 And it came to pass in the first month of the second year, on the first *day* of the month, *that* the [a]tabernacle was raised up.

18 So Moses raised up the tabernacle, fastened its sockets, set up its boards, put in its bars, and raised up its pillars.

19 And he spread out the tent over the tabernacle and put the covering of the tent on top of it, as the LORD had commanded Moses.

20 He took [a]the Testimony and put *it* into the ark, inserted the poles through the rings of the ark, and put the mercy seat on top of the ark.

21 And he brought the ark into the tabernacle, [a]hung up the veil of the covering, and partitioned off the ark of the Testimony, as the LORD had commanded Moses.

22 [a]He put the table in the tabernacle of meeting, on the north side of the tabernacle, outside the veil;

23 [a]and he set the bread in order upon it before the LORD, as the LORD had commanded Moses.

24 [a]He put the lampstand in the tabernacle of meeting, across from the table, on the south side of the tabernacle;

25 and [a]he lit the lamps before the LORD, as the LORD had commanded Moses.

26 [a]He put the gold altar in the tabernacle of meeting in front of the veil;

27 [a]and he burned sweet incense on it, as the LORD had commanded Moses.

28 [a]He hung up the screen *at* the door of the tabernacle.

29 [a]And he put the altar of burnt offering *before* the door of the tabernacle of the tent of meeting, and [b]offered upon it the burnt offering and the grain offering, as the LORD had commanded Moses.

30 [a]He set the laver between the tabernacle of meeting and the altar, and put water there for washing;

31 and Moses, Aaron, and his sons would [a]wash their hands and their feet *with water* from it.

32 Whenever they went into the tabernacle of meeting, and when they came near the altar, they washed, [a]as the LORD had commanded Moses.

33 [a]And he raised up the court all around the tabernacle and the altar, and hung up the screen of the court gate. So Moses [b]finished the work.

The Cloud and the Glory
(Ex. 13:21, 22; Num. 9:15–23)

34 [a]Then the [b]cloud covered the tabernacle of meeting, and the [c]glory of the LORD filled the tabernacle.

35 And Moses [a]was not able to enter the tabernacle of meeting, because the cloud rested above it, and the glory of the LORD filled the tabernacle.

36 [a]Whenever the cloud was taken up from above the tabernacle, the children of Israel would go onward in all their journeys.

37 But [a]if the cloud was not taken up, then

KJV

they journeyed not till the day that it was taken
up.
38 For [a]the cloud of the LORD *was* upon the
tabernacle by day, and fire was on it by night, in
the sight of all the house of Israel, throughout all
their journeys.

38 [a]Ex. 13:21; Num. 9:15; Ps. 78:14; Is. 4:5

NKJV

they did not journey till the day that it was taken
up.
38 For [a]the cloud of the LORD *was* above the
tabernacle by day, and fire was over it by night,
in the sight of all the house of Israel, throughout
all their journeys.

KJV

THE THIRD BOOK OF MOSES CALLED

LEVITICUS

The Burnt Offering

1 And the LORD [a]called unto Moses, and spake
unto him [b]out of the tabernacle of the congregation, saying,
2 Speak unto the children of Israel, and
say unto them, [a]If any man of you bring an offering unto the LORD, ye shall bring your offering of the cattle, *even* of the herd, and of the
flock.
3 If his offering *be* a burnt sacrifice of the
herd, let him offer a male [a]without blemish: he
shall offer it of his own voluntary will at the door
of the tabernacle of the congregation before the
LORD.
4 [a]And he shall put his hand upon the head
of the burnt offering; and it shall be [b]accepted
for him [c]to make atonement for him.
5 And he shall kill the [a]bullock before the
LORD: [b]and the priests, Aaron's sons, shall bring
the blood, [c]and sprinkle the blood round about
upon the altar that *is by* the door of the tabernacle
of the congregation.
6 And he shall [a]flay the burnt offering, and
cut it into his pieces.
7 And the sons of Aaron the priest shall put
[a]fire upon the altar, and [b]lay the wood in order
upon the fire:
8 And the priests, Aaron's sons, shall lay
the parts, the head, and the fat, in order upon
the wood that *is* on the fire which *is* upon the
altar:
9 But his inwards and his legs shall he wash
in water: and the priest shall burn all on the altar,
to be a burnt sacrifice, an offering made by fire,
of a [a]sweet savour unto the LORD.
10 And if his offering *be* of the flocks,
namely, of the sheep, or of the goats, for a burnt
sacrifice; he shall bring it a male [a]without
blemish.
11 [a]And he shall kill it on the side of the altar
northward before the LORD: and the priests, Aaron's sons, shall sprinkle his blood round about
upon the altar.
12 And he shall cut it into his pieces, with
his head and his fat: and the priest shall lay them
in order on the wood that *is* on the fire which *is*
upon the altar:
13 But he shall wash the inwards and the legs
with water: and the priest shall bring *it* all, and
burn *it* upon the altar: it *is* a burnt sacrifice, an
[a]offering made by fire, of a sweet savour unto
the LORD.
14 And if the burnt sacrifice for his offering to the LORD *be* of fowls, then he shall
bring his offering of [a]turtledoves, or of young
pigeons.
15 And the priest shall bring it unto the altar,
and wring off his head, and burn *it* on the altar;
and the blood thereof shall be wrung out at the
side of the altar:
16 And he shall pluck away his crop with his
feathers, and cast it [a]beside the altar on the east
part, by the place of the ashes:
17 And he shall cleave it with the wings
thereof, *but* [a]shall not divide *it* asunder: and the
priest shall burn it upon the altar, upon the wood

CHAPTER 1

1 [a]Ex. 19:3; 25:22; Num. 7:89 [b]Ex. 40:34
2 [a]Lev. 22:18, 19
3 [a]Ex. 12:5; Lev. 22:20–24; Deut. 15:21; Eph. 5:27; Heb. 9:14; 1 Pet. 1:19
4 [a]Ex. 29:10, 15, 19; Lev. 3:2, 8, 13; 4:15 [b][Rom. 12:1]; Phil. 4:18 [c]Lev. 4:20, 26, 31; 2 Chr. 29:23, 24
5 [a]Mic. 6:6 [b]2 Chr. 35:11 [c]Lev. 1:11; 3:2, 8, 13; [Heb. 12:24; 1 Pet. 1:2]
6 [a]Lev. 7:8
7 [a]Lev. 6:8–13; Mal. 1:10 [b]Gen. 22:9
9 [a]Gen. 8:21; [Ezek. 20:28, 41; 2 Cor. 2:15]
10 [a]Ex. 12:5; Lev. 1:3; Ezek. 43:22; [1 Pet. 1:19]
11 [a]Ex. 24:6; 40:22; Lev. 1:5; Ezek. 8:5
13 [a]Num. 15:4–7; 28:12–14
14 [a]Gen. 15:9; Lev. 5:7, 11; 12:8; Luke 2:24
16 [a]Lev. 6:10
17 [a]Gen. 15:10; Lev. 5:8

NKJV

THE THIRD BOOK OF MOSES CALLED

LEVITICUS

The Burnt Offering

1 Now the LORD [a]called to Moses, and spoke
to him [b]from the tabernacle of meeting,
saying,
2 "Speak to the children of Israel, and say
to them: [a]'When any one of you brings an offering
to the LORD, you shall bring your offering of the
livestock—of the herd and of the flock.
3 'If his offering *is* a burnt sacrifice of the
herd, let him offer a male [a]without blemish; he
shall offer it of his own free will at the door of
the tabernacle of meeting before the LORD.
4 [a]'Then he shall put his hand on the head
of the burnt offering, and it will be [b]accepted on
his behalf [c]to make atonement for him.
5 'He shall kill the [a]bull before the LORD;
[b]and the priests, Aaron's sons, shall bring the
blood [c]and sprinkle the blood all around on the
altar that *is by* the door of the tabernacle of
meeting.
6 'And he shall [a]skin the burnt offering and
cut it into its pieces.
7 'The sons of Aaron the priest shall put
[a]fire on the altar, and [b]lay the wood in order on
the fire.
8 'Then the priests, Aaron's sons, shall lay
the parts, the head, and the fat in order on the
wood that *is* on the fire upon the altar;
9 'but he shall wash its entrails and its legs
with water. And the priest shall burn all on the
altar as a burnt sacrifice, an offering made by fire,
a [a]sweet aroma to the LORD.
10 'If his offering *is* of the flocks—of the
sheep or of the goats—as a burnt sacrifice, he shall
bring a male [a]without blemish.
11 [a]'He shall kill it on the north side of the
altar before the LORD; and the priests, Aaron's
sons, shall sprinkle its blood all around on the
altar.
12 'And he shall cut it into its pieces, with
its head and its fat; and the priest shall lay them
in order on the wood that *is* on the fire upon the
altar;
13 'but he shall wash the entrails and the legs
with water. Then the priest shall bring *it* all and
burn *it* on the altar; it *is* a burnt sacrifice, an [a]offer-
ing made by fire, a sweet aroma to the LORD.
14 'And if the burnt sacrifice of his offering
to the LORD *is* of birds, then he shall bring his
offering of [a]turtledoves or young pigeons.
15 'The priest shall bring it to the altar, wring
off its head, and burn *it* on the altar; its blood
shall be drained out at the side of the altar.
16 'And he shall remove its crop with its
feathers and cast it [a]beside the altar on the east
side, into the place for ashes.
17 'Then he shall split it at its wings, *but*
[a]shall not divide *it* completely; and the priest shall
burn it on the altar, on the wood that *is* on the

KJV

that *is* upon the fire: [b]it *is* a burnt sacrifice, an offering made by fire, of a sweet savour unto the LORD.

The Grain Offering

2 And when any will offer [a]a meat offering unto the LORD, his offering shall be *of* fine flour; and he shall pour oil upon it, and put [b]frankincense thereon:

2 And he shall bring it to Aaron's sons the priests: and he shall take thereout his handful of the flour thereof, and of the oil thereof, with all the frankincense thereof; and the priest shall burn [a]the memorial of it upon the altar, *to be* an offering made by fire, of a sweet savour unto the LORD:

3 And [a]the remnant of the meat offering *shall be* Aaron's and his [b]sons': [c]*it is* a thing most holy of the offerings of the LORD made by fire.

4 And if thou bring an oblation of a meat offering baken in the oven, *it shall be* unleavened cakes of fine flour mingled with oil, or unleavened wafers [a]anointed with oil.

5 And if thy oblation *be* a meat offering *baken* in a pan, it shall be *of* fine flour unleavened, mingled with oil.

6 Thou shalt part it in pieces, and pour oil thereon: it *is* a meat offering.

7 And if thy oblation *be* a meat offering *baken* in the [a]fryingpan, it shall be made *of* fine flour with oil.

8 And thou shalt bring the meat offering that is made of these things unto the LORD: and when it is presented unto the priest, he shall bring it unto the altar.

9 And the priest shall take from the meat offering [a]a memorial thereof, and shall burn *it* upon the altar: *it is* an [b]offering made by fire, of a sweet savour unto the LORD.

10 And [a]that which is left of the meat offering *shall be* Aaron's and his sons': *it is* a thing most holy of the offerings of the LORD made by fire.

11 No meat offering, which ye shall bring unto the LORD, shall be made with [a]leaven: for ye shall burn no leaven, nor any honey, in any offering of the LORD made by fire.

12 [a]As for the oblation of the firstfruits, ye shall offer them unto the LORD: but they shall not be burnt on the altar for a sweet savour.

13 And every oblation of thy meat offering [a]shalt thou season with salt; neither shalt thou suffer [b]the salt of the covenant of thy God to be lacking from thy meat offering: [c]with all thine offerings thou shalt offer salt.

14 And if thou offer a meat offering of thy firstfruits unto the LORD, [a]thou shalt offer for the meat offering of thy firstfruits green ears of corn dried by the fire, *even* corn beaten out of [b]full ears.

15 And [a]thou shalt put oil upon it, and lay frankincense thereon: it *is* a meat offering.

16 And the priest shall burn [a]the memorial of it, *part* of the beaten corn thereof, and *part* of the oil thereof, with all the frankincense thereof: *it is* an offering made by fire unto the LORD.

The Peace Offering

3 And if his oblation *be* a [a]sacrifice of peace offering, if he offer *it* of the herd; whether *it be* a male or female, he shall offer it [b]without blemish before the LORD.

2 And [a]he shall lay his hand upon the head of his offering, and kill it *at* the door of the tabernacle of the congregation: and Aaron's sons the priests shall [b]sprinkle the blood upon the altar round about.

3 And he shall offer of the sacrifice of the peace offering an offering made by fire unto the LORD; [a]the fat that covereth the inwards, and all the fat that *is* upon the inwards,

4 And the two kidneys, and the fat that *is* on them, which *is* by the flanks, and the caul above the liver, with the kidneys, it shall he take away.

---

17 [b]Lev. 1:9, 13

CHAPTER 2

1 [a]Lev. 6:14; 9:17; Num. 15:4 [b]Lev. 5:11
2 [a]Lev. 2:9; 5:12; 6:15; 24:7; Acts 10:4
3 [a]Lev. 7:9 [b]Lev. 6:6; 10:12, 13 [c]Ex. 29:37; Num. 18:9
4 [a]Ex. 29:2
7 [a]Lev. 7:9
9 [a]Lev. 2:2, 16; 5:12; 6:15 [b]Ex. 29:18
10 [a]Lev. 2:3; 6:16
11 [a]Ex. 23:18; 34:25; Lev. 6:16, 17; [Matt. 16:12; Mark 8:15; Luke 12:1; 1 Cor. 5:8; Gal. 5:9]
12 [a]Ex. 22:29; 34:22; Lev. 23:10, 11, 17, 18
13 [a][Mark 9:49, 50; Col. 4:6] [b]Num. 18:19; 2 Chr. 13:5 [c]Ezek. 43:24
14 [a]Lev. 23:10, 14 [b]2 Kin. 4:42
15 [a]Lev. 2:1
16 [a]Lev. 2:2

CHAPTER 3

1 [a]Lev. 7:11, 29 [b]Lev. 1:3; 22:20–24
2 [a]Ex. 29:10, 11, 16, 20; Lev. 1:4, 5; 16:21 [b]Lev. 1:5
3 [a]Ex. 29:13, 22; Lev. 1:8; 3:16; 4:8, 9

NKJV

fire. [b]It *is* a burnt sacrifice, an offering made by fire, a sweet aroma to the LORD.

The Grain Offering

2 'When anyone offers [a]a grain offering to the LORD, his offering shall be *of* fine flour. And he shall pour oil on it, and put [b]frankincense on it.

2 'He shall bring it to Aaron's sons, the priests, one of whom shall take from it his handful of fine flour and oil with all the frankincense. And the priest shall burn [a]*it as* a memorial on the altar, an offering made by fire, a sweet aroma to the LORD.

3 [a]'The rest of the grain offering *shall be* Aaron's and his [b]sons'. [c]*It is* most holy of the offerings to the LORD made by fire.

4 'And if you bring as an offering a grain offering baked in the oven, *it shall be* unleavened cakes of fine flour mixed with oil, or unleavened wafers [a]anointed with oil.

5 'But if your offering *is* a grain offering *baked* in a pan, *it shall be of* fine flour, unleavened, mixed with oil.

6 'You shall break it in pieces and pour oil on it; it *is* a grain offering.

7 'If your offering *is* a grain offering *baked* in a [a]covered pan, it shall be made *of* fine flour with oil.

8 'You shall bring the grain offering that is made of these things to the LORD. And when it is presented to the priest, he shall bring it to the altar.

9 'Then the priest shall take from the grain offering [a]a memorial portion, and burn *it* on the altar. *It is* an [b]offering made by fire, a sweet aroma to the LORD.

10 'And [a]what is left of the grain offering *shall be* Aaron's and his sons'. *It is* most holy of the offerings to the LORD made by fire.

11 'No grain offering which you bring to the LORD shall be made with [a]leaven, for you shall burn no leaven nor any honey in any offering to the LORD made by fire.

12 [a]'As for the offering of the firstfruits, you shall offer them to the LORD, but they shall not be burned on the altar for a sweet aroma.

13 'And every offering of your grain offering [a]you shall season with salt; you shall not allow [b]the salt of the covenant of your God to be lacking from your grain offering. [c]With all your offerings you shall offer salt.

14 'If you offer a grain offering of your firstfruits to the LORD, [a]you shall offer for the grain offering of your firstfruits green heads of grain roasted on the fire, grain beaten from [b]full heads.

15 'And [a]you shall put oil on it, and lay frankincense on it. It *is* a grain offering.

16 'Then the priest shall burn [a]the memorial portion: *part* of its beaten grain and *part* of its oil, with all the frankincense, as an offering made by fire to the LORD.

The Peace Offering

3 'When his offering *is* a [a]sacrifice of a peace offering, if he offers *it* of the herd, whether male or female, he shall offer it [b]without blemish before the LORD.

2 'And [a]he shall lay his hand on the head of his offering, and kill it *at* the door of the tabernacle of meeting; and Aaron's sons, the priests, shall [b]sprinkle the blood all around on the altar.

3 'Then he shall offer from the sacrifice of the peace offering an offering made by fire to the LORD. [a]The fat that covers the entrails and all the fat that *is* on the entrails,

4 'the two kidneys and the fat that *is* on them by the flanks, and the fatty lobe *attached* to the liver above the kidneys, he shall remove;

KJV

5 And Aaron's sons [a]shall burn it on the altar upon the [b]burnt sacrifice, which *is* upon the wood that *is* on the fire: *it is* an [c]offering made by fire, of a [d]sweet savour unto the LORD.

6 And if his offering for a sacrifice of peace offering unto the LORD *be* of the flock; male or female, [a]he shall offer it without blemish.

7 If he offer a [a]lamb for his offering, then shall he [b]offer it [c]before the LORD.

8 And he shall lay his hand upon the head of his offering, and kill it before the tabernacle of the congregation: and Aaron's sons shall sprinkle the blood thereof round about upon the altar.

9 And he shall offer of the sacrifice of the peace offering an offering made by fire unto the LORD; the fat thereof, *and* the whole rump, it shall he take off hard by the backbone; and the fat that covereth the inwards, and all the fat that *is* upon the inwards,

10 And the two kidneys, and the fat that *is* upon them, which *is* by the flanks, and the caul above the liver, with the kidneys, it shall he take away.

11 And the priest shall burn it upon the altar: *it is* [a]the food of the offering made by fire unto the LORD.

12 And if his [a]offering *be* a goat, then [b]he shall offer it before the LORD.

13 And he shall lay his hand upon the head of it, and kill it before the tabernacle of the congregation: and the sons of Aaron shall sprinkle the blood thereof upon the altar round about.

14 And he shall offer thereof his offering, *even* an offering made by fire unto the LORD; the fat that covereth the inwards, and all the fat that *is* upon the inwards,

15 And the two kidneys, and the fat that *is* upon them, which *is* by the flanks, and the caul above the liver, with the kidneys, it shall he take away.

16 And the priest shall burn them upon the altar: *it is* the food of the offering made by fire for a sweet savour: [a]all the fat *is* the LORD's.

17 *It shall be* a [a]perpetual statute for your generations throughout all your dwellings, that ye eat neither fat nor [b]blood.

The Sin Offering

4 And the LORD spake unto Moses, saying,

2 Speak unto the children of Israel, saying, [a]If a soul shall sin through ignorance against any of the commandments of the LORD *concerning things* which ought not to be done, and shall do against any of them:

3 [a]If the priest that is anointed do sin according to the sin of the people; then let him bring for his sin, which he hath sinned, [b]a young bullock without blemish unto the LORD for a [c]sin offering.

4 And he shall bring the bullock [a]unto the door of the tabernacle of the congregation before the LORD; and shall lay his hand upon the bullock's head, and kill the bullock before the LORD.

5 And the priest that is anointed [a]shall take of the bullock's blood, and bring it to the tabernacle of the congregation:

6 And the priest shall dip his finger in the blood, and sprinkle of the blood seven times before the LORD, before the [a]vail of the sanctuary.

7 And the priest shall [a]put *some* of the blood upon the horns of the altar of sweet incense before the LORD, which *is* in the tabernacle of the congregation; and shall pour [b]all the blood of the bullock at the bottom of the altar of the burnt offering, which *is at* the door of the tabernacle of the congregation.

8 And he shall take off from it all the fat of the bullock for the sin offering; the fat that covereth the inwards, and all the fat that *is* upon the inwards,

9 And the two kidneys, and the fat that *is* upon them, which *is* by the flanks, and the caul

---

5 [a]Ex. 29:13; Lev. 6:12; 7:28–34 [b]2 Chr. 35:14 [c]Num. 28:3–10 [d]Num. 15:8–10
6 [a]Lev. 3:1; 22:20–24
7 [a]Num. 15:4, 5 [b]1 Kin. 8:62 [c]Lev. 17:8, 9
11 [a]Lev. 21:6, 8, 17, 21, 22; 22:25; Num. 28:2; [Ezek. 44:7; Mal. 1:7, 12]
12 [a]Num. 15:6–11 [b]Lev. 3:1, 7
16 [a]Lev. 7:23–25; 1 Sam. 2:15; 2 Chr. 7:7
17 [a]Lev. 6:18; 7:36; 17:7; 23:14 [b]Gen. 9:4; Lev. 7:23, 26; 17:10, 14; 1 Sam. 14:33

CHAPTER 4

2 [a]Lev. 5:15–18; Num. 15:22–30; 1 Sam. 14:27; Acts 3:17
3 [a]Ex. 40:15; Lev. 8:12 [b]Lev. 3:1; 9:2 [c]Lev. 9:7
4 [a]Lev. 1:3, 4; 4:15; Num. 8:12
5 [a]Lev. 16:14; Num. 19:4
6 [a]Ex. 40:21, 26
7 [a]Lev. 4:18, 25, 30, 34; 8:15; 9:9; 16:18 [b]Lev. 5:9; Ex. 40:5, 6

NKJV

5 'and Aaron's sons [a]shall burn it on the altar upon the [b]burnt sacrifice, which *is* on the wood that *is* on the fire, *as* an [c]offering made by fire, a [d]sweet aroma to the LORD.

6 'If his offering as a sacrifice of a peace offering to the LORD *is* of the flock, *whether* male or female, [a]he shall offer it without blemish.

7 'If he offers a [a]lamb as his offering, then he shall [b]offer it [c]before the LORD.

8 'And he shall lay his hand on the head of his offering, and kill it before the tabernacle of meeting; and Aaron's sons shall sprinkle its blood all around on the altar.

9 'Then he shall offer from the sacrifice of the peace offering, as an offering made by fire to the LORD, its fat *and* the whole fat tail which he shall remove close to the backbone. And the fat that covers the entrails and all the fat that *is* on the entrails,

10 'the two kidneys and the fat that *is* on them by the flanks, and the fatty lobe *attached* to the liver above the kidneys, he shall remove;

11 'and the priest shall burn *them* on the altar *as* [a]food, an offering made by fire to the LORD.

12 'And if his [a]offering *is* a goat, then [b]he shall offer it before the LORD.

13 'He shall lay his hand on its head and kill it before the tabernacle of meeting; and the sons of Aaron shall sprinkle its blood all around on the altar.

14 'Then he shall offer from it his offering, as an offering made by fire to the LORD. The fat that covers the entrails and all the fat that *is* on the entrails,

15 'the two kidneys and the fat that *is* on them by the flanks, and the fatty lobe *attached* to the liver above the kidneys, he shall remove;

16 'and the priest shall burn them on the altar *as* food, an offering made by fire for a sweet aroma; [a]all the fat *is* the LORD's.

17 '*This shall be* a [a]perpetual statute throughout your generations in all your dwellings: you shall eat neither fat nor [b]blood.' "

The Sin Offering

4 Now the LORD spoke to Moses, saying,

2 "Speak to the children of Israel, saying: [a]'If a person sins unintentionally against any of the commandments of the LORD *in anything* which ought not to be done, and does any of them,

3 [a]'if the anointed priest sins, bringing guilt on the people, then let him offer to the LORD for his sin which he has sinned [b]a young bull without blemish as a [c]sin offering.

4 'He shall bring the bull [a]to the door of the tabernacle of meeting before the LORD, lay his hand on the bull's head, and kill the bull before the LORD.

5 'Then the anointed priest [a]shall take some of the bull's blood and bring it to the tabernacle of meeting.

6 'The priest shall dip his finger in the blood and sprinkle some of the blood seven times before the LORD, in front of the [a]veil of the sanctuary.

7 'And the priest shall [a]put some of the blood on the horns of the altar of sweet incense before the LORD, which is in the tabernacle of meeting; and he shall pour [b]the remaining blood of the bull at the base of the altar of the burnt offering, which is at the door of the tabernacle of meeting.

8 'He shall take from it all the fat of the bull as the sin offering. The fat that covers the entrails and all the fat which *is* on the entrails,

9 'the two kidneys and the fat that *is* on them by the flanks, and the fatty lobe *attached*

KJV

above the liver, with the kidneys, it shall he take away,

10 [a]As it was taken off from the bullock of the sacrifice of peace offerings: and the priest shall burn them upon the altar of the burnt offering.

11 [a]And the skin of the bullock, and all his flesh, with his head, and with his legs, and his inwards, and his dung,

12 Even the whole bullock shall he carry forth without the camp unto a clean place, [a]where the ashes are poured out, and [b]burn him on the wood with fire: where the ashes are poured out shall he be burnt.

13 And [a]if the whole congregation of Israel sin through ignorance, [b]and the thing be hid from the eyes of the assembly, and they have done *somewhat against* any of the commandments of the LORD *concerning things* which should not be done, and are guilty;

14 When the sin, which they have sinned against it, is known, then the congregation shall offer a young bullock for the sin, and bring him before the tabernacle of the congregation.

15 And the elders of the congregation [a]shall lay their hands upon the head of the bullock before the LORD: and the bullock shall be killed before the LORD.

16 [a]And the priest that is anointed shall bring of the bullock's blood to the tabernacle of the congregation:

17 And the priest shall dip his finger *in some* of the blood, and sprinkle *it* seven times before the LORD, *even* before the vail.

18 And he shall put *some* of the blood upon the horns of the altar which *is* before the LORD, that *is* in the tabernacle of the congregation, and shall pour out all the blood at the bottom of the altar of the burnt offering, which *is at* the door of the tabernacle of the congregation.

19 And he shall take all his fat from him, and burn *it* upon the altar.

20 And he shall do with the bullock as he did [a]with the bullock for a sin offering, so shall he do with this: [b]and the priest shall make an atonement for them, and it shall be forgiven them.

21 And he shall carry forth the bullock without the camp, and burn him as he burned the first bullock: it *is* a sin offering for the congregation.

22 When a ruler hath sinned, and [a]done *somewhat* through ignorance *against* any of the commandments of the LORD his God *concerning things* which should not be done, and is guilty;

23 Or [a]if his sin, wherein he hath sinned, come to his knowledge; he shall bring his offering, a kid of the goats, a male without blemish:

24 And [a]he shall lay his hand upon the head of the goat, and kill it in the place where they kill the burnt offering before the LORD: it *is* a sin offering.

25 [a]And the priest shall take of the blood of the sin offering with his finger, and put *it* upon the horns of the altar of burnt offering, and shall pour out his blood at the bottom of the altar of burnt offering.

26 And he shall burn all his fat upon the altar, as [a]the fat of the sacrifice of peace offerings: [b]and the priest shall make an atonement for him as concerning his sin, and it shall be forgiven him.

27 And [a]if any one of the common people sin through ignorance, while he doeth *somewhat against* any of the commandments of the LORD *concerning things* which ought not to be done, and be guilty;

28 Or [a]if his sin, which he hath sinned, come to his knowledge: then he shall bring his offering, a kid of the goats, a female without blemish, for his sin which he hath sinned.

29 [a]And he shall lay his hand upon the head of the sin offering, and slay the sin offering in the place of the burnt offering.

30 And the priest shall take of the blood

10 [a]Lev. 3:3–5
11 [a]Ex. 29:14; Lev. 9:11; Num. 19:5
12 [a]Lev. 4:21; 6:10, 11; 16:27 [b][Heb. 13:11, 12]
13 [a]Num. 15:24–26; Josh. 7:11 [b]Lev. 5:2–4, 17
15 [a]Lev. 1:3, 4
16 [a]Lev. 4:5; [Heb. 9:12–14]
20 [a]Lev. 4:3 [b]Lev. 1:4; Num. 15:25
22 [a]Lev. 4:2, 13, 27
23 [a]Lev. 4:14; 5:4
24 [a]Lev. 4:4; [Is. 53:6]
25 [a]Lev. 4:7, 18, 30, 34
26 [a]Lev. 3:3–5 [b]Lev. 4:20; Num. 15:28
27 [a]Lev. 4:2; Num. 15:27
28 [a]Lev. 4:23
29 [a]Lev. 1:4; 4:4, 24

NKJV

to the liver above the kidneys, he shall remove,

10 [a]'as it was taken from the bull of the sacrifice of the peace offering; and the priest shall burn them on the altar of the burnt offering.

11 [a]'But the bull's hide and all its flesh, with its head and legs, its entrails and offal—

12 'the whole bull he shall carry outside the camp to a clean place, [a]where the ashes are poured out, and [b]burn it on wood with fire; where the ashes are poured out it shall be burned.

13 'Now [a]if the whole congregation of Israel sins unintentionally, [b]and the thing is hidden from the eyes of the assembly, and they have done *something against* any of the commandments of the LORD *in anything* which should not be done, and are guilty;

14 'when the sin which they have committed becomes known, then the assembly shall offer a young bull for the sin, and bring it before the tabernacle of meeting.

15 'And the elders of the congregation [a]shall lay their hands on the head of the bull before the LORD. Then the bull shall be killed before the LORD.

16 [a]'The anointed priest shall bring some of the bull's blood to the tabernacle of meeting.

17 'Then the priest shall dip his finger in the blood and sprinkle *it* seven times before the LORD, in front of the veil.

18 'And he shall put *some* of the blood on the horns of the altar which *is* before the LORD, which *is* in the tabernacle of meeting; and he shall pour the remaining blood at the base of the altar of burnt offering, which is at the door of the tabernacle of meeting.

19 'He shall take all the fat from it and burn *it* on the altar.

20 'And he shall do [a]with the bull as he did with the bull as a sin offering; thus he shall do with it. [b]So the priest shall make atonement for them, and it shall be forgiven them.

21 'Then he shall carry the bull outside the camp, and burn it as he burned the first bull. It *is* a sin offering for the assembly.

22 'When a ruler has sinned, and [a]done *something* unintentionally *against* any of the commandments of the LORD his God *in anything* which should not be done, and is guilty,

23 'or [a]if his sin which he has committed comes to his knowledge, he shall bring as his offering a kid of the goats, a male without blemish.

24 'And [a]he shall lay his hand on the head of the goat, and kill it at the place where they kill the burnt offering before the LORD. It *is* a sin offering.

25 [a]'The priest shall take some of the blood of the sin offering with his finger, put *it* on the horns of the altar of burnt offering, and pour its blood at the base of the altar of burnt offering.

26 'And he shall burn all its fat on the altar, like [a]the fat of the sacrifice of the peace offering. [b]So the priest shall make atonement for him concerning his sin, and it shall be forgiven him.

27 [a]'If anyone of the common people sins unintentionally by doing *something against* any of the commandments of the LORD *in anything* which ought not to be done, and is guilty,

28 'or [a]if his sin which he has committed comes to his knowledge, then he shall bring as his offering a kid of the goats, a female without blemish, for his sin which he has committed.

29 [a]'And he shall lay his hand on the head of the sin offering, and kill the sin offering at the place of the burnt offering.

30 'Then the priest shall take *some* of its

KJV

thereof with his finger, and put *it* upon the horns of the altar of burnt offering, and shall pour out all the blood thereof at the bottom of the altar.

31 And [a]he shall take away all the fat thereof, [b]as the fat is taken away from off the sacrifice of peace offerings; and the priest shall burn *it* upon the altar for a [c]sweet savour unto the LORD; [d]and the priest shall make an atonement for him, and it shall be forgiven him.

32 And if he bring a lamb for a sin offering, [a]he shall bring it a female without blemish.

33 And he shall [a]lay his hand upon the head of the sin offering, and slay it for a sin offering in the place where they kill the burnt offering.

34 And the priest shall take of the blood of the sin offering with his finger, and put *it* upon the horns of the altar of burnt offering, and shall pour out all the blood thereof at the bottom of the altar:

35 And he shall take away all the fat thereof, as the fat of the lamb is taken away from the sacrifice of the peace offerings; and the priest shall burn them upon the altar, [a]according to the offerings made by fire unto the LORD: [b]and the priest shall make an atonement for his sin that he hath committed, and it shall be forgiven him.

The Trespass Offering

5 And if a soul sin, and [a]hear the voice of swearing, and *is* a witness, whether he hath seen or known *of it;* if he do not utter *it,* then he shall [b]bear his iniquity.

2 Or [a]if a soul touch any unclean thing, whether *it be* a carcase of an unclean beast, or a carcase of unclean cattle, or the carcase of unclean creeping things, and *if* it be hidden from him; he also shall be unclean, and [b]guilty.

3 Or if he touch [a]the uncleanness of man, whatsoever uncleanness *it be* that a man shall be defiled withal, and it be hid from him; when he knoweth *of it,* then he shall be guilty.

4 Or if a soul swear, pronouncing with *his* lips [a]to do evil, or [b]to do good, whatsoever *it be* that a man shall pronounce with an oath, and it be hid from him; when he knoweth *of it,* then he shall be guilty in one of these.

5 And it shall be, when he shall be guilty in one of these *things,* that he shall [a]confess that he hath sinned in that *thing:*

6 And he shall bring his trespass offering unto the LORD for his sin which he hath sinned, a female from the flock, a lamb or a kid of the goats, for a sin offering; and the priest shall make an atonement for him concerning his sin.

7 And [a]if he be not able to bring a lamb, then he shall bring for his trespass, which he hath committed, two [b]turtledoves, or two young pigeons, unto the LORD; one for a sin offering, and the other for a burnt offering.

8 And he shall bring them unto the priest, who shall offer *that* which *is* for the sin offering first, and [a]wring off his head from his neck, but shall not divide *it* asunder:

9 And he shall sprinkle of the blood of the sin offering upon the side of the altar; and the [a]rest of the blood shall be wrung out at the bottom of the altar: it *is* a sin offering.

10 And he shall offer the second *for* a burnt offering, according to the [a]manner: and [b]the priest shall make an atonement for him for his sin which he hath sinned, and it shall be forgiven him.

11 But if he be [a]not able to bring two turtledoves, or two young pigeons, then he that sinned shall bring for his offering the tenth part of an ephah of fine flour for a sin offering; [b]he shall put no oil upon it, neither shall he put *any* frankincense thereon: for it *is* a sin offering.

12 Then shall he bring it to the priest, and the priest shall take his handful of it, [a]*even* a memorial thereof, and burn *it* on the altar, [b]ac-

31 [a]Lev. 3:14 [b]Lev. 3:3, 4 [c]Gen. 8:21; Ex. 29:18; Lev. 1:9, 13; 2:2, 9, 12 [d]Lev. 4:26
32 [a]Lev. 4:28
33 [a]Lev. 1:4; Num. 8:12
35 [a]Lev. 3:5 [b]Lev. 4:26, 31

CHAPTER 5

1 [a]Prov. 29:24; [Jer. 23:10] [b]Lev. 5:17; 7:18; 17:16; 19:8; 20:17; Num. 9:13
2 [a]Lev. 11:24, 28, 31, 39; Num. 19:11–16; Deut. 14:8 [b]Lev. 5:17
3 [a]Lev. 5:12, 13, 15
4 [a]1 Sam. 25:22; Acts 23:12 [b][Matt. 5:33–37]; Mark 6:23; [James 5:12]
5 [a]Lev. 16:21; 26:40; Num. 5:7; Ezra 10:11, 12; Ps. 32:5; Prov. 28:13
7 [a]Lev. 12:6, 8; 14:21 [b]Lev. 1:14
8 [a]Lev. 1:15–17
9 [a]Lev. 4:7, 18, 30, 34
10 [a]Lev. 1:14–17 [b]Lev. 4:20, 26; 5:13, 16
11 [a]Lev. 14:21–32 [b]Lev. 2:1, 2; 6:15; Num. 5:15
12 [a]Lev. 2:2 [b]Lev. 4:35

NKJV

blood with his finger, put *it* on the horns of the altar of burnt offering, and pour all *the remaining* blood at the base of the altar.

31 [a]'He shall remove all its fat, [b]as fat is removed from the sacrifice of the peace offering; and the priest shall burn it on the altar for a [c]sweet aroma to the LORD. [d]So the priest shall make atonement for him, and it shall be forgiven him.

32 'If he brings a lamb as his sin offering, [a]he shall bring a female without blemish.

33 'Then he shall [a]lay his hand on the head of the sin offering, and kill it as a sin offering at the place where they kill the burnt offering.

34 'The priest shall take *some* of the blood of the sin offering with his finger, put *it* on the horns of the altar of burnt offering, and pour all *the remaining* blood at the base of the altar.

35 'He shall remove all its fat, as the fat of the lamb is removed from the sacrifice of the peace offering. Then the priest shall burn it on the altar, [a]according to the offerings made by fire to the LORD. [b]So the priest shall make atonement for his sin that he has committed, and it shall be forgiven him.

The Trespass Offering

5 'If a person sins in [a]hearing the utterance of an oath, and *is* a witness, whether he has seen or known *of the matter*—if he does not tell *it,* he [b]bears guilt.

2 'Or [a]if a person touches any unclean thing, whether *it is* the carcass of an unclean beast, or the carcass of unclean livestock, or the carcass of unclean creeping things, and he is unaware of it, he also shall be unclean and [b]guilty.

3 'Or if he touches [a]human uncleanness—whatever uncleanness with which a man may be defiled, and he is unaware of it—when he realizes *it,* then he shall be guilty.

4 'Or if a person swears, speaking thoughtlessly with *his* lips [a]to do evil or [b]to do good, whatever *it is* that a man may pronounce by an oath, and he is unaware of it—when he realizes *it,* then he shall be guilty in any of these *matters.*

5 'And it shall be, when he is guilty in any of these *matters,* that he shall [a]confess that he has sinned in that *thing;*

6 'and he shall bring his trespass offering to the LORD for his sin which he has committed, a female from the flock, a lamb or a kid of the goats as a sin offering. So the priest shall make atonement for him concerning his sin.

7 [a]'If he is not able to bring a lamb, then he shall bring to the LORD, for his trespass which he has committed, two [b]turtledoves or two young pigeons: one as a sin offering and the other as a burnt offering.

8 'And he shall bring them to the priest, who shall offer *that* which *is* for the sin offering first, and [a]wring off its head from its neck, but shall not divide *it* completely.

9 'Then he shall sprinkle *some* of the blood of the sin offering on the side of the altar, and the [a]rest of the blood shall be drained out at the base of the altar. It *is* a sin offering.

10 'And he shall offer the second *as* a burnt offering according to the [a]prescribed manner. So [b]the priest shall make atonement on his behalf for his sin which he has committed, and it shall be forgiven him.

11 'But if he is [a]not able to bring two turtledoves or two young pigeons, then he who sinned shall bring for his offering one-tenth of an ephah of fine flour as a sin offering. [b]He shall put no oil on it, nor shall he put frankincense on it, for it *is* a sin offering.

12 'Then he shall bring it to the priest, and the priest shall take his handful of it [a]as a memorial portion, and burn *it* on the altar [b]according

KJV

cording to the offerings made by fire unto the LORD: it *is* a sin offering.

13 [a]And the priest shall make an atonement for him as touching his sin that he hath sinned in one of these, and it shall be forgiven him: and [b]*the remnant* shall be the priest's, as a meat offering.

Offerings with Restitution

14 And the LORD spake unto Moses, saying,

15 [a]If a soul commit a trespass, and sin through ignorance, in the holy things of the LORD; then [b]he shall bring for his trespass unto the LORD a ram without blemish out of the flocks, with thy estimation by shekels of silver, after [c]the shekel of the sanctuary, for a trespass offering:

16 And he shall make amends for the harm that he hath done in the holy thing, and [a]shall add the fifth part thereto, and give it unto the priest: [b]and the priest shall make an atonement for him with the ram of the trespass offering, and it shall be forgiven him.

17 And if a soul sin, and commit any of these things which are forbidden to be done by the commandments of the LORD; [a]though he wist *it* not, yet is he [b]guilty, and shall bear his iniquity.

18 [a]And he shall bring a ram without blemish out of the flock, with thy estimation, for a trespass offering, unto the priest: and the priest shall make an atonement for him concerning his ignorance wherein he erred and wist *it* not, and it shall be forgiven him.

19 It *is* a trespass offering: [a]he hath certainly trespassed against the LORD.

6 And the LORD spake unto Moses, saying,

2 If a soul sin, and [a]commit a trespass against the LORD, and [b]lie unto his neighbour in that [c]which was delivered him to keep, or in fellowship, or in a thing taken away by violence, or hath [d]deceived his neighbour;

3 Or [a]have found that which was lost, and lieth concerning it, and [b]sweareth falsely; in any of all these that a man doeth, sinning therein:

4 Then it shall be, because he hath sinned, and is guilty, that he shall restore [a]that which he took violently away, or the thing which he hath deceitfully gotten, or that which was delivered him to keep, or the lost thing which he found,

5 Or all that about which he hath sworn falsely; he shall even [a]restore it in the principal, and shall add the fifth part more thereto, *and* give it unto him to whom it appertaineth, in the day of his trespass offering.

6 And he shall bring his trespass offering unto the LORD, [a]a ram without blemish out of the flock, with thy estimation, for a trespass offering, unto the priest:

7 [a]And the priest shall make an atonement for him before the LORD: and it shall be forgiven him for any thing of all that he hath done in trespassing therein.

The Law of the Burnt Offering

8 And the LORD spake unto Moses, saying,

9 Command Aaron and his sons, saying, This *is* the [a]law of the burnt offering: It *is* the burnt offering, because of the burning upon the altar all night unto the morning, and the fire of the altar shall be burning in it.

10 [a]And the priest shall put on his linen garment, and his linen breeches shall he put upon his flesh, and take up the ashes which the fire hath consumed with the burnt offering on the altar, and he shall put them [b]beside the altar.

11 And [a]he shall put off his garments, and put on other garments, and carry forth the ashes without the camp [b]unto a clean place.

12 And the fire upon the altar shall be burning in it; it shall not be put out: and the priest shall burn wood on it every morning, and lay the

13 [a]Lev. 4:26 [b]Lev. 2:3; 6:17, 26
15 [a]Lev. 4:2; 22:14; Num. 5:5–8 [b]Ezra 10:19 [c]Ex. 30:13; Lev. 27:25
16 [a]Lev. 6:5; 22:14; 27:13, 15, 27, 31; Num. 5:7 [b]Lev. 4:26
17 [a]Lev. 4:2, 13, 22, 27 [b]Lev. 5:1, 2
18 [a]Lev. 5:15
19 [a]Ezra 10:2

CHAPTER 6
2 [a]Num. 5:6 [b]Lev. 19:11; Acts 5:4; Col. 3:9 [c]Ex. 22:7, 10 [d]Prov. 24:28
3 [a]Ex. 23:4; Deut. 22:1–4 [b]Ex. 22:11; Lev. 19:12; Jer. 7:9; Zech. 5:4
4 [a]Lev. 24:18, 21
5 [a]Lev. 5:16; Num. 5:7, 8; 2 Sam. 12:6
6 [a]Lev. 1:3; 5:15
7 [a]Lev. 4:26
9 [a]Ex. 29:38–42; Num. 28:3–10
10 [a]Ex. 28:39–43; Lev. 16:4; Ezek. 44:17, 18 [b]Lev. 1:16
11 [a]Ezek. 44:19 [b]Lev. 4:12

NKJV

to the offerings made by fire to the LORD. It *is* a sin offering.

13 [a]'The priest shall make atonement for him, for his sin that he has committed in any of these matters; and it shall be forgiven him. [b]*The rest* shall be the priest's as a grain offering.' "

Offerings with Restitution

14 Then the LORD spoke to Moses, saying:

15 [a]"If a person commits a trespass, and sins unintentionally in regard to the holy things of the LORD, then [b]he shall bring to the LORD as his trespass offering a ram without blemish from the flocks, with your valuation in shekels of silver according to [c]the shekel of the sanctuary, as a trespass offering.

16 "And he shall make restitution for the harm that he has done in regard to the holy thing, [a]and shall add one-fifth to it and give it to the priest. [b]So the priest shall make atonement for him with the ram of the trespass offering, and it shall be forgiven him.

17 "If a person sins, and commits any of these things which are forbidden to be done by the commandments of the LORD, [a]though he does not know *it,* yet he is [b]guilty and shall bear his iniquity.

18 [a]"And he shall bring to the priest a ram without blemish from the flock, with your valuation, as a trespass offering. So the priest shall make atonement for him regarding his ignorance in which he erred and did not know *it,* and it shall be forgiven him.

19 "It is a trespass offering; [a]he has certainly trespassed against the LORD."

6 And the LORD spoke to Moses, saying:

2 "If a person sins and [a]commits a trespass against the LORD by [b]lying to his neighbor about [c]what was delivered to him for safekeeping, or about a pledge, or about a robbery, or if he has [d]extorted from his neighbor,

3 "or if he [a]has found what was lost and lies concerning it, and [b]swears falsely—in any one of these things that a man may do in which he sins:

4 "then it shall be, because he has sinned and is guilty, that he shall restore [a]what he has stolen, or the thing which he has extorted, or what was delivered to him for safekeeping, or the lost thing which he found,

5 "or all that about which he has sworn falsely. He shall [a]restore its full value, add one-fifth more to it, *and* give it to whomever it belongs, on the day of his trespass offering.

6 "And he shall bring his trespass offering to the LORD, [a]a ram without blemish from the flock, with your valuation, as a trespass offering, to the priest.

7 [a]"So the priest shall make atonement for him before the LORD, and he shall be forgiven for any one of these things that he may have done in which he trespasses."

The Law of the Burnt Offering

8 Then the LORD spoke to Moses, saying,

9 "Command Aaron and his sons, saying, 'This *is* the [a]law of the burnt offering: The burnt offering *shall be* on the hearth upon the altar all night until morning, and the fire of the altar shall be kept burning on it.

10 [a]'And the priest shall put on his linen garment, and his linen trousers he shall put on his body, and take up the ashes of the burnt offering which the fire has consumed on the altar, and he shall put them [b]beside the altar.

11 'Then [a]he shall take off his garments, put on other garments, and carry the ashes outside the camp [b]to a clean place.

12 'And the fire on the altar shall be kept burning on it; it shall not be put out. And the priest shall burn wood on it every morning, and lay the

KJV

burnt offering in order upon it; and he shall burn thereon [a]the fat of the peace offerings.

13 The fire shall ever be burning upon the [a]altar; it shall never go out.

The Law of the Grain Offering

14 And this *is* the law of the meat offering: the sons of Aaron shall offer it before the LORD, before the altar.

15 And he shall take of it his handful, of the flour of the meat offering, and of the oil thereof, and all the frankincense which *is* upon the meat offering, and shall burn *it* upon the altar *for* a sweet savour, *even* the memorial of it, unto the LORD.

16 And the remainder thereof shall Aaron and his sons eat: with unleavened bread shall it be eaten in the holy place; in the court of the tabernacle of the congregation they shall eat it.

17 It shall not be baken with leaven. I have given it *unto them for* their portion of my offerings made by fire; it *is* most holy, as *is* the sin offering, and as the [a]trespass offering.

18 [a]All the males among the children of Aaron shall eat of it. [b]*It shall be* a statute for ever in your generations concerning the offerings of the LORD made by fire: [c]every one that toucheth them shall be holy.

19 And the LORD spake unto Moses, saying,

20 [a]This *is* the offering of Aaron and of his sons, which they shall offer unto the LORD in the day when he is anointed; the tenth part of an [b]ephah of fine flour for a meat offering perpetual, half of it in the morning, and half thereof at night.

21 In a [a]pan it shall be made with oil; *and when it is* baken, thou shalt bring it in: *and* the baken pieces of the meat offering shalt thou offer *for* a sweet savour unto the LORD.

22 And the priest of his sons [a]that is anointed in his stead shall offer it: *it is* a statute for ever unto the LORD; [b]it shall be wholly burnt.

23 For every meat offering for the priest shall be wholly burnt: it shall not be eaten.

The Law of the Sin Offering

24 And the LORD spake unto Moses, saying,

25 Speak unto Aaron and to his sons, saying, This *is* the law of the sin offering: [a]In the place where the burnt offering is killed shall the sin offering be killed before the LORD: it *is* most holy.

26 [a]The priest that offereth it for sin shall eat it: in the holy place shall it be eaten, in the court of the tabernacle of the congregation.

27 [a]Whatsoever shall touch the flesh thereof shall be holy: and when there is sprinkled of the blood thereof upon any garment, thou shalt wash that whereon it was sprinkled in the holy place.

28 But the earthen vessel wherein it is sodden [a]shall be broken: and if it be sodden in a brasen pot, it shall be both scoured, and rinsed in water.

29 All the males among the priests shall eat thereof: it *is* most holy.

30 [a]And no sin offering, whereof *any* of the blood is brought into the tabernacle of the congregation to reconcile *withal* in the holy [b]*place,* shall be [c]eaten: it shall be [d]burnt in the fire.

The Law of the Trespass Offering

7 Likewise [a]this *is* the law of the trespass offering: it *is* most holy.

2 In the place where they kill the burnt offering shall they kill the trespass offering: and the blood thereof shall he sprinkle round about upon the altar.

3 And he shall offer of it all the fat thereof; the rump, and the fat that covereth the inwards,

4 And the two kidneys, and the fat that *is* on them, which *is* by the flanks, and the caul *that is* above the liver, with the kidneys, it shall he take away:

5 And the priest shall burn them upon the

---

12 [a]Lev. 3:3, 5, 9, 14
13 [a]Lev. 1:7
17 [a]Lev. 7:7
18 [a]Lev. 6:29; 7:6; Num. 18:10; 1 Cor. 9:13 [b]Lev. 3:17 [c]Ex. 29:37; Lev. 22:3–7; Num. 4:15; Hag. 2:11–13
20 [a]Ex. 29:2 [b]Ex. 16:36
21 [a]Lev. 2:5; 7:9
22 [a]Lev. 4:3 [b]Ex. 29:25
25 [a]Lev. 1:1, 3, 5, 11
26 [a][Lev. 10:17, 18]; Num. 18:9, 10; [Ezek. 44:28, 29]
27 [a]Ex. 29:37; Num. 4:15; Hag. 2:11–13
28 [a]Lev. 11:33; 15:12
30 [a]Lev. 4:7, 11, 12, 18, 21; 10:18; 16:27; [Heb. 13:11, 12] [b]Ex. 26:33 [c]Lev. 6:16, 23, 26 [d]Lev. 16:27

CHAPTER 7
1 [a]Lev. 5:14—6:7

NKJV

burnt offering in order on it; and he shall burn on it [a]the fat of the peace offerings.

13 'A fire shall always be burning on the [a]altar; it shall never go out.

The Law of the Grain Offering

14 'This *is* the law of the grain offering: The sons of Aaron shall offer it on the altar before the LORD.

15 'He shall take from it his handful of the fine flour of the grain offering, with its oil, and all the frankincense which *is* on the grain offering, and shall burn *it* on the altar *for* a sweet aroma, as a memorial to the LORD.

16 'And the remainder of it Aaron and his sons shall eat; with unleavened bread it shall be eaten in a holy place; in the court of the tabernacle of meeting they shall eat it.

17 'It shall not be baked with leaven. I have given it *as* their portion of My offerings made by fire; it *is* most holy, like the sin offering and the [a]trespass offering.

18 [a]'All the males among the children of Aaron may eat it. [b]*It shall be* a statute forever in your generations concerning the offerings made by fire to the LORD. [c]Everyone who touches them must be holy.' "

19 And the LORD spoke to Moses, saying,

20 [a]"This *is* the offering of Aaron and his sons, which they shall offer to the LORD, *beginning* on the day when he is anointed: one-tenth of an [b]ephah of fine flour as a daily grain offering, half of it in the morning and half of it at night.

21 "It shall be made in a [a]pan with oil. *When it is* mixed, you shall bring it in. The baked pieces of the grain offering you shall offer *for* a sweet aroma to the LORD.

22 "The priest from among his sons, [a]who is anointed in his place, shall offer it. *It is* a statute forever to the LORD. [b]It shall be wholly burned.

23 "For every grain offering for the priest shall be wholly burned. It shall not be eaten."

The Law of the Sin Offering

24 Also the LORD spoke to Moses, saying,

25 "Speak to Aaron and to his sons, saying, 'This *is* the law of the sin offering: [a]In the place where the burnt offering is killed, the sin offering shall be killed before the LORD. It *is* most holy.

26 [a]'The priest who offers it for sin shall eat it. In a holy place it shall be eaten, in the court of the tabernacle of meeting.

27 [a]'Everyone who touches its flesh must be holy. And when its blood is sprinkled on any garment, you shall wash that on which it was sprinkled, in a holy place.

28 'But the earthen vessel in which it is boiled [a]shall be broken. And if it is boiled in a bronze pot, it shall be both scoured and rinsed in water.

29 'All the males among the priests may eat it. It *is* most holy.

30 [a]'But no sin offering from which *any* of the blood is brought into the tabernacle of meeting, to make atonement in *the holy [b]*place,* shall be [c]eaten. It shall be [d]burned in the fire.

The Law of the Trespass Offering

7 'Likewise [a]this *is* the law of the trespass offering (it *is* most holy):

2 'In the place where they kill the burnt offering they shall kill the trespass offering. And its blood he shall sprinkle all around on the altar.

3 'And he shall offer from it all its fat. The fat tail and the fat that covers the entrails,

4 'the two kidneys and the fat that *is* on them by the flanks, and the fatty lobe *attached* to the liver above the kidneys, he shall remove;

5 'and the priest shall burn them on the altar

---

*6:30 The Most Holy Place when capitalized

KJV

altar *for* an offering made by fire unto the LORD: it *is* a trespass offering.

6 [a]Every male among the priests shall eat thereof: it shall be eaten in the holy place: [b]it *is* most holy.

7 As the sin offering *is*, so *is* [a]the trespass offering: *there is* one law for them: the priest that maketh atonement therewith shall have *it*.

8 And the priest that offereth any man's burnt offering, *even* the priest shall have to himself the skin of the burnt offering which he hath offered.

9 And [a]all the meat offering that is baken in the oven, and all that is dressed in the fryingpan, and in the pan, shall be the priest's that offereth it.

10 And every meat offering, mingled with oil, and dry, shall all the sons of Aaron have, one *as much* as another.

The Law of Peace Offerings

11 And [a]this *is* the law of the sacrifice of peace offerings, which he shall offer unto the LORD.

12 If he offer it for a thanksgiving, then he shall offer with the sacrifice of thanksgiving unleavened cakes mingled with oil, and unleavened wafers [a]anointed with oil, and cakes mingled with oil, of fine flour, fried.

13 Besides the cakes, he shall offer *for* his offering [a]leavened bread with the sacrifice of thanksgiving of his peace offerings.

14 And of it he shall offer one out of the whole oblation *for* an heave offering unto the LORD, [a]*and* it shall be the priest's that sprinkleth the blood of the peace offerings.

15 [a]And the flesh of the sacrifice of his peace offerings for thanksgiving shall be eaten the same day that it is offered; he shall not leave any of it until the morning.

16 But [a]if the sacrifice of his offering *be* a vow, or a voluntary offering, it shall be eaten the same day that he offereth his sacrifice: and on the morrow also the remainder of it shall be eaten:

17 But the remainder of the flesh of the sacrifice on the third day shall be burnt with fire.

18 And if *any* of the flesh of the sacrifice of his peace offerings be eaten at all on the third day, it shall not be accepted, neither shall it be [a]imputed unto him that offereth it: it shall be an [b]abomination, and the soul that eateth of it shall bear his iniquity.

19 And the flesh that toucheth any unclean *thing* shall not be eaten; it shall be burnt with fire: and as for the flesh, all that be clean shall eat thereof.

20 But the soul that eateth *of* the flesh of the sacrifice of peace offerings, that *pertain* unto the [a]LORD, [b]having his uncleanness upon him, even that soul [c]shall be cut off from his people.

21 Moreover the soul that shall touch any unclean *thing, as* [a]the uncleanness of man, or *any* [b]unclean beast, or any [c]abominable unclean *thing*, and eat of the flesh of the sacrifice of peace offerings, which *pertain* unto the LORD, even that soul [d]shall be cut off from his people.

Fat and Blood May Not Be Eaten

22 And the LORD spake unto Moses, saying,

23 Speak unto the children of Israel, saying, [a]Ye shall eat no manner of fat, of ox, or of sheep, or of goat.

24 And the fat of the beast that dieth of itself, and the fat of that which is torn with beasts, may be used in any other use: but ye shall in no wise eat of it.

25 For whosoever eateth the fat of the beast, of which men offer an offering made by fire unto the LORD, even the soul that eateth *it* shall be cut off from his people.

26 [a]Moreover ye shall eat no manner of

---

6 [a]Lev. 6:16–18, 29; Num. 18:9 [b]Lev. 2:3
7 [a]Lev. 6:24–30; 14:13
9 [a]Lev. 2:3, 10; Num. 18:9; Ezek. 44:29
11 [a]Lev. 3:1; 22:18, 21; Ezek. 45:15
12 [a]Lev. 2:4; Num. 6:15
13 [a]Lev. 2:12; 23:17, 18; Amos 4:5
14 [a]Num. 18:8, 11, 19
15 [a]Lev. 22:29, 30
16 [a]Lev. 19:5–8
18 [a]Num. 18:27 [b]Lev. 11:10, 11, 41; 19:7; [Prov. 15:8]
20 [a][Heb. 2:17] [b]Lev. 5:3; 15:3; 22:3–7; Num. 19:13; [1 Cor. 11:28] [c]Gen. 17:14; Ex. 31:14
21 [a]Lev. 5:2, 3, 5 [b]Lev. 11:24, 28 [c]Ezek. 4:14 [d]Lev. 7:20
23 [a]Lev. 3:17; 17:10–15; Deut. 14:21; Ezek. 4:14; 44:31
26 [a]Gen. 9:4; Lev. 3:17; 17:10–16; 19:26; Deut. 12:23; 1 Sam. 14:33; Ezek. 33:25; [John 6:53]; Acts 15:20, 29

NKJV

as an offering made by fire to the LORD. It *is* a trespass offering.

6 [a]'Every male among the priests may eat it. It shall be eaten in a holy place. [b]It *is* most holy.

7 [a]'The trespass offering *is* like the sin offering; *there is* one law for them both: the priest who makes atonement with it shall have *it*.

8 'And the priest who offers anyone's burnt offering, that priest shall have for himself the skin of the burnt offering which he has offered.

9 'Also [a]every grain offering that is baked in the oven and all that is prepared in the covered pan, or in a pan, shall be the priest's who offers it.

10 'Every grain offering, *whether* mixed with oil or dry, shall belong to all the sons of Aaron, to one *as much* as the other.

The Law of Peace Offerings

11 [a]'This *is* the law of the sacrifice of peace offerings which he shall offer to the LORD:

12 'If he offers it for a thanksgiving, then he shall offer, with the sacrifice of thanksgiving, unleavened cakes mixed with oil, unleavened wafers [a]anointed with oil, or cakes of blended flour mixed with oil.

13 'Besides the cakes, *as* his offering he shall offer [a]leavened bread with the sacrifice of thanksgiving of his peace offering.

14 'And from it he shall offer one cake from each offering *as* a heave offering to the LORD. [a]It shall belong to the priest who sprinkles the blood of the peace offering.

15 [a]'The flesh of the sacrifice of his peace offering for thanksgiving shall be eaten the same day it is offered. He shall not leave any of it until morning.

16 'But [a]if the sacrifice of his offering *is* a vow or a voluntary offering, it shall be eaten the same day that he offers his sacrifice; but on the next day the remainder of it also may be eaten;

17 'the remainder of the flesh of the sacrifice on the third day must be burned with fire.

18 'And if *any* of the flesh of the sacrifice of his peace offering is eaten at all on the third day, it shall not be accepted, nor shall it be [a]imputed to him; it shall be an [b]abomination *to* him who offers it, and the person who eats of it shall bear guilt.

19 'The flesh that touches any unclean thing shall not be eaten. It shall be burned with fire. And as for the *clean* flesh, all who are clean may eat of it.

20 'But the person who eats the flesh of the sacrifice of the peace offering that *belongs* to the [a]LORD, [b]while he is unclean, that person [c]shall be cut off from his people.

21 'Moreover the person who touches any unclean thing, *such as* [a]human uncleanness, *an* [b]unclean animal, or any [c]abominable* unclean thing, and who eats the flesh of the sacrifice of the peace offering that *belongs* to the LORD, that person [d]shall be cut off from his people.' "

Fat and Blood May Not Be Eaten

22 And the LORD spoke to Moses, saying,

23 "Speak to the children of Israel, saying: [a]'You shall not eat any fat, of ox or sheep or goat.

24 'And the fat of an animal that dies *naturally*, and the fat of what is torn by wild beasts, may be used in any other way; but you shall by no means eat it.

25 'For whoever eats the fat of the animal of which men offer an offering made by fire to the LORD, the person who eats *it* shall be cut off from his people.

26 [a]'Moreover you shall not eat any blood

---

*7:21 So with MT, LXX, Vg.; Sam., Syr., Tg. *swarming thing* (cf. 5:2)

KJV

blood, *whether it be* of fowl or of beast, in any
of your dwellings.
27 Whatsoever soul *it be* that eateth any
manner of blood, even that soul shall be cut off
from his people.

The Portion of Aaron and His Sons

28 And the LORD spake unto Moses, saying,
29 Speak unto the children of Israel, saying,
[a]He that offereth the sacrifice of his peace offerings unto the LORD shall bring his oblation unto
the LORD of the sacrifice of his peace offerings.
30 [a]His own hands shall bring the offerings
of the LORD made by fire, the fat with the breast,
it shall he bring, that the [b]breast may be waved
for a wave offering before the LORD.
31 [a]And the priest shall burn the fat upon
the altar: but the [b]breast shall be Aaron's and his
sons'.
32 And [a]the right shoulder shall ye give unto
the priest *for* an heave offering of the sacrifices
of your peace offerings.
33 He among the sons of Aaron, that offereth
the blood of the peace offerings, and the fat, shall
have the right shoulder for *his* part.
34 For [a]the wave breast and the heave shoulder have I taken of the children of Israel from
off the sacrifices of their peace offerings, and have
given them unto Aaron the priest and unto his
sons by a statute for ever from among the children
of Israel.
35 This *is the portion* of the anointing of
Aaron, and of the anointing of his sons, out of
the offerings of the LORD made by fire, in the day
when he presented them to minister unto the LORD
in the priest's office;
36 Which the LORD commanded to be given
them of the children of Israel, [a]in the day that
he anointed them, *by* a statute for ever throughout
their generations.
37 This *is* the law [a]of the burnt offering, [b]of
the meat offering, [c]and of the sin offering, [d]and
of the trespass offering, [e]and of the consecrations,
and [f]of the sacrifice of the peace offerings;
38 Which the LORD commanded Moses in
mount Sinai, in the day that he commanded the
children of Israel [a]to offer their oblations unto the
LORD, in the wilderness of Sinai.

Aaron and His Sons Consecrated
(Ex. 29:1–37)

8 And the LORD spake unto Moses, saying,
2 [a]Take Aaron and his sons with him, and
[b]the garments, and [c]the anointing oil, and a [d]bull-
ock for the sin offering, and two [e]rams, and a
basket of unleavened bread;
3 And gather thou all the congregation together unto the door of the tabernacle of the
congregation.
4 And Moses did as the LORD commanded
him; and the assembly was gathered together unto
the door of the tabernacle of the congregation.
5 And Moses said unto the congregation,
This *is* the thing which the LORD commanded to
be done.
6 And Moses brought Aaron and his sons,
and [a]washed them with water.
7 And he [a]put upon him the coat, and girded
him with the girdle, and clothed him with the robe,
and put the ephod upon him, and he girded him
with the curious girdle of the ephod, and bound
it unto him therewith.
8 And he put the breastplate upon him: also
he [a]put in the breastplate the Urim and the
Thummim.
9 [a]And he put the mitre upon his head; also
upon the mitre, *even* upon his forefront, did he
put the golden plate, the holy crown; as the LORD
commanded Moses.
10 [a]And Moses took the anointing oil, and
anointed the tabernacle and all that *was* therein,
and sanctified them.

29 [a]Lev. 3:1; 22:21; Ezek. 45:15
30 [a]Lev. 3:3, 4, 9, 14 [b]Ex. 29:24, 27; Lev. 8:27; 9:21; Num. 6:20
31 [a]Lev. 3:5, 11, 16 [b]Num. 18:11; Deut. 18:3
32 [a]Ex. 29:27; Lev. 7:34; 9:21; Num. 6:20
34 [a]Ex. 29:28; Lev. 10:14, 15; Num. 18:18, 19; Deut. 18:3
36 [a]Ex. 40:13–15; Lev. 8:12, 30
37 [a]Lev. 6:9 [b]Lev. 6:14 [c]Lev. 6:25 [d]Lev. 7:1 [e]Ex. 29:1; Lev. 6:20 [f]Lev. 7:11
38 [a]Lev. 1:1, 2; Deut. 4:5

CHAPTER 8

2 [a]Ex. 29:1–3 [b]Ex. 28:2, 4 [c]Ex. 30:24, 25 [d]Ex. 29:10 [e]Ex. 29:15, 19
6 [a]Ex. 30:20; Heb. 10:22
7 [a]Ex. 39:1–31
8 [a]Ex. 28:30; Num. 27:21; Deut. 33:8; 1 Sam. 28:6; Ezra 2:63; Neh. 7:65
9 [a]Ex. 28:36, 37; 29:6
10 [a]Ex. 30:26–29; 40:10, 11; Lev. 8:2

*8:8 Lit. *Lights and the Perfections,* Ex. 28:30

NKJV

in any of your dwellings, *whether* of bird or beast.
27 'Whoever eats any blood, that person shall
be cut off from his people.' "

The Portion of Aaron and His Sons

28 Then the LORD spoke to Moses, saying,
29 "Speak to the children of Israel, saying:
[a]'He who offers the sacrifice of his peace offering
to the LORD shall bring his offering to the LORD
from the sacrifice of his peace offering.
30 [a]'His own hands shall bring the offerings
made by fire to the LORD. The fat with the breast
he shall bring, that the [b]breast may be waved *as*
a wave offering before the LORD.
31 [a]'And the priest shall burn the fat on the
altar, but the [b]breast shall be Aaron's and his
sons'.
32 [a]'Also the right thigh you shall give to the
priest *as* a heave offering from the sacrifices of
your peace offerings.
33 'He among the sons of Aaron, who offers
the blood of the peace offering and the fat, shall
have the right thigh for *his* part.
34 'For [a]the breast of the wave offering and
the thigh of the heave offering I have taken from
the children of Israel, from the sacrifices of their
peace offerings, and I have given them to Aaron
the priest and to his sons from the children of
Israel by a statute forever.' "
35 This *is* the consecrated portion for Aaron
and his sons, from the offerings made by fire to
the LORD, on the day when *Moses* presented them
to minister to the LORD as priests.
36 The LORD commanded this to be given to
them by the children of Israel, [a]on the day that
He anointed them, *by* a statute forever throughout
their generations.
37 This *is* the law [a]of the burnt offering, [b]the
grain offering, [c]the sin offering, [d]the trespass offering, [e]the consecrations, and [f]the sacrifice of the
peace offering,
38 which the LORD commanded Moses on
Mount Sinai, on the day when He commanded
the children of Israel [a]to offer their offerings to
the LORD in the Wilderness of Sinai.

Aaron and His Sons Consecrated
(Ex. 29:1–37)

8 And the LORD spoke to Moses, saying:
2 [a]"Take Aaron and his sons with him, and
[b]the garments, [c]the anointing oil, a [d]bull as the
sin offering, two [e]rams, and a basket of unleavened bread;
3 "and gather all the congregation together
at the door of the tabernacle of meeting."
4 So Moses did as the LORD commanded
him. And the congregation was gathered together
at the door of the tabernacle of meeting.
5 And Moses said to the congregation, "This
is what the LORD commanded to be done."
6 Then Moses brought Aaron and his sons
and [a]washed them with water.
7 And he [a]put the tunic on him, girded him
with the sash, clothed him with the robe, and put
the ephod on him; and he girded him with the
intricately woven band of the ephod, and with it
tied *the ephod* on him.
8 Then he put the breastplate on him, and
he [a]put the *Urim and the Thummim in the
breastplate.
9 [a]And he put the turban on his head. Also
on the turban, on its front, he put the golden plate,
the holy crown, as the LORD had commanded
Moses.
10 [a]Also Moses took the anointing oil, and
anointed the tabernacle and all that *was* in it, and
consecrated them.

KJV

11 And he sprinkled thereof upon the altar
seven times, and anointed the altar and all his
vessels, both the laver and his foot, to sanctify
them.
12 And he [a]poured of the anointing oil upon
Aaron's head, and anointed him, to sanctify him.
13 [a]And Moses brought Aaron's sons, and
put coats upon them, and girded them with girdles, and put bonnets upon them; as the LORD
commanded Moses.
14 [a]And he brought the bullock for the sin
offering: and Aaron and his sons [b]laid their hands
upon the head of the bullock for the sin offering.
15 And he slew *it;* [a]and Moses took the
blood, and put *it* upon the horns of the altar round
about with his finger, and purified the altar, and
poured the blood at the bottom of the altar, and
sanctified it, to make reconciliation upon it.
16 [a]And he took all the fat that *was* upon
the inwards, and the caul *above* the liver, and the
two kidneys, and their fat, and Moses burned *it*
upon the altar.
17 But the bullock, and his hide, his flesh,
and his dung, he burnt with fire without the camp;
as the LORD [a]commanded Moses.
18 [a]And he brought the ram for the burnt offering: and Aaron and his sons laid their hands
upon the head of the ram.
19 And he killed *it;* and Moses sprinkled the
blood upon the altar round about.
20 And he cut the ram into pieces; and Moses
[a]burnt the head, and the pieces, and the fat.
21 And he washed the inwards and the legs
in water; and Moses burnt the whole ram upon
the altar: it *was* a burnt sacrifice for a sweet savour, *and* an offering made by fire unto the LORD;
[a]as the LORD commanded Moses.
22 And [a]he brought the other ram, the ram
of consecration: and Aaron and his sons laid their
hands upon the head of the ram.
23 And he slew *it;* and Moses took of the
[a]blood of it, and put *it* upon the tip of Aaron's
right ear, and upon the thumb of his right hand,
and upon the great toe of his right foot.
24 And he brought Aaron's sons, and Moses
put of the [a]blood upon the tip of their right ear,
and upon the thumbs of their right hands, and
upon the great toes of their right feet: and Moses
sprinkled the blood upon the altar round about.
25 [a]And he took the fat, and the rump, and
all the fat that *was* upon the inwards, and the
caul *above* the liver, and the two kidneys, and
their fat, and the right shoulder:
26 [a]And out of the basket of unleavened
bread, that *was* before the LORD, he took one unleavened cake, and a cake of oiled bread, and one
wafer, and put *them* on the fat, and upon the right
shoulder:
27 And he put all [a]upon Aaron's hands, and
upon his sons' hands, and waved them *for* a wave
offering before the LORD.
28 [a]And Moses took them from off their
hands, and burnt *them* on the altar upon the burnt
offering: they *were* consecrations for a sweet
savour: it *is* an offering made by fire unto the
LORD.
29 And [a]Moses took the [b]breast, and waved
it *for* a wave offering before the LORD: *for* of the
ram of consecration it was Moses' [c]part; as the
LORD commanded Moses.
30 And [a]Moses took of the anointing oil, and
of the blood which *was* upon the altar, and sprinkled *it* upon Aaron, *and* upon his garments, and
upon his sons, and upon his sons' garments with
him; and sanctified Aaron, *and* his garments, and
his sons, and his sons' garments with him.
31 And Moses said unto Aaron and to his
sons, [a]Boil the flesh *at* the door of the tabernacle
of the congregation: and there eat it with the
bread that *is* in the basket of consecrations, as I
commanded, saying, Aaron and his sons shall eat
it.

12 [a]Ex. 29:7; 30:30; Lev. 21:10, 12; Ps. 133:2
13 [a]Ex. 29:8, 9
14 [a]Ex. 29:10; Ps. 66:15; Ezek. 43:19 [b]Lev. 4:4
15 [a]Ex. 29:12, 36; Lev. 4:7; Ezek. 43:20, 26; [Heb. 9:22]
16 [a]Ex. 29:13; Lev. 4:8
17 [a]Ex. 29:14; Lev. 4:11, 12
18 [a]Ex. 29:15
20 [a]Lev. 1:8
21 [a]Ex. 29:18
22 [a]Ex. 29:19, 31; Lev. 8:2
23 [a]Ex. 29:20, 21; Lev. 14:14
24 [a][Heb. 9:13, 14, 18–23]
25 [a]Ex. 29:22
26 [a]Ex. 29:23
27 [a]Ex. 29:24; Lev. 7:30, 34
28 [a]Ex. 29:25
29 [a]Ps. 99:6 [b]Ex. 29:27 [c]Ex. 29:26
30 [a]Ex. 29:21; 30:30; Num. 3:3
31 [a]Ex. 29:31, 32

NKJV

11 He sprinkled some of it on the altar seven
times, anointed the altar and all its utensils, and
the laver and its base, to consecrate them.
12 And he [a]poured some of the anointing oil
on Aaron's head and anointed him, to consecrate
him.
13 [a]Then Moses brought Aaron's sons and
put tunics on them, girded them with sashes, and
put hats on them, as the LORD had commanded
Moses.
14 [a]And he brought the bull for the sin offering. Then Aaron and his sons [b]laid their hands
on the head of the bull for the sin offering,
15 and Moses killed *it.* [a]Then he took the
blood, and put *some* on the horns of the altar all
around with his finger, and purified the altar. And
he poured the blood at the base of the altar, and
consecrated it, to make atonement for it.
16 [a]Then he took all the fat that *was* on the
entrails, the fatty lobe *attached to* the liver, and
the two kidneys with their fat, and Moses burned
them on the altar.
17 But the bull, its hide, its flesh, and its offal,
he burned with fire outside the camp, as the LORD
[a]had commanded Moses.
18 [a]Then he brought the ram as the burnt
offering. And Aaron and his sons laid their hands
on the head of the ram,
19 and Moses killed *it.* Then he sprinkled the
blood all around on the altar.
20 And he cut the ram into pieces; and Moses
[a]burned the head, the pieces, and the fat.
21 Then he washed the entrails and the legs
in water. And Moses burned the whole ram on
the altar. It *was* a burnt sacrifice for a sweet
aroma, an offering made by fire to the LORD, [a]as
the LORD had commanded Moses.
22 And [a]he brought the second ram, the ram
of consecration. Then Aaron and his sons laid
their hands on the head of the ram,
23 and Moses killed *it.* Also he took *some*
of [a]its blood and put it on the tip of Aaron's right
ear, on the thumb of his right hand, and on the
big toe of his right foot.
24 Then he brought Aaron's sons. And Moses
put *some* of the [a]blood on the tips of their right
ears, on the thumbs of their right hands, and on
the big toes of their right feet. And Moses sprinkled the blood all around on the altar.
25 [a]Then he took the fat and the fat tail, all
the fat that *was* on the entrails, the fatty lobe
attached to the liver, the two kidneys and their
fat, and the right thigh;
26 [a]and from the basket of unleavened bread
that was before the LORD he took one unleavened
cake, a cake of bread *anointed with* oil, and one
wafer, and put *them* on the fat and on the right
thigh;
27 and he put all *these* [a]in Aaron's hands and
in his sons' hands, and waved them *as* a wave
offering before the LORD.
28 [a]Then Moses took them from their hands
and burned *them* on the altar, on the burnt offering. They *were* consecration offerings for a sweet
aroma. That *was* an offering made by fire to the
LORD.
29 And [a]Moses took the [b]breast and waved
it *as* a wave offering before the LORD. It was Moses' [c]part of the ram of consecration, as the LORD
had commanded Moses.
30 Then [a]Moses took some of the anointing
oil and some of the blood which *was* on the altar,
and sprinkled *it* on Aaron, on his garments, on
his sons, and on the garments of his sons with
him; and he consecrated Aaron, his garments, his
sons, and the garments of his sons with him.
31 And Moses said to Aaron and his sons,
[a]"Boil the flesh *at* the door of the tabernacle of
meeting, and eat it there with the bread that *is*
in the basket of consecration offerings, as I commanded, saying, 'Aaron and his sons shall eat it.'

KJV

32 [a]And that which remaineth of the flesh and of the bread shall ye burn with fire.

33 And ye shall not go out of the door of the tabernacle of the congregation *in* seven days, until the days of your consecration be at an end: for [a]seven days shall he consecrate you.

34 [a]As he hath done this day, *so* the LORD hath commanded to do, to make an atonement for you.

35 Therefore shall ye abide *at* the door of the tabernacle of the congregation day and night seven days, and [a]keep the charge of the LORD, that ye die not: for so I am commanded.

36 So Aaron and his sons did all things which the LORD commanded by the hand of Moses.

The Priestly Ministry Begins

9 And [a]it came to pass on the eighth day, *that* Moses called Aaron and his sons, and the elders of Israel;

2 And he said unto Aaron, Take thee a young [a]calf for a sin offering, and a ram for a burnt offering, without blemish, and offer *them* before the LORD.

3 And unto the children of Israel thou shalt speak, saying, [a]Take ye a kid of the goats for a sin offering; and a calf and a lamb, *both* of the first year, without blemish, for a burnt offering;

4 Also a bullock and a ram for peace offerings, to sacrifice before the LORD; and [a]a meat offering mingled with oil: for [b]to day the LORD will appear unto you.

5 And they brought *that* which Moses commanded before the tabernacle of the congregation: and all the congregation drew near and stood before the LORD.

6 And Moses said, This *is* the thing which the LORD commanded that ye should do: and the glory of the LORD shall appear unto you.

7 And Moses said unto Aaron, Go unto the altar, and [a]offer thy sin offering, and thy burnt offering, and make an atonement for thyself, and for the people: and [b]offer the offering of the people, and make an atonement for them; as the LORD commanded.

8 Aaron therefore went unto the altar, and slew the calf of the sin offering, which *was* for himself.

9 And the sons of Aaron brought the blood unto him: and he dipped his finger in the blood, and put *it* upon the horns of the altar, and poured out the blood at the bottom of the altar:

10 [a]But the fat, and the kidneys, and the caul above the liver of the sin offering, he burnt upon the altar; as the LORD commanded Moses.

11 [a]And the flesh and the hide he burnt with fire without the camp.

12 And he slew the burnt offering; and Aaron's sons presented unto him the blood, [a]which he sprinkled round about upon the altar.

13 [a]And they presented the burnt offering unto him, with the pieces thereof, and the head: and he burnt *them* upon the altar.

14 [a]And he did wash the inwards and the legs, and burnt *them* upon the burnt offering on the altar.

15 [a]And he brought the people's offering, and took the goat, which *was* the sin offering for the people, and slew it, and offered it for sin, as the first.

16 And he brought the burnt offering, and offered it [a]according to the manner.

17 And he brought the meat offering, and took an handful thereof, and burnt *it* upon the altar, [a]beside the burnt sacrifice of the morning.

18 He slew also the bullock and the ram *for* [a]a sacrifice of peace offerings, which *was* for the people: and Aaron's sons presented unto him the blood, which he sprinkled upon the altar round about,

19 And the fat of the bullock and of the ram,

32 [a]Ex. 29:34
33 [a]Ex. 29:30, 35; Lev. 10:7; Ezek. 43:25, 26
34 [a][Heb. 7:16]
35 [a]Num. 1:53; 3:7; 9:19; Deut. 11:1; 1 Kin. 2:3; Ezek. 48:11

CHAPTER 9

1 [a]Ezek. 43:27
2 [a]Ex. 29:21; Lev. 4:1–12
3 [a]Lev. 4:23, 28; Ezra 6:17; 10:19
4 [a]Lev. 2:4 [b]Ex. 29:43; Lev. 9:6, 23
7 [a]Lev. 4:3; 1 Sam. 3:14; [Heb. 5:3–5; 7:27] [b]Lev. 4:16, 20; Heb. 5:1
10 [a]Ex. 23:18; Lev. 8:16
11 [a]Lev. 4:11, 12; 8:17
12 [a]Lev. 1:5; 8:19
13 [a]Lev. 8:20
14 [a]Lev. 8:21
15 [a][Is. 53:10; Heb. 2:17; 5:3]
16 [a]Lev. 1:1–13
17 [a]Ex. 29:38, 39
18 [a]Lev. 3:1–11

NKJV

32 [a]"What remains of the flesh and of the bread you shall burn with fire.

33 "And you shall not go outside the door of the tabernacle of meeting *for* seven days, until the days of your consecration are ended. For [a]seven days he shall consecrate you.

34 [a]"As he has done this day, *so* the LORD has commanded to do, to make atonement for you.

35 "Therefore you shall stay *at* the door of the tabernacle of meeting day and night for seven days, and [a]keep the charge of the LORD, so that you may not die; for so I have been commanded."

36 So Aaron and his sons did all the things that the LORD had commanded by the hand of Moses.

The Priestly Ministry Begins

9 It came to pass on the [a]eighth day that Moses called Aaron and his sons and the elders of Israel.

2 And he said to Aaron, "Take for yourself a young [a]bull as a sin offering and a ram as a burnt offering, without blemish, and offer *them* before the LORD.

3 "And to the children of Israel you shall speak, saying, [a]'Take a kid of the goats as a sin offering, and a calf and a lamb, *both* of the first year, without blemish, as a burnt offering,

4 'also a bull and a ram as peace offerings, to sacrifice before the LORD, and [a]a grain offering mixed with oil; for [b]today the LORD will appear to you.'"

5 So they brought what Moses commanded before the tabernacle of meeting. And all the congregation drew near and stood before the LORD.

6 Then Moses said, "This *is* the thing which the LORD commanded you to do, and the glory of the LORD will appear to you."

7 And Moses said to Aaron, "Go to the altar, [a]offer your sin offering and your burnt offering, and make atonement for yourself and for the people. [b]Offer the offering of the people, and make atonement for them, as the LORD commanded."

8 Aaron therefore went to the altar and killed the calf of the sin offering, which *was* for himself.

9 Then the sons of Aaron brought the blood to him. And he dipped his finger in the blood, put *it* on the horns of the altar, and poured the blood at the base of the altar.

10 [a]But the fat, the kidneys, and the fatty lobe from the liver of the sin offering he burned on the altar, as the LORD had commanded Moses.

11 [a]The flesh and the hide he burned with fire outside the camp.

12 And he killed the burnt offering; and Aaron's sons presented to him the blood, [a]which he sprinkled all around on the altar.

13 [a]Then they presented the burnt offering to him, with its pieces and head, and he burned *them* on the altar.

14 [a]And he washed the entrails and the legs, and burned *them* with the burnt offering on the altar.

15 [a]Then he brought the people's offering, and took the goat, which *was* the sin offering for the people, and killed it and offered it for sin, like the first one.

16 And he brought the burnt offering and offered it [a]according to the prescribed manner.

17 Then he brought the grain offering, took a handful of it, and burned *it* on the altar, [a]besides the burnt sacrifice of the morning.

18 He also killed the bull and the ram *as* [a]sacrifices of peace offerings, which *were* for the people. And Aaron's sons presented to him the blood, which he sprinkled all around on the altar,

19 and the fat from the bull and the ram—

KJV

the rump, and that which covereth *the inwards*,
and the kidneys, and the caul *above* the liver:
20 And they put the fat upon the breasts,
[a]and he burnt the fat upon the altar:
21 And the breasts and the right shoulder
Aaron waved [a]*for* a wave offering before the
LORD; as Moses commanded.
22 And Aaron lifted up his hand toward the
people, and [a]blessed them, and came down from
offering of the sin offering, and the burnt offering,
and peace offerings.
23 And Moses and Aaron went into the tabernacle of the congregation, and came out, and
blessed the people: and the glory of the LORD appeared unto all the people.
24 And [a]there came a fire out from before
the LORD, and consumed upon the altar the burnt
offering and the fat: *which* when all the people
saw, they [b]shouted, and fell on their [c]faces.

The Profane Fire of Nadab and Abihu

10 And [a]Nadab and Abihu, the sons of Aaron,
[b]took either of them his censer, and put fire
therein, and put incense thereon, and offered
[c]strange fire before the LORD, which he commanded them not.
2 And there [a]went out fire from the LORD,
and devoured them, and they died before the
LORD.
3 Then Moses said unto Aaron, This *is it*
that the LORD spake, saying, I will be sanctified
in them [a]that come nigh me, and before all the
people I will be glorified. And Aaron held his
peace.
4 And Moses called Mishael and Elzaphan,
and the sons of Uzziel the uncle of Aaron, and
said unto them, Come near, [a]carry your brethren
from before the sanctuary out of the camp.
5 So they went near, and carried them in
their coats out of the camp; as Moses had said.
6 And Moses said unto Aaron, and unto
Eleazar and unto Ithamar, his sons, Uncover not
your heads, neither rend your clothes; lest ye die,
and [a]lest wrath come upon all the people: but let
your brethren, the whole house of Israel, bewail
the burning which the LORD hath kindled.
7 [a]And ye shall not go out from the door
of the tabernacle of the congregation, lest ye die:
[b]for the anointing oil of the LORD *is* upon you.
And they did according to the word of Moses.

Conduct Prescribed for Priests

8 And the LORD spake unto Aaron, saying,
9 [a]Do not drink wine nor strong drink, thou,
nor thy sons with thee, when ye go into the tabernacle of the congregation, lest ye die: *it shall be*
a statute for ever throughout your generations:
10 And that ye may [a]put difference between
holy and unholy, and between unclean and clean;
11 [a]And that ye may teach the children of
Israel all the statutes which the LORD hath spoken
unto them by the hand of Moses.
12 And Moses spake unto Aaron, and unto
Eleazar and unto Ithamar, his sons that were left,
Take [a]the meat offering that remaineth of the offerings of the LORD made by fire, and eat it without
leaven beside the altar: for [b]it *is* most holy:
13 And ye shall eat it in the [a]holy place, because it *is* thy due, and thy sons' due, of the sacrifices of the LORD made by fire: for [b]so I am
commanded.
14 And [a]the wave breast and heave shoulder
shall ye eat in a clean place; thou, and thy sons,
and thy [b]daughters with thee: for *they be* thy due,
and thy sons' [c]due, *which* are given out of the
sacrifices of peace offerings of the children of
Israel.
15 [a]The heave shoulder and the wave breast
shall they bring with the offerings made by fire
of the fat, to wave *it for* a wave offering before

20 [a]Lev. 3:5, 16
21 [a]Ex. 29:24, 26, 27; Lev. 7:30–34
22 [a]Num. 6:22–26; Deut. 21:5; Luke 24:50
24 [a]Gen. 4:4; Judg. 6:21; 2 Chr. 7:1; Ps. 20:3 [b]Ezra 3:11 [c]1 Kin. 18:38, 39

CHAPTER 10

1 [a]Ex. 24:1, 9; Num. 3:2–4; 1 Chr. 24:2 [b]Lev. 16:12 [c]Ex. 30:9; 1 Sam. 2:17
2 [a]Gen. 19:24; Num. 11:1; 16:35; Rev. 20:9
3 [a]Ex. 19:22; Lev. 21:6; Is. 52:11; Ezek. 20:41
4 [a]Acts 5:6, 10
6 [a]Num. 1:53; 16:22, 46; 18:5; Josh. 7:1; 22:18, 20; 2 Sam. 24:1
7 [a]Lev. 8:33; 21:12 [b]Lev. 8:30
9 [a]Gen. 9:21; [Prov. 20:1; 31:5]; Is. 28:7; Ezek. 44:21; Hos. 4:11; Luke 1:15; [Eph. 5:18]; 1 Tim. 3:3; Titus 1:7
10 [a]Lev. 11:47; 20:25; Ezek. 22:26; 44:23
11 [a]Deut. 24:8; Neh. 8:2, 8; Jer. 18:18; Mal. 2:7
12 [a]Num. 18:9 [b]Lev. 21:22
13 [a]Num. 18:10 [b]Lev. 2:3; 6:16
14 [a]Ex. 29:24, 26, 27; Lev. 7:30–34; Num. 18:11 [b]Lev. 22:13 [c]Num. 18:10
15 [a]Lev. 7:29, 30, 34

NKJV

the fatty tail, what covers *the entrails* and the kidneys, and the fatty lobe *attached to* the liver;
20 and they put the fat on the breasts. [a]Then
he burned the fat on the altar;
21 but the breasts and the right thigh Aaron
waved [a]*as* a wave offering before the LORD, as
Moses had commanded.
22 Then Aaron lifted his hand toward the
people, [a]blessed them, and came down from offering the sin offering, the burnt offering, and peace
offerings.
23 And Moses and Aaron went into the tabernacle of meeting, and came out and blessed the
people. Then the glory of the LORD appeared to
all the people,
24 and [a]fire came out from before the LORD
and consumed the burnt offering and the fat on
the altar. When all the people saw *it*, they
[b]shouted and fell on their [c]faces.

The Profane Fire of Nadab and Abihu

10 Then [a]Nadab and Abihu, the sons of Aaron,
[b]each took his censer and put fire in it, put
incense on it, and offered [c]profane fire before the
LORD, which He had not commanded them.
2 So [a]fire went out from the LORD and devoured them, and they died before the LORD.
3 And Moses said to Aaron, "This is what
the LORD spoke, saying:

'By those [a]who come near Me
I must be regarded as holy;
And before all the people
I must be glorified.' "

So Aaron held his peace.
4 Then Moses called Mishael and Elzaphan,
the sons of Uzziel the uncle of Aaron, and said
to them, "Come near, [a]carry your brethren from
before the sanctuary out of the camp."
5 So they went near and carried them by
their tunics out of the camp, as Moses had said.
6 And Moses said to Aaron, and to Eleazar
and Ithamar, his sons, "Do not uncover your
heads nor tear your clothes, lest you die, and
[a]wrath come upon all the people. But let your
brethren, the whole house of Israel, bewail the
burning which the LORD has kindled.
7 [a]"You shall not go out from the door of
the tabernacle of meeting, lest you die, [b]for the
anointing oil of the LORD *is* upon you." And they
did according to the word of Moses.

Conduct Prescribed for Priests

8 Then the LORD spoke to Aaron, saying:
9 [a]"Do not drink wine or intoxicating drink,
you, nor your sons with you, when you go into
the tabernacle of meeting, lest you die. *It shall
be* a statute forever throughout your generations,
10 "that you may [a]distinguish between holy
and unholy, and between unclean and clean,
11 [a]"and that you may teach the children of
Israel all the statutes which the LORD has spoken
to them by the hand of Moses."
12 And Moses spoke to Aaron, and to Eleazar
and Ithamar, his sons who were left: [a]"Take the
grain offering that remains of the offerings made
by fire to the LORD, and eat it without leaven beside the altar; [b]for it *is* most holy.
13 "You shall eat it in a [a]holy place, because
it *is* your due and your sons' due, of the sacrifices
made by fire to the LORD; for [b]so I have been
commanded.
14 [a]"The breast of the wave offering and the
thigh of the heave offering you shall eat in a clean
place, you, your sons, and your [b]daughters with
you; for *they are* your due and your sons' [c]due,
which are given from the sacrifices of peace offerings of the children of Israel.
15 [a]"The thigh of the heave offering and the
breast of the wave offering they shall bring with
the offerings of fat made by fire, to offer *as* a wave

KJV

the LORD; and it shall be thine, and thy sons' with
thee, by a statute for ever; as the LORD hath
commanded.
16 And Moses diligently sought [a]the goat of
the sin offering, and, behold, it was burnt: and
he was angry with Eleazar and Ithamar, the sons
of Aaron *which were* left *alive*, saying,
17 [a]Wherefore have ye not eaten the sin offering in the holy place, seeing it *is* most holy,
and *God* hath given it you to bear [b]the iniquity
of the congregation, to make atonement for them
before the LORD?
18 Behold, [a]the blood of it was not brought
in within the holy *place:* ye should indeed have
eaten it in the holy *place,* [b]as I commanded.
19 And Aaron said unto Moses, Behold, [a]this
day have they offered their sin offering and their
burnt offering before the LORD; and such things
have befallen me: and *if* I had eaten the sin offering to day, [b]should it have been accepted in the
sight of the LORD?
20 And when Moses heard *that,* he was content.

Foods Permitted and Forbidden *(Deut. 14:3–21)*

11 And the LORD spake unto Moses and to
Aaron, saying unto them,
2 Speak unto the children of Israel, saying,
[a]These *are* the beasts which ye shall eat among
all the beasts that *are* on the earth.
3 Whatsoever parteth the hoof, and is
clovenfooted, *and* cheweth the cud, among the
beasts, that shall ye eat.
4 Nevertheless these shall ye [a]not eat of
them that chew the cud, or of them that divide
the hoof: *as* the camel, because he cheweth the
cud, but divideth not the hoof; he *is* unclean unto
you.
5 And the coney, because he cheweth the
cud, but divideth not the hoof; he *is* unclean unto
you.
6 And the hare, because he cheweth the cud,
but divideth not the hoof; he *is* unclean unto you.
7 And the swine, though he divide the hoof,
and be clovenfooted, yet he cheweth not the cud;
[a]he *is* unclean to you.
8 Of their flesh shall ye not eat, and their
carcase shall ye not touch; [a]they *are* unclean to
you.
9 [a]These shall ye eat of all that *are* in the
waters: whatsoever hath fins and scales in the waters, in the seas, and in the rivers, them shall ye
eat.
10 And all that have not fins and scales in
the seas, and in the rivers, of all that move in
the waters, and of any living thing which *is* in
the waters, they *shall be* an [a]abomination unto
you:
11 They shall be even an abomination unto
you; ye shall not eat of their flesh, but ye shall
have their carcases in abomination.
12 Whatsoever hath no fins nor scales in the
waters, that *shall be* an abomination unto you.
13 [a]And these *are they which* ye shall have
in abomination among the fowls; they shall not
be eaten, they *are* an abomination: the eagle, and
the ossifrage, and the ospray,
14 And the vulture, and the kite after his
kind;
15 Every raven after his kind;
16 And the owl, and the night hawk, and the
cuckow, and the hawk after his kind,
17 And the little owl, and the cormorant, and
the great owl,
18 And the swan, and the pelican, and the
gier eagle,
19 And the stork, the heron after her kind,
and the lapwing, and the bat.
20 All fowls that creep, going upon *all* four,
shall be an abomination unto you.
21 Yet these may ye eat of every flying creep-

16 [a]Lev. 9:3, 15
17 [a]Lev. 6:24–30 [b]Ex. 28:38; Lev. 22:16; Num. 18:1
18 [a]Lev. 6:30 [b]Lev. 6:26, 30
19 [a]Lev. 9:8, 12 [b][Is. 1:11–15]; Jer. 6:20; 14:12; Hos. 9:4; [Mal. 1:10, 13; 3:1–4]

CHAPTER 11
2 [a]Deut. 14:4; Ezek. 4:14; Dan. 1:8; [Matt. 15:11]; Acts 10:12, 14; [Rom. 14:14; Heb. 9:10; 13:9]
4 [a]Acts 10:14
7 [a]Is. 65:4; 66:3, 17; Mark 5:1–17
8 [a]Is. 52:11; [Mark 7:2, 15, 18]; Acts 10:14, 15; 15:29
9 [a]Deut. 14:9
10 [a]Lev. 7:18, 21; Deut. 14:3
13 [a]Deut. 14:12–19; Is. 66:17

*

10:18 The Most Holy Place when capitalized

NKJV

offering before the LORD. And it shall be yours
and your sons' with you, by a statute forever, as
the LORD has commanded."
16 Then Moses made careful inquiry about
[a]the goat of the sin offering, and there it was—
burned up. And he was angry with Eleazar and
Ithamar, the sons of Aaron *who were* left, saying,
17 [a]"Why have you not eaten the sin offering
in a holy place, since it *is* most holy, and *God*
has given it to you to bear [b]the guilt of the congregation, to make atonement for them before the
LORD?
18 "See! [a]Its blood was not brought inside
*the holy *place;* indeed you should have eaten it
in a holy *place,* [b]as I commanded."
19 And Aaron said to Moses, "Look, [a]this
day they have offered their sin offering and their
burnt offering before the LORD, and such things
have befallen me! *If* I had eaten the sin offering
today, [b]would it have been accepted in the sight
of the LORD?"
20 So when Moses heard *that,* he was content.

Foods Permitted and Forbidden *(Deut. 14:3–21)*

11 Now the LORD spoke to Moses and Aaron,
saying to them,
2 "Speak to the children of Israel, saying,
[a]'These *are* the animals which you may eat among
all the animals that *are* on the earth:
3 'Among the animals, whatever divides the
hoof, having cloven hooves *and* chewing the
cud—that you may eat.
4 'Nevertheless these you shall [a]not eat
among those that chew the cud or those that have
cloven hooves: the camel, because it chews the
cud but does not have cloven hooves, is unclean
to you;
5 'the rock hyrax, because it chews the cud
but does not have cloven hooves, *is* unclean to
you;
6 'the hare, because it chews the cud but
does not have cloven hooves, *is* unclean to you;
7 'and the swine, though it divides the hoof,
having cloven hooves, yet does not chew the cud,
[a]*is* unclean to you.
8 'Their flesh you shall not eat, and their
carcasses you shall not touch. [a]They *are* unclean
to you.
9 [a]'These you may eat of all that *are* in the
water: whatever in the water has fins and scales,
whether in the seas or in the rivers—that you may
eat.
10 'But all in the seas or in the rivers that
do not have fins and scales, all that move in the
water or any living thing which *is* in the water,
they *are* an [a]abomination to you.
11 'They shall be an abomination to you; you
shall not eat their flesh, but you shall regard their
carcasses as an abomination.
12 'Whatever in the water does not have fins
or scales—that *shall be* an abomination to you.
13 [a]'And these you shall regard as an abomination among the birds; they shall not be eaten,
they *are* an abomination: the eagle, the vulture,
the buzzard,
14 'the kite, and the falcon after its kind;
15 'every raven after its kind,
16 'the ostrich, the short-eared owl, the sea
gull, and the hawk after its kind;
17 'the little owl, the fisher owl, and the
screech owl;
18 'the white owl, the jackdaw, and the carrion vulture;
19 'the stork, the heron after its kind, the hoopoe, and the bat.
20 'All flying insects that creep on *all* fours
shall be an abomination to you.
21 'Yet these you may eat of every flying

KJV

ing thing that goeth upon *all* four, which have
legs above their feet, to leap withal upon the earth;
22 *Even* these of them ye may eat; [a]the locust
after his kind, and the bald locust after his kind,
and the beetle after his kind, and the grasshopper
after his kind.
23 But all *other* flying creeping things, which
have four feet, *shall be* an abomination unto you.

Unclean Animals

24 And for these ye shall be unclean: whosoever toucheth the carcase of them shall be
unclean until the even.
25 And whosoever beareth *ought* of the carcase of them [a]shall wash his clothes, and be unclean until the even.
26 *The carcases* of every beast which divideth the hoof, and *is* not clovenfooted, nor cheweth
the cud, *are* unclean unto you: every one that
toucheth them shall be unclean.
27 And whatsoever goeth upon his paws,
among all manner of beasts that go on *all* four,
those *are* unclean unto you: whoso toucheth their
carcase shall be unclean until the even.
28 And he that beareth the carcase of them
shall wash his clothes, and be unclean until the
even: they *are* unclean unto you.
29 These also *shall be* unclean unto you
among the creeping things that creep upon the
earth; the weasel, and [a]the mouse, and the tortoise
after his kind,
30 And the ferret, and the chameleon, and
the lizard, and the snail, and the mole.
31 These *are* unclean to you among all that
creep: whosoever doth [a]touch them, when they
be dead, shall be unclean until the even.
32 And upon whatsoever *any* of them, when
they are dead, doth fall, it shall be unclean;
whether *it be* any vessel of wood, or raiment, or
skin, or sack, whatsoever vessel *it be*, wherein
any work is done, [a]it must be put into water, and
it shall be unclean until the even; so it shall be
cleansed.
33 And every [a]earthen vessel, whereinto *any*
of them falleth, whatsoever *is* in it shall be unclean; and [b]ye shall break it.
34 Of all meat which may be eaten, *that* on
which *such* water cometh shall be unclean: and
all drink that may be drunk in every *such* vessel
shall be unclean.
35 And every *thing* whereupon *any part* of
their carcase falleth shall be unclean; *whether it
be* oven, or ranges for pots, they shall be broken
down: *for* they *are* unclean, and shall be unclean
unto you.
36 Nevertheless a fountain or pit, *wherein
there is* plenty of water, shall be clean: but that
which toucheth their carcase shall be unclean.
37 And if *any part* of their carcase fall upon
any sowing seed which is to be sown, it *shall be*
clean.
38 But if *any* water be put upon the seed, and
any part of their carcase fall thereon, it *shall be*
unclean unto you.
39 And if any beast, of which ye may eat,
die; he that toucheth the carcase thereof shall be
[a]unclean until the even.
40 And [a]he that eateth of the carcase of it
shall wash his clothes, and be unclean until
the even: he also that beareth the carcase of it
shall wash his clothes, and be unclean until the
even.
41 And every creeping thing that creepeth
upon the earth *shall be* an abomination; it shall
not be eaten.
42 Whatsoever goeth upon the belly, and
whatsoever goeth upon *all* four, or whatsoever
hath more feet among all creeping things that
creep upon the earth, them ye shall not eat; for
they *are* an abomination.
43 [a]Ye shall not make your selves abominable with any creeping thing that creepeth, neither

22 [a]Matt. 3:4; Mark 1:6
25 [a]Lev. 14:8; 15:5; Num. 19:10, 21, 22; 31:24; Zech. 13:1; [Heb. 9:10; 10:22; Rev. 7:14]
29 [a]Is. 66:17
31 [a]Hag. 2:13
32 [a]Lev. 15:12
33 [a]Lev. 6:28 [b]Lev. 15:12; Ps. 2:9; Jer. 48:38; [2 Tim. 2:21]; Rev. 2:27
39 [a]Hag. 2:11–13
40 [a]Ex. 22:31; Lev. 17:15; 22:8; Deut. 14:21; Ezek. 4:14; 44:31
43 [a]Lev. 20:25

NKJV

insect that creeps on *all* fours: those which have
jointed legs above their feet with which to leap
on the earth.
22 'These you may eat: [a]the locust after its
kind, the destroying locust after its kind, the
cricket after its kind, and the grasshopper after
its kind.
23 'But all *other* flying insects which have
four feet *shall be* an abomination to you.

Unclean Animals

24 'By these you shall become unclean;
whoever touches the carcass of any of them shall
be unclean until evening;
25 'whoever carries part of the carcass of any
of them [a]shall wash his clothes and be unclean
until evening:
26 '*The carcass* of any animal which divides
the foot, but is not cloven-hoofed or does not chew
the cud, *is* unclean to you. Everyone who touches
it shall be unclean.
27 'And whatever goes on its paws, among
all kinds of animals that go on *all* fours, those
are unclean to you. Whoever touches any such
carcass shall be unclean until evening.
28 'Whoever carries *any such* carcass shall
wash his clothes and be unclean until evening. It
is unclean to you.
29 'These also *shall be* unclean to you among
the creeping things that creep on the earth: the
mole, [a]the mouse, and the large lizard after its
kind;
30 'the gecko, the monitor lizard, the sand
reptile, the sand lizard, and the chameleon.
31 'These *are* unclean to you among all that
creep. Whoever [a]touches them when they are
dead shall be unclean until evening.
32 'Anything on which *any* of them falls,
when they are dead shall be unclean, whether *it
is* any item of wood or clothing or skin or sack,
whatever item *it is*, in which *any* work is done,
[a]it must be put in water. And it shall be unclean
until evening; then it shall be clean.
33 'Any [a]earthen vessel into which *any* of
them falls [b]you shall break; and whatever *is* in it
shall be unclean:
34 'in such a vessel, any edible food upon
which water falls becomes unclean, and any drink
that may be drunk from it becomes unclean.
35 'And everything on which *a part* of *any
such* carcass falls shall be unclean; *whether it is*
an oven or cooking stove, it shall be broken down;
for they *are* unclean, and shall be unclean to you.
36 'Nevertheless a spring or a cistern, *in
which there is* plenty of water, shall be clean, but
whatever touches any such carcass becomes
unclean.
37 'And if a part of *any such* carcass falls
on any planting seed which is to be sown, it *remains* clean.
38 'But if water is put on the seed, and if *a
part* of *any such* carcass falls on it, it *becomes*
unclean to you.
39 'And if any animal which you may eat
dies, he who touches its carcass shall be [a]unclean
until evening.
40 [a]'He who eats of its carcass shall wash
his clothes and be unclean until evening. He also
who carries its carcass shall wash his clothes and
be unclean until evening.
41 'And every creeping thing that creeps on
the earth *shall be* an abomination. It shall not be
eaten.
42 'Whatever crawls on its belly, whatever
goes on *all* fours, or whatever has many feet
among all creeping things that creep on the
earth—these you shall not eat, for they *are* an
abomination.
43 [a]'You shall not make yourselves abominable with any creeping thing that creeps; nor shall

KJV

shall ye make yourselves unclean with them, that ye should be defiled thereby.

44 For I *am* the LORD your [a]God: ye shall therefore sanctify yourselves, and [b]ye shall be holy; for I *am* holy: neither shall ye defile yourselves with any manner of creeping thing that creepeth upon the earth.

45 [a]For I *am* the LORD that bringeth you up out of the land of Egypt, to be your God: [b]ye shall therefore be holy, for I *am* holy.

46 This *is* the law of the beasts, and of the fowl, and of every living creature that moveth in the waters, and of every creature that creepeth upon the earth:

47 [a]To make a difference between the unclean and the clean, and between the beast that may be eaten and the beast that may not be eaten.

The Ritual After Childbirth *(cf. Luke 2:22–24)*

12 And the LORD spake unto Moses, saying,

2 Speak unto the children of Israel, saying, If a [a]woman have conceived seed, and born a man child: then [b]she shall be unclean seven days; [c]according to the days of the separation for her infirmity shall she be unclean.

3 And in the [a]eighth day the flesh of his foreskin shall be circumcised.

4 And she shall then continue in the blood of her purifying three and thirty days; she shall touch no hallowed thing, nor come into the sanctuary, until the days of her purifying be fulfilled.

5 But if she bear a maid child, then she shall be unclean two weeks, as in her separation: and she shall continue in the blood of her purifying threescore and six days.

6 And [a]when the days of her purifying are fulfilled, for a son, or for a daughter, she shall bring a [b]lamb of the first year for a burnt offering, and a young pigeon, or a turtledove, for a [c]sin offering, unto the door of the tabernacle of the congregation, unto the priest:

7 Who shall offer it before the LORD, and make an atonement for her; and she shall be cleansed from the issue of her blood. This *is* the law for her that hath born a male or a female.

8 [a]And if she be not able to bring a lamb, then she shall bring two turtles, or two young pigeons; the one for the burnt offering, and the other for a sin offering: [b]and the priest shall make an atonement for her, and she shall be clean.

The Law Concerning Leprosy

13 And the LORD spake unto Moses and Aaron, saying,

2 When a man shall have in the skin of his flesh a rising, [a]a scab, or bright spot, and it be in the skin of his flesh *like* the plague of leprosy; [b]then he shall be brought unto Aaron the priest, or unto one of his sons the priests:

3 And the priest shall look on the plague in the skin of the flesh: and *when* the hair in the plague is turned white, and the plague in sight *be* deeper than the skin of his flesh, it *is* a plague of leprosy: and the priest shall look on him, and pronounce him unclean.

4 If the bright spot *be* white in the skin of his flesh, and in sight *be* not deeper than the skin, and the hair thereof be not turned white; then the priest shall shut up *him that hath* the plague [a]seven days:

5 And the priest shall look on him the seventh day: and, behold, *if* the plague in his sight be at a stay, *and* the plague spread not in the skin; then the priest shall shut him up seven days more:

6 And the priest shall look on him again the seventh day: and, behold, *if* the plague *be* somewhat dark, *and* the plague spread not in the skin,

44 [a]Ex. 6:7; Lev. 22:33; 25:38; 26:45 [b]Ex. 19:6; Lev. 19:2; 20:7, 26; [Amos 3:3]; Matt. 5:48; 1 Thess. 4:7; 1 Pet. 1:15, 16; [Rev. 22:11, 14]
45 [a]Ex. 6:7; 20:2; Lev. 22:33; 25:38; 26:45; Ps. 105:43–45; Hos. 11:1 [b]Lev. 11:44
47 [a]Lev. 10:10; Ezek. 44:23; Mal. 3:18

CHAPTER 12

2 [a]Lev. 15:19; [Job 14:4; Ps. 51:5] [b]Ex. 22:30; Lev. 8:33; 13:4; Luke 2:22 [c]Lev. 18:19
3 [a]Gen. 17:12; Luke 1:59; 2:21; John 7:22, 23; Gal. 5:3
6 [a]Luke 2:22 [b][John 1:29; 1 Pet. 1:18, 19] [c]Lev. 5:7
8 [a]Lev. 5:7; Luke 2:22–24 [b]Lev. 4:26

CHAPTER 13

2 [a]Deut. 28:27; Is. 3:17 [b]Deut. 17:8, 9; 24:8; Mal. 2:7; Luke 17:14
4 [a]Lev. 14:8

*

13:2 Heb. *saraath*, disfiguring skin diseases, including leprosy, and so in vv. 2–46 and 14:1–32

NKJV

you make yourselves unclean with them, lest you be defiled by them.

44 'For I *am* the LORD your [a]God. You shall therefore consecrate yourselves, and [b]you shall be holy; for I *am* holy. Neither shall you defile yourselves with any creeping thing that creeps on the earth.

45 [a]'For I *am* the LORD who brings you up out of the land of Egypt, to be your God. [b]You shall therefore be holy, for I *am* holy.

46 'This *is* the law of the animals and the birds and every living creature that moves in the waters, and of every creature that creeps on the earth,

47 [a]'to distinguish between the unclean and the clean, and between the animal that may be eaten and the animal that may not be eaten.' "

The Ritual After Childbirth *(cf. Luke 2:22–24)*

12 Then the LORD spoke to Moses, saying,

2 "Speak to the children of Israel, saying: 'If a [a]woman has conceived, and borne a male child, then [b]she shall be unclean seven days; [c]as in the days of her customary impurity she shall be unclean.

3 'And on the [a]eighth day the flesh of his foreskin shall be circumcised.

4 'She shall then continue in the blood of *her* purification thirty-three days. She shall not touch any hallowed thing, nor come into the sanctuary until the days of her purification are fulfilled.

5 'But if she bears a female child, then she shall be unclean two weeks, as in her customary impurity, and she shall continue in the blood of *her* purification sixty-six days.

6 [a]'When the days of her purification are fulfilled, whether for a son or a daughter, she shall bring to the priest a [b]lamb of the first year as a burnt offering, and a young pigeon or a turtledove as a [c]sin offering, to the door of the tabernacle of meeting.

7 'Then he shall offer it before the LORD, and make atonement for her. And she shall be clean from the flow of her blood. This *is* the law for her who has borne a male or a female.

8 [a]'And if she is not able to bring a lamb, then she may bring two turtledoves or two young pigeons—one as a burnt offering and the other as a sin offering. [b]So the priest shall make atonement for her, and she will be clean.' "

The Law Concerning Leprosy

13 And the LORD spoke to Moses and Aaron, saying:

2 "When a man has on the skin of his body a swelling, [a]a scab, or a bright spot, and it becomes on the skin of his body *like* a *leprous sore, [b]then he shall be brought to Aaron the priest or to one of his sons the priests.

3 "The priest shall examine the sore on the skin of the body; and if the hair on the sore has turned white, and the sore appears *to be* deeper than the skin of his body, it *is* a leprous sore. Then the priest shall examine him, and pronounce him unclean.

4 "But if the bright spot *is* white on the skin of his body, and does not appear *to be* deeper than the skin, and its hair has not turned white, then the priest shall isolate *the one who has* the sore [a]seven days.

5 "And the priest shall examine him on the seventh day; and indeed *if* the sore appears to be as it was, *and* the sore has not spread on the skin, then the priest shall isolate him another seven days.

6 "Then the priest shall examine him again on the seventh day; and indeed *if* the sore has faded, *and* the sore has not spread on the skin, then the priest shall pronounce him clean; it *is*

KJV

the priest shall pronounce him clean: it *is but* a scab: and he [a]shall wash his clothes, and be clean.

7 But if the scab spread much abroad in the skin, after that he hath been seen of the priest for his cleansing, he shall be seen of the priest again:

8 And *if* the priest see that, behold, the scab spreadeth in the skin, then the priest shall pronounce him unclean: it *is* a leprosy.

9 When the plague of leprosy is in a man, then he shall be brought unto the priest;

10 [a]And the priest shall see *him:* and, behold, *if* the rising *be* white in the skin, and it have turned the hair white, and *there be* quick raw flesh in the rising;

11 It *is* an old leprosy in the skin of his flesh, and the priest shall pronounce him unclean, and shall not shut him up: for he *is* unclean.

12 And if a leprosy break out abroad in the skin, and the leprosy cover all the skin of *him that hath* the plague from his head even to his foot, wheresoever the priest looketh;

13 Then the priest shall consider: and, behold, *if* the leprosy have covered all his flesh, he shall pronounce *him* clean *that hath* the plague: it is all turned [a]white: he *is* clean.

14 But when raw flesh appeareth in him, he shall be unclean.

15 And the priest shall see the raw flesh, and pronounce him to be unclean: *for* the raw flesh *is* unclean: it *is* a leprosy.

16 Or if the raw flesh turn again, and be changed unto white, he shall come unto the priest;

17 And the priest shall see him: and, behold, *if* the plague be turned into white; then the priest shall pronounce *him* clean *that hath* the plague: he *is* clean.

18 The flesh also, in which, *even* in the skin thereof, was a [a]boil, and is healed,

19 And in the place of the boil there be a white rising, or a bright spot, white, and somewhat reddish, and it be shewed to the priest;

20 And if, when the priest seeth it, behold, it *be* in sight lower than the skin, and the hair thereof be turned white; the priest shall pronounce him unclean: it *is* a plague of leprosy broken out of the boil.

21 But if the priest look on it, and, behold, *there be* no white hairs therein, and *if* it *be* not lower than the skin, but *be* somewhat dark; then the priest shall shut him up seven days:

22 And if it spread much abroad in the skin, then the priest shall pronounce him unclean: it *is* a plague.

23 But if the bright spot stay in his place, *and* spread not, it *is* a burning boil; and the priest shall pronounce him clean.

24 Or if there be *any* flesh, in the skin whereof *there is* a hot [a]burning, and the quick *flesh* that burneth have a white bright spot, somewhat reddish, or white;

25 Then the priest shall look upon it: and, behold, *if* the hair in the bright spot be turned white, and it *be in* sight deeper than the skin; it *is* a leprosy broken out of the burning: wherefore the priest shall pronounce him unclean: it *is* the plague of leprosy.

26 But if the priest look on it, and, behold, *there be* no white hair in the bright spot, and it *be* no lower than the *other* skin, but *be* somewhat dark; then the priest shall shut him up seven days:

27 And the priest shall look upon him the seventh day: *and* if it be spread much abroad in the skin, then the priest shall pronounce him unclean: it *is* the plague of leprosy.

28 And if the bright spot stay in his place, *and* spread not in the skin, but it *be* somewhat dark; it *is* a rising of the burning, and the priest shall pronounce him clean: for it *is* an inflammation of the burning.

29 If a man or woman have a plague upon the head or the beard;

6 [a]Lev. 11:25; 14:8; [John 13:8, 10]
10 [a]Num. 12:10, 12; 2 Kin. 5:27; 2 Chr. 26:19, 20
13 [a]Ex. 4:6
18 [a]Ex. 9:9; 15:26
24 [a]Is. 3:24

NKJV

only a scab, and he [a]shall wash his clothes and be clean.

7 "But if the scab should at all spread over the skin, after he has been seen by the priest for his cleansing, he shall be seen by the priest again.

8 "And *if* the priest sees that the scab has indeed spread on the skin, then the priest shall pronounce him unclean. It *is* leprosy.

9 "When the leprous sore is on a person, then he shall be brought to the priest.

10 [a]"And the priest shall examine *him;* and indeed *if* the swelling on the skin *is* white, and it has turned the hair white, and *there is* a spot of raw flesh in the swelling,

11 "it *is* an old leprosy on the skin of his body. The priest shall pronounce him unclean, and shall not isolate him, for he *is* unclean.

12 "And if leprosy breaks out all over the skin, and the leprosy covers all the skin of *the one who has* the sore, from his head to his foot, wherever the priest looks,

13 "then the priest shall consider; and indeed *if* the leprosy has covered all his body, he shall pronounce *him* clean *who has* the sore. It has all turned [a]white. He *is* clean.

14 "But when raw flesh appears on him, he shall be unclean.

15 "And the priest shall examine the raw flesh and pronounce him to be unclean; *for* the raw flesh *is* unclean. It *is* leprosy.

16 "Or if the raw flesh changes and turns white again, he shall come to the priest.

17 "And the priest shall examine him; and indeed *if* the sore has turned white, then the priest shall pronounce *him* clean *who has* the sore. He *is* clean.

18 "If the body develops a [a]boil in the skin, and it is healed,

19 "and in the place of the boil there comes a white swelling or a bright spot, reddish-white, then it shall be shown to the priest;

20 "and *if,* when the priest sees it, it indeed *appears* deeper than the skin, and its hair has turned white, the priest shall pronounce him unclean. It *is* a leprous sore which has broken out of the boil.

21 "But if the priest examines it, and indeed *there are* no white hairs in it, and it *is* not deeper than the skin, but has faded, then the priest shall isolate him seven days;

22 "and if it should at all spread over the skin, then the priest shall pronounce him unclean. It *is* a leprous sore.

23 "But if the bright spot stays in one place, *and* has not spread, it *is* the scar of the boil; and the priest shall pronounce him clean.

24 "Or if the body receives a [a]burn on its skin by fire, and the raw *flesh* of the burn becomes a bright spot, reddish-white or white,

25 "then the priest shall examine it; and indeed *if* the hair of the bright spot has turned white, and it appears deeper than the skin, it *is* leprosy broken out in the burn. Therefore the priest shall pronounce him unclean. It *is* a leprous sore.

26 "But if the priest examines it, and indeed *there are* no white hairs in the bright spot, and it *is* not deeper than the skin, but has faded, then the priest shall isolate him seven days.

27 "And the priest shall examine him on the seventh day. If it has at all spread over the skin, then the priest shall pronounce him unclean. It *is* a leprous sore.

28 "But if the bright spot stays in one place, *and* has not spread on the skin, but has faded, it *is* a swelling from the burn. The priest shall pronounce him clean, for it *is* the scar from the burn.

29 "If a man or woman has a sore on the head or the beard,

KJV

30 Then the priest shall see the plague: and, behold, if it *be* in sight deeper than the skin; *and there be* in it a yellow thin hair; then the priest shall pronounce him unclean: it *is* a dry scall, *even* a leprosy upon the head or beard.

31 And if the priest look on the plague of the scall, and, behold, it *be* not in sight deeper than the skin, and *that there is* no black hair in it; then the priest shall shut up *him that hath* the plague of the scall seven days:

32 And in the seventh day the priest shall look on the plague: and, behold, *if* the scall spread not, and there be in it no yellow hair, and the scall *be* not in sight deeper than the skin;

33 He shall be shaven, but the scall shall he not shave; and the priest shall shut up *him that hath* the scall seven days more:

34 And in the seventh day the priest shall look on the scall: and, behold, *if* the scall be not spread in the skin, nor *be* in sight deeper than the skin; then the priest shall pronounce him clean: and he shall wash his clothes, and be clean.

35 But if the scall spread much in the skin after his cleansing;

36 Then the priest shall look on him: and, behold, if the scall be spread in the skin, the priest shall not seek for yellow hair; he *is* unclean.

37 But if the scall be in his sight at a stay, and *that* there is black hair grown up therein; the scall is healed, he *is* clean: and the priest shall pronounce him clean.

38 If a man also or a woman have in the skin of their flesh bright spots, *even* white bright spots;

39 Then the priest shall look: and, behold, *if* the bright spots in the skin of their flesh *be* darkish white; it *is* a freckled spot *that* groweth in the skin; he *is* clean.

40 And the man whose hair is fallen off his head, he *is* bald; *yet is* he clean.

41 And he that hath his hair fallen off from the part of his head toward his face, he *is* forehead bald: *yet is* he clean.

42 And if there be in the bald head, or bald [a]forehead, a white reddish sore; it *is* a leprosy sprung up in his bald head, or his bald forehead.

43 Then the priest shall look upon it: and, behold, *if* the rising of the sore *be* white reddish in his bald head, or in his bald forehead, as the leprosy appeareth in the skin of the flesh;

44 He is a leprous man, he *is* unclean: the priest shall pronounce him utterly unclean; his plague *is* in his [a]head.

45 And the leper in whom the plague *is*, his clothes shall be rent, and his head [a]bare, and he shall [b]put a covering upon his upper lip, and shall cry, [c]Unclean, unclean.

46 All the days wherein the plague *shall be* in him he shall be defiled; he *is* unclean: he shall dwell alone; [a]without the camp *shall* his habitation *be*.

The Law Concerning Leprous Garments

47 The garment also that the plague of leprosy is in, *whether it be* a woollen garment, or a linen garment;

48 Whether *it be* in the warp, or woof; of linen, or of woollen; whether in a skin, or in any thing made of skin;

49 And if the plague be greenish or reddish in the garment, or in the skin, either in the warp, or in the woof, or in any thing of skin; it *is* a plague of leprosy, and shall be shewed unto the priest:

50 And the priest shall look upon the plague, and shut up *it that hath* the plague seven days:

51 And he shall look on the plague on the seventh day: if the plague be spread in the garment, either in the warp, or in the woof, or in a skin, *or* in any work that is made of skin; the plague *is* [a]a fretting leprosy; it *is* unclean.

52 He shall therefore burn that garment,

42 [a]2 Chr. 26:19
44 [a]Is. 1:5
45 [a]Lev. 10:6; 21:10 [b]Ezek. 24:17, 22; Mic. 3:7 [c]Is. 6:5; 64:6; Lam. 4:15; Luke 5:8
46 [a]Num. 5:1–4; 12:14; 2 Kin. 7:3; 15:5; 2 Chr. 26:21; Ps. 38:11; Luke 17:12
51 [a]Lev. 14:44

NKJV

30 "then the priest shall examine the sore; and indeed if it appears deeper than the skin, *and there is* in it thin yellow hair, then the priest shall pronounce him unclean. It *is* a scaly leprosy of the head or beard.

31 "But if the priest examines the scaly sore, and indeed it does not appear deeper than the skin, and *there is* no black hair in it, then the priest shall isolate *the one who has* the scale seven days.

32 "And on the seventh day the priest shall examine the sore; and indeed *if* the scale has not spread, and there is no yellow hair in it, and the scale does not appear deeper than the skin,

33 "he shall shave himself, but the scale he shall not shave. And the priest shall isolate *the one who has* the scale another seven days.

34 "On the seventh day the priest shall examine the scale; and indeed *if* the scale has not spread over the skin, and does not appear deeper than the skin, then the priest shall pronounce him clean. He shall wash his clothes and be clean.

35 "But if the scale should at all spread over the skin after his cleansing,

36 "then the priest shall examine him; and indeed *if* the scale has spread over the skin, the priest need not seek for yellow hair. He *is* unclean.

37 "But if the scale appears to be at a standstill, and there is black hair grown up in it, the scale has healed. He *is* clean, and the priest shall pronounce him clean.

38 "If a man or a woman has bright spots on the skin of the body, *specifically* white bright spots,

39 "then the priest shall look; and indeed *if* the bright spots on the skin of the body *are* dull white, it *is* a white spot *that* grows on the skin. He *is* clean.

40 "As for the man whose hair has fallen from his head, he *is* bald, *but* he *is* clean.

41 "He whose hair has fallen from his forehead, he *is* bald on the forehead, *but* he *is* clean.

42 "And if there is on the bald head or bald [a]forehead a reddish-white sore, it *is* leprosy breaking out on his bald head or his bald forehead.

43 "Then the priest shall examine it; and indeed *if* the swelling of the sore *is* reddish-white on his bald head or on his bald forehead, as the appearance of leprosy on the skin of the body,

44 "he is a leprous man. He *is* unclean. The priest shall surely pronounce him unclean; his sore *is* on his [a]head.

45 "Now the leper on whom the sore *is*, his clothes shall be torn and his head [a]bare; and he shall [b]cover his mustache, and cry, [c]'Unclean! Unclean!'

46 "He shall be unclean. All the days he has the sore he shall be unclean. He *is* unclean, and he shall dwell alone; his dwelling *shall be* [a]outside the camp.

The Law Concerning Leprous Garments

47 "Also, if a garment has a *leprous plague in it, *whether it is* a woolen garment or a linen garment,

48 "whether *it is* in the warp or woof of linen or wool, whether in leather or in anything made of leather,

49 "and if the plague is greenish or reddish in the garment or in the leather, whether in the warp or in the woof, or in anything made of leather, it *is* a leprous plague and shall be shown to the priest.

50 "The priest shall examine the plague and isolate *that which has* the plague seven days.

51 "And he shall examine the plague on the seventh day. If the plague has spread in the garment, either in the warp or in the woof, in the leather *or* in anything made of leather, the plague *is* [a]an active leprosy. It *is* unclean.

52 "He shall therefore burn that garment in

*_____

13:47 A mold, fungus, or similar infestation, and so in vv. 47–59

KJV

whether warp or woof, in woollen or in linen, or any thing of skin, wherein the plague is: for it *is* a fretting leprosy; it shall be burnt in the fire.

53 And if the priest shall look, and, behold, the plague be not spread in the garment, either in the warp, or in the woof, or in any thing of skin;

54 Then the priest shall command that they wash *the thing* wherein the plague *is*, and he shall shut it up seven days more:

55 And the priest shall look on the plague, after that it is washed: and, behold, *if* the plague have not changed his colour, and the plague be not spread; it *is* unclean; thou shalt burn it in the fire; it *is* fret inward, *whether* it *be* bare within or without.

56 And if the priest look, and, behold, the plague *be* somewhat dark after the washing of it; then he shall rend it out of the garment, or out of the skin, or out of the warp, or out of the woof:

57 And if it appear still in the garment, either in the warp, or in the woof, or in any thing of skin; it *is* a spreading *plague:* thou shalt burn that wherein the plague *is* with fire.

58 And the garment, either warp, or woof, or whatsoever thing of skin *it be,* which thou shalt wash, if the plague be departed from them, then it shall be washed the second time, and shall be clean.

59 This *is* the law of the plague of leprosy in a garment of woollen or linen, either in the warp, or woof, or any thing of skins, to pronounce it clean, or to pronounce it unclean.

The Ritual for Cleansing Healed Lepers *(cf. Matt. 8:1–4; Luke 5:12–14)*

14 And the LORD spake unto Moses, saying,

2 This shall be the law of the leper in the day of his cleansing: He [a]shall be brought unto the priest:

3 And the priest shall go forth out of the camp; and the priest shall look, and, behold, *if* the plague of leprosy be healed in the leper;

4 Then shall the priest command to take for him that is to be cleansed two birds alive *and* clean, and [a]cedar wood, and [b]scarlet, and [c]hyssop:

5 And the priest shall command that one of the birds be killed in an earthen vessel over running water:

6 As for the living bird, he shall take it, and the cedar wood, and the scarlet, and the hyssop, and shall dip them and the living bird in the blood of the bird *that was* killed over the running water:

7 And he shall [a]sprinkle upon him that is to be cleansed from the leprosy [b]seven times, and shall pronounce him clean, and shall let the living bird loose into the open field.

8 And he that is to be cleansed [a]shall wash his clothes, and shave off all his hair, and [b]wash himself in water, that he may be clean: and after that he shall come into the camp, and [c]shall tarry abroad out of his tent seven days.

9 But it shall be on the [a]seventh day, that he shall shave all his hair off his head and his beard and his eyebrows, even all his hair he shall shave off: and he shall wash his clothes, also he shall wash his flesh in water, and he shall be clean.

10 And on the eighth day [a]he shall take two he lambs without blemish, and one ewe lamb of the first year without blemish, and three tenth deals of fine flour *for* [b]a meat offering, mingled with oil, and one log of oil.

11 And the priest that maketh *him* clean shall present the man that is to be made clean, and those things, before the LORD, *at* the door of the tabernacle of the congregation:

12 And the priest shall take one he lamb, and [a]offer him for a trespass offering, and the log of

CHAPTER 14

2 [a]Matt. 8:2, 4; Mark 1:40, 44; Luke 5:12, 14; 17:14
4 [a]Lev. 14:6, 49, 51, 52; Num. 19:6; Heb. 9:19 [b]Ex. 25:4 [c]Ex. 12:22; Ps. 51:7
7 [a]Num. 19:18, 19; [Heb. 9:13, 21; 12:24] [b]2 Kin. 5:10, 14; Ps. 51:2
8 [a]Lev. 11:25; 13:6; Num. 8:7 [b]Lev. 11:25; [Eph. 5:26; Heb. 10:22; Rev. 1:5, 6] [c]Lev. 13:5; Num. 5:2, 3; 12:14, 15; 2 Chr. 26:21
9 [a]Num. 19:19
10 [a]Matt. 8:4; Mark 1:44; Luke 5:14 [b]Lev. 2:1; Num. 15:4
12 [a]Lev. 5:6, 18; 6:6; 14:19

NKJV

which is the plague, whether warp or woof, in wool or in linen, or anything of leather, for it *is* an active leprosy; *the garment* shall be burned in the fire.

53 "But if the priest examines *it,* and indeed the plague has not spread in the garment, either in the warp or in the woof, or in anything made of leather,

54 "then the priest shall command that they wash *the thing* in which *is* the plague; and he shall isolate it another seven days.

55 "Then the priest shall examine the plague after it has been washed; and indeed *if* the plague has not changed its color, though the plague has not spread, it *is* unclean, and you shall burn it in the fire; it continues eating away, *whether* the damage *is* outside or inside.

56 "If the priest examines *it,* and indeed the plague has faded after washing it, then he shall tear it out of the garment, whether out of the warp or out of the woof, or out of the leather.

57 "But if it appears again in the garment, either in the warp or in the woof, or in anything made of leather, it *is* a spreading *plague;* you shall burn with fire that in which is the plague.

58 "And if you wash the garment, either warp or woof, or whatever is made of leather, if the plague has disappeared from it, then it shall be washed a second time, and shall be clean.

59 "This *is* the law of the leprous plague in a garment of wool or linen, either in the warp or woof, or in anything made of leather, to pronounce it clean or to pronounce it unclean."

The Ritual for Cleansing Healed Lepers *(cf. Matt. 8:1–4; Luke 5:12–14)*

14 Then the LORD spoke to Moses, saying,

2 "This shall be the law of the leper for the day of his cleansing: He [a]shall be brought to the priest.

3 "And the priest shall go out of the camp, and the priest shall examine *him;* and indeed, *if* the leprosy is healed in the leper,

4 "then the priest shall command to take for him who is to be cleansed two living *and* clean birds, [a]cedar wood, [b]scarlet, and [c]hyssop.

5 "And the priest shall command that one of the birds be killed in an earthen vessel over running water.

6 "As for the living bird, he shall take it, the cedar wood and the scarlet and the hyssop, and dip them and the living bird in the blood of the bird *that was* killed over the running water.

7 "And he shall [a]sprinkle it [b]seven times on him who is to be cleansed from the leprosy, and shall pronounce him clean, and shall let the living bird loose in the open field.

8 "He who is to be cleansed [a]shall wash his clothes, shave off all his hair, and [b]wash himself in water, that he may be clean. After that he shall come into the camp, and [c]shall stay outside his tent seven days.

9 "But on the [a]seventh day he shall shave all the hair off his head and his beard and his eyebrows—all his hair he shall shave off. He shall wash his clothes and wash his body in water, and he shall be clean.

10 "And on the eighth day [a]he shall take two male lambs without blemish, one ewe lamb of the first year without blemish, three-tenths *of an ephah* of fine flour mixed with oil as [b]a grain offering, and one log of oil.

11 "Then the priest who makes *him* clean shall present the man who is to be made clean, and those things, before the LORD, *at* the door of the tabernacle of meeting.

12 "And the priest shall take one male lamb and [a]offer it as a trespass offering, and the log

KJV

oil, and [b]wave them *for* a wave offering before
the LORD:
13 And he shall slay the lamb [a]in the place
where he shall kill the sin offering and the burnt
offering, in the holy place: for [b]as the sin offering
is the priest's, *so is* the trespass offering: [c]it *is*
most holy:
14 And the priest shall take *some* of the blood
of the trespass offering, and the priest shall put
it [a]upon the tip of the right ear of him that is to
be cleansed, and upon the thumb of his right hand,
and upon the great toe of his right foot:
15 And the priest shall take *some* of the log
of oil, and pour *it* into the palm of his own left
hand:
16 And the priest shall dip his right finger
in the oil that *is* in his left hand, and shall [a]sprin-
kle of the oil with his finger seven times before
the LORD:
17 And of the rest of the oil that *is* in his hand
shall the priest put upon the tip of the right ear
of him that is to be cleansed, and upon the thumb
of his right hand, and upon the great toe of
his right foot, upon the blood of the trespass
offering:
18 And the remnant of the oil that *is* in the
priest's hand he shall pour upon the head of him
that is to be cleansed: [a]and the priest shall make
an atonement for him before the LORD.
19 And the priest shall offer [a]the sin offering,
and make an atonement for him that is to be
cleansed from his uncleanness; and afterward he
shall kill the burnt offering:
20 And the priest shall offer the burnt offering and the meat offering upon the altar: and the
priest shall make an atonement for him, and he
shall be [a]clean.
21 And [a]if he *be* poor, and cannot get so
much; then he shall take one lamb *for* a trespass
offering to be waved, to make an atonement for
him, and one tenth deal of fine flour mingled with
oil for a meat offering, and a log of oil;
22 [a]And two turtledoves, or two young pigeons, such as he is able to get; and the one shall
be a sin offering, and the other a burnt offering.
23 [a]And he shall bring them on the eighth
day for his cleansing unto the priest, unto the door
of the tabernacle of the congregation, before the
LORD.
24 [a]And the priest shall take the lamb of the
trespass offering, and the log of oil, and the priest
shall wave them *for* a wave offering before the
LORD:
25 And he shall kill the lamb of the trespass
offering, [a]and the priest shall take *some* of the
blood of the trespass offering, and put *it* upon
the tip of the right ear of him that is to be cleansed,
and upon the thumb of his right hand, and upon
the great toe of his right foot:
26 And the priest shall pour of the oil into
the palm of his own left hand:
27 And the priest shall sprinkle with his right
finger *some* of the oil that *is* in his left hand seven
times before the LORD:
28 And the priest shall put of the oil that *is*
in his hand upon the tip of the right ear of him
that is to be cleansed, and upon the thumb of his
right hand, and upon the great toe of his right
foot, upon the place of the blood of the trespass
offering:
29 And the rest of the oil that *is* in the priest's
hand he shall put upon the head of him that is to
be cleansed, to make an atonement for him before
the LORD.
30 And he shall offer the one of [a]the turtledoves, or of the young pigeons, such as he can
get;
31 *Even* such as he is able to get, the one
for a sin offering, and the other *for* a burnt offering, with the meat offering: and the priest shall
make an atonement for him that is to be cleansed
before the LORD.

12 [b]Ex. 29:22–24, 26
13 [a]Ex. 29:11; Lev. 1:5, 11; 4:4, 24 [b]Lev. 6:24–30; 7:7 [c]Lev. 2:3; 7:6; 21:22
14 [a]Ex. 29:20; Lev. 8:23, 24
16 [a]Lev. 4:6
18 [a]Lev. 4:26; 5:6; Num. 15:28; [Heb. 2:17]
19 [a]Lev. 5:1, 6; 12:7; [2 Cor. 5:21]
20 [a]Lev. 14:8, 9
21 [a]Lev. 5:7, 11; 12:8; 27:8
22 [a]Lev. 12:8; 15:14, 15
23 [a]Lev. 14:10, 11
24 [a]Lev. 14:12
25 [a]Lev. 14:14, 17
30 [a]Lev. 14:22; 15:14, 15

NKJV

of oil, and [b]wave them *as* a wave offering before
the LORD.
13 "Then he shall kill the lamb [a]in the place
where he kills the sin offering and the burnt offering, in a holy place; for [b]as the sin offering *is*
the priest's, so *is* the trespass offering. [c]It *is* most
holy.
14 "The priest shall take *some* of the blood
of the trespass offering, and the priest shall put
it [a]on the tip of the right ear of him who is to be
cleansed, on the thumb of his right hand, and on
the big toe of his right foot.
15 "And the priest shall take *some* of the log
of oil, and pour *it* into the palm of his own left
hand.
16 "Then the priest shall dip his right finger
in the oil that *is* in his left hand, and shall [a]sprin-
kle some of the oil with his finger seven times
before the LORD.
17 "And of the rest of the oil in his hand,
the priest shall put *some* on the tip of the right
ear of him who is to be cleansed, on the thumb
of his right hand, and on the big toe of his right
foot, on the blood of the trespass offering.
18 "The rest of the oil that *is* in the priest's
hand he shall put on the head of him who is to
be cleansed. [a]So the priest shall make atonement
for him before the LORD.
19 "Then the priest shall offer [a]the sin offering, and make atonement for him who is to be
cleansed from his uncleanness. Afterward he shall
kill the burnt offering.
20 "And the priest shall offer the burnt offering and the grain offering on the altar. So the
priest shall make atonement for him, and he shall
be [a]clean.
21 "But [a]if he *is* poor and cannot afford it,
then he shall take one male lamb *as* a trespass
offering to be waved, to make atonement for him,
one-tenth *of an ephah* of fine flour mixed with
oil as a grain offering, a log of oil,
22 [a]"and two turtledoves or two young pigeons, such as he is able to afford: one shall be
a sin offering and the other a burnt offering.
23 [a]"He shall bring them to the priest on the
eighth day for his cleansing, to the door of the
tabernacle of meeting, before the LORD.
24 [a]"And the priest shall take the lamb of
the trespass offering and the log of oil, and the
priest shall wave them *as* a wave offering before
the LORD.
25 "Then he shall kill the lamb of the trespass
offering, [a]and the priest shall take *some* of the
blood of the trespass offering and put *it* on the
tip of the right ear of him who is to be cleansed,
on the thumb of his right hand, and on the big
toe of his right foot.
26 "And the priest shall pour some of the oil
into the palm of his own left hand.
27 "Then the priest shall sprinkle with his
right finger *some* of the oil that *is* in his left hand
seven times before the LORD.
28 "And the priest shall put *some* of the oil
that *is* in his hand on the tip of the right ear of
him who is to be cleansed, on the thumb of the
right hand, and on the big toe of his right foot,
on the place of the blood of the trespass offering.
29 "The rest of the oil that *is* in the priest's
hand he shall put on the head of him who is to
be cleansed, to make atonement for him before
the LORD.
30 "And he shall offer one of [a]the turtledoves
or young pigeons, such as he can afford—
31 "such as he is able to afford, the one *as* a
sin offering and the other *as* a burnt offering, with
the grain offering. So the priest shall make atonement for him who is to be cleansed before the
LORD.

KJV

32 This *is* the law *of him* in whom *is* the plague of leprosy, whose hand is not able to get [a]*that which pertaineth* to his cleansing.

The Law Concerning Leprous Houses

33 And the LORD spake unto Moses and unto Aaron, saying,

34 [a]When ye be come into the land of Canaan, which I give to you for a possession, and [b]I put the plague of leprosy in a house of the land of your possession;

35 And he that owneth the house shall come and tell the priest, saying, It seemeth to me *there is* as it were [a]a plague in the house:

36 Then the priest shall command that they empty the house, before the priest go *into it* to see the plague, that all that *is* in the house be not made unclean: and afterward the priest shall go in to see the house:

37 And he shall look on the plague, and, behold, *if* the plague *be* in the walls of the house with hollow strakes, greenish or reddish, which in sight *are* lower than the wall;

38 Then the priest shall go out of the house to the door of the house, and shut up the house seven days:

39 And the priest shall come again the seventh day, and shall look: and, behold, *if* the plague be spread in the walls of the house;

40 Then the priest shall command that they take away the stones in which the plague *is*, and they shall cast them into an unclean place without the city:

41 And he shall cause the house to be scraped within round about, and they shall pour out the dust that they scrape off without the city into an unclean place:

42 And they shall take other stones, and put *them* in the place of those stones; and he shall take other morter, and shall plaister the house.

43 And if the plague come again, and break out in the house, after that he hath taken away the stones, and after he hath scraped the house, and after it is plaistered;

44 Then the priest shall come and look, and, behold, *if* the plague be spread in the house, it *is* [a]a fretting leprosy in the house: it *is* unclean.

45 And he shall break down the house, the stones of it, and the timber thereof, and all the morter of the house; and he shall carry *them* forth out of the city into an unclean place.

46 Moreover he that goeth into the house all the while that it is shut up shall be unclean [a]until the even.

47 And he that lieth in the house shall [a]wash his clothes; and he that eateth in the house shall wash his clothes.

48 And if the priest shall come in, and look *upon it*, and, behold, the plague hath not spread in the house, after the house was plaistered: then the priest shall pronounce the house clean, because the plague is healed.

49 And [a]he shall take to cleanse the house two birds, and cedar wood, and scarlet, and hyssop:

50 And he shall kill the one of the birds in an earthen vessel over running water:

51 And he shall take the cedar wood, and the hyssop, and the scarlet, and the living bird, and dip them in the blood of the slain bird, and in the running water, and sprinkle the house seven times:

52 And he shall cleanse the house with the blood of the bird, and with the running water, and with the living bird, and with the cedar wood, and with the hyssop, and with the scarlet:

53 But he shall let go the living bird out of the city into the open fields, and [a]make an atonement for the house: and it shall be clean.

54 This *is* the law for all manner of [a]plague of leprosy, and scall,

32 [a]Lev. 14:10
34 [a]Gen. 12:7; 13:17; 17:8; Num. 32:22; Deut. 7:1; 32:49 [b][Prov. 3:33]
35 [a][Ps. 91:9, 10; Prov. 3:33; Zech. 5:4]
44 [a]Lev. 13:51; [Zech. 5:4]
46 [a]Lev. 11:24; 15:5
47 [a]Lev. 14:8
49 [a]Lev. 14:4
53 [a]Lev. 14:20
54 [a]Lev. 13:30; 26:21

NKJV

32 "This *is* the law *for one* who had a leprous sore, who cannot afford [a]the usual cleansing."

The Law Concerning Leprous Houses

33 And the LORD spoke to Moses and Aaron, saying:

34 [a]"When you have come into the land of Canaan, which I give you as a possession, and [b]I put the *leprous plague in a house in the land of your possession,

35 "and he who owns the house comes and tells the priest, saying, 'It seems to me that *there is* [a]some plague in the house,'

36 "then the priest shall command that they empty the house, before the priest goes *into it* to examine the plague, that all that *is* in the house may not be made unclean; and afterward the priest shall go in to examine the house.

37 "And he shall examine the plague; and indeed *if* the plague *is* on the walls of the house with ingrained streaks, greenish or reddish, which appear to be deep in the wall,

38 "then the priest shall go out of the house, to the door of the house, and shut up the house seven days.

39 "And the priest shall come again on the seventh day and look; and indeed *if* the plague has spread on the walls of the house,

40 "then the priest shall command that they take away the stones in which *is* the plague, and they shall cast them into an unclean place outside the city.

41 "And he shall cause the house to be scraped inside, all around, and the dust that they scrape off they shall pour out in an unclean place outside the city.

42 "Then they shall take other stones and put *them* in the place of *those* stones, and he shall take other mortar and plaster the house.

43 "Now if the plague comes back and breaks out in the house, after he has taken away the stones, after he has scraped the house, and after it is plastered,

44 "then the priest shall come and look; and indeed *if* the plague has spread in the house, it *is* [a]an active leprosy in the house. It *is* unclean.

45 "And he shall break down the house, its stones, its timber, and all the plaster of the house, and he shall carry *them* outside the city to an unclean place.

46 "Moreover he who goes into the house at all while it is shut up shall be unclean [a]until evening.

47 "And he who lies down in the house shall [a]wash his clothes, and he who eats in the house shall wash his clothes.

48 "But if the priest comes in and examines *it*, and indeed the plague has not spread in the house after the house was plastered, then the priest shall pronounce the house clean, because the plague is healed.

49 "And [a]he shall take, to cleanse the house, two birds, cedar wood, scarlet, and hyssop.

50 "Then he shall kill one of the birds in an earthen vessel over running water;

51 "and he shall take the cedar wood, the hyssop, the scarlet, and the living bird, and dip them in the blood of the slain bird and in the running water, and sprinkle the house seven times.

52 "And he shall cleanse the house with the blood of the bird and the running water and the living bird, with the cedar wood, the hyssop, and the scarlet.

53 "Then he shall let the living bird loose outside the city in the open field, and [a]make atonement for the house, and it shall be clean.

54 "This *is* the law for any [a]leprous sore and scale,

*

14:34 Decomposition by mildew, mold, dry rot, etc., and so in vv. 34–53

KJV

55 And for the [a]leprosy of a garment, [b]and of a house,

56 And [a]for a rising, and for a scab, and for a bright spot:

57 To [a]teach when *it is* unclean, and when *it is* clean: this *is* the law of leprosy.

The Law Concerning Bodily Discharges

15 And the LORD spake unto Moses and to Aaron, saying,

2 Speak unto the children of Israel, and say unto them, [a]When any man hath a running issue out of his flesh, *because of* his issue he *is* unclean.

3 And this shall be his uncleanness in his issue: whether his flesh run with his issue, or his flesh be stopped from his issue, it *is* his uncleanness.

4 Every bed, whereon he lieth that hath the issue, is unclean: and every thing, whereon he sitteth, shall be unclean.

5 And whosoever [a]toucheth his bed shall [b]wash his clothes, [c]and bathe *himself* in water, and be unclean until the even.

6 And he that sitteth on *any* thing whereon he sat that hath the [a]issue shall wash his clothes, and bathe *himself* in water, and be unclean until the even.

7 And he that toucheth the flesh of him that hath the issue shall wash his clothes, and bathe *himself* in water, and be unclean until the even.

8 And if he that hath the issue [a]spit upon him that is clean; then he shall wash his clothes, and bathe *himself* in water, and be unclean until the even.

9 And what saddle soever he rideth upon that hath the issue shall be unclean.

10 And whosoever toucheth any thing that was under him shall be unclean until the even: and he that beareth *any of* those things shall wash his clothes, and bathe *himself* in water, and be unclean until the even.

11 And whomsoever he toucheth that hath the issue, and hath not rinsed his hands in water, he shall wash his clothes, and bathe *himself* in water, and be unclean until the even.

12 And the [a]vessel of earth, that he toucheth which hath the issue, shall be broken: and every vessel of wood shall be rinsed in water.

13 And when he that hath an issue is cleansed of his issue; then [a]he shall number to himself seven days for his cleansing, and wash his clothes, and bathe his flesh in running water, and shall be clean.

14 And on the eighth day he shall take to him [a]two turtledoves, or two young pigeons, and come before the LORD unto the door of the tabernacle of the congregation, and give them unto the priest:

15 And the priest shall offer them, [a]the one *for* a sin offering, and the other *for* a burnt offering; [b]and the priest shall make an atonement for him before the LORD for his issue.

16 And [a]if any man's seed of copulation go out from him, then he shall wash all his flesh in water, and be unclean until the even.

17 And every garment, and every skin, whereon is the seed of copulation, shall be washed with water, and be unclean until the even.

18 The woman also with whom man shall lie *with* seed of copulation, they shall *both* bathe *themselves* in water, and [a]be unclean until the even.

19 And [a]if a woman have an issue, *and* her issue in her flesh be blood, she shall be put apart seven days: and whosoever toucheth her shall be unclean until the even.

20 And every thing that she lieth upon in her separation shall be unclean: every thing also that she sitteth upon shall be unclean.

21 And whosoever toucheth her bed shall wash his clothes, and bathe *himself* in water, and be unclean until the even.

55 [a]Lev. 13:47–52 [b]Lev. 14:34
56 [a]Lev. 13:2
57 [a]Lev. 11:47; 20:25; Deut. 24:8; Ezek. 44:23

CHAPTER 15

2 [a]Lev. 22:4; Num. 5:2; 2 Sam. 3:29
5 [a]Lev. 5:2; 14:46 [b]Lev. 14:8, 47 [c]Lev. 11:25; 17:15
6 [a]Lev. 15:10; Deut. 23:10
8 [a]Num. 12:14
12 [a]Lev. 6:28; 11:32, 33
13 [a]Lev. 14:8; 15:28; Num. 19:11, 12
14 [a]Lev. 14:22, 23, 30, 31
15 [a]Lev. 14:30, 31 [b]Lev. 14:19, 31
16 [a]Lev. 22:4; Deut. 23:10, 11
18 [a][Ex. 19:15; 1 Sam. 21:4; 1 Cor. 6:18]
19 [a]Lev. 12:2

NKJV

55 "for the [a]leprosy of a garment [b]and of a house,

56 [a]"for a swelling and a scab and a bright spot,

57 "to [a]teach when *it is* unclean and when *it is* clean. This *is* the law of leprosy."

The Law Concerning Bodily Discharges

15 And the LORD spoke to Moses and Aaron, saying,

2 "Speak to the children of Israel, and say to them: [a]'When any man has a discharge from his body, his discharge *is* unclean.

3 'And this shall be his uncleanness in regard to his discharge—whether his body runs with his discharge, or his body is stopped up by his discharge, it *is* his uncleanness.

4 'Every bed is unclean on which he who has the discharge lies, and everything on which he sits shall be unclean.

5 'And whoever [a]touches his bed shall [b]wash his clothes and [c]bathe in water, and be unclean until evening.

6 'He who sits on anything on which he who has the [a]discharge sat shall wash his clothes and bathe in water, and be unclean until evening.

7 'And he who touches the body of him who has the discharge shall wash his clothes and bathe in water, and be unclean until evening.

8 'If he who has the discharge [a]spits on him who is clean, then he shall wash his clothes and bathe in water, and be unclean until evening.

9 'Any saddle on which he who has the discharge rides shall be unclean.

10 'Whoever touches anything that was under him shall be unclean until evening. He who carries *any of* those things shall wash his clothes and bathe in water, and be unclean until evening.

11 'And whomever the one who has the discharge touches, and has not rinsed his hands in water, he shall wash his clothes and bathe in water, and be unclean until evening.

12 'The [a]vessel of earth that he who has the discharge touches shall be broken, and every vessel of wood shall be rinsed in water.

13 'And when he who has a discharge is cleansed of his discharge, then [a]he shall count for himself seven days for his cleansing, wash his clothes, and bathe his body in running water; then he shall be clean.

14 'On the eighth day he shall take for himself [a]two turtledoves or two young pigeons, and come before the LORD, to the door of the tabernacle of meeting, and give them to the priest.

15 'Then the priest shall offer them, [a]the one *as* a sin offering and the other *as* a burnt offering. [b]So the priest shall make atonement for him before the LORD because of his discharge.

16 [a]'If any man has an emission of semen, then he shall wash all his body in water, and be unclean until evening.

17 'And any garment and any leather on which there is semen, it shall be washed with water, and be unclean until evening.

18 'Also, when a woman lies with a man, and *there is* an emission of semen, they shall bathe in water, and [a]be unclean until evening.

19 [a]'If a woman has a discharge, *and* the discharge from her body is blood, she shall be set apart seven days; and whoever touches her shall be unclean until evening.

20 'Everything that she lies on during her impurity shall be unclean; also everything that she sits on shall be unclean.

21 'Whoever touches her bed shall wash his clothes and bathe in water, and be unclean until evening.

KJV

22 And whosoever toucheth any thing that
she sat upon shall wash his clothes, and bathe
himself in water, and be unclean until the even.
23 And if it *be* on *her* bed, or on any thing
whereon she sitteth, when he toucheth it, he shall
be unclean until the even.
24 And [a]if any man lie with her at all, and
her flowers be upon him, he shall be unclean
seven days; and all the bed whereon he lieth shall
be unclean.
25 And if [a]a woman have an issue of her
blood many days out of the time of her separation,
or if it run beyond the time of her separation; all
the days of the issue of her uncleanness shall be
as the days of her separation: she *shall be* unclean.
26 Every bed whereon she lieth all the days
of her issue shall be unto her as the bed of her
separation: and whatsoever she sitteth upon shall
be unclean, as the uncleanness of her separation.
27 And whosoever toucheth those things
shall be unclean, and shall wash his clothes, and
bathe *himself* in water, and be unclean until the
even.
28 But [a]if she be cleansed of her issue, then
she shall number to herself seven days, and after
that she shall be clean.
29 And on the eighth day she shall take unto
her two turtles, or two young pigeons, and bring
them unto the priest, to the door of the tabernacle
of the congregation.
30 And the priest shall offer the one *for* a sin
offering, and the other *for* a [a]burnt offering; and
the priest shall make an atonement for her before
the LORD for the issue of her uncleanness.
31 Thus shall ye [a]separate the children of Israel from their uncleanness; that they die not in
their uncleanness, when they [b]defile my tabernacle that *is* among them.
32 [a]This *is* the law of him that hath an issue,
[b]and *of him* whose seed goeth from him, and is
defiled therewith;
33 [a]And of her that is sick of her flowers,
and of him that hath an issue, of the man, [b]and
of the woman, [c]and of him that lieth with her that
is unclean.

The Day of Atonement

16 And the LORD spake unto Moses after [a]the
death of the two sons of Aaron, when they
offered before the LORD, and died;
2 And the LORD said unto Moses, Speak
unto Aaron thy brother, that he [a]come not at all
times into the holy *place* within the vail before
the mercy seat, which *is* upon the ark; that he
die not: for [b]I will appear in the cloud upon the
mercy seat.
3 Thus shall Aaron [a]come into the holy
place: [b]with a young bullock for a sin offering,
and a ram for a burnt offering.
4 He shall put on the [a]holy linen coat, and
he shall have the linen breeches upon his flesh,
and shall be girded with a linen girdle, and with
the linen mitre shall he be attired: these *are* holy
garments; therefore [b]shall he wash his flesh in
water, and *so* put them on.
5 And he shall take of [a]the congregation of
the children of Israel two kids of the goats for a
sin offering, and one ram for a burnt offering.
6 And Aaron shall offer his bullock of the
sin offering, which *is* for himself, and [a]make an
atonement for himself, and for his house.
7 And he shall take the two goats, and present them before the LORD *at* the door of the tabernacle of the congregation.
8 And Aaron shall cast lots upon the two
goats; one lot for the LORD, and the other lot for
the scapegoat.
9 And Aaron shall bring the goat upon
which the LORD's lot fell, and offer him *for* a sin
offering.
10 But the goat, on which the lot fell to be

24 [a]Lev. 18:19; 20:18
25 [a]Matt. 9:20; Mark 5:25; Luke 8:43
28 [a]Lev. 15:13–15
30 [a]Lev. 5:7
31 [a]Lev. 11:47; 14:57; 22:2; Deut. 24:8; Ezek. 44:23; [Heb. 12:15] [b]Lev. 20:3; Num. 5:3; 19:13, 20; Ezek. 5:11; 23:38; 36:17
32 [a]Lev. 15:2 [b]Lev. 15:16
33 [a]Lev. 15:19 [b]Lev. 15:25 [c]Lev. 15:24

CHAPTER 16

1 [a]Lev. 10:1, 2; 2 Sam. 6:6–8
2 [a]Ex. 30:10; Lev. 16:34; 23:27; [Heb. 6:19; 9:7, 8, 12; 10:19] [b]Ex. 25:21, 22; 40:34; 1 Kin. 8:10–12
3 [a]Lev. 4:1–12; 16:6; [Heb. 9:7, 12, 24, 25] [b]Lev. 4:3
4 [a]Ex. 28:39, 42, 43; Lev. 6:10; Ezek. 44:17, 18 [b]Ex. 30:20; Lev. 8:6, 7
5 [a]Lev. 4:14; Num. 29:11; 2 Chr. 29:21; Ezra 6:17; Ezek. 45:22, 23
6 [a]Lev. 9:7; [Heb. 5:3; 7:27, 28; 9:7]

NKJV

22 'And whoever touches anything that she
sat on shall wash his clothes and bathe in water,
and be unclean until evening.
23 'If *anything* is on *her* bed or on anything
on which she sits, when he touches it, he shall
be unclean until evening.
24 'And [a]if any man lies with her at all, so
that her impurity is on him, he shall be unclean
seven days; and every bed on which he lies shall
be unclean.
25 'If [a]a woman has a discharge of blood for
many days, other than at the time of her *custom-*
ary impurity, or if it runs beyond her *usual time*
of impurity, all the days of her unclean discharge
shall be as the days of her *customary* impurity.
She *shall be* unclean.
26 'Every bed on which she lies all the days
of her discharge shall be to her as the bed of her
impurity; and whatever she sits on shall be unclean, as the uncleanness of her impurity.
27 'Whoever touches those things shall be
unclean; he shall wash his clothes and bathe in
water, and be unclean until evening.
28 'But [a]if she is cleansed of her discharge,
then she shall count for herself seven days, and
after that she shall be clean.
29 'And on the eighth day she shall take for
herself two turtledoves or two young pigeons, and
bring them to the priest, to the door of the tabernacle of meeting.
30 'Then the priest shall offer the one *as* a
sin offering and the other *as* a [a]burnt offering,
and the priest shall make atonement for her
before the LORD for the discharge of her uncleanness.
31 'Thus you shall [a]separate the children of
Israel from their uncleanness, lest they die in their
uncleanness when they [b]defile My tabernacle that
is among them.
32 [a]'This *is* the law for one who has a discharge, [b]and *for him* who emits semen and is unclean thereby,
33 [a]'and for her who is indisposed because
of her *customary* impurity, and for one who has
a discharge, either man [b]or woman, [c]and for him
who lies with her who is unclean.' "

The Day of Atonement

16 Now the LORD spoke to Moses after [a]the
death of the two sons of Aaron, when they
offered *profane fire* before the LORD, and died;
2 and the LORD said to Moses: "Tell Aaron
your brother [a]not to come at *just* any time into
the Holy *Place* inside the veil, before the mercy
seat which *is* on the ark, lest he die; for [b]I will
appear in the cloud above the mercy seat.
3 "Thus Aaron shall [a]come into the Holy
Place: [b]with *the blood of* a young bull as a sin
offering, and *of* a ram as a burnt offering.
4 "He shall put the [a]holy linen tunic and
the linen trousers on his body; he shall be girded
with a linen sash, and with the linen turban he
shall be attired. These *are* holy garments. Therefore [b]he shall wash his body in water, and put
them on.
5 "And he shall take from [a]the congregation
of the children of Israel two kids of the goats as
a sin offering, and one ram as a burnt offering.
6 "Aaron shall offer the bull as a sin offering, which *is* for himself, and [a]make atonement
for himself and for his house.
7 "He shall take the two goats and present
them before the LORD *at* the door of the tabernacle
of meeting.
8 "Then Aaron shall cast lots for the two
goats: one lot for the LORD and the other lot for
the scapegoat.
9 "And Aaron shall bring the goat on which
the LORD's lot fell, and offer it *as* a sin offering.
10 "But the goat on which the lot fell to be

KJV

the scapegoat, shall be presented alive before the LORD, to make [a]an atonement with him, *and* to let him go for a scapegoat into the wilderness.

11 And Aaron shall bring the bullock of the sin offering, which *is* for [a]himself, and shall make an atonement for himself, and for his house, and shall kill the bullock of the sin offering which *is* for himself:

12 And he shall take [a]a censer full of burning coals of fire from off the altar before the LORD, and his hands full of [b]sweet incense beaten small, and bring *it* within the vail:

13 [a]And he shall put the incense upon the fire before the LORD, that the cloud of the incense may cover the [b]mercy seat that *is* upon the testimony, that he [c]die not:

14 And [a]he shall take of the blood of the bullock, and [b]sprinkle *it* with his finger upon the mercy seat eastward; and before the mercy seat shall he sprinkle of the blood with his finger seven times.

15 [a]Then shall he kill the goat of the sin offering, that *is* for the people, and bring his blood [b]within the vail, and do with that blood as he did with the blood of the bullock, and sprinkle it upon the mercy seat, and before the mercy seat:

16 And he shall [a]make an atonement for the holy *place*, because of the uncleanness of the children of Israel, and because of their transgressions in all their sins: and so shall he do for the tabernacle of the congregation, that remaineth among them in the midst of their uncleanness.

17 And there shall be [a]no man in the tabernacle of the congregation when he goeth in to make an atonement in the holy *place*, until he come out, and have made an atonement for himself, and for his household, and for all the congregation of Israel.

18 And he shall go out unto the altar that *is* before the LORD, and make an atonement for [a]it; and shall take of the blood of the bullock, and of the blood of the goat, and put *it* upon the horns of the altar round about.

19 And he shall sprinkle of the blood upon it with his finger seven times, and cleanse it, and [a]hallow it from the uncleanness of the children of Israel.

20 And when he hath made an end of reconciling the holy *place*, and the tabernacle of the congregation, and the altar, he shall bring the live goat:

21 And Aaron shall lay both his hands upon the head of the live goat, and [a]confess over him all the iniquities of the children of Israel, and all their transgressions in all their sins, [b]putting them upon the head of the goat, and shall send *him* away by the hand of a fit man into the wilderness:

22 And the goat shall [a]bear upon him all their iniquities unto a land not inhabited: and he shall [b]let go the goat in the wilderness.

23 And Aaron shall come into the tabernacle of the congregation, [a]and shall put off the linen garments, which he put on when he went into the holy *place*, and shall leave them there:

24 And he shall wash his flesh with water in the holy place, and put on his garments, and come forth, and offer his burnt offering, and the burnt offering of the people, and make an atonement for himself, and for the people.

25 And [a]the fat of the sin offering shall he burn upon the altar.

26 And he that let go the goat for the scapegoat shall wash his clothes, [a]and bathe his flesh in water, and afterward come into the camp.

27 [a]And the bullock *for* the sin offering, and the goat *for* the sin offering, whose blood was brought in to make atonement in the holy *place*, shall *one* carry forth without the camp; and they shall burn in the fire their skins, and their flesh, and their dung.

28 And he that burneth them shall wash his

10 [a][Is. 53:5, 6; Rom. 3:25; Heb. 7:27; 9:23, 24; 1 John 2:2]
11 [a][Heb. 7:27; 9:7]
12 [a]Lev. 10:1; Num. 16:7, 18; Is. 6:6, 7; Rev. 8:5 [b]Ex. 30:34–38
13 [a]Ex. 30:7, 8; Num. 16:7, 18, 46 [b]Ex. 25:21 [c]Ex. 28:43; Lev. 22:9; Num. 4:15, 20
14 [a]Lev. 4:5; [Heb. 9:25; 10:4] [b]Lev. 4:6, 17
15 [a][Heb. 2:17] [b][Heb. 6:19; 7:27; 9:3, 7, 12]
16 [a]Ex. 29:36; 30:10; Ezek. 45:18; [Heb. 9:22–24]
17 [a]Ex. 34:3; Luke 1:10
18 [a]Ex. 29:36
19 [a]Lev. 16:14; Ezek. 43:20
21 [a]Lev. 5:5; 26:40 [b][Is. 53:6]
22 [a]Lev. 8:14; [Is. 53:6, 11, 12; John 1:29; Heb. 9:28; 1 Pet. 2:24] [b]Lev. 14:7
23 [a]Lev. 6:11; 16:4; Ezek. 42:14; 44:19
25 [a]Lev. 1:8; 4:10
26 [a]Lev. 15:5
27 [a]Lev. 4:12, 21; 6:30; Heb. 13:11

NKJV

the scapegoat shall be presented alive before the LORD, to make [a]atonement upon it, *and* to let it go as the scapegoat into the wilderness.

11 "And Aaron shall bring the bull of the sin offering, which is for [a]himself, and make atonement for himself and for his house, and shall kill the bull as the sin offering which *is* for himself.

12 "Then he shall take [a]a censer full of burning coals of fire from the altar before the LORD, with his hands full of [b]sweet incense beaten fine, and bring *it* inside the veil.

13 [a]"And he shall put the incense on the fire before the LORD, that the cloud of incense may cover the [b]mercy seat that *is* on the Testimony, lest he [c]die.

14 [a]"He shall take some of the blood of the bull and [b]sprinkle *it* with his finger on the mercy seat on the east *side;* and before the mercy seat he shall sprinkle some of the blood with his finger seven times.

15 [a]"Then he shall kill the goat of the sin offering, which *is* for the people, bring its blood [b]inside the veil, do with that blood as he did with the blood of the bull, and sprinkle it on the mercy seat and before the mercy seat.

16 "So he shall [a]make atonement for the Holy *Place,* because of the uncleanness of the children of Israel, and because of their transgressions, for all their sins; and so he shall do for the tabernacle of meeting which remains among them in the midst of their uncleanness.

17 "There shall be [a]no man in the tabernacle of meeting when he goes in to make atonement in the Holy *Place,* until he comes out, that he may make atonement for himself, for his household, and for all the assembly of Israel.

18 "And he shall go out to the altar that *is* before the LORD, and make atonement for [a]it, and shall take some of the blood of the bull and some of the blood of the goat, and put it on the horns of the altar all around.

19 "Then he shall sprinkle some of the blood on it with his finger seven times, cleanse it, and [a]consecrate it from the uncleanness of the children of Israel.

20 "And when he has made an end of atoning for the Holy *Place,* the tabernacle of meeting, and the altar, he shall bring the live goat.

21 "Aaron shall lay both his hands on the head of the live goat, [a]confess over it all the iniquities of the children of Israel, and all their transgressions, concerning all their sins, [b]putting them on the head of the goat, and shall send *it* away into the wilderness by the hand of a suitable man.

22 "The goat shall [a]bear on itself all their iniquities to an uninhabited land; and he shall [b]release the goat in the wilderness.

23 "Then Aaron shall come into the tabernacle of meeting, [a]shall take off the linen garments which he put on when he went into the Holy *Place,* and shall leave them there.

24 "And he shall wash his body with water in a holy place, put on his garments, come out and offer his burnt offering and the burnt offering of the people, and make atonement for himself and for the people.

25 [a]"The fat of the sin offering he shall burn on the altar.

26 "And he who released the goat as the scapegoat shall wash his clothes [a]and bathe his body in water, and afterward he may come into the camp.

27 [a]"The bull *for* the sin offering and the goat *for* the sin offering, whose blood was brought in to make atonement in the Holy *Place,* shall be carried outside the camp. And they shall burn in the fire their skins, their flesh, and their offal.

28 "Then he who burns them shall wash his

KJV

clothes, and bathe his flesh in water, and afterward he shall come into the camp.
29 And *this* shall be a statute for ever unto
you: *that* [a]in the seventh month, on the tenth *day*
of the month, ye shall afflict your souls, and do
no work at all, *whether it be* one of your own
country, or a stranger that sojourneth among you:
30 For on that day shall *the priest* make an
atonement for you, to [a]cleanse you, *that* ye may
be clean from all your sins before the LORD.
31 [a]It *shall be* a sabbath of rest unto you, and
ye shall afflict your souls, by a statute for ever.
32 [a]And the priest, whom he shall anoint,
and whom he shall [b]consecrate to minister in the
priest's office in his father's stead, shall make the
atonement, and shall put on the linen clothes, *even*
the holy garments:
33 And he shall make an atonement for the
holy sanctuary, and he shall make an atonement
for the tabernacle of the congregation, and for
the altar, and he shall make an atonement for the
priests, and for all the people of the congregation.
34 [a]And this shall be an everlasting statute
unto you, to make an atonement for the children
of Israel for all their sins [b]once a year. And he
did as the LORD commanded Moses.

The Sanctity of Blood

17 And the LORD spake unto Moses, saying,
2 Speak unto Aaron, and unto his sons,
and unto all the children of Israel, and say unto
them; This *is* the thing which the LORD hath commanded, saying,
3 What man soever *there be* of the house
of Israel, [a]that killeth an ox, or lamb, or goat, in
the camp, or that killeth *it* out of the camp,
4 And bringeth it not unto the door of the
tabernacle of the congregation, to offer an offering unto the LORD before the tabernacle of the
LORD; blood shall be [a]imputed unto that man; he
hath shed blood; and that man shall be cut off
from among his people:
5 To the end that the children of Israel may
bring their sacrifices, [a]which they offer in the
open field, even that they may bring them unto
the LORD, unto the door of the tabernacle of the
congregation, unto the priest, and offer them *for*
peace offerings unto the LORD.
6 And the priest [a]shall sprinkle the blood
upon the altar of the LORD *at* the door of the tabernacle of the congregation, and [b]burn the fat for
a sweet savour unto the LORD.
7 And they shall no more offer their sacrifices [a]unto devils, after whom they [b]have gone a
whoring. This shall be a statute for ever unto them
throughout their generations.
8 And thou shalt say unto them, Whatsoever man *there be* of the house of Israel, or of
the strangers which sojourn among you, [a]that offereth a burnt offering or sacrifice,
9 And bringeth it not unto the door of the
tabernacle of the [a]congregation, to offer it unto
the LORD; even that man shall be cut off from
among his people.
10 [a]And whatsoever man *there be* of the
house of Israel, or of the strangers that sojourn
among you, that eateth any manner of blood; [b]I
will even set my face against that soul that eateth
blood, and will cut him off from among his people.
11 For the [a]life of the flesh *is* in the blood:
and I have given it to you upon the altar [b]to make
an atonement for your souls: for [c]it *is* the blood
that maketh an atonement for the soul.
12 Therefore I said unto the children of Israel, No soul of you shall eat blood, neither shall
any stranger that sojourneth among you eat
blood.
13 And whatsoever man *there be* of the children of Israel, or of the strangers that sojourn
among you, which hunteth and catcheth any
[a]beast or fowl that may be eaten; he shall even

29 [a]Ex. 30:10; Lev. 23:27–32; Num. 29:7
30 [a]Ps. 51:2; Jer. 33:8; [Eph. 5:26; Heb. 9:13, 14; 1 John 1:7, 9]
31 [a]Lev. 23:27, 32; Ezra 8:21; Is. 58:3, 5; Dan. 10:12
32 [a]Lev. 4:3, 5, 16; 21:10 [b]Ex. 29:29, 30; Num. 20:26, 28
34 [a]Lev. 23:31; Num. 29:7 [b]Ex. 30:10; [Heb. 9:7, 25, 28]

CHAPTER 17

3 [a]Deut. 12:5, 15, 21
4 [a]Rom. 5:13
5 [a]Gen. 21:33; 22:2; 31:54; Deut. 12:1–27; Ezek. 20:28
6 [a]Lev. 3:2 [b]Ex. 29:13, 18; Num. 18:17
7 [a]Ex. 22:20; 32:8; 34:15; Deut. 32:17; 2 Chr. 11:15; Ps. 106:37; 1 Cor. 10:20 [b]Ex. 34:15; Deut. 31:16; Ezek. 23:8
8 [a]Lev. 1:2, 3; 18:26
9 [a]Lev. 14:23
10 [a]Gen. 9:4; Lev. 3:17; 7:26, 27; Deut. 12:16, 23–25; 15:23; 1 Sam. 14:33 [b]Lev. 20:3, 5, 6
11 [a]Gen. 9:4; Lev. 17:14 [b][Matt. 26:28; Rom. 3:25; Eph. 1:7; Col. 1:14, 20; 1 Pet. 1:2; 1 John 1:7] [c][Heb. 9:22]
13 [a]Lev. 7:26

NKJV

clothes and bathe his body in water, and afterward he may come into the camp.
29 "*This* shall be a statute forever for you:
[a]In the seventh month, on the tenth *day* of the
month, you shall afflict your souls, and do no
work at all, *whether* a native of your own country
or a stranger who dwells among you.
30 "For on that day *the priest* shall make
atonement for you, to [a]cleanse you, *that* you may
be clean from all your sins before the LORD.
31 [a]"It *is* a sabbath of solemn rest for you,
and you shall afflict your souls. *It is* a statute
forever.
32 [a]"And the priest, who is anointed and
[b]consecrated to minister as priest in his father's
place, shall make atonement, and put on the linen
clothes, the holy garments;
33 "then he shall make atonement for *the
Holy Sanctuary, and he shall make atonement for
the tabernacle of meeting and for the altar, and
he shall make atonement for the priests and for
all the people of the assembly.
34 [a]"This shall be an everlasting statute for
you, to make atonement for the children of Israel,
for all their sins, [b]once a year." And he did as
the LORD commanded Moses.

The Sanctity of Blood

17 And the LORD spoke to Moses, saying,
2 "Speak to Aaron, to his sons, and to
all the children of Israel, and say to them, 'This
is the thing which the LORD has commanded,
saying:
3 "Whatever man of the house of Israel who
[a]kills an ox or lamb or goat in the camp, or who
kills *it* outside the camp,
4 "and does not bring it to the door of the
tabernacle of meeting to offer an offering to the
LORD before the tabernacle of the LORD, the guilt
of bloodshed shall be [a]imputed to that man. He
has shed blood; and that man shall be cut off from
among his people,
5 "to the end that the children of Israel may
bring their sacrifices [a]which they offer in the open
field, that they may bring them to the LORD at
the door of the tabernacle of meeting, to the priest,
and offer them *as* peace offerings to the LORD.
6 "And the priest [a]shall sprinkle the blood
on the altar of the LORD *at* the door of the tabernacle of meeting, and [b]burn the fat for a sweet
aroma to the LORD.
7 "They shall no more offer their sacrifices
[a]to demons, after whom they [b]have played the
harlot. This shall be a statute forever for them
throughout their generations." '
8 "Also you shall say to them: 'Whatever
man of the house of Israel, or of the strangers
who dwell among you, [a]who offers a burnt offering or sacrifice,
9 'and does not [a]bring it to the door of the
tabernacle of meeting, to offer it to the LORD, that
man shall be cut off from among his people.
10 [a]'And whatever man of the house of Israel, or of the strangers who dwell among you,
who eats any blood, [b]I will set My face against
that person who eats blood, and will cut him off
from among his people.
11 'For the [a]life of the flesh *is* in the blood,
and I have given it to you upon the altar [b]to make
atonement for your souls; for [c]it *is* the blood *that*
makes atonement for the soul.'
12 "Therefore I said to the children of Israel,
'No one among you shall eat blood, nor shall any
stranger who dwells among you eat blood.'
13 "Whatever man of the children of Israel,
or of the strangers who dwell among you, who
[a]hunts and catches any animal or bird that may

*16:33 The Most Holy Place

KJV

[b]pour out the blood thereof, and [c]cover it with dust.

14 [a]For *it is* the life of all flesh; the blood of it *is* for the life thereof: therefore I said unto the children of Israel, Ye shall eat the blood of no manner of flesh: for the life of all flesh *is* the blood thereof: whosoever eateth it shall be cut off.

15 [a]And every soul that eateth that which died *of itself,* or that which was torn *with beasts, whether it be* one of your own country, or a stranger, [b]he shall both wash his clothes, and [c]bathe *himself* in water, and be unclean until the even: then shall he be clean.

16 But if he wash *them* not, nor bathe his flesh; then [a]he shall bear his iniquity.

Laws of Sexual Morality

18 And the LORD spake unto Moses, saying,
2 Speak unto the children of Israel, and
say unto them, [a]I am the LORD your God.

3 [a]After the doings of the land of Egypt, wherein ye dwelt, shall ye not do: and [b]after the doings of the land of Canaan, whither I bring you, shall ye not do: neither shall ye walk in their ordinances.

4 [a]Ye shall do my judgments, and keep mine ordinances, to walk therein: I *am* the LORD your God.

5 Ye shall therefore keep my statutes, and my judgments: which if a man do, he shall live in them: I *am* the LORD.

6 None of you shall approach to any that is near of kin to him, to uncover *their* nakedness: I *am* the LORD.

7 The nakedness of thy father, or the nakedness of thy mother, shalt thou not uncover: she *is* thy mother; thou shalt not uncover her nakedness.

8 The nakedness of thy [a]father's wife shalt thou not uncover: it *is* thy father's nakedness.

9 [a]The nakedness of thy sister, the daughter of thy father, or daughter of thy mother, *whether she be* born at home, or born abroad, *even* their nakedness thou shalt not uncover.

10 The nakedness of thy son's daughter, or of thy daughter's daughter, *even* their nakedness thou shalt not uncover: for their's *is* thine own nakedness.

11 The nakedness of thy father's wife's daughter, begotten of thy father, she *is* thy sister, thou shalt not uncover her nakedness.

12 [a]Thou shalt not uncover the nakedness of thy father's sister: she *is* thy father's near kinswoman.

13 Thou shalt not uncover the nakedness of thy mother's sister: for she *is* thy mother's near kinswoman.

14 [a]Thou shalt not uncover the nakedness of thy father's brother, thou shalt not approach to his wife: she *is* thine aunt.

15 Thou shalt not uncover the nakedness of thy daughter in law: she *is* thy son's wife; thou shalt not uncover her nakedness.

16 Thou shalt not uncover the nakedness of thy brother's wife: it *is* thy brother's nakedness.

17 Thou shalt not uncover the nakedness of a woman and her [a]daughter, neither shalt thou take her son's daughter, or her daughter's daughter, to uncover her nakedness; *for* they *are* her near kinswomen: it *is* wickedness.

18 Neither shalt thou take a wife to her sister, [a]to vex *her,* to uncover her nakedness, beside the other in her life *time.*

19 Also thou shalt not approach unto a woman to uncover her nakedness, as [a]long as she is put apart for her [b]uncleanness.

20 [a]Moreover thou shalt not lie carnally with thy [b]neighbour's wife, to defile thyself with her.

21 And thou shalt not let any of thy seed [a]pass through [b]*the fire* to [c]Molech, neither shalt thou profane the name of thy God: I *am* the LORD.

13 [b]Deut. 12:16, 24 [c]Ezek. 24:7
14 [a]Gen. 9:4; Lev. 17:11; Deut. 12:23
15 [a]Ex. 22:31; Lev. 7:24; 22:8; Deut. 14:21; Ezek. 4:14; 44:31 [b]Lev. 11:25 [c]Lev. 15:5
16 [a]Lev. 5:1

CHAPTER 18

2 [a]Ex. 6:7; Lev. 11:44, 45; 19:3; Ezek. 20:5, 7, 19, 20
3 [a]Josh. 24:14; Ezek. 20:7, 8 [b]Ex. 23:24; Lev. 18:24–30; 20:23; Deut. 12:30, 31
4 [a]Ezek. 20:19
8 [a]Gen. 35:22
9 [a]Lev. 18:11; 20:17; Deut. 27:22
12 [a]Lev. 20:19
14 [a]Lev. 20:20
17 [a]Lev. 20:14
18 [a]1 Sam. 1:6, 8
19 [a]Ezek. 18:6 [b]Lev. 15:24; 20:18
20 [a][Prov. 6:25–33] [b]Ex. 20:14; Lev. 20:10; [Matt. 5:27, 28; 1 Cor. 6:9; Heb. 13:4]
21 [a]Lev. 20:2–5; Deut. 12:31 [b]2 Kin. 16:3 [c]1 Kin. 11:7, 33; Acts 7:43

NKJV

be eaten, he shall [b]pour out its blood and [c]cover it with dust;

14 [a]"for *it is* the life of all flesh. Its blood sustains its life. Therefore I said to the children of Israel, 'You shall not eat the blood of any flesh, for the life of all flesh is its blood. Whoever eats it shall be cut off.'

15 [a]"And every person who eats what died *naturally* or what was torn *by beasts, whether he is* a native of your own country or a stranger, [b]he shall both wash his clothes and [c]bathe in water, and be unclean until evening. Then he shall be clean.

16 "But if he does not wash *them* or bathe his body, then [a]he shall bear his guilt."

Laws of Sexual Morality

18 Then the LORD spoke to Moses, saying,
2 "Speak to the children of Israel, and
say to them: [a]'I am the LORD your God.

3 [a]'According to the doings of the land of Egypt, where you dwelt, you shall not do; and [b]according to the doings of the land of Canaan, where I am bringing you, you shall not do; nor shall you walk in their ordinances.

4 [a]'You shall observe My judgments and keep My ordinances, to walk in them: I *am* the LORD your God.

5 'You shall therefore keep My statutes and My judgments, which if a man does, he shall live by them: I *am* the LORD.

6 'None of you shall approach anyone who is near of kin to him, to uncover his nakedness: I *am* the LORD.

7 'The nakedness of your father or the nakedness of your mother you shall not uncover. She *is* your mother; you shall not uncover her nakedness.

8 'The nakedness of your [a]father's wife you shall not uncover; it *is* your father's nakedness.

9 [a]'The nakedness of your sister, the daughter of your father, or the daughter of your mother, *whether* born at home or elsewhere, their nakedness you shall not uncover.

10 'The nakedness of your son's daughter or your daughter's daughter, their nakedness you shall not uncover; for theirs *is* your own nakedness.

11 'The nakedness of your father's wife's daughter, begotten by your father—she *is* your sister—you shall not uncover her nakedness.

12 [a]'You shall not uncover the nakedness of your father's sister; she *is* near of kin to your father.

13 'You shall not uncover the nakedness of your mother's sister, for she *is* near of kin to your mother.

14 [a]'You shall not uncover the nakedness of your father's brother. You shall not approach his wife; she *is* your aunt.

15 'You shall not uncover the nakedness of your daughter-in-law—she *is* your son's wife—you shall not uncover her nakedness.

16 'You shall not uncover the nakedness of your brother's wife; it *is* your brother's nakedness.

17 'You shall not uncover the nakedness of a woman and her [a]daughter, nor shall you take her son's daughter or her daughter's daughter, to uncover her nakedness. They *are* near of kin to her. It *is* wickedness.

18 'Nor shall you take a woman [a]as a rival to her sister, to uncover her nakedness while the other is alive.

19 'Also you shall not approach a woman to uncover her nakedness as [a]long as she is in her [b]*customary* impurity.

20 [a]'Moreover you shall not lie carnally with your [b]neighbor's wife, to defile yourself with her.

21 'And you shall not let any of your descendants [a]pass through [b]*the fire* to [c]Molech, nor shall you profane the name of your God: I *am* the LORD.

KJV

22 Thou shalt not lie with [a]mankind, as with womankind: it *is* abomination.

23 Neither shalt thou lie with any [a]beast to defile thyself therewith: neither shall any woman stand before a beast to lie down thereto: it *is* confusion.

24 [a]Defile not ye yourselves in any of these things: [b]for in all these the nations are defiled which I cast out before you:

25 And [a]the land is defiled: therefore I do [b]visit the iniquity thereof upon it, and the land itself [c]vomiteth out her inhabitants.

26 [a]Ye shall therefore keep my statutes and my judgments, and shall not commit *any* of these abominations; *neither* any of your own nation, nor any stranger that sojourneth among you:

27 (For all these abominations have the men of the land done, which *were* before you, and the land is defiled;)

28 That [a]the land spue not you out also, when ye defile it, as it spued out the nations that *were* before you.

29 For whosoever shall commit any of these abominations, even the souls that commit *them* shall be cut off from among their people.

30 Therefore shall ye keep mine ordinance, [a]that *ye* commit not *any one* of these abominable customs, which were committed before you, and that ye defile not yourselves therein: [b]I *am* the LORD your God.

Moral and Ceremonial Laws

19 And the LORD spake unto Moses, saying,
2 Speak unto all the congregation of the children of Israel, and say unto them, [a]Ye shall be holy: for I the LORD your God *am* holy.

3 [a]Ye shall fear every man his mother, and his father, and [b]keep my sabbaths: I *am* the LORD your God.

4 [a]Turn ye not unto idols, [b]nor make to yourselves molten gods: I *am* the LORD your God.

5 And [a]if ye offer a sacrifice of peace offerings unto the LORD, ye shall offer it at your own will.

6 It shall be eaten the same day ye offer it, and on the morrow: and if ought remain until the third day, it shall be burnt in the fire.

7 And if it be eaten at all on the third day, it *is* abominable; it shall not be accepted.

8 Therefore *every one* that eateth it shall bear his iniquity, because he hath profaned the hallowed thing of the LORD: and that soul shall be cut off from among his people.

9 And [a]when ye reap the harvest of your land, thou shalt not wholly reap the corners of thy field, neither shalt thou gather the gleanings of thy harvest.

10 And thou shalt not glean thy vineyard, neither shalt thou gather *every* grape of thy vineyard; thou shalt leave them for the poor and stranger: I *am* the LORD your God.

11 [a]Ye shall not steal, neither deal falsely, [b]neither lie one to another.

12 And ye shall not [a]swear by my name falsely, [b]neither shalt thou profane the name of thy God: I *am* the LORD.

13 [a]Thou shalt not defraud thy neighbour, neither rob *him:* [b]the wages of him that is hired shall not abide with thee all night until the morning.

14 Thou shalt not curse the deaf, [a]nor put a stumblingblock before the blind, but shalt fear thy God: I *am* the LORD.

15 Ye shall do no unrighteousness in [a]judgment: thou shalt not [b]respect the person of the poor, nor honour the person of the mighty: *but* in righteousness shalt thou judge thy neighbour.

16 Thou shalt not go up and down *as* a [a]talebearer among thy people: neither shalt thou [b]stand against the blood of thy neighbour: I *am* the LORD.

17 [a]Thou shalt not hate thy brother in thine

22 [a]Lev. 20:13; Rom. 1:27
23 [a]Ex. 22:19; Lev. 20:15, 16; Deut. 27:21
24 [a]Matt. 15:18–20; 1 Cor. 3:17 [b]Lev. 18:3; 20:23; Deut. 18:12
25 [a]Num. 35:33, 34; Ezek. 36:17 [b]Is. 26:21; Jer. 5:9 [c]Lev. 18:28; 20:22
26 [a]Lev. 18:5, 30
28 [a]Jer. 9:19
30 [a]Lev. 18:3; 22:9 [b]Lev. 18:2

CHAPTER 19

2 [a]Ex. 19:6; Lev. 11:44; 20:7, 26; [Eph. 1:4]; 1 Pet. 1:16
3 [a]Ex. 20:12; Deut. 5:16; Matt. 15:4; Eph. 6:2 [b]Ex. 16:23; 20:8; 31:13
4 [a]Ex. 20:4; Ps. 96:5; 115:4–7; 1 Cor. 10:14; [Col. 3:5] [b]Ex. 34:17
5 [a]Lev. 7:16
9 [a]Lev. 23:22; Deut. 24:19–22
11 [a]Ex. 20:15, 16 [b]Jer. 9:3–5; Eph. 4:25
12 [a]Ex. 20:7; Deut. 5:11; [Matt. 5:33–37; James 5:12] [b]Lev. 18:21
13 [a]Ex. 22:7–15, 21–27; Mark 10:19 [b]Deut. 24:15; Mal. 3:5; James 5:4
14 [a]Deut. 27:18
15 [a]Deut. 16:19 [b]Ex. 23:3, 6; Deut. 1:17; 10:17; Ps. 82:2
16 [a]Prov. 11:13; 18:8; 20:19 [b]Ex. 23:7; Deut. 27:25; 1 Kin. 21:7–19
17 [a][1 John 2:9, 11; 3:15]

NKJV

22 'You shall not lie with [a]a male as with a woman. It *is* an abomination.

23 'Nor shall you mate with any [a]animal, to defile yourself with it. Nor shall any woman stand before an animal to mate with it. It *is* perversion.

24 [a]'Do not defile yourselves with any of these things; [b]for by all these the nations are defiled, which I am casting out before you.

25 'For [a]the land is defiled; therefore I [b]visit the punishment of its iniquity upon it, and the land [c]vomits out its inhabitants.

26 [a]'You shall therefore keep My statutes and My judgments, and shall not commit *any* of these abominations, *either* any of your own nation or any stranger who dwells among you

27 '(for all these abominations the men of the land have done, who *were* before you, and thus the land is defiled),

28 'lest [a]the land vomit you out also when you defile it, as it vomited out the nations that *were* before you.

29 'For whoever commits any of these abominations, the persons who commit *them* shall be cut off from among their people.

30 'Therefore you shall keep My ordinance, so [a]that *you* do not commit *any* of these abominable customs which were committed before you, and that you do not defile yourselves by them: [b]I *am* the LORD your God.' "

Moral and Ceremonial Laws

19 And the LORD spoke to Moses, saying,
2 "Speak to all the congregation of the children of Israel, and say to them: [a]'You shall be holy, for I the LORD your God *am* holy.

3 [a]'Every one of you shall revere his mother and his father, and [b]keep My Sabbaths: I *am* the LORD your God.

4 [a]'Do not turn to idols, [b]nor make for yourselves molded gods: I *am* the LORD your God.

5 'And [a]if you offer a sacrifice of a peace offering to the LORD, you shall offer it of your own free will.

6 'It shall be eaten the same day you offer *it*, and on the next day. And if any remains until the third day, it shall be burned in the fire.

7 'And if it is eaten at all on the third day, it *is* an abomination. It shall not be accepted.

8 'Therefore *everyone* who eats it shall bear his iniquity, because he has profaned the hallowed *offering* of the LORD; and that person shall be cut off from his people.

9 [a]'When you reap the harvest of your land, you shall not wholly reap the corners of your field, nor shall you gather the gleanings of your harvest.

10 'And you shall not glean your vineyard, nor shall you gather *every* grape of your vineyard; you shall leave them for the poor and the stranger: I *am* the LORD your God.

11 [a]'You shall not steal, nor deal falsely, [b]nor lie to one another.

12 'And you shall not [a]swear by My name falsely, [b]nor shall you profane the name of your God: I *am* the LORD.

13 [a]'You shall not cheat your neighbor, nor rob *him.* [b]The wages of him who is hired shall not remain with you all night until morning.

14 'You shall not curse the deaf, [a]nor put a stumbling block before the blind, but shall fear your God: I *am* the LORD.

15 'You shall do no injustice in [a]judgment. You shall not [b]be partial to the poor, nor honor the person of the mighty. In righteousness you shall judge your neighbor.

16 'You shall not go about *as* a [a]talebearer among your people; nor shall you [b]take a stand against the life of your neighbor: I *am* the LORD.

17 [a]'You shall not hate your brother in your

KJV

heart: [b]thou shalt in any wise rebuke thy neighbour, and not suffer sin upon him.
18 [a]Thou shalt not avenge, nor bear any
grudge against the children of thy people, [b]but
thou shalt love thy neighbour as thyself: I *am* the
LORD.
19 Ye shall keep my statutes. Thou shalt not
let thy cattle gender with a diverse kind: thou
shalt not sow thy field with mingled seed: neither
shall a garment mingled of linen and woollen
come upon thee.
20 And whosoever lieth carnally with a
woman, that *is* a [a]bondmaid, betrothed to an husband, and not at all redeemed, nor freedom given
her; she shall be scourged; they shall not be put
to death, because she was not free.
21 And he shall bring his trespass offering
unto the LORD, unto the door of the tabernacle of
the congregation, *even* a ram for a trespass
offering.
22 And the priest shall make an atonement
for him with the ram of the trespass offering before the LORD for his sin which he hath done: and
the sin which he hath done shall be forgiven him.
23 And when ye shall come into the land, and
shall have planted all manner of trees for food,
then ye shall count the fruit thereof as uncircumcised: three years shall it be as uncircumcised
unto you: it shall not be eaten of.
24 But in the fourth year all the fruit thereof
shall be holy to praise the LORD *withal.*
25 And in the fifth year shall ye eat of the
fruit thereof, that it may yield unto you the increase thereof: I *am* the LORD your God.
26 Ye shall not eat *any thing* with the blood:
neither shall ye use enchantment, nor observe
times.
27 Ye shall not round the corners of your
heads, neither shalt thou mar the corners of thy
beard.
28 Ye shall not [a]make any cuttings in your
flesh for the dead, nor print any marks upon you:
I *am* the LORD.
29 [a]Do not prostitute thy daughter, to cause
her to be a whore; lest the land fall to whoredom,
and the land become full of wickedness.
30 Ye shall keep my sabbaths, and [a]rever-
ence my sanctuary: I *am* the LORD.
31 Regard not them that have familiar spirits,
neither seek after [a]wizards, to be defiled by them:
I *am* the LORD your God.
32 [a]Thou shalt rise up before the hoary head,
and honour the face of the old man, and [b]fear
thy God: I *am* the LORD.
33 And [a]if a stranger sojourn with thee in
your land, ye shall not vex him.
34 [a]*But* the stranger that dwelleth with you
shall be unto you as one born among you, and
[b]thou shalt love him as thyself; for ye were strangers in the land of Egypt: I *am* the LORD your God.
35 Ye shall do no unrighteousness in judgment, in meteyard, in weight, or in measure.
36 [a]Just balances, just weights, a just ephah,
and a just hin, shall ye have: I *am* the LORD your
God, which brought you out of the land of Egypt.
37 [a]Therefore shall ye observe all my statutes, and all my judgments, and do them: I *am*
the LORD.

17 [b]Matt. 18:15; [Luke 17:3]; Eph. 5:11
18 [a][Deut. 32:35; 1 Sam. 24:12; Rom. 12:19; Heb. 10:30] [b]Matt. 5:43; 19:19; Mark 12:31; Luke 10:27; [Rom. 13:9; Gal. 5:14]; James 2:8
20 [a]Deut. 22:23–27
28 [a]1 Kin. 18:28; Jer. 16:6
29 [a]Lev. 21:9; Deut. 22:21; 23:17, 18
30 [a]Lev. 26:2; Eccl. 5:1
31 [a]Lev. 20:6, 27; Deut. 18:11; 1 Sam. 28:3; Is. 8:19
32 [a]Prov. 23:22; Lam. 5:12; 1 Tim. 5:1 [b]Lev. 19:14
33 [a]Ex. 22:21; Deut. 24:17, 18
34 [a]Ex. 12:48 [b]Deut. 10:19
36 [a]Deut. 25:13–15; Prov. 20:10
37 [a]Lev. 18:4, 5; Deut. 4:5, 6; 5:1; 6:25

NKJV

heart. [b]You shall surely rebuke your neighbor,
and not bear sin because of him.
18 [a]'You shall not take vengeance, nor bear
any grudge against the children of your people,
[b]but you shall love your neighbor as yourself: I
am the LORD.
19 'You shall keep My statutes. You shall not
let your livestock breed with another kind. You
shall not sow your field with mixed seed. Nor shall
a garment of mixed linen and wool come upon
you.
20 'Whoever lies carnally with a woman who
is [a]betrothed to a man as a concubine, and who
has not at all been redeemed nor given her freedom, for this there shall be scourging; *but* they
shall not be put to death, because she was not
free.
21 'And he shall bring his trespass offering
to the LORD, to the door of the tabernacle of meeting, a ram as a trespass offering.
22 'The priest shall make atonement for him
with the ram of the trespass offering before the
LORD for his sin which he has committed. And
the sin which he has committed shall be forgiven
him.
23 'When you come into the land, and have
planted all kinds of trees for food, then you shall
count their fruit as uncircumcised. Three years it
shall be as uncircumcised to you. *It* shall not be
eaten.
24 'But in the fourth year all its fruit shall
be holy, a praise to the LORD.
25 'And in the fifth year you may eat its fruit,
that it may yield to you its increase: I *am* the LORD
your God.
26 'You shall not eat *anything* with the blood,
nor shall you practice divination or soothsaying.
27 'You shall not shave around the sides of
your head, nor shall you disfigure the edges of
your beard.
28 'You shall not [a]make any cuttings in your
flesh for the dead, nor tattoo any marks on you:
I *am* the LORD.
29 [a]'Do not prostitute your daughter, to
cause her to be a harlot, lest the land fall into
harlotry, and the land become full of wickedness.
30 'You shall keep My Sabbaths and [a]rever-
ence My sanctuary: I *am* the LORD.
31 'Give no regard to mediums and familiar
spirits; do not seek after [a]them, to be defiled by
them: I *am* the LORD your God.
32 [a]'You shall rise before the gray headed
and honor the presence of an old man, and [b]fear
your God: I *am* the LORD.
33 'And [a]if a stranger dwells with you in your
land, you shall not mistreat him.
34 [a]'The stranger who dwells among you
shall be to you as one born among you, and [b]you
shall love him as yourself; for you were strangers
in the land of Egypt: I *am* the LORD your God.
35 'You shall do no injustice in judgment, in
measurement of length, weight, or volume.
36 'You shall have [a]honest scales, honest
weights, an honest ephah, and an honest hin: I
am the LORD your God, who brought you out of
the land of Egypt.
37 [a]'Therefore you shall observe all My statutes and all My judgments, and perform them: I
am the LORD.' "

Penalties for Breaking the Law

20 And the LORD spake unto Moses, saying,
2 [a]Again, thou shalt say to the children
of Israel, [b]Whosoever *he be* of the children of Israel, or of the strangers that sojourn in Israel, that
giveth *any* of his seed unto Molech; he shall surely
be put to death: the people of the land shall [c]stone
him with stones.
3 And [a]I will set my face against that man,
and will cut him off from among his people; because he hath given of his seed unto Molech, to

CHAPTER 20
2 [a]Lev. 18:2 [b]Lev. 18:21; 2 Kin. 23:10; 2 Chr. 33:6; Jer. 7:31 [c]Deut. 17:2–5
3 [a]Lev. 17:10

Penalties for Breaking the Law

20 Then the LORD spoke to Moses, saying,
2 [a]"Again, you shall say to the children
of Israel: [b]'Whoever of the children of Israel, or
of the strangers who dwell in Israel, who gives
any of his descendants to Molech, he shall surely
be put to death. The people of the land shall [c]stone
him with stones.
3 [a]'I will set My face against that man, and
will cut him off from his people, because he has

KJV

defile my sanctuary, and to profane my holy name.

4 And if the people of the land do any ways hide their eyes from the man, when he giveth of his seed unto Molech, and kill him not:

5 Then I will set my face against that man, and against his family, and will cut him off, and all that go a whoring after him, to commit whoredom with Molech, from among their people.

6 And [a]the soul that turneth after such as have familiar spirits, and after wizards, to go a whoring after them, I will even set my face against that soul, and will cut him off from among his people.

7 [a]Sanctify yourselves therefore, and be ye holy: for I *am* the LORD your God.

8 And ye shall keep [a]my statutes, and do them: [b]I *am* the LORD which sanctify you.

9 For [a]every one that curseth his father or his mother shall be surely put to death: he hath cursed his father or his mother; [b]his blood *shall be* upon him.

10 And [a]the man that committeth adultery with *another* man's wife, *even he* that committeth adultery with his neighbour's wife, the adulterer and the adulteress shall surely be put to death.

11 And the man that lieth with his [a]father's wife hath uncovered his father's nakedness: both of them shall surely be put to death; their blood *shall be* upon them.

12 And if a man lie with his [a]daughter in law, both of them shall surely be put to death: they have wrought confusion; their blood *shall be* upon them.

13 [a]If a man also lie with mankind, as he lieth with a woman, both of them have committed an abomination: they shall surely be put to death; their blood *shall be* upon them.

14 And if a man take a wife and her [a]mother, it *is* wickedness: they shall be burnt with fire, both he and they; that there be no wickedness among you.

15 And if a man lie with a [a]beast, he shall surely be put to death: and ye shall slay the beast.

16 And if a woman approach unto any beast, and lie down thereto, thou shalt kill the woman, and the beast: they shall surely be put to death; their blood *shall be* upon them.

17 And if a man shall take his [a]sister, his father's daughter, or his mother's daughter, and see her nakedness, and she see his nakedness; it *is* a wicked thing; and they shall be cut off in the sight of their people: he hath uncovered his sister's nakedness; he shall bear his iniquity.

18 [a]And if a man shall lie with a woman having her sickness, and shall uncover her nakedness; he hath discovered her fountain, and she hath uncovered the fountain of her blood: and both of them shall be cut off from among their people.

19 And thou shalt not uncover the nakedness of thy [a]mother's sister, nor of thy [b]father's sister: for he uncovereth his near kin: they shall bear their iniquity.

20 And if a man shall lie with his [a]uncle's wife, he hath uncovered his uncle's nakedness: they shall bear their sin; they shall die childless.

21 And if a man shall take his [a]brother's wife, it *is* an unclean thing: he hath uncovered his brother's nakedness; they shall be childless.

22 Ye shall therefore keep all my [a]statutes, and all my judgments, and do them: that the land, whither I bring you to dwell therein, [b]spue you not out.

23 [a]And ye shall not walk in the manners of the nation, which I cast out before you: for they committed all these things, and [b]therefore I abhorred them.

24 But [a]I have said unto you, Ye shall inherit their land, and I will give it unto you to possess it, a land that floweth with milk and honey: I *am*

6 [a]Lev. 19:31; 1 Sam. 28:7–25
7 [a]Lev. 19:2; Heb. 12:14
8 [a]Lev. 19:19, 37 [b]Ex. 31:13; Deut. 14:2; Ezek. 37:28
9 [a]Ex. 21:17; Deut. 27:16; Prov. 20:20; Matt. 15:4 [b]2 Sam. 1:16
10 [a]Ex. 20:14; Lev. 18:20; Deut. 5:18; 22:22; John 8:4, 5
11 [a]Lev. 18:7, 8; Deut. 27:20
12 [a]Lev. 18:15
13 [a]Lev. 18:22; Deut. 23:17; Judg. 19:22
14 [a]Lev. 18:17
15 [a]Lev. 18:23; Deut. 27:21
17 [a]Lev. 18:9; Deut. 27:22
18 [a]Lev. 15:24; 18:19
19 [a]Lev. 18:13 [b]Lev. 18:12
20 [a]Lev. 18:14
21 [a]Lev. 18:16; Matt. 14:3, 4
22 [a]Lev. 18:26; 19:37 [b]Lev. 18:25, 28; 2 Chr. 36:14–16
23 [a]Lev. 18:3, 24 [b]Deut. 9:5
24 [a]Ex. 3:17; 6:8; 13:5; 33:1–3

NKJV

given *some* of his descendants to Molech, to defile My sanctuary and profane My holy name.

4 'And if the people of the land should in any way hide their eyes from the man, when he gives *some* of his descendants to Molech, and they do not kill him,

5 'then I will set My face against that man and against his family; and I will cut him off from his people, and all who prostitute themselves with him to commit harlotry with Molech.

6 'And [a]the person who turns to mediums and familiar spirits, to prostitute himself with them, I will set My face against that person and cut him off from his people.

7 [a]'Consecrate yourselves therefore, and be holy, for I *am* the LORD your God.

8 'And you shall keep [a]My statutes, and perform them: [b]I *am* the LORD who sanctifies you.

9 'For [a]everyone who curses his father or his mother shall surely be put to death. He has cursed his father or his mother. [b]His blood *shall be* upon him.

10 [a]'The man who commits adultery with *another* man's wife, *he* who commits adultery with his neighbor's wife, the adulterer and the adulteress, shall surely be put to death.

11 'The man who lies with his [a]father's wife has uncovered his father's nakedness; both of them shall surely be put to death. Their blood *shall be* upon them.

12 'If a man lies with his [a]daughter-in-law, both of them shall surely be put to death. They have committed perversion. Their blood *shall be* upon them.

13 [a]'If a man lies with a male as he lies with a woman, both of them have committed an abomination. They shall surely be put to death. Their blood *shall be* upon them.

14 'If a man marries a woman and her [a]mother, it *is* wickedness. They shall be burned with fire, both he and they, that there may be no wickedness among you.

15 'If a man mates with an [a]animal, he shall surely be put to death, and you shall kill the animal.

16 'If a woman approaches any animal and mates with it, you shall kill the woman and the animal. They shall surely be put to death. Their blood *is* upon them.

17 'If a man takes his [a]sister, his father's daughter or his mother's daughter, and sees her nakedness and she sees his nakedness, it *is* a wicked thing. And they shall be cut off in the sight of their people. He has uncovered his sister's nakedness. He shall bear his guilt.

18 [a]'If a man lies with a woman during her sickness and uncovers her nakedness, he has exposed her flow, and she has uncovered the flow of her blood. Both of them shall be cut off from their people.

19 'You shall not uncover the nakedness of your [a]mother's sister nor of your [b]father's sister, for that would uncover his near of kin. They shall bear their guilt.

20 'If a man lies with his [a]uncle's wife, he has uncovered his uncle's nakedness. They shall bear their sin; they shall die childless.

21 'If a man takes his [a]brother's wife, it *is* an unclean thing. He has uncovered his brother's nakedness. They shall be childless.

22 'You shall therefore keep all My [a]statutes and all My judgments, and perform them, that the land where I am bringing you to dwell [b]may not vomit you out.

23 [a]'And you shall not walk in the statutes of the nation which I am casting out before you; for they commit all these things, and [b]therefore I abhor them.

24 'But [a]I have said to you, "You shall inherit their land, and I will give it to you to possess, a land flowing with milk and honey." I *am* the LORD

KJV

the LORD your God, [b]which have separated you
from *other* people.
25 [a]Ye shall therefore put difference between
clean beasts and unclean, and between unclean
fowls and clean: [b]and ye shall not make your
souls abominable by beast, or by fowl, or by any
manner of living thing that creepeth on the
ground, which I have separated from you as
unclean.
26 And ye shall be holy unto me: [a]for I the
LORD *am* holy, and have severed you from *other*
people, that ye should be mine.
27 [a]A man also or woman that hath a familiar spirit, or that is a wizard, shall surely be put
to death: they shall stone them with stones: their
blood *shall be* upon them.

Regulations for Conduct of Priests
(cf. Ezek. 44:15–31)

21 And the LORD said unto Moses, Speak unto
the priests the sons of Aaron, and say unto
them, [a]There shall none be defiled for the dead
among his people:
2 But for his kin, that is near unto him, *that
is,* for his mother, and for his father, and for his
son, and for his daughter, and for his brother,
3 And for his sister a virgin, that is nigh unto
him, which hath had no husband; for her may
he be defiled.
4 *But* he shall not defile himself, *being* a
chief man among his people, to profane himself.
5 [a]They shall not make baldness upon their
head, neither shall they shave off the corner of
their beard, nor make any cuttings in their flesh.
6 They shall be [a]holy unto their God, and
not profane the name of their God: for the offerings of the LORD made by fire, *and* the [b]bread of
their God, they do offer: [c]therefore they shall be
holy.
7 [a]They shall not take a wife *that is* a
whore, or profane; neither shall they take a
woman [b]put away from her husband: for he *is*
holy unto his God.
8 Thou shalt sanctify him therefore; for he
offereth the bread of thy God: he shall be holy
unto thee: for [a]I the LORD, which [b]sanctify you,
am holy.
9 And the daughter of any priest, if she profane herself by playing the whore, she profaneth
her father: she shall be [a]burnt with fire.
10 And *he that is* the high priest among his
brethren, upon whose head the anointing oil was
[a]poured, and that is consecrated to put on the garments, shall not [b]uncover his head, nor rend his
clothes;
11 Neither shall he go [a]in to any dead body,
nor defile himself for his father, or for his mother;
12 [a]Neither shall he go out of the sanctuary,
nor profane the sanctuary of his God; for the
[b]crown of the anointing oil of his God *is* upon
him: I *am* the LORD.
13 And he shall take a wife in her virginity.
14 A widow, or a divorced woman, or profane, *or* an harlot, these shall he not take: but he
shall take a virgin of his own people to wife.
15 Neither shall he profane his seed among
his people: for I the LORD do sanctify him.
16 And the LORD spake unto Moses, saying,
17 Speak unto Aaron, saying, Whosoever *he
be* of thy seed in their generations that hath *any*
blemish, let him not approach to offer the bread
of his God.
18 For whatsoever man *he be* that hath a
[a]blemish, he shall not approach: a blind man, or
a lame, or he that hath a flat nose, or any thing
[b]superfluous,
19 Or a man that is brokenfooted, or brokenhanded,
20 Or crookbackt, or a dwarf, or that hath a
blemish in his eye, or be scurvy, or scabbed, or
hath his stones broken;
21 No man that hath a blemish of the seed

24 [b]Ex. 19:5; 33:16; Lev. 20:26; Deut. 7:6; 14:2; 1 Kin. 8:53
25 [a]Lev. 10:10; 11:1–47; Deut. 14:3–21 [b]Lev. 11:43
26 [a]Lev. 19:2; 1 Pet. 1:16
27 [a]Lev. 19:31; 1 Sam. 28:9

CHAPTER 21

1 [a]Lev. 19:28; Ezek. 44:25
5 [a]Lev. 19:27; Deut. 14:1; Ezek. 44:20
6 [a]Ex. 22:31 [b]Lev. 3:11 [c]Is. 52:11
7 [a]Ezek. 44:22 [b]Deut. 24:1, 2
8 [a]Lev. 11:44, 45 [b]Lev. 8:12, 30
9 [a]Deut. 22:21
10 [a]Lev. 8:12 [b]Lev. 10:6, 7
11 [a]Num. 19:14
12 [a]Lev. 10:7 [b]Ex. 29:6, 7
18 [a]Lev. 22:19–25 [b]Lev. 22:23

*———

21:7 Lit. *he*

NKJV

your God, [b]who has separated you from the
peoples.
25 [a]'You shall therefore distinguish between
clean animals and unclean, between unclean birds
and clean, [b]and you shall not make yourselves
abominable by beast or by bird, or by any kind
of living thing that creeps on the ground, which
I have separated from you as unclean.
26 'And you shall be holy to Me, [a]for I the
LORD *am* holy, and have separated you from the
peoples, that you should be Mine.
27 [a]'A man or a woman who is a medium,
or who has familiar spirits, shall surely be put to
death; they shall stone them with stones. Their
blood *shall be* upon them.' "

Regulations for Conduct of Priests
(cf. Ezek. 44:15–31)

21 And the LORD said to Moses, "Speak to the
priests, the sons of Aaron, and say to them:
[a]'None shall defile himself for the dead among
his people,
2 'except for his relatives who are nearest
to him: his mother, his father, his son, his daughter, and his brother;
3 'also his virgin sister who is near to him,
who has had no husband, for her he may defile
himself.
4 '*Otherwise* he shall not defile himself, *being* a chief man among his people, to profane
himself.
5 [a]'They shall not make any bald *place* on
their heads, nor shall they shave the edges of their
beards nor make any cuttings in their flesh.
6 'They shall be [a]holy to their God and not
profane the name of their God, for they offer the
offerings of the LORD made by fire, *and* the [b]bread
of their God; [c]therefore they shall be holy.
7 [a]'They shall not take a wife *who is* a harlot
or a defiled woman, nor shall they take a woman
[b]divorced from her husband; for **the priest* is
holy to his God.
8 'Therefore you shall consecrate him, for
he offers the bread of your God. He shall be holy
to you, for [a]I the LORD, who [b]sanctify you, *am*
holy.
9 'The daughter of any priest, if she profanes herself by playing the harlot, she profanes
her father. She shall be [a]burned with fire.
10 '*He who is* the high priest among his
brethren, on whose head the anointing oil was
[a]poured and who is consecrated to wear the garments, shall not [b]uncover his head nor tear his
clothes;
11 'nor shall he go [a]near any dead body, nor
defile himself for his father or his mother;
12 [a]'nor shall he go out of the sanctuary, nor
profane the sanctuary of his God; for the [b]consecration of the anointing oil of his God *is* upon
him: I *am* the LORD.
13 'And he shall take a wife in her virginity.
14 'A widow or a divorced woman or a defiled woman *or* a harlot—these he shall not marry;
but he shall take a virgin of his own people as
wife.
15 'Nor shall he profane his posterity among
his people, for I the LORD sanctify him.' "
16 And the LORD spoke to Moses, saying,
17 "Speak to Aaron, saying: 'No man of your
descendants in *succeeding* generations, who has
any defect, may approach to offer the bread of
his God.
18 'For any man who has a [a]defect shall not
approach: a man blind or lame, who has a marred
face or any *limb* [b]too long,
19 'a man who has a broken foot or broken
hand,
20 'or is a hunchback or a dwarf, or *a man*
who has a defect in his eye, or eczema or scab,
or is a eunuch.
21 'No man of the descendants of Aaron the

KJV

of Aaron the priest shall come nigh to offer the offerings of the LORD made by fire: he hath a blemish; he shall not come nigh to offer the bread of his God.

22 He shall eat the bread of his God, *both* of the most holy, and of the holy.

23 Only he shall not go in unto the [a]vail, nor come nigh unto the altar, because he hath a blemish; that [b]he profane not my sanctuaries: for I the LORD do sanctify them.

24 And Moses told *it* unto Aaron, and to his sons, and unto all the children of Israel.

22 And the LORD spake unto Moses, saying,
2 Speak unto Aaron and to his sons, that they [a]separate themselves from the holy things of the children of Israel, and that they [b]profane not my holy name *in those things* which they [c]hallow unto me: I *am* the LORD.

3 Say unto them, Whosoever *he be* of all your seed among your generations, that goeth unto the holy things, which the children of Israel hallow unto the LORD, [a]having his uncleanness upon him, that soul shall be cut off from my presence: I *am* the LORD.

4 What man soever of the seed of Aaron *is* a [a]leper, or hath [b]a running issue; he shall not eat of the holy things, [c]until he be clean. And [d]whoso toucheth any thing *that is* unclean *by* the dead, or [e]a man whose seed goeth from him;

5 Or [a]whosoever toucheth any creeping thing, whereby he may be made unclean, or [b]a man of whom he may take uncleanness, whatsoever uncleanness he hath;

6 The soul which hath touched any such shall be unclean until even, and shall not eat of the holy things, unless he [a]wash his flesh with water.

7 And when the sun is down, he shall be clean, and shall afterward eat of the holy things; because [a]it *is* his food.

8 [a]That which dieth of itself, or is torn *with beasts*, he shall not eat to defile himself therewith: I *am* the LORD.

9 They shall therefore keep [a]mine ordinance, [b]lest they bear sin for it, and die therefore, if they profane it: I the LORD do sanctify them.

10 [a]There shall no stranger eat *of* the holy thing: a sojourner of the priest, or an hired servant, shall not eat *of* the holy thing.

11 But if the priest [a]buy *any* soul with his money, he shall eat of it, and he that is born in his house: they shall eat of his meat.

12 If the priest's daughter also be *married* unto a stranger, she may not eat of an offering of the holy things.

13 But if the priest's daughter be a widow, or divorced, and have no child, and is returned unto her father's house, as in her youth, she shall eat of her father's meat: but there shall no stranger eat thereof.

14 And if a man eat *of* the holy thing unwittingly, then he shall put the fifth *part* thereof unto it, and shall give *it* unto the priest with the holy thing.

15 And they shall not profane the [a]holy things of the children of Israel, which they offer unto the LORD;

16 Or suffer them to bear the iniquity of trespass, when they eat their holy things: for I the LORD do sanctify them.

Offerings Accepted and Not Accepted

17 And the LORD spake unto Moses, saying,

18 Speak unto Aaron, and to his sons, and unto all the children of Israel, and say unto them, [a]Whatsoever *he be* of the house of Israel, or of the strangers in Israel, that will offer his oblation for all his vows, and for all his freewill offerings, which they will offer unto the LORD for a burnt offering;

19 [a]*Ye shall offer* at your own will a male

---

23 [a]Lev. 16:2 [b]Lev. 21:12

CHAPTER 22

2 [a]Num. 6:3 [b]Lev. 18:21 [c]Ex. 28:38; Lev. 16:19; 25:10; Num. 18:32; Deut. 15:19
3 [a]Lev. 7:20, 21; Num. 19:13
4 [a]Num. 5:2 [b]Lev. 15:2 [c]Lev. 14:2; 15:13 [d]Lev. 11:24–28, 39, 40; Num. 19:11 [e]Lev. 15:16, 17
5 [a]Lev. 11:23–28 [b]Lev. 15:7, 19
6 [a]Lev. 15:5
7 [a]Lev. 21:22; Num. 18:11, 13
8 [a]Ex. 22:31; Lev. 7:24; 11:39, 40; 17:15; Ezek. 44:31
9 [a]Lev. 18:30 [b]Ex. 28:43; Lev. 22:16; Num. 18:22
10 [a]Ex. 29:33; Lev. 22:13; Num. 3:10
11 [a]Ex. 12:44
15 [a]Num. 18:32
18 [a]Lev. 1:2, 3, 10
19 [a]Lev. 1:3; Deut. 15:21

NKJV

priest, who has a defect, shall come near to offer the offerings made by fire to the LORD. He has a defect; he shall not come near to offer the bread of his God.

22 'He may eat the bread of his God, *both* the most holy and the holy;

23 'only he shall not go near the [a]veil or approach the altar, because he has a defect, lest [b]he profane My sanctuaries; for I the LORD sanctify them.' "

24 And Moses told *it* to Aaron and his sons, and to all the children of Israel.

22 Then the LORD spoke to Moses, saying,
2 "Speak to Aaron and his sons, that they [a]separate themselves from the holy things of the children of Israel, and that they [b]do not profane My holy name *by* what they [c]dedicate to Me: I *am* the LORD.

3 "Say to them: 'Whoever of all your descendants throughout your generations, who goes near the holy things which the children of Israel dedicate to the LORD, [a]while he has uncleanness upon him, that person shall be cut off from My presence: I *am* the LORD.

4 'Whatever man of the descendants of Aaron, who *is* a [a]leper or has [b]a discharge, shall not eat the holy offerings [c]until he is clean. And [d]whoever touches anything made unclean *by* a corpse, or [e]a man who has had an emission of semen,

5 'or [a]whoever touches any creeping thing by which he would be made unclean, or [b]any person by whom he would become unclean, whatever his uncleanness may be—

6 'the person who has touched any such thing shall be unclean until evening, and shall not eat the holy *offerings* unless he [a]washes his body with water.

7 'And when the sun goes down he shall be clean; and afterward he may eat the holy *offerings*, because [a]it *is* his food.

8 [a]'Whatever dies *naturally* or is torn *by beasts* he shall not eat, to defile himself with it: I *am* the LORD.

9 'They shall therefore keep [a]My ordinance, [b]lest they bear sin for it and die thereby, if they profane it: I the LORD sanctify them.

10 [a]'No outsider shall eat the holy *offering;* one who dwells with the priest, or a hired servant, shall not eat the holy thing.

11 'But if the priest [a]buys a person with his money, he may eat it; and one who is born in his house may eat his food.

12 'If the priest's daughter is married to an outsider, she may not eat of the holy offerings.

13 'But if the priest's daughter is a widow or divorced, and has no child, and has returned to her father's house as in her youth, she may eat her father's food; but no outsider shall eat it.

14 'And if a man eats the holy *offering* unintentionally, then he shall restore a holy *offering* to the priest, and add one-fifth to it.

15 'They shall not profane the [a]holy *offerings* of the children of Israel, which they offer to the LORD,

16 'or allow them to bear the guilt of trespass when they eat their holy *offerings;* for I the LORD sanctify them.' "

Offerings Accepted and Not Accepted

17 And the LORD spoke to Moses, saying,

18 "Speak to Aaron and his sons, and to all the children of Israel, and say to them: [a]'Whatever man of the house of Israel, or of the strangers in Israel, who offers his sacrifice for any of his vows or for any of his freewill offerings, which they offer to the LORD as a burnt offering—

19 [a]'*you shall offer* of your own free will a

KJV

without blemish, of the beeves, of the sheep, or of the goats.

20 [a]*But* whatsoever hath a blemish, *that* shall ye not offer: for it shall not be acceptable for you.

21 And [a]whosoever offereth a sacrifice of peace offerings unto the LORD [b]to accomplish *his* vow, or a freewill offering in beeves or sheep, it shall be perfect to be accepted; there shall be no blemish therein.

22 [a]Blind, or broken, or maimed, or having a wen, or scurvy, or scabbed, ye shall not offer these unto the LORD, nor make [b]an offering by fire of them upon the altar unto the LORD.

23 Either a bullock or a lamb that hath any thing [a]superfluous or lacking in his parts, that mayest thou offer *for* a freewill offering; but for a vow it shall not be accepted.

24 Ye shall not offer unto the LORD that which is bruised, or crushed, or broken, or cut; neither shall ye make *any offering thereof* in your land.

25 Neither [a]from a stranger's hand shall ye offer [b]the bread of your God of any of these; because their [c]corruption *is* in them, *and* blemishes *be* in them: they shall not be accepted for you.

26 And the LORD spake unto Moses, saying,

27 [a]When a bullock, or a sheep, or a goat, is brought forth, then it shall be seven days under the dam; and from the eighth day and thenceforth it shall be accepted for an offering made by fire unto the LORD.

28 And *whether it be* cow or ewe, ye shall not kill it [a]and her young both in one day.

29 And when ye will [a]offer a sacrifice of thanksgiving unto the LORD, offer *it* at your own will.

30 On the same day it shall be eaten up; ye shall leave [a]none of it until the morrow: I *am* the LORD.

31 [a]Therefore shall ye keep my commandments, and do them: I *am* the LORD.

32 [a]Neither shall ye profane my holy name; but [b]I will be hallowed among the children of Israel: I *am* the LORD which [c]hallow you,

33 [a]That brought you out of the land of Egypt, to be your God: I *am* the LORD.

Feasts of the LORD

23 And the LORD spake unto Moses, saying,

2 Speak unto the children of Israel, and say unto them, *Concerning* the feasts of the LORD, which ye shall proclaim *to be* [a]holy convocations, *even* these *are* my feasts.

The Sabbath

3 [a]Six days shall work be done: but the seventh day *is* the sabbath of rest, an holy convocation; ye shall do no work *therein:* it *is* the sabbath of the LORD in all your dwellings.

The Passover and Unleavened Bread (*Num. 28:16–25*)

4 [a]These *are* the feasts of the LORD, *even* holy convocations, which ye shall proclaim in their seasons.

5 [a]In the fourteenth *day* of the first month at even *is* the LORD's passover.

6 And on the fifteenth day of the same month *is* the feast of unleavened bread unto the LORD: seven days ye must eat unleavened bread.

7 [a]In the first day ye shall have an holy convocation: ye shall do no servile work therein.

8 But ye shall offer an offering made by fire unto the LORD seven days: in the seventh day *is* an holy convocation: ye shall do no servile work *therein.*

The Feast of Firstfruits

9 And the LORD spake unto Moses, saying,

10 Speak unto the children of Israel, and say

---

20 [a]Deut. 15:21; 17:1; Mal. 1:8, 14; [Eph. 5:27; Heb. 9:14; 1 Pet. 1:19] **21** [a]Lev. 3:1, 6 [b]Num. 15:3, 8; Ps. 61:8; 65:1; Eccl. 5:4, 5 **22** [a]Lev. 22:20; Mal. 1:8 [b]Lev. 1:9, 13; 3:3, 5 **23** [a]Lev. 21:18 **25** [a]Num. 15:15, 16 [b]Lev. 21:6, 17 [c]Mal. 1:14 **27** [a]Ex. 22:30 **28** [a]Deut. 22:6, 7 **29** [a]Lev. 7:12; Ps. 107:22; 116:17; Amos 4:5 **30** [a]Lev. 7:15 **31** [a]Lev. 19:37; Num. 15:40; Deut. 4:40 **32** [a]Lev. 18:21 [b]Lev. 10:3; Matt. 6:9; Luke 11:2 [c]Lev. 20:8 **33** [a]Lev. 19:36, 37; Num. 15:40; Deut. 4:40

CHAPTER 23

2 [a]Ex. 12:16 **3** [a]Ex. 20:9; 23:12; 31:15; Lev. 19:3; Deut. 5:13, 14; Luke 13:14 **4** [a]Ex. 23:14–16; Lev. 23:2, 37 **5** [a]Ex. 12:1–28; Num. 9:1–5; 28:16–25; Deut. 16:1–8; Josh. 5:10 **7** [a]Ex. 12:16; Num. 28:18, 25

NKJV

male without blemish from the cattle, from the sheep, or from the goats.

20 [a]'Whatever has a defect, you shall not offer, for it shall not be acceptable on your behalf.

21 'And [a]whoever offers a sacrifice of a peace offering to the LORD, [b]to fulfill *his* vow, or a freewill offering from the cattle or the sheep, it must be perfect to be accepted; there shall be no defect in it.

22 [a]'Those *that are* blind or broken or maimed, or have an ulcer or eczema or scabs, you shall not offer to the LORD, nor make [b]an offering by fire of them on the altar to the LORD.

23 'Either a bull or a lamb that has any limb [a]too long or too short you may offer *as* a freewill offering, but for a vow it shall not be accepted.

24 'You shall not offer to the LORD what is bruised or crushed, or torn or cut; nor shall you make *any offering of them* in your land.

25 'Nor [a]from a foreigner's hand shall you offer any of these as [b]the bread of your God, because their [c]corruption *is* in them, *and* defects *are* in them. They shall not be accepted on your behalf.' "

26 And the LORD spoke to Moses, saying:

27 [a]"When a bull or a sheep or a goat is born, it shall be seven days with its mother; and from the eighth day and thereafter it shall be accepted as an offering made by fire to the LORD.

28 "*Whether it is* a cow or ewe, do not kill both her [a]and her young on the same day.

29 "And when you [a]offer a sacrifice of thanksgiving to the LORD, offer *it* of your own free will.

30 "On the same day it shall be eaten; you shall leave [a]none of it until morning: I *am* the LORD.

31 [a]"Therefore you shall keep My commandments, and perform them: I *am* the LORD.

32 [a]"You shall not profane My holy name, but [b]I will be hallowed among the children of Israel. I *am* the LORD who [c]sanctifies you,

33 [a]"who brought you out of the land of Egypt, to be your God: I *am* the LORD."

Feasts of the LORD

23 And the LORD spoke to Moses, saying,

2 "Speak to the children of Israel, and say to them: 'The feasts of the LORD, which you shall proclaim *to be* [a]holy convocations, these *are* My feasts.

The Sabbath

3 [a]'Six days shall work be done, but the seventh day *is* a Sabbath of solemn rest, a holy convocation. You shall do no work *on it;* it *is* the Sabbath of the LORD in all your dwellings.

The Passover and Unleavened Bread (*Num. 28:16–25*)

4 [a]'These *are* the feasts of the LORD, holy convocations which you shall proclaim at their appointed times.

5 [a]'On the fourteenth *day* of the first month at twilight *is* the LORD's Passover.

6 'And on the fifteenth day of the same month *is* the Feast of Unleavened Bread to the LORD; seven days you must eat unleavened bread.

7 [a]'On the first day you shall have a holy convocation; you shall do no customary work on it.

8 'But you shall offer an offering made by fire to the LORD for seven days. The seventh day *shall be* a holy convocation; you shall do no customary work *on it.*' "

The Feast of Firstfruits

9 And the LORD spoke to Moses, saying,

10 "Speak to the children of Israel, and say

KJV

unto them, [a]When ye be come into the land which I give unto you, and shall reap the harvest thereof, then ye shall bring a sheaf of [b]the firstfruits of your harvest unto the priest:

11 And he shall [a]wave the sheaf before the LORD, to be accepted for you: on the morrow after the sabbath the priest shall wave it.

12 And ye shall offer that day when ye wave the sheaf an he lamb without blemish of the first year for a burnt offering unto the LORD.

13 And the meat offering thereof *shall be* two tenth deals of fine flour mingled with oil, an offering made by fire unto the LORD *for* a sweet savour: and the drink offering thereof *shall be* of wine, the fourth *part* of an hin.

14 And ye shall eat neither bread, nor parched corn, nor green ears, until the selfsame day that ye have brought an offering unto your God: *it shall be* a statute for ever throughout your generations in all your dwellings.

The Feast of Weeks
(Ex. 34:22; Num. 28:26–31; Deut. 16:9, 10)

15 And ye shall count unto you from the morrow after the sabbath, from the day that ye brought the sheaf of the wave offering; seven sabbaths shall be complete:

16 Even unto the morrow after the seventh sabbath shall ye number [a]fifty days; and ye shall offer [b]a new meat offering unto the LORD.

17 Ye shall bring out of your habitations two wave loaves of two tenth deals: they shall be of fine flour; they shall be baken with leaven; *they are* [a]the firstfruits unto the LORD.

18 And ye shall offer with the bread seven lambs without blemish of the first year, and one young bullock, and two rams: they shall be *for* a burnt offering unto the LORD, with their meat offering, and their drink offerings, *even* an offering made by fire, of sweet savour unto the LORD.

19 Then ye shall sacrifice [a]one kid of the goats for a sin offering, and two lambs of the first year for a sacrifice of [b]peace offerings.

20 And the priest shall wave them with the bread of the firstfruits *for* a wave offering before the LORD, with the two lambs: [a]they shall be holy to the LORD for the priest.

21 And ye shall proclaim on the selfsame day, *that* it may be an holy convocation unto you: ye shall do no servile work *therein: it shall be* a statute for ever in all your dwellings throughout your generations.

22 And [a]when ye reap the harvest of your land, thou shalt not make clean riddance of the corners of thy field when thou reapest, neither shalt thou gather any gleaning of thy harvest: thou shalt leave them unto the poor, and to the stranger: I *am* the LORD your God.

The Feast of Trumpets
(Num. 29:1–6)

23 And the LORD spake unto Moses, saying,

24 Speak unto the children of Israel, saying, In the [a]seventh month, in the first *day* of the month, shall ye have a sabbath, [b]a memorial of blowing of trumpets, an holy convocation.

25 Ye shall do no servile work *therein:* but ye shall offer an offering made by fire unto the LORD.

The Day of Atonement
(Num. 29:7–11)

26 And the LORD spake unto Moses, saying,

27 [a]Also on the tenth *day* of this seventh month *there shall be* a day of atonement: it shall be an holy convocation unto you; and ye shall afflict your souls, and offer an offering made by fire unto the LORD.

28 And ye shall do no work in that same day: for it *is* a day of atonement, [a]to make an atonement for you before the LORD your God.

10 [a]Ex. 23:19; 34:26 [b][Rom. 11:16]; James 1:18; Rev. 14:4
11 [a]Ex. 29:24
16 [a]Acts 2:1 [b]Num. 28:26
17 [a]Ex. 23:16, 19; Num. 15:17–21
19 [a]Lev. 4:23, 28; Num. 28:30; [2 Cor. 5:21] [b]Lev. 3:1
20 [a]Lev. 14:13; Num. 18:12; Deut. 18:4
22 [a]Lev. 19:9, 10; Deut. 24:19–22; Ruth 2:2, 15
24 [a]Num. 29:1 [b]Lev. 25:9
27 [a]Lev. 16:1–34; 25:9; Num. 29:7
28 [a]Lev. 16:34

NKJV

to them: [a]'When you come into the land which I give to you, and reap its harvest, then you shall bring a sheaf of [b]the firstfruits of your harvest to the priest.

11 'He shall [a]wave the sheaf before the LORD, to be accepted on your behalf; on the day after the Sabbath the priest shall wave it.

12 'And you shall offer on that day, when you wave the sheaf, a male lamb of the first year, without blemish, as a burnt offering to the LORD.

13 'Its grain offering *shall be* two-tenths *of an ephah* of fine flour mixed with oil, an offering made by fire to the LORD, for a sweet aroma; and its drink offering *shall be* of wine, one-fourth of a hin.

14 'You shall eat neither bread nor parched grain nor fresh grain until the same day that you have brought an offering to your God; *it shall be* a statute forever throughout your generations in all your dwellings.

The Feast of Weeks
(Ex. 34:22; Num. 28:26–31; Deut. 16:9, 10)

15 'And you shall count for yourselves from the day after the Sabbath, from the day that you brought the sheaf of the wave offering: seven Sabbaths shall be completed.

16 'Count [a]fifty days to the day after the seventh Sabbath; then you shall offer [b]a new grain offering to the LORD.

17 'You shall bring from your dwellings two wave *loaves* of two-tenths *of an ephah.* They shall be of fine flour; they shall be baked with leaven. *They are* [a]the firstfruits to the LORD.

18 'And you shall offer with the bread seven lambs of the first year, without blemish, one young bull, and two rams. They shall be *as* a burnt offering to the LORD, with their grain offering and their drink offerings, an offering made by fire for a sweet aroma to the LORD.

19 'Then you shall sacrifice [a]one kid of the goats as a sin offering, and two male lambs of the first year as a sacrifice of a [b]peace offering.

20 'The priest shall wave them with the bread of the firstfruits *as* a wave offering before the LORD, with the two lambs. [a]They shall be holy to the LORD for the priest.

21 'And you shall proclaim on the same day *that* it is a holy convocation to you. You shall do no customary work *on it. It shall be* a statute forever in all your dwellings throughout your generations.

22 [a]'When you reap the harvest of your land, you shall not wholly reap the corners of your field when you reap, nor shall you gather any gleaning from your harvest. You shall leave them for the poor and for the stranger: I *am* the LORD your God.' "

The Feast of Trumpets
(Num. 29:1–6)

23 Then the LORD spoke to Moses, saying,

24 "Speak to the children of Israel, saying: 'In the [a]seventh month, on the first *day* of the month, you shall have a sabbath-*rest,* [b]a memorial of blowing of trumpets, a holy convocation.

25 'You shall do no customary work *on it;* and you shall offer an offering made by fire to the LORD.' "

The Day of Atonement
(Num. 29:7–11)

26 And the LORD spoke to Moses, saying:

27 [a]"Also the tenth *day* of this seventh month *shall be* the Day of Atonement. It shall be a holy convocation for you; you shall afflict your souls, and offer an offering made by fire to the LORD.

28 "And you shall do no work on that same day, for it *is* the Day of Atonement, [a]to make atonement for you before the LORD your God.

KJV

29 For whatsoever soul *it be* that shall not be [a]afflicted in that same day, [b]he shall be cut off from among his people.
30 And whatsoever soul *it be* that doeth any work in that same day, [a]the same soul will I destroy from among his people.
31 Ye shall do no manner of work: *it shall be* a statute for ever throughout your generations in all your dwellings.
32 It *shall be* unto you a sabbath of rest, and ye shall afflict your souls: in the ninth *day* of the month at even, from even unto even, shall ye celebrate your sabbath.

The Feast of Tabernacles
(Num. 29:12–40; Deut. 16:13–17)

33 And the LORD spake unto Moses, saying,
34 Speak unto the children of Israel, saying, [a]The fifteenth day of this seventh month *shall be* the feast of tabernacles *for* seven days unto the LORD.
35 On the first day *shall be* an holy convocation: ye shall do no servile work *therein.*
36 Seven days ye shall offer an [a]offering made by fire unto the LORD: [b]on the eighth day shall be an holy convocation unto you; and ye shall offer an offering made by fire unto the LORD: it *is* a [c]solemn assembly; *and* ye shall do no servile work *therein.*
37 [a]These *are* the feasts of the LORD, which ye shall proclaim *to be* holy convocations, to offer an offering made by fire unto the LORD, a burnt offering, and a meat offering, a sacrifice, and drink offerings, every thing upon his day:
38 [a]Beside the sabbaths of the LORD, and beside your gifts, and beside all your vows, and beside all your freewill offerings, which ye give unto the LORD.
39 Also in the fifteenth day of the seventh month, when ye have [a]gathered in the fruit of the land, ye shall keep a feast unto the LORD seven days: on the first day *shall be* a sabbath, and on the eighth day *shall be* a sabbath.
40 And [a]ye shall take you on the first day the boughs of goodly trees, branches of palm trees, and the boughs of thick trees, and willows of the brook; [b]and ye shall rejoice before the LORD your God seven days.
41 [a]And ye shall keep it a feast unto the LORD seven days in the year. *It shall be* a statute for ever in your generations: ye shall celebrate it in the seventh month.
42 [a]Ye shall dwell in booths seven days; [b]all that are Israelites born shall dwell in booths:
43 [a]That your generations may [b]know that I made the children of Israel to dwell in booths, when [c]I brought them out of the land of Egypt: I *am* the LORD your God.
44 And Moses [a]declared unto the children of Israel the feasts of the LORD.

Care of the Tabernacle Lamps
(Ex. 27:20, 21)

24 And the LORD spake unto Moses, saying,
2 [a]Command the children of Israel, that they bring unto thee pure oil olive beaten for the light, to cause the lamps to burn continually.
3 Without the vail of the testimony, in the tabernacle of the congregation, shall Aaron order it from the evening unto the morning before the LORD continually: *it shall be* a statute for ever in your generations.
4 He shall order the lamps upon [a]the pure candlestick before the LORD continually.

The Bread of the Tabernacle

5 And thou shalt take fine flour, and bake twelve [a]cakes thereof: two tenth deals shall be in one cake.

29 [a]Is. 22:12; Jer. 31:9; Ezek. 7:16 [b]Gen. 17:14; Lev. 13:46; Num. 5:2
30 [a]Lev. 20:3–6
34 [a]Ex. 23:16; Num. 29:12; Deut. 16:13–16; Ezra 3:4; Neh. 8:14; Zech. 14:16–19; John 7:2
36 [a]Num. 29:12–34 [b]Num. 29:35–38; Neh. 8:18; John 7:37 [c]Deut. 16:8; 2 Chr. 7:8
37 [a]Lev. 23:2, 4
38 [a]Num. 29:39
39 [a]Ex. 23:16; Deut. 16:13
40 [a]Neh. 8:15 [b]Deut. 12:7; 16:14, 15
41 [a]Num. 29:12; Neh. 8:18
42 [a][Is. 4:6] [b]Neh. 8:14–16
43 [a]Ex. 13:14; Deut. 31:13; Ps. 78:5 [b]Ex. 10:2 [c]Lev. 22:33
44 [a]Lev. 23:2

CHAPTER 24
2 [a]Ex. 27:20, 21
4 [a]Ex. 25:31; 31:8; 37:17
5 [a]Ex. 25:30; 39:36; 40:23

NKJV

29 "For any person who is not [a]afflicted *in soul* on that same day [b]shall be cut off from his people.
30 "And any person who does any work on that same day, [a]that person I will destroy from among his people.
31 "You shall do no manner of work; *it shall be* a statute forever throughout your generations in all your dwellings.
32 "It *shall be* to you a sabbath of *solemn* rest, and you shall afflict your souls; on the ninth *day* of the month at evening, from evening to evening, you shall celebrate your sabbath."

The Feast of Tabernacles
(Num. 29:12–40; Deut. 16:13–17)

33 Then the LORD spoke to Moses, saying,
34 "Speak to the children of Israel, saying: [a]'The fifteenth day of this seventh month *shall be* the Feast of Tabernacles *for* seven days to the LORD.
35 'On the first day *there shall be* a holy convocation. You shall do no customary work *on it.*
36 '*For* seven days you shall offer an [a]offering made by fire to the LORD. [b]On the eighth day you shall have a holy convocation, and you shall offer an offering made by fire to the LORD. It *is* a [c]sacred assembly, *and* you shall do no customary work *on it.*
37 [a]'These *are* the feasts of the LORD which you shall proclaim *to be* holy convocations, to offer an offering made by fire to the LORD, a burnt offering and a grain offering, a sacrifice and drink offerings, everything on its day—
38 [a]'besides the Sabbaths of the LORD, besides your gifts, besides all your vows, and besides all your freewill offerings which you give to the LORD.
39 'Also on the fifteenth day of the seventh month, when you have [a]gathered in the fruit of the land, you shall keep the feast of the LORD *for* seven days; on the first day *there shall be* a sabbath-*rest,* and on the eighth day a sabbath-*rest.*
40 'And [a]you shall take for yourselves on the first day the fruit of beautiful trees, branches of palm trees, the boughs of leafy trees, and willows of the brook; [b]and you shall rejoice before the LORD your God for seven days.
41 [a]'You shall keep it as a feast to the LORD for seven days in the year. *It shall be* a statute forever in your generations. You shall celebrate it in the seventh month.
42 [a]'You shall dwell in booths for seven days. [b]All who are native Israelites shall dwell in booths,
43 [a]'that your generations may [b]know that I made the children of Israel dwell in booths when [c]I brought them out of the land of Egypt: I *am* the LORD your God.' "
44 So Moses [a]declared to the children of Israel the feasts of the LORD.

Care of the Tabernacle Lamps
(Ex. 27:20, 21)

24 Then the LORD spoke to Moses, saying:
2 [a]"Command the children of Israel that they bring to you pure oil of pressed olives for the light, to make the lamps burn continually.
3 "Outside the veil of the Testimony, in the tabernacle of meeting, Aaron shall be in charge of it from evening until morning before the LORD continually; *it shall be* a statute forever in your generations.
4 "He shall be in charge of the lamps on [a]the pure *gold* lampstand before the LORD continually.

The Bread of the Tabernacle

5 "And you shall take fine flour and bake twelve [a]cakes with it. Two-tenths *of an ephah* shall be in each cake.

KJV

6 And thou shalt set them in two rows, six
on a row, [a]upon the pure table before the LORD.
7 And thou shalt put pure frankincense
upon *each* row, that it may be on the bread for a
[a]memorial, *even* an offering made by fire unto
the LORD.
8 [a]Every sabbath he shall set it in order before the LORD continually, *being taken* from the
children of Israel by an everlasting covenant.
9 And [a]it shall be Aaron's and his sons';
[b]and they shall eat it in the holy place: for it *is*
most holy unto him of the offerings of the LORD
made by fire by a perpetual statute.

The Penalty for Blasphemy

10 And the son of an Israelitish woman,
whose father *was* an Egyptian, went out among
the children of Israel: and this son of the Israelitish *woman* and a man of Israel strove together
in the camp;
11 And the Israelitish woman's son [a]blas-
phemed the name *of the LORD,* and [b]cursed. And
they [c]brought him unto Moses: (and his mother's
name *was* Shelomith, the daughter of Dibri, of
the tribe of Dan:)
12 And they [a]put him in ward, [b]that the mind
of the LORD might be shewed them.
13 And the LORD spake unto Moses, saying,
14 Bring forth him that hath cursed without
the camp; and let all that heard *him* [a]lay their
hands upon his head, and let all the congregation
stone him.
15 And thou shalt speak unto the children
of Israel, saying, Whosoever curseth his God
[a]shall bear his sin.
16 And he that [a]blasphemeth the name of the
LORD, he shall surely be put to death, *and* all the
congregation shall certainly stone him: as well
the stranger, as he that is born in the land, when
he blasphemeth the name *of the LORD,* shall be
put to death.
17 [a]And he that killeth any man shall surely
be put to death.
18 [a]And he that killeth a beast shall make it
good; beast for beast.
19 And if a man cause a blemish in his neighbour; as [a]he hath done, so shall it be done to him;
20 Breach for [a]breach, [b]eye for eye, tooth for
tooth: as he hath caused a blemish in a man, so
shall it be done to him *again.*
21 And he that killeth a beast, he shall restore
it: and he that killeth a man, he shall be put to
death.
22 Ye shall have [a]one manner of law, as well
for the stranger, as for one of your own country:
for I *am* the LORD your God.
23 And Moses spake to the children of Israel,
that they should bring forth him that had cursed
out of the camp, and stone him with stones. And
the children of Israel did as the LORD commanded
Moses.

The Sabbath of the Seventh Year
(Deut. 15:1–11)

25 And the LORD spake unto Moses in mount
[a]Sinai, saying,
2 Speak unto the children of Israel, and say
unto them, When ye come into the land which I
give you, then shall the land [a]keep a sabbath unto
the LORD.
3 Six years thou shalt sow thy field, and six
years thou shalt prune thy vineyard, and gather
in the fruit thereof;
4 But in the [a]seventh year shall be a sabbath
of [b]rest unto the land, a sabbath for the LORD:
thou shalt neither sow thy field, nor prune thy
vineyard.
5 [a]That which groweth of its own accord
of thy harvest thou shalt not reap, neither gather
the grapes of thy vine undressed: *for* it is a year
of rest unto the land.
6 And the sabbath of the land shall be meat

6 [a]Ex. 25:23, 24; 1 Kin. 7:48; 2 Chr. 4:19; 13:11; Heb. 9:2 **7** [a]Lev. 2:2, 9, 16 **8** [a]Num. 4:7; 1 Chr. 9:32; 2 Chr. 2:4; Matt. 12:4, 5 **9** [a]1 Sam. 21:6; Matt. 12:4; Mark 2:26; Luke 6:4 [b]Ex. 29:33; Lev. 8:31 **11** [a]Ex. 22:28 [b]Job 1:5, 11, 22; Is. 8:21 [c]Ex. 18:22, 26 **12** [a]Num. 15:34 [b]Num. 27:5 **14** [a]Deut. 13:9; 17:7 **15** [a]Lev. 20:17; Num. 9:13 **16** [a]Ex. 20:7; 1 Kin. 21:10, 13; [Matt. 12:31; Mark 3:28, 29] **17** [a]Gen. 9:6; Ex. 21:12; Num. 35:30, 31; Deut. 19:11, 12; 27:24 **18** [a]Lev. 24:21 **19** [a]Ex. 21:24 **20** [a]Ex. 21:23; Deut. 19:21 [b][Matt. 5:38, 39] **22** [a]Ex. 12:49; Lev. 19:33–37; Num. 9:14; 15:15, 16, 29

CHAPTER 25

1 [a]Lev. 26:46 **2** [a]Lev. 26:34, 35 **4** [a]Deut. 15:1; Neh. 10:31 [b][Heb. 4:9] **5** [a]2 Kin. 19:29

NKJV

6 "You shall set them in two rows, six in a
row, [a]on the pure *gold* table before the LORD.
7 "And you shall put pure frankincense on
each row, that it may be on the bread for a [a]me-
morial, an offering made by fire to the LORD.
8 [a]"Every Sabbath he shall set it in order
before the LORD continually, *being taken* from the
children of Israel by an everlasting covenant.
9 "And [a]it shall be for Aaron and his sons,
[b]and they shall eat it in a holy place; for it *is* most
holy to him from the offerings of the LORD made
by fire, by a perpetual statute."

The Penalty for Blasphemy

10 Now the son of an Israelite woman, whose
father *was* an Egyptian, went out among the children of Israel; and this Israelite *woman's* son and
a man of Israel fought each other in the camp.
11 And the Israelite woman's son [a]blas-
phemed the name *of the LORD* and [b]cursed; and
so they [c]brought him to Moses. (His mother's
name *was* Shelomith the daughter of Dibri, of the
tribe of Dan.)
12 Then they [a]put him in custody, [b]that the
mind of the LORD might be shown to them.
13 And the LORD spoke to Moses, saying,
14 "Take outside the camp him who has
cursed; then let all who heard *him* [a]lay their hands
on his head, and let all the congregation stone
him.
15 "Then you shall speak to the children of
Israel, saying: 'Whoever curses his God [a]shall
bear his sin.
16 'And whoever [a]blasphemes the name of
the LORD shall surely be put to death. All the congregation shall certainly stone him, the stranger
as well as him who is born in the land. When he
blasphemes the name *of the LORD,* he shall be put
to death.
17 [a]'Whoever kills any man shall surely be
put to death.
18 [a]'Whoever kills an animal shall make it
good, animal for animal.
19 'If a man causes disfigurement of his
neighbor, as [a]he has done, so shall it be done to
him—
20 'fracture for [a]fracture, [b]eye for eye, tooth
for tooth; as he has caused disfigurement of a
man, so shall it be done to him.
21 'And whoever kills an animal shall restore
it; but whoever kills a man shall be put to death.
22 'You shall have [a]the same law for the
stranger and for one from your own country; for
I *am* the LORD your God.' "
23 Then Moses spoke to the children of Israel; and they took outside the camp him who
had cursed, and stoned him with stones. So the
children of Israel did as the LORD commanded
Moses.

The Sabbath of the Seventh Year
(Deut. 15:1–11)

25 And the LORD spoke to Moses on Mount
[a]Sinai, saying,
2 "Speak to the children of Israel, and say
to them: 'When you come into the land which I
give you, then the land shall [a]keep a sabbath to
the LORD.
3 'Six years you shall sow your field, and
six years you shall prune your vineyard, and
gather its fruit;
4 'but in the [a]seventh year there shall be a
sabbath of solemn [b]rest for the land, a sabbath
to the LORD. You shall neither sow your field nor
prune your vineyard.
5 [a]'What grows of its own accord of your
harvest you shall not reap, nor gather the grapes
of your untended vine, *for* it is a year of rest for
the land.
6 'And the sabbath *produce* of the land shall

KJV

for you; for thee, and for thy servant, and for thy
maid, and for thy hired servant, and for thy
stranger that sojourneth with thee,
7 And for thy cattle, and for the beast that
are in thy land, shall all the increase thereof be
meat.

The Year of Jubilee

8 And thou shalt number seven sabbaths of
years unto thee, seven times seven years; and the
space of the seven sabbaths of years shall be unto
thee forty and nine years.
9 Then shalt thou cause the trumpet of the
jubile to sound on the tenth *day* of the seventh
month, [a]in the day of atonement shall ye make
the trumpet sound throughout all your land.
10 And ye shall hallow the fiftieth year, and
[a]proclaim liberty throughout *all* the land unto all
the inhabitants thereof: it shall be a jubile unto
you; [b]and ye shall return every man unto his possession, and ye shall return every man unto his
family.
11 A jubile shall that fiftieth year be unto
you: [a]ye shall not sow, neither reap that which
groweth of itself in it, nor gather *the grapes* in it
of thy vine undressed.
12 For it *is* the jubile; it shall be holy unto
you: [a]ye shall eat the increase thereof out of the
field.
13 [a]In the year of this jubile ye shall return
every man unto his possession.
14 And if thou sell ought unto thy neighbour,
or buyest *ought* of thy neighbour's hand, ye shall
not [a]oppress one another:
15 [a]According to the number of years after
the jubile thou shalt buy of thy neighbour, *and*
according unto the number of years of the fruits
he shall sell unto thee:
16 According to the multitude of years thou
shalt increase the price thereof, and according to
the fewness of years thou shalt diminish the price
of it: for *according* to the number *of the years* of
the fruits doth he sell unto thee.
17 [a]Ye shall not therefore oppress one another; [b]but thou shalt fear thy God: for I *am* the
LORD your God.

Provisions for the Seventh Year

18 [a]Wherefore ye shall do my statutes, and
keep my judgments, and do them; [b]and ye shall
dwell in the land in safety.
19 And the land shall yield her fruit, and [a]ye
shall eat your fill, and dwell therein in safety.
20 And if ye shall say, [a]What shall we eat
the seventh year? behold, [b]we shall not sow, nor
gather in our increase:
21 Then I will [a]command my blessing upon
you in the [b]sixth year, and it shall bring forth
fruit for three years.
22 [a]And ye shall sow the eighth year, and
eat *yet* of [b]old fruit until the ninth year; until her
fruits come in ye shall eat *of* the old *store*.

Redemption of Property

23 The land shall not be sold for ever: for
[a]the land *is* mine; for ye *are* [b]strangers and sojourners with me.
24 And in all the land of your possession ye
shall grant a redemption for the land.
25 [a]If thy brother be waxen poor, and hath
sold away *some* of his possession, and if [b]any of
his kin come to redeem it, then shall he redeem
that which his brother sold.
26 And if the man have none to redeem it,
and himself be able to redeem it;
27 Then [a]let him count the years of the sale
thereof, and restore the overplus unto the man
to whom he sold it; that he may return unto his
possession.
28 But if he be not able to restore *it* to him,
then that which is sold shall remain in the hand
of him that hath bought it until the year of jubile:

9 [a]Lev. 23:24, 27
10 [a]Is. 61:2; 63:4; Jer. 34:8, 15, 17; [Luke 4:19] [b]Lev. 25:13, 28, 54; Num. 36:4
11 [a]Lev. 25:5
12 [a]Lev. 25:6, 7
13 [a]Lev. 25:10; 27:24; Num. 36:4
14 [a]Lev. 19:13
15 [a]Lev. 27:18, 23
17 [a]Lev. 25:14; Prov. 14:31; 22:22; Jer. 7:5, 6; 1 Thess. 4:6 [b]Lev. 19:14, 32; 25:43
18 [a]Lev. 19:37 [b]Lev. 26:5; Deut. 12:10; Ps. 4:8; Jer. 23:6
19 [a]Lev. 26:5; Ezek. 34:25
20 [a]Matt. 6:25, 31 [b]Lev. 25:4, 5
21 [a]Deut. 28:8 [b]Ex. 16:29
22 [a]2 Kin. 19:29 [b]Lev. 26:10; Josh. 5:11
23 [a]Ex. 19:5; 2 Chr. 7:20 [b]Gen. 23:4; Ex. 6:4; 1 Chr. 29:15; Ps. 39:12; Heb. 11:13; 1 Pet. 2:11
25 [a]Ruth 2:20; 4:4, 6 [b]Num. 5:8; Ruth 3:2, 9, 12; [Job 19:25]; Jer. 32:7, 8
27 [a]Lev. 25:50–52

NKJV

be food for you: for you, your male and female
servants, your hired man, and the stranger who
dwells with you,
7 'for your livestock and the beasts that *are*
in your land—all its produce shall be for food.

The Year of Jubilee

8 'And you shall count seven sabbaths of
years for yourself, seven times seven years; and
the time of the seven sabbaths of years shall be
to you forty-nine years.
9 'Then you shall cause the trumpet of the
Jubilee to sound on the tenth *day* of the seventh
month; [a]on the Day of Atonement you shall make
the trumpet to sound throughout all your land.
10 'And you shall consecrate the fiftieth year,
and [a]proclaim liberty throughout *all* the land to
all its inhabitants. It shall be a Jubilee for you;
[b]and each of you shall return to his possession,
and each of you shall return to his family.
11 'That fiftieth year shall be a Jubilee to you;
in it [a]you shall neither sow nor reap what grows
of its own accord, nor gather *the grapes* of your
untended vine.
12 'For it *is* the Jubilee; it shall be holy to
you; [a]you shall eat its produce from the field.
13 [a]'In this Year of Jubilee, each of you shall
return to his possession.
14 'And if you sell anything to your neighbor
or buy from your neighbor's hand, you shall not
[a]oppress one another.
15 [a]'According to the number of years after
the Jubilee you shall buy from your neighbor, and
according to the number of years of crops he shall
sell to you.
16 'According to the multitude of years you
shall increase its price, and according to the fewer
number of years you shall diminish its price; for
he sells to you *according* to the number *of the*
years of the crops.
17 'Therefore [a]you shall not oppress one another, [b]but you shall fear your God; for I *am* the
LORD your God.

Provisions for the Seventh Year

18 [a]'So you shall observe My statutes and
keep My judgments, and perform them; [b]and you
will dwell in the land in safety.
19 'Then the land will yield its fruit, and [a]you
will eat your fill, and dwell there in safety.
20 'And if you say, [a]"What shall we eat in
the seventh year, since [b]we shall not sow nor
gather in our produce?"
21 'Then I will [a]command My blessing on
you in the [b]sixth year, and it will bring forth produce enough for three years.
22 [a]'And you shall sow in the eighth year,
and eat [b]old produce until the ninth year; until
its produce comes in, you shall eat *of* the old *har-*
vest.

Redemption of Property

23 'The land shall not be sold permanently,
for [a]the land *is* Mine; for you *are* [b]strangers and
sojourners with Me.
24 'And in all the land of your possession you
shall grant redemption of the land.
25 [a]'If one of your brethren becomes poor,
and has sold *some* of his possession, and if [b]his
redeeming relative comes to redeem it, then he
may redeem what his brother sold.
26 'Or if the man has no one to redeem it,
but he himself becomes able to redeem it,
27 'then [a]let him count the years since its
sale, and restore the remainder to the man to
whom he sold it, that he may return to his
possession.
28 'But if he is not able to have *it* restored
to himself, then what was sold shall remain in
the hand of him who bought it until the Year of

KJV

[a]and in the jubile it shall go out, and he shall return unto his possession.
29 And if a man sell a dwelling house in a
walled city, then he may redeem it within a whole
year after it is sold; *within* a full year may he
redeem it.
30 And if it be not redeemed within the space
of a full year, then the house that *is* in the walled
city shall be established for ever to him that
bought it throughout his generations: it shall not
go out in the jubile.
31 But the houses of the villages which have
no wall round about them shall be counted as the
fields of the country: they may be redeemed, and
they shall go out in the jubile.
32 Notwithstanding [a]the cities of the Levites,
and the houses of the cities of their possession,
may the Levites redeem at any time.
33 And if a man purchase of the Levites, then
the house that was sold, and the city of his possession, shall go out in *the year of* jubile: for the
houses of the cities of the Levites *are* their possession among the children of Israel.
34 But [a]the field of the suburbs of their cities
may not be [b]sold; for it *is* their perpetual possession.

Lending to the Poor

35 And if thy brother be waxen poor, and
fallen in decay with thee; then thou shalt [a]relieve
him: *yea, though he be* a stranger, or a sojourner;
that he may live with thee.
36 [a]Take thou no usury of him, or increase:
but [b]fear thy God; that thy brother may live with
thee.
37 Thou shalt not give him thy money upon
usury, nor lend him thy victuals for increase.
38 [a]I *am* the LORD your God, which brought
you forth out of the land of Egypt, to give you
the land of Canaan, *and* to be your God.

The Law Concerning Slavery

39 And if thy brother *that dwelleth* by thee
be waxen poor, and be sold unto thee; thou shalt
not compel him to serve as a bondservant:
40 *But* as an hired servant, *and* as a sojourner, he shall be with thee, *and* shall serve thee
unto the year of jubile:
41 And *then* shall he depart from thee, *both*
he and his children [a]with him, and shall return
unto his own family, and unto the possession of
his fathers shall he return.
42 For they *are* [a]my servants, which I
brought forth out of the land of Egypt: they shall
not be sold as bondmen.
43 [a]Thou shalt not rule over him [b]with rigour; but [c]shalt fear thy God.
44 Both thy bondmen, and thy bondmaids,
which thou shalt have, *shall be* of the heathen
that are round about you; of them shall ye buy
bondmen and bondmaids.
45 Moreover of [a]the children of the strangers
that do sojourn among you, of them shall ye buy,
and of their families that *are* with you, which they
begat in your land: and they shall be your
possession.
46 And [a]ye shall take them as an inheritance
for your children after you, to inherit *them for* a
possession; they shall be your bondmen for ever:
but over your brethren the children of Israel, ye
shall not rule one over another with rigour.
47 And if a sojourner or stranger wax rich
by thee, and thy brother *that dwelleth* by him
wax poor, and sell himself unto the stranger *or*
sojourner by thee, or to the stock of the stranger's
family:
48 After that he is sold he may be redeemed
again; one of his brethren may redeem him:
49 Either his uncle, or his uncle's son, may
redeem him, or *any* that is nigh of kin unto him
of his family may redeem him; or if he be able,
he may redeem himself.

28 [a]Lev. 25:10, 13
32 [a]Num. 35:1–8; Josh. 21:2
34 [a]Num. 35:2–5 [b]Acts 4:36, 37
35 [a]Deut. 15:7–11; 24:14, 15; Luke 6:35; 1 John 3:17
36 [a]Ex. 22:25; Deut. 23:19, 20 [b]Neh. 5:9
38 [a]Lev. 11:45; 22:32, 33
41 [a]Ex. 21:3
42 [a]Lev. 25:55; [Rom. 6:22; 1 Cor. 7:22, 23]
43 [a]Eph. 6:9; Col. 4:1 [b]Ex. 1:13, 14; Lev. 25:46, 53; Ezek. 34:4 [c]Ex. 1:17; Deut. 25:18; Mal. 3:5
45 [a][Is. 56:3, 6, 7]
46 [a]Is. 14:2

NKJV

Jubilee; [a]and in the Jubilee it shall be released,
and he shall return to his possession.
29 'If a man sells a house in a walled city,
then he may redeem it within a whole year after
it is sold; *within* a full year he may redeem it.
30 'But if it is not redeemed within the space
of a full year, then the house in the walled city
shall belong permanently to him who bought it,
throughout his generations. It shall not be released in the Jubilee.
31 'However the houses of villages which
have no wall around them shall be counted as
the fields of the country. They may be redeemed,
and they shall be released in the Jubilee.
32 'Nevertheless [a]the cities of the Levites,
and the houses in the cities of their possession,
the Levites may redeem at any time.
33 'And if a man purchases a house from the
Levites, then the house that was sold in the city
of his possession shall be released in the Jubilee;
for the houses in the cities of the Levites *are* their
possession among the children of Israel.
34 'But [a]the field of the common-land of their
cities may not be [b]sold, for it *is* their perpetual
possession.

Lending to the Poor

35 'If one of your brethren becomes poor, and
falls into poverty among you, then you shall [a]help
him, like a stranger or a sojourner, that he may
live with you.
36 [a]'Take no usury or interest from him; but
[b]fear your God, that your brother may live with
you.
37 'You shall not lend him your money for
usury, nor lend him your food at a profit.
38 [a]'I *am* the LORD your God, who brought
you out of the land of Egypt, to give you the land
of Canaan *and* to be your God.

The Law Concerning Slavery

39 'And if *one of* your brethren *who dwells*
by you becomes poor, and sells himself to you,
you shall not compel him to serve as a slave.
40 'As a hired servant *and* a sojourner he
shall be with you, *and* shall serve you until the
Year of Jubilee.
41 'And *then* he shall depart from you—he
and his children [a]with him—and shall return to
his own family. He shall return to the possession
of his fathers.
42 'For they *are* [a]My servants, whom I
brought out of the land of Egypt; they shall not
be sold as slaves.
43 [a]'You shall not rule over him [b]with rigor,
but you [c]shall fear your God.
44 'And as for your male and female slaves
whom you may have—from the nations that are
around you, from them you may buy male and
female slaves.
45 'Moreover you may buy [a]the children of
the strangers who dwell among you, and their
families who are with you, which they beget in
your land; and they shall become your property.
46 'And [a]you may take them as an inheritance for your children after you, to inherit *them*
as a possession; they shall be your permanent
slaves. But regarding your brethren, the children
of Israel, you shall not rule over one another with
rigor.
47 'Now if a sojourner or stranger close to
you becomes rich, and *one of* your brethren *who*
dwells by him becomes poor, and sells himself to
the stranger *or* sojourner close to you, or to a
member of the stranger's family,
48 'after he is sold he may be redeemed
again. One of his brothers may redeem him;
49 'or his uncle or his uncle's son may redeem him; or *anyone* who is near of kin to him
in his family may redeem him; or if he is able he
may redeem himself.

KJV

50 And he shall reckon with him that bought him from the year that he was sold to him unto the year of jubile: and the price of his sale shall be according unto the number of years, [a]according to the time of an hired servant shall it be with him.

51 If *there be* yet many years *behind,* according unto them he shall give again the price of his redemption out of the money that he was bought for.

52 And if there remain but few years unto the year of jubile, then he shall count with him, *and* according unto his years shall he give him again the price of his redemption.

53 *And* as a yearly hired servant shall he be with him: *and the other* shall not rule with rigour over him in thy sight.

54 And if he be not redeemed in these *years,* then he shall go out in the year of jubile, *both* he, and his children with him.

55 For unto me the children of Israel *are* servants; they *are* my servants whom I brought forth out of the land of Egypt: I *am* the LORD your God.

Promise of Blessing and Retribution
(Deut. 7:12–24; 28:1–68)

26 Ye shall make you [a]no idols nor graven image, neither rear you up a standing image, neither shall ye set up *any* image of stone in your land, to bow down unto it: for I *am* the LORD your God.

2 [a]Ye shall keep my sabbaths, and reverence my sanctuary: I *am* the LORD.

3 [a]If ye walk in my statutes, and keep my commandments, and do them;

4 [a]Then I will give you rain in due season, [b]and the land shall yield her increase, and the trees of the field shall yield their fruit.

5 [a]And your threshing shall reach unto the vintage, and the vintage shall reach unto the sowing time: and ye shall eat your bread to the full, and [b]dwell in your land safely.

6 And [a]I will give peace in the land, and [b]ye shall lie down, and none shall make *you* afraid: and I will rid [c]evil beasts out of the land, neither shall [d]the sword go through your land.

7 And ye shall chase your enemies, and they shall fall before you by the sword.

8 And [a]five of you shall chase an hundred, and an hundred of you shall put ten thousand to flight: and your enemies shall fall before you by the sword.

9 For I will [a]have respect unto you, and [b]make you fruitful, and multiply you, and establish my [c]covenant with you.

10 And ye shall eat [a]old store, and bring forth the old because of the new.

11 [a]And I will set my tabernacle among you: and my soul shall not abhor you.

12 [a]And I will walk among you, and will be your God, and ye shall be my people.

13 I *am* the LORD your God, which brought you forth out of the land of Egypt, that ye should not be their bondmen; and I have broken the bands of your [a]yoke, and made you go upright.

14 But if ye will not hearken unto me, and will not do all these commandments;

15 And if ye shall despise my statutes, or if your soul abhor my judgments, so that ye will not do all my commandments, *but* that ye break my covenant:

16 I also will do this unto you; I will even

50 [a]Job 7:1; Is. 16:14

CHAPTER 26

1 [a]Ex. 20:4, 5; Deut. 4:15–18; 5:8
2 [a]Lev. 19:30
3 [a]Deut. 28:1–14
4 [a]Is. 30:23 [b]Ps. 67:6
5 [a]Deut. 11:15; Joel 2:19, 26; Amos 9:13 [b]Lev. 25:18, 19; Ezek. 34:25
6 [a]Is. 45:7 [b]Job 11:19; Ps. 4:8; Zeph. 3:13 [c]2 Kin. 17:25; Hos. 2:18 [d]Ezek. 14:17
8 [a]Deut. 32:30; Judg. 7:7–12
9 [a]Ex. 2:25; 2 Kin. 13:23 [b]Gen. 17:6, 7; Ps. 107:38 [c]Gen. 17:1–7
10 [a]Lev. 25:22
11 [a]Ex. 25:8; 29:45, 46; Josh. 22:19; Ps. 76:2; Ezek. 37:26; Rev. 21:3
12 [a]Deut. 23:14; [2 Cor. 6:16]
13 [a]Gen. 27:40

NKJV

50 'Thus he shall reckon with him who bought him: The price of his release shall be according to the number of years, from the year that he was sold to him until the Year of Jubilee; *it shall be* [a]according to the time of a hired servant for him.

51 'If *there are* still many years *remaining,* according to them he shall repay the price of his redemption from the money with which he was bought.

52 'And if there remain but a few years until the Year of Jubilee, then he shall reckon with him, *and* according to his years he shall repay him the price of his redemption.

53 'He shall be with him as a yearly hired servant, and he shall not rule with rigor over him in your sight.

54 'And if he is not redeemed in these *years,* then he shall be released in the Year of Jubilee—he and his children with him.

55 'For the children of Israel *are* servants to Me; they *are* My servants whom I brought out of the land of Egypt: I *am* the LORD your God.

Promise of Blessing and Retribution
(Deut. 7:12–24; 28:1–68)

26 'You shall [a]not make idols for yourselves;
neither a carved image nor a *sacred* pillar
shall you rear up for yourselves;
nor shall you set up an engraved stone in
your land, to bow down to it;
for I *am* the LORD your God.
2 [a]You shall keep My Sabbaths and
reverence My sanctuary:
I *am* the LORD.

3 [a]'If you walk in My statutes and keep My
commandments, and perform them,
4 [a]then I will give you rain in its season, [b]the
land shall yield its produce, and the
trees of the field shall yield their fruit.
5 [a]Your threshing shall last till the time of
vintage, and the vintage shall last till the
time of sowing;
you shall eat your bread to the full, and
[b]dwell in your land safely.
6 [a]I will give peace in the land, and [b]you shall
lie down, and none will make *you*
afraid;
I will rid the land of [c]evil beasts,
and [d]the sword will not go through your
land.
7 You will chase your enemies, and they
shall fall by the sword before you.
8 [a]Five of you shall chase a hundred, and a
hundred of you shall put ten thousand
to flight;
your enemies shall fall by the sword
before you.

9 'For I will [a]look on you favorably and
[b]make you fruitful, multiply you and
confirm My [c]covenant with you.
10 You shall eat the [a]old harvest, and clear
out the old because of the new.
11 [a]I will set My tabernacle among you, and
My soul shall not abhor you.
12 [a]I will walk among you and be your God,
and you shall be My people.
13 I *am* the LORD your God, who brought you
out of the land of Egypt, that *you* should
not be their slaves;
I have broken the bands of your [a]yoke and
made you walk upright.

14 'But if you do not obey Me, and do not
observe all these commandments,
15 and if you despise My statutes, or if your
soul abhors My judgments, so that you
do not perform all My commandments,
but break My covenant,
16 I also will do this to you:

KJV

appoint over you terror, [a]consumption, and the
burning ague, that shall [b]consume the eyes, and
[c]cause sorrow of heart: and [d]ye shall sow your
seed in vain, for your enemies shall eat it.
17 And I will set [a]my face against you, and
[b]ye shall be slain before your enemies: [c]they that
hate you shall reign over you; and ye shall [d]flee
when none pursueth you.
18 And if ye will not yet for all this hearken
unto me, then I will punish you [a]seven times more
for your sins.
19 And I will [a]break the pride of your power;
and I [b]will make your heaven as iron, and your
earth as brass:
20 And your [a]strength shall be spent in vain:
for your [b]land shall not yield her increase, neither
shall the trees of the land yield their fruits.
21 And if ye walk contrary unto me, and will
not hearken unto me; I will bring seven times
more plagues upon you according to your sins.
22 [a]I will also send wild beasts among you,
which shall rob you of your children, and destroy
your cattle, and make you few in number; and
[b]your *high* ways shall be desolate.
23 And if ye [a]will not be reformed by me by
these things, but will walk contrary unto me;
24 [a]Then will I also walk contrary unto you,
and will punish you yet seven times for your sins.
25 And [a]I will bring a sword upon you, that
shall avenge the quarrel of *my* covenant: and
when ye are gathered together within your cities,
[b]I will send the pestilence among you; and ye shall
be delivered into the hand of the enemy.
26 [a]*And* when I have broken the staff of your
bread, ten women shall bake your bread in one
oven, and they shall deliver *you* your bread again
by weight: and [b]ye shall eat, and not be satisfied.
27 And if ye will not for all this hearken unto
me, but walk contrary unto me;
28 Then I will walk contrary unto you also
in fury; and I, even I, will chastise you seven times
for your sins.
29 [a]And ye shall eat the flesh of your sons,
and the flesh of your daughters shall ye eat.
30 And [a]I will destroy your high places, and
cut down your images, and cast your carcases
upon the carcases of your idols, and my soul shall
abhor you.
31 And I will make your [a]cities waste, and
[b]bring your sanctuaries unto desolation, and I will
not [c]smell the savour of your sweet odours.
32 [a]And I will bring the land into desolation:
and your enemies which dwell therein shall be
astonished at it.
33 And [a]I will scatter you among the
heathen, and will draw out a sword after you: and
your land shall be desolate, and your cities waste.
34 [a]Then shall the land enjoy her sabbaths,
as long as it lieth desolate, and ye *be* in your enemies' land; *even* then shall the land rest, and enjoy
her sabbaths.

16 [a]Deut. 28:22 [b]1 Sam. 2:33 [c]Ezek. 24:23; 33:10 [d]Judg. 6:3–6; Job 31:8; Mic. 6:15
17 [a]Ps. 34:16 [b]Deut. 28:25; 1 Sam. 4:10; 31:1 [c]Ps. 106:41 [d]Prov. 28:1
18 [a]1 Sam. 2:5
19 [a]Is. 25:11 [b]Deut. 28:23
20 [a]Ps. 127:1; Is. 17:10, 11; 49:4; Jer. 12:13 [b]Gen. 4:12; Deut. 11:17
22 [a]Deut. 32:24; Ezek. 14:21 [b]Judg. 5:6; 2 Chr. 15:5; Zech. 7:14
23 [a]Jer. 2:30; Amos 4:6–12
24 [a]Lev. 26:28, 41; Ps. 18:26
25 [a]Ezek. 5:17 [b]Num. 16:49; Deut. 28:21; 2 Sam. 24:15
26 [a]Ps. 105:16; Is. 3:1; Ezek. 4:16, 17; 5:16 [b]Mic. 6:14; Hag. 1:6
29 [a]Deut. 28:53; 2 Kin. 6:28, 29
30 [a]1 Kin. 13:2; 2 Chr. 34:3; Is. 27:9; Ezek. 6:3–6, 13
31 [a]2 Kin. 25:4, 10 [b]2 Chr. 36:19; Ps. 74:7 [c]Is. 1:11–15
32 [a]Jer. 9:11; 18:16
33 [a]Deut. 4:27; Ps. 44:11; Ezek. 12:15; 20:23; 22:15; Zech. 7:14
34 [a]Lev. 26:43; 2 Chr. 36:21

NKJV

I will even appoint terror over you,
[a]wasting disease and fever which shall
[b]consume the eyes and [c]cause sorrow
of heart.
And [d]you shall sow your seed in vain, for
your enemies shall eat it.
17 I will set [a]My face against you, and [b]you
shall be defeated by your enemies.
[c]Those who hate you shall reign over you,
and you shall [d]flee when no one pursues
you.

18 'And after all this, if you do not obey Me,
then I will punish you [a]seven times
more for your sins.
19 I will [a]break the pride of your power;
I [b]will make your heavens like iron and
your earth like bronze.
20 And your [a]strength shall be spent in vain;
for your [b]land shall not yield its produce,
nor shall the trees of the land yield their
fruit.

21 'Then, if you walk contrary to Me, and are
not willing to obey Me, I will bring on
you seven times more plagues,
according to your sins.
22 [a]I will also send wild beasts among you,
which shall rob you of your children,
destroy your livestock, and make you
few in number;
and [b]your highways shall be desolate.

23 'And if [a]by these things you are not
reformed by Me, but walk contrary to
Me,
24 [a]then I also will walk contrary to you, and
I will punish you yet seven times for
your sins.
25 And [a]I will bring a sword against you that
will execute the vengeance of the
covenant;
when you are gathered together within
your cities [b]I will send pestilence among
you;
and you shall be delivered into the hand
of the enemy.
26 [a]When I have cut off your supply of bread,
ten women shall bake your bread in one
oven, and they shall bring back your
bread by weight, [b]and you shall eat and
not be satisfied.

27 'And after all this, if you do not obey Me,
but walk contrary to Me,
28 then I also will walk contrary to you in
fury;
and I, even I, will chastise you seven times
for your sins.
29 [a]You shall eat the flesh of your sons, and
you shall eat the flesh of your daughters.
30 [a]I will destroy your high places, cut down
your incense altars, and cast your
carcasses on the lifeless forms of your
idols;
and My soul shall abhor you.
31 I will lay your [a]cities waste and [b]bring
your sanctuaries to desolation, and I
will not [c]smell the fragrance of your
sweet aromas.
32 [a]I will bring the land to desolation, and
your enemies who dwell in it shall be
astonished at it.
33 [a]I will scatter you among the nations and
draw out a sword after you;
your land shall be desolate and your cities
waste.
34 [a]Then the land shall enjoy its sabbaths as
long as it lies desolate and you *are* in
your enemies' land;
then the land shall rest and enjoy its
sabbaths.

KJV

35 As long as it lieth desolate it shall rest; because it did not rest in your [a]sabbaths, when ye dwelt upon it.

36 And upon them that are left *alive* of you I will send a [a]faintness into their hearts in the lands of their enemies; and the sound of a shaken leaf shall chase them; and they shall flee, as fleeing from a sword; and they shall fall when none pursueth.

37 And [a]they shall fall one upon another, as it were before a sword, when none pursueth: and [b]ye shall have no power to stand before your enemies.

38 And ye shall [a]perish among the heathen, and the land of your enemies shall eat you up.

39 And they that are left of you [a]shall pine away in their iniquity in your enemies' lands; and also in the iniquities of their [b]fathers shall they pine away with them.

40 [a]If they shall confess their iniquity, and the iniquity of their fathers, with their trespass which they trespassed against me, and that also they have walked contrary unto me;

41 And *that* I also have walked contrary unto them, and have brought them into the land of their enemies; if then their [a]uncircumcised hearts be [b]humbled, and they then [c]accept of the punishment of their iniquity:

42 Then will I [a]remember my covenant with Jacob, and also my covenant with Isaac, and also my covenant with Abraham will I remember; and I will [b]remember the land.

43 [a]The land also shall be left of them, and shall enjoy her sabbaths, while she lieth desolate without them: and they shall accept of the punishment of their iniquity: because, even because they [b]despised my judgments, and because their soul abhorred my statutes.

44 And yet for all that, when they be in the land of their enemies, [a]I will not cast them away, neither will I abhor them, to destroy them utterly, and to break my covenant with them: for I *am* the LORD their God.

45 But I will [a]for their sakes remember the covenant of their ancestors, [b]whom I brought forth out of the land of Egypt [c]in the sight of the heathen, that I might be their God: I *am* the LORD.

46 [a]These *are* the statutes and judgments and laws, which the LORD made between him and the children of Israel [b]in mount Sinai by the hand of Moses.

Redeeming Persons and Property Dedicated to God

27 And the LORD spake unto Moses, saying,

2 Speak unto the children of Israel, and say unto them, [a]When a man shall make a singular vow, the persons *shall be* for the LORD by thy estimation.

3 And thy estimation shall be of the male from twenty years old even unto sixty years old, even thy estimation shall be fifty shekels of silver, [a]after the shekel of the sanctuary.

4 And if it *be* a female, then thy estimation shall be thirty shekels.

5 And if *it be* from five years old even unto twenty years old, then thy estimation shall be of the male twenty shekels, and for the female ten shekels.

35 [a]Lev. 25:2
36 [a]Is. 30:17; Lam. 1:3, 6; 4:19; Ezek. 21:7, 12, 15
37 [a]Judg. 7:22; 1 Sam. 14:15, 16; Is. 10:4 [b]Josh. 7:12, 13; Judg. 2:14
38 [a]Deut. 4:26
39 [a]Deut. 28:65; Ezek. 4:17; 33:10; Zech. 10:9 [b]Ex. 34:7
40 [a]Num. 5:7; 1 Kin. 8:33, 34; Neh. 9:2; Luke 15:18; [1 John 1:9]
41 [a]Acts 7:51; Rom. 2:29 [b]2 Chr. 12:6, 7, 12; 1 Pet. 5:5, 6 [c]Ps. 39:9; 51:3, 4; Dan. 9:7
42 [a]Ex. 2:24; 6:5; Ps. 106:45; Ezek. 16:60 [b]Ps. 136:23
43 [a]Lev. 26:34, 35 [b]Lev. 26:15
44 [a]Deut. 4:31; 2 Kin. 13:23; Jer. 30:11; [Rom. 11:1–36]
45 [a][Rom. 11:28] [b]Lev. 22:33; 25:38 [c]Ps. 98:2; Ezek. 20:9, 14, 22
46 [a]Lev. 27:34; Deut. 6:1; 12:1; [John 1:17] [b]Lev. 25:1

CHAPTER 27
2 [a]Lev. 7:16; Num. 6:2; Deut. 23:21–23; Judg. 11:30, 31, 39
3 [a]Ex. 30:13; Lev. 27:25; Num. 3:47; 18:16

NKJV

35 As long as *it* lies desolate it shall rest—
for the time it did not rest on your
[a]sabbaths when you dwelt in it.

36 'And as for those of you who are left, I
will send [a]faintness into their hearts in
the lands of their enemies;
the sound of a shaken leaf shall cause
them to flee;
they shall flee as though fleeing from a
sword, and they shall fall when no one
pursues.
37 [a]They shall stumble over one another, as
it were before a sword, when no one
pursues;
and [b]you shall have no *power* to stand
before your enemies.
38 You shall [a]perish among the nations, and
the land of your enemies shall eat you
up.
39 And those of you who are left [a]shall waste
away in their iniquity in your enemies'
lands;
also in their [b]fathers' iniquities, which are
with them, they shall waste away.

40 '*But* [a]if they confess their iniquity and the
iniquity of their fathers, with their
unfaithfulness in which they were
unfaithful to Me, and that they also have
walked contrary to Me,
41 and *that* I also have walked contrary to
them and have brought them into the
land of their enemies;
if their [a]uncircumcised hearts are
[b]humbled, and they [c]accept their guilt—
42 then I will [a]remember My covenant with
Jacob, and My covenant with Isaac and
My covenant with Abraham I will
remember;
I will [b]remember the land.
43 [a]The land also shall be left empty by them,
and will enjoy its sabbaths while it lies
desolate without them;
they will accept their guilt, because they
[b]despised My judgments and because
their soul abhorred My statutes.
44 Yet for all that, when they are in the land
of their enemies, [a]I will not cast them
away, nor shall I abhor them, to utterly
destroy them and break My covenant
with them;
for I *am* the LORD their God.
45 But [a]for their sake I will remember the
covenant of their ancestors, [b]whom I
brought out of the land of Egypt [c]in the
sight of the nations, that I might be their
God:
I *am* the LORD.' "

46 [a]These *are* the statutes and judgments and laws which the LORD made between Himself and the children of Israel [b]on Mount Sinai by the hand of Moses.

Redeeming Persons and Property Dedicated to God

27 Now the LORD spoke to Moses, saying,

2 "Speak to the children of Israel, and say to them: [a]'When a man consecrates by a vow certain persons to the LORD, according to your valuation,

3 'if your valuation is of a male from twenty years old up to sixty years old, then your valuation shall be fifty shekels of silver, [a]according to the shekel of the sanctuary.

4 'If it *is* a female, then your valuation shall be thirty shekels;

5 'and if from five years old up to twenty years old, then your valuation for a male shall be twenty shekels, and for a female ten shekels;

KJV

6 And if *it be* from a month old even unto five years old, then thy estimation shall be of the male five shekels of silver, and for the female thy estimation *shall be* three shekels of silver.

7 And if *it be* from sixty years old and above; if *it be* a male, then thy estimation shall be fifteen shekels, and for the female ten shekels.

8 But if he be poorer than thy estimation, then he shall present himself before the priest, and the priest shall value [a]him; according to his ability that vowed shall the priest value him.

9 And if *it be* a beast, whereof men bring an offering unto the LORD, all that *any man* giveth of such unto the LORD shall be holy.

10 He shall not alter it, nor change it, a good for a bad, or a bad for a good: and if he shall at all change beast for beast, then it and the exchange thereof shall be [a]holy.

11 And if *it be* any unclean beast, of which they do not offer a sacrifice unto the LORD, then he shall present the beast before the priest:

12 And the priest shall value it, whether it be good or bad: as thou valuest it, *who art* the priest, so shall it be.

13 [a]But if he will at all redeem it, then he shall add a fifth *part* thereof unto thy estimation.

14 And when a man shall sanctify his house *to be* holy unto the LORD, then the priest shall estimate it, whether it be good or bad: as the priest shall estimate it, so shall it stand.

15 And if he that sanctified it will redeem his house, then he shall add the fifth *part* of the money of thy estimation unto it, and it shall be his.

16 And if a man shall sanctify unto the LORD *some part* of a field of his possession, then thy estimation shall be according to the seed thereof: an homer of barley seed *shall be valued* at fifty shekels of silver.

17 If he sanctify his field from the year of jubile, according to thy estimation it shall stand.

18 But if he sanctify his field after the jubile, then the priest shall [a]reckon unto him the money according to the years that remain, even unto the year of the jubile, and it shall be abated from thy estimation.

19 And if he that sanctified the field will in any wise redeem it, then he shall add the fifth *part* of the money of thy estimation unto it, and it shall be assured to him.

20 And if he will not redeem the field, or if he have sold the field to another man, it shall not be redeemed any more.

21 But the field, [a]when it goeth out in the jubile, shall be holy unto the LORD, as a field [b]devoted; [c]the possession thereof shall be the priest's.

22 And if *a man* sanctify unto the LORD a field which he hath bought, which *is* not of the fields of [a]his possession;

23 Then the priest shall reckon unto him the worth of thy estimation, *even* unto the year of the jubile: and he shall give thine estimation in that day, *as* a holy thing unto the LORD.

24 [a]In the year of the jubile the field shall return unto him of whom it was bought, *even* to him to whom the possession of the land *did belong*.

25 And all thy estimations shall be according to the shekel of the sanctuary: [a]twenty gerahs shall be the shekel.

26 Only the [a]firstling of the beasts, which should be the LORD's firstling, no man shall sanctify it; whether *it be* ox, or sheep: it *is* the LORD's.

27 And if *it be* of an unclean beast, then he shall redeem *it* according to thine estimation, and [a]shall add a fifth *part* of it thereto: or if it be not redeemed, then it shall be sold according to thy estimation.

28 [a]Notwithstanding no devoted thing, that a man shall devote unto the LORD of all that he hath, *both* of man and beast, and of the field of

8 [a]Lev. 5:11; 14:21–24
10 [a]Lev. 27:33
13 [a]Lev. 6:5; 22:14; 27:15, 19
18 [a]Lev. 25:15, 16, 28
21 [a]Lev. 25:10, 28, 31 [b]Lev. 27:28 [c]Num. 18:14; Ezek. 44:29
22 [a]Lev. 25:10, 25
24 [a]Lev. 25:10–13, 28
25 [a]Ex. 30:13; Lev. 27:3; Num. 3:47; 18:16; Ezek. 45:12
26 [a]Ex. 13:2, 12; 22:30
27 [a]Lev. 27:11, 12
28 [a]Lev. 27:21; Num. 18:14; Josh. 6:17–19

NKJV

6 'and if from a month old up to five years old, then your valuation for a male shall be five shekels of silver, and for a female your valuation shall be three shekels of silver;

7 'and if from sixty years old and above, if *it is* a male, then your valuation shall be fifteen shekels, and for a female ten shekels.

8 'But if he is too poor to pay your valuation, then he shall present himself before the priest, and the priest shall set a value for [a]him; according to the ability of him who vowed, the priest shall value him.

9 'If *it is* an animal that men may bring as an offering to the LORD, all that *anyone* gives to the LORD shall be holy.

10 'He shall not substitute it or exchange it, good for bad or bad for good; and if he at all exchanges animal for animal, then both it and the one exchanged for it shall be [a]holy.

11 'If *it is* an unclean animal which they do not offer as a sacrifice to the LORD, then he shall present the animal before the priest;

12 'and the priest shall set a value for it, whether it is good or bad; as you, the priest, value it, so it shall be.

13 [a]'But if he *wants* at all *to* redeem it, then he must add one-fifth to your valuation.

14 'And when a man dedicates his house *to be* holy to the LORD, then the priest shall set a value for it, whether it is good or bad; as the priest values it, so it shall stand.

15 'If he who dedicated it *wants to* redeem his house, then he must add one-fifth of the money of your valuation to it, and it shall be his.

16 'If a man dedicates to the LORD *part* of a field of his possession, then your valuation shall be according to the seed for it. A homer of barley seed *shall be valued* at fifty shekels of silver.

17 'If he dedicates his field from the Year of Jubilee, according to your valuation it shall stand.

18 'But if he dedicates his field after the Jubilee, then the priest shall [a]reckon to him the money due according to the years that remain till the Year of Jubilee, and it shall be deducted from your valuation.

19 'And if he who dedicates the field ever wishes to redeem it, then he must add one-fifth of the money of your valuation to it, and it shall belong to him.

20 'But if he does not want to redeem the field, or if he has sold the field to another man, it shall not be redeemed anymore;

21 'but the field, [a]when it is released in the Jubilee, shall be holy to the LORD, as a [b]devoted field; it shall be [c]the possession of the priest.

22 'And if a man dedicates to the LORD a field which he has bought, which is not the field of [a]his possession,

23 'then the priest shall reckon to him the worth of your valuation, up to the Year of Jubilee, and he shall give your valuation on that day *as* a holy *offering* to the LORD.

24 [a]'In the Year of Jubilee the field shall return to him from whom it was bought, to the one who *owned* the land as a possession.

25 'And all your valuations shall be according to the shekel of the sanctuary: [a]twenty gerahs to the shekel.

26 'But the [a]firstborn of the animals, which should be the LORD's firstborn, no man shall dedicate; whether *it is* an ox or sheep, it *is* the LORD's.

27 'And if *it is* an unclean animal, then he shall redeem *it* according to your valuation, and [a]shall add one-fifth to it; or if it is not redeemed, then it shall be sold according to your valuation.

28 [a]'Nevertheless no devoted *offering* that a man may devote to the LORD of all that he has, *both* man and beast, or the field of his possession,

KJV

his possession, shall be sold or redeemed: every devoted thing *is* most holy unto the LORD.

29 [a]None devoted, which shall be devoted of men, shall be redeemed; *but* shall surely be put to death.

30 And [a]all the tithe of the land, *whether* of the seed of the land, *or* of the fruit of the tree, *is* the LORD'S: *it is* holy unto the LORD.

31 [a]And if a man will at all redeem *ought* of his tithes, he shall add thereto the fifth *part* thereof.

32 And concerning the tithe of the herd, or of the flock, *even* of whatsoever [a]passeth under the rod, the tenth shall be holy unto the LORD.

33 He shall not search whether it be good or bad, [a]neither shall he change it: and if he change it at all, then both it and the change thereof shall be holy; it shall not be redeemed.

34 [a]These *are* the commandments, which the LORD commanded Moses for the children of Israel in mount [b]Sinai.

29 [a]Num. 21:2
30 [a]Gen. 28:22; Num. 18:21, 24; 2 Chr. 31:5, 6, 12; Neh. 13:12; Mal. 3:8
31 [a]Lev. 27:13
32 [a]Jer. 33:13; Ezek. 20:37; Mic. 7:14
33 [a]Lev. 27:10
34 [a]Lev. 26:46; Deut. 4:5; Mal. 4:4 [b]Ex. 19:1–6, 25; [Heb. 12:18–29]

NKJV

shall be sold or redeemed; every devoted *offering is* most holy to the LORD.

29 [a]'No person under the ban, who may become doomed to destruction among men, shall be redeemed, *but* shall surely be put to death.

30 'And [a]all the tithe of the land, *whether* of the seed of the land *or* of the fruit of the tree, *is* the LORD's. It *is* holy to the LORD.

31 [a]'If a man wants at all to redeem *any* of his tithes, he shall add one-fifth to it.

32 'And concerning the tithe of the herd or the flock, of whatever [a]passes under the rod, the tenth one shall be holy to the LORD.

33 'He shall not inquire whether it is good or bad, [a]nor shall he exchange it; and if he exchanges it at all, then both it and the one exchanged for it shall be holy; it shall not be redeemed.' "

34 [a]These *are* the commandments which the LORD commanded Moses for the children of Israel on Mount [b]Sinai.

KJV

THE FOURTH BOOK OF MOSES CALLED

NUMBERS

The First Census of Israel
(cf. 2 Sam. 24:1–9; 1 Chr. 21:1–6)

1 And the LORD spake unto Moses [a]in the wilderness of Sinai, [b]in the tabernacle of the congregation, on the [c]first *day* of the second month, in the second year after they were come out of the land of Egypt, saying,

2 [a]Take ye the sum of all the congregation of the children of Israel, after their families, by the house of their fathers, with the number of *their* names, every male [b]by their polls;

3 From [a]twenty years old and upward, all that are able to go forth to war in Israel: thou and Aaron shall number them by their armies.

4 And with you there shall be a man of every tribe; every one head of the house of his fathers.

5 And these *are* the names of the men that shall stand with you: of *the tribe of* Reuben; Elizur the son of Shedeur.

6 Of Simeon; Shelumiel the son of Zurishaddai.

7 Of Judah; Nahshon the son of Amminadab.

8 Of Issachar; Nethaneel the son of Zuar.

9 Of Zebulun; Eliab the son of Helon.

10 Of the children of Joseph: of Ephraim; Elishama the son of Ammihud: of Manasseh; Gamaliel the son of Pedahzur.

11 Of Benjamin; Abidan the son of Gideoni.

12 Of Dan; Ahiezer the son of Ammishaddai.

13 Of Asher; Pagiel the son of Ocran.

14 Of Gad; Eliasaph the son of [a]Deuel.

15 Of Naphtali; Ahira the son of Enan.

16 [a]These *were* the [b]renowned of the congregation, princes of the tribes of their fathers, [c]heads of thousands in Israel.

17 And Moses and Aaron took these men which are expressed [a]by *their* names:

18 And they assembled all the congregation together on the first *day* of the second month, and they declared their [a]pedigrees after their families, by the house of their fathers, according to the number of the names, from twenty years old and upward, by their polls.

19 As the LORD commanded Moses, so he numbered them in the wilderness of Sinai.

20 And the [a]children of Reuben, Israel's eldest son, by their generations, after their families, by the house of their fathers, according to the number of the names, by their polls, every male from twenty years old and upward, all that were able to go forth to war;

21 Those that were numbered of them, *even* of the tribe of Reuben, *were* forty and six thousand and five hundred.

22 Of the [a]children of Simeon, by their generations, after their families, by the house of their fathers, those that were numbered of them, according to the number of the names, by their polls, every male from twenty years old and upward, all that were able to go forth to war;

23 Those that were numbered of them, *even* of the tribe of Simeon, *were* fifty and nine thousand and three hundred.

24 Of the [a]children of Gad, by their genera-

CHAPTER 1

1 [a]Ex. 19:1; Num. 10:11, 12 [b]Ex. 25:22 [c]Ex. 40:2, 17; Num. 9:1; 10:11
2 [a]Ex. 30:12; Num. 26:2, 63, 64; 2 Sam. 24:2; 1 Chr. 21:2 [b]Ex. 30:12, 13; 38:26
3 [a]Ex. 30:14; 38:26
14 [a]Num. 7:42
16 [a]Ex. 18:21; Num. 7:2; 1 Chr. 27:16–22 [b]Num. 16:2 [c]Ex. 18:21, 25; Jer. 5:5; Mic. 3:1, 9; 5:2
17 [a]Is. 43:1
18 [a]Ezra 2:59; Heb. 7:3
20 [a]Num. 2:10, 11; 26:5–11; 32:6, 15, 21, 29
22 [a]Num. 2:12, 13; 26:12–14
24 [a]Gen. 30:11; Num. 26:15–18; Josh. 4:12; Jer. 49:1

NKJV

THE FOURTH BOOK OF MOSES CALLED

NUMBERS

The First Census of Israel
(cf. 2 Sam. 24:1–9; 1 Chr. 21:1–6)

1 Now the LORD spoke to Moses [a]in the Wilderness of Sinai, [b]in the tabernacle of meeting, on the [c]first *day* of the second month, in the second year after they had come out of the land of Egypt, saying:

2 [a]"Take a census of all the congregation of the children of Israel, by their families, by their fathers' houses, according to the number of names, every male [b]individually,

3 "from [a]twenty years old and above—all who *are able to* go to war in Israel. You and Aaron shall number them by their armies.

4 "And with you there shall be a man from every tribe, each one the head of his father's house.

5 "These are the names of the men who shall stand with you: from Reuben, Elizur the son of Shedeur;

6 "from Simeon, Shelumiel the son of Zurishaddai;

7 "from Judah, Nahshon the son of Amminadab;

8 "from Issachar, Nethanel the son of Zuar;

9 "from Zebulun, Eliab the son of Helon;

10 "from the sons of Joseph: from Ephraim, Elishama the son of Ammihud; from Manasseh, Gamaliel the son of Pedahzur;

11 "from Benjamin, Abidan the son of Gideoni;

12 "from Dan, Ahiezer the son of Ammishaddai;

13 "from Asher, Pagiel the son of Ocran;

14 "from Gad, Eliasaph the son of [a]Deuel;*

15 "from Naphtali, Ahira the son of Enan."

16 [a]These *were* [b]chosen from the congregation, leaders of their fathers' tribes, [c]heads of the divisions in Israel.

17 Then Moses and Aaron took these men who had been mentioned [a]by name,

18 and they assembled all the congregation together on the first *day* of the second month; and they recited their [a]ancestry by families, by their fathers' houses, according to the number of names, from twenty years old and above, each one individually.

19 As the LORD commanded Moses, so he numbered them in the Wilderness of Sinai.

20 Now the [a]children of Reuben, Israel's oldest son, their genealogies by their families, by their fathers' house, according to the number of names, every male individually, from twenty years old and above, all who *were able to* go to war:

21 those who were numbered of the tribe of Reuben *were* forty-six thousand five hundred.

22 From the [a]children of Simeon, their genealogies by their families, by their fathers' house, of those who were numbered, according to the number of names, every male individually, from twenty years old and above, all who *were able to* go to war:

23 those who were numbered of the tribe of Simeon *were* fifty-nine thousand three hundred.

24 From the [a]children of Gad, their genealo-

---

*1:14 *Reuel,* Num. 2:14

KJV

tions, after their families, by the house of their fathers, according to the number of the names, from twenty years old and upward, all that were able to go forth to war;

25 Those that were numbered of them, *even* of the tribe of Gad, *were* forty and five thousand six hundred and fifty.

26 Of the [a]children of Judah, by their generations, after their families, by the house of their fathers, according to the number of the names, from twenty years old and upward, all that were able to go forth to war;

27 Those that were numbered of them, *even* of the tribe of Judah, *were* [a]threescore and fourteen thousand and six hundred.

28 Of the [a]children of Issachar, by their generations, after their families, by the house of their fathers, according to the number of the names, from twenty years old and upward, all that were able to go forth to war;

29 Those that were numbered of them, *even* of the tribe of Issachar, *were* fifty and four thousand and four hundred.

30 Of the [a]children of Zebulun, by their generations, after their families, by the house of their fathers, according to the number of the names, from twenty years old and upward, all that were able to go forth to war;

31 Those that were numbered of them, *even* of the tribe of Zebulun, *were* fifty and seven thousand and four hundred.

32 Of the children of Joseph, *namely*, of the [a]children of Ephraim, by their generations, after their families, by the house of their fathers, according to the number of the names, from twenty years old and upward, all that were able to go forth to war;

33 Those that were numbered of them, *even* of the tribe of Ephraim, *were* forty thousand and five hundred.

34 Of the [a]children of Manasseh, by their generations, after their families, by the house of their fathers, according to the number of the names, from twenty years old and upward, all that were able to go forth to war;

35 Those that were numbered of them, *even* of the tribe of Manasseh, *were* thirty and two thousand and two hundred.

36 Of the [a]children of Benjamin, by their generations, after their families, by the house of their fathers, according to the number of the names, from twenty years old and upward, all that were able to go forth to war;

37 Those that were numbered of them, *even* of the tribe of Benjamin, *were* thirty and five thousand and four hundred.

38 Of the [a]children of Dan, by their generations, after their families, by the house of their fathers, according to the number of the names, from twenty years old and upward, all that were able to go forth to war;

39 Those that were numbered of them, *even* of the tribe of Dan, *were* threescore and two thousand and seven hundred.

40 Of the [a]children of Asher, by their generations, after their families, by the house of their fathers, according to the number of the names, from twenty years old and upward, all that were able to go forth to war;

41 Those that were numbered of them, *even* of the tribe of Asher, *were* forty and one thousand and five hundred.

42 Of the children of Naphtali, throughout their generations, after their families, by the house of their fathers, according to the number of the names, from twenty years old and upward, all that were able to go forth to war;

43 Those that were numbered of them, *even* of the tribe of Naphtali, *were* fifty and three thousand and four hundred.

44 [a]These *are* those that were numbered, which Moses and Aaron numbered, and the

26 [a]Gen. 29:35; Num. 26:19–22; 2 Sam. 24:9; Ps. 78:68; Matt. 1:2
27 [a]2 Chr. 17:14
28 [a]Num. 2:5, 6
30 [a]Num. 2:7, 8; 26:26, 27
32 [a]Gen. 48:1–22; Num. 26:28–37; Deut. 33:13–17; Jer. 7:15; Obad. 19
34 [a]Num. 2:20, 21; 26:28–34
36 [a]Gen. 49:27; Num. 26:38–41; 2 Chr. 17:17; Rev. 7:8
38 [a]Gen. 30:6; 46:23; Num. 2:25, 26; 26:42, 43
40 [a]Num. 2:27, 28; 26:44–47
44 [a]Num. 26:64

NKJV

gies by their families, by their fathers' house, according to the number of names, from twenty years old and above, all who *were able to* go to war:

25 those who were numbered of the tribe of Gad *were* forty-five thousand six hundred and fifty.

26 From the [a]children of Judah, their genealogies by their families, by their fathers' house, according to the number of names, from twenty years old and above, all who *were able to* go to war:

27 those who were numbered of the tribe of Judah *were* [a]seventy-four thousand six hundred.

28 From the [a]children of Issachar, their genealogies by their families, by their fathers' house, according to the number of names, from twenty years old and above, all who *were able to* go to war:

29 those who were numbered of the tribe of Issachar *were* fifty-four thousand four hundred.

30 From the [a]children of Zebulun, their genealogies by their families, by their fathers' house, according to the number of names, from twenty years old and above, all who *were able to* go to war:

31 those who were numbered of the tribe of Zebulun *were* fifty-seven thousand four hundred.

32 From the sons of Joseph, the [a]children of Ephraim, their genealogies by their families, by their fathers' house, according to the number of names, from twenty years old and above, all who *were able to* go to war:

33 those who were numbered of the tribe of Ephraim *were* forty thousand five hundred.

34 From the [a]children of Manasseh, their genealogies by their families, by their fathers' house, according to the number of names, from twenty years old and above, all who *were able to* go to war:

35 those who were numbered of the tribe of Manasseh *were* thirty-two thousand two hundred.

36 From the [a]children of Benjamin, their genealogies by their families, by their fathers' house, according to the number of names, from twenty years old and above, all who *were able to* go to war:

37 those who were numbered of the tribe of Benjamin *were* thirty-five thousand four hundred.

38 From the [a]children of Dan, their genealogies by their families, by their fathers' house, according to the number of names, from twenty years old and above, all who *were able to* go to war:

39 those who were numbered of the tribe of Dan *were* sixty-two thousand seven hundred.

40 From the [a]children of Asher, their genealogies by their families, by their fathers' house, according to the number of names, from twenty years old and above, all who *were able to* go to war:

41 those who were numbered of the tribe of Asher *were* forty-one thousand five hundred.

42 From the children of Naphtali, their genealogies by their families, by their fathers' house, according to the number of names, from twenty years old and above, all who *were able to* go to war:

43 those who were numbered of the tribe of Naphtali *were* fifty-three thousand four hundred.

44 [a]These are the ones who were numbered, whom Moses and Aaron numbered, with the

KJV

princes of Israel, *being* twelve men: each one was for the house of his fathers.

45 So were all those that were numbered of the children of Israel, by the house of their fathers, from twenty years old and upward, all that were able to go forth to war in Israel;

46 Even all they that were numbered were [a]six hundred thousand and three thousand and five hundred and fifty.

47 But [a]the Levites after the tribe of their fathers were not numbered among them.

48 For the LORD had spoken unto Moses, saying,

49 [a]Only thou shalt not number the tribe of Levi, neither take the sum of them among the children of Israel:

50 [a]But thou shalt appoint the Levites over the tabernacle of testimony, and over all the vessels thereof, and over all things that *belong* to it: they shall bear the tabernacle, and all the vessels thereof; and they shall minister unto it, [b]and shall encamp round about the tabernacle.

51 [a]And when the tabernacle setteth forward, the Levites shall take it down: and when the tabernacle is to be pitched, the Levites shall set it [b]up: [c]and the stranger that cometh nigh shall be put to death.

52 And the children of Israel shall pitch their tents, [a]every man by his own camp, and every man by his own standard, throughout their hosts.

53 [a]But the Levites shall pitch round about the tabernacle of testimony, that there be no [b]wrath upon the congregation of the children of Israel: and the Levites shall [c]keep the charge of the tabernacle of testimony.

54 And the children of Israel did according to all that the LORD commanded Moses, so did they.

The Tribes and Leaders by Armies

2 And the LORD spake unto Moses and unto Aaron, saying,

2 [a]Every man of the children of Israel shall pitch by his own standard, with the ensign of their father's house: [b]far off about the tabernacle of the congregation shall they pitch.

3 And on the [a]east side toward the rising of the sun shall they of the standard of the camp of Judah pitch throughout their armies: and [b]Nahshon the son of Amminadab *shall be* captain of the children of Judah.

4 And his host, and those that were numbered of them, *were* threescore and fourteen thousand and six hundred.

5 And those that do pitch next unto him *shall be* the tribe of Issachar: and Nethaneel the son of Zuar *shall be* captain of the children of Issachar.

6 And his host, and those that were numbered thereof, *were* fifty and four thousand and four hundred.

7 *Then* the tribe of Zebulun: and Eliab the son of Helon *shall be* captain of the children of Zebulun.

8 And his host, and those that were numbered thereof, *were* fifty and seven thousand and four hundred.

9 All that were numbered in the camp of Judah *were* an hundred thousand and fourscore thousand and six thousand and four hundred, throughout their armies. [a]These shall first set forth.

10 On the [a]south side *shall be* the standard of the camp of Reuben according to their armies: and the captain of the children of Reuben *shall be* Elizur the son of Shedeur.

11 And his host, and those that were numbered thereof, *were* forty and six thousand and five hundred.

12 And those which pitch by him *shall be* the tribe of Simeon: and the captain of the children

---

46 [a]Ex. 12:37; 38:26; Num. 2:32; 26:51, 63; Heb. 11:12; Rev. 7:4–8
47 [a]Num. 2:33; 3:14–22; 26:57–62; 1 Chr. 6:1–47; 21:6
49 [a]Num. 2:33; 26:62
50 [a]Ex. 38:21; Num. 3:7, 8; 4:15, 25–27, 33 [b]Num. 3:23, 29, 35, 38
51 [a]Num. 4:5–15; 10:17, 21 [b]Num. 10:21 [c]Num. 3:10, 38; 4:15, 19, 20; 18:22
52 [a]Num. 2:2, 34; 24:2
53 [a]Num. 1:50 [b]Lev. 10:6; Num. 8:19; 16:46; 18:5; 1 Sam. 6:19 [c]Num. 8:24; 18:2–4; 1 Chr. 23:32

CHAPTER 2

2 [a]Num. 1:52; 24:2 [b]Josh. 3:4
3 [a]Num. 10:5 [b]Num. 1:7; 7:12; 10:14; Ruth 4:20; 1 Chr. 2:10; Matt. 1:4; Luke 3:32, 33
9 [a]Num. 10:14
10 [a]Num. 10:6

NKJV

leaders of Israel, twelve men, each one representing his father's house.

45 So all who were numbered of the children of Israel, by their fathers' houses, from twenty years old and above, all who *were able to* go to war in Israel—

46 all who were numbered were [a]six hundred and three thousand five hundred and fifty.

47 But [a]the Levites were not numbered among them by their fathers' tribe;

48 for the LORD had spoken to Moses, saying:

49 [a]"Only the tribe of Levi you shall not number, nor take a census of them among the children of Israel;

50 [a]"but you shall appoint the Levites over the tabernacle of the Testimony, over all its furnishings, and over all things that belong to it; they shall carry the tabernacle and all its furnishings; they shall attend to it [b]and camp around the tabernacle.

51 [a]"And when the tabernacle is to go forward, the Levites shall take it down; and when the tabernacle is to be set up, the Levites shall set it [b]up. [c]The outsider who comes near shall be put to death.

52 "The children of Israel shall pitch their tents, [a]everyone by his own camp, everyone by his own standard, according to their armies;

53 [a]"but the Levites shall camp around the tabernacle of the Testimony, that there may be no [b]wrath on the congregation of the children of Israel; and the Levites shall [c]keep charge of the tabernacle of the Testimony."

54 Thus the children of Israel did; according to all that the LORD commanded Moses, so they did.

The Tribes and Leaders by Armies

2 And the LORD spoke to Moses and Aaron, saying:

2 [a]"Everyone of the children of Israel shall camp by his own standard, beside the emblems of his father's house; they shall camp [b]some distance from the tabernacle of meeting.

3 "On the [a]east side, toward the rising of the sun, those of the standard of the forces with Judah shall camp according to their armies; and [b]Nahshon the son of Amminadab *shall be* the leader of the children of Judah."

4 And his army was numbered at seventy-four thousand six hundred.

5 "Those who camp next to him *shall be* the tribe of Issachar, and Nethanel the son of Zuar *shall be* the leader of the children of Issachar."

6 And his army was numbered at fifty-four thousand four hundred.

7 "Then *comes* the tribe of Zebulun, and Eliab the son of Helon *shall be* the leader of the children of Zebulun."

8 And his army was numbered at fifty-seven thousand four hundred.

9 "All who were numbered according to their armies of the forces with Judah, one hundred and eighty-six thousand four hundred—[a]these shall break camp first.

10 "On the [a]south side *shall be* the standard of the forces with Reuben according to their armies, and the leader of the children of Reuben *shall be* Elizur the son of Shedeur."

11 And his army was numbered at forty-six thousand five hundred.

12 "Those who camp next to him *shall be* the tribe of Simeon, and the leader of the children of

KJV

of Simeon *shall be* Shelumiel the son of Zurishaddai.

13 And his host, and those that were numbered of them, *were* fifty and nine thousand and three hundred.

14 Then the tribe of Gad: and the captain of the sons of Gad *shall be* Eliasaph the son of Reuel.

15 And his host, and those that were numbered of them, *were* forty and five thousand and six hundred and fifty.

16 All that were numbered in the camp of Reuben *were* an hundred thousand and fifty and one thousand and four hundred and fifty, throughout their armies. [a]And they shall set forth in the second rank.

17 [a]Then the tabernacle of the congregation shall set forward with the camp of the Levites [b]in the midst of the camp: as they encamp, so shall they set forward, every man in his place by their standards.

18 On the west side *shall be* the standard of the camp of Ephraim according to their armies: and the captain of the sons of Ephraim *shall be* Elishama the son of Ammihud.

19 And his host, and those that were numbered of them, *were* forty thousand and five hundred.

20 And by him *shall be* the tribe of Manasseh: and the captain of the children of Manasseh *shall be* Gamaliel the son of Pedahzur.

21 And his host, and those that were numbered of them, *were* thirty and two thousand and two hundred.

22 Then the tribe of Benjamin: and the captain of the sons of Benjamin *shall be* Abidan the son of Gideoni.

23 And his host, and those that were numbered of them, *were* thirty and five thousand and four hundred.

24 All that were numbered of the camp of Ephraim *were* an hundred thousand and eight thousand and an hundred, throughout their armies. [a]And they shall go forward in the third rank.

25 The standard of the camp of Dan *shall be* on the north side by their armies: and the captain of the children of Dan *shall be* Ahiezer the son of Ammishaddai.

26 And his host, and those that were numbered of them, *were* threescore and two thousand and seven hundred.

27 And those that encamp by him *shall be* the tribe of Asher: and the captain of the children of Asher *shall be* Pagiel the son of Ocran.

28 And his host, and those that were numbered of them, *were* forty and one thousand and five hundred.

29 Then the tribe of Naphtali: and the captain of the children of Naphtali *shall be* Ahira the son of Enan.

30 And his host, and those that were numbered of them, *were* fifty and three thousand and four hundred.

31 All they that were numbered in the camp of Dan *were* an hundred thousand and fifty and seven thousand and six hundred. [a]They shall go hindmost with their standards.

32 These *are* those which were numbered of the children of Israel by the house of their fathers: [a]all those that were numbered of the camps throughout their hosts *were* six hundred thousand and three thousand and five hundred and fifty.

33 But [a]the Levites were not numbered among the children of Israel; as the LORD commanded Moses.

34 And the children of Israel [a]did according to all that the LORD commanded Moses: [b]so they pitched by their standards, and so they set forward, every one after their families, according to the house of their fathers.

16 [a]Num. 10:18
17 [a]Num. 10:17, 21 [b]Num. 1:53
24 [a]Num. 10:22
31 [a]Num. 10:25
32 [a]Ex. 38:26; Num. 1:46; 11:21
33 [a]Num. 1:47; 26:57–62
34 [a]Num. 1:54 [b]Num. 24:2, 5, 6

***2:14** *Deuel,* Num. 1:14; 7:42

NKJV

Simeon *shall be* Shelumiel the son of Zurishaddai."

13 And his army was numbered at fifty-nine thousand three hundred.

14 "Then *comes* the tribe of Gad, and the leader of the children of Gad *shall be* Eliasaph the son of *Reuel."

15 And his army was numbered at forty-five thousand six hundred and fifty.

16 "All who were numbered according to their armies of the forces with Reuben, one hundred and fifty-one thousand four hundred and fifty—[a]they shall be the second to break camp.

17 [a]"And the tabernacle of meeting shall move out with the camp of the Levites [b]in the middle of the camps; as they camp, so they shall move out, everyone in his place, by their standards.

18 "On the west side *shall be* the standard of the forces with Ephraim according to their armies, and the leader of the children of Ephraim *shall be* Elishama the son of Ammihud."

19 And his army was numbered at forty thousand five hundred.

20 "Next to him *comes* the tribe of Manasseh, and the leader of the children of Manasseh *shall be* Gamaliel the son of Pedahzur."

21 And his army was numbered at thirty-two thousand two hundred.

22 "Then *comes* the tribe of Benjamin, and the leader of the children of Benjamin *shall be* Abidan the son of Gideoni."

23 And his army was numbered at thirty-five thousand four hundred.

24 "All who were numbered according to their armies of the forces with Ephraim, one hundred and eight thousand one hundred—[a]they shall be the third to break camp.

25 "The standard of the forces with Dan *shall be* on the north side according to their armies, and the leader of the children of Dan *shall be* Ahiezer the son of Ammishaddai."

26 And his army was numbered at sixty-two thousand seven hundred.

27 "Those who camp next to him *shall be* the tribe of Asher, and the leader of the children of Asher *shall be* Pagiel the son of Ocran."

28 And his army was numbered at forty-one thousand five hundred.

29 "Then *comes* the tribe of Naphtali, and the leader of the children of Naphtali *shall be* Ahira the son of Enan."

30 And his army was numbered at fifty-three thousand four hundred.

31 "All who were numbered of the forces with Dan, one hundred and fifty-seven thousand six hundred—[a]they shall break camp last, with their standards."

32 These *are* the ones who were numbered of the children of Israel by their fathers' houses. [a]All who were numbered according to their armies of the forces *were* six hundred and three thousand five hundred and fifty.

33 But [a]the Levites were not numbered among the children of Israel, just as the LORD commanded Moses.

34 Thus the children of Israel [a]did according to all that the LORD commanded Moses; [b]so they camped by their standards and so they broke camp, each one by his family, according to their fathers' houses.

KJV

The Sons of Aaron
(Lev. 10:1–7)

3 These also *are* the [a]generations of Aaron and Moses in the day *that* the LORD spake with Moses in mount Sinai.

2 And these *are* the names of the sons of Aaron; Nadab the [a]firstborn, and [b]Abihu, Eleazar, and Ithamar.

3 These *are* the names of the sons of Aaron, [a]the priests which were anointed, whom he consecrated to minister in the priest's office.

4 [a]And Nadab and Abihu died before the LORD, when they offered strange fire before the LORD, in the wilderness of Sinai, and they had no children: and Eleazar and Ithamar ministered in the priest's office in the sight of Aaron their father.

The Levites Serve in the Tabernacle

5 And the LORD spake unto Moses, saying,

6 [a]Bring the tribe of Levi near, and present them before Aaron the priest, that they may minister unto him.

7 And they shall keep his charge, and the charge of the whole congregation before the tabernacle of the congregation, to do [a]the service of the tabernacle.

8 And they shall keep all the instruments of the tabernacle of the congregation, and the charge of the children of Israel, to do the service of the tabernacle.

9 And [a]thou shalt give the Levites unto Aaron and to his sons: they *are* wholly given unto him out of the children of Israel.

10 And thou shalt appoint Aaron and his sons, [a]and they shall wait on their priest's office: [b]and the stranger that cometh nigh shall be put to death.

11 And the LORD spake unto Moses, saying,

12 And I, behold, [a]I have taken the Levites from among the children of Israel instead of all the firstborn that openeth the matrix among the children of Israel: therefore the Levites shall be [b]mine;

13 Because [a]all the firstborn *are* mine; [b]*for* on the day that I smote all the firstborn in the land of Egypt I hallowed unto me all the firstborn in Israel, both man and beast: mine shall they be: I *am* the LORD.

Census of the Levites Commanded
(cf. Num. 1:47–54)

14 And the LORD spake unto Moses in the wilderness of Sinai, saying,

15 Number the children of Levi after the house of their fathers, by their families: [a]every male from a month old and upward shalt thou number them.

16 And Moses numbered them according to the word of the LORD, as he was commanded.

17 [a]And these were the sons of Levi by their names; Gershon, and Kohath, and Merari.

18 And these *are* the names of the sons of [a]Gershon by their families; [b]Libni, and Shimei.

19 And the sons of [a]Kohath by their families; [b]Amram, and Izehar, Hebron, and Uzziel.

20 [a]And the sons of Merari by their families; Mahli, and Mushi. These *are* the families of the Levites according to the house of their fathers.

21 Of Gershon *was* the family of the Libnites, and the family of the Shimites: these *are* the families of the Gershonites.

22 Those that were numbered of them, according to the number of all the males, from a month old and upward, *even* those that were numbered of them *were* seven thousand and five hundred.

23 [a]The families of the Gershonites shall pitch behind the tabernacle westward.

24 And the chief of the house of the father of the Gershonites *shall be* Eliasaph the son of Lael.

CHAPTER 3
1 [a]Ex. 6:16–27
2 [a]Ex. 6:23 [b]Lev. 10:1, 2; Num. 26:60, 61; 1 Chr. 24:2
3 [a]Ex. 28:41; Lev. 8
4 [a]Lev. 10:1, 2; Num. 26:61; 1 Chr. 24:2
6 [a]Num. 8:6–22; 18:1–7; Deut. 10:8; 33:8–11
7 [a]Num. 1:50; 8:11, 15, 24, 26
9 [a]Num. 8:19; 18:6, 7
10 [a]Ex. 29:9; Num. 18:7 [b]Num. 1:51; 3:38; 16:40
12 [a]Num. 3:41; 8:16; 18:6 [b]Ex. 13:2; Num. 3:45; 8:14
13 [a]Ex. 13:2; Lev. 27:26; Num. 8:16, 17; Neh. 10:36; Luke 2:23 [b]Ex. 13:12, 15; Num. 8:17
15 [a]Num. 3:39; 26:62
17 [a]Gen. 46:11; Ex. 6:16–22; Num. 26:57; 1 Chr. 6:1, 16; 23:6
18 [a]Num. 4:38–41 [b]Ex. 6:17
19 [a]Num. 4:34–37 [b]Ex. 6:18
20 [a]Ex. 6:19; Num. 4:42–45
23 [a]Num. 1:53

*
3:9 Sam., LXX *Me*

NKJV

The Sons of Aaron
(Lev. 10:1–7)

3 Now these *are* the [a]records of Aaron and Moses when the LORD spoke with Moses on Mount Sinai.

2 And these *are* the names of the sons of Aaron: Nadab, the [a]firstborn, and [b]Abihu, Eleazar, and Ithamar.

3 These *are* the names of the sons of Aaron, [a]the anointed priests, whom he consecrated to minister as priests.

4 [a]Nadab and Abihu had died before the LORD when they offered profane fire before the LORD in the Wilderness of Sinai; and they had no children. So Eleazar and Ithamar ministered as priests in the presence of Aaron their father.

The Levites Serve in the Tabernacle

5 And the LORD spoke to Moses, saying:

6 [a]"Bring the tribe of Levi near, and present them before Aaron the priest, that they may serve him.

7 "And they shall attend to his needs and the needs of the whole congregation before the tabernacle of meeting, to do [a]the work of the tabernacle.

8 "Also they shall attend to all the furnishings of the tabernacle of meeting, and to the needs of the children of Israel, to do the work of the tabernacle.

9 "And [a]you shall give the Levites to Aaron and his sons; they *are* given entirely to *him from among the children of Israel.

10 "So you shall appoint Aaron and his sons, [a]and they shall attend to their priesthood; [b]but the outsider who comes near shall be put to death."

11 Then the LORD spoke to Moses, saying:

12 "Now behold, [a]I Myself have taken the Levites from among the children of Israel instead of every firstborn who opens the womb among the children of Israel. Therefore the Levites shall be [b]Mine,

13 "because [a]all the firstborn *are* Mine. [b]On the day that I struck all the firstborn in the land of Egypt, I sanctified to Myself all the firstborn in Israel, both man and beast. They shall be Mine: I *am* the LORD."

Census of the Levites Commanded
(cf. Num. 1:47–54)

14 Then the LORD spoke to Moses in the Wilderness of Sinai, saying:

15 "Number the children of Levi by their fathers' houses, by their families; you shall number [a]every male from a month old and above."

16 So Moses numbered them according to the word of the LORD, as he was commanded.

17 [a]These were the sons of Levi by their names: Gershon, Kohath, and Merari.

18 And these *are* the names of the sons of [a]Gershon by their families: [b]Libni and Shimei.

19 And the sons of [a]Kohath by their families: [b]Amram, Izehar, Hebron, and Uzziel.

20 [a]And the sons of Merari by their families: Mahli and Mushi. These *are* the families of the Levites by their fathers' houses.

21 From Gershon *came* the family of the Libnites and the family of the Shimites; these *were* the families of the Gershonites.

22 Those who were numbered, according to the number of all the males from a month old and above—of those who were numbered *there were* seven thousand five hundred.

23 [a]The families of the Gershonites were to camp behind the tabernacle westward.

24 And the leader of the father's house of the Gershonites *was* Eliasaph the son of Lael.

KJV

25 And [a]the charge of the sons of Gershon in the tabernacle of the congregation *shall be* [b]the tabernacle, and [c]the tent, [d]the covering thereof, and [e]the hanging for the door of the tabernacle of the congregation,

26 And [a]the hangings of the court, and [b]the curtain for the door of the court, which *is* by the tabernacle, and by the altar round about, and [c]the cords of it for all the service thereof.

27 [a]And of Kohath *was* the family of the Amramites, and the family of the Izeharites, and the family of the Hebronites, and the family of the Uzzielites: these *are* the families of the Kohathites.

28 In the number of all the males, from a month old and upward, *were* eight thousand and six hundred, keeping the charge of the sanctuary.

29 [a]The families of the sons of Kohath shall pitch on the side of the tabernacle southward.

30 And the chief of the house of the father of the families of the Kohathites *shall be* Elizaphan the son of [a]Uzziel.

31 And [a]their charge *shall be* [b]the ark, and [c]the table, and [d]the candlestick, and [e]the altars, and the vessels of the sanctuary wherewith they minister, and [f]the hanging, and all the service thereof.

32 And Eleazar the son of Aaron the priest *shall be* chief over the chief of the Levites, *and have* the oversight of them that keep the charge of the sanctuary.

33 Of Merari *was* the family of the Mahlites, and the family of the Mushites: these *are* the families of Merari.

34 And those that were numbered of them, according to the number of all the males, from a month old and upward, *were* six thousand and two hundred.

35 And the chief of the house of the father of the families of Merari *was* Zuriel the son of Abihail: [a]*these* shall pitch on the side of the tabernacle northward.

36 And [a]*under* the custody and charge of the sons of Merari *shall be* the boards of the tabernacle, and the bars thereof, and the pillars thereof, and the sockets thereof, and all the vessels thereof, and all that serveth thereto,

37 And the pillars of the court round about, and their sockets, and their pins, and their cords.

38 [a]But those that encamp before the tabernacle toward the east, *even* before the tabernacle of the congregation eastward, *shall be* Moses, and Aaron and his sons, [b]keeping the charge of the sanctuary [c]for the charge of the children of Israel; and [d]the stranger that cometh nigh shall be put to death.

39 [a]All that were numbered of the Levites, which Moses and Aaron numbered at the commandment of the LORD, throughout their families, all the males from a month old and upward, *were* twenty and two thousand.

Levites Dedicated Instead of the Firstborn

40 And the LORD said unto Moses, [a]Number all the firstborn of the males of the children of Israel from a month old and upward, and take the number of their names.

41 [a]And thou shalt take the Levites for me (I *am* the LORD) instead of all the firstborn among the children of Israel; and the cattle of the Levites instead of all the firstlings among the cattle of the children of Israel.

42 And Moses numbered, as the LORD commanded him, all the firstborn among the children of Israel.

43 And all the firstborn males by the number of names, from a month old and upward, of those that were numbered of them, were twenty and two thousand two hundred and threescore and thirteen.

44 And the LORD spake unto Moses, saying,

45 [a]Take the Levites instead of all the

25 [a]Num. 4:24–26 [b]Ex. 25:9 [c]Ex. 26:1 [d]Ex. 26:7, 14 [e]Ex. 26:36
26 [a]Ex. 27:9, 12, 14, 15 [b]Ex. 27:16 [c]Ex. 35:18
27 [a]1 Chr. 26:23
29 [a]Ex. 6:18; Num. 1:53
30 [a]Lev. 10:4
31 [a]Num. 4:15 [b]Ex. 25:10 [c]Ex. 25:23 [d]Ex. 25:31 [e]Ex. 27:1; 30:1 [f]Ex. 26:31–33
35 [a]Num. 1:53; 2:25
36 [a]Num. 4:31, 32
38 [a]Num. 1:53 [b]Num. 18:5 [c]Num. 3:7, 8 [d]Num. 3:10
39 [a]Num. 3:43; 4:48; 26:62
40 [a]Num. 3:15
41 [a]Num. 3:12, 45
45 [a]Num. 3:12, 41

NKJV

25 [a]The duties of the children of Gershon in the tabernacle of meeting *included* [b]the tabernacle, [c]the tent with [d]its covering, [e]the screen for the door of the tabernacle of meeting,

26 [a]the screen for the door of the court, [b]the hangings of the court which *are* around the tabernacle and the altar, and [c]their cords, according to all the work relating to them.

27 [a]From Kohath *came* the family of the Amramites, the family of the Izharites, the family of the Hebronites, and the family of the Uzzielites; these *were* the families of the Kohathites.

28 According to the number of all the males, from a month old and above, *there were* eight thousand *six hundred keeping charge of the sanctuary.

29 [a]The families of the children of Kohath were to camp on the south side of the tabernacle.

30 And the leader of the fathers' house of the families of the Kohathites *was* Elizaphan the son of [a]Uzziel.

31 [a]Their duty *included* [b]the ark, [c]the table, [d]the lampstand, [e]the altars, the utensils of the sanctuary with which they ministered, [f]the screen, and all the work relating to them.

32 And Eleazar the son of Aaron the priest *was to be* chief over the leaders of the Levites, *with* oversight of those who kept charge of the sanctuary.

33 From Merari *came* the family of the Mahlites and the family of the Mushites; these *were* the families of Merari.

34 And those who were numbered, according to the number of all the males from a month old and above, *were* six thousand two hundred.

35 The leader of the fathers' house of the families of Merari *was* Zuriel the son of Abihail. [a]These *were* to camp on the north side of the tabernacle.

36 And [a]the appointed duty of the children of Merari *included* the boards of the tabernacle, its bars, its pillars, its sockets, its utensils, all the work relating to them,

37 and the pillars of the court all around, with their sockets, their pegs, and their cords.

38 [a]Moreover those who were to camp before the tabernacle on the east, before the tabernacle of meeting, *were* Moses, Aaron, and his sons, [b]keeping charge of the sanctuary, [c]to meet the needs of the children of Israel; but [d]the outsider who came near was to be put to death.

39 [a]All who were numbered of the Levites, whom Moses and Aaron numbered at the commandment of the LORD, by their families, all the males from a month old and above, *were* twenty-two thousand.

Levites Dedicated Instead of the Firstborn

40 Then the LORD said to Moses: [a]"Number all the firstborn males of the children of Israel from a month old and above, and take the number of their names.

41 [a]"And you shall take the Levites for Me—I *am* the LORD—instead of all the firstborn among the children of Israel, and the livestock of the Levites instead of all the firstborn among the livestock of the children of Israel."

42 So Moses numbered all the firstborn among the children of Israel, as the LORD commanded him.

43 And all the firstborn males, according to the number of names from a month old and above, of those who were numbered of them, were twenty-two thousand two hundred and seventy-three.

44 Then the LORD spoke to Moses, saying:

45 [a]"Take the Levites instead of all the

*

3:28 Some LXX mss. *three*

KJV

firstborn among the children of Israel, and the cattle of the Levites instead of their cattle; and the Levites shall be mine: I *am* the LORD.

46 And for those that are to be [a]redeemed of the two hundred and threescore and thirteen of the firstborn of the children of Israel, [b]which are more than the Levites;

47 Thou shalt even take [a]five shekels apiece [b]by the poll, after the shekel of the sanctuary shalt thou take *them:* [c](the shekel *is* twenty gerahs:)

48 And thou shalt give the money, wherewith the odd number of them is to be redeemed, unto Aaron and to his sons.

49 And Moses took the redemption money of them that were over and above them that were redeemed by the Levites:

50 Of the firstborn of the children of Israel took he the money; [a]a thousand three hundred and threescore and five *shekels,* after the shekel of the sanctuary:

51 And Moses [a]gave the money of them that were redeemed unto Aaron and to his sons, according to the word of the LORD, as the LORD commanded Moses.

Duties of the Sons of Kohath

4 And the LORD spake unto Moses and unto Aaron, saying,

2 Take the sum of the sons of [a]Kohath from among the sons of Levi, after their families, by the house of their fathers,

3 [a]From thirty years old and upward even until fifty years old, all that enter into the host, to do the work in the tabernacle of the congregation.

4 [a]This *shall be* the service of the sons of Kohath in the tabernacle of the congregation, *about* [b]the most holy things:

5 And when the camp setteth forward, Aaron shall come, and his sons, and they shall take down [a]the covering vail, and cover the [b]ark of testimony with it:

6 And shall put thereon the covering of badgers' skins, and shall spread over *it* a cloth wholly of [a]blue, and shall put in [b]the staves thereof.

7 And upon the [a]table of shewbread they shall spread a cloth of blue, and put thereon the dishes, and the spoons, and the bowls, and covers to cover withal: and the [b]continual bread shall be thereon:

8 And they shall spread upon them a cloth of scarlet, and cover the same with a covering of badgers' skins, and shall put in the staves thereof.

9 And they shall take a cloth of blue, and cover the [a]candlestick of the light, [b]and his lamps, and his tongs, and his snuffdishes, and all the oil vessels thereof, wherewith they minister unto it:

10 And they shall put it and all the vessels thereof within a covering of badgers' skins, and shall put *it* upon a bar.

11 And upon [a]the golden altar they shall spread a cloth of blue, and cover it with a covering of badgers' skins, and shall put to the staves thereof:

12 And they shall take all the [a]instruments of ministry, wherewith they minister in the sanctuary, and put *them* in a cloth of blue, and cover them with a covering of badgers' skins, and shall put *them* on a bar:

13 And they shall take away the ashes from the altar, and spread a purple cloth thereon:

14 And they shall put upon it all the vessels thereof, wherewith they minister about it, *even* the censers, the fleshhooks, and the shovels, and the basons, all the vessels of the altar; and they shall spread upon it a covering of badgers' skins, and put to the staves of it.

15 And when Aaron and his sons have made an end of covering the sanctuary, and all the vessels of the sanctuary, as the camp is to set forward; after that, [a]the sons of Kohath shall come

46 [a]Ex. 13:13, 15; Num. 18:15, 16 [b]Num. 3:39, 43
47 [a]Lev. 27:6; Num. 18:16 [b]Num. 1:2, 18, 20 [c]Ex. 30:13
50 [a]Num. 3:46, 47
51 [a]Num. 3:48

CHAPTER 4
2 [a]Num. 3:27–32
3 [a]Num. 4:23, 30, 35; 8:24; 1 Chr. 23:3, 24, 27; Ezra 3:8
4 [a]Num. 4:15 [b]Num. 4:19
5 [a]Ex. 26:31; Heb. 9:3 [b]Ex. 25:10, 16
6 [a]Ex. 39:1 [b]Ex. 25:13; 1 Kin. 8:7, 8
7 [a]Ex. 25:23, 29, 30 [b]Lev. 24:5–9
9 [a]Ex. 25:31 [b]Ex. 25:37, 38
11 [a]Ex. 30:1–5
12 [a]Ex. 25:9; 1 Chr. 9:29
15 [a]Num. 7:9; 10:21; Deut. 31:9; Josh. 4:10; 2 Sam. 6:13; 1 Chr. 15:2, 15

NKJV

firstborn among the children of Israel, and the livestock of the Levites instead of their livestock. The Levites shall be Mine: I *am* the LORD.

46 "And for [a]the redemption of the two hundred and seventy-three of the firstborn of the children of Israel, [b]who are more than the number of the Levites,

47 "you shall take [a]five shekels for each one [b]individually; you shall take *them* in the currency of the shekel of the sanctuary, [c]the shekel of twenty gerahs.

48 "And you shall give the money, with which the excess number of them is redeemed, to Aaron and his sons."

49 So Moses took the redemption money from those who were over and above those who were redeemed by the Levites.

50 From the firstborn of the children of Israel he took the money, [a]one thousand three hundred and sixty-five *shekels,* according to the shekel of the sanctuary.

51 And Moses [a]gave their redemption money to Aaron and his sons, according to the word of the LORD, as the LORD commanded Moses.

Duties of the Sons of Kohath

4 Then the LORD spoke to Moses and Aaron, saying:

2 "Take a census of the sons of [a]Kohath from among the children of Levi, by their families, by their fathers' house,

3 [a]"from thirty years old and above, even to fifty years old, all who enter the service to do the work in the tabernacle of meeting.

4 [a]"This *is* the service of the sons of Kohath in the tabernacle of meeting, *relating to* [b]the most holy things:

5 "When the camp prepares to journey, Aaron and his sons shall come, and they shall take down [a]the covering veil and cover the [b]ark of the Testimony with it.

6 "Then they shall put on it a covering of badger skins, and spread over *that* a cloth entirely of [a]blue; and they shall insert [b]its poles.

7 "On the [a]table of showbread they shall spread a blue cloth, and put on it the dishes, the pans, the bowls, and the pitchers for pouring; and the [b]showbread* shall be on it.

8 "They shall spread over them a scarlet cloth, and cover the same with a covering of badger skins; and they shall insert its poles.

9 "And they shall take a blue cloth and cover the [a]lampstand of the light, [b]with its lamps, its wick-trimmers, its trays, and all its oil vessels, with which they service it.

10 "Then they shall put it with all its utensils in a covering of badger skins, and put *it* on a carrying beam.

11 "Over [a]the golden altar they shall spread a blue cloth, and cover it with a covering of badger skins; and they shall insert its poles.

12 "Then they shall take all the [a]utensils of service with which they minister in the sanctuary, put *them* in a blue cloth, cover them with a covering of badger skins, and put *them* on a carrying beam.

13 "Also they shall take away the ashes from the altar, and spread a purple cloth over it.

14 "They shall put on it all its implements with which they minister there—the firepans, the forks, the shovels, the basins, and all the utensils of the altar—and they shall spread on it a covering of badger skins, and insert its poles.

15 "And when Aaron and his sons have finished covering the sanctuary and all the furnishings of the sanctuary, when the camp is set to go, then [a]the sons of Kohath shall come to carry

*———

4:7 Lit. *continual bread*

KJV

to bear *it:* [b]but they shall not touch *any* holy thing,
lest they die. [c]These *things are* the burden of the
sons of Kohath in the tabernacle of the congregation.
16 And to the office of Eleazar the son of
Aaron the priest *pertaineth* [a]the oil for the light,
and the [b]sweet incense, and [c]the daily meat offering, and the [d]anointing oil, *and* the oversight of
all the tabernacle, and of all that therein *is,* in
the sanctuary, and in the vessels thereof.
17 And the LORD spake unto Moses and unto
Aaron, saying,
18 Cut ye not off the tribe of the families of
the Kohathites from among the Levites:
19 But thus do unto them, that they may live,
and not die, when they approach unto [a]the most
holy things: Aaron and his sons shall go in, and
appoint them every one to his service and to his
burden:
20 [a]But they shall not go in to see when the
holy things are covered, lest they die.

Duties of the Sons of Gershon

21 And the LORD spake unto Moses, saying,
22 Take also the sum of the sons of [a]Gershon,
throughout the houses of their fathers, by their
families;
23 [a]From thirty years old and upward until
fifty years old shalt thou number them; all that
enter in to perform the service, to do the work in
the tabernacle of the congregation.
24 This *is* the [a]service of the families of the
Gershonites, to serve, and for burdens:
25 [a]And they shall bear the [b]curtains of the
tabernacle, and the tabernacle of the congregation, his covering, and the covering of the [c]bad-
gers' skins that *is* above upon it, and the hanging
for the door of the tabernacle of the congregation,
26 And the hangings of the court, and the
hanging for the door of the gate of the court,
which *is* by the tabernacle and by the altar round
about, and their cords, and all the instruments of
their service, and all that is made for them: so
shall they serve.
27 At the appointment of Aaron and his sons
shall be all the service of the sons of the Gershonites, in all their burdens, and in all their service:
and ye shall appoint unto them in charge all their
burdens.
28 This *is* the service of the families of the
sons of Gershon in the tabernacle of the congregation: and their charge *shall be* [a]under the hand
of Ithamar the son of Aaron the priest.

Duties of the Sons of Merari

29 As for the sons of [a]Merari, thou shalt number them after their families, by the house of their
fathers;
30 [a]From thirty years old and upward even
unto fifty years old shalt thou number them, every
one that entereth into the service, to do the work
of the tabernacle of the congregation.
31 And [a]this *is* the charge of their [b]burden,
according to all their service in the tabernacle of
the congregation; [c]the boards of the tabernacle,
and the bars thereof, and the pillars thereof, and
sockets thereof,
32 And the pillars of the court round about,
and their sockets, and their pins, and their cords,
with all their instruments, and with all their service: and by name ye shall [a]reckon the instruments of the charge of their burden.
33 This *is* the service of the families of the
sons of Merari, according to all their service, in
the tabernacle of the congregation, under the
hand of Ithamar the son of Aaron the priest.

Census of the Levites

34 [a]And Moses and Aaron and the chief of
the congregation numbered the sons of the Kohathites after their families, and after the house
of their fathers,

15 [b]2 Sam. 6:6, 7; 1 Chr. 13:9, 10 [c]Num. 3:31
16 [a]Ex. 25:6; Lev. 24:2 [b]Ex. 30:34 [c]Ex. 29:38 [d]Ex. 30:23–25
19 [a]Num. 4:4
20 [a]Ex. 19:21; 1 Sam. 6:19
22 [a]Num. 3:22
23 [a]Num. 4:3; 1 Chr. 23:3, 24, 27
24 [a]Num. 7:7
25 [a]Num. 3:25, 26 [b]Ex. 36:8 [c]Ex. 26:14
28 [a]Num. 4:33
29 [a]Num. 3:33–37
30 [a]Num. 4:3; 8:24–26
31 [a]Num. 3:36, 37 [b]Num. 7:8 [c]Ex. 26:15
32 [a]Ex. 25:9; 38:21
34 [a]Num. 4:2

NKJV

them; [b]but they shall not touch any holy thing,
lest they die. [c]These *are* the things in the tabernacle of meeting which the sons of Kohath are to
carry.
16 "The appointed duty of Eleazar the son
of Aaron the priest *is* [a]the oil for the light, the
[b]sweet incense, [c]the daily grain offering, the
[d]anointing oil, the oversight of all the tabernacle,
of all that *is* in it, with the sanctuary and its
furnishings."
17 Then the LORD spoke to Moses and Aaron,
saying:
18 "Do not cut off the tribe of the families
of the Kohathites from among the Levites;
19 "but do this in regard to them, that they
may live and not die when they approach [a]the
most holy things: Aaron and his sons shall go in
and appoint each of them to his service and his
task.
20 [a]"But they shall not go in to watch while
the holy things are being covered, lest they die."

Duties of the Sons of Gershon

21 Then the LORD spoke to Moses, saying:
22 "Also take a census of the sons of [a]Ger-
shon, by their fathers' house, by their families.
23 [a]"From thirty years old and above, even
to fifty years old, you shall number them, all who
enter to perform the service, to do the work in
the tabernacle of meeting.
24 "This *is* the [a]service of the families of the
Gershonites, in serving and carrying:
25 [a]"They shall carry the [b]curtains of the tabernacle and the tabernacle of meeting *with* its
covering, the covering of [c]badger skins that *is* on
it, the screen for the door of the tabernacle of
meeting,
26 "the screen for the door of the gate of the
court, the hangings of the court which *are* around
the tabernacle and altar, and their cords, all the
furnishings for their service and all that is made
for these things: so shall they serve.
27 "Aaron and his sons shall assign all the
service of the sons of the Gershonites, all their
tasks and all their service. And you shall appoint
to them all their tasks as their duty.
28 "This *is* the service of the families of the
sons of Gershon in the tabernacle of meeting. And
their duties *shall be* [a]under the *authority of Ithamar the son of Aaron the priest.

Duties of the Sons of Merari

29 "*As for* the sons of [a]Merari, you shall
number them by their families and by their fathers' house.
30 [a]"From thirty years old and above, even
to fifty years old, you shall number them, everyone who enters the service to do the work of the
tabernacle of meeting.
31 "And [a]this *is* [b]what they must carry as
all their service for the tabernacle of meeting: [c]the
boards of the tabernacle, its bars, its pillars, its
sockets,
32 "and the pillars around the court with
their sockets, pegs, and cords, with all their furnishings and all their service; and you shall [a]as-
sign *to each man* by name the items he must
carry.
33 "This *is* the service of the families of the
sons of Merari, as all their service for the tabernacle of meeting, under the *authority of Ithamar
the son of Aaron the priest."

Census of the Levites

34 [a]And Moses, Aaron, and the leaders of the
congregation numbered the sons of the Kohathites by their families and by their fathers' house,

---

*4:28 Lit. *hand*
4:33 Lit. *hand*

KJV

35 From thirty [a]years old and upward even
unto fifty years old, every one that entereth into
the service, for the work in the tabernacle of the
congregation:
36 And those that were numbered of them
by their families were two thousand seven hundred and fifty.
37 These *were* they that were numbered of
the families of the Kohathites, all that might do
service in the tabernacle of the congregation,
which Moses and Aaron did number according
to the commandment of the LORD by the hand of
Moses.
38 And those that were numbered of the sons
of Gershon, throughout their families, and by the
house of their fathers,
39 From thirty years old and upward even
unto fifty years old, every one that entereth into
the service, for the work in the tabernacle of the
congregation,
40 Even those that were numbered of them,
throughout their families, by the house of their
fathers, were two thousand and six hundred and
thirty.
41 [a]These *are* they that were numbered of
the families of the sons of Gershon, of all that
might do service in the tabernacle of the congregation, whom Moses and Aaron did number according to the commandment of the LORD.
42 And those that were numbered of the families of the sons of Merari, throughout their families, by the house of their fathers,
43 From thirty years old and upward even
unto fifty years old, every one that entereth into
the service, for the work in the tabernacle of the
congregation,
44 Even those that were numbered of them
after their families, were three thousand and two
hundred.
45 These *be* those that were numbered of the
families of the sons of Merari, whom Moses and
Aaron numbered [a]according to the word of the
LORD by the hand of Moses.
46 All those that were [a]numbered of the Levites, whom Moses and Aaron and the chief of
Israel numbered, after their families, and after the
house of their fathers,
47 [a]From thirty years old and upward even
unto fifty years old, every one that came to do
the service of the ministry, and the service of the
burden in the tabernacle of the congregation,
48 Even those that were numbered of them,
were eight thousand and five hundred and
fourscore.
49 According to the commandment of the
LORD they were numbered by the hand of Moses,
[a]every one according to his service, and according
to his burden: thus were they numbered of him,
[b]as the LORD commanded Moses.

Ceremonially Unclean Persons Isolated
(cf. Lev. 15:1–33)

5 And the LORD spake unto Moses, saying,
2 Command the children of Israel, that they
put out of the camp every [a]leper, and every one
that hath an [b]issue, and whosoever is [c]defiled by
the dead:
3 Both male and female shall ye put out,
without the camp shall ye put them; that they
defile not their camps, [a]in the midst whereof I
dwell.
4 And the children of Israel did so, and put
them out without the camp: as the LORD spake
unto Moses, so did the children of Israel.

Confession and Restitution
(Lev. 6:1–7)

5 And the LORD spake unto Moses, saying,
6 Speak unto the children of Israel, [a]When
a man or woman shall commit any sin that men
commit, to do a trespass against the LORD, and
that person be guilty;

35 [a]Num. 4:47
41 [a]Num. 4:22
45 [a]Num. 4:29
46 [a]Num. 3:39; 26:57–62; 1 Chr. 23:3–23
47 [a]Num. 4:3, 23, 30
49 [a]Num. 4:15, 24, 31 [b]Num. 4:1, 21

CHAPTER 5
2 [a]Lev. 13:3, 8, 46; Num. 12:10, 14, 15 [b]Lev. 15:2 [c]Lev. 21:1; Num. 9:6, 10; 19:11, 13; 31:19
3 [a]Lev. 26:11, 12; Num. 35:34; [2 Cor. 6:16]
6 [a]Lev. 5:14—6:7

NKJV

35 from thirty [a]years old and above, even to
fifty years old, everyone who entered the service
for work in the tabernacle of meeting;
36 and those who were numbered by their
families were two thousand seven hundred and
fifty.
37 These *were* the ones who were numbered
of the families of the Kohathites, all who might
serve in the tabernacle of meeting, whom Moses
and Aaron numbered according to the commandment of the LORD by the hand of Moses.
38 And those who were numbered of the sons
of Gershon, by their families and by their fathers'
house,
39 from thirty years old and above, even to
fifty years old, everyone who entered the service
for work in the tabernacle of meeting—
40 those who were numbered by their families, by their fathers' house, were two thousand
six hundred and thirty.
41 [a]These *are* the ones who were numbered
of the families of the sons of Gershon, of all who
might serve in the tabernacle of meeting, whom
Moses and Aaron numbered according to the
commandment of the LORD.
42 Those of the families of the sons of Merari
who were numbered, by their families, by their
fathers' house,
43 from thirty years old and above, even to
fifty years old, everyone who entered the service
for work in the tabernacle of meeting—
44 those who were numbered by their families were three thousand two hundred.
45 These *are* the ones who were numbered
of the families of the sons of Merari, whom Moses
and Aaron numbered [a]according to the word of
the LORD by the hand of Moses.
46 All who were [a]numbered of the Levites,
whom Moses, Aaron, and the leaders of Israel
numbered, by their families and by their fathers'
houses,
47 [a]from thirty years old and above, even to
fifty years old, everyone who came to do the work
of service and the work of bearing burdens in the
tabernacle of meeting—
48 those who were numbered were eight
thousand five hundred and eighty.
49 According to the commandment of the
LORD they were numbered by the hand of Moses,
[a]each according to his service and according to
his task; thus were they numbered by him, [b]as
the LORD commanded Moses.

Ceremonially Unclean Persons Isolated
(cf. Lev. 15:1–33)

5 And the LORD spoke to Moses, saying:
2 "Command the children of Israel that they
put out of the camp every [a]leper, everyone who
has a [b]discharge, and whoever becomes [c]defiled
by a corpse.
3 "You shall put out both male and female;
you shall put them outside the camp, that they
may not defile their camps [a]in the midst of which
I dwell."
4 And the children of Israel did so, and put
them outside the camp; as the LORD spoke to Moses, so the children of Israel did.

Confession and Restitution
(Lev. 6:1–7)

5 Then the LORD spoke to Moses, saying,
6 "Speak to the children of Israel: [a]'When
a man or woman commits any sin that men commit in unfaithfulness against the LORD, and that
person is guilty,

KJV

7 [a]Then they shall confess their sin which they have done: and he shall recompense his trespass [b]with the principal thereof, and add unto it the fifth *part* thereof, and give *it* unto *him* against whom he hath trespassed.

8 But if the man have no kinsman to recompense the trespass unto, let the trespass be recompensed unto the LORD, *even* to the priest; beside [a]the ram of the atonement, whereby an atonement shall be made for him.

9 And every [a]offering of all the holy things of the children of Israel, which they bring unto the priest, shall be [b]his.

10 And every man's hallowed things shall be his: whatsoever any man giveth the priest, it shall be [a]his.

Concerning Unfaithful Wives

11 And the LORD spake unto Moses, saying,

12 Speak unto the children of Israel, and say unto them, If any man's wife go aside, and commit a trespass against him,

13 And a man [a]lie with her carnally, and it be hid from the eyes of her husband, and be kept close, and she be defiled, and *there be* no witness against her, neither she be [b]taken *with the manner;*

14 And the spirit of jealousy come upon him, and he be [a]jealous of his wife, and she be defiled: or if the spirit of jealousy come upon him, and he be jealous of his wife, and she be not defiled:

15 Then shall the man bring his wife unto the priest, and he shall [a]bring her offering for her, the tenth *part* of an ephah of barley meal; he shall pour no oil upon it, nor put frankincense thereon; for it *is* an offering of jealousy, an offering of memorial, [b]bringing iniquity to remembrance.

16 And the priest shall bring her near, and set her before the LORD:

17 And the priest shall take holy water in an earthen vessel; and of the dust that is in the floor of the tabernacle the priest shall take, and put *it* into the water:

18 And the priest shall set the woman before the [a]LORD, and uncover the woman's head, and put the offering of memorial in her hands, which *is* the jealousy offering: and the priest shall have in his hand the bitter water that causeth the curse:

19 And the priest shall charge her by an oath, and say unto the woman, If no man have lain with thee, and if thou hast not gone aside to uncleanness *with another* instead of thy husband, be thou free from this bitter water that causeth the curse:

20 But if thou hast gone aside *to another* instead of thy husband, and if thou be defiled, and some man have lain with thee beside thine husband:

21 Then the priest shall [a]charge the woman with an oath of cursing, and the priest shall say unto the woman, [b]The LORD make thee a curse and an oath among thy people, when the LORD doth make thy thigh to rot, and thy belly to swell;

22 And this water that causeth the curse [a]shall go into thy bowels, to make *thy* belly to swell, and *thy* thigh to rot: [b]And the woman shall say, Amen, amen.

23 And the priest shall write these curses in a book, and he shall blot *them* out with the bitter water:

24 And he shall cause the woman to drink the bitter water that causeth the curse: and the water that causeth the curse shall enter into her, *and become* bitter.

25 [a]Then the priest shall take the jealousy offering out of the woman's hand, and shall [b]wave the offering before the LORD, and offer it upon the altar:

26 And the priest shall take an handful of the offering, [a]*even* the memorial thereof, and burn *it* upon the altar, and afterward shall cause the woman to drink the water.

27 And when he hath made her to drink the

7 [a]Lev. 5:5; 26:40, 41; Josh. 7:19; Ps. 32:5; 1 John 1:9 [b]Lev. 6:4, 5
8 [a]Lev. 5:15; 6:6, 7; 7:7
9 [a]Ex. 29:28; Lev. 6:17, 18, 26; 7:6–14 [b]Lev. 7:32–34; 10:14, 15
10 [a]Lev. 10:13
13 [a]Lev. 18:20; 20:10 [b]John 8:4
14 [a]Prov. 6:34; Song 8:6
15 [a]Lev. 5:11 [b]1 Kin. 17:18; Ezek. 29:16; Heb. 10:3
18 [a]Heb. 13:4
21 [a]Josh. 6:26; 1 Sam. 14:24; Neh. 10:29 [b]Jer. 29:22
22 [a]Ps. 109:18 [b]Deut. 27:15–26
25 [a]Lev. 8:27 [b]Lev. 2:2, 9
26 [a]Lev. 2:2, 9

NKJV

7 [a]'then he shall confess the sin which he has committed. He shall make restitution for his trespass [b]in full, plus one-fifth of it, and give *it* to the one he has wronged.

8 'But if the man has no relative to whom restitution may be made for the wrong, the restitution for the wrong *must go* to the LORD for the priest, in addition to [a]the ram of the atonement with which atonement is made for him.

9 'Every [a]offering of all the holy things of the children of Israel, which they bring to the priest, shall be [b]his.

10 'And every man's holy things shall be his; whatever any man gives the priest shall be [a]his.' "

Concerning Unfaithful Wives

11 And the LORD spoke to Moses, saying,

12 "Speak to the children of Israel, and say to them: 'If any man's wife goes astray and behaves unfaithfully toward him,

13 'and a man [a]lies with her carnally, and it is hidden from the eyes of her husband, and it is concealed that she has defiled herself, and *there was* no witness against her, nor was she [b]caught—

14 'if the spirit of jealousy comes upon him and he becomes [a]jealous of his wife, who has defiled herself; or if the spirit of jealousy comes upon him and he becomes jealous of his wife, although she has not defiled herself—

15 'then the man shall bring his wife to the priest. He shall [a]bring the offering required for her, one-tenth of an ephah of barley meal; he shall pour no oil on it and put no frankincense on it, because it *is* a grain offering of jealousy, an offering for remembering, for [b]bringing iniquity to remembrance.

16 'And the priest shall bring her near, and set her before the LORD.

17 'The priest shall take holy water in an earthen vessel, and take some of the dust that is on the floor of the tabernacle and put *it* into the water.

18 'Then the priest shall stand the woman before the [a]LORD, uncover the woman's head, and put the offering for remembering in her hands, which *is* the grain offering of jealousy. And the priest shall have in his hand the bitter water that brings a curse.

19 'And the priest shall put her under oath, and say to the woman, "If no man has lain with you, and if you have not gone astray to uncleanness *while* under your husband's *authority,* be free from this bitter water that brings a curse.

20 "But if you have gone astray *while* under your husband's *authority,* and if you have defiled yourself and some man other than your husband has lain with you"—

21 'then the priest shall [a]put the woman under the oath of the curse, and he shall say to the woman—[b]"the LORD make you a curse and an oath among your people, when the LORD makes your thigh rot and your belly swell;

22 "and may this water that causes the curse [a]go into your stomach, and make *your* belly swell and *your* thigh rot." [b]Then the woman shall say, "Amen, so be it."

23 'Then the priest shall write these curses in a book, and he shall scrape *them* off into the bitter water.

24 'And he shall make the woman drink the bitter water that brings a curse, and the water that brings the curse shall enter her *to become* bitter.

25 [a]'Then the priest shall take the grain offering of jealousy from the woman's hand, shall [b]wave the offering before the LORD, and bring it to the altar;

26 'and the priest shall take a handful of the offering, [a]as its memorial portion, burn *it* on the altar, and afterward make the woman drink the water.

27 'When he has made her drink the water,

KJV

water, then it shall come to pass, *that*, if she be
defiled, and have done trespass against her husband, that the water that causeth the [a]curse shall
enter into her, *and become* bitter, and her belly
shall swell, and her thigh shall rot: and the woman
[b]shall be a curse among her people.
28 And if the woman be not defiled, but be
clean; then she shall be free, and shall conceive
seed.
29 This *is* the law of jealousies, when a wife
goeth aside *to another* [a]instead of her husband,
and is defiled;
30 Or when the spirit of jealousy cometh
upon him, and he be jealous over his wife, and
shall set the woman before the LORD, and the
priest shall execute upon her all this law.
31 Then shall the man be guiltless from iniquity, and this woman [a]shall bear her iniquity.

The Law of the Nazirite

6 And the LORD spake unto Moses, saying,
2 Speak unto the children of Israel, and say
unto them, When either man or woman shall
[a]separate *themselves* to vow a vow of a Nazarite,
to separate *themselves* unto the LORD:
3 [a]He shall separate *himself* from wine and
strong drink, and shall drink no vinegar of wine,
or vinegar of strong drink, neither shall he drink
any liquor of grapes, nor eat moist grapes, or
dried.
4 All the days of his separation shall he eat
nothing that is made of the vine tree, from the
kernels even to the husk.
5 All the days of the vow of his separation
there shall no [a]razor come upon his head: until
the days be fulfilled, in the which he separateth
himself unto the LORD, he shall be holy, *and* shall
let the locks of the hair of his head grow.
6 All the days that he separateth *himself*
unto the LORD [a]he shall come at no dead body.
7 [a]He shall not make himself unclean for
his father, or for his mother, for his brother, or
for his sister, when they die: because the consecration of his God *is* upon his head.
8 [a]All the days of his separation he *is* holy
unto the LORD.
9 And if any man die very suddenly by
him, and he hath defiled the head of his consecration; then he shall [a]shave his head in the day of
his cleansing, on the seventh day shall he shave
it.
10 And [a]on the eighth day he shall bring two
turtles, or two young pigeons, to the priest, to the
door of the tabernacle of the congregation:
11 And the priest shall offer the one for a
sin offering, and the other for a burnt offering,
and make an atonement for him, for that he
sinned by the dead, and shall hallow his head that
same day.
12 And he shall consecrate unto the LORD the
days of his separation, and shall bring a lamb of
the first year [a]for a trespass offering: but the days
that were before shall be lost, because his separation was defiled.
13 And this *is* the law of the Nazarite, [a]when
the days of his separation are fulfilled: he shall
be brought unto the door of the tabernacle of the
congregation:
14 And he shall offer his offering unto the
LORD, one he lamb of the first year without blemish for a burnt offering, and one ewe lamb of the
first year without blemish [a]for a sin offering, and
one ram without blemish [b]for peace offerings,
15 And a basket of unleavened bread, [a]cakes
of fine flour mingled with oil, and wafers of unleavened bread [b]anointed with oil, and their meat
offering, and their [c]drink offerings.
16 And the priest shall bring *them* before the
LORD, and shall offer his sin offering, and his burnt
offering:
17 And he shall offer the ram *for* a sacrifice
of peace offerings unto the LORD, with the basket

27 [a]Deut. 28:37; Is. 65:15; Jer. 24:9; 29:18, 22; 42:18 [b]Num. 5:21
29 [a]Num. 5:19
31 [a]Lev. 20:17, 19, 20

CHAPTER 6

2 [a]Lev. 27:2; Judg. 13:5; [Lam. 4:7; Amos 2:11, 12]; Acts 21:23; Rom. 1:1
3 [a]Lev. 10:9; Amos 2:12; Luke 1:15
5 [a]Judg. 13:5; 16:17; 1 Sam. 1:11
6 [a]Lev. 21:1–3, 11; Num. 19:11–22
7 [a]Lev. 21:1, 2, 11; Num. 9:6
8 [a][2 Cor. 6:17, 18]
9 [a]Lev. 14:8, 9; Acts 18:18; 21:24
10 [a]Lev. 5:7; 14:22; 15:14, 29
12 [a]Lev. 5:6
13 [a]Acts 21:26
14 [a]Lev. 4:2, 27, 32 [b]Lev. 3:6
15 [a]Lev. 2:4 [b]Ex. 29:2 [c]Num. 15:5, 7, 10

NKJV

then it shall be, if she has defiled herself and behaved unfaithfully toward her husband, that the
water that brings a [a]curse will enter her *and be-*
come bitter, and her belly will swell, her thigh
will rot, and the woman [b]will become a curse
among her people.
28 'But if the woman has not defiled herself,
and is clean, then she shall be free and may conceive children.
29 'This *is* the law of jealousy, when a wife,
while under her husband's *authority*, [a]goes astray
and defiles herself,
30 'or when the spirit of jealousy comes upon
a man, and he becomes jealous of his wife; then
he shall stand the woman before the LORD, and
the priest shall execute all this law upon her.
31 'Then the man shall be free from iniquity,
but that woman [a]shall bear her guilt.' "

The Law of the Nazirite

6 Then the LORD spoke to Moses, saying,
2 "Speak to the children of Israel, and say
to them: 'When either a man or woman consecrates an offering to take the vow of a Nazirite,
[a]to separate himself to the LORD,
3 [a]'he shall separate himself from wine and
similar drink; he shall drink neither vinegar made
from wine nor vinegar made from *similar* drink;
neither shall he drink any grape juice, nor eat
fresh grapes or raisins.
4 'All the days of his separation he shall eat
nothing that is produced by the grapevine, from
seed to skin.
5 'All the days of the vow of his separation
no [a]razor shall come upon his head; until the days
are fulfilled for which he separated himself to the
LORD, he shall be holy. *Then* he shall let the locks
of the hair of his head grow.
6 'All the days that he separates himself to
the LORD [a]he shall not go near a dead body.
7 [a]'He shall not make himself unclean even
for his father or his mother, for his brother or
his sister, when they die, because his separation
to God *is* on his head.
8 [a]'All the days of his separation he shall
be holy to the LORD.
9 'And if anyone dies very suddenly beside
him, and he defiles his consecrated head, then he
shall [a]shave his head on the day of his cleansing;
on the seventh day he shall shave it.
10 'Then [a]on the eighth day he shall bring
two turtledoves or two young pigeons to the
priest, to the door of the tabernacle of meeting;
11 'and the priest shall offer one as a sin offering and *the* other as a burnt offering, and make
atonement for him, because he sinned in regard
to the corpse; and he shall sanctify his head that
same day.
12 'He shall consecrate to the LORD the days
of his separation, and bring a male lamb in its
first year [a]as a trespass offering; but the former
days shall be lost, because his separation was
defiled.
13 'Now this *is* the law of the Nazirite: [a]When
the days of his separation are fulfilled, he shall
be brought to the door of the tabernacle of
meeting.
14 'And he shall present his offering to the
LORD: one male lamb in its first year without blemish as a burnt offering, one ewe lamb in its first
year without blemish [a]as a sin offering, one ram
without blemish [b]as a peace offering,
15 'a basket of unleavened bread, [a]cakes of
fine flour mixed with oil, unleavened wafers
[b]anointed with oil, and their grain offering with
their [c]drink offerings.
16 'Then the priest shall bring *them* before
the LORD and offer his sin offering and his burnt
offering;
17 'and he shall offer the ram as a sacrifice
of a peace offering to the LORD, with the basket

KJV

of unleavened bread: the priest shall offer also
his meat offering, and his drink offering.
18 [a]And the Nazarite shall shave the head
of his separation *at* the door of the tabernacle of
the congregation, and shall take the hair of the
head of his separation, and put *it* in the fire which
is under the sacrifice of the peace offerings.
19 And the priest shall take the [a]sodden
shoulder of the ram, and one [b]unleavened cake
out of the basket, and one unleavened wafer, and
[c]shall put *them* upon the hands of the Nazarite,
after *the hair of* his separation is shaven:
20 And the priest shall wave them *for* a wave
offering before the LORD: [a]this *is* holy for the
priest, with the wave breast and heave shoulder:
and after that the Nazarite may drink wine.
21 This *is* the law of the Nazarite who hath
vowed, *and of* his offering unto the LORD for his
separation, beside *that* that his hand shall get:
according to the vow which he vowed, so he must
do after the law of his separation.

The Priestly Blessing

22 And the LORD spake unto Moses, saying,
23 Speak unto Aaron and unto his sons, saying, On this wise ye shall bless the children of
Israel, saying unto them,
24 The LORD [a]bless thee, and [b]keep thee:
25 The LORD [a]make his face shine upon thee,
and [b]be gracious unto thee:
26 [a]The LORD lift up his countenance upon
thee, and [b]give thee peace.
27 [a]And they shall put my name upon the
children of Israel; and [b]I will bless them.

Offerings of the Leaders

7 And it came to pass on the day that Moses
had fully [a]set up the tabernacle, and had
[b]anointed it, and sanctified it, and all the instruments thereof, both the altar and all the vessels
thereof, and had anointed them, and sanctified
them;
2 That [a]the princes of Israel, heads of the
house of their fathers, who *were* the princes of
the tribes, and were over them that were numbered, offered:
3 And they brought their offering before the
LORD, six covered wagons, and twelve oxen; a
wagon for two of the princes, and for each one
an ox: and they brought them before the
tabernacle.
4 And the LORD spake unto Moses, saying,
5 Take *it* of them, that they may be to do
the service of the tabernacle of the congregation;
and thou shalt give them unto the Levites, to every
man according to his service.
6 And Moses took the wagons and the oxen,
and gave them unto the Levites.
7 Two wagons and four oxen [a]he gave unto
the sons of Gershon, according to their service:
8 [a]And four wagons and eight oxen he gave
unto the sons of Merari, according unto their service, under the hand of Ithamar the son of Aaron
the priest.
9 But unto the sons of Kohath he gave none:
because [a]the service of the sanctuary belonging
unto them [b]*was that* they should bear upon their
shoulders.
10 And the princes offered for [a]dedicating of
the altar in the day that it was anointed, even the
princes offered their offering before the altar.
11 And the LORD said unto Moses, They shall
offer their offering, each prince on his day, for
the dedicating of the altar.
12 And he that offered his offering the first
day was [a]Nahshon the son of Amminadab, of the
tribe of Judah:
13 And his offering *was* one silver charger,
the weight thereof *was* an hundred and thirty

---

18 [a]Num. 6:9; Acts 21:23, 24
19 [a]1 Sam. 2:15 [b]Ex. 29:23, 24 [c]Lev. 7:30
20 [a]Ex. 29:27, 28
24 [a]Deut. 28:3–6 [b]Ps. 121:7; John 7:11
25 [a]Ps. 31:16; 67:1; 80:3, 7, 19; 119:135; Dan. 9:17 [b]Gen. 43:29; Ex. 33:19; Mal. 1:9
26 [a]Ps. 4:6; 89:15 [b]Lev. 26:6; Is. 26:3, 12; John 14:27; Phil. 4:7
27 [a]Deut. 28:10; 2 Sam. 7:23; 2 Chr. 7:14; Is. 43:7; Dan. 9:18, 19 [b]Ex. 20:24; Num. 23:20; Ps. 5:12; 67:7; 115:12, 13; Eph. 1:3

CHAPTER 7

1 [a]Ex. 40:17–33 [b]Lev. 8:10, 11
2 [a]Num. 1:4
7 [a]Num. 4:24–28
8 [a]Num. 4:29–33
9 [a]Num. 4:15 [b]Num. 4:6–14
10 [a]Num. 7:1; Deut. 20:5; 1 Kin. 8:63; 2 Chr. 7:5, 9; Ezra 6:16; Neh. 12:27
12 [a]Num. 2:3

*7:8 Lit. *hand*

NKJV

of unleavened bread; the priest shall also offer
its grain offering and its drink offering.
18 [a]'Then the Nazirite shall shave his consecrated head *at* the door of the tabernacle of meeting, and shall take the hair from his consecrated
head and put *it* on the fire which is under the
sacrifice of the peace offering.
19 'And the priest shall take the [a]boiled
shoulder of the ram, one [b]unleavened cake from
the basket, and one unleavened wafer, and [c]put
them upon the hands of the Nazirite after he has
shaved his consecrated *hair,*
20 'and the priest shall wave them as a wave
offering before the LORD; [a]they *are* holy for the
priest, together with the breast of the wave offering and the thigh of the heave offering. After that
the Nazirite may drink wine.'
21 "This is the law of the Nazirite who vows
to the LORD the offering for his separation, and
besides that, whatever else his hand is able to provide; according to the vow which he takes, so he
must do according to the law of his separation."

The Priestly Blessing

22 And the LORD spoke to Moses, saying:
23 "Speak to Aaron and his sons, saying,
'This is the way you shall bless the children of
Israel. Say to them:

24 "The LORD [a]bless you and [b]keep you;
25 The LORD [a]make His face shine upon you,
And [b]be gracious to you;
26 [a]The LORD lift up His countenance upon
you,
And [b]give you peace." '

27 [a]"So they shall put My name on the children of Israel, and [b]I will bless them."

Offerings of the Leaders

7 Now it came to pass, when Moses had finished
[a]setting up the tabernacle, that he [b]anointed
it and consecrated it and all its furnishings, and
the altar and all its utensils; so he anointed them
and consecrated them.
2 Then [a]the leaders of Israel, the heads of
their fathers' houses, who *were* the leaders of the
tribes and over those who were numbered, made
an offering.
3 And they brought their offering before the
LORD, six covered carts and twelve oxen, a cart
for *every* two of the leaders, and for each one an
ox; and they presented them before the tabernacle.
4 Then the LORD spoke to Moses, saying,
5 "Accept *these* from them, that they may
be used in doing the work of the tabernacle of
meeting; and you shall give them to the Levites,
to every man according to his service."
6 So Moses took the carts and the oxen, and
gave them to the Levites.
7 Two carts and four oxen [a]he gave to the
sons of Gershon, according to their service;
8 [a]and four carts and eight oxen he gave
to the sons of Merari, according to their service,
under the *authority of Ithamar the son of Aaron
the priest.
9 But to the sons of Kohath he gave none,
because theirs *was* [a]the service of the holy things,
[b]*which* they carried on their shoulders.
10 Now the leaders offered [a]the dedication
offering for the altar when it was anointed; so the
leaders offered their offering before the altar.
11 For the LORD said to Moses, "They shall
offer their offering, one leader each day, for the
dedication of the altar."
12 And the one who offered his offering on
the first day *was* [a]Nahshon the son of Amminadab, from the tribe of Judah.
13 His offering *was* one silver platter, the
weight of which *was* one hundred and thirty

KJV

shekels, one silver bowl of seventy shekels, after [a]the shekel of the sanctuary; both of them *were* full of fine flour mingled with oil for a [b]meat offering:

14 One spoon of ten *shekels* of gold, full of [a]incense:

15 [a]One young bullock, one ram, one lamb [b]of the first year, for a burnt offering:

16 One kid of the goats for a [a]sin offering:

17 And for [a]a sacrifice of peace offerings, two oxen, five rams, five he goats, five lambs of the first year: this *was* the offering of Nahshon the son of Amminadab.

18 On the second day Nethaneel the son of Zuar, prince of Issachar, did offer:

19 He offered *for* his offering one silver charger, the weight whereof *was* an hundred and thirty *shekels,* one silver bowl of seventy shekels, after the shekel of the sanctuary; both of them full of fine flour mingled with oil for a meat offering:

20 One spoon of gold of ten *shekels,* full of incense:

21 One young bullock, one ram, one lamb of the first year, for a burnt offering:

22 One kid of the goats for a sin offering:

23 And for a sacrifice of peace offerings, two oxen, five rams, five he goats, five lambs of the first year: this *was* the offering of Nethaneel the son of Zuar.

24 On the third day Eliab the son of Helon, prince of the children of Zebulun, *did offer:*

25 His offering *was* one silver charger, the weight whereof *was* an hundred and thirty *shekels,* one silver bowl of seventy shekels, after the shekel of the sanctuary; both of them full of fine flour mingled with oil for a meat offering:

26 One golden spoon of ten *shekels,* full of incense:

27 One young bullock, one ram, one lamb of the first year, for a burnt offering:

28 One kid of the goats for a sin offering:

29 And for a sacrifice of peace offerings, two oxen, five rams, five he goats, five lambs of the first year: this *was* the offering of Eliab the son of Helon.

30 On the fourth day [a]Elizur the son of Shedeur, prince of the children of Reuben, *did offer:*

31 His offering *was* one silver charger of the weight of an hundred and thirty *shekels,* one silver bowl of seventy shekels, after the shekel of the sanctuary; both of them full of fine flour mingled with oil for a meat offering:

32 One golden spoon of ten *shekels,* full of incense:

33 One young bullock, one ram, one lamb of the first year, for a burnt offering:

34 One kid of the goats for a sin offering:

35 And for a sacrifice of peace offerings, two oxen, five rams, five he goats, five lambs of the first year: this *was* the offering of Elizur the son of Shedeur.

36 On the fifth day [a]Shelumiel the son of Zurishaddai, prince of the children of Simeon, *did offer:*

37 His offering *was* one silver charger, the weight whereof *was* an hundred and thirty *shekels,* one silver bowl of seventy shekels, after the shekel of the sanctuary; both of them full of fine flour mingled with oil for a meat offering:

38 One golden spoon of ten *shekels,* full of incense:

39 One young bullock, one ram, one lamb of the first year, for a burnt offering:

40 One kid of the goats for a sin offering:

41 And for a sacrifice of peace offerings, two oxen, five rams, five he goats, five lambs of the

13 [a]Ex. 30:13 [b]Lev. 2:1
14 [a]Ex. 30:34
15 [a]Lev. 1:2 [b]Ex. 12:5
16 [a]Lev. 4:23
17 [a]Lev. 3:1
30 [a]Num. 1:5; 2:10
36 [a]Num. 1:6; 2:12; 7:41

NKJV

shekels, and one silver bowl of seventy shekels, according to [a]the shekel of the sanctuary, both of them full of fine flour mixed with oil as a [b]grain offering;

14 one gold pan of ten *shekels,* full of [a]incense;

15 [a]one young bull, one ram, and one male lamb [b]in its first year, as a burnt offering;

16 one kid of the goats as a [a]sin offering;

17 and for [a]the sacrifice of peace offerings: two oxen, five rams, five male goats, and five male lambs in their first year. This *was* the offering of Nahshon the son of Amminadab.

18 On the second day Nethanel the son of Zuar, leader of Issachar, presented *an offering.*

19 *For* his offering he offered one silver platter, the weight of which *was* one hundred and thirty *shekels,* and one silver bowl of seventy shekels, according to the shekel of the sanctuary, both of them full of fine flour mixed with oil as a grain offering;

20 one gold pan of ten *shekels,* full of incense;

21 one young bull, one ram, and one male lamb in its first year, as a burnt offering;

22 one kid of the goats as a sin offering;

23 and as the sacrifice of peace offerings: two oxen, five rams, five male goats, and five male lambs in their first year. This *was* the offering of Nethanel the son of Zuar.

24 On the third day Eliab the son of Helon, leader of the children of Zebulun, *presented an offering.*

25 His offering *was* one silver platter, the weight of which *was* one hundred and thirty *shekels,* and one silver bowl of seventy shekels, according to the shekel of the sanctuary, both of them full of fine flour mixed with oil as a grain offering;

26 one gold pan of ten *shekels,* full of incense;

27 one young bull, one ram, and one male lamb in its first year, as a burnt offering;

28 one kid of the goats as a sin offering;

29 and for the sacrifice of peace offerings: two oxen, five rams, five male goats, and five male lambs in their first year. This *was* the offering of Eliab the son of Helon.

30 On the fourth day [a]Elizur the son of Shedeur, leader of the children of Reuben, *presented an offering.*

31 His offering *was* one silver platter, the weight of which *was* one hundred and thirty *shekels,* and one silver bowl of seventy shekels, according to the shekel of the sanctuary, both of them full of fine flour mixed with oil as a grain offering;

32 one gold pan of ten *shekels,* full of incense;

33 one young bull, one ram, and one male lamb in its first year, as a burnt offering;

34 one kid of the goats as a sin offering;

35 and as the sacrifice of peace offerings: two oxen, five rams, five male goats, and five male lambs in their first year. This *was* the offering of Elizur the son of Shedeur.

36 On the fifth day [a]Shelumiel the son of Zurishaddai, leader of the children of Simeon, *presented an offering.*

37 His offering *was* one silver platter, the weight of which *was* one hundred and thirty *shekels,* and one silver bowl of seventy shekels, according to the shekel of the sanctuary, both of them full of fine flour mixed with oil as a grain offering;

38 one gold pan of ten *shekels,* full of incense;

39 one young bull, one ram, and one male lamb in its first year, as a burnt offering;

40 one kid of the goats as a sin offering;

41 and as the sacrifice of peace offerings: two oxen, five rams, five male goats, and five male

KJV

first year: this *was* the offering of Shelumiel the son of Zurishaddai.

42 On the sixth day [a]Eliasaph the son of Deuel, prince of the children of Gad, *offered:*

43 His offering *was* one silver charger of the weight of an hundred and thirty *shekels,* a silver bowl of seventy shekels, after the shekel of the sanctuary; both of them full of fine flour mingled with oil for a meat offering:

44 One golden spoon of ten *shekels,* full of incense:

45 One young bullock, one ram, one lamb of the first year, for [a]a burnt offering:

46 One kid of the goats for a sin offering:

47 And for a sacrifice of peace offerings, two oxen, five rams, five he goats, five lambs of the first year: this *was* the offering of Eliasaph the son of Deuel.

48 On the seventh day [a]Elishama the son of Ammihud, prince of the children of Ephraim, *offered:*

49 His offering *was* one silver charger, the weight whereof *was* an hundred and thirty *shekels,* one silver bowl of seventy shekels, after the shekel of the sanctuary; both of them full of fine flour mingled with oil for a meat offering:

50 One golden spoon of ten *shekels,* full of incense:

51 One young bullock, one ram, one lamb of the first year, for a burnt offering:

52 One kid of the goats for a sin offering:

53 And for a sacrifice of peace offerings, two oxen, five rams, five he goats, five lambs of the first year: this *was* the offering of Elishama the son of Ammihud.

54 On the eighth day *offered* [a]Gamaliel the son of Pedahzur, prince of the children of Manasseh:

55 His offering *was* one silver charger of the weight of an hundred and thirty *shekels,* one silver bowl of seventy shekels, after the shekel of the sanctuary; both of them full of fine flour mingled with oil for a meat offering:

56 One golden spoon of ten *shekels,* full of incense:

57 One young bullock, one ram, one lamb of the first year, for a burnt offering:

58 One kid of the goats for a sin offering:

59 And for a sacrifice of peace offerings, two oxen, five rams, five he goats, five lambs of the first year: this *was* the offering of Gamaliel the son of Pedahzur.

60 On the ninth day [a]Abidan the son of Gideoni, prince of the children of Benjamin, *offered:*

61 His offering *was* one silver charger, the weight whereof *was* an hundred and thirty *shekels,* one silver bowl of seventy shekels, after the shekel of the sanctuary; both of them full of fine flour mingled with oil for a meat offering:

62 One golden spoon of ten *shekels,* full of incense:

63 One young bullock, one ram, one lamb of the first year, for a burnt offering:

64 One kid of the goats for a sin offering:

65 And for a sacrifice of peace offerings, two oxen, five rams, five he goats, five lambs of the first year: this *was* the offering of Abidan the son of Gideoni.

66 On the tenth day [a]Ahiezer the son of Ammishaddai, prince of the children of Dan, *offered:*

67 His offering *was* one silver charger, the weight whereof *was* an hundred and thirty *shekels,* one silver bowl of seventy shekels, after the shekel of the sanctuary; both of them full

42 [a]Num. 1:14; 2:14; 10:20
45 [a]Ps. 40:6
48 [a]Num. 1:10; 2:18; 1 Chr. 7:26
54 [a]Num. 1:10; 2:20
60 [a]Num. 1:11; 2:22
66 [a]Num. 1:12; 2:25

NKJV

lambs in their first year. This *was* the offering of Shelumiel the son of Zurishaddai.

42 On the sixth day [a]Eliasaph the son of *Deuel, leader of the children of Gad, *presented an offering.*

43 His offering *was* one silver platter, the weight of which *was* one hundred and thirty *shekels,* and one silver bowl of seventy shekels, according to the shekel of the sanctuary, both of them full of fine flour mixed with oil as a grain offering;

44 one gold pan of ten *shekels,* full of incense;

45 one young bull, one ram, and one male lamb in its first year, as [a]a burnt offering;

46 one kid of the goats as a sin offering;

47 and as the sacrifice of peace offerings: two oxen, five rams, five male goats, and five male lambs in their first year. This *was* the offering of Eliasaph the son of Deuel.

48 On the seventh day [a]Elishama the son of Ammihud, leader of the children of Ephraim, *presented an offering.*

49 His offering *was* one silver platter, the weight of which *was* one hundred and thirty *shekels,* and one silver bowl of seventy shekels, according to the shekel of the sanctuary, both of them full of fine flour mixed with oil as a grain offering;

50 one gold pan of ten *shekels,* full of incense;

51 one young bull, one ram, and one male lamb in its first year, as a burnt offering;

52 one kid of the goats as a sin offering;

53 and as the sacrifice of peace offerings: two oxen, five rams, five male goats, and five male lambs in their first year. This *was* the offering of Elishama the son of Ammihud.

54 On the eighth day [a]Gamaliel the son of Pedahzur, leader of the children of Manasseh, *presented an offering.*

55 His offering *was* one silver platter, the weight of which *was* one hundred and thirty *shekels,* and one silver bowl of seventy shekels, according to the shekel of the sanctuary, both of them full of fine flour mixed with oil as a grain offering;

56 one gold pan of ten *shekels,* full of incense;

57 one young bull, one ram, and one male lamb in its first year, as a burnt offering;

58 one kid of the goats as a sin offering;

59 and as the sacrifice of peace offerings: two oxen, five rams, five male goats, and five male lambs in their first year. This *was* the offering of Gamaliel the son of Pedahzur.

60 On the ninth day [a]Abidan the son of Gideoni, leader of the children of Benjamin, *presented an offering.*

61 His offering *was* one silver platter, the weight of which *was* one hundred and thirty *shekels,* and one silver bowl of seventy shekels, according to the shekel of the sanctuary, both of them full of fine flour mixed with oil as a grain offering;

62 one gold pan of ten *shekels,* full of incense;

63 one young bull, one ram, and one male lamb in its first year, as a burnt offering;

64 one kid of the goats as a sin offering;

65 and as the sacrifice of peace offerings: two oxen, five rams, five male goats, and five male lambs in their first year. This *was* the offering of Abidan the son of Gideoni.

66 On the tenth day [a]Ahiezer the son of Ammishaddai, leader of the children of Dan, *presented an offering.*

67 His offering *was* one silver platter, the weight of which *was* one hundred and thirty *shekels,* and one silver bowl of seventy shekels, according to the shekel of the sanctuary, both of

*

7:42 *Reuel,* Num. 2:14

KJV

of fine flour mingled with oil for a meat offering:
68 One golden spoon of ten *shekels,* full of
incense:
69 One young bullock, one ram, one lamb of
the first year, for a burnt offering:
70 One kid of the goats for a sin offering:
71 And for a sacrifice of peace offerings, two
oxen, five rams, five he goats, five lambs of the
first year: this *was* the offering of Ahiezer the son
of Ammishaddai.
72 On the eleventh day [a]Pagiel the son of
Ocran, prince of the children of Asher, *offered:*
73 His offering *was* one silver charger, the
weight whereof *was* an hundred and thirty *shekels,* one silver bowl of seventy shekels, after the
shekel of the sanctuary; both of them full of fine
flour mingled with oil for a meat offering:
74 One golden spoon of ten *shekels,* full of
incense:
75 One young bullock, one ram, one lamb of
the first year, for a burnt offering:
76 One kid of the goats for a sin offering:
77 And for a sacrifice of peace offerings, two
oxen, five rams, five he goats, five lambs of the
first year: this *was* the offering of Pagiel the son
of Ocran.
78 On the twelfth day [a]Ahira the son of Enan,
prince of the children of Naphtali, *offered:*
79 His offering *was* one silver charger, the
weight whereof *was* an hundred and thirty *shekels,* one silver bowl of seventy shekels, after the
shekel of the sanctuary; both of them full of fine
flour mingled with oil for a meat offering:
80 One golden spoon of ten *shekels,* full of
incense:
81 One young bullock, one ram, one lamb of
the first year, for a burnt offering:
82 One kid of the goats for a sin offering:
83 And for a sacrifice of peace offerings, two
oxen, five rams, five he goats, five lambs of the
first year: this *was* the offering of Ahira the son
of Enan.
84 This *was* [a]the dedication of the altar, in
the day when it was anointed, by the princes of
Israel: twelve chargers of silver, twelve silver
bowls, twelve spoons of gold:
85 Each charger of silver *weighing* an hundred and thirty *shekels,* each bowl seventy: all
the silver vessels *weighed* two thousand and four
hundred *shekels,* after the shekel of the sanctuary:
86 The golden spoons *were* twelve, full of incense, *weighing* ten *shekels* apiece, after the
shekel of the sanctuary: all the gold of the spoons
was an hundred and twenty *shekels.*
87 All the oxen for the burnt offering *were*
twelve bullocks, the rams twelve, the lambs of the
first year twelve, with their meat offering: and the
kids of the goats for sin offering twelve.
88 And all the oxen for the sacrifice of the
peace offerings *were* twenty and four bullocks,
the rams sixty, the he goats sixty, the lambs of
the first year sixty. This *was* the dedication of the
altar, after that it was [a]anointed.
89 And when Moses was gone into the tabernacle of the congregation [a]to speak with him, then
he heard [b]the voice of one speaking unto him
from off the mercy seat that *was* upon the ark of
testimony, from [c]between the two cherubims: and
he spake unto him.

Arrangement of the Lamps
(Ex. 25:31–40)

8 And the LORD spake unto Moses, saying,
2 Speak unto Aaron, and say unto him,

72 [a]Num. 1:13; 2:27
78 [a]Num. 1:15; 2:29
84 [a]Num. 7:10
88 [a]Num. 7:1, 10
89 [a][Ex. 33:9, 11]; Num. 12:8 [b]Ex. 25:21, 22 [c]Ps. 80:1; 99:1

NKJV

them full of fine flour mixed with oil as a grain
offering;
68 one gold pan of ten *shekels,* full of
incense;
69 one young bull, one ram, and one male
lamb in its first year, as a burnt offering;
70 one kid of the goats as a sin offering;
71 and as the sacrifice of peace offerings: two
oxen, five rams, five male goats, and five male
lambs in their first year. This *was* the offering of
Ahiezer the son of Ammishaddai.
72 On the eleventh day [a]Pagiel the son of
Ocran, leader of the children of Asher, *presented
an offering.*
73 His offering *was* one silver platter, the
weight of which *was* one hundred and thirty *shekels,* and one silver bowl of seventy shekels, according to the shekel of the sanctuary, both of
them full of fine flour mixed with oil as a grain
offering;
74 one gold pan of ten *shekels,* full of
incense;
75 one young bull, one ram, and one male
lamb in its first year, as a burnt offering;
76 one kid of the goats as a sin offering;
77 and as the sacrifice of peace offerings: two
oxen, five rams, five male goats, and five male
lambs in their first year. This *was* the offering of
Pagiel the son of Ocran.
78 On the twelfth day [a]Ahira the son of Enan,
leader of the children of Naphtali, *presented an
offering.*
79 His offering *was* one silver platter, the
weight of which *was* one hundred and thirty *shekels,* and one silver bowl of seventy shekels, according to the shekel of the sanctuary, both of
them full of fine flour mixed with oil as a grain
offering;
80 one gold pan of ten *shekels,* full of incense;
81 one young bull, one ram, and one male
lamb in its first year, as a burnt offering;
82 one kid of the goats as a sin offering;
83 and as the sacrifice of peace offerings: two
oxen, five rams, five male goats, and five male
lambs in their first year. This *was* the offering of
Ahira the son of Enan.
84 This *was* [a]the dedication *offering* for the
altar from the leaders of Israel, when it was
anointed: twelve silver platters, twelve silver
bowls, and twelve gold pans.
85 Each silver platter *weighed* one hundred
and thirty *shekels* and each bowl seventy *shekels.*
All the silver of the vessels *weighed* two thousand
four hundred *shekels,* according to the shekel of
the sanctuary.
86 The twelve gold pans full of incense
weighed ten *shekels* apiece, according to the
shekel of the sanctuary; all the gold of the pans
weighed one hundred and twenty *shekels.*
87 All the oxen for the burnt offering *were*
twelve young bulls, the rams twelve, the male
lambs in their first year twelve, with their grain
offering, and the kids of the goats as a sin offering
twelve.
88 And all the oxen for the sacrifice of peace
offerings were twenty-four bulls, the rams sixty,
the male goats sixty, and the lambs in their first
year sixty. This *was* the dedication *offering* for
the altar after it was [a]anointed.
89 Now when Moses went into the tabernacle
of meeting [a]to speak with Him, he heard [b]the
voice of One speaking to him from above the
mercy seat that *was* on the ark of the Testimony,
from [c]between the two cherubim; thus He spoke
to him.

Arrangement of the Lamps
(Ex. 25:31–40)

8 And the LORD spoke to Moses, saying:
2 "Speak to Aaron, and say to him, 'When

KJV

When thou [a]lightest the lamps, the seven [b]lamps
shall give light over against the candlestick.
3 And Aaron did so; he lighted the lamps
thereof over against the candlestick, as the LORD
commanded Moses.
4 [a]And this work of the candlestick *was of*
beaten gold, unto the shaft thereof, unto the flowers thereof, *was* [b]beaten work: [c]according unto
the pattern which the LORD had shewed Moses,
so he made the candlestick.

Cleansing and Dedication of the Levites

5 And the LORD spake unto Moses, saying,
6 Take the Levites from among the children
of Israel, and cleanse them.
7 And thus shalt thou do unto them, to
cleanse them: Sprinkle [a]water of purifying upon
them, and [b]let them shave all their flesh, and let
them wash their clothes, and *so* make themselves
clean.
8 Then let them take a young bullock with
[a]his meat offering, *even* fine flour mingled with
oil, and another young bullock shalt thou take for
a sin offering.
9 [a]And thou shalt bring the Levites before
the tabernacle of the congregation: [b]and thou
shalt gather the whole assembly of the children
of Israel together:
10 And thou shalt bring the Levites before
the LORD: and the children of Israel [a]shall put their
hands upon the Levites:
11 And Aaron shall offer the Levites before
the LORD *for* an [a]offering of the children of Israel,
that they may execute the service of the LORD.
12 [a]And the Levites shall lay their hands
upon the heads of the bullocks: and thou shalt
offer the one *for* a sin offering, and the other *for*
a burnt offering, unto the LORD, to make an atonement for the Levites.
13 And thou shalt set the Levites before
Aaron, and before his sons, and offer them *for*
an offering unto the LORD.
14 Thus shalt thou [a]separate the Levites from
among the children of Israel: and the Levites shall
be [b]mine.
15 And after that shall the Levites go in to
do the service of the tabernacle of the congregation: and thou shalt cleanse them, and [a]offer them
for an offering.
16 For they *are* [a]wholly given unto me from
among the children of Israel; [b]instead of such as
open every womb, *even instead of* the firstborn
of all the children of Israel, have I taken them
unto me.
17 [a]For all the firstborn of the children of Israel *are* mine, *both* man and beast: on the day
that I smote every firstborn in the land of Egypt
I sanctified them for myself.
18 And I have taken the Levites for all the
firstborn of the children of Israel.
19 And [a]I have given the Levites *as* a gift to
Aaron and to his sons from among the children
of Israel, to do the service of the children of Israel
in the tabernacle of the congregation, and to make
an atonement for the children of Israel: [b]that there
be no plague among the children of Israel, when
the children of Israel come nigh unto the
sanctuary.
20 And Moses, and Aaron, and all the congregation of the children of Israel, did to the Levites according unto all that the LORD commanded
Moses concerning the Levites, so did the children
of Israel unto them.
21 [a]And the Levites were purified, and they
washed their clothes; and Aaron offered them *as*
an offering before the LORD; and Aaron made an
atonement for them to cleanse them.
22 [a]And after that went the Levites in to do
their service in the tabernacle of the congregation
before Aaron, and before his sons: [b]as the LORD
had commanded Moses concerning the Levites,
so did they unto them.

CHAPTER 8
2 [a]Lev. 24:2–4 [b]Ex. 25:37; 40:25
4 [a]Ex. 25:31 [b]Ex. 25:18 [c]Ex. 25:40; Acts 7:44
7 [a]Num. 19:9, 13, 17, 20; Ps. 51:2, 7; [Heb. 9:13, 14] [b]Lev. 14:8, 9
8 [a]Lev. 2:1; Num. 15:8–10
9 [a]Ex. 29:4; 40:12 [b]Lev. 8:3
10 [a]Lev. 1:4
11 [a]Num. 18:6
12 [a]Ex. 29:10
14 [a]Num. 16:9 [b]Num. 3:12, 45; 16:9
15 [a]Num. 8:11, 13
16 [a]Num. 3:9 [b]Ex. 13:2; Num. 3:12, 45
17 [a]Ex. 12:2, 12, 13, 15; Num. 3:13; Luke 2:23
19 [a]Num. 3:9 [b]Num. 1:53; 16:46; 18:5; 2 Chr. 26:16
21 [a]Num. 8:7
22 [a]Num. 8:15 [b]Num. 8:5

NKJV

you [a]arrange the lamps, the seven [b]lamps shall
give light in front of the lampstand.' "
3 And Aaron did so; he arranged the lamps
to face toward the front of the lampstand, as the
LORD commanded Moses.
4 [a]Now this workmanship of the lampstand
was hammered gold; from its shaft to its flowers
it *was* [b]hammered work. [c]According to the pattern which the LORD had shown Moses, so he
made the lampstand.

Cleansing and Dedication of the Levites

5 Then the LORD spoke to Moses, saying:
6 "Take the Levites from among the children of Israel and cleanse them *ceremonially*.
7 "Thus you shall do to them to cleanse
them: Sprinkle [a]water of purification on them,
and [b]let them shave all their body, and let them
wash their clothes, and *so* make themselves clean.
8 "Then let them take a young bull with [a]its
grain offering of fine flour mixed with oil, and
you shall take another young bull as a sin offering.
9 [a]"And you shall bring the Levites before
the tabernacle of meeting, [b]and you shall gather
together the whole congregation of the children
of Israel.
10 "So you shall bring the Levites before the
LORD, and the children of Israel [a]shall lay their
hands on the Levites;
11 "and Aaron shall offer the Levites before
the LORD, *like* a [a]wave offering from the children
of Israel, that they may perform the work of the
LORD.
12 [a]"Then the Levites shall lay their hands
on the heads of the young bulls, and you shall
offer one as a sin offering and the other as a burnt
offering to the LORD, to make atonement for the
Levites.
13 "And you shall stand the Levites before
Aaron and his sons, and then offer them *like* a
wave offering to the LORD.
14 "Thus you shall [a]separate the Levites
from among the children of Israel, and the Levites
shall be [b]Mine.
15 "After that the Levites shall go in to service the tabernacle of meeting. So you shall
cleanse them and [a]offer them, *like* a wave
offering.
16 "For they *are* [a]wholly given to Me from
among the children of Israel; I have taken them
for Myself [b]instead of all who open the womb,
the firstborn of all the children of Israel.
17 [a]"For all the firstborn among the children
of Israel *are* Mine, *both* man and beast; on the
day that I struck all the firstborn in the land of
Egypt I sanctified them to Myself.
18 "I have taken the Levites instead of all
the firstborn of the children of Israel.
19 "And [a]I have given the Levites as a gift
to Aaron and his sons from among the children
of Israel, to do the work for the children of Israel
in the tabernacle of meeting, and to make atonement for the children of Israel, [b]that there be no
plague among the children of Israel when the children of Israel come near the sanctuary."
20 Thus Moses and Aaron and all the congregation of the children of Israel did to the Levites;
according to all that the LORD commanded Moses
concerning the Levites, so the children of Israel
did to them.
21 [a]And the Levites purified themselves and
washed their clothes; then Aaron presented them,
like a wave offering before the LORD, and Aaron
made atonement for them to cleanse them.
22 [a]After that the Levites went in to do their
work in the tabernacle of meeting before Aaron
and his sons; [b]as the LORD commanded Moses
concerning the Levites, so they did to them.

KJV

23 And the LORD spake unto Moses, saying,
24 This *is it* that *belongeth* unto the Levites:
[a]from twenty and five years old and upward they
shall go in to wait upon the service of the tabernacle of the congregation:
25 And from the age of fifty years they shall
cease waiting upon the service *thereof,* and shall
serve no more:
26 But shall minister with their brethren in
the tabernacle of the congregation, [a]to keep the
charge, and shall do no service. Thus shalt thou
do unto the Levites touching their charge.

The Second Passover
(Ex. 12:1–20)

9 And the LORD spake unto Moses in the wilderness of Sinai, in the first month of the second
year after they were come out of the land of Egypt,
saying,
2 Let the children of Israel also keep [a]the
passover at his appointed [b]season.
3 In the fourteenth day of this month, at
even, ye shall keep it in his appointed season: according to all the rites of it, and according to all
the ceremonies thereof, shall ye keep it.
4 And Moses spake unto the children of Israel, that they should keep the passover.
5 And [a]they kept the passover on the fourteenth day of the first month at even in the wilderness of Sinai: according to all that the LORD commanded Moses, so did the children of Israel.
6 And there were certain men, who were [a]de-
filed by the dead body of a man, that they could
not keep the passover on that day: [b]and they came
before Moses and before Aaron on that day:
7 And those men said unto him, We *are* defiled by the dead body of a man: wherefore are
we kept back, that we may not offer an offering
of the LORD in his appointed season among the
children of Israel?
8 And Moses said unto them, Stand still, and
[a]I will hear what the LORD will command concerning you.
9 And the LORD spake unto Moses, saying,
10 Speak unto the children of Israel, saying,
If any man of you or of your posterity shall be
unclean by reason of a dead body, or *be* in a journey afar off, yet he shall keep the passover unto
the LORD.
11 [a]The fourteenth day of the second month
at even they shall keep it, *and* [b]eat it with unleavened bread and bitter *herbs.*
12 [a]They shall leave none of it unto the morning, [b]nor break any bone of it: [c]according to all
the ordinances of the passover they shall keep it.
13 But the man that *is* clean, and is not in a
journey, and forbeareth to keep the passover,
even the same soul [a]shall be cut off from among
his people: because he [b]brought not the offering
of the LORD in his appointed season, that man
shall [c]bear his sin.
14 And if a stranger shall sojourn among
you, and will keep the passover unto the LORD;
according to the ordinance of the passover, and
according to the manner thereof, so shall he do:
[a]ye shall have one ordinance, both for the
stranger, and for him that was born in the land.

The Cloud and the Fire
(Ex. 13:21, 22; 40:34–38)

15 And [a]on the day that the tabernacle was
reared up the cloud [b]covered the tabernacle,
namely, the tent of the testimony: and [c]at even
there was upon the tabernacle as it were the appearance of fire, until the morning.
16 So it was alway: the cloud covered it *by
day,* and the appearance of fire by night.
17 And when the cloud [a]was taken up from
the tabernacle, then after that the children of Israel journeyed: and in the place where the cloud
abode, there the children of Israel pitched their
tents.

24 [a]Num. 4:3; 1 Chr. 23:3, 24, 27
26 [a]Num. 1:53

CHAPTER 9
2 [a]Ex. 12:1–16; Lev. 23:5; Num. 28:16; Deut. 16:1, 2 [b]2 Chr. 30:1–15; Luke 22:7; [1 Cor. 5:7, 8]
5 [a]Josh. 5:10
6 [a]Num. 5:2; 19:11–22; John 18:28 [b]Ex. 18:15, 19, 26; Num. 27:2
8 [a]Ex. 18:22; Num. 27:5
11 [a]2 Chr. 30:2, 15 [b]Ex. 12:8
12 [a]Ex. 12:10 [b]Ex. 12:46; [John 19:36] [c]Ex. 12:43
13 [a]Gen. 17:14; Ex. 12:15, 47 [b]Num. 9:7 [c]Num. 5:31
14 [a]Ex. 12:49; Lev. 24:22; Num. 15:15, 16, 29
15 [a]Ex. 40:33, 34; Neh. 9:12, 19; Ps. 78:14 [b]Is. 4:5 [c]Ex. 13:21, 22; 40:38
17 [a]Ex. 40:36–38; Num. 10:11, 12, 33, 34; Ps. 80:1

NKJV

23 Then the LORD spoke to Moses, saying,
24 "This *is* what *pertains* to the Levites:
[a]From twenty-five years old and above one may enter to perform service in the work of the tabernacle of meeting;
25 "and at the age of fifty years they must
cease performing this work, and shall work no
more.
26 "They may minister with their brethren
in the tabernacle of meeting, [a]to attend to needs,
but they *themselves* shall do no work. Thus you
shall do to the Levites regarding their duties."

The Second Passover
(Ex. 12:1–20)

9 Now the LORD spoke to Moses in the Wilderness of Sinai, in the first month of the second
year after they had come out of the land of Egypt,
saying:
2 "Let the children of Israel keep [a]the Passover at its appointed [b]time.
3 "On the fourteenth day of this month, at
twilight, you shall keep it at its appointed time.
According to all its rites and ceremonies you shall
keep it."
4 So Moses told the children of Israel that
they should keep the Passover.
5 And [a]they kept the Passover on the fourteenth day of the first month, at twilight, in the
Wilderness of Sinai; according to all that the LORD
commanded Moses, so the children of Israel did.
6 Now there were *certain* men who were
[a]defiled by a human corpse, so that they could
not keep the Passover on that day; [b]and they came
before Moses and Aaron that day.
7 And those men said to him, "We *became*
defiled by a human corpse. Why are we kept from
presenting the offering of the LORD at its appointed time among the children of Israel?"
8 And Moses said to them, "Stand still, that
[a]I may hear what the LORD will command concerning you."
9 Then the LORD spoke to Moses, saying,
10 "Speak to the children of Israel, saying:
'If anyone of you or your posterity is unclean because of a corpse, or *is* far away on a journey,
he may still keep the LORD's Passover.
11 'On [a]the fourteenth day of the second
month, at twilight, they may keep it. They shall
[b]eat it with unleavened bread and bitter herbs.
12 [a]'They shall leave none of it until morning,
[b]nor break one of its bones. [c]According to all the
ordinances of the Passover they shall keep it.
13 'But the man who *is* clean and is not on
a journey, and ceases to keep the Passover, that
same person [a]shall be cut off from among his people, because he [b]did not bring the offering of the
LORD at its appointed time; that man shall [c]bear
his sin.
14 'And if a stranger dwells among you, and
would keep the LORD's Passover, he must do so
according to the rite of the Passover and according to its ceremony; [a]you shall have one ordinance, both for the stranger and the native of the
land.' "

The Cloud and the Fire
(Ex. 13:21, 22; 40:34–38)

15 Now [a]on the day that the tabernacle was
raised up, the cloud [b]covered the tabernacle, the
tent of the Testimony; [c]from evening until morning it was above the tabernacle like the appearance of fire.
16 So it was always: the cloud covered it *by
day,* and the appearance of fire by night.
17 Whenever the cloud [a]was taken up from
above the tabernacle, after that the children of
Israel would journey; and in the place where the
cloud settled, there the children of Israel would
pitch their tents.

KJV

18 At the commandment of the LORD the children of Israel journeyed, and at the commandment of the LORD they pitched: [a]as long as the cloud abode upon the tabernacle they rested in their tents.

19 And when the cloud tarried long upon the tabernacle many days, then the children of Israel [a]kept the charge of the LORD, and journeyed not.

20 And *so* it was, when the cloud was a few days upon the tabernacle; according to the commandment of the LORD they abode in their tents, and according to the commandment of the LORD they journeyed.

21 And *so* it was, when the cloud abode from even unto the morning, and *that* the cloud was taken up in the morning, then they journeyed: whether *it was* by day or by night that the cloud was taken up, they journeyed.

22 Or *whether it were* two days, or a month, or a year, that the cloud tarried upon the tabernacle, remaining thereon, the children of Israel [a]abode in their tents, and journeyed not: but when it was taken up, they journeyed.

23 At the commandment of the LORD they rested in the tents, and at the commandment of the LORD they journeyed: they [a]kept the charge of the LORD, at the commandment of the LORD by the hand of Moses.

Two Silver Trumpets

10 And the LORD spake unto Moses, saying,
2 Make thee two trumpets of silver; of a whole piece shalt thou make them: that thou mayest use them for the [a]calling of the assembly, and for the journeying of the camps.

3 And when [a]they shall blow with them, all the assembly shall assemble themselves to thee at the door of the tabernacle of the congregation.

4 And if they blow *but* with one *trumpet,* then the princes, *which are* [a]heads of the thousands of Israel, shall gather themselves unto thee.

5 When ye blow an [a]alarm, then [b]the camps that lie on the east parts shall go forward.

6 When ye blow an alarm the second time, then the camps that lie [a]on the south side shall take their journey: they shall blow an alarm for their journeys.

7 But when the congregation is to be gathered together, [a]ye shall blow, but ye shall not [b]sound an alarm.

8 [a]And the sons of Aaron, the priests, shall blow with the trumpets; and they shall be to you for an ordinance for ever throughout your generations.

9 And [a]if ye go to war in your land against the enemy that [b]oppresseth you, then ye shall blow an alarm with the trumpets; and ye shall be [c]remembered before the LORD your God, and ye shall be saved from your enemies.

10 Also [a]in the day of your gladness, and in your solemn days, and in the beginnings of your months, ye shall blow with the trumpets over your burnt offerings, and over the sacrifices of your peace offerings; that they may be to you [b]for a memorial before your God: I *am* the LORD your God.

Departure from Sinai

11 And it came to pass on the twentieth *day* of the second month, in the second year, that the cloud [a]was taken up from off the tabernacle of the testimony.

12 And the children of Israel took [b]their journeys out of the [a]wilderness of Sinai; and the cloud rested in the [c]wilderness of Paran.

13 And they first took their journey [a]according to the commandment of the LORD by the hand of Moses.

14 [a]In the first *place* went the standard of the camp of the children of Judah according to

18 [a]1 Cor. 10:1
19 [a]Num. 1:53; 3:8
22 [a]Ex. 40:36, 37
23 [a]Num. 9:19

CHAPTER 10
2 [a]Is. 1:13
3 [a]Jer. 4:5; Joel 2:15
4 [a]Ex. 18:21; Num. 1:16; 7:2
5 [a]Joel 2:1 [b]Num. 2:3
6 [a]Num. 2:10
7 [a]Num. 10:3 [b]Joel 2:1
8 [a]Num. 31:6; Josh. 6:4; 1 Chr. 15:24; 2 Chr. 13:12
9 [a]Num. 31:6; Josh. 6:5; 2 Chr. 13:14 [b]Judg. 2:18; 4:3; 6:9; 10:8, 12 [c]Gen. 8:1; Ps. 106:4
10 [a]Lev. 23:24; Num. 29:1; 1 Chr. 15:24; 2 Chr. 5:12; Ps. 81:3 [b]Lev. 23:24; Num. 10:9
11 [a]Num. 9:17
12 [a]Ex. 19:1; Num. 1:1; 9:5 [b]Ex. 40:36 [c]Gen. 21:21; Num. 12:16; Deut. 1:1
13 [a]Num. 10:5, 6
14 [a]Num. 2:3–9

NKJV

18 At the command of the LORD the children of Israel would journey, and at the command of the LORD they would camp; [a]as long as the cloud stayed above the tabernacle they remained encamped.

19 Even when the cloud continued long, many days above the tabernacle, the children of Israel [a]kept the charge of the LORD and did not journey.

20 So it was, when the cloud was above the tabernacle a few days: according to the command of the LORD they would remain encamped, and according to the command of the LORD they would journey.

21 So it was, when the cloud remained only from evening until morning: when the cloud was taken up in the morning, then they would journey; whether by day or by night, whenever the cloud was taken up, they would journey.

22 *Whether it was* two days, a month, or a year that the cloud remained above the tabernacle, the children of Israel [a]would remain encamped and not journey; but when it was taken up, they would journey.

23 At the command of the LORD they remained encamped, and at the command of the LORD they journeyed; they [a]kept the charge of the LORD, at the command of the LORD by the hand of Moses.

Two Silver Trumpets

10 And the LORD spoke to Moses, saying:
2 "Make two silver trumpets for yourself; you shall make them of hammered work; you shall use them for [a]calling the congregation and for directing the movement of the camps.

3 "When [a]they blow both of them, all the congregation shall gather before you at the door of the tabernacle of meeting.

4 "But if they blow *only* one, then the leaders, the [a]heads of the divisions of Israel, shall gather to you.

5 "When you sound the [a]advance, [b]the camps that lie on the east side shall then begin their journey.

6 "When you sound the advance the second time, then the camps that lie [a]on the south side shall begin their journey; they shall sound the call for them to begin their journeys.

7 "And when the assembly is to be gathered together, [a]you shall blow, but not [b]sound the advance.

8 [a]"The sons of Aaron, the priests, shall blow the trumpets; and these shall be to you as an ordinance forever throughout your generations.

9 [a]"When you go to war in your land against the enemy who [b]oppresses you, then you shall sound an alarm with the trumpets, and you will be [c]remembered before the LORD your God, and you will be saved from your enemies.

10 "Also [a]in the day of your gladness, in your appointed feasts, and at the beginning of your months, you shall blow the trumpets over your burnt offerings and over the sacrifices of your peace offerings; and they shall be [b]a memorial for you before your God: I *am* the LORD your God."

Departure from Sinai

11 Now it came to pass on the twentieth *day* of the second month, in the second year, that the cloud [a]was taken up from above the tabernacle of the Testimony.

12 And the children of Israel set out from the [a]Wilderness of Sinai on [b]their journeys; then the cloud settled down in the [c]Wilderness of Paran.

13 So they started out for the first time [a]according to the command of the LORD by the hand of Moses.

14 The standard of the camp of the children of Judah [a]set out first according to their armies;

KJV

their armies: and over his host *was* [b]Nahshon the son of Amminadab.

15 And over the host of the tribe of the children of Issachar *was* Nethaneel the son of Zuar.

16 And over the host of the tribe of the children of Zebulun *was* Eliab the son of Helon.

17 And [a]the tabernacle was taken down; and the sons of Gershon and the sons of Merari set forward, [b]bearing the tabernacle.

18 And [a]the standard of the camp of Reuben set forward according to their armies: and over his host *was* Elizur the son of Shedeur.

19 And over the host of the tribe of the children of Simeon *was* Shelumiel the son of Zurishaddai.

20 And over the host of the tribe of the children of Gad *was* Eliasaph the son of Deuel.

21 And the Kohathites set forward, bearing the [a]sanctuary: and *the other* did set up the tabernacle against they came.

22 And [a]the standard of the camp of the children of Ephraim set forward according to their armies: and over his host *was* Elishama the son of Ammihud.

23 And over the host of the tribe of the children of Manasseh *was* Gamaliel the son of Pedahzur.

24 And over the host of the tribe of the children of Benjamin *was* Abidan the son of Gideoni.

25 And [a]the standard of the camp of the children of Dan set forward, *which was* the rereward of all the camps throughout their hosts: and over his host *was* Ahiezer the son of Ammishaddai.

26 And over the host of the tribe of the children of Asher *was* Pagiel the son of Ocran.

27 And over the host of the tribe of the children of Naphtali *was* Ahira the son of Enan.

28 [a]Thus *were* the journeyings of the children of Israel according to their armies, when they set forward.

29 And Moses said unto [a]Hobab, the son of [b]Raguel the Midianite, Moses' father in law, We are journeying unto the place of which the LORD said, [c]I will give it you: come thou with us, and [d]we will do thee good: for [e]the LORD hath spoken good concerning Israel.

30 And he said unto him, I will not go; but I will depart to mine own land, and to my kindred.

31 And he said, Leave us not, I pray thee; forasmuch as thou knowest how we are to encamp in the wilderness, and thou mayest be to us [a]instead of eyes.

32 And it shall be, if thou go with us, yea, it shall be, that [a]what goodness the LORD shall do unto us, the same will we do unto thee.

33 And they departed from [a]the mount of the LORD three days' journey: and the ark of the covenant of the LORD [b]went before them in the three days' journey, to search out a resting place for them.

34 And [a]the cloud of the LORD *was* upon them by day, when they went out of the camp.

35 And it came to pass, when the ark set forward, that Moses said, [a]Rise up, LORD, and let thine enemies be scattered; and let them that hate thee flee before thee.

36 And when it rested, he said, Return, O LORD, unto the many thousands of Israel.

The People Complain

11 And [a]*when* the people complained, it displeased the LORD: and the LORD heard *it;* [b]and his anger was kindled; and the [c]fire of the LORD burnt among them, and consumed *them that were* in the uttermost parts of the camp.

2 And the people [a]cried unto Moses; and when Moses [b]prayed unto the LORD, the fire was quenched.

3 And he called the name of the place Tab-

---

14 [b]Num. 1:7
17 [a]Num. 1:51 [b]Num. 4:21–32; 7:7–9
18 [a]Num. 2:10–16
21 [a]Num. 4:4–20; 7:9
22 [a]Num. 2:18–24
25 [a]Num. 2:25–31; Josh. 6:9
28 [a]Num. 2:34
29 [a]Judg. 4:11 [b]Ex. 2:18; 3:1; 18:12 [c]Gen. 12:7; Ex. 6:4–8 [d]Judg. 1:16 [e]Gen. 32:12; Ex. 3:8
31 [a]Job 29:15
32 [a]Ex. 18:9; Lev. 19:34; Judg. 1:16
33 [a]Ex. 3:1; Deut. 1:6 [b]Deut. 1:33; Josh. 3:3–6; Ezek. 20:6
34 [a]Ex. 13:21; Neh. 9:12, 19
35 [a]Ps. 68:1, 2; 132:8; Is. 17:12–14

CHAPTER 11

1 [a]Num. 14:2; 16:11; 17:5; Deut. 9:22 [b]Ps. 78:21 [c]Lev. 10:2; 2 Kin. 1:12
2 [a]Num. 12:11, 13; 21:7 [b][James 5:16]

*

10:29 *Jethro,* Ex. 3:1; LXX *Raguel*
11:3 Lit. *Burning*

NKJV

over their army was [b]Nahshon the son of Amminadab.

15 Over the army of the tribe of the children of Issachar *was* Nethanel the son of Zuar.

16 And over the army of the tribe of the children of Zebulun *was* Eliab the son of Helon.

17 Then [a]the tabernacle was taken down; and the sons of Gershon and the sons of Merari set out, [b]carrying the tabernacle.

18 And [a]the standard of the camp of Reuben set out according to their armies; over their army *was* Elizur the son of Shedeur.

19 Over the army of the tribe of the children of Simeon *was* Shelumiel the son of Zurishaddai.

20 And over the army of the tribe of the children of Gad *was* Eliasaph the son of Deuel.

21 Then the Kohathites set out, carrying the [a]holy things. (The tabernacle would be prepared for their arrival.)

22 And [a]the standard of the camp of the children of Ephraim set out according to their armies; over their army *was* Elishama the son of Ammihud.

23 Over the army of the tribe of the children of Manasseh *was* Gamaliel the son of Pedahzur.

24 And over the army of the tribe of the children of Benjamin *was* Abidan the son of Gideoni.

25 Then [a]the standard of the camp of the children of Dan (the rear guard of all the camps) set out according to their armies; over their army *was* Ahiezer the son of Ammishaddai.

26 Over the army of the tribe of the children of Asher *was* Pagiel the son of Ocran.

27 And over the army of the tribe of the children of Naphtali *was* Ahira the son of Enan.

28 [a]Thus *was* the order of march of the children of Israel, according to their armies, when they began their journey.

29 Now Moses said to [a]Hobab the son of [b]*Reuel the Midianite, Moses' father-in-law, "We are setting out for the place of which the LORD said, [c]'I will give it to you.' Come with us, and [d]we will treat you well; for [e]the LORD has promised good things to Israel."

30 And he said to him, "I will not go, but I will depart to my *own* land and to my relatives."

31 So *Moses* said, "Please do not leave, inasmuch as you know how we are to camp in the wilderness, and you can be our [a]eyes.

32 "And it shall be, if you go with us—indeed it shall be—that [a]whatever good the LORD will do to us, the same we will do to you."

33 So they departed from [a]the mountain of the LORD on a journey of three days; and the ark of the covenant of the LORD [b]went before them for the three days' journey, to search out a resting place for them.

34 And [a]the cloud of the LORD *was* above them by day when they went out from the camp.

35 So it was, whenever the ark set out, that Moses said:

[a]"Rise up, O LORD!
Let Your enemies be scattered,
And let those who hate You flee before You."

36 And when it rested, he said:

"Return, O LORD,
To the many thousands of Israel."

The People Complain

11 Now [a]*when* the people complained, it displeased the LORD; [b]for the LORD heard *it,* and His anger was aroused. So the [c]fire of the LORD burned among them, and consumed *some* in the outskirts of the camp.

2 Then the people [a]cried out to Moses, and when Moses [b]prayed to the LORD, the fire was quenched.

3 So he called the name of the place *Tab-

KJV

erah: because the fire of the LORD burnt among them.

4 And the [a]mixt multitude that *was* among them fell a [b]lusting: and the children of Israel also wept again, and said, [c]Who shall give us flesh to eat?

5 [a]We remember the fish, which we did eat in Egypt freely; the cucumbers, and the melons, and the leeks, and the onions, and the garlick:

6 But now [a]our soul *is* dried away: *there is* nothing at all, beside this manna, *before* our eyes.

7 And [a]the manna *was* as coriander seed, and the colour thereof as the colour of bdellium.

8 *And* the people went about, and gathered *it*, and ground *it* in mills, or beat *it* in a mortar, and baked *it* in pans, and made cakes of it: and [a]the taste of it was as the taste of fresh oil.

9 And [a]when the dew fell upon the camp in the night, the manna fell upon it.

10 Then Moses heard the people weep throughout their families, every man in the door of his tent: and [a]the anger of the LORD was kindled greatly; Moses also was displeased.

11 [a]And Moses said unto the LORD, Wherefore hast thou afflicted thy servant? and wherefore have I not found favour in thy sight, that thou layest the burden of all this people upon me?

12 Have I conceived all this people? have I begotten them, that thou shouldest say unto me, [a]Carry them in thy bosom, as a [b]nursing father beareth the sucking child, unto the land which thou [c]swarest unto their fathers?

13 [a]Whence should I have flesh to give unto all this people? for they weep unto me, saying, Give us flesh, that we may eat.

14 [a]I am not able to bear all this people alone, because *it is* too heavy for me.

15 And if thou deal thus with me, kill me, I pray thee, out of hand, if I have found favour in thy sight; and let me not [a]see my wretchedness.

The Seventy Elders

16 And the LORD said unto Moses, Gather unto me [a]seventy men of the elders of Israel, whom thou knowest to be the elders of the people, and [b]officers over them; and bring them unto the tabernacle of the congregation, that they may stand there with thee.

17 And I will come down and talk with thee there: and [a]I will take of the spirit which *is* upon thee, and will put *it* upon them; and they shall bear the burden of the people with thee, that thou bear *it* not thyself alone.

18 And say thou unto the people, Sanctify yourselves against to morrow, and ye shall eat flesh: for ye have wept [a]in the ears of the LORD, saying, Who shall give us flesh to eat? for *it was* well with us in Egypt: therefore the LORD will give you flesh, and ye shall eat.

19 Ye shall not eat one day, nor two days, nor five days, neither ten days, nor twenty days;

20 [a]*But* even a whole month, until it come out at your nostrils, and it be loathsome unto you: because that ye have [b]despised the LORD which *is* among you, and have wept before him, saying, [c]Why came we forth out of Egypt?

21 And Moses said, [a]The people, among whom I *am, are* six hundred thousand footmen; and thou hast said, I will give them flesh, that they may eat a whole month.

22 [a]Shall the flocks and the herds be slain for them, to suffice them? or shall all the fish of the sea be gathered together for them, to suffice them?

23 And the LORD said unto Moses, [a]Is the LORD's hand waxed short? thou shalt see now whether my [b]word shall come to pass unto thee or not.

24 And Moses went out, and told the people the words of the LORD, and [a]gathered the seventy men of the elders of the people, and set them round about the tabernacle.

4 [a]Ex. 12:38 [b]1 Cor. 10:6 [c][Ps. 78:18]
5 [a]Ex. 16:3
6 [a]Num. 21:5
7 [a]Ex. 16:14, 31
8 [a]Ex. 16:31
9 [a]Ex. 16:13, 14
10 [a]Ps. 78:21
11 [a]Ex. 5:22; Deut. 1:12
12 [a]Is. 40:11 [b]Is. 49:23; 1 Thess. 2:7 [c]Gen. 26:3
13 [a]Matt. 15:33; Mark 8:4
14 [a]Ex. 18:18; Deut. 1:12
15 [a]Rev. 3:17
16 [a]Ex. 18:25; 24:1, 9 [b]Deut. 16:18
17 [a]1 Sam. 10:6; 2 Kin. 2:15; [Joel 2:28]
18 [a]Ex. 16:7
20 [a]Ps. 78:29; 106:15 [b]1 Sam. 10:19 [c]Num. 21:5
21 [a]Gen. 12:2; Ex. 12:37; Num. 1:46; 2:32
22 [a]2 Kin. 7:2
23 [a]Is. 50:2; 59:1 [b]Num. 23:19
24 [a]Num. 11:16

NKJV

erah, because the fire of the LORD had burned among them.

4 Now the [a]mixed multitude who were among them yielded to [b]intense craving; so the children of Israel also wept again and said: [c]"Who will give us meat to eat?

5 [a]"We remember the fish which we ate freely in Egypt, the cucumbers, the melons, the leeks, the onions, and the garlic;

6 "but now [a]our whole being *is* dried up; *there is* nothing at all except this manna *before* our eyes!"

7 Now [a]the manna *was* like coriander seed, and its color like the color of bdellium.

8 The people went about and gathered *it*, ground *it* on millstones or beat *it* in the mortar, cooked *it* in pans, and made cakes of it; and [a]its taste was like the taste of pastry prepared with oil.

9 And [a]when the dew fell on the camp in the night, the manna fell on it.

10 Then Moses heard the people weeping throughout their families, everyone at the door of his tent; and [a]the anger of the LORD was greatly aroused; Moses also was displeased.

11 [a]So Moses said to the LORD, "Why have You afflicted Your servant? And why have I not found favor in Your sight, that You have laid the burden of all these people on me?

12 "Did I conceive all these people? Did I beget them, that You should say to me, [a]'Carry them in your bosom, as a [b]guardian carries a nursing child,' to the land which You [c]swore to their fathers?

13 [a]"Where am I to get meat to give to all these people? For they weep all over me, saying, 'Give us meat, that we may eat.'

14 [a]"I am not able to bear all these people alone, because the burden *is* too heavy for me.

15 "If You treat me like this, please kill me here and now—if I have found favor in Your sight—and [a]do not let me see my wretchedness!"

The Seventy Elders

16 So the LORD said to Moses: "Gather to Me [a]seventy men of the elders of Israel, whom you know to be the elders of the people and [b]officers over them; bring them to the tabernacle of meeting, that they may stand there with you.

17 "Then I will come down and talk with you there. [a]I will take of the Spirit that *is* upon you and will put *the same* upon them; and they shall bear the burden of the people with you, that you may not bear *it* yourself alone.

18 "Then you shall say to the people, 'Consecrate yourselves for tomorrow, and you shall eat meat; for you have wept [a]in the hearing of the LORD, saying, "Who will give us meat to eat? For *it was* well with us in Egypt." Therefore the LORD will give you meat, and you shall eat.

19 'You shall eat, not one day, nor two days, nor five days, nor ten days, nor twenty days,

20 [a]'but *for* a whole month, until it comes out of your nostrils and becomes loathsome to you, because you have [b]despised the LORD who is among you, and have wept before Him, saying, [c]"Why did we ever come up out of Egypt?" ' "

21 And Moses said, [a]"The people whom I *am* among *are* six hundred thousand men on foot; yet You have said, 'I will give them meat, that they may eat *for* a whole month.'

22 [a]"Shall flocks and herds be slaughtered for them, to provide enough for them? Or shall all the fish of the sea be gathered together for them, to provide enough for them?"

23 And the LORD said to Moses, [a]"Has the LORD's arm been shortened? Now you shall see whether [b]what I say will happen to you or not."

24 So Moses went out and told the people the words of the LORD, and he [a]gathered the seventy men of the elders of the people and placed them around the tabernacle.

KJV

25 And the LORD came down in a cloud, and
spake unto him, and took of the spirit that *was*
upon him, and gave *it* unto the seventy elders:
and it came to pass, *that,* [a]when the spirit rested
upon them, [b]they prophesied, and did not cease.
26 But there remained two *of the* men in the
camp, the name of the one *was* Eldad, and the
name of the other Medad: and the spirit rested
upon them; and they *were* of them that were written, but [a]went not out unto the tabernacle: and
they prophesied in the camp.
27 And there ran a young man, and told Moses, and said, Eldad and Medad do prophesy in
the camp.
28 And Joshua the son of Nun, the servant
of Moses, *one* of his young men, answered and
said, My lord Moses, [a]forbid them.
29 And Moses said unto him, Enviest thou
for my sake? [a]would God that all the LORD's people were prophets, *and* that the LORD would put
his spirit upon them!
30 And Moses gat him into the camp, he and
the elders of Israel.

The LORD Sends Quail

31 And there went forth a [a]wind from the
LORD, and brought quails from the sea, and let
them fall by the camp, as it were a day's journey
on this side, and as it were a day's journey on
the other side, round about the camp, and as it
were two cubits *high* upon the face of the earth.
32 And the people stood up all that day, and
all *that* night, and all the next day, and they gathered the quails: he that gathered least gathered
ten [a]homers: and they spread *them* all abroad for
themselves round about the camp.
33 And while the [a]flesh *was* yet between
their teeth, ere it was chewed, the wrath of the
LORD was kindled against the people, and the
LORD smote the people with a very great plague.
34 And he called the name of that place
Kibroth–hattaavah: because there they buried the
people that lusted.
35 [a]*And* the people journeyed from Kibroth–
hattaavah unto Hazeroth; and abode at Hazeroth.

Dissension of Aaron and Miriam

12 And [a]Miriam and Aaron spake [b]against
Moses because of the Ethiopian woman
whom he had married: for [c]he had married an
Ethiopian woman.
2 And they said, Hath the LORD indeed spoken only by [a]Moses? [b]hath he not spoken also
by us? And the LORD [c]heard *it.*
3 (Now the man Moses *was* very meek,
above all the men which *were* upon the face of
the earth.)
4 [a]And the LORD spake suddenly unto Moses, and unto Aaron, and unto Miriam, Come out
ye three unto the tabernacle of the congregation.
And they three came out.
5 [a]And the LORD came down in the pillar
of the cloud, and stood *in* the door of the tabernacle, and called Aaron and Miriam: and they both
came forth.
6 And he said, Hear now my words: If there
be a prophet among you, *I* the LORD will make
myself known unto him [a]in a vision, *and* will
speak unto him [b]in a dream.
7 [a]My servant Moses *is* not so, [b]who *is* faithful in all [c]mine house.
8 With him will I speak [a]mouth to mouth,
even [b]apparently, and not in dark speeches; and
[c]the similitude of the LORD shall he behold: wherefore then [d]were ye not afraid to speak against
my servant Moses?
9 And the anger of the LORD was kindled
against them; and he departed.

25 [a]2 Kin. 2:15 [b]1 Sam. 10:5, 6, 10; Joel 2:28; Acts 2:17, 18; 1 Cor. 14:1
26 [a]Jer. 36:5
28 [a][Mark 9:38–40; Luke 9:49]
29 [a]1 Cor. 14:5
31 [a]Ex. 16:13; Ps. 78:26–28; 105:40
32 [a]Ex. 16:36; Ezek. 45:11
33 [a]Ps. 78:29–31; 106:15
35 [a]Num. 33:17

CHAPTER 12

1 [a]Ex. 15:20, 21; Num. 20:1 [b]Num. 11:1 [c]Ex. 2:21
2 [a]Num. 16:3 [b]Ex. 15:20; Mic. 6:4 [c]Gen. 29:33; Num. 11:1; 2 Kin. 19:4; Is. 37:4; Ezek. 35:12, 13
4 [a][Ps. 76:9]
5 [a]Ex. 19:9; 34:5; Num. 11:25; 16:19
6 [a]Gen. 46:2; 1 Sam. 3:15; Job 33:15; Ezek. 1:1; Dan. 8:2; Luke 1:11; Acts 10:11, 17; 22:17, 18 [b]Gen. 31:10; 1 Kin. 3:5, 15; Matt. 1:20
7 [a]Josh. 1:1; Ps. 105:26 [b]Heb. 3:2, 5 [c]1 Tim. 1:12
8 [a]Ex. 33:11; Deut. 34:10; Hos. 12:13 [b][1 Cor. 13:12] [c]Ex. 33:19–23 [d]2 Pet. 2:10; Jude 8

*

11:25 Tg., Vg. *and they did not cease*
11:34 Lit. *Graves of Craving*

NKJV

25 Then the LORD came down in the cloud,
and spoke to him, and took of the Spirit that *was*
upon him, and placed *the same* upon the seventy
elders; and it happened, [a]when the Spirit rested
upon them, that [b]they prophesied, *although they
never did *so* again.
26 But two men had remained in the camp:
the name of one *was* Eldad, and the name of the
other Medad. And the Spirit rested upon them.
Now they *were* among those listed, but who [a]had
not gone out to the tabernacle; yet they prophesied in the camp.
27 And a young man ran and told Moses, and
said, "Eldad and Medad are prophesying in the
camp."
28 So Joshua the son of Nun, Moses' assistant, *one* of his choice men, answered and said,
"Moses my lord, [a]forbid them!"
29 Then Moses said to him, "Are you zealous
for my sake? [a]Oh, that all the LORD's people were
prophets *and* that the LORD would put His Spirit
upon them!"
30 And Moses returned to the camp, *both* he
and the elders of Israel.

The LORD Sends Quail

31 Now a [a]wind went out from the LORD, and
it brought quail from the sea and left *them* flutter-
ing near the camp, about a day's journey on this
side and about a day's journey on the other side,
all around the camp, and about two cubits above
the surface of the ground.
32 And the people stayed up all that day, all
night, and all the next day, and gathered the quail
(he who gathered least gathered ten [a]homers);
and they spread *them* out for themselves all
around the camp.
33 But while the [a]meat *was* still between
their teeth, before it was chewed, the wrath of
the LORD was aroused against the people, and the
LORD struck the people with a very great plague.
34 So he called the name of that place *Kibroth Hattaavah, because there they buried the
people who had yielded to craving.
35 [a]From Kibroth Hattaavah the people
moved to Hazeroth, and camped at Hazeroth.

Dissension of Aaron and Miriam

12 Then [a]Miriam and Aaron spoke [b]against
Moses because of the Ethiopian woman
whom he had married; for [c]he had married an
Ethiopian woman.
2 So they said, "Has the LORD indeed spoken only through [a]Moses? [b]Has He not spoken
through us also?" And the LORD [c]heard *it.*
3 (Now the man Moses *was* very humble,
more than all men who *were* on the face of the
earth.)
4 [a]Suddenly the LORD said to Moses, Aaron,
and Miriam, "Come out, you three, to the tabernacle of meeting!" So the three came out.
5 [a]Then the LORD came down in the pillar
of cloud and stood *in* the door of the tabernacle,
and called Aaron and Miriam. And they both went
forward.
6 Then He said,

"Hear now My words:
If there is a prophet among you,
I, the LORD, make Myself known to him
[a]in a vision;
I speak to him [b]in a dream.
7 Not so with [a]My servant Moses;
[b]He *is* faithful in all [c]My house.
8 I speak with him [a]face to face,
Even [b]plainly, and not in dark sayings;
And he sees [c]the form of the LORD.
Why then [d]were you not afraid
To speak against My servant Moses?"

9 So the anger of the LORD was aroused
against them, and He departed.

KJV

10 And the cloud departed from off the tabernacle; and, [a]behold, Miriam *became* [b]leprous, *white* as snow: and Aaron looked upon Miriam, and, behold, *she was* leprous.

11 And Aaron said unto Moses, Alas, my lord, I beseech thee, [a]lay not the sin upon us, wherein we have done foolishly, and wherein we have sinned.

12 Let her not be [a]as one dead, of whom the flesh is half consumed when he cometh out of his mother's womb.

13 And Moses cried unto the LORD, saying, [a]Heal her now, O God, I beseech thee.

14 And the LORD said unto Moses, If her father had but [a]spit in her face, should she not be ashamed seven days? let her be [b]shut out from the camp seven days, and after that let her be received in *again.*

15 [a]And Miriam was shut out from the camp seven days: and the people journeyed not till Miriam was brought in *again.*

16 And afterward the people removed from [a]Hazeroth, and pitched in the wilderness of Paran.

Spies Sent into Canaan
(*Deut. 1:19–33*)

13 And the LORD spake unto Moses, saying,

2 [a]Send thou men, that they may search the land of Canaan, which I give unto the children of Israel: of every tribe of their fathers shall ye send a man, every one a ruler among them.

3 And Moses by the commandment of the LORD sent them [a]from the wilderness of Paran: all those men *were* heads of the children of Israel.

4 And these *were* their names: of the tribe of Reuben, Shammua the son of Zaccur.

5 Of the tribe of Simeon, Shaphat the son of Hori.

6 [a]Of the tribe of Judah, [b]Caleb the son of Jephunneh.

7 Of the tribe of Issachar, Igal the son of Joseph.

8 Of the tribe of Ephraim, Oshea the son of Nun.

9 Of the tribe of Benjamin, Palti the son of Raphu.

10 Of the tribe of Zebulun, Gaddiel the son of Sodi.

11 Of the tribe of Joseph, *namely,* of the tribe of Manasseh, Gaddi the son of Susi.

12 Of the tribe of Dan, Ammiel the son of Gemalli.

13 Of the tribe of Asher, Sethur the son of Michael.

14 Of the tribe of Naphtali, Nahbi the son of Vophsi.

15 Of the tribe of Gad, Geuel the son of Machi.

16 These *are* the names of the men which Moses sent to spy out the land. And Moses called [a]Oshea the son of Nun Jehoshua.

17 And Moses sent them to spy out the land of Canaan, and said unto them, Get you up this *way* southward, and go up into [a]the mountain:

18 And see the land, what it *is;* and the people that dwelleth therein, whether they *be* strong or weak, few or many;

19 And what the land *is* that they dwell in, whether it *be* good or bad; and what cities *they be* that they dwell in, whether in tents, or in strong holds;

20 And what the land *is,* whether it *be* fat or lean, whether there be wood therein, or not. And [a]be ye of good courage, and bring of the fruit of the land. Now the time *was* the time of the firstripe grapes.

21 So they went up, and searched the land [a]from the wilderness of Zin unto [b]Rehob, as men come to [c]Hamath.

22 And they ascended by the south, and came unto [a]Hebron; where Ahiman, Sheshai, and Tal-

10 [a]Deut. 24:9 [b]Ex. 4:6; 2 Kin. 5:27; 15:5; 2 Chr. 26:19, 20
11 [a]2 Sam. 19:19; 24:10
12 [a]Ps. 88:4
13 [a]Ps. 103:3
14 [a]Deut. 25:9; Job 30:10; Is. 50:6 [b]Lev. 13:46; Num. 5:1–4
15 [a]Deut. 24:9; 2 Chr. 26:20, 21
16 [a]Num. 11:35; 33:17, 18

CHAPTER 13

2 [a]Num. 32:8; Deut. 1:22; 9:23
3 [a]Num. 12:16; 32:8; Deut. 1:19; 9:23
6 [a]Num. 34:19 [b]Num. 14:6, 30; Josh. 14:6, 7; Judg. 1:12; 1 Chr. 4:15
16 [a]Ex. 17:9; Deut. 32:44
17 [a]Judg. 1:9
20 [a]Deut. 31:6, 7, 23
21 [a]Num. 20:1; 27:14; 33:36; Josh. 15:1 [b]Josh. 19:28 [c]Num. 34:8; Josh. 13:5
22 [a]Josh. 15:13, 14; Judg. 1:10

*

13:8 LXX, Vg. *Oshea*
13:16 LXX, Vg. *Oshea*

NKJV

10 And when the cloud departed from above the tabernacle, [a]suddenly Miriam *became* [b]leprous, as *white as* snow. Then Aaron turned toward Miriam, and there she was, a leper.

11 So Aaron said to Moses, "Oh, my lord! Please [a]do not lay *this* sin on us, in which we have done foolishly and in which we have sinned.

12 "Please [a]do not let her be as one dead, whose flesh is half consumed when he comes out of his mother's womb!"

13 So Moses cried out to the LORD, saying, "Please [a]heal her, O God, I pray!"

14 Then the LORD said to Moses, "If her father had but [a]spit in her face, would she not be shamed seven days? Let her be [b]shut out of the camp seven days, and afterward she may be received *again.*"

15 [a]So Miriam was shut out of the camp seven days, and the people did not journey till Miriam was brought in *again.*

16 And afterward the people moved from [a]Hazeroth and camped in the Wilderness of Paran.

Spies Sent into Canaan
(*Deut. 1:19–33*)

13 And the LORD spoke to Moses, saying,

2 [a]"Send men to spy out the land of Canaan, which I am giving to the children of Israel; from each tribe of their fathers you shall send a man, every one a leader among them."

3 So Moses sent them [a]from the Wilderness of Paran according to the command of the LORD, all of them men who *were* heads of the children of Israel.

4 Now these *were* their names: from the tribe of Reuben, Shammua the son of Zaccur;

5 from the tribe of Simeon, Shaphat the son of Hori;

6 [a]from the tribe of Judah, [b]Caleb the son of Jephunneh;

7 from the tribe of Issachar, Igal the son of Joseph;

8 from the tribe of Ephraim, *Hoshea the son of Nun;

9 from the tribe of Benjamin, Palti the son of Raphu;

10 from the tribe of Zebulun, Gaddiel the son of Sodi;

11 from the tribe of Joseph, *that is,* from the tribe of Manasseh, Gaddi the son of Susi;

12 from the tribe of Dan, Ammiel the son of Gemalli;

13 from the tribe of Asher, Sethur the son of Michael;

14 from the tribe of Naphtali, Nahbi the son of Vophsi;

15 from the tribe of Gad, Geuel the son of Machi.

16 These *are* the names of the men whom Moses sent to spy out the land. And Moses called [a]Hoshea* the son of Nun, Joshua.

17 Then Moses sent them to spy out the land of Canaan, and said to them, "Go up this *way* into the South, and go up to [a]the mountains,

18 "and see what the land is like: whether the people who dwell in it *are* strong or weak, few or many;

19 "whether the land they dwell in *is* good or bad; whether the cities they inhabit *are* like camps or strongholds;

20 "whether the land *is* rich or poor; and whether there are forests there or not. [a]Be of good courage. And bring some of the fruit of the land." Now the time *was* the season of the first ripe grapes.

21 So they went up and spied out the land [a]from the Wilderness of Zin as far as [b]Rehob, near the entrance of [c]Hamath.

22 And they went up through the South and came to [a]Hebron; Ahiman, Sheshai, and Talmai,

KJV

mai, the children of [b]Anak, *were.* (Now Hebron was built seven years before Zoan in Egypt.)

23 [a]And they came unto the brook of Eshcol, and cut down from thence a branch with one cluster of grapes, and they bare it between two upon a staff; and *they brought* of the pomegranates, and of the figs.

24 The place was called the brook Eshcol, because of the cluster of grapes which the children of Israel cut down from thence.

25 And they returned from searching of the land after forty days.

26 And they went and came to Moses, and to Aaron, and to all the congregation of the children of Israel, unto the wilderness of Paran, to [a]Kadesh; and brought back word unto them, and unto all the congregation, and shewed them the fruit of the land.

27 And they told him, and said, We came unto the land whither thou sentest us, and surely it floweth with [a]milk and honey; [b]and this *is* the fruit of it.

28 Nevertheless the [a]people *be* strong that dwell in the land, and the cities *are* walled, *and* very great: and moreover we saw the children of [b]Anak there.

29 [a]The Amalekites dwell in the land of the south: and the Hittites, and the Jebusites, and the Amorites, dwell in the mountains: and the Canaanites dwell by the sea, and by the coast of Jordan.

30 And [a]Caleb stilled the people before Moses, and said, Let us go up at once, and possess it; for we are well able to overcome it.

31 [a]But the men that went up with him said, We be not able to go up against the people; for they *are* stronger than we.

32 And they [a]brought up an evil report of the land which they had searched unto the children of Israel, saying, The land, through which we have gone to search it, *is* a land that eateth up the inhabitants thereof; and [b]all the people that we saw in it *are* men of a great stature.

33 And there we saw the giants, [a]the sons of Anak, *which come* of the giants: and we were in our own sight [b]as grasshoppers, and so we were [c]in their sight.

Israel Refuses to Enter Canaan

14 And all the congregation lifted up their voice, and cried; and the people [a]wept that night.

2 [a]And all the children of Israel murmured against Moses and against Aaron: and the whole congregation said unto them, Would God that we had died in the land of Egypt! or would God we had died in this wilderness!

3 And wherefore hath the LORD brought us unto this land, to fall by the sword, that our wives and our [a]children should be a prey? were it not better for us to return into Egypt?

4 And they said one to another, [a]Let us make a captain, and [b]let us return into Egypt.

5 Then Moses and Aaron fell on their faces before all the assembly of the congregation of the children of Israel.

6 And Joshua the son of Nun, and Caleb the son of Jephunneh, *which were* of them that searched the land, rent their clothes:

7 And they spake unto all the company of the children of Israel, saying, [a]The land, which we passed through to search it, *is* an exceeding good land.

8 If the LORD [a]delight in us, then he will bring us into this land, and give it us; [b]a land which floweth with milk and honey.

9 Only [a]rebel not ye against the LORD, [b]neither fear ye the people of the land; for [c]they *are* bread for us: their defence is departed from them, [d]and the LORD *is* with us: fear them not.

10 [a]But all the congregation bade stone them with stones. And [b]the glory of the LORD appeared

---

22 [b]Josh. 11:21, 22
23 [a]Gen. 14:13; Num. 13:24; 32:9; Deut. 1:24, 25
26 [a]Num. 20:1, 16; 32:8; 33:36; Deut. 1:19; Josh. 14:6
27 [a]Ex. 3:8, 17; 13:5; 33:3 [b]Deut. 1:25
28 [a]Deut. 1:28; 9:1, 2 [b]Josh. 11:21, 22
29 [a]Ex. 17:8; Judg. 6:3
30 [a]Num. 14:6, 24
31 [a]Num. 32:9; Deut. 1:28; 9:1–3; Josh. 14:8
32 [a]Num. 14:36, 37; Ps. 106:24 [b]Amos 2:9
33 [a]Deut. 1:28; 9:2; Josh. 11:21 [b]Is. 40:22 [c]1 Sam. 17:42

CHAPTER 14

1 [a]Num. 11:4; Deut. 1:45
2 [a]Ex. 16:2; 17:3; Num. 16:41; Ps. 106:25; 1 Cor. 10:10
3 [a]Num. 14:31; Deut. 1:39
4 [a]Neh. 9:17 [b]Deut. 17:16; Acts 7:39
7 [a]Num. 13:27; Deut. 1:25
8 [a]Deut. 10:15; 2 Sam. 15:25, 26; 1 Kin. 10:9; Ps. 147:11 [b]Ex. 3:8; Num. 13:27
9 [a]Deut. 1:26; 9:7, 23, 24; 1 Sam. 15:23 [b]Deut. 7:18 [c]Num. 24:8 [d]Gen. 48:21; Ex. 33:16; Deut. 20:1, 3, 4; 31:6–8; Josh. 1:5; Judg. 1:22; 2 Chr. 13:12; Ps. 46:7, 11; Zech. 8:23; Matt. 28:20; Heb. 13:5
10 [a]Ex. 17:4 [b]Ex. 16:10; Lev. 9:23

*

13:24 Lit. *Cluster*
13:33 Heb. *nephilim*

NKJV

the descendants of [b]Anak, *were* there. (Now Hebron was built seven years before Zoan in Egypt.)

23 [a]Then they came to the Valley of Eshcol, and there cut down a branch with one cluster of grapes; they carried it between two of them on a pole. *They* also *brought* some of the pomegranates and figs.

24 The place was called the Valley of *Eshcol, because of the cluster which the men of Israel cut down there.

25 And they returned from spying out the land after forty days.

26 Now they departed and came back to Moses and Aaron and all the congregation of the children of Israel in the Wilderness of Paran, at [a]Kadesh; they brought back word to them and to all the congregation, and showed them the fruit of the land.

27 Then they told him, and said: "We went to the land where you sent us. It truly flows with [a]milk and honey, [b]and this *is* its fruit.

28 "Nevertheless the [a]people who dwell in the land *are* strong; the cities *are* fortified *and* very large; moreover we saw the descendants of [b]Anak there.

29 [a]"The Amalekites dwell in the land of the South; the Hittites, the Jebusites, and the Amorites dwell in the mountains; and the Canaanites dwell by the sea and along the banks of the Jordan."

30 Then [a]Caleb quieted the people before Moses, and said, "Let us go up at once and take possession, for we are well able to overcome it."

31 [a]But the men who had gone up with him said, "We are not able to go up against the people, for they *are* stronger than we."

32 And they [a]gave the children of Israel a bad report of the land which they had spied out, saying, "The land through which we have gone as spies *is* a land that devours its inhabitants, and [b]all the people whom we saw in it *are* men of *great* stature.

33 "There we saw the *giants ([a]the descendants of Anak came from the giants); and we were [b]like grasshoppers in our own sight, and so we were [c]in their sight."

Israel Refuses to Enter Canaan

14 So all the congregation lifted up their voices and cried, and the people [a]wept that night.

2 [a]And all the children of Israel complained against Moses and Aaron, and the whole congregation said to them, "If only we had died in the land of Egypt! Or if only we had died in this wilderness!

3 "Why has the LORD brought us to this land to fall by the sword, that our wives and [a]children should become victims? Would it not be better for us to return to Egypt?"

4 So they said to one another, [a]"Let us select a leader and [b]return to Egypt."

5 Then Moses and Aaron fell on their faces before all the assembly of the congregation of the children of Israel.

6 But Joshua the son of Nun and Caleb the son of Jephunneh, *who were* among those who had spied out the land, tore their clothes;

7 and they spoke to all the congregation of the children of Israel, saying: [a]"The land we passed through to spy out *is* an exceedingly good land.

8 "If the LORD [a]delights in us, then He will bring us into this land and give it to us, [b]'a land which flows with milk and honey.'

9 "Only [a]do not rebel against the LORD, [b]nor fear the people of the land, for [c]they *are* our bread; their protection has departed from them, [d]and the LORD *is* with us. Do not fear them."

10 [a]And all the congregation said to stone them with stones. Now [b]the glory of the LORD ap-

KJV

in the tabernacle of the congregation before all the children of Israel.

Moses Intercedes for the People

11 And the LORD said unto Moses, How long will this people [a]provoke me? and how long will it be ere they [b]believe me, for all the signs which I have shewed among them?

12 I will smite them with the pestilence, and disinherit them, and will [a]make of thee a greater nation and mightier than they.

13 And [a]Moses said unto the LORD, [b]Then the Egyptians shall hear *it*, (for thou broughtest up this people in thy might from among them;)

14 And they will tell *it* to the inhabitants of this land: *for* they have [a]heard that thou LORD *art* among this people, that thou LORD art seen face to face, and *that* thy cloud standeth over them, and *that* thou goest before them, by daytime in a pillar of a cloud, and in a pillar of fire by night.

15 Now *if* thou shalt kill *all* this people as one man, then the nations which have heard the fame of thee will speak, saying,

16 Because the LORD was not [a]able to bring this people into the land which he sware unto them, therefore he hath slain them in the wilderness.

17 And now, I beseech thee, let the power of my Lord be great, according as thou hast spoken, saying,

18 The LORD *is* [a]longsuffering, and of great mercy, forgiving iniquity and transgression, and by no means clearing *the guilty*, [b]visiting the iniquity of the fathers upon the children unto the third and fourth *generation*.

19 [a]Pardon, I beseech thee, the iniquity of this people [b]according unto the greatness of thy mercy, and [c]as thou hast forgiven this people, from Egypt even until now.

20 And the LORD said, I have pardoned [a]according to thy word:

21 But *as* truly *as* I live, [a]all the earth shall be filled with the glory of the LORD.

22 [a]Because all those men which have seen my glory, and my miracles, which I did in Egypt and in the wilderness, and have tempted me now [b]these ten times, and have not hearkened to my voice;

23 Surely they shall not [a]see the land which I sware unto their fathers, neither shall any of them that provoked me see it:

24 But my servant [a]Caleb, because he had another spirit with him, and [b]hath followed me fully, him will I bring into the land whereinto he went; and his seed shall possess it.

25 (Now the Amalekites and the Canaanites dwelt in the valley.) To morrow turn you, and [a]get you into the wilderness by the way of the Red sea.

Death Sentence on the Rebels

26 And the LORD spake unto Moses and unto Aaron, saying,

27 [a]How long *shall I bear with* this evil congregation, which murmur against me? [b]I have heard the murmurings of the children of Israel, which they murmur against me.

28 Say unto them, [a]*As truly as* I live, saith the LORD, as ye have spoken in mine ears, so will I do to you:

29 Your carcases shall fall in this wilderness; and [a]all that were numbered of you, according to your whole number, from twenty years old and upward, which have murmured against me,

30 Doubtless ye shall not come into the land, *concerning* which I sware to make you dwell therein, [a]save Caleb the son of Jephunneh, and Joshua the son of Nun.

31 [a]But your little ones, which ye said should be a prey, them will I bring in, and they shall know the land which [b]ye have despised.

11 [a]Ps. 95:8; Heb. 3:8 [b]Deut. 9:23; [John 12:37]
12 [a]Ex. 32:10
13 [a]Ps. 106:23 [b]Ex. 32:12; Deut. 9:26–28; 32:27
14 [a]Deut. 2:25
16 [a]Deut. 9:28
18 [a]Ex. 34:6, 7; Deut. 5:10; 7:9; Ps. 103:8; 145:8; Jon. 4:2 [b]Ex. 20:5; Deut. 5:9
19 [a]Ex. 32:32; 34:9 [b]Ps. 51:1; 106:45 [c]Ps. 78:38
20 [a]2 Sam. 12:13; Mic. 7:18–20; [1 John 5:14–16]
21 [a]Ps. 72:19; Is. 6:3; 66:18, 19; Hab. 2:14
22 [a]Deut. 1:35; 1 Cor. 10:5; Heb. 3:17 [b]Gen. 31:7
23 [a]Num. 26:65; 32:11; Heb. 3:18
24 [a]Josh. 14:6, 8, 9 [b]Num. 32:12
25 [a]Num. 21:4; Deut. 1:40
27 [a]Ex. 16:28 [b]Ex. 16:12
28 [a]Deut. 1:35; 2:14, 15; Heb. 3:16–19
29 [a]Num. 1:45, 46; 26:64; Josh. 5:6
30 [a]Num. 26:65; 32:12; Deut. 1:36–38; Josh. 14:6–15
31 [a]Num. 14:3; Deut. 1:39 [b]Ps. 106:24

NKJV

peared in the tabernacle of meeting before all the children of Israel.

Moses Intercedes for the People

11 Then the LORD said to Moses: "How long will these people [a]reject Me? And how long will they not [b]believe Me, with all the signs which I have performed among them?

12 "I will strike them with the pestilence and disinherit them, and I will [a]make of you a nation greater and mightier than they."

13 And [a]Moses said to the LORD: [b]"Then the Egyptians will hear *it*, for by Your might You brought these people up from among them,

14 "and they will tell *it* to the inhabitants of this land. They have [a]heard that You, LORD, *are* among these people; that You, LORD, are seen face to face and Your cloud stands above them, and You go before them in a pillar of cloud by day and in a pillar of fire by night.

15 "Now *if* You kill these people as one man, then the nations which have heard of Your fame will speak, saying,

16 'Because the LORD was not [a]able to bring this people to the land which He swore to give them, therefore He killed them in the wilderness.'

17 "And now, I pray, let the power of my Lord be great, just as You have spoken, saying,

18 [a]'The LORD is longsuffering and abundant in mercy, forgiving iniquity and transgression; but He by no means clears *the guilty*, [b]visiting the iniquity of the fathers on thechildren to the third and fourth *generation*.'

19 [a]"Pardon the iniquity of this people, I pray, [b]according to the greatness of Your mercy, just [c]as You have forgiven this people, from Egypt even until now."

20 Then the LORD said: "I have pardoned, [a]according to your word;

21 "but truly, as I live, [a]all the earth shall be filled with the glory of the LORD—

22 [a]"because all these men who have seen My glory and the signs which I did in Egypt and in the wilderness, and have put Me to the test now [b]these ten times, and have not heeded My voice,

23 "they certainly shall not [a]see the land of which I swore to their fathers, nor shall any of those who rejected Me see it.

24 "But My servant [a]Caleb, because he has a different spirit in him and [b]has followed Me fully, I will bring into the land where he went, and his descendants shall inherit it.

25 "Now the Amalekites and the Canaanites dwell in the valley; tomorrow turn and [a]move out into the wilderness by the Way of the Red Sea."

Death Sentence on the Rebels

26 And the LORD spoke to Moses and Aaron, saying,

27 [a]"How long *shall I bear with* this evil congregation who complain against Me? [b]I have heard the complaints which the children of Israel make against Me.

28 "Say to them, [a]'As I live,' says the LORD, 'just as you have spoken in My hearing, so I will do to you:

29 'The carcasses of you who have complained against Me shall fall in this wilderness, [a]all of you who were numbered, according to your entire number, from twenty years old and above.

30 [a]'Except for Caleb the son of Jephunneh and Joshua the son of Nun, you shall by no means enter the land which I swore I would make you dwell in.

31 [a]'But your little ones, whom you said would be victims, I will bring in, and they shall know the land which [b]you have despised.

KJV

32 But *as for* you, [a]your carcases, they shall
fall in this wilderness.
33 And your children shall [a]wander in the
wilderness [b]forty years, and [c]bear your whoredoms, until your carcases be wasted in the
wilderness.
34 [a]After the number of the days in which
ye searched the land, *even* [b]forty days, each day
for a year, shall ye bear your iniquities, *even* forty
years, [c]and ye shall know my breach of promise.
35 [a]I the LORD have said, I will surely do it
unto all [b]this evil congregation, that are gathered
together against me: in this wilderness they shall
be consumed, and there they shall die.
36 And the men, which Moses sent to search
the land, who returned, and made all the congregation to murmur against him, by bringing up a
slander upon the land,
37 Even those men that did bring up the evil
report upon the land, [a]died by the plague before
the LORD.
38 [a]But Joshua the son of Nun, and Caleb
the son of Jephunneh, *which were* of the men that
went to search the land, lived *still*.

A Futile Invasion Attempt
(*Deut. 1:41–45*)

39 And Moses told these sayings unto all the
children of Israel: [a]and the people mourned
greatly.
40 And they rose up early in the morning,
and gat them up into the top of the mountain,
saying, Lo, [a]we *be here*, and will go up unto the
place which the LORD hath promised: for we have
sinned.
41 And Moses said, Wherefore now do ye
transgress the commandment of the LORD? but it
shall not prosper.
42 [a]Go not up, for the LORD *is* not among you;
that ye be not smitten before your enemies.
43 For the Amalekites and the Canaanites
are there before you, and ye shall fall by the
sword: [a]because ye are turned away from the
LORD, therefore the LORD will not be with you.
44 [a]But they presumed to go up unto the hill
top: nevertheless the ark of the covenant of the
LORD, and Moses, departed not out of the camp.
45 Then the Amalekites came down, and the
Canaanites which dwelt in that hill, and smote
them, and discomfited them, *even* unto [a]Hormah.

Laws of Grain and Drink Offerings

15 And the LORD spake unto Moses, saying,
2 [a]Speak unto the children of Israel, and
say unto them, When ye be come into the land
of your habitations, which I give unto you,
3 And [a]will make an offering by fire unto
the LORD, a burnt offering, or a sacrifice [b]in performing a vow, or in a freewill offering, or [c]in
your solemn feasts, to make a [d]sweet savour unto
the LORD, of the herd, or of the flock:
4 Then [a]shall he that offereth his offering
unto the LORD bring [b]a meat offering of a tenth
deal of flour mingled [c]with the fourth *part* of an
hin of oil.
5 [a]And the fourth *part* of an hin of wine
for a drink offering shalt thou prepare with the
burnt offering or sacrifice, for one [b]lamb.
6 [a]Or for a ram, thou shalt prepare *for* a
meat offering two tenth deals of flour mingled
with the third *part* of an hin of oil.
7 And for a drink offering thou shalt offer
the third *part* of an hin of wine, *for* a sweet savour
unto the LORD.
8 And when thou preparest a bullock *for* a
burnt offering, or *for* a sacrifice in performing a
vow, or [a]peace offerings unto the LORD:
9 Then shall he bring [a]with a bullock a meat
offering of three tenth deals of flour mingled with
half an hin of oil.
10 And thou shalt bring for a drink offering

32 [a]Num. 26:64, 65; 32:13; 1 Cor. 10:5
33 [a]Num. 32:13; Ps. 107:40 [b]Deut. 2:14 [c]Ezek. 23:35
34 [a]Num. 13:25 [b]Ps. 95:10; Ezek. 4:6 [c]1 Kin. 8:56; [Heb. 4:1]
35 [a]Num. 23:19 [b]1 Cor. 10:5
37 [a]Num. 16:49; [1 Cor. 10:10]; Heb. 3:17, 18
38 [a]Josh. 14:6, 10
39 [a]Ex. 33:4
40 [a]Deut. 1:41–44
42 [a]Deut. 1:42; 31:17
43 [a]2 Chr. 15:2
44 [a]Deut. 1:43
45 [a]Num. 21:3

CHAPTER 15
2 [a]Lev. 23:10; Num. 15:18; Deut. 7:1
3 [a]Lev. 1:2, 3 [b]Lev. 7:16; 22:18, 21 [c]Lev. 23:2, 8, 12, 38; Num. 28:18, 19, 27; Deut. 16:10 [d]Gen. 8:21; Ex. 29:18; Lev. 1:9
4 [a]Lev. 2:1; 6:14 [b]Ex. 29:40; Lev. 23:13 [c]Lev. 14:10; Num. 28:5
5 [a]Num. 28:7, 14 [b]Lev. 1:10; 3:6; Num. 15:11; 28:4, 5
6 [a]Num. 28:12, 14
8 [a]Lev. 7:11
9 [a]Num. 28:12, 14

NKJV

32 'But *as for* you, [a]your carcasses shall fall
in this wilderness.
33 'And your sons shall [a]be shepherds in the
wilderness [b]forty years, and [c]bear the brunt of
your infidelity, until your carcasses are consumed
in the wilderness.
34 [a]'According to the number of the days in
which you spied out the land, [b]forty days, for each
day you shall bear your guilt one year, *namely*
forty years, [c]and you shall know My rejection.
35 [a]'I the LORD have spoken this. I will surely
do so to all [b]this evil congregation who are gathered together against Me. In this wilderness they
shall be consumed, and there they shall die.' "
36 Now the men whom Moses sent to spy out
the land, who returned and made all the congregation complain against him by bringing a bad report of the land,
37 those very men who brought the evil report about the land, [a]died by the plague before
the LORD.
38 [a]But Joshua the son of Nun and Caleb the
son of Jephunneh remained alive, of the men who
went to spy out the land.

A Futile Invasion Attempt
(*Deut. 1:41–45*)

39 Then Moses told these words to all the
children of Israel, [a]and the people mourned
greatly.
40 And they rose early in the morning and
went up to the top of the mountain, saying, [a]"Here
we are, and we will go up to the place which the
LORD has promised, for we have sinned!"
41 And Moses said, "Now why do you transgress the command of the LORD? For this will not
succeed.
42 [a]"Do not go up, lest you be defeated by
your enemies, for the LORD *is* not among you.
43 "For the Amalekites and the Canaanites
are there before you, and you shall fall by the
sword; [a]because you have turned away from the
LORD, the LORD will not be with you."
44 [a]But they presumed to go up to the mountaintop. Nevertheless, neither the ark of the covenant of the LORD nor Moses departed from the
camp.
45 Then the Amalekites and the Canaanites
who dwelt in that mountain came down and attacked them, and drove them back as far as
[a]Hormah.

Laws of Grain and Drink Offerings

15 And the LORD spoke to Moses, saying,
2 [a]"Speak to the children of Israel, and
say to them: 'When you have come into the land
you are to inhabit, which I am giving to you,
3 'and you [a]make an offering by fire to the
LORD, a burnt offering or a sacrifice, [b]to fulfill a
vow or as a freewill offering or [c]in your appointed
feasts, to make a [d]sweet aroma to the LORD, from
the herd or the flock,
4 'then [a]he who presents his offering to the
LORD shall bring [b]a grain offering of one-tenth *of
an ephah* of fine flour mixed [c]with one-fourth of
a hin of oil;
5 [a]'and one-fourth of a hin of wine as a
drink offering you shall prepare with the burnt
offering or the sacrifice, for each [b]lamb.
6 [a]'Or for a ram you shall prepare as a grain
offering two-tenths *of an ephah* of fine flour mixed
with one-third of a hin of oil;
7 'and as a drink offering you shall offer
one-third of a hin of wine as a sweet aroma to
the LORD.
8 'And when you prepare a young bull as a
burnt offering, or as a sacrifice to fulfill a vow,
or as a [a]peace offering to the LORD,
9 'then shall be offered [a]with the young bull
a grain offering of three-tenths *of an ephah* of fine
flour mixed with half a hin of oil;
10 'and you shall bring as the drink offering

KJV

half an hin of wine, *for* an offering made by fire, of a sweet savour unto the LORD.

11 [a]Thus shall it be done for one bullock, or for one ram, or for a lamb, or a kid.

12 According to the number that ye shall prepare, so shall ye do to every one according to their number.

13 All that are born of the country shall do these things after this manner, in offering an offering made by fire, of a sweet savour unto the LORD.

14 And if a stranger sojourn with you, or whosoever *be* among you in your generations, and will offer an offering made by fire, of a sweet savour unto the LORD; as ye do, so he shall do.

15 [a]One ordinance *shall be both* for you of the congregation, and also for the stranger that sojourneth *with you,* an ordinance for ever in your generations: as ye *are,* so shall the stranger be before the LORD.

16 One law and one manner shall be for you, and for the stranger that sojourneth with you.

17 And the LORD spake unto Moses, saying,

18 [a]Speak unto the children of Israel, and say unto them, When ye come into the land whither I bring you,

19 Then it shall be, that, when ye eat of [a]the bread of the land, ye shall offer up an heave offering unto the LORD.

20 [a]Ye shall offer up a cake of the first of your dough *for* an heave offering: as *ye do* [b]the heave offering of the threshingfloor, so shall ye heave it.

21 Of the first of your dough ye shall give unto the LORD an heave offering in your generations.

Laws Concerning Unintentional Sin

22 And [a]if ye have erred, and not observed all these commandments, which the LORD hath spoken unto Moses,

23 *Even* all that the LORD hath commanded you by the hand of Moses, from the day that the LORD commanded *Moses,* and henceforward among your generations;

24 Then it shall be, [a]if *ought* be committed by ignorance without the knowledge of the congregation, that all the congregation shall offer one young bullock for a burnt offering, for a sweet savour unto the LORD, [b]with his meat offering, and his drink offering, according to the manner, and [c]one kid of the goats for a sin offering.

25 [a]And the priest shall make an atonement for all the congregation of the children of Israel, and it shall be forgiven them; for it *is* ignorance: and they shall bring their offering, a sacrifice made by fire unto the LORD, and their sin offering before the LORD, for their ignorance:

26 And it shall be forgiven all the congregation of the children of Israel, and the stranger that sojourneth among them; seeing all the people *were* in ignorance.

27 And [a]if any soul sin through ignorance, then he shall bring a she goat of the first year for a sin offering.

28 [a]And the priest shall make an atonement for the soul that sinneth ignorantly, when he sinneth by ignorance before the LORD, to make an atonement for him; and it shall be forgiven him.

29 [a]Ye shall have one law for him that sinneth through ignorance, *both for* him that is born among the children of Israel, and for the stranger that sojourneth among them.

Law Concerning Presumptuous Sin

30 [a]But the soul that doeth *ought* presumptuously, *whether he be* born in the land, or a stranger, the same reproacheth the LORD; and that soul shall be cut off from among his people.

31 Because he hath [a]despised the word of the LORD, and hath broken his commandment, that

11 [a]Num. 28
15 [a]Ex. 12:49; Num. 9:14; 15:29
18 [a]Num. 15:2; Deut. 26:1
19 [a]Josh. 5:11, 12
20 [a]Ex. 34:26; Lev. 23:10, 14, 17; Deut. 26:2, 10; Prov. 3:9, 10 [b]Lev. 2:14; 23:10, 16
22 [a]Lev. 4:2
24 [a]Lev. 4:13 [b]Num. 15:8–10 [c]Lev. 4:23
25 [a]Lev. 4:20; [Heb. 2:17]
27 [a]Lev. 4:27–31
28 [a]Lev. 4:35
29 [a]Num. 15:15
30 [a]Num. 14:40–44; Deut. 1:43; 17:12; Ps. 19:13; Heb. 10:26
31 [a]2 Sam. 12:9; Prov. 13:13

NKJV

half a hin of wine as an offering made by fire, a sweet aroma to the LORD.

11 [a]'Thus it shall be done for each young bull, for each ram, or for each lamb or young goat.

12 'According to the number that you prepare, so you shall do with everyone according to their number.

13 'All who are native-born shall do these things in this manner, in presenting an offering made by fire, a sweet aroma to the LORD.

14 'And if a stranger dwells with you, or whoever *is* among you throughout your generations, and would present an offering made by fire, a sweet aroma to the LORD, just as you do, so shall he do.

15 [a]'One ordinance *shall be* for you of the assembly and for the stranger who dwells *with you,* an ordinance forever throughout your generations; as you are, so shall the stranger be before the LORD.

16 'One law and one custom shall be for you and for the stranger who dwells with you.' "

17 Again the LORD spoke to Moses, saying,

18 [a]"Speak to the children of Israel, and say to them: 'When you come into the land to which I bring you,

19 'then it will be, when you eat of [a]the bread of the land, that you shall offer up a heave offering to the LORD.

20 [a]'You shall offer up a cake of the first of your ground meal *as* a heave offering; as [b]a heave offering of the threshing floor, so shall you offer it up.

21 'Of the first of your ground meal you shall give to the LORD a heave offering throughout your generations.

Laws Concerning Unintentional Sin

22 [a]'If you sin unintentionally, and do not observe all these commandments which the LORD has spoken to Moses—

23 'all that the LORD has commanded you by the hand of Moses, from the day the LORD gave commandment and onward throughout your generations—

24 'then it will be, [a]if it is unintentionally committed, without the knowledge of the congregation, that the whole congregation shall offer one young bull as a burnt offering, as a sweet aroma to the LORD, [b]with its grain offering and its drink offering, according to the ordinance, and [c]one kid of the goats as a sin offering.

25 [a]'So the priest shall make atonement for the whole congregation of the children of Israel, and it shall be forgiven them, for it was unintentional; they shall bring their offering, an offering made by fire to the LORD, and their sin offering before the LORD, for their unintended sin.

26 'It shall be forgiven the whole congregation of the children of Israel and the stranger who dwells among them, because all the people *did it* unintentionally.

27 'And [a]if a person sins unintentionally, then he shall bring a female goat in its first year as a sin offering.

28 [a]'So the priest shall make atonement for the person who sins unintentionally, when he sins unintentionally before the LORD, to make atonement for him; and it shall be forgiven him.

29 [a]'You shall have one law for him who sins unintentionally, *for* him who is native-born among the children of Israel and for the stranger who dwells among them.

Law Concerning Presumptuous Sin

30 [a]'But the person who does *anything* presumptuously, *whether he is* native-born or a stranger, that one brings reproach on the LORD, and he shall be cut off from among his people.

31 'Because he has [a]despised the word of the LORD, and has broken His commandment, that

KJV

soul shall utterly be cut off; his iniquity *shall be*
upon him.

Penalty for Violating the Sabbath
(Ex. 31:12–17)

32 And while the children of Israel were in
the wilderness, [a]they found a man that gathered
sticks upon the sabbath day.
33 And they that found him gathering sticks
brought him unto Moses and Aaron, and unto all
the congregation.
34 And they put him [a]in ward, because it was
not declared what should be done to him.
35 And the LORD said unto Moses, [a]The
man shall be surely put to death: all the congregation shall [b]stone him with stones without the
camp.
36 And all the congregation brought him
without the camp, and stoned him with stones,
and he died; as the LORD commanded Moses.

Tassels on Garments

37 And the LORD spake unto Moses, saying,
38 Speak unto the children of Israel, and bid
[a]them that they make them fringes in the borders
of their garments throughout their generations,
and that they put upon the fringe of the borders
a ribband of blue:
39 And it shall be unto you for a fringe, that
ye may look upon it, and [a]remember all the commandments of the LORD, and do them; and that
ye [b]seek not after your own heart and your own
eyes, after which ye use [c]to go a whoring:
40 That ye may remember, and do all my
commandments, and be [a]holy unto your God.
41 I *am* the LORD your God, which brought
you out of the land of Egypt, to be your God: I
am the LORD your God.

Rebellion Against Moses and Aaron

16 Now [a]Korah, the son of Izhar, the son of
Kohath, the son of Levi, and [b]Dathan and
Abiram, the sons of Eliab, and On, the son of Peleth, sons of Reuben, took *men:*
2 And they rose up before Moses, with certain of the children of Israel, two hundred and
fifty princes of the assembly, [a]famous in the congregation, men of renown:
3 And [a]they gathered themselves together
against Moses and against Aaron, and said unto
them, *Ye take* too much upon you, seeing [b]all the
congregation *are* holy, every one of them, [c]and
the LORD *is* among them: wherefore then lift ye
up yourselves above the congregation of the
LORD?
4 And when Moses heard *it,* he [a]fell upon
his face:
5 And he spake unto Korah and unto all his
company, saying, Even to morrow the LORD will
shew who *are* [a]his, and *who is* [b]holy; and will
cause *him* to come near unto him: even *him* whom
he hath chosen will he cause to [c]come near unto
him.
6 This do; Take you censers, Korah, and all
his company;
7 And put fire therein, and put incense in
them before the LORD to morrow: and it shall be
that the man whom the LORD doth choose, he *shall
be* holy: *ye take* too much upon you, ye sons of
Levi.
8 And Moses said unto Korah, Hear, I pray
you, ye sons of Levi:
9 *Seemeth it but* [a]a small thing unto you,
that the God of Israel hath [b]separated you from
the congregation of Israel, to bring you near to
himself to do the service of the tabernacle of the
LORD, and to stand before the congregation to
minister unto them?
10 And he hath brought thee near *to him,*
and all thy brethren the sons of Levi with thee:
and seek ye the priesthood also?
11 For which cause *both* thou and all thy

32 [a]Ex. 31:14, 15; 35:2, 3
34 [a]Lev. 24:12
35 [a]Ex. 31:14, 15 [b]Lev. 24:14; Deut. 21:21; 1 Kin. 21:13; Acts 7:58
38 [a]Deut. 22:12; Matt. 23:5
39 [a]Ps. 103:18 [b]Deut. 29:19 [c]Ps. 73:27; 106:39; James 4:4
40 [a][Lev. 11:44, 45; Rom. 12:1; Col. 1:22; 1 Pet. 1:15, 16]

CHAPTER 16

1 [a]Ex. 6:21 [b]Num. 26:9; Deut. 11:6
2 [a]Num. 1:16; 26:9
3 [a]Num. 12:2; 14:2; Ps. 106:16 [b]Ex. 19:6 [c]Ex. 29:45
4 [a]Num. 14:5; 20:6
5 [a][2 Tim. 2:19] [b]Lev. 21:6–8, 12 [c]Ezek. 40:46; 44:15, 16
9 [a]1 Sam. 18:23; Is. 7:13 [b]Num. 3:41, 45; 8:13–16; Deut. 10:8

NKJV

person shall be completely cut off; his guilt *shall
be* upon him.' "

Penalty for Violating the Sabbath
(Ex. 31:12–17)

32 Now while the children of Israel were in
the wilderness, [a]they found a man gathering
sticks on the Sabbath day.
33 And those who found him gathering sticks
brought him to Moses and Aaron, and to all the
congregation.
34 They put him [a]under guard, because it had
not been explained what should be done to him.
35 Then the LORD said to Moses, [a]"The man
must surely be put to death; all the congregation
shall [b]stone him with stones outside the camp."
36 So, as the LORD commanded Moses, all the
congregation brought him outside the camp and
stoned him with stones, and he died.

Tassels on Garments

37 Again the LORD spoke to Moses, saying,
38 "Speak to the children of Israel: Tell
[a]them to make tassels on the corners of their garments throughout their generations, and to put a
blue thread in the tassels of the corners.
39 "And you shall have the tassel, that you
may look upon it and [a]remember all the commandments of the LORD and do them, and that
you [b]*may* not [c]follow the harlotry to which your
own heart and your own eyes are inclined,
40 "and that you may remember and do all
My commandments, and be [a]holy for your God.
41 "I *am* the LORD your God, who brought
you out of the land of Egypt, to be your God: I
am the LORD your God."

Rebellion Against Moses and Aaron

16 Now [a]Korah the son of Izhar, the son of
Kohath, the son of Levi, with [b]Dathan and
Abiram the sons of Eliab, and On the son of Peleth, sons of Reuben, took *men;*
2 and they rose up before Moses with some
of the children of Israel, two hundred and fifty
leaders of the congregation, [a]representatives of
the congregation, men of renown.
3 [a]They gathered together against Moses
and Aaron, and said to them, "*You take* too much
upon yourselves, for [b]all the congregation *is* holy,
every one of them, [c]and the LORD *is* among them.
Why then do you exalt yourselves above the assembly of the LORD?"
4 So when Moses heard *it,* he [a]fell on his
face;
5 and he spoke to Korah and all his company, saying, "Tomorrow morning the LORD will
show who *is* [a]His and *who is* [b]holy, and will cause
him to come near to Him. That one whom He
chooses He will cause to [c]come near to Him.
6 "Do this: Take censers, Korah and all your
company;
7 "put fire in them and put incense in them
before the LORD tomorrow, and it shall be *that*
the man whom the LORD chooses *is* the holy one.
You take too much upon yourselves, you sons of
Levi!"
8 Then Moses said to Korah, "Hear now,
you sons of Levi:
9 "*Is it* [a]a small thing to you that the God
of Israel has [b]separated you from the congregation of Israel, to bring you near to Himself, to do
the work of the tabernacle of the LORD, and to
stand before the congregation to serve them;
10 "and that He has brought you near *to
Himself,* you and all your brethren, the sons of
Levi, with you? And are you seeking the priesthood also?
11 "Therefore you and all your company *are*

KJV

company *are* gathered together against the LORD:
[a]and what *is* Aaron, that ye murmur against him?
12 And Moses sent to call Dathan and Abiram, the sons of Eliab: which said, We will not
come up:
13 *Is it* a small thing that thou hast brought
us up out of a [a]land that floweth with milk and
honey, to kill us in the wilderness, except thou
[b]make thyself altogether a prince over us?
14 Moreover [a]thou hast not brought us into
[b]a land that floweth with milk and honey, or given
us inheritance of fields and vineyards: wilt thou
put out the eyes of these men? we will not come
up.
15 And Moses was very wroth, and said unto
the LORD, [a]Respect not thou their offering: [b]I have
not taken one ass from them, neither have I hurt
one of them.
16 And Moses said unto Korah, Be thou and
all thy company [a]before the LORD, thou, and they,
and Aaron, to morrow:
17 And take every man his censer, and put
incense in them, and bring ye before the LORD
every man his censer, two hundred and fifty censers; thou also, and Aaron, each *of you* his censer.
18 And they took every man his censer, and
put fire in them, and laid incense thereon, and
stood in the door of the tabernacle of the congregation with Moses and Aaron.
19 And Korah gathered all the congregation
against them unto the door of the tabernacle of
the congregation: and [a]the glory of the LORD appeared unto all the congregation.
20 And the LORD spake unto Moses and unto
Aaron, saying,
21 [a]Separate yourselves from among this
congregation, that I may [b]consume them in a
moment.
22 And they [a]fell upon their faces, and said,
O God, [b]the God of the spirits of all flesh, shall
one man sin, and wilt thou be wroth with all the
[c]congregation?
23 And the LORD spake unto Moses, saying,
24 Speak unto the congregation, saying, Get
you up from about the tabernacle of Korah, Dathan, and Abiram.
25 And Moses rose up and went unto Dathan
and Abiram; and the elders of Israel followed him.
26 And he spake unto the congregation, saying, [a]Depart, I pray you, from the tents of these
wicked men, and touch nothing of their's, lest ye
be consumed in all their sins.
27 So they gat up from the tabernacle of Korah, Dathan, and Abiram, on every side: and Dathan and Abiram came out, and stood in the door
of their tents, and their wives, and their sons, and
their little [a]children.
28 And Moses said, [a]Hereby ye shall know
that the LORD hath sent me to do all these works;
for *I have* not *done them* [b]of mine own mind.
29 If these men die the common death of all
men, or if they be [a]visited after the visitation of
all men; *then* the LORD hath not sent me.
30 But if the LORD make [a]a new thing, and
the earth open her mouth, and swallow them up,
with all that *appertain* unto them, and they [b]go
down quick into the pit; then ye shall understand
that these men have provoked the LORD.
31 [a]And it came to pass, as he had made an
end of speaking all these words, that the ground
clave asunder that *was* under them:
32 And the earth opened her mouth, and
swallowed them up, and their houses, and [a]all the
men that *appertained* unto Korah, and all *their*
goods.
33 They, and all that *appertained* to them,
went down alive into the pit, and the earth closed
upon them: and they perished from among the
congregation.
34 And all Israel that *were* round about them
fled at the cry of them: for they said, Lest the
earth swallow us up *also*.

11 [a]Ex. 16:7, 8
13 [a]Ex. 16:3; Num. 11:4–6 [b]Ex. 2:14; Acts 7:27, 35
14 [a]Num. 14:1–4 [b]Ex. 3:8; Lev. 20:24
15 [a]Gen. 4:4, 5 [b]1 Sam. 12:3; Acts 20:33
16 [a]1 Sam. 12:3, 7
19 [a]Ex. 16:7, 10; Lev. 9:6, 23; Num. 14:10
21 [a]Gen. 19:17; Jer. 51:6 [b]Ex. 32:10; 33:5
22 [a]Num. 14:5 [b]Num. 27:16; Job 12:10; Eccl. 12:7; Heb. 12:9 [c]Gen. 18:23–32; 20:4
26 [a]Gen. 19:12, 14, 15, 17
27 [a]Ex. 20:5; Num. 26:11
28 [a]Ex. 3:12; John 5:36 [b]Num. 24:13; John 5:30
29 [a]Ex. 20:5; Job 35:15; Is. 10:3
30 [a]Job 31:3; Is. 28:21 [b][Ps. 55:15]
31 [a]Num. 26:10; Ps. 106:17
32 [a]Num. 26:11; 1 Chr. 6:22, 37

NKJV

gathered together against the LORD. [a]And what
is Aaron that you complain against him?"
12 And Moses sent to call Dathan and Abiram the sons of Eliab, but they said, "We will
not come up!
13 "*Is it* a small thing that you have brought
us up out of [a]a land flowing with milk and honey,
to kill us in the wilderness, that you should [b]keep
acting like a prince over us?
14 "Moreover [a]you have not brought us into
[b]a land flowing with milk and honey, nor given
us inheritance of fields and vineyards. Will you
put out the eyes of these men? We will not come
up!"
15 Then Moses was very angry, and said to
the LORD, [a]"Do not respect their offering. [b]I have
not taken one donkey from them, nor have I hurt
one of them."
16 And Moses said to Korah, "Tomorrow,
you and all your company be present [a]before the
LORD—you and they, as well as Aaron.
17 "Let each take his censer and put incense
in it, and each of you bring his censer before the
LORD, two hundred and fifty censers; both you
and Aaron, each *with* his censer."
18 So every man took his censer, put fire in
it, laid incense on it, and stood at the door of the
tabernacle of meeting with Moses and Aaron.
19 And Korah gathered all the congregation
against them at the door of the tabernacle of meeting. Then [a]the glory of the LORD appeared to all
the congregation.
20 And the LORD spoke to Moses and Aaron,
saying,
21 [a]"Separate yourselves from among this
congregation, that I may [b]consume them in a
moment."
22 Then they [a]fell on their faces, and said,
"O God, [b]the God of the spirits of all flesh, shall
one man sin, and You be angry with all the
[c]congregation?"
23 So the LORD spoke to Moses, saying,
24 "Speak to the congregation, saying, 'Get
away from the tents of Korah, Dathan, and
Abiram.'"
25 Then Moses rose and went to Dathan and
Abiram, and the elders of Israel followed him.
26 And he spoke to the congregation, saying,
[a]"Depart now from the tents of these wicked men!
Touch nothing of theirs, lest you be consumed in
all their sins."
27 So they got away from around the tents
of Korah, Dathan, and Abiram; and Dathan and
Abiram came out and stood at the door of their
tents, with their wives, their sons, and their little
[a]children.
28 And Moses said: [a]"By this you shall know
that the LORD has sent me to do all these works,
for *I have* not *done them* [b]of my own will.
29 "If these men die naturally like all men,
or if they are [a]visited by the common fate of all
men, *then* the LORD has not sent me.
30 "But if the LORD creates [a]a new thing, and
the earth opens its mouth and swallows them up
with all that belongs to them, and they [b]go down
alive into the pit, then you will understand that
these men have rejected the LORD."
31 [a]Now it came to pass, as he finished
speaking all these words, that the ground split
apart under them,
32 and the earth opened its mouth and swallowed them up, with their households and [a]all the
men with Korah, with all *their* goods.
33 So they and all those with them went
down alive into the pit; the earth closed over them,
and they perished from among the assembly.
34 Then all Israel who *were* around them fled
at their cry, for they said, "Lest the earth swallow
us up *also!*"

KJV

35 And there [a]came out a fire from the LORD,
and consumed the two hundred and fifty men that
offered incense.
36 And the LORD spake unto Moses, saying,
37 Speak unto Eleazar the son of Aaron the
priest, that he take up the censers out of the burning, and scatter thou the fire yonder; for [a]they
are hallowed.
38 The censers of these [a]sinners against their
own souls, let them make them broad plates *for*
a covering of the altar: for they offered them
before the LORD, therefore they are hallowed:
[b]and they shall be a sign unto the children of
Israel.
39 And Eleazar the priest took the brasen
censers, wherewith they that were burnt had offered; and they were made broad *plates for* a covering of the altar:
40 *To be* a memorial unto the children of Israel, [a]that no stranger, which *is* not of the seed
of Aaron, come near to offer incense before the
LORD; that he be not as Korah, and as his company: as the LORD said to him by the hand of Moses.

Complaints of the People

41 But on the morrow [a]all the congregation
of the children of Israel murmured against Moses
and against Aaron, saying, Ye have killed the people of the LORD.
42 And it came to pass, when the congregation was gathered against Moses and against
Aaron, that they looked toward the tabernacle of
the congregation: and, behold, [a]the cloud covered
it, and the glory of the LORD appeared.
43 And Moses and Aaron came before the
tabernacle of the congregation.
44 And the LORD spake unto Moses, saying,
45 Get you up from among this congregation,
that I may consume them as in a moment. And
they fell upon their faces.
46 And Moses said unto Aaron, Take a censer, and put fire therein from off the altar, and
put on incense, and go quickly unto the congregation, and make an atonement for them: [a]for there
is wrath gone out from the LORD; the plague is
begun.
47 And Aaron took as Moses commanded,
and ran into the midst of the congregation; and,
behold, the plague was begun among the people:
and he put on incense, and made an atonement
for the people.
48 And he stood between the dead and the
living; and [a]the plague was stayed.
49 Now they that died in the plague were
fourteen thousand and seven hundred, beside
them that died about the matter of Korah.
50 And Aaron returned unto Moses unto the
door of the tabernacle of the congregation: and
the plague was stayed.

The Budding of Aaron's Rod

17 And the LORD spake unto Moses, saying,
2 Speak unto the children of Israel, and
take of every one of them a rod according to the
house of *their* fathers, of all their princes according to the house of their fathers twelve rods: write
thou every man's name upon his rod.
3 And thou shalt write Aaron's name upon
the rod of Levi: for one rod *shall be* for the head
of the house of their fathers.
4 And thou shalt lay them up in the tabernacle of the congregation before the [a]testimony,
[b]where I will meet with you.
5 And it shall come to pass, *that* the man's
rod, [a]whom I shall choose, shall blossom: and I
will make to cease from me the murmurings of
the children of Israel, [b]whereby they murmur
against you.
6 And Moses spake unto the children of Israel, and every one of their princes gave him a
rod apiece, for each prince one, according to their

35 [a]Lev. 10:2; Num. 11:1–3; 26:10; Ps. 106:18
37 [a]Lev. 27:28
38 [a]Prov. 20:2; Hab. 2:10 [b]Num. 17:10; Ezek. 14:8
40 [a]Num. 3:10; 2 Chr. 26:18
41 [a]Num. 14:2; Ps. 106:25
42 [a]Ex. 40:34
46 [a]Lev. 10:6; Num. 18:5
48 [a]Num. 25:8; Ps. 106:30

CHAPTER 17
4 [a]Ex. 25:16 [b]Ex. 25:22; 29:42, 43; 30:36; Num. 17:7
5 [a]Num. 16:5 [b]Num. 16:11

NKJV

35 And [a]a fire came out from the LORD and
consumed the two hundred and fifty men who
were offering incense.
36 Then the LORD spoke to Moses, saying:
37 "Tell Eleazar, the son of Aaron the priest,
to pick up the censers out of the blaze, for [a]they
are holy, and scatter the fire some distance away.
38 "The censers of [a]these men who sinned
against their own souls, let them be made into
hammered plates as a covering for the altar. Because they presented them before the LORD, therefore they are holy; [b]and they shall be a sign to
the children of Israel."
39 So Eleazar the priest took the bronze censers, which those who were burned up had presented, and they were hammered out as a covering on the altar,
40 *to be* a memorial to the children of Israel
[a]that no outsider, who *is* not a descendant of
Aaron, should come near to offer incense before
the LORD, that he might not become like Korah
and his companions, just as the LORD had said to
him through Moses.

Complaints of the People

41 On the next day [a]all the congregation of
the children of Israel complained against Moses
and Aaron, saying, "You have killed the people
of the LORD."
42 Now it happened, when the congregation
had gathered against Moses and Aaron, that they
turned toward the tabernacle of meeting; and suddenly [a]the cloud covered it, and the glory of the
LORD appeared.
43 Then Moses and Aaron came before the
tabernacle of meeting.
44 And the LORD spoke to Moses, saying,
45 "Get away from among this congregation,
that I may consume them in a moment." And they
fell on their faces.
46 So Moses said to Aaron, "Take a censer
and put fire in it from the altar, put incense *on
it,* and take it quickly to the congregation and
make atonement for them; [a]for wrath has gone
out from the LORD. The plague has begun."
47 Then Aaron took *it* as Moses commanded,
and ran into the midst of the assembly; and already the plague had begun among the people.
So he put in the incense and made atonement for
the people.
48 And he stood between the dead and the
living; so [a]the plague was stopped.
49 Now those who died in the plague were
fourteen thousand seven hundred, besides those
who died in the Korah incident.
50 So Aaron returned to Moses at the door
of the tabernacle of meeting, for the plague had
stopped.

The Budding of Aaron's Rod

17 And the LORD spoke to Moses, saying:
2 "Speak to the children of Israel, and
get from them a rod from each father's house,
all their leaders according to their fathers'
houses—twelve rods. Write each man's name on
his rod.
3 "And you shall write Aaron's name on the
rod of Levi. For there shall be one rod for the
head of *each* father's house.
4 "Then you shall place them in the tabernacle of meeting before [a]the Testimony, [b]where I
meet with you.
5 "And it shall be *that* the rod of the man
[a]whom I choose will blossom; thus I will rid Myself of the complaints of the children of Israel,
[b]which they make against you."
6 So Moses spoke to the children of Israel,
and each of their leaders gave him a rod apiece,
for each leader according to their fathers' houses,

KJV

fathers' houses, *even* twelve rods: and the rod of
Aaron *was* among their rods.
7 And Moses laid up the rods before the
LORD in [a]the tabernacle of witness.
8 And it came to pass, that on the morrow
Moses went into the tabernacle of witness; and,
behold, the [a]rod of Aaron for the house of Levi
was budded, and brought forth buds, and bloomed
blossoms, and yielded almonds.
9 And Moses brought out all the rods from
before the LORD unto all the children of Israel:
and they looked, and took every man his rod.
10 And the LORD said unto Moses, Bring
[a]Aaron's rod again before the testimony, to be
kept [b]for a token against the rebels; [c]and thou
shalt quite take away their murmurings from me,
that they die not.
11 And Moses did *so:* as the LORD commanded him, so did he.
12 And the children of Israel spake unto Moses, saying, Behold, we die, we perish, we all
perish.
13 [a]Whosoever cometh any thing near unto
the tabernacle of the LORD shall die: shall we be
consumed with dying?

Duties of Priests and Levites

18 And the LORD said unto Aaron, [a]Thou and
thy sons and thy father's house with thee
shall [b]bear the iniquity of the sanctuary: and thou
and thy sons with thee shall bear the iniquity of
your priesthood.
2 And thy brethren also of the [a]tribe of Levi,
the tribe of thy father, bring thou with thee, that
they may be [b]joined unto thee, and minister unto
thee: but thou and thy sons with thee *shall minister* before the tabernacle of witness.
3 And they shall keep thy charge, and [a]the
charge of all the tabernacle: [b]only they shall not
come nigh the vessels of the sanctuary and the
altar, [c]that neither they, nor ye also, die.
4 And they shall be joined unto thee, and
keep the charge of the tabernacle of the congregation, for all the service of the tabernacle: [a]and a
stranger shall not come nigh unto you.
5 And ye shall keep [a]the charge of the sanctuary, and the charge of the altar: [b]that there be
no wrath any more upon the children of Israel.
6 And I, behold, I have [a]taken your brethren
the Levites from among the children of Israel: [b]to
you *they are* given *as* a gift for the LORD, to do
the service of the tabernacle of the congregation.
7 Therefore [a]thou and thy sons with thee
shall keep your priest's office for every thing of
the altar, and [b]within the vail; and ye shall serve:
I have given your priest's office *unto you as* a
[c]service of gift: and the stranger that cometh nigh
shall be put to death.

Offerings for Support of the Priests

8 And the LORD spake unto Aaron, Behold,
[a]I also have given thee the charge of mine heave
offerings of all the hallowed things of the children
of Israel; unto thee have I given them [b]by reason
of the anointing, and to thy sons, by an ordinance
for ever.
9 This shall be thine of the most holy things,
reserved from the fire: every oblation of their's,
every [a]meat offering of their's, and every [b]sin offering of their's, and every [c]trespass offering of
their's, which they shall render unto me, *shall be*
most holy for thee and for thy sons.
10 [a]In the most holy *place* shalt thou eat it;
every male shall eat it: it shall be holy unto thee.
11 And this *is* thine; [a]the heave offering of
their gift, with all the wave offerings of the children of Israel: I have given them unto thee, and
to thy sons and to thy daughters with thee, by a
statute for ever: [b]every one that is clean in thy
house shall eat of it.
12 [a]All the best of the oil, and all the best of
the wine, and of the wheat, [b]the firstfruits of them

7 [a]Ex. 38:21; Num. 1:50, 51; 9:15; 18:2; Acts 7:44
8 [a][Ezek. 17:24]; Heb. 9:4
10 [a]Heb. 9:4 [b]Num. 16:38; Deut. 9:7, 24 [c]Num. 17:5
13 [a]Num. 1:51, 53; 18:4, 7

CHAPTER 18

1 [a]Num. 17:13 [b]Ex. 28:38; Lev. 10:17; 22:16
2 [a]Gen. 29:34; Num. 1:47 [b]Num. 3:5–10
3 [a]Num. 3:25, 31, 36 [b]Num. 16:40 [c]Num. 4:15
4 [a]Num. 3:10
5 [a]Ex. 27:21; 30:7; Lev. 24:3 [b]Num. 8:19; 16:46
6 [a]Num. 3:12, 45 [b]Num. 3:9
7 [a]Num. 3:10; 18:5 [b]Heb. 9:3, 6 [c]Matt. 10:8; 1 Pet. 5:2, 3
8 [a]Lev. 6:16, 18; 7:28–34; Num. 5:9 [b]Ex. 29:29; 40:13, 15
9 [a]Lev. 2:2, 3; 10:12, 13 [b]Lev. 6:25, 26 [c]Lev. 7:7; Num. 5:8–10
10 [a]Lev. 6:16, 26
11 [a]Ex. 29:27, 28; Deut. 18:3–5 [b]Lev. 22:1–16
12 [a]Ex. 23:19; Neh. 10:35, 36 [b]Ex. 22:29; Lev. 23:20

NKJV

twelve rods; and the rod of Aaron *was* among
their rods.
7 And Moses placed the rods before the
LORD in [a]the tabernacle of witness.
8 Now it came to pass on the next day that
Moses went into the tabernacle of witness, and
behold, the [a]rod of Aaron, of the house of Levi,
had sprouted and put forth buds, had produced
blossoms and yielded ripe almonds.
9 Then Moses brought out all the rods from
before the LORD to all the children of Israel; and
they looked, and each man took his rod.
10 And the LORD said to Moses, "Bring [a]Aar-
on's rod back before the Testimony, to be kept
[b]as a sign against the rebels, [c]that you may put
their complaints away from Me, lest they die."
11 Thus did Moses; just as the LORD had commanded him, so he did.
12 So the children of Israel spoke to Moses,
saying, "Surely we die, we perish, we all perish!
13 [a]"Whoever even comes near the tabernacle of the LORD must die. Shall we all utterly die?"

Duties of Priests and Levites

18 Then the LORD said to Aaron: [a]"You and
your sons and your father's house with you
shall [b]bear the iniquity *related to* the sanctuary,
and you and your sons with you shall bear the
iniquity *associated with* your priesthood.
2 "Also bring with you your brethren of the
[a]tribe of Levi, the tribe of your father, that they
may be [b]joined with you and serve you while you
and your sons *are* with you before the tabernacle
of witness.
3 "They shall attend to your needs and [a]all
the needs of the tabernacle; [b]but they shall not
come near the articles of the sanctuary and the
altar, [c]lest they die—they and you also.
4 "They shall be joined with you and attend
to the needs of the tabernacle of meeting, for all
the work of the tabernacle; [a]but an outsider shall
not come near you.
5 "And you shall attend to [a]the duties of the
sanctuary and the duties of the altar, [b]that there
may be no more wrath on the children of Israel.
6 "Behold, I Myself have [a]taken your brethren the Levites from among the children of Israel;
[b]*they are* a gift to you, given by the LORD, to do
the work of the tabernacle of meeting.
7 "Therefore [a]you and your sons with you
shall attend to your priesthood for everything at
the altar and [b]behind the veil; and you shall serve.
I give your priesthood *to you* as a [c]gift for service,
but the outsider who comes near shall be put to
death."

Offerings for Support of the Priests

8 And the LORD spoke to Aaron: "Here, [a]I
Myself have also given you charge of My heave
offerings, all the holy gifts of the children of Israel; I have given them [b]as a portion to you and
your sons, as an ordinance forever.
9 "This shall be yours of the most holy
things *reserved* from the fire: every offering of
theirs, every [a]grain offering and every [b]sin offering and every [c]trespass offering which they render to Me, *shall be* most holy for you and your
sons.
10 [a]"In a most holy *place* you shall eat it;
every male shall eat it. It shall be holy to you.
11 "This also *is* yours: [a]the heave offering
of their gift, with all the wave offerings of the
children of Israel; I have given them to you, and
your sons and daughters with you, as an ordinance forever. [b]Everyone who is clean in your
house may eat it.
12 [a]"All the best of the oil, all the best of
the new wine and the grain, [b]their firstfruits

KJV

which they shall offer unto the LORD, them have I given thee.

13 *And* whatsoever is first ripe in the land, [a]which they shall bring unto the LORD, shall be thine; every one that is clean in thine house shall eat *of* it.

14 [a]Every thing devoted in Israel shall be thine.

15 Every thing that openeth [a]the matrix in all flesh, which they bring unto the LORD, *whether it be* of men or beasts, shall be thine: nevertheless [b]the firstborn of man shalt thou surely redeem, and the firstling of unclean beasts shalt thou redeem.

16 And those that are to be redeemed from a month old shalt thou redeem, [a]according to thine estimation, for the money of five shekels, after the shekel of the sanctuary, which *is* [b]twenty gerahs.

17 [a]But the firstling of a cow, or the firstling of a sheep, or the firstling of a goat, thou shalt not redeem; they *are* holy: [b]thou shalt sprinkle their blood upon the altar, and shalt burn their fat *for* an offering made by fire, for a sweet savour unto the LORD.

18 And the flesh of them shall be thine, as the [a]wave breast and as the right shoulder are thine.

19 All the heave offerings of the holy things, which the children of Israel offer unto the LORD, have I given thee, and thy sons and thy daughters with thee, by a statute for ever: [a]it *is* a covenant of salt for ever before the LORD unto thee and to thy seed with thee.

20 And the LORD spake unto Aaron, Thou shalt have [a]no inheritance in their land, neither shalt thou have any part among them: [b]I *am* thy part and thine inheritance among the children of Israel.

Tithes for Support of the Levites

21 And, behold, [a]I have given the children of Levi all the tenth in Israel for an inheritance, for their service which they serve, *even* [b]the service of the tabernacle of the congregation.

22 [a]Neither must the children of Israel henceforth come nigh the tabernacle of the congregation, [b]lest they bear sin, and die.

23 But the Levites shall do the service of the tabernacle of the congregation, and they shall bear their iniquity: *it shall be* a statute for ever throughout your generations, that among the children of Israel they have no inheritance.

24 But the tithes of the children of Israel, which they offer *as* an heave offering unto the LORD, I have given to the Levites to inherit: therefore I have said unto them, Among the children of Israel they shall have no inheritance.

The Tithe of the Levites

25 And the LORD spake unto Moses, saying,

26 Thus speak unto the Levites, and say unto them, When ye take of the children of Israel the tithes which I have given you from them for your inheritance, then ye shall offer up an heave offering of it for the LORD, [a]*even* a tenth *part* of the tithe.

27 And *this* your heave offering shall be reckoned unto you, as though *it were* the corn of the [a]threshingfloor, and as the fulness of the winepress.

28 Thus ye also shall offer an heave offering unto the LORD of all your tithes, which ye receive of the children of Israel; and ye shall give thereof the LORD's heave offering to Aaron the priest.

29 Out of all your gifts ye shall offer every heave offering of the LORD, of all the best thereof, *even* the hallowed part thereof out of it.

30 Therefore thou shalt say unto them, When ye have heaved the best thereof from it, then it shall be counted unto the Levites as the increase

13 [a]Ex. 22:29; 23:19; 34:26
14 [a]Lev. 27:1–33
15 [a]Ex. 13:2 [b]Ex. 13:12–15; Num. 3:46; Luke 2:22–24
16 [a]Lev. 27:6 [b]Ex. 30:13
17 [a]Deut. 15:19 [b]Lev. 3:2, 5
18 [a]Ex. 29:26–28; Lev. 7:31–36
19 [a]Lev. 2:13; 2 Chr. 13:5; [Mark 9:49, 50]
20 [a]Deut. 10:8, 9; 12:12; 14:27–29; 18:1, 2; Josh. 13:14, 33 [b]Ps. 16:5; Ezek. 44:28
21 [a]Lev. 27:30–33; Deut. 14:22–29; Neh. 10:37; 12:44; Mal. 3:8–10; [Heb. 7:4–10] [b]Num. 3:7, 8
22 [a]Num. 1:51 [b]Lev. 22:9
26 [a]Neh. 10:38
27 [a]Num. 15:20; [2 Cor. 8:12]

NKJV

which they offer to the LORD, I have given them to you.

13 "Whatever first ripe fruit is in their land, [a]which they bring to the LORD, shall be yours. Everyone who is clean in your house may eat it.

14 [a]"Every devoted thing in Israel shall be yours.

15 "Everything that first opens [a]the womb of all flesh, which they bring to the LORD, whether man or beast, shall be yours; nevertheless [b]the firstborn of man you shall surely redeem, and the firstborn of unclean animals you shall redeem.

16 "And those redeemed of the devoted things you shall redeem when one month old, [a]according to your valuation, for five shekels of silver, according to the shekel of the sanctuary, which *is* [b]twenty gerahs.

17 [a]"But the firstborn of a cow, the firstborn of a sheep, or the firstborn of a goat you shall not redeem; they *are* holy. [b]You shall sprinkle their blood on the altar, and burn their fat *as* an offering made by fire for a sweet aroma to the LORD.

18 "And their flesh shall be yours, just as the [a]wave breast and the right thigh are yours.

19 "All the heave offerings of the holy things, which the children of Israel offer to the LORD, I have given to you and your sons and daughters with you as an ordinance forever; [a]it *is* a covenant of salt forever before the LORD with you and your descendants with you."

20 Then the LORD said to Aaron: "You shall have [a]no inheritance in their land, nor shall you have any portion among them; [b]I *am* your portion and your inheritance among the children of Israel.

Tithes for Support of the Levites

21 "Behold, [a]I have given the children of Levi all the tithes in Israel as an inheritance in return for the work which they perform, [b]the work of the tabernacle of meeting.

22 [a]"Hereafter the children of Israel shall not come near the tabernacle of meeting, [b]lest they bear sin and die.

23 "But the Levites shall perform the work of the tabernacle of meeting, and they shall bear their iniquity; *it shall be* a statute forever, throughout your generations, that among the children of Israel they shall have no inheritance.

24 "For the tithes of the children of Israel, which they offer up *as* a heave offering to the LORD, I have given to the Levites as an inheritance; therefore I have said to them, 'Among the children of Israel they shall have no inheritance.' "

The Tithe of the Levites

25 Then the LORD spoke to Moses, saying,

26 "Speak thus to the Levites, and say to them: 'When you take from the children of Israel the tithes which I have given you from them as your inheritance, then you shall offer up a heave offering of it to the LORD, [a]a tenth of the tithe.

27 'And your heave offering shall be reckoned to you as though *it were* the grain of the [a]threshing floor and as the fullness of the winepress.

28 'Thus you shall also offer a heave offering to the LORD from all your tithes which you receive from the children of Israel, and you shall give the LORD's heave offering from it to Aaron the priest.

29 'Of all your gifts you shall offer up every heave offering due to the LORD, from all the best of them, the consecrated part of them.'

30 "Therefore you shall say to them: 'When you have lifted up the best of it, then *the rest* shall be accounted to the Levites as the produce

KJV

of the threshingfloor, and as the increase of the winepress.

31 And ye shall eat it in every place, ye and your households: for it *is* [a]your reward for your service in the tabernacle of the congregation.

32 And ye shall [a]bear no sin by reason of it, when ye have heaved from it the best of it: neither shall ye [b]pollute the holy things of the children of Israel, lest ye die.

Laws of Purification

19 And the LORD spake unto Moses and unto Aaron, saying,

2 This *is* the ordinance of the law which the LORD hath commanded, saying, Speak unto the children of Israel, that they bring thee a red heifer without spot, wherein *is* no [a]blemish, [b]*and* upon which never came yoke:

3 And ye shall give her unto Eleazar the priest, that he may bring her [a]forth without the camp, and *one* shall slay her before his face:

4 And Eleazar the priest shall take of her blood with his finger, and [a]sprinkle of her blood directly before the tabernacle of the congregation seven times:

5 And *one* shall burn the heifer in his sight; [a]her skin, and her flesh, and her blood, with her dung, shall he burn:

6 And the priest shall take [a]cedar wood, and [b]hyssop, and scarlet, and cast *it* into the midst of the burning of the heifer.

7 [a]Then the priest shall wash his clothes, and he shall bathe his flesh in water, and afterward he shall come into the camp, and the priest shall be unclean until the even.

8 And he that burneth her shall wash his clothes in water, and bathe his flesh in water, and shall be unclean until the even.

9 And a man *that is* clean shall gather up [a]the ashes of the heifer, and lay *them* up without the camp in a clean place, and it shall be kept for the congregation of the children of Israel [b]for a water of separation: it *is* a purification for sin.

10 And he that gathereth the ashes of the heifer shall wash his clothes, and be unclean until the even: and it shall be unto the children of Israel, and unto the stranger that sojourneth among them, for a statute for ever.

11 [a]He that toucheth the dead body of any man shall be unclean seven days.

12 [a]He shall purify himself with it on the third day, and on the seventh day he shall be clean: but if he purify not himself the third day, then the seventh day he shall not be clean.

13 Whosoever toucheth the dead body of any man that is dead, and purifieth [a]not himself, [b]defileth the tabernacle of the LORD; and that soul shall be cut off from Israel: because [c]the water of separation was not sprinkled upon him, he shall be unclean; [d]his uncleanness *is* yet upon him.

14 This *is* the law, when a man dieth in a tent: all that come into the tent, and all that *is* in the tent, shall be unclean seven days.

15 And every [a]open vessel, which hath no covering bound upon it, *is* unclean.

16 And [a]whosoever toucheth one that is slain with a sword in the open fields, or a dead body, or a bone of a man, or a grave, shall be unclean seven days.

17 And for an unclean *person* they shall take of the [a]ashes of the burnt heifer of purification for sin, and running water shall be put thereto in a vessel:

18 And a clean person shall take [a]hyssop, and dip *it* in the water, and sprinkle *it* upon the tent, and upon all the vessels, and upon the persons that were there, and upon him that touched a bone, or one slain, or one dead, or a grave:

19 And the clean *person* shall sprinkle upon the unclean on the third day, and on the seventh

31 [a][Matt. 10:10; Luke 10:7]; 1 Cor. 9:13; [1 Tim. 5:18]
32 [a]Lev. 19:8; 22:16; Ezek. 22:26 [b]Lev. 22:2, 15

CHAPTER 19

2 [a]Lev. 22:20–25 [b]Deut. 21:3; 1 Sam. 6:7
3 [a]Lev. 4:12, 21; Num. 19:9; Heb. 13:11
4 [a]Lev. 4:6; Heb. 9:13
5 [a]Ex. 29:14; Lev. 4:11, 12; 9:11
6 [a]Lev. 14:4, 6, 49 [b]Ex. 12:22; 1 Kin. 4:33
7 [a]Lev. 11:25; 15:5; 16:26, 28
9 [a][Heb. 9:13, 14] [b]Num. 19:13, 20, 21
11 [a]Lev. 21:1, 11; Num. 5:2; 6:6; 9:6, 10; 31:19; Lam. 4:14; Hag. 2:13
12 [a]Num. 19:19; 31:19
13 [a]Lev. 22:3–7 [b]Lev. 15:31 [c]Num. 8:7; 19:9 [d]Lev. 7:20; 22:3
15 [a]Lev. 11:32; Num. 31:20
16 [a]Num. 19:11; 31:19
17 [a]Num. 19:9
18 [a]Ps. 51:7

*
19:9 Lit. *impurity*

NKJV

of the threshing floor and as the produce of the winepress.

31 'You may eat it in any place, you and your households, for it *is* [a]your reward for your work in the tabernacle of meeting.

32 'And you shall [a]bear no sin because of it, when you have lifted up the best of it. But you shall not [b]profane the holy gifts of the children of Israel, lest you die.' "

Laws of Purification

19 Now the LORD spoke to Moses and Aaron, saying,

2 "This *is* the ordinance of the law which the LORD has commanded, saying: 'Speak to the children of Israel, that they bring you a red heifer without blemish, in which there *is* no [a]defect [b]*and* on which a yoke has never come.

3 'You shall give it to Eleazar the priest, that he may take it [a]outside the camp, and it shall be slaughtered before him;

4 'and Eleazar the priest shall take some of its blood with his finger, and [a]sprinkle some of its blood seven times directly in front of the tabernacle of meeting.

5 'Then the heifer shall be burned in his sight: [a]its hide, its flesh, its blood, and its offal shall be burned.

6 'And the priest shall take [a]cedar wood and [b]hyssop and scarlet, and cast *them* into the midst of the fire burning the heifer.

7 [a]'Then the priest shall wash his clothes, he shall bathe in water, and afterward he shall come into the camp; the priest shall be unclean until evening.

8 'And the one who burns it shall wash his clothes in water, bathe in water, and shall be unclean until evening.

9 'Then a man *who is* clean shall gather up [a]the ashes of the heifer, and store *them* outside the camp in a clean place; and they shall be kept for the congregation of the children of Israel [b]for the water of *purification; it *is* for purifying from sin.

10 'And the one who gathers the ashes of the heifer shall wash his clothes, and be unclean until evening. It shall be a statute forever to the children of Israel and to the stranger who dwells among them.

11 [a]'He who touches the dead body of anyone shall be unclean seven days.

12 [a]'He shall purify himself with the water on the third day and on the seventh day; *then* he will be clean. But if he does not purify himself on the third day and on the seventh day, he will not be clean.

13 'Whoever touches the body of anyone who has died, and [a]does not purify himself, [b]defiles the tabernacle of the LORD. That person shall be cut off from Israel. He shall be unclean, because [c]the water of purification was not sprinkled on him; [d]his uncleanness *is* still on him.

14 'This *is* the law when a man dies in a tent: All who come into the tent and all who *are* in the tent shall be unclean seven days;

15 'and every [a]open vessel, which has no cover fastened on it, *is* unclean.

16 [a]'Whoever in the open field touches one who is slain by a sword or who has died, or a bone of a man, or a grave, shall be unclean seven days.

17 'And for an unclean *person* they shall take some of the [a]ashes of the heifer burnt for purification from sin, and running water shall be put on them in a vessel.

18 'A clean person shall take [a]hyssop and dip *it* in the water, sprinkle *it* on the tent, on all the vessels, on the persons who were there, or on the one who touched a bone, the slain, the dead, or a grave.

19 'The clean *person* shall sprinkle the unclean on the third day and on the seventh day;

KJV

day: [a]and on the seventh day he shall purify himself, and wash his clothes, and bathe himself in water, and shall be clean at even.

20 But the man that shall be unclean, and shall not purify himself, that soul shall be cut off from among the congregation, because he hath [a]defiled the sanctuary of the LORD: the water of separation hath not been sprinkled upon him; he *is* unclean.

21 And it shall be a perpetual statute unto them, that he that sprinkleth the water of separation shall wash his clothes; and he that toucheth the water of separation shall be unclean until even.

22 And [a]whatsoever the unclean *person* toucheth shall be unclean; and [b]the soul that toucheth *it* shall be unclean until even.

Moses' Error at Kadesh
(Ex. 17:1–7)

20 Then [a]came the children of Israel, *even* the whole congregation, into the desert of Zin in the first month: and the people abode in [b]Kadesh; and [c]Miriam died there, and was buried there.

2 [a]And there was no water for the congregation: [b]and they gathered themselves together against Moses and against Aaron.

3 And the people [a]chode with Moses, and spake, saying, Would God that we had died [b]when our brethren died before the LORD!

4 And [a]why have ye brought up the congregation of the LORD into this wilderness, that we and our cattle should die there?

5 And wherefore have ye made us to come up out of Egypt, to bring us in unto this evil place? it *is* no place of seed, or of figs, or of vines, or of pomegranates; neither *is* there any water to drink.

6 And Moses and Aaron went from the presence of the assembly unto the door of the tabernacle of the congregation, and [a]they fell upon their faces: and [b]the glory of the LORD appeared unto them.

7 And the LORD spake unto Moses, saying,

8 [a]Take the rod, and gather thou the assembly together, thou, and Aaron thy brother, and speak ye unto the rock before their eyes; and it shall give forth his water, and [b]thou shalt bring forth to them water out of the rock: so thou shalt give the congregation and their beasts drink.

9 And Moses took the rod [a]from before the LORD, as he commanded him.

10 And Moses and Aaron gathered the congregation together before the rock, and he said unto them, [a]Hear now, ye rebels; must we fetch you water out of this rock?

11 And Moses lifted up his hand, and with his rod he smote the rock twice: and [a]the water came out abundantly, and the congregation drank, and their beasts *also*.

12 And the LORD spake unto Moses and Aaron, Because [a]ye believed me not, to [b]sanctify me in the eyes of the children of Israel, therefore ye shall not bring this congregation into the land which I have given them.

13 [a]This *is* the water of Meribah; because the children of Israel strove with the LORD, and he was sanctified in them.

Passage Through Edom Refused

14 [a]And Moses sent messengers from Kadesh unto the king of [b]Edom, [c]Thus saith thy brother Israel, Thou knowest all the travel that hath befallen us:

15 [a]How our fathers went down into Egypt, [b]and we have dwelt in Egypt a long time; [c]and the Egyptians vexed us, and our fathers:

16 And [a]when we cried unto the LORD, he heard our voice, and [b]sent an angel, and hath brought us forth out of Egypt: and, behold, we *are* in Kadesh, a city in the uttermost of thy border:

---

19 [a]Lev. 14:9 **20** [a]Num. 19:13 **22** [a]Hag. 2:11–13 [b]Lev. 15:5

CHAPTER 20

1 [a]Num. 13:21; 33:36 [b]Num. 13:26 [c]Ex. 15:20; Num. 26:59 **2** [a]Ex. 17:1 [b]Num. 16:19, 42 **3** [a]Ex. 17:2; Num. 14:2 [b]Num. 11:1, 33; 14:37; 16:31–35, 49 **4** [a]Ex. 17:3 **6** [a]Num. 14:5; 16:4, 22, 45 [b]Num. 14:10 **8** [a]Ex. 4:17, 20; 17:5, 6 [b]Neh. 9:15; Ps. 78:15, 16; 105:41; Is. 43:20; 48:21; [1 Cor. 10:4] **9** [a]Num. 17:10 **10** [a]Ps. 106:33 **11** [a]Ex. 17:6; Deut. 8:15; Ps. 78:16; Is. 48:21; [1 Cor. 10:4] **12** [a]Num. 20:28; 27:14; Deut. 1:37; 3:26, 27; 34:5 [b]Lev. 10:3; Ezek. 20:41; 36:23; 1 Pet. 3:15 **13** [a]Deut. 33:8; Ps. 106:32 **14** [a]Judg. 11:16, 17 [b]Gen. 36:31–39 [c]Deut. 2:4; Obad. 10–12 **15** [a]Gen. 46:6; Acts 7:15 [b]Ex. 12:40 [c]Ex. 1:11; Deut. 26:6; Acts 7:19 **16** [a]Ex. 2:23; 3:7 [b]Ex. 3:2; 14:19

*———

20:13 Lit. *Contention*

NKJV

[a]and on the seventh day he shall purify himself, wash his clothes, and bathe in water; and at evening he shall be clean.

20 'But the man who is unclean and does not purify himself, that person shall be cut off from among the assembly, because he has [a]defiled the sanctuary of the LORD. The water of purification has not been sprinkled on him; he *is* unclean.

21 'It shall be a perpetual statute for them. He who sprinkles the water of purification shall wash his clothes; and he who touches the water of purification shall be unclean until evening.

22 [a]'Whatever the unclean *person* touches shall be unclean; and [b]the person who touches *it* shall be unclean until evening.' "

Moses' Error at Kadesh
(Ex. 17:1–7)

20 Then[a] the children of Israel, the whole congregation, came into the Wilderness of Zin in the first month, and the people stayed in [b]Kadesh; and [c]Miriam died there and was buried there.

2 [a]Now there was no water for the congregation; [b]so they gathered together against Moses and Aaron.

3 And the people [a]contended with Moses and spoke, saying: "If only we had died [b]when our brethren died before the LORD!

4 [a]"Why have you brought up the assembly of the LORD into this wilderness, that we and our animals should die here?

5 "And why have you made us come up out of Egypt, to bring us to this evil place? It *is* not a place of grain or figs or vines or pomegranates; nor *is* there any water to drink."

6 So Moses and Aaron went from the presence of the assembly to the door of the tabernacle of meeting, and [a]they fell on their faces. And [b]the glory of the LORD appeared to them.

7 Then the LORD spoke to Moses, saying,

8 [a]"Take the rod; you and your brother Aaron gather the congregation together. Speak to the rock before their eyes, and it will yield its water; thus [b]you shall bring water for them out of the rock, and give drink to the congregation and their animals."

9 So Moses took the rod [a]from before the LORD as He commanded him.

10 And Moses and Aaron gathered the assembly together before the rock; and he said to them, [a]"Hear now, you rebels! Must we bring water for you out of this rock?"

11 Then Moses lifted his hand and struck the rock twice with his rod; [a]and water came out abundantly, and the congregation and their animals drank.

12 Then the LORD spoke to Moses and Aaron, "Because [a]you did not believe Me, to [b]hallow Me in the eyes of the children of Israel, therefore you shall not bring this assembly into the land which I have given them."

13 [a]This *was* the water of *Meribah, because the children of Israel contended with the LORD, and He was hallowed among them.

Passage Through Edom Refused

14 [a]Now Moses sent messengers from Kadesh to the king of [b]Edom. [c]"Thus says your brother Israel: 'You know all the hardship that has befallen us,

15 [a]'how our fathers went down to Egypt, [b]and we dwelt in Egypt a long time, [c]and the Egyptians afflicted us and our fathers.

16 [a]'When we cried out to the LORD, He heard our voice and [b]sent the Angel and brought us up out of Egypt; now here we are in Kadesh, a city on the edge of your border.

KJV

17 [a]Let us pass, I pray thee, through thy country: we will not pass through the fields, or through the vineyards, neither will we drink *of* the water of the wells: we will go by the king's *high* way, we will not turn to the right hand nor to the left, until we have passed thy borders.

18 And [a]Edom said unto him, Thou shalt not pass by me, lest I come out against thee with the sword.

19 And the children of Israel said unto him, We will go by the high way: and if I and my cattle drink of thy water, [a]then I will pay for it: I will only, without *doing* any thing *else,* go through on my feet.

20 And he said, [a]Thou shalt not go through. And Edom came out against him with much people, and with a strong hand.

21 Thus Edom [a]refused to give Israel passage through his border: wherefore Israel [b]turned away from him.

Death of Aaron

22 And the children of Israel, *even* the whole congregation, journeyed from [a]Kadesh, [b]and came unto mount Hor.

23 And the LORD spake unto Moses and Aaron in mount Hor, by the coast of the land of Edom, saying,

24 Aaron shall be [a]gathered unto his people: for he shall not enter into the land which I have given unto the children of Israel, because ye rebelled against my word at the water of Meribah.

25 [a]Take Aaron and Eleazar his son, and bring them up unto mount Hor:

26 And strip Aaron of his garments, and put them upon Eleazar his son: and Aaron shall be gathered *unto his people,* and shall die there.

27 And Moses did as the LORD commanded: and they went up into mount Hor in the sight of all the congregation.

28 And [a]Moses stripped Aaron of his garments, and put them upon Eleazar his son; and [b]Aaron died there in the top of the mount: and Moses and Eleazar came down from the mount.

29 And when all the congregation saw that Aaron was dead, they mourned for Aaron [a]thirty days, *even* all the house of Israel.

Canaanites Defeated at Hormah

21 And *when* [a]king Arad the Canaanite, which dwelt in the south, heard tell that Israel came by the way of the spies; then he fought against Israel, and took *some* of them prisoners.

2 [a]And Israel vowed a vow unto the LORD, and said, If thou wilt indeed deliver this people into my hand, then [b]I will utterly destroy their cities.

3 And the LORD hearkened to the voice of Israel, and delivered up the Canaanites; and they utterly destroyed them and their cities: and he called the name of the place Hormah.

The Bronze Serpent

4 And they journeyed from mount Hor by the way of the Red sea, to [a]compass the land of Edom: and the soul of the people was much discouraged because of the way.

5 And the people [a]spake against God, and against Moses, Wherefore have ye brought us up out of Egypt to die in the wilderness? for *there is* no bread, neither *is there any* water; and our soul loatheth this light bread.

6 And [a]the LORD sent [b]fiery serpents among the people, and they bit the people; and much people of Israel died.

7 [a]Therefore the people came to Moses, and said, We have [b]sinned, for we have spoken against the LORD, and against thee; [c]pray unto the LORD, that he take away the serpents from us. And Moses prayed for the people.

8 And the LORD said unto Moses, [a]Make thee a [b]fiery serpent, and set it upon a pole: and

17 [a]Num. 21:22
18 [a]Num. 24:18; Ps. 137:7; Ezek. 25:12, 13; Obad. 10–15
19 [a]Deut. 2:6, 28
20 [a]Judg. 11:17
21 [a]Deut. 2:27, 30 [b]Deut. 2:8; Judg. 11:18
22 [a]Num. 33:37 [b]Num. 21:4
24 [a]Gen. 25:8; Deut. 32:50
25 [a]Num. 33:38; Deut. 32:50
28 [a]Ex. 29:29, 30; Deut. 10:6 [b]Num. 33:38
29 [a]Gen. 50:3, 10; Deut. 34:8

CHAPTER 21

1 [a]Num. 33:40; Josh. 12:14; Judg. 1:16
2 [a]Gen. 28:20; Judg. 11:30 [b]Deut. 2:34
4 [a]Judg. 11:18
5 [a]Num. 20:4, 5
6 [a]1 Cor. 10:9 [b]Deut. 8:15
7 [a]Num. 11:2; Ps. 78:34; Is. 26:16; Hos. 5:15 [b]Lev. 26:40 [c]Ex. 8:8; 1 Sam. 12:19; 1 Kin. 13:6; Acts 8:24
8 [a][John 3:14, 15] [b]Is. 14:29; 30:6

*

21:3 Lit. *Utter Destruction*

NKJV

17 'Please [a]let us pass through your country. We will not pass through fields or vineyards, nor will we drink water from wells; we will go along the King's Highway; we will not turn aside to the right hand or to the left until we have passed through your territory.' "

18 Then [a]Edom said to him, "You shall not pass through my *land,* lest I come out against you with the sword."

19 So the children of Israel said to him, "We will go by the Highway, and if I or my livestock drink any of your water, [a]then I will pay for it; let me only pass through on foot, nothing *more.*"

20 Then he said, [a]"You shall not pass through." So Edom came out against them with many men and with a strong hand.

21 Thus Edom [a]refused to give Israel passage through his territory; so Israel [b]turned away from him.

Death of Aaron

22 Now the children of Israel, the whole congregation, journeyed from [a]Kadesh [b]and came to Mount Hor.

23 And the LORD spoke to Moses and Aaron in Mount Hor by the border of the land of Edom, saying:

24 "Aaron shall be [a]gathered to his people, for he shall not enter the land which I have given to the children of Israel, because you rebelled against My word at the water of Meribah.

25 [a]"Take Aaron and Eleazar his son, and bring them up to Mount Hor;

26 "and strip Aaron of his garments and put them on Eleazar his son; for Aaron shall be gathered *to his people* and die there."

27 So Moses did just as the LORD commanded, and they went up to Mount Hor in the sight of all the congregation.

28 [a]Moses stripped Aaron of his garments and put them on Eleazar his son; and [b]Aaron died there on the top of the mountain. Then Moses and Eleazar came down from the mountain.

29 Now when all the congregation saw that Aaron was dead, all the house of Israel mourned for Aaron [a]thirty days.

Canaanites Defeated at Hormah

21 The [a]king of Arad, the Canaanite, who dwelt in the South, heard that Israel was coming on the road to Atharim. Then he fought against Israel and took *some* of them prisoners.

2 [a]So Israel made a vow to the LORD, and said, "If You will indeed deliver this people into my hand, then [b]I will utterly destroy their cities."

3 And the LORD listened to the voice of Israel and delivered up the Canaanites, and they utterly destroyed them and their cities. So the name of that place was called *Hormah.

The Bronze Serpent

4 Then they journeyed from Mount Hor by the Way of the Red Sea, to [a]go around the land of Edom; and the soul of the people became very discouraged on the way.

5 And the people [a]spoke against God and against Moses: "Why have you brought us up out of Egypt to die in the wilderness? For *there is* no food and no water, and our soul loathes this worthless bread."

6 So [a]the LORD sent [b]fiery serpents among the people, and they bit the people; and many of the people of Israel died.

7 [a]Therefore the people came to Moses, and said, "We have [b]sinned, for we have spoken against the LORD and against you; [c]pray to the LORD that He take away the serpents from us." So Moses prayed for the people.

8 Then the LORD said to Moses, [a]"Make a [b]fiery *serpent,* and set it on a pole; and it shall

KJV

it shall come to pass, that every one that is bitten, when he looketh upon it, shall live.

9 And [a]Moses made a serpent of brass, and put it upon a pole, and it came to pass, that if a serpent had bitten any man, when he beheld the serpent of brass, he lived.

From Mount Hor to Moab

10 And the children of Israel set forward, and [a]pitched in Oboth.

11 And they journeyed from Oboth, and pitched at Ije–abarim, in the wilderness which *is* before Moab, toward the sunrising.

12 [a]From thence they removed, and pitched in the valley of Zared.

13 From thence they removed, and pitched on the other side of Arnon, which *is* in the wilderness that cometh out of the coasts of the Amorites: for [a]Arnon *is* the border of Moab, between Moab and the Amorites.

14 Wherefore it is said in the book of the wars of the LORD, What he did in the Red sea, and in the brooks of Arnon,

15 And at the stream of the brooks that goeth down to the dwelling of [a]Ar, and lieth upon the border of Moab.

16 And from thence *they went* [a]to Beer: that *is* the well whereof the LORD spake unto Moses, Gather the people together, and I will give them water.

17 [a]Then Israel sang this song, Spring up, O well; sing ye unto it:

18 The princes digged the well, the nobles of the people digged it, by *the direction of* the [a]lawgiver, with their staves. And from the wilderness *they went* to Mattanah:

19 And from Mattanah to Nahaliel: and from Nahaliel to Bamoth:

20 And from Bamoth *in* the valley, that *is* in the country of Moab, to the top of Pisgah, which looketh [a]toward Jeshimon.

King Sihon Defeated
(Deut. 2:26–37)

21 And [a]Israel sent messengers unto Sihon king of the Amorites, saying,

22 [a]Let me pass through thy land: we will not turn into the fields, or into the vineyards; we will not drink *of* the waters of the well: *but* we will go along by the king's *high* way, until we be past thy borders.

23 [a]And Sihon would not suffer Israel to pass through his border: but Sihon gathered all his people together, and went out against Israel into the wilderness: [b]and he came to Jahaz, and fought against Israel.

24 And [a]Israel smote him with the edge of the sword, and possessed his land from Arnon unto Jabbok, even unto the children of Ammon: for the border of the children of Ammon *was* strong.

25 And Israel took all these cities: and Israel [a]dwelt in all the cities of the Amorites, in Heshbon, and in all the villages thereof.

26 For Heshbon *was* the city of Sihon the king of the Amorites, who had fought against the former king of Moab, and taken all his land out of his hand, even unto Arnon.

27 Wherefore they that speak in proverbs say, Come into Heshbon, let the city of Sihon be built and prepared:

28 For there is [a]a fire gone out of Heshbon, a flame from the city of Sihon: it hath consumed

9 [a]2 Kin. 18:4; John 3:14, 15
10 [a]Num. 33:43, 44
12 [a]Deut. 2:13
13 [a]Num. 22:36; Judg. 11:18
15 [a]Num. 21:28; Deut. 2:9, 18, 29
16 [a]Judg. 9:21
17 [a]Ex. 15:1
18 [a]Is. 33:22
20 [a]Num. 23:28
21 [a]Num. 32:33; Deut. 2:26–37; Judg. 11:19
22 [a]Num. 20:16, 17
23 [a]Deut. 29:7 [b]Deut. 2:32; Judg. 11:20
24 [a]Deut. 2:33; Josh. 12:1; Neh. 9:22; Ps. 135:10; 136:19; Amos 2:9
25 [a]Amos 2:10
28 [a]Jer. 48:45, 46

NKJV

be that everyone who is bitten, when he looks at it, shall live."

9 So [a]Moses made a bronze serpent, and put it on a pole; and so it was, if a serpent had bitten anyone, when he looked at the bronze serpent, he lived.

From Mount Hor to Moab

10 Now the children of Israel moved on and [a]camped in Oboth.

11 And they journeyed from Oboth and camped at Ije Abarim, in the wilderness which *is* east of Moab, toward the sunrise.

12 [a]From there they moved and camped in the Valley of Zered.

13 From there they moved and camped on the other side of the Arnon, which *is* in the wilderness that extends from the border of the Amorites; for [a]the Arnon *is* the border of Moab, between Moab and the Amorites.

14 Therefore it is said in the Book of the Wars of the LORD:

*"Waheb in Suphah,
The brooks of the Arnon,
15 And the slope of the brooks
That reaches to the dwelling of [a]Ar,
And lies on the border of Moab."

16 From there *they went* [a]to Beer, which *is* the well where the LORD said to Moses, "Gather the people together, and I will give them water."

17 [a]Then Israel sang this song:

"Spring up, O well!
All of you sing to it—
18 The well the leaders sank,
Dug by the nation's nobles,
By the [a]lawgiver, with their staves."

And from the wilderness *they went* to Mattanah,

19 from Mattanah to Nahaliel, from Nahaliel to Bamoth,

20 and from Bamoth, *in* the valley that *is* in the country of Moab, to the top of Pisgah which looks [a]down on the *wasteland.

King Sihon Defeated
(Deut. 2:26–37)

21 Then [a]Israel sent messengers to Sihon king of the Amorites, saying,

22 [a]"Let me pass through your land. We will not turn aside into fields or vineyards; we will not drink water from wells. We will go by the King's Highway until we have passed through your territory."

23 [a]But Sihon would not allow Israel to pass through his territory. So Sihon gathered all his people together and went out against Israel in the wilderness, [b]and he came to Jahaz and fought against Israel.

24 Then [a]Israel defeated him with the edge of the sword, and took possession of his land from the Arnon to the Jabbok, as far as the people of Ammon; for the border of the people of Ammon *was* fortified.

25 So Israel took all these cities, and Israel [a]dwelt in all the cities of the Amorites, in Heshbon and in all its villages.

26 For Heshbon *was* the city of Sihon king of the Amorites, who had fought against the former king of Moab, and had taken all his land from his hand as far as the Arnon.

27 Therefore those who speak in proverbs say:

"Come to Heshbon, let it be built;
Let the city of Sihon be repaired.

28 "For [a]fire went out from Heshbon,
A flame from the city of Sihon;

*———

21:14 Ancient unknown places; Vg. *What He did in the Red Sea*
21:20 Heb. *Jeshimon*

KJV

[b]Ar of Moab, *and* the lords of the [c]high places of
Arnon.
29 Woe to thee, [a]Moab! thou art undone, O
people of [b]Chemosh: he hath given his [c]sons that
escaped, and his [d]daughters, into captivity unto
Sihon king of the Amorites.
30 We have shot at them; Heshbon is perished even [a]unto Dibon, and we have laid them
waste even unto Nophah, which *reacheth* unto
[b]Medeba.
31 Thus Israel dwelt in the land of the
Amorites.
32 And Moses sent to spy out [a]Jaazer, and
they took the villages thereof, and drove out the
Amorites that *were* there.

King Og Defeated
(Deut. 3:1–22)

33 [a]And they turned and went up by the way
of [b]Bashan: and Og the king of Bashan went out
against them, he, and all his people, to the battle
[c]at Edrei.
34 And the LORD said unto Moses, [a]Fear him
not: for I have delivered him into thy hand, and
all his people, and his land; and [b]thou shalt do
to him as thou didst unto Sihon king of the Amorites, which dwelt at Heshbon.
35 [a]So they smote him, and his sons, and all
his people, until there was none left him alive:
and they possessed his land.

Balak Sends for Balaam

22 And [a]the children of Israel set forward, and
pitched in the plains of Moab on this side
Jordan *by* Jericho.
2 And [a]Balak the son of Zippor saw all that
Israel had done to the Amorites.
3 And [a]Moab was sore afraid of the people,
because they *were* many: and Moab was distressed because of the children of Israel.
4 And Moab said unto [a]the elders of Midian,
Now shall this company lick up all *that are* round
about us, as the ox licketh up the grass of the
field. And Balak the son of Zippor *was* king of
the Moabites at that time.
5 [a]He sent messengers therefore unto Balaam the son of Beor to [b]Pethor, which *is* by the
river of the land of the children of his people, to
call him, saying, Behold, there is a people come
out from Egypt: behold, they cover the face of
the earth, and they abide over against me:
6 [a]Come now therefore, I pray thee, [b]curse
me this people; for they *are* too mighty for me:
peradventure I shall prevail, *that* we may smite
them, and *that* I may drive them out of the land:
for I wot that he whom thou blessest *is* blessed,
and he whom thou cursest is cursed.
7 And the elders of Moab and the elders of
Midian departed with [a]the rewards of divination
in their hand; and they came unto Balaam, and
spake unto him the words of Balak.
8 And he said unto them, [a]Lodge here this
night, and I will bring you word again, as the LORD
shall speak unto me: and the princes of Moab
abode with Balaam.
9 [a]And God came unto Balaam, and said,
What men *are* these with thee?
10 And Balaam said unto God, Balak the son
of Zippor, king of Moab, hath sent unto me,
saying,
11 Behold, *there is* a people come out of
Egypt, which covereth the face of the earth: come
now, curse me them; peradventure I shall be able
to overcome them, and drive them out.
12 And God said unto Balaam, Thou shalt not
go with them; thou shalt not curse the people:
for [a]they *are* blessed.
13 And Balaam rose up in the morning, and

28 [b]Deut. 2:9, 18; Is. 15:1 [c]Num. 22:41; 33:52
29 [a]Jer. 48:46 [b]Judg. 11:24; 1 Kin. 11:33; 2 Kin. 23:13 [c]Is. 15:2, 5 [d]Is. 16:2
30 [a]Num. 32:3, 34; Jer. 48:18, 22 [b]Is. 15:2
32 [a]Num. 32:1, 3, 35; Jer. 48:32
33 [a]Deut. 29:7 [b]Deut. 3:1 [c]Josh. 13:12
34 [a]Deut. 3:2 [b]Num. 21:24; Ps. 135:10; 136:20
35 [a]Deut. 3:3, 4; 29:7; Josh. 13:12

CHAPTER 22

1 [a]Num. 33:48, 49
2 [a]Josh. 24:9; Judg. 11:25; Mic. 6:5; Rev. 2:14
3 [a]Ex. 15:15
4 [a]Num. 25:15–18; 31:1–3; Josh. 13:21
5 [a]Num. 31:8, 16; Deut. 23:4; Josh. 13:22; 24:9; Neh. 13:1, 2; Mic. 6:5; 2 Pet. 2:15; Jude 11; Rev. 2:14 [b]Deut. 23:4
6 [a]Num. 22:17; 23:7, 8 [b]Num. 22:12; 24:9
7 [a]1 Sam. 9:7, 8
8 [a]Num. 22:19
9 [a]Gen. 20:3
12 [a]Num. 23:20; [Rom. 11:28]

*
22:5 The Euphrates • Or *the people of Amau*

NKJV

It consumed [b]Ar of Moab,
The lords of the [c]heights of the Arnon.
29 Woe to you, [a]Moab!
You have perished, O people of
[b]Chemosh!
He has given his [c]sons as fugitives,
And his [d]daughters into captivity,
To Sihon king of the Amorites.

30 "But we have shot at them;
Heshbon has perished [a]as far as Dibon.
Then we laid waste as far as Nophah,
Which *reaches* to [b]Medeba."

31 Thus Israel dwelt in the land of the
Amorites.
32 Then Moses sent to spy out [a]Jazer; and
they took its villages and drove out the Amorites
who *were* there.

King Og Defeated
(Deut. 3:1–22)

33 [a]And they turned and went up by the way
to [b]Bashan. So Og king of Bashan went out
against them, he and all his people, to battle [c]at
Edrei.
34 Then the LORD said to Moses, [a]"Do not
fear him, for I have delivered him into your hand,
with all his people and his land; and [b]you shall
do to him as you did to Sihon king of the Amorites, who dwelt at Heshbon."
35 [a]So they defeated him, his sons, and all
his people, until there was no survivor left him;
and they took possession of his land.

Balak Sends for Balaam

22 Then [a]the children of Israel moved, and
camped in the plains of Moab on the side
of the Jordan *across from* Jericho.
2 Now [a]Balak the son of Zippor saw all that
Israel had done to the Amorites.
3 And [a]Moab was exceedingly afraid of the
people because they *were* many, and Moab was
sick with dread because of the children of Israel.
4 So Moab said to [a]the elders of Midian,
"Now this company will lick up everything
around us, as an ox licks up the grass of the field."
And Balak the son of Zippor *was* king of the Moabites at that time.
5 Then [a]he sent messengers to Balaam the
son of Beor at [b]Pethor, which *is* near *the River
in the land of *the sons of his people, to call him,
saying: "Look, a people has come from Egypt.
See, they cover the face of the earth, and are set-
tling next to me!
6 [a]"Therefore please come at once, [b]curse
this people for me, for they *are* too mighty for
me. Perhaps I shall be able to defeat them and
drive them out of the land, for I know that he
whom you bless *is* blessed, and he whom you
curse is cursed."
7 So the elders of Moab and the elders of
Midian departed with [a]the diviner's fee in their
hand, and they came to Balaam and spoke to him
the words of Balak.
8 And he said to them, [a]"Lodge here tonight, and I will bring back word to you, as the
LORD speaks to me." So the princes of Moab
stayed with Balaam.
9 [a]Then God came to Balaam and said,
"Who *are* these men with you?"
10 So Balaam said to God, "Balak the son
of Zippor, king of Moab, has sent to me, *saying,*
11 'Look, a people has come out of Egypt,
and they cover the face of the earth. Come now,
curse them for me; perhaps I shall be able to overpower them and drive them out.' "
12 And God said to Balaam, "You shall not
go with them; you shall not curse the people, for
[a]they *are* blessed."
13 So Balaam rose in the morning and said

KJV

said unto the princes of Balak, Get you into your land: for the LORD refuseth to give me leave to go with you.

14 And the princes of Moab rose up, and they went unto Balak, and said, Balaam refuseth to come with us.

15 And Balak sent yet again princes, more, and more honourable than they.

16 And they came to Balaam, and said to him, Thus saith Balak the son of Zippor, Let nothing, I pray thee, hinder thee from coming unto me:

17 For I will [a]promote thee unto very great honour, and I will do whatsoever thou sayest unto me: [b]come therefore, I pray thee, curse me this people.

18 And Balaam answered and said unto the servants of Balak, [a]If Balak would give me his house full of silver and gold, [b]I cannot go beyond the word of the LORD my God, to do less or more.

19 Now therefore, I pray you, [a]tarry ye also here this night, that I may know what the LORD will say unto me more.

20 [a]And God came unto Balaam at night, and said unto him, If the men come to call thee, rise up, *and* go with them; but [b]yet the word which I shall say unto thee, that shalt thou do.

21 And Balaam rose up in the morning, and saddled his ass, and went with the princes of Moab.

Balaam, the Donkey, and the Angel

22 And God's anger was kindled because he went: [a]and the angel of the LORD stood in the way for an adversary against him. Now he was riding upon his ass, and his two servants *were* with him.

23 And [a]the ass saw the angel of the LORD standing in the way, and his sword drawn in his hand: and the ass turned aside out of the way, and went into the field: and Balaam smote the ass, to turn her into the way.

24 But the angel of the LORD stood in a path of the vineyards, a wall *being* on this side, and a wall on that side.

25 And when the ass saw the angel of the LORD, she thrust herself unto the wall, and crushed Balaam's foot against the wall: and he smote her again.

26 And the angel of the LORD went further, and stood in a narrow place, where *was* no way to turn either to the right hand or to the left.

27 And when the ass saw the angel of the LORD, she fell down under Balaam: and Balaam's anger was kindled, and he smote the ass with a staff.

28 And the LORD [a]opened the mouth of the ass, and she said unto Balaam, What have I done unto thee, that thou hast smitten me these three times?

29 And Balaam said unto the ass, Because thou hast mocked me: I would there were a sword in mine hand, [a]for now would I kill thee.

30 [a]And the ass said unto Balaam, *Am* not I thine ass, upon which thou hast ridden ever since *I was* thine unto this day? was I ever wont to do so unto thee? And he said, Nay.

31 Then the LORD [a]opened the eyes of Balaam, and he saw the angel of the LORD standing in the way, and his sword drawn in his hand: and he bowed down his head, and fell flat on his face.

32 And the angel of the LORD said unto him, Wherefore hast thou smitten thine ass these three times? behold, I went out to withstand thee, because *thy* way is [a]perverse before me:

33 And the ass saw me, and turned from me these three times: unless she had turned from me, surely now also I had slain thee, and saved her alive.

34 And Balaam said unto the angel of the LORD, [a]I have sinned; for I knew not that thou stoodest in the way against me: now therefore, if it displease thee, I will get me back again.

17 [a]Num. 24:11 [b]Num. 22:6
18 [a]Num. 22:38; 24:13 [b]1 Kin. 22:14; 2 Chr. 18:13
19 [a]Num. 22:8
20 [a]Num. 22:9 [b]Num. 22:35; 23:5, 12, 16, 26; 24:13
22 [a]Ex. 4:24
23 [a]Josh. 5:13; 2 Kin. 6:17; Dan. 10:7; Acts 22:9
28 [a]2 Pet. 2:16
29 [a][Prov. 12:10; Matt. 15:19]
30 [a]2 Pet. 2:16
31 [a]Gen. 21:19; 2 Kin. 6:17; Luke 24:16, 31
32 [a][2 Pet. 2:14, 15]
34 [a]1 Sam. 15:24, 30; 26:21; 2 Sam. 12:13

NKJV

to the princes of Balak, "Go back to your land, for the LORD has refused to give me permission to go with you."

14 And the princes of Moab rose and went to Balak, and said, "Balaam refuses to come with us."

15 Then Balak again sent princes, more numerous and more honorable than they.

16 And they came to Balaam and said to him, "Thus says Balak the son of Zippor: 'Please let nothing hinder you from coming to me;

17 'for I will certainly [a]honor you greatly, and I will do whatever you say to me. [b]Therefore please come, curse this people for me.' "

18 Then Balaam answered and said to the servants of Balak, [a]"Though Balak were to give me his house full of silver and gold, [b]I could not go beyond the word of the LORD my God, to do less or more.

19 "Now therefore, please, you also [a]stay here tonight, that I may know what more the LORD will say to me."

20 [a]And God came to Balaam at night and said to him, "If the men come to call you, rise *and* go with them; but [b]only the word which I speak to you—that you shall do."

21 So Balaam rose in the morning, saddled his donkey, and went with the princes of Moab.

Balaam, the Donkey, and the Angel

22 Then God's anger was aroused because he went, [a]and the Angel of the LORD took His stand in the way as an adversary against him. And he was riding on his donkey, and his two servants *were* with him.

23 Now [a]the donkey saw the Angel of the LORD standing in the way with His drawn sword in His hand, and the donkey turned aside out of the way and went into the field. So Balaam struck the donkey to turn her back onto the road.

24 Then the Angel of the LORD stood in a narrow path between the vineyards, *with* a wall on this side and a wall on that side.

25 And when the donkey saw the Angel of the LORD, she pushed herself against the wall and crushed Balaam's foot against the wall; so he struck her again.

26 Then the Angel of the LORD went further, and stood in a narrow place where there *was* no way to turn either to the right hand or to the left.

27 And when the donkey saw the Angel of the LORD, she lay down under Balaam; so Balaam's anger was aroused, and he struck the donkey with his staff.

28 Then the LORD [a]opened the mouth of the donkey, and she said to Balaam, "What have I done to you, that you have struck me these three times?"

29 And Balaam said to the donkey, "Because you have abused me. I wish there were a sword in my hand, [a]for now I would kill you!"

30 [a]So the donkey said to Balaam, "*Am* I not your donkey on which you have ridden, ever since *I became* yours, to this day? Was I ever disposed to do this to you?" And he said, "No."

31 Then the LORD [a]opened Balaam's eyes, and he saw the Angel of the LORD standing in the way with His drawn sword in His hand; and he bowed his head and fell flat on his face.

32 And the Angel of the LORD said to him, "Why have you struck your donkey these three times? Behold, I have come out to stand against you, because *your* way is [a]perverse before Me.

33 "The donkey saw Me and turned aside from Me these three times. If she had not turned aside from Me, surely I would also have killed you by now, and let her live."

34 And Balaam said to the Angel of the LORD, [a]"I have sinned, for I did not know You stood in the way against me. Now therefore, if it displeases You, I will turn back."

KJV

35 And the angel of the LORD said unto Balaam, Go with the men: [a]but only the word that I
shall speak unto thee, that thou shalt speak. So
Balaam went with the princes of Balak.
36 And when Balak heard that Balaam was
come, [a]he went out to meet him unto a city of
Moab, [b]which *is* in the border of Arnon, which
is in the utmost coast.
37 And Balak said unto Balaam, Did I not
earnestly send unto thee to call thee? wherefore
camest thou not unto me? am I not able indeed
[a]to promote thee to honour?
38 And Balaam said unto Balak, Lo, I am
come unto thee: have I now any power at all to
say any thing? [a]the word that God putteth in my
mouth, that shall I speak.
39 And Balaam went with Balak, and they
came unto Kirjath–huzoth.
40 And Balak offered oxen and sheep, and
sent to Balaam, and to the princes that *were* with
him.

Balaam's First Prophecy

41 And it came to pass on the morrow, that
Balak took Balaam, and brought him up into the
[a]high places of Baal, that thence he might see the
utmost *part* of the people.

23 And Balaam said unto Balak, [a]Build me
here seven altars, and prepare me here
seven oxen and seven rams.
2 And Balak did as Balaam had spoken; and
Balak and Balaam [a]offered on *every* altar a bullock and a ram.
3 And Balaam said unto Balak, [a]Stand by
thy burnt offering, and I will go: peradventure the
LORD will come [b]to meet me: and whatsoever he
sheweth me I will tell thee. And he went to an
high place.
4 [a]And God met Balaam: and he said unto
him, I have prepared seven altars, and I have offered upon *every* altar a bullock and a ram.
5 And the LORD [a]put a word in Balaam's
mouth, and said, Return unto Balak, and thus thou
shalt speak.
6 And he returned unto him and, lo, he
stood by his burnt sacrifice, he, and all the princes
of Moab.
7 And he [a]took up his parable, and said, Balak the king of Moab hath brought me from Aram,
out of the mountains of the east, *saying*, [b]Come,
curse me Jacob, and come, [c]defy Israel.
8 [a]How shall I curse, *whom* God hath not
cursed? or how shall I defy, *whom* the LORD hath
not defied?
9 For from the top of the rocks I see him,
and from the hills I behold him: lo, [a]the people
shall dwell alone, and [b]shall not be reckoned
among the nations.
10 [a]Who can count the dust of Jacob, and
the number of the fourth *part* of Israel? Let me
die [b]the death of the righteous, and let my last
end be like his!
11 And Balak said unto Balaam, What hast
thou done unto me? [a]I took thee to curse mine
enemies, and, behold, thou hast blessed *them*
altogether.
12 And he answered and said, [a]Must I not
take heed to speak that which the LORD hath put
in my mouth?

Balaam's Second Prophecy

13 And Balak said unto him, Come, I pray
thee, with me unto another place, from whence
thou mayest see them: thou shalt see but the

35 [a]Num. 22:20
36 [a]Gen. 14:17 [b]Num. 21:13
37 [a]Num. 22:17; 24:11
38 [a]Num. 23:26; 24:13; 1 Kin. 22:14; 2 Chr. 18:13
41 [a]Num. 21:28; Deut. 12:2

CHAPTER 23

1 [a]Num. 23:29
2 [a]Num. 23:14, 30
3 [a]Num. 23:15 [b]Num. 23:4, 16
4 [a]Num. 23:16
5 [a]Num. 22:20, 35, 38; 23:16; Deut. 18:18; Jer. 1:9
7 [a]Deut. 23:4; Job 27:1; 29:1; Ps. 78:2 [b]Num. 22:6, 11, 17 [c]1 Sam. 17:10
8 [a]Num. 22:12
9 [a]Deut. 32:8; 33:28; Josh. 11:23 [b]Ex. 33:16; Ezra 9:2; [Eph. 2:14]
10 [a]Gen. 13:16; 22:17; 28:14; 2 Chr. 1:9 [b]Ps.116:15
11 [a]Num. 22:11
12 [a]Num. 22:38

*
23:10 Or *dust cloud*

NKJV

35 Then the Angel of the LORD said to Balaam, "Go with the men, [a]but only the word that
I speak to you, that you shall speak." So Balaam
went with the princes of Balak.
36 Now when Balak heard that Balaam was
coming, [a]he went out to meet him at the city of
Moab, [b]which *is* on the border at the Arnon, the
boundary of the territory.
37 Then Balak said to Balaam, "Did I not earnestly send to you, calling for you? Why did you
not come to me? Am I not able [a]to honor you?"
38 And Balaam said to Balak, "Look, I have
come to you! Now, have I any power at all to say
anything? [a]The word that God puts in my mouth,
that I must speak."
39 So Balaam went with Balak, and they
came to Kirjath Huzoth.
40 Then Balak offered oxen and sheep, and
he sent *some* to Balaam and to the princes who
were with him.

Balaam's First Prophecy

41 So it was, the next day, that Balak took
Balaam and brought him up to the [a]high places
of Baal, that from there he might observe the extent of the people.

23 Then Balaam said to Balak, [a]"Build seven
altars for me here, and prepare for me here
seven bulls and seven rams."
2 And Balak did just as Balaam had spoken,
and Balak and Balaam [a]offered a bull and a ram
on *each* altar.
3 Then Balaam said to Balak, [a]"Stand by
your burnt offering, and I will go; perhaps the
LORD will come [b]to meet me, and whatever He
shows me I will tell you." So he went to a desolate
height.
4 [a]And God met Balaam, and he said to
Him, "I have prepared the seven altars, and I have
offered on *each* altar a bull and a ram."
5 Then the LORD [a]put a word in Balaam's
mouth, and said, "Return to Balak, and thus you
shall speak."
6 So he returned to him, and there he was,
standing by his burnt offering, he and all the
princes of Moab.
7 And he [a]took up his oracle and said:

"Balak the king of Moab has brought me
from Aram,
From the mountains of the east.
[b]'Come, curse Jacob for me,
And come, [c]denounce Israel!'

8 "How[a] shall I curse whom God has not
cursed?
And how shall I denounce *whom* the LORD
has not denounced?
9 For from the top of the rocks I see him,
And from the hills I behold him;
There! [a]A people dwelling alone,
[b]Not reckoning itself among the nations.

10 "Who[a] can count the *dust of Jacob,
Or number one-fourth of Israel?
Let me die [b]the death of the righteous,
And let my end be like his!"

11 Then Balak said to Balaam, "What
have you done to me? [a]I took you to curse my
enemies, and look, you have blessed *them* bountifully!"
12 So he answered and said, [a]"Must I not
take heed to speak what the LORD has put in my
mouth?"

Balaam's Second Prophecy

13 Then Balak said to him, "Please come
with me to another place from which you may
see them; you shall see only the outer part of

KJV

utmost part of them, and shalt not see them all:
and curse me them from thence.
14 And he brought him into the field of Zophim, to the top of Pisgah, [a]and built seven altars,
and offered a bullock and a ram on *every* altar.
15 And he said unto Balak, Stand here by
thy burnt offering, while I meet *the* LORD yonder.
16 And the LORD met Balaam, and [a]put a
word in his mouth, and said, Go again unto Balak,
and say thus.
17 And when he came to him, behold, he
stood by his burnt offering, and the princes of
Moab with him. And Balak said unto him, What
hath the LORD spoken?
18 And he took up his parable, and said,
[a]Rise up, Balak, and hear; hearken unto me, thou
son of Zippor:
19 [a]God *is* not a man, that he should lie; neither the son of man, that he should repent: hath
he [b]said, and shall he not do *it?* or hath he spoken,
and shall he not make it good?
20 Behold, I have received *commandment* to
bless: and [a]he hath blessed; and I cannot reverse
it.
21 [a]He hath not beheld iniquity in Jacob, neither hath he seen perverseness in Israel: the LORD
his God *is* with him, [b]and the shout of a king *is*
among them.
22 [a]God brought them out of Egypt; he hath
as it were [b]the strength of an unicorn.
23 Surely *there is* no enchantment against
Jacob, neither *is there* any divination against Israel: according to this time it shall be said of Jacob
and of Israel, [a]What hath God wrought!
24 Behold, the people shall rise up [a]as a great
lion, and lift up himself as a young lion: [b]he shall
not lie down until he eat *of* the prey, and drink
the blood of the slain.
25 And Balak said unto Balaam, Neither
curse them at all, nor bless them at all.
26 But Balaam answered and said unto Balak, Told not I thee, saying, [a]All that the LORD
speaketh, that I must do?

Balaam's Third Prophecy

27 And Balak said unto Balaam, Come, I pray
thee, I will bring thee unto another place; peradventure it will please God that thou mayest curse
me them from thence.
28 And Balak brought Balaam unto the top
of Peor, that looketh [a]toward Jeshimon.
29 And Balaam said unto Balak, Build me
here seven altars, and prepare me here seven bullocks and seven rams.
30 And Balak did as Balaam had said, and
offered a bullock and a ram on *every* altar.

14 [a]Num. 23:1, 2
16 [a]Num. 22:35; 23:5
18 [a]Judg. 3:20
19 [a]1 Sam. 15:29; Mal. 3:6; James 1:17 [b]Num. 11:23; 1 Kin. 8:56
20 [a]Gen. 12:2; 22:17; Num. 22:12
21 [a]Ps. 32:2; [Rom. 4:7, 8] [b]Ps. 89:15–18
22 [a]Num. 24:8 [b]Deut. 33:17; Job 39:10
23 [a]Ps. 31:19; 44:1
24 [a]Gen. 49:9 [b]Gen. 49:27; Josh. 11:23
26 [a]Num. 22:38
28 [a]Num. 21:20

NKJV

them, and shall not see them all; curse them for
me from there."
14 So he brought him to the field of Zophim,
to the top of Pisgah, [a]and built seven altars, and
offered a bull and a ram on *each* altar.
15 And he said to Balak, "Stand here by your
burnt offering while I *meet *the* LORD over there."
16 Then the LORD met Balaam, and [a]put a
word in his mouth, and said, "Go back to Balak,
and thus you shall speak."
17 So he came to him, and there he was,
standing by his burnt offering, and the princes
of Moab were with him. And Balak said to him,
"What has the LORD spoken?"
18 Then he took up his oracle and said:

[a]"Rise up, Balak, and hear!
Listen to me, son of Zippor!

19 "God[a] *is* not a man, that He should lie,
Nor a son of man, that He should repent.
Has He [b]said, and will He not do?
Or has He spoken, and will He not make it good?
20 Behold, I have received *a command* to bless;
[a]He has blessed, and I cannot reverse it.

21 "He[a] has not observed iniquity in Jacob,
Nor has He seen wickedness in Israel.
The LORD his God *is* with him,
[b]And the shout of a King *is* among them.
22 [a]God brings them out of Egypt;
He has [b]strength like a wild ox.

23 "For *there is* no sorcery against Jacob,
Nor any divination against Israel.
It now must be said of Jacob
And of Israel, 'Oh, [a]what God has done!'
24 Look, a people rises [a]like a lioness,
And lifts itself up like a lion;
[b]It shall not lie down until it devours the prey,
And drinks the blood of the slain."

25 Then Balak said to Balaam, "Neither
curse them at all, nor bless them at all!"
26 So Balaam answered and said to Balak,
"Did I not tell you, saying, [a]'All that the LORD
speaks, that I must do'?"

Balaam's Third Prophecy

27 Then Balak said to Balaam, "Please come,
I will take you to another place; perhaps it will
please God that you may curse them for me from
there."
28 So Balak took Balaam to the top of Peor,
that [a]overlooks *the wasteland.
29 Then Balaam said to Balak, "Build for me
here seven altars, and prepare for me here seven
bulls and seven rams."
30 And Balak did as Balaam had said, and
offered a bull and a ram on *every* altar.

KJV

24 And when Balaam saw that it pleased the
LORD to bless Israel, he went not, as at
[a]other times, to seek for enchantments, but he set
his face toward the wilderness.
2 And Balaam lifted up his eyes, and he saw
Israel [a]abiding *in his tents* according to their
tribes; and [b]the spirit of God came upon him.
3 [a]And he took up his parable, and said, Balaam the son of Beor hath said, and the man
whose eyes are open hath said:
4 He hath said, which heard the words of
God, which saw the vision of the Almighty, [a]fall-
ing *into a trance,* but having his eyes open:
5 How goodly are thy tents, O Jacob, *and*
thy tabernacles, O Israel!

CHAPTER 24
1 [a]Num. 23:3, 15
2 [a]Num. 2:2, 34 [b]Num. 11:25; 1 Sam. 10:10; 19:20, 23; 2 Chr. 15:1
3 [a]Num. 23:7, 18
4 [a]Ezek. 1:28

*
23:15 So with MT, Tg., Vg.; Syr. *call;* LXX *go and ask God*
23:28 Heb. *Jeshimon*

NKJV

24 Now when Balaam saw that it pleased the
LORD to bless Israel, he did not go as at
[a]other times, to seek to use sorcery, but he set
his face toward the wilderness.
2 And Balaam raised his eyes, and saw Israel [a]encamped according to their tribes; and [b]the
Spirit of God came upon him.
3 [a]Then he took up his oracle and said:

"The utterance of Balaam the son of Beor,
The utterance of the man whose eyes are opened,
4 The utterance of him who hears the words of God,
Who sees the vision of the Almighty,
Who [a]falls down, with eyes wide open:

5 "How lovely are your tents, O Jacob!
Your dwellings, O Israel!

KJV

6 As the valleys are they spread forth, as gardens by the river's side, [a]as the trees of lign aloes [b]which the LORD hath planted, *and* as cedar trees beside the waters.

7 He shall pour the water out of his buckets, and his seed *shall be* [a]in many waters, and his king shall be higher than [b]Agag, and his [c]kingdom shall be exalted.

8 [a]God brought him forth out of Egypt; he hath as it were the strength of an unicorn: he shall [b]eat up the nations his enemies, and shall [c]break their bones, and [d]pierce *them* through with his arrows.

9 [a]He couched, he lay down as a lion, and as a great lion: who shall stir him up? [b]Blessed *is* he that blesseth thee, and cursed *is* he that curseth thee.

10 And Balak's anger was kindled against Balaam, and he [a]smote his hands together: and Balak said unto Balaam, [b]I called thee to curse mine enemies, and, behold, thou hast altogether blessed *them* these three times.

11 Therefore now flee thou to thy place: [a]I thought to promote thee unto great honour; but, lo, the LORD hath kept thee back from honour.

12 And Balaam said unto Balak, Spake I not also to thy messengers which thou sentest unto me, saying,

13 If Balak would give me his house full of silver and gold, I cannot go beyond the commandment of the LORD, to do *either* good or bad of mine own mind; *but* what the LORD saith, that will I speak?

14 And now, behold, I go unto my people: come *therefore, and* [a]I will advertise thee what this people shall do to thy people in the [b]latter days.

Balaam's Fourth Prophecy

15 And he took up his parable, and said, Balaam the son of Beor hath said, and the man whose eyes are open hath said:

16 He hath said, which heard the words of God, and knew the knowledge of the most High, *which* saw the vision of the Almighty, falling *into a trance,* but having his eyes open:

17 [a]I shall see him, but not now: I shall behold him, but not nigh: there shall come [b]a Star out of Jacob, and [c]a Sceptre shall rise out of Israel, and shall smite the corners of Moab, and destroy all the children of Sheth.

18 And [a]Edom shall be a possession, Seir also shall be a possession for his enemies; and Israel shall do valiantly.

19 [a]Out of Jacob shall come he that shall have dominion, and shall destroy him that remaineth of the city.

20 And when he looked on Amalek, he took up his parable, and said, Amalek *was* the first of the nations; but his latter end *shall be* that he perish for ever.

21 And he looked on the Kenites, and took up his parable, and said, Strong is thy dwellingplace, and thou puttest thy nest in a rock.

22 Nevertheless the Kenite shall be wasted, until Asshur shall carry thee away captive.

6 [a]Ps. 1:3; Jer. 17:8 [b]Ps. 104:16
7 [a]Jer. 51:13; Rev. 17:1, 15 [b]1 Sam. 15:8, 9 [c]2 Sam. 5:12; 1 Chr. 14:2
8 [a]Num. 23:22 [b]Num. 14:9; 23:24 [c]Ps. 2:9; Jer. 50:17 [d]Ps. 45:5
9 [a]Gen. 49:9; Num. 23:24 [b]Gen. 12:3; 27:29
10 [a]Ezek. 21:14, 17 [b]Num. 23:11; Neh. 13:2
11 [a]Num. 22:17, 37
14 [a][Mic. 6:5] [b]Gen. 49:1; Deut. 4:30; Dan. 2:28
17 [a]Rev. 1:7; Matt. 1:2; Luke 3:34 [b]Matt. 2:2 [c]Gen. 49:10
18 [a]2 Sam. 8:14
19 [a]Gen. 49:10; Amos 9:11, 12

*______
24:17 Heb. *Sheth,* Jer. 48:45

NKJV

6 Like valleys that stretch out,
Like gardens by the riverside,
[a]Like aloes [b]planted by the LORD,
Like cedars beside the waters.
7 He shall pour water from his buckets,
And his seed *shall be* [a]in many waters.

"His king shall be higher than [b]Agag,
And his [c]kingdom shall be exalted.

8 "God[a] brings him out of Egypt;
He has strength like a wild ox;
He shall [b]consume the nations, his enemies;
He shall [c]break their bones
And [d]pierce *them* with his arrows.
9 'He[a] bows down, he lies down as a lion;
And as a lion, who shall rouse him?'

[b]"Blessed *is* he who blesses you,
And cursed *is* he who curses you."

10 Then Balak's anger was aroused against Balaam, and he [a]struck his hands together; and Balak said to Balaam, [b]"I called you to curse my enemies, and look, you have bountifully blessed *them* these three times!

11 "Now therefore, flee to your place. [a]I said I would greatly honor you, but in fact, the LORD has kept you back from honor."

12 So Balaam said to Balak, "Did I not also speak to your messengers whom you sent to me, saying,

13 'If Balak were to give me his house full of silver and gold, I could not go beyond the word of the LORD, to do good or bad of my own will. What the LORD says, that I must speak'?

14 "And now, indeed, I am going to my people. Come, [a]I will advise you what this people will do to your people in the [b]latter days."

Balaam's Fourth Prophecy

15 So he took up his oracle and said:

"The utterance of Balaam the son of Beor,
And the utterance of the man whose eyes are opened;
16 The utterance of him who hears the words of God,
And has the knowledge of the Most High,
Who sees the vision of the Almighty,
Who falls down, with eyes wide open:

17 "I[a] see Him, but not now;
I behold Him, but not near;
[b]A Star shall come out of Jacob;
[c]A Scepter shall rise out of Israel,
And batter the brow of Moab,
And destroy all the sons of *tumult.

18 "And [a]Edom shall be a possession;
Seir also, his enemies, shall be a possession,
While Israel does valiantly.
19 [a]Out of Jacob One shall have dominion,
And destroy the remains of the city."

20 Then he looked on Amalek, and he took up his oracle and said:

"Amalek *was* first among the nations,
But *shall be* last until he perishes."

21 Then he looked on the Kenites, and he took up his oracle and said:

"Firm is your dwelling place,
And your nest is set in the rock;
22 Nevertheless Kain shall be burned.
How long until Asshur carries you away captive?"

KJV

23 And he took up his parable, and said, Alas, who shall live when God doeth this!
24 And ships *shall come* from the coast of [a]Chittim, and shall afflict Asshur, and shall afflict [b]Eber, and he also shall perish for ever.
25 And Balaam rose up, and went and [a]returned to his place: and Balak also went his way.

Israel's Harlotry in Moab

25 And Israel abode in [a]Shittim, and the [b]people began to commit whoredom with the daughters of Moab.
2 And [a]they called the people unto [b]the sacrifices of their gods: and the people did eat, and [c]bowed down to their gods.
3 And Israel joined himself unto Baal–peor: and [a]the anger of the LORD was kindled against Israel.
4 And the LORD said unto Moses, [a]Take all the heads of the people, and hang them up before the LORD against the sun, [b]that the fierce anger of the LORD may be turned away from Israel.
5 And Moses said unto [a]the judges of Israel, [b]Slay ye every one his men that were joined unto Baal–peor.
6 And, behold, one of the children of Israel came and brought unto his brethren a Midianitish woman in the sight of Moses, and in the sight of all the congregation of the children of Israel, [a]who *were* weeping *before* the door of the tabernacle of the congregation.
7 And [a]when Phinehas, [b]the son of Eleazar, the son of Aaron the priest, saw *it,* he rose up from among the congregation, and took a javelin in his hand;
8 And he went after the man of Israel into the tent, and thrust both of them through, the man of Israel, and the woman through her belly. So [a]the plague was [b]stayed from the children of Israel.
9 And [a]those that died in the plague were twenty and four thousand.
10 And the LORD spake unto Moses, saying,
11 [a]Phinehas, the son of Eleazar, the son of Aaron the priest, hath turned my wrath away from the children of Israel, while he was zealous for my sake among them, that I consumed not the children of Israel in [b]my jealousy.
12 Wherefore say, [a]Behold, I give unto him my [b]covenant of peace:
13 And he shall have it, and [a]his seed after him, *even* the covenant of [b]an everlasting priesthood; because he was [c]zealous for his God, and [d]made an atonement for the children of Israel.
14 Now the name of the Israelite that was slain, *even* that was slain with the Midianitish woman, *was* Zimri, the son of Salu, a prince of a chief house among the Simeonites.
15 And the name of the Midianitish woman that was slain *was* Cozbi, the daughter of [a]Zur; he *was* head over a people, *and* of a chief house in Midian.
16 And the LORD spake unto Moses, saying,
17 [a]Vex the Midianites, and smite them:
18 For they vex you with their [a]wiles, wherewith they have beguiled you in the matter of Peor, and in the matter of Cozbi, the daughter of a prince of Midian, their sister, which was slain in the day of the plague for Peor's sake.

The Second Census of Israel

26 And it came to pass after the [a]plague, that the LORD spake unto Moses and unto Eleazar the son of Aaron the priest, saying,
2 [a]Take the sum of all the congregation of the children of Israel, [b]from twenty years old and upward, throughout their fathers' house, all that are able to go to war in Israel.

---

24 [a]Gen. 10:4; Ezek. 27:6; Dan. 11:30 [b]Gen. 10:21, 25
25 [a]Num. 21:34; 31:8

CHAPTER 25

1 [a]Num. 33:49; Josh. 2:1 [b]Rev. 2:14
2 [a]Josh. 22:17; Hos. 9:10 [b]Ex. 34:15; Deut. 32:38; 1 Cor. 10:20 [c]Ex. 20:5
3 [a]Ps. 106:28, 29
4 [a]Deut. 4:3 [b]Num. 25:11; Deut. 13:17
5 [a]Ex. 18:21 [b]Deut. 13:6, 9
6 [a]Joel 2:17
7 [a]Ps. 106:30 [b]Ex. 6:25
8 [a]Ps. 106:30 [b]Num. 16:46–48
9 [a]Deut. 4:3
11 [a]Ps. 106:30 [b][Ex. 20:5]; Deut. 32:16, 21; 1 Kin. 14:22; Ps. 78:58; Ezek. 16:38
12 [a][Mal. 2:4, 5; 3:1] [b]Is. 54:10; Ezek. 34:25; 37:26; Mal. 2:5
13 [a]1 Chr. 6:4 [b]Ex. 40:15 [c]Acts 22:3; Rom. 10:2 [d][Heb. 2:17]
15 [a]Num. 31:8; Josh. 13:21
17 [a]Num. 31:1–3
18 [a]Num. 31:16; Rev. 2:14

CHAPTER 26

1 [a]Num. 25:9
2 [a]Ex. 30:12; 38:25, 26; Num. 1:2; 14:29 [b]Num. 1:3

*

24:24 Heb. *Kittim* • Lit. *he* or *that one*
25:1 Heb. *Shittim*

NKJV

23 Then he took up his oracle and said:

"Alas! Who shall live when God does this?
24 But ships *shall come* from the coasts of
[a]Cyprus,*
And they shall afflict Asshur and afflict
[b]Eber,
And so shall **Amalek,* until he perishes."

25 So Balaam rose and departed and [a]returned to his place; Balak also went his way.

Israel's Harlotry in Moab

25 Now Israel remained in [a]Acacia Grove,* and the [b]people began to commit harlotry with the women of Moab.
2 [a]They invited the people to [b]the sacrifices of their gods, and the people ate and [c]bowed down to their gods.
3 So Israel was joined to Baal of Peor, and [a]the anger of the LORD was aroused against Israel.
4 Then the LORD said to Moses, [a]"Take all the leaders of the people and hang the offenders before the LORD, out in the sun, [b]that the fierce anger of the LORD may turn away from Israel."
5 So Moses said to [a]the judges of Israel, [b]"Every one of you kill his men who were joined to Baal of Peor."
6 And indeed, one of the children of Israel came and presented to his brethren a Midianite woman in the sight of Moses and in the sight of all the congregation of the children of Israel, [a]who *were* weeping at the door of the tabernacle of meeting.
7 Now [a]when Phinehas [b]the son of Eleazar, the son of Aaron the priest, saw *it,* he rose from among the congregation and took a javelin in his hand;
8 and he went after the man of Israel into the tent and thrust both of them through, the man of Israel, and the woman through her body. So [a]the plague was [b]stopped among the children of Israel.
9 And [a]those who died in the plague were twenty-four thousand.
10 Then the LORD spoke to Moses, saying:
11 [a]"Phinehas the son of Eleazar, the son of Aaron the priest, has turned back My wrath from the children of Israel, because he was zealous with My zeal among them, so that I did not consume the children of Israel in [b]My zeal.
12 "Therefore say, [a]'Behold, I give to him My [b]covenant of peace;
13 'and it shall be to him and [a]his descendants after him a covenant of [b]an everlasting priesthood, because he was [c]zealous for his God, and [d]made atonement for the children of Israel.' "
14 Now the name of the Israelite who was killed, who was killed with the Midianite woman, *was* Zimri the son of Salu, a leader of a father's house among the Simeonites.
15 And the name of the Midianite woman who was killed *was* Cozbi the daughter of [a]Zur; he *was* head of the people of a father's house in Midian.
16 Then the LORD spoke to Moses, saying:
17 [a]"Harass the Midianites, and attack them;
18 "for they harassed you with their [a]schemes by which they seduced you in the matter of Peor and in the matter of Cozbi, the daughter of a leader of Midian, their sister, who was killed in the day of the plague because of Peor."

The Second Census of Israel

26 And it came to pass, after the [a]plague, that the LORD spoke to Moses and Eleazar the son of Aaron the priest, saying:
2 [a]"Take a census of all the congregation of the children of Israel [b]from twenty years old and above, by their fathers' houses, all who are able to go to war in Israel."

KJV

3 And Moses and Eleazar the priest spake with them [a]in the plains of Moab by Jordan *near* Jericho, saying,

4 *Take the sum of the people,* from twenty years old and upward; as the LORD [a]commanded Moses and the children of Israel, which went forth out of the land of Egypt.

5 [a]Reuben, the eldest son of Israel: the children of Reuben; Hanoch, *of whom cometh* the family of the Hanochites: of Pallu, the family of the Palluites:

6 Of Hezron, the family of the Hezronites: of Carmi, the family of the Carmites.

7 These *are* the families of the Reubenites: and they that were numbered of them were forty and three thousand and seven hundred and thirty.

8 And the sons of Pallu; Eliab.

9 And the sons of Eliab; Nemuel, and Dathan, and Abiram. This *is that* Dathan and Abiram, *which were* [a]famous in the congregation, who strove against Moses and against Aaron in the company of Korah, when they strove against the LORD:

10 [a]And the earth opened her mouth, and swallowed them up together with Korah, when that company died, what time the fire devoured two hundred and fifty men: [b]and they became a sign.

11 Notwithstanding [a]the children of Korah died not.

12 The sons of Simeon after their families: of Nemuel, the family of the Nemuelites: of Jamin, the family of the Jaminites: of Jachin, the family of the Jachinites:

13 Of Zerah, the family of the Zarhites: of Shaul, the family of the Shaulites.

14 These *are* the families of the Simeonites, twenty and two thousand and two hundred.

15 The children of Gad after their families: of Zephon, the family of the Zephonites: of Haggi, the family of the Haggites: of Shuni, the family of the Shunites:

16 Of Ozni, the family of the Oznites: of Eri, the family of the Erites:

17 Of Arod, the family of the Arodites: of Areli, the family of the Arelites.

18 These *are* the families of the children of Gad according to those that were numbered of them, forty thousand and five hundred.

19 [a]The sons of Judah *were* Er and Onan: and Er and Onan died in the land of Canaan.

20 And [a]the sons of Judah after their families were; of Shelah, the family of the Shelanites: of Pharez, the family of the Pharzites: of Zerah, the family of the Zarhites.

21 And the sons of Pharez were; of Hezron, the family of the Hezronites: of Hamul, the family of the Hamulites.

22 These *are* the families of Judah according to those that were numbered of them, threescore and sixteen thousand and five hundred.

23 *Of* the sons of Issachar after their families: *of* Tola, the family of the Tolaites: of Pua, the family of the Punites:

24 Of Jashub, the family of the Jashubites: of Shimron, the family of the Shimronites.

25 These *are* the families of Issachar according to those that were numbered of them, threescore and four thousand and three hundred.

26 [a]*Of* the sons of Zebulun after their families: of Sered, the family of the Sardites: of Elon, the family of the Elonites: of Jahleel, the family of the Jahleelites.

27 These *are* the families of the Zebulunites according to those that were numbered of them, threescore thousand and five hundred.

28 [a]The sons of Joseph after their families *were* Manasseh and Ephraim.

29 Of the sons of [a]Manasseh: of [b]Machir, the family of the Machirites: and Machir begat Gilead: of Gilead *come* the family of the Gileadites.

30 These *are* the sons of Gilead: *of* Jeezer,

3 [a]Num. 22:1; 31:12; 33:48; 35:1
4 [a]Num. 1:1
5 [a]Gen. 46:8; Ex. 6:14; 1 Chr. 5:1–3
9 [a]Num. 1:16; 16:1, 2
10 [a]Num. 16:32–35 [b]Num. 16:38–40; 1 Cor. 10:6; 2 Pet. 2:6
11 [a]Ex. 6:24; 1 Chr. 6:22, 23
19 [a]Gen. 38:2; 46:12
20 [a]1 Chr. 2:3
26 [a]Gen. 46:14
28 [a]Gen. 46:20; Deut. 33:16
29 [a]Josh. 17:1 [b]1 Chr. 7:14, 15

*———

26:12 *Jemuel,* Gen. 46:10; Ex. 6:15 • *Jarib,* 1 Chr. 4:24
26:13 *Zohar,* Gen. 46:10
26:15 *Ziphion,* Gen. 46:16
26:16 *Ezbon,* Gen. 46:16
26:17 Sam., Syr. *Arodi* and Gen. 46:16
26:23 So with Sam., LXX, Syr., Vg.; Heb. *Puvah,* Gen. 46:13; 1 Chr. 7:1 • Sam., LXX, Syr., Vg. *Puaites*
26:30 *Abiezer,* Josh. 17:2

NKJV

3 So Moses and Eleazar the priest spoke with them [a]in the plains of Moab by the Jordan, *across from* Jericho, saying:

4 "*Take a census of the people* from twenty years old and above, just as the LORD [a]commanded Moses and the children of Israel who came out of the land of Egypt."

5 [a]Reuben *was* the firstborn of Israel. The children of Reuben *were: of* Hanoch, the family of the Hanochites; *of* Pallu, the family of the Palluites;

6 *of* Hezron, the family of the Hezronites; *of* Carmi, the family of the Carmites.

7 These *are* the families of the Reubenites: those who were numbered of them were forty-three thousand seven hundred and thirty.

8 And the son of Pallu *was* Eliab.

9 The sons of Eliab *were* Nemuel, Dathan, and Abiram. These *are* the Dathan and Abiram, [a]representatives of the congregation, who contended against Moses and Aaron in the company of Korah, when they contended against the LORD;

10 [a]and the earth opened its mouth and swallowed them up together with Korah when that company died, when the fire devoured two hundred and fifty men; [b]and they became a sign.

11 Nevertheless [a]the children of Korah did not die.

12 The sons of Simeon according to their families *were: of* *Nemuel, the family of the Nemuelites; *of* Jamin, the family of the Jaminites; *of* *Jachin, the family of the Jachinites;

13 *of* *Zerah, the family of the Zarhites; *of* Shaul, the family of the Shaulites.

14 These *are* the families of the Simeonites: twenty-two thousand two hundred.

15 The sons of Gad according to their families *were: of* *Zephon, the family of the Zephonites; *of* Haggi, the family of the Haggites; *of* Shuni, the family of the Shunites;

16 *of* *Ozni, the family of the Oznites; *of* Eri, the family of the Erites;

17 *of* *Arod, the family of the Arodites; *of* Areli, the family of the Arelites.

18 These *are* the families of the sons of Gad according to those who were numbered of them: forty thousand five hundred.

19 [a]The sons of Judah *were* Er and Onan; and Er and Onan died in the land of Canaan.

20 And [a]the sons of Judah according to their families were: *of* Shelah, the family of the Shelanites; *of* Perez, the family of the Parzites; *of* Zerah, the family of the Zarhites.

21 And the sons of Perez were: *of* Hezron, the family of the Hezronites; *of* Hamul, the family of the Hamulites.

22 These *are* the families of Judah according to those who were numbered of them: seventy-six thousand five hundred.

23 The sons of Issachar according to their families *were: of* Tola, the family of the Tolaites; of *Puah, the family of the *Punites;

24 of Jashub, the family of the Jashubites; of Shimron, the family of the Shimronites.

25 These *are* the families of Issachar according to those who were numbered of them: sixty-four thousand three hundred.

26 [a]The sons of Zebulun according to their families *were:* of Sered, the family of the Sardites; of Elon, the family of the Elonites; of Jahleel, the family of the Jahleelites.

27 These *are* the families of the Zebulunites according to those who were numbered of them: sixty thousand five hundred.

28 [a]The sons of Joseph according to their families, by Manasseh and Ephraim, *were:*

29 The sons of [a]Manasseh: of [b]Machir, the family of the Machirites; and Machir begot Gilead; of Gilead, the family of the Gileadites.

30 These *are* the sons of Gilead: *of* *Jeezer,

KJV

the family of the Jeezerites: of Helek, the family of the Helekites:

31 And *of* Asriel, the family of the Asrielites: and *of* Shechem, the family of the Shechemites:

32 And *of* Shemida, the family of the Shemidaites: and *of* Hepher, the family of the Hepherites.

33 And [a]Zelophehad the son of Hepher had no sons, but daughters: and the names of the daughters of Zelophehad *were* Mahlah, and Noah, Hoglah, Milcah, and Tirzah.

34 These *are* the families of Manasseh, and those that were numbered of them, fifty and two thousand and seven hundred.

35 These *are* the sons of Ephraim after their families: of Shuthelah, the family of the Shuthalhites: of Becher, the family of the Bachrites: of Tahan, the family of the Tahanites.

36 And these *are* the sons of Shuthelah: of Eran, the family of the Eranites.

37 These *are* the families of the sons of Ephraim according to those that were numbered of them, thirty and two thousand and five hundred. These *are* the sons of Joseph after their families.

38 [a]The sons of Benjamin after their families: of Bela, the family of the Belaites: of Ashbel, the family of the Ashbelites: of [b]Ahiram, the family of the Ahiramites:

39 Of [a]Shupham, the family of the Shuphamites: of Hupham, the family of the Huphamites.

40 And the sons of Bela were Ard and Naaman: [a]*of Ard,* the family of the Ardites: *and* of Naaman, the family of the Naamites.

41 These *are* the sons of Benjamin after their families: and they that were numbered of them *were* forty and five thousand and six hundred.

42 These *are* the sons of Dan after their families: of Shuham, the family of the Shuhamites. These *are* the families of Dan after their families.

43 All the families of the Shuhamites, according to those that were numbered of them, *were* threescore and four thousand and four hundred.

44 [a]*Of* the children of Asher after their families: of Jimna, the family of the Jimnites: of Jesui, the family of the Jesuites: of Beriah, the family of the Beriites.

45 Of the sons of Beriah: of Heber, the family of the Heberites: of Malchiel, the family of the Malchielites.

46 And the name of the daughter of Asher *was* Sarah.

47 These *are* the families of the sons of Asher according to those that were numbered of them; *who were* fifty and three thousand and four hundred.

48 [a]*Of* the sons of Naphtali after their families: of Jahzeel, the family of the Jahzeelites: of Guni, the family of the Gunites:

49 Of Jezer, the family of the Jezerites: of [a]Shillem, the family of the Shillemites.

50 These *are* the families of Naphtali according to their families: and they that were numbered of them *were* forty and five thousand and four hundred.

51 [a]These *were* the numbered of the children of Israel, six hundred thousand and a thousand seven hundred and thirty.

52 And the LORD spake unto Moses, saying,

53 [a]Unto these the land shall be [b]divided for an inheritance according to the number of names.

54 [a]To many thou shalt give the more inheritance, and to few thou shalt give the less inheritance: to every one shall his inheritance be given according to those that were numbered of him.

55 Notwithstanding the land shall be [a]divided by lot: according to the names of the tribes of their fathers they shall inherit.

56 According to the lot shall the possession thereof be divided between many and few.

---

33 [a]Num. 27:1; 36:11
38 [a]Gen. 46:21; 1 Chr. 7:6 [b]Gen. 46:21; 1 Chr. 8:1, 2
39 [a]1 Chr. 7:12
40 [a]1 Chr. 8:3
44 [a]Gen. 46:17; 1 Chr. 7:30
48 [a]Gen. 46:24; 1 Chr. 7:13
49 [a]1 Chr. 7:13
51 [a]Ex. 12:37; 38:26; Num. 1:46; 11:21
53 [a]Josh. 11:23; 14:1 [b]Num. 33:54
54 [a]Num. 33:54
55 [a]Num. 33:54; 54:13; Josh. 11:23; 14:2

NKJV

the family of the Jeezerites; of Helek, the family of the Helekites;

31 *of* Asriel, the family of the Asrielites; *of* Shechem, the family of the Shechemites;

32 *of* Shemida, the family of the Shemidaites; *of* Hepher, the family of the Hepherites.

33 Now [a]Zelophehad the son of Hepher had no sons, but daughters; and the names of the daughters of Zelophehad *were* Mahlah, Noah, Hoglah, Milcah, and Tirzah.

34 These *are* the families of Manasseh; and those who were numbered of them *were* fifty-two thousand seven hundred.

35 These *are* the sons of Ephraim according to their families: of Shuthelah, the family of the Shuthalhites; of *Becher, the family of the Bachrites; of Tahan, the family of the Tahanites.

36 And these *are* the sons of Shuthelah: of Eran, the family of the Eranites.

37 These *are* the families of the sons of Ephraim according to those who were numbered of them: thirty-two thousand five hundred. These *are* the sons of Joseph according to their families.

38 [a]The sons of Benjamin according to their families were: of Bela, the family of the Belaites; of Ashbel, the family of the Ashbelites; of [b]Ahiram, the family of the Ahiramites;

39 of [a]Shupham,* the family of the Shuphamites; of *Hupham, the family of the Huphamites.

40 And the sons of Bela were *Ard and Naaman: [a]*of Ard,* the family of the Ardites; of Naaman, the family of the Naamites.

41 These *are* the sons of Benjamin according to their families; and those who were numbered of them *were* forty-five thousand six hundred.

42 These *are* the sons of Dan according to their families: of *Shuham, the family of the Shuhamites. These *are* the families of Dan according to their families.

43 All the families of the Shuhamites, according to those who were numbered of them, *were* sixty-four thousand four hundred.

44 [a]The sons of Asher according to their families *were:* of Jimna, the family of the Jimnites; of Jesui, the family of the Jesuites; of Beriah, the family of the Beriites.

45 Of the sons of Beriah: of Heber, the family of the Heberites; of Malchiel, the family of the Malchielites.

46 And the name of the daughter of Asher *was* Serah.

47 These *are* the families of the sons of Asher according to those who were numbered of them: fifty-three thousand four hundred.

48 [a]The sons of Naphtali according to their families *were:* of *Jahzeel, the family of the Jahzeelites; of Guni, the family of the Gunites;

49 of Jezer, the family of the Jezerites; of [a]Shillem, the family of the Shillemites.

50 These *are* the families of Naphtali according to their families; and those who were numbered of them *were* forty-five thousand four hundred.

51 [a]These *are* those who were numbered of the children of Israel: six hundred and one thousand seven hundred and thirty.

52 Then the LORD spoke to Moses, saying:

53 [a]"To these the land shall be [b]divided as an inheritance, according to the number of names.

54 [a]"To a large *tribe* you shall give a larger inheritance, and to a small *tribe* you shall give a smaller inheritance. Each shall be given its inheritance according to those who were numbered of them.

55 "But the land shall be [a]divided by lot; they shall inherit according to the names of the tribes of their fathers.

56 "According to the lot their inheritance shall be divided between the larger and the smaller."

---

*

26:35 *Bered,* 1 Chr. 7:20
26:39 MT *Shephupham; Shephuphan,* 1 Chr. 8:5
• *Huppim,* Gen. 46:21
26:40 *Addar,* 1 Chr. 8:3
26:42 *Hushim,* Gen. 46:23
26:48 *Jahziel,* 1 Chr. 7:13

KJV

57 [a]And these *are* they that were numbered of the Levites after their families: of Gershon, the family of the Gershonites: of Kohath, the family of the Kohathites: of Merari, the family of the Merarites.

58 These *are* the families of the Levites: the family of the Libnites, the family of the Hebronites, the family of the Mahlites, the family of the Mushites, the family of the Korathites. And Kohath begat Amram.

59 And the name of Amram's wife *was* [a]Jochebed, the daughter of Levi, whom *her mother* bare to Levi in Egypt: and she bare unto Amram Aaron and Moses, and Miriam their sister.

60 [a]And unto Aaron was born Nadab, and Abihu, Eleazar, and Ithamar.

61 And [a]Nadab and Abihu died, when they offered strange fire before the LORD.

62 [a]And those that were numbered of them were twenty and three thousand, all males from a month old and upward: [b]for they were not numbered among the children of Israel, because there was [c]no inheritance given them among the children of Israel.

63 These *are* they that were numbered by Moses and Eleazar the priest, who numbered the children of Israel [a]in the plains of Moab by Jordan *near* Jericho.

64 [a]But among these there was not a man of them whom Moses and Aaron the priest numbered, when they numbered the children of Israel in the [b]wilderness of Sinai.

65 For the LORD had said of them, They [a]shall surely die in the wilderness. And there was not left a man of them, [b]save Caleb the son of Jephunneh, and Joshua the son of Nun.

Inheritance Laws

27 Then came the daughters of [a]Zelophehad, the son of Hepher, the son of Gilead, the son of Machir, the son of Manasseh, of the families of Manasseh the son of Joseph: and these *are* the names of his daughters; Mahlah, Noah, and Hoglah, and Milcah, and Tirzah.

2 And they stood before Moses, and before Eleazar the priest, and before the princes and all the congregation, *by* the door of the tabernacle of the congregation, saying,

3 Our father [a]died in the wilderness, and he was not in the company of them that gathered themselves together against the LORD [b]in the company of Korah; but died in his own sin, and had no sons.

4 Why should the name of our father be [a]done away from among his family, because he hath no son? [b]Give unto us *therefore* a possession among the brethren of our father.

5 And Moses [a]brought their cause before the LORD.

6 And the LORD spake unto Moses, saying,

7 The daughters of Zelophehad speak right: [a]thou shalt surely give them a possession of an inheritance among their father's brethren; and thou shalt cause the inheritance of their father to pass unto them.

8 And thou shalt speak unto the children of Israel, saying, If a man die, and have no son, then ye shall cause his inheritance to pass unto his daughter.

9 And if he have no daughter, then ye shall give his inheritance unto his brethren.

10 And if he have no brethren, then ye shall give his inheritance unto his father's brethren.

11 And if his father have no brethren, then ye shall give his inheritance unto his kinsman that is next to him of his family, and he shall possess it: and it shall be unto the children of Israel [a]a statute of judgment, as the LORD commanded Moses.

57 [a]Gen. 46:11; Ex. 6:16–19; Num. 3:15; 1 Chr. 6:1, 16
59 [a]Ex. 2:1, 2; 6:20
60 [a]Num. 3:2
61 [a]Lev. 10:1, 2; Num. 3:3, 4; 1 Chr. 24:2
62 [a]Num. 3:39 [b]Num. 1:49 [c]Num. 18:20, 23, 24
63 [a]Num. 26:3
64 [a]Num. 14:29–35; Deut. 2:14–16; Heb. 3:17 [b]Num. 1:1–46
65 [a]Num. 14:26–35; [1 Cor. 10:5, 6] [b]Num. 14:30

CHAPTER 27

1 [a]Num. 26:33; 36:1, 11; Josh. 17:3
3 [a]Num. 14:35; 26:64, 65 [b]Num. 16:1, 2
4 [a]Deut. 25:6 [b]Josh. 17:4
5 [a]Ex. 18:13–26
7 [a]Num. 36:2; Josh. 17:4
11 [a]Num. 35:29

NKJV

57 [a]And these *are* those who were numbered of the Levites according to their families: of Gershon, the family of the Gershonites; of Kohath, the family of the Kohathites; of Merari, the family of the Merarites.

58 These *are* the families of the Levites: the family of the Libnites, the family of the Hebronites, the family of the Mahlites, the family of the Mushites, and the family of the Korathites. And Kohath begot Amram.

59 The name of Amram's wife *was* [a]Jochebed the daughter of Levi, who was born to Levi in Egypt; and to Amram she bore Aaron and Moses and their sister Miriam.

60 [a]To Aaron were born Nadab and Abihu, Eleazar and Ithamar.

61 And [a]Nadab and Abihu died when they offered profane fire before the LORD.

62 [a]Now those who were numbered of them were twenty-three thousand, every male from a month old and above; [b]for they were not numbered among the other children of Israel, because there was [c]no inheritance given to them among the children of Israel.

63 These *are* those who were numbered by Moses and Eleazar the priest, who numbered the children of Israel [a]in the plains of Moab by the Jordan, *across from* Jericho.

64 [a]But among these there was not a man of those who were numbered by Moses and Aaron the priest when they numbered the children of Israel in the [b]Wilderness of Sinai.

65 For the LORD had said of them, "They [a]shall surely die in the wilderness." So there was not left a man of them, [b]except Caleb the son of Jephunneh and Joshua the son of Nun.

Inheritance Laws

27 Then came the daughters of [a]Zelophehad the son of Hepher, the son of Gilead, the son of Machir, the son of Manasseh, from the families of Manasseh the son of Joseph; and these *were* the names of his daughters: Mahlah, Noah, Hoglah, Milcah, and Tirzah.

2 And they stood before Moses, before Eleazar the priest, and before the leaders and all the congregation, *by* the doorway of the tabernacle of meeting, saying:

3 "Our father [a]died in the wilderness; but he was not in the company of those who gathered together against the LORD, [b]in company with Korah, but he died in his own sin; and he had no sons.

4 "Why should the name of our father be [a]removed from among his family because he had no son? [b]Give us a possession among our father's brothers."

5 So Moses [a]brought their case before the LORD.

6 And the LORD spoke to Moses, saying:

7 "The daughters of Zelophehad speak *what is* right; [a]you shall surely give them a possession of inheritance among their father's brothers, and cause the inheritance of their father to pass to them.

8 "And you shall speak to the children of Israel, saying: 'If a man dies and has no son, then you shall cause his inheritance to pass to his daughter.

9 'If he has no daughter, then you shall give his inheritance to his brothers.

10 'If he has no brothers, then you shall give his inheritance to his father's brothers.

11 'And if his father has no brothers, then you shall give his inheritance to the relative closest to him in his family, and he shall possess it.' " And it shall be to the children of Israel [a]a statute of judgment, just as the LORD commanded Moses.

KJV

Joshua the Next Leader of Israel
(Deut. 31:1–8)

12 And the LORD said unto Moses, [a]Get thee up into this mount Abarim, and see the land which I have given unto the children of Israel.
13 And when thou hast seen it, thou also [a]shalt be gathered unto thy people, as Aaron thy brother was gathered.
14 For ye [a]rebelled against my commandment in the desert of Zin, in the strife of the congregation, to sanctify me at the water before their eyes: that *is* the [b]water of Meribah in Kadesh in the wilderness of Zin.
15 And Moses spake unto the LORD, saying,
16 Let the LORD, [a]the God of the spirits of all flesh, set a man over the congregation,
17 [a]Which may go out before them, and which may go in before them, and which may lead them out, and which may bring them in; that the congregation of the LORD be not [b]as sheep which have no shepherd.
18 And the LORD said unto Moses, Take thee Joshua the son of Nun, a man [a]in whom *is* the spirit, and [b]lay thine hand upon him;
19 And set him before Eleazar the priest, and before all the congregation; and [a]give him a charge in their sight.
20 And [a]thou shalt put *some* of thine honour upon him, that all the congregation of the children of Israel [b]may be obedient.
21 [a]And he shall stand before Eleazar the priest, who shall ask *counsel* for him [b]after the judgment of Urim before the LORD: [c]at his word shall they go out, and at his word they shall come in, *both* he, and all the children of Israel with him, even all the congregation.
22 And Moses did as the LORD commanded him: and he took Joshua, and set him before Eleazar the priest, and before all the congregation:
23 And he laid his hands upon him, [a]and gave him a charge, as the LORD commanded by the hand of Moses.

Daily Offerings
(Ex. 29:38–46)

28 And the LORD spake unto Moses, saying,
2 Command the children of Israel, and say unto them, My offering, *and* [a]my bread for my sacrifices made by fire, *for* a sweet savour unto me, shall ye observe to offer unto me in their due season.
3 And thou shalt say unto them, [a]This *is* the offering made by fire which ye shall offer unto the LORD; two lambs of the first year without spot day by day, *for* a continual burnt offering.
4 The one lamb shalt thou offer in the morning, and the other lamb shalt thou offer at even;
5 And [a]a tenth *part* of an ephah of flour for a [b]meat offering, mingled with the fourth *part* of an hin of beaten oil.
6 *It is* [a]a continual burnt offering, which was ordained in mount Sinai for a sweet savour, a sacrifice made by fire unto the LORD.
7 And the drink offering thereof *shall be* the fourth *part* of an hin for the one lamb: [a]in the holy *place* shalt thou cause the strong wine to be poured unto the LORD *for* a drink offering.
8 And the other lamb shalt thou offer at even: as the meat offering of the morning, and as the drink offering thereof, thou shalt offer *it*, a sacrifice made by fire, of a sweet savour unto the LORD.

Sabbath Offerings

9 And on the sabbath day two lambs of the first year without spot, and two tenth deals of flour *for* a meat offering, mingled with oil, and the drink offering thereof:
10 *This is* [a]the burnt offering of every sabbath, beside the continual burnt offering, and his drink offering.

12 [a]Num. 33:47; Deut. 3:23–27; 32:48–52; 34:1–4
13 [a]Num. 20:12, 24, 28; 31:2; Deut. 10:6; 34:5, 6
14 [a]Num. 20:12, 24; Deut. 1:37; 32:51; Ps. 106:32, 33 [b]Ex. 17:7
16 [a]Num. 16:22; Heb. 12:9
17 [a]Deut. 31:2; 1 Sam. 8:20; 18:13; 2 Chr. 1:10 [b]1 Kin. 22:17; Zech. 10:2; Matt. 9:36; Mark 6:34
18 [a]Gen. 41:38; Judg. 3:10; 1 Sam. 16:13, 18 [b]Deut. 34:9
19 [a]Deut. 3:28; 31:3, 7, 8, 23
20 [a]Num. 11:17 [b]Josh. 1:16–18
21 [a]Judg. 20:18, 23, 26; 1 Sam. 23:9; 30:7 [b]Ex. 28:30; 1 Sam. 28:6 [c]Josh. 9:14; 1 Sam. 22:10
23 [a]Deut. 3:28; 31:7, 8

CHAPTER 28

2 [a]Lev. 3:11; 21:6, 8; [Mal. 1:7, 12]
3 [a]Ex. 29:38–42
5 [a]Ex. 16:36; Num. 15:4 [b]Lev. 2:1
6 [a]Ex. 29:42; Amos 5:25
7 [a]Ex. 29:42
10 [a]Ezek. 46:4

NKJV

Joshua the Next Leader of Israel
(Deut. 31:1–8)

12 Now the LORD said to Moses: [a]"Go up into this Mount Abarim, and see the land which I have given to the children of Israel.
13 "And when you have seen it, you also [a]shall be gathered to your people, as Aaron your brother was gathered.
14 "For in the Wilderness of Zin, during the strife of the congregation, you [a]rebelled against My command to hallow Me at the waters before their eyes." (These *are* the [b]waters of Meribah, at Kadesh in the Wilderness of Zin.)
15 Then Moses spoke to the LORD, saying:
16 "Let the LORD, [a]the God of the spirits of all flesh, set a man over the congregation,
17 [a]"who may go out before them and go in before them, who may lead them out and bring them in, that the congregation of the LORD may not be [b]like sheep which have no shepherd."
18 And the LORD said to Moses: "Take Joshua the son of Nun with you, a man [a]in whom *is* the Spirit, and [b]lay your hand on him;
19 "set him before Eleazar the priest and before all the congregation, and [a]inaugurate him in their sight.
20 "And [a]you shall give *some* of your authority to him, that all the congregation of the children of Israel [b]may be obedient.
21 [a]"He shall stand before Eleazar the priest, who shall inquire before the LORD for him [b]by the judgment of the Urim. [c]At his word they shall go out, and at his word they shall come in, he and all the children of Israel with him—all the congregation."
22 So Moses did as the LORD commanded him. He took Joshua and set him before Eleazar the priest and before all the congregation.
23 And he laid his hands on him [a]and inaugurated him, just as the LORD commanded by the hand of Moses.

Daily Offerings
(Ex. 29:38–46)

28 Now the LORD spoke to Moses, saying,
2 "Command the children of Israel, and say to them, 'My offering, [a]My food for My offerings made by fire as a sweet aroma to Me, you shall be careful to offer to Me at their appointed time.'
3 "And you shall say to them, [a]'This *is* the offering made by fire which you shall offer to the LORD: two male lambs in their first year without blemish, day by day, as a regular burnt offering.
4 'The one lamb you shall offer in the morning, the other lamb you shall offer in the evening,
5 'and [a]one-tenth of an ephah of fine flour as a [b]grain offering mixed with one-fourth of a hin of pressed oil.
6 '*It is* [a]a regular burnt offering which was ordained at Mount Sinai for a sweet aroma, an offering made by fire to the LORD.
7 'And its drink offering *shall be* one-fourth of a hin for each lamb; [a]in a holy *place* you shall pour out the drink to the LORD as an offering.
8 'The other lamb you shall offer in the evening; as the morning grain offering and its drink offering, you shall offer *it* as an offering made by fire, a sweet aroma to the LORD.

Sabbath Offerings

9 'And on the Sabbath day two lambs in their first year, without blemish, and two-tenths *of an ephah* of fine flour as a grain offering, mixed with oil, with its drink offering—
10 '*this is* [a]the burnt offering for every Sabbath, besides the regular burnt offering with its drink offering.

KJV

Monthly Offerings

11 And [a]in the beginnings of your months ye shall offer a burnt offering unto the LORD; two young bullocks, and one ram, seven lambs of the first year without spot;
12 And [a]three tenth deals of flour *for* a meat offering, mingled with oil, for one bullock; and two tenth deals of flour *for* a meat offering, mingled with oil, for one ram;
13 And a several tenth deal of flour mingled with oil *for* a meat offering unto one lamb; *for* a burnt offering of a sweet savour, a sacrifice made by fire unto the LORD.
14 And their drink offerings shall be half an hin of wine unto a bullock, and the third *part* of an hin unto a ram, and a fourth *part* of an hin unto a lamb: this *is* the burnt offering of every month throughout the months of the year.
15 And [a]one kid of the goats for a sin offering unto the LORD shall be offered, beside the continual burnt offering, and his drink offering.

Offerings at Passover
(Lev. 23:5–14)

16 [a]And in the fourteenth day of the first month *is* the passover of the LORD.
17 [a]And in the fifteenth day of this month *is* the feast: seven days shall unleavened bread be eaten.
18 In the [a]first day *shall be* an holy convocation; ye shall do no manner of servile work *therein:*
19 But ye shall offer a sacrifice made by fire *for* a burnt offering unto the LORD; two young bullocks, and one ram, and seven lambs of the first year: [a]they shall be unto you without blemish:
20 And their meat offering *shall be of* flour mingled with oil: three tenth deals shall ye offer for a bullock, and two tenth deals for a ram;
21 A several tenth deal shalt thou offer for every lamb, throughout the seven lambs:
22 And [a]one goat *for* a sin offering, to make an atonement for you.
23 Ye shall offer these beside the burnt offering in the morning, which *is* for a continual burnt offering.
24 After this manner ye shall offer daily, throughout the seven days, the meat of the sacrifice made by fire, of a sweet savour unto the LORD: it shall be offered beside the continual burnt offering, and his drink offering.
25 And [a]on the seventh day ye shall have an holy convocation; ye shall do no servile work.

Offerings at the Feast of Weeks
(Lev. 23:15–22)

26 Also [a]in the day of the firstfruits, when ye bring a new meat offering unto the LORD, after your weeks *be out*, ye shall have an holy convocation; ye shall do no servile work:
27 But ye shall offer the burnt offering for a sweet savour unto the LORD; [a]two young bullocks, one ram, seven lambs of the first year;
28 And their meat offering of flour mingled with oil, three tenth deals unto one bullock, two tenth deals unto one ram,
29 A several tenth deal unto one lamb, throughout the seven lambs;
30 *And* one kid of the goats, to make an atonement for you.
31 Ye shall offer *them* beside the continual burnt offering, and his meat offering, ([a]they shall be unto you without blemish) and their drink offerings.

Offerings at the Feast of Trumpets
(Lev. 23:23–25)

29 And in the seventh month, on the first *day* of the month, ye shall have an holy convocation; ye shall do no servile work: [a]it is a day of blowing the trumpets unto you.

---

11 [a]Num. 10:10; 1 Sam. 20:5; 1 Chr. 23:31; 2 Chr. 2:4; Ezra 3:5; Neh. 10:33; Is. 1:13, 14; Ezek. 45:17; 46:6, 7; Hos. 2:11; Col. 2:16
12 [a]Num. 15:4–12
15 [a]Num. 15:24; 28:3, 22
16 [a]Ex. 12:1–20; Lev. 23:5–8; Num. 9:2–5; Deut. 16:1–8; Ezek. 45:21
17 [a]Lev. 23:6
18 [a]Ex. 12:16; Lev. 23:7
19 [a]Lev. 22:20; Num. 28:31; 29:8; Deut. 15:21
22 [a]Num. 28:15
25 [a]Ex. 12:16; 13:6; Lev. 23:8
26 [a]Ex. 23:16; 34:22; Lev. 23:10–21; Deut. 16:9–12; Acts 2:1
27 [a]Lev. 23:18, 19
31 [a]Num. 28:3, 19

CHAPTER 29
1 [a]Ex. 23:16; 34:22; Lev. 23:23–25

NKJV

Monthly Offerings

11 [a]'At the beginnings of your months you shall present a burnt offering to the LORD: two young bulls, one ram, and seven lambs in their first year, without blemish;
12 [a]'three-tenths *of an ephah* of fine flour as a grain offering, mixed with oil, for each bull; two-tenths *of an ephah* of fine flour as a grain offering, mixed with oil, for the one ram;
13 'and one-tenth *of an ephah* of fine flour, mixed with oil, as a grain offering for each lamb, as a burnt offering of sweet aroma, an offering made by fire to the LORD.
14 'Their drink offering shall be half a hin of wine for a bull, one-third of a hin for a ram, and one-fourth of a hin for a lamb; this *is* the burnt offering for each month throughout the months of the year.
15 'Also [a]one kid of the goats as a sin offering to the LORD shall be offered, besides the regular burnt offering and its drink offering.

Offerings at Passover
(Lev. 23:5–14)

16 [a]'On the fourteenth day of the first month *is* the Passover of the LORD.
17 [a]'And on the fifteenth day of this month *is* the feast; unleavened bread shall be eaten for seven days.
18 'On the [a]first day *you shall have* a holy convocation. You shall do no customary work.
19 'And you shall present an offering made by fire as a burnt offering to the LORD: two young bulls, one ram, and seven lambs in their first year. [a]Be sure they are without blemish.
20 'Their grain offering shall be of fine flour mixed with oil: three-tenths *of an ephah* you shall offer for a bull, and two-tenths for a ram;
21 'you shall offer one-tenth *of an ephah* for each of the seven lambs;
22 'also [a]one goat *as* a sin offering, to make atonement for you.
23 'You shall offer these besides the burnt offering of the morning, which *is* for a regular burnt offering.
24 'In this manner you shall offer the food of the offering made by fire daily for seven days, as a sweet aroma to the LORD; it shall be offered besides the regular burnt offering and its drink offering.
25 'And [a]on the seventh day you shall have a holy convocation. You shall do no customary work.

Offerings at the Feast of Weeks
(Lev. 23:15–22)

26 'Also [a]on the day of the firstfruits, when you bring a new grain offering to the LORD at your *Feast of* Weeks, you shall have a holy convocation. You shall do no customary work.
27 'You shall present a burnt offering as a sweet aroma to the LORD: [a]two young bulls, one ram, and seven lambs in their first year,
28 'with their grain offering of fine flour mixed with oil: three-tenths *of an ephah* for each bull, two-tenths for the one ram,
29 'and one-tenth for each of the seven lambs;
30 '*also* one kid of the goats, to make atonement for you.
31 [a]'Be sure they are without blemish. You shall present *them* with their drink offerings, besides the regular burnt offering with its grain offering.

Offerings at the Feast of Trumpets
(Lev. 23:23–25)

29 'And in the seventh month, on the first *day* of the month, you shall have a holy convocation. You shall do no customary work. For you [a]it is a day of blowing the trumpets.

KJV

2 And ye shall offer a burnt offering for a sweet savour unto the LORD; one young bullock, one ram, *and* seven lambs of the first year without blemish:

3 And their meat offering *shall be of* flour mingled with oil, three tenth deals for a bullock, *and* two tenth deals for a ram,

4 And one tenth deal for one lamb, throughout the seven lambs:

5 And one kid of the goats *for* a sin offering, to make an atonement for you:

6 Beside [a]the burnt offering of the month, and his meat offering, and [b]the daily burnt offering, and his meat offering, and their drink offerings, [c]according unto their manner, for a sweet savour, a sacrifice made by fire unto the LORD.

Offerings on the Day of Atonement
(Lev. 23:26–32)

7 And [a]ye shall have on the tenth *day* of this seventh month an holy convocation; and ye shall [b]afflict your souls: ye shall not do any work *therein:*

8 But ye shall offer a burnt offering unto the LORD *for* a sweet savour; one young bullock, one ram, *and* seven lambs of the first year; [a]they shall be unto you without blemish:

9 And their meat offering *shall be of* flour mingled with oil, three tenth deals to a bullock, *and* two tenth deals to one ram,

10 A several tenth deal for one lamb, throughout the seven lambs:

11 One kid of the goats *for* a sin offering; beside [a]the sin offering of atonement, and the continual burnt offering, and the meat offering of it, and their drink offerings.

Offerings at the Feast of Tabernacles
(Lev. 23:33–44)

12 And [a]on the fifteenth day of the seventh month ye shall have an holy convocation; ye shall do no servile work, and ye shall keep a feast unto the LORD seven days:

13 And [a]ye shall offer a burnt offering, a sacrifice made by fire, of a sweet savour unto the LORD; thirteen young bullocks, two rams, *and* fourteen lambs of the first year; they shall be without blemish:

14 And their meat offering *shall be of* flour mingled with oil, three tenth deals unto every bullock of the thirteen bullocks, two tenth deals to each ram of the two rams,

15 And a several tenth deal to each lamb of the fourteen lambs:

16 And one kid of the goats *for* a sin offering; beside the continual burnt offering, his meat offering, and his drink offering.

17 And on the [a]second day *ye shall offer* twelve young bullocks, two rams, fourteen lambs of the first year without spot:

18 And their meat offering and their drink offerings for the bullocks, for the rams, and for the lambs, *shall be* according to their number, [a]after the manner:

19 And one kid of the goats *for* a sin offering; beside the continual burnt offering, and the meat offering thereof, and their drink offerings.

20 And on the third day eleven bullocks, two rams, fourteen lambs of the first year without blemish;

21 And their meat offering and their drink offerings for the bullocks, for the rams, and for the lambs, *shall be* according to their number, [a]after the manner:

22 And one goat *for* a sin offering; beside the continual burnt offering, and his meat offering, and his drink offering.

23 And on the fourth day ten bullocks, two rams, *and* fourteen lambs of the first year without blemish:

24 Their meat offering and their drink offerings for the bullocks, for the rams, and for the

6 [a]Num. 28:11–15 [b]Num. 28:3 [c]Num. 15:11, 12
7 [a]Lev. 16:29–34; 23:26–32 [b]Ps. 35:13; Is. 58:5
8 [a]Num. 28:19
11 [a]Lev. 16:3, 5
12 [a]Lev. 23:33–35; Deut. 16:13–15; Ezek. 45:25
13 [a]Ezra 3:4
17 [a]Lev. 23:36
18 [a]Num. 15:12; 28:7, 14; 29:3, 4, 9, 10
21 [a]Num. 29:18

NKJV

2 'You shall offer a burnt offering as a sweet aroma to the LORD: one young bull, one ram, *and* seven lambs in their first year, without blemish.

3 'Their grain offering *shall be* fine flour mixed with oil: three-tenths *of an ephah* for the bull, two-tenths for the ram,

4 'and one-tenth for each of the seven lambs;

5 'also one kid of the goats *as* a sin offering, to make atonement for you;

6 'besides [a]the burnt offering with its grain offering for the New Moon, [b]the regular burnt offering with its grain offering, and their drink offerings, [c]according to their ordinance, as a sweet aroma, an offering made by fire to the LORD.

Offerings on the Day of Atonement
(Lev. 23:26–32)

7 [a]'On the tenth *day* of this seventh month you shall have a holy convocation. You shall [b]afflict your souls; you shall not do any work.

8 'You shall present a burnt offering to the LORD *as* a sweet aroma: one young bull, one ram, *and* seven lambs in their first year. [a]Be sure they are without blemish.

9 'Their grain offering *shall be of* fine flour mixed with oil: three-tenths *of an ephah* for the bull, two-tenths for the one ram,

10 'and one-tenth for each of the seven lambs;

11 'also one kid of the goats *as* a sin offering, besides [a]the sin offering for atonement, the regular burnt offering with its grain offering, and their drink offerings.

Offerings at the Feast of Tabernacles
(Lev. 23:33–44)

12 [a]'On the fifteenth day of the seventh month you shall have a holy convocation. You shall do no customary work, and you shall keep a feast to the LORD seven days.

13 [a]'You shall present a burnt offering, an offering made by fire as a sweet aroma to the LORD: thirteen young bulls, two rams, *and* fourteen lambs in their first year. They shall be without blemish.

14 'Their grain offering *shall be of* fine flour mixed with oil: three-tenths *of an ephah* for each of the thirteen bulls, two-tenths for each of the two rams,

15 'and one-tenth for each of the fourteen lambs;

16 'also one kid of the goats *as* a sin offering, besides the regular burnt offering, its grain offering, and its drink offering.

17 'On the [a]second day *present* twelve young bulls, two rams, fourteen lambs in their first year without blemish,

18 'and their grain offering and their drink offerings for the bulls, for the rams, and for the lambs, by their number, [a]according to the ordinance;

19 'also one kid of the goats *as* a sin offering, besides the regular burnt offering with its grain offering, and their drink offerings.

20 'On the third day *present* eleven bulls, two rams, fourteen lambs in their first year without blemish,

21 'and their grain offering and their drink offerings for the bulls, for the rams, and for the lambs, by their number, [a]according to the ordinance;

22 'also one goat *as* a sin offering, besides the regular burnt offering, its grain offering, and its drink offering.

23 'On the fourth day *present* ten bulls, two rams, *and* fourteen lambs in their first year, without blemish,

24 'and their grain offering and their drink offerings for the bulls, for the rams, and for the

KJV

lambs, *shall be* according to their number, after the manner:

25 And one kid of the goats *for* a sin offering; beside the continual burnt offering, his meat offering, and his drink offering.

26 And on the fifth day nine bullocks, two rams, *and* fourteen lambs of the first year without spot:

27 And their meat offering and their drink offerings for the bullocks, for the rams, and for the lambs, *shall be* according to their number, after the manner:

28 And one goat *for* a sin offering; beside the continual burnt offering, and his meat offering, and his drink offering.

29 And on the sixth day eight bullocks, two rams, *and* fourteen lambs of the first year without blemish:

30 And their meat offering and their drink offerings for the bullocks, for the rams, and for the lambs, *shall be* according to their number, after the manner:

31 And one goat *for* a sin offering; beside the continual burnt offering, his meat offering, and his drink offering.

32 And on the seventh day seven bullocks, two rams, *and* fourteen lambs of the first year without blemish:

33 And their meat offering and their drink offerings for the bullocks, for the rams, and for the lambs, *shall be* according to their number, after the manner:

34 And one goat *for* a sin offering; beside the continual burnt offering, his meat offering, and his drink offering.

35 On the eighth day ye shall have a [a]solemn assembly: ye shall do no servile work *therein:*

36 But ye shall offer a burnt offering, a sacrifice made by fire, of a sweet savour unto the LORD: one bullock, one ram, seven lambs of the first year without blemish:

37 Their meat offering and their drink offerings for the bullock, for the ram, and for the lambs, *shall be* according to their number, after the manner:

38 And one goat *for* a sin offering; beside the continual burnt offering, and his meat offering, and his drink offering.

39 These *things* ye shall do unto the LORD in your [a]set feasts, beside your [b]vows, and your freewill offerings, for your burnt offerings, and for your meat offerings, and for your drink offerings, and for your peace offerings.

40 And Moses told the children of Israel according to all that the LORD commanded Moses.

35 [a]Lev. 23:36
39 [a]Lev. 23:1–44; 1 Chr. 23:31; 2 Chr. 31:3; Ezra 3:5; Neh. 10:33; Is. 1:14 [b]Lev. 7:16; 22:18, 21, 23; 23:38

NKJV

lambs, by their number, according to the ordinance;

25 'also one kid of the goats *as* a sin offering, besides the regular burnt offering, its grain offering, and its drink offering.

26 'On the fifth day *present* nine bulls, two rams, *and* fourteen lambs in their first year without blemish,

27 'and their grain offering and their drink offerings for the bulls, for the rams, and for the lambs, by their number, according to the ordinance;

28 'also one goat *as* a sin offering, besides the regular burnt offering, its grain offering, and its drink offering.

29 'On the sixth day *present* eight bulls, two rams, *and* fourteen lambs in their first year without blemish,

30 'and their grain offering and their drink offerings for the bulls, for the rams, and for the lambs, by their number, according to the ordinance;

31 'also one goat *as* a sin offering, besides the regular burnt offering, its grain offering, and its drink offering.

32 'On the seventh day *present* seven bulls, two rams, *and* fourteen lambs in their first year without blemish,

33 'and their grain offering and their drink offerings for the bulls, for the rams, and for the lambs, by their number, according to the ordinance;

34 'also one goat *as* a sin offering, besides the regular burnt offering, its grain offering, and its drink offering.

35 'On the eighth day you shall have a [a]sacred assembly. You shall do no customary work.

36 'You shall present a burnt offering, an offering made by fire as a sweet aroma to the LORD: one bull, one ram, seven lambs in their first year without blemish,

37 'and their grain offering and their drink offerings for the bull, for the ram, and for the lambs, by their number, according to the ordinance;

38 'also one goat *as* a sin offering, besides the regular burnt offering, its grain offering, and its drink offering.

39 'These you shall present to the LORD at your [a]appointed feasts (besides your [b]vowed offerings and your freewill offerings) as your burnt offerings and your grain offerings, as your drink offerings and your peace offerings.' "

40 So Moses told the children of Israel everything, just as the LORD commanded Moses.

KJV

The Law Concerning Vows

30 And Moses spake unto [a]the heads of the tribes concerning the children of Israel, saying, This *is* the thing which the LORD hath commanded.

2 [a]If a man vow a vow unto the LORD, or [b]swear an oath to bind his soul with a bond; he shall not break his word, he shall [c]do according to all that proceedeth out of his mouth.

3 If a woman also vow a vow unto the LORD, and bind *herself* by a bond, *being* in her father's house in her youth;

4 And her father hear her vow, and her bond wherewith she hath bound her soul, and her father shall hold his peace at her: then all her vows shall stand, and every bond wherewith she hath bound her soul shall stand.

5 But if her father disallow her in the day that he heareth; not any of her vows, or of her bonds wherewith she hath bound her soul, shall stand: and the LORD shall forgive her, because her father disallowed her.

6 And if she had at all an husband, when she vowed, or uttered ought out of her lips, wherewith she bound her soul;

CHAPTER 30

1 [a]Num. 1:4, 16; 7:2
2 [a]Lev. 27:2; Deut. 23:21–23; Judg. 11:30, 31, 35; Eccl. 5:4 [b]Lev. 5:4; Matt. 14:9; Acts 23:14 [c]Job 22:27; Ps. 22:25; 50:14; 66:13, 14; Nah. 1:15

NKJV

The Law Concerning Vows

30 Then Moses spoke to [a]the heads of the tribes concerning the children of Israel, saying, "This *is* the thing which the LORD has commanded:

2 [a]"If a man makes a vow to the LORD, or [b]swears an oath to bind himself by some agreement, he shall not break his word; he shall [c]do according to all that proceeds out of his mouth.

3 "Or if a woman makes a vow to the LORD, and binds *herself* by some agreement while in her father's house in her youth,

4 "and her father hears her vow and the agreement by which she has bound herself, and her father holds his peace, then all her vows shall stand, and every agreement with which she has bound herself shall stand.

5 "But if her father overrules her on the day that he hears, then none of her vows nor her agreements by which she has bound herself shall stand; and the LORD will release her, because her father overruled her.

6 "If indeed she takes a husband, while bound by her vows or by a rash utterance from her lips by which she bound herself,

KJV

7 And her husband heard *it,* and held his peace at her in the day that he heard *it:* then her vows shall stand, and her bonds wherewith she bound her soul shall stand.

8 But if her husband [a]disallowed her on the day that he heard *it;* then he shall make her vow which she vowed, and that which she uttered with her lips, wherewith she bound her soul, of none effect: and the LORD shall forgive her.

9 But every vow of a widow, and of her that is divorced, wherewith they have bound their souls, shall stand against her.

10 And if she vowed in her husband's house, or bound her soul by a bond with an oath;

11 And her husband heard *it,* and held his peace at her, *and* disallowed her not: then all her vows shall stand, and every bond wherewith she bound her soul shall stand.

12 But if her husband hath utterly made them void on the day he heard *them; then* whatsoever proceeded out of her lips concerning her vows, or concerning the bond of her soul, shall not stand: her husband hath made them void; and the LORD shall forgive her.

13 Every vow, and every binding oath to afflict the soul, her husband may establish it, or her husband may make it void.

14 But if her husband altogether hold his peace at her from day to day; then he establisheth all her vows, or all her bonds, which *are* upon her: he confirmeth them, because he held his peace at her in the day that he heard *them.*

15 But if he shall any ways make them void after that he hath heard *them;* then he shall bear her iniquity.

16 These *are* the statutes, which the LORD commanded Moses, between a man and his wife, between the father and his daughter, *being yet* in her youth in her father's house.

Vengeance on the Midianites

31 And the LORD spake unto Moses, saying,
2 [a]Avenge the children of Israel of the Midianites: afterward shalt thou [b]be gathered unto thy people.

3 And Moses spake unto the people, saying, Arm some of yourselves unto the war, and let them go against the Midianites, and avenge the LORD of [a]Midian.

4 Of every tribe a thousand, throughout all the tribes of Israel, shall ye send to the war.

5 So there were delivered out of the thousands of Israel, a thousand of *every* tribe, twelve thousand armed for war.

6 And Moses sent them to the war, a thousand of *every* tribe, them and Phinehas the son of Eleazar the priest, to the war, with the holy instruments, and [a]the trumpets to blow in his hand.

7 And they warred against the Midianites, as the LORD commanded Moses; and [a]they slew all the [b]males.

8 And they slew the kings of Midian, beside the rest of them that were slain; *namely,* [a]Evi, and Rekem, and [b]Zur, and Hur, and Reba, five kings of Midian: [c]Balaam also the son of Beor they slew with the sword.

9 And the children of Israel took *all* the women of Midian captives, and their little ones, and took the spoil of all their cattle, and all their flocks, and all their goods.

10 And they burnt all their cities wherein they dwelt, and all their goodly castles, with fire.

11 And [a]they took all the spoil, and all the prey, *both* of men and of beasts.

Return from the War

12 And they brought the captives, and the prey, and the spoil, unto Moses, and Eleazar the priest, and unto the congregation of the children of Israel, unto the camp at the plains of Moab, which *are* by Jordan *near* Jericho.

8 [a][Gen. 3:16]

CHAPTER 31

2 [a]Num. 25:17 [b]Num. 25:12, 13
3 [a]Josh. 13:21
6 [a]Num. 10:9
7 [a]Deut. 20:13; Judg. 21:11; 1 Sam. 27:9; 1 Kin. 11:15, 16 [b]Gen. 34:25
8 [a]Josh. 13:21 [b]Num. 25:15 [c]Num. 31:16; Josh. 13:22
11 [a]Deut. 20:14

NKJV

7 "and her husband hears *it,* and makes no response to her on the day that he hears, then her vows shall stand, and her agreements by which she bound herself shall stand.

8 "But if her husband [a]overrules her on the day that he hears *it,* he shall make void her vow which she took and what she uttered with her lips, by which she bound herself, and the LORD will release her.

9 "Also any vow of a widow or a divorced woman, by which she has bound herself, shall stand against her.

10 "If she vowed in her husband's house, or bound herself by an agreement with an oath,

11 "and her husband heard *it,* and made no response to her *and* did not overrule her, then all her vows shall stand, and every agreement by which she bound herself shall stand.

12 "But if her husband truly made them void on the day he heard *them,* then whatever proceeded from her lips concerning her vows or concerning the agreement binding her, it shall not stand; her husband has made them void, and the LORD will release her.

13 "Every vow and every binding oath to afflict her soul, her husband may confirm it, or her husband may make it void.

14 "Now if her husband makes no response whatever to her from day to day, then he confirms all her vows or all the agreements that bind her; he confirms them, because he made no response to her on the day that he heard *them.*

15 "But if he does make them void after he has heard *them,* then he shall bear her guilt."

16 These *are* the statutes which the LORD commanded Moses, between a man and his wife, and between a father and his daughter in her youth in her father's house.

Vengeance on the Midianites

31 And the LORD spoke to Moses, saying:
2 [a]"Take vengeance on the Midianites for the children of Israel. Afterward you shall [b]be gathered to your people."

3 So Moses spoke to the people, saying, "Arm some of yourselves for war, and let them go against the Midianites to take vengeance for the LORD on [a]Midian.

4 "A thousand from each tribe of all the tribes of Israel you shall send to the war."

5 So there were recruited from the divisions of Israel one thousand from *each* tribe, twelve thousand armed for war.

6 Then Moses sent them to the war, one thousand from *each* tribe; he sent them to the war with Phinehas the son of Eleazar the priest, with the holy articles and [a]the signal trumpets in his hand.

7 And they warred against the Midianites, just as the LORD commanded Moses, and [a]they killed all the [b]males.

8 They killed the kings of Midian with *the rest of* those who were killed—[a]Evi, Rekem, [b]Zur, Hur, and Reba, the five kings of Midian. [c]Balaam the son of Beor they also killed with the sword.

9 And the children of Israel took the women of Midian captive, with their little ones, and took as spoil all their cattle, all their flocks, and all their goods.

10 They also burned with fire all the cities where they dwelt, and all their forts.

11 And [a]they took all the spoil and all the booty—of man and beast.

Return from the War

12 Then they brought the captives, the booty, and the spoil to Moses, to Eleazar the priest, and to the congregation of the children of Israel, to the camp in the plains of Moab by the Jordan, *across from* Jericho.

KJV

13 And Moses, and Eleazar the priest, and all the princes of the congregation, went forth to meet them without the camp.

14 And Moses was wroth with the officers of the host, *with* the captains over thousands, and captains over hundreds, which came from the battle.

15 And Moses said unto them, Have ye saved [a]all the women alive?

16 Behold, [a]these caused the children of Israel, through the [b]counsel of Balaam, to commit trespass against the LORD in the matter of Peor, and [c]there was a plague among the congregation of the LORD.

17 Now therefore [a]kill every male among the little ones, and kill every woman that hath known man by lying with him.

18 But all the women children, that have not known a man by lying with him, keep alive [a]for yourselves.

19 And [a]do ye abide without the camp seven days: whosoever hath killed any person, and [b]whosoever hath touched any slain, purify *both* yourselves and your captives on the third day, and on the seventh day.

20 And purify all *your* raiment, and all that is made of skins, and all work of goats' *hair*, and all things made of wood.

21 And Eleazar the priest said unto the men of war which went to the battle, This *is* the ordinance of the law which the LORD commanded Moses;

22 Only the gold, and the silver, the brass, the iron, the tin, and the lead,

23 Every thing that may abide the fire, ye shall make *it* go through the fire, and it shall be clean: nevertheless it shall be purified [a]with the water of separation: and all that abideth not the fire ye shall make go through the water.

24 [a]And ye shall wash your clothes on the seventh day, and ye shall be clean, and afterward ye shall come into the camp.

Division of the Plunder

25 And the LORD spake unto Moses, saying,

26 Take the sum of the prey that was taken, *both* of man and of beast, thou, and Eleazar the priest, and the chief fathers of the congregation:

27 And [a]divide the prey into two parts; between them that took the war upon them, who went out to battle, and between all the congregation:

28 And levy a tribute unto the LORD of the men of war which went out to battle: [a]one soul of five hundred, *both* of the persons, and of the beeves, and of the asses, and of the sheep:

29 Take *it* of their half, and [a]give *it* unto Eleazar the priest, *for* an heave offering of the LORD.

30 And of the children of Israel's half, thou shalt take [a]one portion of fifty, of the persons, of the beeves, of the asses, and of the flocks, of all manner of beasts, and give them unto the Levites, [b]which keep the charge of the tabernacle of the LORD.

31 And Moses and Eleazar the priest did as the LORD commanded Moses.

32 And the booty, *being* the rest of the prey which the men of war had caught, was six hundred thousand and seventy thousand and five thousand sheep,

33 And threescore and twelve thousand beeves,

34 And threescore and one thousand asses,

35 And thirty and two thousand persons in all, of women that had not known man by lying with him.

36 And the half, *which was* the portion of them that went out to war, was in number three hundred thousand and seven and thirty thousand and five hundred sheep:

15 [a]Deut. 20:14
16 [a]Num. 25:2 [b]Num. 24:14; 2 Pet. 2:15; Rev. 2:14 [c]Num. 25:9
17 [a]Deut. 7:2; 20:16–18; Judg. 21:11
18 [a]Deut. 21:10–14
19 [a]Num. 5:2 [b]Num. 19:11–22
23 [a]Num. 19:9, 17
24 [a]Lev. 11:25
27 [a]Josh. 22:8; 1 Sam. 30:24
28 [a]Num. 31:30, 47
29 [a]Deut. 18:1–5
30 [a]Num. 31:42–47 [b]Num. 3:7, 8, 25, 31, 36; 18:3, 4

NKJV

13 And Moses, Eleazar the priest, and all the leaders of the congregation, went to meet them outside the camp.

14 But Moses was angry with the officers of the army, *with* the captains over thousands and captains over hundreds, who had come from the battle.

15 And Moses said to them: "Have you kept [a]all the women alive?

16 "Look, [a]these *women* caused the children of Israel, through the [b]counsel of Balaam, to trespass against the LORD in the incident of Peor, and [c]there was a plague among the congregation of the LORD.

17 "Now therefore, [a]kill every male among the little ones, and kill every woman who has known a man intimately.

18 "But keep alive [a]for yourselves all the young girls who have not known a man intimately.

19 "And as for you, [a]remain outside the camp seven days; whoever has killed any person, and [b]whoever has touched any slain, purify yourselves and your captives on the third day and on the seventh day.

20 "Purify every garment, everything made of leather, everything woven of goats' *hair*, and everything made of wood."

21 Then Eleazar the priest said to the men of war who had gone to the battle, "This *is* the ordinance of the law which the LORD commanded Moses:

22 "Only the gold, the silver, the bronze, the iron, the tin, and the lead,

23 "everything that can endure fire, you shall put through the fire, and it shall be clean; and it shall be purified [a]with the water of purification. But all that cannot endure fire you shall put through water.

24 [a]"And you shall wash your clothes on the seventh day and be clean, and afterward you may come into the camp."

Division of the Plunder

25 Now the LORD spoke to Moses, saying:

26 "Count up the plunder that was taken—of man and beast—you and Eleazar the priest and the chief fathers of the congregation;

27 "and [a]divide the plunder into two parts, between those who took part in the war, who went out to battle, and all the congregation.

28 "And levy a tribute for the LORD on the men of war who went out to battle: [a]one of every five hundred of the persons, the cattle, the donkeys, and the sheep;

29 "take *it* from their half, and [a]give *it* to Eleazar the priest as a heave offering to the LORD.

30 "And from the children of Israel's half you shall take [a]one of every fifty, drawn from the persons, the cattle, the donkeys, and the sheep, from all the livestock, and give them to the Levites [b]who keep charge of the tabernacle of the LORD."

31 So Moses and Eleazar the priest did as the LORD commanded Moses.

32 The booty remaining from the plunder, which the men of war had taken, was six hundred and seventy-five thousand sheep,

33 seventy-two thousand cattle,

34 sixty-one thousand donkeys,

35 and thirty-two thousand persons in all, of women who had not known a man intimately.

36 And the half, the portion for those who had gone out to war, was in number three hundred and thirty-seven thousand five hundred sheep;

KJV

37 And the LORD's tribute of the sheep was
six hundred and threescore and fifteen.
38 And the beeves *were* thirty and six thousand; of which the LORD's tribute *was* threescore
and twelve.
39 And the asses *were* thirty thousand and
five hundred; of which the LORD's tribute *was*
threescore and one.
40 And the persons *were* sixteen thousand;
of which the LORD's tribute *was* thirty and two
persons.
41 And Moses gave the tribute, *which was*
the LORD's heave offering, unto Eleazar the priest,
[a]as the LORD commanded Moses.
42 And of the children of Israel's half, which
Moses divided from the men that warred,
43 (Now the half *that pertained unto* the congregation was three hundred thousand and thirty
thousand *and* seven thousand and five hundred
sheep,
44 And thirty and six thousand beeves,
45 And thirty thousand asses and five
hundred,
46 And sixteen thousand persons;)
47 Even [a]of the children of Israel's half, Moses took one portion of fifty, *both* of man and of
beast, and gave them unto the Levites, which kept
the charge of the tabernacle of the LORD; as the
LORD commanded Moses.
48 And the officers which *were* over thousands of the host, the captains of thousands, and
captains of hundreds, came near unto Moses:
49 And they said unto Moses, Thy servants
have taken the sum of the men of war which *are*
under our charge, and there lacketh not one man
of us.
50 We have therefore brought an oblation for
the LORD, what every man hath gotten, of jewels
of gold, chains, and bracelets, rings, earrings, and
tablets, [a]to make an atonement for our souls before the LORD.
51 And Moses and Eleazar the priest took the
gold of them, *even* all wrought jewels.
52 And all the gold of the offering that they
offered up to the LORD, of the captains of thousands, and of the captains of hundreds, was sixteen thousand seven hundred and fifty shekels.
53 (*For* [a]the men of war had taken spoil, every man for himself.)
54 And Moses and Eleazar the priest took the
gold of the captains of thousands and of hundreds,
and brought it into the tabernacle of the congregation, [a]*for* a memorial for the children of Israel before the LORD.

The Tribes Settling East of the Jordan
(Deut. 3:12–22)

32 Now the children of Reuben and the children of Gad had a very great multitude of
cattle: and when they saw the land of [a]Jazer, and
the land of [b]Gilead, that, behold, the place *was* a
place for cattle;
2 The children of Gad and the children of
Reuben came and spake unto Moses, and to Eleazar the priest, and unto the princes of the congregation, saying,
3 Ataroth, and Dibon, and Jazer, and [a]Nim-
rah, and [b]Heshbon, and Elealeh, and [c]Shebam,
and Nebo, and [d]Beon,
4 *Even* the country [a]which the LORD smote
before the congregation of Israel, *is* a land for
cattle, and thy servants have cattle:
5 Wherefore, said they, if we have found
grace in thy sight, let this land be given unto thy
servants for a possession, *and* bring us not over
Jordan.
6 And Moses said unto the children of Gad
and to the children of Reuben, Shall your brethren
go to war, and shall ye sit here?
7 And wherefore [a]discourage ye the heart
of the children of Israel from going over into the
land which the LORD hath given them?

41 [a]Num. 5:9, 10; 18:8, 19
47 [a]Num. 31:30
50 [a]Ex. 30:12–16
53 [a]Num. 31:32; Deut. 20:14
54 [a]Ex. 30:16

CHAPTER 32
1 [a]Num. 21:32; Josh. 13:25; 2 Sam. 24:5 [b]Deut. 3:13
3 [a]Num. 32:36 [b]Josh. 13:17, 26 [c]Num. 32:38 [d]Num. 32:38
4 [a]Num. 21:24, 34, 35
7 [a]Num. 13:27—14:4

NKJV

37 and the LORD's tribute of the sheep was
six hundred and seventy-five.
38 The cattle *were* thirty-six thousand, of
which the LORD's tribute *was* seventy-two.
39 The donkeys *were* thirty thousand five
hundred, of which the LORD's tribute *was* sixty-
one.
40 The persons *were* sixteen thousand, of
which the LORD's tribute *was* thirty-two persons.
41 So Moses gave the tribute *which was* the
LORD's heave offering to Eleazar the priest, [a]as
the LORD commanded Moses.
42 And from the children of Israel's half,
which Moses separated from the men who
fought—
43 now the half belonging to the congregation was three hundred and thirty-seven thousand
five hundred sheep,
44 thirty-six thousand cattle,
45 thirty thousand five hundred donkeys,
46 and sixteen thousand persons—
47 and [a]from the children of Israel's half Moses took one of every fifty, drawn from man and
beast, and gave them to the Levites, who kept
charge of the tabernacle of the LORD, as the LORD
commanded Moses.
48 Then the officers who *were* over thousands of the army, the captains of thousands and
captains of hundreds, came near to Moses;
49 and they said to Moses, "Your servants
have taken a count of the men of war who *are*
under our command, and not a man of us is
missing.
50 "Therefore we have brought an offering
for the LORD, what every man found of ornaments
of gold: armlets and bracelets and signet rings
and earrings and necklaces, [a]to make atonement
for ourselves before the LORD."
51 So Moses and Eleazar the priest received
the gold from them, all the fashioned ornaments.
52 And all the gold of the offering that they
offered to the LORD, from the captains of thousands and captains of hundreds, was sixteen thousand seven hundred and fifty shekels.
53 [a](The men of war had taken spoil, every
man for himself.)
54 And Moses and Eleazar the priest received the gold from the captains of thousands
and of hundreds, and brought it into the tabernacle of meeting [a]as a memorial for the children of
Israel before the LORD.

The Tribes Settling East of the Jordan
(Deut. 3:12–22)

32 Now the children of Reuben and the children of Gad had a very great multitude of
livestock; and when they saw the land of [a]Jazer
and the land of [b]Gilead, that indeed the region
was a place for livestock,
2 the children of Gad and the children of
Reuben came and spoke to Moses, to Eleazar the
priest, and to the leaders of the congregation,
saying,
3 "Ataroth, Dibon, Jazer, [a]Nimrah, [b]Hesh-
bon, Elealeh, [c]Shebam, Nebo, and [d]Beon,
4 "the country [a]which the LORD defeated before the congregation of Israel, *is* a land for livestock, and your servants have livestock."
5 Therefore they said, "If we have found favor in your sight, let this land be given to your
servants as a possession. Do not take us over the
Jordan."
6 And Moses said to the children of Gad and
to the children of Reuben: "Shall your brethren
go to war while you sit here?
7 "Now why will you [a]discourage the heart
of the children of Israel from going over into the
land which the LORD has given them?

KJV

8 Thus did your fathers, [a]when I sent them from Kadesh–barnea [b]to see the land.

9 For [a]when they went up unto the valley of Eshcol, and saw the land, they discouraged the heart of the children of Israel, that they should not go into the land which the LORD had given them.

10 [a]And the LORD's anger was kindled the same time, and he sware, saying,

11 Surely none of the men that came up out of Egypt, [a]from twenty years old and upward, shall see the land which I sware unto Abraham, unto Isaac, and unto Jacob; because [b]they have not wholly followed me:

12 Save Caleb the son of Jephunneh the Kenezite, and Joshua the son of Nun: [a]for they have wholly followed the LORD.

13 And the LORD's anger was kindled against Israel, and he made them [a]wander in the wilderness forty years, until [b]all the generation, that had done evil in the sight of the LORD, was consumed.

14 And, behold, ye are risen up in your fathers' stead, an increase of sinful men, to augment yet the [a]fierce anger of the LORD toward Israel.

15 For if ye [a]turn away from after him, he will yet again leave them in the wilderness; and ye shall destroy all this people.

16 And they came near unto him, and said, We will build sheepfolds here for our cattle, and cities for our little ones:

17 But [a]we ourselves will go ready armed before the children of Israel, until we have brought them unto their place: and our little ones shall dwell in the fenced cities because of the inhabitants of the land.

18 [a]We will not return unto our houses, until the children of Israel have inherited every man his inheritance.

19 For we will not inherit with them on yonder side Jordan, or forward; [a]because our inheritance is fallen to us on this side Jordan eastward.

20 And [a]Moses said unto them, If ye will do this thing, if ye will go armed before the LORD to war,

21 And will go all of you armed over Jordan before the LORD, until he hath driven out his enemies from before him,

22 And [a]the land be subdued before the LORD: then afterward [b]ye shall return, and be guiltless before the LORD, and before Israel; and [c]this land shall be your possession before the LORD.

23 But if ye will not do so, behold, ye have sinned against the LORD: and be sure [a]your sin will find you out.

24 [a]Build you cities for your little ones, and folds for your sheep; and do that which hath proceeded out of your mouth.

25 And the children of Gad and the children of Reuben spake unto Moses, saying, Thy servants will do as my lord commandeth.

26 [a]Our little ones, our wives, our flocks, and all our cattle, shall be there in the cities of Gilead:

27 [a]But thy servants will pass over, every man armed for war, before the LORD to battle, as my lord saith.

28 So [a]concerning them Moses commanded Eleazar the priest, and Joshua the son of Nun, and the chief fathers of the tribes of the children of Israel:

29 And Moses said unto them, If the children of Gad and the children of Reuben will pass with you over Jordan, every man armed to battle, before the LORD, and the land shall be subdued before you; then ye shall give them the land of Gilead for a possession:

30 But if they will not pass over with you armed, they shall have possessions among you in the land of Canaan.

31 And the children of Gad and the children

8 [a]Num. 13:3, 26 [b]Deut. 1:19–25
9 [a]Num. 13:24, 31; Deut. 1:24, 28
10 [a]Num. 14:11; Deut. 1:34–36
11 [a]Num. 14:28, 29; 26:63–65; Deut. 1:35 [b]Num. 14:24, 30
12 [a]Num. 14:6–9, 24, 30; Deut. 1:36; Josh. 14:8, 9
13 [a]Num. 14:33–35 [b]Num. 26:64, 65
14 [a]Num. 11:1; Deut. 1:34
15 [a]Deut. 30:17, 18; Josh. 22:16–18; 2 Chr. 7:19; 15:2
17 [a]Josh. 4:12, 13
18 [a]Josh. 22:1–4
19 [a]Josh. 12:1; 13:8
20 [a]Deut. 3:18; Josh. 1:14
22 [a]Deut. 3:20; Josh. 11:23 [b]Josh. 22:4 [c]Deut. 3:12, 15, 16, 18; Josh. 1:15; 13:8, 32; 22:4, 9
23 [a]Gen. 4:7; 44:16; Josh. 7:1–26; Is. 59:12; [Gal. 6:7]
24 [a]Num. 32:16
26 [a]Josh. 1:14
27 [a]Josh. 4:12
28 [a]Josh. 1:13

NKJV

8 "Thus your fathers did [a]when I sent them away from Kadesh Barnea [b]to see the land.

9 "For [a]when they went up to the Valley of Eshcol and saw the land, they discouraged the heart of the children of Israel, so that they did not go into the land which the LORD had given them.

10 [a]"So the LORD's anger was aroused on that day, and He swore an oath, saying,

11 'Surely none of the men who came up from Egypt, [a]from twenty years old and above, shall see the land of which I swore to Abraham, Isaac, and Jacob, because [b]they have not wholly followed Me,

12 'except Caleb the son of Jephunneh, the Kenizzite, and Joshua the son of Nun, [a]for they have wholly followed the LORD.'

13 "So the LORD's anger was aroused against Israel, and He made them [a]wander in the wilderness forty years, until [b]all the generation that had done evil in the sight of the LORD was gone.

14 "And look! You have risen in your fathers' place, a brood of sinful men, to increase still more the [a]fierce anger of the LORD against Israel.

15 "For if you [a]turn away from following Him, He will once again leave them in the wilderness, and you will destroy all these people."

16 Then they came near to him and said: "We will build sheepfolds here for our livestock, and cities for our little ones,

17 "but [a]we ourselves will be armed, ready *to go* before the children of Israel until we have brought them to their place; and our little ones will dwell in the fortified cities because of the inhabitants of the land.

18 [a]"We will not return to our homes until every one of the children of Israel has received his inheritance.

19 "For we will not inherit with them on the other side of the Jordan and beyond, [a]because our inheritance has fallen to us on this eastern side of the Jordan."

20 Then [a]Moses said to them: "If you do this thing, if you arm yourselves before the LORD for the war,

21 "and all your armed men cross over the Jordan before the LORD until He has driven out His enemies from before Him,

22 "and [a]the land is subdued before the LORD, then afterward [b]you may return and be blameless before the LORD and before Israel; and [c]this land shall be your possession before the LORD.

23 "But if you do not do so, then take note, you have sinned against the LORD; and be sure [a]your sin will find you out.

24 [a]"Build cities for your little ones and folds for your sheep, and do what has proceeded out of your mouth."

25 And the children of Gad and the children of Reuben spoke to Moses, saying: "Your servants will do as my lord commands.

26 [a]"Our little ones, our wives, our flocks, and all our livestock will be there in the cities of Gilead;

27 [a]"but your servants will cross over, every man armed for war, before the LORD to battle, just as my lord says."

28 So Moses gave command [a]concerning them to Eleazar the priest, to Joshua the son of Nun, and to the chief fathers of the tribes of the children of Israel.

29 And Moses said to them: "If the children of Gad and the children of Reuben cross over the Jordan with you, every man armed for battle before the LORD, and the land is subdued before you, then you shall give them the land of Gilead as a possession.

30 "But if they do not cross over armed with you, they shall have possessions among you in the land of Canaan."

31 Then the children of Gad and the children

KJV

of Reuben answered, saying, As the LORD hath said unto thy servants, so will we do.

32 We will pass over armed before the LORD into the land of Canaan, that the possession of our inheritance on this side Jordan *may be* our's.

33 And [a]Moses gave unto them, *even* to the children of Gad, and to the children of Reuben, and unto half the tribe of Manasseh the son of Joseph, [b]the kingdom of Sihon king of the Amorites, and the kingdom of Og king of Bashan, the land, with the cities thereof in the coasts, *even* the cities of the country round about.

34 And the children of Gad built [a]Dibon, and Ataroth, and [b]Aroer,

35 And Atroth, Shophan, and [a]Jaazer, and Jogbehah,

36 And [a]Beth–nimrah, and Beth–haran, [b]fenced cities: and folds for sheep.

37 And the children of Reuben [a]built Heshbon, and Elealeh, and Kirjathaim,

38 And [a]Nebo, and [b]Baal–meon, [c](their names being changed,) and Shibmah: and gave other names unto the cities which they builded.

39 And the children of [a]Machir the son of Manasseh went to Gilead, and took it, and dispossessed the Amorite which *was* in it.

40 And Moses [a]gave Gilead unto Machir the son of Manasseh; and he dwelt therein.

41 And [a]Jair the son of Manasseh went and took the small towns thereof, and called them [b]Havoth–jair.

42 And Nobah went and took Kenath, and the villages thereof, and called it Nobah, after his own name.

Israel's Journey from Egypt Reviewed

33 These *are* the journeys of the children of Israel, which went forth out of the land of Egypt with their armies under the [a]hand of Moses and Aaron.

2 And Moses wrote their goings out according to their journeys by the commandment of the LORD: and these *are* their journeys according to their goings out.

3 And they [a]departed from Rameses in [b]the first month, on the fifteenth day of the first month; on the morrow after the passover the children of Israel went out [c]with an high hand in the sight of all the Egyptians.

4 For the Egyptians buried all *their* firstborn, [a]which the LORD had smitten among them: [b]upon their gods also the LORD executed judgments.

5 [a]And the children of Israel removed from Rameses, and pitched in Succoth.

6 And they departed from [a]Succoth, and pitched in Etham, which *is* in the edge of the wilderness.

7 And [a]they removed from Etham, and turned again unto Pi–hahiroth, which *is* before Baal–zephon: and they pitched before Migdol.

8 And they departed from before Pi–hahiroth, and [a]passed through the midst of the sea into the wilderness, and went three days' journey in the wilderness of Etham, and pitched in Marah.

9 And they removed from Marah, and [a]came unto Elim: and in Elim *were* twelve fountains of water, and threescore and ten palm trees; and they pitched there.

10 And they removed from Elim, and encamped by the Red sea.

11 And they removed from the Red sea, and encamped in the [a]wilderness of Sin.

12 And they took their journey out of the wilderness of Sin, and encamped in Dophkah.

13 And they departed from Dophkah, and encamped in Alush.

14 And they removed from Alush, and encamped at [a]Rephidim, where was no water for the people to drink.

15 And they departed from Rephidim, and pitched in the [a]wilderness of Sinai.

33 [a]Deut. 3:8–17; 29:8; Josh. 12:1–6; 13:8–31; 22:4 [b]Num. 21:24, 33, 35
34 [a]Num. 33:45, 46 [b]Deut. 2:36
35 [a]Num. 32:1, 3
36 [a]Num. 32:3 [b]Num. 32:24
37 [a]Num. 21:27
38 [a]Is. 46:1 [b]Ezek. 25:9 [c]Ex. 23:13; Josh. 23:7
39 [a]Gen. 50:23; Num. 27:1; 36:1
40 [a]Deut. 3:12, 13, 15; Josh. 13:31
41 [a]Deut. 3:14; Josh. 13:30 [b]Judg. 10:4; 1 Kin. 4:13

CHAPTER 33
1 [a]Ps. 77:20
3 [a]Ex. 12:37 [b]Ex. 12:2; 13:4 [c]Ex. 14:8
4 [a]Ex. 12:29 [b][Ex. 12:12; 18:11]; Is. 19:1
5 [a]Ex. 12:37
6 [a]Ex. 13:20
7 [a]Ex. 14:1, 2, 9
8 [a]Ex. 14:22; 15:22, 23
9 [a]Ex. 15:27
11 [a]Ex. 16:1
14 [a]Ex. 17:1; 19:2
15 [a]Ex. 16:1; 19:1, 2

NKJV

of Reuben answered, saying: "As the LORD has said to your servants, so we will do.

32 "We will cross over armed before the LORD into the land of Canaan, but the possession of our inheritance *shall remain* with us on this side of the Jordan."

33 So [a]Moses gave to the children of Gad, to the children of Reuben, and to half the tribe of Manasseh the son of Joseph, [b]the kingdom of Sihon king of the Amorites and the kingdom of Og king of Bashan, the land with its cities within the borders, the cities of the surrounding country.

34 And the children of Gad built [a]Dibon and Ataroth and [b]Aroer,

35 Atroth and Shophan and [a]Jazer and Jogbehah,

36 [a]Beth Nimrah and Beth Haran, [b]fortified cities, and folds for sheep.

37 And the children of Reuben built [a]Heshbon and Elealeh and Kirjathaim,

38 [a]Nebo and [b]Baal Meon [c](*their* names being changed) and Shibmah; and they gave *other* names to the cities which they built.

39 And the children of [a]Machir the son of Manasseh went to Gilead and took it, and dispossessed the Amorites who *were* in it.

40 So Moses [a]gave Gilead to Machir the son of Manasseh, and he dwelt in it.

41 Also [a]Jair the son of Manasseh went and took its small towns, and called them [b]Havoth Jair.*

42 Then Nobah went and took Kenath and its villages, and he called it Nobah, after his own name.

Israel's Journey from Egypt Reviewed

33 These *are* the journeys of the children of Israel, who went out of the land of Egypt by their armies under the [a]hand of Moses and Aaron.

2 Now Moses wrote down the starting points of their journeys at the command of the LORD. And these *are* their journeys according to their starting points:

3 They [a]departed from Rameses in [b]the first month, on the fifteenth day of the first month; on the day after the Passover the children of Israel went out [c]with boldness in the sight of all the Egyptians.

4 For the Egyptians were burying all *their* firstborn, [a]whom the LORD had killed among them. Also [b]on their gods the LORD had executed judgments.

5 [a]Then the children of Israel moved from Rameses and camped at Succoth.

6 They departed from [a]Succoth and camped at Etham, which *is* on the edge of the wilderness.

7 [a]They moved from Etham and turned back to Pi Hahiroth, which *is* east of Baal Zephon; and they camped near Migdol.

8 They departed *from before Hahiroth and [a]passed through the midst of the sea into the wilderness, went three days' journey in the Wilderness of Etham, and camped at Marah.

9 They moved from Marah and [a]came to Elim. At Elim *were* twelve springs of water and seventy palm trees; so they camped there.

10 They moved from Elim and camped by the Red Sea.

11 They moved from the Red Sea and camped in the [a]Wilderness of Sin.

12 They journeyed from the Wilderness of Sin and camped at Dophkah.

13 They departed from Dophkah and camped at Alush.

14 They moved from Alush and camped at [a]Rephidim, where there was no water for the people to drink.

15 They departed from Rephidim and camped in the [a]Wilderness of Sinai.

*

32:41 Lit. *Towns of Jair*
33:8 Many Heb. mss., Sam., Syr., Tg., Vg. *from Pi Hahiroth;* cf. Num. 33:7

KJV

16 And they removed from the desert of Sinai, and pitched [a]at Kibroth–hattaavah.

17 And they departed from Kibroth–hattaavah, and [a]encamped at Hazeroth.

18 And they departed from Hazeroth, and pitched in [a]Rithmah.

19 And they departed from Rithmah, and pitched at Rimmon–parez.

20 And they departed from Rimmon–parez, and pitched in Libnah.

21 And they removed from Libnah, and pitched at Rissah.

22 And they journeyed from Rissah, and pitched in Kehelathah.

23 And they went from Kehelathah, and pitched in mount Shapher.

24 And they removed from mount Shapher, and encamped in Haradah.

25 And they removed from Haradah, and pitched in Makheloth.

26 And they removed from Makheloth, and encamped at Tahath.

27 And they departed from Tahath, and pitched at Tarah.

28 And they removed from Tarah, and pitched in Mithcah.

29 And they went from Mithcah, and pitched in Hashmonah.

30 And they departed from Hashmonah, and [a]encamped at Moseroth.

31 And they departed from Moseroth, and pitched in Bene–jaakan.

32 And they removed from [a]Bene–jaakan, and [b]encamped at Hor–hagidgad.

33 And they went from Hor–hagidgad, and pitched in Jotbathah.

34 And they removed from Jotbathah, and encamped at Ebronah.

35 And they departed from Ebronah, [a]and encamped at Ezion–gaber.

36 And they removed from Ezion–gaber, and pitched in the [a]wilderness of Zin, which *is* Kadesh.

37 And they removed from [a]Kadesh, and pitched in mount Hor, in the edge of the land of Edom.

38 And [a]Aaron the priest went up into mount Hor at the commandment of the LORD, and died there, in the fortieth year after the children of Israel were come out of the land of Egypt, in the first *day* of the fifth month.

39 And Aaron *was* an hundred and twenty and three years old when he died in mount Hor.

40 And [a]king Arad the Canaanite, which dwelt in the south in the land of Canaan, heard of the coming of the children of Israel.

41 And they departed from mount Hor, and pitched in Zalmonah.

42 And they departed from Zalmonah, and pitched in Punon.

43 And they departed from Punon, and [a]pitched in Oboth.

44 And [a]they departed from Oboth, and pitched in Ije–abarim, in the border of Moab.

45 And they departed from Iim, and pitched [a]in Dibon–gad.

46 And they removed from Dibon–gad, and encamped in [a]Almon–diblathaim.

47 And they removed from Almon–diblathaim, [a]and pitched in the mountains of Abarim, before Nebo.

48 And they departed from the mountains of Abarim, and [a]pitched in the plains of Moab by Jordan *near* Jericho.

49 And they pitched by Jordan, from Beth–jesimoth *even* unto [a]Abel–shittim in the plains of Moab.

Instructions for the Conquest of Canaan

50 And the LORD spake unto Moses in the plains of Moab by Jordan, *near* Jericho, saying,

16 [a]Num. 11:34
17 [a]Num. 11:35
18 [a]Num. 12:16
30 [a]Deut. 10:6
32 [a]Deut. 10:6 [b]Deut. 10:7
35 [a]Deut. 2:8; 1 Kin. 9:26; 22:48
36 [a]Num. 20:1; 27:14
37 [a]Num. 20:22, 23; 21:4
38 [a]Num. 20:25, 28; Deut. 10:6; 32:50
40 [a]Num. 21:1
43 [a]Num. 21:10
44 [a]Num. 21:11
45 [a]Num. 32:34
46 [a]Jer. 48:22; Ezek. 6:14
47 [a]Num. 21:20; Deut. 32:49
48 [a]Num. 22:1; 31:12; 35:1
49 [a]Num. 25:1; Josh. 2:1

*______

33:45 Same as *Ije Abarim,* v. 44
33:49 Heb. *Abel Shittim*

NKJV

16 They moved from the Wilderness of Sinai and camped [a]at Kibroth Hattaavah.

17 They departed from Kibroth Hattaavah and [a]camped at Hazeroth.

18 They departed from Hazeroth and camped at [a]Rithmah.

19 They departed from Rithmah and camped at Rimmon Perez.

20 They departed from Rimmon Perez and camped at Libnah.

21 They moved from Libnah and camped at Rissah.

22 They journeyed from Rissah and camped at Kehelathah.

23 They went from Kehelathah and camped at Mount Shepher.

24 They moved from Mount Shepher and camped at Haradah.

25 They moved from Haradah and camped at Makheloth.

26 They moved from Makheloth and camped at Tahath.

27 They departed from Tahath and camped at Terah.

28 They moved from Terah and camped at Mithkah.

29 They went from Mithkah and camped at Hashmonah.

30 They departed from Hashmonah and [a]camped at Moseroth.

31 They departed from Moseroth and camped at Bene Jaakan.

32 They moved from [a]Bene Jaakan and [b]camped at Hor Hagidgad.

33 They went from Hor Hagidgad and camped at Jotbathah.

34 They moved from Jotbathah and camped at Abronah.

35 They departed from Abronah [a]and camped at Ezion Geber.

36 They moved from Ezion Geber and camped in the [a]Wilderness of Zin, which *is* Kadesh.

37 They moved from [a]Kadesh and camped at Mount Hor, on the boundary of the land of Edom.

38 Then [a]Aaron the priest went up to Mount Hor at the command of the LORD, and died there in the fortieth year after the children of Israel had come out of the land of Egypt, on the first *day* of the fifth month.

39 Aaron *was* one hundred and twenty-three years old when he died on Mount Hor.

40 Now [a]the king of Arad, the Canaanite, who dwelt in the South in the land of Canaan, heard of the coming of the children of Israel.

41 So they departed from Mount Hor and camped at Zalmonah.

42 They departed from Zalmonah and camped at Punon.

43 They departed from Punon and [a]camped at Oboth.

44 [a]They departed from Oboth and camped at Ije Abarim, at the border of Moab.

45 They departed from *Ijim and camped [a]at Dibon Gad.

46 They moved from Dibon Gad and camped at [a]Almon Diblathaim.

47 They moved from Almon Diblathaim [a]and camped in the mountains of Abarim, before Nebo.

48 They departed from the mountains of Abarim and [a]camped in the plains of Moab by the Jordan, *across from* Jericho.

49 They camped by the Jordan, from Beth Jesimoth as far as the [a]Abel Acacia Grove* in the plains of Moab.

Instructions for the Conquest of Canaan

50 Now the LORD spoke to Moses in the plains of Moab by the Jordan, *across from* Jericho, saying,

KJV

51 Speak unto the children of Israel, and say unto them, [a]When ye are passed over Jordan into the land of Canaan;

52 [a]Then ye shall drive out all the inhabitants of the land from before you, and destroy all their pictures, and destroy all their molten images, and quite pluck down all their high places:

53 And ye shall dispossess *the inhabitants of* the land, and dwell therein: for I have given you the land to [a]possess it.

54 And [a]ye shall divide the land by lot for an inheritance among your families: *and* to the more ye shall give the more inheritance, and to the fewer ye shall give the less inheritance: every man's *inheritance* shall be in the place where his lot falleth; according to the tribes of your fathers ye shall inherit.

55 But if ye will not drive out the inhabitants of the land from before you; then it shall come to pass, that those which ye let remain of them *shall be* [a]pricks in your eyes, and thorns in your sides, and shall vex you in the land wherein ye dwell.

56 Moreover it shall come to pass, *that* I shall do unto you, as I thought to do unto them.

The Appointed Boundaries of Canaan

34 And the LORD spake unto Moses, saying,

2 Command the children of Israel, and say unto them, When ye come into [a]the land of Canaan; (this *is* the land that shall fall unto you for an inheritance, *even* the land of Canaan with the coasts thereof:)

3 Then [a]your south quarter shall be from the wilderness of Zin along by the coast of Edom, and your south border shall be the outmost coast of [b]the salt sea eastward:

4 And your border shall turn from the south [a]to the ascent of Akrabbim, and pass on to Zin: and the going forth thereof shall be from the south [b]to Kadesh–barnea, and shall go on to [c]Hazar–addar, and pass on to Azmon:

5 And the border shall fetch a compass from Azmon [a]unto the river of Egypt, and the goings out of it shall be at the sea.

6 And *as for* the [a]western border, ye shall even have the great sea for a border: this shall be your west border.

7 And this shall be your north border: from the great sea ye shall point out for you [a]mount Hor:

8 From mount Hor ye shall point out *your border* [a]unto the entrance of Hamath; and the goings forth of the border shall be to [b]Zedad:

9 And the border shall go on to Ziphron, and the goings out of it shall be at [a]Hazar–enan: this shall be your north border.

10 And ye shall point out your east border from Hazar–enan to Shepham:

11 And the coast shall go down from Shepham [a]to Riblah, on the east side of Ain; and the border shall descend, and shall reach unto the side of the sea [b]of Chinnereth eastward:

12 And the border shall go down to Jordan, and the goings out of it shall be at [a]the salt sea: this shall be your land with the coasts thereof round about.

13 And Moses commanded the children of Israel, saying, [a]This *is* the land which ye shall inherit by lot, which the LORD commanded to give unto the nine tribes, and to the half tribe:

14 [a]For the tribe of the children of Reuben according to the house of their fathers, and the tribe of the children of Gad according to the house of their fathers, have received *their inheritance;* and half the tribe of Manasseh have received their inheritance:

15 The two tribes and the half tribe have received their inheritance on this side Jordan *near* Jericho eastward, toward the sunrising.

51 [a]Deut. 7:1, 2; 9:1; Josh. 3:17
52 [a]Ex. 23:24, 33; 34:13; Deut. 7:2, 5; 12:3; Judg. 2:2; Ps. 106:34–36
53 [a]Deut. 11:31; Josh. 21:43
54 [a]Num. 26:53–56
55 [a]Josh. 23:13; Judg. 2:3

CHAPTER 34
2 [a]Gen. 17:8; Deut. 1:7, 8; Ps. 78:54, 55; 105:11
3 [a]Josh. 15:1–3; Ezek. 47:13, 19 [b]Gen. 14:3; Josh. 15:2
4 [a]Josh. 15:3 [b]Num. 13:26; 32:8 [c]Josh. 15:3, 4
5 [a]Gen. 15:18; Josh. 15:4, 47; 1 Kin. 8:65; Is. 27:12
6 [a]Ex. 23:31; Josh. 15:12; Ezek. 47:20
7 [a]Num. 33:37
8 [a]Num. 13:21; Josh. 13:5; 2 Kin. 14:25 [b]Ezek. 47:15
9 [a]Ezek. 47:17
11 [a]2 Kin. 23:33; Jer. 39:5, 6 [b]Deut. 3:17; Josh. 11:2; 12:3; 13:27; 19:35; Matt. 14:34; Luke 5:1
12 [a]Num. 34:3
13 [a]Gen. 15:18; Num. 26:52–56; Deut. 11:24; Josh. 14:1–5
14 [a]Num. 32:33

NKJV

51 "Speak to the children of Israel, and say to them: [a]'When you have crossed the Jordan into the land of Canaan,

52 [a]'then you shall drive out all the inhabitants of the land from before you, destroy all their engraved stones, destroy all their molded images, and demolish all their high places;

53 'you shall dispossess *the inhabitants of* the land and dwell in it, for I have given you the land to [a]possess.

54 'And [a]you shall divide the land by lot as an inheritance among your families; to the larger you shall give a larger inheritance, and to the smaller you shall give a smaller inheritance; there everyone's *inheritance* shall be whatever falls to him by lot. You shall inherit according to the tribes of your fathers.

55 'But if you do not drive out the inhabitants of the land from before you, then it shall be that those whom you let remain *shall be* [a]irritants in your eyes and thorns in your sides, and they shall harass you in the land where you dwell.

56 'Moreover it shall be *that* I will do to you as I thought to do to them.' "

The Appointed Boundaries of Canaan

34 Then the LORD spoke to Moses, saying,

2 "Command the children of Israel, and say to them: 'When you come into [a]the land of Canaan, this *is* the land that shall fall to you as an inheritance—the land of Canaan to its boundaries.

3 [a]'Your southern border shall be from the Wilderness of Zin along the border of Edom; then your southern border shall extend eastward to the end of [b]the Salt Sea;

4 'your border shall turn from the southern side of [a]the Ascent of Akrabbim, continue to Zin, and be on the south of [b]Kadesh Barnea; then it shall go on to [c]Hazar Addar, and continue to Azmon;

5 'the border shall turn from Azmon [a]to the Brook of Egypt, and it shall end at the Sea.

6 'As for the [a]western border, you shall have the Great Sea for a border; this shall be your western border.

7 'And this shall be your northern border: From the Great Sea you shall mark out your *border* line to [a]Mount Hor;

8 'from Mount Hor you shall mark out *your border* [a]to the entrance of Hamath; then the direction of the border shall be toward [b]Zedad;

9 'the border shall proceed to Ziphron, and it shall end at [a]Hazar Enan. This shall be your northern border.

10 'You shall mark out your eastern border from Hazar Enan to Shepham;

11 'the border shall go down from Shepham [a]to Riblah on the east side of Ain; the border shall go down and reach to the eastern side of the Sea [b]of Chinnereth;

12 'the border shall go down along the Jordan, and it shall end at [a]the Salt Sea. This shall be your land with its surrounding boundaries.' "

13 Then Moses commanded the children of Israel, saying: [a]"This *is* the land which you shall inherit by lot, which the LORD has commanded to give to the nine tribes and to the half-tribe.

14 [a]"For the tribe of the children of Reuben according to the house of their fathers, and the tribe of the children of Gad according to the house of their fathers, have received *their inheritance;* and the half-tribe of Manasseh has received its inheritance.

15 "The two tribes and the half-tribe have received their inheritance on this side of the Jordan, *across from* Jericho eastward, toward the sunrise."

KJV

The Leaders Appointed to Divide the Land

16 And the LORD spake unto Moses, saying,

17 These *are* the names of the men which shall divide the land unto you: [a]Eleazar the priest, and Joshua the son of Nun.

18 And ye shall take one [a]prince of every tribe, to divide the land by inheritance.

19 And the names of the men *are* these: Of the tribe of Judah, Caleb the son of Jephunneh.

20 And of the tribe of the children of Simeon, Shemuel the son of Ammihud.

21 Of the tribe of Benjamin, Elidad the son of Chislon.

22 And the prince of the tribe of the children of Dan, Bukki the son of Jogli.

23 The prince of the children of Joseph, for the tribe of the children of Manasseh, Hanniel the son of Ephod.

24 And the prince of the tribe of the children of Ephraim, Kemuel the son of Shiphtan.

25 And the prince of the tribe of the children of Zebulun, Elizaphan the son of Parnach.

26 And the prince of the tribe of the children of Issachar, Paltiel the son of Azzan.

27 And the prince of the tribe of the children of Asher, Ahihud the son of Shelomi.

28 And the prince of the tribe of the children of Naphtali, Pedahel the son of Ammihud.

29 These *are they* whom the LORD commanded to divide the inheritance unto the children of Israel in the land of Canaan.

Cities for the Levites

35 And the LORD spake unto Moses in [a]the plains of Moab by Jordan *near* Jericho, saying,

2 [a]Command the children of Israel, that they give unto the Levites of the inheritance of their possession cities to dwell in; and ye shall give *also* unto the Levites [b]suburbs for the cities round about them.

3 And the cities shall they have to dwell in; and the suburbs of them shall be for their cattle, and for their goods, and for all their beasts.

4 And the suburbs of the cities, which ye shall give unto the Levites, *shall reach* from the wall of the city and outward a thousand cubits round about.

5 And ye shall measure from without the city on the east side two thousand cubits, and on the south side two thousand cubits, and on the west side two thousand cubits, and on the north side two thousand cubits; and the city *shall be* in the midst: this shall be to them the suburbs of the cities.

6 And among the cities which ye shall give unto the Levites *there shall be* [a]six cities for refuge, which ye shall appoint for the manslayer, that he may flee thither: and to them ye shall add forty and two cities.

7 *So* all the cities which ye shall give to the Levites *shall be* [a]forty and eight cities: them *shall ye give* with their suburbs.

8 And the cities which ye shall give *shall be* [a]of the possession of the children of Israel: [b]from *them that have* many ye shall give many; but from *them that have* few ye shall give few: every one shall give of his cities unto the Levites according to his inheritance which he inheriteth.

Cities of Refuge
(Deut. 19:1–13; Josh. 20:1–9)

9 And the LORD spake unto Moses, saying,

10 Speak unto the children of Israel, and say unto them, [a]When ye be come over Jordan into the land of Canaan;

11 Then [a]ye shall appoint you cities to be cities of refuge for you; that the slayer may flee thither, which killeth any person at unawares.

12 [a]And they shall be unto you cities for refuge from the avenger; that the manslayer die not,

17 [a]Josh. 14:1, 2; 19:51
18 [a]Num. 1:4, 16

CHAPTER 35

1 [a]Num. 33:50
2 [a]Josh. 14:3, 4; 21:2, 3; Ezek. 45:1; 48:10–20 [b]Lev. 25:32–34
6 [a]Deut. 4:41; Josh. 20:2, 7, 8; 21:3, 13
7 [a]Josh. 21:41
8 [a]Josh. 21:3 [b]Num. 26:54; 33:54
10 [a]Deut. 19:2; Josh. 20:1–9
11 [a]Ex. 21:13; Num. 35:22–25; Deut. 19:1–13
12 [a]Deut. 19:6; Josh. 20:3, 5, 6

NKJV

The Leaders Appointed to Divide the Land

16 And the LORD spoke to Moses, saying,

17 "These *are* the names of the men who shall divide the land among you as an inheritance: [a]Eleazar the priest and Joshua the son of Nun.

18 "And you shall take one [a]leader of every tribe to divide the land for the inheritance.

19 "These *are* the names of the men: from the tribe of Judah, Caleb the son of Jephunneh;

20 "from the tribe of the children of Simeon, Shemuel the son of Ammihud;

21 "from the tribe of Benjamin, Elidad the son of Chislon;

22 "a leader from the tribe of the children of Dan, Bukki the son of Jogli;

23 "from the sons of Joseph: a leader from the tribe of the children of Manasseh, Hanniel the son of Ephod,

24 "and a leader from the tribe of the children of Ephraim, Kemuel the son of Shiphtan;

25 "a leader from the tribe of the children of Zebulun, Elizaphan the son of Parnach;

26 "a leader from the tribe of the children of Issachar, Paltiel the son of Azzan;

27 "a leader from the tribe of the children of Asher, Ahihud the son of Shelomi;

28 "and a leader from the tribe of the children of Naphtali, Pedahel the son of Ammihud."

29 These *are* the ones the LORD commanded to divide the inheritance among the children of Israel in the land of Canaan.

Cities for the Levites

35 And the LORD spoke to Moses in [a]the plains of Moab by the Jordan *across from* Jericho, saying:

2 [a]"Command the children of Israel that they give the Levites cities to dwell in from the inheritance of their possession, and you shall *also* give the Levites [b]common-land around the cities.

3 "They shall have the cities to dwell in; and their common-land shall be for their cattle, for their herds, and for all their animals.

4 "The common-land of the cities which you will give the Levites *shall extend* from the wall of the city outward a thousand cubits all around.

5 "And you shall measure outside the city on the east side two thousand cubits, on the south side two thousand cubits, on the west side two thousand cubits, and on the north side two thousand cubits. The city *shall be* in the middle. This shall belong to them as common-land for the cities.

6 "Now among the cities which you will give to the Levites *you shall appoint* [a]six cities of refuge, to which a manslayer may flee. And to these you shall add forty-two cities.

7 "So all the cities you will give to the Levites *shall be* [a]forty-eight; these *you shall give* with their common-land.

8 "And the cities which you will give *shall be* [a]from the possession of the children of Israel; [b]from the larger *tribe* you shall give many, from the smaller you shall give few. Each shall give some of its cities to the Levites, in proportion to the inheritance that each receives."

Cities of Refuge
(Deut. 19:1–13; Josh. 20:1–9)

9 Then the LORD spoke to Moses, saying,

10 "Speak to the children of Israel, and say to them: [a]'When you cross the Jordan into the land of Canaan,

11 'then [a]you shall appoint cities to be cities of refuge for you, that the manslayer who kills any person accidentally may flee there.

12 [a]'They shall be cities of refuge for you from the avenger, that the manslayer may not die

KJV

until he stand before the congregation in judgment.

13 And of these cities which ye shall give [a]six cities shall ye have for refuge.

14 [a]Ye shall give three cities on this side Jordan, and three cities shall ye give in the land of Canaan, *which* shall be cities of refuge.

15 These six cities shall be a refuge, *both* for the children of Israel, and [a]for the stranger, and for the sojourner among them: that every one that killeth any person unawares may flee thither.

16 [a]And if he smite him with an instrument of iron, so that he die, he *is* a murderer: the murderer shall surely be put to death.

17 And if he smite him with throwing a stone, wherewith he may die, and he die, he *is* a murderer: the murderer shall surely be put to death.

18 Or *if* he smite him with an hand weapon of wood, wherewith he may die, and he die, he *is* a murderer: the murderer shall surely be put to death.

19 [a]The revenger of blood himself shall slay the murderer: when he meeteth him, he shall slay him.

20 But [a]if he thrust him of hatred, or hurl at him [b]by laying of wait, that he die;

21 Or in enmity smite him with his hand, that he die: he that smote *him* shall surely be put to death; *for* he *is* a murderer: the revenger of blood shall slay the murderer, when he meeteth him.

22 But if he thrust him suddenly [a]without enmity, or have cast upon him any thing without laying of wait,

23 Or with any stone, wherewith a man may die, seeing *him* not, and cast *it* upon him, that he die, and *was* not his enemy, neither sought his harm:

24 Then [a]the congregation shall judge between the slayer and the revenger of blood according to these judgments:

25 And the congregation shall deliver the slayer out of the hand of the revenger of blood, and the congregation shall restore him to the city of his refuge, whither he was fled: and [a]he shall abide in it unto the death of the high priest, [b]which was anointed with the holy oil.

26 But if the slayer shall at any time come without the border of the city of his refuge, whither he was fled;

27 And the revenger of blood find him without the borders of the city of his refuge, and the revenger of blood kill the slayer; he shall not be guilty of blood:

28 Because he should have remained in the city of his refuge until the death of the high priest: but after the death of the high priest the slayer shall return into the land of his possession.

29 So these *things* shall be for [a]a statute of judgment unto you throughout your generations in all your dwellings.

30 Whoso killeth any person, the murderer shall be put to death by the [a]mouth of witnesses: but one witness shall not testify against any person *to cause him* to die.

31 Moreover ye shall take no satisfaction for the life of a murderer, which *is* guilty of death: but he shall be surely put to death.

32 And ye shall take no satisfaction for him that is fled to the city of his refuge, that he should come again to dwell in the land, until the death of the priest.

33 So ye shall not pollute the land wherein ye *are*: for blood [a]it defileth the land: and the land cannot be cleansed of the blood that is shed therein, but [b]by the blood of him that shed it.

34 [a]Defile not therefore the land which ye shall inhabit, wherein I dwell: for [b]I the LORD dwell among the children of Israel.

13 [a]Num. 35:6
14 [a]Deut. 4:41; Josh. 20:8
15 [a]Num. 15:16
16 [a]Ex. 21:12, 14; Lev. 24:17; Deut. 19:11, 12
19 [a]Num. 35:21, 24, 27; Deut. 19:6, 12
20 [a]Gen. 4:8; 2 Sam. 3:27; 20:10; 1 Kin. 2:31, 32 [b]Ex. 21:14; Deut. 19:11, 12
22 [a]Ex. 21:13
24 [a]Num. 35:12; Josh. 20:6
25 [a]Josh. 20:6 [b]Ex. 29:7; Lev. 4:3; 21:10
29 [a]Num. 27:11
30 [a]Deut. 17:6; 19:15; Matt. 18:16; John 7:51; 8:17, 18; 2 Cor. 13:1; Heb. 10:28
33 [a]Deut. 21:7, 8; Ps. 106:38 [b]Gen. 9:6
34 [a]Lev. 18:24, 25; Deut. 21:23 [b]Ex. 29:45, 46

NKJV

until he stands before the congregation in judgment.

13 'And of the cities which you give, you shall have [a]six cities of refuge.

14 [a]'You shall appoint three cities on this side of the Jordan, and three cities you shall appoint in the land of Canaan, *which* will be cities of refuge.

15 'These six cities shall be for refuge for the children of Israel, [a]for the stranger, and for the sojourner among them, that anyone who kills a person accidentally may flee there.

16 [a]'But if he strikes him with an iron implement, so that he dies, he *is* a murderer; the murderer shall surely be put to death.

17 'And if he strikes him with a stone in the hand, by which one could die, and he does die, he *is* a murderer; the murderer shall surely be put to death.

18 'Or *if* he strikes him with a wooden hand weapon, by which one could die, and he does die, he *is* a murderer; the murderer shall surely be put to death.

19 [a]'The avenger of blood himself shall put the murderer to death; when he meets him, he shall put him to death.

20 [a]'If he pushes him out of hatred or, [b]while lying in wait, hurls something at him so that he dies,

21 'or in enmity he strikes him with his hand so that he dies, the one who struck *him* shall surely be put to death. He *is* a murderer. The avenger of blood shall put the murderer to death when he meets him.

22 'However, if he pushes him suddenly [a]without enmity, or throws anything at him without lying in wait,

23 'or uses a stone, by which a man could die, throwing *it* at him without seeing *him*, so that he dies, while he was not his enemy or seeking his harm,

24 'then [a]the congregation shall judge between the manslayer and the avenger of blood according to these judgments.

25 'So the congregation shall deliver the manslayer from the hand of the avenger of blood, and the congregation shall return him to the city of refuge where he had fled, and [a]he shall remain there until the death of the high priest [b]who was anointed with the holy oil.

26 'But if the manslayer at any time goes outside the limits of the city of refuge where he fled,

27 'and the avenger of blood finds him outside the limits of his city of refuge, and the avenger of blood kills the manslayer, he shall not be guilty of blood,

28 'because he should have remained in his city of refuge until the death of the high priest. But after the death of the high priest the manslayer may return to the land of his possession.

29 'And these *things* shall be [a]a statute of judgment to you throughout your generations in all your dwellings.

30 'Whoever kills a person, the murderer shall be put to death on the [a]testimony of witnesses; but one witness is not *sufficient* testimony against a person for the death *penalty*.

31 'Moreover you shall take no ransom for the life of a murderer who *is* guilty of death, but he shall surely be put to death.

32 'And you shall take no ransom for him who has fled to his city of refuge, that he may return to dwell in the land before the death of the priest.

33 'So you shall not pollute the land where you *are*; for blood [a]defiles the land, and no atonement can be made for the land, for the blood that is shed on it, except [b]by the blood of him who shed it.

34 'Therefore [a]do not defile the land which you inhabit, in the midst of which I dwell; for [b]I the LORD dwell among the children of Israel.' "

KJV

Marriage of Female Heirs

36 And the chief fathers of the families of the [a]children of Gilead, the son of Machir, the son of Manasseh, of the families of the sons of Joseph, came near, and [b]spake before Moses, and before the princes, the chief fathers of the children of Israel:

2 And they said, [a]The LORD commanded my lord to give the land for an inheritance by lot to the children of Israel: and [b]my lord was commanded by the LORD to give the inheritance of Zelophehad our brother unto his daughters.

3 And if they be married to any of the sons of the *other* tribes of the children of Israel, then shall their inheritance be [a]taken from the inheritance of our fathers, and shall be put to the inheritance of the tribe whereunto they are received: so shall it be taken from the lot of our inheritance.

4 And when [a]the jubile of the children of Israel shall be, then shall their inheritance be put unto the inheritance of the tribe whereunto they are received: so shall their inheritance be taken away from the inheritance of the tribe of our fathers.

5 And Moses commanded the children of Israel according to the word of the LORD, saying, The tribe of the sons of Joseph [a]hath said well.

6 This *is* the thing which the LORD doth command concerning the daughters of Zelophehad, saying, Let them marry to whom they think best; [a]only to the family of the tribe of their father shall they marry.

7 So shall not the inheritance of the children of Israel remove from tribe to tribe: for every one of the children of Israel shall [a]keep himself to the inheritance of the tribe of his fathers.

8 And [a]every daughter, that possesseth an inheritance in any tribe of the children of Israel, shall be wife unto one of the family of the tribe of her father, that the children of Israel may enjoy every man the inheritance of his fathers.

9 Neither shall the inheritance remove from *one* tribe to another tribe; but every one of the tribes of the children of Israel shall keep himself to his own inheritance.

10 Even as the LORD commanded Moses, so did the daughters of Zelophehad:

11 [a]For Mahlah, Tirzah, and Hoglah, and Milcah, and Noah, the daughters of Zelophehad, were married unto their father's brothers' sons:

12 *And* they were married into the families of the sons of Manasseh the son of Joseph, and their inheritance remained in the tribe of the family of their father.

13 These *are* the commandments and the judgments, which the LORD commanded by the hand of Moses unto the children of Israel [a]in the plains of Moab by Jordan *near* Jericho.

CHAPTER 36

1 [a]Num. 26:29 [b]Num. 27:1–11
2 [a]Num. 26:55; 33:54; Josh. 17:4 [b]Num. 27:1, 5–7
3 [a]Num. 27:4
4 [a]Lev. 25:10
5 [a]Num. 27:7
6 [a]Num. 36:11, 12
7 [a]1 Kin. 21:3
8 [a]1 Chr. 23:22
11 [a]Num. 26:33; 27:1
13 [a]Num. 26:3; 33:50

NKJV

Marriage of Female Heirs

36 Now the chief fathers of the families of the [a]children of Gilead the son of Machir, the son of Manasseh, of the families of the sons of Joseph, came near and [b]spoke before Moses and before the leaders, the chief fathers of the children of Israel.

2 And they said: [a]"The LORD commanded my lord *Moses* to give the land as an inheritance by lot to the children of Israel, and [b]my lord was commanded by the LORD to give the inheritance of our brother Zelophehad to his daughters.

3 "Now if they are married to any of the sons of the *other* tribes of the children of Israel, then their inheritance will be [a]taken from the inheritance of our fathers, and it will be added to the inheritance of the tribe into which they marry; so it will be taken from the lot of our inheritance.

4 "And when [a]the Jubilee of the children of Israel comes, then their inheritance will be added to the inheritance of the tribe into which they marry; so their inheritance will be taken away from the inheritance of the tribe of our fathers."

5 Then Moses commanded the children of Israel according to the word of the LORD, saying: [a]"What the tribe of the sons of Joseph speaks is right.

6 "This *is* what the LORD commands concerning the daughters of Zelophehad, saying, 'Let them marry whom they think best, [a]but they may marry only within the family of their father's tribe.'

7 "So the inheritance of the children of Israel shall not change hands from tribe to tribe, for every one of the children of Israel shall [a]keep the inheritance of the tribe of his fathers.

8 "And [a]every daughter who possesses an inheritance in any tribe of the children of Israel shall be the wife of one of the family of her father's tribe, so that the children of Israel each may possess the inheritance of his fathers.

9 "Thus no inheritance shall change hands from *one* tribe to another, but every tribe of the children of Israel shall keep its own inheritance."

10 Just as the LORD commanded Moses, so did the daughters of Zelophehad;

11 [a]for Mahlah, Tirzah, Hoglah, Milcah, and Noah, the daughters of Zelophehad, were married to the sons of their father's brothers.

12 They were married into the families of the children of Manasseh the son of Joseph, and their inheritance remained in the tribe of their father's family.

13 These *are* the commandments and the judgments which the LORD commanded the children of Israel by the hand of Moses [a]in the plains of Moab by the Jordan, *across from* Jericho.

KJV

THE FIFTH BOOK OF MOSES CALLED

DEUTERONOMY

The Previous Command to Enter Canaan

1 These *be* the words which Moses spake unto all Israel [a]on this side Jordan in the wilderness, in the plain over against the Red *sea*, between Paran, and Tophel, and Laban, and Hazeroth, and Dizahab.

2 (*There are* eleven days' *journey* from Horeb by the way of mount Seir [a]unto Kadesh–barnea.)

3 And it came to pass [a]in the fortieth year, in the eleventh month, on the first *day* of the month, *that* Moses spake unto the children of Israel, according unto all that the LORD had given him in commandment unto them;

4 [a]After he had slain Sihon the king of the Amorites, which dwelt in Heshbon, and Og the king of Bashan, which dwelt at Astaroth [b]in Edrei:

5 On this side Jordan, in the land of Moab, began Moses to declare this law, saying,

6 The LORD our God spake unto us [a]in Horeb, saying, Ye have dwelt long [b]enough in this mount:

7 Turn you, and take your journey, and go to the mount of the Amorites, and unto all *the places* nigh thereunto, in the plain, in the hills, and in the vale, and in the south, and by the sea side, to the land of the Canaanites, and unto Lebanon, unto the great river, the river Euphrates.

8 Behold, I have set the land before you: go in and possess the land which the LORD sware unto your fathers, [a]Abraham, Isaac, and Jacob, to give unto them and to their seed after them.

Tribal Leaders Appointed
(Ex. 18:13–27)

9 And [a]I spake unto you at that time, saying, I am not able to bear you myself alone:

10 The LORD your God hath multiplied you, and, behold, [a]ye *are* this day as the stars of heaven for multitude.

11 ([a]The LORD God of your fathers make you a thousand times so many more as ye *are*, and bless you, [b]as he hath promised you!)

12 [a]How can I myself alone bear your cumbrance, and your burden, and your strife?

13 Take you wise men, and understanding, and known among your tribes, and I will make them rulers over you.

14 And ye answered me, and said, The thing which thou hast spoken *is* good *for us* to do.

15 So I took [a]the chief of your tribes, wise men, and known, and made them heads over you, captains over thousands, and captains over hundreds, and captains over fifties, and captains over tens, and officers among your tribes.

16 And I charged your judges at that time, saying, Hear *the causes* between your brethren, and [a]judge righteously between *every* man and his [b]brother, and the stranger *that is* with him.

17 [a]Ye shall not respect persons in judgment; *but* ye shall hear the small as well as the great; ye shall not be afraid of the face of man; for [b]the judgment *is* God's: and the cause that is too hard for you, [c]bring *it* unto me, and I will hear it.

18 And I commanded you at that time all the things which ye should do.

CHAPTER 1

1 [a]Deut. 4:44–46; Josh. 9:1, 10
2 [a]Num. 13:26; 32:8; Deut. 9:23
3 [a]Num. 33:38
4 [a]Num. 21:23, 24, 33–35; Deut. 2:26–35; Josh. 13:10; Neh. 9:22 [b]Josh. 13:12
6 [a]Ex. 3:1, 12 [b]Ex. 19:1, 2
8 [a]Gen. 12:7; 15:5; 22:17; 26:3; 28:13; Ex. 33:1; Num. 14:23; 32:11
9 [a]Ex. 18:18, 24; Num. 11:14, 24
10 [a]Gen. 15:5; 22:17; Ex. 32:13; Deut. 7:7; 10:22; 26:5; 28:62
11 [a]2 Sam. 24:3 [b]Gen. 15:5
12 [a]1 Kin. 3:8, 9
15 [a]Ex. 18:25
16 [a]Deut. 16:18; John 7:24 [b]Lev. 24:22
17 [a]Lev. 19:15; Deut. 10:17; 16:19; 24:17; 1 Sam. 16:7; Prov. 24:23–26; Acts 10:34; James 2:1, 9 [b]2 Chr. 19:6 [c]Ex. 18:22, 26

*

1:1 Heb. *arabah* • One LXX ms., Tg., Vg. *Red Sea*
1:4 LXX, Syr., Vg. *and;* cf. Josh. 12:4
1:7 Heb. *arabah*

NKJV

THE FIFTH BOOK OF MOSES CALLED

DEUTERONOMY

The Previous Command to Enter Canaan

1 These *are* the words which Moses spoke to all Israel [a]on this side of the Jordan in the wilderness, in the *plain opposite *Suph, between Paran, Tophel, Laban, Hazeroth, and Dizahab.

2 *It is* eleven days' *journey* from Horeb by way of Mount Seir [a]to Kadesh Barnea.

3 Now it came to pass [a]in the fortieth year, in the eleventh month, on the first *day* of the month, *that* Moses spoke to the children of Israel according to all that the LORD had given him as commandments to them,

4 [a]after he had killed Sihon king of the Amorites, who dwelt in Heshbon, and Og king of Bashan, who dwelt at Ashtaroth [b]in* Edrei.

5 On this side of the Jordan in the land of Moab, Moses began to explain this law, saying,

6 "The LORD our God spoke to us [a]in Horeb, saying: 'You have dwelt long [b]enough at this mountain.

7 'Turn and take your journey, and go to the mountains of the Amorites, to all the neighboring *places* in the *plain, in the mountains and in the lowland, in the South and on the seacoast, to the land of the Canaanites and to Lebanon, as far as the great river, the River Euphrates.

8 'See, I have set the land before you; go in and possess the land which the LORD swore to your fathers—to [a]Abraham, Isaac, and Jacob—to give to them and their descendants after them.'

Tribal Leaders Appointed
(Ex. 18:13–27)

9 "And [a]I spoke to you at that time, saying: 'I alone am not able to bear you.

10 'The LORD your God has multiplied you, [a]and here you *are* today, as the stars of heaven in multitude.

11 [a]'May the LORD God of your fathers make you a thousand times more numerous than you are, and bless you [b]as He has promised you!

12 [a]'How can I alone bear your problems and your burdens and your complaints?

13 'Choose wise, understanding, and knowledgeable men from among your tribes, and I will make them heads over you.'

14 "And you answered me and said, 'The thing which you have told *us* to do *is* good.'

15 "So I took [a]the heads of your tribes, wise and knowledgeable men, and made them heads over you, leaders of thousands, leaders of hundreds, leaders of fifties, leaders of tens, and officers for your tribes.

16 "Then I commanded your judges at that time, saying, 'Hear *the cases* between your brethren, and [a]judge righteously between a man and his [b]brother or the stranger who is with him.

17 [a]'You shall not show partiality in judgment; you shall hear the small as well as the great; you shall not be afraid in any man's presence, for [b]the judgment *is* God's. The case that is too hard for you, [c]bring to me, and I will hear it.'

18 "And I commanded you at that time all the things which you should do.

KJV

Israel's Refusal to Enter the Land
(Num. 13:1–33)

19 And when we departed from Horeb, [a]we went through all that great and terrible wilderness, which ye saw by the way of the mountain of the Amorites, as the LORD our God commanded us; and [b]we came to Kadesh–barnea.

20 And I said unto you, Ye are come unto the mountain of the Amorites, which the LORD our God doth give unto us.

21 Behold, the LORD thy God hath set the land before thee: go up *and* possess *it,* as the LORD God of thy fathers hath said unto thee; [a]fear not, neither be discouraged.

22 And ye came near unto me every one of you, and said, We will send men before us, and they shall search us out the land, and bring us word again by what way we must go up, and into what cities we shall come.

23 And the saying pleased me well: and [a]I took twelve men of you, one of a tribe:

24 [a]And they turned and went up into the mountain, and came unto the valley of Eshcol, and searched it out.

25 And they took of the fruit of the land in their hands, and brought *it* down unto us, and brought us word again, and said, *It is* a [a]good land which the LORD our God doth give us.

26 [a]Notwithstanding ye would not go up, but rebelled against the commandment of the LORD your God:

27 And ye [a]murmured in your tents, and said, Because the LORD [b]hated us, he hath brought us forth out of the land of Egypt, to deliver us into the hand of the Amorites, to destroy us.

28 Whither shall we go up? our brethren have discouraged our heart, saying, [a]The people *is* greater and taller than we; the cities *are* great and walled up to heaven; and moreover we have seen the sons of the [b]Anakims there.

29 Then I said unto you, Dread not, [a]neither be afraid of them.

30 [a]The LORD your God which goeth before you, he shall fight for you, according to all that he did for you in Egypt before your eyes;

31 And in the wilderness, where thou hast seen how that the LORD thy God bare thee, as a [a]man doth bear his son, in all the way that ye went, until ye came into this place.

32 Yet in this thing [a]ye did not believe the LORD your God,

33 [a]Who went in the way before you, [b]to search you out a place to pitch your tents *in,* in fire by night, to shew you by what way ye should go, and in a cloud by day.

The Penalty for Israel's Rebellion
(Num. 14:20–45)

34 And the LORD heard the voice of your words, and was wroth, [a]and sware, saying,

35 [a]Surely there shall not one of these men of this evil generation see that good land, which I sware to give unto your fathers,

36 [a]Save Caleb the son of Jephunneh; he shall see it, and to him will I give the land that he hath trodden upon, and to his children, because [b]he hath wholly followed the LORD.

37 [a]Also the LORD was angry with me for your sakes, saying, Thou also shalt not go in thither.

38 [a]*But* Joshua the son of Nun, [b]which standeth before thee, he shall go in thither: [c]encourage him: for he shall cause Israel to inherit it.

39 [a]Moreover your little ones, which [b]ye said should be a prey, and your children, which in that day [c]had no knowledge between good and evil, they shall go in thither, and unto them will I give it, and they shall possess it.

40 [a]But *as for* you, turn you, and take your journey into the wilderness by the way of the Red sea.

19 [a]Num. 10:12; Deut. 2:7; 8:15; 32:10; Jer. 2:6 [b]Num. 13:26
21 [a]Josh. 1:6, 9
23 [a]Num. 13:2, 3
24 [a]Num. 13:21–25
25 [a]Num. 13:27
26 [a]Num. 14:1–4; Ps. 106:24
27 [a]Ps. 106:25 [b]Deut. 9:28
28 [a]Num. 13:28, 31–33; Deut. 9:1, 2 [b]Num. 13:28
29 [a]Num. 14:9; Deut. 7:18
30 [a]Ex. 14:14; Deut. 3:22; 20:4; Neh. 4:20
31 [a]Deut. 32:10–12; Is. 46:3, 4; 63:9; Hos. 11:3
32 [a]Num. 14:11; 20:12; Ps. 106:24; Heb. 3:9, 10, 16–19; 4:1, 2; Jude 5
33 [a]Ex. 13:21; Num. 9:15–23; Neh. 9:12; Ps. 78:14 [b]Num. 10:33; Ezek. 20:6
34 [a]Deut. 2:14, 15
35 [a]Num. 14:22, 23; Ps. 95:10, 11
36 [a]Num. 14:24; [Josh. 14:9] [b]Num. 32:11, 12
37 [a]Num. 20:12; 27:14; Deut. 3:26; 4:21; 34:4; Ps. 106:32
38 [a]Num. 14:30 [b]Ex. 24:13; 33:11; 1 Sam. 16:22 [c]Num. 27:18, 19; Deut. 31:7, 23; Josh. 11:23
39 [a]Num. 14:31 [b]Num. 14:3 [c]Is. 7:15, 16
40 [a]Num. 14:25

NKJV

Israel's Refusal to Enter the Land
(Num. 13:1–33)

19 "So we departed from Horeb, [a]and went through all that great and terrible wilderness which you saw on the way to the mountains of the Amorites, as the LORD our God had commanded us. Then [b]we came to Kadesh Barnea.

20 "And I said to you, 'You have come to the mountains of the Amorites, which the LORD our God is giving us.

21 'Look, the LORD your God has set the land before you; go up *and* possess *it,* as the LORD God of your fathers has spoken to you; [a]do not fear or be discouraged.'

22 "And every one of you came near to me and said, 'Let us send men before us, and let them search out the land for us, and bring back word to us of the way by which we should go up, and of the cities into which we shall come.'

23 "The plan pleased me well; so [a]I took twelve of your men, one man from *each* tribe.

24 [a]"And they departed and went up into the mountains, and came to the Valley of Eshcol, and spied it out.

25 "They also took *some* of the fruit of the land in their hands and brought *it* down to us; and they brought back word to us, saying, *'It is* a [a]good land which the LORD our God is giving us.'

26 [a]"Nevertheless you would not go up, but rebelled against the command of the LORD your God;

27 "and you [a]complained in your tents, and said, 'Because the LORD [b]hates us, He has brought us out of the land of Egypt to deliver us into the hand of the Amorites, to destroy us.

28 'Where can we go up? Our brethren have discouraged our hearts, saying, [a]"The people *are* greater and taller than we; the cities *are* great and fortified up to heaven; moreover we have seen the sons of the [b]Anakim there." '

29 "Then I said to you, 'Do not be terrified, [a]or afraid of them.

30 [a]'The LORD your God, who goes before you, He will fight for you, according to all He did for you in Egypt before your eyes,

31 'and in the wilderness where you saw how the LORD your God carried you, as a [a]man carries his son, in all the way that you went until you came to this place.'

32 "Yet, for all that, [a]you did not believe the LORD your God,

33 [a]"who went in the way before you [b]to search out a place for you to pitch your tents, to show you the way you should go, in the fire by night and in the cloud by day.

The Penalty for Israel's Rebellion
(Num. 14:20–45)

34 "And the LORD heard the sound of your words, and was angry, [a]and took an oath, saying,

35 [a]'Surely not one of these men of this evil generation shall see that good land of which I swore to give to your fathers,

36 [a]'except Caleb the son of Jephunneh; he shall see it, and to him and his children I am giving the land on which he walked, because [b]he wholly followed the LORD.'

37 [a]"The LORD was also angry with me for your sakes, saying, 'Even you shall not go in there.

38 [a]'Joshua the son of Nun, [b]who stands before you, he shall go in there. [c]Encourage him, for he shall cause Israel to inherit it.

39 [a]'Moreover your little ones and your children, who [b]you say will be victims, who today [c]have no knowledge of good and evil, they shall go in there; to them I will give it, and they shall possess it.

40 [a]'But *as for* you, turn and take your journey into the wilderness by the Way of the Red Sea.'

KJV

41 Then ye answered and said unto me, [a]We have sinned against the LORD, we will go up and fight, according to all that the LORD our God commanded us. And when ye had girded on every man his weapons of war, ye were ready to go up into the hill.

42 And the LORD said unto me, Say unto them, [a]Go not up, neither fight; for I *am* not among you; lest ye be smitten before your enemies.

43 So I spake unto you; and ye would not hear, but [a]rebelled against the commandment of the LORD, and [b]went presumptuously up into the hill.

44 And the Amorites, which dwelt in that mountain, came out against you, and chased you, [a]as bees do, and destroyed you in Seir, *even* unto Hormah.

45 And ye returned and wept before the LORD; but the LORD would not hearken to your voice, nor give ear unto you.

46 [a]So ye abode in Kadesh many days, according unto the days that ye abode *there.*

The Desert Years

2 Then we turned, and [a]took our journey into the wilderness by the way of the Red sea, [b]as the LORD spake unto me: and we compassed mount Seir many days.

2 And the LORD spake unto me, saying,

3 Ye have compassed this mountain [a]long enough: turn you northward.

4 And command thou the people, saying, [a]Ye *are* to pass through the coast of [b]your brethren the children of Esau, which dwell in Seir; and they shall be afraid of you: take ye good heed unto yourselves therefore:

5 Meddle not with them; for I will not give you of their land, no, not so much as a footbreadth; [a]because I have given mount Seir unto Esau *for* a possession.

6 Ye shall buy meat of them for money, that ye may eat; and ye shall also buy water of them for money, that ye may drink.

7 For the LORD thy God hath blessed thee in all the works of thy hand: he knoweth thy walking through this great wilderness: [a]these forty years the LORD thy God *hath been* with thee; thou hast lacked nothing.

8 And when we passed by from our brethren the children of Esau, which dwelt in Seir, through the way of the plain from [a]Elath, and from Ezion–gaber, we [b]turned and passed by the way of the wilderness of Moab.

9 And the LORD said unto me, Distress not the Moabites, neither contend with them in battle: for I will not give thee of their land *for* a possession; because I have given [a]Ar unto [b]the children of Lot *for* a possession.

10 [a]The Emims dwelt therein in times past, a people great, and many, and tall, as [b]the Anakims;

11 Which also were accounted giants, as the Anakims; but the Moabites call them Emims.

12 [a]The Horims also dwelt in Seir beforetime; but the children of Esau succeeded them, when they had destroyed them from before them, and dwelt in their stead; as Israel did unto the land of his possession, which the LORD gave unto them.

13 Now rise up, *said I,* and get you over [a]the brook Zered. And we went over the brook Zered.

14 And the space in which we came [a]from Kadesh–barnea, until we were come over the brook Zered, *was* thirty and eight years; [b]until all the generation of the men of war were wasted out from among the host, [c]as the LORD sware unto them.

15 For indeed the hand of the LORD was against them, to destroy them from among the host, until they were consumed.

41 [a]Num. 14:40
42 [a]Num. 14:41–43
43 [a]Num. 14:44 [b]Deut. 17:12, 13
44 [a]Num. 14:45; Ps. 118:12
46 [a]Num. 13:25; 20:1, 22; Deut. 2:7, 14

CHAPTER 2

1 [a]Deut. 1:40 [b]Num. 14:25
3 [a]Deut. 2:7, 14
4 [a]Num. 20:14–21 [b]Deut. 23:7
5 [a]Gen. 36:8; Josh. 24:4
7 [a]Deut. 8:2–4; [Matt. 6:8, 32]
8 [a]Judg. 11:18; 1 Kin. 9:26 [b]Num. 21:4
9 [a]Num. 21:15, 28; Deut. 2:18, 29 [b]Gen. 19:36–38
10 [a]Gen. 14:5 [b]Num. 13:22, 33; Deut. 9:2
12 [a]Gen. 14:6; 36:20; Deut. 2:22
13 [a]Num. 21:12
14 [a]Num. 13:26 [b]Num. 14:33; 26:64; Deut. 1:34, 35 [c]Num. 14:35; Ezek. 20:15

NKJV

41 "Then you answered and said to me, [a]'We have sinned against the LORD; we will go up and fight, just as the LORD our God commanded us.' And when everyone of you had girded on his weapons of war, you were ready to go up into the mountain.

42 "And the LORD said to me, 'Tell them, [a]"Do not go up nor fight, for I *am* not among you; lest you be defeated before your enemies." '

43 "So I spoke to you; yet you would not listen, but [a]rebelled against the command of the LORD, and [b]presumptuously went up into the mountain.

44 "And the Amorites who dwelt in that mountain came out against you and chased you [a]as bees do, and drove you back from Seir to Hormah.

45 "Then you returned and wept before the LORD, but the LORD would not listen to your voice nor give ear to you.

46 [a]"So you remained in Kadesh many days, according to the days that you spent *there.*

The Desert Years

2 "Then we turned and [a]journeyed into the wilderness of the Way of the Red Sea, [b]as the LORD spoke to me, and we skirted Mount Seir for many days.

2 "And the LORD spoke to me, saying:

3 'You have skirted this mountain [a]long enough; turn northward.

4 'And command the people, saying, [a]"You *are about to* pass through the territory of [b]your brethren, the descendants of Esau, who live in Seir; and they will be afraid of you. Therefore watch yourselves carefully.

5 "Do not meddle with them, for I will not give you *any* of their land, no, not so much as one footstep, [a]because I have given Mount Seir to Esau *as* a possession.

6 "You shall buy food from them with money, that you may eat; and you shall also buy water from them with money, that you may drink.

7 "For the LORD your God has blessed you in all the work of your hand. He knows your trudging through this great wilderness. [a]These forty years the LORD your God *has been* with you; you have lacked nothing." '

8 "And when we passed beyond our brethren, the descendants of Esau who dwell in Seir, away from the road of the plain, away from [a]Elath and Ezion Geber, we [b]turned and passed by way of the Wilderness of Moab.

9 "Then the LORD said to me, 'Do not harass Moab, nor contend with them in battle, for I will not give you *any* of their land *as* a possession, because I have given [a]Ar to [b]the descendants of Lot *as* a possession.' "

10 [a](The Emim had dwelt there in times past, a people as great and numerous and tall as [b]the Anakim.

11 They were also regarded as *giants, like the Anakim, but the Moabites call them Emim.

12 [a]The Horites formerly dwelt in Seir, but the descendants of Esau dispossessed them and destroyed them from before them, and dwelt in their place, just as Israel did to the land of their possession which the LORD gave them.)

13 " 'Now rise and cross over [a]the Valley of the Zered.' So we crossed over the Valley of the Zered.

14 "And the time we took to come [a]from Kadesh Barnea until we crossed over the Valley of the Zered *was* thirty-eight years, [b]until all the generation of the men of war was consumed from the midst of the camp, [c]just as the LORD had sworn to them.

15 "For indeed the hand of the LORD was against them, to destroy them from the midst of the camp until they were consumed.

*2:11 Heb. *rephaim*

KJV

16 So it came to pass, when all the men of war were consumed and dead from among the people,

17 That the LORD spake unto me, saying,

18 Thou art to pass over through Ar, the coast of Moab, this day:

19 And *when* thou comest nigh over against the children of Ammon, distress them not, nor meddle with them: for I will not give thee of the land of the children of Ammon *any* possession; because I have given it unto [a]the children of Lot *for* a possession.

20 (That also was accounted a land of giants: giants dwelt therein in old time; and the Ammonites call them [a]Zamzummims;

21 [a]A people great, and many, and tall, as the Anakims; but the LORD destroyed them before them; and they succeeded them, and dwelt in their stead:

22 As he did to the children of Esau, [a]which dwelt in Seir, when he destroyed [b]the Horims from before them; and they succeeded them, and dwelt in their stead even unto this day:

23 And [a]the Avims which dwelt in Hazerim, *even* unto Azzah, [b]the Caphtorims, which came forth out of Caphtor, destroyed them, and dwelt in their stead.)

24 Rise ye up, take your journey, and [a]pass over the river Arnon: behold, I have given into thine hand [b]Sihon the Amorite, king of Heshbon, and his land: begin to possess *it*, and contend with him in battle.

25 [a]This day will I begin to put the dread of thee and the fear of thee upon the nations *that are* under the whole heaven, who shall hear report of thee, and shall [b]tremble, and be in anguish because of thee.

King Sihon Defeated
(*Num. 21:21–32*)

26 And I [a]sent messengers out of the wilderness of Kedemoth unto Sihon king of Heshbon [b]with words of peace, saying,

27 [a]Let me pass through thy land: I will go along by the high way, I will neither turn unto the right hand nor to the left.

28 Thou shalt sell me meat for money, that I may eat; and give me water for money, that I may drink: [a]only I will pass through on my feet;

29 ([a]As the children of Esau which dwell in Seir, and the Moabites which dwell in Ar, did unto me;) until I shall pass over Jordan into the land which the LORD our God giveth us.

30 [a]But Sihon king of Heshbon would not let us pass by him: for [b]the LORD thy God [c]hardened his spirit, and made his heart obstinate, that he might deliver him into thy hand, as *appeareth* this day.

31 And the LORD said unto me, Behold, I have begun to [a]give Sihon and his land before thee: begin to possess, that thou mayest inherit his land.

32 [a]Then Sihon came out against us, he and all his people, to fight at Jahaz.

33 And [a]the LORD our God delivered him before us; and [b]we smote him, and his sons, and all his people.

34 And we took all his cities at that time, and [a]utterly destroyed the men, and the women, and the little ones, of every city, we left none to remain:

35 Only the cattle we took for a prey unto ourselves, and the spoil of the cities which we took.

36 [a]From Aroer, which *is* by the brink of the river of Arnon, and *from* the [b]city that *is* by the river, even unto Gilead, there was not one city too strong for us: [c]the LORD our God delivered all unto us:

37 Only unto the land of the children of Ammon thou camest not, *nor* unto any place of the river [a]Jabbok, nor unto the cities in the moun-

NKJV

16 "So it was, when all the men of war had finally perished from among the people,

17 "that the LORD spoke to me, saying:

18 'This day you are to cross over at Ar, the boundary of Moab.

19 'And *when* you come near the people of Ammon, do not harass them or meddle with them, for I will not give you *any* of the land of the people of Ammon *as* a possession, because I have given it to [a]the descendants of Lot *as* a possession.' "

20 (That was also regarded as a land of *giants; giants formerly dwelt there. But the Ammonites call them [a]Zamzummim,

21 [a]a people as great and numerous and tall as the Anakim. But the LORD destroyed them before them, and they dispossessed them and dwelt in their place,

22 just as He had done for the descendants of Esau, [a]who dwelt in Seir, when He destroyed [b]the Horites from before them. They dispossessed them and dwelt in their place, even to this day.

23 And [a]the Avim, who dwelt in villages as far as Gaza—[b]the Caphtorim, who came from Caphtor, destroyed them and dwelt in their place.)

24 " 'Rise, take your journey, and [a]cross over the River Arnon. Look, I have given into your hand [b]Sihon the Amorite, king of Heshbon, and his land. Begin to possess *it*, and engage him in battle.

25 [a]'This day I will begin to put the dread and fear of you upon the nations under the whole heaven, who shall hear the report of you, and shall [b]tremble and be in anguish because of you.'

King Sihon Defeated
(*Num. 21:21–32*)

26 "And I [a]sent messengers from the Wilderness of Kedemoth to Sihon king of Heshbon, [b]with words of peace, saying,

27 [a]'Let me pass through your land; I will keep strictly to the road, and I will turn neither to the right nor to the left.

28 'You shall sell me food for money, that I may eat, and give me water for money, that I may drink; [a]only let me pass through on foot,

29 [a]'just as the descendants of Esau who dwell in Seir and the Moabites who dwell in Ar did for me, until I cross the Jordan to the land which the LORD our God is giving us.'

30 [a]"But Sihon king of Heshbon would not let us pass through, for [b]the LORD your God [c]hardened his spirit and made his heart obstinate, that He might deliver him into your hand, as *it is* this day.

31 "And the LORD said to me, 'See, I have begun to [a]give Sihon and his land over to you. Begin to possess *it*, that you may inherit his land.'

32 [a]"Then Sihon and all his people came out against us to fight at Jahaz.

33 "And [a]the LORD our God delivered him over to us; so [b]we defeated him, his sons, and all his people.

34 "We took all his cities at that time, and we [a]utterly destroyed the men, women, and little ones of every city; we left none remaining.

35 "We took only the livestock as plunder for ourselves, with the spoil of the cities which we took.

36 [a]"From Aroer, which *is* on the bank of the River Arnon, and *from* [b]the city that *is* in the ravine, as far as Gilead, there was not one city too strong for us; [c]the LORD our God delivered all to us.

37 "Only you did not go near the land of the people of Ammon—anywhere along the River [a]Jabbok, or to the cities of the mountains,

19 [a]Gen. 19:38; Num. 21:24
20 [a]Gen. 14:5
21 [a]Deut. 2:10
22 [a]Gen. 36:8; Deut. 2:5 [b]Gen. 14:6; 36:20–30
23 [a]Josh. 13:3 [b]Gen. 10:14; 1 Chr. 1:12; Jer. 47:4; Amos 9:7
24 [a]Num. 21:13, 14; Judg. 11:18 [b]Deut. 1:4
25 [a]Ex. 23:27; Deut. 11:25; Josh. 2:9 [b]Ex. 15:14–16
26 [a]Num. 21:21–32; Deut. 1:4; Judg. 11:19–21 [b]Deut. 20:10
27 [a]Num. 21:21, 22; Judg. 11:19
28 [a]Num. 20:19
29 [a]Num. 20:18; Deut. 23:3, 4; Judg. 11:17
30 [a]Num. 21:23 [b]Josh. 11:20 [c]Ex. 4:21
31 [a]Deut. 1:3, 8
32 [a]Num. 21:23
33 [a]Ex. 23:31; Deut. 7:2 [b]Num. 21:24
34 [a]Lev. 27:28
36 [a]Deut. 3:12; 4:48; Josh. 13:9 [b]Josh. 13:9, 16 [c]Ps. 44:3
37 [a]Gen. 32:22; Num. 21:24; Deut. 3:16

*

2:20 Heb. *rephaim*

KJV

tains, nor unto [b]whatsoever the LORD our God forbad us.

King Og Defeated
(Num. 21:33–35)

3 Then we turned, and went up the way to
Bashan: and [a]Og the king of Bashan came out
against us, he and all his people, to battle [b]at
Edrei.
2 And the LORD said unto me, Fear him not:
for I will deliver him, and all his people, and his
land, into thy hand; and thou shalt do unto him
as thou didst unto [a]Sihon king of the Amorites,
which dwelt at Heshbon.
3 So the LORD our God delivered into our
hands Og also, the king of Bashan, and all his
people: and we smote him until none was left to
him remaining.
4 And we took all his cities at that time,
there was not a city which we took not from them,
threescore cities, [a]all the region of Argob, the
kingdom of Og in Bashan.
5 All these cities *were* fenced with high
walls, gates, and bars; beside unwalled towns a
great many.
6 And we utterly destroyed them, as we did
unto Sihon king [a]of Heshbon, utterly destroying
the men, women, and children, of every city.
7 But all the cattle, and the spoil of the cities,
we took for a prey to ourselves.
8 And we took at that time out of the hand
of the two kings of the Amorites the [a]land that
was on this side Jordan, from the river of Arnon
unto mount [b]Hermon;
9 (*Which* [a]Hermon the Sidonians call Sirion; and the Amorites call it Shenir;)
10 [a]All the cities of the plain, and all Gilead,
and [b]all Bashan, unto Salchah and Edrei, cities
of the kingdom of Og in Bashan.
11 [a]For only Og king of Bashan remained of
the remnant of [b]giants; behold, his bedstead *was*
a bedstead of iron; *is* it not in [c]Rabbath of the
children of Ammon? nine cubits *was* the length
thereof, and four cubits the breadth of it, after
the cubit of a man.

The Land East of the Jordan Divided

12 And this [a]land, *which* we possessed at that
time, [b]from Aroer, which *is* by the river Arnon,
and half mount Gilead, and [c]the cities thereof,
gave I unto the Reubenites and to the Gadites.
13 [a]And the rest of Gilead, and all Bashan,
being the kingdom of Og, gave I unto the half
tribe of Manasseh; all the region of Argob, with
all Bashan, which was called the land of giants.
14 [a]Jair the son of Manasseh took all the
country of Argob [b]unto the coasts of Geshuri and
Maachathi; and [c]called them after his own name,
Bashan–havoth–jair, unto this day.
15 And I gave [a]Gilead unto Machir.
16 And unto the Reubenites [a]and unto the
Gadites I gave from Gilead even unto the river
Arnon half the valley, and the border even unto
the river Jabbok, [b]*which is* the border of the children of Ammon;
17 The plain also, and Jordan, and the coast
thereof, from Chinnereth [a]even unto the sea of
the plain, [b]*even* the salt sea, under Ashdoth–
pisgah eastward.
18 And I commanded you at that time, saying, The LORD your God hath given you this land
to possess it: [a]ye shall pass over armed before
your brethren the children of Israel, all *that are*
meet for the war.
19 But your wives, and your little ones, and
your cattle, (*for* I know that ye have much cattle,)
shall abide in your cities which I have given
you;
20 Until the LORD have given [a]rest unto your
brethren, as well as unto you, and *until* they also
possess the land which the LORD your God hath
given them beyond Jordan: and *then* shall ye

37 [b]Deut. 2:5, 9, 19

CHAPTER 3

1 [a]Num. 21:33–35; Deut. 29:7 [b]Deut. 1:4
2 [a]Num. 21:34; Josh. 13:21
4 [a]Deut. 3:13, 14
6 [a]Deut. 2:24, 34, 35
8 [a]Num. 32:33; Josh. 12:6; 13:8–12 [b]Deut. 4:48; 1 Chr. 5:23
9 [a]1 Chr. 5:23
10 [a]Deut. 4:49 [b]Josh. 12:5; 13:11
11 [a]Amos 2:9 [b]Gen. 14:5; Deut. 2:11, 20 [c]2 Sam. 12:26; Jer. 49:2; Ezek. 21:20
12 [a]Num. 32:33; Josh. 12:6; 13:8–12 [b]Deut. 2:36; Josh. 12:2 [c]Num. 34:14
13 [a]Josh. 13:29–31; 17:1
14 [a]1 Chr. 2:22 [b]Josh. 13:13; 2 Sam. 3:3; 10:6 [c]Num. 32:41
15 [a]Num. 32:39, 40
16 [a]2 Sam. 24:5 [b]Num. 21:24; Deut. 2:37; Josh. 12:2
17 [a]Num. 34:11, 12; Deut. 4:49; Josh. 12:3 [b]Gen. 14:3; Josh. 3:16
18 [a]Num. 32:20; Josh. 4:12, 13
20 [a]Deut. 12:9, 10

*———

3:11 Heb. *rephaim*
3:13 Heb. *rephaim*
3:14 Lit. *Towns of Jair*

NKJV

or [b]wherever the LORD our God had forbidden
us.

King Og Defeated
(Num. 21:33–35)

3 "Then we turned and went up the road to
Bashan; and [a]Og king of Bashan came out
against us, he and all his people, to battle [b]at
Edrei.
2 "And the LORD said to me, 'Do not fear
him, for I have delivered him and all his people
and his land into your hand; you shall do to him
as you did to [a]Sihon king of the Amorites, who
dwelt at Heshbon.'
3 "So the LORD our God also delivered into
our hands Og king of Bashan, with all his people,
and we attacked him until he had no survivors
remaining.
4 "And we took all his cities at that time;
there was not a city which we did not take from
them: sixty cities, [a]all the region of Argob, the
kingdom of Og in Bashan.
5 "All these cities *were* fortified with high
walls, gates, and bars, besides a great many rural
towns.
6 "And we utterly destroyed them, as we
did to Sihon king [a]of Heshbon, utterly destroying
the men, women, and children of every city.
7 "But all the livestock and the spoil of the
cities we took as booty for ourselves.
8 "And at that time we took the [a]land from
the hand of the two kings of the Amorites who
were on this side of the Jordan, from the River
Arnon to Mount [b]Hermon
9 "(the Sidonians call [a]Hermon Sirion, and
the Amorites call it Senir),
10 [a]"all the cities of the plain, all Gilead, and
[b]all Bashan, as far as Salcah and Edrei, cities of
the kingdom of Og in Bashan.
11 [a]"For only Og king of Bashan remained
of the remnant of [b]the *giants. Indeed his bedstead *was* an iron bedstead. (*Is* it not in [c]Rabbah
of the people of Ammon?) Nine cubits *is* its length
and four cubits its width, according to the standard cubit.

The Land East of the Jordan Divided

12 "And this [a]land, *which* we possessed at
that time, [b]from Aroer, which *is* by the River Arnon, and half the mountains of Gilead and [c]its
cities, I gave to the Reubenites and the Gadites.
13 [a]"The rest of Gilead, and all Bashan, the
kingdom of Og, I gave to half the tribe of Manasseh. (All the region of Argob, with all Bashan,
was called the land of the *giants.
14 [a]"Jair the son of Manasseh took all the
region of Argob, [b]as far as the border of the Geshurites and the Maachathites, and [c]called Bashan
after his own name, *Havoth Jair, to this day.)
15 "Also I gave [a]Gilead to Machir.
16 "And to the Reubenites [a]and the Gadites
I gave from Gilead as far as the River Arnon, the
middle of the river as *the* border, as far as the
River Jabbok, [b]the border of the people of
Ammon;
17 "the plain also, with the Jordan as *the* border, from Chinnereth [a]as far as the east side of
the Sea of the Arabah [b](the Salt Sea), below the
slopes of Pisgah.
18 "Then I commanded you at that time, saying: 'The LORD your God has given you this land
to possess. [a]All you men of valor shall cross over
armed before your brethren, the children of Israel.
19 'But your wives, your little ones, and your
livestock (I know that you have much livestock)
shall stay in your cities which I have given you,
20 'until the LORD has given [a]rest to your
brethren as to you, and they also possess the land
which the LORD your God is giving them beyond

KJV

[b]return every man unto his possession, which I have given you.

21 And [a]I commanded Joshua at that time, saying, Thine eyes have seen all that the LORD your God hath done unto these two kings: so shall the LORD do unto all the kingdoms whither thou passest.

22 Ye shall not fear them: for [a]the LORD your God he shall fight for you.

Moses Forbidden to Enter the Land

23 And [a]I besought the LORD at that time, saying,

24 O Lord GOD, thou hast begun to shew thy servant [a]thy greatness, and thy mighty hand: for [b]what God *is there* in heaven or in earth, that can do according to thy works, and according to thy might?

25 I pray thee, let me go over, and see [a]the good land that *is* beyond Jordan, that goodly mountain, and Lebanon.

26 But the LORD [a]was wroth with me for your sakes, and would not hear me: and the LORD said unto me, Let it suffice thee; speak no more unto me of this matter.

27 [a]Get thee up into the top of Pisgah, and lift up thine eyes westward, and northward, and southward, and eastward, and behold *it* with thine eyes: for thou shalt not go over this Jordan.

28 But [a]charge Joshua, and encourage him, and strengthen him: for he shall go over before this people, and he shall cause them to inherit the land which thou shalt see.

29 So we abode in [a]the valley over against Beth–peor.

Moses Commands Obedience

4 Now therefore hearken, O Israel, unto [a]the statutes and unto the judgments, which I teach you, for to do *them,* that ye may live, and go in and possess the land which the LORD God of your fathers giveth you.

2 [a]Ye shall not add unto the word which I command you, neither shall ye diminish *ought* from it, that ye may keep the commandments of the LORD your God which I command you.

3 Your eyes have seen what the LORD did because of [a]Baal–peor: for all the men that followed Baal–peor, the LORD thy God hath destroyed them from among you.

4 But ye that did cleave unto the LORD your God *are* alive every one of you this day.

5 Behold, I have taught you statutes and judgments, even as the LORD my God commanded me, that ye should do so in the land whither ye go to possess it.

6 Keep therefore and do *them;* for this *is* [a]your wisdom and your understanding in the sight of the nations, which shall hear all these statutes, and say, Surely this great nation *is* a wise and understanding people.

7 For [a]what nation *is there so* great, who *hath* [b]God *so* nigh unto them, as the LORD our God *is* in all *things that* we call upon him *for?*

8 And what nation *is there so* great, that hath statutes and judgments *so* righteous as all this law, which I set before you this day?

9 Only take heed to thyself, and [a]keep thy soul diligently, lest thou [b]forget the things which thine eyes have seen, and lest they depart from thy heart all the days of thy life: but [c]teach them thy sons, and thy sons' sons;

10 *Specially* [a]the day that thou stoodest before the LORD thy God in Horeb, when the LORD said unto me, Gather me the people together, and I will make them hear my words, that they may learn to fear me all the days that they shall live upon the earth, and *that* they may teach their children.

11 And ye came near and stood under the mountain; and the mountain burned with fire unto

20 [b]Josh. 22:4
21 [a][Num. 27:22, 23]; Josh. 11:23
22 [a]Ex. 14:14; Deut. 1:30; 20:4; Neh. 4:20
23 [a][2 Cor. 12:8, 9]
24 [a]Deut. 5:24; 11:2 [b]Ex. 8:10; 15:11; 2 Sam. 7:22; Ps. 71:19; 86:8
25 [a]Ex. 3:8; Deut. 4:22
26 [a]Num. 20:12; 27:14; Deut. 1:37; 31:2; 32:51, 52; 34:4
27 [a]Num. 23:14; 27:12
28 [a]Num. 27:18, 23; Deut. 31:3, 7, 8, 23
29 [a]Deut. 4:46; 34:6

CHAPTER 4

1 [a]Lev. 19:37; 20:8; 22:31; Deut. 5:1; 8:1; Ezek. 20:11; [Rom. 10:5]
2 [a]Deut. 12:32; [Josh. 1:7]; Prov. 30:6; [Rev. 22:18, 19]
3 [a]Num. 25:1–9; Josh. 22:17; Ps. 106:28
6 [a]Deut. 30:19, 20; 32:46, 47; Job 28:28; Ps. 19:7; 111:10; Prov. 1:7; [2 Tim. 3:15]
7 [a][Deut. 4:32–34; 2 Sam. 7:23] [b][Ps. 46:1; Is. 55:6]
9 [a]Prov. 4:23 [b]Deut. 29:2–8 [c]Gen. 18:19; Deut. 4:10; 6:7, 20–25; Ps. 78:5, 6; Prov. 22:6; Eph. 6:4
10 [a]Ex. 19:9, 16, 17

NKJV

the Jordan. Then each of you may [b]return to his possession which I have given you.'

21 "And [a]I commanded Joshua at that time, saying, 'Your eyes have seen all that the LORD your God has done to these two kings; so will the LORD do to all the kingdoms through which you pass.

22 'You must not fear them, for [a]the LORD your God Himself fights for you.'

Moses Forbidden to Enter the Land

23 "Then [a]I pleaded with the LORD at that time, saying:

24 'O Lord GOD, You have begun to show Your servant [a]Your greatness and Your mighty hand, for [b]what god *is there* in heaven or on earth who can do *anything* like Your works and Your mighty *deeds?*

25 'I pray, let me cross over and see [a]the good land beyond the Jordan, those pleasant mountains, and Lebanon.'

26 "But the LORD [a]was angry with me on your account, and would not listen to me. So the LORD said to me: 'Enough of that! Speak no more to Me of this matter.

27 [a]'Go up to the top of Pisgah, and lift your eyes toward the west, the north, the south, and the east; behold *it* with your eyes, for you shall not cross over this Jordan.

28 'But [a]command Joshua, and encourage him and strengthen him; for he shall go over before this people, and he shall cause them to inherit the land which you will see.'

29 "So we stayed in [a]the valley opposite Beth Peor.

Moses Commands Obedience

4 "Now, O Israel, listen to [a]the statutes and the judgments which I teach you to observe, that you may live, and go in and possess the land which the LORD God of your fathers is giving you.

2 [a]"You shall not add to the word which I command you, nor take from it, that you may keep the commandments of the LORD your God which I command you.

3 "Your eyes have seen what the LORD did at [a]Baal Peor; for the LORD your God has destroyed from among you all the men who followed Baal of Peor.

4 "But you who held fast to the LORD your God *are* alive today, every one of you.

5 "Surely I have taught you statutes and judgments, just as the LORD my God commanded me, that you should act according *to them* in the land which you go to possess.

6 "Therefore be careful to observe *them;* for this *is* [a]your wisdom and your understanding in the sight of the peoples who will hear all these statutes, and say, 'Surely this great nation *is* a wise and understanding people.'

7 "For [a]what great nation *is there* that has [b]God so near to it, as the LORD our God *is* to us, for whatever *reason* we may call upon Him?

8 "And what great nation *is there* that has *such* statutes and righteous judgments as are in all this law which I set before you this day?

9 "Only take heed to yourself, and diligently [a]keep yourself, lest you [b]forget the things your eyes have seen, and lest they depart from your heart all the days of your life. And [c]teach them to your children and your grandchildren,

10 "*especially concerning* [a]the day you stood before the LORD your God in Horeb, when the LORD said to me, 'Gather the people to Me, and I will let them hear My words, that they may learn to fear Me all the days they live on the earth, and *that* they may teach their children.'

11 "Then you came near and stood at the foot of the mountain, and the mountain burned with

KJV

the midst of heaven, with darkness, clouds, and
thick darkness.
12 [a]And the LORD spake unto you out of the
midst of the fire: ye heard the voice of the words,
but saw no similitude; [b]only *ye heard* a voice.
13 [a]And he declared unto you his covenant,
which he commanded you to perform, *even* [b]ten
commandments; and [c]he wrote them upon two
tables of stone.
14 And [a]the LORD commanded me at that
time to teach you statutes and judgments, that ye
might do them in the land whither ye go over to
possess it.

Beware of Idolatry

15 [a]Take ye therefore good heed unto yourselves; for ye saw no manner of [b]similitude on
the day *that* the LORD spake unto you in Horeb
out of the midst of the fire:
16 Lest ye [a]corrupt *yourselves,* and [b]make
you a graven image, the similitude of any figure,
[c]the likeness of male or female,
17 The likeness of any beast that *is* on the
earth, the likeness of any winged fowl that flieth
in the air,
18 The likeness of any thing that creepeth
on the ground, the likeness of any fish that *is* in
the waters beneath the earth:
19 And lest thou [a]lift up thine eyes unto
heaven, and when thou seest the sun, and the
moon, and the stars, *even* [b]all the host of heaven,
shouldest be driven to [c]worship them, and serve
them, which the LORD thy God hath divided unto
all nations under the whole heaven.
20 But the LORD hath taken you, and
[a]brought you forth out of the iron furnace, *even*
out of Egypt, to be unto him a [b]people of inheritance, as *ye are* this day.
21 Furthermore [a]the LORD was angry with
me for your sakes, and sware that [b]I should not
go over Jordan, and that I should not go in unto
that good land, which the LORD thy God giveth
thee *for* an inheritance:
22 But [a]I must die in this land, [b]I must not
go over Jordan: but ye shall go over, and possess
[c]that good land.
23 Take heed unto yourselves, lest ye forget
the covenant of the LORD your God, which he
made with you, [a]and make you a graven image,
or the likeness of any *thing,* which the LORD thy
God hath forbidden thee.
24 For [a]the LORD thy God *is* a consuming fire,
even [b]a jealous God.
25 When thou shalt beget children, and children's children, and ye shall have remained long
in the land, and shall corrupt *yourselves,* and
make a graven image, *or* the likeness of any *thing,*
and [a]shall do evil in the sight of the LORD thy
God, to provoke him to anger:
26 [a]I call heaven and earth to witness against
you this day, that ye shall soon utterly perish from
off the land whereunto ye go over Jordan to possess it; ye shall not prolong *your* days upon it,
but shall utterly be destroyed.
27 And the LORD [a]shall scatter you among
the nations, and ye shall be left few in number
among the heathen, whither the LORD shall lead
you.
28 And [a]there ye shall serve gods, the work
of men's hands, wood and stone, [b]which neither
see, nor hear, nor eat, nor smell.
29 [a]But if from thence thou shalt seek the
LORD thy God, thou shalt find *him,* if thou seek
him with all thy heart and with all thy soul.
30 When thou art in tribulation, and all these
things are come upon thee, *even* in the [a]latter
days, if thou [b]turn to the LORD thy God, and shalt
be obedient unto his voice;
31 (For the LORD thy God *is* a merciful God;)
he will not forsake thee, neither [a]destroy thee,
nor forget the covenant of thy fathers which he
sware unto them.

12 [a]Deut. 5:4, 22 [b]Ex. 19:17–19; 20:22; 1 Kin. 19:11–18
13 [a]Deut. 9:9, 11 [b]Ex. 34:28; Deut. 10:4 [c]Ex. 24:12
14 [a]Ex. 21:1
15 [a]Josh. 23:11 [b]Is. 40:18
16 [a]Ex. 32:7; Deut. 9:12; 31:29 [b]Ex. 20:4, 5 [c]Rom. 1:23
19 [a]Deut. 17:3; Job 31:26–28 [b]2 Kin. 21:3 [c][Rom. 1:25]
20 [a]1 Kin. 8:51; Jer. 11:4 [b]Deut. 7:6; 27:9; [Titus 2:14]
21 [a]Num. 20:12; Deut. 1:37; 3:26 [b]Num. 27:13, 14
22 [a]2 Pet. 1:13–15 [b]Deut. 3:27 [c]Deut. 3:25
23 [a]Ex. 20:4, 5; Deut. 4:16
24 [a]Ex. 24:17; Deut. 9:3; Is. 33:14; Heb. 12:29 [b]Ex. 20:5; 34:14
25 [a]2 Kin. 17:17
26 [a]Deut. 30:18, 19; 2 Chr. 36:14–20; Is. 1:2; Mic. 6:2
27 [a]Lev. 26:33; Deut. 28:62; Neh. 1:8
28 [a]Deut. 28:64; 1 Sam. 26:19; Jer. 16:13 [b]Ps. 115:4–7; 135:15–17; Is. 44:9; 46:7
29 [a][Lev. 26:39–45; Deut. 30:1–3; 2 Chr. 15:4; Neh. 1:9]
30 [a]Gen. 49:1; Deut. 31:29; Jer. 23:20; Hos. 3:5 [b]Joel 2:12; Heb. 1:2
31 [a]Lev. 26:44; Jer. 30:11

NKJV

fire to the midst of heaven, with darkness, cloud,
and thick darkness.
12 [a]"And the LORD spoke to you out of the
midst of the fire. You heard the sound of the
words, but saw no form; [b]*you* only *heard* a voice.
13 [a]"So He declared to you His covenant
which He commanded you to perform, [b]the Ten
Commandments; and [c]He wrote them on two tablets of stone.
14 "And [a]the LORD commanded me at that
time to teach you statutes and judgments, that you
might observe them in the land which you cross
over to possess.

Beware of Idolatry

15 [a]"Take careful heed to yourselves, for you
saw no [b]form when the LORD spoke to you at
Horeb out of the midst of the fire,
16 "lest you [a]act corruptly and [b]make for
yourselves a carved image in the form of any figure: [c]the likeness of male or female,
17 "the likeness of any animal that *is* on the
earth or the likeness of any winged bird that flies
in the air,
18 "the likeness of anything that creeps on
the ground or the likeness of any fish that *is* in
the water beneath the earth.
19 "And *take heed,* lest you [a]lift your eyes
to heaven, and *when* you see the sun, the moon,
and the stars, [b]all the host of heaven, you feel
driven to [c]worship them and serve them, which
the LORD your God has given to all the peoples
under the whole heaven as a heritage.
20 "But the LORD has taken you and [a]brought
you out of the iron furnace, out of Egypt, to be
[b]His people, an inheritance, as you are this day.
21 "Furthermore [a]the LORD was angry with
me for your sakes, and swore that [b]I would not
cross over the Jordan, and that I would not enter
the good land which the LORD your God is giving
you as an inheritance.
22 "But [a]I must die in this land, [b]I must not
cross over the Jordan; but you shall cross over
and possess [c]that good land.
23 "Take heed to yourselves, lest you forget
the covenant of the LORD your God which He
made with you, [a]and make for yourselves a
carved image in the form of anything which the
LORD your God has forbidden you.
24 "For [a]the LORD your God *is* a consuming
fire, [b]a jealous God.
25 "When you beget children and grandchildren and have grown old in the land, and act corruptly and make a carved image in the form of
anything, and [a]do evil in the sight of the LORD
your God to provoke Him to anger,
26 [a]"I call heaven and earth to witness
against you this day, that you will soon utterly
perish from the land which you cross over the
Jordan to possess; you will not prolong *your* days
in it, but will be utterly destroyed.
27 "And the LORD [a]will scatter you among
the peoples, and you will be left few in number
among the nations where the LORD will drive you.
28 "And [a]there you will serve gods, the work
of men's hands, wood and stone, [b]which neither
see nor hear nor eat nor smell.
29 [a]"But from there you will seek the LORD
your God, and you will find *Him* if you seek Him
with all your heart and with all your soul.
30 "When you are in distress, and all these
things come upon you in the [a]latter days, when
you [b]turn to the LORD your God and obey His
voice
31 "(for the LORD your God *is* a merciful
God), He will not forsake you nor [a]destroy you,
nor forget the covenant of your fathers which He
swore to them.

KJV

32 For [a]ask now of the days that are past, which were before thee, since the day that God created man upon the earth, and *ask* [b]from the one side of heaven unto the other, whether there hath been *any such thing* as this great thing *is*, or hath been heard like it?

33 [a]Did *ever* people hear the voice of God speaking out of the midst of the fire, as thou hast heard, and live?

34 Or hath God assayed to go *and* take him a nation from the midst of *another* nation, [a]by temptations, [b]by signs, and by wonders, and by war, and [c]by a mighty hand, and [d]by a stretched out arm, [e]and by great terrors, according to all that the LORD your God did for you in Egypt before your eyes?

35 Unto thee it was shewed, that thou mightest know that the LORD he *is* God; [a]*there is* none else beside him.

36 [a]Out of heaven he made thee to hear his voice, that he might instruct thee: and upon earth he shewed thee his great fire; and thou heardest his words out of the midst of the fire.

37 And because [a]he loved thy fathers, therefore he chose their seed after them, and [b]brought thee out in his sight with his mighty power out of Egypt;

38 [a]To drive out nations from before thee greater and mightier than thou *art*, to bring thee in, to give thee their land *for* an inheritance, as *it is* this day.

39 Know therefore this day, and consider *it* in thine heart, that [a]the LORD he *is* God in heaven above, and upon the earth beneath: *there is* none else.

40 [a]Thou shalt keep therefore his statutes, and his commandments, which I command thee this day, that it may go well with thee, and with thy children after thee, and that thou mayest prolong *thy* days upon the earth, which the LORD thy God giveth thee, for ever.

Cities of Refuge East of the Jordan

41 Then Moses [a]severed three cities on this side Jordan toward the sun rising;

42 [a]That the slayer might flee thither, which should kill his neighbour unawares, and hated him not in times past; and that fleeing unto one of these cities he might live:

43 *Namely*, [a]Bezer in the wilderness, in the plain country, of the Reubenites; and Ramoth in Gilead, of the Gadites; and Golan in Bashan, of the Manassites.

Introduction to God's Law

44 And this *is* the law which Moses set before the children of Israel:

45 These *are* the testimonies, and the statutes, and the judgments, which Moses spake unto the children of Israel, after they came forth out of Egypt,

46 On this side Jordan, [a]in the valley over against Beth–peor, in the land of Sihon king of the Amorites, who dwelt at Heshbon, whom Moses and the children of Israel [b]smote, after they were come forth out of Egypt:

47 And they possessed his land, and the land [a]of Og king of Bashan, two kings of the Amorites, which *were* on this side Jordan toward the sun rising;

48 [a]From Aroer, which *is* by the bank of the river Arnon, even unto mount Sion, which *is* [b]Hermon,

49 And all the plain on this side Jordan eastward, even unto the sea of the plain, under the [a]springs of Pisgah.

The Ten Commandments Reviewed
(Ex. 20:1–17)

5 And Moses called all Israel, and said unto them, Hear, O Israel, the statutes and judg-

32 [a]Deut. 32:7; Job 8:8 [b]Deut. 28:64; Matt. 24:31
33 [a]Ex. 20:22; 24:11; Deut. 5:24–26
34 [a]Deut. 7:19 [b]Ex. 7:3 [c]Ex. 13:3 [d]Ex. 6:6 [e]Deut. 26:8
35 [a]Ex. 8:10; 9:14; [Deut. 4:39; 32:12, 39; 1 Sam. 2:2; Is. 43:10–12; 44:6–8; 45:5–7]; Mark 12:32
36 [a]Ex. 19:9, 19; 20:18, 22; Deut. 4:33; Neh. 9:13; Heb. 12:19, 25
37 [a]Deut. 7:7, 8; 10:15; 33:3 [b]Ex. 13:3, 9, 14
38 [a]Deut. 7:1
39 [a]Deut. 4:35; Josh. 2:11
40 [a]Lev. 22:31; Deut. 5:16; 32:46, 47
41 [a]Num. 35:6; Deut. 19:2–13; Josh. 20:7–9
42 [a]Deut. 19:4
43 [a]Josh. 20:8
46 [a]Deut. 3:29 [b]Num. 21:24; Deut. 1:4
47 [a]Num. 21:33–35
48 [a]Deut. 2:36; 3:12 [b]Deut. 3:9; Ps. 133:3
49 [a]Deut. 3:17

*

4:48 Syr. *Sirion*

NKJV

32 "For [a]ask now concerning the days that are past, which were before you, since the day that God created man on the earth, and *ask* [b]from one end of heaven to the other, whether *any* great *thing* like this has happened, or *anything* like it has been heard.

33 [a]"Did *any* people *ever* hear the voice of God speaking out of the midst of the fire, as you have heard, and live?

34 "Or did God *ever* try to go *and* take for Himself a nation from the midst of *another* nation, [a]by trials, [b]by signs, by wonders, by war, [c]by a mighty hand and [d]an outstretched arm, [e]and by great terrors, according to all that the LORD your God did for you in Egypt before your eyes?

35 "To you it was shown, that you might know that the LORD Himself *is* God; [a]*there is* none other besides Him.

36 [a]"Out of heaven He let you hear His voice, that He might instruct you; on earth He showed you His great fire, and you heard His words out of the midst of the fire.

37 "And because [a]He loved your fathers, therefore He chose their descendants after them; and [b]He brought you out of Egypt with His Presence, with His mighty power,

38 [a]"driving out from before you nations greater and mightier than you, to bring you in, to give you their land *as* an inheritance, as *it is* this day.

39 "Therefore know this day, and consider *it* in your heart, that [a]the LORD Himself *is* God in heaven above and on the earth beneath; *there is* no other.

40 [a]"You shall therefore keep His statutes and His commandments which I command you today, that it may go well with you and with your children after you, and that you may prolong *your* days in the land which the LORD your God is giving you for all time."

Cities of Refuge East of the Jordan

41 Then Moses [a]set apart three cities on this side of the Jordan, toward the rising of the sun,

42 [a]that the manslayer might flee there, who kills his neighbor unintentionally, without having hated him in time past, and that by fleeing to one of these cities he might live:

43 [a]Bezer in the wilderness on the plateau for the Reubenites, Ramoth in Gilead for the Gadites, and Golan in Bashan for the Manassites.

Introduction to God's Law

44 Now this *is* the law which Moses set before the children of Israel.

45 These *are* the testimonies, the statutes, and the judgments which Moses spoke to the children of Israel after they came out of Egypt,

46 on this side of the Jordan, [a]in the valley opposite Beth Peor, in the land of Sihon king of the Amorites, who dwelt at Heshbon, whom Moses and the children of Israel [b]defeated after they came out of Egypt.

47 And they took possession of his land and the land [a]of Og king of Bashan, two kings of the Amorites, who *were* on this side of the Jordan, toward the rising of the sun,

48 [a]from Aroer, which *is* on the bank of the River Arnon, even to Mount *Sion (that is, [b]Hermon),

49 and all the plain on the east side of the Jordan as far as the Sea of the Arabah, below the [a]slopes of Pisgah.

The Ten Commandments Reviewed
(Ex. 20:1–17)

5 And Moses called all Israel, and said to them: "Hear, O Israel, the statutes and judgments

KJV

ments which I speak in your ears this day, that ye may learn them, and keep, and do them.

2 [a]The LORD our God made a covenant with us in Horeb.

3 The LORD [a]made not this covenant with our fathers, but with us, *even* us, who *are* all of us here alive this day.

4 [a]The LORD talked with you face to face in the mount out of the midst of the fire,

5 [a](I stood between the LORD and you at that time, to shew you the word of the LORD: for [b]ye were afraid by reason of the fire, and went not up into the mount;) saying,

6 [a]I *am* the LORD thy God, which brought thee out of the land of Egypt, from the house of bondage.

7 [a]Thou shalt have none other gods before me.

8 [a]Thou shalt not make thee *any* graven image, *or* any likeness *of any thing* that *is* in heaven above, or that *is* in the earth beneath, or that *is* in the waters beneath the earth:

9 Thou shalt not [a]bow down thyself unto them, nor serve them: for I the LORD thy God *am* a jealous God, visiting the iniquity of the fathers upon the children unto the third and fourth *generation* of them that hate me,

10 [a]And shewing mercy unto thousands of them that love me and keep my commandments.

11 [a]Thou shalt not take the name of the LORD thy God in vain: for the LORD will not hold *him* guiltless that taketh his name in vain.

12 [a]Keep the sabbath day to sanctify it, as the LORD thy God hath commanded thee.

13 [a]Six days thou shalt labour, and do all thy work:

14 But the seventh day *is* the [a]sabbath of the LORD thy God: *in it* thou shalt not do any work, thou, nor thy son, nor thy daughter, nor thy manservant, nor thy maidservant, nor thine ox, nor thine ass, nor any of thy cattle, nor thy stranger that *is* within thy gates; that thy manservant and thy maidservant may rest as well as thou.

15 [a]And remember that thou wast a servant in the land of Egypt, and *that* the LORD thy God brought thee out thence [b]through a mighty hand and by a stretched out arm: therefore the LORD thy God commanded thee to keep the sabbath day.

16 [a]Honour thy father and thy mother, as the LORD thy God hath commanded thee; [b]that thy days may be prolonged, and that it may go well with [c]thee, in the land which the LORD thy God giveth thee.

17 [a]Thou shalt not kill.

18 [a]Neither shalt thou commit adultery.

19 [a]Neither shalt thou steal.

20 [a]Neither shalt thou bear false witness against thy neighbour.

21 [a]Neither shalt thou desire thy neighbour's wife, neither shalt thou covet thy neighbour's house, his field, or his manservant, or his maidservant, his ox, or his ass, or any *thing* that *is* thy neighbour's.

22 These words the LORD spake unto all your assembly in the mount out of the midst of the fire, of the cloud, and of the thick darkness, with a great voice: and he added no more. And [a]he wrote them in two tables of stone, and delivered them unto me.

CHAPTER 5

2 [a]Ex. 19:5; Deut. 4:23; Mal. 4:4
3 [a]Jer. 31:32; Matt. 13:17; Heb. 8:9
4 [a]Ex. 19:9
5 [a]Ex. 20:21; Gal. 3:19 [b]Ex. 19:16
6 [a]Ex. 20:2–17; Lev. 26:1; Deut. 6:4; Ps. 81:10
7 [a]Ex. 20:2, 3; 23:13; Hos. 13:4
8 [a]Ex. 20:4
9 [a]Ex. 34:7, 14–16; Num. 14:18; Deut. 7:10
10 [a]Num. 14:18; Deut. 7:9; Jer. 32:18; Dan. 9:4
11 [a]Ex. 20:7; Lev. 19:12; Deut. 6:13; 10:20; Matt. 5:33
12 [a]Ex. 20:8; Ezek. 20:12; Mark 2:27
13 [a]Ex. 23:12; 35:2
14 [a][Gen. 2:2]; Ex. 16:29; [Heb. 4:4]
15 [a]Deut. 15:15 [b]Deut. 4:34, 37
16 [a]Ex. 20:12; Lev. 19:3; Matt. 15:4; Eph. 6:2, 3; Col. 3:20 [b]Deut. 6:2 [c]Deut. 4:40
17 [a]Ex. 20:13; Matt. 5:21
18 [a]Ex. 20:14; Mark 10:19; Luke 18:20; [Rom. 13:9]; James 2:11
19 [a]Ex. 20:15; Lev. 19:11; [Rom. 13:9]
20 [a]Ex. 20:16; 23:1; Matt. 19:18
21 [a]Ex. 20:17; [Rom. 7:7; 13:9]
22 [a]Ex. 24:12; 31:18; Deut. 4:13

NKJV

which I speak in your hearing today, that you may learn them and be careful to observe them.

2 [a]"The LORD our God made a covenant with us in Horeb.

3 "The LORD [a]did not make this covenant with our fathers, but with us, those who *are* here today, all of us who *are* alive.

4 [a]"The LORD talked with you face to face on the mountain from the midst of the fire.

5 [a]"I stood between the LORD and you at that time, to declare to you the word of the LORD; for [b]you were afraid because of the fire, and you did not go up the mountain. *He* said:

6 [a]'I *am* the LORD your God who brought you out of the land of Egypt, out of the house of bondage.

7 [a]'You shall have no other gods before Me.

8 [a]'You shall not make for yourself a carved image—any likeness *of anything* that *is* in heaven above, or that *is* in the earth beneath, or that *is* in the water under the earth;

9 you shall not [a]bow down to them nor serve them. For I, the LORD your God, *am* a jealous God, visiting the iniquity of the fathers upon the children to the third and fourth *generations* of those who hate Me,

10 [a]but showing mercy to thousands, to those who love Me and keep My commandments.

11 [a]'You shall not take the name of the LORD your God in vain, for the LORD will not hold *him* guiltless who takes His name in vain.

12 [a]'Observe the Sabbath day, to keep it holy, as the LORD your God commanded you.

13 [a]Six days you shall labor and do all your work,

14 but the seventh day *is* the [a]Sabbath of the LORD your God. *In it* you shall do no work: you, nor your son, nor your daughter, nor your male servant, nor your female servant, nor your ox, nor your donkey, nor any of your cattle, nor your stranger who *is* within your gates, that your male servant and your female servant may rest as well as you.

15 [a]And remember that you were a slave in the land of Egypt, and the LORD your God brought you out from there [b]by a mighty hand and by an outstretched arm; therefore the LORD your God commanded you to keep the Sabbath day.

16 [a]'Honor your father and your mother, as the LORD your God has commanded you, [b]that your days may be long, and that it may be well with [c]you in the land which the LORD your God is giving you.

17 [a]'You shall not murder.

18 [a]'You shall not commit adultery.

19 [a]'You shall not steal.

20 [a]'You shall not bear false witness against your neighbor.

21 [a]'You shall not covet your neighbor's wife; and you shall not desire your neighbor's house, his field, his male servant, his female servant, his ox, his donkey, or anything that *is* your neighbor's.'

22 "These words the LORD spoke to all your assembly, in the mountain from the midst of the fire, the cloud, and the thick darkness, with a loud voice; and He added no more. And [a]He wrote them on two tablets of stone and gave them to me.

KJV

The People Afraid of God's Presence
(Ex. 20:18–21)

23 [a]And it came to pass, when ye heard the voice out of the midst of the darkness, (for the mountain did burn with fire,) that ye came near unto me, *even* all the heads of your tribes, and your elders;

24 And ye said, Behold, the LORD our God hath shewed us his glory and his greatness, and [a]we have heard his voice out of the midst of the fire: we have seen this day that God doth talk with man, and he [b]liveth.

25 Now therefore why should we die? for this great fire will consume us: [a]if we hear the voice of the LORD our God any more, then we shall die.

26 [a]For who *is there of* all flesh, that hath heard the voice of the living God speaking out of the midst of the fire, as we *have,* and lived?

27 Go thou near, and hear all that the LORD our God shall say: and [a]speak thou unto us all that the LORD our God shall speak unto thee; and we will hear *it,* and do *it.*

28 And the LORD heard the voice of your words, when ye spake unto me; and the LORD said unto me, I have heard the voice of the words of this people, which they have spoken unto thee: [a]they have well said all that they have spoken.

29 [a]O that there were such an heart in them, that they would fear me, and [b]keep all my commandments always, [c]that it might be well with them, and with their children for ever!

30 Go say to them, Get you into your tents again.

31 But as for thee, stand thou here by me, [a]and I will speak unto thee all the commandments, and the statutes, and the judgments, which thou shalt teach them, that they may do *them* in the land which I give them to possess it.

32 Ye shall observe to do therefore as the LORD your God hath commanded you: [a]ye shall not turn aside to the right hand or to the left.

33 Ye shall walk in [a]all the ways which the LORD your God hath commanded you, that ye may live, [b]and *that it may be* well with you, and *that* ye may prolong *your* days in the land which ye shall possess.

The Greatest Commandment

6 Now these *are* [a]the commandments, the statutes, and the judgments, which the LORD your God commanded to teach you, that ye might do *them* in the land whither ye go to possess it:

2 [a]That thou mightest fear the LORD thy God, to keep all his statutes and his commandments, which I command thee, thou, and thy son, and thy son's son, all the days of thy life; [b]and that thy days may be prolonged.

3 Hear therefore, O Israel, and observe to do *it;* that it may be well with thee, and that ye may [a]increase mightily, [b]as the LORD God of thy fathers hath promised thee, in [c]the land that floweth with milk and honey.

4 [a]Hear, O Israel: The LORD our God *is* one LORD:

5 And [a]thou shalt love the LORD thy God with all thine heart, and [b]with all thy soul, and with all thy might.

6 And [a]these words, which I command thee this day, shall be in thine heart:

7 And [a]thou shalt teach them diligently unto thy children, and shalt talk of them when thou sittest in thine house, and when thou walkest by the way, and when thou liest down, and when thou risest up.

8 [a]And thou shalt bind them for a sign upon thine hand, and they shall be as frontlets between thine eyes.

9 [a]And thou shalt write them upon the posts of thy house, and on thy gates.

23 [a]Ex. 20:18, 19
24 [a]Ex. 19:19 [b]Deut. 4:33; Judg. 13:22
25 [a]Ex. 20:18, 19; Deut. 18:16
26 [a]Deut. 4:33
27 [a]Ex. 20:19; Heb. 12:19
28 [a]Deut. 18:17
29 [a]Deut. 32:29; Ps. 81:13; Is. 48:18 [b]Deut. 11:1 [c]Deut. 4:40
31 [a][Gal. 3:19]
32 [a]Deut. 17:20; 28:14; Josh. 1:7; 23:6; Prov. 4:27
33 [a]Deut. 10:12; Ps. 119:3; Jer. 7:23; Luke 1:6 [b]Deut. 4:40; Eph. 6:3

CHAPTER 6

1 [a]Deut. 12:1
2 [a]Ex. 20:20; Deut. 10:12, 13; [Ps. 111:10; 128:1; Eccl. 12:13] [b]Deut. 4:40
3 [a]Deut. 7:13 [b]Gen. 22:17 [c]Ex. 3:8, 17
4 [a]Deut. 4:35; Mark 12:29; John 17:3; [1 Cor. 8:4, 6]
5 [a]Matt. 22:37; Mark 12:30; Luke 10:27 [b]2 Kin. 23:25
6 [a]Deut. 11:18–20; Ps. 119:11, 98
7 [a]Deut. 4:9; 11:19; [Eph. 6:4]
8 [a]Ex. 12:14; 13:9, 16; Deut. 11:18; Prov. 3:3; 6:21; 7:3
9 [a]Deut. 11:20; Is. 57:8

* **6:4** Or *The* LORD *is our God, the* LORD *alone,* i.e., the only one

NKJV

The People Afraid of God's Presence
(Ex. 20:18–21)

23 [a]"So it was, when you heard the voice from the midst of the darkness, while the mountain was burning with fire, that you came near to me, all the heads of your tribes and your elders.

24 "And you said: 'Surely the LORD our God has shown us His glory and His greatness, and [a]we have heard His voice from the midst of the fire. We have seen this day that God speaks with man; yet he [b]*still* lives.

25 'Now therefore, why should we die? For this great fire will consume us; [a]if we hear the voice of the LORD our God anymore, then we shall die.

26 [a]'For who *is there* of all flesh who has heard the voice of the living God speaking from the midst of the fire, as we *have,* and lived?

27 'You go near and hear all that the LORD our God may say, and [a]tell us all that the LORD our God says to you, and we will hear and do *it.*'

28 "Then the LORD heard the voice of your words when you spoke to me, and the LORD said to me: 'I have heard the voice of the words of this people which they have spoken to you. [a]They are right *in* all that they have spoken.

29 [a]'Oh, that they had such a heart in them that they would fear Me and [b]always keep all My commandments, [c]that it might be well with them and with their children forever!

30 'Go and say to them, "Return to your tents."

31 'But as for you, stand here by Me, [a]and I will speak to you all the commandments, the statutes, and the judgments which you shall teach them, that they may observe *them* in the land which I am giving them to possess.'

32 "Therefore you shall be careful to do as the LORD your God has commanded you; [a]you shall not turn aside to the right hand or to the left.

33 "You shall walk in [a]all the ways which the LORD your God has commanded you, that you may live [b]and *that it may be* well with you, and *that* you may prolong *your* days in the land which you shall possess.

The Greatest Commandment

6 "Now this *is* [a]the commandment, *and these are* the statutes and judgments which the LORD your God has commanded to teach you, that you may observe *them* in the land which you are crossing over to possess,

2 [a]"that you may fear the LORD your God, to keep all His statutes and His commandments which I command you, you and your son and your grandson, all the days of your life, [b]and that your days may be prolonged.

3 "Therefore hear, O Israel, and be careful to observe *it,* that it may be well with you, and that you may [a]multiply greatly [b]as the LORD God of your fathers has promised you—[c]'a land flowing with milk and honey.'

4 [a]"Hear, O Israel: *The LORD our God, the LORD *is* one!

5 [a]"You shall love the LORD your God with all your heart, [b]with all your soul, and with all your strength.

6 "And [a]these words which I command you today shall be in your heart.

7 [a]"You shall teach them diligently to your children, and shall talk of them when you sit in your house, when you walk by the way, when you lie down, and when you rise up.

8 [a]"You shall bind them as a sign on your hand, and they shall be as frontlets between your eyes.

9 [a]"You shall write them on the doorposts of your house and on your gates.

KJV

Caution Against Disobedience

10 And it shall be, when the LORD thy God shall have brought thee into the land which he sware unto thy fathers, to Abraham, to Isaac, and to Jacob, to give thee great and goodly cities, [a]which thou buildedst not,

11 And houses full of all good *things,* which thou filledst not, and wells digged, which thou diggedst not, vineyards and olive trees, which thou plantedst not; [a]when thou shalt have eaten and be full;

12 *Then* beware lest thou forget the [a]LORD, which brought thee forth out of the land of Egypt, from the house of bondage.

13 Thou shalt [a]fear the LORD thy God, and serve him, and [b]shalt swear by his name.

14 Ye shall not go after other gods, [a]of the gods of the people which *are* round about you;

15 (For [a]the LORD thy God *is* a jealous God [b]among you) lest the anger of the LORD thy God be kindled against thee, and destroy thee from off the face of the earth.

16 [a]Ye shall not tempt the LORD your God, [b]as ye tempted *him* in Massah.

17 Ye shall [a]diligently keep the commandments of the LORD your God, and his testimonies, and his statutes, which he hath commanded thee.

18 And thou [a]shalt do *that which is* right and good in the sight of the LORD: that it may be well with thee, and that thou mayest go in and possess the good land which the LORD sware unto thy fathers,

19 [a]To cast out all thine enemies from before thee, as the LORD hath spoken.

20 *And* [a]when thy son asketh thee in time to come, saying, What *mean* the testimonies, and the statutes, and the judgments, which the LORD our God hath commanded you?

21 Then thou shalt say unto thy son, We were Pharaoh's bondmen in Egypt; and the LORD brought us out of Egypt [a]with a mighty hand:

22 And the LORD shewed signs and wonders, great and sore, upon Egypt, upon Pharaoh, and upon all his household, before our eyes:

23 And he brought us out from thence, that he might bring us in, to give us the land which he sware unto our fathers.

24 And the LORD commanded us to do all these statutes, [a]to fear the LORD our God, [b]for our good always, that [c]he might preserve us alive, as *it is* at this day.

25 And [a]it shall be our righteousness, if we observe to do all these commandments before the LORD our God, as he hath commanded us.

A Chosen People
(Ex. 34:10–16)

7 When the LORD thy God shall bring thee into the land whither thou goest to [a]possess it, and hath cast out many [b]nations before thee, [c]the Hittites, and the Girgashites, and the Amorites, and the Canaanites, and the Perizzites, and the Hivites, and the Jebusites, seven nations greater and mightier than thou;

2 And when the LORD thy God shall deliver [a]them before thee; thou shalt smite them, *and* utterly destroy them; [b]thou shalt make no covenant with them, nor shew mercy unto them:

3 [a]Neither shalt thou make marriages with them; thy daughter thou shalt not give unto his son, nor his daughter shalt thou take unto thy son.

4 For they will turn away thy son from following me, that they may serve other gods: [a]so will the anger of the LORD be kindled against you, and destroy thee suddenly.

5 But thus shall ye deal with them; ye shall [a]destroy their altars, and break down their images, and cut down their groves, and burn their graven images with fire.

6 For thou *art* an holy people unto the LORD thy God: [a]the LORD thy God hath chosen thee to

10 [a]Deut. 9:1; 19:1; Josh. 24:13; Ps. 105:44
11 [a]Deut. 8:10; 11:15; 14:29
12 [a]Deut. 8:11–18
13 [a]Deut. 13:4; Matt. 4:10; Luke 4:8 [b]Deut. 5:11; [Is. 45:23; Jer. 4:2]
14 [a]Deut. 13:7
15 [a]Ex. 20:5; Deut. 4:24 [b]Ex. 33:3
16 [a]Matt. 4:7; Luke 4:12 [b][1 Cor. 10:9]
17 [a]Deut. 11:22; Ps. 119:4
18 [a]Ex. 15:26; Deut. 8:7–10
19 [a]Num. 33:52, 53
20 [a]Ex. 13:8, 14
21 [a]Ex. 13:3
24 [a]Deut. 6:2 [b]Deut. 10:12, 13; Job 35:7, 8; Jer. 32:39 [c]Deut. 4:1
25 [a]Deut. 24:13; [Rom. 10:3, 5]

CHAPTER 7

1 [a]Deut. 6:10 [b]Gen. 15:19–21 [c]Ex. 33:2
2 [a]Num. 31:17; Deut. 20:16–18 [b]Ex. 23:32, 33; Josh. 2:14
3 [a]Ex. 34:15, 16; Josh. 23:12; 1 Kin. 11:2; Ezra 9:2
4 [a]Deut. 6:15
5 [a]Ex. 23:24; 34:13; Deut. 12:3
6 [a]Ex. 19:5, 6; Amos 3:2; 1 Pet. 2:9

*

7:5 Heb. *Asherim,* Canaanite deities

NKJV

Caution Against Disobedience

10 "So it shall be, when the LORD your God brings you into the land of which He swore to your fathers, to Abraham, Isaac, and Jacob, to give you large and beautiful cities [a]which you did not build,

11 "houses full of all good things, which you did not fill, hewn-out wells which you did not dig, vineyards and olive trees which you did not plant—[a]when you have eaten and are full—

12 "*then* beware, lest you forget the [a]LORD who brought you out of the land of Egypt, from the house of bondage.

13 "You shall [a]fear the LORD your God and serve Him, and [b]shall take oaths in His name.

14 "You shall not go after other gods, [a]the gods of the peoples who *are* all around you

15 "(for [a]the LORD your God *is* a jealous God [b]among you), lest the anger of the LORD your God be aroused against you and destroy you from the face of the earth.

16 [a]"You shall not tempt the LORD your God [b]as you tempted *Him* in Massah.

17 "You shall [a]diligently keep the commandments of the LORD your God, His testimonies, and His statutes which He has commanded you.

18 "And you [a]shall do *what is* right and good in the sight of the LORD, that it may be well with you, and that you may go in and possess the good land of which the LORD swore to your fathers,

19 [a]"to cast out all your enemies from before you, as the LORD has spoken.

20 [a]"When your son asks you in time to come, saying, 'What *is the meaning of* the testimonies, the statutes, and the judgments which the LORD our God has commanded you?'

21 "then you shall say to your son: 'We were slaves of Pharaoh in Egypt, and the LORD brought us out of Egypt [a]with a mighty hand;

22 'and the LORD showed signs and wonders before our eyes, great and severe, against Egypt, Pharaoh, and all his household.

23 'Then He brought us out from there, that He might bring us in, to give us the land of which He swore to our fathers.

24 'And the LORD commanded us to observe all these statutes, [a]to fear the LORD our God, [b]for our good always, that [c]He might preserve us alive, as *it is* this day.

25 'Then [a]it will be righteousness for us, if we are careful to observe all these commandments before the LORD our God, as He has commanded us.'

A Chosen People
(Ex. 34:10–16)

7 "When the LORD your God brings you into the land which you go to [a]possess, and has cast out many [b]nations before you, [c]the Hittites and the Girgashites and the Amorites and the Canaanites and the Perizzites and the Hivites and the Jebusites, seven nations greater and mightier than you,

2 "and when the LORD your God delivers [a]them over to you, you shall conquer them *and* utterly destroy them. [b]You shall make no covenant with them nor show mercy to them.

3 [a]"Nor shall you make marriages with them. You shall not give your daughter to their son, nor take their daughter for your son.

4 "For they will turn your sons away from following Me, to serve other gods; [a]so the anger of the LORD will be aroused against you and destroy you suddenly.

5 "But thus you shall deal with them: you shall [a]destroy their altars, and break down their *sacred* pillars, and cut down their *wooden images, and burn their carved images with fire.

6 "For you *are* a holy people to the LORD your God; [a]the LORD your God has chosen you

KJV

be a special people unto himself, above all people that *are* upon the face of the earth.

7 The LORD did not set his [a]love upon you, nor choose you, because ye were more in number than any people; for ye *were* [b]the fewest of all people:

8 But [a]because the LORD loved you, and because he would keep [b]the oath which he had sworn unto your fathers, [c]hath the LORD brought you out with a mighty hand, and redeemed you out of the house of bondmen, from the hand of Pharaoh king of Egypt.

9 Know therefore that the LORD thy God, he *is* God, [a]the faithful God, [b]which keepeth covenant and mercy with them that love him and keep his commandments to a thousand generations;

10 And repayeth them that hate him to their face, to destroy them: he will not be [a]slack to him that hateth him, he will repay him to his face.

11 Thou shalt therefore keep the commandments, and the statutes, and the judgments, which I command thee this day, to do them.

Blessings of Obedience
(Lev. 26:1–13; Deut. 28:1–14)

12 Wherefore it shall come to pass, if ye hearken to these judgments, and keep, and do them, that the LORD thy God shall keep unto thee the covenant and the mercy which he sware unto thy fathers:

13 And he will [a]love thee, and bless thee, and multiply thee: [b]he will also bless the fruit of thy womb, and the fruit of thy land, thy corn, and thy wine, and thine oil, the increase of thy kine, and the flocks of thy sheep, in the land which he sware unto thy fathers to give thee.

14 Thou shalt be blessed above all people: there shall not be male or female [a]barren among you, or among your cattle.

15 And the LORD will take away from thee all sickness, and will put none of the [a]evil diseases of Egypt, which thou knowest, upon thee; but will lay them upon all *them* that hate thee.

16 And thou shalt consume all the people which the LORD thy God shall deliver thee; thine eye shall have no pity upon them: neither shalt thou serve their gods; for that *will* [a]*be* a snare unto thee.

17 If thou shalt say in thine heart, These nations *are* more than I; how can I dispossess them?

18 Thou shalt not be afraid of them: *but* shalt well [a]remember what the LORD thy God did unto Pharaoh, and unto all Egypt;

19 [a]The great temptations which thine eyes saw, and the signs, and the wonders, and the mighty hand, and the stretched out arm, whereby the LORD thy God brought thee out: so shall the LORD thy God do unto all the people of whom thou art afraid.

20 [a]Moreover the LORD thy God will send the hornet among them, until they that are left, and hide themselves from thee, be destroyed.

21 Thou shalt not be affrighted at them: for the LORD thy God *is* among you, a mighty God and terrible.

22 And the LORD thy God will put out those nations before thee [a]by little and little: thou mayest not consume them at once, lest the beasts of the field increase upon thee.

23 But the LORD thy God shall deliver them unto thee, and shall destroy them with a mighty destruction, until they be destroyed.

24 And [a]he shall deliver their kings into thine hand, and thou shalt destroy their name from under heaven: [b]there shall no man be able to stand before thee, until thou have destroyed them.

25 The graven images of their gods shall ye burn with fire: thou shalt not [a]desire the silver or gold *that is* on them, nor take *it* unto thee,

7 [a]Deut. 4:37 [b]Deut. 10:22
8 [a]Deut. 10:15 [b]Luke 1:55, 72, 73 [c]Ex. 13:3, 14
9 [a]1 Cor. 1:9; 2 Thess. 3:3; 2 Tim. 2:13 [b]Ex. 20:6; Deut. 5:10; Neh. 1:5; Dan. 9:4
10 [a][2 Pet. 3:10]
13 [a]Ps. 146:8; Prov. 15:9; John 14:21 [b]Deut. 28:4
14 [a]Ex. 23:26
15 [a]Ex. 9:14; 15:26; Deut. 28:27, 60
16 [a]Ex. 23:33; Judg. 8:27; Ps. 106:36
18 [a]Ps. 105:5
19 [a]Deut. 4:34; 29:3
20 [a]Ex. 23:28; Josh. 24:12
22 [a]Ex. 23:29, 30
24 [a]Josh. 10:24, 42; 12:1–24 [b]Josh. 23:9
25 [a]Prov. 23:6

NKJV

to be a people for Himself, a special treasure above all the peoples on the face of the earth.

7 "The LORD did not set His [a]love on you nor choose you because you were more in number than any other people, for you were [b]the least of all peoples;

8 "but [a]because the LORD loves you, and because He would keep [b]the oath which He swore to your fathers, [c]the LORD has brought you out with a mighty hand, and redeemed you from the house of bondage, from the hand of Pharaoh king of Egypt.

9 "Therefore know that the LORD your God, He *is* God, [a]the faithful God [b]who keeps covenant and mercy for a thousand generations with those who love Him and keep His commandments;

10 "and He repays those who hate Him to their face, to destroy them. He will not be [a]slack with him who hates Him; He will repay him to his face.

11 "Therefore you shall keep the commandment, the statutes, and the judgments which I command you today, to observe them.

Blessings of Obedience
(Lev. 26:1–13; Deut. 28:1–14)

12 "Then it shall come to pass, because you listen to these judgments, and keep and do them, that the LORD your God will keep with you the covenant and the mercy which He swore to your fathers.

13 "And He will [a]love you and bless you and multiply you; [b]He will also bless the fruit of your womb and the fruit of your land, your grain and your new wine and your oil, the increase of your cattle and the offspring of your flock, in the land of which He swore to your fathers to give you.

14 "You shall be blessed above all peoples; there shall not be a male or female [a]barren among you or among your livestock.

15 "And the LORD will take away from you all sickness, and will afflict you with none of the [a]terrible diseases of Egypt which you have known, but will lay *them* on all those who hate you.

16 "Also you shall destroy all the peoples whom the LORD your God delivers over to you; your eye shall have no pity on them; nor shall you serve their gods, for that *will* [a]*be* a snare to you.

17 "If you should say in your heart, 'These nations are greater than I; how can I dispossess them?'—

18 "you shall not be afraid of them, *but* you shall [a]remember well what the LORD your God did to Pharaoh and to all Egypt:

19 [a]"the great trials which your eyes saw, the signs and the wonders, the mighty hand and the outstretched arm, by which the LORD your God brought you out. So shall the LORD your God do to all the peoples of whom you are afraid.

20 [a]"Moreover the LORD your God will send the hornet among them until those who are left, who hide themselves from you, are destroyed.

21 "You shall not be terrified of them; for the LORD your God, the great and awesome God, *is* among you.

22 "And the LORD your God will drive out those nations before you [a]little by little; you will be unable to destroy them at once, lest the beasts of the field become *too* numerous for you.

23 "But the LORD your God will deliver them over to you, and will inflict defeat upon them until they are destroyed.

24 "And [a]He will deliver their kings into your hand, and you will destroy their name from under heaven; [b]no one shall be able to stand against you until you have destroyed them.

25 "You shall burn the carved images of their gods with fire; you shall not [a]covet the silver or gold *that is* on them, nor take *it* for yourselves,

KJV

lest thou be snared therein: for it *is* an abomination to the LORD thy God.

26 Neither shalt thou bring an abomination into thine house, lest thou be a cursed thing like it: *but* thou shalt utterly detest it, and thou shalt utterly abhor it; [a]for it *is* a cursed thing.

Remember the LORD Your God

8 All the commandments which I command thee this day [a]shall ye observe to do, that ye may live, and [b]multiply, and go in and possess the land which the LORD sware unto your fathers.

2 And thou shalt remember all the way which the LORD thy God [a]led thee these forty years in the wilderness, to humble thee, *and* [b]to prove thee, [c]to know what *was* in thine heart, whether thou wouldest keep his commandments, or no.

3 And he humbled thee, and [a]suffered thee to hunger, and [b]fed thee with manna, which thou knewest not, neither did thy fathers know; that he might make thee know that man doth [c]not live by bread only, but by every *word* that proceedeth out of the mouth of the LORD doth man live.

4 [a]Thy raiment waxed not old upon thee, neither did thy foot swell, these forty years.

5 [a]Thou shalt also consider in thine heart, that, as a man chasteneth his son, so the LORD thy God chasteneth thee.

6 Therefore thou shalt keep the commandments of the LORD thy God, [a]to walk in his ways, and to fear him.

7 For the LORD thy God bringeth thee into a good land, [a]a land of brooks of water, of fountains and depths that spring out of valleys and hills;

8 A land of wheat, and barley, and vines, and fig trees, and pomegranates; a land of oil olive, and honey;

9 A land wherein thou shalt eat bread without scarceness, thou shalt not lack any *thing* in it; a land whose stones *are* iron, and out of whose hills thou mayest dig brass.

10 [a]When thou hast eaten and art full, then thou shalt bless the LORD thy God for the good land which he hath given thee.

11 Beware that thou forget not the LORD thy God, in not keeping his commandments, and his judgments, and his statutes, which I command thee this day:

12 [a]Lest *when* thou hast eaten and art full, and hast built goodly houses, and dwelt *therein;*

13 And *when* thy herds and thy flocks multiply, and thy silver and thy gold is multiplied, and all that thou hast is multiplied;

14 [a]Then thine heart be lifted up, and thou [b]forget the LORD thy God, which brought thee forth out of the land of Egypt, from the house of bondage;

15 Who [a]led thee through that great and terrible wilderness, [b]*wherein were* fiery serpents, and scorpions, and drought, where *there was* no water; [c]who brought thee forth water out of the rock of flint;

16 Who fed thee in the wilderness with [a]manna, which thy fathers knew not, that he might humble thee, and that he might prove thee, [b]to do thee good at thy latter end;

17 And thou say in thine heart, My power and the might of *mine* hand hath gotten me this wealth.

18 But thou shalt remember the LORD thy God: [a]for *it is* he that giveth thee power to get wealth, [b]that he may establish his covenant which he sware unto thy fathers, as *it is* this day.

19 And it shall be, if thou do at all forget the LORD thy God, and walk after other gods, and serve them, and worship them, [a]I testify against you this day that ye shall surely perish.

20 As the nations which the LORD destroyeth before your face, [a]so shall ye perish; because ye

26 [a]Deut. 13:17

CHAPTER 8

1 [a]Deut. 4:1; 6:24 [b]Deut. 30:16
2 [a]Deut. 1:3; 2:7; 29:5; Ps. 136:16; Amos 2:10 [b]Ex. 16:4 [c][John 2:25]
3 [a]Ex. 16:2, 3 [b]Ex. 16:12, 14, 35 [c]Matt. 4:4; Luke 4:4
4 [a]Deut. 29:5; Neh. 9:21
5 [a]2 Sam. 7:14; Ps. 89:30–33; Prov. 3:11, 12; Heb. 12:5–11; Rev. 3:19
6 [a][Deut. 5:33]
7 [a]Deut. 11:9–12; Jer. 2:7
10 [a]Deut. 6:11, 12
12 [a]Deut. 28:47; Prov. 30:9; Hos. 13:6
14 [a]1 Cor. 4:7 [b]Deut. 8:11; Ps. 106:21
15 [a]Is. 63:12–14 [b]Num. 21:6 [c]Ex. 17:6; Num. 20:11
16 [a]Ex. 16:15 [b]Jer. 24:5, 6; [Heb. 12:11]
18 [a]Prov. 10:22; Hos. 2:8 [b]Deut. 7:8, 12
19 [a]Deut. 4:26; 30:18
20 [a][Dan. 9:11, 12]

NKJV

lest you be snared by it; for it *is* an abomination to the LORD your God.

26 "Nor shall you bring an abomination into your house, lest you be doomed to destruction like it. You shall utterly detest it and utterly abhor it, [a]for it *is* an accursed thing.

Remember the LORD Your God

8 "Every commandment which I command you today [a]you must be careful to observe, that you may live and [b]multiply, and go in and possess the land of which the LORD swore to your fathers.

2 "And you shall remember that the LORD your God [a]led you all the way these forty years in the wilderness, to humble you *and* [b]test you, [c]to know what *was* in your heart, whether you would keep His commandments or not.

3 "So He humbled you, [a]allowed you to hunger, and [b]fed you with manna which you did not know nor did your fathers know, that He might make you know that man shall [c]not live by bread alone; but man lives by every *word* that proceeds from the mouth of the LORD.

4 [a]"Your garments did not wear out on you, nor did your foot swell these forty years.

5 [a]"You should know in your heart that as a man chastens his son, *so* the LORD your God chastens you.

6 "Therefore you shall keep the commandments of the LORD your God, [a]to walk in His ways and to fear Him.

7 "For the LORD your God is bringing you into a good land, [a]a land of brooks of water, of fountains and springs, that flow out of valleys and hills;

8 "a land of wheat and barley, of vines and fig trees and pomegranates, a land of olive oil and honey;

9 "a land in which you will eat bread without scarcity, in which you will lack nothing; a land whose stones *are* iron and out of whose hills you can dig copper.

10 [a]"When you have eaten and are full, then you shall bless the LORD your God for the good land which He has given you.

11 "Beware that you do not forget the LORD your God by not keeping His commandments, His judgments, and His statutes which I command you today,

12 [a]"lest—*when* you have eaten and are full, and have built beautiful houses and dwell *in them;*

13 "and *when* your herds and your flocks multiply, and your silver and your gold are multiplied, and all that you have is multiplied;

14 [a]"when your heart is lifted up, and you [b]forget the LORD your God who brought you out of the land of Egypt, from the house of bondage;

15 "who [a]led you through that great and terrible wilderness, [b]*in which were* fiery serpents and scorpions and thirsty land where there was no water; [c]who brought water for you out of the flinty rock;

16 "who fed you in the wilderness with [a]manna, which your fathers did not know, that He might humble you and that He might test you, [b]to do you good in the end—

17 "then you say in your heart, 'My power and the might of my hand have gained me this wealth.'

18 "And you shall remember the LORD your God, [a]for *it is* He who gives you power to get wealth, [b]that He may establish His covenant which He swore to your fathers, as *it is* this day.

19 "Then it shall be, if you by any means forget the LORD your God, and follow other gods, and serve them and worship them, [a]I testify against you this day that you shall surely perish.

20 "As the nations which the LORD destroys before you, [a]so you shall perish, because you

KJV

would not be obedient unto the voice of the LORD your God.

Israel's Rebellions Reviewed
(*Ex. 32:1–35*)

9 Hear, O Israel: Thou *art* to pass over Jordan this day, to go in to possess nations greater and mightier than thyself, cities great and fenced up to heaven,

2 A people great and tall, the [a]children of the Anakims, whom thou knowest, and *of whom* thou hast heard *say,* Who can stand before the children of Anak!

3 Understand therefore this day, that the LORD thy God *is* he which [a]goeth over before thee; *as* a [b]consuming fire [c]he shall destroy them, and he shall bring them down before thy face: [d]so shalt thou drive them out, and destroy them quickly, as the LORD hath said unto thee.

4 [a]Speak not thou in thine heart, after that the LORD thy God hath cast them out from before thee, saying, For my righteousness the LORD hath brought me in to possess this land: but [b]for the wickedness of these nations the LORD doth drive them out from before thee.

5 [a]Not for thy righteousness, or for the uprightness of thine heart, dost thou go to possess their land: but for the wickedness of these nations the LORD thy God doth drive them out from before thee, and that he may perform the [b]word which the LORD sware unto thy fathers, Abraham, Isaac, and Jacob.

6 Understand therefore, that the LORD thy God giveth thee not this good land to possess it for thy righteousness; for thou *art* a [a]stiffnecked people.

7 Remember, *and* forget not, how thou [a]provokedst the LORD thy God to wrath in the wilderness: [b]from the day that thou didst depart out of the land of Egypt, until ye came unto this place, ye have been rebellious against the LORD.

8 Also [a]in Horeb ye provoked the LORD to wrath, so that the LORD was angry with you to have destroyed you.

9 [a]When I was gone up into the mount to receive the tables of stone, *even* the tables of the covenant which the LORD made with you, then I abode in the mount forty days and [b]forty nights, I neither did eat bread nor drink water:

10 [a]And the LORD delivered unto me two tables of stone written with the finger of God; and on them *was written* according to all the words, which the LORD spake with you in the mount out of the midst of the fire [b]in the day of the assembly.

11 And it came to pass at the end of forty days and forty nights, *that* the LORD gave me the two tables of stone, *even* the tables of the covenant.

12 And the LORD said unto me, [a]Arise, get thee down quickly from hence; for thy people which thou hast brought forth out of Egypt have corrupted *themselves;* they are [b]quickly turned aside out of the way which I commanded them; they have made them a molten image.

13 Furthermore [a]the LORD spake unto me, saying, I have seen this people, and, behold, [b]it *is* a stiffnecked people:

14 [a]Let me alone, that I may destroy them, and [b]blot out their name from under heaven: [c]and I will make of thee a nation mightier and greater than they.

15 [a]So I turned and came down from the mount, and [b]the mount burned with fire: and the two tables of the covenant *were* in my two hands.

16 And [a]I looked, and, behold, ye had sinned against the LORD your God, *and* had made you a molten calf: ye had turned aside quickly out of the way which the LORD had commanded you.

17 And I took the two tables, and cast them out of my two hands, and [a]brake them before your eyes.

CHAPTER 9

2 [a]Num. 13:22, 28, 33; Josh. 11:21, 22
3 [a]Deut. 1:33; 31:3; Josh. 3:11; 5:14; John 10:4 [b]Deut. 4:24; Heb. 12:29 [c]Deut. 7:24 [d]Ex. 23:31
4 [a]Deut. 8:17; [Rom. 11:6, 20; 1 Cor. 4:4, 7] [b]Gen. 15:16; Lev. 18:3, 24–30; Deut. 12:31; 18:9–14
5 [a][Titus 3:5] [b]Gen. 50:24
6 [a]Ex. 34:9; Deut. 31:27
7 [a]Num. 14:22 [b]Ex. 14:11
8 [a]Ex. 32:1–8; Ps. 106:19
9 [a]Ex. 24:12, 15; Deut. 5:2–22 [b]Ex. 24:18
10 [a]Ex. 31:18; Deut. 4:13 [b]Ex. 19:17
12 [a]Ex. 32:7, 8 [b]Deut. 31:29
13 [a]Ex. 32:9 [b]Deut. 9:6
14 [a]Ex. 32:10 [b]Deut. 29:20 [c]Num. 14:12
15 [a]Ex. 32:15–19 [b]Ex. 19:18
16 [a]Ex. 32:19
17 [a]Ex. 32:19

NKJV

would not be obedient to the voice of the LORD your God.

Israel's Rebellions Reviewed
(*Ex. 32:1–35*)

9 "Hear, O Israel: You *are* to cross over the Jordan today, and go in to dispossess nations greater and mightier than yourself, cities great and fortified up to heaven,

2 "a people great and tall, the [a]descendants of the Anakim, whom you know, and *of whom* you heard *it said,* 'Who can stand before the descendants of Anak?'

3 "Therefore understand today that the LORD your God *is* He who [a]goes over before you *as* a [b]consuming fire. [c]He will destroy them and bring them down before you; [d]so you shall drive them out and destroy them quickly, as the LORD has said to you.

4 [a]"Do not think in your heart, after the LORD your God has cast them out before you, saying, 'Because of my righteousness the LORD has brought me in to possess this land'; but *it is* [b]because of the wickedness of these nations *that* the LORD is driving them out from before you.

5 [a]"*It is* not because of your righteousness or the uprightness of your heart *that* you go in to possess their land, but because of the wickedness of these nations *that* the LORD your God drives them out from before you, and that He may fulfill the [b]word which the LORD swore to your fathers, to Abraham, Isaac, and Jacob.

6 "Therefore understand that the LORD your God is not giving you this good land to possess because of your righteousness, for you *are* a [a]stiff-necked people.

7 "Remember! Do not forget how you [a]provoked the LORD your God to wrath in the wilderness. [b]From the day that you departed from the land of Egypt until you came to this place, you have been rebellious against the LORD.

8 "Also [a]in Horeb you provoked the LORD to wrath, so that the LORD was angry *enough* with you to have destroyed you.

9 [a]"When I went up into the mountain to receive the tablets of stone, the tablets of the covenant which the LORD made with you, then I stayed on the mountain forty days and [b]forty nights. I neither ate bread nor drank water.

10 [a]"Then the LORD delivered to me two tablets of stone written with the finger of God, and on them *were* all the words which the LORD had spoken to you on the mountain from the midst of the fire [b]in the day of the assembly.

11 "And it came to pass, at the end of forty days and forty nights, *that* the LORD gave me the two tablets of stone, the tablets of the covenant.

12 "Then the LORD said to me, [a]'Arise, go down quickly from here, for your people whom you brought out of Egypt have acted corruptly; they have [b]quickly turned aside from the way which I commanded them; they have made themselves a molded image.'

13 "Furthermore [a]the LORD spoke to me, saying, 'I have seen this people, and indeed [b]they are a stiff-necked people.

14 [a]'Let Me alone, that I may destroy them and [b]blot out their name from under heaven; [c]and I will make of you a nation mightier and greater than they.'

15 [a]"So I turned and came down from the mountain, and [b]the mountain burned with fire; and the two tablets of the covenant *were* in my two hands.

16 "And [a]I looked, and behold, you had sinned against the LORD your God—had made for yourselves a molded calf! You had turned aside quickly from the way which the LORD had commanded you.

17 "Then I took the two tablets and threw them out of my two hands and [a]broke them before your eyes.

KJV

18 And I [a]fell down before the LORD, as at the first, forty days and forty nights: I did neither eat bread, nor drink water, because of all your sins which ye sinned, in doing wickedly in the sight of the LORD, to provoke him to anger.

19 [a]For I was afraid of the anger and hot displeasure, wherewith the LORD was wroth against you to destroy you. [b]But the LORD hearkened unto me at that time also.

20 And the LORD was very angry with Aaron to have destroyed him: and I prayed for Aaron also the same time.

21 And I took your sin, the calf which ye had made, and burnt it with fire, and stamped it, *and* ground *it* very small, *even* until it was as small as dust: and I [a]cast the dust thereof into the brook that descended out of the mount.

22 And at [a]Taberah, and at [b]Massah, and at [c]Kibroth–hattaavah, ye provoked the LORD to wrath.

23 Likewise [a]when the LORD sent you from Kadesh–barnea, saying, Go up and possess the land which I have given you; then ye rebelled against the commandment of the LORD your God, and [b]ye believed him not, nor hearkened to his voice.

24 [a]Ye have been rebellious against the LORD from the day that I knew you.

25 [a]Thus I fell down before the LORD forty days and forty nights, as I fell down *at the first;* because the LORD had said he would destroy you.

26 I prayed therefore unto the LORD, and said, O Lord GOD, destroy not thy people and [a]thine inheritance, which thou hast redeemed through thy greatness, which thou hast brought forth out of Egypt with a mighty hand.

27 Remember thy servants, Abraham, Isaac, and Jacob; look not unto the stubbornness of this people, nor to their wickedness, nor to their sin:

28 Lest the land whence thou broughtest us out say, Because the LORD was not able to bring them into the land which he promised them, and because he hated them, he hath brought them out to slay them in the wilderness.

29 Yet they *are* thy people and thine inheritance, which thou broughtest out by thy mighty power and by thy stretched out arm.

The Second Pair of Tablets
(Ex. 34:1–9)

10 At that time the LORD said unto me, Hew thee two tables of stone like unto the first, and come up unto me into the mount, and make thee an [a]ark of wood.

2 And I will write on the tables the words that were in the first tables which thou brakest, and [a]thou shalt put them in the ark.

3 And I made an ark *of* shittim wood, and hewed two tables of stone like unto the first, and went up into the mount, having the two tables in mine hand.

4 And he wrote on the tables, according to the first writing, the ten commandments, [a]which the LORD spake unto you in the mount out of the midst of the fire in the day of the assembly: and the LORD gave them unto me.

5 And I turned myself and [a]came down from the mount, and [b]put the tables in the ark which I had made; [c]and there they be, as the LORD commanded me.

6 And the children of Israel took their journey from Beeroth of the children of Jaakan to Mosera: there Aaron [a]died, and there he was buried; and Eleazar his son ministered in the priest's office in his stead.

7 [a]From thence they journeyed unto Gudgodah; and from Gudgodah to Jotbath, a land of rivers of waters.

8 At that time [a]the LORD separated the tribe of Levi, [b]to bear the ark of the covenant of the LORD, [c]to stand before the LORD to minister unto him, and [d]to bless in his name, unto this day.

18 [a]Ex. 34:28; Ps. 106:23
19 [a]Ex. 32:10, 11; Heb. 12:21 [b]Ex. 32:14
21 [a]Ex. 32:20
22 [a]Num. 11:1, 3 [b]Ex. 17:7 [c]Num. 11:4, 34
23 [a]Num. 13:3 [b]Ps. 106:24, 25
24 [a]Deut. 9:7; 31:27
25 [a]Deut. 9:18
26 [a]Deut. 32:9

CHAPTER 10
1 [a]Ex. 25:10
2 [a]Ex. 25:16, 21
4 [a]Ex. 20:1; 34:28
5 [a]Ex. 34:29 [b]Ex. 40:20 [c]1 Kin. 8:9
6 [a]Num. 20:25–28; 33:38
7 [a]Num. 33:32–34
8 [a]Num. 3:6 [b]Num. 4:5, 15; 10:21 [c]Deut. 18:5 [d]Num. 6:23

NKJV

18 "And I [a]fell down before the LORD, as at the first, forty days and forty nights; I neither ate bread nor drank water, because of all your sin which you committed in doing wickedly in the sight of the LORD, to provoke Him to anger.

19 [a]"For I was afraid of the anger and hot displeasure with which the LORD was angry with you, to destroy you. [b]But the LORD listened to me at that time also.

20 "And the LORD was very angry with Aaron *and* would have destroyed him; so I prayed for Aaron also at the same time.

21 "Then I took your sin, the calf which you had made, and burned it with fire and crushed it *and* ground *it* very small, until it was as fine as dust; and I [a]threw its dust into the brook that descended from the mountain.

22 "Also at [a]Taberah and [b]Massah and [c]Kibroth Hattaavah you provoked the LORD to wrath.

23 "Likewise, [a]when the LORD sent you from Kadesh Barnea, saying, 'Go up and possess the land which I have given you,' then you rebelled against the commandment of the LORD your God, and [b]you did not believe Him nor obey His voice.

24 [a]"You have been rebellious against the LORD from the day that I knew you.

25 [a]"Thus I prostrated myself before the LORD; forty days and forty nights I kept prostrating myself, because the LORD had said He would destroy you.

26 "Therefore I prayed to the LORD, and said: 'O Lord GOD, do not destroy Your people and [a]Your inheritance whom You have redeemed through Your greatness, whom You have brought out of Egypt with a mighty hand.

27 'Remember Your servants, Abraham, Isaac, and Jacob; do not look on the stubbornness of this people, or on their wickedness or their sin,

28 'lest the land from which You brought us should say, "Because the LORD was not able to bring them to the land which He promised them, and because He hated them, He has brought them out to kill them in the wilderness."

29 'Yet they *are* Your people and Your inheritance, whom You brought out by Your mighty power and by Your outstretched arm.'

The Second Pair of Tablets
(Ex. 34:1–9)

10 "At that time the LORD said to me, 'Hew for yourself two tablets of stone like the first, and come up to Me on the mountain and make yourself an [a]ark of wood.

2 'And I will write on the tablets the words that were on the first tablets, which you broke; and [a]you shall put them in the ark.'

3 "So I made an ark of acacia wood, hewed two tablets of stone like the first, and went up the mountain, having the two tablets in my hand.

4 "And He wrote on the tablets according to the first writing, the Ten Commandments, [a]which the LORD had spoken to you in the mountain from the midst of the fire in the day of the assembly; and the LORD gave them to me.

5 "Then I turned and [a]came down from the mountain, and [b]put the tablets in the ark which I had made; [c]and there they are, just as the LORD commanded me."

6 (Now the children of Israel journeyed from the wells of Bene Jaakan to Moserah, where Aaron [a]died, and where he was buried; and Eleazar his son ministered as priest in his stead.

7 [a]From there they journeyed to Gudgodah, and from Gudgodah to Jotbathah, a land of rivers of water.

8 At that time [a]the LORD separated the tribe of Levi [b]to bear the ark of the covenant of the LORD, [c]to stand before the LORD to minister to Him and [d]to bless in His name, to this day.

KJV

9 [a]Wherefore Levi hath no part nor inheritance with his brethren; the LORD *is* his inheritance, according as the LORD thy God promised him.

10 And [a]I stayed in the mount, according to the first time, forty days and forty nights; and [b]the LORD hearkened unto me at that time also, *and* the LORD would not destroy thee.

11 [a]And the LORD said unto me, Arise, take *thy* journey before the people, that they may go in and possess the land, which I sware unto their fathers to give unto them.

The Essence of the Law

12 And now, Israel, [a]what doth the LORD thy God require of thee, but to fear the LORD thy God, to walk in all his ways, and to [b]love him, and to serve the LORD thy God with all thy heart and with all thy soul,

13 To keep the commandments of the LORD, and his statutes, which I command thee this day [a]for thy good?

14 Behold, the heaven and the heaven of heavens *is* the [a]LORD's thy God, the earth *also,* with all that therein *is.*

15 Only the LORD had a delight in thy fathers to love them, and he chose their seed after them, *even* you above all people, as *it is* this day.

16 Circumcise therefore the foreskin of your [a]heart, and be no more [b]stiffnecked.

17 For the LORD your God *is* [a]God of gods, and [b]Lord of lords, a great God, [c]a mighty, and a terrible, which [d]regardeth not persons, nor taketh reward:

18 [a]He doth execute the judgment of the fatherless and widow, and loveth the stranger, in giving him food and raiment.

19 Love ye therefore the stranger: for ye were strangers in the land of Egypt.

20 [a]Thou shalt fear the LORD thy God; him shalt thou serve, and to him shalt thou cleave, and swear by his name.

21 He *is* thy praise, and he *is* thy God, that hath done for thee these great and terrible things, which thine eyes have seen.

22 Thy fathers went down into Egypt with threescore and ten persons; and now the LORD thy God hath made thee as the stars of heaven for multitude.

Love and Obedience Rewarded

11 Therefore thou shalt love the LORD thy God, and keep his charge, and his statutes, and his judgments, and his commandments, alway.

2 And know ye this day: for *I speak* not with your children which have not known, and which have not seen the chastisement of the LORD your God, his greatness, his mighty hand, and his stretched out arm,

3 And his miracles, and his acts, which he did in the midst of Egypt unto Pharaoh the king of Egypt, and unto all his land;

4 And what he did unto the army of Egypt, unto their horses, and to their chariots; [a]how he made the water of the Red sea to overflow them as they pursued after you, and *how* the LORD hath destroyed them unto this day;

5 And what he did unto you in the wilderness, until ye came into this place;

6 And [a]what he did unto Dathan and Abiram, the sons of Eliab, the son of Reuben: how the earth opened her mouth, and swallowed them up, and their households, and their tents, and all the substance that *was* in their possession, in the midst of all Israel:

7 But your eyes have [a]seen all the great acts of the LORD which he did.

8 Therefore shall ye keep all the commandments which I command you this day, that ye may [a]be strong, and go in and possess the land, whither ye go to possess it;

9 And [a]that ye may prolong *your* days in

9 [a]Num. 18:20, 24; Deut. 18:1, 2; Ezek. 44:28
10 [a]Ex. 34:28; Deut. 9:18 [b]Ex. 32:14
11 [a]Ex. 33:1
12 [a]Mic. 6:8 [b]Deut. 6:5; Matt. 22:37; 1 Tim. 1:5
13 [a]Deut. 6:24
14 [a][Neh. 9:6; Ps. 68:33; 115:16]
16 [a]Lev. 26:41; Deut. 30:6; Jer. 4:4; Rom. 2:28, 29 [b]Deut. 9:6, 13
17 [a]Deut. 4:35, 39; Is. 44:8; 46:9; Dan. 2:47; 1 Cor. 8:5, 6 [b]Rev. 19:16 [c]Deut. 7:21 [d]Acts 10:34
18 [a]Ex. 22:22–24; Ps. 68:5; 146:9
20 [a]Matt. 4:10

CHAPTER 11

4 [a]Ex. 14:28; Ps. 106:11
6 [a]Num. 16:1–35; Ps. 106:16–18
7 [a]Deut. 10:21; 29:2
8 [a]Deut. 31:6, 7, 23; Josh. 1:6, 7
9 [a]Deut. 4:40; 5:16, 33; 6:2; Prov. 10:27

NKJV

9 [a]Therefore Levi has no portion nor inheritance with his brethren; the LORD *is* his inheritance, just as the LORD your God promised him.)

10 "As at the first time, [a]I stayed in the mountain forty days and forty nights; [b]the LORD also heard me at that time, *and* the LORD chose not to destroy you.

11 [a]"Then the LORD said to me, 'Arise, begin *your* journey before the people, that they may go in and possess the land which I swore to their fathers to give them.'

The Essence of the Law

12 "And now, Israel, [a]what does the LORD your God require of you, but to fear the LORD your God, to walk in all His ways and to [b]love Him, to serve the LORD your God with all your heart and with all your soul,

13 "*and* to keep the commandments of the LORD and His statutes which I command you today [a]for your good?

14 "Indeed heaven and the highest heavens belong to the [a]LORD your God, *also* the earth with all that *is* in it.

15 "The LORD delighted only in your fathers, to love them; and He chose their descendants after them, you above all peoples, as *it is* this day.

16 "Therefore circumcise the foreskin of your [a]heart, and be [b]stiff-necked no longer.

17 "For the LORD your God *is* [a]God of gods and [b]Lord of lords, the great God, [c]mighty and awesome, who [d]shows no partiality nor takes a bribe.

18 [a]"He administers justice for the fatherless and the widow, and loves the stranger, giving him food and clothing.

19 "Therefore love the stranger, for you were strangers in the land of Egypt.

20 [a]"You shall fear the LORD your God; you shall serve Him, and to Him you shall hold fast, and take oaths in His name.

21 "He *is* your praise, and He *is* your God, who has done for you these great and awesome things which your eyes have seen.

22 "Your fathers went down to Egypt with seventy persons, and now the LORD your God has made you as the stars of heaven in multitude.

Love and Obedience Rewarded

11 "Therefore you shall love the LORD your God, and keep His charge, His statutes, His judgments, and His commandments always.

2 "Know today that *I do* not *speak* with your children, who have not known and who have not seen the chastening of the LORD your God, His greatness and His mighty hand and His outstretched arm—

3 "His signs and His acts which He did in the midst of Egypt, to Pharaoh king of Egypt, and to all his land;

4 "what He did to the army of Egypt, to their horses and their chariots: [a]how He made the waters of the Red Sea overflow them as they pursued you, and *how* the LORD has destroyed them to this day;

5 "what He did for you in the wilderness until you came to this place;

6 "and [a]what He did to Dathan and Abiram the sons of Eliab, the son of Reuben: how the earth opened its mouth and swallowed them up, their households, their tents, and all the substance that *was* in their possession, in the midst of all Israel—

7 "but your eyes have [a]seen every great act of the LORD which He did.

8 "Therefore you shall keep every commandment which I command you today, that you may [a]be strong, and go in and possess the land which you cross over to possess,

9 "and [a]that you may prolong *your* days in

KJV

the land, [b]which the LORD sware unto your fathers
to give unto them and to their seed, [c]a land that
floweth with milk and honey.
10 For the land, whither thou goest in to possess it, *is* not as the land of Egypt, from whence
ye came out, where thou sowedst thy seed, and
wateredst *it* with thy foot, as a garden of herbs:
11 [a]But the land, whither ye go to possess
it, *is* a land of hills and valleys, *and* drinketh water
of the rain of heaven:
12 A land which the LORD thy God careth for:
[a]the eyes of the LORD thy God *are* always upon
it, from the beginning of the year even unto the
end of the year.
13 And it shall come to pass, if ye shall
hearken diligently unto my commandments
which I command you this day, to love the LORD
your God, and to serve him with all your heart
and with all your soul,
14 That [a]I will give *you* the rain of your land
in his due season, [b]the first rain and the latter
rain, that thou mayest gather in thy corn, and thy
wine, and thine oil.
15 [a]And I will send grass in thy fields for thy
cattle, that thou mayest [b]eat and be full.
16 Take heed to yourselves, [a]that your heart
be not deceived, and ye turn aside, and [b]serve
other gods, and worship them;
17 And *then* [a]the LORD's wrath be kindled
against you, and he [b]shut up the heaven, that
there be no rain, and that the land yield not her
fruit; and *lest* [c]ye perish quickly from off the good
land which the LORD giveth you.
18 Therefore [a]shall ye lay up these my words
in your heart and in your [b]soul, and [c]bind them
for a sign upon your hand, that they may be as
frontlets between your eyes.
19 [a]And ye shall teach them your children,
speaking of them when thou sittest in thine house,
and when thou walkest by the way, when thou
liest down, and when thou risest up.
20 [a]And thou shalt write them upon the door
posts of thine house, and upon thy gates:
21 That [a]your days may be multiplied, and
the days of your children, in the land which the
LORD sware unto your fathers to give them, as
[b]the days of heaven upon the earth.
22 For if [a]ye shall diligently keep all these
commandments which I command you, to do
them, to love the LORD your God, to walk in all
his ways, and [b]to cleave unto him;
23 Then will the LORD [a]drive out all these nations from before you, and ye shall [b]possess
greater nations and mightier than yourselves.
24 [a]Every place whereon the soles of your
feet shall tread shall be your's: [b]from the wilderness and Lebanon, from the river, the river Euphrates, even unto the uttermost sea shall your
coast be.
25 There shall no man be able to [a]stand before you: *for* the LORD your God shall lay the fear
of you and the [b]dread of you upon all the land
that ye shall tread upon, as he hath said unto you.
26 [a]Behold, I set before you this day a blessing and a curse;
27 [a]A blessing, if ye obey the commandments
of the LORD your God, which I command you this
day:
28 And a [a]curse, if ye will not obey the commandments of the LORD your God, but turn aside
out of the way which I command you this day,
to go after other gods, which ye have not known.
29 And it shall come to pass, when the LORD
thy God hath brought thee in unto the land
whither thou goest to possess it, that thou shalt
put the [a]blessing upon mount Gerizim, and the
[b]curse upon mount Ebal.
30 *Are* they not on the other side Jordan, by
the way where the sun goeth down, in the land
of the Canaanites, which dwell in the champaign
over against Gilgal, [a]beside the plains of Moreh?
31 For ye shall pass over Jordan to go in to

9 [b]Deut. 9:5 [c]Ex. 3:8
11 [a]Deut. 8:7
12 [a]1 Kin. 9:3
14 [a]Lev. 26:4; Deut. 28:12 [b]Joel 2:23; James 5:7
15 [a]Ps. 104:14 [b]Deut. 6:11; Joel 2:19
16 [a]Deut. 29:18; Job 31:27 [b]Deut. 8:19
17 [a]Deut. 6:15; 9:19 [b]Deut. 28:24; 1 Kin. 8:35; 2 Chr. 6:26; 7:13 [c]Deut. 4:26; 2 Chr. 36:14–20
18 [a]Deut. 6:6–9 [b]Ps. 119:2, 34 [c]Deut. 6:8
19 [a]Deut. 4:9, 10; 6:7; Prov. 22:6
20 [a]Deut. 6:9
21 [a]Deut. 4:40 [b]Ps. 72:5; 89:29; Prov. 3:2; 4:10; 9:11
22 [a]Deut. 11:1 [b]Deut. 10:20
23 [a]Deut. 4:38 [b]Deut. 9:1
24 [a]Josh. 1:3; 14:9 [b]Gen. 15:18; Ex. 23:31; Deut. 1:7, 8
25 [a]Deut. 7:24 [b]Ex. 23:27; Deut. 2:25; Josh. 2:9–11
26 [a]Deut. 30:1, 15, 19
27 [a]Deut. 28:1–14
28 [a]Deut. 28:15–68
29 [a]Deut. 27:12, 13; Josh. 8:33 [b]Deut. 27:13–26
30 [a]Gen. 12:6

NKJV

the land [b]which the LORD swore to give your fathers, to them and their descendants, [c]'a land
flowing with milk and honey.'
10 "For the land which you go to possess *is*
not like the land of Egypt from which you have
come, where you sowed your seed and watered
it by foot, as a vegetable garden;
11 [a]"but the land which you cross over to
possess *is* a land of hills and valleys, which drinks
water from the rain of heaven,
12 "a land for which the LORD your God
cares; [a]the eyes of the LORD your God *are* always
on it, from the beginning of the year to the very
end of the year.
13 'And it shall be that if you earnestly obey
My commandments which I command you today,
to love the LORD your God and serve Him with
all your heart and with all your soul,
14 'then [a]I* will give *you* the rain for your
land in its season, [b]the early rain and the latter
rain, that you may gather in your grain, your new
wine, and your oil.
15 [a]'And I will send grass in your fields for
your livestock, that you may [b]eat and be filled.'
16 "Take heed to yourselves, [a]lest your heart
be deceived, and you turn aside and [b]serve other
gods and worship them,
17 "lest [a]the LORD's anger be aroused against
you, and He [b]shut up the heavens so that there
be no rain, and the land yield no produce, and
[c]you perish quickly from the good land which the
LORD is giving you.
18 "Therefore [a]you shall lay up these words
of mine in your heart and in your [b]soul, and [c]bind
them as a sign on your hand, and they shall be
as frontlets between your eyes.
19 [a]"You shall teach them to your children,
speaking of them when you sit in your house,
when you walk by the way, when you lie down,
and when you rise up.
20 [a]"And you shall write them on the doorposts of your house and on your gates,
21 "that [a]your days and the days of your children may be multiplied in the land of which the
LORD swore to your fathers to give them, like [b]the
days of the heavens above the earth.
22 "For if [a]you carefully keep all these commandments which I command you to do—to love
the LORD your God, to walk in all His ways, and
[b]to hold fast to Him—
23 "then the LORD will [a]drive out all these
nations from before you, and you will [b]dispossess
greater and mightier nations than yourselves.
24 [a]"Every place on which the sole of your
foot treads shall be yours: [b]from the wilderness
and Lebanon, from the river, the River Euphrates,
even to the *Western Sea, shall be your territory.
25 "No man shall be able to [a]stand against
you; the LORD your God will put the [b]dread of
you and the fear of you upon all the land where
you tread, just as He has said to you.
26 [a]"Behold, I set before you today a blessing
and a curse:
27 [a]"the blessing, if you obey the commandments of the LORD your God which I command
you today;
28 "and the [a]curse, if you do not obey the
commandments of the LORD your God, but turn
aside from the way which I command you today,
to go after other gods which you have not known.
29 "Now it shall be, when the LORD your God
has brought you into the land which you go to
possess, that you shall put the [a]blessing on Mount
Gerizim and the [b]curse on Mount Ebal.
30 "*Are* they not on the other side of the Jordan, toward the setting sun, in the land of the
Canaanites who dwell in the plain opposite Gilgal,
[a]beside the terebinth trees of Moreh?
31 "For you will cross over the Jordan and

11:14 So with MT, Tg.; Sam., LXX, Vg. *He*
11:24 Mediterranean

KJV

possess the land which the LORD your God giveth you, and ye shall possess it, and dwell therein.

32 And ye shall observe to do all the statutes and judgments which I set before you this day.

A Prescribed Place of Worship

12 These [a]*are* the statutes and judgments, which ye shall observe to do in the land, which the LORD God of thy fathers giveth thee to possess it, [b]all the days that ye live upon the earth.

2 [a]Ye shall utterly destroy all the places, wherein the nations which ye shall possess served their gods, [b]upon the high mountains, and upon the hills, and under every green tree:

3 And [a]ye shall overthrow their altars, and break their pillars, and burn their groves with fire; and ye shall hew down the graven images of their gods, and destroy the names of them out of that place.

4 Ye shall not do [a]so unto the LORD your God.

5 But unto the [a]place which the LORD your God shall choose out of all your tribes to put his name there, *even* unto his [b]habitation shall ye seek, and thither thou shalt come:

6 And [a]thither ye shall bring your burnt offerings, and your sacrifices, and your tithes, and heave offerings of your hand, and your vows, and your freewill offerings, and the [b]firstlings of your herds and of your flocks:

7 And [a]there ye shall eat before the LORD your God, and [b]ye shall rejoice in all that ye put your hand unto, ye and your households, wherein the LORD thy God hath blessed thee.

8 Ye shall not do after all *the things* that we do here this day, [a]every man whatsoever *is* right in his own eyes.

9 For ye are not as yet come to the [a]rest and to the inheritance, which the LORD your God giveth you.

10 But *when* ye go over Jordan, and dwell in the land which the LORD your God giveth you to inherit, and *when* he giveth you [a]rest from all your enemies round about, so that ye dwell in safety;

11 Then there shall be a place which the LORD your God shall choose to cause his name to dwell there; thither shall ye bring all that I command you; your burnt offerings, and your sacrifices, your tithes, and the heave offering of your hand, and all your choice vows which ye vow unto the LORD:

12 And [a]ye shall rejoice before the LORD your God, ye, and your sons, and your daughters, and your menservants, and your maidservants, and the [b]Levite that *is* within your gates; forasmuch as he hath no part nor inheritance with you.

13 Take heed to thyself that thou offer not thy burnt offerings in every place that thou seest:

14 But in the place which the LORD shall choose in one of thy tribes, there thou shalt offer thy burnt offerings, and there thou shalt do all that I command thee.

15 Notwithstanding [a]thou mayest kill and eat flesh in all thy gates, whatsoever thy soul lusteth after, according to the blessing of the LORD thy God which he hath given thee: [b]the unclean and the clean may eat thereof, [c]as of the roebuck, and as of the hart.

16 [a]Only ye shall not eat the blood; ye shall pour it upon the earth as water.

17 Thou mayest not eat within thy gates the tithe of thy corn, or of thy wine, or of thy oil, or the firstlings of thy herds or of thy flock, nor any of thy vows which thou vowest, nor thy freewill offerings, or heave offering of thine hand:

18 But thou must eat them before the LORD thy God in the place which the LORD thy God shall

CHAPTER 12

1 [a]Deut. 6:1 [b]Deut. 4:9, 10; 1 Kin. 8:40
2 [a]Ex. 34:13 [b]2 Kin. 16:4; 17:10, 11
3 [a]Num. 33:52; Deut. 7:5; Judg. 2:2
4 [a]Deut. 12:31
5 [a]Ex. 20:24 [b]Ex. 15:13; 1 Sam. 2:29
6 [a]Lev. 17:3, 4 [b]Deut. 14:23
7 [a]Deut. 14:26 [b]Deut. 12:12, 18
8 [a]Judg. 17:6; 21:25
9 [a]Deut. 3:20; 25:19; Ps. 95:11
10 [a]Josh. 11:23
12 [a]Deut. 12:18; 26:11 [b]Deut. 10:9; 14:29
15 [a]Deut. 12:21 [b]Deut. 12:22 [c]Deut. 14:5
16 [a]Gen. 9:4; Lev. 7:26; 17:10–12; 1 Sam. 14:33; Acts 15:20, 29

NKJV

go in to possess the land which the LORD your God is giving you, and you will possess it and dwell in it.

32 "And you shall be careful to observe all the statutes and judgments which I set before you today.

A Prescribed Place of Worship

12 "These [a]*are* the statutes and judgments which you shall be careful to observe in the land which the LORD God of your fathers is giving you to possess, [b]all the days that you live on the earth.

2 [a]"You shall utterly destroy all the places where the nations which you shall dispossess served their gods, [b]on the high mountains and on the hills and under every green tree.

3 "And [a]you shall destroy their altars, break their *sacred* pillars, and burn their wooden images with fire; you shall cut down the carved images of their gods and destroy their names from that place.

4 "You shall not [a]worship the LORD your God *with* such *things*.

5 "But you shall seek the [a]place where the LORD your God chooses, out of all your tribes, to put His name for His [b]dwelling place; and there you shall go.

6 [a]"There you shall take your burnt offerings, your sacrifices, your tithes, the heave offerings of your hand, your vowed offerings, your freewill offerings, and the [b]firstborn of your herds and flocks.

7 "And [a]there you shall eat before the LORD your God, and [b]you shall rejoice in all to which you have put your hand, you and your households, in which the LORD your God has blessed you.

8 "You shall not at all do as we are doing here today—[a]every man doing whatever *is* right in his own eyes—

9 "for as yet you have not come to the [a]rest and the inheritance which the LORD your God is giving you.

10 "But *when* you cross over the Jordan and dwell in the land which the LORD your God is giving you to inherit, and He gives you [a]rest from all your enemies round about, so that you dwell in safety,

11 "then there will be the place where the LORD your God chooses to make His name abide. There you shall bring all that I command you: your burnt offerings, your sacrifices, your tithes, the heave offerings of your hand, and all your choice offerings which you vow to the LORD.

12 "And [a]you shall rejoice before the LORD your God, you and your sons and your daughters, your male and female servants, and the [b]Levite who *is* within your gates, since he has no portion nor inheritance with you.

13 "Take heed to yourself that you do not offer your burnt offerings in every place that you see;

14 "but in the place which the LORD chooses, in one of your tribes, there you shall offer your burnt offerings, and there you shall do all that I command you.

15 "However, [a]you may slaughter and eat meat within all your gates, whatever your heart desires, according to the blessing of the LORD your God which He has given you; [b]the unclean and the clean may eat of it, [c]of the gazelle and the deer alike.

16 [a]"Only you shall not eat the blood; you shall pour it on the earth like water.

17 "You may not eat within your gates the tithe of your grain or your new wine or your oil, of the firstborn of your herd or your flock, of any of your offerings which you vow, of your freewill offerings, or of the heave offering of your hand.

18 "But you must eat them before the LORD your God in the place which the LORD your God

KJV

choose, thou, and thy son, and thy daughter, and thy manservant, and thy maidservant, and the Levite that *is* within thy gates: and thou shalt rejoice before the LORD thy God in all that thou puttest thine hands unto.

19 Take heed to thyself that thou forsake not the Levite as long as thou livest upon the earth.

20 When the LORD thy God shall [a]enlarge thy border, as he hath promised thee, and thou shalt say, I will eat flesh, because thy soul longeth to eat flesh; thou mayest eat flesh, whatsoever thy soul lusteth after.

21 If the place which the LORD thy God hath chosen to put his name there be too far from [a]thee, then thou shalt kill of thy herd and of thy flock, which the LORD hath given thee, as I have commanded thee, and thou shalt eat in thy gates whatsoever thy soul lusteth after.

22 Even as the roebuck and the hart is eaten, so thou shalt eat them: the unclean and the clean shall eat *of* them alike.

23 Only be sure that thou eat not the blood: [a]for the blood *is* the life; and thou mayest not eat the life with the flesh.

24 Thou shalt not eat it; thou shalt pour it upon the earth as water.

25 Thou shalt not eat it; [a]that it may go well with thee, and with thy children after thee, [b]when thou shalt do *that which is* right in the sight of the LORD.

26 Only thy [a]holy things which thou hast, and thy vows, thou shalt take, and go unto the place which the LORD shall choose:

27 And [a]thou shalt offer thy burnt offerings, the flesh and the blood, upon the altar of the LORD thy God: and the blood of thy sacrifices shall be poured out upon the altar of the LORD thy God, and thou shalt eat the flesh.

28 Observe and hear all these words which I command thee, [a]that it may go well with thee, and with thy children after thee for ever, when thou doest *that which is* good and right in the sight of the LORD thy God.

Beware of False Gods

29 When [a]the LORD thy God shall cut off the nations from before thee, whither thou goest to possess them, and thou succeedest them, and dwellest in their land;

30 Take heed to thyself that thou be not snared by following them, after that they be destroyed from before thee; and that thou enquire not after their gods, saying, How did these nations serve their gods? even so will I do likewise.

31 [a]Thou shalt not do so unto the LORD thy God: for every abomination to the LORD, which he hateth, have they done unto their gods; for [b]even their sons and their daughters they have burnt in the fire to their gods.

32 What thing soever I command you, observe to do it: [a]thou shalt not add thereto, nor diminish from it.

Punishment of Apostates

13 If there arise among you a prophet, or a [a]dreamer of dreams, [b]and giveth thee a sign or a wonder,

2 And [a]the sign or the wonder come to pass, whereof he spake unto thee, saying, Let us go after other gods, which thou hast not known, and let us serve them;

3 Thou shalt not hearken unto the words of that prophet, or that dreamer of dreams: for the LORD your God [a]proveth you, to know whether ye love the LORD your God with all your heart and with all your soul.

4 Ye shall [a]walk after the LORD your God, and fear him, and keep his commandments, and obey his voice, and ye shall serve him, and [b]cleave unto him.

5 And [a]that prophet, or that dreamer of dreams, shall be put to death; because he hath

---

20 [a]Gen. 15:18; Ex. 34:24; Deut. 11:24; 19:8
21 [a]Deut. 14:24
23 [a]Gen. 9:4; Lev. 17:10–14; Deut. 12:16
25 [a]Deut. 4:40; 6:18; Is. 3:10 [b]Ex. 15:26; 1 Kin. 11:38
26 [a]Num. 5:9, 10; 18:19
27 [a]Lev. 1:5, 9, 13, 17
28 [a]Deut. 12:25
29 [a]Ex. 23:23; Deut. 19:1; Josh. 23:4
31 [a]Lev. 18:3, 26, 30; 20:1, 2 [b]Deut. 18:10; Ps. 106:37; Jer. 32:35
32 [a]Deut. 4:2; 13:18; Josh. 1:7; Prov. 30:6; Rev. 22:18, 19

CHAPTER 13

1 [a]Num. 12:6; Jer. 23:28; Zech. 10:2 [b]Matt. 24:24; Mark 13:22; 2 Thess. 2:9
2 [a]Deut. 18:22
3 [a]Ex. 20:20; Deut. 8:2, 16
4 [a]Deut. 10:12, 20; 2 Kin. 23:3 [b]Deut. 30:20
5 [a]Deut. 18:20; Jer. 14:15

NKJV

chooses, you and your son and your daughter, your male servant and your female servant, and the Levite who *is* within your gates; and you shall rejoice before the LORD your God in all to which you put your hands.

19 "Take heed to yourself that you do not forsake the Levite as long as you live in your land.

20 "When the LORD your God [a]enlarges your border as He has promised you, and you say, 'Let me eat meat,' because you long to eat meat, you may eat as much meat as your heart desires.

21 "If the place where the LORD your God chooses to put His name is too far from [a]you, then you may slaughter from your herd and from your flock which the LORD has given you, just as I have commanded you, and you may eat within your gates as much as your heart desires.

22 "Just as the gazelle and the deer are eaten, so you may eat them; the unclean and the clean alike may eat them.

23 "Only be sure that you do not eat the blood, [a]for the blood *is* the life; you may not eat the life with the meat.

24 "You shall not eat it; you shall pour it on the earth like water.

25 "You shall not eat it, [a]that it may go well with you and your children after you, [b]when you do *what is* right in the sight of the LORD.

26 "Only the [a]holy things which you have, and your vowed offerings, you shall take and go to the place which the LORD chooses.

27 "And [a]you shall offer your burnt offerings, the meat and the blood, on the altar of the LORD your God; and the blood of your sacrifices shall be poured out on the altar of the LORD your God, and you shall eat the meat.

28 "Observe and obey all these words which I command you, [a]that it may go well with you and your children after you forever, when you do *what is* good and right in the sight of the LORD your God.

Beware of False Gods

29 "When [a]the LORD your God cuts off from before you the nations which you go to dispossess, and you displace them and dwell in their land,

30 "take heed to yourself that you are not ensnared to follow them, after they are destroyed from before you, and that you do not inquire after their gods, saying, 'How did these nations serve their gods? I also will do likewise.'

31 [a]"You shall not worship the LORD your God in that way; for every abomination to the LORD which He hates they have done to their gods; for [b]they burn even their sons and daughters in the fire to their gods.

32 "Whatever I command you, be careful to observe it; [a]you shall not add to it nor take away from it.

Punishment of Apostates

13 "If there arises among you a prophet or a [a]dreamer of dreams, [b]and he gives you a sign or a wonder,

2 "and [a]the sign or the wonder comes to pass, of which he spoke to you, saying, 'Let us go after other gods'—which you have not known—'and let us serve them,'

3 "you shall not listen to the words of that prophet or that dreamer of dreams, for the LORD your God [a]is testing you to know whether you love the LORD your God with all your heart and with all your soul.

4 "You shall [a]walk after the LORD your God and fear Him, and keep His commandments and obey His voice; you shall serve Him and [b]hold fast to Him.

5 "But [a]that prophet or that dreamer of dreams shall be put to death, because he has spo-

KJV

spoken to turn *you* away from the LORD your God, which brought you out of the land of Egypt, and redeemed you out of the house of bondage, to thrust thee out of the way which the LORD thy God commanded thee to walk in. [b]So shalt thou put the evil away from the midst of thee.

6 [a]If thy brother, the son of thy mother, or thy son, or thy daughter, or [b]the wife of thy bosom, or thy friend, [c]which *is* as thine own soul, entice thee secretly, saying, Let us go and serve other gods, which thou hast not known, thou, nor thy fathers;

7 *Namely,* of the gods of the people which *are* round about you, nigh unto thee, or far off from thee, from the *one* end of the earth even unto the *other* end of the earth;

8 Thou shalt [a]not consent unto him, nor hearken unto him; neither shall thine eye pity him, neither shalt thou spare, neither shalt thou conceal him:

9 But thou shalt surely kill him; thine hand shall be first upon him to put him to [a]death, and afterwards the hand of all the people.

10 And thou shalt stone him with stones, that he die; because he hath sought to thrust thee away from the LORD thy God, which brought thee out of the land of Egypt, from the house of bondage.

11 And all Israel shall hear, and [a]fear, and shall do no more any such wickedness as this is among you.

12 [a]If thou shalt hear *say* in one of thy cities, which the LORD thy God hath given thee to dwell there, saying,

13 *Certain* men, the children of Belial, are gone out from among you, and have withdrawn the inhabitants of their city, saying, Let us go and serve other gods, which ye have not known;

14 Then shalt thou enquire, and make search, and ask diligently; and, behold, *if it be* truth, *and* the thing certain, *that* such abomination is wrought among you;

15 Thou shalt surely smite the inhabitants of that city with the edge of the sword, destroying it utterly, and all that *is* therein, and the cattle thereof, with the edge of the sword.

16 And thou shalt gather all the spoil of it into the midst of the street thereof, and shalt [a]burn with fire the city, and all the spoil thereof every whit, for the LORD thy God: and it shall be [b]an heap for ever; it shall not be built again.

17 And [a]there shall cleave nought of the cursed thing to thine hand: that the LORD may [b]turn from the fierceness of his anger, and shew thee mercy, and have compassion upon thee, and multiply thee, as he hath sworn unto thy fathers;

18 When thou shalt hearken to the voice of the LORD thy God, [a]to keep all his commandments which I command thee this day, to do *that which is* right in the eyes of the LORD thy God.

Improper Mourning

14 Ye *are* [a]the children of the LORD your God: [b]ye shall not cut yourselves, nor make any baldness between your eyes for the dead.

2 [a]For thou *art* an holy people unto the LORD thy God, and the LORD hath chosen thee to be a peculiar people unto himself, above all the nations that *are* upon the earth.

Clean and Unclean Meat
(*Lev. 11:1–47*)

3 [a]Thou shalt not eat any abominable thing.

4 [a]These *are* the beasts which ye shall eat: the ox, the sheep, and the goat,

5 The hart, and the roebuck, and the fallow deer, and the wild goat, and the pygarg, and the wild ox, and the chamois.

6 And every beast that parteth the hoof, and cleaveth the cleft into two claws, *and* cheweth the cud among the beasts, that ye shall eat.

7 Nevertheless these ye shall not eat of them that chew the cud, or of them that divide the

5 [b]Deut. 17:5, 7; 1 Cor. 5:13
6 [a]Deut. 17:2 [b]Gen. 16:5 [c]1 Sam. 18:1, 3
8 [a]Deut. 7:16; Prov. 1:10
9 [a]Lev. 24:14; Deut. 17:7
11 [a]Deut. 17:13
12 [a]Judg. 20:1–48
16 [a]Josh. 6:24 [b]Josh. 8:28; Is. 17:1; 25:2; Jer 49:2
17 [a]Josh. 6:18 [b]Josh. 7:26
18 [a]Deut. 12:25, 28, 32

CHAPTER 14
1 [a][Rom. 8:16; Gal. 3:26] [b]Lev. 19:28; 21:1–5
2 [a]Lev. 20:26; Deut. 7:6; [Rom. 12:1]
3 [a]Ezek. 4:14
4 [a]Lev. 11:2–45

*14:5 Or *addax*

NKJV

ken in order to turn *you* away from the LORD your God, who brought you out of the land of Egypt and redeemed you from the house of bondage, to entice you from the way in which the LORD your God commanded you to walk. [b]So you shall put away the evil from your midst.

6 [a]"If your brother, the son of your mother, your son or your daughter, [b]the wife of your bosom, or your friend [c]who is as your own soul, secretly entices you, saying, 'Let us go and serve other gods,' which you have not known, neither you nor your fathers,

7 "of the gods of the people which *are* all around you, near to you or far off from you, from *one* end of the earth to the *other* end of the earth,

8 "you shall [a]not consent to him or listen to him, nor shall your eye pity him, nor shall you spare him or conceal him;

9 "but you shall surely kill him; your hand shall be first against him to put him to [a]death, and afterward the hand of all the people.

10 "And you shall stone him with stones until he dies, because he sought to entice you away from the LORD your God, who brought you out of the land of Egypt, from the house of bondage.

11 "So all Israel shall hear and [a]fear, and not again do such wickedness as this among you.

12 [a]"If you hear someone in one of your cities, which the LORD your God gives you to dwell in, saying,

13 'Corrupt men have gone out from among you and enticed the inhabitants of their city, saying, "Let us go and serve other gods" '—which you have not known—

14 "then you shall inquire, search out, and ask diligently. And *if it is* indeed true *and* certain *that* such an abomination was committed among you,

15 "you shall surely strike the inhabitants of that city with the edge of the sword, utterly destroying it, all that is in it and its livestock—with the edge of the sword.

16 "And you shall gather all its plunder into the middle of the street, and completely [a]burn with fire the city and all its plunder, for the LORD your God. It shall be [b]a heap forever; it shall not be built again.

17 [a]"So none of the accursed things shall remain in your hand, that the LORD may [b]turn from the fierceness of His anger and show you mercy, have compassion on you and multiply you, just as He swore to your fathers,

18 "because you have listened to the voice of the LORD your God, [a]to keep all His commandments which I command you today, to do *what is* right in the eyes of the LORD your God.

Improper Mourning

14 "You *are* [a]the children of the LORD your God; [b]you shall not cut yourselves nor shave the front of your head for the dead.

2 [a]"For you *are* a holy people to the LORD your God, and the LORD has chosen you to be a people for Himself, a special treasure above all the peoples who *are* on the face of the earth.

Clean and Unclean Meat
(*Lev. 11:1–47*)

3 [a]"You shall not eat any detestable thing.

4 [a]"These *are* the animals which you may eat: the ox, the sheep, the goat,

5 "the deer, the gazelle, the roe deer, the wild goat, the *mountain goat, the antelope, and the mountain sheep.

6 "And you may eat every animal with cloven hooves, having the hoof split into two parts, *and that* chews the cud, among the animals.

7 "Nevertheless, of those that chew the cud or have cloven hooves, you shall not eat, *such as*

KJV

cloven hoof; *as* the camel, and the hare, and the
coney: for they chew the cud, but divide not the
hoof; *therefore* they *are* unclean unto you.
8 And the swine, because it divideth the
hoof, yet cheweth not the cud, it *is* unclean unto
you: ye shall not eat of their flesh, [a]nor touch their
dead carcase.
9 [a]These ye shall eat of all that *are* in the
waters: all that have fins and scales shall ye eat:
10 And whatsoever hath not fins and scales
ye may not eat; it *is* unclean unto you.
11 *Of* all clean birds ye shall eat.
12 [a]But these *are they* of which ye shall not
eat: the eagle, and the ossifrage, and the ospray,
13 And the glede, and the kite, and the vulture after his kind,
14 And every raven after his kind,
15 And the owl, and the night hawk, and the
cuckow, and the hawk after his kind,
16 The little owl, and the great owl, and the
swan,
17 And the pelican, and the gier eagle, and
the cormorant,
18 And the stork, and the heron after her
kind, and the lapwing, and the bat.
19 And [a]every creeping thing that flieth *is*
unclean unto you: [b]they shall not be eaten.
20 *But of* all clean fowls ye may eat.
21 [a]Ye shall not eat *of* any thing that dieth
of itself: thou shalt give it unto the stranger that
is in thy gates, that he may eat it; or thou mayest
sell it unto an alien: [b]for thou *art* an holy people
unto the LORD thy God. [c]Thou shalt not seethe a
kid in his mother's milk.

Tithing Principles

22 [a]Thou shalt truly tithe all the increase of
thy seed, that the field bringeth forth year by year.
23 [a]And thou shalt eat before the LORD thy
God, in the place which he shall choose to place
his name there, the tithe of thy corn, of thy wine,
and of thine oil, and [b]the firstlings of thy herds
and of thy flocks; that thou mayest learn to fear
the LORD thy God always.
24 And if the way be too long for thee, so
that thou art not able to carry it; *or* [a]if the place
be too far from thee, which the LORD thy God shall
choose to set his name there, when the LORD thy
God hath blessed thee:
25 Then shalt thou turn *it* into money, and
bind up the money in thine hand, and shalt go
unto the place which the LORD thy God shall
choose:
26 And thou shalt bestow that money for
whatsoever thy soul lusteth after, for oxen, or for
sheep, or for wine, or for strong drink, or for
whatsoever thy soul desireth: and thou shalt eat
there before the LORD thy God, and thou shalt [a]re-
joice, thou, and thine household,
27 And the [a]Levite that *is* within thy gates;
thou shalt not forsake him; for he hath no part
nor inheritance with thee.
28 [a]At the end of three years thou shalt bring
forth all the [b]tithe of thine increase the same year,
and shalt lay *it* up within thy gates:
29 And the Levite, (because he hath no part
nor inheritance with thee,) and the stranger, and
the fatherless, and the widow, which *are* within
thy gates, shall come, and shall eat and be satisfied; that the LORD thy God may bless thee in all
the work of thine hand which thou doest.

Debts Canceled Every Seven Years
(Ex. 21:1–11; Lev. 25:1–7)

15 At the end of [a]*every* seven years thou shalt
make a release.
2 And this *is* the manner of the release: Every creditor that lendeth *ought* unto his neighbour
shall release *it;* he shall not exact *it* of his neighbour, or of his brother; because it is called the
LORD's release.
3 Of a foreigner thou mayest exact *it again:*

8 [a]Lev. 11:26, 27
9 [a]Lev. 11:9
12 [a]Lev. 11:13
19 [a]Lev. 11:20 [b]Lev. 11:23
21 [a]Lev. 17:15; 22:8; Ezek. 4:14; 44:31 [b]Deut. 14:2 [c]Ex. 23:19; 34:26
22 [a]Lev. 27:30; Deut. 12:6, 17; Neh. 10:37
23 [a]Deut. 12:5–7 [b]Deut. 15:19, 20
24 [a]Deut. 12:5, 21
26 [a]Deut. 12:7
27 [a]Deut. 12:12
28 [a]Deut. 26:12; Amos 4:4 [b]Num. 18:21–24

CHAPTER 15

1 [a]Ex. 21:2; 23:10, 11; Lev. 25:4; Jer. 34:14

NKJV

these: the camel, the hare, and the rock hyrax;
for they chew the cud but do not have cloven
hooves; they *are* unclean for you.
8 "Also the swine is unclean for you, because it has cloven hooves, yet *does* not *chew* the
cud; you shall not eat their flesh [a]or touch their
dead carcasses.
9 [a]"These you may eat of all that *are* in the
waters: you may eat all that have fins and scales.
10 "And whatever does not have fins and
scales you shall not eat; it *is* unclean for you.
11 "All clean birds you may eat.
12 [a]"But these you shall not eat: the eagle,
the vulture, the buzzard,
13 "the red kite, the falcon, and the kite after
their kinds;
14 "every raven after its kind;
15 "the ostrich, the short-eared owl, the sea
gull, and the hawk after their kinds;
16 "the little owl, the screech owl, the white
owl,
17 "the jackdaw, the carrion vulture, the
fisher owl,
18 "the stork, the heron after its kind, and
the hoopoe and the bat.
19 "Also [a]every creeping thing that flies is
unclean for you; [b]they shall not be eaten.
20 "You may eat all clean birds.
21 [a]"You shall not eat anything that dies *of*
itself; you may give it to the alien who *is* within
your gates, that he may eat it, or you may sell it
to a foreigner; [b]for you *are* a holy people to the
LORD your God. [c]You shall not boil a young goat
in its mother's milk.

Tithing Principles

22 [a]"You shall truly tithe all the increase of
your grain that the field produces year by year.
23 [a]"And you shall eat before the LORD your
God, in the place where He chooses to make His
name abide, the tithe of your grain and your new
wine and your oil, of [b]the firstborn of your herds
and your flocks, that you may learn to fear the
LORD your God always.
24 "But if the journey is too long for you, so
that you are not able to carry *the tithe, or* [a]if the
place where the LORD your God chooses to put
His name is too far from you, when the LORD your
God has blessed you,
25 "then you shall exchange *it* for money,
take the money in your hand, and go to the place
which the LORD your God chooses.
26 "And you shall spend that money for
whatever your heart desires: for oxen or sheep,
for wine or similar drink, for whatever your heart
desires; you shall eat there before the LORD your
God, and you shall [a]rejoice, you and your
household.
27 "You shall not forsake the [a]Levite who *is*
within your gates, for he has no part nor inheritance with you.
28 [a]"At the end of *every* third year you shall
bring out the [b]tithe of your produce of that year
and store *it* up within your gates.
29 "And the Levite, because he has no portion nor inheritance with you, and the stranger
and the fatherless and the widow who *are* within
your gates, may come and eat and be satisfied,
that the LORD your God may bless you in all the
work of your hand which you do.

Debts Canceled Every Seven Years
(Ex. 21:1–11; Lev. 25:1–7)

15 "At the end of [a]*every* seven years you shall
grant a release *of debts.*
2 "And this *is* the form of the release: Every
creditor who has lent *anything* to his neighbor
shall release *it;* he shall not require *it* of his neighbor or his brother, because it is called the LORD's
release.
3 "Of a foreigner you may require *it;* but

KJV

but *that* which is thine with thy brother thine
hand shall release;
4 Save when there shall be no poor among
you; for the LORD shall greatly [a]bless thee in the
land which the LORD thy God giveth thee *for* an
inheritance to possess it:
5 Only if thou carefully hearken unto the
voice of the LORD thy God, to observe to do all
these commandments which I command thee this
day.
6 For the LORD thy God blesseth thee, as he
promised thee: and [a]thou shalt lend unto many
nations, but thou shalt not borrow; and thou shalt
reign over many nations, but they shall not reign
over thee.

Generosity to the Poor

7 If there be among you a poor man of one
of thy brethren within any of thy gates in thy land
which the LORD thy God giveth thee, [a]thou shalt
not harden thine heart, nor shut thine hand from
thy poor brother:
8 But [a]thou shalt open thine hand wide unto
him, and shalt surely lend him sufficient for his
need, *in that* which he wanteth.
9 Beware that there be not a thought in thy
wicked heart, saying, The seventh year, the year
of release, is at hand; and thine [a]eye be evil
against thy poor brother, and thou givest him
nought; and [b]he cry unto the LORD against thee,
and [c]it be sin unto thee.
10 Thou shalt surely give him, and [a]thine
heart shall not be grieved when thou givest unto
him: because that [b]for this thing the LORD thy God
shall bless thee in all thy works, and in all that
thou puttest thine hand unto.
11 For [a]the poor shall never cease out of the
land: therefore I command thee, saying, Thou
shalt open thine hand wide unto thy brother, to
thy poor, and to thy needy, in thy land.

The Law Concerning Bondservants

12 *And* [a]if thy brother, an Hebrew man, or
an Hebrew woman, be [b]sold unto thee, and serve
thee six years; then in the seventh year thou shalt
let him go free from thee.
13 And when thou sendest him out free from
thee, thou shalt not let him go away empty:
14 Thou shalt furnish him liberally out of thy
flock, and out of thy floor, and out of thy winepress: *of that* wherewith the LORD thy God hath
[a]blessed thee thou shalt give unto him.
15 And [a]thou shalt remember that thou wast
a bondman in the land of Egypt, and the LORD
thy God redeemed thee: therefore I command thee
this thing to day.
16 And it shall be, [a]if he say unto thee, I will
not go away from thee; because he loveth thee
and thine house, because he is well with thee;
17 Then thou shalt take an aul, and thrust *it*
through his ear unto the door, and he shall be
thy servant for ever. And also unto thy maidservant thou shalt do likewise.
18 It shall not seem hard unto thee, when
thou sendest him away free from thee; for he hath
been worth [a]a double hired servant *to thee,* in
serving thee six years: and the LORD thy God shall
bless thee in all that thou doest.

The Law Concerning Firstborn Animals

19 [a]All the firstling males that come of thy
herd and of thy flock thou shalt sanctify unto the
LORD thy God: thou shalt do no work with the
firstling of thy bullock, nor shear the firstling of
thy sheep.
20 [a]Thou shalt eat *it* before the LORD thy God
year by year in the place which the LORD shall
choose, thou and thy household.
21 [a]And if there be *any* blemish therein, *as
if it be* lame, or blind, *or have* any ill blemish,
thou shalt not sacrifice it unto the LORD thy God.
22 Thou shalt eat it within thy gates: [a]the

4 [a]Deut. 7:13
6 [a]Deut. 28:12, 44
7 [a]Ex. 23:6; Lev. 25:35–37; Deut. 24:12–14; [1 John 3:17]
8 [a]Matt. 5:42; Gal. 2:10
9 [a]Deut. 28:54, 56 [b]Ex. 22:23; Deut. 24:15; Job 34:28; Ps. 12:5; James 5:4 [c][Matt. 25:41, 42]
10 [a]2 Cor. 9:5, 7 [b]Deut. 14:29; Ps. 41:1; Prov. 22:9
11 [a]Matt. 26:11; Mark 14:7; John 12:8
12 [a]Ex. 21:2–6; Jer. 34:14 [b]Lev. 25:39–46
14 [a]Prov. 10:22
15 [a]Deut. 5:15
16 [a]Ex. 21:5, 6
18 [a]Is. 16:14
19 [a]Ex. 13:2, 12
20 [a]Lev. 7:15–18; Deut. 12:5; 14:23
21 [a]Lev. 22:19–25; Deut. 17:1
22 [a]Deut. 12:15, 16, 22

NKJV

you shall give up your claim to what is owed by
your brother,
4 "except when there may be no poor
among you; for the LORD will greatly [a]bless you
in the land which the LORD your God is giving
you to possess *as* an inheritance—
5 "only if you carefully obey the voice of
the LORD your God, to observe with care all these
commandments which I command you today.
6 "For the LORD your God will bless you just
as He promised you; [a]you shall lend to many nations, but you shall not borrow; you shall reign
over many nations, but they shall not reign over
you.

Generosity to the Poor

7 "If there is among you a poor man of your
brethren, within any of the gates in your land
which the LORD your God is giving you, [a]you shall
not harden your heart nor shut your hand from
your poor brother,
8 "but [a]you shall open your hand wide to
him and willingly lend him sufficient for his need,
whatever he needs.
9 "Beware lest there be a wicked thought
in your heart, saying, 'The seventh year, the year
of release, is at hand,' and your [a]eye be evil
against your poor brother and you give him nothing, and [b]he cry out to the LORD against you, and
[c]it become sin among you.
10 "You shall surely give to him, and [a]your
heart should not be grieved when you give to him,
because [b]for this thing the LORD your God will
bless you in all your works and in all to which
you put your hand.
11 "For [a]the poor will never cease from the
land; therefore I command you, saying, 'You shall
open your hand wide to your brother, to your poor
and your needy, in your land.'

The Law Concerning Bondservants

12 [a]"If your brother, a Hebrew man, or a Hebrew woman, is [b]sold to you and serves you six
years, then in the seventh year you shall let him
go free from you.
13 "And when you send him away free from
you, you shall not let him go away empty-handed;
14 "you shall supply him liberally from your
flock, from your threshing floor, and from your
winepress. *From what* the LORD has [a]blessed you
with, you shall give to him.
15 [a]"You shall remember that you were a
slave in the land of Egypt, and the LORD your God
redeemed you; therefore I command you this
thing today.
16 "And [a]if it happens that he says to you,
'I will not go away from you,' because he loves
you and your house, since he prospers with you,
17 "then you shall take an awl and thrust *it*
through his ear to the door, and he shall be your
servant forever. Also to your female servant you
shall do likewise.
18 "It shall not seem hard to you when you
send him away free from you; for he has been
worth [a]a double hired servant in serving you six
years. Then the LORD your God will bless you in
all that you do.

The Law Concerning Firstborn Animals

19 [a]"All the firstborn males that come from
your herd and your flock you shall sanctify to the
LORD your God; you shall do no work with the
firstborn of your herd, nor shear the firstborn of
your flock.
20 [a]"You and your household shall eat *it* before the LORD your God year by year in the place
which the LORD chooses.
21 [a]"But if there is a defect in it, *if it is* lame
or blind *or has* any serious defect, you shall not
sacrifice it to the LORD your God.
22 "You may eat it within your gates; [a]the

KJV

unclean and the clean *person shall eat it* alike, as the roebuck, and as the hart.

23 Only thou shalt not eat the blood thereof; thou shalt pour it upon the ground as water.

The Passover Reviewed
(Ex. 12:1–20; 23:14–19; 34:18–26)

16 Observe the [a]month of Abib, and keep the passover unto the LORD thy God: for [b]in the month of Abib the LORD thy God brought thee forth out of Egypt by night.

2 Thou shalt therefore sacrifice the passover unto the LORD thy God, of the flock and [a]the herd, in the [b]place which the LORD shall choose to place his name there.

3 Thou shalt eat no leavened bread with it; [a]seven days shalt thou eat unleavened bread therewith, *even* the bread of affliction; for thou camest forth out of the land of Egypt in haste: that thou mayest [b]remember the day when thou camest forth out of the land of Egypt all the days of thy life.

4 [a]And there shall be no leavened bread seen with thee in all thy coast seven days; neither shall there *any thing* of the flesh, which thou sacrificedst the first day at even, remain all night until the [b]morning.

5 Thou mayest not sacrifice the passover within any of thy gates, which the LORD thy God giveth thee:

6 But at the place which the LORD thy God shall choose to place his name in, there thou shalt sacrifice the passover [a]at even, at the going down of the sun, at the season that thou camest forth out of Egypt.

7 And thou shalt roast and eat *it* [a]in the place which the LORD thy God shall choose: and thou shalt turn in the morning, and go unto thy tents.

8 Six days thou shalt eat unleavened bread: and [a]on the seventh day *shall be* a solemn assembly to the LORD thy God: thou shalt do no work *therein.*

The Feast of Weeks Reviewed
(Ex. 34:22; Lev. 23:15–21; Num. 28:26–31)

9 Seven weeks shalt thou number unto thee: begin to number the seven weeks from *such time as* thou beginnest *to put* the sickle to the corn.

10 And thou shalt keep the [a]feast of weeks unto the LORD thy God with a tribute of a freewill offering of thine hand, which thou shalt give *unto the LORD thy God,* [b]according as the LORD thy God hath blessed thee:

11 And [a]thou shalt rejoice before the LORD thy God, thou, and thy son, and thy daughter, and thy manservant, and thy maidservant, and the Levite that *is* within thy gates, and the stranger, and the fatherless, and the widow, that *are* among you, in the place which the LORD thy God hath chosen to place his name there.

12 [a]And thou shalt remember that thou wast a bondman in Egypt: and thou shalt observe and do these statutes.

The Feast of Tabernacles Reviewed
(Lev. 23:33–43; Num. 29:12–40)

13 [a]Thou shalt observe the feast of tabernacles seven days, after that thou hast gathered in thy corn and thy wine:

14 And [a]thou shalt rejoice in thy feast, thou, and thy son, and thy daughter, and thy manservant, and thy maidservant, and the Levite, the stranger, and the fatherless, and the widow, that *are* within thy gates.

15 [a]Seven days shalt thou keep a solemn feast unto the LORD thy God in the place which the LORD shall choose: because the LORD thy God shall bless thee in all thine increase, and in all the works of thine hands, therefore thou shalt surely rejoice.

16 [a]Three times in a year shall all thy males

CHAPTER 16

1 [a]Ex. 12:2 [b]Ex. 13:4
2 [a]Num. 28:19 [b]Deut. 12:5, 26; 15:20
3 [a]Num. 29:12 [b]Ex. 13:3; Deut. 4:9
4 [a]Ex. 13:7 [b]Num. 9:12
6 [a]Ex. 12:7–10
7 [a]2 Kin. 23:23
8 [a]Ex. 12:16; 13:6; Lev. 23:8, 36
10 [a]Ex. 34:22; Lev. 23:15, 16; Num. 28:26 [b]1 Cor. 16:2
11 [a]Deut. 16:14
12 [a]Deut. 15:15
13 [a]Ex. 23:16
14 [a]Neh. 8:9
15 [a]Lev. 23:39–41
16 [a]Ex. 23:14–17; 34:22–24

NKJV

unclean and the clean *person* alike *may eat it,* as *if it were* a gazelle or a deer.

23 "Only you shall not eat its blood; you shall pour it on the ground like water.

The Passover Reviewed
(Ex. 12:1–20; 23:14–19; 34:18–26)

16 "Observe the [a]month of Abib, and keep the Passover to the LORD your God, for [b]in the month of Abib the LORD your God brought you out of Egypt by night.

2 "Therefore you shall sacrifice the Passover to the LORD your God, from the flock and [a]the herd, in the [b]place where the LORD chooses to put His name.

3 "You shall eat no leavened bread with it; [a]seven days you shall eat unleavened bread with it, *that is,* the bread of affliction (for you came out of the land of Egypt in haste), that you may [b]remember the day in which you came out of the land of Egypt all the days of your life.

4 [a]"And no leaven shall be seen among you in all your territory for seven days, nor shall *any* of the meat which you sacrifice the first day at twilight remain overnight until [b]morning.

5 "You may not sacrifice the Passover within any of your gates which the LORD your God gives you;

6 "but at the place where the LORD your God chooses to make His name abide, there you shall sacrifice the Passover [a]at twilight, at the going down of the sun, at the time you came out of Egypt.

7 "And you shall roast and eat *it* [a]in the place which the LORD your God chooses, and in the morning you shall turn and go to your tents.

8 "Six days you shall eat unleavened bread, and [a]on the seventh day there *shall be* a sacred assembly to the LORD your God. You shall do no work *on it.*

The Feast of Weeks Reviewed
(Ex. 34:22; Lev. 23:15–21; Num. 28:26–31)

9 "You shall count seven weeks for yourself; begin to count the seven weeks from *the time* you begin *to put* the sickle to the grain.

10 "Then you shall keep the [a]Feast of Weeks to the LORD your God with the tribute of a freewill offering from your hand, which you shall give [b]as the LORD your God blesses you.

11 [a]"You shall rejoice before the LORD your God, you and your son and your daughter, your male servant and your female servant, the Levite who *is* within your gates, the stranger and the fatherless and the widow who *are* among you, at the place where the LORD your God chooses to make His name abide.

12 [a]"And you shall remember that you were a slave in Egypt, and you shall be careful to observe these statutes.

The Feast of Tabernacles Reviewed
(Lev. 23:33–43; Num. 29:12–40)

13 [a]"You shall observe the Feast of Tabernacles seven days, when you have gathered from your threshing floor and from your winepress.

14 "And [a]you shall rejoice in your feast, you and your son and your daughter, your male servant and your female servant and the Levite, the stranger and the fatherless and the widow, who *are* within your gates.

15 [a]"Seven days you shall keep a sacred feast to the LORD your God in the place which the LORD chooses, because the LORD your God will bless you in all your produce and in all the work of your hands, so that you surely rejoice.

16 [a]"Three times a year all your males shall

KJV

appear before the LORD thy God in the place which he shall choose; in the feast of unleavened bread, and in the feast of weeks, and in the feast of tabernacles: and [b]they shall not appear before the LORD empty:

17 Every man *shall give* as he is able, [a]according to the blessing of the LORD thy God which he hath given thee.

Justice Must Be Administered

18 [a]Judges and officers shalt thou make thee in all thy gates, which the LORD thy God giveth thee, throughout thy tribes: and they shall judge the people with just judgment.

19 [a]Thou shalt not wrest judgment; [b]thou shalt not respect persons, [c]neither take a gift: for a gift doth blind the eyes of the wise, and pervert the words of the righteous.

20 That which is altogether just shalt thou follow, that thou mayest [a]live, and inherit the land which the LORD thy God giveth thee.

21 [a]Thou shalt not plant thee a grove of any trees near unto the altar of the LORD thy God, which thou shalt make thee.

22 [a]Neither shalt thou set thee up *any* image; which the LORD thy God hateth.

17 Thou [a]shalt not sacrifice unto the LORD thy God *any* bullock, or sheep, wherein is blemish, *or* any evilfavouredness: for that *is* an abomination unto the LORD thy God.

2 [a]If there be found among you, within any of thy gates which the LORD thy God giveth thee, man or woman, that hath wrought wickedness in the sight of the LORD thy God, [b]in transgressing his covenant,

3 And hath gone and served other gods, and worshipped them, either [a]the sun, or moon, or any of the host of heaven, [b]which I have not commanded;

4 [a]And it be told thee, and thou hast heard *of it*, and enquired diligently, and, behold, *it be* true, *and* the thing certain, *that* such abomination is wrought in Israel:

5 Then shalt thou bring forth that man or that woman, which have committed that wicked thing, unto thy gates, *even* that man or that woman, and [a]shalt stone them with stones, till they [b]die.

6 At the mouth of two witnesses, or three [a]witnesses, shall he that is worthy of death be put to death; *but* at the mouth of one witness he shall not be put to death.

7 The hands of the witnesses shall be first upon him to put him to death, and afterward the hands of all the people. So thou shalt put the evil away from among [a]you.

8 [a]If there arise a matter too hard for thee in judgment, between blood and blood, between plea and plea, and between stroke and stroke, *being* matters of controversy within thy gates: then shalt thou arise, and get thee up into the [b]place which the LORD thy God shall choose;

9 And [a]thou shalt come unto the priests the Levites, and [b]unto the judge that shall be in those days, and enquire; [c]and they shall shew thee the sentence of judgment:

10 And thou shalt do according to the sentence, which they of that place which the LORD shall choose shall shew thee; and thou shalt observe to do according to all that they inform thee:

11 According to the sentence of the law which they shall teach thee, and according to the judgment which they shall tell thee, thou shalt do: thou shalt not decline from the sentence which they shall shew thee, *to* the right hand, nor *to* the left.

12 And [a]the man that will do presumptuously, and will not hearken unto the priest that standeth to minister there before the LORD thy God, or unto the judge, even that man shall die: and thou shalt put away the evil from Israel.

16 [b]Ex. 23:15
17 [a]Lev. 14:30, 31; Deut. 16:10
18 [a]Ex. 23:1–8; Deut. 1:16, 17; John 7:24
19 [a]Ex. 23:2, 6 [b]Deut. 1:17 [c]Ex. 23:8
20 [a]Ezek. 18:5–9
21 [a]Ex. 34:13
22 [a]Lev. 26:1

CHAPTER 17
1 [a]Deut. 15:21; Mal. 1:8, 13
2 [a]Deut. 13:6 [b]Josh. 7:11
3 [a]Deut. 4:19 [b]Jer. 7:22
4 [a]Deut. 13:12, 14
5 [a]Lev. 24:14–16; Josh. 7:25 [b]Deut. 13:6–18
6 [a]Num. 35:30; Deut. 19:15; Matt. 18:16; John 8:17; 2 Cor. 13:1; 1 Tim. 5:19; Heb. 10:28
7 [a]Deut. 13:5; 19:19; 1 Cor. 5:13
8 [a]Deut. 1:17; 2 Chr. 19:10 [b]Deut. 12:5; 16:2
9 [a]Jer. 18:18 [b]Deut. 19:17–19 [c]Ezek. 44:24
12 [a]Num. 15:30; Deut. 1:43

NKJV

appear before the LORD your God in the place which He chooses: at the Feast of Unleavened Bread, at the Feast of Weeks, and at the Feast of Tabernacles; and [b]they shall not appear before the LORD empty-handed.

17 "Every man *shall give* as he is able, [a]according to the blessing of the LORD your God which He has given you.

Justice Must Be Administered

18 "You shall appoint [a]judges and officers in all your gates, which the LORD your God gives you, according to your tribes, and they shall judge the people with just judgment.

19 [a]"You shall not pervert justice; [b]you shall not show partiality, [c]nor take a bribe, for a bribe blinds the eyes of the wise and twists the words of the righteous.

20 "You shall follow what is altogether just, that you may [a]live and inherit the land which the LORD your God is giving you.

21 [a]"You shall not plant for yourself any tree, as a wooden image, near the altar which you build for yourself to the LORD your God.

22 [a]"You shall not set up a sacred pillar, which the LORD your God hates.

17 "You [a]shall not sacrifice to the LORD your God a bull or sheep which has any blemish *or* defect, for that *is* an abomination to the LORD your God.

2 [a]"If there is found among you, within any of your gates which the LORD your God gives you, a man or a woman who has been wicked in the sight of the LORD your God, [b]in transgressing His covenant,

3 "who has gone and served other gods and worshiped them, either [a]the sun or moon or any of the host of heaven, [b]which I have not commanded,

4 [a]"and it is told you, and you hear *of it*, then you shall inquire diligently. And if *it is* indeed true *and* certain that such an abomination has been committed in Israel,

5 "then you shall bring out to your gates that man or woman who has committed that wicked thing, and [a]shall stone [b]to death that man or woman with stones.

6 "Whoever is deserving of death shall be put to death on the testimony of two or three [a]witnesses; he shall not be put to death on the testimony of one witness.

7 "The hands of the witnesses shall be the first against him to put him to death, and afterward the hands of all the people. So you shall put away the evil from among [a]you.

8 [a]"If a matter arises which is too hard for you to judge, between degrees of guilt for bloodshed, between one judgment or another, or between one punishment or another, matters of controversy within your gates, then you shall arise and go up to the [b]place which the LORD your God chooses.

9 "And [a]you shall come to the priests, the Levites, and [b]to the judge *there* in those days, and inquire *of them;* [c]they shall pronounce upon you the sentence of judgment.

10 "You shall do according to the sentence which they pronounce upon you in that place which the LORD chooses. And you shall be careful to do according to all that they order you.

11 "According to the sentence of the law in which they instruct you, according to the judgment which they tell you, you shall do; you shall not turn aside *to* the right hand or *to* the left from the sentence which they pronounce upon you.

12 "Now [a]the man who acts presumptuously and will not heed the priest who stands to minister there before the LORD your God, or the judge, that man shall die. So you shall put away the evil from Israel.

KJV

13 [a]And all the people shall hear, and fear, and do no more presumptuously.

Principles Governing Kings

14 When thou art come unto the land which the LORD thy God giveth thee, and shalt possess it, and shalt dwell therein, and shalt say, [a]I will set a king over me, like as all the nations that *are* about me;

15 Thou shalt in any wise set *him* king over thee, [a]whom the LORD thy God shall choose: *one* [b]from among thy brethren shalt thou set king over thee: thou mayest not set a stranger over thee, which *is* not thy brother.

16 But he shall not multiply [a]horses to himself, nor cause the people [b]to return to Egypt, to the end that he should multiply horses: forasmuch as [c]the LORD hath said unto you, [d]Ye shall henceforth return no more that way.

17 Neither shall he multiply wives to himself, that his heart turn not away: neither shall he greatly multiply to himself silver and [a]gold.

18 And it shall be, when he sitteth upon the throne of his kingdom, that he shall write him a copy of this law in a book out of *that which is* [a]before the priests the Levites:

19 And [a]it shall be with him, and he shall read therein all the days of his life: that he may learn to fear the LORD his God, to keep all the words of this law and these statutes, to do them:

20 That his heart be not lifted up above his brethren, and that he [a]turn not aside from the commandment, *to* the right hand, or *to* the left: to the end that he may prolong *his* days in his kingdom, he, and his children, in the midst of Israel.

The Portion of the Priests and Levites

18 The priests the Levites, *and* all the tribe of Levi, shall have no part nor [a]inheritance with Israel: they shall eat the offerings of the LORD made by fire, and his inheritance.

2 Therefore shall they have no inheritance among their brethren: the LORD *is* their inheritance, as he hath said unto them.

3 And this shall be the priest's [a]due from the people, from them that offer a sacrifice, whether *it be* ox or sheep; and they shall give unto the priest the shoulder, and the two cheeks, and the maw.

4 [a]The firstfruit *also* of thy corn, of thy wine, and of thine oil, and the first of the fleece of thy sheep, shalt thou give him.

5 For [a]the LORD thy God hath chosen him out of all thy tribes, [b]to stand to minister in the name of the LORD, him and his sons for ever.

6 And if a Levite come from any of thy gates out of all Israel, where he [a]sojourned, and come with all the desire of his mind [b]unto the place which the LORD shall choose;

7 Then he shall minister in the name of the LORD his God, [a]as all his brethren the Levites *do*, which stand there before the LORD.

8 They shall have like [a]portions to eat, beside that which cometh of the sale of his patrimony.

Avoid Wicked Customs

9 When thou art come into the land which the LORD thy God giveth thee, [a]thou shalt not learn to do after the abominations of those nations.

10 There shall not be found among you *any one* that maketh his son or his daughter [a]to pass through the fire, [b]*or* that useth divination, *or* an observer of times, or an enchanter, or a witch,

11 [a]Or a charmer, or a consulter with familiar spirits, or a wizard, or a [b]necromancer.

12 For all that do these things *are* an abomination unto the LORD: and [a]because of these abominations the LORD thy God doth drive them out from before thee.

13 [a]Deut. 13:11
14 [a]1 Sam. 8:5, 19, 20; 10:19
15 [a]1 Sam. 9:15, 16; 10:24; 16:12, 13; 1 Chr. 22:8–10; Hos. 8:4 [b]Jer. 30:21
16 [a]1 Kin. 4:26; 10:26–29; Ps. 20:7 [b]Is. 31:1; Ezek. 17:15 [c]Ex. 13:17, 18; Hos. 11:5 [d]Deut. 28:68
17 [a]1 Kin. 10:14
18 [a]Deut. 31:24–26
19 [a]Ps. 119:97, 98
20 [a]Deut. 5:32; 1 Kin. 15:5

CHAPTER 18
1 [a]Deut. 10:9; 1 Cor. 9:13
3 [a]Lev. 7:32–34; Num. 18:11, 12; 1 Sam. 2:13–16, 29
4 [a]Ex. 22:29
5 [a]Ex. 28:1 [b]Deut. 10:8
6 [a]Num. 35:2 [b]Deut. 12:5; 14:23
7 [a]Num. 1:50; 2 Chr. 31:2
8 [a]Lev. 27:30–33; Num. 18:21–24; 2 Chr. 31:4; Neh. 12:44
9 [a]Lev. 18:26, 27, 30; Deut. 12:29, 30; 20:16–18
10 [a]Lev. 18:21; Deut. 12:31 [b]Ex. 22:18; Lev. 19:26, 31; 20:6, 27; Is. 8:19
11 [a]Lev. 20:27 [b]1 Sam. 28:7
12 [a]Lev. 18:24; Deut. 9:4

NKJV

13 [a]"And all the people shall hear and fear, and no longer act presumptuously.

Principles Governing Kings

14 "When you come to the land which the LORD your God is giving you, and possess it and dwell in it, and say, [a]'I will set a king over me like all the nations that *are* around me,'

15 "you shall surely set a king over you [a]whom the LORD your God chooses; *one* [b]from among your brethren you shall set as king over you; you may not set a foreigner over you, who *is* not your brother.

16 "But he shall not multiply [a]horses for himself, nor cause the people [b]to return to Egypt to multiply horses, for [c]the LORD has said to you, [d]'You shall not return that way again.'

17 "Neither shall he multiply wives for himself, lest his heart turn away; nor shall he greatly multiply silver and [a]gold for himself.

18 "Also it shall be, when he sits on the throne of his kingdom, that he shall write for himself a copy of this law in a book, from *the one* [a]before the priests, the Levites.

19 "And [a]it shall be with him, and he shall read it all the days of his life, that he may learn to fear the LORD his God and be careful to observe all the words of this law and these statutes,

20 "that his heart may not be lifted above his brethren, that he [a]may not turn aside from the commandment *to* the right hand or *to* the left, and that he may prolong *his* days in his kingdom, he and his children in the midst of Israel.

The Portion of the Priests and Levites

18 "The priests, the Levites—all the tribe of Levi—shall have no part nor [a]inheritance with Israel; they shall eat the offerings of the LORD made by fire, and His portion.

2 "Therefore they shall have no inheritance among their brethren; the LORD is their inheritance, as He said to them.

3 "And this shall be the priest's [a]due from the people, from those who offer a sacrifice, whether *it is* bull or sheep: they shall give to the priest the shoulder, the cheeks, and the stomach.

4 [a]"The firstfruits of your grain and your new wine and your oil, and the first of the fleece of your sheep, you shall give him.

5 "For [a]the LORD your God has chosen him out of all your tribes [b]to stand to minister in the name of the LORD, him and his sons forever.

6 "So if a Levite comes from any of your gates, from where he [a]dwells among all Israel, and comes with all the desire of his mind [b]to the place which the LORD chooses,

7 "then he may serve in the name of the LORD his God [a]as all his brethren the Levites *do,* who stand there before the LORD.

8 "They shall have equal [a]portions to eat, besides what comes from the sale of his inheritance.

Avoid Wicked Customs

9 "When you come into the land which the LORD your God is giving you, [a]you shall not learn to follow the abominations of those nations.

10 "There shall not be found among you *anyone* who makes his son or his daughter [a]pass through the fire, [b]*or one* who practices witchcraft, *or* a soothsayer, or one who interprets omens, or a sorcerer,

11 [a]"or one who conjures spells, or a medium, or a spiritist, or [b]one who calls up the dead.

12 "For all who do these things *are* an abomination to the LORD, and [a]because of these abominations the LORD your God drives them out from before you.

KJV

13 Thou shalt be perfect with the LORD thy God.

14 For these nations, which thou shalt possess, hearkened unto observers of times, and unto diviners: but as for thee, the LORD thy God hath not suffered thee so *to do.*

A New Prophet Like Moses

15 [a]The LORD thy God will raise up unto thee a Prophet from the midst of thee, of thy brethren, like unto me; unto him ye shall hearken;

16 According to all that thou desiredst of the LORD thy God in Horeb [a]in the day of the assembly, saying, [b]Let me not hear again the voice of the LORD my God, neither let me see this great fire any more, that I die not.

17 And the LORD said unto me, [a]They have well *spoken that* which they have spoken.

18 [a]I will raise them up a Prophet from among their brethren, like unto thee, and [b]will put my words in his mouth; [c]and he shall speak unto them all that I shall command him.

19 [a]And it shall come to pass, *that* whosoever will not hearken unto my words which he shall speak in my name, I will require *it* of him.

20 But [a]the prophet, which shall presume to speak a word in my name, which I have not commanded him to speak, or [b]that shall speak in the name of other gods, even that prophet shall die.

21 And if thou say in thine heart, How shall we know the word which the LORD hath not spoken?

22 [a]When a prophet speaketh in the name of the LORD, [b]if the thing follow not, nor come to pass, that *is* the thing which the LORD hath not spoken, *but* the prophet hath spoken it [c]presumptuously: thou shalt not be afraid of him.

Three Cities of Refuge
(Num. 35:9–28; Josh. 20:1–9)

19 When the LORD thy God [a]hath cut off the nations, whose land the LORD thy God giveth thee, and thou succeedest them, and dwellest in their cities, and in their houses;

2 [a]Thou shalt separate three cities for thee in the midst of thy land, which the LORD thy God giveth thee to possess it.

3 Thou shalt prepare thee a way, and divide the coasts of thy land, which the LORD thy God giveth thee to inherit, into three parts, that every slayer may flee thither.

4 And [a]this *is* the case of the slayer, which shall flee thither, that he may live: Whoso killeth his neighbour ignorantly, whom he hated not in time past;

5 As when a man goeth into the wood with his neighbour to hew wood, and his hand fetcheth a stroke with the axe to cut down the tree, and the head slippeth from the helve, and lighteth upon his neighbour, that he die; he shall flee unto one of those cities, and live:

6 [a]Lest the avenger of the blood pursue the slayer, while his heart is hot, and overtake him, because the way is long, and slay him; whereas he *was* not worthy of death, inasmuch as he hated him not in time past.

7 Wherefore I command thee, saying, Thou shalt separate three cities for thee.

8 And if the LORD thy God [a]enlarge thy coast, as he hath sworn unto thy [b]fathers, and give thee all the land which he promised to give unto thy fathers;

9 If thou shalt keep all these commandments to do them, which I command thee this day, to love the LORD thy God, and to walk ever in his ways; [a]then shalt thou add three cities more for thee, beside these three:

10 That [a]innocent blood be not shed in thy land, which the LORD thy God giveth thee *for* an inheritance, and *so* blood be upon thee.

11 But [a]if any man hate his neighbour, and

15 [a]Matt. 21:11; Luke 1:76; 2:25–34; 7:16; 24:19; Acts 3:22
16 [a]Deut. 5:23–27 [b]Ex. 20:18, 19; Heb. 12:19
17 [a]Deut. 5:28
18 [a]Deut. 34:10; John 1:45; Acts 3:22 [b]Num. 23:5; Is. 49:2; 51:16; John 17:8 [c][John 4:25; 8:28]
19 [a]Acts 3:23; [Heb. 12:25]
20 [a]Deut. 13:5; Jer. 14:14, 15; Zech. 13:2–5 [b]Deut. 13:1–3; Jer. 2:8
22 [a]Jer. 28:9 [b]Deut. 13:2 [c]Deut. 18:20

CHAPTER 19

1 [a]Deut. 12:29
2 [a]Ex. 21:13; Num. 35:10–15; Deut. 4:41; Josh. 20:2
4 [a]Num. 35:9–34; Deut. 4:42
6 [a]Num. 35:12
8 [a]Deut. 12:20 [b]Gen. 15:18–21
9 [a]Josh. 20:7–9
10 [a]Num. 35:33; Deut. 21:1–9
11 [a]Num. 35:16, 24; Deut. 27:24; [1 John 3:15]

NKJV

13 "You shall be blameless before the LORD your God.

14 "For these nations which you will dispossess listened to soothsayers and diviners; but as for you, the LORD your God has not appointed such for you.

A New Prophet Like Moses

15 [a]"The LORD your God will raise up for you a Prophet like me from your midst, from your brethren. Him you shall hear,

16 "according to all you desired of the LORD your God in Horeb [a]in the day of the assembly, saying, [b]'Let me not hear again the voice of the LORD my God, nor let me see this great fire anymore, lest I die.'

17 "And the LORD said to me: [a]'What they have spoken is good.

18 [a]'I will raise up for them a Prophet like you from among their brethren, and [b]will put My words in His mouth, [c]and He shall speak to them all that I command Him.

19 [a]'And it shall be *that* whoever will not hear My words, which He speaks in My name, I will require *it* of him.

20 'But [a]the prophet who presumes to speak a word in My name, which I have not commanded him to speak, or [b]who speaks in the name of other gods, that prophet shall die.'

21 "And if you say in your heart, 'How shall we know the word which the LORD has not spoken?'—

22 [a]"when a prophet speaks in the name of the LORD, [b]if the thing does not happen or come to pass, that *is* the thing which the LORD has not spoken; the prophet has spoken it [c]presumptuously; you shall not be afraid of him.

Three Cities of Refuge
(Num. 35:9–28; Josh. 20:1–9)

19 "When the LORD your God [a]has cut off the nations whose land the LORD your God is giving you, and you dispossess them and dwell in their cities and in their houses,

2 [a]"you shall separate three cities for yourself in the midst of your land which the LORD your God is giving you to possess.

3 "You shall prepare roads for yourself, and divide into three parts the territory of your land which the LORD your God is giving you to inherit, that any manslayer may flee there.

4 "And [a]this *is* the case of the manslayer who flees there, that he may live: Whoever kills his neighbor unintentionally, not having hated him in time past—

5 "as when *a man* goes to the woods with his neighbor to cut timber, and his hand swings a stroke with the ax to cut down the tree, and the head slips from the handle and strikes his neighbor so that he dies—he shall flee to one of these cities and live;

6 [a]"lest the avenger of blood, while his anger is hot, pursue the manslayer and overtake him, because the way is long, and kill him, though he *was* not deserving of death, since he had not hated the victim in time past.

7 "Therefore I command you, saying, 'You shall separate three cities for yourself.'

8 "Now if the LORD your God [a]enlarges your territory, as He swore to [b]your fathers, and gives you the land which He promised to give to your fathers,

9 "and if you keep all these commandments and do them, which I command you today, to love the LORD your God and to walk always in His ways, [a]then you shall add three more cities for yourself besides these three,

10 [a]"lest innocent blood be shed in the midst of your land which the LORD your God is giving you *as* an inheritance, and *thus* guilt of bloodshed be upon you.

11 "But [a]if anyone hates his neighbor, lies

KJV

lie in wait for him, and rise up against him, and
smite him mortally that he die, and fleeth into
one of these cities:
12 Then the elders of his city shall send and
fetch him thence, and deliver him into the hand
of the avenger of blood, that he may die.
13 [a]Thine eye shall not pity him, [b]but thou
shalt put away *the guilt of* innocent blood from
Israel, that it may go well with thee.

Property Boundaries

14 [a]Thou shalt not remove thy neighbour's
landmark, which they of old time have set in thine
inheritance, which thou shalt inherit in the land
that the LORD thy God giveth thee to possess it.

The Law Concerning Witnesses

15 [a]One witness shall not rise up against a
man for any iniquity, or for any sin, in any sin
that he sinneth: at the mouth of two witnesses,
or at the mouth of three witnesses, shall the matter be established.
16 If a false witness [a]rise up against any man
to testify against him *that which is* wrong;
17 Then both the men, between whom the
controversy *is*, shall stand before the LORD, [a]be-
fore the priests and the judges, which shall be in
those days;
18 And the judges shall make diligent inquisition: and, behold, *if* the witness *be* a false
witness, *and* hath testified falsely against his
brother;
19 [a]Then shall ye do unto him, as he had
thought to have done unto his brother: so [b]shalt
thou put the evil away from among you.
20 [a]And those which remain shall hear, and
fear, and shall henceforth commit no more any
such evil among you.
21 [a]And thine eye shall not pity; *but* [b]life
shall go for life, eye for eye, tooth for tooth, hand
for hand, foot for foot.

Principles Governing Warfare

20 When thou goest out to battle against thine
enemies, and seest [a]horses, and chariots,
and a people more than thou, be not [b]afraid of
them: for the LORD thy God *is* [c]with thee, which
brought thee up out of the land of Egypt.
2 And it shall be, when ye are come nigh
unto the battle, that the priest shall approach and
speak unto the people,
3 And shall say unto them, Hear, O Israel,
ye approach this day unto battle against your enemies: let not your hearts faint, fear not, and do
not tremble, neither be ye terrified because of
them;
4 For the LORD your God *is* he that goeth
with you, [a]to fight for you against your enemies,
to save you.
5 And the officers shall speak unto the people, saying, What man *is there* that hath built a
new house, and hath not [a]dedicated it? let him
go and return to his house, lest he die in the battle,
and another man dedicate it.
6 And what man *is he* that hath planted a
vineyard, and hath not *yet* eaten of it? let him
also go and return unto his house, lest he die in
the battle, and another man eat of it.
7 [a]And what man *is there* that hath betrothed a wife, and hath not taken her? let him
go and return unto his house, lest he die in the
battle, and another man take her.
8 And the officers shall speak further unto
the people, and they shall say, [a]What man *is there*
that is fearful and fainthearted? let him go and
return unto his house, lest his brethren's heart
faint as well as his heart.
9 And it shall be, when the officers have
made an end of speaking unto the people, that
they shall make captains of the armies to lead
the people.

13 [a]Deut. 13:8 [b]Num. 35:33, 34; 1 Kin. 2:31 **14** [a]Deut. 27:17; Job 24:2; Prov. 22:28; Hos. 5:10 **15** [a]Num. 35:30; Deut. 17:6; Matt. 18:16; John 8:17; 2 Cor. 13:1; 1 Tim. 5:19; Heb. 10:28 **16** [a]Ex. 23:1; Ps. 27:12; 35:11 **17** [a]Deut. 17:8–11; 21:5 **19** [a]Prov. 19:5; Dan. 6:24 [b]Deut. 13:5; 17:7; 21:21; 22:21 **20** [a]Deut. 17:13; 21:21 **21** [a]Deut. 19:13 [b]Ex. 21:23, 24; Lev. 24:20; Matt. 5:38, 39

CHAPTER 20

1 [a]Ps. 20:7; Is. 31:1 [b]Deut. 7:18 [c]Num. 23:21; Deut. 5:6; 31:6, 8; 2 Chr. 13:12; 32:7, 8; Ps. 23:4; Is. 41:10 **4** [a]Deut. 1:30; 3:22; Josh. 23:10 **5** [a]Neh. 12:27 **7** [a]Deut. 24:5 **8** [a]Judg. 7:3

*

20:8 So with MT, Tg.; Sam., LXX, Syr., Vg. *lest he make his brother's heart faint*

NKJV

in wait for him, rises against him and strikes him
mortally, so that he dies, and he flees to one of
these cities,
12 "then the elders of his city shall send and
bring him from there, and deliver him over to the
hand of the avenger of blood, that he may die.
13 [a]"Your eye shall not pity him, [b]but you
shall put away *the guilt of* innocent blood from
Israel, that it may go well with you.

Property Boundaries

14 [a]"You shall not remove your neighbor's
landmark, which the men of old have set, in your
inheritance which you will inherit in the land that
the LORD your God is giving you to possess.

The Law Concerning Witnesses

15 [a]"One witness shall not rise against a man
concerning any iniquity or any sin that he commits; by the mouth of two or three witnesses the
matter shall be established.
16 "If a false witness [a]rises against any man
to testify against him of wrongdoing,
17 "then both men in the controversy shall
stand before the LORD, [a]before the priests and the
judges who serve in those days.
18 "And the judges shall make careful in-
quiry, and indeed, *if* the witness *is* a false witness,
who has testified falsely against his brother,
19 [a]"then you shall do to him as he thought
to have done to his brother; so [b]you shall put
away the evil from among you.
20 [a]"And those who remain shall hear and
fear, and hereafter they shall not again commit
such evil among you.
21 [a]"Your eye shall not pity: [b]life *shall be*
for life, eye for eye, tooth for tooth, hand for hand,
foot for foot.

Principles Governing Warfare

20 "When you go out to battle against your
enemies, and see [a]horses and chariots *and*
people more numerous than you, do not be [b]afraid
of them; for the LORD your God *is* [c]with you, who
brought you up from the land of Egypt.
2 "So it shall be, when you are on the verge
of battle, that the priest shall approach and speak
to the people.
3 "And he shall say to them, 'Hear, O Israel:
Today you are on the verge of battle with your
enemies. Do not let your heart faint, do not be
afraid, and do not tremble or be terrified because
of them;
4 'for the LORD your God *is* He who goes
with you, [a]to fight for you against your enemies,
to save you.'
5 "Then the officers shall speak to the people, saying: 'What man *is there* who has built a
new house and has not [a]dedicated it? Let him go
and return to his house, lest he die in the battle
and another man dedicate it.
6 'Also what man *is there* who has planted
a vineyard and has not eaten of it? Let him go
and return to his house, lest he die in the battle
and another man eat of it.
7 [a]'And what man *is there* who is betrothed
to a woman and has not married her? Let him
go and return to his house, lest he die in the battle
and another man marry her.'
8 "The officers shall speak further to the
people, and say, [a]'What man *is there who is* fearful and fainthearted? Let him go and return to
his house, *lest the heart of his brethren faint like
his heart.'
9 "And so it shall be, when the officers have
finished speaking to the people, that they shall
make captains of the armies to lead the people.

KJV

10 When thou comest nigh unto a city to fight against it, [a]then proclaim peace unto it.

11 And it shall be, if it make thee answer of peace, and open unto thee, then it shall be, *that* all the people *that is* found therein shall be tributaries unto thee, and they shall serve thee.

12 And if it will make no peace with thee, but will make war against thee, then thou shalt besiege it:

13 And when the LORD thy God hath delivered it into thine hands, [a]thou shalt smite every male thereof with the edge of the sword:

14 But the women, and the little ones, and [a]the cattle, and all that is in the city, *even* all the spoil thereof, shalt thou take unto thyself; and [b]thou shalt eat the spoil of thine enemies, which the LORD thy God hath given thee.

15 Thus shalt thou do unto all the cities *which are* very far off from thee, which *are* not of the cities of these nations.

16 But [a]of the cities of these people, which the LORD thy God doth give thee *for* an inheritance, thou shalt save alive nothing that breatheth:

17 But thou shalt utterly destroy them; *namely,* the Hittites, and the Amorites, the Canaanites, and the Perizzites, the Hivites, and the Jebusites; as the LORD thy God hath commanded thee:

18 That [a]they teach you not to do after all their abominations, which they have done unto their gods; so should ye [b]sin against the LORD your God.

19 When thou shalt besiege a city a long time, in making war against it to take it, thou shalt not destroy the trees thereof by forcing an ax against them: for thou mayest eat of them, and thou shalt not cut them down (for the tree of the field *is* man's *life*) to employ *them* in the siege:

20 Only the trees which thou knowest that they *be* not trees for meat, thou shalt destroy and cut them down; and thou shalt build bulwarks against the city that maketh war with thee, until it be subdued.

The Law Concerning Unsolved Murder

21 If *one* be found slain in the land which the LORD thy God giveth thee to possess it, lying in the field, *and* it be not known who hath slain him:

2 Then thy elders and thy judges shall come forth, and they shall measure unto the cities which *are* round about him that is slain:

3 And it shall be, *that* the city *which is* next unto the slain man, even the elders of that city shall take an heifer, which hath not been wrought with, *and* which hath not drawn in the [a]yoke;

4 And the elders of that city shall bring down the heifer unto a rough valley, which is neither eared nor sown, and shall strike off the heifer's neck there in the valley:

5 And the priests the sons of Levi shall come near; for [a]them the LORD thy God hath chosen to minister unto him, and to bless in the name of the LORD; and [b]by their word shall every controversy and every stroke be *tried:*

6 And all the elders of that city, *that are* next unto the slain *man,* [a]shall wash their hands over the heifer that is beheaded in the valley:

7 And they shall answer and say, Our hands have not shed this blood, neither have our eyes seen *it.*

8 Be merciful, O LORD, unto thy people Israel, whom thou hast redeemed, [a]and lay not innocent blood unto thy people of Israel's charge. And the blood shall be forgiven them.

9 So [a]shalt thou put away the *guilt of* innocent blood from among you, when thou shalt do *that which is* right in the sight of the LORD.

10 [a]2 Sam. 10:19
13 [a]Num. 31:7
14 [a]Josh. 8:2 [b]1 Sam. 14:30
16 [a]Ex. 23:31–33; Num. 21:2, 3; Deut. 7:1–5; Josh. 11:14
18 [a]Ex. 34:12–16; Deut. 7:4; 12:30; 18:9 [b]Ex. 23:33; 2 Kin. 21:3–15; Ps. 106:34–41

CHAPTER 21

3 [a]Num. 19:2
5 [a]Deut. 10:8; 1 Chr. 23:13 [b]Deut. 17:8, 9
6 [a]Ps. 19:12; 26:6; Matt. 27:24
8 [a]Deut. 19:10, 13; Jon. 1:14
9 [a]Deut. 19:13

NKJV

10 "When you go near a city to fight against it, [a]then proclaim an offer of peace to it.

11 "And it shall be that if they accept your offer of peace, and open to you, then all the people *who are* found in it shall be placed under tribute to you, and serve you.

12 "Now if *the city* will not make peace with you, but makes war against you, then you shall besiege it.

13 "And when the LORD your God delivers it into your hands, [a]you shall strike every male in it with the edge of the sword.

14 "But the women, the little ones, [a]the livestock, and all that is in the city, all its spoil, you shall plunder for yourself; and [b]you shall eat the enemies' plunder which the LORD your God gives you.

15 "Thus you shall do to all the cities *which are* very far from you, which *are* not of the cities of these nations.

16 "But [a]of the cities of these peoples which the LORD your God gives you *as* an inheritance, you shall let nothing that breathes remain alive,

17 "but you shall utterly destroy them: the Hittite and the Amorite and the Canaanite and the Perizzite and the Hivite and the Jebusite, just as the LORD your God has commanded you,

18 "lest [a]they teach you to do according to all their abominations which they have done for their gods, and you [b]sin against the LORD your God.

19 "When you besiege a city for a long time, while making war against it to take it, you shall not destroy its trees by wielding an ax against them; if you can eat of them, do not cut them down to use in the siege, for the tree of the field *is* man's *food.*

20 "Only the trees which you know *are* not trees for food you may destroy and cut down, to build siegeworks against the city that makes war with you, until it is subdued.

The Law Concerning Unsolved Murder

21 "If *anyone* is found slain, lying in the field in the land which the LORD your God is giving you to possess, *and* it is not known who killed him,

2 "then your elders and your judges shall go out and measure *the distance* from the slain man to the surrounding cities.

3 "And it shall be *that* the elders of the city nearest to the slain man will take a heifer which has not been worked *and* which has not pulled with a [a]yoke.

4 "The elders of that city shall bring the heifer down to a valley with flowing water, which is neither plowed nor sown, and they shall break the heifer's neck there in the valley.

5 "Then the priests, the sons of Levi, shall come near, for [a]the LORD your God has chosen them to minister to Him and to bless in the name of the LORD; [b]by their word every controversy and every assault shall be *settled.*

6 "And all the elders of that city nearest to the slain *man* [a]shall wash their hands over the heifer whose neck was broken in the valley.

7 "Then they shall answer and say, 'Our hands have not shed this blood, nor have our eyes seen *it.*

8 'Provide atonement, O LORD, for Your people Israel, whom You have redeemed, [a]and do not lay innocent blood to the charge of Your people Israel.' And atonement shall be provided on their behalf for the blood.

9 "So [a]you shall put away the *guilt of* innocent blood from among you when you do *what is* right in the sight of the LORD.

KJV

Female Captives

10 When thou goest forth to war against thine enemies, and the LORD thy God hath delivered them into thine hands, and thou hast taken them captive,

11 And seest among the captives a beautiful woman, and hast a desire unto her, that thou wouldest have her to thy [a]wife;

12 Then thou shalt bring her home to thine house; and she shall [a]shave her head, and pare her nails;

13 And she shall put the raiment of her captivity from off her, and shall remain in thine house, and [a]bewail her father and her mother a full month: and after that thou shalt go in unto her, and be her husband, and she shall be thy wife.

14 And it shall be, if thou have no delight in her, then thou shalt let her go whither she will; but thou shalt not sell her at all for money, thou shalt not make merchandise of her, because thou hast [a]humbled her.

Firstborn Inheritance Rights

15 If a man have two wives, one beloved, [a]and another hated, and they have born him children, *both* the beloved and the hated; and *if* the firstborn son be her's that was hated:

16 Then it shall be, [a]when he maketh his sons to inherit *that* which he hath, *that* he may not make the son of the beloved firstborn before the son of the hated, *which is indeed* the firstborn:

17 But he shall acknowledge the son of the hated *for* the firstborn, [a]by giving him a double portion of all that he hath: for he [b]*is* the beginning of his strength; [c]the right of the firstborn *is* his.

The Rebellious Son

18 If a man have a stubborn and rebellious son, which will not obey the voice of his father, or the voice of his mother, and *that*, when they have chastened him, will not hearken unto them:

19 Then shall his father and his mother lay hold on him, and bring him out unto the elders of his city, and unto the gate of his place;

20 And they shall say unto the elders of his city, This our son *is* stubborn and rebellious, he will not obey our voice; *he is* a glutton, and a drunkard.

21 And all the men of his city shall stone him with stones, that he die: [a]so shalt thou put evil away from among you; [b]and all Israel shall hear, and fear.

Miscellaneous Laws

22 And if a man have committed a sin [a]worthy of death, and he be to be put to death, and thou hang him on a tree:

23 [a]His body shall not remain all night upon the tree, but thou shalt in any wise bury him that day; (for [c]he that is hanged *is* accursed of God;) that [b]thy land be not defiled, which the LORD thy God giveth thee *for* an inheritance.

22 Thou [a]shalt not see thy brother's ox or his sheep go astray, and hide thyself from them: thou shalt in any case bring them again unto thy brother.

2 And if thy brother *be* not nigh unto thee, or if thou know him not, then thou shalt bring it unto thine own house, and it shall be with thee until thy brother seek after it, and thou shalt restore it to him again.

3 In like manner shalt thou do with his ass; and so shalt thou do with his raiment; and with all lost thing of thy brother's, which he hath lost, and thou hast found, shalt thou do likewise: thou mayest not hide thyself.

4 [a]Thou shalt not see thy brother's ass or his ox fall down by the way, and hide thyself from them: thou shalt surely help him to lift *them* up again.

11 [a]Num. 31:18
12 [a]Lev. 14:8, 9; Num. 6:9
13 [a]Ps. 45:10
14 [a]Gen. 34:2; Deut. 22:29; Judg. 19:24
15 [a]Gen. 29:33
16 [a]1 Chr. 5:2; 26:10
17 [a]2 Kin. 2:9 [b]Gen. 49:3 [c]Gen. 25:31, 33
21 [a]Deut. 13:5; 19:19, 20; 22:21, 24 [b]Deut. 13:11
22 [a]Deut. 22:26; Matt. 26:66; Mark 14:64; Acts 23:29
23 [a]Josh. 8:29; 10:26, 27; John 19:31 [b]Lev. 18:25; Num. 35:34 [c]Gal. 3:13

CHAPTER 22
1 [a]Ex. 23:4
4 [a]Ex. 23:5

NKJV

Female Captives

10 "When you go out to war against your enemies, and the LORD your God delivers them into your hand, and you take them captive,

11 "and you see among the captives a beautiful woman, and desire her and would take her for your [a]wife,

12 "then you shall bring her home to your house, and she shall [a]shave her head and trim her nails.

13 "She shall put off the clothes of her captivity, remain in your house, and [a]mourn her father and her mother a full month; after that you may go in to her and be her husband, and she shall be your wife.

14 "And it shall be, if you have no delight in her, then you shall set her free, but you certainly shall not sell her for money; you shall not treat her brutally, because you have [a]humbled her.

Firstborn Inheritance Rights

15 "If a man has two wives, one loved [a]and the other unloved, and they have borne him children, *both* the loved and the unloved, and *if* the firstborn son is of her who is unloved,

16 "then it shall be, [a]on the day he bequeaths his possessions to his sons, *that* he must not bestow firstborn status on the son of the loved wife in preference to the son of the unloved, the *true* firstborn.

17 "But he shall acknowledge the son of the unloved wife *as* the firstborn [a]by giving him a double portion of all that he has, for he [b]*is* the beginning of his strength; [c]the right of the firstborn *is* his.

The Rebellious Son

18 "If a man has a stubborn and rebellious son who will not obey the voice of his father or the voice of his mother, and *who*, when they have chastened him, will not heed them,

19 "then his father and his mother shall take hold of him and bring him out to the elders of his city, to the gate of his city.

20 "And they shall say to the elders of his city, 'This son of ours is stubborn and rebellious; he will not obey our voice; he is a glutton and a drunkard.'

21 "Then all the men of his city shall stone him to death with stones; [a]so you shall put away the evil from among you, [b]and all Israel shall hear and fear.

Miscellaneous Laws

22 "If a man has committed a sin [a]deserving of death, and he is put to death, and you hang him on a tree,

23 [a]"his body shall not remain overnight on the tree, but you shall surely bury him that day, so that [b]you do not defile the land which the LORD your God is giving you *as* an inheritance; for [c]he who is hanged *is* accursed of God.

22 "You [a]shall not see your brother's ox or his sheep going astray, and hide yourself from them; you shall certainly bring them back to your brother.

2 "And if your brother *is* not near you, or if you do not know him, then you shall bring it to your own house, and it shall remain with you until your brother seeks it; then you shall restore it to him.

3 "You shall do the same with his donkey, and so shall you do with his garment; with any lost thing of your brother's, which he has lost and you have found, you shall do likewise; you must not hide yourself.

4 [a]"You shall not see your brother's donkey or his ox fall down along the road, and hide yourself from them; you shall surely help him lift *them* up again.

KJV

5 The woman shall not wear that which pertaineth unto a man, neither shall a man put on a woman's garment: for all that do so *are* abomination unto the LORD thy God.

6 If a bird's nest chance to be before thee in the way in any tree, or on the ground, *whether they be* young ones, or eggs, and the dam sitting upon the young, or upon the eggs, [a]thou shalt not take the dam with the young:

7 *But* thou shalt in any wise let the dam go, and take the young to thee; [a]that it may be well with thee, and *that* thou mayest prolong *thy* days.

8 When thou buildest a new house, then thou shalt make a battlement for thy roof, that thou bring not blood upon thine house, if any man fall from thence.

9 [a]Thou shalt not sow thy vineyard with divers seeds: lest the fruit of thy seed which thou hast sown, and the fruit of thy vineyard, be defiled.

10 [a]Thou shalt not plow with an ox and an ass together.

11 [a]Thou shalt not wear a garment of divers sorts, *as* of woollen and linen together.

12 Thou shalt make thee [a]fringes upon the four quarters of thy vesture, wherewith thou coverest *thyself*.

Laws of Sexual Morality

13 If any man take a wife, and go in unto her, and [a]hate her,

14 And give occasions of speech against her, and bring up an evil name upon her, and say, I took this woman, and when I came to her, I found her not a maid:

15 Then shall the father of the damsel, and her mother, take and bring forth *the tokens of* the damsel's virginity unto the elders of the city in the gate:

16 And the damsel's father shall say unto the elders, I gave my daughter unto this man to wife, and he hateth her;

17 And, lo, he hath given occasions of speech *against her*, saying, I found not thy daughter a maid; and yet these *are the tokens of* my daughter's virginity. And they shall spread the cloth before the elders of the city.

18 And the elders of that city shall take that man and chastise him;

19 And they shall amerce him in an hundred *shekels* of silver, and give *them* unto the father of the damsel, because he hath brought up an evil name upon a virgin of Israel: and she shall be his wife; he may not put her away all his days.

20 But if this thing be true, *and the tokens of* virginity be not found for the damsel:

21 Then they shall bring out the damsel to the door of her father's house, and the men of her city shall stone her with [a]stones that she die: because she hath [b]wrought folly in Israel, to play the whore in her father's house: [c]so shalt thou put evil away from among you.

22 [a]If a man be found lying with a woman married to an husband, then they shall both of them die, *both* the man that lay with the woman, and the woman: so shalt thou put away evil from Israel.

23 If a damsel *that is* a virgin be [a]betrothed unto an husband, and a man find her in the city, and lie with her;

24 Then ye shall bring them both out unto the gate of that city, and ye shall stone them with stones that they die; the damsel, because she cried not, *being* in the city; and the man, because he hath [a]humbled his neighbour's wife: [b]so thou shalt put away evil from among you.

25 But if a man find a betrothed damsel in the field, and the man force her, and lie with her: then the man only that lay with her shall die:

26 But unto the damsel thou shalt do nothing; *there is* in the damsel no sin *worthy* of death: for as when a man riseth against his

6 [a]Lev. 22:28
7 [a]Deut. 4:40
9 [a]Lev. 19:19
10 [a][2 Cor. 6:14–16]
11 [a]Lev. 19:19
12 [a]Num. 15:37–41; Matt. 23:5
13 [a]Deut. 21:15; 24:3
21 [a]Deut. 21:21 [b]Gen. 34:7; Judg. 20:5–10; 2 Sam. 13:12, 13 [c]Deut. 13:5
22 [a]Lev. 20:10; Num. 5:22–27; Ezek. 16:38; [Matt. 5:27, 28]; John 8:5; [1 Cor. 6:9; Heb. 13:4]
23 [a]Lev. 19:20–22; Matt. 1:18, 19
24 [a]Deut. 21:14 [b]Deut. 22:21, 22; 1 Cor. 5:2, 13

NKJV

5 "A woman shall not wear anything that pertains to a man, nor shall a man put on a woman's garment, for all who do so *are* an abomination to the LORD your God.

6 "If a bird's nest happens to be before you along the way, in any tree or on the ground, with young ones or eggs, with the mother sitting on the young or on the eggs, [a]you shall not take the mother with the young;

7 "you shall surely let the mother go, and take the young for yourself, [a]that it may be well with you and *that* you may prolong *your* days.

8 "When you build a new house, then you shall make a parapet for your roof, that you may not bring guilt of bloodshed on your household if anyone falls from it.

9 [a]"You shall not sow your vineyard with different kinds of seed, lest the yield of the seed which you have sown and the fruit of your vineyard be defiled.

10 [a]"You shall not plow with an ox and a donkey together.

11 [a]"You shall not wear a garment of different sorts, *such as* wool and linen mixed together.

12 "You shall make [a]tassels on the four corners of the clothing with which you cover *yourself*.

Laws of Sexual Morality

13 "If any man takes a wife, and goes in to her, and [a]detests her,

14 "and charges her with shameful conduct, and brings a bad name on her, and says, 'I took this woman, and when I came to her I found she *was* not a virgin,'

15 "then the father and mother of the young woman shall take and bring out *the evidence of* the young woman's virginity to the elders of the city at the gate.

16 "And the young woman's father shall say to the elders, 'I gave my daughter to this man as wife, and he detests her.

17 'Now he has charged her with shameful conduct, saying, "I found your daughter *was* not a virgin," and yet these *are the evidences of* my daughter's virginity.' And they shall spread the cloth before the elders of the city.

18 "Then the elders of that city shall take that man and punish him;

19 "and they shall fine him one hundred *shekels* of silver and give *them* to the father of the young woman, because he has brought a bad name on a virgin of Israel. And she shall be his wife; he cannot divorce her all his days.

20 "But if the thing is true, *and evidences of* virginity are not found for the young woman,

21 "then they shall bring out the young woman to the door of her father's house, and the men of her city shall stone her to death with [a]stones, because she has [b]done a disgraceful thing in Israel, to play the harlot in her father's house. [c]So you shall put away the evil from among you.

22 [a]"If a man is found lying with a woman married to a husband, then both of them shall die—the man that lay with the woman, and the woman; so you shall put away the evil from Israel.

23 "If a young woman *who is* a virgin is [a]betrothed to a husband, and a man finds her in the city and lies with her,

24 "then you shall bring them both out to the gate of that city, and you shall stone them to death with stones, the young woman because she did not cry out in the city, and the man because he [a]humbled his neighbor's wife; [b]so you shall put away the evil from among you.

25 "But if a man finds a betrothed young woman in the countryside, and the man forces her and lies with her, then only the man who lay with her shall die.

26 "But you shall do nothing to the young woman; *there is* in the young woman no sin *deserving* of death, for just as when a man rises

KJV

neighbour, and slayeth him, even so *is* this matter:
27 For he found her in the field, *and* the betrothed damsel cried, and *there was* none to save
her.
28 [a]If a man find a damsel *that is* a virgin,
which is not betrothed, and lay hold on her, and
lie with her, and they be found;
29 Then the man that lay with her shall give
unto the damsel's father [a]fifty *shekels* of silver,
and she shall be his wife; [b]because he hath humbled her, he may not put her away all his days.
30 [a]A man shall not take his father's wife,
nor [b]discover his father's skirt.

Those Excluded from the Congregation

23 He that is wounded in the stones, or hath
his privy member cut off, shall [a]not enter
into the congregation of the LORD.
2 A bastard shall not enter into the congregation of the LORD; even to his tenth generation
shall he not enter into the congregation of the
LORD.
3 [a]An Ammonite or Moabite shall not enter
into the congregation of the LORD; even to their
tenth generation shall they not enter into the congregation of the LORD for ever:
4 [a]Because they met you not with bread and
with water in the way, when ye came forth out
of Egypt; and [b]because they hired against thee
Balaam the son of Beor of Pethor of Mesopotamia,
to curse thee.
5 Nevertheless the LORD thy God would not
hearken unto Balaam; but the LORD thy God
turned the curse into a blessing unto thee, because
the LORD thy God [a]loved thee.
6 [a]Thou shalt not seek their peace nor their
prosperity all thy days for ever.
7 Thou shalt not abhor an Edomite; [a]for he
is thy brother: thou shalt not abhor an Egyptian;
because [b]thou wast a stranger in his land.
8 The children that are begotten of them
shall enter into the congregation of the LORD in
their third generation.

Cleanliness of the Camp Site

9 When the host goeth forth against thine
enemies, then keep thee from every wicked thing.
10 [a]If there be among you any man, that is
not clean by reason of uncleanness that chanceth
him by night, then shall he go abroad out of the
camp, he shall not come within the camp:
11 But it shall be, when evening cometh on,
[a]he shall wash *himself* with water: and when the
sun is down, he shall come into the camp *again.*
12 Thou shalt have a place also without the
camp, whither thou shalt go forth abroad:
13 And thou shalt have a paddle upon thy
weapon; and it shall be, when thou wilt ease thyself abroad, thou shalt dig therewith, and shalt
turn back and cover that which cometh from thee:
14 For the LORD thy God [a]walketh in the
midst of thy camp, to deliver thee, and to give
up thine enemies before thee; therefore shall thy
camp be holy: that he see no unclean thing in
thee, and turn away from thee.

Miscellaneous Laws

15 [a]Thou shalt not deliver unto his master
the servant which is escaped from his master unto
thee:
16 He shall dwell with thee, *even* among you,
in that place which he shall choose in one of thy
gates, where it liketh him best: [a]thou shalt not
oppress him.
17 There shall be no whore [a]of the daughters
of Israel, nor [b]a sodomite of the sons of Israel.
18 Thou shalt not bring the hire of a whore,
or the price of a dog, into the house of the LORD
thy God for any vow: for even both these *are*
abomination unto the LORD thy God.

28 [a]Ex. 22:16, 17
29 [a]Ex. 22:16, 17 [b]Deut. 22:24
30 [a]Lev. 18:8; 20:11; Deut. 27:20; 1 Cor. 5:1 [b]Ruth 3:9; Ezek. 16:8

CHAPTER 23

1 [a]Lev. 21:20; 22:24
3 [a]Neh. 13:1, 2
4 [a]Deut. 2:27–30 [b]Num. 22:5, 6; 23:7; Josh. 24:9; 2 Pet. 2:15; Jude 11
5 [a]Deut. 4:37
6 [a]Ezra 9:12
7 [a]Gen. 25:24–26; Deut. 2:4, 8; Amos 1:11; Obad. 10, 12 [b]Ex. 22:21; 23:9; Lev. 19:34; Deut. 10:19
10 [a]Lev. 15:16
11 [a]Lev. 15:5
14 [a]Lev. 26:12; Deut. 7:21
15 [a]1 Sam. 30:15
16 [a]Ex. 22:21; Prov. 22:22
17 [a]Lev. 19:29; Deut. 22:21 [b]Gen. 19:5; 2 Kin. 23:7

*———

23:4 Heb. *Aram Naharaim*
23:17 Heb. *qedeshah,* fem. of *qadesh* (see following note) • Heb. *qadesh,* one practicing sodomy and prostitution in religious rituals

NKJV

against his neighbor and kills him, even so *is* this
matter.
27 "For he found her in the countryside, *and*
the betrothed young woman cried out, but *there
was* no one to save her.
28 [a]"If a man finds a young woman *who is*
a virgin, who is not betrothed, and he seizes her
and lies with her, and they are found out,
29 "then the man who lay with her shall give
to the young woman's father [a]fifty *shekels* of silver, and she shall be his wife [b]because he has
humbled her; he shall not be permitted to divorce
her all his days.
30 [a]"A man shall not take his father's wife,
nor [b]uncover his father's bed.

Those Excluded from the Congregation

23 "He who is emasculated by crushing or mutilation shall [a]not enter the assembly of the
LORD.
2 "One of illegitimate birth shall not enter
the assembly of the LORD; even to the tenth generation none of his *descendants* shall enter the
assembly of the LORD.
3 [a]"An Ammonite or Moabite shall not enter the assembly of the LORD; even to the tenth
generation none of his *descendants* shall enter the
assembly of the LORD forever,
4 [a]"because they did not meet you with
bread and water on the road when you came out
of Egypt, and [b]because they hired against you Balaam the son of Beor from Pethor of *Mesopotamia, to curse you.
5 "Nevertheless the LORD your God would
not listen to Balaam, but the LORD your God
turned the curse into a blessing for you, because
the LORD your God [a]loves you.
6 [a]"You shall not seek their peace nor their
prosperity all your days forever.
7 "You shall not abhor an Edomite, [a]for he
is your brother. You shall not abhor an Egyptian,
because [b]you were an alien in his land.
8 "The children of the third generation born
to them may enter the assembly of the LORD.

Cleanliness of the Camp Site

9 "When the army goes out against your enemies, then keep yourself from every wicked
thing.
10 [a]"If there is any man among you who becomes unclean by some occurrence in the night,
then he shall go outside the camp; he shall not
come inside the camp.
11 "But it shall be, when evening comes, that
[a]he shall wash with water; and when the sun sets,
he may come into the camp.
12 "Also you shall have a place outside the
camp, where you may go out;
13 "and you shall have an implement among
your equipment, and when you sit down outside,
you shall dig with it and turn and cover your
refuse.
14 "For the LORD your God [a]walks in the
midst of your camp, to deliver you and give your
enemies over to you; therefore your camp shall
be holy, that He may see no unclean thing among
you, and turn away from you.

Miscellaneous Laws

15 [a]"You shall not give back to his master
the slave who has escaped from his master to you.
16 "He may dwell with you in your midst,
in the place which he chooses within one of your
gates, where it seems best to him; [a]you shall not
oppress him.
17 "There shall be no *ritual* *harlot [a]of the
daughters of Israel, or a [b]perverted* one of the
sons of Israel.
18 "You shall not bring the wages of a harlot
or the price of a dog to the house of the LORD
your God for any vowed offering, for both of these
are an abomination to the LORD your God.

KJV

19 [a]Thou shalt not lend upon usury to thy brother; usury of money, usury of victuals, usury of any thing that is lent upon usury:

20 [a]Unto a stranger thou mayest lend upon usury; but unto thy brother thou shalt not lend upon usury: [b]that the LORD thy God may bless thee in all that thou settest thine hand to in the land whither thou goest to possess it.

21 [a]When thou shalt vow a vow unto the LORD thy God, thou shalt not slack to pay it: for the LORD thy God will surely require it of thee; and it would be sin in thee.

22 But if thou shalt forbear to vow, it shall be no sin in thee.

23 [a]That which is gone out of thy lips thou shalt keep and perform; *even* a freewill offering, according as thou hast vowed unto the LORD thy God, which thou hast promised with thy mouth.

24 When thou comest into thy neighbour's vineyard, then thou mayest eat grapes thy fill at thine own pleasure; but thou shalt not put *any* in thy vessel.

25 When thou comest into the standing corn of thy neighbour, [a]then thou mayest pluck the ears with thine hand; but thou shalt not move a sickle unto thy neighbour's standing corn.

Law Concerning Divorce

24 When a [a]man hath taken a wife, and married her, and it come to pass that she find no favour in his eyes, because he hath found some uncleanness in her: then let him write her a [b]bill of divorcement, and give *it* in her hand, and send her out of his house.

2 And when she is departed out of his house, she may go and be another man's *wife*.

3 And *if* the latter husband hate her, and write her a bill of divorcement, and giveth *it* in her hand, and sendeth her out of his house; or if the latter husband die, which took her *to be* his wife;

4 [a]Her former husband, which sent her away, may not take her again to be his wife, after that she is defiled; for that *is* abomination before the LORD: and thou shalt not cause the land to sin, which the LORD thy God giveth thee *for* an inheritance.

Miscellaneous Laws

5 [a]When a man hath taken a new wife, he shall not go out to war, neither shall he be charged with any business: *but* he shall be free at home one year, and shall [b]cheer up his wife which he hath taken.

6 No man shall take the nether or the upper millstone to pledge: for he taketh *a man's* life to pledge.

7 If a man be [a]found stealing any of his brethren of the children of Israel, and maketh merchandise of him, or selleth him; then that thief shall die; [b]and thou shalt put evil away from among you.

8 Take heed in [a]the plague of leprosy, that thou observe diligently, and do according to all that the priests the Levites shall teach you: as I commanded them, *so* ye shall observe to do.

9 [a]Remember what the LORD thy God did [b]unto Miriam by the way, after that ye were come forth out of Egypt.

10 When thou dost [a]lend thy brother any thing, thou shalt not go into his house to fetch his pledge.

11 Thou shalt stand abroad, and the man to whom thou dost lend shall bring out the pledge abroad unto thee.

12 And if the man *be* poor, thou shalt not sleep with his pledge:

13 [a]In any case thou shalt deliver him the pledge again when the sun goeth down, that he may sleep in his own raiment, and [b]bless thee: and [c]it shall be righteousness unto thee before the LORD thy God.

19 [a]Ex. 22:25; Lev. 25:35–37; Neh. 5:2–7; Ps. 15:5
20 [a]Deut. 15:3 [b]Deut. 15:10
21 [a]Num. 30:1, 2; Job 22:27; Ps. 61:8; Eccl. 5:4, 5; Matt. 5:33
23 [a]Num. 30:2; Ps. 66:13, 14
25 [a]Matt. 12:1; Mark 2:23; Luke 6:1

CHAPTER 24

1 [a][Matt. 5:31; 19:7; Mark 10:4] [b][Jer. 3:8]
4 [a][Jer. 3:1]
5 [a]Deut. 20:7 [b]Prov. 5:18
7 [a]Ex. 21:16 [b]Deut. 19:19
8 [a]Lev. 13:2; 14:2
9 [a][1 Cor. 10:6] [b]Num. 12:10
10 [a]Matt. 5:42
13 [a]Ex. 22:26; Ezek. 18:7 [b]Job 29:11; 2 Tim. 1:18 [c]Deut. 6:25; Ps. 106:31; Dan. 4:27

NKJV

19 [a]"You shall not charge interest to your brother—interest on money *or* food *or* anything that is lent out at interest.

20 [a]"To a foreigner you may charge interest, but to your brother you shall not charge interest, [b]that the LORD your God may bless you in all to which you set your hand in the land which you are entering to possess.

21 [a]"When you make a vow to the LORD your God, you shall not delay to pay it; for the LORD your God will surely require it of you, and it would be sin to you.

22 "But if you abstain from vowing, it shall not be sin to you.

23 [a]"That which has gone from your lips you shall keep and perform, for you voluntarily vowed to the LORD your God what you have promised with your mouth.

24 "When you come into your neighbor's vineyard, you may eat your fill of grapes at your pleasure, but you shall not put *any* in your container.

25 "When you come into your neighbor's standing grain, [a]you may pluck the heads with your hand, but you shall not use a sickle on your neighbor's standing grain.

Law Concerning Divorce

24 "When a [a]man takes a wife and marries her, and it happens that she finds no favor in his eyes because he has found some uncleanness in her, and he writes her a [b]certificate of divorce, puts *it* in her hand, and sends her out of his house,

2 "when she has departed from his house, and goes and becomes another man's *wife,*

3 "*if* the latter husband detests her and writes her a certificate of divorce, puts *it* in her hand, and sends her out of his house, or if the latter husband dies who took her as his wife,

4 [a]"*then* her former husband who divorced her must not take her back to be his wife after she has been defiled; for that *is* an abomination before the LORD, and you shall not bring sin on the land which the LORD your God is giving you *as* an inheritance.

Miscellaneous Laws

5 [a]"When a man has taken a new wife, he shall not go out to war or be charged with any business; he shall be free at home one year, and [b]bring happiness to his wife whom he has taken.

6 "No man shall take the lower or the upper millstone in pledge, for he takes *one's* living in pledge.

7 "If a man is [a]found kidnapping any of his brethren of the children of Israel, and mistreats him or sells him, then that kidnapper shall die; [b]and you shall put away the evil from among you.

8 "Take heed in [a]an outbreak of leprosy, that you carefully observe and do according to all that the priests, the Levites, shall teach you; just as I commanded them, *so* you shall be careful to do.

9 [a]"Remember what the LORD your God did [b]to Miriam on the way when you came out of Egypt!

10 "When you [a]lend your brother anything, you shall not go into his house to get his pledge.

11 "You shall stand outside, and the man to whom you lend shall bring the pledge out to you.

12 "And if the man *is* poor, you shall not keep his pledge overnight.

13 [a]"You shall in any case return the pledge to him again when the sun goes down, that he may sleep in his own garment and [b]bless you; and [c]it shall be righteousness to you before the LORD your God.

KJV

14 Thou shalt not [a]oppress an hired servant *that is* poor and needy, *whether he be* of thy brethren, or of thy strangers that *are* in thy land within thy gates:

15 At his day [a]thou shalt give *him* his hire, neither shall the sun go down upon it; for he *is* poor, and setteth his heart upon it: [b]lest he cry against thee unto the LORD, and it be sin unto thee.

16 [a]The fathers shall not be put to death for the children, neither shall the children be put to death for the fathers: every man shall be put to death for his own sin.

17 [a]Thou shalt not pervert the judgment of the stranger, *nor* of the fatherless; [b]nor take a widow's raiment to pledge:

18 But [a]thou shalt remember that thou wast a bondman in Egypt, and the LORD thy God redeemed thee thence: therefore I command thee to do this thing.

19 [a]When thou cuttest down thine harvest in thy field, and hast forgot a sheaf in the field, thou shalt not go again to fetch it: it shall be for the stranger, for the fatherless, and for the widow: that the LORD thy God may [b]bless thee in all the work of thine hands.

20 When thou beatest thine olive tree, thou shalt not go over the boughs again: it shall be for the stranger, for the fatherless, and for the widow.

21 When thou gatherest the grapes of thy vineyard, thou shalt not glean *it* afterward: it shall be for the stranger, for the fatherless, and for the widow.

22 And thou shalt remember that thou wast a bondman in the land of Egypt: therefore I command thee to do this thing.

25 If there be a [a]controversy between men, and they come unto judgment, that *the judges* may judge them; then they [b]shall justify the righteous, and condemn the wicked.

2 And it shall be, if the wicked man *be* [a]worthy to be beaten, that the judge shall cause him to lie down, [b]and to be beaten before his face, according to his fault, by a certain number.

3 [a]Forty stripes he may give him, *and* not exceed: lest, *if* he should exceed, and beat him above these with many stripes, then thy brother should [b]seem vile unto thee.

4 [a]Thou shalt not muzzle the ox when he treadeth out *the corn.*

Marriage Duty of the Surviving Brother

5 [a]If brethren dwell together, and one of them die, and have no child, the wife of the dead shall not marry without unto a stranger: her husband's brother shall go in unto her, and take her to him to wife, and perform the duty of an husband's brother unto her.

6 And it shall be, *that* the firstborn which she beareth [a]shall succeed in the name of his brother *which is* dead, that [b]his name be not put out of Israel.

7 And if the man like not to take his brother's wife, then let his brother's wife go up to the [a]gate unto the elders, and say, My husband's brother refuseth to raise up unto his brother a name in Israel, he will not perform the duty of my husband's brother.

8 Then the elders of his city shall call him, and speak unto him: and *if* he stand *to it,* and say, [a]I like not to take her;

9 Then shall his brother's wife come unto him in the presence of the elders, and [a]loose his shoe from off his foot, and spit in his face, and shall answer and say, So shall it be done unto that man that will not [b]build up his brother's house.

10 And his name shall be called in Israel, The house of him that hath his shoe loosed.

14 [a]Lev. 19:13; Deut. 15:7–18; [Prov. 14:31]; Amos 4:1; [Mal. 3:5; 1 Tim. 5:18]
15 [a]Lev. 19:13; Jer. 22:13 [b]Ex. 22:23; Deut. 15:9; Job 35:9; James 5:4
16 [a]2 Kin. 14:6; 2 Chr. 25:4; Jer. 31:29, 30; Ezek. 18:20
17 [a]Ex. 23:6 [b]Ex. 22:26
18 [a]Deut. 24:22
19 [a]Lev. 19:9, 10 [b]Deut. 15:10; Ps. 41:1; Prov. 19:17

CHAPTER 25
1 [a]Deut. 17:8–13; 19:17; Ezek. 44:24 [b]Prov. 17:15
2 [a]Prov. 19:29; Luke 12:48 [b]Matt. 10:17
3 [a]2 Cor. 11:24 [b]Job 18:3
4 [a][Prov. 12:10; 1 Cor. 9:9; 1 Tim. 5:18]
5 [a]Matt. 22:24; Mark 12:19; Luke 20:28
6 [a]Gen. 38:9 [b]Ruth 4:5, 10
7 [a]Ruth 4:1, 2
8 [a]Ruth 4:6
9 [a]Ruth 4:7, 8 [b]Ruth 4:11

NKJV

14 "You shall not [a]oppress a hired servant *who is* poor and needy, *whether* one of your brethren or one of the aliens who *is* in your land within your gates.

15 "Each day [a]you shall give *him* his wages, and not let the sun go down on it, for he *is* poor and has set his heart on it; [b]lest he cry out against you to the LORD, and it be sin to you.

16 [a]"Fathers shall not be put to death for *their* children, nor shall children be put to death for *their* fathers; a person shall be put to death for his own sin.

17 [a]"You shall not pervert justice due the stranger or the fatherless, [b]nor take a widow's garment as a pledge.

18 "But [a]you shall remember that you were a slave in Egypt, and the LORD your God redeemed you from there; therefore I command you to do this thing.

19 [a]"When you reap your harvest in your field, and forget a sheaf in the field, you shall not go back to get it; it shall be for the stranger, the fatherless, and the widow, that the LORD your God may [b]bless you in all the work of your hands.

20 "When you beat your olive trees, you shall not go over the boughs again; it shall be for the stranger, the fatherless, and the widow.

21 "When you gather the grapes of your vineyard, you shall not glean *it* afterward; it shall be for the stranger, the fatherless, and the widow.

22 "And you shall remember that you were a slave in the land of Egypt; therefore I command you to do this thing.

25 "If there is a [a]dispute between men, and they come to court, that *the judges* may judge them, and they [b]justify the righteous and condemn the wicked,

2 "then it shall be, if the wicked man [a]deserves to be beaten, that the judge will cause him to lie down [b]and be beaten in his presence, according to his guilt, with a certain number of blows.

3 [a]"Forty blows he may give him *and* no more, lest he should exceed this and beat him with many blows above these, and your brother [b]be humiliated in your sight.

4 [a]"You shall not muzzle an ox while it treads out *the grain.*

Marriage Duty of the Surviving Brother

5 [a]"If brothers dwell together, and one of them dies and has no son, the widow of the dead man shall not be *married* to a stranger outside *the family;* her husband's brother shall go in to her, take her as his wife, and perform the duty of a husband's brother to her.

6 "And it shall be *that* the firstborn son which she bears [a]will succeed to the name of his dead brother, that [b]his name may not be blotted out of Israel.

7 "But if the man does not want to take his brother's wife, then let his brother's wife go up to the [a]gate to the elders, and say, 'My husband's brother refuses to raise up a name to his brother in Israel; he will not perform the duty of my husband's brother.'

8 "Then the elders of his city shall call him and speak to him. But *if* he stands firm and says, [a]'I do not want to take her,'

9 "then his brother's wife shall come to him in the presence of the elders, [a]remove his sandal from his foot, spit in his face, and answer and say, 'So shall it be done to the man who will not [b]build up his brother's house.'

10 "And his name shall be called in Israel, 'The house of him who had his sandal removed.'

KJV

Miscellaneous Laws

11 When men strive together one with another, and the wife of the one draweth near for
to deliver her husband out of the hand of him
that smiteth him, and putteth forth her hand, and
taketh him by the secrets:
12 Then thou shalt cut off her hand, [a]thine
eye shall not pity *her.*
13 [a]Thou shalt not have in thy bag divers
weights, a great and a small.
14 Thou shalt not have in thine house divers
measures, a great and a small.
15 *But* thou shalt have a perfect and just
weight, a perfect and just measure shalt thou
have: [a]that thy days may be lengthened in the
land which the LORD thy God giveth thee.
16 For [a]all that do such things, *and* all that
do unrighteously, *are* an abomination unto the
LORD thy God.

Destroy the Amalekites

17 [a]Remember what Amalek did unto thee
by the way, when ye were come forth out of
Egypt;
18 How he met thee by the way, and smote
the hindmost of thee, *even* all *that were* feeble
behind thee, when thou *wast* faint and weary; and
he [a]feared not God.
19 Therefore it shall be, [a]when the LORD thy
God hath given thee rest from all thine enemies
round about, in the land which the LORD thy God
giveth thee *for* an inheritance to possess it, *that*
thou shalt [b]blot out the remembrance of Amalek
from under heaven; thou shalt not forget *it.*

Offerings of Firstfruits and Tithes

26 And it shall be, when thou *art* come in unto
the land which the LORD thy God giveth
thee *for* an inheritance, and possessest it, and
dwellest therein;
2 [a]That thou shalt take of the first of all the
fruit of the earth, which thou shalt bring of thy
land that the LORD thy God giveth thee, and shalt
put *it* in a basket, and shalt [b]go unto the place
which the LORD thy God shall choose to place his
name there.
3 And thou shalt go unto the priest that shall
be in those days, and say unto him, I profess this
day unto the LORD thy God, that I am come unto
the country which the LORD sware unto our fathers for to give us.
4 And the priest shall take the basket out
of thine hand, and set it down before the altar of
the LORD thy God.
5 And thou shalt speak and say before the
LORD thy God, [a]A Syrian [b]ready to perish *was*
my father, and [c]he went down into Egypt, and
sojourned there with a [d]few, and became there a
nation, [e]great, mighty, and populous:
6 And the [a]Egyptians evil entreated us, and
afflicted us, and laid upon us hard bondage:
7 And [a]when we cried unto the LORD God
of our fathers, the LORD heard our voice, and
looked on our affliction, and our labour, and our
oppression:
8 And [a]the LORD brought us forth out of
Egypt with a mighty hand, and with an outstretched arm, and [b]with great terribleness, and
with signs, and with wonders:
9 And he hath brought us into this place,
and hath given us this land, *even* [a]a land that floweth with milk and honey.
10 And now, behold, I have brought the firstfruits of the land, which thou, O LORD, hast given
me. And thou shalt set it before the LORD thy God,
and worship before the LORD thy God:
11 And [a]thou shalt rejoice in every good
thing which the LORD thy God hath given unto
thee, and unto thine house, thou, and the Levite,
and the stranger that *is* among you.
12 When thou hast made an end of tithing

12 [a]Deut. 7:2; 19:13 **13** [a]Lev. 19:35–37; Prov. 11:1; 20:23; Ezek. 45:10; Mic. 6:11 **15** [a]Ex. 20:12 **16** [a]Prov. 11:1; [1 Thess. 4:6] **17** [a]Ex. 17:8–16; 1 Sam. 15:1–3 **18** [a][Ps. 36:1]; Rom. 3:18 **19** [a]1 Sam. 15:3 [b]Ex. 17:14

CHAPTER 26

2 [a]Ex. 22:29; 23:16, 19; Num. 18:13; Deut. 16:10; Prov. 3:9 [b]Deut. 12:5 **5** [a]Gen. 25:20; Hos. 12:12 [b]Gen. 43:1, 2; 45:7, 11 [c]Gen. 46:1, 6; Acts 7:15 [d]Gen. 46:27; Deut. 10:22 [e]Deut. 1:10 **6** [a]Ex. 1:8–11, 14 **7** [a]Ex. 2:23–25; 3:9; 4:31 **8** [a]Ex. 12:37, 51; 13:3, 14, 16; Deut. 5:15 [b]Deut. 4:34; 34:11, 12 **9** [a]Ex. 3:8, 17 **11** [a]Deut. 12:7; 16:11; Eccl. 3:12, 13; 5:18–20

NKJV

Miscellaneous Laws

11 "If *two* men fight together, and the wife
of one draws near to rescue her husband from
the hand of the one attacking him, and puts out
her hand and seizes him by the genitals,
12 "then you shall cut off her hand; [a]your
eye shall not pity *her.*
13 [a]"You shall not have in your bag differing
weights, a heavy and a light.
14 "You shall not have in your house differing measures, a large and a small.
15 "You shall have a perfect and just weight,
a perfect and just measure, [a]that your days may
be lengthened in the land which the LORD your
God is giving you.
16 "For [a]all who do such things, all who behave unrighteously, *are* an abomination to the
LORD your God.

Destroy the Amalekites

17 [a]"Remember what Amalek did to you on
the way as you were coming out of Egypt,
18 "how he met you on the way and attacked
your rear ranks, all the stragglers at your rear,
when you *were* tired and weary; and he [a]did not
fear God.
19 "Therefore it shall be, [a]when the LORD
your God has given you rest from your enemies
all around, in the land which the LORD your God
is giving you to possess *as* an inheritance, *that*
you will [b]blot out the remembrance of Amalek
from under heaven. You shall not forget.

Offerings of Firstfruits and Tithes

26 "And it shall be, when you come into the
land which the LORD your God is giving you
as an inheritance, and you possess it and dwell
in it,
2 [a]"that you shall take some of the first of
all the produce of the ground, which you shall
bring from your land that the LORD your God is
giving you, and put *it* in a basket and [b]go to the
place where the LORD your God chooses to make
His name abide.
3 "And you shall go to the one who is priest
in those days, and say to him, 'I declare today to
the LORD *your God that I have come to the country which the LORD swore to our fathers to give
us.'
4 "Then the priest shall take the basket out
of your hand and set it down before the altar of
the LORD your God.
5 "And you shall answer and say before the
LORD your God: 'My father *was* [a]a *Syrian, [b]about
to perish, and [c]he went down to Egypt and dwelt
there, [d]few in number; and there he became a nation, [e]great, mighty, and populous.
6 'But the [a]Egyptians mistreated us, afflicted us, and laid hard bondage on us.
7 [a]'Then we cried out to the LORD God of
our fathers, and the LORD heard our voice and
looked on our affliction and our labor and our
oppression.
8 'So [a]the LORD brought us out of Egypt with
a mighty hand and with an outstretched arm,
[b]with great terror and with signs and wonders.
9 'He has brought us to this place and has
given us this land, [a]"a land flowing with milk and
honey";
10 'and now, behold, I have brought the firstfruits of the land which you, O LORD, have given
me.' Then you shall set it before the LORD your
God, and worship before the LORD your God.
11 "So [a]you shall rejoice in every good *thing*
which the LORD your God has given to you and
your house, you and the Levite and the stranger
who *is* among you.
12 "When you have finished laying aside all

*———

26:3 LXX *my*
26:5 Or *Aramean*

KJV

all the [a]tithes of thine increase the third year, *which is* [b]the year of tithing, and hast given *it* unto the Levite, the stranger, the fatherless, and the widow, that they may eat within thy gates, and be filled;

13 Then thou shalt say before the LORD thy God, I have brought away the hallowed things out of *mine* house, and also have given them unto the Levite, and unto the stranger, to the fatherless, and to the widow, according to all thy commandments which thou hast commanded me: I have not transgressed thy commandments, [a]neither have I forgotten *them:*

14 [a]I have not eaten thereof in my mourning, neither have I taken away *ought* thereof for *any* unclean *use,* nor given *ought* thereof for the dead: *but* I have hearkened to the voice of the LORD my God, *and* have done according to all that thou hast commanded me.

15 [a]Look down from thy holy habitation, from heaven, and bless thy people Israel, and the land which thou hast given us, as thou swarest unto our fathers, [b]a land that floweth with milk and honey.

A Special People of God

16 This day the LORD thy God hath commanded thee to do these statutes and judgments: thou shalt therefore keep and do them with all thine heart, and with all thy soul.

17 Thou hast [a]avouched the LORD this day to be thy God, and to walk in his ways, and to keep his statutes, and his commandments, and his judgments, and to [b]hearken unto his voice:

18 And [a]the LORD hath avouched thee this day to be his peculiar people, as he hath promised thee, and that *thou* shouldest keep all his commandments;

19 And to make thee [a]high above all nations which he hath made, in praise, and in name, and in honour; and that thou mayest be [b]an holy people unto the LORD thy God, as he hath spoken.

The Law Inscribed on Stones

27 And Moses with the elders of Israel commanded the people, saying, Keep all the commandments which I command you this day.

2 And it shall be on the day [a]when ye shall pass over Jordan unto the land which the LORD thy God giveth thee, that [b]thou shalt set thee up great stones, and plaister them with plaister:

3 And thou shalt write upon them all the words of this law, when thou art passed over, that thou mayest go in unto the land which the LORD thy God giveth thee, [a]a land that floweth with milk and honey; as the LORD God of thy fathers hath promised thee.

4 Therefore it shall be when ye be gone over Jordan, *that* ye shall set up these stones, which I command you this day, [a]in mount Ebal, and thou shalt plaister them with plaister.

5 And there shalt thou build an altar unto the LORD thy God, an altar of stones: [a]thou shalt not lift up *any* iron *tool* upon them.

6 Thou shalt build the altar of the LORD thy God of whole stones: and thou shalt offer burnt offerings thereon unto the LORD thy God:

7 And thou shalt offer peace offerings, and shalt eat there, and [a]rejoice before the LORD thy God.

8 And thou shalt [a]write upon the stones all the words of this law very plainly.

9 And Moses and the priests the Levites spake unto all Israel, saying, Take heed, and hearken, O Israel; [a]this day thou art become the people of the LORD thy God.

10 Thou shalt therefore obey the voice of the LORD thy God, and do his commandments and his statutes, which I command thee this day.

---

12 [a]Lev. 27:30; Num. 18:24 [b]Deut. 14:28, 29
13 [a]Ps. 119:141, 153, 176
14 [a]Lev. 7:20; Jer. 16:7; Hos. 9:4
15 [a]Ps. 80:14; Is. 63:15; Zech. 2:13 [b]Ex. 3:8
17 [a]Ex. 20:19 [b]Deut. 15:5
18 [a]Ex. 6:7; 19:5; Deut. 7:6; 14:2; 28:9; [Titus 2:14; 1 Pet. 2:9]
19 [a]Deut. 4:7, 8; 28:1 [b]Ex. 19:6; Deut. 7:6; 28:9; Is. 62:12; [1 Pet. 2:9]

CHAPTER 27

2 [a]Josh. 4:1 [b]Josh. 8:32
3 [a]Ex. 3:8
4 [a]Deut. 11:29; Josh. 8:30, 31
5 [a]Ex. 20:25; Josh. 8:31
7 [a]Deut. 26:11
8 [a]Josh. 8:32
9 [a]Deut. 26:18

NKJV

the [a]tithe of your increase in the third year—[b]the year of tithing—and have given *it* to the Levite, the stranger, the fatherless, and the widow, so that they may eat within your gates and be filled,

13 "then you shall say before the LORD your God: 'I have removed the holy *tithe* from *my* house, and also have given them to the Levite, the stranger, the fatherless, and the widow, according to all Your commandments which You have commanded me; I have not transgressed Your commandments, [a]nor have I forgotten *them.*

14 [a]'I have not eaten any of it when in mourning, nor have I removed *any* of it for an unclean *use,* nor given *any* of it for the dead. I have obeyed the voice of the LORD my God, and have done according to all that You have commanded me.

15 [a]'Look down from Your holy habitation, from heaven, and bless Your people Israel and the land which You have given us, just as You swore to our fathers, [b]"a land flowing with milk and honey." '

A Special People of God

16 "This day the LORD your God commands you to observe these statutes and judgments; therefore you shall be careful to observe them with all your heart and with all your soul.

17 "Today you have [a]proclaimed the LORD to be your God, and that you will walk in His ways and keep His statutes, His commandments, and His judgments, and that you will [b]obey His voice.

18 "Also today [a]the LORD has proclaimed you to be His special people, just as He promised you, that *you* should keep all His commandments,

19 "and that He will set you [a]high above all nations which He has made, in praise, in name, and in honor, and that you may be [b]a holy people to the LORD your God, just as He has spoken."

The Law Inscribed on Stones

27 Now Moses, with the elders of Israel, commanded the people, saying: "Keep all the commandments which I command you today.

2 "And it shall be, on the day [a]when you cross over the Jordan to the land which the LORD your God is giving you, that [b]you shall set up for yourselves large stones, and whitewash them with lime.

3 "You shall write on them all the words of this law, when you have crossed over, that you may enter the land which the LORD your God is giving you, [a]'a land flowing with milk and honey,' just as the LORD God of your fathers promised you.

4 "Therefore it shall be, when you have crossed over the Jordan, *that* [a]on Mount Ebal you shall set up these stones, which I command you today, and you shall whitewash them with lime.

5 "And there you shall build an altar to the LORD your God, an altar of stones; [a]you shall not use an iron *tool* on them.

6 "You shall build with whole stones the altar of the LORD your God, and offer burnt offerings on it to the LORD your God.

7 "You shall offer peace offerings, and shall eat there, and [a]rejoice before the LORD your God.

8 "And you shall [a]write very plainly on the stones all the words of this law."

9 Then Moses and the priests, the Levites, spoke to all Israel, saying, "Take heed and listen, O Israel: [a]This day you have become the people of the LORD your God.

10 "Therefore you shall obey the voice of the LORD your God, and observe His commandments and His statutes which I command you today."

KJV

Curses Pronounced from Mount Ebal

11 And Moses charged the people the same day, saying,
12 These shall stand [a]upon mount Gerizim to bless the people, when ye are come over Jordan; Simeon, and Levi, and Judah, and Issachar, and Joseph, and Benjamin:
13 And [a]these shall stand upon mount Ebal to curse; Reuben, Gad, and Asher, and Zebulun, Dan, and Naphtali.
14 And [a]the Levites shall speak, and say unto all the men of Israel with a loud voice,
15 [a]Cursed *be* the man that maketh *any* graven or molten image, an abomination unto the LORD, the work of the hands of the craftsman, and putteth *it* in *a* secret *place.* [b]And all the people shall answer and say, Amen.
16 [a]Cursed *be* he that setteth light by his father or his mother. And all the people shall say, Amen.
17 [a]Cursed *be* he that removeth his neighbour's landmark. And all the people shall say, Amen.
18 [a]Cursed *be* he that maketh the blind to wander out of the way. And all the people shall say, Amen.
19 [a]Cursed *be* he that perverteth the judgment of the stranger, fatherless, and widow. And all the people shall say, Amen.
20 [a]Cursed *be* he that lieth with his father's wife; because he uncovereth his father's skirt. And all the people shall say, Amen.
21 [a]Cursed *be* he that lieth with any manner of beast. And all the people shall say, Amen.
22 [a]Cursed *be* he that lieth with his sister, the daughter of his father, or the daughter of his mother. And all the people shall say, Amen.
23 [a]Cursed *be* he that lieth with his mother in law. And all the people shall say, Amen.
24 [a]Cursed *be* he that smiteth his neighbour secretly. And all the people shall say, Amen.
25 [a]Cursed *be* he that taketh reward to slay an innocent person. And all the people shall say, Amen.
26 [a]Cursed *be* he that confirmeth not *all* the words of this law to do them. And all the people shall say, Amen.

Blessings on Obedience
(Lev. 26:1–13; Deut. 7:12–24)

28 And it shall come to pass, [a]if thou shalt hearken diligently unto the voice of the LORD thy God, to observe *and* to do all his commandments which I command thee this day, that the LORD thy God [b]will set thee on high above all nations of the earth:
2 And all these blessings shall come on thee, and [a]overtake thee, if thou shalt hearken unto the voice of the LORD thy God.
3 [a]Blessed *shalt* thou *be* in the city, and blessed *shalt* thou *be* [b]in the field.
4 Blessed *shall be* [a]the fruit of thy body, and the fruit of thy ground, and the fruit of thy cattle, the increase of thy kine, and the flocks of thy sheep.
5 Blessed *shall be* thy basket and thy store.
6 [a]Blessed *shalt* thou *be* when thou comest in, and blessed *shalt* thou *be* when thou goest out.
7 The LORD [a]shall cause thine enemies that rise up against thee to be smitten before thy face: they shall come out against thee one way, and flee before thee seven ways.
8 The LORD shall [a]command the blessing upon thee in thy storehouses, and in all that thou

12 [a]Deut. 11:29; Josh. 8:33; Judg. 9:7
13 [a]Deut. 11:29; Josh. 8:33
14 [a]Deut. 33:10; Josh. 8:33; Dan. 9:11
15 [a]Ex. 20:4, 23; 34:17; Lev. 19:4; 26:1; Deut. 4:16, 23; Is. 44:9; Hos. 13:2 [b]Num. 5:22; Jer. 11:5; 1 Cor. 14:16
16 [a]Ex. 20:12; Lev. 19:3; 20:9; Deut. 5:16; 21:18–21; Ezek. 22:7
17 [a]Deut. 19:14; Prov. 22:28
18 [a]Lev. 19:14
19 [a]Ex. 22:21, 22; 23:9; Lev. 19:33; Deut. 10:18; 24:17
20 [a]Lev. 18:8; 20:11; Deut. 22:30; 1 Cor. 5:1
21 [a]Ex. 22:19; Lev. 18:23; 20:15, 16
22 [a]Lev. 18:9
23 [a]Lev. 18:17; 20:14
24 [a]Ex. 20:13; 21:12; Lev. 24:17; Num. 35:30, 31
25 [a]Ex. 23:7; Ps. 15:5; Ezek. 22:12
26 [a]Ps. 119:21; Jer. 11:3; Gal. 3:10

CHAPTER 28

1 [a]Ex. 15:26; Lev. 26:3–13; Deut. 7:12–26; 11:13 [b]Deut. 26:19; 1 Chr. 14:2
2 [a]Deut. 28:15
3 [a]Ps. 128:1, 4 [b]Gen. 39:5
4 [a]Gen. 22:17
6 [a]Ps. 121:8
7 [a]Lev. 26:7, 8
8 [a]Lev. 25:21

NKJV

Curses Pronounced from Mount Ebal

11 And Moses commanded the people on the same day, saying,
12 "These shall stand [a]on Mount Gerizim to bless the people, when you have crossed over the Jordan: Simeon, Levi, Judah, Issachar, Joseph, and Benjamin;
13 "and [a]these shall stand on Mount Ebal to curse: Reuben, Gad, Asher, Zebulun, Dan, and Naphtali.
14 "And [a]the Levites shall speak with a loud voice and say to all the men of Israel:
15 [a]'Cursed *is* the one who makes a carved or molded image, an abomination to the LORD, the work of the hands of the craftsman, and sets *it* up in secret.'
[b]"And all the people shall answer and say, 'Amen!'
16 [a]'Cursed *is* the one who treats his father or his mother with contempt.'
"And all the people shall say, 'Amen!'
17 [a]'Cursed *is* the one who moves his neighbor's landmark.'
"And all the people shall say, 'Amen!'
18 [a]'Cursed *is* the one who makes the blind to wander off the road.'
"And all the people shall say, 'Amen!'
19 [a]'Cursed *is* the one who perverts the justice due the stranger, the fatherless, and widow.'
"And all the people shall say, 'Amen!'
20 [a]'Cursed *is* the one who lies with his father's wife, because he has uncovered his father's bed.'
"And all the people shall say, 'Amen!'
21 [a]'Cursed *is* the one who lies with any kind of animal.'
"And all the people shall say, 'Amen!'
22 [a]'Cursed *is* the one who lies with his sister, the daughter of his father or the daughter of his mother.'
"And all the people shall say, 'Amen!'
23 [a]'Cursed *is* the one who lies with his mother-in-law.'
"And all the people shall say, 'Amen!'
24 [a]'Cursed *is* the one who attacks his neighbor secretly.'
"And all the people shall say, 'Amen!'
25 [a]'Cursed *is* the one who takes a bribe to slay an innocent person.'
"And all the people shall say, 'Amen!'
26 [a]'Cursed *is* the one who does not confirm *all* the words of this law.'
"And all the people shall say, 'Amen!'

Blessings on Obedience
(Lev. 26:1–13; Deut. 7:12–24)

28 "Now it shall come to pass, [a]if you diligently obey the voice of the LORD your God, to observe carefully all His commandments which I command you today, that the LORD your God [b]will set you high above all nations of the earth.
2 "And all these blessings shall come upon you and [a]overtake you, because you obey the voice of the LORD your God:
3 [a]"Blessed *shall* you *be* in the city, and blessed *shall* you *be* [b]in the country.
4 "Blessed *shall be* [a]the fruit of your body, the produce of your ground and the increase of your herds, the increase of your cattle and the offspring of your flocks.
5 "Blessed *shall be* your basket and your kneading bowl.
6 [a]"Blessed *shall* you *be* when you come in, and blessed *shall* you *be* when you go out.
7 "The LORD [a]will cause your enemies who rise against you to be defeated before your face; they shall come out against you one way and flee before you seven ways.
8 "The LORD will [a]command the blessing on you in your storehouses and in all to which you

KJV

[b]settest thine hand unto; and he shall bless thee
in the land which the LORD thy God giveth thee.
9 [a]The LORD shall establish thee an holy
people unto himself, as he hath sworn unto thee,
if thou shalt keep the commandments of the LORD
thy God, and walk in his ways.
10 And all people of the earth shall see that
thou art [a]called by the name of the LORD; and
they shall be [b]afraid of thee.
11 And [a]the LORD shall make thee plenteous
in goods, in the fruit of thy body, and in the fruit
of thy cattle, and in the fruit of thy ground, in
the land which the LORD sware unto thy fathers
to give thee.
12 The LORD shall open unto thee his good
treasure, the heaven [a]to give the rain unto thy
land in his season, and [b]to bless all the work of
thine hand: and [c]thou shalt lend unto many nations, and thou shalt not borrow.
13 And the LORD shall make [a]thee the head,
and not the tail; and thou shalt be above only,
and thou shalt not be beneath; if that thou
hearken unto the commandments of the LORD thy
God, which I command thee this day, to observe
and to do *them:*
14 [a]And thou shalt not go aside from any of
the words which I command thee this day, *to* the
right hand, or *to* the left, to go after other gods
to serve them.

Curses on Disobedience
(Lev. 26:14–46)

15 But it shall come to pass, [a]if thou wilt not
hearken unto the voice of the LORD thy God, to
observe to do all his commandments and his statutes which I command thee this day; that all these
curses shall come upon thee, and overtake thee:
16 Cursed *shalt* thou *be* in the city, and
cursed *shalt* thou *be* in the field.
17 Cursed *shall be* thy basket and thy store.
18 Cursed *shall be* the fruit of thy body, and
the fruit of thy land, the increase of thy kine, and
the flocks of thy sheep.
19 Cursed *shalt* thou *be* when thou comest
in, and cursed *shalt* thou *be* when thou goest out.
20 The LORD shall send upon thee [a]cursing,
[b]vexation, and [c]rebuke, in all that thou settest
thine hand unto for to do, until thou be destroyed,
and until thou perish quickly; because of the wickedness of thy doings, whereby thou hast forsaken
me.
21 The LORD shall make the pestilence cleave
unto thee, until he have consumed thee from off
the land, whither thou goest to possess it.
22 [a]The LORD shall smite thee with a consumption, and with a fever, and with an inflammation, and with an extreme burning, and with
the sword, and with [b]blasting, and with mildew;
and they shall pursue thee until thou perish.
23 And [a]thy heaven that *is* over thy head
shall be brass, and the earth that *is* under thee
shall be iron.
24 The LORD shall make the rain of thy land
powder and dust: from heaven shall it come down
upon thee, until thou be destroyed.
25 [a]The LORD shall cause thee to be smitten
before thine enemies: thou shalt go out one way
against them, and flee seven ways before them:
and shalt be removed into all the kingdoms of
the earth.
26 And [a]thy carcase shall be meat unto all
fowls of the air, and unto the beasts of the earth,
and no man shall fray *them* away.
27 The LORD will smite thee with [a]the botch
of Egypt, and with [b]the emerods, and with the
scab, and with the itch, whereof thou canst not
be healed.
28 The LORD shall smite thee with madness,
and blindness, and [a]astonishment of heart:
29 And thou shalt [a]grope at noonday, as the
blind gropeth in darkness, and thou shalt not
prosper in thy ways: and thou shalt be only op-

8 [b]Deut. 15:10
9 [a]Ex. 19:5, 6
10 [a]Num. 6:27; 2 Chr. 7:14; Is. 63:19; Dan. 9:18, 19 [b]Deut. 11:25
11 [a]Deut. 30:9
12 [a]Lev. 26:4; Deut. 11:14 [b]Deut. 14:29 [c]Deut. 15:6
13 [a][Is. 9:14, 15]
14 [a]Deut. 5:32; Josh. 1:7
15 [a]Lev. 26:14–39; Josh. 23:15; Dan. 9:10–14; Mal. 2:2
20 [a]Mal. 2:2 [b]Is. 65:14 [c]Ps. 80:16; Is. 30:17
22 [a]Lev. 26:16 [b]Amos 4:9
23 [a]Lev. 26:19
25 [a]Deut. 32:30
26 [a]1 Sam. 17:44; Ps. 79:2
27 [a]Ex. 15:26 [b]1 Sam. 5:6
28 [a]Jer. 4:9
29 [a]Job 5:14

NKJV

[b]set your hand, and He will bless you in the land
which the LORD your God is giving you.
9 [a]"The LORD will establish you as a holy
people to Himself, just as He has sworn to you,
if you keep the commandments of the LORD your
God and walk in His ways.
10 "Then all peoples of the earth shall see
that you are [a]called by the name of the LORD, and
they shall be [b]afraid of you.
11 "And [a]the LORD will grant you plenty of
goods, in the fruit of your body, in the increase
of your livestock, and in the produce of your
ground, in the land of which the LORD swore to
your fathers to give you.
12 "The LORD will open to you His good treasure, the heavens, [a]to give the rain to your land
in its season, and [b]to bless all the work of your
hand. [c]You shall lend to many nations, but you
shall not borrow.
13 "And the LORD will make [a]you the head
and not the tail; you shall be above only, and not
be beneath, if you heed the commandments of the
LORD your God, which I command you today, and
are careful to observe *them.*
14 [a]"So you shall not turn aside from any
of the words which I command you this day, *to*
the right or the left, to go after other gods to serve
them.

Curses on Disobedience
(Lev. 26:14–46)

15 "But it shall come to pass, [a]if you do not
obey the voice of the LORD your God, to observe
carefully all His commandments and His statutes
which I command you today, that all these curses
will come upon you and overtake you:
16 "Cursed *shall* you *be* in the city, and
cursed *shall* you *be* in the country.
17 "Cursed *shall be* your basket and your
kneading bowl.
18 "Cursed *shall be* the fruit of your body
and the produce of your land, the increase of your
cattle and the offspring of your flocks.
19 "Cursed *shall* you *be* when you come in,
and cursed *shall* you *be* when you go out.
20 "The LORD will send on you [a]cursing,
[b]confusion, and [c]rebuke in all that you set your
hand to do, until you are destroyed and until you
perish quickly, because of the wickedness of your
doings in which you have forsaken Me.
21 "The LORD will make the plague cling to
you until He has consumed you from the land
which you are going to possess.
22 [a]"The LORD will strike you with consumption, with fever, with inflammation, with severe
burning fever, with the sword, with [b]scorching,
and with mildew; they shall pursue you until you
perish.
23 "And [a]your heavens which *are* over your
head shall be bronze, and the earth which is under
you *shall be* iron.
24 "The LORD will change the rain of your
land to powder and dust; from the heaven it shall
come down on you until you are destroyed.
25 [a]"The LORD will cause you to be defeated
before your enemies; you shall go out one way
against them and flee seven ways before them;
and you shall become troublesome to all the kingdoms of the earth.
26 [a]"Your carcasses shall be food for all the
birds of the air and the beasts of the earth, and
no one shall frighten *them* away.
27 "The LORD will strike you with [a]the boils
of Egypt, with [b]tumors, with the scab, and with
the itch, from which you cannot be healed.
28 "The LORD will strike you with madness
and blindness and [a]confusion of heart.
29 "And you shall [a]grope at noonday, as a
blind man gropes in darkness; you shall not prosper in your ways; you shall be only oppressed

KJV

pressed and spoiled evermore, and no man shall save *thee.*

30 [a]Thou shalt betroth a wife, and another man shall lie with her: [b]thou shalt build an house, and thou shalt not dwell therein: [c]thou shalt plant a vineyard, and shalt not gather the grapes thereof.

31 Thine ox *shall be* slain before thine eyes, and thou shalt not eat thereof: thine ass *shall be* violently taken away from before thy face, and shall not be restored to thee: thy sheep *shall be* given unto thine enemies, and thou shalt have none to rescue *them.*

32 Thy sons and thy daughters *shall be* given unto [a]another people, and thine eyes shall look, and [b]fail *with longing* for them all the day long: and *there shall be* no might in thine [c]hand.

33 [a]The fruit of thy land, and all thy labours, shall a nation which thou knowest not eat up; and thou shalt be only oppressed and crushed alway:

34 So that thou shalt be mad for the sight of thine eyes which thou shalt see.

35 The LORD shall smite thee in the knees, and in the legs, with a sore botch that cannot be healed, from the sole of thy foot unto the top of thy head.

36 The LORD shall [a]bring thee, and thy king which thou shalt set over thee, unto a nation which neither thou nor thy fathers have known; and [b]there shalt thou serve other gods, wood and stone.

37 And thou shalt become [a]an astonishment, a proverb, [b]and a byword, among all nations whither the LORD shall lead thee.

38 [a]Thou shalt carry much seed out into the field, and shalt gather *but* little in; for [b]the locust shall consume it.

39 Thou shalt plant vineyards, and dress *them,* but shalt neither drink *of* the [a]wine, nor gather *the grapes;* for the worms shall eat them.

40 Thou shalt have olive trees throughout all thy coasts, but thou shalt not anoint *thyself* with the oil; for thine olive shall cast *his fruit.*

41 Thou shalt beget sons and daughters, but thou shalt not enjoy them; for [a]they shall go into captivity.

42 All thy trees and fruit of thy land shall the locust consume.

43 The stranger that *is* within thee shall get up above thee very high; and thou shalt come down very low.

44 He shall lend to thee, and thou shalt not lend to him: he shall be the head, and thou shalt be the tail.

45 Moreover all these curses shall come upon thee, and shall pursue thee, and overtake thee, till thou be destroyed; because thou hearkenedst not unto the voice of the LORD thy God, to keep his commandments and his statutes which he commanded thee:

46 And they shall be upon [a]thee for a sign and for a wonder, and upon thy seed for ever.

47 [a]Because thou servedst not the LORD thy God with joyfulness, and with gladness of heart, [b]for the abundance of all *things;*

48 Therefore shalt thou serve thine enemies which the LORD shall send against thee, in [a]hunger, and in thirst, and in nakedness, and in want of all *things:* and he [b]shall put a yoke of iron upon thy neck, until he have destroyed thee.

49 [a]The LORD shall bring a nation against thee from far, from the end of the earth, [b]*as swift* as the eagle flieth; a nation whose tongue thou shalt not understand;

50 A nation of fierce countenance, [a]which shall not regard the person of the old, nor shew favour to the young:

51 And he shall eat the fruit of thy cattle, and the fruit of thy land, until thou be destroyed: which *also* shall not leave thee *either* corn, wine, or oil, *or* the increase of thy kine, or flocks of thy sheep, until he have destroyed thee.

30 [a]2 Sam. 12:11; Job 31:10; Jer. 8:10 [b]Amos 5:11; Zeph. 1:13 [c]Deut. 20:6; Job 31:8; Jer. 12:13; Mic. 6:15
32 [a]2 Chr. 29:9 [b]Ps. 119:82 [c]Neh. 5:5
33 [a]Lev. 26:16; Jer. 5:15, 17
36 [a]2 Kin. 17:4, 6; 24:12, 14; 25:7, 11; 2 Chr. 36:1–21; Jer. 39:1–9 [b]Deut. 4:28; Jer. 16:13
37 [a]1 Kin. 9:7, 8; Jer. 24:9; 25:9 [b]Ps. 44:14
38 [a]Mic. 6:15; Hag. 1:6 [b]Ex. 10:4; Joel 1:4
39 [a]Zeph. 1:13
41 [a]Lam. 1:5
46 [a]Num. 26:10; Is. 8:18; Ezek. 14:8
47 [a]Deut. 12:7; Neh. 9:35–37 [b]Deut. 32:15
48 [a]Lam. 4:4–6 [b]Jer. 28:13, 14
49 [a]Is. 5:26–30; 7:18–20; Jer. 5:15 [b]Jer. 48:40; 49:22; Lam. 4:19; Hos. 8:1
50 [a]2 Chr. 36:17

NKJV

and plundered continually, and no one shall save *you.*

30 [a]"You shall betroth a wife, but another man shall lie with her; [b]you shall build a house, but you shall not dwell in it; [c]you shall plant a vineyard, but shall not gather its grapes.

31 "Your ox *shall be* slaughtered before your eyes, but you shall not eat of it; your donkey *shall be* violently taken away from before you, and shall not be restored to you; your sheep *shall be* given to your enemies, and you shall have no one to rescue *them.*

32 "Your sons and your daughters *shall be* given to [a]another people, and your eyes shall look and [b]fail *with longing* for them all day long; and *there shall be* no strength in your [c]hand.

33 "A nation whom you have not known shall eat [a]the fruit of your land and the produce of your labor, and you shall be only oppressed and crushed continually.

34 "So you shall be driven mad because of the sight which your eyes see.

35 "The LORD will strike you in the knees and on the legs with severe boils which cannot be healed, and from the sole of your foot to the top of your head.

36 "The LORD will [a]bring you and the king whom you set over you to a nation which neither you nor your fathers have known, and [b]there you shall serve other gods—wood and stone.

37 "And you shall become [a]an astonishment, a proverb, [b]and a byword among all nations where the LORD will drive you.

38 [a]"You shall carry much seed out to the field but gather little in, for [b]the locust shall consume it.

39 "You shall plant vineyards and tend *them,* but you shall neither drink *of* the [a]wine nor gather the *grapes;* for the worms shall eat them.

40 "You shall have olive trees throughout all your territory, but you shall not anoint *yourself* with the oil; for your olives shall drop off.

41 "You shall beget sons and daughters, but they shall not be yours; for [a]they shall go into captivity.

42 "Locusts shall consume all your trees and the produce of your land.

43 "The alien who *is* among you shall rise higher and higher above you, and you shall come down lower and lower.

44 "He shall lend to you, but you shall not lend to him; he shall be the head, and you shall be the tail.

45 "Moreover all these curses shall come upon you and pursue and overtake you, until you are destroyed, because you did not obey the voice of the LORD your God, to keep His commandments and His statutes which He commanded you.

46 "And they shall be upon [a]you for a sign and a wonder, and on your descendants forever.

47 [a]"Because you did not serve the LORD your God with joy and gladness of heart, [b]for the abundance of everything,

48 "therefore you shall serve your enemies, whom the LORD will send against you, in [a]hunger, in thirst, in nakedness, and in need of everything; and He [b]will put a yoke of iron on your neck until He has destroyed you.

49 [a]"The LORD will bring a nation against you from afar, from the end of the earth, [b]*as swift* as the eagle flies, a nation whose language you will not understand,

50 "a nation of fierce countenance, [a]which does not respect the elderly nor show favor to the young.

51 "And they shall eat the increase of your livestock and the produce of your land, until you are destroyed; they shall not leave you grain or new wine or oil, *or* the increase of your cattle or the offspring of your flocks, until they have destroyed you.

KJV

52 And he shall [a]besiege thee in all thy gates,
until thy high and fenced walls come down,
wherein thou trustedst, throughout all thy land:
and he shall besiege thee in all thy gates throughout all thy land, which the LORD thy God hath
given thee.
53 And [a]thou shalt eat the fruit of thine own
body, the flesh of thy sons and of thy daughters,
which the LORD thy God hath given thee, in the
siege, and in the straitness, wherewith thine enemies shall distress thee:
54 *So that* the man *that is* tender among you,
and very delicate, [a]his eye shall be evil toward
his brother, and toward [b]the wife of his bosom,
and toward the remnant of his children which he
shall leave:
55 So that he will not give to any of them of
the flesh of his children whom he shall eat: because he hath nothing left him in the siege, and
in the straitness, wherewith thine enemies shall
distress thee in all thy gates.
56 The tender and delicate woman among
you, which would not adventure to set the sole
of her foot upon the ground for delicateness and
tenderness, her eye shall be evil toward the husband of her bosom, and toward her son, and toward her daughter,
57 And toward her young one that cometh
out [a]from between her feet, and toward her children which she shall bear: for she shall eat them
for want of all *things* secretly in the siege and
straitness, wherewith thine enemy shall distress
thee in thy gates.
58 If thou wilt not observe to do all the words
of this law that are written in this book, that thou
mayest fear [a]this glorious and fearful name, THE
LORD THY GOD;
59 Then the LORD will make thy plagues
[a]wonderful, and the plagues of thy seed, *even*
great plagues, and of long continuance, and sore
sicknesses, and of long continuance.
60 Moreover he will bring upon thee all [a]the
diseases of Egypt, which thou wast afraid of; and
they shall cleave unto thee.
61 Also every sickness, and every plague,
which *is* not written in the book of this law, them
will the LORD bring upon thee, until thou be
destroyed.
62 And ye [a]shall be left few in number,
whereas ye were [b]as the stars of heaven for multitude; because thou wouldest not obey the voice
of the LORD thy God.
63 And it shall come to pass, *that* as the LORD
[a]rejoiced over you to do you good, and to multiply
you; so the LORD [b]will rejoice over you to destroy
you, and to bring you to nought; and ye shall be
[c]plucked from off the land whither thou goest to
possess it.
64 And the LORD [a]shall scatter thee among
all people, from the one end of the earth even
unto the other; and [b]there thou shalt serve other
gods, which neither thou nor thy fathers have
known, *even* wood and stone.
65 And [a]among these nations shalt thou find
no ease, neither shall the sole of thy foot have
rest: [b]but the LORD shall give thee there a trembling heart, and failing of eyes, and [c]sorrow of
mind:
66 And thy life shall hang in doubt before
thee; and thou shalt fear day and night, and shalt
have none assurance of thy life:
67 [a]In the morning thou shalt say, Would
God it were even! and at even thou shalt say,
Would God it were morning! for the fear of thine
heart wherewith thou shalt fear, and [b]for the sight
of thine eyes which thou shalt see.
68 And the LORD [a]shall bring thee into
Egypt again with ships, by the way whereof I
spake unto thee, [b]Thou shalt see it no more again:
and there ye shall be sold unto your enemies for
bondmen and bondwomen, and no man shall buy
you.

52 [a]2 Kin. 25:1, 2, 4
53 [a]Lev. 26:29; 2 Kin. 6:28, 29; Jer. 19:9; Lam. 2:20; 4:10
54 [a]Deut. 15:9 [b]Deut. 13:6
57 [a]Gen. 49:10
58 [a]Ex. 6:3
59 [a]Dan. 9:12
60 [a]Deut. 7:15
62 [a]Deut. 4:27 [b]Deut. 10:22; Neh. 9:23
63 [a]Deut. 30:9; Jer. 32:41 [b]Prov. 1:26; [Is. 1:24] [c]Jer. 12:14; 45:4
64 [a]Lev. 26:33; Deut. 4:27, 28; Neh. 1:8; Jer. 16:13; Amos 9:9 [b]Deut. 28:36
65 [a]Lam. 1:3; Amos 9:4 [b]Lev. 26:36 [c]Lev. 26:16
67 [a]Job 7:4 [b]Deut. 28:34
68 [a]Jer. 43:7; Hos. 8:13 [b]Deut. 17:16

NKJV

52 "They shall [a]besiege you at all your gates
until your high and fortified walls, in which you
trust, come down throughout all your land; and
they shall besiege you at all your gates throughout
all your land which the LORD your God has given
you.
53 [a]"You shall eat the fruit of your own body,
the flesh of your sons and your daughters whom
the LORD your God has given you, in the siege
and desperate straits in which your enemy shall
distress you.
54 "The sensitive and very refined man
among you [a]will be hostile toward his brother,
toward [b]the wife of his bosom, and toward the
rest of his children whom he leaves behind,
55 "so that he will not give any of them the
flesh of his children whom he will eat, because
he has nothing left in the siege and desperate
straits in which your enemy shall distress you at
all your gates.
56 "The tender and delicate woman among
you, who would not venture to set the sole of her
foot on the ground because of her delicateness
and sensitivity, *will refuse to the husband of her
bosom, and to her son and her daughter,
57 "her placenta which comes out [a]from between her feet and her children whom she bears;
for she will eat them secretly for lack of everything in the siege and desperate straits in which
your enemy shall distress you at all your gates.
58 "If you do not carefully observe all the
words of this law that are written in this book,
that you may fear [a]this glorious and awesome
name, THE LORD YOUR GOD,
59 "then the LORD will bring upon you and
your descendants [a]extraordinary plagues—great
and prolonged plagues—and serious and prolonged sicknesses.
60 "Moreover He will bring back on you all
[a]the diseases of Egypt, of which you were afraid,
and they shall cling to you.
61 "Also every sickness and every plague,
which *is* not written in this Book of the Law, will
the LORD bring upon you until you are destroyed.
62 "You [a]shall be left few in number,
whereas you were [b]as the stars of heaven in multitude, because you would not obey the voice of
the LORD your God.
63 "And it shall be, *that* just as the LORD [a]re-
joiced over you to do you good and multiply you,
so the LORD [b]will rejoice over you to destroy you
and bring you to nothing; and you shall be
[c]plucked from off the land which you go to
possess.
64 "Then the LORD [a]will scatter you among
all peoples, from one end of the earth to the other,
and [b]there you shall serve other gods, which neither you nor your fathers have known—wood and
stone.
65 "And [a]among those nations you shall find
no rest, nor shall the sole of your foot have a resting place; [b]but there the LORD will give you a trembling heart, failing eyes, and [c]anguish of soul.
66 "Your life shall hang in doubt before you;
you shall fear day and night, and have no assurance of life.
67 [a]"In the morning you shall say, 'Oh, that
it were evening!' And at evening you shall say,
'Oh, that it were morning!' because of the fear
which terrifies your heart, and [b]because of the
sight which your eyes see.
68 "And the LORD [a]will take you back to
Egypt in ships, by the way of which I said to you,
[b]'You shall never see it again.' And there you shall
be offered for sale to your enemies as male and
female slaves, but no one will buy *you*."

*———
28:56 Lit. *her eye shall be evil toward*

KJV

The Covenant Renewed in Moab

29 These *are* the words of the covenant, which
the LORD commanded Moses to make with
the children of Israel in the land of Moab, beside
the [a]covenant which he made with them in Horeb.
2 And Moses called unto all Israel, and said
unto them, [a]Ye have seen all that the LORD did
before your eyes in the land of Egypt unto Pharaoh, and unto all his servants, and unto all his
land;
3 [a]The great temptations which thine eyes
have seen, the signs, and those great miracles:
4 Yet [a]the LORD hath not given you an heart
to perceive, and eyes to see, and ears to hear, unto
this day.
5 [a]And I have led you forty years in the wilderness: [b]your clothes are not waxen old upon
you, and thy shoe is not waxen old upon thy foot.
6 [a]Ye have not eaten bread, neither have
ye drunk wine or strong drink: that ye might
know that I *am* the LORD your God.
7 And when ye came unto this place, [a]Sihon
the king of Heshbon, and Og the king of Bashan,
came out against us unto battle, and we smote
them:
8 And we took their land, and [a]gave it for
an inheritance unto the Reubenites, and to the
Gadites, and to the half tribe of Manasseh.
9 [a]Keep therefore the words of this covenant, and do them, that ye may [b]prosper in all
that ye do.
10 Ye stand this day all of you before the
LORD your God; your captains of your tribes, your
elders, and your officers, *with* all the men of
Israel,
11 Your little ones, your wives, and thy
stranger that *is* in thy camp, from [a]the hewer of
thy wood unto the drawer of thy water:
12 That thou shouldest enter into covenant
with the LORD thy God, and [a]into his oath, which
the LORD thy God maketh with thee this day:
13 That he may [a]establish thee to day for a
people unto himself, and *that* he may be unto thee
a God, [b]as he hath said unto thee, and [c]as he hath
sworn unto thy fathers, to Abraham, to Isaac, and
to Jacob.
14 Neither with you only [a]do I make this covenant and this oath;
15 But with *him* that standeth here with us
this day before the LORD our God, [a]and also with
him that *is* not here with us this day:
16 (For ye know how we have dwelt in the
land of Egypt; and how we came through the nations which ye passed by;
17 And ye have seen their abominations, and
their idols, wood and stone, silver and gold, which
were among them:)
18 Lest there should be among you man, or
woman, or family, or tribe, [a]whose heart turneth
away this day from the LORD our God, to go *and*
serve the gods of these nations; [b]lest there should
be among you a root that beareth [c]gall and
wormwood;
19 And it come to pass, when he heareth the
words of this curse, that he bless himself in his
heart, saying, I shall have peace, though I walk
[a]in the imagination of mine heart, [b]to add drunkenness to thirst:
20 [a]The LORD will not spare him, but then
[b]the anger of the LORD and [c]his jealousy shall
smoke against that man, and all the curses that
are written in this book shall lie upon him, and
the LORD [d]shall blot out his name from under
heaven.
21 And the LORD [a]shall separate him unto
evil out of all the tribes of Israel, according to all
the curses of the covenant that are written in this
book of the [b]law:
22 So that the generation to come of your
children that shall rise up after you, and the
stranger that shall come from a far land, shall

CHAPTER 29
1 [a]Lev. 26:46; Deut. 5:2, 3
2 [a]Ex. 19:4; Deut. 11:7
3 [a]Deut. 4:34; 7:19
4 [a][Is. 6:9, 10; Ezek. 12:2]; Matt. 13:14; [Acts 28:26, 27]; Rom. 11:8; [Eph. 4:18]
5 [a]Deut. 1:3; 8:2 [b]Deut. 8:4
6 [a]Ex. 16:12; Deut. 8:3
7 [a]Num. 21:23, 24; Deut. 2:26—3:3
8 [a]Num. 32:33; Deut. 3:12, 13
9 [a]Deut. 4:6; 1 Kin. 2:3 [b]Josh. 1:7
11 [a]Josh. 9:21, 23, 27
12 [a]Neh. 10:29
13 [a]Deut. 28:9 [b]Ex. 6:7 [c]Gen. 17:7, 8
14 [a][Jer. 31:31; Heb. 8:7, 8]
15 [a]Acts 2:39
18 [a]Deut. 11:16 [b]Heb. 12:15 [c]Deut. 32:32; Acts 8:23
19 [a]Jer. 3:17; 7:24 [b]Is. 30:1
20 [a]Ezek. 14:7 [b]Ps. 74:1 [c]Ps. 79:5; Ezek. 23:25 [d]Ex. 32:33; Deut. 9:14; 2 Kin. 14:27
21 [a][Matt. 24:51] [b]Deut. 30:10

*

29:19 *walk in the stubbornness* or *imagination*

NKJV

The Covenant Renewed in Moab

29 These *are* the words of the covenant which
the LORD commanded Moses to make with
the children of Israel in the land of Moab, besides
the [a]covenant which He made with them in Horeb.
2 Now Moses called all Israel and said to
them: [a]"You have seen all that the LORD did before your eyes in the land of Egypt, to Pharaoh
and to all his servants and to all his land—
3 [a]"the great trials which your eyes have
seen, the signs, and those great wonders.
4 "Yet [a]the LORD has not given you a heart
to perceive and eyes to see and ears to hear, to
this *very* day.
5 [a]"And I have led you forty years in the
wilderness. [b]Your clothes have not worn out on
you, and your sandals have not worn out on your
feet.
6 [a]"You have not eaten bread, nor have you
drunk wine or *similar* drink, that you may know
that I *am* the LORD your God.
7 "And when you came to this place, [a]Sihon
king of Heshbon and Og king of Bashan came
out against us to battle, and we conquered them.
8 "We took their land and [a]gave it as an
inheritance to the Reubenites, to the Gadites, and
to half the tribe of Manasseh.
9 "Therefore [a]keep the words of this covenant, and do them, that you may [b]prosper in all
that you do.
10 "All of you stand today before the LORD
your God: your leaders and your tribes and your
elders and your officers, all the men of Israel,
11 "your little ones and your wives—also the
stranger who *is* in your camp, from [a]the one who
cuts your wood to the one who draws your water—
12 "that you may enter into covenant with
the LORD your God, and [a]into His oath, which the
LORD your God makes with you today,
13 "that He may [a]establish you today as a
people for Himself, and *that* He may be God to
you, [b]just as He has spoken to you, and [c]just as
He has sworn to your fathers, to Abraham, Isaac,
and Jacob.
14 "I make this covenant and this oath, [a]not
with you alone,
15 "but with *him* who stands here with us
today before the LORD our God, [a]as well as with
him who *is* not here with us today
16 (for you know that we dwelt in the land
of Egypt and that we came through the nations
which you passed by,
17 and you saw their abominations and their
idols which *were* among them—wood and stone
and silver and gold);
18 "so that there may not be among you man
or woman or family or tribe, [a]whose heart turns
away today from the LORD our God, to go *and*
serve the gods of these nations, [b]and that there
may not be among you a root bearing [c]bitterness
or wormwood;
19 "and so it may not happen, when he hears
the words of this curse, that he blesses himself
in his heart, saying, 'I shall have peace, even
though I *follow the [a]dictates of my heart'—[b]as
though the drunkard could be included with the
sober.
20 [a]"The LORD would not spare him; for then
[b]the anger of the LORD and [c]His jealousy would
burn against that man, and every curse that is
written in this book would settle on him, and the
LORD [d]would blot out his name from under
heaven.
21 "And the LORD [a]would separate him from
all the tribes of Israel for adversity, according to
all the curses of the covenant that are written in
this Book of the [b]Law,
22 "so that the coming generation of your
children who rise up after you, and the foreigner
who comes from a far land, would say, when they

KJV

say, when they [a]see the plagues of that land, and
the sicknesses which the LORD hath laid upon it;
23 *And that* the whole land thereof *is* brimstone, [a]and salt, *and* burning, *that* it is not sown,
nor beareth, nor any grass groweth therein, [b]like
the overthrow of Sodom, and Gomorrah, Admah,
and Zeboim, which the LORD overthrew in his anger, and in his wrath:
24 Even all nations shall say, [a]Wherefore
hath the LORD done thus unto this land? what
meaneth the heat of this great anger?
25 Then men shall say, Because they have
forsaken the covenant of the LORD God of their
fathers, which he made with them when he
brought them forth out of the land of Egypt:
26 For they went and served other gods, and
worshipped them, gods whom they knew not, and
whom he had not given unto them:
27 And the anger of the LORD was kindled
against this land, [a]to bring upon it all the curses
that are written in this book:
28 And the LORD [a]rooted them out of their
land in anger, and in wrath, and in great indignation, and cast them into another land, as *it is* this
day.
29 The secret *things belong* unto the LORD
our God: but those *things which are* revealed *belong* unto us and to our children for ever, that
we may do all the words of this law.

The Blessing of Returning to God

30 And [a]it shall come to pass, when [b]all these
things are come upon thee, the blessing and
the [c]curse, which I have set before thee, and [d]thou
shalt call *them* to mind among all the nations,
whither the LORD thy God hath driven thee,
2 And shalt [a]return unto the LORD thy God,
and shalt obey his voice according to all that I
command thee this day, thou and thy children,
with all thine heart, and with all thy soul;
3 [a]That then the LORD thy God will turn thy
captivity, and have compassion upon thee, and
will return and [b]gather thee from all the nations,
whither the LORD thy God hath scattered thee.
4 [a]If *any* of thine be driven out unto the outmost *parts* of heaven, from thence will the LORD
thy God gather thee, and from thence will he fetch
thee:
5 And the LORD thy God will bring thee into
the land which thy fathers possessed, and thou
shalt possess it; and he will do thee good, and
multiply thee above thy fathers.
6 And [a]the LORD thy God will circumcise
thine heart, and the heart of thy seed, to love the
LORD thy God with all thine heart, and with all
thy soul, that thou mayest live.
7 And the LORD thy God will put all these
[a]curses upon thine enemies, and on them that hate
thee, which persecuted thee.
8 And thou shalt [a]return and obey the voice
of the LORD, and do all his commandments which
I command thee this day.
9 [a]And the LORD thy God will make thee
plenteous in every work of thine hand, in the fruit
of thy body, and in the fruit of thy cattle, and in
the fruit of thy land, for good: for the LORD will
again [b]rejoice over thee for good, as he rejoiced
over thy fathers:
10 If thou shalt hearken unto the voice of the
LORD thy God, to keep his commandments and
his statutes which are written in this book of the
law, *and* if thou turn unto the LORD thy God with
all thine heart, and with all thy soul.

The Choice of Life or Death

11 For this commandment which I command
thee this day, [a]it *is* not hidden from thee, neither
is it far off.
12 [a]It *is* not in heaven, that thou shouldest
say, Who shall go up for us to heaven, and bring
it unto us, that we may hear it, and do it?
13 Neither *is* it beyond the sea, that thou

---

22 [a]Jer. 19:8; 49:17; 50:13
23 [a]Jer. 17:6; Zeph. 2:9 [b]Gen. 19:24, 25; Is. 1:9; Jer. 20:16; Hos. 11:8
24 [a]1 Kin. 9:8; Jer. 22:8
27 [a]Dan. 9:11
28 [a]1 Kin. 14:15; 2 Chr. 7:20; Ps. 52:5; Prov. 2:22

CHAPTER 30
1 [a]Lev. 26:40 [b]Deut. 28:2 [c]Deut. 28:15–45 [d]Deut. 4:29, 30
2 [a]Deut. 4:29, 30; Neh. 1:9; Is. 55:7; Lam. 3:40; Joel 2:12
3 [a]Ps. 106:45; Jer. 29:14; Lam. 3:22, 32 [b]Ps. 147:2; Jer. 32:37; Ezek. 34:13
4 [a]Deut. 28:64; Neh. 1:9; Is. 62:11
6 [a]Deut. 10:16; Jer. 32:39; Ezek. 11:19
7 [a]Is. 54:15–17; Jer. 30:16, 20
8 [a]Zeph. 3:20
9 [a]Deut. 28:11 [b]Deut. 28:63; Jer. 32:41
11 [a]Is. 45:19
12 [a]Prov. 30:4; Rom. 10:6–8

NKJV

[a]see the plagues of that land and the sicknesses
which the LORD has laid on it:
23 'The whole land *is* brimstone, [a]salt, and
burning; it is not sown, nor does it bear, nor does
any grass grow there, [b]like the overthrow of
Sodom and Gomorrah, Admah, and Zeboiim,
which the LORD overthrew in His anger and His
wrath.'
24 "All nations would say, [a]'Why has the
LORD done so to this land? What does the heat
of this great anger mean?'
25 "Then *people* would say: 'Because they
have forsaken the covenant of the LORD God of
their fathers, which He made with them when He
brought them out of the land of Egypt;
26 'for they went and served other gods and
worshiped them, gods that they did not know and
that He had not given to them.
27 'Then the anger of the LORD was aroused
against this land, [a]to bring on it every curse that
is written in this book.
28 'And the LORD [a]uprooted them from their
land in anger, in wrath, and in great indignation,
and cast them into another land, as *it is* this day.'
29 "The secret *things belong* to the LORD our
God, but those *things which are* revealed *belong*
to us and to our children forever, that *we* may
do all the words of this law.

The Blessing of Returning to God

30 "Now [a]it shall come to pass, when [b]all
these things come upon you, the blessing
and the [c]curse which I have set before you, and
[d]you call *them* to mind among all the nations
where the LORD your God drives you,
2 "and you [a]return to the LORD your God
and obey His voice, according to all that I command you today, you and your children, with all
your heart and with all your soul,
3 [a]"that the LORD your God will bring you
back from captivity, and have compassion on you,
and [b]gather you again from all the nations where
the LORD your God has scattered you.
4 [a]"If *any* of you are driven out to the farthest *parts* under heaven, from there the LORD
your God will gather you, and from there He will
bring you.
5 "Then the LORD your God will bring you
to the land which your fathers possessed, and you
shall possess it. He will prosper you and multiply
you more than your fathers.
6 "And [a]the LORD your God will circumcise
your heart and the heart of your descendants, to
love the LORD your God with all your heart and
with all your soul, that you may live.
7 "Also the LORD your God will put all these
[a]curses on your enemies and on those who hate
you, who persecuted you.
8 "And you will [a]again obey the voice of
the LORD and do all His commandments which I
command you today.
9 [a]"The LORD your God will make you
abound in all the work of your hand, in the fruit
of your body, in the increase of your livestock,
and in the produce of your land for good. For the
LORD will again [b]rejoice over you for good as He
rejoiced over your fathers,
10 "if you obey the voice of the LORD your
God, to keep His commandments and His statutes
which are written in this Book of the Law, *and* if
you turn to the LORD your God with all your heart
and with all your soul.

The Choice of Life or Death

11 "For this commandment which I command you today [a]*is* not *too* mysterious for you,
nor *is* it far off.
12 [a]"It *is* not in heaven, that you should say,
'Who will ascend into heaven for us and bring it
to us, that we may hear it and do it?'
13 "Nor *is* it beyond the sea, that you should

KJV

shouldest say, Who shall go over the sea for us, and bring it unto us, that we may hear it, and do it?

14 But the word *is* very nigh unto thee, in thy [a]mouth, and in thy heart, that thou mayest do it.

15 See, [a]I have set before thee this day life and good, and death and evil;

16 In that I command thee this day to love the LORD thy God, to walk in his ways, and to keep his commandments and his statutes and his judgments, that thou mayest live and multiply: and the LORD thy God shall bless thee in the land whither thou goest to possess it.

17 But if thine heart turn away, so that thou wilt not hear, but shalt be drawn away, and worship other gods, and serve them;

18 [a]I denounce unto you this day, that ye shall surely perish, *and that* ye shall not prolong *your* days upon the land, whither thou passest over Jordan to go to possess it.

19 [a]I call heaven and earth to record this day against you, *that* [b]I have set before you life and death, blessing and cursing: therefore choose life, that both thou and thy seed may live:

20 That thou mayest love the LORD thy God, *and* that thou mayest obey his voice, and that thou mayest cleave unto him: for he *is* thy [a]life, and the length of thy days: that thou mayest dwell in the land which the LORD sware unto thy fathers, to Abraham, to Isaac, and to Jacob, to give them.

Joshua the New Leader of Israel
(Num. 27:12–23)

31 And Moses went and spake these words unto all Israel.

2 And he said unto them, I [a]*am* an hundred and twenty years old this day; I can no more [b]go out and come in: also the LORD hath said unto me, [c]Thou shalt not go over this Jordan.

3 The LORD thy God, [a]he will go over before thee, *and* he will destroy these nations from before thee, and thou shalt possess them: *and* [b]Joshua, he shall go over before thee, [c]as the LORD hath said.

4 [a]And the LORD shall do unto them [b]as he did to Sihon and to Og, kings of the Amorites, and unto the land of them, whom he destroyed.

5 And [a]the LORD shall give them up before your face, that ye may do unto them according unto all the commandments which I have commanded you.

6 [a]Be strong and of a good courage, [b]fear not, nor be afraid of them: for the LORD thy God, [c]he *it is* that doth go with thee; [d]he will not fail thee, nor forsake thee.

7 And Moses called unto Joshua, and said unto him in the sight of all Israel, [a]Be strong and of a good courage: for thou must go with this people unto the land which the LORD hath sworn unto their fathers to give them; and thou shalt cause them to inherit it.

8 And the LORD, [a]he *it is* that doth go before thee; [b]he will be with thee, he will not fail thee, neither forsake thee: fear not, neither be dismayed.

The Law to Be Read Every Seven Years

9 And Moses wrote this law, [a]and delivered it unto the priests the sons of Levi, [b]which bare the ark of the covenant of the LORD, and unto all the elders of Israel.

10 And Moses commanded them, saying, At the end of *every* seven years, in the solemnity of the [a]year of release, [b]in the feast of tabernacles,

11 When all Israel is come to [a]appear before the LORD thy God in the [b]place which he shall choose, [c]thou shalt read this law before all Israel in their hearing.

12 [a]Gather the people together, men, and women, and children, and thy stranger that *is* within thy gates, that they may hear, and that they

14 [a]Rom. 10:8
15 [a]Deut. 30:1, 19
18 [a]Deut. 4:26; 8:19
19 [a]Deut. 4:26 [b]Deut. 30:15
20 [a]Ps. 27:1; [John 11:25; 14:6; Col. 3:4]

CHAPTER 31
2 [a]Ex. 7:7; Deut. 34:7 [b]Num. 27:17; 1 Kin. 3:7 [c]Num. 20:12
3 [a]Deut. 9:3; Josh. 11:23 [b]Num. 27:18 [c]Num. 27:21
4 [a]Deut. 3:21 [b]Num. 21:24, 33
5 [a]Deut. 7:2; 20:10–20
6 [a]Josh. 10:25; 1 Chr. 22:13 [b]Deut. 1:29 [c]Deut. 20:4 [d]Josh. 1:5; Heb. 13:5
7 [a]Num. 27:19; Deut. 31:23; Josh. 1:6
8 [a]Ex. 13:21 [b]Deut. 31:6; Josh. 1:5; 1 Chr. 28:20; Heb. 13:5
9 [a]Deut. 17:18; 31:25, 26 [b]Num. 4:5, 6, 15; Deut. 10:8; 31:25, 26; Josh. 3:3
10 [a]Deut. 15:1, 2 [b]Lev. 23:34; Deut. 16:13
11 [a]Deut. 16:16 [b]Deut. 12:5 [c]Josh. 8:34; 2 Kin. 23:2
12 [a]Deut. 4:10

NKJV

say, 'Who will go over the sea for us and bring it to us, that we may hear it and do it?'

14 "But the word *is* very near you, [a]in your mouth and in your heart, that you may do it.

15 "See, [a]I have set before you today life and good, death and evil,

16 "in that I command you today to love the LORD your God, to walk in His ways, and to keep His commandments, His statutes, and His judgments, that you may live and multiply; and the LORD your God will bless you in the land which you go to possess.

17 "But if your heart turns away so that you do not hear, and are drawn away, and worship other gods and serve them,

18 [a]"I announce to you today that you shall surely perish; you shall not prolong *your* days in the land which you cross over the Jordan to go in and possess.

19 [a]"I call heaven and earth as witnesses today against you, *that* [b]I have set before you life and death, blessing and cursing; therefore choose life, that both you and your descendants may live;

20 "that you may love the LORD your God, that you may obey His voice, and that you may cling to Him, for He *is* your [a]life and the length of your days; and that you may dwell in the land which the LORD swore to your fathers, to Abraham, Isaac, and Jacob, to give them."

Joshua the New Leader of Israel
(Num. 27:12–23)

31 Then Moses went and spoke these words to all Israel.

2 And he said to them: "I [a]*am* one hundred and twenty years old today. I can no longer [b]go out and come in. Also the LORD has said to me, [c]'You shall not cross over this Jordan.'

3 "The LORD your God [a]Himself crosses over before you; He will destroy these nations from before you, and you shall dispossess them. [b]Joshua himself crosses over before you, just [c]as the LORD has said.

4 [a]"And the LORD will do to them [b]as He did to Sihon and Og, the kings of the Amorites and their land, when He destroyed them.

5 [a]"The LORD will give them over to you, that you may do to them according to every commandment which I have commanded you.

6 [a]"Be strong and of good courage, [b]do not fear nor be afraid of them; for the LORD your God, [c]He *is* the One who goes with you. [d]He will not leave you nor forsake you."

7 Then Moses called Joshua and said to him in the sight of all Israel, [a]"Be strong and of good courage, for you must go with this people to the land which the LORD has sworn to their fathers to give them, and you shall cause them to inherit it.

8 "And the LORD, [a]He *is* the One who goes before you. [b]He will be with you, He will not leave you nor forsake you; do not fear nor be dismayed."

The Law to Be Read Every Seven Years

9 So Moses wrote this law [a]and delivered it to the priests, the sons of Levi, [b]who bore the ark of the covenant of the LORD, and to all the elders of Israel.

10 And Moses commanded them, saying: "At the end of *every* seven years, at the appointed time in the [a]year of release, [b]at the Feast of Tabernacles,

11 "when all Israel comes to [a]appear before the LORD your God in the [b]place which He chooses, [c]you shall read this law before all Israel in their hearing.

12 [a]"Gather the people together, men and women and little ones, and the stranger who *is* within your gates, that they may hear and that

KJV

may learn, and fear the LORD your God, and observe to do all the words of this law:

13 And *that* their children, [a]which have not known *any thing*, [b]may hear, and learn to fear the LORD your God, as long as ye live in the land whither ye go over Jordan to possess it.

Prediction of Israel's Rebellion

14 And the LORD said unto Moses, [a]Behold, thy days approach that thou must die: call Joshua, and present yourselves in the tabernacle of the congregation, that [b]I may give him a charge. And Moses and Joshua went, and presented themselves in the tabernacle of the congregation.

15 And [a]the LORD appeared in the tabernacle in a pillar of a cloud: and the pillar of the cloud stood over the door of the tabernacle.

16 And the LORD said unto Moses, Behold, thou shalt sleep with thy fathers; and this people will [a]rise up, and [b]go a whoring after the gods of the strangers of the land, whither they go *to be* among them, and will [c]forsake me, and [d]break my covenant which I have made with them.

17 Then my anger shall be [a]kindled against them in that day, and [b]I will forsake them, and I will [c]hide my face from them, and they shall be devoured, and many evils and troubles shall befall them; so that they will say in that day, [d]Are not these evils come upon us, because our God *is* [e]not among us?

18 And [a]I will surely hide my face in that day for all the evils which they shall have wrought, in that they are turned unto other gods.

19 Now therefore write ye this song for you, and teach it the children of Israel: put it in their mouths, that this song may be [a]a witness for me against the children of Israel.

20 For when I shall have brought them into the land which I sware unto their fathers, that floweth with milk and honey; and they shall have eaten and filled themselves, [a]and waxen fat; [b]then will they turn unto other gods, and serve them, and provoke me, and break my covenant.

21 And it shall come to pass, [a]when many evils and troubles are befallen them, that this song shall testify against them as a witness; for it shall not be forgotten out of the mouths of their seed: for [b]I know their imagination [c]which they go about, even now, before I have brought them into the land which I sware.

22 Moses therefore wrote this song the same day, and taught it the children of Israel.

23 [a]And he gave Joshua the son of Nun a charge, and said, [b]Be strong and of a good courage: for thou shalt bring the children of Israel into the land which I sware unto them: and I will be with thee.

24 And it came to pass, when Moses had made an end of writing the words of this law in a book, until they were finished,

25 That Moses commanded the Levites, which bare the ark of the covenant of the LORD, saying,

26 Take this book of the law, [a]and put it in the side of the ark of the covenant of the LORD your God, that it may be there [b]for a witness against thee.

27 [a]For I know thy rebellion, and thy [b]stiff neck: behold, while I am yet alive with you this day, ye have been rebellious against the LORD; and how much more after my death?

28 Gather unto me all the elders of your tribes, and your officers, that I may speak these words in their ears, [a]and call heaven and earth to record against them.

29 For I know that after my death ye will utterly [a]corrupt *yourselves*, and turn aside from the way which I have commanded you; and [b]evil will befall you [c]in the latter days; because ye will do evil in the sight of the LORD, to provoke him to anger through the work of your hands.

13 [a]Deut. 11:2 [b]Ps. 78:6, 7
14 [a]Num. 27:13 [b]Num. 27:19; Deut. 3:28
15 [a]Ex. 33:9
16 [a]Deut. 29:22 [b]Ex. 34:15; Deut. 4:25–28; Judg. 2:11, 12, 17 [c]Deut. 32:15 [d]Judg. 2:20
17 [a]Judg. 2:14; 6:13 [b]2 Chr. 15:2 [c]Deut. 32:20 [d]Judg. 6:13 [e]Num. 14:42
18 [a]Deut. 31:17; [Is. 1:15, 16]
19 [a]Deut. 31:22, 26
20 [a]Deut. 32:15–17 [b]Deut. 31:16
21 [a]Deut. 31:17 [b]Hos. 5:3 [c]Amos 5:25, 26
23 [a]Num. 27:23; Deut. 31:14 [b]Deut. 31:7
26 [a]2 Kin. 22:8 [b]Deut. 31:19
27 [a]Deut. 9:7, 24 [b]Ex. 32:9; Deut. 9:6, 13
28 [a]Deut. 30:19
29 [a]Deut. 32:5; Judg. 2:19; [Acts 20:29, 30] [b]Deut. 28:15 [c]Gen. 49:1; Deut. 4:30

NKJV

they may learn to fear the LORD your God and carefully observe all the words of this law,

13 "and *that* their children, [a]who have not known it, [b]may hear and learn to fear the LORD your God as long as you live in the land which you cross the Jordan to possess."

Prediction of Israel's Rebellion

14 Then the LORD said to Moses, [a]"Behold, the days approach when you must die; call Joshua, and present yourselves in the tabernacle of meeting, that [b]I may inaugurate him." So Moses and Joshua went and presented themselves in the tabernacle of meeting.

15 Now [a]the LORD appeared at the tabernacle in a pillar of cloud, and the pillar of cloud stood above the door of the tabernacle.

16 And the LORD said to Moses: "Behold, you will rest with your fathers; and this people will [a]rise and [b]play the harlot with the gods of the foreigners of the land, where they go *to be* among them, and they will [c]forsake Me and [d]break My covenant which I have made with them.

17 "Then My anger shall be [a]aroused against them in that day, and [b]I will forsake them, and I will [c]hide My face from them, and they shall be devoured. And many evils and troubles shall befall them, so that they will say in that day, [d]'Have not these evils come upon us because our God *is* [e]not among us?'

18 "And [a]I will surely hide My face in that day because of all the evil which they have done, in that they have turned to other gods.

19 "Now therefore, write down this song for yourselves, and teach it to the children of Israel; put it in their mouths, that this song may be [a]a witness for Me against the children of Israel.

20 "When I have brought them to the land flowing with milk and honey, of which I swore to their fathers, and they have eaten and filled themselves [a]and grown fat, [b]then they will turn to other gods and serve them; and they will provoke Me and break My covenant.

21 "Then it shall be, [a]when many evils and troubles have come upon them, that this song will testify against them as a witness; for it will not be forgotten in the mouths of their descendants, for [b]I know the inclination [c]of their behavior today, even before I have brought them to the land of which I swore *to give them*."

22 Therefore Moses wrote this song the same day, and taught it to the children of Israel.

23 [a]Then He inaugurated Joshua the son of Nun, and said, [b]"Be strong and of good courage; for you shall bring the children of Israel into the land of which I swore to them, and I will be with you."

24 So it was, when Moses had completed writing the words of this law in a book, when they were finished,

25 that Moses commanded the Levites, who bore the ark of the covenant of the LORD, saying:

26 "Take this Book of the Law, [a]and put it beside the ark of the covenant of the LORD your God, that it may be there [b]as a witness against you;

27 [a]"for I know your rebellion and your [b]stiff neck. *If* today, while I am yet alive with you, you have been rebellious against the LORD, then how much more after my death?

28 "Gather to me all the elders of your tribes, and your officers, that I may speak these words in their hearing [a]and call heaven and earth to witness against them.

29 "For I know that after my death you will [a]become utterly corrupt, and turn aside from the way which I have commanded you. And [b]evil will befall you [c]in the latter days, because you will do evil in the sight of the LORD, to provoke Him to anger through the work of your hands."

KJV

The Song of Moses

30 And Moses spake in the ears of all the congregation of Israel the words of this song, until they were ended.

32 Give [a]ear, O ye heavens, and I will speak; and hear, O [b]earth, the words of my mouth.
2 [a]My doctrine shall drop as the rain, my speech shall distil as the dew, [b]as the small rain upon the tender herb, and as the showers upon the grass:
3 Because I will publish the [a]name of the LORD: [b]ascribe ye greatness unto our God.
4 *He is* [a]the Rock, [b]his work *is* perfect: for all his ways *are* judgment: [c]a God of truth and [d]without iniquity, just and right *is* he.
5 [a]They have corrupted themselves, their spot *is* not *the spot* of his children: *they are* a [b]perverse and crooked generation.
6 Do ye thus [a]requite the LORD, O foolish people and unwise? *is* not he [b]thy father *that* hath [c]bought thee? Hath he not [d]made thee, and established thee?
7 [a]Remember the days of old, consider the years of many generations: [b]ask thy father, and he will shew thee; thy elders, and they will tell thee.
8 When the Most High [a]divided to the nations their inheritance, when he [b]separated the sons of Adam, he set the bounds of the people according to the number of the children of Israel.
9 For [a]the LORD's portion *is* his people; Jacob *is* the lot of his inheritance.
10 He found him [a]in a desert land, and in the waste howling wilderness; he led him about, he instructed him, he [b]kept him as the apple of his eye.
11 [a]As an eagle stirreth up her nest, fluttereth over her young, spreadeth abroad her wings, taketh them, beareth them on her wings:
12 *So* the LORD alone did lead him, and *there was* no strange god with him.
13 [a]He made him ride on the high places of the earth, that he might eat the increase of the fields; and he made him to suck honey out of the rock, and oil out of the flinty rock;
14 Butter of kine, and milk of sheep, [a]with fat of lambs, and rams of the breed of Bashan, and goats, with the fat of kidneys of wheat; and thou didst drink the pure [b]blood of the grape.
15 But Jeshurun waxed fat, and kicked: [a]thou art waxen fat, thou art grown thick, thou art covered *with fatness;* then he [b]forsook God *which* [c]made him, and lightly esteemed the [d]Rock of his salvation.
16 [a]They provoked him to jealousy with strange *gods,* with abominations provoked they him to anger.
17 [a]They sacrificed unto devils, not to God; to gods whom they knew not, to new *gods that*

CHAPTER 32
1 [a]Deut. 4:26; Ps. 50:4; Is. 1:2 [b]Jer. 6:19
2 [a]Is. 55:10, 11 [b]Ps. 72:6
3 [a]Deut. 28:58 [b]1 Chr. 29:11
4 [a]Deut. 32:15, 18, 30; Ps. 18:2 [b]2 Sam. 22:31 [c]Deut. 7:9; Is. 65:16; Jer. 10:10 [d]Job 34:10
5 [a]Deut. 4:25; 31:29 [b]Phil. 2:15
6 [a]Ps. 116:12 [b]Ex. 4:22; Deut. 1:31; Is. 63:16 [c]Ps. 74:2 [d]Deut. 32:15
7 [a]Ps. 44:1 [b]Ex. 12:26; 13:14; Ps. 78:5–8
8 [a]Acts 17:26 [b]Gen. 11:8
9 [a]Ex. 19:5
10 [a]Jer. 2:6; Hos. 13:5 [b]Ps. 17:8; Prov. 7:2; Zech. 2:8
11 [a]Is. 31:5
13 [a]Is. 58:14
14 [a]Ps. 81:16 [b]Gen. 49:11
15 [a]Deut. 31:20 [b]Is. 1:4 [c]Is. 51:13 [d]Ps. 95:1
16 [a]Ps. 78:58; 1 Cor. 10:22
17 [a]Rev. 9:20

NKJV

The Song of Moses

30 Then Moses spoke in the hearing of all the assembly of Israel the words of this song until they were ended:

32 "Give [a]ear, O heavens, and I will speak;
And hear, O [b]earth, the words of my mouth.
2 Let [a]my teaching drop as the rain,
My speech distill as the dew,
[b]As raindrops on the tender herb,
And as showers on the grass.
3 For I proclaim the [a]name of the LORD:
[b]Ascribe greatness to our God.
4 *He is* [a]the Rock, [b]His work *is* perfect;
For all His ways *are* justice,
[c]A God of truth and [d]without injustice;
Righteous and upright *is* He.

5 "They[a] have corrupted themselves;
They are not His children,
Because of their blemish:
A [b]perverse and crooked generation.
6 Do you thus [a]deal with the LORD,
O foolish and unwise people?
Is He not [b]your Father, *who* [c]bought you?
Has He not [d]made you and established you?

7 "Remember[a] the days of old,
Consider the years of many generations.
[b]Ask your father, and he will show you;
Your elders, and they will tell you:
8 When the Most High [a]divided their inheritance to the nations,
When He [b]separated the sons of Adam,
He set the boundaries of the peoples
According to the number of the children of Israel.
9 For [a]the LORD's portion *is* His people;
Jacob *is* the place of His inheritance.

10 "He found him [a]in a desert land
And in the wasteland, a howling wilderness;
He encircled him, He instructed him,
He [b]kept him as the apple of His eye.
11 [a]As an eagle stirs up its nest,
Hovers over its young,
Spreading out its wings, taking them up,
Carrying them on its wings,
12 So the LORD alone led him,
And *there was* no foreign god with him.

13 "He[a] made him ride in the heights of the earth,
That he might eat the produce of the fields;
He made him draw honey from the rock,
And oil from the flinty rock;
14 Curds from the cattle, and milk of the flock,
[a]With fat of lambs;
And rams of the breed of Bashan, and goats,
With the choicest wheat;
And you drank wine, the [b]blood of the grapes.

15 "But Jeshurun grew fat and kicked;
[a]You grew fat, you grew thick,
You are obese!
Then he [b]forsook God *who* [c]made him,
And scornfully esteemed the [d]Rock of his salvation.
16 [a]They provoked Him to jealousy with foreign *gods;*
With abominations they provoked Him to anger.
17 [a]They sacrificed to demons, not to God,
To gods they did not know,

KJV

came newly up, whom your fathers feared not.

18 [a]Of the Rock *that* begat thee thou art unmindful, and hast [b]forgotten God that formed thee.

19 [a]And when the LORD saw *it*, he abhorred *them*, because of the provoking of his sons, and of his daughters.

20 And he said, I will hide my face from them, I will see what their end *shall be:* for they *are* a very froward generation, [a]children in whom *is* no faith.

21 [a]They have moved me to jealousy with *that which is* not God; they have provoked me to anger [b]with their vanities: and [c]I will move them to jealousy with *those which are* not a people; I will provoke them to anger with a foolish nation.

22 For [a]a fire is kindled in mine anger, and shall burn unto the lowest hell, and shall consume the earth with her increase, and set on fire the foundations of the mountains.

23 I will [a]heap mischiefs upon them; [b]I will spend mine arrows upon them.

24 *They shall be* burnt with hunger, and devoured with burning heat, and with bitter destruction: I will also send the [a]teeth of beasts upon them, with the poison of serpents of the dust.

25 The sword without, and terror within, shall destroy both the young man and the virgin, the suckling *also* with the man of gray hairs.

26 [a]I said, I would scatter them into corners, I would make the remembrance of them to cease from among men:

27 Were it not that I feared the wrath of the enemy, lest their adversaries should behave themselves strangely, *and* lest they should say, [a]Our hand *is* high, and the LORD hath not done all this.

28 For they *are* a nation void of counsel, neither *is there any* understanding in them.

29 [a]O that they were wise, *that* they understood this, *that* they would consider their [b]latter end!

30 How should one chase a thousand, and two put ten thousand to flight, except their Rock [a]had sold them, and the LORD had shut them up?

31 For their rock *is* not as our Rock, [a]even our enemies themselves *being* judges.

32 For [a]their vine *is* of the vine of Sodom, and of the fields of Gomorrah: their grapes *are* grapes of gall, their clusters *are* bitter:

33 Their wine *is* [a]the poison of dragons, and the cruel [b]venom of asps.

34 *Is* not this [a]laid up in store with me, *and* sealed up among my treasures?

35 [a]To me *belongeth* vengeance, and recompence; their foot shall slide in *due* time: [b]for the day of their calamity *is* at hand, and the things that shall come upon them make haste.

18 [a]Is. 17:10 [b]Jer. 2:32
19 [a]Judg. 2:14
20 [a]Matt. 17:17
21 [a]Ps. 78:58 [b]Ps. 31:6 [c]Rom. 10:19
22 [a]Num. 16:33–35; Ps. 18:7, 8; Lam. 4:11
23 [a]Ex. 32:12; Deut. 29:21, 24 [b]Ps. 7:12, 13
24 [a]Lev. 26:22
26 [a]Ezek. 20:23
27 [a]Is. 10:12–15
29 [a]Ps. 81:13; [Luke 19:42] [b]Deut. 31:29
30 [a]Judg. 2:14; Ps. 44:12
31 [a][1 Sam. 4:7, 8; Jer. 40:2, 3]
32 [a]Is. 1:8–10
33 [a]Ps. 58:4 [b]Rom. 3:13
34 [a][Jer. 2:22]
35 [a]Ps. 94:1; Rom. 12:19; Heb. 10:30 [b]2 Pet. 2:3

NKJV

To new *gods*, new arrivals
That your fathers did not fear.
18 [a]Of the Rock *who* begot you, you are unmindful,
And have [b]forgotten the God who fathered you.

19 "And[a] when the LORD saw *it*, He spurned *them*,
Because of the provocation of His sons and His daughters.
20 And He said: 'I will hide My face from them,
I will see what their end *will be*,
For they *are* a perverse generation,
[a]Children in whom *is* no faith.
21 [a]They have provoked Me to jealousy by *what* is not God;
They have moved Me to anger [b]by their foolish idols.
But [c]I will provoke them to jealousy by *those who are* not a nation;
I will move them to anger by a foolish nation.
22 For [a]a fire is kindled in My anger,
And shall burn to the lowest hell;
It shall consume the earth with her increase,
And set on fire the foundations of the mountains.

23 'I will [a]heap disasters on them;
[b]I will spend My arrows on them.
24 *They shall be* wasted with hunger,
Devoured by pestilence and bitter destruction;
I will also send against them the [a]teeth of beasts,
With the poison of serpents of the dust.
25 The sword shall destroy outside;
There shall be terror within
For the young man and virgin,
The nursing child with the man of gray hairs.
26 [a]I would have said, "I will dash them in pieces,
I will make the memory of them to cease from among men,"
27 Had I not feared the wrath of the enemy,
Lest their adversaries should misunderstand,
Lest they should say, [a]"Our hand *is* high;
And it is not the LORD who has done all this." '

28 "For they *are* a nation void of counsel,
Nor *is there any* understanding in them.
29 [a]Oh, that they were wise, *that* they understood this,
That they would consider their [b]latter end!
30 How could one chase a thousand,
And two put ten thousand to flight,
Unless their Rock [a]had sold them,
And the LORD had surrendered them?
31 For their rock *is* not like our Rock,
[a]Even our enemies themselves *being* judges.
32 For [a]their vine *is* of the vine of Sodom
And of the fields of Gomorrah;
Their grapes *are* grapes of gall,
Their clusters *are* bitter.
33 Their wine *is* [a]the poison of serpents,
And the cruel [b]venom of cobras.

34 '*Is* this not [a]laid up in store with Me,
Sealed up among My treasures?
35 [a]Vengeance is Mine, and recompense;
Their foot shall slip in *due* time;
[b]For the day of their calamity *is* at hand,
And the things to come hasten upon them.'

KJV

36 [a]For the LORD shall judge his people, [b]and
repent himself for his servants, when he seeth that
their power is gone, and [c]*there is* none shut up,
or left.
37 And he shall say, [a]Where *are* their gods,
their rock in whom they trusted,
38 Which did eat the fat of their sacrifices,
and drank the wine of their drink offerings? Let
them rise up and help you, *and* be your protection.
39 See now that [a]I, *even* I, *am* he, and [b]*there
is* no god with me: [c]I kill, and I make alive; I
wound, and I heal: neither *is there any* that can
deliver out of my hand.
40 For I lift up my hand to heaven, and say,
I live for ever.
41 [a]If I whet my glittering sword, and mine
hand take hold on judgment; I will render vengeance to mine enemies, and will reward them
that hate me.
42 I will make mine arrows drunk with blood,
and my sword shall devour flesh; *and that* with
the blood of the slain and of the captives, from
the beginning of revenges upon the enemy.
43 [a]Rejoice, O ye nations, *with* his people:
for he will [b]avenge the blood of his servants, and
will render vengeance to his adversaries, and [c]will
be merciful unto his land, *and* to his people.
44 And Moses came and spake all the words
of this song in the ears of the people, he, and
Hoshea the son of Nun.
45 And Moses made an end of speaking all
these words to all Israel:
46 And he said unto them, [a]Set your hearts
unto all the words which I testify among you this
day, which ye shall command your [b]children to
observe to do, all the words of this law.
47 For it *is* not a vain thing for you; because
it *is* your [a]life: and through this thing ye shall
prolong *your* days in the land, whither ye go over
Jordan to possess it.

Moses to Die on Mount Nebo

48 And the LORD spake unto Moses that selfsame day, saying,
49 [a]Get thee up into this mountain Abarim,
unto mount Nebo, which *is* in the land of Moab,
that *is* over against Jericho; and behold the land
of Canaan, which I give unto the children of Israel
for a possession:
50 And die in the mount whither thou goest
up, and be gathered unto thy people; as [a]Aaron
thy brother died in mount Hor, and was gathered
unto his people:
51 Because [a]ye trespassed against me among
the children of Israel at the waters of Meribah-
Kadesh, in the wilderness of Zin; because ye
[b]sanctified me not in the midst of the children of
Israel.
52 [a]Yet thou shalt see the land before *thee;*
but thou shalt not go thither unto the land which
I give the children of Israel.

Moses' Final Blessing on Israel

33 And this *is* [a]the blessing, wherewith Moses
[b]the man of God blessed the children of
Israel before his death.
2 And he said, [a]The LORD came from Sinai,
and rose up from [b]Seir unto them; he shined
forth from [c]mount Paran, and he came with

36 [a]Ps. 135:14; Heb. 10:30 [b]Ps. 106:45; Jer. 31:20 [c]2 Kin. 14:26
37 [a]Judg. 10:14; Jer. 2:28
39 [a]Is. 41:4; 43:10 [b]Deut. 32:12; Is. 45:5 [c]1 Sam. 2:6; Ps. 68:20
41 [a]Is. 1:24; 66:16; Jer. 50:28–32
43 [a]Rom. 15:10 [b]2 Kin. 9:7; Rev. 6:10; 19:2 [c]Ps. 65:3; 79:9; 85:1
46 [a]Ezek. 40:4; 44:5 [b]Deut. 11:19
47 [a]Deut. 8:3; 30:15–20
49 [a]Num. 27:12–14; Deut. 3:27
50 [a]Num. 20:25, 28; 33:38
51 [a]Num. 20:11–13 [b]Lev. 10:3
52 [a]Num. 27:12; Deut. 34:1–5

CHAPTER 33

1 [a]Gen. 49:28 [b]Ps. 90
2 [a]Ex. 19:18, 20; Ps. 68:8, 17; Hab. 3:3 [b]Deut. 2:1, 4 [c]Num. 10:12

*______________

32:43 DSS fragment adds *And let all the gods (angels) worship Him;* cf. LXX and Heb. 1:6
32:44 Heb. *Hoshea,* Num. 13:8, 16

NKJV

36 "For[a] the LORD will judge His people
[b]And have compassion on His servants,
When He sees that *their* power is gone,
And [c]*there is* no one *remaining,* bond or
free.
37 He will say: [a]'Where *are* their gods,
The rock in which they sought refuge?
38 Who ate the fat of their sacrifices,
And drank the wine of their drink
offering?
Let them rise and help you,
And be your refuge.

39 'Now see that [a]I, *even* I, *am* He,
And [b]*there is* no God besides Me;
[c]I kill and I make alive;
I wound and I heal;
Nor *is there any* who can deliver from My
hand.
40 For I raise My hand to heaven,
And say, "*As* I live forever,
41 [a]If I whet My glittering sword,
And My hand takes hold on judgment,
I will render vengeance to My enemies,
And repay those who hate Me.
42 I will make My arrows drunk with blood,
And My sword shall devour flesh,
With the blood of the slain and the
captives,
From the heads of the leaders of the
enemy." '

43 "Rejoice,[a] O Gentiles, *with* His *people;
For He will [b]avenge the blood of His
servants,
And render vengeance to His adversaries;
He [c]will provide atonement for His land
and His people."

44 So Moses came with *Joshua the son of
Nun and spoke all the words of this song in the
hearing of the people.
45 Moses finished speaking all these words
to all Israel,
46 and he said to them: [a]"Set your hearts on
all the words which I testify among you today,
which you shall command your [b]children to be
careful to observe—all the words of this law.
47 "For it *is* not a futile thing for you, because
it *is* your [a]life, and by this word you shall prolong
your days in the land which you cross over the
Jordan to possess."

Moses to Die on Mount Nebo

48 Then the LORD spoke to Moses that very
same day, saying:
49 [a]"Go up this mountain of the Abarim,
Mount Nebo, which *is* in the land of Moab, across
from Jericho; view the land of Canaan, which I
give to the children of Israel as a possession;
50 "and die on the mountain which you ascend, and be gathered to your people, just as
[a]Aaron your brother died on Mount Hor and was
gathered to his people;
51 "because [a]you trespassed against Me
among the children of Israel at the waters of Meribah Kadesh, in the Wilderness of Zin, because
you [b]did not hallow Me in the midst of the children of Israel.
52 [a]"Yet you shall see the land before *you,*
though you shall not go there, into the land which
I am giving to the children of Israel."

Moses' Final Blessing on Israel

33 Now this *is* [a]the blessing with which Moses
[b]the man of God blessed the children of
Israel before his death.
2 And he said:

[a]"The LORD came from Sinai,
And dawned on them from [b]Seir;
He shone forth from [c]Mount Paran,

KJV

[d]ten thousands of saints: from his right hand *went*
a fiery law for them.
3 Yea, [a]he loved the people; [b]all his saints
are in thy hand: and they [c]sat down at thy feet;
every one shall [d]receive of thy words.
4 [a]Moses commanded us a law, [b]*even* the
inheritance of the congregation of Jacob.
5 And he was [a]king in [b]Jeshurun, when the
heads of the people *and* the tribes of Israel were
gathered together.
6 Let [a]Reuben live, and not die; and let *not*
his men be few.
7 And this *is the blessing* of [a]Judah: and
he said, Hear, LORD, the voice of Judah, and bring
him unto his people: [b]let his hands be sufficient
for him; and be thou [c]an help *to him* from his
enemies.
8 And of [a]Levi he said, [b]*Let* thy Thummim
and thy Urim *be* with thy holy one, [c]whom thou
didst prove at Massah, *and with* whom thou didst
strive at the waters of Meribah;
9 [a]Who said unto his father and to his
mother, I have not [b]seen him; [c]neither did he acknowledge his brethren, nor knew his own children: for [d]they have observed thy word, and kept
thy covenant.
10 [a]They shall teach Jacob thy judgments,
and Israel thy law: they shall put incense before
thee, [b]and whole burnt sacrifice upon thine altar.
11 Bless, LORD, his substance, and [a]accept
the work of his hands: smite through the loins of
them that rise against him, and of them that hate
him, that they rise not again.
12 *And* of Benjamin he said, The beloved of
the LORD shall dwell in safety by him; *and the
LORD* shall cover him all the day long, and he shall
dwell between his shoulders.
13 And of Joseph he said, [a]Blessed of the
LORD *be* his land, for the precious things of
heaven, for the [b]dew, and for the deep that couch-
eth beneath,
14 And for the precious fruits *brought forth*
by the sun, and for the precious things put forth
by the moon,
15 And for the chief things of [a]the ancient
mountains, and for the precious things [b]of the
lasting hills,
16 And for the precious things of the earth
and fulness thereof, and *for* the good will of [a]him
that dwelt in the bush: let *the blessing* [b]come upon
the head of Joseph, and upon the top of the head
of him *that was* separated from his brethren.
17 His glory *is like* the [a]firstling of his bullock, and his horns *are like* the [b]horns of unicorns:

2 [d]Dan. 7:10; Acts 7:53; Rev. 5:11
3 [a]Ps. 47:4; Hos. 11:1 [b]1 Sam. 2:9 [c][Luke 10:39] [d]Prov. 2:1
4 [a]Deut. 4:2; John 1:17; 7:19 [b]Ps. 119:111
5 [a]Ex. 15:18 [b]Deut. 32:15
6 [a]Gen. 49:3, 4
7 [a]Gen. 49:8–12 [b]Gen. 49:8 [c]Ps. 146:5
8 [a]Gen. 49:5 [b]Ex. 28:30; Lev. 8:8 [c]Num. 20:2–13; Deut. 6:2, 3, 16; Ps. 81:7
9 [a][Num. 25:5–8; Matt. 10:37; 19:29] [b][Gen. 29:32] [c]Ex. 32:26–28 [d]Mal. 2:5, 6
10 [a]Lev. 10:11; Deut. 31:9–13; Mal. 2:7 [b]Lev. 1:9; Ps. 51:19
11 [a]2 Sam. 24:23; Ezek. 20:40
13 [a]Gen. 49:22–26 [b]Gen. 27:28
15 [a]Gen. 49:26 [b]Hab. 3:6
16 [a]Ex. 3:2–4; Acts 7:30–35 [b]Gen. 49:26
17 [a]1 Chr. 5:1 [b]Num. 23:22

NKJV

And He came with [d]ten thousands of
saints;
From His right hand
Came a fiery law for them.
3 Yes, [a]He loves the people;
[b]All His saints *are* in Your hand;
They [c]sit down at Your feet;
Everyone [d]receives Your words.
4 [a]Moses commanded a law for us,
[b]A heritage of the congregation of Jacob.
5 And He was [a]King in [b]Jeshurun,
When the leaders of the people were
gathered,
All the tribes of Israel together.

6 "Let [a]Reuben live, and not die,
Nor let his men be few."

7 And this he said of [a]Judah:

"Hear, LORD, the voice of Judah,
And bring him to his people;
[b]Let his hands be sufficient for him,
And may You be [c]a help against his
enemies."

8 And of [a]Levi he said:

[b]"*Let* Your Thummim and Your Urim *be*
with Your holy one,
[c]Whom You tested at Massah,
And with whom You contended at the
waters of Meribah,
9 [a]Who says of his father and mother,
'I have not [b]seen them';
[c]Nor did he acknowledge his brothers,
Or know his own children;
For [d]they have observed Your word
And kept Your covenant.
10 [a]They shall teach Jacob Your judgments,
And Israel Your law.
They shall put incense before You,
[b]And a whole burnt sacrifice on Your altar.
11 Bless his substance, LORD,
And [a]accept the work of his hands;
Strike the loins of those who rise against
him,
And of those who hate him, that they rise
not again."

12 Of Benjamin he said:

"The beloved of the LORD shall dwell in
safety by Him,
Who shelters him all the day long;
And he shall dwell between His
shoulders."

13 And of Joseph he said:

[a]"Blessed of the LORD *is* his land,
With the precious things of heaven, with
the [b]dew,
And the deep lying beneath,
14 With the precious fruits of the sun,
With the precious produce of the months,
15 With the best things of [a]the ancient
mountains,
With the precious things [b]of the
everlasting hills,
16 With the precious things of the earth and
its fullness,
And the favor of [a]Him who dwelt in the
bush.
Let *the blessing* come [b]'on the head of
Joseph,
And on the crown of the head of him *who
was* separate from his brothers.'
17 His glory *is like* a [a]firstborn bull,
And his horns *like* the [b]horns of the wild
ox;
Together with them

KJV

with them [c]he shall push the people together to
the ends of the earth: and [d]they *are* the ten thousands of Ephraim, and they *are* the thousands of
Manasseh.
18 And of Zebulun he said, [a]Rejoice, Zebulun, in thy going out; and, Issachar, in thy tents.
19 They shall [a]call the people unto the mountain; there [b]they shall offer sacrifices of righteousness: for they shall suck *of* the abundance of the
seas, and *of* treasures hid in the sand.
20 And of Gad he said, Blessed *be* he that
[a]enlargeth Gad: he dwelleth as a lion, and teareth
the arm with the crown of the head.
21 And [a]he provided the first part for himself,
because there, *in* a portion of the lawgiver, *was*
he seated; and [b]he came with the heads of the
people, he executed the justice of the LORD, and
his judgments with Israel.
22 And of Dan he said, Dan *is* a lion's whelp:
[a]he shall leap from Bashan.
23 And of Naphtali he said, O Naphtali, [a]satis-
fied with favour, and full with the blessing of
the LORD: [b]possess thou the west and the south.
24 And of Asher he said, [a]*Let* Asher *be*
blessed with children; let him be acceptable to
his brethren, and let him [b]dip his foot in oil.
25 Thy shoes *shall be* [a]iron and brass; and
as thy days, *so shall* thy strength *be*.
26 *There is* [a]none like unto the God of [b]Jeshu-
run, [c]*who* rideth upon the heaven in thy help,
and in his excellency on the sky.
27 The eternal God *is thy* [a]refuge, and underneath *are* the everlasting arms: and [b]he shall
thrust out the enemy from before thee; and shall
say, Destroy *them*.
28 [a]Israel then shall dwell in safety [c]alone:
[b]the fountain of Jacob *shall be* upon a land of
corn and wine; also his [d]heavens shall drop down
dew.
29 [a]Happy *art* thou, O Israel: [b]who *is* like
unto thee, O people saved by the LORD, [c]the shield
of thy help, and who *is* the sword of thy excellency! And thine enemies [d]shall be found liars
unto thee; and [e]thou shalt tread upon their high
places.

Moses Dies on Mount Nebo

34 And Moses went up from the plains of
Moab [a]unto the mountain of Nebo, to the
top of Pisgah, that *is* over against Jericho. And
the LORD shewed him all the land of Gilead, unto
Dan,
2 And all Naphtali, and the land of Ephraim,
and Manasseh, and all the land of Judah, unto
the utmost sea,
3 And the south, and the plain of the valley
of Jericho, [a]the city of palm trees, unto Zoar.

---

17 [c]1 Kin. 22:11; Ps. 44:5 [d]Gen. 48:19
18 [a]Gen. 49:13–15
19 [a]Ex. 15:17; Ps. 2:6; Is. 2:3 [b]Ps. 4:5; 51:19
20 [a]1 Chr. 12:8
21 [a]Num. 32:16, 17 [b]Josh. 4:12
22 [a]Gen. 49:16, 17; Josh. 19:47
23 [a]Gen. 49:21 [b]Josh. 19:32
24 [a]Gen. 49:20 [b]Job 29:6
25 [a]Deut. 8:9
26 [a]Ex. 15:11; Deut. 4:35; Ps. 86:8; Jer. 10:6 [b]Deut. 32:15 [c]Deut. 10:14; Ps. 68:3, 33, 34; 104:3
27 [a][Ps. 90:1; 91:2, 9] [b]Deut. 9:3–5
28 [a]Deut. 33:12; Jer. 23:6; 33:16 [b]Deut. 8:7, 8 [c]Num. 23:9 [d]Gen. 27:28
29 [a]Ps. 144:15 [b]Deut. 4:32–34; 2 Sam. 7:23 [c]Gen. 15:1; Ps. 115:9 [d]Ps. 18:44; 66:3 [e]Num. 33:52

CHAPTER 34
1 [a]Num. 27:12; Deut. 32:49
3 [a]2 Chr. 28:15

*______
34:2 Mediterranean

NKJV

[c]He shall push the peoples
To the ends of the earth;
[d]They *are* the ten thousands of Ephraim,
And they *are* the thousands of Manasseh."

18 And of Zebulun he said:

[a]"Rejoice, Zebulun, in your going out,
And Issachar in your tents!
19 They shall [a]call the peoples *to* the mountain;
There [b]they shall offer sacrifices of righteousness;
For they shall partake *of* the abundance of the seas
And *of* treasures hidden in the sand."

20 And of Gad he said:

"Blessed *is* he who [a]enlarges Gad;
He dwells as a lion,
And tears the arm and the crown of his head.
21 [a]He provided the first *part* for himself,
Because a lawgiver's portion was reserved there.
[b]He came *with* the heads of the people;
He administered the justice of the LORD,
And His judgments with Israel."

22 And of Dan he said:

"Dan *is* a lion's whelp;
[a]He shall leap from Bashan."

23 And of Naphtali he said:

"O Naphtali, [a]satisfied with favor,
And full of the blessing of the LORD,
[b]Possess the west and the south."

24 And of Asher he said:

[a]"Asher *is* most blessed of sons;
Let him be favored by his brothers,
And let him [b]dip his foot in oil.
25 Your sandals *shall be* [a]iron and bronze;
As your days, *so shall* your strength *be*.

26 "*There is* [a]no one like the God of [b]Jeshurun,
[c]*Who* rides the heavens to help you,
And in His excellency on the clouds.
27 The eternal God *is your* [a]refuge,
And underneath *are* the everlasting arms;
[b]He will thrust out the enemy from before you,
And will say, 'Destroy!'
28 Then [a]Israel shall dwell in safety,
[b]The fountain of Jacob [c]alone,
In a land of grain and new wine;
His [d]heavens shall also drop dew.
29 [a]Happy *are* you, O Israel!
[b]Who *is* like you, a people saved by the LORD,
[c]The shield of your help
And the sword of your majesty!
Your enemies [d]shall submit to you,
And [e]you shall tread down their high places."

Moses Dies on Mount Nebo

34 Then Moses went up from the plains of
Moab [a]to Mount Nebo, to the top of Pisgah,
which is across from Jericho. And the LORD
showed him all the land of Gilead as far as
Dan,
2 all Naphtali and the land of Ephraim and
Manasseh, all the land of Judah as far as the
*Western Sea,
3 the South, and the plain of the Valley of
Jericho, [a]the city of palm trees, as far as Zoar.

KJV

4 And the LORD said unto him, [a]This *is* the
land which I sware unto Abraham, unto Isaac,
and unto Jacob, saying, I will give it unto thy seed:
[b]I have caused thee to see *it* with thine eyes, but
thou shalt not go over thither.
5 [a]So Moses the servant of the LORD died
there in the land of Moab, according to the word
of the LORD.
6 And he buried him in a valley in the land
of Moab, over against Beth–peor: but [a]no man
knoweth of his sepulchre unto this day.
7 [a]And Moses *was* an hundred and twenty
years old when he died: [b]his eye was not dim,
nor his natural force abated.
8 And the children of Israel wept for Moses
in the plains of Moab [a]thirty days: so the days
of weeping *and* mourning for Moses were ended.
9 And Joshua the son of Nun was full of
the [a]spirit of wisdom; for [b]Moses had laid his
hands upon him: and the children of Israel hearkened unto him, and did as the LORD commanded
Moses.
10 And there [a]arose not a prophet since in
Israel like unto Moses, [b]whom the LORD knew face
to face,
11 In all [a]the signs and the wonders, which
the LORD sent him to do in the land of Egypt to
Pharaoh, and to all his servants, and to all his
land,
12 And in all that mighty hand, and in all
the great terror which Moses shewed in the sight
of all Israel.

4 [a]Gen. 12:7 [b]Deut. 3:27
5 [a]Num. 20:12; Deut. 32:50; Josh. 1:1, 2
6 [a]Jude 9
7 [a]Deut. 31:2 [b]Gen. 27:1; 48:10
8 [a]Gen. 50:3, 10
9 [a]Is. 11:2 [b]Num. 27:18, 23
10 [a]Deut. 18:15, 18 [b]Ex. 33:11; Num. 12:8; Deut. 5:4
11 [a]Deut. 7:19

NKJV

4 Then the LORD said to him, [a]"This *is* the
land of which I swore to give Abraham, Isaac,
and Jacob, saying, 'I will give it to your descendants.' [b]I have caused you to see *it* with your eyes,
but you shall not cross over there."
5 [a]So Moses the servant of the LORD died
there in the land of Moab, according to the word
of the LORD.
6 And He buried him in a valley in the land
of Moab, opposite Beth Peor; but [a]no one knows
his grave to this day.
7 [a]Moses *was* one hundred and twenty
years old when he died. [b]His eyes were not dim
nor his natural vigor diminished.
8 And the children of Israel wept for Moses
in the plains of Moab [a]thirty days. So the days
of weeping *and* mourning for Moses ended.
9 Now Joshua the son of Nun was full of
the [a]spirit of wisdom, for [b]Moses had laid his
hands on him; so the children of Israel heeded
him, and did as the LORD had commanded Moses.
10 But since then there [a]has not arisen in Israel a prophet like Moses, [b]whom the LORD knew
face to face,
11 in all [a]the signs and wonders which the
LORD sent him to do in the land of Egypt, before
Pharaoh, before all his servants, and in all his
land,
12 and by all that mighty power and all the
great terror which Moses performed in the sight
of all Israel.

KJV

THE BOOK OF

JOSHUA

God's Commission to Joshua

1 Now after the death of Moses the servant of the LORD it came to pass, that the LORD spake unto Joshua the son of Nun, Moses' [a]minister, saying,

2 [a]Moses my servant is dead; now therefore arise, go over this Jordan, thou, and all this people, unto the land which I do give to them, *even* to the children of Israel.

3 [a]Every place that the sole of your foot shall tread upon, that have I given unto you, as I said unto Moses.

4 [a]From the wilderness and this Lebanon even unto the great river, the river Euphrates, all the land of the Hittites, and unto the great sea toward the going down of the sun, shall be your coast.

5 [a]There shall not any man be able to stand before thee all the days of thy life: [b]as I was with Moses, *so* [c]I will be with thee: [d]I will not fail thee, nor forsake thee.

6 [a]Be strong and of a good courage: for unto this people shalt thou divide for an inheritance the land, which I sware unto their fathers to give them.

7 Only be thou strong and very courageous, that thou mayest observe to do according to all the law, [a]which Moses my servant commanded thee: [b]turn not from it *to* the right hand or *to* the left, that thou mayest prosper whithersoever thou goest.

8 [a]This book of the law shall not depart out of thy mouth; but [b]thou shalt meditate therein day and night, that thou mayest observe to do according to all that is written therein: for then thou shalt make thy way prosperous, and then thou shalt have good success.

9 [a]Have not I commanded thee? Be strong and of a good courage; [b]be not afraid, neither be thou dismayed: for the LORD thy God *is* with thee whithersoever thou goest.

The Order to Cross the Jordan

10 Then Joshua commanded the officers of the people, saying,

11 Pass through the host, and command the people, saying, Prepare you victuals; for [a]within three days ye shall pass over this Jordan, to go in to possess the land, which the LORD your God giveth you to possess it.

12 And to the Reubenites, and to the Gadites, and to half the tribe of Manasseh, spake Joshua, saying,

13 Remember [a]the word which Moses the servant of the LORD commanded you, saying, The LORD your God hath given you rest, and hath given you this land.

14 Your wives, your little ones, and your cattle, shall remain in the land which Moses gave you on this side Jordan; but ye shall pass before your brethren armed, all the mighty men of valour, and help them;

15 Until the LORD have given your brethren rest, as *he hath given* you, and they also have possessed the land which the LORD your God giveth them: [a]then ye shall return unto the land of

CHAPTER 1

1 [a]Ex. 24:13; Num. 13:16; 14:6, 29, 30, 37, 38; Deut. 1:38; Acts 7:45
2 [a]Num. 12:7; Deut. 34:5
3 [a]Deut. 11:24; Josh. 11:23
4 [a]Gen. 15:18; Ex. 23:31; Num. 34:3–12
5 [a]Deut. 7:24 [b]Ex. 3:12 [c]Deut. 31:8, 23 [d]Deut. 31:6, 7; Heb. 13:5
6 [a]Deut. 31:7, 23
7 [a]Num. 27:23; Deut. 31:7; Josh. 11:15 [b]Deut. 5:32
8 [a]Deut. 17:18, 19; 31:24, 26; Josh. 8:34 [b]Deut. 29:9; Ps. 1:1–3
9 [a]Deut. 31:7 [b]Ps. 27:1
11 [a]Deut. 9:1; Josh. 3:17
13 [a]Num. 32:20–28
15 [a]Josh. 22:1–4

NKJV

THE BOOK OF

JOSHUA

God's Commission to Joshua

1 After the death of Moses the servant of the LORD, it came to pass that the LORD spoke to Joshua the son of Nun, Moses' [a]assistant, saying:

2 [a]"Moses My servant is dead. Now therefore, arise, go over this Jordan, you and all this people, to the land which I am giving to them—the children of Israel.

3 [a]"Every place that the sole of your foot will tread upon I have given you, as I said to Moses.

4 [a]"From the wilderness and this Lebanon as far as the great river, the River Euphrates, all the land of the Hittites, and to the Great Sea toward the going down of the sun, shall be your territory.

5 [a]"No man shall *be able to* stand before you all the days of your life; [b]as I was with Moses, *so* [c]I will be with you. [d]I will not leave you nor forsake you.

6 [a]"Be strong and of good courage, for to this people you shall divide as an inheritance the land which I swore to their fathers to give them.

7 "Only be strong and very courageous, that you may observe to do according to all the law [a]which Moses My servant commanded you; [b]do not turn from it to the right hand or to the left, that you may prosper wherever you go.

8 [a]"This Book of the Law shall not depart from your mouth, but [b]you shall meditate in it day and night, that you may observe to do according to all that is written in it. For then you will make your way prosperous, and then you will have good success.

9 [a]"Have I not commanded you? Be strong and of good courage; [b]do not be afraid, nor be dismayed, for the LORD your God *is* with you wherever you go."

The Order to Cross the Jordan

10 Then Joshua commanded the officers of the people, saying,

11 "Pass through the camp and command the people, saying, 'Prepare provisions for yourselves, for [a]within three days you will cross over this Jordan, to go in to possess the land which the LORD your God is giving you to possess.' "

12 And to the Reubenites, the Gadites, and half the tribe of Manasseh Joshua spoke, saying,

13 "Remember [a]the word which Moses the servant of the LORD commanded you, saying, 'The LORD your God is giving you rest and is giving you this land.'

14 "Your wives, your little ones, and your livestock shall remain in the land which Moses gave you on this side of the Jordan. But you shall pass before your brethren armed, all your mighty men of valor, and help them,

15 "until the LORD has given your brethren rest, as He *gave* you, and they also have taken possession of the land which the LORD your God is giving them. [a]Then you shall return to the land

KJV

your possession, and enjoy it, which Moses the LORD's servant gave you on this side Jordan toward the sunrising.

16 And they answered Joshua, saying, All that thou commandest us we will do, and whithersoever thou sendest us, we will go.

17 According as we hearkened unto Moses in all things, so will we hearken unto thee: only the LORD thy God [a]be with thee, as he was with Moses.

18 Whosoever *he be* that doth rebel against thy commandment, and will not hearken unto thy words in all that thou commandest him, he shall be put to death: only be strong and of a good courage.

Rahab Hides the Spies
(Heb. 11:31)

2 And Joshua the son of Nun sent [a]out of Shittim two men to spy secretly, saying, Go view the land, even Jericho. And they went, and [b]came into an harlot's house, named [c]Rahab, and lodged there.

2 And [a]it was told the king of Jericho, saying, Behold, there came men in hither to night of the children of Israel to search out the country.

3 And the king of Jericho sent unto Rahab, saying, Bring forth the men that are come to thee, which are entered into thine house: for they be come to search out all the country.

4 [a]And the woman took the two men, and hid them, and said thus, There came men unto me, but I wist not whence they *were:*

5 And it came to pass *about the time* of shutting of the gate, when it was dark, that the men went out: whither the men went I wot not: pursue after them quickly; for ye shall overtake them.

6 But [a]she had brought them up to the roof of the house, and hid them with the stalks of flax, which she had laid in order upon the roof.

7 And the men pursued after them the way to Jordan unto the fords: and as soon as they which pursued after them were gone out, they shut the gate.

8 And before they were laid down, she came up unto them upon the roof;

9 And she said unto the men, [a]I know that the LORD hath given you the land, and that [b]your terror is fallen upon us, and that all the inhabitants of the land [c]faint because of you.

10 For we have heard how the LORD [a]dried up the water of the Red sea for you, when ye came out of Egypt; and [b]what ye did unto the two kings of the Amorites, that *were* on the other side Jordan, Sihon and Og, whom ye [c]utterly destroyed.

11 And as soon as we had [a]heard *these things,* [b]our hearts did melt, neither did there remain any more courage in any man, because of you: for [c]the LORD your God, he *is* God in heaven above, and in earth beneath.

12 Now therefore, I pray you, [a]swear unto me by the LORD, since I have shewed you kindness, that ye will also shew kindness unto [b]my father's house, and [c]give me a true token:

13 And *that* ye will save [a]alive my father, and my mother, and my brethren, and my sisters, and all that they have, and deliver our lives from death.

14 And the men answered her, Our life for your's, if ye utter not this our business. And it shall be, when the LORD hath given us the land, that [a]we will deal kindly and truly with thee.

15 Then she [a]let them down by a cord through the window: for her house *was* upon the town wall, and she dwelt upon the wall.

16 And she said unto them, Get you to the mountain, lest the pursuers meet you; and hide yourselves there three days, until the pursuers be returned: and afterward may ye go your way.

17 And the men said unto her, We *will be*

---

17 [a]1 Sam. 20:13; 1 Kin. 1:37

CHAPTER 2

1 [a]Num. 25:1; Josh. 3:1 [b]Heb. 11:31; James 2:25 [c]Matt. 1:5
2 [a]Josh. 2:22
4 [a]2 Sam. 17:19, 20
6 [a]Ex. 1:17; 2 Sam. 17:19
9 [a]Deut. 1:8 [b]Gen. 35:5; Ex. 23:27; Deut. 2:25; 11:25; Josh. 9:9, 10 [c]Ex. 15:15; Josh. 5:1
10 [a]Ex. 14:21; Josh. 4:23 [b]Num. 21:21–35 [c]Deut. 20:17; Josh. 6:21
11 [a]Ex. 15:14, 15 [b]Josh. 5:1; 7:5; Ps. 22:14; Is. 13:7 [c]Deut. 4:39
12 [a]1 Sam. 20:14, 15, 17 [b]1 Tim. 5:8 [c]Ex. 12:13; Josh. 2:18
13 [a]Josh. 6:23–25
14 [a]Gen. 47:29; Judg. 1:24; [Matt. 5:7]
15 [a]Acts 9:25

*
2:1 Heb. *Shittim*

NKJV

of your possession and enjoy it, which Moses the LORD's servant gave you on this side of the Jordan toward the sunrise."

16 So they answered Joshua, saying, "All that you command us we will do, and wherever you send us we will go.

17 "Just as we heeded Moses in all things, so we will heed you. Only the LORD your God [a]be with you, as He was with Moses.

18 "Whoever rebels against your command and does not heed your words, in all that you command him, shall be put to death. Only be strong and of good courage."

Rahab Hides the Spies
(Heb. 11:31)

2 Now Joshua the son of Nun sent out two men [a]from *Acacia Grove to spy secretly, saying, "Go, view the land, especially Jericho." So they went, and [b]came to the house of a harlot named [c]Rahab, and lodged there.

2 And [a]it was told the king of Jericho, saying, "Behold, men have come here tonight from the children of Israel to search out the country."

3 So the king of Jericho sent to Rahab, saying, "Bring out the men who have come to you, who have entered your house, for they have come to search out all the country."

4 [a]Then the woman took the two men and hid them. So she said, "Yes, the men came to me, but I did not know where they *were* from.

5 "And it happened as the gate was being shut, when it was dark, that the men went out. Where the men went I do not know; pursue them quickly, for you may overtake them."

6 (But [a]she had brought them up to the roof and hidden them with the stalks of flax, which she had laid in order on the roof.)

7 Then the men pursued them by the road to the Jordan, to the fords. And as soon as those who pursued them had gone out, they shut the gate.

8 Now before they lay down, she came up to them on the roof,

9 and said to the men: [a]"I know that the LORD has given you the land, that [b]the terror of you has fallen on us, and that all the inhabitants of the land [c]are fainthearted because of you.

10 "For we have heard how the LORD [a]dried up the water of the Red Sea for you when you came out of Egypt, and [b]what you did to the two kings of the Amorites who *were* on the other side of the Jordan, Sihon and Og, whom you [c]utterly destroyed.

11 "And as soon as we [a]heard *these things,* [b]our hearts melted; neither did there remain any more courage in anyone because of you, for [c]the LORD your God, He *is* God in heaven above and on earth beneath.

12 "Now therefore, I beg you, [a]swear to me by the LORD, since I have shown you kindness, that you also will show kindness to [b]my father's house, and [c]give me a true token,

13 "and [a]spare my father, my mother, my brothers, my sisters, and all that they have, and deliver our lives from death."

14 So the men answered her, "Our lives for yours, if none of you tell this business of ours. And it shall be, when the LORD has given us the land, that [a]we will deal kindly and truly with you."

15 Then she [a]let them down by a rope through the window, for her house *was* on the city wall; she dwelt on the wall.

16 And she said to them, "Get to the mountain, lest the pursuers meet you. Hide there three days, until the pursuers have returned. Afterward you may go your way."

17 So the men said to her: "We *will be*

KJV

[a]blameless of this thine oath which thou hast made us swear.

18 [a]Behold, *when* we come into the land, thou shalt bind this line of scarlet thread in the window which thou didst let us down by: [b]and thou shalt bring thy father, and thy mother, and thy brethren, and all thy father's household, home unto thee.

19 And it shall be, *that* whosoever shall go out of the doors of thy house into the street, his blood *shall be* upon his head, and we *will be* guiltless: and whosoever shall be with thee in the house, [a]his blood *shall be* on our head, if *any* hand be upon him.

20 And if thou utter this our business, then we will be quit of thine oath which thou hast made us to swear.

21 And she said, According unto your words, so *be* it. And she sent them away, and they departed: and she bound the scarlet line in the window.

22 And they went, and came unto the mountain, and abode there three days, until the pursuers were returned: and the pursuers sought *them* throughout all the way, but found *them* not.

23 So the two men returned, and descended from the mountain, and passed over, and came to Joshua the son of Nun, and told him all *things* that befell them:

24 And they said unto Joshua, Truly [a]the LORD hath delivered into our hands all the land; for even all the inhabitants of the country do faint because of us.

Israel Crosses the Jordan

3 And Joshua rose early in the morning; and they removed [a]from Shittim, and came to Jordan, he and all the children of Israel, and lodged there before they passed over.

2 And it came to pass [a]after three days, that the officers went through the host;

3 And they commanded the people, saying, [a]When ye see the ark of the covenant of the LORD your God, [b]and the priests the Levites bearing it, then ye shall remove from your place, and go after it.

4 [a]Yet there shall be a space between you and it, about two thousand cubits by measure: come not near unto it, that ye may know the way by which ye must go: for ye have not passed *this* way heretofore.

5 And Joshua said unto the people, [a]Sanctify yourselves: for to morrow the LORD will do wonders among you.

6 And Joshua spake unto the priests, saying, [a]Take up the ark of the covenant, and pass over before the people. And they took up the ark of the covenant, and went before the people.

7 And the LORD said unto Joshua, This day will I begin to [a]magnify thee in the sight of all Israel, that they may know that, [b]as I was with Moses, *so* I will be with thee.

8 And thou shalt command [a]the priests that bear the ark of the covenant, saying, When ye are come to the brink of the water of Jordan, [b]ye shall stand still in Jordan.

9 And Joshua said unto the children of Israel, Come hither, and hear the words of the LORD your God.

10 And Joshua said, Hereby ye shall know that [a]the living God *is* among you, and *that* he will without fail [b]drive out from before you the [c]Canaanites, and the Hittites, and the Hivites, and the Perizzites, and the Girgashites, and the Amorites, and the Jebusites.

11 Behold, the ark of the covenant of [a]the Lord of all the earth passeth over before you into Jordan.

12 Now therefore [a]take you twelve men out of the tribes of Israel, out of every tribe a man.

13 And it shall come to pass, [a]as soon as the

17 [a]Ex. 20:7
18 [a]Josh. 2:12 [b]Josh. 6:23
19 [a]1 Kin. 2:32; Matt. 27:25
24 [a]Ex. 23:31; Josh. 6:2; 21:44

CHAPTER 3
1 [a]Josh. 2:1
2 [a]Josh. 1:10, 11
3 [a]Num. 10:33 [b]Deut. 31:9, 25
4 [a]Ex. 19:12
5 [a]Ex. 19:10, 14, 15; Lev. 20:7; Num. 11:18; Josh. 7:13; 1 Sam. 16:5; Job 1:5; Joel 2:16
6 [a]Num. 4:15
7 [a]Josh. 4:14; 1 Chr. 29:25; 2 Chr. 1:1 [b]Josh. 1:5, 9
8 [a]Josh. 3:3 [b]Josh. 3:17
10 [a]Deut. 5:26; Josh. 11:23; 1 Sam. 17:26; 2 Kin. 19:4; Hos. 1:10; Matt. 16:16; 1 Thess. 1:9 [b]Ex. 33:2; Deut. 7:1; 18:12; Ps. 44:2 [c]Acts 13:19
11 [a]Josh. 3:13; Job 41:11; Ps. 24:1; Mic. 4:13; Zech. 4:14; 6:5
12 [a]Josh. 4:2, 4
13 [a]Josh. 3:15, 16

NKJV

[a]blameless of this oath of yours which you have made us swear,

18 [a]"unless, *when* we come into the land, you bind this line of scarlet cord in the window through which you let us down, [b]and unless you bring your father, your mother, your brothers, and all your father's household to your own home.

19 "So it shall be *that* whoever goes outside the doors of your house into the street, his blood *shall be* on his own head, and we *will be* guiltless. And whoever is with you in the house, [a]his blood *shall be* on our head if a hand is laid on him.

20 "And if you tell this business of ours, then we will be free from your oath which you made us swear."

21 Then she said, "According to your words, so *be* it." And she sent them away, and they departed. And she bound the scarlet cord in the window.

22 They departed and went to the mountain, and stayed there three days until the pursuers returned. The pursuers sought *them* all along the way, but did not find *them*.

23 So the two men returned, descended from the mountain, and crossed over; and they came to Joshua the son of Nun, and told him all that had befallen them.

24 And they said to Joshua, "Truly [a]the LORD has delivered all the land into our hands, for indeed all the inhabitants of the country are fainthearted because of us."

Israel Crosses the Jordan

3 Then Joshua rose early in the morning; and they set out [a]from *Acacia Grove and came to the Jordan, he and all the children of Israel, and lodged there before they crossed over.

2 So it was, [a]after three days, that the officers went through the camp;

3 and they commanded the people, saying, [a]"When you see the ark of the covenant of the LORD your God, [b]and the priests, the Levites, bearing it, then you shall set out from your place and go after it.

4 [a]"Yet there shall be a space between you and it, about two thousand cubits by measure. Do not come near it, that you may know the way by which you must go, for you have not passed *this* way before."

5 And Joshua said to the people, [a]"Sanctify yourselves, for tomorrow the LORD will do wonders among you."

6 Then Joshua spoke to the priests, saying, [a]"Take up the ark of the covenant and cross over before the people." So they took up the ark of the covenant and went before the people.

7 And the LORD said to Joshua, "This day I will begin to [a]exalt you in the sight of all Israel, that they may know that, [b]as I was with Moses, so I will be with you.

8 "You shall command [a]the priests who bear the ark of the covenant, saying, 'When you have come to the edge of the water of the Jordan, [b]you shall stand in the Jordan.' "

9 So Joshua said to the children of Israel, "Come here, and hear the words of the LORD your God."

10 And Joshua said, "By this you shall know that [a]the living God *is* among you, and *that* He will without fail [b]drive out from before you the [c]Canaanites and the Hittites and the Hivites and the Perizzites and the Girgashites and the Amorites and the Jebusites:

11 "Behold, the ark of the covenant of [a]the Lord of all the earth is crossing over before you into the Jordan.

12 "Now therefore, [a]take for yourselves twelve men from the tribes of Israel, one man from every tribe.

13 "And it shall come to pass, [a]as soon as

*3:1 Heb. *Shittim*

KJV

soles of the feet of the priests that bear the ark
of the LORD, [b]the Lord of all the earth, shall rest
in the waters of Jordan, *that* the waters of Jordan
shall be cut off *from* the waters that come down
from above; and they [c]shall stand upon an heap.
14 And it came to pass, when the people removed from their tents, to pass over Jordan, and
the priests bearing the [a]ark of the covenant before
the people;
15 And as they that bare the ark were come
unto Jordan, and [a]the feet of the priests that bare
the ark were dipped in the brim of the water, (for
[b]Jordan overfloweth all his banks [c]all the time
of harvest,)
16 That the waters which came down from
above stood *and* rose up upon an heap very far
from the city Adam, that *is* beside [a]Zaretan: and
those that came down [b]toward the sea of the plain,
even [c]the salt sea, failed, *and* were cut off: and
the people passed over right against Jericho.
17 And the priests that bare the ark of the
covenant of the LORD stood firm on dry ground
in the midst of Jordan, [a]and all the Israelites
passed over on dry ground, until all the people
were passed clean over Jordan.

The Memorial Stones

4 And it came to pass, when all the people were
clean passed [a]over Jordan, that the LORD
spake unto Joshua, saying,
2 [a]Take you twelve men out of the people,
out of every tribe a man,
3 And command ye them, saying, Take you
hence out of the midst of Jordan, out of the place
where [a]the priests' feet stood firm, twelve stones,
and ye shall carry them over with you, and leave
them in [b]the lodging place, where ye shall lodge
this night.
4 Then Joshua called the twelve men, whom
he had prepared of the children of Israel, out of
every tribe a man:
5 And Joshua said unto them, Pass over before the ark of the LORD your God into the midst
of Jordan, and take you up every man of you a
stone upon his shoulder, according unto the number of the tribes of the children of Israel:
6 That this may be [a]a sign among you, *that*
[b]when your children ask *their fathers* in time to
come, saying, What *mean* ye by these stones?
7 Then ye shall answer them, That [a]the waters of Jordan were cut off before the ark of the
covenant of the LORD; when it passed over Jordan,
the waters of Jordan were cut off: and these stones
shall be for [b]a memorial unto the children of Israel
for ever.
8 And the children of Israel did so as Joshua
commanded, and took up twelve stones out of the
midst of Jordan, as the LORD spake unto Joshua,
according to the number of the tribes of the children of Israel, and carried them over with them
unto the place where they lodged, and laid them
down there.
9 And Joshua set up twelve stones in the
midst of Jordan, in the place where the feet of
the priests which bare the ark of the covenant
stood: and they are there unto this day.
10 For the priests which bare the ark stood
in the midst of Jordan, until every thing was finished that the LORD commanded Joshua to speak
unto the people, according to all that Moses commanded Joshua: and the people hasted and passed
over.
11 And it came to pass, when all the people
were clean passed over, that the [a]ark of the LORD
passed over, and the priests, in the presence of
the people.
12 And [a]the children of Reuben, and the children of Gad, and half the tribe of Manasseh,
passed over armed before the children of Israel,
as Moses spake unto them:
13 About forty thousand prepared for war

13 [b]Josh. 3:11 [c]Ps. 78:13; 114:3
14 [a]Ps. 132:8; Acts 7:44, 45
15 [a]Josh. 3:13 [b]1 Chr. 12:15; Jer. 12:5; 49:19 [c]Josh. 4:18; 5:10, 12
16 [a]1 Kin. 4:12; 7:46 [b]Deut. 3:17 [c]Gen. 14:3; Num. 34:3
17 [a]Gen. 50:24; Ex. 3:8; 6:1–8; 14:21, 22, 29; 33:1; Deut. 6:10; Heb. 11:29

CHAPTER 4
1 [a]Deut. 27:2; Josh. 3:17
2 [a]Josh. 3:12
3 [a]Josh. 3:13 [b]Josh. 4:19, 20
6 [a]Deut. 27:2; Ps. 103:2 [b]Ex. 12:26; 13:14; Deut. 6:20
7 [a]Josh. 3:13, 16 [b]Ex. 12:14; Num. 16:40
11 [a]Josh. 3:11; 6:11
12 [a]Num. 32:17, 20, 27, 28; Josh. 1:14

NKJV

the soles of the feet of the priests who bear the
ark of the LORD, [b]the Lord of all the earth, shall
rest in the waters of the Jordan, *that* the waters
of the Jordan shall be cut off, the waters that come
down from upstream, and they [c]shall stand as a
heap."
14 So it was, when the people set out from
their camp to cross over the Jordan, with the
priests bearing the [a]ark of the covenant before
the people,
15 and as those who bore the ark came to
the Jordan, and [a]the feet of the priests who bore
the ark dipped in the edge of the water (for the
[b]Jordan overflows all its banks [c]during the whole
time of harvest),
16 that the waters which came down from
upstream stood *still, and* rose in a heap very far
away at Adam, the city that *is* beside [a]Zaretan.
So the waters that went down [b]into the Sea of
the Arabah, [c]the Salt Sea, failed, *and* were cut
off; and the people crossed over opposite Jericho.
17 Then the priests who bore the ark of the
covenant of the LORD stood firm on dry ground
in the midst of the Jordan; [a]and all Israel crossed
over on dry ground, until all the people had
crossed completely over the Jordan.

The Memorial Stones

4 And it came to pass, when all the people had
completely crossed [a]over the Jordan, that the
LORD spoke to Joshua, saying:
2 [a]"Take for yourselves twelve men from
the people, one man from every tribe,
3 "and command them, saying, 'Take for
yourselves twelve stones from here, out of the
midst of the Jordan, from the place where [a]the
priests' feet stood firm. You shall carry them over
with you and leave them in [b]the lodging place
where you lodge tonight.' "
4 Then Joshua called the twelve men whom
he had appointed from the children of Israel, one
man from every tribe;
5 and Joshua said to them: "Cross over before the ark of the LORD your God into the midst
of the Jordan, and each one of you take up a stone
on his shoulder, according to the number of the
tribes of the children of Israel,
6 "that this may be [a]a sign among you
[b]when your children ask in time to come, saying,
'What do these stones *mean* to you?'
7 "Then you shall answer them that [a]the
waters of the Jordan were cut off before the ark
of the covenant of the LORD; when it crossed over
the Jordan, the waters of the Jordan were cut off.
And these stones shall be for [b]a memorial to the
children of Israel forever."
8 And the children of Israel did so, just as
Joshua commanded, and took up twelve stones
from the midst of the Jordan, as the LORD had
spoken to Joshua, according to the number of the
tribes of the children of Israel, and carried them
over with them to the place where they lodged,
and laid them down there.
9 Then Joshua set up twelve stones in the
midst of the Jordan, in the place where the feet
of the priests who bore the ark of the covenant
stood; and they are there to this day.
10 So the priests who bore the ark stood in
the midst of the Jordan until everything was finished that the LORD had commanded Joshua to
speak to the people, according to all that Moses
had commanded Joshua; and the people hurried
and crossed over.
11 Then it came to pass, when all the people
had completely crossed over, that the [a]ark of the
LORD and the priests crossed over in the presence
of the people.
12 And [a]the men of Reuben, the men of Gad,
and half the tribe of Manasseh crossed over
armed before the children of Israel, as Moses had
spoken to them.
13 About forty thousand prepared for war

KJV

passed over before the LORD unto battle, to the
plains of Jericho.
14 On that day the LORD [a]magnified Joshua
in the sight of all Israel; and they feared him, as
they feared Moses, all the days of his life.
15 And the LORD spake unto Joshua, saying,
16 Command the priests that bear [a]the ark
of the testimony, that they come up out of Jordan.
17 Joshua therefore commanded the priests,
saying, Come ye up out of Jordan.
18 And it came to pass, when the priests that
bare the ark of the covenant of the LORD were
come up out of the midst of Jordan, *and* the soles
of the priests' feet were lifted up unto the dry land,
that the waters of Jordan returned unto their
place, [a]and flowed over all his banks, as *they did*
before.
19 And the people came up out of Jordan on
the tenth *day* of the first month, and encamped
[a]in Gilgal, in the east border of Jericho.
20 And [a]those twelve stones, which they took
out of Jordan, did Joshua pitch in Gilgal.
21 And he spake unto the children of Israel,
saying, [a]When your children shall ask their fathers in time to come, saying, What *mean* these
stones?
22 Then ye shall let your children know, saying, [a]Israel came over this Jordan on [b]dry land.
23 For the LORD your God dried up the waters
of Jordan from before you, until ye were passed
over, as the LORD your God did to the Red sea,
[a]which he dried up from before us, until we were
gone over:
24 [a]That all the people of the earth might
know the hand of the LORD, that it *is* [b]mighty:
that ye might [c]fear the LORD your God for ever.

The Second Generation Circumcised

5 And it came to pass, when all the kings of
the Amorites, which *were* on the side of Jordan westward, and all the kings of the Canaanites,
[a]which *were* by the sea, [b]heard that the LORD had
dried up the waters of Jordan from before the children of Israel, until we were passed over, that
their heart melted, [c]neither was there spirit in
them any more, because of the children of Israel.
2 At that time the LORD said unto Joshua,
Make thee [a]sharp knives, and circumcise again
the children of Israel the second time.
3 And Joshua made him sharp knives, and
circumcised the children of Israel at the hill of
the foreskins.
4 And this *is* the cause why Joshua did circumcise: [a]All the people that came out of Egypt,
that were males, *even* all the men of war, died
in the wilderness by the way, after they came out
of Egypt.
5 Now all the people that came out were circumcised: but all the people *that were* born in
the wilderness by the way as they came forth out
of Egypt, *them* they had not circumcised.
6 For the children of Israel walked [a]forty
years in the wilderness, till all the people *that
were* men of war, which came out of Egypt, were
consumed, because they obeyed not the voice of
the LORD: unto whom the LORD sware that [b]he
would not shew them the land, which the LORD
sware unto their fathers that he would give us,
[c]a land that floweth with milk and honey.
7 And [a]their children, *whom* he raised up
in their stead, them Joshua circumcised: for they
were uncircumcised, because they had not circumcised them by the way.
8 And it came to pass, when they had done
circumcising all the people, that they abode in
their places in the camp, [a]till they were whole.
9 And the LORD said unto Joshua, This day
have I rolled away [a]the reproach of Egypt from
off you. Wherefore the name of the place is called
[b]Gilgal unto this day.
10 And the children of Israel encamped in
Gilgal, and kept the passover [a]on the fourteenth

14 [a]Josh. 3:7; 1 Chr. 29:25
16 [a]Ex. 25:16, 22
18 [a]Josh. 3:15; 1 Chr. 12:15
19 [a]Josh. 5:9
20 [a]Deut. 11:30; Josh. 4:3; 5:9, 10
21 [a]Josh. 4:6
22 [a]Ex. 12:26, 27; 13:8–14; Deut. 26:5–9 [b]Josh. 3:17
23 [a]Ex. 14:21
24 [a]1 Kin. 8:42; 2 Kin. 19:19; Ps. 106:8 [b]Ex. 15:16; 1 Chr. 29:12; Ps. 89:13 [c]Ex. 14:31; Deut. 6:2; Ps. 76:7; Jer. 10:7

CHAPTER 5

1 [a]Num. 13:29 [b]Ex. 15:14, 15 [c]Josh. 2:10, 11; 9:9; 1 Kin. 10:5
2 [a]Ex. 4:25
4 [a]Num. 14:29; 26:64, 65; Deut. 2:14–16
6 [a]Num. 14:33; Deut. 1:3; 29:5 [b]Num. 14:23, 29–35; 26:23–65; Heb. 3:11 [c]Ex. 3:8
7 [a]Num. 14:31; Deut. 1:39
8 [a]Gen. 34:25
9 [a]Gen. 34:14 [b]Josh. 4:19
10 [a]Ex. 12:6; Num. 9:5

NKJV

crossed over before the LORD for battle, to the
plains of Jericho.
14 On that day the LORD [a]exalted Joshua in
the sight of all Israel; and they feared him, as they
had feared Moses, all the days of his life.
15 Then the LORD spoke to Joshua, saying,
16 "Command the priests who bear [a]the ark
of the Testimony to come up from the Jordan."
17 Joshua therefore commanded the priests,
saying, "Come up from the Jordan."
18 And it came to pass, when the priests who
bore the ark of the covenant of the LORD had come
from the midst of the Jordan, *and* the soles of
the priests' feet touched the dry land, that the waters of the Jordan returned to their place [a]and
overflowed all its banks as before.
19 Now the people came up from the Jordan
on the tenth *day* of the first month, and they
camped [a]in Gilgal on the east border of Jericho.
20 And [a]those twelve stones which they took
out of the Jordan, Joshua set up in Gilgal.
21 Then he spoke to the children of Israel,
saying: [a]"When your children ask their fathers
in time to come, saying, 'What *are* these stones?'
22 "then you shall let your children know,
saying, [a]'Israel crossed over this Jordan on [b]dry
land';
23 "for the LORD your God dried up the waters of the Jordan before you until you had
crossed over, as the LORD your God did to the
Red Sea, [a]which He dried up before us until we
had crossed over,
24 [a]"that all the peoples of the earth may
know the hand of the LORD, that it *is* [b]mighty,
that you may [c]fear the LORD your God forever."

The Second Generation Circumcised

5 So it was, when all the kings of the Amorites
who *were* on the west side of the Jordan, and
all the kings of the Canaanites [a]who *were* by the
sea, [b]heard that the LORD had dried up the waters
of the Jordan from before the children of Israel
until *we had crossed over, that their heart
melted; [c]and there was no spirit in them any
longer because of the children of Israel.
2 At that time the LORD said to Joshua,
"Make [a]flint knives for yourself, and circumcise
the sons of Israel again the second time."
3 So Joshua made flint knives for himself,
and circumcised the sons of Israel at *the hill of
the foreskins.
4 And this *is* the reason why Joshua circumcised them: [a]All the people who came out of Egypt
who were males, all the men of war, had died in
the wilderness on the way, after they had come
out of Egypt.
5 For all the people who came out had been
circumcised, but all the people born in the wilderness, on the way as they came out of Egypt, had
not been circumcised.
6 For the children of Israel walked [a]forty
years in the wilderness, till all the people *who
were* men of war, who came out of Egypt, were
consumed, because they did not obey the voice
of the LORD—to whom the LORD swore that [b]He
would not show them the land which the LORD
had sworn to their fathers that He would give us,
[c]"a land flowing with milk and honey."
7 Then Joshua circumcised [a]their sons
whom He raised up in their place; for they were
uncircumcised, because they had not been circumcised on the way.
8 So it was, when they had finished circumcising all the people, that they stayed in their
places in the camp [a]till they were healed.
9 Then the LORD said to Joshua, "This day
I have rolled away [a]the reproach of Egypt from
you." Therefore the name of the place is called
[b]Gilgal* to this day.
10 Now the children of Israel camped in Gilgal, and kept the Passover [a]on the fourteenth day

*———

5:1 So with Kt.; Qr., some Heb. mss. and editions, LXX, Syr., Tg., Vg. *they*
5:3 Heb. *Gibeath Haaraloth*
5:9 Lit. *Rolling*

KJV

day of the month at even in the plains of Jericho.
11 And they did eat of the old corn of the
land on the morrow after the passover, unleavened cakes, and parched *corn* in the selfsame day.
12 And [a]the manna ceased on the morrow
after they had eaten of the old corn of the land;
neither had the children of Israel manna any
more; but they did eat of the fruit of the land of
Canaan that year.

The Commander of the Army of the LORD

13 And it came to pass, when Joshua was by
Jericho, that he lifted up his eyes and looked, and,
behold, there stood [a]a man over against him [b]with
his sword drawn in his hand: and Joshua went
unto him, and said unto him, *Art* thou for us, or
for our adversaries?
14 And he said, Nay; but *as* captain of the
host of the LORD am I now come. And Joshua [a]fell
on his face to the earth, and did [b]worship, and
said unto him, What saith my lord unto his
servant?
15 And the captain of the LORD's host said
unto Joshua, [a]Loose thy shoe from off thy foot;
for the place whereon thou standest *is* holy. And
Joshua did so.

The Destruction of Jericho

6 Now [a]Jericho was straitly shut up because of
the children of Israel: none went out, and none
came in.
2 And the LORD said unto Joshua, See, [a]I
have given into thine hand Jericho, and the [b]king
thereof, *and* the mighty men of valour.
3 And ye shall compass the city, all *ye* men
of war, *and* go round about the city once. Thus
shalt thou do six days.
4 And seven priests shall bear before the
ark seven [a]trumpets of rams' horns: and the seventh day ye shall compass the city [b]seven times,
and [c]the priests shall blow with the trumpets.
5 And it shall come to pass, that when they
make a long *blast* with the ram's horn, *and* when
ye hear the sound of the trumpet, all the people
shall shout with a great shout; and the wall of
the city shall fall down flat, and the people shall
ascend up every man straight before him.
6 And Joshua the son of Nun called the
priests, and said unto them, Take up the ark of
the covenant, and let seven priests bear seven
trumpets of rams' horns before the ark of the
LORD.
7 And he said unto the people, Pass on, and
compass the city, and let him that is armed pass
on before the ark of the LORD.
8 And it came to pass, when Joshua had
spoken unto the people, that the seven priests
bearing the seven trumpets of rams' horns passed
on before the LORD, and blew with the trumpets:
and the ark of the covenant of the LORD followed
them.
9 And the armed men went before the
priests that blew with the trumpets, [a]and the rereward came after the ark, *the priests* going on,
and blowing with the trumpets.
10 And Joshua had commanded the people,
saying, Ye shall not shout, nor make any noise
with your voice, neither shall *any* word proceed
out of your mouth, until the day I bid you shout;
then shall ye shout.
11 So the [a]ark of the LORD compassed the
city, going about *it* once: and they came into the
camp, and lodged in the camp.
12 And Joshua rose early in the morning,
[a]and the priests took up the ark of the LORD.
13 And seven priests bearing seven trumpets
of rams' horns before the ark of the LORD went
on continually, and blew with the trumpets: and
the armed men went before them; but the rereward came after the ark of the LORD, *the priests*
going on, and blowing with the trumpets.
14 And the second day they compassed the

12 [a]Ex. 16:35
13 [a]Gen. 18:1, 2; 32:24, 30; Ex. 23:23; Num. 22:31; Zech. 1:8; Acts 1:10 [b]Num. 22:23; 1 Chr. 21:16
14 [a]Gen. 17:3; Num. 20:6 [b]Ex. 34:8
15 [a]Ex. 3:5; Acts 7:33

CHAPTER 6

1 [a]Josh. 2:1
2 [a]Josh. 2:9, 24; 8:1 [b]Deut. 7:24
4 [a]Lev. 25:9; Judg. 7:16, 22 [b]1 Kin. 18:43; 2 Kin. 4:35; 5:10 [c]Num. 10:8
9 [a]Num. 10:25
11 [a]Josh. 4:11
12 [a]Deut. 31:25

NKJV

of the month at twilight on the plains of Jericho.
11 And they ate of the produce of the land
on the day after the Passover, unleavened bread
and parched grain, on the very same day.
12 Then [a]the manna ceased on the day after
they had eaten the produce of the land; and the
children of Israel no longer had manna, but they
ate the food of the land of Canaan that year.

The Commander of the Army of the LORD

13 And it came to pass, when Joshua was by
Jericho, that he lifted his eyes and looked, and
behold, [a]a Man stood opposite him [b]with His
sword drawn in His hand. And Joshua went to
Him and said to Him, "*Are* You for us or for our
adversaries?"
14 So He said, "No, but *as* Commander of
the army of the LORD I have now come." And
Joshua [a]fell on his face to the earth and [b]wor-
shiped, and said to Him, "What does my Lord say
to His servant?"
15 Then the Commander of the LORD's army
said to Joshua, [a]"Take your sandal off your foot,
for the place where you stand *is* holy." And
Joshua did so.

The Destruction of Jericho

6 Now [a]Jericho was securely shut up because
of the children of Israel; none went out, and
none came in.
2 And the LORD said to Joshua: "See! [a]I have
given Jericho into your hand, its [b]king, *and* the
mighty men of valor.
3 "You shall march around the city, all *you*
men of war; you shall go all around the city once.
This you shall do six days.
4 "And seven priests shall bear seven
[a]trumpets of rams' horns before the ark. But the
seventh day you shall march around the city
[b]seven times, and [c]the priests shall blow the
trumpets.
5 "It shall come to pass, when they make a
long *blast* with the ram's horn, *and* when you hear
the sound of the trumpet, that all the people shall
shout with a great shout; then the wall of the city
will fall down flat. And the people shall go up
every man straight before him."
6 Then Joshua the son of Nun called the
priests and said to them, "Take up the ark of the
covenant, and let seven priests bear seven trumpets of rams' horns before the ark of the LORD."
7 And he said to the people, "Proceed, and
march around the city, and let him who is armed
advance before the ark of the LORD."
8 So it was, when Joshua had spoken to the
people, that the seven priests bearing the seven
trumpets of rams' horns before the LORD advanced and blew the trumpets, and the ark of the
covenant of the LORD followed them.
9 The armed men went before the priests
who blew the trumpets, [a]and the rear guard came
after the ark, while *the priests* continued blowing
the trumpets.
10 Now Joshua had commanded the people,
saying, "You shall not shout or make any noise
with your voice, nor shall a word proceed out of
your mouth, until the day I say to you, 'Shout!'
Then you shall shout."
11 So he had [a]the ark of the LORD circle the
city, going around *it* once. Then they came into
the camp and lodged in the camp.
12 And Joshua rose early in the morning,
[a]and the priests took up the ark of the LORD.
13 Then seven priests bearing seven trumpets of rams' horns before the ark of the LORD
went on continually and blew with the trumpets.
And the armed men went before them. But the
rear guard came after the ark of the LORD, while
the priests continued blowing the trumpets.
14 And the second day they marched around

KJV

city once, and returned into the camp: so they
did six days.
15 And it came to pass on the seventh day,
that they rose early about the dawning of the day,
and compassed the city after the same manner
seven times: only on that day they compassed the
city seven times.
16 And it came to pass at the seventh time,
when the priests blew with the trumpets, Joshua
said unto the people, Shout; for the LORD hath
given you the city.
17 And the city shall be [a]accursed, *even* it,
and all that *are* therein, to the LORD: only [b]Rahab
the harlot shall live, she and all that *are* with her
in the house, because [c]she hid the messengers that
we sent.
18 And ye, [a]in any wise keep *yourselves* from
the accursed thing, lest ye make *yourselves* accursed, when ye take of the accursed thing, and
make the camp of Israel a curse, [b]and trouble it.
19 But all the silver, and gold, and vessels
of brass and iron, *are* consecrated unto the LORD:
they shall come into the treasury of the LORD.
20 So the people shouted when *the priests*
blew with the trumpets: and it came to pass, when
the people heard the sound of the trumpet, and
the people shouted with a great shout, that [a]the
wall fell down flat, so that the people went up
into the city, every man straight before him, and
they took the city.
21 And they [a]utterly destroyed all that *was*
in the city, both man and woman, young and old,
and ox, and sheep, and ass, with the edge of the
sword.
22 But Joshua had said unto the two men that
had spied out the country, Go into the harlot's
house, and bring out thence the woman, and all
that she hath, [a]as ye sware unto her.
23 And the young men that were spies went
in, and brought out Rahab, [a]and her father, and
her mother, and her brethren, and all that she
had; and they brought out all her kindred, and
left them without the camp of Israel.
24 And they burnt the city with fire, and all
that *was* therein: only the silver, and the gold,
and the vessels of brass and of iron, they put into
the treasury of the house of the LORD.
25 And Joshua saved Rahab the harlot alive,
and her father's household, and all that she had;
and [a]she dwelleth in Israel *even* unto this day;
because she hid the messengers, which Joshua
sent to spy out Jericho.
26 And Joshua adjured *them* at that time,
saying, [a]Cursed *be* the man before the LORD, that
riseth up and buildeth this city Jericho: he shall
lay the foundation thereof in his firstborn, and
in his youngest *son* shall he set up the gates of
it.
27 So the LORD was with Joshua; and his
fame was *noised* throughout all the country.

Defeat at Ai

7 But the children of Israel committed a [a]tres-
pass in the [b]accursed thing: for [c]Achan, the
son of Carmi, the son of Zabdi, the son of Zerah,
of the tribe of Judah, took of the accursed thing:
and the anger of the LORD was kindled against
the children of Israel.
2 And Joshua sent men from Jericho to Ai,
which *is* beside Beth–aven, on the east side of
Beth–el, and spake unto them, saying, Go up and
view the country. And the men went up and
viewed Ai.
3 And they returned to Joshua, and said
unto him, Let not all the people go up; but let
about two or three thousand men go up and smite
Ai; *and* make not all the people to labour thither;
for they *are but* few.
4 So there went up thither of the people
about three thousand men: [a]and they fled before
the men of Ai.
5 And the men of Ai smote of them about

17 [a]Deut. 13:17; Josh. 7:1 [b]Josh. 2:1; Matt. 1:5 [c]Josh. 2:4, 6
18 [a]Deut. 7:26 [b]Josh. 7:1, 12, 25; 1 Kin. 18:17, 18; [Jon. 1:12]
20 [a]Heb. 11:30
21 [a]Deut. 7:2; 20:16, 17
22 [a]Josh. 2:12–19; Heb. 11:31
23 [a]Josh. 2:13
25 [a][Matt. 1:5]
26 [a]1 Kin. 16:34

CHAPTER 7

1 [a]Josh. 7:20, 21 [b]Josh. 6:17–19 [c]Josh. 22:20
4 [a]Lev. 26:17; Deut. 28:25

*

7:1 *Zimri*, 1 Chr. 2:6

NKJV

the city once and returned to the camp. So they
did six days.
15 But it came to pass on the seventh day
that they rose early, about the dawning of the day,
and marched around the city seven times in the
same manner. On that day only they marched
around the city seven times.
16 And the seventh time it happened, when
the priests blew the trumpets, that Joshua said
to the people: "Shout, for the LORD has given you
the city!
17 "Now the city shall be [a]doomed by the
LORD to destruction, it and all who *are* in it. Only
[b]Rahab the harlot shall live, she and all who *are*
with her in the house, because [c]she hid the messengers that we sent.
18 "And you, [a]by all means abstain from the
accursed things, lest you become accursed when
you take of the accursed things, and make the
camp of Israel a curse, [b]and trouble it.
19 "But all the silver and gold, and vessels
of bronze and iron, *are* consecrated to the LORD;
they shall come into the treasury of the LORD."
20 So the people shouted when *the priests*
blew the trumpets. And it happened when the people heard the sound of the trumpet, and the people
shouted with a great shout, that [a]the wall fell
down flat. Then the people went up into the city,
every man straight before him, and they took the
city.
21 And they [a]utterly destroyed all that *was*
in the city, both man and woman, young and old,
ox and sheep and donkey, with the edge of the
sword.
22 But Joshua had said to the two men who
had spied out the country, "Go into the harlot's
house, and from there bring out the woman and
all that she has, [a]as you swore to her."
23 And the young men who had been spies
went in and brought out Rahab, [a]her father, her
mother, her brothers, and all that she had. So they
brought out all her relatives and left them outside
the camp of Israel.
24 But they burned the city and all that *was*
in it with fire. Only the silver and gold, and the
vessels of bronze and iron, they put into the treasury of the house of the LORD.
25 And Joshua spared Rahab the harlot, her
father's household, and all that she had. So [a]she
dwells in Israel to this day, because she hid the
messengers whom Joshua sent to spy out Jericho.
26 Then Joshua charged *them* at that time,
saying, [a]"Cursed *be* the man before the LORD who
rises up and builds this city Jericho; he shall lay
its foundation with his firstborn, and with his
youngest he shall set up its gates."
27 So the LORD was with Joshua, and his
fame spread throughout all the country.

Defeat at Ai

7 But the children of Israel committed a [a]tres-
pass regarding the [b]accursed things, for
[c]Achan the son of Carmi, the son of *Zabdi, the
son of Zerah, of the tribe of Judah, took of the
accursed things; so the anger of the LORD burned
against the children of Israel.
2 Now Joshua sent men from Jericho to Ai,
which *is* beside Beth Aven, on the east side of
Bethel, and spoke to them, saying, "Go up and
spy out the country." So the men went up and
spied out Ai.
3 And they returned to Joshua and said to
him, "Do not let all the people go up, but let about
two or three thousand men go up and attack Ai.
Do not weary all the people there, for *the people
of Ai are* few."
4 So about three thousand men went up
there from the people, [a]but they fled before the
men of Ai.
5 And the men of Ai struck down about

KJV

thirty and six men: for they chased them *from* before the gate *even* unto Shebarim, and smote them in the going down: wherefore [a]the hearts of the people melted, and became as water.

6 And Joshua [a]rent his clothes, and fell to the earth upon his face before the ark of the LORD until the eventide, he and the elders of Israel, and [b]put dust upon their heads.

7 And Joshua said, Alas, O Lord GOD, [a]wherefore hast thou at all brought this people over Jordan, to deliver us into the hand of the Amorites, to destroy us? would to God we had been content, and dwelt on the other side Jordan!

8 O Lord, what shall I say, when Israel turneth their backs before their enemies!

9 For the Canaanites and all the inhabitants of the land shall hear of *it,* and shall environ us round, and [a]cut off our name from the earth: and [b]what wilt thou do unto thy great name?

The Sin of Achan

10 And the LORD said unto Joshua, Get thee up; wherefore liest thou thus upon thy face?

11 Israel hath sinned, and they have also transgressed my covenant which I commanded them: [a]for they have even taken of the accursed thing, and have also stolen, and [b]dissembled also, and they have put *it* even among their own stuff.

12 [a]Therefore the children of Israel could not stand before their enemies, *but* turned *their* backs before their enemies, because [b]they were accursed: neither will I be with you any more, except ye destroy the accursed from among you.

13 Up, [a]sanctify the people, and say, [b]Sanctify yourselves against to morrow: for thus saith the LORD God of Israel, *There is* an accursed thing in the midst of thee, O Israel: thou canst not stand before thine enemies, until ye take away the accursed thing from among you.

14 In the morning therefore ye shall be brought according to your tribes: and it shall be, *that* the tribe which [a]the LORD taketh shall come according to the families *thereof;* and the family which the LORD shall take shall come by households; and the household which the LORD shall take shall come man by man.

15 [a]And it shall be, *that* he that is taken with the accursed thing shall be burnt with fire, he and all that he hath: because he hath [b]transgressed the covenant of the LORD, and because he [c]hath wrought folly in Israel.

16 So Joshua rose up early in the morning, and brought Israel by their tribes; and the tribe of Judah was taken:

17 And he brought the family of Judah; and he took the family of the Zarhites: and he brought the family of the Zarhites man by man; and Zabdi was taken:

18 And he brought his household man by man; and Achan, the son of Carmi, the son of Zabdi, the son of Zerah, of the tribe of Judah, [a]was taken.

19 And Joshua said unto Achan, My son, [a]give, I pray thee, glory to the LORD God of Israel, [b]and make confession unto him; and [c]tell me now what thou hast done; hide *it* not from me.

20 And Achan answered Joshua, and said, Indeed [a]I have sinned against the LORD God of Israel, and thus and thus have I done:

21 When I saw among the spoils a goodly Babylonish garment, and two hundred shekels of silver, and a wedge of gold of fifty shekels weight, then I coveted them, and took them; and, behold, they *are* hid in the earth in the midst of my tent, and the silver under it.

22 So Joshua sent messengers, and they ran unto the tent; and, behold, *it was* hid in his tent, and the silver under it.

23 And they took them out of the midst of the tent, and brought them unto Joshua, and unto

5 [a]Lev. 26:36; Josh. 2:9, 11
6 [a]Gen. 37:29, 34 [b]1 Sam. 4:12
7 [a]Ex. 17:3; Num. 21:5
9 [a]Deut. 32:26 [b]Ex. 32:12; Num. 14:13
11 [a]Josh. 6:17–19 [b]Acts 5:1, 2
12 [a]Judg. 2:14 [b]Deut. 7:26; [Hag. 2:13, 14]
13 [a]Ex. 19:10 [b]Josh. 3:5
14 [a][Prov. 16:33]
15 [a]1 Sam. 14:38, 39 [b]Josh. 7:11 [c]Gen. 34:7; Judg. 20:6
18 [a]1 Sam. 14:42
19 [a]1 Sam. 6:5; Jer. 13:16; John 9:24 [b]Num. 5:6, 7; 2 Chr. 30:22; Ezra 10:10, 11; Ps. 32:5; Prov. 28:13; Jer. 3:12, 13; Dan. 9:4 [c]1 Sam. 14:43
20 [a]Num. 22:34; 1 Sam. 15:24

NKJV

thirty-six men, for they chased them *from* before the gate as far as Shebarim, and struck them down on the descent; therefore [a]the hearts of the people melted and became like water.

6 Then Joshua [a]tore his clothes, and fell to the earth on his face before the ark of the LORD until evening, he and the elders of Israel; and they [b]put dust on their heads.

7 And Joshua said, "Alas, Lord GOD, [a]why have You brought this people over the Jordan at all—to deliver us into the hand of the Amorites, to destroy us? Oh, that we had been content, and dwelt on the other side of the Jordan!

8 "O Lord, what shall I say when Israel turns its back before its enemies?

9 "For the Canaanites and all the inhabitants of the land will hear *it,* and surround us, and [a]cut off our name from the earth. Then [b]what will You do for Your great name?"

The Sin of Achan

10 So the LORD said to Joshua: "Get up! Why do you lie thus on your face?

11 "Israel has sinned, and they have also transgressed My covenant which I commanded them. [a]For they have even taken some of the accursed things, and have both stolen and [b]deceived; and they have also put *it* among their own stuff.

12 [a]"Therefore the children of Israel could not stand before their enemies, *but* turned *their* backs before their enemies, because [b]they have become doomed to destruction. Neither will I be with you anymore, unless you destroy the accursed from among you.

13 "Get up, [a]sanctify the people, and say, [b]'Sanctify yourselves for tomorrow, because thus says the LORD God of Israel: "*There is* an accursed thing in your midst, O Israel; you cannot stand before your enemies until you take away the accursed thing from among you."

14 'In the morning therefore you shall be brought according to your tribes. And it shall be *that* the tribe which [a]the LORD takes shall come according to families; and the family which the LORD takes shall come by households; and the household which the LORD takes shall come man by man.

15 [a]'Then it shall be *that* he who is taken with the accursed thing shall be burned with fire, he and all that he has, because he has [b]transgressed the covenant of the LORD, and because he [c]has done a disgraceful thing in Israel.' "

16 So Joshua rose early in the morning and brought Israel by their tribes, and the tribe of Judah was taken.

17 He brought the clan of Judah, and he took the family of the Zarhites; and he brought the family of the Zarhites man by man, and Zabdi was taken.

18 Then he brought his household man by man, and Achan the son of Carmi, the son of Zabdi, the son of Zerah, of the tribe of Judah, [a]was taken.

19 Now Joshua said to Achan, "My son, I beg you, [a]give glory to the LORD God of Israel, [b]and make confession to Him, and [c]tell me now what you have done; do not hide *it* from me."

20 And Achan answered Joshua and said, "Indeed [a]I have sinned against the LORD God of Israel, and this is what I have done:

21 "When I saw among the spoils a beautiful Babylonian garment, two hundred shekels of silver, and a wedge of gold weighing fifty shekels, I coveted them and took them. And there they are, hidden in the earth in the midst of my tent, with the silver under it."

22 So Joshua sent messengers, and they ran to the tent; and there it was, hidden in his tent, with the silver under it.

23 And they took them from the midst of the tent, brought them to Joshua and to all the

KJV

all the children of Israel, and laid them out before
the LORD.
24 And Joshua, and all Israel with him, took
Achan the son of Zerah, and the silver, and
the garment, and the wedge of gold, and his
sons, and his daughters, and his oxen, and his
asses, and his sheep, and his tent, and [a]all that
he had: and they brought them unto [b]the valley
of Achor.
25 And Joshua said, [a]Why hast thou troubled
us? the LORD shall trouble thee this day. [b]And all
Israel stoned him with stones, and burned them
with fire, after they had stoned them with stones.
26 And they [a]raised over him a great heap
of stones unto this day. So [b]the LORD turned from
the fierceness of his anger. Wherefore the name
of that place was called, [c]The valley of Achor,
unto this day.

The Fall of Ai

8 And the LORD said unto Joshua, [a]Fear not, neither be thou dismayed: take all the people of
war with thee, and arise, go up to Ai: see, [b]I have
given into thy hand the king of Ai, and his people,
and his city, and his land:
2 And thou shalt do to Ai and her king as
thou didst unto [a]Jericho and her king: only [b]the
spoil thereof, and the cattle thereof, shall ye take
for a prey unto yourselves: lay thee an ambush
for the city behind it.
3 So Joshua arose, and all the people of war,
to go up against Ai: and Joshua chose out thirty
thousand mighty men of valour, and sent them
away by night.
4 And he commanded them, saying, Behold,
[a]ye shall lie in wait against the city, *even* behind
the city: go not very far from the city, but be ye
all ready:
5 And I, and all the people that *are* with me,
will approach unto the city: and it shall come to
pass, when they come out against us, as at the
first, that [a]we will flee before them,
6 (For they will come out after us) till we
have drawn them from the city; for they will say,
They flee before us, as at the first: therefore we
will flee before them.
7 Then ye shall rise up from the ambush,
and seize upon the city: for the LORD your God
will deliver it into your hand.
8 And it shall be, when ye have taken the
city, *that* ye shall set the city on fire: according
to the commandment of the LORD shall ye do.
[a]See, I have commanded you.
9 Joshua therefore sent them forth: and
they went to lie in ambush, and abode between
Beth–el and Ai, on the west side of Ai: but Joshua
lodged that night among the people.
10 And Joshua rose up early in the morning,
and numbered the people, and went up, he and
the elders of Israel, before the people to Ai.
11 [a]And all the people, *even the people* of
war that *were* with him, went up, and drew nigh,
and came before the city, and pitched on the north
side of Ai: now *there was* a valley between them
and Ai.
12 And he took about five thousand men, and
set them to lie in ambush between Beth–el and
Ai, on the west side of the city.
13 And when they had set the people, *even*
all the host that *was* on the north of the city, and
their liers in wait on the west of the city, Joshua
went that night into the midst of the valley.
14 And it came to pass, when the king of Ai
saw *it,* that they hasted and rose up early, and
the men of the city went out against Israel to battle, he and all his people, at a time appointed, before the plain; but he [a]wist not that *there were*
liers in ambush against him behind the city.
15 And Joshua and all Israel [a]made as if they
were beaten before them, and fled by the way of
the wilderness.
16 And all the people that *were* in Ai were

24 [a]Num. 16:32, 33; Dan. 6:24 [b]Josh. 7:26; 15:7
25 [a]Josh. 6:18; 1 Chr. 2:7; [Gal. 5:12] [b]Deut. 17:5
26 [a]Josh. 8:29; 2 Sam. 18:17; Lam. 3:53 [b]Deut. 13:17 [c]Josh. 7:24; Is. 65:10; Hos. 2:15

CHAPTER 8

1 [a]Deut. 1:21; 7:18; 31:8; Josh. 1:9; 10:8 [b]Josh. 6:2
2 [a]Josh. 6:21 [b]Deut. 20:14; Josh. 8:27
4 [a]Judg. 20:29
5 [a]Josh. 7:5; Judg. 20:32
8 [a]2 Sam. 13:28
11 [a]Josh. 8:5
14 [a]Judg. 20:34; Eccl. 9:12
15 [a]Judg. 20:36

*7:26 Lit. *Trouble*

NKJV

children of Israel, and laid them out before the
LORD.
24 Then Joshua, and all Israel with him, took
Achan the son of Zerah, the silver, the garment,
the wedge of gold, his sons, his daughters, his
oxen, his donkeys, his sheep, his tent, and [a]all
that he had, and they brought them to [b]the Valley
of Achor.
25 And Joshua said, [a]"Why have you troubled us? The LORD will trouble you this day." [b]So
all Israel stoned him with stones; and they burned
them with fire after they had stoned them with
stones.
26 Then they [a]raised over him a great heap
of stones, still there to this day. So [b]the LORD
turned from the fierceness of His anger. Therefore
the name of that place has been called [c]the Valley
of *Achor to this day.

The Fall of Ai

8 Now the LORD said to Joshua: [a]"Do not be
afraid, nor be dismayed; take all the people
of war with you, and arise, go up to Ai. See, [b]I
have given into your hand the king of Ai, his people, his city, and his land.
2 "And you shall do to Ai and its king as
you did to [a]Jericho and its king. Only [b]its spoil
and its cattle you shall take as booty for yourselves. Lay an ambush for the city behind it."
3 So Joshua arose, and all the people of war,
to go up against Ai; and Joshua chose thirty thousand mighty men of valor and sent them away
by night.
4 And he commanded them, saying: "Behold, [a]you shall lie in ambush against the city,
behind the city. Do not go very far from the city,
but all of you be ready.
5 "Then I and all the people who *are* with
me will approach the city; and it will come about,
when they come out against us as at the first, that
[a]we shall flee before them.
6 "For they will come out after us till we
have drawn them from the city, for they will say,
'*They are* fleeing before us as at the first.' Therefore we will flee before them.
7 "Then you shall rise from the ambush and
seize the city, for the LORD your God will deliver
it into your hand.
8 "And it will be, when you have taken the
city, *that* you shall set the city on fire. According
to the commandment of the LORD you shall do.
[a]See, I have commanded you."
9 Joshua therefore sent them out; and they
went to lie in ambush, and stayed between Bethel
and Ai, on the west side of Ai; but Joshua lodged
that night among the people.
10 Then Joshua rose up early in the morning
and mustered the people, and went up, he and
the elders of Israel, before the people to Ai.
11 [a]And all the people of war who *were* with
him went up and drew near; and they came before
the city and camped on the north side of Ai. Now
a valley *lay* between them and Ai.
12 So he took about five thousand men and
set them in ambush between Bethel and Ai, on
the west side of the city.
13 And when they had set the people, all the
army that *was* on the north of the city, and its
rear guard on the west of the city, Joshua went
that night into the midst of the valley.
14 Now it happened, when the king of Ai saw
it, that the men of the city hurried and rose early
and went out against Israel to battle, he and all
his people, at an appointed place before the plain.
But he [a]did not know that *there was* an ambush
against him behind the city.
15 And Joshua and all Israel [a]made as if they
were beaten before them, and fled by the way of
the wilderness.
16 So all the people who *were* in Ai were

KJV

called together to pursue after them: and they pursued after Joshua, and were drawn away from the city.

17 And there was not a man left in Ai or Beth–el, that went not out after Israel: and they left the city open, and pursued after Israel.

18 And the LORD said unto Joshua, Stretch out the spear that *is* in thy hand toward Ai; for I will give it into thine hand. And Joshua stretched out the spear that *he had* in his hand toward the city.

19 And the ambush arose quickly out of their place, and they ran as soon as he had stretched out his hand: and they entered into the city, and took it, and hasted and set the city on fire.

20 And when the men of Ai looked behind them, they saw, and, behold, the smoke of the city ascended up to heaven, and they had no power to flee this way or that way: and the people that fled to the wilderness turned back upon the pursuers.

21 And when Joshua and all Israel saw that the ambush had taken the city, and that the smoke of the city ascended, then they turned again, and slew the men of Ai.

22 And the other issued out of the city against them; so they were in the midst of Israel, some on this side, and some on that side: and they smote them, so that they [a]let none of them remain or escape.

23 And the king of Ai they took alive, and brought him to Joshua.

24 And it came to pass, when Israel had made an end of slaying all the inhabitants of Ai in the field, in the wilderness wherein they chased them, and when they were all fallen on the edge of the sword, until they were consumed, that all the Israelites returned unto Ai, and smote it with the edge of the sword.

25 And *so* it was, *that* all that fell that day, both of men and women, *were* twelve thousand, *even* all the men of Ai.

26 For Joshua drew not his hand back, wherewith he stretched out the spear, until he had [a]utterly destroyed all the inhabitants of Ai.

27 [a]Only the cattle and the spoil of that city Israel took for a prey unto themselves, according unto the word of the LORD which he [b]commanded Joshua.

28 And Joshua burnt Ai, and made it [a]an heap for ever, *even* a desolation unto this day.

29 [a]And the king of Ai he hanged on a tree until eventide: [b]and as soon as the sun was down, Joshua commanded that they should take his carcase down from the tree, and cast it at the entering of the gate of the city, and [c]raise thereon a great heap of stones, *that remaineth* unto this day.

Joshua Renews the Covenant *(cf. Deut. 27:4, 5)*

30 Then Joshua built an altar unto the LORD God of Israel [a]in mount Ebal,

31 As Moses the servant of the LORD commanded the children of Israel, as it is written in the book of the law of Moses, [a]an altar of whole stones, over which no man hath lift up *any* iron: and [b]they offered thereon burnt offerings unto the LORD, and sacrificed peace offerings.

32 And [a]he wrote there upon the stones a copy of the law of Moses, which he wrote in the presence of the children of Israel.

33 And all Israel, and their elders, and officers, and their judges, stood on this side the ark and on that side before the priests the Levites, [a]which bare the ark of the covenant of the LORD, as well [b]the stranger, as he that was born among them; half of them over against mount Gerizim, and half of them over against mount Ebal; [c]as Moses the servant of the LORD had commanded before, that they should bless the people of Israel.

34 And afterward [a]he read all the words of

---

22 [a]Deut. 7:2
26 [a]Josh. 6:21
27 [a]Num. 31:22, 26 [b]Josh. 8:2
28 [a]Deut. 13:16
29 [a]Josh. 10:26 [b]Deut. 21:22, 23; Josh. 10:27 [c]Josh. 7:26; 10:27
30 [a]Deut. 27:4–8
31 [a]Ex. 20:25; Deut. 27:5, 6 [b]Ex. 20:24
32 [a]Deut. 27:2, 3, 8
33 [a]Deut. 31:9, 25 [b]Deut. 31:12 [c]Deut. 11:29; 27:12
34 [a]Deut. 31:11; Neh. 8:3

NKJV

called together to pursue them. And they pursued Joshua and were drawn away from the city.

17 There was not a man left in Ai or Bethel who did not go out after Israel. So they left the city open and pursued Israel.

18 Then the LORD said to Joshua, "Stretch out the spear that *is* in your hand toward Ai, for I will give it into your hand." And Joshua stretched out the spear that *was* in his hand toward the city.

19 So *those in* ambush arose quickly out of their place; they ran as soon as he had stretched out his hand, and they entered the city and took it, and hurried to set the city on fire.

20 And when the men of Ai looked behind them, they saw, and behold, the smoke of the city ascended to heaven. So they had no power to flee this way or that way, and the people who had fled to the wilderness turned back on the pursuers.

21 Now when Joshua and all Israel saw that the ambush had taken the city and that the smoke of the city ascended, they turned back and struck down the men of Ai.

22 Then the others came out of the city against them; so they were *caught* in the midst of Israel, some on this side and some on that side. And they struck them down, so that they [a]let none of them remain or escape.

23 But the king of Ai they took alive, and brought him to Joshua.

24 And it came to pass when Israel had made an end of slaying all the inhabitants of Ai in the field, in the wilderness where they pursued them, and when they all had fallen by the edge of the sword until they were consumed, that all the Israelites returned to Ai and struck it with the edge of the sword.

25 So it was *that* all who fell that day, both men and women, *were* twelve thousand—all the people of Ai.

26 For Joshua did not draw back his hand, with which he stretched out the spear, until he had [a]utterly destroyed all the inhabitants of Ai.

27 [a]Only the livestock and the spoil of that city Israel took as booty for themselves, according to the word of the LORD which He had [b]commanded Joshua.

28 So Joshua burned Ai and made it [a]a heap forever, a desolation to this day.

29 [a]And the king of Ai he hanged on a tree until evening. [b]And as soon as the sun was down, Joshua commanded that they should take his corpse down from the tree, cast it at the entrance of the gate of the city, and [c]raise over it a great heap of stones *that remains* to this day.

Joshua Renews the Covenant *(cf. Deut. 27:4, 5)*

30 Now Joshua built an altar to the LORD God of Israel [a]in Mount Ebal,

31 as Moses the servant of the LORD had commanded the children of Israel, as it is written in the Book of the Law of Moses: [a]"an altar of whole stones over which no man has wielded an iron *tool*." And [b]they offered on it burnt offerings to the LORD, and sacrificed peace offerings.

32 And there, in the presence of the children of Israel, [a]he wrote on the stones a copy of the law of Moses, which he had written.

33 Then all Israel, with their elders and officers and judges, stood on either side of the ark before the priests, the Levites, [a]who bore the ark of the covenant of the LORD, [b]the stranger as well as he who was born among them. Half of them *were* in front of Mount Gerizim and half of them in front of Mount Ebal, [c]as Moses the servant of the LORD had commanded before, that they should bless the people of Israel.

34 And afterward [a]he read all the words of

KJV

the law, [b]the blessings and cursings, according to all that is written in the [c]book of the law.

35 There was not a word of all that Moses commanded, which Joshua read not before all the congregation of Israel, [a]with the women, and the little ones, [b]and the strangers that were conversant among them.

The Treaty with the Gibeonites

9 And it came to pass, when [a]all the kings which *were* on this side Jordan, in the hills, and in the valleys, and in all the coasts of [b]the great sea over against Lebanon, [c]the Hittite, and the Amorite, the Canaanite, the Perizzite, the Hivite, and the Jebusite, heard *thereof;*

2 That they [a]gathered themselves together, to fight with Joshua and with Israel, with one accord.

3 And when the inhabitants of [a]Gibeon [b]heard what Joshua had done unto Jericho and to Ai,

4 They did work wilily, and went and made as if they had been ambassadors, and took old sacks upon their asses, and wine bottles, old, and rent, and bound up;

5 And old shoes and clouted upon their feet, and old garments upon them; and all the bread of their provision was dry *and* mouldy.

6 And they went to Joshua [a]unto the camp at Gilgal, and said unto him, and to the men of Israel, We be come from a far country: now therefore make ye a league with us.

7 And the men of Israel said unto the [a]Hivites, Peradventure ye dwell among us; and [b]how shall we make a league with you?

8 And they said unto Joshua, [a]We *are* thy servants. And Joshua said unto them, Who *are* ye? and from whence come ye?

9 And they said unto him, [a]From a very far country thy servants are come because of the name of the LORD thy God: for we have [b]heard the fame of him, and all that he did in Egypt,

10 And [a]all that he did to the two kings of the Amorites, that *were* beyond Jordan, to Sihon king of Heshbon, and to Og king of Bashan, which *was* at Ashtaroth.

11 Wherefore our elders and all the inhabitants of our country spake to us, saying, Take victuals with you for the journey, and go to meet them, and say unto them, We *are* your servants: therefore now make ye a league with us.

12 This our bread we took hot *for* our provision out of our houses on the day we came forth to go unto you; but now, behold, it is dry, and it is mouldy:

13 And these bottles of wine, which we filled, *were* new; and, behold, they be rent: and these our garments and our shoes are become old by reason of the very long journey.

14 And the men took of their victuals, [a]and asked not *counsel* at the mouth of the LORD.

15 And Joshua [a]made peace with them, and made a league with them, to let them live: and the princes of the congregation sware unto them.

16 And it came to pass at the end of three days after they had made a league with them, that they heard that they *were* their neighbours, and *that* they dwelt among them.

17 And the children of Israel journeyed, and came unto their cities on the third day. Now their cities *were* [a]Gibeon, and Chephirah, and Beeroth, and Kirjath–jearim.

18 And the children of Israel smote them not, [a]because the princes of the congregation had sworn unto them by the LORD God of Israel. And all the congregation murmured against the princes.

19 But all the princes said unto all the congregation, We have sworn unto them by the LORD God of Israel: now therefore we may not touch them.

20 This we will do to them; we will even let

34 [b]Deut. 28:2, 15, 45; 29:20, 21; 30:19 [c]Josh. 1:8
35 [a]Ex. 12:38; Deut. 31:12 [b]Josh. 8:33

CHAPTER 9

1 [a]Num. 13:29; Josh. 3:10 [b]Num. 34:6 [c]Ex. 3:17; 23:23
2 [a]Josh. 10:5; Ps. 83:3, 5
3 [a]Josh. 9:17, 22; 10:2; 21:17; 2 Sam. 21:1, 2 [b]Josh. 6:27
6 [a]Josh. 5:10
7 [a]Josh. 9:1; 11:19 [b]Ex. 23:32; Deut. 7:2
8 [a]Deut. 20:11; 2 Kin. 10:5
9 [a]Deut. 20:15 [b]Ex. 15:14; Josh. 2:9, 10; 5:1
10 [a]Num. 21:24, 33
14 [a]Num. 27:21; Is. 30:1
15 [a]2 Sam. 21:2
17 [a]Josh. 18:25
18 [a]Ps. 15:4

NKJV

the law, [b]the blessings and the cursings, according to all that is written in the [c]Book of the Law.

35 There was not a word of all that Moses had commanded which Joshua did not read before all the assembly of Israel, [a]with the women, the little ones, [b]and the strangers who were living among them.

The Treaty with the Gibeonites

9 And it came to pass when [a]all the kings who *were* on this side of the Jordan, in the hills and in the lowland and in all the coasts of [b]the Great Sea toward Lebanon—[c]the Hittite, the Amorite, the Canaanite, the Perizzite, the Hivite, and the Jebusite—heard *about it,*

2 that they [a]gathered together to fight with Joshua and Israel with one accord.

3 But when the inhabitants of [a]Gibeon [b]heard what Joshua had done to Jericho and Ai,

4 they worked craftily, and went and pretended to be ambassadors. And they took old sacks on their donkeys, old wineskins torn and mended,

5 old and patched sandals on their feet, and old garments on themselves; and all the bread of their provision was dry *and* moldy.

6 And they went to Joshua, [a]to the camp at Gilgal, and said to him and to the men of Israel, "We have come from a far country; now therefore, make a covenant with us."

7 Then the men of Israel said to the [a]Hivites, "Perhaps you dwell among us; so [b]how can we make a covenant with you?"

8 But they said to Joshua, [a]"We *are* your servants." And Joshua said to them, "Who *are* you, and where do you come from?"

9 So they said to him: [a]"From a very far country your servants have come, because of the name of the LORD your God; for we have [b]heard of His fame, and all that He did in Egypt,

10 "and [a]all that He did to the two kings of the Amorites who *were* beyond the Jordan—to Sihon king of Heshbon, and Og king of Bashan, who was at Ashtaroth.

11 "Therefore our elders and all the inhabitants of our country spoke to us, saying, 'Take provisions with you for the journey, and go to meet them, and say to them, "We *are* your servants; now therefore, make a covenant with us." '

12 "This bread of ours we took hot *for* our provision from our houses on the day we departed to come to you. But now look, it is dry and moldy.

13 "And these wineskins which we filled *were* new, and see, they are torn; and these our garments and our sandals have become old because of the very long journey."

14 Then the men of Israel took some of their provisions; [a]but they did not ask counsel of the LORD.

15 So Joshua [a]made peace with them, and made a covenant with them to let them live; and the rulers of the congregation swore to them.

16 And it happened at the end of three days, after they had made a covenant with them, that they heard that they *were* their neighbors who dwelt near them.

17 Then the children of Israel journeyed and came to their cities on the third day. Now their cities *were* [a]Gibeon, Chephirah, Beeroth, and Kirjath Jearim.

18 But the children of Israel did not attack them, [a]because the rulers of the congregation had sworn to them by the LORD God of Israel. And all the congregation complained against the rulers.

19 Then all the rulers said to all the congregation, "We have sworn to them by the LORD God of Israel; now therefore, we may not touch them.

20 "This we will do to them: We will let them

KJV

them live, lest [a]wrath be upon us, because of the
oath which we sware unto them.
21 And the princes said unto them, Let them
live; but let them be [a]hewers of wood and drawers
of water unto all the congregation; as the princes
had [b]promised them.
22 And Joshua called for them, and he spake
unto them, saying, Wherefore have ye beguiled
us, saying, [a]We *are* very far from you; when [b]ye
dwell among us?
23 Now therefore ye *are* [a]cursed, and there
shall none of you be freed from being bondmen,
and hewers of wood and drawers of water for the
house of my God.
24 And they answered Joshua, and said, Because it was certainly told thy servants, how that
the LORD thy God [a]commanded his servant Moses
to give you all the land, and to destroy all the
inhabitants of the land from before you, therefore
[b]we were sore afraid of our lives because of you,
and have done this thing.
25 And now, behold, we *are* [a]in thine hand:
as it seemeth good and right unto thee to do unto
us, do.
26 And so did he unto them, and delivered
them out of the hand of the children of Israel,
that they slew them not.
27 And Joshua made them that day [a]hewers
of wood and drawers of water for the congregation, and for the altar of the LORD, even unto this
day, [b]in the place which he should choose.

The Sun Stands Still

10 Now it came to pass, when Adoni–zedek
king of Jerusalem had [a]heard how Joshua
had taken [b]Ai, and had utterly destroyed it; [c]as
he had done to Jericho and her king, so he had
done to [d]Ai and her king; and [e]how the inhabitants of Gibeon had made peace with Israel, and
were among them;
2 That they [a]feared greatly, because Gibeon
was a great city, as one of the royal cities, and
because it *was* greater than Ai, and all the men
thereof *were* mighty.
3 Wherefore Adoni–zedek king of Jerusalem sent unto Hoham king of Hebron, and unto
Piram king of Jarmuth, and unto Japhia king of
Lachish, and unto Debir king of Eglon, saying,
4 Come up unto me, and help me, that we
may smite Gibeon: for [a]it hath made peace with
Joshua and with the children of Israel.
5 Therefore the five kings of the [a]Amorites,
the king of Jerusalem, the king of Hebron, the
king of Jarmuth, the king of Lachish, the king of
Eglon, [b]gathered themselves together, and went
up, they and all their hosts, and encamped before
Gibeon, and made war against it.
6 And the men of Gibeon sent unto Joshua
to the camp [a]to Gilgal, saying, Slack not thy hand
from thy servants; come up to us quickly, and save
us, and help us: for all the kings of the Amorites
that dwell in the mountains are gathered together
against us.
7 So Joshua ascended from Gilgal, he, and
[a]all the people of war with him, and all the mighty
men of valour.
8 And the LORD said unto Joshua, [a]Fear
them not: for I have delivered them into thine
hand; [b]there shall not a man of them [c]stand before
thee.
9 Joshua therefore came unto them suddenly, *and* went up from Gilgal all night.
10 And the LORD [a]discomfited them before
Israel, and slew them with a great slaughter at
Gibeon, and chased them along the way that
goeth up [b]to Beth–horon, and smote them to
[c]Azekah, and unto Makkedah.
11 And it came to pass, as they fled from before Israel, *and* were in the going down to Beth–
horon, [a]that the LORD cast down great stones from
heaven upon them unto Azekah, and they died:
they were more which died with hailstones than

20 [a]2 Sam. 21:1, 2, 6; Ezek. 17:13, 15
21 [a]Deut. 29:11 [b]Josh. 9:15
22 [a]Josh. 9:6, 9 [b]Josh. 9:16
23 [a]Gen. 9:25
24 [a]Ex. 23:31–33; Deut. 7:1, 2 [b]Ex. 15:14
25 [a]Gen. 16:6
27 [a]Josh. 9:21, 23 [b]Deut. 12:5

CHAPTER 10
1 [a]Josh. 9:1 [b]Josh. 8:1 [c]Josh. 6:21 [d]Josh. 8:22, 26, 28 [e]Josh. 9:15
2 [a]Ex. 15:14–16; Deut. 11:25; 1 Chr. 14:17
4 [a]Josh. 9:15; 10:1
5 [a]Num. 13:29 [b]Josh. 9:2
6 [a]Josh. 5:10; 9:6
7 [a]Josh. 8:1
8 [a]Josh. 11:6; Judg. 4:14 [b]Josh. 1:5, 9 [c]Josh. 21:44
10 [a]Judg. 4:15; 1 Sam. 7:10, 12; Is. 28:21 [b]Josh. 16:3, 5 [c]Josh. 15:35
11 [a]Is. 30:30; Rev. 16:21

NKJV

live, lest [a]wrath be upon us because of the oath
which we swore to them."
21 And the rulers said to them, "Let them
live, but let them be [a]woodcutters and water carriers for all the congregation, as the rulers had
[b]promised them."
22 Then Joshua called for them, and he spoke
to them, saying, "Why have you deceived us, saying, [a]'We *are* very far from you,' when [b]you dwell
near us?
23 "Now therefore, you *are* [a]cursed, and
none of you shall be freed from being slaves—
woodcutters and water carriers for the house of
my God."
24 So they answered Joshua and said, "Because your servants were clearly told that the
LORD your God [a]commanded His servant Moses
to give you all the land, and to destroy all the
inhabitants of the land from before you; therefore
[b]we were very much afraid for our lives because
of you, and have done this thing.
25 "And now, here we are, [a]in your hands;
do with us as it seems good and right to do to
us."
26 So he did to them, and delivered them out
of the hand of the children of Israel, so that they
did not kill them.
27 And that day Joshua made them [a]wood-
cutters and water carriers for the congregation
and for the altar of the LORD, [b]in the place which
He would choose, even to this day.

The Sun Stands Still

10 Now it came to pass when Adoni-Zedek
king of Jerusalem [a]heard how Joshua had
taken [b]Ai and had utterly destroyed it—[c]as he had
done to Jericho and its king, so he had done to
[d]Ai and its king—and [e]how the inhabitants of
Gibeon had made peace with Israel and were
among them,
2 that they [a]feared greatly, because Gibeon
was a great city, like one of the royal cities, and
because it *was* greater than Ai, and all its men
were mighty.
3 Therefore Adoni-Zedek king of Jerusalem
sent to Hoham king of Hebron, Piram king of Jarmuth, Japhia king of Lachish, and Debir king of
Eglon, saying,
4 "Come up to me and help me, that we may
attack Gibeon, for [a]it has made peace with Joshua
and with the children of Israel."
5 Therefore the five kings of the [a]Amorites,
the king of Jerusalem, the king of Hebron, the
king of Jarmuth, the king of Lachish, *and* the king
of Eglon, [b]gathered together and went up, they
and all their armies, and camped before Gibeon
and made war against it.
6 And the men of Gibeon sent to Joshua at
the camp [a]at Gilgal, saying, "Do not forsake your
servants; come up to us quickly, save us and help
us, for all the kings of the Amorites who dwell
in the mountains have gathered together against
us."
7 So Joshua ascended from Gilgal, he and
[a]all the people of war with him, and all the mighty
men of valor.
8 And the LORD said to Joshua, [a]"Do not
fear them, for I have delivered them into your
hand; [b]not a man of them shall [c]stand before
you."
9 Joshua therefore came upon them suddenly, having marched all night from Gilgal.
10 So the LORD [a]routed them before Israel,
killed them with a great slaughter at Gibeon,
chased them along the road that goes [b]to Beth
Horon, and struck them down as far as [c]Azekah
and Makkedah.
11 And it happened, as they fled before Israel *and* were on the descent of Beth Horon,
[a]that the LORD cast down large hailstones from
heaven on them as far as Azekah, and they died.
There were more who died from the hailstones

KJV

they whom the children of Israel slew with the
sword.
12 Then spake Joshua to the LORD in the day
when the LORD delivered up the Amorites before
the children of Israel, and he said in the sight of
Israel, [a]Sun, stand thou still upon Gibeon; and
thou, Moon, in the valley of [b]Ajalon.
13 And the sun stood still, and the moon
stayed, until the people had avenged themselves
upon their enemies. [a]*Is* not this written in the
book of Jasher? So the sun stood still in the midst
of heaven, and hasted not to go down about a
whole day.
14 And there was [a]no day like that before it
or after it, that the LORD hearkened unto the voice
of a man: for [b]the LORD fought for Israel.
15 [a]And Joshua returned, and all Israel with
him, unto the camp to Gilgal.

The Amorite Kings Executed

16 But these five kings fled, and hid themselves in a cave at Makkedah.
17 And it was told Joshua, saying, The five
kings are found hid in a cave at Makkedah.
18 And Joshua said, Roll great stones upon
the mouth of the cave, and set men by it for to
keep them:
19 And stay ye not, *but* pursue after your enemies, and smite the hindmost of them; suffer
them not to enter into their cities: for the LORD
your God hath delivered them into your hand.
20 And it came to pass, when Joshua and the
children of Israel had made an end of slaying
them with a very great slaughter, till they were
consumed, that the rest *which* remained of them
entered into fenced cities.
21 And all the people returned to the camp
to Joshua at Makkedah in peace: [a]none moved
his tongue against any of the children of Israel.
22 Then said Joshua, Open the mouth of the
cave, and bring out those five kings unto me out
of the cave.
23 And they did so, and brought forth those
five kings unto him out of the cave, the king of
Jerusalem, the king of Hebron, the king of Jarmuth, the king of Lachish, *and* the king of Eglon.
24 And it came to pass, when they brought
out those kings unto Joshua, that Joshua called
for all the men of Israel, and said unto the captains
of the men of war which went with him, Come
near, put your feet upon the necks of these kings.
And they came near, and [a]put their feet upon the
necks of them.
25 And Joshua said unto them, [a]Fear not, nor
be dismayed, be strong and of good courage: for
[b]thus shall the LORD do to all your enemies against
whom ye fight.
26 And afterward Joshua smote them, and
slew them, and hanged them on five trees: and
they [a]were hanging upon the trees until the
evening.
27 And it came to pass at the time of the going down of the sun, *that* Joshua commanded,
and they [a]took them down off the trees, and cast
them into the cave wherein they had been hid,
and laid great stones in the cave's mouth, *which
remain* until this very day.

Conquest of the Southland

28 And that day Joshua took Makkedah, and
smote it with the edge of the sword, and the king
thereof he utterly [a]destroyed, them, and all the
souls that *were* therein; he let none remain: and
he did to the king of Makkedah [b]as he did unto
the king of Jericho.
29 Then Joshua passed from Makkedah, and
all Israel with him, unto [a]Libnah, and fought
against Libnah:
30 And the LORD delivered it also, and the

12 [a]Is. 28:21; Hab. 3:11 [b]Judg. 12:12
13 [a]2 Sam. 1:18
14 [a]Is. 38:7, 8 [b]Ex. 14:14; Deut. 1:30; 20:4; Josh. 10:42; 23:3
15 [a]Josh. 10:43
21 [a]Ex. 11:7
24 [a]Ps. 107:40; Is. 26:5, 6; Mal. 4:3
25 [a]Deut. 31:6–8; Josh. 1:9 [b]Deut. 3:21; 7:19
26 [a]Josh. 8:29; 2 Sam. 21:9
27 [a]Deut. 21:22, 23; Josh. 8:29
28 [a]Deut. 7:2, 16 [b]Josh. 6:21
29 [a]Josh. 15:42; 21:13; 2 Kin. 8:22; 19:8

NKJV

than the children of Israel killed with the
sword.
12 Then Joshua spoke to the LORD in the day
when the LORD delivered up the Amorites before
the children of Israel, and he said in the sight of
Israel:

> [a]"Sun, stand still over Gibeon;
> And Moon, in the Valley of [b]Aijalon."
> 13 So the sun stood still,
> And the moon stopped,
> Till the people had revenge
> Upon their enemies.

[a]*Is* this not written in the Book of Jasher? So the
sun stood still in the midst of heaven, and did
not hasten to go *down* for about a whole day.
14 And there has been [a]no day like that, before it or after it, that the LORD heeded the voice
of a man; for [b]the LORD fought for Israel.
15 [a]Then Joshua returned, and all Israel with
him, to the camp at Gilgal.

The Amorite Kings Executed

16 But these five kings had fled and hidden
themselves in a cave at Makkedah.
17 And it was told Joshua, saying, "The five
kings have been found hidden in the cave at
Makkedah."
18 So Joshua said, "Roll large stones against
the mouth of the cave, and set men by it to guard
them.
19 "And do not stay *there* yourselves, *but*
pursue your enemies, and attack their rear *guard.*
Do not allow them to enter their cities, for the
LORD your God has delivered them into your
hand."
20 Then it happened, while Joshua and the
children of Israel made an end of slaying them
with a very great slaughter, till they had finished,
that those who escaped entered fortified cities.
21 And all the people returned to the camp,
to Joshua at Makkedah, in peace. [a]No one moved
his tongue against any of the children of Israel.
22 Then Joshua said, "Open the mouth of the
cave, and bring out those five kings to me from
the cave."
23 And they did so, and brought out those
five kings to him from the cave: the king of Jerusalem, the king of Hebron, the king of Jarmuth,
the king of Lachish, *and* the king of Eglon.
24 So it was, when they brought out those
kings to Joshua, that Joshua called for all the men
of Israel, and said to the captains of the men of
war who went with him, "Come near, put your
feet on the necks of these kings." And they drew
near and [a]put their feet on their necks.
25 Then Joshua said to them, [a]"Do not be
afraid, nor be dismayed; be strong and of good
courage, for [b]thus the LORD will do to all your
enemies against whom you fight."
26 And afterward Joshua struck them and
killed them, and hanged them on five trees; and
they [a]were hanging on the trees until evening.
27 So it was at the time of the going down
of the sun *that* Joshua commanded, and they
[a]took them down from the trees, cast them into
the cave where they had been hidden, and laid
large stones against the cave's mouth, *which remain* until this very day.

Conquest of the Southland

28 On that day Joshua took Makkedah, and
struck it and its king with the edge of the sword.
He utterly [a]destroyed *them—all the people who
were in it. He let none remain. He also did to the
king of Makkedah [b]as he had done to the king
of Jericho.
29 Then Joshua passed from Makkedah, and
all Israel with him, to [a]Libnah; and they fought
against Libnah.
30 And the LORD also delivered it and its king

*

10:28 So with MT and most authorities; many Heb. mss., some LXX mss., and some Tg. mss. *it*

KJV

king thereof, into the hand of Israel; and he smote
it with the edge of the sword, and all the souls
that *were* therein; he let none remain in it; but
did unto the king thereof as he did unto the king
of Jericho.
31 And Joshua passed from Libnah, and all
Israel with him, unto Lachish, and encamped
against it, and fought against it:
32 And the LORD delivered Lachish into the
hand of Israel, which took it on the second day,
and smote it with the edge of the sword, and all
the souls that *were* therein, according to all that
he had done to Libnah.
33 Then Horam king of Gezer came up to
help Lachish; and Joshua smote him and his people, until he had left him none remaining.
34 And from Lachish Joshua passed unto
Eglon, and all Israel with him; and they encamped
against it, and fought against it:
35 And they took it on that day, and smote
it with the edge of the sword, and all the souls
that *were* therein he utterly destroyed that day,
according to all that he had done to Lachish.
36 And Joshua went up from Eglon, and all
Israel with him, unto [a]Hebron; and they fought
against it:
37 And they took it, and smote it with the
edge of the sword, and the king thereof, and all
the cities thereof, and all the souls that *were*
therein; he left none remaining, according to all
that he had done to Eglon; but destroyed it utterly,
and all the souls that *were* therein.
38 And Joshua returned, and all Israel with
him, to [a]Debir; and fought against it:
39 And he took it, and the king thereof, and
all the cities thereof; and they smote them with
the edge of the sword, and utterly destroyed all
the souls that *were* therein; he left none remaining: as he had done to Hebron, so he did to Debir,
and to the king thereof; as he had done also to
Libnah, and to her king.
40 So Joshua smote all the [a]country of the
hills, and of the south, and of the vale, and of
the springs, and [b]all their kings: he left none remaining, but [c]utterly destroyed all that breathed,
as the LORD God of Israel commanded.
41 And Joshua smote them from [a]Kadesh–
barnea even unto [b]Gaza, [c]and all the country of
Goshen, even unto Gibeon.
42 And all these kings and their land did
Joshua take at one time, [a]because the LORD God
of Israel fought for Israel.
43 And Joshua returned, and all Israel with
him, unto the camp to Gilgal.

The Northern Conquest

11 And it came to pass, when Jabin king of
Hazor had heard *those things,* that he [a]sent
to Jobab king of Madon, and to the king [b]of Shimron, and to the king of Achshaph,
2 And to the kings that *were* on the north
of the mountains, and of the plains south of [a]Chin-
neroth, and in the valley, and in the borders [b]of
Dor on the west,
3 *And to* the Canaanite on the east and on
the west, and *to* the [a]Amorite, and the Hittite, and
the Perizzite, and the Jebusite in the mountains,
[b]and *to* the Hivite under [c]Hermon [d]in the land
of Mizpeh.
4 And they went out, they and all their hosts
with them, much people, [a]even as the sand that
is upon the sea shore in multitude, with horses
and chariots very many.
5 And when all these kings were met together, they came and pitched together at the waters of Merom, to fight against Israel.
6 And the LORD said unto Joshua, [a]Be not
afraid because of them: for to morrow about this
time will I deliver them up all slain before Israel:
thou shalt [b]hough their horses, and burn their
chariots with fire.
7 So Joshua came, and all the people of war

NKJV

into the hand of Israel; he struck it and all the
people who *were* in it with the edge of the sword.
He let none remain in it, but did to its king as he
had done to the king of Jericho.
31 Then Joshua passed from Libnah, and all
Israel with him, to Lachish; and they encamped
against it and fought against it.
32 And the LORD delivered Lachish into the
hand of Israel, who took it on the second day,
and struck it and all the people who *were* in it
with the edge of the sword, according to all that
he had done to Libnah.
33 Then Horam king of Gezer came up to
help Lachish; and Joshua struck him and his people, until he left him none remaining.
34 From Lachish Joshua passed to Eglon,
and all Israel with him; and they encamped
against it and fought against it.
35 They took it on that day and struck it with
the edge of the sword; all the people who *were*
in it he utterly destroyed that day, according to
all that he had done to Lachish.
36 So Joshua went up from Eglon, and all
Israel with him, to [a]Hebron; and they fought
against it.
37 And they took it and struck it with the
edge of the sword—its king, all its cities, and all
the people who *were* in it; he left none remaining,
according to all that he had done to Eglon, but
utterly destroyed it and all the people who *were*
in it.
38 Then Joshua returned, and all Israel with
him, to [a]Debir; and they fought against it.
39 And he took it and its king and all its cities; they struck them with the edge of the sword
and utterly destroyed all the people who *were* in
it. He left none remaining; as he had done to Hebron, so he did to Debir and its king, as he had
done also to Libnah and its king.
40 So Joshua conquered all the land: the
[a]mountain country and the *South and the lowland
and the wilderness slopes, and [b]all their kings;
he left none remaining, but [c]utterly destroyed all
that breathed, as the LORD God of Israel had
commanded.
41 And Joshua conquered them from [a]Ka-
desh Barnea as far as [b]Gaza, [c]and all the country
of Goshen, even as far as Gibeon.
42 All these kings and their land Joshua took
at one time, [a]because the LORD God of Israel
fought for Israel.
43 Then Joshua returned, and all Israel with
him, to the camp at Gilgal.

The Northern Conquest

11 And it came to pass, when Jabin king of
Hazor heard *these things,* that he [a]sent to
Jobab king of Madon, to the king [b]of Shimron,
to the king of Achshaph,
2 and to the kings who *were* from the north,
in the mountains, in the plain south of [a]Chinne-
roth, in the lowland, and in the heights [b]of Dor
on the west,
3 to the Canaanites in the east and in the
west, the [a]Amorite, the Hittite, the Perizzite, the
Jebusite in the mountains, [b]and the Hivite below
[c]Hermon [d]in the land of Mizpah.
4 So they went out, they and all their armies
with them, *as* many people [a]*as* the sand that *is*
on the seashore in multitude, with very many
horses and chariots.
5 And when all these kings had met together, they came and camped together at the waters of Merom to fight against Israel.
6 But the LORD said to Joshua, [a]"Do not be
afraid because of them, for tomorrow about this
time I will deliver all of them slain before Israel.
You shall [b]hamstring their horses and burn their
chariots with fire."
7 So Joshua and all the people of war with

36 [a]Num. 13:22; Josh. 14:13–15; 15:13; Judg. 1:10, 20; 2 Sam. 5:1, 3, 5, 13; 2 Chr. 11:10
38 [a]Josh. 15:15; Judg. 1:11; 1 Chr. 6:58
40 [a]Deut. 1:7 [b]Deut. 7:24 [c]Deut. 20:16, 17
41 [a]Num. 13:26; Deut. 9:23 [b]Gen. 10:19; Josh. 11:22 [c]Josh. 11:16; 15:51
42 [a]Josh. 10:14

CHAPTER 11
1 [a]Josh. 10:3 [b]Josh. 19:15
2 [a]Num. 34:11 [b]Josh. 17:11; Judg. 1:27; 1 Kin. 4:11
3 [a]Josh. 9:1 [b]Deut. 7:1; Judg. 3:3, 5; 1 Kin. 9:20 [c]Josh. 11:17; 13:5, 11 [d]Gen. 31:49
4 [a]Gen. 22:17; 32:12; Judg. 7:12; 1 Sam. 13:5
6 [a]Josh. 10:8 [b]2 Sam. 8:4

* **10:40** Heb. *Negev,* and so throughout the book

KJV

with him, against them by the waters of Merom
suddenly; and they fell upon them.
8 And the LORD delivered them into the
hand of Israel, who smote them, and chased them
unto great [a]Zidon, and unto [b]Misrephoth–maim,
and unto the valley of Mizpeh eastward; and they
smote them, until they left them none remaining.
9 And Joshua did unto them as the LORD
bade him: he houghed their horses, and burnt
their chariots with fire.
10 And Joshua at that time turned back, and
took Hazor, and smote the king thereof with the
sword: for Hazor beforetime was the head of all
those kingdoms.
11 And they smote all the souls that *were*
therein with the edge of the sword, [a]utterly destroying *them:* there was not any left to [b]breathe:
and he burnt Hazor with fire.
12 And all the cities of those kings, and all
the kings of them, did Joshua take, and smote
them with the edge of the sword, *and* he utterly
destroyed them, [a]as Moses the servant of the LORD
commanded.
13 But *as for* the cities that stood still in their
strength, Israel burned none of them, save Hazor
only; *that* did Joshua burn.
14 And all the [a]spoil of these cities, and the
cattle, the children of Israel took for a prey unto
themselves; but every man they smote with the
edge of the sword, until they had destroyed them,
neither left they any to breathe.
15 [a]As the LORD commanded Moses his servant, so [b]did Moses command Joshua, and [c]so
did Joshua; he left nothing undone of all that the
LORD commanded Moses.

Summary of Joshua's Conquests

16 So Joshua took all that land, [a]the hills,
and all the south country, [b]and all the land of
Goshen, and the valley, and the plain, and the
mountain of Israel, and the valley of the same;
17 [a]*Even* from the mount Halak, that goeth
up to Seir, even unto Baal–gad in the valley of
Lebanon under mount Hermon: and [b]all their
kings he took, and smote them, and slew them.
18 Joshua made war a long time with all
those kings.
19 There was not a city that made peace with
the children of Israel, save [a]the Hivites the inhabitants of Gibeon: all *other* they took in battle.
20 For [a]it was of the LORD to harden their
hearts, that they should come against Israel in battle, that he might destroy them utterly, *and* that
they might have no favour, but that he might destroy them, [b]as the LORD commanded Moses.
21 And at that time came Joshua, and cut off
[a]the Anakims from the mountains, from Hebron,
from Debir, from Anab, and from all the mountains of Judah, and from all the mountains of Israel: Joshua destroyed them utterly with their
cities.
22 There was none of the Anakims left in the
land of the children of Israel: only [a]in Gaza, in
Gath, [b]and in Ashdod, there remained.
23 So Joshua took the whole land, [a]accord-
ing to all that the LORD said unto Moses; and
Joshua gave it for an inheritance unto Israel [b]ac-
cording to their divisions by their tribes. And the
land [c]rested from war.

The Kings Conquered by Moses
(cf. Num. 21:21–35)

12 Now these *are* the kings of the land, which
the children of Israel smote, and possessed
their land on the other side Jordan toward the
rising of the sun, [a]from the river Arnon [b]unto
mount Hermon, and all the plain on the east:
2 [a]Sihon king of the Amorites, who dwelt
in Heshbon, *and* ruled from Aroer, which *is* upon
the bank of the river Arnon, and from the middle
of the river, and from half Gilead, even unto the

8 [a]Gen. 49:13 [b]Josh. 13:6
11 [a]Deut. 20:16 [b]Josh. 10:40
12 [a]Num. 33:50–56; Deut. 7:2; 20:16
14 [a]Deut. 20:14–18
15 [a]Ex. 34:10–17 [b]Deut. 31:7, 8 [c]Josh. 1:7
16 [a]Josh. 12:8 [b]Josh. 10:40, 41
17 [a]Josh. 12:7 [b]Deut. 7:24
19 [a]Josh. 9:3–7
20 [a]Deut. 2:30 [b]Deut. 20:16, 17
21 [a]Num. 13:22, 33; Deut. 1:28; 9:2; Josh. 15:13, 14
22 [a]1 Sam. 17:4 [b]Josh. 15:46; 1 Sam. 5:1; Is. 20:1
23 [a]Ex. 33:2; Num. 34:2–15 [b]Num. 26:53; Josh. 14; 15 [c]Deut. 12:9, 10; 25:19; [Heb. 4:8]

CHAPTER 12

1 [a]Num. 21:24 [b]Deut. 3:8
2 [a]Num. 21:24; Deut. 2:24–27

*

11:8 Heb. *Misrephoth Maim,* lit. *Burnings of Water*
11:13 Heb. *tel,* a heap of successive city ruins
11:16 Heb. *arabah*

NKJV

him came against them suddenly by the waters
of Merom, and they attacked them.
8 And the LORD delivered them into the
hand of Israel, who defeated them and chased
them to Greater [a]Sidon, to the *Brook [b]Misre-
photh, and to the Valley of Mizpah eastward; they
attacked them until they left none of them
remaining.
9 So Joshua did to them as the LORD had
told him: he hamstrung their horses and burned
their chariots with fire.
10 Joshua turned back at that time and took
Hazor, and struck its king with the sword; for Hazor was formerly the head of all those kingdoms.
11 And they struck all the people who *were*
in it with the edge of the sword, [a]utterly destroying *them.* There was none left [b]breathing. Then
he burned Hazor with fire.
12 So all the cities of those kings, and all their
kings, Joshua took and struck with the edge of
the sword. He utterly destroyed them, [a]as Moses
the servant of the LORD had commanded.
13 But *as for* the cities that stood on their
*mounds, Israel burned none of them, except Ha-
zor only, *which* Joshua burned.
14 And all the [a]spoil of these cities and the
livestock, the children of Israel took as booty for
themselves; but they struck every man with the
edge of the sword until they had destroyed them,
and they left none breathing.
15 [a]As the LORD had commanded Moses his
servant, so [b]Moses commanded Joshua, and [c]so
Joshua did. He left nothing undone of all that the
LORD had commanded Moses.

Summary of Joshua's Conquests

16 Thus Joshua took all this land: [a]the mountain country, all the South, [b]all the land of
Goshen, the lowland, and the Jordan *plain—the
mountains of Israel and its lowlands,
17 [a]from Mount Halak and the ascent to Seir,
even as far as Baal Gad in the Valley of Lebanon
below Mount Hermon. He captured [b]all their
kings, and struck them down and killed them.
18 Joshua made war a long time with all
those kings.
19 There was not a city that made peace with
the children of Israel, except [a]the Hivites, the inhabitants of Gibeon. All *the others* they took in
battle.
20 For [a]it was of the LORD to harden their
hearts, that they should come against Israel in battle, that He might utterly destroy them, *and* that
they might receive no mercy, but that He might
destroy them, [b]as the LORD had commanded
Moses.
21 And at that time Joshua came and cut off
[a]the Anakim from the mountains: from Hebron,
from Debir, from Anab, from all the mountains
of Judah, and from all the mountains of Israel;
Joshua utterly destroyed them with their cities.
22 None of the Anakim were left in the land
of the children of Israel; they remained only [a]in
Gaza, in Gath, [b]and in Ashdod.
23 So Joshua took the whole land, [a]accord-
ing to all that the LORD had said to Moses; and
Joshua gave it as an inheritance to Israel [b]accord-
ing to their divisions by their tribes. Then the land
[c]rested from war.

The Kings Conquered by Moses
(cf. Num. 21:21–35)

12 These *are* the kings of the land whom the
children of Israel defeated, and whose land
they possessed on the other side of the Jordan
toward the rising of the sun, [a]from the River Arnon [b]to Mount Hermon, and all the eastern Jordan
plain:
2 *One king was* [a]Sihon king of the Amorites,
who dwelt in Heshbon *and* ruled half of Gilead,
from Aroer, which is on the bank of the River
Arnon, from the middle of that river, even as far

KJV

river Jabbok, *which is* the border of the children
of Ammon;
3 And [a]from the plain to the sea of Chinneroth on the east, and unto the sea of the plain,
even the salt sea on the east, [b]the way to Beth–
jeshimoth; and from the south, under [c]Ashdoth–
pisgah:
4 And [a]the coast of Og king of Bashan,
which was of [b]the remnant of the giants, [c]that
dwelt at Ashtaroth and at Edrei,
5 And reigned in [a]mount Hermon, [b]and in
Salcah, and in all Bashan, [c]unto the border of the
Geshurites and the Maachathites, and half Gilead,
the border of Sihon king of Heshbon.
6 [a]Them did Moses the servant of the LORD
and the children of Israel smite: and [b]Moses the
servant of the LORD gave it *for* a possession unto
the Reubenites, and the Gadites, and the half tribe
of Manasseh.

The Kings Conquered by Joshua

7 And these *are* the kings of the country
[a]which Joshua and the children of Israel smote on
this side Jordan on the west, from Baal–gad in
the valley of Lebanon even unto the mount Halak,
that goeth up to [b]Seir; which Joshua [c]gave unto
the tribes of Israel *for* a possession according to
their divisions;
8 [a]In the mountains, and in the valleys, and
in the plains, and in the springs, and in the wilderness, and in the south country; [b]the Hittites, the
Amorites, and the Canaanites, the Perizzites, the
Hivites, and the Jebusites:
9 [a]The king of Jericho, one; [b]the king of Ai,
which *is* beside Beth–el, one;
10 [a]The king of Jerusalem, one; the king of
Hebron, one;
11 The king of Jarmuth, one; the king of
Lachish, one;
12 The king of Eglon, one; [a]the king of Gezer,
one;
13 [a]The king of Debir, one; the king of Geder,
one;
14 The king of Hormah, one; the king of Arad,
one;
15 [a]The king of Libnah, one; the king of Adullam, one;
16 [a]The king of Makkedah, one; [b]the king of
Beth–el, one;
17 The king of Tappuah, one; [a]the king of Hepher, one;
18 The king of Aphek, one; the king of La-
sharon, one;
19 The king of Madon, one; [a]the king of Hazor, one;
20 The king of [a]Shimron–meron, one; the
king of Achshaph, one;
21 The king of Taanach, one; the king of Megiddo, one;
22 [a]The king of Kedesh, one; the king of Jokneam of Carmel, one;
23 The king of Dor in the [a]coast of Dor, one;
the king of [b]the nations of Gilgal, one;
24 The king of Tirzah, one: [a]all the kings
thirty and one.

Remaining Land to Be Conquered

13 Now Joshua [a]was old *and* stricken in years;
and the LORD said unto him, Thou art old
and stricken in years, and there remaineth yet
very much land to be possessed.
2 [a]This *is* the land that yet remaineth: [b]all
the borders of the Philistines, and all [c]Geshuri,
3 [a]From Sihor, which *is* before Egypt, even
unto the borders of Ekron northward, *which* is
counted to the Canaanite: [b]five lords of the Philistines; the Gazathites, and the Ashdothites, the
Eshkalonites, the Gittites, and the Ekronites; also
[c]the Avites:
4 From the south, all the land of the Canaan-

3 [a]Deut. 3:17 [b]Josh. 13:20 [c]Deut. 3:17; 4:49
4 [a]Num. 21:33; Deut. 3:4, 10 [b]Deut. 3:11; Josh. 13:12 [c]Deut. 1:4
5 [a]Deut. 3:8 [b]Deut. 3:10; Josh. 13:11; 1 Chr. 5:11 [c]Deut. 3:14; 1 Sam. 27:8
6 [a]Num. 21:24, 35 [b]Num. 32:29–33; Deut. 3:12; Josh. 13:8
7 [a]Josh. 11:17 [b]Gen. 14:6; 32:3; Deut. 2:1, 4 [c]Josh. 11:23
8 [a]Josh. 10:40; 11:16 [b]Ex. 3:8; 23:23; Josh. 9:1
9 [a]Josh. 6:2 [b]Josh. 8:29
10 [a]Josh. 10:23
12 [a]Josh. 10:33
13 [a]Josh. 10:38, 39
15 [a]Josh. 10:29, 30
16 [a]Josh. 10:28 [b]Josh. 8:17; Judg. 1:22
17 [a]1 Kin. 4:10
19 [a]Josh. 11:10
20 [a]Josh. 11:1; 19:15
22 [a]Josh. 19:37; 20:7; 21:32
23 [a]Josh. 11:2 [b]Gen. 14:1, 2; Is. 9:1
24 [a]Deut. 7:24

CHAPTER 13
1 [a]Josh. 14:10; 23:1, 2
2 [a]Judg. 3:1–3 [b]Joel 3:4 [c]Josh. 13:13; 2 Sam. 3:3
3 [a]1 Chr. 13:5; Jer. 2:18 [b]Judg. 3:3 [c]Deut. 2:23

NKJV

as the River Jabbok, *which is* the border of the
Ammonites,
3 and [a]the eastern Jordan plain from the
Sea of Chinneroth as far as the Sea of the Arabah
(the Salt Sea), [b]the road to Beth Jeshimoth, and
southward below [c]the slopes of Pisgah.
4 *The other king was* [a]Og king of Bashan
and his territory, *who was* of [b]the remnant of the
giants, [c]who dwelt at Ashtaroth and at Edrei,
5 and reigned over [a]Mount Hermon, [b]over
Salcah, over all Bashan, [c]as far as the border of
the Geshurites and the Maachathites, and over
half of Gilead *to* the border of Sihon king of
Heshbon.
6 [a]These Moses the servant of the LORD and
the children of Israel had conquered; and [b]Moses
the servant of the LORD had given it *as* a possession to the Reubenites, the Gadites, and half the
tribe of Manasseh.

The Kings Conquered by Joshua

7 And these *are* the kings of the country
[a]which Joshua and the children of Israel conquered
on this side of the Jordan, on the west, from Baal
Gad in the Valley of Lebanon as far as Mount
Halak and the ascent to [b]Seir, which Joshua [c]gave
to the tribes of Israel *as* a possession according
to their divisions,
8 [a]in the mountain country, in the lowlands,
in the *Jordan* plain, in the slopes, in the wilderness, and in the South—[b]the Hittites, the Amorites, the Canaanites, the Perizzites, the Hivites,
and the Jebusites:
9 [a]the king of Jericho, one; [b]the king of Ai,
which *is* beside Bethel, one;
10 [a]the king of Jerusalem, one; the king of
Hebron, one;
11 the king of Jarmuth, one; the king of Lachish, one;
12 the king of Eglon, one; [a]the king of Gezer,
one;
13 [a]the king of Debir, one; the king of Geder,
one;
14 the king of Hormah, one; the king of Arad,
one;
15 [a]the king of Libnah, one; the king of
Adullam, one;
16 [a]the king of Makkedah, one; [b]the king of
Bethel, one;
17 the king of Tappuah, one; [a]the king of
Hepher, one;
18 the king of Aphek, one; the king of La-
sharon, one;
19 the king of Madon, one; [a]the king of Hazor, one;
20 the king of [a]Shimron Meron, one; the king
of Achshaph, one;
21 the king of Taanach, one; the king of Megiddo, one;
22 [a]the king of Kedesh, one; the king of Jokneam in Carmel, one;
23 the king of Dor in the [a]heights of Dor,
one; the king of [b]the people of Gilgal, one;
24 the king of Tirzah, one—[a]all the kings,
thirty-one.

Remaining Land to Be Conquered

13 Now Joshua [a]was old, advanced in years.
And the LORD said to him: "You are old,
advanced in years, and there remains very much
land yet to be possessed.
2 [a]"This is the land that yet remains: [b]all
the territory of the Philistines and all [c]*that of* the
Geshurites,
3 [a]"from Sihor, which *is* east of Egypt, as
far as the border of Ekron northward (*which* is
counted as Canaanite); the [b]five lords of the Philistines—the Gazites, the Ashdodites, the Ashke-
lonites, the Gittites, and the Ekronites; also [c]the
Avites;
4 "from the south, all the land of the Ca-

KJV

ites, and Mearah that *is* beside the Sidonians, [a]unto Aphek, to the borders of [b]the Amorites:

5 And the land of [a]the Giblites, and all Lebanon, toward the sunrising, [b]from Baal–gad under mount Hermon unto the entering into Hamath.

6 All the inhabitants of the hill country from Lebanon unto [a]Misrephoth–maim, *and* all the Sidonians, them [b]will I drive out from before the children of Israel: only [c]divide thou it by lot unto the Israelites for an inheritance, as I have commanded thee.

7 Now therefore divide this land for an inheritance unto the nine tribes, and the half tribe of Manasseh,

The Land Divided East of the Jordan

8 With whom the Reubenites and the Gadites have received their inheritance, [a]which Moses gave them, [b]beyond Jordan eastward, *even* as Moses the servant of the LORD gave them;

9 From Aroer, that *is* upon the bank of the river Arnon, and the city that *is* in the midst of the river, [a]and all the plain of Medeba unto Dibon;

10 And [a]all the cities of Sihon king of the Amorites, which reigned in Heshbon, unto the border of the children of Ammon;

11 [a]And Gilead, and the border of the Geshurites and Maachathites, and all mount Hermon, and all Bashan unto Salcah;

12 All the kingdom of Og in Bashan, which reigned in Ashtaroth and in Edrei, who remained of [a]the remnant of the giants: [b]for these did Moses smite, and cast them out.

13 Nevertheless the children of Israel expelled [a]not the Geshurites, nor the Maachathites: but the Geshurites and the Maachathites dwell among the Israelites until this day.

14 [a]Only unto the tribe of Levi he gave none inheritance; the sacrifices of the LORD God of Israel made by fire *are* their inheritance, [b]as he said unto them.

The Land of Reuben

15 [a]And Moses gave unto the tribe of the children of Reuben *inheritance* according to their families.

16 And their coast was [a]from Aroer, that *is* on the bank of the river Arnon, [b]and the city that *is* in the midst of the river, [c]and all the plain by Medeba;

17 [a]Heshbon, and all her cities that *are* in the plain; Dibon, and Bamoth–baal, and Beth–baal–meon,

18 [a]And Jahaza, and Kedemoth, and Mephaath,

19 [a]And Kirjathaim, and [b]Sibmah, and Zareth–shahar in the mount of the valley,

20 And Beth–peor, and [a]Ashdoth–pisgah, and Beth–jeshimoth,

21 [a]And all the cities of the plain, and all the kingdom of Sihon king of the Amorites, which reigned in Heshbon, [b]whom Moses smote [c]with the princes of Midian, Evi, and Rekem, and Zur, and Hur, and Reba, *which were* dukes of Sihon, dwelling in the country.

22 [a]Balaam also the son of Beor, the soothsayer, did the children of Israel slay with the sword among them that were slain by them.

23 And the border of the children of Reuben was Jordan, and the border *thereof.* This *was* the inheritance of the children of Reuben after their families, the cities and the villages thereof.

The Land of Gad

24 [a]And Moses gave *inheritance* unto the tribe of Gad, *even* unto the children of Gad according to their families.

25 [a]And their coast was Jazer, and all the cities of Gilead, [b]and half the land of the children of Ammon, unto Aroer that *is* before [c]Rabbah;

26 And from Heshbon unto Ramath–mizpeh,

NKJV

naanites, and Mearah that belongs to the Sidonians [a]as far as Aphek, to the border of [b]the Amorites;

5 "the land of [a]the *Gebalites, and all Lebanon, toward the sunrise, [b]from Baal Gad below Mount Hermon as far as the entrance to Hamath;

6 "all the inhabitants of the mountains from Lebanon as far as [a]the *Brook Misrephoth, *and* all the Sidonians—them [b]I will drive out from before the children of Israel; only [c]divide it by lot to Israel as an inheritance, as I have commanded you.

7 "Now therefore, divide this land as an inheritance to the nine tribes and half the tribe of Manasseh."

The Land Divided East of the Jordan

8 With the other half-tribe the Reubenites and the Gadites received their inheritance, [a]which Moses had given them, [b]beyond the Jordan eastward, as Moses the servant of the LORD had given them:

9 from Aroer which *is* on the bank of the River Arnon, and the town that *is* in the midst of the ravine, [a]and all the plain of Medeba as far as Dibon;

10 [a]all the cities of Sihon king of the Amorites, who reigned in Heshbon, as far as the border of the children of Ammon;

11 [a]Gilead, and the border of the Geshurites and Maachathites, all Mount Hermon, and all Bashan as far as Salcah;

12 all the kingdom of Og in Bashan, who reigned in Ashtaroth and Edrei, who remained of [a]the remnant of the giants; [b]for Moses had defeated and cast out these.

13 Nevertheless the children of Israel [a]did not drive out the Geshurites or the Maachathites, but the Geshurites and the Maachathites dwell among the Israelites until this day.

14 [a]Only to the tribe of Levi he had given no inheritance; the sacrifices of the LORD God of Israel made by fire *are* their inheritance, [b]as He said to them.

The Land of Reuben

15 [a]And Moses had given to the tribe of the children of Reuben *an inheritance* according to their families.

16 Their territory was [a]from Aroer, which *is* on the bank of the River Arnon, [b]and the city that *is* in the midst of the ravine, [c]and all the plain by Medeba;

17 [a]Heshbon and all its cities that *are* in the plain: Dibon, Bamoth Baal, Beth Baal Meon,

18 [a]Jahaza, Kedemoth, Mephaath,

19 [a]Kirjathaim, [b]Sibmah, Zereth Shahar on the mountain of the valley,

20 Beth Peor, [a]the slopes of Pisgah, and Beth Jeshimoth—

21 [a]all the cities of the plain and all the kingdom of Sihon king of the Amorites, who reigned in Heshbon, [b]whom Moses had struck [c]with the princes of Midian: Evi, Rekem, Zur, Hur, and Reba, who *were* princes of Sihon dwelling in the country.

22 The children of Israel also killed with the sword [a]Balaam the son of Beor, the soothsayer, among those who were killed by them.

23 And the border of the children of Reuben was the bank of the Jordan. This *was* the inheritance of the children of Reuben according to their families, the cities and their villages.

The Land of Gad

24 [a]Moses also had given *an inheritance* to the tribe of Gad, to the children of Gad according to their families.

25 [a]Their territory was Jazer, and all the cities of Gilead, [b]and half the land of the Ammonites as far as Aroer, which *is* before [c]Rabbah,

26 and from Heshbon to Ramath Mizpah and

---

4 [a]Josh. 12:18; 19:30; 1 Sam. 4:1; 1 Kin. 20:26, 30 [b]Judg. 1:34
5 [a]1 Kin. 5:18; Ezek. 27:9 [b]Josh. 12:7
6 [a]Josh. 11:8 [b]Josh. 23:13; Judg. 2:21, 23 [c]Josh. 14:1, 2
8 [a]Num. 32:33; Deut. 3:12, 13; Josh. 22:4 [b]Josh. 12:1–6
9 [a]Num. 21:30; Josh. 13:16
10 [a]Num. 21:24, 25
11 [a]Num. 32:1; Josh. 12:5
12 [a]Deut. 3:11; Josh. 12:4 [b]Num. 21:24, 34, 35
13 [a]Josh. 13:11
14 [a]Num. 18:20, 23, 24; Deut. 18:1; Josh. 14:3, 4 [b]Josh. 13:33
15 [a]Num. 34:14; Josh. 13:15–23
16 [a]Josh. 12:2 [b]Num. 21:28 [c]Num. 21:30; Josh. 13:9
17 [a]Num. 21:28, 30
18 [a]Num. 21:23; Judg. 11:20; Is. 15:4; Jer. 48:34
19 [a]Num. 32:37; Jer. 48:1, 23; Ezek. 25:9 [b]Num. 32:38
20 [a]Deut. 3:17; Josh. 12:3
21 [a]Deut. 3:10 [b]Num. 21:24 [c]Num. 31:8
22 [a]Num. 22:5; 31:8
24 [a]Num. 34:14; 1 Chr. 5:11
25 [a]Num. 32:1, 35 [b]Judg. 11:13, 15 [c]Deut. 3:11; 2 Sam. 11:1; 12:26

*

13:5 Or *Giblites*
13:6 Heb. *Misrephoth Maim,* lit. *Burnings of Water*

KJV

and Betonim; and from Mahanaim unto the border of Debir;

27 And in the valley, [a]Beth–aram, and Beth–nimrah, [b]and Succoth, and Zaphon, the rest of the kingdom of Sihon king of Heshbon, Jordan and *his* border, *even* unto the edge [c]of the sea of Chinnereth on the other side Jordan eastward.

28 This *is* the inheritance of the children of Gad after their families, the cities, and their villages.

Half the Tribe of Manasseh (East)

29 [a]And Moses gave *inheritance* unto the half tribe of Manasseh: and *this* was *the possession* of the half tribe of the children of Manasseh by their families.

30 And their coast was from Mahanaim, all Bashan, all the kingdom of Og king of Bashan, and [a]all the towns of Jair, which *are* in Bashan, threescore cities:

31 And half Gilead, and [a]Ashtaroth, and Edrei, cities of the kingdom of Og in Bashan, *were pertaining* unto the [b]children of Machir the son of Manasseh, *even* to the one half of the children of Machir by their families.

32 These *are the countries* which Moses did distribute for inheritance in the plains of Moab, on the other side Jordan, by Jericho, eastward.

33 [a]But unto the tribe of Levi Moses gave not *any* inheritance: the LORD God of Israel *was* their inheritance, [b]as he said unto them.

The Land Divided West of the Jordan

14 And these *are the countries* which the children of Israel inherited in the land of Canaan, [a]which Eleazar the priest, and Joshua the son of Nun, and the heads of the fathers of the tribes of the children of Israel, distributed for inheritance to them.

2 [a]By lot *was* their inheritance, as the LORD commanded by the hand of Moses, for the nine tribes, and *for* the half tribe.

3 [a]For Moses had given the inheritance of two tribes and an half tribe on the other side Jordan: but unto the Levites he gave none inheritance among them.

4 For [a]the children of Joseph were two tribes, Manasseh and Ephraim: therefore they gave no part unto the Levites in the land, save [b]cities to dwell *in*, with their suburbs for their cattle and for their substance.

5 [a]As the LORD commanded Moses, so the children of Israel did, and they divided the land.

Caleb Inherits Hebron

6 Then the children of Judah came unto Joshua in Gilgal: and Caleb the son of Jephunneh the [a]Kenezite said unto him, Thou knowest [b]the thing that the LORD said unto Moses the man of God concerning me and [c]thee in Kadesh–barnea.

7 Forty years old *was* I when Moses the servant of the LORD [a]sent me from Kadesh–barnea to espy out the land; and I brought him word again as *it was* in mine heart.

8 Nevertheless [a]my brethren that went up with me made the heart of the people melt: but I wholly [b]followed the LORD my God.

9 And Moses sware on that day, saying, [a]Surely the land [b]whereon thy feet have trodden shall be thine inheritance, and thy children's for ever, because thou hast wholly followed the LORD my God.

10 And now, behold, the LORD hath kept me [a]alive, [b]as he said, these forty and five years, even since the LORD spake this word unto Moses, while *the children of* Israel wandered in the wilderness: and now, lo, I *am* this day fourscore and five years old.

11 [a]As yet I *am as* strong this day as *I was* in the day that Moses sent me: as my strength

27 [a]Num. 32:36 [b]Gen. 33:17; 1 Kin. 7:46 [c]Num. 34:11; Deut. 3:17
29 [a]Num. 34:14; 1 Chr. 5:23
30 [a]Num. 32:41; 1 Chr. 2:23
31 [a]Josh. 9:10; 12:4; 13:12; 1 Chr. 6:71 [b]Num. 32:39, 40; Josh. 17:1
33 [a]Deut. 18:1; Josh. 13:14; 18:7 [b]Num. 18:20; Deut. 10:9; 18:1, 2

CHAPTER 14

1 [a]Num. 34:16–29
2 [a]Num. 26:55; 33:54; 34:13; Ps. 16:5
3 [a]Num. 32:33; Josh. 13:8, 32, 33
4 [a]Gen. 41:51; 46:20; 48:1, 5; Num. 26:28; 2 Chr. 30:1 [b]Num. 35:2–8; Josh. 21:1–42
5 [a]Num. 35:2; Josh. 21:2
6 [a]Num. 32:11, 12 [b]Num. 14:24, 30 [c]Num. 13:26
7 [a]Num. 13:6, 17; 14:6
8 [a]Num. 13:31, 32; Deut. 1:28 [b]Num. 14:24; Deut. 1:36
9 [a]Num. 14:23, 24 [b]Num. 13:22; Deut. 1:36
10 [a]Num. 14:24, 30, 38 [b]Josh. 5:6; Neh. 9:21
11 [a]Deut. 34:7

NKJV

Betonim, and from Mahanaim to the border of Debir,

27 and in the valley [a]Beth Haram, Beth Nimrah, [b]Succoth, and Zaphon, the rest of the kingdom of Sihon king of Heshbon, with the Jordan as *its* border, as far as the edge [c]of the Sea of Chinnereth, on the other side of the Jordan eastward.

28 This *is* the inheritance of the children of Gad according to their families, the cities and their villages.

Half the Tribe of Manasseh (East)

29 [a]Moses also had given *an inheritance* to half the tribe of Manasseh; it was for half the tribe of the children of Manasseh according to their families:

30 Their territory was from Mahanaim, all Bashan, all the kingdom of Og king of Bashan, and [a]all the towns of Jair which are in Bashan, sixty cities;

31 half of Gilead, and [a]Ashtaroth and Edrei, cities of the kingdom of Og in Bashan, *were* for the [b]children of Machir the son of Manasseh, for half of the children of Machir according to their families.

32 These *are the areas* which Moses had distributed as an inheritance in the plains of Moab on the other side of the Jordan, by Jericho eastward.

33 [a]But to the tribe of Levi Moses had given no inheritance; the LORD God of Israel *was* their inheritance, [b]as He had said to them.

The Land Divided West of the Jordan

14 These *are the areas* which the children of Israel inherited in the land of Canaan, [a]which Eleazar the priest, Joshua the son of Nun, and the heads of the fathers of the tribes of the children of Israel distributed as an inheritance to them.

2 Their inheritance *was* [a]by lot, as the LORD had commanded by the hand of Moses, for the nine tribes and the half-tribe.

3 [a]For Moses had given the inheritance of the two tribes and the half-tribe on the other side of the Jordan; but to the Levites he had given no inheritance among them.

4 For [a]the children of Joseph were two tribes: Manasseh and Ephraim. And they gave no part to the Levites in the land, except [b]cities to dwell *in*, with their common-lands for their livestock and their property.

5 [a]As the LORD had commanded Moses, so the children of Israel did; and they divided the land.

Caleb Inherits Hebron

6 Then the children of Judah came to Joshua in Gilgal. And Caleb the son of Jephunneh the [a]Kenizzite said to him: "You know [b]the word which the LORD said to Moses the man of God concerning [c]you and me in Kadesh Barnea.

7 "I *was* forty years old when Moses the servant of the LORD [a]sent me from Kadesh Barnea to spy out the land, and I brought back word to him as *it was* in my heart.

8 "Nevertheless [a]my brethren who went up with me made the heart of the people melt, but I wholly [b]followed the LORD my God.

9 "So Moses swore on that day, saying, [a]'Surely the land [b]where your foot has trodden shall be your inheritance and your children's forever, because you have wholly followed the LORD my God.'

10 "And now, behold, the LORD has kept me [a]alive, [b]as He said, these forty-five years, ever since the LORD spoke this word to Moses while Israel wandered in the wilderness; and now, here I am this day, eighty-five years old.

11 [a]"As yet I *am as* strong this day as on the day that Moses sent me; just as my strength

KJV

was then, even so *is* my strength now, for war,
both [b]to go out, and to come in.
12 Now therefore give me this mountain,
whereof the LORD spake in that day; for thou
heardest in that day how [a]the Anakims *were*
there, and *that* the cities *were* great *and* fenced:
[b]if so be the LORD *will be* with me, then [c]I shall
be able to drive them out, as the LORD said.
13 And Joshua [a]blessed him, [b]and gave unto
Caleb the son of Jephunneh Hebron for an
inheritance.
14 [a]Hebron therefore became the inheritance
of Caleb the son of Jephunneh the Kenezite unto
this day, because that he [b]wholly followed the
LORD God of Israel.
15 And [a]the name of Hebron before *was* Kirjath–arba; *which Arba was* a great man among
the Anakims. [b]And the land had rest from war.

The Land of Judah

15 *This* then was the lot of the tribe of the children of Judah by their families; [a]*even* to
the border of Edom the [b]wilderness of Zin southward *was* the uttermost part of the south coast.
2 And their [a]south border was from the
shore of the salt sea, from the bay that looketh
southward:
3 And it went out to the south side [a]to Maa-
leh–acrabbim, and passed along to Zin, and ascended up on the south side unto Kadesh–barnea,
and passed along to Hezron, and went up to Adar,
and fetched a compass to Karkaa:
4 *From thence* it passed [a]toward Azmon,
and went out unto the river of Egypt; and the goings out of that coast were at the sea: this shall
be your south coast.
5 And the east border *was* the salt sea, *even*
unto the end of Jordan. And *their* [a]border in the
north quarter *was* from the bay of the sea at the
uttermost part of Jordan:
6 And the border went up to [a]Beth–hogla,
and passed along by the north of Beth–arabah;
and the border went up [b]to the stone of Bohan
the son of Reuben:
7 And the border went up toward [a]Debir
from [b]the valley of Achor, and so northward,
looking toward Gilgal, that *is* before the going up
to Adummim, which *is* on the south side of the
river: and the border passed toward the waters
of En–shemesh, and the goings out thereof were
at [c]En–rogel:
8 And the border went up [a]by the valley of
the son of Hinnom unto the south side of the [b]Jebu-
site; the same *is* Jerusalem: and the border went
up to the top of the mountain that *lieth* before
the valley of Hinnom westward, which *is* at the
end of the valley [c]of the giants northward:
9 And the border was drawn from the top
of the hill unto [a]the fountain of the water of Nephtoah, and went out to the cities of mount Ephron;
and the border was drawn [b]to Baalah, which *is*
[c]Kirjath–jearim:
10 And the border compassed from Baalah
westward unto mount Seir, and passed along unto
the side of mount Jearim, which *is* Chesalon, on
the north side, and went down to Beth–shemesh,
and passed on to [a]Timnah:
11 And the border went out unto the side of
[a]Ekron northward: and the border was drawn to
Shicron, and passed along to mount Baalah, and
went out unto Jabneel; and the goings out of the
border were at the sea.
12 And the west border *was* [a]to the great sea,
and the coast *thereof*. This *is* the coast of the children of Judah round about according to their families.

Caleb Occupies Hebron and Debir
(Judg. 1:11–15)

13 [a]And unto Caleb the son of Jephunneh he
gave a part among the children of [b]Judah, according to the commandment of the LORD to Joshua,

11 [b]Deut. 31:2
12 [a]Num. 13:28, 33 [b]Rom. 8:31 [c]Josh. 15:14; Judg. 1:20
13 [a]Josh. 22:6 [b]Josh. 10:37; 15:13
14 [a]Josh. 21:12 [b]Josh. 14:8, 9
15 [a]Gen. 23:2; Josh. 15:13 [b]Josh. 11:23

CHAPTER 15

1 [a]Num. 34:3 [b]Num. 33:36
2 [a]Num. 34:3, 4
3 [a]Num. 34:4
4 [a]Num. 34:5
5 [a]Josh. 18:15–19
6 [a]Josh. 18:19, 21 [b]Josh. 18:17
7 [a]Josh. 13:26 [b]Josh. 7:26 [c]2 Sam. 17:17; 1 Kin. 1:9
8 [a]Josh. 18:16; 2 Kin. 23:10; Jer. 19:2, 6 [b]Josh. 15:63; 18:28; Judg. 1:21; 19:10 [c]Josh. 18:16
9 [a]Josh. 18:15 [b]1 Chr. 13:6 [c]Judg. 18:12
10 [a]Gen. 38:13; Judg. 14:1
11 [a]Josh. 19:43
12 [a]Num. 34:6, 7; Josh. 15:47
13 [a]Josh. 14:13 [b]Num. 13:6

NKJV

was then, so now *is* my strength for war, both
[b]for going out and for coming in.
12 "Now therefore, give me this mountain of
which the LORD spoke in that day; for you heard
in that day how [a]the Anakim *were* there, and *that*
the cities *were* great *and* fortified. [b]It may be that
the LORD *will be* with me, and [c]I shall be able to
drive them out as the LORD said."
13 And Joshua [a]blessed him, [b]and gave Hebron to Caleb the son of Jephunneh as an
inheritance.
14 [a]Hebron therefore became the inheritance
of Caleb the son of Jephunneh the Kenizzite to
this day, because he [b]wholly followed the LORD
God of Israel.
15 And [a]the name of Hebron formerly was
Kirjath Arba (*Arba was* the greatest man among
the Anakim). [b]Then the land had rest from war.

The Land of Judah

15 So *this* was the lot of the tribe of the children of Judah according to their families:
[a]The border of Edom at the [b]Wilderness of Zin
southward *was* the extreme southern boundary.
2 And their [a]southern border began at the
shore of the Salt Sea, from the bay that faces
southward.
3 Then it went out to the southern side of
[a]the Ascent of Akrabbim, passed along to Zin,
ascended on the south side of Kadesh Barnea,
passed along to Hezron, went up to Adar, and
went around to Karkaa.
4 *From there* it passed [a]toward Azmon and
went out to the Brook of Egypt; and the border
ended at the sea. This shall be your southern
border.
5 The east border *was* the Salt Sea as far
as the mouth of the Jordan. And the [a]border on
the northern quarter *began* at the bay of the sea
at the mouth of the Jordan.
6 The border went up to [a]Beth Hoglah and
passed north of Beth Arabah; and the border went
up [b]to the stone of Bohan the son of Reuben.
7 Then the border went up toward [a]Debir
from [b]the Valley of Achor, and it turned northward toward Gilgal, which *is* before the Ascent
of Adummim, which *is* on the south side of the
valley. The border continued toward the waters
of En Shemesh and ended at [c]En Rogel.
8 And the border went up [a]by the Valley
of the Son of Hinnom to the southern slope of
the [b]Jebusite *city* (which *is* Jerusalem). The border went up to the top of the mountain that *lies*
before the Valley of Hinnom westward, which *is*
at the end of the Valley [c]of *Rephaim northward.
9 Then the border went around from the top
of the hill to [a]the fountain of the water of Nephtoah, and extended to the cities of Mount Ephron.
And the border went around [b]to Baalah (which
is [c]Kirjath Jearim).
10 Then the border turned westward from
Baalah to Mount Seir, passed along to the side
of Mount Jearim on the north (which *is* Chesalon),
went down to Beth Shemesh, and passed on to
[a]Timnah.
11 And the border went out to the side of
[a]Ekron northward. Then the border went around
to Shicron, passed along to Mount Baalah, and
extended to Jabneel; and the border ended at the
sea.
12 The west border *was* [a]the coastline of the
Great Sea. This *is* the boundary of the children
of Judah all around according to their families.

Caleb Occupies Hebron and Debir
(Judg. 1:11–15)

13 [a]Now to Caleb the son of Jephunneh he
gave a share among the children of [b]Judah, according to the commandment of the LORD to

*———
15:8 Lit. *Giants*

KJV

even [c]the city of Arba the father of Anak, which *city is* Hebron.

14 And Caleb drove thence [a]the three sons of Anak, [b]Sheshai, and Ahiman, and Talmai, the children of Anak.

15 And [a]he went up thence to the inhabitants of Debir: and the name of Debir before *was* Kirjath–sepher.

16 [a]And Caleb said, He that smiteth Kirjath–sepher, and taketh it, to him will I give Achsah my daughter to wife.

17 And [a]Othniel the [b]son of Kenaz, the brother of Caleb, took it: and he gave him [c]Achsah his daughter to wife.

18 [a]And it came to pass, as she came *unto him,* that she moved him to ask of her father a field: and [b]she lighted off *her* ass; and Caleb said unto her, What wouldest thou?

19 Who answered, Give me a [a]blessing; for thou hast given me a south land; give me also springs of water. And he gave her the upper springs, and the nether springs.

The Cities of Judah

20 This *is* the inheritance of the tribe of the children of Judah according to their families.

21 And the uttermost cities of the tribe of the children of Judah toward the coast of Edom southward were Kabzeel, and [a]Eder, and Jagur,

22 And Kinah, and Dimonah, and Adadah,

23 And Kedesh, and Hazor, and Ithnan,

24 [a]Ziph, and Telem, and Bealoth,

25 And Hazor, Hadattah, and Kerioth, *and* Hezron, which *is* Hazor,

26 Amam, and Shema, and Moladah,

27 And Hazar–gaddah, and Heshmon, and Beth–palet,

28 And Hazar–shual, and [a]Beer–sheba, and Bizjothjah,

29 Baalah, and Iim, and Azem,

30 And Eltolad, and Chesil, and [a]Hormah,

31 And [a]Ziklag, and Madmannah, and Sansannah,

32 And Lebaoth, and Shilhim, and Ain, and [a]Rimmon: all the cities *are* twenty and nine, with their villages:

33 *And* in the valley, [a]Eshtaol, and Zoreah, and Ashnah,

34 And Zanoah, and En–gannim, Tappuah, and Enam,

35 Jarmuth, and [a]Adullam, Socoh, and Azekah,

36 And Sharaim, and Adithaim, and Gederah, and Gederothaim; fourteen cities with their villages:

37 Zenan, and Hadashah, and Migdal–gad,

38 And Dilean, and Mizpeh, [a]and Joktheel,

39 [a]Lachish, and Bozkath, and [b]Eglon,

40 And Cabbon, and Lahmam, and Kithlish,

41 And Gederoth, Beth–dagon, and Naamah, and Makkedah; sixteen cities with their villages:

42 [a]Libnah, and Ether, and Ashan,

43 And Jiphtah, and Ashnah, and Nezib,

44 And Keilah, and Achzib, and Mareshah; nine cities with their villages:

45 Ekron, with her towns and her villages:

46 From Ekron even unto the sea, all that *lay* near [a]Ashdod, with their villages:

47 Ashdod with her towns and her villages, Gaza with her towns and her villages, unto [a]the river of Egypt, and [b]the great sea, and the border *thereof:*

48 And in the mountains, Shamir, and Jattir, and Socoh,

49 And Dannah, and Kirjath–sannah, which *is* Debir,

50 And Anab, and Eshtemoh, and Anim,

51 [a]And Goshen, and Holon, and Giloh; eleven cities with their villages:

52 Arab, and Dumah, and Eshean,

53 And Janum, and Beth–tappuah, and Aphekah,

NKJV

Joshua, *namely,* [c]Kirjath Arba, which *is* Hebron (*Arba was* the father of Anak).

14 Caleb drove out [a]the three sons of Anak from there: [b]Sheshai, Ahiman, and Talmai, the children of Anak.

15 Then [a]he went up from there to the inhabitants of Debir (formerly the name of Debir *was* Kirjath Sepher).

16 [a]And Caleb said, "He who attacks Kirjath Sepher and takes it, to him I will give Achsah my daughter as wife."

17 So [a]Othniel the [b]son of Kenaz, the brother of Caleb, took it; and he gave him [c]Achsah his daughter as wife.

18 [a]Now it was so, when she came *to him,* that she persuaded him to ask her father for a field. So [b]she dismounted from *her* donkey, and Caleb said to her, "What do you wish?"

19 She answered, "Give me a [a]blessing; since you have given me land in the South, give me also springs of water." So he gave her the upper springs and the lower springs.

The Cities of Judah

20 This *was* the inheritance of the tribe of the children of Judah according to their families:

21 The cities at the limits of the tribe of the children of Judah, toward the border of Edom in the South, were Kabzeel, [a]Eder, Jagur,

22 Kinah, Dimonah, Adadah,

23 Kedesh, Hazor, Ithnan,

24 [a]Ziph, Telem, Bealoth,

25 Hazor, Hadattah, Kerioth, Hezron (which *is* Hazor),

26 Amam, Shema, Moladah,

27 Hazar Gaddah, Heshmon, Beth Pelet,

28 Hazar Shual, [a]Beersheba, Bizjothjah,

29 Baalah, Ijim, Ezem,

30 Eltolad, Chesil, [a]Hormah,

31 [a]Ziklag, Madmannah, Sansannah,

32 Lebaoth, Shilhim, Ain, and [a]Rimmon: all the cities *are* twenty-nine, with their villages.

33 In the lowland: [a]Eshtaol, Zorah, Ashnah,

34 Zanoah, En Gannim, Tappuah, Enam,

35 Jarmuth, [a]Adullam, Socoh, Azekah,

36 Sharaim, Adithaim, Gederah, and Gederothaim: fourteen cities with their villages;

37 Zenan, Hadashah, Migdal Gad,

38 Dilean, Mizpah, [a]Joktheel,

39 [a]Lachish, Bozkath, [b]Eglon,

40 Cabbon, *Lahmas, Kithlish,

41 Gederoth, Beth Dagon, Naamah, and Makkedah: sixteen cities with their villages;

42 [a]Libnah, Ether, Ashan,

43 Jiphtah, Ashnah, Nezib,

44 Keilah, Achzib, and Mareshah: nine cities with their villages;

45 Ekron, with its towns and villages;

46 from Ekron to the sea, all that *lay* near [a]Ashdod, with their villages;

47 Ashdod with its towns and villages, Gaza with its towns and villages—as far as [a]the Brook of Egypt and [b]the Great Sea with *its* coastline.

48 And in the mountain country: Shamir, Jattir, Sochoh,

49 Dannah, Kirjath Sannah (which *is* Debir),

50 Anab, Eshtemoh, Anim,

51 [a]Goshen, Holon, and Giloh: eleven cities with their villages;

52 Arab, Dumah, Eshean,

53 Janum, Beth Tappuah, Aphekah,

13 [c]Josh. 14:15
14 [a]Judg. 1:10, 20 [b]Num. 13:22
15 [a]Josh. 10:38; Judg. 1:11
16 [a]Judg. 1:12
17 [a]Judg. 1:13; 3:9 [b]Num. 32:12; Josh. 14:6 [c]Judg. 1:12
18 [a]Judg. 1:14 [b]Gen. 24:64; 1 Sam. 25:23
19 [a]Gen. 33:11
21 [a]Gen. 35:21
24 [a]1 Sam. 23:14
28 [a]Gen. 21:31; Josh. 19:2
30 [a]Josh. 19:4
31 [a]Josh. 19:5; 1 Sam. 27:6; 30:1
32 [a]Judg. 20:45, 47
33 [a]Judg. 13:25; 16:31
35 [a]1 Sam. 22:1
38 [a]2 Kin. 14:7
39 [a]2 Kin. 14:19 [b]Josh. 10:3
42 [a]Josh. 21:13
46 [a]Josh. 11:22
47 [a]Josh. 15:4 [b]Num. 34:6
51 [a]Josh. 10:41; 11:16

*________

15:40 Or *Lahmam*

KJV

54 And Humtah, and [a]Kirjath–arba, which *is*
Hebron, and Zior; nine cities with their villages:
55 [a]Maon, Carmel, and Ziph, and Juttah,
56 And Jezreel, and Jokdeam, and Zanoah,
57 Cain, Gibeah, and Timnah; ten cities with
their villages:
58 Halhul, Beth–zur, and Gedor,
59 And Maarath, and Beth–anoth, and Eltekon; six cities with their villages:
60 [a]Kirjath–baal, which *is* Kirjath–jearim,
and Rabbah; two cities with their villages:
61 In the wilderness, Beth–arabah, Middin,
and Secacah,
62 And Nibshan, and the city of Salt, and
[a]En–gedi; six cities with their villages.
63 As for the Jebusites the inhabitants of Jerusalem, [a]the children of Judah could not drive
them out: [b]but the Jebusites dwell with the children of Judah at Jerusalem unto this day.

Ephraim and West Manasseh

16 And the lot of the children of Joseph fell
from Jordan by Jericho, unto the water of
Jericho on the east, to the [a]wilderness that goeth
up from Jericho throughout mount Beth–el,
2 And goeth out from [a]Beth–el to Luz, and
passeth along unto the borders of Archi to
Ataroth,
3 And goeth down westward to the coast
of Japhleti, [a]unto the coast of Beth–horon the
nether, and to [b]Gezer: and the goings out thereof
are at the sea.
4 [a]So the children of Joseph, Manasseh and
Ephraim, took their inheritance.

The Land of Ephraim

5 [a]And the border of the children of
Ephraim according to their families was *thus:*
even the border of their inheritance on the east
side was [b]Ataroth–addar, [c]unto Beth–horon the
upper;
6 And the border went out toward the sea
to [a]Michmethah on the north side; and the border
went about eastward unto Taanath–shiloh, and
passed by it on the east to Janohah;
7 And it went down from Janohah to Ataroth, and to Naarath, and came to Jericho, and
went out at Jordan.
8 The border went out from [a]Tappuah westward unto the [b]river Kanah; and the goings out
thereof were at the sea. This *is* the inheritance
of the tribe of the children of Ephraim by their
families.
9 And [a]the separate cities for the children
of Ephraim *were* among the inheritance of the
children of Manasseh, all the cities with their
villages.
10 [a]And they drave not out the Canaanites
that dwelt in Gezer: but the Canaanites dwell
among the Ephraimites unto this day, and serve
under tribute.

The Other Half-Tribe of Manasseh (West)

17 There was also a lot for the tribe of Manasseh; for he *was* the [a]firstborn of Joseph;
to wit, for [b]Machir the firstborn of Manasseh, the
father of Gilead: because he was a man of war,
therefore he had [c]Gilead and Bashan.
2 There was also *a lot* for [a]the rest of the
children of Manasseh by their families; [b]for the
children of Abiezer, and for the children of Helek,
[c]and for the children of Asriel, and for the children of Shechem, [d]and for the children of Hepher,
and for the children of Shemida: these *were* the
male children of Manasseh the son of Joseph by
their families.
3 But [a]Zelophehad, the son of Hepher, the
son of Gilead, the son of Machir, the son of Manasseh, had no sons, but daughters: and these *are*
the names of his daughters, Mahlah, and Noah,
Hoglah, Milcah, and Tirzah.
4 And they came near before [a]Eleazar the

54 [a]Josh. 14:15
55 [a]1 Sam. 23:24, 25
60 [a]Josh. 18:14; 1 Sam. 7:1, 2
62 [a]1 Sam. 23:29; Ezek. 47:10
63 [a]Judg. 1:8, 21; 2 Sam. 5:6; 1 Chr. 11:4
[b]Judg. 1:21

CHAPTER 16

1 [a]Josh. 8:15; 18:12
2 [a]Josh. 18:13; Judg. 1:26
3 [a]Josh. 18:13; 1 Kin. 9:17; 2 Chr. 8:5 [b]Josh. 21:21; 1 Kin. 9:15; 1 Chr. 7:28
4 [a]Josh. 17:14
5 [a]Judg. 1:29; 1 Chr. 7:28, 29
[b]Josh. 18:13
[c]2 Chr. 8:5
6 [a]Josh. 17:7
8 [a]Josh. 17:8
[b]Josh. 17:9
9 [a]Josh. 17:9
10 [a]Josh. 15:63; 17:12, 13; Judg. 1:29; 1 Kin. 9:16

CHAPTER 17

1 [a]Gen. 41:51; 46:20; 48:18
[b]Gen. 50:23; Judg. 5:14
[c]Deut. 3:15
2 [a]Num. 26:29–33
[b]1 Chr. 7:18
[c]Num. 26:31
[d]Num. 26:32
3 [a]Num. 26:33; 27:1; 36:2
4 [a]Josh. 14:1

*

16:2 LXX *to Bethel*
16:7 *Naaran,* 1 Chr. 7:28
17:2 *Jeezer,* Num. 26:30

NKJV

54 Humtah, [a]Kirjath Arba (which *is* Hebron),
and Zior: nine cities with their villages;
55 [a]Maon, Carmel, Ziph, Juttah,
56 Jezreel, Jokdeam, Zanoah,
57 Kain, Gibeah, and Timnah: ten cities with
their villages;
58 Halhul, Beth Zur, Gedor,
59 Maarath, Beth Anoth, and Eltekon: six cities with their villages;
60 [a]Kirjath Baal (which *is* Kirjath Jearim)
and Rabbah: two cities with their villages.
61 In the wilderness: Beth Arabah, Middin,
Secacah,
62 Nibshan, the City of Salt, and [a]En Gedi:
six cities with their villages.
63 As for the Jebusites, the inhabitants of Jerusalem, [a]the children of Judah could not drive
them out; [b]but the Jebusites dwell with the children of Judah at Jerusalem to this day.

Ephraim and West Manasseh

16 The lot fell to the children of Joseph from
the Jordan, by Jericho, to the waters of Jericho on the east, to the [a]wilderness that goes up
from Jericho through the mountains to Bethel,
2 then went out *from [a]Bethel to Luz,
passed along to the border of the Archites at
Ataroth,
3 and went down westward to the boundary
of the Japhletites, [a]as far as the boundary of
Lower Beth Horon to [b]Gezer; and it ended at the
sea.
4 [a]So the children of Joseph, Manasseh and
Ephraim, took their inheritance.

The Land of Ephraim

5 [a]The border of the children of Ephraim,
according to their families, was *thus:* The border
of their inheritance on the east side was [b]Ataroth
Addar [c]as far as Upper Beth Horon.
6 And the border went out toward the sea
on the north side of [a]Michmethath; then the border went around eastward to Taanath Shiloh, and
passed by it on the east of Janohah.
7 Then it went down from Janohah to Ataroth and *Naarah, reached to Jericho, and came
out at the Jordan.
8 The border went out from [a]Tappuah westward to the [b]Brook Kanah, and it ended at the
sea. This *was* the inheritance of the tribe of the
children of Ephraim according to their families.
9 [a]The separate cities for the children of
Ephraim *were* among the inheritance of the children of Manasseh, all the cities with their villages.
10 [a]And they did not drive out the Canaanites who dwelt in Gezer; but the Canaanites dwell
among the Ephraimites to this day and have become forced laborers.

The Other Half-Tribe of Manasseh (West)

17 There was also a lot for the tribe of Manasseh, for he *was* the [a]firstborn of Joseph:
namely for [b]Machir the firstborn of Manasseh, the
father of Gilead, because he was a man of war;
therefore he was given [c]Gilead and Bashan.
2 And there was *a lot* for [a]the rest of the
children of Manasseh according to their families:
[b]for the children of *Abiezer, the children of Helek, [c]the children of Asriel, the children of Shechem, [d]the children of Hepher, and the children
of Shemida; these *were* the male children of Manasseh the son of Joseph according to their
families.
3 But [a]Zelophehad the son of Hepher, the
son of Gilead, the son of Machir, the son of Manasseh, had no sons, but only daughters. And
these *are* the names of his daughters: Mahlah,
Noah, Hoglah, Milcah, and Tirzah.
4 And they came near before [a]Eleazar the

KJV

priest, and before Joshua the son of Nun, and before the princes, saying, [b]The LORD commanded Moses to give us an inheritance among our brethren. Therefore according to the commandment of the LORD he gave them an inheritance among the brethren of their father.

5 And there fell ten portions to [a]Manasseh, beside the land of Gilead and Bashan, which *were* on the other side Jordan;

6 Because the daughters of Manasseh had an inheritance among his sons: and the rest of Manasseh's sons had the land of Gilead.

7 And the coast of Manasseh was from Asher to [a]Michmethah, that *lieth* before Shechem; and the border went along on the right hand unto the inhabitants of En–tappuah.

8 *Now* Manasseh had the land of Tappuah: but [a]Tappuah on the border of Manasseh *belonged* to the children of Ephraim;

9 And the coast descended unto the river Kanah, southward of the river: [a]these cities of Ephraim *are* among the cities of Manasseh: the coast of Manasseh also *was* on the north side of the river, and the outgoings of it were at the sea:

10 Southward *it was* Ephraim's, and northward *it was* Manasseh's, and the sea is his border; and they met together in Asher on the north, and in Issachar on the east.

11 [a]And Manasseh had in Issachar and in Asher [b]Beth–shean and her towns, and Ibleam and her towns, and the inhabitants of Dor and her towns, and the inhabitants of En–dor and her towns, and the inhabitants of Taanach and her towns, and the inhabitants of Megiddo and her towns, *even* three countries.

12 Yet [a]the children of Manasseh could not drive out *the inhabitants of* those cities; but the Canaanites would dwell in that land.

13 Yet it came to pass, when the children of Israel were waxen strong, that they put the Canaanites to [a]tribute; but did not utterly drive them out.

More Land for Ephraim and Manasseh

14 [a]And the children of Joseph spake unto Joshua, saying, Why hast thou given me *but* [b]one lot and one portion to inherit, seeing I *am* [c]a great people, forasmuch as the LORD hath blessed me hitherto?

15 And Joshua answered them, If thou *be* a great people, *then* get thee up to the wood *country*, and cut down for thyself there in the land of the Perizzites and of the giants, if mount Ephraim be too narrow for thee.

16 And the children of Joseph said, The hill is not enough for us: and all the Canaanites that dwell in the land of the valley have [a]chariots of iron, *both they* who *are* of Beth–shean and her towns, and *they* who *are* [b]of the valley of Jezreel.

17 And Joshua spake unto the house of Joseph, *even* to Ephraim and to Manasseh, saying, Thou *art* a great people, and hast great power: thou shalt not have one lot *only:*

18 But the mountain shall be thine; for it *is* a wood, and thou shalt cut it down: and the outgoings of it shall be thine: for thou shalt drive out the Canaanites, [a]though they have iron chariots, *and* though they *be* strong.

The Remainder of the Land Divided

18 And the whole congregation of the children of Israel assembled together [a]at Shiloh, and [b]set up the tabernacle of the congregation there. And the land was subdued before them.

2 And there remained among the children of Israel seven tribes, which had not yet received their inheritance.

3 And Joshua said unto the children of Israel, [a]How long *are* ye slack to go to possess the land, which the LORD God of your fathers hath given you?

4 Give out from among you three men for

---

4 [b]Num. 27:2–11
5 [a]Josh. 22:7
7 [a]Josh. 16:6
8 [a]Josh. 16:8
9 [a]Josh. 16:9
11 [a]1 Chr. 7:29 [b]Judg. 1:27; 1 Sam. 31:10; 1 Kin. 4:12
12 [a]Judg. 1:19, 27, 28
13 [a]Josh. 16:10
14 [a]Josh. 16:4 [b]Gen. 48:22 [c]Gen. 48:19; Num. 26:34, 37
16 [a]Josh. 17:18; Judg. 1:19; 4:3 [b]Josh. 19:18; 1 Kin. 4:12
18 [a]Deut. 20:1

CHAPTER 18

1 [a]Josh. 19:51; 21:2; 22:9; Jer. 7:12 [b]Judg. 18:31; 1 Sam. 1:3, 24; 4:3, 4
3 [a]Judg. 18:9

NKJV

priest, before Joshua the son of Nun, and before the rulers, saying, [b]"The LORD commanded Moses to give us an inheritance among our brothers." Therefore, according to the commandment of the LORD, he gave them an inheritance among their father's brothers.

5 Ten shares fell to [a]Manasseh, besides the land of Gilead and Bashan, which *were* on the other side of the Jordan,

6 because the daughters of Manasseh received an inheritance among his sons; and the rest of Manasseh's sons had the land of Gilead.

7 And the territory of Manasseh was from Asher to [a]Michmethath, that *lies* east of Shechem; and the border went along south to the inhabitants of En Tappuah.

8 Manasseh had the land of Tappuah, but [a]Tappuah on the border of Manasseh *belonged* to the children of Ephraim.

9 And the border descended to the Brook Kanah, southward to the brook. [a]These cities of Ephraim *are* among the cities of Manasseh. The border of Manasseh *was* on the north side of the brook; and it ended at the sea.

10 Southward *it was* Ephraim's, northward *it was* Manasseh's, and the sea was its border. Manasseh's territory was adjoining Asher on the north and Issachar on the east.

11 And in Issachar and in Asher, [a]Manasseh had [b]Beth Shean and its towns, Ibleam and its towns, the inhabitants of Dor and its towns, the inhabitants of En Dor and its towns, the inhabitants of Taanach and its towns, and the inhabitants of Megiddo and its towns—three hilly regions.

12 Yet [a]the children of Manasseh could not drive out *the inhabitants of* those cities, but the Canaanites were determined to dwell in that land.

13 And it happened, when the children of Israel grew strong, that they put the Canaanites to [a]forced labor, but did not utterly drive them out.

More Land for Ephraim and Manasseh

14 [a]Then the children of Joseph spoke to Joshua, saying, "Why have you given us *only* [b]one lot and one share to inherit, since we *are* [c]a great people, inasmuch as the LORD has blessed us until now?"

15 So Joshua answered them, "If you *are* a great people, *then* go up to the forest *country* and clear a place for yourself there in the land of the Perizzites and the giants, since the mountains of Ephraim are too confined for you."

16 But the children of Joseph said, "The mountain country is not enough for us; and all the Canaanites who dwell in the land of the valley have [a]chariots of iron, *both those* who *are* of Beth Shean and its towns and *those* who *are* [b]of the Valley of Jezreel."

17 And Joshua spoke to the house of Joseph—to Ephraim and Manasseh—saying, "You *are* a great people and have great power; you shall not have *only* one lot,

18 "but the mountain country shall be yours. Although it *is* wooded, you shall cut it down, and its farthest extent shall be yours; for you shall drive out the Canaanites, [a]though they have iron chariots *and* are strong."

The Remainder of the Land Divided

18 Now the whole congregation of the children of Israel assembled together [a]at Shiloh, and [b]set up the tabernacle of meeting there. And the land was subdued before them.

2 But there remained among the children of Israel seven tribes which had not yet received their inheritance.

3 Then Joshua said to the children of Israel: [a]"How long will you neglect to go and possess the land which the LORD God of your fathers has given you?

4 "Pick out from among you three men for

KJV

each tribe: and I will send them, and they shall rise, and go through the land, and describe it according to the inheritance of them; and they shall come *again* to me.

5 And they shall divide it into seven parts: [a]Judah shall abide in their coast on the south, and the [b]house of Joseph shall abide in their coasts on the north.

6 Ye shall therefore describe the land *into* seven parts, and bring *the description* hither to me, [a]that I may cast lots for you here before the LORD our God.

7 [a]But the Levites have no part among you; for the priesthood of the LORD *is* their inheritance: [b]and Gad, and Reuben, and half the tribe of Manasseh, have received their inheritance beyond Jordan on the east, which Moses the servant of the LORD gave them.

8 And the men arose, and went away: and Joshua charged them that went to describe the land, saying, Go and walk [a]through the land, and describe it, and come again to me, that I may here cast lots for you before the LORD in Shiloh.

9 And the men went and passed through the land, and described it by cities into seven parts in a book, and came *again* to Joshua to the host at Shiloh.

10 And Joshua cast [a]lots for them in Shiloh before the LORD: and there [b]Joshua divided the land unto the children of Israel according to their divisions.

The Land of Benjamin

11 [a]And the lot of the tribe of the children of Benjamin came up according to their families: and the coast of their lot came forth between the children of Judah and the children of Joseph.

12 [a]And their border on the north side was from Jordan; and the border went up to the side of Jericho on the north side, and went up through the mountains westward; and the goings out thereof were at the wilderness of Beth-aven.

13 And the border went over from thence toward Luz, to the side of Luz, [a]which *is* Beth-el, southward: and the border descended to Ataroth-adar, near the hill that *lieth* on the south side [b]of the nether Beth-horon.

14 And the border was drawn *thence*, and compassed the corner of the sea southward, from the hill that *lieth* before Beth-horon southward; and the goings out thereof were at [a]Kirjath-baal, which *is* Kirjath-jearim, a city of the children of Judah: this *was* the west quarter.

15 And the south quarter *was* from the end of Kirjath-jearim, and the border went out on the west, and went out to [a]the well of waters of Nephtoah:

16 And the border came down to the end of the mountain that *lieth* before [a]the valley of the son of Hinnom, *and* which *is* in the valley of the giants on the north, and descended to the valley of Hinnom, to the side of Jebusi on the south, and descended to [b]En-rogel,

17 And was drawn from the north, and went forth to En-shemesh, and went forth toward Geliloth, which *is* over against the going up of Adummim, and descended to [a]the stone of Bohan the son of Reuben,

18 And passed along toward the side over against Arabah northward, and went down unto Arabah:

19 And the border passed along to the side of Beth-hoglah northward: and the outgoings of the border were at the north bay of the [a]salt sea at the south end of Jordan: this *was* the south coast.

20 And Jordan was the border of it on the east side. This *was* the inheritance of the children of Benjamin, by the coasts thereof round about, according to their families.

21 Now the cities of the tribe of the children

5 [a]Josh. 15:1 [b]Josh. 16:1—17:18
6 [a]Josh. 14:2; 18:10
7 [a]Num. 18:7, 20; Josh. 13:33 [b]Josh. 13:8
8 [a]Gen. 13:17
10 [a]Acts 13:19 [b]Num. 34:16–29; Josh. 19:51
11 [a]Judg. 1:21
12 [a]Josh. 16:1
13 [a]Gen. 28:19; Josh. 16:2; Judg. 1:23 [b]Josh. 16:3
14 [a]Josh. 15:9
15 [a]Josh. 15:9
16 [a]Josh. 15:8 [b]Josh. 15:7
17 [a]Josh. 15:6
19 [a]Josh. 15:2, 5

NKJV

each tribe, and I will send them; they shall rise and go through the land, survey it according to their inheritance, and come *back* to me.

5 "And they shall divide it into seven parts. [a]Judah shall remain in their territory on the south, and the [b]house of Joseph shall remain in their territory on the north.

6 "You shall therefore survey the land in seven parts and bring *the survey* here to me, [a]that I may cast lots for you here before the LORD our God.

7 [a]"But the Levites have no part among you, for the priesthood of the LORD *is* their inheritance. [b]And Gad, Reuben, and half the tribe of Manasseh have received their inheritance beyond the Jordan on the east, which Moses the servant of the LORD gave them."

8 Then the men arose to go away; and Joshua charged those who went to survey the land, saying, "Go, walk [a]through the land, survey it, and come back to me, that I may cast lots for you here before the LORD in Shiloh."

9 So the men went, passed through the land, and wrote the survey in a book in seven parts by cities; and they came to Joshua at the camp in Shiloh.

10 Then Joshua cast [a]lots for them in Shiloh before the LORD, and there [b]Joshua divided the land to the children of Israel according to their divisions.

The Land of Benjamin

11 [a]Now the lot of the tribe of the children of Benjamin came up according to their families, and the territory of their lot came out between the children of Judah and the children of Joseph.

12 [a]Their border on the north side began at the Jordan, and the border went up to the side of Jericho on the north, and went up through the mountains westward; it ended at the Wilderness of Beth Aven.

13 The border went over from there toward Luz, to the side of Luz [a](which *is* Bethel) southward; and the border descended to Ataroth Addar, near the hill that *lies* on the south side [b]of Lower Beth Horon.

14 Then the border extended around the west side to the south, from the hill that *lies* before Beth Horon southward; and it ended at [a]Kirjath Baal (which *is* Kirjath Jearim), a city of the children of Judah. This *was* the west side.

15 The south side *began* at the end of Kirjath Jearim, and the border extended on the west and went out to [a]the spring of the waters of Nephtoah.

16 Then the border came down to the end of the mountain that *lies* before [a]the Valley of the Son of Hinnom, which *is* in the Valley of the *Rephaim on the north, descended to the Valley of Hinnom, to the side of the Jebusite *city* on the south, and descended to [b]En Rogel.

17 And it went around from the north, went out to En Shemesh, and extended toward Geliloth, which is before the Ascent of Adummim, and descended to [a]the stone of Bohan the son of Reuben.

18 Then it passed along toward the north side of *Arabah, and went down to Arabah.

19 And the border passed along to the north side of Beth Hoglah; then the border ended at the north bay at the [a]Salt Sea, at the south end of the Jordan. This *was* the southern boundary.

20 The Jordan was its border on the east side. This *was* the inheritance of the children of Benjamin, according to its boundaries all around, according to their families.

21 Now the cities of the tribe of the children

*

18:16 Lit. *Giants*
18:18 *Beth Arabah,* Josh. 15:6; 18:22

KJV

of Benjamin according to their families were Jericho, and Beth–hoglah, and the valley of Keziz,

22 And Beth–arabah, and Zemaraim, and Beth–el,

23 And Avim, and Parah, and Ophrah,

24 And Chephar–haammonai, and Ophni, and Gaba; twelve cities with their villages:

25 [a]Gibeon, and [b]Ramah, and Beeroth,

26 And Mizpeh, and Chephirah, and Mozah,

27 And Rekem, and Irpeel, and Taralah,

28 And Zelah, Eleph, and [a]Jebusi, which *is* Jerusalem, Gibeath, *and* Kirjath; fourteen cities with their villages. This *is* the inheritance of the children of Benjamin according to their families.

Simeon's Inheritance with Judah

19 And the [a]second lot came forth to Simeon, *even* for the tribe of the children of Simeon according to their families: [b]and their inheritance was within the inheritance of the children of Judah.

2 And [a]they had in their inheritance Beer–sheba, or Sheba, and Moladah,

3 And Hazar–shual, and Balah, and Azem,

4 And Eltolad, and Bethul, and Hormah,

5 And Ziklag, and Beth–marcaboth, and Hazar–susah,

6 And Beth–lebaoth, and Sharuhen; thirteen cities and their villages:

7 Ain, Remmon, and Ether, and Ashan; four cities and their villages:

8 And all the villages that *were* round about these cities to Baalath–beer, [a]Ramath of the south. This *is* the inheritance of the tribe of the children of Simeon according to their families.

9 Out of the portion of the children of Judah *was* the inheritance of the children of Simeon: for the part of the children of Judah was too much for them: [a]therefore the children of Simeon had their inheritance within the inheritance of them.

The Land of Zebulun

10 And the third lot came up for the children of Zebulun according to their families: and the border of their inheritance was unto Sarid:

11 [a]And their border went up toward the sea, and Maralah, and reached to Dabbasheth, and reached to the river that *is* [b]before Jokneam;

12 And turned from Sarid eastward toward the sunrising unto the border of Chisloth–tabor, and then goeth out to [a]Daberath, and goeth up to Japhia,

13 And from thence passeth on along on the east to [a]Gittah–hepher, to Ittah–kazin, and goeth out to Remmon–methoar to Neah;

14 And the border compasseth it on the north side to Hannathon: and the outgoings thereof are in the valley of Jiphthah–el:

15 And Kattath, and Nahallal, and Shimron, and Idalah, and Beth–lehem: twelve cities with their villages.

16 This *is* the inheritance of the children of Zebulun according to their families, these cities with their villages.

The Land of Issachar

17 *And* the fourth lot came out to Issachar, for the children of Issachar according to their families.

18 And their border was toward Jezreel, and Chesulloth, and Shunem,

19 And Haphraim, and Shihon, and Anaharath,

20 And Rabbith, and Kishion, and Abez,

21 And Remeth, and En–gannim, and En–haddah, and Beth–pazzez;

22 And the coast reacheth to Tabor, and Shahazimah, and [a]Beth–shemesh; and the outgoings of their border were at Jordan: sixteen cities with their villages.

23 This *is* the inheritance of the tribe of the

---

25 [a]Josh. 11:19; 21:17; 1 Kin. 3:4, 5 [b]Jer. 31:15
28 [a]Josh. 15:8, 63

CHAPTER 19

1 [a]Judg. 1:3 [b]Josh. 19:9
2 [a]1 Chr. 4:28
8 [a]1 Sam. 30:27
9 [a]Josh. 19:1
11 [a]Gen. 49:13 [b]Josh. 12:22
12 [a]1 Chr. 6:72
13 [a]2 Kin. 14:25
22 [a]Josh. 15:10; Judg. 1:33

NKJV

of Benjamin, according to their families, were Jericho, Beth Hoglah, Emek Keziz,

22 Beth Arabah, Zemaraim, Bethel,

23 Avim, Parah, Ophrah,

24 Chephar Haammoni, Ophni, and Gaba: twelve cities with their villages;

25 [a]Gibeon, [b]Ramah, Beeroth,

26 Mizpah, Chephirah, Mozah,

27 Rekem, Irpeel, Taralah,

28 Zelah, Eleph, [a]Jebus (which *is* Jerusalem), Gibeath, *and* Kirjath: fourteen cities with their villages. This was the inheritance of the children of Benjamin according to their families.

Simeon's Inheritance with Judah

19 The [a]second lot came out for Simeon, for the tribe of the children of Simeon according to their families. [b]And their inheritance was within the inheritance of the children of Judah.

2 [a]They had in their inheritance Beersheba (Sheba), Moladah,

3 Hazar Shual, Balah, Ezem,

4 Eltolad, Bethul, Hormah,

5 Ziklag, Beth Marcaboth, Hazar Susah,

6 Beth Lebaoth, and Sharuhen: thirteen cities and their villages;

7 Ain, Rimmon, Ether, and Ashan: four cities and their villages;

8 and all the villages that *were* all around these cities as far as Baalath Beer, [a]Ramah of the South. This *was* the inheritance of the tribe of the children of Simeon according to their families.

9 The inheritance of the children of Simeon *was included* in the share of the children of Judah, for the share of the children of Judah was too much for them. [a]Therefore the children of Simeon had *their* inheritance within the inheritance of that people.

The Land of Zebulun

10 The third lot came out for the children of Zebulun according to their families, and the border of their inheritance was as far as Sarid.

11 [a]Their border went toward the west and to Maralah, went to Dabbasheth, and extended along the brook that is [b]east of Jokneam.

12 Then from Sarid it went eastward toward the sunrise along the border of Chisloth Tabor, and went out toward [a]Daberath, bypassing Japhia.

13 And from there it passed along on the east of [a]Gath Hepher, toward Eth Kazin, and extended to Rimmon, which borders on Neah.

14 Then the border went around it on the north side of Hannathon, and it ended in the Valley of Jiphthah El.

15 Included were Kattath, Nahallal, Shimron, Idalah, and Bethlehem: twelve cities with their villages.

16 This *was* the inheritance of the children of Zebulun according to their families, these cities with their villages.

The Land of Issachar

17 The fourth lot came out to Issachar, for the children of Issachar according to their families.

18 And their territory went to Jezreel, and *included* Chesulloth, Shunem,

19 Haphraim, Shion, Anaharath,

20 Rabbith, Kishion, Abez,

21 Remeth, En Gannim, En Haddah, and Beth Pazzez.

22 And the border reached to Tabor, Shahazimah, and [a]Beth Shemesh; their border ended at the Jordan: sixteen cities with their villages.

23 This *was* the inheritance of the tribe of

KJV

children of Issachar according to their families,
the cities and their villages.

The Land of Asher

24 [a]And the fifth lot came out for the tribe
of the children of Asher according to their
families.
25 And their border was Helkath, and Hali,
and Beten, and Achshaph,
26 And Alammelech, and Amad, and Mish-
eal; and reacheth to [a]Carmel westward, and to
Shihor–libnath;
27 And turneth toward the sunrising to Beth–
dagon, and reacheth to Zebulun, and to the valley
of Jiphthah–el toward the north side of Beth–
emek, and Neiel, and goeth out to [a]Cabul on the
left hand,
28 And Hebron, and Rehob, and Hammon,
and Kanah, [a]*even* unto great Zidon;
29 And *then* the coast turneth to Ramah, and
to the strong city Tyre; and the coast turneth to
Hosah; and the outgoings thereof are at the sea
from the coast to [a]Achzib:
30 Ummah also, and Aphek, and Rehob:
twenty and two cities with their villages.
31 This *is* the inheritance of the tribe of the
children of Asher according to their families,
these cities with their villages.

The Land of Naphtali

32 [a]The sixth lot came out to the children of
Naphtali, *even* for the children of Naphtali according to their families.
33 And their coast was from Heleph, from
Allon to Zaanannim, and Adami, Nekeb, and Jabneel, unto Lakum; and the outgoings thereof were
at Jordan:
34 And *then* [a]the coast turneth westward to
Aznoth–tabor, and goeth out from thence to Hukkok, and reacheth to Zebulun on the south side,
and reacheth to Asher on the west side, and to
Judah upon Jordan toward the sunrising.
35 And the fenced cities *are* Ziddim, Zer, and
Hammath, Rakkath, and Chinnereth,
36 And Adamah, and Ramah, and Hazor,
37 And [a]Kedesh, and Edrei, and En–hazor,
38 And Iron, and Migdal–el, Horem, and
Beth–anath, and Beth–shemesh; nineteen cities
with their villages.
39 This *is* the inheritance of the tribe of the
children of Naphtali according to their families,
the cities and their villages.

The Land of Dan

40 [a]*And* the seventh lot came out for the tribe
of the children of Dan according to their families.
41 And the coast of their inheritance was Zorah, and [a]Eshtaol, and Ir–shemesh,
42 And [a]Shaalabbin, and [b]Ajalon, and
Jethlah,
43 And Elon, and Thimnathah, and [a]Ekron,
44 And Eltekeh, and Gibbethon, and Baalath,
45 And Jehud, and Bene–berak, and Gath–
rimmon,
46 And Me–jarkon, and Rakkon, with the
border before Japho.
47 And the [a]coast of the children of Dan went
out *too little* for them: therefore the children of
Dan went up to fight against Leshem, and took
it, and smote it with the edge of the sword, and
possessed it, and dwelt therein, and called
Leshem, [b]Dan, after the name of Dan their father.
48 This *is* the inheritance of the tribe of the
children of Dan according to their families, these
cities with their villages.

Joshua's Inheritance

49 When they had made an end of dividing
the land for inheritance by their coasts, the children of Israel gave an inheritance to Joshua the
son of Nun among them:
50 According to the word of the LORD they

24 [a]Judg. 1:31, 32
26 [a]1 Sam. 15:12; 1 Kin. 18:20; Is. 33:9; 35:2; Jer. 46:18
27 [a]1 Kin. 9:13
28 [a]Gen. 10:19; Josh. 11:8; Judg. 1:31; Acts 27:3
29 [a]Judg. 1:31
32 [a]Josh. 19:32–39; Judg. 1:33
34 [a]Deut. 33:23
37 [a]Josh. 20:7
40 [a]Josh. 19:40–48; Judg. 1:34–36
41 [a]Josh. 15:33
42 [a]Judg. 1:35; 1 Kin. 4:9 [b]Josh. 10:12; 21:24
43 [a]Josh. 15:11; Judg. 1:18
47 [a]Judg. 18 [b]Judg. 18:29

NKJV

the children of Issachar according to their families, the cities and their villages.

The Land of Asher

24 [a]The fifth lot came out for the tribe of the
children of Asher according to their families.
25 And their territory included Helkath, Hali,
Beten, Achshaph,
26 Alammelech, Amad, and Mishal; it
reached to [a]Mount Carmel westward, along *the
Brook* Shihor Libnath.
27 It turned toward the sunrise to Beth Dagon; and it reached to Zebulun and to the Valley
of Jiphthah El, then northward beyond Beth Emek
and Neiel, bypassing [a]Cabul *which was* on the
left,
28 including *Ebron, Rehob, Hammon, and
Kanah, [a]as far as Greater Sidon.
29 And the border turned to Ramah and to
the fortified city of Tyre; then the border turned
to Hosah, and ended at the sea by the region of
[a]Achzib.
30 Also Ummah, Aphek, and Rehob *were included:* twenty-two cities with their villages.
31 This *was* the inheritance of the tribe of
the children of Asher according to their families,
these cities with their villages.

The Land of Naphtali

32 [a]The sixth lot came out to the children of
Naphtali, for the children of Naphtali according
to their families.
33 And their border began at Heleph, enclos-
ing the territory from the terebinth tree in Zaanannim, Adami Nekeb, and Jabneel, as far as
Lakkum; it ended at the Jordan.
34 [a]From Heleph the border extended westward to Aznoth Tabor, and went out from there
toward Hukkok; it adjoined Zebulun on the south
side and Asher on the west side, and ended at
Judah by the Jordan toward the sunrise.
35 And the fortified cities *are* Ziddim, Zer,
Hammath, Rakkath, Chinnereth,
36 Adamah, Ramah, Hazor,
37 [a]Kedesh, Edrei, En Hazor,
38 Iron, Migdal El, Horem, Beth Anath, and
Beth Shemesh: nineteen cities with their villages.
39 This *was* the inheritance of the tribe of
the children of Naphtali according to their families, the cities and their villages.

The Land of Dan

40 [a]The seventh lot came out for the tribe of
the children of Dan according to their families.
41 And the territory of their inheritance was
Zorah, [a]Eshtaol, Ir Shemesh,
42 [a]Shaalabbin, [b]Aijalon, Jethlah,
43 Elon, Timnah, [a]Ekron,
44 Eltekeh, Gibbethon, Baalath,
45 Jehud, Bene Berak, Gath Rimmon,
46 Me Jarkon, and Rakkon, with the region
near Joppa.
47 And the [a]border of the children of Dan
went beyond these, because the children of Dan
went up to fight against Leshem and took it; and
they struck it with the edge of the sword, took
possession of it, and dwelt in it. They called
Leshem, [b]Dan, after the name of Dan their father.
48 This *is* the inheritance of the tribe of the
children of Dan according to their families, these
cities with their villages.

Joshua's Inheritance

49 When they had made an end of dividing
the land as an inheritance according to their borders, the children of Israel gave an inheritance
among them to Joshua the son of Nun.
50 According to the word of the LORD they

*

19:28 So with MT, Tg., Vg.; a few Heb. mss. *Abdon* (cf. 21:30 and 1 Chr. 6:74)

KJV

gave him the city which he asked, *even* [a]Timnath–[b]serah in mount Ephraim: and he built the city, and dwelt therein.

51 [a]These *are* the inheritances, which Eleazar the priest, and Joshua the son of Nun, and the heads of the fathers of the tribes of the children of Israel, divided for an inheritance by lot [b]in Shiloh before the LORD, at the door of the tabernacle of the congregation. So they made an end of dividing the country.

The Cities of Refuge
(Num. 35:9–28; Deut. 19:1–13)

20 The LORD also spake unto Joshua, saying,
2 Speak to the children of Israel, saying, [a]Appoint out for you cities of refuge, whereof I spake unto you by the hand of Moses:

3 That the slayer that killeth *any* person unawares *and* unwittingly may flee thither: and they shall be your refuge from the avenger of blood.

4 And when he that doth flee unto one of those cities shall stand at the entering of the gate of the city, and shall declare his cause in the ears of the elders of that city, they shall take him into the city unto them, and give him a place, that he may dwell among them.

5 [a]And if the avenger of blood pursue after him, then they shall not deliver the slayer up into his hand; because he smote his neighbour unwittingly, and hated him not beforetime.

6 And he shall dwell in that city, [a]until he stand before the congregation for judgment, *and* until the death of the high priest that shall be in those days: then shall the slayer return, and come unto his own city, and unto his own house, unto the city from whence he fled.

7 And they appointed [a]Kedesh in Galilee in mount Naphtali, and [b]Shechem in mount Ephraim, and [c]Kirjath–arba, which *is* Hebron, in [d]the mountain of Judah.

8 And on the other side Jordan by Jericho eastward, they assigned [a]Bezer in the wilderness upon the plain out of the tribe of Reuben, and [b]Ramoth in Gilead out of the tribe of Gad, and [c]Golan in Bashan out of the tribe of Manasseh.

9 [a]These were the cities appointed for all the children of Israel, and for the stranger that sojourneth among them, that whosoever killeth *any* person at unawares might flee thither, and not die by the hand of the avenger of blood, [b]until he stood before the congregation.

Cities of the Levites
(1 Chr. 6:54–81)

21 Then came near the heads of the fathers of the [a]Levites unto [b]Eleazar the priest, and unto Joshua the son of Nun, and unto the heads of the fathers of the tribes of the children of Israel;

2 And they spake unto them at [a]Shiloh in the land of Canaan, saying, [b]The LORD commanded by the hand of Moses to give us cities to dwell in, with the suburbs thereof for our cattle.

3 And the children of Israel gave unto the Levites out of their inheritance, at the commandment of the LORD, these cities and their suburbs.

4 And the lot came out for the families of the Kohathites: and [a]the children of Aaron the priest, *which were* of the Levites, [b]had by lot out of the tribe of Judah, and out of the tribe of Simeon, and out of the tribe of Benjamin, thirteen cities.

5 And [a]the rest of the children of Kohath *had* by lot out of the families of the tribe of Ephraim, and out of the tribe of Dan, and out of the half tribe of Manasseh, ten cities.

6 And [a]the children of Gershon *had* by lot out of the families of the tribe of Issachar, and out of the tribe of Asher, and out of the tribe of Naphtali, and out of the half tribe of Manasseh in Bashan, thirteen cities.

7 [a]The children of Merari by their families *had* out of the tribe of Reuben, and out of the

50 [a]Josh. 24:30 [b]1 Chr. 7:24
51 [a]Num. 34:17; Josh. 14:1 [b]Josh. 18:1, 10

CHAPTER 20

2 [a]Ex. 21:13; Num. 35:6–34; Deut. 19:2, 9
5 [a]Num. 35:12
6 [a]Num. 35:12, 24, 25
7 [a]Josh. 21:32; 1 Chr. 6:76 [b]Josh. 21:21; 2 Chr. 10:1 [c]Josh. 14:15; 21:11, 13 [d]Luke 1:39
8 [a]Deut. 4:43; Josh. 21:36; 1 Chr. 6:78 [b]Josh. 21:38; 1 Kin. 22:3 [c]Josh. 21:27
9 [a]Num. 35:15 [b]Josh. 20:6

CHAPTER 21

1 [a]Num. 35:1–8 [b]Num. 34:16–29; Josh. 14:1; 17:4
2 [a]Josh. 18:1 [b]Num. 35:2
4 [a]Josh. 21:8, 19 [b]Josh. 19:51
5 [a]Josh. 21:20
6 [a]Josh. 21:27
7 [a]Josh. 21:34

NKJV

gave him the city which he asked for, [a]Timnath [b]Serah in the mountains of Ephraim; and he built the city and dwelt in it.

51 [a]These *were* the inheritances which Eleazar the priest, Joshua the son of Nun, and the heads of the fathers of the tribes of the children of Israel divided as an inheritance by lot [b]in Shiloh before the LORD, at the door of the tabernacle of meeting. So they made an end of dividing the country.

The Cities of Refuge
(Num. 35:9–28; Deut. 19:1–13)

20 The LORD also spoke to Joshua, saying,
2 "Speak to the children of Israel, saying: [a]'Appoint for yourselves cities of refuge, of which I spoke to you through Moses,

3 'that the slayer who kills a person accidentally *or* unintentionally may flee there; and they shall be your refuge from the avenger of blood.

4 'And when he flees to one of those cities, and stands at the entrance of the gate of the city, and declares his case in the hearing of the elders of that city, they shall take him into the city as one of them, and give him a place, that he may dwell among them.

5 [a]'Then if the avenger of blood pursues him, they shall not deliver the slayer into his hand, because he struck his neighbor unintentionally, but did not hate him beforehand.

6 'And he shall dwell in that city [a]until he stands before the congregation for judgment, *and* until the death of the one who is high priest in those days. Then the slayer may return and come to his own city and his own house, to the city from which he fled.' "

7 So they appointed [a]Kedesh in Galilee, in the mountains of Naphtali, [b]Shechem in the mountains of Ephraim, and [c]Kirjath Arba (which *is* Hebron) in [d]the mountains of Judah.

8 And on the other side of the Jordan, by Jericho eastward, they assigned [a]Bezer in the wilderness on the plain, from the tribe of Reuben, [b]Ramoth in Gilead, from the tribe of Gad, and [c]Golan in Bashan, from the tribe of Manasseh.

9 [a]These were the cities appointed for all the children of Israel and for the stranger who dwelt among them, that whoever killed a person accidentally might flee there, and not die by the hand of the avenger of blood [b]until he stood before the congregation.

Cities of the Levites
(1 Chr. 6:54–81)

21 Then the heads of the fathers' *houses* of the [a]Levites came near to [b]Eleazar the priest, to Joshua the son of Nun, and to the heads of the fathers' *houses* of the tribes of the children of Israel.

2 And they spoke to them at [a]Shiloh in the land of Canaan, saying, [b]"The LORD commanded through Moses to give us cities to dwell in, with their common-lands for our livestock."

3 So the children of Israel gave to the Levites from their inheritance, at the commandment of the LORD, these cities and their common-lands:

4 Now the lot came out for the families of the Kohathites. And [a]the children of Aaron the priest, *who were* of the Levites, [b]had thirteen cities by lot from the tribe of Judah, from the tribe of Simeon, and from the tribe of Benjamin.

5 [a]The rest of the children of Kohath had ten cities by lot from the families of the tribe of Ephraim, from the tribe of Dan, and from the half-tribe of Manasseh.

6 And [a]the children of Gershon had thirteen cities by lot from the families of the tribe of Issachar, from the tribe of Asher, from the tribe of Naphtali, and from the half-tribe of Manasseh in Bashan.

7 [a]The children of Merari according to their families had twelve cities from the tribe of Reu-

KJV

tribe of Gad, and out of the tribe of Zebulun,
twelve cities.
8 [a]And the children of Israel gave by lot
unto the Levites these cities with their suburbs,
[b]as the LORD commanded by the hand of Moses.
9 And they gave out of the tribe of the children of Judah, and out of the tribe of the children
of Simeon, these cities which are *here* mentioned
by name.
10 Which the children of Aaron, *being* of the
families of the Kohathites, *who were* of the children of Levi, had: for theirs was the first lot.
11 [a]And they gave them the city of Arba the
father of [b]Anak, [c]which *city is* Hebron, in the hill
country of Judah, with the suburbs thereof round
about it.
12 But [a]the fields of the city, and the villages
thereof, gave they to Caleb the son of Jephunneh
for his possession.
13 Thus [a]they gave to the children of Aaron
the priest [b]Hebron with her suburbs, *to be* a city
of refuge for the slayer; [c]and Libnah with her
suburbs,
14 And [a]Jattir with her suburbs, [b]and Eshtemoa with her suburbs,
15 And [a]Holon with her suburbs, [b]and Debir
with her suburbs,
16 And [a]Ain with her suburbs, [b]and Juttah
with her suburbs, *and* [c]Beth–shemesh with her
suburbs; nine cities out of those two tribes.
17 And out of the tribe of Benjamin, [a]Gibeon
with her suburbs, [b]Geba with her suburbs,
18 Anathoth with her suburbs, and [a]Almon
with her suburbs; four cities.
19 All the cities of the children of Aaron, the
priests, *were* thirteen cities with their suburbs.
20 [a]And the families of the children of Kohath, the Levites which remained of the children
of Kohath, even they had the cities of their lot
out of the tribe of Ephraim.
21 For they gave them [a]Shechem with her
suburbs in mount Ephraim, *to be* a city of refuge
for the slayer; and [b]Gezer with her suburbs,
22 And Kibzaim with her suburbs, and Beth–
horon with her suburbs; four cities.
23 And out of the tribe of Dan, Eltekeh with
her suburbs, Gibbethon with her suburbs,
24 [a]Aijalon with her suburbs, Gath–rimmon
with her suburbs; four cities.
25 And out of the half tribe of Manasseh, Ta-
nach with her suburbs, and Gath–rimmon with
her suburbs; two cities.
26 All the cities *were* ten with their suburbs
for the families of the children of Kohath that
remained.
27 [a]And unto the children of Gershon, of the
families of the Levites, out of the *other* half tribe
of Manasseh *they gave* [b]Golan in Bashan with
her suburbs, *to be* a city of refuge for the slayer;
and Beesh–terah with her suburbs; two cities.
28 And out of the tribe of Issachar, Kishon
with her suburbs, Dabareh with her suburbs,
29 Jarmuth with her suburbs, En–gannim
with her suburbs; four cities.
30 And out of the tribe of Asher, Mishal with
her suburbs, Abdon with her suburbs,
31 Helkath with her suburbs, and Rehob with
her suburbs; four cities.
32 And out of the tribe of Naphtali, [a]Kedesh
in Galilee with her suburbs, *to be* a city of refuge
for the slayer; and Hammoth–dor with her suburbs, and Kartan with her suburbs; three cities.
33 All the cities of the Gershonites according
to their families *were* thirteen cities with their
suburbs.

8 [a]Josh. 21:3 [b]Num. 35:2
11 [a]Josh. 20:7; 1 Chr. 6:55 [b]Josh. 14:15; 15:13, 14 [c]Josh. 20:7; Luke 1:39
12 [a]Josh. 14:14; 1 Chr. 6:56
13 [a]1 Chr. 6:57 [b]Josh. 15:54; 20:2, 7 [c]Josh. 15:42; 2 Kin. 8:22
14 [a]Josh. 15:48 [b]Josh. 15:50
15 [a]1 Chr. 6:58 [b]Josh. 15:49
16 [a]1 Chr. 6:59 [b]Josh. 15:55 [c]Josh. 15:10
17 [a]Josh. 18:25 [b]Josh. 18:24
18 [a]1 Chr. 6:60
20 [a]1 Chr. 6:66
21 [a]Josh. 20:7 [b]Judg. 1:29
24 [a]Josh. 10:12
27 [a]Josh. 21:6; 1 Chr. 6:71 [b]Josh. 20:8
32 [a]Josh. 20:7

NKJV

ben, from the tribe of Gad, and from the tribe of
Zebulun.
8 [a]And the children of Israel gave these cities with their common-lands by lot to the Levites,
[b]as the LORD had commanded by the hand of
Moses.
9 So they gave from the tribe of the children
of Judah and from the tribe of the children of
Simeon these cities which are designated by
name,
10 which were for the children of Aaron, one
of the families of the Kohathites, *who were* of the
children of Levi; for the lot was theirs first.
11 [a]And they gave them Kirjath Arba (*Arba
was* the father of [b]Anak), [c]which *is* Hebron, in
the mountains of Judah, with the common-land
surrounding it.
12 But [a]the fields of the city and its villages
they gave to Caleb the son of Jephunneh as his
possession.
13 Thus [a]to the children of Aaron the priest
they gave [b]Hebron with its common-land (a city
of refuge for the slayer), [c]Libnah with its common-land,
14 [a]Jattir with its common-land, [b]Eshtemoa
with its common-land,
15 [a]Holon with its common-land, [b]Debir with
its common-land,
16 [a]Ain with its common-land, [b]Juttah with
its common-land, and [c]Beth Shemesh with its
common-land: nine cities from those two tribes;
17 and from the tribe of Benjamin, [a]Gibeon
with its common-land, [b]Geba with its common-
land,
18 Anathoth with its common-land, and [a]Al-
mon with its common-land: four cities.
19 All the cities of the children of Aaron, the
priests, *were* thirteen cities with their common-
lands.
20 [a]And the families of the children of
Kohath, the Levites, the rest of the children of
Kohath, even they had the cities of their lot
from the tribe of Ephraim.
21 For they gave them [a]Shechem with its
common-land in the mountains of Ephraim (a city
of refuge for the slayer), [b]Gezer with its common-
land,
22 Kibzaim with its common-land, and Beth
Horon with its common-land: four cities;
23 and from the tribe of Dan, Eltekeh with
its common-land, Gibbethon with its common-
land,
24 [a]Aijalon with its common-land, *and* Gath
Rimmon with its common-land: four cities;
25 and from the half-tribe of Manasseh, Ta-
nach with its common-land and Gath Rimmon
with its common-land: two cities.
26 All the ten cities with their common-lands
were for the rest of the families of the children
of Kohath.
27 [a]Also to the children of Gershon, of the
families of the Levites, from the *other* half-tribe
of Manasseh, *they gave* [b]Golan in Bashan with
its common-land (a city of refuge for the slayer),
and Be Eshterah with its common-land: two cities;
28 and from the tribe of Issachar, Kishion
with its common-land, Daberath with its common-
land,
29 Jarmuth with its common-land, *and* En
Gannim with its common-land: four cities;
30 and from the tribe of Asher, Mishal with
its common-land, Abdon with its common-land,
31 Helkath with its common-land, and Rehob
with its common-land: four cities;
32 and from the tribe of Naphtali, [a]Kedesh
in Galilee with its common-land (a city of refuge
for the slayer), Hammoth Dor with its common-
land, and Kartan with its common-land: three
cities.
33 All the cities of the Gershonites according
to their families *were* thirteen cities with their
common-lands.

KJV

34 [a]And unto the families of the children of
Merari, the rest of the Levites, out of the tribe of
Zebulun, Jokneam with her suburbs, and Kartah
with her suburbs,
35 Dimnah with her suburbs, Nahalal with
her suburbs; four cities.
36 And out of the tribe of Reuben, [a]Bezer
with her suburbs, and Jahazah with her suburbs,
37 Kedemoth with her suburbs, and Mephaath with her suburbs; four cities.
38 And out of the tribe of Gad, [a]Ramoth in
Gilead with her suburbs, *to be* a city of refuge
for the slayer; and Mahanaim with her suburbs,
39 Heshbon with her suburbs, Jazer with her
suburbs; four cities in all.
40 So all the cities for the children of Merari
by their families, which were remaining of the
families of the Levites, were *by* their lot twelve
cities.
41 [a]All the cities of the Levites within the
possession of the children of Israel *were* forty and
eight cities with their suburbs.
42 These cities were every one with their suburbs round about them: thus *were* all these cities.

The Promise Fulfilled

43 And the LORD gave unto Israel [a]all the
land which he sware to give unto their fathers;
and they [b]possessed it, and dwelt therein.
44 [a]And the LORD gave them [b]rest round
about, according to all that he sware unto their
fathers: and [c]there stood not a man of all their
enemies before them; the LORD delivered all their
enemies into their hand.
45 [a]There failed not ought of any good thing
which the LORD had spoken unto the house of Israel; all came to pass.

Eastern Tribes Return to Their Lands

22 Then Joshua called the Reubenites, and the
Gadites, and the half tribe of Manasseh,
2 And said unto them, Ye have kept [a]all that
Moses the servant of the LORD commanded you,
[b]and have obeyed my voice in all that I commanded you:
3 Ye have not left your brethren these many
days unto this day, but have kept the charge of
the commandment of the LORD your God.
4 And now the LORD your God hath given
[a]rest unto your brethren, as he promised them:
therefore now return ye, and get you unto your
tents, *and* unto the land of your possession,
[b]which Moses the servant of the LORD gave you
on the other side Jordan.
5 But [a]take diligent heed to do the commandment and the law, which Moses the servant
of the LORD charged you, [b]to love the LORD your
God, and to walk in all his ways, and to keep his
commandments, and to cleave unto him, and to
serve him with all your heart and with all your
soul.
6 So Joshua [a]blessed them, and sent them
away: and they went unto their tents.
7 Now to the *one* half of the tribe of Manasseh Moses had given *possession* in Bashan: [a]but
unto the *other* half thereof gave Joshua among
their brethren on this side Jordan westward. And
when Joshua sent them away also unto their tents,
then he blessed them,
8 And he spake unto them, saying, Return
with much riches unto your tents, and with very
much cattle, with silver, and with gold, and with
brass, and with iron, and with very much raiment:
[a]divide the spoil of your enemies with your
brethren.
9 And the children of Reuben and the children of Gad and the half tribe of Manasseh returned, and departed from the children of Israel
out of Shiloh, which *is* in the land of Canaan, to
go unto [a]the country of Gilead, to the land of their
possession, whereof they were possessed, according to the word of the LORD by the hand of Moses.

34 [a]Josh. 21:7; 1 Chr. 6:77–81
36 [a]Deut. 4:43; Josh. 20:8
38 [a]Josh. 20:8
41 [a]Num. 35:7
43 [a]Gen. 12:7; 26:3, 4; 28:4, 13, 14 [b]Num. 33:53; Josh. 1:11
44 [a]Deut. 7:23, 24; Josh. 11:23; 22:4 [b]Josh. 1:13, 15; 11:23 [c]Deut. 7:24
45 [a][Num. 23:19]; Josh. 23:14; 1 Kin. 8:56

CHAPTER 22
2 [a]Num. 32:20–22; Deut. 3:18 [b]Josh. 1:12–18
4 [a]Josh. 21:44 [b]Num. 32:33
5 [a]Deut. 6:6, 17; 11:22; Jer. 12:16 [b]Deut. 10:12; 11:13, 22
6 [a]Gen. 47:7; Ex. 39:43; Josh. 14:13; 2 Sam. 6:18; Luke 24:50
7 [a]Josh. 17:1–13
8 [a]Num. 31:27; 1 Sam. 30:24
9 [a]Num. 32:1, 26, 29

*__________
21:36 So with LXX, Vg. (cf. 1 Chr. 6:78, 79); MT, Bg., Tg. omit vv. 36, 37

NKJV

34 [a]And to the families of the children of
Merari, the rest of the Levites, from the tribe of
Zebulun, Jokneam with its common-land, Kartah
with its common-land,
35 Dimnah with its common-land, *and* Nahalal with its common-land: four cities;
36 *and from the tribe of Reuben, [a]Bezer with
its common-land, Jahaz with its common-land,
37 Kedemoth with its common-land, and
Mephaath with its common-land: four cities;
38 and from the tribe of Gad, [a]Ramoth in Gilead with its common-land (a city of refuge for
the slayer), Mahanaim with its common-land,
39 Heshbon with its common-land, *and* Jazer
with its common-land: four cities in all.
40 So all the cities for the children of Merari
according to their families, the rest of the families
of the Levites, were *by* their lot twelve cities.
41 [a]All the cities of the Levites within the
possession of the children of Israel *were* forty-
eight cities with their common-lands.
42 Every one of these cities had its common-
land surrounding it; thus *were* all these cities.

The Promise Fulfilled

43 So the LORD gave to Israel [a]all the land
of which He had sworn to give to their fathers,
and they [b]took possession of it and dwelt in it.
44 [a]The LORD gave them [b]rest all around, according to all that He had sworn to their fathers.
And [c]not a man of all their enemies stood against
them; the LORD delivered all their enemies into
their hand.
45 [a]Not a word failed of any good thing
which the LORD had spoken to the house of Israel.
All came to pass.

Eastern Tribes Return to Their Lands

22 Then Joshua called the Reubenites, the
Gadites, and half the tribe of Manasseh,
2 and said to them: "You have kept [a]all that
Moses the servant of the LORD commanded you,
[b]and have obeyed my voice in all that I commanded you.
3 "You have not left your brethren these
many days, up to this day, but have kept the
charge of the commandment of the LORD your
God.
4 "And now the LORD your God has given
[a]rest to your brethren, as He promised them; now
therefore, return and go to your tents *and* to the
land of your possession, [b]which Moses the servant of the LORD gave you on the other side of
the Jordan.
5 "But [a]take careful heed to do the commandment and the law which Moses the servant
of the LORD commanded you, [b]to love the LORD
your God, to walk in all His ways, to keep His
commandments, to hold fast to Him, and to serve
Him with all your heart and with all your soul."
6 So Joshua [a]blessed them and sent them
away, and they went to their tents.
7 Now to half the tribe of Manasseh Moses
had given a possession in Bashan, [a]but to the
other half of it Joshua gave *a possession* among
their brethren on this side of the Jordan, westward. And indeed, when Joshua sent them away
to their tents, he blessed them,
8 and spoke to them, saying, "Return with
much riches to your tents, with very much livestock, with silver, with gold, with bronze, with
iron, and with very much clothing. [a]Divide the
spoil of your enemies with your brethren."
9 So the children of Reuben, the children
of Gad, and half the tribe of Manasseh returned,
and departed from the children of Israel at Shiloh,
which *is* in the land of Canaan, to go to [a]the country of Gilead, to the land of their possession,
which they had obtained according to the word
of the LORD by the hand of Moses.

KJV

An Altar by the Jordan

10 And when they came unto the borders of
Jordan, that *are* in the land of Canaan, the children of Reuben and the children of Gad and the
half tribe of Manasseh built there an altar by Jordan, a great altar to see to.
11 And the children of Israel [a]heard say, Behold, the children of Reuben and the children of
Gad and the half tribe of Manasseh have built
an altar over against the land of Canaan, in the
borders of Jordan, at the passage of the children
of Israel.
12 And when the children of Israel heard *of
it,* [a]the whole congregation of the children of Israel gathered themselves together at Shiloh, to
go up to war against them.
13 And the children of Israel [a]sent unto the
children of Reuben, and to the children of Gad,
and to the half tribe of Manasseh, into the land
of Gilead, [b]Phinehas the son of Eleazar the priest,
14 And with him ten princes, of each chief
house a prince throughout all the tribes of Israel;
and [a]each one *was* an head of the house of their
fathers among the thousands of Israel.
15 And they came unto the children of Reuben, and to the children of Gad, and to the half
tribe of Manasseh, unto the land of Gilead, and
they spake with them, saying,
16 Thus saith the whole congregation of the
LORD, What [a]trespass *is* this that ye have committed against the God of Israel, to turn away this
day from following the LORD, in that ye have
builded you an altar, [b]that ye might rebel this day
against the LORD?
17 *Is* the iniquity [a]of Peor too little for us,
from which we are not cleansed until this day,
although there was a plague in the congregation
of the LORD,
18 But that ye must turn away this day from
following the LORD? and it will be, *seeing* ye rebel
to day against the LORD, that to morrow [a]he will
be wroth with the whole congregation of Israel.
19 Notwithstanding, if the land of your possession *be* unclean, *then* pass ye over unto the
land of the possession of the LORD, [a]wherein the
LORD's tabernacle dwelleth, and take possession
among us: but rebel not against the LORD, nor
rebel against us, in building you an altar beside
the altar of the LORD our God.
20 [a]Did not Achan the son of Zerah commit
a trespass in the accursed thing, and wrath fell
on all the congregation of Israel? and that man
perished not alone in his iniquity.
21 Then the children of Reuben and the children of Gad and the half tribe of Manasseh answered, and said unto the heads of the thousands
of Israel,
22 The LORD [a]God of gods, the LORD God of
gods, he [b]knoweth, and Israel he shall know; if
it be in rebellion, or if in transgression against
the LORD, (save us not this day,)
23 That we have built us an altar to turn from
following the LORD, or if to offer thereon burnt
offering or meat offering, or if to offer peace offerings thereon, let the LORD himself [a]require *it;*
24 And if we have not *rather* done it for fear
of *this* thing, saying, In time to come your children
might speak unto our children, saying, What have
ye to do with the LORD God of Israel?
25 For the LORD hath made Jordan a border
between us and you, ye children of Reuben and
children of Gad; ye have no part in the LORD: so
shall your children make our children cease from
fearing the LORD.
26 Therefore we said, Let us now prepare to
build us an altar, not for burnt offering, nor for
sacrifice:
27 But *that* it *may be* [a]a witness between us,
and you, and our generations after us, that we
might [b]do the service of the LORD before him with
our burnt offerings, and with our sacrifices, and

NKJV

An Altar by the Jordan

10 And when they came to the region of the
Jordan which *is* in the land of Canaan, the children of Reuben, the children of Gad, and half the
tribe of Manasseh built an altar there by the Jordan—a great, impressive altar.
11 Now the children of Israel [a]heard *someone* say, "Behold, the children of Reuben, the children of Gad, and half the tribe of Manasseh have
built an altar on the frontier of the land of Canaan,
in the region of the Jordan—on the children of
Israel's side."
12 And when the children of Israel heard *of
it,* [a]the whole congregation of the children of Israel gathered together at Shiloh to go to war
against them.
13 Then the children of Israel [a]sent [b]Phin-
ehas the son of Eleazar the priest to the children
of Reuben, to the children of Gad, and to half the
tribe of Manasseh, into the land of Gilead,
14 and with him ten rulers, one ruler each
from the chief house of every tribe of Israel; and
[a]each one *was* the head of the house of his father
among the *divisions of Israel.
15 Then they came to the children of Reuben,
to the children of Gad, and to half the tribe of
Manasseh, to the land of Gilead, and they spoke
with them, saying,
16 "Thus says the whole congregation of the
LORD: 'What [a]treachery *is* this that you have committed against the God of Israel, to turn away this
day from following the LORD, in that you have
built for yourselves an altar, [b]that you might rebel
this day against the LORD?
17 '*Is* the iniquity [a]of Peor not enough for
us, from which we are not cleansed till this day,
although there was a plague in the congregation
of the LORD,
18 'but that you must turn away this day from
following the LORD? And it shall be, if you rebel
today against the LORD, that tomorrow [a]He will
be angry with the whole congregation of Israel.
19 'Nevertheless, if the land of your possession *is* unclean, *then* cross over to the land of the
possession of the LORD, [a]where the LORD's tabernacle stands, and take possession among us; but
do not rebel against the LORD, nor rebel against
us, by building yourselves an altar besides the altar of the LORD our God.
20 [a]'Did not Achan the son of Zerah commit
a trespass in the accursed thing, and wrath fell
on all the congregation of Israel? And that man
did not perish alone in his iniquity.' "
21 Then the children of Reuben, the children
of Gad, and half the tribe of Manasseh answered
and said to the heads of the *divisions of Israel:
22 "The LORD [a]God of gods, the LORD God
of gods, He [b]knows, and let Israel itself know—
if *it is* in rebellion, or if in treachery against the
LORD, do not save us this day.
23 "If we have built ourselves an altar to turn
from following the LORD, or if to offer on it burnt
offerings or grain offerings, or if to offer peace
offerings on it, let the LORD Himself [a]require *an
account.*
24 "But in fact we have done it for fear, for
a reason, saying, 'In time to come your descendants may speak to our descendants, saying,
"What have you to do with the LORD God of Israel?
25 "For the LORD has made the Jordan a border between you and us, *you* children of Reuben
and children of Gad. You have no part in the
LORD." So your descendants would make our descendants cease fearing the LORD.'
26 "Therefore we said, 'Let us now prepare
to build ourselves an altar, not for burnt offering
nor for sacrifice,
27 'but *that* it *may be* [a]a witness between you
and us and our generations after us, that we may
[b]perform the service of the LORD before Him with
our burnt offerings, with our sacrifices, and with

11 [a]Deut. 13:12–18; Judg. 20:12, 13
12 [a]Josh. 18:1; Judg. 20:1
13 [a]Deut. 13:14; Judg. 20:12 [b]Ex. 6:25; Num. 25:7, 11–13
14 [a]Num. 1:4
16 [a]Deut. 12:5–14 [b]Lev. 17:8, 9
17 [a]Num. 25:1–9; Deut. 4:3
18 [a]Num. 16:22
19 [a]Josh. 18:1
20 [a]Josh. 7:1–26
22 [a]Deut. 4:35; 10:17; Is. 44:8; 45:5; 46:9; [1 Cor. 8:5, 6] [b][Job 10:7; 23:10; Jer. 12:3; 2 Cor. 11:11, 31]
23 [a]Deut. 18:19; 1 Sam. 20:16
27 [a]Gen. 31:48; Josh. 22:34; 24:27 [b]Deut. 12:5, 14

*
22:14 Lit. *thousands*
22:21 Lit. *thousands*

KJV

with our peace offerings; that your children may not say to our children in time to come, Ye have no part in the LORD.

28 Therefore said we, that it shall be, when they should *so* say to us or to our generations in time to come, that we may say *again,* Behold the pattern of the altar of the LORD, which our fathers made, not for burnt offerings, nor for sacrifices; but it *is* a witness between us and you.

29 God forbid that we should rebel against the LORD, and turn this day from following the LORD, [a]to build an altar for burnt offerings, for meat offerings, or for sacrifices, beside the altar of the LORD our God that *is* before his tabernacle.

30 And when Phinehas the priest, and the princes of the congregation and heads of the thousands of Israel which *were* with him, heard the words that the children of Reuben and the children of Gad and the children of Manasseh spake, it pleased them.

31 And Phinehas the son of Eleazar the priest said unto the children of Reuben, and to the children of Gad, and to the children of Manasseh, This day we perceive that the LORD *is* [a]among us, because ye have not committed this trespass against the LORD: now ye have delivered the children of Israel out of the hand of the LORD.

32 And Phinehas the son of Eleazar the priest, and the princes, returned from the children of Reuben, and from the children of Gad, out of the land of Gilead, unto the land of Canaan, to the children of Israel, and brought them word again.

33 And the thing pleased the children of Israel; and the children of Israel [a]blessed God, and did not intend to go up against them in battle, to destroy the land wherein the children of Reuben and Gad dwelt.

34 And the children of Reuben and the children of Gad called the altar *Ed:* for it *shall be* a witness between us that the LORD *is* God.

Joshua's Farewell Address

23 And it came to pass a long time after that the LORD [a]had given rest unto Israel from all their enemies round about, that Joshua [b]waxed old *and* stricken in age.

2 And Joshua [a]called for all Israel, *and* for their elders, and for their heads, and for their judges, and for their officers, and said unto them, I am old *and* stricken in age:

3 And ye have seen all that the [a]LORD your God hath done unto all these nations because of you; for the [b]LORD your God *is* he that hath fought for you.

4 Behold, [a]I have divided unto you by lot these nations that remain, to be an inheritance for your tribes, from Jordan, with all the nations that I have cut off, even unto the great sea westward.

5 And the LORD your God, [a]he shall expel them from before you, and drive them from out of your sight; and ye shall possess their land, [b]as the LORD your God hath promised unto you.

6 [a]Be ye therefore very courageous to keep and to do all that is written in the book of the law of Moses, [b]that ye turn not aside therefrom *to* the right hand or *to* the left;

7 That ye [a]come not among these nations, these that remain among you; neither [b]make mention of the name of their gods, nor cause to [c]swear *by them,* neither [d]serve them, nor bow yourselves unto them:

8 But [a]cleave unto the LORD your God, as ye have done unto this day.

9 [a]For the LORD hath driven out from before you great nations and strong: but *as for* you, no man hath been able to stand before you unto this day.

10 [a]One man of you shall chase a thousand: for the LORD your God, he *it is* that fighteth for you, [b]as he hath promised you.

29 [a]Deut. 12:13, 14
31 [a]Ex. 25:8; Lev. 26:11, 12; 2 Chr. 15:2; Zech. 8:23
33 [a]1 Chr. 29:20; Neh. 8:6; Dan. 2:19; Luke 2:28

CHAPTER 23

1 [a]Josh. 21:44; 22:4 [b]Josh. 13:1; 24:29
2 [a]Deut. 31:28
3 [a]Ps. 44:3 [b]Ex. 14:14; Deut. 1:30; Josh. 10:14, 42
4 [a]Josh. 13:2, 6; 18:10
5 [a]Ex. 23:30; 33:2 [b]Num. 33:53
6 [a]Josh. 1:7 [b]Deut. 5:32
7 [a]Ex. 23:33; Deut. 7:2, 3; [Prov. 4:14; Eph. 5:11] [b]Ex. 23:13; Ps. 16:4; Jer. 5:7; Hos. 2:17 [c]Deut. 6:13; 10:20 [d]Ex. 20:5
8 [a]Deut. 10:20
9 [a]Deut. 7:24; 11:23; Josh. 1:5
10 [a]Lev. 26:8; Deut. 28:7; Is. 30:17 [b]Ex. 14:14

*

22:30 Lit. *thousands*
22:34 LXX adds *and half the tribe of Manasseh*

NKJV

our peace offerings; that your descendants may not say to our descendants in time to come, "You have no part in the LORD." '

28 "Therefore we said that it will be, when they say *this* to us or to our generations in time to come, that we may say, 'Here is the replica of the altar of the LORD which our fathers made, though not for burnt offerings nor for sacrifices; but it *is* a witness between you and us.'

29 "Far be it from us that we should rebel against the LORD, and turn from following the LORD this day, [a]to build an altar for burnt offerings, for grain offerings, or for sacrifices, besides the altar of the LORD our God which *is* before His tabernacle."

30 Now when Phinehas the priest and the rulers of the congregation, the heads of the *divisions of Israel who *were* with him, heard the words that the children of Reuben, the children of Gad, and the children of Manasseh spoke, it pleased them.

31 Then Phinehas the son of Eleazar the priest said to the children of Reuben, the children of Gad, and the children of Manasseh, "This day we perceive that the LORD *is* [a]among us, because you have not committed this treachery against the LORD. Now you have delivered the children of Israel out of the hand of the LORD."

32 And Phinehas the son of Eleazar the priest, and the rulers, returned from the children of Reuben and the children of Gad, from the land of Gilead to the land of Canaan, to the children of Israel, and brought back word to them.

33 So the thing pleased the children of Israel, and the children of Israel [a]blessed God; they spoke no more of going against them in battle, to destroy the land where the children of Reuben and Gad dwelt.

34 The children of Reuben and the children of *Gad called the altar, *Witness,* "For *it is* a witness between us that the LORD *is* God."

Joshua's Farewell Address

23 Now it came to pass, a long time after the LORD [a]had given rest to Israel from all their enemies round about, that Joshua [b]was old, advanced in age.

2 And Joshua [a]called for all Israel, for their elders, for their heads, for their judges, and for their officers, and said to them: "I am old, advanced in age.

3 "You have seen all that the [a]LORD your God has done to all these nations because of you, for the [b]LORD your God *is* He who has fought for you.

4 "See, [a]I have divided to you by lot these nations that remain, to be an inheritance for your tribes, from the Jordan, with all the nations that I have cut off, as far as the Great Sea westward.

5 "And the LORD your God [a]will expel them from before you and drive them out of your sight. So you shall possess their land, [b]as the LORD your God promised you.

6 [a]"Therefore be very courageous to keep and to do all that is written in the Book of the Law of Moses, [b]lest you turn aside from it to the right hand or to the left,

7 "*and* lest you [a]go among these nations, these who remain among you. You shall not [b]make mention of the name of their gods, nor cause *anyone* to [c]swear *by them;* you shall not [d]serve them nor bow down to them,

8 "but you shall [a]hold fast to the LORD your God, as you have done to this day.

9 [a]"For the LORD has driven out from before you great and strong nations; but *as for* you, no one has been able to stand against you to this day.

10 [a]"One man of you shall chase a thousand, for the LORD your God *is* He who fights for you, [b]as He promised you.

KJV

11 [a]Take good heed therefore unto yourselves, that ye love the LORD your God.

12 Else if ye do in any wise [a]go back, and cleave unto the remnant of these nations, *even* these that remain among you, and shall [b]make marriages with them, and go in unto them, and they to you:

13 Know for a certainty that [a]the LORD your God will no more drive out *any of* these nations from before you; [b]but they shall be snares and traps unto you, and scourges in your sides, and thorns in your eyes, until ye perish from off this good land which the LORD your God hath given you.

14 And, behold, this day [a]I *am* going the way of all the earth: and ye know in all your hearts and in all your souls, that [b]not one thing hath failed of all the good things which the LORD your God spake concerning you; all are come to pass unto you, *and* not one thing hath failed thereof.

15 [a]Therefore it shall come to pass, *that* as all good things are come upon you, which the LORD your God promised you; so shall the LORD bring upon you [b]all evil things, until he have destroyed you from off this good land which the LORD your God hath given you.

16 When ye have transgressed the covenant of the LORD your God, which he commanded you, and have gone and served other gods, and bowed yourselves to them; then shall the [a]anger of the LORD be kindled against you, and ye shall perish quickly from off the good land which he hath given unto you.

The Covenant at Shechem
(cf. Ex. 24:9–18)

24 And Joshua gathered all the tribes of Israel to [a]Shechem, and [b]called for the elders of Israel, and for their heads, and for their judges, and for their officers; and they [c]presented themselves before God.

2 And Joshua said unto all the people, Thus saith the LORD God of Israel, [a]Your fathers dwelt on the other side of the flood in old time, *even* Terah, the father of Abraham, and the father of Nachor: and [b]they served other gods.

3 And [a]I took your father Abraham from the other side of the flood, and led him throughout all the land of Canaan, and multiplied his seed, and [b]gave him Isaac.

4 And I gave unto Isaac [a]Jacob and Esau: and I gave unto [b]Esau mount Seir, to possess it; [c]but Jacob and his children went down into Egypt.

5 [a]I sent Moses also and Aaron, and [b]I plagued Egypt, according to that which I did among them: and afterward I brought you out.

6 And I [a]brought your fathers out of Egypt: and ye came unto the sea; and the Egyptians pursued after your fathers with chariots and horsemen unto the Red sea.

7 And when they cried unto the LORD, he put [a]darkness between you and the Egyptians, and brought the sea upon them, and covered them; and [b]your eyes have seen what I have done in Egypt: and ye dwelt in the wilderness [c]a long season.

8 And I brought you into the land of the Amorites, which dwelt on the other side Jordan; [a]and they fought with you: and I gave them into your hand, that ye might possess their land; and I destroyed them from before you.

9 Then [a]Balak the son of Zippor, king of Moab, arose and warred against Israel, and [b]sent and called Balaam the son of Beor to curse you:

10 [a]But I would not hearken unto Balaam; [b]therefore he blessed you still: so I delivered you out of his hand.

11 And [a]ye went over Jordan, and came unto Jericho: and [b]the men of Jericho fought against you, the Amorites, and the Perizzites, and the Canaanites, and the Hittites, and the Girgashites, the

11 [a]Josh. 22:5 **12** [a][2 Pet. 2:20, 21] [b]Deut. 7:3, 4; Ezra 9:2; Neh. 13:25 **13** [a]Judg. 2:3 [b]Ex. 23:33; 34:12; Deut. 7:16 **14** [a]1 Kin. 2:2 [b]Josh. 21:45; [Luke 21:33] **15** [a]Deut. 28:63 [b]Lev. 26:14–39; Deut. 28:15–68 **16** [a]Deut. 4:24–28

CHAPTER 24

1 [a]Gen. 35:4 [b]Josh. 23:2 [c]1 Sam. 10:19 **2** [a]Gen. 11:7–32 [b]Josh. 24:14 **3** [a]Gen. 12:1; Acts 7:2, 3 [b]Gen. 21:1–8; [Ps. 127:3] **4** [a]Gen. 25:24–26 [b]Gen. 36:8; Deut. 2:5 [c]Gen. 46:1, 3, 6 **5** [a]Ex. 3:10 [b]Ex. 7—10 **6** [a]Ex. 12:37, 51; 14:2–31 **7** [a]Ex. 14:20 [b]Deut. 4:34 [c]Josh. 5:6 **8** [a]Num. 21:21–35 **9** [a]Judg. 11:25 [b]Num. 22:2–14 **10** [a]Deut. 23:5 [b]Num. 23:11, 20; 24:10 **11** [a]Josh. 3:14, 17 [b]Josh. 6:1; 10:1

*———————
24:2 The Euphrates

NKJV

11 [a]"Therefore take careful heed to yourselves, that you love the LORD your God.

12 "Or else, if indeed you do [a]go back, and cling to the remnant of these nations—these that remain among you—and [b]make marriages with them, and go in to them and they to you,

13 "know for certain that [a]the LORD your God will no longer drive out these nations from before you. [b]But they shall be snares and traps to you, and scourges on your sides and thorns in your eyes, until you perish from this good land which the LORD your God has given you.

14 "Behold, this day [a]I *am* going the way of all the earth. And you know in all your hearts and in all your souls that [b]not one thing has failed of all the good things which the LORD your God spoke concerning you. All have come to pass for you; not one word of them has failed.

15 [a]"Therefore it shall come to pass, that as all the good things have come upon you which the LORD your God promised you, so the LORD will bring upon you [b]all harmful things, until He has destroyed you from this good land which the LORD your God has given you.

16 "When you have transgressed the covenant of the LORD your God, which He commanded you, and have gone and served other gods, and bowed down to them, then the [a]anger of the LORD will burn against you, and you shall perish quickly from the good land which He has given you."

The Covenant at Shechem
(cf. Ex. 24:9–18)

24 Then Joshua gathered all the tribes of Israel to [a]Shechem and [b]called for the elders of Israel, for their heads, for their judges, and for their officers; and they [c]presented themselves before God.

2 And Joshua said to all the people, "Thus says the LORD God of Israel: [a]'Your fathers, *including* Terah, the father of Abraham and the father of Nahor, dwelt on the other side of *the River in old times; and [b]they served other gods.

3 [a]'Then I took your father Abraham from the other side of the River, led him throughout all the land of Canaan, and multiplied his descendants and [b]gave him Isaac.

4 'To Isaac I gave [a]Jacob and Esau. To [b]Esau I gave the mountains of Seir to possess, [c]but Jacob and his children went down to Egypt.

5 [a]'Also I sent Moses and Aaron, and [b]I plagued Egypt, according to what I did among them. Afterward I brought you out.

6 'Then I [a]brought your fathers out of Egypt, and you came to the sea; and the Egyptians pursued your fathers with chariots and horsemen to the Red Sea.

7 'So they cried out to the LORD; and He put [a]darkness between you and the Egyptians, brought the sea upon them, and covered them. And [b]your eyes saw what I did in Egypt. Then you dwelt in the wilderness [c]a long time.

8 'And I brought you into the land of the Amorites, who dwelt on the other side of the Jordan, [a]and they fought with you. But I gave them into your hand, that you might possess their land, and I destroyed them from before you.

9 'Then [a]Balak the son of Zippor, king of Moab, arose to make war against Israel, and [b]sent and called Balaam the son of Beor to curse you.

10 [a]'But I would not listen to Balaam; [b]therefore he continued to bless you. So I delivered you out of his hand.

11 'Then [a]you went over the Jordan and came to Jericho. And [b]the men of Jericho fought against you—*also* the Amorites, the Perizzites, the Canaanites, the Hittites, the Girgashites, the

KJV

Hivites, and the Jebusites; and I delivered them
into your hand.
12 And [a]I sent the hornet before you, which
drave them out from before you, *even* the two
kings of the Amorites; *but* [b]not with thy sword,
nor with thy bow.
13 And I have given you a land for which
ye did not labour, and [a]cities which ye built not,
and ye dwell in them; of the vineyards and oliveyards which ye planted not do ye eat.
14 [a]Now therefore fear the LORD, and serve
him in [b]sincerity and in truth: and [c]put away the
gods which your fathers served on the other side
of the flood, and [d]in Egypt; and serve ye the LORD.
15 And if it seem evil unto you to serve the
LORD, [a]choose you this day whom ye will serve;
whether [b]the gods which your fathers served that
were on the other side of the flood, or [c]the gods
of the Amorites, in whose land ye dwell: [d]but as
for me and my house, we will serve the LORD.
16 And the people answered and said, God
forbid that we should forsake the LORD, to serve
other gods;
17 For the LORD our God, he *it is* that brought
us up and our fathers out of the land of Egypt,
from the house of bondage, and which did those
great signs in our sight, and preserved us in all
the way wherein we went, and among all the people through whom we passed:
18 And the LORD drave out from before us
all the people, even the Amorites which dwelt in
the land: [a]*therefore* will we also serve the LORD;
for he *is* our God.
19 And Joshua said unto the people, [a]Ye cannot serve the LORD: for he *is* an [b]holy God; he is
[c]a jealous God; [d]he will not forgive your transgressions nor your sins.
20 [a]If ye forsake the LORD, and serve strange
gods, [b]then he will turn and do you hurt, and consume you, after that he hath done you good.
21 And the people said unto Joshua, Nay; but
we will serve the LORD.
22 And Joshua said unto the people, Ye *are*
witnesses against yourselves that [a]ye have chosen
you the LORD, to serve him. And they said, *We*
are witnesses.
23 Now therefore [a]put away, *said he,* the
strange gods which *are* among you, and [b]incline
your heart unto the LORD God of Israel.
24 And the people [a]said unto Joshua, The
LORD our God will we serve, and his voice will
we obey.
25 So Joshua [a]made a covenant with the people that day, and set them a statute and an ordinance [b]in Shechem.
26 And Joshua [a]wrote these words in the
book of the law of God, and took [b]a great stone,
and [c]set it up there [d]under an oak, that *was* by
the sanctuary of the LORD.
27 And Joshua said unto all the people, Behold, this stone shall be [a]a witness unto us; for
[b]it hath heard all the words of the LORD which
he spake unto us: it shall be therefore a witness
unto you, lest ye deny your God.
28 So [a]Joshua let the people depart, every
man unto his inheritance.

Death of Joshua and Eleazar

29 [a]And it came to pass after these things,
that Joshua the son of Nun, the servant of the
LORD, died, *being* an hundred and ten years old.
30 And they buried him in the border of his
inheritance in [a]Timnath-serah, which *is* in mount
Ephraim, on the north side of the hill of Gaash.
31 And [a]Israel served the LORD all the days
of Joshua, and all the days of the elders that over-
lived Joshua, and which had [b]known all the works
of the LORD, that he had done for Israel.
32 And [a]the bones of Joseph, which the children of Israel brought up out of Egypt, buried they

12 [a]Ex. 23:28; Deut. 7:20 [b]Ps. 44:3
13 [a]Deut. 6:10, 11
14 [a]Deut. 10:12, 13; 1 Sam. 12:24 [b]2 Cor. 1:12 [c]Josh. 24:2, 23; Ezek. 20:18 [d]Ezek. 20:7, 8
15 [a]Ruth 1:15; 1 Kin. 18:21 [b]Josh. 24:2; Ezek. 20:39 [c]Ex. 23:24, 32 [d]Gen. 18:19; Ps. 101:2; [1 Tim. 3:4, 5]
18 [a]Ps. 116:16
19 [a]Matt. 6:24 [b]Lev. 11:44, 45; 1 Sam. 6:20 [c]Ex. 20:5 [d]Ex. 23:21
20 [a]1 Chr. 28:9; Ezra 8:22; Is. 1:28; 63:10; 65:11, 12; Jer. 17:13 [b]Deut. 4:24–26; Josh. 23:15
22 [a]Ps. 119:173
23 [a]Gen. 35:2; Josh. 24:14; Judg. 10:15, 16; 1 Sam. 7:3 [b]1 Kin. 8:57, 58; Ps. 119:36; 141:4
24 [a]Ex. 19:8; 24:3, 7; Deut. 5:24–27
25 [a]Ex. 15:25 [b]Josh. 24:1
26 [a]Deut. 31:24 [b]Judg. 9:6 [c]Gen. 28:18 [d]Gen. 35:4
27 [a]Gen. 31:48 [b]Deut. 32:1
28 [a]Judg. 2:6, 7
29 [a]Judg. 2:8
30 [a]Josh. 19:50; Judg. 2:9
31 [a]Judg. 2:7 [b]Deut. 11:2
32 [a]Gen. 50:25; Ex. 13:19; Heb. 11:22

NKJV

Hivites, and the Jebusites. But I delivered them
into your hand.
12 [a]'I sent the hornet before you which drove
them out from before you, *also* the two kings of
the Amorites, *but* [b]not with your sword or with
your bow.
13 'I have given you a land for which you
did not labor, and [a]cities which you did not build,
and you dwell in them; you eat of the vineyards
and olive groves which you did not plant.'
14 [a]"Now therefore, fear the LORD, serve Him
in [b]sincerity and in truth, and [c]put away the gods
which your fathers served on the other side of
the River and [d]in Egypt. Serve the LORD!
15 "And if it seems evil to you to serve the
LORD, [a]choose for yourselves this day whom you
will serve, whether [b]the gods which your fathers
served that *were* on the other side of the River,
or [c]the gods of the Amorites, in whose land you
dwell. [d]But as for me and my house, we will serve
the LORD."
16 So the people answered and said: "Far be
it from us that we should forsake the LORD to serve
other gods;
17 "for the LORD our God *is* He who brought
us and our fathers up out of the land of Egypt,
from the house of bondage, who did those great
signs in our sight, and preserved us in all the way
that we went and among all the people through
whom we passed.
18 "And the LORD drove out from before us
all the people, including the Amorites who dwelt
in the land. [a]We also will serve the LORD, for He
is our God."
19 But Joshua said to the people, [a]"You cannot serve the LORD, for He *is* a [b]holy God. He *is*
[c]a jealous God; [d]He will not forgive your transgressions nor your sins.
20 [a]"If you forsake the LORD and serve foreign gods, [b]then He will turn and do you harm
and consume you, after He has done you good."
21 And the people said to Joshua, "No, but
we will serve the LORD!"
22 So Joshua said to the people, "You *are*
witnesses against yourselves that [a]you have chosen the LORD for yourselves, to serve Him." And
they said, "*We are* witnesses!"
23 "Now therefore," *he said,* [a]"put away the
foreign gods which *are* among you, and [b]incline
your heart to the LORD God of Israel."
24 And the people [a]said to Joshua, "The
LORD our God we will serve, and His voice we
will obey!"
25 So Joshua [a]made a covenant with the people that day, and made for them a statute and an
ordinance [b]in Shechem.
26 Then Joshua [a]wrote these words in the
Book of the Law of God. And he took [b]a large
stone, and [c]set it up there [d]under the oak that
was by the sanctuary of the LORD.
27 And Joshua said to all the people, "Behold, this stone shall be [a]a witness to us, for [b]it
has heard all the words of the LORD which He
spoke to us. It shall therefore be a witness to you,
lest you deny your God."
28 So [a]Joshua let the people depart, each to
his own inheritance.

Death of Joshua and Eleazar

29 [a]Now it came to pass after these things
that Joshua the son of Nun, the servant of the
LORD, died, *being* one hundred and ten years old.
30 And they buried him within the border of
his inheritance at [a]Timnath Serah, which *is* in the
mountains of Ephraim, on the north side of Mount
Gaash.
31 [a]Israel served the LORD all the days of
Joshua, and all the days of the elders who outlived
Joshua, who had [b]known all the works of the
LORD which He had done for Israel.
32 [a]The bones of Joseph, which the children
of Israel had brought up out of Egypt, they buried

KJV

in Shechem, in a parcel of ground [b]which Jacob bought of the sons of Hamor the father of Shechem for an hundred pieces of silver: and it became the inheritance of the children of Joseph.
33 And [a]Eleazar the son of Aaron died; and they buried him in a hill *that pertained to* [b]Phinehas his son, which was given him in mount Ephraim.

32 [b]Gen. 33:19; John 4:5
33 [a]Ex. 28:1; Num. 20:28; Josh. 14:1
[b]Ex. 6:25

NKJV

at Shechem, in the plot of ground [b]which Jacob had bought from the sons of Hamor the father of Shechem for one hundred pieces of silver, and which had become an inheritance of the children of Joseph.
33 And [a]Eleazar the son of Aaron died. They buried him in a hill *belonging to* [b]Phinehas his son, which was given to him in the mountains of Ephraim.

KJV

THE BOOK OF

JUDGES

The Continuing Conquest of Canaan (*Josh. 15:13–19*)

1 Now after the [a]death of Joshua it came to
pass, that the children of Israel [b]asked the
LORD, saying, Who shall go up for us against the
[c]Canaanites first, to fight against them?
2 And the LORD said, [a]Judah shall go up:
behold, I have delivered the land into his hand.
3 And Judah said unto [a]Simeon his brother,
Come up with me into my lot, that we may fight
against the Canaanites; and [b]I likewise will go
with thee into thy lot. So Simeon went with him.
4 And Judah went up; and the LORD delivered the Canaanites and the Perizzites into their
hand: and they slew of them in [a]Bezek ten thousand men.
5 And they found Adoni–bezek in Bezek:
and they fought against him, and they slew the
Canaanites and the Perizzites.
6 But Adoni–bezek fled; and they pursued
after him, and caught him, and cut off his thumbs
and his great toes.
7 And Adoni–bezek said, Threescore and
ten kings, having their thumbs and their great toes
cut off, gathered *their meat* under my table: [a]as
I have done, so God hath requited me. And they
brought him to Jerusalem, and there he died.
8 Now [a]the children of Judah had fought
against Jerusalem, and had taken it, and smitten
it with the edge of the sword, and set the city on
fire.
9 [a]And afterward the children of Judah
went down to fight against the Canaanites, that
dwelt in the mountain, and in the south, and in
the valley.
10 And Judah went against the Canaanites
that dwelt in [a]Hebron: (now the name of Hebron
before *was* [b]Kirjath–arba:) and they slew Sheshai,
and Ahiman, and Talmai.
11 [a]And from thence he went against the inhabitants of Debir: and the name of Debir before
was Kirjath–sepher:
12 [a]And Caleb said, He that smiteth Kirjath–
sepher, and taketh it, to him will I give Achsah
my daughter to wife.
13 And Othniel the son of Kenaz, [a]Caleb's
younger brother, took it: and he gave him Achsah
his daughter to wife.
14 [a]And it came to pass, when she came *to*
him, that she moved him to ask of her father a
field: and she lighted from off *her* ass; and Caleb
said unto her, What wilt thou?
15 And she said unto him, [a]Give me a blessing: for thou hast given me a south land; give me
also springs of water. And Caleb gave her the upper springs and the nether springs.
16 [a]And the children of the Kenite, Moses'
father in law, went up out [b]of the city of palm
trees with the children of Judah into the wilderness of Judah, which *lieth* in the south of [c]Arad;
[d]and they went and dwelt among the people.
17 [a]And Judah went with Simeon his
brother, and they slew the Canaanites that inhabited Zephath, and utterly destroyed it. And the
name of the city was called [b]Hormah.
18 Also Judah took [a]Gaza with the coast

CHAPTER 1

1 [a]Josh. 24:29 [b]Num. 27:21; Judg. 20:18 [c]Josh. 17:12, 13
2 [a]Gen. 49:8, 9; Rev. 5:5
3 [a]Josh. 19:1 [b]Judg. 1:17
4 [a]1 Sam. 11:8
7 [a]Lev. 24:19; 1 Sam. 15:33; [James 2:13]
8 [a]Josh. 15:63; Judg. 1:21
9 [a]Josh. 10:36; 11:21; 15:13
10 [a]Josh. 15:13–19 [b]Josh. 14:15
11 [a]Josh. 15:15
12 [a]Josh. 15:16, 17
13 [a]Judg. 3:9
14 [a]Josh. 15:18, 19
15 [a]Gen. 33:11
16 [a]Num. 10:29–32; Judg. 4:11, 17; 1 Sam. 15:6; 1 Chr. 2:55 [b]Deut. 34:3; Judg. 3:13 [c]Josh. 12:14 [d]1 Sam. 15:6
17 [a]Judg. 1:3 [b]Num. 21:3; Josh. 19:4
18 [a]Josh. 11:22

*

1:9 Heb. *Negev,* and so throughout the book
1:14 LXX, Vg. *he urged her*

NKJV

THE BOOK OF

JUDGES

The Continuing Conquest of Canaan (*Josh. 15:13–19*)

1 Now after the [a]death of Joshua it came to pass
that the children of Israel [b]asked the LORD,
saying, "Who shall be first to go up for us against
the [c]Canaanites to fight against them?"
2 And the LORD said, [a]"Judah shall go up.
Indeed I have delivered the land into his hand."
3 So Judah said to [a]Simeon his brother,
"Come up with me to my allotted territory, that
we may fight against the Canaanites; and [b]I will
likewise go with you to your allotted territory."
And Simeon went with him.
4 Then Judah went up, and the LORD delivered the Canaanites and the Perizzites into their
hand; and they killed ten thousand men at [a]Bezek.
5 And they found Adoni-Bezek in Bezek,
and fought against him; and they defeated the Canaanites and the Perizzites.
6 Then Adoni-Bezek fled, and they pursued
him and caught him and cut off his thumbs and
big toes.
7 And Adoni-Bezek said, "Seventy kings
with their thumbs and big toes cut off used to
gather *scraps* under my table; [a]as I have done,
so God has repaid me." Then they brought him
to Jerusalem, and there he died.
8 Now [a]the children of Judah fought against
Jerusalem and took it; they struck it with the edge
of the sword and set the city on fire.
9 [a]And afterward the children of Judah
went down to fight against the Canaanites who
dwelt in the mountains, in the *South, and in the
lowland.
10 Then Judah went against the Canaanites
who dwelt in [a]Hebron. (Now the name of Hebron
was formerly [b]Kirjath Arba.) And they killed
Sheshai, Ahiman, and Talmai.
11 [a]From there they went against the inhabitants of Debir. (The name of Debir *was* formerly
Kirjath Sepher.)
12 [a]Then Caleb said, "Whoever attacks Kirjath Sepher and takes it, to him I will give my
daughter Achsah as wife."
13 And Othniel the son of Kenaz, [a]Caleb's
younger brother, took it; so he gave him his
daughter Achsah as wife.
14 [a]Now it happened, when she came *to him,*
that *she urged him to ask her father for a field.
And she dismounted from *her* donkey, and Caleb
said to her, "What do you wish?"
15 So she said to him, [a]"Give me a blessing;
since you have given me land in the South, give
me also springs of water." And Caleb gave her
the upper springs and the lower springs.
16 [a]Now the children of the Kenite, Moses'
father-in-law, went up [b]from the City of Palms
with the children of Judah into the Wilderness
of Judah, which *lies* in the South *near* [c]Arad; [d]and
they went and dwelt among the people.
17 [a]And Judah went with his brother Simeon, and they attacked the Canaanites who inhabited Zephath, and utterly destroyed it. So the
name of the city was called [b]Hormah.
18 Also Judah took [a]Gaza with its territory,

KJV

thereof, and Askelon with the coast thereof, and
Ekron with the coast thereof.
19 And the LORD was with Judah; and he
drave out *the inhabitants of* the mountain; but
could not drive out the inhabitants of the valley,
because they had [a]chariots of iron.
20 [a]And they gave Hebron unto Caleb, as
Moses said: and he expelled thence the [b]three
sons of Anak.
21 [a]And the children of Benjamin did not
drive out the Jebusites that inhabited Jerusalem;
but the Jebusites dwell with the children of Benjamin in Jerusalem unto this day.
22 And the house of Joseph, they also went
up against Beth–el: [a]and the LORD *was* with them.
23 And the house of Joseph [a]sent to descry
Beth–el. (Now the name of the city before *was*
[b]Luz.)
24 And the spies saw a man come forth out
of the city, and they said unto him, Shew us, we
pray thee, the entrance into the city, and [a]we will
shew thee mercy.
25 And when he shewed them the entrance
into the city, they smote the city with the edge
of the sword; but they let go the man and all his
family.
26 And the man went into the land of the Hittites, and built a city, and called the name thereof
Luz: which *is* the name thereof unto this day.

Incomplete Conquest of the Land

27 [a]Neither did Manasseh drive out *the inhabitants of* Beth–shean and her towns, nor [b]Taa-
nach and her towns, nor the inhabitants of [c]Dor
and her towns, nor the inhabitants of Ibleam and
her towns, nor the inhabitants of Megiddo and
her towns: but the Canaanites would dwell in that
land.
28 And it came to pass, when Israel was
strong, that they put the Canaanites to tribute,
and did not utterly drive them out.
29 [a]Neither did Ephraim drive out the Canaanites that dwelt in Gezer; but the Canaanites
dwelt in Gezer among them.
30 Neither did [a]Zebulun drive out the inhabitants of Kitron, nor the inhabitants of Nahalol;
but the Canaanites dwelt among them, and became tributaries.
31 [a]Neither did Asher drive out the inhabitants of Accho, nor the inhabitants of Zidon, nor
of Ahlab, nor of Achzib, nor of Helbah, nor of
Aphik, nor of Rehob:
32 But the Asherites [a]dwelt among the Canaanites, the inhabitants of the land: for they did
not drive them out.
33 [a]Neither did Naphtali drive out the inhabitants of Beth–shemesh, nor the inhabitants of
Beth–anath; but he dwelt among the Canaanites,
the inhabitants of the land: nevertheless the inhabitants of Beth–shemesh and of Beth–anath became tributaries unto them.
34 And the Amorites forced the children of
Dan into the mountain: for they would not suffer
them to come down to the valley:
35 But the Amorites would dwell in mount
Heres [a]in Aijalon, and in Shaalbim: yet the hand
of the house of Joseph prevailed, so that they became tributaries.
36 And the coast of the Amorites *was* [a]from
the going up to Akrabbim, from the rock, and upward.

Israel's Disobedience

2 And an angel of the LORD came up from Gilgal
to Bochim, and said, [a]I made you to go up
out of Egypt, and [b]have brought you unto the land
which I sware unto your fathers; and [c]I said, I
will never break my covenant with you.
2 And [a]ye shall make no league with the
inhabitants of this land; [b]ye shall throw down
their altars: [c]but ye have not obeyed my voice:
why have ye done this?

19 [a]Josh. 17:16, 18; Judg. 4:3, 13
20 [a]Num. 14:24; Josh. 14:9, 14 [b]Josh. 15:14; Judg. 1:10
21 [a]Josh. 15:63; Judg. 1:8
22 [a]Judg. 1:19
23 [a]Josh. 2:1; 7:2 [b]Gen. 28:19
24 [a]Josh. 2:12, 14
27 [a]Josh. 17:11–13 [b]Josh. 21:25 [c]Josh. 17:11
29 [a]Josh. 16:10; 1 Kin. 9:16
30 [a]Josh. 19:10–16
31 [a]Josh. 19:24–31
32 [a]Ps. 106:34, 35
33 [a]Josh. 19:32–39
35 [a]Josh. 19:42
36 [a]Num. 34:4; Josh. 15:3

CHAPTER 2

1 [a]Ex. 20:2; Judg. 6:8, 9 [b]Deut. 1:8 [c]Gen. 17:7, 8; Lev. 26:42, 44; Deut. 7:9; Ps. 89:34
2 [a]Ex. 23:32; Deut. 7:2 [b]Ex. 34:12, 13; Deut. 12:3 [c]Ps. 106:34

*

1:35 *Shaalabbin,* Josh. 19:42

NKJV

Ashkelon with its territory, and Ekron with its
territory.
19 So the LORD was with Judah. And they
drove out the mountaineers, but they could not
drive out the inhabitants of the lowland, because
they had [a]chariots of iron.
20 [a]And they gave Hebron to Caleb, as Moses had said. Then he expelled from there the
[b]three sons of Anak.
21 [a]But the children of Benjamin did not
drive out the Jebusites who inhabited Jerusalem;
so the Jebusites dwell with the children of Benjamin in Jerusalem to this day.
22 And the house of Joseph also went up
against Bethel, [a]and the LORD *was* with them.
23 So the house of Joseph [a]sent men to spy
out Bethel. (The name of the city *was* formerly
[b]Luz.)
24 And when the spies saw a man coming
out of the city, they said to him, "Please show us
the entrance to the city, and [a]we will show you
mercy."
25 So he showed them the entrance to the
city, and they struck the city with the edge of the
sword; but they let the man and all his family
go.
26 And the man went to the land of the Hittites, built a city, and called its name Luz, which
is its name to this day.

Incomplete Conquest of the Land

27 [a]However, Manasseh did not drive out *the
inhabitants of* Beth Shean and its villages, or
[b]Taanach and its villages, or the inhabitants of
[c]Dor and its villages, or the inhabitants of Ibleam
and its villages, or the inhabitants of Megiddo and
its villages; for the Canaanites were determined
to dwell in that land.
28 And it came to pass, when Israel was
strong, that they put the Canaanites under tribute,
but did not completely drive them out.
29 [a]Nor did Ephraim drive out the Canaanites who dwelt in Gezer; so the Canaanites dwelt
in Gezer among them.
30 Nor did [a]Zebulun drive out the inhabitants of Kitron or the inhabitants of Nahalol; so
the Canaanites dwelt among them, and were put
under tribute.
31 [a]Nor did Asher drive out the inhabitants
of Acco or the inhabitants of Sidon, or of Ahlab,
Achzib, Helbah, Aphik, or Rehob.
32 So the Asherites [a]dwelt among the Canaanites, the inhabitants of the land; for they did
not drive them out.
33 [a]Nor did Naphtali drive out the inhabitants of Beth Shemesh or the inhabitants of Beth
Anath; but they dwelt among the Canaanites, the
inhabitants of the land. Nevertheless the inhabitants of Beth Shemesh and Beth Anath were put
under tribute to them.
34 And the Amorites forced the children of
Dan into the mountains, for they would not allow
them to come down to the valley;
35 and the Amorites were determined to
dwell in Mount Heres, [a]in Aijalon, and in *Shaalbim; yet when the strength of the house of Joseph
became greater, they were put under tribute.
36 Now the boundary of the Amorites *was*
[a]from the Ascent of Akrabbim, from Sela, and
upward.

Israel's Disobedience

2 Then the Angel of the LORD came up from Gilgal to Bochim, and said: [a]"I led you up from
Egypt and [b]brought you to the land of which I
swore to your fathers; and [c]I said, 'I will never
break My covenant with you.
2 'And [a]you shall make no covenant with
the inhabitants of this land; [b]you shall tear down
their altars.' [c]But you have not obeyed My voice.
Why have you done this?

KJV

3 Wherefore I also said, I will not drive them out from before you; but they shall be [a]*as thorns* in your sides, and [b]their gods shall be a [c]snare unto you.

4 And it came to pass, when the angel of the LORD spake these words unto all the children of Israel, that the people lifted up their voice, and wept.

5 And they called the name of that place Bochim: and they sacrificed there unto the LORD.

6 And when [a]Joshua had let the people go, the children of Israel went every man unto his inheritance to possess the land.

Death of Joshua *(Josh. 24:29–31)*

7 [a]And the people served the LORD all the days of Joshua, and all the days of the elders that outlived Joshua, who had seen all the great works of the LORD, that he did for Israel.

8 And [a]Joshua the son of Nun, the servant of the LORD, died, *being* an hundred and ten years old.

9 [a]And they buried him in the border of his inheritance in [b]Timnath–heres, in the mount of Ephraim, on the north side of the hill Gaash.

10 And also all that generation were gathered unto their fathers: and there arose another generation after them, which [a]knew not the LORD, nor yet the works which he had done for Israel.

Israel's Unfaithfulness

11 And the children of Israel did [a]evil in the sight of the LORD, and served Baalim:

12 And they [a]forsook the LORD God of their fathers, which brought them out of the land of Egypt, and followed [b]other gods, of the gods of the people that *were* round about them, and [c]bowed themselves unto them, and provoked the LORD to anger.

13 And they forsook the LORD, [a]and served Baal and Ashtaroth.

14 [a]And the anger of the LORD was hot against Israel, and he [b]delivered them into the hands of spoilers that spoiled them, and [c]he sold them into the hands of their enemies round about, so that they [d]could not any longer stand before their enemies.

15 Whithersoever they went out, the hand of the LORD was against them for evil, as the LORD had said, and as the LORD had [a]sworn unto them: and they were greatly distressed.

16 Nevertheless [a]the LORD raised up judges, which delivered them out of the hand of those that spoiled them.

17 And yet they would not hearken unto their judges, but they [a]went a whoring after other gods, and bowed themselves unto them: they turned quickly out of the way which their fathers walked in, obeying the commandments of the LORD; *but* they did not so.

18 And when the LORD raised them up judges, then [a]the LORD was with the judge, and delivered them out of the hand of their enemies all the days of the judge: [b]for it repented the LORD because of their groanings by reason of them that oppressed them and vexed them.

19 And it came to pass, [a]when the judge was dead, *that* they returned, and corrupted *themselves* more than their fathers, in following other gods to serve them, and to bow down unto them; they ceased not from their own doings, nor from their stubborn way.

20 And the anger of the LORD was hot against Israel; and he said, Because that this people hath [a]transgressed my covenant which I commanded their fathers, and have not hearkened unto my voice:

21 I also will not henceforth drive out any from before them of the nations which Joshua [a]left when he died:

22 [a]That through them I may [b]prove Israel,

3 [a]Num. 33:55; Josh. 23:13 [b]Judg. 3:6 [c]Ex. 23:33; Deut. 7:16; Ps. 106:36
6 [a]Josh. 22:6; 24:28–31
7 [a]Josh. 24:31
8 [a]Josh. 24:29
9 [a]Josh. 24:30 [b]Josh. 19:49, 50
10 [a]Ex. 5:2; 1 Sam. 2:12; Gal. 4:8; [Titus 1:16]
11 [a]Judg. 3:7, 12; 4:1; 6:1
12 [a]Deut. 31:16; Judg. 8:33; 10:6 [b]Deut. 6:14 [c]Ex. 20:5
13 [a]Judg. 10:6; Ps. 106:36
14 [a]Deut. 31:17; Judg. 3:8; Ps. 106:40–42 [b]2 Kin. 17:20 [c]Is. 50:1 [d]Lev. 26:37; Josh. 7:12, 13
15 [a]Lev. 26:14–26; Deut. 28:15–68
16 [a]Judg. 3:9, 10, 15; Ps. 106:43–45
17 [a]Ex. 34:15
18 [a]Josh. 1:5 [b]Gen. 6:6
19 [a]Judg. 3:12
20 [a][Josh. 23:16]
21 [a]Josh. 23:4, 5, 13
22 [a]Judg. 3:1, 4 [b]Deut. 8:2, 16; 13:3

NKJV

3 "Therefore I also said, 'I will not drive them out before you; but they shall be [a]*thorns** in your side, and [b]their gods shall be a [c]snare to you.' "

4 So it was, when the Angel of the LORD spoke these words to all the children of Israel, that the people lifted up their voices and wept.

5 Then they called the name of that place *Bochim; and they sacrificed there to the LORD.

6 And when [a]Joshua had dismissed the people, the children of Israel went each to his own inheritance to possess the land.

Death of Joshua *(Josh. 24:29–31)*

7 [a]So the people served the LORD all the days of Joshua, and all the days of the elders who outlived Joshua, who had seen all the great works of the LORD which He had done for Israel.

8 Now [a]Joshua the son of Nun, the servant of the LORD, died *when he was* one hundred and ten years old.

9 [a]And they buried him within the border of his inheritance at [b]Timnath Heres, in the mountains of Ephraim, on the north side of Mount Gaash.

10 When all that generation had been gathered to their fathers, another generation arose after them who [a]did not know the LORD nor the work which He had done for Israel.

Israel's Unfaithfulness

11 Then the children of Israel did [a]evil in the sight of the LORD, and served the Baals;

12 and they [a]forsook the LORD God of their fathers, who had brought them out of the land of Egypt; and they followed [b]other gods from *among* the gods of the people who *were* all around them, and they [c]bowed down to them; and they provoked the LORD to anger.

13 They forsook the LORD [a]and served Baal and the *Ashtoreths.

14 [a]And the anger of the LORD was hot against Israel. So He [b]delivered them into the hands of plunderers who despoiled them; and [c]He sold them into the hands of their enemies all around, so that they [d]could no longer stand before their enemies.

15 Wherever they went out, the hand of the LORD was against them for calamity, as the LORD had said, and as the LORD had [a]sworn to them. And they were greatly distressed.

16 Nevertheless, [a]the LORD raised up judges who delivered them out of the hand of those who plundered them.

17 Yet they would not listen to their judges, but they [a]played the harlot with other gods, and bowed down to them. They turned quickly from the way in which their fathers walked, in obeying the commandments of the LORD; they did not do so.

18 And when the LORD raised up judges for them, [a]the LORD was with the judge and delivered them out of the hand of their enemies all the days of the judge; [b]for the LORD was moved to pity by their groaning because of those who oppressed them and harassed them.

19 And it came to pass, [a]when the judge was dead, that they reverted and behaved more corruptly than their fathers, by following other gods, to serve them and bow down to them. They did not cease from their own doings nor from their stubborn way.

20 Then the anger of the LORD was hot against Israel; and He said, "Because this nation has [a]transgressed My covenant which I commanded their fathers, and has not heeded My voice,

21 "I also will no longer drive out before them any of the nations which Joshua [a]left when he died,

22 "so [a]that through them I may [b]test Israel,

*———

2:3 LXX, Tg., Vg. *enemies to you*
2:5 Lit. *Weeping*
2:13 Canaanite goddesses

KJV

whether they will keep the way of the LORD to walk therein, as their fathers did keep *it*, or not.
23 Therefore the LORD left those nations, without driving them out hastily; neither delivered he them into the hand of Joshua.

The Nations Remaining in the Land

3 Now these *are* [a]the nations which the LORD left, to prove Israel by them, *even* as many *of Israel* as had not known all the wars of Canaan;
2 Only that the generations of the children of Israel might know, to teach them war, at the least such as before knew nothing thereof;
3 *Namely*, [a]five lords of the Philistines, and all the Canaanites, and the Sidonians, and the Hivites that dwelt in mount Lebanon, from mount Baal–hermon unto the entering in of Hamath.
4 And they were to prove Israel by them, to know whether they would hearken unto the commandments of the LORD, which he commanded their fathers by the hand of Moses.
5 [a]And the children of Israel dwelt among the Canaanites, Hittites, and Amorites, and Perizzites, and Hivites, and Jebusites:
6 And [a]they took their daughters to be their wives, and gave their daughters to their sons, and served their gods.

Othniel

7 And the children of Israel did [a]evil in the sight of the LORD, and [b]forgat the LORD their God, and served Baalim and the groves.
8 Therefore the anger of the LORD was hot against Israel, and he [a]sold them into the hand of [b]Chushan–rishathaim king of Mesopotamia: and the children of Israel served Chushan–rishathaim eight years.
9 And when the children of Israel [a]cried unto the LORD, the LORD [b]raised up a deliverer to the children of Israel, who delivered them, *even* [c]Othniel the son of Kenaz, Caleb's younger brother.
10 And [a]the spirit of the LORD came upon him, and he judged Israel, and went out to war: and the LORD delivered Chushan–rishathaim king of Mesopotamia into his hand; and his hand prevailed against Chushan–rishathaim.
11 And the land had rest forty years. And Othniel the son of Kenaz died.

Ehud

12 [a]And the children of Israel did evil again in the sight of the LORD: and the LORD strengthened [b]Eglon the king of Moab against Israel, because they had done evil in the sight of the LORD.
13 And he gathered unto him the children of Ammon and [a]Amalek, and went and smote Israel, and possessed [b]the city of palm trees.
14 So the children of Israel [a]served Eglon the king of Moab eighteen years.
15 But when the children of Israel [a]cried unto the LORD, the LORD raised them up a deliverer, Ehud the son of Gera, a Benjamite, a man [b]lefthanded: and by him the children of Israel sent a present unto Eglon the king of Moab.
16 But Ehud made him a dagger which had two edges, of a cubit length; and he did gird it under his raiment upon his right thigh.
17 And he brought the present unto Eglon king of Moab: and Eglon *was* a very fat man.
18 And when he had made an end to offer the present, he sent away the people that bare the present.
19 But he himself turned again [a]from the quarries that *were* by Gilgal, and said, I have a secret errand unto thee, O king: who said, Keep silence. And all that stood by him went out from him.
20 And Ehud came unto him; and he was sitting in a summer parlour, which he had for

CHAPTER 3

1 [a]Judg. 1:1; 2:21, 22
3 [a]Josh. 13:3
5 [a]Ps. 106:35
6 [a]Ex. 34:15, 16; Deut. 7:3, 4; Josh. 23:12
7 [a]Judg. 2:11 [b]Deut. 32:18
8 [a]Deut. 32:30; Judg. 2:14 [b]Hab. 3:7
9 [a]Judg. 3:15 [b]Judg. 2:16 [c]Judg. 1:13
10 [a]Num. 27:18; 1 Sam. 11:6; 2 Chr. 15:1
12 [a]Judg. 2:19 [b]1 Sam. 12:9
13 [a]Judg. 5:14 [b]Deut. 34:3; Judg. 1:16; 2 Chr. 28:15
14 [a]Deut. 28:48
15 [a]Ps. 78:34 [b]Judg. 20:16
19 [a]Josh. 4:20

*______

3:7 Name or symbol for Canaanite goddesses

NKJV

whether they will keep the ways of the LORD, to walk in them as their fathers kept *them*, or not."
23 Therefore the LORD left those nations, without driving them out immediately; nor did He deliver them into the hand of Joshua.

The Nations Remaining in the Land

3 Now these *are* [a]the nations which the LORD left, that He might test Israel by them, *that is*, all who had not known any of the wars in Canaan
2 (*this was* only so that the generations of the children of Israel might be taught to know war, at least those who had not formerly known it),
3 *namely*, [a]five lords of the Philistines, all the Canaanites, the Sidonians, and the Hivites who dwelt in Mount Lebanon, from Mount Baal Hermon to the entrance of Hamath.
4 And they were *left, that He might* test Israel by them, to know whether they would obey the commandments of the LORD, which He had commanded their fathers by the hand of Moses.
5 [a]Thus the children of Israel dwelt among the Canaanites, the Hittites, the Amorites, the Perizzites, the Hivites, and the Jebusites.
6 And [a]they took their daughters to be their wives, and gave their daughters to their sons; and they served their gods.

Othniel

7 So the children of Israel did [a]evil in the sight of the LORD. They [b]forgot the LORD their God, and served the Baals and *Asherahs.
8 Therefore the anger of the LORD was hot against Israel, and He [a]sold them into the hand of [b]Cushan-Rishathaim king of Mesopotamia; and the children of Israel served Cushan-Rishathaim eight years.
9 When the children of Israel [a]cried out to the LORD, the LORD [b]raised up a deliverer for the children of Israel, who delivered them: [c]Othniel the son of Kenaz, Caleb's younger brother.
10 [a]The Spirit of the LORD came upon him, and he judged Israel. He went out to war, and the LORD delivered Cushan-Rishathaim king of Mesopotamia into his hand; and his hand prevailed over Cushan-Rishathaim.
11 So the land had rest for forty years. Then Othniel the son of Kenaz died.

Ehud

12 [a]And the children of Israel again did evil in the sight of the LORD. So the LORD strengthened [b]Eglon king of Moab against Israel, because they had done evil in the sight of the LORD.
13 Then he gathered to himself the people of Ammon and [a]Amalek, went and defeated Israel, and took possession of [b]the City of Palms.
14 So the children of Israel [a]served Eglon king of Moab eighteen years.
15 But when the children of Israel [a]cried out to the LORD, the LORD raised up a deliverer for them: Ehud the son of Gera, the Benjamite, a [b]left-handed man. By him the children of Israel sent tribute to Eglon king of Moab.
16 Now Ehud made himself a dagger (it was double-edged and a cubit in length) and fastened it under his clothes on his right thigh.
17 So he brought the tribute to Eglon king of Moab. (Now Eglon *was* a very fat man.)
18 And when he had finished presenting the tribute, he sent away the people who had carried the tribute.
19 But he himself turned back [a]from the stone images that *were* at Gilgal, and said, "I have a secret message for you, O king." He said, "Keep silence!" And all who attended him went out from him.
20 So Ehud came to him (now he was sitting upstairs in his cool private chamber). Then Ehud

KJV

himself alone. And Ehud said, I have a message from God unto thee. And he arose out of *his* seat.

21 And Ehud put forth his left hand, and took the dagger from his right thigh, and thrust it into his belly:

22 And the haft also went in after the blade; and the fat closed upon the blade, so that he could not draw the dagger out of his belly; and the dirt came out.

23 Then Ehud went forth through the porch, and shut the doors of the parlour upon him, and locked them.

24 When he was gone out, his servants came; and when they saw that, behold, the doors of the parlour *were* locked, they said, Surely he [a]covereth his feet in his summer chamber.

25 And they tarried till they were [a]ashamed: and, behold, he opened not the doors of the parlour; therefore they took a key, and opened *them*: and, behold, their lord *was* fallen down dead on the earth.

26 And Ehud escaped while they tarried, and passed beyond the quarries, and escaped unto Seirath.

27 And it came to pass, when he was come, that [a]he blew a trumpet in the [b]mountain of Ephraim, and the children of Israel went down with him from the mount, and he before them.

28 And he said unto them, Follow after me: for [a]the LORD hath delivered your enemies the Moabites into your hand. And they went down after him, and took the [b]fords of Jordan toward Moab, and suffered not a man to pass over.

29 And they slew of Moab at that time about ten thousand men, all lusty, and all men of valour; and there escaped not a man.

30 So Moab was subdued that day under the hand of Israel. And [a]the land had rest fourscore years.

Shamgar

31 And after him was [a]Shamgar the son of Anath, which slew of the Philistines six hundred men [b]with an ox goad: [c]and he also delivered [d]Israel.

Deborah

4 And [a]the children of Israel again did [b]evil in the sight of the LORD, when Ehud was dead.

2 And the LORD [a]sold them into the hand of Jabin king of Canaan, that reigned in [b]Hazor; the captain of whose host *was* [c]Sisera, which dwelt in [d]Harosheth of the Gentiles.

3 And the children of Israel cried unto the LORD: for he had nine hundred [a]chariots of iron; and twenty years [b]he mightily oppressed the children of Israel.

4 And Deborah, a prophetess, the wife of Lapidoth, she judged Israel at that time.

5 [a]And she dwelt under the palm tree of Deborah between Ramah and Beth–el in mount Ephraim: and the children of Israel came up to her for judgment.

6 And she sent and called [a]Barak the son of Abinoam out [b]of Kedesh–naphtali, and said unto him, Hath not the LORD God of Israel commanded, *saying*, Go and draw toward mount [c]Tabor, and take with thee ten thousand men of the children of Naphtali and of the children of Zebulun?

7 And [a]I will draw unto thee to the [b]river Kishon, Sisera, the captain of Jabin's army, with his chariots and his multitude; and I will deliver him into thine hand.

8 And Barak said unto her, If thou wilt go with me, then I will go: but if thou wilt not go with me, *then* I will not go.

9 And she said, I will surely go with thee: notwithstanding the journey that thou takest shall not be for thine honour; for the LORD shall [a]sell Sisera into the hand of a woman. And Deborah arose, and went with Barak to Kedesh.

24 [a]1 Sam. 24:3
25 [a]2 Kin. 2:17; 8:11
27 [a]Judg. 6:34; 1 Sam. 13:3 [b]Josh. 17:15
28 [a]Judg. 7:9, 15; 1 Sam. 17:47 [b]Josh. 2:7; Judg. 12:5
30 [a]Judg. 3:11
31 [a]Judg. 5:6 [b]1 Sam. 17:47 [c]Judg. 2:16 [d]1 Sam. 4:1

CHAPTER 4

1 [a]Judg. 2:19 [b]Judg. 2:11
2 [a]Judg. 2:14 [b]Josh. 11:1, 10 [c]1 Sam. 12:9; Ps. 83:9 [d]Judg. 4:13, 16
3 [a]Deut. 20:1; Judg. 1:19 [b]Ps. 106:42
5 [a]Gen. 35:8
6 [a]Heb. 11:32 [b]Josh. 19:37; 21:32 [c]Judg. 8:18
7 [a]Ex. 14:4 [b]Judg. 5:21; 1 Kin. 18:40; Ps. 83:9, 10
9 [a]Judg. 2:14

*———

3:24 Lit. *his*

NKJV

said, "I have a message from God for you." So he arose from *his* seat.

21 Then Ehud reached with his left hand, took the dagger from his right thigh, and thrust it into his belly.

22 Even the hilt went in after the blade, and the fat closed over the blade, for he did not draw the dagger out of his belly; and his entrails came out.

23 Then Ehud went out through the porch and shut the doors of the upper room behind him and locked them.

24 When he had gone out, *Eglon's* servants came to look, and *to their* surprise, the doors of the upper room were locked. So they said, "He is probably [a]attending to his needs in the cool chamber."

25 So they waited till they were [a]embarrassed, and still he had not opened the doors of the upper room. Therefore they took the key and opened *them*. And there was their master, fallen dead on the floor.

26 But Ehud had escaped while they delayed, and passed beyond the stone images and escaped to Seirah.

27 And it happened, when he arrived, that [a]he blew the trumpet in the [b]mountains of Ephraim, and the children of Israel went down with him from the mountains; and he led them.

28 Then he said to them, "Follow *me*, for [a]the LORD has delivered your enemies the Moabites into your hand." So they went down after him, seized the [b]fords of the Jordan leading to Moab, and did not allow anyone to cross over.

29 And at that time they killed about ten thousand men of Moab, all stout men of valor; not a man escaped.

30 So Moab was subdued that day under the hand of Israel. And [a]the land had rest for eighty years.

Shamgar

31 After him was [a]Shamgar the son of Anath, who killed six hundred men of the Philistines [b]with an ox goad; [c]and he also delivered [d]Israel.

Deborah

4 When Ehud was dead, [a]the children of Israel again did [b]evil in the sight of the LORD.

2 So the LORD [a]sold them into the hand of Jabin king of Canaan, who reigned in [b]Hazor. The commander of his army *was* [c]Sisera, who dwelt in [d]Harosheth Hagoyim.

3 And the children of Israel cried out to the LORD; for Jabin had nine hundred [a]chariots of iron, and for twenty years [b]he had harshly oppressed the children of Israel.

4 Now Deborah, a prophetess, the wife of Lapidoth, was judging Israel at that time.

5 [a]And she would sit under the palm tree of Deborah between Ramah and Bethel in the mountains of Ephraim. And the children of Israel came up to her for judgment.

6 Then she sent and called for [a]Barak the son of Abinoam from [b]Kedesh in Naphtali, and said to him, "Has not the LORD God of Israel commanded, 'Go and deploy *troops* at Mount [c]Tabor; take with you ten thousand men of the sons of Naphtali and of the sons of Zebulun;

7 'and against you [a]I will deploy Sisera, the commander of Jabin's army, with his chariots and his multitude at the [b]River Kishon; and I will deliver him into your hand'?"

8 And Barak said to her, "If you will go with me, then I will go; but if you will not go with me, I will not go!"

9 So she said, "I will surely go with you; nevertheless there will be no glory for you in the journey you are taking, for the LORD will [a]sell Sisera into the hand of a woman." Then Deborah arose and went with Barak to Kedesh.

KJV

10 And Barak called [a]Zebulun and Naphtali
to Kedesh; and he went up with ten thousand men
[b]at his feet: and Deborah went up with him.
11 Now Heber [a]the Kenite, *which was* of the
children of [b]Hobab the father in law of Moses,
had severed himself from the Kenites, and pitched
his tent unto the plain of Zaanaim, [c]which *is* by
Kedesh.
12 And they shewed Sisera that Barak the
son of Abinoam was gone up to mount Tabor.
13 And Sisera gathered together all his chariots, *even* nine hundred chariots of iron, and all
the people that *were* with him, from Harosheth
of the Gentiles unto the river of Kishon.
14 And Deborah said unto Barak, Up; for this
is the day in which the LORD hath delivered Sisera
into thine hand: [a]is not the LORD gone out before
thee? So Barak went down from mount Tabor,
and ten thousand men after him.
15 And the LORD discomfited Sisera, and all
his chariots, and all *his* host, with the edge of the
sword before Barak; so that Sisera lighted down
off *his* chariot, and fled away on his feet.
16 But Barak pursued after the chariots, and
after the host, unto Harosheth of the Gentiles: and
all the host of Sisera fell upon the edge of the
sword; *and* there was not a man [a]left.
17 Howbeit Sisera fled away on his feet to
the tent of [a]Jael the wife of Heber the Kenite: for
there was peace between Jabin the king of Hazor
and the house of Heber the Kenite.
18 And Jael went out to meet Sisera, and said
unto him, Turn in, my lord, turn in to me; fear
not. And when he had turned in unto her into
the tent, she covered him with a mantle.
19 And he said unto her, Give me, I pray thee,
a little water to drink; for I am thirsty. And she
opened [a]a bottle of milk, and gave him drink, and
covered him.
20 Again he said unto her, Stand in the door
of the tent, and it shall be, when any man doth
come and enquire of thee, and say, Is there any
man here? that thou shalt say, No.
21 Then Jael Heber's wife [a]took a nail of the
tent, and took an hammer in her hand, and went
softly unto him, and smote the nail into his temples, and fastened it into the ground: for he was
fast asleep and weary. So he died.
22 And, behold, as Barak pursued Sisera,
Jael came out to meet him, and said unto him,
Come, and I will shew thee the man whom thou
seekest. And when he came into her *tent*, behold,
Sisera lay dead, and the nail *was* in his temples.
23 So God subdued on that day Jabin the
king of Canaan before the children of Israel.
24 And the hand of the children of Israel
prospered, and prevailed against Jabin the king
of Canaan, until they had destroyed Jabin king
of Canaan.

The Song of Deborah

5 Then [a]sang Deborah and Barak the son of
Abinoam on that day, saying,
2 Praise ye the LORD for the [a]avenging of
Israel, [b]when the people willingly offered
themselves.
3 [a]Hear, O ye kings; give ear, O ye princes;
I, *even* [b]I, will sing unto the LORD; I will sing *praise*
to the LORD God of Israel.
4 LORD, [a]when thou wentest out of Seir,
when thou marchedst out of [b]the field of Edom,
the earth trembled, and the heavens dropped, the
clouds also dropped water.
5 [a]The mountains melted from before the
LORD, *even* [b]that Sinai from before the LORD God
of Israel.

10 [a]Judg. 5:18 [b]Ex. 11:8; 1 Kin. 20:10 **11** [a]Judg. 1:16 [b]Num. 10:29 [c]Judg. 4:6 **14** [a]Deut. 9:3; 31:3; 2 Sam. 5:24; Ps. 68:7; Is. 52:12 **16** [a]Ex. 14:28; Ps. 83:9 **17** [a]Judg. 5:6 **19** [a]Judg. 5:24–27 **21** [a]Judg. 5:24–27

CHAPTER 5

1 [a]Ex. 15:1; Judg. 4:4 **2** [a]Ps. 18:47 [b]2 Chr. 17:16 **3** [a]Deut. 32:1, 3 [b]Ps. 27:6 **4** [a]Deut. 33:2; Ps. 68:7 [b]Ps. 68:8 **5** [a]Ps. 97:5 [b]Ex. 19:18

*

4:10 Lit. *at his feet*

NKJV

10 And Barak called [a]Zebulun and Naphtali
to Kedesh; he went up with ten thousand men
[b]under* his command, and Deborah went up with
him.
11 Now Heber [a]the Kenite, of the children
of [b]Hobab the father-in-law of Moses, had separated himself from the Kenites and pitched his
tent near the terebinth tree at Zaanaim, [c]which
is beside Kedesh.
12 And they reported to Sisera that Barak the
son of Abinoam had gone up to Mount Tabor.
13 So Sisera gathered together all his chariots, nine hundred chariots of iron, and all the people who *were* with him, from Harosheth Hagoyim
to the River Kishon.
14 Then Deborah said to Barak, "Up! For this
is the day in which the LORD has delivered Sisera
into your hand. [a]Has not the LORD gone out before
you?" So Barak went down from Mount Tabor
with ten thousand men following him.
15 And the LORD routed Sisera and all *his*
chariots and all *his* army with the edge of the
sword before Barak; and Sisera alighted from *his*
chariot and fled away on foot.
16 But Barak pursued the chariots and the
army as far as Harosheth Hagoyim, and all the
army of Sisera fell by the edge of the sword; not
a man was [a]left.
17 However, Sisera had fled away on foot to
the tent of [a]Jael, the wife of Heber the Kenite;
for *there was* peace between Jabin king of Hazor
and the house of Heber the Kenite.
18 And Jael went out to meet Sisera, and said
to him, "Turn aside, my lord, turn aside to me;
do not fear." And when he had turned aside with
her into the tent, she covered him with a blanket.
19 Then he said to her, "Please give me a
little water to drink, for I am thirsty." So she
opened [a]a jug of milk, gave him a drink, and covered him.
20 And he said to her, "Stand at the door of
the tent, and if any man comes and inquires of
you, and says, 'Is there any man here?' you shall
say, 'No.' "
21 Then Jael, Heber's wife, [a]took a tent peg
and took a hammer in her hand, and went softly
to him and drove the peg into his temple, and it
went down into the ground; for he was fast asleep
and weary. So he died.
22 And then, as Barak pursued Sisera, Jael
came out to meet him, and said to him, "Come, I
will show you the man whom you seek." And
when he went into her *tent*, there lay Sisera, dead
with the peg in his temple.
23 So on that day God subdued Jabin king
of Canaan in the presence of the children of Israel.
24 And the hand of the children of Israel
grew stronger and stronger against Jabin king of
Canaan, until they had destroyed Jabin king of
Canaan.

The Song of Deborah

5 Then Deborah and Barak the son of Abinoam
[a]sang on that day, saying:

2 "When leaders [a]lead in Israel,
[b]When the people willingly offer
themselves,
Bless the LORD!

3 "Hear,[a] O kings! Give ear, O princes!
I, *even* [b]I, will sing to the LORD;
I will sing praise to the LORD God of Israel.

4 "LORD, [a]when You went out from Seir,
When You marched from [b]the field of
Edom,
The earth trembled and the heavens
poured,
The clouds also poured water;
5 [a]The mountains gushed before the LORD,
[b]This Sinai, before the LORD God of Israel.

KJV

6 In the days of [a]Shamgar the son of Anath, in the days of [b]Jael, [c]the highways were unoccupied, and the travellers walked through byways.

7 *The inhabitants of* the villages ceased, they ceased in Israel, until that I Deborah arose, that I arose a mother in Israel.

8 They chose [a]new gods; then *was* war in the gates: was there a shield or spear seen among forty thousand in Israel?

9 My heart *is* toward the governors of Israel, that offered themselves willingly among the people. Bless ye the LORD.

10 Speak, ye that ride on white [a]asses, ye that sit in judgment, and walk by the way.

11 *They that are delivered* from the noise of archers in the places of drawing water, there shall they rehearse the righteous acts of the LORD, *even* the righteous acts *toward the inhabitants* of his villages in Israel: then shall the people of the LORD go down to the gates.

12 [a]Awake, awake, Deborah: awake, awake, utter a song: arise, Barak, and lead thy captivity captive, thou son of Abinoam.

13 Then he made him that remaineth have dominion over the nobles among the people: the LORD made me have dominion over the mighty.

14 Out of Ephraim *was there* a root of them against [a]Amalek; after thee, Benjamin, among thy people; out of Machir came down governors, and out of Zebulun they that handle the pen of the writer.

15 And the princes of Issachar *were* with Deborah; even Issachar, and also Barak: he was sent on foot into the valley. For the divisions of Reuben *there were* great thoughts of heart.

16 Why abodest thou among the sheepfolds, to hear the bleatings of the flocks? For the divisions of Reuben *there were* great searchings of heart.

17 [a]Gilead abode beyond Jordan: and why did Dan remain in ships? [b]Asher continued on the sea shore, and abode in his breaches.

18 [a]Zebulun and Naphtali *were* a people *that* jeoparded their lives unto the death in the high places of the field.

19 The kings came *and* fought, then fought the kings of Canaan in [a]Taanach by the waters of Megiddo; they took no gain of money.

20 They fought from heaven; the stars in their courses fought against Sisera.

21 [a]The river of Kishon swept them away, that ancient river, the river Kishon. O my soul, thou hast trodden down strength.

22 Then were the horsehoofs broken by the means of the pransings, the pransings of their mighty ones.

23 Curse ye Meroz, said the angel of the LORD, curse ye bitterly the inhabitants thereof; be-

6 [a]Judg. 3:31
[b]Judg. 4:17
[c]Is. 33:8
8 [a]Deut. 32:17
10 [a]Judg. 10:4; 12:14
12 [a]Ps. 57:8
14 [a]Judg. 3:13
17 [a]Josh. 22:9
[b]Josh. 19:29, 31
18 [a]Judg. 4:6, 10
19 [a]Judg. 1:27
21 [a]Judg. 4:7

NKJV

6 "In the days of [a]Shamgar, son of Anath,
In the days of [b]Jael,
[c]The highways were deserted,
And the travelers walked along the byways.
7 Village life ceased, it ceased in Israel,
Until I, Deborah, arose,
Arose a mother in Israel.
8 They chose [a]new gods;
Then *there was* war in the gates;
Not a shield or spear was seen among forty thousand in Israel.
9 My heart *is* with the rulers of Israel
Who offered themselves willingly with the people.
Bless the LORD!

10 "Speak, you who ride on white [a]donkeys,
Who sit in judges' attire,
And who walk along the road.
11 Far from the noise of the archers, among the watering places,
There they shall recount the righteous acts of the LORD,
The righteous acts *for* His villagers in Israel;
Then the people of the LORD shall go down to the gates.

12 "Awake,[a] awake, Deborah!
Awake, awake, sing a song!
Arise, Barak, and lead your captives away,
O son of Abinoam!

13 "Then the survivors came down, the people against the nobles;
The LORD came down for me against the mighty.
14 From Ephraim *were* those whose roots were in [a]Amalek.
After you, Benjamin, with your peoples,
From Machir rulers came down,
And from Zebulun those who bear the recruiter's staff.
15 And *the princes of Issachar *were* with Deborah;
As Issachar, so *was* Barak
Sent into the valley *under his command;
Among the divisions of Reuben
There were great resolves of heart.
16 Why did you sit among the sheepfolds,
To hear the pipings for the flocks?
The divisions of Reuben have great searchings of heart.
17 [a]Gilead stayed beyond the Jordan,
And why did Dan remain *on ships?
[b]Asher continued at the seashore,
And stayed by his inlets.
18 [a]Zebulun *is* a people *who* jeopardized their lives to the point of death,
Naphtali also, on the heights of the battlefield.

19 "The kings came *and* fought,
Then the kings of Canaan fought
In [a]Taanach, by the waters of Megiddo;
They took no spoils of silver.
20 They fought from the heavens;
The stars from their courses fought against Sisera.
21 [a]The torrent of Kishon swept them away,
That ancient torrent, the torrent of Kishon.
O my soul, march on in strength!
22 Then the horses' hooves pounded,
The galloping, galloping of his steeds.
23 'Curse Meroz,' said the *angel of the LORD,
'Curse its inhabitants bitterly,
Because they did not come to the help of the LORD,

*

5:15 So with LXX, Syr., Tg., Vg.; MT *And my princes in Issachar* • Lit. *at his feet*
5:17 Or *at ease*
5:23 Or *Angel*

KJV

cause they came not to the help of the LORD, to
the help of the LORD against the mighty.
24 Blessed above women shall Jael the wife
of Heber the Kenite be, [a]blessed shall she be
above women in the tent.
25 He asked water, *and* she gave *him* milk;
she brought forth butter in a lordly dish.
26 She put her hand to the nail, and her right
hand to the workmen's hammer; and with the
hammer she smote Sisera, she smote off his head,
when she had pierced and stricken through his
temples.
27 At her feet he bowed, he fell, he lay down:
at her feet he bowed, he fell: where he bowed,
there he fell down [a]dead.
28 The mother of Sisera looked out at a window, and cried through the lattice, Why is his
chariot *so* long in coming? why tarry the wheels
of his chariots?
29 Her wise ladies answered her, yea, she returned answer to herself,
30 Have they not sped? have they *not* divided
the prey; to every man a damsel *or* two; to Sisera
a prey of divers colours, a prey of divers colours
of needlework, of divers colours of needlework
on both sides, *meet* for the necks of *them that*
take the spoil?
31 So let all thine enemies [a]perish, O LORD:
but *let* them that love him *be* [b]as the [c]sun when
he goeth forth in his [d]might. And the land had
rest forty years.

Midianites Oppress Israel

6 And the children of Israel did [a]evil in the sight
of the LORD: and the LORD delivered them into
the hand of [b]Midian seven years.
2 And the hand of Midian prevailed against
Israel: *and* because of the Midianites the children
of Israel made them the dens which *are* in the
mountains, and [a]caves, and strong holds.
3 And *so* it was, when Israel had sown, that
the Midianites came up, and the Amalekites, and
the [a]children of the east, even they came up
against them;
4 And they encamped against them, and
[a]destroyed the increase of the earth, till thou come
unto Gaza, and left no sustenance for Israel, neither sheep, nor ox, nor [b]ass.
5 For they came up with their cattle and
their tents, and they came as grasshoppers for
multitude; *for* both they and their camels were
without number: and they entered into the land
to destroy it.
6 And Israel was greatly impoverished because of the Midianites; and the children of Israel
[a]cried unto the LORD.
7 And it came to pass, when the children
of Israel cried unto the LORD because of the
Midianites,
8 That the LORD sent a prophet unto the children of Israel, which said unto them, Thus saith
the LORD God of Israel, I brought you up from
Egypt, and brought you forth out of the [a]house
of bondage;
9 And I delivered you out of the hand of
the Egyptians, and out of the hand of all that oppressed you, and [a]drave them out from before
you, and gave you their land;
10 And I said unto you, I *am* the LORD your
God; [a]fear not the gods of the Amorites, in whose
land ye dwell: but ye have not obeyed my [b]voice.

Gideon

11 And there came an angel of the LORD, and
sat under an oak which *was* in Ophrah, that

24 [a][Luke 1:28]
27 [a]Judg. 4:18–21
31 [a]Ps. 92:9 [b]2 Sam. 23:4 [c]Ps. 37:6; 89:36, 37 [d]Ps. 19:5

CHAPTER 6

1 [a]Judg. 2:11 [b]Num. 22:4; 31:1–3
2 [a]1 Sam. 13:6; Heb. 11:38
3 [a]Judg. 7:12
4 [a]Lev. 26:16 [b]Deut. 28:31
6 [a]Ps. 50:15; Hos. 5:15
8 [a]Josh. 24:17
9 [a]Ps. 44:2, 3
10 [a]2 Kin. 17:35, 37, 38; Jer. 10:2 [b]Judg. 2:1, 2

NKJV

To the help of the LORD against the
mighty.'

24 "Most blessed among women is Jael,
The wife of Heber the Kenite;
[a]Blessed is she among women in tents.
25 He asked for water, she gave milk;
She brought out cream in a lordly bowl.
26 She stretched her hand to the tent peg,
Her right hand to the workmen's hammer;
She pounded Sisera, she pierced his head,
She split and struck through his temple.
27 At her feet he sank, he fell, he lay still;
At her feet he sank, he fell;
Where he sank, there he fell [a]dead.

28 "The mother of Sisera looked through the
window,
And cried out through the lattice,
'Why is his chariot *so* long in coming?
Why tarries the clatter of his chariots?'
29 Her wisest ladies answered her,
Yes, she answered herself,
30 'Are they not finding and dividing the
spoil:
To every man a girl *or* two;
For Sisera, plunder of dyed garments,
Plunder of garments embroidered and
dyed,
Two pieces of dyed embroidery for the
neck of the looter?'

31 "Thus let all Your enemies [a]perish, O LORD!
But *let* those who love Him *be* [b]like the
[c]sun
When it comes out in full [d]strength."

So the land had rest for forty years.

Midianites Oppress Israel

6 Then the children of Israel did [a]evil in the
sight of the LORD. So the LORD delivered them
into the hand of [b]Midian for seven years,
2 and the hand of Midian prevailed against
Israel. Because of the Midianites, the children of
Israel made for themselves the dens, [a]the caves,
and the strongholds which *are* in the mountains.
3 So it was, whenever Israel had sown, Midianites would come up; also Amalekites and the
[a]people of the East would come up against them.
4 Then they would encamp against them
and [a]destroy the produce of the earth as far as
Gaza, and leave no sustenance for Israel, neither
sheep nor ox nor [b]donkey.
5 For they would come up with their livestock and their tents, coming in as numerous as
locusts; both they and their camels were without
number; and they would enter the land to destroy
it.
6 So Israel was greatly impoverished because of the Midianites, and the children of Israel
[a]cried out to the LORD.
7 And it came to pass, when the children
of Israel cried out to the LORD because of the
Midianites,
8 that the LORD sent a prophet to the children of Israel, who said to them, "Thus says the
LORD God of Israel: 'I brought you up from Egypt
and brought you out of the [a]house of bondage;
9 'and I delivered you out of the hand of
the Egyptians and out of the hand of all who oppressed you, and [a]drove them out before you and
gave you their land.
10 'Also I said to you, "I *am* the LORD your
God; [a]do not fear the gods of the Amorites, in
whose land you dwell." But you have not obeyed
My [b]voice.' "

Gideon

11 Now the Angel of the LORD came and sat
under the terebinth tree which *was* in Ophrah,

KJV

pertained unto Joash [a]the Abi–ezrite: and his
son [b]Gideon threshed wheat by the winepress, to
hide *it* from the Midianites.
12 And the [a]angel of the LORD appeared unto
him, and said unto him, The LORD *is* [b]with thee,
thou mighty man of valour.
13 And Gideon said unto him, Oh my Lord,
if the LORD be with us, why then is all this befallen
us? and [a]where *be* all his miracles [b]which our
fathers told us of, saying, Did not the LORD bring
us up from Egypt? but now the LORD hath [c]for-
saken us, and delivered us into the hands of the
Midianites.
14 And the LORD looked upon him, and said,
[a]Go in this thy might, and thou shalt save Israel
from the hand of the Midianites: [b]have not I sent
thee?
15 And he said unto him, Oh my Lord,
wherewith shall I save Israel? behold, [a]my family
is poor in Manasseh, and I *am* the least in my
father's house.
16 And the LORD said unto him, [a]Surely I will
be with thee, and thou shalt smite the Midianites
as one man.
17 And he said unto him, If now I have found
grace in thy sight, then [a]shew me a sign that thou
talkest with me.
18 [a]Depart not hence, I pray thee, until I
come unto thee, and bring forth my present, and
set *it* before thee. And he said, I will tarry until
thou come again.
19 [a]And Gideon went in, and made ready a
kid, and unleavened cakes of an ephah of flour:
the flesh he put in a basket, and he put the broth
in a pot, and brought *it* out unto him under the
oak, and presented *it*.
20 And the angel of God said unto him, Take
the flesh and the unleavened cakes, and [a]lay *them*
upon this rock, and [b]pour out the broth. And he
did so.
21 Then the angel of the LORD put forth the
end of the staff that *was* in his hand, and touched
the flesh and the unleavened cakes; and [a]there
rose up fire out of the rock, and consumed the
flesh and the unleavened cakes. Then the angel
of the LORD departed out of his sight.
22 And when Gideon [a]perceived that he *was*
an angel of the LORD, Gideon said, Alas, O Lord
GOD! [b]for because I have seen an angel of the
LORD face to face.
23 And the LORD said unto him, [a]Peace *be*
unto thee; fear not: thou shalt not die.
24 Then Gideon built an altar there unto the
LORD, and called it Jehovah–shalom: unto this day
it *is* yet [a]in Ophrah of the Abi–ezrites.
25 And it came to pass the same night, that
the LORD said unto him, Take thy father's young
bullock, even the second bullock of seven years
old, and [a]throw down the altar of [b]Baal that thy
father hath, and [c]cut down the grove that *is* by
it:
26 And build an altar unto the LORD thy God
upon the top of this rock, in the ordered place,
and take the second bullock, and offer a burnt
sacrifice with the wood of the grove which thou
shalt cut down.
27 Then Gideon took ten men of his servants,
and did as the LORD had said unto him: and *so* it
was, because he feared his father's household,
and the men of the city, that he could not do *it*
by day, that he did *it* by night.

Gideon Destroys the Altar of Baal

28 And when the men of the city arose early
in the morning, behold, the altar of Baal was cast
down, and the grove was cut down that *was* by
it, and the second bullock was offered upon the
altar *that was* built.
29 And they said one to another, Who hath
done this thing? And when they enquired and
asked, they said, Gideon the son of Joash hath
done this thing.

11 [a]Josh. 17:2; Judg. 6:15 [b]Judg. 7:1; Heb. 11:32
12 [a]Judg. 13:3; Luke 1:11, 28 [b]Josh. 1:5
13 [a][Is. 59:1] [b]Josh. 4:6, 21; Ps. 44:1 [c]Deut. 31:17; 2 Chr. 15:2; Ps. 44:9–16
14 [a]1 Sam. 12:11 [b]Josh. 1:9
15 [a]1 Sam. 9:21
16 [a]Ex. 3:12; Josh. 1:5
17 [a]Judg. 6:36, 37; 2 Kin. 20:8; Ps. 86:17; Is. 7:11; 38:7, 8
18 [a]Gen. 18:3, 5
19 [a]Gen. 18:6–8
20 [a]Judg. 13:19 [b]1 Kin. 18:33, 34
21 [a]Lev. 9:24
22 [a]Gen. 32:30; Ex. 33:20; Judg. 13:21, 22 [b]Gen. 16:13
23 [a]Dan. 10:19
24 [a]Judg. 8:32
25 [a]Judg. 2:2 [b]Judg. 3:7 [c]Ex. 34:13; Deut. 7:5

*———

6:13 Heb. *adoni*, used of man
6:15 Heb. *Adonai*, used of God
6:24 Heb. *YHWH Shalom*
6:25 Heb. *Asherah*, a Canaanite goddess

NKJV

which *belonged* to Joash [a]the Abiezrite, while his
son [b]Gideon threshed wheat in the winepress, in
order to hide *it* from the Midianites.
12 And the [a]Angel of the LORD appeared to
him, and said to him, "The LORD *is* [b]with you,
you mighty man of valor!"
13 Gideon said to Him, "O *my lord, if the
LORD is with us, why then has all this happened
to us? And [a]where *are* all His miracles [b]which
our fathers told us about, saying, 'Did not the
LORD bring us up from Egypt?' But now the LORD
has [c]forsaken us and delivered us into the hands
of the Midianites."
14 Then the LORD turned to him and said,
[a]"Go in this might of yours, and you shall save
Israel from the hand of the Midianites. [b]Have I
not sent you?"
15 So he said to Him, "O *my Lord, how can
I save Israel? Indeed [a]my clan *is* the weakest in
Manasseh, and I *am* the least in my father's
house."
16 And the LORD said to him, [a]"Surely I will
be with you, and you shall defeat the Midianites
as one man."
17 Then he said to Him, "If now I have found
favor in Your sight, then [a]show me a sign that it
is You who talk with me.
18 [a]"Do not depart from here, I pray, until I
come to You and bring out my offering and set
it before You." And He said, "I will wait until
you come back."
19 [a]So Gideon went in and prepared a young
goat, and unleavened bread from an ephah of
flour. The meat he put in a basket, and he put
the broth in a pot; and he brought *them* out to
Him under the terebinth tree and presented *them*.
20 The Angel of God said to him, "Take the
meat and the unleavened bread and [a]lay *them*
on this rock, and [b]pour out the broth." And he
did so.
21 Then the Angel of the LORD put out the
end of the staff that *was* in His hand, and touched
the meat and the unleavened bread; and [a]fire rose
out of the rock and consumed the meat and the
unleavened bread. And the Angel of the LORD departed out of his sight.
22 Now Gideon [a]perceived that He *was* the
Angel of the LORD. So Gideon said, "Alas, O Lord
GOD! [b]For I have seen the Angel of the LORD face
to face."
23 Then the LORD said to him, [a]"Peace *be*
with you; do not fear, you shall not die."
24 So Gideon built an altar there to the LORD,
and called it *The-LORD-*Is*-Peace. To this day it
is still [a]in Ophrah of the Abiezrites.
25 Now it came to pass the same night that
the LORD said to him, "Take your father's young
bull, the second bull of seven years old, and [a]tear
down the altar of [b]Baal that your father has, and
[c]cut down the *wooden image that *is* beside it;
26 "and build an altar to the LORD your God
on top of this rock in the proper arrangement,
and take the second bull and offer a burnt sacrifice with the wood of the image which you shall
cut down."
27 So Gideon took ten men from among his
servants and did as the LORD had said to him.
But because he feared his father's household and
the men of the city too much to do *it* by day, he
did *it* by night.

Gideon Destroys the Altar of Baal

28 And when the men of the city arose early
in the morning, there was the altar of Baal, torn
down; and the wooden image that *was* beside it
was cut down, and the second bull was being offered on the altar *which had been* built.
29 So they said to one another, "Who has
done this thing?" And when they had inquired
and asked, they said, "Gideon the son of Joash
has done this thing."

KJV

30 Then the men of the city said unto Joash, Bring out thy son, that he may die: because he hath cast down the altar of Baal, and because he hath cut down the grove that *was* by it.

31 And Joash said unto all that stood against him, Will ye plead for Baal? will ye save him? he that will plead for him, let him be put to death whilst *it is yet* morning: if he *be* a god, let him plead for himself, because *one* hath cast down his altar.

32 Therefore on that day he called him [a]Jerubbaal, saying, Let Baal plead against him, because he hath thrown down his altar.

33 Then all [a]the Midianites and the Amalekites and the children of the east were gathered together, and went over, and pitched in [b]the valley of Jezreel.

34 But [a]the Spirit of the LORD came upon Gideon, and he [b]blew a trumpet; and Abi–ezer was gathered after him.

35 And he sent messengers throughout all Manasseh; who also was gathered after him: and he sent messengers unto [a]Asher, and unto [b]Zebulun, and unto Naphtali; and they came up to meet them.

The Sign of the Fleece

36 And Gideon said unto God, If thou wilt save Israel by mine hand, as thou hast said,

37 [a]Behold, I will put a fleece of wool in the floor; *and* if the dew be on the fleece only, and *it be* dry upon all the earth *beside,* then shall I know that thou wilt save Israel by mine hand, as thou hast said.

38 And it was so: for he rose up early on the morrow, and thrust the fleece together, and wringed the dew out of the fleece, a bowl full of water.

39 And Gideon said unto God, [a]Let not thine anger be hot against me, and I will speak but this once: let me prove, I pray thee, but this once with the fleece; let it now be dry only upon the fleece, and upon all the ground let there be dew.

40 And God did so that night: for it was dry upon the fleece only, and there was dew on all the ground.

Gideon's Valiant Three Hundred

7 Then [a]Jerubbaal, who *is* Gideon, and all the people that *were* with him, rose up early, and pitched beside the well of Harod: so that the host of the Midianites were on the north side of them, by the hill of Moreh, in the valley.

2 And the LORD said unto Gideon, The people that *are* with thee *are* too many for me to give the Midianites into their hands, lest Israel [a]vaunt themselves against me, saying, Mine own hand hath saved me.

3 Now therefore go to, proclaim in the ears of the people, saying, [a]Whosoever *is* fearful and afraid, let him return and depart early from mount Gilead. And there returned of the people twenty and two thousand; and there remained ten thousand.

4 And the LORD said unto Gideon, The people *are* yet *too* many; bring them down unto the water, and I will try them for thee there: and it shall be, *that* of whom I say unto thee, This shall go with thee, the same shall go with thee; and of whomsoever I say unto thee, This shall not go with thee, the same shall not go.

5 So he brought down the people unto the water: and the LORD said unto Gideon, Every one that lappeth of the water with his tongue, as a dog lappeth, him shalt thou set by himself; likewise every one that boweth down upon his knees to drink.

6 And the number of them that lapped, *putting* their hand to their mouth, were three hundred men: but all the rest of the people bowed down upon their knees to drink water.

7 And the LORD said unto Gideon, [a]By the

32 [a]Judg. 7:1; 1 Sam. 12:11; 2 Sam. 11:21
33 [a]Judg. 6:3 [b]Josh. 17:16; Hos. 1:5
34 [a]Judg. 3:10; 1 Chr. 12:18; 2 Chr. 24:20 [b]Num. 10:3; Judg. 3:27
35 [a]Judg. 5:17; 7:23 [b]Judg. 4:6, 10; 5:18
37 [a][Ex. 4:3–7]
39 [a]Gen. 18:32

CHAPTER 7

1 [a]Judg. 6:32
2 [a]Deut. 8:17; Is. 10:13
3 [a]Deut. 20:8
7 [a]1 Sam. 14:6

NKJV

30 Then the men of the city said to Joash, "Bring out your son, that he may die, because he has torn down the altar of Baal, and because he has cut down the wooden image that *was* beside it."

31 But Joash said to all who stood against him, "Would you plead for Baal? Would you save him? Let the one who would plead for him be put to death by morning! If he *is* a god, let him plead for himself, because his altar has been torn down!"

32 Therefore on that day he called him [a]Jerubbaal,* saying, "Let Baal plead against him, because he has torn down his altar."

33 Then all [a]the Midianites and Amalekites, the people of the East, gathered together; and they crossed over and encamped in [b]the Valley of Jezreel.

34 But [a]the Spirit of the LORD came upon Gideon; then he [b]blew the trumpet, and the Abiezrites gathered behind him.

35 And he sent messengers throughout all Manasseh, who also gathered behind him. He also sent messengers to [a]Asher, [b]Zebulun, and Naphtali; and they came up to meet them.

The Sign of the Fleece

36 So Gideon said to God, "If You will save Israel by my hand as You have said—

37 [a]"look, I shall put a fleece of wool on the threshing floor; if there is dew on the fleece only, and *it is* dry on all the ground, then I shall know that You will save Israel by my hand, as You have said."

38 And it was so. When he rose early the next morning and squeezed the fleece together, he wrung the dew out of the fleece, a bowlful of water.

39 Then Gideon said to God, [a]"Do not be angry with me, but let me speak just once more: Let me test, I pray, just once more with the fleece; let it now be dry only on the fleece, but on all the ground let there be dew."

40 And God did so that night. It was dry on the fleece only, but there was dew on all the ground.

Gideon's Valiant Three Hundred

7 Then [a]Jerubbaal (that *is,* Gideon) and all the people who *were* with him rose early and encamped beside the well of Harod, so that the camp of the Midianites was on the north side of them by the hill of Moreh in the valley.

2 And the LORD said to Gideon, "The people who *are* with you *are* too many for Me to give the Midianites into their hands, lest Israel [a]claim glory for itself against Me, saying, 'My own hand has saved me.'

3 "Now therefore, proclaim in the hearing of the people, saying, [a]'Whoever *is* fearful and afraid, let him turn and depart at once from Mount Gilead.' " And twenty-two thousand of the people returned, and ten thousand remained.

4 But the LORD said to Gideon, "The people *are* still *too* many; bring them down to the water, and I will test them for you there. Then it will be, *that* of whom I say to you, 'This one shall go with you,' the same shall go with you; and of whomever I say to you, 'This one shall not go with you,' the same shall not go."

5 So he brought the people down to the water. And the LORD said to Gideon, "Everyone who laps from the water with his tongue, as a dog laps, you shall set apart by himself; likewise everyone who gets down on his knees to drink."

6 And the number of those who lapped, *putting* their hand to their mouth, was three hundred men; but all the rest of the people got down on their knees to drink water.

7 Then the LORD said to Gideon, [a]"By the

*6:32 Lit. *Let Baal Plead*

KJV

three hundred men that lapped will I save you,
and deliver the Midianites into thine hand: and
let all the *other* people go every man unto his
place.
8 So the people took victuals in their hand,
and their trumpets: and he sent all *the rest of* Israel every man unto his tent, and retained those
three hundred men: and the host of Midian was
beneath him in the valley.
9 And it came to pass the same [a]night, that
the LORD said unto him, Arise, get thee down unto
the host; for I have delivered it into thine hand.
10 But if thou fear to go down, go thou with
Phurah thy servant down to the host:
11 And thou shalt [a]hear what they say; and
afterward shall thine hands be strengthened to
go down unto the host. Then went he down with
Phurah his servant unto the outside of the armed
men that *were* in the host.
12 And the Midianites and the Amalekites
and [a]all the children of the east lay along in the
valley like grasshoppers for [b]multitude; and their
camels *were* without number, as the sand by the
sea side for multitude.
13 And when Gideon was come, behold,
there was a man that told a dream unto his fellow,
and said, Behold, I dreamed a dream, and, lo, a
cake of barley bread tumbled into the host of
Midian, and came unto a tent, and smote it that
it fell, and overturned it, that the tent lay along.
14 And his fellow answered and said, This
is nothing else save the sword of Gideon the son
of Joash, a man of Israel: *for* into his hand hath
[a]God delivered Midian, and all the host.
15 And it was *so*, when Gideon heard the telling of the dream, and the interpretation thereof,
that he worshipped, and returned into the host
of Israel, and said, Arise; for the LORD hath delivered into your hand the host of Midian.
16 And he divided the three hundred men
into three companies, and he put a trumpet in
every man's hand, with empty pitchers, and lamps
within the pitchers.
17 And he said unto them, Look on me, and
do likewise: and, behold, when I come to the outside of the camp, it shall be *that*, as I do, so shall
ye do.
18 When I blow with a trumpet, I and all that
are with me, then blow ye the trumpets also on
every side of all the camp, and say, *The sword*
of the LORD, and of Gideon.
19 So Gideon, and the hundred men that
were with him, came unto the outside of the camp
in the beginning of the middle watch; and they
had but newly set the watch: and they blew the
trumpets, and brake the pitchers that *were* in their
hands.
20 And the three companies blew the trumpets, and brake the pitchers, and held the lamps
in their left hands, and the trumpets in their right
hands to blow *withal*: and they cried, The sword
of the LORD, and of Gideon.
21 And they [a]stood every man in his place
round about the camp: [b]and all the host ran, and
cried, and fled.
22 And the three hundred [a]blew the trumpets, and [b]the LORD set [c]every man's sword
against his fellow, even throughout all the host:
and the host fled to Beth–shittah in Zererath, *and*
to the border of [d]Abel–meholah, unto Tabbath.
23 And the men of Israel gathered themselves together out of [a]Naphtali, and out of Asher,
and out of all Manasseh, and pursued after the
Midianites.
24 And Gideon sent messengers throughout
all [a]mount Ephraim, saying, Come down against
the Midianites, and take before them the waters
unto Beth–barah and Jordan. Then all the men
of Ephraim gathered themselves together, and
[b]took the waters unto [c]Beth–barah and Jordan.
25 And they took [a]two princes of the Midianites, [b]Oreb and Zeeb; and they slew Oreb upon

9 [a]Gen. 46:2, 3; Judg. 6:25
11 [a]Gen. 24:14; 1 Sam. 14:9, 10
12 [a]Judg. 6:3, 33; 8:10 [b]Judg. 6:5
14 [a]Judg. 6:14, 16
21 [a]Ex. 14:13, 14; 2 Chr. 20:17 [b]2 Kin. 7:7
22 [a]Josh. 6:4, 16, 20 [b]Ps. 83:9; Is. 9:4 [c]1 Sam. 14:20; 2 Chr. 20:23 [d]1 Kin. 4:12
23 [a]Judg. 6:35
24 [a]Judg. 3:27 [b]Judg. 3:28 [c]John 1:28
25 [a]Judg. 8:3 [b]Ps. 83:11; Is. 10:26

NKJV

three hundred men who lapped I will save you,
and deliver the Midianites into your hand. Let all
the *other* people go, every man to his place."
8 So the people took provisions and their
trumpets in their hands. And he sent away all *the
rest of* Israel, every man to his tent, and retained
those three hundred men. Now the camp of Midian was below him in the valley.
9 It happened on the same [a]night that the
LORD said to him, "Arise, go down against the
camp, for I have delivered it into your hand.
10 "But if you are afraid to go down, go down
to the camp with Purah your servant,
11 "and you shall [a]hear what they say; and
afterward your hands shall be strengthened to go
down against the camp." Then he went down with
Purah his servant to the outpost of the armed men
who *were* in the camp.
12 Now the Midianites and Amalekites, [a]all
the people of the East, were lying in the valley
[b]as numerous as locusts; and their camels *were*
without number, as the sand by the seashore in
multitude.
13 And when Gideon had come, there was a
man telling a dream to his companion. He said,
"I have had a dream: *To my* surprise, a loaf of
barley bread tumbled into the camp of Midian; it
came to a tent and struck it so that it fell and
overturned, and the tent collapsed."
14 Then his companion answered and said,
"This *is* nothing else but the sword of Gideon the
son of Joash, a man of Israel! Into his hand [a]God
has delivered Midian and the whole camp."
15 And so it was, when Gideon heard the telling of the dream and its interpretation, that he
worshiped. He returned to the camp of Israel, and
said, "Arise, for the LORD has delivered the camp
of Midian into your hand."
16 Then he divided the three hundred men
into three companies, and he put a trumpet into
every man's hand, with empty pitchers, and
torches inside the pitchers.
17 And he said to them, "Look at me and
do likewise; watch, and when I come to the edge
of the camp you shall do as I do:
18 "When I blow the trumpet, I and all who
are with me, then you also blow the trumpets on
every side of the whole camp, and say, '*The sword
of* the LORD and of Gideon!' "
19 So Gideon and the hundred men who *were*
with him came to the outpost of the camp at the
beginning of the middle watch, just as they had
posted the watch; and they blew the trumpets and
broke the pitchers that *were* in their hands.
20 Then the three companies blew the trumpets and broke the pitchers—they held the torches
in their left hands and the trumpets in their right
hands for blowing—and they cried, "The sword
of the LORD and of Gideon!"
21 And [a]every man stood in his place all
around the camp; [b]and the whole army ran and
cried out and fled.
22 When the three hundred [a]blew the trumpets, [b]the LORD set [c]every man's sword against
his companion throughout the whole camp; and
the army fled to *Beth Acacia, toward Zererah,
as far as the border of [d]Abel Meholah, by
Tabbath.
23 And the men of Israel gathered together
from [a]Naphtali, Asher, and all Manasseh, and
pursued the Midianites.
24 Then Gideon sent messengers throughout
all the [a]mountains of Ephraim, saying, "Come
down against the Midianites, and seize from them
the watering places as far as Beth Barah and the
Jordan." Then all the men of Ephraim gathered
together and [b]seized the watering places as far
as [c]Beth Barah and the Jordan.
25 And they captured [a]two princes of the
Midianites, [b]Oreb and Zeeb. They killed Oreb at

*
7:22 Heb. *Beth Shittah*

KJV

the rock Oreb, and Zeeb they slew at the winepress of Zeeb, and pursued Midian, and brought
the heads of Oreb and Zeeb to Gideon on the
[c]other side Jordan.

Gideon Subdues the Midianites

8 And [a]the men of Ephraim said unto him, Why
hast thou served us thus, that thou calledst
us not, when thou wentest to fight with the Midianites? And they did chide with him sharply.
2 And he said unto them, What have I done
now in comparison of you? *Is* not the gleaning
of the grapes of Ephraim better than the vintage
of [a]Abi–ezer?
3 [a]God hath delivered into your hands the
princes of Midian, Oreb and Zeeb: and what was
I able to do in comparison of you? Then their [b]an-
ger was abated toward him, when he had said that.
4 And Gideon came [a]to Jordan, *and* passed
over, he, and [b]the three hundred men that *were*
with him, faint, yet pursuing *them*.
5 And he said unto the men of [a]Succoth,
Give, I pray you, loaves of bread unto the people
that follow me; for they *be* faint, and I am pursuing after Zebah and Zalmunna, kings of Midian.
6 And the princes of Succoth said, [a]*Are* the
hands of Zebah and Zalmunna now in thine hand,
that [b]we should give bread unto thine army?
7 And Gideon said, Therefore when the
LORD hath delivered Zebah and Zalmunna into
mine hand, [a]then I will tear your flesh with the
thorns of the wilderness and with briers.
8 And he went up thence [a]to Penuel, and
spake unto them likewise: and the men of Penuel
answered him as the men of Succoth had answered *him*.
9 And he spake also unto the men of Penuel,
saying, When I [a]come again in peace, [b]I will break
down this tower.
10 Now Zebah and Zalmunna *were* in Kar-
kor, and their hosts with them, about fifteen thousand *men*, all that were left of [a]all the hosts of
the children of the east: for there fell [b]an hundred
and twenty thousand men that drew sword.
11 And Gideon went up by the way of them
that dwelt in tents on the east of [a]Nobah and Jogbehah, and smote the host: for the host was
[b]secure.
12 And when Zebah and Zalmunna fled, he
pursued after them, and [a]took the two kings of
Midian, Zebah and Zalmunna, and discomfited all
the host.
13 And Gideon the son of Joash returned
from battle before the sun *was up*,
14 And caught a young man of the men of
Succoth, and enquired of him: and he described
unto him the princes of Succoth, and the elders
thereof, *even* threescore and seventeen men.
15 And he came unto the men of Succoth,
and said, Behold Zebah and Zalmunna, with
whom ye did [a]upbraid me, saying, *Are* the hands
of Zebah and Zalmunna now in thine hand, that
we should give bread unto thy men *that are*
weary?
16 [a]And he took the elders of the city, and
thorns of the wilderness and briers, and with them
he taught the men of Succoth.
17 [a]And he beat down the tower of [b]Penuel,
and slew the men of the city.
18 Then said he unto Zebah and Zalmunna,
What manner of men *were they* whom ye slew
at [a]Tabor? And they answered, As thou *art*, so
were they; each one resembled the children of a
king.
19 And he said, They *were* my brethren, *even*
the sons of my mother: *as* the LORD liveth, if ye
had saved them alive, I would not slay you.
20 And he said unto Jether his firstborn, Up,
and slay them. But the youth drew not his sword:
for he feared, because he *was* yet a youth.
21 Then Zebah and Zalmunna said, Rise
thou, and fall upon us: for as the man *is*, *so is*

25 [c]Judg. 8:4

CHAPTER 8

1 [a]Judg. 12:1; 2 Sam. 19:41
2 [a]Judg. 6:11
3 [a]Judg. 7:24, 25 [b]Prov. 15:1
4 [a]Judg. 7:25 [b]Judg. 7:6
5 [a]Gen. 33:17; Ps. 60:6
6 [a]1 Kin. 20:11; Judg. 8:15 [b]1 Sam. 25:11
7 [a]Judg. 8:16
8 [a]Gen. 32:30, 31; 1 Kin. 12:25
9 [a]1 Kin. 22:27 [b]Judg. 8:17
10 [a]Judg. 7:12 [b]Judg. 6:5
11 [a]Num. 32:35, 42 [b]Judg. 18:27; [1 Thess. 5:3]
12 [a]Ps. 83:11
15 [a]Judg. 8:6
16 [a]Judg. 8:7
17 [a]Judg. 8:9 [b]1 Kin. 12:25
18 [a]Judg. 4:6; Ps. 89:12

NKJV

the rock of Oreb, and Zeeb they killed at the winepress of Zeeb. They pursued Midian and brought
the heads of Oreb and Zeeb to Gideon on the
[c]other side of the Jordan.

Gideon Subdues the Midianites

8 Now [a]the men of Ephraim said to him, "Why
have you done this to us by not calling us
when you went to fight with the Midianites?" And
they reprimanded him sharply.
2 So he said to them, "What have I done
now in comparison with you? *Is* not the gleaning
of the grapes of Ephraim better than the vintage
of [a]Abiezer?
3 [a]"God has delivered into your hands the
princes of Midian, Oreb and Zeeb. And what was
I able to do in comparison with you?" Then their
[b]anger toward him subsided when he said that.
4 When Gideon came [a]to the Jordan, he and
[b]the three hundred men who *were* with him
crossed over, exhausted but still in pursuit.
5 Then he said to the men of [a]Succoth,
"Please give loaves of bread to the people who
follow me, for they are exhausted, and I am pursuing Zebah and Zalmunna, kings of Midian."
6 And the leaders of Succoth said, [a]"*Are* the
hands of Zebah and Zalmunna now in your hand,
that [b]we should give bread to your army?"
7 So Gideon said, "For this cause, when the
LORD has delivered Zebah and Zalmunna into my
hand, [a]then I will tear your flesh with the thorns
of the wilderness and with briers!"
8 Then he went up from there [a]to Penuel
and spoke to them in the same way. And the men
of Penuel answered him as the men of Succoth
had answered.
9 So he also spoke to the men of Penuel,
saying, "When I [a]come back in peace, [b]I will tear
down this tower!"
10 Now Zebah and Zalmunna *were* at Kar-
kor, and their armies with them, about fifteen
thousand, all who were left of [a]all the army of
the people of the East; for [b]one hundred and
twenty thousand men who drew the sword had
fallen.
11 Then Gideon went up by the road of those
who dwell in tents on the east of [a]Nobah and Jogbehah; and he attacked the army while the camp
felt [b]secure.
12 When Zebah and Zalmunna fled, he pursued them; and he [a]took the two kings of Midian,
Zebah and Zalmunna, and routed the whole army.
13 Then Gideon the son of Joash returned
from battle, from the Ascent of Heres.
14 And he caught a young man of the men
of Succoth and interrogated him; and he wrote
down for him the leaders of Succoth and its elders,
seventy-seven men.
15 Then he came to the men of Succoth and
said, "Here are Zebah and Zalmunna, about
whom you [a]ridiculed me, saying, '*Are* the hands
of Zebah and Zalmunna now in your hand, that
we should give bread to your weary men?' "
16 [a]And he took the elders of the city, and
thorns of the wilderness and briers, and with them
he taught the men of Succoth.
17 [a]Then he tore down the tower of [b]Penuel
and killed the men of the city.
18 And he said to Zebah and Zalmunna,
"What kind of men *were they* whom you killed
at [a]Tabor?" So they answered, "As you *are*, so
were they; each one resembled the son of a king."
19 Then he said, "They *were* my brothers,
the sons of my mother. *As* the LORD lives, if you
had let them live, I would not kill you."
20 And he said to Jether his firstborn, "Rise,
kill them!" But the youth would not draw his
sword; for he was afraid, because he *was* still a
youth.
21 So Zebah and Zalmunna said, "Rise your-
self, and kill us; for as a man *is*, *so is* his strength."

KJV

his strength. And Gideon arose, and [a]slew Zebah
and Zalmunna, and took away the ornaments that
were on their camels' necks.

Gideon's Ephod

22 Then the men of Israel said unto Gideon,
[a]Rule thou over us, both thou, and thy son, and
thy son's son also: for thou hast [b]delivered us
from the hand of Midian.
23 And Gideon said unto them, I will not rule
over you, neither shall my son rule over you: [a]the
LORD shall rule over you.
24 And Gideon said unto them, I would desire
a request of you, that ye would give me every
man the earrings of his prey. (For they had golden
earrings, [a]because they *were* Ishmaelites.)
25 And they answered, We will willingly give
them. And they spread a garment, and did cast
therein every man the earrings of his prey.
26 And the weight of the golden earrings that
he requested was a thousand and seven hundred
shekels of gold; beside ornaments, and collars,
and purple raiment that *was* on the kings of Midian, and beside the chains that *were* about their
camels' necks.
27 And Gideon [a]made an ephod thereof, and
put it in his city, *even* [b]in Ophrah: and all Israel
[c]went thither a whoring after it: which thing became [d]a snare unto Gideon, and to his house.
28 Thus was Midian subdued before the children of Israel, so that they lifted up their heads
no more. [a]And the country was in quietness forty
years in the days of Gideon.

Death of Gideon

29 And [a]Jerubbaal the son of Joash went and
dwelt in his own house.
30 And Gideon had [a]threescore and ten sons
of his body begotten: for he had many wives.
31 [a]And his concubine that *was* in Shechem,
she also bare him a son, whose name he called
Abimelech.
32 And Gideon the son of Joash died [a]in a
good old age, and was buried in the sepulchre of
Joash his father, [b]in Ophrah of the Abi–ezrites.
33 And it came to pass, [a]as soon as Gideon
was dead, that the children of Israel turned again,
and [b]went a whoring after Baalim, [c]and made
Baal–berith their god.
34 And the children of Israel [a]remembered
not the LORD their God, who had delivered them
out of the hands of all their enemies on every side:
35 [a]Neither shewed they kindness to the
house of Jerubbaal, *namely,* Gideon, according to
all the goodness which he had shewed unto Israel.

Abimelech's Conspiracy

9 And Abimelech the son of Jerubbaal went to
Shechem unto [a]his mother's brethren, and
communed with them, and with all the family of
the house of his mother's father, saying,
2 Speak, I pray you, in the ears of all the
men of Shechem, Whether *is* better for you, either
that all the sons of Jerubbaal, *which are* [a]three-
score and ten persons, reign over you, or that one
reign over you? remember also that I *am* your
[b]bone and your flesh.
3 And his mother's brethren spake of him
in the ears of all the men of Shechem all these
words: and their hearts inclined to follow Abimelech; for they said, He *is* our [a]brother.
4 And they gave him threescore and ten
pieces of silver out of the house of [a]Baal–berith,
wherewith Abimelech hired [b]vain and light persons, which followed him.
5 And he went unto his father's house [a]at
Ophrah, and [b]slew his brethren the sons of Jerubbaal, *being* threescore and ten persons, upon one
stone: notwithstanding yet Jotham the youngest
son of Jerubbaal was left; for he hid himself.
6 And all the men of Shechem gathered to-

21 [a]Ps. 83:11
22 [a][Judg. 9:8] [b]Judg. 3:9; 9:17
23 [a]1 Sam. 8:7; 10:19; 12:12; Ps. 10:16
24 [a]Gen. 37:25, 28
27 [a]Judg. 17:5 [b]Judg. 6:11, 24 [c][Ps. 106:39] [d]Deut. 7:16
28 [a]Judg. 5:31
29 [a]Judg. 6:32; 7:1
30 [a]Judg. 9:2, 5
31 [a]Judg. 9:1
32 [a]Gen. 25:8; Job 5:26 [b]Judg. 6:24; 8:27
33 [a]Judg. 2:19 [b]Judg. 2:17 [c]Judg. 9:4, 46
34 [a]Deut. 4:9; Judg. 3:7; Ps. 78:11, 42; 106:13, 21
35 [a]Judg. 9:16–18

CHAPTER 9
1 [a]Judg. 8:31, 35
2 [a]Judg. 8:30; 9:5, 18 [b]Gen. 29:14
3 [a]Gen. 29:15
4 [a]Judg. 8:33 [b]Judg. 11:3; 2 Chr. 13:7; Acts 17:5
5 [a]Judg. 6:24 [b]Judg. 8:30; 9:2, 18; 2 Kin. 11:1, 2

NKJV

So Gideon arose and [a]killed Zebah and Zalmunna, and took the crescent ornaments that
were on their camels' necks.

Gideon's Ephod

22 Then the men of Israel said to Gideon,
[a]"Rule over us, both you and your son, and your
grandson also; for you have [b]delivered us from
the hand of Midian."
23 But Gideon said to them, "I will not rule
over you, nor shall my son rule over you; [a]the
LORD shall rule over you."
24 Then Gideon said to them, "I would like
to make a request of you, that each of you would
give me the earrings from his plunder." For they
had golden earrings, [a]because they *were* Ishmaelites.
25 So they answered, "We will gladly give
them." And they spread out a garment, and each
man threw into it the earrings from his plunder.
26 Now the weight of the gold earrings that
he requested was one thousand seven hundred
shekels of gold, besides the crescent ornaments,
pendants, and purple robes which *were* on the
kings of Midian, and besides the chains that *were*
around their camels' necks.
27 Then Gideon [a]made it into an ephod and
set it up in his city, [b]Ophrah. And all Israel
[c]played the harlot with it there. It became [d]a snare
to Gideon and to his house.
28 Thus Midian was subdued before the children of Israel, so that they lifted their heads no
more. [a]And the country was quiet for forty years
in the days of Gideon.

Death of Gideon

29 Then [a]Jerubbaal the son of Joash went
and dwelt in his own house.
30 Gideon had [a]seventy sons who were his
own offspring, for he had many wives.
31 [a]And his concubine who *was* in Shechem
also bore him a son, whose name he called Abimelech.
32 Now Gideon the son of Joash died [a]at a
good old age, and was buried in the tomb of Joash
his father, [b]in Ophrah of the Abiezrites.
33 So it was, [a]as soon as Gideon was dead,
that the children of Israel again [b]played the harlot
with the Baals, [c]and made Baal-Berith their god.
34 Thus the children of Israel [a]did not remember the LORD their God, who had delivered
them from the hands of all their enemies on every
side;
35 [a]nor did they show kindness to the house
of Jerubbaal (Gideon) in accordance with the
good he had done for Israel.

Abimelech's Conspiracy

9 Then Abimelech the son of Jerubbaal went
to Shechem, to [a]his mother's brothers, and
spoke with them and with all the family of the
house of his mother's father, saying,
2 "Please speak in the hearing of all the men
of Shechem: 'Which is better for you, that all
[a]seventy of the sons of Jerubbaal reign over you,
or that one reign over you?' Remember that I
am your own flesh and [b]bone."
3 And his mother's brothers spoke all these
words concerning him in the hearing of all the
men of Shechem; and their heart was inclined to
follow Abimelech, for they said, "He is our
[a]brother."
4 So they gave him seventy *shekels* of silver
from the temple of [a]Baal-Berith, with which
Abimelech hired [b]worthless and reckless men;
and they followed him.
5 Then he went to his father's house [a]at
Ophrah and [b]killed his brothers, the seventy sons
of Jerubbaal, on one stone. But Jotham the youngest son of Jerubbaal was left, because he hid
himself.
6 And all the men of Shechem gathered to-

KJV

gether, and all the house of Millo, and went, and made Abimelech king, by the plain of the pillar that *was* in Shechem.

The Parable of the Trees

7 And when they told *it* to Jotham, he went and stood in the top of [a]mount Gerizim, and lifted up his voice, and cried, and said unto them, Hearken unto me, ye men of Shechem, that God may hearken unto you.

8 [a]The trees went forth *on a time* to anoint a king over them; and they said unto the olive tree, [b]Reign thou over us.

9 But the olive tree said unto them, Should I leave my fatness, [a]wherewith by me they honour God and man, and go to be promoted over the trees?

10 And the trees said to the fig tree, Come thou, *and* reign over us.

11 But the fig tree said unto them, Should I forsake my sweetness, and my good fruit, and go to be promoted over the trees?

12 Then said the trees unto the vine, Come thou, *and* reign over us.

13 And the vine said unto them, Should I leave my wine, [a]which cheereth God and man, and go to be promoted over the trees?

14 Then said all the trees unto the bramble, Come thou, *and* reign over us.

15 And the bramble said unto the trees, If in truth ye anoint me king over you, *then* come *and* put your trust in my [a]shadow: and if not, [b]let fire come out of the bramble, and devour the [c]cedars of Lebanon.

16 Now therefore, if ye have done truly and sincerely, in that ye have made Abimelech king, and if ye have dealt well with Jerubbaal and his house, and have done unto him [a]according to the deserving of his hands;

17 (For my [a]father fought for you, and adventured his life far, and [b]delivered you out of the hand of Midian:

18 [a]And ye are risen up against my father's house this day, and have slain his sons, threescore and ten persons, upon one stone, and have made Abimelech, the son of his [b]maidservant, king over the men of Shechem, because he *is* your brother;)

19 If ye then have dealt truly and sincerely with Jerubbaal and with his house this day, *then* [a]rejoice ye in Abimelech, and let him also rejoice in you:

20 But if not, [a]let fire come out from Abimelech, and devour the men of Shechem, and the house of Millo; and let fire come out from the men of Shechem, and from the house of Millo, and devour Abimelech.

21 And Jotham ran away, and fled, and went to [a]Beer, and dwelt there, for fear of Abimelech his brother.

Downfall of Abimelech

22 When Abimelech had reigned three years over Israel,

23 Then [a]God sent an [b]evil spirit between Abimelech and the men of Shechem; and the men of Shechem [c]dealt treacherously with Abimelech:

24 [a]That the cruelty *done* to the threescore and ten sons of Jerubbaal might come, and their [b]blood be laid upon Abimelech their brother, which slew them; and upon the men of Shechem, which aided him in the killing of his brethren.

25 And the men of Shechem set liers in wait for him in the top of the mountains, and they robbed all that came along that way by them: and it was told Abimelech.

26 And Gaal the son of Ebed came with his

7 [a]Deut. 11:29; 27:12; Josh. 8:33; John 4:20
8 [a]2 Kin. 14:9 [b]Judg. 8:22, 23
9 [a][John 5:23]
13 [a]Ps. 104:15
15 [a]Is. 30:2; Dan. 4:12; Hos. 14:7 [b]Num. 21:28; Judg. 9:20; Ezek. 19:14 [c]2 Kin. 14:9; Is. 2:13; Ezek. 31:3
16 [a]Judg. 8:35
17 [a]Judg. 7 [b]Judg. 8:22
18 [a]Judg. 8:30, 35; 9:2, 5, 6 [b]Judg. 8:31
19 [a]Is. 8:6; [Phil. 3:3]
20 [a]Judg. 9:15, 45, 56, 57
21 [a]Num. 21:16
23 [a]1 Kin. 12:15; Is. 19:14 [b]1 Sam. 16:14; 18:9, 10; 1 Kin. 22:22; 2 Chr. 18:22 [c]Is. 33:1
24 [a]1 Kin. 2:32; Esth. 9:25; Matt. 23:35, 36 [b]Num. 35:33

NKJV

gether, all of Beth Millo, and they went and made Abimelech king beside the terebinth tree at the pillar that *was* in Shechem.

The Parable of the Trees

7 Now when they told Jotham, he went and stood on top of [a]Mount Gerizim, and lifted his voice and cried out. And he said to them:

"Listen to me, you men of Shechem,
That God may listen to you!

8 "The[a] trees once went forth to anoint a king over them.
And they said to the olive tree,
[b]'Reign over us!'
9 But the olive tree said to them,
'Should I cease giving my oil,
[a]With which they honor God and men,
And go to sway over trees?'

10 "Then the trees said to the fig tree,
'You come *and* reign over us!'
11 But the fig tree said to them,
'Should I cease my sweetness and my good fruit,
And go to sway over trees?'

12 "Then the trees said to the vine,
'You come *and* reign over us!'
13 But the vine said to them,
'Should I cease my new wine,
[a]Which cheers *both* God and men,
And go to sway over trees?'

14 "Then all the trees said to the bramble,
'You come *and* reign over us!'
15 And the bramble said to the trees,
'If in truth you anoint me as king over you,
Then come *and* take shelter in my [a]shade;
But if not, [b]let fire come out of the bramble
And devour the [c]cedars of Lebanon!'

16 "Now therefore, if you have acted in truth and sincerity in making Abimelech king, and if you have dealt well with Jerubbaal and his house, and have done to him [a]as he deserves—

17 "for my [a]father fought for you, risked his life, and [b]delivered you out of the hand of Midian;

18 [a]"but you have risen up against my father's house this day, and killed his seventy sons on one stone, and made Abimelech, the son of his [b]female servant, king over the men of Shechem, because he is your brother—

19 "if then you have acted in truth and sincerity with Jerubbaal and with his house this day, *then* [a]rejoice in Abimelech, and let him also rejoice in you.

20 "But if not, [a]let fire come from Abimelech and devour the men of Shechem and Beth Millo; and let fire come from the men of Shechem and from Beth Millo and devour Abimelech!"

21 And Jotham ran away and fled; and he went to [a]Beer and dwelt there, for fear of Abimelech his brother.

Downfall of Abimelech

22 After Abimelech had reigned over Israel three years,

23 [a]God sent a [b]spirit of ill will between Abimelech and the men of Shechem; and the men of Shechem [c]dealt treacherously with Abimelech,

24 [a]that the crime *done* to the seventy sons of Jerubbaal might be settled and their [b]blood be laid on Abimelech their brother, who killed them, and on the men of Shechem, who aided him in the killing of his brothers.

25 And the men of Shechem set men in ambush against him on the tops of the mountains, and they robbed all who passed by them along that way; and it was told Abimelech.

26 Now Gaal the son of Ebed came with his

KJV

brethren, and went over to Shechem: and the men of Shechem put their confidence in him.

27 And they went out into the fields, and gathered their vineyards, and trode *the grapes,* and made merry, and went into [a]the house of their god, and did eat and drink, and cursed Abimelech.

28 And Gaal the son of Ebed said, [a]Who *is* Abimelech, and who *is* Shechem, that we should serve him? *is* not *he* the son of Jerubbaal? and Zebul his officer? serve the men of [b]Hamor the father of Shechem: for why should we serve him?

29 And [a]would to God this people were under my hand! then would I remove Abimelech. And he said to Abimelech, Increase thine army, and come out.

30 And when Zebul the ruler of the city heard the words of Gaal the son of Ebed, his anger was kindled.

31 And he sent messengers unto Abimelech privily, saying, Behold, Gaal the son of Ebed and his brethren be come to Shechem; and, behold, they fortify the city against thee.

32 Now therefore up by night, thou and the people that *is* with thee, and lie in wait in the field:

33 And it shall be, *that* in the morning, as soon as the sun is up, thou shalt rise early, and set upon the city: and, behold, *when* he and the people that *is* with him come out against thee, then mayest thou do to them as thou shalt find occasion.

34 And Abimelech rose up, and all the people that *were* with him, by night, and they laid wait against Shechem in four companies.

35 And Gaal the son of Ebed went out, and stood in the entering of the gate of the city: and Abimelech rose up, and the people that *were* with him, from lying in wait.

36 And when Gaal saw the people, he said to Zebul, Behold, there come people down from the top of the mountains. And Zebul said unto him, Thou seest the shadow of the mountains as *if they were* men.

37 And Gaal spake again and said, See there come people down by the middle of the land, and another company come along by the plain of Meonenim.

38 Then said Zebul unto him, Where *is* now thy mouth, wherewith thou [a]saidst, Who *is* Abimelech, that we should serve him? *is* not this the people that thou hast despised? go out, I pray now, and fight with them.

39 And Gaal went out before the men of Shechem, and fought with Abimelech.

40 And Abimelech chased him, and he fled before him, and many were overthrown *and* wounded, *even* unto the entering of the gate.

41 And Abimelech dwelt at Arumah: and Zebul thrust out Gaal and his brethren, that they should not dwell in Shechem.

42 And it came to pass on the morrow, that the people went out into the field; and they told Abimelech.

43 And he took the people, and divided them into three companies, and laid wait in the field, and looked, and, behold, the people *were* come forth out of the city; and he rose up against them, and smote them.

44 And Abimelech, and the company that *was* with him, rushed forward, and stood in the entering of the gate of the city: and the two *other* companies ran upon all *the people* that *were* in the fields, and slew them.

45 And Abimelech fought against the city all that day; and [a]he took the city, and slew the people that *was* therein, and [b]beat down the city, and sowed it with salt.

46 And when all the men of the tower of Shechem heard *that,* they entered into an hold of the house [a]of the god Berith.

47 And it was told Abimelech, that all the

27 [a]Judg. 9:4
28 [a]1 Sam. 25:10; 1 Kin. 12:16 [b]Gen. 34:2, 6; Josh. 24:32
29 [a]2 Sam. 15:4
38 [a]Judg. 9:28, 29
45 [a]Judg. 9:20 [b]Deut. 29:23; 2 Kin. 3:25
46 [a]Judg. 8:33

NKJV

brothers and went over to Shechem; and the men of Shechem put their confidence in him.

27 So they went out into the fields, and gathered *grapes* from their vineyards and trod *them,* and made merry. And they went into [a]the house of their god, and ate and drank, and cursed Abimelech.

28 Then Gaal the son of Ebed said, [a]"Who *is* Abimelech, and who *is* Shechem, that we should serve him? *Is he* not the son of Jerubbaal, and *is not* Zebul his officer? Serve the men of [b]Hamor the father of Shechem; but why should we serve him?

29 [a]"If only this people were under my *authority! Then I would remove Abimelech." So *he said to Abimelech, "Increase your army and come out!"

30 When Zebul, the ruler of the city, heard the words of Gaal the son of Ebed, his anger was aroused.

31 And he sent messengers to Abimelech secretly, saying, "Take note! Gaal the son of Ebed and his brothers have come to Shechem; and here they are, fortifying the city against you.

32 "Now therefore, get up by night, you and the people who *are* with you, and lie in wait in the field.

33 "And it shall be, as soon as the sun is up in the morning, *that* you shall rise early and rush upon the city; and *when* he and the people who are with him come out against you, you may then do to them as you find opportunity."

34 So Abimelech and all the people who *were* with him rose by night, and lay in wait against Shechem in four companies.

35 When Gaal the son of Ebed went out and stood in the entrance to the city gate, Abimelech and the people who *were* with him rose from lying in wait.

36 And when Gaal saw the people, he said to Zebul, "Look, people are coming down from the tops of the mountains!" But Zebul said to him, "You see the shadows of the mountains as *if they were* men."

37 So Gaal spoke again and said, "See, people are coming down from the center of the land, and another company is coming from the *Diviners' Terebinth Tree."

38 Then Zebul said to him, "Where indeed *is* your mouth now, with which you [a]said, 'Who is Abimelech, that we should serve him?' *Are* not these the people whom you despised? Go out, if you will, and fight with them now."

39 So Gaal went out, leading the men of Shechem, and fought with Abimelech.

40 And Abimelech chased him, and he fled from him; and many fell wounded, to the *very* entrance of the gate.

41 Then Abimelech dwelt at Arumah, and Zebul drove out Gaal and his brothers, so that they would not dwell in Shechem.

42 And it came about on the next day that the people went out into the field, and they told Abimelech.

43 So he took his people, divided them into three companies, and lay in wait in the field. And he looked, and there were the people, coming out of the city; and he rose against them and attacked them.

44 Then Abimelech and the company that *was* with him rushed forward and stood at the entrance of the gate of the city; and the *other* two companies rushed upon all who *were* in the fields and killed them.

45 So Abimelech fought against the city all that day; [a]he took the city and killed the people who *were* in it; and he [b]demolished the city and sowed it with salt.

46 Now when all the men of the tower of Shechem had heard *that,* they entered the stronghold of the temple [a]of the god Berith.

47 And it was told Abimelech that all the

---

*

9:29 Lit. *hand* • So with MT, Tg.; DSS *they;* LXX *I*
9:37 Heb. *Meonenim*

KJV

men of the tower of Shechem were gathered together.

48 And Abimelech gat him up to mount [a]Zalmon, he and all the people that *were* with him; and Abimelech took an axe in his hand, and cut down a bough from the trees, and took it, and laid *it* on his shoulder, and said unto the people that *were* with him, What ye have seen me do, make haste, *and* do as I *have done.*

49 And all the people likewise cut down every man his bough, and followed Abimelech, and put *them* to the hold, and set the hold on fire upon them; so that all the men of the tower of Shechem died also, about a thousand men and women.

50 Then went Abimelech to Thebez, and encamped against Thebez, and took it.

51 But there was a strong tower within the city, and thither fled all the men and women, and all they of the city, and shut *it* to them, and gat them up to the top of the tower.

52 And Abimelech came unto the tower, and fought against it, and went hard unto the door of the tower to burn it with fire.

53 And a certain woman [a]cast a piece of a millstone upon Abimelech's head, and all to brake his skull.

54 Then [a]he called hastily unto the young man his armourbearer, and said unto him, Draw thy sword, and slay me, that men say not of me, A woman slew him. And his young man thrust him through, and he died.

55 And when the men of Israel saw that Abimelech was dead, they departed every man unto his place.

56 [a]Thus God rendered the wickedness of Abimelech, which he did unto his father, in slaying his seventy brethren:

57 And all the evil of the men of Shechem did God render upon their heads: and upon them came [a]the curse of Jotham the son of Jerubbaal.

Tola

10 And after Abimelech there [a]arose to defend Israel Tola the son of Puah, the son of Dodo, a man of Issachar; and he dwelt in Shamir in mount Ephraim.

2 And he judged Israel twenty and three years, and died, and was buried in Shamir.

Jair

3 And after him arose Jair, a Gileadite, and judged Israel twenty and two years.

4 And he had thirty sons that [a]rode on thirty ass colts, and they had thirty cities, [b]which are called Havoth–jair unto this day, which *are* in the land of Gilead.

5 And Jair died, and was buried in Camon.

Israel Oppressed Again

6 And [a]the children of Israel did evil again in the sight of the LORD, and [b]served Baalim, and Ashtaroth, and [c]the gods of Syria, and the gods of [d]Zidon, and the gods of Moab, and the gods of the children of Ammon, and the gods of the Philistines, and forsook the LORD, and served not him.

7 And the anger of the LORD was hot against Israel, and he [a]sold them into the hands of the [b]Philistines, and into the hands of the children of [c]Ammon.

8 And that year they vexed and oppressed the children of Israel: eighteen years, all the children of Israel that *were* on the other side Jordan in the [a]land of the Amorites, which *is* in Gilead.

9 Moreover the children of Ammon passed over Jordan to fight also against Judah, and against Benjamin, and against the house of Ephraim; so that Israel was sore distressed.

10 [a]And the children of Israel cried unto the LORD, saying, We have [b]sinned against thee, both

48 [a]Ps. 68:14 **53** [a]2 Sam. 11:21 **54** [a]1 Sam. 31:4 **56** [a]Judg. 9:24; Job 31:3; Prov. 5:22 **57** [a]Judg. 9:20

CHAPTER 10

1 [a]Judg. 2:16 **4** [a]Judg. 5:10; 12:14 [b]Deut. 3:14 **6** [a]Judg. 2:11; 3:7; 6:1; 13:1 [b]Judg. 2:13 [c]Judg. 2:12 [d]1 Kin. 11:33; Ps. 106:36 **7** [a]Judg. 2:14; 4:2; 1 Sam. 12:9 [b]Judg. 13:1 [c]Judg. 3:13 **8** [a]Num. 32:33 **10** [a]Judg. 6:6; 1 Sam. 12:10 [b]Deut. 1:41

*

10:4 Lit. *Towns of Jair,* Num. 32:41; Deut. 3:14

NKJV

men of the tower of Shechem were gathered together.

48 Then Abimelech went up to Mount [a]Zalmon, he and all the people who *were* with him. And Abimelech took an ax in his hand and cut down a bough from the trees, and took it and laid *it* on his shoulder; then he said to the people who were with him, "What you have seen me do, make haste *and* do as I *have done.*"

49 So each of the people likewise cut down his own bough and followed Abimelech, put *them* against the stronghold, and set the stronghold on fire above them, so that all the people of the tower of Shechem died, about a thousand men and women.

50 Then Abimelech went to Thebez, and he encamped against Thebez and took it.

51 But there was a strong tower in the city, and all the men and women—all the people of the city—fled there and shut themselves in; then they went up to the top of the tower.

52 So Abimelech came as far as the tower and fought against it; and he drew near the door of the tower to burn it with fire.

53 But a certain woman [a]dropped an upper millstone on Abimelech's head and crushed his skull.

54 Then [a]he called quickly to the young man, his armorbearer, and said to him, "Draw your sword and kill me, lest men say of me, 'A woman killed him.'" So his young man thrust him through, and he died.

55 And when the men of Israel saw that Abimelech was dead, they departed, every man to his place.

56 [a]Thus God repaid the wickedness of Abimelech, which he had done to his father by killing his seventy brothers.

57 And all the evil of the men of Shechem God returned on their own heads, and on them came [a]the curse of Jotham the son of Jerubbaal.

Tola

10 After Abimelech there [a]arose to save Israel Tola the son of Puah, the son of Dodo, a man of Issachar; and he dwelt in Shamir in the mountains of Ephraim.

2 He judged Israel twenty-three years; and he died and was buried in Shamir.

Jair

3 After him arose Jair, a Gileadite; and he judged Israel twenty-two years.

4 Now he had thirty sons who [a]rode on thirty donkeys; they also had thirty towns, [b]which are called *"Havoth Jair" to this day, which *are* in the land of Gilead.

5 And Jair died and was buried in Camon.

Israel Oppressed Again

6 Then [a]the children of Israel again did evil in the sight of the LORD, and [b]served the Baals and the Ashtoreths, [c]the gods of Syria, the gods of [d]Sidon, the gods of Moab, the gods of the people of Ammon, and the gods of the Philistines; and they forsook the LORD and did not serve Him.

7 So the anger of the LORD was hot against Israel; and He [a]sold them into the hands of the [b]Philistines and into the hands of the people of [c]Ammon.

8 From that year they harassed and oppressed the children of Israel for eighteen years—all the children of Israel who *were* on the other side of the Jordan in the [a]land of the Amorites, in Gilead.

9 Moreover the people of Ammon crossed over the Jordan to fight against Judah also, against Benjamin, and against the house of Ephraim, so that Israel was severely distressed.

10 [a]And the children of Israel cried out to the LORD, saying, "We have [b]sinned against You,

KJV

because we have forsaken our God, and also
served Baalim.
11 And the LORD said unto the children of
Israel, *Did* not *I deliver you* [a]from the Egyptians,
and [b]from the Amorites, [c]from the children of
Ammon, and [d]from the Philistines?
12 [a]The Zidonians also, [b]and the Amalekites,
and the Maonites, [c]did oppress you; and ye cried
to me, and I delivered you out of their hand.
13 [a]Yet ye have forsaken me, and served
other gods: wherefore I will deliver you no more.
14 Go and [a]cry unto the gods which ye have
chosen; let them deliver you in the time of your
tribulation.
15 And the children of Israel said unto the
LORD, We have sinned: [a]do thou unto us whatsoever seemeth good unto thee; deliver us only, we
pray thee, this day.
16 [a]And they put away the strange gods from
among them, and served the LORD: and [b]his soul
was grieved for the misery of Israel.
17 Then the children of Ammon were gathered together, and encamped in Gilead. And the
children of Israel assembled themselves together,
and encamped in [a]Mizpeh.
18 And the people *and* princes of Gilead said
one to another, What man *is he* that will begin
to fight against the children of Ammon? he shall
[a]be head over all the inhabitants of Gilead.

Jephthah

11 Now [a]Jephthah the Gileadite was [b]a
mighty man of valour, and he *was* the son
of an harlot: and Gilead begat Jephthah.
2 And Gilead's wife bare him sons; and his
wife's sons grew up, and they thrust out Jephthah,
and said unto him, Thou shalt [a]not inherit in our
father's house; for thou *art* the son of a strange
woman.
3 Then Jephthah fled from his brethren, and
dwelt in the land of [a]Tob: and there were gathered
[b]vain men to Jephthah, and went out with him.
4 And it came to pass in process of time,
that the [a]children of Ammon made war against
Israel.
5 And it was so, that when the children of
Ammon made war against Israel, the elders of
Gilead went to fetch Jephthah out of the land of
Tob:
6 And they said unto Jephthah, Come, and
be our captain, that we may fight with the children
of Ammon.
7 And Jephthah said unto the elders of Gilead, [a]Did not ye hate me, and expel me out of
my father's house? and why are ye come unto
me now when ye are in distress?
8 [a]And the elders of Gilead said unto Jephthah, Therefore we [b]turn again to thee now, that
thou mayest go with us, and fight against the children of Ammon, and be [c]our head over all the
inhabitants of Gilead.
9 And Jephthah said unto the elders of Gilead, If ye bring me home again to fight against
the children of Ammon, and the LORD deliver them
before me, shall I be your head?
10 And the elders of Gilead said unto Jephthah, [a]The LORD be witness between us, if we
do not so according to thy words.
11 Then Jephthah went with the elders of
Gilead, and the people made him [a]head and captain over them: and Jephthah uttered all his words
[b]before the LORD in Mizpeh.
12 And Jephthah sent messengers unto the
king of the children of Ammon, saying, [a]What
hast thou to do with me, that thou art come
against me to fight in my land?
13 And the king of the children of Ammon
answered unto the messengers of Jephthah, [a]Be-
cause Israel took away my land, when they came
up out of Egypt, from [b]Arnon even unto [c]Jabbok,
and unto Jordan: now therefore restore those
lands again peaceably.

11 [a]Ex. 14:30 [b]Num. 21:21, 24, 25 [c]Judg. 3:12, 13 [d]Judg. 3:31
12 [a]Judg. 1:31; 5:19 [b]Judg. 6:3; 7:12 [c]Ps. 106:42, 43
13 [a][Deut. 32:15; Judg. 2:12; Jer. 2:13]
14 [a]Deut. 32:37, 38
15 [a]1 Sam. 3:18; 2 Sam. 15:26
16 [a]2 Chr. 7:14; Jer. 18:7, 8 [b]Ps. 106:44, 45; Is. 63:9
17 [a]Gen. 31:49; Judg. 11:11, 29
18 [a]Judg. 11:8, 11

CHAPTER 11
1 [a]Heb. 11:32 [b]Judg. 6:12; 2 Kin. 5:1
2 [a]Gen. 21:10; Deut. 23:2
3 [a]2 Sam. 10:6, 8 [b]1 Sam. 22:2
4 [a]Judg. 10:9, 17
7 [a]Gen. 26:27
8 [a]Judg. 10:18 [b][Luke 17:4] [c]Judg. 10:18
10 [a]Gen. 31:49, 50; Jer. 29:23; 42:5
11 [a]Judg. 11:8 [b]Judg. 10:17; 20:1; 1 Sam. 10:17
12 [a]2 Sam. 16:10
13 [a]Num. 21:24–26 [b]Josh. 13:9 [c]Gen. 32:22

*———
10:12 LXX mss. *Midianites*

NKJV

because we have both forsaken our God and
served the Baals!"
11 So the LORD said to the children of Israel,
"*Did I* not *deliver you* [a]from the Egyptians and
[b]from the Amorites and [c]from the people of Ammon and [d]from the Philistines?
12 "Also [a]the Sidonians [b]and Amalekites
and *Maonites [c]oppressed you; and you cried out
to Me, and I delivered you from their hand.
13 [a]"Yet you have forsaken Me and served
other gods. Therefore I will deliver you no more.
14 "Go and [a]cry out to the gods which you
have chosen; let them deliver you in your time
of distress."
15 And the children of Israel said to the LORD,
"We have sinned! [a]Do to us whatever seems best
to You; only deliver us this day, we pray."
16 [a]So they put away the foreign gods from
among them and served the LORD. And [b]His soul
could no longer endure the misery of Israel.
17 Then the people of Ammon gathered together and encamped in Gilead. And the children
of Israel assembled together and encamped in
[a]Mizpah.
18 And the people, the leaders of Gilead, said
to one another, "Who *is* the man who will begin
the fight against the people of Ammon? He shall
[a]be head over all the inhabitants of Gilead."

Jephthah

11 Now [a]Jephthah the Gileadite was [b]a
mighty man of valor, but he *was* the son
of a harlot; and Gilead begot Jephthah.
2 Gilead's wife bore sons; and when his
wife's sons grew up, they drove Jephthah out, and
said to him, "You shall have [a]no inheritance in
our father's house, for you *are* the son of another
woman."
3 Then Jephthah fled from his brothers and
dwelt in the land of [a]Tob; and [b]worthless men
banded together with Jephthah and went out *raiding* with him.
4 It came to pass after a time that the [a]peo-
ple of Ammon made war against Israel.
5 And so it was, when the people of Ammon
made war against Israel, that the elders of Gilead
went to get Jephthah from the land of Tob.
6 Then they said to Jephthah, "Come and
be our commander, that we may fight against the
people of Ammon."
7 So Jephthah said to the elders of Gilead,
[a]"Did you not hate me, and expel me from my
father's house? Why have you come to me now
when you are in distress?"
8 [a]And the elders of Gilead said to Jephthah, "That is why we have [b]turned again to you
now, that you may go with us and fight against
the people of Ammon, and be [c]our head over all
the inhabitants of Gilead."
9 So Jephthah said to the elders of Gilead,
"If you take me back home to fight against the
people of Ammon, and the LORD delivers them
to me, shall I be your head?"
10 And the elders of Gilead said to Jephthah,
[a]"The LORD will be a witness between us, if we
do not do according to your words."
11 Then Jephthah went with the elders of
Gilead, and the people made him [a]head and commander over them; and Jephthah spoke all his
words [b]before the LORD in Mizpah.
12 Now Jephthah sent messengers to the
king of the people of Ammon, saying, [a]"What do
you have against me, that you have come to fight
against me in my land?"
13 And the king of the people of Ammon answered the messengers of Jephthah, [a]"Because
Israel took away my land when they came up out
of Egypt, from [b]the Arnon as far as [c]the Jabbok,
and to the Jordan. Now therefore, restore those
lands peaceably."

KJV

14 And Jephthah sent messengers again unto
the king of the children of Ammon:
15 And said unto him, Thus saith Jephthah,
[a]Israel took not away the land of Moab, nor the
land of the children of Ammon:
16 But when Israel came up from Egypt, and
walked through the wilderness unto the Red sea,
and [a]came to Kadesh;
17 Then [a]Israel sent messengers unto the
king of Edom, saying, Let me, I pray thee, pass
through thy land: [b]but the king of Edom would
not hearken *thereto*. And in like manner they sent
unto the [c]king of Moab: but he would not *consent*:
and Israel [d]abode in Kadesh.
18 Then they [a]went along through the wilderness, and [b]compassed the land of Edom, and
the land of Moab, and came by the east side of
the land of Moab, and pitched on the other side
of Arnon, but came not within the border of Moab:
for Arnon *was* the border of Moab.
19 And [a]Israel sent messengers unto Sihon
king of the Amorites, the king of Heshbon; and
Israel said unto him, [b]Let us pass, we pray thee,
through thy land into my place.
20 [a]But Sihon trusted not Israel to pass
through his coast: but Sihon gathered all his people together, and pitched in Jahaz, and fought
against Israel.
21 And the LORD God of Israel [a]delivered Sihon and all his people into the hand of Israel, and
they [b]smote them: so Israel possessed all the land
of the Amorites, the inhabitants of that country.
22 And they possessed [a]all the coasts of the
Amorites, from Arnon even unto Jabbok, and
from the wilderness even unto Jordan.
23 So now the LORD God of Israel hath dispossessed the Amorites from before his people
Israel, and shouldest thou possess it?
24 Wilt not thou possess that which [a]Che-
mosh thy god giveth thee to possess? So whomsoever [b]the LORD our God shall drive out from
before us, them will we possess.
25 And now *art* thou any thing better than
[a]Balak the son of Zippor, king of Moab? did he
ever strive against Israel, or did he ever fight
against them,
26 While Israel dwelt in [a]Heshbon and her
towns, and in [b]Aroer and her towns, and in all
the cities that *be* along by the coasts of Arnon,
three hundred years? why therefore did ye not
recover *them* within that time?
27 Wherefore I have not sinned against thee,
but thou doest me wrong to war against me: the
LORD [a]the Judge [b]be judge this day between the
children of Israel and the children of Ammon.
28 Howbeit the king of the children of Ammon hearkened not unto the words of Jephthah
which he sent him.

Jephthah's Vow and Victory

29 Then [a]the Spirit of the LORD came upon
Jephthah, and he passed over Gilead, and Manasseh, and passed over Mizpeh of Gilead, and from
Mizpeh of Gilead he passed over *unto* the children
of Ammon.
30 And Jephthah [a]vowed a vow unto the
LORD, and said, If thou shalt without fail deliver
the children of Ammon into mine hands,
31 Then it shall be, that whatsoever cometh
forth of the doors of my house to meet me, when
I return in peace from the children of Ammon,
[a]shall surely be the LORD's, [b]and I will offer it up
for a burnt offering.
32 So Jephthah passed over unto the children
of Ammon to fight against them; and the LORD
delivered them into his hands.
33 And he smote them from Aroer, even till
thou come to [a]Minnith, *even* twenty cities, and
unto the plain of the vineyards, with a very great

15 [a]Deut. 2:9, 19
16 [a]Num. 13:26; 20:1
17 [a]Num. 20:14 [b]Num. 20:14–21 [c]Josh. 24:9 [d]Num. 20:1
18 [a]Deut. 2:9, 18, 19 [b]Num. 21:4
19 [a]Num. 21:21; Deut. 2:26–36 [b]Num. 21:22; Deut. 2:27
20 [a]Num. 21:23; Deut. 2:27
21 [a]Josh. 24:8 [b]Num. 21:24, 25
22 [a]Deut. 2:36, 37
24 [a]Num. 21:29; 1 Kin. 11:7; Jer. 48:7 [b][Deut. 9:4, 5; Josh. 3:10]
25 [a]Num. 22:2; Josh. 24:9; Mic. 6:5
26 [a]Num. 21:25, 26 [b]Deut. 2:36
27 [a]Gen. 18:25 [b]Gen. 16:5; 31:53; [1 Sam. 24:12, 15]
29 [a]Judg. 3:10
30 [a]Gen. 28:20; Num. 30:2; 1 Sam. 1:11
31 [a]Lev. 27:2, 3, 28; 1 Sam. 1:11 [b]Ps. 66:13
33 [a]Ezek. 27:17

*
11:33 Lit. *Plain of Vineyards*

NKJV

14 So Jephthah again sent messengers to the
king of the people of Ammon,
15 and said to him, "Thus says Jephthah:
[a]'Israel did not take away the land of Moab, nor
the land of the people of Ammon;
16 'for when Israel came up from Egypt, they
walked through the wilderness as far as the Red
Sea and [a]came to Kadesh.
17 'Then [a]Israel sent messengers to the king
of Edom, saying, "Please let me pass through your
land." [b]But the king of Edom would not heed. And
in like manner they sent to the [c]king of Moab,
but he would not *consent*. So Israel [d]remained
in Kadesh.
18 'And they [a]went along through the wilderness and [b]bypassed the land of Edom and the land
of Moab, came to the east side of the land of Moab,
and encamped on the other side of the Arnon.
But they did not enter the border of Moab, for
the Arnon *was* the border of Moab.
19 'Then [a]Israel sent messengers to Sihon
king of the Amorites, king of Heshbon; and Israel
said to him, "Please [b]let us pass through your land
into our place."
20 [a]'But Sihon did not trust Israel to pass
through his territory. So Sihon gathered all his
people together, encamped in Jahaz, and fought
against Israel.
21 'And the LORD God of Israel [a]delivered Sihon and all his people into the hand of Israel, and
they [b]defeated them. Thus Israel gained possession of all the land of the Amorites, who inhabited
that country.
22 'They took possession of [a]all the territory
of the Amorites, from the Arnon to the Jabbok
and from the wilderness to the Jordan.
23 'And now the LORD God of Israel has dispossessed the Amorites from before His people
Israel; should you then possess it?
24 'Will you not possess whatever [a]Chemosh
your god gives you to possess? So whatever [b]the
LORD our God takes possession of before us, we
will possess.
25 'And now, *are* you any better than [a]Balak
the son of Zippor, king of Moab? Did he ever
strive against Israel? Did he ever fight against
them?
26 'While Israel dwelt in [a]Heshbon and its
villages, in [b]Aroer and its villages, and in all the
cities along the banks of the Arnon, for three hundred years, why did you not recover *them* within
that time?
27 'Therefore I have not sinned against you,
but you wronged me by fighting against me. May
the LORD, [a]the Judge, [b]render judgment this day
between the children of Israel and the people of
Ammon.'"
28 However, the king of the people of Ammon did not heed the words which Jephthah sent
him.

Jephthah's Vow and Victory

29 Then [a]the Spirit of the LORD came upon
Jephthah, and he passed through Gilead and Manasseh, and passed through Mizpah of Gilead;
and from Mizpah of Gilead he advanced *toward*
the people of Ammon.
30 And Jephthah [a]made a vow to the LORD,
and said, "If You will indeed deliver the people
of Ammon into my hands,
31 "then it will be that whatever comes out
of the doors of my house to meet me, when I return in peace from the people of Ammon, [a]shall
surely be the LORD's, [b]and I will offer it up as a
burnt offering."
32 So Jephthah advanced toward the people
of Ammon to fight against them, and the LORD
delivered them into his hands.
33 And he defeated them from Aroer as far
as [a]Minnith—twenty cities—and to *Abel Ker-
amim, with a very great slaughter. Thus the

KJV

slaughter. Thus the children of Ammon were subdued before the children of Israel.

Jephthah's Daughter

34 And Jephthah came to [a]Mizpeh unto his
house, and, behold, [b]his daughter came out to
meet him with timbrels and with dances: and she
was his only child; beside her he had neither son
nor daughter.
35 And it came to pass, when he saw her,
that he [a]rent his clothes, and said, Alas, my
daughter! thou hast brought me very low, and
thou art one of them that trouble me: for I [b]have
opened my mouth unto the LORD, and [c]I cannot
go back.
36 And she said unto him, My father, *if* thou
hast opened thy mouth unto the LORD, [a]do to me
according to that which hath proceeded out of thy
mouth; forasmuch as [b]the LORD hath taken vengeance for thee of thine enemies, *even* of the children of Ammon.
37 And she said unto her father, Let this
thing be done for me: let me alone two months,
that I may go up and down upon the mountains,
and bewail my virginity, I and my fellows.
38 And he said, Go. And he sent her away
for two months: and she went with her companions, and bewailed her virginity upon the
mountains.
39 And it came to pass at the end of two
months, that she returned unto her father, who
[a]did with her *according* to his vow which he had
vowed: and she knew no man. And it was a custom in Israel,
40 *That* the daughters of Israel went yearly
to lament the daughter of Jephthah the Gileadite
four days in a year.

Jephthah's Conflict with Ephraim

12 And [a]the men of Ephraim gathered themselves together, and went northward, and
said unto Jephthah, Wherefore passedst thou over
to fight against the children of Ammon, and didst
not call us to go with thee? we will burn thine
house upon thee with fire.
2 And Jephthah said unto them, I and my
people were at great strife with the children of
Ammon; and when I called you, ye delivered me
not out of their hands.
3 And when I saw that ye delivered *me* not,
I [a]put my life in my hands, and passed over
against the children of Ammon, and the LORD delivered them into my hand: wherefore then are
ye come up unto me this day, to fight against me?
4 Then Jephthah gathered together all the
men of Gilead, and fought with Ephraim: and the
men of Gilead smote Ephraim, because they said,
Ye Gileadites [a]*are* fugitives of Ephraim among
the Ephraimites, *and* among the Manassites.
5 And the Gileadites took the [a]passages of
Jordan before the Ephraimites: and it was *so,* that
when those Ephraimites which were escaped said,
Let me go over; that the men of Gilead said unto
him, *Art* thou an Ephraimite? If he said, Nay;
6 Then said they unto him, Say now [a]Shibbo-
leth: and he said Sibboleth: for he could not
frame to pronounce *it* right. Then they took him,
and slew him at the passages of Jordan: and there
fell at that time of the Ephraimites forty and two
thousand.
7 And Jephthah judged Israel six years.
Then died Jephthah the Gileadite, and was buried
in *one of* the cities of Gilead.

Ibzan, Elon, and Abdon

8 And after him Ibzan of Beth–lehem judged
Israel.
9 And he had thirty sons, and thirty daughters, *whom* he sent abroad, and took in thirty
daughters from abroad for his sons. And he
judged Israel seven years.

34 [a]Judg. 10:17; 11:11 [b]Ex. 15:20; 1 Sam. 18:6; Ps. 68:25; Jer. 31:4
35 [a]Gen. 37:29, 34 [b]Eccl. 5:2, 4, 5 [c]Num. 30:2
36 [a]Num. 30:2 [b]2 Sam. 18:19, 31
39 [a]Judg. 11:31

CHAPTER 12

1 [a]Judg. 8:1
3 [a]1 Sam. 19:5; 28:21; Job 13:14
4 [a]1 Sam. 25:10
5 [a]Josh. 22:11
6 [a]Ps. 69:2, 15

NKJV

people of Ammon were subdued before the children of Israel.

Jephthah's Daughter

34 When Jephthah came to his house at
[a]Mizpah, there was [b]his daughter, coming out to
meet him with timbrels and dancing; and she *was*
his only child. Besides her he had neither son nor
daughter.
35 And it came to pass, when he saw her,
that he [a]tore his clothes, and said, "Alas, my
daughter! You have brought me very low! You
are among those who trouble me! For I [b]have
given my word to the LORD, and [c]I cannot go back
on it."
36 So she said to him, "My father, *if* you have
given your word to the LORD, [a]do to me according
to what has gone out of your mouth, because [b]the
LORD has avenged you of your enemies, the people
of Ammon."
37 Then she said to her father, "Let this thing
be done for me: let me alone for two months, that
I may go and wander on the mountains and bewail
my virginity, my friends and I."
38 So he said, "Go." And he sent her away
for two months; and she went with her friends,
and bewailed her virginity on the mountains.
39 And it was so at the end of two months
that she returned to her father, and he [a]carried
out his vow with her which he had vowed. She
knew no man. And it became a custom in Israel
40 *that* the daughters of Israel went four
days each year to lament the daughter of Jephthah the Gileadite.

Jephthah's Conflict with Ephraim

12 Then [a]the men of Ephraim gathered together, crossed over toward Zaphon, and
said to Jephthah, "Why did you cross over to fight
against the people of Ammon, and did not call
us to go with you? We will burn your house down
on you with fire!"
2 And Jephthah said to them, "My people
and I were in a great struggle with the people of
Ammon; and when I called you, you did not deliver me out of their hands.
3 "So when I saw that you would not deliver
me, I [a]took my life in my hands and crossed over
against the people of Ammon; and the LORD delivered them into my hand. Why then have you come
up to me this day to fight against me?"
4 Now Jephthah gathered together all the
men of Gilead and fought against Ephraim. And
the men of Gilead defeated Ephraim, because they
said, "You Gileadites [a]*are* fugitives of Ephraim
among the Ephraimites *and* among the Manassites."
5 The Gileadites seized the [a]fords of the Jordan before the Ephraimites *arrived.* And when
any Ephraimite who escaped said, "Let me cross
over," the men of Gilead would say to him, "*Are*
you an Ephraimite?" If he said, "No,"
6 then they would say to him, "Then say,
[a]'Shibboleth'!" And he would say, "Sibboleth,"
for he could not pronounce *it* right. Then they
would take him and kill him at the fords of the
Jordan. There fell at that time forty-two thousand
Ephraimites.
7 And Jephthah judged Israel six years.
Then Jephthah the Gileadite died and was buried
in among the cities of Gilead.

Ibzan, Elon, and Abdon

8 After him, Ibzan of Bethlehem judged
Israel.
9 He had thirty sons. And he gave away
thirty daughters in marriage, and brought in thirty
daughters from elsewhere for his sons. He judged
Israel seven years.

KJV

10 Then died Ibzan, and was buried at Bethlehem.

11 And after him Elon, a Zebulonite, judged Israel; and he judged Israel ten years.

12 And Elon the Zebulonite died, and was buried in Aijalon in the country of Zebulun.

13 And after him Abdon the son of Hillel, a Pirathonite, judged Israel.

14 And he had forty sons and thirty nephews, that [a]rode on three-score and ten ass colts: and he judged Israel eight years.

15 And Abdon the son of Hillel the Pirathonite died, and was buried in Pirathon in the land of Ephraim, [a]in the mount of the Amalekites.

The Birth of Samson
(cf. Num. 6:1–21)

13 And the children of Israel [a]did evil again in the sight of the LORD; and the LORD delivered them [b]into the hand of the Philistines forty years.

2 And there was a certain man of [a]Zorah, of the family of the Danites, whose name *was* Manoah; and his wife *was* barren, and bare not.

3 And the [a]angel of the LORD appeared unto the woman, and said unto her, Behold now, thou *art* barren, and bearest not: but thou shalt conceive, and bear a son.

4 Now therefore beware, I pray thee, and [a]drink not wine nor strong drink, and eat not any unclean *thing:*

5 For, lo, thou shalt conceive, and bear a son; and no [a]razor shall come on his head: for the child shall be [b]a Nazarite unto God from the womb: and he shall [c]begin to deliver Israel out of the hand of the Philistines.

6 Then the woman came and told her husband, saying, [a]A man of God came unto me, and his [b]countenance *was* like the countenance of an angel of God, very terrible: but I [c]asked him not whence he *was*, neither told he me his name:

7 But he said unto me, Behold, thou shalt conceive, and bear a son; and now drink no wine nor strong drink, neither eat any unclean *thing:* for the child shall be a Nazarite to God from the womb to the day of his death.

8 Then Manoah intreated the LORD, and said, O my Lord, let the man of God which thou didst send come again unto us, and teach us what we shall do unto the child that shall be born.

9 And God hearkened to the voice of Manoah; and the angel of God came again unto the woman as she sat in the field: but Manoah her husband *was* not with her.

10 And the woman made haste, and ran, and shewed her husband, and said unto him, Behold, the man hath appeared unto me, that came unto me the *other* day.

11 And Manoah arose, and went after his wife, and came to the man, and said unto him, *Art* thou the man that spakest unto the woman? And he said, I *am.*

12 And Manoah said, Now let thy words come to pass. How shall we order the child, and *how* shall we do unto him?

13 And the angel of the LORD said unto Manoah, Of all that I said unto the woman let her beware.

14 She may not eat of any *thing* that cometh of the vine, [a]neither let her drink wine or strong drink, nor eat any unclean *thing:* all that I commanded her let her observe.

15 And Manoah said unto the angel of the LORD, I pray thee, [a]let us detain thee, until we shall have made ready a kid for thee.

16 And the angel of the LORD said unto Manoah, Though thou detain me, I will not eat of thy bread: and if thou wilt offer a burnt offering, thou must offer it unto the LORD. For Manoah knew not that he *was* an angel of the LORD.

17 And Manoah said unto the angel of the

---

14 [a]Judg. 5:10; 10:4
15 [a]Judg. 3:13, 27; 5:14

CHAPTER 13

1 [a]Judg. 2:11 [b]Judg. 10:7; 1 Sam. 12:9
2 [a]Josh. 19:41; Judg. 16:31
3 [a]Judg. 6:12
4 [a]Num. 6:2, 3, 20; Judg. 13:4; Luke 1:15
5 [a]Num. 6:5; 1 Sam. 1:11 [b]Num. 6:2 [c]1 Sam. 7:13; 2 Sam. 8:1; 1 Chr. 18:1
6 [a]Gen. 32:24–30 [b]Matt. 28:3; Luke 9:29; Acts 6:15 [c]Judg. 13:17, 18
14 [a]Num. 6:3, 4; Judg. 13:4
15 [a]Gen. 18:5; Judg. 6:18

NKJV

10 Then Ibzan died and was buried at Bethlehem.

11 After him, Elon the Zebulunite judged Israel. He judged Israel ten years.

12 And Elon the Zebulunite died and was buried at Aijalon in the country of Zebulun.

13 After him, Abdon the son of Hillel the Pirathonite judged Israel.

14 He had forty sons and thirty grandsons, who [a]rode on seventy young donkeys. He judged Israel eight years.

15 Then Abdon the son of Hillel the Pirathonite died and was buried in Pirathon in the land of Ephraim, [a]in the mountains of the Amalekites.

The Birth of Samson
(cf. Num. 6:1–21)

13 Again the children of Israel [a]did evil in the sight of the LORD, and the LORD delivered them [b]into the hand of the Philistines for forty years.

2 Now there was a certain man from [a]Zorah, of the family of the Danites, whose name *was* Manoah; and his wife *was* barren and had no children.

3 And the [a]Angel of the LORD appeared to the woman and said to her, "Indeed now, you are barren and have borne no children, but you shall conceive and bear a son.

4 "Now therefore, please be careful [a]not to drink wine or *similar* drink, and not to eat anything unclean.

5 "For behold, you shall conceive and bear a son. And no [a]razor shall come upon his head, for the child shall be [b]a Nazirite to God from the womb; and he shall [c]begin to deliver Israel out of the hand of the Philistines."

6 So the woman came and told her husband, saying, [a]"A Man of God came to me, and His [b]countenance *was* like the countenance of the Angel of God, very awesome; but I [c]did not ask Him where He *was* from, and He did not tell me His name.

7 "And He said to me, 'Behold, you shall conceive and bear a son. Now drink no wine or *similar* drink, nor eat anything unclean, for the child shall be a Nazirite to God from the womb to the day of his death.' "

8 Then Manoah prayed to the LORD, and said, "O my Lord, please let the Man of God whom You sent come to us again and teach us what we shall do for the child who will be born."

9 And God listened to the voice of Manoah, and the Angel of God came to the woman again as she was sitting in the field; but Manoah her husband *was* not with her.

10 Then the woman ran in haste and told her husband, and said to him, "Look, the Man who came to me the *other* day has just now appeared to me!"

11 So Manoah arose and followed his wife. When he came to the Man, he said to Him, "Are You the Man who spoke to this woman?" And He said, "I *am.*"

12 Manoah said, "Now let Your words come *to pass!* What will be the boy's rule of life, and his work?"

13 So the Angel of the LORD said to Manoah, "Of all that I said to the woman let her be careful.

14 "She may not eat anything that comes from the vine, [a]nor may she drink wine or *similar* drink, nor eat anything unclean. All that I commanded her let her observe."

15 Then Manoah said to the Angel of the LORD, "Please [a]let us detain You, and we will prepare a young goat for You."

16 And the Angel of the LORD said to Manoah, "Though you detain Me, I will not eat your food. But if you offer a burnt offering, you must offer it to the LORD." (For Manoah did not know He *was* the Angel of the LORD.)

17 Then Manoah said to the Angel of the

KJV

LORD, What *is* thy name, that when thy sayings
come to pass we may do thee honour?
18 And the angel of the LORD said unto him,
[a]Why askest thou thus after my name, seeing it
is secret?
19 So Manoah took a kid with a meat offering, [a]and offered *it* upon a rock unto the LORD:
and *the angel* did wonderously; and Manoah and
his wife looked on.
20 For it came to pass, when the flame went
up toward heaven from off the altar, that the angel
of the LORD ascended in the flame of the altar.
And Manoah and his wife looked on *it,* and [a]fell
on their faces to the ground.
21 But the angel of the LORD did no more appear to Manoah and to his wife. [a]Then Manoah
knew that he *was* an angel of the LORD.
22 And Manoah said unto his wife, [a]We shall
surely die, because we have seen God.
23 But his wife said unto him, If the LORD
were pleased to kill us, he would not have received a burnt offering and a meat offering at our
hands, neither would he have shewed us all these
things, nor would as at this time have told us *such
things* as these.
24 And the woman bare a son, and called his
name [a]Samson: and [b]the child grew, and the LORD
blessed him.
25 [a]And the Spirit of the LORD began to move
him at times in the camp of Dan [b]between Zorah
and [c]Eshtaol.

Samson's Philistine Wife

14 And Samson went down [a]to Timnath, and
[b]saw a woman in Timnath of the daughters
of the Philistines.
2 And he came up, and told his father and
his mother, and said, I have seen a woman in Timnath of the daughters of the Philistines: now
therefore [a]get her for me to wife.
3 Then his father and his mother said unto
him, *Is there* never a woman among the daughters
of [a]thy brethren, or among all my people, that
thou goest to take a wife of the [b]uncircumcised
Philistines? And Samson said unto his father, Get
her for me; for she pleaseth me well.
4 But his father and his mother knew not
that it *was* [a]of the LORD, that he sought an occasion against the Philistines: for at that time [b]the
Philistines had dominion over Israel.
5 Then went Samson down, and his father
and his mother, to Timnath, and came to the vineyards of Timnath: and, behold, a young lion
roared against him.
6 And [a]the Spirit of the LORD came mightily
upon him, and he rent him as he would have rent
a kid, and *he had* nothing in his hand: but he told
not his father or his mother what he had done.
7 And he went down, and talked with the
woman; and she pleased Samson well.
8 And after a time he returned to take her,
and he turned aside to see the carcase of the lion:
and, behold, *there was* a swarm of bees and honey
in the carcase of the lion.
9 And he took thereof in his hands, and
went on eating, and came to his father and
mother, and gave them, and they did eat: but he
told not them that he had taken the honey out of
the [a]carcase of the lion.
10 So his father went down unto the woman:
and Samson made there a feast; for so used the
young men to do.
11 And it came to pass, when they saw him,
that they brought thirty companions to be with
him.
12 And Samson said unto them, I will now
[a]put forth a riddle unto you: if ye can certainly
declare it me [b]within the seven days of the feast,
and find *it* out, then I will give you thirty sheets
and thirty [c]change of garments:

18 [a]Gen. 32:29
19 [a]Judg. 6:19–21
20 [a]Lev. 9:24; 1 Chr. 21:16; Ezek. 1:28; Matt. 17:6
21 [a]Judg. 6:22
22 [a]Gen. 32:30; Ex. 33:20; Deut. 5:26; Judg. 6:22, 23
24 [a]Heb. 11:32 [b]1 Sam. 3:19; Luke 1:80
25 [a]Judg. 3:10; 1 Sam. 11:6; Matt. 4:1 [b]Josh. 15:33; Judg. 18:11 [c]Judg. 16:31

CHAPTER 14

1 [a]Gen. 38:13; Josh. 15:10, 57 [b]Gen. 34:2
2 [a]Gen. 21:21
3 [a]Gen. 24:3, 4 [b]Gen. 34:14; Ex. 34:16; Deut. 7:3
4 [a]Josh. 11:20; 1 Kin. 12:15; 2 Kin. 6:33; 2 Chr. 10:15 [b]Deut. 28:48; Judg. 13:1
6 [a]Judg. 3:10
9 [a]Lev. 11:27
12 [a]1 Kin. 10:1; Ezek. 17:2 [b]Gen. 29:27 [c]Gen. 45:22; 2 Kin. 5:22

*________

13:25 Lit. *Camp of Dan,* Judg. 18:12

NKJV

LORD, "What *is* Your name, that when Your words
come *to pass* we may honor You?"
18 And the Angel of the LORD said to him,
[a]"Why do you ask My name, seeing it *is* wonderful?"
19 So Manoah took the young goat with the
grain offering, [a]and offered it upon the rock to
the LORD. And He did a wondrous thing while Manoah and his wife looked on—
20 it happened as the flame went up toward
heaven from the altar—the Angel of the LORD ascended in the flame of the altar! When Manoah
and his wife saw *this,* they [a]fell on their faces to
the ground.
21 When the Angel of the LORD appeared no
more to Manoah and his wife, [a]then Manoah
knew that He *was* the Angel of the LORD.
22 And Manoah said to his wife, [a]"We shall
surely die, because we have seen God!"
23 But his wife said to him, "If the LORD had
desired to kill us, He would not have accepted a
burnt offering and a grain offering from our
hands, nor would He have shown us all these
things, nor would He have told us *such things* as
these at this time."
24 So the woman bore a son and called his
name [a]Samson; and [b]the child grew, and the LORD
blessed him.
25 [a]And the Spirit of the LORD began to move
upon him at *Mahaneh Dan [b]between Zorah and
[c]Eshtaol.

Samson's Philistine Wife

14 Now Samson went down [a]to Timnah, and
[b]saw a woman in Timnah of the daughters
of the Philistines.
2 So he went up and told his father and
mother, saying, "I have seen a woman in Timnah
of the daughters of the Philistines; now therefore,
[a]get her for me as a wife."
3 Then his father and mother said to him,
"*Is there* no woman among the daughters of [a]your
brethren, or among all my people, that you must
go and get a wife from the [b]uncircumcised Philistines?" And Samson said to his father, "Get her
for me, for she pleases me well."
4 But his father and mother did not know
that it was [a]of the LORD—that He was seeking an
occasion to move against the Philistines. For at
that time [b]the Philistines had dominion over
Israel.
5 So Samson went down to Timnah with his
father and mother, and came to the vineyards of
Timnah.
Now *to his* surprise, a young lion *came*
roaring against him.
6 And [a]the Spirit of the LORD came mightily
upon him, and he tore the lion apart as one would
have torn apart a young goat, though *he had* nothing in his hand. But he did not tell his father or
his mother what he had done.
7 Then he went down and talked with the
woman; and she pleased Samson well.
8 After some time, when he returned to get
her, he turned aside to see the carcass of the lion.
And behold, a swarm of bees and honey *were* in
the carcass of the lion.
9 He took some of it in his hands and went
along, eating. When he came to his father and
mother, he gave *some* to them, and they also ate.
But he did not tell them that he had taken the
honey out of the [a]carcass of the lion.
10 So his father went down to the woman.
And Samson gave a feast there, for young men
used to do so.
11 And it happened, when they saw him, that
they brought thirty companions to be with him.
12 Then Samson said to them, "Let me [a]pose
a riddle to you. If you can correctly solve and explain it to me [b]within the seven days of the feast,
then I will give you thirty linen garments and
thirty [c]changes of clothing.

KJV

13 But if ye cannot declare *it* me, then shall
ye give me thirty sheets and thirty change of garments. And they said unto him, [a]Put forth thy riddle, that we may hear it.
14 And he said unto them, Out of the eater
came forth meat, and out of the strong came forth
sweetness. And they could not in three days ex-
pound the riddle.
15 And it came to pass on the seventh day,
that they said unto Samson's wife, [a]Entice thy
husband, that he may declare unto us the riddle,
[b]lest we burn thee and thy father's house with
fire: have ye called us to take that we have? *is it*
not *so?*
16 And Samson's wife wept before him, and
said, [a]Thou dost but hate me, and lovest me not:
thou hast put forth a riddle unto the children of
my people, and hast not told *it* me. And he said
unto her, Behold, I have not told *it* my father nor
my mother, and shall I tell *it* thee?
17 And she wept before him the seven days,
while their feast lasted: and it came to pass on
the seventh day, that he told her, because she lay
sore upon him: and she told the riddle to the children of her people.
18 And the men of the city said unto him on
the seventh day before the sun went down, What
is sweeter than honey? And what *is* stronger than
a lion? And he said unto them, If ye had not
plowed with my heifer, ye had not found out my
riddle.
19 And [a]the Spirit of the LORD came upon
him, and he went down to Ashkelon, and slew
thirty men of them, and took their spoil, and gave
change of garments unto them which expounded
the riddle. And his anger was kindled, and he
went up to his father's house.
20 But Samson's wife [a]was *given* to his companion, whom he had used as [b]his friend.

13 [a]Ezek. 17:2
15 [a]Judg. 16:5 [b]Judg. 15:6
16 [a]Judg. 16:15
19 [a]Judg. 3:10; 13:25
20 [a]Judg. 15:2 [b]John 3:29

NKJV

13 "But if you cannot explain *it* to me, then
you shall give me thirty linen garments and thirty
changes of clothing." And they said to him,
[a]"Pose your riddle, that we may hear it."
14 So he said to them:

"Out of the eater came something to eat,
And out of the strong came something
sweet."

Now for three days they could not explain the
riddle.
15 But it came to pass on the *seventh day
that they said to Samson's wife, [a]"Entice your
husband, that he may explain the riddle to us,
[b]or else we will burn you and your father's house
with fire. Have you invited us in order to take
what is ours? *Is that* not *so?*"
16 Then Samson's wife wept on him, and
said, [a]"You only hate me! You do not love me!
You have posed a riddle to the sons of my people, but you have not explained *it* to me." And he
said to her, "Look, I have not explained *it* to my
father or my mother; so should I explain *it* to
you?"
17 Now she had wept on him the seven days
while their feast lasted. And it happened on the
seventh day that he told her, because she pressed
him so much. Then she explained the riddle to
the sons of her people.
18 So the men of the city said to him on the
seventh day before the sun went down:

"What *is* sweeter than honey?
And what *is* stronger than a lion?"

And he said to them:

"If you had not plowed with my heifer,
You would not have solved my riddle!"

19 Then [a]the Spirit of the LORD came upon
him mightily, and he went down to Ashkelon and
killed thirty of their men, took their apparel, and
gave the changes *of clothing* to those who had
explained the riddle. So his anger was aroused,
and he went back up to his father's house.
20 And Samson's wife [a]was *given* to his companion, who had been [b]his best man.

KJV

Samson Defeats the Philistines

15 But it came to pass within a while after, in
the time of wheat harvest, that Samson visited his wife with a [a]kid; and he said, I will go in
to my wife into the chamber. But her father would
not suffer him to go in.
2 And her father said, I verily thought that
thou hadst utterly [a]hated her; therefore I gave her
to thy companion: *is* not her younger sister fairer
than she? take her, I pray thee, instead of her.
3 And Samson said concerning them, Now
shall I be more blameless than the Philistines,
though I do them a displeasure.
4 And Samson went and caught three hundred foxes, and took firebrands, and turned tail
to tail, and put a firebrand in the midst between
two tails.
5 And when he had set the brands on fire,
he let *them* go into the standing corn of the Philistines, and burnt up both the shocks, and also the
standing corn, with the vineyards *and* olives.
6 Then the Philistines said, Who hath done
this? And they answered, Samson, the son in law
of the Timnite, because he had taken his wife,
and given her to his companion. [a]And the Philistines came up, and burnt her and her father with
fire.
7 And Samson said unto them, Though ye
have done this, yet will I be avenged of you, and
after that I will cease.
8 And he smote them hip and thigh with a

CHAPTER 15

1 [a]Gen. 38:17
2 [a]Judg. 14:20
6 [a]Judg. 14:15

*14:15 So with MT, Tg., Vg.; LXX, Syr. *fourth*

NKJV

Samson Defeats the Philistines

15 After a while, in the time of wheat harvest,
it happened that Samson visited his wife
with a [a]young goat. And he said, "Let me go in
to my wife, into *her* room." But her father would
not permit him to go in.
2 Her father said, "I really thought that you
thoroughly [a]hated her; therefore I gave her to
your companion. *Is* not her younger sister better
than she? Please, take her instead."
3 And Samson said to them, "This time I
shall be blameless regarding the Philistines if I
harm them!"
4 Then Samson went and caught three hundred foxes; and he took torches, turned *the foxes*
tail to tail, and put a torch between each pair of
tails.
5 When he had set the torches on fire, he
let *the foxes* go into the standing grain of the Philistines, and burned up both the shocks and the
standing grain, as well as the vineyards *and* olive
groves.
6 Then the Philistines said, "Who has done
this?" And they answered, "Samson, the son-in-
law of the Timnite, because he has taken his wife
and given her to his companion." [a]So the Philistines came up and burned her and her father with
fire.
7 Samson said to them, "Since you would
do a thing like this, I will surely take revenge on
you, and after that I will cease."
8 So he attacked them hip and thigh with

KJV

great slaughter: and he went down and dwelt in the top of the rock [a]Etam.

9 Then the Philistines went up, and pitched in Judah, and spread themselves [a]in Lehi.

10 And the men of Judah said, Why are ye come up against us? And they answered, To bind Samson are we come up, to do to him as he hath done to us.

11 Then three thousand men of Judah went to the top of the rock Etam, and said to Samson, Knowest thou not that the Philistines *are* [a]rulers over us? what *is* this *that* thou hast done unto us? And he said unto them, As they did unto me, so have I done unto them.

12 And they said unto him, We are come down to bind thee, that we may deliver thee into the hand of the Philistines. And Samson said unto them, Swear unto me, that ye will not fall upon me yourselves.

13 And they spake unto him, saying, No; but we will bind thee fast, and deliver thee into their hand: but surely we will not kill thee. And they bound him with two [a]new cords, and brought him up from the rock.

14 *And* when he came unto Lehi, the Philistines shouted against him: and [a]the Spirit of the LORD came mightily upon him, and the cords that *were* upon his arms became as flax that was burnt with fire, and his bands loosed from off his hands.

15 And he found a new jawbone of an ass, and put forth his hand, and took it, and [a]slew a thousand men therewith.

16 And Samson said, With the jawbone of an ass, heaps upon heaps, with the jaw of an ass have I slain a thousand men.

17 And it came to pass, when he had made an end of speaking, that he cast away the jawbone out of his hand, and called that place Ramath–lehi.

18 And he was sore athirst, and called on the LORD, and said, [a]Thou hast given this great deliverance into the hand of thy servant: and now shall I die for thirst, and fall into the hand of the uncircumcised?

19 But God clave an hollow place that *was* in the jaw, and there came water thereout; and when he had drunk, [a]his spirit came again, and he revived: wherefore he called the name thereof En–hakkore, which *is* in Lehi unto this day.

20 And [a]he judged Israel [c]in the days of the Philistines [b]twenty years.

Samson and Delilah

16 Then went Samson to [a]Gaza, and saw there an harlot, and went in unto her.

2 *And it was told* the Gazites, saying, Samson is come hither. And they [a]compassed *him* in, and laid wait for him all night in the gate of the city, and were quiet all the night, saying, In the morning, when it is day, we shall kill him.

3 And Samson lay till midnight, and arose at midnight, and took the doors of the gate of the city, and the two posts, and went away with them, bar and all, and put *them* upon his shoulders, and carried them up to the top of an hill that *is* before Hebron.

4 And it came to pass afterward, that he loved a woman in the valley of Sorek, whose name *was* Delilah.

5 And the [a]lords of the Philistines came up unto her, and said unto her, [b]Entice him, and see wherein his great strength *lieth*, and by what *means* we may prevail against him, that we may bind him to afflict him: and we will give thee every one of us eleven hundred *pieces* of silver.

6 And Delilah said to Samson, Tell me, I pray thee, wherein thy great strength *lieth*, and wherewith thou mightest be bound to afflict thee.

8 [a]2 Chr. 11:6
9 [a]Judg. 15:19
11 [a]Lev. 26:25; Deut. 28:43; Judg. 13:1; 14:4; Ps. 106:40–42
13 [a]Judg. 16:11, 12
14 [a]Judg. 3:10; 14:6
15 [a]Lev. 26:8; Josh. 23:10; Judg. 3:31
18 [a]Ps. 3:7
19 [a]Gen. 45:27; Is. 40:29
20 [a]Judg. 10:2; 12:7–14
[b]Judg. 16:31
[c]Judg. 13:1

CHAPTER 16
1 [a]Josh. 15:47
2 [a]1 Sam. 23:26; Ps. 118:10–12
5 [a]Josh. 13:3
[b]Judg. 14:15

* 15:17 Lit. *Jawbone Height*
15:19 Lit. *Jawbone*, Judg. 15:14
• Lit. *Spring of the Caller*

NKJV

a great slaughter; then he went down and dwelt in the cleft of the rock of [a]Etam.

9 Now the Philistines went up, encamped in Judah, and deployed themselves [a]against Lehi.

10 And the men of Judah said, "Why have you come up against us?" So they answered, "We have come up to arrest Samson, to do to him as he has done to us."

11 Then three thousand men of Judah went down to the cleft of the rock of Etam, and said to Samson, "Do you not know that the Philistines [a]rule over us? What *is* this you have done to us?" And he said to them, "As they did to me, so I have done to them."

12 But they said to him, "We have come down to arrest you, that we may deliver you into the hand of the Philistines." Then Samson said to them, "Swear to me that you will not kill me yourselves."

13 So they spoke to him, saying, "No, but we will tie you securely and deliver you into their hand; but we will surely not kill you." And they bound him with two [a]new ropes and brought him up from the rock.

14 When he came to Lehi, the Philistines came shouting against him. Then [a]the Spirit of the LORD came mightily upon him; and the ropes that *were* on his arms became like flax that is burned with fire, and his bonds broke loose from his hands.

15 He found a fresh jawbone of a donkey, reached out his hand and took it, and [a]killed a thousand men with it.

16 Then Samson said:

"With the jawbone of a donkey,
Heaps upon heaps,
With the jawbone of a donkey
I have slain a thousand men!"

17 And so it was, when he had finished speaking, that he threw the jawbone from his hand, and called that place *Ramath Lehi.

18 Then he became very thirsty; so he cried out to the LORD and said, [a]"You have given this great deliverance by the hand of Your servant; and now shall I die of thirst and fall into the hand of the uncircumcised?"

19 So God split the hollow place that *is* in *Lehi, and water came out, and he drank; and [a]his spirit returned, and he revived. Therefore he called its name *En Hakkore, which is in Lehi to this day.

20 And [a]he judged Israel [b]twenty years [c]in the days of the Philistines.

Samson and Delilah

16 Now Samson went to [a]Gaza and saw a harlot there, and went in to her.

2 *When* the Gazites *were told*, "Samson has come here!" they [a]surrounded *the place* and lay in wait for him all night at the gate of the city. They were quiet all night, saying, "In the morning, when it is daylight, we will kill him."

3 And Samson lay *low* till midnight; then he arose at midnight, took hold of the doors of the gate of the city and the two gateposts, pulled them up, bar and all, put *them* on his shoulders, and carried them to the top of the hill that faces Hebron.

4 Afterward it happened that he loved a woman in the Valley of Sorek, whose name *was* Delilah.

5 And the [a]lords of the Philistines came up to her and said to her, [b]"Entice him, and find out where his great strength *lies*, and by what *means* we may overpower him, that we may bind him to afflict him; and every one of us will give you eleven hundred *pieces* of silver."

6 So Delilah said to Samson, "Please tell me where your great strength *lies*, and with what you may be bound to afflict you."

KJV

7 And Samson said unto her, If they bind me with seven green withs that were never dried, then shall I be weak, and be as another man.

8 Then the lords of the Philistines brought up to her seven green withs which had not been dried, and she bound him with them.

9 Now *there were* men lying in wait, abiding with her in the chamber. And she said unto him, The Philistines *be* upon thee, Samson. And he brake the withs, as a thread of tow is broken when it toucheth the fire. So his strength was not known.

10 And Delilah said unto Samson, Behold, thou hast mocked me, and told me lies: now tell me, I pray thee, wherewith thou mightest be bound.

11 And he said unto her, If they bind me fast with [a]new ropes that never were occupied, then shall I be weak, and be as another man.

12 Delilah therefore took new ropes, and bound him therewith, and said unto him, The Philistines *be* upon thee, Samson. And *there were* liers in wait abiding in the chamber. And he brake them from off his arms like a thread.

13 And Delilah said unto Samson, Hitherto thou hast mocked me, and told me lies: tell me wherewith thou mightest be bound. And he said unto her, If thou weavest the seven locks of my head with the web.

14 And she fastened *it* with the pin, and said unto him, The Philistines *be* upon thee, Samson. And he awaked out of his sleep, and went away with the pin of the beam, and with the web.

15 And she said unto him, [a]How canst thou say, I love thee, when thine heart *is* not with me? thou hast mocked me these three times, and hast not told me wherein thy great strength *lieth*.

16 And it came to pass, when she pressed him daily with her words, and urged him, *so* that his soul was vexed unto death;

17 That he [a]told her all his heart, and said unto her, [b]There hath not come a razor upon mine head; for I *have been* a Nazarite unto God from my mother's womb: if I be shaven, then my strength will go from me, and I shall become weak, and be like any *other* man.

18 And when Delilah saw that he had told her all his heart, she sent and called for the lords of the Philistines, saying, Come up this once, for he hath shewed me all his heart. Then the lords of the Philistines came up unto her, and brought money in their hand.

19 [a]And she made him sleep upon her knees; and she called for a man, and she caused him to shave off the seven locks of his head; and she began to afflict him, and his strength went from him.

20 And she said, The Philistines *be* upon thee, Samson. And he awoke out of his sleep, and said, I will go out as at other times before, and shake myself. And he wist not that the LORD [a]was departed from him.

21 But the Philistines took him, and put out his [a]eyes, and brought him down to Gaza, and bound him with fetters of brass; and he did grind in the prison house.

22 Howbeit the hair of his head began to grow again after he was shaven.

Samson Dies with the Philistines

23 Then the lords of the Philistines gathered them together for to offer a great sacrifice unto [a]Dagon their god, and to rejoice: for they said, Our god hath delivered Samson our enemy into our hand.

24 And when the people saw him, they [a]praised their god: for they said, Our god hath

NKJV

7 And Samson said to her, "If they bind me with seven fresh bowstrings, not yet dried, then I shall become weak, and be like any *other* man."

8 So the lords of the Philistines brought up to her seven fresh bowstrings, not yet dried, and she bound him with them.

9 Now *men were* lying in wait, staying with her in the room. And she said to him, "The Philistines *are* upon you, Samson!" But he broke the bowstrings as a strand of yarn breaks when it touches fire. So the secret of his strength was not known.

10 Then Delilah said to Samson, "Look, you have mocked me and told me lies. Now, please tell me what you may be bound with."

11 So he said to her, "If they bind me securely with [a]new ropes that have never been used, then I shall become weak, and be like any *other* man."

12 Therefore Delilah took new ropes and bound him with them, and said to him, "The Philistines *are* upon you, Samson!" And *men were* lying in wait, staying in the room. But he broke them off his arms like a thread.

13 Delilah said to Samson, "Until now you have mocked me and told me lies. Tell me what you may be bound with." And he said to her, "If you weave the seven locks of my head into the web of the loom"—

14 So she wove *it* tightly with the batten of the loom, and said to him, "The Philistines *are* upon you, Samson!" But he awoke from his sleep, and pulled out the batten and the web from the loom.

15 Then she said to him, [a]"How can you say, 'I love you,' when your heart *is* not with me? You have mocked me these three times, and have not told me where your great strength *lies*."

16 And it came to pass, when she pestered him daily with her words and pressed him, *so* that his soul was vexed to death,

17 that he [a]told her all his heart, and said to her, [b]"No razor has ever come upon my head, for I *have been* a Nazirite to God from my mother's womb. If I am shaven, then my strength will leave me, and I shall become weak, and be like any *other* man."

18 When Delilah saw that he had told her all his heart, she sent and called for the lords of the Philistines, saying, "Come up once more, for he has told me all his heart." So the lords of the Philistines came up to her and brought the money in their hand.

19 [a]Then she lulled him to sleep on her knees, and called for a man and had him shave off the seven locks of his head. Then *she began to torment him, and his strength left him.

20 And she said, "The Philistines *are* upon you, Samson!" So he awoke from his sleep, and said, "I will go out as before, at other times, and shake myself free!" But he did not know that the LORD [a]had departed from him.

21 Then the Philistines took him and put out his [a]eyes, and brought him down to Gaza. They bound him with bronze fetters, and he became a grinder in the prison.

22 However, the hair of his head began to grow again after it had been shaven.

Samson Dies with the Philistines

23 Now the lords of the Philistines gathered together to offer a great sacrifice to [a]Dagon their god, and to rejoice. And they said:

"Our god has delivered into our hands
Samson our enemy!"

24 When the people saw him, they [a]praised their god; for they said:

"Our god has delivered into our hands our
enemy,

---

11 [a]Judg. 15:13
15 [a]Judg. 14:16
17 [a][Mic. 7:5] [b]Num. 6:5; Judg. 13:5
19 [a]Prov. 7:26, 27
20 [a]Num. 14:9, 42, 43; [Josh. 7:12]; 1 Sam. 16:14; 18:12; 28:15, 16; 2 Chr. 15:2
21 [a]2 Kin. 25:7
23 [a]1 Sam. 5:2
24 [a]Dan. 5:4

*______

16:19 So with MT, Tg., Vg.; LXX *he began to be weak,*

KJV

delivered into our hands our enemy, and the destroyer of our country, which slew many of us.

25 And it came to pass, when their hearts were [a]merry, that they said, Call for Samson, that he may make us sport. And they called for Samson out of the prison house; and he made them sport: and they set him between the pillars.

26 And Samson said unto the lad that held him by the hand, Suffer me that I may feel the pillars whereupon the house standeth, that I may lean upon them.

27 Now the house was full of men and women; and all the lords of the Philistines *were* there; and *there were* upon the [a]roof about three thousand men and women, that beheld while Samson made sport.

28 And Samson called unto the LORD, and said, O Lord GOD, [a]remember me, I pray thee, and strengthen me, I pray thee, only this once, O God, that I may be at once avenged of the Philistines for my two eyes.

29 And Samson took hold of the two middle pillars upon which the house stood, and on which it was borne up, of the one with his right hand, and of the other with his left.

30 And Samson said, Let me die with the Philistines. And he bowed himself with *all his* might; and the house fell upon the lords, and upon all the people that *were* therein. So the dead which he slew at his death were more than *they* which he slew in his life.

31 Then his brethren and all the house of his father came down, and took him, and brought *him* up, and [a]buried him between Zorah and Eshtaol in the buryingplace of Manoah his father. And he judged Israel [b]twenty years.

Micah's Idolatry

17 And there was a man of mount Ephraim, whose name *was* [a]Micah.

2 And he said unto his mother, The eleven hundred *shekels* of silver that were taken from thee, about which thou [a]cursedst, and spakest of also in mine ears, behold, the silver *is* with me; I took it. And his mother said, [b]Blessed *be thou* of the LORD, my son.

3 And when he had restored the eleven hundred *shekels* of silver to his mother, his mother said, I had wholly dedicated the silver unto the LORD from my hand for my son, to [a]make a graven image and a molten image: now therefore I will restore it unto thee.

4 Yet he restored the money unto his mother; and his mother [a]took two hundred *shekels* of silver, and gave them to the founder, who made thereof a graven image and a molten image: and they were in the house of Micah.

5 And the man Micah had an [a]house of gods, and made an [b]ephod, and [c]teraphim, and consecrated one of his sons, who became his priest.

6 [a]In those days *there was* no king in Israel, [b]*but* every man did *that which was* right in his own eyes.

7 And there was a young man out of [a]Bethlehem–judah of the family of Judah, who *was* a Levite, and he [b]sojourned there.

8 And the man departed out of the city from Beth–lehem–judah to sojourn where he could find *a place*: and he came to mount Ephraim to the house of Micah, as he journeyed.

9 And Micah said unto him, Whence comest thou? And he said unto him, I *am* a Levite of Beth–lehem–judah, and I go to sojourn where I may find *a place*.

10 And Micah said unto him, Dwell with me, [a]and be unto me a [b]father and a priest, and I will give thee ten *shekels* of silver by the year, and a suit of apparel, and thy victuals. So the Levite went in.

11 And the Levite was content to dwell with

25 [a]Judg. 9:27
27 [a]Deut. 22:8
28 [a]Jer. 15:15
31 [a]Judg. 13:25 [b]Judg. 15:20

CHAPTER 17

1 [a]Judg. 18:2
2 [a]Lev. 5:1 [b]Gen. 14:19
3 [a]Ex. 20:4, 23; 34:17; Lev. 19:4
4 [a]Is. 46:6
5 [a]Judg. 18:24 [b]Judg. 8:27; 18:14 [c]Gen. 31:19, 30; Hos. 3:4
6 [a]Judg. 18:1; 19:1 [b]Deut. 12:8; Judg. 21:25
7 [a]Josh. 19:15; Judg. 19:1; Ruth 1:1, 2; Mic. 5:2; Matt. 2:1, 5, 6 [b]Deut. 18:6
10 [a]Judg. 18:19 [b]Gen. 45:8; Job 29:16

*———
17:5 Heb. *teraphim*

NKJV

The destroyer of our land,
And the one who multiplied our dead."

25 So it happened, when their hearts were [a]merry, that they said, "Call for Samson, that he may perform for us." So they called for Samson from the prison, and he performed for them. And they stationed him between the pillars.

26 Then Samson said to the lad who held him by the hand, "Let me feel the pillars which support the temple, so that I can lean on them."

27 Now the temple was full of men and women. All the lords of the Philistines *were* there—about three thousand men and women on the [a]roof watching while Samson performed.

28 Then Samson called to the LORD, saying, "O Lord GOD, [a]remember me, I pray! Strengthen me, I pray, just this once, O God, that I may with one *blow* take vengeance on the Philistines for my two eyes!"

29 And Samson took hold of the two middle pillars which supported the temple, and he braced himself against them, one on his right and the other on his left.

30 Then Samson said, "Let me die with the Philistines!" And he pushed with *all his* might, and the temple fell on the lords and all the people who *were* in it. So the dead that he killed at his death were more than he had killed in his life.

31 And his brothers and all his father's household came down and took him, and brought *him* up and [a]buried him between Zorah and Eshtaol in the tomb of his father Manoah. He had judged Israel [b]twenty years.

Micah's Idolatry

17 Now there was a man from the mountains of Ephraim, whose name *was* [a]Micah.

2 And he said to his mother, "The eleven hundred *shekels* of silver that were taken from you, and on which you [a]put a curse, even saying it in my ears—here *is* the silver with me; I took it." And his mother said, [b]"*May you be* blessed by the LORD, my son!"

3 So when he had returned the eleven hundred *shekels* of silver to his mother, his mother said, "I had wholly dedicated the silver from my hand to the LORD for my son, to [a]make a carved image and a molded image; now therefore, I will return it to you."

4 Thus he returned the silver to his mother. Then his mother [a]took two hundred *shekels* of silver and gave them to the silversmith, and he made it into a carved image and a molded image; and they were in the house of Micah.

5 The man Micah had a [a]shrine, and made an [b]ephod and [c]household* idols; and he consecrated one of his sons, who became his priest.

6 [a]In those days *there was* no king in Israel; [b]everyone did *what was* right in his own eyes.

7 Now there was a young man from [a]Bethlehem in Judah, of the family of Judah; he *was* a Levite, and [b]was staying there.

8 The man departed from the city of Bethlehem in Judah to stay wherever he could find *a place*. Then he came to the mountains of Ephraim, to the house of Micah, as he journeyed.

9 And Micah said to him, "Where do you come from?" So he said to him, "I *am* a Levite from Bethlehem in Judah, and I am on my way to find *a place* to stay."

10 Micah said to him, "Dwell with me, [a]and be a [b]father and a priest to me, and I will give you ten *shekels* of silver per year, a suit of clothes, and your sustenance." So the Levite went in.

11 Then the Levite was content to dwell with

KJV

the man; and the young man was unto him as
one of his sons.
12 And Micah [a]consecrated the Levite; and
the young man [b]became his priest, and was in
the house of Micah.
13 Then said Micah, Now know I that the
LORD will do me good, seeing I have a Levite to
my [a]priest.

The Danites Adopt Micah's Idolatry

18 In [a]those days *there was* no king in Israel:
and in those days [b]the tribe of the Danites
sought them an inheritance to dwell in; for unto
that day *all their* inheritance had not fallen unto
them among the tribes of Israel.
2 And the children of Dan sent of their family five men from their coasts, men of valour, from
[a]Zorah, and from Eshtaol, [b]to spy out the land,
and to search it; and they said unto them, Go,
search the land: who when they came to mount
Ephraim, to the [c]house of Micah, they lodged
there.
3 When they *were* by the house of Micah,
they knew the voice of the young man the Levite:
and they turned in thither, and said unto him,
Who brought thee hither? and what makest thou
in this *place?* and what hast thou here?
4 And he said unto them, Thus and thus
dealeth Micah with me, and hath [a]hired me, and
I am his priest.
5 And they said unto him, [a]Ask counsel, we
pray thee, [b]of God, that we may know whether
our way which we go shall be prosperous.
6 And the priest said unto them, [a]Go in
peace: before the LORD *is* your way wherein ye
go.
7 Then the five men departed, and came to
[a]Laish, and saw the people that *were* therein,
[b]how they dwelt careless, after the manner of the
Zidonians, quiet and secure; and *there was* no
magistrate in the land, that might put *them* to
shame in *any* thing; and they *were* far from the
[c]Zidonians, and had no business with *any* man.
8 And they came unto their brethren to [a]Zo-
rah and Eshtaol: and their brethren said unto
them, What *say* ye?
9 And they said, [a]Arise, that we may go up
against them: for we have seen the land, and, behold, it *is* very good: and *are* ye [b]still? be not slothful to go, *and* to enter to possess the land.
10 When ye go, ye shall come unto a people
[a]secure, and to a large land: for God hath given
it into your hands; [b]a place where *there is* no want
of any thing that *is* in the earth.
11 And there went from thence of the family
of the Danites, out of Zorah and out of Eshtaol,
six hundred men appointed with weapons of war.
12 And they went up, and pitched in [a]Kir-
jath–jearim, in Judah: wherefore they called that
place [b]Mahaneh–dan unto this day: behold, *it is*
behind Kirjath–jearim.
13 And they passed thence unto mount
Ephraim, and came unto [a]the house of Micah.
14 [a]Then answered the five men that went
to spy out the country of Laish, and said unto
their brethren, Do ye know that [b]there is in these
houses an ephod, and teraphim, and a graven image, and a molten image? now therefore consider
what ye have to do.
15 And they turned thitherward, and came
to the house of the young man the Levite, *even*
unto the house of Micah, and saluted him.
16 And the [a]six hundred men appointed with
their weapons of war, which *were* of the children
of Dan, stood by the entering of the gate.
17 And [a]the five men that went to spy out
the land went up, *and* came in thither, *and* took
[b]the graven image, and the ephod, and the teraphim, and the molten image: and the priest stood
in the entering of the gate with the six hundred
men *that were* appointed with weapons of war.
18 And these went into Micah's house, and

12 [a]Judg. 17:5 [b]Judg. 18:30
13 [a]Judg. 18:4

CHAPTER 18

1 [a]Judg. 17:6; 19:1; 21:25 [b]Josh. 19:40–48
2 [a]Judg. 13:25 [b]Num. 13:17; Josh. 2:1 [c]Judg. 17:1
4 [a]Judg. 17:10, 12
5 [a]1 Kin. 22:5; [Is. 30:1]; Hos. 4:12 [b]Judg. 1:1; 17:5; 18:14
6 [a]1 Kin. 22:6
7 [a]Josh. 19:47 [b]Judg. 18:27–29 [c]Judg. 10:12
8 [a]Judg. 18:2
9 [a]Num. 13:30; Josh. 2:23, 24 [b]1 Kin. 22:3
10 [a]Judg. 18:7, 27 [b]Deut. 8:9
12 [a]Josh. 15:60 [b]Judg. 13:25
13 [a]Judg. 18:2
14 [a]1 Sam. 14:28 [b]Judg. 17:5
16 [a]Judg. 18:11
17 [a]Judg. 18:2, 14 [b]Judg. 17:4, 5

*

18:7 So with MT, Tg., Vg.; LXX *with* Syria
18:12 Lit. *Camp of Dan*

NKJV

the man; and the young man became like one of
his sons to him.
12 So Micah [a]consecrated the Levite, and the
young man [b]became his priest, and lived in the
house of Micah.
13 Then Micah said, "Now I know that the
LORD will be good to me, since I have a Levite as
[a]priest!"

The Danites Adopt Micah's Idolatry

18 In [a]those days *there was* no king in Israel.
And in those days [b]the tribe of the Danites
was seeking an inheritance for itself to dwell in;
for until that day *their* inheritance among the
tribes of Israel had not fallen to them.
2 So the children of Dan sent five men of
their family from their territory, men of valor from
[a]Zorah and Eshtaol, [b]to spy out the land and
search it. They said to them, "Go, search the
land." So they went to the mountains of Ephraim,
to the [c]house of Micah, and lodged there.
3 While they *were* at the house of Micah,
they recognized the voice of the young Levite.
They turned aside and said to him, "Who brought
you here? What are you doing in this *place?* What
do you have here?"
4 He said to them, "Thus and so Micah did
for me. He has [a]hired me, and I have become his
priest."
5 So they said to him, "Please [a]inquire [b]of
God, that we may know whether the journey on
which we go will be prosperous."
6 And the priest said to them, [a]"Go in peace.
The presence of the LORD *be* with you on your
way."
7 So the five men departed and went to
[a]Laish. They saw the people who *were* there,
[b]how they dwelt safely, in the manner of the Sidonians, quiet and secure. *There were* no rulers
in the land who might put *them* to shame for anything. They *were* far from the [c]Sidonians, and
they had no ties *with anyone.
8 Then *the spies* came back to their brethren at [a]Zorah and Eshtaol, and their brethren said
to them, "What *is* your *report?*"
9 So they said, [a]"Arise, let us go up against
them. For we have seen the land, and indeed it
is very good. *Would* you [b]*do* nothing? Do not hesitate to go, *and* enter to possess the land.
10 "When you go, you will come to a [a]secure
people and a large land. For God has given it into
your hands, [b]a place where *there is* no lack of
anything that *is* on the earth."
11 And six hundred men of the family of the
Danites went from there, from Zorah and Eshtaol,
armed with weapons of war.
12 Then they went up and encamped in [a]Kir-
jath Jearim in Judah. (Therefore they call that
place [b]Mahaneh Dan* to this day. There *it is,* west
of Kirjath Jearim.)
13 And they passed from there to the mountains of Ephraim, and came to [a]the house of
Micah.
14 [a]Then the five men who had gone to spy
out the country of Laish answered and said to
their brethren, "Do you know that [b]there are in
these houses an ephod, household idols, a carved
image, and a molded image? Now therefore, consider what you should do."
15 So they turned aside there, and came to
the house of the young Levite man—to the house
of Micah—and greeted him.
16 The [a]six hundred men armed with their
weapons of war, who *were* of the children of Dan,
stood by the entrance of the gate.
17 Then [a]the five men who had gone to spy
out the land went up. Entering there, they took
[b]the carved image, the ephod, the household idols,
and the molded image. The priest stood at the entrance of the gate with the six hundred men *who
were* armed with weapons of war.
18 When these went into Micah's house and

KJV

fetched the carved image, the ephod, and the teraphim, and the molten image. Then said the priest unto them, What do ye?

19 And they said unto him, Hold thy peace, [a]lay thine hand upon thy mouth, and go with us, [b]and be to us a father and a priest: *is it* better for thee to be a priest unto the house of one man, or that thou be a priest unto a tribe and a family in Israel?

20 And the priest's heart was glad, and he took the ephod, and the teraphim, and the graven image, and went in the midst of the people.

21 So they turned and departed, and put the little ones and the cattle and the carriage before them.

22 *And* when they were a good way from the house of Micah, the men that *were* in the houses near to Micah's house were gathered together, and overtook the children of Dan.

23 And they cried unto the children of Dan. And they turned their faces, and said unto Micah, [a]What aileth thee, that thou comest with such a company?

24 And he said, Ye have [a]taken away my gods which I made, and the priest, and ye are gone away: and what have I more? and what *is* this *that* ye say unto me, What aileth thee?

25 And the children of Dan said unto him, Let not thy voice be heard among us, lest angry fellows run upon thee, and thou lose thy life, with the lives of thy household.

26 And the children of Dan went their way: and when Micah saw that they *were* too strong for him, he turned and went back unto his house.

Danites Settle in Laish

27 And they took *the things* which Micah had made, and the priest which he had, and came unto Laish, unto a people *that were* at quiet and secure: [a]and they smote them with the edge of the sword, and burnt the city with fire.

28 And *there was* no deliverer, because it *was* [a]far from Zidon, and they had no business with *any* man; and it was in the valley that *lieth* [b]by Beth–rehob. And they built a city, and dwelt therein.

29 And [a]they called the name of the city [b]Dan, after the name of Dan their father, who was born unto Israel: howbeit the name of the city *was* Laish at the first.

30 And the children of Dan set up the graven image: and Jonathan, the son of Gershom, the son of Manasseh, he and his sons were priests to the tribe of Dan [a]until the day of the captivity of the land.

31 And they set them up Micah's graven image, which he made, [a]all the time that the house of God was in Shiloh.

The Levite's Concubine

19 And it came to pass in those days, [a]when *there was* no king in Israel, that there was a certain Levite sojourning on the side of mount Ephraim, who took to him a concubine out of [b]Beth–lehem–judah.

2 And his concubine played the whore against him, and went away from him unto her father's house to Beth–lehem–judah, and was there four whole months.

3 And her husband arose, and went after her, to [a]speak friendly unto her, *and* to bring her again, having his servant with him, and a couple of asses: and she brought him into her father's house: and when the father of the damsel saw him, he rejoiced to meet him.

4 And his father in law, the damsel's father, retained him; and he abode with him three days: so they did eat and drink, and lodged there.

5 And it came to pass on the fourth day, when they arose early in the morning, that he rose up to depart: and the damsel's father said unto

NKJV

took the carved image, the ephod, the household idols, and the molded image, the priest said to them, "What are you doing?"

19 And they said to him, "Be quiet, [a]put your hand over your mouth, and come with us; [b]be a father and a priest to us. *Is it* better for you to be a priest to the household of one man, or that you be a priest to a tribe and a family in Israel?"

20 So the priest's heart was glad; and he took the ephod, the household idols, and the carved image, and took his place among the people.

21 Then they turned and departed, and put the little ones, the livestock, and the goods in front of them.

22 When they were a good way from the house of Micah, the men who *were* in the houses near Micah's house gathered together and overtook the children of Dan.

23 And they called out to the children of Dan. So they turned around and said to Micah, [a]"What ails you, that you have gathered such a company?"

24 So he said, "You have [a]taken away my gods which I made, and the priest, and you have gone away. Now what more do I have? How can you say to me, 'What ails you?' "

25 And the children of Dan said to him, "Do not let your voice be heard among us, lest angry men fall upon you, and you lose your life, with the lives of your household!"

26 Then the children of Dan went their way. And when Micah saw that they *were* too strong for him, he turned and went back to his house.

Danites Settle in Laish

27 So they took *the things* Micah had made, and the priest who had belonged to him, and went to Laish, to a people quiet and secure; [a]and they struck them with the edge of the sword and burned the city with fire.

28 *There was* no deliverer, because it *was* [a]far from Sidon, and they had no ties with anyone. It was in the valley that belongs [b]to Beth Rehob. So they rebuilt the city and dwelt there.

29 And [a]they called the name of the city [b]Dan, after the name of Dan their father, who was born to Israel. However, the name of the city formerly *was* Laish.

30 Then the children of Dan set up for themselves the carved image; and Jonathan the son of Gershom, the son of *Manasseh, and his sons were priests to the tribe of Dan [a]until the day of the captivity of the land.

31 So they set up for themselves Micah's carved image which he made, [a]all the time that the house of God was in Shiloh.

The Levite's Concubine

19 And it came to pass in those days, [a]when *there was* no king in Israel, that there was a certain Levite staying in the remote mountains of Ephraim. He took for himself a concubine from [b]Bethlehem in Judah.

2 But his concubine played the harlot against him, and went away from him to her father's house at Bethlehem in Judah, and was there four whole months.

3 Then her husband arose and went after her, to [a]speak kindly to her *and* bring her back, having his servant and a couple of donkeys with him. So she brought him into her father's house; and when the father of the young woman saw him, he was glad to meet him.

4 Now his father-in-law, the young woman's father, detained him; and he stayed with him three days. So they ate and drank and lodged there.

5 Then it came to pass on the fourth day that they arose early in the morning, and he stood to depart; but the young woman's father said to

---

19 [a]Job 21:5; 29:9; 40:4; Mic. 7:16 [b]Judg. 17:10 **23** [a]2 Kin. 6:28 **24** [a]Gen. 31:30; Judg. 17:5 **27** [a]Josh. 19:47 **28** [a]Judg. 18:7 [b]Num. 13:21; 2 Sam. 10:6 **29** [a]Josh. 19:47 [b]Judg. 20:1; 1 Kin. 12:29, 30; 15:20 **30** [a]2 Kin. 15:29 **31** [a]Deut. 12:1–32; Josh. 18:1, 8; Judg. 19:18; 21:12

CHAPTER 19

1 [a]Judg. 17:6; 18:1; 21:25 [b]Judg. 17:7; Ruth 1:1 **3** [a]Gen. 34:3; 50:21

*

18:30 LXX, Vg. *Moses*

KJV

his son in law, [a]Comfort thine heart with a morsel
of bread, and afterward go your way.
6 And they sat down, and did eat and drink
both of them together: for the damsel's father had
said unto the man, Be content, I pray thee, and
tarry all night, and let thine heart be merry.
7 And when the man rose up to depart, his
father in law urged him: therefore he lodged there
again.
8 And he arose early in the morning on the
fifth day to depart: and the damsel's father said,
Comfort thine heart, I pray thee. And they tarried
until afternoon, and they did eat both of them.
9 And when the man rose up to depart, he,
and his concubine, and his servant, his father in
law, the damsel's father, said unto him, Behold,
now the day draweth toward evening, I pray you
tarry all night: behold, the day groweth to an end,
lodge here, that thine heart may be merry; and
to morrow get you early on your way, that thou
mayest go home.
10 But the man would not tarry that night,
but he rose up and departed, and came over
against [a]Jebus, which *is* Jerusalem; and *there*
were with him two asses saddled, his concubine
also *was* with him.
11 *And* when they *were* by Jebus, the day
was far spent; and the servant said unto his master, Come, I pray thee, and let us turn in into this
city [a]of the Jebusites, and lodge in it.
12 And his master said unto him, We will not
turn aside hither into the city of a stranger, that
is not of the children of Israel; we will pass over
[a]to Gibeah.
13 And he said unto his servant, Come, and
let us draw near to one of these places to lodge
all night, in Gibeah, or in [a]Ramah.
14 And they passed on and went their way;
and the sun went down upon them *when they*
were by Gibeah, which *belongeth* to Benjamin.
15 And they turned aside thither, to go in *and*
to lodge in Gibeah: and when he went in, he sat
him down in a street of the city: for *there was*
no man that [a]took them into his house to lodging.
16 And, behold, there came an old man from
[a]his work out of the field at even, which *was* also
of mount Ephraim; and he sojourned in Gibeah:
but the men of the place *were* Benjamites.
17 And when he had lifted up his eyes, he
saw a wayfaring man in the street of the city: and
the old man said, Whither goest thou? and whence
comest thou?
18 And he said unto him, We *are* passing
from Beth–lehem–judah toward the side of mount
Ephraim; from thence *am* I: and I went to Beth–
lehem–judah, but I *am now* going to [a]the house
of the LORD; and there *is* no man that receiveth
me to house.
19 Yet there is both straw and provender for
our asses; and there is bread and wine also for
me, and for thy handmaid, and for the young man
which is with thy servants: *there is* no want of
any thing.
20 And the old man said, [a]Peace *be* with thee;
howsoever *let* all thy wants *lie* upon me; [b]only
lodge not in the street.
21 [a]So he brought him into his house, and
gave provender unto the asses: [b]and they washed
their feet, and did eat and drink.

Gibeah's Crime

22 *Now* as they were making their [a]hearts
merry, behold, [b]the men of the city, certain [c]sons
of Belial, beset the house round about, *and* beat
at the door, and spake to the master of the house,
the old man, saying, [d]Bring forth the man that
came into thine house, that we may know him.
23 And [a]the man, the master of the house,
went out unto them, and said unto them, Nay, my
brethren, *nay,* I pray you, do not *so* wickedly;

5 [a]Gen. 18:5; Judg. 19:8; Ps. 104:15
10 [a]Josh. 18:28; 1 Chr. 11:4, 5
11 [a]Josh. 15:8, 63; Judg. 1:21; 2 Sam. 5:6
12 [a]Josh. 18:28
13 [a]Josh. 18:25
15 [a]Matt. 25:43
16 [a]Ps. 104:23
18 [a]Josh. 18:1; Judg. 18:31; 20:18; 1 Sam. 1:3, 7
20 [a]Gen. 43:23; Judg. 6:23; 1 Sam. 25:6 [b]Gen. 19:2
21 [a]Gen. 24:32; 43:24 [b]Gen. 18:4; John 13:5
22 [a]Judg. 16:25; 19:6, 9 [b]Gen. 19:4, 5; Judg. 20:5; Hos. 9:9; 10:9 [c]Deut. 13:13; 1 Sam. 2:12; 1 Kin. 21:10; [2 Cor. 6:15] [d]Gen. 19:5; [Rom. 1:26, 27]
23 [a]Gen. 19:6, 7

NKJV

his son-in-law, [a]"Refresh your heart with a morsel
of bread, and afterward go your way."
6 So they sat down, and the two of them
ate and drank together. Then the young woman's
father said to the man, "Please be content to stay
all night, and let your heart be merry."
7 And when the man stood to depart,
his father-in-law urged him; so he lodged there
again.
8 Then he arose early in the morning on the
fifth day to depart, but the young woman's father
said, "Please refresh your heart." So they delayed
until afternoon; and both of them ate.
9 And when the man stood to depart—he
and his concubine and his servant—his father-in-
law, the young woman's father, said to him,
"Look, the day is now drawing toward evening;
please spend the night. See, the day is coming to
an end; lodge here, that your heart may be merry.
Tomorrow go your way early, so that you may
get home."
10 However, the man was not willing to
spend that night; so he rose and departed, and
came to opposite [a]Jebus (that *is,* Jerusalem). With
him were the two saddled donkeys; his concubine
was also with him.
11 They *were* near Jebus, and the day was
far spent; and the servant said to his master,
"Come, please, and let us turn aside into this city
[a]of the Jebusites and lodge in it."
12 But his master said to him, "We will not
turn aside here into a city of foreigners, who *are*
not of the children of Israel; we will go on [a]to
Gibeah."
13 So he said to his servant, "Come, let us
draw near to one of these places, and spend the
night in Gibeah or in [a]Ramah."
14 And they passed by and went their way;
and the sun went down on them near Gibeah,
which belongs to Benjamin.
15 They turned aside there to go in to lodge
in Gibeah. And when he went in, he sat down in
the open square of the city, for no one would [a]take
them into *his* house to spend the night.
16 Just then an old man came in from [a]his
work in the field at evening, who also *was* from
the mountains of Ephraim; he was staying in
Gibeah, whereas the men of the place *were*
Benjamites.
17 And when he raised his eyes, he saw the
traveler in the open square of the city; and the
old man said, "Where are you going, and where
do you come from?"
18 So he said to him, "We *are* passing from
Bethlehem in Judah toward the remote mountains
of Ephraim; I *am* from there. I went to Bethlehem
in Judah; *now* I am going to [a]the house of the
LORD. But there *is* no one who will take me into
his house,
19 "although we have both straw and fodder
for our donkeys, and bread and wine for myself,
for your female servant, and for the young man
who is with your servant; *there is* no lack of
anything."
20 And the old man said, [a]"Peace *be* with
you! However, *let* all your needs *be* my responsibility; [b]only do not spend the night in the open
square."
21 [a]So he brought him into his house, and
gave fodder to the donkeys. [b]And they washed
their feet, and ate and drank.

Gibeah's Crime

22 As they were [a]enjoying themselves, suddenly [b]certain men of the city, [c]perverted* men,
surrounded the house *and* beat on the door. They
spoke to the master of the house, the old man,
saying, [d]"Bring out the man who came to your
house, that we may know him *carnally!*"
23 But [a]the man, the master of the house,
went out to them and said to them, "No, my brethren! I beg you, do not act *so* wickedly! Seeing

***19:22** Lit. *sons of Belial*

KJV

seeing that this man is come into mine house, [b]do not this folly.

24 [a]Behold, *here is* my daughter a maiden, and his concubine; them I will bring out now, and [b]humble ye them, and do with them what seemeth good unto you: but unto this man do not so vile a thing.

25 But the men would not hearken to him: so the man took his concubine, and brought her forth unto them; and they [a]knew her, and abused her all the night until the morning: and when the day began to spring, they let her go.

26 Then came the woman in the dawning of the day, and fell down at the door of the man's house where her lord *was,* till it was light.

27 And her lord rose up in the morning, and opened the doors of the house, and went out to go his way: and, behold, the woman his concubine was fallen down *at* the door of the house, and her hands *were* upon the threshold.

28 And he said unto her, Up, and let us be going. But [a]none answered. Then the man took her *up* upon an ass, and the man rose up, and gat him unto his place.

29 And when he was come into his house, he took a knife, and laid hold on his concubine, and [a]divided her, *together* with her bones, into twelve pieces, and sent her into all the coasts of Israel.

30 And it was so, that all that saw it said, There was no such deed done nor seen from the day that the children of Israel came up out of the land of Egypt unto this day: consider of it, [a]take advice, and speak *your minds.*

Israel's War with the Benjamites

20 Then [a]all the children of Israel went out, and the congregation was gathered together as one man, from [b]Dan even to [c]Beer-sheba, with the land of Gilead, unto the LORD [d]in Mizpeh.

2 And the chief of all the people, *even* of all the tribes of Israel, presented themselves in the assembly of the people of God, four hundred thousand footmen [a]that drew sword.

3 (Now the children of Benjamin heard that the children of Israel were gone up to Mizpeh.) Then said the children of Israel, Tell *us,* how was this wickedness?

4 And the Levite, the husband of the woman that was slain, answered and said, [a]I came into Gibeah that *belongeth* to Benjamin, I and my concubine, to lodge.

5 [a]And the men of Gibeah rose against me, and beset the house round about upon me by night, *and* thought to have slain me: [b]and my concubine have they forced, that she is dead.

6 And [a]I took my concubine, and cut her in pieces, and sent her throughout all the country of the inheritance of Israel: for they [b]have committed lewdness and folly in Israel.

7 Behold, ye *are* all children of Israel; [a]give here your advice and counsel.

8 And all the people arose as one man, saying, We will not any *of us* go to his tent, neither will we any *of us* turn into his house.

9 But now this *shall be* the thing which we will do to Gibeah; *we will go up* [a]by lot against it;

10 And we will take ten men of an hundred throughout all the tribes of Israel, and an hundred of a thousand, and a thousand out of ten thousand, to fetch victual for the people, that they may do, when they come to Gibeah of Benjamin, according to all the folly that they have wrought in Israel.

11 So all the men of Israel were gathered against the city, knit together as one man.

12 [a]And the tribes of Israel sent men through all the tribe of Benjamin, saying, What wickedness *is* this that is done among you?

13 Now therefore deliver *us* the men, [a]the children of Belial, which *are* in Gibeah, that we

23 [b]Gen. 34:7; Deut. 22:21; Judg. 20:6, 10; 2 Sam. 13:12
24 [a]Gen. 19:8 [b]Gen. 34:2; Deut. 21:14
25 [a]Gen. 4:1
28 [a]Judg. 20:5
29 [a]Judg. 20:6; 1 Sam. 11:7
30 [a]Judg. 20:7; Prov. 13:10

CHAPTER 20

1 [a]Josh. 22:12; Judg. 20:11; 21:5 [b]Judg. 18:29; 1 Sam. 3:20; 2 Sam. 3:10; 24:2 [c]Josh. 19:2 [d]Judg. 10:17; 1 Sam. 7:5
2 [a]Judg. 8:10
4 [a]Judg. 19:15
5 [a]Judg. 19:22 [b]Judg. 19:25, 26
6 [a]Judg. 19:29 [b]Josh. 7:15
7 [a]Judg. 19:30
9 [a]Judg. 1:3
12 [a]Deut. 13:14; Josh. 22:13, 16
13 [a]Deut. 13:13; Judg. 19:22

*______

19:24 Lit. *his*
19:29 Lit. *with her bones*
20:13 Lit. *sons of Belial*

NKJV

this man has come into my house, [b]do not commit this outrage.

24 [a]"Look, *here is* my virgin daughter and **the man's* concubine; let me bring them out now. [b]Humble them, and do with them as you please; but to this man do not do such a vile thing!"

25 But the men would not heed him. So the man took his concubine and brought *her* out to them. And they [a]knew her and abused her all night until morning; and when the day began to break, they let her go.

26 Then the woman came as the day was dawning, and fell down at the door of the man's house where her master *was,* till it was light.

27 When her master arose in the morning, and opened the doors of the house and went out to go his way, there was his concubine, fallen *at* the door of the house with her hands on the threshold.

28 And he said to her, "Get up and let us be going." But [a]there was no answer. So the man lifted her onto the donkey; and the man got up and went to his place.

29 When he entered his house he took a knife, laid hold of his concubine, and [a]divided her into twelve pieces, *limb by limb, and sent her throughout all the territory of Israel.

30 And so it was that all who saw it said, "No such deed has been done or seen from the day that the children of Israel came up from the land of Egypt until this day. Consider it, [a]confer, and speak up!"

Israel's War with the Benjamites

20 So [a]all the children of Israel came out, from [b]Dan to [c]Beersheba, as well as from the land of Gilead, and the congregation gathered together as one man before the LORD [d]at Mizpah.

2 And the leaders of all the people, all the tribes of Israel, presented themselves in the assembly of the people of God, four hundred thousand foot soldiers [a]who drew the sword.

3 (Now the children of Benjamin heard that the children of Israel had gone up to Mizpah.) Then the children of Israel said, "Tell *us,* how did this wicked deed happen?"

4 So the Levite, the husband of the woman who was murdered, answered and said, "My concubine and [a]I went into Gibeah, which belongs to Benjamin, to spend the night.

5 [a]"And the men of Gibeah rose against me, and surrounded the house at night because of me. They intended to kill me, [b]but instead they ravished my concubine so that she died.

6 "So [a]I took hold of my concubine, cut her in pieces, and sent her throughout all the territory of the inheritance of Israel, because they [b]committed lewdness and outrage in Israel.

7 "Look! All of you *are* children of Israel; [a]give your advice and counsel here and now!"

8 So all the people arose as one man, saying, "None *of us* will go to his tent, nor will any turn back to his house;

9 "but now this *is* the thing which we will do to Gibeah: *We will go up* [a]against it by lot.

10 "We will take ten men out of *every* hundred throughout all the tribes of Israel, a hundred out of *every* thousand, and a thousand out of *every* ten thousand, to make provisions for the people, that when they come to Gibeah in Benjamin, they may repay all the vileness that they have done in Israel."

11 So all the men of Israel were gathered against the city, united together as one man.

12 [a]Then the tribes of Israel sent men through all the tribe of Benjamin, saying, "What *is* this wickedness that has occurred among you?

13 "Now therefore, deliver up the men, [a]the *perverted men who *are* in Gibeah, that we may

KJV

may put them to death, and [b]put away evil from Israel. But the children of Benjamin would not hearken to the voice of their brethren the children of Israel:

14 But the children of Benjamin gathered themselves together out of the cities unto Gibeah, to go out to battle against the children of Israel.

15 And the [a]children of Benjamin were numbered at that time out of the cities twenty and six thousand men that drew sword, beside the inhabitants of Gibeah, which were numbered seven hundred chosen men.

16 Among all this people *there were* seven hundred chosen men [a]lefthanded; every one could sling stones at an hair *breadth*, and not miss.

17 And the men of Israel, beside Benjamin, were numbered four hundred thousand men that drew sword: all these *were* men of war.

18 And the children of Israel arose, and [a]went up to the house of God, and [b]asked counsel of God, and said, Which of us shall go up first to the battle against the children of Benjamin? And the LORD said, [c]Judah *shall go up* first.

19 And the children of Israel rose up in the morning, and encamped against Gibeah.

20 And the men of Israel went out to battle against Benjamin; and the men of Israel put themselves in array to fight against them at Gibeah.

21 And [a]the children of Benjamin came forth out of Gibeah, and destroyed down to the ground of the Israelites that day twenty and two thousand men.

22 And the people the men of Israel encouraged themselves, and set their battle again in array in the place where they put themselves in array the first day.

23 ([a]And the children of Israel went up and wept before the LORD until even, and asked counsel of the LORD, saying, Shall I go up again to battle against the children of Benjamin my brother? And the LORD said, Go up against him.)

24 And the children of Israel came near against the children of Benjamin the second day.

25 And [a]Benjamin went forth against them out of Gibeah the second day, and destroyed down to the ground of the children of Israel again eighteen thousand men; all these drew the sword.

26 Then all the children of Israel, and all the people, [a]went up, and came unto the house of God, and wept, and sat there before the LORD, and fasted that day until even, and offered burnt offerings and peace offerings before the LORD.

27 And the children of Israel enquired of the LORD, (for [a]the ark of the covenant of God *was* there in those days,

28 [a]And Phinehas, the son of Eleazar, the son of Aaron, [b]stood before it in those days,) saying, Shall I yet again go out to battle against the children of Benjamin my brother, or shall I cease? And the LORD said, Go up; for to morrow I will deliver them into thine hand.

29 And Israel [a]set liers in wait round about Gibeah.

30 And the children of Israel went up against the children of Benjamin on the third day, and put themselves in array against Gibeah, as at other times.

31 And the children of Benjamin went out against the people, *and* were drawn away from the city; and they began to smite of the people, *and* kill, as at other times, in the highways, of which [a]one goeth up to the house of God, and the other to Gibeah in the field, about thirty men of Israel.

32 And the children of Benjamin said, They *are* smitten down before us, as at the first. But the children of Israel said, Let us flee, and draw them from the city unto the highways.

33 And all the men of Israel rose up out of

NKJV

put them to death and [b]remove the evil from Israel!" But the children of Benjamin would not listen to the voice of their brethren, the children of Israel.

14 Instead, the children of Benjamin gathered together from their cities to Gibeah, to go to battle against the children of Israel.

15 And from their cities at that time [a]the children of Benjamin numbered twenty-six thousand men who drew the sword, besides the inhabitants of Gibeah, who numbered seven hundred select men.

16 Among all this people *were* seven hundred select men *who were* [a]left-handed; every one could sling a stone at a hair's *breadth* and not miss.

17 Now besides Benjamin, the men of Israel numbered four hundred thousand men who drew the sword; all of these *were* men of war.

18 Then the children of Israel arose and [a]went up to *the house of God to [b]inquire of God. They said, "Which of us shall go up first to battle against the children of Benjamin?" The LORD said, [c]"Judah first!"

19 So the children of Israel rose in the morning and encamped against Gibeah.

20 And the men of Israel went out to battle against Benjamin, and the men of Israel put themselves in battle array to fight against them at Gibeah.

21 Then [a]the children of Benjamin came out of Gibeah, and on that day cut down to the ground twenty-two thousand men of the Israelites.

22 And the people, that is, the men of Israel, encouraged themselves and again formed the battle line at the place where they had put themselves in array on the first day.

23 [a]Then the children of Israel went up and wept before the LORD until evening, and asked counsel of the LORD, saying, "Shall I again draw near for battle against the children of my brother Benjamin?" And the LORD said, "Go up against him."

24 So the children of Israel approached the children of Benjamin on the second day.

25 And [a]Benjamin went out against them from Gibeah on the second day, and cut down to the ground eighteen thousand more of the children of Israel; all these drew the sword.

26 Then all the children of Israel, that is, all the people, [a]went up and came to *the house of God and wept. They sat there before the LORD and fasted that day until evening; and they offered burnt offerings and peace offerings before the LORD.

27 So the children of Israel inquired of the LORD ([a]the ark of the covenant of God *was* there in those days,

28 [a]and Phinehas the son of Eleazar, the son of Aaron, [b]stood before it in those days), saying, "Shall I yet again go out to battle against the children of my brother Benjamin, or shall I cease?" And the LORD said, "Go up, for tomorrow I will deliver them into your hand."

29 Then Israel [a]set men in ambush all around Gibeah.

30 And the children of Israel went up against the children of Benjamin on the third day, and put themselves in battle array against Gibeah as at the other times.

31 So the children of Benjamin went out against the people, *and* were drawn away from the city. They began to strike down *and* kill some of the people, as at the other times, in the highways [a](one of which goes up to Bethel and the other to Gibeah) and in the field, about thirty men of Israel.

32 And the children of Benjamin said, "They *are* defeated before us, as at first." But the children of Israel said, "Let us flee and draw them away from the city to the highways."

33 So all the men of Israel rose from their

---

13 [b]Deut. 17:12; 1 Cor. 5:13
15 [a]Num. 1:36, 37; 2:23; 26:41
16 [a]Judg. 3:15; 1 Chr. 12:2
18 [a]Judg. 20:23, 26 [b]Num. 27:21 [c]Judg. 1:1, 2
21 [a][Gen. 49:27]
23 [a]Judg. 20:26, 27
25 [a]Judg. 20:21
26 [a]Judg. 20:18, 23; 21:2
27 [a]Josh. 18:1; 1 Sam. 1:3; 3:3; 4:3, 4
28 [a]Num. 25:7, 13; Josh. 24:33 [b]Deut. 10:8; 18:5
29 [a]Josh. 8:4
31 [a]Judg. 21:19

*
20:18 Or *Bethel*
20:26 Or *Bethel*

KJV

their place, and put themselves in array at Baal-
tamar: and the liers in wait of Israel came forth
out of their places, *even* out of the meadows of
Gibeah.
34 And there came against Gibeah ten thousand chosen men out of all Israel, and the battle
was sore: [a]but they knew not that evil *was* near
them.
35 And the LORD smote Benjamin before Israel: and the children of Israel destroyed of the
Benjamites that day twenty and five thousand and
an hundred men: all these drew the sword.
36 So the children of Benjamin saw that they
were smitten: [a]for the men of Israel gave place
to the Benjamites, because they trusted unto the
liers in wait which they had set beside Gibeah.
37 [a]And the liers in wait hasted, and rushed
upon Gibeah; and the liers in wait drew *themselves* along, and smote all the city with the edge
of the sword.
38 Now there was an appointed sign between
the men of Israel and the liers in wait, that they
should make a great flame with [a]smoke rise up
out of the city.
39 And when the men of Israel retired in the
battle, Benjamin began to smite *and* kill of the
men of Israel about thirty persons: for they said,
Surely they are smitten down before us, as *in* the
first battle.
40 But when the flame began to arise up out
of the city with a pillar of smoke, the Benjamites
[a]looked behind them, and, behold, the flame of
the city ascended up to heaven.
41 And when the men of Israel turned again,
the men of Benjamin were amazed: for they saw
that evil was come upon them.
42 Therefore they turned *their backs* before
the men of Israel unto the way of the wilderness;
but the battle overtook them; and them which
came out of the cities they destroyed in the midst
of them.
43 *Thus* they inclosed the Benjamites round
about, *and* chased them, *and* trode them down
with ease over against Gibeah toward the
sunrising.
44 And there fell of Benjamin eighteen thousand men; all these *were* men of valour.
45 And they turned and fled toward the wilderness unto the rock of [a]Rimmon: and they
gleaned of them in the highways five thousand
men; and pursued hard after them unto Gidom,
and slew two thousand men of them.
46 So that all which fell that day of Benjamin
were twenty and five thousand men that drew the
sword; all these *were* men of valour.
47 [a]But six hundred men turned and fled to
the wilderness unto the rock Rimmon, and abode
in the rock Rimmon four months.
48 And the men of Israel turned again upon
the children of Benjamin, and smote them with
the edge of the sword, as well the men of *every*
city, as the beast, and all that came to hand: also
they set on fire all the cities that they came to.

Wives Provided for the Benjamites

21 Now [a]the men of Israel had sworn in
Mizpeh, saying, There shall not any of us
give his daughter unto Benjamin to wife.
2 And the people came [a]to the house of God,
and abode there till even before God, and lifted
up their voices, and wept sore;
3 And said, O LORD God of Israel, why is
this come to pass in Israel, that there should be
to day one tribe lacking in Israel?
4 And it came to pass on the morrow,
that the people rose early, and [a]built there an altar, and offered burnt offerings and peace
offerings.
5 And the children of Israel said, Who *is
there* among all the tribes of Israel that came not
up with the congregation unto the LORD? [a]For they
had made a great oath concerning him that came

34 [a]Josh. 8:14; Job 21:13; Is. 47:11
36 [a]Josh. 8:15
37 [a]Josh. 8:19
38 [a]Josh. 8:20
40 [a]Josh. 8:20
45 [a]Josh. 15:32; 1 Chr. 6:77; Zech. 14:10
47 [a]Judg. 21:13

CHAPTER 21
1 [a]Judg. 20:1
2 [a]Judg. 20:18, 26
4 [a]Deut. 12:5; 2 Sam. 24:25
5 [a]Judg. 20:1–3

*
20:34 Lit. *they*
20:45 LXX *the rest*
21:2 Or *Bethel*

NKJV

place and put themselves in battle array at Baal
Tamar. Then Israel's men in ambush burst forth
from their position in the plain of Geba.
34 And ten thousand select men from all Israel came against Gibeah, and the battle was
fierce. [a]But **the Benjamites* did not know that
disaster *was* upon them.
35 The LORD defeated Benjamin before Israel. And the children of Israel destroyed that day
twenty-five thousand one hundred Benjamites; all
these drew the sword.
36 So the children of Benjamin saw that they
were defeated. [a]The men of Israel had given
ground to the Benjamites, because they relied on
the men in ambush whom they had set against
Gibeah.
37 [a]And the men in ambush quickly rushed
upon Gibeah; the men in ambush spread out and
struck the whole city with the edge of the sword.
38 Now the appointed signal between the
men of Israel and the men in ambush was that
they would make a great cloud of [a]smoke rise
up from the city,
39 whereupon the men of Israel would turn
in battle. Now Benjamin had begun to strike *and*
kill about thirty of the men of Israel. For they said,
"Surely they are defeated before us, as *in* the first
battle."
40 But when the cloud began to rise from the
city in a column of smoke, the Benjamites [a]looked
behind them, and there was the whole city going
up *in smoke* to heaven.
41 And when the men of Israel turned back,
the men of Benjamin panicked, for they saw that
disaster had come upon them.
42 Therefore they turned *their backs* before
the men of Israel in the direction of the wilderness; but the battle overtook them, and whoever
came out of the cities they destroyed in their
midst.
43 They surrounded the Benjamites, chased
them, *and* easily trampled them down as far as
the front of Gibeah toward the east.
44 And eighteen thousand men of Benjamin
fell; all these *were* men of valor.
45 Then *they turned and fled toward the wilderness to the rock of [a]Rimmon; and they cut
down five thousand of them on the highways.
Then they pursued them relentlessly up to Gidom,
and killed two thousand of them.
46 So all who fell of Benjamin that day were
twenty-five thousand men who drew the sword;
all these *were* men of valor.
47 [a]But six hundred men turned and fled toward the wilderness to the rock of Rimmon, and
they stayed at the rock of Rimmon for four
months.
48 And the men of Israel turned back against
the children of Benjamin, and struck them down
with the edge of the sword—from *every* city, men
and beasts, all who were found. They also set fire
to all the cities they came to.

Wives Provided for the Benjamites

21 Now [a]the men of Israel had sworn an oath
at Mizpah, saying, "None of us shall give
his daughter to Benjamin as a wife."
2 Then the people came [a]to *the house of
God, and remained there before God till evening.
They lifted up their voices and wept bitterly,
3 and said, "O LORD God of Israel, why has
this come to pass in Israel, that today there should
be one tribe *missing* in Israel?"
4 So it was, on the next morning, that the
people rose early and [a]built an altar there, and
offered burnt offerings and peace offerings.
5 The children of Israel said, "Who *is there*
among all the tribes of Israel who did not come
up with the assembly to the LORD?" [a]For they had
made a great oath concerning anyone who had

KJV

not up to the LORD to Mizpeh, saying, He shall surely be put to death.

6 And the children of Israel repented them for Benjamin their brother, and said, There is one tribe cut off from Israel this day.

7 How shall we do for wives for them that remain, seeing we have sworn by the LORD that we will not give them of our daughters to wives?

8 And they said, What one *is there* of the tribes of Israel that came not up to Mizpeh to the LORD? And, behold, there came none to the camp from [a]Jabesh–gilead to the assembly.

9 For the people were numbered, and, behold, *there were* none of the inhabitants of Jabesh–gilead there.

10 And the congregation sent thither twelve thousand men of the valiantest, and commanded them, saying, [a]Go and smite the inhabitants of Jabesh–gilead with the edge of the sword, with the women and the children.

11 And this *is* the thing that ye shall do, [a]Ye shall utterly destroy every male, and every woman that hath lain by man.

12 And they found among the inhabitants of Jabesh–gilead four hundred young virgins, that had known no man by lying with any male: and they brought them unto the camp to [a]Shiloh, which *is* in the land of Canaan.

13 And the whole congregation sent *some* to speak to the children of Benjamin [a]that were in the rock Rimmon, and to call peaceably unto them.

14 And Benjamin came again at that time; and they gave them wives which they had saved alive of the women of Jabesh–gilead: and yet so they sufficed them not.

15 And the people [a]repented them for Benjamin, because that the LORD had made a breach in the tribes of Israel.

16 Then the elders of the congregation said, How shall we do for wives for them that remain, seeing the women are destroyed out of Benjamin?

17 And they said, *There must be* an inheritance for them that be escaped of Benjamin, that a tribe be not destroyed out of Israel.

18 Howbeit we may not give them wives of our daughters: [a]for the children of Israel have sworn, saying, Cursed *be* he that giveth a wife to Benjamin.

19 Then they said, Behold, *there is* a [a]feast of the LORD in [b]Shiloh yearly *in a place* which *is* on the north side of Beth–el, on the east side of the [c]highway that goeth up from Beth–el to Shechem, and on the south of Lebonah.

20 Therefore they commanded the children of Benjamin, saying, Go and lie in wait in the vineyards;

21 And see, and, behold, if the daughters of Shiloh come out [a]to dance in dances, then come ye out of the vineyards, and catch you every man his wife of the daughters of Shiloh, and go to the land of Benjamin.

22 And it shall be, when their fathers or their brethren come unto us to complain, that we will say unto them, Be favourable unto them for our sakes: because we reserved not to each man his wife in the war: for ye did not give unto them at this time, *that* ye should be guilty.

23 And the children of Benjamin did so, and took *them* wives, according to their number, of them that danced, whom they caught: and they went and returned unto their inheritance, and [a]repaired the cities, and dwelt in them.

24 And the children of Israel departed thence at that time, every man to his tribe and to his family, and they went out from thence every man to his inheritance.

25 [a]In those days *there was* no king in Israel: [b]every man did *that which was* right in his own eyes.

NKJV

not come up to the LORD at Mizpah, saying, "He shall surely be put to death."

6 And the children of Israel grieved for Benjamin their brother, and said, "One tribe is cut off from Israel today.

7 "What shall we do for wives for those who remain, seeing we have sworn by the LORD that we will not give them our daughters as wives?"

8 And they said, "What one *is there* from the tribes of Israel who did not come up to Mizpah to the LORD?" And, in fact, no one had come to the camp from [a]Jabesh Gilead to the assembly.

9 For when the people were counted, indeed, not one of the inhabitants of Jabesh Gilead *was* there.

10 So the congregation sent out there twelve thousand of their most valiant men, and commanded them, saying, [a]"Go and strike the inhabitants of Jabesh Gilead with the edge of the sword, including the women and children.

11 "And this *is* the thing that you shall do: [a]You shall utterly destroy every male, and every woman who has known a man intimately."

12 So they found among the inhabitants of Jabesh Gilead four hundred young virgins who had not known a man intimately; and they brought them to the camp at [a]Shiloh, which is in the land of Canaan.

13 Then the whole congregation sent *word* to the children of Benjamin [a]who *were* at the rock of Rimmon, and announced peace to them.

14 So Benjamin came back at that time, and they gave them the women whom they had saved alive of the women of Jabesh Gilead; and yet they had not found enough for them.

15 And the people [a]grieved for Benjamin, because the LORD had made a void in the tribes of Israel.

16 Then the elders of the congregation said, "What shall we do for wives for those who remain, since the women of Benjamin have been destroyed?"

17 And they said, "*There must be* an inheritance for the survivors of Benjamin, that a tribe may not be destroyed from Israel.

18 "However, we cannot give them wives from our daughters, [a]for the children of Israel have sworn an oath, saying, 'Cursed *be* the one who gives a wife to Benjamin.'"

19 Then they said, "In fact, *there is* a yearly [a]feast of the LORD in [b]Shiloh, which *is* north of Bethel, on the east side of the [c]highway that goes up from Bethel to Shechem, and south of Lebonah."

20 Therefore they instructed the children of Benjamin, saying, "Go, lie in wait in the vineyards,

21 "and watch; and just when the daughters of Shiloh come out [a]to perform their dances, then come out from the vineyards, and every man catch a wife for himself from the daughters of Shiloh; then go to the land of Benjamin.

22 "Then it shall be, when their fathers or their brothers come to us to complain, that we will say to them, 'Be kind to them for our sakes, because we did not take a wife for any of them in the war; for *it is* not *as though* you have given the *women* to them at this time, making yourselves guilty of your oath.'"

23 And the children of Benjamin did so; they took enough wives for their number from those who danced, whom they caught. Then they went and returned to their inheritance, and they [a]rebuilt the cities and dwelt in them.

24 So the children of Israel departed from there at that time, every man to his tribe and family; they went out from there, every man to his inheritance.

25 [a]In those days *there was* no king in Israel; [b]everyone did *what was* right in his own eyes.

---

8 [a]1 Sam. 11:1; 31:11 **10** [a]Num. 31:17; Judg. 5:23; 1 Sam. 11:7 **11** [a]Num. 31:17; Deut. 20:13, 14 **12** [a]Josh. 18:1; Judg. 18:31 **13** [a]Judg. 20:47 **15** [a]Judg. 21:6 **18** [a]Judg. 11:35; 21:1 **19** [a]Lev. 23:2 [b]Deut. 12:5; Josh. 18:1; Judg. 18:31; 1 Sam. 1:3 [c]Judg. 20:31 **21** [a]Ex. 15:20; Judg. 11:34; 1 Sam. 18:6 **23** [a]Judg. 20:48 **25** [a]Judg. 17:6; 18:1; 19:1 [b]Deut. 12:8; Judg. 17:6

KJV

THE BOOK OF

RUTH

Elimelech's Family Goes to Moab

1 Now it came to pass in the days when [a]the
judges ruled, that there was [b]a famine in the
land. And a certain man of [c]Beth–lehem–judah
went to sojourn in the country of [d]Moab, he, and
his wife, and his two sons.
2 And the name of the man *was* Elimelech,
and the name of his wife Naomi, and the name
of his two sons Mahlon and Chilion, [a]Ephrathites
of Beth–lehem–judah. And they came [b]into the
country of Moab, and continued there.
3 And Elimelech Naomi's husband died;
and she was left, and her two sons.
4 And they took them wives of the women
of Moab; the name of the one *was* Orpah, and
the name of the other Ruth: and they dwelled
there about ten years.
5 And Mahlon and Chilion died also both
of them; and the woman was left of her two sons
and her husband.

Naomi Returns with Ruth

6 Then she arose with her daughters in law,
that she might return from the country of Moab:
for she had heard in the country of Moab how
that the LORD had [a]visited his people in [b]giving
them bread.
7 Wherefore she went forth out of the place
where she was, and her two daughters in law with
her; and they went on the way to return unto the
land of Judah.
8 And Naomi said unto her two daughters
in law, [a]Go, return each to her mother's house:
[b]the LORD deal kindly with you, as ye have dealt
[c]with the dead, and with me.
9 The LORD grant you that ye may find [a]rest,
each *of you* in the house of her husband. Then
she kissed them; and they lifted up their voice,
and wept.
10 And they said unto her, Surely we will return with thee unto thy people.
11 And Naomi said, Turn again, my daughters: why will ye go with me? *are* there yet *any*
more sons in my womb, [a]that they may be your
husbands?
12 Turn again, my daughters, go *your way;*
for I am too old to have an husband. If I should
say, I have hope, *if* I should have an husband also
to night, and should also bear sons;
13 Would ye tarry for them till they were
grown? would ye stay for them from having husbands? nay, my daughters; for it grieveth me
much for your sakes that [a]the hand of the LORD
is gone out against me.
14 And they lifted up their voice, and wept
again: and Orpah kissed her mother in law; but
Ruth [a]clave unto her.
15 And she said, Behold, thy sister in law is
gone back unto [a]her people, and unto her gods:
[b]return thou after thy sister in law.
16 And Ruth said, [a]Intreat me not to leave
thee, *or* to return from following after thee: for
whither thou goest, I will go; and where thou lodg-
est, I will lodge: [b]thy people *shall be* my people,
and thy God my God:

CHAPTER 1

1 [a]Judg. 2:16–18 [b]Gen. 12:10; 26:1; 2 Kin. 8:1 [c]Judg. 17:8; Mic. 5:2 [d]Gen. 19:37
2 [a]Gen. 35:19; 1 Sam. 1:1; 1 Kin. 11:26 [b]Judg. 3:30
6 [a]Ex. 3:16; 4:31; Jer. 29:10; Zeph. 2:7; Luke 1:68 [b]Ps. 132:15; Matt. 6:11
8 [a]Josh. 24:15 [b]2 Tim. 1:16–18 [c]Ruth 2:20
9 [a]Ruth 3:1
11 [a]Gen. 38:11; Deut. 25:5
13 [a]Judg. 2:15; Job 19:21; Ps. 32:4; 38:2
14 [a][Prov. 17:17]
15 [a]Judg. 11:24 [b]Josh. 1:15
16 [a]2 Kin. 2:2, 4, 6 [b]Ruth 2:11, 12

NKJV

THE BOOK OF

RUTH

Elimelech's Family Goes to Moab

1 Now it came to pass, in the days when [a]the
judges ruled, that there was [b]a famine in the
land. And a certain man of [c]Bethlehem, Judah,
went to dwell in the country of [d]Moab, he and
his wife and his two sons.
2 The name of the man *was* Elimelech, the
name of his wife *was* Naomi, and the names of
his two sons *were* Mahlon and Chilion—[a]Ephrath-
ites of Bethlehem, Judah. And they went [b]to the
country of Moab and remained there.
3 Then Elimelech, Naomi's husband, died;
and she was left, and her two sons.
4 Now they took wives of the women of
Moab: the name of the one *was* Orpah, and the
name of the other Ruth. And they dwelt there
about ten years.
5 Then both Mahlon and Chilion also died;
so the woman survived her two sons and her husband.

Naomi Returns with Ruth

6 Then she arose with her daughters-in-law
that she might return from the country of Moab,
for she had heard in the country of Moab that
the LORD had [a]visited His people by [b]giving them
bread.
7 Therefore she went out from the place
where she was, and her two daughters-in-law with
her; and they went on the way to return to the
land of Judah.
8 And Naomi said to her two daughters-in-
law, [a]"Go, return each to her mother's house.
[b]The LORD deal kindly with you, as you have dealt
[c]with the dead and with me.
9 "The LORD grant that you may find [a]rest,
each in the house of her husband." So she kissed
them, and they lifted up their voices and wept.
10 And they said to her, "Surely we will return with you to your people."
11 But Naomi said, "Turn back, my daughters; why will you go with me? *Are* there still sons
in my womb, [a]that they may be your husbands?
12 "Turn back, my daughters, go—for I am
too old to have a husband. If I should say I have
hope, *if* I should have a husband tonight and
should also bear sons,
13 "would you wait for them till they were
grown? Would you restrain yourselves from having husbands? No, my daughters; for it grieves
me very much for your sakes that [a]the hand of
the LORD has gone out against me!"
14 Then they lifted up their voices and wept
again; and Orpah kissed her mother-in-law, but
Ruth [a]clung to her.
15 And she said, "Look, your sister-in-law
has gone back to [a]her people and to her gods;
[b]return after your sister-in-law."
16 But Ruth said:

[a]"Entreat me not to leave you,
Or to turn back from following after you;
For wherever you go, I will go;
And wherever you lodge, I will lodge;
[b]Your people *shall be* my people,
And your God, my God.

KJV

17 Where thou diest, will I die, and there will I be buried: [a]the LORD do so to me, and more also, *if ought* but death part thee and me.

18 [a]When she saw that she was stedfastly minded to go with her, then she left speaking unto her.

19 So they two went until they came to Beth–lehem. And it came to pass, when they were come to Beth–lehem, that [a]all the city was moved about them, and they said, [b]*Is* this Naomi?

20 And she said unto them, Call me not Naomi, call me Mara: for the Almighty hath dealt very bitterly with me.

21 I went out full, [a]and the LORD hath brought me home again empty: why *then* call ye me Naomi, seeing the LORD hath testified against me, and the Almighty hath afflicted me?

22 So Naomi returned, and Ruth the Moabitess, her daughter in law, with her, which returned out of the country of Moab: and they came to Beth–lehem [a]in the beginning of barley harvest.

Ruth Meets Boaz

2 And Naomi had a [a]kinsman of her husband's, a mighty man of wealth, of the family of [b]Elimelech; and his name *was* [c]Boaz.

2 And Ruth the Moabitess said unto Naomi, Let me now go to the [a]field, and glean ears of corn after *him* in whose sight I shall find grace. And she said unto her, Go, my daughter.

3 And she went, and came, and gleaned in the field after the reapers: and her hap was to light on a part of the field *belonging* unto Boaz, who *was* of the kindred of Elimelech.

4 And, behold, Boaz came from [a]Beth–lehem, and said unto the reapers, [b]The LORD *be* with you. And they answered him, The LORD bless thee.

5 Then said Boaz unto his servant that was set over the reapers, Whose damsel *is* this?

6 And the servant that was set over the reapers answered and said, It *is* the Moabitish damsel [a]that came back with Naomi out of the country of Moab:

7 And she said, I pray you, let me glean and gather after the reapers among the sheaves: so she came, and hath continued even from the morning until now, that she tarried a little in the house.

8 Then said Boaz unto Ruth, Hearest thou not, my daughter? Go not to glean in another field, neither go from hence, but abide here fast by my maidens:

9 *Let* thine eyes *be* on the field that they do reap, and go thou after them: have I not charged the young men that they shall not touch thee? and when thou art athirst, go unto the vessels, and drink of *that* which the young men have drawn.

10 Then she [a]fell on her face, and bowed herself to the ground, and said unto him, Why have I found [b]grace in thine eyes, that thou shouldest take knowledge of me, seeing I *am* a stranger?

11 And Boaz answered and said unto her, It hath fully been shewed me, [a]all that thou hast done unto thy mother in law since the death of thine husband: and *how* thou hast left thy father and thy mother, and the land of thy nativity, and art come unto a people which thou knewest not heretofore.

12 [a]The LORD recompense thy work, and a full reward be given thee of the LORD God of Israel, [b]under whose wings thou art come to trust.

13 Then she said, [a]Let me find favour in thy sight, my lord; for that thou hast comforted me, and for that thou hast spoken friendly unto thine handmaid, [b]though I be not like unto one of thine handmaidens.

14 And Boaz said unto her, At mealtime come thou hither, and eat of the bread, and dip thy morsel in the vinegar. And she sat beside the

17 [a]1 Sam. 3:17; 2 Sam. 19:13; 2 Kin. 6:31
18 [a]Acts 21:14
19 [a]Matt. 21:10 [b]Is. 23:7; Lam. 2:15
21 [a]Job 1:21
22 [a]Ruth 2:23; 2 Sam. 21:9

CHAPTER 2

1 [a]Ruth 3:2, 12 [b]Ruth 1:2 [c]Ruth 4:21
2 [a]Lev. 19:9, 10; 23:22; Deut. 24:19
4 [a]Ruth 1:1 [b]Ps. 129:7, 8; Luke 1:28; 2 Thess. 3:16
6 [a]Ruth 1:22
10 [a]1 Sam. 25:23 [b]1 Sam. 1:18
11 [a]Ruth 1:14–18
12 [a]1 Sam. 24:19; Ps. 58:11 [b]Ruth 1:16; Ps. 17:8; 36:7; 57:1; 61:4; 63:7; 91:4
13 [a]Gen. 33:15; 1 Sam. 1:18 [b]1 Sam. 25:41

*

1:20 Lit. *Pleasant* • Lit. *Bitter*

NKJV

17 Where you die, I will die,
And there will I be buried.
[a]The LORD do so to me, and more also,
If *anything but* death parts you and me."

18 [a]When she saw that she was determined to go with her, she stopped speaking to her.

19 Now the two of them went until they came to Bethlehem. And it happened, when they had come to Bethlehem, that [a]all the city was excited because of them; and the women said, [b]"*Is* this Naomi?"

20 But she said to them, "Do not call me *Naomi; call me *Mara, for the Almighty has dealt very bitterly with me.

21 "I went out full, [a]and the LORD has brought me home again empty. Why do you call me Naomi, since the LORD has testified against me, and the Almighty has afflicted me?"

22 So Naomi returned, and Ruth the Moabitess her daughter-in-law with her, who returned from the country of Moab. Now they came to Bethlehem [a]at the beginning of barley harvest.

Ruth Meets Boaz

2 There was a [a]relative of Naomi's husband, a man of great wealth, of the family of [b]Elimelech. His name *was* [c]Boaz.

2 So Ruth the Moabitess said to Naomi, "Please let me go to the [a]field, and glean heads of grain after *him* in whose sight I may find favor." And she said to her, "Go, my daughter."

3 Then she left, and went and gleaned in the field after the reapers. And she happened to come to the part of the field *belonging* to Boaz, who *was* of the family of Elimelech.

4 Now behold, Boaz came from [a]Bethlehem, and said to the reapers, [b]"The LORD *be* with you!" And they answered him, "The LORD bless you!"

5 Then Boaz said to his servant who was in charge of the reapers, "Whose young woman *is* this?"

6 So the servant who was in charge of the reapers answered and said, "It *is* the young Moabite woman [a]who came back with Naomi from the country of Moab.

7 "And she said, 'Please let me glean and gather after the reapers among the sheaves.' So she came and has continued from morning until now, though she rested a little in the house."

8 Then Boaz said to Ruth, "You will listen, my daughter, will you not? Do not go to glean in another field, nor go from here, but stay close by my young women.

9 "*Let* your eyes *be* on the field which they reap, and go after them. Have I not commanded the young men not to touch you? And when you are thirsty, go to the vessels and drink from what the young men have drawn."

10 So she [a]fell on her face, bowed down to the ground, and said to him, "Why have I found [b]favor in your eyes, that you should take notice of me, since I *am* a foreigner?"

11 And Boaz answered and said to her, "It has been fully reported to me, [a]all that you have done for your mother-in-law since the death of your husband, and *how* you have left your father and your mother and the land of your birth, and have come to a people whom you did not know before.

12 [a]"The LORD repay your work, and a full reward be given you by the LORD God of Israel, [b]under whose wings you have come for refuge."

13 Then she said, [a]"Let me find favor in your sight, my lord; for you have comforted me, and have spoken kindly to your maidservant, [b]though I am not like one of your maidservants."

14 Now Boaz said to her at mealtime, "Come here, and eat of the bread, and dip your piece of bread in the vinegar." So she sat beside the

KJV

reapers: and he reached her parched *corn,* and she did eat, and [a]was sufficed, and left.

15 And when she was risen up to glean, Boaz commanded his young men, saying, Let her glean even among the sheaves, and reproach her not:

16 And let fall also *some* of the handfuls of purpose for her, and leave *them,* that she may glean *them,* and rebuke her not.

17 So she gleaned in the field until even, and beat out that she had gleaned: and it was about an ephah of [a]barley.

18 And she took *it* up, and went into the city: and her mother in law saw what she had gleaned: and she brought forth, and gave to her [a]that she had reserved after she was sufficed.

19 And her mother in law said unto her, Where hast thou gleaned to day? and where wroughtest thou? blessed be he that did [a]take knowledge of thee. And she shewed her mother in law with whom she had wrought, and said, The man's name with whom I wrought to day *is* Boaz.

20 And Naomi said unto her daughter in law, [a]Blessed *be* he of the LORD, who [b]hath not left off his kindness to the living and to the dead. And Naomi said unto her, The man *is* near of kin unto us, [c]one of our next kinsmen.

21 And Ruth the Moabitess said, He said unto me also, Thou shalt keep fast by my young men, until they have ended all my harvest.

22 And Naomi said unto Ruth her daughter in law, *It is* good, my daughter, that thou go out with his maidens, that they meet thee not in any other field.

23 So she kept fast by the maidens of Boaz to glean unto the end of barley harvest and of wheat harvest; and dwelt with her mother in law.

Ruth's Redemption Assured

3 Then Naomi her mother in law said unto her, My daughter, [a]shall I not seek [b]rest for thee, that it may be well with thee?

2 And now *is* not Boaz of our kindred, [a]with whose maidens thou wast? Behold, he winnoweth barley to night in the threshingfloor.

3 Wash thyself therefore, [a]and anoint thee, and put thy raiment upon thee, and get thee down to the floor: *but* make not thyself known unto the man, until he shall have done eating and drinking.

4 And it shall be, when he lieth down, that thou shalt mark the place where he shall lie, and thou shalt go in, and uncover his feet, and lay thee down; and he will tell thee what thou shalt do.

5 And she said unto her, All that thou sayest unto me I will do.

6 And she went down unto the floor, and did according to all that her mother in law bade her.

7 And when Boaz had eaten and drunk, and [a]his heart was merry, he went to lie down at the end of the heap of corn: and she came softly, and uncovered his feet, and laid her down.

8 And it came to pass at midnight, that the man was afraid, and turned himself: and, behold, a woman lay at his feet.

9 And he said, Who *art* thou? And she answered, I *am* Ruth thine handmaid: [a]spread therefore thy skirt over thine handmaid; for thou *art* [b]a near kinsman.

10 And he said, [a]Blessed *be* thou of the LORD, my daughter: *for* thou hast shewed more kindness in the latter end than [b]at the beginning, inasmuch as thou followedst not young men, whether poor or rich.

11 And now, my daughter, fear not; I will do to thee all that thou requirest: for all the city of my people doth know that thou *art* [a]a virtuous woman.

12 And now it is true that I *am thy* [a]near kinsman: howbeit [b]there is a kinsman nearer than I.

14 [a]Ruth 2:18
17 [a]Ruth 1:22
18 [a]Ruth 2:14
19 [a]Ruth 2:10; [Ps. 41:1]
20 [a]Ruth 3:10; 2 Sam. 2:5 [b]Prov. 17:17 [c]Ruth 3:9; 4:4, 6

CHAPTER 3

1 [a]1 Cor. 7:36; 1 Tim. 5:8 [b]Ruth 1:9
2 [a]Ruth 2:3, 8
3 [a]2 Sam. 14:2
7 [a]Judg. 19:6, 9, 22; 2 Sam. 13:28; Esth. 1:10
9 [a]Ezek. 16:8 [b]Ruth 2:20; 3:12
10 [a]Ruth 2:20 [b]Ruth 1:8
11 [a]Prov. 12:4; 31:10–31
12 [a]Ruth 3:9 [b]Ruth 4:1

NKJV

reapers, and he passed parched *grain* to her; and she ate and [a]was satisfied, and kept some back.

15 And when she rose up to glean, Boaz commanded his young men, saying, "Let her glean even among the sheaves, and do not reproach her.

16 "Also let *grain* from the bundles fall purposely for her; leave *it* that she may glean, and do not rebuke her."

17 So she gleaned in the field until evening, and beat out what she had gleaned, and it was about an ephah of [a]barley.

18 Then she took *it* up and went into the city, and her mother-in-law saw what she had gleaned. So she brought out and gave to her [a]what she had kept back after she had been satisfied.

19 And her mother-in-law said to her, "Where have you gleaned today? And where did you work? Blessed be the one who [a]took notice of you." So she told her mother-in-law with whom she had worked, and said, "The man's name with whom I worked today *is* Boaz."

20 Then Naomi said to her daughter-in-law, [a]"Blessed *be* he of the LORD, who [b]has not forsaken His kindness to the living and the dead!" And Naomi said to her, "This man *is* a relation of ours, [c]one of our close relatives."

21 Ruth the Moabitess said, "He also said to me, 'You shall stay close by my young men until they have finished all my harvest.' "

22 And Naomi said to Ruth her daughter-in-law, "*It is* good, my daughter, that you go out with his young women, and that people do not meet you in any other field."

23 So she stayed close by the young women of Boaz, to glean until the end of barley harvest and wheat harvest; and she dwelt with her mother-in-law.

Ruth's Redemption Assured

3 Then Naomi her mother-in-law said to her, "My daughter, [a]shall I not seek [b]security for you, that it may be well with you?

2 "Now Boaz, [a]whose young women you were with, *is he* not our relative? In fact, he is winnowing barley tonight at the threshing floor.

3 "Therefore wash yourself and [a]anoint yourself, put on your *best* garment and go down to the threshing floor; *but* do not make yourself known to the man until he has finished eating and drinking.

4 "Then it shall be, when he lies down, that you shall notice the place where he lies; and you shall go in, uncover his feet, and lie down; and he will tell you what you should do."

5 And she said to her, "All that you say to me I will do."

6 So she went down to the threshing floor and did according to all that her mother-in-law instructed her.

7 And after Boaz had eaten and drunk, and [a]his heart was cheerful, he went to lie down at the end of the heap of grain; and she came softly, uncovered his feet, and lay down.

8 Now it happened at midnight that the man was startled, and turned himself; and there, a woman was lying at his feet.

9 And he said, "Who *are* you?" So she answered, "I *am* Ruth, your maidservant. [a]Take* your maidservant under your wing, for you are [b]a close relative."

10 Then he said, [a]"Blessed *are* you of the LORD, my daughter! For you have shown more kindness at the end than [b]at the beginning, in that you did not go after young men, whether poor or rich.

11 "And now, my daughter, do not fear. I will do for you all that you request, for all the people of my town know that you *are* [a]a virtuous woman.

12 "Now it is true that I *am* a [a]close relative; however, [b]there is a relative closer than I.

*3:9 Or *Spread the corner of your garment over your maidservant*

KJV

13 Tarry this night, and it shall be in the morning, *that* if he will [a]perform unto thee the part of a kinsman, well; let him do the kinsman's part: but if he will not do the part of a kinsman to thee, then will I do the part of a kinsman to thee, [b]*as* the LORD liveth: lie down until the morning.

14 And she lay at his feet until the morning: and she rose up before one could know another. And he said, [a]Let it not be known that a woman came into the floor.

15 Also he said, Bring the vail that *thou hast* upon thee, and hold it. And when she held it, he measured six *measures* of barley, and laid *it* on her: and she went into the city.

16 And when she came to her mother in law, she said, Who *art* thou, my daughter? And she told her all that the man had done to her.

17 And she said, These six *measures* of barley gave he me; for he said to me, Go not empty unto thy mother in law.

18 Then said she, [a]Sit still, my daughter, until thou know how the matter will fall: for the man will not be in rest, until he have finished the thing this day.

Boaz Redeems Ruth

4 Then went Boaz up to the gate, and sat him down there: and, behold, [a]the kinsman of whom Boaz spake came by; unto whom he said, Ho, such a one! turn aside, sit down here. And he turned aside, and sat down.

2 And he took ten men of [a]the elders of the city, and said, Sit ye down here. And they sat down.

3 And he said unto the kinsman, Naomi, that is come again out of the country of Moab, selleth a parcel of land, [a]which *was* our brother Elimelech's:

4 And I thought to advertise thee, saying, [a]Buy *it* [b]before the inhabitants, and before the elders of my people. If thou wilt redeem *it*, redeem *it*: but if thou wilt not redeem *it*, *then* tell me, that I may know: [c]for *there is* none to redeem *it* beside thee; and I *am* after thee. And he said, I will redeem *it*.

5 Then said Boaz, What day thou buyest the field of the hand of Naomi, thou must buy *it* also of Ruth the Moabitess, the wife of the dead, [a]to raise up the name of the dead upon his inheritance.

6 [a]And the kinsman said, I cannot redeem *it* for myself, lest I mar mine own inheritance: redeem thou my right to thyself; for I cannot redeem *it*.

7 [a]Now this *was the manner* in former time in Israel concerning redeeming and concerning changing, for to confirm all things; a man plucked off his shoe, and gave *it* to his neighbour: and this *was* a testimony in Israel.

8 Therefore the kinsman said unto Boaz, Buy *it* for thee. So he drew off his shoe.

9 And Boaz said unto the elders, and *unto* all the people, Ye *are* witnesses this day, that I have bought all that *was* Elimelech's, and all that *was* Chilion's and Mahlon's, of the hand of Naomi.

10 Moreover Ruth the Moabitess, the wife of Mahlon, have I purchased to be my wife, to raise up the name of the dead upon his inheritance, [a]that the name of the dead be not cut off from among his brethren, and from the gate of his place: ye *are* witnesses this day.

11 And all the people that *were* in the gate, and the elders, said, *We are* witnesses. [a]The LORD make the woman that is come into thine house like Rachel and like Leah, which two did [b]build the house of Israel: and do thou worthily in [c]Ephratah, and be famous in [d]Beth–lehem:

12 And let thy house be like the house of [a]Pharez, [b]whom Tamar bare unto Judah, of [c]the seed which the LORD shall give thee of this young woman.

NKJV

13 "Stay this night, and in the morning it shall be *that* if he will [a]perform the duty of a close relative for you—good; let him do it. But if he does not want to perform the duty for you, then I will perform the duty for you, [b]*as* the LORD lives! Lie down until morning."

14 So she lay at his feet until morning, and she arose before one could recognize another. Then he said, [a]"Do not let it be known that the woman came to the threshing floor."

15 Also he said, "Bring the shawl that *is* on you and hold it." And when she held it, he measured six *ephahs* of barley, and laid *it* on her. Then *she went into the city.

16 When she came to her mother-in-law, she said, "*Is* that you, my daughter?" Then she told her all that the man had done for her.

17 And she said, "These six *ephahs* of barley he gave me; for he said to me, 'Do not go empty-handed to your mother-in-law.' "

18 Then she said, [a]"Sit still, my daughter, until you know how the matter will turn out; for the man will not rest until he has concluded the matter this day."

Boaz Redeems Ruth

4 Now Boaz went up to the gate and sat down there; and behold, [a]the close relative of whom Boaz had spoken came by. So Boaz said, "Come aside, *friend, sit down here." So he came aside and sat down.

2 And he took ten men of [a]the elders of the city, and said, "Sit down here." So they sat down.

3 Then he said to the close relative, "Naomi, who has come back from the country of Moab, sold the piece of land [a]which *belonged* to our brother Elimelech.

4 "And I thought to inform you, saying, [a]'Buy *it* back [b]in the presence of the inhabitants and the elders of my people. If you will redeem *it*, redeem *it;* but if *you will not redeem *it, then* tell me, that I may know; [c]for *there is* no one but you to redeem *it*, and I *am* next after you.' " And he said, "I will redeem *it*."

5 Then Boaz said, "On the day you buy the field from the hand of Naomi, you must also buy *it* from Ruth the Moabitess, the wife of the dead, [a]to *perpetuate the name of the dead through his inheritance."

6 [a]And the close relative said, "I cannot redeem *it* for myself, lest I ruin my own inheritance. You redeem my right of redemption for yourself, for I cannot redeem *it*."

7 [a]Now this *was the custom* in former times in Israel concerning redeeming and exchanging, to confirm anything: one man took off his sandal and gave *it* to the other, and this *was* a confirmation in Israel.

8 Therefore the close relative said to Boaz, "Buy *it* for yourself." So he took off his sandal.

9 And Boaz said to the elders and all the people, "You *are* witnesses this day that I have bought all that was Elimelech's, and all that *was* Chilion's and Mahlon's, from the hand of Naomi.

10 "Moreover, Ruth the Moabitess, the widow of Mahlon, I have acquired as my wife, to perpetuate the name of the dead through his inheritance, [a]that the name of the dead may not be cut off from among his brethren and from *his position at the gate. You *are* witnesses this day."

11 And all the people who *were* at the gate, and the elders, said, "*We are* witnesses. [a]The LORD make the woman who is coming to your house like Rachel and Leah, the two who [b]built the house of Israel; and may you prosper in [c]Ephrathah and be famous in [d]Bethlehem.

12 "May your house be like the house of [a]Perez, [b]whom Tamar bore to Judah, because of [c]the offspring which the LORD will give you from this young woman."

---

13 [a]Deut. 25:5–10; Ruth 4:5, 10; Matt. 22:24 [b]Judg. 8:19; Jer. 4:2; 12:16
14 [a][Rom. 12:17; 14:16; 1 Cor. 10:32; 2 Cor. 8:21; 1 Thess. 5:22]
18 [a][Ps. 37:3, 5]

CHAPTER 4

1 [a]Ruth 3:12
2 [a]1 Kin. 21:8; Prov. 31:23
3 [a]Lev. 25:25
4 [a]Jer. 32:7, 8 [b]Gen. 23:18 [c]Lev. 25:25
5 [a]Gen. 38:8; Deut. 25:5, 6; Ruth 3:13; Matt. 22:24
6 [a]Ruth 3:12, 13; Job 19:14
7 [a]Deut. 25:7–10
10 [a]Deut. 25:6
11 [a]Ps. 127:3; 128:3 [b]Gen. 29:25–30; Deut. 25:9 [c]Gen. 35:16–18 [d]1 Sam. 16:4–13; Mic. 5:2; Matt. 2:1–8
12 [a]1 Chr. 2:4; Matt. 1:3 [b]Gen. 38:6–29 [c]1 Sam. 2:20

---

*

3:15 Many Heb. mss., Syr., Vg. *she;* MT, LXX, Tg. *he*
4:1 Heb. *peloni almoni,* lit. *so and so*
4:4 So with many Heb. mss., LXX, Syr., Tg., Vg.; MT *he*
4:5 Lit. *raise up*
4:10 Probably his civic office

KJV

Descendants of Boaz and Ruth
(Matt. 1:2–6)

13 So Boaz [a]took Ruth, and she was his wife:
and when he went in unto her, [b]the LORD gave
her conception, and she bare a son.
14 And [a]the women said unto Naomi,
Blessed *be* the LORD, which hath not left thee this
day without a kinsman, that his name may be famous in Israel.
15 And he shall be unto thee a restorer of
thy life, and a nourisher of thine old age: for thy
daughter in law, which loveth thee, which is [a]bet-
ter to thee than seven sons, hath born him.
16 And Naomi took the child, and laid it in
her bosom, and became nurse unto it.
17 [a]And the women her neighbours gave it
a name, saying, There is a son born to Naomi;
and they called his name Obed: he *is* the father
of Jesse, the father of David.
18 [a]Now these *are* the generations of Pharez:
[b]Pharez begat Hezron,
19 And Hezron begat Ram, and Ram begat
Amminadab,
20 And Amminadab begat [a]Nahshon, and
Nahshon begat [b]Salmon,
21 And Salmon begat Boaz, and Boaz begat
Obed,
22 And Obed begat Jesse, and Jesse begat
[a]David.

13 [a]Ruth 3:11 [b]Gen. 29:31; 33:5; Matt. 1:5
14 [a]Luke 1:58; [Rom. 12:15]
15 [a]1 Sam. 1:8
17 [a]Luke 1:58
18 [a]1 Chr. 2:4, 5; Matt. 1:1–7 [b]Num. 26:20, 21
20 [a]Num. 1:7 [b]Matt. 1:4
22 [a]1 Chr. 2:15; Matt. 1:6

***4:20** Heb. *Salmah*

NKJV

Descendants of Boaz and Ruth
(Matt. 1:2–6)

13 So Boaz [a]took Ruth and she became his
wife; and when he went in to her, [b]the LORD gave
her conception, and she bore a son.
14 Then [a]the women said to Naomi, "Blessed
be the LORD, who has not left you this day without
a close relative; and may his name be famous in
Israel!
15 "And may he be to you a restorer of life
and a nourisher of your old age; for your daughter-in-law, who loves you, who is [a]better to you
than seven sons, has borne him."
16 Then Naomi took the child and laid him
on her bosom, and became a nurse to him.
17 [a]Also the neighbor women gave him a
name, saying, "There is a son born to Naomi."
And they called his name Obed. He *is* the father
of Jesse, the father of David.
18 [a]Now this *is* the genealogy of Perez: [b]Pe-
rez begot Hezron;
19 Hezron begot Ram, and Ram begot Amminadab;
20 Amminadab begot [a]Nahshon, and Nahshon begot [b]Salmon;*
21 Salmon begot Boaz, and Boaz begot Obed;
22 Obed begot Jesse, and Jesse begot [a]David.

KJV

THE FIRST BOOK OF

SAMUEL

The Family of Elkanah

1 Now there was a certain man of Ramathaim–
zophim, of [a]mount Ephraim, and his name
was [b]Elkanah, the son of Jeroham, the son of
Elihu, the son of Tohu, the son of Zuph, [c]an
Ephrathite:
2 And he had [a]two wives; the name of the
one *was* Hannah, and the name of the other Peninnah: and Peninnah had children, but Hannah
had no children.
3 And this man went up out of his city
[a]yearly [b]to worship and to sacrifice unto the
LORD of hosts in [c]Shiloh. And the two sons of Eli,
Hophni and Phinehas, the priests of the LORD,
were there.
4 And when the time was that Elkanah [a]of-
fered, he gave to Peninnah his wife, and to all
her sons and her daughters, portions:
5 But unto Hannah he gave a worthy portion; for he loved Hannah: [a]but the LORD had shut
up her womb.
6 And her adversary also [a]provoked her
sore, for to make her fret, because the LORD had
shut up her womb.
7 And *as* he did so year by year, when she
went up to the house of the LORD, so she provoked
her; therefore she wept, and did not eat.

Hannah's Vow

8 Then said Elkanah her husband to her,
Hannah, why weepest thou? and why eatest thou
not? and why is thy heart grieved? *am* not I [a]better
to thee than ten sons?
9 So Hannah rose up after they had eaten
in Shiloh, and after they had drunk. Now Eli the
priest sat upon a seat by a post of [a]the temple of
the LORD.
10 [a]And she *was* in bitterness of soul, and
prayed unto the LORD, and wept sore.
11 And she [a]vowed a vow, and said, O LORD
of hosts, if thou wilt indeed [b]look on the affliction
of thine handmaid, and [c]remember me, and not
forget thine handmaid, but wilt give unto thine
handmaid a man child, then I will give him unto
the LORD all the days of his life, and there [d]shall
no razor come upon his head.
12 And it came to pass, as she continued
praying before the LORD, that Eli marked her
mouth.
13 Now Hannah, she spake in her heart; only
her lips moved, but her voice was not heard:
therefore Eli thought she had been drunken.
14 And Eli said unto her, How long wilt thou
be drunken? put away thy wine from thee.
15 And Hannah answered and said, No, my
lord, I *am* a woman of a sorrowful spirit: I have
drunk neither wine nor strong drink, but have
[a]poured out my soul before the LORD.
16 Count not thine handmaid for a daughter
of [a]Belial: for out of the abundance of my complaint and grief have I spoken hitherto.
17 Then Eli answered and said, [a]Go in peace:
and [b]the God of Israel grant *thee* thy petition that
thou hast asked of him.
18 And she said, [a]Let thine handmaid find
grace in thy sight. So the woman [b]went her way,

CHAPTER 1

1 [a]Josh. 17:17, 18; 24:33 [b]1 Chr. 6:27, 33–38 [c]Ruth 1:2
2 [a]Deut. 21:15–17
3 [a]Ex. 34:14, 23; Judg. 21:19; 1 Sam. 1:21; Luke 2:41 [b]Deut. 12:5–7; 16:16 [c]Josh. 18:1
4 [a]Deut. 12:17, 18
5 [a]Gen. 16:1; 30:1, 2
6 [a]Job 24:21
8 [a]Ruth 4:15
9 [a]1 Sam. 3:3
10 [a]Job 7:11
11 [a]Gen. 28:20; Num. 30:6–11 [b]Ps. 25:18 [c]Gen. 8:1 [d]Num. 6:5; Judg. 13:5
15 [a]Job 30:16; Ps. 42:4; 62:8; Lam. 2:19
16 [a]Deut. 13:13
17 [a]Judg. 18:6; 1 Sam. 25:35; 2 Kin. 5:19; Mark 5:34; Luke 7:50 [b]Ps. 20:3–5
18 [a]Gen. 33:15; Ruth 2:13 [b]Prov. 15:13; Eccl. 9:7; Rom. 15:13

*

1:1 *Eliel,* 1 Chr. 6:34 • *Toah,* 1 Chr. 6:34
1:9 *palace* or *temple,* Heb. *heykal*
1:16 Lit. *daughter of Belial*

NKJV

THE FIRST BOOK OF

SAMUEL

The Family of Elkanah

1 Now there was a certain man of Ramathaim
Zophim, of the [a]mountains of Ephraim, and
his name *was* [b]Elkanah the son of Jeroham, the
son of *Elihu, the son of *Tohu, the son of Zuph,
[c]an Ephraimite.
2 And he had [a]two wives: the name of one
was Hannah, and the name of the other Peninnah.
Peninnah had children, but Hannah had no
children.
3 This man went up from his city [a]yearly
[b]to worship and sacrifice to the LORD of hosts in
[c]Shiloh. Also the two sons of Eli, Hophni and
Phinehas, the priests of the LORD, *were* there.
4 And whenever the time came for Elkanah
to make an [a]offering, he would give portions to
Peninnah his wife and to all her sons and
daughters.
5 But to Hannah he would give a double
portion, for he loved Hannah, [a]although the LORD
had closed her womb.
6 And her rival also [a]provoked her severely,
to make her miserable, because the LORD had
closed her womb.
7 So it was, year by year, when she went
up to the house of the LORD, that she provoked
her; therefore she wept and did not eat.

Hannah's Vow

8 Then Elkanah her husband said to her,
"Hannah, why do you weep? Why do you not eat?
And why is your heart grieved? *Am* I not [a]better
to you than ten sons?"
9 So Hannah arose after they had finished
eating and drinking in Shiloh. Now Eli the priest
was sitting on the seat by the doorpost of [a]the
*tabernacle of the LORD.
10 [a]And she *was* in bitterness of soul, and
prayed to the LORD and wept in anguish.
11 Then she [a]made a vow and said, "O LORD
of hosts, if You will indeed [b]look on the affliction
of Your maidservant and [c]remember me, and not
forget Your maidservant, but will give Your maidservant a male child, then I will give him to the
LORD all the days of his life, and [d]no razor shall
come upon his head."
12 And it happened, as she continued praying before the LORD, that Eli watched her mouth.
13 Now Hannah spoke in her heart; only her
lips moved, but her voice was not heard. Therefore Eli thought she was drunk.
14 So Eli said to her, "How long will you be
drunk? Put your wine away from you!"
15 But Hannah answered and said, "No, my
lord, I *am* a woman of sorrowful spirit. I have
drunk neither wine nor intoxicating drink, but
have [a]poured out my soul before the LORD.
16 "Do not consider your maidservant a
[a]wicked* woman, for out of the abundance of my
complaint and grief I have spoken until now."
17 Then Eli answered and said, [a]"Go in
peace, and [b]the God of Israel grant your petition
which you have asked of Him."
18 And she said, [a]"Let your maidservant
find favor in your sight." So the woman [b]went

KJV

and did eat, and her countenance was no more
sad.

Samuel Is Born and Dedicated

19 And they rose up in the morning early,
and worshipped before the LORD, and returned,
and came to their house to Ramah: and Elkanah
[a]knew Hannah his wife; and the LORD [b]remem-
bered her.
20 Wherefore it came to pass, when the time
was come about after Hannah had conceived, that
she bare a son, and called his name Samuel, *saying,* Because I have asked him of the LORD.
21 And the man Elkanah, and all his house,
[a]went up to offer unto the LORD the yearly sacrifice, and his vow.
22 But Hannah went not up; for she said unto
her husband, *I will not go up* until the child be
weaned, and *then* I will [a]bring him, that he may
appear before the LORD, and there [b]abide [c]for
ever.
23 And [a]Elkanah her husband said unto her,
Do what seemeth thee good; tarry until thou have
weaned him; only the LORD establish his word.
So the woman abode, and gave her son suck until
she weaned him.
24 And when she had weaned him, she [a]took
him up with her, with three bullocks, and one
ephah of flour, and a bottle of wine, and brought
him unto [b]the house of the LORD in Shiloh: and
the child *was* young.
25 And they slew a bullock, and [a]brought the
child to Eli.
26 And she said, Oh my lord, [a]*as* thy soul
liveth, my lord, I *am* the woman that stood by
thee here, praying unto the LORD.
27 [a]For this child I prayed; and the LORD hath
given me my petition which I asked of him:
28 Therefore also I have lent him to the LORD;
as long as he liveth he shall be lent to the LORD.
And he [a]worshipped the LORD there.

Hannah's Prayer
(cf. Luke 1:46–55)

2 And Hannah [a]prayed, and said, [b]My heart rejoiceth in the LORD, [c]mine horn is exalted in
the LORD: my mouth is enlarged over mine enemies; because I [d]rejoice in thy salvation.
2 [a]*There is* none holy as the LORD: for *there
is* [b]none beside thee: neither *is there* any [c]rock
like our God.
3 Talk no more so exceeding proudly; [a]let
not arrogancy come out of your mouth: for the
LORD *is* a God of [b]knowledge, and by him actions
are weighed.
4 [a]The bows of the mighty men *are* broken,
and they that stumbled are girded with strength.
5 *They that were* full have hired out themselves for bread; and *they that were* hungry
ceased: so that [a]the barren hath born seven; and
[b]she that hath many children is waxed feeble.
6 [a]The LORD killeth, and maketh alive: he
bringeth down to the grave, and bringeth up.
7 The LORD [a]maketh poor, and maketh rich:
[b]he bringeth low, and lifteth up.
8 [a]He raiseth up the poor out of the dust,
and lifteth up the beggar from the dunghill, [b]to
set *them* among princes, and to make them inherit

19 [a]Gen. 4:1 [b]Gen. 21:1; 30:22
21 [a]Deut. 12:11; 1 Sam. 1:3
22 [a]Luke 2:22 [b]1 Sam. 1:11, 28 [c]Ex. 21:6
23 [a]Num. 30:7, 10, 11
24 [a]Num. 15:9, 10; Deut. 12:5, 6 [b]Josh. 18:1; 1 Sam. 4:3, 4
25 [a]Luke 2:22
26 [a]2 Kin. 2:2, 4, 6; 4:30
27 [a][Matt. 7:7]
28 [a]Gen. 24:26, 52

CHAPTER 2

1 [a]Phil. 4:6 [b]1 Sam. 2:1–10; Ps. 97:11, 12; Luke 1:46–55 [c]Ps. 75:10; 89:17, 24; 92:10; 112:9 [d]Ps. 9:14; 13:5; 35:9; Is. 12:2, 3
2 [a]Ex. 15:11; Ps. 86:8; Rev. 15:4 [b]Deut. 4:35 [c]Deut. 32:4, 30, 31; 2 Sam. 22:32; Ps. 18:2
3 [a]Ps. 94:4 [b]1 Sam. 16:7
4 [a]Ps. 37:15; 46:9
5 [a]Ps. 113:9 [b]Is. 54:1; Jer. 15:9
6 [a]Deut. 32:39; 2 Kin. 5:7; Job 5:18; [Rev. 1:18]
7 [a]Deut. 8:17, 18; Job 1:21 [b]Job 5:11; Ps. 75:7; James 4:10
8 [a]Job 42:10–12; Ps. 75:7; 113:7; Luke 1:52 [b]Job 36:7; Ps. 113:8

*———

1:20 Lit. *Heard by God*
1:23 So with MT, Tg., Vg.; DSS, LXX, Syr. *your*
1:24 DSS, LXX, Syr. *a three-year-old bull*
2:1 Strength

NKJV

her way and ate, and her face was no longer
sad.

Samuel Is Born and Dedicated

19 Then they rose early in the morning and
worshiped before the LORD, and returned and
came to their house at Ramah. And Elkanah
[a]knew Hannah his wife, and the LORD [b]remem-
bered her.
20 So it came to pass in the process of time
that Hannah conceived and bore a son, and called
his name *Samuel, *saying,* "Because I have asked
for him from the LORD."
21 Now the man Elkanah and all his house
[a]went up to offer to the LORD the yearly sacrifice
and his vow.
22 But Hannah did not go up, for she said
to her husband, "*Not* until the child is weaned;
then I will [a]take him, that he may appear before
the LORD and [b]remain there [c]forever."
23 So [a]Elkanah her husband said to her, "Do
what seems best to you; wait until you have
weaned him. Only let the LORD establish *His
word." Then the woman stayed and nursed her
son until she had weaned him.
24 Now when she had weaned him, she [a]took
him up with her, with *three bulls, one ephah of
flour, and a skin of wine, and brought him to [b]the
house of the LORD in Shiloh. And the child *was*
young.
25 Then they slaughtered a bull, and
[a]brought the child to Eli.
26 And she said, "O my lord! [a]As your soul
lives, my lord, I *am* the woman who stood by you
here, praying to the LORD.
27 [a]"For this child I prayed, and the LORD
has granted me my petition which I asked of
Him.
28 "Therefore I also have lent him to the
LORD; as long as he lives he shall be lent to the
LORD." So they [a]worshiped the LORD there.

Hannah's Prayer
(cf. Luke 1:46–55)

2 And Hannah [a]prayed and said:

[b]"My heart rejoices in the LORD;
[c]My *horn is exalted in the LORD.
I smile at my enemies,
Because I [d]rejoice in Your salvation.

2 "No[a] one is holy like the LORD,
For *there is* [b]none besides You,
Nor *is there* any [c]rock like our God.

3 "Talk no more so very proudly;
[a]Let no arrogance come from your mouth,
For the LORD *is* the God of [b]knowledge;
And by Him actions are weighed.

4 "The[a] bows of the mighty men *are* broken,
And those who stumbled are girded with
strength.
5 *Those who were* full have hired
themselves out for bread,
And the hungry have ceased *to hunger.*
Even [a]the barren has borne seven,
And [b]she who has many children has
become feeble.

6 "The[a] LORD kills and makes alive;
He brings down to the grave and brings
up.
7 The LORD [a]makes poor and makes rich;
[b]He brings low and lifts up.
8 [a]He raises the poor from the dust
And lifts the beggar from the ash heap,
[b]To set *them* among princes
And make them inherit the throne of
glory.

KJV

the throne of glory: [c]for the pillars of the earth
are the LORD's, and he hath set the world upon
them.
9 [a]He will keep the feet of his saints, and
the [b]wicked shall be silent in darkness; for by
strength shall no man prevail.
10 The adversaries of the LORD shall be [a]bro-
ken to pieces; [b]out of heaven shall he thunder
upon them: [c]the LORD shall judge the ends of the
earth; and [d]he shall give [e]strength unto his king,
and [f]exalt the horn of his anointed.
11 And Elkanah went to Ramah to his house.
And the child did minister unto the LORD before
Eli the priest.

The Wicked Sons of Eli

12 Now the sons of Eli *were* [a]sons of Belial;
[b]they knew not the LORD.
13 And the priest's custom with the people
was, that, when any man offered sacrifice, the
priest's servant came, while the flesh was in seething, with a fleshhook of three teeth in his hand;
14 And he struck *it* into the pan, or kettle,
or caldron, or pot; all that the fleshhook brought
up the priest took for himself. So they did in [a]Shi-
loh unto all the Israelites that came thither.
15 Also before they [a]burnt the fat, the priest's
servant came, and said to the man that sacrificed,
Give flesh to roast for the priest; for he will not
have sodden flesh of thee, but raw.
16 And *if* any man said unto him, Let them
not fail to burn the fat presently, and *then* take
as much as thy soul desireth; then he would answer him, *Nay;* but thou shalt give *it me* now:
and if not, I will take *it* by force.
17 Wherefore the sin of the young men was
very great [a]before the LORD: for men [b]abhorred
the offering of the LORD.

Samuel's Childhood Ministry

18 [a]But Samuel ministered before the LORD,
being a child, [b]girded with a linen ephod.
19 Moreover his mother made him a little
coat, and brought *it* to him from year to year,
when she [a]came up with her husband to offer the
yearly sacrifice.
20 And Eli [a]blessed Elkanah and his wife,
and said, The LORD give thee seed of this woman
for the loan which is [b]lent to the LORD. And they
went unto their own home.
21 And the LORD [a]visited Hannah, so that she
conceived, and bare three sons and two daughters. And the child Samuel [b]grew before the LORD.

Prophecy Against Eli's Household

22 Now Eli was very old, and heard all that
his sons did unto all Israel; and how they lay with
[a]the women that assembled *at* the door of the tabernacle of the congregation.
23 And he said unto them, Why do ye such
things? for I hear of your evil dealings by all this
people.
24 Nay, my sons; for *it is* no good report that
I hear: ye make the LORD's people to transgress.
25 If one man sin against another, the [a]judge
shall judge him: but if a man [b]sin against the
LORD, who shall intreat for him? Notwithstanding
they hearkened not unto the voice of their father,
[c]because the LORD would slay them.
26 And the child Samuel [a]grew on, and was
[b]in favour both with the LORD, and also with men.
27 And there came a [a]man of God unto Eli,
and said unto him, Thus saith the LORD, [b]Did I

8 [c]Job 38:4–6; Ps. 75:3; 104:5
9 [a]Ps. 37:23, 24; 91:11, 12; 94:18; 121:3; Prov. 3:26; [1 Pet. 1:5] [b][Rom. 3:19]
10 [a]Ex. 15:6; Ps. 2:9 [b]1 Sam. 7:10; 2 Sam. 22:14, 15; Ps. 18:13, 14 [c]Ps. 96:13; 98:9; [Matt. 25:31, 32] [d][Matt. 28:18] [e]Ps. 21:1, 7 [f]Ps. 89:24
12 [a]Deut. 13:13 [b]Judg. 2:10; [Rom. 1:28]
14 [a]1 Sam. 1:3
15 [a]Lev. 3:3–5, 16
17 [a]Gen. 6:11 [b][Mal. 2:7–9]
18 [a]1 Sam. 2:11; 3:1 [b]Ex. 28:4
19 [a]1 Sam. 1:3, 21
20 [a]Gen. 14:19 [b]1 Sam. 1:11, 27, 28
21 [a]Gen. 21:1 [b]Judg. 13:24; 1 Sam. 2:26; 3:19–21; Luke 1:80; 2:40
22 [a]Ex. 38:8
25 [a]Deut. 1:17; 25:1, 2 [b]Num. 15:30 [c]Josh. 11:20
26 [a]1 Sam. 2:21 [b]Prov. 3:4
27 [a]Deut. 33:1; Judg. 13:6; 1 Sam. 9:6; 1 Kin. 13:1 [b]Ex. 4:14–16; 12:1

NKJV

[c]"For the pillars of the earth *are* the LORD's,
And He has set the world upon them.
9 [a]He will guard the feet of His saints,
But the [b]wicked shall be silent in
darkness.

"For by strength no man shall prevail.
10 The adversaries of the LORD shall be
[a]broken in pieces;
[b]From heaven He will thunder against
them.
[c]The LORD will judge the ends of the earth.

[d]"He will give [e]strength to His king,
And [f]exalt the horn of His anointed."

11 Then Elkanah went to his house at Ramah. But the child ministered to the LORD before
Eli the priest.

The Wicked Sons of Eli

12 Now the sons of Eli *were* [a]corrupt;* [b]they
did not know the LORD.
13 And the priests' custom with the people
was that when any man offered a sacrifice, the
priest's servant would come with a three-pronged
fleshhook in his hand while the meat was boiling.
14 Then he would thrust *it* into the pan, or
kettle, or caldron, or pot; and the priest would
take for himself all that the fleshhook brought up.
So they did in [a]Shiloh to all the Israelites who
came there.
15 Also, before they [a]burned the fat, the
priest's servant would come and say to the man
who sacrificed, "Give meat for roasting to the
priest, for he will not take boiled meat from you,
but raw."
16 And *if* the man said to him, "They should
really burn the fat first; *then* you may take *as
much* as your heart desires," he would then answer him, "*No,* but you must give *it* now; and if
not, I will take *it* by force."
17 Therefore the sin of the young men was
very great [a]before the LORD, for men [b]abhorred
the offering of the LORD.

Samuel's Childhood Ministry

18 [a]But Samuel ministered before the LORD,
even as a child, [b]wearing a linen ephod.
19 Moreover his mother used to make him a
little robe, and bring *it* to him year by year when
she [a]came up with her husband to offer the yearly
sacrifice.
20 And Eli [a]would bless Elkanah and his
wife, and say, "The LORD give you descendants
from this woman for the loan that was [b]given to
the LORD." Then they would go to their own home.
21 And the LORD [a]visited Hannah, so that she
conceived and bore three sons and two daughters.
Meanwhile the child Samuel [b]grew before the
LORD.

Prophecy Against Eli's Household

22 Now Eli was very old; and he heard everything his sons did to all Israel, *and how they lay
with [a]the women who assembled at the door of
the tabernacle of meeting.
23 So he said to them, "Why do you do such
things? For I hear of your evil dealings from all
the people.
24 "No, my sons! For *it is* not a good report
that I hear. You make the LORD's people transgress.
25 "If one man sins against another, [a]God
will judge him. But if a man [b]sins against the
LORD, who will intercede for him?" Nevertheless
they did not heed the voice of their father, [c]be-
cause the LORD desired to kill them.
26 And the child Samuel [a]grew in stature,
and [b]in favor both with the LORD and men.
27 Then a [a]man of God came to Eli and said
to him, "Thus says the LORD: [b]'Did I not clearly

2:12 Lit. *sons of Belial*
2:22 So with MT, Tg., Vg.; DSS, LXX omit rest of verse

KJV

plainly appear unto the house of thy father, when they were in Egypt in Pharaoh's house?
28 And did I [a]choose him out of all the tribes of Israel *to be* my priest, to offer upon mine altar, to burn incense, to wear an ephod before me? and [b]did I give unto the house of thy father all the offerings made by fire of the children of Israel?
29 Wherefore [a]kick ye at my sacrifice and at mine offering, which I have commanded *in my* [b]habitation; and honourest thy sons above [c]me, to make yourselves fat with the chiefest of all the offerings of Israel my people?
30 Wherefore the LORD God of Israel saith, [a]I said indeed *that* thy house, and the house of thy father, should walk before me for ever: but now the LORD saith, [b]Be it far from me; for them that honour me I will honour, and [c]they that despise me shall be lightly esteemed.
31 Behold, [a]the days come, that I will cut off thine arm, and the arm of thy father's house, that there shall not be an old man in thine house.
32 And thou shalt see an enemy *in my* habitation, in all *the wealth* which *God* shall give Israel: and there shall not be [a]an old man in thine house for ever.
33 And the man of thine, *whom* I shall not cut off from mine altar, *shall be* to consume thine eyes, and to grieve thine heart: and all the increase of thine house shall die in the flower of their age.
34 And this *shall be* [a]a sign unto thee, that shall come upon thy two sons, on Hophni and Phinehas; [b]in one day they shall die both of them.
35 And [a]I will raise me up a faithful priest, *that* shall do according to *that* which *is* in mine heart and in my mind: and [b]I will build him a sure house; and he shall walk before [c]mine anointed for ever.
36 [a]And it shall come to pass, *that* every one that is left in thine house shall come *and* crouch to him for a piece of silver and a morsel of bread, and shall say, Put me, I pray thee, into one of the priests' offices, that I may eat a piece of bread.

Samuel's First Prophecy

3 And [a]the child Samuel ministered unto the LORD before Eli. And [b]the word of the LORD was precious in those days; *there was* no open vision.
2 And it came to pass at that time, when Eli *was* laid down in his place, and his eyes began to wax [a]dim, *that* he could not see;
3 And ere [a]the lamp of God went out in the temple of the LORD, where the ark of God *was,* and Samuel was laid down *to sleep;*
4 That the LORD called Samuel: and he answered, Here *am* I.
5 And he ran unto Eli, and said, Here *am* I; for thou calledst me. And he said, I called not; lie down again. And he went and lay down.
6 And the LORD called yet again, Samuel. And Samuel arose and went to Eli, and said, Here *am* I; for thou didst call me. And he answered, I called not, my son; lie down again.
7 Now Samuel [a]did not yet know the LORD, neither was the word of the LORD yet revealed unto him.
8 And the LORD called Samuel again the third time. And he arose and went to Eli, and said, Here *am* I; for thou didst call me. And Eli perceived that the LORD had called the child.
9 Therefore Eli said unto Samuel, Go, lie down: and it shall be, if he call thee, that thou shalt say, [a]Speak, LORD; for thy servant heareth. So Samuel went and lay down in his place.
10 And the LORD came, and stood, and called as at other times, Samuel, Samuel. Then Samuel answered, Speak; for thy servant heareth.
11 And the LORD said to Samuel, Behold, I

28 [a]Ex. 28:1, 4; Num. 16:5 [b]Lev. 2:3, 10; 6:16; 7:7, 8, 34, 35; Num. 5:9
29 [a]Deut. 32:15 [b]Deut. 12:5; Ps. 26:8 [c]Matt. 10:37
30 [a]Ex. 29:9; Num. 25:13 [b]Jer. 18:9, 10 [c]Ps. 91:14; Mal. 2:9–12
31 [a]1 Sam. 4:11–18; 22:18, 19; 1 Kin. 2:27, 35
32 [a]Zech. 8:4
34 [a]1 Sam. 10:7–9; 1 Kin. 13:3 [b]1 Sam. 4:11, 17
35 [a]1 Kin. 2:35; Ezek. 44:15; [Heb. 2:17; 7:26–28] [b]2 Sam. 7:11, 27; 1 Kin. 11:38 [c]Ps. 18:50
36 [a]1 Kin. 2:27

CHAPTER 3

1 [a]1 Sam. 2:11, 18 [b]Ps. 74:9; Ezek. 7:26; Amos 8:11, 12
2 [a]Gen. 27:1; 48:10; 1 Sam. 4:15
3 [a]Ex. 27:20, 21
7 [a]1 Sam. 2:12; Acts 19:2; 1 Cor. 13:11
9 [a]1 Kin. 2:17

*———

3:3 *palace* or *temple*

NKJV

reveal Myself to the house of your father when they were in Egypt in Pharaoh's house?
28 'Did I not [a]choose him out of all the tribes of Israel *to be* My priest, to offer upon My altar, to burn incense, and to wear an ephod before Me? And [b]did I not give to the house of your father all the offerings of the children of Israel made by fire?
29 'Why do you [a]kick at My sacrifice and My offering which I have commanded *in My* [b]dwelling place, and honor your sons more than [c]Me, to make yourselves fat with the best of all the offerings of Israel My people?'
30 "Therefore the LORD God of Israel says: [a]'I said indeed *that* your house and the house of your father would walk before Me forever.' But now the LORD says: [b]'Far be it from Me; for those who honor Me I will honor, and [c]those who despise Me shall be lightly esteemed.
31 'Behold, [a]the days are coming that I will cut off your arm and the arm of your father's house, so that there will not be an old man in your house.
32 'And you will see an enemy *in My* dwelling place, *despite* all the good which God does for Israel. And there shall not be [a]an old man in your house forever.
33 'But any of your men *whom* I do not cut off from My altar shall consume your eyes and grieve your heart. And all the descendants of your house shall die in the flower of their age.
34 'Now this *shall be* [a]a sign to you that will come upon your two sons, on Hophni and Phinehas: [b]in one day they shall die, both of them.
35 'Then [a]I will raise up for Myself a faithful priest *who* shall do according to what *is* in My heart and in My mind. [b]I will build him a sure house, and he shall walk before [c]My anointed forever.
36 [a]'And it shall come to pass that everyone who is left in your house will come *and* bow down to him for a piece of silver and a morsel of bread, and say, "Please, put me in one of the priestly positions, that I may eat a piece of bread." ' "

Samuel's First Prophecy

3 Now [a]the boy Samuel ministered to the LORD before Eli. And [b]the word of the LORD was rare in those days; *there was* no widespread revelation.
2 And it came to pass at that time, while Eli *was* lying down in his place, and when his eyes had begun to grow [a]so dim that he could not see,
3 and before [a]the lamp of God went out in the *tabernacle of the LORD where the ark of God *was,* and while Samuel was lying down,
4 that the LORD called Samuel. And he answered, "Here I am!"
5 So he ran to Eli and said, "Here I am, for you called me." And he said, "I did not call; lie down again." And he went and lay down.
6 Then the LORD called yet again, "Samuel!" So Samuel arose and went to Eli, and said, "Here I am, for you called me." He answered, "I did not call, my son; lie down again."
7 (Now Samuel [a]did not yet know the LORD, nor was the word of the LORD yet revealed to him.)
8 And the LORD called Samuel again the third time. So he arose and went to Eli, and said, "Here I am, for you did call me." Then Eli perceived that the LORD had called the boy.
9 Therefore Eli said to Samuel, "Go, lie down; and it shall be, if He calls you, that you must say, [a]'Speak, LORD, for Your servant hears.' " So Samuel went and lay down in his place.
10 Now the LORD came and stood and called as at other times, "Samuel! Samuel!" And Samuel answered, "Speak, for Your servant hears."
11 Then the LORD said to Samuel: "Behold, I

KJV

will do a thing in Israel, [a]at which both the ears
of every one that heareth it shall tingle.
12 In that day I will perform against Eli [a]all
things which I have spoken concerning his house:
when I begin, I will also make an end.
13 [a]For I have told him that I will [b]judge his
house for ever for the iniquity which he knoweth;
because [c]his sons made themselves vile, and he
[d]restrained them not.
14 And therefore I have sworn unto the
house of Eli, that the iniquity of Eli's house [a]shall
not be purged with sacrifice nor offering for ever.
15 And Samuel lay until the morning, and
opened the doors of the house of the LORD. And
Samuel feared to shew Eli the vision.
16 Then Eli called Samuel, and said, Samuel,
my son. And he answered, Here *am* I.
17 And he said, What *is* the thing that *the*
LORD hath said unto thee? I pray thee hide *it* not
from me: [a]God do so to thee, and more also, if
thou hide *any* thing from me of all the things that
he said unto thee.
18 And Samuel told him every whit, and hid
nothing from him. And he said, [a]It *is* the LORD:
let him do what seemeth him good.
19 And Samuel [a]grew, and [b]the LORD was
with him, [c]and did let none of his words fall to
the ground.
20 And all Israel [a]from Dan even to Beer–
sheba knew that Samuel *was* established *to be* a
prophet of the LORD.
21 And the LORD appeared again in Shiloh:
for the LORD revealed himself to Samuel in Shiloh
by [a]the word of the LORD.

4 And the word of Samuel came to all Israel.

The Ark of God Captured

Now Israel went out against the Philistines to battle, and pitched beside [a]Eben–ezer: and the Philistines pitched in Aphek.
2 And the [a]Philistines put themselves in array against Israel: and when they joined battle,
Israel was smitten before the Philistines: and they
slew of the army in the field about four thousand
men.
3 And when the people were come into the
camp, the elders of Israel said, Wherefore hath
the LORD smitten us to day before the Philistines?
[a]Let us fetch the ark of the covenant of the LORD
out of Shiloh unto us, that, when it cometh among
us, it may save us out of the hand of our enemies.
4 So the people sent to Shiloh, that they
might bring from thence the ark of the covenant
of the LORD of hosts, [a]which dwelleth *between*
[b]the cherubims: and the [c]two sons of Eli, Hophni
and Phinehas, *were* there with the ark of the covenant of God.
5 And when the ark of the covenant of the
LORD came into the camp, all Israel shouted with
a great shout, so that the earth rang again.
6 And when the Philistines heard the noise
of the shout, they said, What *meaneth* the noise
of this great shout in the camp of the Hebrews?
And they understood that the ark of the LORD was
come into the camp.
7 And the Philistines were afraid, for they
said, God is come into the camp. And they said,
[a]Woe unto us! for there hath not been such a thing
heretofore.
8 Woe unto us! who shall deliver us out of
the hand of these mighty Gods? these *are* the Gods
that smote the Egyptians with all the plagues in
the wilderness.
9 [a]Be strong, and quit yourselves like men,
O ye Philistines, that ye be not servants unto the
Hebrews, [b]as they have been to you: quit yourselves like men, and fight.
10 And the Philistines fought, and [a]Israel
was smitten, and they fled every man into his tent:
and there was a very great slaughter; for there
fell of Israel thirty thousand footmen.

NKJV

will do something in Israel [a]at which both ears
of everyone who hears it will tingle.
12 "In that day I will perform against Eli [a]all
that I have spoken concerning his house, from
beginning to end.
13 [a]"For I have told him that I will [b]judge
his house forever for the iniquity which he knows,
because [c]his sons made themselves vile, and he
[d]did not restrain them.
14 "And therefore I have sworn to the house
of Eli that the iniquity of Eli's house [a]shall not
be atoned for by sacrifice or offering forever."
15 So Samuel lay down until *morning, and
opened the doors of the house of the LORD. And
Samuel was afraid to tell Eli the vision.
16 Then Eli called Samuel and said, "Samuel,
my son!" He answered, "Here I am."
17 And he said, "What *is* the word that *the*
LORD spoke to you? Please do not hide *it* from
me. [a]God do so to you, and more also, if you hide
anything from me of all the things that He said
to you."
18 Then Samuel told him everything, and hid
nothing from him. And he said, [a]"It *is* the LORD.
Let Him do what seems good to Him."
19 So Samuel [a]grew, and [b]the LORD was with
him [c]and let none of his words fall to the ground.
20 And all Israel [a]from Dan to Beersheba
knew that Samuel *had been* established as a
prophet of the LORD.
21 Then the LORD appeared again in Shiloh.
For the LORD revealed Himself to Samuel in Shiloh
by [a]the word of the LORD.

4 And the word of Samuel came to all *Israel.

The Ark of God Captured

Now Israel went out to battle against the Philistines, and encamped beside [a]Ebenezer; and the
Philistines encamped in Aphek.
2 Then the [a]Philistines put themselves in
battle array against Israel. And when they joined
battle, Israel was defeated by the Philistines, who
killed about four thousand men of the army in
the field.
3 And when the people had come into the
camp, the elders of Israel said, "Why has the LORD
defeated us today before the Philistines? [a]Let us
bring the ark of the covenant of the LORD from
Shiloh to us, that when it comes among us it may
save us from the hand of our enemies."
4 So the people sent to Shiloh, that they
might bring from there the ark of the covenant
of the LORD of hosts, [a]who dwells *between* [b]the
cherubim. And the [c]two sons of Eli, Hophni and
Phinehas, *were* there with the ark of the covenant
of God.
5 And when the ark of the covenant of the
LORD came into the camp, all Israel shouted so
loudly that the earth shook.
6 Now when the Philistines heard the noise
of the shout, they said, "What *does* the sound of
this great shout in the camp of the Hebrews
mean?" Then they understood that the ark of the
LORD had come into the camp.
7 So the Philistines were afraid, for they
said, "God has come into the camp!" And they
said, [a]"Woe to us! For such a thing has never happened before.
8 "Woe to us! Who will deliver us from the
hand of these mighty gods? These *are* the gods
who struck the Egyptians with all the plagues in
the wilderness.
9 [a]"Be strong and conduct yourselves like
men, you Philistines, that you do not become servants of the Hebrews, [b]as they have been to you.
Conduct yourselves like men, and fight!"
10 So the Philistines fought, and [a]Israel was
defeated, and every man fled to his tent. There
was a very great slaughter, and there fell of Israel
thirty thousand foot soldiers.

11 [a]2 Kin. 21:12; Jer. 19:3
12 [a]1 Sam. 2:27–36; Ezek. 12:25; Luke 21:33
13 [a]1 Sam. 2:29–31 [b]1 Sam. 2:22; Ezek. 7:3; 18:30 [c]1 Sam. 2:12, 17, 22 [d]1 Sam. 2:23, 25
14 [a]Num. 15:30, 31; Is. 22:14; Heb. 10:4, 26–31
17 [a]Ruth 1:17
18 [a]Gen. 24:50; Ex. 34:5–7; Lev. 10:3; Is. 39:8; Acts 5:39
19 [a]1 Sam. 2:21 [b]Gen. 21:22; 28:15; 39:2, 21, 23 [c]1 Sam. 9:6
20 [a]Judg. 20:1
21 [a]1 Sam. 3:1, 4

CHAPTER 4
1 [a]1 Sam. 7:12
2 [a]1 Sam. 12:9
3 [a]Num. 10:35; Josh. 6:6–21
4 [a]Ex. 25:18–21; 1 Sam. 6:2; Ps. 80:1 [b]Num. 7:89 [c]1 Sam. 2:12
7 [a]Ex. 15:14
9 [a]1 Cor. 16:13 [b]Judg. 13:1; 1 Sam. 14:21
10 [a]Lev. 26:17; Deut. 28:15, 25; 1 Sam. 4:2; 2 Sam. 18:17; 19:8; 2 Kin. 14:12; 2 Chr. 25:22

*
3:15 So with MT, Tg., Vg.; LXX adds *and he arose in the morning*
4:1 So with MT, Tg.; LXX, Vg. add *And it came to pass in those days that the Philistines gathered themselves together to fight;* LXX adds further *against Israel*

KJV

11 And [a]the ark of God was taken; and [b]the
two sons of Eli, Hophni and Phinehas, were slain.

Death of Eli

12 And there ran a man of Benjamin out of
the army, and [a]came to Shiloh the same day with
his clothes rent, and [b]with earth upon his head.
13 And when he came, lo, Eli sat upon [a]a
seat by the wayside watching: for his heart trembled for the ark of God. And when the man came
into the city, and told *it*, all the city cried out.
14 And when Eli heard the noise of the crying, he said, What *meaneth* the noise of this tumult? And the man came in hastily, and told Eli.
15 Now Eli was ninety and eight years old;
and [a]his eyes were dim, that he could not see.
16 And the man said unto Eli, I *am* he that
came out of the army, and I fled to day out of
the army. And he said, [a]What is there done, my
son?
17 And the messenger answered and said, Israel is fled before the Philistines, and there hath
been also a great slaughter among the people, and
thy two sons also, Hophni and Phinehas, are dead,
and the ark of God is taken.
18 And it came to pass, when he made mention of the ark of God, that he fell from off the
seat backward by the side of the gate, and his
neck brake, and he died: for he was an old man,
and heavy. And he had judged Israel forty years.

Ichabod

19 And his daughter in law, Phinehas' wife,
was with child, *near* to be delivered: and when
she heard the tidings that the ark of God was
taken, and that her father in law and her husband
were dead, she bowed herself and travailed; for
her pains came upon her.
20 And about the time of her death [a]the
women that stood by her said unto her, Fear not;
for thou hast born a son. But she answered not,
neither did she regard *it*.
21 And she named the child [a]I–chabod, saying, [b]The glory is departed from Israel: because
the ark of God was taken, and because of her father in law and her husband.
22 And she said, The glory is departed from
Israel: for the ark of God is taken.

The Philistines and the Ark

5 And the Philistines took the ark of God, and
brought it [a]from Eben–ezer unto Ashdod.
2 When the Philistines took the ark of God,
they brought it into the house of [a]Dagon, and set
it by Dagon.
3 And when they of Ashdod arose early on
the morrow, behold, Dagon *was* [a]fallen upon his
face to the earth before the ark of the LORD. And
they took Dagon, and [b]set him in his place again.
4 And when they arose early on the morrow
morning, behold, Dagon *was* fallen upon his face
to the ground before the ark of the LORD; and [a]the
head of Dagon and both the palms of his hands
were cut off upon the threshold; only *the stump*
of Dagon was left to him.
5 Therefore neither the priests of Dagon,
nor any that come into Dagon's house, [a]tread on
the threshold of Dagon in Ashdod unto this day.
6 But the [a]hand of the LORD was heavy upon
them of Ashdod, and he [b]destroyed them, and
smote them with [c]emerods, *even* Ashdod and the
[d]coasts thereof.
7 And when the men of Ashdod saw that *it*
was so, they said, The ark of the [a]God of Israel
shall not abide with us: for his hand is sore upon
us, and upon Dagon our god.
8 They sent therefore and gathered all the
[a]lords of the Philistines unto them, and said, What
shall we do with the ark of the God of Israel?
And they answered, Let the ark of the God of Is-

---

11 [a]1 Sam. 2:32; Ps. 78:60, 61 [b]1 Sam. 2:34; Ps. 78:64
12 [a]2 Sam. 1:2 [b]Josh. 7:6; 2 Sam. 13:19; 15:32; Neh. 9:1; Job 2:12
13 [a]1 Sam. 1:9; 4:18
15 [a]1 Sam. 3:2; 1 Kin. 14:4
16 [a]2 Sam. 1:4
20 [a]Gen. 35:16–19
21 [a]1 Sam. 14:3 [b]Ps. 26:8; 78:61; [Jer. 2:11]

CHAPTER 5

1 [a]1 Sam. 4:1; 7:12
2 [a]Judg. 16:23–30; 1 Chr. 10:8–10
3 [a]Is. 19:1; 46:1, 2 [b]Is. 46:7
4 [a]Jer. 50:2; Ezek. 6:4, 6; Mic. 1:7
5 [a]Zeph. 1:9
6 [a]Ex. 9:3; Deut. 2:15; 1 Sam. 5:7; 7:13; Ps. 32:4; 145:20; 147:6 [b]1 Sam. 6:5 [c]Deut. 28:27; Ps. 78:66 [d]Josh. 15:46, 47
7 [a]1 Sam. 6:5
8 [a]1 Sam. 6:4

*

4:13 So with MT, Vg.; LXX *beside the gate watching the road*
4:21 Lit. *Inglorious*
5:2 A Philistine idol
5:4 So with LXX, Syr., Tg., Vg.; MT *Dagon*
5:6 Probably bubonic plague. LXX, Vg. add *And in the midst of their land rats sprang up, and there was a great death panic in the city.*

NKJV

11 Also [a]the ark of God was captured; and
[b]the two sons of Eli, Hophni and Phinehas, died.

Death of Eli

12 Then a man of Benjamin ran from the battle line the same day, and [a]came to Shiloh with
his clothes torn and [b]dirt on his head.
13 Now when he came, there was Eli, sitting
on [a]a seat *by the wayside watching, for his heart
trembled for the ark of God. And when the man
came into the city and told *it*, all the city cried
out.
14 When Eli heard the noise of the outcry,
he said, "What *does* the sound of this tumult
mean?" And the man came quickly and told Eli.
15 Eli was ninety-eight years old, and [a]his
eyes were so dim that he could not see.
16 Then the man said to Eli, "I *am* he who
came from the battle. And I fled today from the
battle line." And he said, [a]"What happened, my
son?"
17 So the messenger answered and said, "Israel has fled before the Philistines, and there has
been a great slaughter among the people. Also
your two sons, Hophni and Phinehas, are dead;
and the ark of God has been captured."
18 Then it happened, when he made mention
of the ark of God, that Eli fell off the seat backward by the side of the gate; and his neck was
broken and he died, for the man was old and
heavy. And he had judged Israel forty years.

Ichabod

19 Now his daughter-in-law, Phinehas' wife,
was with child, *due* to be delivered; and when she
heard the news that the ark of God was captured,
and that her father-in-law and her husband were
dead, she bowed herself and gave birth, for her
labor pains came upon her.
20 And about the time of her death [a]the
women who stood by her said to her, "Do not
fear, for you have borne a son." But she did not
answer, nor did she regard *it*.
21 Then she named the child [a]Ichabod,* saying, [b]"The glory has departed from Israel!" because the ark of God had been captured and
because of her father-in-law and her husband.
22 And she said, "The glory has departed
from Israel, for the ark of God has been captured."

The Philistines and the Ark

5 Then the Philistines took the ark of God and
brought it [a]from Ebenezer to Ashdod.
2 When the Philistines took the ark of God,
they brought it into the house of [a]Dagon* and set
it by Dagon.
3 And when the people of Ashdod arose
early in the morning, there was Dagon, [a]fallen
on its face to the earth before the ark of the
LORD. So they took Dagon and [b]set it in its place
again.
4 And when they arose early the next morning, there was Dagon, fallen on its face to the
ground before the ark of the LORD. [a]The head of
Dagon and both the palms of its hands *were* broken off on the threshold; only *Dagon's torso was
left of it.
5 Therefore neither the priests of Dagon nor
any who come into Dagon's house [a]tread on the
threshold of Dagon in Ashdod to this day.
6 But the [a]hand of the LORD was heavy on
the people of Ashdod, and He [b]ravaged them and
struck them with [c]tumors,* *both* Ashdod and its
[d]territory.
7 And when the men of Ashdod saw how
it was, they said, "The ark of the [a]God of Israel
must not remain with us, for His hand is harsh
toward us and Dagon our god."
8 Therefore they sent and gathered to themselves all the [a]lords of the Philistines, and said,
"What shall we do with the ark of the God of
Israel?" And they answered, "Let the ark of the

KJV

rael be carried about unto [b]Gath. And they carried the ark of the God of Israel about *thither*.

9 And it was so, that, after they had carried it about, [a]the hand of the LORD was against the city with a very great destruction: and he smote the men of the city, both small and great, and they had emerods in their secret parts.

10 Therefore they sent the ark of God to Ekron. And it came to pass, as the ark of God came to Ekron, that the Ekronites cried out, saying, They have brought about the ark of the God of Israel to us, to slay us and our people.

11 So they sent and gathered together all the lords of the Philistines, and said, Send away the ark of the God of Israel, and let it go again to his own place, that it slay us not, and our people: for there was a deadly destruction throughout all the city; the hand of God was very heavy there.

12 And the men that died not were smitten with the emerods: and the [a]cry of the city went up to heaven.

The Ark Returned to Israel

6 And the ark of the LORD was in the country of the Philistines seven months.

2 And the Philistines [a]called for the priests and the diviners, saying, What shall we do to the ark of the LORD? tell us wherewith we shall send it to his place.

3 And they said, If ye send away the ark of the God of Israel, send it not [a]empty; but in any wise return him [b]a trespass offering: then ye shall be healed, and it shall be known to you why his hand is not removed from you.

4 Then said they, What *shall be* the trespass offering which we shall return to him? They answered, [a]Five golden emerods, and five golden mice, *according to* the number of the lords of the Philistines: for one plague *was* on you all, and on your lords.

5 Wherefore ye shall make images of your emerods, and images of your mice that [a]mar the land; and ye shall [b]give glory unto the God of Israel: peradventure he will [c]lighten his hand from off you, and from off [d]your gods, and from off your land.

6 Wherefore then do ye harden your hearts, [a]as the Egyptians and Pharaoh hardened their hearts? when he had wrought wonderfully among them, [b]did they not let the people go, and they departed?

7 Now therefore make [a]a new cart, and take two milch kine, [b]on which there hath come no yoke, and tie the kine to the cart, and bring their calves home from them:

8 And take the ark of the LORD, and lay it upon the cart; and put [a]the jewels of gold, which ye return him *for* a trespass offering, in a coffer by the side thereof; and send it away, that it may go.

9 And see, if it goeth up by the way of his own coast to [a]Beth–shemesh, *then* he hath done us this great evil: but if not, then [b]we shall know that *it is* not his hand *that* smote us; it *was* a chance *that* happened to us.

10 And the men did so; and took two milch kine, and tied them to the cart, and shut up their calves at home:

11 And they laid the ark of the LORD upon the cart, and the coffer with the mice of gold and the images of their emerods.

12 And the kine took the straight way to the way of Beth–shemesh, *and* went along the [a]highway, lowing as they went, and turned not aside *to* the right hand or *to* the left; and the lords of the Philistines went after them unto the border of Beth–shemesh.

13 And *they of* Beth–shemesh *were* reaping their [a]wheat harvest in the valley: and they lifted up their eyes, and saw the ark, and rejoiced to see *it*.

8 [b]Josh. 11:22
9 [a]Deut. 2:15; 1 Sam. 5:11; 7:13; 12:15
12 [a]1 Sam. 9:16; Jer. 14:2

CHAPTER 6

2 [a]Gen. 41:8; Ex. 7:11; Is. 2:6; 47:13; Dan. 2:2; 5:7
3 [a]Ex. 23:15; Deut. 16:16 [b]Lev. 5:15, 16
4 [a]1 Sam. 5:6, 9, 12; 6:17
5 [a]1 Sam. 5:6 [b]Josh. 7:19; 1 Chr. 16:28, 29; Is. 42:12; Jer. 13:16; Mal. 2:2; Rev. 14:7 [c]1 Sam. 5:6, 11; Ps. 39:10 [d]1 Sam. 5:3, 4, 7
6 [a]Ex. 7:13; 8:15; 9:34; 14:17 [b]Ex. 12:31
7 [a]2 Sam. 6:3 [b]Num. 19:2; Deut. 21:3, 4
8 [a]1 Sam. 6:4, 5
9 [a]Josh. 15:10; 21:16 [b]1 Sam. 6:3
12 [a]Num. 20:19
13 [a]1 Sam. 12:17

NKJV

God of Israel be carried away to [b]Gath." So they carried the ark of the God of Israel away.

9 So it was, after they had carried it away, that [a]the hand of the LORD was against the city with a very great destruction; and He struck the men of the city, both small and great, and tumors broke out on them.

10 Therefore they sent the ark of God to Ekron. So it was, as the ark of God came to Ekron, that the Ekronites cried out, saying, "They have brought the ark of the God of Israel to us, to kill us and our people!"

11 So they sent and gathered together all the lords of the Philistines, and said, "Send away the ark of the God of Israel, and let it go back to its own place, so that it does not kill us and our people." For there was a deadly destruction throughout all the city; the hand of God was very heavy there.

12 And the men who did not die were stricken with the tumors, and the [a]cry of the city went up to heaven.

The Ark Returned to Israel

6 Now the ark of the LORD was in the country of the Philistines seven months.

2 And the Philistines [a]called for the priests and the diviners, saying, "What shall we do with the ark of the LORD? Tell us how we should send it to its place."

3 So they said, "If you send away the ark of the God of Israel, do not send it [a]empty; but by all means return *it* to Him *with* [b]a trespass offering. Then you will be healed, and it will be known to you why His hand is not removed from you."

4 Then they said, "What *is* the trespass offering which we shall return to Him?" They answered, [a]"Five golden tumors and five golden rats, *according to* the number of the lords of the Philistines. For the same plague *was* on all of you and on your lords.

5 "Therefore you shall make images of your tumors and images of your rats that [a]ravage the land, and you shall [b]give glory to the God of Israel; perhaps He will [c]lighten His hand from you, from [d]your gods, and from your land.

6 "Why then do you harden your hearts [a]as the Egyptians and Pharaoh hardened their hearts? When He did mighty things among them, [b]did they not let the people go, that they might depart?

7 "Now therefore, make [a]a new cart, take two milk cows [b]which have never been yoked, and hitch the cows to the cart; and take their calves home, away from them.

8 "Then take the ark of the LORD and set it on the cart; and put [a]the articles of gold which you are returning to Him *as* a trespass offering in a chest by its side. Then send it away, and let it go.

9 "And watch: if it goes up the road to its own territory, to [a]Beth Shemesh, *then* He has done us this great evil. But if not, then [b]we shall know that *it is* not His hand *that* struck us—it happened to us by chance."

10 Then the men did so; they took two milk cows and hitched them to the cart, and shut up their calves at home.

11 And they set the ark of the LORD on the cart, and the chest with the gold rats and the images of their tumors.

12 Then the cows headed straight for the road to Beth Shemesh, *and* went along the [a]highway, lowing as they went, and did not turn aside to the right hand or the left. And the lords of the Philistines went after them to the border of Beth Shemesh.

13 Now *the people of* Beth Shemesh *were* reaping their [a]wheat harvest in the valley; and they lifted their eyes and saw the ark, and rejoiced to see *it*.

KJV

14 And the cart came into the field of Joshua,
a Beth–shemite, and stood there, where *there was*
a great stone: and they clave the wood of the cart,
and offered the kine a burnt offering unto the
LORD.
15 And the Levites took down the ark of the
LORD, and the coffer that *was* with it, wherein the
jewels of gold *were*, and put *them* on the great
stone: and the men of Beth–shemesh offered burnt
offerings and sacrificed sacrifices the same day
unto the LORD.
16 And when [a]the five lords of the Philistines
had seen *it*, they returned to Ekron the same day.
17 [a]And these *are* the golden emerods which
the Philistines returned *for* a trespass offering
unto the LORD; for Ashdod one, for Gaza one, for
Askelon one, for [b]Gath one, for Ekron one;
18 And the golden mice, *according to* the
number of all the cities of the Philistines *belonging*
to the five lords, *both* of fenced cities, and of country villages, even unto the great *stone of* Abel,
whereon they set down the ark of the LORD: *which*
stone remaineth unto this day in the field of
Joshua, the Beth–shemite.
19 And [a]he smote the men of Beth–shemesh,
because they had looked into the ark of the LORD,
even he [b]smote of the people fifty thousand and
threescore and ten men: and the people lamented,
because the LORD had smitten *many* of the people
with a great slaughter.

The Ark at Kirjath Jearim

20 And the men of Beth–shemesh said, [a]Who
is able to stand before this holy LORD God? and
to whom shall he go up from us?
21 And they sent messengers to the inhabitants of [a]Kirjath–jearim, saying, The Philistines
have brought again the ark of the LORD; come ye
down, *and* fetch it up to you.

7 And the men of [a]Kirjath–jearim came, and
fetched up the ark of the LORD, and brought
it into the house of [b]Abinadab in the hill, and
[c]sanctified Eleazar his son to keep the ark of the
LORD.

Samuel Judges Israel

2 And it came to pass, while the ark abode
in Kirjath–jearim, that the time was long; for it
was twenty years: and all the house of Israel lamented after the LORD.
3 And Samuel spake unto all the house of
Israel, saying, If ye do [a]return unto the LORD with
all your hearts, *then* [b]put away the strange gods
and [c]Ashtaroth from among you, and [d]prepare
your hearts unto the LORD, and [e]serve him only:
and he will deliver you out of the hand of the
Philistines.
4 Then the children of Israel did put away
[a]Baalim and Ashtaroth, and served the LORD only.
5 And Samuel said, [a]Gather all Israel to
Mizpeh, and [b]I will pray for you unto the LORD.
6 And they gathered together to Mizpeh,
[a]and drew water, and poured *it* out before the
LORD, and [b]fasted on that day, and said there, [c]We
have sinned against the LORD. And Samuel judged
the children of Israel in Mizpeh.
7 And when the Philistines heard that the
children of Israel were gathered together to
Mizpeh, the lords of the Philistines went up
against Israel. And when the children of Israel
heard *it*, they were afraid of the Philistines.
8 And the children of Israel said to Samuel,
[a]Cease not to cry unto the LORD our God for us,
that he will save us out of the hand of the
Philistines.
9 And Samuel took a [a]sucking lamb, and
offered *it for* a burnt offering wholly unto the
LORD: and [b]Samuel cried unto the LORD for Israel;
and the LORD heard him.
10 And as Samuel was offering up the burnt
offering, the Philistines drew near to battle

NKJV

14 Then the cart came into the field of Joshua
of Beth Shemesh, and stood there; a large stone
was there. So they split the wood of the cart and
offered the cows as a burnt offering to the LORD.
15 The Levites took down the ark of the LORD
and the chest that *was* with it, in which *were* the
articles of gold, and put *them* on the large stone.
Then the men of Beth Shemesh offered burnt offerings and made sacrifices the same day to the
LORD.
16 So when [a]the five lords of the Philistines
had seen *it*, they returned to Ekron the same day.
17 [a]These *are* the golden tumors which the
Philistines returned *as* a trespass offering to the
LORD: one for Ashdod, one for Gaza, one for Ashkelon, one for [b]Gath, one for Ekron;
18 and the golden rats, *according to* the number of all the cities of the Philistines *belonging*
to the five lords, *both* fortified cities and country
villages, even as far as the large *stone of* Abel
on which they set the ark of the LORD, *which stone*
remains to this day in the field of Joshua of Beth
Shemesh.
19 Then [a]He struck the men of Beth Shemesh, because they had looked into the ark of
the LORD. *He [b]struck fifty thousand and seventy
men of the people, and the people lamented because the LORD had struck the people with a great
slaughter.

The Ark at Kirjath Jearim

20 And the men of Beth Shemesh said,
[a]"Who is able to stand before this holy LORD God?
And to whom shall it go up from us?"
21 So they sent messengers to the inhabitants
of [a]Kirjath Jearim, saying, "The Philistines have
brought back the ark of the LORD; come down
and take it up with you."

7 Then the men of [a]Kirjath Jearim came and
took the ark of the LORD, and brought it into
the house of [b]Abinadab on the hill, and [c]conse-
crated Eleazar his son to keep the ark of the LORD.

Samuel Judges Israel

2 So it was that the ark remained in Kirjath
Jearim a long time; it was there twenty years. And
all the house of Israel lamented after the LORD.
3 Then Samuel spoke to all the house of Israel, saying, "If you [a]return to the LORD with all
your hearts, *then* [b]put away the foreign gods and
the [c]Ashtoreths* from among you, and [d]prepare
your hearts for the LORD, and [e]serve Him only;
and He will deliver you from the hand of the
Philistines."
4 So the children of Israel put away the
[a]Baals and the *Ashtoreths, and served the LORD
only.
5 And Samuel said, [a]"Gather all Israel to
Mizpah, and [b]I will pray to the LORD for you."
6 So they gathered together at Mizpah,
[a]drew water, and poured *it* out before the LORD.
And they [b]fasted that day, and said there, [c]"We
have sinned against the LORD." And Samuel
judged the children of Israel at Mizpah.
7 Now when the Philistines heard that the
children of Israel had gathered together at
Mizpah, the lords of the Philistines went up
against Israel. And when the children of Israel
heard *of it*, they were afraid of the Philistines.
8 So the children of Israel said to Samuel,
[a]"Do not cease to cry out to the LORD our God
for us, that He may save us from the hand of the
Philistines."
9 And Samuel took a [a]suckling lamb and
offered *it as* a whole burnt offering to the LORD.
Then [b]Samuel cried out to the LORD for Israel,
and the LORD answered him.
10 Now as Samuel was offering up the burnt
offering, the Philistines drew near to battle

---

16 [a]Josh. 13:3; Judg. 3:3 **17** [a]1 Sam. 6:4 [b]1 Sam. 5:8 **19** [a]Ex. 19:21; Num. 4:5, 15, 16, 20 [b]2 Sam. 6:7 **20** [a]Lev. 11:44, 45; Ps. 24:3, 4; Mal. 3:2; Rev. 6:17 **21** [a]Josh. 9:17; 15:9, 60; 18:14; Judg. 18:12; 1 Chr. 13:5, 6

CHAPTER 7

1 [a]1 Sam. 6:21; Ps. 132:6 [b]2 Sam. 6:3, 4 [c]Lev. 21:8 **3** [a]Deut. 30:2–10; 1 Kin. 8:48; Is. 55:7; Hos. 6:1; Joel 2:12–14 [b]Gen. 35:2; Josh. 24:14, 23; Judg. 10:16 [c]Judg. 2:13; 1 Sam. 31:10 [d]2 Chr. 30:19; Job 11:13 [e]Deut. 6:13; 10:20; 13:4; Josh. 24:14; Matt. 4:10; Luke 4:8 **4** [a]Judg. 2:11; 10:16 **5** [a]Judg. 10:17; 20:1; 1 Sam. 10:17 [b]1 Sam. 12:17–19 **6** [a]2 Sam. 14:14 [b]Judg. 20:26; Neh. 9:1, 2; Dan. 9:3–5; Joel 2:12 [c]Judg. 10:10; 1 Sam. 12:10; 1 Kin. 8:47; Ps. 106:6 **8** [a]1 Sam. 12:19–24; Is. 37:4 **9** [a]Lev. 22:27 [b]1 Sam. 12:18; Ps. 99:6; Jer. 15:1

*

6:19 Or *He struck seventy men of the people and fifty oxen of a man*
7:3 Images of Canaanite goddesses
7:4 Images of Canaanite goddesses

KJV

against Israel: [a]but the LORD thundered with a great thunder on that day upon the Philistines, and discomfited them; and they were smitten before Israel.

11 And the men of Israel went out of Mizpeh, and pursued the Philistines, and smote them, until *they came* under Beth–car.

12 Then Samuel [a]took a stone, and set *it* between Mizpeh and Shen, and called the name of it Eben–ezer, saying, Hitherto hath the LORD helped us.

13 [a]So the Philistines were subdued, and they [b]came no more into the coast of Israel: and the hand of the LORD was against the Philistines all the days of Samuel.

14 And the cities which the Philistines had taken from Israel were restored to Israel, from Ekron even unto Gath; and the coasts thereof did Israel deliver out of the hands of the Philistines. And there was peace between Israel and the Amorites.

15 And Samuel [a]judged Israel all the days of his life.

16 And he went from year to year in circuit to Beth–el, and Gilgal, and Mizpeh, and judged Israel in all those places.

17 And [a]his return *was* to Ramah; for there *was* his house; and there he judged Israel; and there he [b]built an altar unto the LORD.

Israel Demands a King

8 And it came to pass, when Samuel was [a]old, that he [b]made his [c]sons judges over Israel.

2 Now the name of his firstborn was Joel; and the name of his second, Abiah: *they were* judges in Beer–sheba.

3 And his sons [a]walked not in his ways, but turned aside [b]after lucre, and [c]took bribes, and perverted judgment.

4 Then all the elders of Israel gathered themselves together, and came to Samuel unto Ramah,

5 And said unto him, Behold, thou art old, and thy sons walk not in thy ways: now [a]make us a king to judge us like all the nations.

6 But the thing [a]displeased Samuel, when they said, Give us a king to judge us. And Samuel [b]prayed unto the LORD.

7 And the LORD said unto Samuel, Hearken unto the voice of the people in all that they say unto thee: for [a]they have not rejected thee, but [b]they have rejected me, that I should not reign over them.

8 According to all the works which they have done since the day that I brought them up out of Egypt even unto this day, wherewith they have forsaken me, and served other gods, so do they also unto thee.

9 Now therefore hearken unto their voice: howbeit yet protest solemnly unto them, and [a]shew them the manner of the king that shall reign over them.

10 And Samuel told all the words of the LORD unto the people that asked of him a king.

11 And he said, [a]This will be the manner of the king that shall reign over you: He will take your [b]sons, and appoint *them* for himself, for his [c]chariots, and *to be* his horsemen; and *some* shall run before his chariots.

12 And he will [a]appoint him captains over thousands, and captains over fifties; and *will set them* to ear his ground, and to reap his harvest, and to make his instruments of war, and instruments of his chariots.

13 And he will take your daughters *to be* confectionaries, and *to be* cooks, and *to be* bakers.

14 And [a]he will take your fields, and your vineyards, and your oliveyards, *even* the best *of them,* and give *them* to his servants.

15 And he will take the tenth of your seed, and of your vineyards, and give to his officers, and to his servants.

10 [a]Josh. 10:10; 2 Sam. 22:14, 15; Ps. 18:13, 14
12 [a]Gen. 28:18; 35:14; Josh. 4:9; 24:26
13 [a]Judg. 13:1 [b]1 Sam. 13:5
15 [a]1 Sam. 12:11
17 [a]1 Sam. 8:4 [b]Judg. 21:4

CHAPTER 8

1 [a]1 Sam. 12:2 [b]Deut. 16:18, 19; 2 Chr. 19:5 [c]Judg. 10:4
3 [a]Jer. 22:15–17 [b]Ex. 18:21 [c]Ex. 23:6–8; Deut. 16:19; 1 Sam. 12:3
5 [a]Deut. 17:14, 15; Hos. 13:10, 11; Acts 13:21
6 [a]1 Sam. 12:17 [b]1 Sam. 7:9
7 [a]Ex. 16:8 [b]1 Sam. 10:19
9 [a]1 Sam. 8:11–18
11 [a]Deut. 17:14–20 [b]1 Sam. 14:52 [c]2 Sam. 15:1
12 [a]1 Sam. 22:7
14 [a]1 Kin. 21:7; [Ezek. 46:18]

*

7:12 Lit. *Stone of Help*

NKJV

against Israel. [a]But the LORD thundered with a loud thunder upon the Philistines that day, and so confused them that they were overcome before Israel.

11 And the men of Israel went out of Mizpah and pursued the Philistines, and drove them back as far as below Beth Car.

12 Then Samuel [a]took a stone and set *it* up between Mizpah and Shen, and called its name *Ebenezer, saying, "Thus far the LORD has helped us."

13 [a]So the Philistines were subdued, and they [b]did not come anymore into the territory of Israel. And the hand of the LORD was against the Philistines all the days of Samuel.

14 Then the cities which the Philistines had taken from Israel were restored to Israel, from Ekron to Gath; and Israel recovered its territory from the hands of the Philistines. Also there was peace between Israel and the Amorites.

15 And Samuel [a]judged Israel all the days of his life.

16 He went from year to year on a circuit to Bethel, Gilgal, and Mizpah, and judged Israel in all those places.

17 But [a]he always returned to Ramah, for his home *was* there. There he judged Israel, and there he [b]built an altar to the LORD.

Israel Demands a King

8 Now it came to pass when Samuel was [a]old that he [b]made his [c]sons judges over Israel.

2 The name of his firstborn was Joel, and the name of his second, Abijah; *they were* judges in Beersheba.

3 But his sons [a]did not walk in his ways; they turned aside [b]after dishonest gain, [c]took bribes, and perverted justice.

4 Then all the elders of Israel gathered together and came to Samuel at Ramah,

5 and said to him, "Look, you are old, and your sons do not walk in your ways. Now [a]make us a king to judge us like all the nations."

6 But the thing [a]displeased Samuel when they said, "Give us a king to judge us." So Samuel [b]prayed to the LORD.

7 And the LORD said to Samuel, "Heed the voice of the people in all that they say to you; for [a]they have not rejected you, but [b]they have rejected Me, that I should not reign over them.

8 "According to all the works which they have done since the day that I brought them up out of Egypt, even to this day—with which they have forsaken Me and served other gods—so they are doing to you also.

9 "Now therefore, heed their voice. However, you shall solemnly forewarn them, and [a]show them the behavior of the king who will reign over them."

10 So Samuel told all the words of the LORD to the people who asked him for a king.

11 And he said, [a]"This will be the behavior of the king who will reign over you: He will take your [b]sons and appoint *them* for his own [c]chariots and *to be* his horsemen, and *some* will run before his chariots.

12 "He will [a]appoint captains over his thousands and captains over his fifties, *will set some* to plow his ground and reap his harvest, and *some* to make his weapons of war and equipment for his chariots.

13 "He will take your daughters *to be* perfumers, cooks, and bakers.

14 "And [a]he will take the best of your fields, your vineyards, and your olive groves, and give *them* to his servants.

15 "He will take a tenth of your grain and your vintage, and give it to his officers and servants.

KJV

16 And he will take your menservants, and
your maidservants, and your goodliest young
men, and your asses, and put *them* to his work.
17 He will take the tenth of your sheep: and
ye shall be his servants.
18 And ye shall cry out in that day because
of your king which ye shall have chosen you; and
the LORD [a]will not hear you in that day.
19 Nevertheless the people [a]refused to obey
the voice of Samuel; and they said, Nay; but we
will have a king over us;
20 That we also may be [a]like all the nations;
and that our king may judge us, and go out before
us, and fight our battles.
21 And Samuel heard all the words of the
people, and he rehearsed them in the ears of the
LORD.
22 And the LORD said to Samuel, [a]Hearken
unto their voice, and make them a king. And Samuel said unto the men of Israel, Go ye every man
unto his city.

Saul Chosen to Be King

9 Now there was a man of Benjamin, whose
name *was* [a]Kish, the son of Abiel, the son of
Zeror, the son of Bechorath, the son of Aphiah,
a Benjamite, a mighty man of power.
2 And he had a son, whose name *was* Saul,
a choice young man, and a goodly: and *there was*
not among the children of Israel a goodlier person
than he: [a]from his shoulders and upward *he was*
higher than any of the people.
3 And the asses of Kish Saul's father were
lost. And Kish said to Saul his son, Take now one
of the servants with thee, and arise, go seek the
asses.
4 And he passed through mount Ephraim,
and passed through the land of [a]Shalisha, but they
found *them* not: then they passed through the
land of Shalim, and *there they were* not: and he
passed through the land of the Benjamites, but
they found *them* not.
5 *And* when they were come to the land of
[a]Zuph, Saul said to his servant that *was* with him,
Come, and let [b]us return; lest my father leave *car-*
ing for the asses, and take thought for us.
6 And he said unto him, Behold now, *there*
is in this city [a]a man of God, and *he is* an honourable man; [b]all that he saith cometh surely to pass:
now let us go thither; peradventure he can shew
us our way that we should go.
7 Then said Saul to his servant, But, behold,
if we go, [a]what shall we bring the man? for the
bread is spent in our vessels, and *there is* not a
present to bring to the man of God: what have
we?
8 And the servant answered Saul again, and
said, Behold, I have here at hand the fourth part
of a shekel of silver: *that* will I give to the man
of God, to tell us our way.
9 (Beforetime in Israel, when a man [a]went
to enquire of God, thus he spake, Come, and let
us go to the seer: for *he that is* now *called* a
Prophet was beforetime called [b]a Seer.)
10 Then said Saul to his servant, Well said;
come, let us go. So they went unto the city where
the man of God *was*.
11 *And* as they went up the hill to the city,
[a]they found young maidens going out to draw water, and said unto them, Is the seer here?
12 And they answered them, and said, He is;
behold, *he is* before you: make haste now, for he
came to day to the city; for [a]*there is* a sacrifice
of the people to day [b]in the high place:
13 As soon as ye be come into the city, ye
shall straightway find him, before he go up to the
high place to eat: for the people will not eat until
he come, because he doth bless the sacrifice; *and*
afterwards they eat that be bidden. Now therefore
get you up; for about this time ye shall find him.
14 And they went up into the city: *and* when
they were come into the city, behold, Samuel

18 [a]Prov. 1:25–28; Is. 1:15; Mic. 3:4
19 [a]Is. 66:4; Jer. 44:16
20 [a]1 Sam. 8:5
22 [a]1 Sam. 8:7; Hos. 13:11

CHAPTER 9

1 [a]1 Sam. 14:51; 1 Chr. 8:33; 9:36–39
2 [a]1 Sam. 10:23
4 [a]2 Kin. 4:42
5 [a]1 Sam. 1:1 [b]1 Sam. 10:2
6 [a]Deut. 33:1; 1 Kin. 13:1; 2 Kin. 5:8 [b]1 Sam. 3:19
7 [a]Judg. 6:18; 13:17; 1 Kin. 14:3; 2 Kin. 4:42; 8:8
9 [a]Gen. 25:22 [b]2 Sam. 24:11; 2 Kin. 17:13; 1 Chr. 26:28; 29:29; 2 Chr. 16:7, 10; Is. 30:10; Amos 7:12
11 [a]Gen. 24:11, 15; 29:8, 9; Ex. 2:16
12 [a]Gen. 31:54; 1 Sam. 16:2 [b]1 Sam. 7:17; 10:5; 1 Kin. 3:2

*———
8:16 LXX *cattle*

NKJV

16 "And he will take your male servants,
your female servants, your finest *young men, and
your donkeys, and put *them* to his work.
17 "He will take a tenth of your sheep. And
you will be his servants.
18 "And you will cry out in that day because
of your king whom you have chosen for yourselves, and the LORD [a]will not hear you in that
day."
19 Nevertheless the people [a]refused to obey
the voice of Samuel; and they said, "No, but we
will have a king over us,
20 "that we also may be [a]like all the nations,
and that our king may judge us and go out before
us and fight our battles."
21 And Samuel heard all the words of the
people, and he repeated them in the hearing of
the LORD.
22 So the LORD said to Samuel, [a]"Heed their
voice, and make them a king." And Samuel said
to the men of Israel, "Every man go to his city."

Saul Chosen to Be King

9 There was a man of Benjamin whose name
was [a]Kish the son of Abiel, the son of Zeror,
the son of Bechorath, the son of Aphiah, a Benjamite, a mighty man of power.
2 And he had a choice and handsome son
whose name *was* Saul. *There was* not a more
handsome person than he among the children of
Israel. [a]From his shoulders upward *he was* taller
than any of the people.
3 Now the donkeys of Kish, Saul's father,
were lost. And Kish said to his son Saul, "Please
take one of the servants with you, and arise, go
and look for the donkeys."
4 So he passed through the mountains of
Ephraim and through the land of [a]Shalisha, but
they did not find *them*. Then they passed through
the land of Shaalim, and *they were* not *there*.
Then he passed through the land of the Benjamites, but they did not find *them*.
5 When they had come to the land of [a]Zuph,
Saul said to his servant who *was* with him,
"Come, let [b]us return, lest my father cease *caring*
about the donkeys and become worried about us."
6 And he said to him, "Look now, *there is*
in this city [a]a man of God, and *he is* an honorable
man; [b]all that he says surely comes to pass. So
let us go there; perhaps he can show us the way
that we should go."
7 Then Saul said to his servant, "But look,
if we go, [a]what shall we bring the man? For the
bread in our vessels is all gone, and *there is* no
present to bring to the man of God. What do we
have?"
8 And the servant answered Saul again and
said, "Look, I have here at hand one-fourth of a
shekel of silver. I will give *that* to the man of
God, to tell us our way."
9 (Formerly in Israel, when a man [a]went to
inquire of God, he spoke thus: "Come, let us go
to the seer"; for *he who is* now *called* a prophet
was formerly called [b]a seer.)
10 Then Saul said to his servant, "Well said;
come, let us go." So they went to the city where
the man of God *was*.
11 As they went up the hill to the city, [a]they
met some young women going out to draw water,
and said to them, "Is the seer here?"
12 And they answered them and said, "Yes,
there he is, just ahead of you. Hurry now; for today he came to this city, because [a]there is a sacrifice of the people today [b]on the high place.
13 "As soon as you come into the city, you
will surely find him before he goes up to the high
place to eat. For the people will not eat until he
comes, because he must bless the sacrifice; afterward those who are invited will eat. Now therefore, go up, for about this time you will find him."
14 So they went up to the city. As they were
coming into the city, there was Samuel, coming

KJV

came out against them, for to go up to the high place.

15 [a]Now the LORD had told Samuel in his ear a day before Saul came, saying,

16 To morrow about this time [a]I will send thee a man out of the land of Benjamin, [b]and thou shalt anoint him *to be* captain over my people Israel, that he may save my people out of the hand of the Philistines: for I have [c]looked upon my people, because their cry is come unto me.

17 And when Samuel saw Saul, the LORD said unto him, [a]Behold the man whom I spake to thee of! this same shall reign over my people.

18 Then Saul drew near to Samuel in the gate, and said, Tell me, I pray thee, where the seer's house *is*.

19 And Samuel answered Saul, and said, I *am* the seer: go up before me unto the high place; for ye shall eat with me to day, and to morrow I will let thee go, and will tell thee all that *is* in thine heart.

20 And as for [a]thine asses that were lost three days ago, set not thy mind on them; for they are found. And on whom [b]*is* all the desire of Israel? *Is it* not on thee, and on all thy father's house?

21 And Saul answered and said, [a]*Am* not I a Benjamite, of the [b]smallest of the tribes of Israel? and [c]my family the least of all the families of the tribe of Benjamin? wherefore then speakest thou so to me?

22 And Samuel took Saul and his servant, and brought them into the parlour, and made them sit in the chiefest place among them that were bidden, which *were* about thirty persons.

23 And Samuel said unto the cook, Bring the portion which I gave thee, of which I said unto thee, Set it by thee.

24 And the cook took up [a]the shoulder, and *that* which *was* upon it, and set *it* before Saul. And *Samuel* said, Behold that which is left! set *it* before thee, *and* eat: for unto this time hath it been kept for thee since I said, I have invited the people. So Saul did eat with Samuel that day.

25 And when they were come down from the high place into the city, *Samuel* communed with Saul upon [a]the top of the house.

26 And they arose early: and it came to pass about the spring of the day, that Samuel called Saul to the top of the house, saying, Up, that I may send thee away. And Saul arose, and they went out both of them, he and Samuel, abroad.

Saul Anointed King

27 *And* as they were going down to the end of the city, Samuel said to Saul, Bid the servant pass on before us, (and he passed on,) but stand thou still a while, that I may shew thee the word of God.

10 Then [a]Samuel took a vial of oil, and poured *it* upon his head, [b]and kissed him, and said, *Is it* not because [c]the LORD hath anointed thee *to be* captain over [d]his inheritance?

2 When thou art departed from me to day, then thou shalt find two men by [a]Rachel's sepulchre in the border of Benjamin [b]at Zelzah; and they will say unto thee, The asses which thou wentest to seek are found: and, lo, thy father hath left the care of the asses, and sorroweth for [c]you, saying, What shall I do for my son?

3 Then shalt thou go on forward from thence, and thou shalt come to the plain of Tabor, and there shall meet thee three men going up [a]to God to Beth–el, one carrying three kids, and another carrying three loaves of bread, and another carrying a bottle of wine:

4 And they will salute thee, and give thee two *loaves* of bread; which thou shalt receive of their hands.

5 After that thou shalt come to the hill of

15 [a]1 Sam. 15:1
16 [a]Deut. 17:15 [b]1 Sam. 10:1 [c]Ex. 2:23–25; 3:7, 9
17 [a]1 Sam. 16:12; Hos. 13:11
20 [a]1 Sam. 9:3 [b]1 Sam. 8:5, 19; 12:13
21 [a]1 Sam. 15:17 [b]Judg. 20:46–48; Ps. 68:27 [c]Judg. 6:15
24 [a]Ex. 29:22, 27; Lev. 7:32, 33; Num. 18:18; Ezek. 24:4
25 [a]Deut. 22:8; 2 Sam. 11:2; Luke 5:19; Acts 10:9

CHAPTER 10

1 [a]Ex. 30:23–33; 1 Sam. 9:16; 16:13; 2 Kin. 9:3, 6 [b]Ps. 2:12 [c]2 Sam. 5:2; Acts 13:21 [d]Ex. 34:9; Deut. 32:9; Ps. 78:71
2 [a]Gen. 35:16–20; 48:7 [b]Josh. 18:28 [c]1 Sam. 9:3–5
3 [a]Gen. 28:22; 35:1, 3, 7

*———————

9:21 Lit. *tribes*
9:25 So with MT, Tg.; LXX omits *He spoke with Saul on top of the house;* LXX, Vg. afterward add *And he prepared a bed for Saul on top of the house, and he slept.*
10:1 So with MT, Tg., Vg.; LXX *people Israel; and you shall rule the people of the Lord;* LXX, Vg. add *And you shall deliver His people from the hands of their enemies all around them. And this shall be a sign to you, that God has anointed you to be a prince.*

NKJV

out toward them on his way up to the high place.

15 [a]Now the LORD had told Samuel in his ear the day before Saul came, saying,

16 "Tomorrow about this time [a]I will send you a man from the land of Benjamin, [b]and you shall anoint him commander over My people Israel, that he may save My people from the hand of the Philistines; for I have [c]looked upon My people, because their cry has come to Me."

17 So when Samuel saw Saul, the LORD said to him, [a]"There he is, the man of whom I spoke to you. This one shall reign over My people."

18 Then Saul drew near to Samuel in the gate, and said, "Please tell me, where *is* the seer's house?"

19 Samuel answered Saul and said, "I *am* the seer. Go up before me to the high place, for you shall eat with me today; and tomorrow I will let you go and will tell you all that *is* in your heart.

20 "But as for [a]your donkeys that were lost three days ago, do not be anxious about them, for they have been found. And on whom [b]*is* all the desire of Israel? *Is it* not on you and on all your father's house?"

21 And Saul answered and said, [a]"*Am* I not a Benjamite, of the [b]smallest of the tribes of Israel, and [c]my family the least of all the families of the *tribe of Benjamin? Why then do you speak like this to me?"

22 Now Samuel took Saul and his servant and brought them into the hall, and had them sit in the place of honor among those who were invited; there *were* about thirty persons.

23 And Samuel said to the cook, "Bring the portion which I gave you, of which I said to you, 'Set it apart.' "

24 So the cook took up [a]the thigh with its upper part and set *it* before Saul. And *Samuel* said, "Here it is, what was kept back. *It* was set apart for you. Eat; for until this time it has been kept for you, since I said I invited the people." So Saul ate with Samuel that day.

25 When they had come down from the high place into the city, **Samuel* spoke with Saul on [a]the top of the house.

26 They arose early; and it was about the dawning of the day that Samuel called to Saul on the top of the house, saying, "Get up, that I may send you on your way." And Saul arose, and both of them went outside, he and Samuel.

Saul Anointed King

27 As they were going down to the outskirts of the city, Samuel said to Saul, "Tell the servant to go on ahead of us." And he went on. "But you stand here awhile, that I may announce to you the word of God."

10 Then [a]Samuel took a flask of oil and poured *it* on his head, [b]and kissed him and said: "*Is it* not because [c]the LORD has anointed you commander over [d]His *inheritance?

2 "When you have departed from me today, you will find two men by [a]Rachel's tomb in the territory of Benjamin [b]at Zelzah; and they will say to you, 'The donkeys which you went to look for have been found. And now your father has ceased caring about the donkeys and is worrying about [c]you, saying, "What shall I do about my son?" '

3 "Then you shall go on forward from there and come to the terebinth tree of Tabor. There three men going up [a]to God at Bethel will meet you, one carrying three young goats, another carrying three loaves of bread, and another carrying a skin of wine.

4 "And they will greet you and give you two *loaves* of bread, which you shall receive from their hands.

5 "After that you shall come to the hill of

KJV

God, [a]where *is* the garrison of the Philistines: and it shall come to pass, when thou art come thither to the city, that thou shalt meet a company of prophets coming down [b]from the high place with a psaltery, and a tabret, and a pipe, and a harp, before them; [c]and they shall prophesy:

6 And [a]the Spirit of the LORD will come upon thee, and [b]thou shalt prophesy with them, and shalt be turned into another man.

7 And let it be, when these [a]signs are come unto thee, *that* thou do as occasion serve thee; for [b]God *is* with thee.

8 And thou shalt go down before me [a]to Gilgal; and, behold, I will come down unto thee, to offer burnt offerings, *and* to sacrifice sacrifices of peace offerings: [b]seven days shalt thou tarry, till I come to thee, and shew thee what thou shalt do.

9 And it was *so*, that when he had turned his back to go from Samuel, God gave him another heart: and all those signs came to pass that day.

10 And [a]when they came thither to the hill, behold, [b]a company of prophets met him; and the Spirit of God came upon him, and he prophesied among them.

11 And it came to pass, when all that knew him beforetime saw that, behold, he prophesied among the prophets, then the people said one to another, What *is* this *that* is come unto the son of Kish? [a]*Is* Saul also among the prophets?

12 And one of the same place answered and said, But [a]who *is* their father? Therefore it became a proverb, *Is* Saul also among the prophets?

13 And when he had made an end of prophesying, he came to the high place.

14 And Saul's [a]uncle said unto him and to his servant, Whither went ye? And he said, To seek the asses: and when we saw that *they were* no where, we came to Samuel.

15 And Saul's uncle said, Tell me, I pray thee, what Samuel said unto you.

16 And Saul said unto his uncle, He told us plainly that the asses were [a]found. But of the matter of the kingdom, whereof Samuel spake, he told him not.

Saul Proclaimed King

17 And Samuel called the people together [a]unto the LORD [b]to Mizpeh;

18 And said unto the children of Israel, [a]Thus saith the LORD God of Israel, I brought up Israel out of Egypt, and delivered you out of the hand of the Egyptians, and out of the hand of all kingdoms, *and* of them that oppressed you:

19 [a]And ye have this day rejected your God, who himself saved you out of all your adversities and your tribulations; and ye have said unto him, *Nay*, but set a king over us. Now therefore present yourselves before the LORD by your tribes, and by your thousands.

20 And when Samuel had [a]caused all the tribes of Israel to come near, the tribe of Benjamin was taken.

21 When he had caused the tribe of Benjamin to come near by their families, the family of Matri was taken, and Saul the son of Kish was taken: and when they sought him, he could not be found.

22 Therefore they [a]enquired of the LORD further, if the man should yet come thither. And the LORD answered, Behold, he hath hid himself among the stuff.

23 And they ran and fetched him thence: and when he stood among the people, [a]he was higher than any of the people from his shoulders and upward.

24 And Samuel said to all the people, See ye him [a]whom the LORD hath chosen, that *there is* none like him among all the people? And all the people shouted, and said, [b]God save the king.

25 Then Samuel told the people [a]the manner of the kingdom, and wrote *it* in a book, and laid

5 [a]1 Sam. 13:2, 3 [b]1 Sam. 19:12, 20; 2 Kin. 2:3, 5, 15 [c]Ex. 15:20, 21; 2 Kin. 3:15; 1 Chr. 25:1–6; 1 Cor. 14:1
6 [a]Num. 11:25, 29; Judg. 14:6; 1 Sam. 16:13 [b]1 Sam. 10:10; 19:23, 24
7 [a]Ex. 4:8; Luke 2:12 [b]Josh. 1:5; Judg. 6:12; 1 Sam. 3:19; [Heb. 13:5]
8 [a]1 Sam. 11:14, 15; 13:8 [b]1 Sam. 13:8–10
10 [a]1 Sam. 10:5 [b]1 Sam. 19:20
11 [a]1 Sam. 19:24; Amos 7:14, 15; Matt. 13:54–57; John 7:15; Acts 4:13
12 [a]John 5:30, 36
14 [a]1 Sam. 14:50
16 [a]1 Sam. 9:20
17 [a]Judg. 20:1 [b]1 Sam. 7:5, 6
18 [a]Judg. 6:8, 9; 1 Sam. 8:8; 12:6, 8
19 [a]1 Sam. 8:7, 19; 12:12
20 [a]Acts 1:24, 26
22 [a]1 Sam. 23:2, 4, 10, 11
23 [a]1 Sam. 9:2
24 [a]Deut. 17:15; 1 Sam. 9:16; 2 Sam. 21:6 [b]1 Kin. 1:25, 39
25 [a]Deut. 17:14–20; 1 Sam. 8:11–18

NKJV

God [a]where the Philistine garrison *is*. And it will happen, when you have come there to the city, that you will meet a group of prophets coming down [b]from the high place with a stringed instrument, a tambourine, a flute, and a harp before them; [c]and they will be prophesying.

6 "Then [a]the Spirit of the LORD will come upon you, and [b]you will prophesy with them and be turned into another man.

7 "And let it be, when these [a]signs come to you, *that* you do as the occasion demands; for [b]God *is* with you.

8 "You shall go down before me [a]to Gilgal; and surely I will come down to you to offer burnt offerings *and* make sacrifices of peace offerings. [b]Seven days you shall wait, till I come to you and show you what you should do."

9 So it was, when he had turned his back to go from Samuel, that God gave him another heart; and all those signs came to pass that day.

10 [a]When they came there to the hill, there was [b]a group of prophets to meet him; then the Spirit of God came upon him, and he prophesied among them.

11 And it happened, when all who knew him formerly saw that he indeed prophesied among the prophets, that the people said to one another, "What *is* this *that* has come upon the son of Kish? [a]*Is* Saul also among the prophets?"

12 Then a man from there answered and said, "But [a]who *is* their father?" Therefore it became a proverb: "*Is* Saul also among the prophets?"

13 And when he had finished prophesying, he went to the high place.

14 Then Saul's [a]uncle said to him and his servant, "Where did you go?" So he said, "To look for the donkeys. When we saw that *they were* nowhere *to be found*, we went to Samuel."

15 And Saul's uncle said, "Tell me, please, what Samuel said to you."

16 So Saul said to his uncle, "He told us plainly that the donkeys had been [a]found." But about the matter of the kingdom, he did not tell him what Samuel had said.

Saul Proclaimed King

17 Then Samuel called the people together [a]to the LORD [b]at Mizpah,

18 and said to the children of Israel, [a]"Thus says the LORD God of Israel: 'I brought up Israel out of Egypt, and delivered you from the hand of the Egyptians *and* from the hand of all kingdoms and from those who oppressed you.'

19 [a]"But you have today rejected your God, who Himself saved you from all your adversities and your tribulations; and you have said to Him, 'No, set a king over us!' Now therefore, present yourselves before the LORD by your tribes and by your *clans."

20 And when Samuel had [a]caused all the tribes of Israel to come near, the tribe of Benjamin was chosen.

21 When he had caused the tribe of Benjamin to come near by their families, the family of Matri was chosen. And Saul the son of Kish was chosen. But when they sought him, he could not be found.

22 Therefore they [a]inquired of the LORD further, "Has the man come here yet?" And the LORD answered, "There he is, hidden among the equipment."

23 So they ran and brought him from there; and when he stood among the people, [a]he was taller than any of the people from his shoulders upward.

24 And Samuel said to all the people, "Do you see him [a]whom the LORD has chosen, that *there is* no one like him among all the people?" So all the people shouted and said, [b]"Long live the king!"

25 Then Samuel explained to the people [a]the behavior of royalty, and wrote *it* in a book and

---

***10:19** Lit. *thousands*

KJV

it up before the LORD. And Samuel sent all the
people away, every man to his house.
26 And Saul also went home [a]to Gibeah; and
there went with him a band of men, whose hearts
God had touched.
27 [a]But the [b]children of Belial said, How
shall this man save us? And they despised him,
[c]and brought him no presents. But he held his
peace.

Saul Saves Jabesh Gilead

11 Then [a]Nahash the Ammonite came up, and
encamped against [b]Jabesh–gilead: and all
the men of Jabesh said unto Nahash, [c]Make a
covenant with us, and we will serve thee.
2 And Nahash the Ammonite answered
them, On this *condition* will I make *a covenant*
with you, that I may thrust out all your right eyes,
and lay it *for* [a]a reproach upon all Israel.
3 And the elders of Jabesh said unto him,
Give us seven days' respite, that we may send
messengers unto all the coasts of Israel: and then,
if *there be* no man to save us, we will come out
to thee.
4 Then came the messengers [a]to Gibeah of
Saul, and told the tidings in the ears of the people:
and [b]all the people lifted up their voices, and wept.
5 And, behold, Saul came after the herd out
of the field; and Saul said, What *aileth* the people
that they weep? And they told him the tidings of
the men of Jabesh.
6 [a]And the Spirit of God came upon Saul
when he heard those tidings, and his anger was
kindled greatly.
7 And he took a yoke of oxen, and [a]hewed
them in pieces, and sent *them* throughout all the
coasts of Israel by the hands of messengers, saying, [b]Whosoever cometh not forth after Saul and
after Samuel, so shall it be done unto his oxen.
And the fear of the LORD fell on the people, and
they came out with one consent.
8 And when he numbered them in [a]Bezek,
the children [b]of Israel were three hundred thousand, and the men of Judah thirty thousand.
9 And they said unto the messengers that
came, Thus shall ye say unto the men of Jabesh–
gilead, To morrow, by *that time* the sun be hot,
ye shall have help. And the messengers came and
shewed *it* to the men of Jabesh; and they were
glad.
10 Therefore the men of Jabesh said, To morrow we will come out unto you, and ye shall do
with us all that seemeth good unto you.
11 And it was *so* on the morrow, that [a]Saul
put the people [b]in three companies; and they
came into the midst of the host in the morning
watch, and slew the Ammonites until the heat of
the day: and it came to pass, that they which remained were scattered, so that two of them were
not left together.
12 And the people said unto Samuel, [a]Who
is he that said, Shall Saul reign over us? [b]bring
the men, that we may put them to death.
13 And Saul said, [a]There shall not a man be
put to death this day: for to day [b]the LORD hath
wrought salvation in Israel.
14 Then said Samuel to the people, Come,
and let us go [a]to Gilgal, and renew the kingdom
there.
15 And all the people went to Gilgal; and
there they made Saul king [a]before the LORD in
Gilgal; and [b]there they sacrificed sacrifices of
peace offerings before the LORD; and there Saul
and all the men of Israel rejoiced greatly.

Samuel's Address at Saul's Coronation

12 And Samuel said unto all Israel, Behold,
I have hearkened unto [a]your voice in all
that ye said unto me, and [b]have made a king over
you.
2 And now, behold, the king [a]walketh before you: [b]and I am old and grayheaded; and,

26 [a]Judg. 20:14
27 [a]1 Sam. 11:12 [b]Deut. 13:13; 1 Sam. 25:17 [c]2 Sam. 8:2; 1 Kin. 4:21; 10:25; 2 Chr. 17:5; Matt. 2:11

CHAPTER 11

1 [a]1 Sam. 12:12 [b]Judg. 21:8; 1 Sam. 31:11 [c]Gen. 26:28; 1 Kin. 20:34; Job 41:4; Ezek. 17:13
2 [a]Gen. 34:14; 1 Sam. 17:26; Ps. 44:13
4 [a]1 Sam. 10:26; 15:34; 2 Sam. 21:6 [b]Gen. 27:38; Judg. 2:4; 20:23, 26; 21:2; 1 Sam. 30:4
6 [a]Judg. 3:10; 6:34; 11:29; 13:25; 14:6; 1 Sam. 10:10; 16:13
7 [a]Judg. 19:29 [b]Judg. 21:5, 8, 10
8 [a]Judg. 1:5 [b]2 Sam. 24:9
11 [a]1 Sam. 31:11 [b]Judg. 7:16, 20
12 [a]1 Sam. 10:27 [b]Luke 19:27
13 [a]1 Sam. 10:27; 2 Sam. 19:22 [b]Ex. 14:13, 30; 1 Sam. 19:5
14 [a]1 Sam. 7:16; 10:8
15 [a]1 Sam. 10:17 [b]Josh. 8:31; 1 Sam. 10:8

CHAPTER 12

1 [a]1 Sam. 8:5, 7, 9, 20, 22 [b]1 Sam. 10:24; 11:14, 15
2 [a]Num. 27:17; 1 Sam. 8:20 [b]1 Sam. 8:1, 5

NKJV

laid *it* up before the LORD. And Samuel sent all
the people away, every man to his house.
26 And Saul also went home [a]to Gibeah; and
valiant *men* went with him, whose hearts God had
touched.
27 [a]But some [b]rebels said, "How can this
man save us?" So they despised him, [c]and
brought him no presents. But he held his peace.

Saul Saves Jabesh Gilead

11 Then [a]Nahash the Ammonite came up and
encamped against [b]Jabesh Gilead; and all
the men of Jabesh said to Nahash, [c]"Make a covenant with us, and we will serve you."
2 And Nahash the Ammonite answered
them, "On this *condition* I will make *a covenant*
with you, that I may put out all your right eyes,
and bring [a]reproach on all Israel."
3 Then the elders of Jabesh said to him,
"Hold off for seven days, that we may send messengers to all the territory of Israel. And then, if
there is no one to save us, we will come out to
you."
4 So the messengers came [a]to Gibeah of
Saul and told the news in the hearing of the people. And [b]all the people lifted up their voices and
wept.
5 Now there was Saul, coming behind the
herd from the field; and Saul said, "What *troubles*
the people, that they weep?" And they told him
the words of the men of Jabesh.
6 [a]Then the Spirit of God came upon Saul
when he heard this news, and his anger was
greatly aroused.
7 So he took a yoke of oxen and [a]cut them
in pieces, and sent *them* throughout all the territory of Israel by the hands of messengers, saying,
[b]"Whoever does not go out with Saul and Samuel
to battle, so it shall be done to his oxen." And
the fear of the LORD fell on the people, and they
came out with one consent.
8 When he numbered them in [a]Bezek, the
children [b]of Israel were three hundred thousand,
and the men of Judah thirty thousand.
9 And they said to the messengers who
came, "Thus you shall say to the men of Jabesh
Gilead: 'Tomorrow, by *the time* the sun is hot,
you shall have help.'" Then the messengers came
and reported *it* to the men of Jabesh, and they
were glad.
10 Therefore the men of Jabesh said, "Tomorrow we will come out to you, and you may
do with us whatever seems good to you."
11 So it was, on the next day, that [a]Saul put
the people [b]in three companies; and they came
into the midst of the camp in the morning watch,
and killed Ammonites until the heat of the day.
And it happened that those who survived were
scattered, so that no two of them were left
together.
12 Then the people said to Samuel, [a]"Who
is he who said, 'Shall Saul reign over us?' [b]Bring
the men, that we may put them to death."
13 But Saul said, [a]"Not a man shall be put
to death this day, for today [b]the LORD has accomplished salvation in Israel."
14 Then Samuel said to the people, "Come,
let us go [a]to Gilgal and renew the kingdom there."
15 So all the people went to Gilgal, and there
they made Saul king [a]before the LORD in Gilgal.
[b]There they made sacrifices of peace offerings before the LORD, and there Saul and all the men of
Israel rejoiced greatly.

Samuel's Address at Saul's Coronation

12 Now Samuel said to all Israel: "Indeed I
have heeded [a]your voice in all that you said
to me, and [b]have made a king over you.
2 "And now here is the king, [a]walking before you; [b]and I am old and grayheaded, and look,

KJV

behold, my sons *are* with you: and I have walked before you from my childhood unto this day.

3 Behold, here I *am:* witness against me before the LORD, and before [a]his anointed: [b]whose ox have I taken? or whose ass have I taken? or whom have I defrauded? whom have I oppressed? or of whose hand have I received *any* [c]bribe to [d]blind mine eyes therewith? and I will restore it you.

4 And they said, [a]Thou hast not defrauded us, nor oppressed us, neither hast thou taken ought of any man's hand.

5 And he said unto them, The LORD *is* witness against you, and his anointed *is* witness this day, [a]that ye have not found ought [b]in my hand. And they answered, *He is* witness.

6 And Samuel said unto the people, [a]*It is* the LORD that advanced Moses and Aaron, and that brought your fathers up out of the land of Egypt.

7 Now therefore stand still, that I may [a]reason with you before the LORD of all the [b]righteous acts of the LORD, which he did to you and to your fathers.

8 [a]When Jacob was come into Egypt, and your fathers [b]cried unto the LORD, then the LORD [c]sent Moses and Aaron, which brought forth your fathers out of Egypt, and made them dwell in this place.

9 And when they [a]forgat the LORD their God, he sold them into the hand of [b]Sisera, captain of the host of Hazor, and into the hand of the [c]Philistines, and into the hand of the king of [d]Moab, and they fought against them.

10 And they cried unto the LORD, and said, [a]We have sinned, because we have forsaken the LORD, [b]and have served Baalim and Ashtaroth: but now deliver us out of the hand of our enemies, and we will serve thee.

11 And the LORD sent Jerubbaal, and Bedan, and [a]Jephthah, and [b]Samuel, and delivered you out of the hand of your enemies on every side, and ye dwelled safe.

12 And when ye saw that [a]Nahash the king of the children of Ammon came against you, [b]ye said unto me, Nay; but a king shall reign over us: when [c]the LORD your God *was* your king.

13 Now therefore [a]behold the king [b]whom ye have chosen, *and* whom ye have desired! and, behold, [c]the LORD hath set a king over you.

14 If ye will [a]fear the LORD, and serve him, and obey his voice, and not rebel against the commandment of the LORD then shall both ye and also the king that reigneth over you continue following the LORD your God:

15 But if ye will [a]not obey the voice of the LORD, but [b]rebel against the commandment of the LORD, then shall the hand of the LORD be against you, as *it was* against your fathers.

16 Now therefore [a]stand and see this great thing, which the LORD will do before your eyes.

17 *Is it* not [a]wheat harvest to day? [b]I will call unto the LORD, and he shall send thunder and [c]rain; that ye may perceive and see that [d]your wickedness *is* great, which ye have done in the sight of the LORD, in asking you a king.

18 So Samuel called unto the LORD; and the LORD sent thunder and rain that day: and [a]all the people greatly feared the LORD and Samuel.

19 And all the people said unto Samuel, [a]Pray for thy servants unto the LORD thy God, that we die not: for we have added unto all our sins *this* evil, to ask us a king.

20 And Samuel said unto the people, Fear not: ye have done all this wickedness: [a]yet turn not aside from following the LORD, but serve the LORD with all your heart;

21 And [a]turn ye not aside: [b]for *then should ye go* after vain *things,* which cannot profit nor deliver; for they *are* vain.

22 For [a]the LORD will not forsake [b]his people

NKJV

my sons *are* with you. I have walked before you from my childhood to this day.

3 "Here I am. Witness against me before the LORD and before [a]His anointed: [b]Whose ox have I taken, or whose donkey have I taken, or whom have I cheated? Whom have I oppressed, or from whose hand have I received *any* [c]bribe with which to [d]blind my eyes? I will restore *it* to you."

4 And they said, [a]"You have not cheated us or oppressed us, nor have you taken anything from any man's hand."

5 Then he said to them, "The LORD *is* witness against you, and His anointed *is* witness this day, [a]that you have not found anything [b]in my hand." And they answered, "*He is* witness."

6 Then Samuel said to the people, [a]"*It is* the LORD who raised up Moses and Aaron, and who brought your fathers up from the land of Egypt.

7 "Now therefore, stand still, that I may [a]reason with you before the LORD concerning all the [b]righteous acts of the LORD which He did to you and your fathers:

8 [a]"When Jacob had gone into *Egypt, and your fathers [b]cried out to the LORD, then the LORD [c]sent Moses and Aaron, who brought your fathers out of Egypt and made them dwell in this place.

9 "And when they [a]forgot the LORD their God, He sold them into the hand of [b]Sisera, commander of the army of Hazor, into the hand of the [c]Philistines, and into the hand of the king of [d]Moab; and they fought against them.

10 "Then they cried out to the LORD, and said, [a]'We have sinned, because we have forsaken the LORD [b]and served the Baals and *Ashtoreths; but now deliver us from the hand of our enemies, and we will serve You.'

11 "And the LORD sent *Jerubbaal, *Bedan, [a]Jephthah, and [b]Samuel,* and delivered you out of the hand of your enemies on every side; and you dwelt in safety.

12 "And when you saw that [a]Nahash king of the Ammonites came against you, [b]you said to me, 'No, but a king shall reign over us,' when [c]the LORD your God *was* your king.

13 "Now therefore, [a]here is the king [b]whom you have chosen *and* whom you have desired. And take note, [c]the LORD has set a king over you.

14 "If you [a]fear the LORD and serve Him and obey His voice, and do not rebel against the commandment of the LORD, then both you and the king who reigns over you will continue following the LORD your God.

15 "However, if you do [a]not obey the voice of the LORD, but [b]rebel against the commandment of the LORD, then the hand of the LORD will be against you, as *it was* against your fathers.

16 "Now therefore, [a]stand and see this great thing which the LORD will do before your eyes:

17 "*Is* today not the [a]wheat harvest? [b]I will call to the LORD, and He will send thunder and [c]rain, that you may perceive and see that [d]your wickedness *is* great, which you have done in the sight of the LORD, in asking a king for yourselves."

18 So Samuel called to the LORD, and the LORD sent thunder and rain that day; and [a]all the people greatly feared the LORD and Samuel.

19 And all the people said to Samuel, [a]"Pray for your servants to the LORD your God, that we may not die; for we have added to all our sins the evil of asking a king for ourselves."

20 Then Samuel said to the people, "Do not fear. You have done all this wickedness; [a]yet do not turn aside from following the LORD, but serve the LORD with all your heart.

21 "And [a]do not turn aside; [b]for *then you would go* after empty things which cannot profit or deliver, for they *are* nothing.

22 "For [a]the LORD will not forsake [b]His peo-

---

3 [a]1 Sam. 10:1; 24:6 [b]Num. 16:15 [c]Ex. 23:8 [d]Deut. 16:19
4 [a]Lev. 19:13
5 [a]Acts 23:9; 24:20 [b]Ex. 22:4
6 [a]Mic. 6:4
7 [a]Is. 1:18 [b]Judg. 5:11
8 [a]Gen. 46:5, 6 [b]Ex. 2:23–25 [c]Ex. 3:10; 4:14–16
9 [a]Judg. 3:7 [b]Judg. 4:2 [c]Judg. 3:31; 10:7; 13:1 [d]Judg. 3:12–30
10 [a]Judg. 10:10 [b]Judg. 2:13; 3:7
11 [a]Judg. 11:1 [b]1 Sam. 7:13
12 [a]1 Sam. 11:1, 2 [b]1 Sam. 8:5, 19, 20 [c]Judg. 8:23
13 [a]1 Sam. 10:24 [b]1 Sam. 8:5; 12:17, 19 [c]Hos. 13:11
14 [a]Josh. 24:14
15 [a]Deut. 28:15 [b]Is. 1:20
16 [a]Ex. 14:13, 31
17 [a]Gen. 30:14 [b][James5:16–18] [c]Ezra 10:9 [d]1 Sam. 8:7
18 [a]Ex. 14:31
19 [a]Ex. 9:28
20 [a]Deut. 11:16
21 [a]2 Chr. 25:15 [b]Is. 41:29
22 [a]Deut. 31:6 [b]Is. 43:21

*

12:8 So with MT, Tg., Vg.; LXX adds *and the Egyptians afflicted them* **12:10** Images of Canaanite goddesses **12:11** Gideon, cf. Judg. 6:25–32; Syr. *Deborah;* Tg. *Gideon* • LXX, Syr. *Barak;* Tg. *Simson* • Syr. *Simson*

KJV

[c]for his great name's sake: because [d]it hath
pleased the LORD to make you his people.
23 Moreover as for me, God forbid that I
should sin against the LORD [a]in ceasing to pray
for you: but [b]I will teach you the [c]good and the
right way:
24 [a]Only fear the LORD, and serve him in
truth with all your heart: for [b]consider how [c]great
things he hath done for you.
25 But if ye shall still do wickedly, [a]ye shall
be consumed, [b]both ye and your king.

Saul's Unlawful Sacrifice

13 Saul reigned one year; and when he had
reigned two years over Israel,
2 Saul chose him three thousand *men* of Israel; *whereof* two thousand were with Saul in
[a]Michmash and in mount Beth–el, and a thousand
were with [b]Jonathan in [c]Gibeah of Benjamin: and
the rest of the people he sent every man to his
tent.
3 And Jonathan smote [a]the garrison of the
Philistines that *was* in [b]Geba, and the Philistines
heard *of it*. And Saul blew the trumpet throughout
all the land, saying, Let the Hebrews hear.
4 And all Israel heard say *that* Saul had
smitten a garrison of the Philistines, and *that* Israel also was had in abomination with the Philistines. And the people were called together after
Saul to Gilgal.
5 And the Philistines gathered themselves
together to fight with Israel, thirty thousand chariots, and six thousand horsemen, and people [a]as
the sand which *is* on the sea shore in multitude:
and they came up, and pitched in Michmash, eastward from [b]Beth–aven.
6 When the men of Israel saw that they were
in a strait, (for the people were distressed,) then
the people [a]did hide themselves in caves, and in
thickets, and in rocks, and in high places, and in
pits.
7 And *some of* the Hebrews went over Jordan to the [a]land of Gad and Gilead. As for Saul,
he *was* yet in Gilgal, and all the people followed
him trembling.
8 [a]And he tarried seven days, according to
the set time that Samuel *had appointed:* but Samuel came not to Gilgal; and the people were scattered from him.
9 And Saul said, Bring hither a burnt offering to me, and peace offerings. And he offered
the burnt offering.
10 And it came to pass, that as soon as he
had made an end of offering the burnt offering,
behold, Samuel came; and Saul went out to meet
him, that he might salute him.
11 And Samuel said, What hast thou done?
And Saul said, Because I saw that the people
were scattered from me, and *that* thou camest
not within the days appointed, and *that* the Philistines gathered themselves together at Michmash;
12 Therefore said I, The Philistines will come
down now upon me to Gilgal, and I have not made
supplication unto the LORD: I forced myself therefore, and offered a burnt offering.
13 And Samuel said to Saul, [a]Thou hast done
foolishly: [b]thou hast not kept the commandment
of the LORD thy God, which he commanded thee:
for now would the LORD have established thy
kingdom upon Israel for ever.
14 [a]But now thy kingdom shall not continue:
[b]the LORD hath sought him a man [c]after his
own heart, and the LORD hath commanded him
to be captain over his people, because thou hast
[d]not kept *that* which the LORD commanded
thee.
15 And Samuel arose, and gat him up from
Gilgal unto Gibeah of Benjamin. And Saul numbered the people *that were* present with him,
[a]about six hundred men.

22 [c]Jer. 14:21 [d]Deut. 7:6–11
23 [a]Rom. 1:9 [b]Ps. 34:11 [c]1 Kin. 8:36
24 [a]Eccl. 12:13 [b]Is. 5:12 [c]Deut. 10:21
25 [a]Josh. 24:20 [b]Deut. 28:36

CHAPTER 13

2 [a]1 Sam. 14:5, 31 [b]1 Sam. 14:1 [c]1 Sam. 10:26
3 [a]1 Sam. 10:5 [b]2 Sam. 5:25
5 [a]Judg. 7:12 [b]Josh. 7:2
6 [a]Judg. 6:2
7 [a]Num. 32:1–42
8 [a]1 Sam. 10:8
13 [a]2 Chr. 16:9 [b]1 Sam. 15:11, 22, 28
14 [a]1 Sam. 15:28; 31:6 [b]1 Sam. 16:1 [c]Acts 7:46; 13:22 [d]1 Sam. 15:11, 19
15 [a]1 Sam. 13:2, 6, 7; 14:2

*

13:1 Heb. is difficult; cf. 2 Sam. 5:4; 2 Kin. 14:2; see also 2 Sam. 2:10; Acts 13:21
13:5 So with MT, LXX, Tg., Vg.; Syr. and some mss. of LXX *three thousand*
13:15 So with MT, Tg.; LXX, Vg. add *And the rest of the people went up after Saul to meet the people who fought against them, going from Gilgal to Gibeah in the hill of Benjamin.*

NKJV

ple, [c]for His great name's sake, because [d]it has
pleased the LORD to make you His people.
23 "Moreover, as for me, far be it from me
that I should sin against the LORD [a]in ceasing to
pray for you; but [b]I will teach you the [c]good and
the right way.
24 [a]"Only fear the LORD, and serve Him in
truth with all your heart; for [b]consider what
[c]great things He has done for you.
25 "But if you still do wickedly, [a]you shall
be swept away, [b]both you and your king."

Saul's Unlawful Sacrifice

13 Saul *reigned one year; and when he had
reigned two years over Israel,
2 Saul chose for himself three thousand
men of Israel. Two thousand were with Saul in
[a]Michmash and in the mountains of Bethel, and
a thousand were with [b]Jonathan in [c]Gibeah of
Benjamin. The rest of the people he sent away,
every man to his tent.
3 And Jonathan attacked [a]the garrison of
the Philistines that *was* in [b]Geba, and the Philistines heard *of it*. Then Saul blew the trumpet
throughout all the land, saying, "Let the Hebrews
hear!"
4 Now all Israel heard it said *that* Saul had
attacked a garrison of the Philistines, and *that*
Israel had also become an abomination to the
Philistines. And the people were called together
to Saul at Gilgal.
5 Then the Philistines gathered together to
fight with Israel, *thirty thousand chariots and six
thousand horsemen, and people [a]as the sand
which *is* on the seashore in multitude. And they
came up and encamped in Michmash, to the east
of [b]Beth Aven.
6 When the men of Israel saw that they were
in danger (for the people were distressed), then
the people [a]hid in caves, in thickets, in rocks, in
holes, and in pits.
7 And *some of* the Hebrews crossed over
the Jordan to the [a]land of Gad and Gilead. As
for Saul, he *was* still in Gilgal, and all the people
followed him trembling.
8 [a]Then he waited seven days, according to
the time set by Samuel. But Samuel did not come
to Gilgal; and the people were scattered from him.
9 So Saul said, "Bring a burnt offering and
peace offerings here to me." And he offered the
burnt offering.
10 Now it happened, as soon as he had finished presenting the burnt offering, that Samuel
came; and Saul went out to meet him, that he
might greet him.
11 And Samuel said, "What have you done?"
Saul said, "When I saw that the people were scattered from me, and *that* you did not come within
the days appointed, and *that* the Philistines gathered together at Michmash,
12 "then I said, 'The Philistines will now
come down on me at Gilgal, and I have not made
supplication to the LORD.' Therefore I felt compelled, and offered a burnt offering."
13 And Samuel said to Saul, [a]"You have
done foolishly. [b]You have not kept the commandment of the LORD your God, which He commanded
you. For now the LORD would have established
your kingdom over Israel forever.
14 [a]"But now your kingdom shall not continue. [b]The LORD has sought for Himself a man
[c]after His own heart, and the LORD has commanded him *to be* commander over His people,
because you have [d]not kept what the LORD commanded you."
15 Then Samuel arose and went up from Gilgal to Gibeah of *Benjamin. And Saul numbered
the people present with him, [a]about six hundred
men.

KJV

No Weapons for the Army

16 And Saul, and Jonathan his son, and the people *that were* present with them, abode in Gibeah of Benjamin: but the Philistines encamped in Michmash.

17 And the spoilers came out of the camp of the Philistines in three companies: one company turned unto the way *that leadeth to* [a]Ophrah, unto the land of Shual:

18 And another company turned the way *to* [a]Beth–horon: and another company turned *to* the way of the border that looketh to the valley of [b]Zeboim toward the wilderness.

19 Now [a]there was no smith found throughout all the land of Israel: for the Philistines said, Lest the Hebrews make *them* swords or spears:

20 But all the Israelites went down to the Philistines, to sharpen every man his share, and his coulter, and his ax, and his mattock.

21 Yet they had a file for the mattocks, and for the coulters, and for the forks, and for the axes, and to sharpen the goads.

22 So it came to pass in the day of battle, that [a]there was neither sword nor spear found in the hand of any of the people that *were* with Saul and Jonathan: but with Saul and with Jonathan his son was there found.

23 [a]And the garrison of the Philistines went out to the passage of Michmash.

Jonathan Defeats the Philistines

14 Now it came to pass upon a day, that Jonathan the son of Saul said unto the young man that bare his armour, Come, and let us go over to the Philistines' garrison, that *is* on the other side. But he told not his father.

2 And Saul tarried in the uttermost part of [a]Gibeah under a pomegranate tree which *is* in Migron: and the people that *were* with him *were* about six hundred men;

3 And [a]Ahiah, the son of Ahitub, [b]I–chabod's brother, the son of Phinehas, the son of Eli, the LORD's priest in Shiloh, [c]wearing an ephod. And the people knew not that Jonathan was gone.

4 And between the passages, by which Jonathan sought to go over [a]unto the Philistines' garrison, *there was* a sharp rock on the one side, and a sharp rock on the other side: and the name of the one *was* Bozez, and the name of the other Seneh.

5 The forefront of the one *was* situate northward over against Michmash, and the other southward over against Gibeah.

6 And Jonathan said to the young man that bare his armour, Come, and let us go over unto the garrison of these [a]uncircumcised: it may be that the LORD will work for us: for *there is* no restraint to the LORD [b]to save by many or by few.

7 And his armourbearer said unto him, Do all that *is* in thine heart: turn thee; behold, I *am* with thee according to thy heart.

8 Then said Jonathan, Behold, we will pass over unto *these* men, and we will discover ourselves unto them.

9 If they say thus unto us, Tarry until we come to you; then we will stand still in our place, and will not go up unto them.

10 But if they say thus, Come up unto us; then we will go up: for the LORD hath delivered them into our hand: and [a]this *shall be* a sign unto us.

11 And both of them discovered themselves unto the garrison of the Philistines: and the Philistines said, Behold, the Hebrews come forth out of the holes where they had [a]hid themselves.

12 And the men of the garrison answered Jonathan and his armourbearer, and said, Come up to us, and we will shew you a thing. And Jonathan said unto his armourbearer, Come up after me: for the LORD hath delivered them into the hand of Israel.

13 And Jonathan climbed up upon his hands

17 [a]Josh. 18:23
18 [a]Josh. 16:3; 18:13, 14 [b]Gen. 14:2; Neh. 11:34
19 [a]Judg. 5:8; 2 Kin. 24:14; Jer. 24:1; 29:2
22 [a]Judg. 5:8
23 [a]1 Sam. 14:1, 4

CHAPTER 14

2 [a]1 Sam. 13:15, 16
3 [a]1 Sam. 22:9, 11, 20 [b]1 Sam. 4:21 [c]1 Sam. 2:28
4 [a]1 Sam. 13:23
6 [a]1 Sam. 17:26, 36; Jer. 9:25, 26 [b]Judg. 7:4, 7; 1 Sam. 17:46, 47; 2 Chr. 14:11; [Ps. 115:3; 135:6; Zech. 4:6; Matt. 19:26; Rom. 8:31]
10 [a]Gen. 24:14; Judg. 6:36–40
11 [a]1 Sam. 13:6; 14:22

*

13:21 About two-thirds shekel weight

NKJV

No Weapons for the Army

16 Saul, Jonathan his son, and the people present with them remained in Gibeah of Benjamin. But the Philistines encamped in Michmash.

17 Then raiders came out of the camp of the Philistines in three companies. One company turned onto the road to [a]Ophrah, to the land of Shual,

18 another company turned to the road *to* [a]Beth Horon, and another company turned *to* the road of the border that overlooks the Valley of [b]Zeboim toward the wilderness.

19 Now [a]there was no blacksmith to be found throughout all the land of Israel, for the Philistines said, "Lest the Hebrews make swords or spears."

20 But all the Israelites would go down to the Philistines to sharpen each man's plowshare, his mattock, his ax, and his sickle;

21 and the charge for a sharpening was a *pim for the plowshares, the mattocks, the forks, and the axes, and to set the points of the goads.

22 So it came about, on the day of battle, that [a]there was neither sword nor spear found in the hand of any of the people who *were* with Saul and Jonathan. But they were found with Saul and Jonathan his son.

23 [a]And the garrison of the Philistines went out to the pass of Michmash.

Jonathan Defeats the Philistines

14 Now it happened one day that Jonathan the son of Saul said to the young man who bore his armor, "Come, let us go over to the Philistines' garrison that *is* on the other side." But he did not tell his father.

2 And Saul was sitting in the outskirts of [a]Gibeah under a pomegranate tree which *is* in Migron. The people who *were* with him *were* about six hundred men.

3 [a]Ahijah the son of Ahitub, [b]Ichabod's brother, the son of Phinehas, the son of Eli, the LORD's priest in Shiloh, was [c]wearing an ephod. But the people did not know that Jonathan had gone.

4 Between the passes, by which Jonathan sought to go over [a]to the Philistines' garrison, *there was* a sharp rock on one side and a sharp rock on the other side. And the name of one *was* Bozez, and the name of the other Seneh.

5 The front of one faced northward opposite Michmash, and the other southward opposite Gibeah.

6 Then Jonathan said to the young man who bore his armor, "Come, let us go over to the garrison of these [a]uncircumcised; it may be that the LORD will work for us. For nothing restrains the LORD [b]from saving by many or by few."

7 So his armorbearer said to him, "Do all that is in your heart. Go then; here I am with you, according to your heart."

8 Then Jonathan said, "Very well, let us cross over to *these* men, and we will show ourselves to them.

9 "If they say thus to us, 'Wait until we come to you,' then we will stand still in our place and not go up to them.

10 "But if they say thus, 'Come up to us,' then we will go up. For the LORD has delivered them into our hand, and [a]this *will be* a sign to us."

11 So both of them showed themselves to the garrison of the Philistines. And the Philistines said, "Look, the Hebrews are coming out of the holes where they have [a]hidden."

12 Then the men of the garrison called to Jonathan and his armorbearer, and said, "Come up to us, and we will show you something." Jonathan said to his armorbearer, "Come up after me, for the LORD has delivered them into the hand of Israel."

13 And Jonathan climbed up on his hands

KJV

and upon his feet, and his armourbearer after him: and they [a]fell before Jonathan; and his armourbearer slew after him.

14 And that first slaughter, which Jonathan and his armourbearer made, was about twenty men, within as it were an half acre of land, *which* a yoke *of oxen might plow.*

15 And [a]there was trembling in the host, in the field, and among all the people: the garrison, and [b]the spoilers, they also trembled, and the earth quaked: so it was [c]a very great trembling.

16 And the watchmen of Saul in Gibeah of Benjamin looked; and, behold, the multitude melted away, and they [a]went on beating down *one another.*

17 Then said Saul unto the people that *were* with him, Number now, and see who is gone from us. And when they had numbered, behold, Jonathan and his armourbearer *were* not *there.*

18 And Saul said unto Ahiah, Bring hither the ark of God. For the ark of God was at that time with the children of Israel.

19 And it came to pass, while Saul [a]talked unto the priest, that the noise that *was* in the host of the Philistines went on and increased: and Saul said unto the priest, Withdraw thine hand.

20 And Saul and all the people that *were* with him assembled themselves, and they came to the battle: and, behold, [a]every man's sword was against his fellow, *and there was* a very great discomfiture.

21 Moreover the Hebrews *that* were with the Philistines before that time, which went up with them into the camp *from the country* round about, even they also *turned* to be with the Israelites that *were* with Saul and Jonathan.

22 Likewise all the men of Israel which [a]had hid themselves in mount Ephraim, *when* they heard that the Philistines fled, even they also followed hard after them in the battle.

23 [a]So the LORD saved Israel that day: and the battle passed over [b]unto Beth–aven.

Saul's Rash Oath

24 And the men of Israel were distressed that day: for Saul had [a]adjured the people, saying, Cursed *be* the man that eateth *any* food until evening, that I may be avenged on mine enemies. So none of the people tasted *any* food.

25 [a]And all *they of* the land came to a wood; and there was [b]honey upon the ground.

26 And when the people were come into the wood, behold, the honey dropped; but no man put his hand to his mouth: for the people feared the oath.

27 But Jonathan heard not when his father charged the people with the oath: wherefore he put forth the end of the rod that *was* in his hand, and dipped it in an honeycomb, and put his hand to his mouth; and his eyes were enlightened.

28 Then answered one of the people, and said, Thy father straitly charged the people with an oath, saying, Cursed *be* the man that eateth *any* food this day. And the people were faint.

29 Then said Jonathan, My father hath troubled the land: see, I pray you, how mine eyes have been enlightened, because I tasted a little of this honey.

30 How much more, if haply the people had eaten freely to day of the spoil of their enemies which they found? for had there not been now a much greater slaughter among the Philistines?

31 And they smote the Philistines that day from Michmash to Aijalon: and the people were very faint.

32 And the people flew upon the spoil, and took sheep, and oxen, and calves, and slew *them* on the ground: and the people did eat *them* [a]with the blood.

33 Then they told Saul, saying, Behold, the people sin against the LORD, in that they eat with

13 [a]Lev. 26:8; Josh. 23:10
15 [a]Deut. 28:7; 2 Kin. 7:6, 7; Job 18:11 [b]1 Sam. 13:17 [c]Gen. 35:5
16 [a]1 Sam. 14:20
19 [a]Num. 27:21
20 [a]Judg. 7:22; 2 Chr. 20:23
22 [a]1 Sam. 13:6
23 [a]Ex. 14:30; 2 Chr. 32:22; Hos. 1:7 [b]1 Sam. 13:5
24 [a]Josh. 6:26
25 [a]Deut. 9:28; Matt. 3:5 [b]Ex. 3:8; Num. 13:27; Matt. 3:4
32 [a]Gen. 9:4; Lev. 3:17; 17:10–14; 19:26; Deut. 12:16, 23, 24; Acts 15:20

NKJV

and knees with his armorbearer after him; and they [a]fell before Jonathan. And as he came after him, his armorbearer killed them.

14 That first slaughter which Jonathan and his armorbearer made was about twenty men within about *half an acre of land.

15 And [a]there was trembling in the camp, in the field, and among all the people. The garrison and [b]the raiders also trembled; and the earth quaked, so that it was [c]a very great trembling.

16 Now the watchmen of Saul in Gibeah of Benjamin looked, and *there* was the multitude, melting away; and they [a]went here and there.

17 Then Saul said to the people who *were* with him, "Now call the roll and see who has gone from us." And when they had called the roll, surprisingly, Jonathan and his armorbearer *were* not *there.*

18 And Saul said to Ahijah, "Bring the *ark of God here" (for at that time the *ark of God was with the children of Israel).

19 Now it happened, while Saul [a]talked to the priest, that the noise which *was* in the camp of the Philistines continued to increase; so Saul said to the priest, "Withdraw your hand."

20 Then Saul and all the people who *were* with him assembled, and they went to the battle; and indeed [a]every man's sword was against his neighbor, *and there was* very great confusion.

21 Moreover the Hebrews *who* were with the Philistines before that time, who went up with them into the camp *from the* surrounding *country,* they also joined the Israelites who *were* with Saul and Jonathan.

22 Likewise all the men of Israel who [a]had hidden in the mountains of Ephraim, *when* they heard that the Philistines fled, they also followed hard after them in the battle.

23 [a]So the LORD saved Israel that day, and the battle shifted [b]to Beth Aven.

Saul's Rash Oath

24 And the men of Israel were distressed that day, for Saul had [a]placed the people under oath, saying, "Cursed *is* the man who eats *any* food until evening, before I have taken vengeance on my enemies." So none of the people tasted food.

25 [a]Now all *the people* of the land came to a forest; and there was [b]honey on the ground.

26 And when the people had come into the woods, there was the honey, dripping; but no one put his hand to his mouth, for the people feared the oath.

27 But Jonathan had not heard his father charge the people with the oath; therefore he stretched out the end of the rod that *was* in his hand and dipped it in a honeycomb, and put his hand to his mouth; and his countenance brightened.

28 Then one of the people said, "Your father strictly charged the people with an oath, saying, 'Cursed *is* the man who eats food this day.' " And the people were faint.

29 But Jonathan said, "My father has troubled the land. Look now, how my countenance has brightened because I tasted a little of this honey.

30 "How much better if the people had eaten freely today of the spoil of their enemies which they found! For now would there not have been a much greater slaughter among the Philistines?"

31 Now they had driven back the Philistines that day from Michmash to Aijalon. So the people were very faint.

32 And the people rushed on the spoil, and took sheep, oxen, and calves, and slaughtered *them* on the ground; and the people ate *them* [a]with the blood.

33 Then they told Saul, saying, "Look, the people are sinning against the LORD by eating with

---

14:14 Lit. *half the area plowed by a yoke* of oxen in a day
14:18 So with MT, Tg., Vg.; LXX *ephod* • See preceding note

KJV

the blood. And he said, Ye have transgressed: roll a great stone unto me this day.

34 And Saul said, Disperse yourselves among the people, and say unto them, Bring me hither every man his ox, and every man his sheep, and slay *them* here, and eat; and sin not against the LORD in eating with the blood. And all the people brought every man his ox with him that night, and slew *them* there.

35 And Saul [a]built an altar unto the LORD: the same was the first altar that he built unto the LORD.

36 And Saul said, Let us go down after the Philistines by night, and spoil them until the morning light, and let us not leave a man of them. And they said, Do whatsoever seemeth good unto thee. Then said the priest, Let us draw near hither unto God.

37 And Saul [a]asked counsel of God, Shall I go down after the Philistines? wilt thou deliver them into the hand of Israel? But [b]he answered him not that day.

38 And Saul said, [a]Draw ye near hither, all the chief of the people: and know and see wherein this sin hath been this day.

39 For, [a]*as* the LORD liveth, which saveth Israel, though it be in Jonathan my son, he shall surely die. But *there was* not a man among all the people *that* answered him.

40 Then said he unto all Israel, Be ye on one side, and I and Jonathan my son will be on the other side. And the people said unto Saul, Do what seemeth good unto thee.

41 Therefore Saul said unto the LORD God of Israel, [a]Give a perfect *lot.* [b]And Saul and Jonathan were taken: but the people escaped.

42 And Saul said, Cast *lots* between me and Jonathan my son. And Jonathan was taken.

43 Then Saul said to Jonathan, [a]Tell me what thou hast done. And Jonathan told him, and said, [b]I did but taste a little honey with the end of the rod that *was* in mine hand, *and,* lo, I must die.

44 And Saul answered, [a]God do so and more also: [b]for thou shalt surely die, Jonathan.

45 And the people said unto Saul, Shall Jonathan die, who hath wrought this great salvation in Israel? God forbid: [a]*as* the LORD liveth, there shall not one hair of his head fall to the ground; for he hath wrought [b]with God this day. So the people rescued Jonathan, that he died not.

46 Then Saul went up from following the Philistines: and the Philistines went to their own place.

Saul's Continuing Wars

47 So Saul took the kingdom over Israel, and fought against all his enemies on every side, against Moab, and against the children of [a]Ammon, and against Edom, and against the kings of [b]Zobah, and against the Philistines: and whithersoever he turned himself, he vexed *them.*

48 And he gathered an host, and [a]smote the Amalekites, and delivered Israel out of the hands of them that spoiled them.

49 Now [a]the sons of Saul were Jonathan, and Ishui, and Melchi-shua: and the names of his two daughters *were these;* the name of the firstborn Merab, and the name of the younger [b]Michal:

50 And the name of Saul's wife *was* Ahinoam, the daughter of Ahimaaz: and the name of the captain of his host *was* Abner, the son of Ner, Saul's [a]uncle.

51 [a]And Kish *was* the father of Saul; and Ner the father of Abner *was* the son of Abiel.

52 And there was sore war against the Philistines all the days of Saul: and when Saul saw any strong man, or any valiant man, [a]he took him unto him.

Saul Spares King Agag

15 Samuel also said unto Saul, [a]The LORD sent me to anoint thee *to be* king over his peo-

---

35 [a]1 Sam. 7:12, 17; 2 Sam. 24:25
37 [a]Judg. 20:18 [b]1 Sam. 28:6
38 [a]Josh. 7:14; 1 Sam. 10:19
39 [a]1 Sam. 14:24, 44; 2 Sam. 12:5
41 [a]Prov. 16:33; Acts 1:24–26 [b]Josh. 7:16; 1 Sam. 10:20, 21
43 [a]Josh. 7:19 [b]1 Sam. 14:27
44 [a]Ruth 1:17; 1 Sam. 25:22 [b]1 Sam. 14:39
45 [a]2 Sam. 14:11; 1 Kin. 1:52; Luke 21:18; Acts 27:34 [b][2 Cor. 6:1; Phil. 2:12, 13]
47 [a]1 Sam. 11:1–13 [b]2 Sam. 10:6
48 [a]Ex. 17:16; 1 Sam. 15:3–7
49 [a]1 Sam. 31:2; 1 Chr. 8:33 [b]1 Sam. 18:17–20, 27; 19:12
50 [a]1 Sam. 10:14
51 [a]1 Sam. 9:1, 21
52 [a]1 Sam. 8:11

CHAPTER 15

1 [a]1 Sam. 9:16; 10:1

*

14:41 So with MT, Tg.; LXX, Vg. *Why do You not answer Your servant today? If the injustice is with me or Jonathan my son, O LORD God of Israel, give proof; and if You say it is with Your people Israel, give holiness.*
14:47 LXX, Vg. *prospered*
14:49 *Abinadab,* 1 Chr. 8:33; 9:39

NKJV

the blood!" So he said, "You have dealt treacherously; roll a large stone to me this day."

34 Then Saul said, "Disperse yourselves among the people, and say to them, 'Bring me here every man's ox and every man's sheep, slaughter *them* here, and eat; and do not sin against the LORD by eating with the blood.' " So every one of the people brought his ox with him that night, and slaughtered *it* there.

35 Then Saul [a]built an altar to the LORD. This was the first altar that he built to the LORD.

36 Now Saul said, "Let us go down after the Philistines by night, and plunder them until the morning light; and let us not leave a man of them." And they said, "Do whatever seems good to you." Then the priest said, "Let us draw near to God here."

37 So Saul [a]asked counsel of God, "Shall I go down after the Philistines? Will You deliver them into the hand of Israel?" But [b]He did not answer him that day.

38 And Saul said, [a]"Come over here, all you chiefs of the people, and know and see what this sin was today.

39 "For [a]*as* the LORD lives, who saves Israel, though it be in Jonathan my son, he shall surely die." But not a man among all the people answered him.

40 Then he said to all Israel, "You be on one side, and my son Jonathan and I will be on the other side." And the people said to Saul, "Do what seems good to you."

41 Therefore Saul said to the LORD God of Israel, [a]"Give* a perfect *lot.*" [b]So Saul and Jonathan were taken, but the people escaped.

42 And Saul said, "Cast *lots* between my son Jonathan and me." So Jonathan was taken.

43 Then Saul said to Jonathan, [a]"Tell me what you have done." And Jonathan told him, and said, [b]"I only tasted a little honey with the end of the rod that *was* in my hand. So now I must die!"

44 Saul answered, [a]"God do so and more also; [b]for you shall surely die, Jonathan."

45 But the people said to Saul, "Shall Jonathan die, who has accomplished this great deliverance in Israel? Certainly not! [a]*As* the LORD lives, not one hair of his head shall fall to the ground, for he has worked [b]with God this day." So the people rescued Jonathan, and he did not die.

46 Then Saul returned from pursuing the Philistines, and the Philistines went to their own place.

Saul's Continuing Wars

47 So Saul established his sovereignty over Israel, and fought against all his enemies on every side, against Moab, against the people of [a]Ammon, against Edom, against the kings of [b]Zobah, and against the Philistines. Wherever he turned, he *harassed *them.*

48 And he gathered an army and [a]attacked the Amalekites, and delivered Israel from the hands of those who plundered them.

49 [a]The sons of Saul were Jonathan, *Jishui, and Malchishua. And the names of his two daughters *were these:* the name of the firstborn Merab, and the name of the younger [b]Michal.

50 The name of Saul's wife *was* Ahinoam the daughter of Ahimaaz. And the name of the commander of his army *was* Abner the son of Ner, Saul's [a]uncle.

51 [a]Kish *was* the father of Saul, and Ner the father of Abner *was* the son of Abiel.

52 Now there was fierce war with the Philistines all the days of Saul. And when Saul saw any strong man or any valiant man, [a]he took him for himself.

Saul Spares King Agag

15 Samuel also said to Saul, [a]"The LORD sent me to anoint you king over His people, over

KJV

ple, over Israel: now therefore hearken thou unto the voice of the words of the LORD.

2 Thus saith the LORD of hosts, I remember *that* which Amalek did to Israel, [a]how he laid *wait* for him in the way, when he came up from Egypt.

3 Now go and [a]smite Amalek, and [b]utterly destroy all that they have, and spare them not; but slay both man and woman, infant and suckling, ox and sheep, camel and ass.

4 And Saul gathered the people together, and numbered them in Telaim, two hundred thousand footmen, and ten thousand men of Judah.

5 And Saul came to a city of Amalek, and laid wait in the valley.

6 And Saul said unto [a]the Kenites, [b]Go, depart, get you down from among the Amalekites, lest I destroy you with them: for [c]ye shewed kindness to all the children of Israel, when they came up out of Egypt. So the Kenites departed from among the Amalekites.

7 [a]And Saul smote the Amalekites from [b]Havilah *until* thou comest to [c]Shur, that *is* over against Egypt.

8 And [a]he took Agag the king of the Amalekites alive, and [b]utterly destroyed all the people with the edge of the sword.

9 But Saul and the people [a]spared Agag, and the best of the sheep, and of the oxen, and of the fatlings, and the lambs, and all *that was* good, and would not utterly destroy them: but every thing *that was* vile and refuse, that they destroyed utterly.

Saul Rejected as King

10 Then came the word of the LORD unto Samuel, saying,

11 [a]It repenteth me that I have set up Saul *to be* king: for he is [b]turned back from following me, [c]and hath not performed my commandments. And it [d]grieved Samuel; and he cried unto the LORD all night.

12 And when Samuel rose early to meet Saul in the morning, it was told Samuel, saying, Saul came to [a]Carmel, and, behold, he set him up a place, and is gone about, and passed on, and gone down to Gilgal.

13 And Samuel came to Saul: and Saul said unto him, [a]Blessed *be* thou of the LORD: I have performed the commandment of the LORD.

14 And Samuel said, What *meaneth* then this bleating of the sheep in mine ears, and the lowing of the oxen which I hear?

15 And Saul said, They have brought them from the Amalekites: [a]for the people spared the best of the sheep and of the oxen, to sacrifice unto the LORD thy God; and the rest we have utterly destroyed.

16 Then Samuel said unto Saul, Stay, and I will tell thee what the LORD hath said to me this night. And he said unto him, Say on.

17 And Samuel said, [a]When thou *wast* little in thine own sight, *wast* thou not *made* the head of the tribes of Israel, and the LORD anointed thee king over Israel?

18 And the LORD sent thee on a journey, and said, Go and utterly destroy the sinners the Amalekites, and fight against them until they be consumed.

19 Wherefore then didst thou not obey the voice of the LORD, but didst fly upon the spoil, and didst evil in the sight of the LORD?

20 And Saul said unto Samuel, Yea, [a]I have obeyed the voice of the LORD, and have gone the way which the LORD sent me, and have brought Agag the king of Amalek, and have utterly destroyed the Amalekites.

21 [a]But the people took of the spoil, sheep and oxen, the chief of the things which should have been utterly destroyed, to sacrifice unto the LORD thy God in Gilgal.

22 And Samuel said, [a]Hath the LORD *as great*

2 [a]Ex. 17:8, 14; Num. 24:20; Deut. 25:17–19
3 [a]Deut. 25:19 [b]Lev. 27:28, 29; Num. 24:20; Deut. 20:16–18; Josh. 6:17–21
6 [a]Num. 24:21; Judg. 1:16; 4:11–22; 1 Chr. 2:55 [b]Gen. 18:25; 19:12, 14; Rev. 18:4 [c]Ex. 18:10, 19; Num. 10:29, 32
7 [a]1 Sam. 14:48 [b]Gen. 2:11; 25:17, 18 [c]Gen. 16:7; Ex. 15:22; 1 Sam. 27:8
8 [a]1 Sam. 15:32, 33 [b]1 Sam. 27:8, 9
9 [a]1 Sam. 15:3, 15, 19
11 [a]Gen. 6:6, 7; 1 Sam. 15:35; 2 Sam. 24:16 [b]Josh. 22:16; 1 Kin. 9:6 [c]1 Sam. 13:13; 15:3, 9 [d]1 Sam. 15:35; 16:1
12 [a]Josh. 15:55; 1 Sam. 25:2
13 [a]Gen. 14:19; Judg. 17:2; Ruth 3:10; 2 Sam. 2:5
15 [a][Gen. 3:12, 13; Ex. 32:22, 23]; 1 Sam. 15:9, 21; [Prov. 28:13]
17 [a]1 Sam. 9:21; 10:22
20 [a]1 Sam. 15:13; [Prov. 28:13]
21 [a]1 Sam. 15:15
22 [a]Ps. 50:8, 9; 51:16, 17; [Prov. 21:3; Is. 1:11–17; Jer. 7:22, 23; Mic. 6:6–8; Heb. 10:4–10]

NKJV

Israel. Now therefore, heed the voice of the words of the LORD.

2 "Thus says the LORD of hosts: 'I will punish Amalek *for* what he did to Israel, [a]how he ambushed him on the way when he came up from Egypt.

3 'Now go and [a]attack Amalek, and [b]utterly destroy all that they have, and do not spare them. But kill both man and woman, infant and nursing child, ox and sheep, camel and donkey.' "

4 So Saul gathered the people together and numbered them in Telaim, two hundred thousand foot soldiers and ten thousand men of Judah.

5 And Saul came to a city of Amalek, and lay in wait in the valley.

6 Then Saul said to [a]the Kenites, [b]"Go, depart, get down from among the Amalekites, lest I destroy you with them. For [c]you showed kindness to all the children of Israel when they came up out of Egypt." So the Kenites departed from among the Amalekites.

7 [a]And Saul attacked the Amalekites, from [b]Havilah all the way to [c]Shur, which is east of Egypt.

8 [a]He also took Agag king of the Amalekites alive, and [b]utterly destroyed all the people with the edge of the sword.

9 But Saul and the people [a]spared Agag and the best of the sheep, the oxen, the fatlings, the lambs, and all *that was* good, and were unwilling to utterly destroy them. But everything despised and worthless, that they utterly destroyed.

Saul Rejected as King

10 Now the word of the LORD came to Samuel, saying,

11 [a]"I greatly regret that I have set up Saul *as* king, for he has [b]turned back from following Me, [c]and has not performed My commandments." And it [d]grieved Samuel, and he cried out to the LORD all night.

12 So when Samuel rose early in the morning to meet Saul, it was told Samuel, saying, "Saul went to [a]Carmel, and indeed, he set up a monument for himself; and he has gone on around, passed by, and gone down to Gilgal."

13 Then Samuel went to Saul, and Saul said to him, [a]"Blessed *are* you of the LORD! I have performed the commandment of the LORD."

14 But Samuel said, "What then *is* this bleating of the sheep in my ears, and the lowing of the oxen which I hear?"

15 And Saul said, "They have brought them from the Amalekites; [a]for the people spared the best of the sheep and the oxen, to sacrifice to the LORD your God; and the rest we have utterly destroyed."

16 Then Samuel said to Saul, "Be quiet! And I will tell you what the LORD said to me last night." And he said to him, "Speak on."

17 So Samuel said, [a]"When you *were* little in your own eyes, *were* you not head of the tribes of Israel? And did not the LORD anoint you king over Israel?

18 "Now the LORD sent you on a mission, and said, 'Go, and utterly destroy the sinners, the Amalekites, and fight against them until they are consumed.'

19 "Why then did you not obey the voice of the LORD? Why did you swoop down on the spoil, and do evil in the sight of the LORD?"

20 And Saul said to Samuel, [a]"But I have obeyed the voice of the LORD, and gone on the mission on which the LORD sent me, and brought back Agag king of Amalek; I have utterly destroyed the Amalekites.

21 [a]"But the people took of the plunder, sheep and oxen, the best of the things which should have been utterly destroyed, to sacrifice to the LORD your God in Gilgal."

22 So Samuel said:

KJV

delight in burnt offerings and sacrifices, as in
obeying the voice of the LORD? Behold, [b]to obey
is better than sacrifice, *and* to hearken than the
fat of rams.
23 For rebellion *is as* the sin of witchcraft,
and stubbornness *is as* iniquity and idolatry. Because thou hast rejected the word of the LORD,
[a]he hath also rejected thee from *being* king.
24 [a]And Saul said unto Samuel, I have
sinned: for I have transgressed the commandment
of the LORD, and thy words: because I [b]feared the
people, and obeyed their voice.
25 Now therefore, I pray thee, pardon my sin,
and turn again with me, that I may worship the
LORD.
26 And Samuel said unto Saul, I will not return with thee: [a]for thou hast rejected the word
of the LORD, and the LORD hath rejected thee from
being king over Israel.
27 And as Samuel turned about to go away,
[a]he laid hold upon the skirt of his mantle, and it
rent.
28 And Samuel said unto him, [a]The LORD
hath rent the kingdom of Israel from thee this day,
and hath given it to a neighbour of thine, *that is*
better than thou.
29 And also the Strength of Israel [a]will not
lie nor repent: for he *is* not a man, that he should
repent.
30 Then he said, I have sinned: *yet* [a]honour
me now, I pray thee, before the elders of my people, and before Israel, and turn again with me,
that I may worship the LORD thy God.
31 So Samuel turned again after Saul; and
Saul worshipped the LORD.
32 Then said Samuel, Bring ye hither to me
Agag the king of the Amalekites. And Agag came
unto him delicately. And Agag said, Surely the
bitterness of death is past.
33 And Samuel said, [a]As thy sword hath
made women childless, so shall thy mother be
childless among women. And Samuel hewed
Agag in pieces before the LORD in Gilgal.
34 Then Samuel went to [a]Ramah; and Saul
went up to his house to [b]Gibeah of Saul.
35 And [a]Samuel came no more to see Saul
until the day of his death: nevertheless Samuel
mourned for Saul: and the LORD repented that he
had made Saul king over Israel.

David Anointed King

16 And the LORD said unto Samuel, [a]How long
wilt thou mourn for Saul, seeing I have rejected him from reigning over Israel? [b]fill thine
horn with oil, and go, I will send thee to [c]Jesse
the Beth–lehemite: for [d]I have provided me a king
among his sons.
2 And Samuel said, How can I go? if Saul
hear *it*, he will kill me. And the LORD said, Take
an heifer with thee, and say, [a]I am come to sacrifice to the LORD.
3 And call Jesse to the sacrifice, and I will
shew thee what thou shalt do: and thou shalt
anoint unto me *him* whom I name unto thee.
4 And Samuel did that which the LORD
spake, and came to Beth–lehem. And the elders
of the town [a]trembled at his coming, and said,
[b]Comest thou peaceably?
5 And he said, Peaceably: I am come to sacrifice unto the LORD: [a]sanctify yourselves, and
come with me to the sacrifice. And he sanctified
Jesse and his sons, and called them to the
sacrifice.
6 And it came to pass, when they were
come, that he looked on [a]Eliab, and [b]said, Surely
the LORD's anointed *is* before him.
7 But the LORD said unto Samuel, [a]Look not
on his countenance, or on the height of his stature;
because I have refused him: [b]for *the LORD seeth*

---

22 [a]Ps. 50:8, 9; 51:16, 17; [Prov. 21:3; Is. 1:11–17; Jer. 7:22, 23; Mic. 6:6–8; Heb. 10:4–10] [b][Eccl. 5:1; Hos. 6:6; Matt. 5:24; 9:13; 12:7; Mark 12:33]
23 [a]1 Sam. 13:14; 16:1
24 [a]Num. 22:34; Josh. 7:20; 1 Sam. 26:21; 2 Sam. 12:13; Ps. 51:4 [b][Ex. 23:2; Prov. 29:25; Is. 51:12, 13]
26 [a]1 Sam. 2:30
27 [a]1 Kin. 11:30, 31
28 [a]1 Sam. 28:17, 18; 1 Kin. 11:31
29 [a]Num. 23:19; Ezek. 24:14; 2 Tim. 2:13; Titus 1:2
30 [a][John 5:44; 12:43]
33 [a][Gen. 9:6]; Num. 14:45; Judg. 1:7; [Matt. 7:2]
34 [a]1 Sam. 7:17 [b]1 Sam. 11:4
35 [a]1 Sam. 19:24

CHAPTER 16

1 [a]1 Sam. 15:23, 35 [b]1 Sam. 9:16; 10:1; 2 Kin. 9:1 [c]Ruth 4:18–22 [d]Ps. 78:70, 71; Acts 13:22
2 [a]1 Sam. 9:12
4 [a]1 Sam. 21:1 [b]1 Kin. 2:13; 2 Kin. 9:22
5 [a]Gen. 35:2; Ex. 19:10
6 [a]1 Sam. 17:13, 28 [b]1 Kin. 12:26
7 [a]Ps. 147:10 [b]Is. 55:8, 9

*

16:7 LXX *For God does not see as man sees*; Tg. *It is not by the appearance of a man*; Vg. *Nor do I judge according to the looks of a man*

NKJV

[a]"Has the LORD *as great* delight in burnt
offerings and sacrifices,
As in obeying the voice of the LORD?
Behold, [b]to obey is better than sacrifice,
And to heed than the fat of rams.
23 For rebellion *is as* the sin of witchcraft,
And stubbornness *is as* iniquity and
idolatry.
Because you have rejected the word of the
LORD,
[a]He also has rejected you from *being* king."

24 [a]Then Saul said to Samuel, "I have sinned,
for I have transgressed the commandment of the
LORD and your words, because I [b]feared the people and obeyed their voice.
25 "Now therefore, please pardon my
sin, and return with me, that I may worship the
LORD."
26 But Samuel said to Saul, "I will not return
with you, [a]for you have rejected the word of the
LORD, and the LORD has rejected you from being
king over Israel."
27 And as Samuel turned around to go away,
[a]*Saul* seized the edge of his robe, and it tore.
28 So Samuel said to him, [a]"The LORD has
torn the kingdom of Israel from you today, and
has given it to a neighbor of yours, *who is* better
than you.
29 "And also the Strength of Israel [a]will not
lie nor relent. For He *is* not a man, that He should
relent."
30 Then he said, "I have sinned; *yet* [a]honor
me now, please, before the elders of my people
and before Israel, and return with me, that I may
worship the LORD your God."
31 So Samuel turned back after Saul, and
Saul worshiped the LORD.
32 Then Samuel said, "Bring Agag king of
the Amalekites here to me." So Agag came to him
cautiously. And Agag said, "Surely the bitterness
of death is past."
33 But Samuel said, [a]"As your sword has
made women childless, so shall your mother be
childless among women." And Samuel hacked
Agag in pieces before the LORD in Gilgal.
34 Then Samuel went to [a]Ramah, and Saul
went up to his house at [b]Gibeah of Saul.
35 And [a]Samuel went no more to see Saul
until the day of his death. Nevertheless Samuel
mourned for Saul, and the LORD regretted that He
had made Saul king over Israel.

David Anointed King

16 Now the LORD said to Samuel, [a]"How long
will you mourn for Saul, seeing I have rejected him from reigning over Israel? [b]Fill your
horn with oil, and go; I am sending you to [c]Jesse
the Bethlehemite. For [d]I have provided Myself a
king among his sons."
2 And Samuel said, "How can I go? If Saul
hears *it*, he will kill me." But the LORD said, "Take
a heifer with you, and say, [a]'I have come to sacrifice to the LORD.'
3 "Then invite Jesse to the sacrifice, and I
will show you what you shall do; you shall anoint
for Me the one I name to you."
4 So Samuel did what the LORD said, and
went to Bethlehem. And the elders of the town
[a]trembled at his coming, and said, [b]"Do you come
peaceably?"
5 And he said, "Peaceably; I have come to
sacrifice to the LORD. [a]Sanctify yourselves, and
come with me to the sacrifice." Then he consecrated Jesse and his sons, and invited them to
the sacrifice.
6 So it was, when they came, that he looked
at [a]Eliab and [b]said, "Surely the LORD's anointed
is before Him!"
7 But the LORD said to Samuel, [a]"Do not
look at his appearance or at his physical stature,
because I have refused him. [b]For* *the LORD does*

KJV

not as man seeth; for man [c]looketh on the outward appearance, but the LORD looketh on the
[d]heart.
8 Then Jesse called Abinadab, and made
him pass before Samuel. And he said, Neither
hath the LORD chosen this.
9 Then Jesse made Shammah to pass by.
And he said, Neither hath the LORD chosen this.
10 Again, Jesse made seven of his sons to
pass before Samuel. And Samuel said unto Jesse,
The LORD hath not chosen these.
11 And Samuel said unto Jesse, Are here all
thy children? And he said, There remaineth yet
the youngest, and, behold, he keepeth the [a]sheep.
And Samuel said unto Jesse, Send and fetch him:
for we will not sit down till he come hither.
12 And he sent, and brought him in. Now he
was [a]ruddy, *and* withal of a [b]beautiful countenance, and goodly to look to. [c]And the LORD said,
Arise, anoint him: for this *is* he.
13 Then Samuel took the horn of oil, and
anointed him in the midst of his brethren: and
[a]the Spirit of the LORD came upon David from
that day forward. So Samuel rose up, and went
to Ramah.

A Distressing Spirit Troubles Saul

14 [a]But the Spirit of the LORD departed from
Saul, and [b]an evil spirit from the LORD troubled
him.
15 And Saul's servants said unto him, Behold
now, an evil spirit from God troubleth thee.
16 Let our lord now command thy servants,
which are before thee, to seek out a man, *who is*
a cunning player on an harp: and it shall come
to pass, when the evil spirit from God is upon
thee, that he shall [a]play with his hand, and thou
shalt be well.
17 And Saul said unto his servants, Provide
me now a man that can play well, and bring *him*
to me.
18 Then answered one of the servants, and
said, Behold, I have seen a son of Jesse the Bethlehemite, *that is* cunning in playing, and a mighty
valiant man, and a man of war, and prudent in
matters, and a comely person, and [a]the LORD *is*
with him.
19 Wherefore Saul sent messengers unto
Jesse, and said, Send me David thy son, which
is with the sheep.
20 And Jesse [a]took an ass *laden* with bread,
and a bottle of wine, and a kid, and sent *them*
by David his son unto Saul.
21 And David came to Saul, and [a]stood before him: and he loved him greatly; and he
became his armourbearer.
22 And Saul sent to Jesse, saying, Let David,
I pray thee, stand before me; for he hath found
favour in my sight.
23 And it came to pass, when the *evil* spirit
from God was upon Saul, that David took an harp,
and played with his hand: so Saul was refreshed,
and was well, and the evil spirit departed from
him.

David and Goliath

17 Now the Philistines gathered together their
armies to battle, and were gathered together at [a]Shochoh, which *belongeth* to Judah,
and pitched between Shochoh and Azekah, in
Ephes-dammim.
2 And Saul and the men of Israel were gathered together, and pitched by the valley of Elah,
and set the battle in array against the Philistines.
3 And the Philistines stood on a mountain
on the one side, and Israel stood on a mountain
on the other side: and *there was* a valley between
them.
4 And there went out a champion out of the
camp of the Philistines, named [a]Goliath, of [b]Gath,
whose height *was* six cubits and a span.
5 And *he had* an helmet of brass upon his

7 [c]2 Cor. 10:7 [d]1 Kin. 8:39
11 [a]2 Sam. 7:8; Ps. 78:70–72
12 [a]1 Sam. 17:42 [b]Gen. 39:6; Ex. 2:2; Acts 7:20 [c]1 Sam. 9:17
13 [a]Num. 27:18; 1 Sam. 10:6, 9, 10
14 [a]Judg. 16:20; 1 Sam. 11:6; 18:12; 28:15 [b]Judg. 9:23; 1 Sam. 16:15, 16; 18:10; 19:9; 1 Kin. 22:19–22
16 [a]1 Sam. 18:10; 19:9; 2 Kin. 3:15
18 [a]1 Sam. 3:19; 18:12, 14
20 [a]1 Sam. 10:4, 27; Prov. 18:16
21 [a]Gen. 41:46; Prov. 22:29

CHAPTER 17
1 [a]Josh. 15:35; 2 Chr. 28:18
4 [a]2 Sam. 21:19 [b]Josh. 11:21, 22

NKJV

not *see* as man sees; for man [c]looks at the outward
appearance, but the LORD looks at the [d]heart."
8 So Jesse called Abinadab, and made him
pass before Samuel. And he said, "Neither has
the LORD chosen this one."
9 Then Jesse made Shammah pass by. And
he said, "Neither has the LORD chosen this one."
10 Thus Jesse made seven of his sons pass
before Samuel. And Samuel said to Jesse, "The
LORD has not chosen these."
11 And Samuel said to Jesse, "Are all the
young men here?" Then he said, "There remains
yet the youngest, and there he is, keeping the
[a]sheep." And Samuel said to Jesse, "Send and
bring him. For we will not *sit down till he comes
here."
12 So he sent and brought him in. Now he
was [a]ruddy, [b]with bright eyes, and good-looking.
[c]And the LORD said, "Arise, anoint him; for this
is the one!"
13 Then Samuel took the horn of oil and
anointed him in the midst of his brothers; and
[a]the Spirit of the LORD came upon David from
that day forward. So Samuel arose and went to
Ramah.

A Distressing Spirit Troubles Saul

14 [a]But the Spirit of the LORD departed from
Saul, and [b]a distressing spirit from the LORD troubled him.
15 And Saul's servants said to him, "Surely,
a distressing spirit from God is troubling you.
16 "Let our master now command your servants, *who are* before you, to seek out a man *who
is* a skillful player on the harp. And it shall be
that he will [a]play it with his hand when the distressing spirit from God is upon you, and you shall
be well."
17 So Saul said to his servants, "Provide me
now a man who can play well, and bring *him* to
me."
18 Then one of the servants answered and
said, "Look, I have seen a son of Jesse the Bethlehemite, *who is* skillful in playing, a mighty man
of valor, a man of war, prudent in speech, and a
handsome person; and [a]the LORD *is* with him."
19 Therefore Saul sent messengers to Jesse,
and said, "Send me your son David, who *is* with
the sheep."
20 And Jesse [a]took a donkey *loaded with*
bread, a skin of wine, and a young goat, and sent
them by his son David to Saul.
21 So David came to Saul and [a]stood before
him. And he loved him greatly, and he became
his armorbearer.
22 Then Saul sent to Jesse, saying, "Please
let David stand before me, for he has found favor
in my sight."
23 And so it was, whenever the spirit from
God was upon Saul, that David would take a harp
and play *it* with his hand. Then Saul would become refreshed and well, and the distressing spirit
would depart from him.

David and Goliath

17 Now the Philistines gathered their armies
together to battle, and were gathered at
[a]Sochoh, which *belongs* to Judah; they encamped
between Sochoh and Azekah, in Ephes Dammim.
2 And Saul and the men of Israel were gathered together, and they encamped in the Valley
of Elah, and drew up in battle array against the
Philistines.
3 The Philistines stood on a mountain on
one side, and Israel stood on a mountain on the
other side, with a valley between them.
4 And a champion went out from the camp
of the Philistines, named [a]Goliath, from [b]Gath,
whose height *was* six cubits and a span.
5 *He had* a bronze helmet on his head, and

* **16:11** So with LXX, Vg.; MT *turn around;* Tg., Syr. *turn away*

KJV

head, and he *was* armed with a coat of mail; and the weight of the coat *was* five thousand shekels of brass.

6 And *he had* greaves of brass upon his legs, and a target of brass between his shoulders.

7 And the staff of his spear *was* like a weaver's beam; and his spear's head *weighed* six hundred shekels of iron: and one bearing a shield went before him.

8 And he stood and cried unto the armies of Israel, and said unto them, Why are ye come out to set *your* battle in array? *am* not I a Philistine, and ye [a]servants to Saul? choose you a man for you, and let him come down to me.

9 If he be able to fight with me, and to kill me, then will we be your servants: but if I prevail against him, and kill him, then shall ye be our servants, and [a]serve us.

10 And the Philistine said, I [a]defy the armies of Israel this day; give me a man, that we may fight together.

11 When Saul and all Israel heard those words of the Philistine, they were dismayed, and greatly afraid.

12 Now David *was* [a]the son of that [b]Ephrathite of Beth–lehem–judah, whose name *was* Jesse; and he had [c]eight sons: and the man went among men *for* an old man in the days of Saul.

13 And the three eldest sons of Jesse went *and* followed Saul to the battle: and the [a]names of his three sons that went to the battle *were* Eliab the first born, and next unto him Abinadab, and the third Shammah.

14 And David *was* the youngest: and the three eldest followed Saul.

15 But David went and returned from Saul [a]to feed his father's sheep at Beth–lehem.

16 And the Philistine drew near morning and evening, and presented himself forty days.

17 And Jesse said unto David his son, Take now for thy brethren an ephah of this parched *corn,* and these ten loaves, and run to the camp to thy brethren;

18 And carry these ten cheeses unto the captain of *their* thousand, and [a]look how thy brethren fare, and take their pledge.

19 Now Saul, and they, and all the men of Israel, *were* in the valley of Elah, fighting with the Philistines.

20 And David rose up early in the morning, and left the sheep with a keeper, and took, and went, as Jesse had commanded him; and he came to the trench, as the host was going forth to the fight, and shouted for the battle.

21 For Israel and the Philistines had put the battle in array, army against army.

22 And David left his carriage in the hand of the keeper of the carriage, and ran into the army, and came and saluted his brethren.

23 And as he talked with them, behold, there came up the champion, the Philistine of Gath, Goliath by name, out of the armies of the Philistines, and spake [a]according to the same words: and David heard *them.*

24 And all the men of Israel, when they saw the man, fled from him, and were sore afraid.

25 And the men of Israel said, Have ye seen this man that is come up? surely to defy Israel is he come up: and it shall be, *that* the man who killeth him, the king will enrich him with great riches, and [a]will give him his daughter, and make his father's house free in Israel.

26 And David spake to the men that stood by him, saying, What shall be done to the man that killeth this Philistine, and taketh away [a]the reproach from Israel? for who *is* this [b]uncircumcised Philistine, that he should [c]defy the armies of [d]the living God?

27 And the people answered him after this manner, saying, [a]So shall it be done to the man that killeth him.

8 [a]1 Sam. 8:17
9 [a]1 Sam. 11:1
10 [a]1 Sam. 17:26, 36, 45; 2 Sam. 21:21
12 [a]Ruth 4:22; 1 Sam. 16:1, 18; 17:58 [b]Gen. 35:19 [c]1 Sam. 16:10, 11; 1 Chr. 2:13–15
13 [a]1 Sam. 16:6, 8, 9; 1 Chr. 2:13
15 [a]1 Sam. 16:11, 19; 2 Sam. 7:8
18 [a]Gen. 37:13, 14
23 [a]1 Sam. 17:8–10
25 [a]Josh. 15:16
26 [a]1 Sam. 11:2 [b]1 Sam. 14:6; 17:36; Jer. 9:25, 26 [c]1 Sam. 17:10 [d]Deut. 5:26; 2 Kin. 19:4; Jer. 10:10
27 [a]1 Sam. 17:25

NKJV

he *was* armed with a coat of mail, and the weight of the coat *was* five thousand shekels of bronze.

6 And *he had* bronze armor on his legs and a bronze javelin between his shoulders.

7 Now the staff of his spear *was* like a weaver's beam, and his iron spearhead *weighed* six hundred shekels; and a shield-bearer went before him.

8 Then he stood and cried out to the armies of Israel, and said to them, "Why have you come out to line up for battle? *Am* I not a Philistine, and you the [a]servants of Saul? Choose a man for yourselves, and let him come down to me.

9 "If he is able to fight with me and kill me, then we will be your servants. But if I prevail against him and kill him, then you shall be our servants and [a]serve us."

10 And the Philistine said, "I [a]defy the armies of Israel this day; give me a man, that we may fight together."

11 When Saul and all Israel heard these words of the Philistine, they were dismayed and greatly afraid.

12 Now David *was* [a]the son of that [b]Ephrathite of Bethlehem Judah, whose name *was* Jesse, and who had [c]eight sons. And the man was old, advanced *in years,* in the days of Saul.

13 The three oldest sons of Jesse had gone to follow Saul to the battle. The [a]names of his three sons who went to the battle *were* Eliab the firstborn, next to him Abinadab, and the third Shammah.

14 David *was* the youngest. And the three oldest followed Saul.

15 But David occasionally went and returned from Saul [a]to feed his father's sheep at Bethlehem.

16 And the Philistine drew near and presented himself forty days, morning and evening.

17 Then Jesse said to his son David, "Take now for your brothers an ephah of this dried *grain* and these ten loaves, and run to your brothers at the camp.

18 "And carry these ten cheeses to the captain of *their* thousand, and [a]see how your brothers fare, and bring back news of them."

19 Now Saul and they and all the men of Israel *were* in the Valley of Elah, fighting with the Philistines.

20 So David rose early in the morning, left the sheep with a keeper, and took *the things* and went as Jesse had commanded him. And he came to the camp as the army was going out to the fight and shouting for the battle.

21 For Israel and the Philistines had drawn up in battle array, army against army.

22 And David left his supplies in the hand of the supply keeper, ran to the army, and came and greeted his brothers.

23 Then as he talked with them, there was the champion, the Philistine of Gath, Goliath by name, coming up from the armies of the Philistines; and he spoke [a]according to the same words. So David heard *them.*

24 And all the men of Israel, when they saw the man, fled from him and were dreadfully afraid.

25 So the men of Israel said, "Have you seen this man who has come up? Surely he has come up to defy Israel; and it shall be *that* the man who kills him the king will enrich with great riches, [a]will give him his daughter, and give his father's house exemption *from taxes* in Israel."

26 Then David spoke to the men who stood by him, saying, "What shall be done for the man who kills this Philistine and takes away [a]the reproach from Israel? For who *is* this [b]uncircumcised Philistine, that he should [c]defy the armies of [d]the living God?"

27 And the people answered him in this manner, saying, [a]"So shall it be done for the man who kills him."

KJV

28 And Eliab his eldest brother heard when he spake unto the men; and Eliab's [a]anger was kindled against David, and he said, Why camest thou down hither? and with whom hast thou left those few sheep in the wilderness? I know thy pride, and the naughtiness of thine heart; for thou art come down that thou mightest see the battle.

29 And David said, What have I now done? [a]*Is there* not a cause?

30 And he turned from him toward another, and [a]spake after the same manner: and the people answered him again after the former manner.

31 And when the words were heard which David spake, they rehearsed *them* before Saul: and he sent for him.

32 And David said to Saul, [a]Let no man's heart fail because of him; [b]thy servant will go and fight with this Philistine.

33 And Saul said to David, [a]Thou art not able to go against this Philistine to fight with him: for thou *art but* a youth, and he a man of war from his youth.

34 And David said unto Saul, Thy servant kept his father's sheep, and there came a [a]lion, and a bear, and took a lamb out of the flock:

35 And I went out after him, and smote him, and delivered *it* out of his mouth: and when he arose against me, I caught *him* by his beard, and smote him, and slew him.

36 Thy servant slew both the lion and the bear: and this uncircumcised Philistine shall be as one of them, seeing he hath defied the armies of the living God.

37 David said moreover, [a]The LORD that delivered me out of the paw of the lion, and out of the paw of the bear, he will deliver me out of the hand of this Philistine. And Saul said unto David, Go, and [b]the LORD be with thee.

38 And Saul armed David with his armour, and he put an helmet of brass upon his head; also he armed him with a coat of mail.

39 And David girded his sword upon his armour, and he assayed to go; for he had not proved *it*. And David said unto Saul, I cannot go with these; for I have not proved *them*. And David put them off him.

40 And he took his staff in his hand, and chose him five smooth stones out of the brook, and put them in a shepherd's bag which he had, even in a scrip; and his sling *was* in his hand: and he drew near to the Philistine.

41 And the Philistine came on and drew near unto David; and the man that bare the shield *went* before him.

42 And when the Philistine looked about, and saw David, he [a]disdained him: for he was *but* a youth, and [b]ruddy, and of a fair countenance.

43 And the Philistine said unto David, [a]*Am* I a dog, that thou comest to me with staves? And the Philistine cursed David by his gods.

44 And the Philistine [a]said to David, Come to me, and I will give thy flesh unto the fowls of the air, and to the beasts of the field.

45 Then said David to the Philistine, Thou comest to me with a sword, and with a spear, and with a shield: [a]but I come to thee in the name of the LORD of hosts, the God of the armies of Israel, whom thou hast [b]defied.

46 This day will the LORD deliver thee into mine hand; and I will smite thee, and take thine head from thee; and I will give [a]the carcases of the host of the Philistines this day unto the fowls of the air, and to the wild beasts of the earth; [b]that all the earth may know that there is a God in Israel.

47 And all this assembly shall know that the LORD [a]saveth not with sword and spear: for [b]the battle *is* the LORD's, and he will give you into our hands.

48 And it came to pass, when the Philistine arose, and came and drew nigh to meet David,

28 [a]Gen. 37:4, 8–36; [Prov. 18:19; Matt. 10:36]
29 [a]1 Sam. 17:17
30 [a]1 Sam. 17:26, 27
32 [a]Deut. 20:1–4
[b]1 Sam. 16:18
33 [a]Num. 13:31; Deut. 9:2
34 [a]Judg. 14:5
37 [a][2 Cor. 1:10; 2 Tim. 4:17, 18]
[b]1 Sam. 20:13; 1 Chr. 22:11, 16
42 [a][Ps. 123:4; Prov. 16:18; 1 Cor. 1:27, 28] [b]1 Sam. 16:12
43 [a]1 Sam. 24:14; 2 Sam. 3:8; 9:8; 16:9; 2 Kin. 8:13
44 [a]1 Sam. 17:46; 1 Kin. 20:10, 11
45 [a]2 Sam. 22:33, 35; 2 Chr. 32:8; Ps. 124:8; [2 Cor. 10:4]; Heb. 11:33, 34
[b]1 Sam. 17:10
46 [a]Deut. 28:26 [b]Josh. 4:24; 1 Kin. 8:43; 18:36; 2 Kin. 19:19; Is. 52:10
47 [a]1 Sam. 14:6; 2 Chr. 14:11; 20:15; Ps. 44:6; Hos. 1:7; Zech. 4:6
[b]2 Chr. 20:15

NKJV

28 Now Eliab his oldest brother heard when he spoke to the men; and Eliab's [a]anger was aroused against David, and he said, "Why did you come down here? And with whom have you left those few sheep in the wilderness? I know your pride and the insolence of your heart, for you have come down to see the battle."

29 And David said, "What have I done now? [a]*Is there* not a cause?"

30 Then he turned from him toward another and [a]said the same thing; and these people answered him as the first ones *did*.

31 Now when the words which David spoke were heard, they reported *them* to Saul; and he sent for him.

32 Then David said to Saul, [a]"Let no man's heart fail because of him; [b]your servant will go and fight with this Philistine."

33 And Saul said to David, [a]"You are not able to go against this Philistine to fight with him; for you *are* a youth, and he a man of war from his youth."

34 But David said to Saul, "Your servant used to keep his father's sheep, and when a [a]lion or a bear came and took a lamb out of the flock,

35 I went out after it and struck it, and delivered *the lamb* from its mouth; and when it arose against me, I caught *it* by its beard, and struck and killed it.

36 "Your servant has killed both lion and bear; and this uncircumcised Philistine will be like one of them, seeing he has defied the armies of the living God."

37 Moreover David said, [a]"The LORD, who delivered me from the paw of the lion and from the paw of the bear, He will deliver me from the hand of this Philistine." And Saul said to David, [b]"Go, and the LORD be with you!"

38 So Saul clothed David with his armor, and he put a bronze helmet on his head; he also clothed him with a coat of mail.

39 David fastened his sword to his armor and tried to walk, for he had not tested *them*. And David said to Saul, "I cannot walk with these, for I have not tested *them*." So David took them off.

40 Then he took his staff in his hand; and he chose for himself five smooth stones from the brook, and put them in a shepherd's bag, in a pouch which he had, and his sling was in his hand. And he drew near to the Philistine.

41 So the Philistine came, and began drawing near to David, and the man who bore the shield *went* before him.

42 And when the Philistine looked about and saw David, he [a]disdained him; for he was *only* a youth, [b]ruddy and good-looking.

43 So the Philistine [a]said to David, "*Am* I a dog, that you come to me with sticks?" And the Philistine cursed David by his gods.

44 And the Philistine [a]said to David, "Come to me, and I will give your flesh to the birds of the air and the beasts of the field!"

45 Then David said to the Philistine, "You come to me with a sword, with a spear, and with a javelin. [a]But I come to you in the name of the LORD of hosts, the God of the armies of Israel, whom you have [b]defied.

46 "This day the LORD will deliver you into my hand, and I will strike you and take your head from you. And this day I will give [a]the carcasses of the camp of the Philistines to the birds of the air and the wild beasts of the earth, [b]that all the earth may know that there is a God in Israel.

47 "Then all this assembly shall know that the LORD [a]does not save with sword and spear; for [b]the battle *is* the LORD's, and He will give you into our hands."

48 So it was, when the Philistine arose and came and drew near to meet David, that David

KJV

that David hasted, and [a]ran toward the army to meet the Philistine.

49 And David put his hand in his bag, and took thence a stone, and slang *it,* and smote the Philistine in his forehead, that the stone sunk into his forehead; and he fell upon his face to the earth.

50 So David prevailed over the Philistine with a [a]sling and with a stone, and smote the Philistine, and slew him; but *there was* no sword in the hand of David.

51 Therefore David ran, and stood upon the Philistine, and took his [a]sword, and drew it out of the sheath thereof, and slew him, and cut off his head therewith. And when the Philistines saw their champion was dead, [b]they fled.

52 And the men of Israel and of Judah arose, and shouted, and pursued the Philistines, until thou come to the valley, and to the gates of Ekron. And the wounded of the Philistines fell down by the way to [a]Shaaraim, even unto Gath, and unto Ekron.

53 And the children of Israel returned from chasing after the Philistines, and they spoiled their tents.

54 And David took the head of the Philistine, and brought it to Jerusalem; but he put his armour in his tent.

55 And when Saul saw David go forth against the Philistine, he said unto [a]Abner, the captain of the host, Abner, [b]whose son *is* this youth? And Abner said, *As* thy soul liveth, O king, I cannot tell.

56 And the king said, Enquire thou whose son the stripling *is.*

57 And as David returned from the slaughter of the Philistine, Abner took him, and brought him before Saul [a]with the head of the Philistine in his hand.

58 And Saul said to him, Whose son *art* thou, *thou* young man? And David answered, [a]*I am* the son of thy servant Jesse the Beth–lehemite.

Saul Resents David

18 And it came to pass, when he had made an end of speaking unto Saul, that [a]the soul of Jonathan was knit with the soul of David, [b]and Jonathan loved him as his own soul.

2 And Saul took him that day, [a]and would let him go no more home to his father's house.

3 Then Jonathan and David made a [a]covenant, because he loved him as his own soul.

4 And Jonathan stripped himself of the robe that *was* upon him, and gave it to David, and his garments, even to his sword, and to his bow, and to his girdle.

5 And David went out whithersoever Saul sent him, *and* behaved himself wisely: and Saul set him over the men of war, and he was accepted in the sight of all the people, and also in the sight of Saul's servants.

6 And it came to pass as they came, when David was returned from the slaughter of the Philistine, that [a]the women came out of all cities of Israel, singing and dancing, to meet king Saul, with tabrets, with joy, and with instruments of musick.

7 And the women [a]answered *one another* as they played, and said, [b]Saul hath slain his thousands, and David his ten thousands.

8 And Saul was very wroth, and the saying [a]displeased him; and he said, They have ascribed unto David ten thousands, and to me they have ascribed *but* thousands: and *what* can he have more but [b]the kingdom?

9 And Saul eyed David from that day and forward.

10 And it came to pass on the morrow, that [a]the evil spirit from God came upon Saul, [b]and he prophesied in the midst of the house: and Da-

48 [a]Ps. 27:3
50 [a]Judg. 3:31; 15:15; 20:16
51 [a]1 Sam. 21:9; 2 Sam. 23:21 [b]Heb. 11:34
52 [a]Josh. 15:36
55 [a]1 Sam. 14:50 [b]1 Sam. 16:21, 22
57 [a]1 Sam. 17:54
58 [a]1 Sam. 17:12

CHAPTER 18

1 [a]Gen. 44:30 [b]Deut. 13:6; 1 Sam. 20:17; 2 Sam. 1:26
2 [a]1 Sam. 17:15
3 [a]1 Sam. 20:8–17
6 [a]Ex. 15:20, 21; Judg. 11:34; Ps. 68:25; 149:3
7 [a]Ex. 15:21 [b]1 Sam. 21:11; 29:5
8 [a]Eccl. 4:4 [b]1 Sam. 15:28
10 [a]1 Sam. 16:14 [b]1 Sam. 19:24; 1 Kin. 18:29; Acts 16:16

NKJV

hurried and [a]ran toward the army to meet the Philistine.

49 Then David put his hand in his bag and took out a stone; and he slung *it* and struck the Philistine in his forehead, so that the stone sank into his forehead, and he fell on his face to the earth.

50 So David prevailed over the Philistine with a [a]sling and a stone, and struck the Philistine and killed him. But *there was* no sword in the hand of David.

51 Therefore David ran and stood over the Philistine, took his [a]sword and drew it out of its sheath and killed him, and cut off his head with it. And when the Philistines saw that their champion was dead, [b]they fled.

52 Now the men of Israel and Judah arose and shouted, and pursued the Philistines as far as the entrance of *the valley and to the gates of Ekron. And the wounded of the Philistines fell along the road to [a]Shaaraim, even as far as Gath and Ekron.

53 Then the children of Israel returned from chasing the Philistines, and they plundered their tents.

54 And David took the head of the Philistine and brought it to Jerusalem, but he put his armor in his tent.

55 When Saul saw David going out against the Philistine, he said to [a]Abner, the commander of the army, "Abner, [b]whose son *is* this youth?" And Abner said, "As your soul lives, O king, I do not know."

56 So the king said, "Inquire whose son this young man *is.*"

57 Then, as David returned from the slaughter of the Philistine, Abner took him and brought him before Saul [a]with the head of the Philistine in his hand.

58 And Saul said to him, "Whose son *are* you, young man?" So David answered, [a]"*I am* the son of your servant Jesse the Bethlehemite."

Saul Resents David

18 Now when he had finished speaking to Saul, [a]the soul of Jonathan was knit to the soul of David, [b]and Jonathan loved him as his own soul.

2 Saul took him that day, [a]and would not let him go home to his father's house anymore.

3 Then Jonathan and David made a [a]covenant, because he loved him as his own soul.

4 And Jonathan took off the robe that *was* on him and gave it to David, with his armor, even to his sword and his bow and his belt.

5 So David went out wherever Saul sent him, *and* behaved wisely. And Saul set him over the men of war, and he was accepted in the sight of all the people and also in the sight of Saul's servants.

6 Now it had happened as they were coming *home,* when David was returning from the slaughter of the Philistine, that [a]the women had come out of all the cities of Israel, singing and dancing, to meet King Saul, with tambourines, with joy, and with musical instruments.

7 So the women [a]sang as they danced, and said:

[b]"Saul has slain his thousands,
And David his ten thousands."

8 Then Saul was very angry, and the saying [a]displeased him; and he said, "They have ascribed to David ten thousands, and to me they have ascribed *only* thousands. Now *what* more can he have but [b]the kingdom?"

9 So Saul eyed David from that day forward.

10 And it happened on the next day that [a]the distressing spirit from God came upon Saul, [b]and he prophesied inside the house. So David

*

17:52 So with MT, Syr., Tg., Vg.; LXX *Gath*

KJV

vid [c]played with his hand, as at other times: [d]and
there was a javelin in Saul's hand.
11 And Saul [a]cast the javelin; for he said, I
will smite David even to the wall *with it.* And
David avoided out of his presence twice.
12 And Saul was [a]afraid of David, because
[b]the LORD was with him, and was [c]departed from
Saul.
13 Therefore Saul removed him from him,
and made him his captain over a thousand; and
[a]he went out and came in before the people.
14 And David behaved himself wisely in all
his ways; and [a]the LORD *was* with him.
15 Wherefore when Saul saw that he behaved himself very wisely, he was afraid of him.
16 But [a]all Israel and Judah loved David, because he went out and came in before them.

David Marries Michal

17 And Saul said to David, Behold my elder
daughter Merab, [a]her will I give thee to wife: only
be thou valiant for me, and fight [b]the LORD's battles. For Saul said, [c]Let not mine hand be upon
him, but let the hand of the Philistines be upon
him.
18 And David said unto Saul, [a]Who *am* I?
and what *is* my life, *or* my father's family in Israel,
that I should be son in law to the king?
19 But it came to pass at the time when
Merab Saul's daughter should have been given
to David, that she was given unto [a]Adriel the [b]Me-
holathite to wife.
20 [a]And Michal Saul's daughter loved David:
and they told Saul, and the thing pleased him.
21 And Saul said, I will give him her, that
she may be a snare to him, and that [a]the hand
of the Philistines may be against him. Wherefore
Saul said to David, Thou shalt [b]this day be my
son in law in *the one of* the twain.
22 And Saul commanded his servants, *saying,* Commune with David secretly, and say, Behold, the king hath delight in thee, and all his
servants love thee: now therefore be the king's
son in law.
23 And Saul's servants spake those words in
the ears of David. And David said, Seemeth it to
you *a* light *thing* to be a king's son in law, seeing
that I *am* a poor man, and lightly esteemed?
24 And the servants of Saul told him, saying,
On this manner spake David.
25 And Saul said, Thus shall ye say to David,
The king desireth not any [a]dowry, but an hundred
foreskins of the Philistines, to be [b]avenged of the
king's enemies. But Saul [c]thought to make David
fall by the hand of the Philistines.
26 And when his servants told David these
words, it pleased David well to be the king's son
in law: and [a]the days were not expired.
27 Wherefore David arose and went, he and
[a]his men, and slew of the Philistines two hundred
men; and [b]David brought their foreskins, and they
gave them in full tale to the king, that he might
be the king's son in law. And Saul gave him Michal his daughter to wife.
28 And Saul saw and knew that the LORD *was*
with David, and *that* Michal Saul's daughter
loved him.
29 And Saul was yet the more afraid of David; and Saul became David's enemy continually.
30 Then the princes of the Philistines [a]went
forth: and it came to pass, after they went forth,
that David [b]behaved himself more wisely than
all the servants of Saul; so that his name was
much set by.

Saul Persecutes David

19 And Saul spake to Jonathan his son, and
to all his servants, that they should kill
[a]David.

---

10 [c]1 Sam. 16:23 [d]1 Sam. 19:9, 10
11 [a]1 Sam. 19:10; 20:33
12 [a]1 Sam. 18:15, 29 [b]1 Sam. 16:13, 18 [c]1 Sam. 16:14; 28:15
13 [a]Num. 27:17; 1 Sam. 18:16; 29:6; 2 Sam. 5:2
14 [a]Gen. 39:2, 3, 23; Josh. 6:27; 1 Sam. 16:18
16 [a]Num. 27:16, 17; 1 Sam. 18:5; 2 Sam. 5:2; 1 Kin. 3:7
17 [a]1 Sam. 14:49; 17:25 [b]Num. 32:20, 27, 29; 1 Sam. 25:28 [c]1 Sam. 18:21, 25; 2 Sam. 12:9
18 [a]1 Sam. 9:21; 18:23; 2 Sam. 7:18
19 [a]2 Sam. 21:8 [b]Judg. 7:22; 2 Sam. 21:8; 1 Kin. 19:16
20 [a]1 Sam. 18:28
21 [a]1 Sam. 18:17 [b]1 Sam. 18:26
25 [a]Gen. 34:12; Ex. 22:17 [b]1 Sam. 14:24 [c]1 Sam. 18:17
26 [a]1 Sam. 18:21
27 [a]1 Sam. 18:13 [b]2 Sam. 3:14
30 [a]2 Sam. 11:1 [b]1 Sam. 18:5

CHAPTER 19

1 [a]1 Sam. 8:8, 9 [b]1 Sam. 18:1

NKJV

[c]played *music* with his hand, as at other times;
[d]but *there was* a spear in Saul's hand.
11 And Saul [a]cast the spear, for he said, "I
will pin David to the wall!" But David escaped
his presence twice.
12 Now Saul was [a]afraid of David, because
[b]the LORD was with him, but had [c]departed from
Saul.
13 Therefore Saul removed him from his
presence, and made him his captain over a thousand; and [a]he went out and came in before the
people.
14 And David behaved wisely in all his ways,
and [a]the LORD *was* with him.
15 Therefore, when Saul saw that he behaved
very wisely, he was afraid of him.
16 But [a]all Israel and Judah loved David, because he went out and came in before them.

David Marries Michal

17 Then Saul said to David, "Here is my older
daughter Merab; [a]I will give her to you as a wife.
Only be valiant for me, and fight [b]the LORD's battles." For Saul thought, [c]"Let my hand not be
against him, but let the hand of the Philistines
be against him."
18 So David said to Saul, [a]"Who *am* I, and
what *is* my life *or* my father's family in Israel,
that I should be son-in-law to the king?"
19 But it happened at the time when Merab,
Saul's daughter, should have been given to David,
that she was given to [a]Adriel the [b]Meholathite
as a wife.
20 [a]Now Michal, Saul's daughter, loved David. And they told Saul, and the thing pleased him.
21 So Saul said, "I will give her to him, that
she may be a snare to him, and that [a]the hand
of the Philistines may be against him." Therefore
Saul said to David a second time, [b]"You shall be
my son-in-law today."
22 And Saul commanded his servants, "Communicate with David secretly, and say, 'Look, the
king has delight in you, and all his servants love
you. Now therefore, become the king's son-in-
law.' "
23 So Saul's servants spoke those words in
the hearing of David. And David said, "Does it
seem to you *a* light *thing* to be a king's son-in-
law, seeing I *am* a poor and lightly esteemed
man?"
24 And the servants of Saul told him, saying,
"In this manner David spoke."
25 Then Saul said, "Thus you shall say to David: 'The king does not desire any [a]dowry but one
hundred foreskins of the Philistines, to take [b]ven-
geance on the king's enemies.' " But Saul [c]thought
to make David fall by the hand of the Philistines.
26 So when his servants told David these
words, it pleased David well to become the king's
son-in-law. Now [a]the days had not expired;
27 therefore David arose and went, he and
[a]his men, and killed two hundred men of the Philistines. And [b]David brought their foreskins, and
they gave them in full count to the king, that he
might become the king's son-in-law. Then Saul
gave him Michal his daughter as a wife.
28 Thus Saul saw and knew that the LORD
was with David, and *that* Michal, Saul's daughter,
loved him;
29 and Saul was still more afraid of David.
So Saul became David's enemy continually.
30 Then the princes of the Philistines [a]went
out *to war.* And so it was, whenever they went
out, *that* David [b]behaved more wisely than all
the servants of Saul, so that his name became
highly esteemed.

Saul Persecutes David

19 Now Saul spoke to Jonathan his son and
to all his servants, that they should kill
[a]David; but Jonathan, Saul's son, [b]delighted
greatly in David.

KJV

2 But Jonathan Saul's son [a]delighted much in David: and Jonathan told David, saying, Saul my father seeketh to kill thee: now therefore, I pray thee, take heed to thyself until the morning, and abide in a secret *place,* and hide thyself:

3 And I will go out and stand beside my father in the field where thou *art,* and I will commune with my father of thee; and what I see, that I will tell [a]thee.

4 And Jonathan [a]spake good of David unto Saul his father, and said unto him, Let not the king [b]sin against his servant, against David; because he hath not sinned against thee, and because his works *have been* to thee-ward very good:

5 For he did put his [a]life in his hand, and [b]slew the Philistine, and [c]the LORD wrought a great salvation for all Israel: thou sawest *it,* and didst rejoice: [d]wherefore then wilt thou [e]sin against innocent blood, to slay David without a cause?

6 And Saul hearkened unto the voice of Jonathan: and Saul sware, *As* the LORD liveth, he shall not be slain.

7 And Jonathan called David, and Jonathan shewed him all those things. And Jonathan brought David to Saul, and he was in his presence, [a]as in times past.

8 And there was war again: and David went out, and fought with the Philistines, and [a]slew them with a great slaughter; and they fled from him.

9 And [a]the evil spirit from the LORD was upon Saul, as he sat in his house with his javelin in his hand: and David played with *his* hand.

10 And Saul sought to smite David even to the wall with the javelin; but he slipped away out of Saul's presence, and he smote the javelin into the wall: and David fled, and escaped that night.

11 [a]Saul also sent messengers unto David's house, to watch him, and to slay him in the morning: and Michal David's wife told him, saying, If thou save not thy life to night, to morrow thou shalt be slain.

12 So Michal [a]let David down through a window: and he went, and fled, and escaped.

13 And Michal took an image, and laid *it* in the bed, and put a pillow of goats' *hair* for his bolster, and covered *it* with a cloth.

14 And when Saul sent messengers to take David, she said, He *is* sick.

15 And Saul sent the messengers *again* to see David, saying, Bring him up to me in the bed, that I may slay him.

16 And when the messengers were come in, behold, *there was* an image in the bed, with a pillow of goats' *hair* for his bolster.

17 And Saul said unto Michal, Why hast thou deceived me so, and sent away mine enemy, that he is escaped? And Michal answered Saul, He said unto me, Let me go; [a]why should I kill thee?

18 So David fled, and escaped, and came to [a]Samuel to [b]Ramah, and told him all that Saul had done to him. And he and Samuel went and dwelt in Naioth.

19 And it was told Saul, saying, Behold, David *is* at Naioth in Ramah.

20 And [a]Saul sent messengers to take David: [b]and when they saw the company of the prophets prophesying, and Samuel standing *as* appointed over them, the Spirit of God was upon the messengers of Saul, and they also [c]prophesied.

21 And when it was told Saul, he sent other messengers, and they prophesied likewise. And Saul sent messengers again the third time, and they prophesied also.

22 Then went he also to Ramah, and came to a great well that *is* in Sechu: and he asked and said, Where *are* Samuel and David? And *one* said, Behold, *they be* at Naioth in Ramah.

23 And he went thither to Naioth in Ramah: and [a]the Spirit of God was upon him also, and

2 [a]1 Sam. 18:1
3 [a]1 Sam. 20:8–13
4 [a]1 Sam. 20:32; [Prov. 31:8, 9] [b]Gen. 42:22; [Prov. 17:13]; Jer. 18:20
5 [a]Judg. 9:17; 12:3 [b]1 Sam. 17:49, 50 [c]1 Sam. 11:13; 1 Chr. 11:14 [d]1 Sam. 20:32 [e][Deut. 19:10–13]
7 [a]1 Sam. 16:21; 18:2, 10, 13
8 [a]1 Sam. 18:27; 23:5
9 [a]1 Sam. 16:14; 18:10, 11
11 [a]Judg. 16:2; Ps. 59:title
12 [a]Josh. 2:15; Acts 9:25; 2 Cor. 11:33
17 [a]2 Sam. 2:22
18 [a]1 Sam. 16:13 [b]1 Sam. 7:17
20 [a]1 Sam. 19:11, 14; John 7:32 [b]1 Sam. 10:5, 6, 10; [1 Cor. 14:3, 24, 25] [c]Num. 11:25; Joel 2:28
23 [a]1 Sam. 10:10

NKJV

2 So Jonathan told David, saying, "My father Saul seeks to kill you. Therefore please be on your guard until morning, and stay in a secret *place* and hide.

3 "And I will go out and stand beside my father in the field where you *are,* and I will speak with my father about you. Then what I observe, I will tell [a]you."

4 Thus Jonathan [a]spoke well of David to Saul his father, and said to him, "Let not the king [b]sin against his servant, against David, because he has not sinned against you, and because his works *have been* very good toward you.

5 "For he took his [a]life in his hands and [b]killed the Philistine, and [c]the LORD brought about a great deliverance for all Israel. You saw *it* and rejoiced. [d]Why then will you [e]sin against innocent blood, to kill David without a cause?"

6 So Saul heeded the voice of Jonathan, and Saul swore, "As the LORD lives, he shall not be killed."

7 Then Jonathan called David, and Jonathan told him all these things. So Jonathan brought David to Saul, and he was in his presence [a]as in times past.

8 And there was war again; and David went out and fought with the Philistines, [a]and struck them with a mighty blow, and they fled from him.

9 Now [a]the distressing spirit from the LORD came upon Saul as he sat in his house with his spear in his hand. And David was playing *music* with *his* hand.

10 Then Saul sought to pin David to the wall with the spear, but he slipped away from Saul's presence; and he drove the spear into the wall. So David fled and escaped that night.

11 [a]Saul also sent messengers to David's house to watch him and to kill him in the morning. And Michal, David's wife, told him, saying, "If you do not save your life tonight, tomorrow you will be killed."

12 So Michal [a]let David down through a window. And he went and fled and escaped.

13 And Michal took an image and laid *it* in the bed, put a cover of goats' *hair* for his head, and covered *it* with clothes.

14 So when Saul sent messengers to take David, she said, "He *is* sick."

15 Then Saul sent the messengers *back* to see David, saying, "Bring him up to me in the bed, that I may kill him."

16 And when the messengers had come in, there was the image in the bed, with a cover of goats' *hair* for his head.

17 Then Saul said to Michal, "Why have you deceived me like this, and sent my enemy away, so that he has escaped?" And Michal answered Saul, "He said to me, 'Let me go! [a]Why should I kill you?' "

18 So David fled and escaped, and went to [a]Samuel at [b]Ramah, and told him all that Saul had done to him. And he and Samuel went and stayed in Naioth.

19 Now it was told Saul, saying, "Take note, David *is* at Naioth in Ramah!"

20 Then [a]Saul sent messengers to take David. [b]And when they saw the group of prophets prophesying, and Samuel standing *as* leader over them, the Spirit of God came upon the messengers of Saul, and they also [c]prophesied.

21 And when Saul was told, he sent other messengers, and they prophesied likewise. Then Saul sent messengers again the third time, and they prophesied also.

22 Then he also went to Ramah, and came to the great well that *is* at Sechu. So he asked, and said, "Where *are* Samuel and David?" And *someone* said, "Indeed *they are* at Naioth in Ramah."

23 So he went there to Naioth in Ramah. Then [a]the Spirit of God was upon him also, and

KJV

he went on, and prophesied, until he came to Naioth in Ramah.

24 [a]And he stripped off his clothes also, and prophesied before Samuel in like manner, and lay down [b]naked all that day and all that night. Wherefore they say, [c]*Is* Saul also among the prophets?

Jonathan's Loyalty to David

20 And David fled from Naioth in Ramah, and came and said before Jonathan, What have I done? what *is* mine iniquity? and what *is* my sin before thy father, that he seeketh my life?

2 And he said unto him, God forbid; thou shalt not die: behold, my father will do nothing either great or small, but that he will shew it me: and why should my father hide this thing from me? it *is* not *so*.

3 And David sware moreover, and said, Thy father certainly knoweth that I have found grace in thine eyes; and he saith, Let not Jonathan know this, lest he be grieved: but [a]truly *as* the LORD liveth, and *as* thy soul liveth, *there is* but a step between me and death.

4 Then said Jonathan unto David, Whatsoever thy soul desireth, I will even do *it* for thee.

5 And David said unto Jonathan, Behold, to morrow *is* the [a]new moon, and I should not fail to sit with the king at meat: but let me go, that I may [b]hide myself in the field unto the third *day* at even.

6 If thy father at all miss me, then say, David earnestly asked *leave* of me that he might run [a]to Beth–lehem his city: for *there is* a yearly sacrifice there for all the family.

7 [a]If he say thus, *It is* well; thy servant shall have peace: but if he be very wroth, *then* be sure that [b]evil is determined by him.

8 Therefore thou shalt [a]deal kindly with thy servant; for [b]thou hast brought thy servant into a covenant of the LORD with thee: notwithstanding, [c]if there be in me iniquity, slay me thyself; for why shouldest thou bring me to thy father?

9 And Jonathan said, Far be it from thee: for if I knew certainly that evil were determined by my father to come upon thee, then would not I tell it thee?

10 Then said David to Jonathan, Who shall tell me? or what *if* thy father answer thee roughly?

11 And Jonathan said unto David, Come, and let us go out into the field. And they went out both of them into the field.

12 And Jonathan said unto David, O LORD God of Israel, when I have sounded my father about to morrow any time, *or* the third *day*, and, behold, *if there be* good toward David, and I then send not unto thee, and shew it thee;

13 [a]The LORD do so and much more to Jonathan: but if it please my father *to do* thee evil, then I will shew it thee, and send thee away, that thou mayest go in peace: and [b]the LORD be with thee, as he hath [c]been with my father.

14 And thou shalt not only while yet I live shew me the kindness of the LORD, that I die not:

15 But *also* [a]thou shalt not cut off thy kindness from my house for ever: no, not when the LORD hath cut off the enemies of David every one from the face of the earth.

16 So Jonathan made *a covenant* with the house of David, *saying*, [a]Let the LORD even require *it* at the hand of David's enemies.

17 And Jonathan caused David to swear again, because he loved him: [a]for he loved him as he loved his own soul.

18 Then Jonathan said to David, [a]To morrow *is* the new moon: and thou shalt be missed, because thy seat will be empty.

19 And *when* thou hast stayed three days, *then* thou shalt go down quickly, and come to [a]the place where thou didst hide thyself when the

---

24 [a]Is. 20:2 [b]Mic. 1:8 [c]1 Sam. 10:10–12

CHAPTER 20

3 [a]1 Sam. 27:1; 2 Kin. 2:6
5 [a]Num. 10:10; 28:11–15 [b]1 Sam. 19:2, 3
6 [a]1 Sam. 16:4; 17:12; John 7:42
7 [a]Deut. 1:23; 2 Sam. 17:4 [b]1 Sam. 25:17; Esth. 7:7
8 [a]Josh. 2:14 [b]1 Sam. 18:3; 20:16; 23:18 [c]2 Sam. 14:32
13 [a]Ruth 1:17; 1 Sam. 3:17 [b]Josh. 1:5; 1 Sam. 17:37; 18:12; 1 Chr. 22:11, 16 [c]1 Sam. 10:7
15 [a]1 Sam. 24:21; 2 Sam. 9:1, 3, 7; 21:7
16 [a]Deut. 23:21; 1 Sam. 25:22; 31:2; 2 Sam. 4:7; 21:8
17 [a]1 Sam. 18:1
18 [a]1 Sam. 20:5, 24
19 [a]1 Sam. 19:2

NKJV

he went on and prophesied until he came to Naioth in Ramah.

24 [a]And he also stripped off his clothes and prophesied before Samuel in like manner, and lay down [b]naked all that day and all that night. Therefore they say, [c]"*Is* Saul also among the prophets?"

Jonathan's Loyalty to David

20 Then David fled from Naioth in Ramah, and went and said to Jonathan, "What have I done? What *is* my iniquity, and what *is* my sin before your father, that he seeks my life?"

2 So Jonathan said to him, "By no means! You shall not die! Indeed, my father will do nothing either great or small without first telling me. And why should my father hide this thing from me? It *is* not *so!*"

3 Then David took an oath again, and said, "Your father certainly knows that I have found favor in your eyes, and he has said, 'Do not let Jonathan know this, lest he be grieved.' But [a]truly, *as* the LORD lives and *as* your soul lives, *there is* but a step between me and death."

4 So Jonathan said to David, "Whatever you yourself desire, I will do *it* for you."

5 And David said to Jonathan, "Indeed tomorrow *is* the [a]New Moon, and I should not fail to sit with the king to eat. But let me go, that I may [b]hide in the field until the third *day* at evening.

6 "If your father misses me at all, then say, 'David earnestly asked *permission* of me that he might run over [a]to Bethlehem, his city, for *there is* a yearly sacrifice there for all the family.'

7 [a]"If he says thus: '*It is* well,' your servant will be safe. But if he is very angry, be sure that [b]evil is determined by him.

8 "Therefore you shall [a]deal kindly with your servant, for [b]you have brought your servant into a covenant of the LORD with you. Nevertheless, [c]if there is iniquity in me, kill me yourself, for why should you bring me to your father?"

9 But Jonathan said, "Far be it from you! For if I knew certainly that evil was determined by my father to come upon you, then would I not tell you?"

10 Then David said to Jonathan, "Who will tell me, or what *if* your father answers you roughly?"

11 And Jonathan said to David, "Come, let us go out into the field." So both of them went out into the field.

12 Then Jonathan said to David: "The LORD God of Israel *is witness!* When I have sounded out my father sometime tomorrow, *or* the third *day*, and indeed *there is* good toward David, and I do not send to you and tell you,

13 "may [a]the LORD do so and much more to Jonathan. But if it pleases my father *to do* you evil, then I will report it to you and send you away, that you may go in safety. And [b]the LORD be with you as He has [c]been with my father.

14 "And you shall not only show me the kindness of the LORD while I still live, that I may not die;

15 "but [a]you shall not cut off your kindness from my house forever, no, not when the LORD has cut off every one of the enemies of David from the face of the earth."

16 So Jonathan made *a covenant* with the house of David, *saying*, [a]"Let the LORD require *it* at the hand of David's enemies."

17 Now Jonathan again caused David to vow, because he loved him; [a]for he loved him as he loved his own soul.

18 Then Jonathan said to David, [a]"Tomorrow *is* the New Moon; and you will be missed, because your seat will be empty.

19 "And *when* you have stayed three days, go down quickly and come to [a]the place where

KJV

business was *in hand,* and shalt remain by the stone Ezel.

20 And I will shoot three arrows on the side *thereof,* as though I shot at a mark.

21 And, behold, I will send a lad, *saying,* Go, find out the arrows. If I expressly say unto the lad, Behold, the arrows *are* on this side of thee, take them; then come thou: for *there is* peace to thee, and no hurt; [a]*as* the LORD liveth.

22 But if I say thus unto the young man, Behold, the arrows *are* beyond thee; go thy way: for the LORD hath sent thee away.

23 And *as touching* [a]the matter which thou and I have spoken of, behold, the LORD *be* between thee and me for ever.

24 So David hid himself in the field: and when the new moon was come, the king sat him down to eat meat.

25 And the king sat upon his seat, as at other times, *even* upon a seat by the wall: and Jonathan arose, and Abner sat by Saul's side, and David's place was empty.

26 Nevertheless Saul spake not any thing that day: for he thought, Something hath befallen him, he *is* not clean; surely he *is* [a]not clean.

27 And it came to pass on the morrow, *which was* the second *day* of the month, that David's place was empty: and Saul said unto Jonathan his son, Wherefore cometh not the son of Jesse to meat, neither yesterday, nor to day?

28 And Jonathan [a]answered Saul, David earnestly asked *leave* of me *to go* to Beth–lehem:

29 And he said, Let me go, I pray thee; for our family hath a sacrifice in the city; and my brother, he hath commanded me *to be there:* and now, if I have found favour in thine eyes, let me get away, I pray thee, and see my brethren. Therefore he cometh not unto the king's table.

30 Then Saul's anger was kindled against Jonathan, and he said unto him, Thou son of the perverse rebellious *woman,* do not I know that thou hast chosen the son of Jesse to thine own confusion, and unto the confusion of thy mother's nakedness?

31 For as long as the son of Jesse liveth upon the ground, thou shalt not be established, nor thy kingdom. Wherefore now send and fetch him unto me, for he shall surely die.

32 And Jonathan answered Saul his father, and said unto him, [a]Wherefore shall he be slain? what hath he done?

33 And Saul [a]cast a javelin at him to smite him: [b]whereby Jonathan knew that it was determined of his father to slay David.

34 So Jonathan arose from the table in fierce anger, and did eat no meat the second day of the month: for he was grieved for David, because his father had done him shame.

35 And it came to pass in the morning, that Jonathan went out into the field at the time appointed with David, and a little lad with him.

36 And he said unto his lad, Run, find out now the arrows which I shoot. *And* as the lad ran, he shot an arrow beyond him.

37 And when the lad was come to the place of the arrow which Jonathan had shot, Jonathan cried after the lad, and said, *Is* not the arrow beyond thee?

38 And Jonathan cried after the lad, Make speed, haste, stay not. And Jonathan's lad gathered up the arrows, and came to his master.

39 But the lad knew not any thing: only Jonathan and David knew the matter.

40 And Jonathan gave his artillery unto his lad, and said unto him, Go, carry *them* to the city.

41 *And* as soon as the lad was gone, David arose out of *a place* toward the south, and fell on his face to the ground, and bowed himself three times: and they kissed one another, and wept one with another, until David exceeded.

42 And Jonathan said to David, [a]Go in peace,

21 [a]Jer. 4:2
23 [a]1 Sam. 20:14, 15
26 [a]Lev. 7:20, 21; 15:5
28 [a]1 Sam. 20:6
32 [a]Gen. 31:36; 1 Sam. 19:5; [Prov. 31:9]; Matt. 27:23; Luke 23:22
33 [a]1 Sam. 18:11; 19:10 [b]1 Sam. 20:7
42 [a]1 Sam. 1:17

NKJV

you hid on the day of the deed; and remain by the stone Ezel.

20 "Then I will shoot three arrows to the side, as though I shot at a target;

21 "and there I will send a lad, *saying,* 'Go, find the arrows.' If I expressly say to the lad, 'Look, the arrows *are* on this side of you; get them and come'—then, [a]as the LORD lives, *there is* safety for you and no harm.

22 "But if I say thus to the young man, 'Look, the arrows *are* beyond you'—go your way, for the LORD has sent you away.

23 "And as for [a]the matter which you and I have spoken of, indeed the LORD *be* between you and me forever."

24 Then David hid in the field. And when the New Moon had come, the king sat down to eat the feast.

25 Now the king sat on his seat, as at other times, on a seat by the wall. And *Jonathan arose, and Abner sat by Saul's side, but David's place was empty.

26 Nevertheless Saul did not say anything that day, for he thought, "Something has happened to him; he *is* unclean, surely he *is* [a]unclean."

27 And it happened the next day, the second *day* of the month, that David's place was empty. And Saul said to Jonathan his son, "Why has the son of Jesse not come to eat, either yesterday or today?"

28 So Jonathan [a]answered Saul, "David earnestly asked *permission* of me *to go* to Bethlehem.

29 "And he said, 'Please let me go, for our family has a sacrifice in the city, and my brother has commanded me *to be there.* And now, if I have found favor in your eyes, please let me get away and see my brothers.' Therefore he has not come to the king's table."

30 Then Saul's anger was aroused against Jonathan, and he said to him, "You son of a perverse, rebellious *woman!* Do I not know that you have chosen the son of Jesse to your own shame and to the shame of your mother's nakedness?

31 "For as long as the son of Jesse lives on the earth, you shall not be established, nor your kingdom. Now therefore, send and bring him to me, for he shall surely die."

32 And Jonathan answered Saul his father, and said to him, [a]"Why should he be killed? What has he done?"

33 Then Saul [a]cast a spear at him to kill him, [b]by which Jonathan knew that it was determined by his father to kill David.

34 So Jonathan arose from the table in fierce anger, and ate no food the second day of the month, for he was grieved for David, because his father had treated him shamefully.

35 And so it was, in the morning, that Jonathan went out into the field at the time appointed with David, and a little lad *was* with him.

36 Then he said to his lad, "Now run, find the arrows which I shoot." As the lad ran, he shot an arrow beyond him.

37 When the lad had come to the place where the arrow was which Jonathan had shot, Jonathan cried out after the lad and said, "*Is* not the arrow beyond you?"

38 And Jonathan cried out after the lad, "Make haste, hurry, do not delay!" So Jonathan's lad gathered up the arrows and came back to his master.

39 But the lad did not know anything. Only Jonathan and David knew of the matter.

40 Then Jonathan gave his weapons to his lad, and said to him, "Go, carry *them* to the city."

41 As soon as the lad had gone, David arose from *a place* toward the south, fell on his face to the ground, and bowed down three times. And they kissed one another; and they wept together, but David more so.

42 Then Jonathan said to David, [a]"Go in

***20:25** So with MT, Syr., Tg., Vg.; LXX *he sat across from Jonathan*

KJV

forasmuch as we have sworn both of us in the name of the LORD, saying, The LORD be between me and thee, and between my seed and thy seed for ever. And he arose and departed: and Jonathan went into the city.

David and the Holy Bread

21 Then came David to Nob to Ahimelech the priest: and [a]Ahimelech was [b]afraid at the meeting of David, and said unto him, Why *art* thou alone, and no man with thee?

2 And David said unto Ahimelech the priest, The king hath commanded me a business, and hath said unto me, Let no man know any thing of the business whereabout I send thee, and what I have commanded thee: and I have appointed *my* servants to such and such a place.

3 Now therefore what is under thine hand? give *me* five *loaves of* bread in mine hand, or what there is present.

4 And the priest answered David, and said, *There is* no common bread under mine hand, but there is [a]hallowed bread; [b]if the young men have kept themselves at least from women.

5 And David answered the priest, and said unto him, Of a truth women *have been* kept from us about these three days, since I came out, and the [a]vessels of the young men are holy, and *the bread is* in a manner common, yea, though it were sanctified this day [b]in the vessel.

6 So the priest [a]gave him hallowed *bread:* for there was no bread there but the shewbread, [b]that was taken from before the LORD, to put hot bread in the day when it was taken away.

7 Now a certain man of the servants of Saul *was* there that day, detained before the LORD; and his name *was* [a]Doeg, an Edomite, the chiefest of the herdmen that *belonged* to Saul.

8 And David said unto Ahimelech, And is there not here under thine hand spear or sword? for I have neither brought my sword nor my weapons with me, because the king's business required haste.

9 And the priest said, The sword of Goliath the Philistine, whom thou slewest in [a]the valley of Elah, [b]behold, it *is here* wrapped in a cloth behind the ephod: if thou wilt take that, take *it:* for *there is* no other save that here. And David said, *There is* none like that; give it me.

David Flees to Gath

10 And David arose, and fled that day for fear of Saul, and went to Achish the king of Gath.

11 And [a]the servants of Achish said unto him, *Is* not this David the king of the land? did they not sing one to another of him in dances, saying, [b]Saul hath slain his thousands, and David his ten thousands?

12 And David [a]laid up these words in his heart, and was sore afraid of Achish the king of Gath.

13 And [a]he changed his behaviour before them, and feigned himself mad in their hands, and scrabbled on the doors of the gate, and let his spittle fall down upon his beard.

14 Then said Achish unto his servants, Lo, ye see the man is mad: wherefore *then* have ye brought him to me?

15 Have I need of mad men, that ye have brought this *fellow* to play the mad man in my presence? shall this *fellow* come into my house?

David's Four Hundred Men

22 David therefore departed thence, and [a]escaped [b]to the cave Adullam: and when his brethren and all his father's house heard *it,* they went down thither to him.

2 [a]And every one *that was* in distress, and every one that *was* in debt, and every one *that was* discontented, gathered themselves unto him;

CHAPTER 21

1 [a]1 Sam. 14:3; Mark 2:26 [b]1 Sam. 16:4
4 [a]Ex. 25:30; Lev. 24:5–9; Matt. 12:4 [b]Ex. 19:15
5 [a]Ex. 19:14, 15; 1 Thess. 4:4 [b]Lev. 8:26
6 [a]Matt. 12:3, 4; Mark 2:25, 26; Luke 6:3, 4 [b]Lev. 24:8, 9
7 [a]1 Sam. 14:47; 22:9; Ps. 52:title
9 [a]1 Sam. 17:2, 50 [b]1 Sam. 31:10
11 [a]Ps. 56:title [b]1 Sam. 18:6–8; 29:5
12 [a]Luke 2:19
13 [a]Ps. 34:title

CHAPTER 22

1 [a]Ps. 57:title; 142:title [b]Josh. 12:15; 15:35; 2 Sam. 23:13
2 [a]Judg. 11:3

NKJV

peace, since we have both sworn in the name of the LORD, saying, 'May the LORD be between you and me, and between your descendants and my descendants, forever.' " So he arose and departed, and Jonathan went into the city.

David and the Holy Bread

21 Now David came to Nob, to Ahimelech the priest. And [a]Ahimelech was [b]afraid when he met David, and said to him, "Why *are* you alone, and no one is with you?"

2 So David said to Ahimelech the priest, "The king has ordered me on some business, and said to me, 'Do not let anyone know anything about the business on which I send you, or what I have commanded you.' And I have directed *my* young men to such and such a place.

3 "Now therefore, what have you on hand? Give *me* five *loaves of* bread in my hand, or whatever can be found."

4 And the priest answered David and said, "*There is* no common bread on hand; but there is [a]holy bread, [b]if the young men have at least kept themselves from women."

5 Then David answered the priest, and said to him, "Truly, women *have been* kept from us about three days since I came out. And the [a]vessels of the young men are holy, and *the bread is* in effect common, even though it was consecrated [b]in the vessel this day."

6 So the priest [a]gave him holy *bread;* for there was no bread there but the showbread [b]which had been taken from before the LORD, in order to put hot bread *in its place* on the day when it was taken away.

7 Now a certain man of the servants of Saul *was* there that day, detained before the LORD. And his name *was* [a]Doeg, an Edomite, the chief of the herdsmen who *belonged* to Saul.

8 And David said to Ahimelech, "Is there not here on hand a spear or a sword? For I have brought neither my sword nor my weapons with me, because the king's business required haste."

9 So the priest said, "The sword of Goliath the Philistine, whom you killed in [a]the Valley of Elah, [b]there it is, wrapped in a cloth behind the ephod. If you will take that, take *it.* For *there is* no other except that one here." And David said, "*There is* none like it; give it to me."

David Flees to Gath

10 Then David arose and fled that day from before Saul, and went to Achish the king of Gath.

11 And [a]the servants of Achish said to him, "*Is* this not David the king of the land? Did they not sing of him to one another in dances, saying:

[b]'Saul has slain his thousands,
And David his ten thousands'?"

12 Now David [a]took these words to heart, and was very much afraid of Achish the king of Gath.

13 So [a]he changed his behavior before them, pretended madness in their hands, scratched on the doors of the gate, and let his saliva fall down on his beard.

14 Then Achish said to his servants, "Look, you see the man is insane. Why have you brought him to me?

15 "Have I need of madmen, that you have brought this *fellow* to play the madman in my presence? Shall this *fellow* come into my house?"

David's Four Hundred Men

22 David therefore departed from there and [a]escaped [b]to the cave of Adullam. So when his brothers and all his father's house heard *it,* they went down there to him.

2 [a]And everyone *who was* in distress, everyone who *was* in debt, and everyone *who was* discontented gathered to him. So he became captain

KJV

and he became a captain over them: and there
were with him about [b]four hundred men.
3 And David went thence to Mizpeh of
[a]Moab: and he said unto the king of Moab, Let
my father and my mother, I pray thee, come forth,
and be with you, till I know what God will do
for me.
4 And he brought them before the king of
Moab: and they dwelt with him all the while that
David was in the hold.
5 And the prophet [a]Gad said unto David,
Abide not in the hold; depart, and get thee into
the land of Judah. Then David departed, and came
into the forest of Hareth.

Saul Murders the Priests

6 When Saul heard that David was discovered, and the men that *were* with him, (now Saul
abode in [a]Gibeah under a tree in Ramah, having
his spear in his hand, and all his servants *were*
standing about him;)
7 Then Saul said unto his servants that
stood about him, Hear now, ye Benjamites; will
the son of Jesse [a]give every one of you fields and
vineyards, *and* make you all captains of thousands, and captains of hundreds;
8 That all of you have conspired against me,
and *there is* none that sheweth me that [a]my
son hath made a league with the son of Jesse,
and *there is* none of you that is sorry for me, or
sheweth unto me that my son hath stirred up
my servant against me, to lie in wait, as at this
day?
9 Then answered [a]Doeg the Edomite, which
was set over the servants of Saul, and said, I saw
the son of Jesse coming to Nob, to [b]Ahimelech
the son of [c]Ahitub.
10 [a]And he enquired of the LORD for him, and
[b]gave him victuals, and gave him the sword of
Goliath the Philistine.
11 Then the king sent to call Ahimelech the
priest, the son of Ahitub, and all his father's
house, the priests that *were* in Nob: and they came
all of them to the king.
12 And Saul said, Hear now, thou son of Ahitub. And he answered, Here I *am*, my lord.
13 And Saul said unto him, Why have ye conspired against me, thou and the son of Jesse, in
that thou hast given him bread, and a sword, and
hast enquired of God for him, that he should rise
against me, to lie in wait, as at this day?
14 Then Ahimelech answered the king, and
said, And who *is so* [a]faithful among all thy servants as David, which is the king's son in law,
and goeth at thy bidding, and is honourable in
thine house?
15 Did I then begin to enquire of God for
him? be it far from me: let not the king impute
any thing unto his servant, *nor* to all the house
of my father: for thy servant knew nothing of all
this, less or more.
16 And the king said, Thou shalt surely die,
Ahimelech, thou, and all [a]thy father's house.
17 And the king said unto the footmen that
stood about him, Turn, and slay the priests of the
LORD; because their hand also *is* with David, and
because they knew when he fled, and did not shew
it to me. But the servants of the king [a]would not
put forth their hand to fall upon the priests of
the LORD.
18 And the king said to Doeg, Turn thou, and
fall upon the priests. And Doeg the Edomite
turned, and he fell upon the priests, and [a]slew
on that day fourscore and five persons that did
wear a linen ephod.
19 [a]And Nob, the city of the priests, smote
he with the edge of the sword, both men and
women, children and sucklings, and oxen, and
asses, and sheep, with the edge of the sword.
20 [a]And one of the sons of Ahimelech the
son of Ahitub, named Abiathar, [b]escaped, and fled
after David.

2 [b]1 Sam. 25:13
3 [a]2 Sam. 8:2
5 [a]2 Sam. 24:11; 1 Chr. 21:9; 29:29; 2 Chr. 29:25
6 [a]1 Sam. 15:34
7 [a]1 Sam. 8:14
8 [a]1 Sam. 18:3; 20:16, 30
9 [a]1 Sam. 21:7; 22:22; Ps. 52:title [b]1 Sam. 21:1 [c]1 Sam. 14:3
10 [a]Num. 27:21; 1 Sam. 10:22 [b]1 Sam. 21:6, 9
14 [a]1 Sam. 19:4, 5; 20:32; 24:11
16 [a]Deut. 24:16
17 [a]Ex. 1:17
18 [a]1 Sam. 2:31
19 [a]Josh. 21:1–45; 1 Sam. 22:9, 11
20 [a]1 Sam. 23:6, 9; 30:7; 1 Kin. 2:26, 27 [b]1 Sam. 2:33

NKJV

over them. And there were about [b]four hundred
men with him.
3 Then David went from there to Mizpah
of [a]Moab; and he said to the king of Moab,
"Please let my father and mother come here with
you, till I know what God will do for me."
4 So he brought them before the king of
Moab, and they dwelt with him all the time that
David was in the stronghold.
5 Now the prophet [a]Gad said to David, "Do
not stay in the stronghold; depart, and go to the
land of Judah." So David departed and went into
the forest of Hereth.

Saul Murders the Priests

6 When Saul heard that David and the men
who *were* with him had been discovered—now
Saul was staying in [a]Gibeah under a tamarisk tree
in Ramah, with his spear in his hand, and all his
servants standing about him—
7 then Saul said to his servants who stood
about him, "Hear now, you Benjamites! Will the
son of Jesse [a]give every one of you fields and
vineyards, *and* make you all captains of thousands and captains of hundreds?
8 "All of you have conspired against [a]me,
and *there is* no one who reveals to me that [a]my
son has made a covenant with the son of Jesse;
and *there is* not one of you who is sorry for me
or reveals to me that my son has stirred up my
servant against me, to lie in wait, as *it is* this day."
9 Then answered [a]Doeg the Edomite, who
was set over the servants of Saul, and said, "I
saw the son of Jesse going to Nob, to [b]Ahimelech
the son of [c]Ahitub.
10 [a]"And he inquired of the LORD for him,
[b]gave him provisions, and gave him the sword
of Goliath the Philistine."
11 So the king sent to call Ahimelech the
priest, the son of Ahitub, and all his father's
house, the priests who *were* in Nob. And they all
came to the king.
12 And Saul said, "Hear now, son of Ahitub!"
He answered, "Here I am, my lord."
13 Then Saul said to him, "Why have you
conspired against me, you and the son of Jesse,
in that you have given him bread and a sword,
and have inquired of God for him, that he should
rise against me, to lie in wait, as it is this day?"
14 So Ahimelech answered the king and said,
"And who among all your servants *is as* [a]faithful
as David, who is the king's son-in-law, who goes
at your bidding, and is honorable in your house?
15 "Did I then begin to inquire of God for
him? Far be it from me! Let not the king impute
anything to his servant, *or* to any in the house of
my father. For your servant knew nothing of all
this, little or much."
16 And the king said, "You shall surely die,
Ahimelech, you and all [a]your father's house!"
17 Then the king said to the guards who
stood about him, "Turn and kill the priests of the
LORD, because their hand also *is* with David, and
because they knew when he fled and did not tell
it to me." But the servants of the king [a]would not
lift their hands to strike the priests of the LORD.
18 And the king said to Doeg, "You turn and
kill the priests!" So Doeg the Edomite turned and
struck the priests, and [a]killed on that day eighty-
five men who wore a linen ephod.
19 [a]Also Nob, the city of the priests, he struck
with the edge of the sword, both men and women,
children and nursing infants, oxen and donkeys
and sheep—with the edge of the sword.
20 [a]Now one of the sons of Ahimelech the
son of Ahitub, named Abiathar, [b]escaped and fled
after David.

KJV

21 And Abiathar shewed David that Saul had slain the LORD's priests.
22 And David said unto Abiathar, I knew *it* that day, when Doeg the Edomite *was* there, that he would surely tell Saul: I have occasioned *the death* of all the persons of thy father's house.
23 Abide thou with me, fear not: [a]for he that seeketh my life seeketh thy life: but with me thou *shalt be* in safeguard.

David Saves the City of Keilah

23 Then they told David, saying, Behold, the Philistines fight against [a]Keilah, and they rob the threshingfloors.
2 Therefore David [a]enquired of the LORD, saying, Shall I go and smite these Philistines? And the LORD said unto David, Go, and smite the Philistines, and save Keilah.
3 And David's men said unto him, Behold, we be afraid here in Judah: how much more then if we come to Keilah against the armies of the Philistines?
4 Then David enquired of the LORD yet again. And the LORD answered him and said, Arise, go down to Keilah; for I will deliver the Philistines into thine hand.
5 So David and his men went to Keilah, and [a]fought with the Philistines, and brought away their cattle, and smote them with a great slaughter. So David saved the inhabitants of Keilah.
6 And it came to pass, when Abiathar the son of Ahimelech [a]fled to David to Keilah, *that* he came down *with* an ephod in his hand.
7 And it was told Saul that David was come to Keilah. And Saul said, God hath delivered him into mine hand; for he is shut in, by entering into a town that hath gates and bars.
8 And Saul called all the people together to war, to go down to Keilah, to besiege David and his men.
9 And David knew that Saul secretly practised mischief against him; and [a]he said to Abiathar the priest, Bring hither the ephod.
10 Then said David, O LORD God of Israel, thy servant hath certainly heard that Saul seeketh to come to Keilah, [a]to destroy the city for my sake.
11 Will the men of Keilah deliver me up into his hand? will Saul come down, as thy servant hath heard? O LORD God of Israel, I beseech thee, tell thy servant. And the LORD said, He will come down.
12 Then said David, Will the men of Keilah deliver me and my men into the hand of Saul? And the LORD said, They will deliver *thee* up.
13 Then David and his men, [a]*which were* about six hundred, arose and departed out of Keilah, and went whithersoever they could go. And it was told Saul that David was escaped from Keilah; and he forbare to go forth.

David in Wilderness Strongholds

14 And David abode in the wilderness in strong holds, and remained in [a]a mountain in the wilderness of [b]Ziph. And Saul [c]sought him every day, but God delivered him not into his hand.
15 And David saw that Saul was come out to seek his life: and David *was* in the wilderness of Ziph in a wood.
16 And Jonathan Saul's son arose, and went to David into the wood, and strengthened his hand in God.
17 And he said unto him, [a]Fear not: for the hand of Saul my father shall not find thee; and thou shalt be king over Israel, and I shall be next unto thee; and [b]that also Saul my father knoweth.
18 And they two [a]made a covenant before the LORD: and David abode in the wood, and Jonathan went to his house.
19 Then [a]came up the Ziphites to Saul to Gibeah, saying, Doth not David hide himself with us in strong holds in the wood, in the hill of Hachilah, which *is* on the south of Jeshimon?

23 [a]1 Kin. 2:26

CHAPTER 23

1 [a]Josh. 15:44; Neh. 3:17, 18
2 [a]1 Sam. 22:10; 23:4, 6, 9; 28:6; 30:8; 2 Sam. 5:19, 23
5 [a]1 Sam. 19:8; 2 Sam. 5:20
6 [a]1 Sam. 22:20
9 [a]Num. 27:21; 1 Sam. 23:6; 30:7
10 [a]1 Sam. 22:19
13 [a]1 Sam. 22:2; 25:13
14 [a]Ps. 11:1 [b]Josh. 15:55; 2 Chr. 11:8 [c]Ps. 32:7; 54:3, 4
17 [a][Ps. 27:1–3; Heb. 13:6] [b]1 Sam. 20:31; 24:20
18 [a]1 Sam. 18:3; 20:12–17, 42; 2 Sam. 9:1; 21:7
19 [a]1 Sam. 26:1; Ps. 54:title

NKJV

21 And Abiathar told David that Saul had killed the LORD's priests.
22 So David said to Abiathar, "I knew that day, when Doeg the Edomite *was* there, that he would surely tell Saul. I have caused *the death* of all the persons of your father's house.
23 "Stay with me; do not fear. [a]For he who seeks my life seeks your life, but with me you *shall be* safe."

David Saves the City of Keilah

23 Then they told David, saying, "Look, the Philistines are fighting against [a]Keilah, and they are robbing the threshing floors."
2 Therefore David [a]inquired of the LORD, saying, "Shall I go and attack these Philistines?" And the LORD said to David, "Go and attack the Philistines, and save Keilah."
3 But David's men said to him, "Look, we are afraid here in Judah. How much more then if we go to Keilah against the armies of the Philistines?"
4 Then David inquired of the LORD once again. And the LORD answered him and said, "Arise, go down to Keilah. For I will deliver the Philistines into your hand."
5 And David and his men went to Keilah and [a]fought with the Philistines, struck them with a mighty blow, and took away their livestock. So David saved the inhabitants of Keilah.
6 Now it happened, when Abiathar the son of Ahimelech [a]fled to David at Keilah, *that* he went down *with* an ephod in his hand.
7 And Saul was told that David had gone to Keilah. So Saul said, "God has delivered him into my hand, for he has shut himself in by entering a town that has gates and bars."
8 Then Saul called all the people together for war, to go down to Keilah to besiege David and his men.
9 When David knew that Saul plotted evil against him, [a]he said to Abiathar the priest, "Bring the ephod here."
10 Then David said, "O LORD God of Israel, Your servant has certainly heard that Saul seeks to come to Keilah [a]to destroy the city for my sake.
11 "Will the men of Keilah deliver me into his hand? Will Saul come down, as Your servant has heard? O LORD God of Israel, I pray, tell Your servant." And the LORD said, "He will come down."
12 Then David said, "Will the men of Keilah deliver me and my men into the hand of Saul?" And the LORD said, "They will deliver *you*."
13 So David and his men, [a]about six hundred, arose and departed from Keilah and went wherever they could go. Then it was told Saul that David had escaped from Keilah; so he halted the expedition.

David in Wilderness Strongholds

14 And David stayed in strongholds in the wilderness, and remained in [a]the mountains in the Wilderness of [b]Ziph. Saul [c]sought him every day, but God did not deliver him into his hand.
15 So David saw that Saul had come out to seek his life. And David *was* in the Wilderness of Ziph *in a forest.
16 Then Jonathan, Saul's son, arose and went to David in the woods and strengthened his hand in God.
17 And he said to him, [a]"Do not fear, for the hand of Saul my father shall not find you. You shall be king over Israel, and I shall be next to you. [b]Even my father Saul knows that."
18 So the two of them [a]made a covenant before the LORD. And David stayed in the woods, and Jonathan went to his own house.
19 Then the Ziphites [a]came up to Saul at Gibeah, saying, "Is David not hiding with us in strongholds in the woods, in the hill of Hachilah, which *is* on the south of Jeshimon?

*23:15 Or *in Horesh*

KJV

20 Now therefore, O king, come down according to all the desire of thy soul to come down;
and [a]our part *shall be* to deliver him into the
king's hand.
21 And Saul said, Blessed *be* ye of the LORD;
for ye have compassion on me.
22 Go, I pray you, prepare yet, and know and
see his place where his haunt is, *and* who hath
seen him there: for it is told me *that* he dealeth
very subtilly.
23 See therefore, and take knowledge of all
the lurking places where he hideth himself, and
come ye again to me with the certainty, and I will
go with you: and it shall come to pass, if he be
in the land, that I will search him out throughout
all the thousands of Judah.
24 And they arose, and went to Ziph before
Saul: but David and his men *were* in the wilderness [a]of Maon, in the plain on the south of
Jeshimon.
25 Saul also and his men went to seek *him*.
And they told David: wherefore he came down
into a rock, and abode in the wilderness of Maon.
And when Saul heard *that*, he pursued after David in the wilderness of Maon.
26 And Saul went on this side of the mountain, and David and his men on that side of the
mountain: [a]and David made haste to get away
for fear of Saul; for Saul and his men [b]compassed
David and his men round about to take them.
27 [a]But there came a messenger unto Saul,
saying, Haste thee, and come; for the Philistines
have invaded the land.
28 Wherefore Saul returned from pursuing
after David, and went against the Philistines:
therefore they called that place Sela–hammahlekoth.
29 And David went up from thence, and
dwelt in strong holds at [a]En–gedi.

David Spares Saul

24 And it came to pass, [a]when Saul was returned from following the Philistines, that
it was told him, saying, Behold, David *is* in the
wilderness of En–gedi.
2 Then Saul took three thousand chosen
men out of all Israel, and [a]went to seek David
and his men upon the rocks of the wild goats.
3 And he came to the sheepcotes by the
way, where *was* a cave; and [a]Saul went in to
[b]cover his feet: and [c]David and his men remained
in the sides of the cave.
4 [a]And the men of David said unto him, Behold the day of which the LORD said unto thee,
Behold, I will deliver thine enemy into thine hand,
that thou mayest do to him as it shall seem good
unto thee. Then David arose, and cut off the skirt
of Saul's robe privily.
5 And it came to pass afterward, that [a]Da-
vid's heart smote him, because he had cut off
Saul's skirt.
6 And he said unto his men, [a]The LORD forbid that I should do this thing unto my master,
the LORD's anointed, to stretch forth mine hand
against him, seeing he *is* the anointed of the
LORD.
7 So David [a]stayed his servants with these
words, and suffered them not to rise against Saul.
But Saul rose up out of the cave, and went on
his way.
8 David also arose afterward, and went out
of the cave, and cried after Saul, saying, My lord
the king. And when Saul looked behind him, David stooped with his face to the earth, and bowed
himself.
9 And David said to Saul, [a]Wherefore hearest thou men's words, saying, Behold, David seeketh thy hurt?
10 Behold, this day thine eyes have seen how
that the LORD had delivered thee to day into mine
hand in the cave: and *some* bade *me* kill thee:
but *mine eye* spared thee; and I said, I will not

20 [a]Ps. 54:3
24 [a]Josh. 15:55; 1 Sam. 25:2
26 [a]Ps. 31:22 [b]Ps. 17:9
27 [a]2 Kin. 19:9
29 [a]Josh. 15:62; 2 Chr. 20:2

CHAPTER 24

1 [a]1 Sam. 23:19, 28, 29
2 [a]1 Sam. 26:2; Ps. 38:12
3 [a]1 Sam. 24:10 [b]Judg. 3:24 [c]Ps. 57:title; 142:title
4 [a]1 Sam. 26:8–11
5 [a]2 Sam. 24:10
6 [a]1 Sam. 26:11
7 [a]Ps. 7:4; [Matt. 5:44; Rom. 12:17, 19]
9 [a]Ps. 141:6; [Prov. 16:28; 17:9]

*______

23:23 Lit. *thousands*
23:28 Heb. *Sela Hammahlekoth*

NKJV

20 "Now therefore, O king, come down according to all the desire of your soul to come
down; and [a]our part *shall be* to deliver him into
the king's hand."
21 And Saul said, "Blessed *are* you of the
LORD, for you have compassion on me.
22 "Please go and find out for sure, and see
the place where his hideout is, *and* who has seen
him there. For I am told he is very crafty.
23 "See therefore, and take knowledge of all
the lurking places where he hides; and come back
to me with certainty, and I will go with you. And
it shall be, if he is in the land, that I will search
for him throughout all the *clans of Judah."
24 So they arose and went to Ziph before
Saul. But David and his men *were* in the Wilderness [a]of Maon, in the plain on the south of
Jeshimon.
25 When Saul and his men went to seek *him*,
they told David. Therefore he went down to the
rock, and stayed in the Wilderness of Maon. And
when Saul heard *that*, he pursued David in the
Wilderness of Maon.
26 Then Saul went on one side of the mountain, and David and his men on the other side of
the mountain. [a]So David made haste to get away
from Saul, for Saul and his men [b]were encircling
David and his men to take them.
27 [a]But a messenger came to Saul, saying,
"Hurry and come, for the Philistines have invaded
the land!"
28 Therefore Saul returned from pursuing
David, and went against the Philistines; so they
called that place *the Rock of Escape.
29 Then David went up from there and dwelt
in strongholds at [a]En Gedi.

David Spares Saul

24 Now it happened, [a]when Saul had returned
from following the Philistines, that it was
told him, saying, "Take note! David *is* in the Wilderness of En Gedi."
2 Then Saul took three thousand chosen
men from all Israel, and [a]went to seek David and
his men on the Rocks of the Wild Goats.
3 So he came to the sheepfolds by the road,
where there *was* a cave; and [a]Saul went in to [b]at-
tend to his needs. ([c]David and his men were staying in the recesses of the cave.)
4 [a]Then the men of David said to him, "This
is the day of which the LORD said to you, 'Behold,
I will deliver your enemy into your hand, that you
may do to him as it seems good to you.' " And
David arose and secretly cut off a corner of Saul's
robe.
5 Now it happened afterward that [a]David's
heart troubled him because he had cut Saul's *robe*.
6 And he said to his men, [a]"The LORD forbid
that I should do this thing to my master, the
LORD's anointed, to stretch out my hand against
him, seeing he *is* the anointed of the LORD."
7 So David [a]restrained his servants with
these words, and did not allow them to rise
against Saul. And Saul got up from the cave and
went on *his* way.
8 David also arose afterward, went out of
the cave, and called out to Saul, saying, "My lord
the king!" And when Saul looked behind him, David stooped with his face to the earth, and bowed
down.
9 And David said to Saul: [a]"Why do you
listen to the words of men who say, 'Indeed David
seeks your harm'?
10 "Look, this day your eyes have seen that
the LORD delivered you today into my hand in the
cave, and *someone* urged *me* to kill you. But *my
eye* spared you, and I said, 'I will not stretch out

KJV

put forth mine hand against my lord; for he *is*
the LORD's anointed.
11 Moreover, my father, see, yea, see the
skirt of thy robe in my hand: for in that I cut off
the skirt of thy robe, and killed thee not, know
thou and see that *there is* [a]neither evil nor transgression in mine hand, and I have not sinned
against thee; yet thou [b]huntest my soul to take
it.
12 [a]The LORD judge between me and thee,
and the LORD avenge me of thee: but mine hand
shall not be upon thee.
13 As saith the proverb of the ancients,
[a]Wickedness proceedeth from the wicked: but
mine hand shall not be upon thee.
14 After whom is the king of Israel come out?
after whom dost thou pursue? [a]after a dead dog,
after [b]a flea.
15 [a]The LORD therefore be judge, and judge
between me and thee, and [b]see, and [c]plead my
cause, and deliver me out of thine hand.
16 And it came to pass, when David had
made an end of speaking these words unto Saul,
that Saul said, [a]*Is* this thy voice, my son David?
And Saul lifted up his voice, and wept.
17 [a]And he said to David, Thou *art* [b]more
righteous than I: for [c]thou hast rewarded me
good, whereas I have rewarded thee evil.
18 And thou hast shewed this day how that
thou hast dealt well with me: forasmuch as when
[a]the LORD had delivered me into thine hand, thou
killedst me not.
19 For if a man find his enemy, will he let
him go well away? wherefore the LORD reward
thee good for that thou hast done unto me this
day.
20 And now, behold, [a]I know well that thou
shalt surely be king, and that the kingdom of Israel shall be established in thine hand.
21 [a]Swear now therefore unto me by the
LORD, [b]that thou wilt not cut off my seed after
me, and that thou wilt not destroy my name out
of my father's house.
22 And David sware unto Saul. And Saul
went home; but David and his men gat them up
unto [a]the hold.

Death of Samuel

25 And [a]Samuel died; and all the Israelites
were gathered together, and [b]lamented
him, and buried him in his house at Ramah. And
David arose, and went down [c]to the wilderness
of Paran.

David and the Wife of Nabal

2 And *there was* a man [a]in Maon, whose
possessions *were* in [b]Carmel; and the man *was*
very great, and he had three thousand sheep, and
a thousand goats: and he was shearing his sheep
in Carmel.
3 Now the name of the man *was* Nabal; and
the name of his wife Abigail: and *she was* a
woman of good understanding, and of a beautiful
countenance: but the man *was* churlish and evil
in his doings; and he *was* of the house of [a]Caleb.
4 And David heard in the wilderness that
Nabal did [a]shear his sheep.
5 And David sent out ten young men, and
David said unto the young men, Get you up to
Carmel, and go to Nabal, and greet him in my
name:
6 And thus shall ye say to him that liveth
in prosperity, [a]Peace *be* both to thee, and peace
be to thine house, and peace *be* unto all that thou
hast.
7 And now I have heard that thou hast
shearers: now thy shepherds which were with us,
we hurt them not, [a]neither was there ought missing unto them, all the while they were in Carmel.
8 Ask thy young men, and they will shew
thee. Wherefore let the young men find favour
in thine eyes: for we come in [a]a good day: give,

11 [a]Judg. 11:27; Ps. 7:3; 35:7 [b]1 Sam. 26:20
12 [a]Gen. 16:5; Judg. 11:27; 1 Sam. 26:10–23; Job 5:8
13 [a][Matt. 7:16–20]
14 [a]1 Sam. 17:43; 2 Sam. 9:8 [b]1 Sam. 26:20
15 [a]1 Sam. 24:12 [b]2 Chr. 24:22 [c]Ps. 35:1; 43:1; 119:154; Mic. 7:9
16 [a]1 Sam. 26:17
17 [a]1 Sam. 26:21 [b]Gen. 38:26 [c][Matt. 5:44]
18 [a]1 Sam. 26:23
20 [a]1 Sam. 23:17
21 [a]Gen. 21:23; 1 Sam. 20:14–17 [b]2 Sam. 21:6–8
22 [a]1 Sam. 23:29

CHAPTER 25

1 [a]1 Sam. 28:3 [b]Num. 20:29; Deut. 34:8 [c]Gen. 21:21; Num. 10:12; 13:3
2 [a]1 Sam. 23:24 [b]Josh. 15:55
3 [a]Josh. 15:13; 1 Sam. 30:14
4 [a]Gen. 38:13; 2 Sam. 13:23
6 [a]Judg. 19:20; 1 Chr. 12:18; Ps. 122:7; Luke 10:5
7 [a]1 Sam. 25:15, 21
8 [a]Neh. 8:10–12; Esth. 8:17; 9:19, 22

NKJV

my hand against my lord, for he *is* the LORD's
anointed.'
11 "Moreover, my father, see! Yes, see the
corner of your robe in my hand! For in that I cut
off the corner of your robe, and did not kill you,
know and see that *there is* [a]neither evil nor rebellion in my hand, and I have not sinned against
you. Yet you [b]hunt my life to take it.
12 [a]"Let the LORD judge between you and me,
and let the LORD avenge me on you. But my hand
shall not be against you.
13 "As the proverb of the ancients says,
[a]'Wickedness proceeds from the wicked.' But my
hand shall not be against you.
14 "After whom has the king of Israel come
out? Whom do you pursue? [a]A dead dog? [b]A flea?
15 [a]"Therefore let the LORD be judge, and
judge between you and me, and [b]see and [c]plead
my case, and deliver me out of your hand."
16 So it was, when David had finished speaking these words to Saul, that Saul said, [a]"*Is* this
your voice, my son David?" And Saul lifted up
his voice and wept.
17 [a]Then he said to David: "You *are* [b]more
righteous than I; for [c]you have rewarded me with
good, whereas I have rewarded you with evil.
18 "And you have shown this day how you
have dealt well with me; for when [a]the LORD delivered me into your hand, you did not kill me.
19 "For if a man finds his enemy, will he let
him get away safely? Therefore may the LORD reward you with good for what you have done to
me this day.
20 "And now [a]I know indeed that you shall
surely be king, and that the kingdom of Israel
shall be established in your hand.
21 [a]"Therefore swear now to me by the LORD
[b]that you will not cut off my descendants after
me, and that you will not destroy my name from
my father's house."
22 So David swore to Saul. And Saul went
home, but David and his men went up to [a]the
stronghold.

Death of Samuel

25 Then [a]Samuel died; and the Israelites gathered together and [b]lamented for him, and
buried him at his home in Ramah. And David
arose and went down [c]to the Wilderness of
*Paran.

David and the Wife of Nabal

2 Now *there was* a man [a]in Maon whose
business *was* in [b]Carmel, and the man *was* very
rich. He had three thousand sheep and a thousand
goats. And he was shearing his sheep in Carmel.
3 The name of the man *was* Nabal, and the
name of his wife Abigail. And *she was* a woman
of good understanding and beautiful appearance;
but the man *was* harsh and evil in *his* doings. He
was of the house of [a]Caleb.
4 When David heard in the wilderness that
Nabal was [a]shearing his sheep,
5 David sent ten young men; and David said
to the young men, "Go up to Carmel, go to Nabal,
and greet him in my name.
6 "And thus you shall say to him who lives
in prosperity: [a]'Peace *be* to you, peace to your
house, and peace to all that you have!
7 'Now I have heard that you have shearers.
Your shepherds were with us, and we did not hurt
them, [a]nor was there anything missing from them
all the while they were in Carmel.
8 'Ask your young men, and they will tell
you. Therefore let *my* young men find favor in
your eyes, for we come on [a]a feast day. Please

*

25:1 So with MT, Syr., Tg., Vg.; LXX *Maon*

KJV

I pray thee, whatsoever cometh to thine hand unto thy servants, and to thy son David.

9 And when David's young men came, they spake to Nabal according to all those words in the name of David, and ceased.

10 And Nabal answered David's servants, and said, [a]Who *is* David? and who *is* the son of Jesse? there be many servants now a days that break away every man from his master.

11 [a]Shall I then take my bread, and my water, and my flesh that I have killed for my shearers, and give *it* unto men, whom I know not whence they *be?*

12 So David's young men turned their way, and went again, and came and told him all those sayings.

13 And David said unto his men, Gird ye on every man his sword. And they girded on every man his sword; and David also girded on his sword: and there went up after David about four hundred men; and two hundred [a]abode by the stuff.

14 But one of the young men told Abigail, Nabal's wife, saying, Behold, David sent messengers out of the wilderness to salute our master; and he railed on them.

15 But the men *were* very good unto us, and [a]we were not hurt, neither missed we any thing, as long as we were conversant with them, when we were in the fields:

16 They were [a]a wall unto us both by night and day, all the while we were with them keeping the sheep.

17 Now therefore know and consider what thou wilt do; for [a]evil is determined against our master, and against all his household: for he *is such* a son of [b]Belial, that *a man* cannot speak to him.

18 Then Abigail made haste, and [a]took two hundred loaves, and two bottles of wine, and five sheep ready dressed, and five measures of parched *corn,* and an hundred clusters of raisins, and two hundred cakes of figs, and laid *them* on asses.

19 And she said unto her servants, [a]Go on before me; behold, I come after you. But she told not her husband Nabal.

20 And it was *so, as* she rode on the ass, that she came down by the covert of the hill, and, behold, David and his men came down against her; and she met them.

21 Now David had said, Surely in vain have I kept all that this *fellow* hath in the wilderness, so that nothing was missed of all that *pertained* unto him: and he hath [a]requited me evil for good.

22 [a]So and more also do God unto the enemies of David, if I [b]leave of all that *pertain* to him by the morning light [c]any that pisseth against the wall.

23 And when Abigail saw David, she hasted, and [a]lighted off the ass, and fell before David on her face, and bowed herself to the ground,

24 And fell at his feet, and said, Upon me, my lord, *upon* me *let this* iniquity *be:* and let thine handmaid, I pray thee, speak in thine audience, and hear the words of thine handmaid.

25 Let not my lord, I pray thee, regard this man of Belial, *even* Nabal: for as his name *is,* so *is* he; Nabal *is* his name, and folly *is* with him: but I thine handmaid saw not the young men of my lord, whom thou didst send.

26 Now therefore, my lord, [a]*as* the LORD liveth, and *as* thy soul liveth, seeing the LORD hath [b]withholden thee from coming to *shed* blood, and from [c]avenging thyself with thine own hand, now [d]let thine enemies, and they that seek evil to my lord, be as Nabal.

27 And now [a]this blessing which thine handmaid hath brought unto my lord, let it even be given unto the young men that follow my lord.

28 I pray thee, forgive the trespass of thine handmaid: for [a]the LORD will certainly make my

NKJV

give whatever comes to your hand to your servants and to your son David.' "

9 So when David's young men came, they spoke to Nabal according to all these words in the name of David, and waited.

10 Then Nabal answered David's servants, and said, [a]"Who *is* David, and who *is* the son of Jesse? There are many servants nowadays who break away each one from his master.

11 [a]"Shall I then take my bread and my water and my meat that I have killed for my shearers, and give *it* to men when I do not know where they *are* from?"

12 So David's young men turned on their heels and went back; and they came and told him all these words.

13 Then David said to his men, "Every man gird on his sword." So every man girded on his sword, and David also girded on his sword. And about four hundred men went with David, and two hundred [a]stayed with the supplies.

14 Now one of the young men told Abigail, Nabal's wife, saying, "Look, David sent messengers from the wilderness to greet our master; and he reviled them.

15 "But the men *were* very good to us, and [a]we were not hurt, nor did we miss anything as long as we accompanied them, when we were in the fields.

16 "They were [a]a wall to us both by night and day, all the time we were with them keeping the sheep.

17 "Now therefore, know and consider what you will do, for [a]harm is determined against our master and against all his household. For he *is such* a [b]scoundrel* that *one* cannot speak to him."

18 Then Abigail made haste and [a]took two hundred *loaves* of bread, two skins of wine, five sheep already dressed, five seahs of roasted *grain,* one hundred clusters of raisins, and two hundred cakes of figs, and loaded *them* on donkeys.

19 And she said to her servants, [a]"Go on before me; see, I am coming after you." But she did not tell her husband Nabal.

20 So it was, *as* she rode on the donkey, that she went down under cover of the hill; and there were David and his men, coming down toward her, and she met them.

21 Now David had said, "Surely in vain I have protected all that this *fellow* has in the wilderness, so that nothing was missed of all that *belongs* to him. And he has [a]repaid me evil for good.

22 [a]"May God do so, and more also, to the enemies of David, if I [b]leave [c]one male of all who *belong* to him by morning light."

23 Now when Abigail saw David, she [a]dismounted quickly from the donkey, fell on her face before David, and bowed down to the ground.

24 So she fell at his feet and said: "On me, my lord, *on* me *let* this iniquity *be!* And please let your maidservant speak in your ears, and hear the words of your maidservant.

25 "Please, let not my lord regard this scoundrel Nabal. For as his name *is,* so *is* he: *Nabal *is* his name, and folly *is* with him! But I, your maidservant, did not see the young men of my lord whom you sent.

26 "Now therefore, my lord, [a]*as* the LORD lives and *as* your soul lives, since the LORD has [b]held you back from coming to bloodshed and from [c]avenging yourself with your own hand, now then, [d]let your enemies and those who seek harm for my lord be as Nabal.

27 "And now [a]this present which your maidservant has brought to my lord, let it be given to the young men who follow my lord.

28 "Please forgive the trespass of your maidservant. For [a]the LORD will certainly make for my

10 [a]Judg. 9:28
11 [a]Judg. 8:6, 15
13 [a]1 Sam. 30:24
15 [a]1 Sam. 25:7, 21
16 [a]Ex. 14:22; Job 1:10
17 [a]1 Sam. 20:7 [b]Deut. 13:13; Judg. 19:22
18 [a]Gen. 32:13; [Prov. 18:16; 21:14]
19 [a]Gen. 32:16, 20
21 [a]1 Sam. 24:17; Ps. 109:5; [Prov. 17:13]
22 [a]Ruth 1:17; 1 Sam. 3:17; 20:13, 16 [b]1 Sam. 25:34 [c]1 Kin. 14:10; 21:21; 2 Kin. 9:8
23 [a]Josh. 15:18; Judg. 1:14
26 [a]2 Kin. 2:2 [b]Gen. 20:6; 1 Sam. 25:33 [c][Rom. 12:19] [d]2 Sam. 18:32
27 [a]Gen. 33:11; 1 Sam. 30:26; 2 Kin. 5:15
28 [a]2 Sam. 7:11–16, 27; 1 Kin. 9:5; 1 Chr. 17:10, 25

*

25:17 Lit. *son of Belial*
25:25 Lit. *Fool*

KJV

lord a sure house; because my lord [b]fighteth the battles of the LORD, and [c]evil hath not been found in thee *all* thy days.

29 Yet a man is risen to pursue thee, and to seek thy soul: but the soul of my lord shall be [a]bound in the bundle of life with the LORD thy God; and the souls of thine enemies, them shall he [b]sling out, *as out* of the middle of a sling.

30 And it shall come to pass, when the LORD shall have done to my lord according to all the good that he hath spoken concerning thee, and shall have appointed thee [a]ruler over Israel;

31 That this shall be no grief unto thee, nor offence of heart unto my lord, either that thou hast shed blood causeless, or that my lord hath avenged himself: but when the LORD shall have dealt well with my lord, then remember thine handmaid.

32 And David said to Abigail, [a]Blessed *be* the LORD God of Israel, which sent thee this day to meet me:

33 And blessed *be* thy advice, and blessed *be* thou, which hast [a]kept me this day from coming to *shed* blood, and from avenging myself with mine own hand.

34 For in very deed, *as* the LORD God of Israel liveth, which hath [a]kept me back from hurting thee, except thou hadst hasted and come to meet me, surely there had [b]not been left unto Nabal by the morning light any that pisseth against the wall.

35 So David received of her hand *that* which she had brought him, and said unto her, [a]Go up in peace to thine house; see, I have hearkened to thy voice, and have [b]accepted thy person.

36 And Abigail came to Nabal; and, behold, [a]he held a feast in his house, like the feast of a king; and Nabal's heart *was* merry within him, for he *was* very drunken: wherefore she told him nothing, less or more, until the morning light.

37 But it came to pass in the morning, when the wine was gone out of Nabal, and his wife had told him these things, that his heart died within him, and he became *as* a stone.

38 And it came to pass about ten days *after*, that the LORD [a]smote Nabal, that he died.

39 And when David heard that Nabal was dead, he said, [a]Blessed *be* the LORD, that hath [b]pleaded the cause of my reproach from the hand of Nabal, and hath [c]kept his servant from evil: for the LORD hath [d]returned the wickedness of Nabal upon his own head. And David sent and communed with Abigail, to take her to him to wife.

40 And when the servants of David were come to Abigail to Carmel, they spake unto her, saying, David sent us unto thee, to take thee to him to wife.

41 And she arose, and bowed herself on *her* face to the earth, and said, Behold, *let* thine handmaid *be* a servant to [a]wash the feet of the servants of my lord.

42 And Abigail hasted, and arose, and rode upon an ass, with five damsels of her's that went after her; and she went after the messengers of David, and became his wife.

43 David also took Ahinoam [a]of Jezreel; [b]and they were also both of them his wives.

44 But Saul had given [a]Michal his daughter, David's wife, to Phalti the son of Laish, which *was* of [b]Gallim.

David Spares Saul a Second Time

26 And the Ziphites came unto Saul to Gibeah, saying, [a]Doth not David hide himself in the hill of Hachilah, *which is* before Jeshimon?

2 Then Saul arose, and went down to the wilderness of Ziph, having [a]three thousand chosen men of Israel with him, to seek David in the wilderness of Ziph.

3 And Saul pitched in the hill of Hachilah, which *is* before Jeshimon, by the way. But David

---

28 [b]1 Sam. 18:17 [c]1 Sam. 24:11; Ps. 7:3
29 [a][Ps. 66:9; Col. 3:3] [b]Jer. 10:18
30 [a]1 Sam. 13:14; 15:28
32 [a]Gen. 24:27; Ex. 18:10; 1 Kin. 1:48; Ps. 41:13; 72:18; 106:48; Luke 1:68
33 [a]1 Sam. 25:26
34 [a]1 Sam. 25:26 [b]1 Sam. 25:22
35 [a]1 Sam. 20:42; 2 Sam. 15:9; 2 Kin. 5:19; Luke 7:50; 8:48 [b]Gen. 19:21
36 [a]2 Sam. 13:28; Prov. 20:1; Is. 5:11; Dan. 5:1; [Hos. 4:11]
38 [a]1 Sam. 26:10; 2 Sam. 6:7; Ps. 104:29
39 [a]1 Sam. 25:32 [b]1 Sam. 24:15; Prov. 22:23 [c]1 Sam. 25:26, 34 [d]1 Kin. 2:44
41 [a][Prov. 15:33]; Luke 7:38, 44
43 [a]Josh. 15:56 [b]1 Sam. 27:3; 30:5
44 [a]1 Sam. 18:20; 2 Sam. 3:14 [b]Is. 10:30

CHAPTER 26

1 [a]1 Sam. 23:19; Ps. 54:title
2 [a]1 Sam. 13:2; 24:2

*

25:44 *Paltiel,* 2 Sam. 3:15

NKJV

lord an enduring house, because my lord [b]fights the battles of the LORD, [c]and evil is not found in you throughout your days.

29 "Yet a man has risen to pursue you and seek your life, but the life of my lord shall be [a]bound in the bundle of the living with the LORD your God; and the lives of your enemies He shall [b]sling out, *as from* the pocket of a sling.

30 "And it shall come to pass, when the LORD has done for my lord according to all the good that He has spoken concerning you, and has appointed you [a]ruler over Israel,

31 "that this will be no grief to you, nor offense of heart to my lord, either that you have shed blood without cause, or that my lord has avenged himself. But when the LORD has dealt well with my lord, then remember your maidservant."

32 Then David said to Abigail: [a]"Blessed *is* the LORD God of Israel, who sent you this day to meet me!

33 "And blessed *is* your advice and blessed *are* you, because you have [a]kept me this day from coming to bloodshed and from avenging myself with my own hand.

34 "For indeed, *as* the LORD God of Israel lives, who has [a]kept me back from hurting you, unless you had hurried and come to meet me, surely [b]by morning light no males would have been left to Nabal!"

35 So David received from her hand what she had brought him, and said to her, [a]"Go up in peace to your house. See, I have heeded your voice and [b]respected your person."

36 Now Abigail went to Nabal, and there he was, [a]holding a feast in his house, like the feast of a king. And Nabal's heart *was* merry within him, for he *was* very drunk; therefore she told him nothing, little or much, until morning light.

37 So it was, in the morning, when the wine had gone from Nabal, and his wife had told him these things, that his heart died within him, and he became *like* a stone.

38 Then it happened, *after* about ten days, that the LORD [a]struck Nabal, and he died.

39 So when David heard that Nabal was dead, he said, [a]"Blessed *be* the LORD, who has [b]pleaded the cause of my reproach from the hand of Nabal, and has [c]kept His servant from evil! For the LORD has [d]returned the wickedness of Nabal on his own head." And David sent and proposed to Abigail, to take her as his wife.

40 When the servants of David had come to Abigail at Carmel, they spoke to her saying, "David sent us to you, to ask you to become his wife."

41 Then she arose, bowed her face to the earth, and said, "Here is your maidservant, a servant to [a]wash the feet of the servants of my lord."

42 So Abigail rose in haste and rode on a donkey, attended by five of her maidens; and she followed the messengers of David, and became his wife.

43 David also took Ahinoam [a]of Jezreel, [b]and so both of them were his wives.

44 But Saul had given [a]Michal his daughter, David's wife, to *Palti the son of Laish, who *was* from [b]Gallim.

David Spares Saul a Second Time

26 Now the Ziphites came to Saul at Gibeah, saying, [a]"Is David not hiding in the hill of Hachilah, opposite Jeshimon?"

2 Then Saul arose and went down to the Wilderness of Ziph, having [a]three thousand chosen men of Israel with him, to seek David in the Wilderness of Ziph.

3 And Saul encamped in the hill of Hachilah, which *is* opposite Jeshimon, by the road. But

KJV

abode in the wilderness, and he saw that Saul
came after him into the wilderness.
4 David therefore sent out spies, and understood that Saul was come in very deed.
5 And David arose, and came to the place
where Saul had pitched: and David beheld the
place where Saul lay, and [a]Abner the son of Ner,
the captain of his host: and Saul lay in the trench,
and the people pitched round about him.
6 Then answered David and said to Ahimelech the Hittite, and to Abishai [a]the son of Zeruiah, brother to [b]Joab, saying, Who will [c]go down
with me to Saul to the camp? And [d]Abishai said,
I will go down with thee.
7 So David and Abishai came to the people
by night; and, behold, Saul lay sleeping within
the trench, and his spear stuck in the ground at
his bolster: but Abner and the people lay round
about him.
8 Then said Abishai to David, [a]God hath delivered thine enemy into thine hand this day: now
therefore let me smite him, I pray thee, with the
spear even to the earth at once, and I will not
smite him the second time.
9 And David said to Abishai, Destroy him
not: [a]for who can stretch forth his hand against
the LORD's anointed, and be guiltless?
10 David said furthermore, *As* the LORD liveth, [a]the LORD shall smite him; or [b]his day shall
come to die; or he shall [c]descend into battle, and
perish.
11 [a]The LORD forbid that I should stretch
forth mine hand against the LORD's anointed: but,
I pray thee, take thou now the spear that *is* at
his bolster, and the cruse of water, and let us go.
12 So David took the spear and the cruse of
water from Saul's bolster; and they gat them
away, and no man saw *it*, nor knew *it*, neither
awaked: for they *were* all asleep; because [a]a deep
sleep from the LORD was fallen upon them.
13 Then David went over to the other side,
and stood on the top of an hill afar off; a great
space *being* between them:
14 And David cried to the people, and to Abner the son of Ner, saying, Answerest thou not,
Abner? Then Abner answered and said, Who *art*
thou *that* criest to the king?
15 And David said to Abner, *Art* not thou a
valiant man? and who *is* like to thee in Israel?
wherefore then hast thou not kept thy lord the
king? for there came one of the people in to destroy the king thy lord.
16 This thing *is* not good that thou hast done.
As the LORD liveth, ye *are* worthy to die, because
ye have not kept your master, the LORD's
anointed. And now see where the king's spear *is*,
and the cruse of water that *was* at his bolster.
17 And Saul knew David's voice, and said,
[a]*Is* this thy voice, my son David? And David said,
It is my voice, my lord, O king.
18 And he said, [a]Wherefore doth my lord
thus pursue after his servant? for what have I
done? or what evil *is* in mine hand?
19 Now therefore, I pray thee, let my lord the
king hear the words of his servant. If the LORD
have [a]stirred thee up against me, let him accept
an offering: but if *they be* the children of men,
cursed *be* they before the LORD; [b]for they have
driven me out this day from abiding in the [c]inheri-
tance of the LORD, saying, Go, serve other gods.
20 Now therefore, let not my blood fall to the
earth before the face of the LORD: for the king of
Israel is come out to seek [a]a flea, as when one
doth hunt a partridge in the mountains.
21 Then said Saul, [a]I have sinned: return, my
son David: for I will no more do thee harm, because my soul was precious in thine eyes this day:
behold, I have played the fool, and have erred
exceedingly.
22 And David answered and said, Behold the

5 [a]1 Sam. 14:50, 51; 17:55
6 [a]1 Chr. 2:16 [b]2 Sam. 2:13 [c]Judg. 7:10, 11 [d]2 Sam. 2:18, 24
8 [a]1 Sam. 24:4
9 [a]1 Sam. 24:6, 7; 2 Sam. 1:14, 16
10 [a][Deut. 32:35]; 1 Sam. 25:26, 38; [Luke 18:7; Rom. 12:19; Heb. 10:30] [b]Gen. 47:29; Deut. 31:14; [Job 7:1; 14:5]; Ps. 37:13 [c]1 Sam. 31:6
11 [a]1 Sam. 24:6–12; [Rom. 12:17, 19]
12 [a]Gen. 2:21; 15:12; Is. 29:10
17 [a]1 Sam. 24:16
18 [a]1 Sam. 24:9, 11–14
19 [a]2 Sam. 16:11; 24:1 [b]Deut. 4:27, 28 [c]2 Sam. 14:16; 20:19
20 [a]1 Sam. 24:14
21 [a]Ex. 9:27; 1 Sam. 15:24, 30; 24:17; 2 Sam. 12:13

NKJV

David stayed in the wilderness, and he saw that
Saul came after him into the wilderness.
4 David therefore sent out spies, and understood that Saul had indeed come.
5 So David arose and came to the place
where Saul had encamped. And David saw the
place where Saul lay, and [a]Abner the son of Ner,
the commander of his army. Now Saul lay within
the camp, with the people encamped all around
him.
6 Then David answered, and said to Ahimelech the Hittite and to Abishai [a]the son of Zeruiah,
brother of [b]Joab, saying, "Who will [c]go down
with me to Saul in the camp?" And [d]Abishai said,
"I will go down with you."
7 So David and Abishai came to the people
by night; and there Saul lay sleeping within the
camp, with his spear stuck in the ground by his
head. And Abner and the people lay all around
him.
8 Then Abishai said to David, [a]"God has delivered your enemy into your hand this day. Now
therefore, please, let me strike him at once with
the spear, right to the earth; and I will not *have
to strike* him a second time!"
9 But David said to Abishai, "Do not destroy
him; [a]for who can stretch out his hand against
the LORD's anointed, and be guiltless?"
10 David said furthermore, "*As* the LORD
lives, [a]the LORD shall strike him, or [b]his day shall
come to die, or he shall [c]go out to battle and
perish.
11 [a]"The LORD forbid that I should stretch
out my hand against the LORD's anointed. But
please, take now the spear and the jug of water
that *are* by his head, and let us go."
12 So David took the spear and the jug of
water *by* Saul's head, and they got away; and no
man saw or knew *it* or awoke. For they *were* all
asleep, because [a]a deep sleep from the LORD had
fallen on them.
13 Now David went over to the other side,
and stood on the top of a hill afar off, a great
distance *being* between them.
14 And David called out to the people and
to Abner the son of Ner, saying, "Do you not answer, Abner?" Then Abner answered and said,
"Who *are* you, calling out to the king?"
15 So David said to Abner, "*Are* you not a
man? And who *is* like you in Israel? Why then
have you not guarded your lord the king? For one
of the people came in to destroy your lord the
king.
16 "This thing that you have done *is* not
good. *As* the LORD lives, you deserve to die, because you have not guarded your master, the
LORD's anointed. And now see where the king's
spear *is*, and the jug of water that *was* by his
head."
17 Then Saul knew David's voice, and said,
[a]"*Is* that your voice, my son David?" David said,
"*It is* my voice, my lord, O king."
18 And he said, [a]"Why does my lord thus
pursue his servant? For what have I done, or what
evil *is* in my hand?
19 "Now therefore, please, let my lord the
king hear the words of his servant: If the LORD
has [a]stirred you up against me, let Him accept
an offering. But if *it is* the children of men, *may*
they *be* cursed before the LORD, [b]for they have
driven me out this day from sharing in the [c]inheri-
tance of the LORD, saying, 'Go, serve other gods.'
20 "So now, do not let my blood fall to the
earth before the face of the LORD. For the king
of Israel has come out to seek [a]a flea, as when
one hunts a partridge in the mountains."
21 Then Saul said, [a]"I have sinned. Return,
my son David. For I will harm you no more, because my life was precious in your eyes this day.
Indeed I have played the fool and erred exceedingly."
22 And David answered and said, "Here is

KJV

king's spear! and let one of the young men come over and fetch it.

23 [a]The LORD [b]render to every man his righteousness and his faithfulness: for the LORD delivered thee into *my* hand to day, but I would not stretch forth mine hand against the LORD's anointed.

24 And, behold, as thy life was much set by this day in mine eyes, so let my life be much set by in the eyes of the LORD, and let him deliver me out of all tribulation.

25 Then Saul said to David, Blessed *be* thou, my son David: thou shalt both do great *things*, and also shalt still [a]prevail. So David went on his way, and Saul returned to his place.

David Allied with the Philistines

27 And David said in his heart, I shall now perish one day by the hand of Saul: *there is* nothing better for me than that I should speedily escape into the land of the Philistines; and Saul shall despair of me, to seek me any more in any coast of Israel: so shall I escape out of his hand.

2 And David arose, [a]and he passed over with the six hundred men that *were* with him [b]unto Achish, the son of Maoch, king of Gath.

3 And David dwelt with Achish at Gath, he and his men, every man with his household, *even* David [a]with his two wives, Ahinoam the Jezreelitess, and Abigail the Carmelitess, Nabal's wife.

4 And it was told Saul that David was fled to Gath: and he sought no more again for him.

5 And David said unto Achish, If I have now found grace in thine eyes, let them give me a place in some town in the country, that I may dwell there: for why should thy servant dwell in the royal city with thee?

6 Then Achish gave him Ziklag that day: wherefore [a]Ziklag pertaineth unto the kings of Judah unto this day.

7 And the time that David [a]dwelt in the country of the Philistines was a full year and four months.

8 And David and his men went up, and invaded [a]the Geshurites, [b]and the Gezrites, and the [c]Amalekites: for those *nations were* of old the inhabitants of the land, [d]as thou goest to Shur, even unto the land of Egypt.

9 And David smote the land, and left neither man nor woman alive, and took away the sheep, and the oxen, and the asses, and the camels, and the apparel, and returned, and came to Achish.

10 And Achish said, Whither have ye made a road to day? And David said, Against the south of Judah, and against the south of [a]the Jerahmeelites, and against the south of [b]the Kenites.

11 And David saved neither man nor woman alive, to bring *tidings* to Gath, saying, Lest they should tell on us, saying, So did David, and so *will be* his manner all the while he dwelleth in the country of the Philistines.

12 And Achish believed David, saying, He hath made his people Israel utterly to abhor him; therefore he shall be my servant for ever.

28 And [a]it came to pass in those days, that the Philistines gathered their armies together for warfare, to fight with Israel. And Achish said unto David, Know thou assuredly, that thou shalt go out with me to battle, thou and thy men.

2 And David said to Achish, Surely thou shalt know what thy servant can do. And Achish said to David, Therefore will I make thee keeper of mine head for ever.

Saul Consults a Medium
(cf. Deut. 18:9–14)

3 Now [a]Samuel was dead, and all Israel had lamented him, and buried him in [b]Ramah, even in his own city. And Saul had put away [c]those

23 [a]1 Sam. 24:19; Ps. 7:8; 18:20; 62:12 [b]2 Sam. 22:21
25 [a]Gen. 32:28; 1 Sam. 24:20

CHAPTER 27

2 [a]1 Sam. 25:13 [b]1 Sam. 21:10; 1 Kin. 2:39
3 [a]1 Sam. 25:42, 43
6 [a]Josh. 15:31; 19:5; 1 Chr. 12:1; Neh. 11:28
7 [a]1 Sam. 29:3
8 [a]Josh. 13:2, 13 [b]Josh. 16:10; Judg. 1:29 [c]Ex. 17:8, 16; 1 Sam. 15:7, 8 [d]Gen. 25:18; Ex. 15:22
10 [a]1 Chr. 2:9, 25 [b]Judg. 1:16

CHAPTER 28

1 [a]1 Sam. 29:1, 2
3 [a]1 Sam. 25:1 [b]1 Sam. 1:19 [c]Ex. 22:18; Lev. 19:31; 20:27; Deut. 18:10, 11; 1 Sam. 15:23; 28:9

*

27:8 Or *Gezrites*

NKJV

the king's spear. Let one of the young men come over and get it.

23 [a]"May the LORD [b]repay every man *for* his righteousness and his faithfulness; for the LORD delivered you into *my* hand today, but I would not stretch out my hand against the LORD's anointed.

24 "And indeed, as your life was valued much this day in my eyes, so let my life be valued much in the eyes of the LORD, and let Him deliver me out of all tribulation."

25 Then Saul said to David, "*May* you *be* blessed, my son David! You shall both do great things and also still [a]prevail." So David went on his way, and Saul returned to his place.

David Allied with the Philistines

27 And David said in his heart, "Now I shall perish someday by the hand of Saul. *There is* nothing better for me than that I should speedily escape to the land of the Philistines; and Saul will despair of me, to seek me anymore in any part of Israel. So I shall escape out of his hand."

2 Then David arose [a]and went over with the six hundred men who *were* with him [b]to Achish the son of Maoch, king of Gath.

3 So David dwelt with Achish at Gath, he and his men, each man with his household, *and* David [a]with his two wives, Ahinoam the Jezreelitess, and Abigail the Carmelitess, Nabal's widow.

4 And it was told Saul that David had fled to Gath; so he sought him no more.

5 Then David said to Achish, "If I have now found favor in your eyes, let them give me a place in some town in the country, that I may dwell there. For why should your servant dwell in the royal city with you?"

6 So Achish gave him Ziklag that day. Therefore [a]Ziklag has belonged to the kings of Judah to this day.

7 Now the time that David [a]dwelt in the country of the Philistines was one full year and four months.

8 And David and his men went up and raided [a]the Geshurites, [b]the *Girzites, and the [c]Amalekites. For those nations were the inhabitants of the land from of old, [d]as you go to Shur, even as far as the land of Egypt.

9 Whenever David attacked the land, he left neither man nor woman alive, but took away the sheep, the oxen, the donkeys, the camels, and the apparel, and returned and came to Achish.

10 Then Achish would say, "Where have you made a raid today?" And David would say, "Against the southern *area* of Judah, or against the southern *area* of [a]the Jerahmeelites, or against the southern *area* of [b]the Kenites."

11 David would save neither man nor woman alive, to bring *news* to Gath, saying, "Lest they should inform on us, saying, 'Thus David did.'" And thus *was* his behavior all the time he dwelt in the country of the Philistines.

12 So Achish believed David, saying, "He has made his people Israel utterly abhor him; therefore he will be my servant forever."

28 Now [a]it happened in those days that the Philistines gathered their armies together for war, to fight with Israel. And Achish said to David, "You assuredly know that you will go out with me to battle, you and your men."

2 So David said to Achish, "Surely you know what your servant can do." And Achish said to David, "Therefore I will make you one of my chief guardians forever."

Saul Consults a Medium
(cf. Deut. 18:9–14)

3 Now [a]Samuel had died, and all Israel had lamented for him and buried him in [b]Ramah, in

KJV

that had familiar spirits, and the wizards, out of the land.

4 And the Philistines gathered themselves together, and came and pitched in [a]Shunem: and Saul gathered all Israel together, and they pitched in [b]Gilboa.

5 And when Saul saw the host of the Philistines, he was [a]afraid, and his heart greatly trembled.

6 And when Saul enquired of the LORD, [a]the LORD answered him not, neither by [b]dreams, nor [c]by Urim, nor by prophets.

7 Then said Saul unto his servants, Seek me a woman that hath a familiar spirit, [a]that I may go to her, and enquire of her. And his servants said to him, Behold, *there is* a woman that hath a familiar spirit at En–dor.

8 And Saul disguised himself, and put on other raiment, and he went, and two men with him, and they came to the woman by night: and [a]he said, I pray thee, divine unto me by the familiar spirit, and bring me *him* up, whom I shall name unto thee.

9 And the woman said unto him, Behold, thou knowest what Saul hath done, how he hath [a]cut off those that have familiar spirits, and the wizards, out of the land: wherefore then layest thou a snare for my life, to cause me to die?

10 And Saul sware to her by the LORD, saying, *As* the LORD liveth, there shall no punishment happen to thee for this thing.

11 Then said the woman, Whom shall I bring up unto thee? And he said, Bring me up Samuel.

12 And when the woman saw Samuel, she cried with a loud voice: and the woman spake to Saul, saying, Why hast thou deceived me? for thou *art* Saul.

13 And the king said unto her, Be not afraid: for what sawest thou? And the woman said unto Saul, I saw [a]gods ascending out of the earth.

14 And he said unto her, What form *is* he of? And she said, An old man cometh up; and he *is* covered with [a]a mantle. And Saul perceived that it *was* Samuel, and he stooped with *his* face to the ground, and bowed himself.

15 And Samuel said to Saul, Why hast thou [a]disquieted me, to bring me up? And Saul answered, I am sore distressed; for the Philistines make war against me, and [b]God is departed from me, and [c]answereth me no more, neither by prophets, nor by dreams: therefore I have called thee, that thou mayest make known unto me what I shall do.

16 Then said Samuel, Wherefore then dost thou ask of me, seeing the LORD is departed from thee, and is become thine enemy?

17 And the LORD hath done to him, [a]as he spake by me: for the LORD hath rent the kingdom out of thine hand, and given it to thy neighbour, *even* to David:

18 [a]Because thou obeyedst not the voice of the LORD, nor executedst his fierce wrath upon [b]Amalek, therefore hath the LORD done this thing unto thee this day.

19 Moreover the LORD will also deliver Israel with thee into the hand of the Philistines: and to morrow *shalt* thou and thy sons *be* with [a]me: the LORD also shall deliver the host of Israel into the hand of the Philistines.

20 Then Saul fell straightway all along on the earth, and was sore afraid, because of the words of Samuel: and there was no strength in him; for he had eaten no bread all the day, nor all the night.

21 And the woman came unto Saul, and saw that he was sore troubled, and said unto him, Behold, thine handmaid hath obeyed thy voice, and I have [a]put my life in my hand, and have hearkened unto thy words which thou spakest unto me.

22 Now therefore, I pray thee, hearken thou also unto the voice of thine handmaid, and let me

NKJV

his own city. And Saul had put [c]the mediums and the spiritists out of the land.

4 Then the Philistines gathered together, and came and encamped at [a]Shunem. So Saul gathered all Israel together, and they encamped at [b]Gilboa.

5 When Saul saw the army of the Philistines, he was [a]afraid, and his heart trembled greatly.

6 And when Saul inquired of the LORD, [a]the LORD did not answer him, either by [b]dreams or [c]by Urim or by the prophets.

7 Then Saul said to his servants, "Find me a woman who is a medium, [a]that I may go to her and inquire of her." And his servants said to him, "In fact, *there is* a woman who is a medium at En Dor."

8 So Saul disguised himself and put on other clothes, and he went, and two men with him; and they came to the woman by night. And [a]he said, "Please conduct a séance for me, and bring up for me the one I shall name to you."

9 Then the woman said to him, "Look, you know what Saul has done, how he has [a]cut off the mediums and the spiritists from the land. Why then do you lay a snare for my life, to cause me to die?"

10 And Saul swore to her by the LORD, saying, "*As* the LORD lives, no punishment shall come upon you for this thing."

11 Then the woman said, "Whom shall I bring up for you?" And he said, "Bring up Samuel for me."

12 When the woman saw Samuel, she cried out with a loud voice. And the woman spoke to Saul, saying, "Why have you deceived me? For you *are* Saul!"

13 And the king said to her, "Do not be afraid. What did you see?" And the woman said to Saul, "I saw [a]a* spirit ascending out of the earth."

14 So he said to her, "What *is* his form?" And she said, "An old man is coming up, and he *is* covered with [a]a mantle." And Saul perceived that it *was* Samuel, and he stooped with *his* face to the ground and bowed down.

15 Now Samuel said to Saul, "Why have you [a]disturbed me by bringing me up?" And Saul answered, "I am deeply distressed; for the Philistines make war against me, and [b]God has departed from me and [c]does not answer me anymore, neither by prophets nor by dreams. Therefore I have called you, that you may reveal to me what I should do."

16 Then Samuel said: "So why do you ask me, seeing the LORD has departed from you and has become your enemy?

17 "And the LORD has done for *Himself [a]as He spoke by me. For the LORD has torn the kingdom out of your hand and given it to your neighbor, David.

18 [a]"Because you did not obey the voice of the LORD nor execute His fierce wrath upon [b]Amalek, therefore the LORD has done this thing to you this day.

19 "Moreover the LORD will also deliver Israel with you into the hand of the Philistines. And tomorrow you and your sons *will be* with [a]me. The LORD will also deliver the army of Israel into the hand of the Philistines."

20 Immediately Saul fell full length on the ground, and was dreadfully afraid because of the words of Samuel. And there was no strength in him, for he had eaten no food all day or all night.

21 And the woman came to Saul and saw that he was severely troubled, and said to him, "Look, your maidservant has obeyed your voice, and I have [a]put my life in my hands and heeded the words which you spoke to me.

22 "Now therefore, please, heed also the voice of your maidservant, and let me set a piece

---

3 [c]Ex. 22:18; Lev. 19:31; 20:27; Deut. 18:10, 11; 1 Sam. 15:23; 28:9
4 [a]Josh. 19:18; 1 Sam. 28:4; 1 Kin. 1:3; 2 Kin. 4:8 [b]1 Sam. 31:1
5 [a]Job 18:11; [Is. 57:20]
6 [a]1 Sam. 14:37; Prov. 1:28; Lam. 2:9 [b]Num. 12:6; Joel 2:28 [c]Ex. 28:30; Num. 27:21; Deut. 33:8
7 [a]1 Chr. 10:13
8 [a]Deut. 18:10, 11; 1 Chr. 10:13; Is. 8:19
9 [a]1 Sam. 28:3
13 [a]Ex. 22:28; Ps. 138:1
14 [a]1 Sam. 15:27; 2 Kin. 2:8, 13
15 [a]Is. 14:9 [b]1 Sam. 16:14; 18:12 [c]1 Sam. 28:6
17 [a]1 Sam. 15:28
18 [a]1 Sam. 13:9–13; 15:1–26; 1 Kin. 20:42; 1 Chr. 10:13; Jer. 48:10 [b]1 Sam. 15:3–9
19 [a]1 Sam. 31:1–6; Job 3:17–19
21 [a]Judg. 12:3; 1 Sam. 19:5; Job 13:14

*

28:13 Heb. *elohim*
28:17 Or *him*, David

KJV

set a morsel of bread before thee; and eat, that thou mayest have strength, when thou goest on thy way.

23 But he refused, and said, I will not eat. But his servants, together with the woman, compelled him; and he hearkened unto their voice. So he arose from the earth, and sat upon the bed.

24 And the woman had a fat calf in the house; and she hasted, and killed it, and took flour, and kneaded *it*, and did bake unleavened bread thereof:

25 And she brought *it* before Saul, and before his servants; and they did eat. Then they rose up, and went away that night.

The Philistines Reject David

29 Now [a]the Philistines gathered together all their armies [b]to Aphek: and the Israelites pitched by a fountain which *is* in Jezreel.

2 And the [a]lords of the Philistines passed on by hundreds, and by thousands: but [b]David and his men passed on in the rereward with Achish.

3 Then said the princes of the Philistines, What *do* these Hebrews *here?* And Achish said unto the princes of the Philistines, *Is* not this David, the servant of Saul the king of Israel, which hath been with me [a]these days, or these years, and I have [b]found no fault in him since he fell *unto me* unto this day?

4 And the princes of the Philistines were wroth with him; and the princes of the Philistines said unto him, [a]Make this fellow return, that he may go again to his place which thou hast appointed him, and let him not go down with us to [b]battle, lest [c]in the battle he be an adversary to us: for wherewith should he reconcile himself unto his master? *should it* not *be* with the heads of these [d]men?

5 *Is* not this David, [a]of whom they sang one to another in dances, saying, [b]Saul slew his thousands, and David his ten thousands?

6 Then Achish called David, and said unto him, Surely, *as* the LORD liveth, thou hast been upright, and [a]thy going out and thy coming in with me in the host *is* good in my sight: for [b]I have not found evil in thee since the day of thy coming unto me unto this day: nevertheless the lords favour thee not.

7 Wherefore now return, and go in peace, that thou displease not the lords of the Philistines.

8 And David said unto Achish, But what have I done? and what hast thou found in thy servant so long as I have been with thee unto this day, that I may not go fight against the enemies of my lord the king?

9 And Achish answered and said to David, I know that thou *art* good in my sight, [a]as an angel of God: notwithstanding [b]the princes of the Philistines have said, He shall not go up with us to the battle.

10 Wherefore now rise up early in the morning with thy master's servants [a]that are come with thee: and as soon as ye be up early in the morning, and have light, depart.

11 So David and his men rose up early to depart in the morning, to return into the land of the Philistines. [a]And the Philistines went up to Jezreel.

David's Conflict with the Amalekites

30 And it came to pass, when David and his men were come to [a]Ziklag on the third day, that the [b]Amalekites had invaded the south, and Ziklag, and smitten Ziklag, and burned it with fire;

2 And had taken the [a]women captives, that *were* therein: they slew not any, either great or small, but carried *them* away, and went on their way.

NKJV

of bread before you; and eat, that you may have strength when you go on *your* way."

23 But he refused and said, "I will not eat." So his servants, together with the woman, urged him; and he heeded their voice. Then he arose from the ground and sat on the bed.

24 Now the woman had a fatted calf in the house, and she hastened to kill it. And she took flour and kneaded *it*, and baked unleavened bread from it.

25 So she brought *it* before Saul and his servants, and they ate. Then they rose and went away that night.

The Philistines Reject David

29 Then [a]the Philistines gathered together all their armies [b]at Aphek, and the Israelites encamped by a fountain which *is* in Jezreel.

2 And the [a]lords of the Philistines passed in review by hundreds and by thousands, but [b]David and his men passed in review at the rear with Achish.

3 Then the princes of the Philistines said, "What *are* these Hebrews *doing here?*" And Achish said to the princes of the Philistines, "*Is* this not David, the servant of Saul king of Israel, who has been with me [a]these days, or these years? And to this day I have [b]found no fault in him since he defected *to me.*"

4 But the princes of the Philistines were angry with him; so the princes of the Philistines said to him, [a]"Make this fellow return, that he may go back to the place which you have appointed for him, and do not let him go down with us to [b]battle, lest [c]in the battle he become our adversary. For with what could he reconcile himself to his master, if not with the heads of these [d]men?

5 "*Is* this not David, [a]of whom they sang to one another in dances, saying:

[b]'Saul has slain his thousands,
And David his ten thousands'?"

6 Then Achish called David and said to him, "Surely, *as* the LORD lives, you have been upright, and [a]your going out and your coming in with me in the army *is* good in my sight. For to this day [b]I have not found evil in you since the day of your coming to me. Nevertheless the lords do not favor you.

7 "Therefore return now, and go in peace, that you may not displease the lords of the Philistines."

8 So David said to Achish, "But what have I done? And to this day what have you found in your servant as long as I have been with you, that I may not go and fight against the enemies of my lord the king?"

9 Then Achish answered and said to David, "I know that you *are* as good in my sight [a]as an angel of God; nevertheless [b]the princes of the Philistines have said, 'He shall not go up with us to the battle.'

10 "Now therefore, rise early in the morning with your master's servants [a]who have come with *you. And as soon as you are up early in the morning and have light, depart."

11 So David and his men rose early to depart in the morning, to return to the land of the Philistines. [a]And the Philistines went up to Jezreel.

David's Conflict with the Amalekites

30 Now it happened, when David and his men came to [a]Ziklag, on the third day, that the [b]Amalekites had invaded the South and Ziklag, attacked Ziklag and burned it with fire,

2 and had taken captive the [a]women and those who *were* there, from small to great; they did not kill anyone, but carried *them* away and went their way.

CHAPTER 29

1 [a]1 Sam. 28:1 [b]Josh. 12:18; 19:30; 1 Sam. 4:1; 1 Kin. 20:30
2 [a]1 Sam. 6:4; 7:7 [b]1 Sam. 28:1, 2
3 [a]1 Sam. 27:7 [b]1 Sam. 27:1–6; 1 Chr. 12:19, 20; Dan. 6:5
4 [a]1 Sam. 27:6 [b]1 Sam. 14:21 [c]1 Sam. 29:9 [d]1 Chr. 12:19, 20
5 [a]1 Sam. 21:11 [b]1 Sam. 18:7
6 [a]2 Sam. 3:25; 2 Kin. 19:27 [b]1 Sam. 29:3
9 [a]2 Sam. 14:17, 20; 19:27 [b]1 Sam. 29:4
10 [a]1 Chr. 12:19, 22
11 [a]2 Sam. 4:4

CHAPTER 30

1 [a]1 Sam. 27:6 [b]1 Sam. 15:7; 27:8
2 [a]1 Sam. 27:2, 3

*

29:10 So with MT, Tg., Vg.; LXX adds *and go to the place which I have selected for you there; and set no bothersome word in your heart, for you are good before me. And rise on your way*

KJV

3 So David and his men came to the city, and, behold, *it was* burned with fire; and their wives, and their sons, and their daughters, were taken captives.

4 Then David and the people that *were* with him lifted up their voice and wept, until they had no more power to weep.

5 And David's two [a]wives were taken captives, Ahinoam the Jezreelitess, and Abigail the wife of Nabal the Carmelite.

6 And David was greatly distressed; for [a]the people spake of stoning him, because the soul of all the people was grieved, every man for his sons and for his daughters: [b]but David encouraged himself in the LORD his God.

7 [a]And David said to Abiathar the priest, Ahimelech's son, I pray thee, bring me hither the ephod. And [b]Abiathar brought thither the ephod to David.

8 [a]And David enquired at the LORD, saying, Shall I pursue after this troop? shall I overtake them? And he answered him, Pursue: for thou shalt surely overtake *them,* and without fail recover *all.*

9 So David went, he and the six hundred men that *were* with him, and came to the brook Besor, where those that were left behind stayed.

10 But David pursued, he and four hundred men: [a]for two hundred abode behind, which were so faint that they could not go over the brook Besor.

11 And they found an Egyptian in the field, and brought him to David, and gave him bread, and he did eat; and they made him drink water;

12 And they gave him a piece of [a]a cake of figs, and two clusters of raisins: and [b]when he had eaten, his spirit came again to him: for he had eaten no bread, nor drunk *any* water, three days and three nights.

13 And David said unto him, To whom *belongest* thou? and whence *art* thou? And he said, I *am* a young man of Egypt, servant to an Amalekite; and my master left me, because three days agone I fell sick.

14 We made an invasion *upon* the south of [a]the Cherethites, and upon *the coast* which *belongeth* to Judah, and upon the south [b]of Caleb; and we burned Ziklag with fire.

15 And David said to him, Canst thou bring me down to this company? And he said, Swear unto me by God, that thou wilt neither kill me, nor deliver me into the hands of my [a]master, and I will bring thee down to this company.

16 And when he had brought him down, behold, *they were* spread abroad upon all the earth, [a]eating and drinking, and dancing, because of all the great spoil that they had taken out of the land of the Philistines, and out of the land of Judah.

17 And David smote them from the twilight even unto the evening of the next day: and there escaped not a man of them, save four hundred young men, which rode upon camels, and fled.

18 And David recovered all that the Amalekites had carried away: and David rescued his two wives.

19 And there was nothing lacking to them, neither small nor great, neither sons nor daughters, neither spoil, nor any *thing* that they had taken to them: [a]David recovered all.

20 And David took all the flocks and the herds, *which* they drave before those *other* cattle, and said, This *is* David's spoil.

21 And David came to the [a]two hundred men, which were so faint that they could not follow David, whom they had made also to abide at the brook Besor: and they went forth to meet David, and to meet the people that *were* with him: and when David came near to the people, he saluted them.

22 Then answered all the wicked men and *men* [a]of Belial, of those that went with David, and said, Because they went not with us, we will not

NKJV

3 So David and his men came to the city, and there it was, burned with fire; and their wives, their sons, and their daughters had been taken captive.

4 Then David and the people who *were* with him lifted up their voices and wept, until they had no more power to weep.

5 And David's two [a]wives, Ahinoam the Jezreelitess, and Abigail the widow of Nabal the Carmelite, had been taken captive.

6 Now David was greatly distressed, for [a]the people spoke of stoning him, because the soul of all the people was grieved, every man for his sons and his daughters. [b]But David strengthened himself in the LORD his God.

7 [a]Then David said to Abiathar the priest, Ahimelech's son, "Please bring the ephod here to me." And [b]Abiathar brought the ephod to David.

8 [a]So David inquired of the LORD, saying, "Shall I pursue this troop? Shall I overtake them?" And He answered him, "Pursue, for you shall surely overtake *them* and without fail recover *all.*"

9 So David went, he and the six hundred men who *were* with him, and came to the Brook Besor, where those stayed who were left behind.

10 But David pursued, he and four hundred men; [a]for two hundred stayed *behind,* who were so weary that they could not cross the Brook Besor.

11 Then they found an Egyptian in the field, and brought him to David; and they gave him bread and he ate, and they let him drink water.

12 And they gave him a piece of [a]a cake of figs and two clusters of raisins. So [b]when he had eaten, his strength came back to him; for he had eaten no bread nor drunk water for three days and three nights.

13 Then David said to him, "To whom do you *belong,* and where *are* you from?" And he said, "I *am* a young man from Egypt, servant of an Amalekite; and my master left me behind, because three days ago I fell sick.

14 "We made an invasion of the southern *area* of [a]the Cherethites, in the *territory* which *belongs* to Judah, and of the southern *area* [b]of Caleb; and we burned Ziklag with fire."

15 And David said to him, "Can you take me down to this troop?" So he said, "Swear to me by God that you will neither kill me nor deliver me into the hands of my [a]master, and I will take you down to this troop."

16 And when he had brought him down, there they were, spread out over all the land, [a]eating and drinking and dancing, because of all the great spoil which they had taken from the land of the Philistines and from the land of Judah.

17 Then David attacked them from twilight until the evening of the next day. Not a man of them escaped, except four hundred young men who rode on camels and fled.

18 So David recovered all that the Amalekites had carried away, and David rescued his two wives.

19 And nothing of theirs was lacking, either small or great, sons or daughters, spoil or anything which they had taken from them; [a]David recovered all.

20 Then David took all the flocks and herds they had driven before those *other* livestock, and said, "This *is* David's spoil."

21 Now David came to the [a]two hundred men who had been so weary that they could not follow David, whom they also had made to stay at the Brook Besor. So they went out to meet David and to meet the people who *were* with him. And when David came near the people, he greeted them.

22 Then all the wicked and [a]worthless* men of those who went with David answered and said, "Because they did not go with us, we will not give

5 [a]1 Sam. 25:42, 43
6 [a]Ex. 17:4; John 8:59 [b]1 Sam. 23:16; Is. 25:4; Hab. 3:17–19
7 [a]1 Sam. 23:2–9 [b]1 Sam. 23:6
8 [a]1 Sam. 23:2, 4; Ps. 50:15; 91:15
10 [a]1 Sam. 30:9, 21
12 [a]1 Sam. 25:18; 1 Kin. 20:7 [b]Judg. 15:19; 1 Sam. 14:27
14 [a]2 Sam. 8:18; 1 Kin. 1:38, 44; Ezek. 25:16; Zeph. 2:5 [b]Josh. 14:13; 15:13
15 [a]Deut. 23:15
16 [a]1 Thess. 5:3
19 [a]1 Sam. 30:8
21 [a]1 Sam. 30:10
22 [a]Deut. 13:13; Judg. 19:22

*30:22 Lit. *men of Belial*

KJV

give them *ought* of the spoil that we have recovered, save to every man his wife and his children,
that they may lead *them* away, and depart.
23 Then said David, Ye shall not do so, my
brethren, with that which the LORD hath given us,
who hath preserved us, and delivered the company that came against us into our hand.
24 For who will hearken unto you in this matter? but [a]as his part *is* that goeth down to the
battle, so *shall* his part *be* that tarrieth by the stuff:
they shall part alike.
25 And it was *so* from that day forward, that
he made it a statute and an ordinance for Israel
unto this day.
26 And when David came to Ziklag, he sent
of the spoil unto the elders of Judah, *even* to his
friends, saying, Behold a present for you of the
spoil of the enemies of the LORD;
27 To *them* which *were* in Beth–el, and to
them which *were* in [a]south Ramoth, and to *them*
which *were* in [b]Jattir,
28 And to *them* which *were* in [a]Aroer, and
to *them* which *were* in [b]Siphmoth, and to *them*
which *were* in [c]Eshtemoa,
29 And to *them* which *were* in Rachal, and
to *them* which *were* in the cities of [a]the Jerahmeelites, and to *them* which *were* in the cities of
the [b]Kenites,
30 And to *them* which *were* in [a]Hormah, and
to *them* which *were* in Chor–ashan, and to *them*
which *were* in Athach,
31 And to *them* which *were* in [a]Hebron, and
to all the places where David himself and his men
were wont to [b]haunt.

The Tragic End of Saul and His Sons
(1 Chr. 10:1–14)

31 Now [a]the Philistines fought against Israel:
and the men of Israel fled from before
the Philistines, and fell down slain in mount
[b]Gilboa.
2 And the Philistines followed hard upon
Saul and upon his sons; and the Philistines slew
[a]Jonathan, and Abinadab, and Melchi–shua,
Saul's sons.
3 And [a]the battle went sore against Saul,
and the archers hit him; and he was sore wounded
of the archers.
4 [a]Then said Saul unto his armourbearer,
Draw thy sword, and thrust me through therewith; lest [b]these uncircumcised come and thrust
me through, and abuse me. But his armourbearer
would not; [c]for he was sore afraid. Therefore Saul
took a sword, and [d]fell upon it.
5 And when his armourbearer saw that Saul
was dead, he fell likewise upon his sword, and
died with him.
6 So Saul died, and his three sons, and his
armourbearer, and all his men, that same day
together.
7 And when the men of Israel that *were* on
the other side of the valley, and *they* that *were*
on the other side Jordan, saw that the men of Israel fled, and that Saul and his sons were dead,
they forsook the cities, and fled; and the Philistines came and dwelt in them.
8 And it came to pass on the morrow, when
the Philistines came to strip the slain, that they
found Saul and his three sons fallen in mount
Gilboa.
9 And they cut off his head, and stripped
off his armour, and sent into the land of the Philistines round about, to [a]publish *it in* the house of
their idols, and among the people.
10 [a]And they put his armour in the house of
[b]Ashtaroth: and [c]they fastened his body to the
wall of [d]Beth–shan.
11 [a]And when the inhabitants of Jabesh–
gilead heard of that which the Philistines had
done to Saul;
12 [a]All the valiant men arose, and went all
night, and took the body of Saul and the bodies

24 [a]Num. 31:27; Josh. 22:8
27 [a]Josh. 19:8 [b]Josh. 15:48; 21:14
28 [a]Josh. 13:16 [b]1 Chr. 27:27 [c]Josh. 15:50
29 [a]1 Sam. 27:10 [b]Judg. 1:16; 1 Sam. 15:6; 27:10
30 [a]Num. 14:45; 21:3; Josh. 12:14; 15:30; 19:4; Judg. 1:17
31 [a]Num. 13:22; Josh. 14:13–15; 21:11–13; 2 Sam. 2:1 [b]1 Sam. 23:22

CHAPTER 31

1 [a]1 Chr. 10:1–12 [b]1 Sam. 28:4
2 [a]1 Sam. 14:49; 1 Chr. 8:33
3 [a]2 Sam. 1:6
4 [a]Judg. 9:54; 1 Chr. 10:4 [b]Judg. 14:3; 1 Sam. 14:6; 17:26, 36 [c]2 Sam. 1:14 [d]2 Sam. 1:6, 10
9 [a]Judg. 16:23, 24; 2 Sam. 1:20
10 [a]1 Sam. 21:9 [b]Judg. 2:13; 1 Sam. 7:3 [c]2 Sam. 21:12 [d]Judg. 1:27
11 [a]1 Sam. 11:1–13
12 [a]1 Sam. 11:1–11; 2 Sam. 2:4–7

NKJV

them *any* of the spoil that we have recovered, except for every man's wife and children, that they
may lead *them* away and depart."
23 But David said, "My brethren, you shall
not do so with what the LORD has given us, who
has preserved us and delivered into our hand the
troop that came against us.
24 "For who will heed you in this matter? But
[a]as his part *is* who goes down to the battle, so
shall his part *be* who stays by the supplies; they
shall share alike."
25 So it was, from that day forward; he made
it a statute and an ordinance for Israel to this day.
26 Now when David came to Ziklag, he sent
some of the spoil to the elders of Judah, to his
friends, saying, "Here is a present for you from
the spoil of the enemies of the LORD"—
27 to *those* who *were* in Bethel, *those* who
were in [a]Ramoth of the South, *those* who *were*
in [b]Jattir,
28 *those* who *were* in [a]Aroer, *those* who
were in [b]Siphmoth, *those* who *were* in [c]Eshtemoa,
29 *those* who *were* in Rachal, *those* who
were in the cities of [a]the Jerahmeelites, *those* who
were in the cities of the [b]Kenites,
30 *those* who *were* in [a]Hormah, *those* who
were in *Chorashan, *those* who *were* in Athach,
31 *those* who *were* in [a]Hebron, and to all the
places where David himself and his men were accustomed to [b]rove.

The Tragic End of Saul and His Sons
(1 Chr. 10:1–14)

31 Now [a]the Philistines fought against Israel;
and the men of Israel fled from before the
Philistines, and fell slain on Mount [b]Gilboa.
2 Then the Philistines followed hard after
Saul and his sons. And the Philistines killed [a]Jon-
athan, Abinadab, and Malchishua, Saul's sons.
3 [a]The battle became fierce against Saul.
The archers hit him, and he was severely
wounded by the archers.
4 [a]Then Saul said to his armorbearer,
"Draw your sword, and thrust me through with
it, lest [b]these uncircumcised men come and thrust
me through and abuse me." But his armorbearer
would not, [c]for he was greatly afraid. Therefore
Saul took a sword and [d]fell on it.
5 And when his armorbearer saw that Saul
was dead, he also fell on his sword, and died with
him.
6 So Saul, his three sons, his armorbearer,
and all his men died together that same day.
7 And when the men of Israel who *were* on
the other side of the valley, and *those* who *were*
on the other side of the Jordan, saw that the men
of Israel had fled and that Saul and his sons were
dead, they forsook the cities and fled; and the
Philistines came and dwelt in them.
8 So it happened the next day, when the
Philistines came to strip the slain, that they found
Saul and his three sons fallen on Mount Gilboa.
9 And they cut off his head and stripped off
his armor, and sent *word* throughout the land of
the Philistines, to [a]proclaim *it in* the temple of
their idols and among the people.
10 [a]Then they put his armor in the temple
of the [b]Ashtoreths, and [c]they fastened his body
to the wall of [d]Beth* Shan.
11 [a]Now when the inhabitants of Jabesh Gilead heard what the Philistines had done to Saul,
12 [a]all the valiant men arose and traveled all
night, and took the body of Saul and the bodies

*______

30:30 Or *Borashan*
31:10 *Beth Shean*, Josh. 17:11

KJV

of his sons from the wall of Beth–shan, and came
to Jabesh, and [b]burnt them there.
13 And they took their bones, and [a]buried
them under a tree at Jabesh, [b]and fasted seven
days.

12 [b]2 Chr. 16:14; Jer. 34:5; Amos 6:10
13 [a]2 Sam. 2:4, 5; 21:12–14 [b]Gen. 50:10

NKJV

of his sons from the wall of Beth Shan; and they
came to Jabesh and [b]burned them there.
13 Then they took their bones and [a]buried
them under the tamarisk tree at Jabesh, [b]and
fasted seven days.

KJV

THE SECOND BOOK OF

SAMUEL

The Report of Saul's Death

1 Now it came to pass after the [a]death of Saul, when David was returned from [b]the slaughter of the Amalekites, and David had abode two days in Ziklag;

2 It came even to pass on the third day, that, behold, [a]a man came out of the camp from Saul [b]with his clothes rent, and earth upon his head: and *so* it was, when he came to David, that he [c]fell to the earth, and did obeisance.

3 And David said unto him, From whence comest thou? And he said unto him, Out of the camp of Israel am I escaped.

4 And David said unto him, [a]How went the matter? I pray thee, tell me. And he answered, That the people are fled from the battle, and many of the people also are fallen and dead; and Saul and [b]Jonathan his son are dead also.

5 And David said unto the young man that told him, How knowest thou that Saul and Jonathan his son be dead?

6 And the young man that told him said, As I happened by chance upon [a]mount Gilboa, behold, [b]Saul leaned upon his spear; and, lo, the chariots and horsemen followed hard after him.

7 And when he looked behind him, he saw me, and called unto me. And I answered, Here *am* I.

8 And he said unto me, Who *art* thou? And I answered him, I *am* an Amalekite.

9 He said unto me again, Stand, I pray thee, upon me, and slay me: for anguish is come upon me, because my life *is* yet whole in me.

10 So I stood upon him, and [a]slew him, because I was sure that he could not live after that he was fallen: and I took the crown that *was* upon his head, and the bracelet that *was* on his arm, and have brought them hither unto my lord.

11 Then David took hold on his clothes, and [a]rent them; and likewise all the men that *were* with him:

12 And they [a]mourned, and wept, and [b]fasted until even, for Saul, and for Jonathan his son, and for the [c]people of the LORD, and for the house of Israel; because they were fallen by the sword.

13 And David said unto the young man that told him, Whence *art* thou? And he answered, I *am* the son of a stranger, an Amalekite.

14 And David said unto him, How [a]wast thou not [b]afraid to [c]stretch forth thine hand to destroy the LORD's anointed?

15 And [a]David called one of the young men, and said, Go near, *and* fall upon him. And he smote him that he died.

16 And David said unto him, [a]Thy blood *be* upon thy head; for [b]thy mouth hath testified against thee, saying, I have slain the LORD's anointed.

The Song of the Bow

17 And David lamented with this lamentation over Saul and over Jonathan his son:

18 ([a]Also he bade them teach the children of Judah *the use of* the bow: behold, *it is* written [b]in the book of Jasher.)

CHAPTER 1

1 [a]1 Sam. 31:6 [b]1 Sam. 30:1, 17, 26
2 [a]2 Sam. 4:10 [b]1 Sam. 4:12 [c]1 Sam. 25:23
4 [a]1 Sam. 4:16; 31:3 [b]1 Sam. 31:2
6 [a]1 Sam. 31:1 [b]1 Sam. 31:2–4
10 [a]Judg. 9:54; 2 Kin. 11:12
11 [a]2 Sam. 3:31; 13:31
12 [a]2 Sam. 3:31 [b]1 Sam. 31:13 [c]2 Sam. 6:21
14 [a]Num. 12:8 [b]1 Sam. 31:4 [c]1 Sam. 24:6; 26:9
15 [a]2 Sam. 4:10, 12
16 [a]1 Sam. 26:9; 2 Sam. 3:28; 1 Kin. 2:32–37 [b]2 Sam. 1:10; Luke 19:22
18 [a]1 Sam. 31:3 [b]Josh. 10:13

NKJV

THE SECOND BOOK OF

SAMUEL

The Report of Saul's Death

1 Now it came to pass after the [a]death of Saul, when David had returned from [b]the slaughter of the Amalekites, and David had stayed two days in Ziklag,

2 on the third day, behold, it happened that [a]a man came from Saul's camp [b]with his clothes torn and dust on his head. So it was, when he came to David, that he [c]fell to the ground and prostrated himself.

3 And David said to him, "Where have you come from?" So he said to him, "I have escaped from the camp of Israel."

4 Then David said to him, [a]"How did the matter go? Please tell me." And he answered, "The people have fled from the battle, many of the people are fallen and dead, and Saul and [b]Jonathan his son are dead also."

5 So David said to the young man who told him, "How do you know that Saul and Jonathan his son are dead?"

6 Then the young man who told him said, "As I happened by chance *to be* on [a]Mount Gilboa, there was [b]Saul, leaning on his spear; and indeed the chariots and horsemen followed hard after him.

7 "Now when he looked behind him, he saw me and called to me. And I answered, 'Here I am.'

8 "And he said to me, 'Who *are* you?' So I answered him, 'I *am* an Amalekite.'

9 "He said to me again, 'Please stand over me and kill me, for anguish has come upon me, but my life still *remains* in me.'

10 "So I stood over him and [a]killed him, because I was sure that he could not live after he had fallen. And I took the crown that *was* on his head and the bracelet that *was* on his arm, and have brought them here to my lord."

11 Therefore David took hold of his own clothes and [a]tore them, and *so did* all the men who *were* with him.

12 And they [a]mourned and wept and [b]fasted until evening for Saul and for Jonathan his son, for the [c]people of the LORD and for the house of Israel, because they had fallen by the sword.

13 Then David said to the young man who told him, "Where *are* you from?" And he answered, "I *am* the son of an alien, an Amalekite."

14 So David said to him, "How [a]was it you were not [b]afraid to [c]put forth your hand to destroy the LORD's anointed?"

15 Then [a]David called one of the young men and said, "Go near, *and* execute him!" And he struck him so that he died.

16 So David said to him, [a]"Your blood *is* on your own head, for [b]your own mouth has testified against you, saying, 'I have killed the LORD's anointed.' "

The Song of the Bow

17 Then David lamented with this lamentation over Saul and over Jonathan his son,

18 [a]and he told *them* to teach the children of Judah *the Song of* the Bow; indeed *it is* written [b]in the Book of Jasher:

KJV

19 The beauty of Israel is slain upon thy high places: [a]how are the mighty fallen!

20 [a]Tell *it* not in Gath, publish *it* not in the streets of [b]Askelon; lest [c]the daughters of the Philistines rejoice, lest the daughters of [d]the uncircumcised triumph.

21 Ye [a]mountains of Gilboa, [b]*let there be* no dew, neither *let there be* rain, upon you, nor fields of offerings: for there the shield of the mighty is vilely cast away, the shield of Saul, *as though he had* not *been* [c]anointed with oil.

22 From the blood of the slain, from the fat of the mighty, [a]the bow of Jonathan turned not back, and the sword of Saul returned not empty.

23 Saul and Jonathan *were* lovely and pleasant in their lives, and in their [a]death they were not divided: they were swifter than eagles, they were [b]stronger than lions.

24 Ye daughters of Israel, weep over Saul, who clothed you in scarlet, with *other* delights, who put on ornaments of gold upon your apparel.

25 How are the mighty fallen in the midst of the battle! O Jonathan, *thou wast* slain in thine high places.

26 I am distressed for thee, my brother Jonathan: very pleasant hast thou been unto me: [a]thy love to me was wonderful, passing the love of women.

27 [a]How are the mighty fallen, and the weapons of war perished!

David Anointed King of Judah

2 And it came to pass after this, that David [a]enquired of the LORD, saying, Shall I go up into any of the cities of Judah? And the LORD said unto him, Go up. And David said, Whither shall I go up? And he said, Unto [b]Hebron.

2 So David went up thither, and his [a]two wives also, Ahinoam the Jezreelitess, and Abigail Nabal's wife the Carmelite.

3 And [a]his men that *were* with him did David bring up, every man with his household: and they dwelt in the cities of Hebron.

4 [a]And the men of Judah came, and there they [b]anointed David king over the house of Judah. And they told David, saying, *That* [c]the men of Jabesh–gilead *were they* that buried Saul.

5 And David sent messengers unto the men of Jabesh–gilead, and said unto them, [a]Blessed *be* ye of the LORD, that ye have shewed this kindness unto your lord, *even* unto Saul, and have buried him.

6 And now [a]the LORD shew kindness and truth unto you: and I also will requite you this kindness, because ye have done this thing.

7 Therefore now let your hands be strengthened, and be ye valiant: for your master Saul is dead, and also the house of Judah have anointed me king over them.

Ishbosheth Made King of Israel

8 But [a]Abner the son of Ner, captain of Saul's host, took Ish–bosheth the son of Saul, and brought him over to [b]Mahanaim;

9 And made him king over [a]Gilead, and over the [b]Ashurites, and over [c]Jezreel, and over Ephraim, and over Benjamin, and over all Israel.

---

19 [a]2 Sam. 1:27
20 [a]1 Sam. 27:2; 31:8–13; Mic. 1:10 [b]1 Sam. 6:17; Jer. 25:20 [c]Ex. 15:20; Judg. 11:34; 1 Sam. 18:6 [d]1 Sam. 31:4
21 [a]1 Sam. 31:1 [b]Ezek. 31:15 [c]1 Sam. 10:1
22 [a]Deut. 32:42; 1 Sam. 18:4
23 [a]1 Sam. 31:2–4 [b]Judg. 14:18
26 [a]1 Sam. 18:1–4; 19:2; 20:17
27 [a]2 Sam. 1:19, 25

CHAPTER 2

1 [a]Judg. 1:1; 1 Sam. 23:2, 4, 9; 30:7, 8 [b]1 Sam. 30:31; 2 Sam. 2:11; 5:1–3; 1 Kin. 2:11
2 [a]1 Sam. 25:42, 43; 30:5
3 [a]1 Sam. 27:2, 3; 30:1; 1 Chr. 12:1
4 [a]1 Sam. 30:26; 2 Sam. 2:11; 5:5; 19:14, 41–43 [b]1 Sam. 16:13; 2 Sam. 5:3 [c]1 Sam. 31:11–13
5 [a]Ruth 2:20; 3:10
6 [a]Ex. 34:6; 2 Tim. 1:16, 18
8 [a]1 Sam. 14:50; 2 Sam. 3:6 [b]Gen. 32:2; Josh. 21:38; 2 Sam. 17:24
9 [a]Josh. 22:9 [b]Judg. 1:32 [c]1 Sam. 29:1

***2:8** *Esh-Baal,* 1 Chr. 8:33; 9:39

NKJV

19 "The beauty of Israel is slain on your high places!
[a]How the mighty have fallen!
20 [a]Tell *it* not in Gath,
Proclaim *it* not in the streets of [b]Ashkelon—
Lest [c]the daughters of the Philistines rejoice,
Lest the daughters of [d]the uncircumcised triumph.

21 "O [a]mountains of Gilboa,
[b]*Let there be* no dew nor rain upon you,
Nor fields of offerings.
For the shield of the mighty is cast away there!
The shield of Saul, not [c]anointed with oil.
22 From the blood of the slain,
From the fat of the mighty,
[a]The bow of Jonathan did not turn back,
And the sword of Saul did not return empty.

23 "Saul and Jonathan *were* beloved and pleasant in their lives,
And in their [a]death they were not divided;
They were swifter than eagles,
They were [b]stronger than lions.

24 "O daughters of Israel, weep over Saul,
Who clothed you in scarlet, with luxury;
Who put ornaments of gold on your apparel.

25 "How the mighty have fallen in the midst of the battle!
Jonathan *was* slain in your high places.
26 I am distressed for you, my brother Jonathan;
You have been very pleasant to me;
[a]Your love to me was wonderful,
Surpassing the love of women.

27 "How[a] the mighty have fallen,
And the weapons of war perished!"

David Anointed King of Judah

2 It happened after this that David [a]inquired of the LORD, saying, "Shall I go up to any of the cities of Judah?" And the LORD said to him, "Go up." David said, "Where shall I go up?" And He said, "To [b]Hebron."

2 So David went up there, and his [a]two wives also, Ahinoam the Jezreelitess, and Abigail the widow of Nabal the Carmelite.

3 And David brought up [a]the men who *were* with him, every man with his household. So they dwelt in the cities of Hebron.

4 [a]Then the men of Judah came, and there they [b]anointed David king over the house of Judah. And they told David, saying, [c]"The men of Jabesh Gilead *were the ones* who buried Saul."

5 So David sent messengers to the men of Jabesh Gilead, and said to them, [a]"You *are* blessed of the LORD, for you have shown this kindness to your lord, to Saul, and have buried him.

6 "And now may [a]the LORD show kindness and truth to you. I also will repay you this kindness, because you have done this thing.

7 "Now therefore, let your hands be strengthened, and be valiant; for your master Saul is dead, and also the house of Judah has anointed me king over them."

Ishbosheth Made King of Israel

8 But [a]Abner the son of Ner, commander of Saul's army, took *Ishbosheth the son of Saul and brought him over to [b]Mahanaim;

9 and he made him king over [a]Gilead, over the [b]Ashurites, over [c]Jezreel, over Ephraim, over Benjamin, and over all Israel.

KJV

10 Ish–bosheth Saul's son *was* forty years old when he began to reign over Israel, and reigned two years. But the house of Judah followed David.

11 And [a]the time that David was king in Hebron over the house of Judah was seven years and six months.

Israel and Judah at War

12 And Abner the son of Ner, and the servants of Ish–bosheth the son of Saul, went out from Mahanaim to [a]Gibeon.

13 And [a]Joab the son of Zeruiah, and the servants of David, went out, and met together by [b]the pool of Gibeon: and they sat down, the one on the one side of the pool, and the other on the other side of the pool.

14 And Abner said to Joab, Let the young men now arise, and play before us. And Joab said, Let them arise.

15 Then there arose and went over by number twelve of Benjamin, which *pertained* to Ish–bosheth the son of Saul, and twelve of the servants of David.

16 And they caught every one his fellow by the head, and *thrust* his sword in his fellow's side; so they fell down together: wherefore that place was called Helkath–hazzurim, which *is* in Gibeon.

17 And there was a very sore battle that day; and Abner was beaten, and the men of Israel, before the servants of David.

18 And there were [a]three sons of Zeruiah there, Joab, and Abishai, and Asahel: and Asahel *was* [b]*as* light of foot [c]as a wild roe.

19 And Asahel pursued after Abner; and in going he turned not to the right hand nor to the left from following Abner.

20 Then Abner looked behind him, and said, *Art* thou Asahel? And he answered, I *am*.

21 And Abner said to him, Turn thee aside to thy right hand or to thy left, and lay thee hold on one of the young men, and take thee his armour. But Asahel would not turn aside from following of him.

22 And Abner said again to Asahel, Turn thee aside from following me: wherefore should I smite thee to the ground? how then should I hold up my face to Joab thy brother?

23 Howbeit he refused to turn aside: wherefore Abner with the hinder end of his spear smote him [a]under the fifth *rib*, that the spear came out behind him; and he fell down there, and died in the same place: and it came to pass, *that* as many as came to the place where Asahel fell down and died stood [b]still.

24 Joab also and Abishai pursued after Abner: and the sun went down when they were come to the hill of Ammah, that *lieth* before Giah by the way of the wilderness of Gibeon.

25 And the children of Benjamin gathered themselves together after Abner, and became one troop, and stood on the top of an hill.

26 Then Abner called to Joab, and said, Shall the sword devour for ever? knowest thou not that it will be bitterness in the latter end? how long shall it be then, ere thou bid the people return from following their brethren?

27 And Joab said, *As* God liveth, unless [a]thou hadst spoken, surely then in the morning the people had gone up every one from following his brother.

28 So Joab blew a trumpet, and all the people stood still, and pursued after Israel no more, neither fought they any more.

29 And Abner and his men walked all that night through the plain, and passed over Jordan, and went through all Bithron, and they came to Mahanaim.

30 And Joab returned from following Abner: and when he had gathered all the people together, there lacked of David's servants nineteen men and Asahel.

11 [a]2 Sam. 5:5; 1 Kin. 2:11
12 [a]Josh. 10:2–12; 18:25
13 [a]1 Sam. 26:6; 2 Sam. 8:16; 1 Chr. 2:16; 11:6 [b]Jer. 41:12
18 [a]1 Chr. 2:16 [b]1 Chr. 12:8; Hab. 3:19 [c]Ps. 18:33
23 [a]2 Sam. 3:27; 4:6; 20:10 [b]2 Sam. 20:12
27 [a]2 Sam. 2:14

NKJV

10 Ishbosheth, Saul's son, *was* forty years old when he began to reign over Israel, and he reigned two years. Only the house of Judah followed David.

11 And [a]the time that David was king in Hebron over the house of Judah was seven years and six months.

Israel and Judah at War

12 Now Abner the son of Ner, and the servants of Ishbosheth the son of Saul, went out from Mahanaim to [a]Gibeon.

13 And [a]Joab the son of Zeruiah, and the servants of David, went out and met them by [b]the pool of Gibeon. So they sat down, one on one side of the pool and the other on the other side of the pool.

14 Then Abner said to Joab, "Let the young men now arise and compete before us." And Joab said, "Let them arise."

15 So they arose and went over by number, twelve from Benjamin, *followers* of Ishbosheth the son of Saul, and twelve from the servants of David.

16 And each one grasped his opponent by the head and *thrust* his sword in his opponent's side; so they fell down together. Therefore that place was called *the Field of Sharp Swords, which *is* in Gibeon.

17 So there was a very fierce battle that day, and Abner and the men of Israel were beaten before the servants of David.

18 Now the [a]three sons of Zeruiah were there: Joab and Abishai and Asahel. And Asahel *was* [b]*as* fleet of foot [c]as a wild gazelle.

19 So Asahel pursued Abner, and in going he did not turn to the right hand or to the left from following Abner.

20 Then Abner looked behind him and said, "*Are* you Asahel?" He answered, "I *am*."

21 And Abner said to him, "Turn aside to your right hand or to your left, and lay hold on one of the young men and take his armor for yourself." But Asahel would not turn aside from following him.

22 So Abner said again to Asahel, "Turn aside from following me. Why should I strike you to the ground? How then could I face your brother Joab?"

23 However, he refused to turn aside. Therefore Abner struck him [a]in the stomach with the blunt end of the spear, so that the spear came out of his back; and he fell down there and died on the spot. So it was *that* as many as came to the place where Asahel fell down and died, stood [b]still.

24 Joab and Abishai also pursued Abner. And the sun was going down when they came to the hill of Ammah, which *is* before Giah by the road to the Wilderness of Gibeon.

25 Now the children of Benjamin gathered together behind Abner and became a unit, and took their stand on top of a hill.

26 Then Abner called to Joab and said, "Shall the sword devour forever? Do you not know that it will be bitter in the latter end? How long will it be then until you tell the people to return from pursuing their brethren?"

27 And Joab said, "*As* God lives, unless [a]you had spoken, surely then by morning all the people would have given up pursuing their brethren."

28 So Joab blew a trumpet; and all the people stood still and did not pursue Israel anymore, nor did they fight anymore.

29 Then Abner and his men went on all that night through the plain, crossed over the Jordan, and went through all Bithron; and they came to Mahanaim.

30 So Joab returned from pursuing Abner. And when he had gathered all the people together, there were missing of David's servants nineteen men and Asahel.

*———
2:16 Heb. *Helkath Hazzurim*

KJV

31 But the servants of David had smitten of Benjamin, and of Abner's men, *so that* three hundred and threescore men died.

32 And they took up Asahel, and buried him in the sepulchre of his father, which *was in* [a]Beth–lehem. And Joab and his men went all night, and they came to Hebron at break of day.

3 Now there was long [a]war between the house of Saul and the house of David: but David waxed stronger and stronger, and the house of Saul waxed weaker and weaker.

Sons of David

2 And [a]unto David were sons born in Hebron: and his firstborn was Amnon, [b]of Ahinoam the Jezreelitess;

3 And his second, Chileab, of Abigail the wife of Nabal the Carmelite; and the third, [a]Absalom the son of Maacah the daughter of Talmai king [b]of Geshur;

4 And the fourth, [a]Adonijah the son of Haggith; and the fifth, Shephatiah the son of Abital;

5 And the sixth, Ithream, by Eglah David's wife. These were born to David in Hebron.

Abner Joins Forces with David

6 And it came to pass, while there was war between the house of Saul and the house of David, that Abner made himself strong for the house of Saul.

7 And Saul had a concubine, whose name *was* [a]Rizpah, the daughter of Aiah: and *Ish–bosheth* said to Abner, Wherefore hast thou [b]gone in unto my father's concubine?

8 Then was Abner very wroth for the words of Ish–bosheth, and said, *Am* I [a]a dog's head, which against Judah do shew kindness this day unto the house of Saul thy father, to his brethren, and to his friends, and have not delivered thee into the hand of David, that thou chargest me to day with a fault concerning this woman?

9 [a]So do God to Abner, and more also, except, [b]as the LORD hath sworn to David, even so I do to him;

10 To translate the kingdom from the house of Saul, and to set up the throne of David over Israel and over Judah, [a]from Dan even to Beer–sheba.

11 And he could not answer Abner a word again, because he feared him.

12 And Abner sent messengers to David on his behalf, saying, Whose *is* the land? saying *also*, Make thy league with me, and, behold, my hand *shall be* with thee, to bring about all Israel unto thee.

13 And he said, Well; I will make a league with thee: but one thing I require of thee, that is, [a]Thou shalt not see my face, except thou first bring [b]Michal Saul's daughter, when thou comest to see my face.

14 And David sent messengers to [a]Ish–bosheth Saul's son, saying, Deliver *me* my wife Michal, which I espoused to me [b]for an hundred foreskins of the Philistines.

15 And Ish–bosheth sent, and took her from *her* husband, *even* from Phaltiel the son of Laish.

16 And her husband went with her along weeping behind her to [a]Bahurim. Then said Abner unto him, Go, return. And he returned.

17 And Abner had communication with the elders of Israel, saying, Ye sought for David in times past *to be* king over you:

18 Now then do *it*: [a]for the LORD hath spoken of David, saying, By the hand of my servant David I will save my people Israel out of the hand of the Philistines, and out of the hand of all their enemies.

19 And Abner also spake in the ears of [a]Benjamin: and Abner went also to speak in the ears of David in Hebron all that seemed good to Israel,

---

32 [a]1 Sam. 20:6

CHAPTER 3

1 [a]1 Kin. 14:30; [Ps. 46:9]
2 [a]1 Chr. 3:1–4 [b]1 Sam. 25:42, 43
3 [a]2 Sam. 15:1–10 [b]Josh. 13:13; 1 Sam. 27:8; 2 Sam. 13:37; 14:32; 15:8
4 [a]1 Kin. 1:5
7 [a]2 Sam. 21:8–11 [b]2 Sam. 16:21
8 [a]Deut. 23:18; 1 Sam. 24:14; 2 Sam. 9:8; 16:9
9 [a]Ruth 1:17; 1 Kin. 19:2 [b]1 Sam. 15:28; 16:1, 12; 28:17; 1 Chr. 12:23
10 [a]Judg. 20:1; 1 Sam. 3:20; 2 Sam. 17:11; 1 Kin. 4:25
13 [a]Gen. 43:3 [b]1 Sam. 18:20; 19:11; 25:44; 2 Sam. 6:16
14 [a]2 Sam. 2:10 [b]1 Sam. 18:25–27
16 [a]2 Sam. 16:5; 19:16
18 [a]2 Sam. 3:9
19 [a]1 Sam. 10:20, 21; 1 Chr. 12:29

*

3:15 *Palti,* 1 Sam. 25:44
3:18 So with many Heb. mss., LXX, Syr., Tg.; MT *he*

NKJV

31 But the servants of David had struck down, of Benjamin and Abner's men, three hundred and sixty men who died.

32 Then they took up Asahel and buried him in his father's tomb, which *was in* [a]Bethlehem. And Joab and his men went all night, and they came to Hebron at daybreak.

3 Now there was a long [a]war between the house of Saul and the house of David. But David grew stronger and stronger, and the house of Saul grew weaker and weaker.

Sons of David

2 Sons were born [a]to David in Hebron: His firstborn was Amnon [b]by Ahinoam the Jezreelitess;

3 his second, Chileab, by Abigail the widow of Nabal the Carmelite; the third, [a]Absalom the son of Maacah, the daughter of Talmai, king [b]of Geshur;

4 the fourth, [a]Adonijah the son of Haggith; the fifth, Shephatiah the son of Abital;

5 and the sixth, Ithream, by David's wife Eglah. These were born to David in Hebron.

Abner Joins Forces with David

6 Now it was so, while there was war between the house of Saul and the house of David, that Abner was strengthening *his hold* on the house of Saul.

7 And Saul had a concubine, whose name *was* [a]Rizpah, the daughter of Aiah. So *Ishbosheth* said to Abner, "Why have you [b]gone in to my father's concubine?"

8 Then Abner became very angry at the words of Ishbosheth, and said, "*Am* I [a]a dog's head that belongs to Judah? Today I show loyalty to the house of Saul your father, to his brothers, and to his friends, and have not delivered you into the hand of David; and you charge me today with a fault concerning this woman?

9 [a]"May God do so to Abner, and more also, if I do not do for David [b]as the LORD has sworn to him—

10 "to transfer the kingdom from the house of Saul, and set up the throne of David over Israel and over Judah, [a]from Dan to Beersheba."

11 And he could not answer Abner another word, because he feared him.

12 Then Abner sent messengers on his behalf to David, saying, "Whose *is* the land?" saying *also*, "Make your covenant with me, and indeed my hand *shall be* with you to bring all Israel to you."

13 And *David* said, "Good, I will make a covenant with you. But one thing I require of you: [a]you shall not see my face unless you first bring [b]Michal, Saul's daughter, when you come to see my face."

14 So David sent messengers to [a]Ishbosheth, Saul's son, saying, "Give *me* my wife Michal, whom I betrothed to myself [b]for a hundred foreskins of the Philistines."

15 And Ishbosheth sent and took her from *her* husband, from *Paltiel the son of Laish.

16 Then her husband went along with her to [a]Bahurim, weeping behind her. So Abner said to him, "Go, return!" And he returned.

17 Now Abner had communicated with the elders of Israel, saying, "In time past you were seeking for David *to be* king over you.

18 "Now then, do *it!* [a]For the LORD has spoken of David, saying, 'By the hand of My servant David, *I will save My people Israel from the hand of the Philistines and the hand of all their enemies.' "

19 And Abner also spoke in the hearing of [a]Benjamin. Then Abner also went to speak in the

KJV

and that seemed good to the whole house of Benjamin.

20 So Abner came to David to Hebron, and twenty men with him. And David made Abner and the men that *were* with him a feast.

21 And Abner said unto David, I will arise and go, and [a]will gather all Israel unto my lord the king, that they may make a league with thee, and that thou mayest [b]reign over all that thine heart desireth. And David sent Abner away; and he went in peace.

Joab Murders Abner

22 And, behold, the servants of David and Joab came from *pursuing* a troop, and brought in a great spoil with them: but Abner *was* not with David in Hebron; for he had sent him away, and he was gone in peace.

23 When Joab and all the host that *was* with him were come, they told Joab, saying, Abner the son of Ner came to the king, and he hath sent him away, and he is gone in peace.

24 Then Joab came to the king, and said, What hast thou done? behold, Abner came unto thee; why *is* it *that* thou hast sent him away, and he is quite gone?

25 Thou knowest Abner the son of Ner, that he came to deceive thee, and to know [a]thy going out and thy coming in, and to know all that thou doest.

26 And when Joab was come out from David, he sent messengers after Abner, which brought him again from the well of Sirah: but David knew *it* not.

27 And when Abner was returned to Hebron, Joab [a]took him aside in the gate to speak with him quietly, and smote him there [b]under the fifth *rib,* that he died, for the blood of [c]Asahel his brother.

28 And afterward when David heard *it,* he said, I and my kingdom *are* guiltless before the LORD for ever from the blood of Abner the son of Ner:

29 [a]Let it rest on the head of Joab, and on all his father's house; and let there not fail from the house of Joab one [b]that hath an issue, or that is a leper, or that leaneth on a staff, or that falleth on the sword, or that lacketh bread.

30 So Joab and Abishai his brother slew Abner, because he had slain their brother [a]Asahel at Gibeon in the battle.

David's Mourning for Abner

31 And David said to Joab, and to all the people that *were* with him, [a]Rend your clothes, and [b]gird you with sackcloth, and mourn before Abner. And king David *himself* followed the bier.

32 And they buried Abner in Hebron: and the king lifted up his voice, and wept at the grave of Abner; and all the people wept.

33 And the king lamented over Abner, and said, Died Abner as a [a]fool dieth?

34 Thy hands *were* not bound, nor thy feet put into fetters: as a man falleth before wicked men, *so* fellest thou. And all the people wept again over him.

35 And when all the people came [a]to cause David to eat meat while it was yet day, David sware, saying, [b]So do God to me, and more also, if I taste bread, or ought else, [c]till the sun be down.

36 And all the people took notice *of it,* and it pleased them: as whatsoever the king did pleased all the people.

37 For all the people and all Israel understood that day that it was not of the king to slay Abner the son of Ner.

38 And the king said unto his servants, Know ye not that there is a prince and a great man fallen this day in Israel?

21 [a]2 Sam. 3:10, 12 [b]1 Kin. 11:37
25 [a]Deut. 28:6; 1 Sam. 29:6; Is. 37:28
27 [a]2 Sam. 20:9, 10; 1 Kin. 2:5 [b]2 Sam. 4:6 [c]2 Sam. 2:23
29 [a]Deut. 21:6–9; 1 Kin. 2:32, 33 [b]Lev. 15:2
30 [a]2 Sam. 2:23
31 [a]Josh. 7:6; 2 Sam. 1:2, 11 [b]Gen. 37:34
33 [a]2 Sam. 13:12, 13
35 [a]2 Sam. 12:17; Jer. 16:7, 8 [b]Ruth 1:17 [c]Judg. 20:26; 2 Sam. 1:12

NKJV

hearing of David in Hebron all that seemed good to Israel and the whole house of Benjamin.

20 So Abner and twenty men with him came to David at Hebron. And David made a feast for Abner and the men who *were* with him.

21 Then Abner said to David, "I will arise and go, and [a]gather all Israel to my lord the king, that they may make a covenant with you, and that you may [b]reign over all that your heart desires." So David sent Abner away, and he went in peace.

Joab Murders Abner

22 At that moment the servants of David and Joab came from a raid and brought much spoil with them. But Abner *was* not with David in Hebron, for he had sent him away, and he had gone in peace.

23 When Joab and all the troops that *were* with him had come, they told Joab, saying, "Abner the son of Ner came to the king, and he sent him away, and he has gone in peace."

24 Then Joab came to the king and said, "What have you done? Look, Abner came to you; why *is* it *that* you sent him away, and he has already gone?

25 "Surely you realize that Abner the son of Ner came to deceive you, to know [a]your going out and your coming in, and to know all that you are doing."

26 And when Joab had gone from David's presence, he sent messengers after Abner, who brought him back from the well of Sirah. But David did not know *it.*

27 Now when Abner had returned to Hebron, Joab [a]took him aside in the gate to speak with him privately, and there stabbed him [b]in the stomach, so that he died for the blood of [c]Asahel his brother.

28 Afterward, when David heard *it,* he said, "My kingdom and I *are* guiltless before the LORD forever of the blood of Abner the son of Ner.

29 [a]"Let it rest on the head of Joab and on all his father's house; and let there never fail to be in the house of Joab one [b]who has a discharge or is a leper, who leans on a staff or falls by the sword, or who lacks bread."

30 So Joab and Abishai his brother killed Abner, because he had killed their brother [a]Asahel at Gibeon in the battle.

David's Mourning for Abner

31 Then David said to Joab and to all the people who were with him, [a]"Tear your clothes, [b]gird yourselves with sackcloth, and mourn for Abner." And King David followed the coffin.

32 So they buried Abner in Hebron; and the king lifted up his voice and wept at the grave of Abner, and all the people wept.

33 And the king sang *a lament* over Abner and said:

"Should Abner die as a [a]fool dies?
34 Your hands were not bound
Nor your feet put into fetters;
As a man falls before wicked men, *so*
you fell."

Then all the people wept over him again.

35 And when all the people came [a]to persuade David to eat food while it was still day, David took an oath, saying, [b]"God do so to me, and more also, if I taste bread or anything else [c]till the sun goes down!"

36 Now all the people took note *of it,* and it pleased them, since whatever the king did pleased all the people.

37 For all the people and all Israel understood that day that it had not been the king's *intent* to kill Abner the son of Ner.

38 Then the king said to his servants, "Do you not know that a prince and a great man has fallen this day in Israel?

KJV

39 And I *am* this day weak, though anointed king; and these men the sons of Zeruiah [a]*be* too hard for me: [b]the LORD shall reward the doer of evil according to his wickedness.

Ishbosheth Is Murdered

4 And when Saul's son heard that Abner was dead in Hebron, [a]his hands were feeble, and all the Israelites were [b]troubled.

2 And Saul's son had two men *that were* captains of bands: the name of the one *was* Baanah, and the name of the other Rechab, the sons of Rimmon a Beerothite, of the children of Benjamin: (for [a]Beeroth also was reckoned to Benjamin.

3 And the Beerothites fled to [a]Gittaim, and were sojourners there until this day.)

4 And [a]Jonathan, Saul's son, had a son *that was* lame of *his* feet. He was five years old when the tidings came of Saul and Jonathan [b]out of Jezreel, and his nurse took him up, and fled: and it came to pass, as she made haste to flee, that he fell, and became lame. And his name *was* [c]Mephibosheth.

5 And the sons of Rimmon the Beerothite, Rechab and Baanah, went, and came about the heat of the day to the [a]house of Ish–bosheth, who lay on a bed at noon.

6 And they came thither into the midst of the house, *as though* they would have fetched wheat; and they smote him [a]under the fifth *rib:* and Rechab and Baanah his brother escaped.

7 For when they came into the house, he lay on his bed in his bedchamber, and they smote him, and slew him, and beheaded him, and took his head, and gat them away through the plain all night.

8 And they brought the head of Ish–bosheth unto David to Hebron, and said to the king, Behold the head of Ish–bosheth the son of Saul thine enemy, [a]which sought thy life; and the LORD hath avenged my lord the king this day of Saul, and of his seed.

9 And David answered Rechab and Baanah his brother, the sons of Rimmon the Beerothite, and said unto them, *As* the LORD liveth, [a]who hath redeemed my soul out of all adversity,

10 When [a]one told me, saying, Behold, Saul is dead, thinking to have brought good tidings, I took hold of him, and slew him in Ziklag, who *thought* that I would have given him a reward for his tidings:

11 How much more, when wicked men have slain a righteous person in his own house upon his bed? shall I not therefore now [a]require his blood of your hand, and take you away from the earth?

12 And David [a]commanded his young men, and they slew them, and cut off their hands and their feet, and hanged *them* up over the pool in Hebron. But they took the head of Ish–bosheth, and buried *it* in the [b]sepulchre of Abner in Hebron.

David Reigns over All Israel
(1 Chr. 11:1–3)

5 Then [a]came all the tribes of Israel to David unto Hebron, and spake, saying, Behold, [b]we *are* thy bone and thy flesh.

2 Also in time past, when Saul was king over us, [a]thou wast he that leddest out and broughtest in Israel: and the LORD said to thee, [b]Thou shalt feed my people Israel, and thou shalt be a captain over Israel.

3 [a]So all the elders of Israel came to the king to Hebron; [b]and king David made a league with them in Hebron [c]before the LORD: and they anointed David king over Israel.

4 David *was* [a]thirty years old when he began to reign, [b]*and* he reigned forty years.

5 In Hebron he reigned over Judah [a]seven years and six months: and in Jerusalem he

---

39 [a]2 Sam. 19:5–7 [b]1 Kin. 2:5, 6, 32–34; 2 Tim. 4:14

CHAPTER 4

1 [a]Ezra 4:4; Is. 13:7 [b]Matt. 2:3
2 [a]Josh. 18:25
3 [a]Neh. 11:33
4 [a]2 Sam. 9:3 [b]1 Sam. 29:1, 11 [c]2 Sam. 9:6
5 [a]2 Sam. 2:8, 9
6 [a]2 Sam. 2:23; 20:10
8 [a]1 Sam. 19:2, 10, 11; 23:15; 25:29
9 [a]Gen. 48:16; 1 Kin. 1:29; Ps. 31:7
10 [a]2 Sam. 1:2–16
11 [a][Gen. 9:5, 6; Ps. 9:12]
12 [a]2 Sam. 1:15 [b]2 Sam. 3:32

CHAPTER 5

1 [a]1 Chr. 11:1–3 [b]Gen. 29:14; Judg. 9:2; 2 Sam. 19:12, 13
2 [a]1 Sam. 18:5, 13, 16 [b]1 Sam. 16:1
3 [a]2 Sam. 3:17; 1 Chr. 11:3 [b]2 Sam. 2:4; 3:21; 2 Kin. 11:17 [c]Judg. 11:11; 1 Sam. 23:18
4 [a]Gen. 41:46; Num. 4:3; Luke 3:23 [b]1 Kin. 2:11; 1 Chr. 26:31; 29:27
5 [a]2 Sam. 2:11; 1 Chr. 3:4; 29:27

*

4:1 Ishbosheth
4:4 *Merib-Baal,* 1 Chr. 8:34; 9:40

NKJV

39 "And I *am* weak today, though anointed king; and these men, the sons of Zeruiah, [a]*are* too harsh for me. [b]The LORD shall repay the evildoer according to his wickedness."

Ishbosheth Is Murdered

4 When Saul's *son heard that Abner had died in Hebron, [a]he lost heart, and all Israel was [b]troubled.

2 Now Saul's son *had* two men *who were* captains of troops. The name of one *was* Baanah and the name of the other Rechab, the sons of Rimmon the Beerothite, of the children of Benjamin. (For [a]Beeroth also was *part* of Benjamin,

3 because the Beerothites fled to [a]Gittaim and have been sojourners there until this day.)

4 [a]Jonathan, Saul's son, had a son *who was* lame in *his* feet. He was five years old when the news about Saul and Jonathan came [b]from Jezreel; and his nurse took him up and fled. And it happened, as she made haste to flee, that he fell and became lame. His name *was* [c]Mephibosheth.*

5 Then the sons of Rimmon the Beerothite, Rechab and Baanah, set out and came at about the heat of the day to the [a]house of Ishbosheth, who was lying on his bed at noon.

6 And they came there, all the way into the house, *as though* to get wheat, and they stabbed him [a]in the stomach. Then Rechab and Baanah his brother escaped.

7 For when they came into the house, he was lying on his bed in his bedroom; then they struck him and killed him, beheaded him and took his head, and were all night escaping through the plain.

8 And they brought the head of Ishbosheth to David at Hebron, and said to the king, "Here is the head of Ishbosheth, the son of Saul your enemy, [a]who sought your life; and the LORD has avenged my lord the king this day of Saul and his descendants."

9 But David answered Rechab and Baanah his brother, the sons of Rimmon the Beerothite, and said to them, "*As* the LORD lives, [a]who has redeemed my life from all adversity,

10 "when [a]someone told me, saying, 'Look, Saul is dead,' thinking to have brought good news, I arrested him and had him executed in Ziklag—the one who *thought* I would give him a reward for *his* news.

11 "How much more, when wicked men have killed a righteous person in his own house on his bed? Therefore, shall I not now [a]require his blood at your hand and remove you from the earth?"

12 So David [a]commanded his young men, and they executed them, cut off their hands and feet, and hanged *them* by the pool in Hebron. But they took the head of Ishbosheth and buried *it* in the [b]tomb of Abner in Hebron.

David Reigns over All Israel
(1 Chr. 11:1–3)

5 Then all the tribes of Israel [a]came to David at Hebron and spoke, saying, "Indeed [b]we *are* your bone and your flesh.

2 "Also, in time past, when Saul was king over us, [a]you were the one who led Israel out and brought them in; and the LORD said to you, [b]'You shall shepherd My people Israel, and be ruler over Israel.' "

3 [a]Therefore all the elders of Israel came to the king at Hebron, [b]and King David made a covenant with them at Hebron [c]before the LORD. And they anointed David king over Israel.

4 David *was* [a]thirty years old when he began to reign, *and* [b]he reigned forty years.

5 In Hebron he reigned over Judah [a]seven years and six months, and in Jerusalem he

KJV

reigned thirty and three years over all Israel and
Judah.

The Conquest of Jerusalem
(1 Chr. 11:4–9; 14:1–7)

6 [a]And the king and his men went to Jerusalem unto [b]the Jebusites, the inhabitants of the
land: which spake unto David, saying, Except
thou take away the blind and the lame, thou shalt
not come in hither: thinking, David cannot come
in hither.
7 Nevertheless David took the strong hold
of Zion: [a]the same *is* the city of David.
8 And David said on that day, Whosoever
getteth up to the gutter, and smiteth the Jebusites,
and the lame and the blind, *that are* hated of David's soul, [a]*he shall be chief and captain.* Wherefore they said, The blind and the lame shall not
come into the house.
9 So David dwelt in the fort, and called it
[a]the city of David. And David built round about
from Millo and inward.
10 And David went on, and grew great, and
[a]the LORD God of hosts *was* with [b]him.
11 And [a]Hiram [b]king of Tyre sent messengers to David, and cedar trees, and carpenters,
and masons: and they built David an house.
12 And David perceived that the LORD had
established him king over Israel, and that he had
[a]exalted his kingdom for his people Israel's [b]sake.
13 And [a]David took *him* more concubines
and wives out of Jerusalem, after he was come
from Hebron: and there were yet sons and daughters born to David.
14 And [a]these *be* the names of those that
were born unto him in Jerusalem; Shammuah,
and Shobab, and Nathan, and [b]Solomon,
15 Ibhar also, and Elishua, and Nepheg, and
Japhia,
16 And Elishama, and Eliada, and Eliphalet.

The Philistines Defeated
(1 Chr. 14:8–17)

17 [a]But when the Philistines heard that they
had anointed David king over Israel, all the Philistines came up to seek David; and David heard *of*
it, [b]and went down to the hold.
18 The Philistines also came and spread
themselves in [a]the valley of Rephaim.
19 And David [a]enquired of the LORD, saying,
Shall I go up to the Philistines? wilt thou deliver
them into mine hand? And the LORD said unto
David, Go up: for I will doubtless deliver the Philistines into thine hand.
20 And David came to [a]Baal–perazim, and
David smote them there, and said, The LORD hath
broken forth upon mine enemies before me, as
the breach of waters. Therefore he called the
name of that place Baal–perazim.
21 And there they left their images, and David and his men [a]burned them.
22 [a]And the Philistines came up yet again,
and spread themselves in the valley of Rephaim.
23 And when [a]David enquired of the LORD,
he said, Thou shalt not go up; *but* fetch a compass
behind them, and come upon them over against
the mulberry trees.
24 And let it be, when thou [a]hearest the
sound of a going in the tops of the mulberry trees,
that then thou shalt bestir thyself: for then [b]shall
the LORD go out before thee, to smite the host of
the Philistines.
25 And David did so, as the LORD had commanded him; and smote the Philistines from
[a]Geba until thou come to [b]Gazer.

The Ark Brought to Jerusalem
(1 Chr. 13:1–14; 15:25—16:3)

6 Again, David gathered together all *the* chosen
men of Israel, thirty thousand.
2 And [a]David arose, and went with all the
people that *were* with him from Baale of Judah,

6 [a]Judg. 1:21 [b]Josh. 15:63; Judg. 1:8; 19:11, 12
7 [a]2 Sam. 6:12, 16; 1 Kin. 2:10; 8:1; 9:24
8 [a]1 Chr. 11:6–9
9 [a]2 Sam. 5:7; 1 Kin. 9:15, 24
10 [a]1 Sam. 17:45 [b]1 Sam. 18:12, 28
11 [a]1 Kin. 5:1–18 [b]1 Chr. 14:1
12 [a]Num. 24:7 [b]Is. 45:4
13 [a][Deut. 17:17]; 1 Chr. 3:9
14 [a]1 Chr. 3:5–8 [b]2 Sam. 12:24
17 [a]1 Chr. 11:16 [b]2 Sam. 23:14
18 [a]Gen. 14:5; Josh. 15:8; 1 Chr. 11:15; Is. 17:5
19 [a]1 Sam. 23:2; 2 Sam. 2:1
20 [a]1 Chr. 14:11; Is. 28:21
21 [a]Deut. 7:5, 25
22 [a]1 Chr. 14:13
23 [a]2 Sam. 5:19
24 [a]2 Kin. 7:6; 1 Chr. 14:15 [b]Judg. 4:14
25 [a]1 Chr. 14:16 [b]Josh. 16:10

CHAPTER 6

2 [a]1 Chr. 13:5, 6

*

5:9 Lit. *The Landfill*
5:14 *Shimea,* 1 Chr. 3:5
5:15 *Elishama,* 1 Chr. 3:6
5:20 Lit. *Master of Breakthroughs*
5:25 So with MT, Tg., Vg.; LXX *Gibeon*

NKJV

reigned thirty-three years over all Israel and Judah.

The Conquest of Jerusalem
(1 Chr. 11:4–9; 14:1–7)

6 [a]And the king and his men went to Jerusalem against [b]the Jebusites, the inhabitants of the
land, who spoke to David, saying, "You shall not
come in here; but the blind and the lame will repel
you," thinking, "David cannot come in here."
7 Nevertheless David took the stronghold of
Zion [a](that *is,* the City of David).
8 Now David said on that day, "Whoever
climbs up by way of the water shaft and defeats
the Jebusites (the lame and the blind, *who are*
hated by David's soul), [a]*he shall be chief and cap-*
tain." Therefore they say, "The blind and the lame
shall not come into the house."
9 Then David dwelt in the stronghold, and
called it [a]the City of David. And David built all
around from *the Millo and inward.
10 So David went on and became great, and
[a]the LORD God of hosts *was* with [b]him.
11 Then [a]Hiram [b]king of Tyre sent messengers to David, and cedar trees, and carpenters and
masons. And they built David a house.
12 So David knew that the LORD had established him as king over Israel, and that He had
[a]exalted His kingdom [b]for the sake of His people
Israel.
13 And [a]David took more concubines and
wives from Jerusalem, after he had come from
Hebron. Also more sons and daughters were born
to David.
14 Now [a]these *are* the names of those who
were born to him in Jerusalem: *Shammua, Shobab, Nathan, [b]Solomon,
15 Ibhar, *Elishua, Nepheg, Japhia,
16 Elishama, Eliada, and Eliphelet.

The Philistines Defeated
(1 Chr. 14:8–17)

17 [a]Now when the Philistines heard that they
had anointed David king over Israel, all the Philistines went up to search for David. And David
heard *of it* [b]and went down to the stronghold.
18 The Philistines also went and deployed
themselves in [a]the Valley of Rephaim.
19 So David [a]inquired of the LORD, saying,
"Shall I go up against the Philistines? Will You
deliver them into my hand?" And the LORD said
to David, "Go up, for I will doubtless deliver the
Philistines into your hand."
20 So David went to [a]Baal Perazim, and David defeated them there; and he said, "The LORD
has broken through my enemies before me, like
a breakthrough of water." Therefore he called the
name of that place *Baal Perazim.
21 And they left their images there, and David and his men [a]carried them away.
22 [a]Then the Philistines went up once again
and deployed themselves in the Valley of Rephaim.
23 Therefore [a]David inquired of the LORD,
and He said, "You shall not go up; circle around
behind them, and come upon them in front of the
mulberry trees.
24 "And it shall be, when you [a]hear the
sound of marching in the tops of the mulberry
trees, then you shall advance quickly. For then
[b]the LORD will go out before you to strike the camp
of the Philistines."
25 And David did so, as the LORD commanded him; and he drove back the Philistines
from [a]Geba* as far as [b]Gezer.

The Ark Brought to Jerusalem
(1 Chr. 13:1–14; 15:25—16:3)

6 Again David gathered all *the* choice *men* of
Israel, thirty thousand.
2 And [a]David arose and went with all the
people who *were* with him from Baale Judah to

KJV

to bring up from thence the ark of God, whose
name is called by the name of the LORD of hosts
[b]that dwelleth *between* the cherubims.
3 And they set the ark of God upon a new
cart, and brought it out of the house of Abinadab
that *was* in [a]Gibeah: and Uzzah and Ahio, the
sons of Abinadab, drave the new cart.
4 And they brought it out of [a]the house of
Abinadab which *was* at Gibeah, accompanying
the ark of God: and Ahio went before the ark.
5 And David and all the house of Israel
[a]played before the LORD on all manner of *instru-*
ments made of fir wood, even on harps, and on
psalteries, and on timbrels, and on cornets, and
on cymbals.
6 And when they came to [a]Nachon's threshingfloor, Uzzah put forth *his* [b]*hand* to the ark of
God, and took hold of it; for the oxen shook *it*.
7 And the anger of the LORD was kindled
against Uzzah; and God smote him there for *his*
error; and there he died by the ark of God.
8 And David was displeased, because the
LORD had made a breach upon Uzzah: and he
called the name of the place Perez–uzzah to this
day.
9 And [a]David was afraid of the LORD that
day, and said, How shall the ark of the LORD come
to me?
10 So David would not remove the ark of the
LORD unto him into the [a]city of David: but David
carried it aside into the house of Obed–edom the
[b]Gittite.
11 [a]And the ark of the LORD continued in the
house of Obed–edom the Gittite three months: and
the LORD [b]blessed Obed–edom, and all his
household.
12 And it was told king David, saying, The
LORD hath blessed the house of Obed–edom, and
all that *pertaineth* unto him, because of the ark
of God. [a]So David went and brought up the ark
of God from the house of Obed–edom into the
city of David with gladness.
13 And it was *so*, that when [a]they that bare
the ark of the LORD had gone six paces, he sacrificed [b]oxen and fatlings.
14 And David [a]danced before the LORD with
all *his* might; and David *was* girded [b]with a linen
ephod.
15 [a]So David and all the house of Israel
brought up the ark of the LORD with shouting, and
with the sound of the trumpet.
16 And as the ark of the LORD came into the
city of David, [a]Michal Saul's daughter looked
through a window, and saw king David leaping
and dancing before the LORD; and she despised
him in her heart.
17 And [a]they brought in the ark of the LORD,
and set it in [b]his place, in the midst of the tabernacle that David had pitched for it: and David [c]of-
fered burnt offerings and peace offerings before
the LORD.
18 And as soon as David had made an end
of offering burnt offerings and peace offerings,
[a]he blessed the people in the name of the LORD
of hosts.
19 [a]And he dealt among all the people, *even*
among the whole multitude of Israel, as well to
the women as men, to every one a cake of bread,
and a good piece *of flesh*, and a flagon *of wine*.
So all the people departed every one to his house.
20 [a]Then David returned to bless his household. And Michal the daughter of Saul came out
to meet David, and said, How glorious was the
king of Israel to day, who [b]uncovered himself to
day in the eyes of the handmaids of his servants,
as one of the [c]vain fellows shamelessly uncovereth himself!
21 And David said unto Michal, *It was* before
the LORD, [a]which chose me before thy father, and
before all his house, to appoint me ruler over the
[b]people of the LORD, over Israel: therefore will I
play before the LORD.

2 [b]Ex. 25:22; 1 Sam. 4:4; Ps. 80:1
3 [a]1 Sam. 26:1
4 [a]1 Sam. 7:1; 1 Chr. 13:7
5 [a]1 Sam. 18:6, 7
6 [a]1 Chr. 13:9 [b]Num. 4:15, 19, 20
9 [a]Deut. 9:19; Ps. 119:120; Luke 5:8
10 [a]2 Sam. 5:7 [b]1 Chr. 13:13; 26:4–8
11 [a]1 Chr. 13:14 [b]Gen. 30:27; 39:5
12 [a]1 Chr. 15:25—16:3
13 [a]Num. 4:15; Josh. 3:3; 1 Sam. 6:15; 2 Sam. 15:24; 1 Chr. 15:2, 15 [b]1 Kin. 8:5
14 [a]Ps. 30:11; 149:3 [b]1 Sam. 2:18, 28
15 [a]1 Chr. 15:28
16 [a]2 Sam. 3:14
17 [a]1 Chr. 16:1 [b]1 Chr. 15:1; 2 Chr. 1:4 [c]1 Kin. 8:5, 62, 63
18 [a]1 Kin. 8:14, 15, 55
19 [a]1 Chr. 16:3
20 [a]Ps. 30:title [b]2 Sam. 6:14, 16 [c]Judg. 9:4
21 [a]1 Sam. 13:14; 15:28 [b]2 Kin. 11:17

NKJV

bring up from there the ark of God, whose name
is called *by the Name, the LORD of Hosts, [b]who
dwells *between* the cherubim.
3 So they set the ark of God on a new cart,
and brought it out of the house of Abinadab,
which *was* on [a]the hill; and Uzzah and Ahio, the
sons of Abinadab, drove the new *cart.
4 And they brought it out of [a]the house of
Abinadab, which *was* on the hill, accompanying
the ark of God; and Ahio went before the ark.
5 Then David and all the house of Israel
[a]played *music* before the LORD on all kinds of
instruments of fir wood, on harps, on stringed
instruments, on tambourines, on sistrums, and
on cymbals.
6 And when they came to [a]Nachon's threshing floor, Uzzah put out *his* [b]*hand* to the ark of
God and took hold of it, for the oxen stumbled.
7 Then the anger of the LORD was aroused
against Uzzah, and God struck him there for *his*
error; and he died there by the ark of God.
8 And David became angry because of the
LORD's outbreak against Uzzah; and he called the
name of the place *Perez Uzzah to this day.
9 [a]David was afraid of the LORD that day;
and he said, "How can the ark of the LORD come
to me?"
10 So David would not move the ark of the
LORD with him into the [a]City of David; but David
took it aside into the house of Obed-Edom the
[b]Gittite.
11 [a]The ark of the LORD remained in the
house of Obed-Edom the Gittite three months.
And the LORD [b]blessed Obed-Edom and all his
household.
12 Now it was told King David, saying, "The
LORD has blessed the house of Obed-Edom and
all that *belongs* to him, because of the ark of God."
[a]So David went and brought up the ark of God
from the house of Obed-Edom to the City of David
with gladness.
13 And so it was, when [a]those bearing the
ark of the LORD had gone six paces, that he sacrificed [b]oxen and fatted sheep.
14 Then David [a]danced before the LORD with
all *his* might; and David *was* wearing [b]a linen
ephod.
15 [a]So David and all the house of Israel
brought up the ark of the LORD with shouting and
with the sound of the trumpet.
16 Now as the ark of the LORD came into the
City of David, [a]Michal, Saul's daughter, looked
through a window and saw King David leaping
and whirling before the LORD; and she despised
him in her heart.
17 So [a]they brought the ark of the LORD, and
set it in [b]its place in the midst of the tabernacle
that David had erected for it. Then David [c]offered
burnt offerings and peace offerings before the
LORD.
18 And when David had finished offering
burnt offerings and peace offerings, [a]he blessed
the people in the name of the LORD of hosts.
19 [a]Then he distributed among all the people,
among the whole multitude of Israel, both the
women and the men, to everyone a loaf of bread,
a piece *of meat*, and a cake of raisins. So all the
people departed, everyone to his house.
20 [a]Then David returned to bless his household. And Michal the daughter of Saul came out
to meet David, and said, "How glorious was the
king of Israel today, [b]uncovering himself today
in the eyes of the maids of his servants, as one
of the [c]base fellows shamelessly uncovers
himself!"
21 So David said to Michal, "*It was* before
the LORD, [a]who chose me instead of your father
and all his house, to appoint me ruler over the
[b]people of the LORD, over Israel. Therefore I will
play *music* before the LORD.

*
6:2 LXX, Tg., Vg. omit *by the Name;* many Heb. mss., Syr. *there*
6:3 LXX adds *with the ark*
6:8 Lit. *Outburst Against Uzzah*

KJV

22 And I will yet be more vile than thus, and will be base in mine own sight: and of the maidservants which thou hast spoken of, of them shall I be had in honour.

23 Therefore Michal the daughter of Saul had no child [a]unto the day of her death.

God's Covenant with David
(1 Chr. 17:1–15)

7 And it came to pass, [a]when the king sat in his house, and the LORD had given him rest round about from all his enemies;

2 That the king said unto Nathan the prophet, See now, I dwell in [a]an house of cedar, [b]but the ark of God dwelleth within [c]curtains.

3 And Nathan said to the king, Go, do all that *is* in thine [a]heart; for the LORD *is* with thee.

4 And it came to pass that night, that the word of the LORD came unto Nathan, saying,

5 Go and tell my servant David, Thus saith the LORD, [a]Shalt thou build me an house for me to dwell in?

6 Whereas I have not dwelt in *any* house [a]since the time that I brought up the children of Israel out of Egypt, even to this day, but have walked in [b]a tent and in a tabernacle.

7 In all *the places* wherein I have [a]walked with all the children of Israel spake I a word with any of the tribes of Israel, whom I commanded [b]to feed my people Israel, saying, Why build ye not me an house of cedar?

8 Now therefore so shalt thou say unto my servant David, Thus saith the LORD of hosts, [a]I took thee from the sheepcote, from following the sheep, to be ruler over my people, over Israel:

9 And [a]I was with thee whithersoever thou wentest, [b]and have cut off all thine enemies out of thy sight, and have made thee a great name, like unto the name of the great *men* that *are* in the earth.

10 Moreover I will appoint a place for my people Israel, and will [a]plant them, that they may dwell in a place of their own, and move no more; [b]neither shall the children of wickedness afflict them any more, as beforetime,

11 And as [a]since the time that I commanded judges *to be* over my people Israel, and have caused thee to rest from all thine enemies. Also the LORD telleth thee [b]that he will make thee an house.

12 And [a]when thy days be fulfilled, and thou [b]shalt sleep with thy fathers, [c]I will set up thy seed after thee, which shall proceed out of thy bowels, and I will establish his kingdom.

13 [a]He shall build an house for my name, and I will [b]stablish the throne of his kingdom for ever.

14 [a]I will be his father, and he shall be [b]my son. If he commit iniquity, I will chasten him with the rod of men, and with the stripes of the children of men:

15 But my mercy shall not depart away from him, [a]as I took *it* from Saul, whom I put away before thee.

16 And [a]thine house and thy kingdom shall be established for ever before thee: thy throne shall be established for ever.

17 According to all these words, and according to all this vision, so did Nathan speak unto David.

David's Thanksgiving to God
(1 Chr. 17:16–27)

18 Then went king David in, and sat before the LORD, and he said, [a]Who *am* I, O Lord GOD? and what *is* my house, that thou hast brought me hitherto?

19 And this was yet a small thing in thy sight, O Lord GOD; but thou hast spoken also of thy servant's house for a great while to come. [a]And *is* this the manner of man, O Lord GOD?

20 And what can David say more unto thee? for thou, Lord GOD, [a]knowest thy servant.

---

23 [a]1 Sam. 15:35; Is. 22:14

CHAPTER 7

1 [a]1 Chr. 17:1–27
2 [a]2 Sam. 5:11 [b]Acts 7:46 [c]Ex. 26:1
3 [a]1 Kin. 8:17, 18; 1 Chr. 22:7
5 [a]1 Kin. 5:3, 4; 8:19; 1 Chr. 22:8
6 [a]Josh. 18:1; 1 Kin. 8:16 [b]Ex. 40:18, 34
7 [a]Lev. 26:11, 12 [b]2 Sam. 5:2; [Acts 20:28]
8 [a]1 Sam. 16:11, 12; Ps. 78:70, 71
9 [a]1 Sam. 18:14; 2 Sam. 5:10 [b]1 Sam. 31:6
10 [a]Ex. 15:17; Ps. 44:2; 80:8; Jer. 24:6 [b]Ps. 89:22, 23; Is. 60:18
11 [a]Judg. 2:14–16 [b]Ex. 1:21; 1 Sam. 25:28; 2 Sam. 7:27
12 [a]1 Kin. 2:1 [b]Deut. 31:16; Acts 13:36 [c]1 Kin. 8:20; Ps. 132:11; Matt. 1:6; Luke 3:31
13 [a]1 Kin. 5:5; 8:19; 2 Chr. 6:2 [b]2 Sam. 7:16; [Is. 9:7; 49:8]
14 [a][Heb. 1:5] [b][Ps. 2:7; 89:26, 27, 30]; Matt. 3:17
15 [a]1 Sam. 15:23, 28; 16:14
16 [a]2 Sam. 7:13; Ps. 89:36, 37; Matt. 25:31; John 12:34
18 [a]Gen. 32:10; Ex. 3:11; 1 Sam. 18:18
19 [a][Is. 55:8, 9]
20 [a][1 Sam. 16:7]; Ps. 139:1; John 21:17

---

*
7:11 Royal dynasty
7:16 LXX *Me*

NKJV

22 "And I will be even more undignified than this, and will be humble in my own sight. But as for the maidservants of whom you have spoken, by them I will be held in honor."

23 Therefore Michal the daughter of Saul had no children [a]to the day of her death.

God's Covenant with David
(1 Chr. 17:1–15)

7 Now it came to pass [a]when the king was dwelling in his house, and the LORD had given him rest from all his enemies all around,

2 that the king said to Nathan the prophet, "See now, I dwell in [a]a house of cedar, [b]but the ark of God dwells inside tent [c]curtains."

3 Then Nathan said to the king, "Go, do all that *is* in your [a]heart, for the LORD *is* with you."

4 But it happened that night that the word of the LORD came to Nathan, saying,

5 "Go and tell My servant David, 'Thus says the LORD: [a]"Would you build a house for Me to dwell in?

6 "For I have not dwelt in a house [a]since the time that I brought the children of Israel up from Egypt, even to this day, but have moved about in [b]a tent and in a tabernacle.

7 "Wherever I have [a]moved about with all the children of Israel, have I ever spoken a word to anyone from the tribes of Israel, whom I commanded [b]to shepherd My people Israel, saying, 'Why have you not built Me a house of cedar?' " '

8 "Now therefore, thus shall you say to My servant David, 'Thus says the LORD of hosts: [a]"I took you from the sheepfold, from following the sheep, to be ruler over My people, over Israel.

9 "And [a]I have been with you wherever you have gone, [b]and have cut off all your enemies from before you, and have made you a great name, like the name of the great men who *are* on the earth.

10 "Moreover I will appoint a place for My people Israel, and will [a]plant them, that they may dwell in a place of their own and move no more; [b]nor shall the sons of wickedness oppress them anymore, as previously,

11 [a]"since the time that I commanded judges *to be* over My people Israel, and have caused you to rest from all your enemies. Also the LORD tells you [b]that He will make you a *house.

12 [a]"When your days are fulfilled and you [b]rest with your fathers, [c]I will set up your seed after you, who will come from your body, and I will establish his kingdom.

13 [a]"He shall build a house for My name, and I will [b]establish the throne of his kingdom forever.

14 [a]"I will be his Father, and he shall be [b]My son. If he commits iniquity, I will chasten him with the rod of men and with the blows of the sons of men.

15 "But My mercy shall not depart from him, [a]as I took *it* from Saul, whom I removed from before you.

16 "And [a]your house and your kingdom shall be established forever before *you. Your throne shall be established forever." ' "

17 According to all these words and according to all this vision, so Nathan spoke to David.

David's Thanksgiving to God
(1 Chr. 17:16–27)

18 Then King David went in and sat before the LORD; and he said: [a]"Who *am* I, O Lord GOD? And what is my house, that You have brought me this far?

19 "And yet this was a small thing in Your sight, O Lord GOD; and You have also spoken of Your servant's house for a great while to come. [a]*Is* this the manner of man, O Lord GOD?

20 "Now what more can David say to You? For You, Lord GOD, [a]know Your servant.

KJV

21 For thy word's sake, and according to thine own heart, hast thou done all these great things, to make thy servant know *them.*

22 Wherefore [a]thou art great, O LORD God: for [b]*there is* none like thee, neither *is there any* God beside thee, according to all that we have heard with our [c]ears.

23 And [a]what one nation in the earth *is* like thy people, *even* like Israel, whom God went to redeem for a people to himself, and to make him a name, and to do for you great things and terrible, for thy land, before [b]thy people, which thou redeemedst to thee from Egypt, *from* the nations and their gods?

24 For [a]thou hast confirmed to thyself thy people Israel *to be* a people unto thee for ever: [b]and thou, LORD, art become their God.

25 And now, O LORD God, the word that thou hast spoken concerning thy servant, and concerning his house, establish *it* for ever, and do as thou hast said.

26 And let thy name be magnified for ever, saying, The LORD of hosts *is* the God over Israel: and let the house of thy servant David be established before thee.

27 For thou, O LORD of hosts, God of Israel, hast revealed to thy servant, saying, I will build thee an house: therefore hath thy servant found in his heart to pray this prayer unto thee.

28 And now, O Lord GOD, thou *art* that God, and [a]thy words be true, and thou hast promised this goodness unto thy servant:

29 Therefore now let it please thee to bless the house of thy servant, that it may continue for ever before thee: for thou, O Lord GOD, hast spoken *it:* and with thy blessing let the house of thy servant be blessed [a]for ever.

David's Further Conquests
(*1 Chr. 18:1–13*)

8 And after this it came to pass, that David smote the Philistines, and subdued them: and David took Metheg–ammah out of the hand of the Philistines.

2 And [a]he smote Moab, and measured them with a line, casting them down to the ground; even with two lines measured he to put to death, and with one full line to keep alive. And so the Moabites became David's [b]servants, *and* [c]brought gifts.

3 David smote also Hadadezer, the son of Rehob, king of [a]Zobah, as he went to recover [b]his border at the river Euphrates.

4 And David took from him a thousand *chariots,* and seven hundred horsemen, and twenty thousand footmen: and David [a]houghed all the chariot *horses,* but reserved of them *for* an hundred chariots.

5 [a]And when the Syrians of Damascus came to succour Hadadezer king of Zobah, David slew of the Syrians two and twenty thousand men.

6 Then David put garrisons in Syria of Damascus: and the Syrians became servants to David, *and* brought gifts. [a]And the LORD preserved David whithersoever he went.

7 And David took [a]the shields of gold that were on the servants of Hadadezer, and brought them to Jerusalem.

8 And from Betah, and from [a]Berothai, cities of Hadadezer, king David took exceeding much brass.

9 When Toi king of [a]Hamath heard that David had smitten all the host of Hadadezer,

10 Then Toi sent Joram his son unto king David, to salute him, and to bless him, because he had fought against Hadadezer, and smitten him: for Hadadezer had wars with Toi. And *Joram* brought with him vessels of silver, and vessels of gold, and vessels of brass:

11 Which also king David [a]did dedicate unto

22 [a]Deut. 10:17; 1 Chr. 16:25; 2 Chr. 2:5; Ps. 86:10; Jer. 10:6 [b]Ex. 15:11; Deut. 3:24; 4:35; 32:39 [c]Ex. 10:2; Ps. 44:1
23 [a]Ps. 147:20 [b]Deut. 9:26; 33:29
24 [a]Gen. 17:7, 8; Ex. 6:7; [Deut. 26:18] [b]Ps. 48:14
28 [a]Ex. 34:6; Josh. 21:45; John 17:17
29 [a]2 Sam. 22:51

CHAPTER 8

2 [a]Num. 24:17 [b]2 Sam. 12:31 [c]1 Sam. 10:27; 1 Kin. 4:21
3 [a]1 Sam. 14:47; 2 Sam. 10:16, 19 [b]Gen. 15:18; 2 Sam. 10:15–19
4 [a]Josh. 11:6, 9
5 [a]1 Kin. 11:23–25
6 [a]2 Sam. 7:9; 8:14
7 [a]1 Kin. 10:16
8 [a]Ezek. 47:16
9 [a]1 Kin. 8:65; 2 Kin. 14:28; 2 Chr. 8:4
11 [a]1 Kin. 7:51

NKJV

21 "For Your word's sake, and according to Your own heart, You have done all these great things, to make Your servant know *them.*

22 "Therefore [a]You are great, *O Lord GOD. For [b]*there is* none like You, nor *is there any* God besides You, according to all that we have heard with our [c]ears.

23 "And who *is* like Your people, like Israel, [a]the one nation on the earth whom God went to redeem for Himself as a people, to make for Himself a name—and to do for Yourself great and awesome deeds for Your land—before [b]Your people whom You redeemed for Yourself from Egypt, the nations, and their gods?

24 "For [a]You have made Your people Israel Your very own people forever; [b]and You, LORD, have become their God.

25 "Now, O LORD God, the word which You have spoken concerning Your servant and concerning his house, establish *it* forever and do as You have said.

26 "So let Your name be magnified forever, saying, 'The LORD of hosts *is* the God over Israel.' And let the house of Your servant David be established before You.

27 "For You, O LORD of hosts, God of Israel, have revealed *this* to Your servant, saying, 'I will build you a house.' Therefore Your servant has found it in his heart to pray this prayer to You.

28 "And now, O Lord GOD, You are God, and [a]Your words are true, and You have promised this goodness to Your servant.

29 "Now therefore, let it please You to bless the house of Your servant, that it may continue before You forever; for You, O Lord GOD, have spoken *it,* and with Your blessing let the house of Your servant be blessed [a]forever."

David's Further Conquests
(*1 Chr. 18:1–13*)

8 After this it came to pass that David attacked the Philistines and subdued them. And David took Metheg Ammah from the hand of the Philistines.

2 Then [a]he defeated Moab. Forcing them down to the ground, he measured them off with a line. With two lines he measured off those to be put to death, and with one full line those to be kept alive. So the Moabites became David's [b]servants, *and* [c]brought tribute.

3 David also defeated Hadadezer the son of Rehob, king of [a]Zobah, as he went to recover [b]his territory at the River Euphrates.

4 David took from him one thousand *chariots,* *seven hundred horsemen, and twenty thousand foot soldiers. Also David [a]hamstrung all the chariot horses, except that he spared *enough* of them for one hundred chariots.

5 [a]When the Syrians of Damascus came to help Hadadezer king of Zobah, David killed twenty-two thousand of the Syrians.

6 Then David put garrisons in Syria of Damascus; and the Syrians became David's servants, *and* brought tribute. So [a]the LORD preserved David wherever he went.

7 And David took [a]the shields of gold that had belonged to the servants of Hadadezer, and brought them to Jerusalem.

8 Also from *Betah and from [a]Berothai, cities of Hadadezer, King David took a large amount of bronze.

9 When *Toi king of [a]Hamath heard that David had defeated all the army of Hadadezer,

10 then Toi sent *Joram his son to King David, to greet him and bless him, because he had fought against Hadadezer and defeated him (for Hadadezer had been at war with Toi); and *Joram* brought with him articles of silver, articles of gold, and articles of bronze.

11 King David also [a]dedicated these to the LORD, along with the silver and gold that he had

*

7:22 Tg., Syr. *O LORD God*
8:4 *seven thousand,* 1 Chr. 18:4
8:8 *Tibhath,* 1 Chr. 18:8
8:9 *Tou,* 1 Chr. 18:9
8:10 *Hadoram,* 1 Chr. 18:10

KJV

the LORD, with the silver and gold that he had
dedicated of all nations which he subdued;
12 Of Syria, and of Moab, and of the children
of Ammon, and of the [a]Philistines, and of Amalek,
and of the spoil of Hadadezer, son of Rehob, king
of Zobah.
13 And David gat *him* a [a]name when he returned from smiting of the Syrians in [c]the valley
of salt, [b]*being* eighteen thousand *men*.
14 And he put garrisons in Edom; throughout
all Edom put he garrisons, and [a]all they of Edom
became David's servants. And the LORD preserved
David whithersoever he went.

David's Administration
(1 Chr. 18:14–17)

15 And David reigned over all Israel; and David executed judgment and justice unto all his
people.
16 [a]And Joab the son of Zeruiah *was* over
the host; and [b]Jehoshaphat the son of Ahilud *was*
recorder;
17 And [a]Zadok the son of Ahitub, and Ahimelech the son of Abiathar, *were* the priests; and
Seraiah *was* the scribe;
18 [a]And Benaiah the son of Jehoiada *was*
over both the [b]Cherethites and the Pelethites; and
David's sons were chief rulers.

David's Kindness to Mephibosheth

9 And David said, Is there yet any that is left
of the house of Saul, that I may [a]shew him
kindness for Jonathan's sake?
2 And *there was* of the house of Saul a servant whose name *was* [a]Ziba. And when they had
called him unto David, the king said unto him,
Art thou Ziba? And he said, Thy servant *is he*.
3 And the king said, *Is* there not yet any of
the house of Saul, that I may shew [a]the kindness
of God unto him? And Ziba said unto the king,
Jonathan hath yet a son, *which is* [b]lame on *his*
feet.
4 And the king said unto him, Where *is* he?
And Ziba said unto the king, Behold, he *is* in the
house of [a]Machir, the son of Ammiel, in Lo–debar.
5 Then king David sent, and fetched him out
of the house of Machir, the son of Ammiel, from
Lo–debar.
6 Now when [a]Mephibosheth, the son of Jonathan, the son of Saul, was come unto David, he
fell on his face, and did reverence. And David
said, Mephibosheth. And he answered, Behold thy
servant!
7 And David said unto him, Fear not: for I
will surely shew thee kindness for Jonathan thy
father's sake, and will restore thee all the land
of Saul thy father; and thou shalt eat bread at
my table continually.
8 And he bowed himself, and said, What *is*
thy servant, that thou shouldest look upon such
[a]a dead dog as I *am*?
9 Then the king called to Ziba, Saul's servant, and said unto him, [a]I have given unto thy
master's son all that pertained to Saul and to all
his house.
10 Thou therefore, and thy sons, and thy servants, shall till the land for him, and thou shalt
bring in *the fruits*, that thy master's son may have
food to eat: but Mephibosheth thy master's son
[a]shall eat bread alway at my table. Now Ziba had
[b]fifteen sons and twenty servants.
11 Then said Ziba unto the king, According
to all that my lord the king hath commanded his
servant, so shall thy servant do. As for Mephibosheth, *said the king*, he shall eat at my table,
as one of the king's sons.
12 And Mephibosheth had a young son,
[a]whose name *was* Micha. And all that dwelt in
the house of Ziba *were* servants unto Mephibosheth.
13 So Mephibosheth dwelt in Jerusalem: [a]for

---

12 [a]2 Sam. 5:17–25
13 [a]2 Sam. 7:9 [b]2 Kin. 14:7 [c]1 Chr. 18:12; Ps. 60:title
14 [a]Gen. 27:29, 37–40; Num. 24:18; 1 Kin. 11:15
16 [a]2 Sam. 19:13; 20:23; 1 Chr. 11:6 [b]1 Kin. 4:3
17 [a]1 Chr. 6:4–8; 24:3
18 [a]1 Kin. 1:8; 1 Chr. 18:17 [b]1 Sam. 30:14; 1 Kin. 1:38

CHAPTER 9

1 [a]1 Sam. 18:3; 20:14–16; 2 Sam. 21:7; [Prov. 27:10]
2 [a]2 Sam. 16:1–4; 19:17, 29
3 [a]1 Sam. 20:14 [b]2 Sam. 4:4
4 [a]2 Sam. 17:27–29
6 [a]2 Sam. 16:4; 19:24–30
8 [a]2 Sam. 16:9
9 [a]2 Sam. 16:4; 19:29
10 [a]2 Sam. 9:7, 11, 13; 19:28 [b]2 Sam. 19:17
12 [a]1 Chr. 8:34
13 [a]2 Sam. 9:7, 10, 11; 1 Kin. 2:7; 2 Kin. 25:29

NKJV

dedicated from all the nations which he had subdued—
12 from *Syria, from Moab, from the people
of Ammon, from the [a]Philistines, from Amalek,
and from the spoil of Hadadezer the son of Rehob,
king of Zobah.
13 And David made *himself* a [a]name when
he returned from killing [b]eighteen thousand *Syrians in [c]the Valley of Salt.
14 He also put garrisons in Edom; throughout all Edom he put garrisons, and [a]all the Edomites became David's servants. And the LORD preserved David wherever he went.

David's Administration
(1 Chr. 18:14–17)

15 So David reigned over all Israel; and David administered judgment and justice to all his
people.
16 [a]Joab the son of Zeruiah *was* over the
army; [b]Jehoshaphat the son of Ahilud *was*
recorder;
17 [a]Zadok the son of Ahitub and Ahimelech
the son of Abiathar *were* the priests; *Seraiah *was*
the scribe;
18 [a]Benaiah the son of Jehoiada *was over*
both the [b]Cherethites and the Pelethites; and David's sons were chief ministers.

David's Kindness to Mephibosheth

9 Now David said, "Is there still anyone who
is left of the house of Saul, that I may [a]show
him kindness for Jonathan's sake?"
2 And *there was* a servant of the house of
Saul whose name *was* [a]Ziba. So when they had
called him to David, the king said to him, "*Are*
you Ziba?" He said, "At your service!"
3 Then the king said, "*Is* there not still
someone of the house of Saul, to whom I may
show [a]the kindness of God?" And Ziba said to
the king, "There is still a son of Jonathan *who is*
[b]lame in *his* feet."
4 So the king said to him, "Where *is* he?"
And Ziba said to the king, "Indeed he *is* in the
house of [a]Machir the son of Ammiel, in Lo
Debar."
5 Then King David sent and brought him
out of the house of Machir the son of Ammiel,
from Lo Debar.
6 Now when [a]Mephibosheth the son of Jonathan, the son of Saul, had come to David, he
fell on his face and prostrated himself. Then David said, "Mephibosheth?" And he answered,
"Here is your servant!"
7 So David said to him, "Do not fear, for I
will surely show you kindness for Jonathan your
father's sake, and will restore to you all the land
of Saul your grandfather; and you shall eat bread
at my table continually."
8 Then he bowed himself, and said, "What
is your servant, that you should look upon such
[a]a dead dog as I?"
9 And the king called to Ziba, Saul's servant, and said to him, [a]"I have given to your master's son all that belonged to Saul and to all his
house.
10 "You therefore, and your sons and your
servants, shall work the land for him, and
you shall bring in *the harvest*, that your master's
son may have food to eat. But Mephibosheth your
master's son [a]shall eat bread at my table always."
Now Ziba had [b]fifteen sons and twenty servants.
11 Then Ziba said to the king, "According
to all that my lord the king has commanded his
servant, so will your servant do." "As for Mephibosheth," *said the king*, "he shall eat at *my table
like one of the king's sons."
12 Mephibosheth had a young son [a]whose
name *was* Micha. And all who dwelt in the house
of Ziba *were* servants of Mephibosheth.
13 So Mephibosheth dwelt in Jerusalem, [a]for

---

*

8:12 LXX, Syr., Heb. mss. *Edom*
8:13 LXX, Syr., Heb. mss. *Edomites* and 1 Chr. 18:12
8:17 *Shavsha,* 1 Chr. 18:16
9:11 LXX *David's table*

KJV

he did eat continually at the king's table; and [b]was
lame on both his feet.

The Ammonites and Syrians Defeated
(1 Chr. 19:1–19)

10 And it came to pass after this, that the [a]king
of the children of Ammon died, and Hanun
his son reigned in his stead.
2 Then said David, I will shew [a]kindness
unto Hanun the son of [b]Nahash, as his father
shewed kindness unto me. And David sent to comfort him by the hand of his servants for his father.
And David's servants came into the land of the
children of Ammon.
3 And the princes of the children of Ammon
said unto Hanun their lord, Thinkest thou that David doth honour thy father, that he hath sent comforters unto thee? hath not David *rather* sent his
servants unto thee, to search the city, and to spy
it out, and to overthrow it?
4 Wherefore Hanun took David's servants,
and shaved off the one half of their beards, and
cut off their garments in the middle, [a]*even* to their
buttocks, and sent them away.
5 When they told *it* unto David, he sent to
meet them, because the men were greatly
ashamed: and the king said, Tarry at Jericho until
your beards be grown, and *then* return.
6 And when the children of Ammon saw
that they [a]stank before David, the children of Ammon sent and hired [b]the Syrians of [c]Beth–rehob,
and the Syrians of Zoba, twenty thousand footmen, and of king [d]Maacah a thousand men, and
of [e]Ish–tob twelve thousand men.
7 And when David heard of *it*, he sent Joab,
and all the host of [a]the mighty men.
8 And the children of Ammon came out, and
put the battle in array at the entering in of the
gate: and [a]the Syrians of Zoba, and of Rehob, and
Ish–tob, and Maacah, *were* by themselves in the
field.
9 When Joab saw that the front of the battle
was against him before and behind, he chose of
all the choice *men* of Israel, and put *them* in array
against the Syrians:
10 And the rest of the people he delivered
into the hand of [a]Abishai his brother, that he
might put *them* in array against the children of
Ammon.
11 And he said, If the Syrians be too strong
for me, then thou shalt help me: but if the children
of Ammon be too strong for thee, then I will come
and help thee.
12 [a]Be of good courage, and let us [b]play the
men for our people, and for the cities of our God:
and [c]the LORD do that which seemeth him good.
13 And Joab drew nigh, and the people that
were with him, unto the battle against the Syrians:
and they fled before him.
14 And when the children of Ammon saw
that the Syrians were fled, then fled they also before Abishai, and entered into the city. So Joab
returned from the children of Ammon, and came
to [a]Jerusalem.
15 And when the Syrians saw that they were
smitten before Israel, they gathered themselves
together.
16 And Hadarezer sent, and brought out the
Syrians that *were* beyond the river: and they came
to Helam; and Shobach the captain of the host
of Hadarezer *went* before them.
17 And when it was told David, he gathered
all Israel together, and passed over Jordan, and
came to Helam. And the Syrians set themselves
in array against David, and fought with him.
18 And the Syrians fled before Israel; and
David slew *the men of* seven hundred chariots
of the Syrians, and forty thousand [a]horsemen,
and smote Shobach the captain of their host, who
died there.
19 And when all the kings *that were* servants
to Hadarezer saw that they were smitten before

13 [b]2 Sam. 9:3
CHAPTER 10
1 [a]2 Sam. 11:1; 1 Chr. 19:1
2 [a]2 Sam. 9:1; 1 Kin. 2:7
[b]1 Sam. 11:1
4 [a]Is. 20:4; 47:2
6 [a]Gen. 34:30; Ex. 5:21
[b]2 Sam. 8:3, 5
[c]Judg. 18:28
[d]Deut. 3:14; Josh. 13:11, 13
[e]Judg. 11:3, 5
7 [a]2 Sam. 23:8
8 [a]2 Sam. 10:6
10 [a]1 Sam. 26:6; 2 Sam. 3:30
12 [a]Deut. 31:6; Josh. 1:6, 7, 9; Neh. 4:14
[b]1 Sam. 4:9; 1 Cor. 16:13
[c]1 Sam. 3:18
14 [a]2 Sam. 11:1
18 [a]1 Chr. 19:18

*________

10:16 Heb. *Hadarezer*
• The Euphrates
10:19 Heb. *Hadarezer*

NKJV

he ate continually at the king's table. And he [b]was
lame in both his feet.

The Ammonites and Syrians Defeated
(1 Chr. 19:1–19)

10 It happened after this that the [a]king of the
people of Ammon died, and Hanun his son
reigned in his place.
2 Then David said, "I will show [a]kindness
to Hanun the son of [b]Nahash, as his father
showed kindness to me." So David sent by the
hand of his servants to comfort him concerning
his father. And David's servants came into the
land of the people of Ammon.
3 And the princes of the people of Ammon
said to Hanun their lord, "Do you think that David
really honors your father because he has sent
comforters to you? Has David not *rather* sent his
servants to you to search the city, to spy it out,
and to overthrow it?"
4 Therefore Hanun took David's servants,
shaved off half of their beards, cut off their garments in the middle, [a]at their buttocks, and sent
them away.
5 When they told David, he sent to meet
them, because the men were greatly ashamed.
And the king said, "Wait at Jericho until your
beards have grown, and *then* return."
6 When the people of Ammon saw that they
[a]had made themselves repulsive to David, the
people of Ammon sent and hired [b]the Syrians of
[c]Beth Rehob and the Syrians of Zoba, twenty
thousand foot soldiers; and from the king of
[d]Maacah one thousand men, and from [e]Ish-Tob
twelve thousand men.
7 Now when David heard *of it*, he sent Joab
and all the army of [a]the mighty men.
8 Then the people of Ammon came out and
put themselves in battle array at the entrance of
the gate. And [a]the Syrians of Zoba, Beth Rehob,
Ish-Tob, and Maacah *were* by themselves in the
field.
9 When Joab saw that the battle line was
against him before and behind, he chose some
of Israel's best and put *them* in battle array
against the Syrians.
10 And the rest of the people he put under
the command of [a]Abishai his brother, that he
might set *them* in battle array against the people
of Ammon.
11 Then he said, "If the Syrians are too
strong for me, then you shall help me; but if the
people of Ammon are too strong for you, then I
will come and help you.
12 [a]"Be of good courage, and let us [b]be
strong for our people and for the cities of our God.
And may [c]the LORD do *what is* good in His sight."
13 So Joab and the people who *were* with
him drew near for the battle against the Syrians,
and they fled before him.
14 When the people of Ammon saw that the
Syrians were fleeing, they also fled before
Abishai, and entered the city. So Joab returned
from the people of Ammon and went to [a]Jeru-
salem.
15 When the Syrians saw that they had been
defeated by Israel, they gathered together.
16 Then *Hadadezer sent and brought out the
Syrians who *were* beyond *the River, and they
came to Helam. And Shobach the commander of
Hadadezer's army *went* before them.
17 When it was told David, he gathered all
Israel, crossed over the Jordan, and came to Helam. And the Syrians set themselves in battle array against David and fought with him.
18 Then the Syrians fled before Israel; and
David killed seven hundred charioteers and forty
thousand [a]horsemen of the Syrians, and struck
Shobach the commander of their army, who died
there.
19 And when all the kings *who were* servants
to *Hadadezer saw that they were defeated by Is-

KJV

Israel, they made peace with Israel, and [a]served them. So the Syrians feared to help the children of Ammon any more.

David, Bathsheba, and Uriah

11 And it came to pass, after the year was expired, at the [a]time when kings go forth *to battle*, that [b]David sent Joab, and his servants with him, and all Israel; and they destroyed the children of Ammon, and besieged [c]Rabbah. But David tarried still at Jerusalem.

2 And it came to pass in an eveningtide, that David arose from off his bed, [a]and walked upon the roof of the king's house: and from the roof he [b]saw a woman washing herself; and the woman *was* very beautiful to look upon.

3 And David sent and enquired after the woman. And *one* said, *Is* not this Bath–sheba, the daughter of Eliam, the wife [a]of Uriah the [b]Hittite?

4 And David sent messengers, and took her; and she came in unto him, and [a]he lay with her; for she was [b]purified from her uncleanness: and she returned unto her house.

5 And the woman conceived, and sent and told David, and said, I *am* with child.

6 And David sent to Joab, *saying*, Send me Uriah the Hittite. And Joab sent Uriah to David.

7 And when Uriah was come unto him, David demanded *of him* how Joab did, and how the people did, and how the war prospered.

8 And David said to Uriah, Go down to thy house, and [a]wash thy feet. And Uriah departed out of the king's house, and there followed him a mess *of meat* from the king.

9 But Uriah slept at the [a]door of the king's house with all the servants of his lord, and went not down to his house.

10 And when they had told David, saying, Uriah went not down unto his house, David said unto Uriah, Camest thou not from *thy* journey? why *then* didst thou not go down unto thine house?

11 And Uriah said unto David, [a]The ark, and Israel, and Judah, abide in tents; and [b]my lord Joab, and the servants of my lord, are encamped in the open fields; shall I then go into mine house, to eat and to drink, and to lie with my wife? *as* thou livest, and *as* thy soul liveth, I will not do this thing.

12 And David said to Uriah, Tarry here to day also, and to morrow I will let thee depart. So Uriah abode in Jerusalem that day, and the morrow.

13 And when David had called him, he did eat and drink before him; and he made him [a]drunk: and at even he went out to lie on his bed [b]with the servants of his lord, but went not down to his house.

14 And it came to pass in the morning, that David [a]wrote a letter to Joab, and sent *it* by the hand of Uriah.

15 And he wrote in the letter, saying, Set ye Uriah in the forefront of the hottest battle, and retire ye from him, that he may [a]be smitten, and die.

16 And it came to pass, when Joab observed the city, that he assigned Uriah unto a place where he knew that valiant men *were*.

17 And the men of the city went out, and fought with Joab: and there fell *some* of the people of the servants of David; and Uriah the Hittite died also.

18 Then Joab sent and told David all the things concerning the war;

19 And charged the messenger, saying, When thou hast made an end of telling the matters of the war unto the king,

20 And if so be that the king's wrath arise, and he say unto thee, Wherefore approached ye so nigh unto the city when ye did fight? knew ye not that they would shoot from the wall?

19 [a]2 Sam. 8:6

CHAPTER 11

1 [a]1 Kin. 20:22–26 [b]1 Chr. 20:1 [c]2 Sam. 12:26; Jer. 49:2, 3; Amos 1:14
2 [a]Deut. 22:8; 1 Sam. 9:25; Matt. 24:17; Acts 10:9 [b]Gen. 34:2; [Ex. 20:17]; Job 31:1; [Matt. 5:28]
3 [a]2 Sam. 23:39 [b]1 Sam. 26:6
4 [a][Lev. 20:10; Deut. 22:22]; Ps. 51:title; [James 1:14, 15] [b]Lev. 15:19, 28
8 [a]Gen. 18:4; 19:2
9 [a]1 Kin. 14:27, 28
11 [a]2 Sam. 7:2, 6 [b]2 Sam. 20:6–22
13 [a]Gen. 19:33, 35 [b]2 Sam. 11:9
14 [a]1 Kin. 21:8, 9
15 [a]2 Sam. 12:9

NKJV

rael, they made peace with Israel and [a]served them. So the Syrians were afraid to help the people of Ammon anymore.

David, Bathsheba, and Uriah

11 It happened in the spring of the year, at the [a]time when kings go out *to battle*, that [b]David sent Joab and his servants with him, and all Israel; and they destroyed the people of Ammon and besieged [c]Rabbah. But David remained at Jerusalem.

2 Then it happened one evening that David arose from his bed [a]and walked on the roof of the king's house. And from the roof he [b]saw a woman bathing, and the woman *was* very beautiful to behold.

3 So David sent and inquired about the woman. And *someone* said, "*Is* this not Bathsheba, the daughter of Eliam, the wife [a]of Uriah the [b]Hittite?"

4 Then David sent messengers, and took her; and she came to him, and [a]he lay with her, for she was [b]cleansed from her impurity; and she returned to her house.

5 And the woman conceived; so she sent and told David, and said, "I *am* with child."

6 Then David sent to Joab, *saying*, "Send me Uriah the Hittite." And Joab sent Uriah to David.

7 When Uriah had come to him, David asked how Joab was doing, and how the people were doing, and how the war prospered.

8 And David said to Uriah, "Go down to your house and [a]wash your feet." So Uriah departed from the king's house, and a gift *of food* from the king followed him.

9 But Uriah slept at the [a]door of the king's house with all the servants of his lord, and did not go down to his house.

10 So when they told David, saying, "Uriah did not go down to his house," David said to Uriah, "Did you not come from a journey? Why did you not go down to your house?"

11 And Uriah said to David, [a]"The ark and Israel and Judah are dwelling in tents, and [b]my lord Joab and the servants of my lord are encamped in the open fields. Shall I then go to my house to eat and drink, and to lie with my wife? *As* you live, and *as* your soul lives, I will not do this thing."

12 Then David said to Uriah, "Wait here today also, and tomorrow I will let you depart." So Uriah remained in Jerusalem that day and the next.

13 Now when David called him, he ate and drank before him; and he made him [a]drunk. And at evening he went out to lie on his bed [b]with the servants of his lord, but he did not go down to his house.

14 In the morning it happened that David [a]wrote a letter to Joab and sent *it* by the hand of Uriah.

15 And he wrote in the letter, saying, "Set Uriah in the forefront of the hottest battle, and retreat from him, that he may [a]be struck down and die."

16 So it was, while Joab besieged the city, that he assigned Uriah to a place where he knew there *were* valiant men.

17 Then the men of the city came out and fought with Joab. And *some* of the people of the servants of David fell; and Uriah the Hittite died also.

18 Then Joab sent and told David all the things concerning the war,

19 and charged the messenger, saying, "When you have finished telling the matters of the war to the king,

20 "if it happens that the king's wrath rises, and he says to you: 'Why did you approach so near to the city when you fought? Did you not know that they would shoot from the wall?

KJV

21 Who smote [a]Abimelech the son of Jerub-
besheth? did not a woman cast a piece of a millstone upon him from the wall, that he died in Thebez? why went ye nigh the wall? then say thou,
Thy servant Uriah the Hittite is dead also.
22 So the messenger went, and came and
shewed David all that Joab had sent him for.
23 And the messenger said unto David,
Surely the men prevailed against us, and came
out unto us into the field, and we were upon them
even unto the entering of the gate.
24 And the shooters shot from off the wall
upon thy servants; and *some* of the king's servants be dead, and thy servant Uriah the Hittite
is dead also.
25 Then David said unto the messenger, Thus
shalt thou say unto Joab, Let not this thing displease thee, for the sword devoureth one as well
as another: make thy battle more strong against
the city, and overthrow it: and encourage thou
him.
26 And when the wife of Uriah heard that
Uriah her husband was dead, she mourned for
her husband.
27 And when the mourning was past, David
sent and fetched her to his house, and she [a]be-
came his wife, and bare him a son. But the thing
that David had done [b]displeased the LORD.

Nathan's Parable and David's Confession

12 And the LORD sent Nathan unto David. And
[a]he came unto him, and [b]said unto him,
There were two men in one city; the one rich,
and the other poor.
2 The rich *man* had exceeding many flocks
and herds:
3 But the poor *man* had nothing, save one
little ewe lamb, which he had bought and nourished up: and it grew up together with him, and
with his children; it did eat of his own meat, and
drank of his own cup, and lay in his bosom, and
was unto him as a daughter.
4 And there came a traveller unto the rich
man, and he spared to take of his own flock and
of his own herd, to dress for the wayfaring man
that was come unto him; but took the poor man's
lamb, and dressed it for the man that was come
to him.
5 And David's anger was greatly kindled
against the man; and he said to Nathan, *As* the
LORD liveth, the man that hath done this *thing*
shall surely die:
6 And he shall restore the lamb [a]fourfold,
because he did this thing, and because he had no
pity.
7 And Nathan said to David, Thou *art* the
man. Thus saith the LORD God of Israel, I
[a]anointed thee king over Israel, and I delivered
thee out of the hand of Saul;
8 And I gave thee thy master's house, and
thy master's wives into thy bosom, and gave thee
the house of Israel and of Judah; and if *that had
been* too little, I would moreover have given unto
thee such and such things.
9 [a]Wherefore hast thou [b]despised the commandment of the LORD, to do evil in his sight?
[c]thou hast killed Uriah the Hittite with the sword,
and hast taken his wife *to be* thy wife, and hast
slain him with the sword of the children of
Ammon.
10 Now therefore [a]the sword shall never depart from thine house; because thou hast despised
me, and hast taken the wife of Uriah the Hittite
to be thy wife.
11 Thus saith the LORD, Behold, I will raise
up evil against thee out of thine own house, and
I will [a]take thy wives before thine eyes, and give
them unto thy neighbour, and he shall lie with
thy wives in the sight of this sun.
12 For thou didst *it* secretly: [a]but I will do
this thing before all Israel, and before the sun.
13 [a]And David said unto Nathan, [b]I have

21 [a]Judg. 9:50–54
27 [a]2 Sam. 12:9 [b]1 Chr. 21:7; [Heb. 13:4]

CHAPTER 12
1 [a]Ps. 51:title [b]1 Kin. 20:35–41
6 [a][Ex. 22:1]; Luke 19:8
7 [a]1 Sam. 16:13; 2 Sam. 5:3
9 [a]1 Sam. 15:19 [b]Num. 15:31 [c]2 Sam. 11:14–17, 27
10 [a]2 Sam. 13:28; 18:14; 1 Kin. 2:25; [Amos 7:9]
11 [a]Deut. 28:30; 2 Sam. 16:21, 22
12 [a]2 Sam. 16:22
13 [a]1 Sam. 15:24 [b]2 Sam. 24:10; Job 7:20; Ps. 51; Luke 18:13

*______

11:21 Gideon; *Jerubbaal,* Judg. 6:32ff.

NKJV

21 'Who struck [a]Abimelech the son of *Jer-
ubbesheth? Was it not a woman who cast a piece
of a millstone on him from the wall, so that he
died in Thebez? Why did you go near the wall?'—
then you shall say, 'Your servant Uriah the Hittite
is dead also.' "
22 So the messenger went, and came and told
David all that Joab had sent by him.
23 And the messenger said to David, "Surely
the men prevailed against us and came out to us
in the field; then we drove them back as far as
the entrance of the gate.
24 "The archers shot from the wall at your
servants; and *some* of the king's servants are
dead, and your servant Uriah the Hittite is dead
also."
25 Then David said to the messenger, "Thus
you shall say to Joab: 'Do not let this thing displease you, for the sword devours one as well as
another. Strengthen your attack against the city,
and overthrow it.' So encourage him."
26 When the wife of Uriah heard that Uriah
her husband was dead, she mourned for her
husband.
27 And when her mourning was over, David
sent and brought her to his house, and she [a]be-
came his wife and bore him a son. But the thing
that David had done [b]displeased the LORD.

Nathan's Parable and David's Confession

12 Then the LORD sent Nathan to David. And
[a]he came to him, and [b]said to him: "There
were two men in one city, one rich and the other
poor.
2 "The rich *man* had exceedingly many
flocks and herds.
3 "But the poor *man* had nothing, except
one little ewe lamb which he had bought and
nourished; and it grew up together with him and
with his children. It ate of his own food and drank
from his own cup and lay in his bosom; and it
was like a daughter to him.
4 "And a traveler came to the rich man, who
refused to take from his own flock and from his
own herd to prepare one for the wayfaring man
who had come to him; but he took the poor man's
lamb and prepared it for the man who had come
to him."
5 So David's anger was greatly aroused
against the man, and he said to Nathan, "*As* the
LORD lives, the man who has done this shall surely
die!
6 "And he shall restore [a]fourfold for the
lamb, because he did this thing and because he
had no pity."
7 Then Nathan said to David, "You *are* the
man! Thus says the LORD God of Israel: 'I
[a]anointed you king over Israel, and I delivered
you from the hand of Saul.
8 'I gave you your master's house and your
master's wives into your keeping, and gave you
the house of Israel and Judah. And if *that had
been* too little, I also would have given you much
more!
9 [a]'Why have you [b]despised the commandment of the LORD, to do evil in His sight? [c]You
have killed Uriah the Hittite with the sword; you
have taken his wife *to be* your wife, and have
killed him with the sword of the people of
Ammon.
10 'Now therefore, [a]the sword shall never depart from your house, because you have despised
Me, and have taken the wife of Uriah the Hittite
to be your wife.'
11 "Thus says the LORD: 'Behold, I will raise
up adversity against you from your own house;
and I will [a]take your wives before your eyes and
give *them* to your neighbor, and he shall lie with
your wives in the sight of this sun.
12 'For you did *it* secretly, [a]but I will do this
thing before all Israel, before the sun.' "
13 [a]So David said to Nathan, [b]"I have sinned

KJV

sinned against the LORD. And Nathan said unto David, The LORD also hath [c]put away thy sin; thou shalt not die.

14 Howbeit, because by this deed thou hast given great occasion to the enemies of the LORD [a]to blaspheme, the child also *that is* born unto thee shall surely die.

15 And Nathan departed unto his house.

The Death of David's Son

And the [a]LORD struck the child that Uriah's wife bare unto David, and it was very sick.

16 David therefore besought God for the child; and David fasted, and went in, and [a]lay all night upon the earth.

17 And the elders of his house arose, *and went* to him, to raise him up from the earth: but he would not, neither did he eat bread with them.

18 And it came to pass on the seventh day, that the child died. And the servants of David feared to tell him that the child was dead: for they said, Behold, while the child was yet alive, we spake unto him, and he would not hearken unto our voice: how will he then vex himself, if we tell him that the child is dead?

19 But when David saw that his servants whispered, David perceived that the child was dead: therefore David said unto his servants, Is the child dead? And they said, He is dead.

20 Then David arose from the earth, and washed, and [a]anointed *himself,* and changed his apparel, and came into the house of the LORD, and [b]worshipped: then he came to his own house; and when he required, they set bread before him, and he did eat.

21 Then said his servants unto him, What thing *is* this that thou hast done? thou didst fast and weep for the child, *while it was* alive; but when the child was dead, thou didst rise and eat bread.

22 And he said, While the child was yet alive, I fasted and wept: [a]for I said, Who can tell *whether* GOD will be gracious to me, that the child may live?

23 But now he is dead, wherefore should I fast? can I bring him back again? I shall go [a]to him, but [b]he shall not return to me.

Solomon Is Born

24 And David comforted Bath–sheba his wife, and went in unto her, and lay with her: and [a]she bare a son, and [b]he called his name Solomon: and the LORD loved him.

25 And he sent by the hand of Nathan the prophet; and he called his name Jedidiah, because of the LORD.

Rabbah Is Captured
(1 Chr. 20:1–3)

26 And [a]Joab fought against [b]Rabbah of the children of Ammon, and took the royal city.

27 And Joab sent messengers to David, and said, I have fought against Rabbah, and have taken the city of waters.

28 Now therefore gather the rest of the people together, and encamp against the city, and take it: lest I take the city, and it be called after my name.

29 And David gathered all the people together, and went to Rabbah, and fought against it, and took it.

30 [a]And he took their king's crown from off his head, the weight whereof *was* a talent of gold with the precious stones: and it was *set* on David's head. And he brought forth the spoil of the city in great abundance.

31 And he brought forth the people that *were* therein, and put *them* under saws, and under harrows of iron, and under axes of iron, and made them pass through the brickkiln: and thus did he unto all the cities of the children of Ammon. So David and all the people returned unto Jerusalem.

13 [c]2 Sam. 24:10; Job 7:21; [Ps. 32:1–5; Prov. 28:13; Mic. 7:18]; Zech. 3:4
14 [a]Is. 52:5; [Ezek. 36:20, 23]; Rom. 2:24
15 [a]1 Sam. 25:38
16 [a]2 Sam. 13:31
20 [a]Ruth 3:3; Matt. 6:17 [b]Job 1:20
22 [a]Is. 38:1–5; Joel 2:14; Jon. 3:9
23 [a]Gen. 37:35 [b]Job 7:8–10
24 [a]Matt. 1:6 [b]1 Chr. 22:9
26 [a]1 Chr. 20:1 [b]Deut. 3:11; 2 Sam. 11:1
30 [a]1 Chr. 20:2

NKJV

against the LORD." And Nathan said to David, "The LORD also has [c]put away your sin; you shall not die.

14 "However, because by this deed you have given great occasion to the enemies of the LORD [a]to blaspheme, the child also *who is* born to you shall surely die."

15 Then Nathan departed to his house.

The Death of David's Son

And the [a]LORD struck the child that Uriah's wife bore to David, and it became ill.

16 David therefore pleaded with God for the child, and David fasted and went in and [a]lay all night on the ground.

17 So the elders of his house arose *and went* to him, to raise him up from the ground. But he would not, nor did he eat food with them.

18 Then on the seventh day it came to pass that the child died. And the servants of David were afraid to tell him that the child was dead. For they said, "Indeed, while the child was alive, we spoke to him, and he would not heed our voice. How can we tell him that the child is dead? He may do some harm!"

19 When David saw that his servants were whispering, David perceived that the child was dead. Therefore David said to his servants, "Is the child dead?" And they said, "He is dead."

20 So David arose from the ground, washed and [a]anointed himself, and changed his clothes; and he went into the house of the LORD and [b]worshiped. Then he went to his own house; and when he requested, they set food before him, and he ate.

21 Then his servants said to him, "What *is* this that you have done? You fasted and wept for the child *while he was* alive, but when the child died, you arose and ate food."

22 And he said, "While the child was alive, I fasted and wept; [a]for I said, 'Who can tell *whether* *the LORD will be gracious to me, that the child may live?'

23 "But now he is dead; why should I fast? Can I bring him back again? I shall go [a]to him, but [b]he shall not return to me."

Solomon Is Born

24 Then David comforted Bathsheba his wife, and went in to her and lay with her. So [a]she bore a son, and [b]he* called his name Solomon. Now the LORD loved him,

25 and He sent *word* by the hand of Nathan the prophet: So *he called his name *Jedidiah, because of the LORD.

Rabbah Is Captured
(1 Chr. 20:1–3)

26 Now [a]Joab fought against [b]Rabbah of the people of Ammon, and took the royal city.

27 And Joab sent messengers to David, and said, "I have fought against Rabbah, and I have taken the city's water *supply.*

28 "Now therefore, gather the rest of the people together and encamp against the city and take it, lest I take the city and it be called after my name."

29 So David gathered all the people together and went to Rabbah, fought against it, and took it.

30 [a]Then he took their king's crown from his head. Its weight *was* a talent of gold, with precious stones. And it was *set* on David's head. Also he brought out the spoil of the city in great abundance.

31 And he brought out the people who *were* in it, and put *them to work* with saws and iron picks and iron axes, and made them cross over to the brick works. So he did to all the cities of the people of Ammon. Then David and all the people returned to Jerusalem.

12:22 Heb. mss., Syr. *God*
12:24 So with Kt., LXX, Vg.; Qr., a few Heb. mss., Syr., Tg. *she*
12:25 Qr., some Heb. mss., Syr., Tg. *she* • Lit. *Beloved of the LORD*

KJV

Amnon and Tamar

13 And it came to pass after this, [a]that Absalom the son of David had a fair sister, whose name *was* [b]Tamar; and [c]Amnon the son of David loved her.

2 And Amnon was so vexed, that he fell sick for his sister Tamar; for she *was* a virgin; and Amnon thought it hard for him to do any thing to her.

3 But Amnon had a friend, whose name *was* Jonadab, [a]the son of Shimeah David's brother: and Jonadab *was* a very subtil man.

4 And he said unto him, Why *art* thou, *being* the king's son, lean from day to day? wilt thou not tell me? And Amnon said unto him, I love Tamar, my brother Absalom's sister.

5 And Jonadab said unto him, Lay thee down on thy bed, and make thyself sick: and when thy father cometh to see thee, say unto him, I pray thee, let my sister Tamar come, and give me meat, and dress the meat in my sight, that I may see *it*, and eat *it* at her hand.

6 So Amnon lay down, and made himself sick: and when the king was come to see him, Amnon said unto the king, I pray thee, let Tamar my sister come, and [a]make me a couple of cakes in my sight, that I may eat at her hand.

7 Then David sent home to Tamar, saying, Go now to thy brother Amnon's house, and dress him meat.

8 So Tamar went to her brother Amnon's house; and he was laid down. And she took flour, and kneaded *it*, and made cakes in his sight, and did bake the cakes.

9 And she took a pan, and poured *them* out before him; but he refused to eat. And Amnon said, [a]Have out all men from me. And they went out every man from him.

10 And Amnon said unto Tamar, Bring the meat into the chamber, that I may eat of thine hand. And Tamar took the cakes which she had made, and brought *them* into the chamber to Amnon her brother.

11 And when she had brought *them* unto him to eat, [a]he took hold of her, and said unto her, Come lie with me, my sister.

12 And she answered him, Nay, my brother, do not force me; for [a]no such thing ought to be done in Israel: do not thou this [b]folly.

13 And I, whither shall I cause my shame to go? and as for thee, thou shalt be as one of the fools in Israel. Now therefore, I pray thee, speak unto the king; [a]for he will not withhold me from thee.

14 Howbeit he would not hearken unto her voice: but, being stronger than she, [a]forced her, and lay with her.

15 Then Amnon hated her exceedingly; so that the hatred wherewith he hated her *was* greater than the love wherewith he had loved her. And Amnon said unto her, Arise, be gone.

16 And she said unto him, *There is* no cause: this evil in sending me away *is* greater than the other that thou didst unto me. But he would not hearken unto her.

17 Then he called his servant that ministered unto him, and said, Put now this *woman* out from me, and bolt the door after her.

18 And *she had* [a]a garment of divers colours upon her: for with such robes were the king's daughters *that were* virgins apparelled. Then his servant brought her out, and bolted the door after her.

19 And Tamar put [a]ashes on her head, and rent her garment of divers colours that *was* on her, and [b]laid her hand on her head, and went on crying.

20 And Absalom her brother said unto her, Hath Amnon thy brother been with thee? but hold now thy peace, my sister: he *is* thy brother; regard

CHAPTER 13

1 [a]2 Sam. 3:2, 3; 1 Chr. 3:2 [b]1 Chr. 3:9 [c]2 Sam. 3:2
3 [a]1 Sam. 16:9
6 [a]Gen. 18:6
9 [a]Gen. 45:1
11 [a]Gen. 39:12; [Deut. 27:22]; Ezek. 22:11
12 [a][Lev. 18:9–11; 20:17] [b]Gen. 34:7; Judg. 19:23; 20:6
13 [a]Gen. 20:12
14 [a]Lev. 18:9; [Deut. 22:25; 27:22]; 2 Sam. 12:11
18 [a]Gen. 37:3; Judg. 5:30; Ps. 45:13, 14
19 [a]Josh. 7:6; 2 Sam. 1:2; Job 2:12; 42:6 [b]Jer. 2:37

NKJV

Amnon and Tamar

13 After this [a]Absalom the son of David had a lovely sister, whose name *was* [b]Tamar; and [c]Amnon the son of David loved her.

2 Amnon was so distressed over his sister Tamar that he became sick; for she *was* a virgin. And it was improper for Amnon to do anything to her.

3 But Amnon had a friend whose name *was* Jonadab [a]the son of Shimeah, David's brother. Now Jonadab *was* a very crafty man.

4 And he said to him, "Why *are* you, the king's son, becoming thinner day after day? Will you not tell me?" Amnon said to him, "I love Tamar, my brother Absalom's sister."

5 So Jonadab said to him, "Lie down on your bed and pretend to be ill. And when your father comes to see you, say to him, 'Please let my sister Tamar come and give me food, and prepare the food in my sight, that I may see *it* and eat it from her hand.' "

6 Then Amnon lay down and pretended to be ill; and when the king came to see him, Amnon said to the king, "Please let Tamar my sister come and [a]make a couple of cakes for me in my sight, that I may eat from her hand."

7 And David sent home to Tamar, saying, "Now go to your brother Amnon's house, and prepare food for him."

8 So Tamar went to her brother Amnon's house; and he was lying down. Then she took flour and kneaded *it*, made cakes in his sight, and baked the cakes.

9 And she took the pan and placed *them* out before him, but he refused to eat. Then Amnon said, [a]"Have everyone go out from me." And they all went out from him.

10 Then Amnon said to Tamar, "Bring the food into the bedroom, that I may eat from your hand." And Tamar took the cakes which she had made, and brought *them* to Amnon her brother in the bedroom.

11 Now when she had brought *them* to him to eat, [a]he took hold of her and said to her, "Come, lie with me, my sister."

12 But she answered him, "No, my brother, do not force me, for [a]no such thing should be done in Israel. Do not do this [b]disgraceful thing!

13 "And I, where could I take my shame? And as for you, you would be like one of the fools in Israel. Now therefore, please speak to the king; [a]for he will not withhold me from you."

14 However, he would not heed her voice; and being stronger than she, he [a]forced her and lay with her.

15 Then Amnon hated her exceedingly, so that the hatred with which he hated her *was* greater than the love with which he had loved her. And Amnon said to her, "Arise, be gone!"

16 So she said to him, "No, indeed! This evil of sending me away *is* worse than the other that you did to me." But he would not listen to her.

17 Then he called his servant who attended him, and said, "Here! Put this *woman* out, away from me, and bolt the door behind her."

18 Now she had on [a]a robe of many colors, for the king's virgin daughters wore such apparel. And his servant put her out and bolted the door behind her.

19 Then Tamar put [a]ashes on her head, and tore her robe of many colors that *was* on her, and [b]laid her hand on her head and went away crying bitterly.

20 And Absalom her brother said to her, "Has Amnon your brother been with you? But now hold your peace, my sister. He *is* your

KJV

not this thing. So Tamar remained desolate in her brother Absalom's house.

21 But when king David heard of all these things, he was very wroth.

22 And Absalom spake unto his brother Amnon [a]neither good nor bad: for Absalom [b]hated Amnon, because he had forced his sister Tamar.

Absalom Murders Amnon

23 And it came to pass after two full years, that Absalom [a]had sheepshearers in Baal–hazor, which *is* beside Ephraim: and Absalom invited all the king's sons.

24 And Absalom came to the king, and said, Behold now, thy servant hath sheepshearers; let the king, I beseech thee, and his servants go with thy servant.

25 And the king said to Absalom, Nay, my son, let us not all now go, lest we be chargeable unto thee. And he pressed him: howbeit he would not go, but blessed him.

26 Then said Absalom, If not, I pray thee, let my brother Amnon go with us. And the king said unto him, Why should he go with thee?

27 But Absalom pressed him, that he let Amnon and all the king's sons go with him.

28 Now Absalom had commanded his servants, saying, Mark ye now when Amnon's [a]heart is merry with wine, and when I say unto you, Smite Amnon; then kill him, fear not: have not I commanded you? be courageous, and be valiant.

29 And the servants of Absalom [a]did unto Amnon as Absalom had commanded. Then all the king's sons arose, and every man gat him up upon [b]his mule, and fled.

30 And it came to pass, while they were in the way, that tidings came to David, saying, Absalom hath slain all the king's sons, and there is not one of them left.

31 Then the king arose, and [a]tare his garments, and [b]lay on the earth; and all his servants stood by with their clothes rent.

32 And [a]Jonadab, the son of Shimeah David's brother, answered and said, Let not my lord suppose *that* they have slain all the young men the king's sons; for Amnon only is dead: for by the appointment of Absalom this hath been determined from the day that he forced his sister Tamar.

33 Now therefore [a]let not my lord the king take the thing to his heart, to think that all the king's sons are dead: for Amnon only is dead.

Absalom Flees to Geshur

34 [a]But Absalom fled. And the young man that kept the watch lifted up his eyes, and looked, and, behold, there came much people by the way of the hill side behind him.

35 And Jonadab said unto the king, Behold, the king's sons come: as thy servant said, so it is.

36 And it came to pass, as soon as he had made an end of speaking, that, behold, the king's sons came, and lifted up their voice and wept: and the king also and all his servants wept very sore.

37 But Absalom fled, and went to [a]Talmai, the son of Ammihud, king of Geshur. And *David* mourned for his son every day.

38 So Absalom fled, and went to [a]Geshur, and was there three years.

39 And *the soul of* king David longed to go forth unto Absalom: for he was [a]comforted concerning Amnon, seeing he was dead.

Absalom Returns to Jerusalem

14 Now Joab the son of Zeruiah perceived that the king's heart *was* [a]toward Absalom.

2 And Joab sent to [a]Tekoah, and fetched thence a wise woman, and said unto her, I pray thee, feign thyself to be a mourner, [b]and put on

22 [a]Gen. 24:50; 31:24 [b][Lev. 19:17, 18; 1 John 2:9, 11; 3:10, 12, 15]
23 [a]Gen. 38:12, 13; 1 Sam. 25:4
28 [a]Judg. 19:6, 9, 22; Ruth 3:7; 1 Sam. 25:36; Esth. 1:10
29 [a]2 Sam. 12:10 [b]2 Sam. 18:9; 1 Kin. 1:33, 38
31 [a]2 Sam. 1:11 [b]2 Sam. 12:16
32 [a]2 Sam. 13:3–5
33 [a]2 Sam. 19:19
34 [a]2 Sam. 13:37, 38
37 [a]2 Sam. 3:3; 1 Chr. 3:2
38 [a]2 Sam. 14:23, 32; 15:8
39 [a]Gen. 38:12; 2 Sam. 12:19, 23

CHAPTER 14

1 [a]2 Sam. 13:39
2 [a]2 Sam. 23:26; 2 Chr. 11:6; Amos 1:1 [b]Ruth 3:3

*

13:34 LXX adds *And the watchman went and told the king, and said, "I see men from the way of Horonaim, from the regions of the mountains."*
13:39 So with MT, Syr., Vg.; LXX *the spirit of the king;* Tg. *the soul of King David* • So with MT, Tg.; LXX, Vg. *ceased to pursue after*

NKJV

brother; do not take this thing to heart." So Tamar remained desolate in her brother Absalom's house.

21 But when King David heard of all these things, he was very angry.

22 And Absalom spoke to his brother Amnon [a]neither good nor bad. For Absalom [b]hated Amnon, because he had forced his sister Tamar.

Absalom Murders Amnon

23 And it came to pass, after two full years, that Absalom [a]had sheepshearers in Baal Hazor, which *is* near Ephraim; so Absalom invited all the king's sons.

24 Then Absalom came to the king and said, "Kindly note, your servant has sheepshearers; please, let the king and his servants go with your servant."

25 But the king said to Absalom, "No, my son, let us not all go now, lest we be a burden to you." Then he urged him, but he would not go; and he blessed him.

26 Then Absalom said, "If not, please let my brother Amnon go with us." And the king said to him, "Why should he go with you?"

27 But Absalom urged him; so he let Amnon and all the king's sons go with him.

28 Now Absalom had commanded his servants, saying, "Watch now, when Amnon's [a]heart is merry with wine, and when I say to you, 'Strike Amnon!' then kill him. Do not be afraid. Have I not commanded you? Be courageous and valiant."

29 So the servants of Absalom [a]did to Amnon as Absalom had commanded. Then all the king's sons arose, and each one got on [b]his mule and fled.

30 And it came to pass, while they were on the way, that news came to David, saying, "Absalom has killed all the king's sons, and not one of them is left!"

31 So the king arose and [a]tore his garments and [b]lay on the ground, and all his servants stood by with their clothes torn.

32 Then [a]Jonadab the son of Shimeah, David's brother, answered and said, "Let not my lord suppose they have killed all the young men, the king's sons, for only Amnon is dead. For by the command of Absalom this has been determined from the day that he forced his sister Tamar.

33 "Now therefore, [a]let not my lord the king take the thing to his heart, to think that all the king's sons are dead. For only Amnon is dead."

Absalom Flees to Geshur

34 [a]Then Absalom fled. And the young man who was keeping watch lifted his eyes and looked, and there, many people were coming from the road on the hillside behind *him.

35 And Jonadab said to the king, "Look, the king's sons are coming; as your servant said, so it is."

36 So it was, as soon as he had finished speaking, that the king's sons indeed came, and they lifted up their voice and wept. Also the king and all his servants wept very bitterly.

37 But Absalom fled and went to [a]Talmai the son of Ammihud, king of Geshur. And *David* mourned for his son every day.

38 So Absalom fled and went to [a]Geshur, and was there three years.

39 And *King David *longed to go to Absalom. For he had been [a]comforted concerning Amnon, because he was dead.

Absalom Returns to Jerusalem

14 So Joab the son of Zeruiah perceived that the king's heart *was* concerned [a]about Absalom.

2 And Joab sent to [a]Tekoa and brought from there a wise woman, and said to her, "Please pretend to be a mourner, [b]and put on mourning

KJV

now mourning apparel, and anoint not thyself
with oil, but be as a woman that had a long time
mourned for the dead:
3 And come to the king, and speak on this
manner unto him. So Joab [a]put the words in her
mouth.
4 And when the woman of Tekoah
spake to the king, she [a]fell on her face to the
ground, and did obeisance, and said, [b]Help, O
king.
5 And the king said unto her, What aileth
thee? And she answered, [a]I *am* indeed a widow
woman, and mine husband is dead.
6 And thy handmaid had two sons, and they
two strove together in the field, and *there was*
none to part them, but the one smote the other,
and slew him.
7 And, behold, the whole family is risen
against thine handmaid, and they said, Deliver
him that smote his brother, that we may kill him,
[a]for the life of his brother whom he slew; and
we will destroy the heir also: and so they shall
quench my coal which is left, and shall not leave
to my husband *neither* name nor remainder upon
the earth.
8 And the king said unto the woman, Go
to thine house, and I will give charge concerning
thee.
9 And the woman of Tekoah said unto the
king, My lord, O king, [a]the iniquity *be* on me,
and on my father's house: [b]and the king and his
throne *be* guiltless.
10 And the king said, Whosoever saith *ought*
unto thee, bring him to me, and he shall not touch
thee any more.
11 Then said she, I pray thee, let the king
remember the LORD thy God, that thou wouldest
not suffer [a]the revengers of blood to destroy any
more, lest they destroy my son. And he said, [b]*As*
the LORD liveth, there shall not one hair of thy
son fall to the earth.
12 Then the woman said, Let thine handmaid, I pray thee, speak *one* word unto my lord
the king. And he said, Say on.
13 And the woman said, Wherefore then hast
thou thought such a thing against [a]the people of
God? for the king doth speak this thing as one
which is faulty, in that the king doth not fetch
home again [b]his banished.
14 For we [a]must needs die, and *are* as water
spilt on the ground, which cannot be gathered up
again; neither doth God [b]respect *any* person: yet
doth he [c]devise means, that his banished be not
expelled from him.
15 Now therefore that I am come to speak
of this thing unto my lord the king, *it is* because
the people have made me afraid: and thy handmaid said, I will now speak unto the king; it may
be that the king will perform the request of his
handmaid.
16 For the king will hear, to deliver his handmaid out of the hand of the man *that would* destroy me and my son together out of the [a]inheri-
tance of God.
17 Then thine handmaid said, The word of
my lord the king shall now be comfortable: for
[a]as an angel of God, so *is* my lord the king to
[b]discern good and bad: therefore the LORD thy
God will be with thee.
18 Then the king answered and said unto the
woman, Hide not from me, I pray thee, the thing
that I shall ask thee. And the woman said, Let
my lord the king now speak.
19 And the king said, *Is not* the hand of Joab
with thee in all this? And the woman answered
and said, *As* thy soul liveth, my lord the king,
none can turn to the right hand or to the left from
ought that my lord the king hath spoken: for thy
servant Joab, he bade me, and [a]he put all these
words in the mouth of thine handmaid:
20 To fetch about this form of speech hath
thy servant Joab done this thing: and my lord *is*

3 [a]Ex. 4:15; 2 Sam. 14:19
4 [a]1 Sam. 20:41; 25:23; 2 Sam. 1:2 [b]2 Kin. 6:26, 28
5 [a][Zech. 7:10]
7 [a]Num. 35:19; Deut. 19:12, 13
9 [a]Gen. 27:13; 43:9; 1 Sam. 25:24; Matt. 27:25 [b]2 Sam. 3:28, 29; 1 Kin. 2:33
11 [a]Num. 35:19, 21; [Deut. 19:4–10] [b]1 Sam. 14:45; 1 Kin. 1:52; Matt. 10:30; Acts 27:34
13 [a]Judg. 20:2 [b]2 Sam. 13:37, 38
14 [a]Job 30:23; 34:15; [Heb. 9:27] [b]Job 34:19; Matt. 22:16; Acts 10:34; Rom. 2:11 [c]Num. 35:15
16 [a]Deut. 32:9; 1 Sam. 26:19; 2 Sam. 20:19
17 [a]1 Sam. 29:9; 2 Sam. 19:27 [b]1 Kin. 3:9
19 [a]2 Sam. 14:3

*14:4 Many Heb. mss., LXX, Syr., Vg. *came*

NKJV

apparel; do not anoint yourself with oil, but act
like a woman who has been mourning a long time
for the dead.
3 "Go to the king and speak to him in this
manner." So Joab [a]put the words in her mouth.
4 And when the woman of Tekoa *spoke to
the king, she [a]fell on her face to the ground and
prostrated herself, and said, [b]"Help, O king!"
5 Then the king said to her, "What troubles
you?" And she answered, [a]"Indeed I *am* a widow,
my husband is dead.
6 "Now your maidservant had two sons;
and the two fought with each other in the field,
and *there was* no one to part them, but the one
struck the other and killed him.
7 "And now the whole family has risen up
against your maidservant, and they said, 'Deliver
him who struck his brother, that we may execute
him [a]for the life of his brother whom he killed;
and we will destroy the heir also.' So they would
extinguish my ember that is left, and leave to my
husband *neither* name nor remnant on the earth."
8 Then the king said to the woman, "Go to
your house, and I will give orders concerning
you."
9 And the woman of Tekoa said to the king,
"My lord, O king, *let* [a]the iniquity *be* on me and
on my father's house, [b]and the king and his throne
be guiltless."
10 So the king said, "Whoever says *anything*
to you, bring him to me, and he shall not touch
you anymore."
11 Then she said, "Please let the king remember the LORD your God, and do not permit [a]the
avenger of blood to destroy anymore, lest they
destroy my son." And he said, [b]"*As* the LORD lives,
not one hair of your son shall fall to the ground."
12 Therefore the woman said, "Please, let
your maidservant speak *another* word to my lord
the king." And he said, "Say on."
13 So the woman said: "Why then have you
schemed such a thing against [a]the people of God?
For the king speaks this thing as one who is guilty,
in that the king does not bring [b]his banished one
home again.
14 "For we [a]will surely die and *become* like
water spilled on the ground, which cannot be
gathered up again. Yet God does not [b]take away
a life; but He [c]devises means, so that His banished
ones are not expelled from Him.
15 "Now therefore, I have come to speak of
this thing to my lord the king because the people
have made me afraid. And your maidservant said,
'I will now speak to the king; it may be that the
king will perform the request of his maidservant.
16 'For the king will hear and deliver his
maidservant from the hand of the man *who would*
destroy me and my son together from the [a]inheri-
tance of God.'
17 "Your maidservant said, 'The word of my
lord the king will now be comforting; for [a]as the
angel of God, so *is* my lord the king in [b]discerning
good and evil. And may the LORD your God be
with you.' "
18 Then the king answered and said to the
woman, "Please do not hide from me anything
that I ask you." And the woman said, "Please,
let my lord the king speak."
19 So the king said, "*Is* the hand of Joab with
you in all this?" And the woman answered and
said, "*As* you live, my lord the king, no one can
turn to the right hand or to the left from anything
that my lord the king has spoken. For your servant
Joab commanded me, and [a]he put all these words
in the mouth of your maidservant.
20 "To bring about this change of affairs your
servant Joab has done this thing; but my lord *is*

KJV

wise, [a]according to the wisdom of an angel of God, to know all *things* that *are* in the earth.

21 And the king said unto Joab, Behold now, I have done this thing: go therefore, bring the young man Absalom again.

22 And Joab fell to the ground on his face, and bowed himself, and thanked the king: and Joab said, To day thy servant knoweth that I have found grace in thy sight, my lord, O king, in that the king hath fulfilled the request of his servant.

23 So Joab arose [a]and went to Geshur, and brought Absalom to Jerusalem.

24 And the king said, Let him turn to his own house, and let him [a]not see my face. So Absalom returned to his own house, and saw not the king's face.

David Forgives Absalom

25 But in all Israel there was none to be so much praised as Absalom for his beauty: [a]from the sole of his foot even to the crown of his head there was no blemish in him.

26 And when he polled his head, (for it was at every year's end that he polled *it:* because *the hair* was heavy on him, therefore he polled it:) he weighed the hair of his head at two hundred shekels after the king's weight.

27 And [a]unto Absalom there were born three sons, and one daughter, whose name *was* Tamar: she was a woman of a fair countenance.

28 So Absalom dwelt two full years in Jerusalem, [a]and saw not the king's face.

29 Therefore Absalom sent for Joab, to have sent him to the king; but he would not come to him: and when he sent again the second time, he would not come.

30 Therefore he said unto his servants, See, Joab's field is near mine, and he hath barley there; go and set it on fire. And Absalom's servants set the field on fire.

31 Then Joab arose, and came to Absalom unto *his* house, and said unto him, Wherefore have thy servants set my field on fire?

32 And Absalom answered Joab, Behold, I sent unto thee, saying, Come hither, that I may send thee to the king, to say, Wherefore am I come from Geshur? *it had been* good for me *to have been* there still: now therefore let me see the king's face; and [a]if there be *any* iniquity in me, let him kill me.

33 So Joab came to the king, and told him: and when he had called for Absalom, he came to the king, and bowed himself on his face to the ground before the king: and the king [a]kissed Absalom.

Absalom's Treason

15 And [a]it came to pass after this, that Absalom [b]prepared him chariots and horses, and fifty men to run before him.

2 And Absalom rose up early, and stood beside the way of the gate: and it was *so,* that when any man that had a [a]controversy came to the king for judgment, then Absalom called unto him, and said, Of what city *art* thou? And he said, Thy servant *is* of one of the tribes of Israel.

3 And Absalom said unto him, See, thy matters *are* good and right; but *there is* no man *deputed* of the king to hear thee.

4 Absalom said moreover, [a]Oh that I were made judge in the land, that every man which hath any suit or cause might come unto me, and I would do him justice!

5 And it was *so,* that when any man came nigh *to him* to do him obeisance, he put forth his hand, and took him, and [a]kissed him.

6 And on this manner did Absalom to all Israel that came to the king for judgment: [a]so Absalom stole the hearts of the men of Israel.

7 And it came to pass [a]after forty years, that Absalom said unto the king, I pray thee, let me

20 [a]2 Sam. 14:17; 19:27
23 [a]2 Sam. 13:37, 38
24 [a]Gen. 43:3; 2 Sam. 3:13
25 [a]Deut. 28:35; Job 2:7; Is. 1:6
27 [a]2 Sam. 13:1; 18:18
28 [a]2 Sam. 14:24
32 [a]1 Sam. 20:8; [Prov. 28:13]
33 [a]Gen. 33:4; 45:15; Luke 15:20

CHAPTER 15
1 [a]2 Sam. 12:11 [b]1 Kin. 1:5
2 [a]Deut. 19:17
4 [a]Judg. 9:29
5 [a]2 Sam. 14:33; 20:9
6 [a][Rom. 16:18]
7 [a][Deut. 23:21]

*———
15:7 LXX mss., Syr., Josephus *four*

NKJV

wise, [a]according to the wisdom of the angel of God, to know everything that *is* in the earth."

21 And the king said to Joab, "All right, I have granted this thing. Go therefore, bring back the young man Absalom."

22 Then Joab fell to the ground on his face and bowed himself, and thanked the king. And Joab said, "Today your servant knows that I have found favor in your sight, my lord, O king, in that the king has fulfilled the request of his servant."

23 So Joab arose [a]and went to Geshur, and brought Absalom to Jerusalem.

24 And the king said, "Let him return to his own house, but [a]do not let him see my face." So Absalom returned to his own house, but did not see the king's face.

David Forgives Absalom

25 Now in all Israel there was no one who was praised as much as Absalom for his good looks. [a]From the sole of his foot to the crown of his head there was no blemish in him.

26 And when he cut the hair of his head—at the end of every year he cut *it* because it was heavy on him—when he cut it, he weighed the hair of his head at two hundred shekels according to the king's standard.

27 [a]To Absalom were born three sons, and one daughter whose name *was* Tamar. She was a woman of beautiful appearance.

28 And Absalom dwelt two full years in Jerusalem, [a]but did not see the king's face.

29 Therefore Absalom sent for Joab, to send him to the king, but he would not come to him. And when he sent again the second time, he would not come.

30 So he said to his servants, "See, Joab's field is near mine, and he has barley there; go and set it on fire." And Absalom's servants set the field on fire.

31 Then Joab arose and came to Absalom's house, and said to him, "Why have your servants set my field on fire?"

32 And Absalom answered Joab, "Look, I sent to you, saying, 'Come here, so that I may send you to the king, to say, "Why have I come from Geshur? *It would be* better for me *to be* there still." ' Now therefore, let me see the king's face; but [a]if there is iniquity in me, let him execute me."

33 So Joab went to the king and told him. And when he had called for Absalom, he came to the king and bowed himself on his face to the ground before the king. Then the king [a]kissed Absalom.

Absalom's Treason

15 After this [a]it happened that Absalom [b]provided himself with chariots and horses, and fifty men to run before him.

2 Now Absalom would rise early and stand beside the way to the gate. *So* it was, whenever anyone who had a [a]lawsuit came to the king for a decision, that Absalom would call to him and say, "What city *are* you from?" And he would say, "Your servant *is* from such and such a tribe of Israel."

3 Then Absalom would say to him, "Look, your case *is* good and right; but *there is* no deputy of the king to hear you."

4 Moreover Absalom would say, [a]"Oh, that I were made judge in the land, and everyone who has any suit or cause would come to me; then I would give him justice."

5 And *so* it was, whenever anyone came near to bow down to him, that he would put out his hand and take him and [a]kiss him.

6 In this manner Absalom acted toward all Israel who came to the king for judgment. [a]So Absalom stole the hearts of the men of Israel.

7 Now it came to pass [a]after *forty years that Absalom said to the king, "Please, let me go

KJV

go and pay my vow, which I have vowed unto the LORD, in [b]Hebron.

8 [a]For thy servant [b]vowed a vow [c]while I abode at Geshur in Syria, saying, If the LORD shall bring me again indeed to Jerusalem, then I will serve the LORD.

9 And the king said unto him, Go in peace. So he arose, and went to Hebron.

10 But Absalom sent spies throughout all the tribes of Israel, saying, As soon as ye hear the sound of the trumpet, then ye shall say, Absalom [a]reigneth in Hebron.

11 And with Absalom went two hundred men out of Jerusalem, *that were* [a]called; and they [b]went in their simplicity, and they knew not any thing.

12 And Absalom sent for Ahithophel the Gilonite, [a]David's counsellor, from his city, *even* from [b]Giloh, while he offered sacrifices. And the conspiracy was strong; for the people [c]increased continually with Absalom.

David Escapes from Jerusalem

13 And there came a messenger to David, saying, [a]The hearts of the men of Israel are after Absalom.

14 And David said unto all his servants that *were* with him at Jerusalem, Arise, and let us [a]flee; for we shall not *else* escape from Absalom: make speed to depart, lest he overtake us suddenly, and bring evil upon us, and smite the city with the edge of the sword.

15 And the king's servants said unto the king, Behold, thy servants *are ready to do* whatsoever my lord the king shall appoint.

16 And [a]the king went forth, and all his household after him. And the king left [b]ten women, *which were* concubines, to keep the house.

17 And the king went forth, and all the people after him, and tarried in a place that was far off.

18 And all his servants passed on beside him; [a]and all the Cherethites, and all the Pelethites, and all the Gittites, [b]six hundred men which came after him from Gath, passed on before the king.

19 Then said the king to [a]Ittai the Gittite, Wherefore goest thou also with us? return to thy place, and abide with the king: for thou *art* a stranger, and also an exile.

20 Whereas thou camest *but* yesterday, should I this day make thee go up and down with us? seeing I go [a]whither I may, return thou, and take back thy brethren: mercy and truth *be* with thee.

21 And Ittai answered the king, and said, [a]*As* the LORD liveth, and *as* my lord the king liveth, surely in what place my lord the king shall be, whether in death or life, even there also will thy servant be.

22 And David said to Ittai, Go and pass over. And Ittai the Gittite passed over, and all his men, and all the little ones that *were* with him.

23 And all the country wept with a loud voice, and all the people passed over: the king also himself passed over the brook Kidron, and all the people passed over, toward the way of the [a]wilderness.

24 And lo [a]Zadok also, and all the Levites *were* with him, bearing the [b]ark of the covenant of God: and they set down the ark of God; and [c]Abiathar went up, until all the people had done passing out of the city.

25 And the king said unto Zadok, Carry back the ark of God into the city: if I shall find favour in the eyes of the LORD, he [a]will bring me again, and shew me *both* it, and [b]his habitation:

26 But if he thus say, I have no [a]delight in thee; behold, *here am* I, [b]let him do to me as seemeth good unto him.

27 The king said also unto Zadok the priest, *Art not* thou a [a]seer? return into the city in peace,

7 [b]2 Sam. 3:2, 3
8 [a]1 Sam. 16:2 [b]Gen. 28:20, 21 [c]2 Sam. 13:38
10 [a]1 Kin. 1:34; 2 Kin. 9:13
11 [a]1 Sam. 16:3, 5 [b]Gen. 20:5
12 [a]2 Sam. 16:15; 1 Chr. 27:33; Ps. 41:9; 55:12–14 [b]Josh. 15:51 [c]Ps. 3:1
13 [a]Judg. 9:3; 2 Sam. 15:6
14 [a]2 Sam. 12:11; Ps. 3:title
16 [a]Ps. 3:title [b]2 Sam. 12:11; 16:21, 22
18 [a]2 Sam. 8:18 [b]1 Sam. 23:13; 25:13; 30:1, 9
19 [a]2 Sam. 18:2
20 [a]1 Sam. 23:13
21 [a]Ruth 1:16, 17; [Prov. 17:17]
23 [a]2 Sam. 15:28; 16:2
24 [a]2 Sam. 8:17 [b]Num. 4:15; 1 Sam. 4:4 [c]1 Sam. 22:20
25 [a][Ps. 43:3] [b]Ex. 15:13; Jer. 25:30
26 [a]Num. 14:8; 2 Sam. 22:20; 1 Kin. 10:9; 2 Chr. 9:8; Is. 62:4 [b]1 Sam. 3:18
27 [a]1 Sam. 9:6–9

NKJV

to [b]Hebron and pay the vow which I made to the LORD.

8 [a]"For your servant [b]took a vow [c]while I dwelt at Geshur in Syria, saying, 'If the LORD indeed brings me back to Jerusalem, then I will serve the LORD.' "

9 And the king said to him, "Go in peace." So he arose and went to Hebron.

10 Then Absalom sent spies throughout all the tribes of Israel, saying, "As soon as you hear the sound of the trumpet, then you shall say, 'Absalom [a]reigns in Hebron!' "

11 And with Absalom went two hundred men [a]invited from Jerusalem, and they [b]went along innocently and did not know anything.

12 Then Absalom sent for Ahithophel the Gilonite, [a]David's counselor, from his city—from [b]Giloh—while he offered sacrifices. And the conspiracy grew strong, for the people with Absalom [c]continually increased in number.

David Escapes from Jerusalem

13 Now a messenger came to David, saying, [a]"The hearts of the men of Israel are with Absalom."

14 So David said to all his servants who *were* with him at Jerusalem, "Arise, and let us [a]flee, or we shall not escape from Absalom. Make haste to depart, lest he overtake us suddenly and bring disaster upon us, and strike the city with the edge of the sword."

15 And the king's servants said to the king, "We *are* your servants, *ready to do* whatever my lord the king commands."

16 Then [a]the king went out with all his household after him. But the king left [b]ten women, concubines, to keep the house.

17 And the king went out with all the people after him, and stopped at the outskirts.

18 Then all his servants passed before him; [a]and all the Cherethites, all the Pelethites, and all the Gittites, [b]six hundred men who had followed him from Gath, passed before the king.

19 Then the king said to [a]Ittai the Gittite, "Why are you also going with us? Return and remain with the king. For you *are* a foreigner and also an exile from your own place.

20 "In fact, you came *only* yesterday. Should I make you wander up and down with us today, since I go [a]I know not where? Return, and take your brethren back. Mercy and truth *be* with you."

21 But Ittai answered the king and said, [a]"*As* the LORD lives, and *as* my lord the king lives, surely in whatever place my lord the king shall be, whether in death or life, even there also your servant will be."

22 So David said to Ittai, "Go, and cross over." Then Ittai the Gittite and all his men and all the little ones who *were* with him crossed over.

23 And all the country wept with a loud voice, and all the people crossed over. The king himself also crossed over the Brook Kidron, and all the people crossed over toward the way of the [a]wilderness.

24 There was [a]Zadok also, and all the Levites with him, bearing the [b]ark of the covenant of God. And they set down the ark of God, and [c]Abiathar went up until all the people had finished crossing over from the city.

25 Then the king said to Zadok, "Carry the ark of God back into the city. If I find favor in the eyes of the LORD, He [a]will bring me back and show me *both* it and [b]His dwelling place.

26 "But if He says thus: 'I have no [a]delight in you,' here I am, [b]let Him do to me as seems good to Him."

27 The king also said to Zadok the priest, "*Are* you *not* a [a]seer? Return to the city in peace,

KJV

and [b]your two sons with you, Ahimaaz thy son, and Jonathan the son of Abiathar.

28 See, [a]I will tarry in the plain of the wilderness, until there come word from you to certify me.

29 Zadok therefore and Abiathar carried the ark of God again to Jerusalem: and they tarried there.

30 And David went up by the ascent of *mount* Olivet, and wept as he went up, and [a]had his head covered, and he went [b]barefoot: and all the people that *was* with him [c]covered every man his head, and they went up, [d]weeping as they went up.

31 And *one* told David, saying, [a]Ahithophel *is* among the conspirators with Absalom. And David said, O LORD, I pray thee, [b]turn the counsel of Ahithophel into foolishness.

32 And it came to pass, that *when* David was come to the top *of the mount,* where he worshipped God, behold, Hushai the [a]Archite came to meet him [b]with his coat rent, and earth upon his head:

33 Unto whom David said, If thou passest on with me, then thou shalt be [a]a burden unto me:

34 But if thou return to the city, and say unto Absalom, [a]I will be thy servant, O king; *as* I *have been* thy father's servant hitherto, so *will* I now also *be* thy servant: then mayest thou for me defeat the counsel of Ahithophel.

35 And *hast thou* not there with thee Zadok and Abiathar the priests? therefore it shall be, *that* what thing soever thou shalt hear out of the king's house, thou shalt tell *it* to [a]Zadok and Abiathar the priests.

36 Behold, *they have* there [a]with them their two sons, Ahimaaz Zadok's *son,* and Jonathan Abiathar's *son;* and by them ye shall send unto me every thing that ye can hear.

37 So Hushai [a]David's friend came into the city, [b]and Absalom came into Jerusalem.

Mephibosheth's Servant

16 And [a]when David was a little past the top *of the hill,* behold, [b]Ziba the servant of Mephibosheth met him, with a couple of asses saddled, and upon them two hundred *loaves* of bread, and an hundred bunches of raisins, and an hundred of summer fruits, and a bottle of wine.

2 And the king said unto Ziba, What meanest thou by these? And Ziba said, The asses *be* for the king's household to ride on; and the bread and summer fruit for the young men to eat; and the wine, [a]that such as be faint in the wilderness may drink.

3 And the king said, And where *is* thy [a]master's son? [b]And Ziba said unto the king, Behold, he abideth at Jerusalem: for he said, To day shall the house of Israel restore me the kingdom of my father.

4 Then said the king to Ziba, Behold, thine *are* all that *pertained* unto Mephibosheth. And Ziba said, I humbly beseech thee *that* I may find grace in thy sight, my lord, O king.

Shimei Curses David

5 And when king David came to [a]Bahurim, behold, thence came out a man of the family of the house of Saul, whose name *was* [b]Shimei, the son of Gera: he came forth, and cursed still as he came.

6 And he cast stones at David, and at all the servants of king David: and all the people and all the mighty men *were* on his right hand and on his left.

7 And thus said Shimei when he cursed, Come out, come out, thou bloody man, and thou [a]man of Belial:

8 The LORD hath [a]returned upon thee all [b]the blood of the house of Saul, in whose stead thou hast reigned; and the LORD hath delivered the kingdom into the hand of Absalom thy son:

27 [b]2 Sam. 17:17–20
28 [a]Josh. 5:10; 2 Sam. 17:16
30 [a]2 Sam. 19:4; Esth. 6:12; Ezek. 24:17, 23 [b]Is. 20:2–4 [c]Jer. 14:3, 4 [d][Ps. 126:6]
31 [a]Ps. 3:1, 2; 55:12 [b]2 Sam. 16:23; 17:14, 23
32 [a]Josh. 16:2 [b]2 Sam. 1:2
33 [a]2 Sam. 19:35
34 [a]2 Sam. 16:19
35 [a]2 Sam. 17:15, 16
36 [a]2 Sam. 15:27
37 [a]2 Sam. 16:16; 1 Chr. 27:33 [b]2 Sam. 16:15

CHAPTER 16
1 [a]2 Sam. 15:30, 32 [b]2 Sam. 9:2; 19:17, 29
2 [a]2 Sam. 15:23; 17:29
3 [a]2 Sam. 9:9, 10 [b]2 Sam. 19:27
5 [a]2 Sam. 3:16 [b]2 Sam. 19:21; 1 Kin. 2:8, 9, 44–46
7 [a]Deut. 13:13
8 [a]Judg. 9:24, 56, 57; 1 Kin. 2:32, 33 [b]2 Sam. 1:16; 3:28, 29; 4:11, 12

NKJV

and [b]your two sons with you, Ahimaaz your son, and Jonathan the son of Abiathar.

28 "See, [a]I will wait in the plains of the wilderness until word comes from you to inform me."

29 Therefore Zadok and Abiathar carried the ark of God back to Jerusalem. And they remained there.

30 So David went up by the Ascent of the *Mount of* Olives, and wept as he went up; and he [a]had his head covered and went [b]barefoot. And all the people who *were* with him [c]covered their heads and went up, [d]weeping as they went up.

31 Then *someone* told David, saying, [a]"Ahithophel *is* among the conspirators with Absalom." And David said, "O LORD, I pray, [b]turn the counsel of Ahithophel into foolishness!"

32 Now it happened when David had come to the top *of the mountain,* where he worshiped God—there was Hushai the [a]Archite coming to meet him [b]with his robe torn and dust on his head.

33 David said to him, "If you go on with me, then you will become [a]a burden to me.

34 "But if you return to the city, and say to Absalom, [a]'I will be your servant, O king; *as* I *was* your father's servant previously, so I *will* now also *be* your servant,' then you may defeat the counsel of Ahithophel for me.

35 "And *do* you not *have* Zadok and Abiathar the priests with you there? Therefore it will be *that* whatever you hear from the king's house, you shall tell to [a]Zadok and Abiathar the priests.

36 "Indeed *they have* there [a]with them their two sons, Ahimaaz, Zadok's *son,* and Jonathan, Abiathar's *son;* and by them you shall send me everything you hear."

37 So Hushai, [a]David's friend, went into the city. [b]And Absalom came into Jerusalem.

Mephibosheth's Servant

16 When[a] David was a little past the top *of the mountain,* there was [b]Ziba the servant of Mephibosheth, who met him with a couple of saddled donkeys, and on them two hundred *loaves* of bread, one hundred clusters of raisins, one hundred summer fruits, and a skin of wine.

2 And the king said to Ziba, "What do you mean to do with these?" So Ziba said, "The donkeys *are* for the king's household to ride on, the bread and summer fruit for the young men to eat, and the wine for [a]those who are faint in the wilderness to drink."

3 Then the king said, "And where *is* your [a]master's son?" [b]And Ziba said to the king, "Indeed he is staying in Jerusalem, for he said, 'Today the house of Israel will restore the kingdom of my father to me.' "

4 So the king said to Ziba, "Here, all that *belongs* to Mephibosheth *is* yours." And Ziba said, "I humbly bow before you, *that* I may find favor in your sight, my lord, O king!"

Shimei Curses David

5 Now when King David came to [a]Bahurim, there was a man from the family of the house of Saul, whose name *was* [b]Shimei the son of Gera, coming from there. He came out, cursing continuously as he came.

6 And he threw stones at David and at all the servants of King David. And all the people and all the mighty men *were* on his right hand and on his left.

7 Also Shimei said thus when he cursed: "Come out! Come out! You bloodthirsty man, [a]you rogue!

8 "The LORD has [a]brought upon you all [b]the blood of the house of Saul, in whose place you have reigned; and the LORD has delivered the kingdom into the hand of Absalom your son. So

KJV

and, behold, thou *art taken* in thy mischief, because thou *art* a bloody man.
9 Then said Abishai the son of Zeruiah unto
the king, Why should this [a]dead dog [b]curse my
lord the king? let me go over, I pray thee, and
take off his head.
10 And the king said, [a]What have I to do with
you, ye sons of Zeruiah? so let him curse, because
[b]the LORD hath said unto him, Curse David.
[c]Who shall then say, Wherefore hast thou done
so?
11 And David said to Abishai, and to all his
servants, Behold, [a]my son, which [b]came forth of
my bowels, seeketh my life: how much more now
may this Benjamite *do it?* let him alone, and let
him curse; for the LORD hath bidden him.
12 It may be that the LORD will look on mine
affliction, and that the LORD will [a]requite me
[b]good for his cursing this day.
13 And as David and his men went by the
way, Shimei went along on the hill's side over
against him, and cursed as he went, and threw
stones at him, and cast dust.
14 And the king, and all the people that *were*
with him, came weary, and refreshed themselves
there.

The Advice of Ahithophel

15 And [a]Absalom, and all the people the men
of Israel, came to Jerusalem, and Ahithophel with
him.
16 And it came to pass, when Hushai the Archite, [a]David's friend, was come unto Absalom,
that [b]Hushai said unto Absalom, God save the
king, God save the king.
17 And Absalom said to Hushai, *Is* this thy
kindness to thy friend? [a]why wentest thou not
with thy friend?
18 And Hushai said unto Absalom, Nay; but
whom the LORD, and this people, and all the men
of Israel, choose, his will I be, and with him will
I abide.
19 And again, [a]whom should I serve? *should*
I not *serve* in the presence of his son? as I have
served in thy father's presence, so will I be in thy
presence.
20 Then said Absalom to [a]Ahithophel, Give
counsel among you what we shall do.
21 And Ahithophel said unto Absalom, Go
in unto thy father's [a]concubines, which he hath
left to keep the house; and all Israel shall hear
that thou [b]art abhorred of thy father: then shall
[c]the hands of all that *are* with thee be strong.
22 So they spread Absalom a tent upon the
top of the house; and Absalom went in unto his
father's concubines [a]in the sight of all Israel.
23 And the counsel of Ahithophel, which he
counselled in those days, *was* as if a man had
enquired at the oracle of God: so *was* all the counsel of Ahithophel [a]both with David and with Absalom.

17 Moreover Ahithophel said unto Absalom,
Let me now choose out twelve thousand
men, and I will arise and pursue after David this
night:
2 And I will come upon him while he *is*
[a]weary and weak handed, and will make him
afraid: and all the people that *are* with him shall
flee; and I will [b]smite the king only:
3 And I will bring back all the people unto
thee: the man whom thou seekest *is* as if all returned: *so* all the people shall be in peace.
4 And the saying pleased Absalom well, and
all the [a]elders of Israel.

The Advice of Hushai

5 Then said Absalom, Call now Hushai the
Archite also, and let us hear likewise what he
[a]saith.
6 And when Hushai was come to Absalom,
Absalom spake unto him, saying, Ahithophel hath

9 [a]1 Sam. 24:14; 2 Sam. 9:8 [b]Ex. 22:28
10 [a]2 Sam. 3:39; 19:22; [1 Pet. 2:23] [b]2 Kin. 18:25; [Lam. 3:38] [c][Rom. 9:20]
11 [a]2 Sam. 12:11 [b]Gen. 15:4
12 [a]Deut. 23:5; Neh. 13:2; Prov. 20:22 [b]Deut. 23:5; [Rom. 8:28; Heb. 12:10, 11]
15 [a]2 Sam. 15:12, 37
16 [a]2 Sam. 15:37 [b]2 Sam. 15:34
17 [a]2 Sam. 19:25; [Prov. 17:17]
19 [a]2 Sam. 15:34
20 [a]2 Sam. 15:12
21 [a]2 Sam. 15:16; 20:3 [b]Gen. 34:30; 1 Sam. 13:4 [c]2 Sam. 2:7; Zech. 8:13
22 [a]2 Sam. 12:11, 12
23 [a]2 Sam. 15:12

CHAPTER 17
2 [a]Deut. 25:18; 2 Sam. 16:14 [b]Zech. 13:7
4 [a]2 Sam. 5:3; 19:11
5 [a]2 Sam. 15:32–34

NKJV

now you *are caught* in your own evil, because
you are a bloodthirsty man!"
9 Then Abishai the son of Zeruiah said to
the king, "Why should this [a]dead dog [b]curse my
lord the king? Please, let me go over and take
off his head!"
10 But the king said, [a]"What have I to do
with you, you sons of Zeruiah? So let him curse,
because [b]the LORD has said to him, 'Curse David.'
[c]Who then shall say, 'Why have you done so?' "
11 And David said to Abishai and all his servants, "See how [a]my son who [b]came from my
own body seeks my life. How much more now
may this Benjamite? Let him alone, and let him
curse; for so the LORD has ordered him.
12 "It may be that the LORD will look on *my
affliction, and that the LORD will [a]repay me with
[b]good for his cursing this day."
13 And as David and his men went along the
road, Shimei went along the hillside opposite him
and cursed as he went, threw stones at him and
kicked up dust.
14 Now the king and all the people who *were*
with him became weary; so they refreshed themselves there.

The Advice of Ahithophel

15 Meanwhile [a]Absalom and all the people,
the men of Israel, came to Jerusalem; and Ahithophel *was* with him.
16 And so it was, when Hushai the Archite,
[a]David's friend, came to Absalom, that [b]Hushai
said to Absalom, "*Long* live the king! *Long* live
the king!"
17 So Absalom said to Hushai, "*Is* this your
loyalty to your friend? [a]Why did you not go with
your friend?"
18 And Hushai said to Absalom, "No, but
whom the LORD and this people and all the men
of Israel choose, his I will be, and with him I will
remain.
19 "Furthermore, [a]whom should I serve?
Should I not *serve* in the presence of his son? As
I have served in your father's presence, so will I
be in your presence."
20 Then Absalom said to [a]Ahithophel, "Give
advice as to what we should do."
21 And Ahithophel said to Absalom, "Go in
to your father's [a]concubines, whom he has left
to keep the house; and all Israel will hear that
you [b]are abhorred by your father. Then [c]the
hands of all who are with you will be strong."
22 So they pitched a tent for Absalom on the
top of the house, and Absalom went in to his father's concubines [a]in the sight of all Israel.
23 Now the advice of Ahithophel, which he
gave in those days, *was* as if one had inquired at
the oracle of God. So *was* all the advice of Ahithophel [a]both with David and with Absalom.

17 Moreover Ahithophel said to Absalom,
"Now let me choose twelve thousand men,
and I will arise and pursue David tonight.
2 "I will come upon him while he *is* [a]weary
and weak, and make him afraid. And all the people who *are* with him will flee, and I will [b]strike
only the king.
3 "Then I will bring back all the people to
you. When all return except the man whom you
seek, all the people will be at peace."
4 And the saying pleased Absalom and all
the [a]elders of Israel.

The Advice of Hushai

5 Then Absalom said, "Now call Hushai the
Archite also, and let us hear what he [a]says too."
6 And when Hushai came to Absalom, Absalom spoke to him, saying, "Ahithophel has spo-

*
16:12 So with Kt., LXX, Syr., Vg.; Qr. *my eyes;* Tg. *tears of my eyes*

KJV

spoken after this manner: shall we do *after* his
saying? if not; speak thou.
7 And Hushai said unto Absalom, The counsel that Ahithophel hath given *is* not good at this
time.
8 For, said Hushai, thou knowest thy father
and his men, that they *be* mighty men, and they
be chafed in their minds, as [a]a bear robbed of
her whelps in the field: and thy father *is* a man
of war, and will not lodge with the people.
9 Behold, he is hid now in some pit, or in
some *other* place: and it will come to pass, when
some of them be overthrown at the first, that whosoever heareth it will say, There is a slaughter
among the people that follow Absalom.
10 And he also *that is* valiant, whose heart
is as the heart of a lion, shall utterly [a]melt: for
all Israel knoweth that thy father *is* a mighty man,
and *they* which *be* with him *are* valiant men.
11 Therefore I counsel that all Israel be generally gathered unto thee, [a]from Dan even to
Beer–sheba, [b]as the sand that *is* by the sea for
multitude; and that thou go to battle in thine own
person.
12 So shall we come upon him in some place
where he shall be found, and we will light upon
him as the dew falleth on the ground: and of him
and of all the men that *are* with him there shall
not be left so much as one.
13 Moreover, if he be gotten into a city, then
shall all Israel bring ropes to that city, and we
will [a]draw it into the river, until there be not one
small stone found there.
14 And Absalom and all the men of Israel
said, The counsel of Hushai the Archite *is* better
than the counsel of Ahithophel. For [a]the LORD had
appointed to defeat the good counsel of Ahithophel, to the intent that the LORD might bring evil
upon Absalom.

Hushai Warns David to Escape

15 [a]Then said Hushai unto Zadok and to Abiathar the priests, Thus and thus did Ahithophel
counsel Absalom and the elders of Israel; and thus
and thus have I counselled.
16 Now therefore send quickly, and tell David, saying, Lodge not this night [a]in the plains of
the wilderness, but speedily pass over; lest the
king be swallowed up, and all the people that *are*
with him.
17 [a]Now Jonathan and Ahimaaz [b]stayed by
[c]En–rogel; for they might not be seen to come
into the city: and a wench went and told them;
and they went and told king David.
18 Nevertheless a lad saw them, and told Absalom: but they went both of them away quickly,
and came to a man's house [a]in Bahurim, which
had a well in his court; whither they went down.
19 [a]And the woman took and spread a covering over the well's mouth, and spread ground corn
thereon; and the thing was not known.
20 And when Absalom's servants came to the
woman to the house, they said, Where *is* Ahimaaz
and Jonathan? And [a]the woman said unto them,
They be gone over the brook of water. And when
they had sought and could not find *them*, they
returned to Jerusalem.
21 And it came to pass, after they were departed, that they came up out of the well, and
went and told king David, and said unto David,
[a]Arise, and pass quickly over the water: for thus
hath Ahithophel counselled against you.
22 Then David arose, and all the people that
were with him, and they passed over Jordan: by
the morning light there lacked not one of them
that was not gone over Jordan.
23 And when Ahithophel saw that his counsel was not followed, he saddled *his* ass, and
arose, and gat him home to [a]his house, to his city,
and put his [b]household in order, and [c]hanged
himself, and died, and was buried in the sepulchre
of his father.

8 [a]Hos. 13:8
10 [a]Josh. 2:11
11 [a]Judg. 20:1; 2 Sam. 3:10 [b]Gen. 22:17; Josh. 11:4; 1 Kin. 20:10
13 [a]Mic. 1:6
14 [a]2 Sam. 15:31, 34
15 [a]2 Sam. 15:35, 36
16 [a]2 Sam. 15:28
17 [a]2 Sam. 15:27, 36; 1 Kin. 1:42, 43 [b]Josh. 2:4–6 [c]Josh. 15:7; 18:16
18 [a]2 Sam. 3:16; 16:5
19 [a]Josh. 2:4–6
20 [a]Ex. 1:19; [Lev. 19:11]; Josh. 2:3–5
21 [a]2 Sam. 17:15, 16
23 [a]2 Sam. 15:12 [b]2 Kin. 20:1 [c]Matt. 27:5

NKJV

ken in this manner. Shall we do as he says? If
not, speak up."
7 So Hushai said to Absalom: "The advice
that Ahithophel has given *is* not good at this time.
8 "For," said Hushai, "you know your father
and his men, that they *are* mighty men, and they
are enraged in their minds, like [a]a bear robbed
of her cubs in the field; and your father *is* a man
of war, and will not camp with the people.
9 "Surely by now he is hidden in some pit,
or in some *other* place. And it will be, when some
of them are overthrown at the first, that whoever
hears *it* will say, 'There is a slaughter among the
people who follow Absalom.'
10 "And even he *who is* valiant, whose heart
is like the heart of a lion, will [a]melt completely.
For all Israel knows that your father *is* a mighty
man, and *those* who *are* with him *are* valiant men.
11 "Therefore I advise that all Israel be fully
gathered to you, [a]from Dan to Beersheba, [b]like
the sand that *is* by the sea for multitude, and that
you go to battle in person.
12 "So we will come upon him in some place
where he may be found, and we will fall on him
as the dew falls on the ground. And of him and
all the men who *are* with him there shall not be
left so much as one.
13 "Moreover, if he has withdrawn into a
city, then all Israel shall bring ropes to that city;
and we will [a]pull it into the river, until there is
not one small stone found there."
14 So Absalom and all the men of Israel said,
"The advice of Hushai the Archite *is* better than
the advice of Ahithophel." For [a]the LORD had purposed to defeat the good advice of Ahithophel,
to the intent that the LORD might bring disaster
on Absalom.

Hushai Warns David to Escape

15 [a]Then Hushai said to Zadok and Abiathar
the priests, "Thus and so Ahithophel advised Absalom and the elders of Israel, and thus and so I
have advised.
16 "Now therefore, send quickly and tell David, saying, 'Do not spend this night [a]in the plains
of the wilderness, but speedily cross over, lest the
king and all the people who *are* with him be swallowed up.'"
17 [a]Now Jonathan and Ahimaaz [b]stayed at
[c]En Rogel, for they dared not be seen coming into
the city; so a female servant would come and tell
them, and they would go and tell King David.
18 Nevertheless a lad saw them, and told Absalom. But both of them went away quickly and
came to a man's house [a]in Bahurim, who had a
well in his court; and they went down into it.
19 [a]Then the woman took and spread a covering over the well's mouth, and spread ground
grain on it; and the thing was not known.
20 And when Absalom's servants came to the
woman at the house, they said, "Where *are* Ahimaaz and Jonathan?" So [a]the woman said to
them, "They have gone over the water brook."
And when they had searched and could not find
them, they returned to Jerusalem.
21 Now it came to pass, after they had departed, that they came up out of the well and went
and told King David, and said to David, [a]"Arise
and cross over the water quickly. For thus has
Ahithophel advised against you."
22 So David and all the people who *were* with
him arose and crossed over the Jordan. By morning light not one of them was left who had not
gone over the Jordan.
23 Now when Ahithophel saw that his advice
was not followed, he saddled a donkey, and arose
and went home to [a]his house, to his city. Then
he put his [b]household in order, and [c]hanged himself, and died; and he was buried in his father's
tomb.

KJV

24 Then David came to [a]Mahanaim. And Absalom passed over Jordan, he and all the men of Israel with him.

25 And Absalom made [a]Amasa captain of the host instead of Joab: which Amasa *was* a man's son, whose name *was* Ithra an Israelite, that went in to [b]Abigail the daughter of Nahash, sister to Zeruiah Joab's mother.

26 So Israel and Absalom pitched in the land of Gilead.

27 And it came to pass, when David was come to Mahanaim, that [a]Shobi the son of Nahash of Rabbah of the children of Ammon, and [b]Machir the son of Ammiel of Lo–debar, and [c]Barzillai the Gileadite of Rogelim,

28 Brought beds, and basons, and earthen vessels, and wheat, and barley, and flour, and parched *corn,* and beans, and lentiles, and parched *pulse,*

29 And honey, and butter, and sheep, and cheese of kine, for David, and for the people that *were* with him, to eat: for they said, The people *is* hungry, and weary, and thirsty, [a]in the wilderness.

Absalom's Defeat and Death

18 And David numbered the people that *were* with him, and [a]set captains of thousands and captains of hundreds over them.

2 And David sent forth a third part of the people under the hand of Joab, [a]and a third part under the hand of Abishai the son of Zeruiah, Joab's brother, and a third part under the hand of [b]Ittai the Gittite. And the king said unto the people, I will surely go forth with you myself also.

3 [a]But the people answered, Thou shalt not go forth: for if we flee away, they will not care for us; neither if half of us die, will they care for us: but now *thou art* worth ten thousand of us: therefore now *it is* better that thou succour us out of the city.

4 And the king said unto them, What seemeth you best I will do. And the king stood by the gate side, and all the people came out by hundreds and by thousands.

5 And the king commanded Joab and Abishai and Ittai, saying, *Deal* gently for my sake with the young man, *even* with Absalom. [a]And all the people heard when the king gave all the captains charge concerning Absalom.

6 So the people went out into the field against Israel: and the battle was in the [a]wood of Ephraim;

7 Where the people of Israel were slain before the servants of David, and there was there a great slaughter that day of twenty thousand *men.*

8 For the battle was there scattered over the face of all the country: and the wood devoured more people that day than the sword devoured.

9 And Absalom met the servants of David. And Absalom rode upon a mule, and the mule went under the thick boughs of a great oak, and [a]his head caught hold of the oak, and he was taken up between the heaven and the earth; and the mule that *was* under him went away.

10 And a certain man saw *it,* and told Joab, and said, Behold, I saw Absalom hanged in an oak.

11 And Joab said unto the man that told him, And, behold, thou sawest *him,* and why didst thou not smite him there to the ground? and I would have given thee ten *shekels* of silver, and a girdle.

12 And the man said unto Joab, Though I should receive a thousand *shekels* of silver in mine hand, *yet* would I not put forth mine hand against the king's son: [a]for in our hearing the king charged thee and Abishai and Ittai, saying, Beware that none *touch* the young man Absalom.

13 Otherwise I should have wrought falsehood against mine own life: for there is no matter

24 [a]Gen. 32:2; Josh. 13:26; 2 Sam. 2:8; 19:32
25 [a]2 Sam. 19:13; 20:9–12; 1 Kin. 2:5, 32 [b]1 Chr. 2:16
27 [a]1 Sam. 11:1; 2 Sam. 10:1; 12:29 [b]2 Sam. 9:4 [c]2 Sam. 19:31, 32; 1 Kin. 2:7
29 [a]2 Sam. 16:2, 14

CHAPTER 18
1 [a]Ex. 18:25; Num. 31:14; 1 Sam. 22:7
2 [a]Judg. 7:16; 1 Sam. 11:11 [b]2 Sam. 15:19–22
3 [a]2 Sam. 21:17
5 [a]2 Sam. 18:12
6 [a]Josh. 17:15, 18; 2 Sam. 17:26
9 [a]2 Sam. 14:26
12 [a]2 Sam. 18:5

*———
17:25 *Jether,* 1 Chr. 2:17 • So with MT, some LXX mss., Tg.; some LXX mss. *Ishmaelite* (cf. 1 Chr. 2:17); Vg. *of Jezrael*
18:12 Vss. *'Protect the young man Absalom for me!'*

NKJV

24 Then David went to [a]Mahanaim. And Absalom crossed over the Jordan, he and all the men of Israel with him.

25 And Absalom made [a]Amasa captain of the army instead of Joab. This Amasa *was* the son of a man whose name *was* *Jithra, an *Israelite, who had gone in to [b]Abigail the daughter of Nahash, sister of Zeruiah, Joab's mother.

26 So Israel and Absalom encamped in the land of Gilead.

27 Now it happened, when David had come to Mahanaim, that [a]Shobi the son of Nahash from Rabbah of the people of Ammon, [b]Machir the son of Ammiel from Lo Debar, and [c]Barzillai the Gileadite from Rogelim,

28 brought beds and basins, earthen vessels and wheat, barley and flour, parched *grain* and beans, lentils and parched *seeds,*

29 honey and curds, sheep and cheese of the herd, for David and the people who *were* with him to eat. For they said, "The people are hungry and weary and thirsty [a]in the wilderness."

Absalom's Defeat and Death

18 And David numbered the people who *were* with him, and [a]set captains of thousands and captains of hundreds over them.

2 Then David sent out one third of the people under the hand of Joab, [a]one third under the hand of Abishai the son of Zeruiah, Joab's brother, and one third under the hand of [b]Ittai the Gittite. And the king said to the people, "I also will surely go out with you myself."

3 [a]But the people answered, "You shall not go out! For if we flee away, they will not care about us; nor if half of us die, will they care about us. But *you are* worth ten thousand of us now. For you are now more help to us in the city."

4 Then the king said to them, "Whatever seems best to you I will do." So the king stood beside the gate, and all the people went out by hundreds and by thousands.

5 Now the king had commanded Joab, Abishai, and Ittai, saying, "*Deal* gently for my sake with the young man Absalom." [a]And all the people heard when the king gave all the captains orders concerning Absalom.

6 So the people went out into the field of battle against Israel. And the battle was in the [a]woods of Ephraim.

7 The people of Israel were overthrown there before the servants of David, and a great slaughter of twenty thousand took place there that day.

8 For the battle there was scattered over the face of the whole countryside, and the woods devoured more people that day than the sword devoured.

9 Then Absalom met the servants of David. Absalom rode on a mule. The mule went under the thick boughs of a great terebinth tree, and [a]his head caught in the terebinth; so he was left hanging between heaven and earth. And the mule which *was* under him went on.

10 Now a certain man saw *it* and told Joab, and said, "I just saw Absalom hanging in a terebinth tree!"

11 So Joab said to the man who told him, "You just saw *him!* And why did you not strike him there to the ground? I would have given you ten *shekels* of silver and a belt."

12 But the man said to Joab, "Though I were to receive a thousand *shekels* of silver in my hand, I would not raise my hand against the king's son. [a]For in our hearing the king commanded you and Abishai and Ittai, saying, *'Beware lest anyone *touch* the young man Absalom!'

13 "Otherwise I would have dealt falsely against my own life. For there is nothing hidden

KJV

hid from the king, and thou thyself wouldest have set thyself against *me.*

14 Then said Joab, I may not tarry thus with thee. And he took three darts in his hand, and thrust them through the heart of Absalom, while he *was* yet alive in the midst of the oak.

15 And ten young men that bare Joab's armour compassed about and smote Absalom, and slew him.

16 And Joab blew the trumpet, and the people returned from pursuing after Israel: for Joab held back the people.

17 And they took Absalom, and cast him into a great pit in the wood, and [a]laid a very great heap of stones upon him: and all Israel [b]fled every one to his tent.

18 Now Absalom in his lifetime had taken and reared up for himself a pillar, which *is* in [a]the king's dale: for he said, [b]I have no son to keep my name in remembrance: and he called the pillar after his own name: and it is called unto this day, Absalom's place.

David Hears of Absalom's Death

19 Then said [a]Ahimaaz the son of Zadok, Let me now run, and bear the king tidings, how that the LORD hath avenged him of his enemies.

20 And Joab said unto him, Thou shalt not bear tidings this day, but thou shalt bear tidings another day: but this day thou shalt bear no tidings, because the king's son is dead.

21 Then said Joab to Cushi, Go tell the king what thou hast seen. And Cushi bowed himself unto Joab, and ran.

22 Then said Ahimaaz the son of Zadok yet again to Joab, But howsoever, let me, I pray thee, also run after Cushi. And Joab said, Wherefore wilt thou run, my son, seeing that thou hast no tidings ready?

23 But howsoever, *said he,* let me run. And he said unto him, Run. Then Ahimaaz ran by the way of the plain, and overran Cushi.

24 And David sat between the [a]two gates: and the watchman went up to the roof over the gate unto the wall, and lifted up his eyes, and looked, and behold a man running alone.

25 And the watchman cried, and told the king. And the king said, If he *be* alone, *there is* tidings in his mouth. And he came apace, and drew near.

26 And the watchman saw another man running: and the watchman called unto the porter, and said, Behold *another* man running alone. And the king said, He also bringeth tidings.

27 And the watchman said, Me thinketh the running of the foremost is like the running of Ahimaaz the son of Zadok. And the king said, He *is* a good man, and cometh with [a]good tidings.

28 And Ahimaaz called, and said unto the king, All is well. And he fell down to the earth upon his face before the king, and said, [a]Blessed *be* the LORD thy God, which hath delivered up the men that lifted up their hand against my lord the king.

29 And the king said, Is the young man Absalom safe? And Ahimaaz answered, When Joab sent the king's servant, and *me* thy servant, I saw a great tumult, but I knew not what *it was.*

30 And the king said *unto him,* Turn aside, *and* stand here. And he turned aside, and stood still.

31 And, behold, Cushi came; and Cushi said, Tidings, my lord the king: for the LORD hath avenged thee this day of all them that rose up against thee.

32 And the king said unto Cushi, *Is* the young man Absalom safe? And Cushi answered, The enemies of my lord the king, and all that rise against thee to do *thee* hurt, be as *that* young man *is.*

17 [a]Deut. 21:20, 21; Josh. 7:26; 8:29 [b]2 Sam. 19:8; 20:1, 22
18 [a]Gen. 14:17 [b]2 Sam. 14:27
19 [a]2 Sam. 15:36; 17:17
24 [a]Judg. 5:11; 2 Sam. 13:34; 2 Kin. 9:17
27 [a]1 Kin. 1:42
28 [a]2 Sam. 16:12

NKJV

from the king, and you yourself would have set yourself against *me.*"

14 Then Joab said, "I cannot linger with you." And he took three spears in his hand and thrust them through Absalom's heart, while he was *still* alive in the midst of the terebinth tree.

15 And ten young men who bore Joab's armor surrounded Absalom, and struck and killed him.

16 So Joab blew the trumpet, and the people returned from pursuing Israel. For Joab held back the people.

17 And they took Absalom and cast him into a large pit in the woods, and [a]laid a very large heap of stones over him. Then all Israel [b]fled, everyone to his tent.

18 Now Absalom in his lifetime had taken and set up a pillar for himself, which *is* in [a]the King's Valley. For he said, [b]"I have no son to keep my name in remembrance." He called the pillar after his own name. And to this day it is called Absalom's Monument.

David Hears of Absalom's Death

19 Then [a]Ahimaaz the son of Zadok said, "Let me run now and take the news to the king, how the LORD has avenged him of his enemies."

20 And Joab said to him, "You shall not take the news this day, for you shall take the news another day. But today you shall take no news, because the king's son is dead."

21 Then Joab said to the Cushite, "Go, tell the king what you have seen." So the Cushite bowed himself to Joab and ran.

22 And Ahimaaz the son of Zadok said again to Joab, "But whatever happens, please let me also run after the Cushite." So Joab said, "Why will you run, my son, since you have no news ready?"

23 "But whatever happens," *he said,* "let me run." So he said to him, "Run." Then Ahimaaz ran by way of the plain, and outran the Cushite.

24 Now David was sitting between the [a]two gates. And the watchman went up to the roof over the gate, to the wall, lifted his eyes and looked, and there was a man, running alone.

25 Then the watchman cried out and told the king. And the king said, "If he *is* alone, *there is* news in his mouth." And he came rapidly and drew near.

26 Then the watchman saw *another* man running, and the watchman called to the gatekeeper and said, "There is *another* man, running alone!" And the king said, "He also brings news."

27 So the watchman said, "I think the running of the first is like the running of Ahimaaz the son of Zadok." And the king said, "He *is* a good man, and comes with [a]good news."

28 So Ahimaaz called out and said to the king, "All is well!" Then he bowed down with his face to the earth before the king, and said, [a]"Blessed *be* the LORD your God, who has delivered up the men who raised their hand against my lord the king!"

29 The king said, "Is the young man Absalom safe?" Ahimaaz answered, "When Joab sent the king's servant and *me* your servant, I saw a great tumult, but I did not know what *it was about.*"

30 And the king said, "Turn aside *and* stand here." So he turned aside and stood still.

31 Just then the Cushite came, and the Cushite said, "There is good news, my lord the king! For the LORD has avenged you this day of all those who rose against you."

32 And the king said to the Cushite, "Is the young man Absalom safe?" So the Cushite answered, "May the enemies of my lord the king, and all who rise against you to do harm, be like *that* young man!"

KJV

David's Mourning for Absalom

33 And the king was much moved, and went up to the chamber over the gate, and wept: and as he went, thus he said, [a]O my son Absalom, my son, my son Absalom! would God I had died for thee, O Absalom, my son, [b]my son!

19 And it was told Joab, Behold, the king weepeth and [a]mourneth for Absalom.

2 And the victory that day was *turned* into [a]mourning unto all the people: for the people heard say that day how the king was grieved for his son.

3 And the people gat them by stealth that day [a]into the city, as people being ashamed steal away when they flee in battle.

4 But the king [a]covered his face, and the king cried with a loud voice, [b]O my son Absalom, O Absalom, my son, my son!

5 And [a]Joab came into the house to the king, and said, Thou hast shamed this day the faces of all thy servants, which this day have saved thy life, and the lives of thy sons and of thy daughters, and the lives of thy wives, and the lives of thy concubines;

6 In that thou lovest thine enemies, and hatest thy friends. For thou hast declared this day, that thou regardest neither princes nor servants: for this day I perceive, that if Absalom had lived, and all we had died this day, then it had pleased thee well.

7 Now therefore arise, go forth, and speak comfortably unto thy servants: for I swear by the LORD, if thou go not forth, there will not tarry one with thee this night: and that will be worse unto thee than all the evil that befell thee from thy youth until now.

8 Then the king arose, and sat in the [a]gate. And they told unto all the people, saying, Behold, the king doth sit in the gate. And all the people came before the king: for Israel had [b]fled every man to his tent.

David Returns to Jerusalem

9 And all the people were at strife throughout all the tribes of Israel, saying, The king saved us out of the hand of our [a]enemies, and he delivered us out of the hand of the [b]Philistines; and now he is [c]fled out of the land for Absalom.

10 And Absalom, whom we anointed over us, is dead in battle. Now therefore why speak ye not a word of bringing the king back?

11 And king David sent to [a]Zadok and to Abiathar the priests, saying, Speak unto the elders of Judah, saying, Why are ye the last to bring the king back to his house? seeing the speech of all Israel is come to the king, *even* to his house.

12 Ye *are* my brethren, ye *are* [a]my bones and my flesh: wherefore then are ye the last to bring back the king?

13 [a]And say ye to Amasa, *Art* thou not of my bone, and of my flesh? [b]God do so to me, and more also, if thou be not captain of the host before me continually in the room of Joab.

14 And he bowed the heart of all the men of Judah, [a]even as *the heart of* one man; so that they sent *this word* unto the king, Return thou, and all thy servants.

15 So the king returned, and came to Jordan. And Judah came to [a]Gilgal, to go to meet the king, to conduct the king [b]over Jordan.

16 And [a]Shimei the son of Gera, a Benjamite, which *was* of Bahurim, hasted and came down with the men of Judah to meet king David.

17 And *there were* a thousand men of [a]Benjamin with him, and [b]Ziba the servant of the house of Saul, and his fifteen sons and his twenty servants with him; and they went over Jordan before the king.

18 And there went over a ferry boat to carry

33 [a]2 Sam. 12:10 [b]2 Sam. 19:4

CHAPTER 19

1 [a]Jer. 14:2
2 [a]Esth. 4:3
3 [a]2 Sam. 17:24, 27; 19:32
4 [a]2 Sam. 15:30 [b]2 Sam. 18:33
5 [a]2 Sam. 18:14
8 [a]2 Sam. 15:2; 18:24 [b]2 Sam. 18:17
9 [a]2 Sam. 8:1–14 [b]2 Sam. 3:18 [c]2 Sam. 15:14
11 [a]2 Sam. 15:24
12 [a]2 Sam. 5:1; 1 Chr. 11:1
13 [a]2 Sam. 17:25; 1 Chr. 2:17 [b]Ruth 1:17
14 [a]Judg. 20:1
15 [a]Josh. 5:9; 1 Sam. 11:14, 15 [b]2 Sam. 17:22
16 [a]2 Sam. 16:5; 1 Kin. 2:8
17 [a]2 Sam. 3:19; 1 Kin. 12:21 [b]2 Sam. 9:2, 10; 16:1, 2

NKJV

David's Mourning for Absalom

33 Then the king was deeply moved, and went up to the chamber over the gate, and wept. And as he went, he said thus: [a]"O my son Absalom—my son, my son Absalom—if only I had died in your place! O Absalom my son, [b]my son!"

19 And Joab was told, "Behold, the king is weeping and [a]mourning for Absalom."

2 So the victory that day was *turned* into [a]mourning for all the people. For the people heard it said that day, "The king is grieved for his son."

3 And the people stole back [a]into the city that day, as people who are ashamed steal away when they flee in battle.

4 But the king [a]covered his face, and the king cried out with a loud voice, [b]"O my son Absalom! O Absalom, my son, my son!"

5 Then [a]Joab came into the house to the king, and said, "Today you have disgraced all your servants who today have saved your life, the lives of your sons and daughters, the lives of your wives and the lives of your concubines,

6 "in that you love your enemies and hate your friends. For you have declared today that you regard neither princes nor servants; for today I perceive that if Absalom had lived and all of us had died today, then it would have pleased you well.

7 "Now therefore, arise, go out and speak comfort to your servants. For I swear by the LORD, if you do not go out, not one will stay with you this night. And that will be worse for you than all the evil that has befallen you from your youth until now."

8 Then the king arose and sat in the [a]gate. And they told all the people, saying, "There is the king, sitting in the gate." So all the people came before the king. For everyone of Israel had [b]fled to his tent.

David Returns to Jerusalem

9 Now all the people were in a dispute throughout all the tribes of Israel, saying, "The king saved us from the hand of our [a]enemies, he delivered us from the hand of the [b]Philistines, and now he has [c]fled from the land because of Absalom.

10 "But Absalom, whom we anointed over us, has died in battle. Now therefore, why do you say nothing about bringing back the king?"

11 So King David sent to [a]Zadok and Abiathar the priests, saying, "Speak to the elders of Judah, saying, 'Why are you the last to bring the king back to his house, since the words of all Israel have come to the king, to his *very* house?

12 'You *are* my brethren, you *are* [a]my bone and my flesh. Why then are you the last to bring back the king?'

13 [a]"And say to Amasa, '*Are* you not my bone and my flesh? [b]God do so to me, and more also, if you are not commander of the army before me continually in place of Joab.' "

14 So he swayed the hearts of all the men of Judah, [a]just as *the heart of* one man, so that they sent *this word* to the king: "Return, you and all your servants!"

15 Then the king returned and came to the Jordan. And Judah came to [a]Gilgal, to go to meet the king, to escort the king [b]across the Jordan.

16 And [a]Shimei the son of Gera, a Benjamite, who *was* from Bahurim, hurried and came down with the men of Judah to meet King David.

17 *There were* a thousand men of [a]Benjamin with him, and [b]Ziba the servant of the house of Saul, and his fifteen sons and his twenty servants with him; and they went over the Jordan before the king.

18 Then a ferryboat went across to carry over

KJV

over the king's household, and to do what he
thought good.

David's Mercy to Shimei

And Shimei the son of Gera fell down before the
king, as he was come over Jordan;
19 And said unto the king, [a]Let not my lord
impute iniquity unto me, neither do thou remember [b]that which thy servant did perversely the day
that my lord the king went out of Jerusalem, that
the king should [c]take it to his heart.
20 For thy servant doth know that I have
sinned: therefore, behold, I am come the first this
day of all [a]the house of Joseph to go down to
meet my lord the king.
21 But Abishai the son of Zeruiah answered
and said, Shall not Shimei be put to death for this,
[a]because he [b]cursed the LORD's anointed?
22 And David said, [a]What have I to do with
you, ye sons of Zeruiah, that ye should this day
be adversaries unto me? [b]shall there any man be
put to death this day in Israel? for do not I know
that I *am* this day king over Israel?
23 Therefore [a]the king said unto Shimei,
Thou shalt not die. And the king sware unto him.

David and Mephibosheth Meet

24 And [a]Mephibosheth the son of Saul came
down to meet the king, and had neither dressed
his feet, nor trimmed his beard, nor washed his
clothes, from the day the king departed until the
day he came *again* in peace.
25 And it came to pass, when he was come
to Jerusalem to meet the king, that the king said
unto him, [a]Wherefore wentest not thou with me,
Mephibosheth?
26 And he answered, My lord, O king, my
servant deceived me: for thy servant said, I will
saddle me an ass, that I may ride thereon, and
go to the king; because thy servant *is* lame.
27 And [a]he hath slandered thy servant unto
my lord the king; [b]but my lord the king *is* as an
angel of God: do therefore *what is* good in thine
eyes.
28 For all *of* my father's house were but dead
men before my lord the king: [a]yet didst thou set
thy servant among them that did eat at thine own
table. What right therefore have I yet to cry any
more unto the king?
29 And the king said unto him, Why speakest
thou any more of thy matters? I have said, Thou
and Ziba divide the land.
30 And Mephibosheth said unto the king,
Yea, let him take all, forasmuch as my lord the
king is come again in peace unto his own house.

David's Kindness to Barzillai

31 And [a]Barzillai the Gileadite came down
from Rogelim, and went over Jordan with the
king, to conduct him over Jordan.
32 Now Barzillai was a very aged man, *even*
fourscore years old: and [a]he had provided the
king of sustenance while he lay at Mahanaim; for
he *was* a very great man.
33 And the king said unto Barzillai, Come
thou over with me, and I will feed thee with me
in Jerusalem.
34 And Barzillai said unto the king, How long
have I to live, that I should go up with the king
unto Jerusalem?
35 I *am* this day [a]fourscore years old: *and*
can I discern between good and evil? can thy servant taste what I eat or what I drink? can I hear
any more the voice of singing men and singing
women? wherefore then should thy servant be yet
a burden unto my lord the king?
36 Thy servant will go a little way over Jordan with the king: and why should the king recompense it me with such a reward?
37 Let thy servant, I pray thee, turn back
again, that I may die in mine own city, *and be
buried* by the grave of my father and of my

19 [a]1 Sam. 22:15 [b]2 Sam. 16:5, 6 [c]2 Sam. 13:33
20 [a]Judg. 1:22; 1 Kin. 11:28
21 [a][Ex. 22:28] [b][1 Sam. 26:9]
22 [a]2 Sam. 3:39; 16:10 [b]1 Sam. 11:13
23 [a]1 Kin. 2:8, 9, 37, 46
24 [a]2 Sam. 9:6; 21:7
25 [a]2 Sam. 16:7
27 [a]2 Sam. 16:3, 4 [b]2 Sam. 14:17, 20
28 [a]2 Sam. 9:7–13
31 [a]2 Sam. 17:27–29; 1 Kin. 2:7
32 [a]2 Sam. 17:27–29
35 [a]Ps. 90:10

NKJV

the king's household, and to do what he thought
good.

David's Mercy to Shimei

Now Shimei the son of Gera fell down before the king when he had crossed the Jordan.
19 Then he said to the king, [a]"Do not let my
lord impute iniquity to me, or remember what
[b]wrong your servant did on the day that my lord
the king left Jerusalem, that the king should [c]take
it to heart.
20 "For I, your servant, know that I have
sinned. Therefore here I am, the first to come today of all [a]the house of Joseph to go down to
meet my lord the king."
21 But Abishai the son of Zeruiah answered
and said, "Shall not Shimei be put to death for
this, [a]because he [b]cursed the LORD's anointed?"
22 And David said, [a]"What have I to do with
you, you sons of Zeruiah, that you should be adversaries to me today? [b]Shall any man be put to
death today in Israel? For do I not know that today
I *am* king over Israel?"
23 Therefore [a]the king said to Shimei, "You
shall not die." And the king swore to him.

David and Mephibosheth Meet

24 Now [a]Mephibosheth the son of Saul came
down to meet the king. And he had not cared for
his feet, nor trimmed his mustache, nor washed
his clothes, from the day the king departed until
the day he returned in peace.
25 So it was, when he had come to Jerusalem
to meet the king, that the king said to him, [a]"Why
did you not go with me, Mephibosheth?"
26 And he answered, "My lord, O king, my
servant deceived me. For your servant said, 'I will
saddle a donkey for myself, that I may ride on it
and go to the king,' because your servant *is* lame.
27 "And [a]he has slandered your servant to
my lord the king, [b]but my lord the king *is* like
the angel of God. Therefore do *what is* good in
your eyes.
28 "For all my father's house were but dead
men before my lord the king. [a]Yet you set your
servant among those who eat at your own table.
Therefore what right have I still to cry out anymore to the king?"
29 So the king said to him, "Why do you
speak anymore of your matters? I have said, 'You
and Ziba divide the land.' "
30 Then Mephibosheth said to the king,
"Rather, let him take it all, inasmuch as my lord
the king has come back in peace to his own
house."

David's Kindness to Barzillai

31 And [a]Barzillai the Gileadite came down
from Rogelim and went across the Jordan with
the king, to escort him across the Jordan.
32 Now Barzillai was a very aged man,
eighty years old. And [a]he had provided the king
with supplies while he stayed at Mahanaim, for
he *was* a very rich man.
33 And the king said to Barzillai, "Come
across with me, and I will provide for you while
you are with me in Jerusalem."
34 But Barzillai said to the king, "How long
have I to live, that I should go up with the king
to Jerusalem?
35 "I *am* today [a]eighty years old. Can I discern between the good and bad? Can your servant
taste what I eat or what I drink? Can I hear any
longer the voice of singing men and singing
women? Why then should your servant be a further burden to my lord the king?
36 "Your servant will go a little way across
the Jordan with the king. And why should the
king repay me *with* such a reward?
37 "Please let your servant turn back again,
that I may die in my own city, near the grave of
my father and mother. But here is your servant

KJV

mother. But behold thy servant [a]Chimham; let him go over with my lord the king; and do to him what shall seem good unto thee.

38 And the king answered, Chimham shall go over with me, and I will do to him that which shall seem good unto thee: and whatsoever thou shalt require of me, *that* will I do for thee.

39 And all the people went over Jordan. And when the king was come over, the king [a]kissed Barzillai, and blessed him; and he returned unto his own place.

The Quarrel About the King

40 Then the king went on to Gilgal, and Chimham went on with him: and all the people of Judah conducted the king, and also half the people of Israel.

41 And, behold, all the men of Israel came to the king, and said unto the king, Why have our brethren the men of Judah stolen thee away, and [a]have brought the king, and his household, and all David's men with him, over Jordan?

42 And all the men of Judah answered the men of Israel, Because the king *is* [a]near of kin to us: wherefore then be ye angry for this matter? have we eaten at all of the king's *cost?* or hath he given us any gift?

43 And the men of Israel answered the men of Judah, and said, We have [a]ten parts in the king, and we have also more *right* in David than ye: why then did ye despise us, that our advice should not be first had in bringing back our king? And [b]the words of the men of Judah were fiercer than the words of the men of Israel.

The Rebellion of Sheba

20 And there happened to be there a man of Belial, whose name *was* Sheba, the son of Bichri, a Benjamite: and he blew a trumpet, and said, [a]We have no part in David, neither have we inheritance in the son of Jesse: [b]every man to his tents, O Israel.

2 So every man of Israel went up from after David, *and* followed Sheba the son of Bichri: but the [a]men of Judah clave unto their king, from Jordan even to Jerusalem.

3 And David came to his house at Jerusalem; and the king took the ten women [a]*his* concubines, whom he had left to keep the house, and put them in ward, and fed them, but went not in unto them. So they were shut up unto the day of their death, living in widowhood.

4 Then said the king to Amasa, [a]Assemble me the men of Judah within three days, and be thou here present.

5 So Amasa went to assemble *the men of* Judah: but he tarried longer than the set time which he had appointed him.

6 And David said to [a]Abishai, Now shall Sheba the son of Bichri do us more harm than *did* Absalom: take thou [b]thy lord's servants, and pursue after him, lest he get him fenced cities, and escape us.

7 And there went out after him Joab's men, and the [a]Cherethites, and the Pelethites, and [b]all the mighty men: and they went out of Jerusalem, to pursue after Sheba the son of Bichri.

8 When they *were* at the great stone which *is* in Gibeon, Amasa went before them. And Joab's garment that he had put on was girded unto him, and upon it a girdle *with* a sword fastened upon his loins in the sheath thereof; and as he went forth it fell out.

9 And Joab said to Amasa, *Art* thou in health, my brother? [a]And Joab took Amasa by the beard with the right hand to kiss him.

10 But Amasa took no heed to the sword that *was* in Joab's hand: so [a]he smote him therewith [b]in the fifth *rib,* and shed out his bowels to the ground, and struck him not again; and he died.

---

37 [a]2 Sam. 19:40; Jer. 41:17
39 [a]Gen. 31:55; Ruth 1:14; 2 Sam. 14:33
41 [a]2 Sam. 19:15
42 [a]2 Sam. 19:12
43 [a]1 Kin. 11:30, 31 [b]Judg. 8:1; 12:1

CHAPTER 20

1 [a]2 Sam. 19:43; 1 Kin. 12:16 [b]1 Sam. 13:2; 2 Sam. 18:17; 2 Chr. 10:16
2 [a]2 Sam. 19:14
3 [a]2 Sam. 15:16; 16:21, 22
4 [a]2 Sam. 17:25; 19:13
6 [a]2 Sam. 21:17 [b]2 Sam. 11:11; 1 Kin. 1:33
7 [a]2 Sam. 8:18; 1 Kin. 1:38, 44 [b]2 Sam. 15:18
9 [a]Matt. 26:49; Luke 22:47
10 [a]2 Sam. 3:27; 1 Kin. 2:5 [b]2 Sam. 2:23

*
19:40 MT *Chimhan*
20:1 Lit. *man of Belial*

NKJV

[a]Chimham; let him cross over with my lord the king, and do for him what seems good to you."

38 And the king answered, "Chimham shall cross over with me, and I will do for him what seems good to you. Now whatever you request of me, I will do for you."

39 Then all the people went over the Jordan. And when the king had crossed over, the king [a]kissed Barzillai and blessed him, and he returned to his own place.

The Quarrel About the King

40 Now the king went on to Gilgal, and *Chimham went on with him. And all the people of Judah escorted the king, and also half the people of Israel.

41 Just then all the men of Israel came to the king, and said to the king, "Why have our brethren, the men of Judah, stolen you away and [a]brought the king, his household, and all David's men with him across the Jordan?"

42 So all the men of Judah answered the men of Israel, "Because the king *is* [a]a close relative of ours. Why then are you angry over this matter? Have we ever eaten at the king's *expense?* Or has he given us any gift?"

43 And the men of Israel answered the men of Judah, and said, "We have [a]ten shares in the king; therefore we also have more *right* to David than you. Why then do you despise us—were we not the first to advise bringing back our king?" Yet [b]the words of the men of Judah were fiercer than the words of the men of Israel.

The Rebellion of Sheba

20 And there happened to be there a *rebel, whose name *was* Sheba the son of Bichri, a Benjamite. And he blew a trumpet, and said:

[a]"We have no share in David,
Nor do we have inheritance in the son of Jesse;
[b]Every man to his tents, O Israel!"

2 So every man of Israel deserted David, *and* followed Sheba the son of Bichri. But the [a]men of Judah, from the Jordan as far as Jerusalem, remained loyal to their king.

3 Now David came to his house at Jerusalem. And the king took the ten women, [a]his concubines whom he had left to keep the house, and put them in seclusion and supported them, but did not go in to them. So they were shut up to the day of their death, living in widowhood.

4 And the king said to Amasa, [a]"Assemble the men of Judah for me within three days, and be present here yourself."

5 So Amasa went to assemble *the men of* Judah. But he delayed longer than the set time which David had appointed him.

6 And David said to [a]Abishai, "Now Sheba the son of Bichri will do us more harm than Absalom. Take [b]your lord's servants and pursue him, lest he find for himself fortified cities, and escape us."

7 So Joab's men, with the [a]Cherethites, the Pelethites, and [b]all the mighty men, went out after him. And they went out of Jerusalem to pursue Sheba the son of Bichri.

8 When they *were* at the large stone which *is* in Gibeon, Amasa came before them. Now Joab was dressed in battle armor; on it was a belt *with* a sword fastened in its sheath at his hips; and as he was going forward, it fell out.

9 Then Joab said to Amasa, "*Are* you in health, my brother?" [a]And Joab took Amasa by the beard with his right hand to kiss him.

10 But Amasa did not notice the sword that *was* in Joab's hand. And [a]he struck him with it [b]in the stomach, and his entrails poured out on the ground; and he did not *strike* him again. Thus

KJV

So Joab and Abishai his brother pursued after Sheba the son of Bichri.

11 And one of Joab's men stood by him, and said, He that favoureth Joab, and he that *is* for David, *let him* go after Joab.

12 And Amasa wallowed in blood in the midst of the highway. And when the man saw that all the people stood still, he removed Amasa out of the highway into the field, and cast a cloth upon him, when he saw that every one that came by him stood still.

13 When he was removed out of the highway, all the people went on after Joab, to pursue after Sheba the son of Bichri.

14 And he went through all the tribes of Israel unto [a]Abel, and to Beth–maachah, and all the Berites: and they were gathered together, and went also after him.

15 And they came and besieged him in Abel of Beth–maachah, and they [a]cast up a bank against the city, and it stood in the trench: and all the people that *were* with Joab battered the wall, to throw it down.

16 Then cried a wise woman out of the city, Hear, hear; say, I pray you, unto Joab, Come near hither, that I may speak with thee.

17 And when he was come near unto her, the woman said, *Art* thou Joab? And he answered, I *am he*. Then she said unto him, Hear the words of thine handmaid. And he answered, I do hear.

18 Then she spake, saying, They were wont to speak in old time, saying, They shall surely ask *counsel* at Abel: and so they ended *the matter*.

19 I *am one of them that are* peaceable *and* faithful in Israel: thou seekest to destroy a city and a mother in Israel: why wilt thou swallow up [a]the inheritance of the LORD?

20 And Joab answered and said, Far be it, far be it from me, that I should swallow up or destroy.

21 The matter *is* not so: but a man of mount Ephraim, Sheba the son of Bichri by name, hath lifted up his hand against the king, *even* against David: deliver him only, and I will depart from the city. And the woman said unto Joab, Behold, his head shall be thrown to thee over the wall.

22 Then the woman went unto all the people [a]in her wisdom. And they cut off the head of Sheba the son of Bichri, and cast *it* out to Joab. And he blew a trumpet, and they retired from the city, every man to his tent. And Joab returned to Jerusalem unto the king.

David's Government Officers

23 Now [a]Joab *was* over all the host of Israel: and Benaiah the son of Jehoiada *was* over the Cherethites and over the Pelethites:

24 And Adoram *was* [a]over the tribute: and [b]Jehoshaphat the son of Ahilud *was* recorder:

25 And Sheva *was* scribe: and [a]Zadok and Abiathar *were* the priests:

26 [a]And Ira also the Jairite was a chief ruler about David.

David Avenges the Gibeonites

21 Then there was a famine in the days of David three years, year after year; and David [a]enquired of the LORD. And the LORD answered, *It is* for Saul, and for *his* bloody house, because he slew the Gibeonites.

2 And the king called the Gibeonites, and said unto them; (now the Gibeonites *were* not of the children of Israel, but [a]of the remnant of the Amorites; and the children of Israel had sworn unto them: and Saul sought to slay them [b]in his zeal to the children of Israel and Judah.)

3 Wherefore David said unto the Gibeonites, What shall I do for you? and wherewith shall I make the atonement, that ye may bless [a]the inheritance of the LORD?

---

14 [a]1 Kin. 15:20; 2 Kin. 15:29; 2 Chr. 16:4
15 [a]2 Kin. 19:32; Ezek. 4:2
19 [a]1 Sam. 26:19; 2 Sam. 14:16; 21:3
22 [a]2 Sam. 20:16; [Eccl. 9:13–16]
23 [a]2 Sam. 8:16–18; 1 Kin. 4:3–6
24 [a]1 Kin. 4:6 [b]2 Sam. 8:16; 1 Kin. 4:3
25 [a]2 Sam. 8:17; 1 Kin. 4:4
26 [a]2 Sam. 8:18

CHAPTER 21

1 [a]Num. 27:21; 2 Sam. 5:19
2 [a]Josh. 9:3, 15–20 [b][Ex. 34:11–16]
3 [a]1 Sam. 26:19; 2 Sam. 20:19

*

20:14 Lit. *him*

NKJV

he died. Then Joab and Abishai his brother pursued Sheba the son of Bichri.

11 Meanwhile one of Joab's men stood near Amasa, and said, "Whoever favors Joab and whoever *is* for David—follow Joab!"

12 But Amasa wallowed in *his* blood in the middle of the highway. And when the man saw that all the people stood still, he moved Amasa from the highway to the field and threw a garment over him, when he saw that everyone who came upon him halted.

13 When he was removed from the highway, all the people went on after Joab to pursue Sheba the son of Bichri.

14 And he went through all the tribes of Israel to [a]Abel and Beth Maachah and all the Berites. So they were gathered together and also went after **Sheba*.

15 Then they came and besieged him in Abel of Beth Maachah; and they [a]cast up a siege mound against the city, and it stood by the rampart. And all the people who *were* with Joab battered the wall to throw it down.

16 Then a wise woman cried out from the city, "Hear, hear! Please say to Joab, 'Come nearby, that I may speak with you.' "

17 When he had come near to her, the woman said, "*Are* you Joab?" He answered, "I *am*." Then she said to him, "Hear the words of your maidservant." And he answered, "I am listening."

18 So she spoke, saying, "They used to talk in former times, saying, 'They shall surely seek *guidance* at Abel,' and so they would end *disputes*.

19 "I *am among the* peaceable *and* faithful in Israel. You seek to destroy a city and a mother in Israel. Why would you swallow up [a]the inheritance of the LORD?"

20 And Joab answered and said, "Far be it, far be it from me, that I should swallow up or destroy!

21 "That *is* not so. But a man from the mountains of Ephraim, Sheba the son of Bichri by name, has raised his hand against the king, against David. Deliver him only, and I will depart from the city." So the woman said to Joab, "Watch, his head will be thrown to you over the wall."

22 Then the woman [a]in her wisdom went to all the people. And they cut off the head of Sheba the son of Bichri, and threw *it* out to Joab. Then he blew a trumpet, and they withdrew from the city, every man to his tent. So Joab returned to the king at Jerusalem.

David's Government Officers

23 And [a]Joab *was* over all the army of Israel; Benaiah the son of Jehoiada *was* over the Cherethites and the Pelethites;

24 Adoram *was* [a]in charge of revenue; [b]Jehoshaphat the son of Ahilud *was* recorder;

25 Sheva *was* scribe; [a]Zadok and Abiathar *were* the priests;

26 [a]and Ira the Jairite was a chief minister under David.

David Avenges the Gibeonites

21 Now there was a famine in the days of David for three years, year after year; and David [a]inquired of the LORD. And the LORD answered, "*It is* because of Saul and *his* bloodthirsty house, because he killed the Gibeonites."

2 So the king called the Gibeonites and spoke to them. Now the Gibeonites *were* not of the children of Israel, but [a]of the remnant of the Amorites; the children of Israel had sworn protection to them, but Saul had sought to kill them [b]in his zeal for the children of Israel and Judah.

3 Therefore David said to the Gibeonites, "What shall I do for you? And with what shall I make atonement, that you may bless [a]the inheritance of the LORD?"

KJV

4 And the Gibeonites said unto him, We will have no silver nor gold of Saul, nor of his house; neither for us shalt thou kill any man in Israel. And he said, What ye shall say, *that* will I do for you.

5 And they answered the king, The man that consumed us, and that devised against us *that* we should be destroyed from remaining in any of the coasts of Israel,

6 Let seven men of his sons be delivered [a]unto us, and we will hang them up unto the LORD [b]in Gibeah of Saul, [c]*whom* the LORD did choose. And the king said, I will give *them*.

7 But the king spared [a]Mephibosheth, the son of Jonathan the son of Saul, because of [b]the LORD's oath that *was* between them, between David and Jonathan the son of Saul.

8 But the king took the two sons of [a]Rizpah the daughter of Aiah, whom she bare unto Saul, Armoni and Mephibosheth; and the five sons of Michal the daughter of Saul, whom she brought up for Adriel the son of Barzillai the Meholathite:

9 And he delivered them into the hands of the Gibeonites, and they hanged them in the hill [a]before the LORD: and they fell *all* seven together, and were put to death in the days of harvest, in the first *days*, in the beginning of barley harvest.

10 And [a]Rizpah the daughter of Aiah took sackcloth, and spread it for her upon the rock, [b]from the beginning of harvest until water dropped upon them out of heaven, and suffered neither the birds of the air to rest on them by day, nor the beasts of the field by night.

11 And it was told David what Rizpah the daughter of Aiah, the concubine of Saul, had done.

12 And David went and took the bones of Saul and the bones of Jonathan his son from the men of [a]Jabesh–gilead, which had stolen them from the street of Beth–shan, where the [b]Philistines had hanged them, when the Philistines had slain Saul in Gilboa:

13 And he brought up from thence the bones of Saul and the bones of Jonathan his son; and they gathered the bones of them that were hanged.

14 And the bones of Saul and Jonathan his son buried they in the country of Benjamin in [a]Zelah, in the sepulchre of Kish his father: and they performed all that the king commanded. And after that [b]God was intreated for the land.

Philistine Giants Destroyed
(*1 Chr. 20:4–8*)

15 Moreover the Philistines had yet war again with Israel; and David went down, and his servants with him, and fought against the Philistines: and David waxed faint.

16 And Ishbi–benob, which *was* of the sons of the [a]giant, the weight of whose spear *weighed* three hundred *shekels* of brass in weight, he being girded with a new *sword*, thought to have slain David.

17 But [a]Abishai the son of Zeruiah succoured him, and smote the Philistine, and killed him. Then the men of David sware unto him, saying, [b]Thou shalt go no more out with us to battle, that thou quench not the [c]light of Israel.

18 [a]And it came to pass after this, that there was again a battle with the Philistines at Gob: then [b]Sibbechai the Hushathite slew Saph, which *was* of the sons of the giant.

19 And there was again a battle in Gob with the Philistines, where [a]Elhanan the son of Jaare–oregim, a Beth–lehemite, slew [b]*the brother of* Goliath the Gittite, the staff of whose spear *was* like a weaver's beam.

20 And [a]there was yet a battle in Gath, where was a man of *great* stature, that had on every hand six fingers, and on every foot six toes, four and twenty in number; and he also was born to the giant.

6 [a]Num. 25:4 [b]1 Sam. 10:26 [c]1 Sam. 10:24; [Hos. 13:11]
7 [a]2 Sam. 4:4; 9:10 [b]1 Sam. 18:3; 20:12–17; 23:18; 2 Sam. 9:1–7
8 [a]2 Sam. 3:7
9 [a]2 Sam. 6:17
10 [a]2 Sam. 3:7; 21:8 [b]Deut. 21:23
12 [a]1 Sam. 31:11–13 [b]1 Sam. 31:8
14 [a]Josh. 18:28 [b]Josh. 7:26; 2 Sam. 24:25
16 [a]Num. 13:22, 28; Josh. 15:14; 2 Sam. 21:18–22
17 [a]2 Sam. 20:6–10 [b]2 Sam. 18:3 [c]2 Sam. 22:29; 1 Kin. 11:36
18 [a]1 Chr. 20:4–8 [b]1 Chr. 11:29; 27:11
19 [a]2 Sam. 23:24 [b]1 Sam. 17:4; 1 Chr. 20:5
20 [a]1 Chr. 20:6

*______

21:8 *Merab*, 1 Sam. 18:19; 25:44; 2 Sam. 3:14; 6:23
21:12 *Beth Shean*, Josh. 17:11
21:18 *Sippai*, 1 Chr. 20:4
21:19 *Jair*, 1 Chr. 20:5

NKJV

4 And the Gibeonites said to him, "We will have no silver or gold from Saul or from his house, nor shall you kill any man in Israel for us." So he said, "Whatever you say, I will do for you."

5 Then they answered the king, "As for the man who consumed us and plotted against us, *that* we should be destroyed from remaining in any of the territories of Israel,

6 "let seven men of his descendants be delivered [a]to us, and we will hang them before the LORD [b]in Gibeah of Saul, [c]*whom* the LORD chose." And the king said, "I will give *them*."

7 But the king spared [a]Mephibosheth the son of Jonathan, the son of Saul, because of [b]the LORD's oath that *was* between them, between David and Jonathan the son of Saul.

8 So the king took Armoni and Mephibosheth, the two sons of [a]Rizpah the daughter of Aiah, whom she bore to Saul, and the five sons of *Michal the daughter of Saul, whom she brought up for Adriel the son of Barzillai the Meholathite;

9 and he delivered them into the hands of the Gibeonites, and they hanged them on the hill [a]before the LORD. So they fell, *all* seven together, and were put to death in the days of harvest, in the first *days*, in the beginning of barley harvest.

10 Now [a]Rizpah the daughter of Aiah took sackcloth and spread it for herself on the rock, [b]from the beginning of harvest until the late rains poured on them from heaven. And she did not allow the birds of the air to rest on them by day nor the beasts of the field by night.

11 And David was told what Rizpah the daughter of Aiah, the concubine of Saul, had done.

12 Then David went and took the bones of Saul, and the bones of Jonathan his son, from the men of [a]Jabesh Gilead who had stolen them from the street of *Beth Shan, where the [b]Philistines had hung them up, after the Philistines had struck down Saul in Gilboa.

13 So he brought up the bones of Saul and the bones of Jonathan his son from there; and they gathered the bones of those who had been hanged.

14 They buried the bones of Saul and Jonathan his son in the country of Benjamin in [a]Zelah, in the tomb of Kish his father. So they performed all that the king commanded. And after that [b]God heeded the prayer for the land.

Philistine Giants Destroyed
(*1 Chr. 20:4–8*)

15 When the Philistines were at war again with Israel, David and his servants with him went down and fought against the Philistines; and David grew faint.

16 Then Ishbi-Benob, who *was* one of the sons of the [a]giant, the weight of whose bronze spear *was* three hundred *shekels*, who was bearing a new *sword*, thought he could kill David.

17 But [a]Abishai the son of Zeruiah came to his aid, and struck the Philistine and killed him. Then the men of David swore to him, saying, [b]"You shall go out no more with us to battle, lest you quench the [c]lamp of Israel."

18 [a]Now it happened afterward that there was again a battle with the Philistines at Gob. Then [b]Sibbechai the Hushathite killed *Saph, who *was* one of the sons of the giant.

19 Again there was war at Gob with the Philistines, where [a]Elhanan the son of *Jaare-Oregim the Bethlehemite killed [b]*the brother of* Goliath the Gittite, the shaft of whose spear *was* like a weaver's beam.

20 Yet again [a]there was war at Gath, where there was a man of *great* stature, who had six fingers on each hand and six toes on each foot, twenty-four in number; and he also was born to the giant.

KJV

21 And when he [a]defied Israel, Jonathan the
son of Shimeah the brother of David slew him.
22 [a]These four were born to the giant in
Gath, and fell by the hand of David, and by the
hand of his servants.

Praise for God's Deliverance
(Ps. 18:1–50)

22 And David [a]spake unto the LORD the words
of this song, in the day *that* the LORD had
[b]delivered him out of the hand of all his enemies,
and out of the hand of Saul:
2 And he [a]said, [b]The LORD *is* my rock, and
my [c]fortress, and my deliverer;
3 The God of my rock; [a]in him will I trust:
he is my [b]shield, and the [c]horn of my salvation,
my [d]high tower, and my [e]refuge, my saviour; thou
savest me from violence.
4 I will call on the LORD, *who is* worthy to
be praised: so shall I be saved from mine enemies.
5 When the waves of death compassed me,
the floods of ungodly men made me afraid;
6 The [a]sorrows of hell compassed me about;
the snares of death prevented me;
7 In my distress [a]I called upon the LORD,
and cried to my God: and he did [b]hear my voice
out of his temple, and my cry *did enter* into his
ears.
8 Then [a]the earth shook and trembled; [b]the
foundations of heaven moved and shook, because
he was wroth.
9 There went up a smoke out of his nostrils,
and [a]fire out of his mouth devoured: coals were
kindled by it.
10 He [a]bowed the heavens also, and came
down; and [b]darkness *was* under his feet.
11 And he rode upon a cherub, and did fly:
and he was seen [a]upon the wings of the wind.
12 And he made [a]darkness pavilions round
about him, dark waters, *and* thick clouds of the
skies.
13 Through the brightness before him were
coals of fire kindled.
14 The LORD [a]thundered from heaven, and
the most High uttered his voice.
15 And he sent out [a]arrows, and scattered
them; lightning, and discomfited them.
16 And the channels of the sea [a]appeared,
the foundations of the world were discovered, at
the [b]rebuking of the LORD, at the blast of the
breath of his nostrils.
17 [a]He sent from above, he took me; he drew
me out of many waters;
18 He delivered me from my strong enemy,
and from them that hated me: for they were too
strong for me.
19 They prevented me in the day of my calamity:
but the LORD was my [a]stay.
20 [a]He brought me forth also into a large
place: he delivered me, because he [b]delighted in
me.
21 [a]The LORD rewarded me according to my
righteousness: according to the [b]cleanness of my
hands hath he recompensed me.
22 For I have [a]kept the ways of the LORD,
and have not wickedly departed from my God.
23 For all his [a]judgments *were* before me:

21 [a]1 Sam. 17:10
22 [a]1 Chr. 20:8

CHAPTER 22

1 [a]Ex. 15:1; Deut. 31:30; Judg. 5:1 [b]Ps. 18:title; 34:19
2 [a]Ps. 18 [b]Deut. 32:4; 1 Sam. 2:2 [c]Ps. 91:2
3 [a]Ps. 7:1; Heb. 2:13 [b]Gen. 15:1; Deut. 33:29; Ps. 84:11 [c]Luke 1:69 [d]Prov. 18:10 [e]Ps. 9:9; 46:1, 7, 11; Jer. 16:19
6 [a]Ps. 116:3
7 [a]Ps. 116:4; 120:1 [b]Ex. 3:7; Ps. 34:6, 15
8 [a]Judg. 5:4; Ps. 77:18; 97:4 [b]Job 26:11
9 [a]Deut. 32:22; Ps. 97:3, 4; Heb. 12:29
10 [a]Ex. 19:16–20; Is. 64:1 [b]Ex. 20:21
11 [a]Ps. 104:3
12 [a]Job 36:29; Ps. 97:2
14 [a]1 Sam. 2:10; Job 37:2–5; Ps. 29:3
15 [a]Deut. 32:23; Josh. 10:10; 1 Sam. 7:10; Ps. 7:13
16 [a]Nah. 1:4 [b]Ex. 15:8
17 [a]Ps. 144:7; Is. 43:2
19 [a]Is. 10:20
20 [a]Ps. 31:8; 118:5 [b]2 Sam. 15:26
21 [a]1 Sam. 26:23; [Ps. 7:8] [b][Job 17:9]; Ps. 24:4
22 [a]Gen. 18:19; 2 Chr. 34:33; Ps. 119:3
23 [a][Deut. 6:6–9; 7:12]; Ps. 119:30, 102

*———

21:21 *Shammah,* 1 Sam. 16:9 and elsewhere
22:8 So with MT, LXX, Tg.; Syr., Vg. *hills* (cf. Ps. 18:7)
22:11 So with MT, LXX; many Heb. mss., Syr., Vg. *flew* (cf. Ps. 18:10); Tg. *spoke with power*

NKJV

21 So when he [a]defied Israel, Jonathan the
son of *Shimea, David's brother, killed him.
22 [a]These four were born to the giant in
Gath, and fell by the hand of David and by the
hand of his servants.

Praise for God's Deliverance
(Ps. 18:1–50)

22 Then David [a]spoke to the LORD the words
of this song, on the day when the LORD had
[b]delivered him from the hand of all his enemies,
and from the hand of Saul.
2 And he [a]said:

[b]"The LORD *is* my rock and my [c]fortress and
my deliverer;
3 The God of my strength, [a]in whom I will
trust;
My [b]shield and the [c]horn of my salvation,
My [d]stronghold and my [e]refuge;
My Savior, You save me from violence.
4 I will call upon the LORD, *who is worthy*
to be praised;
So shall I be saved from my enemies.

5 "When the waves of death surrounded me,
The floods of ungodliness made me afraid.
6 The [a]sorrows of Sheol surrounded me;
The snares of death confronted me.
7 In my distress [a]I called upon the LORD,
And cried out to my God;
He [b]heard my voice from His temple,
And my cry *entered* His ears.

8 "Then [a]the earth shook and trembled;
[b]The foundations of *heaven quaked and
were shaken,
Because He was angry.
9 Smoke went up from His nostrils,
And devouring [a]fire from His mouth;
Coals were kindled by it.
10 He [a]bowed the heavens also, and came
down
With [b]darkness under His feet.
11 He rode upon a cherub, and flew;
And He *was seen [a]upon the wings of the
wind.
12 He made [a]darkness canopies around Him,
Dark waters *and* thick clouds of the skies.
13 From the brightness before Him
Coals of fire were kindled.

14 "The LORD [a]thundered from heaven,
And the Most High uttered His voice.
15 He sent out [a]arrows and scattered them;
Lightning bolts, and He vanquished them.
16 Then the channels of the sea [a]were seen,
The foundations of the world were
uncovered,
At the [b]rebuke of the LORD,
At the blast of the breath of His nostrils.

17 "He[a] sent from above, He took me,
He drew me out of many waters.
18 He delivered me from my strong enemy,
From those who hated me;
For they were too strong for me.
19 They confronted me in the day of my
calamity,
But the LORD was my [a]support.
20 [a]He also brought me out into a broad place;
He delivered me because He [b]delighted in
me.

21 "The[a] LORD rewarded me according to my
righteousness;
According to the [b]cleanness of my hands
He has recompensed me.
22 For I have [a]kept the ways of the LORD,
And have not wickedly departed from my
God.
23 For all His [a]judgments *were* before me;

KJV

and *as for* his statutes, I did not depart from them.

24 I was also [a]upright before him, and have kept myself from mine iniquity.

25 Therefore [a]the LORD hath recompensed me according to my righteousness; according to my cleanness in his eye sight.

26 With [a]the merciful thou wilt shew thyself merciful, *and* with the upright man thou wilt shew thyself upright.

27 With the pure thou wilt shew thyself pure; and [a]with the froward thou wilt shew thyself unsavoury.

28 And the [a]afflicted people thou wilt save: but thine eyes *are* upon [b]the haughty, *that* thou mayest bring *them* down.

29 For thou *art* my [a]lamp, O LORD: and the LORD will lighten my darkness.

30 For by thee I have run through a troop: by my God have I leaped over a [a]wall.

31 *As for* God, [a]his way *is* perfect; [b]the word of the LORD *is* tried: he *is* a buckler to all them that trust in him.

32 For [a]who *is* God, save the LORD? and who *is* a rock, save our God?

33 God *is* my [a]strength *and* power: and he [b]maketh my way [c]perfect.

34 He maketh my feet [a]like hinds' *feet:* and [b]setteth me upon my high places.

35 He teacheth my hands to war; so that a bow of steel is broken by mine arms.

36 Thou hast also given me the shield of thy salvation: and thy gentleness hath made me great.

37 Thou hast [a]enlarged my steps under me; so that my feet did not slip.

38 I have pursued mine enemies, and destroyed them; and turned not again until I had consumed them.

39 And I have consumed them, and wounded them, that they could not arise: yea, they are fallen [a]under my feet.

40 For thou hast [a]girded me with strength to battle: [b]them that rose up against me hast thou subdued under me.

41 Thou hast also given me the [a]necks of mine enemies, that I might destroy them that hate me.

42 They looked, but *there was* none to save; *even* [a]unto the LORD, but he answered them not.

43 Then did I beat them as small [a]as the dust of the earth: I did stamp them [b]as the mire of the street, *and* did spread them abroad.

44 [a]Thou also hast delivered me from the strivings of my people, thou hast kept me *to be* [b]head of the heathen: [c]a people *which* I knew not shall serve me.

45 Strangers shall submit themselves unto me: as soon as they hear, they shall be obedient unto me.

46 Strangers shall fade away, and they shall be afraid [a]out of their close places.

47 The LORD liveth; and blessed *be* my rock; and exalted be the God of the [a]rock of my salvation.

24 [a][Eph. 1:4] **25** [a]2 Sam. 22:21 **26** [a][Matt. 5:7] **27** [a][Lev. 26:23, 24] **28** [a]Ps. 72:12 [b]Job 40:11 **29** [a]Ps. 119:105; 132:17 **30** [a]2 Sam. 5:6–8 **31** [a][Matt. 5:48] [b]Ps. 12:6 **32** [a]Is. 45:5, 6 **33** [a]Ps. 27:1 [b][Heb. 13:21] [c]Ps. 101:2, 6 **34** [a]2 Sam. 2:18 [b]Is. 33:16 **37** [a]Prov. 4:12 **39** [a]Mal. 4:3 **40** [a][Ps. 18:32] [b][Ps. 44:5] **41** [a]Gen. 49:8 **42** [a]1 Sam. 28:6 **43** [a]Ps. 18:42 [b]Is. 10:6 **44** [a]2 Sam. 3:1 [b]Deut. 28:13 [c][Is. 55:5] **46** [a][Mic. 7:17] **47** [a]Ps. 89:26

*

22:25 LXX, Syr., Vg. *the cleanness of my hands in His sight* (cf. Ps. 18:24); Tg. *my cleanness before His word*
22:33 DSS, LXX, Syr., Vg. *It is God who arms me with strength* (cf. Ps. 18:32); Tg *It is God who sustains me with strength* • So with Qr., LXX, Syr., Tg., Vg. (cf. Ps. 18:32); Kt. *His*
22:34 So with Qr., LXX, Syr., Tg., Vg. (cf. Ps. 18:33); Kt. *His*
22:46 So with LXX, Tg., Vg. (cf. Ps. 18:45); MT *gird themselves*

NKJV

And *as for* His statutes, I did not depart
from them.
24 I was also [a]blameless before Him,
And I kept myself from my iniquity.
25 Therefore [a]the LORD has recompensed me
according to my righteousness,
According to *my cleanness in His eyes.

26 "With [a]the merciful You will show Yourself
merciful;
With a blameless man You will show
Yourself blameless;
27 With the pure You will show Yourself
pure;
And [a]with the devious You will show
Yourself shrewd.
28 You will save the [a]humble people;
But Your eyes *are* on [b]the haughty, *that*
You may bring *them* down.

29 "For You *are* my [a]lamp, O LORD;
The LORD shall enlighten my darkness.
30 For by You I can run against a troop;
By my God I can leap over a [a]wall.
31 *As for* God, [a]His way *is* perfect;
[b]The word of the LORD *is* proven;
He *is* a shield to all who trust in Him.

32 "For [a]who *is* God, except the LORD?
And who *is* a rock, except our God?
33 *God *is* my [a]strength *and* power,
And He [b]makes *my way [c]perfect.
34 He makes *my feet [a]like the *feet* of deer,
And [b]sets me on my high places.
35 He teaches my hands to make war,
So that my arms can bend a bow of
bronze.

36 "You have also given me the shield of Your
salvation;
Your gentleness has made me great.
37 You [a]enlarged my path under me;
So my feet did not slip.

38 "I have pursued my enemies and destroyed
them;
Neither did I turn back again till they were
destroyed.
39 And I have destroyed them and wounded
them,
So that they could not rise;
They have fallen [a]under my feet.
40 For You have [a]armed me with strength
for the battle;
You have subdued under me [b]those who
rose against me.
41 You have also given me the [a]necks of my
enemies,
So that I destroyed those who hated me.
42 They looked, but *there was* none to save;
Even [a]to the LORD, but He did not answer
them.
43 Then I beat them as fine [a]as the dust of
the earth;
I trod them [b]like dirt in the streets,
And I spread them out.

44 "You[a] have also delivered me from the
strivings of my people;
You have kept me as the [b]head of the
nations.
[c]A people I have not known shall serve me.
45 The foreigners submit to me;
As soon as they hear, they obey me.
46 The foreigners fade away,
And *come frightened [a]from their
hideouts.

47 "The LORD lives!
Blessed *be* my Rock!
Let God be exalted,
The [a]Rock of my salvation!

KJV

48 It *is* God that avengeth me, and that
[a]bringeth down the people under me,
49 And that bringeth me forth from mine enemies: thou also hast lifted me up on high above
them that rose up against me: thou hast delivered
me from the [a]violent man.
50 Therefore I will give thanks unto thee, O
LORD, among [a]the heathen, and I will sing praises
unto thy [b]name.
51 [a]*He is* the tower of salvation for his king:
and sheweth mercy to his [b]anointed, unto David,
and [c]to his seed for evermore.

David's Last Words

23 Now these *be* the last words of David. David the son of Jesse said, [a]and the man *who*
was raised up on high, [b]the anointed of the God
of Jacob, and the sweet psalmist of Israel, said,
2 [a]The Spirit of the LORD spake by me, and
his word *was* in my tongue.
3 The God of Israel said, [a]the Rock of Israel
spake to me, He that ruleth over men *must be*
just, ruling [b]in the fear of God.
4 And [a]*he shall be* as the light of the morning, *when* the sun riseth, *even* a morning without
clouds; *as* the tender grass *springing* out of the
earth by clear shining after rain.
5 Although my house *be* not so with God;
[a]yet he hath made with me an everlasting covenant, ordered in all *things*, and sure: for *this is*
all my salvation, and all *my* desire, although he
make *it* not to grow.
6 But *the sons* of Belial *shall be* all of them
as thorns thrust away, because they cannot be
taken with hands:
7 But the man *that* shall touch them must
be fenced with iron and the staff of a spear; and
they shall be utterly burned with fire in the *same*
place.

David's Mighty Men
(*1 Chr. 11:10–47*)

8 These *be* the names of the mighty men
whom David had: The Tachmonite that sat in the
seat, chief among the captains; the same *was*
Adino the Eznite: *he lift up his spear* against eight
hundred, whom he slew at one time.
9 And after him *was* [a]Eleazar the son of
Dodo the Ahohite, *one* of the three mighty men
with David, when they defied the Philistines *that*
were there gathered together to battle, and the
men of Israel were gone away:
10 He arose, and smote the Philistines until
his hand was [a]weary, and his hand clave unto
the sword: and the LORD wrought a great victory
that day; and the people returned after him only
to [b]spoil.
11 And after him *was* [a]Shammah the son of
Agee the Hararite. [b]And the Philistines were gathered together into a troop, where was a piece of
ground full of lentiles: and the people fled from
the Philistines.
12 But he stood in the midst of the ground,
and defended it, and slew the Philistines: and the
LORD wrought a great victory.
13 And [a]three of the thirty chief went down,
and came to David in the harvest time unto [b]the
cave of Adullam: and the troop of the Philistines
pitched in [c]the valley of Rephaim.

48 [a]1 Sam. 24:12; Ps. 144:2
49 [a]Ps. 140:1, 4, 11
50 [a]2 Sam. 8:1–14 [b]Ps. 57:7; Rom. 15:9
51 [a]Ps. 144:10 [b]Ps. 89:20 [c]2 Sam. 7:12–16; Ps. 89:29

CHAPTER 23

1 [a]2 Sam. 7:8, 9; Ps. 78:70, 71 [b]1 Sam. 16:12, 13; Ps. 89:20
2 [a]Matt. 22:43; [2 Pet. 1:21]
3 [a][Deut. 32:4] [b]Ex. 18:21; [Is. 11:1–5]
4 [a]Ps. 89:36; Is. 60:1
5 [a]2 Sam. 7:12; Ps. 89:29; Is. 55:3
9 [a]1 Chr. 11:12; 27:4
10 [a]Judg. 8:4 [b]1 Sam. 30:24, 25
11 [a]1 Chr. 11:27 [b]1 Chr. 11:13, 14
13 [a]1 Chr. 11:15 [b]1 Sam. 22:1 [c]2 Sam. 5:18

*———

23:8 Lit. *One Who Sits in the Seat* (1 Chr. 11:11) • So with MT, Tg.; LXX, Vg. *the three*
23:9 *Dodai*, 1 Chr. 27:4

NKJV

48 *It is* God who avenges me,
And [a]subdues the peoples under me;
49 He delivers me from my enemies.
You also lift me up above those who rise
against me;
You have delivered me from the [a]violent
man.
50 Therefore I will give thanks to You, O
LORD, among [a]the Gentiles,
And sing praises to Your [b]name.

51 "He[a] *is* the tower of salvation to His king,
And shows mercy to His [b]anointed,
To David and [c]his descendants
forevermore."

David's Last Words

23 Now these *are* the last words of David.
Thus says David the son of Jesse;
Thus says [a]the man raised up on high,
[b]The anointed of the God of Jacob,
And the sweet psalmist of Israel:

2 "The[a] Spirit of the LORD spoke by me,
And His word *was* on my tongue.
3 The God of Israel said,
[a]The Rock of Israel spoke to me:
'He who rules over men *must be* just,
Ruling [b]in the fear of God.
4 And [a]*he shall be* like the light of the
morning *when* the sun rises,
A morning without clouds,
Like the tender grass *springing* out of the
earth,
By clear shining after rain.'

5 "Although my house *is* not so with God,
[a]Yet He has made with me an everlasting
covenant,
Ordered in all *things* and secure.
For *this is* all my salvation and all *my*
desire;
Will He not make *it* increase?
6 But *the sons* of rebellion *shall* all *be* as
thorns thrust away,
Because they cannot be taken with hands.
7 But the man *who* touches them
Must be armed with iron and the shaft of
a spear,
And they shall be utterly burned with fire
in *their* place."

David's Mighty Men
(*1 Chr. 11:10–47*)

8 These *are* the names of the mighty men
whom David had: *Josheb-Basshebeth the Tachmonite, chief among *the captains. He was
called Adino the Eznite, because he had killed
eight hundred men at one time.
9 And after him *was* [a]Eleazar the son of
*Dodo, the Ahohite, *one* of the three mighty men
with David when they defied the Philistines *who*
were gathered there for battle, and the men of
Israel had retreated.
10 He arose and attacked the Philistines until
his hand was [a]weary, and his hand stuck to the
sword. The LORD brought about a great victory
that day; and the people returned after him only
to [b]plunder.
11 And after him *was* [a]Shammah the son of
Agee the Hararite. [b]The Philistines had gathered
together into a troop where there was a piece of
ground full of lentils. So the people fled from the
Philistines.
12 But he stationed himself in the middle of
the field, defended it, and killed the Philistines.
So the LORD brought about a great victory.
13 Then [a]three of the thirty chief men went
down at harvest time and came to David at [b]the
cave of Adullam. And the troop of Philistines encamped in [c]the Valley of Rephaim.

KJV

14 And David *was* then in [a]an hold, and the garrison of the Philistines *was* then *in* Beth–lehem.

15 And David longed, and said, Oh that one would give me drink of the water of the well of Beth–lehem, which *is* by the gate!

16 And the three mighty men brake through the host of the Philistines, and drew water out of the well of Beth–lehem, that *was* by the gate, and took *it*, and brought *it* to David: nevertheless he would not drink thereof, but poured it out unto the LORD.

17 And he said, Be it far from me, O LORD, that I should do this: *is not this* [a]the blood of the men that went in jeopardy of their lives? therefore he would not drink it. These things did these three mighty men.

18 And [a]Abishai, the brother of Joab, the son of Zeruiah, was chief among three. And he lifted up his spear against three hundred, *and* slew *them*, and had the name among three.

19 Was he not most honourable of three? therefore he was their captain: howbeit he attained not unto the *first* three.

20 And Benaiah the son of Jehoiada, the son of a valiant man, of [a]Kabzeel, who had done many acts, [b]he slew two lionlike men of Moab: he went down also and slew a lion in the midst of a pit in time of snow:

21 And he slew an Egyptian, a goodly man: and the Egyptian had a spear in his hand; but he went down to him with a staff, and plucked the spear out of the Egyptian's hand, and slew him with his own spear.

22 These *things* did Benaiah the son of Jehoiada, and had the name among three mighty men.

23 He was more honourable than the thirty, but he attained not to the *first* three. And David set him [a]over his guard.

24 [a]Asahel the brother of Joab *was* one of the thirty; Elhanan the son of Dodo of Beth–lehem,

25 [a]Shammah the Harodite, Elika the Harodite,

26 Helez the Paltite, Ira the son of Ikkesh the Tekoite,

27 Abiezer the Anethothite, Mebunnai the Hushathite,

28 Zalmon the Ahohite, Maharai the Netophathite,

29 Heleb the son of Baanah, a Netophathite, Ittai the son of Ribai out of Gibeah of the children of Benjamin,

30 Benaiah the Pirathonite, Hiddai of the brooks of [a]Gaash,

31 Abi–albon the Arbathite, Azmaveth the Barhumite,

32 Eliahba the Shaalbonite, of the sons of Jashen, Jonathan,

33 [a]Shammah the Hararite, Ahiam the son of Sharar the Hararite,

34 Eliphelet the son of Ahasbai, the son of the Maachathite, Eliam the son of [a]Ahithophel the Gilonite,

35 Hezrai the Carmelite, Paarai the Arbite,

36 Igal the son of Nathan of [a]Zobah, Bani the Gadite,

37 Zelek the Ammonite, Nahari the Beerothite, armourbearer to Joab the son of Zeruiah,

38 [a]Ira an Ithrite, Gareb an Ithrite,

39 [a]Uriah the Hittite: thirty and seven in all.

David's Census of Israel and Judah
(1 Chr. 21:1–6)

24 And [a]again the anger of the LORD was kindled against Israel, and he moved David against them to say, [b]Go, number Israel and Judah.

2 For the king said to Joab the captain of the host, which *was* with him, Go now through all the tribes of Israel, [a]from Dan even to Beer–

---

14 [a]1 Sam. 22:4, 5
17 [a][Lev. 17:10]
18 [a]2 Sam. 21:17; 1 Chr. 11:20
20 [a]Josh. 15:21 [b]Ex. 15:15
23 [a]2 Sam. 8:18; 20:23
24 [a]2 Sam. 2:18; 1 Chr. 27:7
25 [a]1 Chr. 11:27
30 [a]Judg. 2:9
33 [a]2 Sam. 23:11
34 [a]2 Sam. 15:12
36 [a]2 Sam. 8:3
38 [a]1 Cor. 11:28
39 [a]2 Sam. 11:3, 6

CHAPTER 24

1 [a]2 Sam. 21:1, 2 [b]Num. 26:2; 1 Chr. 27:23, 24
2 [a]Judg. 20:1; 2 Sam. 3:10

*

23:18 So with MT, LXX, Vg.; some Heb. mss., Syr. *thirty;* Tg. *the mighty men*
23:35 *Hezro,* 1 Chr. 11:37

NKJV

14 David *was* then in [a]the stronghold, and the garrison of the Philistines *was* then *in* Bethlehem.

15 And David said with longing, "Oh, that someone would give me a drink of the water from the well of Bethlehem, which *is* by the gate!"

16 So the three mighty men broke through the camp of the Philistines, drew water from the well of Bethlehem that *was* by the gate, and took it and brought *it* to David. Nevertheless he would not drink it, but poured it out to the LORD.

17 And he said, "Far be it from me, O LORD, that I should do this! Is *this not* [a]the blood of the men who went in *jeopardy of* their lives?" Therefore he would not drink it. These things were done by the three mighty men.

18 Now [a]Abishai the brother of Joab, the son of Zeruiah, was chief of **another* three. He lifted his spear against three hundred *men,* killed *them,* and won a name among *these* three.

19 Was he not the most honored of three? Therefore he became their captain. However, he did not attain to the *first* three.

20 Benaiah *was* the son of Jehoiada, the son of a valiant man from [a]Kabzeel, who had done many deeds. [b]He had killed two lion-like heroes of Moab. He also had gone down and killed a lion in the midst of a pit on a snowy day.

21 And he killed an Egyptian, a spectacular man. The Egyptian *had* a spear in his hand; so he went down to him with a staff, wrested the spear out of the Egyptian's hand, and killed him with his own spear.

22 These *things* Benaiah the son of Jehoiada did, and won a name among three mighty men.

23 He was more honored than the thirty, but he did not attain to the *first* three. And David appointed him [a]over his guard.

24 [a]Asahel the brother of Joab *was* one of the thirty; Elhanan the son of Dodo of Bethlehem,

25 [a]Shammah the Harodite, Elika the Harodite,

26 Helez the Paltite, Ira the son of Ikkesh the Tekoite,

27 Abiezer the Anathothite, Mebunnai the Hushathite,

28 Zalmon the Ahohite, Maharai the Netophathite,

29 Heleb the son of Baanah (the Netophathite), Ittai the son of Ribai from Gibeah of the children of Benjamin,

30 Benaiah a Pirathonite, Hiddai from the brooks of [a]Gaash,

31 Abi-Albon the Arbathite, Azmaveth the Barhumite,

32 Eliahba the Shaalbonite (of the sons of Jashen), Jonathan,

33 [a]Shammah the Hararite, Ahiam the son of Sharar the Hararite,

34 Eliphelet the son of Ahasbai, the son of the Maachathite, Eliam the son of [a]Ahithophel the Gilonite,

35 *Hezrai the Carmelite, Paarai the Arbite,

36 Igal the son of Nathan of [a]Zobah, Bani the Gadite,

37 Zelek the Ammonite, Naharai the Beerothite (armorbearer of Joab the son of Zeruiah),

38 [a]Ira the Ithrite, Gareb the Ithrite,

39 *and* [a]Uriah the Hittite: thirty-seven in all.

David's Census of Israel and Judah
(1 Chr. 21:1–6)

24 Again [a]the anger of the LORD was aroused against Israel, and He moved David against them to say, [b]"Go, number Israel and Judah."

2 So the king said to Joab the commander of the army who *was* with him, "Now go throughout all the tribes of Israel, [a]from Dan to Be-

KJV

sheba, and number ye the people, that [b]I may
know the number of the people.
3 And Joab said unto the king, Now the
LORD thy God [a]add unto the people, how many
soever they be, an hundredfold, and that the eyes
of my lord the king may see *it:* but why doth my
lord the king delight in this thing?
4 Notwithstanding the king's word prevailed against Joab, and against the captains of
the host. And Joab and the captains of the host
went out from the presence of the king, to number
the people of Israel.
5 And they passed over Jordan, and pitched
in [a]Aroer, on the right side of the city that *lieth*
in the midst of the river of Gad, and toward
[b]Jazer:
6 Then they came to Gilead, and to the land
of Tahtim–hodshi; and they came to [a]Dan–jaan,
and about to [b]Zidon,
7 And came to the strong hold of [a]Tyre, and
to all the cities of the [b]Hivites, and of the Canaanites: and they went out to the south of Judah, *even*
to Beer–sheba.
8 So when they had gone through all the
land, they came to Jerusalem at the end of nine
months and twenty days.
9 And Joab gave up the sum of the number
of the people unto the king: [a]and there were in
Israel eight hundred thousand valiant men that
drew the sword; and the men of Judah *were* five
hundred thousand men.

The Judgment on David's Sin
(1 Chr. 21:7–17)

10 And [a]David's heart smote him after that
he had numbered the people. And [b]David said
unto the LORD, [c]I have sinned greatly in that I
have done: and now, I beseech thee, O LORD, take
away the iniquity of thy servant; for I have [d]done
very foolishly.
11 For when David was up in the morning,
the word of the LORD came unto the prophet [a]Gad,
David's [b]seer, saying,
12 Go and say unto David, Thus saith the
LORD, I offer thee three *things;* choose thee one
of them, that I may *do it* unto thee.
13 So Gad came to David, and told him, and
said unto him, Shall [a]seven years of famine come
unto thee in thy land? or wilt thou flee three
months before thine enemies, while they pursue
thee? or that there be three days' pestilence in
thy land? now advise, and see what answer I shall
return to him that sent me.
14 And David said unto Gad, I am in a great
strait: let us fall now into the hand of the LORD;
[a]for his mercies *are* great: and [b]let me not fall
into the hand of man.
15 So [a]the LORD sent a pestilence upon Israel
from the morning even to the time appointed: and
there died of the people from Dan even to Beer–
sheba seventy thousand men.
16 [a]And when the angel stretched out his
hand upon Jerusalem to destroy it, [b]the LORD repented him of the evil, and said to the angel that
destroyed the people, It is enough: stay now thine
hand. And the angel of the LORD was by the
threshingplace of Araunah the Jebusite.
17 And David spake unto the LORD when he
saw the angel that smote the people, and said,
Lo, [a]I have sinned, and I have done wickedly: but
these sheep, what have they done? let thine hand,
I pray thee, be against me, and against my father's
house.

The Altar on the Threshing Floor
(1 Chr. 21:18–27)

18 And Gad came that day to David, and said
unto him, [a]Go up, rear an altar unto the LORD in
the threshingfloor of Araunah the Jebusite.
19 And David, according to the saying of
Gad, went up as the LORD commanded.

2 [b][Jer. 17:5]
3 [a]Deut. 1:11
5 [a]Deut. 2:36; Josh. 13:9, 16 [b]Num. 32:1, 3
6 [a]Josh. 19:47; Judg. 18:29 [b]Josh. 19:28; Judg. 18:28
7 [a]Josh. 19:29 [b]Josh. 11:3; Judg. 3:3
9 [a]1 Chr. 21:5
10 [a]1 Sam. 24:5 [b]2 Sam. 23:1 [c]2 Sam. 12:13 [d]1 Sam. 13:13; [2 Chr. 16:9]
11 [a]1 Sam. 22:5 [b]1 Sam. 9:9; 1 Chr. 29:29
13 [a]Ezek. 14:21
14 [a][Ps. 51:1; 103:8, 13, 14; 119:156; 130:4, 7] [b][Is. 47:6; Zech. 1:15]
15 [a]1 Chr. 21:14
16 [a]Ex. 12:23; 2 Kin. 19:35; Acts 12:23 [b]Gen. 6:6; 1 Sam. 15:11
17 [a]2 Sam. 7:8; 1 Chr. 21:17; Ps. 74:1
18 [a]1 Chr. 21:18

*______

24:13 So with MT, Syr., Tg., Vg.; LXX *three* (cf. 1 Chr. 21:12)
24:16 Or *Angel* • *Ornan,* 1 Chr. 21:15

NKJV

ersheba, and count the people, that [b]I may know
the number of the people."
3 And Joab said to the king, "Now may the
LORD your God [a]add to the people a hundred times
more than there are, and may the eyes of my lord
the king see *it.* But why does my lord the king
desire this thing?"
4 Nevertheless the king's word prevailed
against Joab and against the captains of the army.
Therefore Joab and the captains of the army went
out from the presence of the king to count the
people of Israel.
5 And they crossed over the Jordan and
camped in [a]Aroer, on the right side of the town
which *is* in the midst of the ravine of Gad, and
toward [b]Jazer.
6 Then they came to Gilead and to the land
of Tahtim Hodshi; they came to [a]Dan Jaan and
around to [b]Sidon;
7 and they came to the stronghold of [a]Tyre
and to all the cities of the [b]Hivites and the Canaanites. Then they went out to South Judah *as
far as* Beersheba.
8 So when they had gone through all the
land, they came to Jerusalem at the end of nine
months and twenty days.
9 Then Joab gave the sum of the number
of the people to the king. [a]And there were in Israel
eight hundred thousand valiant men who drew
the sword, and the men of Judah were five hundred thousand men.

The Judgment on David's Sin
(1 Chr. 21:7–17)

10 And [a]David's heart condemned him after
he had numbered the people. So [b]David said to
the LORD, [c]"I have sinned greatly in what I have
done; but now, I pray, O LORD, take away the iniquity of Your servant, for I have [d]done very
foolishly."
11 Now when David arose in the morning,
the word of the LORD came to the prophet [a]Gad,
David's [b]seer, saying,
12 "Go and tell David, 'Thus says the LORD:
"I offer you three *things;* choose one of them for
yourself, that I may do *it* to you." ' "
13 So Gad came to David and told him; and
he said to him, "Shall [a]seven* years of famine
come to you in your land? Or shall you flee three
months before your enemies, while they pursue
you? Or shall there be three days' plague in your
land? Now consider and see what answer I should
take back to Him who sent me."
14 And David said to Gad, "I am in great distress. Please let us fall into the hand of the LORD,
[a]for His mercies *are* great; but [b]do not let me fall
into the hand of man."
15 So [a]the LORD sent a plague upon Israel
from the morning till the appointed time. From
Dan to Beersheba seventy thousand men of the
people died.
16 [a]And when the *angel stretched out His
hand over Jerusalem to destroy it, [b]the LORD relented from the destruction, and said to the angel
who was destroying the people, "It is enough; now
restrain your hand." And the angel of the LORD
was by the threshing floor of *Araunah the
Jebusite.
17 Then David spoke to the LORD when he
saw the angel who was striking the people, and
said, "Surely [a]I have sinned, and I have done
wickedly; but these sheep, what have they done?
Let Your hand, I pray, be against me and against
my father's house."

The Altar on the Threshing Floor
(1 Chr. 21:18–27)

18 And Gad came that day to David and said
to him, [a]"Go up, erect an altar to the LORD on
the threshing floor of Araunah the Jebusite."
19 So David, according to the word of Gad,
went up as the LORD commanded.

KJV

20 And Araunah looked, and saw the king
and his servants coming on toward him: and
Araunah went out, and bowed himself before the
king on his face upon the ground.
21 And Araunah said, Wherefore is my lord
the king come to his servant? [a]And David said,
To buy the threshingfloor of thee, to build an altar
unto the LORD, that [b]the plague may be stayed
from the people.
22 And Araunah said unto David, Let my
lord the king take and offer up what *seemeth* good
unto him: [a]behold, *here be* oxen for burnt sacrifice, and threshing instruments and *other* instruments of the oxen for wood.
23 All these *things* did Araunah, *as* a king,
give unto the king. And Araunah said unto the
king, The LORD thy God [a]accept thee.
24 And the king said unto Araunah, Nay; but
I will surely buy *it* of thee at a price: neither will
I offer burnt offerings unto the LORD my God of
that which doth cost me nothing. So [a]David
bought the threshingfloor and the oxen for fifty
shekels of silver.
25 And David built there an altar unto the
LORD, and offered burnt offerings and peace offerings. [a]So the LORD was intreated for the land, and
[b]the plague was stayed from Israel.

21 [a]Gen. 23:8–16 [b]Num. 16:48, 50
22 [a]1 Sam. 6:14; 1 Kin. 19:21
23 [a][Ezek. 20:40, 41]
24 [a]1 Chr. 21:24, 25
25 [a]2 Sam. 21:14 [b]2 Sam. 24:21

NKJV

20 Now Araunah looked, and saw the king
and his servants coming toward him. So Araunah
went out and bowed before the king with his face
to the ground.
21 Then Araunah said, "Why has my lord the
king come to his servant?" [a]And David said, "To
buy the threshing floor from you, to build an altar
to the LORD, that [b]the plague may be withdrawn
from the people."
22 Now Araunah said to David, "Let my lord
the king take and offer up whatever *seems* good
to him. [a]Look, *here are* oxen for burnt sacrifice,
and threshing implements and the yokes of the
oxen for wood.
23 "All these, O king, Araunah has given to
the king." And Araunah said to the king, "May
the LORD your God [a]accept you."
24 Then the king said to Araunah, "No, but
I will surely buy *it* from you for a price; nor will
I offer burnt offerings to the LORD my God with
that which costs me nothing." So [a]David bought
the threshing floor and the oxen for fifty shekels
of silver.
25 And David built there an altar to the LORD,
and offered burnt offerings and peace offerings.
[a]So the LORD heeded the prayers for the land, and
[b]the plague was withdrawn from Israel.

KJV

THE FIRST BOOK OF THE

KINGS

Adonijah Presumes to Be King

1 Now king David was [a]old *and* stricken in
years; and they covered him with clothes, but
he gat no heat.
2 Wherefore his servants said unto him, Let
there be sought for my lord the king a young virgin: and let her stand before the king, and let her
cherish him, and let her lie in thy bosom, that
my lord the king may get heat.
3 So they sought for a fair damsel throughout all the coasts of Israel, and found [a]Abishag a
[b]Shunammite, and brought her to the king.
4 And the damsel *was* very fair, and cherished the king, and ministered to him: but the king
knew her not.
5 Then [a]Adonijah the son of Haggith exalted himself, saying, I will be king: and [b]he prepared him chariots and horsemen, and fifty men
to run before him.
6 And his father had not displeased him at
any time in saying, Why hast thou done so? and
he also *was a* very goodly *man;* [a]and *his mother*
bare him after Absalom.
7 And he conferred with [a]Joab the son of
Zeruiah, and with [b]Abiathar the priest: and [c]they
following Adonijah helped *him.*
8 But [a]Zadok the priest, and [b]Benaiah the
son of Jehoiada, and [c]Nathan the prophet, and
[d]Shimei, and Rei, and [e]the mighty men which *be-*
longed to David, were not with Adonijah.
9 And Adonijah slew sheep and oxen and
fat cattle by the stone of Zoheleth, which *is* by
[a]En–rogel, and called all his brethren the king's
sons, and all the men of Judah the king's servants:
10 But Nathan the prophet, and Benaiah, and
the mighty men, and [a]Solomon his brother, he
called not.
11 Wherefore Nathan spake unto Bath–
sheba the mother of Solomon, saying, Hast
thou not heard that Adonijah the son of [a]Hag-
gith doth reign, and David our lord knoweth *it*
not?
12 Now therefore come, let me, I pray thee,
give thee counsel, that thou mayest save thine
own life, and the life of thy son Solomon.
13 Go and get thee in unto king David, and
say unto him, Didst not thou, my lord, O king,
swear unto thine handmaid, saying, [a]Assuredly
Solomon thy son shall reign after me, and he shall
sit upon my throne? why then doth Adonijah
reign?
14 Behold, while thou yet talkest there with
the king, I also will come in after thee, and confirm thy words.
15 And Bath–sheba went in unto the king
into the chamber: and the king was very old; and
Abishag the Shunammite ministered unto the
king.
16 And Bath–sheba bowed, and did obeisance unto the king. And the king said, What
wouldest thou?
17 And she said unto him, My lord, [a]thou
swarest by the LORD thy God unto thine handmaid, *saying,* Assuredly Solomon thy son
shall reign after me, and he shall sit upon my
throne.

CHAPTER 1

1 [a]1 Chr. 23:1
3 [a]1 Kin. 2:17 [b]Josh. 19:18; 1 Sam. 28:4
5 [a]2 Sam. 3:4 [b]2 Sam. 15:1
6 [a]2 Sam. 3:3, 4; 1 Chr. 3:2
7 [a]1 Chr. 11:6 [b]2 Sam. 20:25 [c]1 Kin. 2:22, 28
8 [a]1 Kin. 2:35 [b]1 Kin. 2:25; 2 Sam. 8:18 [c]2 Sam. 12:1 [d]1 Kin. 4:18 [e]2 Sam. 23:8
9 [a]Josh. 15:7; 18:16; 2 Sam. 17:17
10 [a]2 Sam. 12:24
11 [a]2 Sam. 3:4
13 [a]1 Kin. 1:30; 1 Chr. 22:9–13
17 [a]1 Kin. 1:13, 30

NKJV

THE FIRST BOOK OF THE

KINGS

Adonijah Presumes to Be King

1 Now King David was [a]old, advanced in
years; and they put covers on him, but he
could not get warm.
2 Therefore his servants said to him, "Let
a young woman, a virgin, be sought for our lord
the king, and let her stand before the king, and
let her care for him; and let her lie in your bosom,
that our lord the king may be warm."
3 So they sought for a lovely young woman
throughout all the territory of Israel, and found
[a]Abishag the [b]Shunammite, and brought her to
the king.
4 The young woman *was* very lovely; and
she cared for the king, and served him; but the
king did not know her.
5 Then [a]Adonijah the son of Haggith exalted himself, saying, "I will be king"; and [b]he
prepared for himself chariots and horsemen, and
fifty men to run before him.
6 (And his father had not rebuked him at
any time by saying, "Why have you done so?"
He *was* also very good-looking. [a]*His mother* had
borne him after Absalom.)
7 Then he conferred with [a]Joab the son of
Zeruiah and with [b]Abiathar the priest, and [c]they
followed and helped Adonijah.
8 But [a]Zadok the priest, [b]Benaiah the son
of Jehoiada, [c]Nathan the prophet, [d]Shimei, Rei,
and [e]the mighty men who *belonged* to David were
not with Adonijah.
9 And Adonijah sacrificed sheep and oxen
and fattened cattle by the stone of Zoheleth,
which *is* by [a]En Rogel; he also invited all his
brothers, the king's sons, and all the men of Judah, the king's servants.
10 But he did not invite Nathan the prophet,
Benaiah, the mighty men, or [a]Solomon his
brother.
11 So Nathan spoke to Bathsheba the mother
of Solomon, saying, "Have you not heard that
Adonijah the son of [a]Haggith has become king,
and David our lord does not know *it?*
12 "Come, please, let me now give you advice, that you may save your own life and the
life of your son Solomon.
13 "Go immediately to King David and say
to him, 'Did you not, my lord, O king, swear to
your maidservant, saying, [a]"Assuredly your son
Solomon shall reign after me, and he shall sit on
my throne"? Why then has Adonijah become
king?'
14 "Then, while you are still talking there
with the king, I also will come in after you and
confirm your words."
15 So Bathsheba went into the chamber to
the king. (Now the king was very old, and Abishag
the Shunammite was serving the king.)
16 And Bathsheba bowed and did homage to
the king. Then the king said, "What is your wish?"
17 Then she said to him, "My lord, [a]you
swore by the LORD your God to your maidservant,
saying, 'Assuredly Solomon your son shall reign
after me, and he shall sit on my throne.'

KJV

18 And now, behold, Adonijah reigneth; and
now, my lord the king, thou knowest *it* not:
19 [a]And he hath slain oxen and fat cattle and
sheep in abundance, and hath called all the sons
of the king, and Abiathar the priest, and Joab the
captain of the host: but Solomon thy servant hath
he not called.
20 And thou, my lord, O king, the eyes of
all Israel *are* upon thee, that thou shouldest tell
them who shall sit on the throne of my lord the
king after him.
21 Otherwise it shall come to pass, when my
lord the king [a]shall sleep with his fathers, that I
and my son Solomon shall be counted offenders.
22 And, lo, while she yet talked with the king,
Nathan the prophet also came in.
23 And they told the king, saying, Behold Nathan the prophet. And when he was come in before the king, he bowed himself before the king
with his face to the ground.
24 And Nathan said, My lord, O king, hast
thou said, Adonijah shall reign after me, and he
shall sit upon my throne?
25 [a]For he is gone down this day, and hath
slain oxen and fat cattle and sheep in abundance,
and hath called all the king's sons, and the captains of the host, and Abiathar the priest; and,
behold, they eat and drink before him, and say,
[b]God save king Adonijah.
26 But me, *even* me thy servant, and Zadok
the priest, and Benaiah the son of Jehoiada, and
thy servant Solomon, hath he not called.
27 Is this thing done by my lord the king,
and thou hast not shewed *it* unto thy servant, who
should sit on the throne of my lord the king after
him?

David Proclaims Solomon King
(1 Chr. 29:22–25)

28 Then king David answered and said, Call
me Bath–sheba. And she came into the king's
presence, and stood before the king.
29 And the king sware, and said, [a]*As* the
LORD liveth, that hath redeemed my soul out of
all distress,
30 [a]Even as I sware unto thee by the LORD
God of Israel, saying, Assuredly Solomon thy son
shall reign after me, and he shall sit upon my
throne in my stead; even so will I certainly do
this day.
31 Then Bath–sheba bowed with *her* face to
the earth, and did reverence to the king, and said,
[a]Let my lord king David live for ever.
32 And king David said, Call me Zadok the
priest, and Nathan the prophet, and Benaiah the
son of Jehoiada. And they came before the king.
33 The king also said unto them, [a]Take with
you the servants of your lord, and cause Solomon
my son to ride upon mine own [b]mule, and bring
him down to [c]Gihon:
34 And let Zadok the priest and Nathan the
prophet [a]anoint him there king over Israel: and
[b]blow ye with the trumpet, and say, God save king
Solomon.
35 Then ye shall come up after him, that he
may come and sit upon my throne; for he shall
be king in my stead: and I have appointed him
to be ruler over Israel and over Judah.
36 And Benaiah the son of Jehoiada answered the king, and said, [a]Amen: the LORD God
of my lord the king say so *too*.
37 [a]As the LORD hath been with my lord the
king, even so be he with Solomon, and [b]make
his throne greater than the throne of my lord king
David.
38 So Zadok the priest, and Nathan the
prophet, [a]and Benaiah the son of Jehoiada, and
the [b]Cherethites, and the Pelethites, went down,
and caused Solomon to ride upon king David's
mule, and brought him to Gihon.
39 And Zadok the priest took an horn of [a]oil

19 [a]1 Kin. 1:7–9, 25
21 [a]Deut. 31:16; 2 Sam. 7:12; 1 Kin. 2:10
25 [a]1 Kin. 1:9, 19 [b]1 Sam. 10:24
29 [a]2 Sam. 4:9; 12:5
30 [a]1 Kin. 1:13, 17
31 [a]Neh. 2:3; Dan. 2:4; 3:9
33 [a]2 Sam. 20:6 [b]Esth. 6:8 [c]2 Chr. 32:30; 33:14
34 [a]1 Sam. 10:1; 16:3, 12; 2 Sam. 2:4; 5:3; 1 Kin. 19:16; 2 Kin. 9:3; 11:12; 1 Chr. 29:22 [b]2 Sam. 15:10; 2 Kin. 9:13; 11:14
36 [a]Jer. 28:6
37 [a]Josh. 1:5, 17; 1 Sam. 20:13 [b]1 Kin. 1:47
38 [a]2 Sam. 8:18; 23:20–23 [b]2 Sam. 20:7; 1 Chr. 18:17
39 [a]Ex. 30:23, 25, 32; Ps. 89:20

NKJV

18 "So now, look! Adonijah has become
king; and now, my lord the king, you do not know
about *it*.
19 [a]"He has sacrificed oxen and fattened cattle and sheep in abundance, and has invited all
the sons of the king, Abiathar the priest, and Joab
the commander of the army; but Solomon your
servant he has not invited.
20 "And as for you, my lord, O king, the eyes
of all Israel *are* on you, that you should tell them
who will sit on the throne of my lord the king
after him.
21 "Otherwise it will happen, when my lord
the king [a]rests with his fathers, that I and my son
Solomon will be counted as offenders."
22 And just then, while she was still talking
with the king, Nathan the prophet also came in.
23 So they told the king, saying, "Here is Nathan the prophet." And when he came in before
the king, he bowed down before the king with
his face to the ground.
24 And Nathan said, "My lord, O king, have
you said, 'Adonijah shall reign after me, and he
shall sit on my throne'?
25 [a]"For he has gone down today, and has
sacrificed oxen and fattened cattle and sheep in
abundance, and has invited all the king's sons,
and the commanders of the army, and Abiathar
the priest; and look! They are eating and drinking
before him; and they say, [b]'*Long* live King
Adonijah!'
26 "But he has not invited me—me your servant—nor Zadok the priest, nor Benaiah the son
of Jehoiada, nor your servant Solomon.
27 "Has this thing been done by my lord the
king, and you have not told your servant who
should sit on the throne of my lord the king after
him?"

David Proclaims Solomon King
(1 Chr. 29:22–25)

28 Then King David answered and said,
"Call Bathsheba to me." So she came into the
king's presence and stood before the king.
29 And the king took an oath and said, [a]"*As*
the LORD lives, who has redeemed my life from
every distress,
30 [a]"just as I swore to you by the LORD God
of Israel, saying, 'Assuredly Solomon your son
shall be king after me, and he shall sit on my
throne in my place,' so I certainly will do this
day."
31 Then Bathsheba bowed with *her* face to
the earth, and paid homage to the king, and said,
[a]"Let my lord King David live forever!"
32 And King David said, "Call to me Zadok
the priest, Nathan the prophet, and Benaiah the
son of Jehoiada." So they came before the king.
33 The king also said to them, [a]"Take with
you the servants of your lord, and have Solomon
my son ride on my own [b]mule, and take him down
to [c]Gihon.
34 "There let Zadok the priest and Nathan
the prophet [a]anoint him king over Israel; and
[b]blow the horn, and say, '*Long* live King
Solomon!'
35 "Then you shall come up after him, and
he shall come and sit on my throne, and he shall
be king in my place. For I have appointed him to
be ruler over Israel and Judah."
36 Benaiah the son of Jehoiada answered the
king and said, [a]"Amen! May the LORD God of my
lord the king say so *too*.
37 [a]"As the LORD has been with my lord the
king, even so may He be with Solomon, and
[b]make his throne greater than the throne of my
lord King David."
38 So Zadok the priest, Nathan the prophet,
[a]Benaiah the son of Jehoiada, the [b]Cherethites,
and the Pelethites went down and had Solomon
ride on King David's mule, and took him to Gihon.
39 Then Zadok the priest took a horn of [a]oil

KJV

out of the tabernacle, and [b]anointed Solomon. And they blew the trumpet; [c]and all the people said, God save king Solomon.

40 And all the people came up after him, and the people piped with pipes, and rejoiced with great joy, so that the earth rent with the sound of them.

41 And Adonijah and all the guests that *were* with him heard *it* as they had made an end of eating. And when Joab heard the sound of the trumpet, he said, Wherefore *is this* noise of the city being in an uproar?

42 And while he yet spake, behold, [a]Jonathan the son of Abiathar the priest came: and Adonijah said unto him, Come in; for [b]thou *art* a valiant man, and bringest good tidings.

43 And Jonathan answered and said to Adonijah, Verily our lord king David hath made Solomon king.

44 And the king hath sent with him Zadok the priest, and Nathan the prophet, and Benaiah the son of Jehoiada, and the Cherethites, and the Pelethites, and they have caused him to ride upon the king's mule:

45 And Zadok the priest and Nathan the prophet have anointed him king in Gihon: and they are come up from thence rejoicing, so that the city rang again. This *is* the noise that ye have heard.

46 And also Solomon [a]sitteth on the throne of the kingdom.

47 And moreover the king's servants came to bless our lord king David, saying, [a]God make the name of Solomon better than thy name, and make his throne greater than thy throne. [b]And the king bowed himself upon the bed.

48 And also thus said the king, Blessed *be* the LORD God of Israel, which hath [a]given *one* to sit on my throne this day, mine eyes even seeing [b]*it*.

49 And all the guests that *were* with Adonijah were afraid, and rose up, and went every man his way.

50 And Adonijah feared because of Solomon, and arose, and went, and [a]caught hold on the horns of the altar.

51 And it was told Solomon, saying, Behold, Adonijah feareth king Solomon: for, lo, he hath caught hold on the horns of the altar, saying, Let king Solomon swear unto me to day that he will not slay his servant with the sword.

52 And Solomon said, If he will shew himself a worthy man, [a]there shall not an hair of him fall to the earth: but if wickedness shall be found in him, he shall die.

53 So king Solomon sent, and they brought him down from the altar. And he came and bowed himself to king Solomon: and Solomon said unto him, Go to thine house.

David's Instructions to Solomon

2 Now [a]the days of David drew nigh that he should die; and he charged Solomon his son, saying,

2 [a]I go the way of all the earth: [b]be thou strong therefore, and shew thyself a man;

3 And keep the charge of the LORD thy God, to walk in his ways, to keep his statutes, and his commandments, and his judgments, and his testimonies, as it is written in the law of Moses, that thou mayest [a]prosper in all that thou doest, and whithersoever thou turnest thyself:

4 That the LORD may [a]continue his word which he spake concerning me, saying, [b]If thy children take heed to their way, to [c]walk before me in truth with all their heart and with all their soul, [d]there shall not fail thee (said he) a man on the throne of Israel.

5 Moreover thou knowest also what Joab the son of Zeruiah [a]did to me, *and* what he did to the two captains of the hosts of Israel, unto [b]Abner the son of Ner, and unto [c]Amasa the son

39 [b]1 Chr. 29:22 [c]1 Sam. 10:24
42 [a]2 Sam. 17:17, 20 [b]2 Sam. 18:27
46 [a]1 Kin. 2:12; 1 Chr. 29:23
47 [a]1 Kin. 1:37 [b]Gen. 47:31
48 [a]1 Kin. 3:6; [Ps. 132:11, 12] [b]2 Sam. 7:12
50 [a]Ex. 27:2; 30:10; 1 Kin. 2:28
52 [a]1 Sam. 14:45; 2 Sam. 14:11; Acts 27:34

CHAPTER 2

1 [a]Gen. 47:29; Deut. 31:14
2 [a]Josh. 23:14 [b]Deut. 31:7, 23; 1 Chr. 22:13
3 [a][Deut. 29:9; Josh. 1:7]; 1 Chr. 22:12, 13
4 [a]2 Sam. 7:25 [b][Ps. 132:12] [c]2 Kin. 20:3 [d]2 Sam. 7:12, 13; 1 Kin. 8:25
5 [a]2 Sam. 3:39; 18:5, 12, 14 [b]2 Sam. 3:27; 1 Kin. 2:32 [c]2 Sam. 20:10

NKJV

from the tabernacle and [b]anointed Solomon. And they blew the horn, [c]and all the people said, *"Long* live King Solomon!"

40 And all the people went up after him; and the people played the flutes and rejoiced with great joy, so that the earth *seemed to* split with their sound.

41 Now Adonijah and all the guests who *were* with him heard *it* as they finished eating. And when Joab heard the sound of the horn, he said, "Why *is* the city in such a noisy uproar?"

42 While he was still speaking, there came [a]Jonathan, the son of Abiathar the priest. And Adonijah said to him, "Come in, for [b]you *are* a prominent man, and bring good news."

43 Then Jonathan answered and said to Adonijah, "No! Our lord King David has made Solomon king.

44 "The king has sent with him Zadok the priest, Nathan the prophet, Benaiah the son of Jehoiada, the Cherethites, and the Pelethites; and they have made him ride on the king's mule.

45 "So Zadok the priest and Nathan the prophet have anointed him king at Gihon; and they have gone up from there rejoicing, so that the city is in an uproar. This *is* the noise that you have heard.

46 "Also Solomon [a]sits on the throne of the kingdom.

47 "And moreover the king's servants have gone to bless our lord King David, saying, [a]'May God make the name of Solomon better than your name, and may He make his throne greater than your throne.' [b]Then the king bowed himself on the bed.

48 "Also the king said thus, 'Blessed *be* the LORD God of Israel, who has [a]given *one* to sit on my throne this day, while my eyes see [b]*it!*' "

49 So all the guests who were with Adonijah were afraid, and arose, and each one went his way.

50 Now Adonijah was afraid of Solomon; so he arose, and went and [a]took hold of the horns of the altar.

51 And it was told Solomon, saying, "Indeed Adonijah is afraid of King Solomon; for look, he has taken hold of the horns of the altar, saying, 'Let King Solomon swear to me today that he will not put his servant to death with the sword.' "

52 Then Solomon said, "If he proves himself a worthy man, [a]not one hair of him shall fall to the earth; but if wickedness is found in him, he shall die."

53 So King Solomon sent them to bring him down from the altar. And he came and fell down before King Solomon; and Solomon said to him, "Go to your house."

David's Instructions to Solomon

2 Now [a]the days of David drew near that he should die, and he charged Solomon his son, saying:

2 [a]"I go the way of all the earth; [b]be strong, therefore, and prove yourself a man.

3 "And keep the charge of the LORD your God: to walk in His ways, to keep His statutes, His commandments, His judgments, and His testimonies, as it is written in the Law of Moses, that you may [a]prosper in all that you do and wherever you turn;

4 "that the LORD may [a]fulfill His word which He spoke concerning me, saying, [b]'If your sons take heed to their way, to [c]walk before Me in truth with all their heart and with all their soul,' He said, [d]'you shall not lack a man on the throne of Israel.'

5 "Moreover you know also what Joab the son of Zeruiah [a]did to me, *and* what he did to the two commanders of the armies of Israel, to [b]Abner the son of Ner and [c]Amasa the son of

KJV

of Jether, whom he slew, and shed the blood of war in peace, and put the blood of war upon his girdle that *was* about his loins, and in his shoes that *were* on his feet.

6 Do therefore [a]according to thy wisdom, and let not his hoar head go down to the grave in peace.

7 But shew kindness unto the sons of [a]Barzillai the Gileadite, and let them be of those that [b]eat at thy table: for so [c]they came to me when I fled because of Absalom thy brother.

8 And, behold, *thou hast* with thee [a]Shimei the son of Gera, a Benjamite of Bahurim, which cursed me with a grievous curse in the day when I went to Mahanaim: but [b]he came down to meet me at Jordan, and [c]I sware to him by the LORD, saying, I will not put thee to death with the sword.

9 Now therefore [a]hold him not guiltless: for thou *art* a wise man, and knowest what thou oughtest to do unto him; but his hoar head [b]bring thou down to the grave with blood.

Death of David
(1 Chr. 3:4; 29:26–28)

10 So [a]David slept with his fathers, and was buried in [b]the city of David.

11 And the days that David [a]reigned over Israel *were* forty years: seven years reigned he in Hebron, and thirty and three years reigned he in Jerusalem.

12 [a]Then sat Solomon upon the throne of David his father; and his kingdom was [b]established greatly.

Solomon Executes Adonijah

13 And Adonijah the son of Haggith came to Bath–sheba the mother of Solomon. And she said, [a]Comest thou peaceably? And he said, Peaceably.

14 He said moreover, I have somewhat to say unto thee. And she said, Say on.

15 And he said, Thou knowest that the kingdom was [a]mine, and *that* all Israel set their faces on me, that I should reign: howbeit the kingdom is turned about, and is become my brother's: for [b]it was his from the LORD.

16 And now I ask one petition of thee, deny me not. And she said unto him, Say on.

17 And he said, Speak, I pray thee, unto Solomon the king, (for he will not say thee nay,) that he give me [a]Abishag the Shunammite to wife.

18 And Bath–sheba said, Well; I will speak for thee unto the king.

19 Bath–sheba therefore went unto king Solomon, to speak unto him for Adonijah. And the king rose up to meet her, and [a]bowed himself unto her, and sat down on his throne, and caused a seat to be set for the king's mother; [b]and she sat on his right hand.

20 Then she said, I desire one small petition of thee; *I pray thee,* say me not nay. And the king said unto her, Ask on, my mother: for I will not say thee nay.

21 And she said, Let Abishag the Shunammite be given to Adonijah thy brother to wife.

22 And king Solomon answered and said unto his mother, And why dost thou ask Abishag the Shunammite for Adonijah? ask for him the kingdom also; for he *is* mine [a]elder brother; even for him, and for [b]Abiathar the priest, and for Joab the son of Zeruiah.

23 Then king Solomon sware by the LORD, saying, [a]God do so to me, and more also, if Adonijah have not spoken this word against his own life.

24 Now therefore, *as* the LORD liveth, which hath established me, and set me on the throne of David my father, and who hath made me an house, as he [a]promised, Adonijah shall be put to death this day.

25 And king Solomon sent by the hand of

6 [a]1 Kin. 2:9; Prov. 20:26
7 [a]2 Sam. 19:31–39 [b]2 Sam. 9:7, 10; 19:28 [c]2 Sam. 17:17–29
8 [a]2 Sam. 16:5–13 [b]2 Sam. 19:18 [c]2 Sam. 19:23
9 [a]Ex. 20:7; Job 9:28 [b]Gen. 42:38; 44:31
10 [a]1 Kin. 1:21; Acts 2:29; 13:36 [b]2 Sam. 5:7; 1 Kin. 3:1
11 [a]2 Sam. 5:4, 5; 1 Chr. 3:4; 29:26, 27
12 [a]1 Kin. 1:46; 1 Chr. 29:23 [b]1 Kin. 2:46; 2 Chr. 1:1
13 [a]1 Sam. 16:4, 5
15 [a]1 Kin. 1:11, 18 [b]1 Chr. 22:9, 10; 28:5–7; [Dan. 2:21]
17 [a]1 Kin. 1:3, 4
19 [a][Ex. 20:12] [b]Ps. 45:9
22 [a]1 Kin. 1:6; 2:15; 1 Chr. 3:2, 5 [b]1 Kin. 1:7
23 [a]Ruth 1:17
24 [a]2 Sam. 7:11, 13; 1 Chr. 22:10

NKJV

Jether, whom he killed. And he shed the blood of war in peacetime, and put the blood of war on his belt that *was* around his waist, and on his sandals that *were* on his feet.

6 "Therefore do [a]according to your wisdom, and do not let his gray hair go down to the grave in peace.

7 "But show kindness to the sons of [a]Barzillai the Gileadite, and let them be among those who [b]eat at your table, for so [c]they came to me when I fled from Absalom your brother.

8 "And see, *you have* with you [a]Shimei the son of Gera, a Benjamite from Bahurim, who cursed me with a malicious curse in the day when I went to Mahanaim. But [b]he came down to meet me at the Jordan, and [c]I swore to him by the LORD, saying, 'I will not put you to death with the sword.'

9 "Now therefore, [a]do not hold him guiltless, for you *are* a wise man and know what you ought to do to him; but [b]bring his gray hair down to the grave with blood."

Death of David
(1 Chr. 3:4; 29:26–28)

10 So [a]David rested with his fathers, and was buried in [b]the City of David.

11 The period that David [a]reigned over Israel *was* forty years; seven years he reigned in Hebron, and in Jerusalem he reigned thirty-three years.

12 [a]Then Solomon sat on the throne of his father David; and his kingdom was [b]firmly established.

Solomon Executes Adonijah

13 Now Adonijah the son of Haggith came to Bathsheba the mother of Solomon. So she said, [a]"Do you come peaceably?" And he said, "Peaceably."

14 Moreover he said, "I have something *to say* to you." And she said, "Say it."

15 Then he said, "You know that the kingdom was [a]mine, and all Israel had set their expectations on me, that I should reign. However, the kingdom has been turned over, and has become my brother's; for [b]it was his from the LORD.

16 "Now I ask one petition of you; do not deny me." And she said to him, "Say it."

17 Then he said, "Please speak to King Solomon, for he will not refuse you, that he may give me [a]Abishag the Shunammite as wife."

18 So Bathsheba said, "Very well, I will speak for you to the king."

19 Bathsheba therefore went to King Solomon, to speak to him for Adonijah. And the king rose up to meet her and [a]bowed down to her, and sat down on his throne and had a throne set for the king's mother; [b]so she sat at his right hand.

20 Then she said, "I desire one small petition of you; do not refuse me." And the king said to her, "Ask it, my mother, for I will not refuse you."

21 So she said, "Let Abishag the Shunammite be given to Adonijah your brother as wife."

22 And King Solomon answered and said to his mother, "Now why do you ask Abishag the Shunammite for Adonijah? Ask for him the kingdom also—for he *is* my [a]older brother—for him, and for [b]Abiathar the priest, and for Joab the son of Zeruiah."

23 Then King Solomon swore by the LORD, saying, [a]"May God do so to me, and more also, if Adonijah has not spoken this word against his own life!

24 "Now therefore, *as* the LORD lives, who has confirmed me and set me on the throne of David my father, and who has established a *house for me, as He [a]promised, Adonijah shall be put to death today!"

25 So King Solomon sent by the hand of

*2:24 Royal dynasty

KJV

[a]Benaiah the son of Jehoiada; and he fell upon him that he died.

Abiathar Exiled, Joab Executed

26 And unto Abiathar the priest said the king, Get thee to [a]Anathoth, unto thine own fields; for thou *art* worthy of death: but I will not at this time put thee to death, [b]because thou barest the ark of the Lord GOD before David my father, and because thou hast been afflicted in all wherein my father was afflicted.
27 So Solomon thrust out Abiathar from being priest unto the LORD; that he might [a]fulfil the word of the LORD, which he spake concerning the house of Eli in Shiloh.
28 Then tidings came to Joab: for Joab [a]had turned after Adonijah, though he turned not after Absalom. And Joab fled unto the tabernacle of the LORD, and [b]caught hold on the horns of the altar.
29 And it was told king Solomon that Joab was fled unto the tabernacle of the LORD; and, behold, *he is* by the altar. Then Solomon sent Benaiah the son of Jehoiada, saying, Go, [a]fall upon him.
30 And Benaiah came to the tabernacle of the LORD, and said unto him, Thus saith the king, [a]Come forth. And he said, Nay; but I will die here. And Benaiah brought the king word again, saying, Thus said Joab, and thus he answered me.
31 And the king said unto him, [a]Do as he hath said, and fall upon him, and bury him; [b]that thou mayest take away the innocent blood, which Joab shed, from me, and from the house of my father.
32 And the LORD [a]shall return his blood upon his own head, who fell upon two men more righteous [b]and better than he, and slew them with the sword, my father David not knowing *thereof, to wit,* [c]Abner the son of Ner, captain of the host of Israel, and [d]Amasa the son of Jether, captain of the host of Judah.
33 Their blood shall therefore return upon the head of Joab, and [a]upon the head of his seed for ever: [b]but upon David, and upon his seed, and upon his house, and upon his throne, shall there be peace for ever from the LORD.
34 So Benaiah the son of Jehoiada went up, and fell upon him, and slew him: and he was buried in his own house in the wilderness.
35 And the king put Benaiah the son of Jehoiada in his room over the host: and [a]Zadok the priest did the king put in the room of [b]Abiathar.

Shimei Executed

36 And the king sent and called for [a]Shimei, and said unto him, Build thee an house in Jerusalem, and dwell there, and go not forth thence any whither.
37 For it shall be, *that* on the day thou goest out, and passest over [a]the brook Kidron, thou shalt know for certain that thou shalt surely die: [b]thy blood shall be upon thine own head.
38 And Shimei said unto the king, The saying *is* good: as my lord the king hath said, so will thy servant do. And Shimei dwelt in Jerusalem many days.
39 And it came to pass at the end of three years, that two of the servants of Shimei ran away unto [a]Achish son of Maachah king of Gath. And they told Shimei, saying, Behold, thy servants *be* in Gath.
40 And Shimei arose, and saddled his ass, and went to Gath to Achish to seek his servants: and Shimei went, and brought his servants from Gath.
41 And it was told Solomon that Shimei had gone from Jerusalem to Gath, and was come again.
42 And the king sent and called for Shimei, and said unto him, Did I not make thee to swear

25 [a]2 Sam. 8:18; 1 Kin. 4:4
26 [a]Josh. 21:18; Jer. 1:1 [b]1 Sam. 22:23; 23:6; 2 Sam. 15:14, 29
27 [a]1 Sam. 2:31–35
28 [a]1 Kin. 1:7 [b]1 Kin. 1:50
29 [a]1 Kin. 2:5, 6
30 [a][Ex. 21:14]
31 [a][Ex. 21:14] [b][Num. 35:33; Deut. 19:13; 21:8, 9]
32 [a][Gen. 9:6]; Judg. 9:24, 57 [b]2 Chr. 21:13, 14 [c]2 Sam. 3:27 [d]2 Sam. 20:9, 10
33 [a]2 Sam. 3:29 [b][Prov. 25:5]
35 [a]1 Sam. 2:35; 1 Kin. 4:4; 1 Chr. 6:53; 24:3; 29:22 [b]1 Kin. 2:27
36 [a]2 Sam. 16:5–13; 1 Kin. 2:8
37 [a]2 Sam. 15:23; 2 Kin. 23:6; John 18:1 [b]Lev. 20:9; Josh. 2:19; 2 Sam. 1:16; Ezek. 18:13
39 [a]1 Sam. 27:2

NKJV

[a]Benaiah the son of Jehoiada; and he struck him down, and he died.

Abiathar Exiled, Joab Executed

26 And to Abiathar the priest the king said, "Go to [a]Anathoth, to your own fields, for you *are* deserving of death; but I will not put you to death at this time, [b]because you carried the ark of the Lord GOD before my father David, and because you were afflicted every time my father was afflicted."
27 So Solomon removed Abiathar from being priest to the LORD, that he might [a]fulfill the word of the LORD which He spoke concerning the house of Eli at Shiloh.
28 Then news came to Joab, for Joab [a]had defected to Adonijah, though he had not defected to Absalom. So Joab fled to the tabernacle of the LORD, and [b]took hold of the horns of the altar.
29 And King Solomon was told, "Joab has fled to the tabernacle of the LORD; there *he is,* by the altar." Then Solomon sent Benaiah the son of Jehoiada, saying, "Go, [a]strike him down."
30 So Benaiah went to the tabernacle of the LORD, and said to him, "Thus says the king, [a]'Come out!' " And he said, "No, but I will die here." And Benaiah brought back word to the king, saying, "Thus said Joab, and thus he answered me."
31 Then the king said to him, [a]"Do as he has said, and strike him down and bury him, [b]that you may take away from me and from the house of my father the innocent blood which Joab shed.
32 "So the LORD [a]will return his blood on his head, because he struck down two men more righteous [b]and better than he, and killed them with the sword—[c]Abner the son of Ner, the commander of the army of Israel, and [d]Amasa the son of Jether, the commander of the army of Judah—though my father David did not know *it.*
33 "Their blood shall therefore return upon the head of Joab and [a]upon the head of his descendants forever. [b]But upon David and his descendants, upon his house and his throne, there shall be peace forever from the LORD."
34 So Benaiah the son of Jehoiada went up and struck and killed him; and he was buried in his own house in the wilderness.
35 The king put Benaiah the son of Jehoiada in his place over the army, and the king put [a]Zadok the priest in the place of [b]Abiathar.

Shimei Executed

36 Then the king sent and called for [a]Shimei, and said to him, "Build yourself a house in Jerusalem and dwell there, and do not go out from there anywhere.
37 "For it shall be, on the day you go out and cross [a]the Brook Kidron, know for certain you shall surely die; [b]your blood shall be on your own head."
38 And Shimei said to the king, "The saying *is* good. As my lord the king has said, so your servant will do." So Shimei dwelt in Jerusalem many days.
39 Now it happened at the end of three years, that two slaves of Shimei ran away to [a]Achish the son of Maachah, king of Gath. And they told Shimei, saying, "Look, your slaves *are* in Gath!"
40 So Shimei arose, saddled his donkey, and went to Achish at Gath to seek his slaves. And Shimei went and brought his slaves from Gath.
41 And Solomon was told that Shimei had gone from Jerusalem to Gath and had come back.
42 Then the king sent and called for Shimei, and said to him, "Did I not make you swear by

KJV

by the LORD, and protested unto thee, saying,
Know for a certain, on the day thou goest out,
and walkest abroad any whither, that thou shalt
surely die? and thou saidst unto me, The word
that I have heard *is* good.
43 Why then hast thou not kept the oath of
the LORD, and the commandment that I have
charged thee with?
44 The king said moreover to Shimei, Thou
knowest [a]all the wickedness which thine heart is
privy to, that thou didst to David my father: therefore the LORD shall [b]return thy wickedness upon
thine own head;
45 And king Solomon *shall be* blessed, and
[a]the throne of David shall be established before
the LORD for ever.
46 So the king commanded Benaiah the son
of Jehoiada; which went out, and fell upon him,
that he died. And the [a]kingdom was established
in the hand of Solomon.

Solomon Requests Wisdom
(2 Chr. 1:2–13)

3 And [a]Solomon made affinity with Pharaoh
king of Egypt, and took Pharaoh's daughter,
and brought her [b]into the city of David, until he
had made an end of building his [c]own house, and
[d]the house of the LORD, and [e]the wall of Jerusalem
round about.
2 [a]Only the people sacrificed in high places,
because there was no house built unto the name
of the LORD, until those days.
3 And Solomon [a]loved the LORD, [b]walking
in the statutes of David his father: only he sacrificed and burnt incense in high places.
4 And [a]the king went to Gibeon to sacrifice
there; [b]for that *was* the great high place: a thousand burnt offerings did Solomon offer upon that
altar.
5 [a]In Gibeon the LORD appeared to Solomon
[b]in a dream by night: and God said, Ask what I
shall give thee.
6 [a]And Solomon said, Thou hast shewed
unto thy servant David my father great mercy,
according as he [b]walked before thee in truth, and
in righteousness, and in uprightness of heart with
thee; and thou hast kept for him this great kindness, that thou [c]hast given him a son to sit on
his throne, as *it is* this day.
7 And now, O LORD my God, thou hast made
thy servant king instead of David my father: and
I *am but* a [a]little child: I know not *how* [b]to go
out or come in.
8 And thy servant *is* in the midst of thy people which thou [a]hast chosen, a great people, [b]that
cannot be numbered nor counted for multitude.
9 [a]Give therefore thy servant an understanding heart [b]to judge thy people, that I may
[c]discern between good and bad: for who is able
to judge this thy so great a people?
10 And the speech pleased the LORD, that Solomon had asked this thing.
11 And God said unto him, Because thou hast
asked this thing, and hast [a]not asked for thyself
long life; neither hast asked riches for thyself, nor
hast asked the life of thine enemies; but hast
asked for thyself understanding to discern
judgment;
12 [a]Behold, I have done according to thy
words: [b]lo, I have given thee a wise and an understanding heart; so that there was none like thee
before thee, neither after thee shall any arise like
unto thee.
13 And I have also [a]given thee that which
thou hast not asked, both [b]riches, and honour:
so that there shall not be any among the kings
like unto thee all thy days.
14 And [a]if thou wilt walk in my ways, to keep
my statutes and my commandments, [b]as thy father David did walk, then I will [c]lengthen thy
days.
15 And Solomon [a]awoke; and, behold, *it was*

44 [a]2 Sam. 16:5–13 [b]1 Sam. 25:39; 2 Kin. 11:1, 12–16; Ps. 7:16; Ezek. 17:19
45 [a]2 Sam. 7:13; [Prov. 25:5]
46 [a]1 Kin. 2:12; 2 Chr. 1:1

CHAPTER 3

1 [a]1 Kin. 7:8; 9:24 [b]2 Sam. 5:7 [c]1 Kin. 7:1 [d]1 Kin. 6 [e]1 Kin. 9:15, 19
2 [a][Deut. 12:2–5, 13, 14]; 1 Kin. 11:7; 22:43
3 [a][Rom. 8:28] [b][1 Kin. 3:6, 14]
4 [a]1 Kin. 9:2; 2 Chr. 1:3 [b]1 Chr. 16:39; 21:29
5 [a]1 Kin. 9:2; 11:9; 2 Chr. 1:7 [b]Num. 12:6; Matt. 1:20; 2:13
6 [a]2 Chr. 1:8 [b]1 Kin. 2:4; 9:4; 2 Kin. 20:3 [c]2 Sam. 7:8–17; 1 Kin. 1:48
7 [a]1 Chr. 22:5; Jer. 1:6, 7 [b]Num. 27:17; 2 Sam. 5:2
8 [a][Ex. 19:6; Deut. 7:6] [b]Gen. 13:6; 15:5; 22:17
9 [a]2 Chr. 1:10; [James 1:5] [b]Ps. 72:1, 2 [c]2 Sam. 14:17; Is. 7:15; [Heb. 5:14]
11 [a][James 4:3]
12 [a][1 John 5:14, 15] [b]1 Kin. 4:29–31; 5:12; 10:24; Eccl. 1:16
13 [a][Matt. 6:33; Eph. 3:20] [b]1 Kin. 4:21, 24; 10:23; 1 Chr. 29:12
14 [a][1 Kin. 6:12] [b]1 Kin. 15:5 [c]Ps. 91:16; Prov. 3:2
15 [a]Gen. 41:7

NKJV

the LORD, and warn you, saying, 'Know for certain
that on the day you go out and travel anywhere,
you shall surely die'? And you said to me, 'The
word I have heard *is* good.'
43 "Why then have you not kept the oath of
the LORD and the commandment that I gave you?"
44 The king said moreover to Shimei, "You
know, as your heart acknowledges, [a]all the wickedness that you did to my father David; therefore
the LORD will [b]return your wickedness on your
own head.
45 "But King Solomon *shall be* blessed, and
[a]the throne of David shall be established before
the LORD forever."
46 So the king commanded Benaiah the son
of Jehoiada; and he went out and struck him
down, and he died. Thus the [a]kingdom was established in the hand of Solomon.

Solomon Requests Wisdom
(2 Chr. 1:2–13)

3 Now [a]Solomon made a treaty with Pharaoh
king of Egypt, and married Pharaoh's daughter; then he brought her [b]to the City of David until
he had finished building his [c]own house, and [d]the
house of the LORD, and [e]the wall all around
Jerusalem.
2 [a]Meanwhile the people sacrificed at the
high places, because there was no house built for
the name of the LORD until those days.
3 And Solomon [a]loved the LORD, [b]walking
in the statutes of his father David, except that he
sacrificed and burned incense at the high places.
4 Now [a]the king went to Gibeon to sacrifice
there, [b]for that *was* the great high place: Solomon
offered a thousand burnt offerings on that altar.
5 [a]At Gibeon the LORD appeared to Solomon
[b]in a dream by night; and God said, "Ask! What
shall I give you?"
6 [a]And Solomon said: "You have shown
great mercy to Your servant David my father, because he [b]walked before You in truth, in righteousness, and in uprightness of heart with You;
You have continued this great kindness for him,
and You [c]have given him a son to sit on his
throne, as *it is* this day.
7 "Now, O LORD my God, You have made
Your servant king instead of my father David, but
I *am* a [a]little child; I do not know *how* [b]to go out
or come in.
8 "And Your servant *is* in the midst of Your
people whom You [a]have chosen, a great people,
[b]too numerous to be numbered or counted.
9 [a]"Therefore give to Your servant an understanding heart [b]to judge Your people, that I
may [c]discern between good and evil. For who is
able to judge this great people of Yours?"
10 The speech pleased the LORD, that Solomon had asked this thing.
11 Then God said to him: "Because you have
asked this thing, and have [a]not asked long life
for yourself, nor have asked riches for yourself,
nor have asked the life of your enemies, but have
asked for yourself understanding to discern
justice,
12 [a]"behold, I have done according to your
words; [b]see, I have given you a wise and understanding heart, so that there has not been anyone
like you before you, nor shall any like you arise
after you.
13 "And I have also [a]given you what you
have not asked: both [b]riches and honor, so that
there shall not be anyone like you among the
kings all your days.
14 "So [a]if you walk in My ways, to keep My
statutes and My commandments, [b]as your father
David walked, then I will [c]lengthen your days."
15 Then Solomon [a]awoke; and indeed it had

KJV

a dream. And he came to Jerusalem, and stood
before the ark of the covenant of the LORD, and
offered up burnt offerings, and offered peace offerings, and [b]made a feast to all his servants.

Solomon's Wise Judgment

16 Then came there two women, *that were*
harlots, unto the king, and [a]stood before him.
17 And the one woman said, O my lord, I and
this woman dwell in one house; and I was delivered of a child with her in the house.
18 And it came to pass the third day after
that I was delivered, that this woman was delivered also: and we *were* together; *there was* no
stranger with us in the house, save we two in the
house.
19 And this woman's child died in the night;
because she overlaid it.
20 And she arose at midnight, and took my
son from beside me, while thine handmaid slept,
and laid it in her bosom, and laid her dead child
in my bosom.
21 And when I rose in the morning to give
my child suck, behold, it was dead: but when I
had considered it in the morning, behold, it was
not my son, which I did bear.
22 And the other woman said, Nay; but the
living *is* my son, and the dead *is* thy son. And
this said, No; but the dead *is* thy son, and the
living *is* my son. Thus they spake before the king.
23 Then said the king, The one saith, This *is*
my son that liveth, and thy son *is* the dead: and
the other saith, Nay; but thy son *is* the dead, and
my son *is* the living.
24 And the king said, Bring me a sword. And
they brought a sword before the king.
25 And the king said, Divide the living child
in two, and give half to the one, and half to the
other.
26 Then spake the woman whose the living
child *was* unto the king, for [a]her bowels yearned
upon her son, and she said, O my lord, give her
the living child, and in no wise slay it. But the
other said, Let it be neither mine nor thine, *but*
divide *it*.
27 Then the king answered and said, Give
her the living child, and in no wise slay it: she *is*
the mother thereof.
28 And all Israel heard of the judgment
which the king had judged; and they feared the
king: for they saw that the [a]wisdom of God *was*
in him, to do judgment.

Solomon's Administration

4 So king Solomon was king over all Israel.
2 And these *were* the princes which he had;
Azariah the son of Zadok the priest,
3 Elihoreph and Ahiah, the sons of Shisha,
scribes; [a]Jehoshaphat the son of Ahilud, the
recorder.
4 And [a]Benaiah the son of Jehoiada *was*
over the host: and Zadok and [b]Abiathar *were* the
priests:
5 And Azariah the son of Nathan *was* over
[a]the officers: and Zabud the son of Nathan *was*
[b]principal officer, *and* [c]the king's friend:
6 And Ahishar *was* over the household: and
[a]Adoniram the son of Abda *was* over the tribute.
7 And Solomon had twelve officers over all
Israel, which provided victuals for the king and
his household: each man his month in a year made
provision.
8 And these *are* their names: The son of
Hur, in mount Ephraim:
9 The son of Dekar, in Makaz, and in Shaalbim, and Beth–shemesh, and Elon–beth–hanan:
10 The son of Hesed, in Aruboth; to him *pertained* Sochoh, and all the land of Hepher:
11 The son of Abinadab, in all the region of
Dor; which had Taphath the daughter of Solomon
to wife:
12 Baana the son of Ahilud; *to him pertained*

15 [b]Gen. 40:20; 1 Kin. 8:65; Esth. 1:3; Dan. 5:1; Mark 6:21
16 [a]Num. 27:2
26 [a]Gen. 43:30; Is. 49:15; Jer. 31:20; Hos. 11:8
28 [a]1 Kin. 3:9, 11, 12; 2 Chr. 1:12; Dan. 1:17; [Col. 2:2, 3]

CHAPTER 4

3 [a]2 Sam. 8:16; 20:24
4 [a]1 Kin. 2:35 [b]1 Kin. 2:27
5 [a]1 Kin. 4:7 [b]2 Sam. 8:18; 20:26 [c]2 Sam. 15:37; 16:16; 1 Chr. 27:33
6 [a]1 Kin. 5:14

*

4:8 Lit. *Son of Hur*
4:9 Lit. *Son of Deker*
4:10 Lit. *Son of Hesed*
4:11 Lit. *Son of Abinadab*

NKJV

been a dream. And he came to Jerusalem and
stood before the ark of the covenant of the LORD,
offered up burnt offerings, offered peace offerings,
and [b]made a feast for all his servants.

Solomon's Wise Judgment

16 Now two women *who were* harlots came
to the king, and [a]stood before him.
17 And one woman said, "O my lord, this
woman and I dwell in the same house; and I gave
birth while she *was* in the house.
18 "Then it happened, the third day after I
had given birth, that this woman also gave birth.
And we *were* together; no one *was* with us in the
house, except the two of us in the house.
19 "And this woman's son died in the night,
because she lay on him.
20 "So she arose in the middle of the night
and took my son from my side, while your maidservant slept, and laid him in her bosom, and laid
her dead child in my bosom.
21 "And when I rose in the morning to nurse
my son, there he was, dead. But when I had examined him in the morning, indeed, he was not my
son whom I had borne."
22 Then the other woman said, "No! But the
living one *is* my son, and the dead one *is* your
son." And the first woman said, "No! But the dead
one *is* your son, and the living one *is* my son."
Thus they spoke before the king.
23 And the king said, "The one says, 'This
is my son, who lives, and your son *is* the dead
one'; and the other says, 'No! But your son *is* the
dead one, and my son *is* the living one.' "
24 Then the king said, "Bring me a sword."
So they brought a sword before the king.
25 And the king said, "Divide the living child
in two, and give half to one, and half to the other."
26 Then the woman whose son *was* living
spoke to the king, for [a]she yearned with compassion for her son; and she said, "O my lord, give
her the living child, and by no means kill him!"
But the other said, "Let him be neither mine nor
yours, *but* divide *him*."
27 So the king answered and said, "Give the
first woman the living child, and by no means
kill him; she *is* his mother."
28 And all Israel heard of the judgment
which the king had rendered; and they feared the
king, for they saw that the [a]wisdom of God *was*
in him to administer justice.

Solomon's Administration

4 So King Solomon was king over all Israel.
2 And these *were* his officials: Azariah the
son of Zadok, the priest;
3 Elihoreph and Ahijah, the sons of Shisha,
scribes; [a]Jehoshaphat the son of Ahilud, the
recorder;
4 [a]Benaiah the son of Jehoiada, over the
army; Zadok and [b]Abiathar, the priests;
5 Azariah the son of Nathan, over [a]the officers; Zabud the son of Nathan, [b]a priest *and* [c]the
king's friend;
6 Ahishar, over the household; and [a]Adoni-
ram the son of Abda, over the labor force.
7 And Solomon had twelve governors over
all Israel, who provided food for the king and his
household; each one made provision for one
month of the year.
8 These *are* their names: *Ben-Hur, in the
mountains of Ephraim;
9 *Ben-Deker, in Makaz, Shaalbim, Beth
Shemesh, and Elon Beth Hanan;
10 *Ben-Hesed, in Arubboth; to him *belonged*
Sochoh and all the land of Hepher;
11 *Ben-Abinadab, *in* all the regions of Dor;
he had Taphath the daughter of Solomon as wife;
12 Baana the son of Ahilud, *in* Taanach,

KJV

Taanach and Megiddo, and all Beth–shean, which
is by Zartanah beneath Jezreel, from Beth–shean
to Abel–meholah, *even* unto *the place that is* beyond Jokneam:
13 The son of Geber, in Ramoth–gilead; to
him *pertained* [a]the towns of Jair the son of Manasseh, which *are* in Gilead; to him *also pertained*
[b]the region of Argob, which *is* in Bashan, threescore great cities with walls and brasen bars:
14 Ahinadab the son of Iddo *had* Mahanaim:
15 [a]Ahimaaz *was* in Naphtali; he also took
Basmath the daughter of Solomon to wife:
16 Baanah the son of [a]Hushai *was* in Asher
and in Aloth:
17 Jehoshaphat the son of Paruah, in
Issachar:
18 [a]Shimei the son of Elah, in Benjamin:
19 Geber the son of Uri *was* in the country
of Gilead, *in* [a]the country of Sihon king of the
Amorites, and of Og king of Bashan; and *he was*
the only officer which *was* in the land.

Prosperity and Wisdom of Solomon's Reign

20 Judah and Israel *were* many, [a]as the sand
which *is* by the sea in multitude, [b]eating and
drinking, and making merry.
21 And [a]Solomon reigned over all kingdoms
from [b]the river unto the land of the Philistines,
and unto the border of Egypt: [c]they brought presents, and served Solomon all the days of his life.
22 [a]And Solomon's provision for one day
was thirty measures of fine flour, and threescore
measures of meal,
23 Ten fat oxen, and twenty oxen out of the
pastures, and an hundred sheep, beside harts, and
roebucks, and fallowdeer, and fatted fowl.
24 For he had dominion over all *the region*
on this side the river, from Tiphsah even to Azzah,
over [a]all the kings on this side the river: and [b]he
had peace on all sides round about him.
25 And Judah and Israel [a]dwelt safely,
[b]every man under his vine and under his fig tree,
[c]from Dan even to Beer–sheba, all the days of
Solomon.
26 And [a]Solomon had forty thousand stalls
of [b]horses for his chariots, and twelve thousand
horsemen.
27 And [a]those officers provided victual for
king Solomon, and for all that came unto king
Solomon's table, every man in his month: they
lacked nothing.
28 Barley also and straw for the horses and
dromedaries brought they unto the place where
the officers were, every man according to his
charge.
29 And [a]God gave Solomon wisdom and understanding exceeding much, and largeness of
heart, even as the sand that *is* on the sea shore.
30 And Solomon's wisdom excelled the wisdom of all the children [a]of the east country, and
all [b]the wisdom of Egypt.
31 For he was [a]wiser than all men; [b]than
Ethan the Ezrahite, [c]and Heman, and Chalcol, and
Darda, the sons of Mahol: and his fame was in
all nations round about.
32 And [a]he spake three thousand proverbs:
and his [b]songs were a thousand and five.
33 And he spake of trees, from the cedar tree
that *is* in Lebanon even unto the hyssop that
springeth out of the wall: he spake also of beasts,
and of fowl, and of creeping things, and of fishes.
34 And [a]there came of all people to hear the
wisdom of Solomon, from all kings of the earth,
which had heard of his wisdom.

Solomon Prepares to Build the Temple
(2 Chr. 2:1–18)

5 And [a]Hiram king of Tyre sent his servants
unto Solomon; for he had heard that they had
anointed him king in the room of his father: [b]for
Hiram was ever a lover of David.
2 And [a]Solomon sent to Hiram, saying,

13 [a]Num. 32:41; 1 Chr. 2:22 [b]Deut. 3:4
15 [a]2 Sam. 15:27
16 [a]2 Sam. 15:32; 1 Chr. 27:33
18 [a]1 Kin. 1:8
19 [a]Deut. 3:8–10
20 [a]Gen. 22:17; 32:12; 1 Kin. 3:8; [Prov. 14:28] [b]Ps. 72:3, 7; Mic. 4:4
21 [a]Ex. 34:24; 2 Chr. 9:26; Ps. 72:8 [b]Gen. 15:18; Josh. 1:4 [c]Ps. 68:29
22 [a]Neh. 5:18
24 [a]Ps. 72:11 [b]1 Kin. 5:4; 1 Chr. 22:9
25 [a][Jer. 23:6] [b][Mic. 4:4; Zech. 3:10] [c]Judg. 20:1
26 [a]1 Kin. 10:26; 2 Chr. 1:14 [b][Deut. 17:16]
27 [a]1 Kin. 4:7
29 [a]1 Kin. 3:12
30 [a]Gen. 25:6 [b]Is. 19:11, 12; Acts 7:22
31 [a]1 Kin. 3:12 [b]1 Chr. 15:19; Ps. 89:title [c]1 Chr. 2:6; Ps. 88:title
32 [a]Prov. 1:1; 10:1; 25:1; Eccl. 12:9 [b]Song 1:1
34 [a]1 Kin. 10:1; 2 Chr. 9:1, 23

CHAPTER 5

1 [a]1 Kin. 5:10, 18; 2 Chr. 2:3 [b]2 Sam. 5:11; 1 Chr. 14:1
2 [a]2 Chr. 2:3

*

4:13 Lit. *Son of Geber*
4:21 The Euphrates
4:24 The Euphrates
4:26 So with MT, most other authorities; some LXX mss. *four thousand;* cf. 2 Chr. 9:25

NKJV

Megiddo, and all Beth Shean, which *is* beside Zaretan below Jezreel, from Beth Shean to Abel Meholah, as far as the other side of Jokneam;
13 *Ben-Geber, in Ramoth Gilead; to him *belonged* [a]the towns of Jair the son of Manasseh,
in Gilead; to him *also belonged* [b]the region of Argob in Bashan—sixty large cities with walls and
bronze gate-bars;
14 Ahinadab the son of Iddo, *in* Mahanaim;
15 [a]Ahimaaz, in Naphtali; he also took Basemath the daughter of Solomon as wife;
16 Baanah the son of [a]Hushai, in Asher and
Aloth;
17 Jehoshaphat the son of Paruah, in Issachar;
18 [a]Shimei the son of Elah, in Benjamin;
19 Geber the son of Uri, in the land of Gilead,
in [a]the country of Sihon king of the Amorites,
and of Og king of Bashan. *He was* the only governor who *was* in the land.

Prosperity and Wisdom of Solomon's Reign

20 Judah and Israel *were* as numerous [a]as
the sand by the sea in multitude, [b]eating and
drinking and rejoicing.
21 So [a]Solomon reigned over all kingdoms
from [b]the* River *to* the land of the Philistines, as
far as the border of Egypt. [c]*They* brought tribute
and served Solomon all the days of his life.
22 [a]Now Solomon's provision for one day
was thirty kors of fine flour, sixty kors of meal,
23 ten fatted oxen, twenty oxen from the pastures, and one hundred sheep, besides deer, gazelles, roebucks, and fatted fowl.
24 For he had dominion over all *the region*
on this side of *the River from Tiphsah even to
Gaza, namely over [a]all the kings on this side of
the River; and [b]he had peace on every side all
around him.
25 And Judah and Israel [a]dwelt safely, [b]each
man under his vine and his fig tree, [c]from Dan
as far as Beersheba, all the days of Solomon.
26 [a]Solomon had *forty thousand stalls of
[b]horses for his chariots, and twelve thousand
horsemen.
27 And [a]these governors, each man in his
month, provided food for King Solomon and for
all who came to King Solomon's table. There was
no lack in their supply.
28 They also brought barley and straw to the
proper place, for the horses and steeds, each man
according to his charge.
29 And [a]God gave Solomon wisdom and exceedingly great understanding, and largeness of
heart like the sand on the seashore.
30 Thus Solomon's wisdom excelled the wisdom of all the men [a]of the East and all [b]the wisdom of Egypt.
31 For he was [a]wiser than all men—[b]than
Ethan the Ezrahite, [c]and Heman, Chalcol, and
Darda, the sons of Mahol; and his fame was in
all the surrounding nations.
32 [a]He spoke three thousand proverbs, and
his [b]songs were one thousand and five.
33 Also he spoke of trees, from the cedar tree
of Lebanon even to the hyssop that springs out
of the wall; he spoke also of animals, of birds, of
creeping things, and of fish.
34 And men of all nations, from all the kings
of the earth who had heard of his wisdom, [a]came
to hear the wisdom of Solomon.

Solomon Prepares to Build the Temple
(2 Chr. 2:1–18)

5 Now [a]Hiram king of Tyre sent his servants
to Solomon, because he heard that they had
anointed him king in place of his father, [b]for
Hiram had always loved David.
2 Then [a]Solomon sent to Hiram, saying:

KJV

3 [a]Thou knowest how that David my father could not build an house unto the name of the LORD his God [b]for the wars which were about him on every side, until the LORD put them under the soles of his feet.

4 But now the LORD my God hath given me [a]rest on every side, *so that there is* neither adversary nor evil occurrent.

5 [a]And, behold, I purpose to build an house unto the name of the LORD my God, [b]as the LORD spake unto David my father, saying, Thy son, whom I will set upon thy throne in thy room, he shall build an house unto my name.

6 Now therefore command thou that they hew me [a]cedar trees out of Lebanon; and my servants shall be with thy servants: and unto thee will I give hire for thy servants according to all that thou shalt appoint: for thou knowest that *there is* not among us any that can skill to hew timber like unto the Sidonians.

7 And it came to pass, when Hiram heard the words of Solomon, that he rejoiced greatly, and said, Blessed *be* the LORD this day, which hath given unto David a wise son over this great people.

8 And Hiram sent to Solomon, saying, I have considered the things which thou sentest to me for: *and* I will do all thy desire concerning timber of cedar, and concerning timber of fir.

9 My servants shall bring *them* down [a]from Lebanon unto the sea: and I will convey them by sea in floats unto the place that thou shalt appoint me, and will cause them to be discharged there, and thou shalt receive *them:* and thou shalt accomplish my desire, [b]in giving food for my household.

10 So Hiram gave Solomon cedar trees and fir trees *according to* all his desire.

11 [a]And Solomon gave Hiram twenty thousand measures of wheat *for* food to his household, and twenty measures of pure oil: thus gave Solomon to Hiram year by year.

12 And the LORD gave Solomon wisdom, [a]as he promised him: and there was peace between Hiram and Solomon; and they two made a league together.

13 And king Solomon raised a levy out of all Israel; and the levy was thirty thousand men.

14 And he sent them to Lebanon, ten thousand a month by courses: a month they were in Lebanon, *and* two months at home: and [a]Adoniram *was* over the levy.

15 [a]And Solomon had threescore and ten thousand that bare burdens, and fourscore thousand hewers in the mountains;

16 Beside the [a]chief of Solomon's officers which *were* over the work, three thousand and three hundred, which ruled over the people that wrought in the work.

17 And the king commanded, and they brought great stones, costly stones, *and* [a]hewed stones, to lay the foundation of the house.

18 And Solomon's builders and Hiram's builders did hew *them,* and the stonesquarers: so they prepared timber and stones to build the house.

Solomon Builds the Temple
(2 Chr. 3:1–14)

6 And [a]it came to pass in the four hundred and eightieth year after the children of Israel were come out of the land of Egypt, in the fourth year of Solomon's reign over Israel, in the month Zif, which *is* the second month, that [b]he began to build the house of the LORD.

2 And [a]the house which king Solomon built

---

3 [a]1 Chr. 28:2, 3 [b]1 Chr. 22:8; 28:3
4 [a]1 Kin. 4:24; 1 Chr. 22:9
5 [a]2 Chr. 2:4 [b]2 Sam. 7:12, 13; 1 Kin. 6:38; 1 Chr. 17:12; 22:10; 28:6; 2 Chr. 6:2
6 [a]2 Chr. 2:8, 10
9 [a]Ezra 3:7 [b]Ezek. 27:17; Acts 12:20
11 [a]2 Chr. 2:10
12 [a]1 Kin. 3:12
14 [a]1 Kin. 12:18
15 [a]1 Kin. 9:20–22; 2 Chr. 2:17, 18
16 [a]1 Kin. 9:23
17 [a]1 Kin. 6:7; 1 Chr. 22:2

CHAPTER 6
1 [a]2 Chr. 3:1, 2 [b]Acts 7:47
2 [a]Ezek. 41:1

*———

5:3 Lit. *them*
5:11 So with MT, Tg., Vg.; LXX, Syr. *twenty thousand kors*
5:16 So with MT, Tg., Vg.; LXX *six hundred*
5:17 Lit. *house*
6:1 So with MT, Tg., Vg.; LXX *fortieth*

NKJV

3 [a]You know how my father David could not build a house for the name of the LORD his God [b]because of the wars which were fought against him on every side, until the LORD put *his foes* under the soles of his feet.

4 But now the LORD my God has given me [a]rest on every side; *there is* neither adversary nor evil occurrence.

5 [a]And behold, I propose to build a house for the name of the LORD my God, [b]as the LORD spoke to my father David, saying, "Your son, whom I will set on your throne in your place, he shall build the house for My name."

6 Now therefore, command that they cut down [a]cedars for me from Lebanon; and my servants will be with your servants, and I will pay you wages for your servants according to whatever you say. For you know *there is* none among us who has skill to cut timber like the Sidonians.

7 So it was, when Hiram heard the words of Solomon, that he rejoiced greatly and said,

Blessed *be* the LORD this day, for He has given David a wise son over this great people!

8 Then Hiram sent to Solomon, saying:

I have considered *the message* which you sent me, *and* I will do all you desire concerning the cedar and cypress logs.

9 My servants shall bring *them* down [a]from Lebanon to the sea; I will float them in rafts by sea to the place you indicate to me, and will have them broken apart there; then you can take *them* away. And you shall fulfill my desire [b]by giving food for my household.

10 Then Hiram gave Solomon cedar and cypress logs *according to* all his desire.

11 [a]And Solomon gave Hiram twenty thousand kors of wheat *as* food for his household, and *twenty kors of pressed oil. Thus Solomon gave to Hiram year by year.

12 So the LORD gave Solomon wisdom, [a]as He had promised him; and there was peace between Hiram and Solomon, and the two of them made a treaty together.

13 Then King Solomon raised up a labor force out of all Israel; and the labor force was thirty thousand men.

14 And he sent them to Lebanon, ten thousand a month in shifts: they were one month in Lebanon *and* two months at home; [a]Adoniram *was* in charge of the labor force.

15 [a]Solomon had seventy thousand who carried burdens, and eighty thousand who quarried *stone* in the mountains,

16 besides three thousand *three hundred from the [a]chiefs of Solomon's deputies, who supervised the people who labored in the work.

17 And the king commanded them to quarry large stones, costly stones, *and* [a]hewn stones, to lay the foundation of the *temple.

18 So Solomon's builders, Hiram's builders, and the Gebalites quarried *them;* and they prepared timber and stones to build the temple.

Solomon Builds the Temple
(2 Chr. 3:1–14)

6 And [a]it came to pass in the four hundred and *eightieth year after the children of Israel had come out of the land of Egypt, in the fourth year of Solomon's reign over Israel, in the month of Ziv, which *is* the second month, [b]that he began to build the house of the LORD.

2 Now [a]the house which King Solomon built

KJV

for the LORD, the length thereof *was* threescore cubits, and the breadth thereof twenty *cubits*, and the height thereof thirty cubits.

3 And the porch before the temple of the house, twenty cubits *was* the length thereof, according to the breadth of the house; *and* ten cubits *was* the breadth thereof before the house.

4 And for the house he made [a]windows of narrow lights.

5 And against the wall of the house he built [a]chambers round about, *against* the walls of the house round about, *both* of the temple [b]and of the oracle: and he made chambers round about:

6 The nethermost chamber *was* five cubits broad, and the middle *was* six cubits broad, and the third *was* seven cubits broad: for without *in the wall* of the house he made narrowed rests round about, that *the beams* should not be fastened in the walls of the house.

7 And [a]the house, when it was in building, was built of stone made ready before it was brought thither: so that there was neither hammer nor axe *nor* any tool of iron heard in the house, while it was in building.

8 The door for the middle chamber *was* in the right side of the house: and they went up with winding stairs into the middle *chamber*, and out of the middle into the third.

9 [a]So he built the house, and finished it; and covered the house with beams and boards of cedar.

10 And *then* he built chambers against all the house, five cubits high: and they rested on the house with timber of cedar.

11 And the word of the LORD came to Solomon, saying,

12 *Concerning* this house which thou art in building, [a]if thou wilt walk in my statutes, and execute my judgments, and keep all my commandments to walk in them; then will I perform my word with thee, [b]which I spake unto David thy father:

13 And [a]I will dwell among the children of Israel, and will not [b]forsake my people Israel.

14 So Solomon built the house, and finished it.

15 And he built the walls of the house within with boards of cedar, both the floor of the house, and the walls of the cieling: *and* he covered *them* on the inside with wood, and covered the floor of the house with planks of fir.

16 And he built twenty cubits on the sides of the house, both the floor and the walls with boards of cedar: he even built *them* for it within, *even* for the oracle, *even* for the [a]most holy *place*.

17 And the house, that *is*, the temple before it, was forty cubits *long*.

18 And the cedar of the house within *was* carved with knops and open flowers: all *was* cedar; there was no stone seen.

19 And the oracle he prepared in the house within, to set there the ark of the covenant of the LORD.

20 And the oracle in the forepart *was* twenty cubits in length, and twenty cubits in breadth, and twenty cubits in the height thereof: and he overlaid it with pure gold; and *so* covered the altar *which was of* cedar.

21 So Solomon overlaid the house within with pure gold: and he made a partition by the chains of gold before the oracle; and he overlaid it with gold.

22 And the whole house he overlaid with gold, until he had finished all the house: also [a]the whole altar that *was* by the oracle he overlaid with gold.

23 And within the oracle [a]he made two cherubims *of* olive tree, *each* ten cubits high.

24 And five cubits *was* the one wing of the cherub, and five cubits the other wing of the cherub: from the uttermost part of the one wing unto the uttermost part of the other *were* ten cubits.

4 [a]Ezek. 40:16; 41:16
5 [a]Ezek. 41:6 [b]1 Kin. 6:16, 19–21, 31
7 [a]Ex. 20:25; Deut. 27:5, 6
9 [a]1 Kin. 6:14, 38
12 [a]1 Kin. 2:4; 9:4 [b][2 Sam. 7:13; 1 Chr. 22:10]
13 [a]Ex. 25:8; Lev. 26:11; [2 Cor. 6:16; Rev. 21:3] [b][Deut. 31:6]
16 [a]Ex. 26:33; Lev. 16:2; 1 Kin. 8:6; 2 Chr. 3:8; Ezek. 45:3; Heb. 9:3
22 [a]Ex. 30:1, 3, 6
23 [a]Ex. 37:7–9; 2 Chr. 3:10–12

NKJV

for the LORD, its length *was* sixty cubits, its width twenty, and its height thirty cubits.

3 The vestibule in front of the *sanctuary of the house *was* twenty cubits long across the width of the house, *and* the width of **the vestibule extended* ten cubits from the front of the house.

4 And he made for the house [a]windows with beveled frames.

5 Against the wall of the temple he built [a]chambers all around, *against* the walls of the temple, all around the sanctuary [b]and the *inner sanctuary. Thus he made side chambers all around it.

6 The lowest chamber *was* five cubits wide, the middle *was* six cubits wide, and the third *was* seven cubits wide; for he made narrow ledges around the outside of the temple, so that *the support beams* would not be fastened into the walls of the temple.

7 And [a]the temple, when it was being built, was built with stone finished at the quarry, so that no hammer or chisel *or* any iron tool was heard in the temple while it was being built.

8 The doorway for the *middle story *was* on the right side of the temple. They went up by stairs to the middle *story*, and from the middle to the third.

9 [a]So he built the temple and finished it, and he paneled the temple with beams and boards of cedar.

10 And he built side chambers against the entire temple, each five cubits high; they were attached to the temple with cedar beams.

11 Then the word of the LORD came to Solomon, saying:

12 "*Concerning* this temple which you are building, [a]if you walk in My statutes, execute My judgments, keep all My commandments, and walk in them, then I will perform My word with you, [b]which I spoke to your father David.

13 "And [a]I will dwell among the children of Israel, and will not [b]forsake My people Israel."

14 So Solomon built the temple and finished it.

15 And he built the inside walls of the temple with cedar boards; from the floor of the temple to the ceiling he paneled the inside with wood; and he covered the floor of the temple with planks of cypress.

16 Then he built the twenty-cubit room at the rear of the temple, from floor to ceiling, with cedar boards; he built *it* inside as the inner sanctuary, as the [a]Most Holy *Place*.

17 And in front of it the temple sanctuary was forty cubits *long*.

18 The inside of the temple was cedar, carved with ornamental buds and open flowers. All *was* cedar; there was no stone *to be* seen.

19 And he prepared the inner sanctuary inside the temple, to set the ark of the covenant of the LORD there.

20 The inner sanctuary *was* twenty cubits long, twenty cubits wide, and twenty cubits high. He overlaid it with pure gold, and overlaid the altar of cedar.

21 So Solomon overlaid the inside of the temple with pure gold. He stretched gold chains across the front of the inner sanctuary, and overlaid it with gold.

22 The whole temple he overlaid with gold, until he had finished all the temple; also he overlaid with gold [a]the entire altar that *was* by the inner sanctuary.

23 Inside the inner sanctuary [a]he made two cherubim *of* olive wood, *each* ten cubits high.

24 One wing of the cherub *was* five cubits, and the other wing of the cherub five cubits: ten cubits from the tip of one wing to the tip of the other.

6:3 Heb. *heykal;* here the main room of the temple; elsewhere called the holy place, Ex. 26:33; Ezek. 41:1 • Lit. *it*
6:5 Heb. *debir;* here the inner room of the temple; elsewhere called the Most Holy Place, v. 16
6:8 So with MT, Vg.; LXX *upper story;* Tg. *ground story*

KJV

25 And the other cherub *was* ten cubits: both the cherubims *were* of one measure and one size.
26 The height of the one cherub *was* ten cubits, and so *was it* of the other cherub.
27 And he set the cherubims within the inner house: and [a]they stretched forth the wings of the cherubims, so that the wing of the one touched the *one* wall, and the wing of the other cherub touched the other wall; and their wings touched one another in the midst of the house.
28 And he overlaid the cherubims with gold.
29 And he carved all the walls of the house round about with carved [a]figures of cherubims and palm trees and open flowers, within and without.
30 And the floor of the house he overlaid with gold, within and without.
31 And for the entering of the oracle he made doors *of* olive tree: the lintel *and* side posts *were* a fifth part *of the wall.*
32 The two doors also *were of* olive tree; and he carved upon them carvings of cherubims and palm trees and open flowers, and overlaid *them* with gold, and spread gold upon the cherubims, and upon the palm trees.
33 So also made he for the door of the temple posts *of* olive tree, a fourth part *of the wall.*
34 And the two doors *were of* fir tree: the [a]two leaves of the one door *were* folding, and the two leaves of the other door *were* folding.
35 And he carved *thereon* cherubims and palm trees and open flowers: and covered *them* with gold fitted upon the carved work.
36 And he built the [a]inner court with three rows of hewed stone, and a row of cedar beams.
37 [a]In the fourth year was the foundation of the house of the LORD laid, in the month Zif:
38 And in the eleventh year, in the month Bul, which *is* the eighth month, was the house finished throughout all the parts thereof, and according to all the fashion of it. So was he [a]seven years in building it.

Solomon's Other Buildings

7 But Solomon was building his own house [a]thirteen years, and he finished all his house.
2 He built also the [a]house of the forest of Lebanon; the length thereof *was* an hundred cubits, and the breadth thereof fifty cubits, and the height thereof thirty cubits, upon four rows of cedar pillars, with cedar beams upon the pillars.
3 And *it was* covered with cedar above upon the beams, that *lay* on forty five pillars, fifteen *in* a row.
4 And *there were* windows *in* three rows, and light *was* against light *in* three ranks.
5 And all the doors and posts *were* square, with the windows: and light *was* against light *in* three ranks.
6 And he made a porch of pillars; the length thereof *was* fifty cubits, and the breadth thereof thirty cubits: and the porch *was* before them: and the *other* pillars and the thick beam *were* before them.
7 Then he made a porch for the throne where he might judge, *even* the porch of judgment: and *it was* covered with cedar from one side of the floor to the other.
8 And his house where he dwelt *had* another court within the porch, *which* was of the like work. Solomon made also an house for Pharaoh's daughter, [a]whom he had taken *to wife,* like unto this porch.
9 All these *were of* costly stones, according to the measures of hewed stones, sawed with saws, within and without, even from the foundation unto the coping, and *so* on the outside toward the great court.
10 And the foundation *was of* costly stones, even great stones, stones of ten cubits, and stones of eight cubits.

27 [a]Ex. 25:20; 37:9; 1 Kin. 8:7; 2 Chr. 5:8
29 [a]Ex. 36:8, 35
34 [a]Ezek. 41:23–25
36 [a]1 Kin. 7:12; Jer. 36:10
37 [a]1 Kin. 6:1
38 [a]2 Sam. 7:13; 1 Kin. 5:5; 6:1; 8:19

CHAPTER 7
1 [a]1 Kin. 3:1; 9:10; 2 Chr. 8:1
2 [a]1 Kin. 10:17, 21; 2 Chr. 9:16
8 [a]1 Kin. 3:1; 9:24; 11:1; 2 Chr. 8:11

*________
6:27 Lit. *house*
7:7 Lit. *floor* of the upper level

NKJV

25 And the other cherub *was* ten cubits; both cherubim *were* of the same size and shape.
26 The height of one cherub *was* ten cubits, and so *was* the other cherub.
27 Then he set the cherubim inside the inner *room; and [a]they stretched out the wings of the cherubim so that the wing of the one touched *one* wall, and the wing of the other cherub touched the other wall. And their wings touched each other in the middle of the room.
28 Also he overlaid the cherubim with gold.
29 Then he carved all the walls of the temple all around, both the inner and outer *sanctuaries,* with carved [a]figures of cherubim, palm trees, and open flowers.
30 And the floor of the temple he overlaid with gold, both the inner and outer *sanctuaries.*
31 For the entrance of the inner sanctuary he made doors *of* olive wood; the lintel *and* doorposts *were* one-fifth *of the wall.*
32 The two doors *were of* olive wood; and he carved on them figures of cherubim, palm trees, and open flowers, and overlaid *them* with gold; and he spread gold on the cherubim and on the palm trees.
33 So for the door of the sanctuary he also made doorposts *of* olive wood, one-fourth *of the wall.*
34 And the two doors *were of* cypress wood; [a]two panels *comprised* one folding door, and two panels *comprised* the other folding door.
35 Then he carved cherubim, palm trees, and open flowers *on them,* and overlaid *them* with gold applied evenly on the carved work.
36 And he built the [a]inner court with three rows of hewn stone and a row of cedar beams.
37 [a]In the fourth year the foundation of the house of the LORD was laid, in the month of Ziv.
38 And in the eleventh year, in the month of Bul, which is the eighth month, the house was finished in all its details and according to all its plans. So he was [a]seven years in building it.

Solomon's Other Buildings

7 But Solomon took [a]thirteen years to build his own house; so he finished all his house.
2 He also built the [a]House of the Forest of Lebanon; its length *was* one hundred cubits, its width fifty cubits, and its height thirty cubits, with four rows of cedar pillars, and cedar beams on the pillars.
3 And *it was* paneled with cedar above the beams that *were* on forty-five pillars, fifteen *to* a row.
4 *There were* windows *with beveled frames in* three rows, and window *was* opposite window *in* three tiers.
5 And all the doorways and doorposts *had* rectangular frames; and window *was* opposite window *in* three tiers.
6 He also made the Hall of Pillars: its length *was* fifty cubits, and its width thirty cubits; and in front of them *was* a portico with pillars, and a canopy *was* in front of them.
7 Then he made a hall for the throne, the Hall of Judgment, where he might judge; and *it was* paneled with cedar from floor to *ceiling.
8 And the house where he dwelt *had* another court inside the hall, of like workmanship. Solomon also made a house like this hall for Pharaoh's daughter, [a]whom he had taken *as wife.*
9 All these *were of* costly stones cut to size, trimmed with saws, inside and out, from the foundation to the eaves, and also on the outside to the great court.
10 The foundation *was of* costly stones, large stones, some ten cubits and some eight cubits.

KJV

11 And above *were* costly stones, after the measures of hewed stones, and cedars.

12 And the great court round about *was* with three rows of hewed stones, and a row of cedar beams, both for the [a]inner court of the house of the LORD, [b]and for the porch of the house.

Hiram the Craftsman

13 And king Solomon sent and fetched Hiram out of Tyre.

14 [a]He *was* a widow's son of the tribe of Naphtali, and [b]his father *was* a man of Tyre, a worker in brass: and [c]he was filled with wisdom, and understanding, and cunning to work all works in brass. And he came to king Solomon, and wrought all his work.

The Bronze Pillars for the Temple
(2 Chr. 3:15–17)

15 For he cast [a]two pillars of brass, of eighteen cubits high apiece: and a line of twelve cubits did compass either of them about.

16 And he made two chapiters *of* molten brass, to set upon the tops of the pillars: the height of the one chapiter *was* five cubits, and the height of the other chapiter *was* five cubits:

17 *And* nets of checker work, and wreaths of chain work, for the chapiters which *were* upon the top of the pillars; seven for the one chapiter, and seven for the other chapiter.

18 And he made the pillars, and two rows round about upon the one network, to cover the chapiters that *were* upon the top, with pomegranates: and so did he for the other chapiter.

19 And the chapiters that *were* upon the top of the pillars *were* of lily work in the porch, four cubits.

20 And the chapiters upon the two pillars *had pomegranates* also above, over against the belly which *was* by the network: and the pomegranates *were* [a]two hundred in rows round about upon the other chapiter.

21 [a]And he set up the pillars in the porch of the temple: and he set up the right pillar, and called the name thereof Jachin: and he set up the left pillar, and called the name thereof Boaz.

22 And upon the top of the pillars *was* lily work: so was the work of the pillars finished.

The Sea and the Oxen

23 And he made [a]a molten sea, ten cubits from the one brim to the other: *it was* round all about, and his height *was* five cubits: and a line of thirty cubits did compass it round about.

24 And under the brim of it round about *there were* knops compassing it, ten in a cubit, [a]compassing the sea round about: the knops *were* cast in two rows, when it was cast.

25 It stood upon [a]twelve oxen, three looking toward the north, and three looking toward the west, and three looking toward the south, and three looking toward the east: and the sea *was set* above upon them, and all their hinder parts *were* inward.

26 And it *was* an hand breadth thick, and the brim thereof was wrought like the brim of a cup, with flowers of lilies: it contained two thousand baths.

The Carts and the Lavers

27 And he made ten bases of brass; four cubits *was* the length of one base, and four cubits the breadth thereof, and three cubits the height of it.

28 And the work of the bases *was* on this *manner:* they had borders, and the borders *were* between the ledges:

29 And on the borders that *were* between the ledges *were* lions, oxen, and cherubims: and upon the ledges *there was* a base above: and beneath the lions and oxen *were* certain additions made of thin work.

12 [a]1 Kin. 6:36 [b]John 10:23; Acts 3:11
14 [a]2 Chr. 2:14 [b]2 Chr. 4:16 [c]Ex. 31:3; 36:1
15 [a]2 Kin. 25:17; 2 Chr. 3:15; 4:12; Jer. 52:21
20 [a]2 Chr. 3:16; 4:13; Jer. 52:23
21 [a]2 Chr. 3:17
23 [a]2 Kin. 25:13; 2 Chr. 4:2; Jer. 52:17
24 [a]2 Chr. 4:3
25 [a]2 Chr. 4:4, 5; Jer. 52:20

NKJV

11 And above *were* costly stones, hewn to size, and cedar wood.

12 The great court *was* enclosed with three rows of hewn stones and a row of cedar beams. So were the [a]inner court of the house of the LORD [b]and the vestibule of the temple.

Hiram the Craftsman

13 Now King Solomon sent and brought *Huram from Tyre.

14 [a]He *was* the son of a widow from the tribe of Naphtali, and [b]his father *was* a man of Tyre, a bronze worker; [c]he was filled with wisdom and understanding and skill in working with all kinds of bronze work. So he came to King Solomon and did all his work.

The Bronze Pillars for the Temple
(2 Chr. 3:15–17)

15 And he cast [a]two pillars of bronze, each one eighteen cubits high, and a line of twelve cubits measured the circumference of each.

16 Then he made two capitals *of* cast bronze, to set on the tops of the pillars. The height of one capital *was* five cubits, and the height of the other capital *was* five cubits.

17 *He made* a lattice network, with wreaths of chainwork, for the capitals which *were* on top of the pillars: seven chains for one capital and seven for the other capital.

18 So he made the pillars, and two rows of pomegranates above the network all around to cover the capitals that *were* on top; and thus he did for the other capital.

19 The capitals which *were* on top of the pillars in the hall *were* in the shape of lilies, four cubits.

20 The capitals on the two pillars also *had pomegranates* above, by the convex surface which *was* next to the network; and there *were* [a]two hundred such pomegranates in rows on each of the capitals all around.

21 [a]Then he set up the pillars by the vestibule of the temple; he set up the pillar on the right and called its name Jachin, and he set up the pillar on the left and called its name Boaz.

22 The tops of the pillars were in the shape of lilies. So the work of the pillars was finished.

The Sea and the Oxen

23 And he made [a]the Sea of cast bronze, ten cubits from one brim to the other; *it was* completely round. Its height *was* five cubits, and a line of thirty cubits measured its circumference.

24 Below its brim *were* ornamental buds encircling it all around, ten to a cubit, [a]all the way around the Sea. The ornamental buds *were* cast in two rows when it was cast.

25 It stood on [a]twelve oxen: three looking toward the north, three looking toward the west, three looking toward the south, and three looking toward the east; the Sea *was set* upon them, and all their back parts *pointed* inward.

26 It *was* a handbreadth thick; and its brim was shaped like the brim of a cup, *like* a lily blossom. It contained *two thousand baths.

The Carts and the Lavers

27 He also made ten carts of bronze; four cubits *was* the length of each cart, four cubits its width, and three cubits its height.

28 And this *was* the design of the carts: They had panels, and the panels *were* between frames;

29 on the panels that *were* between the frames *were* lions, oxen, and cherubim. And on the frames *was* a pedestal on top. Below the lions and oxen *were* wreaths of plaited work.

*

7:13 Heb. *Hiram;* cf. 2 Chr. 2:13, 14
7:26 About 12,000 gallons; *three thousand;* cf. 2 Chr. 4:5

KJV

30 And every base had four brasen wheels, and plates of brass: and the four corners thereof had undersetters: under the laver *were* undersetters molten, at the side of every addition.

31 And the mouth of it within the chapiter and above *was* a cubit: but the mouth thereof *was* round *after* the work of the base, a cubit and an half: and also upon the mouth of it *were* gravings with their borders, foursquare, not round.

32 And under the borders *were* four wheels; and the axletrees of the wheels *were joined* to the base: and the height of a wheel *was* a cubit and half a cubit.

33 And the work of the wheels *was* like the work of a chariot wheel: their axletrees, and their naves, and their felloes, and their spokes, *were* all molten.

34 And *there were* four undersetters to the four corners of one base: *and* the undersetters *were* of the very base itself.

35 And in the top of the base *was there* a round compass of half a cubit high: and on the top of the base the ledges thereof and the borders thereof *were* of the same.

36 For on the plates of the ledges thereof, and on the borders thereof, he graved cherubims, lions, and palm trees, according to the proportion of every one, and additions round about.

37 After this *manner* he made the ten bases: all of them had one casting, one measure, *and* one size.

38 Then [a]made he ten lavers of brass: one laver contained forty baths: *and* every laver was four cubits: *and* upon every one of the ten bases one laver.

39 And he put five bases on the right side of the house, and five on the left side of the house: and he set the sea on the right side of the house eastward over against the south.

Furnishings of the Temple
(*2 Chr. 4:11–18*)

40 [a]And Hiram made the lavers, and the shovels, and the basons. So Hiram made an end of doing all the work that he made king Solomon for the house of the LORD:

41 The two pillars, and the *two* bowls of the chapiters that *were* on the top of the two pillars; and the two [a]networks, to cover the two bowls of the chapiters which *were* upon the top of the pillars;

42 And [a]four hundred pomegranates for the two networks, *even* two rows of pomegranates for one network, to cover the two bowls of the chapiters that *were* upon the pillars;

43 And the ten bases, and ten lavers on the bases;

44 And one sea, and twelve oxen under the sea;

45 [a]And the pots, and the shovels, and the basons: and all these vessels, which Hiram made to king Solomon for the house of the LORD, *were of* bright brass.

46 [a]In the plain of Jordan did the king cast them, in the clay ground between [b]Succoth and [c]Zarthan.

47 And Solomon left all the vessels *unweighed,* because they were exceeding many: neither was the weight of the brass found [a]out.

48 And Solomon made all the vessels that *pertained* unto the house of the LORD: [a]the altar of gold, and [b]the table of gold, whereupon [c]the shewbread *was,*

49 And the candlesticks of pure gold, five on the right *side,* and five on the left, before the oracle, with the flowers, and the lamps, and the tongs *of* gold,

50 And the bowls, and the snuffers, and the basons, and the spoons, and the censers *of* pure gold; and the hinges *of* gold, *both* for the doors of the inner house, the most holy *place, and* for the doors of the house, *to wit,* of the temple.

38 [a]Ex. 30:18; 2 Chr. 4:6
40 [a]2 Chr. 4:11—5:1
41 [a]1 Kin. 7:17, 18
42 [a]1 Kin. 7:20
45 [a]Ex. 27:3; 2 Chr. 4:16
46 [a]2 Chr. 4:17 [b]Gen. 33:17; Josh. 13:27 [c]Josh. 3:16
47 [a]1 Chr. 22:3, 14
48 [a]Ex. 37:25, 26; 2 Chr. 4:8 [b]Ex. 37:10, 11 [c]Lev. 24:5–8

NKJV

30 Every cart had four bronze wheels and axles of bronze, and its four feet had supports. Under the laver *were* supports of cast *bronze* beside each wreath.

31 Its opening inside the crown at the top *was* one cubit in diameter; and the opening *was* round, shaped *like* a pedestal, one and a half cubits in outside diameter; and also on the opening *were* engravings, but the panels were square, not round.

32 Under the panels *were* the four wheels, and the axles of the wheels *were joined* to the cart. The height of a wheel *was* one and a half cubits.

33 The workmanship of the wheels *was* like the workmanship of a chariot wheel; their axle pins, their rims, their spokes, and their hubs *were* all of cast *bronze.*

34 And *there were* four supports at the four corners of each cart; its supports *were* part of the cart itself.

35 On the top of the cart, at the height of half a cubit, *it was* perfectly round. And on the top of the cart, its flanges and its panels *were* of the same casting.

36 On the plates of its flanges and on its panels he engraved cherubim, lions, and palm trees, wherever there was a clear space on each, with wreaths all around.

37 Thus he made the ten carts. All of them were of the same mold, one measure, *and* one shape.

38 Then [a]he made ten lavers of bronze; each laver contained forty baths, *and* each laver *was* four cubits. On each of the ten carts *was* a laver.

39 And he put five carts on the right side of the house, and five on the left side of the house. He set the Sea on the right side of the house, toward the southeast.

Furnishings of the Temple
(*2 Chr. 4:11–18*)

40 [a]Huram* made the lavers and the shovels and the bowls. So Huram finished doing all the work that he was to do for King Solomon *for* the house of the LORD:

41 the two pillars, the *two* bowl-shaped capitals that *were* on top of the two pillars; the two [a]networks covering the two bowl-shaped capitals which *were* on top of the pillars;

42 [a]four hundred pomegranates for the two networks (two rows of pomegranates for each network, to cover the two bowl-shaped capitals that *were* on top of the pillars);

43 the ten carts, and ten lavers on the carts;

44 one Sea, and twelve oxen under the Sea;

45 [a]the pots, the shovels, and the bowls. All these articles which *Huram made for King Solomon *for* the house of the LORD *were of* burnished bronze.

46 [a]In the plain of Jordan the king had them cast in clay molds, between [b]Succoth and [c]Zaretan.

47 And Solomon did not weigh all the articles, because *there were* so many; the weight of the bronze was not [a]determined.

48 Thus Solomon had all the furnishings made for the house of the LORD: [a]the altar of gold, and [b]the table of gold on which *was* [c]the showbread;

49 the lampstands of pure gold, five on the right *side* and five on the left in front of the inner sanctuary, with the flowers and the lamps and the wick-trimmers of gold;

50 the basins, the trimmers, the bowls, the ladles, and the censers of pure gold; and the hinges of gold, *both* for the doors of the inner room (the Most Holy *Place*) *and* for the doors of the main hall of the temple.

*———

7:40 Heb. *Hiram;* cf. 2 Chr. 2:13, 14
7:45 Heb. *Hiram;* cf. 2 Chr. 2:13, 14

KJV

51 So was ended all the work that king
Solomon made for the house of the LORD. And
Solomon brought in the things [a]which David his
father had dedicated; *even* the silver, and the
gold, and the vessels, did he put among the treasures of the house of the LORD.

The Ark Brought into the Temple
(2 Chr. 5:2—6:2)

8 Then [a]Solomon assembled the elders of Israel,
and all the heads of the tribes, the chief of
the fathers of the children of Israel, unto king Solomon in Jerusalem, [b]that they might bring [c]up
the ark of the covenant of the LORD out of the
city of David, which *is* Zion.
2 And all the men of Israel assembled themselves unto king Solomon at the [a]feast in the
month Ethanim, which *is* the seventh month.
3 And all the elders of Israel came, [a]and the
priests took up the ark.
4 And they brought up the ark of the LORD,
[a]and the tabernacle of the congregation, and all
the holy vessels that *were* in the tabernacle, even
those did the priests and the Levites bring up.
5 And king Solomon, and all the congregation of Israel, that were assembled unto him, *were*
with him before the ark, [a]sacrificing sheep and
oxen, that could not be told nor numbered for
multitude.
6 And the priests [a]brought in the ark of the
covenant of the LORD unto [b]his place, into the oracle of the house, to the most holy *place, even* [c]un-
der the wings of the cherubims.
7 For the cherubims spread forth *their* two
wings over the place of the ark, and the cherubims
covered the ark and the staves thereof above.
8 And they [a]drew out the staves, that the
ends of the staves were seen out in the holy *place*
before the oracle, and they were not seen without:
and there they are unto this day.
9 [a]*There was* nothing in the ark [b]save the
two tables of stone, which Moses [c]put there at
Horeb, [d]when the LORD made *a covenant* with the
children of Israel, when they came out of the land
of Egypt.
10 And it came to pass, when the priests were
come out of the holy *place,* that the cloud [a]filled
the house of the LORD,
11 So that the priests could not stand to minister because of the cloud: for the [a]glory of the
LORD had filled the house of the LORD.
12 [a]Then spake Solomon, The LORD said that
he would dwell [b]in the thick darkness.
13 [a]I have surely built thee an house to dwell
in, [b]a settled place for thee to abide in for ever.

Solomon's Speech at Completion of the Work
(2 Chr. 6:3–11)

14 And the king turned his face about, and
[a]blessed all the congregation of Israel: (and all
the congregation of Israel stood;)
15 And he said, [a]Blessed *be* the LORD God
of Israel, which [b]spake with his mouth unto David
my father, and hath with his hand fulfilled *it,*
saying,
16 Since the day that I brought forth my people Israel out of Egypt, I chose no city out of all
the tribes of Israel to build an house, that [a]my
name might be therein; but I chose [b]David to be
over my people Israel.
17 And [a]it was in the heart of David my father to build an house for the name of the LORD
God of Israel.
18 [a]And the LORD said unto David my father,
Whereas it was in thine heart to build an house
unto my name, thou didst well that it was in thine
heart.
19 Nevertheless [a]thou shalt not build the
house; but thy son that shall come forth out of
thy loins, he shall build the house unto my name.

51 [a]2 Sam. 8:11; 1 Chr. 18:11; 2 Chr. 5:1

CHAPTER 8

1 [a]Num. 1:4; 7:2; 2 Chr. 5:2–14 [b]2 Sam. 6:12–17; 1 Chr. 15:25–29 [c]2 Sam. 5:7; 6:12, 16
2 [a]Lev. 23:34; 1 Kin. 8:65; 2 Chr. 7:8–10
3 [a]Num. 4:15; 7:9; Deut. 31:9; Josh. 3:3, 6
4 [a]1 Kin. 3:4; 2 Chr. 1:3
5 [a]2 Sam. 6:13; 2 Chr. 1:6
6 [a]2 Sam. 6:17 [b]Ex. 26:33, 34; 1 Kin. 6:19 [c]1 Kin. 6:27
8 [a]Ex. 25:13–15; 37:4, 5
9 [a]Ex. 25:21; Deut. 10:2 [b]Ex. 25:16; Deut. 10:5; Heb. 9:4 [c]Ex. 24:7, 8; 40:20; Deut. 4:13 [d]Ex. 34:27, 28
10 [a]Ex. 40:34, 35; 2 Chr. 7:1, 2
11 [a]2 Chr. 7:1, 2
12 [a]2 Chr. 6:1 [b]Lev. 16:2; Ps. 18:11; 97:2
13 [a]2 Sam. 7:13 [b][Ex. 15:17]; Ps. 132:14
14 [a]2 Sam. 6:18; 1 Kin. 8:55
15 [a]1 Chr. 29:10, 20; Neh. 9:5; Luke 1:68 [b]2 Sam. 7:2, 12, 13, 25; 1 Chr. 22:10
16 [a]Deut. 12:5; 1 Kin. 8:29 [b]1 Sam. 16:1; 2 Sam. 7:8; 1 Chr. 28:4
17 [a]2 Sam. 7:2, 3; 1 Chr. 17:1, 2
18 [a]2 Chr. 6:8, 9
19 [a]2 Sam. 7:5, 12, 13; 1 Kin. 5:3, 5; 6:38; 1 Chr. 17:11, 12; 22:8–10; 2 Chr. 6:2

*__________

8:17 Lit. *house,* and so in vv. 18–20

NKJV

51 So all the work that King Solomon had
done for the house of the LORD was finished; and
Solomon brought in the things [a]which his father
David had dedicated: the silver and the gold and
the furnishings. He put them in the treasuries of
the house of the LORD.

The Ark Brought into the Temple
(2 Chr. 5:2—6:2)

8 Now [a]Solomon assembled the elders of Israel
and all the heads of the tribes, the chief fathers of the children of Israel, to King Solomon
in Jerusalem, [b]that they might bring [c]up the ark
of the covenant of the LORD from the City of David, which *is* Zion.
2 Therefore all the men of Israel assembled
with King Solomon at the [a]feast in the month of
Ethanim, which *is* the seventh month.
3 So all the elders of Israel came, [a]and the
priests took up the ark.
4 Then they brought up the ark of the LORD,
[a]the tabernacle of meeting, and all the holy furnishings that *were* in the tabernacle. The priests
and the Levites brought them up.
5 Also King Solomon, and all the congregation of Israel who were assembled with him, *were*
with him before the ark, [a]sacrificing sheep and
oxen that could not be counted or numbered for
multitude.
6 Then the priests [a]brought in the ark of
the covenant of the LORD to [b]its place, into the
inner sanctuary of the temple, to the Most Holy
Place, [c]under the wings of the cherubim.
7 For the cherubim spread *their* two wings
over the place of the ark, and the cherubim overshadowed the ark and its poles.
8 The poles [a]extended so that the ends of
the poles could be seen from the holy *place,* in
front of the inner sanctuary; but they could not
be seen from outside. And they are there to this
day.
9 [a]Nothing *was* in the ark [b]except the two
tablets of stone which Moses [c]put there at Horeb,
[d]when the LORD made *a covenant* with the children of Israel, when they came out of the land of
Egypt.
10 And it came to pass, when the priests
came out of the holy *place,* that the cloud [a]filled
the house of the LORD,
11 so that the priests could not continue ministering because of the cloud; for the [a]glory of
the LORD filled the house of the LORD.
12 [a]Then Solomon spoke:

"The LORD said He would dwell [b]in the
dark cloud.
13 [a]I have surely built You an exalted house,
[b]And a place for You to dwell in forever."

Solomon's Speech at Completion of the Work
(2 Chr. 6:3–11)

14 Then the king turned around and [a]blessed
the whole assembly of Israel, while all the assembly of Israel was standing.
15 And he said: [a]"Blessed *be* the LORD God
of Israel, who [b]spoke with His mouth to my father
David, and with His hand has fulfilled *it,* saying,
16 'Since the day that I brought My people
Israel out of Egypt, I have chosen no city from
any tribe of Israel *in which* to build a house, that
[a]My name might be there; but I chose [b]David to
be over My people Israel.'
17 "Now [a]it was in the heart of my father
David to build a *temple for the name of the LORD
God of Israel.
18 [a]"But the LORD said to my father David,
'Whereas it was in your heart to build a temple
for My name, you did well that it was in your
heart.
19 'Nevertheless [a]you shall not build the temple, but your son who will come from your body,
he shall build the temple for My name.'

KJV

20 And the LORD hath performed his word that he spake, and I am risen up in the room of David my father, and sit on the throne of Israel, [a]as the LORD promised, and have built an house for the name of the LORD God of Israel.

21 And I have set there a place for the ark, wherein *is* [a]the covenant of the LORD, which he made with our fathers, when he brought them out of the land of Egypt.

Solomon's Prayer of Dedication
(*2 Chr. 6:12–39*)

22 And Solomon stood before [a]the altar of the LORD in the presence of all the congregation of Israel, and [b]spread forth his hands toward heaven:

23 And he said, LORD God of Israel, [a]*there is* no God like thee, in heaven above, or on earth beneath, [b]who keepest covenant and mercy with thy servants that [c]walk before thee with all their heart:

24 Who hast kept with thy servant David my father that thou promisedst him: thou spakest also with thy mouth, and hast fulfilled *it* with thine hand, as *it is* this day.

25 Therefore now, LORD God of Israel, keep with thy servant David my father that thou promisedst him, saying, [a]There shall not fail thee a man in my sight to sit on the throne of Israel; so that thy children take heed to their way, that they walk before me as thou hast walked before me.

26 [a]And now, O God of Israel, let thy word, I pray thee, be verified, which thou spakest unto thy servant David my father.

27 But [a]will God indeed dwell on the earth? behold, the heaven and heaven of [b]heavens cannot contain thee; how much less this house that I have builded?

28 Yet have thou respect unto the prayer of thy servant, and to his supplication, O LORD my God, to hearken unto the cry and to the prayer, which thy servant prayeth before thee to day:

29 That thine eyes may be open toward this house night and day, *even* toward the place of which thou hast said, [a]My name shall be [b]there: that thou mayest hearken unto the prayer which thy servant shall make [c]toward this place.

30 [a]And hearken thou to the supplication of thy servant, and of thy people Israel, when they shall pray toward this place: and hear thou in heaven thy dwelling place: and when thou hearest, forgive.

31 If any man trespass against his neighbour, and [a]an oath be laid upon him to cause him to swear, and the oath come before thine altar in this house:

32 Then hear thou in heaven, and do, and judge thy servants, [a]condemning the wicked, to bring his way upon his head; and justifying the righteous, to give him according to his righteousness.

33 [a]When thy people Israel be smitten down before the enemy, because they have sinned against thee, and [b]shall turn again to thee, and confess thy name, and pray, and make supplication unto thee in this house:

34 Then hear thou in heaven, and forgive the sin of thy people Israel, and bring them again unto the land which thou gavest unto their [a]fathers.

35 [a]When heaven is shut up, and there is no rain, because they have sinned against thee; if they pray toward this place, and confess thy name, and turn from their sin, when thou afflictest them:

36 Then hear thou in heaven, and forgive the sin of thy servants, and of thy people Israel, that thou [a]teach them [b]the good way wherein they should walk, and give rain upon thy land, which thou hast given to thy people for an inheritance.

37 [a]If there be in the land famine, if there be pestilence, blasting, mildew, locust, *or* if there be caterpiller; if their enemy besiege them in the

20 [a]1 Chr. 28:5, 6
21 [a]Deut. 31:26; 1 Kin. 8:9
22 [a]1 Kin. 8:54; 2 Chr. 6:12 [b]Ex. 9:33; Ezra 9:5
23 [a]Ex. 15:11; 2 Sam. 7:22 [b][Deut. 7:9; Neh. 1:5; Dan. 9:4] [c][Gen. 17:1; 1 Kin. 3:6]; 2 Kin. 20:3
25 [a]2 Sam. 7:12, 16; 1 Kin. 2:4; 9:5
26 [a]2 Sam. 7:25
27 [a][2 Chr. 2:6; Is. 66:1; Acts 7:49; 17:24] [b]2 Cor. 12:2
29 [a]Deut. 12:11 [b]1 Kin. 9:3; 2 Chr. 7:15 [c]Dan. 6:10
30 [a]Neh. 1:6
31 [a]Ex. 22:8–11
32 [a]Deut. 25:1
33 [a]Lev. 26:17; Deut. 28:25 [b]Lev. 26:39, 40
34 [a][Lev. 26:40–42; Deut. 30:1–3]
35 [a]Lev. 26:19; Deut. 28:23
36 [a]Ps. 25:4; 27:11; 94:12 [b]1 Sam. 12:23
37 [a]Lev. 26:16, 25, 26; Deut. 28:21, 22, 27, 38, 42, 52

NKJV

20 "So the LORD has fulfilled His word which He spoke; and I have filled the position of my father David, and sit on the throne of Israel, [a]as the LORD promised; and I have built a temple for the name of the LORD God of Israel.

21 "And there I have made a place for the ark, in which *is* [a]the covenant of the LORD which He made with our fathers, when He brought them out of the land of Egypt."

Solomon's Prayer of Dedication
(*2 Chr. 6:12–39*)

22 Then Solomon stood before [a]the altar of the LORD in the presence of all the assembly of Israel, and [b]spread out his hands toward heaven;

23 and he said: "LORD God of Israel, [a]*there is* no God in heaven above or on earth below like You, [b]who keep *Your* covenant and mercy with Your servants who [c]walk before You with all their hearts.

24 "You have kept what You promised Your servant David my father; You have both spoken with Your mouth and fulfilled *it* with Your hand, as *it is* this day.

25 "Therefore, LORD God of Israel, now keep what You promised Your servant David my father, saying, [a]'You shall not fail to have a man sit before Me on the throne of Israel, only if your sons take heed to their way, that they walk before Me as you have walked before Me.'

26 [a]"And now I pray, O God of Israel, let Your word come true, which You have spoken to Your servant David my father.

27 "But [a]will God indeed dwell on the earth? Behold, heaven and the [b]heaven of heavens cannot contain You. How much less this temple which I have built!

28 "Yet regard the prayer of Your servant and his supplication, O LORD my God, and listen to the cry and the prayer which Your servant is praying before You today:

29 "that Your eyes may be open toward this temple night and day, toward the place of which You said, [a]'My name shall be [b]there,' that You may hear the prayer which Your servant makes [c]toward this place.

30 [a]"And may You hear the supplication of Your servant and of Your people Israel, when they pray toward this place. Hear in heaven Your dwelling place; and when You hear, forgive.

31 "When anyone sins against his neighbor, and is forced to take [a]an oath, and comes *and* takes an oath before Your altar in this temple,

32 "then hear in heaven, and act, and judge Your servants, [a]condemning the wicked, bringing his way on his head, and justifying the righteous by giving him according to his righteousness.

33 [a]"When Your people Israel are defeated before an enemy because they have sinned against You, and [b]when they turn back to You and confess Your name, and pray and make supplication to You in this temple,

34 "then hear in heaven, and forgive the sin of Your people Israel, and bring them back to the land which You gave to their [a]fathers.

35 [a]"When the heavens are shut up and there is no rain because they have sinned against You, when they pray toward this place and confess Your name, and turn from their sin because You afflict them,

36 "then hear in heaven, and forgive the sin of Your servants, Your people Israel, that You may [a]teach them [b]the good way in which they should walk; and send rain on Your land which You have given to Your people as an inheritance.

37 [a]"When there is famine in the land, pestilence *or* blight *or* mildew, locusts *or* grasshoppers; when their enemy besieges them in the land of

KJV

land of their cities; whatsoever plague, whatsoever sickness *there be;*

38 What prayer and supplication soever be *made* by any man, *or* by all thy people Israel, which shall know every man the plague of his own heart, and spread forth his hands toward this house:

39 Then hear thou in heaven thy dwelling place, and forgive, and do, and give to every man according to his ways, whose heart thou knowest; (for thou, *even* thou only, [a]knowest the hearts of all the children of men;)

40 [a]That they may fear thee all the days that they live in the land which thou gavest unto our fathers.

41 Moreover concerning a stranger, that *is* not of thy people Israel, but cometh out of a far country for thy name's sake;

42 (For they shall hear of thy great name, and of thy [a]strong hand, and of thy stretched out arm;) when he shall come and pray toward this house;

43 Hear thou in heaven thy dwelling place, and do according to all that the stranger calleth to thee for: [a]that all people of the earth may know thy name, to [b]fear thee, as *do* thy people Israel; and that they may know that this house, which I have builded, is called by thy name.

44 If thy people go out to battle against their enemy, whithersoever thou shalt send them, and shall pray unto the LORD toward the city which thou hast chosen, and *toward* the house that I have built for thy name:

45 Then hear thou in heaven their prayer and their supplication, and maintain their cause.

46 If they sin against thee, [a](for *there is* no man that sinneth not,) and thou be angry with them, and deliver them to the enemy, so that they carry them away captives [b]unto the land of the enemy, far or near;

47 [a]*Yet* if they shall bethink themselves in the land whither they were carried captives, and repent, and make supplication unto thee in the land of them that carried them captives, [b]saying, We have sinned, and have done perversely, we have committed wickedness;

48 And *so* [a]return unto thee with all their heart, and with all their soul, in the land of their enemies, which led them away captive, and [b]pray unto thee toward their land, which thou gavest unto their fathers, the city which thou hast chosen, and the house which I have built for thy name:

49 Then hear thou their prayer and their supplication in heaven thy dwelling place, and maintain their cause,

50 And forgive thy people that have sinned against thee, and all their transgressions wherein they have transgressed against thee, and [a]give them compassion before them who carried them captive, that they may have compassion on them:

51 For [a]they *be* thy people, and thine inheritance, which thou broughtest forth out of Egypt, [b]from the midst of the furnace of iron:

52 [a]That thine eyes may be open unto the supplication of thy servant, and unto the supplication of thy people Israel, to hearken unto them in all that they call for unto thee.

53 For thou didst separate them from among all the people of the earth, *to be* thine inheritance, [a]as thou spakest by the hand of Moses thy servant, when thou broughtest our fathers out of Egypt, O Lord GOD.

Solomon Blesses the Assembly
(2 Chr. 6:40–42)

54 [a]And it was *so,* that when Solomon had made an end of praying all this prayer and supplication unto the LORD, he arose from before the altar of the LORD, from kneeling on his knees with his hands spread up to heaven.

55 And he stood, [a]and blessed all the congregation of Israel with a loud voice, saying,

39 [a][1 Sam. 16:7; 1 Chr. 28:9; Jer. 17:10]; Acts 1:24
40 [a][Ps. 130:4]
42 [a]Ex. 13:3; Deut. 3:24
43 [a][Ex. 9:16; 1 Sam. 17:46; 2 Kin. 19:19] [b]Ps. 102:15
46 [a]2 Chr. 6:36; Ps. 130:3; Prov. 20:9; Eccl. 7:20; [Rom. 3:23; 1 John 1:8, 10] [b]Lev. 26:34, 44; Deut. 28:36, 64; 2 Kin. 17:6, 18; 25:21
47 [a][Lev. 26:40–42]; Neh. 9:2 [b]Ezra 9:6, 7; Neh. 1:6; Ps. 106:6; Dan. 9:5
48 [a]Jer. 29:12–14 [b]Dan. 6:10; Jon. 2:4
50 [a][2 Chr. 30:9]; Ezra 7:6; Ps. 106:46; Acts 7:10
51 [a]Ex. 32:11, 12; Deut. 9:26–29; Neh. 1:10; [Rom. 11:28, 29] [b]Deut. 4:20; Jer. 11:4
52 [a]1 Kin. 8:29
53 [a]Ex. 19:5, 6
54 [a]2 Chr. 7:1
55 [a]Num. 6:23–26; 2 Sam. 6:18; 1 Kin. 8:14

NKJV

their cities; whatever plague or whatever sickness *there is;*

38 "whatever prayer, whatever supplication is made by anyone, *or* by all Your people Israel, when each one knows the plague of his own heart, and spreads out his hands toward this temple:

39 "then hear in heaven Your dwelling place, and forgive, and act, and give to everyone according to all his ways, whose heart You know (for You alone [a]know the hearts of all the sons of men),

40 [a]"that they may fear You all the days that they live in the land which You gave to our fathers.

41 "Moreover, concerning a foreigner, who *is* not of Your people Israel, but has come from a far country for Your name's sake

42 "(for they will hear of Your great name and Your [a]strong hand and Your outstretched arm), when he comes and prays toward this temple,

43 "hear in heaven Your dwelling place, and do according to all for which the foreigner calls to You, [a]that all peoples of the earth may know Your name and [b]fear You, as *do* Your people Israel, and that they may know that this temple which I have built is called by Your name.

44 "When Your people go out to battle against their enemy, wherever You send them, and when they pray to the LORD toward the city which You have chosen and the temple which I have built for Your name,

45 "then hear in heaven their prayer and their supplication, and maintain their cause.

46 "When they sin against You [a](for *there is* no one who does not sin), and You become angry with them and deliver them to the enemy, and they take them captive [b]to the land of the enemy, far or near;

47 [a]"*yet* when they come to themselves in the land where they were carried captive, and repent, and make supplication to You in the land of those who took them captive, [b]saying, 'We have sinned and done wrong, we have committed wickedness';

48 "and *when* they [a]return to You with all their heart and with all their soul in the land of their enemies who led them away captive, and [b]pray to You toward their land which You gave to their fathers, the city which You have chosen and the temple which I have built for Your name:

49 "then hear in heaven Your dwelling place their prayer and their supplication, and maintain their cause,

50 "and forgive Your people who have sinned against You, and all their transgressions which they have transgressed against You; and [a]grant them compassion before those who took them captive, that they may have compassion on them

51 "(for [a]they *are* Your people and Your inheritance, whom You brought out of Egypt, [b]out of the iron furnace),

52 [a]"that Your eyes may be open to the supplication of Your servant and the supplication of Your people Israel, to listen to them whenever they call to You.

53 "For You separated them from among all the peoples of the earth *to be* Your inheritance, [a]as You spoke by Your servant Moses, when You brought our fathers out of Egypt, O Lord GOD."

Solomon Blesses the Assembly
(2 Chr. 6:40–42)

54 [a]And so it was, when Solomon had finished praying all this prayer and supplication to the LORD, that he arose from before the altar of the LORD, from kneeling on his knees with his hands spread up to heaven.

55 Then he stood [a]and blessed all the assembly of Israel with a loud voice, saying:

KJV

56 Blessed *be* the LORD, that hath given [a]rest unto his people Israel, according to all that he promised: [b]there hath not failed one word of all his good promise, which he promised by the hand of Moses his servant.

57 The LORD our God be with us, as he was with our fathers: [a]let him not leave us, nor forsake us:

58 That he may [a]incline our hearts unto him, to walk in all his ways, and to keep his commandments, and his statutes, and his judgments, which he commanded our fathers.

59 And let these my words, wherewith I have made supplication before the LORD, be nigh unto the LORD our God day and night, that he maintain the cause of his servant, and the cause of his people Israel at all times, as the matter shall require:

60 [a]That all the people of the earth may know that [b]the LORD *is* God, *and that there is* none else.

61 Let your [a]heart therefore be perfect with the LORD our God, to walk in his statutes, and to keep his commandments, as at this day.

Solomon Dedicates the Temple
(2 Chr. 7:4–11)

62 And [a]the king, and all Israel with him, offered sacrifice before the LORD.

63 And Solomon offered a sacrifice of peace offerings, which he offered unto the LORD, two and twenty thousand oxen, and an hundred and twenty thousand sheep. So the king and all the children of Israel dedicated the house of the LORD.

64 [a]The same day did the king hallow the middle of the court that *was* before the house of the LORD: for there he offered burnt offerings, and meat offerings, and the fat of the peace offerings: because the [b]brasen altar that *was* before the LORD *was* too little to receive the burnt offerings, and meat offerings, and the fat of the peace offerings.

65 And at that time Solomon held [a]a feast, and all Israel with him, a great congregation, from [b]the entering in of Hamath unto [c]the river of Egypt, before the LORD our God, [d]seven days and seven days, *even* fourteen days.

66 [a]On the eighth day he sent the people away: and they blessed the king, and went unto their tents joyful and glad of heart for all the goodness that the LORD had done for David his servant, and for Israel his people.

God's Second Appearance to Solomon
(2 Chr. 7:12–22)

9 And [a]it came to pass, when Solomon had finished the building of the house of the LORD, [b]and the king's house, and [c]all Solomon's desire which he was pleased to do,

2 That the LORD appeared to Solomon the second time, [a]as he had appeared unto him at Gibeon.

3 And the LORD said unto him, [a]I have heard thy prayer and thy supplication, that thou hast made before me: I have hallowed this house, which thou hast built, [b]to put my name there for ever; [c]and mine eyes and mine heart shall be there perpetually.

4 And if thou wilt [a]walk before me, [b]as David thy father walked, in integrity of heart, and in uprightness, to do according to all that I have commanded thee, *and* wilt [c]keep my statutes and my judgments:

5 Then I will establish the throne of thy kingdom upon Israel for ever, [a]as I promised to David thy father, saying, There shall not fail thee a man upon the throne of Israel.

6 [a]*But* if ye shall at all turn from following me, ye or your children, and will not keep my commandments *and* my statutes which I have set before you, but go and serve other gods, and worship them:

7 [a]Then will I cut off Israel out of the land

56 [a]1 Chr. 22:18 [b]Deut. 12:10; Josh. 21:45; 23:14
57 [a]Deut. 31:6; Josh. 1:5; 1 Sam. 12:22; [Rom. 8:31–37]; Heb. 13:5
58 [a]Ps. 119:36; Jer. 31:33
60 [a]Josh. 4:24; 1 Sam. 17:46; 1 Kin. 8:43; 2 Kin. 19:19 [b]Deut. 4:35, 39; 1 Kin. 18:39; [Jer. 10:10–12]
61 [a]Deut. 18:13; 1 Kin. 11:4; 15:3, 14; 2 Kin. 20:3
62 [a]2 Chr. 7:4–10
64 [a]2 Chr. 7:7 [b]2 Chr. 4:1
65 [a]Lev. 23:34; 1 Kin. 8:2 [b]Num. 34:8; Josh. 13:5; Judg. 3:3; 2 Kin. 14:25 [c]Gen. 15:18; Ex. 23:31; Num. 34:5 [d]2 Chr. 7:8
66 [a]2 Chr. 7:9

CHAPTER 9

1 [a]2 Chr. 7:11 [b]1 Kin. 7:1 [c]2 Chr. 8:6
2 [a]1 Kin. 3:5; 11:9; 2 Chr. 1:7
3 [a]2 Kin. 20:5; Ps. 10:17 [b]1 Kin. 8:29 [c]Deut. 11:12
4 [a]Gen. 17:1 [b]1 Kin. 11:4, 6; 15:5 [c]1 Kin. 8:61
5 [a]2 Sam. 7:12, 16; 1 Kin. 2:4; 6:12; 8:25; 1 Chr. 22:10; Matt. 1:6; 25:31
6 [a]2 Sam. 7:14–16; 2 Chr. 7:19, 20; Ps. 89:30
7 [a][Lev. 18:24–29]; Deut. 4:26; 2 Kin. 17:23; 25:21

NKJV

56 "Blessed *be* the LORD, who has given [a]rest to His people Israel, according to all that He promised. [b]There has not failed one word of all His good promise, which He promised through His servant Moses.

57 "May the LORD our God be with us, as He was with our fathers. [a]May He not leave us nor forsake us,

58 "that He may [a]incline our hearts to Himself, to walk in all His ways, and to keep His commandments and His statutes and His judgments, which He commanded our fathers.

59 "And may these words of mine, with which I have made supplication before the LORD, be near the LORD our God day and night, that He may maintain the cause of His servant and the cause of His people Israel, as each day may require,

60 [a]"that all the peoples of the earth may know that [b]the LORD *is* God; *there is* no other.

61 "Let your [a]heart therefore be loyal to the LORD our God, to walk in His statutes and keep His commandments, as at this day."

Solomon Dedicates the Temple
(2 Chr. 7:4–11)

62 Then [a]the king and all Israel with him offered sacrifices before the LORD.

63 And Solomon offered a sacrifice of peace offerings, which he offered to the LORD, twenty-two thousand bulls and one hundred and twenty thousand sheep. So the king and all the children of Israel dedicated the house of the LORD.

64 On [a]the same day the king consecrated the middle of the court that *was* in front of the house of the LORD; for there he offered burnt offerings, grain offerings, and the fat of the peace offerings, because the [b]bronze altar that *was* before the LORD *was* too small to receive the burnt offerings, the grain offerings, and the fat of the peace offerings.

65 At that time Solomon held [a]a feast, and all Israel with him, a great assembly from [b]the entrance of Hamath to [c]the Brook of Egypt, before the LORD our God, [d]seven days and seven *more* days—fourteen days.

66 [a]On the eighth day he sent the people away; and they blessed the king, and went to their tents joyful and glad of heart for all the good that the LORD had done for His servant David, and for Israel His people.

God's Second Appearance to Solomon
(2 Chr. 7:12–22)

9 And [a]it came to pass, when Solomon had finished building the house of the LORD [b]and the king's house, and [c]all Solomon's desire which he wanted to do,

2 that the LORD appeared to Solomon the second time, [a]as He had appeared to him at Gibeon.

3 And the LORD said to him: [a]"I have heard your prayer and your supplication that you have made before Me; I have consecrated this house which you have built [b]to put My name there forever, [c]and My eyes and My heart will be there perpetually.

4 "Now if you [a]walk before Me [b]as your father David walked, in integrity of heart and in uprightness, to do according to all that I have commanded you, *and* if you [c]keep My statutes and My judgments,

5 "then I will establish the throne of your kingdom over Israel forever, [a]as I promised David your father, saying, 'You shall not fail to have a man on the throne of Israel.'

6 [a]"*But* if you or your sons at all turn from following Me, and do not keep My commandments *and* My statutes which I have set before you, but go and serve other gods and worship them,

7 [a]"then I will cut off Israel from the land

KJV

which I have given them; and this house, which
I have hallowed [b]for my name, will I cast out of
my sight; [c]and Israel shall be a proverb and a
byword among all people:
8 And [a]at this house, *which* is high, every
one that passeth by it shall be astonished, and
shall hiss; and they shall say, [b]Why hath the LORD
done thus unto this land, and to this house?
9 And they shall answer, Because they forsook the LORD their God, who brought forth their
fathers out of the land of Egypt, and have taken
hold upon other gods, and have worshipped them,
and served them: therefore hath the LORD brought
upon them all this [a]evil.

Solomon and Hiram Exchange Gifts

10 And [a]it came to pass at the end of twenty
years, when Solomon had built the two houses,
the house of the LORD, and the king's house,
11 [a](*Now* Hiram the king of Tyre had furnished Solomon with cedar trees and fir trees, and
with gold, according to all his desire,) that then
king Solomon gave Hiram twenty cities in the
land of Galilee.
12 And Hiram came out from Tyre to see the
cities which Solomon had given him; and they
pleased him not.
13 And he said, What cities *are* these which
thou hast given me, my brother? [a]And he called
them the land of Cabul unto this day.
14 And Hiram sent to the king sixscore talents of gold.

Solomon's Additional Achievements
(2 Chr. 8:3–16)

15 And this *is* the reason of [a]the levy which
king Solomon raised; for to build the house of
the LORD, and his own house, and [b]Millo, and the
wall of Jerusalem, and [c]Hazor, and [d]Megiddo, and
[e]Gezer.
16 *For* Pharaoh king of Egypt had gone up,
and taken Gezer, and burnt it with fire, [a]and slain
the Canaanites that dwelt in the city, and given
it *for* a present unto his daughter, Solomon's wife.
17 And Solomon built Gezer, and [a]Beth–horon the nether,
18 And [a]Baalath, and Tadmor in the wilderness, in the land,
19 And all the cities of store that Solomon
had, and cities for [a]his chariots, and cities for his
[b]horsemen, and that which Solomon [c]desired to
build in Jerusalem, and in Lebanon, and in all
the land of his dominion.
20 [a]*And* all the people *that were* left of the
Amorites, Hittites, Perizzites, Hivites, and Jebusites, which *were* not of the children of Israel,
21 Their children [a]that were left after them
in the land, [b]whom the children of Israel also were
not able utterly to destroy, [c]upon those did Solomon levy a tribute of [d]bondservice unto this day.
22 But of the children of Israel did Solomon
[a]make no bondmen: but they *were* men of war,
and his servants, and his princes, and his captains,
and rulers of his chariots, and his horsemen.
23 These *were* the chief of the officers that
were over Solomon's work, [a]five hundred and
fifty, which bare rule over the people that wrought
in the work.
24 But [a]Pharaoh's daughter came up out of
the city of David unto [b]her house which *Solomon*
had built for her: [c]then did he build Millo.
25 [a]And three times in a year did Solomon
offer burnt offerings and peace offerings upon the
altar which he built unto the LORD, and he burnt
incense upon the altar that *was* before the LORD.
So he finished the house.
26 And [a]king Solomon made a navy of ships
in [b]Ezion–geber, which *is* beside Eloth, on the
shore of the Red sea, in the land of Edom.
27 [a]And Hiram sent in the navy his servants,
shipmen that had knowledge of the sea, with the
servants of Solomon.

7 [b][Jer. 7:4–14] [c]Deut. 28:37; Ps. 44:14; Jer. 24:9
8 [a]2 Chr. 7:21 [b][Deut. 29:24–26]; Jer. 22:8, 9
9 [a][Deut. 29:25–28]
10 [a]1 Kin. 6:37, 38; 7:1; 2 Chr. 8:1
11 [a]1 Kin. 5:1
13 [a]Josh. 19:27
15 [a]1 Kin. 5:13 [b]2 Sam. 5:9; 1 Kin. 9:24 [c]Josh. 11:1; 19:36 [d]Josh. 17:11 [e]Josh. 16:10
16 [a]Josh. 16:10; Judg. 1:29
17 [a]Josh. 10:10; 16:3; 21:22; 2 Chr. 8:5
18 [a]Josh. 19:44; 2 Chr. 8:4
19 [a]1 Kin. 10:26; 2 Chr. 1:14 [b]1 Kin. 4:26 [c]1 Kin. 9:1
20 [a]2 Chr. 8:7
21 [a]Judg. 1:21–36; 3:1 [b]Josh. 15:63; 17:12, 13 [c]Judg. 1:28, 35 [d]Ezra 2:55, 58; Neh. 7:57
22 [a][Lev. 25:39]
23 [a]2 Chr. 8:10
24 [a]1 Kin. 3:1 [b]1 Kin. 7:8 [c]2 Sam. 5:9; 1 Kin. 11:27; 2 Chr. 32:5
25 [a]Ex. 23:14–17; Deut. 16:16; 2 Chr. 8:12, 13
26 [a]2 Chr. 8:17, 18 [b]Num. 33:35; Deut. 2:8; 1 Kin. 22:48
27 [a]1 Kin. 5:6, 9; 10:11

*________

9:13 Lit. *Good for Nothing*
9:15 Lit. *The Landfill*
9:24 Lit. *he;* cf. 2 Chr. 8:11
9:26 Heb. *Eloth*

NKJV

which I have given them; and this house which I
have consecrated [b]for My name I will cast out of
My sight. [c]Israel will be a proverb and a byword
among all peoples.
8 "And *as for* [a]this house, *which* is exalted,
everyone who passes by it will be astonished and
will hiss, and say, [b]'Why has the LORD done thus
to this land and to this house?'
9 "Then they will answer, 'Because they forsook the LORD their God, who brought their fathers out of the land of Egypt, and have embraced
other gods, and worshiped them and served them;
therefore the LORD has brought all this [a]calamity
on them.' "

Solomon and Hiram Exchange Gifts

10 Now [a]it happened at the end of twenty
years, when Solomon had built the two houses,
the house of the LORD and the king's house
11 [a](Hiram the king of Tyre had supplied Solomon with cedar and cypress and gold, as much
as he desired), *that* King Solomon then gave
Hiram twenty cities in the land of Galilee.
12 Then Hiram went from Tyre to see the cities which Solomon had given him, but they did
not please him.
13 So he said, "What *kind of* cities *are* these
which you have given me, my brother?" [a]And he
called them the land of *Cabul, as they are to this
day.
14 Then Hiram sent the king one hundred
and twenty talents of gold.

Solomon's Additional Achievements
(2 Chr. 8:3–16)

15 And this *is* the reason for [a]the labor force
which King Solomon raised: to build the house
of the LORD, his own house, *the [b]Millo, the wall
of Jerusalem, [c]Hazor, [d]Megiddo, and [e]Gezer.
16 (Pharaoh king of Egypt had gone up and
taken Gezer and burned it with fire, [a]had killed
the Canaanites who dwelt in the city, and had
given it *as* a dowry to his daughter, Solomon's
wife.)
17 And Solomon built Gezer, Lower [a]Beth
Horon,
18 [a]Baalath, and Tadmor in the wilderness,
in the land *of Judah,*
19 all the storage cities that Solomon had,
cities for [a]his chariots and cities for his [b]cavalry,
and whatever Solomon [c]desired to build in Jerusalem, in Lebanon, and in all the land of his
dominion.
20 [a]All the people *who were* left of the Amorites, Hittites, Perizzites, Hivites, and Jebusites,
who *were* not of the children of Israel—
21 that is, their descendants [a]who were left
in the land after them, [b]whom the children of Israel had not been able to destroy completely—
[c]from these Solomon raised [d]forced labor, as it
is to this day.
22 But of the children of Israel Solomon
[a]made no forced laborers, because they *were* men
of war and his servants: his officers, his captains,
commanders of his chariots, and his cavalry.
23 Others *were* chiefs of the officials who
were over Solomon's work: [a]five hundred and
fifty, who ruled over the people who did the work.
24 But [a]Pharaoh's daughter came up from
the City of David to [b]her house which **Solomon*
had built for her. [c]Then he built the Millo.
25 [a]Now three times a year Solomon offered
burnt offerings and peace offerings on the altar
which he had built for the LORD, and he burned
incense with them *on the altar* that *was* before
the LORD. So he finished the temple.
26 [a]King Solomon also built a fleet of ships
at [b]Ezion Geber, which *is* near *Elath on the shore
of the Red Sea, in the land of Edom.
27 [a]Then Hiram sent his servants with the
fleet, seamen who knew the sea, to work with the
servants of Solomon.

KJV

28 And they came to [a]Ophir, and fetched
from thence gold, four hundred and twenty talents, and brought *it* to king Solomon.

The Queen of Sheba's Praise of Solomon
(2 Chr. 9:1–28)

10 And when the [a]queen of Sheba heard of
the fame of Solomon concerning the name
of the LORD, she came [b]to prove him with hard
questions.
2 And she came to Jerusalem with a very
great train, with camels that bare spices, and very
much gold, and precious stones: and when she
was come to Solomon, she communed with him
of all that was in her heart.
3 And Solomon told her all her questions:
there was not *any* thing hid from the king, which
he told her not.
4 And when the queen of Sheba had seen
all Solomon's wisdom, and the house that he had
built,
5 And the meat of his table, and the sitting
of his servants, and the attendance of his ministers, and their apparel, and his cupbearers, [a]and
his ascent by which he went up unto the house
of the LORD; there was no more spirit in her.
6 And she said to the king, It was a true
report that I heard in mine own land of thy acts
and of thy wisdom.
7 Howbeit I believed not the words, until I
came, and mine eyes had seen *it*: and, behold,
the half was not told me: thy wisdom and prosperity exceedeth the fame which I heard.
8 [a]Happy *are* thy men, happy *are* these thy
servants, which stand continually before thee, *and*
that hear thy wisdom.
9 [a]Blessed be the LORD thy God, which [b]de-
lighted in thee, to set thee on the throne of Israel:
because the LORD loved Israel for ever, therefore
made he thee king, [c]to do judgment and justice.
10 And she [a]gave the king an hundred and
twenty talents of gold, and of spices very great
store, and precious stones: there came no more
such abundance of spices as these which the
queen of Sheba gave to king Solomon.
11 [a]And the navy also of Hiram, that brought
gold from Ophir, brought in from Ophir great
plenty of almug trees, and precious stones.
12 [a]And the king made of the almug trees
pillars for the house of the LORD, and for the king's
house, harps also and psalteries for singers: there
came no such [b]almug trees, nor were seen unto
this day.
13 And king Solomon gave unto the queen
of Sheba all her desire, whatsoever she asked,
beside *that* which Solomon gave her of his royal
bounty. So she turned and went to her own country, she and her servants.

Solomon's Great Wealth

14 Now the weight of gold that came to Solomon in one year was six hundred threescore and
six talents of gold,
15 Beside *that he had* of the [a]merchantmen,
and of the traffick of the spice merchants, and
[b]of all the kings of Arabia, and of the governors
of the country.
16 And king Solomon made two hundred targets *of* beaten gold: six hundred *shekels* of gold
went to one target.
17 And *he made* [a]three hundred shields *of*
beaten gold; three pound of gold went to one
shield: and the king put them in the [b]house of
the forest of Lebanon.
18 [a]Moreover the king made a great throne
of ivory, and overlaid it with the best gold.
19 The throne had six steps, and the top of
the throne *was* round behind: and *there were*
stays on either side on the place of the seat, and
two lions stood beside the stays.
20 And twelve lions stood there on the one

28 [a]Job 22:24

CHAPTER 10

1 [a]2 Chr. 9:1; Matt. 12:42; Luke 11:31 [b]Judg. 14:12; Ps. 49:4; Prov. 1:6
5 [a]1 Chr. 26:16; 2 Chr. 9:4
8 [a]Prov. 8:34
9 [a]1 Kin. 5:7 [b]2 Sam. 22:20 [c]2 Sam. 8:15; Ps. 72:2; [Prov. 8:15]
10 [a]Ps. 72:10, 15
11 [a]1 Kin. 9:27, 28; Job 22:24
12 [a]2 Chr. 9:11 [b]2 Chr. 9:10
15 [a]2 Chr. 1:16 [b]2 Chr. 9:24; Ps. 72:10
17 [a]1 Kin. 14:26 [b]1 Kin. 7:2
18 [a]1 Kin. 10:22; 2 Chr. 9:17; Ps. 45:8

***10:11** *algum*, 2 Chr. 9:10, 11

NKJV

28 And they went to [a]Ophir, and acquired
four hundred and twenty talents of gold from
there, and brought *it* to King Solomon.

The Queen of Sheba's Praise of Solomon
(2 Chr. 9:1–28)

10 Now when the [a]queen of Sheba heard of
the fame of Solomon concerning the name
of the LORD, she came [b]to test him with hard
questions.
2 She came to Jerusalem with a very great
retinue, with camels that bore spices, very much
gold, and precious stones; and when she came to
Solomon, she spoke with him about all that was
in her heart.
3 So Solomon answered all her questions;
there was nothing so difficult for the king that
he could not explain *it* to her.
4 And when the queen of Sheba had seen
all the wisdom of Solomon, the house that he had
built,
5 the food on his table, the seating of his
servants, the service of his waiters and their apparel, his cupbearers, [a]and his entryway by which
he went up to the house of the LORD, there was
no more spirit in her.
6 Then she said to the king: "It was a true
report which I heard in my own land about your
words and your wisdom.
7 "However I did not believe the words until
I came and saw with my own eyes; and indeed
the half was not told me. Your wisdom and prosperity exceed the fame of which I heard.
8 [a]"Happy *are* your men and happy *are*
these your servants, who stand continually before
you *and* hear your wisdom!
9 [a]"Blessed be the LORD your God, who [b]de-
lighted in you, setting you on the throne of Israel!
Because the LORD has loved Israel forever, therefore He made you king, [c]to do justice and
righteousness."
10 Then she [a]gave the king one hundred and
twenty talents of gold, spices in great quantity,
and precious stones. There never again came such
abundance of spices as the queen of Sheba gave
to King Solomon.
11 [a]Also, the ships of Hiram, which brought
gold from Ophir, brought great *quantities* of *almug wood and precious stones from Ophir.
12 [a]And the king made steps of the almug
wood for the house of the LORD and for the king's
house, also harps and stringed instruments for
singers. There never again came such [b]almug
wood, nor has the like been seen to this day.
13 Now King Solomon gave the queen of
Sheba all she desired, whatever she asked, besides what Solomon had given her according to
the royal generosity. So she turned and went to
her own country, she and her servants.

Solomon's Great Wealth

14 The weight of gold that came to Solomon
yearly was six hundred and sixty-six talents of
gold,
15 besides *that* from the [a]traveling merchants, from the income of traders, [b]from all the
kings of Arabia, and from the governors of the
country.
16 And King Solomon made two hundred
large shields *of* hammered gold; six hundred
shekels of gold went into each shield.
17 He also *made* [a]three hundred shields *of*
hammered gold; three minas of gold went into
each shield. The king put them in the [b]House of
the Forest of Lebanon.
18 [a]Moreover the king made a great throne
of ivory, and overlaid it with pure gold.
19 The throne had six steps, and the top of
the throne *was* round at the back; *there were* armrests on either side of the place of the seat, and
two lions stood beside the armrests.
20 Twelve lions stood there, one on each side

KJV

side and on the other upon the six steps: there
was not the like made in any kingdom.
21 [a]And all king Solomon's drinking vessels
were of gold, and all the vessels of the house of
the forest of Lebanon *were of* pure gold; none
were of silver: it was nothing accounted of in the
days of Solomon.
22 For the king had at sea a navy of [a]Thar-
shish with the navy of Hiram: once in three years
came the [b]navy of Tharshish, bringing gold, and
silver, ivory, and apes, and peacocks.
23 So [a]king Solomon exceeded all the kings
of the earth for riches and for wisdom.
24 And all the earth sought to Solomon, to
hear his wisdom, which God had put in his heart.
25 And they brought every man his present,
vessels of silver, and vessels of gold, and garments, and armour, and spices, horses, and mules,
a rate year by year.
26 [a]And Solomon [b]gathered together chariots and horsemen: and he had a thousand and
four hundred chariots, and twelve thousand
horsemen, whom he bestowed in the cities for
chariots, and with the king at Jerusalem.
27 [a]And the king made silver *to be* in Jerusalem as stones, and cedars made he *to be* as the
sycomore trees that *are* in the vale, for abundance.
28 [a]And Solomon had horses brought out of
Egypt, and linen yarn: the king's merchants received the linen yarn at a price.
29 And a chariot came up and went out of
Egypt for six hundred *shekels* of silver, and an
horse for an hundred and fifty: [a]and so for all
the kings of the Hittites, and for the kings of Syria,
did they bring *them* out by their means.

Solomon's Heart Turns from the LORD

11 But [a]king Solomon loved [b]many strange
women, together with the daughter of Pharaoh, women of the Moabites, Ammonites, Edomites, Zidonians, *and* Hittites;
2 Of the nations *concerning* which the LORD
said unto the children of Israel, [a]Ye shall not go
in to them, neither shall they come in unto you:
for surely they will turn away your heart after
their gods: Solomon clave unto these in love.
3 And he had seven hundred wives, prin-
cesses, and three hundred concubines: and his
wives turned away his heart.
4 For it came to pass, when Solomon was
old, [a]*that* his wives turned away his heart after
other gods: and his [b]heart was not perfect with
the LORD his God, [c]as *was* the heart of David his
father.
5 For Solomon went after [a]Ashtoreth the
goddess of the Zidonians, and after [b]Milcom the
abomination of the [c]Ammonites.
6 And Solomon did evil in the sight of the
LORD, and went not fully after the LORD, as *did*
David his father.
7 [a]Then did Solomon build an high place
for [b]Chemosh, the abomination of Moab, in [c]the
hill that *is* before Jerusalem, and for Molech, the
abomination of the children of Ammon.
8 And likewise did he for all his strange
wives, which burnt incense and sacrificed unto
their gods.
9 And the LORD was angry with Solomon,
because his heart was turned from the LORD God
of Israel, [a]which had appeared unto him twice,
10 And [a]had commanded him concerning
this thing, that he should not go after other gods:
but he kept not that which the LORD commanded.
11 Wherefore the LORD said unto Solomon,
Forasmuch as this is done of thee, and thou hast
not kept my covenant and my statutes, which I
have commanded thee, [a]I will surely rend the
kingdom from thee, and will give it to thy
[b]servant.
12 Notwithstanding in thy days I will not do
it for David thy father's sake: *but* I will rend it
out of the hand of thy son.

21 [a]2 Chr. 9:20
22 [a]Gen. 10:4; 2 Chr. 20:36 [b]1 Kin. 9:26–28; 22:48; Ps. 72:10
23 [a]1 Kin. 3:12, 13; 4:30; 2 Chr. 1:12
26 [a]1 Kin. 4:26; 2 Chr. 1:14; 9:25 [b][Deut. 17:16]; 1 Kin. 9:19
27 [a][Deut. 17:17]; 2 Chr. 1:15–17
28 [a][Deut. 17:16]; 2 Chr. 1:16; 9:28
29 [a]Josh. 1:4; 2 Kin. 7:6, 7

CHAPTER 11

1 [a][Neh. 13:26] [b][Deut. 17:17]; 1 Kin. 3:1
2 [a]Ex. 34:16; [Deut. 7:3, 4]
4 [a][Deut. 17:17; Neh. 13:26] [b]1 Kin. 8:61 [c]1 Kin. 9:4
5 [a]Judg. 2:13; 1 Kin. 11:33 [b][Lev. 20:2–5] [c]2 Kin. 23:13
7 [a]Num. 33:52 [b]Num. 21:29; Judg. 11:24 [c]2 Kin. 23:13
9 [a]1 Kin. 3:5; 9:2
10 [a]1 Kin. 6:12; 9:6, 7
11 [a]1 Kin. 11:31; 12:15, 16 [b]1 Kin. 11:31, 37

*

10:22 Lit. *ships of Tarshish,* deep-sea vessels • Or *peacocks*
10:26 So with LXX, Syr., Tg., Vg. (cf. 2 Chr. 9:25); MT *led*
10:29 Lit. *by their hands*

NKJV

of the six steps; nothing like *this* had been made
for any *other* kingdom.
21 [a]All King Solomon's drinking vessels
were gold, and all the vessels of the House of the
Forest of Lebanon *were* pure gold. Not *one was*
silver, for this was accounted as nothing in the
days of Solomon.
22 For the king had [a]merchant* ships at sea
with the fleet of Hiram. Once every three years
the merchant [b]ships came bringing gold, silver,
ivory, apes, and *monkeys.
23 So [a]King Solomon surpassed all the kings
of the earth in riches and wisdom.
24 Now all the earth sought the presence of
Solomon to hear his wisdom, which God had put
in his heart.
25 Each man brought his present: articles of
silver and gold, garments, armor, spices, horses,
and mules, at a set rate year by year.
26 [a]And Solomon [b]gathered chariots and
horsemen; he had one thousand four hundred
chariots and twelve thousand horsemen, whom
he *stationed in the chariot cities and with the
king at Jerusalem.
27 [a]The king made silver *as common* in Jerusalem as stones, and he made cedar trees as abundant as the sycamores which *are* in the lowland.
28 [a]Also Solomon had horses imported from
Egypt and Keveh; the king's merchants bought
them in Keveh at the *current* price.
29 Now a chariot that was imported from
Egypt cost six hundred *shekels* of silver, and a
horse one hundred and fifty; [a]and *thus, through
their agents, they exported *them* to all the kings
of the Hittites and the kings of Syria.

Solomon's Heart Turns from the LORD

11 But [a]King Solomon loved [b]many foreign
women, as well as the daughter of Pharaoh:
women of the Moabites, Ammonites, Edomites,
Sidonians, *and* Hittites—
2 from the nations of whom the LORD had
said to the children of Israel, [a]"You shall not inter-
marry with them, nor they with you. Surely they
will turn away your hearts after their gods." Solomon clung to these in love.
3 And he had seven hundred wives, prin-
cesses, and three hundred concubines; and his
wives turned away his heart.
4 For it was so, when Solomon was old,
[a]that his wives turned his heart after other gods;
and his [b]heart was not loyal to the LORD his God,
[c]as *was* the heart of his father David.
5 For Solomon went after [a]Ashtoreth the
goddess of the Sidonians, and after [b]Milcom the
abomination of the [c]Ammonites.
6 Solomon did evil in the sight of the LORD,
and did not fully follow the LORD, as *did* his father
David.
7 [a]Then Solomon built a high place for
[b]Chemosh the abomination of Moab, on [c]the hill
that *is* east of Jerusalem, and for Molech the
abomination of the people of Ammon.
8 And he did likewise for all his foreign
wives, who burned incense and sacrificed to their
gods.
9 So the LORD became angry with Solomon,
because his heart had turned from the LORD God
of Israel, [a]who had appeared to him twice,
10 and [a]had commanded him concerning this
thing, that he should not go after other gods; but
he did not keep what the LORD had commanded.
11 Therefore the LORD said to Solomon, "Because you have done this, and have not kept My
covenant and My statutes, which I have commanded you, [a]I will surely tear the kingdom away
from you and give it to your [b]servant.
12 "Nevertheless I will not do it in your days,
for the sake of your father David; I will tear it
out of the hand of your son.

KJV

13 [a]Howbeit I will not rend away all the kingdom; *but* will give [b]one tribe to thy son [c]for David my servant's sake, and for Jerusalem's sake [d]which I have chosen.

Adversaries of Solomon

14 And the LORD [a]stirred up an adversary unto Solomon, Hadad the Edomite: he *was* of the king's seed in Edom.

15 [a]For it came to pass, when David was in Edom, and Joab the captain of the host was gone up to bury the slain, [b]after he had smitten every male in Edom;

16 (For six months did Joab remain there with all Israel, until he had cut off every male in Edom:)

17 That Hadad fled, he and certain Edomites of his father's servants with him, to go into Egypt; Hadad *being* yet a little child.

18 And they arose out of Midian, and came to Paran: and they took men with them out of Paran, and they came to Egypt, unto Pharaoh king of Egypt; which gave him an house, and appointed him victuals, and gave him land.

19 And Hadad found great favour in the sight of Pharaoh, so that he gave him to wife the sister of his own wife, the sister of Tahpenes the queen.

20 And the sister of Tahpenes bare him Genubath his son, whom Tahpenes weaned in Pharaoh's house: and Genubath was in Pharaoh's household among the sons of Pharaoh.

21 [a]And when Hadad heard in Egypt that David slept with his fathers, and that Joab the captain of the host was dead, Hadad said to Pharaoh, Let me depart, that I may go to mine own country.

22 Then Pharaoh said unto him, But what hast thou lacked with me, that, behold, thou seekest to go to thine own country? And he answered, Nothing: howbeit let me go in any wise.

23 And God stirred him up *another* adversary, Rezon the son of Eliadah, which fled from his lord [a]Hadadezer king of Zobah:

24 And he gathered men unto him, and became captain over a band, [a]when David slew them *of Zobah:* and they went to Damascus, and dwelt therein, and reigned in Damascus.

25 And he was an adversary to Israel all the days of Solomon, beside the mischief that Hadad *did:* and he abhorred Israel, and reigned over Syria.

Jeroboam's Rebellion

26 And [a]Jeroboam the son of Nebat, an Ephrathite of Zereda, Solomon's servant, whose mother's name *was* Zeruah, a widow woman, [b]even he [c]lifted up *his* hand against the king.

27 And this *was* the cause that he lifted up *his* hand against the king: [a]Solomon built Millo, *and* repaired the breaches of the city of David his father.

28 And the man Jeroboam *was* a mighty man of valour: and Solomon seeing the young man that he was [a]industrious, he made him ruler over all the charge of the house of Joseph.

29 And it came to pass at that time when Jeroboam went out of Jerusalem, that the prophet [a]Ahijah the Shilonite found him in the way; and he had clad himself with a new garment; and they two *were* alone in the field:

30 And Ahijah caught the new garment that *was* on him, and [a]rent it *in* twelve pieces:

31 And he said to Jeroboam, Take thee ten pieces: for [a]thus saith the LORD, the God of Israel, Behold, I will rend the kingdom out of the hand of Solomon, and will give ten tribes to thee:

32 (But he shall have one tribe for my servant David's sake, and for Jerusalem's sake, the city which I have chosen out of all the tribes of Israel:)

13 [a]2 Sam. 7:15; 1 Chr. 17:13; Ps. 89:33 [b]1 Kin. 12:20 [c]2 Sam. 7:15, 16 [d]Deut. 12:11; 1 Kin. 9:3; 14:21
14 [a]1 Chr. 5:26
15 [a]2 Sam. 8:14; 1 Chr. 18:12, 13 [b]Num. 24:18, 19; [Deut. 20:13]
21 [a]1 Kin. 2:10, 34
23 [a]2 Sam. 8:3; 10:16
24 [a]2 Sam. 8:3; 10:8, 18
26 [a]1 Kin. 12:2 [b]1 Kin. 11:11; 2 Chr. 13:6 [c]2 Sam. 20:21
27 [a]1 Kin. 9:15, 24
28 [a][Prov. 22:29]
29 [a]1 Kin. 12:15; 14:2; 2 Chr. 9:29
30 [a]1 Sam. 15:27, 28; 24:5
31 [a]1 Kin. 11:11, 13

NKJV

13 [a]"However I will not tear away the whole kingdom; I will give [b]one tribe to your son [c]for the sake of my servant David, and for the sake of Jerusalem [d]which I have chosen."

Adversaries of Solomon

14 Now the LORD [a]raised up an adversary against Solomon, Hadad the Edomite; he *was* a descendant of the king in Edom.

15 [a]For it happened, when David was in Edom, and Joab the commander of the army had gone up to bury the slain, [b]after he had killed every male in Edom

16 (because for six months Joab remained there with all Israel, until he had cut down every male in Edom),

17 that Hadad fled to go to Egypt, he and certain Edomites of his father's servants with him. Hadad *was* still a little child.

18 Then they arose from Midian and came to Paran; and they took men with them from Paran and came to Egypt, to Pharaoh king of Egypt, who gave him a house, apportioned food for him, and gave him land.

19 And Hadad found great favor in the sight of Pharaoh, so that he gave him as wife the sister of his own wife, that is, the sister of Queen Tahpenes.

20 Then the sister of Tahpenes bore him Genubath his son, whom Tahpenes weaned in Pharaoh's house. And Genubath was in Pharaoh's household among the sons of Pharaoh.

21 [a]So when Hadad heard in Egypt that David rested with his fathers, and that Joab the commander of the army was dead, Hadad said to Pharaoh, "Let me depart, that I may go to my own country."

22 Then Pharaoh said to him, "But what have you lacked with me, that suddenly you seek to go to your own country?" So he answered, "Nothing, but do let me go anyway."

23 And God raised up *another* adversary against him, Rezon the son of Eliadah, who had fled from his lord, [a]Hadadezer king of Zobah.

24 So he gathered men to him and became captain over a band *of raiders,* [a]when David killed those *of Zobah.* And they went to Damascus and dwelt there, and reigned in Damascus.

25 He was an adversary of Israel all the days of Solomon (besides the trouble that Hadad *caused*); and he abhorred Israel, and reigned over Syria.

Jeroboam's Rebellion

26 Then Solomon's servant, [a]Jeroboam the son of Nebat, an Ephraimite from Zereda, whose mother's name *was* Zeruah, a widow, [b]also [c]rebelled against the king.

27 And this *is* what caused him to rebel against the king: [a]Solomon had built the Millo *and* repaired the damages to the City of David his father.

28 The man Jeroboam *was* a mighty man of valor; and Solomon, seeing that the young man was [a]industrious, made him the officer over all the labor force of the house of Joseph.

29 Now it happened at that time, when Jeroboam went out of Jerusalem, that the prophet [a]Ahijah the Shilonite met him on the way; and he had clothed himself with a new garment, and the two *were* alone in the field.

30 Then Ahijah took hold of the new garment that *was* on him, and [a]tore it *into* twelve pieces.

31 And he said to Jeroboam, "Take for yourself ten pieces, for [a]thus says the LORD, the God of Israel: 'Behold, I will tear the kingdom out of the hand of Solomon and will give ten tribes to you

32 '(but he shall have one tribe for the sake of My servant David, and for the sake of Jerusalem, the city which I have chosen out of all the tribes of Israel),

KJV

33 [a]Because that they have forsaken me, and have worshipped Ashtoreth the goddess of the Zidonians, Chemosh the god of the Moabites, and Milcom the god of the children of Ammon, and have not walked in my ways, to do *that which is* right in mine eyes, and *to keep* my statutes and my judgments, as *did* David his father.

34 Howbeit I will not take the whole kingdom out of his hand: but I will make him prince all the days of his life for David my servant's sake, whom I chose, because he kept my commandments and my statutes:

35 But [a]I will take the kingdom out of his son's hand, and will give it unto thee, *even* ten tribes.

36 And unto his son will I give one tribe, that [a]David my servant may have a light alway before me in Jerusalem, the city which I have chosen me to put my name there.

37 And I will take thee, and thou shalt reign according to all that thy soul desireth, and shalt be king over Israel.

38 And it shall be, if thou wilt hearken unto all that I command thee, and wilt walk in my ways, and do *that is* right in my sight, to keep my statutes and my commandments, as David my servant did; that [a]I will be with thee, and [b]build thee a sure house, as I built for David, and will give Israel unto thee.

39 And I will for this afflict the seed of David, but not for ever.

40 Solomon sought therefore to kill Jeroboam. And Jeroboam arose, and fled into Egypt, unto [a]Shishak king of Egypt, and was in Egypt until the death of Solomon.

Death of Solomon
(*2 Chr. 9:29–31*)

41 And [a]the rest of the acts of Solomon, and all that he did, and his wisdom, *are* they not written in the book of the acts of Solomon?

42 [a]And the time that Solomon reigned in Jerusalem over all Israel *was* forty years.

43 [a]And Solomon slept with his fathers, and was buried in the city of David his father: and Rehoboam his son reigned in his [b]stead.

The Revolt Against Rehoboam
(*2 Chr. 10:1–19; 11:1–4*)

12 And [a]Rehoboam went to [b]Shechem: for all Israel were come to Shechem to make him king.

2 And it came to pass, when [a]Jeroboam the son of Nebat, who was yet in [b]Egypt, heard *of it*, (for he was fled from the presence of king Solomon, and Jeroboam dwelt in Egypt;)

3 That they sent and called him. And Jeroboam and all the congregation of Israel came, and spake unto Rehoboam, saying,

4 Thy father made our [a]yoke grievous: now therefore make thou the grievous service of thy father, and his heavy yoke which he put upon us, lighter, and we will serve thee.

5 And he said unto them, Depart yet *for* three days, then come again to me. And the people departed.

6 And king Rehoboam consulted with the old men, that stood before Solomon his father while he yet lived, and said, How do ye advise that I may answer this people?

7 And they spake unto him, saying, [a]If thou wilt be a servant unto this people this day, and wilt serve them, and answer them, and speak good words to them, then they will be thy servants for ever.

8 But he forsook the counsel of the old men, which they had given him, and consulted with the young men that were grown up with him, *and* which stood before him:

9 And he said unto them, What counsel give ye that we may answer this people, who have spo-

NKJV

33 [a]'because *they have forsaken Me, and worshiped Ashtoreth the goddess of the Sidonians, Chemosh the god of the Moabites, and Milcom the god of the people of Ammon, and have not walked in My ways to do *what is* right in My eyes and *keep* My statutes and My judgments, as *did* his father David.

34 'However I will not take the whole kingdom out of his hand, because I have made him ruler all the days of his life for the sake of My servant David, whom I chose because he kept My commandments and My statutes.

35 'But [a]I will take the kingdom out of his son's hand and give it to you—ten tribes.

36 'And to his son I will give one tribe, that [a]My servant David may always have a lamp before Me in Jerusalem, the city which I have chosen for Myself, to put My name there.

37 'So I will take you, and you shall reign over all your heart desires, and you shall be king over Israel.

38 'Then it shall be, if you heed all that I command you, walk in My ways, and do *what is* right in My sight, to keep My statutes and My commandments, as My servant David did, then [a]I will be with you and [b]build for you an enduring house, as I built for David, and will give Israel to you.

39 'And I will afflict the descendants of David because of this, but not forever.' "

40 Solomon therefore sought to kill Jeroboam. But Jeroboam arose and fled to Egypt, to [a]Shishak king of Egypt, and was in Egypt until the death of Solomon.

Death of Solomon
(*2 Chr. 9:29–31*)

41 Now [a]the rest of the acts of Solomon, all that he did, and his wisdom, *are* they not written in the book of the acts of Solomon?

42 [a]And the period that Solomon reigned in Jerusalem over all Israel *was* forty years.

43 [a]Then Solomon rested with his fathers, and was buried in the City of David his father. And Rehoboam his son reigned in his [b]place.

The Revolt Against Rehoboam
(*2 Chr. 10:1–19; 11:1–4*)

12 And [a]Rehoboam went to [b]Shechem, for all Israel had gone to Shechem to make him king.

2 So it happened, when [a]Jeroboam the son of Nebat heard *it* (he was still in [b]Egypt, for he had fled from the presence of King Solomon and had been dwelling in Egypt),

3 that they sent and called him. Then Jeroboam and the whole assembly of Israel came and spoke to Rehoboam, saying,

4 "Your father made our [a]yoke heavy; now therefore, lighten the burdensome service of your father, and his heavy yoke which he put on us, and we will serve you."

5 So he said to them, "Depart *for* three days, then come back to me." And the people departed.

6 Then King Rehoboam consulted the elders who stood before his father Solomon while he still lived, and he said, "How do you advise *me* to answer these people?"

7 And they spoke to him, saying, [a]"If you will be a servant to these people today, and serve them, and answer them, and speak good words to them, then they will be your servants forever."

8 But he rejected the advice which the elders had given him, and consulted the young men who had grown up with him, who stood before him.

9 And he said to them, "What advice do you give? How should we answer this people who

33 [a]1 Sam. 7:3; 1 Kin. 11:5–8
35 [a]1 Kin. 12:16, 17
36 [a][1 Kin. 15:4; 2 Kin. 8:19]
38 [a]Deut. 31:8; Josh. 1:5 [b]2 Sam. 7:11, 27
40 [a]1 Kin. 11:17; 14:25; 2 Chr. 12:2–9
41 [a]2 Chr. 9:29
42 [a]2 Chr. 9:30
43 [a]1 Kin. 2:10; 2 Chr. 9:31 [b]1 Kin. 14:21; 2 Chr. 10:1

CHAPTER 12

1 [a]2 Chr. 10:1 [b]Judg. 9:6
2 [a]1 Kin. 11:26 [b]1 Kin. 11:40
4 [a]1 Sam. 8:11–18; 1 Kin. 4:7; 5:13–15
7 [a]2 Chr. 10:7; [Prov. 15:1]

*______

11:33 So with MT, Tg.; LXX, Syr., Vg. *he has*

KJV

ken to me, saying, Make the yoke which thy father did put upon us lighter?

10 And the young men that were grown up with him spake unto him, saying, Thus shalt thou speak unto this people that spake unto thee, saying, Thy father made our yoke heavy, but make thou *it* lighter unto us; thus shalt thou say unto them, My little *finger* shall be thicker than my father's loins.

11 And now whereas my father did lade you with a heavy yoke, I will add to your yoke: my father hath chastised you with whips, but I will chastise you with scorpions.

12 So Jeroboam and all the people came to Rehoboam the third day, as the king had appointed, saying, Come to me again the third day.

13 And the king answered the people roughly, and forsook the old men's counsel that they gave him;

14 And spake to them after the counsel of the young men, saying, My father made your yoke heavy, and I will add to your yoke: my father *also* chastised you with whips, but I will chastise you with scorpions.

15 Wherefore the king hearkened not unto the people; for [a]the cause was from the LORD, that he might perform his saying, which the LORD [b]spake by Ahijah the Shilonite unto Jeroboam the son of Nebat.

16 So when all Israel saw that the king hearkened not unto them, the people answered the king, saying, [a]What portion have we in David? neither *have we* inheritance in the son of Jesse: to your tents, O Israel: now see to thine own house, David. So Israel departed unto their tents.

17 But [a]*as for* the children of Israel which dwelt in the cities of Judah, Rehoboam reigned over them.

18 Then king Rehoboam [a]sent Adoram, who *was* over the tribute; and all Israel stoned him with stones, that he died. Therefore king Rehoboam made speed to get him up to his chariot, to flee to Jerusalem.

19 So [a]Israel rebelled against the house of David unto this day.

20 And it came to pass, when all Israel heard that Jeroboam was come again, that they sent and called him unto the congregation, and made him king over all [a]Israel: there was none that followed the house of David, but the tribe of Judah [b]only.

21 And when [a]Rehoboam was come to Jerusalem, he assembled all the house of Judah, with the tribe of [b]Benjamin, an hundred and fourscore thousand chosen men, which were warriors, to fight against the house of Israel, to bring the kingdom again to Rehoboam the son of Solomon.

22 But [a]the word of God came unto Shemaiah the man of God, saying,

23 Speak unto Rehoboam, the son of Solomon, king of Judah, and unto all the house of Judah and Benjamin, and to the remnant of the people, saying,

24 Thus saith the LORD, Ye shall not go up, nor fight against your brethren the children of Israel: return every man to his house; [a]for this thing is from me. They hearkened therefore to the word of the LORD, and returned to depart, according to the word of the LORD.

Jeroboam's Gold Calves

25 Then Jeroboam [a]built Shechem in mount Ephraim, and dwelt therein; and went out from thence, and built [b]Penuel.

26 And Jeroboam said in his heart, Now shall the kingdom return to the house of David:

27 If this people [a]go up to do sacrifice in the house of the LORD at Jerusalem, then shall the heart of this people turn again unto their lord,

15 [a]Deut. 2:30; Judg. 14:4; 1 Kin. 12:24; 2 Chr. 10:15 [b]1 Kin. 11:11, 29, 31
16 [a]2 Sam. 20:1
17 [a]1 Kin. 11:13, 36; 2 Chr. 11:14–17
18 [a]1 Kin. 4:6; 5:14
19 [a]2 Kin. 17:21
20 [a]2 Kin. 17:21 [b]1 Kin. 11:13, 32, 36
21 [a]2 Chr. 11:1–4 [b]2 Sam. 19:17
22 [a]2 Chr. 11:2; 12:5–7
24 [a]1 Kin. 12:15
25 [a]Gen. 12:6; Judg. 9:45–49; 1 Kin. 12:1 [b]Gen. 32:30, 31; Judg. 8:8, 17
27 [a][Deut. 12:5–7, 14]

NKJV

have spoken to me, saying, 'Lighten the yoke which your father put on us'?"

10 Then the young men who had grown up with him spoke to him, saying, "Thus you should speak to this people who have spoken to you, saying, 'Your father made our yoke heavy, but you make *it* lighter on us'—thus you shall say to them: 'My little *finger* shall be thicker than my father's waist!

11 'And now, whereas my father put a heavy yoke on you, I will add to your yoke; my father chastised you with whips, but I will chastise you with *scourges!' "

12 So Jeroboam and all the people came to Rehoboam the third day, as the king had directed, saying, "Come back to me the third day."

13 Then the king answered the people roughly, and rejected the advice which the elders had given him;

14 and he spoke to them according to the advice of the young men, saying, "My father made your yoke heavy, but I will add to your yoke; my father chastised you with whips, but I will chastise you with *scourges!"

15 So the king did not listen to the people; for [a]the turn *of events* was from the LORD, that He might fulfill His word, which the LORD had [b]spoken by Ahijah the Shilonite to Jeroboam the son of Nebat.

16 Now when all Israel saw that the king did not listen to them, the people answered the king, saying:

> [a]"What share have we in David?
> *We have* no inheritance in the son of
> Jesse.
> To your tents, O Israel!
> Now, see to your own house, O David!"

So Israel departed to their tents.

17 But Rehoboam reigned over [a]the children of Israel who dwelt in the cities of Judah.

18 Then King Rehoboam [a]sent Adoram, who *was* in charge of the revenue; but all Israel stoned him with stones, and he died. Therefore King Rehoboam mounted his chariot in haste to flee to Jerusalem.

19 So [a]Israel has been in rebellion against the house of David to this day.

20 Now it came to pass when all Israel heard that Jeroboam had come back, they sent for him and called him to the congregation, and made him king over all [a]Israel. There was none who followed the house of David, but the tribe of Judah [b]only.

21 And when [a]Rehoboam came to Jerusalem, he assembled all the house of Judah with the tribe of [b]Benjamin, one hundred and eighty thousand chosen *men* who were warriors, to fight against the house of Israel, that he might restore the kingdom to Rehoboam the son of Solomon.

22 But [a]the word of God came to Shemaiah the man of God, saying,

23 "Speak to Rehoboam the son of Solomon, king of Judah, to all the house of Judah and Benjamin, and to the rest of the people, saying,

24 'Thus says the LORD: "You shall not go up nor fight against your brethren the children of Israel. Let every man return to his house, [a]for this thing is from Me." ' " Therefore they obeyed the word of the LORD, and turned back, according to the word of the LORD.

Jeroboam's Gold Calves

25 Then Jeroboam [a]built Shechem in the mountains of Ephraim, and dwelt there. Also he went out from there and built [b]Penuel.

26 And Jeroboam said in his heart, "Now the kingdom may return to the house of David:

27 "If these people [a]go up to offer sacrifices in the house of the LORD at Jerusalem, then the heart of this people will turn back to their lord,

*
12:11 Scourges with points or barbs, lit. *scorpions*
12:14 Lit. *scorpions*

KJV

even unto Rehoboam king of Judah, and they shall kill me, and go again to Rehoboam king of Judah.

28 Whereupon the king took counsel, and [a]made two calves *of* gold, and said unto them, It is too much for you to go up to Jerusalem: [b]behold thy gods, O Israel, which brought thee up out of the land of Egypt.

29 And he set the one in [a]Beth–el, and the other put he in [b]Dan.

30 And this thing became [a]a sin: for the people went *to worship* before the one, *even* unto Dan.

31 And he made an house of high places, [a]and made priests of the lowest of the people, which were not of the sons of Levi.

32 And Jeroboam ordained a feast in the eighth month, on the fifteenth day of the month, like unto [a]the feast that *is* in Judah, and he offered upon the altar. So did he in Beth–el, sacrificing unto the calves that he had made: [b]and he placed in Beth–el the priests of the high places which he had made.

33 So he offered upon the altar which he had made in Beth–el the fifteenth day of the eighth month, *even* in the month which he had [a]devised of his own heart; and ordained a feast unto the children of Israel: and he offered upon the altar, and [b]burnt incense.

The Message of the Man of God

13 And, behold, there [a]came a man of God out of Judah by the word of the LORD unto Beth–el: [b]and Jeroboam stood by the altar to burn incense.

2 And he cried against the altar in the word of the LORD, and said, O altar, altar, thus saith the LORD; Behold, a child shall be born unto the house of David, [a]Josiah by name; and upon thee shall he offer the priests of the high places that burn incense upon thee, and men's bones shall be [b]burnt upon thee.

3 And he gave [a]a sign the same day, saying, This *is* the sign which the LORD hath spoken; Behold, the altar shall be rent, and the ashes that *are* upon it shall be poured out.

4 And it came to pass, when king Jeroboam heard the saying of the man of God, which had cried against the altar in Beth–el, that he put forth his hand from the altar, saying, Lay hold on him. And his hand, which he put forth against him, dried up, so that he could not pull it in again to him.

5 The altar also was rent, and the ashes poured out from the altar, according to the sign which the man of God had given by the word of the LORD.

6 And the king answered and said unto the man of God, [a]Intreat now the face of the LORD thy God, and pray for me, that my hand may be restored me again. And the man of God besought the LORD, and the king's hand was restored him again, and became as *it was* before.

7 And the king said unto the man of God, Come home with me, and refresh thyself, and [a]I will give thee a reward.

8 And the man of God said unto the king, [a]If thou wilt give me half thine house, I will not go in with thee, neither will I eat bread nor drink water in this place:

9 For so was it charged me by the word of the LORD, saying, [a]Eat no bread, nor drink water, nor turn again by the same way that thou camest.

10 So he went another way, and returned not by the way that he came to Beth–el.

Death of the Man of God

11 Now there dwelt an [a]old prophet in Beth–el; and his sons came and told him all the works that the man of God had done that day in Beth–el: the words which he had spoken unto the king, them they told also to their father.

12 And their father said unto them, What

---

28 [a]2 Kin. 10:29; 17:16; [Hos. 8:4–7] [b]Ex. 32:4, 8
29 [a]Gen. 28:19 [b]Judg. 18:26–31
30 [a]1 Kin. 13:34; 2 Kin. 17:21
31 [a][Num. 3:10; 17:1–11]; Judg. 17:5; 1 Kin. 13:33; 2 Kin. 17:32; 2 Chr. 11:14, 15
32 [a]Lev. 23:33, 34; Num. 29:12; 1 Kin. 8:2, 5 [b]Amos 7:10–13
33 [a]Num. 15:39 [b]1 Kin. 13:1

CHAPTER 13

1 [a]2 Kin. 23:17 [b]1 Kin. 12:32, 33
2 [a]2 Kin. 23:15, 16 [b][Lev. 26:30]
3 [a]Ex. 4:1–5; Judg. 6:17; Is. 7:14; 38:7; John 2:18; 1 Cor. 1:22
6 [a]Ex. 8:8; 9:28; 10:17; Num. 21:7; Jer. 37:3; Acts 8:24; [James 5:16]
7 [a]1 Sam. 9:7; 2 Kin. 5:15
8 [a]Num. 22:18; 24:13; 1 Kin. 13:16, 17
9 [a][1 Cor. 5:11]
11 [a]1 Kin. 13:25

*

12:31 Lit. *a house;* cf. 1 Kin. 13:32, lit. houses

NKJV

Rehoboam king of Judah, and they will kill me and go back to Rehoboam king of Judah."

28 Therefore the king asked advice, [a]made two calves of gold, and said to the people, "It is too much for you to go up to Jerusalem. [b]Here are your gods, O Israel, which brought you up from the land of Egypt!"

29 And he set up one in [a]Bethel, and the other he put in [b]Dan.

30 Now this thing became [a]a sin, for the people went *to worship* before the one as far as Dan.

31 He made *shrines on the high places, [a]and made priests from every class of people, who were not of the sons of Levi.

32 Jeroboam ordained a feast on the fifteenth day of the eighth month, like [a]the feast that *was* in Judah, and offered sacrifices on the altar. So he did at Bethel, sacrificing to the calves that he had made. [b]And at Bethel he installed the priests of the high places which he had made.

33 So he made offerings on the altar which he had made at Bethel on the fifteenth day of the eighth month, in the month which he had [a]devised in his own heart. And he ordained a feast for the children of Israel, and offered sacrifices on the altar and [b]burned incense.

The Message of the Man of God

13 And behold, [a]a man of God went from Judah to Bethel by the word of the LORD, [b]and Jeroboam stood by the altar to burn incense.

2 Then he cried out against the altar by the word of the LORD, and said, "O altar, altar! Thus says the LORD: 'Behold, a child, [a]Josiah by name, shall be born to the house of David; and on you he shall sacrifice the priests of the high places who burn incense on you, and men's bones shall be [b]burned on you.' "

3 And he gave [a]a sign the same day, saying, "This *is* the sign which the LORD has spoken: Surely the altar shall split apart, and the ashes on it shall be poured out."

4 So it came to pass when King Jeroboam heard the saying of the man of God, who cried out against the altar in Bethel, that he stretched out his hand from the altar, saying, "Arrest him!" Then his hand, which he stretched out toward him, withered, so that he could not pull it back to himself.

5 The altar also was split apart, and the ashes poured out from the altar, according to the sign which the man of God had given by the word of the LORD.

6 Then the king answered and said to the man of God, "Please [a]entreat the favor of the LORD your God, and pray for me, that my hand may be restored to me." So the man of God entreated the LORD, and the king's hand was restored to him, and became as before.

7 Then the king said to the man of God, "Come home with me and refresh yourself, and [a]I will give you a reward."

8 But the man of God said to the king, [a]"If you were to give me half your house, I would not go in with you; nor would I eat bread nor drink water in this place.

9 "For so it was commanded me by the word of the LORD, saying, [a]'You shall not eat bread, nor drink water, nor return by the same way you came.' "

10 So he went another way and did not return by the way he came to Bethel.

Death of the Man of God

11 Now an [a]old prophet dwelt in Bethel, and his sons came and told him all the works that the man of God had done that day in Bethel; they also told their father the words which he had spoken to the king.

12 And their father said to them, "Which way

KJV

way went he? For his sons had seen what way the man of God went, which came from Judah.

13 And he said unto his sons, Saddle me the ass. So they saddled him the ass: and he rode thereon,

14 And went after the man of God, and found him sitting under an oak: and he said unto him, *Art* thou the man of God that camest from Judah? And he said, I *am*.

15 Then he said unto him, Come home with me, and eat bread.

16 And he said, [a]I may not return with thee, nor go in with thee: neither will I eat bread nor drink water with thee in this place:

17 For it was said to me [a]by the word of the LORD, Thou shalt eat no bread nor drink water there, nor turn again to go by the way that thou camest.

18 He said unto him, I *am* a prophet also as thou *art;* and an angel spake unto me by the word of the LORD, saying, Bring him back with thee into thine house, that he may eat bread and drink water. *But* he lied unto him.

19 So he went back with him, and did eat bread in his house, and drank water.

20 And it came to pass, as they sat at the table, that the word of the LORD came unto the prophet that brought him back:

21 And he cried unto the man of God that came from Judah, saying, Thus saith the LORD, Forasmuch as thou hast disobeyed the mouth of the LORD, and hast not kept the commandment which the LORD thy God commanded thee,

22 But camest back, and hast eaten bread and drunk water in the [a]place, of the which *the LORD* did say to thee, Eat no bread, and drink no water; thy carcase shall not come unto the sepulchre of thy fathers.

23 And it came to pass, after he had eaten bread, and after he had drunk, that he saddled for him the ass, *to wit,* for the prophet whom he had brought back.

24 And when he was gone, [a]a lion met him by the way, and slew him: and his carcase was cast in the way, and the ass stood by it, the lion also stood by the carcase.

25 And, behold, men passed by, and saw the carcase cast in the way, and the lion standing by the carcase: and they came and told *it* in the city where the old prophet dwelt.

26 And when the prophet that brought him back from the way heard *thereof,* he said, It *is* the man of God, who was disobedient unto the word of the LORD: therefore the LORD hath delivered him unto the lion, which hath torn him, and slain him, according to the word of the LORD, which he spake unto him.

27 And he spake to his sons, saying, Saddle me the ass. And they saddled *him.*

28 And he went and found his carcase cast in the way, and the ass and the lion standing by the carcase: the lion had not eaten the carcase, nor torn the ass.

29 And the prophet took up the carcase of the man of God, and laid it upon the ass, and brought it back: and the old prophet came to the city, to mourn and to bury him.

30 And he laid his carcase in his own grave; and they mourned over him, *saying,* [a]Alas, my brother!

31 And it came to pass, after he had buried him, that he spake to his sons, saying, When I am dead, then bury me in the sepulchre wherein the man of God *is* buried; [a]lay my bones beside his bones:

32 [a]For the saying which he cried by the word of the LORD against the altar in Beth–el, and against all the houses of the high places which *are* in the cities of [b]Samaria, shall surely come to pass.

33 [a]After this thing Jeroboam returned not from his evil way, but made again of the lowest

16 [a]1 Kin. 13:8, 9
17 [a]1 Kin. 20:35; 1 Thess. 4:15
22 [a]1 Kin. 13:9
24 [a]1 Kin. 20:36
30 [a]Jer. 22:18
31 [a]Ruth 1:17; 2 Kin. 23:17, 18
32 [a]1 Kin. 13:2; 2 Kin. 23:16, 19
[b]1 Kin. 16:24; John 4:5; Acts 8:14
33 [a]1 Kin. 12:31, 32; 2 Chr. 11:15; 13:9

NKJV

did he go?" For his sons *had seen which way the man of God went who came from Judah.

13 Then he said to his sons, "Saddle the donkey for me." So they saddled the donkey for him; and he rode on it,

14 and went after the man of God, and found him sitting under an oak. Then he said to him, "*Are* you the man of God who came from Judah?" And he said, "I *am.*"

15 Then he said to him, "Come home with me and eat bread."

16 And he said, [a]"I cannot return with you nor go in with you; neither can I eat bread nor drink water with you in this place.

17 "For I have been told [a]by the word of the LORD, 'You shall not eat bread nor drink water there, nor return by going the way you came.' "

18 He said to him, "I too *am* a prophet as you *are,* and an angel spoke to me by the word of the LORD, saying, 'Bring him back with you to your house, that he may eat bread and drink water.' " (He was lying to him.)

19 So he went back with him, and ate bread in his house, and drank water.

20 Now it happened, as they sat at the table, that the word of the LORD came to the prophet who had brought him back;

21 and he cried out to the man of God who came from Judah, saying, "Thus says the LORD: 'Because you have disobeyed the word of the LORD, and have not kept the commandment which the LORD your God commanded you,

22 'but you came back, ate bread, and drank water in the [a]place of which *the LORD* said to you, "Eat no bread and drink no water," your corpse shall not come to the tomb of your fathers.' "

23 So it was, after he had eaten bread and after he had drunk, that he saddled the donkey for him, the prophet whom he had brought back.

24 When he was gone, [a]a lion met him on the road and killed him. And his corpse was thrown on the road, and the donkey stood by it. The lion also stood by the corpse.

25 And there, men passed by and saw the corpse thrown on the road, and the lion standing by the corpse. Then they went and told *it* in the city where the old prophet dwelt.

26 Now when the prophet who had brought him back from the way heard *it,* he said, "It *is* the man of God who was disobedient to the word of the LORD. Therefore the LORD has delivered him to the lion, which has torn him and killed him, according to the word of the LORD which He spoke to him."

27 And he spoke to his sons, saying, "Saddle the donkey for me." So they saddled *it.*

28 Then he went and found his corpse thrown on the road, and the donkey and the lion standing by the corpse. The lion had not eaten the corpse nor torn the donkey.

29 And the prophet took up the corpse of the man of God, laid it on the donkey, and brought it back. So the old prophet came to the city to mourn, and to bury him.

30 Then he laid the corpse in his own tomb; and they mourned over him, *saying,* [a]"Alas, my brother!"

31 So it was, after he had buried him, that he spoke to his sons, saying, "When I am dead, then bury me in the tomb where the man of God *is* buried; [a]lay my bones beside his bones.

32 [a]"For the saying which he cried out by the word of the LORD against the altar in Bethel, and against all the *shrines on the high places which *are* in the cities of [b]Samaria, will surely come to pass."

33 [a]After this event Jeroboam did not turn from his evil way, but again he made priests from

*

13:12 LXX, Syr., Tg., Vg. *showed him*
13:32 Lit. *houses*

KJV

of the people priests of the high places: whosoever
would, he consecrated him, and he became *one*
of the priests of the high places.
34 [a]And this thing became sin unto the house
of Jeroboam, even [b]to cut *it* off, and to destroy
it from off the face of the earth.

Judgment on the House of Jeroboam

14 At that time Abijah the son of Jeroboam
fell sick.
2 And Jeroboam said to his wife, Arise, I
pray thee, and disguise thyself, that thou be not
known to be the wife of Jeroboam; and get thee
to Shiloh: behold, there *is* Ahijah the prophet,
which told me that [a]*I should be* king over this
people.
3 [a]And take with thee ten loaves, and crack-
nels, and a cruse of honey, and go to him: he shall
tell thee what shall become of the child.
4 And Jeroboam's wife did so, and arose,
[a]and went to Shiloh, and came to the house of
Ahijah. But Ahijah could not see; for his eyes were
set by reason of his age.
5 And the LORD said unto Ahijah, Behold,
the wife of Jeroboam cometh to ask a thing of
thee for her son; for he *is* sick: thus and thus shalt
thou say unto her: for it shall be, when she cometh
in, that she shall feign herself *to be* another
woman.
6 And it was *so,* when Ahijah heard the
sound of her feet, as she came in at the door, that
he said, Come in, thou wife of Jeroboam; why
feignest thou thyself *to be* another? for I *am* sent
to thee *with* heavy *tidings.*
7 Go, tell Jeroboam, Thus saith the LORD
God of Israel, [a]Forasmuch as I exalted thee from
among the people, and made thee prince over my
people Israel,
8 And [a]rent the kingdom away from the
house of David, and gave it thee: and *yet* thou
hast not been as my servant David, [b]who kept
my commandments, and who followed me with
all his heart, to do *that* only *which was* right in
mine eyes;
9 But hast done evil above all that were before thee: [a]for thou hast gone and made thee other
gods, and molten images, to provoke me to anger,
and [b]hast cast me behind thy back:
10 Therefore, behold, [a]I will bring evil upon
the house of Jeroboam, and [b]will cut off from Jeroboam him that pisseth against the wall, [c]*and* him
that is shut up and left in Israel, and will take
away the remnant of the house of Jeroboam, as
a man taketh away dung, till it be all gone.
11 [a]Him that dieth of Jeroboam in the city
shall the dogs eat; and him that dieth in the field
shall the fowls of the air eat: for the LORD hath
spoken *it.*
12 Arise thou therefore, get thee to thine own
house: *and* [a]when thy feet enter into the city, the
child shall die.
13 And all Israel shall mourn for him, and
bury him: for he only of Jeroboam shall come to
the grave, because in him [a]there is found *some*
good thing toward the LORD God of Israel in the
house of Jeroboam.
14 [a]Moreover the LORD shall raise him up a
king over Israel, who shall cut off the house of
Jeroboam that day: but what? even now.
15 For the LORD shall smite Israel, as a reed
is shaken in the water, and he shall [a]root up Israel
out of this [b]good land, which he gave to their fathers, and shall scatter them [c]beyond the river,
[d]because they have made their groves, provoking
the LORD to anger.
16 And he shall give Israel up because of the
sins of Jeroboam, [a]who did sin, and who made
Israel to sin.
17 And Jeroboam's wife arose, and departed,
and came to [a]Tirzah: *and* [b]when she came to the
threshold of the door, the child died;
18 And they buried him; and all Israel

34 [a]1 Kin. 12:30; 2 Kin. 17:21 [b][1 Kin. 14:10; 15:29, 30]

CHAPTER 14

2 [a]1 Kin. 11:29–31
3 [a]1 Sam. 9:7, 8; 1 Kin. 13:7; 2 Kin. 4:42
4 [a]1 Kin. 11:29
7 [a]2 Sam. 12:7, 8; 1 Kin. 16:2
8 [a]1 Kin. 11:31 [b]1 Kin. 11:33, 38; 15:5
9 [a]1 Kin. 12:28; 2 Chr. 11:15 [b]2 Chr. 29:6; Neh. 9:26; Ps. 50:17
10 [a]1 Kin. 15:29 [b]1 Kin. 21:21; 2 Kin. 9:8 [c]Deut. 32:36; 2 Kin. 14:26
11 [a]1 Kin. 16:4; 21:24
12 [a]1 Kin. 14:17
13 [a]2 Chr. 12:12; 19:3
14 [a]1 Kin. 15:27–29
15 [a]Deut. 29:28; 2 Kin. 17:6; Ps. 52:5 [b][Josh. 23:15, 16] [c]2 Kin. 15:29 [d][Ex. 34:13, 14; Deut. 12:3]
16 [a]1 Kin. 12:30; 13:34; 15:30, 34; 16:2
17 [a]1 Kin. 15:21, 33; 16:6, 8, 15, 23; Song 6:4 [b]1 Kin. 14:12

NKJV

every class of people for the high places; whoever
wished, he consecrated him, and he became *one*
of the priests of the high places.
34 [a]And this thing was the sin of the house
of Jeroboam, so as [b]to exterminate and destroy
it from the face of the earth.

Judgment on the House of Jeroboam

14 At that time Abijah the son of Jeroboam
became sick.
2 And Jeroboam said to his wife, "Please
arise, and disguise yourself, that they may not recognize you as the wife of Jeroboam, and go to
Shiloh. Indeed, Ahijah the prophet *is* there, who
told me that [a]*I would be* king over this people.
3 [a]"Also take with you ten loaves, *some*
cakes, and a jar of honey, and go to him; he will
tell you what will become of the child."
4 And Jeroboam's wife did so; she arose
[a]and went to Shiloh, and came to the house of
Ahijah. But Ahijah could not see, for his eyes were
glazed by reason of his age.
5 Now the LORD had said to Ahijah, "Here
is the wife of Jeroboam, coming to ask you something about her son, for he *is* sick. Thus and thus
you shall say to her; for it will be, when she comes
in, that she will pretend *to be* another *woman.*"
6 And so it was, when Ahijah heard the
sound of her footsteps as she came through the
door, he said, "Come in, wife of Jeroboam. Why
do you pretend *to be* another *person?* For I *have
been* sent to you *with* bad *news.*
7 "Go, tell Jeroboam, 'Thus says the LORD
God of Israel: [a]"Because I exalted you from
among the people, and made you ruler over My
people Israel,
8 "and [a]tore the kingdom away from the
house of David, and gave it to you; and *yet* you
have not been as My servant David, [b]who kept
My commandments and who followed Me with
all his heart, to do only *what was* right in My
eyes;
9 "but you have done more evil than all who
were before you, [a]for you have gone and made
for yourself other gods and molded images to provoke Me to anger, and [b]have cast Me behind your
back—
10 "therefore behold! [a]I will bring disaster
on the house of Jeroboam, and [b]will cut off from
Jeroboam every male in Israel, [c]bond and free; I
will take away the remnant of the house of Jeroboam, as one takes away refuse until it is all gone.
11 "The dogs shall eat [a]whoever belongs to
Jeroboam and dies in the city, and the birds of
the air shall eat whoever dies in the field; for the
LORD has spoken!" '
12 "Arise therefore, go to your own house.
[a]When your feet enter the city, the child shall die.
13 "And all Israel shall mourn for him and
bury him, for he is the only one of Jeroboam who
shall come to the grave, because in him [a]there is
found something good toward the LORD God of
Israel in the house of Jeroboam.
14 [a]"Moreover the LORD will raise up for
Himself a king over Israel who shall cut off the
house of Jeroboam; this is the day. What? Even
now!
15 "For the LORD will strike Israel, as a reed
is shaken in the water. He will [a]uproot Israel from
this [b]good land which He gave to their fathers,
and will scatter them [c]beyond *the River, [d]be-
cause they have made their *wooden images, provoking the LORD to anger.
16 "And He will give Israel up because of the
sins of Jeroboam, [a]who sinned and who made Israel sin."
17 Then Jeroboam's wife arose and departed,
and came to [a]Tirzah. [b]When she came to the
threshold of the house, the child died.
18 And they buried him; and all Israel

*
14:15 The Euphrates • Heb. *Asherim,* Canaanite deities

KJV

mourned for him, [a]according to the word of the
LORD, which he spake by the hand of his servant
Ahijah the prophet.

Death of Jeroboam

19 And the rest of the acts of Jeroboam, how
he [a]warred, and how he reigned, behold, they *are*
written in the book of the chronicles of the kings
of Israel.
20 And the days which Jeroboam reigned
were two and twenty years: and he slept with his
fathers, and [a]Nadab his son reigned in his stead.

Rehoboam Reigns in Judah
(2 Chr. 11:5—12:16)

21 And Rehoboam the son of Solomon
reigned in Judah. [a]Rehoboam *was* forty and one
years old when he began to reign, and he reigned
seventeen years in Jerusalem, the city [b]which the
LORD did choose out of all the tribes of Israel, to
put his name there. [c]And his mother's name *was*
Naamah an Ammonitess.
22 [a]And Judah did evil in the sight of the
LORD, and they [b]provoked him to jealousy with
their sins which they had committed, above all
that their fathers had done.
23 For they also built them [a]high places, and
[b]images, [c]and groves, on every high hill, and [d]under every green tree.
24 [a]And there were also sodomites in the
land: *and* they did according to all the [b]abominations of the nations which the LORD cast out before the children of [c]Israel.
25 [a]And it came to pass in the fifth year of
king Rehoboam, *that* Shishak king of Egypt came
up against Jerusalem:
26 [a]And he took away the treasures of the
house of the LORD, and the treasures of the king's
house; he even took away all: and he took away
all the shields of gold [b]which Solomon had made.
27 And king Rehoboam made in their stead
brasen shields, and committed *them* unto the
hands of the chief of the guard, which kept the
door of the king's house.
28 And it was *so*, when the king went into
the house of the LORD, that the guard bare them,
and brought them back into the guard chamber.
29 [a]Now the rest of the acts of Rehoboam,
and all that he did, *are* they not written in the
book of the chronicles of the kings of Judah?
30 And there was [a]war between Rehoboam
and Jeroboam all *their* days.
31 [a]And Rehoboam slept with his fathers,
and was buried with his fathers in the city of David. [b]And his mother's name *was* Naamah an Ammonitess. And [c]Abijam his son reigned in his
stead.

Abijam Reigns in Judah
(2 Chr. 13:1—14:1)

15 Now [a]in the eighteenth year of king Jeroboam the son of Nebat reigned Abijam over
Judah.
2 Three years reigned he in Jerusalem.
[a]And his mother's name *was* [b]Maachah, the
daughter of [c]Abishalom.
3 And he walked in all the sins of his father,
which he had done before him: and [a]his heart
was not perfect with the LORD his God, as the
heart of David his father.
4 Nevertheless [a]for David's sake did the
LORD his God give him a lamp in Jerusalem, to
set up his son after him, and to establish
Jerusalem:
5 Because David [a]did *that which was* right
in the eyes of the LORD, and turned not aside from
any *thing* that he commanded him all the days
of his life, [b]save only in the matter of Uriah the
Hittite.
6 [a]And there was war between Rehoboam
and Jeroboam all the days of his life.

18 [a]1 Kin. 14:13
19 [a]1 Kin. 14:30; 2 Chr. 13:2–20
20 [a]1 Kin. 15:25
21 [a]2 Chr. 12:13 [b]1 Kin. 11:32, 36 [c]1 Kin. 14:31
22 [a]2 Chr. 12:1, 14 [b]Deut. 32:21; Ps. 78:58; 1 Cor. 10:22
23 [a]Deut. 12:2; Ezek. 16:24, 25 [b][Deut. 16:22] [c][2 Kin. 17:9, 10] [d]Is. 57:5; Jer. 2:20
24 [a]Gen. 19:5; Deut. 23:17; 1 Kin. 15:12; 22:46; 2 Kin. 23:7 [b]Deut. 20:18 [c][Deut. 9:4, 5]
25 [a]1 Kin. 11:40; 2 Chr. 12:2
26 [a]1 Kin. 15:18; 2 Chr. 12:9–11 [b]1 Kin. 10:17
29 [a]2 Chr. 12:15, 16
30 [a]1 Kin. 12:21–24; 15:6
31 [a]2 Chr. 12:16 [b]1 Kin. 14:21 [c]2 Chr. 12:16

CHAPTER 15

1 [a]2 Chr. 13:1
2 [a]2 Chr. 11:20–22 [b]2 Chr. 13:2 [c]2 Chr. 11:21
3 [a]1 Kin. 11:4; Ps. 119:80
4 [a]2 Sam. 21:17; 1 Kin. 11:32, 36; 2 Chr. 21:7
5 [a]1 Kin. 9:4; 14:8; Luke 1:6 [b]2 Sam. 11:3, 15–17; 12:9, 10
6 [a]1 Kin. 14:30; 2 Chr. 12:15—13:20

*

14:24 Heb. *qadesh*, one practicing sodomy and prostitution in religious rituals
14:31 *Abijah*, 2 Chr. 12:16
15:6 So with MT, LXX, Tg., Vg.; some Heb. mss., Syr. *Abijam*

NKJV

mourned for him, [a]according to the word of the
LORD which He spoke through His servant Ahijah
the prophet.

Death of Jeroboam

19 Now the rest of the acts of Jeroboam, how
he [a]made war and how he reigned, indeed they
are written in the book of the chronicles of the
kings of Israel.
20 The period that Jeroboam reigned *was*
twenty-two years. So he rested with his fathers.
Then [a]Nadab his son reigned in his place.

Rehoboam Reigns in Judah
(2 Chr. 11:5—12:16)

21 And Rehoboam the son of Solomon
reigned in Judah. [a]Rehoboam *was* forty-one years
old when he became king. He reigned seventeen
years in Jerusalem, the city [b]which the LORD had
chosen out of all the tribes of Israel, to put His
name there. [c]His mother's name *was* Naamah, an
Ammonitess.
22 [a]Now Judah did evil in the sight of the
LORD, and they [b]provoked Him to jealousy with
their sins which they committed, more than all
that their fathers had done.
23 For they also built for themselves [a]high
places, [b]*sacred* pillars, and [c]wooden images on
every high hill and [d]under every green tree.
24 [a]And there were also *perverted persons
in the land. They did according to all the [b]abominations of the nations which the LORD had cast
out before the children of [c]Israel.
25 [a]It happened in the fifth year of King Rehoboam *that* Shishak king of Egypt came up
against Jerusalem.
26 [a]And he took away the treasures of the
house of the LORD and the treasures of the king's
house; he took away everything. He also took
away all the gold shields [b]which Solomon had
made.
27 Then King Rehoboam made bronze
shields in their place, and committed *them* to the
hands of the captains of the guard, who guarded
the doorway of the king's house.
28 And whenever the king entered the house
of the LORD, the guards carried them, then brought
them back into the guardroom.
29 [a]Now the rest of the acts of Rehoboam,
and all that he did, *are* they not written in the
book of the chronicles of the kings of Judah?
30 And there was [a]war between Rehoboam
and Jeroboam all *their* days.
31 [a]So Rehoboam rested with his fathers,
and was buried with his fathers in the City of David. [b]His mother's name *was* Naamah, an Ammonitess. Then [c]Abijam* his son reigned in his
place.

Abijam Reigns in Judah
(2 Chr. 13:1—14:1)

15 [a]In the eighteenth year of King Jeroboam the son of Nebat, Abijam became king over
Judah.
2 He reigned three years in Jerusalem. [a]His
mother's name *was* [b]Maachah the granddaughter
of [c]Abishalom.
3 And he walked in all the sins of his father,
which he had done before him; [a]his heart was
not loyal to the LORD his God, as was the heart
of his father David.
4 Nevertheless [a]for David's sake the LORD
his God gave him a lamp in Jerusalem, by setting
up his son after him and by establishing
Jerusalem;
5 because David [a]did *what was* right in the
eyes of the LORD, and had not turned aside from
anything that He commanded him all the days
of his life, [b]except in the matter of Uriah the
Hittite.
6 [a]And there was war between *Rehoboam
and Jeroboam all the days of his life.

KJV

7 [a]Now the rest of the acts of Abijam, and
all that he did, *are* they not written in the book
of the chronicles of the kings of Judah? And there
was war between Abijam and Jeroboam.
8 [a]And Abijam slept with his fathers; and
they buried him in the city of David: and Asa his
son reigned in his stead.

Asa Reigns in Judah
(*2 Chr. 14:1—16:14*)

9 And in the twentieth year of Jeroboam
king of Israel reigned Asa over Judah.
10 And forty and one years reigned he in Jerusalem. And his mother's name *was* Maachah,
the daughter of Abishalom.
11 [a]And Asa did *that which was* right in the
eyes of the LORD, as *did* David his father.
12 [a]And he took away the sodomites out of
the land, and removed all the idols that his fathers
had made.
13 And also [a]Maachah his mother, even her
he removed from *being* queen, because she had
made an idol in a grove; and Asa destroyed her
idol, and [b]burnt *it* by the brook Kidron.
14 [a]But the high places were not removed:
nevertheless Asa's [b]heart was perfect with the
LORD all his days.
15 And he brought in the things which his
father [a]had dedicated, and the things which himself had dedicated, into the house of the LORD,
silver, and gold, and vessels.
16 And there was war between Asa and Baasha king of Israel all their days.
17 And [a]Baasha king of Israel went up
against Judah, and built [b]Ramah, [c]that he might
not suffer any to go out or come in to Asa king
of Judah.
18 Then Asa took all the silver and the gold
that were left in the treasures of the house of the
LORD, and the treasures of the king's house, and
delivered them into the hand of his servants: and
king Asa sent them to [a]Ben–hadad, the son of
Tabrimon, the son of Hezion, king of Syria, that
dwelt at [b]Damascus, saying,
19 *There is* a league between me and thee,
and between my father and thy father: behold, I
have sent unto thee a present of silver and gold;
come and break thy league with Baasha king of
Israel, that he may depart from me.
20 So Ben–hadad hearkened unto king Asa,
and [a]sent the captains of the hosts which he had
against the cities of Israel, and smote [b]Ijon, and
[c]Dan, and [d]Abel–beth–maachah, and all Cinne-
roth, with all the land of Naphtali.
21 And it came to pass, when Baasha heard
thereof, that he left off building of Ramah, and
dwelt in [a]Tirzah.
22 [a]Then king Asa made a proclamation
throughout all Judah; none *was* exempted: and
they took away the stones of Ramah, and the timber thereof, wherewith Baasha had builded; and
king Asa built with them [b]Geba of Benjamin, and
[c]Mizpah.
23 The rest of all the acts of Asa, and all his
might, and all that he did, and the cities which
he built, *are* they not written in the book of the
chronicles of the kings of Judah? Nevertheless [a]in
the time of his old age he was diseased in his
feet.
24 And Asa slept with his fathers, and was
buried with his fathers in the city of David his
father: [a]and [b]Jehoshaphat his son reigned in his
stead.

Nadab Reigns in Israel

25 And [a]Nadab the son of Jeroboam began
to reign over Israel in the second year of Asa king
of Judah, and reigned over Israel two years.
26 And he did evil in the sight of the LORD,
and walked in the way of his father, and in [a]his
sin wherewith he made Israel to sin.
27 [a]And Baasha the son of Ahijah, of the

7 [a]2 Chr. 13:2–22
8 [a]2 Chr. 14:1
11 [a]2 Chr. 14:2
12 [a]Deut. 23:17; 1 Kin. 14:24; 22:46
13 [a]2 Chr. 15:16–18 [b]Ex. 32:20
14 [a]1 Kin. 3:2; 22:43; 2 Kin. 12:3; 2 Chr. 15:17, 18 [b][1 Sam. 16:7]; 1 Kin. 8:61; 15:3
15 [a]1 Kin. 7:51
17 [a]2 Chr. 16:1–6 [b]Josh. 18:25; 1 Kin. 15:21, 22 [c]1 Kin. 12:26–29
18 [a]2 Kin. 12:17, 18; 2 Chr. 16:2 [b]Gen. 14:15; 1 Kin. 11:23, 24
20 [a]1 Kin. 20:1 [b]2 Kin. 15:29 [c]Judg. 18:29; 1 Kin. 12:29 [d]2 Sam. 20:14, 15
21 [a]1 Kin. 14:17; 16:15–18
22 [a]2 Chr. 16:6 [b]Josh. 21:17 [c]Josh. 18:26
23 [a]2 Chr. 16:11–14
24 [a]2 Chr. 17:1 [b]1 Kin. 22:41–44; Matt. 1:8
25 [a]1 Kin. 14:20
26 [a]1 Kin. 12:28–33; 14:16
27 [a]1 Kin. 14:14

15:12 Heb. *qedeshim*, those practicing sodomy and prostitution in religious rituals
15:13 A Canaanite goddess

NKJV

7 [a]Now the rest of the acts of Abijam, and
all that he did, *are* they not written in the book
of the chronicles of the kings of Judah? And there
was war between Abijam and Jeroboam.
8 [a]So Abijam rested with his fathers, and
they buried him in the City of David. Then Asa
his son reigned in his place.

Asa Reigns in Judah
(*2 Chr. 14:1—16:14*)

9 In the twentieth year of Jeroboam king
of Israel, Asa became king over Judah.
10 And he reigned forty-one years in Jerusalem. His grandmother's name *was* Maachah the
granddaughter of Abishalom.
11 [a]Asa did *what was* right in the eyes of
the LORD, as *did* his father David.
12 [a]And he banished the *perverted persons
from the land, and removed all the idols that his
fathers had made.
13 Also he removed [a]Maachah his grandmother from *being* queen mother, because she
had made an obscene image of *Asherah. And
Asa cut down her obscene image and [b]burned *it*
by the Brook Kidron.
14 [a]But the high places were not removed.
Nevertheless Asa's [b]heart was loyal to the LORD
all his days.
15 He also brought into the house of the LORD
the things which his father [a]had dedicated, and
the things which he himself had dedicated: silver
and gold and utensils.
16 Now there was war between Asa and Baasha king of Israel all their days.
17 And [a]Baasha king of Israel came up
against Judah, and built [b]Ramah, [c]that he might
let none go out or come in to Asa king of Judah.
18 Then Asa took all the silver and gold *that
was* left in the treasuries of the house of the LORD
and the treasuries of the king's house, and delivered them into the hand of his servants. And King
Asa sent them to [a]Ben-Hadad the son of Tabrim-
mon, the son of Hezion, king of Syria, who dwelt
in [b]Damascus, saying,
19 "*Let there be* a treaty between you and
me, as there was between my father and your father. See, I have sent you a present of silver and
gold. Come and break your treaty with Baasha
king of Israel, so that he will withdraw from me."
20 So Ben-Hadad heeded King Asa, and
[a]sent the captains of his armies against the cities
of Israel. He attacked [b]Ijon, [c]Dan, [d]Abel Beth
Maachah, and all Chinneroth, with all the land
of Naphtali.
21 Now it happened, when Baasha heard *it*,
that he stopped building Ramah, and remained
in [a]Tirzah.
22 [a]Then King Asa made a proclamation
throughout all Judah; none *was* exempted. And
they took away the stones and timber of Ramah,
which Baasha had used for building; and with
them King Asa built [b]Geba of Benjamin, and
[c]Mizpah.
23 The rest of all the acts of Asa, all his
might, all that he did, and the cities which he built,
are they not written in the book of the chronicles
of the kings of Judah? But [a]in the time of his old
age he was diseased in his feet.
24 So Asa rested with his fathers, and was
buried with his fathers in the City of David his
father. [a]Then [b]Jehoshaphat his son reigned in his
place.

Nadab Reigns in Israel

25 Now [a]Nadab the son of Jeroboam became
king over Israel in the second year of Asa king
of Judah, and he reigned over Israel two years.
26 And he did evil in the sight of the LORD,
and walked in the way of his father, and in [a]his
sin by which he had made Israel sin.
27 [a]Then Baasha the son of Ahijah, of the

KJV

house of Issachar, conspired against him; and Baasha smote him at [b]Gibbethon, which *belonged* to the Philistines; for Nadab and all Israel laid siege to Gibbethon.

28 Even in the third year of Asa king of Judah did Baasha slay him, and reigned in his stead.

29 And it came to pass, when he reigned, *that* he smote all the house of Jeroboam; he left not to Jeroboam any that breathed, until he had destroyed him, according unto [a]the saying of the LORD, which he spake by his servant Ahijah the Shilonite:

30 [a]Because of the sins of Jeroboam which he sinned, and which he made Israel sin, by his provocation wherewith he provoked the LORD God of Israel to anger.

31 Now the rest of the acts of Nadab, and all that he did, *are* they not written in the book of the chronicles of the kings of Israel?

32 [a]And there was war between Asa and Baasha king of Israel all their days.

Baasha Reigns in Israel

33 In the third year of Asa king of Judah began Baasha the son of Ahijah to reign over all Israel in Tirzah, twenty and four years.

34 And he did evil in the sight of the LORD, and walked in [a]the way of Jeroboam, and in his sin wherewith he made Israel to sin.

16 Then the word of the LORD came to [a]Jehu the son of [b]Hanani against [c]Baasha, saying,

2 [a]Forasmuch as I exalted thee out of the dust, and made thee prince over my people Israel; and [b]thou hast walked in the way of Jeroboam, and hast made my people Israel to sin, to provoke me to anger with their sins;

3 Behold, I will [a]take away the posterity of Baasha, and the posterity of his house; and will make thy house like [b]the house of Jeroboam the son of Nebat.

4 [a]Him that dieth of Baasha in the city shall the dogs eat; and him that dieth of his in the fields shall the fowls of the air eat.

5 Now the rest of the acts of Baasha, and what he did, and his might, [a]*are* they not written in the book of the chronicles of the kings of Israel?

6 So Baasha slept with his fathers, and was buried in [a]Tirzah: and Elah his son reigned in his stead.

7 And also by the hand of the prophet [a]Jehu the son of Hanani came the word of the LORD against Baasha, and against his house, even for all the evil that he did in the sight of the LORD, in provoking him to anger with the work of his hands, in being like the house of Jeroboam; and because [b]he killed him.

Elah Reigns in Israel

8 In the twenty and sixth year of Asa king of Judah began Elah the son of Baasha to reign over Israel in Tirzah, two years.

9 [a]And his servant Zimri, captain of half *his* chariots, conspired against him, as he was in Tirzah, drinking himself drunk in the house of Arza [b]steward of *his* house in Tirzah.

10 And Zimri went in and smote him, and killed him, in the twenty and seventh year of Asa king of Judah, and reigned in his stead.

11 And it came to pass, when he began to reign, as soon as he sat on his throne, *that* he slew all the house of Baasha: he left him [a]not one that pisseth against a wall, neither of his kinsfolks, nor of his friends.

12 Thus did Zimri destroy all the house of Baasha, [a]according to the word of the LORD, which he spake against Baasha by Jehu the prophet,

13 For all the sins of Baasha, and the sins of Elah his son, by which they sinned, and by which

27 [b]Josh. 19:44; 21:23; 1 Kin. 16:15
29 [a]1 Kin. 14:10–14
30 [a]1 Kin. 14:9, 16
32 [a]1 Kin. 15:16
34 [a]1 Kin. 13:33; 14:16

CHAPTER 16
1 [a]1 Kin. 16:7; 2 Chr. 19:2; 20:34 [b]2 Chr. 16:7–10 [c]1 Kin. 15:27
2 [a]1 Sam. 2:8; 1 Kin. 14:7 [b]1 Kin. 12:25–33; 15:34
3 [a]1 Kin. 16:11; 21:21 [b]1 Kin. 14:10; 15:29
4 [a]1 Kin. 14:11; 21:24
5 [a]2 Chr. 16:11
6 [a]1 Kin. 14:17; 15:21
7 [a]1 Kin. 16:1 [b]1 Kin. 15:27, 29
9 [a]2 Kin. 9:30–33 [b]Gen. 24:2; 39:4; 1 Kin. 18:3
11 [a]1 Sam. 25:22
12 [a]1 Kin. 16:3

NKJV

house of Issachar, conspired against him. And Baasha killed him at [b]Gibbethon, which *belonged* to the Philistines, while Nadab and all Israel laid siege to Gibbethon.

28 Baasha killed him in the third year of Asa king of Judah, and reigned in his place.

29 And it was so, when he became king, *that* he killed all the house of Jeroboam. He did not leave to Jeroboam anyone that breathed, until he had destroyed him, according to [a]the word of the LORD which He had spoken by His servant Ahijah the Shilonite,

30 [a]because of the sins of Jeroboam, which he had sinned and by which he had made Israel sin, because of his provocation with which he had provoked the LORD God of Israel to anger.

31 Now the rest of the acts of Nadab, and all that he did, *are* they not written in the book of the chronicles of the kings of Israel?

32 [a]And there was war between Asa and Baasha king of Israel all their days.

Baasha Reigns in Israel

33 In the third year of Asa king of Judah, Baasha the son of Ahijah became king over all Israel in Tirzah, and *reigned* twenty-four years.

34 He did evil in the sight of the LORD, and walked in [a]the way of Jeroboam, and in his sin by which he had made Israel sin.

16 Then the word of the LORD came to [a]Jehu the son of [b]Hanani, against [c]Baasha, saying:

2 [a]"Inasmuch as I lifted you out of the dust and made you ruler over My people Israel, and [b]you have walked in the way of Jeroboam, and have made My people Israel sin, to provoke Me to anger with their sins,

3 "surely I will [a]take away the posterity of Baasha and the posterity of his house, and I will make your house like [b]the house of Jeroboam the son of Nebat.

4 "The dogs shall eat [a]whoever belongs to Baasha and dies in the city, and the birds of the air shall eat whoever dies in the fields."

5 Now the rest of the acts of Baasha, what he did, and his might, [a]*are* they not written in the book of the chronicles of the kings of Israel?

6 So Baasha rested with his fathers and was buried in [a]Tirzah. Then Elah his son reigned in his place.

7 And also the word of the LORD came by the prophet [a]Jehu the son of Hanani against Baasha and his house, because of all the evil that he did in the sight of the LORD in provoking Him to anger with the work of his hands, in being like the house of Jeroboam, and because [b]he killed them.

Elah Reigns in Israel

8 In the twenty-sixth year of Asa king of Judah, Elah the son of Baasha became king over Israel, *and reigned* two years in Tirzah.

9 [a]Now his servant Zimri, commander of half *his* chariots, conspired against him as he was in Tirzah drinking himself drunk in the house of Arza, [b]steward of *his* house in Tirzah.

10 And Zimri went in and struck him and killed him in the twenty-seventh year of Asa king of Judah, and reigned in his place.

11 Then it came to pass, when he began to reign, as soon as he was seated on his throne, *that* he killed all the household of Baasha; he [a]did not leave him one male, neither of his relatives nor of his friends.

12 Thus Zimri destroyed all the household of Baasha, [a]according to the word of the LORD, which He spoke against Baasha by Jehu the prophet,

13 for all the sins of Baasha and the sins of Elah his son, by which they had sinned and by

KJV

they made Israel to sin, in provoking the LORD God of Israel to anger [a]with their vanities.

14 Now the rest of the acts of Elah, and all that he did, *are* they not written in the book of the chronicles of the kings of Israel?

Zimri Reigns in Israel

15 In the twenty and seventh year of Asa king of Judah did Zimri reign seven days in Tirzah. And the people *were* encamped [a]against Gibbethon, which *belonged* to the Philistines.

16 And the people *that were* encamped heard say, Zimri hath conspired, and hath also slain the king: wherefore all Israel made Omri, the captain of the host, king over Israel that day in the camp.

17 And Omri went up from Gibbethon, and all Israel with him, and they besieged Tirzah.

18 And it came to pass, when Zimri saw that the city was taken, that he went into the palace of the king's house, and burnt the king's house over him with fire, and died,

19 For his sins which he sinned in doing evil in the sight of the LORD, [a]in walking in the [b]way of Jeroboam, and in his sin which he did, to make Israel to sin.

20 Now the rest of the acts of Zimri, and his treason that he wrought, *are* they not written in the book of the chronicles of the kings of Israel?

Omri Reigns in Israel

21 Then were the people of Israel divided into two parts: half of the people followed Tibni the son of Ginath, to make him king; and half followed Omri.

22 But the people that followed Omri prevailed against the people that followed Tibni the son of Ginath: so Tibni died, and Omri reigned.

23 In the thirty and first year of Asa king of Judah began Omri to reign over Israel, twelve years: six years reigned he in [a]Tirzah.

24 And he bought the hill Samaria of Shemer for two talents of silver, and built on the hill, and called the name of the city which he built, after the name of Shemer, owner of the hill, [a]Samaria.

25 But [a]Omri wrought evil in the eyes of the LORD, and did worse than all that *were* before him.

26 For he [a]walked in all the way of Jeroboam the son of Nebat, and in his sin wherewith he made Israel to sin, to provoke the LORD God of Israel to anger with their [b]vanities.

27 Now the rest of the acts of Omri which he did, and his might that he shewed, *are* they not written in the book of the chronicles of the kings of Israel?

28 So Omri slept with his fathers, and was buried in Samaria: and Ahab his son reigned in his stead.

Ahab Reigns in Israel

29 And in the thirty and eighth year of Asa king of Judah began Ahab the son of Omri to reign over Israel: and Ahab the son of Omri reigned over Israel in Samaria twenty and two years.

30 And Ahab the son of Omri did evil in the sight of the LORD above all that *were* before him.

31 And it came to pass, as if it had been a light thing for him to walk in the sins of Jeroboam the son of Nebat, [a]that he took to wife Jezebel the daughter of Ethbaal king of the [b]Zidonians, [c]and went and served Baal, and worshipped him.

32 And he reared up an altar for Baal in [a]the house of Baal, which he had built in Samaria.

33 [a]And Ahab made a grove; and Ahab [b]did more to provoke the LORD God of Israel to anger than all the kings of Israel that were before him.

34 In his days did Hiel the Beth–elite build Jericho: he laid the foundation thereof in Abiram

13 [a]Deut. 32:21; 1 Sam. 12:21; [Is. 41:29; Jon. 2:8; 1 Cor. 8:4; 10:19]
15 [a]1 Kin. 15:27
19 [a]1 Kin. 15:26, 34 [b]1 Kin. 12:25–33
23 [a]1 Kin. 15:21; 2 Kin. 15:14
24 [a]1 Kin. 13:32; 2 Kin. 17:24; John 4:4
25 [a]Mic. 6:16
26 [a]1 Kin. 16:19 [b]1 Kin. 16:13
31 [a]Deut. 7:3 [b]Judg. 18:7; 1 Kin. 11:1–5 [c]1 Kin. 21:25, 26; 2 Kin. 10:18; 17:16
32 [a]2 Kin. 10:21, 26, 27
33 [a]2 Kin. 13:6 [b]1 Kin. 14:9; 16:29, 30; 21:25

NKJV

which they had made Israel sin, in provoking the LORD God of Israel to anger [a]with their idols.

14 Now the rest of the acts of Elah, and all that he did, *are* they not written in the book of the chronicles of the kings of Israel?

Zimri Reigns in Israel

15 In the twenty-seventh year of Asa king of Judah, Zimri had reigned in Tirzah seven days. And the people *were* encamped [a]against Gibbethon, which *belonged* to the Philistines.

16 Now the people *who were* encamped heard it said, "Zimri has conspired and also has killed the king." So all Israel made Omri, the commander of the army, king over Israel that day in the camp.

17 Then Omri and all Israel with him went up from Gibbethon, and they besieged Tirzah.

18 And it happened, when Zimri saw that the city was taken, that he went into the citadel of the king's house and burned the king's house down upon himself with fire, and died,

19 because of the sins which he had committed in doing evil in the sight of the LORD, [a]in walking in the [b]way of Jeroboam, and in his sin which he had committed to make Israel sin.

20 Now the rest of the acts of Zimri, and the treason he committed, *are* they not written in the book of the chronicles of the kings of Israel?

Omri Reigns in Israel

21 Then the people of Israel were divided into two parts: half of the people followed Tibni the son of Ginath, to make him king, and half followed Omri.

22 But the people who followed Omri prevailed over the people who followed Tibni the son of Ginath. So Tibni died and Omri reigned.

23 In the thirty-first year of Asa king of Judah, Omri became king over Israel, *and reigned* twelve years. Six years he reigned in [a]Tirzah.

24 And he bought the hill of Samaria from Shemer for two talents of silver; then he built on the hill, and called the name of the city which he built, [a]Samaria, after the name of Shemer, owner of the hill.

25 [a]Omri did evil in the eyes of the LORD, and did worse than all who *were* before him.

26 For he [a]walked in all the ways of Jeroboam the son of Nebat, and in his sin by which he had made Israel sin, provoking the LORD God of Israel to anger with their [b]idols.

27 Now the rest of the acts of Omri which he did, and the might that he showed, *are* they not written in the book of the chronicles of the kings of Israel?

28 So Omri rested with his fathers and was buried in Samaria. Then Ahab his son reigned in his place.

Ahab Reigns in Israel

29 In the thirty-eighth year of Asa king of Judah, Ahab the son of Omri became king over Israel; and Ahab the son of Omri reigned over Israel in Samaria twenty-two years.

30 Now Ahab the son of Omri did evil in the sight of the LORD, more than all who *were* before him.

31 And it came to pass, as though it had been a trivial thing for him to walk in the sins of Jeroboam the son of Nebat, [a]that he took as wife Jezebel the daughter of Ethbaal, king of the [b]Sidonians; [c]and he went and served Baal and worshiped him.

32 Then he set up an altar for Baal in [a]the temple of Baal, which he had built in Samaria.

33 [a]And Ahab made a *wooden image. Ahab [b]did more to provoke the LORD God of Israel to anger than all the kings of Israel who were before him.

34 In his days Hiel of Bethel built Jericho. He laid its foundation with Abiram his firstborn,

*

16:33 Heb. *Asherah*, a Canaanite goddess

KJV

his firstborn, and set up the gates thereof in his youngest *son* Segub, [a]according to the word of the LORD, which he spake by Joshua the son of Nun.

Elijah Proclaims a Drought

17 And Elijah the Tishbite, *who was* of the [a]inhabitants of Gilead, said unto Ahab, [b]*As* the LORD God of Israel liveth, [c]before whom I stand, [d]there shall not be dew nor rain [e]these years, but according to my word.

2 And the word of the LORD came unto him, saying,

3 Get thee hence, and turn thee eastward, and hide thyself by the brook Cherith, that *is* before Jordan.

4 And it shall be, *that* thou shalt drink of the brook; and I have commanded the [a]ravens to feed thee there.

5 So he went and did according unto the word of the LORD: for he went and dwelt by the brook Cherith, that *is* before Jordan.

6 And the ravens brought him bread and flesh in the morning, and bread and flesh in the evening; and he drank of the brook.

7 And it came to pass after a while, that the brook dried up, because there had been no rain in the land.

Elijah and the Widow

8 And the word of the LORD came unto him, saying,

9 Arise, get thee to [a]Zarephath, which *belongeth* to [b]Zidon, and dwell there: behold, I have commanded a widow woman there to sustain thee.

10 So he arose and went to Zarephath. And when he came to the gate of the city, behold, the widow woman *was* there gathering of sticks: and he called to her, and said, Fetch me, I pray thee, a little water in a vessel, that I may drink.

11 And as she was going to fetch *it,* he called to her, and said, Bring me, I pray thee, a morsel of bread in thine hand.

12 And she said, *As* the LORD thy God liveth, I have not a cake, but an handful of meal in a barrel, and a little oil in a cruse: and, behold, I *am* gathering two sticks, that I may go in and dress it for me and my son, that we may eat it, and [a]die.

13 And Elijah said unto her, Fear not; go *and* do as thou hast said: but make me thereof a little cake first, and bring *it* unto me, and after make for thee and for thy son.

14 For thus saith the LORD God of Israel, The barrel of meal shall not waste, neither shall the cruse of oil fail, until the day *that* the LORD sendeth rain upon the earth.

15 And she went and did according to the saying of Elijah: and she, and he, and her house, did eat *many* days.

16 *And* the barrel of meal wasted not, neither did the cruse of oil fail, according to the word of the LORD, which he spake by Elijah.

Elijah Revives the Widow's Son

17 And it came to pass after these things, *that* the son of the woman, the mistress of the house, fell sick; and his sickness was so sore, that there was no breath left in him.

18 And she said unto Elijah, [a]What have I to do with thee, O thou man of God? art thou come unto me to call my sin to remembrance, and to slay my son?

19 And he said unto her, Give me thy son. And he took him out of her bosom, and carried him up into a loft, where he abode, and laid him upon his own bed.

20 And he cried unto the LORD, and said, O LORD my God, hast thou also brought evil upon the widow with whom I sojourn, by slaying her son?

34 [a]Josh. 6:26

CHAPTER 17

1 [a]Judg. 12:4 [b]1 Kin. 18:10; 22:14; 2 Kin. 3:14; 5:20 [c]Deut. 10:8 [d]1 Kin. 18:1; James 5:17 [e]Luke 4:25
4 [a]Job 38:41
9 [a]Obad. 20; Luke 4:25, 26 [b]2 Sam. 24:6
12 [a]Deut. 28:23, 24
18 [a]Luke 5:8

NKJV

and with his youngest *son* Segub he set up its gates, [a]according to the word of the LORD, which He had spoken through Joshua the son of Nun.

Elijah Proclaims a Drought

17 And Elijah the Tishbite, of the [a]inhabitants of Gilead, said to Ahab, [b]"As the LORD God of Israel lives, [c]before whom I stand, [d]there shall not be dew nor rain [e]these years, except at my word."

2 Then the word of the LORD came to him, saying,

3 "Get away from here and turn eastward, and hide by the Brook Cherith, which flows into the Jordan.

4 "And it will be *that* you shall drink from the brook, and I have commanded the [a]ravens to feed you there."

5 So he went and did according to the word of the LORD, for he went and stayed by the Brook Cherith, which flows into the Jordan.

6 The ravens brought him bread and meat in the morning, and bread and meat in the evening; and he drank from the brook.

7 And it happened after a while that the brook dried up, because there had been no rain in the land.

Elijah and the Widow

8 Then the word of the LORD came to him, saying,

9 "Arise, go to [a]Zarephath, which *belongs* to [b]Sidon, and dwell there. See, I have commanded a widow there to provide for you."

10 So he arose and went to Zarephath. And when he came to the gate of the city, indeed a widow *was* there gathering sticks. And he called to her and said, "Please bring me a little water in a cup, that I may drink."

11 And as she was going to get *it,* he called to her and said, "Please bring me a morsel of bread in your hand."

12 So she said, "As the LORD your God lives, I do not have bread, only a handful of flour in a bin, and a little oil in a jar; and see, I *am* gathering a couple of sticks that I may go in and prepare it for myself and my son, that we may eat it, and [a]die."

13 And Elijah said to her, "Do not fear; go *and* do as you have said, but make me a small cake from it first, and bring *it* to me; and afterward make *some* for yourself and your son.

14 "For thus says the LORD God of Israel: 'The bin of flour shall not be used up, nor shall the jar of oil run dry, until the day the LORD sends rain on the earth.' "

15 So she went away and did according to the word of Elijah; and she and he and her household ate for *many* days.

16 The bin of flour was not used up, nor did the jar of oil run dry, according to the word of the LORD which He spoke by Elijah.

Elijah Revives the Widow's Son

17 Now it happened after these things *that* the son of the woman who owned the house became sick. And his sickness was so serious that there was no breath left in him.

18 So she said to Elijah, [a]"What have I to do with you, O man of God? Have you come to me to bring my sin to remembrance, and to kill my son?"

19 And he said to her, "Give me your son." So he took him out of her arms and carried him to the upper room where he was staying, and laid him on his own bed.

20 Then he cried out to the LORD and said, "O LORD my God, have You also brought tragedy on the widow with whom I lodge, by killing her son?"

KJV

21 [a]And he stretched himself upon the child three times, and cried unto the LORD, and said, O LORD my God, I pray thee, let this child's soul come into him again.

22 And the LORD heard the voice of Elijah; and the soul of the child came into him again, and he [a]revived.

23 And Elijah took the child, and brought him down out of the chamber into the house, and delivered him unto his mother: and Elijah said, See, thy son liveth.

24 And the woman said to Elijah, Now by this [a]I know that thou *art* a man of God, *and* that the word of the LORD in thy mouth *is* truth.

Elijah's Message to Ahab

18 And it came to pass *after* [a]many days, that the word of the LORD came to Elijah in the third year, saying, Go, shew thyself unto Ahab; and [b]I will send rain upon the earth.

2 And Elijah went to shew himself unto Ahab. And *there was* a sore famine in Samaria.

3 And Ahab called Obadiah, which *was* the governor of *his* house. (Now Obadiah feared the LORD greatly:

4 For it was *so*, when Jezebel cut off the prophets of the LORD, that Obadiah took an hundred prophets, and hid them by fifty in a cave, and fed them with bread and water.)

5 And Ahab said unto Obadiah, Go into the land, unto all fountains of water, and unto all brooks: peradventure we may find grass to save the horses and mules alive, that we lose not all the beasts.

6 So they divided the land between them to pass throughout it: Ahab went one way by himself, and Obadiah went another way by himself.

7 And as Obadiah was in the way, behold, Elijah met him: and he [a]knew him, and fell on his face, and said, *Art* thou that my lord Elijah?

8 And he answered him, I *am:* go, tell thy lord, Behold, Elijah *is here.*

9 And he said, What have I sinned, that thou wouldest deliver thy servant into the hand of Ahab, to slay me?

10 *As* the LORD thy God liveth, there is no nation or kingdom, whither my lord hath not sent to seek thee: and when they said, *He is* not *there;* he took an oath of the kingdom and nation, that they found thee not.

11 And now thou sayest, Go, tell thy lord, Behold, Elijah *is here.*

12 And it shall come to pass, *as soon as* I am gone from thee, that [a]the Spirit of the LORD shall carry thee whither I know not; and *so* when I come and tell Ahab, and he cannot find thee, he shall slay me: but I thy servant fear the LORD from my youth.

13 Was it not told my lord what I did when Jezebel slew the prophets of the LORD, how I hid an hundred men of the LORD's prophets by fifty in a cave, and fed them with bread and water?

14 And now thou sayest, Go, tell thy lord, Behold, Elijah *is here:* and he shall slay me.

15 And Elijah said, *As* the LORD of hosts liveth, before whom I stand, I will surely shew myself unto him to day.

16 So Obadiah went to meet Ahab, and told him: and Ahab went to meet Elijah.

17 And it came to pass, when Ahab saw Elijah, that Ahab said unto him, [a]*Art* thou he that [b]troubleth Israel?

18 And he answered, I have not troubled Israel; but thou, and thy father's house, [a]in that ye have forsaken the commandments of the LORD, and thou hast followed Baalim.

19 Now therefore send, *and* gather to me all Israel unto mount [a]Carmel, and the prophets of Baal four hundred and fifty, [b]and the prophets of the groves four hundred, which eat at Jezebel's table.

---

21 [a]2 Kin. 4:34, 35; Acts 20:10
22 [a]Luke 7:14, 15; Heb. 11:35
24 [a]John 2:11; 3:2; 16:30

CHAPTER 18

1 [a]1 Kin. 17:1; Luke 4:25; James 5:17 [b]Deut. 28:12
7 [a]2 Kin. 1:6–8
12 [a]2 Kin. 2:16; Ezek. 3:12, 14; Matt. 4:1; Acts 8:39
17 [a]1 Kin. 21:20 [b]Josh. 7:25; Acts 16:20
18 [a]1 Kin. 16:30–33; [2 Chr. 15:2]
19 [a]Josh. 19:26; 2 Kin. 2:25 [b]1 Kin. 16:33

*

18:19 A Canaanite goddess

NKJV

21 [a]And he stretched himself out on the child three times, and cried out to the LORD and said, "O LORD my God, I pray, let this child's soul come back to him."

22 Then the LORD heard the voice of Elijah; and the soul of the child came back to him, and he [a]revived.

23 And Elijah took the child and brought him down from the upper room into the house, and gave him to his mother. And Elijah said, "See, your son lives!"

24 Then the woman said to Elijah, "Now by this [a]I know that you *are* a man of God, *and* that the word of the LORD in your mouth *is* the truth."

Elijah's Message to Ahab

18 And it came to pass *after* [a]many days that the word of the LORD came to Elijah, in the third year, saying, "Go, present yourself to Ahab, and [b]I will send rain on the earth."

2 So Elijah went to present himself to Ahab; and *there was* a severe famine in Samaria.

3 And Ahab had called Obadiah, who *was* in charge of *his* house. (Now Obadiah feared the LORD greatly.

4 For so it was, while Jezebel massacred the prophets of the LORD, that Obadiah had taken one hundred prophets and hidden them, fifty to a cave, and had fed them with bread and water.)

5 And Ahab had said to Obadiah, "Go into the land to all the springs of water and to all the brooks; perhaps we may find grass to keep the horses and mules alive, so that we will not have to kill any livestock."

6 So they divided the land between them to explore it; Ahab went one way by himself, and Obadiah went another way by himself.

7 Now as Obadiah was on his way, suddenly Elijah met him; and he [a]recognized him, and fell on his face, and said, "*Is* that you, my lord Elijah?"

8 And he answered him, "*It is* I. Go, tell your master, 'Elijah *is here.*' "

9 So he said, "How have I sinned, that you are delivering your servant into the hand of Ahab, to kill me?

10 "*As* the LORD your God lives, there is no nation or kingdom where my master has not sent someone to hunt for you; and when they said, '*He is* not *here,*' he took an oath from the kingdom or nation that they could not find you.

11 "And now you say, 'Go, tell your master, "Elijah *is here*" '!

12 "And it shall come to pass, *as soon as* I am gone from you, that [a]the Spirit of the LORD will carry you to a place I do not know; so when I go and tell Ahab, and he cannot find you, he will kill me. But I your servant have feared the LORD from my youth.

13 "Was it not reported to my lord what I did when Jezebel killed the prophets of the LORD, how I hid one hundred men of the LORD's prophets, fifty to a cave, and fed them with bread and water?

14 "And now you say, 'Go, tell your master, "Elijah *is here.*" ' He will kill me!"

15 Then Elijah said, "*As* the LORD of hosts lives, before whom I stand, I will surely present myself to him today."

16 So Obadiah went to meet Ahab, and told him; and Ahab went to meet Elijah.

17 Then it happened, when Ahab saw Elijah, that Ahab said to him, [a]"*Is that* you, O [b]troubler of Israel?"

18 And he answered, "I have not troubled Israel, but you and your father's house *have,* [a]in that you have forsaken the commandments of the LORD and have followed the Baals.

19 "Now therefore, send *and* gather all Israel to me on [a]Mount Carmel, the four hundred and fifty prophets of Baal, [b]and the four hundred prophets of *Asherah, who eat at Jezebel's table."

KJV

Elijah's Mount Carmel Victory

20 So Ahab sent unto all the children of Israel, and [a]gathered the prophets together unto mount Carmel.

21 And Elijah came unto all the people, and said, [a]How long halt ye between two opinions? if the LORD *be* God, follow him: but if Baal, [b]*then* follow him. And the people answered him not a word.

22 Then said Elijah unto the people, [a]I, *even* I only, remain a prophet of the LORD; [b]but Baal's prophets *are* four hundred and fifty men.

23 Let them therefore give us two bullocks; and let them choose one bullock for themselves, and cut it in pieces, and lay *it* on wood, and put no fire *under:* and I will dress the other bullock, and lay *it* on wood, and put no fire *under:*

24 And call ye on the name of your gods, and I will call on the name of the LORD: and the God that [a]answereth by fire, let him be God. And all the people answered and said, It is well spoken.

25 And Elijah said unto the prophets of Baal, Choose you one bullock for yourselves, and dress *it* first; for ye *are* many; and call on the name of your gods, but put no fire *under.*

26 And they took the bullock which was given them, and they dressed *it,* and called on the name of Baal from morning even until noon, saying, O Baal, hear us. But *there was* [a]no voice, nor any that answered. And they leaped upon the altar which was made.

27 And it came to pass at noon, that Elijah mocked them, and said, Cry aloud: for he *is* a god; either he is talking, or he is pursuing, or he is in a journey, *or* peradventure he sleepeth, and must be awaked.

28 And they cried aloud, and [a]cut themselves after their manner with knives and lancets, till the blood gushed out upon them.

29 And it came to pass, when midday was past, [a]and they prophesied until the *time* of the offering of the *evening* sacrifice, that *there was* [b]neither voice, nor any to answer, nor any that regarded.

30 And Elijah said unto all the people, Come near unto me. And all the people came near unto him. [a]And he repaired the altar of the LORD *that was* broken down.

31 And Elijah took twelve stones, according to the number of the tribes of the sons of Jacob, unto whom the word of the LORD came, saying, [a]Israel shall be thy name:

32 And with the stones he built an altar [a]in the name of the LORD: and he made a trench about the altar, as great as would contain two measures of seed.

33 And he [a]put the wood in order, and cut the bullock in pieces, and laid *him* on the wood, and said, Fill four barrels with water, and [b]pour *it* on the burnt sacrifice, and on the wood.

34 And he said, Do *it* the second time. And they did *it* the second time. And he said, Do *it* the third time. And they did *it* the third time.

35 And the water ran round about the altar; and he filled [a]the trench also with water.

36 And it came to pass at *the time of* the offering of the *evening* sacrifice, that Elijah the prophet came near, and said, LORD [a]God of Abraham, Isaac, and of Israel, [b]let it be known this day that thou *art* God in Israel, and *that* I *am* thy servant, and *that* [c]I have done all these things at thy word.

37 Hear me, O LORD, hear me, that this people may know that thou *art* the LORD God, and *that* thou hast turned their heart back again.

38 Then [a]the fire of the LORD fell, and consumed the burnt sacrifice, and the wood, and the stones, and the dust, and licked up the water that *was* in the trench.

39 And when all the people saw *it,* they fell

20 [a]1 Kin. 22:6
21 [a]2 Kin. 17:41; [Matt. 6:24] [b]Josh. 24:15
22 [a]1 Kin. 19:10, 14 [b]1 Kin. 18:19
24 [a]1 Kin. 18:38; 1 Chr. 21:26
26 [a]Ps. 115:5; Jer. 10:5; [1 Cor. 8:4]
28 [a][Lev. 19:28; Deut. 14:1]
29 [a]Ex. 29:39, 41 [b]1 Kin. 18:26
30 [a]1 Kin. 19:10, 14; 2 Chr. 33:16
31 [a]Gen. 32:28; 35:10; 2 Kin. 17:34
32 [a][Ex. 20:25; Col. 3:17]
33 [a]Gen. 22:9; Lev. 1:6–8 [b]Judg. 6:20
35 [a]1 Kin. 18:32, 38
36 [a]Gen. 28:13; Ex. 3:6; 4:5; [Matt. 22:32] [b]1 Kin. 8:43; 2 Kin. 19:19 [c]Num. 16:28
38 [a]Gen. 15:17; Lev. 9:24; 10:1, 2; Judg. 6:21; 2 Kin. 1:12; 1 Chr. 21:26; 2 Chr. 7:1; Job 1:16

NKJV

Elijah's Mount Carmel Victory

20 So Ahab sent for all the children of Israel, and [a]gathered the prophets together on Mount Carmel.

21 And Elijah came to all the people, and said, [a]"How long will you falter between two opinions? If the LORD *is* God, follow Him; but if Baal, [b]follow him." But the people answered him not a word.

22 Then Elijah said to the people, [a]"I alone am left a prophet of the LORD; [b]but Baal's prophets *are* four hundred and fifty men.

23 "Therefore let them give us two bulls; and let them choose one bull for themselves, cut it in pieces, and lay *it* on the wood, but put no fire *under it;* and I will prepare the other bull, and lay *it* on the wood, but put no fire *under it.*

24 "Then you call on the name of your gods, and I will call on the name of the LORD; and the God who [a]answers by fire, He is God." So all the people answered and said, "It is well spoken."

25 Now Elijah said to the prophets of Baal, "Choose one bull for yourselves and prepare *it* first, for you *are* many; and call on the name of your god, but put no fire *under it.*"

26 So they took the bull which was given them, and they prepared *it,* and called on the name of Baal from morning even till noon, saying, "O Baal, hear us!" But *there was* [a]no voice; no one answered. Then they leaped about the altar which they had made.

27 And so it was, at noon, that Elijah mocked them and said, "Cry aloud, for he *is* a god; either he is meditating, or he is busy, or he is on a journey, *or* perhaps he is sleeping and must be awakened."

28 So they cried aloud, and [a]cut themselves, as was their custom, with knives and lances, until the blood gushed out on them.

29 And when midday was past, [a]they prophesied until the *time* of the offering of the *evening* sacrifice. But *there was* [b]no voice; no one answered, no one paid attention.

30 Then Elijah said to all the people, "Come near to me." So all the people came near to him. [a]And he repaired the altar of the LORD *that was* broken down.

31 And Elijah took twelve stones, according to the number of the tribes of the sons of Jacob, to whom the word of the LORD had come, saying, [a]"Israel shall be your name."

32 Then with the stones he built an altar [a]in the name of the LORD; and he made a trench around the altar large enough to hold two seahs of seed.

33 And he [a]put the wood in order, cut the bull in pieces, and laid *it* on the wood, and said, "Fill four waterpots with water, and [b]pour *it* on the burnt sacrifice and on the wood."

34 Then he said, "Do *it* a second time," and they did *it* a second time; and he said, "Do *it* a third time," and they did *it* a third time.

35 So the water ran all around the altar; and he also filled [a]the trench with water.

36 And it came to pass, at *the time of* the offering of the *evening* sacrifice, that Elijah the prophet came near and said, "LORD [a]God of Abraham, Isaac, and Israel, [b]let it be known this day that You *are* God in Israel and I *am* Your servant, and *that* [c]I have done all these things at Your word.

37 "Hear me, O LORD, hear me, that this people may know that You *are* the LORD God, and *that* You have turned their hearts back *to You* again."

38 Then [a]the fire of the LORD fell and consumed the burnt sacrifice, and the wood and the stones and the dust, and it licked up the water that *was* in the trench.

39 Now when all the people saw *it,* they fell

KJV

on their faces: and they said, [a]The LORD, he *is* the God; the LORD, he *is* the God.

40 And Elijah said unto them, [a]Take the prophets of Baal; let not one of them escape. And they took them: and Elijah brought them down to the brook [b]Kishon, and [c]slew them there.

The Drought Ends

41 And Elijah said unto Ahab, Get thee up, eat and drink; for *there is* a sound of abundance of rain.

42 So Ahab went up to eat and to drink. And Elijah went up to the top of Carmel; [a]and he cast himself down upon the earth, and put his face between his knees,

43 And said to his servant, Go up now, look toward the sea. And he went up, and looked, and said, *There is* nothing. And he said, Go again seven times.

44 And it came to pass at the seventh time, that he said, Behold, there ariseth a little cloud out of the sea, like a man's hand. And he said, Go up, say unto Ahab, Prepare *thy chariot,* and get thee down, that the rain stop thee not.

45 And it came to pass in the mean while, that the heaven was black with clouds and wind, and there was a great rain. And Ahab rode, and went to Jezreel.

46 And the [a]hand of the LORD was on Elijah; and he [b]girded up his loins, and ran before Ahab to the entrance of Jezreel.

Elijah Escapes from Jezebel

19 And Ahab told Jezebel all that Elijah had done, and withal how he had [a]slain all the prophets with the sword.

2 Then Jezebel sent a messenger unto Elijah, saying, [a]So let the gods do *to me,* and more also, if I make not thy life as the life of one of them by to morrow about this time.

3 And when he saw *that,* he arose, and went for his life, and came to Beer–sheba, which *belongeth* to Judah, and left his servant there.

4 But he himself went a day's journey into the wilderness, and came and sat down under a juniper tree: and he [a]requested for himself that he might die; and said, It is enough; now, O LORD, take away my life; for I *am* not better than my fathers.

5 And as he lay and slept under a juniper tree, behold, then an angel touched him, and said unto him, Arise *and* eat.

6 And he looked, and, behold, *there was* a cake baken on the coals, and a cruse of water at his head. And he did eat and drink, and laid him down again.

7 And the [a]angel of the LORD came again the second time, and touched him, and said, Arise *and* eat; because the journey *is* too great for thee.

8 And he arose, and did eat and drink, and went in the strength of that meat forty days and [a]forty nights unto [b]Horeb the mount of God.

9 And he came thither unto a cave, and lodged there; and, behold, the word of the LORD *came* to him, and he said unto him, What doest thou here, Elijah?

10 And he said, [a]I have been very [b]jealous for the LORD God of hosts: for the children of Israel have forsaken thy covenant, thrown down thine altars, and [c]slain thy prophets with the sword; and [d]I, *even* I only, am left; and they seek my life, to take it away.

God's Revelation to Elijah

11 And he said, Go forth, and stand [a]upon the mount before the LORD. And, behold, the LORD [b]passed by, and [c]a great and strong wind rent the mountains, and brake in pieces the rocks before the LORD; *but* the LORD *was* not in the wind: and after the wind an earthquake; *but* the LORD *was* not in the earthquake:

39 [a]1 Kin. 18:21, 24
40 [a]2 Kin. 10:25 [b]Judg. 4:7; 5:21 [c][Deut. 13:5; 18:20]
42 [a]James 5:17, 18
46 [a]2 Kin. 3:15; Is. 8:11; Ezek. 3:14 [b]2 Kin. 4:29; 9:1; Jer. 1:17; 1 Pet. 1:13

CHAPTER 19

1 [a]1 Kin. 18:40
2 [a]Ruth 1:17; 1 Kin. 20:10; 2 Kin. 6:31
4 [a]Num. 11:15; Jer. 20:14–18; Jon. 4:3, 8
8 [a]Ex. 24:18; 34:28; Deut. 9:9–11, 18; Matt. 4:2 [b]Ex. 3:1; 4:27
10 [a]Rom. 11:3 [b]Num. 25:11, 13; Ps. 69:9 [c]1 Kin. 18:4 [d]1 Kin. 18:22; Rom. 11:3
11 [a]Ex. 19:20; 24:12, 18 [b]Ex. 33:21, 22 [c]Ezek. 1:4; 37:7

NKJV

on their faces; and they said, [a]"The LORD, He *is* God! The LORD, He *is* God!"

40 And Elijah said to them, [a]"Seize the prophets of Baal! Do not let one of them escape!" So they seized them; and Elijah brought them down to the Brook [b]Kishon and [c]executed them there.

The Drought Ends

41 Then Elijah said to Ahab, "Go up, eat and drink; for *there is* the sound of abundance of rain."

42 So Ahab went up to eat and drink. And Elijah went up to the top of Carmel; [a]then he bowed down on the ground, and put his face between his knees,

43 and said to his servant, "Go up now, look toward the sea." So he went up and looked, and said, "*There is* nothing." And seven times he said, "Go again."

44 Then it came to pass the seventh *time,* that he said, "There is a cloud, as small as a man's hand, rising out of the sea!" So he said, "Go up, say to Ahab, 'Prepare *your chariot,* and go down before the rain stops you.' "

45 Now it happened in the meantime that the sky became black with clouds and wind, and there was a heavy rain. So Ahab rode away and went to Jezreel.

46 Then the [a]hand of the LORD came upon Elijah; and he [b]girded up his loins and ran ahead of Ahab to the entrance of Jezreel.

Elijah Escapes from Jezebel

19 And Ahab told Jezebel all that Elijah had done, also how he had [a]executed all the prophets with the sword.

2 Then Jezebel sent a messenger to Elijah, saying, [a]"So let the gods do *to me,* and more also, if I do not make your life as the life of one of them by tomorrow about this time."

3 And when he saw *that,* he arose and ran for his life, and went to Beersheba, which *belongs* to Judah, and left his servant there.

4 But he himself went a day's journey into the wilderness, and came and sat down under a broom tree. And he [a]prayed that he might die, and said, "It is enough! Now, LORD, take my life, for I *am* no better than my fathers!"

5 Then as he lay and slept under a broom tree, suddenly an *angel touched him, and said to him, "Arise *and* eat."

6 Then he looked, and there by his head *was* a cake baked on coals, and a jar of water. So he ate and drank, and lay down again.

7 And the *angel of the LORD came back the second time, and touched him, and said, "Arise *and* eat, because the journey *is* too great for you."

8 So he arose, and ate and drank; and he went in the strength of that food forty days and [a]forty nights as far as [b]Horeb, the mountain of God.

9 And there he went into a cave, and spent the night in that place; and behold, the word of the LORD *came* to him, and He said to him, "What are you doing here, Elijah?"

10 So he said, [a]"I have been very [b]zealous for the LORD God of hosts; for the children of Israel have forsaken Your covenant, torn down Your altars, and [c]killed Your prophets with the sword. [d]I alone am left; and they seek to take my life."

God's Revelation to Elijah

11 Then He said, "Go out, and stand [a]on the mountain before the LORD." And behold, the LORD [b]passed by, and [c]a great and strong wind tore into the mountains and broke the rocks in pieces before the LORD, *but* the LORD *was* not in the wind; and after the wind an earthquake, *but* the LORD *was* not in the earthquake;

*19:5 Or *Angel*
19:7 Or *Angel*

KJV

12 And after the earthquake a fire; *but* the
LORD *was* not in the fire: and after the fire a still
small voice.
13 And it was *so*, when Elijah heard *it*, that
[a]he wrapped his face in his mantle, and went out,
and stood in the entering in of the cave. [b]And,
behold, *there came* a voice unto him, and said,
What dost thou here, Elijah?
14 [a]And he said, I have been very jealous for
the LORD God of hosts: because the children of
Israel have forsaken thy covenant, thrown down
thine altars, and slain thy prophets with the
sword; and I, *even* I only, am left; and they seek
my life, to take it away.
15 And the LORD said unto him, Go, return
on thy way to the wilderness of Damascus: [a]and
when thou comest, anoint Hazael *to be* king over
Syria:
16 And [a]Jehu the son of Nimshi shalt thou
anoint *to be* king over Israel: and [b]Elisha the son
of Shaphat of Abel–meholah shalt thou anoint *to
be* prophet in thy room.
17 And [a]it shall come to pass, *that* him that
escapeth the sword of Hazael shall Jehu [b]slay:
and him that escapeth from the sword of Jehu
[c]shall Elisha slay.
18 [a]Yet I have left *me* seven thousand in Israel, all the knees which have not bowed unto
Baal, [b]and every mouth which hath not kissed
him.

Elisha Follows Elijah

19 So he departed thence, and found Elisha
the son of Shaphat, who *was* plowing *with* twelve
yoke *of oxen* before him, and he with the twelfth:
and Elijah passed by him, and cast his [a]mantle
upon him.
20 And he left the oxen, and ran after Elijah,
and said, [a]Let me, I pray thee, kiss my father and
my mother, and *then* I will follow thee. And he
said unto him, Go back again: for what have I
done to thee?
21 And he returned back from him, and took
a yoke of oxen, and slew them, and [a]boiled their
flesh with the instruments of the oxen, and gave
unto the people, and they did eat. Then he arose,
and went after Elijah, and ministered unto him.

Ahab Defeats the Syrians

20 And [a]Ben–hadad the king of Syria gathered
all his host together: and *there were* thirty
and two kings with him, and horses, and chariots:
and he went up and besieged [b]Samaria, and
warred against it.
2 And he sent messengers to Ahab king of
Israel into the city, and said unto him, Thus saith
Ben–hadad,
3 Thy silver and thy gold *is* mine; thy wives
also and thy children, *even* the goodliest, *are*
mine.
4 And the king of Israel answered and said,
My lord, O king, according to thy saying, I *am*
thine, and all that I have.
5 And the messengers came again, and said,
Thus speaketh Ben–hadad, saying, Although I
have sent unto thee, saying, Thou shalt deliver
me thy silver, and thy gold, and thy wives, and
thy children;
6 Yet I will send my servants unto thee to
morrow about this time, and they shall search
thine house, and the houses of thy servants; and
it shall be, *that* whatsoever is pleasant in thine
eyes, they shall put *it* in their hand, and take *it*
away.
7 Then the king of Israel called all the elders
of the land, and said, Mark, I pray you, and see
how this *man* seeketh mischief: for he sent unto
me for my wives, and for my children, and for
my silver, and for my gold; and I denied him not.
8 And all the elders and all the people said
unto him, Hearken not *unto him*, nor consent.
9 Wherefore he said unto the messengers

13 [a]Ex. 3:6; Is. 6:2 [b]1 Kin. 19:9
14 [a]1 Kin. 19:10
15 [a]2 Kin. 8:8–15
16 [a]2 Kin. 9:1–10 [b]1 Kin. 19:19–21; 2 Kin. 2:9–15
17 [a]2 Kin. 8:12; 13:3, 22 [b]2 Kin. 9:14—10:28 [c][Hos. 6:5]
18 [a]Rom. 11:4 [b]Hos. 13:2
19 [a]1 Sam. 28:14; 2 Kin. 2:8, 13, 14
20 [a][Matt. 8:21, 22; Luke 9:61, 62]; Acts 20:37
21 [a]2 Sam. 24:22

CHAPTER 20
1 [a]1 Kin. 15:18, 20; 2 Kin. 6:24 [b]1 Kin. 16:24; 2 Kin. 6:24

NKJV

12 and after the earthquake a fire, *but* the
LORD *was* not in the fire; and after the fire a still
small voice.
13 So it was, when Elijah heard *it*, that [a]he
wrapped his face in his mantle and went out and
stood in the entrance of the cave. [b]Suddenly a
voice *came* to him, and said, "What are you doing
here, Elijah?"
14 [a]And he said, "I have been very zealous
for the LORD God of hosts; because the children
of Israel have forsaken Your covenant, torn down
Your altars, and killed Your prophets with the
sword. I alone am left; and they seek to take my
life."
15 Then the LORD said to him: "Go, return
on your way to the Wilderness of Damascus; [a]and
when you arrive, anoint Hazael *as* king over
Syria.
16 "Also you shall anoint [a]Jehu the son of
Nimshi *as* king over Israel. And [b]Elisha the son
of Shaphat of Abel Meholah you shall anoint *as*
prophet in your place.
17 [a]"It shall be *that* whoever escapes the
sword of Hazael, Jehu will [b]kill; and whoever escapes the sword of Jehu, [c]Elisha will kill.
18 [a]"Yet I have reserved seven thousand in
Israel, all whose knees have not bowed to Baal,
[b]and every mouth that has not kissed him."

Elisha Follows Elijah

19 So he departed from there, and found Elisha the son of Shaphat, who *was* plowing *with*
twelve yoke *of oxen* before him, and he was with
the twelfth. Then Elijah passed by him and threw
his [a]mantle on him.
20 And he left the oxen and ran after Elijah,
and said, [a]"Please let me kiss my father and my
mother, and *then* I will follow you." And he said
to him, "Go back again, for what have I done to
you?"
21 So *Elisha* turned back from him, and took
a yoke of oxen and slaughtered them and [a]boiled
their flesh, using the oxen's equipment, and gave
it to the people, and they ate. Then he arose and
followed Elijah, and became his servant.

Ahab Defeats the Syrians

20 Now [a]Ben-Hadad the king of Syria gathered all his forces together; thirty-two
kings *were* with him, with horses and chariots.
And he went up and besieged [b]Samaria, and made
war against it.
2 Then he sent messengers into the city to
Ahab king of Israel, and said to him, "Thus says
Ben-Hadad:
3 'Your silver and your gold *are* mine; your
loveliest wives and children are mine.' "
4 And the king of Israel answered and said,
"My lord, O king, just as you say, I and all that I
have *are* yours."
5 Then the messengers came back and said,
"Thus speaks Ben-Hadad, saying, 'Indeed I have
sent to you, saying, "You shall deliver to me your
silver and your gold, your wives and your
children";
6 'but I will send my servants to you tomorrow about this time, and they shall search your
house and the houses of your servants. And it
shall be, *that* whatever is pleasant in your eyes,
they will put in their hands and take *it*.' "
7 So the king of Israel called all the elders
of the land, and said, "Notice, please, and see how
this *man* seeks trouble, for he sent to me for my
wives, my children, my silver, and my gold; and
I did not deny him."
8 And all the elders and all the people said
to him, "Do not listen or consent."
9 Therefore he said to the messengers of

KJV

of Ben–hadad, Tell my lord the king, All that thou didst send for to thy servant at the first I will do: but this thing I may not do. And the messengers departed, and brought him word again.

10 And Ben–hadad sent unto him, and said, [a]The gods do so unto me, and more also, if the dust of Samaria shall suffice for handfuls for all the people that follow me.

11 And the king of Israel answered and said, Tell *him,* Let not him that girdeth on *his harness* [a]boast himself as he that putteth it off.

12 And it came to pass, when *Ben–hadad* heard this message, as he *was* [a]drinking, he and the kings in the pavilions, that he said unto his servants, Set *yourselves in array.* And they set *themselves in array* against the city.

13 And, behold, there came a prophet unto Ahab king of Israel, saying, Thus saith the LORD, Hast thou seen all this great multitude? behold, [a]I will deliver it into thine hand this day; and thou shalt know that I *am* the LORD.

14 And Ahab said, By whom? And he said, Thus saith the LORD, *Even* by the young men of the princes of the provinces. Then he said, Who shall order the battle? And he answered, Thou.

15 Then he numbered the young men of the princes of the provinces, and they were two hundred and thirty two: and after them he numbered all the people, *even* all the children of Israel, *being* seven thousand.

16 And they went out at noon. But Ben–hadad *was* [a]drinking himself drunk in the pavilions, he and the kings, the thirty and two kings that helped him.

17 And the young men of the princes of the provinces went out first; and Ben–hadad sent out, and they told him, saying, There are men come out of Samaria.

18 And he said, Whether they be come out for peace, take them alive; or whether they be come out for war, take them alive.

19 So these young men of the princes of the provinces came out of the city, and the army which followed them.

20 And they slew every one his man: and the Syrians fled; and Israel pursued them: and Ben–hadad the king of Syria escaped on an horse with the horsemen.

21 And the king of Israel went out, and smote the horses and chariots, and slew the Syrians with a great slaughter.

22 And the prophet came to the king of Israel, and said unto him, Go, strengthen thyself, and mark, and see what thou doest: [a]for at the return of the year the king of Syria will come up against thee.

The Syrians Again Defeated

23 And the servants of the king of Syria said unto him, Their gods *are* gods of the hills; therefore they were stronger than we; but let us fight against them in the plain, and surely we shall be stronger than they.

24 And do this thing, Take the kings away, every man out of his place, and put captains in their rooms:

25 And number thee an army, like the army that thou hast lost, horse for horse, and chariot for chariot: and we will fight against them in the plain, *and* surely we shall be stronger than they. And he hearkened unto their voice, and did so.

26 And it came to pass at the return of the year, that Ben–hadad numbered the Syrians, and went up to [a]Aphek, to fight against Israel.

27 And the children of Israel were numbered, and were all present, and went against them: and the children of Israel pitched before them like two little flocks of kids; but the Syrians filled the [a]country.

28 And there came a [a]man of God, and spake unto the king of Israel, and said, Thus saith the LORD, Because the Syrians have said, The LORD

10 [a]1 Kin. 19:2; 2 Kin. 6:31
11 [a]Prov. 27:1; [Eccl. 7:8]
12 [a]1 Kin. 20:16
13 [a]1 Kin. 20:28
16 [a]1 Kin. 16:9; 20:12; [Prov. 20:1]
22 [a]2 Sam. 11:1; 1 Kin. 20:26
26 [a]Josh. 13:4; 2 Kin. 13:17
27 [a]Judg. 6:3–5; 1 Sam. 13:5–8
28 [a]1 Kin. 17:18

NKJV

Ben-Hadad, "Tell my lord the king, 'All that you sent for to your servant the first time I will do, but this thing I cannot do.' " And the messengers departed and brought back word to him.

10 Then Ben-Hadad sent to him and said, [a]"The gods do so to me, and more also, if enough dust is left of Samaria for a handful for each of the people who follow me."

11 So the king of Israel answered and said, "Tell *him,* 'Let not the one who puts on *his armor* [a]boast like the one who takes *it off.'* "

12 And it happened when *Ben-Hadad* heard this message, as he and the kings *were* [a]drinking at the command post, that he said to his servants, "Get ready." And they got ready to attack the city.

13 Suddenly a prophet approached Ahab king of Israel, saying, "Thus says the LORD: 'Have you seen all this great multitude? Behold, [a]I will deliver it into your hand today, and you shall know that I *am* the LORD.' "

14 So Ahab said, "By whom?" And he said, "Thus says the LORD: 'By the young leaders of the provinces.' " Then he said, "Who will set the battle in order?" And he answered, "You."

15 Then he mustered the young leaders of the provinces, and there were two hundred and thirty-two; and after them he mustered all the people, all the children of Israel—seven thousand.

16 So they went out at noon. Meanwhile Ben-Hadad and the thirty-two kings helping him were [a]getting drunk at the command post.

17 The young leaders of the provinces went out first. And Ben-Hadad sent out *a patrol,* and they told him, saying, "Men are coming out of Samaria!"

18 So he said, "If they have come out for peace, take them alive; and if they have come out for war, take them alive."

19 Then these young leaders of the provinces went out of the city with the army which followed them.

20 And each one killed his man; so the Syrians fled, and Israel pursued them; and Ben-Hadad the king of Syria escaped on a horse with the cavalry.

21 Then the king of Israel went out and attacked the horses and chariots, and killed the Syrians with a great slaughter.

22 And the prophet came to the king of Israel and said to him, "Go, strengthen yourself; take note, and see what you should do, [a]for in the spring of the year the king of Syria will come up against you."

The Syrians Again Defeated

23 Then the servants of the king of Syria said to him, "Their gods *are* gods of the hills. Therefore they were stronger than we; but if we fight against them in the plain, surely we will be stronger than they.

24 "So do this thing: Dismiss the kings, each from his position, and put captains in their places;

25 "and you shall muster an army like the army that you have lost, horse for horse and chariot for chariot. Then we will fight against them in the plain; surely we will be stronger than they." And he listened to their voice and did so.

26 So it was, in the spring of the year, that Ben-Hadad mustered the Syrians and went up to [a]Aphek to fight against Israel.

27 And the children of Israel were mustered and given provisions, and they went against them. Now the children of Israel encamped before them like two little flocks of goats, while the Syrians filled the [a]countryside.

28 Then a [a]man of God came and spoke to the king of Israel, and said, "Thus says the LORD: 'Because the Syrians have said, "The LORD *is* God

KJV

is God of the hills, but he is not God of the valleys, therefore [b]will I deliver all this great multitude into thine hand, and ye shall know that I am the LORD.

29 And they pitched one over against the other seven days. And so it was, that in the seventh day the battle was joined: and the children of Israel slew of the Syrians an hundred thousand footmen in one day.

30 But the rest fled to Aphek, into the city; and there a wall fell upon twenty and seven thousand of the men that were left. And Ben–hadad fled, and came into the city, into an inner chamber.

Ahab's Treaty with Ben-Hadad

31 And his servants said unto him, Behold now, we have heard that the kings of the house of Israel are merciful kings: let us, I pray thee, [a]put sackcloth on our loins, and ropes upon our heads, and go out to the king of Israel: peradventure he will save thy life.

32 So they girded sackcloth on their loins, and put ropes on their heads, and came to the king of Israel, and said, Thy servant Ben–hadad saith, I pray thee, let me live. And he said, Is he yet alive? he is my brother.

33 Now the men did diligently observe whether any thing would come from him, and did hastily catch it: and they said, Thy brother Ben–hadad. Then he said, Go ye, bring him. Then Ben–hadad came forth to him; and he caused him to come up into the chariot.

34 And Ben–hadad said unto him, [a]The cities, which my father took from thy father, I will restore; and thou shalt make streets for thee in Damascus, as my father made in Samaria. Then said Ahab, I will send thee away with this covenant. So he made a covenant with him, and sent him away.

Ahab Condemned

35 And a certain man of [a]the sons of the prophets said unto his neighbour [b]in the word of the LORD,Smite me, I pray thee. And the man refused to smite him.

36 Then said he unto him, Because thou hast not obeyed the voice of the LORD, behold, as soon as thou art departed from me, a lion shall slay thee. And as soon as he was departed from him, [a]a lion found him, and slew him.

37 Then he found another man, and said, Smite me, I pray thee. And the man smote him, so that in smiting he wounded him.

38 So the prophet departed, and waited for the king by the way, and disguised himself with ashes upon his face.

39 And [a]as the king passed by, he cried unto the king: and he said, Thy servant went out into the midst of the battle; and, behold, a man turned aside, and brought a man unto me, and said, Keep this man: if by any means he be missing, then [b]shall thy life be for his life, or else thou shalt pay a talent of silver.

40 And as thy servant was busy here and there, he was gone. And the king of Israel said unto him, So shall thy judgment be; thyself hast decided it.

41 And he hasted, and took the ashes away from his face; and the king of Israel discerned him that he was of the prophets.

42 And he said unto him, Thus saith the LORD, [a]Because thou hast let go out of thy hand a man whom I appointed to utter destruction, therefore thy life shall go for his life, and thy people for his people.

43 And the king of Israel [a]went to his house heavy and displeased, and came to Samaria.

Naboth Is Murdered for His Vineyard

21 And it came to pass after these things, that Naboth the Jezreelite had a vineyard,

28 [b]1 Kin. 20:13
31 [a]Gen. 37:34; 2 Sam. 3:31
34 [a]1 Kin. 15:20
35 [a]2 Kin. 2:3, 5, 7, 15 [b]1 Kin. 13:17, 18
36 [a]1 Kin. 13:24
39 [a]2 Sam. 12:1 [b]2 Kin. 10:24
42 [a]1 Kin. 22:31–37
43 [a]1 Kin. 21:4

NKJV

of the hills, but He is not God of the valleys," therefore [b]I will deliver all this great multitude into your hand, and you shall know that I am the LORD.' "

29 And they encamped opposite each other for seven days. So it was that on the seventh day the battle was joined; and the children of Israel killed one hundred thousand foot soldiers of the Syrians in one day.

30 But the rest fled to Aphek, into the city; then a wall fell on twenty-seven thousand of the men who were left. And Ben-Hadad fled and went into the city, into an inner chamber.

Ahab's Treaty with Ben-Hadad

31 Then his servants said to him, "Look now, we have heard that the kings of the house of Israel are merciful kings. Please, let us [a]put sackcloth around our waists and ropes around our heads, and go out to the king of Israel; perhaps he will spare your life."

32 So they wore sackcloth around their waists and put ropes around their heads, and came to the king of Israel and said, "Your servant Ben-Hadad says, 'Please let me live.' " And he said, "Is he still alive? He is my brother."

33 Now the men were watching closely to see whether any sign of mercy would come from him; and they quickly grasped at this word and said, "Your brother Ben-Hadad." So he said, "Go, bring him." Then Ben-Hadad came out to him; and he had him come up into the chariot.

34 So Ben-Hadad said to him, [a]"The cities which my father took from your father I will restore; and you may set up marketplaces for yourself in Damascus, as my father did in Samaria." Then Ahab said, "I will send you away with this treaty." So he made a treaty with him and sent him away.

Ahab Condemned

35 Now a certain man of [a]the sons of the prophets said to his neighbor [b]by the word of the LORD, "Strike me, please." And the man refused to strike him.

36 Then he said to him, "Because you have not obeyed the voice of the LORD, surely, as soon as you depart from me, a lion shall kill you." And as soon as he left him, [a]a lion found him and killed him.

37 And he found another man, and said, "Strike me, please." So the man struck him, inflicting a wound.

38 Then the prophet departed and waited for the king by the road, and disguised himself with a bandage over his eyes.

39 Now [a]as the king passed by, he cried out to the king and said, "Your servant went out into the midst of the battle; and there, a man came over and brought a man to me, and said, 'Guard this man; if by any means he is missing, [b]your life shall be for his life, or else you shall pay a talent of silver.'

40 "While your servant was busy here and there, he was gone." Then the king of Israel said to him, "So shall your judgment be; you yourself have decided it."

41 And he hastened to take the bandage away from his eyes; and the king of Israel recognized him as one of the prophets.

42 Then he said to him, "Thus says the LORD: [a]'Because you have let slip out of your hand a man whom I appointed to utter destruction, therefore your life shall go for his life, and your people for his people.' "

43 So the king of Israel [a]went to his house sullen and displeased, and came to Samaria.

Naboth Is Murdered for His Vineyard

21 And it came to pass after these things that Naboth the Jezreelite had a vineyard which

KJV

which *was* in [a]Jezreel, hard by the palace of Ahab
king of Samaria.
2 And Ahab spake unto Naboth, saying,
Give me thy [a]vineyard, that I may have it for a
garden of herbs, because it *is* near unto my house:
and I will give thee for it a better vineyard than
it; *or,* if it seem good to thee, I will give thee the
worth of it in money.
3 And Naboth said to Ahab, The LORD forbid it me, [a]that I should give the inheritance of
my fathers unto thee.
4 And Ahab came into his house heavy and
displeased because of the word which Naboth the
Jezreelite had spoken to him: for he had said, I
will not give thee the inheritance of my fathers.
And he laid him down upon his bed, and turned
away his face, and would eat no bread.
5 But [a]Jezebel his wife came to him, and
said unto him, Why is thy spirit so sad, that thou
eatest no bread?
6 And he said unto her, Because I spake
unto Naboth the Jezreelite, and said unto him,
Give me thy vineyard for money; or else, if it
please thee, I will give thee *another* vineyard for
it: and he answered, I will not give thee my
vineyard.
7 And Jezebel his wife said unto him, Dost
thou now govern the kingdom of Israel? arise, *and*
eat bread, and let thine heart be merry: I will give
thee the vineyard of Naboth the Jezreelite.
8 So she wrote letters in Ahab's name, and
sealed *them* with his seal, and sent the letters unto
the elders and to the nobles that *were* in his city,
dwelling with Naboth.
9 And she wrote in the letters, saying, Proclaim a fast, and set Naboth on high among the
people:
10 And set two men, sons of Belial, before
him, to bear witness against him, saying, Thou
didst [a]blaspheme God and the king. And *then*
carry him out, and [b]stone him, that he may die.
11 And the men of his city, *even* the elders
and the nobles who were the inhabitants in his
city, did as Jezebel had sent unto them, *and* as it
was written in the letters which she had sent unto
them.
12 [a]They proclaimed a fast, and set Naboth
on high among the people.
13 And there came in two men, children of
Belial, and sat before him: and the men of Belial
[a]witnessed against him, *even* against Naboth, in
the presence of the people, saying, Naboth did
blaspheme God and the king. [b]Then they carried
him forth out of the city, and stoned him with
stones, that he died.
14 Then they sent to Jezebel, saying, Naboth
is stoned, and is dead.
15 And it came to pass, when Jezebel heard
that Naboth was stoned, and was dead, that Jezebel said to Ahab, Arise, take possession of the
vineyard of Naboth the Jezreelite, which he refused to give thee for money: for Naboth is not
alive, but dead.
16 And it came to pass, when Ahab heard
that Naboth was dead, that Ahab rose up to go
down to the vineyard of Naboth the Jezreelite,
to take possession of it.

The LORD Condemns Ahab

17 [a]And the word of the LORD came to [b]Elijah
the Tishbite, saying,
18 Arise, go down to meet Ahab king of Israel, [a]which *is* in Samaria: behold, *he is* in the
vineyard of Naboth, whither he is gone down to
possess it.
19 And thou shalt speak unto him, saying,
Thus saith the LORD, Hast thou killed, and also
taken possession? And thou shalt speak unto him,
saying, Thus saith the LORD, [a]In the place where
dogs licked the blood of Naboth shall dogs lick
thy blood, even thine.
20 And Ahab said to Elijah, [a]Hast thou found

CHAPTER 21

1 [a]Judg. 6:33; 1 Kin. 18:45, 46
2 [a]1 Sam. 8:14
3 [a][Lev. 25:23; Num. 36:7; Ezek. 46:18]
5 [a]1 Kin. 19:1, 2
10 [a][Ex. 22:28; Lev. 24:15, 16]; Acts 6:11 [b][Lev. 24:14]
12 [a]Is. 58:4
13 [a][Ex. 20:16; 23:1, 7] [b]2 Kin. 9:26; 2 Chr. 24:21; Acts 7:58, 59; Heb. 11:37
17 [a][Ps. 9:12] [b]1 Kin. 19:1
18 [a]1 Kin. 13:32; 2 Chr. 22:9
19 [a]1 Kin. 22:38; 2 Kin. 9:26
20 [a]1 Kin. 18:17

NKJV

was in [a]Jezreel, next to the palace of Ahab king
of Samaria.
2 So Ahab spoke to Naboth, saying, "Give
me your [a]vineyard, that I may have it for a vegetable garden, because it *is* near, next to my house;
and for it I will give you a vineyard better than
it. *Or,* if it seems good to you, I will give you its
worth in money."
3 But Naboth said to Ahab, "The LORD forbid [a]that I should give the inheritance of my fathers to you!"
4 So Ahab went into his house sullen and
displeased because of the word which Naboth the
Jezreelite had spoken to him; for he had said, "I
will not give you the inheritance of my fathers."
And he lay down on his bed, and turned away
his face, and would eat no food.
5 But [a]Jezebel his wife came to him, and
said to him, "Why is your spirit so sullen that
you eat no food?"
6 He said to her, "Because I spoke to Naboth
the Jezreelite, and said to him, 'Give me your vineyard for money; or else, if it pleases you, I will
give you *another* vineyard for it.' And he answered, 'I will not give you my vineyard.' "
7 Then Jezebel his wife said to him, "You
now exercise authority over Israel! Arise, eat
food, and let your heart be cheerful; I will give
you the vineyard of Naboth the Jezreelite."
8 And she wrote letters in Ahab's name,
sealed *them* with his seal, and sent the letters to
the elders and the nobles who *were* dwelling in
the city with Naboth.
9 She wrote in the letters, saying,

Proclaim a fast, and seat Naboth with high
honor among the people;
10 and seat two men, scoundrels, before him
to bear witness against him, saying, "You
have [a]blasphemed God and the king."
Then take him out, and [b]stone him, that
he may die.

11 So the men of his city, the elders and nobles who were inhabitants of his city, did as Jezebel had sent to them, as it *was* written in the letters
which she had sent to them.
12 [a]They proclaimed a fast, and seated Naboth with high honor among the people.
13 And two men, scoundrels, came in and sat
before him; and the scoundrels [a]witnessed against
him, against Naboth, in the presence of the people, saying, "Naboth has blasphemed God and the
king!" [b]Then they took him outside the city and
stoned him with stones, so that he died.
14 Then they sent to Jezebel, saying, "Naboth has been stoned and is dead."
15 And it came to pass, when Jezebel heard
that Naboth had been stoned and was dead, that
Jezebel said to Ahab, "Arise, take possession of
the vineyard of Naboth the Jezreelite, which he
refused to give you for money; for Naboth is not
alive, but dead."
16 So it was, when Ahab heard that Naboth
was dead, that Ahab got up and went down to
take possession of the vineyard of Naboth the
Jezreelite.

The LORD Condemns Ahab

17 [a]Then the word of the LORD came to [b]Eli-
jah the Tishbite, saying,
18 "Arise, go down to meet Ahab king of Israel, [a]who *lives* in Samaria. There *he is,* in the
vineyard of Naboth, where he has gone down to
take possession of it.
19 "You shall speak to him, saying, 'Thus
says the LORD: "Have you murdered and also
taken possession?" ' And you shall speak to him,
saying, 'Thus says the LORD: [a]"In the place where
dogs licked the blood of Naboth, dogs shall lick
your blood, even yours." ' "
20 So Ahab said to Elijah, [a]"Have you found

KJV

me, O mine enemy? And he answered, I have found *thee:* because [b]thou hast sold thyself to work evil in the sight of the LORD.

21 Behold, [a]I will bring evil upon thee, and will take away thy [b]posterity, and will cut off from Ahab [c]him that pisseth against the wall, and [d]him that is shut up and left in Israel,

22 And will make thine house like the house of [a]Jeroboam the son of Nebat, and like the house of [b]Baasha the son of Ahijah, for the provocation wherewith thou hast provoked *me* to anger, and made Israel to sin.

23 And [a]of Jezebel also spake the LORD, saying, The dogs shall eat Jezebel by the wall of Jezreel.

24 [a]Him that dieth of Ahab in the city the dogs shall eat; and him that dieth in the field shall the fowls of the air eat.

25 But [a]there was none like unto Ahab, which did sell himself to work wickedness in the sight of the LORD, [b]whom Jezebel his wife stirred up.

26 And he did very abominably in following idols, according to all *things* [a]as did the Amorites, whom the LORD cast out before the children of Israel.

27 And it came to pass, when Ahab heard those words, that he rent his clothes, and [a]put sackcloth upon his flesh, and fasted, and lay in sackcloth, and went softly.

28 And the word of the LORD came to Elijah the Tishbite, saying,

29 Seest thou how Ahab humbleth himself before me? because he [a]humbleth himself before me, I will not bring the evil in his days: *but* [b]in his son's days will I bring the evil upon his house.

Micaiah Warns Ahab
(2 Chr. 18:1–27)

22 And they continued three years without war between Syria and Israel.

2 And it came to pass in the third year, that [a]Jehoshaphat the king of Judah came down to the king of Israel.

3 And the king of Israel said unto his servants, Know ye that [a]Ramoth in Gilead *is* our's, and we *be* still, *and* take it not out of the hand of the king of Syria?

4 And he said unto Jehoshaphat, Wilt thou go with me to battle to Ramoth–gilead? And Jehoshaphat said to the king of Israel, [a]I *am* as thou *art,* my people as thy people, my horses as thy horses.

5 And Jehoshaphat said unto the king of Israel, [a]Enquire, I pray thee, at the word of the LORD to day.

6 Then the king of Israel [a]gathered the prophets together, about four hundred men, and said unto them, Shall I go against Ramoth–gilead to battle, or shall I forbear? And they said, Go up; for the Lord shall deliver *it* into the hand of the king.

7 And [a]Jehoshaphat said, *Is there* not here a prophet of the LORD besides, that we might enquire of him?

8 And the king of Israel said unto Jehoshaphat, *There is* yet one man, Micaiah the son of Imlah, by whom we may enquire of the LORD: but I hate him; for he doth not prophesy good concerning me, but evil. And Jehoshaphat said, Let not the king say so.

9 Then the king of Israel called an officer, and said, Hasten *hither* Micaiah the son of Imlah.

10 And the king of Israel and Jehoshaphat the king of Judah sat each on his throne, having put on their robes, in a void place in the entrance of the gate of Samaria; and all the prophets prophesied before them.

11 And Zedekiah the son of Chenaanah made him [a]horns of iron: and he said, Thus saith the LORD, With these shalt thou [b]push the Syrians, until thou have consumed them.

---

20 [b]1 Kin. 21:25; 2 Kin. 17:17; [Rom. 7:14]
21 [a]1 Kin. 14:10; 2 Kin. 9:8 [b]2 Kin. 10:10 [c]1 Sam. 25:22 [d]1 Kin. 14:10
22 [a]1 Kin. 15:29 [b]1 Kin. 16:3, 11
23 [a]2 Kin. 9:10, 30–37
24 [a]1 Kin. 14:11; 16:4
25 [a]1 Kin. 16:30–33; 21:20 [b]1 Kin. 16:31
26 [a]Gen. 15:16; [Lev. 18:25–30]; 2 Kin. 21:11
27 [a]Gen. 37:34; 2 Sam. 3:31; 2 Kin. 6:30
29 [a][2 Kin. 22:19] [b]2 Kin. 9:25; 10:11, 17

CHAPTER 22

2 [a]1 Kin. 15:24; 2 Chr. 18:2
3 [a]Deut. 4:43; Josh. 21:38; 1 Kin. 4:13
4 [a]2 Kin. 3:7
5 [a]2 Kin. 3:11
6 [a]1 Kin. 18:19
7 [a]2 Kin. 3:11
11 [a]Zech. 1:18–21 [b]Deut. 33:17

*

21:23 So with MT, LXX; some Heb. mss., Syr., Tg., Vg. *plot of ground* instead of *wall* (cf. 2 Kin. 9:36)
22:7 Or *him*

NKJV

me, O my enemy?" And he answered, "I have found *you,* because [b]you have sold yourself to do evil in the sight of the LORD:

21 'Behold, [a]I will bring calamity on you. I will take away your [b]posterity, and will cut off from Ahab [c]every male in Israel, both [d]bond and free.

22 'I will make your house like the house of [a]Jeroboam the son of Nebat, and like the house of [b]Baasha the son of Ahijah, because of the provocation with which you have provoked *Me* to anger, and made Israel sin.'

23 "And [a]concerning Jezebel the LORD also spoke, saying, 'The dogs shall eat Jezebel by the *wall of Jezreel.'

24 "The dogs shall eat [a]whoever belongs to Ahab and dies in the city, and the birds of the air shall eat whoever dies in the field."

25 But [a]there was no one like Ahab who sold himself to do wickedness in the sight of the LORD, [b]because Jezebel his wife stirred him up.

26 And he behaved very abominably in following idols, according to all [a]*that* the Amorites had done, whom the LORD had cast out before the children of Israel.

27 So it was, when Ahab heard those words, that he tore his clothes and [a]put sackcloth on his body, and fasted and lay in sackcloth, and went about mourning.

28 And the word of the LORD came to Elijah the Tishbite, saying,

29 "See how Ahab has humbled himself before Me? Because he [a]has humbled himself before Me, I will not bring the calamity in his days. [b]In the days of his son I will bring the calamity on his house."

Micaiah Warns Ahab
(2 Chr. 18:1–27)

22 Now three years passed without war between Syria and Israel.

2 Then it came to pass, in the third year, that [a]Jehoshaphat the king of Judah went down to *visit* the king of Israel.

3 And the king of Israel said to his servants, "Do you know that [a]Ramoth in Gilead *is* ours, but we hesitate to take it out of the hand of the king of Syria?"

4 So he said to Jehoshaphat, "Will you go with me to fight at Ramoth Gilead?" Jehoshaphat said to the king of Israel, [a]"I *am* as you *are,* my people as your people, my horses as your horses."

5 Also Jehoshaphat said to the king of Israel, [a]"Please inquire for the word of the LORD today."

6 Then the king of Israel [a]gathered the prophets together, about four hundred men, and said to them, "Shall I go against Ramoth Gilead to fight, or shall I refrain?" So they said, "Go up, for the Lord will deliver *it* into the hand of the king."

7 And [a]Jehoshaphat said, "*Is there* not still a prophet of the LORD here, that we may inquire of *Him?"

8 So the king of Israel said to Jehoshaphat, "*There is* still one man, Micaiah the son of Imlah, by whom we may inquire of the LORD; but I hate him, because he does not prophesy good concerning me, but evil." And Jehoshaphat said, "Let not the king say such things!"

9 Then the king of Israel called an officer and said, "Bring Micaiah the son of Imlah quickly!"

10 The king of Israel and Jehoshaphat the king of Judah, having put on *their* robes, sat each on his throne, at a threshing floor at the entrance of the gate of Samaria; and all the prophets prophesied before them.

11 Now Zedekiah the son of Chenaanah had made [a]horns of iron for himself; and he said, "Thus says the LORD: 'With these you shall [b]gore the Syrians until they are destroyed.' "

KJV

12 And all the prophets prophesied so, saying, Go up to Ramoth–gilead, and prosper: for the LORD shall deliver *it* into the king's hand.

13 And the messenger that was gone to call Micaiah spake unto him, saying, Behold now, the words of the prophets *declare* good unto the king with one mouth: let thy word, I pray thee, be like the word of one of them, and speak *that which is* good.

14 And Micaiah said, *As* the LORD liveth, [a]what the LORD saith unto me, that will I speak.

15 So he came to the king. And the king said unto him, Micaiah, shall we go against Ramoth–gilead to battle, or shall we forbear? And he answered him, Go, and prosper: for the LORD shall deliver *it* into the hand of the king.

16 And the king said unto him, How many times shall I adjure thee that thou tell me nothing but *that which is* true in the name of the LORD?

17 And he said, I saw all Israel [a]scattered upon the hills, as sheep that have not a shepherd: and the LORD said, These have no master: let them return every man to his house in peace.

18 And the king of Israel said unto Jehoshaphat, Did I not tell thee that he would prophesy no good concerning me, but evil?

19 And he said, Hear thou therefore the word of the LORD: [a]I saw the LORD sitting on his throne, [b]and all the host of heaven standing by him on his right hand and on his left.

20 And the LORD said, Who shall persuade Ahab, that he may go up and fall at Ramoth–gilead? And one said on this manner, and another said on that manner.

21 And there came forth a spirit, and stood before the LORD, and said, I will persuade him.

22 And the LORD said unto him, Wherewith? And he said, I will go forth, and I will be a lying spirit in the mouth of all his prophets. And he said, [a]Thou shalt persuade *him,* and prevail also: go forth, and do so.

23 [a]Now therefore, behold, the LORD hath put a lying spirit in the mouth of all these thy prophets, and the LORD hath spoken evil concerning thee.

24 But Zedekiah the son of Chenaanah went near, and [a]smote Micaiah on the cheek, and said, [b]Which way went the Spirit of the LORD from me to speak unto thee?

25 And Micaiah said, Behold, thou shalt see in that day, when thou shalt go into an [a]inner chamber to hide thyself.

26 And the king of Israel said, Take Micaiah, and carry him back unto Amon the governor of the city, and to Joash the king's son;

27 And say, Thus saith the king, Put this *fellow* in the [a]prison, and feed him with bread of affliction and with water of affliction, until I come in peace.

28 And Micaiah said, If thou return at all in peace, [a]the LORD hath not spoken by me. And he said, Hearken, O people, every one of you.

Ahab Dies in Battle
(2 Chr. 18:28–34)

29 So the king of Israel and Jehoshaphat the king of Judah went up to Ramoth–gilead.

30 And the king of Israel said unto Jehoshaphat, I will disguise myself, and enter into the battle; but put thou on thy robes. And the king of Israel [a]disguised himself, and went into the battle.

31 But the [a]king of Syria commanded his thirty and two [b]captains that had rule over his chariots, saying, Fight neither with small nor great, save only with the king of Israel.

32 And it came to pass, when the captains of the chariots saw Jehoshaphat, that they said, Surely it *is* the king of Israel. And they turned aside to fight against him: and Jehoshaphat [a]cried out.

33 And it came to pass, when the captains

14 [a]Num. 22:38; 24:13
17 [a]Num. 27:17; 1 Kin. 22:34–36; 2 Chr. 18:16; Matt. 9:36; Mark 6:34
19 [a]Is. 6:1; Ezek. 1:26–28; Dan. 7:9 [b]Job 1:6; 2:1; Ps. 103:20; Dan. 7:10; Zech. 1:10; [Matt. 18:10; Heb. 1:7, 14]
22 [a]Judg. 9:23; 1 Sam. 16:14; 18:10; 19:9; Job 12:16; [Ezek. 14:9; 2 Thess. 2:11]
23 [a][Ezek. 14:9]
24 [a]Jer. 20:2 [b]2 Chr. 18:23
25 [a]1 Kin. 20:30
27 [a]2 Chr. 16:10; 18:25–27
28 [a]Num. 16:29; Deut. 18:20–22
30 [a]2 Chr. 35:22
31 [a]1 Kin. 20:1 [b]1 Kin. 20:24; 2 Chr. 18:30
32 [a]2 Chr. 18:31

NKJV

12 And all the prophets prophesied so, saying, "Go up to Ramoth Gilead and prosper, for the LORD will deliver *it* into the king's hand."

13 Then the messenger who had gone to call Micaiah spoke to him, saying, "Now listen, the words of the prophets with one accord encourage the king. Please, let your word be like the word of one of them, and speak encouragement."

14 And Micaiah said, "*As* the LORD lives, [a]whatever the LORD says to me, that I will speak."

15 Then he came to the king; and the king said to him, "Micaiah, shall we go to war against Ramoth Gilead, or shall we refrain?" And he answered him, "Go and prosper, for the LORD will deliver *it* into the hand of the king!"

16 So the king said to him, "How many times shall I make you swear that you tell me nothing but the truth in the name of the LORD?"

17 Then he said, "I saw all Israel [a]scattered on the mountains, as sheep that have no shepherd. And the LORD said, 'These have no master. Let each return to his house in peace.' "

18 And the king of Israel said to Jehoshaphat, "Did I not tell you he would not prophesy good concerning me, but evil?"

19 Then *Micaiah* said, "Therefore hear the word of the LORD: [a]I saw the LORD sitting on His throne, [b]and all the host of heaven standing by, on His right hand and on His left.

20 "And the LORD said, 'Who will persuade Ahab to go up, that he may fall at Ramoth Gilead?' So one spoke in this manner, and another spoke in that manner.

21 "Then a spirit came forward and stood before the LORD, and said, 'I will persuade him.'

22 "The LORD said to him, 'In what way?' So he said, 'I will go out and be a lying spirit in the mouth of all his prophets.' And the LORD said, [a]'You shall persuade *him,* and also prevail. Go out and do so.'

23 [a]"Therefore look! The LORD has put a lying spirit in the mouth of all these prophets of yours, and the LORD has declared disaster against you."

24 Now Zedekiah the son of Chenaanah went near and [a]struck Micaiah on the cheek, and said, [b]"Which way did the spirit from the LORD go from me to speak to you?"

25 And Micaiah said, "Indeed, you shall see on that day when you go into an [a]inner chamber to hide!"

26 So the king of Israel said, "Take Micaiah, and return him to Amon the governor of the city and to Joash the king's son;

27 "and say, 'Thus says the king: "Put this *fellow* in [a]prison, and feed him with bread of affliction and water of affliction, until I come in peace." ' "

28 But Micaiah said, "If you ever return in peace, [a]the LORD has not spoken by me." And he said, "Take heed, all you people!"

Ahab Dies in Battle
(2 Chr. 18:28–34)

29 So the king of Israel and Jehoshaphat the king of Judah went up to Ramoth Gilead.

30 And the king of Israel said to Jehoshaphat, "I will disguise myself and go into battle; but you put on your robes." So the king of Israel [a]disguised himself and went into battle.

31 Now the [a]king of Syria had commanded the thirty-two [b]captains of his chariots, saying, "Fight with no one small or great, but only with the king of Israel."

32 So it was, when the captains of the chariots saw Jehoshaphat, that they said, "Surely it *is* the king of Israel!" Therefore they turned aside to fight against him, and Jehoshaphat [a]cried out.

33 And it happened, when the captains of the

KJV

of the chariots perceived that it *was* not the king of Israel, that they turned back from pursuing him.

34 And a *certain* man drew a bow at a venture, and smote the king of Israel between the joints of the harness: wherefore he said unto the driver of his chariot, Turn thine hand, and carry me out of the host; for I am wounded.

35 And the battle increased that day: and the king was stayed up in his chariot against the Syrians, and died at even: and the blood ran out of the wound into the midst of the chariot.

36 And there went a proclamation throughout the host about the going down of the sun, saying, Every man to his city, and every man to his own country.

37 So the king died, and was brought to Samaria; and they buried the king in Samaria.

38 And *one* washed the chariot in the pool of Samaria; and the dogs licked up his blood; and they washed his armour; according [a]unto the word of the LORD which he spake.

39 Now the rest of the acts of Ahab, and all that he did, and [a]the ivory house which he made, and all the cities that he built, *are* they not written in the book of the chronicles of the kings of Israel?

40 So Ahab slept with his fathers; and [a]Ahaziah his son reigned in his stead.

Jehoshaphat Reigns in Judah

(2 Chr. 20:31—21:1)

41 And [a]Jehoshaphat the son of Asa began to reign over Judah in the fourth year of Ahab king of Israel.

42 Jehoshaphat *was* thirty and five years old when he began to reign; and he reigned twenty and five years in Jerusalem. And his mother's name *was* Azubah the daughter of Shilhi.

43 And [a]he walked in all the ways of Asa his father; he turned not aside from it, doing *that which was* right in the eyes of the LORD: nevertheless [b]the high places were not taken away; *for* the people offered and burnt incense yet in the high places.

44 And [a]Jehoshaphat made [b]peace with the king of Israel.

45 Now the rest of the acts of Jehoshaphat, and his might that he shewed, and how he warred, *are* they not written [a]in the book of the chronicles of the kings of Judah?

46 [a]And the remnant of the sodomites, which remained in the days of his father Asa, he took out of the land.

47 [a]*There was* then no king in Edom: a deputy *was* king.

48 [a]Jehoshaphat [b]made ships of Tharshish to go to [c]Ophir for gold: [d]but they went not; for the ships were broken at [e]Ezion-geber.

49 Then said Ahaziah the son of Ahab unto Jehoshaphat, Let my servants go with thy servants in the ships. But Jehoshaphat would not.

50 And [a]Jehoshaphat slept with his fathers, and was buried with his fathers in the city of David his father: and Jehoram his son reigned in his stead.

Ahaziah Reigns in Israel

51 [a]Ahaziah the son of Ahab began to reign over Israel in Samaria the seventeenth year of Jehoshaphat king of Judah, and reigned two years over Israel.

52 And he did evil in the sight of the LORD, and [a]walked in the way of his father, and in the way of his mother, and in the way of Jeroboam the son of Nebat, who made Israel to sin:

53 For [a]he served Baal, and worshipped him, and provoked to anger the LORD God of Israel, [b]according to all that his father had done.

38 [a]1 Kin. 21:19
39 [a]Ps. 45:8; Amos 3:15
40 [a]2 Kin. 1:2, 18
41 [a]2 Chr. 20:31
43 [a]2 Chr. 17:3; 20:32, 33 [b]1 Kin. 14:23; 15:14; 2 Kin. 12:3
44 [a]2 Chr. 19:2 [b]2 Chr. 18:1
45 [a]2 Chr. 20:34
46 [a]Gen. 19:5; Deut. 23:17; 1 Kin. 14:24; 15:12; 2 Kin. 23:7; Jude 7
47 [a]2 Sam. 8:14; 2 Kin. 3:9; 8:20
48 [a]2 Chr. 20:35–37 [b]1 Kin. 10:22 [c]1 Kin. 9:28 [d]2 Chr. 20:37 [e]1 Kin. 9:26
50 [a]2 Chr. 21:1
51 [a]1 Kin. 22:40
52 [a]1 Kin. 15:26; 21:25
53 [a]Judg. 2:11 [b]1 Kin. 16:30–32

*
22:38 Tg., Syr. *they washed his armor*
22:46 Heb. *qadesh,* one practicing sodomy and prostitution in religious rituals
22:48 Or *ships of Tarshish*

NKJV

chariots saw that it *was* not the king of Israel, that they turned back from pursuing him.

34 Now a *certain* man drew a bow at random, and struck the king of Israel between the joints of his armor. So he said to the driver of his chariot, "Turn around and take me out of the battle, for I am wounded."

35 The battle increased that day; and the king was propped up in his chariot, facing the Syrians, and died at evening. The blood ran out from the wound onto the floor of the chariot.

36 Then, as the sun was going down, a shout went throughout the army, saying, "Every man to his city, and every man to his own country!"

37 So the king died, and was brought to Samaria. And they buried the king in Samaria.

38 Then *someone* washed the chariot at a pool in Samaria, and the dogs licked up his blood while *the harlots bathed, according [a]to the word of the LORD which He had spoken.

39 Now the rest of the acts of Ahab, and all that he did, [a]the ivory house which he built and all the cities that he built, *are* they not written in the book of the chronicles of the kings of Israel?

40 So Ahab rested with his fathers. Then [a]Ahaziah his son reigned in his place.

Jehoshaphat Reigns in Judah

(2 Chr. 20:31—21:1)

41 [a]Jehoshaphat the son of Asa had become king over Judah in the fourth year of Ahab king of Israel.

42 Jehoshaphat *was* thirty-five years old when he became king, and he reigned twenty-five years in Jerusalem. His mother's name *was* Azubah the daughter of Shilhi.

43 And [a]he walked in all the ways of his father Asa. He did not turn aside from them, doing *what was* right in the eyes of the LORD. Nevertheless [b]the high places were not taken away, *for* the people offered sacrifices and burned incense on the high places.

44 Also [a]Jehoshaphat made [b]peace with the king of Israel.

45 Now the rest of the acts of Jehoshaphat, the might that he showed, and how he made war, *are* they not written [a]in the book of the chronicles of the kings of Judah?

46 [a]And the rest of the *perverted persons, who remained in the days of his father Asa, he banished from the land.

47 [a]*There was* then no king in Edom, only a deputy of the king.

48 [a]Jehoshaphat [b]made *merchant ships to go to [c]Ophir for gold; [d]but they never sailed, for the ships were wrecked at [e]Ezion Geber.

49 Then Ahaziah the son of Ahab said to Jehoshaphat, "Let my servants go with your servants in the ships." But Jehoshaphat would not.

50 And [a]Jehoshaphat rested with his fathers, and was buried with his fathers in the City of David his father. Then Jehoram his son reigned in his place.

Ahaziah Reigns in Israel

51 [a]Ahaziah the son of Ahab became king over Israel in Samaria in the seventeenth year of Jehoshaphat king of Judah, and reigned two years over Israel.

52 He did evil in the sight of the LORD, and [a]walked in the way of his father and in the way of his mother and in the way of Jeroboam the son of Nebat, who had made Israel sin;

53 for [a]he served Baal and worshiped him, and provoked the LORD God of Israel to anger, [b]according to all that his father had done.

KJV

THE SECOND BOOK OF THE

KINGS

God Judges Ahaziah

1 Then Moab [a]rebelled against Israel [b]after the
death of Ahab.
2 And [a]Ahaziah fell down through a lattice
in his upper chamber that *was* in Samaria, and
was sick: and he sent messengers, and said unto
them, Go, enquire of [b]Baal–zebub the god of [c]Ek-
ron whether I shall recover of this disease.
3 But the angel of the LORD said to Elijah
the Tishbite, Arise, go up to meet the messengers
of the king of Samaria, and say unto them, *Is*
it not because *there is* not a God in Israel,
that ye go to enquire of Baal–zebub the god of
Ekron?
4 Now therefore thus saith the LORD, Thou
shalt not come down from that bed on which thou
art gone up, but shalt surely die. And Elijah
departed.
5 And when the messengers turned back
unto him, he said unto them, Why are ye now
turned back?
6 And they said unto him, There came a
man up to meet us, and said unto us, Go, turn
again unto the king that sent you, and say unto
him, Thus saith the LORD, *Is it* not because *there*
is not a God in Israel, *that* thou sendest to enquire
of Baal–zebub the god of Ekron? therefore thou
shalt not come down from that bed on which thou
art gone up, but shalt surely die.
7 And he said unto them, What manner of
man *was he* which came up to meet you, and told
you these words?
8 And they answered him, *He was* [a]an hairy
man, and girt with a girdle of leather about his
loins. And he said, [b]It *is* Elijah the Tishbite.
9 Then the king sent unto him a captain of
fifty with his fifty. And he went up to him: and,
behold, he sat on the top of an hill. And he spake
unto him, Thou man of God, the king hath said,
Come down.
10 And Elijah answered and said to the captain of fifty, If I *be* a man of God, then [a]let fire
come down from heaven, and consume thee and
thy fifty. And there came down fire from heaven,
and consumed him and his fifty.
11 Again also he sent unto him another captain of fifty with his fifty. And he answered and
said unto him, O man of God, thus hath the king
said, Come down quickly.
12 And Elijah answered and said unto them,
If I *be* a man of God, let fire come down from
heaven, and consume thee and thy fifty. And the
fire of God came down from heaven, and consumed him and his fifty.
13 And he sent again a captain of the third
fifty with his fifty. And the third captain of fifty
went up, and came and fell on his knees before
Elijah, and besought him, and said unto him, O
man of God, I pray thee, let my life, and the life
of these fifty thy servants, [a]be precious in thy
sight.
14 Behold, there came fire down from
heaven, and burnt up the two captains of the former fifties with their fifties: therefore let my life
now be precious in thy sight.
15 And the angel of the LORD said unto Elijah,

CHAPTER 1

1 [a]2 Sam. 8:2 [b]2 Kin. 3:5 **2** [a]1 Kin. 22:40 [b]2 Kin. 1:3, 6, 16; Matt. 10:25; Mark 3:22 [c]1 Sam. 5:10 **8** [a]Zech. 13:4; Matt. 3:4; Mark 1:6 [b]1 Kin. 18:7 **10** [a]1 Kin. 18:36–38; Luke 9:54 **13** [a]1 Sam. 26:21; Ps. 72:14

*

1:3 Or *Angel*
1:15 Or *Angel*

NKJV

THE SECOND BOOK OF THE

KINGS

God Judges Ahaziah

1 Moab [a]rebelled against Israel [b]after the
death of Ahab.
2 Now [a]Ahaziah fell through the lattice of
his upper room in Samaria, and was injured; so
he sent messengers and said to them, "Go, inquire
of [b]Baal-Zebub, the god of [c]Ekron, whether I shall
recover from this injury."
3 But the *angel of the LORD said to Elijah
the Tishbite, "Arise, go up to meet the messengers
of the king of Samaria, and say to them, '*Is it*
because *there is* no God in Israel *that* you are
going to inquire of Baal-Zebub, the god of Ekron?'
4 "Now therefore, thus says the LORD: 'You
shall not come down from the bed to which you
have gone up, but you shall surely die.' " So Elijah
departed.
5 And when the messengers returned to
him, he said to them, "Why have you come back?"
6 So they said to him, "A man came up to
meet us, and said to us, 'Go, return to the king
who sent you, and say to him, "Thus says the
LORD: '*Is it* because *there is* no God in Israel *that*
you are sending to inquire of Baal-Zebub, the god
of Ekron? Therefore you shall not come down
from the bed to which you have gone up, but you
shall surely die.' " ' "
7 Then he said to them, "What kind of man
was it who came up to meet you and told you
these words?"
8 So they answered him, [a]"A hairy man
wearing a leather belt around his waist." And he
said, [b]"It *is* Elijah the Tishbite."
9 Then the king sent to him a captain of fifty
with his fifty men. So he went up to him; and
there he was, sitting on the top of a hill. And he
spoke to him: "Man of God, the king has said,
'Come down!' "
10 So Elijah answered and said to the captain
of fifty, "If I *am* a man of God, then [a]let fire come
down from heaven and consume you and your
fifty men." And fire came down from heaven and
consumed him and his fifty.
11 Then he sent to him another captain of
fifty with his fifty men. And he answered and said
to him: "Man of God, thus has the king said,
'Come down quickly!' "
12 So Elijah answered and said to them, "If
I *am* a man of God, let fire come down from
heaven and consume you and your fifty men."
And the fire of God came down from heaven and
consumed him and his fifty.
13 Again, he sent a third captain of fifty with
his fifty men. And the third captain of fifty went
up, and came and fell on his knees before Elijah,
and pleaded with him, and said to him: "Man of
God, please let my life and the life of these fifty
servants of yours [a]be precious in your sight.
14 "Look, fire has come down from heaven
and burned up the first two captains of fifties with
their fifties. But let my life now be precious in
your sight."
15 And the *angel of the LORD said to Elijah,

KJV

Go down with him: be not afraid of him. And he
arose, and went down with him unto the king.
16 And he said unto him, Thus saith the
LORD, Forasmuch as thou hast sent messengers
to enquire of Baal–zebub the god of Ekron, *is it*
not because *there is* no God in Israel to enquire
of his word? therefore thou shalt not come down
off that bed on which thou art gone up, but shalt
surely die.
17 So he died according to the word of the
LORD which Elijah had spoken. And [a]Jehoram
reigned in his stead in the second year of Jehoram
the son of Jehoshaphat king of Judah; because
he had no son.
18 Now the rest of the acts of Ahaziah which
he did, *are* they not written in the book of the
chronicles of the kings of Israel?

Elijah Ascends to Heaven

2 And it came to pass, when the LORD would
[a]take up Elijah into heaven by a whirlwind,
that Elijah went with [b]Elisha from Gilgal.
2 And Elijah said unto Elisha, [a]Tarry here,
I pray thee; for the LORD hath sent me to Beth–el.
And Elisha said *unto him, As* the LORD liveth,
and [b]*as* thy soul liveth, I will not leave thee. So
they went down to Beth–el.
3 And [a]the sons of the prophets that *were*
at Beth–el came forth to Elisha, and said unto him,
Knowest thou that the LORD will take away thy
master from thy head to day? And he said, Yea,
I know *it;* hold ye your peace.
4 And Elijah said unto him, Elisha, tarry
here, I pray thee; for the LORD hath sent me to
Jericho. And he said, *As* the LORD liveth, and *as*
thy soul liveth, I will not leave thee. So they came
to Jericho.
5 And the sons of the prophets that *were*
at Jericho came to Elisha, and said unto him,
Knowest thou that the LORD will take away thy
master from thy head to day? And he answered,
Yea, I know *it;* hold ye your peace.
6 And Elijah said unto him, Tarry, I pray
thee, here; for the LORD hath sent me to Jordan.
And he said, *As* the LORD liveth, and *as* thy soul
liveth, I will not leave thee. And they two went
on.
7 And fifty men of the sons of the prophets
went, and stood to view afar off: and they two
stood by Jordan.
8 And Elijah took his mantle, and wrapped
it together, and smote the waters, and [a]they were
divided hither and thither, so that they two went
over on dry [b]ground.
9 And it came to pass, when they were gone
over, that Elijah said unto Elisha, Ask what I shall
do for thee, before I be taken away from thee.
And Elisha said, I pray thee, let a double portion
of thy spirit be upon me.
10 And he said, Thou hast asked a hard
thing: *nevertheless,* if thou see me *when I am*
taken from thee, it shall be so unto thee; but if
not, it shall not be so.
11 And it came to pass, as they still went on,
and talked, that, behold, *there appeared* [a]a chariot
of fire, and horses of fire, and parted them both
asunder; and Elijah [b]went up by a whirlwind into
heaven.
12 And Elisha saw *it,* and he cried, [a]My father, my father, the chariot of Israel, and the
horsemen thereof. And he saw him no more: and
he took hold of his own clothes, and rent them
in two pieces.
13 He took up also the mantle of Elijah that
fell from him, and went back, and stood by the
bank of Jordan;
14 And he took the mantle of Elijah that fell
from him, and smote the waters, and said, Where
is the LORD God of Elijah? and when he also had
smitten the waters, [a]they parted hither and
thither: and Elisha went over.
15 And when the sons of the prophets which

17 [a]1 Kin. 22:50; 2 Kin. 8:16; Matt. 1:8

CHAPTER 2

1 [a]Gen. 5:24; [Heb. 11:5] [b]1 Kin. 19:16–21
2 [a]Ruth 1:15, 16 [b]1 Sam. 1:26; 2 Kin. 2:4, 6; 4:30
3 [a]1 Kin. 20:35; 2 Kin. 2:5, 7, 15; 4:1, 38; 9:1
8 [a]Ex. 14:21, 22; Josh. 3:16; 2 Kin. 2:14 [b]Josh. 3:17
11 [a]2 Kin. 6:17; Ps. 104:4 [b]Gen. 5:24; Heb. 11:5
12 [a]2 Kin. 13:14
14 [a]2 Kin. 2:8

NKJV

"Go down with him; do not be afraid of him."
So he arose and went down with him to the king.
16 Then he said to him, "Thus says the LORD:
'Because you have sent messengers to inquire of
Baal-Zebub, the god of Ekron, *is it* because *there*
is no God in Israel to inquire of His word? Therefore you shall not come down from the bed to
which you have gone up, but you shall surely
die.'"
17 So *Ahaziah* died according to the word
of the LORD which Elijah had spoken. Because
he had no son, [a]Jehoram* became king in his
place, in the second year of Jehoram the son of
Jehoshaphat, king of Judah.
18 Now the rest of the acts of Ahaziah which
he did, *are* they not written in the book of the
chronicles of the kings of Israel?

Elijah Ascends to Heaven

2 And it came to pass, when the LORD was about
to [a]take up Elijah into heaven by a whirlwind,
that Elijah went with [b]Elisha from Gilgal.
2 Then Elijah said to Elisha, [a]"Stay here,
please, for the LORD has sent me on to Bethel."
But Elisha said, "*As* the LORD lives, and [b]*as* your
soul lives, I will not leave you!" So they went
down to Bethel.
3 Now [a]the sons of the prophets who *were*
at Bethel came out to Elisha, and said to him, "Do
you know that the LORD will take away your master from over you today?" And he said, "Yes, I
know; keep silent!"
4 Then Elijah said to him, "Elisha, stay here,
please, for the LORD has sent me on to Jericho."
But he said, "*As* the LORD lives, and *as* your soul
lives, I will not leave you!" So they came to
Jericho.
5 Now the sons of the prophets who *were*
at Jericho came to Elisha and said to him, "Do
you know that the LORD will take away your master from over you today?" So he answered, "Yes,
I know; keep silent!"
6 Then Elijah said to him, "Stay here,
please, for the LORD has sent me on to the Jordan."
But he said, "*As* the LORD lives, and *as* your soul
lives, I will not leave you!" So the two of them
went on.
7 And fifty men of the sons of the prophets
went and stood facing *them* at a distance, while
the two of them stood by the Jordan.
8 Now Elijah took his mantle, rolled *it* up,
and struck the water; and [a]it was divided this way
and that, so that the two of them crossed over
on dry [b]ground.
9 And so it was, when they had crossed
over, that Elijah said to Elisha, "Ask! What may
I do for you, before I am taken away from you?"
Elisha said, "Please let a double portion of your
spirit be upon me."
10 So he said, "You have asked a hard thing.
Nevertheless, if you see me *when I am* taken from
you, it shall be so for you; but if not, it shall not
be so."
11 Then it happened, as they continued on
and talked, that suddenly [a]a chariot of fire *ap-*
peared with horses of fire, and separated the two
of them; and Elijah [b]went up by a whirlwind into
heaven.
12 And Elisha saw *it,* and he cried out, [a]"My
father, my father, the chariot of Israel and its
horsemen!" So he saw him no more. And he took
hold of his own clothes and tore them into two
pieces.
13 He also took up the mantle of Elijah that
had fallen from him, and went back and stood
by the bank of the Jordan.
14 Then he took the mantle of Elijah that had
fallen from him, and struck the water, and said,
"Where *is* the LORD God of Elijah?" And when
he also had struck the water, [a]it was divided this
way and that; and Elisha crossed over.
15 Now when the sons of the prophets who

---

*
1:17 The son of Ahab king of Israel, 2 Kin. 3:1

KJV

were [a]to view at Jericho saw him, they said, The
spirit of Elijah doth rest on Elisha. And they came
to meet him, and bowed themselves to the ground
before him.
16 And they said unto him, Behold now,
there be with thy servants fifty strong men; let
them go, we pray thee, and seek thy master: [a]lest
peradventure the Spirit of the LORD hath taken
him up, and cast him upon some mountain, or
into some valley. And he said, Ye shall not send.
17 And when they urged him till he was
[a]ashamed, he said, Send. They sent therefore fifty
men; and they sought three days, but found him
not.
18 And when they came again to him, (for
he tarried at Jericho,) he said unto them, Did I
not say unto you, Go not?

Elisha Performs Miracles

19 And the men of the city said unto Elisha,
Behold, I pray thee, the situation of this city *is*
pleasant, as my lord seeth: but the water *is*
naught, and the ground barren.
20 And he said, Bring me a new cruse, and
put salt therein. And they brought *it* to him.
21 And he went forth unto the spring of the
waters, and [a]cast the salt in there, and said, Thus
saith the LORD, I have healed these waters; there
shall not be from thence any more death or barren
land.
22 So the waters were [a]healed unto this day,
according to the saying of Elisha which he spake.
23 And he went up from thence unto Beth–el:
and as he was going up by the way, there came
forth little children out of the city, and mocked
him, and said unto him, Go up, thou bald head;
go up, thou bald head.
24 And he turned back, and looked on them,
and [a]cursed them in the name of the LORD. And
there came forth two she bears out of the wood,
and tare forty and two children of them.
25 And he went from thence to [a]mount Carmel, and from thence he returned to Samaria.

Moab Rebels Against Israel

3 Now [a]Jehoram the son of Ahab began to reign
over Israel in Samaria the eighteenth year of
Jehoshaphat king of Judah, and reigned twelve
years.
2 And he wrought evil in the sight of the
LORD; but not like his father, and like his mother:
for he put away the image of Baal [a]that his father
had made.
3 Nevertheless he cleaved unto [a]the sins of
Jeroboam the son of Nebat, which made Israel
to sin; he departed not therefrom.
4 And Mesha king of Moab was a sheep-
master, and [a]rendered unto the king of Israel an
hundred thousand [b]lambs, and an hundred thousand rams, with the wool.
5 But it came to pass, when [a]Ahab was
dead, that the king of Moab rebelled against the
king of Israel.
6 And king Jehoram went out of Samaria
the same time, and numbered all Israel.
7 And he went and sent to Jehoshaphat the
king of Judah, saying, The king of Moab hath rebelled against me: wilt thou go with me against
Moab to battle? And he said, I will go up: [a]I *am*
as thou *art*, my people as thy people, *and* my
horses as thy horses.
8 And he said, Which way shall we go up?
And he answered, The way through the wilderness of Edom.
9 So the king of Israel went, and the king
of Judah, and the king of Edom: and they fetched
a compass of seven days' journey: and there was
no water for the host, and for the cattle that followed them.
10 And the king of Israel said, Alas! that the
LORD hath called these three kings together, to
deliver them into the hand of Moab!

15 [a]2 Kin. 2:7
16 [a]1 Kin. 18:12; Ezek. 8:3; Acts 8:39
17 [a]2 Kin. 8:11
21 [a]Ex. 15:25, 26; 2 Kin. 4:41; 6:6; John 9:6
22 [a]Ezek. 47:8, 9
24 [a]Deut. 27:13–26
25 [a]1 Kin. 18:19, 20; 2 Kin. 4:25

CHAPTER 3

1 [a]2 Kin. 1:17
2 [a]1 Kin. 16:31, 32
3 [a]1 Kin. 12:28–32
4 [a]2 Sam. 8:2 [b]Is. 16:1, 2
5 [a]2 Kin. 1:1
7 [a]1 Kin. 22:4

NKJV

were [a]from Jericho saw him, they said, "The spirit
of Elijah rests on Elisha." And they came to meet
him, and bowed to the ground before him.
16 Then they said to him, "Look now, there
are fifty strong men with your servants. Please
let them go and search for your master, [a]lest perhaps the Spirit of the LORD has taken him up and
cast him upon some mountain or into some valley." And he said, "You shall not send anyone."
17 But when they urged him till he was
[a]ashamed, he said, "Send *them!*" Therefore they
sent fifty men, and they searched for three days
but did not find him.
18 And when they came back to him, for he
had stayed in Jericho, he said to them, "Did I not
say to you, 'Do not go'?"

Elisha Performs Miracles

19 Then the men of the city said to Elisha,
"Please notice, the situation of this city *is* pleasant, as my lord sees; but the water *is* bad, and
the ground barren."
20 And he said, "Bring me a new bowl, and
put salt in it." So they brought *it* to him.
21 Then he went out to the source of the water, and [a]cast in the salt there, and said, "Thus
says the LORD: 'I have healed this water; from it
there shall be no more death or barrenness.' "
22 So the water remains [a]healed to this day,
according to the word of Elisha which he spoke.
23 Then he went up from there to Bethel; and
as he was going up the road, some youths came
from the city and mocked him, and said to him,
"Go up, you baldhead! Go up, you baldhead!"
24 So he turned around and looked at them,
and [a]pronounced a curse on them in the name
of the LORD. And two female bears came out of
the woods and mauled forty-two of the youths.
25 Then he went from there to [a]Mount Carmel, and from there he returned to Samaria.

Moab Rebels Against Israel

3 Now [a]Jehoram the son of Ahab became king
over Israel at Samaria in the eighteenth year
of Jehoshaphat king of Judah, and reigned twelve
years.
2 And he did evil in the sight of the LORD,
but not like his father and mother; for he put away
the *sacred* pillar of Baal [a]that his father had made.
3 Nevertheless he persisted in [a]the sins of
Jeroboam the son of Nebat, who had made Israel
sin; he did not depart from them.
4 Now Mesha king of Moab was a sheep-
breeder, and he [a]regularly paid the king of Israel
one hundred thousand [b]lambs and the wool of
one hundred thousand rams.
5 But it happened, when [a]Ahab died, that
the king of Moab rebelled against the king of
Israel.
6 So King Jehoram went out of Samaria at
that time and mustered all Israel.
7 Then he went and sent to Jehoshaphat
king of Judah, saying, "The king of Moab has rebelled against me. Will you go with me to fight
against Moab?" And he said, "I will go up; [a]I *am*
as you *are*, my people as your people, my horses
as your horses."
8 Then he said, "Which way shall we go
up?" And he answered, "By way of the Wilderness of Edom."
9 So the king of Israel went with the king
of Judah and the king of Edom, and they marched
on that roundabout route seven days; and there
was no water for the army, nor for the animals
that followed them.
10 And the king of Israel said, "Alas! For the
LORD has called these three kings together to deliver them into the hand of Moab."

KJV

11 But [a]Jehoshaphat said, *Is there* not here a prophet of the LORD, that we may enquire of the LORD by him? And one of the king of Israel's servants answered and said, Here *is* Elisha the son of Shaphat, which [b]poured water on the hands of Elijah.

12 And Jehoshaphat said, The word of the LORD is with him. So the king of Israel and Jehoshaphat and the king of Edom [a]went down to him.

13 And Elisha said unto the king of Israel, [a]What have I to do with thee? [b]get thee to [c]the prophets of thy father, and to the [d]prophets of thy mother. And the king of Israel said unto him, Nay: for the LORD hath called these three kings together, to deliver them into the hand of Moab.

14 And Elisha said, [a]*As* the LORD of hosts liveth, before whom I stand, surely, were it not that I regard the presence of Jehoshaphat the king of Judah, I would not look toward thee, nor see thee.

15 But now bring me [a]a minstrel. And it came to pass, when the minstrel [b]played, that [c]the hand of the LORD came upon him.

16 And he said, Thus saith the LORD, [a]Make this valley full of ditches.

17 For thus saith the LORD, Ye shall not see wind, neither shall ye see rain; yet that valley shall be filled with water, that ye may drink, both ye, and your cattle, and your beasts.

18 And this is *but* a light thing in the sight of the LORD: he will deliver the Moabites also into your hand.

19 And ye shall smite every fenced city, and every choice city, and shall fell every good tree, and stop all wells of water, and mar every good piece of land with stones.

20 And it came to pass in the morning, when [a]the meat offering was offered, that, behold, there came water by the way of Edom, and the country was filled with water.

21 And when all the Moabites heard that the kings were come up to fight against them, they gathered all that were able to put on armour, and upward, and stood in the border.

22 And they rose up early in the morning, and the sun shone upon the water, and the Moabites saw the water on the other side *as* red as blood:

23 And they said, This *is* blood: the kings are surely slain, and they have smitten one another: now therefore, Moab, to the spoil.

24 And when they came to the camp of Israel, the Israelites rose up and smote the Moabites, so that they fled before them: but they went forward smiting the Moabites, even in *their* country.

25 And they beat down the cities, and on every good piece of land cast every man his stone, and filled it; and they stopped all the wells of water, and felled all the good trees: only in [a]Kir-haraseth left they the stones thereof; howbeit the slingers went about *it,* and smote it.

26 And when the king of Moab saw that the battle was too sore for him, he took with him seven hundred men that drew swords, to break through *even* unto the king of Edom: but they could not.

27 Then [a]he took his eldest son that should have reigned in his stead, and offered him *for* a burnt offering upon the wall. And there was great indignation against Israel: [b]and they departed from him, and returned to *their own* land.

Elisha and the Widow's Oil
(*cf. 1 Kin. 17:14–16*)

4 Now there cried a certain woman of the wives of [a]the sons of the prophets unto Elisha, saying, Thy servant my husband is dead; and thou knowest that thy servant did fear the LORD: and the creditor is come [b]to take unto him my two sons to be bondmen.

2 And Elisha said unto her, What shall I do for thee? tell me, what hast thou in the house?

11 [a]1 Kin. 22:7 [b]1 Kin. 19:21; [John 13:4, 5, 13, 14]
12 [a]2 Kin. 2:25
13 [a][Ezek. 14:3] [b]Judg. 10:14; Ruth 1:15 [c]1 Kin. 22:6–11 [d]1 Kin. 18:19
14 [a]1 Kin. 17:1; 2 Kin. 5:16
15 [a]1 Sam. 10:5 [b]1 Sam. 16:16, 23; 1 Chr. 25:1 [c]Ezek. 1:3; 3:14, 22; 8:1
16 [a]Jer. 14:3
20 [a]Ex. 29:39, 40
25 [a]Is. 16:7, 11; Jer. 48:31, 36
27 [a][Deut. 18:10; Amos 2:1; Mic. 6:7] [b]2 Kin. 8:20

CHAPTER 4
1 [a]1 Kin. 20:35; 2 Kin. 2:3 [b][Lev. 25:39–41, 48]; 1 Sam. 22:2; Neh. 5:2–5; Matt. 18:25

NKJV

11 But [a]Jehoshaphat said, "*Is there* no prophet of the LORD here, that we may inquire of the LORD by him?" So one of the servants of the king of Israel answered and said, "Elisha the son of Shaphat *is* here, who [b]poured water on the hands of Elijah."

12 And Jehoshaphat said, "The word of the LORD is with him." So the king of Israel and Jehoshaphat and the king of Edom [a]went down to him.

13 Then Elisha said to the king of Israel, [a]"What have I to do with you? [b]Go to [c]the prophets of your father and the [d]prophets of your mother." But the king of Israel said to him, "No, for the LORD has called these three kings *together* to deliver them into the hand of Moab."

14 And Elisha said, [a]"*As* the LORD of hosts lives, before whom I stand, surely were it not that I regard the presence of Jehoshaphat king of Judah, I would not look at you, nor see you.

15 "But now bring me [a]a musician." Then it happened, when the musician [b]played, that [c]the hand of the LORD came upon him.

16 And he said, "Thus says the LORD: [a]'Make this valley full of ditches.'

17 "For thus says the LORD: 'You shall not see wind, nor shall you see rain; yet that valley shall be filled with water, so that you, your cattle, and your animals may drink.'

18 "And this is a simple matter in the sight of the LORD; He will also deliver the Moabites into your hand.

19 "Also you shall attack every fortified city and every choice city, and shall cut down every good tree, and stop up every spring of water, and ruin every good piece of land with stones."

20 Now it happened in the morning, when [a]the grain offering was offered, that suddenly water came by way of Edom, and the land was filled with water.

21 And when all the Moabites heard that the kings had come up to fight against them, all who were able to bear arms and older were gathered; and they stood at the border.

22 Then they rose up early in the morning, and the sun was shining on the water; and the Moabites saw the water on the other side *as* red as blood.

23 And they said, "This is blood; the kings have surely struck swords and have killed one another; now therefore, Moab, to the spoil!"

24 So when they came to the camp of Israel, Israel rose up and attacked the Moabites, so that they fled before them; and they entered *their* land, killing the Moabites.

25 Then they destroyed the cities, and each man threw a stone on every good piece of land and filled it; and they stopped up all the springs of water and cut down all the good trees. But they left the stones of [a]Kir Haraseth *intact.* However the slingers surrounded and attacked it.

26 And when the king of Moab saw that the battle was too fierce for him, he took with him seven hundred men who drew swords, to break through to the king of Edom, but they could not.

27 Then [a]he took his eldest son who would have reigned in his place, and offered him *as* a burnt offering upon the wall; and there was great indignation against Israel. [b]So they departed from him and returned to *their own* land.

Elisha and the Widow's Oil
(*cf. 1 Kin. 17:14–16*)

4 A certain woman of the wives of [a]the sons of the prophets cried out to Elisha, saying, "Your servant my husband is dead, and you know that your servant feared the LORD. And the creditor is coming [b]to take my two sons to be his slaves."

2 So Elisha said to her, "What shall I do for you? Tell me, what do you have in the house?"

KJV

And she said, Thine handmaid hath not any thing in the house, save a pot of oil.

3 Then he said, Go, borrow thee vessels abroad of all thy neighbours, *even* empty vessels; [a]borrow not a few.

4 And when thou art come in, thou shalt shut the door upon thee and upon thy sons, and shalt pour out into all those vessels, and thou shalt set aside that which is full.

5 So she went from him, and shut the door upon her and upon her sons, who brought *the vessels* to her; and she poured out.

6 And it came to pass, when the vessels were full, that she said unto her son, Bring me yet a vessel. And he said unto her, *There is* not a vessel more. And the oil stayed.

7 Then she came and told the man of God. And he said, Go, sell the oil, and pay thy debt, and live thou and thy children of the rest.

Elisha Raises the Shunammite's Son
(*cf. 1 Kin. 17:17–24*)

8 And it fell on a day, that Elisha passed to [a]Shunem, where *was* a great woman; and she constrained him to eat bread. And *so* it was, *that* as oft as he passed by, he turned in thither to eat bread.

9 And she said unto her husband, Behold now, I perceive that this *is* an holy man of God, which passeth by us continually.

10 Let us make a little chamber, I pray thee, on the wall; and let us set for him there a bed, and a table, and a stool, and a candlestick: and it shall be, when he cometh to us, that he shall turn in thither.

11 And it fell on a day, that he came thither, and he turned into the chamber, and lay there.

12 And he said to [a]Gehazi his servant, Call this Shunammite. And when he had called her, she stood before him.

13 And he said unto him, Say now unto her, Behold, thou hast been careful for us with all this care; what *is* to be done for thee? wouldest thou be spoken for to the king, or to the captain of the host? And she answered, I dwell among mine own people.

14 And he said, What then *is* to be done for her? And Gehazi answered, Verily she hath no child, and her husband is old.

15 And he said, Call her. And when he had called her, she stood in the door.

16 And he said, About this season, according to the time of life, thou shalt embrace a son. And she said, Nay, my lord, *thou* man of God, [a]do not lie unto thine handmaid.

17 And the woman conceived, and bare a son at that season that Elisha had said unto her, according to the time of life.

18 And when the child was grown, it fell on a day, that he went out to his father to the reapers.

19 And he said unto his father, My head, my head. And he said to a lad, Carry him to his mother.

20 And when he had taken him, and brought him to his mother, he sat on her knees till noon, and *then* died.

21 And she went up, and laid him on the bed of the man of God, and shut *the door* upon him, and went out.

22 And she called unto her husband, and said, Send me, I pray thee, one of the young men, and one of the asses, that I may run to the man of God, and come again.

23 And he said, Wherefore wilt thou go to him to day? *it is* neither [a]new moon, nor sabbath. And she said, *It shall be* well.

24 Then she saddled an ass, and said to her servant, Drive, and go forward; slack not *thy* riding for me, except I bid thee.

25 So she went and came unto the man of God [a]to mount Carmel. And it came to pass, when

3 [a]2 Kin. 3:16
8 [a]Josh. 19:18
12 [a]2 Kin. 4:29–31; 5:20–27; 8:4, 5
16 [a]2 Kin. 4:28
23 [a]Num. 10:10; 28:11; 1 Chr. 23:31
25 [a]2 Kin. 2:25

NKJV

And she said, "Your maidservant has nothing in the house but a jar of oil."

3 Then he said, "Go, borrow vessels from everywhere, from all your neighbors—empty vessels; [a]do not gather just a few.

4 "And when you have come in, you shall shut the door behind you and your sons; then pour it into all those vessels, and set aside the full ones."

5 So she went from him and shut the door behind her and her sons, who brought *the vessels* to her; and she poured *it* out.

6 Now it came to pass, when the vessels were full, that she said to her son, "Bring me another vessel." And he said to her, "*There is* not another vessel." So the oil ceased.

7 Then she came and told the man of God. And he said, "Go, sell the oil and pay your debt; and you *and* your sons live on the rest."

Elisha Raises the Shunammite's Son
(*cf. 1 Kin. 17:17–24*)

8 Now it happened one day that Elisha went to [a]Shunem, where there *was* a notable woman, and she persuaded him to eat some food. So it was, as often as he passed by, he would turn in there to eat some food.

9 And she said to her husband, "Look now, I know that this *is* a holy man of God, who passes by us regularly.

10 "Please, let us make a small upper room on the wall; and let us put a bed for him there, and a table and a chair and a lampstand; so it will be, whenever he comes to us, he can turn in there."

11 And it happened one day that he came there, and he turned in to the upper room and lay down there.

12 Then he said to [a]Gehazi his servant, "Call this Shunammite woman." When he had called her, she stood before him.

13 And he said to him, "Say now to her, 'Look, you have been concerned for us with all this care. What *can I* do for you? Do you want me to speak on your behalf to the king or to the commander of the army?' " She answered, "I dwell among my own people."

14 So he said, "What then *is* to be done for her?" And Gehazi answered, "Actually, she has no son, and her husband is old."

15 So he said, "Call her." When he had called her, she stood in the doorway.

16 Then he said, "About this time next year you shall embrace a son." And she said, "No, my lord. Man of God, [a]do not lie to your maidservant!"

17 But the woman conceived, and bore a son when the appointed time had come, of which Elisha had told her.

18 And the child grew. Now it happened one day that he went out to his father, to the reapers.

19 And he said to his father, "My head, my head!" So he said to a servant, "Carry him to his mother."

20 When he had taken him and brought him to his mother, he sat on her knees till noon, and *then* died.

21 And she went up and laid him on the bed of the man of God, shut *the door* upon him, and went out.

22 Then she called to her husband, and said, "Please send me one of the young men and one of the donkeys, that I may run to the man of God and come back."

23 So he said, "Why are you going to him today? *It is* neither the [a]New Moon nor the Sabbath." And she said, "*It is* well."

24 Then she saddled a donkey, and said to her servant, "Drive, and go forward; do not slacken the pace for me unless I tell you."

25 And so she departed, and went to the man of God [a]at Mount Carmel.

KJV

the man of God saw her afar off, that he said to Gehazi his servant, Behold, *yonder is* that Shunammite:

26 Run now, I pray thee, to meet her, and say unto her, *Is it* well with thee? *is it* well with thy husband? *is it* well with the child? And she answered, *It is* well.

27 And when she came to the man of God to the hill, she caught him by the feet: but Gehazi came near to thrust her away. And the man of God said, Let her alone; for her soul *is* vexed within her: and the LORD hath hid *it* from me, and hath not told me.

28 Then she said, Did I desire a son of my lord? [a]did I not say, Do not deceive me?

29 Then he said to Gehazi, [a]Gird up thy loins, and take my staff in thine hand, and go thy way: if thou meet any man, [b]salute him not; and if any salute thee, answer him not again: and [c]lay my staff upon the face of the child.

30 And the mother of the child said, [a]*As* the LORD liveth, and *as* thy soul liveth, I will not [b]leave thee. And he arose, and followed her.

31 And Gehazi passed on before them, and laid the staff upon the face of the child; but *there was* neither voice, nor hearing. Wherefore he went again to meet him, and told him, saying, The child is [a]not awaked.

32 And when Elisha was come into the house, behold, the child was dead, *and* laid upon his bed.

33 He [a]went in therefore, and shut the door upon them twain, [b]and prayed unto the LORD.

34 And he went up, and lay upon the child, and put his mouth upon his mouth, and his eyes upon his eyes, and his hands upon his hands: and [a]he stretched himself upon the child; and the flesh of the child waxed warm.

35 Then he returned, and walked in the house to and fro; and went up, [a]and stretched himself upon him: and [b]the child sneezed seven times, and the child opened his eyes.

36 And he called Gehazi, and said, Call this Shunammite. So he called her. And when she was come in unto him, he said, Take up thy son.

37 Then she went in, and fell at his feet, and bowed herself to the ground, and [a]took up her son, and went out.

Elisha Purifies the Pot of Stew

38 And Elisha came again to [a]Gilgal: and *there was* a [b]dearth in the land; and the sons of the prophets *were* [c]sitting before him: and he said unto his servant, Set on the great pot, and seethe pottage for the sons of the prophets.

39 And one went out into the field to gather herbs, and found a wild vine, and gathered thereof wild gourds his lap full, and came and shred *them* into the pot of pottage: for they knew *them* not.

40 So they poured out for the men to eat. And it came to pass, as they were eating of the pottage, that they cried out, and said, O *thou* man of God, *there is* [a]death in the pot. And they could not eat *thereof.*

41 But he said, Then bring meal. And [a]he cast *it* into the pot; and he said, Pour out for the people, that they may eat. And there was no harm in the pot.

Elisha Feeds One Hundred Men
(cf. Matt. 14:13–21; 15:32–39)

42 And there came a man from [a]Baal–shalisha, [b]and brought the man of God bread of the firstfruits, twenty loaves of barley, and full ears of corn in the husk thereof. And he said, Give unto the people, that they may eat.

43 And his servitor said, [a]What, should I set this before an hundred men? He said again, Give the people, that they may eat: for thus saith the LORD, [b]They shall eat, and shall leave *thereof.*

28 [a]2 Kin. 4:16
29 [a]1 Kin. 18:46; 2 Kin. 9:1 [b]Luke 10:4 [c]Ex. 7:19; 14:16; 2 Kin. 2:8, 14; Acts 19:12
30 [a]2 Kin. 2:2 [b]2 Kin. 2:4
31 [a]John 11:11
33 [a]2 Kin. 4:4; [Matt. 6:6]; Luke 8:51 [b]1 Kin. 17:20
34 [a]1 Kin. 17:21–23; Acts 20:10
35 [a]1 Kin. 17:21 [b]2 Kin. 8:1, 5
37 [a]1 Kin. 17:23; [Heb. 11:35]
38 [a]2 Kin. 2:1 [b]2 Kin. 8:1 [c]Luke 10:39; Acts 22:3
40 [a]Ex. 10:17
41 [a]Ex. 15:25; 2 Kin. 2:21
42 [a]1 Sam. 9:4 [b]1 Sam. 9:7; [1 Cor. 9:11; Gal. 6:6]
43 [a]Luke 9:13; John 6:9 [b]Luke 9:17; John 6:11

NKJV

So it was, when the man of God saw her afar off, that he said to his servant Gehazi, "Look, the Shunammite woman!

26 "Please run now to meet her, and say to her, '*Is it* well with you? *Is it* well with your husband? *Is it* well with the child?' " And she answered, "*It is* well."

27 Now when she came to the man of God at the hill, she caught him by the feet, but Gehazi came near to push her away. But the man of God said, "Let her alone; for her soul *is* in deep distress, and the LORD has hidden *it* from me, and has not told me."

28 So she said, "Did I ask a son of my lord? [a]Did I not say, 'Do not deceive me'?"

29 Then he said to Gehazi, [a]"Get yourself ready, and take my staff in your hand, and be on your way. If you meet anyone, [b]do not greet him; and if anyone greets you, do not answer him; but [c]lay my staff on the face of the child."

30 And the mother of the child said, [a]"*As* the LORD lives, and *as* your soul lives, I will not [b]leave you." So he arose and followed her.

31 Now Gehazi went on ahead of them, and laid the staff on the face of the child; but *there was* neither voice nor hearing. Therefore he went back to meet him, and told him, saying, "The child has [a]not awakened."

32 When Elisha came into the house, there was the child, lying dead on his bed.

33 He [a]went in therefore, shut the door behind the two of them, [b]and prayed to the LORD.

34 And he went up and lay on the child, and put his mouth on his mouth, his eyes on his eyes, and his hands on his hands; and [a]he stretched himself out on the child, and the flesh of the child became warm.

35 He returned and walked back and forth in the house, and again went up [a]and stretched himself out on him; then [b]the child sneezed seven times, and the child opened his eyes.

36 And he called Gehazi and said, "Call this Shunammite woman." So he called her. And when she came in to him, he said, "Pick up your son."

37 So she went in, fell at his feet, and bowed to the ground; then she [a]picked up her son and went out.

Elisha Purifies the Pot of Stew

38 And Elisha returned to [a]Gilgal, and *there was* a [b]famine in the land. Now the sons of the prophets *were* [c]sitting before him; and he said to his servant, "Put on the large pot, and boil stew for the sons of the prophets."

39 So one went out into the field to gather herbs, and found a wild vine, and gathered from it a lapful of wild gourds, and came and sliced *them* into the pot of stew, though they did not know *what they were.*

40 Then they served it to the men to eat. Now it happened, as they were eating the stew, that they cried out and said, "Man of God, *there is* [a]death in the pot!" And they could not eat *it.*

41 So he said, "Then bring some flour." And [a]he put *it* into the pot, and said, "Serve *it* to the people, that they may eat." And there was nothing harmful in the pot.

Elisha Feeds One Hundred Men
(cf. Matt. 14:13–21; 15:32–39)

42 Then a man came from [a]Baal Shalisha, [b]and brought the man of God bread of the firstfruits, twenty loaves of barley bread, and newly ripened grain in his knapsack. And he said, "Give *it* to the people, that they may eat."

43 But his servant said, [a]"What? Shall I set this before one hundred men?" He said again, "Give it to the people, that they may eat; for thus says the LORD: [b]'They shall eat and have *some* left over.' "

KJV

44 So he set *it* before them, and they did eat,
[a]and left *thereof*, according to the word of the
LORD.

Naaman's Leprosy Healed

5 Now [a]Naaman, captain of the host of the king
of Syria, was [b]a great man with his master,
and honourable, because by him the LORD had
given deliverance unto Syria: he was also a
mighty man in valour, *but he was* a leper.
2 And the Syrians had gone out [a]by companies, and had brought away captive out of the land
of Israel a little maid; and she waited on Naaman's
wife.
3 And she said unto her mistress, Would
God my lord *were* with the prophet that *is* in Samaria! for he would recover him of his leprosy.
4 And *one* went in, and told his lord, saying,
Thus and thus said the maid that *is* of the land
of Israel.
5 And the king of Syria said, Go to, go, and
I will send a letter unto the king of Israel. And
he departed, and [a]took with him ten talents of
silver, and six thousand *pieces* of gold, and ten
changes of raiment.
6 And he brought the letter to the king of
Israel, saying, Now when this letter is come unto
thee, behold, I have *therewith* sent Naaman my
servant to thee, that thou mayest recover him of
his leprosy.
7 And it came to pass, when the king of Israel had read the letter, that he rent his clothes,
and said, *Am* I [a]God, to kill and to make alive,
that this man doth send unto me to recover a man
of his leprosy? wherefore consider, I pray you,
and see how he seeketh a quarrel against me.
8 And it was *so*, when Elisha the man of
God had heard that the king of Israel had rent
his clothes, that he sent to the king, saying,
Wherefore hast thou rent thy clothes? let him
come now to me, and he shall know that there is
a prophet in Israel.
9 So Naaman came with his horses and with
his chariot, and stood at the door of the house of
Elisha.
10 And Elisha sent a messenger unto him,
saying, Go and [a]wash in Jordan seven times, and
thy flesh shall come again to thee, and thou shalt
be clean.
11 But Naaman was wroth, and went away,
and said, Behold, I thought, He will surely come
out to me, and stand, and call on the name of
the LORD his God, and strike his hand over the
place, and recover the leper.
12 *Are* not Abana and Pharpar, rivers of Damascus, better than all the waters of Israel? may
I not wash in them, and be clean? So he turned
and went away in a rage.
13 And his [a]servants came near, and spake
unto him, and said, My father, *if* the prophet had
bid thee *do some* great thing, wouldest thou not
have done *it*? how much rather then, when he
saith to thee, Wash, and be clean?
14 Then went he down, and dipped himself
seven times in Jordan, according to the saying
of the man of God: and his [a]flesh came again like
unto the flesh of a little child, and [b]he was clean.
15 And he returned to the man of God, he
and all his company, and came, and stood before
him: and he said, Behold, now I know that *there*
is [a]no God in all the earth, but in Israel: now therefore, I pray thee, take [b]a blessing of thy servant.
16 But he said, [a]*As* the LORD liveth, before
whom I stand, [b]I will receive none. And he urged
him to take *it*; but he refused.
17 And Naaman said, Shall there not then, I
pray thee, be given to thy servant two mules' burden of earth? for thy servant will henceforth offer
neither burnt offering nor sacrifice unto other
gods, but unto the LORD.
18 In this thing the LORD pardon thy servant,
that when my master goeth into the house of Rim-

44 [a]Matt. 14:20; 15:37; John 6:13

CHAPTER 5

1 [a]Luke 4:27 [b]Ex. 11:3
2 [a]2 Kin. 6:23; 13:20
5 [a]1 Sam. 9:8; 2 Kin. 8:8, 9
7 [a][Gen. 30:2; Deut. 32:39; 1 Sam. 2:6]
10 [a]2 Kin. 4:41; John 9:7
13 [a]1 Sam. 28:23
14 [a]2 Kin. 5:10; Job 33:25 [b]Luke 4:27; 5:13
15 [a]Dan. 2:47; 3:29; 6:26, 27 [b]Gen. 33:11
16 [a]2 Kin. 3:14 [b]Gen. 14:22, 23; 2 Kin. 5:20, 26; [Matt. 10:8]; Acts 8:18, 20

*

5:12 So with Kt., LXX, Vg.; Qr., Syr., Tg. *Amanah*

NKJV

44 So he set *it* before them; and they ate [a]and
had *some* left over, according to the word of the
LORD.

Naaman's Leprosy Healed

5 Now [a]Naaman, commander of the army of the
king of Syria, was [b]a great and honorable man
in the eyes of his master, because by him the LORD
had given victory to Syria. He was also a mighty
man of valor, *but* a leper.
2 And the Syrians had gone out [a]on raids,
and had brought back captive a young girl from
the land of Israel. She waited on Naaman's wife.
3 Then she said to her mistress, "If only my
master *were* with the prophet who *is* in Samaria!
For he would heal him of his leprosy."
4 And *Naaman* went in and told his master,
saying, "Thus and thus said the girl who *is* from
the land of Israel."
5 Then the king of Syria said, "Go now, and
I will send a letter to the king of Israel." So he
departed and [a]took with him ten talents of silver,
six thousand *shekels* of gold, and ten changes of
clothing.
6 Then he brought the letter to the king of
Israel, which said,

> Now be advised, when this letter comes
> to you, that I have sent Naaman my
> servant to you, that you may heal him of
> his leprosy.

7 And it happened, when the king of Israel
read the letter, that he tore his clothes and said,
"*Am* I [a]God, to kill and make alive, that this man
sends a man to me to heal him of his leprosy?
Therefore please consider, and see how he seeks
a quarrel with me."
8 So it was, when Elisha the man of God
heard that the king of Israel had torn his clothes,
that he sent to the king, saying, "Why have you
torn your clothes? Please let him come to me, and
he shall know that there is a prophet in Israel."
9 Then Naaman went with his horses and
chariot, and he stood at the door of Elisha's house.
10 And Elisha sent a messenger to him, saying, "Go and [a]wash in the Jordan seven times,
and your flesh shall be restored to you, and *you*
shall be clean."
11 But Naaman became furious, and went
away and said, "Indeed, I said to myself, 'He will
surely come out *to me*, and stand and call on the
name of the LORD his God, and wave his hand
over the place, and heal the leprosy.'
12 "*Are* not the *Abanah and the Pharpar,
the rivers of Damascus, better than all the waters
of Israel? Could I not wash in them and be clean?"
So he turned and went away in a rage.
13 And his [a]servants came near and spoke
to him, and said, "My father, *if* the prophet had
told you *to do* something great, would you not
have done *it*? How much more then, when he says
to you, 'Wash, and be clean'?"
14 So he went down and dipped seven times
in the Jordan, according to the saying of the man
of God; and his [a]flesh was restored like the flesh
of a little child, and [b]he was clean.
15 And he returned to the man of God, he
and all his aides, and came and stood before him;
and he said, "Indeed, now I know that *there is*
[a]no God in all the earth, except in Israel; now
therefore, please take [b]a gift from your servant."
16 But he said, [a]"*As* the LORD lives, before
whom I stand, [b]I will receive nothing." And he
urged him to take *it*, but he refused.
17 So Naaman said, "Then, if not, please let
your servant be given two mule-loads of earth;
for your servant will no longer offer either burnt
offering or sacrifice to other gods, but to the LORD.
18 "Yet in this thing may the LORD pardon
your servant: when my master goes into the tem-

KJV

mon to worship there, and [a]he leaneth on my hand, and I bow myself in the house of Rimmon: when I bow down myself in the house of Rimmon, the LORD pardon thy servant in this thing.

19 And he said unto him, Go in peace. So he departed from him a little way.

Gehazi's Greed

20 But [a]Gehazi, the servant of Elisha the man of God, said, Behold, my master hath spared Naaman this Syrian, in not receiving at his hands that which he brought: but, *as* the LORD liveth, I will run after him, and take somewhat of him.

21 So Gehazi followed after Naaman. And when Naaman saw *him* running after him, he lighted down from the chariot to meet him, and said, *Is* all well?

22 And he said, All *is* [a]well. My master hath sent me, saying, Behold, even now there be come to me from mount Ephraim two young men of the sons of the prophets: give them, I pray thee, a talent of silver, and two changes of garments.

23 And Naaman said, Be content, take two talents. And he urged him, and bound two talents of silver in two bags, with two changes of garments, and laid *them* upon two of his servants; and they bare *them* before him.

24 And when he came to the tower, he took *them* from their hand, and bestowed *them* in the house: and he let the men go, and they departed.

25 But he went in, and stood before his master. And Elisha said unto him, Whence *comest thou,* Gehazi? And he said, Thy servant went no whither.

26 And he said unto him, Went not mine heart *with thee,* when the man turned again from his chariot to meet thee? *Is it* a [a]time to receive money, and to receive garments, and oliveyards, and vineyards, and sheep, and oxen, and menservants, and maidservants?

27 The leprosy therefore of Naaman [a]shall cleave unto thee, and unto thy seed for ever. And he went out from his presence [b]a leper *as white* as snow.

The Floating Ax Head

6 And [a]the sons of the prophets said unto Elisha, Behold now, the place where we dwell with thee is too strait for us.

2 Let us go, we pray thee, unto Jordan, and take thence every man a beam, and let us make us a place there, where we may dwell. And he answered, Go ye.

3 And one said, Be [a]content, I pray thee, and go with thy servants. And he answered, I will go.

4 So he went with them. And when they came to Jordan, they cut down wood.

5 But as one was felling a beam, the ax head fell into the water: and he cried, and said, Alas, master! for it was [a]borrowed.

6 And the man of God said, Where fell it? And he shewed him the place. And [a]he cut down a stick, and cast *it* in thither; and the iron did swim.

7 Therefore said he, Take *it* up to thee. And he put out his hand, and took it.

The Blinded Syrians Captured

8 Then the [a]king of Syria warred against Israel, and took counsel with his servants, saying, In such and such a place *shall be* my camp.

9 And the man of God sent unto the king of Israel, saying, Beware that thou pass not such a place; for thither the Syrians are come down.

10 And the king of Israel sent to the place which the man of God told him and warned him of, and saved himself there, not once nor twice.

11 Therefore the heart of the king of Syria was sore troubled for this thing; and he called

18 [a]2 Kin. 7:2, 17
20 [a]2 Kin. 4:12; 8:4, 5
22 [a]2 Kin. 4:26
26 [a][Eccl. 3:1, 6]
27 [a][1 Tim. 6:10] [b]Ex. 4:6; Num. 12:10; 2 Kin. 15:5

CHAPTER 6

1 [a]2 Kin. 4:38
3 [a]2 Kin. 5:23
5 [a][Ex. 22:14]
6 [a]Ex. 15:25; 2 Kin. 2:21; 4:41
8 [a]2 Kin. 8:28, 29

NKJV

ple of Rimmon to worship there, and [a]he leans on my hand, and I bow down in the temple of Rimmon—when I bow down in the temple of Rimmon, may the LORD please pardon your servant in this thing."

19 Then he said to him, "Go in peace." So he departed from him a short distance.

Gehazi's Greed

20 But [a]Gehazi, the servant of Elisha the man of God, said, "Look, my master has spared Naaman this Syrian, while not receiving from his hands what he brought; but *as* the LORD lives, I will run after him and take something from him."

21 So Gehazi pursued Naaman. When Naaman saw *him* running after him, he got down from the chariot to meet him, and said, "*Is* all well?"

22 And he said, "All *is* [a]well. My master has sent me, saying, 'Indeed, just now two young men of the sons of the prophets have come to me from the mountains of Ephraim. Please give them a talent of silver and two changes of garments.' "

23 So Naaman said, "Please, take two talents." And he urged him, and bound two talents of silver in two bags, with two changes of garments, and handed *them* to two of his servants; and they carried *them* on ahead of him.

24 When he came to the citadel, he took *them* from their hand, and stored *them* away in the house; then he let the men go, and they departed.

25 Now he went in and stood before his master. Elisha said to him, "Where *did you go,* Gehazi?" And he said, "Your servant did not go anywhere."

26 Then he said to him, "Did not my heart go *with you* when the man turned back from his chariot to meet you? *Is it* [a]time to receive money and to receive clothing, olive groves and vineyards, sheep and oxen, male and female servants?

27 "Therefore the leprosy of Naaman [a]shall cling to you and your descendants forever." And he went out from his presence [b]leprous, *as white* as snow.

The Floating Ax Head

6 And [a]the sons of the prophets said to Elisha, "See now, the place where we dwell with you is too small for us.

2 "Please, let us go to the Jordan, and let every man take a beam from there, and let us make there a place where we may dwell." So he answered, "Go."

3 Then one said, [a]"Please consent to go with your servants." And he answered, "I will go."

4 So he went with them. And when they came to the Jordan, they cut down trees.

5 But as one was cutting down a tree, the iron *ax head* fell into the water; and he cried out and said, "Alas, master! For it was [a]borrowed."

6 So the man of God said, "Where did it fall?" And he showed him the place. So [a]he cut off a stick, and threw *it* in there; and he made the iron float.

7 Therefore he said, "Pick *it* up for yourself." So he reached out his hand and took it.

The Blinded Syrians Captured

8 Now the [a]king of Syria was making war against Israel; and he consulted with his servants, saying, "My camp *will be* in such and such a place."

9 And the man of God sent to the king of Israel, saying, "Beware that you do not pass this place, for the Syrians are coming down there."

10 Then the king of Israel sent *someone* to the place of which the man of God had told him. Thus he warned him, and he was watchful there, not just once or twice.

11 Therefore the heart of the king of Syria was greatly troubled by this thing; and he called

KJV

his servants, and said unto them, Will ye not shew
me which of us *is* for the king of Israel?
12 And one of his servants said, None, my
lord, O king: but Elisha, the prophet that *is* in
Israel, telleth the king of Israel the words that thou
speakest in thy bedchamber.
13 And he said, Go and spy where he *is,* that
I may send and fetch him. And it was told him,
saying, Behold, *he is* in [a]Dothan.
14 Therefore sent he thither horses, and
chariots, and a great host: and they came by night,
and compassed the city about.
15 And when the servant of the man of God
was risen early, and gone forth, behold, an host
compassed the city both with horses and chariots.
And his servant said unto him, Alas, my master!
how shall we do?
16 And he answered, [a]Fear not: for [b]they that
be with us *are* more than they that *be* with them.
17 And Elisha prayed, and said, LORD, I pray
thee, open his eyes, that he may see. And the LORD
[a]opened the eyes of the young man; and he saw:
and, behold, the mountain *was* full of [b]horses and
chariots of fire round about Elisha.
18 And when they came down to him, Elisha
prayed unto the LORD, and said, Smite this people,
I pray thee, with blindness. And [a]he smote them
with blindness according to the word of Elisha.
19 And Elisha said unto them, This *is* not the
way, neither *is* this the city: follow me, and I will
bring you to the man whom ye seek. But he led
them to Samaria.
20 And it came to pass, when they were come
into Samaria, that Elisha said, LORD, open the eyes
of these *men,* that they may see. And the LORD
opened their eyes, and they saw; and, behold, *they
were* in the midst of Samaria.
21 And the king of Israel said unto Elisha,
when he saw them, My [a]father, shall I smite *them?*
shall I smite *them?*
22 And he answered, Thou shalt not smite
them: wouldest thou smite those whom thou hast
taken captive with thy sword and with thy bow?
[a]set bread and water before them, that they may
eat and drink, and go to their master.
23 And he prepared great provision for them:
and when they had eaten and drunk, he sent them
away, and they went to their master. So [a]the
bands of Syria came no more into the land of Israel.

Syria Besieges Samaria in Famine

24 And it came to pass after this, that [a]Ben-
hadad king of Syria gathered all his host, and
went up, and besieged Samaria.
25 And there was a great [a]famine in Samaria:
and, behold, they besieged it, until an ass's head
was *sold* for fourscore *pieces* of silver, and the
fourth part of a cab of dove's dung for five *pieces*
of silver.
26 And as the king of Israel was passing by
upon the wall, there cried a woman unto him, saying, Help, my lord, O king.
27 And he said, If the LORD do not help thee,
whence shall I help thee? out of the barnfloor, or
out of the winepress?
28 And the king said unto her, What aileth
thee? And she answered, This woman said unto
me, Give thy son, that we may eat him to day,
and we will eat my son to morrow.
29 So [a]we boiled my son, and did eat him:
and I said unto her on the next day, Give thy son,
that we may eat him: and she hath hid her son.
30 And it came to pass, when the king heard
the words of the woman, that he [a]rent his clothes;
and he passed by upon the wall, and the people
looked, and, behold, *he had* sackcloth within upon
his flesh.
31 Then he said, [a]God do so and more also

13 [a]Gen. 37:17
16 [a]Ex. 14:13; 1 Kin. 17:13 [b]2 Chr. 32:7; Ps. 55:18; [Rom. 8:31]
17 [a]Num. 22:31; Luke 24:31 [b]2 Kin. 2:11; Ps. 34:7; 68:17; Zech. 1:8; 6:1–7
18 [a]Gen. 19:11; Acts 13:11
21 [a]2 Kin. 2:12; 5:13; 8:9
22 [a][Rom. 12:20]
23 [a]2 Kin. 5:2; 6:8, 9
24 [a]1 Kin. 20:1
25 [a]2 Kin. 4:38; 8:1
29 [a]Lev. 26:27–29; Deut. 28:52–57; Lam. 4:10
30 [a]1 Kin. 21:27
31 [a]Ruth 1:17; 1 Kin. 19:2

NKJV

his servants and said to them, "Will you not show
me which of us *is* for the king of Israel?"
12 And one of his servants said, "None, my
lord, O king; but Elisha, the prophet who *is* in
Israel, tells the king of Israel the words that you
speak in your bedroom."
13 So he said, "Go and see where he *is,* that
I may send and get him." And it was told him,
saying, "Surely *he is* in [a]Dothan."
14 Therefore he sent horses and chariots and
a great army there, and they came by night and
surrounded the city.
15 And when the servant of the man of God
arose early and went out, there was an army, surrounding the city with horses and chariots. And
his servant said to him, "Alas, my master! What
shall we do?"
16 So he answered, [a]"Do not fear, for [b]those
who *are* with us *are* more than those who *are*
with them."
17 And Elisha prayed, and said, "LORD, I
pray, open his eyes that he may see." Then the
LORD [a]opened the eyes of the young man, and
he saw. And behold, the mountain *was* full of
[b]horses and chariots of fire all around Elisha.
18 So when *the Syrians* came down to him,
Elisha prayed to the LORD, and said, "Strike this
people, I pray, with blindness." And [a]He struck
them with blindness according to the word of
Elisha.
19 Now Elisha said to them, "This *is* not the
way, nor *is* this the city. Follow me, and I will
bring you to the man whom you seek." But he
led them to Samaria.
20 So it was, when they had come to Samaria, that Elisha said, "LORD, open the eyes of
these *men,* that they may see." And the LORD
opened their eyes, and they saw; and there *they
were,* inside Samaria!
21 Now when the king of Israel saw them,
he said to Elisha, "My [a]father, shall I kill *them?*
Shall I kill *them?*"
22 But he answered, "You shall not kill *them.*
Would you kill those whom you have taken captive with your sword and your bow? [a]Set food
and water before them, that they may eat and
drink and go to their master."
23 Then he prepared a great feast for them;
and after they ate and drank, he sent them away
and they went to their master. So [a]the bands of
Syrian *raiders* came no more into the land of Israel.

Syria Besieges Samaria in Famine

24 And it happened after this that [a]Ben-Ha-
dad king of Syria gathered all his army, and went
up and besieged Samaria.
25 And there was a great [a]famine in Samaria;
and indeed they besieged it until a donkey's head
was *sold* for eighty *shekels* of silver, and one-
fourth of a kab of dove droppings for five *shekels*
of silver.
26 Then, as the king of Israel was passing
by on the wall, a woman cried out to him, saying,
"Help, my lord, O king!"
27 And he said, "If the LORD does not help
you, where can I find help for you? From the
threshing floor or from the winepress?"
28 Then the king said to her, "What is troubling you?" And she answered, "This woman said
to me, 'Give your son, that we may eat him today,
and we will eat my son tomorrow.'
29 "So [a]we boiled my son, and ate him. And
I said to her on the next day, 'Give your son,
that we may eat him'; but she has hidden her
son."
30 Now it happened, when the king heard the
words of the woman, that he [a]tore his clothes;
and as he passed by on the wall, the people
looked, and there underneath *he had* sackcloth
on his body.
31 Then he said, [a]"God do so to me and more

KJV

to me, if the head of Elisha the son of Shaphat shall stand on him this day.
32 But Elisha sat in his house, and [a]the elders sat with him; and *the king* sent a man from before him: but ere the messenger came to him, he said to the elders, [b]See ye how this son of [c]a murderer hath sent to take away mine head? look, when the messenger cometh, shut the door, and hold him fast at the door: *is* not the sound of his master's feet behind him?
33 And while he yet talked with them, behold, the messenger came down unto him: and he said, Behold, this evil *is* of the LORD; [a]what should I wait for the LORD any longer?

7 Then Elisha said, Hear ye the word of the LORD; Thus saith the LORD, [a]To morrow about this time *shall* a measure of fine flour *be sold* for a shekel, and two measures of barley for a shekel, in the gate of Samaria.
2 [a]Then a lord on whose hand the king leaned answered the man of God, and said, Behold, [b]*if* the LORD would make windows in heaven, might this thing be? And he said, Behold, thou shalt see *it* with thine eyes, but shalt not eat thereof.

The Syrians Flee

3 And there were four leprous men [a]at the entering in of the gate: and they said one to another, Why sit we here until we die?
4 If we say, We will enter into the city, then the famine *is* in the city, and we shall die there: and if we sit still here, we die also. Now therefore come, and let us fall unto the [a]host of the Syrians: if they save us alive, we shall live; and if they kill us, we shall but die.
5 And they rose up in the twilight, to go unto the camp of the Syrians: and when they were come to the uttermost part of the camp of Syria, behold, *there was* no man there.
6 For the Lord had made the host of the Syrians [a]to hear a noise of chariots, and a noise of horses, *even* the noise of a great host: and they said one to another, Lo, the king of Israel hath hired against us [b]the kings of the Hittites, and the kings of the Egyptians, to come upon us.
7 Wherefore they [a]arose and fled in the twilight, and left their tents, and their horses, and their asses, even the camp as it *was*, and fled for their life.
8 And when these lepers came to the uttermost part of the camp, they went into one tent, and did eat and drink, and carried thence silver, and gold, and raiment, and went and hid *it;* and came again, and entered into another tent, and carried thence *also*, and went and hid *it*.
9 Then they said one to another, We do not well: this day *is* a day of good tidings, and we hold our peace: if we tarry till the morning light, some mischief will come upon us: now therefore come, that we may go and tell the king's household.
10 So they came and called unto the porter of the city: and they told them, saying, We came to the camp of the Syrians, and, behold, *there was* no man there, neither voice of man, but horses tied, and asses tied, and the tents as they *were*.
11 And he called the porters; and they told *it* to the king's house within.
12 And the king arose in the night, and said unto his servants, I will now shew you what the Syrians have done to us. They know that we *be* [a]hungry; therefore are they gone out of the camp to hide themselves in the field, saying, When they come out of the city, we shall catch them alive, and get into the city.
13 And one of his servants answered and said, Let *some* take, I pray thee, five of the horses that remain, which are left in the city, (behold,

32 [a]Ezek. 8:1; 14:1; 20:1 [b]Luke 13:32 [c]1 Kin. 18:4, 13, 14; 21:10, 13
33 [a]Job 2:9

CHAPTER 7
1 [a]2 Kin. 7:18, 19
2 [a]2 Kin. 5:18; 7:17, 19, 20 [b]Gen. 7:11; Mal. 3:10
3 [a][Lev. 13:45, 46; Num. 5:2–4; 12:10–14]
4 [a]2 Kin. 6:24
6 [a]2 Sam. 5:24; 2 Kin. 19:7; Job 15:21 [b]1 Kin. 10:29
7 [a]Ps. 48:4–6; [Prov. 28:1]
12 [a]2 Kin. 6:24–29

NKJV

also, if the head of Elisha the son of Shaphat remains on him today!"
32 But Elisha was sitting in his house, and [a]the elders were sitting with him. And *the king* sent a man ahead of him, but before the messenger came to him, he said to the elders, [b]"Do you see how this son of [c]a murderer has sent someone to take away my head? Look, when the messenger comes, shut the door, and hold him fast at the door. *Is* not the sound of his master's feet behind him?"
33 And while he was still talking with them, there was the messenger, coming down to him; and then *the king* said, "Surely this calamity *is* from the LORD; [a]why should I wait for the LORD any longer?"

7 Then Elisha said, "Hear the word of the LORD. Thus says the LORD: [a]'Tomorrow about this time a seah of fine flour *shall be sold* for a shekel, and two seahs of barley for a shekel, at the gate of Samaria.' "
2 [a]So an officer on whose hand the king leaned answered the man of God and said, "Look, [b]*if* the LORD would make windows in heaven, could this thing be?" And he said, "In fact, you shall see *it* with your eyes, but you shall not eat of it."

The Syrians Flee

3 Now there were four leprous men [a]at the entrance of the gate; and they said to one another, "Why are we sitting here until we die?
4 "If we say, 'We will enter the city,' the famine *is* in the city, and we shall die there. And if we sit here, we die also. Now therefore, come, let us surrender to the [a]army of the Syrians. If they keep us alive, we shall live; and if they kill us, we shall only die."
5 And they rose at twilight to go to the camp of the Syrians; and when they had come to the outskirts of the Syrian camp, to their surprise no one *was* there.
6 For the LORD had caused the army of the Syrians [a]to hear the noise of chariots and the noise of horses—the noise of a great army; so they said to one another, "Look, the king of Israel has hired against us [b]the kings of the Hittites and the kings of the Egyptians to attack us!"
7 Therefore they [a]arose and fled at twilight, and left the camp intact—their tents, their horses, and their donkeys—and they fled for their lives.
8 And when these lepers came to the outskirts of the camp, they went into one tent and ate and drank, and carried from it silver and gold and clothing, and went and hid *them;* then they came back and entered another tent, and carried *some* from there *also*, and went and hid *it*.
9 Then they said to one another, "We are not doing right. This day *is* a day of good news, and we remain silent. If we wait until morning light, some punishment will come upon us. Now therefore, come, let us go and tell the king's household."
10 So they went and called to the gatekeepers of the city, and told them, saying, "We went to the Syrian camp, and surprisingly no one *was* there, not a human sound—only horses and donkeys tied, and the tents intact."
11 And the gatekeepers called out, and they told *it* to the king's household inside.
12 So the king arose in the night and said to his servants, "Let me now tell you what the Syrians have done to us. They know that we *are* [a]hungry; therefore they have gone out of the camp to hide themselves in the field, saying, 'When they come out of the city, we shall catch them alive, and get into the city.' "
13 And one of his servants answered and said, "Please, let several *men* take five of the remaining horses which are left in the city. Look,

KJV

they *are* as all the multitude of Israel that are left in it: behold, *I say,* they *are* even as all the multitude of the Israelites that are consumed:) and let us send and see.

14 They took therefore two chariot horses; and the king sent after the host of the Syrians, saying, Go and see.

15 And they went after them unto Jordan: and, lo, all the way *was* full of garments and vessels, which the Syrians had cast away in their haste. And the messengers returned, and told the king.

16 And the people went out, and spoiled the tents of the Syrians. So a measure of fine flour was *sold* for a shekel, and two measures of barley for a shekel, [a]according to the word of the LORD.

17 And the king appointed the lord on whose hand he leaned to have the charge of the gate: and the people trode upon him in the gate, and he died, [a]as the man of God had said, who spake when the king came down to him.

18 And it came to pass as the man of God had spoken to the king, saying, [a]Two measures of barley for a shekel, and a measure of fine flour for a shekel, shall be to morrow about this time in the gate of Samaria:

19 And that lord answered the man of God, and said, Now, behold, *if* the LORD should make windows in heaven, might such a thing be? And he said, Behold, thou shalt see it with thine eyes, but shalt not eat thereof.

20 And so it fell out unto him: for the people trode upon him in the gate, and he died.

The King Restores the Shunammite's Land

8 Then spake Elisha unto the woman, [a]whose son he had restored to life, saying, Arise, and go thou and thine household, and sojourn wheresoever thou canst sojourn: for the LORD [b]hath called for a [c]famine; and it shall also come upon the land seven years.

2 And the woman arose, and did after the saying of the man of God: and she went with her household, and sojourned in the land of the Philistines seven years.

3 And it came to pass at the seven years' end, that the woman returned out of the land of the Philistines: and she went forth to cry unto the king for her house and for her land.

4 And the king talked with [a]Gehazi the servant of the man of God, saying, Tell me, I pray thee, all the great things that Elisha hath done.

5 And it came to pass, as he was telling the king how he had [a]restored a dead body to life, that, behold, the woman, whose son he had restored to life, cried to the king for her house and for her land. And Gehazi said, My lord, O king, this *is* the woman, and this *is* her son, whom Elisha restored to life.

6 And when the king asked the woman, she told him. So the king appointed unto her a certain officer, saying, Restore all that *was* her's, and all the fruits of the field since the day that she left the land, even until now.

Death of Ben-Hadad

7 And Elisha came to Damascus; and [a]Ben–hadad the king of Syria was sick; and it was told him, saying, The man of God is come hither.

8 And the king said unto [a]Hazael, [b]Take a present in thine hand, and go, meet the man of God, and [c]enquire of the LORD by him, saying, Shall I recover of this disease?

9 So [a]Hazael went to meet him, and took a present with him, even of every good thing of Damascus, forty camels' burden, and came and stood before him, and said, Thy son Ben–hadad king of Syria hath sent me to thee, saying, Shall I recover of this disease?

10 And Elisha said unto him, Go, say unto

16 [a]2 Kin. 7:1
17 [a]2 Kin. 6:32; 7:2
18 [a]2 Kin. 7:1

CHAPTER 8

1 [a]2 Kin. 4:18, 31–35 [b]Ps. 105:16; Hag. 1:11 [c]2 Sam. 21:1; 1 Kin. 18:2; 2 Kin. 4:38; 6:25
4 [a]2 Kin. 4:12; 5:20–27
5 [a]2 Kin. 4:35
7 [a]2 Kin. 6:24
8 [a]1 Kin. 19:15 [b]1 Sam. 9:7; 1 Kin. 14:3; 2 Kin. 5:5 [c]2 Kin. 1:2
9 [a]1 Kin. 19:15

NKJV

they *may either become* like all the multitude of Israel that are left in it; or indeed, *I say,* they *may become* like all the multitude of Israel left from those who are consumed; so let us send them and see."

14 Therefore they took two chariots with horses; and the king sent them in the direction of the Syrian army, saying, "Go and see."

15 And they went after them to the Jordan; and indeed all the road *was* full of garments and weapons which the Syrians had thrown away in their haste. So the messengers returned and told the king.

16 Then the people went out and plundered the tents of the Syrians. So a seah of fine flour was *sold* for a shekel, and two seahs of barley for a shekel, [a]according to the word of the LORD.

17 Now the king had appointed the officer on whose hand he leaned to have charge of the gate. But the people trampled him in the gate, and he died, just [a]as the man of God had said, who spoke when the king came down to him.

18 So it happened just as the man of God had spoken to the king, saying, [a]"Two seahs of barley for a shekel, and a seah of fine flour for a shekel, shall be *sold* tomorrow about this time in the gate of Samaria."

19 Then that officer had answered the man of God, and said, "Now look, *if* the LORD would make windows in heaven, could such a thing be?" And he had said, "In fact, you shall see *it* with your eyes, but you shall not eat of it."

20 And so it happened to him, for the people trampled him in the gate, and he died.

The King Restores the Shunammite's Land

8 Then Elisha spoke to the woman [a]whose son he had restored to life, saying, "Arise and go, you and your household, and stay wherever you can; for the LORD [b]has called for a [c]famine, and furthermore, it will come upon the land for seven years."

2 So the woman arose and did according to the saying of the man of God, and she went with her household and dwelt in the land of the Philistines seven years.

3 It came to pass, at the end of seven years, that the woman returned from the land of the Philistines; and she went to make an appeal to the king for her house and for her land.

4 Then the king talked with [a]Gehazi, the servant of the man of God, saying, "Tell me, please, all the great things Elisha has done."

5 Now it happened, as he was telling the king how he had restored the dead to life, that there was the woman whose son he had [a]restored to life, appealing to the king for her house and for her land. And Gehazi said, "My lord, O king, this *is* the woman, and this *is* her son whom Elisha restored to life."

6 And when the king asked the woman, she told him. So the king appointed a certain officer for her, saying, "Restore all that *was* hers, and all the proceeds of the field from the day that she left the land until now."

Death of Ben-Hadad

7 Then Elisha went to Damascus, and [a]Ben-Hadad king of Syria was sick; and it was told him, saying, "The man of God has come here."

8 And the king said to [a]Hazael, [b]"Take a present in your hand, and go to meet the man of God, and [c]inquire of the LORD by him, saying, 'Shall I recover from this disease?' "

9 So [a]Hazael went to meet him and took a present with him, of every good thing of Damascus, forty camel-loads; and he came and stood before him, and said, "Your son Ben-Hadad king of Syria has sent me to you, saying, 'Shall I recover from this disease?' "

10 And Elisha said to him, "Go, say to him,

KJV

him, Thou mayest certainly recover: howbeit the LORD hath shewed me that [a]he shall surely die.

11 And he settled his countenance stedfastly, until he was ashamed: and the man of God [a]wept.

12 And Hazael said, Why weepeth my lord? And he answered, Because I know [a]the evil that thou wilt do unto the children of Israel: their strong holds wilt thou set on fire, and their young men wilt thou slay with the sword, and [b]wilt dash their children, and rip up their women with child.

13 And Hazael said, But what, [a]*is* thy servant a dog, that he should do this great thing? And Elisha answered, [b]The LORD hath shewed me that thou *shalt be* king over Syria.

14 So he departed from Elisha, and came to his master; who said to him, What said Elisha to thee? And he answered, He told me *that* thou shouldest surely recover.

15 And it came to pass on the morrow, that he took a thick cloth, and dipped *it* in water, and spread *it* on his face, so that he died: and Hazael reigned in his stead.

Jehoram Reigns in Judah
(*2 Chr. 21:1–20*)

16 And [a]in the fifth year of Joram the son of Ahab king of Israel, Jehoshaphat *being* then king of Judah, [b]Jehoram the son of Jehoshaphat king of Judah began to reign.

17 [a]Thirty and two years old was he when he began to reign; and he reigned eight years in Jerusalem.

18 And he walked in the way of the kings of Israel, as did the house of Ahab: for [a]the daughter of Ahab was his wife: and he did evil in the sight of the LORD.

19 Yet the LORD would not destroy Judah for David his servant's sake, [a]as he promised him to give him alway a light, *and* to his children.

20 In his days [a]Edom revolted from under the hand of Judah, [b]and made a king over themselves.

21 So Joram went over to Zair, and all the chariots with him: and he rose by night, and smote the Edomites which compassed him about, and the captains of the chariots: and the people fled into their tents.

22 Yet Edom revolted from under the hand of Judah unto this day. [a]Then Libnah revolted at the same time.

23 And the rest of the acts of Joram, and all that he did, *are* they not written in the book of the chronicles of the kings of Judah?

24 And Joram slept with his fathers, and was buried with his fathers in the city of David: and [a]Ahaziah his son reigned in his stead.

Ahaziah Reigns in Judah
(*2 Chr. 22:1–6*)

25 In the twelfth year of Joram the son of Ahab king of Israel did Ahaziah the son of Jehoram king of Judah begin to reign.

26 [a]Two and twenty years old *was* Ahaziah when he began to reign; and he reigned one year in Jerusalem. And his mother's name *was* Athaliah, the daughter of Omri king of Israel.

27 [a]And he walked in the way of the house of Ahab, and did evil in the sight of the LORD, as *did* the house of Ahab: for he *was* the son in law of the house of Ahab.

28 And he went [a]with Joram the son of Ahab to the war against Hazael king of Syria in [b]Ramoth–gilead; and the Syrians wounded Joram.

29 And [a]king Joram went back to be healed in Jezreel of the wounds which the Syrians had given him at Ramah, when he fought against Hazael king of Syria. [b]And Ahaziah the son of Jehoram king of Judah went down to see Joram the son of Ahab in Jezreel, because he was sick.

10 [a]2 Kin. 8:15
11 [a]Luke 19:41
12 [a]2 Kin. 10:32; 12:17; 13:3, 7; Amos 1:3, 4 [b]2 Kin. 15:16; Hos. 13:16; Amos 1:13; Nah. 3:10
13 [a]1 Sam. 17:43; 2 Sam. 9:8 [b]1 Kin. 19:15
16 [a]2 Kin. 1:17; 3:1 [b]2 Chr. 21:3
17 [a]2 Chr. 21:5–10
18 [a]2 Kin. 8:26, 27
19 [a]2 Sam. 7:13; 1 Kin. 11:36; 15:4; 2 Chr. 21:7
20 [a]Gen. 27:40; 2 Chr. 21:8–10 [b]1 Kin. 22:47
22 [a]Josh. 21:13; 2 Kin. 19:8; 2 Chr. 21:10
24 [a]2 Chr. 22:1, 7
26 [a]2 Chr. 22:2
27 [a]2 Chr. 22:3, 4
28 [a]2 Chr. 22:5 [b]1 Kin. 22:3, 29
29 [a]2 Kin. 9:15 [b]2 Kin. 9:16; 2 Chr. 22:6, 7

NKJV

'You shall certainly recover.' However the LORD has shown me that [a]he will really die."

11 Then he set his countenance in a stare until he was ashamed; and the man of God [a]wept.

12 And Hazael said, "Why is my lord weeping?" He answered, "Because I know [a]the evil that you will do to the children of Israel: Their strongholds you will set on fire, and their young men you will kill with the sword; and you [b]will dash their children, and rip open their women with child."

13 So Hazael said, "But what [a]*is* your servant—a dog, that he should do this gross thing?" And Elisha answered, [b]"The LORD has shown me that you *will become* king over Syria."

14 Then he departed from Elisha, and came to his master, who said to him, "What did Elisha say to you?" And he answered, "He told me you would surely recover."

15 But it happened on the next day that he took a thick cloth and dipped *it* in water, and spread *it* over his face so that he died; and Hazael reigned in his place.

Jehoram Reigns in Judah
(*2 Chr. 21:1–20*)

16 Now [a]in the fifth year of Joram the son of Ahab, king of Israel, Jehoshaphat *having been* king of Judah, [b]Jehoram the son of Jehoshaphat began to reign as king of Judah.

17 He was [a]thirty-two years old when he became king, and he reigned eight years in Jerusalem.

18 And he walked in the way of the kings of Israel, just as the house of Ahab had done, for [a]the daughter of Ahab was his wife; and he did evil in the sight of the LORD.

19 Yet the LORD would not destroy Judah, for the sake of his servant David, [a]as He promised him to give a lamp to him *and* his sons forever.

20 In his days [a]Edom revolted against Judah's authority, [b]and made a king over themselves.

21 So *Joram went to Zair, and all his chariots with him. Then he rose by night and attacked the Edomites who had surrounded him and the captains of the chariots; and the troops fled to their tents.

22 Thus Edom has been in revolt against Judah's authority to this day. [a]And Libnah revolted at that time.

23 Now the rest of the acts of Joram, and all that he did, *are* they not written in the book of the chronicles of the kings of Judah?

24 So Joram rested with his fathers, and was buried with his fathers in the City of David. Then [a]Ahaziah his son reigned in his place.

Ahaziah Reigns in Judah
(*2 Chr. 22:1–6*)

25 In the twelfth year of Joram the son of Ahab, king of Israel, Ahaziah the son of Jehoram, king of Judah, began to reign.

26 Ahaziah *was* [a]twenty-two years old when he became king, and he reigned one year in Jerusalem. His mother's name *was* Athaliah the granddaughter of Omri, king of Israel.

27 [a]And he walked in the way of the house of Ahab, and did evil in the sight of the LORD, like the house of Ahab, for he *was* the son-in-law of the house of Ahab.

28 Now he went [a]with Joram the son of Ahab to war against Hazael king of Syria at [b]Ramoth Gilead; and the Syrians wounded Joram.

29 Then [a]King Joram went back to Jezreel to recover from the wounds which the Syrians had inflicted on him at Ramah, when he fought against Hazael king of Syria. [b]And Ahaziah the son of Jehoram, king of Judah, went down to see Joram the son of Ahab in Jezreel, because he was sick.

*———

8:21 *Jehoram,* v. 16

KJV

Jehu Anointed King of Israel

9 And Elisha the prophet called one of [a]the children of the prophets, and said unto him, [b]Gird up thy loins, and take this box of oil in thine hand, [c]and go to Ramoth–gilead:

2 And when thou comest thither, look out there Jehu the son of Jehoshaphat the son of Nimshi, and go in, and make him arise up from among [a]his brethren, and carry him to an inner chamber;

3 Then [a]take the box of oil, and pour *it* on his head, and say, Thus saith the LORD, I have anointed thee king over Israel. Then open the door, and flee, and tarry not.

4 So the young man, *even* the young man the prophet, went to Ramoth–gilead.

5 And when he came, behold, the captains of the host *were* sitting; and he said, I have an errand to thee, O captain. And Jehu said, Unto which of all us? And he said, To thee, O captain.

6 And he arose, and went into the house; and he poured the oil on his head, and said unto him, [a]Thus saith the LORD God of Israel, I have anointed thee king over the people of the LORD, *even* over Israel.

7 And thou shalt smite the house of Ahab thy master, that I may [a]avenge the blood of my servants the prophets, and the blood of all the servants of the LORD, [b]at the hand of Jezebel.

8 For the whole house of Ahab shall perish: and [a]I will cut off from Ahab [b]him that pisseth against the wall, and [c]him that is shut up and left in Israel:

9 And I will make the house of Ahab like the house of [a]Jeroboam the son of Nebat, and like the house of [b]Baasha the son of Ahijah:

10 [a]And the dogs shall eat Jezebel in the portion of Jezreel, and *there shall be* none to bury *her*. And he opened the door, and fled.

11 Then Jehu came forth to the servants of his lord: and *one* said unto him, *Is* all well? wherefore came [a]this mad *fellow* to thee? And he said unto them, Ye know the man, and his communication.

12 And they said, *It is* false; tell us now. And he said, Thus and thus spake he to me, saying, Thus saith the LORD, I have anointed thee king over Israel.

13 Then they hasted, and [a]took every man his garment, and put *it* under him on the top of the stairs, and blew with trumpets, saying, Jehu is king.

Joram of Israel Killed

14 So Jehu the son of Jehoshaphat the son of Nimshi conspired against [a]Joram. (Now Joram had kept Ramoth–gilead, he and all Israel, because of Hazael king of Syria.

15 But [a]king Joram was returned to be healed in Jezreel of the wounds which the Syrians had given him, when he fought with Hazael king of Syria.) And Jehu said, If it be your minds, *then* let none go forth *nor* escape out of the city to go to tell *it* in Jezreel.

16 So Jehu rode in a chariot, and went to Jezreel; for Joram lay there. [a]And Ahaziah king of Judah was come down to see Joram.

17 And there stood a watchman on the tower in Jezreel, and he spied the company of Jehu as he came, and said, I see a company. And Joram said, Take an horseman, and send to meet them, and let him say, *Is it* peace?

18 So there went one on horseback to meet him, and said, Thus saith the king, *Is it* peace? And Jehu said, What hast thou to do with peace? turn thee behind me. And the watchman told, saying, The messenger came to them, but he cometh not again.

19 Then he sent out a second on horseback, which came to them, and said, Thus saith the king, *Is it* peace? And Jehu answered, What hast thou to do with peace? turn thee behind me.

CHAPTER 9

1 [a]1 Kin. 20:35 [b]2 Kin. 4:29; Jer. 1:17 [c]2 Kin. 8:28, 29
2 [a]2 Kin. 9:5, 11
3 [a]1 Kin. 19:16
6 [a]1 Sam. 2:7, 8; 1 Kin. 19:16; 2 Kin. 9:3; 2 Chr. 22:7
7 [a][Deut. 32:35, 41] [b]1 Kin. 18:4; 21:15
8 [a]1 Kin. 14:10; 21:21; 2 Kin. 10:17 [b]1 Sam. 25:22 [c]Deut. 32:36; 2 Kin. 14:26
9 [a]1 Kin. 14:10; 15:29; 21:22 [b]1 Kin. 16:3, 11
10 [a]1 Kin. 21:23; 2 Kin. 9:35, 36
11 [a]Jer. 29:26; Hos. 9:7; Mark 3:21; John 10:20; Acts 26:24; [1 Cor. 4:10]
13 [a]Matt. 21:7, 8; Mark 11:7, 8
14 [a]2 Kin. 8:28
15 [a]2 Kin. 8:29
16 [a]2 Kin. 8:29

NKJV

Jehu Anointed King of Israel

9 And Elisha the prophet called one of [a]the sons of the prophets, and said to him, [b]"Get yourself ready, take this flask of oil in your hand, [c]and go to Ramoth Gilead.

2 "Now when you arrive at that place, look there for Jehu the son of Jehoshaphat, the son of Nimshi, and go in and make him rise up from among [a]his associates, and take him to an inner room.

3 "Then [a]take the flask of oil, and pour *it* on his head, and say, 'Thus says the LORD: "I have anointed you king over Israel." ' Then open the door and flee, and do not delay."

4 So the young man, the servant of the prophet, went to Ramoth Gilead.

5 And when he arrived, there *were* the captains of the army sitting; and he said, "I have a message for you, Commander." Jehu said, "For which *one* of us?" And he said, "For you, Commander."

6 Then he arose and went into the house. And he poured the oil on his head, and said to him, [a]"Thus says the LORD God of Israel: 'I have anointed you king over the people of the LORD, over Israel.

7 'You shall strike down the house of Ahab your master, that I may [a]avenge the blood of My servants the prophets, and the blood of all the servants of the LORD, [b]at the hand of Jezebel.

8 'For the whole house of Ahab shall perish; and [a]I will cut off from Ahab all [b]the males in Israel, both [c]bond and free.

9 'So I will make the house of Ahab like the house of [a]Jeroboam the son of Nebat, and like the house of [b]Baasha the son of Ahijah.

10 [a]'The dogs shall eat Jezebel on the plot *of ground* at Jezreel, and *there shall be* none to bury *her*.' " And he opened the door and fled.

11 Then Jehu came out to the servants of his master, and *one* said to him, "*Is* all well? Why did [a]this madman come to you?" And he said to them, "You know the man and his babble."

12 And they said, "A lie! Tell us now." So he said, "Thus and thus he spoke to me, saying, 'Thus says the LORD: "I have anointed you king over Israel." ' "

13 Then each man hastened [a]to take his garment and put *it* under him on the top of the steps; and they blew trumpets, saying, "Jehu is king!"

Joram of Israel Killed

14 So Jehu the son of Jehoshaphat, the son of Nimshi, conspired against [a]Joram. (Now Joram had been defending Ramoth Gilead, he and all Israel, against Hazael king of Syria.

15 But [a]King Joram had returned to Jezreel to recover from the wounds which the Syrians had inflicted on him when he fought with Hazael king of Syria.) And Jehu said, "If you are so minded, let no one leave *or* escape from the city to go and tell *it* in Jezreel."

16 So Jehu rode in a chariot and went to Jezreel, for Joram was laid up there; [a]and Ahaziah king of Judah had come down to see Joram.

17 Now a watchman stood on the tower in Jezreel, and he saw the company of Jehu as he came, and said, "I see a company of men." And Joram said, "Get a horseman and send him to meet them, and let him say, '*Is it* peace?' "

18 So the horseman went to meet him, and said, "Thus says the king: '*Is it* peace?' " And Jehu said, "What have you to do with peace? Turn around and follow me." So the watchman reported, saying, "The messenger went to them, but is not coming back."

19 Then he sent out a second horseman who came to them, and said, "Thus says the king: '*Is it* peace?' " And Jehu answered, "What have you to do with peace? Turn around and follow me."

KJV

20 And the watchman told, saying, He came even unto them, and cometh not again: and the driving *is* like the driving of Jehu the son of Nimshi; for he driveth furiously.

21 And Joram said, Make ready. And his chariot was made ready. And [a]Joram king of Israel and Ahaziah king of Judah went out, each in his chariot, and they went out against Jehu, and met him [b]in the portion of Naboth the Jezreelite.

22 And it came to pass, when Joram saw Jehu, that he said, *Is it* peace, Jehu? And he answered, What peace, so long as the whoredoms of thy mother Jezebel and her witchcrafts *are so* many?

23 And Joram turned his hands, and fled, and said to Ahaziah, *There is* treachery, O Ahaziah.

24 And Jehu drew a bow with his full strength, and smote Jehoram between his arms, and the arrow went out at his heart, and he sunk down in his chariot.

25 Then said *Jehu* to Bidkar his captain, Take up, *and* cast him in the portion of the field of Naboth the Jezreelite: for remember how that, when I and thou rode together after Ahab his father, [a]the LORD laid this [b]burden upon him;

26 Surely I have seen yesterday the blood of Naboth, and the blood of his sons, saith the LORD; [a]and I will requite thee in this plat, saith the LORD. Now therefore take *and* cast him into the plat *of ground,* according to the word of the LORD.

Ahaziah of Judah Killed
(2 Chr. 22:7–9)

27 But when Ahaziah the king of Judah saw *this,* he fled by the way of the garden house. And Jehu followed after him, and said, Smite him also in the chariot. *And they did so* at the going up to Gur, which *is* by Ibleam. And he fled to [a]Megiddo, and died there.

28 And his servants carried him in a chariot to Jerusalem, and buried him in his sepulchre with his fathers in the city of David.

29 And in the eleventh year of Joram the son of Ahab began Ahaziah to reign over Judah.

Jezebel's Violent Death

30 And when Jehu was come to Jezreel, Jezebel heard *of it;* [a]and she painted her face, and tired her head, and looked out at a window.

31 And as Jehu entered in at the gate, she said, [a]*Had* Zimri peace, who slew his master?

32 And he lifted up his face to the window, and said, Who *is* on my side? who? And there looked out to him two *or* three eunuchs.

33 And he said, Throw her down. So they threw her down: and *some* of her blood was sprinkled on the wall, and on the horses: and he trode her under foot.

34 And when he was come in, he did eat and drink, and said, Go, see now this cursed *woman,* and bury her: for [a]she *is* a king's daughter.

35 And they went to bury her: but they found no more of her than the skull, and the feet, and the palms of *her* hands.

36 Wherefore they came again, and told him. And he said, This *is* the word of the LORD, which he spake by his servant Elijah the Tishbite, saying, [a]In the portion of Jezreel shall dogs eat the flesh of Jezebel:

37 And the carcase of Jezebel shall be [a]as dung upon the face of the field in the portion of Jezreel; *so* that they shall not say, This *is* Jezebel.

Ahab's Seventy Sons Killed

10 And Ahab had seventy sons in Samaria. And Jehu wrote letters, and sent to Samaria, unto the rulers of Jezreel, to the elders, and to them that brought up Ahab's *children,* saying,

21 [a]1 Kin. 19:17; 2 Chr. 22:7 [b]1 Kin. 21:1–14
25 [a]1 Kin. 21:19, 24–29 [b]Is. 13:1
26 [a]1 Kin. 21:13, 19
27 [a]2 Chr. 22:7, 9
30 [a][Jer. 4:30]; Ezek. 23:40
31 [a]1 Kin. 16:9–20; 2 Kin. 9:18–22
34 [a][Ex. 22:28]; 1 Kin. 16:31
36 [a]1 Kin. 21:23
37 [a]Ps. 83:10

NKJV

20 So the watchman reported, saying, "He went up to them and is not coming back; and the driving *is* like the driving of Jehu the son of Nimshi, for he drives furiously!"

21 Then Joram said, "Make ready." And his chariot was made ready. Then [a]Joram king of Israel and Ahaziah king of Judah went out, each in his chariot; and they went out to meet Jehu, and met him [b]on the property of Naboth the Jezreelite.

22 Now it happened, when Joram saw Jehu, that he said, "*Is it* peace, Jehu?" So he answered, "What peace, as long as the harlotries of your mother Jezebel and her witchcraft *are so* many?"

23 Then Joram turned around and fled, and said to Ahaziah, "Treachery, Ahaziah!"

24 Now Jehu drew his bow with full strength and shot Jehoram between his arms; and the arrow came out at his heart, and he sank down in his chariot.

25 Then *Jehu* said to Bidkar his captain, "Pick *him* up, *and* throw him into the tract of the field of Naboth the Jezreelite; for remember, when you and I were riding together behind Ahab his father, that [a]the LORD laid this [b]burden upon him:

26 'Surely I saw yesterday the blood of Naboth and the blood of his sons,' says the LORD, [a]'and I will repay you in this plot,' says the LORD. Now therefore, take *and* throw him on the plot *of ground,* according to the word of the LORD."

Ahaziah of Judah Killed
(2 Chr. 22:7–9)

27 But when Ahaziah king of Judah saw *this,* he fled by the road to *Beth Haggan. So Jehu pursued him, and said, "Shoot him also in the chariot." *And they shot him* at the Ascent of Gur, which is by Ibleam. Then he fled to [a]Megiddo, and died there.

28 And his servants carried him in the chariot to Jerusalem, and buried him in his tomb with his fathers in the City of David.

29 In the eleventh year of Joram the son of Ahab, Ahaziah had become king over Judah.

Jezebel's Violent Death

30 Now when Jehu had come to Jezreel, Jezebel heard *of it;* [a]and she put paint on her eyes and adorned her head, and looked through a window.

31 Then, as Jehu entered at the gate, she said, [a]"*Is it* peace, Zimri, murderer of your master?"

32 And he looked up at the window, and said, "Who *is* on my side? Who?" So two *or* three eunuchs looked out at him.

33 Then he said, "Throw her down." So they threw her down, and *some* of her blood spattered on the wall and on the horses; and he trampled her underfoot.

34 And when he had gone in, he ate and drank. Then he said, "Go now, see to this accursed *woman,* and bury her, for [a]she was a king's daughter."

35 So they went to bury her, but they found no more of her than the skull and the feet and the palms of *her* hands.

36 Therefore they came back and told him. And he said, "This *is* the word of the LORD, which He spoke by His servant Elijah the Tishbite, saying, [a]'On the plot *of ground* at Jezreel dogs shall eat the flesh of Jezebel;

37 'and the corpse of Jezebel shall be [a]as refuse on the surface of the field, in the plot at Jezreel, so that they shall not say, "Here *lies* Jezebel." ' "

Ahab's Seventy Sons Killed

10 Now Ahab had seventy sons in Samaria. And Jehu wrote and sent letters to Samaria, to the rulers of *Jezreel, to the elders, and to those who reared Ahab's *sons,* saying:

---

*

9:27 Lit. *The Garden House*
10:1 So with MT, Syr., Tg.; LXX *Samaria;* Vg. *city*

KJV

2 Now as soon as this letter cometh to you, seeing your master's sons *are* with you, and *there are* with you chariots and horses, a fenced city also, and armour;

3 Look even out the best and meetest of your master's sons, and set *him* on his father's throne, and fight for your master's house.

4 But they were exceedingly afraid, and said, Behold, [a]two kings stood not before him: how then shall we stand?

5 And he that *was* over the house, and he that *was* over the city, the elders also, and the bringers up *of the children*, sent to Jehu, saying, We *are* thy servants, and will do all that thou shalt bid us; we will not make any king: do thou *that which is* good in thine eyes.

6 Then he wrote a letter the second time to them, saying, If ye *be* mine, and *if* ye will hearken unto my voice, take ye the heads of the men your master's sons, and come to me to Jezreel by to morrow this time. Now the king's sons, *being* seventy persons, *were* with the great men of the city, which brought them up.

7 And it came to pass, when the letter came to them, that they took the king's sons, and [a]slew seventy persons, and put their heads in baskets, and sent him *them* to Jezreel.

8 And there came a messenger, and told him, saying, They have brought the heads of the king's sons. And he said, Lay ye them in two heaps at the entering in of the gate until the morning.

9 And it came to pass in the morning, that he went out, and stood, and said to all the people, Ye *be* righteous: behold, [a]I conspired against my master, and slew him: but who slew all these?

10 Know now that there shall [a]fall unto the earth nothing of the word of the LORD, which the LORD spake concerning the house of Ahab: for the LORD hath done *that* which he spake [b]by his servant Elijah.

11 So Jehu slew all that remained of the house of Ahab in Jezreel, and all his great men, and his kinsfolks, and his priests, until he left him none remaining.

Ahaziah's Forty-two Brothers Killed

12 And he arose and departed, and came to Samaria. *And* as he *was* at the shearing house in the way,

13 [a]Jehu met with the brethren of Ahaziah king of Judah, and said, Who *are* ye? And they answered, We *are* the brethren of Ahaziah; and we go down to salute the children of the king and the children of the queen.

14 And he said, Take them alive. And they took them alive, and [a]slew them at the pit of the shearing house, *even* two and forty men; neither left he any of them.

The Rest of Ahab's Family Killed

15 And when he was departed thence, he lighted on [a]Jehonadab the son of [b]Rechab *coming* to meet him: and he saluted him, and said to him, Is thine heart right, as my heart *is* with thy heart? And Jehonadab answered, It is. If it be, [c]give *me* thine hand. And he gave *him* his hand; and he took him up to him into the chariot.

16 And he said, Come with me, and see my [a]zeal for the LORD. So they made him ride in his chariot.

17 And when he came to Samaria, [a]he slew all that remained unto Ahab in Samaria, till he had destroyed him, according to the saying of the LORD, [b]which he spake to Elijah.

Worshipers of Baal Killed

18 And Jehu gathered all the people together, and said unto them, [a]Ahab served Baal a little; *but* Jehu shall serve him much.

CHAPTER 10
4 [a]2 Kin. 9:24, 27
7 [a]Judg. 9:5; 1 Kin. 21:21; 2 Kin. 11:1
9 [a]2 Kin. 9:14–24
10 [a]1 Sam. 3:19; 1 Kin. 8:56; Jer. 44:28 [b]1 Kin. 21:17–24, 29
13 [a]2 Chr. 22:8
14 [a]2 Chr. 22:8
15 [a]Jer. 35:6 [b]1 Chr. 2:55 [c]Ezra 10:19; Ezek. 17:18
16 [a]1 Kin. 19:10
17 [a]2 Kin. 9:8; 2 Chr. 22:8 [b]1 Kin. 21:21, 29
18 [a]1 Kin. 16:31, 32

NKJV

2 Now as soon as this letter comes to you, since your master's sons *are* with you, and you have chariots and horses, a fortified city also, and weapons,

3 choose the best qualified of your master's sons, set *him* on his father's throne, and fight for your master's house.

4 But they were exceedingly afraid, and said, "Look, [a]two kings could not stand up to him; how then can we stand?"

5 And he who *was* in charge of the house, and he who *was* in charge of the city, the elders also, and those who reared *the sons*, sent to Jehu, saying, "We *are* your servants, we will do all you tell us; but we will not make anyone king. Do *what is* good in your sight."

6 Then he wrote a second letter to them, saying:

> If you *are* for me and will obey my voice, take the heads of the men, your master's sons, and come to me at Jezreel by this time tomorrow.

Now the king's sons, seventy persons, *were* with the great men of the city, *who* were rearing them.

7 So it was, when the letter came to them, that they took the king's sons and [a]slaughtered seventy persons, put their heads in baskets and sent *them* to him at Jezreel.

8 Then a messenger came and told him, saying, "They have brought the heads of the king's sons." And he said, "Lay them in two heaps at the entrance of the gate until morning."

9 So it was, in the morning, that he went out and stood, and said to all the people, "You *are* righteous. Indeed [a]I conspired against my master and killed him; but who killed all these?

10 "Know now that nothing shall [a]fall to the earth of the word of the LORD which the LORD spoke concerning the house of Ahab; for the LORD has done what He spoke [b]by His servant Elijah."

11 So Jehu killed all who remained of the house of Ahab in Jezreel, and all his great men and his close acquaintances and his priests, until he left him none remaining.

Ahaziah's Forty-two Brothers Killed

12 And he arose and departed and went to Samaria. On the way, at *Beth Eked of the Shepherds,

13 [a]Jehu met with the brothers of Ahaziah king of Judah, and said, "Who *are* you?" So they answered, "We *are* the brothers of Ahaziah; we have come down to greet the sons of the king and the sons of the queen mother."

14 And he said, "Take them alive!" So they took them alive, and [a]killed them at the well of Beth Eked, forty-two men; and he left none of them.

The Rest of Ahab's Family Killed

15 Now when he departed from there, he met [a]Jehonadab the son of [b]Rechab, *coming* to meet him; and he greeted him and said to him, "Is your heart right, as my heart *is* toward your heart?" And Jehonadab answered, "It is." *Jehu said,* "If it is, [c]give *me* your hand." So he gave *him* his hand, and he took him up to him into the chariot.

16 Then he said, "Come with me, and see my [a]zeal for the LORD." So they had him ride in his chariot.

17 And when he came to Samaria, [a]he killed all who remained to Ahab in Samaria, till he had destroyed them, according to the word of the LORD [b]which He spoke to Elijah.

Worshipers of Baal Killed

18 Then Jehu gathered all the people together, and said to them, [a]"Ahab served Baal a little, Jehu will serve him much.

*

10:12 Or *The Shearing House*

KJV

19 Now therefore call unto me all the [a]prophets of Baal, all his servants, and all his priests;
let none be wanting: for I have a great sacrifice
to do to Baal; whosoever shall be wanting, he
shall not live. But Jehu did *it* in subtilty, to the
intent that he might destroy the worshippers of
Baal.
20 And Jehu said, Proclaim a solemn assembly for Baal. And they proclaimed *it*.
21 And Jehu sent through all Israel: and all
the worshippers of Baal came, so that there was
not a man left that came not. And they came into
the house of Baal; and the [a]house of Baal was
full from one end to another.
22 And he said unto him that *was* over the
vestry, Bring forth vestments for all the worshippers of Baal. And he brought them forth
vestments.
23 And Jehu went, and Jehonadab the son
of Rechab, into the house of Baal, and said unto
the worshippers of Baal, Search, and look that
there be here with you none of the servants of
the LORD, but the worshippers of Baal only.
24 And when they went in to offer sacrifices
and burnt offerings, Jehu appointed fourscore
men without, and said, *If* any of the men whom I
have brought into your hands escape, *he that
letteth him go*, [a]his life *shall be* for the life of
him.
25 And it came to pass, as soon as he had
made an end of offering the burnt offering, that
Jehu said to the guard and to the captains, Go
in, *and* slay them; let none come forth. And they
smote them with the edge of the sword; and the
guard and the captains cast *them* out, and went
to the city of the house of Baal.
26 And they brought forth the [a]images out
of the house of Baal, and burned them.
27 And they brake down the image of Baal,
and brake down the house of Baal, and [a]made it
a draught house unto this day.
28 Thus Jehu destroyed Baal out of Israel.
29 Howbeit *from* the sins of Jeroboam the
son of Nebat, who made Israel to sin, Jehu departed not from after them, *to wit*, [a]the golden
calves that *were* in Beth–el, and that *were* in Dan.
30 And the LORD [a]said unto Jehu, Because
thou hast done well in executing *that which is*
right in mine eyes, *and* hast done unto the house
of Ahab according to all that *was* in mine heart,
[b]thy children of the fourth *generation* shall sit on
the throne of Israel.
31 But Jehu took no heed to walk in the law
of the LORD God of Israel with all his heart: for
he departed not from [a]the sins of Jeroboam,
which made Israel to sin.

Death of Jehu

32 In those days the LORD began to cut Israel
short: and [a]Hazael smote them in all the coasts
of Israel;
33 From Jordan eastward, all the land of
Gilead, the Gadites, and the Reubenites, and the
Manassites, from [a]Aroer, which *is* by the river
Arnon, even [b]Gilead and Bashan.
34 Now the rest of the acts of Jehu, and all
that he did, and all his might, *are* they not written
in the book of the chronicles of the kings of Israel?
35 And Jehu slept with his fathers: and they
buried him in Samaria. And [a]Jehoahaz his son
reigned in his stead.
36 And the time that Jehu reigned over Israel
in Samaria *was* twenty and eight years.

Athaliah Reigns in Judah
(2 Chr. 22:10–12)

11 And when [a]Athaliah [b]the mother of Ahaziah saw that her son was [c]dead, she arose
and destroyed all the seed royal.
2 But Jehosheba, the daughter of king
Joram, sister of [a]Ahaziah, took Joash the son of
Ahaziah, and stole him from among the king's

19 [a]1 Kin. 18:19; 22:6
21 [a]1 Kin. 16:32; 2 Kin. 11:18
24 [a]1 Kin. 20:39
26 [a][Deut. 7:5, 25]; 1 Kin. 14:23; 2 Kin. 3:2
27 [a]Ezra 6:11; Dan. 2:5; 3:29
29 [a]1 Kin. 12:28–30; 13:33, 34
30 [a]2 Kin. 9:6, 7 [b]2 Kin. 13:1, 10; 14:23; 15:8, 12
31 [a]1 Kin. 14:16
32 [a]1 Kin. 19:17; 2 Kin. 8:12; 13:22
33 [a]Deut. 2:36 [b]Amos 1:3–5
35 [a]2 Kin. 13:1

CHAPTER 11

1 [a]2 Chr. 22:10 [b]2 Kin. 8:26 [c]2 Kin. 9:27
2 [a]2 Kin. 8:25

*10:21 Lit. *house*

NKJV

19 "Now therefore, call to me all the [a]prophets of Baal, all his servants, and all his priests.
Let no one be missing, for I have a great sacrifice
for Baal. Whoever is missing shall not live." But
Jehu acted deceptively, with the intent of destroying the worshipers of Baal.
20 And Jehu said, "Proclaim a solemn assembly for Baal." So they proclaimed *it*.
21 Then Jehu sent throughout all Israel; and
all the worshipers of Baal came, so that there was
not a man left who did not come. So they came
into the *temple of Baal, and the [a]temple of Baal
was full from one end to the other.
22 And he said to the one in charge of the
wardrobe, "Bring out vestments for all the worshipers of Baal." So he brought out vestments for
them.
23 Then Jehu and Jehonadab the son of Rechab went into the temple of Baal, and said to
the worshipers of Baal, "Search and see that no
servants of the LORD are here with you, but only
the worshipers of Baal."
24 So they went in to offer sacrifices and
burnt offerings. Now Jehu had appointed for himself eighty men on the outside, and had said, "*If*
any of the men whom I have brought into your
hands escapes, *whoever lets him escape, it shall
be* [a]his life for the life of the other."
25 Now it happened, as soon as he had made
an end of offering the burnt offering, that Jehu
said to the guard and to the captains, "Go in *and*
kill them; let no one come out!" And they killed
them with the edge of the sword; then the guards
and the officers threw *them* out, and went into
the inner room of the temple of Baal.
26 And they brought the [a]*sacred* pillars out
of the temple of Baal and burned them.
27 Then they broke down the *sacred* pillar
of Baal, and tore down the temple of Baal and
[a]made it a refuse dump to this day.
28 Thus Jehu destroyed Baal from Israel.
29 However Jehu did not turn away from the
sins of Jeroboam the son of Nebat, who had made
Israel sin, *that is*, from [a]the golden calves that
were at Bethel and Dan.
30 And the LORD [a]said to Jehu, "Because you
have done well in doing *what is* right in My sight,
and have done to the house of Ahab all that *was*
in My heart, [b]your sons shall sit on the throne of
Israel to the fourth *generation*."
31 But Jehu took no heed to walk in the law
of the LORD God of Israel with all his heart; for
he did not depart from [a]the sins of Jeroboam, who
had made Israel sin.

Death of Jehu

32 In those days the LORD began to cut off
parts of Israel; and [a]Hazael conquered them in
all the territory of Israel
33 from the Jordan eastward: all the land
of Gilead—Gad, Reuben, and Manasseh—from
[a]Aroer, which *is* by the River Arnon, including
[b]Gilead and Bashan.
34 Now the rest of the acts of Jehu, all that
he did, and all his might, *are* they not written in
the book of the chronicles of the kings of Israel?
35 So Jehu rested with his fathers, and they
buried him in Samaria. Then [a]Jehoahaz his son
reigned in his place.
36 And the period that Jehu reigned over Israel in Samaria *was* twenty-eight years.

Athaliah Reigns in Judah
(2 Chr. 22:10–12)

11 When [a]Athaliah [b]the mother of Ahaziah
saw that her son was [c]dead, she arose and
destroyed all the royal heirs.
2 But Jehosheba, the daughter of King
Joram, sister of [a]Ahaziah, took Joash the son of
Ahaziah, and stole him away from among the

KJV

sons *which were* slain; and they hid him, *even* him and his nurse, in the bedchamber from Athaliah, so that he was not slain.

3 And he was with her hid in the house of the LORD six years. And Athaliah did reign over the land.

Joash Crowned King of Judah
(2 Chr. 23:1–11)

4 And [a]the seventh year Jehoiada sent and fetched the rulers over hundreds, with the captains and the guard, and brought them to him into the house of the LORD, and made a covenant with them, and took an oath of them in the house of the LORD, and shewed them the king's son.

5 And he commanded them, saying, This *is* the thing that ye shall do; A third part of you that enter in [a]on the sabbath shall even be keepers of the watch of the king's house;

6 And a third part *shall be* at the gate of Sur; and a third part at the gate behind the guard: so shall ye keep the watch of the house, that it be not broken down.

7 And two parts of all you that go forth on the sabbath, even they shall keep the watch of the house of the LORD about the king.

8 And ye shall compass the king round about, every man with his weapons in his hand: and he that cometh within the ranges, let him be slain: and be ye with the king as he goeth out and as he cometh in.

9 [a]And the captains over the hundreds did according to all *things* that Jehoiada the priest commanded: and they took every man his men that were to come in on the sabbath, with them that should go out on the sabbath, and came to Jehoiada the priest.

10 And to the captains over hundreds did the priest give king David's spears and shields, [a]that *were* in the temple of the LORD.

11 And the guard stood, every man with his weapons in his hand, round about the king, from the right corner of the temple to the left corner of the temple, *along* by the altar and the temple.

12 And he brought forth the king's son, and put the crown upon him, and *gave him* the [a]testimony; and they made him king, and anointed him; and they clapped their hands, and said, [b]God save the king.

Death of Athaliah
(2 Chr. 23:12—24:1)

13 [a]And when Athaliah heard the noise of the guard *and* of the people, she came to the people into the temple of the LORD.

14 And when she looked, behold, the king stood by [a]a pillar, as the manner *was*, and the princes and the trumpeters by the king, and all the people of the land rejoiced, and blew with trumpets: and Athaliah rent her clothes, and cried, Treason, Treason.

15 But Jehoiada the priest commanded the captains of the hundreds, the officers of the host, and said unto them, Have her forth without the ranges: and him that followeth her kill with the sword. For the priest had said, Let her not be slain in the house of the LORD.

16 And they laid hands on her; and she went by the way by the which the horses came into the king's house: and there was she slain.

17 [a]And Jehoiada [b]made a covenant between the LORD and the king and the people, that they should be the LORD's people; [c]between the king also and the people.

18 And all the people of the land went into the [a]house of Baal, and brake it down; his altars and his images [b]brake they in pieces thoroughly, and [c]slew Mattan the priest of Baal before the altars. And [d]the priest appointed officers over the house of the LORD.

4 [a]2 Kin. 12:2; 2 Chr. 23:1
5 [a]1 Chr. 9:25
9 [a]2 Chr. 23:8
10 [a]2 Sam. 8:7; 1 Chr. 18:7
12 [a]Ex. 25:16; 31:18 [b]1 Sam. 10:24
13 [a]2 Kin. 8:26; 2 Chr. 23:12
14 [a]2 Kin. 23:3; 2 Chr. 34:31
17 [a]2 Chr. 23:16 [b]Josh. 24:24, 25; 2 Chr. 15:12–15 [c]2 Sam. 5:3
18 [a]2 Kin. 10:26, 27 [b][Deut. 12:3] [c]1 Kin. 18:40; 2 Kin. 10:11 [d]2 Chr. 23:18

*
11:12 Law, Ex. 25:16, 21; Deut. 31:9

NKJV

king's sons *who were* being murdered; and they hid him and his nurse in the bedroom, from Athaliah, so that he was not killed.

3 So he was hidden with her in the house of the LORD for six years, while Athaliah reigned over the land.

Joash Crowned King of Judah
(2 Chr. 23:1–11)

4 In [a]the seventh year Jehoiada sent and brought the captains of hundreds—of the bodyguards and the escorts—and brought them into the house of the LORD to him. And he made a covenant with them and took an oath from them in the house of the LORD, and showed them the king's son.

5 Then he commanded them, saying, "This *is* what you shall do: One-third of you who come on duty [a]on the Sabbath shall be keeping watch over the king's house,

6 "one-third *shall be* at the gate of Sur, and one-third at the gate behind the escorts. You shall keep the watch of the house, lest it be broken down.

7 "The two contingents of you who go off duty on the Sabbath shall keep the watch of the house of the LORD for the king.

8 "But you shall surround the king on all sides, every man with his weapons in his hand; and whoever comes within range, let him be put to death. You are to be with the king as he goes out and as he comes in."

9 [a]So the captains of the hundreds did according to all that Jehoiada the priest commanded. Each of them took his men who were to be on duty on the Sabbath, with those who were going off duty on the Sabbath, and came to Jehoiada the priest.

10 And the priest gave the captains of hundreds the spears and shields which *had belonged* to King David, [a]that were in the temple of the LORD.

11 Then the escorts stood, every man with his weapons in his hand, all around the king, from the right side of the temple to the left side of the temple, by the altar and the house.

12 And he brought out the king's son, put the crown on him, and *gave him* the [a]Testimony;* they made him king and anointed him, and they clapped their hands and said, [b]"Long live the king!"

Death of Athaliah
(2 Chr. 23:12—24:1)

13 [a]Now when Athaliah heard the noise of the escorts *and* the people, she came to the people *in* the temple of the LORD.

14 When she looked, there was the king standing by [a]a pillar according to custom; and the leaders and the trumpeters were by the king. All the people of the land were rejoicing and blowing trumpets. So Athaliah tore her clothes and cried out, "Treason! Treason!"

15 And Jehoiada the priest commanded the captains of the hundreds, the officers of the army, and said to them, "Take her outside under guard, and slay with the sword whoever follows her." For the priest had said, "Do not let her be killed in the house of the LORD."

16 So they seized her; and she went by way of the horses' entrance *into* the king's house, and there she was killed.

17 [a]Then Jehoiada [b]made a covenant between the LORD, the king, and the people, that they should be the LORD's people, and *also* [c]between the king and the people.

18 And all the people of the land went to the [a]temple of Baal, and tore it down. They thoroughly [b]broke in pieces its altars and images, and [c]killed Mattan the priest of Baal before the altars. And [d]the priest appointed officers over the house of the LORD.

KJV

19 And he took the rulers over hundreds, and the captains, and the guard, and all the people of the land; and they brought down the king from the house of the LORD, and came by the way of the gate of the guard to the king's house. And he sat on the throne of the kings.

20 And all the people of the land rejoiced, and the city was in quiet: and they slew Athaliah with the sword *beside* the king's house.

21 [a]Seven years old *was* Jehoash when he began to reign.

Jehoash Repairs the Temple
(2 Chr. 24:1–14)

12 In the seventh year of Jehu [a]Jehoash began to reign; and forty years reigned he in Jerusalem. And his mother's name *was* Zibiah of Beer–sheba.

2 And Jehoash did *that which was* right in the sight of the LORD all his days wherein [a]Jehoiada the priest instructed him.

3 But [a]the high places were not taken away: the people still sacrificed and burnt incense in the high places.

4 And Jehoash said to the priests, [a]All the money of the dedicated things that is brought into the house of the LORD, *even* [b]the money of every one that passeth *the account,* [c]the money that every man is set at, *and* all the money that [d]cometh into any man's heart to bring into the house of the LORD,

5 Let the priests take *it* to them, every man of his acquaintance: and let them repair the breaches of the house, wheresoever any breach shall be found.

6 But it was *so, that* in the three and twentieth year of king Jehoash [a]the priests had not repaired the breaches of the house.

7 [a]Then king Jehoash called for Jehoiada the priest, and the *other* priests, and said unto them, Why repair ye not the breaches of the house? now therefore receive no *more* money of your acquaintance, but deliver it for the breaches of the house.

8 And the priests consented to receive no *more* money of the people, neither to repair the breaches of the house.

9 But Jehoiada the priest took [a]a chest, and bored a hole in the lid of it, and set it beside the altar, on the right side as one cometh into the house of the LORD: and the priests that kept the door put [b]therein all the money *that was* brought into the house of the LORD.

10 And it was *so,* when they saw that *there was* much money in the chest, that the king's [a]scribe and the high priest came up, and they put up in bags, and told the money that was found in the house of the LORD.

11 And they gave the money, being told, into the hands of them that did the work, that had the oversight of the house of the LORD: and they laid it out to the carpenters and builders, that wrought upon the house of the LORD,

12 And to masons, and hewers of stone, and to buy timber and hewed stone to [a]repair the breaches of the house of the LORD, and for all that was laid out for the house to repair *it.*

13 Howbeit [a]there were not made for the house of the LORD bowls of silver, snuffers, basons, trumpets, any vessels of gold, or vessels of silver, of the money *that was* brought into the house of the LORD:

14 But they gave that to the workmen, and repaired therewith the house of the LORD.

15 Moreover [a]they reckoned not with the men, into whose hand they delivered the money to be bestowed on workmen: for they dealt faithfully.

16 [a]The trespass money and sin money was not brought into the house of the LORD: [b]it was the priests'.

21 [a]2 Chr. 24:1–14

CHAPTER 12

1 [a]2 Chr. 24:1
2 [a]2 Kin. 11:4
3 [a]1 Kin. 15:14; 22:43; 2 Kin. 14:4; 15:35
4 [a]2 Kin. 22:4 [b]Ex. 30:13–16 [c]Lev. 27:2–28 [d]Ex. 35:5; 1 Chr. 29:3–9
6 [a]2 Chr. 24:5
7 [a]2 Chr. 24:6
9 [a]2 Chr. 23:1; 24:8 [b]Mark 12:41; Luke 21:1
10 [a]2 Sam. 8:17; 2 Kin. 19:2; 22:3, 4, 12
12 [a]2 Kin. 22:5, 6
13 [a]2 Chr. 24:14
15 [a]2 Kin. 22:7; [1 Cor. 4:2]; 2 Cor. 8:20
16 [a][Lev. 5:15, 18] [b][Lev. 7:7; Num. 18:9]

NKJV

19 Then he took the captains of hundreds, the bodyguards, the escorts, and all the people of the land; and they brought the king down from the house of the LORD, and went by way of the gate of the escorts to the king's house. Then he sat on the throne of the kings.

20 So all the people of the land rejoiced; and the city was quiet, for they had slain Athaliah with the sword *in* the king's house.

21 Jehoash *was* [a]seven years old when he became king.

Jehoash Repairs the Temple
(2 Chr. 24:1–14)

12 In the seventh year of Jehu, [a]Jehoash* became king, and he reigned forty years in Jerusalem. His mother's name *was* Zibiah of Beersheba.

2 Jehoash did *what was* right in the sight of the LORD all the days in which [a]Jehoiada the priest instructed him.

3 But [a]the high places were not taken away; the people still sacrificed and burned incense on the high places.

4 And Jehoash said to the priests, [a]"All the money of the dedicated gifts that are brought into the house of the LORD—each man's [b]census money, each man's [c]assessment money—*and* all the money that a man [d]purposes in his heart to bring into the house of the LORD,

5 "let the priests take *it* themselves, each from his constituency; and let them repair the damages of the temple, wherever any dilapidation is found."

6 Now it was so, by the twenty-third year of King Jehoash, [a]*that* the priests had not repaired the damages of the temple.

7 [a]So King Jehoash called Jehoiada the priest and the *other* priests, and said to them, "Why have you not repaired the damages of the temple? Now therefore, do not take *more* money from your constituency, but deliver it for repairing the damages of the temple."

8 And the priests agreed that they would neither receive *more* money from the people, nor repair the damages of the temple.

9 Then Jehoiada the priest took [a]a chest, bored a hole in its lid, and set it beside the altar, on the right side as one comes into the house of the LORD; and the priests who kept the door put [b]there all the money brought into the house of the LORD.

10 So it was, whenever they saw that *there was* much money in the chest, that the king's [a]scribe and the high priest came up and put it in bags, and counted the money that was found in the house of the LORD.

11 Then they gave the money, which had been apportioned, into the hands of those who did the work, who had the oversight of the house of the LORD; and they paid it out to the carpenters and builders who worked on the house of the LORD,

12 and to masons and stonecutters, and for buying timber and hewn stone, to [a]repair the damage of the house of the LORD, and for all that was paid out to repair the temple.

13 However [a]there were not made for the house of the LORD basins of silver, trimmers, sprinkling-bowls, trumpets, any articles of gold or articles of silver, from the money brought into the house of the LORD.

14 But they gave that to the workmen, and they repaired the house of the LORD with it.

15 Moreover [a]they did not require an account from the men into whose hand they delivered the money to be paid to workmen, for they dealt faithfully.

16 [a]The money from the trespass offerings and the money from the sin offerings was not brought into the house of the LORD. [b]It belonged to the priests.

* **12:1** *Joash,* 2 Kin. 11:2ff.

KJV

Hazael Threatens Jerusalem

17 Then [a]Hazael king of Syria went up, and
fought against Gath, and took it: and [b]Hazael set
his face to go up to Jerusalem.
18 And Jehoash king of Judah [a]took all the
hallowed things that Jehoshaphat, and Jehoram,
and Ahaziah, his fathers, kings of Judah, had dedicated, and his own hallowed things, and all the
gold *that was* found in the treasures of the house
of the LORD, and in the king's house, and sent *it*
to Hazael king of Syria: and he went away from
Jerusalem.

Death of Joash
(2 Chr. 24:23–27)

19 And the rest of the acts of Joash, and all
that he did, *are* they not written in the book of
the chronicles of the kings of Judah?
20 And [a]his servants arose, and made a conspiracy, and slew Joash in the house of Millo,
which goeth down to Silla.
21 For Jozachar the son of Shimeath, and Jehozabad the son of Shomer, his servants, smote
him, and he died; and they buried him with his
fathers in the city of David: and [a]Amaziah his
son reigned in his stead.

Jehoahaz Reigns in Israel

13 In the three and twentieth year of [a]Joash
the son of Ahaziah king of Judah [b]Jehoa-
haz the son of Jehu began to reign over Israel
in Samaria, *and reigned* seventeen years.
2 And he did *that which was* evil in the sight
of the LORD, and followed the [a]sins of Jeroboam
the son of Nebat, which made Israel to sin; he
departed not therefrom.
3 And [a]the anger of the LORD was kindled
against Israel, and he delivered them into the
hand of [b]Hazael king of Syria, and into the hand
of [c]Ben–hadad the son of Hazael, all *their* days.
4 And Jehoahaz [a]besought the LORD, and
the LORD hearkened unto him: for [b]he saw the
oppression of Israel, because the king of Syria
oppressed them.
5 ([a]And the LORD gave Israel a saviour, so
that they went out from under the hand of the
Syrians: and the children of Israel dwelt in their
tents, as beforetime.
6 Nevertheless they departed not from the
sins of the house of Jeroboam, who made Israel
sin, *but* walked therein: [a]and there remained the
grove also in Samaria.)
7 Neither did he leave of the people to Jehoahaz but fifty horsemen, and ten chariots, and
ten thousand footmen; for the king of Syria had
destroyed them, [a]and had made them [b]like the
dust by threshing.
8 Now the rest of the acts of Jehoahaz, and
all that he did, and his might, *are* they not written
in the book of the chronicles of the kings of Israel?
9 And Jehoahaz slept with his fathers; and
they buried him in Samaria: and Joash his son
reigned in his stead.

Jehoash Reigns in Israel

10 In the thirty and seventh year of Joash
king of Judah began Jehoash the son of Jehoahaz
to reign over Israel in Samaria, *and reigned* sixteen years.
11 And he did *that which was* evil in the sight
of the LORD; he departed not from all the sins of
Jeroboam the son of Nebat, who made Israel sin:
but he walked therein.
12 [a]And the rest of the acts of Joash, and
[b]all that he did, and [c]his might wherewith he
fought against Amaziah king of Judah, *are* they
not written in the book of the chronicles of the
kings of Israel?
13 And Joash [a]slept with his fathers; and Jeroboam sat upon his throne: and Joash was buried
in Samaria with the kings of Israel.

---

17 [a]2 Kin. 8:12 [b]2 Chr. 24:23
18 [a]1 Kin. 15:18; 2 Kin. 16:8; 18:15, 16
20 [a]2 Kin. 14:5; 2 Chr. 24:25
21 [a]2 Chr. 24:27

CHAPTER 13

1 [a]2 Kin. 12:1 [b]2 Kin. 10:35
2 [a]1 Kin. 12:26–33
3 [a]Judg. 2:14 [b]2 Kin. 8:12 [c]Amos 1:4
4 [a][Ps. 78:34] [b][Ex. 3:7, 9; Judg. 2:18]; 2 Kin. 14:26
5 [a]2 Kin. 13:25; 14:25, 27; Neh. 9:27
6 [a]1 Kin. 16:33
7 [a]2 Kin. 10:32 [b][Amos 1:3]
12 [a]2 Kin. 14:8–15 [b]2 Kin. 13:14–19, 25 [c]2 Kin. 14:9; 2 Chr. 25:17–25
13 [a]2 Kin. 14:16

*

12:19 *Jehoash,* vv. 1–18
12:20 Lit. *The Landfill*
12:21 *Zabad,* 2 Chr. 24:26 • *Shimrith,* 2 Chr. 24:26
13:1 *Jehoash,* 2 Kin. 12:1–18
13:6 Heb. *Asherah,* a Canaanite goddess
13:10 *Joash,* v. 9

NKJV

Hazael Threatens Jerusalem

17 [a]Hazael king of Syria went up and fought
against Gath, and took it; then [b]Hazael set his
face to go up to Jerusalem.
18 And Jehoash king of Judah [a]took all the
sacred things that his fathers, Jehoshaphat and
Jehoram and Ahaziah, kings of Judah, had dedicated, and his own sacred things, and all the gold
found in the treasuries of the house of the LORD
and in the king's house, and sent *them* to Hazael
king of Syria. Then he went away from Jerusalem.

Death of Joash
(2 Chr. 24:23–27)

19 Now the rest of the acts of *Joash, and
all that he did, *are* they not written in the book
of the chronicles of the kings of Judah?
20 And [a]his servants arose and formed a conspiracy, and killed Joash in the house of *the
Millo, which goes down to Silla.
21 For *Jozachar the son of Shimeath and Jehozabad the son of *Shomer, his servants, struck
him. So he died, and they buried him with his
fathers in the City of David. Then [a]Amaziah his
son reigned in his place.

Jehoahaz Reigns in Israel

13 In the twenty-third year of [a]Joash* the son
of Ahaziah, king of Judah, [b]Jehoahaz the
son of Jehu became king over Israel in Samaria,
and reigned seventeen years.
2 And he did evil in the sight of the LORD,
and followed the [a]sins of Jeroboam the son of
Nebat, who had made Israel sin. He did not depart
from them.
3 Then [a]the anger of the LORD was aroused
against Israel, and He delivered them into the
hand of [b]Hazael king of Syria, and into the hand
of [c]Ben-Hadad the son of Hazael, all *their* days.
4 So Jehoahaz [a]pleaded with the LORD, and
the LORD listened to him; for [b]He saw the oppression of Israel, because the king of Syria oppressed
them.
5 [a]Then the LORD gave Israel a deliverer,
so that they escaped from under the hand of the
Syrians; and the children of Israel dwelt in their
tents as before.
6 Nevertheless they did not depart from the
sins of the house of Jeroboam, who had made Israel sin, *but* walked in them; [a]and the *wooden
image also remained in Samaria.
7 For He left of the army of Jehoahaz only
fifty horsemen, ten chariots, and ten thousand
foot soldiers; for the king of Syria had destroyed
them [a]and made them [b]like the dust at threshing.
8 Now the rest of the acts of Jehoahaz, all
that he did, and his might, *are* they not written
in the book of the chronicles of the kings of Israel?
9 So Jehoahaz rested with his fathers, and
they buried him in Samaria. Then Joash his son
reigned in his place.

Jehoash Reigns in Israel

10 In the thirty-seventh year of Joash king
of Judah, *Jehoash the son of Jehoahaz became
king over Israel in Samaria, *and reigned* sixteen
years.
11 And he did evil in the sight of the LORD.
He did not depart from all the sins of Jeroboam
the son of Nebat, who made Israel sin, *but* walked
in them.
12 [a]Now the rest of the acts of Joash, [b]all
that he did, and [c]his might with which he fought
against Amaziah king of Judah, *are* they not written in the book of the chronicles of the kings of
Israel?
13 So Joash [a]rested with his fathers. Then
Jeroboam sat on his throne. And Joash was buried
in Samaria with the kings of Israel.

KJV

Death of Elisha

14 Now Elisha was fallen sick of his sickness whereof he died. And Joash the king of Israel came down unto him, and wept over his face, and said, O my father, my father, [a]the chariot of Israel, and the horsemen thereof.

15 And Elisha said unto him, Take bow and arrows. And he took unto him bow and arrows.

16 And he said to the king of Israel, Put thine hand upon the bow. And he put his hand *upon it:* and Elisha put his hands upon the king's hands.

17 And he said, Open the window eastward. And he opened *it.* Then Elisha said, Shoot. And he shot. And he said, The arrow of the LORD's deliverance, and the arrow of deliverance from Syria: for thou shalt smite the Syrians in [a]Aphek, till thou have consumed *them.*

18 And he said, Take the arrows. And he took *them.* And he said unto the king of Israel, Smite upon the ground. And he smote thrice, and stayed.

19 And the man of God was wroth with him, and said, Thou shouldest have smitten five or six times; then hadst thou smitten Syria till thou hadst consumed *it:* [a]whereas now thou shalt smite Syria *but* thrice.

20 And Elisha died, and they buried him. And the [a]bands of the Moabites invaded the land at the coming in of the year.

21 And it came to pass, as they were burying a man, that, behold, they spied a band *of men;* and they cast the man into the sepulchre of Elisha: and when the man was let down, and touched the bones of Elisha, he revived, and stood up on his feet.

Israel Recaptures Cities from Syria

22 But [a]Hazael king of Syria oppressed Israel all the days of Jehoahaz.

23 And the LORD was [a]gracious unto them, and had compassion on them, and [b]had respect unto them, [c]because of his covenant with Abraham, Isaac, and Jacob, and would not destroy them, neither cast he them from his presence as yet.

24 So Hazael king of Syria died; and Ben–hadad his son reigned in his stead.

25 And Jehoash the son of Jehoahaz took again out of the hand of Ben–hadad the son of Hazael the cities, which he had taken out of the hand of Jehoahaz his father by war. [a]Three times did Joash beat him, and recovered the cities of Israel.

Amaziah Reigns in Judah
(2 Chr. 25:1—26:2)

14 In [a]the second year of Joash son of Jehoahaz king of Israel reigned [b]Amaziah the son of Joash king of Judah.

2 He was twenty and five years old when he began to reign, and reigned twenty and nine years in Jerusalem. And his mother's name *was* Jehoaddan of Jerusalem.

3 And he did *that which was* right in the sight of the LORD, yet not like David his father: he did according to all things [a]as Joash his father did.

4 [a]Howbeit the high places were not taken away: as yet the people did sacrifice and burnt incense on the high places.

5 And it came to pass, as soon as the kingdom was confirmed in his hand, that he slew his servants [a]which had slain the king his father.

6 But the children of the murderers he slew not: according unto that which is written in the book of the law of Moses, wherein the LORD commanded, saying, [a]The fathers shall not be put to death for the children, nor the children be put to death for the fathers; but every man shall be put to death for his own sin.

7 [a]He slew of Edom in [b]the valley of salt

14 [a]2 Kin. 2:12
17 [a]1 Kin. 20:26
19 [a]2 Kin. 13:25
20 [a]2 Kin. 3:5; 24:2
22 [a]2 Kin. 8:12, 13
23 [a]2 Kin. 14:27 [b][Ex. 2:24, 25] [c]Gen. 13:16, 17; 17:2–7; Ex. 32:13
25 [a]2 Kin. 13:18, 19

CHAPTER 14

1 [a]2 Kin. 13:10 [b]2 Chr. 25:1, 2
3 [a]2 Kin. 12:2
4 [a]2 Kin. 12:3
5 [a]2 Kin. 12:20
6 [a]Deut. 24:16; [Jer. 31:30; Ezek. 18:4, 20]
7 [a]2 Chr. 25:5–16 [b]2 Sam. 8:13; 1 Chr. 18:12; Ps. 60:title

*________
13:25 *Joash,* vv. 12–14, 25

NKJV

Death of Elisha

14 Elisha had become sick with the illness of which he would die. Then Joash the king of Israel came down to him, and wept over his face, and said, "O my father, my father, [a]the chariots of Israel and their horsemen!"

15 And Elisha said to him, "Take a bow and some arrows." So he took himself a bow and some arrows.

16 Then he said to the king of Israel, "Put your hand on the bow." So he put his hand *on it,* and Elisha put his hands on the king's hands.

17 And he said, "Open the east window"; and he opened *it.* Then Elisha said, "Shoot"; and he shot. And he said, "The arrow of the LORD's deliverance and the arrow of deliverance from Syria; for you must strike the Syrians at [a]Aphek till you have destroyed *them.*"

18 Then he said, "Take the arrows"; so he took *them.* And he said to the king of Israel, "Strike the ground"; so he struck three times, and stopped.

19 And the man of God was angry with him, and said, "You should have struck five or six times; then you would have struck Syria till you had destroyed *it!* [a]But now you will strike Syria *only* three times."

20 Then Elisha died, and they buried him. And the [a]*raiding* bands from Moab invaded the land in the spring of the year.

21 So it was, as they were burying a man, that suddenly they spied a band *of raiders;* and they put the man in the tomb of Elisha; and when the man was let down and touched the bones of Elisha, he revived and stood on his feet.

Israel Recaptures Cities from Syria

22 And [a]Hazael king of Syria oppressed Israel all the days of Jehoahaz.

23 But the LORD was [a]gracious to them, had compassion on them, and [b]regarded them, [c]because of His covenant with Abraham, Isaac, and Jacob, and would not yet destroy them or cast them from His presence.

24 Now Hazael king of Syria died. Then Ben-Hadad his son reigned in his place.

25 And *Jehoash the son of Jehoahaz recaptured from the hand of Ben-Hadad, the son of Hazael, the cities which he had taken out of the hand of Jehoahaz his father by war. [a]Three times Joash defeated him and recaptured the cities of Israel.

Amaziah Reigns in Judah
(2 Chr. 25:1—26:2)

14 In [a]the second year of Joash the son of Jehoahaz, king of Israel, [b]Amaziah the son of Joash, king of Judah, became king.

2 He was twenty-five years old when he became king, and he reigned twenty-nine years in Jerusalem. His mother's name was Jehoaddan of Jerusalem.

3 And he did *what was* right in the sight of the LORD, yet not like his father David; he did everything [a]as his father Joash had done.

4 [a]However the high places were not taken away, and the people still sacrificed and burned incense on the high places.

5 Now it happened, as soon as the kingdom was established in his hand, that he executed his servants [a]who had murdered his father the king.

6 But the children of the murderers he did not execute, according to what is written in the Book of the Law of Moses, in which the LORD commanded, saying, [a]"Fathers shall not be put to death for their children, nor shall children be put to death for their fathers; but a person shall be put to death for his own sin."

7 [a]He killed ten thousand Edomites in [b]the

KJV

ten thousand, and took Selah by war, [c]and called the name of it Joktheel unto this day.

8 [a]Then Amaziah sent messengers to Jehoash, the son of Jehoahaz son of Jehu, king of Israel, saying, Come, let us look one another in the face.

9 And Jehoash the king of Israel sent to Amaziah king of Judah, saying, [a]The thistle that *was* in Lebanon sent to the [b]cedar that *was* in Lebanon, saying, Give thy daughter to my son to wife: and there passed by a wild beast that *was* in Lebanon, and trode down the thistle.

10 Thou hast indeed smitten Edom, and [a]thine heart hath lifted thee up: glory *of this,* and tarry at home: for why shouldest thou meddle to *thy* hurt, that thou shouldest fall, *even* thou, and Judah with thee?

11 But Amaziah would not hear. Therefore Jehoash king of Israel went up; and he and Amaziah king of Judah looked one another in the face at [a]Beth–shemesh, which *belongeth* to Judah.

12 And Judah was put to the worse before Israel; and they fled every man to their tents.

13 And Jehoash king of Israel took Amaziah king of Judah, the son of Jehoash the son of Ahaziah, at Beth–shemesh, and came to Jerusalem, and brake down the wall of Jerusalem from [a]the gate of Ephraim unto [b]the corner gate, four hundred cubits.

14 And he took all [a]the gold and silver, and all the vessels that were found in the house of the LORD, and in the treasures of the king's house, and hostages, and returned to Samaria.

15 [a]Now the rest of the acts of Jehoash which he did, and his might, and how he fought with Amaziah king of Judah, *are* they not written in the book of the chronicles of the kings of Israel?

16 And Jehoash slept with his fathers, and was buried in Samaria with the kings of Israel; and Jeroboam his son reigned in his stead.

17 [a]And Amaziah the son of Joash king of Judah lived after the death of Jehoash son of Jehoahaz king of Israel fifteen years.

18 And the rest of the acts of Amaziah, *are* they not written in the book of the chronicles of the kings of Judah?

19 Now [a]they made a conspiracy against him in Jerusalem: and he fled to [b]Lachish; but they sent after him to Lachish, and slew him there.

20 And they brought him on horses: and he was buried at Jerusalem with his fathers in the city of David.

21 And all the people of Judah took [a]Azariah, which *was* sixteen years old, and made him king instead of his father Amaziah.

22 He built [a]Elath, and restored it to Judah, after that the king slept with his fathers.

Jereboam II Reigns in Israel

23 In the fifteenth year of Amaziah the son of Joash king of Judah Jeroboam the son of Joash king of Israel began to reign in Samaria, *and reigned* forty and one years.

24 And he did *that which was* evil in the sight of the LORD: he departed not from all the [a]sins of Jeroboam the son of Nebat, who made Israel to sin.

25 He [a]restored the coast of Israel [b]from the entering of Hamath unto [c]the sea of the plain, according to the word of the LORD God of Israel, which he spake by the hand of his servant [d]Jonah, the son of Amittai, the prophet, which *was* of [e]Gath–hepher.

26 For the LORD [a]saw the affliction of Israel, *that it was* very bitter: for [b]*there was* not any shut up, nor any left, nor any helper for Israel.

27 [a]And the LORD said not that he would blot out the name of Israel from under heaven: but he saved them by the hand of Jeroboam the son of Joash.

28 Now the rest of the acts of Jeroboam, and all that he did, and his might, how he warred,

---

7 [c]Josh. 15:38 **8** [a]2 Chr. 25:17, 18 **9** [a]Judg. 9:8–15 [b]1 Kin. 4:33 **10** [a]Deut. 8:14; 2 Chr. 32:25; [Ezek. 28:2, 5, 17; Hab. 2:4] **11** [a]Josh. 19:38; 21:16 **13** [a]Neh. 8:16; 12:39 [b]Jer. 31:38; Zech. 14:10 **14** [a]1 Kin. 7:51; 2 Kin. 12:18; 16:8 **15** [a]2 Kin. 13:12, 13 **17** [a]2 Chr. 25:25–28 **19** [a]2 Chr. 25:27 [b]Josh. 10:31 **21** [a]2 Kin. 15:13; 2 Chr. 26:1 **22** [a]1 Kin. 9:26; 2 Kin. 16:6; 2 Chr. 8:17 **24** [a]1 Kin. 12:26–33 **25** [a]2 Kin. 10:32; 13:5, 25 [b]Num. 13:21; 34:8; 1 Kin. 8:65 [c]Deut. 3:17 [d]Jon. 1:1; Matt. 12:39, 40 [e]Josh. 19:13 **26** [a]Ex. 3:7; 2 Kin. 13:4; Ps. 106:44 [b]Deut. 32:36 **27** [a][2 Kin. 13:5, 23]

*

14:8 *Joash,* 2 Kin. 13:9, 12–14, 25; 2 Chr. 25:17ff. **14:21** *Uzziah,* 2 Chr. 26:1ff.; Is. 6:1; etc.

NKJV

Valley of Salt, and took Sela by war, [c]and called its name Joktheel to this day.

8 [a]Then Amaziah sent messengers to *Jehoash the son of Jehoahaz, the son of Jehu, king of Israel, saying, "Come, let us face one another *in battle.*"

9 And Jehoash king of Israel sent to Amaziah king of Judah, saying, [a]"The thistle that *was* in Lebanon sent to the [b]cedar that *was* in Lebanon, saying, 'Give your daughter to my son as wife'; and a wild beast that *was* in Lebanon passed by and trampled the thistle.

10 "You have indeed defeated Edom, and [a]your heart has lifted you up. Glory *in that,* and stay at home; for why should you meddle with trouble so that you fall—you and Judah with you?"

11 But Amaziah would not heed. Therefore Jehoash king of Israel went out; so he and Amaziah king of Judah faced one another at [a]Beth Shemesh, which *belongs* to Judah.

12 And Judah was defeated by Israel, and every man fled to his tent.

13 Then Jehoash king of Israel captured Amaziah king of Judah, the son of Jehoash, the son of Ahaziah, at Beth Shemesh; and he went to Jerusalem, and broke down the wall of Jerusalem from [a]the Gate of Ephraim to [b]the Corner Gate—four hundred cubits.

14 And he took all [a]the gold and silver, all the articles that were found in the house of the LORD and in the treasuries of the king's house, and hostages, and returned to Samaria.

15 [a]Now the rest of the acts of Jehoash which he did—his might, and how he fought with Amaziah king of Judah—*are* they not written in the book of the chronicles of the kings of Israel?

16 So Jehoash rested with his fathers, and was buried in Samaria with the kings of Israel. Then Jeroboam his son reigned in his place.

17 [a]Amaziah the son of Joash, king of Judah, lived fifteen years after the death of Jehoash the son of Jehoahaz, king of Israel.

18 Now the rest of the acts of Amaziah, *are* they not written in the book of the chronicles of the kings of Judah?

19 And [a]they formed a conspiracy against him in Jerusalem, and he fled to [b]Lachish; but they sent after him to Lachish and killed him there.

20 Then they brought him on horses, and he was buried at Jerusalem with his fathers in the City of David.

21 And all the people of Judah took [a]Azariah,* who *was* sixteen years old, and made him king instead of his father Amaziah.

22 He built [a]Elath and restored it to Judah, after the king rested with his fathers.

Jeroboam II Reigns in Israel

23 In the fifteenth year of Amaziah the son of Joash, king of Judah, Jeroboam the son of Joash, king of Israel, became king in Samaria, *and reigned* forty-one years.

24 And he did evil in the sight of the LORD; he did not depart from all the [a]sins of Jeroboam the son of Nebat, who had made Israel sin.

25 He [a]restored the territory of Israel [b]from the entrance of Hamath to [c]the Sea of the Arabah, according to the word of the LORD God of Israel, which He had spoken through His servant [d]Jonah the son of Amittai, the prophet who *was* from [e]Gath Hepher.

26 For the LORD [a]saw *that* the affliction of Israel *was* very bitter; and whether bond or free, [b]there was no helper for Israel.

27 [a]And the LORD did not say that He would blot out the name of Israel from under heaven; but He saved them by the hand of Jeroboam the son of Joash.

28 Now the rest of the acts of Jeroboam, and all that he did—his might, how he made war, and

KJV

and how he recovered [a]Damascus, and Hamath, [b]*which belonged* to Judah, for Israel, *are* they not written in the book of the chronicles of the kings of Israel?

29 And Jeroboam slept with his fathers, *even* with the kings of Israel; and [a]Zachariah his son reigned in his stead.

Azariah Reigns in Judah
(2 Chr. 26:3–23)

15 In the twenty and seventh year of Jeroboam king of Israel began [a]Azariah son of Amaziah king of Judah [b]to reign.

2 Sixteen years old was he when he began to reign, and he reigned two and fifty years in Jerusalem. And his mother's name *was* Jecholiah of Jerusalem.

3 And he did *that which was* right in the sight of the LORD, according to all that his father Amaziah had done;

4 [a]Save that the high places were not removed: the people sacrificed and burnt incense still on the high places.

5 And the LORD [a]smote the king, so that he was a leper unto the day of his [b]death, and [c]dwelt in a several house. And Jotham the king's son *was* over the house, judging the people of the land.

6 And the rest of the acts of Azariah, and all that he did, *are* they not written in the book of the chronicles of the kings of Judah?

7 So Azariah slept with his fathers; and [a]they buried him with his fathers in the city of David: and Jotham his son reigned in his stead.

Zechariah Reigns in Israel

8 In the thirty and eighth year of Azariah king of Judah did [a]Zachariah the son of Jeroboam reign over Israel in Samaria six months.

9 And he did *that which was* evil in the sight of the LORD, [a]as his fathers had done: he departed not from the sins of Jeroboam the son of Nebat, who made Israel to sin.

10 And Shallum the son of Jabesh conspired against him, and [a]smote him before the people, and slew him, and reigned in his stead.

11 And the rest of the acts of Zachariah, behold, they *are* written in the book of the chronicles of the kings of Israel.

12 This *was* the word of the LORD which he spake unto Jehu, saying, [a]Thy sons shall sit on the throne of Israel unto the fourth *generation.* And so it came to pass.

Shallum Reigns in Israel

13 Shallum the son of Jabesh began to reign in the nine and thirtieth year of Uzziah king of Judah; and he reigned a full month in Samaria.

14 For Menahem the son of Gadi went up from [a]Tirzah, and came to Samaria, and smote Shallum the son of Jabesh in Samaria, and slew him, and reigned in his stead.

15 And the rest of the acts of Shallum, and his conspiracy which he made, behold, they *are* written in the book of the chronicles of the kings of Israel.

16 Then Menahem smote [a]Tiphsah, and all that *were* therein, and the coasts thereof from Tirzah: because they opened not *to him,* therefore he smote *it; and* all [b]the women therein that were with child he ripped up.

Menahem Reigns in Israel

17 In the nine and thirtieth year of Azariah king of Judah began Menahem the son of Gadi to reign over Israel, *and reigned* ten years in Samaria.

18 And he did *that which was* evil in the sight of the LORD: he departed not all his days from the sins of Jeroboam the son of Nebat, who made Israel to sin.

19 *And* [a]Pul the king of Assyria came against the land: and Menahem gave Pul a thousand tal-

28 [a]1 Kin. 11:24 [b]2 Sam. 8:6; 1 Kin. 11:24; 2 Chr. 8:3
29 [a]2 Kin. 15:8

CHAPTER 15

1 [a]2 Kin. 15:13, 30 [b]2 Kin. 14:21; 2 Chr. 26:1, 3, 4
4 [a]2 Kin. 12:3; 14:4; 15:35
5 [a]2 Chr. 26:19–23; Ps. 78:31 [b]Is. 6:1 [c][Lev. 13:46]; Num. 12:14
7 [a]2 Chr. 26:23
8 [a]2 Kin. 14:29
9 [a]2 Kin. 14:24
10 [a]Amos 7:9
12 [a]2 Kin. 10:30
14 [a]1 Kin. 14:17; Song 6:4
16 [a]1 Kin. 4:24 [b]2 Kin. 8:12; Hos. 13:16
19 [a]1 Chr. 5:26; 66:19; Hos. 8:9

NKJV

how he recaptured for Israel, from [a]Damascus and Hamath, [b]*what had belonged* to Judah—*are* they not written in the book of the chronicles of the kings of Israel?

29 So Jeroboam rested with his fathers, the kings of Israel. Then [a]Zechariah his son reigned in his place.

Azariah Reigns in Judah
(2 Chr. 26:3–23)

15 In the twenty-seventh year of Jeroboam king of Israel, [a]Azariah the son of Amaziah, king of Judah, [b]became king.

2 He was sixteen years old when he became king, and he reigned fifty-two years in Jerusalem. His mother's name *was* Jecholiah of Jerusalem.

3 And he did *what was* right in the sight of the LORD, according to all that his father Amaziah had done,

4 [a]except that the high places were not removed; the people still sacrificed and burned incense on the high places.

5 Then the LORD [a]struck the king, so that he was a leper until the day of his [b]death; so he [c]dwelt in an isolated house. And Jotham the king's son *was* over the *royal* house, judging the people of the land.

6 Now the rest of the acts of Azariah, and all that he did, *are* they not written in the book of the chronicles of the kings of Judah?

7 So Azariah rested with his fathers, and [a]they buried him with his fathers in the City of David. Then Jotham his son reigned in his place.

Zechariah Reigns in Israel

8 In the thirty-eighth year of Azariah king of Judah, [a]Zechariah the son of Jeroboam reigned over Israel in Samaria six months.

9 And he did evil in the sight of the LORD, [a]as his fathers had done; he did not depart from the sins of Jeroboam the son of Nebat, who had made Israel sin.

10 Then Shallum the son of Jabesh conspired against him, and [a]struck and killed him in front of the people; and he reigned in his place.

11 Now the rest of the acts of Zechariah, indeed they *are* written in the book of the chronicles of the kings of Israel.

12 This *was* the word of the LORD which He spoke to Jehu, saying, [a]"Your sons shall sit on the throne of Israel to the fourth *generation.*" And so it was.

Shallum Reigns in Israel

13 Shallum the son of Jabesh became king in the thirty-ninth year of *Uzziah king of Judah; and he reigned a full month in Samaria.

14 For Menahem the son of Gadi went up from [a]Tirzah, came to Samaria, and struck Shallum the son of Jabesh in Samaria and killed him; and he reigned in his place.

15 Now the rest of the acts of Shallum, and the conspiracy which he led, indeed they *are* written in the book of the chronicles of the kings of Israel.

16 Then from Tirzah, Menahem attacked [a]Tiphsah, all who *were* there, and its territory. Because they did not surrender, therefore he attacked *it.* All [b]the women there who were with child he ripped open.

Menahem Reigns in Israel

17 In the thirty-ninth year of Azariah king of Judah, Menahem the son of Gadi became king over Israel, *and reigned* ten years in Samaria.

18 And he did evil in the sight of the LORD; he did not depart all his days from the sins of Jeroboam the son of Nebat, who had made Israel sin.

19 [a]Pul* king of Assyria came against the land; and Menahem gave Pul a thousand talents

*

15:13 *Azariah,* 2 Kin. 14:21ff.; 15:1ff.
15:19 Tiglath-Pileser III, v. 29

KJV

ents of silver, that his hand might be with him to [b]confirm the kingdom in his hand.

20 And Menahem [a]exacted the money of Israel, *even* of all the mighty men of wealth, of each man fifty shekels of silver, to give to the king of Assyria. So the king of Assyria turned back, and stayed not there in the land.

21 And the rest of the acts of Menahem, and all that he did, *are* they not written in the book of the chronicles of the kings of Israel?

22 And Menahem slept with his fathers; and Pekahiah his son reigned in his stead.

Pekahiah Reigns in Israel

23 In the fiftieth year of Azariah king of Judah Pekahiah the son of Menahem began to reign over Israel in Samaria, *and reigned* two years.

24 And he did *that which was* evil in the sight of the LORD: he departed not from the sins of Jeroboam the son of Nebat, who made Israel to sin.

25 But Pekah the son of Remaliah, a captain of his, conspired against him, and smote him in Samaria, in the [a]palace of the king's house, with Argob and Arieh, and with him fifty men of the Gileadites: and he killed him, and reigned in his room.

26 And the rest of the acts of Pekahiah, and all that he did, behold, they *are* written in the book of the chronicles of the kings of Israel.

Pekah Reigns in Israel

27 In the two and fiftieth year of Azariah king of Judah [a]Pekah the son of Remaliah began to reign over Israel in Samaria, *and reigned* twenty years.

28 And he did *that which was* evil in the sight of the LORD: he departed not from the sins of Jeroboam the son of Nebat, who made Israel to sin.

29 In the days of Pekah king of Israel [a]came Tiglath–pileser king of Assyria, and took [b]Ijon, and Abel–beth–maachah, and Janoah, and Kedesh, and Hazor, and Gilead, and Galilee, all the land of Naphtali, and [c]carried them captive to Assyria.

30 And Hoshea the son of Elah made a conspiracy against Pekah the son of Remaliah, and smote him, and slew him, and [a]reigned in his stead, in the twentieth year of Jotham the son of Uzziah.

31 And the rest of the acts of Pekah, and all that he did, behold, they *are* written in the book of the chronicles of the kings of Israel.

Jotham Reigns in Judah
(*2 Chr. 27:1–9*)

32 In the second year of Pekah the son of Remaliah king of Israel began [a]Jotham the son of Uzziah king of Judah to reign.

33 Five and twenty years old was he when he began to reign, and he reigned sixteen years in Jerusalem. And his mother's name *was* Jerusha, the daughter of Zadok.

34 And he did *that which was* right in the sight of the LORD: he did [a]according to all that his father Uzziah had done.

35 [a]Howbeit the high places were not removed: the people sacrificed and burned incense still in the high places. [b]He built the higher gate of the house of the LORD.

36 Now the rest of the acts of Jotham, and all that he did, *are* they not written in the book of the chronicles of the kings of Judah?

37 In those days the LORD began to send against Judah [a]Rezin the king of Syria, and [b]Pekah the son of Remaliah.

38 And Jotham slept with his fathers, and was buried with his fathers in the city of David his father: and Ahaz his son reigned in his stead.

19 [b]2 Kin. 14:5
20 [a]2 Kin. 23:35
25 [a]1 Kin. 16:18
27 [a]2 Chr. 28:6; Is. 7:1
29 [a]2 Kin. 16:7, 10; 1 Chr. 5:26 [b]1 Kin. 15:20 [c]2 Kin. 17:6
30 [a]2 Kin. 17:1; [Hos. 10:3, 7, 15]
32 [a]2 Chr. 27:1
34 [a]2 Kin. 15:3, 4; 2 Chr. 26:4, 5
35 [a]2 Kin. 15:4 [b]2 Chr. 23:20; 27:3
37 [a]2 Kin. 16:5–9; Is. 7:1–17 [b]2 Kin. 15:26, 27

NKJV

of silver, that his hand might be with him to [b]strengthen the kingdom under his control.

20 And Menahem [a]exacted the money from Israel, from all the very wealthy, from each man fifty shekels of silver, to give to the king of Assyria. So the king of Assyria turned back, and did not stay there in the land.

21 Now the rest of the acts of Menahem, and all that he did, *are* they not written in the book of the chronicles of the kings of Israel?

22 So Menahem rested with his fathers. Then Pekahiah his son reigned in his place.

Pekahiah Reigns in Israel

23 In the fiftieth year of Azariah king of Judah, Pekahiah the son of Menahem became king over Israel in Samaria, *and reigned* two years.

24 And he did evil in the sight of the LORD; he did not depart from the sins of Jeroboam the son of Nebat, who had made Israel sin.

25 Then Pekah the son of Remaliah, an officer of his, conspired against him and killed him in Samaria, in the [a]citadel of the king's house, along with Argob and Arieh; and with him were fifty men of Gilead. He killed him and reigned in his place.

26 Now the rest of the acts of Pekahiah, and all that he did, indeed they *are* written in the book of the chronicles of the kings of Israel.

Pekah Reigns in Israel

27 In the fifty-second year of Azariah king of Judah, [a]Pekah the son of Remaliah became king over Israel in Samaria, *and reigned* twenty years.

28 And he did evil in the sight of the LORD; he did not depart from the sins of Jeroboam the son of Nebat, who had made Israel sin.

29 In the days of Pekah king of Israel, Tiglath-Pileser king of Assyria [a]came and took [b]Ijon, Abel Beth Maachah, Janoah, Kedesh, Hazor, Gilead, and Galilee, all the land of Naphtali; and he [c]carried them captive to Assyria.

30 Then Hoshea the son of Elah led a conspiracy against Pekah the son of Remaliah, and struck and killed him; so he [a]reigned in his place in the twentieth year of Jotham the son of Uzziah.

31 Now the rest of the acts of Pekah, and all that he did, indeed they *are* written in the book of the chronicles of the kings of Israel.

Jotham Reigns in Judah
(*2 Chr. 27:1–9*)

32 In the second year of Pekah the son of Remaliah, king of Israel, [a]Jotham the son of Uzziah, king of Judah, began to reign.

33 He was twenty-five years old when he became king, and he reigned sixteen years in Jerusalem. His mother's name *was* *Jerusha the daughter of Zadok.

34 And he did *what was* right in the sight of the LORD; he did [a]according to all that his father Uzziah had done.

35 [a]However the high places were not removed; the people still sacrificed and burned incense on the high places. [b]He built the Upper Gate of the house of the LORD.

36 Now the rest of the acts of Jotham, and all that he did, *are* they not written in the book of the chronicles of the kings of Judah?

37 In those days the LORD began to send [a]Rezin king of Syria and [b]Pekah the son of Remaliah against Judah.

38 So Jotham rested with his fathers, and was buried with his fathers in the City of David his father. Then Ahaz his son reigned in his place.

**15:33 Jerushah,* 2 Chr. 27:1

KJV

Ahaz Reigns in Judah
(2 Chr. 28:1–27)

16 In the seventeenth year of Pekah the son of Remaliah Ahaz the son of Jotham king of Judah began to reign.

2 Twenty years old *was* Ahaz when he began to reign, and reigned sixteen years in Jerusalem, and did not *that which was* right in the sight of the LORD his God, like David his father.

3 But he walked in the way of the kings of Israel, yea, [a]and made his son to pass through the fire, according to the [b]abominations of the heathen, whom the LORD cast out from before the children of Israel.

4 And he sacrificed and burnt incense in the [a]high places, and [b]on the hills, and under every green tree.

5 [a]Then Rezin king of Syria and Pekah son of Remaliah king of Israel came up to Jerusalem to war: and they besieged Ahaz, but could not overcome *him*.

6 At that time Rezin king of Syria [a]recovered Elath to Syria, and drave the Jews from Elath: and the Syrians came to Elath, and dwelt there unto this day.

7 So Ahaz sent messengers to [a]Tiglath–pileser king of Assyria, saying, I *am* thy servant and thy son: come up, and save me out of the hand of the king of Syria, and out of the hand of the king of Israel, which rise up against me.

8 And Ahaz [a]took the silver and gold that was found in the house of the LORD, and in the treasures of the king's house, and sent *it for* a present to the king of Assyria.

9 And the king of Assyria hearkened unto him: for the king of Assyria went up against [a]Damascus, and [b]took it, and carried *the people of* it captive to [c]Kir, and slew Rezin.

10 And king Ahaz went to Damascus to meet Tiglath–pileser king of Assyria, and saw an altar that *was* at Damascus: and king Ahaz sent to Urijah the priest the fashion of the altar, and the pattern of it, according to all the workmanship thereof.

11 And [a]Urijah the priest built an altar according to all that king Ahaz had sent from Damascus: so Urijah the priest made *it* against king Ahaz came from Damascus.

12 And when the king was come from Damascus, the king saw the altar: and [a]the king approached to the altar, and offered thereon.

13 And he burnt his burnt offering and his meat offering, and poured his drink offering, and sprinkled the blood of his peace offerings, upon the altar.

14 And he brought also [a]the brasen altar, which *was* before the LORD, from the forefront of the house, from between the altar and the house of the LORD, and put it on the north side of the altar.

15 And king Ahaz commanded Urijah the priest, saying, Upon the great altar burn [a]the morning burnt offering, and the evening meat offering, and the king's burnt sacrifice, and his meat offering, with the burnt offering of all the people of the land, and their meat offering, and their drink offerings; and sprinkle upon it all the blood of the burnt offering, and all the blood of the sacrifice: and the brasen altar shall be for me to enquire *by*.

16 Thus did Urijah the priest, according to all that king Ahaz commanded.

17 [a]And king Ahaz cut off [b]the borders of the bases, and removed the laver from off them; and took down [c]the sea from off the brasen oxen that *were* under it, and put it upon a pavement of stones.

18 And the covert for the sabbath that they had built in the house, and the king's entry without, turned he from the house of the LORD for the king of Assyria.

CHAPTER 16

3 [a][Lev. 18:21]; 2 Kin. 17:17; 2 Chr. 28:3; Ps. 106:37, 38; Is. 1:1 [b][Deut. 12:31]; 2 Kin. 21:2, 11
4 [a]2 Kin. 15:34, 35 [b][Deut. 12:2]; 1 Kin. 14:23
5 [a]2 Kin. 15:37; Is. 7:1, 4
6 [a]2 Kin. 14:22; 2 Chr. 26:2
7 [a]2 Kin. 15:29; 1 Chr. 5:26; 2 Chr. 28:20
8 [a]2 Kin. 12:17, 18; 2 Chr. 28:21
9 [a]2 Kin. 14:28 [b]Amos 1:5 [c]Is. 22:6; Amos 9:7
11 [a]Is. 8:2
12 [a]2 Chr. 26:16, 19
14 [a]Ex. 27:1, 2; 40:6, 29; 2 Chr. 4:1
15 [a]Ex. 29:39–41
17 [a]2 Chr. 28:24 [b]1 Kin. 7:27–29 [c]1 Kin. 7:23–25

NKJV

Ahaz Reigns in Judah
(2 Chr. 28:1–27)

16 In the seventeenth year of Pekah the son of Remaliah, Ahaz the son of Jotham, king of Judah, began to reign.

2 Ahaz *was* twenty years old when he became king, and he reigned sixteen years in Jerusalem; and he did not do *what was* right in the sight of the LORD his God, as his father David *had done*.

3 But he walked in the way of the kings of Israel; indeed [a]he made his son pass through the fire, according to the [b]abominations of the nations whom the LORD had cast out from before the children of Israel.

4 And he sacrificed and burned incense on the [a]high places, [b]on the hills, and under every green tree.

5 [a]Then Rezin king of Syria and Pekah the son of Remaliah, king of Israel, came up to Jerusalem to *make* war; and they besieged Ahaz but could not overcome *him*.

6 At that time Rezin king of Syria [a]captured Elath for Syria, and drove the men of Judah from Elath. Then the *Edomites went to Elath, and dwell there to this day.

7 So Ahaz sent messengers to [a]Tiglath-Pileser king of Assyria, saying, "I *am* your servant and your son. Come up and save me from the hand of the king of Syria and from the hand of the king of Israel, who rise up against me."

8 And Ahaz [a]took the silver and gold that was found in the house of the LORD, and in the treasuries of the king's house, and sent *it as* a present to the king of Assyria.

9 So the king of Assyria heeded him; for the king of Assyria went up against [a]Damascus and [b]took it, carried *its people* captive to [c]Kir, and killed Rezin.

10 Now King Ahaz went to Damascus to meet Tiglath-Pileser king of Assyria, and saw an altar that *was* at Damascus; and King Ahaz sent to Urijah the priest the design of the altar and its pattern, according to all its workmanship.

11 Then [a]Urijah the priest built an altar according to all that King Ahaz had sent from Damascus. So Urijah the priest made *it* before King Ahaz came back from Damascus.

12 And when the king came back from Damascus, the king saw the altar; and [a]the king approached the altar and made offerings on it.

13 So he burned his burnt offering and his grain offering; and he poured his drink offering and sprinkled the blood of his peace offerings on the altar.

14 He also brought [a]the bronze altar which *was* before the LORD, from the front of the temple—from between the *new* altar and the house of the LORD—and put it on the north side of the *new* altar.

15 Then King Ahaz commanded Urijah the priest, saying, "On the great *new* altar burn [a]the morning burnt offering, the evening grain offering, the king's burnt sacrifice, and his grain offering, with the burnt offering of all the people of the land, their grain offering, and their drink offerings; and sprinkle on it all the blood of the burnt offering and all the blood of the sacrifice. And the bronze altar shall be for me to inquire *by*."

16 Thus did Urijah the priest, according to all that King Ahaz commanded.

17 [a]And King Ahaz cut off [b]the panels of the carts, and removed the lavers from them; and he took down [c]the Sea from the bronze oxen that *were* under it, and put it on a pavement of stones.

18 Also he removed the Sabbath pavilion which they had built in the temple, and he removed the king's outer entrance from the house of the LORD, on account of the king of Assyria.

*———

16:6 A few ancient mss. *Syrians*

KJV

19 Now the rest of the acts of Ahaz which
he did, *are* they not written in the book of the
chronicles of the kings of Judah?
20 And Ahaz slept with his fathers, and [a]was
buried with his fathers in the city of David: and
Hezekiah his son reigned in his stead.

Hoshea Reigns in Israel

17 In the twelfth year of Ahaz king of Judah
began [a]Hoshea the son of Elah to reign in
Samaria over Israel nine years.
2 And he did *that which was* evil in the sight
of the LORD, but not as the kings of Israel that
were before him.
3 Against him came up [a]Shalmaneser king
of Assyria; and Hoshea [b]became his servant, and
gave him presents.
4 And the king of Assyria found conspiracy
in Hoshea: for he had sent messengers to So king
of Egypt, and brought no present to the king of
Assyria, as *he had done* year by year: therefore
the king of Assyria shut him up, and bound him
in prison.

Israel Carried Captive to Assyria

5 Then [a]the king of Assyria came up
throughout all the land, and went up to Samaria,
and besieged it three years.
6 [a]In the ninth year of Hoshea the king of
Assyria took Samaria, and [b]carried Israel away
into Assyria, [c]and placed them in Halah and in
Habor *by* the river of Gozan, and in the cities of
the Medes.
7 For [a]*so* it was, that the children of Israel
had sinned against the LORD their God, which had
brought them up out of the land of Egypt, from
under the hand of Pharaoh king of Egypt, and
had [b]feared other gods,
8 And [a]walked in the statutes of the
heathen, whom the LORD cast out from before the
children of Israel, and of the kings of Israel, which
they had made.
9 And the children of Israel did secretly
those things that *were* not right against the LORD
their God, and they built them high places in all
their cities, [a]from the tower of the watchmen to
the fenced city.
10 [a]And they set them up images and [b]groves
[c]in every high hill, and under every green tree:
11 And there they burnt incense in all the
high places, as *did* the heathen whom the LORD
carried away before them; and wrought wicked
things to provoke the LORD to anger:
12 For they served idols, [a]whereof the LORD
had said unto them, [b]Ye shall not do this thing.
13 Yet the LORD testified against Israel, and
against Judah, by all the [a]prophets, *and by* all
[b]the seers, saying, [c]Turn ye from your evil ways,
and keep my commandments *and* my statutes, according to all the law which I commanded your
fathers, and which I sent to you by my servants
the prophets.
14 Notwithstanding they would not hear, but
[a]hardened their necks, like to the neck of their
fathers, that [b]did not believe in the LORD their
God.
15 And they [a]rejected his statutes, [b]and his
covenant that he made with their fathers, and his
testimonies which he testified against them; and
they followed [c]vanity, and [d]became vain, and
went after the heathen that *were* round about
them, *concerning* whom the LORD had charged
them, that they should [e]not do like them.
16 And they left all the commandments of
the LORD their God, and [a]made them molten images, *even* two calves, [b]and made a grove, and
worshipped all the [c]host of heaven, [d]and served
Baal.
17 [a]And they caused their sons and their
daughters to pass through the fire, and [b]used divination and enchantments, and [c]sold themselves

20 [a]2 Chr. 28:27

CHAPTER 17

1 [a]2 Kin. 15:30
3 [a]2 Kin. 18:9–12 [b]2 Kin. 24:1
5 [a]2 Kin. 18:9; Hos. 13:16
6 [a]2 Kin. 18:10, 11; Is. 7:7–9; Hos. 1:4; 13:16; Amos 4:2 [b]Lev. 26:32, 33; [Deut. 28:36, 64; 29:27, 28] [c]1 Chr. 5:26
7 [a][Josh. 23:16] [b]Judg. 6:10
8 [a][Lev. 18:3; Deut. 18:9]; 2 Kin. 16:3
9 [a]2 Kin. 18:8
10 [a]1 Kin. 14:23; Is. 57:5 [b][Ex. 34:12–14; Deut. 16:21]; Mic. 5:14 [c][Deut. 12:2]; 2 Kin. 16:4
12 [a][Ex. 20:3–5; Lev. 26:1; Deut. 5:7, 8] [b][Deut. 4:19]
13 [a]Neh. 9:29, 30 [b]1 Sam. 9:9 [c][Jer. 18:11; 25:5; 35:15; Ezek. 18:31]
14 [a]Ex. 32:9; 33:3; Deut. 31:27; [Prov. 29:1; Acts 7:51] [b]Deut. 9:23; Ps. 78:22
15 [a]Jer. 44:3 [b]Ex. 24:6–8; Deut. 29:25 [c]Deut. 32:21; 1 Kin. 16:31; [1 Cor. 8:4] [d]2 Chr. 13:7; Jer. 2:5; [Rom. 1:21–23] [e][Deut. 12:30, 31]
16 [a]Ex. 32:8; 1 Kin. 12:28 [b][1 Kin. 14:15] [c][Deut. 4:19] [d]1 Kin. 16:31; 22:53
17 [a][Lev. 18:21]; 2 Kin. 16:3; Ezek. 23:37 [b][Lev. 19:26; Deut. 18:10–12] [c]1 Kin. 21:20

*

17:10 Heb. *Asherim*, Canaanite deities

NKJV

19 Now the rest of the acts of Ahaz which
he did, *are* they not written in the book of the
chronicles of the kings of Judah?
20 So Ahaz rested with his fathers, and [a]was
buried with his fathers in the City of David. Then
Hezekiah his son reigned in his place.

Hoshea Reigns in Israel

17 In the twelfth year of Ahaz king of Judah,
[a]Hoshea the son of Elah became king of
Israel in Samaria, *and he reigned* nine years.
2 And he did evil in the sight of the LORD,
but not as the kings of Israel who were before
him.
3 [a]Shalmaneser king of Assyria came up
against him; and Hoshea [b]became his vassal, and
paid him tribute money.
4 And the king of Assyria uncovered a conspiracy by Hoshea; for he had sent messengers
to So, king of Egypt, and brought no tribute to
the king of Assyria, as *he had done* year by year.
Therefore the king of Assyria shut him up, and
bound him in prison.

Israel Carried Captive to Assyria

5 Now [a]the king of Assyria went throughout
all the land, and went up to Samaria and besieged
it for three years.
6 [a]In the ninth year of Hoshea, the king of
Assyria took Samaria and [b]carried Israel away
to Assyria, [c]and placed them in Halah and by the
Habor, the River of Gozan, and in the cities of
the Medes.
7 For [a]so it was that the children of Israel
had sinned against the LORD their God, who had
brought them up out of the land of Egypt, from
under the hand of Pharaoh king of Egypt; and
they had [b]feared other gods,
8 and [a]had walked in the statutes of the nations whom the LORD had cast out from before
the children of Israel, and of the kings of Israel,
which they had made.
9 Also the children of Israel secretly did
against the LORD their God things that *were* not
right, and they built for themselves high places
in all their cities, [a]from watchtower to fortified
city.
10 [a]They set up for themselves *sacred* pillars
and [b]wooden images* [c]on every high hill and under every green tree.
11 There they burned incense on all the high
places, like the nations whom the LORD had carried away before them; and they did wicked
things to provoke the LORD to anger,
12 for they served idols, [a]of which the LORD
had said to them, [b]"You shall not do this thing."
13 Yet the LORD testified against Israel and
against Judah, by all of His [a]prophets, [b]every
seer, saying, [c]"Turn from your evil ways, and
keep My commandments *and* My statutes, according to all the law which I commanded your fathers, and which I sent to you by My servants
the prophets."
14 Nevertheless they would not hear, but
[a]stiffened their necks, like the necks of their
fathers, who [b]did not believe in the LORD their
God.
15 And they [a]rejected His statutes [b]and His
covenant that He had made with their fathers, and
His testimonies which He had testified against
them; they followed [c]idols, [d]became idolaters, and
went after the nations who *were* all around them,
concerning whom the LORD had charged them that
they should [e]not do like them.
16 So they left all the commandments of the
LORD their God, [a]made for themselves a molded
image *and* two calves, [b]made a wooden image and
worshiped all the [c]host of heaven, [d]and served
Baal.
17 [a]And they caused their sons and daughters to pass through the fire, [b]practiced witchcraft
and soothsaying, and [c]sold themselves to do evil

KJV

to do evil in the sight of the LORD, to provoke him to anger.

18 Therefore the LORD was very angry with Israel, and removed them out of his sight: there was none left [a]but the tribe of Judah only.

19 Also [a]Judah kept not the commandments of the LORD their God, but walked in the statutes of Israel which they made.

20 And the LORD rejected all the seed of Israel, and afflicted them, and [a]delivered them into the hand of spoilers, until he had cast them out of his [b]sight.

21 For [a]he rent Israel from the house of David; and [b]they made Jeroboam the son of Nebat king: and Jeroboam drave Israel from following the LORD, and made them sin a great sin.

22 For the children of Israel walked in all the sins of Jeroboam which he did; they departed not from them;

23 Until the LORD removed Israel out of his sight, [a]as he had said by all his servants the prophets. [b]So was Israel carried away out of their own land to Assyria unto this day.

Assyria Resettles Samaria

24 [a]And the king of Assyria brought *men* from Babylon, and from Cuthah, and from [b]Ava, and from Hamath, and from Sepharvaim, and placed *them* in the cities of Samaria instead of the children of Israel: and they possessed Samaria, and dwelt in the cities thereof.

25 And *so* it was at the beginning of their dwelling there, *that* they feared not the LORD: therefore the LORD sent lions among them, which slew *some* of them.

26 Wherefore they spake to the king of Assyria, saying, The nations which thou hast removed, and placed in the cities of Samaria, know not the manner of the God of the land: therefore he hath sent lions among them, and, behold, they slay them, because they know not the manner of the God of the land.

27 Then the king of Assyria commanded, saying, Carry thither one of the priests whom ye brought from thence; and let them go and dwell there, and let him teach them the manner of the God of the land.

28 Then one of the priests whom they had carried away from Samaria came and dwelt in Beth–el, and taught them how they should fear the LORD.

29 Howbeit every nation made gods of their own, and put *them* [a]in the houses of the high places which the Samaritans had made, every nation in their cities wherein they dwelt.

30 And the men of [a]Babylon made Succoth–benoth, and the men of Cuth made Nergal, and the men of Hamath made Ashima,

31 [a]And the Avites made Nibhaz and Tartak, and the Sepharvites [b]burnt their children in fire to Adrammelech and Anammelech, the gods of Sepharvaim.

32 So they feared the LORD, [a]and made unto themselves of the lowest of them priests of the high places, which sacrificed for them in the houses of the high places.

33 [a]They feared the LORD, and served their own gods, after the manner of the nations whom they carried away from thence.

34 Unto this day they do after the former manners: they fear not the LORD, neither do they after their statutes, or after their ordinances, or after the law and commandment which the LORD commanded the children of Jacob, [a]whom he named Israel;

35 With whom the LORD had made a covenant, and charged them, saying, [a]Ye shall not fear other gods, nor [b]bow yourselves to them, nor serve them, nor sacrifice to them:

36 But the LORD, who [a]brought you up out of the land of Egypt with great power and [b]a

18 [a]1 Kin. 11:13, 32
19 [a]Jer. 3:8
20 [a]Judg. 2:14; 2 Kin. 13:3; 15:29 [b]2 Kin. 24:20
21 [a]1 Kin. 11:11, 31 [b]1 Kin. 12:20, 28
23 [a]1 Kin. 14:16; Is. 8:4 [b]2 Kin. 17:6
24 [a]Ezra 4:2, 10 [b]2 Kin. 18:34
29 [a]1 Kin. 12:31; 13:32
30 [a]2 Kin. 17:24
31 [a]Ezra 4:9 [b][Lev. 18:21; Deut. 12:31]
32 [a]1 Kin. 12:31; 13:33
33 [a]Zeph. 1:5
34 [a]Gen. 32:28; 35:10
35 [a]Judg. 6:10 [b][Ex. 20:5]
36 [a]Ex. 14:15–30 [b]Ex. 6:6; 9:15

NKJV

in the sight of the LORD, to provoke Him to anger.

18 Therefore the LORD was very angry with Israel, and removed them from His sight; there was none left [a]but the tribe of Judah alone.

19 Also [a]Judah did not keep the commandments of the LORD their God, but walked in the statutes of Israel which they made.

20 And the LORD rejected all the descendants of Israel, afflicted them, and [a]delivered them into the hand of plunderers, until He had cast them from His [b]sight.

21 For [a]He tore Israel from the house of David, and [b]they made Jeroboam the son of Nebat king. Then Jeroboam drove Israel from following the LORD, and made them commit a great sin.

22 For the children of Israel walked in all the sins of Jeroboam which he did; they did not depart from them,

23 until the LORD removed Israel out of His sight, [a]as He had said by all His servants the prophets. [b]So Israel was carried away from their own land to Assyria, *as it is* to this day.

Assyria Resettles Samaria

24 [a]Then the king of Assyria brought *people* from Babylon, Cuthah, [b]Ava, Hamath, and from Sepharvaim, and placed *them* in the cities of Samaria instead of the children of Israel; and they took possession of Samaria and dwelt in its cities.

25 And it was so, at the beginning of their dwelling there, *that* they did not fear the LORD; therefore the LORD sent lions among them, which killed *some* of them.

26 So they spoke to the king of Assyria, saying, "The nations whom you have removed and placed in the cities of Samaria do not know the rituals of the God of the land; therefore He has sent lions among them, and indeed, they are killing them because they do not know the rituals of the God of the land."

27 Then the king of Assyria commanded, saying, "Send there one of the priests whom you brought from there; let him go and dwell there, and let him teach them the rituals of the God of the land."

28 Then one of the priests whom they had carried away from Samaria came and dwelt in Bethel, and taught them how they should fear the LORD.

29 However every nation continued to make gods of its own, and put *them* [a]in the shrines on the high places which the Samaritans had made, *every* nation in the cities where they dwelt.

30 The men of [a]Babylon made Succoth Benoth, the men of Cuth made Nergal, the men of Hamath made Ashima,

31 [a]and the Avites made Nibhaz and Tartak; and the Sepharvites [b]burned their children in fire to Adrammelech and Anammelech, the gods of Sepharvaim.

32 So they feared the LORD, [a]and from every class they appointed for themselves priests of the high places, who sacrificed for them in the shrines of the high places.

33 [a]They feared the LORD, yet served their own gods—according to the rituals of the nations from among whom they were carried away.

34 To this day they continue practicing the former rituals; they do not fear the LORD, nor do they follow their statutes or their ordinances, or the law and commandment which the LORD had commanded the children of Jacob, [a]whom He named Israel,

35 with whom the LORD had made a covenant and charged them, saying: [a]"You shall not fear other gods, nor [b]bow down to them nor serve them nor sacrifice to them;

36 "but the LORD, who [a]brought you up from the land of Egypt with great power and [b]an out-

KJV

stretched out arm, [c]him shall ye fear, and him shall ye worship, and to him shall ye do sacrifice.

37 And the statutes, and the ordinances, and the law, and the commandment, which he wrote for you, [a]ye shall observe to do for evermore; and ye shall not fear other gods.

38 And the covenant that I have made with you [a]ye shall not forget; neither shall ye fear other gods.

39 But the LORD your God ye shall fear; and he shall deliver you out of the hand of all your enemies.

40 Howbeit they did not hearken, but they did after their former manner.

41 [a]So these nations feared the LORD, and served their graven images, both their children, and their children's children: as did their fathers, so do they unto this day.

Hezekiah reigns in Judah
(2 Chr. 29:1, 2; 31:1)

18 Now it came to pass in the third year of [a]Hoshea son of Elah king of Israel, *that* [b]Hezekiah the son of Ahaz king of Judah began to reign.

2 Twenty and five years old was he when he began to reign; and he reigned twenty and nine years in Jerusalem. His mother's name also *was* [a]Abi, the daughter of Zachariah.

3 And he did *that which was* right in the sight of the LORD, according to all that David his father did.

4 [a]He removed the high places, and brake the images, and cut down the groves, and brake in pieces the [b]brasen serpent that Moses had made: for unto those days the children of Israel did burn incense to it: and he called it Nehushtan.

5 He [a]trusted in the LORD God of Israel; [b]so that after him was none like him among all the kings of Judah, nor *any* that were before him.

6 For he [a]clave to the LORD, *and* departed not from following him, but kept his commandments, which the LORD commanded Moses.

7 And the LORD [a]was with him; *and* he [b]prospered whithersoever he went forth: and he [c]rebelled against the king of Assyria, and served him not.

8 [a]He smote the Philistines, *even* unto Gaza, and the borders thereof, [b]from the tower of the watchmen to the fenced city.

9 And [a]it came to pass in the fourth year of king Hezekiah, which *was* the seventh year of Hoshea son of Elah king of Israel, *that* Shalmaneser king of Assyria came up against Samaria, and besieged it.

10 And at the end of three years they took it: *even* in the sixth year of Hezekiah, that *is* [a]the ninth year of Hoshea king of Israel, Samaria was taken.

11 [a]And the king of Assyria did carry away Israel unto Assyria, and put them [b]in Halah and in Habor *by* the river of Gozan, and in the cities of the Medes:

12 Because they obeyed [a]not the voice of the LORD their God, but transgressed his covenant, *and* all that Moses the servant of the LORD commanded, and would not hear *them,* nor do *them.*

13 Now [a]in the fourteenth year of king Hezekiah did Sennacherib king of Assyria come up against all the fenced cities of Judah, and took them.

14 And Hezekiah king of Judah sent to the king of Assyria to Lachish, saying, I have offended; return from me: that which thou puttest on me will I bear. And the king of Assyria appointed unto Hezekiah king of Judah three hundred talents of silver and thirty talents of gold.

15 And Hezekiah [a]gave *him* all the silver that was found in the house of the LORD, and in the treasures of the king's house.

16 At that time did Hezekiah cut off *the gold*

---

36 [c][Deut. 10:20]
37 [a]Deut. 5:32
38 [a]Deut. 4:23; 6:12
41 [a]2 Kin. 17:32, 33

CHAPTER 18

1 [a]2 Kin. 17:1 [b]2 Chr. 28:27; 29:1
2 [a]Is. 38:5
4 [a]2 Chr. 31:1 [b]Num. 21:5–9
5 [a]2 Kin. 19:10; [Job 13:15; Ps. 13:5] [b]2 Kin. 23:25
6 [a]Deut. 10:20; Josh. 23:8
7 [a][2 Chr. 15:2] [b]Gen. 39:2, 3; 1 Sam. 18:5, 14; Ps. 60:12 [c]2 Kin. 16:7
8 [a]1 Chr. 4:41; 2 Chr. 28:18; Is. 14:29 [b]2 Kin. 17:9
9 [a]2 Kin. 17:3
10 [a]2 Kin. 17:6
11 [a]2 Kin. 17:6; Hos. 1:4; Amos 4:2 [b]1 Chr. 5:26
12 [a]2 Kin. 17:7–18
13 [a]2 Chr. 32:1; Is. 36:1—39:8
15 [a]1 Kin. 15:18, 19; 2 Kin. 12:18; 16:8

*

18:2 *Abijah,* 2 Chr. 29:1ff.
18:4 Heb. *Asherah,* a Canaanite goddess • Lit. *Bronze Thing,* also similar to Heb. *nahash, serpent*

NKJV

stretched arm, [c]Him you shall fear, Him you shall worship, and to Him you shall offer sacrifice.

37 "And the statutes, and the ordinances, the law, and the commandment which He wrote for you, [a]you shall be careful to observe forever; you shall not fear other gods.

38 "And the covenant that I have made with you, [a]you shall not forget, nor shall you fear other gods.

39 "But the LORD your God you shall fear; and He will deliver you from the hand of all your enemies."

40 However they did not obey, but they followed their former rituals.

41 [a]So these nations feared the LORD, yet served their carved images; also their children and their children's children have continued doing as their fathers did, even to this day.

Hezekiah Reigns in Judah
(2 Chr. 29:1, 2; 31:1)

18 Now it came to pass in the third year of [a]Hoshea the son of Elah, king of Israel, *that* [b]Hezekiah the son of Ahaz, king of Judah, began to reign.

2 He was twenty-five years old when he became king, and he reigned twenty-nine years in Jerusalem. His mother's name *was* [a]Abi* the daughter of Zechariah.

3 And he did *what was* right in the sight of the LORD, according to all that his father David had done.

4 [a]He removed the high places and broke the *sacred* pillars, cut down the *wooden image and broke in pieces the [b]bronze serpent that Moses had made; for until those days the children of Israel burned incense to it, and called it *Nehushtan.

5 He [a]trusted in the LORD God of Israel, [b]so that after him was none like him among all the kings of Judah, nor who were before him.

6 For he [a]held fast to the LORD; he did not depart from following Him, but kept His commandments, which the LORD had commanded Moses.

7 The LORD [a]was with him; he [b]prospered wherever he went. And he [c]rebelled against the king of Assyria and did not serve him.

8 [a]He subdued the Philistines, as far as Gaza and its territory, [b]from watchtower to fortified city.

9 Now [a]it came to pass in the fourth year of King Hezekiah, which *was* the seventh year of Hoshea the son of Elah, king of Israel, *that* Shalmaneser king of Assyria came up against Samaria and besieged it.

10 And at the end of three years they took it. In the sixth year of Hezekiah, that *is,* [a]the ninth year of Hoshea king of Israel, Samaria was taken.

11 [a]Then the king of Assyria carried Israel away captive to Assyria, and put them [b]in Halah and by the Habor, the River of Gozan, and in the cities of the Medes,

12 because they [a]did not obey the voice of the LORD their God, but transgressed His covenant *and* all that Moses the servant of the LORD had commanded; and they would neither hear nor do *them.*

13 And [a]in the fourteenth year of King Hezekiah, Sennacherib king of Assyria came up against all the fortified cities of Judah and took them.

14 Then Hezekiah king of Judah sent to the king of Assyria at Lachish, saying, "I have done wrong; turn away from me; whatever you impose on me I will pay." And the king of Assyria assessed Hezekiah king of Judah three hundred talents of silver and thirty talents of gold.

15 So Hezekiah [a]gave *him* all the silver that was found in the house of the LORD and in the treasures of the king's house.

16 At that time Hezekiah stripped *the gold*

KJV

from the doors of the temple of the LORD, and *from* the pillars which Hezekiah king of Judah had overlaid, and gave it to the king of Assyria.

Sennacherib Boasts Against the LORD
(Is. 36:2–22; 2 Chr. 32:9–15)

17 And the king of Assyria sent Tartan and Rabsaris and Rab–shakeh from Lachish to king Hezekiah with a great host against Jerusalem. And they went up and came to Jerusalem. And when they were come up, they came and stood by the [a]conduit of the upper pool, [b]which *is* in the highway of the fuller's field.

18 And when they had called to the king, there came out to them [a]Eliakim the son of Hilkiah, which *was* over the household, and Shebna the scribe, and Joah the son of Asaph the recorder.

19 And Rab–shakeh said unto them, Speak ye now to Hezekiah, Thus saith the great king, the king of Assyria, [a]What confidence *is* this wherein thou trustest?

20 Thou sayest, (but *they are but* vain words,) *I have* counsel and strength for the war. Now on whom dost thou trust, that thou rebellest against me?

21 [a]Now, behold, thou trustest upon the staff of this bruised reed, *even* upon Egypt, on which if a man lean, it will go into his hand, and pierce it: so *is* Pharaoh king of Egypt unto all that trust on him.

22 But if ye say unto me, We trust in the LORD our God: *is* not that he, [a]whose high places and whose altars Hezekiah hath taken away, and hath said to Judah and Jerusalem, Ye shall worship before this altar in Jerusalem?

23 Now therefore, I pray thee, give pledges to my lord the king of Assyria, and I will deliver thee two thousand horses, if thou be able on thy part to set riders upon them.

24 How then wilt thou turn away the face of one captain of the least of my master's servants, and put thy trust on Egypt for chariots and for horsemen?

25 Am I now come up without the LORD against this place to destroy it? The LORD said to me, Go up against this land, and destroy it.

26 [a]Then said Eliakim the son of Hilkiah, and Shebna, and Joah, unto Rab–shakeh, Speak, I pray thee, to thy servants in the [b]Syrian language; for we understand *it:* and talk not with us in the Jews' language in the ears of the people that *are* on the wall.

27 But Rab–shakeh said unto them, Hath my master sent me to thy master, and to thee, to speak these words? *hath he* not *sent me* to the men which sit on the wall, that they may eat their own dung, and drink their own piss with you?

28 Then Rab–shakeh stood and cried with a loud voice in the Jews' language, and spake, saying, Hear the word of the great king, the king of Assyria:

29 Thus saith the king, [a]Let not Hezekiah deceive you: for he shall not be able to deliver you out of his hand:

30 Neither let Hezekiah make you trust in the LORD, saying, The LORD will surely deliver us, and this city shall not be delivered into the hand of the king of Assyria.

31 Hearken not to Hezekiah: for thus saith the king of Assyria, Make *an agreement* with me by a present, and come out to me, and *then* eat ye every man of his own [a]vine, and every one of his fig tree, and drink ye every one the waters of his cistern:

32 Until I come and take you away to a land like your own land, [a]a land of corn and wine, a land of bread and vineyards, a land of oil olive and of honey, that ye may live, and not die: and hearken not unto Hezekiah, when he persuadeth you, saying, The LORD will deliver us.

33 [a]Hath any of the gods of the nations deliv-

17 [a]2 Kin. 20:20 [b]Is. 7:3
18 [a]2 Kin. 19:2; Is. 22:20
19 [a]2 Chr. 32:10; [Ps. 118:8, 9]
21 [a]Is. 30:2–7; Ezek. 29:6, 7
22 [a]2 Kin. 18:4; 2 Chr. 31:1; 32:12
26 [a]Is. 36:11—39:8 [b]Ezra 4:7; Dan. 2:4
29 [a]2 Chr. 32:15
31 [a]1 Kin. 4:20, 25
32 [a]Deut. 8:7–9; 11:12
33 [a]2 Kin. 19:12; Is. 10:10, 11

NKJV

from the doors of the temple of the LORD, and *from* the pillars which Hezekiah king of Judah had overlaid, and gave it to the king of Assyria.

Sennacherib Boasts Against the LORD
(Is. 36:2–22; 2 Chr. 32:9–15)

17 Then the king of Assyria sent *the* *Tartan, *the* *Rabsaris, *and the* *Rabshakeh from Lachish, with a great army against Jerusalem, to King Hezekiah. And they went up and came to Jerusalem. When they had come up, they went and stood by the [a]aqueduct from the upper pool, [b]which *was* on the highway to the Fuller's Field.

18 And when they had called to the king, [a]Eliakim the son of Hilkiah, who *was* over the household, Shebna the scribe, and Joah the son of Asaph, the recorder, came out to them.

19 Then *the* Rabshakeh said to them, "Say now to Hezekiah, 'Thus says the great king, the king of Assyria: [a]"What confidence *is* this in which you trust?

20 "You speak of *having* plans and power for war; but *they are* mere words. And in whom do you trust, that you rebel against me?

21 [a]"Now look! You are trusting in the staff of this broken reed, Egypt, on which if a man leans, it will go into his hand and pierce it. So *is* Pharaoh king of Egypt to all who trust in him.

22 "But if you say to me, 'We trust in the LORD our God,' *is* it not He [a]whose high places and whose altars Hezekiah has taken away, and said to Judah and Jerusalem, 'You shall worship before this altar in Jerusalem'?" '

23 "Now therefore, I urge you, give a pledge to my master the king of Assyria, and I will give you two thousand horses—if you are able on your part to put riders on them!

24 "How then will you repel one captain of the least of my master's servants, and put your trust in Egypt for chariots and horsemen?

25 "Have I now come up without the LORD against this place to destroy it? The LORD said to me, 'Go up against this land, and destroy it.' "

26 [a]Then Eliakim the son of Hilkiah, Shebna, and Joah said to *the* Rabshakeh, "Please speak to your servants in [b]Aramaic, for we understand *it;* and do not speak to us in *Hebrew in the hearing of the people who *are* on the wall."

27 But *the* Rabshakeh said to them, "Has my master sent me to your master and to you to speak these words, and not to the men who sit on the wall, who will eat and drink their own waste with you?"

28 Then *the* Rabshakeh stood and called out with a loud voice in Hebrew, and spoke, saying, "Hear the word of the great king, the king of Assyria!

29 "Thus says the king: [a]'Do not let Hezekiah deceive you, for he shall not be able to deliver you from his hand;

30 'nor let Hezekiah make you trust in the LORD, saying, "The LORD will surely deliver us; this city shall not be given into the hand of the king of Assyria." '

31 "Do not listen to Hezekiah; for thus says the king of Assyria: 'Make *peace* with me by a present and come out to me; and every one of you eat from his own [a]vine and every one from his own fig tree, and every one of you drink the waters of his own cistern;

32 'until I come and take you away to a land like your own land, [a]a land of grain and new wine, a land of bread and vineyards, a land of olive groves and honey, that you may live and not die. But do not listen to Hezekiah, lest he persuade you, saying, "The LORD will deliver us."

33 [a]'Has any of the gods of the nations at

*
18:17 A title, probably *Commander in Chief* • A title, probably *Chief Officer* • A title, probably *Chief of Staff* or *Governor*
18:26 Lit. *Judean*

KJV

ered at all his land out of the hand of the king of Assyria?

34 Where *are* the gods of [a]Hamath, and of Arpad? where *are* the gods of Sepharvaim, Hena, and [b]Ivah? have they delivered Samaria out of mine hand?

35 Who *are* they among all the gods of the countries, that have delivered their country out of mine hand, [a]that the LORD should deliver Jerusalem out of mine hand?

36 But the people held their peace, and answered him not a word: for the king's commandment was, saying, Answer him not.

37 Then came Eliakim the son of Hilkiah, which *was* over the household, and Shebna the scribe, and Joah the son of Asaph the recorder, to Hezekiah [a]with *their* clothes rent, and told him the words of Rab–shakeh.

Isaiah Assures Deliverance
(Is. 37:1–7)

19 And [a]it came to pass, when king Hezekiah heard *it*, that he rent his clothes, and covered himself with [b]sackcloth, and went into the house of the LORD.

2 And he sent Eliakim, which *was* over the household, and Shebna the scribe, and the elders of the priests, covered with sackcloth, to Isaiah the prophet the son of Amoz.

3 And they said unto him, Thus saith Hezekiah, This day *is* a day of trouble, and of rebuke, and blasphemy: for the children are come to the birth, and *there is* not strength to bring forth.

4 [a]It may be the LORD thy God will hear all the words of Rab–shakeh, whom the king of Assyria his master hath sent to [b]reproach the living God; and will [c]reprove the words which the LORD thy God hath heard: wherefore lift up *thy* prayer for the remnant that are left.

5 So the servants of king Hezekiah came to Isaiah.

6 [a]And Isaiah said unto them, Thus shall ye say to your master, Thus saith the LORD, Be not [b]afraid of the words which thou hast heard, with which the [c]servants of the king of Assyria have blasphemed me.

7 Behold, I will send [a]a blast upon him, and he shall hear a rumour, and shall return to his own land; and I will cause him to fall by the sword in his own land.

Sennacherib's Threat and Hezekiah's Prayer
(Is. 37:8–20)

8 So Rab–shakeh returned, and found the king of Assyria warring against Libnah: for he had heard that he was departed [a]from Lachish.

9 And [a]when he heard say of Tirhakah king of Ethiopia, Behold, he is come out to fight against thee: he sent messengers again unto Hezekiah, saying,

10 Thus shall ye speak to Hezekiah king of Judah, saying, Let not thy God [a]in whom thou trustest deceive thee, saying, Jerusalem shall not be delivered into the hand of the king of Assyria.

11 Behold, thou hast heard what the kings of Assyria have done to all lands, by destroying them utterly: and shalt thou be delivered?

12 [a]Have the gods of the nations delivered them which my fathers have destroyed; *as* Gozan, and Haran, and Rezeph, and the children of [b]Eden which *were* in Thelasar?

13 [a]Where *is* the king of Hamath, and the king of Arpad, and the king of the city of Sepharvaim, of Hena, and Ivah?

14 [a]And Hezekiah received the letter of the hand of the messengers, and read it: and Hezekiah went up into the house of the LORD, and spread it before the LORD.

15 And Hezekiah prayed before the LORD, and said, O LORD God of Israel, [a]which dwellest *between* the cherubims, [b]thou art the God, *even*

34 [a]2 Kin. 19:13 [b]2 Kin. 17:24
35 [a]Dan. 3:15
37 [a]Is. 33:7

CHAPTER 19

1 [a]2 Kin. 18:13; 2 Chr. 32:20–22; Is. 37:1 [b]Ps. 69:11
4 [a]2 Sam. 16:12 [b]2 Kin. 18:35 [c]Ps. 50:21
6 [a]Is. 37:6 [b][Ps. 112:7] [c]2 Kin. 18:17
7 [a]2 Kin. 19:35–37; Jer. 51:1
8 [a]2 Kin. 18:14, 17
9 [a]1 Sam. 23:27; Is. 37:9
10 [a]2 Kin. 18:5
12 [a]2 Kin. 18:33, 34 [b]Ezek. 27:23
13 [a]2 Kin. 18:34
14 [a]Is. 37:14
15 [a]Ex. 25:22; Ps. 80:1; Is. 37:16 [b][Is. 44:6]

NKJV

all delivered its land from the hand of the king of Assyria?

34 'Where *are* the gods of [a]Hamath and Arpad? Where *are* the gods of Sepharvaim and Hena and [b]Ivah? Indeed, have they delivered Samaria from my hand?

35 'Who among all the gods of the lands have delivered their countries from my hand, [a]that the LORD should deliver Jerusalem from my hand?' "

36 But the people held their peace and answered him not a word; for the king's commandment was, "Do not answer him."

37 Then Eliakim the son of Hilkiah, who *was* over the household, Shebna the scribe, and Joah the son of Asaph, the recorder, came to Hezekiah [a]with *their* clothes torn, and told him the words of *the* Rabshakeh.

Isaiah Assures Deliverance
(Is. 37:1–7)

19 And [a]so it was, when King Hezekiah heard *it*, that he tore his clothes, covered himself with [b]sackcloth, and went into the house of the LORD.

2 Then he sent Eliakim, who *was* over the household, Shebna the scribe, and the elders of the priests, covered with sackcloth, to Isaiah the prophet, the son of Amoz.

3 And they said to him, "Thus says Hezekiah: 'This day *is* a day of trouble, and rebuke, and blasphemy; for the children have come to birth, but *there is* no strength to bring them forth.

4 [a]'It may be that the LORD your God will hear all the words of *the* Rabshakeh, whom his master the king of Assyria has sent to [b]reproach the living God, and will [c]rebuke the words which the LORD your God has heard. Therefore lift up *your* prayer for the remnant that is left.' "

5 So the servants of King Hezekiah came to Isaiah.

6 [a]And Isaiah said to them, "Thus you shall say to your master, 'Thus says the LORD: "Do not be [b]afraid of the words which you have heard, with which the [c]servants of the king of Assyria have blasphemed Me.

7 "Surely I will send [a]a spirit upon him, and he shall hear a rumor and return to his own land; and I will cause him to fall by the sword in his own land." ' "

Sennacherib's Threat and Hezekiah's Prayer
(Is. 37:8–20)

8 Then *the* Rabshakeh returned and found the king of Assyria warring against Libnah, for he heard that he had departed [a]from Lachish.

9 And [a]the king heard concerning Tirhakah king of Ethiopia, "Look, he has come out to make war with you." So he again sent messengers to Hezekiah, saying,

10 "Thus you shall speak to Hezekiah king of Judah, saying: 'Do not let your God [a]in whom you trust deceive you, saying, "Jerusalem shall not be given into the hand of the king of Assyria."

11 'Look! You have heard what the kings of Assyria have done to all lands by utterly destroying them; and shall you be delivered?

12 [a]'Have the gods of the nations delivered those whom my fathers have destroyed, Gozan and Haran and Rezeph, and the people of [b]Eden who *were* in Telassar?

13 [a]'Where *is* the king of Hamath, the king of Arpad, and the king of the city of Sepharvaim, Hena, and Ivah?' "

14 [a]And Hezekiah received the letter from the hand of the messengers, and read it; and Hezekiah went up to the house of the LORD, and spread it before the LORD.

15 Then Hezekiah prayed before the LORD, and said: "O LORD God of Israel, *the One* [a]who dwells *between* the cherubim, [b]You are God, You

KJV

thou alone, of all the kingdoms of the earth; thou
hast made heaven and earth.
16 LORD, [a]bow down thine ear, and hear:
[b]open, LORD, thine eyes, and see: and hear the
words of Sennacherib, [c]which hath sent him to
reproach the living God.
17 Of a truth, LORD, the kings of Assyria have
destroyed the nations and their lands,
18 And have cast their gods into the fire: for
they *were* [a]no gods, but [b]the work of men's hands,
wood and stone: therefore they have destroyed
them.
19 Now therefore, O LORD our God, I beseech
thee, save thou us out of his hand, [a]that all the
kingdoms of the earth may [b]know that thou *art*
the LORD God, *even* thou only.

The Word of the LORD Concerning Sennacherib (Is. 37:21–35)

20 Then Isaiah the son of Amoz sent to Hezekiah, saying, Thus saith the LORD God of Israel,
[a]*That* which thou hast prayed to me against Sennacherib king of Assyria [b]I have heard.
21 This *is* the word that the LORD hath spoken
concerning him; The virgin [a]the daughter of Zion
hath despised thee, *and* laughed thee to scorn;
the daughter of Jerusalem [b]hath shaken her head
at thee.
22 Whom hast thou reproached and blasphemed? and against whom hast thou exalted *thy*
voice, and lifted up thine eyes on high? *even*
against [a]the Holy *One* of Israel.
23 [a]By thy messengers thou hast reproached
the Lord, and hast said, [b]With the multitude of
my chariots I am come up to the height of the
mountains, to the sides of Lebanon, and will cut
down the tall cedar trees thereof, *and* the choice
fir trees thereof: and I will enter into the lodgings
of his borders, *and into* the forest of his Carmel.
24 I have digged and drunk strange waters,
and with the sole of my feet have I [a]dried up all
the rivers of besieged places.
25 Hast thou not heard long ago *how* [a]I have
done it, *and* of ancient times that I have formed
it? now have I brought it to pass, that [b]thou
shouldest be to lay waste fenced cities *into* ruinous heaps.
26 Therefore their inhabitants were of small
power, they were dismayed and confounded; they
were *as* the grass of the field, and *as* the green
herb, *as* [a]the grass on the house tops, and *as corn*
blasted before it be grown up.
27 But [a]I know thy abode, and thy going out,
and thy coming in, and thy rage against me.
28 Because thy rage against me and thy tumult is come up into mine ears, therefore [a]I will
put my hook in thy nose, and my bridle in thy
lips, and I will turn thee back [b]by the way by
which thou camest.
29 And this *shall be* a [a]sign unto thee, Ye
shall eat this year such things as grow of themselves, and in the second year that which spring-

16 [a]Ps. 31:2; Is. 37:17 [b]1 Kin. 8:29; 2 Chr. 6:40 [c]2 Kin. 19:4
18 [a][Is. 44:9–20; Jer. 10:3–5] [b]Ps. 115:4; Jer. 10:3; [Acts 17:29]
19 [a]Ps. 83:18 [b]1 Kin. 8:42, 43
20 [a]Is. 37:21 [b]2 Kin. 20:5; Ps. 65:2
21 [a]Jer. 14:17; Lam. 2:13 [b]Ps. 22:7, 8
22 [a]Jer. 51:5
23 [a]2 Kin. 18:17 [b]Ps. 20:7
24 [a]Is. 19:6
25 [a][Is. 45:7] [b]Is. 10:5, 6
26 [a]Ps. 129:6
27 [a]Ps. 139:1–3; Is. 37:28
28 [a]Job 41:2; Ezek. 29:4; 38:4; Amos 4:2 [b]2 Kin. 19:33, 36
29 [a]Ex. 3:12; 1 Sam. 2:34; 2 Kin. 20:8, 9; Is. 7:11–14; Luke 2:12

NKJV

alone, of all the kingdoms of the earth. You have
made heaven and earth.
16 [a]"Incline Your ear, O LORD, and hear;
[b]open Your eyes, O LORD, and see; and hear
the words of Sennacherib, [c]which he has sent to
reproach the living God.
17 "Truly, LORD, the kings of Assyria have
laid waste the nations and their lands,
18 "and have cast their gods into the fire; for
they *were* [a]not gods, but [b]the work of men's
hands—wood and stone. Therefore they destroyed them.
19 "Now therefore, O LORD our God, I pray,
save us from his hand, [a]that all the kingdoms of
the earth may [b]know that You *are* the LORD God,
You alone."

The Word of the LORD Concerning Sennacherib (Is. 37:21–35)

20 Then Isaiah the son of Amoz sent to Hezekiah, saying, "Thus says the LORD God of Israel:
[a]'Because you have prayed to Me against Sennacherib king of Assyria, [b]I have heard.'
21 "This *is* the word which the LORD has spoken concerning him:

'The virgin, [a]the daughter of Zion,
Has despised you, laughed you to scorn;
The daughter of Jerusalem
[b]Has shaken *her* head behind your back!

22 'Whom have you reproached and
blasphemed?
Against whom have you raised *your* voice,
And lifted up your eyes on high?
Against [a]the Holy *One* of Israel.
23 [a]By your messengers you have reproached
the Lord,
And said: [b]"By the multitude of my
chariots
I have come up to the height of the
mountains,
To the limits of Lebanon;
I will cut down its tall cedars
And its choice cypress trees;
I will enter the extremity of its borders,
To its fruitful forest.
24 I have dug and drunk strange water,
And with the soles of my feet I have [a]dried
up
All the brooks of defense."

25 'Did you not hear long ago
How [a]I made it,
From ancient times that I formed it?
Now I have brought it to pass,
That [b]you should be
For crushing fortified cities *into* heaps of
ruins.
26 Therefore their inhabitants had little
power;
They were dismayed and confounded;
They were *as* the grass of the field
And the green herb,
As [a]the grass on the housetops
And *grain* blighted before it is grown.

27 'But [a]I know your dwelling place,
Your going out and your coming in,
And your rage against Me.
28 Because your rage against Me and your
tumult
Have come up to My ears,
Therefore [a]I will put My hook in your nose
And My bridle in your lips,
And I will turn you back
[b]By the way which you came.

29 'This *shall be* a [a]sign to you:

You shall eat this year such as grows of
itself,

KJV

eth of the same; and in the third year sow ye,
and reap, and plant vineyards, and eat the fruits
thereof.
30 [a]And the remnant that is escaped of the
house of Judah shall yet again take root downward, and bear fruit upward.
31 For out of Jerusalem shall go forth a remnant, and they that escape out of mount Zion: [a]the
zeal of the LORD *of hosts* shall do this.
32 Therefore thus saith the LORD concerning
the king of Assyria, He shall [a]not come into this
city, nor shoot an arrow there, nor come before
it with shield, nor cast a bank against it.
33 By the way that he came, by the same
shall he return, and shall not come into this city,
saith the LORD.
34 For [a]I will [b]defend this city, to save it, for
mine own sake, and [c]for my servant David's sake.

Sennacherib's Defeat and Death
(Is. 37:36–38; 2 Chr. 32:20–23)

35 And [a]it came to pass that night, that the
angel of the LORD went out, and smote in the camp
of the Assyrians an hundred fourscore and five
thousand: and when they arose early in the morning, behold, they *were* all dead corpses.
36 So Sennacherib king of Assyria departed,
and went and returned, and dwelt at [a]Nineveh.
37 And it came to pass, as he was worshipping in the house of Nisroch his god, that [a]Adram-
melech and Sharezer his sons [b]smote him with
the sword: and they escaped into the land of
Armenia. And [c]Esar–haddon his son reigned in
his stead.

Hezekiah's Life Extended
(2 Chr. 32:24–26; Is. 38:1–8)

20 In [a]those days was Hezekiah sick unto
death. And the prophet Isaiah the son of
Amoz came to him, and said unto him, Thus saith
the LORD, Set thine house in order; for thou shalt
die, and not live.
2 Then he turned his face to the wall, and
prayed unto the LORD, saying,
3 I beseech thee, O LORD, [a]remember now
how I have walked before thee in truth and with
a perfect heart, and have done *that which is* good
in thy sight. And Hezekiah wept sore.
4 And it came to pass, afore Isaiah was gone
out into the middle court, that the word of the
LORD came to him, saying,
5 Turn again, and tell Hezekiah [a]the captain
of my people, Thus saith the LORD, the God of
David thy father, [b]I have heard thy prayer, I have
seen [c]thy tears: behold, I will heal thee: on the
third day thou shalt go up unto the house of the
LORD.
6 And I will add unto thy days fifteen years;
and I will deliver thee and this city out of the hand
of the king of Assyria; and [a]I will defend this city
for mine own sake, and for my servant David's
sake.
7 And [a]Isaiah said, Take a lump of figs. And
they took and laid *it* on the boil, and he recovered.
8 And Hezekiah said unto Isaiah, [a]What
shall be the sign that the LORD will heal me, and
that I shall go up into the house of the LORD the
third day?
9 And Isaiah said, [a]This sign shalt thou
have of the LORD, that the LORD will do the thing
that he hath spoken: shall the shadow go forward
ten degrees, or go back ten degrees?

30 [a]2 Kin. 19:4; 2 Chr. 32:22, 23
31 [a]2 Kin. 25:26; Is. 9:7
32 [a]Is. 8:7–10
34 [a]2 Kin. 20:6; 2 Chr. 32:21 [b]Is. 31:5 [c]1 Kin. 11:12, 13
35 [a]Ex. 12:29; Is. 10:12–19; 37:36; Hos. 1:7
36 [a]Gen. 10:11
37 [a]2 Kin. 17:31 [b]2 Kin. 19:7; 2 Chr. 32:21 [c]Ezra 4:2

CHAPTER 20
1 [a]2 Kin. 18:13; 2 Chr. 32:24; Is. 38:1–22
3 [a]2 Kin. 18:3–6; Neh. 13:22
5 [a]1 Sam. 9:16; 10:1 [b]2 Kin. 19:20; Ps. 65:2 [c]Ps. 39:12; 56:8
6 [a]2 Kin. 19:34; 2 Chr. 32:21
7 [a]Is. 38:21
8 [a]Judg. 6:17, 37, 39; Is. 7:11, 14; 38:22
9 [a]Num. 23:19; Is. 38:7, 8

*———
19:31 So with many Heb. mss. and ancient vss. (cf. Is. 37:32); MT omits *of hosts*
19:35 Or *Angel*

NKJV

And in the second year what springs from
the same;
Also in the third year sow and reap,
Plant vineyards and eat the fruit of them.
30 [a]And the remnant who have escaped of the
house of Judah
Shall again take root downward,
And bear fruit upward.
31 For out of Jerusalem shall go a remnant,
And those who escape from Mount Zion.
[a]The zeal of the LORD *of hosts will do this.'

32 "Therefore thus says the LORD concerning
the king of Assyria:

'He shall [a]not come into this city,
Nor shoot an arrow there,
Nor come before it with shield,
Nor build a siege mound against it.
33 By the way that he came,
By the same shall he return;
And he shall not come into this city,'
Says the LORD.
34 'For [a]I will [b]defend this city, to save it
For My own sake and [c]for My servant
David's sake.' "

Sennacherib's Defeat and Death
(Is. 37:36–38; 2 Chr. 32:20–23)

35 And [a]it came to pass on a certain night
that the *angel of the LORD went out, and killed
in the camp of the Assyrians one hundred and
eighty-five thousand; and when *people* arose
early in the morning, there were the corpses—all
dead.
36 So Sennacherib king of Assyria departed
and went away, returned *home,* and remained at
[a]Nineveh.
37 Now it came to pass, as he was worshiping
in the temple of Nisroch his god, that his sons
[a]Adrammelech and Sharezer [b]struck him down
with the sword; and they escaped into the land
of Ararat. Then [c]Esarhaddon his son reigned in
his place.

Hezekiah's Life Extended
(2 Chr. 32:24–26; Is. 38:1–8)

20 In [a]those days Hezekiah was sick and near
death. And Isaiah the prophet, the son of
Amoz, went to him and said to him, "Thus says
the LORD: 'Set your house in order, for you shall
die, and not live.' "
2 Then he turned his face toward the wall,
and prayed to the LORD, saying,
3 [a]"Remember now, O LORD, I pray, how I
have walked before You in truth and with a loyal
heart, and have done *what was* good in Your
sight." And Hezekiah wept bitterly.
4 And it happened, before Isaiah had gone
out into the middle court, that the word of the
LORD came to him, saying,
5 "Return and tell Hezekiah [a]the leader of
My people, 'Thus says the LORD, the God of David
your father: [b]"I have heard your prayer, I have
seen [c]your tears; surely I will heal you. On the
third day you shall go up to the house of the LORD.
6 "And I will add to your days fifteen years.
I will deliver you and this city from the hand of
the king of Assyria; and [a]I will defend this city
for My own sake, and for the sake of My servant
David." ' "
7 Then [a]Isaiah said, "Take a lump of figs."
So they took and laid *it* on the boil, and he
recovered.
8 And Hezekiah said to Isaiah, [a]"What *is*
the sign that the LORD will heal me, and that I
shall go up to the house of the LORD the third
day?"
9 Then Isaiah said, [a]"This is the sign to you
from the LORD, that the LORD will do the thing
which He has spoken: *shall* the shadow go forward ten degrees or go backward ten degrees?"

KJV

10 And Hezekiah answered, It is a light thing for the shadow to go down ten degrees: nay, but let the shadow return backward ten degrees.

11 And Isaiah the prophet cried unto the LORD: and [a]he brought the shadow ten degrees backward, by which it had gone down in the dial of Ahaz.

The Babylonian Envoys
(Is. 39:1–8)

12 [a]At that time Berodach–baladan, the son of Baladan, king of Babylon, sent letters and a present unto Hezekiah: for he had heard that Hezekiah had been sick.

13 And [a]Hezekiah hearkened unto them, and shewed them all the house of his precious things, the silver, and the gold, and the spices, and the precious ointment, and *all* the house of his armour, and all that was found in his treasures: there was nothing in his house, nor in all his dominion, that Hezekiah shewed them not.

14 Then came Isaiah the prophet unto king Hezekiah, and said unto him, What said these men? and from whence came they unto thee? And Hezekiah said, They are come from a far country, *even* from Babylon.

15 And he said, What have they seen in thine house? And Hezekiah answered, [a]All *the things* that *are* in mine house have they seen: there is nothing among my treasures that I have not shewed them.

16 And Isaiah said unto Hezekiah, Hear the word of the LORD.

17 Behold, the days come, that all that *is* in thine house, and that which thy fathers have laid up in store unto this day, [a]shall be carried into Babylon: nothing shall be left, saith the LORD.

18 And of thy sons that shall issue from thee, which thou shalt beget, [a]shall they take away; [b]and they shall be [c]eunuchs in the palace of the king of Babylon.

19 Then said Hezekiah unto Isaiah, [a]Good *is* the word of the LORD which thou hast spoken. And he said, *Is it* not *good,* if peace and truth be in my days?

Death of Hezekiah
(2 Chr. 32:32, 33)

20 [a]And the rest of the acts of Hezekiah, and all his might, and how he [b]made a [c]pool, and a conduit, and [d]brought water into the city, *are* they not written in the book of the chronicles of the kings of Judah?

21 And [a]Hezekiah slept with his fathers: and Manasseh his son reigned in his stead.

Manasseh Reigns in Judah
(2 Chr. 33:1–20)

21 Manasseh [a]*was* twelve years old when he began to reign, and reigned fifty and five years in Jerusalem. And his mother's name *was* Hephzi–bah.

2 And he did *that which was* evil in the sight of the LORD, [a]after the abominations of the heathen, whom the LORD cast out before the children of Israel.

3 For he built up again the high places [a]which Hezekiah his father had destroyed; and he reared up altars for Baal, and made a grove, [b]as did Ahab king of Israel; and [c]worshipped all the host of heaven, and served them.

4 And [a]he built altars in the house of the LORD, of which the LORD said, [b]In Jerusalem will I put my name.

5 And he built altars for all the host of heaven in the [a]two courts of the house of the LORD.

6 [a]And he made his son pass through the fire, and observed [b]times, and used enchantments, and dealt with familiar spirits and wizards: he wrought much wickedness in the sight of the LORD, to provoke *him* to anger.

11 [a]Josh. 10:12–14; Is. 38:8
12 [a]2 Kin. 8:8, 9; 2 Chr. 32:31; Is. 39:1–8
13 [a]2 Kin. 16:9; 2 Chr. 32:27, 31
15 [a]2 Kin. 20:13
17 [a]2 Kin. 24:13; 25:13–15; 2 Chr. 36:10; Jer. 27:21, 22; 52:17
18 [a]2 Kin. 24:12; 2 Chr. 33:11 [b]Dan. 1:3–7 [c]Dan. 1:11, 18
19 [a]1 Sam. 3:18
20 [a]2 Chr. 32:32 [b]Neh. 3:16 [c]2 Kin. 18:17; Is. 7:3 [d]2 Chr. 32:3, 30
21 [a]2 Kin. 16:20; 2 Chr. 32:33

CHAPTER 21

1 [a]2 Chr. 33:1–9
2 [a]2 Kin. 16:3
3 [a]2 Kin. 18:4, 22 [b]1 Kin. 16:31–33 [c][Deut. 4:19; 17:2–5]; 2 Kin. 17:16; 23:5
4 [a]Jer. 7:30; 32:34 [b]1 Kin. 11:13
5 [a]1 Kin. 6:36; 7:12; 2 Kin. 23:12
6 [a][Lev. 18:21; 20:2]; 2 Kin. 16:3; 17:17 [b]Lev. 19:26, 31; [Deut. 18:10–14]; 2 Kin. 17:17

*

20:12 *Merodach-Baladan,* Is. 39:1
20:13 So with many Heb. mss., Syr., Tg.; MT omits *all*
21:3 Heb. *Asherah,* a Canaanite goddess • The gods of the Assyrians

NKJV

10 And Hezekiah answered, "It is an easy thing for the shadow to go down ten degrees; no, but let the shadow go backward ten degrees."

11 So Isaiah the prophet cried out to the LORD, and [a]He brought the shadow ten degrees backward, by which it had gone down on the sundial of Ahaz.

The Babylonian Envoys
(Is. 39:1–8)

12 [a]At that time *Berodach-Baladan the son of Baladan, king of Babylon, sent letters and a present to Hezekiah, for he heard that Hezekiah had been sick.

13 And [a]Hezekiah was attentive to them, and showed them all the house of his treasures—the silver and gold, the spices and precious ointment, and *all his armory—all that was found among his treasures. There was nothing in his house or in all his dominion that Hezekiah did not show them.

14 Then Isaiah the prophet went to King Hezekiah, and said to him, "What did these men say, and from where did they come to you?" So Hezekiah said, "They came from a far country, from Babylon."

15 And he said, "What have they seen in your house?" So Hezekiah answered, [a]"They have seen all that *is* in my house; there is nothing among my treasures that I have not shown them."

16 Then Isaiah said to Hezekiah, "Hear the word of the LORD:

17 'Behold, the days are coming when all that *is* in your house, and what your fathers have accumulated until this day, [a]shall be carried to Babylon; nothing shall be left,' says the LORD.

18 'And [a]they shall take away some of your sons who will descend from you, whom you will beget; [b]and they shall be [c]eunuchs in the palace of the king of Babylon.' "

19 So Hezekiah said to Isaiah, [a]"The word of the LORD which you have spoken *is* good!" For he said, "Will there not be peace and truth at least in my days?"

Death of Hezekiah
(2 Chr. 32:32, 33)

20 [a]Now the rest of the acts of Hezekiah—all his might, and how he [b]made a [c]pool and a tunnel and [d]brought water into the city—*are* they not written in the book of the chronicles of the kings of Judah?

21 So [a]Hezekiah rested with his fathers. Then Manasseh his son reigned in his place.

Manasseh Reigns in Judah
(2 Chr. 33:1–20)

21 Manasseh [a]*was* twelve years old when he became king, and he reigned fifty-five years in Jerusalem. His mother's name *was* Hephzibah.

2 And he did evil in the sight of the LORD, [a]according to the abominations of the nations whom the LORD had cast out before the children of Israel.

3 For he rebuilt the *high places [a]which Hezekiah his father had destroyed; he raised up altars for Baal, and made a *wooden image, [b]as Ahab king of Israel had done; and he [c]worshiped all the host of heaven and served them.

4 [a]He also built altars in the house of the LORD, of which the LORD had said, [b]"In Jerusalem I will put My name."

5 And he built altars for all the host of heaven in the [a]two courts of the house of the LORD.

6 [a]Also he made his son pass through the fire, practiced [b]soothsaying, used witchcraft, and consulted spiritists and mediums. He did much evil in the sight of the LORD, to provoke *Him* to anger.

KJV

7 And he set a graven image of the grove that he had made in the house, of which the LORD said to David, and to Solomon his son, [a]In this house, and in Jerusalem, which I have chosen out of all tribes of Israel, will I put my name for ever:
8 [a]Neither will I make the feet of Israel move any more out of the land which I gave their fathers; only if they will observe to do according to all that I have commanded them, and according to all the law that my servant Moses commanded them.
9 But they hearkened not: and Manasseh [a]seduced them to do more evil than did the nations whom the LORD destroyed before the children of Israel.
10 And the LORD spake [a]by his servants the prophets, saying,
11 [a]Because Manasseh king of Judah hath done these abominations, [b]*and* hath done wickedly above all that the [c]Amorites did, which *were* before him, and [d]hath made Judah also to sin with his idols:
12 Therefore thus saith the LORD God of Israel, Behold, I *am* bringing *such* evil upon Jerusalem and Judah, that whosoever heareth of it, both [a]his ears shall tingle.
13 And I will stretch over Jerusalem [a]the line of Samaria, and the plummet of the house of Ahab: and [b]I will wipe Jerusalem as *a man* wipeth a dish, wiping *it,* and turning *it* upside down.
14 And I will forsake the [a]remnant of mine inheritance, and deliver them into the hand of their enemies; and they shall become a prey and a spoil to all their enemies;
15 Because they have done *that which was* evil in my sight, and have provoked me to anger, since the day their fathers came forth out of Egypt, even unto this day.
16 [a]Moreover Manasseh shed innocent blood very much, till he had filled Jerusalem from one end to another; beside his sin wherewith he made Judah to sin, in doing *that which was* evil in the sight of the LORD.
17 Now [a]the rest of the acts of [b]Manasseh, and all that he did, and his sin that he sinned, *are* they not written in the book of the chronicles of the kings of Judah?
18 And [a]Manasseh slept with his fathers, and was buried in the garden of his own house, in the garden of Uzza: and Amon his son reigned in his stead.

Amon's Reign and Death
(2 Chr. 33:21–25)

19 [a]Amon *was* twenty and two years old when he began to reign, and he reigned two years in Jerusalem. And his mother's name *was* Meshullemeth, the daughter of Haruz of Jotbah.
20 And he did *that which was* evil in the sight of the LORD, [a]as his father Manasseh did.
21 And he walked in all the way that his father walked in, and served the idols that his father served, and worshipped them:
22 And he [a]forsook the LORD God of his fathers, and walked not in the way of the LORD.
23 [a]And the servants of Amon [b]conspired against him, and slew the king in his own house.
24 And the people of the land [a]slew all them that had conspired against king Amon; and the people of the land made Josiah his son king in his stead.
25 Now the rest of the acts of Amon which he did, *are* they not written in the book of the chronicles of the kings of Judah?
26 And he was buried in his sepulchre in the garden of Uzza: and Josiah his son reigned in his stead.

Josiah Reigns in Judah
(2 Chr. 34:1, 2)

22 Josiah [a]*was* eight years old when he began to reign, and he reigned thirty and one

---

7 [a]2 Sam. 7:13; 1 Kin. 8:29; 9:3; 2 Kin. 23:27; 2 Chr. 7:12, 16; Jer. 32:34
8 [a]2 Sam. 7:10; [2 Kin. 18:11, 12]
9 [a][Prov. 29:12]
10 [a]2 Kin. 17:13
11 [a]2 Kin. 23:26, 27; 24:3, 4 [b]1 Kin. 21:26 [c]Gen. 15:16 [d]2 Kin. 21:9
12 [a]1 Sam. 3:11; Jer. 19:3
13 [a]Lam. 2:8; Amos 7:7, 8 [b]2 Kin. 22:16–19; 25:4–11
14 [a]Jer. 6:9
16 [a]2 Kin. 24:4
17 [a]2 Chr. 33:11–19 [b]2 Kin. 20:21
18 [a]2 Chr. 33:20
19 [a]2 Chr. 33:21–23
20 [a]2 Kin. 21:2–6, 11, 16
22 [a]Judg. 2:12, 13; 1 Kin. 11:33; 1 Chr. 28:9
23 [a]1 Chr. 3:14; 2 Chr. 33:24, 25; Matt. 1:10 [b]2 Kin. 12:20; 14:19
24 [a]2 Kin. 14:5

CHAPTER 22

1 [a]1 Kin. 13:2; 2 Chr. 34:1

*

21:7 A Canaanite goddess

NKJV

7 He even set a carved image of *Asherah that he had made, in the house of which the LORD had said to David and to Solomon his son, [a]"In this house and in Jerusalem, which I have chosen out of all the tribes of Israel, I will put My name forever;
8 [a]"and I will not make the feet of Israel wander anymore from the land which I gave their fathers—only if they are careful to do according to all that I have commanded them, and according to all the law that My servant Moses commanded them."
9 But they paid no attention, and Manasseh [a]seduced them to do more evil than the nations whom the LORD had destroyed before the children of Israel.
10 And the LORD spoke [a]by His servants the prophets, saying,
11 [a]"Because Manasseh king of Judah has done these abominations ([b]he has acted more wickedly than all the [c]Amorites who *were* before him, and [d]has also made Judah sin with his idols),
12 "therefore thus says the LORD God of Israel: 'Behold, *I* am bringing *such* calamity upon Jerusalem and Judah, that whoever hears of it, both [a]his ears will tingle.
13 'And I will stretch over Jerusalem [a]the measuring line of Samaria and the plummet of the house of Ahab; [b]I will wipe Jerusalem as *one* wipes a dish, wiping *it* and turning *it* upside down.
14 'So I will forsake the [a]remnant of My inheritance and deliver them into the hand of their enemies; and they shall become victims of plunder to all their enemies,
15 'because they have done evil in My sight, and have provoked Me to anger since the day their fathers came out of Egypt, even to this day.' "
16 [a]Moreover Manasseh shed very much innocent blood, till he had filled Jerusalem from one end to another, besides his sin by which he made Judah sin, in doing evil in the sight of the LORD.
17 Now [a]the rest of the acts of [b]Manasseh—all that he did, and the sin that he committed—*are* they not written in the book of the chronicles of the kings of Judah?
18 So [a]Manasseh rested with his fathers, and was buried in the garden of his own house, in the garden of Uzza. Then his son Amon reigned in his place.

Amon's Reign and Death
(2 Chr. 33:21–25)

19 [a]Amon *was* twenty-two years old when he became king, and he reigned two years in Jerusalem. His mother's name *was* Meshullemeth the daughter of Haruz of Jotbah.
20 And he did evil in the sight of the LORD, [a]as his father Manasseh had done.
21 So he walked in all the ways that his father had walked; and he served the idols that his father had served, and worshiped them.
22 He [a]forsook the LORD God of his fathers, and did not walk in the way of the LORD.
23 [a]Then the servants of Amon [b]conspired against him, and killed the king in his own house.
24 But the people of the land [a]executed all those who had conspired against King Amon. Then the people of the land made his son Josiah king in his place.
25 Now the rest of the acts of Amon which he did, *are* they not written in the book of the chronicles of the kings of Judah?
26 And he was buried in his tomb in the garden of Uzza. Then Josiah his son reigned in his place.

Josiah Reigns in Judah
(2 Chr. 34:1, 2)

22 Josiah [a]*was* eight years old when he became king, and he reigned thirty-one years

KJV

years in Jerusalem. And his mother's name *was* Jedidah, the daughter of Adaiah of [b]Boscath.

2 And he did *that which was* right in the sight of the LORD, and walked in all the way of David his father, and [a]turned not aside to the right hand or to the left.

Hilkiah Finds the Book of the Law
(2 Chr. 34:8–28)

3 [a]And it came to pass in the eighteenth year of king Josiah, *that* the king sent Shaphan the son of Azaliah, the son of Meshullam, the scribe, to the house of the LORD, saying,

4 Go up to Hilkiah the high priest, that he may sum the silver which is [a]brought into the house of the LORD, which [b]the keepers of the door have gathered of the people:

5 And let them [a]deliver it into the hand of the doers of the work, that have the oversight of the house of the LORD: and let them give it to the doers of the work which *is* in the house of the LORD, to repair the breaches of the house,

6 Unto carpenters, and builders, and masons, and to buy timber and hewn stone to repair the house.

7 Howbeit [a]there was no reckoning made with them of the money that was delivered into their hand, because they dealt faithfully.

8 And Hilkiah the high priest said unto Shaphan the scribe, [a]I have found the book of the law in the house of the LORD. And Hilkiah gave the book to Shaphan, and he read it.

9 And Shaphan the scribe came to the king, and brought the king word again, and said, Thy servants have gathered the money that was found in the house, and have delivered it into the hand of them that do the work, that have the oversight of the house of the LORD.

10 And Shaphan the scribe shewed the king, saying, Hilkiah the priest hath delivered me a book. And Shaphan read it before the king.

11 And it came to pass, when the king had heard the words of the book of the law, that he rent his clothes.

12 And the king commanded Hilkiah the priest, and [a]Ahikam the son of Shaphan, and Achbor the son of Michaiah, and Shaphan the scribe, and Asahiah a servant of the king's, saying,

13 Go ye, enquire of the LORD for me, and for the people, and for all Judah, concerning the words of this book that is found: for great *is* [a]the wrath of the LORD that is kindled against us, because our fathers have not hearkened unto the words of this book, to do according unto all that which is written concerning us.

14 So Hilkiah the priest, and Ahikam, and Achbor, and Shaphan, and Asahiah, went unto Huldah the prophetess, the wife of Shallum the son of [a]Tikvah, the son of Harhas, keeper of the ward robe; (now she dwelt in Jerusalem in the college;) and they communed with her.

15 And she said unto them, Thus saith the LORD God of Israel, Tell the man that sent you to me,

16 Thus saith the LORD, Behold, [a]I will bring evil upon this place, and upon the inhabitants thereof, *even* all the words of the book which the king of Judah hath read:

17 [a]Because they have forsaken me, and have burned incense unto other gods, that they might provoke me to anger with all the works of their hands; therefore my wrath shall be kindled against this place, and shall not be quenched.

18 But to [a]the king of Judah which sent you to enquire of the LORD, thus shall ye say to him, Thus saith the LORD God of Israel, *As touching* the words which thou has heard;

19 Because thine [a]heart was tender, and thou hast [b]humbled thyself before the LORD, when thou heardest what I spake against this place, and

1 [b]Josh. 15:39
2 [a]Deut. 5:32; Josh. 1:7
3 [a]2 Chr. 34:8
4 [a]2 Kin. 12:4 [b]2 Kin. 12:9, 10
5 [a]2 Kin. 12:11–14
7 [a]2 Kin. 12:15; [1 Cor. 4:2]
8 [a]Deut. 31:24–26; 2 Chr. 34:14
12 [a]2 Kin. 25:22; Jer. 26:24
13 [a][Deut. 29:23–28; 31:17, 18]
14 [a]2 Chr. 34:22
16 [a]Deut. 29:27; [Dan. 9:11–14]
17 [a]Deut. 29:25–27; 2 Kin. 21:22
18 [a]2 Chr. 34:26
19 [a]1 Sam. 24:5; [Ps. 51:17; Is. 57:15] [b]Ex. 10:3; 1 Kin. 21:29; [2 Chr. 7:14]

NKJV

in Jerusalem. His mother's name *was* Jedidah the daughter of Adaiah of [b]Bozkath.

2 And he did *what was* right in the sight of the LORD, and walked in all the ways of his father David; he [a]did not turn aside to the right hand or to the left.

Hilkiah Finds the Book of the Law
(2 Chr. 34:8–28)

3 [a]Now it came to pass, in the eighteenth year of King Josiah, *that* the king sent Shaphan the scribe, the son of Azaliah, the son of Meshullam, to the house of the LORD, saying:

4 "Go up to Hilkiah the high priest, that he may count the money which has been [a]brought into the house of the LORD, which [b]the doorkeepers have gathered from the people.

5 "And let them [a]deliver it into the hand of those doing the work, who are the overseers in the house of the LORD; let them give it to those who *are* in the house of the LORD doing the work, to repair the damages of the house—

6 "to carpenters and builders and masons—and to buy timber and hewn stone to repair the house.

7 "However [a]there need be no accounting made with them of the money delivered into their hand, because they deal faithfully."

8 Then Hilkiah the high priest said to Shaphan the scribe, [a]"I have found the Book of the Law in the house of the LORD." And Hilkiah gave the book to Shaphan, and he read it.

9 So Shaphan the scribe went to the king, bringing the king word, saying, "Your servants have gathered the money that was found in the house, and have delivered it into the hand of those who do the work, who oversee the house of the LORD."

10 Then Shaphan the scribe showed the king, saying, "Hilkiah the priest has given me a book." And Shaphan read it before the king.

11 Now it happened, when the king heard the words of the Book of the Law, that he tore his clothes.

12 Then the king commanded Hilkiah the priest, [a]Ahikam the son of Shaphan, *Achbor the son of Michaiah, Shaphan the scribe, and Asaiah a servant of the king, saying,

13 "Go, inquire of the LORD for me, for the people and for all Judah, concerning the words of this book that has been found; for great *is* [a]the wrath of the LORD that is aroused against us, because our fathers have not obeyed the words of this book, to do according to all that is written concerning us."

14 So Hilkiah the priest, Ahikam, Achbor, Shaphan, and Asaiah went to Huldah the prophetess, the wife of Shallum the son of [a]Tikvah, the son of Harhas, keeper of the wardrobe. (She dwelt in Jerusalem in the Second Quarter.) And they spoke with her.

15 Then she said to them, "Thus says the LORD God of Israel, 'Tell the man who sent you to Me,

16 "Thus says the LORD: 'Behold, [a]I will bring calamity on this place and on its inhabitants—all the words of the book which the king of Judah has read—

17 [a]'because they have forsaken Me and burned incense to other gods, that they might provoke Me to anger with all the works of their hands. Therefore My wrath shall be aroused against this place and shall not be quenched.' " '

18 "But as for [a]the king of Judah, who sent you to inquire of the LORD, in this manner you shall speak to him, 'Thus says the LORD God of Israel: "*Concerning* the words which you have heard—

19 "because your [a]heart was tender, and you [b]humbled yourself before the LORD when you heard what I spoke against this place and against

*

22:12 *Abdon the son of Micah,* 2 Chr. 34:20

KJV

against the inhabitants thereof, that they should become [c]a desolation and [d]a curse, and hast rent thy clothes, and wept before me; I also have heard *thee,* saith the LORD.

20 Behold therefore, I will gather thee unto thy fathers, and thou [a]shalt be gathered into thy grave in peace; and thine eyes shall not see all the evil which I will bring upon this place. And they brought the king word again.

Josiah Restores True Worship
(2 Chr. 34:29—35:19)

23 And [a]the king sent, and they gathered unto him all the elders of Judah and of Jerusalem.

2 And the king went up into the house of the LORD, and all the men of Judah and all the inhabitants of Jerusalem with him, and the priests, and the prophets, and all the people, both small and great: and he [a]read in their ears all the words of the book of the covenant [b]which was found in the house of the LORD.

3 And the king [a]stood by a pillar, and made a [b]covenant before the LORD, to walk after the LORD, and to keep his commandments and his testimonies and his statutes with all *their* heart and all *their* soul, to perform the words of this covenant that were written in this book. And all the people stood to the covenant.

4 And the king commanded Hilkiah the high priest, and the [a]priests of the second order, and the keepers of the door, to bring [b]forth out of the temple of the LORD all the vessels that were made for Baal, and for the grove, and for all the host of heaven: and he burned them without Jerusalem in the fields of Kidron, and carried the ashes of them unto Beth–el.

5 And he put down the idolatrous priests, whom the kings of Judah had ordained to burn incense in the high places in the cities of Judah, and in the places round about Jerusalem; them also that burned incense unto Baal, to the sun, and to the moon, and to the planets, and to [a]all the host of heaven.

6 And he brought out the [a]grove from the house of the LORD, without Jerusalem, unto the brook Kidron, and burned it at the brook Kidron, and stamped *it* small to [b]powder, and cast the powder thereof upon [c]the graves of the children of the people.

7 And he brake down the houses [a]of the sodomites, that *were* by the house of the LORD, [b]where the [c]women wove hangings for the grove.

8 And he brought all the priests out of the cities of Judah, and defiled the high places where the priests had burned incense, from [a]Geba to Beer–sheba, and brake down the high places of the gates that *were* in the entering in of the gate of Joshua the governor of the city, which *were* on a man's left hand at the gate of the city.

9 [a]Nevertheless the priests of the high places came not up to the altar of the LORD in Jerusalem, [b]but they did eat of the unleavened bread among their brethren.

10 And he defiled [a]Topheth, which *is* in [b]the valley of the children of Hinnom, [c]that no man might make his son or his daughter to [d]pass through the fire to Molech.

11 And he took away the horses that the kings of Judah had given to the sun, at the entering in of the house of the LORD, by the chamber of Nathan–melech the chamberlain, which *was* in the suburbs, and burned the chariots of the sun with fire.

12 And the altars that *were* [a]on the top of the upper chamber of Ahaz, which the kings of Judah had made, and the altars which [b]Manasseh had made in the two courts of the house of the LORD, did the king beat down, and brake *them* down from thence, and cast the dust of them into the brook Kidron.

13 And the high places that *were* before Jeru-

---

19 [c]Lev. 26:31, 32 [d]Jer. 26:6; 44:22
20 [a]2 Kin. 23:30; [Ps. 37:37; Is. 57:1, 2]

CHAPTER 23

1 [a]2 Sam. 19:11; 2 Chr. 34:29, 30
2 [a]Deut. 31:10–13 [b]2 Kin. 22:8
3 [a]2 Kin. 11:14 [b]2 Kin. 11:17
4 [a]2 Kin. 25:18; Jer. 52:24 [b]2 Kin. 21:3–7
5 [a]2 Kin. 21:3
6 [a]2 Kin. 21:7 [b]Ex. 32:20 [c]2 Chr. 34:4
7 [a]1 Kin. 14:24; 15:12 [b]Ex. 35:25, 26; Ezek. 16:16 [c]Ex. 38:8
8 [a]Josh. 21:17; 1 Kin. 15:22
9 [a][Ezek. 44:10–14] [b]1 Sam. 2:36
10 [a]Is. 30:33; Jer. 7:31, 32 [b]Josh. 15:8 [c][Lev. 18:21; Deut. 18:10]; Ezek. 23:37–39 [d]2 Kin. 21:6
12 [a]Jer. 19:13; Zeph. 1:5 [b]2 Kin. 21:5; 2 Chr. 33:5

*

23:4 A Canaanite goddess • The gods of the Assryians
23:6 Heb. *Asherah,* a Canaanite goddess
23:7 Heb. *qedeshim,* those practicing sodomy and prostitution in religious rituals
23:10 Kt. *Sons*

NKJV

its inhabitants, that they would become [c]a desolation and [d]a curse, and you tore your clothes and wept before Me, I also have heard *you,*" says the LORD.

20 "Surely, therefore, I will gather you to your fathers, and you [a]shall be gathered to your grave in peace; and your eyes shall not see all the calamity which I will bring on this place." ' " So they brought back word to the king.

Josiah Restores True Worship
(2 Chr. 34:29—35:19)

23 Now [a]the king sent them to gather all the elders of Judah and Jerusalem to him.

2 The king went up to the house of the LORD with all the men of Judah, and with him all the inhabitants of Jerusalem—the priests and the prophets and all the people, both small and great. And he [a]read in their hearing all the words of the Book of the Covenant [b]which had been found in the house of the LORD.

3 Then the king [a]stood by a pillar and made a [b]covenant before the LORD, to follow the LORD and to keep His commandments and His testimonies and His statutes, with all *his* heart and all *his* soul, to perform the words of this covenant that were written in this book. And all the people took a stand for the covenant.

4 And the king commanded Hilkiah the high priest, the [a]priests of the second order, and the doorkeepers, to bring [b]out of the temple of the LORD all the articles that were made for Baal, for *Asherah, and for all *the host of heaven; and he burned them outside Jerusalem in the fields of Kidron, and carried their ashes to Bethel.

5 Then he removed the idolatrous priests whom the kings of Judah had ordained to burn incense on the high places in the cities of Judah and in the places all around Jerusalem, and those who burned incense to Baal, to the sun, to the moon, to the constellations, and to [a]all the host of heaven.

6 And he brought out the [a]wooden* image from the house of the LORD, to the Brook Kidron outside Jerusalem, burned it at the Brook Kidron and ground *it* to [b]ashes, and threw its ashes on [c]the graves of the common people.

7 Then he tore down the *ritual* booths [a]of the *perverted persons that *were* in the house of the LORD, [b]where the [c]women wove hangings for the wooden image.

8 And he brought all the priests from the cities of Judah, and defiled the high places where the priests had burned incense, from [a]Geba to Beersheba; also he broke down the high places at the gates which *were* at the entrance of the Gate of Joshua the governor of the city, which *were* to the left of the city gate.

9 [a]Nevertheless the priests of the high places did not come up to the altar of the LORD in Jerusalem, [b]but they ate unleavened bread among their brethren.

10 And he defiled [a]Topheth, which *is* in [b]the Valley of the *Son of Hinnom, [c]that no man might make his son or his daughter [d]pass through the fire to Molech.

11 Then he removed the horses that the kings of Judah had dedicated to the sun, at the entrance to the house of the LORD, by the chamber of Nathan-Melech, the officer who *was* in the court; and he burned the chariots of the sun with fire.

12 The altars that *were* [a]on the roof, the upper chamber of Ahaz, which the kings of Judah had made, and the altars which [b]Manasseh had made in the two courts of the house of the LORD, the king broke down and pulverized there, and threw their dust into the Brook Kidron.

13 Then the king defiled the high places that

KJV

salem, which *were* on the right hand of the mount of corruption, which [a]Solomon the king of Israel had builded for Ashtoreth the abomination of the Zidonians, and for Chemosh the abomination of the Moabites, and for Milcom the abomination of the children of Ammon, did the king defile.

14 And he [a]brake in pieces the images, and cut down the groves, and filled their places with the bones of men.

15 Moreover the altar that *was* at Beth–el, *and* the high place [a]which Jeroboam the son of Nebat, who made Israel to sin, had made, both that altar and the high place he brake down, and burned the high place, *and* stamped *it* small to powder, and burned the grove.

16 And as Josiah turned himself, he spied the sepulchres that *were* there in the mount, and sent, and took the bones out of the sepulchres, and burned *them* upon the altar, and polluted it, according to the [a]word of the LORD which the man of God proclaimed, who proclaimed these words.

17 Then he said, What title *is* that that I see? And the men of the city told him, *It is* [a]the sepulchre of the man of God, which came from Judah, and proclaimed these things that thou hast done against the altar of Beth–el.

18 And he said, Let him alone; let no man move his bones. So they let his bones alone, with the bones of [a]the prophet that came out of Samaria.

19 And all the houses also of the high places that *were* [a]in the cities of Samaria, which the kings of Israel had made to provoke *the LORD* to anger, Josiah took away, and did to them according to all the acts that he had done in Beth–el.

20 And [a]he [b]slew all the priests of the high places that *were* there upon the altars, and [c]burned men's bones upon them, and returned to Jerusalem.

21 And the king commanded all the people, saying, [a]Keep the passover unto the LORD your God, [b]as *it is* written in the book of this covenant.

22 Surely [a]there was not holden such a passover from the days of the judges that judged Israel, nor in all the days of the kings of Israel, nor of the kings of Judah;

23 But in the eighteenth year of king Josiah, *wherein* this passover was holden to the LORD in Jerusalem.

24 Moreover the *workers with* familiar spirits, and the wizards, and the images, and the idols, and all the abominations that were spied in the land of Judah and in Jerusalem, did Josiah put away, that he might perform the words of [a]the law which were written in the book [b]that Hilkiah the priest found in the house of the LORD.

25 [a]And like unto him was there no king before him, that turned to the LORD with all his heart, and with all his soul, and with all his might, according to all the law of Moses; neither after him arose there *any* like him.

Impending Judgment on Judah

26 Notwithstanding the LORD turned not from the fierceness of his great wrath, wherewith his anger was kindled against Judah, [a]because of all the provocations that Manasseh had provoked him withal.

27 And the LORD said, I will remove Judah also out of my sight, as [a]I have removed Israel, and will cast off this city Jerusalem which I have chosen, and the house of which I said, [b]My name shall be there.

Josiah Dies in Battle
(2 Chr. 35:20—36:1)

28 Now the rest of the acts of Josiah, and all that he did, *are* they not written in the book of the chronicles of the kings of Judah?

29 [a]In his days Pharaoh–nechoh king of Egypt went up against the king of Assyria to the

---

13 [a]1 Kin. 11:5–7
14 [a][Ex. 23:24; Deut. 7:5–25]
15 [a]1 Kin. 12:28–33
16 [a]1 Kin. 13:2
17 [a]1 Kin. 13:1, 30, 31
18 [a]1 Kin. 13:11, 31
19 [a]2 Chr. 34:6, 7
20 [a]1 Kin. 13:2 [b][Ex. 22:20]; 1 Kin. 18:40; 2 Kin. 10:25; 11:18 [c]2 Chr. 34:5
21 [a]Num. 9:5; Josh. 5:10; 2 Chr. 35:1 [b]Ex. 12:3; Lev. 23:5; Num. 9:2; Deut. 16:2–8
22 [a]2 Chr. 35:18, 19
24 [a][Lev. 19:31; 20:27]; Deut. 18:11 [b]2 Kin. 22:8
25 [a]2 Kin. 18:5
26 [a]2 Kin. 21:11, 12; 24:3, 4; Jer. 15:4
27 [a]2 Kin. 17:18, 20; 18:11; 21:13 [b]1 Kin. 8:29; 9:3; 2 Kin. 21:4, 7
29 [a]2 Chr. 35:20; Jer. 2:16; 46:2

NKJV

were east of Jerusalem, which *were* on the south of the Mount of Corruption, which [a]Solomon king of Israel had built for Ashtoreth the abomination of the Sidonians, for Chemosh the abomination of the Moabites, and for Milcom the abomination of the people of Ammon.

14 And he [a]broke in pieces the *sacred* pillars and cut down the wooden images, and filled their places with the bones of men.

15 Moreover the altar that *was* at Bethel, *and* the high place [a]which Jeroboam the son of Nebat, who made Israel sin, had made, both that altar and the high place he broke down; and he burned the high place *and* crushed *it* to powder, and burned the wooden image.

16 As Josiah turned, he saw the tombs that *were* there on the mountain. And he sent and took the bones out of the tombs and burned *them* on the altar, and defiled it according to the [a]word of the LORD which the man of God proclaimed, who proclaimed these words.

17 Then he said, "What gravestone *is* this that I see?" So the men of the city told him, "*It is* [a]the tomb of the man of God who came from Judah and proclaimed these things which you have done against the altar of Bethel."

18 And he said, "Let him alone; let no one move his bones." So they let his bones alone, with the bones of [a]the prophet who came from Samaria.

19 Now Josiah also took away all the shrines of the high places that *were* [a]in the cities of Samaria, which the kings of Israel had made to provoke *the LORD to anger; and he did to them according to all the deeds he had done in Bethel.

20 [a]He [b]executed all the priests of the high places who *were* there, on the altars, and [c]burned men's bones on them; and he returned to Jerusalem.

21 Then the king commanded all the people, saying, [a]"Keep the Passover to the LORD your God, [b]as *it is* written in this Book of the Covenant."

22 [a]Such a Passover surely had never been held since the days of the judges who judged Israel, nor in all the days of the kings of Israel and the kings of Judah.

23 But in the eighteenth year of King Josiah this Passover was held before the LORD in Jerusalem.

24 Moreover Josiah put away those who consulted mediums and spiritists, the household gods and idols, all the abominations that were seen in the land of Judah and in Jerusalem, that he might perform the words of [a]the law which were written in the book [b]that Hilkiah the priest found in the house of the LORD.

25 [a]Now before him there was no king like him, who turned to the LORD with all his heart, with all his soul, and with all his might, according to all the Law of Moses; nor after him did *any* arise like him.

Impending Judgment on Judah

26 Nevertheless the LORD did not turn from the fierceness of His great wrath, with which His anger was aroused against Judah, [a]because of all the provocations with which Manasseh had provoked Him.

27 And the LORD said, "I will also remove Judah from My sight, as [a]I have removed Israel, and will cast off this city Jerusalem which I have chosen, and the house of which I said, [b]'My name shall be there.' "

Josiah Dies in Battle
(2 Chr. 35:20—36:1)

28 Now the rest of the acts of Josiah, and all that he did, *are* they not written in the book of the chronicles of the kings of Judah?

29 [a]In his days Pharaoh Necho king of Egypt went to the aid of the king of Assyria, to the River

---

*23:19 So with LXX, Syr., Vg.; MT, Tg. omit *the LORD*

KJV

river Euphrates: and king Josiah went against him; and he slew him at [b]Megiddo, when he [c]had seen him.

30 [a]And his servants carried him in a chariot dead from Megiddo, and brought him to Jerusalem, and buried him in his own sepulchre. And [b]the people of the land took Jehoahaz the son of Josiah, and anointed him, and made him king in his father's stead.

The Reign and Captivity of Jehoahaz
(2 Chr. 36:1–4)

31 [a]Jehoahaz *was* twenty and three years old when he began to reign; and he reigned three months in Jerusalem. And his mother's name *was* [b]Hamutal, the daughter of Jeremiah of Libnah.

32 And he did *that which was* evil in the sight of the LORD, according to all that his fathers had done.

33 And Pharaoh–nechoh put him in bands [a]at Riblah in the land of Hamath, that he might not reign in Jerusalem; and put the land to a tribute of an hundred talents of silver, and a talent of gold.

34 And [a]Pharaoh–nechoh made Eliakim the son of Josiah king in the room of Josiah his father, and [b]turned his name to [c]Jehoiakim, and took Jehoahaz away: [d]and he came to Egypt, and died there.

Jehoiakim Reigns in Judah
(2 Chr. 36:5–8)

35 And Jehoiakim gave [a]the silver and the gold to Pharaoh; but he taxed the land to give the money according to the commandment of Pharaoh: he exacted the silver and the gold of the people of the land, of every one according to his taxation, to give *it* unto Pharaoh–nechoh.

36 [a]Jehoiakim *was* twenty and five years old when he began to reign; and he reigned eleven years in Jerusalem. And his mother's name *was* Zebudah, the daughter of Pedaiah of Rumah.

37 And he did *that which was* evil in the sight of the LORD, according to all that his fathers had done.

Judah Overrun by Enemies

24 In [a]his days Nebuchadnezzar king of [b]Babylon came up, and Jehoiakim became his servant three years: then he turned and rebelled against him.

2 [a]And the LORD sent against him bands of the Chaldees, and bands of the Syrians, and bands of the Moabites, and bands of the children of Ammon, and sent them against Judah to destroy it, [b]according to the word of the LORD, which he spake by his servants the prophets.

3 Surely at the commandment of the LORD came *this* upon Judah, to remove *them* out of his sight, [a]for the sins of Manasseh, according to all that he did;

4 [a]And also for the innocent blood that he shed: for he filled Jerusalem with innocent blood; which the LORD would not pardon.

5 Now the rest of the acts of Jehoiakim, and all that he did, *are* they not written in the book of the chronicles of the kings of Judah?

6 [a]So Jehoiakim slept with his fathers: and Jehoiachin his son reigned in his stead.

7 And [a]the king of Egypt came not again any more out of his land: for [b]the king of Babylon had taken from the river of Egypt unto the river Euphrates all that pertained to the king of Egypt.

The Reign and Captivity of Jehoiachin
(2 Chr. 36:9, 10)

8 [a]Jehoiachin *was* eighteen years old when he began to reign, and he reigned in Jerusalem three months. And his mother's name *was* Nehushta, the daughter of Elnathan of Jerusalem.

---

29 [b]Judg. 5:19; Zech. 12:11 [c]2 Kin. 14:8
30 [a]2 Chr. 35:24; 2 Kin. 22:20 [b]2 Chr. 36:1–4
31 [a]1 Chr. 3:15; Jer. 22:11 [b]2 Kin. 24:18
33 [a]2 Kin. 25:6; Jer. 52:27
34 [a]2 Chr. 36:4 [b]2 Kin. 24:17; Dan. 1:7 [c]Matt. 1:11 [d]Jer. 22:11, 12; Ezek. 19:3, 4
35 [a]2 Kin. 23:33
36 [a]2 Chr. 36:5; Jer. 22:18, 19; 26:1

CHAPTER 24

1 [a]2 Chr. 36:6; Jer. 25:1, 9; Dan. 1:1 [b]2 Kin. 20:14
2 [a]Jer. 25:9; 32:28; 35:11; Ezek. 19:8 [b]2 Kin. 20:17; 21:12–14; 23:27
3 [a]2 Kin. 21:2, 11; 23:26
4 [a]2 Kin. 21:16
6 [a]2 Chr. 36:6, 8; Jer. 22:18, 19
7 [a]Jer. 37:57 [b]Jer. 46:2
8 [a]1 Chr. 3:16; 2 Chr. 36:9

NKJV

Euphrates; and King Josiah went against him. And *Pharaoh Necho* killed him at [b]Megiddo when he [c]confronted him.

30 [a]Then his servants moved his body in a chariot from Megiddo, brought him to Jerusalem, and buried him in his own tomb. And [b]the people of the land took Jehoahaz the son of Josiah, anointed him, and made him king in his father's place.

The Reign and Captivity of Jehoahaz
(2 Chr. 36:1–4)

31 [a]Jehoahaz *was* twenty-three years old when he became king, and he reigned three months in Jerusalem. His mother's name *was* [b]Hamutal the daughter of Jeremiah of Libnah.

32 And he did evil in the sight of the LORD, according to all that his fathers had done.

33 Now Pharaoh Necho put him in prison [a]at Riblah in the land of Hamath, that he might not reign in Jerusalem; and he imposed on the land a tribute of one hundred talents of silver and a talent of gold.

34 Then [a]Pharaoh Necho made Eliakim the son of Josiah king in place of his father Josiah, and [b]changed his name to [c]Jehoiakim. And *Pharaoh* took Jehoahaz [d]and went to Egypt, and *he died there.

Jehoiakim Reigns in Judah
(2 Chr. 36:5–8)

35 So Jehoiakim gave [a]the silver and gold to Pharaoh; but he taxed the land to give money according to the command of Pharaoh; he exacted the silver and gold from the people of the land, from every one according to his assessment, to give *it* to Pharaoh Necho.

36 [a]Jehoiakim *was* twenty-five years old when he became king, and he reigned eleven years in Jerusalem. His mother's name *was* Zebudah the daughter of Pedaiah of Rumah.

37 And he did evil in the sight of the LORD, according to all that his fathers had done.

Judah Overrun by Enemies

24 In [a]his days Nebuchadnezzar king of [b]Babylon came up, and Jehoiakim became his vassal *for* three years. Then he turned and rebelled against him.

2 [a]And the LORD sent against him *raiding* bands of Chaldeans, bands of Syrians, bands of Moabites, and bands of the people of Ammon; He sent them against Judah to destroy it, [b]according to the word of the LORD which He had spoken by His servants the prophets.

3 Surely at the commandment of the LORD *this* came upon Judah, to remove *them* from His sight [a]because of the sins of Manasseh, according to all that he had done,

4 [a]and also because of the innocent blood that he had shed; for he had filled Jerusalem with innocent blood, which the LORD would not pardon.

5 Now the rest of the acts of Jehoiakim, and all that he did, *are* they not written in the book of the chronicles of the kings of Judah?

6 [a]So Jehoiakim rested with his fathers. Then Jehoiachin his son reigned in his place.

7 And [a]the king of Egypt did not come out of his land anymore, for [b]the king of Babylon had taken all that belonged to the king of Egypt from the Brook of Egypt to the River Euphrates.

The Reign and Captivity of Jehoiachin
(2 Chr. 36:9, 10)

8 [a]Jehoiachin *was* eighteen years old when he became king, and he reigned in Jerusalem three months. His mother's name *was* Nehushta the daughter of Elnathan of Jerusalem.

---

*23:34 Jehoahaz

KJV

9 And he did *that which was* evil in the sight
of the LORD, according to all that his father had
done.
10 [a]At that time the servants of Nebuchadnezzar king of Babylon came up against Jerusalem, and the city was besieged.
11 And Nebuchadnezzar king of Babylon
came against the city, and his servants did besiege
it.
12 [a]And Jehoiachin the king of Judah went
out to the king of Babylon, he, and his mother,
and his servants, and his princes, and his officers:
and the king of Babylon took him [b]in the eighth
year of his reign.

The Captivity of Jerusalem

13 [a]And he carried out thence all the treasures of the house of the LORD, and the treasures
of the king's house, and [b]cut in pieces all the vessels of gold which Solomon king of Israel had
made in the temple of the LORD, [c]as the LORD had
said.
14 And [a]he carried away all Jerusalem, and
all the princes, and all the mighty men of valour,
[b]*even* ten thousand captives, and [c]all the craftsmen and smiths: none remained, save [d]the poorest
sort of the people of the land.
15 And [a]he carried away Jehoiachin to Babylon, and the king's mother, and the king's wives,
and his officers, and the mighty of the land, *those*
carried he into captivity from Jerusalem to
Babylon.
16 And [a]all the men of might, *even* seven
thousand, and craftsmen and smiths a thousand,
all *that were* strong *and* apt for war, even them
the king of Babylon brought captive to Babylon.

Zedekiah Reigns in Judah
(*2 Chr. 36:11–14; Jer. 52:1–3*)

17 And [a]the king of Babylon made Mattaniah
[b]his father's brother king in his stead, and
[c]changed his name to Zedekiah.
18 [a]Zedekiah *was* twenty and one years old
when he began to reign, and he reigned eleven
years in Jerusalem. And his mother's name *was*
[b]Hamutal, the daughter of Jeremiah of Libnah.
19 [a]And he did *that which was* evil in the
sight of the LORD, according to all that Jehoiakim
had done.
20 For through the anger of the LORD it came
to pass in Jerusalem and Judah, until he had cast
them out from his presence, [a]that Zedekiah rebelled against the king of Babylon.

The Fall and Captivity of Judah
(*2 Chr. 36:15–21; Jer. 52:4–30*)

25 And it came to pass [a]in the ninth year of
his reign, in the tenth month, in the tenth
day of the month, *that* Nebuchadnezzar king of
Babylon came, he, and all his host, against Jerusalem, and pitched against it; and they built forts
against it round about.
2 And the city was besieged unto the eleventh year of king Zedekiah.
3 And on the ninth *day* of the [a]*fourth* month
the famine prevailed in the city, and there was
no bread for the people of the land.
4 And [a]the city was broken up, and all the
men of war *fled* by night by the way of the gate
between two walls, which *is* by the king's garden:
(now the Chaldees *were* against the city round
about:) and [b]*the king* went the way toward the
plain.
5 And the army of the Chaldees pursued after the king, and overtook him in the plains of
Jericho: and all his army were scattered from
him.
6 So they took the king, and brought him
up to the king of Babylon [a]to Riblah; and they
gave judgment upon him.
7 And they slew the sons of Zedekiah before
his eyes, and [a]put out the eyes of Zedekiah, and

10 [a]Dan. 1:1
12 [a]Jer. 22:24–30; 24:1; 29:1, 2; Ezek. 17:12 [b]2 Chr. 36:10
13 [a]2 Kin. 20:17; Is. 39:6 [b]Dan. 5:2, 3 [c]Jer. 20:5
14 [a]Is. 3:2, 3; Jer. 24:1 [b]2 Kin. 24:16; Jer. 52:28 [c]1 Sam. 13:19 [d]2 Kin. 25:12
15 [a]2 Chr. 36:10; Esth. 2:6; Jer. 22:24–28; Ezek. 17:12
16 [a]Jer. 52:28
17 [a]Jer. 37:1 [b]1 Chr. 3:15; 2 Chr. 36:10 [c]2 Chr. 36:4
18 [a]2 Chr. 36:11; Jer. 52:1 [b]2 Kin. 23:31
19 [a]2 Chr. 36:12
20 [a]2 Chr. 36:13; Ezek. 17:15

CHAPTER 25

1 [a]2 Chr. 36:17; Jer. 6:6; 34:2; Ezek. 4:2; 24:1, 2; Hab. 1:6
3 [a]2 Kin. 6:24, 25; Is. 3:1; Jer. 39:2; Lam. 4:9, 10
4 [a]Jer. 39:2 [b]Jer. 39:4–7; Ezek. 12:12
6 [a]2 Kin. 23:33; Jer. 52:9
7 [a]Jer. 39:7; Ezek. 17:16

*

24:17 Lit. *his*
25:4 Lit. *he*
Or *Arabah,* the Jordan Valley

NKJV

9 And he did evil in the sight of the LORD,
according to all that his father had done.
10 [a]At that time the servants of Nebuchadnezzar king of Babylon came up against Jerusalem, and the city was besieged.
11 And Nebuchadnezzar king of Babylon
came against the city, as his servants were besieging it.
12 [a]Then Jehoiachin king of Judah, his
mother, his servants, his princes, and his officers
went out to the king of Babylon; and the king of
Babylon, [b]in the eighth year of his reign, took
him prisoner.

The Captivity of Jerusalem

13 [a]And he carried out from there all the
treasures of the house of the LORD and the treasures of the king's house, and he [b]cut in pieces
all the articles of gold which Solomon king of Israel had made in the temple of the LORD, [c]as the
LORD had said.
14 Also [a]he carried into captivity all Jerusalem: all the captains and all the mighty men of
valor, [b]ten thousand captives, and [c]all the craftsmen and smiths. None remained except [d]the poorest people of the land.
15 And [a]he carried Jehoiachin captive to
Babylon. The king's mother, the king's wives, his
officers, and the mighty of the land he carried into
captivity from Jerusalem to Babylon.
16 [a]All the valiant men, seven thousand, and
craftsmen and smiths, one thousand, all *who were*
strong *and* fit for war, these the king of Babylon
brought captive to Babylon.

Zedekiah Reigns in Judah
(*2 Chr. 36:11–14; Jer. 52:1–3*)

17 Then [a]the king of Babylon made Mattaniah, [b]*Jehoiachin's** uncle, king in his place, and
[c]changed his name to Zedekiah.
18 [a]Zedekiah *was* twenty-one years old
when he became king, and he reigned eleven
years in Jerusalem. His mother's name *was* [b]Ha-
mutal the daughter of Jeremiah of Libnah.
19 [a]He also did evil in the sight of the LORD,
according to all that Jehoiakim had done.
20 For because of the anger of the LORD *this*
happened in Jerusalem and Judah, that He finally
cast them out from His presence. [a]Then Zedekiah
rebelled against the king of Babylon.

The Fall and Captivity of Judah
(*2 Chr. 36:15–21; Jer. 52:4–30*)

25 Now it came to pass [a]in the ninth year of
his reign, in the tenth month, on the tenth
day of the month, *that* Nebuchadnezzar king of
Babylon and all his army came against Jerusalem
and encamped against it; and they built a siege
wall against it all around.
2 So the city was besieged until the eleventh
year of King Zedekiah.
3 By the ninth *day* of the [a]*fourth* month the
famine had become so severe in the city that there
was no food for the people of the land.
4 Then [a]the city wall was broken through,
and all the men of war *fled* at night by way of
the gate between two walls, which was by the
king's garden, even though the Chaldeans *were*
still encamped all around against the city. And
[b]*the king** went by way of the *plain.
5 But the army of the Chaldeans pursued
the king, and they overtook him in the plains of
Jericho. All his army was scattered from him.
6 So they took the king and brought him
up to the king of Babylon [a]at Riblah, and they
pronounced judgment on him.
7 Then they killed the sons of Zedekiah before his eyes, [a]put out the eyes of Zedekiah, bound

KJV

bound him with fetters of brass, and carried him to Babylon.
8 And in the fifth month, [a]on the seventh *day* of the month, which *is* [b]the nineteenth year of king Nebuchadnezzar king of Babylon, [c]came Nebuzar–adan, captain of the guard, a servant of the king of Babylon, unto Jerusalem:
9 [a]And he burnt the house of the LORD, [b]and the king's house, and all the houses of Jerusalem, and every great *man's* house [c]burnt he with fire.
10 And all the army of the Chaldees, that *were with* the captain of the guard, [a]brake down the walls of Jerusalem round about.
11 [a]Now the rest of the people *that were* left in the city, and the fugitives that fell away to the king of Babylon, with the remnant of the multitude, did Nebuzar–adan the captain of the guard carry away.
12 But the captain of the guard [a]left of the poor of the land *to be* vinedressers and husbandmen.
13 And [a]the [b]pillars of brass that *were* in the house of the LORD, and [c]the bases, and [d]the brasen sea that *was* in the house of the LORD, did the Chaldees break in pieces, and [e]carried the brass of them to Babylon.
14 And [a]the pots, and the shovels, and the snuffers, and the spoons, and all the vessels of brass wherewith they ministered, took they away.
15 And the firepans, and the bowls, *and* such things as *were* of gold, *in* gold, and of silver, *in* silver, the captain of the guard took away.
16 The two pillars, one sea, and the bases which Solomon had made for the house of the LORD; [a]the brass of all these vessels was without weight.
17 [a]The height of the one pillar *was* eighteen cubits, and the chapiter upon it *was* brass: and the height of the chapiter three cubits; and the wreathen work, and pomegranates upon the chapiter round about, all of brass: and like unto these had the second pillar with wreathen work.
18 [a]And the captain of the guard took [b]Seraiah the chief priest, and [c]Zephaniah the second priest, and the three keepers of the door:
19 And out of the city he took an officer that was set over the men of war, and [a]five men of them that were in the king's presence, which were found in the city, and the principal scribe of the host, which mustered the people of the land, and threescore men of the people of the land *that were* found in the city:
20 And Nebuzar–adan captain of the guard took these, and brought them to the king of Babylon to Riblah:
21 And the king of Babylon smote them, and slew them at Riblah in the land of Hamath. [a]So Judah was carried away out of their land.

Gedaliah Made Governor of Judah

(Jer. 40:5—41:18)

22 And *as for* [b]the people that remained in the land of Judah, whom Nebuchadnezzar king of Babylon had left, even over them he made Gedaliah the son of [a]Ahikam, the son of Shaphan, ruler.
23 And when all the [a]captains of the armies, they and their men, heard that the king of Babylon had made Gedaliah governor, there came to Gedaliah to Mizpah, even Ishmael the son of Nethaniah, and Johanan the son of Careah, and Seraiah the son of Tanhumeth the Netophathite, and Jaazaniah the son of a Maachathite, they and their men.
24 And Gedaliah sware to them, and to their men, and said unto them, Fear not to be the servants of the Chaldees: dwell in the land, and serve the king of Babylon; and it shall be well with you.
25 But [a]it came to pass in the seventh month, that Ishmael the son of Nethaniah, the son of Elishama, of the seed royal, came, and ten men with

8 [a]Jer. 52:12 [b]2 Kin. 24:12 [c]Jer. 39:9
9 [a]2 Kin. 25:13; 2 Chr. 36:19; Ps. 79:1; Jer. 7:14 [b]Jer. 39:8 [c]Jer. 17:27
10 [a]2 Kin. 14:13; Neh. 1:3
11 [a]Is. 1:9; Jer. 5:19; 39:9
12 [a]2 Kin. 24:14; Jer. 39:10; 40:7; 52:16
13 [a]Jer. 52:17 [b]1 Kin. 7:15 [c]1 Kin. 7:27 [d]1 Kin. 7:23 [e]2 Kin. 20:17; Jer. 27:19–22
14 [a]Ex. 27:3; 1 Kin. 7:45
16 [a]1 Kin. 7:47
17 [a]1 Kin. 7:15–22; Jer. 52:21
18 [a]Jer. 39:9–13; 52:12–16, 24 [b]1 Chr. 6:14; Ezra 7:1 [c]Jer. 21:1; 29:25, 29
19 [a]Esth. 1:14; Jer. 52:25
21 [a]Lev. 26:33; Deut. 28:36, 64; 2 Kin. 23:27
22 [a]2 Kin. 22:12 [b]Is. 1:9; Jer. 40:5
23 [a]Jer. 40:7–9
25 [a]Jer. 41:1–3

NKJV

him with bronze fetters, and took him to Babylon.
8 And in the fifth month, [a]on the seventh *day* of the month (which *was* [b]the nineteenth year of King Nebuchadnezzar king of Babylon), [c]Nebuzaradan the captain of the guard, a servant of the king of Babylon, came to Jerusalem.
9 [a]He burned the house of the LORD [b]and the king's house; all the houses of Jerusalem, that is, all the houses of the great, [c]he burned with fire.
10 And all the army of the Chaldeans who *were with* the captain of the guard [a]broke down the walls of Jerusalem all around.
11 Then Nebuzaradan the captain of the guard carried away captive [a]the rest of the people *who* remained in the city and the defectors who had deserted to the king of Babylon, with the rest of the multitude.
12 But the captain of the guard [a]left *some* of the poor of the land as vinedressers and farmers.
13 [a]The bronze [b]pillars that *were* in the house of the LORD, and [c]the carts and [d]the bronze Sea that *were* in the house of the LORD, the Chaldeans broke in pieces, and [e]carried their bronze to Babylon.
14 They also took away [a]the pots, the shovels, the trimmers, the spoons, and all the bronze utensils with which the priests ministered.
15 The firepans and the basins, the things of solid gold and solid silver, the captain of the guard took away.
16 The two pillars, one Sea, and the carts, which Solomon had made for the house of the LORD, [a]the bronze of all these articles was beyond measure.
17 [a]The height of one pillar *was* eighteen cubits, and the capital on it *was* of bronze. The height of the capital was three cubits, and the network and pomegranates all around the capital were all of bronze. The second pillar was the same, with a network.
18 [a]And the captain of the guard took [b]Seraiah the chief priest, [c]Zephaniah the second priest, and the three doorkeepers.
19 He also took out of the city an officer who had charge of the men of war, [a]five men of the king's close associates who were found in the city, the chief recruiting officer of the army, who mustered the people of the land, and sixty men of the people of the land *who were* found in the city.
20 So Nebuzaradan, captain of the guard, took these and brought them to the king of Babylon at Riblah.
21 Then the king of Babylon struck them and put them to death at Riblah in the land of Hamath. [a]Thus Judah was carried away captive from its own land.

Gedaliah Made Governor of Judah

(Jer. 40:5—41:18)

22 Then he made Gedaliah the son of [a]Ahikam, the son of Shaphan, governor over [b]the people who remained in the land of Judah, whom Nebuchadnezzar king of Babylon had left.
23 Now when all the [a]captains of the armies, they and *their* men, heard that the king of Babylon had made Gedaliah governor, they came to Gedaliah at Mizpah—Ishmael the son of Nethaniah, Johanan the son of Careah, Seraiah the son of Tanhumeth the Netophathite, and *Jaazaniah the son of a Maachathite, they and their men.
24 And Gedaliah took an oath before them and their men, and said to them, "Do not be afraid of the servants of the Chaldeans. Dwell in the land and serve the king of Babylon, and it shall be well with you."
25 But [a]it happened in the seventh month that Ishmael the son of Nethaniah, the son of Elishama, of the royal family, came with ten men

*25:23 *Jezaniah,* Jer. 40:8

KJV

him, and smote Gedaliah, that he died, and the Jews and the Chaldees that were with him at Mizpah.

26 And all the people, both small and great, and the captains of the armies, arose, [a]and came to Egypt: for they were afraid of the Chaldees.

Jehoiachin Released from Prison
(Jer. 52:31–34)

27 [a]And it came to pass in the seven and thirtieth year of the captivity of Jehoiachin king of Judah, in the twelfth month, on the seven and twentieth *day* of the month, *that* Evil–merodach king of Babylon in the year that he began to reign [b]did lift up the head of Jehoiachin king of Judah out of prison;

28 And he spake kindly to him, and set his throne above the throne of the kings that *were* with him in Babylon;

29 And changed his prison garments: and he did [a]eat bread continually before him all the days of his life.

30 And his allowance *was* a continual allowance given him of the king, a daily rate for every day, all the days of his life.

26 [a]2 Kin. 19:31; Jer. 43:4–7
27 [a]2 Kin. 24:12, 15; Jer. 52:31–34
[b]Gen. 40:13, 20
29 [a]2 Sam. 9:7

*

25:27 Lit. *Man of Marduk*

NKJV

and struck and killed Gedaliah, the Jews, as well as the Chaldeans who were with him at Mizpah.

26 And all the people, small and great, and the captains of the armies, arose [a]and went to Egypt; for they were afraid of the Chaldeans.

Jehoiachin Released from Prison
(Jer. 52:31–34)

27 [a]Now it came to pass in the thirty-seventh year of the captivity of Jehoiachin king of Judah, in the twelfth month, on the twenty-seventh *day* of the month, *that* *Evil-Merodach king of Babylon, in the year that he began to reign, [b]released Jehoiachin king of Judah from prison.

28 He spoke kindly to him, and gave him a more prominent seat than those of the kings who *were* with him in Babylon.

29 So Jehoiachin changed from his prison garments, and he [a]ate bread regularly before the king all the days of his life.

30 And as for his provisions, *there was* a regular ration given him by the king, a portion for each day, all the days of his life.

KJV

THE FIRST BOOK OF THE

CHRONICLES

The Family of Adam—Seth to Abraham
(Gen. 5:1–32; 10:1–32; 11:10–26;
Luke 3:34–38)

1 Adam,[a] [b]Sheth, Enosh,
2 Kenan, [a]Mahalaleel, Jered,
3 Henoch, Methuselah, Lamech,
4 [a]Noah, Shem, Ham, and Japheth.
5 [a]The sons of Japheth; Gomer, and Magog,
and Madai, and Javan, and Tubal, and Meshech,
and Tiras.
6 And the sons of Gomer; Ashchenaz, and
Riphath, and Togarmah.
7 And the sons of Javan; Elishah, and
Tarshish, Kittim, and Dodanim.
8 [a]The sons of Ham; Cush, and Mizraim,
Put, and Canaan.
9 And the sons of Cush; Seba, and Havilah,
and Sabta, and Raamah, and Sabtecha. And the
sons of Raamah; Sheba, and Dedan.
10 And Cush [a]begat Nimrod: he began to be
mighty upon the earth.
11 And Mizraim begat Ludim, and Anamim,
and Lehabim, and Napthtuhim,
12 And Pathrusim, and Casluhim, (of whom
came the Philistines,) and [a]Caphthorim.
13 And [a]Canaan begat Zidon his firstborn,
and Heth,
14 The Jebusite also, and the Amorite, and
the Girgashite,
15 And the Hivite, and the Arkite, and the
Sinite,
16 And the Arvadite, and the Zemarite, and
the Hamathite.
17 The sons of [a]Shem; Elam, and Asshur,
and [b]Arphaxad, and Lud, and Aram, and Uz, and
Hul, and Gether, and Meshech.
18 And Arphaxad begat Shelah, and Shelah
begat Eber.
19 And unto Eber were born two sons: the
name of the one *was* Peleg; because in his days
the earth was divided: and his brother's name *was*
Joktan.
20 And [a]Joktan begat Almodad, and Sheleph, and Hazar–maveth, and Jerah,
21 Hadoram also, and Uzal, and Diklah,
22 And Ebal, and Abimael, and Sheba,
23 And Ophir, and Havilah, and Jobab. All
these *were* the sons of Joktan.
24 [a]Shem, Arphaxad, Shelah,
25 [a]Eber, Peleg, Reu,
26 Serug, Nahor, Terah,
27 [a]Abram; the same *is* Abraham.
28 [a]The sons of Abraham; [b]Isaac, and [c]Ish-
mael.

The Family of Ishmael
(Gen. 25:12–16)

29 These *are* their generations: The [a]first-
born of Ishmael, Nebaioth; then Kedar, and Adbeel, and Mibsam,
30 Mishma, and Dumah, Massa, Hadad, and
Tema,
31 Jetur, Naphish, and Kedemah. These are
the sons of Ishmael.

CHAPTER 1

1 [a]Gen. 1:27; 2:7; 5:1, 2, 5 [b]Gen. 4:25, 26; 5:3–9
4 [a]Gen. 5:28—10:1
5 [a]Gen. 10:2–4
8 [a]Gen. 10:6
10 [a]Gen. 10:8–10, 13
12 [a]Deut. 2:23
13 [a]Gen. 9:18, 25–27; 10:15
17 [a]Gen. 10:22–29; 11:10 [b]Luke 3:36
20 [a]Gen. 10:26
24 [a]Gen. 11:10–26; Luke 3:34–36
25 [a]Gen. 11:15
27 [a]Gen. 17:5
28 [a]Gen. 21:2, 3 [b]Gen. 21:2 [c]Gen. 16:11, 15
29 [a]Gen. 25:13–16

*

1:2 Heb. *Qenan*
1:4 So with MT, Vg.; LXX adds *the sons of Noah*
1:6 *Riphath,* Gen. 10:3
1:7 *Tarshish,* Gen. 10:4 • *Dodanim,* Gen. 10:4
1:9 *Sabtah,* Gen. 10:7 • *Raamah,* Gen. 10:7
1:17 *Mash,* Gen. 10:23
1:19 Lit. *Division,* Gen. 10:25
1:22 *Obal,* Gen. 10:28
1:30 *Hadar,* Gen. 25:15

NKJV

THE FIRST BOOK OF THE

CHRONICLES

The Family of Adam—Seth to Abraham
(Gen. 5:1–32; 10:1–32; 11:10–26;
Luke 3:34–38)

1 Adam,[a] [b]Seth, Enosh,
2 *Cainan, Mahalalel, Jared,
3 Enoch, Methuselah, Lamech,
4 [a]Noah,* Shem, Ham, and Japheth.
5 [a]The sons of Japheth *were* Gomer, Magog,
Madai, Javan, Tubal, Meshech, and Tiras.
6 The sons of Gomer *were* Ashkenaz, *Diphath, and Togarmah.
7 The sons of Javan *were* Elishah, *Tar-
shishah, Kittim, and *Rodanim.
8 [a]The sons of Ham *were* Cush, Mizraim,
Put, and Canaan.
9 The sons of Cush *were* Seba, Havilah,
*Sabta, *Raama, and Sabtecha. The sons of
Raama *were* Sheba and Dedan.
10 Cush [a]begot Nimrod; he began to be a
mighty one on the earth.
11 Mizraim begot Ludim, Anamim, Lehabim,
Naphtuhim,
12 Pathrusim, Casluhim (from whom came
the Philistines and the [a]Caphtorim).
13 [a]Canaan begot Sidon, his firstborn, and
Heth;
14 the Jebusite, the Amorite, and the Girgashite;
15 the Hivite, the Arkite, and the Sinite;
16 the Arvadite, the Zemarite, and the
Hamathite.
17 The sons of [a]Shem *were* Elam, Asshur,
[b]Arphaxad, Lud, Aram, Uz, Hul, Gether, and
*Meshech.
18 Arphaxad begot Shelah, and Shelah begot
Eber.
19 To Eber were born two sons: the name
of one *was* *Peleg, for in his days the earth was
divided; and his brother's name *was* Joktan.
20 [a]Joktan begot Almodad, Sheleph, Hazar-
maveth, Jerah,
21 Hadoram, Uzal, Diklah,
22 *Ebal, Abimael, Sheba,
23 Ophir, Havilah, and Jobab. All these *were*
the sons of Joktan.
24 [a]Shem, Arphaxad, Shelah,
25 [a]Eber, Peleg, Reu,
26 Serug, Nahor, Terah,
27 and [a]Abram, who *is* Abraham.
28 [a]The sons of Abraham *were* [b]Isaac and
[c]Ishmael.

The Family of Ishmael
(Gen. 25:12–16)

29 These *are* their genealogies: The [a]first-
born of Ishmael *was* Nebajoth; then Kedar, Adbeel, Mibsam,
30 Mishma, Dumah, Massa, *Hadad, Tema,
31 Jetur, Naphish, and Kedemah. These *were*
the sons of Ishmael.

KJV

The Family of Keturah
(Gen. 25:1–4)

32 Now [a]the sons of Keturah, Abraham's
concubine: she bare Zimran, and Jokshan, and
Medan, and Midian, and Ishbak, and Shuah. And
the sons of Jokshan; Sheba, and Dedan.
33 And the sons of Midian; Ephah, and
Epher, and Henoch, and Abida, and Eldaah. All
these *are* the sons of Keturah.

The Family of Isaac
(Gen. 36:10–14)

34 And [a]Abraham begat Isaac. [b]The sons of
Isaac; Esau and Israel.
35 The sons of [a]Esau; Eliphaz, Reuel, and
Jeush, and Jaalam, and Korah.
36 The sons of Eliphaz; Teman, and Omar,
Zephi, and Gatam, Kenaz, and [a]Timna, and
Amalek.
37 The sons of Reuel; Nahath, Zerah, Shammah, and Mizzah.

The Family of Seir
(Gen. 36:20–28)

38 And [a]the sons of Seir; Lotan, and Shobal,
and Zibeon, and Anah, and Dishon, and Ezar, and
Dishan.
39 And the sons of Lotan; Hori, and Homam:
and Timna *was* Lotan's sister.
40 The sons of Shobal; Alian, and Manahath,
and Ebal, Shephi, and Onam. And the sons of
Zibeon; Aiah, and Anah.
41 The sons of Anah; [a]Dishon. And the sons
of Dishon; Amram, and Eshban, and Ithran, and
Cheran.
42 The sons of Ezer; Bilhan, and Zavan, *and*
Jakan. The sons of Dishan; Uz, and Aran.

The Kings of Edom
(Gen. 36:31–43)

43 Now these *are* the [a]kings that reigned in
the land of Edom before *any* king reigned over
the children of Israel; Bela the son of Beor: and
the name of his city *was* Dinhabah.
44 And when Bela was dead, Jobab the son
of Zerah of Bozrah reigned in his stead.
45 And when Jobab was dead, Husham of
the land of the Temanites reigned in his stead.
46 And when Husham was dead, Hadad the
son of Bedad, which smote Midian in the field of
Moab, reigned in his stead: and the name of his
city *was* Avith.
47 And when Hadad was dead, Samlah of
Masrekah reigned in his stead.
48 [a]And when Samlah was dead, Shaul of
Rehoboth by the river reigned in his stead.
49 And when Shaul was dead, Baal–hanan
the son of Achbor reigned in his stead.
50 And when Baal–hanan was dead, Hadad
reigned in his stead: and the name of his city *was*
Pai; and his wife's name *was* Mehetabel, the
daughter of Matred, the daughter of Mezahab.
51 Hadad died also. And the dukes of Edom
were; duke Timnah, duke Aliah, duke Jetheth,
52 Duke Aholibamah, duke Elah, duke Pinon,
53 Duke Kenaz, duke Teman, duke Mibzar,
54 Duke Magdiel, duke Iram. These *are* the
dukes of Edom.

The Family of Israel
(Gen. 35:23–26; 46:8–25)

2 These *are* the [a]sons of Israel; [b]Reuben, Simeon, Levi, and Judah, Issachar, and Zebulun,
2 Dan, Joseph, and Benjamin, Naphtali,
Gad, and Asher.

From Judah to David
(Ruth 4:18–22; Matt. 1:2–6; Luke 3:31–33)

3 The sons of [a]Judah; Er, and Onan, and
Shelah: *which* three were born unto him of the

32 [a]Gen. 25:1–4
34 [a]Gen. 21:2 [b]Gen. 25:9, 25, 26, 29; 32:28
35 [a]Gen. 36:10–19
36 [a]Gen. 36:12
38 [a]Gen. 36:20–28
41 [a]Gen. 36:25
43 [a]Gen. 36:31–43
48 [a]Gen. 36:37

CHAPTER 2

1 [a]Gen. 29:32–35; 35:23, 26; 46:8–27 [b]Gen. 29:32; 35:22
3 [a]Gen. 38:3–5; 46:12; Num. 26:19

*

1:36 *Zepho,* Gen. 36:11
1:40 *Alvan,* Gen. 36:23
• *Shepho,* Gen. 36:23
1:41 *Hemdan,* Gen. 36:26
1:42 *Akan,* Gen. 36:27
1:50 *Hadar,* Gen. 36:39
• *Pau,* Gen. 36:39
1:51 *Alvah,* Gen. 36:40

NKJV

The Family of Keturah
(Gen. 25:1–4)

32 Now [a]the sons born to Keturah, Abraham's concubine, *were* Zimran, Jokshan, Medan,
Midian, Ishbak, and Shuah. The sons of Jokshan
were Sheba and Dedan.
33 The sons of Midian *were* Ephah, Epher,
Hanoch, Abida, and Eldaah. All these were the
children of Keturah.

The Family of Isaac
(Gen. 36:10–14)

34 And [a]Abraham begot Isaac. [b]The sons of
Isaac *were* Esau and Israel.
35 The sons of [a]Esau *were* Eliphaz, Reuel,
Jeush, Jaalam, and Korah.
36 And the sons of Eliphaz *were* Teman,
Omar, *Zephi, Gatam, *and* Kenaz; and *by* [a]Timna,
Amalek.
37 The sons of Reuel *were* Nahath, Zerah,
Shammah, and Mizzah.

The Family of Seir
(Gen. 36:20–28)

38 [a]The sons of Seir *were* Lotan, Shobal,
Zibeon, Anah, Dishon, Ezer, and Dishan.
39 And the sons of Lotan *were* Hori and
Homam; Lotan's sister *was* Timna.
40 The sons of Shobal *were* *Alian, Manahath, Ebal, *Shephi, and Onam. The sons of
Zibeon *were* Ajah and Anah.
41 The son of Anah *was* [a]Dishon. The sons
of Dishon *were* *Hamran, Eshban, Ithran, and
Cheran.
42 The sons of Ezer *were* Bilhan, Zaavan,
and *Jaakan. The sons of Dishan *were* Uz and
Aran.

The Kings of Edom
(Gen. 36:31–43)

43 Now these *were* the [a]kings who reigned
in the land of Edom before a king reigned over
the children of Israel: Bela the son of Beor, and
the name of his city was Dinhabah.
44 And when Bela died, Jobab the son of
Zerah of Bozrah reigned in his place.
45 When Jobab died, Husham of the land of
the Temanites reigned in his place.
46 And when Husham died, Hadad the son
of Bedad, who attacked Midian in the field of
Moab, reigned in his place. The name of his city
was Avith.
47 When Hadad died, Samlah of Masrekah
reigned in his place.
48 [a]And when Samlah died, Saul of Rehoboth-by-the-River reigned in his place.
49 When Saul died, Baal-Hanan the son of
Achbor reigned in his place.
50 And when Baal-Hanan died, *Hadad
reigned in his place; and the name of his city was
*Pai. His wife's name was Mehetabel the daughter
of Matred, the daughter of Mezahab.
51 Hadad died also. And the chiefs of Edom
were Chief Timnah, Chief *Aliah, Chief Jetheth,
52 Chief Aholibamah, Chief Elah, Chief
Pinon,
53 Chief Kenaz, Chief Teman, Chief Mibzar,
54 Chief Magdiel, and Chief Iram. These
were the chiefs of Edom.

The Family of Israel
(Gen. 35:23–26; 46:8–25)

2 These *were* the [a]sons of Israel: [b]Reuben,
Simeon, Levi, Judah, Issachar, Zebulun,
2 Dan, Joseph, Benjamin, Naphtali, Gad,
and Asher.

From Judah to David
(Ruth 4:18–22; Matt. 1:2–6; Luke 3:31–33)

3 The sons of [a]Judah *were* Er, Onan, and
Shelah. *These* three were born to him by the

KJV

daughter of [b]Shua the Canaanitess. And [c]Er, the
firstborn of Judah, was evil in the sight of the
LORD; and he slew him.
4 And [a]Tamar his daughter in law [b]bare
him Pharez and Zerah. All the sons of Judah *were*
five.
5 The sons of [a]Pharez; Hezron, and Hamul.
6 And the sons of Zerah; Zimri, [a]and Ethan,
and Heman, and Calcol, and Dara: five of them
in all.
7 And the sons of [a]Carmi; Achar, the trou-
bler of Israel, who transgressed in the thing
[b]accursed.
8 And the sons of Ethan; Azariah.
9 The sons also of Hezron, that were born
unto him; Jerahmeel, and Ram, and Chelubai.
10 And Ram [a]begat Amminadab; and Amminadab begat Nahshon, [b]prince of the children
of Judah;
11 And Nahshon begat Salma, and Salma begat Boaz,
12 And Boaz begat Obed, and Obed begat
Jesse,
13 [a]And Jesse begat his firstborn Eliab, and
Abinadab the second, and Shimma the third,
14 Nethaneel the fourth, Raddai the fifth,
15 Ozem the sixth, David the [a]seventh:
16 Whose sisters *were* Zeruiah, and Abigail.
[a]And the sons of Zeruiah; Abishai, and Joab, and
Asahel, three.
17 And Abigail bare Amasa: and the father
of Amasa *was* Jether the Ishmeelite.

The Family of Hezron

18 And Caleb the son of Hezron begat *children* of Azubah *his* wife, and of Jerioth: her sons
are these; Jesher, and Shobab, and Ardon.
19 And when Azubah was dead, Caleb took
unto him [a]Ephrath, which bare him Hur.
20 And Hur begat Uri, and Uri begat [a]Beza-
leel.
21 And afterward Hezron went in to the
daughter of [a]Machir the father of Gilead, whom
he married when he *was* threescore years old; and
she bare him Segub.
22 And Segub begat [a]Jair, who had three and
twenty cities in the land of Gilead.
23 [a]And he took Geshur, and Aram, with the
towns of Jair, from them, with Kenath, and the
towns thereof, *even* threescore cities. All these
belonged to the sons of Machir the father of
Gilead.
24 And after that Hezron was dead in Caleb–
ephratah, then Abiah Hezron's wife bare him
[a]Ashur the father of Tekoa.

The Family of Jerahmeel

25 And the sons of Jerahmeel the firstborn
of Hezron were, Ram the firstborn, and Bunah,
and Oren, and Ozem, *and* Ahijah.
26 Jerahmeel had also another wife, whose
name *was* Atarah; she *was* the mother of Onam.
27 And the sons of Ram the firstborn of Jerahmeel were, Maaz, and Jamin, and Eker.
28 And the sons of Onam were, Shammai,
and Jada. And the sons of Shammai; Nadab, and
Abishur.
29 And the name of the wife of Abishur *was*
Abihail, and she bare him Ahban, and Molid.
30 And the sons of Nadab; Seled, and Appaim: but Seled died without children.
31 And the sons of Appaim; Ishi. And the
sons of Ishi; Sheshan. And [a]the children of
Sheshan; Ahlai.
32 And the sons of Jada the brother of Shammai; Jether, and Jonathan: and Jether died without children.
33 And the sons of Jonathan; Peleth, and
Zaza. These were the sons of Jerahmeel.
34 Now Sheshan had no sons, but daughters.
And Sheshan had a servant, an Egyptian, whose
name *was* Jarha.

3 [b]Gen. 38:2 [c]Gen. 38:7
4 [a]Gen. 38:6 [b]Matt. 1:3
5 [a]Gen. 46:12; Ruth 4:18
6 [a]1 Kin. 4:31
7 [a]1 Chr. 4:1 [b]Josh. 6:18
10 [a]Ruth 4:19–22; Matt. 1:4 [b]Num. 1:7; 2:3
13 [a]1 Sam. 16:6
15 [a]1 Sam. 16:10, 11; 17:12
16 [a]2 Sam. 2:18
19 [a]1 Chr. 2:50
20 [a]Ex. 31:2; 38:22
21 [a]Num. 27:1; Judg. 5:14; 1 Chr. 7:14
22 [a]Judg. 10:3
23 [a]Num. 32:41; Deut. 3:14; Josh. 13:30
24 [a]1 Chr. 4:5
31 [a]1 Chr. 2:34, 35

*

2:7 *Achan,* Josh. 7:1
2:9 *Caleb,* vv. 18, 42
2:11 *Salmon,* Ruth 4:21; Luke 3:32
2:13 *Shammah,* 1 Sam. 16:9
2:17 *Jithra the Israelite,* 2 Sam. 17:25
2:19 Or *Ephrathah*

NKJV

daughter of [b]Shua, the Canaanitess. [c]Er, the firstborn of Judah, was wicked in the sight of the
LORD; so He killed him.
4 And [a]Tamar, his daughter-in-law, [b]bore
him Perez and Zerah. All the sons of Judah *were*
five.
5 The sons of [a]Perez *were* Hezron and Hamul.
6 The sons of Zerah *were* Zimri, [a]Ethan, Heman, Calcol, and Dara—five of them in all.
7 The son of [a]Carmi *was* *Achar, the trou-
bler of Israel, who transgressed in the [b]accursed
thing.
8 The son of Ethan *was* Azariah.
9 Also the sons of Hezron who were born
to him *were* Jerahmeel, Ram, and *Chelubai.
10 Ram [a]begot Amminadab, and Amminadab begot Nahshon, [b]leader of the children of
Judah;
11 Nahshon begot *Salma, and Salma begot
Boaz;
12 Boaz begot Obed, and Obed begot Jesse;
13 [a]Jesse begot Eliab his firstborn, Abinadab
the second, *Shimea the third,
14 Nethanel the fourth, Raddai the fifth,
15 Ozem the sixth, *and* David the [a]seventh.
16 Now their sisters *were* Zeruiah and Abigail. [a]And the sons of Zeruiah *were* Abishai, Joab,
and Asahel—three.
17 Abigail bore Amasa; and the father of
Amasa *was* *Jether the Ishmaelite.

The Family of Hezron

18 Caleb the son of Hezron had children by
Azubah, *his* wife, and by Jerioth. Now these were
her sons: Jesher, Shobab, and Ardon.
19 When Azubah died, Caleb took [a]Ephrath*
as his wife, who bore him Hur.
20 And Hur begot Uri, and Uri begot
[a]Bezalel.
21 Now afterward Hezron went in to the
daughter of [a]Machir the father of Gilead, whom
he married when he *was* sixty years old; and she
bore him Segub.
22 Segub begot [a]Jair, who had twenty-three
cities in the land of Gilead.
23 [a](Geshur and Syria took from them the
towns of Jair, with Kenath and its towns—sixty
towns.) All these *belonged to* the sons of Machir
the father of Gilead.
24 After Hezron died in Caleb Ephrathah,
Hezron's wife Abijah bore him [a]Ashhur the father
of Tekoa.

The Family of Jerahmeel

25 The sons of Jerahmeel, the firstborn of
Hezron, *were* Ram, the firstborn, and Bunah,
Oren, Ozem, *and* Ahijah.
26 Jerahmeel had another wife, whose name
was Atarah; she was the mother of Onam.
27 The sons of Ram, the firstborn of Jerahmeel, were Maaz, Jamin, and Eker.
28 The sons of Onam were Shammai and
Jada. The sons of Shammai *were* Nadab and
Abishur.
29 And the name of the wife of Abishur *was*
Abihail, and she bore him Ahban and Molid.
30 The sons of Nadab *were* Seled and Appaim; Seled died without children.
31 The son of Appaim *was* Ishi, the son of
Ishi *was* Sheshan, and [a]Sheshan's son *was* Ahlai.
32 The sons of Jada, the brother of Shammai,
were Jether and Jonathan; Jether died without
children.
33 The sons of Jonathan *were* Peleth and
Zaza. These were the sons of Jerahmeel.
34 Now Sheshan had no sons, only daughters. And Sheshan had an Egyptian servant whose
name *was* Jarha.

KJV

35 And Sheshan gave his daughter to Jarha
his servant to wife; and she bare him Attai.
36 And Attai begat Nathan, and Nathan begat [a]Zabad,
37 And Zabad begat Ephlal, and Ephlal begat
[a]Obed,
38 And Obed begat Jehu, and Jehu begat
Azariah,
39 And Azariah begat Helez, and Helez begat
Eleasah,
40 And Eleasah begat Sisamai, and Sisamai
begat Shallum,
41 And Shallum begat Jekamiah, and Jekamiah begat Elishama.

The Family of Caleb

42 Now the sons of Caleb the brother of Jerahmeel *were*, Mesha his firstborn, which *was* the
father of Ziph; and the sons of Mareshah the father of Hebron.
43 And the sons of Hebron; Korah, and Tappuah, and Rekem, and Shema.
44 And Shema begat Raham, the father of
Jorkoam: and Rekem begat Shammai.
45 And the son of Shammai *was* Maon: and
Maon *was* the father of Beth–zur.
46 And Ephah, Caleb's concubine, bare
Haran, and Moza, and Gazez: and Haran begat
Gazez.
47 And the sons of Jahdai; Regem, and Jotham, and Gesham, and Pelet, and Ephah, and
Shaaph.
48 Maachah, Caleb's concubine, bare Sheber, and Tirhanah.
49 She bare also Shaaph the father of Madmannah, Sheva the father of Machbenah, and the
father of Gibea: and the daughter of Caleb *was*
[a]Achsa.
50 These were the sons of Caleb the son of
[a]Hur, the firstborn of Ephratah; Shobal the father
of [b]Kirjath–jearim,
51 Salma the father of Beth–lehem, Hareph
the father of Beth–gader.
52 And Shobal the father of Kirjath–jearim
had sons; Haroeh, *and* half of the Manahethites.
53 And the families of Kirjath–jearim; the
Ithrites, and the Puhites, and the Shumathites,
and the Mishraites; of them came the Zareathites,
and the Eshtaulites.
54 The sons of Salma; Beth–lehem, and the
Netophathites, Ataroth, the house of Joab, and
half of the Manahethites, the Zorites.
55 And the families of the scribes which
dwelt at Jabez; the Tirathites, the Shimeathites,
and Suchathites. These *are* the [a]Kenites that came
of Hemath, the father of the house of [b]Rechab.

The Family of David
(Matt. 1:6)

3 Now these were the sons of David, which were
born unto him in Hebron; the firstborn [a]Am-
non, of [b]Ahinoam the [c]Jezreelitess; the second
Daniel, of [d]Abigail the Carmelitess:
2 The third, [a]Absalom the son of Maachah
the daughter of Talmai king of Geshur: the fourth,
[b]Adonijah the son of Haggith:
3 The fifth, Shephatiah of Abital: the sixth,
Ithream by [a]Eglah his wife.
4 *These* six were born unto him in Hebron;
and [a]there he reigned seven years and six months:
and [b]in Jerusalem he reigned thirty and three
years.
5 [a]And these were born unto him in Jerusalem; Shimea, and Shobab, and Nathan, and [b]Sol-
omon, four, of Bath–shua the daughter of Ammiel:
6 Ibhar also, and Elishama, and Eliphelet,
7 And Nogah, and Nepheg, and Japhia,
8 And Elishama, and Eliada, and Eliphelet,
[a]nine.
9 *These were* all the sons of David, beside

NKJV

35 Sheshan gave his daughter to Jarha his
servant as wife, and she bore him Attai.
36 Attai begot Nathan, and Nathan begot
[a]Zabad;
37 Zabad begot Ephlal, and Ephlal begot
[a]Obed;
38 Obed begot Jehu, and Jehu begot Azariah;
39 Azariah begot Helez, and Helez begot
Eleasah;
40 Eleasah begot Sismai, and Sismai begot
Shallum;
41 Shallum begot Jekamiah, and Jekamiah
begot Elishama.

The Family of Caleb

42 The descendants of Caleb the brother of
Jerahmeel *were* Mesha, his firstborn, who was the
father of Ziph, and the sons of Mareshah the father of Hebron.
43 The sons of Hebron *were* Korah, Tappuah,
Rekem, and Shema.
44 Shema begot Raham the father of Jorkoam, and Rekem begot Shammai.
45 And the son of Shammai *was* Maon, and
Maon *was* the father of Beth Zur.
46 Ephah, Caleb's concubine, bore Haran,
Moza, and Gazez; and Haran begot Gazez.
47 And the sons of Jahdai *were* Regem, Jotham, Geshan, Pelet, Ephah, and Shaaph.
48 Maachah, Caleb's concubine, bore Sheber
and Tirhanah.
49 She also bore Shaaph the father of Madmannah, Sheva the father of Machbenah and the
father of Gibea. And the daughter of Caleb *was*
[a]Achsah.
50 These were the descendants of Caleb: The
sons of [a]Hur, the firstborn of Ephrathah, *were*
Shobal the father of [b]Kirjath Jearim,
51 Salma the father of Bethlehem, *and* Hareph the father of Beth Gader.
52 And Shobal the father of Kirjath Jearim
had descendants: Haroeh, *and* half of the **families
of* Manuhoth.
53 The families of Kirjath Jearim *were* the
Ithrites, the Puthites, the Shumathites, and the
Mishraites. From these came the Zorathites and
the Eshtaolites.
54 The sons of Salma *were* Bethlehem, the
Netophathites, Atroth Beth Joab, half of the
Manahethites, and the Zorites.
55 And the families of the scribes who dwelt
at Jabez *were* the Tirathites, the Shimeathites, *and*
the Suchathites. These *were* the [a]Kenites who
came from Hammath, the father of the house of
[b]Rechab.

The Family of David
(Matt. 1:6)

3 Now these were the sons of David who were
born to him in Hebron: The firstborn *was*
[a]Amnon, by [b]Ahinoam the [c]Jezreelitess; the second, *Daniel, by [d]Abigail the Carmelitess;
2 the third, [a]Absalom the son of Maacah,
the daughter of Talmai, king of Geshur; the
fourth, [b]Adonijah the son of Haggith;
3 the fifth, Shephatiah, by Abital; the sixth,
Ithream, by his wife [a]Eglah.
4 *These* six were born to him in Hebron.
[a]There he reigned seven years and six months,
and [b]in Jerusalem he reigned thirty-three years.
5 [a]And these were born to him in Jerusalem: *Shimea, Shobab, Nathan, and [b]Solomon—
four by *Bathshua the daughter of *Ammiel.
6 Also *there* were Ibhar, *Elishama, *Eliphelet,
7 Nogah, Nepheg, Japhia,
8 Elishama, *Eliada, and Eliphelet—[a]nine *in
all.*
9 *These were* all the sons of David, besides

---

36 [a]1 Chr. 11:41
37 [a]2 Chr. 23:1
49 [a]Josh. 15:17
50 [a]1 Chr. 4:4 [b]Josh. 9:17; 18:14
55 [a]Judg. 1:16 [b]2 Kin. 10:15; Jer. 35:2

CHAPTER 3
1 [a]2 Sam. 3:2–5 [b]1 Sam. 25:43 [c]Josh. 15:56 [d]1 Sam. 25:39–42
2 [a]2 Sam. 13:37; 15:1 [b]1 Kin. 1:5
3 [a]2 Sam. 3:5
4 [a]2 Sam. 2:11 [b]2 Sam. 5:5
5 [a]1 Chr. 14:4–7 [b]2 Sam. 12:24, 25
8 [a]2 Sam. 5:14–16

*

2:52 Or *Manuhothites,* same as *Manahethites,* v. 54
3:1 *Chileab,* 2 Sam. 3:3
3:5 *Shammua,* 14:4; 2 Sam. 5:14 • *Bathsheba,* 2 Sam. 11:3 • *Eliam,* 2 Sam. 11:3
3:6 *Elishua,* 14:5; 2 Sam. 5:15 • *Elpelet,* 14:5
3:8 *Beeliada,* 14:7

KJV

the sons of the concubines, and [a]Tamar their sister.

The Family of Solomon
(Matt. 1:7–11)

10 And Solomon's son *was* [a]Rehoboam, Abia
his son, Asa his son, Jehoshaphat his son,
11 Joram his son, Ahaziah his son, Joash his
son,
12 Amaziah his son, Azariah his son, Jotham
his son,
13 Ahaz his son, Hezekiah his son, Manasseh
his son,
14 Amon his son, Josiah his son.
15 And the sons of Josiah *were,* the firstborn
Johanan, the second Jehoiakim, the third Zedekiah, the fourth Shallum.
16 And the sons of [a]Jehoiakim: Jeconiah his
son, Zedekiah his son.

The Family of Jeconiah

17 And the sons of Jeconiah; Assir, Salathiel
[a]his son,
18 Malchiram also, and Pedaiah, and Shena-
zar, Jecamiah, Hoshama, and Nedabiah.
19 And the sons of Pedaiah *were,* Zerubbabel, and Shimei: and the sons of Zerubbabel;
Meshullam, and Hananiah, and Shelomith their
sister:
20 And Hashubah, and Ohel, and Berechiah,
and Hasadiah, Jushab–hesed, five.
21 And the sons of Hananiah; Pelatiah, and
Jesaiah: the sons of Rephaiah, the sons of Arnan,
the sons of Obadiah, the sons of Shechaniah.
22 And the sons of Shechaniah; Shemaiah:
and the sons of Shemaiah; [a]Hattush, and Igeal,
and Bariah, and Neariah, and Shaphat, six.
23 And the sons of Neariah; Elioenai, and
Hezekiah, and Azrikam, three.
24 And the sons of Elioenai *were,* Hodaiah,
and Eliashib, and Pelaiah, and Akkub, and Johanan, and Dalaiah, and Anani, seven.

The Family of Judah

4 The sons of Judah; [a]Pharez, Hezron, and Carmi, and Hur, and Shobal.
2 And Reaiah the son of Shobal begat Jahath; and Jahath begat Ahumai, and Lahad. These
are the families of the Zorathites.
3 And these *were of* the father of Etam;
Jezreel, and Ishma, and Idbash: and the name of
their sister *was* Hazelelponi:
4 And Penuel the father of Gedor, and Ezer
the father of Hushah. These *are* the sons of [a]Hur,
the firstborn of Ephratah, the father of Beth–
lehem.
5 And [a]Ashur the father of Tekoa had two
wives, Helah and Naarah.
6 And Naarah bare him Ahuzam, and Hepher, and Temeni, and Haahashtari. These *were*
the sons of Naarah.
7 And the sons of Helah *were,* Zereth, and
Jezoar, and Ethnan.
8 And Coz begat Anub, and Zobebah, and
the families of Aharhel the son of Harum.
9 And Jabez was [a]more honourable than his
brethren: and his mother called his name Jabez,
saying, Because I bare him with sorrow.
10 And Jabez called on the God of Israel, saying, Oh that thou wouldest bless me indeed, and
enlarge my coast, and that thine hand might be
with me, and that thou wouldest keep *me* from
evil, that it may not grieve me! And God granted
him that which he requested.
11 And Chelub the brother of [a]Shuah begat
Mehir, which *was* the father of Eshton.
12 And Eshton begat Beth–rapha, and Paseah, and Tehinnah the father of Ir–nahash. These
are the men of Rechah.
13 And the sons of Kenaz; [a]Othniel, and Seraiah: and the sons of Othniel; Hathath.
14 And Meonothai begat Ophrah: and Se-

9 [a]2 Sam. 13:1
10 [a]1 Kin. 11:43; Matt. 1:7–10
16 [a]Matt. 1:11
17 [a]Matt. 1:12
22 [a]Ezra 8:2

CHAPTER 4
1 [a]Gen. 38:29; 46:12
4 [a]Ex. 31:2; 1 Chr. 2:50
5 [a]1 Chr. 2:24
9 [a]Gen. 34:19
11 [a]Gen. 38:1–5
13 [a]Josh. 15:17; Judg. 3:9, 11

*
3:10 *Abijam,* 1 Kin. 15:1
3:11 *Jehoram,* 2 Kin. 1:17; 8:16 • *Jehoash,* 2 Kin. 12:1
3:12 *Uzziah,* Is. 6:1
3:15 *Jehoahaz,* 2 Kin. 23:31
3:16 *Mattaniah,* 2 Kin. 24:17
3:17 *Jehoiachin,* 2 Kin. 24:8, or *Coniah,* Jer. 22:24 • Or *the captive were Shealtiel*
4:9 Lit. *He Will Cause Pain*
4:13 LXX, Vg. add *and Meonothai*

NKJV

the sons of the concubines, and [a]Tamar their sister.

The Family of Solomon
(Matt. 1:7–11)

10 Solomon's son *was* [a]Rehoboam; *Abijah
was his son, Asa his son, Jehoshaphat his son,
11 *Joram his son, Ahaziah his son, *Joash
his son,
12 Amaziah his son, *Azariah his son, Jotham his son,
13 Ahaz his son, Hezekiah his son, Manasseh
his son,
14 Amon his son, *and* Josiah his son.
15 The sons of Josiah *were* Johanan the firstborn, the second Jehoiakim, the third Zedekiah,
and the fourth *Shallum.
16 The sons of [a]Jehoiakim *were* Jeconiah his
son *and* *Zedekiah his son.

The Family of Jeconiah

17 And the sons of *Jeconiah **were* Assir,
Shealtiel [a]his son,
18 *and* Malchiram, Pedaiah, Shenazzar,
Jecamiah, Hoshama, and Nedabiah.
19 The sons of Pedaiah *were* Zerubbabel and
Shimei. The sons of Zerubbabel *were* Meshullam,
Hananiah, Shelomith their sister,
20 and Hashubah, Ohel, Berechiah, Hasadiah, and Jushab-Hesed—five *in all.*
21 The sons of Hananiah *were* Pelatiah and
Jeshaiah, the sons of Rephaiah, the sons of Arnan,
the sons of Obadiah, and the sons of Shechaniah.
22 The son of Shechaniah was Shemaiah.
The sons of Shemaiah *were* [a]Hattush, Igal, Bariah, Neariah, and Shaphat—six *in all.*
23 The sons of Neariah *were* Elioenai, Hezekiah, and Azrikam—three *in all.*
24 The sons of Elioenai *were* Hodaviah,
Eliashib, Pelaiah, Akkub, Johanan, Delaiah, and
Anani—seven *in all.*

The Family of Judah

4 The sons of Judah *were* [a]Perez, Hezron,
Carmi, Hur, and Shobal.
2 And Reaiah the son of Shobal begot Jahath, and Jahath begot Ahumai and Lahad. These
were the families of the Zorathites.
3 These *were* the sons *of the father* of Etam:
Jezreel, Ishma, and Idbash; and the name of their
sister *was* Hazelelponi;
4 and Penuel *was* the father of Gedor, and
Ezer *was the* father of Hushah. These *were* the
sons of [a]Hur, the firstborn of Ephrathah the father
of Bethlehem.
5 And [a]Ashhur the father of Tekoa had two
wives, Helah and Naarah.
6 Naarah bore him Ahuzzam, Hepher, Temeni, and Haahashtari. These *were* the sons of
Naarah.
7 The sons of Helah *were* Zereth, Zohar,
and Ethnan;
8 and Koz begot Anub, Zobebah, and the
families of Aharhel the son of Harum.
9 Now Jabez was [a]more honorable than his
brothers, and his mother called his name *Jabez,
saying, "Because I bore *him* in pain."
10 And Jabez called on the God of Israel saying, "Oh, that You would bless me indeed, and
enlarge my territory, that Your hand would be
with me, and that You would keep *me* from evil,
that I may not cause pain!" So God granted him
what he requested.
11 Chelub the brother of [a]Shuhah begot Mehir, who *was* the father of Eshton.
12 And Eshton begot Beth-Rapha, Paseah,
and Tehinnah the father of Ir-Nahash. These *were*
the men of Rechah.
13 The sons of Kenaz *were* [a]Othniel and Seraiah. The sons of Othniel *were* *Hathath,
14 and Meonothai *who* begot Ophrah. Se-

KJV

raiah begat Joab, the father of [a]the valley of Charashim; for they were craftsmen.

15 And the sons of [a]Caleb the son of Jephunneh; Iru, Elah, and Naam: and the sons of Elah, even Kenaz.

16 And the sons of Jehaleleel; Ziph, and Ziphah, Tiria, and Asareel.

17 And the sons of Ezra *were*, Jether, and Mered, and Epher, and Jalon: and she bare Miriam, and Shammai, and Ishbah the father of Eshtemoa.

18 And his wife Jehudijah bare Jered the father of Gedor, and Heber the father of Socho, and Jekuthiel the father of Zanoah. And these *are* the sons of Bithiah the daughter of Pharaoh, which Mered took.

19 And the sons of *his* wife Hodiah the sister of Naham, the father of Keilah the Garmite, and Eshtemoa the [a]Maachathite.

20 And the sons of Shimon *were*, Amnon, and Rinnah, Ben–hanan, and Tilon. And the sons of Ishi *were*, Zoheth, and Ben–zoheth.

21 The sons of [a]Shelah [b]the son of Judah *were*, Er the father of Lecah, and Laadah the father of Mareshah, and the families of the house of them that wrought fine linen, of the house of Ashbea,

22 And Jokim, and the men of Chozeba, and Joash, and Saraph, who had the dominion in Moab, and Jashubi–lehem. And *these are* ancient things.

23 These *were* the potters, and those that dwelt among plants and hedges: there they dwelt with the king for his work.

The Family of Simeon
(*Gen. 46:10*)

24 The [a]sons of Simeon *were*, Nemuel, and Jamin, Jarib, Zerah, *and* Shaul:

25 Shallum his son, Mibsam his son, Mishma his son.

26 And the sons of Mishma; Hamuel his son, Zacchur his son, Shimei his son.

27 And Shimei had sixteen sons and six daughters; but his brethren had not many children, [a]neither did all their family multiply, like to the children of Judah.

28 And they dwelt at Beer–sheba, and Moladah, and Hazar–shual,

29 And at Bilhah, and at Ezem, and at Tolad,

30 And at Bethuel, and at Hormah, and at Ziklag,

31 And at Beth–marcaboth, and Hazar–susim, and at Beth–birei, and at Shaaraim. These *were* their cities unto the reign of David.

32 And their villages *were*, Etam, and Ain, Rimmon, and Tochen, and Ashan, five cities:

33 And all their villages that *were* round about the same cities, unto Baal. These *were* their habitations, and their genealogy.

34 And Meshobab, and Jamlech, and Joshah the son of Amaziah,

35 And Joel, and Jehu the son of Josibiah, the son of Seraiah, the son of Asiel,

36 And Elioenai, and Jaakobah, and Jeshohaiah, and Asaiah, and Adiel, and Jesimiel, and Benaiah,

37 And Ziza the son of Shiphi, the son of Allon, the son of Jedaiah, the son of Shimri, the son of Shemaiah;

38 These mentioned by *their* names *were* princes in their families: and the house of their fathers increased greatly.

39 And they went to the entrance of Gedor, *even* unto the east side of the valley, to seek pasture for their flocks.

40 And they found fat pasture and good, and the land *was* wide, and quiet, and peaceable; for *they* of Ham had dwelt there of old.

41 And these written by name came in the days of Hezekiah king of Judah, and [a]smote their tents, and the habitations that were found there,

14 [a]Neh. 11:35
15 [a]Josh. 14:6, 14; 15:13, 17; 1 Chr. 6:56
19 [a]2 Kin. 25:23
21 [a]Gen. 38:11, 14 [b]Gen. 38:1–5; 46:12
24 [a]Num. 26:12–14
27 [a]Num. 2:9
41 [a]2 Kin. 18:8

*———

4:14 Lit. *Valley of Craftsmen*
4:17 Lit. *she*
4:18 Or *His Judean wife*
4:23 Lit. *Plants* • Lit. *Hedges*
4:24 *Jachin*, Gen. 46:10; Num. 26:12 • *Zohar*, Gen. 46:10; Ex. 6:15
4:33 *Baalath Beer*, Josh. 19:8

NKJV

raiah begot Joab the father of [a]Ge Harashim,* for they were craftsmen.

15 The sons of [a]Caleb the son of Jephunneh *were* Iru, Elah, and Naam. The son of Elah *was* Kenaz.

16 The sons of Jehallelel *were* Ziph, Ziphah, Tiria, and Asarel.

17 The sons of Ezrah *were* Jether, Mered, Epher, and Jalon. And **Mered's wife bore* Miriam, Shammai, and Ishbah the father of Eshtemoa.

18 (*His wife Jehudijah bore Jered the father of Gedor, Heber the father of Sochoh, and Jekuthiel the father of Zanoah.) And these were the sons of Bithiah the daughter of Pharaoh, whom Mered took.

19 The sons of Hodiah's wife, the sister of Naham, *were* the fathers of Keilah the Garmite and of Eshtemoa the [a]Maachathite.

20 And the sons of Shimon *were* Amnon, Rinnah, Ben-Hanan, and Tilon. And the sons of Ishi *were* Zoheth and Ben-Zoheth.

21 The sons of [a]Shelah [b]the son of Judah *were* Er the father of Lecah, Laadah the father of Mareshah, and the families of the house of the linen workers of the house of Ashbea;

22 also Jokim, the men of Chozeba, and Joash; Saraph, who ruled in Moab, and Jashubi-Lehem. Now the records are ancient.

23 These *were* the potters and those who dwell at *Netaim and *Gederah; there they dwelt with the king for his work.

The Family of Simeon
(*Gen. 46:10*)

24 The [a]sons of Simeon *were* Nemuel, Jamin, *Jarib, *Zerah, *and* Shaul,

25 Shallum his son, Mibsam his son, and Mishma his son.

26 And the sons of Mishma *were* Hamuel his son, Zacchur his son, and Shimei his son.

27 Shimei had sixteen sons and six daughters; but his brothers did not have many children, [a]nor did any of their families multiply as much as the children of Judah.

28 They dwelt at Beersheba, Moladah, Hazar Shual,

29 Bilhah, Ezem, Tolad,

30 Bethuel, Hormah, Ziklag,

31 Beth Marcaboth, Hazar Susim, Beth Biri, and at Shaaraim. These *were* their cities until the reign of David.

32 And their villages *were* Etam, Ain, Rimmon, Tochen, and Ashan—five cities—

33 and all the villages that *were* around these cities as far as *Baal. These *were* their dwelling places, and they maintained their genealogy:

34 Meshobab, Jamlech, and Joshah the son of Amaziah;

35 Joel, and Jehu the son of Joshibiah, the son of Seraiah, the son of Asiel;

36 Elioenai, Jaakobah, Jeshohaiah, Asaiah, Adiel, Jesimiel, and Benaiah;

37 Ziza the son of Shiphi, the son of Allon, the son of Jedaiah, the son of Shimri, the son of Shemaiah—

38 these mentioned by name *were* leaders in their families, and their father's house increased greatly.

39 So they went to the entrance of Gedor, as far as the east side of the valley, to seek pasture for their flocks.

40 And they found rich, good pasture, and the land *was* broad, quiet, and peaceful; for some Hamites formerly lived there.

41 These recorded by name came in the days of Hezekiah king of Judah; and they [a]attacked their tents and the Meunites who were found

KJV

and [b]destroyed them utterly unto this day, and dwelt in their rooms: because *there was* pasture there for their flocks.

42 And *some* of them, *even* of the sons of Simeon, five hundred men, went to mount Seir, having for their captains Pelatiah, and Neariah, and Rephaiah, and Uzziel, the sons of Ishi.

43 And they smote [a]the rest of the Amalekites that were escaped, and dwelt there unto this day.

The Family of Reuben
(Gen. 46:8, 9)

5 Now the sons of Reuben the firstborn of Israel, (for [a]he *was* the firstborn; but, forasmuch as he [b]defiled his father's bed, [c]his birthright was given unto the sons of Joseph the son of Israel: and the genealogy is not to be reckoned after the birthright.

2 For [a]Judah prevailed above his brethren, and of him *came* the [b]chief ruler; but the birthright *was* Joseph's:)

3 The sons, *I say,* of [a]Reuben the firstborn of Israel *were,* Hanoch, and Pallu, Hezron, and Carmi.

4 The sons of Joel; Shemaiah his son, Gog his son, Shimei his son,

5 Micah his son, Reaia his son, Baal his son,

6 Beerah his son, whom Tilgath–pilneser king of Assyria [a]carried away *captive:* he *was* prince of the Reubenites.

7 And his brethren by their families, [a]when the genealogy of their generations was reckoned, *were* the chief, Jeiel, and Zechariah,

8 And Bela the son of Azaz, the son of Shema, the son of Joel, who dwelt in [a]Aroer, even unto Nebo and Baal–meon:

9 And eastward he inhabited unto the entering in of the wilderness from the river Euphrates: because their cattle were multiplied [a]in the land of Gilead.

10 And in the days of Saul they made war [a]with the Hagarites, who fell by their hand: and they dwelt in their tents throughout all the east *land* of Gilead.

The Family of Gad

11 And the [a]children of Gad dwelt over against them, in the land of [b]Bashan unto [c]Salchah:

12 Joel the chief, and Shapham the next, and Jaanai, and Shaphat in Bashan.

13 And their brethren of the house of their fathers *were,* Michael, and Meshullam, and Sheba, and Jorai, and Jachan, and Zia, and Heber, seven.

14 These *are* the children of Abihail the son of Huri, the son of Jaroah, the son of Gilead, the son of Michael, the son of Jeshishai, the son of Jahdo, the son of Buz;

15 Ahi the son of Abdiel, the son of Guni, chief of the house of their fathers.

16 And they dwelt in Gilead in Bashan, and in her towns, and in all the suburbs of [a]Sharon, upon their borders.

17 All these were reckoned by genealogies in the days of [a]Jotham king of Judah, and in the days of [b]Jeroboam king of Israel.

18 The sons of Reuben, and the Gadites, and half the tribe of Manasseh, of valiant men, men able to bear buckler and sword, and to shoot with bow, and skilful in war, *were* four and forty thousand seven hundred and threescore, that went out to the war.

19 And they made war with the Hagarites, with [a]Jetur, and Nephish, and Nodab.

20 And [a]they were helped against them, and the Hagarites were delivered into their hand, and all that *were* with them: for they [b]cried to God in the battle, and he was intreated of them; because they [c]put their trust in him.

21 And they took away their cattle; of their

41 [b]2 Kin. 19:11
43 [a]Ex. 17:14; 1 Sam. 15:8; 30:17

CHAPTER 5

1 [a]Gen. 29:32; 49:3 [b]Gen. 35:22; 49:4 [c]Gen. 48:15, 22
2 [a]Gen. 49:8, 10; Ps. 60:7; 108:8 [b]Mic. 5:2; Matt. 2:6
3 [a]Gen. 46:9; Ex. 6:14; Num. 26:5
6 [a]2 Kin. 18:11
7 [a]1 Chr. 5:17
8 [a]Num. 32:34; Josh. 12:2; 13:15, 16
9 [a]Josh. 22:8, 9
10 [a]Gen. 25:12
11 [a]Num. 26:15–18 [b]Josh. 13:11, 24–28 [c]Deut. 3:10
16 [a]1 Chr. 27:29; Song 2:1; Is. 35:2; 65:10
17 [a]2 Kin. 15:5, 32 [b]2 Kin. 14:16, 28
19 [a]Gen. 25:15; 1 Chr. 1:31
20 [a][1 Chr. 5:22] [b]2 Chr. 14:11–13 [c]Ps. 9:10; 20:7, 8; 22:4, 5

NKJV

there, and [b]utterly destroyed them, as it is to this day. So they dwelt in their place, because *there was* pasture for their flocks there.

42 Now *some* of them, five hundred men of the sons of Simeon, went to Mount Seir, having as their captains Pelatiah, Neariah, Rephaiah, and Uzziel, the sons of Ishi.

43 And they defeated [a]the rest of the Amalekites who had escaped. They have dwelt there to this day.

The Family of Reuben
(Gen. 46:8, 9)

5 Now the sons of Reuben the firstborn of Israel—[a]he *was* indeed the firstborn, but because he [b]defiled his father's bed, [c]his birthright was given to the sons of Joseph, the son of Israel, so that the genealogy is not listed according to the birthright;

2 yet [a]Judah prevailed over his brothers, and from him *came* a [b]ruler, although the birthright was Joseph's—

3 the sons of [a]Reuben the firstborn of Israel were Hanoch, Pallu, Hezron, and Carmi.

4 The sons of Joel *were* Shemaiah his son, Gog his son, Shimei his son,

5 Micah his son, Reaiah his son, Baal his son,

6 and Beerah his son, whom *Tiglath-Pileser king of Assyria [a]carried into captivity. He *was* leader of the Reubenites.

7 And his brethren by their families, [a]when the genealogy of their generations was registered: the chief, Jeiel, and Zechariah,

8 and Bela the son of Azaz, the son of Shema, the son of Joel, who dwelt in [a]Aroer, as far as Nebo and Baal Meon.

9 Eastward they settled as far as the entrance of the wilderness this side of the River Euphrates, because their cattle had multiplied [a]in the land of Gilead.

10 Now in the days of Saul they made war [a]with the Hagrites, who fell by their hand; and they dwelt in their tents throughout the entire *area* east of Gilead.

The Family of Gad

11 And the [a]children of Gad dwelt next to them in the land of [b]Bashan as far as [c]Salcah:

12 Joel *was* the chief, Shapham the next, then Jaanai and Shaphat in Bashan,

13 and their brethren of their father's house: Michael, Meshullam, Sheba, Jorai, Jachan, Zia, and Eber—seven *in all.*

14 These *were* the children of Abihail the son of Huri, the son of Jaroah, the son of Gilead, the son of Michael, the son of Jeshishai, the son of Jahdo, the son of Buz;

15 Ahi the son of Abdiel, the son of Guni, *was* chief of their father's house.

16 And *the Gadites* dwelt in Gilead, in Bashan and in its villages, and in all the common-lands of [a]Sharon within their borders.

17 All these were registered by genealogies in the days of [a]Jotham king of Judah, and in the days of [b]Jeroboam king of Israel.

18 The sons of Reuben, the Gadites, and half the tribe of Manasseh *had* forty-four thousand seven hundred and sixty valiant men, men able to bear shield and sword, to shoot with the bow, and skillful in war, who went to war.

19 They made war with the Hagrites, [a]Jetur, Naphish, and Nodab.

20 And [a]they were helped against them, and the Hagrites were delivered into their hand, and all who *were* with them, for they [b]cried out to God in the battle. He heeded their prayer, because they [c]put their trust in Him.

21 Then they took away their livestock—fifty

*

5:6 Heb. *Tilgath-Pilneser*

KJV

camels fifty thousand, and of sheep two hundred and fifty thousand, and of asses two thousand, and of men an hundred thousand.

22 For there fell down many slain, because the war [a]*was* of God. And they dwelt in their steads until [b]the captivity.

The Family of Manasseh (East)

23 And the children of the half tribe of Manasseh dwelt in the land: they increased from Bashan unto Baal–hermon and [a]Senir, and unto mount Hermon.

24 And these *were* the heads of the house of their fathers, even Epher, and Ishi, and Eliel, and Azriel, and Jeremiah, and Hodaviah, and Jahdiel, mighty men of valour, famous men, *and* heads of the house of their fathers.

25 And they transgressed against the God of their fathers, and went a [a]whoring after the gods of the people of the land, whom God destroyed before them.

26 And the God of Israel stirred up the spirit of [a]Pul king of Assyria, and the spirit of [b]Tilgath–pilneser king of Assyria, and he carried them away, even the Reubenites, and the Gadites, and the half tribe of Manasseh, and brought them unto [c]Halah, and Habor, and Hara, and to the river Gozan, unto this day.

The Family of Levi
(Gen. 46:11)

6 The sons of Levi; [a]Gershon, Kohath, and Merari.

2 And the sons of Kohath; Amram, [a]Izhar, and Hebron, and Uzziel.

3 And the children of Amram; Aaron, and Moses, and Miriam. The sons also of Aaron; [a]Nadab, and Abihu, Eleazar, and Ithamar.

4 Eleazar begat Phinehas, Phinehas begat Abishua,

5 And Abishua begat Bukki, and Bukki begat Uzzi,

6 And Uzzi begat Zerahiah, and Zerahiah begat Meraioth,

7 Meraioth begat Amariah, and Amariah begat Ahitub,

8 And [a]Ahitub begat [b]Zadok, and Zadok begat Ahimaaz,

9 And Ahimaaz begat Azariah, and Azariah begat Johanan,

10 And Johanan begat Azariah, (he *it is* [a]that executed the priest's office in the [b]temple that Solomon built in Jerusalem:)

11 And [a]Azariah begat [b]Amariah, and Amariah begat Ahitub,

12 And Ahitub begat Zadok, and Zadok begat Shallum,

13 And Shallum begat Hilkiah, and Hilkiah begat Azariah,

14 And Azariah begat [a]Seraiah, and Seraiah begat Jehozadak,

15 And Jehozadak went *into captivity,* [a]when the LORD carried away Judah and Jerusalem by the hand of Nebuchadnezzar.

16 The sons of Levi; [a]Gershom, Kohath, and Merari.

17 And these *be* the names of the sons of Gershom; Libni, and Shimei.

18 And the sons of Kohath *were,* Amram, and Izhar, and Hebron, and Uzziel.

19 The sons of Merari; Mahli, and Mushi. And these *are* the families of the Levites according to their fathers.

20 Of Gershom; Libni his son, Jahath his son, [a]Zimmah his son,

21 Joah his son, Iddo his son, Zerah his son, Jeaterai his son.

22 The sons of Kohath; Amminadab his son, [a]Korah his son, Assir his son,

23 Elkanah his son, and Ebiasaph his son, and Assir his son,

22 [a][Josh. 23:10; 2 Chr. 32:8; Rom. 8:31] [b]2 Kin. 15:29; 17:6
23 [a]Deut. 3:9
25 [a]2 Kin. 17:7
26 [a]2 Kin. 15:19 [b]2 Kin. 15:29 [c]2 Kin. 17:6; 18:11

CHAPTER 6

1 [a]Gen. 46:11; Ex. 6:16; Num. 26:57; 1 Chr. 23:6
2 [a]1 Chr. 6:18, 22
3 [a]Lev. 10:1, 2
8 [a]2 Sam. 8:17 [b]2 Sam. 15:27
10 [a]2 Chr. 26:17, 18 [b]1 Kin. 6:1; 2 Chr. 3:1
11 [a]Ezra 7:3 [b]2 Chr. 19:11
14 [a]2 Kin. 25:18–21; Neh. 11:11
15 [a]2 Kin. 25:21
16 [a]Gen. 46:11; Ex. 6:16
20 [a]1 Chr. 6:42
22 [a]Num. 16:1

NKJV

thousand of their camels, two hundred and fifty thousand of their sheep, and two thousand of their donkeys—also one hundred thousand of their men;

22 for many fell dead, because the war [a]*was* God's. And they dwelt in their place until [b]the captivity.

The Family of Manasseh (East)

23 So the children of the half-tribe of Manasseh dwelt in the land. Their *numbers* increased from Bashan to Baal Hermon, that is, to [a]Senir, or Mount Hermon.

24 These *were* the heads of their fathers' houses: Epher, Ishi, Eliel, Azriel, Jeremiah, Hodaviah, and Jahdiel. They were mighty men of valor, famous men, *and* heads of their fathers' houses.

25 And they were unfaithful to the God of their fathers, and [a]played the harlot after the gods of the peoples of the land, whom God had destroyed before them.

26 So the God of Israel stirred up the spirit of [a]Pul king of Assyria, that is, [b]Tiglath-Pileser* king of Assyria. He carried the Reubenites, the Gadites, and the half-tribe of Manasseh into captivity. He took them to [c]Halah, Habor, Hara, and the river of Gozan to this day.

The Family of Levi
(Gen. 46:11)

6 The sons of Levi *were* [a]Gershon, Kohath, and Merari.

2 The sons of Kohath *were* Amram, [a]Izhar, Hebron, and Uzziel.

3 The children of Amram *were* Aaron, Moses, and Miriam. And the sons of Aaron *were* [a]Nadab, Abihu, Eleazar, and Ithamar.

4 Eleazar begot Phinehas, *and* Phinehas begot Abishua;

5 Abishua begot Bukki, and Bukki begot Uzzi;

6 Uzzi begot Zerahiah, and Zerahiah begot Meraioth;

7 Meraioth begot Amariah, and Amariah begot Ahitub;

8 [a]Ahitub begot [b]Zadok, and Zadok begot Ahimaaz;

9 Ahimaaz begot Azariah, and Azariah begot Johanan;

10 Johanan begot Azariah (it was he [a]who ministered as priest in the [b]temple that Solomon built in Jerusalem);

11 [a]Azariah begot [b]Amariah, and Amariah begot Ahitub;

12 Ahitub begot Zadok, and Zadok begot Shallum;

13 Shallum begot Hilkiah, and Hilkiah begot Azariah;

14 Azariah begot [a]Seraiah, and Seraiah begot Jehozadak.

15 Jehozadak went *into captivity* [a]when the LORD carried Judah and Jerusalem into captivity by the hand of Nebuchadnezzar.

16 The sons of Levi *were* [a]Gershon,* Kohath, and Merari.

17 These are the names of the sons of Gershon: Libni and Shimei.

18 The sons of Kohath *were* Amram, Izhar, Hebron, and Uzziel.

19 The sons of Merari *were* Mahli and Mushi. Now these *are* the families of the Levites according to their fathers:

20 Of Gershon *were* Libni his son, Jahath his son, [a]Zimmah his son,

21 Joah his son, Iddo his son, Zerah his son, *and* Jeatherai his son.

22 The sons of Kohath *were* Amminadab his son, [a]Korah his son, Assir his son,

23 Elkanah his son, Ebiasaph his son, Assir his son,

*

5:26 Heb. *Tilgath-Pilneser*
6:16 Heb. *Gershom,* an alternate spelling for *Gershon,* vv. 1, 17, 20, 43, 62, 71

KJV

24 Tahath his son, Uriel his son, Uzziah his son, and Shaul his son.
25 And the sons of Elkanah; [a]Amasai, and Ahimoth.
26 *As for* Elkanah: the sons of Elkanah; Zophai his son, and Nahath his son,
27 Eliab his son, Jeroham his son, Elkanah his son.
28 And the sons of Samuel; the firstborn Vashni, and Abiah.
29 The sons of Merari; Mahli, Libni his son, Shimei his son, Uzza his son,
30 Shimea his son, Haggiah his son, Asaiah his son.

Musicians in the House of the LORD

31 And these *are* [a]*they* whom David set over the service of song in the house of the LORD, after that the [b]ark had rest.
32 And they ministered before the dwelling place of the tabernacle of the congregation with singing, until Solomon had built the house of the LORD in Jerusalem: and *then* they waited on their office according to their order.
33 And these *are* they that waited with their children. Of the sons of the [a]Kohathites: Heman a singer, the son of Joel, the son of Shemuel,
34 The son of Elkanah, the son of Jeroham, the son of Eliel, the son of Toah,
35 The son of Zuph, the son of Elkanah, the son of Mahath, the son of Amasai,
36 The son of Elkanah, the son of Joel, the son of Azariah, the son of Zephaniah,
37 The son of Tahath, the son of Assir, the son of [a]Ebiasaph, the son of Korah,
38 The son of Izhar, the son of Kohath, the son of Levi, the son of Israel.
39 And his brother [a]Asaph, who stood on his right hand, *even* Asaph the son of Berachiah, the son of Shimea,
40 The son of Michael, the son of Baaseiah, the son of Malchiah,
41 The son of [a]Ethni, the son of Zerah, the son of Adaiah,
42 The son of Ethan, the son of Zimmah, the son of Shimei,
43 The son of Jahath, the son of Gershom, the son of Levi.
44 And their brethren the sons of Merari *stood* on the left hand: Ethan the son of Kishi, the son of Abdi, the son of Malluch,
45 The son of Hashabiah, the son of Amaziah, the son of Hilkiah,
46 The son of Amzi, the son of Bani, the son of Shamer,
47 The son of Mahli, the son of Mushi, the son of Merari, the son of Levi.
48 Their brethren also the Levites *were* appointed unto all [a]manner of service of the tabernacle of the house of God.

The Family of Aaron

49 [a]But Aaron and his sons offered [b]upon the altar of the burnt offering, and [c]on the altar of incense, *and were appointed* for all the work of the *place* most holy, and to make an atonement for Israel, according to all that Moses the servant of God had commanded.
50 And these *are* the [a]sons of Aaron; Eleazar his son, Phinehas his son, Abishua his son,
51 Bukki his son, Uzzi his son, Zerahiah his son,
52 Meraioth his son, Amariah his son, Ahitub his son,
53 Zadok his son, Ahimaaz his son.

Dwelling Places of the Levites (*Josh. 21:1–42*)

54 [a]Now these *are* their dwelling places throughout their castles in their coasts, of the sons

25 [a]1 Chr. 6:35, 36
31 [a]1 Chr. 15:16–22, 27; 16:4–6 [b]2 Sam. 6:17; 1 Kin. 8:4; 1 Chr. 15:25—16:1
33 [a]Num. 26:57
37 [a]Ex. 6:24
39 [a]2 Chr. 5:12
41 [a]1 Chr. 6:21
48 [a]1 Chr. 9:14–34
49 [a]Ex. 28:1; [Num. 18:1–8] [b]Lev. 1:8, 9 [c]Ex. 30:7
50 [a]1 Chr. 6:4–8; Ezra 7:5
54 [a]Josh. 21

NKJV

24 Tahath his son, Uriel his son, Uzziah his son, and Shaul his son.
25 The sons of Elkanah *were* [a]Amasai and Ahimoth.
26 *As for* Elkanah, the sons of Elkanah *were* *Zophai his son, *Nahath his son,
27 *Eliab his son, Jeroham his son, *and* Elkanah his son.
28 The sons of Samuel *were* **Joel* the firstborn, and Abijah *the second.
29 The sons of Merari *were* Mahli, Libni his son, Shimei his son, Uzzah his son,
30 Shimea his son, Haggiah his son, *and* Asaiah his son.

Musicians in the House of the LORD

31 Now these are [a]the men whom David appointed over the service of song in the house of the LORD, after the [b]ark came to rest.
32 They were ministering with music before the dwelling place of the tabernacle of meeting, until Solomon had built the house of the LORD in Jerusalem, and they served in their office according to their order.
33 And these *are* the ones who ministered with their sons: Of the sons of the [a]Kohathites *were* Heman the singer, the son of Joel, the son of Samuel,
34 the son of Elkanah, the son of Jeroham, the son of *Eliel, the son of *Toah,
35 the son of Zuph, the son of Elkanah, the son of Mahath, the son of Amasai,
36 the son of Elkanah, the son of Joel, the son of Azariah, the son of Zephaniah,
37 the son of Tahath, the son of Assir, the son of [a]Ebiasaph, the son of Korah,
38 the son of Izhar, the son of Kohath, the son of Levi, the son of Israel.
39 And his brother [a]Asaph, who stood at his right hand, *was* Asaph the son of Berachiah, the son of Shimea,
40 the son of Michael, the son of Baaseiah, the son of Malchijah,
41 the son of [a]Ethni, the son of Zerah, the son of Adaiah,
42 the son of Ethan, the son of Zimmah, the son of Shimei,
43 the son of Jahath, the son of Gershon, the son of Levi.
44 Their brethren, the sons of Merari, on the left hand, *were* Ethan the son of Kishi, the son of Abdi, the son of Malluch,
45 the son of Hashabiah, the son of Amaziah, the son of Hilkiah,
46 the son of Amzi, the son of Bani, the son of Shamer,
47 the son of Mahli, the son of Mushi, the son of Merari, the son of Levi.
48 And their brethren, the Levites, *were* appointed to every [a]kind of service of the tabernacle of the house of God.

The Family of Aaron

49 [a]But Aaron and his sons offered sacrifices [b]on the altar of burnt offering and [c]on the altar of incense, for all the work of the Most Holy *Place*, and to make atonement for Israel, according to all that Moses the servant of God had commanded.
50 Now these *are* the [a]sons of Aaron: Eleazar his son, Phinehas his son, Abishua his son,
51 Bukki his son, Uzzi his son, Zerahiah his son,
52 Meraioth his son, Amariah his son, Ahitub his son,
53 Zadok his son, *and* Ahimaaz his son.

Dwelling Places of the Levites (*Josh. 21:1–42*)

54 [a]Now these *are* their dwelling places throughout their settlements in their territory, for

*______

6:26 *Zuph*, v. 35; 1 Sam. 1:1 • *Toah*, v. 34
6:27 *Eliel*, v. 34
6:28 So with LXX, Syr., Arab.; cf. v. 33 and 1 Sam. 8:2 • Heb. *Vasheni*
6:34 *Elihu*, 1 Sam. 1:1 • *Tohu*, 1 Sam. 1:1

KJV

of Aaron, of the families of the Kohathites: for their's was the lot.

55 [a]And they gave them Hebron in the land of Judah, and the suburbs thereof round about it.

56 [a]But the fields of the city, and the villages thereof, they gave to Caleb the son of Jephunneh.

57 And [a]to the sons of Aaron they gave the cities of Judah, *namely,* Hebron, *the city* of refuge, and Libnah with her suburbs, and Jattir, and Eshtemoa, with their suburbs,

58 And Hilen with her suburbs, Debir with her suburbs,

59 And Ashan with her suburbs, and Beth–shemesh with her suburbs:

60 And out of the tribe of Benjamin; Geba with her suburbs, and Alemeth with her suburbs, and Anathoth with her suburbs. All their cities throughout their families *were* thirteen cities.

61 And unto the sons of Kohath, [a]*which were* left of the family of that tribe, *were cities given* out of the half tribe, *namely, out of* the half *tribe* of Manasseh, [b]by lot, ten cities.

62 And to the sons of Gershom throughout their families out of the tribe of Issachar, and out of the tribe of Asher, and out of the tribe of Naphtali, and out of the tribe of Manasseh in Bashan, thirteen cities.

63 Unto the sons of Merari *were given* by lot, throughout their families, out of the tribe of Reuben, and out of the tribe of Gad, and out of the tribe of Zebulun, [a]twelve cities.

64 And the children of Israel gave to the Levites *these* cities with their suburbs.

65 And they gave by lot out of the tribe of the children of Judah, and out of the tribe of the children of Simeon, and out of the tribe of the children of Benjamin, these cities, which are called by *their* names.

66 And [a]*the residue* of the families of the sons of Kohath had cities of their coasts out of the tribe of Ephraim.

67 [a]And they gave unto them, *of* the cities of refuge, Shechem in mount Ephraim with her suburbs; *they gave* also Gezer with her suburbs,

68 And [a]Jokmeam with her suburbs, and Beth–horon with her suburbs,

69 And Aijalon with her suburbs, and Gath–rimmon with her suburbs:

70 And out of the half tribe of Manasseh; Aner with her suburbs, and Bileam with her suburbs, for the family of the remnant of the sons of Kohath.

71 Unto the sons of Gershom *were given* out of the family of the half tribe of Manasseh, Golan in Bashan with her suburbs, and Ashtaroth with her suburbs:

72 And out of the tribe of Issachar; Kedesh with her suburbs, Daberath with her suburbs,

73 And Ramoth with her suburbs, and Anem with her suburbs:

74 And out of the tribe of Asher; Mashal with her suburbs, and Abdon with her suburbs,

75 And Hukok with her suburbs, and Rehob with her suburbs:

76 And out of the tribe of Naphtali; Kedesh in Galilee with her suburbs, and Hammon with her suburbs, and Kirjathaim with her suburbs.

77 Unto the rest of the children of Merari *were given* out of the tribe of Zebulun, Rimmon with her suburbs, Tabor with her suburbs:

78 And on the other side Jordan by Jericho, on the east side of Jordan, *were given them* out of the tribe of Reuben, Bezer in the wilderness with her suburbs, and Jahzah with her suburbs,

79 Kedemoth also with her suburbs, and Mephaath with her suburbs:

80 And out of the tribe of Gad; Ramoth in Gilead with her suburbs, and Mahanaim with her suburbs,

55 [a]Josh. 14:13; 21:11, 12
56 [a]Josh. 14:13; 15:13
57 [a]Josh. 21:13, 19
61 [a]1 Chr. 6:66–70 [b]Josh. 21:5
63 [a]Josh. 21:7, 34–40
66 [a]1 Chr. 6:61
67 [a]Josh. 21:21
68 [a]Josh. 21:22

NKJV

they were *given* by lot to the sons of Aaron, of the family of the Kohathites:

55 [a]They gave them Hebron in the land of Judah, with its surrounding common-lands.

56 [a]But the fields of the city and its villages they gave to Caleb the son of Jephunneh.

57 And [a]to the sons of Aaron they gave *one of* the cities of refuge, Hebron; also Libnah with its common-lands, Jattir, Eshtemoa with its common-lands,

58 *Hilen with its common-lands, Debir with its common-lands,

59 *Ashan with its common-lands, and Beth Shemesh with its common-lands.

60 And from the tribe of Benjamin: Geba with its common-lands, *Alemeth with its common-lands, and Anathoth with its common-lands. All their cities among their families *were* thirteen.

61 [a]To the rest of the family of the tribe of the Kohathites *they gave* [b]by lot ten cities from half the tribe of Manasseh.

62 And to the sons of Gershon, throughout their families, *they gave* thirteen cities from the tribe of Issachar, from the tribe of Asher, from the tribe of Naphtali, and from the tribe of Manasseh in Bashan.

63 To the sons of Merari, throughout their families, *they gave* [a]twelve cities from the tribe of Reuben, from the tribe of Gad, and from the tribe of Zebulun.

64 So the children of Israel gave *these* cities with their common-lands to the Levites.

65 And they gave by lot from the tribe of the children of Judah, from the tribe of the children of Simeon, and from the tribe of the children of Benjamin these cities which are called by *their* names.

66 Now [a]some of the families of the sons of Kohath *were given* cities as their territory from the tribe of Ephraim.

67 [a]And they gave them *one of* the cities of refuge, Shechem with its common-lands, in the mountains of Ephraim, also Gezer with its common-lands,

68 [a]Jokmeam with its common-lands, Beth Horon with its common-lands,

69 Aijalon with its common-lands, and Gath Rimmon with its common-lands.

70 And from the half-tribe of Manasseh: Aner with its common-lands and Bileam with its common-lands, for the rest of the family of the sons of Kohath.

71 From the family of the half-tribe of Manasseh the sons of Gershon *were given* Golan in Bashan with its common-lands and Ashtaroth with its common-lands.

72 And from the tribe of Issachar: Kedesh with its common-lands, Daberath with its common-lands,

73 Ramoth with its common-lands, and Anem with its common-lands.

74 And from the tribe of Asher: Mashal with its common-lands, Abdon with its common-lands,

75 Hukok with its common-lands, and Rehob with its common-lands.

76 And from the tribe of Naphtali: Kedesh in Galilee with its common-lands, Hammon with its common-lands, and Kirjathaim with its common-lands.

77 From the tribe of Zebulun the rest of the children of Merari *were given* *Rimmon with its common-lands and Tabor with its common-lands.

78 And on the other side of the Jordan, across from Jericho, on the east side of the Jordan, *they were given* from the tribe of Reuben: Bezer in the wilderness with its common-lands, Jahzah with its common-lands,

79 Kedemoth with its common-lands, and Mephaath with its common-lands.

80 And from the tribe of Gad: Ramoth in Gilead with its common-lands, Mahanaim with its common-lands,

*

6:58 *Holon,* Josh. 21:15
6:59 *Ain,* Josh. 21:16
6:60 *Almon,* Josh. 21:18
6:77 Heb. *Rimmono,* an alternate spelling of *Rimmon;* 1 Chr. 4:32

KJV

81 And Heshbon with her suburbs, and Jazer
with her suburbs.

The Family of Issachar
(Gen. 46:13)

7 Now the sons of Issachar *were*, [a]Tola, and
Puah, Jashub, and Shimrom, four.
2 And the sons of Tola; Uzzi, and Rephaiah,
and Jeriel, and Jahmai, and Jibsam, and Shemuel,
heads of their father's house, *to wit*, of Tola: *they*
were valiant men of might in their generations;
[a]whose number *was* in the days of David two and
twenty thousand and six hundred.
3 And the sons of Uzzi; Izrahiah: and the
sons of Izrahiah; Michael, and Obadiah, and Joel,
Ishiah, five: all of them chief men.
4 And with them, by their generations, after
the house of their fathers, *were* bands of soldiers
for war, six and thirty thousand *men*: for they
had many wives and sons.
5 And their brethren among all the families
of Issachar *were* valiant men of might, reckoned
in all by their genealogies fourscore and seven
thousand.

The Family of Benjamin
(Gen. 46:21)

6 *The sons* of [a]Benjamin; Bela, and Becher,
and Jediael, three.
7 And the sons of Bela; Ezbon, and Uzzi,
and Uzziel, and Jerimoth, and Iri, five; heads of
the house of *their* fathers, mighty men of valour;
and were reckoned by their genealogies twenty
and two thousand and thirty and four.
8 And the sons of Becher; Zemira, and
Joash, and Eliezer, and Elioenai, and Omri, and
Jerimoth, and Abiah, and Anathoth, and Alameth.
All these *are* the sons of Becher.
9 And the number of them, after their genealogy by their generations, heads of the house
of their fathers, mighty men of valour, *was* twenty
thousand and two hundred.
10 The sons also of Jediael; Bilhan: and the
sons of Bilhan; Jeush, and Benjamin, and Ehud,
and Chenaanah, and Zethan, and Tharshish, and
Ahishahar.
11 All these the sons of Jediael, by the heads of
their fathers, mighty men of valour, *were* seventeen thousand and two hundred *soldiers*, fit to go
out for war *and* battle.
12 Shuppim also, and Huppim, the children
of Ir, *and* Hushim, the sons of Aher.

The Family of Naphtali
(Gen. 46:24)

13 The [a]sons of Naphtali; Jahziel, and Guni,
and Jezer, and Shallum, the sons of Bilhah.

The Family of Manasseh (West)

14 The [a]sons of Manasseh; Ashriel, whom
she bare: (*but* his concubine the Aramitess bare
[b]Machir the father of Gilead:
15 And Machir took to wife *the sister* of Huppim and Shuppim, whose sister's name *was* Maachah;) and the name of the second *was* [a]Zelophe-
had: and Zelophehad had daughters.
16 And Maachah the wife of Machir bare a
son, and she called his name Peresh; and the
name of his brother *was* Sheresh; and his sons
were Ulam and Rakem.
17 And the sons of Ulam; [a]Bedan. These
were the sons of Gilead, the son of Machir, the
son of Manasseh.
18 And his sister Hammoleketh bare Ishod,
and Abiezer, and Mahalah.
19 And the sons of Shemidah were, Ahian,
and Shechem, and Likhi, and Aniam.

The Family of Ephraim

20 And [a]the sons of Ephraim; Shuthelah, and
Bered his son, and Tahath his son, and Eladah
his son, and Tahath his son,

CHAPTER 7
1 [a]Num. 26:23–25
2 [a]2 Sam. 24:1–9; 1 Chr. 27:1
6 [a]Gen. 46:21; Num. 26:38–41; 1 Chr. 8:1
13 [a]Num. 26:48–50
14 [a]Num. 26:29–34 [b]1 Chr. 2:21
15 [a]Num. 26:30–33; 27:1
17 [a]1 Sam. 12:11
20 [a]Num. 26:35–37

*———

7:1 *Puvah*, Gen. 46:13
7:12 *Hupham*, Num. 26:39
7:13 *Jahzeel*, Gen. 46:24 • *Shillem*, Gen. 46:24
7:15 *Hupham*, v. 12; Num. 26:39 • *Shupham*, v. 12; Num. 26:39 • Lit. *the second*

NKJV

81 Heshbon with its common-lands, and
Jazer with its common-lands.

The Family of Issachar
(Gen. 46:13)

7 The sons of Issachar *were* [a]Tola, *Puah, Jashub, and Shimron—four *in all*.
2 The sons of Tola *were* Uzzi, Rephaiah,
Jeriel, Jahmai, Jibsam, and Shemuel, heads of
their father's house. *The sons* of Tola *were* mighty
men of valor in their generations; [a]their number
in the days of David *was* twenty-two thousand
six hundred.
3 The son of Uzzi *was* Izrahiah, and the
sons of Izrahiah *were* Michael, Obadiah, Joel, and
Ishiah. All five of them *were* chief men.
4 And with them, by their generations, according to their fathers' houses, *were* thirty-six
thousand troops ready for war; for they had many
wives and sons.
5 Now their brethren among all the families
of Issachar *were* mighty men of valor, listed by
their genealogies, eighty-seven thousand in all.

The Family of Benjamin
(Gen. 46:21)

6 *The sons* of [a]Benjamin *were* Bela, Becher,
and Jediael—three *in all*.
7 The sons of Bela were Ezbon, Uzzi, Uzziel,
Jerimoth, and Iri—five *in all*. They *were* heads of
their fathers' houses, and they were listed by their
genealogies, twenty-two thousand and thirty-four
mighty men of valor.
8 The sons of Becher *were* Zemirah, Joash,
Eliezer, Elioenai, Omri, Jerimoth, Abijah, Anathoth, and Alemeth. All these *are* the sons of
Becher.
9 And they were recorded by genealogy according to their generations, heads of their fathers' houses, twenty thousand two hundred
mighty men of valor.
10 The son of Jediael *was* Bilhan, and the
sons of Bilhan *were* Jeush, Benjamin, Ehud, Chenaanah, Zethan, Tharshish, and Ahishahar.
11 All these sons of Jediael *were* heads of
their fathers' houses; *there were* seventeen thousand two hundred mighty men of valor fit to go
out for war *and* battle.
12 Shuppim and *Huppim *were* the sons of
Ir, *and* Hushim *was* the son of Aher.

The Family of Naphtali
(Gen. 46:24)

13 The [a]sons of Naphtali *were* *Jahziel, Guni,
Jezer, and *Shallum, the sons of Bilhah.

The Family of Manasseh (West)

14 The [a]descendants of Manasseh: his Syrian
concubine bore him [b]Machir the father of Gilead,
the father of Asriel.
15 Machir took as his wife *the sister* of *Huppim and *Shuppim, whose name *was* Maachah.
The name of *Gilead's* *grandson *was* [a]Zelophe-
had, but Zelophehad begot only daughters.
16 (Maachah the wife of Machir bore a son,
and she called his name Peresh. The name of his
brother *was* Sheresh, and his sons *were* Ulam and
Rakem.
17 The son of Ulam *was* [a]Bedan.) These *were*
the descendants of Gilead the son of Machir, the
son of Manasseh.
18 His sister Hammoleketh bore Ishhod,
Abiezer, and Mahlah.
19 And the sons of Shemida were Ahian,
Shechem, Likhi, and Aniam.

The Family of Ephraim

20 [a]The sons of Ephraim *were* Shuthelah,
Bered his son, Tahath his son, Eladah his son,
Tahath his son,

KJV

21 And Zabad his son, and Shuthelah his son, and Ezer, and Elead, whom the men of Gath *that were* born in *that* land slew, because they came down to take away their cattle.

22 And Ephraim their father mourned many days, and his brethren came to comfort him.

23 And when he went in to his wife, she conceived, and bare a son, and he called his name Beriah, because it went evil with his house.

24 (And his daughter *was* Sherah, who built [a]Beth–horon the nether, and the upper, and Uzzen–sherah.)

25 And Rephah *was* his son, also Resheph, and Telah his son, and Tahan his son,

26 Laadan his son, Ammihud his son, [a]Elishama his son,

27 Non his son, [a]Jehoshuah his son.

28 And their [a]possessions and habitations *were,* Beth–el and the towns thereof, and eastward Naaran, and westward Gezer, with the towns thereof; Shechem also and the towns thereof, unto Gaza and the towns thereof:

29 And by the borders of the children of [a]Manasseh, Beth–shean and her towns, Taanach and her towns, [b]Megiddo and her towns, Dor and her towns. In these dwelt the children of Joseph the son of Israel.

The Family of Asher
(*Gen. 46:17*)

30 [a]The sons of Asher; Imnah, and Isuah, and Ishuai, and Beriah, and Serah their sister.

31 And the sons of Beriah; Heber, and Malchiel, who *is* the father of Birzavith.

32 And Heber begat Japhlet, and Shomer, and Hotham, and Shua their sister.

33 And the sons of Japhlet; Pasach, and Bimhal, and Ashvath. These *are* the children of Japhlet.

34 And the sons of [a]Shamer; Ahi, and Rohgah, Jehubbah, and Aram.

35 And the sons of his brother Helem; Zophah, and Imna, and Shelesh, and Amal.

36 The sons of Zophah; Suah, and Harnepher, and Shual, and Beri, and Imrah,

37 Bezer, and Hod, and Shamma, and Shilshah, and Ithran, and Beera.

38 And the sons of Jether; Jephunneh, and Pispah, and Ara.

39 And the sons of Ulla; Arah, and Haniel, and Rezia.

40 All these *were* the children of Asher, heads of *their* father's house, choice *and* mighty men of valour, chief of the princes. And the number throughout the genealogy of them that were apt to the war *and* to battle *was* twenty and six thousand men.

The Family Tree of King Saul of Benjamin
(*Gen. 46:21*)

8 Now Benjamin begat [a]Bela his firstborn, Ashbel the second, and Aharah the third,

2 Nohah the fourth, and Rapha the fifth.

3 And the sons of Bela were, Addar, and Gera, and Abihud,

4 And Abishua, and Naaman, and Ahoah,

5 And Gera, and Shephuphan, and Huram.

6 And these *are* the sons of Ehud: these are the heads of the fathers of the inhabitants of [a]Geba, and they removed them to [b]Manahath:

7 And Naaman, and Ahiah, and Gera, he removed them, and begat Uzza, and Ahihud.

8 And Shaharaim begat *children* in the country of Moab, after he had sent them away; Hushim and Baara *were* his wives.

9 And he begat of Hodesh his wife, Jobab, and Zibia, and Mesha, and Malcham,

10 And Jeuz, and Shachia, and Mirma. These *were* his sons, heads of the fathers.

11 And of Hushim he begat Abitub, and Elpaal.

---

24 [a]Josh. 16:3, 5; 2 Chr. 8:5
26 [a]Num. 10:22
27 [a]Ex. 17:9, 14; 24:13; 33:11
28 [a]Josh. 16:1–10
29 [a]Gen. 41:51; Josh. 17:7 [b]Josh. 17:11
30 [a]Gen. 46:17; Num. 26:44–47
34 [a]1 Chr. 7:32

CHAPTER 8

1 [a]Gen. 46:21; Num. 26:38; 1 Chr. 7:6
6 [a]1 Chr. 6:60 [b]1 Chr. 2:52

*

7:23 Lit. *In Tragedy*
7:27 Heb. *Non*
7:28 Many Heb. mss., Bg., LXX, Tg., Vg. *Gazza*
7:31 Or *Birzavith* or *Birzoth*
7:32 *Shemer,* v. 34 • *Helem,* v. 35
7:37 *Jether,* v. 38
8:1 *Ahiram,* Num. 26:38
8:3 *Ard,* Num. 26:40

NKJV

21 Zabad his son, Shuthelah his son, and Ezer and Elead. The men of Gath who were born in *that* land killed *them* because they came down to take away their cattle.

22 Then Ephraim their father mourned many days, and his brethren came to comfort him.

23 And when he went in to his wife, she conceived and bore a son; and he called his name *Beriah, because tragedy had come upon his house.

24 Now his daughter *was* Sheerah, who built Lower and Upper [a]Beth Horon and Uzzen Sheerah;

25 and Rephah *was* his son, *as well* as Resheph, and Telah his son, Tahan his son,

26 Laadan his son, Ammihud his son, [a]Elishama his son,

27 *Nun his son, and [a]Joshua his son.

28 Now their [a]possessions and dwelling places *were* Bethel and its towns: to the east Naaran, to the west Gezer and its towns, and Shechem and its towns, as far as *Ayyah and its towns;

29 and by the borders of the children of [a]Manasseh *were* Beth Shean and its towns, Taanach and its towns, [b]Megiddo and its towns, Dor and its towns. In these dwelt the children of Joseph, the son of Israel.

The Family of Asher
(*Gen. 46:17*)

30 [a]The sons of Asher *were* Imnah, Ishvah, Ishvi, Beriah, and their sister Serah.

31 The sons of Beriah *were* Heber and Malchiel, who was the father of *Birzaith.

32 And Heber begot Japhlet, *Shomer, *Hotham, and their sister Shua.

33 The sons of Japhlet *were* Pasach, Bimhal, and Ashvath. These *were* the children of Japhlet.

34 The sons of [a]Shemer *were* Ahi, Rohgah, Jehubbah, and Aram.

35 And the sons of his brother Helem *were* Zophah, Imna, Shelesh, and Amal.

36 The sons of Zophah *were* Suah, Harnepher, Shual, Beri, Imrah,

37 Bezer, Hod, Shamma, Shilshah, *Jithran, and Beera.

38 The sons of Jether *were* Jephunneh, Pispah, and Ara.

39 The sons of Ulla *were* Arah, Haniel, and Rizia.

40 All these *were* the children of Asher, heads of *their* fathers' houses, choice men, mighty men of valor, chief leaders. And they were recorded by genealogies among the army fit for battle; their number *was* twenty-six thousand.

The Family Tree of King Saul of Benjamin
(*Gen. 46:21*)

8 Now Benjamin begot [a]Bela his firstborn, Ashbel the second, *Aharah the third,

2 Nohah the fourth, and Rapha the fifth.

3 The sons of Bela *were* *Addar, Gera, Abihud,

4 Abishua, Naaman, Ahoah,

5 Gera, Shephuphan, and Huram.

6 These *are* the sons of Ehud, who were the heads of the fathers' *houses* of the inhabitants of [a]Geba, and who forced them to move to [b]Manahath:

7 Naaman, Ahijah, and Gera who forced them to move. He begot Uzza and Ahihud.

8 Also Shaharaim had children in the country of Moab, after he had sent away Hushim and Baara his wives.

9 By Hodesh his wife he begot Jobab, Zibia, Mesha, Malcam,

10 Jeuz, Sachiah, and Mirmah. These *were* his sons, heads of their fathers' *houses.*

11 And by Hushim he begot Abitub and Elpaal.

KJV

12 The sons of Elpaal; Eber, and Misham,
and Shamed, who built Ono, and Lod, with the
towns thereof:
13 Beriah also, and [a]Shema, who *were* heads
of the fathers of the inhabitants of Aijalon, who
drove away the inhabitants of Gath:
14 And Ahio, Shashak, and Jeremoth,
15 And Zebadiah, and Arad, and Ader,
16 And Michael, and Ispah, and Joha, the
sons of Beriah;
17 And Zebadiah, and Meshullam, and Hez-
eki, and Heber,
18 Ishmerai also, and Jezliah, and Jobab, the
sons of Elpaal;
19 And Jakim, and Zichri, and Zabdi,
20 And Elienai, and Zilthai, and Eliel,
21 And Adaiah, and Beraiah, and Shimrath,
the sons of Shimhi;
22 And Ishpan, and Heber, and Eliel,
23 And Abdon, and Zichri, and Hanan,
24 And Hananiah, and Elam, and Antothijah,
25 And Iphedeiah, and Penuel, the sons of
Shashak;
26 And Shamsherai, and Shehariah, and
Athaliah,
27 And Jaresiah, and Eliah, and Zichri, the
sons of Jeroham.
28 These *were* heads of the fathers, by their
generations, chief *men*. These dwelt in Jerusalem.
29 And at Gibeon dwelt the father of Gibeon;
whose [a]wife's name *was* Maachah:
30 And his firstborn son Abdon, and Zur, and
Kish, and Baal, and Nadab,
31 And Gedor, and Ahio, and Zacher.
32 And Mikloth begat Shimeah. And these
also dwelt with their brethren in Jerusalem, over
against them.
33 And [a]Ner begat Kish, and Kish begat Saul,
and Saul begat Jonathan, and Malchi–shua, and
Abinadab, and Esh–baal.
34 And the son of Jonathan *was* Merib–baal;
and Merib–baal begat [a]Micah.
35 And the sons of Micah *were*, Pithon, and
Melech, and Tarea, and Ahaz.
36 And Ahaz begat Jehoadah; and Jehoadah
begat Alemeth, and Azmaveth, and Zimri; and
Zimri begat Moza,
37 And Moza begat Binea: Rapha *was* his
son, Eleasah his son, Azel his son:
38 And Azel had six sons, whose names *are*
these, Azrikam, Bocheru, and Ishmael, and Sheariah, and Obadiah, and Hanan. All these *were* the
sons of Azel.
39 And the sons of Eshek his brother *were*,
Ulam his firstborn, Jehush the second, and Eliphelet the third.
40 And the sons of Ulam were mighty men
of valour, archers, and had many sons, and sons'
sons, an hundred and fifty. All these *are* of the
sons of Benjamin.

9 So [a]all Israel were reckoned by genealogies;
and, behold, they *were* written in the book of
the kings of Israel and Judah, *who* were carried
away to Babylon for their transgression.
2 [a]Now the first inhabitants that *dwell* in
their possessions in their cities *were*, the Israelites, the priests, Levites, and [b]the Nethinims.

Dwellers in Jerusalem

3 And in [a]Jerusalem dwelt of the children
of Judah, and of the children of Benjamin, and
of the children of Ephraim, and Manasseh;
4 Uthai the son of Ammihud, the son of
Omri, the son of Imri, the son of Bani, of the children of Pharez the son of Judah.
5 And of the Shilonites; Asaiah the firstborn, and his sons.
6 And of the sons of Zerah; Jeuel, and their
brethren, six hundred and ninety.
7 And of the sons of Benjamin; Sallu the

13 [a]1 Chr. 8:21
29 [a]1 Chr. 9:35–38
33 [a]1 Sam. 14:51
34 [a]2 Sam. 9:12

CHAPTER 9
1 [a]Ezra 2:59
2 [a]Ezra 2:70; Neh. 7:73
[b]Ezra 2:43; 8:20
3 [a]Neh. 11:1, 2

*
8:32 *Shimeam*, 1 Chr. 9:38
8:33 Also the son of Gibeon, 1 Chr. 9:36, 39 • *Jishui*, 1 Sam. 14:49 • *Ish-bosheth*, 2 Sam. 2:8
8:34 *Mephibosheth*, 2 Sam. 4:4
8:36 *Jarah*, 1 Chr. 9:42
8:37 *Rephaiah*, 1 Chr. 9:43

NKJV

12 The sons of Elpaal *were* Eber, Misham,
and Shemed, who built Ono and Lod with its
towns;
13 and Beriah and [a]Shema, who *were* heads
of their fathers' *houses* of the inhabitants of Aijalon, who drove out the inhabitants of Gath.
14 Ahio, Shashak, Jeremoth,
15 Zebadiah, Arad, Eder,
16 Michael, Ispah, and Joha *were* the sons
of Beriah.
17 Zebadiah, Meshullam, Hizki, Heber,
18 Ishmerai, Jizliah, and Jobab *were* the sons
of Elpaal.
19 Jakim, Zichri, Zabdi,
20 Elienai, Zillethai, Eliel,
21 Adaiah, Beraiah, and Shimrath *were* the
sons of Shimei.
22 Ishpan, Eber, Eliel,
23 Abdon, Zichri, Hanan,
24 Hananiah, Elam, Antothijah,
25 Iphdeiah, and Penuel *were* the sons of
Shashak.
26 Shamsherai, Shehariah, Athaliah,
27 Jaareshiah, Elijah, and Zichri *were* the
sons of Jeroham.
28 These *were* heads of the fathers' *houses*
by their generations, chief men. These dwelt in
Jerusalem.
29 Now the father of Gibeon, whose [a]wife's
name *was* Maacah, dwelt at Gibeon.
30 And his firstborn son *was* Abdon, then
Zur, Kish, Baal, Nadab,
31 Gedor, Ahio, Zecher,
32 and Mikloth, *who* begot *Shimeah. They
also dwelt alongside their relatives in Jerusalem,
with their brethren.
33 [a]Ner* begot Kish, Kish begot Saul, and
Saul begot Jonathan, Malchishua, *Abinadab, and
*Esh-Baal.
34 The son of Jonathan *was* *Merib-Baal, and
Merib-Baal begot [a]Micah.
35 The sons of Micah *were* Pithon, Melech,
Tarea, and Ahaz.
36 And Ahaz begot *Jehoaddah; Jehoaddah
begot Alemeth, Azmaveth, and Zimri; and Zimri
begot Moza.
37 Moza begot Binea, *Raphah his son,
Eleasah his son, *and* Azel his son.
38 Azel had six sons whose names *were*
these: Azrikam, Bocheru, Ishmael, Sheariah, Obadiah, and Hanan. All these *were* the sons of Azel.
39 And the sons of Eshek his brother *were*
Ulam his firstborn, Jeush the second, and Eliphelet the third.
40 The sons of Ulam were mighty men of
valor—archers. *They* had many sons and grandsons, one hundred and fifty *in all*. These *were* all
sons of Benjamin.

9 So [a]all Israel was recorded by genealogies,
and indeed, they *were* inscribed in the book
of the kings of Israel. But Judah was carried away
captive to Babylon because of their unfaithfulness.
2 [a]And the first inhabitants who *dwelt* in
their possessions in their cities *were* Israelites,
priests, Levites, and [b]the Nethinim.

Dwellers in Jerusalem

3 Now in [a]Jerusalem the children of Judah
dwelt, and some of the children of Benjamin, and
of the children of Ephraim and Manasseh:
4 Uthai the son of Ammihud, the son of
Omri, the son of Imri, the son of Bani, of the descendants of Perez, the son of Judah.
5 Of the Shilonites: Asaiah the firstborn and
his sons.
6 Of the sons of Zerah: Jeuel, and their
brethren—six hundred and ninety.
7 Of the sons of Benjamin: Sallu the son of

KJV

son of Meshullam, the son of Hodaviah, the son of Hasenuah,

8 And Ibneiah the son of Jeroham, and Elah the son of Uzzi, the son of Michri, and Meshullam the son of Shephathiah, the son of Reuel, the son of Ibnijah;

9 And their brethren, according to their generations, nine hundred and fifty and six. All these men *were* chief of the fathers in the house of their fathers.

The Priests at Jerusalem

10 [a]And of the priests; Jedaiah, and Jehoiarib, and Jachin,

11 And Azariah the son of Hilkiah, the son of Meshullam, the son of Zadok, the son of Meraioth, the son of Ahitub, the [a]ruler of the house of God;

12 And Adaiah the son of Jeroham, the son of Pashur, the son of Malchijah, and Maasiai the son of Adiel, the son of Jahzerah, the son of Meshullam, the son of Meshillemith, the son of Immer;

13 And their brethren, heads of the house of their fathers, a thousand and seven hundred and threescore; very able men for the work of the service of the house of God.

The Levites at Jerusalem

14 And of the Levites; Shemaiah the son of Hasshub, the son of Azrikam, the son of Hashabiah, of the sons of Merari;

15 And Bakbakkar, Heresh, and Galal, and Mattaniah the son of Micah, the son of [a]Zichri, the son of Asaph;

16 And [a]Obadiah the son of [b]Shemaiah, the son of Galal, the son of Jeduthun, and Berechiah the son of Asa, the son of Elkanah, that dwelt in the villages of the Netophathites.

The Levite Gatekeepers

17 And the porters *were*, Shallum, and Akkub, and Talmon, and Ahiman, and their brethren: Shallum *was* the chief;

18 Who hitherto *waited* in the king's gate eastward: they *were* porters in the companies of the children of Levi.

19 And Shallum the son of Kore, the son of Ebiasaph, the son of Korah, and his brethren, of the house of his father, the Korahites, *were* over the work of the service, keepers of the gates of the tabernacle: and their fathers, *being* over the host of the LORD, *were* keepers of the entry.

20 And [a]Phinehas the son of Eleazar was the ruler over them in time past, *and* the LORD *was* with him.

21 *And* [a]Zechariah the son of Meshelemiah *was* porter of the door of the tabernacle of the congregation.

22 All these *which were* chosen to be porters in the gates *were* two hundred and twelve. [a]These were reckoned by their genealogy in their villages, whom David and Samuel [b]the seer did ordain in their set office.

23 So they and their children *had* the oversight of the gates of the house of the LORD, *namely*, the house of the tabernacle, by wards.

24 In four quarters were the porters, toward the east, west, north, and south.

25 And their brethren, *which were* in their villages, *were* to come [a]after seven days from time to time with them.

26 For these Levites, the four chief porters, were in *their* set office, and were over the chambers and treasuries of the house of God.

27 And they lodged round about the house of God, because the [a]charge *was* upon them, and the opening thereof every morning *pertained* to them.

10 [a]Neh. 11:10–14
11 [a]2 Chr. 31:13; Jer. 20:1
15 [a]Neh. 11:17
16 [a]Neh. 11:17 [b]Neh. 11:17
20 [a]Num. 25:6–13; 31:6
21 [a]1 Chr. 26:2, 14
22 [a]1 Chr. 26:1, 2 [b]1 Sam. 9:9
25 [a]2 Kin. 11:4–7; 2 Chr. 23:8
27 [a]1 Chr. 23:30–32

NKJV

Meshullam, the son of Hodaviah, the son of Hassenuah;

8 Ibneiah the son of Jeroham; Elah the son of Uzzi, the son of Michri; Meshullam the son of Shephatiah, the son of Reuel, the son of Ibnijah;

9 and their brethren, according to their generations—nine hundred and fifty-six. All these men *were* heads of a father's *house* in their fathers' houses.

The Priests at Jerusalem

10 [a]Of the priests: Jedaiah, Jehoiarib, and Jachin;

11 Azariah the son of Hilkiah, the son of Meshullam, the son of Zadok, the son of Meraioth, the son of Ahitub, the [a]officer over the house of God;

12 Adaiah the son of Jeroham, the son of Pashur, the son of Malchijah; Maasai the son of Adiel, the son of Jahzerah, the son of Meshullam, the son of Meshillemith, the son of Immer;

13 and their brethren, heads of their fathers' *houses*—one thousand seven hundred and sixty. *They were* very able men for the work of the service of the house of God.

The Levites at Jerusalem

14 Of the Levites: Shemaiah the son of Hasshub, the son of Azrikam, the son of Hashabiah, of the sons of Merari;

15 Bakbakkar, Heresh, Galal, and Mattaniah the son of Micah, the son of [a]Zichri, the son of Asaph;

16 [a]Obadiah the son of [b]Shemaiah, the son of Galal, the son of Jeduthun; and Berechiah the son of Asa, the son of Elkanah, who lived in the villages of the Netophathites.

The Levite Gatekeepers

17 And the gatekeepers *were* Shallum, Akkub, Talmon, Ahiman, and their brethren. Shallum *was* the chief.

18 Until then *they had been* gatekeepers for the camps of the children of Levi at the King's Gate on the east.

19 Shallum the son of Kore, the son of Ebiasaph, the son of Korah, and his brethren, from his father's house, the Korahites, *were* in charge of the work of the service, gatekeepers of the tabernacle. Their fathers had been keepers of the entrance to the camp of the LORD.

20 And [a]Phinehas the son of Eleazar had been the officer over them in time past; the LORD *was* with him.

21 [a]Zechariah the son of Meshelemiah *was* keeper of the door of the tabernacle of meeting.

22 All those chosen as gatekeepers *were* two hundred and twelve. [a]They were recorded by their genealogy, in their villages. David and Samuel [b]the seer had appointed them to their trusted office.

23 So they and their children *were* in charge of the gates of the house of the LORD, the house of the tabernacle, by assignment.

24 The gatekeepers were assigned to the four directions: the east, west, north, and south.

25 And their brethren in their villages *had* to come with them from time to time [a]for seven days.

26 For in this trusted office *were* four chief gatekeepers; they were Levites. And they had charge over the chambers and treasuries of the house of God.

27 And they lodged *all* around the house of God because they *had* the [a]responsibility, and they *were* in charge of opening *it* every morning.

KJV

Other Levite Responsibilities

28 And *certain* of them had the charge of the
ministering vessels, that they should bring them
in and out by tale.
29 *Some* of them also *were* appointed to oversee the vessels, and all the instruments of the
sanctuary, and the [a]fine flour, and the wine, and
the oil, and the frankincense, and the spices.
30 And *some* of the sons of the priests made
[a]the ointment of the spices.
31 And Mattithiah, *one* of the Levites, who
was the firstborn of Shallum the Korahite, had
the set office [a]over the things that were made in
the pans.
32 And *other* of their brethren, of the sons
of the Kohathites, [a]*were* over the shewbread, to
prepare *it* every sabbath.
33 And these *are* [a]the singers, chief of the
fathers of the Levites, *who remaining* in the chambers *were* free: for they were employed in *that*
work day and night.
34 These chief fathers of the Levites *were*
chief throughout their generations; these dwelt at
Jerusalem.

The Family of King Saul

35 And in Gibeon dwelt the father of Gibeon,
Jehiel, whose wife's name *was* [a]Maachah:
36 And his firstborn son Abdon, then Zur,
and Kish, and Baal, and Ner, and Nadab,
37 And Gedor, and Ahio, and Zechariah, and
Mikloth.
38 And Mikloth begat Shimeam. And they
also dwelt with their brethren at Jerusalem, over
against their brethren.
39 [a]And Ner begat Kish; and Kish begat
Saul; and Saul begat Jonathan, and Malchi–shua,
and Abinadab, and Esh–baal.
40 And the son of Jonathan *was* Merib–baal:
and Merib–baal begat Micah.
41 And the sons of Micah *were*, Pithon, and
Melech, and Tahrea, [a]*and Ahaz*.
42 And Ahaz begat Jarah; and Jarah begat
Alemeth, and Azmaveth, and Zimri; and Zimri begat Moza;
43 And Moza begat Binea; and Rephaiah his
son, Eleasah his son, Azel his son.
44 And Azel had six sons, whose names *are*
these, Azrikam, Bocheru, and Ishmael, and Sheariah, and Obadiah, and Hanan: these *were* the
sons of Azel.

Tragic End of Saul and His Sons
(1 Sam. 31:1–13)

10 Now [a]the Philistines fought against Israel;
and the men of Israel fled from before the
Philistines, and fell down slain in mount Gilboa.
2 And the Philistines followed hard after
Saul, and after his sons; and the Philistines slew
Jonathan, and Abinadab, and Malchi–shua, the
sons of Saul.
3 And the battle went sore against Saul, and
the archers hit him, and he was wounded of the
archers.
4 Then said Saul to his armourbearer, Draw
thy sword, and thrust me through therewith; lest
these uncircumcised come and abuse me. But his
armourbearer would not; for he was sore afraid.
So Saul took a sword, and fell upon it.
5 And when his armourbearer saw that Saul
was dead, he fell likewise on the sword, and died.
6 So Saul died, and his three sons, and all
his house died together.
7 And when all the men of Israel that *were*
in the valley saw that they fled, and that Saul and
his sons were dead, then they forsook their cities,
and fled: and the Philistines came and dwelt in
them.
8 And it came to pass on the morrow, when
the Philistines came to strip the slain, that they
found Saul and his sons fallen in mount Gilboa.

29 [a]1 Chr. 23:29
30 [a]Ex. 30:22–25
31 [a]Lev. 2:5; 6:21
32 [a]Lev. 24:5–8
33 [a]1 Chr. 6:31; 25:1
35 [a]1 Chr. 8:29–32
39 [a]1 Chr. 8:33–38
41 [a]1 Chr. 8:35

CHAPTER 10
1 [a]1 Sam. 31:1, 2

*
9:37 *Zecher,* 1 Chr. 8:31
9:38 *Shimeah,* 1 Chr. 8:32
9:41 *Tarea,* 1 Chr. 8:35
• So with Arab., Syr., Tg., Vg. (cf. 8:35); MT, LXX omit *and Ahaz*
9:42 *Jehoaddah,* 1 Chr. 8:36
9:43 *Raphah,* 1 Chr. 8:37

NKJV

Other Levite Responsibilities

28 Now *some* of them were in charge of the
serving vessels, for they brought them in and took
them out by count.
29 *Some* of them *were* appointed over the
furnishings and over all the implements of the
sanctuary, and over the [a]fine flour and the wine
and the oil and the incense and the spices.
30 And *some* of the sons of the priests made
[a]the ointment of the spices.
31 Mattithiah of the Levites, the firstborn of
Shallum the Korahite, had the trusted office [a]over
the things that were baked in the pans.
32 And some of their brethren of the sons
of the Kohathites [a]*were* in charge of preparing
the showbread for every Sabbath.
33 These are [a]the singers, heads of the fathers' *houses* of the Levites, *who lodged* in the
chambers, *and were* free *from other duties;* for
they were employed in *that* work day and night.
34 These heads of the fathers' *houses* of the
Levites *were* heads throughout their generations.
They dwelt at Jerusalem.

The Family of King Saul

35 Jeiel the father of Gibeon, whose wife's
name *was* [a]Maacah, dwelt at Gibeon.
36 His firstborn son *was* Abdon, then Zur,
Kish, Baal, Ner, Nadab,
37 Gedor, Ahio, *Zechariah, and Mikloth.
38 And Mikloth begot *Shimeam. They also
dwelt alongside their relatives in Jerusalem, with
their brethren.
39 [a]Ner begot Kish, Kish begot Saul, and
Saul begot Jonathan, Malchishua, Abinadab, and
Esh-Baal.
40 The son of Jonathan *was* Merib-Baal, and
Merib-Baal begot Micah.
41 The sons of Micah *were* Pithon, Melech,
*Tahrea, [a]*and* Ahaz*.
42 And Ahaz begot *Jarah; Jarah begot Alemeth, Azmaveth, and Zimri; and Zimri begot
Moza;
43 Moza begot Binea, *Rephaiah his son, Eleasah his son, and Azel his son.
44 And Azel had six sons whose names *were*
these: Azrikam, Bocheru, Ishmael, Sheariah, Obadiah, and Hanan; these *were* the sons of Azel.

Tragic End of Saul and His Sons
(1 Sam. 31:1–13)

10 Now [a]the Philistines fought against Israel;
and the men of Israel fled from before the
Philistines, and fell slain on Mount Gilboa.
2 Then the Philistines followed hard after
Saul and his sons. And the Philistines killed Jonathan, Abinadab, and Malchishua, Saul's sons.
3 The battle became fierce against Saul. The
archers hit him, and he was wounded by the
archers.
4 Then Saul said to his armorbearer, "Draw
your sword, and thrust me through with it, lest
these uncircumcised men come and abuse me."
But his armorbearer would not, for he was greatly
afraid. Therefore Saul took a sword and fell on
it.
5 And when his armorbearer saw that Saul
was dead, he also fell on his sword and died.
6 So Saul and his three sons died, and all
his house died together.
7 And when all the men of Israel who *were*
in the valley saw that they had fled and that Saul
and his sons were dead, they forsook their cities
and fled; then the Philistines came and dwelt in
them.
8 So it happened the next day, when the
Philistines came to strip the slain, that they found
Saul and his sons fallen on Mount Gilboa.

KJV

9 And when they had stripped him, they took his head, and his armour, and sent into the land of the Philistines round about, to carry tidings unto their idols, and to the people.

10 [a]And they put his armour in the house of their gods, and fastened his head in the temple of Dagon.

11 And when all Jabesh–gilead heard all that the Philistines had done to Saul,

12 They arose, all the [a]valiant men, and took away the body of Saul, and the bodies of his sons, and brought them to [b]Jabesh, and buried their bones under the oak in Jabesh, and fasted seven days.

13 So Saul died for his transgression which he committed against the LORD, [a]*even* against the word of the LORD, which he kept not, and also for asking *counsel* of *one that had* a familiar spirit, [b]to enquire *of it;*

14 And enquired not of the LORD: therefore he slew him, and [a]turned the kingdom unto David the son of Jesse.

David Made King over All Israel
(2 Sam. 5:1–3)

11 Then [a]all Israel gathered themselves to David unto Hebron, saying, Behold, we *are* thy bone and thy flesh.

2 And moreover in time past, even when Saul was king, thou *wast* he that leddest out and broughtest in Israel: and the LORD thy [a]God said unto thee, Thou shalt [b]feed my people Israel, and thou shalt be ruler over my people Israel.

3 Therefore came all the elders of Israel to the king to Hebron; and David made a covenant with them in Hebron before the LORD; and [a]they anointed David king over Israel, according to the word of the LORD by [b]Samuel.

The City of David
(2 Sam. 5:6–10)

4 And David and all Israel [a]went to Jerusalem, which *is* Jebus; [b]where the Jebusites *were,* the inhabitants of the land.

5 And the inhabitants of Jebus said to David, Thou shalt not come hither. Nevertheless David took the castle of Zion, which *is* the city of David.

6 And David said, Whosoever smiteth the Jebusites first shall be chief and captain. So Joab the son of Zeruiah went first up, and was chief.

7 And David dwelt in the castle; therefore they called it the city of David.

8 And he built the city round about, even from Millo round about: and Joab repaired the rest of the city.

9 So David [a]waxed greater and greater: for the LORD of hosts *was* with [b]him.

The Mighty Men of David
(2 Sam. 23:8–39)

10 [a]These also *are* the chief of the mighty men whom David had, who strengthened themselves with him in his kingdom, *and* with all Israel, to make him king, according to [b]the word of the LORD concerning Israel.

11 And this *is* the number of the mighty men whom David had; [a]Jashobeam, an Hachmonite, the [b]chief of the captains: he lifted up his spear against three hundred slain *by him* at one time.

12 And after him *was* Eleazar the son of [a]Dodo, the Ahohite, who *was one* of the three mighties.

13 He was with David at Pas–dammim, and there the Philistines were gathered together to battle, where was a parcel of ground full of barley; and the people fled from before the Philistines.

14 And they set themselves in the midst of *that* parcel, and delivered it, and slew the Philistines; and the LORD saved *them* by a great deliverance.

10 [a]1 Sam. 31:10
12 [a]1 Sam. 14:52 [b]2 Sam. 21:12
13 [a]1 Sam. 13:13, 14; 15:22–26 [b][Lev. 19:31; 20:6]; 1 Sam. 28:7
14 [a]1 Sam. 15:28; 2 Sam. 3:9, 10; 5:3; 1 Chr. 12:23

CHAPTER 11
1 [a]2 Sam. 5:1
2 [a]1 Sam. 16:1–3; Ps. 78:70–72 [b]2 Sam. 7:7
3 [a]2 Sam. 5:3 [b]1 Sam. 16:1, 4, 12, 13
4 [a]2 Sam. 5:6 [b]Josh. 15:8, 63; Judg. 1:21; 19:10, 11
9 [a]2 Sam. 3:1 [b]1 Sam. 16:18
10 [a]2 Sam. 23:8 [b]1 Sam. 16:1, 12
11 [a]1 Chr. 27:2 [b]1 Chr. 12:18
12 [a]1 Chr. 27:4

*
11:8 Lit. *The Landfill*
11:11 So with Qr.; Kt., LXX, Vg. *the thirty* (cf. 2 Sam. 23:8)

NKJV

9 And they stripped him and took his head and his armor, and sent word *throughout* the land of the Philistines to proclaim the news *in the temple* of their idols and among the people.

10 [a]Then they put his armor in the temple of their gods, and fastened his head in the temple of Dagon.

11 And when all Jabesh Gilead heard all that the Philistines had done to Saul,

12 all the [a]valiant men arose and took the body of Saul and the bodies of his sons; and they brought them to [b]Jabesh, and buried their bones under the tamarisk tree at Jabesh, and fasted seven days.

13 So Saul died for his unfaithfulness which he had committed against the LORD, [a]because he did not keep the word of the LORD, and also because [b]he consulted a medium for guidance.

14 But *he* did not inquire of the LORD; therefore He killed him, and [a]turned the kingdom over to David the son of Jesse.

David Made King over All Israel
(2 Sam 5:1–3)

11 Then [a]all Israel came together to David at Hebron, saying, "Indeed we *are* your bone and your flesh.

2 "Also, in time past, even when Saul was king, you *were* the one who led Israel out and brought them in; and the LORD your [a]God said to you, 'You shall [b]shepherd My people Israel, and be ruler over My people Israel.' "

3 Therefore all the elders of Israel came to the king at Hebron, and David made a covenant with them at Hebron before the LORD. And [a]they anointed David king over Israel, according to the word of the LORD by [b]Samuel.

The City of David
(2 Sam. 5:6–10)

4 And David and all Israel [a]went to Jerusalem, which is Jebus, [b]where the Jebusites *were,* the inhabitants of the land.

5 But the inhabitants of Jebus said to David, "You shall not come in here!" Nevertheless David took the stronghold of Zion (that is, the City of David).

6 Now David said, "Whoever attacks the Jebusites first shall be chief and captain." And Joab the son of Zeruiah went up first, and became chief.

7 Then David dwelt in the stronghold; therefore they called it the City of David.

8 And he built the city around it, from *the Millo to the surrounding area. Joab repaired the rest of the city.

9 So David [a]went on and became great, and the LORD of hosts *was* with [b]him.

The Mighty Men of David
(2 Sam. 23:8–39)

10 Now [a]these *were* the heads of the mighty men whom David had, who strengthened themselves with him in his kingdom, with all Israel, to make him king, according to [b]the word of the LORD concerning Israel.

11 And this *is* the number of the mighty men whom David had: [a]Jashobeam the son of a Hachmonite, [b]chief of *the captains; he had lifted up his spear against three hundred, killed *by him* at one time.

12 After him *was* Eleazar the son of [a]Dodo, the Ahohite, who *was one* of the three mighty men.

13 He was with David at Pasdammim. Now there the Philistines were gathered for battle, and there was a piece of ground full of barley. So the people fled from the Philistines.

14 But they stationed themselves in the middle of *that* field, defended it, and killed the Philistines. So the LORD brought about a great victory.

KJV

15 Now three of the thirty captains [a]went
down to the rock to David, into the cave of Adullam; and the host of the Philistines encamped [b]in
the valley of Rephaim.
16 And David *was* then in the hold, and the
Philistines' garrison *was* then at Beth–lehem.
17 And David longed, and said, Oh that one
would give me drink of the water of the well of
Beth–lehem, that *is* at the gate!
18 And the three brake through the host of
the Philistines, and drew water out of the well of
Beth–lehem, that *was* by the gate, and took *it*,
and brought *it* to David: but David would not
drink *of* it, but poured it out to the LORD,
19 And said, My God forbid it me, that I
should do this thing: shall I drink the blood of
these men that have put their lives in jeopardy?
for with *the jeopardy of* their lives they brought
it. Therefore he would not drink it. These things
did these three mightiest.
20 [a]And Abishai the brother of Joab, he was
chief of the three: for lifting up his spear against
three hundred, he slew *them*, and had a name
among the three.
21 [a]Of the three, he was more honourable
than the two; for he was their captain: howbeit
he attained not to the *first* three.
22 Benaiah the son of Jehoiada, the son of a
valiant man of Kabzeel, who had done many acts;
[a]he slew two lionlike men of Moab: also he went
down and slew a lion in a pit in a snowy day.
23 And he slew an Egyptian, a man of *great*
stature, five cubits high; and in the Egyptian's
hand *was* a spear like a weaver's beam; and he
went down to him with a staff, and plucked the
spear out of the Egyptian's hand, and slew him
with his own spear.
24 These *things* did Benaiah the son of
Jehoiada, and had the name among the three
mighties.
25 Behold, he was honourable among the
thirty, but attained not to the *first* three: and David set him over his guard.
26 Also the valiant men of the armies *were*,
[a]Asahel the brother of Joab, Elhanan the son of
Dodo of Beth–lehem,
27 Shammoth the Harorite, [a]Helez the Pelonite,
28 [a]Ira the son of Ikkesh the Tekoite, [b]Abi-
ezer the Antothite,
29 Sibbecai the Hushathite, Ilai the Ahohite,
30 [a]Maharai the Netophathite, Heled the son
of Baanah the Netophathite,
31 Ithai the son of Ribai of Gibeah, *that pertained* to the children of Benjamin, [a]Benaiah the
Pirathonite,
32 Hurai of the brooks of Gaash, Abiel the
Arbathite,
33 Azmaveth the Baharumite, Eliahba the
Shaalbonite,
34 The sons of Hashem the Gizonite, Jonathan the son of Shage the Hararite,
35 Ahiam the son of Sacar the Hararite, Eli-
phal the son of Ur,
36 Hepher the Mecherathite, Ahijah the Pelonite,
37 Hezro the Carmelite, Naarai the son of
Ezbai,
38 Joel the brother of Nathan, Mibhar the son
of Haggeri,
39 Zelek the Ammonite, Naharai the Bero-
thite, the armourbearer of Joab the son of
Zeruiah,
40 Ira the Ithrite, Gareb the Ithrite,
41 [a]Uriah the Hittite, Zabad the son of
Ahlai,
42 Adina the son of Shiza the Reubenite, a
captain of the Reubenites, and thirty with him,
43 Hanan the son of Maachah, and Joshaphat the Mithnite,
44 Uzzia the Ashterathite, Shama and Jehiel
the sons of Hothan the Aroerite,

15 [a]2 Sam. 23:13 [b]2 Sam. 5:18; 1 Chr. 14:9
20 [a]2 Sam. 23:18; 1 Chr. 18:12
21 [a]2 Sam. 23:19
22 [a]2 Sam. 23:20
26 [a]2 Sam. 23:24
27 [a]2 Sam. 23:26; 1 Chr. 27:10
28 [a]1 Chr. 27:9 [b]1 Chr. 27:12
30 [a]1 Chr. 27:13
31 [a]1 Chr. 27:14
41 [a]2 Sam. 11

*______

11:20 So with MT, LXX, Vg.; Syr. *thirty*
11:27 *Shammah the Harodite*, 2 Sam. 23:25 • *Paltite*, 2 Sam. 23:26
11:30 *Heleb*, 2 Sam. 23:29, or *Heldai*, 1 Chr. 27:15
11:31 *Ittai*, 2 Sam. 23:29
11:32 *Hiddai*, 2 Sam. 23:30 • *Abi-Albon*, 2 Sam. 23:31
11:33 *Barhumite*, 2 Sam. 23:31
11:39 *Beerothite*, 2 Sam. 23:37

NKJV

15 Now three of the thirty chief men [a]went
down to the rock to David, into the cave of Adullam; and the army of the Philistines encamped
[b]in the Valley of Rephaim.
16 David *was* then in the stronghold, and the
garrison of the Philistines *was* then in Bethlehem.
17 And David said with longing, "Oh, that
someone would give me a drink of water from
the well of Bethlehem, which is by the gate!"
18 So the three broke through the camp of
the Philistines, drew water from the well of Bethlehem that *was* by the gate, and took *it* and
brought *it* to David. Nevertheless David would
not drink it, but poured it out to the LORD.
19 And he said, "Far be it from me, O my
God, that I should do this! Shall I drink the blood
of these men *who have put* their lives *in jeopardy?*
For at the risk of their lives they brought it."
Therefore he would not drink it. These things
were done by the three mighty men.
20 [a]Abishai the brother of Joab was chief of
another *three. He had lifted up his spear against
three hundred *men*, killed *them*, and won a name
among *these* three.
21 [a]Of the three he was more honored than
the other two men. Therefore he became their
captain. However he did not attain to the *first*
three.
22 Benaiah was the son of Jehoiada, the son
of a valiant man from Kabzeel, who had done
many deeds. [a]He had killed two lion-like heroes
of Moab. He also had gone down and killed a lion
in the midst of a pit on a snowy day.
23 And he killed an Egyptian, a man of *great*
height, five cubits tall. In the Egyptian's hand
there was a spear like a weaver's beam; and he
went down to him with a staff, wrested the spear
out of the Egyptian's hand, and killed him with
his own spear.
24 These *things* Benaiah the son of Jehoiada
did, and won a name among three mighty men.
25 Indeed he was more honored than the
thirty, but he did not attain to the *first* three. And
David appointed him over his guard.
26 Also the mighty warriors *were* [a]Asahel
the brother of Joab, Elhanan the son of Dodo of
Bethlehem,
27 *Shammoth the Harorite, [a]Helez the *Pelonite,
28 [a]Ira the son of Ikkesh the Tekoite,
[b]Abiezer the Anathothite,
29 Sibbechai the Hushathite, Ilai the Ahohite,
30 [a]Maharai the Netophathite, *Heled the
son of Baanah the Netophathite,
31 *Ithai the son of Ribai of Gibeah, of the
sons of Benjamin, [a]Benaiah the Pirathonite,
32 *Hurai of the brooks of Gaash, *Abiel the
Arbathite,
33 Azmaveth the *Baharumite, Eliahba the
Shaalbonite,
34 the sons of Hashem the Gizonite, Jonathan the son of Shageh the Hararite,
35 Ahiam the son of Sacar the Hararite, Eli-
phal the son of Ur,
36 Hepher the Mecherathite, Ahijah the
Pelonite,
37 Hezro the Carmelite, Naarai the son of
Ezbai,
38 Joel the brother of Nathan, Mibhar the son
of Hagri,
39 Zelek the Ammonite, Naharai the *Beroth-
ite (the armorbearer of Joab the son of Zeruiah),
40 Ira the Ithrite, Gareb the Ithrite,
41 [a]Uriah the Hittite, Zabad the son of Ahlai,
42 Adina the son of Shiza the Reubenite (a
chief of the Reubenites) and thirty with him,
43 Hanan the son of Maachah, Joshaphat the
Mithnite,
44 Uzzia the Ashterathite, Shama and Jeiel
the sons of Hotham the Aroerite,

KJV

45 Jediael the son of Shimri, and Joha his
brother, the Tizite,
46 Eliel the Mahavite, and Jeribai, and Joshaviah, the sons of Elnaam, and Ithmah the Moabite,
47 Eliel, and Obed, and Jasiel the Mesobaite.

The Growth of David's Army
(*1 Sam. 22:1, 2*)

12 Now [a]these *are* they that came to David
to [b]Ziklag, while he yet kept himself close
because of Saul the son of Kish: and they *were*
among the mighty men, helpers of the war.
2 *They were* armed with bows, and could
use both the right hand and [a]the left in *hurling*
stones and *shooting* arrows out of a bow, *even*
of Saul's brethren of Benjamin.
3 The chief *was* Ahiezer, then Joash, the
sons of Shemaah the Gibeathite; and Jeziel, and
Pelet, the sons of Azmaveth; and Berachah, and
Jehu the Antothite,
4 And Ismaiah the Gibeonite, a mighty man
among the thirty, and over the thirty; and Jeremiah, and Jahaziel, and Johanan, and Josabad
the Gederathite,
5 Eluzai, and Jerimoth, and Bealiah, and
Shemariah, and Shephatiah the Haruphite,
6 Elkanah, and Jesiah, and Azareel, and
Joezer, and Jashobeam, the Korhites,
7 And Joelah, and Zebadiah, the sons of
Jeroham of Gedor.
8 And of the Gadites there separated themselves unto David into the hold to the wilderness
men of might, *and* men of war *fit* for the battle,
that could handle shield and buckler, whose faces
were like the faces of lions, and *were* [a]as swift
as the roes upon the mountains;
9 Ezer the first, Obadiah the second, Eliab
the third,
10 Mishmannah the fourth, Jeremiah the
fifth,
11 Attai the sixth, Eliel the seventh,
12 Johanan the eighth, Elzabad the ninth,
13 Jeremiah the tenth, Machbanai the
eleventh.
14 These *were* of the sons of Gad, captains
of the host: one of the least *was* over an hundred,
and the greatest over a [a]thousand.
15 These *are* they that went over Jordan in
the first month, when it had overflown all his
[a]banks; and they put to flight all *them* of the valleys, *both* toward the east, and toward the west.
16 And there came of the children of Benjamin and Judah to the hold unto David.
17 And David went out to meet them, and
answered and said unto them, If ye be come
peaceably unto me to help me, mine heart shall
be knit unto you: but if *ye be come* to betray me
to mine enemies, seeing *there is* no wrong in mine
hands, the God of our fathers look *thereon,* and
rebuke *it.*
18 Then the spirit came upon [a]Amasai, *who
was* chief of the captains, *and he said,* Thine *are
we,* David, and on thy side, thou son of Jesse:
peace, peace *be* unto thee, and peace *be* to thine
helpers; for thy God helpeth thee. Then David received them, and made them captains of the band.
19 And there fell *some* of Manasseh to David,
[a]when he came with the Philistines against Saul
to battle: but they helped them not: for the lords
of the Philistines upon advisement sent him away,
saying, [b]He will fall to his master Saul to *the jeopardy of* our heads.
20 As he went to Ziklag, there fell to him of
Manasseh, Adnah, and Jozabad, and Jediael, and
Michael, and Jozabad, and Elihu, and Zilthai, captains of the thousands that *were* of Manasseh.
21 And they helped David against [a]the band
of the rovers: for they *were* all mighty men of
valour, and were captains in the host.

CHAPTER 12
1 [a]1 Sam. 27:2 [b]1 Sam. 27:6
2 [a]Judg. 3:15; 20:16
8 [a]2 Sam. 2:18
14 [a]1 Sam. 18:13
15 [a]Josh. 3:15; 4:18, 19
18 [a]2 Sam. 17:25
19 [a]1 Sam. 29:2 [b]1 Sam. 29:4
21 [a]1 Sam. 30:1, 9, 10

NKJV

45 Jediael the son of Shimri, and Joha his
brother, the Tizite,
46 Eliel the Mahavite, Jeribai and Joshaviah
the sons of Elnaam, Ithmah the Moabite,
47 Eliel, Obed, and Jaasiel the Mezobaite.

The Growth of David's Army
(*1 Sam. 22:1, 2*)

12 Now [a]these *were* the men who came to David at [b]Ziklag while he was still a fugitive
from Saul the son of Kish; and they *were* among
the mighty men, helpers in the war,
2 armed with bows, using both the right
hand and [a]the left in *hurling* stones and *shooting*
arrows with the bow. *They were* of Benjamin,
Saul's brethren.
3 The chief *was* Ahiezer, then Joash, the
sons of Shemaah the Gibeathite; Jeziel and Pelet
the sons of Azmaveth; Berachah, and Jehu the
Anathothite;
4 Ishmaiah the Gibeonite, a mighty man
among the thirty, and over the thirty; Jeremiah,
Jahaziel, Johanan, and Jozabad the Gederathite;
5 Eluzai, Jerimoth, Bealiah, Shemariah, and
Shephatiah the Haruphite;
6 Elkanah, Jisshiah, Azarel, Joezer, and
Jashobeam, the Korahites;
7 and Joelah and Zebadiah the sons of Jeroham of Gedor.
8 *Some* Gadites joined David at the stronghold in the wilderness, mighty men of valor, men
trained for battle, who could handle shield and
spear, whose faces *were like* the faces of lions,
and *were* [a]as swift as gazelles on the mountains:
9 Ezer the first, Obadiah the second, Eliab
the third,
10 Mishmannah the fourth, Jeremiah the
fifth,
11 Attai the sixth, Eliel the seventh,
12 Johanan the eighth, Elzabad the ninth,
13 Jeremiah the tenth, and Machbanai the
eleventh.
14 These *were* from the sons of Gad, captains
of the army; the least was over a hundred, and
the greatest was over a [a]thousand.
15 These *are* the ones who crossed the Jordan in the first month, when it had overflowed
all its [a]banks; and they put to flight all *those* in
the valleys, to the east and to the west.
16 Then some of the sons of Benjamin and
Judah came to David at the stronghold.
17 And David went out to meet them, and
answered and said to them, "If you have come
peaceably to me to help me, my heart will be
united with you; but if to betray me to my enemies, since *there is* no wrong in my hands, may
the God of our fathers look and bring judgment."
18 Then the Spirit came upon [a]Amasai, chief
of the captains, *and he said:*

"*We are* yours, O David;
We *are* on your side, O son of Jesse!
Peace, peace to you,
And peace to your helpers!
For your God helps you."

So David received them, and made them captains
of the troop.
19 And *some* from Manasseh defected to David [a]when he was going with the Philistines to
battle against Saul; but they did not help them,
for the lords of the Philistines sent him away by
agreement, saying, [b]"He may defect to his master
Saul *and endanger* our heads."
20 When he went to Ziklag, those of Manasseh who defected to him were Adnah, Jozabad,
Jediael, Michael, Jozabad, Elihu, and Zillethai,
captains of the thousands who *were* from
Manasseh.
21 And they helped David against [a]the bands
of raiders, for they *were* all mighty men of valor,
and they were captains in the army.

KJV

22 For at *that* time day by day there came
to David to help him, until *it was* a great host,
[a]like the host of God.

David's Army at Hebron

23 And these *are* the numbers of the bands
that were ready armed to the war, *and* [a]came to
David to [b]Hebron, to [c]turn the kingdom of Saul
to him, [d]according to the word of the LORD.
24 The children of Judah that bare shield and
spear *were* six thousand and eight hundred, ready
armed to the war.
25 Of the children of Simeon, mighty men of
valour for the war, seven thousand and one
hundred.
26 Of the children of Levi four thousand and
six hundred.
27 And Jehoiada *was* the leader of the Aaronites, and with him *were* three thousand and
seven hundred;
28 And [a]Zadok, a young man mighty of valour, and of his father's house twenty and two
captains.
29 And of the children of Benjamin, the kindred of Saul, three thousand: for hitherto [a]the
greatest part of them had kept the ward of the
house of Saul.
30 And of the children of Ephraim twenty
thousand and eight hundred, mighty men of valour, famous throughout the house of their fathers.
31 And of the half tribe of Manasseh eighteen
thousand, which were expressed by name, to
come and make David king.
32 And of the children of Issachar, [a]*which
were men* that had understanding of the times,
to know what Israel ought to do; the heads of
them *were* two hundred; and all their brethren
were at their commandment.
33 Of Zebulun, such as went forth to battle,
expert in war, with all instruments of war, fifty
thousand, which could keep rank: *they were* not
of [a]double heart.
34 And of Naphtali a thousand captains, and
with them with shield and spear thirty and seven
thousand.
35 And of the Danites expert in war twenty
and eight thousand and six hundred.
36 And of Asher, such as went forth to battle,
expert in war, forty thousand.
37 And on the other side of Jordan, of the
Reubenites, and the Gadites, and of the half tribe
of Manasseh, with all manner of instruments of
war for the battle, an hundred and twenty
thousand.
38 All these men of war, that could keep
rank, came with a perfect heart to Hebron, to
make David king over all Israel: and all the rest
also of Israel *were* of [a]one heart to make David
king.
39 And there they were with David three
days, eating and drinking: for their brethren had
prepared for them.
40 Moreover they that were nigh them, *even*
unto Issachar and Zebulun and Naphtali, brought
bread on asses, and on camels, and on mules, and
on oxen, *and* meat, meal, cakes of figs, and
bunches of raisins, and wine, and oil, and oxen,
and sheep abundantly: for *there was* joy in Israel.

The Ark Brought from Kirjath Jearim
(2 Sam. 6:1–11)

13 And David consulted with the [a]captains of
thousands and hundreds, *and* with every
leader.
2 And David said unto all the congregation
of Israel, If *it seem* good unto you, and *that it
be* of the LORD our God, let us send abroad unto
our brethren every where, *that are* [a]left in all the
land of Israel, and with them *also* to the priests
and Levites *which are* in their cities *and* suburbs,
that they may gather themselves unto us:
3 And let us bring again the ark of our God

22 [a]Gen. 32:2; Josh. 5:13–15
23 [a]2 Sam. 2:1–4 [b]1 Chr. 11:1 [c]1 Chr. 10:14 [d]1 Sam. 16:1–4
28 [a]2 Sam. 8:17; 1 Chr. 6:8, 53
29 [a]2 Sam. 2:8, 9
32 [a]Esth. 1:13
33 [a]Ps. 12:2; [James 1:8]
38 [a]2 Chr. 30:12

CHAPTER 13

1 [a]1 Chr. 11:15; 12:34
2 [a]1 Sam. 31:1; Is. 37:4

NKJV

22 For at *that* time they came to David day
by day to help him, until *it was* a great army,
[a]like the army of God.

David's Army at Hebron

23 Now these *were* the numbers of the divisions *that were* equipped for war, *and* [a]came to
David at [b]Hebron to [c]turn *over* the kingdom of
Saul to him, [d]according to the word of the LORD:
24 of the sons of Judah bearing shield and
spear, six thousand eight hundred armed for war;
25 of the sons of Simeon, mighty men of
valor fit for war, seven thousand one hundred;
26 of the sons of Levi four thousand six
hundred;
27 Jehoiada, the leader of the Aaronites, and
with him three thousand seven hundred;
28 [a]Zadok, a young man, a valiant warrior,
and from his father's house twenty-two captains;
29 of the sons of Benjamin, relatives of Saul,
three thousand (until then [a]the greatest part of
them had remained loyal to the house of Saul);
30 of the sons of Ephraim twenty thousand
eight hundred, mighty men of valor, famous men
throughout their father's house;
31 of the half-tribe of Manasseh eighteen
thousand, who were designated by name to come
and make David king;
32 of the sons of Issachar [a]who had understanding of the times, to know what Israel ought
to do, their chiefs were two hundred; and all their
brethren were at their command;
33 of Zebulun there were fifty thousand who
went out to battle, expert in war with all weapons
of war, [a]stouthearted men who could keep ranks;
34 of Naphtali one thousand captains, and
with them thirty-seven thousand with shield and
spear;
35 of the Danites who could keep battle formation, twenty-eight thousand six hundred;
36 of Asher, those who could go out to war,
able to keep battle formation, forty thousand;
37 of the Reubenites and the Gadites and the
half-tribe of Manasseh, from the other side of the
Jordan, one hundred and twenty thousand armed
for battle with every *kind* of weapon of war.
38 All these men of war, who could keep
ranks, came to Hebron with a loyal heart, to make
David king over all Israel; and all the rest of Israel
were of [a]one mind to make David king.
39 And they were there with David three
days, eating and drinking, for their brethren had
prepared for them.
40 Moreover those who were near to them,
from as far away as Issachar and Zebulun and
Naphtali, were bringing food on donkeys and
camels, on mules and oxen—provisions of flour
and cakes of figs and cakes of raisins, wine and
oil and oxen and sheep abundantly, for *there was*
joy in Israel.

The Ark Brought from Kirjath Jearim
(2 Sam. 6:1–11)

13 Then David consulted with the [a]captains of
thousands and hundreds, *and* with every
leader.
2 And David said to all the assembly of Israel, "If *it seems* good to you, and if it is of the
LORD our God, let us send out to our brethren everywhere *who are* [a]left in all the land of Israel,
and with them to the priests and Levites *who are*
in their cities *and* their common-lands, that they
may gather together to us;
3 "and let us bring the ark of our God back

KJV

to us: [a]for we enquired not at it in the days of
Saul.
4 And all the congregation said that they
would do so: for the thing was right in the eyes
of all the people.
5 So [a]David gathered all Israel together,
from [b]Shihor of Egypt even unto the entering of
Hemath, to bring the ark of God [c]from Kirjath–
jearim.
6 And David went up, and all Israel, to
[a]Baalah, *that is,* to Kirjath–jearim, which *be-*
longed to Judah, to bring up thence the ark of
God the LORD, [b]that dwelleth *between* the cherubims, whose name is called *on it.*
7 And they carried the ark of God [a]in a new
cart [b]out of the house of Abinadab: and Uzza and
Ahio drave the cart.
8 [a]And David and all Israel played before
God with all *their* might, and with singing, and
with harps, and with psalteries, and with timbrels,
and with cymbals, and with trumpets.
9 And when they came unto the threshingfloor of Chidon, Uzza put forth his hand to hold
the ark; for the oxen stumbled.
10 And the anger of the LORD was kindled
against Uzza, and he smote him, [a]because he put
his hand to the ark: and there he [b]died before
God.
11 And David was displeased, because the
LORD had made a breach upon Uzza: wherefore
that place is called Perez–uzza to this day.
12 And David was afraid of God that day,
saying, How shall I bring the ark of God *home*
to me?
13 So David brought not the ark *home* to
himself to the city of David, but carried it aside
into the house of Obed–edom the Gittite.
14 [a]And the ark of God remained with the
family of Obed–edom in his house three months.
And the LORD blessed [b]the house of Obed–edom,
and all that he had.

David Established at Jerusalem
(2 Sam. 5:11–16)

14 Now [a]Hiram king of Tyre sent messengers
to David, and timber of cedars, with masons and carpenters, to build him an house.
2 And David perceived that the LORD had
confirmed him king over Israel, for his kingdom
was [a]lifted up on high, because of his people
Israel.
3 And David took more wives at Jerusalem:
and David begat more sons and daughters.
4 Now [a]these *are* the names of *his* children
which he had in Jerusalem; Shammua, and Shobab, Nathan, and Solomon,
5 And Ibhar, and Elishua, and Elpalet,
6 And Nogah, and Nepheg, and Japhia,
7 And Elishama, and Beeliada, and Eliphalet.

The Philistines Defeated
(2 Sam. 5:17–25)

8 And when the Philistines heard that [a]Da-
vid was anointed king over all Israel, all the Philistines went up to seek David. And David heard *of*
it, and went out against them.
9 And the Philistines came and spread
themselves [a]in the valley of Rephaim.
10 And David [a]enquired of God, saying,
Shall I go up against the Philistines? and wilt thou
deliver them into mine hand? And the LORD said
unto him, Go up; for I will deliver them into thine
hand.
11 So they came up to Baal–perazim; and David smote them there. Then David said, God hath
broken in upon mine enemies by mine hand like
the breaking forth of waters: therefore they called
the name of that place Baal–perazim.
12 And when they had left their gods there,
David gave a commandment, and they were
burned with fire.

NKJV

to us, [a]for we have not inquired at it since the
days of Saul."
4 Then all the assembly said that they would
do so, for the thing was right in the eyes of all
the people.
5 So [a]David gathered all Israel together,
from [b]Shihor in Egypt to as far as the entrance
of Hamath, to bring the ark of God [c]from Kirjath
Jearim.
6 And David and all Israel went up to
[a]Baalah,* to Kirjath Jearim, which belonged to
Judah, to bring up from there the ark of God the
LORD, [b]who dwells *between* the cherubim, where
His name is proclaimed.
7 So they carried the ark of God [a]on a new
cart [b]from the house of Abinadab, and Uzza and
Ahio drove the cart.
8 Then [a]David and all Israel played *music*
before God with all *their* might, with singing, on
harps, on stringed instruments, on tambourines,
on cymbals, and with trumpets.
9 And when they came to *Chidon's threshing floor, Uzza put out his hand to hold the ark,
for the oxen stumbled.
10 Then the anger of the LORD was aroused
against Uzza, and He struck him [a]because he put
his hand to the ark; and he [b]died there before
God.
11 And David became angry because of the
LORD's outbreak against Uzza; therefore that
place is called *Perez Uzza to this day.
12 David was afraid of God that day, saying,
"How can I bring the ark of God to me?"
13 So David would not move the ark with
him into the City of David, but took it aside into
the house of Obed-Edom the Gittite.
14 [a]The ark of God remained with the family
of Obed-Edom in his house three months. And
the LORD blessed [b]the house of Obed-Edom and
all that he had.

David Established at Jerusalem
(2 Sam. 5:11–16)

14 Now [a]Hiram king of Tyre sent messengers
to David, and cedar trees, with masons and
carpenters, to build him a house.
2 So David knew that the LORD had established him as king over Israel, for his kingdom
was [a]highly exalted for the sake of His people
Israel.
3 Then David took more wives in Jerusalem, and David begot more sons and daughters.
4 And [a]these are the names of his children
whom he had in Jerusalem: *Shammua, Shobab,
Nathan, Solomon,
5 Ibhar, *Elishua, *Elpelet,
6 Nogah, Nepheg, Japhia,
7 Elishama, *Beeliada, and Eliphelet.

The Philistines Defeated
(2 Sam. 5:17–25)

8 Now when the Philistines heard that [a]Da-
vid had been anointed king over all Israel, all the
Philistines went up to search for David. And David heard *of it* and went out against them.
9 Then the Philistines went and made a raid
[a]on the Valley of Rephaim.
10 And David [a]inquired of God, saying,
"Shall I go up against the Philistines? Will You
deliver them into my hand?" The LORD said to
him, "Go up, for I will deliver them into your
hand."
11 So they went up to Baal Perazim, and David defeated them there. Then David said, "God
has broken through my enemies by my hand like
a breakthrough of water." Therefore they called
the name of that place *Baal Perazim.
12 And when they left their gods there, David
gave a commandment, and they were burned with
fire.

---

3 [a]1 Sam. 7:1, 2
5 [a]1 Sam. 7:5 [b]Josh. 13:3 [c]1 Sam. 6:21; 7:1, 2
6 [a]Josh. 15:9, 60 [b]Ex. 25:22; 1 Sam. 4:4; 2 Kin. 19:15
7 [a]Num. 4:15; 1 Sam. 6:7 [b]1 Sam. 7:1
8 [a]2 Sam. 6:5
10 [a][Num. 4:15]; 1 Chr. 15:13, 15 [b]Lev. 10:2
14 [a]2 Sam. 6:11 [b][Gen. 30:27]; 1 Chr. 26:4–8

CHAPTER 14
1 [a]2 Sam. 5:11; 1 Kin. 5:1
2 [a]Num. 24:7
4 [a]1 Chr. 3:5–8
8 [a]2 Sam. 5:17–21
9 [a]Josh. 17:15; 18:16; 1 Chr. 11:15; 14:13
10 [a]1 Sam. 23:2, 4; 30:8; 2 Sam. 2:1; 5:19, 23; 21:1

*

13:6 *Baale Judah,* 2 Sam. 6:2
13:9 *Nachon,* 2 Sam. 6:6
13:11 Lit. *Outburst Against Uzza*
14:4 *Shimea,* 1 Chr. 3:5
14:5 *Elishama,* 1 Chr. 3:6 • *Eliphelet,* 1 Chr. 3:6
14:7 *Eliada,* 2 Sam. 5:6; 1 Chr. 3:8
14:11 Lit. *Master of Breakthroughs*

KJV

13 [a]And the Philistines yet again spread themselves abroad in the valley.

14 Therefore David enquired again of God; and God said unto him, Go not up after them; turn away from them, [a]and come upon them over against the mulberry trees.

15 And it shall be, when thou shalt hear a sound of going in the tops of the mulberry trees, *that* then thou shalt go out to battle: for God is gone forth before thee to smite the host of the Philistines.

16 David therefore did as God commanded him: and they smote the host of the Philistines from Gibeon even to Gazer.

17 And [a]the fame of David went out into all lands; and the LORD [b]brought the fear of him upon all nations.

The Ark Brought to Jerusalem
(*2 Sam. 6:12–16*)

15 And *David* made him houses in the city of David, and prepared a place for the ark of God, [a]and pitched for it a tent.

2 Then David said, None ought to carry the [a]ark of God but the Levites: for [b]them hath the LORD chosen to carry the ark of God, and to minister unto him for ever.

3 And David [a]gathered all Israel together to Jerusalem, to bring up the ark of the LORD unto his place, which he had prepared for it.

4 And David assembled the children of Aaron, and the Levites:

5 Of the sons of Kohath; Uriel the chief, and his brethren an hundred and twenty:

6 Of the sons of Merari; Asaiah the chief, and his brethren two hundred and twenty:

7 Of the sons of Gershom; Joel the chief, and his brethren an hundred and thirty:

8 Of the sons of [a]Elizaphan; Shemaiah the chief, and his brethren two hundred:

9 Of the sons of [a]Hebron; Eliel the chief, and his brethren fourscore:

10 Of the sons of Uzziel; Amminadab the chief, and his brethren an hundred and twelve.

11 And David called for [a]Zadok and [b]Abiathar the priests, and for the Levites, for Uriel, Asaiah, and Joel, Shemaiah, and Eliel, and Amminadab,

12 And said unto them, Ye *are* the chief of the fathers of the Levites: sanctify yourselves, *both* ye and your brethren, that ye may bring up the ark of the LORD God of Israel unto *the place that* I have prepared for it.

13 For [a]because ye *did it* not at the first, [b]the LORD our God made a breach upon us, for that we sought him not after the due order.

14 So the priests and the Levites sanctified themselves to bring up the ark of the LORD God of Israel.

15 And the children of the Levites bare the ark of God upon their shoulders with the staves thereon, as [a]Moses commanded according to the word of the LORD.

16 And David spake to the chief of the Levites to appoint their brethren *to be* the singers with instruments of musick, psalteries and harps and cymbals, sounding, by lifting up the voice with joy.

17 So the Levites appointed [a]Heman the son of Joel; and of his brethren, [b]Asaph the son of Berechiah; and of the sons of Merari their brethren, [c]Ethan the son of Kushaiah;

18 And with them their brethren of the second *degree*, Zechariah, Ben, and Jaaziel, and Shemiramoth, and Jehiel, and Unni, Eliab, and Benaiah, and Maaseiah, and Mattithiah, and Elipheleh, and Mikneiah, and Obed–edom, and Jeiel, the porters.

19 So the singers, Heman, Asaph, and Ethan, *were appointed* to sound with cymbals of brass;

20 And Zechariah, and Aziel, and Shemira-

---

13 [a]2 Sam. 5:22–25
14 [a]2 Sam. 5:23
17 [a]Josh. 6:27; 2 Chr. 26:8 [b][Ex. 15:14–16; Deut. 2:25; 11:25]; 2 Chr. 20:29

CHAPTER 15

1 [a]1 Chr. 16:1
2 [a][Num. 4:15]; 2 Sam. 6:1–11 [b]Num. 4:2–15; Deut. 10:8; 31:9
3 [a]Ex. 40:20, 21; 2 Sam. 6:12; 1 Kin. 8:1; 1 Chr. 13:5
8 [a]Ex. 6:22
9 [a]Ex. 6:18
11 [a]2 Sam. 8:17; 15:24–29, 35, 36; 18:19, 22, 27; 19:11; 20:25; 1 Chr. 12:28 [b]1 Sam. 22:20–23; 23:6; 30:7; 1 Kin. 2:22, 26, 27; Mark 2:6
13 [a]2 Sam. 6:3 [b]1 Chr. 13:7–11
15 [a]Ex. 25:14; Num. 4:15; 7:9
17 [a]1 Chr. 6:33; 25:1 [b]1 Chr. 6:39 [c]1 Chr. 6:44

*

15:18 So with MT, Vg.; LXX omits *Ben*

NKJV

13 [a]Then the Philistines once again made a raid on the valley.

14 Therefore David inquired again of God, and God said to him, "You shall not go up after them; circle around them, [a]and come upon them in front of the mulberry trees.

15 "And it shall be, when you hear a sound of marching in the tops of the mulberry trees, then you shall go out to battle, for God has gone out before you to strike the camp of the Philistines."

16 So David did as God commanded him, and they drove back the army of the Philistines from Gibeon as far as Gezer.

17 Then [a]the fame of David went out into all lands, and the LORD [b]brought the fear of him upon all nations.

The Ark Brought to Jerusalem
(*2 Sam. 6:12–16*)

15 *David* built houses for himself in the City of David; and he prepared a place for the ark of God, [a]and pitched a tent for it.

2 Then David said, "No one may carry the [a]ark of God but the Levites, for [b]the LORD has chosen them to carry the ark of God and to minister before Him forever."

3 And David [a]gathered all Israel together at Jerusalem, to bring up the ark of the LORD to its place, which he had prepared for it.

4 Then David assembled the children of Aaron and the Levites:

5 of the sons of Kohath, Uriel the chief, and one hundred and twenty of his brethren;

6 of the sons of Merari, Asaiah the chief, and two hundred and twenty of his brethren;

7 of the sons of Gershom, Joel the chief, and one hundred and thirty of his brethren;

8 of the sons of [a]Elizaphan, Shemaiah the chief, and two hundred of his brethren;

9 of the sons of [a]Hebron, Eliel the chief, and eighty of his brethren;

10 of the sons of Uzziel, Amminadab the chief, and one hundred and twelve of his brethren.

11 And David called for [a]Zadok and [b]Abiathar the priests, and for the Levites: for Uriel, Asaiah, Joel, Shemaiah, Eliel, and Amminadab.

12 He said to them, "You *are* the heads of the fathers' *houses* of the Levites; sanctify yourselves, you and your brethren, that you may bring up the ark of the LORD God of Israel to *the place* I have prepared for it.

13 "For [a]because you *did* not *do it* the first *time*, [b]the LORD our God broke out against us, because we did not consult Him about the proper order."

14 So the priests and the Levites sanctified themselves to bring up the ark of the LORD God of Israel.

15 And the children of the Levites bore the ark of God on their shoulders, by its poles, as [a]Moses had commanded according to the word of the LORD.

16 Then David spoke to the leaders of the Levites to appoint their brethren *to be* the singers accompanied by instruments of music, stringed instruments, harps, and cymbals, by raising the voice with resounding joy.

17 So the Levites appointed [a]Heman the son of Joel; and of his brethren, [b]Asaph the son of Berechiah; and of their brethren, the sons of Merari, [c]Ethan the son of Kushaiah;

18 and with them their brethren of the second *rank:* Zechariah, *Ben, Jaaziel, Shemiramoth, Jehiel, Unni, Eliab, Benaiah, Maaseiah, Mattithiah, Elipheleh, Mikneiah, Obed-Edom, and Jeiel, the gatekeepers;

19 the singers, Heman, Asaph, and Ethan, *were* to sound the cymbals of bronze;

20 Zechariah, Aziel, Shemiramoth, Jehiel,

KJV

moth, and Jehiel, and Unni, and Eliab, and Maaseiah, and Benaiah, with psalteries on [a]Alamoth;

21 And Mattithiah, and Elipheleh, and Mikneiah, and Obed–edom, and Jeiel, and Azaziah, with harps on the [a]Sheminith to excel.

22 And Chenaniah, chief of the Levites, *was* for song: he instructed about the song, because he *was* skilful.

23 And Berechiah and Elkanah *were* doorkeepers for the ark.

24 And Shebaniah, and Jehoshaphat, and Nethaneel, and Amasai, and Zechariah, and Benaiah, and Eliezer, the priests, [a]did blow with the trumpets before the ark of God: and [b]Obed–edom and Jehiah *were* doorkeepers for the ark.

25 So [a]David, and the elders of Israel, and the captains over thousands, went to bring up the ark of the covenant of the LORD out of the house of Obed–edom with joy.

26 And it came to pass, when God helped the Levites that bare the ark of the covenant of the LORD, that they offered seven bullocks and seven rams.

27 And David *was* clothed with a robe of fine [a]linen, and all the Levites that bare the ark, and the singers, and Chenaniah the master of the song with the singers: David also *had* upon him an ephod of linen.

28 [a]Thus all Israel brought up the ark of the covenant of the LORD with shouting, and with sound of the cornet, and with trumpets, and with cymbals, making a noise with psalteries and harps.

29 And it came to pass, [a]*as* the ark of the covenant of the LORD came to the city of David, that Michal the daughter of Saul looking out at a window saw king David dancing and playing: and she despised him in her heart.

The Ark Placed in the Tabernacle
(*2 Sam. 6:17–19*)

16 So [a]they brought the ark of God, and set it in the midst of the tent that David had pitched for it: and they offered burnt sacrifices and peace offerings before God.

2 And when David had made an end of offering the burnt offerings and the peace offerings, [a]he blessed the people in the name of the LORD.

3 And he dealt to every one of Israel, both man and woman, to every one a loaf of bread, and a good piece of flesh, and a flagon *of wine*.

4 And he appointed *certain* of the Levites to minister before the ark of the LORD, and to [a]record, and to thank and praise the LORD God of Israel:

5 Asaph the chief, and next to him Zechariah, [a]Jeiel, and Shemiramoth, and Jehiel, and Mattithiah, and Eliab, and Benaiah, and Obed–edom: and Jeiel with psalteries and with harps; but Asaph made a sound with cymbals;

6 Benaiah also and Jahaziel the priests with trumpets continually before the ark of the covenant of God.

David's Song of Thanksgiving
(*Ps. 96:1–13; 105:1–15; 106:1, 47, 48*)

7 Then on that day [a]David delivered [b]first *this psalm* to thank the LORD into the hand of Asaph and his brethren.

8 [a]Give thanks unto the LORD, call upon his name, make known his deeds among the people.

9 Sing unto him, sing psalms unto him, talk ye of all his wondrous works.

10 Glory ye in his holy name: let the heart of them rejoice that seek the LORD.

11 Seek the LORD and his strength, seek his face continually.

20 [a]Ps. 46:title
21 [a]Ps. 6:title
24 [a][Num. 10:8]; Ps. 81:3 [b]1 Chr. 13:13, 14
25 [a]2 Sam. 6:12, 13; 1 Kin. 8:1
27 [a]1 Sam. 2:18, 28
28 [a]Num. 23:21; Josh. 6:20; 1 Chr. 13:8; Zech. 4:7; 1 Thess. 4:16
29 [a]1 Sam. 18:20, 27; 19:11–17; 2 Sam. 3:13, 14; 6:16, 20–23

CHAPTER 16

1 [a]2 Sam. 6:17; 1 Chr. 15:1
2 [a]1 Kin. 8:14
4 [a]Ps. 38:title; 70:title
5 [a]1 Chr. 15:18
7 [a]2 Sam. 22:1; 23:1 [b]Ps. 105:1–15
8 [a]1 Chr. 17:19, 20; Ps. 105:1–15

NKJV

Unni, Eliab, Maaseiah, and Benaiah, with strings according to [a]Alamoth;

21 Mattithiah, Elipheleh, Mikneiah, Obed-Edom, Jeiel, and Azaziah, to direct with harps on the [a]Sheminith;

22 Chenaniah, leader of the Levites, was instructor *in charge of* the music, because he *was* skillful;

23 Berechiah and Elkanah *were* doorkeepers for the ark;

24 Shebaniah, Joshaphat, Nethanel, Amasai, Zechariah, Benaiah, and Eliezer, the priests, [a]were to blow the trumpets before the ark of God; and [b]Obed-Edom and Jehiah, doorkeepers for the ark.

25 So [a]David, the elders of Israel, and the captains over thousands went to bring up the ark of the covenant of the LORD from the house of Obed-Edom with joy.

26 And so it was, when God helped the Levites who bore the ark of the covenant of the LORD, that they offered seven bulls and seven rams.

27 David was clothed with a robe of fine [a]linen, as were all the Levites who bore the ark, the singers, and Chenaniah the music master *with* the singers. David also wore a linen ephod.

28 [a]Thus all Israel brought up the ark of the covenant of the LORD with shouting and with the sound of the horn, with trumpets and with cymbals, making music with stringed instruments and harps.

29 And it happened, [a]*as* the ark of the covenant of the LORD came to the City of David, that Michal, Saul's daughter, looked through a window and saw King David whirling and playing music; and she despised him in her heart.

The Ark Placed in the Tabernacle
(*2 Sam. 6:17–19*)

16 So [a]they brought the ark of God, and set it in the midst of the tabernacle that David had erected for it. Then they offered burnt offerings and peace offerings before God.

2 And when David had finished offering the burnt offerings and the peace offerings, [a]he blessed the people in the name of the LORD.

3 Then he distributed to everyone of Israel, both man and woman, to everyone a loaf of bread, a piece *of meat*, and a cake of raisins.

4 And he appointed some of the Levites to minister before the ark of the LORD, to [a]commemorate, to thank, and to praise the LORD God of Israel:

5 Asaph the chief, and next to him Zechariah, *then* [a]Jeiel, Shemiramoth, Jehiel, Mattithiah, Eliab, Benaiah, and Obed-Edom: Jeiel with stringed instruments and harps, but Asaph made music with cymbals;

6 Benaiah and Jahaziel the priests regularly *blew* the trumpets before the ark of the covenant of God.

David's Song of Thanksgiving
(*Ps. 96:1–13; 105:1–15; 106:1, 47, 48*)

7 On that day [a]David [b]first delivered *this psalm* into the hand of Asaph and his brethren, to thank the LORD:

8 [a]Oh, give thanks to the LORD!
Call upon His name;
Make known His deeds among the peoples!
9 Sing to Him, sing psalms to Him;
Talk of all His wondrous works!
10 Glory in His holy name;
Let the hearts of those rejoice who seek the LORD!
11 Seek the LORD and His strength;
Seek His face evermore!

KJV

12 Remember his marvellous works that he hath done, his wonders, and the judgments of his mouth;
13 O ye seed of Israel his servant, ye children of Jacob, his chosen ones.
14 He *is* the LORD our God; his [a]judgments *are* in all the earth.
15 Be ye mindful always of his covenant; the word *which* he commanded to a thousand generations;
16 *Even of the* [a]*covenant* which he made with Abraham, and of his oath unto Isaac;
17 And hath [a]confirmed the same to [b]Jacob for a law, *and* to Israel *for* an everlasting covenant,
18 Saying, Unto thee will I give the land of Canaan, the lot of your inheritance;
19 When ye were but few, [a]even a few, and strangers in it.
20 And *when* they went from nation to nation, and from *one* kingdom to another people;
21 He suffered no man to do them wrong: yea, he [a]reproved kings for their sakes,
22 *Saying*, [a]Touch not mine anointed, and do my prophets no harm.
23 [a]Sing unto the LORD, all the earth; shew forth from day to day his salvation.
24 Declare his glory among the heathen; his marvellous works among all nations.
25 For great *is* the LORD, and greatly to be praised: he also *is* to be feared above all gods.
26 For all the gods [a]of the people *are* idols: but the LORD made the heavens.
27 Glory and honour *are* in his presence; strength and gladness *are* in his place.
28 Give unto the LORD, ye kindreds of the people, give unto the LORD glory and strength.
29 Give unto the LORD the glory *due* unto his name: bring an offering, and come before him: worship the LORD in the beauty of holiness.
30 Fear before him, all the earth: the world also shall be stable, that it be not moved.
31 Let the heavens be glad, and let the earth rejoice: and let *men* say among the nations, The LORD reigneth.
32 Let the sea roar, and the fulness thereof: let the fields rejoice, and all that *is* therein.
33 Then shall the [a]trees of the wood sing out at the presence of the LORD, because he [b]cometh to judge the earth.
34 [a]O give thanks unto the LORD; for *he is* good; for his mercy *endureth* for ever.
35 [a]And say ye, Save us, O God of our salvation, and gather us together, and deliver us from the heathen, that we may give thanks to thy holy name, *and* glory in thy praise.
36 [a]Blessed *be* the LORD God of Israel for ever and ever. And all [b]the people said, Amen, and praised the LORD.

14 [a]Ps. 48:10; [Is. 26:9]
16 [a]Gen. 17:2; 26:3; 28:13; 35:11
17 [a]Gen. 35:11, 12 [b]Gen. 28:10–15
19 [a]Gen. 34:30; Deut. 7:7
21 [a]Gen. 12:17; 20:3; Ex. 7:15–18
22 [a]Gen. 20:7; Ps. 105:15
23 [a]Ps. 96:1–13
26 [a]Lev. 19:4; [1 Cor. 8:5, 6]
33 [a]Is. 55:12, 13 [b][Joel 3:1–14]; Zech. 14:1–14; [Matt. 25:31–46]
34 [a]2 Chr. 5:13; 7:3; Ezra 3:11; Ps. 106:1; 107:1; 118:1; 136:1; Jer. 33:11
35 [a]Ps. 106:47, 48
36 [a]1 Kin. 8:15, 56; Ps. 72:18 [b]Deut. 27:15; Neh. 8:6

NKJV

12 Remember His marvelous works which
He has done,
His wonders, and the judgments of His
mouth,
13 O seed of Israel His servant,
You children of Jacob, His chosen ones!

14 He *is* the LORD our God;
His [a]judgments *are* in all the earth.
15 Remember His covenant forever,
The word which He commanded, for a
thousand generations,
16 *The* [a]*covenant which* He made with
Abraham,
And His oath to Isaac,
17 And [a]confirmed it to [b]Jacob for a statute,
To Israel *for* an everlasting covenant,
18 Saying, "To you I will give the land of
Canaan
As the allotment of your inheritance,"
19 When you were [a]few in number,
Indeed very few, and strangers in it.

20 When they went from one nation to
another,
And from *one* kingdom to another people,
21 He permitted no man to do them wrong;
Yes, He [a]rebuked kings for their sakes,
22 *Saying*, [a]"Do not touch My anointed ones,
And do My prophets no harm."

23 [a]Sing to the LORD, all the earth;
Proclaim the good news of His salvation
from day to day.
24 Declare His glory among the nations,
His wonders among all peoples.

25 For the LORD *is* great and greatly to be
praised;
He *is* also to be feared above all gods.
26 For all the gods [a]of the peoples *are* idols,
But the LORD made the heavens.
27 Honor and majesty *are* before Him;
Strength and gladness are in His place.

28 Give to the LORD, O families of the
peoples,
Give to the LORD glory and strength.
29 Give to the LORD the glory *due* His name;
Bring an offering, and come before Him.
Oh, worship the LORD in the beauty of
holiness!
30 Tremble before Him, all the earth.
The world also is firmly established,
It shall not be moved.

31 Let the heavens rejoice, and let the earth
be glad;
And let them say among the nations, "The
LORD reigns."
32 Let the sea roar, and all its fullness;
Let the field rejoice, and all that *is* in it.
33 Then the [a]trees of the woods shall rejoice
before the LORD,
For He is [b]coming to judge the earth.

34 [a]Oh, give thanks to the LORD, for *He is*
good!
For His mercy *endures* forever.
35 [a]And say, "Save us, O God of our salvation;
Gather us together, and deliver us from
the Gentiles,
To give thanks to Your holy name,
To triumph in Your praise."

36 [a]Blessed *be* the LORD God of Israel
From everlasting to everlasting!

And all [b]the people said, "Amen!" and praised the LORD.

KJV

Regular Worship Maintained

37 So he left there before the ark of the covenant of the LORD [a]Asaph and his brethren, to minister before the ark continually, as every day's work [b]required:

38 And [a]Obed–edom with their brethren, threescore and eight; Obed–edom also the son of Jeduthun and Hosah *to be* porters:

39 And Zadok the priest, and his brethren the priests, [a]before the tabernacle of the LORD [b]in the high place that *was* at Gibeon,

40 To offer burnt offerings unto the LORD upon the altar of the burnt offering continually [a]morning and evening, and *to do* according to all that is written in the law of the LORD, which he commanded Israel;

41 And with them Heman and Jeduthun, and the rest that were chosen, who were expressed by name, to give thanks to the LORD, [a]because his mercy *endureth* for ever;

42 And with them Heman and Jeduthun with trumpets and cymbals for those that should make a sound, and with musical instruments of God. And the sons of Jeduthun *were* porters.

43 [a]And all the people departed every man to his house: and David returned to bless his house.

God's Covenant with David
(2 Sam. 7:1–29)

17 Now [a]it came to pass, as David sat in his house, that David said to Nathan the prophet, Lo, I dwell in an house of cedars, but the ark of the covenant of the LORD *remaineth* under curtains.

2 Then Nathan said unto David, Do all that *is* in thine heart; for God *is* with thee.

3 And it came to pass the same night, that the word of God came to Nathan, saying,

4 Go and tell David my servant, Thus saith the LORD, Thou shalt [a]not build me an house to dwell in:

5 For I have not dwelt in an house since the day that I brought up Israel unto this day; but have gone from tent to tent, and from *one* tabernacle *to another.*

6 Wheresoever I have walked with all Israel, spake I a word to any of the judges of Israel, whom I commanded to feed my people, saying, Why have ye not built me an house of cedars?

7 Now therefore thus shalt thou say unto my servant David, Thus saith the LORD of hosts, I took thee [a]from the sheepcote, *even* from following the sheep, that thou shouldest be ruler over my people Israel:

8 And I have been with thee whithersoever thou hast walked, and have cut off all thine enemies from before thee, and have made thee a name like the name of the great men that *are* in the earth.

9 Also I will ordain a place for my people Israel, and will [a]plant them, and they shall dwell in their place, and shall be moved no more; neither shall the children of wickedness waste them any more, as at the beginning,

10 And since the time that I commanded judges *to be* over my people Israel. Moreover I will subdue all thine enemies. Furthermore I tell thee that the LORD will build thee an house.

11 And it shall come to pass, when thy days be [a]expired that thou must go *to be* with thy fathers, that I will raise up thy [b]seed after thee, which shall be of thy sons; and I will establish his kingdom.

12 [a]He shall build me an house, and I will stablish his throne for ever.

13 [a]I will be his father, and he shall be my son: and I will not take my mercy away from him, [b]as I took *it* from *him* that was before thee:

14 But [a]I will settle him in mine house and

37 [a]1 Chr. 16:4, 5 [b]2 Chr. 8:14; Ezra 3:4
38 [a]1 Chr. 13:14
39 [a]1 Chr. 21:29; 2 Chr. 1:3 [b]1 Kin. 3:4
40 [a][Ex. 29:38–42; Num. 28:3, 4]
41 [a]1 Chr. 25:1–6; 2 Chr. 5:13; 7:3; Ezra 3:11; Jer. 33:11
43 [a]2 Sam. 6:18–20

CHAPTER 17

1 [a]2 Sam. 7:1; 1 Chr. 14:1
4 [a][1 Chr. 28:2, 3]
7 [a]1 Sam. 16:11–13
9 [a][Deut. 30:1–9; Jer. 16:14–16; 23:5–8; 24:6; Ezek. 37:21–27]; Amos 9:14
11 [a]1 Kin. 2:10; 1 Chr. 29:28 [b]1 Kin. 5:5; 6:12; 8:19–21; [1 Chr. 22:9–13; 28:20]; Matt. 1:6; Luke 3:31
12 [a]1 Kin. 6:38; 2 Chr. 6:2; [Ps. 89:20–37]
13 [a]2 Sam. 7:14, 15; Matt. 3:17; Mark 1:11; Luke 3:22; 2 Cor. 6:18; Heb. 1:5 [b][1 Sam. 15:23–28]; 1 Chr. 10:14
14 [a]Ps. 89:3, 4; Matt. 19:28; 25:31; [Luke 1:31–33]

*

17:10 Royal dynasty

NKJV

Regular Worship Maintained

37 So he left [a]Asaph and his brothers there before the ark of the covenant of the LORD to minister before the ark regularly, as every day's work [b]required;

38 and [a]Obed-Edom with his sixty-eight brethren, including Obed-Edom the son of Jeduthun, and Hosah, *to be* gatekeepers;

39 and Zadok the priest and his brethren the priests, [a]before the tabernacle of the LORD [b]at the high place that *was* at Gibeon,

40 to offer burnt offerings to the LORD on the altar of burnt offering regularly [a]morning and evening, and *to do* according to all that is written in the Law of the LORD which He commanded Israel;

41 and with them Heman and Jeduthun and the rest who were chosen, who were designated by name, to give thanks to the LORD, [a]because His mercy *endures* forever;

42 and with them Heman and Jeduthun, to sound aloud with trumpets and cymbals and the musical instruments of God. Now the sons of Jeduthun *were* gatekeepers.

43 [a]Then all the people departed, every man to his house; and David returned to bless his house.

God's Covenant with David
(2 Sam. 7:1–29)

17 Now [a]it came to pass, when David was dwelling in his house, that David said to Nathan the prophet, "See now, I dwell in a house of cedar, but the ark of the covenant of the LORD *is* under tent curtains."

2 Then Nathan said to David, "Do all that *is* in your heart, for God *is* with you."

3 But it happened that night that the word of God came to Nathan, saying,

4 "Go and tell My servant David, 'Thus says the LORD: "You shall [a]not build Me a house to dwell in.

5 "For I have not dwelt in a house since the time that I brought up Israel, even to this day, but have gone from tent to tent, and from *one* tabernacle *to another.*

6 "Wherever I have moved about with all Israel, have I ever spoken a word to any of the judges of Israel, whom I commanded to shepherd My people, saying, 'Why have you not built Me a house of cedar?' " '

7 "Now therefore, thus shall you say to My servant David, 'Thus says the LORD of hosts: "I took you [a]from the sheepfold, from following the sheep, to be ruler over My people Israel.

8 "And I have been with you wherever you have gone, and have cut off all your enemies from before you, and have made you a name like the name of the great men who *are* on the earth.

9 "Moreover I will appoint a place for My people Israel, and will [a]plant them, that they may dwell in a place of their own and move no more; nor shall the sons of wickedness oppress them anymore, as previously,

10 "since the time that I commanded judges *to be* over My people Israel. Also I will subdue all your enemies. Furthermore I tell you that the LORD will build you a *house.

11 "And it shall be, when your days are [a]fulfilled, when you must go *to be* with your fathers, that I will set up your [b]seed after you, who will be of your sons; and I will establish his kingdom.

12 [a]"He shall build Me a house, and I will establish his throne forever.

13 [a]"I will be his Father, and he shall be My son; and I will not take My mercy away from him, [b]as I took *it* from *him* who was before you.

14 "And [a]I will establish him in My house

KJV

in my kingdom for ever: and his throne shall be established for evermore.

15 According to all these words, and according to all this vision, so did Nathan speak unto David.

16 [a]And David the king came and sat before the LORD, and said, Who *am* I, O LORD God, and what *is* mine house, that thou hast brought me hitherto?

17 And *yet* this was a small thing in thine eyes, O God; for thou hast *also* spoken of thy servant's house for a great while to come, and hast regarded me according to the estate of a man of high degree, O LORD God.

18 What can David *speak* more to thee for the honour of thy servant? for thou knowest thy servant.

19 O LORD, for thy servant's sake, and according to thine own heart, hast thou done all this greatness, in making known all *these* great things.

20 O LORD, *there is* none like thee, neither *is there any* God beside thee, according to all that we have heard with our ears.

21 [a]And what one nation in the earth *is* like thy people Israel, whom God went to redeem *to be* his own people, to make thee a name of greatness and terribleness, by driving out nations from before thy people, whom thou hast redeemed out of Egypt?

22 For thy people Israel didst thou make thine own people for ever; and thou, LORD, becamest their God.

23 Therefore now, LORD, let the thing that thou hast spoken concerning thy servant and concerning his house be established for ever, and do as thou hast said.

24 Let it even be established, that thy name may be magnified for ever, saying, The LORD of hosts *is* the God of Israel, *even* a God to Israel: and *let* the house of David thy servant *be* established before thee.

25 For thou, O my God, hast told thy servant that thou wilt build him an house: therefore thy servant hath found *in his heart* to pray before thee.

26 And now, LORD, thou art God, and hast promised this goodness unto thy servant:

27 Now therefore let it please thee to bless the house of thy servant, that it may be before thee for ever: for thou blessest, O LORD, and *it shall be* blessed for ever.

David's Further Conquests
(2 Sam. 8:1–14)

18 Now after this [a]it came to pass, that David smote the Philistines, and subdued them, and took Gath and her towns out of the hand of the Philistines.

2 And he smote [a]Moab; and the Moabites became David's [b]servants, *and* brought gifts.

3 And [a]David smote Hadarezer king of Zobah unto Hamath, as he went to stablish his dominion by the river Euphrates.

4 And David took from him a thousand chariots, and seven thousand horsemen, and twenty thousand footmen: David also houghed all the chariot *horses,* but reserved of them an hundred chariots.

5 And when the [a]Syrians of Damascus came to help Hadarezer king of Zobah, David slew of the Syrians two and twenty thousand men.

6 Then David put *garrisons* in Syria–damascus; and the Syrians became David's servants, *and* brought gifts. Thus the LORD preserved David whithersoever he went.

7 And David took the shields of gold that were on the servants of Hadarezer, and brought them to Jerusalem.

8 Likewise from Tibhath, and from Chun, cities of Hadarezer, brought David very much

---

16 [a]2 Sam. 7:18
21 [a][Deut. 4:6–8, 33–38]; Ps. 147:20

CHAPTER 18
1 [a]2 Sam. 8:1–18
2 [a]2 Sam. 8:2; Zeph. 2:9 [b]Ps. 60:8
3 [a]2 Sam. 8:3
5 [a]2 Sam. 8:5, 6; 1 Kin. 11:23–25

*
18:3 Heb. *Hadarezer*
18:4 *seven hundred,* 2 Sam. 8:4
18:8 *Betah,* 2 Sam. 8:8

NKJV

and in My kingdom forever; and his throne shall be established forever." ' "

15 According to all these words and according to all this vision, so Nathan spoke to David.

16 [a]Then King David went in and sat before the LORD; and he said: "Who *am* I, O LORD God? And what is my house, that You have brought me this far?

17 "And *yet* this was a small thing in Your sight, O God; and You have *also* spoken of Your servant's house for a great while to come, and have regarded me according to the rank of a man of high degree, O LORD God.

18 "What more can David *say* to You for the honor of Your servant? For You know Your servant.

19 "O LORD, for Your servant's sake, and according to Your own heart, You have done all this greatness, in making known all these great things.

20 "O LORD, *there is* none like You, nor *is there any* God besides You, according to all that we have heard with our ears.

21 [a]"And who *is* like Your people Israel, the one nation on the earth whom God went to redeem for Himself *as* a people—to make for Yourself a name by great and awesome deeds, by driving out nations from before Your people whom You redeemed from Egypt?

22 "For You have made Your people Israel Your very own people forever; and You, LORD, have become their God.

23 "And now, O LORD, the word which You have spoken concerning Your servant and concerning his house, *let it* be established forever, and do as You have said.

24 "So let it be established, that Your name may be magnified forever, saying, 'The LORD of hosts, the God of Israel, *is* Israel's God.' And let the house of Your servant David be established before You.

25 "For You, O my God, have revealed to Your servant that You will build him a house. Therefore Your servant has found it *in his heart* to pray before You.

26 "And now, LORD, You are God, and have promised this goodness to Your servant.

27 "Now You have been pleased to bless the house of Your servant, that it may continue before You forever; for You have blessed it, O LORD, and *it shall be* blessed forever."

David's Further Conquests
(2 Sam. 8:1–14)

18 After this [a]it came to pass that David attacked the Philistines, subdued them, and took Gath and its towns from the hand of the Philistines.

2 Then he defeated [a]Moab, and the Moabites became David's [b]servants, *and* brought tribute.

3 And [a]David defeated *Hadadezer king of Zobah *as far as* Hamath, as he went to establish his power by the River Euphrates.

4 David took from him one thousand chariots, *seven thousand horsemen, and twenty thousand foot soldiers. Also David hamstrung all the chariot *horses,* except that he spared enough of them for one hundred chariots.

5 When the [a]Syrians of Damascus came to help Hadadezer king of Zobah, David killed twenty-two thousand of the Syrians.

6 Then David put *garrisons* in Syria of Damascus; and the Syrians became David's servants, *and* brought tribute. So the LORD preserved David wherever he went.

7 And David took the shields of gold that were on the servants of Hadadezer, and brought them to Jerusalem.

8 Also from *Tibhath and from Chun, cities of Hadadezer, David brought a large amount of

KJV

[a]brass, wherewith [b]Solomon made the brasen sea, and the pillars, and the vessels of brass.

9 Now when Tou king of Hamath heard how David had smitten all the host of Hadarezer king of Zobah;

10 He sent Hadoram his son to king David, to enquire of his welfare, and to congratulate him, because he had fought against Hadarezer, and smitten him; (for Hadarezer had war with Tou;) and *with him* all manner of [a]vessels of gold and silver and brass.

11 Them also king David dedicated unto the LORD, with the silver and the gold that he brought from all *these* nations; from Edom, and from Moab, and from the [a]children of Ammon, and from the [b]Philistines, and from [c]Amalek.

12 Moreover, [a]Abishai the son of Zeruiah slew of the Edomites in the valley of salt [b]eighteen thousand.

13 [a]And he put garrisons in Edom; and all the Edomites became David's servants. Thus the LORD preserved David whithersoever he went.

David's Administration
(2 Sam. 8:15–18)

14 So David reigned over all Israel, and executed judgment and justice among all his people.

15 And Joab the son of Zeruiah *was* over the host; and Jehoshaphat the son of Ahilud, recorder.

16 And Zadok the son of Ahitub, and Abimelech the son of Abiathar, *were* the priests; and Shavsha was scribe;

17 [a]And Benaiah the son of Jehoiada *was* over the Cherethites and the Pelethites; and the sons of David *were* chief about the king.

The Ammonites and Syrians Defeated
(2 Sam. 10:1–19)

19 Now [a]it came to pass after this, that Nahash the king of the children of Ammon died, and his son reigned in his stead.

2 And David said, I will shew kindness unto Hanun the son of Nahash, because his father shewed kindness to me. And David sent messengers to comfort him concerning his father. So the servants of David came into the land of the children of Ammon to Hanun, to comfort him.

3 But the princes of the children of Ammon said to Hanun, Thinkest thou that David doth honour thy father, that he hath sent comforters unto thee? are not his servants come unto thee for to search, and to overthrow, and to spy out the land?

4 Wherefore Hanun took David's servants, and shaved them, and cut off their garments in the midst hard by their [a]buttocks, and sent them away.

5 Then there went *certain,* and told David how the men were served. And he sent to meet them: for the men were greatly ashamed. And the king said, Tarry at Jericho until your beards be grown, and *then* return.

6 And when the children of Ammon saw that they had made themselves odious to David, Hanun and the children of Ammon sent a thousand talents of silver to hire them chariots and horsemen out of Mesopotamia, and out of Syria–maachah, [a]and out of Zobah.

7 So they hired thirty and two thousand chariots, and the king of Maachah and his people; who came and pitched before Medeba. And the children of Ammon gathered themselves together from their cities, and came to battle.

8 And when David heard *of it,* he sent Joab, and all the host of the mighty men.

9 And the children of Ammon came out, and put the battle in array before the gate of the city: and the kings that were come *were* by themselves in the field.

10 Now when Joab saw that the battle was set against him before and behind, he chose out

---

8 [a]2 Sam. 8:8 [b]1 Kin. 7:15, 23; 2 Chr. 4:12, 15, 16
10 [a]2 Sam. 8:10–12
11 [a]2 Sam. 10:12 [b]2 Sam. 5:17–25 [c]2 Sam. 1:1
12 [a]2 Sam. 23:18; 1 Chr. 2:16 [b]2 Sam. 8:13
13 [a]Gen. 27:29–40; Num. 24:18; 2 Sam. 8:14
17 [a]2 Sam. 8:18

CHAPTER 19
1 [a]1 Sam. 11:1; 2 Sam. 10:1–19
4 [a]Is. 20:4
6 [a]1 Chr. 18:5, 9

*
18:9 *Toi,* 2 Sam. 8:9, 10
18:10 *Joram,* 2 Sam. 8:10
18:12 *Syrians,* 2 Sam. 8:13
18:16 *Seraiah,* 2 Sam. 8:17, or *Shisha,* 1 Kin. 4:3
19:6 Heb. *Aram Naharaim* • *Zoba,* 2 Sam. 10:6

NKJV

[a]bronze, with which [b]Solomon made the bronze Sea, the pillars, and the articles of bronze.

9 Now when *Tou king of Hamath heard that David had defeated all the army of Hadadezer king of Zobah,

10 he sent *Hadoram his son to King David, to greet him and bless him, because he had fought against Hadadezer and defeated him (for Hadadezer had been at war with Tou); and *Hadoram brought with him* all kinds of [a]articles of gold, silver, and bronze.

11 King David also dedicated these to the LORD, along with the silver and gold that he had brought from all *these* nations—from Edom, from Moab, from the [a]people of Ammon, from the [b]Philistines, and from [c]Amalek.

12 Moreover [a]Abishai the son of Zeruiah killed [b]eighteen thousand *Edomites in the Valley of Salt.

13 [a]He also put garrisons in Edom, and all the Edomites became David's servants. And the LORD preserved David wherever he went.

David's Administration
(2 Sam. 8:15–18)

14 So David reigned over all Israel, and administered judgment and justice to all his people.

15 Joab the son of Zeruiah *was* over the army; Jehoshaphat the son of Ahilud *was* recorder;

16 Zadok the son of Ahitub and Abimelech the son of Abiathar *were* the priests; *Shavsha *was* the scribe;

17 [a]Benaiah the son of Jehoiada *was* over the Cherethites and the Pelethites; and David's sons *were* chief ministers at the king's side.

The Ammonites and Syrians Defeated
(2 Sam. 10:1–19)

19 It[a] happened after this that Nahash the king of the people of Ammon died, and his son reigned in his place.

2 Then David said, "I will show kindness to Hanun the son of Nahash, because his father showed kindness to me." So David sent messengers to comfort him concerning his father. And David's servants came to Hanun in the land of the people of Ammon to comfort him.

3 And the princes of the people of Ammon said to Hanun, "Do you think that David really honors your father because he has sent comforters to you? Did his servants not come to you to search and to overthrow and to spy out the land?"

4 Therefore Hanun took David's servants, shaved them, and cut off their garments in the middle, at their [a]buttocks, and sent them away.

5 Then *some* went and told David about the men; and he sent to meet them, because the men were greatly ashamed. And the king said, "Wait at Jericho until your beards have grown, and *then* return."

6 When the people of Ammon saw that they had made themselves repulsive to David, Hanun and the people of Ammon sent a thousand talents of silver to hire for themselves chariots and horsemen from *Mesopotamia, from Syrian Maacah, [a]and from *Zobah.

7 So they hired for themselves thirty-two thousand chariots, with the king of Maacah and his people, who came and encamped before Medeba. Also the people of Ammon gathered together from their cities, and came to battle.

8 Now when David heard *of it,* he sent Joab and all the army of the mighty men.

9 Then the people of Ammon came out and put themselves in battle array before the gate of the city, and the kings who had come *were* by themselves in the field.

10 When Joab saw that the battle line was against him before and behind, he chose some

KJV

of all the choice of Israel, and put *them* in array against the Syrians.

11 And the rest of the people he delivered unto the hand of Abishai his brother, and they set *themselves* in array against the children of Ammon.

12 And he said, If the Syrians be too strong for me, then thou shalt help me: but if the children of Ammon be too strong for thee, then I will help thee.

13 Be of good courage, and let us behave ourselves valiantly for our people, and for the cities of our God: and let the LORD do *that which is* good in his sight.

14 So Joab and the people that *were* with him drew nigh before the Syrians unto the battle; and they fled before him.

15 And when the children of Ammon saw that the Syrians were fled, they likewise fled before Abishai his brother, and entered into the city. Then Joab came to Jerusalem.

16 And when the Syrians saw that they were put to the worse before Israel, they sent messengers, and drew forth the Syrians that *were* beyond the river: and Shophach the captain of the host of Hadarezer *went* before them.

17 And it was told David; and he gathered all Israel, and passed over Jordan, and came upon them, and set *the battle* in array against them. So when David had put the battle in array against the Syrians, they fought with him.

18 But the Syrians fled before Israel; and David slew of the Syrians seven thousand *men which fought in* chariots, and forty thousand footmen, and killed Shophach the captain of the host.

19 And when the servants of Hadarezer saw that they were put to the worse before Israel, they made peace with David, and became his servants: neither would the Syrians help the children of Ammon any more.

Rabbah Is Conquered
(2 Sam. 11:1; 12:26–31)

20 And [a]it came to pass, that after the year was expired, at the time that kings go out *to battle,* Joab led forth the power of the army, and wasted the country of the children of Ammon, and came and besieged Rabbah. But [b]David tarried at Jerusalem. And [c]Joab smote Rabbah, and destroyed it.

2 And David [a]took the crown of their king from off his head, and found it to weigh a talent of gold, and *there were* precious stones in it; and it was set upon David's head: and he brought also exceeding much spoil out of the city.

3 And he brought out the people that *were* in it, and cut *them* with saws, and with harrows of iron, and with axes. Even so dealt David with all the cities of the children of Ammon. And David and all the people returned to Jerusalem.

Philistine Giants Destroyed
(2 Sam. 21:15–22)

4 And it came to pass after this, [a]that there arose war at Gezer with the Philistines; at which time [b]Sibbechai the Hushathite slew Sippai, *that was* of the children of the giant: and they were subdued.

5 And there was war again with the Philistines; and Elhanan the son of Jair slew Lahmi the brother of Goliath the Gittite, whose spear staff *was* like a weaver's [a]beam.

6 And yet again [a]there was war at Gath, where was a man of *great* stature, whose fingers and toes *were* four and twenty, six *on each hand,* and six *on each foot:* and he also was the son of the giant.

7 But when he defied Israel, Jonathan the son of Shimea David's brother slew him.

8 These were born unto the giant in Gath; and they fell by the hand of David, and by the hand of his servants.

CHAPTER 20

1 [a]2 Sam. 11:1 [b]2 Sam. 11:2—12:25 [c]2 Sam. 12:26
2 [a]2 Sam. 12:30, 31
4 [a]2 Sam. 21:18 [b]1 Chr. 11:29
5 [a]1 Sam. 17:7; 1 Chr. 11:23
6 [a]1 Sam. 5:8; 2 Sam. 21:20

*__________

19:16 The Euphrates • *Zoba,* 2 Sam. 10:6, or *Shobach,* 2 Sam. 10:16
19:18 *seven hundred,* 2 Sam. 10:18 • *horsemen,* 2 Sam. 10:18
20:3 LXX *cut them with*
20:4 *Saph,* 2 Sam. 21:18
20:5 *Jaare-Oregim,* 2 Sam. 21:19
20:7 *Shammah,* 1 Sam. 16:9 or *Shimeah,* 2 Sam. 21:21

NKJV

of Israel's best and put *them* in battle array against the Syrians.

11 And the rest of the people he put under the command of Abishai his brother, and they set *themselves* in battle array against the people of Ammon.

12 Then he said, "If the Syrians are too strong for me, then you shall help me; but if the people of Ammon are too strong for you, then I will help you.

13 "Be of good courage, and let us be strong for our people and for the cities of our God. And may the LORD do *what is* good in His sight."

14 So Joab and the people who *were* with him drew near for the battle against the Syrians, and they fled before him.

15 When the people of Ammon saw that the Syrians were fleeing, they also fled before Abishai his brother, and entered the city. So Joab went to Jerusalem.

16 Now when the Syrians saw that they had been defeated by Israel, they sent messengers and brought the Syrians who were beyond *the River, and *Shophach the commander of Hadadezer's army *went* before them.

17 When it was told David, he gathered all Israel, crossed over the Jordan and came upon them, and set up in battle array against them. So when David had set up in *battle* array against the Syrians, they fought with him.

18 Then the Syrians fled before Israel; and David killed *seven thousand charioteers and forty thousand *foot soldiers of the Syrians, and killed Shophach the commander of the army.

19 And when the servants of Hadadezer saw that they were defeated by Israel, they made peace with David and became his servants. So the Syrians were not willing to help the people of Ammon anymore.

Rabbah Is Conquered
(2 Sam. 11:1; 12:26–31)

20 It[a] happened in the spring of the year, at the time kings go out *to battle,* that Joab led out the armed forces and ravaged the country of the people of Ammon, and came and besieged Rabbah. But [b]David stayed at Jerusalem. And [c]Joab defeated Rabbah and overthrew it.

2 Then David [a]took their king's crown from his head, and found it to weigh a talent of gold, and *there were* precious stones in it. And it was set on David's head. Also he brought out the spoil of the city in great abundance.

3 And he brought out the people who *were* in it, and *put *them* to work with saws, with iron picks, and with axes. So David did to all the cities of the people of Ammon. Then David and all the people returned *to* Jerusalem.

Philistine Giants Destroyed
(2 Sam. 21:15–22)

4 Now it happened afterward [a]that war broke out at Gezer with the Philistines, at which time [b]Sibbechai the Hushathite killed *Sippai, *who was one* of the sons of the giant. And they were subdued.

5 Again there was war with the Philistines, and Elhanan the son of *Jair killed Lahmi the brother of Goliath the Gittite, the shaft of whose spear *was* like a weaver's [a]beam.

6 Yet again [a]there was war at Gath, where there was a man of *great* stature, with twenty-four fingers and toes, six *on each hand* and six *on each foot;* and he also was born to the giant.

7 So when he defied Israel, Jonathan the son of *Shimea, David's brother, killed him.

8 These were born to the giant in Gath, and they fell by the hand of David and by the hand of his servants.

KJV

The Census of Israel and Judah
(2 Sam. 24:1–25)

21 And [a]Satan stood up against Israel, and provoked David to number Israel.

2 And David said to Joab and to the rulers of the people, Go, number Israel from Beer–sheba even to Dan; [a]and bring the number of them to me, that I may know *it.*

3 And Joab answered, The LORD make his people an hundred times so many more as they *be:* but, my lord the king, *are* they not all my lord's servants? why then doth my lord require this thing? why will he be a cause of trespass to Israel?

4 Nevertheless the king's word prevailed against Joab. Wherefore Joab departed, and went throughout all Israel, and came to Jerusalem.

5 And Joab gave the sum of the number of the people unto David. And all *they of* Israel were a thousand thousand and an hundred thousand men that drew sword: and Judah *was* four hundred threescore and ten thousand men that drew sword.

6 [a]But Levi and Benjamin counted he not among them: for the king's word was abominable to Joab.

7 And God was displeased with this thing; therefore he smote Israel.

8 And David said unto God, [a]I have sinned greatly, because I have done this thing: [b]but now, I beseech thee, do away the iniquity of thy servant; for I have done very foolishly.

9 And the LORD spake unto Gad, David's [a]seer, saying,

10 Go and tell David, [a]saying, Thus saith the LORD, I offer thee three *things:* choose thee one of them, that I may do *it* unto thee.

11 So Gad came to David, and said unto him, Thus saith the LORD, Choose thee

12 [a]Either three years' famine; or three months to be destroyed before thy foes, while that the sword of thine enemies overtaketh *thee;* or else three days the sword of the LORD, even the pestilence, in the land, and the angel of the LORD destroying throughout all the coasts of Israel. Now therefore advise thyself what word I shall bring again to him that sent me.

13 And David said unto Gad, I am in a great strait: let me fall now into the hand of the LORD; for very great *are* his [a]mercies: but let me not fall into the hand of man.

14 So the LORD sent [a]pestilence upon Israel: and there fell of Israel seventy thousand men.

15 And God sent an [a]angel unto Jerusalem to destroy it: and as he was destroying, the LORD beheld, and [b]he repented him of the evil, and said to the angel that destroyed, It is enough, stay now thine hand. And the angel of the LORD stood by the [c]threshingfloor of Ornan the Jebusite.

16 And David lifted up his eyes, and [a]saw the angel of the LORD stand between the earth and the heaven, having a drawn sword in his hand stretched out over Jerusalem. Then David and the elders *of Israel, who were* clothed in sackcloth, fell upon their faces.

17 And David said unto God, *Is it* not I *that* commanded the people to be numbered? even I it is that have sinned and done evil indeed; but *as for* these [a]sheep, what have they done? let thine hand, I pray thee, O LORD my God, be on me, and on my father's house; but not on thy people, that they should be plagued.

18 Then the [a]angel of the LORD commanded Gad to say to David, that David should go up, and set up an altar unto the LORD in the threshingfloor of Ornan the Jebusite.

19 And David went up at the saying of Gad, which he spake in the name of the LORD.

20 And Ornan turned back, and saw the angel; and his four sons with him hid themselves. Now Ornan was threshing wheat.

21 And as David came to Ornan, Ornan

CHAPTER 21

1 [a]2 Sam. 24:1–25; Job 1:6
2 [a]1 Chr. 27:23, 24
6 [a]1 Chr. 27:24
8 [a]2 Sam. 24:10 [b]2 Sam. 12:13
9 [a]1 Sam. 9:9; 2 Kin. 17:13; 1 Chr. 29:29; 2 Chr. 16:7, 10; Is. 30:9, 10; Amos 7:12, 13
10 [a]2 Sam. 24:12–14
12 [a]2 Sam. 24:13
13 [a]Ps. 51:1; 130:4, 7
14 [a]1 Chr. 27:24
15 [a]2 Sam. 24:16 [b]Gen. 6:6 [c]2 Chr. 3:1
16 [a]Josh. 5:13; 2 Chr. 3:1
17 [a]2 Sam. 7:8; Ps. 74:1
18 [a]1 Chr. 21:11, 12; 2 Chr. 3:1

*————

21:12 *seven,* 2 Sam. 24:13 • Or *Angel,* and so throughout the chapter **21:15** Or *He* • Or *Your* • *Araunah,* 2 Sam. 24:16, 18–24

NKJV

The Census of Israel and Judah
(2 Sam. 24:1–25)

21 Now [a]Satan stood up against Israel, and moved David to number Israel.

2 So David said to Joab and to the leaders of the people, "Go, number Israel from Beersheba to Dan, [a]and bring the number of them to me that I may know *it.*"

3 And Joab answered, "May the LORD make His people a hundred times more than they are. But, my lord the king, *are* they not all my lord's servants? Why then does my lord require this thing? Why should he be a cause of guilt in Israel?"

4 Nevertheless the king's word prevailed against Joab. Therefore Joab departed and went throughout all Israel and came to Jerusalem.

5 Then Joab gave the sum of the number of the people to David. All Israel *had* one million one hundred thousand men who drew the sword, and Judah *had* four hundred and seventy thousand men who drew the sword.

6 [a]But he did not count Levi and Benjamin among them, for the king's word was abominable to Joab.

7 And God was displeased with this thing; therefore He struck Israel.

8 So David said to God, [a]"I have sinned greatly, because I have done this thing; [b]but now, I pray, take away the iniquity of Your servant, for I have done very foolishly."

9 Then the LORD spoke to Gad, David's [a]seer, saying,

10 "Go and tell David, [a]saying, 'Thus says the LORD: "I offer you three *things;* choose one of them for yourself, that I may do *it* to you." ' "

11 So Gad came to David and said to him, "Thus says the LORD: 'Choose for yourself,

12 [a]'either *three years of famine, or three months to be defeated by your foes with the sword of your enemies overtaking *you,* or else for three days the sword of the LORD—the plague in the land, with the *angel of the LORD destroying throughout all the territory of Israel.' Now consider what answer I should take back to Him who sent me."

13 And David said to Gad, "I am in great distress. Please let me fall into the hand of the LORD, for His [a]mercies *are* very great; but do not let me fall into the hand of man."

14 So the LORD sent a [a]plague upon Israel, and seventy thousand men of Israel fell.

15 And God sent an [a]angel to Jerusalem to destroy it. As *he was destroying, the LORD looked and [b]relented of the disaster, and said to the angel who was destroying, "It is enough; now restrain *your hand." And the angel of the LORD stood by the [c]threshing floor of *Ornan the Jebusite.

16 Then David lifted his eyes and [a]saw the angel of the LORD standing between earth and heaven, having in his hand a drawn sword stretched out over Jerusalem. So David and the elders, clothed in sackcloth, fell on their faces.

17 And David said to God, "Was it not I who commanded the people to be numbered? I am the one who has sinned and done evil indeed; but these [a]sheep, what have they done? Let Your hand, I pray, O LORD my God, be against me and my father's house, but not against Your people that they should be plagued."

18 Therefore, the [a]angel of the LORD commanded Gad to say to David that David should go and erect an altar to the LORD on the threshing floor of Ornan the Jebusite.

19 So David went up at the word of Gad, which he had spoken in the name of the LORD.

20 Now Ornan turned and saw the angel; and his four sons *who were* with him hid themselves, but Ornan continued threshing wheat.

21 So David came to Ornan, and Ornan

KJV

looked and saw David, and went out of the threshingfloor, and bowed himself to David with *his* face to the ground.

22 Then David said to Ornan, Grant me the place of *this* threshingfloor, that I may build an altar therein unto the LORD: thou shalt grant it me for the full price: that the plague may be stayed from the people.

23 And Ornan said unto David, Take *it* to thee, and let my lord the king do *that which is* good in his eyes: lo, I give *thee* the oxen *also* for burnt offerings, and the threshing instruments for wood, and the wheat for the meat offering; I give it all.

24 And king David said to Ornan, Nay; but I will verily buy it for the full price: for I will not take *that* which *is* thine for the LORD, nor offer burnt offerings without cost.

25 So [a]David gave to Ornan for the place six hundred shekels of gold by weight.

26 And David built there an altar unto the LORD, and offered burnt offerings and peace offerings, and called upon the LORD; and [a]he answered him from heaven by fire upon the altar of burnt offering.

27 And the LORD commanded the angel; and he put up his sword again into the sheath thereof.

28 At that time when David saw that the LORD had answered him in the threshingfloor of Ornan the Jebusite, then he sacrificed there.

29 [a]For the tabernacle of the LORD, which Moses made in the wilderness, and the altar of the burnt offering, *were* at that season in the high place at [b]Gibeon.

30 But David could not go before it to enquire of God: for he was afraid because of the sword of the angel of the LORD.

David Prepares to Build the Temple

22 Then David said, [a]This *is* the house of the LORD God, and this *is* the altar of the burnt offering for Israel.

2 And David commanded to gather together the [a]strangers that *were* in the land of Israel; and he set masons to [b]hew wrought stones to build the house of God.

3 And David prepared iron in abundance for the nails for the doors of the gates, and for the joinings; and brass in abundance [a]without weight;

4 Also cedar trees in abundance: for the [a]Zidonians and they of Tyre brought much cedar wood to David.

5 And David said, [a]Solomon my son *is* young and tender, and the house *that is* to be builded for the LORD *must be* exceeding magnifical, of fame and of glory throughout all countries: I will *therefore* now make preparation for it. So David prepared abundantly before his death.

6 Then he called for Solomon his son, and charged him to build an house for the LORD God of Israel.

7 And David said to Solomon, My son, as for me, [a]it was in my mind to build an house [b]unto the name of the LORD my God:

8 But the word of the LORD came to me, saying, [a]Thou hast shed blood abundantly, and hast made great wars: thou shalt not build an house unto my name, because thou hast shed much blood upon the earth in my sight.

9 [a]Behold, a son shall be born to thee, who shall be a man of rest; and I will give him [b]rest from all his enemies round about: for his name shall be Solomon, and I will give peace and quietness unto Israel in his days.

10 [a]He shall build an house for my name; and [b]he shall be my son, and I *will be* his father; and I will establish the throne of his kingdom over Israel for ever.

11 Now, my son, [a]the LORD be with thee; and prosper thou, and build the house of the LORD thy God, as he hath said of thee.

25 [a]2 Sam. 24:24
26 [a]Lev. 9:24; Judg. 6:21; 1 Kin. 18:36–38; 2 Chr. 3:1; 7:1
29 [a]1 Kin. 3:4; 2 Chr. 1:3 [b]1 Chr. 16:39

CHAPTER 22
1 [a]Deut. 12:5; 2 Sam. 24:18; 1 Chr. 21:18, 19, 26, 28; 2 Chr. 3:1
2 [a]1 Kin. 9:20, 21; 2 Chr. 2:17, 18 [b]1 Kin. 5:17, 18
3 [a]1 Kin. 7:47; 1 Chr. 22:14
4 [a]1 Kin. 5:6–10
5 [a]1 Kin. 3:7; 1 Chr. 29:1, 2
7 [a]2 Sam. 7:1, 2; 1 Kin. 8:17; 1 Chr. 17:1; 28:2 [b]Deut. 12:5, 11
8 [a]2 Sam. 7:5–13; 1 Kin. 5:3; 1 Chr. 28:3
9 [a]1 Chr. 28:5 [b]1 Kin. 4:20, 25; 5:4
10 [a]2 Sam. 7:13; 1 Kin. 5:5; 6:38; 1 Chr. 17:12, 13; 28:6; 2 Chr. 6:2 [b]Heb. 1:5
11 [a]1 Chr. 22:16

NKJV

looked and saw David. And he went out from the threshing floor, and bowed before David with *his* face to the ground.

22 Then David said to Ornan, "Grant me the place of *this* threshing floor, that I may build an altar on it to the LORD. You shall grant it to me at the full price, that the plague may be withdrawn from the people."

23 But Ornan said to David, "Take *it* to yourself, and let my lord the king do *what is* good in his eyes. Look, I *also* give *you* the oxen for burnt offerings, the threshing implements for wood, and the wheat for the grain offering; I give *it* all."

24 Then King David said to Ornan, "No, but I will surely buy *it* for the full price, for I will not take what is yours for the LORD, nor offer burnt offerings with *that which* costs *me* nothing."

25 So [a]David gave Ornan six hundred shekels of gold by weight for the place.

26 And David built there an altar to the LORD, and offered burnt offerings and peace offerings, and called on the LORD; and [a]He answered him from heaven by fire on the altar of burnt offering.

27 So the LORD commanded the angel, and he returned his sword to its sheath.

28 At that time, when David saw that the LORD had answered him on the threshing floor of Ornan the Jebusite, he sacrificed there.

29 [a]For the tabernacle of the LORD and the altar of the burnt offering, which Moses had made in the wilderness, *were* at that time at the high place in [b]Gibeon.

30 But David could not go before it to inquire of God, for he was afraid of the sword of the angel of the LORD.

David Prepares to Build the Temple

22 Then David said, [a]"This *is* the house of the LORD God, and this *is* the altar of burnt offering for Israel."

2 So David commanded to gather the [a]aliens who *were* in the land of Israel; and he appointed masons to [b]cut hewn stones to build the house of God.

3 And David prepared iron in abundance for the nails of the doors of the gates and for the joints, and bronze in abundance [a]beyond measure,

4 and cedar trees in abundance; for the [a]Sidonians and those from Tyre brought much cedar wood to David.

5 Now David said, [a]"Solomon my son *is* young and inexperienced, and the house to be built for the LORD *must be* exceedingly magnificent, famous and glorious throughout all countries. I will now make preparation for it." So David made abundant preparations before his death.

6 Then he called for his son Solomon, and charged him to build a house for the LORD God of Israel.

7 And David said to Solomon: "My son, as for me, [a]it was in my mind to build a house [b]to the name of the LORD my God;

8 "but the word of the LORD came to me, saying, [a]'You have shed much blood and have made great wars; you shall not build a house for My name, because you have shed much blood on the earth in My sight.

9 [a]'Behold, a son shall be born to you, who shall be a man of rest; and I will give him [b]rest from all his enemies all around. His name shall be *Solomon, for I will give peace and quietness to Israel in his days.

10 [a]'He shall build a house for My name, and [b]he shall be My son, and I *will be* his Father; and I will establish the throne of his kingdom over Israel forever.'

11 "Now, my son, may [a]the LORD be with you; and may you prosper, and build the house of the LORD your God, as He has said to you.

---

*22:9 Lit. *Peaceful*

KJV

12 Only the LORD [a]give thee wisdom and understanding, and give thee charge concerning Israel, that thou mayest keep the law of the LORD thy God.

13 [a]Then shalt thou prosper, if thou takest heed to fulfil the statutes and judgments which the LORD charged Moses with concerning Israel: [b]be strong, and of good courage; dread not, nor be dismayed.

14 Now, behold, in my trouble I have prepared for the house of the LORD an hundred thousand talents of gold, and a thousand thousand talents of silver; and of brass and iron [a]without weight; for it is in abundance: timber also and stone have I prepared; and thou mayest add thereto.

15 Moreover *there are* workmen with thee in abundance, hewers and workers of stone and timber, and all manner of cunning men for every manner of work.

16 Of the gold, the silver, and the brass, and the iron, *there is* no number. Arise *therefore,* and be doing, and [a]the LORD be with thee.

17 David also commanded all the [a]princes of Israel to help Solomon his son, *saying,*

18 *Is* not the LORD your God with you? [a]and hath he *not* given you rest on every side? for he hath given the inhabitants of the land into mine hand; and the land is subdued before the LORD, and before his people.

19 Now set your heart and your soul to seek the LORD your God; arise therefore, and build ye the sanctuary of the LORD God, to [a]bring the ark of the covenant of the LORD, and the holy vessels of God, into the house that is to be built [b]to the name of the LORD.

The Divisions of the Levites

23 So when David was old and full of days, he made [a]Solomon his son king over Israel.

2 And he gathered together all the princes of Israel, with the priests and the Levites.

3 Now the Levites were numbered from the age of [a]thirty years and upward: and their number by their polls, man by man, was thirty and eight thousand.

4 Of which, twenty and four thousand *were* to [a]set forward the work of the house of the LORD; and six thousand *were* [b]officers and judges:

5 Moreover four thousand *were* porters; and four thousand [a]praised the LORD with the instruments [b]which I made, *said David,* to praise *therewith.*

6 And [a]David divided them into courses among the sons of Levi, *namely,* Gershon, Kohath, and Merari.

7 Of the [a]Gershonites *were,* Laadan, and Shimei.

8 The sons of Laadan; the chief *was* Jehiel, and Zetham, and Joel, three.

9 The sons of Shimei; Shelomith, and Haziel, and Haran, three. These *were* the chief of the fathers of Laadan.

10 And the sons of Shimei *were,* Jahath, Zina, and Jeush, and Beriah. These four *were* the sons of Shimei.

11 And Jahath was the chief, and Zizah the second: but Jeush and Beriah had not many sons; therefore they were in one reckoning, according to *their* father's house.

12 [a]The sons of Kohath; Amram, Izhar, Hebron, and Uzziel, four.

13 The sons of [a]Amram; Aaron and Moses: and [b]Aaron was separated, that he should sanctify the most holy things, he and his sons for ever, [c]to burn incense before the LORD, [d]to minister unto him, and [e]to bless in his name for ever.

14 Now *concerning* Moses the man of God, [a]his sons were named of the tribe of Levi.

15 [a]The sons of Moses *were,* Gershom, and Eliezer.

---

12 [a]1 Kin. 3:9–12; 2 Chr. 1:10
13 [a][Josh. 1:7, 8]; 1 Chr. 28:7 [b][Deut. 31:7, 8; Josh. 1:6, 7, 9; 1 Chr. 28:20]
14 [a]1 Chr. 22:3
16 [a]1 Chr. 22:11
17 [a]1 Chr. 28:1–6
18 [a]Deut. 12:10; Josh. 22:4; 2 Sam. 7:1; [1 Kin. 5:4; 8:56]
19 [a]1 Kin. 8:1–11; 2 Chr. 5:2–14 [b]1 Kin. 5:3

CHAPTER 23

1 [a]1 Kin. 1:33–40; 1 Chr. 28:4, 5
3 [a]Num. 4:1–3
4 [a]2 Chr. 2:2, 18; Ezra 3:8, 9 [b]Deut. 16:18–20
5 [a]1 Chr. 15:16 [b]2 Chr. 29:25–27
6 [a]Ex. 6:16; Num. 26:57; 2 Chr. 8:14
7 [a]1 Chr. 26:21
12 [a]Ex. 6:18
13 [a]Ex. 6:20 [b]Ex. 28:1; Heb. 5:4 [c]Ex. 30:7; 1 Sam. 2:28 [d][Deut. 21:5] [e]Num. 6:23
14 [a]1 Chr. 26:20–24
15 [a]Ex. 18:3, 4

*

23:7 *Libni,* Ex. 6:17
23:10 LXX, Vg. *Zizah* and v. 11
23:15 Heb. *Gershom,* 1 Chr. 6:16

NKJV

12 "Only may the LORD [a]give you wisdom and understanding, and give you charge concerning Israel, that you may keep the law of the LORD your God.

13 [a]"Then you will prosper, if you take care to fulfill the statutes and judgments with which the LORD charged Moses concerning Israel. [b]Be strong and of good courage; do not fear nor be dismayed.

14 "Indeed I have taken much trouble to prepare for the house of the LORD one hundred thousand talents of gold and one million talents of silver, and bronze and iron [a]beyond measure, for it is so abundant. I have prepared timber and stone also, and you may add to them.

15 "Moreover *there are* workmen with you in abundance: woodsmen and stonecutters, and all types of skillful men for every kind of work.

16 "Of gold and silver and bronze and iron *there is* no limit. Arise and begin working, and [a]the LORD be with you."

17 David also commanded all the [a]leaders of Israel to help Solomon his son, *saying,*

18 "*Is* not the LORD your God with you? [a]And has He *not* given you rest on every side? For He has given the inhabitants of the land into my hand, and the land is subdued before the LORD and before His people.

19 "Now set your heart and your soul to seek the LORD your God. Therefore arise and build the sanctuary of the LORD God, to [a]bring the ark of the covenant of the LORD and the holy articles of God into the house that is to be built [b]for the name of the LORD."

The Divisions of the Levites

23 So when David was old and full of days, he made his son [a]Solomon king over Israel.

2 And he gathered together all the leaders of Israel, with the priests and the Levites.

3 Now the Levites were numbered from the age of [a]thirty years and above; and the number of individual males was thirty-eight thousand.

4 Of these, twenty-four thousand *were* to [a]look after the work of the house of the LORD, six thousand *were* [b]officers and judges,

5 four thousand *were* gatekeepers, and four thousand [a]praised the LORD with *musical* instruments, [b]"which I made," *said David,* "for giving praise."

6 Also [a]David separated them into divisions among the sons of Levi: Gershon, Kohath, and Merari.

7 Of the [a]Gershonites: *Laadan and Shimei.

8 The sons of Laadan: the first Jehiel, then Zetham and Joel—three *in all.*

9 The sons of Shimei: Shelomith, Haziel, and Haran—three *in all.* These were the heads of the fathers' *houses* of Laadan.

10 And the sons of Shimei: Jahath, *Zina, Jeush, and Beriah. These *were* the four sons of Shimei.

11 Jahath was the first and Zizah the second. But Jeush and Beriah did not have many sons; therefore they were assigned as one father's house.

12 [a]The sons of Kohath: Amram, Izhar, Hebron, and Uzziel—four *in all.*

13 The sons of [a]Amram: Aaron and Moses; and [b]Aaron was set apart, he and his sons forever, that he should sanctify the most holy things, [c]to burn incense before the LORD, [d]to minister to Him, and [e]to give the blessing in His name forever.

14 Now [a]the sons of Moses the man of God were reckoned to the tribe of Levi.

15 [a]The sons of Moses *were* *Gershon and Eliezer.

KJV

16 Of the sons of Gershom, [a]Shebuel *was* the chief.

17 And the sons of Eliezer *were*, [a]Rehabiah the chief. And Eliezer had none other sons; but the sons of Rehabiah were very many.

18 Of the sons of Izhar; [a]Shelomith the chief.

19 [a]Of the sons of Hebron; Jeriah the first, Amariah the second, Jahaziel the third, and Jekameam the fourth.

20 Of the sons of Uzziel; Micah the first, and Jesiah the second.

21 [a]The sons of Merari; Mahli, and Mushi. The sons of Mahli; Eleazar, and [b]Kish.

22 And Eleazar died, and [a]had no sons, but daughters: and their brethren the sons of Kish [b]took them.

23 [a]The sons of Mushi; Mahli, and Eder, and Jeremoth, three.

24 These *were* the sons of [a]Levi after the house of their fathers; *even* the chief of the fathers, as they were counted by number of names by their polls, that did the work for the service of the house of the LORD, from the age of [b]twenty years and upward.

25 For David said, The LORD God of Israel [a]hath given rest unto his people, that they may dwell in Jerusalem for ever:

26 And also unto the Levites; they shall no *more* [a]carry the tabernacle, nor any vessels of it for the service thereof.

27 For by the [a]last words of David the Levites *were* numbered from twenty years old and above:

28 Because their office *was* to wait on the sons of Aaron for the service of the house of the LORD, in the courts, and in the chambers, and in the purifying of all holy things, and the work of the service of the house of God;

29 Both for [a]the shewbread, and for [b]the fine flour for meat offering, and for [c]the unleavened cakes, and for [d]*that which is baked in* the pan, and for that which is fried, and for all manner of [e]measure and size;

30 And to stand every morning to thank and praise the LORD, and likewise at even;

31 And to offer all burnt sacrifices unto the LORD [a]in the sabbaths, in the new moons, and on the [b]set feasts, by number, according to the order commanded unto them, continually before the LORD:

32 And that they should [a]keep the [b]charge of the tabernacle of the congregation, and the charge of the holy *place*, and [c]the charge of the sons of Aaron their brethren, in the service of the house of the LORD.

The Divisions of the Priests

24 Now *these are* the divisions of the sons of Aaron. [a]The sons of Aaron; Nadab, and Abihu, Eleazar, and Ithamar.

2 But [a]Nadab and Abihu died before their father, and had no children: therefore Eleazar and Ithamar executed the priest's office.

3 And David distributed them, both Zadok of the sons of Eleazar, and [a]Ahimelech of the sons of Ithamar, according to their offices in their service.

4 And there were more chief men found of the sons of Eleazar than of the sons of Ithamar; and *thus* were they divided. Among the sons of Eleazar *there were* sixteen chief men of the house of *their* fathers, and eight among the sons of Ithamar according to the house of their fathers.

5 Thus were they divided by lot, one sort with another; for the governors of the sanctuary, and governors *of the house* of God, were of the sons of Eleazar, and of the sons of Ithamar.

6 And Shemaiah the son of Nethaneel the scribe, *one* of the Levites, wrote them before the king, and the princes, and Zadok the priest, and Ahimelech the son of Abiathar, and *before* the chief of the fathers of the priests and Levites: one

---

16 [a]1 Chr. 26:24
17 [a]1 Chr. 26:25
18 [a]1 Chr. 24:22
19 [a]1 Chr. 24:23
21 [a]1 Chr. 24:26 [b]1 Chr. 24:29
22 [a]1 Chr. 24:28 [b]Num. 36:6
23 [a]1 Chr. 24:30
24 [a]Num. 10:17, 21 [b]Num. 1:3; Ezra 3:8
25 [a]1 Chr. 22:18
26 [a]Num. 4:5, 15; 7:9; Deut. 10:8
27 [a]2 Sam. 23:1
29 [a]Ex. 25:30 [b]Lev. 6:20 [c]Lev. 2:1, 4 [d]Lev. 2:5, 7 [e]Lev. 19:35
31 [a]Num. 10:10 [b]Lev. 23:2–4
32 [a]2 Chr. 13:10, 11 [b][Num. 1:53]; 1 Chr. 9:27 [c]Num. 3:6–9, 38

CHAPTER 24
1 [a]Lev. 10:1–6; Num. 26:60, 61; 1 Chr. 6:3
2 [a]Num. 3:1–4; 26:61
3 [a]1 Chr. 18:16

NKJV

16 Of the sons of Gershon, [a]Shebuel* *was* the first.

17 Of the descendants of Eliezer, [a]Rehabiah was the first. And Eliezer had no other sons, but the sons of Rehabiah were very many.

18 Of the sons of Izhar, [a]Shelomith *was* the first.

19 [a]Of the sons of Hebron, Jeriah *was* the first, Amariah the second, Jahaziel the third, and Jekameam the fourth.

20 Of the sons of Uzziel, Michah *was* the first and Jesshiah the second.

21 [a]The sons of Merari *were* Mahli and Mushi. The sons of Mahli *were* Eleazar and [b]Kish.

22 And Eleazar died, and [a]had no sons, but only daughters; and their brethren, the sons of Kish, [b]took them *as wives*.

23 [a]The sons of Mushi *were* Mahli, Eder, and Jeremoth—three *in all*.

24 These *were* the sons of [a]Levi by their fathers' houses—the heads of the fathers' *houses* as they were counted individually by the number of their names, who did the work for the service of the house of the LORD, from the age of [b]twenty years and above.

25 For David said, "The LORD God of Israel [a]has given rest to His people, that they may dwell in Jerusalem forever";

26 and also to the Levites, "They shall no longer [a]carry the tabernacle, or any of the articles for its service."

27 For by the [a]last words of David the Levites *were* numbered from twenty years old and above;

28 because their duty *was* to help the sons of Aaron in the service of the house of the LORD, in the courts and in the chambers, in the purifying of all holy things and the work of the service of the house of God,

29 both with [a]the showbread and [b]the fine flour for the grain offering, with [c]the unleavened cakes and [d]*what is baked in* the pan, with what is mixed and with all kinds of [e]measures and sizes;

30 to stand every morning to thank and praise the LORD, and likewise at evening;

31 and at every presentation of a burnt offering to the LORD [a]on the Sabbaths and on the New Moons and on the [b]set feasts, by number according to the ordinance governing them, regularly before the LORD;

32 and that they should [a]attend to the [b]needs of the tabernacle of meeting, the needs of the holy *place*, and the [c]needs of the sons of Aaron their brethren in the work of the house of the LORD.

The Divisions of the Priests

24 Now *these are* the divisions of the sons of Aaron. [a]The sons of Aaron *were* Nadab, Abihu, Eleazar, and Ithamar.

2 And [a]Nadab and Abihu died before their father, and had no children; therefore Eleazar and Ithamar ministered as priests.

3 Then David with Zadok of the sons of Eleazar, and [a]Ahimelech of the sons of Ithamar, divided them according to the schedule of their service.

4 There were more leaders found of the sons of Eleazar than of the sons of Ithamar, and *thus* they were divided. Among the sons of Eleazar *were* sixteen heads of *their* fathers' houses, and eight heads of their fathers' houses among the sons of Ithamar.

5 Thus they were divided by lot, one group as another, for there were officials of the sanctuary and officials *of the house* of God, from the sons of Eleazar and from the sons of Ithamar.

6 And the scribe, Shemaiah the son of Nethanel, *one of* the Levites, wrote them down before the king, the leaders, Zadok the priest, Ahimelech the son of Abiathar, and the heads of the fathers' *houses* of the priests and Levites, one

---

*23:16 *Shubael*, 1 Chr. 24:20

KJV

principal household being taken for Eleazar, and *one* taken for Ithamar.

7 Now the first lot came forth to Jehoiarib, the second to Jedaiah,

8 The third to Harim, the fourth to Seorim,

9 The fifth to Malchijah, the sixth to Mijamin,

10 The seventh to Hakkoz, the eighth to [a]Abijah,

11 The ninth to Jeshua, the tenth to Shecaniah,

12 The eleventh to Eliashib, the twelfth to Jakim,

13 The thirteenth to Huppah, the fourteenth to Jeshebeab,

14 The fifteenth to Bilgah, the sixteenth to Immer,

15 The seventeenth to Hezir, the eighteenth to Aphses,

16 The nineteenth to Pethahiah, the twentieth to Jehezekel,

17 The one and twentieth to Jachin, the two and twentieth to Gamul,

18 The three and twentieth to Delaiah, the four and twentieth to Maaziah.

19 These *were* the orderings of them in their service [a]to come into the house of the LORD, according to their manner, under Aaron their father, as the LORD God of Israel had commanded him.

Other Levites

20 And the rest of the sons of Levi *were these:* Of the sons of Amram; Shubael: of the sons of Shubael; Jehdeiah.

21 Concerning [a]Rehabiah: of the sons of Rehabiah, the first *was* Isshiah.

22 Of the Izharites; Shelomoth: of the sons of Shelomoth; Jahath.

23 And the sons *of [a]Hebron;* Jeriah *the first,* Amariah the second, Jahaziel the third, Jekameam the fourth.

24 *Of* the sons of Uzziel; Michah: of the sons of Michah; Shamir.

25 The brother of Michah *was* Isshiah: of the sons of Isshiah; Zechariah.

26 [a]The sons of Merari *were* Mahli and Mushi: the sons of Jaaziah; Beno.

27 The sons of Merari by Jaaziah; Beno, and Shoham, and Zaccur, and Ibri.

28 Of Mahli *came* Eleazar, [a]who had no sons.

29 Concerning Kish: the son of Kish *was* Jerahmeel.

30 [a]The sons also of Mushi; Mahli, and Eder, and Jerimoth. These *were* the sons of the Levites after the house of their fathers.

31 These likewise cast lots over against their brethren the sons of Aaron in the presence of David the king, and Zadok, and Ahimelech, and the chief of the fathers of the priests and Levites, even the principal fathers over against their younger brethren.

The Musicians

25 Moreover David and the captains of the host separated to the service of the sons of [a]Asaph, and of Heman, and of Jeduthun, who should prophesy with harps, with psalteries, and with cymbals: and the number of the workmen according to their service was:

2 Of the sons of Asaph; Zaccur, and Joseph, and Nethaniah, and Asarelah, the sons of Asaph under the hands of Asaph, which prophesied according to the order of the king.

3 Of [a]Jeduthun: the sons of Jeduthun; Gedaliah, and Zeri, and Jeshaiah, Hashabiah, and Mattithiah, six, under the hands of their father Jeduthun, who prophesied with a harp, to give thanks and to praise the LORD.

4 Of Heman: the sons of Heman; Bukkiah, Mattaniah, Uzziel, Shebuel, and Jerimoth, Hana-

---

10 [a]Neh. 12:4, 17; Luke 1:5
19 [a]1 Chr. 9:25
21 [a]1 Chr. 23:17
23 [a]1 Chr. 23:19; 26:31
26 [a]Ex. 6:19; 1 Chr. 23:21
28 [a]1 Chr. 23:22
30 [a]1 Chr. 23:23

CHAPTER 25
1 [a]1 Chr. 6:30, 33, 39, 44; 2 Chr. 5:12
3 [a]1 Chr. 16:41, 42

*

24:15 LXX, Vg. *Aphses*
24:16 MT *Jehezkel*
24:20 *Shebuel,* 1 Chr. 23:16
24:22 *Shelomith,* 1 Chr. 23:18
24:23 Supplied from 23:19 (following some Heb. mss. and LXX mss.) • See preceding note.
25:2 *Jesharelah,* v. 14
25:3 *Jizri,* v. 11 • So with one Heb. ms., LXX mss. • Shimei is the sixth, v. 17
25:4 *Azarel,* v. 18 • *Shubael,* v. 20 • *Jeremoth,* v. 22

NKJV

father's house taken for Eleazar and *one* for Ithamar.

7 Now the first lot fell to Jehoiarib, the second to Jedaiah,

8 the third to Harim, the fourth to Seorim,

9 the fifth to Malchijah, the sixth to Mijamin,

10 the seventh to Hakkoz, the eighth to [a]Abijah,

11 the ninth to Jeshua, the tenth to Shecaniah,

12 the eleventh to Eliashib, the twelfth to Jakim,

13 the thirteenth to Huppah, the fourteenth to Jeshebeab,

14 the fifteenth to Bilgah, the sixteenth to Immer,

15 the seventeenth to Hezir, the eighteenth to *Happizzez,

16 the nineteenth to Pethahiah, the twentieth to *Jehezekel,

17 the twenty-first to Jachin, the twenty-second to Gamul,

18 the twenty-third to Delaiah, the twenty-fourth to Maaziah.

19 This *was* the schedule of their service [a]for coming into the house of the LORD according to their ordinance by the hand of Aaron their father, as the LORD God of Israel had commanded him.

Other Levites

20 And the rest of the sons of Levi: of the sons of Amram, *Shubael; of the sons of Shubael, Jehdeiah.

21 Concerning [a]Rehabiah, of the sons of Rehabiah, the first *was* Isshiah.

22 Of the Izharites, *Shelomoth; of the sons of Shelomoth, Jahath.

23 Of the sons **of [a]Hebron,* Jeriah **was the first,* Amariah the second, Jahaziel the third, *and* Jekameam the fourth.

24 *Of* the sons of Uzziel, Michah; of the sons of Michah, Shamir.

25 The brother of Michah, Isshiah; of the sons of Isshiah, Zechariah.

26 [a]The sons of Merari *were* Mahli and Mushi; the son of Jaaziah, Beno.

27 The sons of Merari by Jaaziah *were* Beno, Shoham, Zaccur, and Ibri.

28 Of Mahli: Eleazar, [a]who had no sons.

29 Of Kish: the son of Kish, Jerahmeel.

30 Also [a]the sons of Mushi *were* Mahli, Eder, and Jerimoth. These *were* the sons of the Levites according to their fathers' houses.

31 These also cast lots just as their brothers the sons of Aaron did, in the presence of King David, Zadok, Ahimelech, and the heads of the fathers' *houses* of the priests and Levites. The chief fathers *did* just as their younger brethren.

The Musicians

25 Moreover David and the captains of the army separated for the service *some* of the sons of [a]Asaph, of Heman, and of Jeduthun, who *should* prophesy with harps, stringed instruments, and cymbals. And the number of the skilled men performing their service was:

2 Of the sons of Asaph: Zaccur, Joseph, Nethaniah, and *Asharelah; the sons of Asaph *were* under the direction of Asaph, who prophesied according to the order of the king.

3 Of [a]Jeduthun, the sons of Jeduthun: Gedaliah, *Zeri, Jeshaiah, *Shimei, Hashabiah, and Mattithiah, *six, under the direction of their father Jeduthun, who prophesied with a harp to give thanks and to praise the LORD.

4 Of Heman, the sons of Heman: Bukkiah, Mattaniah, *Uzziel, *Shebuel, *Jerimoth, Hana-

KJV

niah, Hanani, Eliathah, Giddalti, and Romamti–ezer, Joshbekashah, Mallothi, Hothir, *and* Mahazioth:

5 All these *were* the sons of Heman the king's seer in the words of God, to lift up the [a]horn. And God gave to Heman fourteen sons and three daughters.

6 All these *were* under the hands of their father for song *in* the house of the LORD, with cymbals, psalteries, and [a]harps, for the service of the house of God, [b]according to the king's order to Asaph, Jeduthun, and Heman.

7 So the [a]number of them, with their brethren that were instructed in the songs of the LORD, *even* all that were cunning, was two hundred fourscore and eight.

8 And they cast lots, ward against *ward,* as well the small as the great, [a]the teacher as the scholar.

9 Now the first lot came forth for Asaph to Joseph: the second to Gedaliah, who with his brethren and sons *were* twelve:

10 The third to Zaccur, *he,* his sons, and his brethren, *were* twelve:

11 The fourth to Izri, *he,* his sons, and his brethren, *were* twelve:

12 The fifth to Nethaniah, *he,* his sons, and his brethren, *were* twelve:

13 The sixth to Bukkiah, *he,* his sons, and his brethren, *were* twelve:

14 The seventh to Jesharelah, *he,* his sons, and his brethren, *were* twelve:

15 The eighth to Jeshaiah, *he,* his sons, and his brethren, *were* twelve:

16 The ninth to Mattaniah, *he,* his sons, and his brethren, *were* twelve:

17 The tenth to Shimei, *he,* his sons, and his brethren, *were* twelve:

18 The eleventh to Azareel, *he,* his sons, and his brethren, *were* twelve:

19 The twelfth to Hashabiah, *he,* his sons, and his brethren, *were* twelve:

20 The thirteenth to Shubael, *he,* his sons, and his brethren, *were* twelve:

21 The fourteenth to Mattithiah, *he,* his sons, and his brethren, *were* twelve:

22 The fifteenth to Jeremoth, *he,* his sons, and his brethren, *were* twelve:

23 The sixteenth to Hananiah, *he,* his sons, and his brethren, *were* twelve:

24 The seventeenth to Joshbekashah, *he,* his sons, and his brethren, *were* twelve:

25 The eighteenth to Hanani, *he,* his sons, and his brethren, *were* twelve:

26 The nineteenth to Mallothi, *he,* his sons, and his brethren, *were* twelve:

27 The twentieth to Eliathah, *he,* his sons, and his brethren, *were* twelve:

28 The one and twentieth to Hothir, *he,* his sons, and his brethren, *were* twelve:

29 The two and twentieth to Giddalti, *he,* his sons, and his brethren, *were* twelve:

30 The three and twentieth to Mahazioth, *he,* his sons, and his brethren, *were* twelve:

31 The four and twentieth to Romamti–ezer, *he,* his sons, and his brethren, *were* twelve.

The Gatekeepers

26 Concerning the divisions of the porters: Of the Korhites *was* Meshelemiah the son of [a]Kore, of the sons of Asaph.

2 And the sons of Meshelemiah *were,* [a]Zechariah the firstborn, Jediael the second, Zebadiah the third, Jathniel the fourth,

3 Elam the fifth, Jehohanan the sixth, Elioenai the seventh.

4 Moreover the sons of [a]Obed–edom *were,* Shemaiah the firstborn, Jehozabad the second, Joah the third, and Sacar the fourth, and Nethaneel the fifth,

5 Ammiel the sixth, Issachar the seventh, Peulthai the eighth: for God blessed him.

5 [a]1 Chr. 16:42
6 [a]1 Chr. 15:16 [b]1 Chr. 15:19; 25:2
7 [a]1 Chr. 23:5
8 [a]2 Chr. 23:13

CHAPTER 26

1 [a]Ps. 42:title
2 [a]1 Chr. 9:21
4 [a]1 Chr. 15:18, 21

*

25:5 Increase his power or influence
25:11 *Zeri,* v. 3
25:14 *Asharelah,* v. 2
25:18 *Uzziel,* v. 4
25:20 *Shebuel,* v. 4
25:22 *Jerimoth,* v. 4

NKJV

niah, Hanani, Eliathah, Giddalti, Romamti-Ezer, Joshbekashah, Mallothi, Hothir, *and* Mahazioth.

5 All these *were* the sons of Heman the king's seer in the words of God, to *exalt his [a]horn. For God gave Heman fourteen sons and three daughters.

6 All these *were* under the direction of their father for the music *in* the house of the LORD, with cymbals, stringed instruments, and [a]harps, for the service of the house of God. Asaph, Jeduthun, and Heman *were* [b]under the authority of the king.

7 So the [a]number of them, with their brethren who were instructed in the songs of the LORD, all who were skillful, *was* two hundred and eighty-eight.

8 And they cast lots for their duty, the small as well as the great, [a]the teacher with the student.

9 Now the first lot for Asaph came out for Joseph; the second for Gedaliah, him with his brethren and sons, twelve;

10 the third for Zaccur, his sons and his brethren, twelve;

11 the fourth for *Jizri, his sons and his brethren, twelve;

12 the fifth for Nethaniah, his sons and his brethren, twelve;

13 the sixth for Bukkiah, his sons and his brethren, twelve;

14 the seventh for *Jesharelah, his sons and his brethren, twelve;

15 the eighth for Jeshaiah, his sons and his brethren, twelve;

16 the ninth for Mattaniah, his sons and his brethren, twelve;

17 the tenth for Shimei, his sons and his brethren, twelve;

18 the eleventh for *Azarel, his sons and his brethren, twelve;

19 the twelfth for Hashabiah, his sons and his brethren, twelve;

20 the thirteenth for *Shubael, his sons and his brethren, twelve;

21 the fourteenth for Mattithiah, his sons and his brethren, twelve;

22 the fifteenth for *Jeremoth, his sons and his brethren, twelve;

23 the sixteenth for Hananiah, his sons and his brethren, twelve;

24 the seventeenth for Joshbekashah, his sons and his brethren, twelve;

25 the eighteenth for Hanani, his sons and his brethren, twelve;

26 the nineteenth for Mallothi, his sons and his brethren, twelve;

27 the twentieth for Eliathah, his sons and his brethren, twelve;

28 the twenty-first for Hothir, his sons and his brethren, twelve;

29 the twenty-second for Giddalti, his sons and his brethren, twelve;

30 the twenty-third for Mahazioth, his sons and his brethren, twelve;

31 the twenty-fourth for Romamti-Ezer, his sons and his brethren, twelve.

The Gatekeepers

26 Concerning the divisions of the gatekeepers: of the Korahites, Meshelemiah the son of [a]Kore, of the sons of Asaph.

2 And the sons of Meshelemiah *were* [a]Zechariah the firstborn, Jediael the second, Zebadiah the third, Jathniel the fourth,

3 Elam the fifth, Jehohanan the sixth, Eliehoenai the seventh.

4 Moreover the sons of [a]Obed-Edom *were* Shemaiah the firstborn, Jehozabad the second, Joah the third, Sacar the fourth, Nethanel the fifth,

5 Ammiel the sixth, Issachar the seventh, Peulthai the eighth; for God blessed him.

KJV

6 Also unto Shemaiah his son were sons born, that ruled throughout the house of their father: for they *were* mighty men of valour.

7 The sons of Shemaiah; Othni, and Rephael, and Obed, Elzabad, whose brethren *were* strong men, Elihu, and Semachiah.

8 All these of the sons of Obed–edom: they and their sons and their brethren, [a]able men for strength for the service, *were* threescore and two of Obed–edom.

9 And Meshelemiah had sons and brethren, strong men, eighteen.

10 Also [a]Hosah, of the children of Merari, had sons; Simri the chief, (for *though* he was not the firstborn, yet his father made him the chief;)

11 Hilkiah the second, Tebaliah the third, Zechariah the fourth: all the sons and brethren of Hosah *were* thirteen.

12 Among these *were* the divisions of the porters, *even* among the chief men, *having* wards one against another, to minister in the house of the LORD.

13 And they [a]cast lots, as well the small as the great, according to the house of their fathers, for every gate.

14 And the lot eastward fell to Shelemiah. Then for Zechariah his son, a wise counsellor, they cast lots; and his lot came out northward.

15 To Obed–edom southward; and to his sons the house of Asuppim.

16 To Shuppim and Hosah *the lot came forth* westward, with the gate Shallecheth, by the causeway of the going [a]up, ward against ward.

17 Eastward *were* six Levites, northward four a day, southward four a day, and toward Asuppim two *and* two.

18 At Parbar westward, four at the causeway, *and* two at Parbar.

19 These *are* the divisions of the porters among the sons of Kore, and among the sons of Merari.

The Treasuries and Other Duties

20 And of the Levites, Ahijah *was* [a]over the treasures of the house of God, and over the treasures of the [b]dedicated things.

21 *As concerning* the sons of Laadan; the sons of the Gershonite Laadan, chief fathers, *even* of Laadan the Gershonite, *were* Jehieli.

22 The sons of Jehieli; Zetham, and Joel his brother, *which were* over the treasures of the house of the LORD.

23 Of the [a]Amramites, *and* the Izharites, the Hebronites, *and* the Uzzielites:

24 And [a]Shebuel the son of Gershom, the son of Moses, *was* ruler of the treasures.

25 And his brethren by Eliezer; Rehabiah his son, and Jeshaiah his son, and Joram his son, and Zichri his son, and [a]Shelomith his son.

26 Which Shelomith and his brethren *were* over all the treasures of the dedicated things, [a]which David the king, and the chief fathers, the captains over thousands and hundreds, and the captains of the host, had dedicated.

27 Out of the spoils won in battles did they dedicate to maintain the house of the LORD.

28 And all that Samuel [a]the seer, and Saul the son of Kish, and Abner the son of Ner, and Joab the son of Zeruiah, had dedicated; *and* whosoever had dedicated *any thing, it was* under the hand of Shelomith, and of his brethren.

29 Of the Izharites, Chenaniah and his sons *were* for the [a]outward business over Israel, for [b]officers and judges.

30 *And* of the Hebronites, [a]Hashabiah and his brethren, men of valour, a thousand and seven hundred, *were* officers among them of Israel on this side Jordan westward in all the business of the LORD, and in the service of the king.

31 Among the Hebronites *was* [a]Jerijah the

8 [a]1 Chr. 9:13
10 [a]1 Chr. 16:38
13 [a]1 Chr. 24:5, 31; 25:8
16 [a]1 Kin. 10:5; 2 Chr. 9:4
20 [a]1 Chr. 9:26 [b]2 Sam. 8:11; 1 Chr. 26:22, 24, 26; 28:12; Ezra 2:69
23 [a]Ex. 6:18; Num. 3:19
24 [a]1 Chr. 23:16
25 [a]1 Chr. 23:18
26 [a]2 Sam. 8:11
28 [a]1 Sam. 9:9
29 [a]Neh. 11:16 [b]1 Chr. 23:4
30 [a]1 Chr. 27:17
31 [a]1 Chr. 23:19

NKJV

6 Also to Shemaiah his son were sons born who governed their fathers' houses, because they *were* men of great ability.

7 The sons of Shemaiah *were* Othni, Rephael, Obed, and Elzabad, whose brothers Elihu and Semachiah *were* able men.

8 All these *were* of the sons of Obed-Edom, they and their sons and their brethren, [a]able men with strength for the work: sixty-two of Obed-Edom.

9 And Meshelemiah had sons and brethren, eighteen able men.

10 Also [a]Hosah, of the children of Merari, had sons: Shimri the first (for *though* he was not the firstborn, his father made him the first),

11 Hilkiah the second, Tebaliah the third, Zechariah the fourth; all the sons and brethren of Hosah *were* thirteen.

12 Among these *were* the divisions of the gatekeepers, among the chief men, *having* duties just like their brethren, to serve in the house of the LORD.

13 And they [a]cast lots for each gate, the small as well as the great, according to their father's house.

14 The lot for the East *Gate* fell to Shelemiah. Then they cast lots *for* his son Zechariah, a wise counselor, and his lot came out for the North Gate;

15 to Obed-Edom the South Gate, and to his sons the *storehouse.

16 To Shuppim and Hosah *the lot came out* for the West Gate, with the Shallecheth Gate on the [a]ascending highway—watchman opposite watchman.

17 On the east were *six* Levites, on the north four each day, on the south four each day, and for the *storehouse two by two.

18 As for the *Parbar on the west, *there were* four on the highway *and* two at the Parbar.

19 These were the divisions of the gatekeepers among the sons of Korah and among the sons of Merari.

The Treasuries and Other Duties

20 Of the Levites, Ahijah *was* [a]over the treasuries of the house of God and over the treasuries of the [b]dedicated things.

21 The sons of Laadan, the descendants of the Gershonites of Laadan, heads of their fathers' *houses*, of Laadan the Gershonite: Jehieli.

22 The sons of Jehieli, Zetham and Joel his brother, *were* over the treasuries of the house of the LORD.

23 Of the [a]Amramites, the Izharites, the Hebronites, and the Uzzielites:

24 [a]Shebuel the son of Gershom, the son of Moses, *was* overseer of the treasuries.

25 And his brethren by Eliezer *were* Rehabiah his son, Jeshaiah his son, Joram his son, Zichri his son, and [a]Shelomith his son.

26 This Shelomith and his brethren *were* over all the treasuries of the dedicated things [a]which King David and the heads of fathers' *houses*, the captains over thousands and hundreds, and the captains of the army, had dedicated.

27 Some of the spoils won in battles they dedicated to maintain the house of the LORD.

28 And all that Samuel [a]the seer, Saul the son of Kish, Abner the son of Ner, and Joab the son of Zeruiah had dedicated, every dedicated *thing*, was under the hand of Shelomith and his brethren.

29 Of the Izharites, Chenaniah and his sons [a]*performed* duties as [b]officials and judges over Israel outside Jerusalem.

30 Of the Hebronites, [a]Hashabiah and his brethren, one thousand seven hundred able men, had the oversight of Israel on the west side of the Jordan for all the business of the LORD, and in the service of the king.

31 Among the Hebronites, [a]Jerijah *was* head

*

26:15 Heb. *asuppim*
26:17 Heb. *asuppim*
26:18 Probably a court or colonnade extending west of the temple

KJV

chief, *even* among the Hebronites, according to the generations of his fathers. In the fortieth year of the reign of David they were sought for, and there were found among them mighty men of valour [b]at Jazer of Gilead.

32 And his brethren, men of valour, *were* two thousand and seven hundred chief fathers, whom king David made rulers over the Reubenites, the Gadites, and the half tribe of Manasseh, for every matter pertaining to God, and [a]affairs of the king.

The Military Divisions

27 Now the children of Israel after their number, *to wit*, the chief fathers and captains of thousands and hundreds, and their officers that served the king in any matter of the courses, which came in and went out month by month throughout all the months of the year, of every course *were* twenty and four thousand.

2 Over the first course for the first month *was* [a]Jashobeam the son of Zabdiel: and in his course *were* twenty and four thousand.

3 Of the children of Perez *was* the chief of all the captains of the host for the first month.

4 And over the course of the second month *was* Dodai an Ahohite, and of his course *was* Mikloth also the ruler: in his course likewise *were* twenty and four thousand.

5 The third captain of the host for the third month *was* [a]Benaiah the son of Jehoiada, a chief priest: and in his course *were* twenty and four thousand.

6 This *is that* Benaiah, *who was* [a]mighty *among* the thirty, and above the thirty: and in his course *was* Ammizabad his son.

7 The fourth *captain* for the fourth month *was* [a]Asahel the brother of Joab, and Zebadiah his son after him: and in his course *were* twenty and four thousand.

8 The fifth captain for the fifth month *was* Shamhuth the Izrahite: and in his course *were* twenty and four thousand.

9 The sixth *captain* for the sixth month *was* [a]Ira the son of Ikkesh the Tekoite: and in his course *were* twenty and four thousand.

10 The seventh *captain* for the seventh month *was* [a]Helez the Pelonite, of the children of Ephraim: and in his course *were* twenty and four thousand.

11 The eighth *captain* for the eighth month *was* [a]Sibbecai the Hushathite, of the Zarhites: and in his course *were* twenty and four thousand.

12 The ninth *captain* for the ninth month *was* [a]Abiezer the Anetothite, of the Benjamites: and in his course *were* twenty and four thousand.

13 The tenth *captain* for the tenth month *was* [a]Maharai the Netophathite, of the Zarhites: and in his course *were* twenty and four thousand.

14 The eleventh *captain* for the eleventh month *was* [a]Benaiah the Pirathonite, of the children of Ephraim: and in his course *were* twenty and four thousand.

15 The twelfth *captain* for the twelfth month *was* Heldai the Netophathite, of Othniel: and in his course *were* twenty and four thousand.

Leaders of Tribes

16 Furthermore over the tribes of Israel: the ruler of the Reubenites *was* Eliezer the son of Zichri: of the Simeonites, Shephatiah the son of Maachah:

17 Of the Levites, [a]Hashabiah the son of Kemuel: of the Aaronites, Zadok:

18 Of Judah, [a]Elihu, *one* of the brethren of David: of Issachar, Omri the son of Michael:

19 Of Zebulun, Ishmaiah the son of Obadiah: of Naphtali, Jerimoth the son of Azriel:

20 Of the children of Ephraim, Hoshea the son of Azaziah: of the half tribe of Manasseh, Joel the son of Pedaiah:

31 [b]Josh. 21:39
32 [a]2 Chr. 19:11

CHAPTER 27

2 [a]1 Chr. 11:11
5 [a]1 Chr. 18:17
6 [a]2 Sam. 23:20–23
7 [a]2 Sam. 23:24; 1 Chr. 11:26
9 [a]1 Chr. 11:28
10 [a]1 Chr. 11:27
11 [a]2 Sam. 21:18; 1 Chr. 11:29; 20:4
12 [a]1 Chr. 11:28
13 [a]2 Sam. 23:28; 1 Chr. 11:30
14 [a]1 Chr. 11:31
17 [a]1 Chr. 26:30
18 [a]1 Sam. 16:6

NKJV

of the Hebronites according to his genealogy of the fathers. In the fortieth year of the reign of David they were sought, and there were found among them capable men [b]at Jazer of Gilead.

32 And his brethren *were* two thousand seven hundred able men, heads of fathers' *houses*, whom King David made officials over the Reubenites, the Gadites, and the half-tribe of Manasseh, for every matter pertaining to God and the [a]affairs of the king.

The Military Divisions

27 And the children of Israel, according to their number, the heads of fathers' *houses*, the captains of thousands and hundreds and their officers, served the king in every matter of the *military* divisions. *These divisions* came in and went out month by month throughout all the months of the year, each division *having* twenty-four thousand.

2 Over the first division for the first month *was* [a]Jashobeam the son of Zabdiel, and in his division *were* twenty-four thousand;

3 *he was* of the children of Perez, and the chief of all the captains of the army for the first month.

4 Over the division of the second month *was* *Dodai an Ahohite, and of his division Mikloth also *was* the leader; in his division *were* twenty-four thousand.

5 The third captain of the army for the third month *was* [a]Benaiah, the son of Jehoiada the priest, who was chief; in his division *were* twenty-four thousand.

6 This was the Benaiah *who was* [a]mighty *among* the thirty, and was over the thirty; in his division *was* Ammizabad his son.

7 The fourth *captain* for the fourth month *was* [a]Asahel the brother of Joab, and Zebadiah his son after him; in his division *were* twenty-four thousand.

8 The fifth *captain* for the fifth month *was* *Shamhuth the Izrahite; in his division were twenty-four thousand.

9 The sixth *captain* for the sixth month *was* [a]Ira the son of Ikkesh the Tekoite; in his division *were* twenty-four thousand.

10 The seventh *captain* for the seventh month *was* [a]Helez the Pelonite, of the children of Ephraim; in his division *were* twenty-four thousand.

11 The eighth *captain* for the eighth month *was* [a]Sibbechai the Hushathite, of the Zarhites; in his division *were* twenty-four thousand.

12 The ninth *captain* for the ninth month *was* [a]Abiezer the Anathothite, of the Benjamites; in his division *were* twenty-four thousand.

13 The tenth *captain* for the tenth month *was* [a]Maharai the Netophathite, of the Zarhites; in his division *were* twenty-four thousand.

14 The eleventh *captain* for the eleventh month *was* [a]Benaiah the Pirathonite, of the children of Ephraim; in his division *were* twenty-four thousand.

15 The twelfth *captain* for the twelfth month *was* *Heldai the Netophathite, of Othniel; in his division *were* twenty-four thousand.

Leaders of Tribes

16 Furthermore, over the tribes of Israel: the officer over the Reubenites *was* Eliezer the son of Zichri; over the Simeonites, Shephatiah the son of Maachah;

17 *over* the Levites, [a]Hashabiah the son of Kemuel; over the Aaronites, Zadok;

18 *over* Judah, [a]Elihu, *one* of David's brothers; *over* Issachar, Omri the son of Michael;

19 *over* Zebulun, Ishmaiah the son of Obadiah; *over* Naphtali, Jerimoth the son of Azriel;

20 *over* the children of Ephraim, Hoshea the son of Azaziah; *over* the half-tribe of Manasseh, Joel the son of Pedaiah;

*———

27:4 Heb. *Dodai,* usually spelled *Dodo,* 2 Sam. 23:9
27:8 *Shammah,* 2 Sam. 23:11, or *Shammoth,* 1 Chr. 11:27
27:15 *Heleb,* 2 Sam. 23:29, or *Heled,* 1 Chr. 11:30

KJV

21 Of the half *tribe* of Manasseh in Gilead,
Iddo the son of Zechariah: of Benjamin, Jaasiel
the son of Abner:
22 Of Dan, Azareel the son of Jeroham.
These *were* the princes of the tribes of Israel.
23 But David took not the number of them
from twenty years old and under: because [a]the
LORD had said he would increase Israel like to
the [b]stars of the heavens.
24 Joab the son of Zeruiah began to number,
but he finished not, because [a]there fell wrath for
it against Israel; neither was the number put in
the account of the Chronicles of king David.

Other State Officials

25 And over the king's treasures *was* Azmaveth the son of Adiel: and over the storehouses
in the fields, in the cities, and in the villages, and
in the castles, *was* Jehonathan the son of Uzziah:
26 And over them that did the work of the
field for tillage of the ground *was* Ezri the son of
Chelub:
27 And over the vineyards *was* Shimei the
Ramathite: over the increase of the vineyards for
the wine cellars *was* Zabdi the Shiphmite:
28 And over the olive trees and the sycomore
trees that *were* in the low plains *was* Baal–hanan
the Gederite: and over the cellars of oil *was* Joash:
29 And over the herds that fed in Sharon *was*
Shitrai the Sharonite: and over the herds *that
were* in the valleys *was* Shaphat the son of
Adlai:
30 Over the camels also *was* Obil the Ishmaelite: and over the asses *was* Jehdeiah the
Meronothite:
31 And over the flocks *was* Jaziz the [a]Hagerite. All these *were* the rulers of the substance which *was* king David's.
32 Also Jonathan David's uncle was a counsellor, a wise man, and a scribe: and Jehiel the
son of Hachmoni *was* with the king's sons:
33 And [a]Ahithophel *was* the king's counsellor: and [b]Hushai the Archite *was* the king's
companion:
34 And after Ahithophel *was* Jehoiada the
son of Benaiah, and [a]Abiathar: and the general
of the king's army *was* [b]Joab.

Solomon Instructed to Build the Temple

28 And David assembled all [a]the princes of
Israel, the princes of the tribes, and [b]the
captains of the companies that ministered to the
king by course, and the captains over the thousands, and captains over the hundreds, and [c]the
stewards over all the substance and possession
of the king, and of his sons, with the officers, and
with [d]the mighty men, and with all the valiant
men, unto Jerusalem.
2 Then David the king stood up upon his
feet, and said, Hear me, my brethren, and my people: *As for me,* [a]I *had* in mine heart to build an
house of rest for the ark of the covenant of the
LORD, and for [b]the footstool of our God, and had
made ready for the building:
3 But God said unto me, [a]Thou shalt not
build an house for my name, because thou *hast
been* a man of war, and hast shed [b]blood.
4 Howbeit the LORD God of Israel [a]chose me
before all the house of my father to be king over
Israel for ever: for he hath chosen [b]Judah *to be*
the ruler; and of the house of Judah, [c]the house
of my father; and [d]among the sons of my father
he liked me to make *me* king over all Israel:
5 [a]And of all my sons, (for the LORD hath
given me many sons,) [b]he hath chosen Solomon
my son to sit upon the throne of the kingdom of
the LORD over Israel.
6 And he said unto me, [a]Solomon thy son,
he shall build my house and my courts: for I have
chosen him *to be* my son, and I will be his father.
7 Moreover I will establish his kingdom

23 [a][Deut. 6:3] [b]Gen. 15:5; 22:17; 26:4; Ex. 32:13; Deut. 1:10
24 [a]2 Sam. 24:12–15; 1 Chr. 21:1–7
31 [a]1 Chr. 5:10
33 [a]2 Sam. 15:12 [b]2 Sam. 15:32–37
34 [a]1 Kin. 1:7 [b]1 Chr. 11:6

CHAPTER 28

1 [a]1 Chr. 27:16 [b]1 Chr. 27:1, 2 [c]1 Chr. 27:25 [d]2 Sam. 23:8–39; 1 Chr. 11:10–47
2 [a]2 Sam. 7:2 [b]Ps. 99:5; 132:7; [Is. 66:1]
3 [a]2 Sam. 7:5, 13; 1 Kin. 5:3 [b][1 Chr. 17:4; 22:8]
4 [a]1 Sam. 16:6–13 [b]Gen. 49:8–10; 1 Chr. 5:2; Ps. 60:7 [c]1 Sam. 16:1 [d]1 Sam. 13:14; 16:12, 13; Acts 13:22
5 [a]1 Chr. 3:1–9; 14:3–7; 23:1 [b]1 Chr. 22:9; 29:1
6 [a]2 Sam. 7:13, 14; 1 Kin. 6:38; 1 Chr. 22:9, 10; 2 Chr. 1:9; 6:2

NKJV

21 *over* the half-*tribe* of Manasseh in Gilead,
Iddo the son of Zechariah; *over* Benjamin, Jaasiel
the son of Abner;
22 *over* Dan, Azarel the son of Jeroham.
These *were* the leaders of the tribes of Israel.
23 But David did not take the number of
those twenty years old and under, because [a]the
LORD had said He would multiply Israel like the
[b]stars of the heavens.
24 Joab the son of Zeruiah began a census,
but he did not finish, for [a]wrath came upon Israel
because of this census; nor was the number recorded in the account of the chronicles of King
David.

Other State Officials

25 And Azmaveth the son of Adiel *was* over
the king's treasuries; and Jehonathan the son of
Uzziah was over the storehouses in the field, in
the cities, in the villages, and in the fortresses.
26 Ezri the son of Chelub was over those who
did the work of the field for tilling the ground.
27 And Shimei the Ramathite *was* over the
vineyards, and Zabdi the Shiphmite was over the
produce of the vineyards for the supply of wine.
28 Baal-Hanan the Gederite was over the
olive trees and the sycamore trees that *were* in
the lowlands, and Joash *was* over the store of oil.
29 And Shitrai the Sharonite *was* over the
herds that fed in Sharon, and Shaphat the son of
Adlai was over the herds *that were* in the valleys.
30 Obil the Ishmaelite *was* over the camels,
Jehdeiah the Meronothite *was* over the donkeys,
31 and Jaziz the [a]Hagrite *was* over the flocks.
All these *were* the officials over King David's
property.
32 Also Jehonathan, David's uncle, *was* a
counselor, a wise man, and a scribe; and Jehiel
the son of Hachmoni *was* with the king's sons.
33 [a]Ahithophel *was* the king's counselor, and
[b]Hushai the Archite *was* the king's companion.
34 After Ahithophel *was* Jehoiada the son of
Benaiah, then [a]Abiathar. And the general of the
king's army *was* [b]Joab.

Solomon Instructed to Build the Temple

28 Now David assembled at Jerusalem all [a]the
leaders of Israel: the officers of the tribes
and [b]the captains of the divisions who served the
king, the captains over thousands and captains
over hundreds, and [c]the stewards over all the substance and possessions of the king and of his sons,
with the officials, the valiant men, and all [d]the
mighty men of valor.
2 Then King David rose to his feet and said,
"Hear me, my brethren and my people: [a]I *had* it
in my heart to build a house of rest for the ark
of the covenant of the LORD, and for [b]the footstool
of our God, and had made preparations to build
it.
3 "But God said to me, [a]'You shall not build
a house for My name, because you *have been* a
man of war and have shed [b]blood.'
4 "However the LORD God of Israel [a]chose
me above all the house of my father to be king
over Israel forever, for He has chosen [b]Judah *to
be* the ruler. And of the house of Judah, [c]the house
of my father, and [d]among the sons of my father,
He was pleased with me to make *me* king over
all Israel.
5 [a]"And of all my sons (for the LORD has
given me many sons) [b]He has chosen my son Solomon to sit on the throne of the kingdom of the
LORD over Israel.
6 "Now He said to me, 'It is [a]your son Solomon *who* shall build My house and My courts;
for I have chosen him *to be* My son, and I will
be his Father.
7 'Moreover I will establish his kingdom

KJV

for ever, [a]if he be constant to do my commandments and my judgments, as at this day.
8 Now therefore, in the sight of all Israel
the congregation of the LORD, and in the audience
of our God, keep and seek for all the commandments of the LORD your God: that ye may possess
this good land, and leave *it* for an inheritance for
your children after you for ever.
9 And thou, Solomon my son, [a]know thou
the God of thy father, and serve him [b]with a perfect heart and with a willing mind: for [c]the LORD
searcheth all hearts, and understandeth all the
imaginations of the thoughts: [d]if thou seek him,
he will be found of thee; but if thou forsake him,
he will [e]cast thee off for ever.
10 Take heed now; [a]for the LORD hath chosen
thee to build an house for the sanctuary: be
strong, and do *it*.
11 Then David gave to Solomon his son [a]the
pattern of the porch, and of the houses thereof,
and of the treasuries thereof, and of the upper
chambers thereof, and of the inner parlours
thereof, and of the place of the mercy seat,
12 And the [a]pattern of all that he had by the
spirit, of the courts of the house of the LORD, and
of all the chambers round about, [b]of the treasuries
of the house of God, and of the treasuries of the
dedicated things:
13 Also for the courses of the priests and the
[a]Levites, and for all the work of the service of
the house of the LORD, and for all the vessels of
service in the house of the LORD.
14 *He gave* of gold by weight for *things* of
gold, for all instruments of all manner of service;
silver also for all instruments of silver by weight,
for all instruments of every kind of service:
15 Even the weight for the [a]candlesticks of
gold, and for their lamps of gold, by weight for
every candlestick, and for the lamps thereof: and
for the candlesticks of silver by weight, *both* for
the candlestick, and *also* for the lamps thereof,
according to the use of every candlestick.
16 And by weight *he gave* gold for the tables
of shewbread, for every [a]table; and *likewise* silver
for the tables of silver:
17 Also pure gold for the fleshhooks, and the
bowls, and the cups: and for the golden basons
he gave gold by weight for every bason; and *likewise silver* by weight for every bason of silver:
18 And for the [a]altar of incense refined gold
by weight; and gold for the pattern of the chariot
of the [b]cherubims, that spread out *their wings*,
and covered the ark of the covenant of the LORD.
19 All *this, said David,* [a]the LORD made me
understand in writing by *his* hand upon me, *even*
all the works of this pattern.
20 And David said to Solomon his son, [a]Be
strong and of good courage, and do *it*: fear not,
nor be dismayed: for the LORD God, *even* my God,
will be with thee; [b]he will not fail thee, nor forsake
thee, until thou hast finished all the work for the
service of the house of the LORD.
21 And, behold, [a]the courses of the priests
and the Levites, *even they shall be with thee* for
all the service of the house of God: and *there shall
be* with thee for all manner of workmanship [b]ev-
ery willing skilful man, for any manner of service:
also the princes and all the people *will be* wholly
at thy commandment.

Offerings for Building the Temple

29 Furthermore David the king said unto all
the congregation, Solomon my son, whom
alone God hath [a]chosen, *is yet* [b]young and tender,
and the work *is* great: for the palace *is* not for
man, but for the LORD God.
2 Now I have prepared with all my might
for the house of my God the gold for *things to
be made* of gold, and the silver for *things* of silver,
and the brass for *things* of brass, the iron for
things of iron, and wood for *things* of wood;
[a]onyx stones, and *stones* to be set, glistering

7 [a]1 Chr. 22:13
9 [a][1 Sam. 12:24]; Jer. 9:24; Hos. 4:1; [John 17:3] [b]2 Kin. 20:3 [c][1 Sam. 16:7; 1 Kin. 8:39; 1 Chr. 29:17]; Jer. 11:20; 17:10; 20:12; Rev. 2:23 [d]2 Chr. 15:2; [Jer. 29:13] [e]Deut. 31:17
10 [a]1 Chr. 22:13; 28:6
11 [a]1 Kin. 6:3; 1 Chr. 28:19
12 [a]Ex. 25:40; Heb. 8:5 [b]1 Chr. 26:20, 28
13 [a]1 Chr. 23:6
15 [a]Ex. 25:31–39; 1 Kin. 7:49
16 [a]1 Kin. 7:48
18 [a]Ex. 30:1–10 [b]Ex. 25:18–22; 1 Sam. 4:4; 1 Kin. 6:23
19 [a]Ex. 25:40; 1 Chr. 28:11, 12
20 [a]Deut. 31:6, 7; [Josh. 1:6–9]; 1 Chr. 22:13 [b]Josh. 1:5; Heb. 13:5
21 [a]1 Chr. 24—26 [b]Ex. 35:25–35; 36:1, 2; 2 Chr. 2:13, 14

CHAPTER 29
1 [a]1 Chr. 28:5 [b]1 Kin. 3:7; 1 Chr. 22:5; Prov. 4:3
2 [a]Is. 54:11, 12; Rev. 21:18

*
29:1 Lit. *palace*

NKJV

forever, [a]if he is steadfast to observe My commandments and My judgments, as it is this day.'
8 "Now therefore, in the sight of all Israel,
the assembly of the LORD, and in the hearing of
our God, be careful to seek out all the commandments of the LORD your God, that you may possess
this good land, and leave *it* as an inheritance for
your children after you forever.
9 "As for you, my son Solomon, [a]know the
God of your father, and serve Him [b]with a loyal
heart and with a willing mind; for [c]the LORD
searches all hearts and understands all the intent
of the thoughts. [d]If you seek Him, He will be found
by you; but if you forsake Him, He will [e]cast you
off forever.
10 "Consider now, [a]for the LORD has chosen
you to build a house for the sanctuary; be strong,
and do it."
11 Then David gave his son Solomon [a]the
plans for the vestibule, its houses, its treasuries,
its upper chambers, its inner chambers, and the
place of the mercy seat;
12 and the [a]plans for all that he had by the
Spirit, of the courts of the house of the LORD, of
all the chambers all around, [b]of the treasuries of
the house of God, and of the treasuries for the
dedicated things;
13 also for the division of the priests and the
[a]Levites, for all the work of the service of the
house of the LORD, and for all the articles of service in the house of the LORD.
14 *He gave* gold by weight for *things* of gold,
for all articles used in every kind of service; also
silver for all articles of silver by weight, for all
articles used in every kind of service;
15 the weight for the [a]lampstands of gold,
and their lamps of gold, by weight for each lampstand and its lamps; for the lampstands of silver
by weight, for the lampstand and its lamps, according to the use of each lampstand.
16 And by weight *he gave* gold for the tables
of the showbread, for each [a]table, and silver for
the tables of silver;
17 also pure gold for the forks, the basins,
the pitchers of pure gold, and the golden bowls—
he gave gold by weight for every bowl; and for
the silver bowls, *silver* by weight for every bowl;
18 and refined gold by weight for the [a]altar
of incense, and for the construction of the chariot,
that is, the gold [b]cherubim that spread *their wings*
and overshadowed the ark of the covenant of the
LORD.
19 "All *this," said David,* [a]"the LORD made
me understand in writing, by *His* hand upon me,
all the works of these plans."
20 And David said to his son Solomon, [a]"Be
strong and of good courage, and do *it;* do not fear
nor be dismayed, for the LORD God—my God—
will be with you. [b]He will not leave you nor forsake you, until you have finished all the work for
the service of the house of the LORD.
21 *"Here are* [a]the divisions of the priests and
the Levites for all the service of the house of God;
and [b]every willing craftsman *will be* with you for
all manner of workmanship, for every kind of service; also the leaders and all the people *will be*
completely at your command."

Offerings for Building the Temple

29 Furthermore King David said to all the assembly: "My son Solomon, whom alone
God has [a]chosen, *is* [b]young and inexperienced;
and the work *is* great, because the *temple *is* not
for man but for the LORD God.
2 "Now for the house of my God I have prepared with all my might: gold for *things to be
made of* gold, silver for *things of* silver, bronze
for *things of* bronze, iron for *things of* iron, wood
for *things of* wood, [a]onyx stones, *stones* to be set,
glistening stones of various colors, all kinds of

KJV

stones, and of divers colours, and all manner of
precious stones, and marble stones in abundance.
3 Moreover, because I have set my affection
to the house of my God, I have of mine own proper
good, of gold and silver, *which* I have given to
the house of my God, over and above all that I
have prepared for the holy house,
4 *Even* three thousand talents of gold, of the
gold of [a]Ophir, and seven thousand talents of refined silver, to overlay the walls of the houses
withal:
5 The gold for *things* of gold, and the silver
for *things* of silver, and for all manner of work
to be made by the hands of artificers. And who
then is [a]willing to consecrate his service this day
unto the LORD?
6 Then [a]the chief of the fathers and princes
of the tribes of Israel, and the captains of thousands and of hundreds, with [b]the rulers of the
king's work, [c]offered willingly,
7 And gave for the service of the house of
God of gold five thousand talents and ten thousand drams, and of silver ten thousand talents,
and of brass eighteen thousand talents, and one
hundred thousand talents of iron.
8 And they with whom *precious* stones were
found gave *them* to the treasure of the house of
the LORD, by the hand of [a]Jehiel the Gershonite.
9 Then the people rejoiced, for that they offered willingly, because with perfect heart they
[a]offered willingly to the LORD: and David the king
also rejoiced with great joy.

David's Praise to God

10 Wherefore David blessed the LORD before
all the congregation: and David said, Blessed *be*
thou, LORD God of Israel our father, for ever and
ever.
11 [a]Thine, O LORD, *is* the greatness, and the
power, and the glory, and the victory, and the majesty: for all *that is* in the heaven and in the earth
is thine; thine *is* the kingdom, O LORD, and thou
art exalted as head above all.
12 [a]Both riches and honour *come* of thee,
and thou reignest over all; and in thine hand *is*
power and might; and in thine hand *it is* to make
great, and to give strength unto all.
13 Now therefore, our God, we thank thee,
and praise thy glorious name.
14 But who *am* I, and what *is* my people, that
we should be able to offer so willingly after this
sort? for all things *come* of thee, and of thine own
have we given thee.
15 For [a]we *are* strangers before thee, and sojourners, as *were* all our fathers: [b]our days on
the earth *are* as a shadow, and *there is* none
abiding.
16 O LORD our God, all this store that we have
prepared to build thee an house for thine holy
name *cometh* of thine hand, and *is* all thine own.
17 I know also, my God, that thou [a]triest the
heart, and [b]hast pleasure in uprightness. As for
me, in the uprightness of mine heart I have willingly offered all these things: and now have I seen
with joy thy people, which are present here, to
offer willingly unto thee.
18 O LORD God of Abraham, Isaac, and of
Israel, our fathers, keep this for ever in the imagination of the thoughts of the heart of thy people,
and prepare their heart unto thee:
19 And [a]give unto Solomon my son a perfect
heart, to keep thy commandments, thy testimo-

4 [a]1 Kin. 9:28
5 [a]2 Chr. 29:31; [2 Cor. 8:5, 12]
6 [a]1 Chr. 27:1; 28:1 [b]1 Chr. 27:25–31 [c]Ex. 35:21–35
8 [a]1 Chr. 23:8
9 [a]Ex. 25:2; 1 Kin. 8:61; 2 Cor. 9:7
11 [a]Matt. 6:13; 1 Tim. 1:17; Rev. 5:13
12 [a]Rom. 11:36
15 [a]Lev. 25:23; Ps. 39:12; Heb. 11:13, 14; 1 Pet. 2:11 [b]Job 14:2; Ps. 90:9
17 [a][1 Sam. 16:7; 1 Chr. 28:9] [b]Prov. 11:20
19 [a][1 Chr. 28:9]; Ps. 72:1

NKJV

precious stones, and marble slabs in abundance.
3 "Moreover, because I have set my affection on the house of my God, I have given to the
house of my God, over and above all that I have
prepared for the holy house, my own special treasure of gold and silver:
4 "three thousand talents of gold, of the gold
of [a]Ophir, and seven thousand talents of refined
silver, to overlay the walls of the houses;
5 "the gold for *things of* gold and the silver
for *things of* silver, and for all kinds of work *to
be done* by the hands of craftsmen. Who *then* is
[a]willing to consecrate himself this day to the
LORD?"
6 Then [a]the leaders of the fathers' *houses,*
leaders of the tribes of Israel, the captains of thousands and of hundreds, with [b]the officers over the
king's work, [c]offered willingly.
7 They gave for the work of the house of
God five thousand talents and ten thousand darics
of gold, ten thousand talents of silver, eighteen
thousand talents of bronze, and one hundred
thousand talents of iron.
8 And whoever had *precious* stones gave
them to the treasury of the house of the LORD,
into the hand of [a]Jehiel* the Gershonite.
9 Then the people rejoiced, for they had offered willingly, because with a loyal heart they
had [a]offered willingly to the LORD; and King David also rejoiced greatly.

David's Praise to God

10 Therefore David blessed the LORD before
all the assembly; and David said:

"Blessed are You, LORD God of Israel, our
Father, forever and ever.
11 [a]Yours, O LORD, *is* the greatness,
The power and the glory,
The victory and the majesty;
For all *that is* in heaven and in earth *is
Yours;*
Yours *is* the kingdom, O LORD,
And You are exalted as head over all.
12 [a]Both riches and honor *come* from You,
And You reign over all.
In Your hand *is* power and might;
In Your hand *it is* to make great
And to give strength to all.

13 "Now therefore, our God,
We thank You
And praise Your glorious name.
14 But who *am* I, and who *are* my people,
That we should be able to offer so
willingly as this?
For all things *come* from You,
And of Your own we have given You.
15 For [a]we *are* aliens and pilgrims before
You,
As *were* all our fathers;
[b]Our days on earth *are* as a shadow,
And without hope.

16 "O LORD our God, all this abundance that
we have prepared to build You a house for Your
holy name is from Your hand, and *is* all Your
own.
17 "I know also, my God, that You [a]test the
heart and [b]have pleasure in uprightness. As for
me, in the uprightness of my heart I have willingly
offered all these *things;* and now with joy I have
seen Your people, who are present here to offer
willingly to You.
18 "O LORD God of Abraham, Isaac, and Israel, our fathers, keep this forever in the intent
of the thoughts of the heart of Your people, and
fix their heart toward You.
19 "And [a]give my son Solomon a loyal heart
to keep Your commandments and Your testimo-

*

29:8 Possibly the same as *Jehieli,* 1 Chr. 26:21, 22

KJV

nies, and thy statutes, and to do all *these things*, and to build the palace, *for* the which [b]I have made provision.

20 And David said to all the congregation, Now bless the LORD your God. And all the congregation blessed the LORD God of their fathers, and bowed down their heads, and worshipped the LORD, and the king.

Solomon Anointed King
(1 Kin. 1:38–40; 2:12)

21 And they sacrificed sacrifices unto the LORD, and offered burnt offerings unto the LORD, on the morrow after that day, *even* a thousand bullocks, a thousand rams, *and* a thousand lambs, with their drink offerings, and [a]sacrifices in abundance for all Israel:

22 And did eat and drink before the LORD on that day with great gladness. And they made Solomon the son of David king the second time, and [a]anointed *him* unto the LORD *to be* the chief governor, and Zadok *to be* priest.

23 Then Solomon sat on the throne of the LORD as king instead of David his father, and prospered; and all Israel obeyed him.

24 And all the princes, and the mighty men, and all the sons likewise of king David, [a]submitted themselves unto Solomon the king.

25 And the LORD magnified Solomon exceedingly in the sight of all Israel, and [a]bestowed upon him *such* royal majesty as had not been on any king before him in Israel.

The Close of David's Reign

26 Thus David the son of Jesse reigned over all Israel.

27 [a]And the time that he reigned over Israel *was* forty years; [b]seven years reigned he in Hebron, and thirty and three *years* reigned he in Jerusalem.

28 And he [a]died in a good old age, [b]full of days, riches, and honour: and Solomon his son reigned in his stead.

29 Now the acts of David the king, first and last, behold, they *are* written in the book of Samuel the seer, and in the book of Nathan the prophet, and in the book of Gad the seer,

30 With all his reign and his might, [a]and the times that went over him, and over Israel, and over all the kingdoms of the countries.

19 [b]1 Chr. 29:1, 2
21 [a]1 Kin. 8:62, 63
22 [a]1 Kin. 1:32–35, 39; 1 Chr. 23:1
24 [a]Eccl. 8:2
25 [a]1 Kin. 3:13; 2 Chr. 1:12; Eccl. 2:9
27 [a]2 Sam. 5:4; 1 Kin. 2:11 [b]2 Sam. 5:5
28 [a]Gen. 25:8 [b]1 Chr. 23:1
30 [a]Dan. 2:21; 4:23, 25

*———————

29:19 Lit. *palace*

NKJV

nies and Your statutes, to do all *these things*, and to build the *temple for which [b]I have made provision."

20 Then David said to all the assembly, "Now bless the LORD your God." So all the assembly blessed the LORD God of their fathers, and bowed their heads and prostrated themselves before the LORD and the king.

Solomon Anointed King
(1 Kin. 1:38–40; 2:12)

21 And they made sacrifices to the LORD and offered burnt offerings to the LORD on the next day: a thousand bulls, a thousand rams, a thousand lambs, with their drink offerings, and [a]sacrifices in abundance for all Israel.

22 So they ate and drank before the LORD with great gladness on that day. And they made Solomon the son of David king the second time, and [a]anointed *him* before the LORD *to be* the leader, and Zadok *to be* priest.

23 Then Solomon sat on the throne of the LORD as king instead of David his father, and prospered; and all Israel obeyed him.

24 All the leaders and the mighty men, and also all the sons of King David, [a]submitted themselves to King Solomon.

25 So the LORD exalted Solomon exceedingly in the sight of all Israel, and [a]bestowed on him *such* royal majesty as had not been on any king before him in Israel.

The Close of David's Reign

26 Thus David the son of Jesse reigned over all Israel.

27 [a]And the period that he reigned over Israel *was* forty years; [b]seven years he reigned in Hebron, and thirty-three *years* he reigned in Jerusalem.

28 So he [a]died in a good old age, [b]full of days and riches and honor; and Solomon his son reigned in his place.

29 Now the acts of King David, first and last, indeed they *are* written in the book of Samuel the seer, in the book of Nathan the prophet, and in the book of Gad the seer,

30 with all his reign and his might, [a]and the events that happened to him, to Israel, and to all the kingdoms of the lands.

KJV

THE SECOND BOOK OF THE
CHRONICLES

Solomon Requests Wisdom
(1 Kin. 3:1–15)

1 And [a]Solomon the son of David was strengthened in his kingdom, and [b]the LORD his God
was with him, and [c]magnified him exceedingly.
2 Then Solomon spake unto all Israel, to
[a]the captains of thousands and of hundreds, and
to the judges, and to every governor in all Israel,
the chief of the fathers.
3 So Solomon, and all the congregation with
him, went to the high place that *was* at [a]Gibeon;
for there was the tabernacle of the congregation
of God, which Moses the servant of the LORD had
[b]made in the wilderness.
4 [a]But the ark of God had David brought
up from Kirjath–jearim to *the place which* David
had prepared for it: for he had pitched a tent for
it at Jerusalem.
5 Moreover [a]the brasen altar, that [b]Bezaleel
the son of Uri, the son of Hur, had made, he put
before the tabernacle of the LORD: and Solomon
and the congregation sought unto it.
6 And Solomon went up thither to the brasen altar before the LORD, which *was* at the tabernacle of the congregation, and [a]offered a thousand burnt offerings upon it.
7 [a]In that night did God appear unto Solomon, and said unto him, Ask what I shall give
thee.
8 And Solomon said unto God, Thou hast
shewed great [a]mercy unto David my father, and
hast made me [b]to reign in his stead.
9 Now, O LORD God, let thy promise unto
David my father be established: [a]for thou hast
made me king over a people like the [b]dust of the
earth in multitude.
10 [a]Give me now wisdom and knowledge,
that I may [b]go out and come in before this people: for who can judge this thy people, *that is* so
great?
11 [a]And God said to Solomon, Because this
was in thine heart, and thou hast not asked riches,
wealth, or honour, nor the life of thine enemies,
neither yet hast asked long life; but hast asked
wisdom and knowledge for thyself, that thou mayest judge my people, over whom I have made thee
king:
12 Wisdom and knowledge *is* granted unto
thee; and I will give thee riches, and wealth, and
honour, such as [a]none of the kings have had that
have been before thee, neither shall there any after thee have the like.

Solomon's Military and Economic Power
(1 Kin. 10:26–29; 2 Chr. 9:25–28)

13 Then Solomon came *from his journey* to
the high place that *was* at Gibeon to Jerusalem,
from before the tabernacle of the congregation,
and reigned over Israel.
14 [a]And Solomon gathered chariots and
horsemen: and he had a thousand and four hundred chariots, and twelve thousand horsemen,
which he placed in the chariot cities, and with
the king at Jerusalem.
15 [a]And the king made silver and gold at Jerusalem *as plenteous* as stones, and cedar trees

CHAPTER 1
1 [a]1 Kin. 2:46 [b]Gen. 39:2 [c]1 Chr. 29:25
2 [a]1 Chr. 27:1–34
3 [a]1 Kin. 3:4; 1 Chr. 16:39; 21:29 [b]Ex. 25—27; 35:4—36:38
4 [a]Ex. 25:10–22; 2 Sam. 6:2–17; 1 Chr. 15:25—16:1
5 [a]Ex. 27:1, 2; 38:1, 2 [b]Ex. 31:2
6 [a]1 Kin. 3:4
7 [a]1 Kin. 3:5–14; 9:2
8 [a]Ps. 18:50 [b]1 Chr. 28:5
9 [a]2 Sam. 7:8–16; 1 Kin. 3:7, 8 [b]Gen. 13:16; Num. 23:10
10 [a]1 Kin. 3:9 [b]Num. 27:17; Deut. 31:2
11 [a]1 Kin. 3:11–13
12 [a]1 Kin. 10:23; 1 Chr. 29:25; 2 Chr. 9:22; Eccl. 2:9
14 [a]1 Kin. 10:26; 2 Chr. 9:25
15 [a]1 Kin. 10:27; 2 Chr. 9:27; Job 22:24

*———

1:5 Some authorities *it was there*

NKJV

THE SECOND BOOK OF THE
CHRONICLES

Solomon Requests Wisdom
(1 Kin. 3:1–15)

1 Now [a]Solomon the son of David was strengthened in his kingdom, and [b]the LORD his
God *was* with him and [c]exalted him exceedingly.
2 And Solomon spoke to all Israel, to [a]the
captains of thousands and of hundreds, to the
judges, and to every leader in all Israel, the heads
of the fathers' *houses.*
3 Then Solomon, and all the assembly with
him, went to the high place that *was* at [a]Gibeon;
for the tabernacle of meeting with God was there,
which Moses the servant of the LORD had [b]made
in the wilderness.
4 [a]But David had brought up the ark of God
from Kirjath Jearim to *the place* David had prepared for it, for he had pitched a tent for it at
Jerusalem.
5 Now [a]the bronze altar that [b]Bezalel the
son of Uri, the son of Hur, had made, *he put before the tabernacle of the LORD; Solomon and the
assembly sought Him *there.*
6 And Solomon went up there to the bronze
altar before the LORD, which *was* at the tabernacle
of meeting, and [a]offered a thousand burnt offerings on it.
7 [a]On that night God appeared to Solomon,
and said to him, "Ask! What shall I give you?"
8 And Solomon said to God: "You have
shown great [a]mercy to David my father, and have
made me [b]king in his place.
9 "Now, O LORD God, let Your promise to
David my father be established, [a]for You have
made me king over a people like the [b]dust of the
earth in multitude.
10 [a]"Now give me wisdom and knowledge,
that I may [b]go out and come in before this people;
for who can judge this great people of Yours?"
11 [a]Then God said to Solomon: "Because this
was in your heart, and you have not asked riches
or wealth or honor or the life of your enemies,
nor have you asked long life—but have asked wisdom and knowledge for yourself, that you may
judge My people over whom I have made you
king—
12 "wisdom and knowledge *are* granted to
you; and I will give you riches and wealth and
honor, such as [a]none of the kings have had who
were before you, nor shall any after you have the
like."

Solomon's Military and Economic Power
(1 Kin. 10:26–29; 2 Chr. 9:25–28)

13 So Solomon came to Jerusalem from the
high place that *was* at Gibeon, from before the
tabernacle of meeting, and reigned over Israel.
14 [a]And Solomon gathered chariots and
horsemen; he had one thousand four hundred
chariots and twelve thousand horsemen, whom
he stationed in the chariot cities and with the king
in Jerusalem.
15 [a]Also the king made silver and gold as
common in Jerusalem as stones, and he made ce-

KJV

made he as the sycomore trees that *are* in the
vale for abundance.
16 [a]And Solomon had horses brought out of
Egypt, and linen yarn: the king's merchants received the linen yarn at a price.
17 And they fetched up, and brought forth
out of Egypt a chariot for six hundred *shekels* of
silver, and an horse for an hundred and fifty: and
so brought they out *horses* for all the kings of
the Hittites, and for the kings of Syria, by their
means.

Solomon Prepares to Build the Temple
(1 Kin. 5:1–18)

2 And Solomon [a]determined to build an house
for the name of the LORD, and an house for
his kingdom.
2 And [a]Solomon told out threescore and ten
thousand men to bear burdens, and fourscore
thousand to hew in the mountain, and three thousand and six hundred to oversee them.
3 And Solomon sent to Huram the king of
Tyre, saying, [a]As thou didst deal with David my
father, and didst send him cedars to build him
an house to dwell therein, *even so deal with me.*
4 Behold, [a]I build an house to the name of
the LORD my God, to dedicate *it* to him, *and* [b]to
burn before him sweet incense, and for [c]the continual shewbread, and for [d]the burnt offerings
morning and evening, on the [e]sabbaths, and on
the new moons, and on the solemn feasts of the
LORD our God. This *is an ordinance* for ever to
Israel.
5 And the house which I build *is* great: for
[a]great *is* our God above all gods.
6 [a]But who is able to build him an house,
seeing the heaven and heaven of heavens cannot
contain him? who *am* I then, that I should build
him an house, save only to burn sacrifice before
him?
7 Send me now therefore a man cunning to
work in gold, and in silver, and in brass, and in
iron, and in purple, and crimson, and blue, and
that can skill to grave with the cunning men that
are with me in Judah and in Jerusalem, [a]whom
David my father did provide.
8 [a]Send me also cedar trees, fir trees, and
algum trees, out of Lebanon: for I know that thy
servants can skill to cut timber in Lebanon; and,
behold, my servants *shall be* with thy servants,
9 Even to prepare me timber in abundance:
for the house which I am about to build *shall be*
wonderful great.
10 [a]And, behold, I will give to thy servants,
the hewers that cut timber, twenty thousand
measures of beaten wheat, and twenty thousand
measures of barley, and twenty thousand baths
of wine, and twenty thousand baths of oil.
11 Then Huram the king of Tyre answered
in writing, which he sent to Solomon, [a]Because
the LORD hath loved his people, he hath made thee
king over them.
12 Huram said moreover, [a]Blessed *be* the
LORD God of Israel, [b]that made heaven and earth,
who hath given to David the king a wise son, endued with prudence and understanding, that
might build an house for the LORD, and an house
for his kingdom.
13 And now I have sent a cunning man, endued with understanding, of Huram my father's,
14 [a]The son of a woman of the daughters of
Dan, and his father *was* a man of Tyre, skilful to

16 [a]1 Kin. 10:28; 22:36; 2 Chr. 9:28

CHAPTER 2

1 [a]1 Kin. 5:5
2 [a]1 Kin. 5:15, 16; 2 Chr. 2:18
3 [a]1 Chr. 14:1
4 [a]2 Chr. 2:1 [b]Ex. 30:7 [c]Ex. 25:30; Lev. 24:8 [d]Ex. 29:38–42 [e]Num. 28:3, 9–11
5 [a]Ps. 135:5; [1 Cor. 8:5, 6]
6 [a]1 Kin. 8:27; 2 Chr. 6:18; Is. 66:1
7 [a]1 Chr. 22:15
8 [a]1 Kin. 5:6
10 [a]1 Kin. 5:11
11 [a]1 Kin. 10:9; 2 Chr. 9:8
12 [a]1 Kin. 5:7 [b]Gen. 1; 2; Acts 4:24; 14:15; Rev. 10:6
14 [a]1 Kin. 7:13, 14

NKJV

dars as abundant as the sycamores which *are* in
the lowland.
16 [a]And Solomon had horses imported from
Egypt and Keveh; the king's merchants bought
them in Keveh at the *current* price.
17 They also acquired and imported from
Egypt a chariot for six hundred *shekels* of silver,
and a horse for one hundred and fifty; thus,
*through their agents, they exported them to all
the kings of the Hittites and the kings of Syria.

Solomon Prepares to Build the Temple
(1 Kin. 5:1–18)

2 Then Solomon [a]determined to build a temple
for the name of the LORD, and a royal house
for himself.
2 [a]Solomon selected seventy thousand men
to bear burdens, eighty thousand to quarry *stone*
in the mountains, and three thousand six hundred
to oversee them.
3 Then Solomon sent to *Hiram king of
Tyre, saying:

[a]As you have dealt with David my father,
and sent him cedars to build himself a
house to dwell in, *so deal with me.*
4 Behold, [a]I am building a temple for the
name of the LORD my God, to dedicate *it*
to Him, [b]to burn before Him sweet
incense, for [c]the continual showbread, for
[d]the burnt offerings morning and evening,
on the [e]Sabbaths, on the New Moons, and
on the set feasts of the LORD our God. This
is an ordinance forever to Israel.
5 And the temple which I build *will be* great,
for [a]our God is greater than all gods.
6 [a]But who is able to build Him a temple,
since heaven and the heaven of heavens
cannot contain Him? Who *am* I then, that
I should build Him a temple, except to
burn sacrifice before Him?
7 Therefore send me at once a man skillful
to work in gold and silver, in bronze and
iron, in purple and crimson and blue, who
has skill to engrave with the skillful men
who are with me in Judah and Jerusalem,
[a]whom David my father provided.
8 [a]Also send me cedar and cypress and
algum logs from Lebanon, for I know that
your servants have skill to cut timber in
Lebanon; and indeed my servants *will be*
with your servants,
9 to prepare timber for me in abundance,
for the temple which I am about to build
shall be great and wonderful.
10 [a]And indeed I will give to your servants,
the woodsmen who cut timber, twenty
thousand kors of ground wheat, twenty
thousand kors of barley, twenty thousand
baths of wine, and twenty thousand baths
of oil.

11 Then Hiram king of Tyre answered in
writing, which he sent to Solomon:

[a]Because the LORD loves His people, He
has made you king over them.

12 *Hiram also said:

[a]Blessed *be* the LORD God of Israel, [b]who
made heaven and earth, for He has given
King David a wise son, endowed with
prudence and understanding, who will
build a temple for the LORD and a royal
house for himself!
13 And now I have sent a skillful man,
endowed with understanding, *Huram my
*master *craftsman*
14 [a](the son of a woman of the daughters of
Dan, and his father was a man of Tyre),

1:17 Lit. *by their hands*
2:3 Heb. *Huram;* cf. 1 Kin. 5:1
2:12 Heb. *Huram;* cf. 1 Kin. 5:1
2:13 *Hiram,* 1 Kin. 7:13 • Lit. *father,* 1 Kin. 7:13, 14

KJV

work in gold, and in silver, in brass, in iron, in
stone, and in timber, in purple, in blue, and in
fine linen, and in crimson; also to grave any manner of graving, and to find out every device which
shall be put to him, with thy cunning men, and
with the cunning men of my lord David thy father.
15 Now therefore the wheat, and the barley,
the oil, and the wine, which [a]my lord hath spoken
of, let him send unto his servants:
16 [a]And we will cut wood out of Lebanon,
as much as thou shalt need: and we will bring it
to thee in flotes by sea to Joppa; and thou shalt
carry it up to Jerusalem.
17 [a]And Solomon numbered all the strangers
that *were* in the land of Israel, after the numbering
wherewith [b]David his father had numbered them;
and they were found an hundred and fifty thousand and three thousand and six hundred.
18 And he set [a]threescore and ten thousand
of them *to be* bearers of burdens, and fourscore
thousand *to be* hewers in the mountain, and three
thousand and six hundred overseers to set the
people a work.

Solomon Builds the Temple
(1 Kin. 6:1–22)

3 Then [a]Solomon began to build the house of
the LORD at [b]Jerusalem in mount Moriah,
where *the LORD* appeared unto David his father,
in the place that David had prepared in the threshingfloor of [c]Ornan the Jebusite.
2 And he began to build in the second *day*
of the second month, in the fourth year of his
reign.
3 Now these *are the things* [a]*wherein* Solomon was instructed for the building of the house
of God. The length by cubits after the first measure *was* threescore cubits, and the breadth
twenty cubits.
4 And the [a]porch that *was* in the front *of
the house,* the length *of it was* according to the
breadth of the house, twenty cubits, and the
height *was* an hundred and twenty: and he overlaid it within with pure gold.
5 And [a]the greater house he [b]cieled with fir
tree, which he overlaid with fine gold, and set
thereon palm trees and chains.
6 And he garnished the house with precious
stones for beauty: and the gold *was* gold of
Parvaim.
7 He overlaid also the house, the beams, the
posts, and the walls thereof, and the doors thereof,
with gold; and graved cherubims on the walls.
8 And he made the [a]most holy house, the
length whereof *was* according to the breadth of
the house, twenty cubits, and the breadth thereof
twenty cubits: and he overlaid it with fine gold,
amounting to six hundred talents.
9 And the weight of the nails *was* fifty shekels of gold. And he overlaid the upper [a]chambers
with gold.
10 [a]And in the most holy house he made two
cherubims of image work, and overlaid them with
gold.
11 And the wings of the cherubims *were*
twenty cubits long: one wing *of the one cherub
was* five cubits, reaching to the wall of the house:
and the other wing *was likewise* five cubits, reaching to the wing of the other cherub.
12 And *one* wing of the other cherub *was* five
cubits, reaching to the wall of the house: and the
other wing *was* five cubits *also,* joining to the
wing of the other cherub.
13 The wings of these cherubims spread
themselves forth twenty cubits: and they stood
on their feet, and their faces *were* inward.
14 And he made the [a]vail *of* blue, and purple,
and crimson, and fine linen, and wrought cherubims thereon.
15 Also he made before the house [a]two pillars of thirty and five cubits high, and the chapiter

15 [a]2 Chr. 2:10
16 [a]1 Kin. 5:8, 9
17 [a]1 Kin. 5:13; 2 Chr. 8:7, 8 [b]1 Chr. 22:2
18 [a]2 Chr. 2:2

CHAPTER 3
1 [a]1 Kin. 6:1 [b]Gen. 22:2–14 [c]1 Chr. 21:18; 22:1
3 [a]1 Kin. 6:2; 1 Chr. 28:11–19
4 [a]1 Kin. 6:3; 1 Chr. 28:11
5 [a]1 Kin. 6:17 [b]1 Kin. 6:15; Jer. 22:14
8 [a]Ex. 26:33; 1 Kin. 6:16
9 [a]1 Chr. 28:11
10 [a]Ex. 25:18–20; 1 Kin. 6:23–28
14 [a]Ex. 26:31; Matt. 27:51; Heb. 9:3
15 [a]1 Kin. 7:15–20; Jer. 52:21

*
3:1 Lit. *He,* following MT, Vg.; LXX *the LORD;* Tg. *the Angel of the LORD* • *Araunah,* 2 Sam. 24:16
3:4 The holy place, the main room of the temple, 1 Kin. 6:3 • So with MT, LXX, Vg.; Arab., some LXX mss., Syr. *twenty*
3:5 Lit. *house*
3:15 Lit. *house* • *eighteen,* 1 Kin. 7:15; 2 Kin. 25:17; Jer. 52:21

NKJV

skilled to work in gold and silver, bronze
and iron, stone and wood, purple and blue,
fine linen and crimson, and to make any
engraving and to accomplish any plan
which may be given to him, with your
skillful men and with the skillful men of
my lord David your father.
15 Now therefore, the wheat, the barley, the
oil, and the wine which [a]my lord has
spoken of, let him send to his servants.
16 [a]And we will cut wood from Lebanon, as
much as you need; we will bring it to you
in rafts by sea to Joppa, and you will carry
it up to Jerusalem.

17 [a]Then Solomon numbered all the aliens
who *were* in the land of Israel, after the census
in which [b]David his father had numbered them;
and there were found to be one hundred and fifty-
three thousand six hundred.
18 And he made [a]seventy thousand of them
bearers of burdens, eighty thousand stonecutters
in the mountain, and three thousand six hundred
overseers to make the people work.

Solomon Builds the Temple
(1 Kin. 6:1–22)

3 Now [a]Solomon began to build the house of
the LORD at [b]Jerusalem on Mount Moriah,
where *the LORD* had appeared to his father David, at the place that David had prepared on the
threshing floor of [c]Ornan* the Jebusite.
2 And he began to build on the second *day*
of the second month in the fourth year of his reign.
3 This is the foundation [a]which Solomon
laid for building the house of God: The length *was*
sixty cubits (by cubits according to the former
measure) and the width twenty cubits.
4 And the [a]vestibule that *was* in front *of
the sanctuary was twenty cubits long across the
width of the house, and the height *was* *one hundred and twenty. He overlaid the inside with pure
gold.
5 [a]The larger *room he [b]paneled with cypress which he overlaid with fine gold, and he
carved palm trees and chainwork on it.
6 And he decorated the house with precious
stones for beauty, and the gold *was* gold from
Parvaim.
7 He also overlaid the house—the beams
and doorposts, its walls and doors—with gold;
and he carved cherubim on the walls.
8 And he made the [a]Most Holy Place. Its
length was according to the width of the house,
twenty cubits, and its width twenty cubits. He
overlaid it with six hundred talents of fine gold.
9 The weight of the nails *was* fifty shekels
of gold; and he overlaid the upper [a]area with gold.
10 [a]In the Most Holy Place he made two
cherubim, fashioned by carving, and overlaid
them with gold.
11 The wings of the cherubim *were* twenty
cubits in *overall* length: one wing *of the one
cherub was* five cubits, touching the wall of the
room, and the other wing *was* five cubits, touching
the wing of the other cherub;
12 *one* wing of the other cherub *was* five cubits, touching the wall of the room, and the other
wing *also was* five cubits, touching the wing of
the other cherub.
13 The wings of these cherubim spanned
twenty cubits overall. They stood on their feet,
and they faced inward.
14 And he made the [a]veil of blue, purple,
crimson, and fine linen, and wove cherubim into
it.
15 Also he made in front of the *temple [a]two
pillars *thirty-five cubits high, and the capital that

KJV

that *was* on the top of each of them *was* five cubits.

16 And he made chains, *as* in the oracle, and put *them* on the heads of the pillars; and made [a]an hundred pomegranates, and put *them* on the chains.

17 And he [a]reared up the pillars before the temple, one on the right hand, and the other on the left; and called the name of that on the right hand Jachin, and the name of that on the left Boaz.

Furnishings of the Temple
(1 Kin. 6:23–38; 7:13–51)

4 Moreover he made [a]an altar of brass, twenty cubits the length thereof, and twenty cubits the breadth thereof, and ten cubits the height thereof.

2 [a]Also he made a molten sea of ten cubits from brim to brim, round in compass, and five cubits the height thereof; and a line of thirty cubits did compass it round about.

3 [a]And under it *was* the similitude of oxen, which did compass it round about: ten in a cubit, compassing the sea round about. Two rows of oxen *were* cast, when it was cast.

4 It stood upon twelve [a]oxen, three looking toward the north, and three looking toward the west, and three looking toward the south, and three looking toward the east: and the sea *was set* above upon them, and all their hinder parts *were* inward.

5 And the thickness of it *was* an handbreadth, and the brim of it like the work of the brim of a cup, with flowers of lilies; *and* it received and held three thousand baths.

6 He made also [a]ten lavers, and put five on the right hand, and five on the left, to wash in them: such things as they offered for the burnt offering they washed in them; but the sea *was* for the [b]priests to wash in.

7 [a]And he made ten candlesticks of gold [b]according to their form, and set *them* in the temple, five on the right hand, and five on the left.

8 [a]He made also ten tables, and placed *them* in the temple, five on the right side, and five on the left. And he made an hundred [b]basons of gold.

9 Furthermore [a]he made the court of the priests, and the [b]great court, and doors for the court, and overlaid the doors of them with brass.

10 And [a]he set the sea on the right side of the east end, over against the south.

11 And [a]Huram made the pots, and the shovels, and the basons. And Huram finished the work that he was to make for king Solomon for the house of God;

12 *To wit,* the two pillars, and [a]the pommels, and the chapiters *which were* on the top of the two pillars, and the two wreaths to cover the two pommels of the chapiters which *were* on the top of the pillars;

13 And [a]four hundred pomegranates on the two wreaths; two rows of pomegranates on each wreath, to cover the two pommels of the chapiters which *were* upon the pillars.

14 He made also [a]bases, and lavers made he upon the bases;

15 One sea, and twelve oxen under it.

16 The pots also, and the shovels, and the fleshhooks, and all their instruments, did [a]Huram his father make to king Solomon for the house of the LORD of bright brass.

17 In the plain of Jordan did the king cast them, in the clay ground between Succoth and Zeredathah.

18 [a]Thus Solomon made all these vessels in great abundance: for the weight of the brass could not be found out.

19 And [a]Solomon made all the vessels that *were for* the house of God, the golden altar also, and the tables whereon [b]the shewbread *was set;*

20 Moreover the candlesticks with their

---

16 [a]1 Kin. 7:20
17 [a]1 Kin. 7:21

CHAPTER 4

1 [a]Ex. 27:1, 2; 2 Kin. 16:14; Ezek. 43:13, 16
2 [a]Ex. 30:17–21; 1 Kin. 7:23–26
3 [a]1 Kin. 7:24–26
4 [a]1 Kin. 7:25
6 [a]1 Kin. 7:38, 40 [b]Ex. 30:19–21
7 [a]1 Kin. 7:49 [b]Ex. 25:31; 1 Chr. 28:12, 19
8 [a]1 Kin. 7:48 [b]1 Chr. 28:17
9 [a]1 Kin. 6:36 [b]2 Kin. 21:5
10 [a]1 Kin. 7:39
11 [a]1 Kin. 7:40–51
12 [a]1 Kin. 7:41
13 [a]1 Kin. 7:20
14 [a]1 Kin. 7:27, 43
16 [a]1 Kin. 7:45; 2 Chr. 2:13
18 [a]1 Kin. 7:47
19 [a]1 Kin. 7:48–50 [b]Ex. 25:30

*

4:5 About 8,000 gallons; *two thousand,* 1 Kin. 7:26
4:16 Lit. *father*
4:17 *Zaretan,* 1 Kin. 7:46

NKJV

was on the top of each of *them* was five cubits.

16 He made wreaths of chainwork, as in the inner sanctuary, and put *them* on top of the pillars; and he made [a]one hundred pomegranates, and put *them* on the wreaths of chainwork.

17 Then he [a]set up the pillars before the temple, one on the right hand and the other on the left; he called the name of the one on the right hand Jachin, and the name of the one on the left Boaz.

Furnishings of the Temple
(1 Kin. 6:23–38; 7:13–51)

4 Moreover he made [a]a bronze altar: twenty cubits was its length, twenty cubits its width, and ten cubits its height.

2 [a]Then he made the Sea of cast *bronze,* ten cubits from one brim to the other; *it was* completely round. Its height *was* five cubits, and a line of thirty cubits measured its circumference.

3 [a]And under it *was* the likeness of oxen encircling it all around, ten to a cubit, all the way around the Sea. The oxen *were* cast in two rows, when it was cast.

4 It stood on twelve [a]oxen: three looking toward the north, three looking toward the west, three looking toward the south, and three looking toward the east; the Sea *was set* upon them, and all their back parts *pointed* inward.

5 It *was* a handbreadth thick; and its brim was shaped like the brim of a cup, *like* a lily blossom. It contained *three thousand baths.

6 He also made [a]ten lavers, and put five on the right side and five on the left, to wash in them; such things as they offered for the burnt offering they would wash in them, but the Sea *was* for the [b]priests to wash in.

7 [a]And he made ten lampstands of gold [b]according to their design, and set *them* in the temple, five on the right side and five on the left.

8 [a]He also made ten tables, and placed *them* in the temple, five on the right side and five on the left. And he made one hundred [b]bowls of gold.

9 Furthermore [a]he made the court of the priests, and the [b]great court and doors for the court; and he overlaid these doors with bronze.

10 [a]He set the Sea on the right side, toward the southeast.

11 Then [a]Huram made the pots and the shovels and the bowls. So Huram finished doing the work that he was to do for King Solomon for the house of God:

12 the two pillars and [a]the bowl-shaped capitals *that were* on top of the two pillars; the two networks covering the two bowl-shaped capitals which *were* on top of the pillars;

13 [a]four hundred pomegranates for the two networks (two rows of pomegranates for each network, to cover the two bowl-shaped capitals that *were* on the pillars);

14 he also made [a]carts and the lavers on the carts;

15 one Sea and twelve oxen under it;

16 also the pots, the shovels, the forks—and all their articles [a]Huram his *master *craftsman* made of burnished bronze for King Solomon for the house of the LORD.

17 In the plain of Jordan the king had them cast in clay molds, between Succoth and *Zeredah.

18 [a]And Solomon had all these articles made in such great abundance that the weight of the bronze was not determined.

19 Thus [a]Solomon had all the furnishings made for the house of God: the altar of gold and the tables on which *was* [b]the showbread;

20 the lampstands with their lamps of pure

KJV

lamps, that they should burn [a]after the manner
before the oracle, of pure gold;
21 And [a]the flowers, and the lamps, and the
tongs, *made he of* gold, *and* that perfect gold;
22 And the snuffers, and the basons, and the
spoons, and the censers, *of* pure gold: and the entry of the house, the inner doors thereof for the
most holy *place,* and the doors of the house of
the temple, *were of* gold.

5 Thus [a]all the work that Solomon made for the
house of the LORD was finished: and Solomon
brought in *all* the things that David his father had
dedicated; and the silver, and the gold, and all
the instruments, put he among the treasures of
the house of God.

The Ark Brought into the Temple (*1 Kin. 8:1–13*)

2 [a]Then Solomon assembled the elders of
Israel, and all the heads of the tribes, the chief
of the fathers of the children of Israel, unto Jerusalem, to bring up the ark of the covenant of the
LORD [b]out of the city of David, which *is* Zion.
3 [a]Wherefore all the men of Israel assembled themselves unto the king [b]in the feast which
was in the seventh month.
4 And all the elders of Israel came; and the
[a]Levites took up the ark.
5 And they brought up the ark, and the tabernacle of the congregation, and all the holy vessels that *were* in the tabernacle, these did the
priests *and* the Levites bring up.
6 Also king Solomon, and all the congregation of Israel that were assembled unto him before
the ark, sacrificed sheep and oxen, which could
not be told nor numbered for multitude.
7 And the priests brought in the ark of the
covenant of the LORD unto his place, to the [a]oracle
of the house, into the most holy *place, even* under
the wings of the cherubims:
8 For the cherubims spread forth *their*
wings over the place of the ark, and the cherubims
covered the ark and the staves thereof above.
9 And they drew out the [a]staves *of the ark,*
that the ends of the staves were seen from the
ark before the oracle; but they were not seen without. And there it is unto this day.
10 *There was* nothing in the ark save the two
tables which Moses [a]put *therein* at Horeb, when
the LORD made *a covenant* with the children of
Israel, when they came out of Egypt.
11 And it came to pass, when the priests were
come out of the holy *place:* (for all the priests
that were present were sanctified, *and* did not
then wait by [a]course:
12 [a]Also the Levites *which were* the singers,
all of them of Asaph, of Heman, of Jeduthun, with
their sons and their brethren, *being* arrayed in
white linen, having cymbals and psalteries and
harps, stood at the east end of the altar, [b]and with
them an hundred and twenty priests sounding
with trumpets:)
13 It came even to pass, as the trumpeters
and singers *were* as one, to make one sound to
be heard in praising and thanking the LORD; and
when they lifted up *their* voice with the trumpets
and cymbals and instruments of musick, and
praised the LORD, *saying,* [a]For *he is* good; for his
mercy *endureth* for ever: that *then* the house was
filled with a cloud, *even* the house of the LORD;
14 So that the priests could not stand to minister by reason of the cloud: [a]for the glory of the
LORD had filled the house of God.

20 [a]Ex. 27:20, 21
21 [a]Ex. 25:31

CHAPTER 5

1 [a]1 Kin. 7:51
2 [a]1 Kin. 8:1–9; Ps. 47:9 [b]2 Sam. 6:12
3 [a]1 Kin. 8:2 [b]Lev. 23:34; 2 Chr. 7:8–10
4 [a]1 Chr. 15:2, 15
7 [a]2 Chr. 4:20
9 [a]Ex. 25:13–15
10 [a]Ex. 25:16; Deut. 10:2, 5; 2 Chr. 6:11; Heb. 9:4
11 [a]1 Chr. 24:1–5
12 [a]Ex. 32:26; 1 Chr. 25:1–7 [b]1 Chr. 13:8; 15:16, 24
13 [a]1 Chr. 16:34, 41; 2 Chr. 7:3; Ezra 3:11; Ps. 100:5; 106:1; 136; Jer. 33:11
14 [a]Ex. 40:35; 1 Kin. 8:11; 2 Chr. 7:2; Ezek. 43:5

NKJV

gold, to burn [a]in the prescribed manner in front
of the inner sanctuary,
21 with [a]the flowers and the lamps and the
wick-trimmers of gold, of purest gold;
22 the trimmers, the bowls, the ladles, and
the censers of pure gold. As for the entry of the
sanctuary, its inner doors to the Most Holy *Place,*
and the doors of the main hall of the temple, *were*
gold.

5 So [a]all the work that Solomon had done for
the house of the LORD was finished; and Solomon brought in the things which his father David
had dedicated: the silver and the gold and all the
furnishings. And he put *them* in the treasuries of
the house of God.

The Ark Brought into the Temple (*1 Kin. 8:1–13*)

2 [a]Now Solomon assembled the elders of Israel and all the heads of the tribes, the chief fathers of the children of Israel, in Jerusalem, that
they might bring the ark of the covenant of
the LORD up [b]from the City of David, which *is*
Zion.
3 [a]Therefore all the men of Israel assembled
with the king [b]at the feast, which *was* in the seventh month.
4 So all the elders of Israel came, and the
[a]Levites took up the ark.
5 Then they brought up the ark, the tabernacle of meeting, and all the holy furnishings that
were in the tabernacle. The priests and the Levites
brought them up.
6 Also King Solomon, and all the congregation of Israel who were assembled with him
before the ark, were sacrificing sheep and oxen
that could not be counted or numbered for
multitude.
7 Then the priests brought in the ark of the
covenant of the LORD to its place, into the [a]inner
sanctuary of the *temple, to the Most Holy *Place,*
under the wings of the cherubim.
8 For the cherubim spread *their* wings over
the place of the ark, and the cherubim overshadowed the ark and its poles.
9 The poles extended so that the ends of the
[a]poles of the ark could be seen from *the holy
place,* in front of the inner sanctuary; but they
could not be seen from outside. And they are there
to this day.
10 Nothing was in the ark except the two tablets which Moses [a]put *there* at Horeb, when the
LORD made *a covenant* with the children of Israel,
when they had come out of Egypt.
11 And it came to pass when the priests came
out of the *Most* Holy *Place* (for all the priests who
were present had sanctified themselves, without
keeping to their [a]divisions),
12 [a]and the Levites *who were* the singers, all
those of Asaph and Heman and Jeduthun, with
their sons and their brethren, stood at the east
end of the altar, clothed in white linen, having
cymbals, stringed instruments and harps, [b]and
with them one hundred and twenty priests sounding with trumpets—
13 indeed it came to pass, when the trumpeters and singers *were* as one, to make one sound
to be heard in praising and thanking the LORD,
and when they lifted up their voice with the trumpets and cymbals and instruments of music, and
praised the LORD, *saying:*

> [a]"*For He is* good,
> For His mercy *endures* forever,"

that the house, the house of the LORD, was filled
with a cloud,
14 so that the priests could not continue ministering because of the cloud; [a]for the glory of
the LORD filled the house of God.

5:7 Lit. *house*

KJV

6 Then [a]said Solomon, The LORD hath said that he would dwell in the [b]thick darkness.

2 But I have built an house of habitation for thee, and a [a]place for thy dwelling for ever.

Solomon's Speech upon Completion of the Work
(1 Kin. 8:14–21)

3 And the king turned his face, and [a]blessed the whole congregation of Israel: and all the congregation of Israel stood.

4 And he said, Blessed *be* the LORD God of Israel, who hath with his hands fulfilled *that* which he spake with his mouth to my father David, [a]saying,

5 Since the day that I brought forth my people out of the land of Egypt I chose no city among all the tribes of Israel to build an house in, that my name might be there; neither chose I any man to be a ruler over my people Israel:

6 [a]But I have chosen Jerusalem, that my name might be there; and [b]have chosen David to be over my people Israel.

7 Now [a]it was in the heart of David my father to build an house for the name of the LORD God of Israel.

8 But the LORD said to David my father, Forasmuch as it was in thine heart to build an house for my name, thou didst well in that it was in thine heart:

9 Notwithstanding thou shalt not build the house; but thy son which shall come forth out of thy loins, he shall build the house for my [a]name.

10 The LORD therefore hath performed his word that he hath spoken: for I am risen up in the room of David my father, and am [a]set on the throne of Israel, as the LORD promised, and have built the house for the name of the LORD God of Israel.

11 And in it have I put the ark, [a]wherein *is* the covenant of the LORD, that he made with the children of Israel.

Solomon's Prayer of Dedication
(1 Kin. 8:22–53)

12 [a]And he stood before the altar of the LORD in the presence of all the congregation of Israel, and spread forth his hands:

13 For Solomon had made a brasen scaffold, of five cubits long, and five cubits broad, and three cubits high, and had set it in the midst of the court: and upon it he stood, and kneeled down upon his knees before all the congregation of Israel, and spread forth his hands toward heaven,

14 And said, O LORD God of Israel, [a]*there is* no God like thee in the heaven, nor in the earth; which keepest [b]covenant, and *shewest* mercy unto thy servants, that walk before thee with all their hearts:

15 [a]Thou which hast kept with thy servant David my father that which thou hast promised him; and spakest with thy mouth, and hast fulfilled *it* with thine hand, as *it is* this day.

16 Now therefore, O LORD God of Israel, keep with thy servant David my father that which thou hast promised him, saying, [a]There shall not fail thee a man in my sight to sit upon the throne of Israel; [b]yet so that thy children take heed to their way to walk in my law, as thou hast walked before me.

17 Now then, O LORD God of Israel, let thy word be verified, which thou hast spoken unto thy servant David.

18 But will God in very deed dwell with men on the earth? [a]behold, heaven and the heaven of heavens cannot contain thee; how much less this house which I have built!

19 Have respect therefore to the prayer of thy servant, and to his supplication, O LORD my God, to hearken unto the cry and the prayer which thy servant prayeth before thee:

20 That thine eyes may be [a]open upon this house day and night, upon the place whereof thou

CHAPTER 6

1 [a]Ex. 19:9; 20:21; 1 Kin. 8:12–21 [b][Lev. 16:2]; Ps. 97:2
2 [a]2 Sam. 7:13; 1 Chr. 17:12; 2 Chr. 7:12
3 [a]2 Sam. 6:18
4 [a]1 Chr. 17:5
6 [a]Deut. 12:5–7; 2 Chr. 12:13; Zech. 2:12 [b]1 Sam. 16:7–13; 1 Chr. 28:4
7 [a]2 Sam. 7:2; 1 Chr. 17:1; 28:2; Ps. 132:1–5
9 [a]1 Chr. 28:3–6
10 [a]1 Kin. 2:12; 10:9
11 [a]2 Chr. 5:7–10
12 [a]1 Kin. 8:22; 2 Chr. 7:7–9
14 [a][Ex. 15:11; Deut. 4:39] [b][Deut. 7:9]
15 [a]1 Chr. 22:9, 10
16 [a]2 Sam. 7:12, 16; 1 Kin. 2:4; 6:12; 2 Chr. 7:18 [b]Ps. 132:12
18 [a][2 Chr. 2:6; Is. 66:1; Acts 7:49]
20 [a]2 Chr. 7:15

*______

6:7 Lit. *house*, and so in vv. 8–10
6:12 Lit. *he*
6:18 Lit. *house*

NKJV

6 Then [a]Solomon spoke:

"The LORD said He would dwell in the
[b]dark cloud.
2 I have surely built You an exalted house,
And [a]a place for You to dwell in forever."

Solomon's Speech upon Completion of the Work
(1 Kin. 8:14–21)

3 Then the king turned around and [a]blessed the whole assembly of Israel, while all the assembly of Israel was standing.

4 And he said: "Blessed *be* the LORD God of Israel, who has fulfilled with His hands *what* He spoke with His mouth to my father David, [a]saying,

5 'Since the day that I brought My people out of the land of Egypt, I have chosen no city from any tribe of Israel *in which* to build a house, that My name might be there, nor did I choose any man to be a ruler over My people Israel.

6 [a]'Yet I have chosen Jerusalem, that My name may be there, and I [b]have chosen David to be over My people Israel.'

7 "Now [a]it was in the heart of my father David to build a *temple for the name of the LORD God of Israel.

8 "But the LORD said to my father David, 'Whereas it was in your heart to build a temple for My name, you did well in that it was in your heart.

9 'Nevertheless you shall not build the temple, but your son who will come from your body, he shall build the temple for My [a]name.'

10 "So the LORD has fulfilled His word which He spoke, and I have filled the position of my father David, and [a]sit on the throne of Israel, as the LORD promised; and I have built the temple for the name of the LORD God of Israel.

11 "And there I have put the ark, [a]in which *is* the covenant of the LORD which He made with the children of Israel."

Solomon's Prayer of Dedication
(1 Kin. 8:22–53)

12 [a]Then *Solomon* stood before the altar of the LORD in the presence of all the assembly of Israel, and spread out his hands

13 (for Solomon had made a bronze platform five cubits long, five cubits wide, and three cubits high, and had set it in the midst of the court; and he stood on it, knelt down on his knees before all the assembly of Israel, and spread out his hands toward heaven);

14 and he said: "LORD God of Israel, [a]*there is* no God in heaven or on earth like You, who keep *Your* [b]covenant and mercy with Your servants who walk before You with all their hearts.

15 [a]"You have kept what You promised Your servant David my father; You have both spoken with Your mouth and fulfilled *it* with Your hand, as *it is* this day.

16 "Therefore, LORD God of Israel, now keep what You promised Your servant David my father, saying, [a]'You shall not fail to have a man sit before Me on the throne of Israel, [b]only if your sons take heed to their way, that they walk in My law as you have walked before Me.'

17 "And now, O LORD God of Israel, let Your word come true, which You have spoken to Your servant David.

18 "But will God indeed dwell with men on the earth? [a]Behold, heaven and the heaven of heavens cannot contain You. How much less this *temple which I have built!

19 "Yet regard the prayer of Your servant and his supplication, O LORD my God, and listen to the cry and the prayer which Your servant is praying before You:

20 "that Your eyes may be [a]open toward this temple day and night, toward the place where *You*

KJV

hast said that thou wouldest put thy name there; to hearken unto the prayer which thy servant prayeth [b]toward this place.

21 Hearken therefore unto the supplications of thy servant, and of thy people Israel, which they shall make toward this place: hear thou from thy dwelling place, *even* from heaven; and when thou hearest, [a]forgive.

22 If a man sin against his neighbour, and an [a]oath be laid upon him to make him swear, and the oath come before thine altar in this house;

23 Then hear thou from heaven, and do, and judge thy servants, by requiting the wicked, by recompensing his way upon his own head; and by justifying the righteous, by giving him according to his [a]righteousness.

24 And if thy people Israel be put to the worse before the [a]enemy, because they have sinned against thee; and shall return and confess thy name, and pray and make supplication before thee in this house;

25 Then hear thou from the heavens, and forgive the sin of thy people Israel, and bring them again unto the land which thou gavest to them and to their fathers.

26 When the [a]heaven is shut up, and there is no rain, because they have sinned against thee; *yet* if they pray toward this place, and confess thy name, and turn from their sin, when thou dost afflict them;

27 Then hear thou from heaven, and forgive the sin of thy servants, and of thy people Israel, when thou hast taught them the good way, wherein they should walk; and send rain upon thy land, which thou hast given unto thy people for an inheritance.

28 If there [a]be dearth in the land, if there be pestilence, if there be blasting, or mildew, locusts, or caterpillers; if their enemies besiege them in the cities of their land; whatsoever sore or whatsoever [b]sickness *there be*:

29 *Then* what prayer *or* what supplication soever shall be made of any man, or of all thy people Israel, when every one shall know his own sore and his own grief, and shall spread forth his hands in this house:

30 Then hear thou from heaven thy dwelling place, and forgive, and render unto every man according unto all his ways, whose heart thou knowest; (for thou only [a]knowest the [b]hearts of the children of men:)

31 That they may fear thee, to walk in thy ways, so long as they live in the land which thou gavest unto our fathers.

32 Moreover concerning the stranger, [a]which is not of thy people Israel, but is come from a far country for thy great name's sake, and thy mighty hand, and thy stretched out arm; if they come and pray in this house;

33 Then hear thou from the heavens, *even* from thy dwelling place, and do according to all that the stranger calleth to thee for; that all people of the earth may know thy name, and fear thee, as *doth* thy people Israel, and may know that this house which I have built is called by thy name.

34 If thy people go out to war against their enemies by the way that thou shalt send them, and they pray unto thee toward this city which thou hast chosen, and the house which I have built for thy name;

35 Then hear thou from the heavens their prayer and their supplication, and maintain their cause.

36 If they sin against thee, (for *there is* [a]no man which sinneth not,) and thou be angry with them, and deliver them over before *their* enemies, and they carry them away [b]captives unto a land far off or near;

37 Yet *if* they bethink themselves in the land whither they are carried captive, and turn and pray unto thee in the land of their captivity,

20 [b]Ps. 5:7; Dan. 6:10
21 [a][Is. 43:25; 44:22; Mic. 7:18]
22 [a]Ex. 22:8–11
23 [a][Job 34:11]
24 [a]2 Kin. 21:14, 15
26 [a]Deut. 28:23, 24; 1 Kin. 17:1
28 [a]2 Chr. 20:9 [b][Mic. 6:13]
30 [a][1 Chr. 28:9; Prov. 21:2; 24:12] [b][1 Sam. 16:7]
32 [a]John 12:20; Acts 8:27
36 [a]Prov. 20:9; Eccl. 7:20; [Rom. 3:9, 19; 5:12; Gal. 3:10]; James 3:2; 1 John 1:8 [b]Deut. 28:63–68

NKJV

said *You would* put Your name, that You may hear the prayer which Your servant makes [b]toward this place.

21 "And may You hear the supplications of Your servant and of Your people Israel, when they pray toward this place. Hear from heaven Your dwelling place, and when You hear, [a]forgive.

22 "If anyone sins against his neighbor, and is forced to take an [a]oath, and comes *and* takes an oath before Your altar in this temple,

23 "then hear from heaven, and act, and judge Your servants, bringing retribution on the wicked by bringing his way on his own head, and justifying the righteous by giving him according to his [a]righteousness.

24 "Or if Your people Israel are defeated before an [a]enemy because they have sinned against You, and return and confess Your name, and pray and make supplication before You in this temple,

25 "then hear from heaven and forgive the sin of Your people Israel, and bring them back to the land which You gave to them and their fathers.

26 "When the [a]heavens are shut up and there is no rain because they have sinned against You, when they pray toward this place and confess Your name, and turn from their sin because You afflict them,

27 "then hear *in* heaven, and forgive the sin of Your servants, Your people Israel, that You may teach them the good way in which they should walk; and send rain on Your land which You have given to Your people as an inheritance.

28 "When there [a]is famine in the land, pestilence or blight or mildew, locusts or grasshoppers; when their enemies besiege them in the land of their cities; whatever plague or whatever [b]sickness *there is;*

29 "whatever prayer, whatever supplication is *made* by anyone, or by all Your people Israel, when each one knows his own burden and his own grief, and spreads out his hands to this temple:

30 "then hear from heaven Your dwelling place, and forgive, and give to everyone according to all his ways, whose heart You know (for You alone [a]know the [b]hearts of the sons of men),

31 "that they may fear You, to walk in Your ways as long as they live in the land which You gave to our fathers.

32 "Moreover, concerning a foreigner, [a]who is not of Your people Israel, but has come from a far country for the sake of Your great name and Your mighty hand and Your outstretched arm, when they come and pray in this temple;

33 "then hear from heaven Your dwelling place, and do according to all for which the foreigner calls to You, that all peoples of the earth may know Your name and fear You, as *do* Your people Israel, and that they may know that this temple which I have built is called by Your name.

34 "When Your people go out to battle against their enemies, wherever You send them, and when they pray to You toward this city which You have chosen and the temple which I have built for Your name,

35 "then hear from heaven their prayer and their supplication, and maintain their cause.

36 "When they sin against You (for *there is* [a]no one who does not sin), and You become angry with them and deliver them to the enemy, and they take them [b]captive to a land far or near;

37 "*yet* when they come to themselves in the land where they were carried captive, and repent, and make supplication to You in the land of their

KJV

saying, We have sinned, we have done amiss, and have dealt wickedly;

38 If they return to thee with all their heart and with all their soul in the land of their captivity, whither they have carried them captives, and pray toward their land, which thou gavest unto their fathers, and *toward* the [a]city which thou hast chosen, and toward the house which I have built for thy name:

39 Then hear thou from the heavens, *even* from thy dwelling place, their prayer and their supplications, and maintain their cause, and forgive thy people which have sinned against thee.

40 Now, my God, let, I beseech thee, thine eyes be [a]open, and *let* thine ears *be* attent unto the prayer *that is made* in this place.

41 Now[a] therefore arise, O LORD God, into thy [b]resting place, thou, and the ark of thy strength: let thy priests, O LORD God, be clothed with salvation, and let thy saints [c]rejoice in goodness.

42 O LORD God, turn not away the face of thine anointed: [a]remember the mercies of David thy servant.

Solomon Dedicates the Temple
(1 Kin. 8:62–66)

7 Now [a]when Solomon had made an end of praying, the [b]fire came down from heaven, and consumed the burnt offering and the sacrifices; and [c]the glory of the LORD filled the house.

2 [a]And the priests could not enter into the house of the LORD, because the glory of the LORD had filled the LORD's house.

3 And when all the children of Israel saw how the fire came down, and the glory of the LORD upon the house, they bowed themselves with their faces to the ground upon the pavement, and worshipped, and praised the LORD, [a]*saying,* For *he is* good; [b]for his mercy *endureth* for ever.

4 [a]Then the king and all the people offered sacrifices before the LORD.

5 And king Solomon offered a sacrifice of twenty and two thousand oxen, and an hundred and twenty thousand sheep: so the king and all the people dedicated the house of God.

6 [a]And the priests waited on their offices: the Levites also with instruments of musick of the LORD, which David the king had made to praise the LORD, because his mercy *endureth* for ever, when David praised by their ministry; and [b]the priests sounded trumpets before them, and all Israel stood.

7 Moreover [a]Solomon hallowed the middle of the court that *was* before the house of the LORD: for there he offered burnt offerings, and the fat of the peace offerings, because the brasen altar which Solomon had made was not able to receive the burnt offerings, and the meat offerings, and the fat.

8 [a]Also at the same time Solomon kept the feast seven days, and all Israel with him, a very great congregation, [b]from the entering in of Hamath unto [c]the river of Egypt.

9 And in the eighth day they made a [a]solemn assembly: for they kept the dedication of the altar seven days, and the feast seven days.

10 And [a]on the three and twentieth day of the seventh month he sent the people away into their tents, glad and merry in heart for the goodness that the LORD had shewed unto David, and to Solomon, and to Israel his people.

11 Thus [a]Solomon finished the house of the LORD, and the king's house: and all that came into

38 [a]Dan. 6:10
40 [a]2 Chr. 6:20
41 [a]Ps. 132:8–10, 16 [b]1 Chr. 28:2 [c]Neh. 9:25
42 [a]2 Sam. 7:15; Ps. 89:49; 132:1, 8–10; Is. 55:3

CHAPTER 7

1 [a]1 Kin. 8:54 [b]Lev. 9:24; Judg. 6:21; 1 Kin. 18:38; 1 Chr. 21:26 [c]1 Kin. 8:10, 11
2 [a]2 Chr. 5:14
3 [a]2 Chr. 5:13; Ps. 106:1; 136:1 [b]1 Chr. 16:41; 2 Chr. 20:21
4 [a]1 Kin. 8:62, 63
6 [a]1 Chr. 15:16 [b]2 Chr. 5:12
7 [a]1 Kin. 8:64–66; 9:3
8 [a]1 Kin. 8:65 [b]1 Kin. 4:21, 24; 2 Kin. 14:25 [c]Josh. 13:3
9 [a]Lev. 23:36
10 [a]1 Kin. 8:66
11 [a]1 Kin. 9:1

*

7:1 Lit. *house*
7:8 The Shihor, 1 Chr. 13:5

NKJV

captivity, saying, 'We have sinned, we have done wrong, and have committed wickedness';

38 "and *when* they return to You with all their heart and with all their soul in the land of their captivity, where they have been carried captive, and pray toward their land which You gave to their fathers, the [a]city which You have chosen, and toward the temple which I have built for Your name:

39 "then hear from heaven Your dwelling place their prayer and their supplications, and maintain their cause, and forgive Your people who have sinned against You.

40 "Now, my God, I pray, let Your eyes be [a]open and *let* Your ears *be* attentive to the prayer *made* in this place.

41 "Now[a] therefore,
Arise, O LORD God, to Your [b]resting place,
You and the ark of Your strength.
Let Your priests, O LORD God, be clothed with salvation,
And let Your saints [c]rejoice in goodness.

42 "O LORD God, do not turn away the face of Your Anointed;
[a]Remember the mercies of Your servant David."

Solomon Dedicates the Temple
(1 Kin. 8:62–66)

7 When [a]Solomon had finished praying, [b]fire came down from heaven and consumed the burnt offering and the sacrifices; and [c]the glory of the LORD filled the *temple.

2 [a]And the priests could not enter the house of the LORD, because the glory of the LORD had filled the LORD's house.

3 When all the children of Israel saw how the fire came down, and the glory of the LORD on the temple, they bowed their faces to the ground on the pavement, and worshiped and praised the LORD, *saying:*

[a]"For *He is* good,
[b]For His mercy *endures* forever."

4 [a]Then the king and all the people offered sacrifices before the LORD.

5 King Solomon offered a sacrifice of twenty-two thousand bulls and one hundred and twenty thousand sheep. So the king and all the people dedicated the house of God.

6 [a]And the priests attended to their services; the Levites also with instruments of the music of the LORD, which King David had made to praise the LORD, saying, "For His mercy *endures* forever," whenever David offered praise by their ministry. [b]The priests sounded trumpets opposite them, while all Israel stood.

7 Furthermore [a]Solomon consecrated the middle of the court that *was* in front of the house of the LORD; for there he offered burnt offerings and the fat of the peace offerings, because the bronze altar which Solomon had made was not able to receive the burnt offerings, the grain offerings, and the fat.

8 [a]At that time Solomon kept the feast seven days, and all Israel with him, a very great assembly [b]from the entrance of Hamath to [c]the* Brook of Egypt.

9 And on the eighth day they held a [a]sacred assembly, for they observed the dedication of the altar seven days, and the feast seven days.

10 [a]On the twenty-third day of the seventh month he sent the people away to their tents, joyful and glad of heart for the good that the LORD had done for David, for Solomon, and for His people Israel.

11 Thus [a]Solomon finished the house of the LORD and the king's house; and Solomon success-

KJV

9 And she gave the king an hundred and
twenty talents of gold, and of spices great abundance, and precious stones: neither was there any
such spice as the queen of Sheba gave king
Solomon.
10 And the servants also of Huram, and
the servants of Solomon, [a]which brought gold
from Ophir, brought algum trees and precious
stones.
11 And the king made *of* the algum trees ter-
races to the house of the LORD, and to the king's
palace, and harps and psalteries for singers: and
there were none such seen before in the land of
Judah.
12 And king Solomon gave to the queen of
Sheba all her desire, whatsoever she asked, beside *that* which she had brought unto the king.
So she turned, and went away to her own land,
she and her servants.

Solomon's Great Wealth
(1 Kin. 10:14–29; 2 Chr. 1:14–17)

13 [a]Now the weight of gold that came to Solomon in one year was six hundred and threescore
and six talents of gold;
14 Beside *that which* chapmen and merchants brought. And all the kings of Arabia and
governors of the country brought gold and silver
to Solomon.
15 And king Solomon made two hundred targets *of* beaten gold: six hundred *shekels* of beaten
gold went to one target.
16 And three hundred shields *made he of*
beaten gold: three hundred *shekels* of gold went
to one shield. And the king put them in the [a]house
of the forest of Lebanon.
17 Moreover the king made a great throne
of ivory, and overlaid it with pure gold.
18 And *there were* six steps to the throne,
with a footstool of gold, *which were* fastened to
the throne, and stays on each side of the sitting
place, and two lions standing by the stays:
19 And twelve lions stood there on the one
side and on the other upon the six steps. There
was not the like made in any kingdom.
20 And all the drinking vessels of king Solomon *were of* gold, and all the vessels of the
house of the forest of Lebanon *were of* pure gold:
none *were of* silver; it was *not* any thing accounted of in the days of Solomon.
21 For the king's ships went to [a]Tarshish
with the servants of Huram: every three years
once came the ships of Tarshish bringing gold,
and silver, ivory, and apes, and peacocks.
22 And king Solomon passed all the kings
of the earth in riches and wisdom.
23 And all the kings of the earth sought the
presence of Solomon, to hear his wisdom, that
God had put in his heart.
24 And they brought every man his present,
vessels of silver, and vessels of gold, and raiment,
[a]harness, and spices, horses, and mules, a rate
year by year.
25 And Solomon [a]had four thousand stalls
for horses and chariots, and twelve thousand
horsemen; whom he bestowed in the chariot cities, and with the king at Jerusalem.
26 [a]And he reigned over all the kings [b]from
the river even unto the land of the Philistines, and
to the border of Egypt.
27 [a]And the king made silver in Jerusalem as
stones, and cedar trees made he as the sycomore trees that *are* in the low plains in [b]abun-
dance.
28 [a]And they brought unto Solomon horses
out of Egypt, and out of all lands.

Death of Solomon
(1 Kin. 11:41–43)

29 [a]Now the rest of the acts of Solomon, first
and last, *are* they not written in the book of Nathan the prophet, and in the prophecy of [b]Ahijah

10 [a]2 Chr. 8:18
13 [a]1 Kin. 10:14–29
16 [a]1 Kin. 7:2
21 [a]2 Chr. 20:36, 37; Ps. 72:10
24 [a]1 Kin. 20:11
25 [a]Deut. 17:16; 1 Kin. 4:26; 10:26; 2 Chr. 1:14; Is. 2:7
26 [a]1 Kin. 4:21 [b]Gen. 15:18; Ps. 72:8
27 [a]1 Kin. 10:27 [b]2 Chr. 1:15–17
28 [a]1 Kin. 10:28; 2 Chr. 1:16
29 [a]1 Kin. 11:41 [b]1 Kin. 11:29

NKJV

9 And she gave the king one hundred and
twenty talents of gold, spices in great abundance,
and precious stones; there never were any spices
such as those the queen of Sheba gave to King
Solomon.
10 Also, the servants of Hiram and the servants of Solomon, [a]who brought gold from Ophir,
brought *algum wood and precious stones.
11 And the king made walkways *of* the *algum wood for the house of the LORD and for the
king's house, also harps and stringed instruments
for singers; and there were none such *as these*
seen before in the land of Judah.
12 Now King Solomon gave to the queen of
Sheba all she desired, whatever she asked, *much
more* than she had brought to the king. So she
turned and went to her own country, she and her
servants.

Solomon's Great Wealth
(1 Kin. 10:14–29; 2 Chr. 1:14–17)

13 [a]The weight of gold that came to Solomon
yearly was six hundred and sixty-six talents of
gold,
14 besides *what* the traveling merchants and
traders brought. And all the kings of Arabia and
governors of the country brought gold and silver
to Solomon.
15 And King Solomon made two hundred
large shields of hammered gold; six hundred
shekels of hammered gold went into each shield.
16 *He* also *made* three hundred shields of
hammered gold; *three hundred *shekels* of gold
went into each shield. The king put them in the
[a]House of the Forest of Lebanon.
17 Moreover the king made a great throne
of ivory, and overlaid it with pure gold.
18 The throne *had* six steps, with a footstool
of gold, *which were* fastened to the throne; there
were armrests on either side of the place of the
seat, and two lions stood beside the armrests.
19 Twelve lions stood there, one on each side
of the six steps; nothing like *this* had been made
for any *other* kingdom.
20 All King Solomon's drinking vessels *were*
gold, and all the vessels of the House of the Forest
of Lebanon *were* pure gold. Not *one was* silver,
for this was accounted as nothing in the days of
Solomon.
21 For the king's ships went to [a]Tarshish
with the servants of *Hiram. Once every three
years the *merchant ships came, bringing gold,
silver, ivory, apes, and *monkeys.
22 So King Solomon surpassed all the kings
of the earth in riches and wisdom.
23 And all the kings of the earth sought the
presence of Solomon to hear his wisdom, which
God had put in his heart.
24 Each man brought his present: articles of
silver and gold, garments, [a]armor, spices, horses,
and mules, at a set rate year by year.
25 Solomon [a]had four thousand stalls for
horses and chariots, and twelve thousand horsemen whom he stationed in the chariot cities and
with the king at Jerusalem.
26 [a]So he reigned over all the kings [b]from
*the River to the land of the Philistines, as far as
the border of Egypt.
27 [a]The king made silver *as common* in Jerusalem as stones, and he made cedar trees [b]as
abundant as the sycamores which *are* in the
lowland.
28 [a]And they brought horses to Solomon
from Egypt and from all lands.

Death of Solomon
(1 Kin. 11:41–43)

29 [a]Now the rest of the acts of Solomon, first
and last, *are* they not written in the book of Nathan the prophet, in the prophecy of [b]Ahijah the

*

9:10 *almug,* 1 Kin. 10:11, 12
9:11 *almug,* 1 Kin. 10:11, 12
9:16 *three minas,* 1 Kin. 10:17
9:21 Heb. *Huram;* cf. 1 Kin. 10:22 • Lit. *ships of Tarshish,* deep-sea vessels • Or *peacocks*
9:26 The Euphrates

KJV

the Shilonite, and in the visions of [c]Iddo the seer against Jeroboam the son of Nebat?

30 [a]And Solomon reigned in Jerusalem over all Israel forty years.

31 And Solomon slept with his fathers, and he was buried in the city of David his father: and Rehoboam his son reigned in his stead.

The Revolt Against Rehoboam
(1 Kin. 12:1–19)

10 And [a]Rehoboam went to Shechem: for to Shechem were all Israel come to make him king.

2 And it came to pass, when Jeroboam the son of Nebat, who *was* in Egypt, [a]whither he had fled from the presence of Solomon the king, heard *it*, that Jeroboam returned out of Egypt.

3 And they sent and called him. So Jeroboam and all Israel came and spake to Rehoboam, saying,

4 Thy father made our yoke grievous: now therefore ease thou somewhat the grievous servitude of thy father, and his heavy yoke that he put upon us, and we will serve thee.

5 And he said unto them, Come again unto me after three days. And the people departed.

6 And king Rehoboam took counsel with the old men that had stood before Solomon his father while he yet lived, saying, What counsel give ye *me* to return answer to this people?

7 And they spake unto him, saying, If thou be kind to this people, and please them, and speak good words to them, they will be thy servants for ever.

8 [a]But he forsook the counsel which the old men gave him, and took counsel with the young men that were brought up with him, that stood before him.

9 And he said unto them, What advice give ye that we may return answer to this people, which have spoken to me, saying, Ease somewhat the yoke that thy father did put upon us?

10 And the young men that were brought up with him spake unto him, saying, Thus shalt thou answer the people that spake unto thee, saying, Thy father made our yoke heavy, but make thou *it* somewhat lighter for us; thus shalt thou say unto them, My little *finger* shall be thicker than my father's loins.

11 For whereas my father put a heavy yoke upon you, I will put more to your yoke: my father chastised you with whips, but I *will chastise you* with scorpions.

12 So [a]Jeroboam and all the people came to Rehoboam on the third day, as the king bade, saying, Come again to me on the third day.

13 And the king answered them roughly; and king Rehoboam forsook the counsel of the old men,

14 And answered them after the advice of the young men, saying, My father made your yoke heavy, but I will add thereto: my father chastised you with whips, but I *will chastise you* with scorpions.

15 So the king hearkened not unto the people: [a]for the cause was of God, that the LORD might perform his [b]word, which he spake by the hand of Ahijah the Shilonite to Jeroboam the son of Nebat.

16 And when all Israel *saw* that the king would not hearken unto them, the people answered the king, saying, What portion have we in David? and *we have* none inheritance in the son of Jesse: every man to your tents, O Israel, *and* now, David, see to thine own house. So all Israel went to their tents.

17 But *as for* the children of Israel that dwelt in the cities of Judah, Rehoboam reigned over them.

18 Then king Rehoboam sent Hadoram that

29 [c]2 Chr. 12:15; 13:22
30 [a]1 Kin. 4:21; 11:42, 43; 1 Chr. 29:28

CHAPTER 10

1 [a]1 Kin. 12:1–20
2 [a]1 Kin. 11:40
8 [a]1 Kin. 12:8–11
12 [a]1 Kin. 12:12–14
15 [a]Judg. 14:4; 1 Chr. 5:22; 2 Chr. 11:4; 22:7 [b]1 Kin. 11:29–39

*

10:11 Scourges with points or barbs, lit. *scorpions*
10:14 So with many Heb. mss., LXX, Syr., Vg. (cf. v. 10; 1 Kin. 12:14); MT *I* • Lit. *scorpions*

NKJV

Shilonite, and in the visions of [c]Iddo the seer concerning Jeroboam the son of Nebat?

30 [a]Solomon reigned in Jerusalem over all Israel forty years.

31 Then Solomon rested with his fathers, and was buried in the City of David his father. And Rehoboam his son reigned in his place.

The Revolt Against Rehoboam
(1 Kin. 12:1–19)

10 And [a]Rehoboam went to Shechem, for all Israel had gone to Shechem to make him king.

2 So it happened, when Jeroboam the son of Nebat heard *it* (he was in Egypt, [a]where he had fled from the presence of King Solomon), that Jeroboam returned from Egypt.

3 Then they sent for him and called him. And Jeroboam and all Israel came and spoke to Rehoboam, saying,

4 "Your father made our yoke heavy; now therefore, lighten the burdensome service of your father and his heavy yoke which he put on us, and we will serve you."

5 So he said to them, "Come back to me after three days." And the people departed.

6 Then King Rehoboam consulted the elders who stood before his father Solomon while he still lived, saying, "How do you advise *me* to answer these people?"

7 And they spoke to him, saying, "If you are kind to these people, and please them, and speak good words to them, they will be your servants forever."

8 [a]But he rejected the advice which the elders had given him, and consulted the young men who had grown up with him, who stood before him.

9 And he said to them, "What advice do you give? How should we answer this people who have spoken to me, saying, 'Lighten the yoke which your father put on us'?"

10 Then the young men who had grown up with him spoke to him, saying, "Thus you should speak to the people who have spoken to you, saying, 'Your father made our yoke heavy, but you make *it* lighter on us'—thus you shall say to them: 'My little *finger* shall be thicker than my father's waist!

11 'And now, whereas my father put a heavy yoke on you, I will add to your yoke; my father chastised you with whips, but I *will chastise you* with *scourges!' "

12 So [a]Jeroboam and all the people came to Rehoboam on the third day, as the king had directed, saying, "Come back to me the third day."

13 Then the king answered them roughly. King Rehoboam rejected the advice of the elders,

14 and he spoke to them according to the advice of the young men, saying, *"My father made your yoke heavy, but I will add to it; my father chastised you with whips, but I *will chastise you* with *scourges!"

15 So the king did not listen to the people; [a]for the turn *of events* was from God, that the LORD might fulfill His [b]word, which He had spoken by the hand of Ahijah the Shilonite to Jeroboam the son of Nebat.

16 Now when all Israel *saw* that the king did not listen to them, the people answered the king, saying:

"What share have we in David?
We have no inheritance in the son of Jesse.
Every man to your tents, O Israel!
Now see to your own house, O David!"

So all Israel departed to their tents.

17 But Rehoboam reigned over the children of Israel who dwelt in the cities of Judah.

18 Then King Rehoboam sent Hadoram, who

KJV

was over the tribute; and the children of Israel
stoned him with stones, that he died. But king
Rehoboam made speed to get him up to *his* chariot, to flee to Jerusalem.
19 [a]And Israel rebelled against the house of
David unto this day.

11 And [a]when Rehoboam was come to Jerusalem, he gathered of the house of Judah and
Benjamin an hundred and fourscore thousand
chosen *men*, which were warriors, to fight against
Israel, that he might bring the kingdom again to
Rehoboam.
2 But the word of the LORD came [a]to Shemaiah the man of God, saying,
3 Speak unto Rehoboam the son of Solomon, king of Judah, and to all Israel in Judah
and Benjamin, saying,
4 Thus saith the LORD, Ye shall not go up,
nor fight against your brethren: return every man
to his house: for this thing is done of me. And
they obeyed the words of the LORD, and returned
from going against Jeroboam.

Rehoboam Fortifies the Cities

5 And Rehoboam dwelt in Jerusalem, and
built cities for defence in Judah.
6 He built even Beth–lehem, and Etam, and
Tekoa,
7 And Beth–zur, and Shoco, and Adullam,
8 And Gath, and Mareshah, and Ziph,
9 And Adoraim, and Lachish, and Azekah,
10 And Zorah, and Aijalon, and Hebron,
which *are* in Judah and in Benjamin fenced cities.
11 And he fortified the strong holds, and put
captains in them, and store of victual, and of oil
and wine.
12 And in every several city *he put* shields
and spears, and made them exceeding strong,
having Judah and Benjamin on his side.

Priests and Levites Move to Judah
(1 Kin. 14:21–24)

13 And the priests and the Levites that *were*
in all Israel resorted to him out of all their coasts.
14 For the Levites left [a]their suburbs and
their possession, and came to Judah and Jerusalem: for [b]Jeroboam and his sons had cast them
off from executing the priest's office unto the
LORD:
15 [a]And he ordained him priests for the high
places, and for [b]the devils, and for [c]the calves
which he had made.
16 [a]And after them out of all the tribes of
Israel such as set their hearts to seek the LORD
God of Israel [b]came to Jerusalem, to sacrifice unto
the LORD God of their fathers.
17 So they [a]strengthened the kingdom of Judah, and made Rehoboam the son of Solomon
strong, three years: for three years they walked
in the way of David and Solomon.

The Family of Rehoboam

18 And Rehoboam took him Mahalath the
daughter of Jerimoth the son of David to wife,
and Abihail the daughter of [a]Eliab the son of
Jesse;
19 Which bare him children; Jeush, and
Shamariah, and Zaham.
20 And after her he took [a]Maachah the
daughter of [b]Absalom; which bare him [c]Abijah,
and Attai, and Ziza, and Shelomith.
21 And Rehoboam loved Maachah the
daughter of Absalom above all his [a]wives and his
concubines: (for he took eighteen wives, and
threescore concubines; and begat twenty and
eight sons, and threescore daughters.)
22 And Rehoboam [a]made [b]Abijah the son of
Maachah the chief, *to be* ruler among his brethren: for *he thought* to make him king.
23 And he dealt wisely, and dispersed of all
his children throughout all the countries of Judah

19 [a]1 Kin. 12:19

CHAPTER 11

1 [a]1 Kin. 12:21–24
2 [a]1 Chr. 12:5; 2 Chr. 12:15
14 [a]Num. 35:2–5 [b]1 Kin. 12:28–33; 2 Chr. 13:9
15 [a]1 Kin. 12:31; 13:33; 14:9; [Hos. 13:2] [b][Lev. 17:7; 1 Cor. 10:20] [c]1 Kin. 12:28
16 [a]2 Chr. 14:7 [b]2 Chr. 15:9, 10; 30:11, 18
17 [a]2 Chr. 12:1, 13
18 [a]1 Sam. 16:6
20 [a]2 Chr. 13:2 [b]1 Kin. 15:2 [c]1 Kin. 14:31
21 [a]Deut. 17:17
22 [a]Deut. 21:15–17 [b]2 Chr. 13:1

NKJV

was in charge of revenue; but the children of Israel stoned him with stones, and he died. Therefore King Rehoboam mounted *his* chariot in haste
to flee to Jerusalem.
19 [a]So Israel has been in rebellion against
the house of David to this day.

11 Now [a]when Rehoboam came to Jerusalem,
he assembled from the house of Judah and
Benjamin one hundred and eighty thousand chosen *men* who were warriors, to fight against
Israel, that he might restore the kingdom to
Rehoboam.
2 But the word of the LORD came [a]to Shemaiah the man of God, saying,
3 "Speak to Rehoboam the son of Solomon,
king of Judah, and to all Israel in Judah and Benjamin, saying,
4 'Thus says the LORD: "You shall not go
up or fight against your brethren! Let every man
return to his house, for this thing is from Me." ' "
Therefore they obeyed the words of the LORD, and
turned back from attacking Jeroboam.

Rehoboam Fortifies the Cities

5 So Rehoboam dwelt in Jerusalem, and
built cities for defense in Judah.
6 And he built Bethlehem, Etam, Tekoa,
7 Beth Zur, Sochoh, Adullam,
8 Gath, Mareshah, Ziph,
9 Adoraim, Lachish, Azekah,
10 Zorah, Aijalon, and Hebron, which are in
Judah and Benjamin, fortified cities.
11 And he fortified the strongholds, and put
captains in them, and stores of food, oil, and wine.
12 Also in every city *he put* shields and
spears, and made them very strong, having Judah
and Benjamin on his side.

Priests and Levites Move to Judah
(1 Kin. 14:21–24)

13 And from all their territories the priests
and the Levites who *were* in all Israel took their
stand with him.
14 For the Levites left [a]their common-lands
and their possessions and came to Judah and Jerusalem, for [b]Jeroboam and his sons had rejected
them from serving as priests to the LORD.
15 [a]Then he appointed for himself priests for
the high places, for [b]the demons, and [c]the calf
idols which he had made.
16 [a]And *after *the Levites left,* those from
all the tribes of Israel, such as set their heart to
seek the LORD God of Israel, [b]came to Jerusalem
to sacrifice to the LORD God of their fathers.
17 So they [a]strengthened the kingdom of Judah, and made Rehoboam the son of Solomon
strong for three years, because they walked in
the way of David and Solomon for three years.

The Family of Rehoboam

18 Then Rehoboam took for himself as wife
Mahalath the daughter of Jerimoth the son of David, *and of* Abihail the daughter of [a]Eliah the son
of Jesse.
19 And she bore him children: Jeush, Shamariah, and Zaham.
20 After her he took [a]Maachah the *granddaughter of [b]Absalom; and she bore him [c]Abijah,
Attai, Ziza, and Shelomith.
21 Now Rehoboam loved Maachah the
granddaughter of Absalom more than all his
[a]wives and his concubines; for he took eighteen
wives and sixty concubines, and begot twenty-
eight sons and sixty daughters.
22 And Rehoboam [a]appointed [b]Abijah the
son of Maachah as chief, *to be* leader among his
brothers; for he *intended* to make him king.
23 He dealt wisely, and dispersed some of his
sons throughout all the territories of Judah and

*

11:16 Lit. *after them*
11:20 Lit. *daughter*, but in the broader sense of granddaughter

KJV

and Benjamin, unto every [a]fenced city: and he gave them victual in abundance. And he desired many wives.

Egypt Attacks Judah
(1 Kin. 14:25–28)

12 And [a]it came to pass, when Rehoboam had established the kingdom, and had strengthened himself, [b]he forsook the law of the LORD, and all Israel with him.

2 [a]And it came to pass, *that* in the fifth year of king Rehoboam Shishak king of Egypt came up against Jerusalem, because they had transgressed against the LORD,

3 With twelve hundred chariots, and threescore thousand horsemen: and the people *were* without number that came with him out of Egypt; [a]the Lubims, the Sukkiims, and the Ethiopians.

4 And he took the fenced cities which *pertained* to Judah, and came to Jerusalem.

5 Then came [a]Shemaiah the prophet to Rehoboam, and *to* the princes of Judah, that were gathered together to Jerusalem because of Shishak, and said unto them, Thus saith the LORD, Ye have forsaken me, and therefore have I also left you in the hand of Shishak.

6 Whereupon the princes of Israel and the king [a]humbled themselves; and they said, [b]The LORD *is* righteous.

7 And when the LORD saw that they humbled themselves, [a]the word of the LORD came to Shemaiah, saying, They have humbled themselves; *therefore* I will not destroy them, but I will grant them some deliverance; and my wrath shall not be poured out upon Jerusalem by the hand of Shishak.

8 Nevertheless [a]they shall be his servants; that they may know [b]my service, and the service of the kingdoms of the countries.

9 [a]So Shishak king of Egypt came up against Jerusalem, and took away the treasures of the house of the LORD, and the treasures of the king's house; he took all: he carried away also the shields of gold which Solomon had [b]made.

10 Instead of which king Rehoboam made shields of brass, and committed *them* [a]to the hands of the chief of the guard, that kept the entrance of the king's house.

11 And when the king entered into the house of the LORD, the guard came and fetched them, and brought them again into the guard chamber.

12 And when he humbled himself, the wrath of the LORD turned from him, that he would not destroy *him* altogether: and also in Judah things went well.

The End of Rehoboam's Reign
(1 Kin. 14:21, 22, 29–31)

13 So king Rehoboam strengthened himself in Jerusalem, and reigned: for [a]Rehoboam *was* one and forty years old when he began to reign, and he reigned seventeen years in Jerusalem, [b]the city which the LORD had chosen out of all the tribes of Israel, to put his name there. And his mother's name *was* Naamah an [c]Ammonitess.

14 And he did evil, because he prepared not his heart to seek the LORD.

15 Now the acts of Rehoboam, first and last, *are* they not written in the book of Shemaiah the prophet, [a]and of Iddo the seer concerning genealogies? [b]And *there were* wars between Rehoboam and Jeroboam continually.

16 And Rehoboam slept with his fathers, and was buried in the city of David: and [a]Abijah his son reigned in his stead.

Abijah Reigns in Judah
(1 Kin. 15:1–8)

13 Now [a]in the eighteenth year of king Jeroboam began Abijah to reign over [b]Judah.

2 He reigned three years in Jerusalem. His

---

23 [a]2 Chr. 11:5

CHAPTER 12

1 [a]2 Chr. 11:17 [b]1 Kin. 14:22–24
2 [a]1 Kin. 11:40; 14:25
3 [a]2 Chr. 16:8; Nah. 3:9
5 [a]2 Chr. 11:2
6 [a][James 4:10] [b]Ex. 9:27; [Dan. 9:14]
7 [a]1 Kin. 21:28, 29
8 [a]Is. 26:13 [b][Deut. 28:47, 48]
9 [a]1 Kin. 14:25, 26 [b]1 Kin. 10:16, 17; 2 Chr. 9:15, 16
10 [a]1 Kin. 14:27
13 [a]1 Kin. 14:21 [b]2 Chr. 6:6 [c]1 Kin. 11:1, 5
15 [a]2 Chr. 9:29; 13:22 [b]1 Kin. 14:30
16 [a]2 Chr. 11:20–22

CHAPTER 13

1 [a]1 Kin. 15:1 [b]1 Kin. 12:17

*

12:16 *Abijam,* 1 Kin. 14:31

NKJV

Benjamin, to every [a]fortified city; and he gave them provisions in abundance. He also sought many wives *for them.*

Egypt Attacks Judah
(1 Kin. 14:25–28)

12 Now [a]it came to pass, when Rehoboam had established the kingdom and had strengthened himself, that [b]he forsook the law of the LORD, and all Israel along with him.

2 [a]And it happened in the fifth year of King Rehoboam *that* Shishak king of Egypt came up against Jerusalem, because they had transgressed against the LORD,

3 with twelve hundred chariots, sixty thousand horsemen, and people without number who came with him out of Egypt—[a]the Lubim and the Sukkiim and the Ethiopians.

4 And he took the fortified cities of Judah and came to Jerusalem.

5 Then [a]Shemaiah the prophet came to Rehoboam and the leaders of Judah, who were gathered together in Jerusalem because of Shishak, and said to them, "Thus says the LORD: 'You have forsaken Me, and therefore I also have left you in the hand of Shishak.' "

6 So the leaders of Israel and the king [a]humbled themselves; and they said, [b]"The LORD *is* righteous."

7 Now when the LORD saw that they humbled themselves, [a]the word of the LORD came to Shemaiah, saying, "They have humbled themselves; *therefore* I will not destroy them, but I will grant them some deliverance. My wrath shall not be poured out on Jerusalem by the hand of Shishak.

8 "Nevertheless [a]they will be his servants, that they may distinguish [b]My service from the service of the kingdoms of the nations."

9 [a]So Shishak king of Egypt came up against Jerusalem, and took away the treasures of the house of the LORD and the treasures of the king's house; he took everything. He also carried away the gold shields which Solomon had [b]made.

10 Then King Rehoboam made bronze shields in their place, and committed *them* [a]to the hands of the captains of the guard, who guarded the doorway of the king's house.

11 And whenever the king entered the house of the LORD, the guard would go and bring them out; then they would take them back into the guardroom.

12 When he humbled himself, the wrath of the LORD turned from him, so as not to destroy *him* completely; and things also went well in Judah.

The End of Rehoboam's Reign
(1 Kin. 14:21, 22, 29–31)

13 Thus King Rehoboam strengthened himself in Jerusalem and reigned. Now [a]Rehoboam *was* forty-one years old when he became king; and he reigned seventeen years in Jerusalem, [b]the city which the LORD had chosen out of all the tribes of Israel, to put His name there. His mother's name *was* Naamah, an [c]Ammonitess.

14 And he did evil, because he did not prepare his heart to seek the LORD.

15 The acts of Rehoboam, first and last, *are* they not written in the book of Shemaiah the prophet, [a]and of Iddo the seer concerning genealogies? [b]And *there were* wars between Rehoboam and Jeroboam all their days.

16 So Rehoboam rested with his fathers, and was buried in the City of David. Then [a]Abijah* his son reigned in his place.

Abijah Reigns in Judah
(1 Kin. 15:1–8)

13 In [a]the eighteenth year of King Jeroboam, Abijah became king over [b]Judah.

2 He reigned three years in Jerusalem. His

KJV

mother's name also *was* Michaiah the daughter of Uriel of Gibeah. And there was war between Abijah and Jeroboam.

3 And Abijah set the battle in array with an army of valiant men of war, *even* four hundred thousand chosen men: Jeroboam also set the battle in array against him with eight hundred thousand chosen men, *being* mighty men of valour.

4 And Abijah stood up upon mount [a]Zemaraim, which *is* in mount Ephraim, and said, Hear me, thou Jeroboam, and all Israel;

5 Ought ye not to know that the LORD God of Israel [a]gave the kingdom over Israel to David for ever, *even* to him and to his sons [b]by a covenant of salt?

6 Yet Jeroboam the son of Nebat, the servant of Solomon the son of David, is risen up, and hath [a]rebelled against his lord.

7 And there are gathered unto him [a]vain men, the children of Belial, and have strengthened themselves against Rehoboam the son of Solomon, when Rehoboam was [b]young and tenderhearted, and could not withstand them.

8 And now ye think to withstand the kingdom of the LORD in the hand of the sons of David; and ye *be* a great multitude, and *there are* with you golden calves, which Jeroboam [a]made you for gods.

9 [a]Have ye not cast out the priests of the LORD, the sons of Aaron, and the Levites, and have made you priests after the manner of the nations of *other* lands? [b]so that whosoever cometh to consecrate himself with a young bullock and seven rams, *the same* may be a priest of [c]*them that are* no gods.

10 But as for us, the LORD *is* our [a]God, and we have not forsaken him; and the priests, which minister unto the LORD, *are* the sons of Aaron, and the Levites *wait* upon *their* business:

11 [a]And they burn unto the LORD every morning and every evening burnt sacrifices and sweet incense: the [b]shewbread also *set they in order* upon the pure table; and the candlestick of gold with the lamps thereof, [c]to burn every evening: for we keep the charge of the LORD our God; but ye have forsaken him.

12 And, behold, God himself *is* with us for *our* [a]captain, [b]and his priests with sounding trumpets to cry alarm against you. O children of Israel, fight ye not against the LORD God of your fathers; for ye shall not prosper.

13 But Jeroboam caused an ambushment to come about behind them: so they were before Judah, and the ambushment *was* behind them.

14 And when Judah looked back, behold, the battle *was* before and behind: and they [a]cried unto the LORD, and the priests sounded with the trumpets.

15 Then the men of Judah gave a shout: and as the men of Judah shouted, it came to pass, that God [a]smote Jeroboam and all Israel before Abijah and Judah.

16 And the children of Israel fled before Judah: and God delivered them into their hand.

17 And Abijah and his people slew them with a great slaughter: so there fell down slain of Israel five hundred thousand chosen men.

18 Thus the children of Israel were brought under at that time, and the children of Judah prevailed, [a]because they relied upon the LORD God of their fathers.

19 And Abijah pursued after Jeroboam, and took cities from him, Beth–el with the towns thereof, and Jeshanah with the towns thereof, and Ephrain with the towns thereof.

20 Neither did Jeroboam recover strength again in the days of Abijah: and the LORD [a]struck him, and [b]he died.

21 But Abijah waxed mighty, and married fourteen wives, and begat twenty and two sons, and sixteen daughters.

22 And the rest of the acts of Abijah, and his

---

4 [a]Josh. 18:22
5 [a]2 Sam. 7:8–16 [b]Lev. 2:13; Num. 18:19
6 [a]1 Kin. 11:28; 12:20
7 [a]Judg. 9:4 [b]2 Chr. 12:13
8 [a]1 Kin. 12:28; 14:9; 2 Chr. 11:15; [Hos. 8:4–6]
9 [a]2 Chr. 11:13–15 [b]Ex. 29:29–33 [c]Jer. 2:11; 5:7
10 [a]Josh. 24:15
11 [a]Ex. 29:38; 2 Chr. 2:4 [b]Ex. 25:30; Lev. 24:5–9 [c]Ex. 27:20, 21; Lev. 24:2, 3
12 [a]Josh. 5:13–15; [Heb. 2:10] [b][Num. 10:8–10]
14 [a]Josh. 24:7; 2 Chr. 6:34, 35; 14:11
15 [a]1 Kin. 14:14; 2 Chr. 14:12
18 [a]1 Chr. 5:20; 2 Chr. 14:11; [Ps. 22:5]
19 [a]Josh. 15:9
20 [a]1 Sam. 2:6; 25:38; Acts 12:23 [b]1 Kin. 14:20

NKJV

mother's name *was* *Michaiah the daughter of Uriel of Gibeah. And there was war between Abijah and Jeroboam.

3 Abijah set the battle in order with an army of valiant warriors, four hundred thousand choice men. Jeroboam also drew up in battle formation against him with eight hundred thousand choice men, mighty men of valor.

4 Then Abijah stood on Mount [a]Zemaraim, which *is* in the mountains of Ephraim, and said, "Hear me, Jeroboam and all Israel:

5 "Should you not know that the LORD God of Israel [a]gave the dominion over Israel to David forever, to him and his sons, [b]by a covenant of salt?

6 "Yet Jeroboam the son of Nebat, the servant of Solomon the son of David, rose up and [a]rebelled against his lord.

7 "Then [a]worthless rogues gathered to him, and strengthened themselves against Rehoboam the son of Solomon, when Rehoboam was [b]young and inexperienced and could not withstand them.

8 "And now you think to withstand the kingdom of the LORD, which is in the hand of the sons of David; and you *are* a great multitude, and with you are the gold calves which Jeroboam [a]made for you as gods.

9 [a]"Have you not cast out the priests of the LORD, the sons of Aaron, and the Levites, and made for yourselves priests, like the peoples of *other* lands, [b]so that whoever comes to consecrate himself with a young bull and seven rams may be a priest of [c]*things that are* not gods?

10 "But as for us, the LORD *is* our [a]God, and we have not forsaken Him; and the priests who minister to the LORD *are* the sons of Aaron, and the Levites *attend* to *their* duties.

11 [a]"And they burn to the LORD every morning and every evening burnt sacrifices and sweet incense; *they* also *set* the [b]showbread *in order on* the pure *gold* table, and the lampstand of gold with its lamps [c]to burn every evening; for we keep the command of the LORD our God, but you have forsaken Him.

12 "Now look, God Himself is with us as *our* [a]head, [b]and His priests with sounding trumpets to sound the alarm against you. O children of Israel, do not fight against the LORD God of your fathers, for you shall not prosper!"

13 But Jeroboam caused an ambush to go around behind them; so they were in front of Judah, and the ambush *was* behind them.

14 And when Judah looked around, to their surprise the battle line *was* at both front and rear; and they [a]cried out to the LORD, and the priests sounded the trumpets.

15 Then the men of Judah gave a shout; and as the men of Judah shouted, it happened that God [a]struck Jeroboam and all Israel before Abijah and Judah.

16 And the children of Israel fled before Judah, and God delivered them into their hand.

17 Then Abijah and his people struck them with a great slaughter; so five hundred thousand choice men of Israel fell slain.

18 Thus the children of Israel were subdued at that time; and the children of Judah prevailed, [a]because they relied on the LORD God of their fathers.

19 And Abijah pursued Jeroboam and took cities from him: Bethel with its villages, Jeshanah with its villages, and [a]Ephrain* with its villages.

20 So Jeroboam did not recover strength again in the days of Abijah; and the LORD [a]struck him, and [b]he died.

21 But Abijah grew mighty, married fourteen wives, and begot twenty-two sons and sixteen daughters.

22 Now the rest of the acts of Abijah, his

---

*

13:2 *Maachah,* 1 Kin. 15:2; 2 Chr. 11:20, 21
13:19 Or *Ephron*

KJV

ways, and his sayings, *are* written in [a]the story of the prophet Iddo.

14 So Abijah slept with his fathers, and they buried him in the city of David: and [a]Asa his son reigned in his stead. In his days the land was quiet ten years.

Asa Reigns in Judah
(1 Kin. 15:9–15)

2 And Asa did *that which was* good and right in the eyes of the LORD his God:

3 For he took away the altars of the strange *gods,* and [a]the high places, and [b]brake down the images, [c]and cut down the groves:

4 And commanded Judah to [a]seek the LORD God of their fathers, and to do the law and the commandment.

5 Also he took away out of all the cities of Judah the high places and the images: and the kingdom was quiet before him.

6 And he built fenced cities in Judah: for the land had rest, and he had no war in those years; because the LORD had given him [a]rest.

7 Therefore he said unto Judah, Let us build these cities, and make about *them* walls, and towers, gates, and bars, *while* the land *is* yet before us; because we have sought the LORD our God, we have sought *him,* and he hath given us rest on every side. So they built and prospered.

8 And Asa had an army *of men* that bare targets and spears, out of Judah three hundred thousand; and out of Benjamin, that bare shields and drew [a]bows, two hundred and fourscore thousand: all these *were* mighty men of [b]valour.

9 [a]And there came out against them Zerah the Ethiopian with an host of a thousand thousand, and three hundred chariots; and came unto [b]Mareshah.

10 Then Asa went out against him, and they set the battle in array in the valley of Zephathah at Mareshah.

11 And Asa [a]cried unto the LORD his God, and said, LORD, *it is* [b]nothing with thee to help, whether with many, or with them that have no power: help us, O LORD our God; for we rest on thee, and [c]in thy name we go against this multitude. O LORD, thou *art* our God; let not man prevail against thee.

12 So the LORD [a]smote the Ethiopians before Asa, and before Judah; and the Ethiopians fled.

13 And Asa and the people that *were* with him pursued them unto [a]Gerar: and the Ethiopians were overthrown, that they could not recover themselves; for they were destroyed before the LORD, and before his host; and they carried away very much spoil.

14 And they smote all the cities round about Gerar; for [a]the fear of the LORD came upon them: and they spoiled all the cities; for there was exceeding much spoil in them.

15 They smote also the tents of cattle, and carried away sheep and camels in abundance, and returned to Jerusalem.

The Reforms of Asa

15 And [a]the Spirit of God came upon Azariah the son of Oded:

2 And he went out to meet Asa, and said unto him, Hear ye me, Asa, and all Judah and Benjamin; [a]The LORD *is* with you, while ye be with him; and [b]if ye seek him, he will be found of you; but [c]if ye forsake him, he will forsake you.

3 Now [a]for a long season Israel *hath been* without the true God, and without a [b]teaching priest, and without [c]law.

4 But [a]when they in their trouble did turn unto the LORD God of Israel, and sought him, he was found of them.

5 And in those times *there was* no peace to him that went out, nor to him that came in,

---

22 [a]2 Chr. 9:29

CHAPTER 14

1 [a]1 Kin. 15:8
3 [a]1 Kin. 15:14; 2 Chr. 15:17 [b][Ex. 34:13] [c]1 Kin. 11:7
4 [a][2 Chr. 7:14]
6 [a]2 Chr. 15:15
8 [a]1 Chr. 12:2 [b]2 Chr. 13:3
9 [a]2 Chr. 12:2, 3; 16:8 [b]Josh. 15:44
11 [a]Ex. 14:10; 2 Chr. 13:14; [Ps. 22:5] [b][1 Sam. 14:6] [c]1 Sam. 17:45; [Prov. 18:10]
12 [a]2 Chr. 13:15
13 [a]Gen. 10:19; 20:1
14 [a]Gen. 35:5; Deut. 11:25; Josh. 2:9; 2 Chr. 17:10

CHAPTER 15

1 [a]Num. 24:2; Judg. 3:10; 2 Chr. 20:14; 24:20
2 [a][James 4:8] [b][1 Chr. 28:9]; 2 Chr. 14:4; 33:12, 13; [Jer. 29:13; Matt. 7:7] [c]2 Chr. 24:20
3 [a]Hos. 3:4 [b]2 Kin. 12:2 [c]Lev. 10:11; 2 Chr. 17:8, 9
4 [a][Deut. 4:29]

NKJV

ways, and his sayings *are* written in [a]the annals of the prophet Iddo.

14 So Abijah rested with his fathers, and they buried him in the City of David. Then [a]Asa his son reigned in his place. In his days the land was quiet for ten years.

Asa Reigns in Judah
(1 Kin. 15:9–15)

2 Asa did *what was* good and right in the eyes of the LORD his God,

3 for he removed the altars of the foreign *gods* and [a]the high places, and [b]broke down the *sacred* pillars [c]and cut down the wooden images.

4 He commanded Judah to [a]seek the LORD God of their fathers, and to observe the law and the commandment.

5 He also removed the high places and the incense altars from all the cities of Judah, and the kingdom was quiet under him.

6 And he built fortified cities in Judah, for the land had rest; he had no war in those years, because the LORD had given him [a]rest.

7 Therefore he said to Judah, "Let us build these cities and make walls around *them,* and towers, gates, and bars, *while* the land *is* yet before us, because we have sought the LORD our God; we have sought *Him,* and He has given us rest on every side." So they built and prospered.

8 And Asa had an army of three hundred thousand from Judah who carried shields and spears, and from Benjamin two hundred and eighty thousand men who carried shields and drew [a]bows; all these *were* mighty men of [b]valor.

9 [a]Then Zerah the Ethiopian came out against them with an army of a million men and three hundred chariots, and he came to [b]Mareshah.

10 So Asa went out against him, and they set the troops in battle array in the Valley of Zephathah at Mareshah.

11 And Asa [a]cried out to the LORD his God, and said, "LORD, *it is* [b]nothing for You to help, whether with many or with those who have no power; help us, O LORD our God, for we rest on You, and [c]in Your name we go against this multitude. O LORD, You *are* our God; do not let man prevail against You!"

12 So the LORD [a]struck the Ethiopians before Asa and Judah, and the Ethiopians fled.

13 And Asa and the people who *were* with him pursued them to [a]Gerar. So the Ethiopians were overthrown, and they could not recover, for they were broken before the LORD and His army. And they carried away very much spoil.

14 Then they defeated all the cities around Gerar, for [a]the fear of the LORD came upon them; and they plundered all the cities, for there was exceedingly much spoil in them.

15 They also attacked the livestock enclosures, and carried off sheep and camels in abundance, and returned to Jerusalem.

The Reforms of Asa

15 Now [a]the Spirit of God came upon Azariah the son of Oded.

2 And he went out to meet Asa, and said to him: "Hear me, Asa, and all Judah and Benjamin. [a]The LORD *is* with you while you are with Him. [b]If you seek Him, He will be found by you; but [c]if you forsake Him, He will forsake you.

3 [a]"For a long time Israel *has been* without the true God, without a [b]teaching priest, and without [c]law;

4 "but [a]when in their trouble they turned to the LORD God of Israel, and sought Him, He was found by them.

5 "And in those times *there was* no peace to the one who went out, nor to the one who came

KJV

but great vexations *were* upon all the inhabitants of the countries.

6 [a]And nation was destroyed of nation, and city of city: for God did vex them with all adversity.

7 Be ye strong therefore, and let not your hands be weak: for your work shall be rewarded.

8 And when Asa heard these words, and the prophecy of Oded the prophet, he took courage, and put away the abominable idols out of all the land of Judah and Benjamin, and out of the cities [a]which he had taken from mount Ephraim, and renewed the altar of the LORD, that *was* before the porch of the LORD.

9 And he gathered all Judah and Benjamin, and [a]the strangers with them out of Ephraim and Manasseh, and out of Simeon: for they fell to him out of Israel in abundance, when they saw that the LORD his God *was* with him.

10 So they gathered themselves together at Jerusalem in the third month, in the fifteenth year of the reign of Asa.

11 [a]And they offered unto the LORD the same time, of the spoil *which* they had brought, seven hundred oxen and seven thousand sheep.

12 And they [a]entered into a covenant to seek the LORD God of their fathers with all their heart and with all their soul;

13 [a]That whosoever would not seek the LORD God of Israel [b]should be put to death, whether small or great, whether man or woman.

14 And they sware unto the LORD with a loud voice, and with shouting, and with trumpets, and with cornets.

15 And all Judah rejoiced at the oath: for they had sworn with all their heart, and [a]sought him with their whole desire; and he was found of them: and the LORD gave them [b]rest round about.

16 And also *concerning* [a]Maachah the mother of Asa the king, he removed her from *being* queen, because she had made an idol in a grove: and Asa cut down her idol, and stamped *it*, and burnt *it* at the brook Kidron.

17 But [a]the high places were not taken away out of Israel: nevertheless the heart of Asa was perfect all his days.

18 And he brought into the house of God the things that his father had dedicated, and that he himself had dedicated, silver, and gold, and vessels.

19 And there was no *more* war unto the five and thirtieth year of the reign of Asa.

Asa's Treaty with Syria
(1 Kin. 15:16–22)

16 In the six and thirtieth year of the reign of Asa [a]Baasha king of Israel came up against Judah, and built Ramah, [b]to the intent that he might let none go out or come in to Asa king of Judah.

2 Then Asa brought out silver and gold out of the treasures of the house of the LORD and of the king's house, and sent to Ben–hadad king of Syria, that dwelt at Damascus, saying,

3 *There is* a league between me and thee, as *there was* between my father and thy father: behold, I have sent thee silver and gold; go, break thy league with Baasha king of Israel, that he may depart from me.

4 And Ben–hadad hearkened unto king Asa, and sent the captains of his armies against the cities of Israel; and they smote Ijon, and Dan, and Abel–maim, and all the store cities of Naphtali.

5 And it came to pass, when Baasha heard *it*, that he left off building of Ramah, and let his work cease.

6 Then Asa the king took all Judah; and they carried away the stones of Ramah, and the timber thereof, wherewith Baasha was building; and he built therewith Geba and Mizpah.

---

6 [a]Matt. 24:7
8 [a]2 Chr. 13:19
9 [a]2 Chr. 11:16
11 [a]2 Chr. 14:13–15
12 [a]2 Kin. 23:3; 2 Chr. 23:16; 34:31; Neh. 10:29
13 [a]Ex. 22:20 [b]Deut. 13:5–15
15 [a]2 Chr. 15:2 [b]2 Chr. 14:7
16 [a]1 Kin. 15:2, 10, 13
17 [a]1 Kin. 15:14; 2 Chr. 14:3, 5

CHAPTER 16

1 [a]1 Kin. 15:17–22 [b]2 Chr. 15:9

*

15:8 So with MT, LXX; Syr., Vg. *Azariah the son of Oded* (cf. v. 1) **15:16** A Canaanite deity

---

NKJV

in, but great turmoil *was* on all the inhabitants of the lands.

6 [a]"So nation was destroyed by nation, and city by city, for God troubled them with every adversity.

7 "But you, be strong and do not let your hands be weak, for your work shall be rewarded!"

8 And when Asa heard these words and the prophecy of *Oded the prophet, he took courage, and removed the abominable idols from all the land of Judah and Benjamin and from the cities [a]which he had taken in the mountains of Ephraim; and he restored the altar of the LORD that *was* before the vestibule of the LORD.

9 Then he gathered all Judah and Benjamin, and [a]those who dwelt with them from Ephraim, Manasseh, and Simeon, for they came over to him in great numbers from Israel when they saw that the LORD his God was with him.

10 So they gathered together at Jerusalem in the third month, in the fifteenth year of the reign of Asa.

11 [a]And they offered to the LORD at that time seven hundred bulls and seven thousand sheep from the spoil they had brought.

12 Then they [a]entered into a covenant to seek the LORD God of their fathers with all their heart and with all their soul;

13 [a]and whoever would not seek the LORD God of Israel [b]was to be put to death, whether small or great, whether man or woman.

14 Then they took an oath before the LORD with a loud voice, with shouting and trumpets and rams' horns.

15 And all Judah rejoiced at the oath, for they had sworn with all their heart and [a]sought Him with all their soul; and He was found by them, and the LORD gave them [b]rest all around.

16 Also he removed [a]Maachah, the mother of Asa the king, from *being* queen mother, because she had made an obscene image of *Asherah; and Asa cut down her obscene image, then crushed and burned *it* by the Brook Kidron.

17 But [a]the high places were not removed from Israel. Nevertheless the heart of Asa was loyal all his days.

18 He also brought into the house of God the things that his father had dedicated and that he himself had dedicated: silver and gold and utensils.

19 And there was no war until the thirty-fifth year of the reign of Asa.

Asa's Treaty with Syria
(1 Kin. 15:16–22)

16 In the thirty-sixth year of the reign of Asa, [a]Baasha king of Israel came up against Judah and built Ramah, [b]that he might let none go out or come in to Asa king of Judah.

2 Then Asa brought silver and gold from the treasuries of the house of the LORD and of the king's house, and sent to Ben-Hadad king of Syria, who dwelt in Damascus, saying,

3 "*Let there be* a treaty between you and me, as there was between my father and your father. See, I have sent you silver and gold; come, break your treaty with Baasha king of Israel, so that he will withdraw from me."

4 So Ben-Hadad heeded King Asa, and sent the captains of his armies against the cities of Israel. They attacked Ijon, Dan, Abel Maim, and all the storage cities of Naphtali.

5 Now it happened, when Baasha heard *it*, that he stopped building Ramah and ceased his work.

6 Then King Asa took all Judah, and they carried away the stones of Ramah, which Baasha had used for building; and with them he built Geba and Mizpah.

KJV

Hanani's Message to Asa

7 And at that time [a]Hanani the seer came to Asa king of Judah, and said unto him, [b]Because thou hast relied on the king of Syria, and not relied on the LORD thy God, therefore is the host of the king of Syria escaped out of thine hand.

8 Were not [a]the Ethiopians and [b]the Lubims a huge host, with very many chariots and horsemen? yet, because thou didst rely on the LORD, he delivered them into thine [c]hand.

9 [a]For the eyes of the LORD run to and fro throughout the whole earth, to shew himself strong in the behalf of *them* whose heart *is* perfect toward him. Herein [b]thou hast done foolishly: therefore from henceforth [c]thou shalt have wars.

10 Then Asa was wroth with the seer, and [a]put him in a prison house; for *he was* in a rage with him because of this *thing.* And Asa oppressed *some* of the people the same time.

Illness and Death of Asa
(1 Kin. 15:23, 24)

11 [a]And, behold, the acts of Asa, first and last, lo, they *are* written in the book of the kings of Judah and Israel.

12 And Asa in the thirty and ninth year of his reign was diseased in his feet, until his disease *was* exceeding *great:* yet in his disease he [a]sought not to the LORD, but to the physicians.

13 [a]And Asa slept with his fathers, and died in the one and fortieth year of his reign.

14 And they buried him in his own sepulchres, which he had made for himself in the city of David, and laid him in the bed which was filled [a]with sweet odours and divers kinds *of spices* prepared by the apothecaries' art: and they made [b]a very great burning for him.

Jehoshaphat Reigns in Judah

17 And [a]Jehoshaphat his son reigned in his stead, and strengthened himself against Israel.

2 And he placed forces in all the fenced cities of Judah, and set garrisons in the land of [a]Judah, and in the cities of Ephraim, [b]which Asa his father had taken.

3 And the LORD was with Jehoshaphat, because he walked in the first ways of his father David, and sought not unto Baalim;

4 But sought to the *LORD* God of his father, and walked in his commandments, and not after [a]the doings of Israel.

5 Therefore the LORD stablished the kingdom in his hand; and all Judah [a]brought to Jehoshaphat presents; [b]and he had riches and honour in abundance.

6 And his heart was lifted up in the ways of the LORD: moreover [a]he took away the high places and groves out of Judah.

7 Also in the third year of his reign he sent to his princes, *even* to Ben–hail, and to Obadiah, and to Zechariah, and to Nethaneel, and to Michaiah, [a]to teach in the cities of Judah.

8 And with them *he sent* Levites, *even* Shemaiah, and Nethaniah, and Zebadiah, and Asahel, and Shemiramoth, and Jehonathan, and Adonijah, and Tobijah, and Tob–adonijah, Levites; and with them Elishama and Jehoram, priests.

9 [a]And they taught in Judah, and *had* the book of the law of the LORD with them, and went about throughout all the cities of Judah, and taught the people.

10 And [a]the fear of the LORD fell upon all the kingdoms of the lands that *were* round about Judah, so that they made no war against Jehoshaphat.

11 Also *some* of the Philistines [a]brought Jehoshaphat presents, and tribute silver; and the Arabians brought him flocks, seven thousand and

---

7 [a]1 Kin. 16:1; 2 Chr. 19:2 [b]2 Chr. 32:8–10; Ps. 118:9; [Is. 31:1; Jer. 17:5]
8 [a]2 Chr. 14:9 [b]2 Chr. 12:3 [c]2 Chr. 13:16, 18
9 [a]Job 34:21; [Prov. 5:21; 15:3; Jer. 16:17; 32:19]; Zech. 4:10 [b]1 Sam. 13:13 [c]1 Kin. 15:32
10 [a]2 Chr. 18:26; Jer. 20:2; Matt. 14:3
11 [a]1 Kin. 15:23, 24; 2 Chr. 14:2
12 [a][Jer. 17:5]
13 [a]1 Kin. 15:24
14 [a]Gen. 50:2; Mark 16:1; John 19:39, 40 [b]2 Chr. 21:19; Jer. 34:5

CHAPTER 17

1 [a]1 Kin. 15:24; 2 Chr. 20:31
2 [a]2 Chr. 11:5 [b]2 Chr. 15:8
4 [a]1 Kin. 12:28
5 [a]1 Sam. 10:27; 1 Kin. 10:25 [b]2 Chr. 18:1
6 [a]1 Kin. 22:43; 2 Chr. 15:17; 19:3; 20:33
7 [a]2 Chr. 15:3; 35:3
9 [a]Deut. 6:4–9; 2 Chr. 35:3; Neh. 8:3, 7
10 [a]Gen. 35:5; 2 Chr. 14:14
11 [a]2 Sam. 8:2; 2 Chr. 9:14; 26:8

*
17:4 LXX *the LORD God*

NKJV

Hanani's Message to Asa

7 And at that time [a]Hanani the seer came to Asa king of Judah, and said to him: [b]"Because you have relied on the king of Syria, and have not relied on the LORD your God, therefore the army of the king of Syria has escaped from your hand.

8 "Were [a]the Ethiopians and [b]the Lubim not a huge army with very many chariots and horsemen? Yet, because you relied on the LORD, He delivered them into your [c]hand.

9 [a]"For the eyes of the LORD run to and fro throughout the whole earth, to show Himself strong on behalf of *those* whose heart *is* loyal to Him. In this [b]you have done foolishly; therefore from now on [c]you shall have wars."

10 Then Asa was angry with the seer, and [a]put him in prison, for *he was* enraged at him because of this. And Asa oppressed *some* of the people at that time.

Illness and Death of Asa
(1 Kin. 15:23, 24)

11 [a]Note that the acts of Asa, first and last, are indeed written in the book of the kings of Judah and Israel.

12 And in the thirty-ninth year of his reign, Asa became diseased in his feet, and his malady was severe; yet in his disease he [a]did not seek the LORD, but the physicians.

13 [a]So Asa rested with his fathers; he died in the forty-first year of his reign.

14 They buried him in his own tomb, which he had made for himself in the City of David; and they laid him in the bed which was filled [a]with spices and various ingredients prepared in a mixture of ointments. They made [b]a very great burning for him.

Jehoshaphat Reigns in Judah

17 Then [a]Jehoshaphat his son reigned in his place, and strengthened himself against Israel.

2 And he placed troops in all the fortified cities of Judah, and set garrisons in the land of [a]Judah and in the cities of Ephraim [b]which Asa his father had taken.

3 Now the LORD was with Jehoshaphat, because he walked in the former ways of his father David; he did not seek the Baals,

4 but sought *the God of his father, and walked in His commandments and not according to [a]the acts of Israel.

5 Therefore the LORD established the kingdom in his hand; and all Judah [a]gave presents to Jehoshaphat, [b]and he had riches and honor in abundance.

6 And his heart took delight in the ways of the LORD; moreover [a]he removed the high places and wooden images from Judah.

7 Also in the third year of his reign he sent his leaders, Ben-Hail, Obadiah, Zechariah, Nethanel, and Michaiah, [a]to teach in the cities of Judah.

8 And with them *he sent* Levites: Shemaiah, Nethaniah, Zebadiah, Asahel, Shemiramoth, Jehonathan, Adonijah, Tobijah, and Tobadonijah—the Levites; and with them Elishama and Jehoram, the priests.

9 [a]So they taught in Judah, and *had* the Book of the Law of the LORD with them; they went throughout all the cities of Judah and taught the people.

10 And [a]the fear of the LORD fell on all the kingdoms of the lands that *were* around Judah, so that they did not make war against Jehoshaphat.

11 Also *some* of the Philistines [a]brought Jehoshaphat presents and silver as tribute; and the Arabians brought him flocks, seven thousand

KJV

seven hundred rams, and seven thousand and seven hundred he goats.

12 And Jehoshaphat waxed great exceedingly; and he built in Judah castles, and cities of store.

13 And he had much business in the cities of Judah: and the men of war, mighty men of valour, *were* in Jerusalem.

14 And these *are* the numbers of them according to the house of their fathers: Of Judah, the captains of thousands; Adnah the chief, and with him mighty men of valour three hundred thousand.

15 And next to him *was* Jehohanan the captain, and with him two hundred and fourscore thousand.

16 And next him *was* Amasiah the son of Zichri, [a]who willingly offered himself unto the LORD; and with him two hundred thousand mighty men of valour.

17 And of Benjamin; Eliada a mighty man of valour, and with him armed men with bow and shield two hundred thousand.

18 And next him *was* Jehozabad, and with him an hundred and fourscore thousand ready prepared for the war.

19 These waited on the king, beside [a]*those* whom the king put in the fenced cities throughout all Judah.

Micaiah Warns Ahab
(*1 Kin. 22:1–28*)

18 Now Jehoshaphat [a]had riches and honour in abundance, and [b]joined affinity with [c]Ahab.

2 [a]And after *certain* years he went down to Ahab to Samaria. And Ahab killed sheep and oxen for him in abundance, and for the people that *he had* with him, and persuaded him to go up *with him* to Ramoth–gilead.

3 And Ahab king of Israel said unto Jehoshaphat king of Judah, Wilt thou go with me to Ramoth–gilead? And he answered him, I *am* as thou *art*, and my people as thy people; and *we will be* with thee in the war.

4 And Jehoshaphat said unto the king of Israel, [a]Enquire, I pray thee, at the word of the LORD to day.

5 Therefore the king of Israel gathered together of prophets four hundred men, and said unto them, Shall we go to Ramoth–gilead to battle, or shall I forbear? And they said, Go up; for God will deliver *it* into the king's hand.

6 But Jehoshaphat said, *Is there* not here a prophet of the LORD besides, that we might enquire of [a]him?

7 And the king of Israel said unto Jehoshaphat, *There is* yet one man, by whom we may enquire of the LORD: but I hate him; for he never prophesied good unto me, but always evil: the same *is* Micaiah the son of Imla. And Jehoshaphat said, Let not the king say so.

8 And the king of Israel called for one *of his* officers, and said, Fetch quickly Micaiah the son of Imla.

9 And the king of Israel and Jehoshaphat king of Judah sat either of them on his throne, clothed in *their* robes, and they sat in a void place at the entering in of the gate of Samaria; and all the prophets prophesied before them.

10 And Zedekiah the son of Chenaanah had made him [a]horns of iron, and said, Thus saith the LORD, With these thou shalt push Syria until they be consumed.

11 And all the prophets prophesied so, saying, Go up to Ramoth–gilead, and prosper: for the LORD shall deliver *it* into the hand of the king.

12 And the messenger that went to call Micaiah spake to him, saying, Behold, the words of the prophets *declare* good to the king with one

16 [a]Judg. 5:2, 9; 1 Chr. 29:9
19 [a]2 Chr. 17:2

CHAPTER 18

1 [a]2 Chr. 17:5
[b]1 Kin. 22:44; 2 Kin. 8:18
[c]1 Kin. 22:40
2 [a][Ex. 23:2]; 1 Kin. 22:2
4 [a]1 Sam. 23:2, 4, 9; 2 Sam. 2:1
6 [a]2 Kin. 3:11
10 [a]Zech. 1:18–21

NKJV

seven hundred rams and seven thousand seven hundred male goats.

12 So Jehoshaphat became increasingly powerful, and he built fortresses and storage cities in Judah.

13 He had much property in the cities of Judah; and the men of war, mighty men of valor, *were* in Jerusalem.

14 These *are* their numbers, according to their fathers' houses. Of Judah, the captains of thousands: Adnah the captain, and with him three hundred thousand mighty men of valor;

15 and next to him *was* Jehohanan the captain, and with him two hundred and eighty thousand;

16 and next to him *was* Amasiah the son of Zichri, [a]who willingly offered himself to the LORD, and with him two hundred thousand mighty men of valor.

17 Of Benjamin: Eliada a mighty man of valor, and with him two hundred thousand men armed with bow and shield;

18 and next to him *was* Jehozabad, and with him one hundred and eighty thousand prepared for war.

19 These served the king, besides [a]those the king put in the fortified cities throughout all Judah.

Micaiah Warns Ahab
(*1 Kin. 22:1–28*)

18 Jehoshaphat [a]had riches and honor in abundance; and by marriage he [b]allied himself with [c]Ahab.

2 [a]After some years he went down to *visit* Ahab in Samaria; and Ahab killed sheep and oxen in abundance for him and the people who were with him, and persuaded him to go up *with him* to Ramoth Gilead.

3 So Ahab king of Israel said to Jehoshaphat king of Judah, "Will you go with me *against* Ramoth Gilead?" And he answered him, "I *am* as you *are*, and my people as your people; *we will be* with you in the war."

4 Also Jehoshaphat said to the king of Israel, [a]"Please inquire for the word of the LORD today."

5 Then the king of Israel gathered the prophets together, four hundred men, and said to them, "Shall we go to war against Ramoth Gilead, or shall I refrain?" So they said, "Go up, for God will deliver it into the king's hand."

6 But Jehoshaphat said, "*Is there* not still a prophet of the LORD here, that we may inquire of [a]Him?"*

7 So the king of Israel said to Jehoshaphat, "*There is* still one man by whom we may inquire of the LORD; but I hate him, because he never prophesies good concerning me, but always evil. He *is* Micaiah the son of Imla." And Jehoshaphat said, "Let not the king say such things!"

8 Then the king of Israel called one *of his* officers and said, "Bring Micaiah the son of Imla quickly!"

9 The king of Israel and Jehoshaphat king of Judah, clothed in *their* robes, sat each on his throne; and they sat at a threshing floor at the entrance of the gate of Samaria; and all the prophets prophesied before them.

10 Now Zedekiah the son of Chenaanah had made [a]horns of iron for himself; and he said, "Thus says the LORD: 'With these you shall gore the Syrians until they are destroyed.' "

11 And all the prophets prophesied so, saying, "Go up to Ramoth Gilead and prosper, for the LORD will deliver *it* into the king's hand."

12 Then the messenger who had gone to call Micaiah spoke to him, saying, "Now listen, the words of the prophets with one accord encourage

* 18:6 Or *him*

KJV

assent; let thy word therefore, I pray thee, be like one of their's, and speak thou good.

13 And Micaiah said, *As* the LORD liveth, [a]even what my God saith, that will I speak.

14 And when he was come to the king, the king said unto him, Micaiah, shall we go to Ramoth–gilead to battle, or shall I forbear? And he said, Go ye up, and prosper, and they shall be delivered into your hand.

15 And the king said to him, How many times shall I adjure thee that thou say nothing but the truth to me in the name of the LORD?

16 Then he said, I did see all Israel [a]scattered upon the mountains, as sheep that have no [b]shepherd: and the LORD said, These have no master; let them return *therefore* every man to his house in peace.

17 And the king of Israel said to Jehoshaphat, Did I not tell thee *that* he would not prophesy good unto me, but evil?

18 Again he said, Therefore hear the word of the LORD; I saw the LORD sitting upon his [a]throne, and all the host of heaven standing on his right hand and *on* his left.

19 And the LORD said, Who shall entice Ahab king of Israel, that he may go up and fall at Ramoth–gilead? And one spake saying after this manner, and another saying after that manner.

20 Then there came out a [a]spirit, and stood before the LORD, and said, I will entice him. And the LORD said unto him, Wherewith?

21 And he said, I will go out, and be a lying spirit in the mouth of all his prophets. And *the LORD* said, Thou shalt entice *him,* and thou shalt also prevail: go out, and do *even* so.

22 Now therefore, behold, [a]the LORD hath put a lying spirit in the mouth of these thy prophets, and the LORD hath spoken evil against thee.

23 Then Zedekiah the son of Chenaanah came near, and [a]smote Micaiah upon the cheek, and said, Which way went the Spirit of the LORD from me to speak unto thee?

24 And Micaiah said, Behold, thou shalt see on that day when thou shalt go into an inner chamber to hide thyself.

25 Then the king of Israel said, Take ye Micaiah, and carry him back to Amon the governor of the city, and to Joash the king's son;

26 And say, Thus saith the king, [a]Put this *fellow* in the prison, and feed him with bread of affliction and with water of affliction, until I return in peace.

27 And Micaiah said, If thou certainly return in peace, *then* hath not the LORD spoken by [a]me. And he said, Hearken, all ye people.

Ahab Dies in Battle
(1 Kin. 22:29–40)

28 So the king of Israel and Jehoshaphat the king of Judah went up to Ramoth–gilead.

29 And the king of Israel said unto Jehoshaphat, I will [a]disguise myself, and will go to the battle; but put thou on thy robes. So the king of Israel disguised himself; and they went to the battle.

30 Now the king of Syria had commanded the captains of the chariots that *were* with him, saying, Fight ye not with small or great, save only with the king of Israel.

31 And it came to pass, when the captains of the chariots saw Jehoshaphat, that they said, It *is* the king of Israel. Therefore they compassed about him to fight: but Jehoshaphat [a]cried out, and the LORD helped him; and God moved them *to depart* from him.

32 For it came to pass, that, when the captains of the chariots perceived that it was not the king of Israel, they turned back again from pursuing him.

33 And a *certain* man drew a bow at a venture, and smote the king of Israel between the joints of the harness: therefore he said to his char-

13 [a]Num. 22:18–20, 35; 23:12, 26; 1 Kin. 22:14
16 [a][Jer. 23:1–8; 31:10] [b]Num. 27:17; 1 Kin. 22:17; [Ezek. 34:5–8]; Matt. 9:36; Mark 6:34
18 [a]Is. 6:1–5; Dan. 7:9, 10
20 [a]Job 1:6; 2 Thess. 2:9
22 [a]Job 12:16, 17; Is. 19:12–14; Ezek. 14:9
23 [a]Jer. 20:2; Mark 14:65; Acts 23:2
26 [a]2 Chr. 16:10
27 [a]Deut. 18:22
29 [a]2 Chr. 35:22
31 [a]2 Chr. 13:14, 15

NKJV

the king. Therefore please let your word be like *the word of* one of them, and speak encouragement."

13 And Micaiah said, "*As* the LORD lives, [a]whatever my God says, that I will speak."

14 Then he came to the king; and the king said to him, "Micaiah, shall we go to war against Ramoth Gilead, or shall I refrain?" And he said, "Go and prosper, and they shall be delivered into your hand!"

15 So the king said to him, "How many times shall I make you swear that you tell me nothing but the truth in the name of the LORD?"

16 Then he said, "I saw all Israel [a]scattered on the mountains, as sheep that have no [b]shepherd. And the LORD said, 'These have no master. Let each return to his house in peace.' "

17 And the king of Israel said to Jehoshaphat, "Did I not tell you he would not prophesy good concerning me, but evil?"

18 Then *Micaiah* said, "Therefore hear the word of the LORD: I saw the LORD sitting on His [a]throne, and all the host of heaven standing on His right hand and His left.

19 "And the LORD said, 'Who will persuade Ahab king of Israel to go up, that he may fall at Ramoth Gilead?' So one spoke in this manner, and another spoke in that manner.

20 "Then a [a]spirit came forward and stood before the LORD, and said, 'I will persuade him.' The LORD said to him, 'In what way?'

21 "So he said, 'I will go out and be a lying spirit in the mouth of all his prophets.' And *the LORD* said, 'You shall persuade *him* and also prevail; go out and do so.'

22 "Therefore look! [a]The LORD has put a lying spirit in the mouth of these prophets of yours, and the LORD has declared disaster against you."

23 Then Zedekiah the son of Chenaanah went near and [a]struck Micaiah on the cheek, and said, "Which way did the spirit from the LORD go from me to speak to you?"

24 And Micaiah said, "Indeed you shall see on that day when you go into an inner chamber to hide!"

25 Then the king of Israel said, "Take Micaiah, and return him to Amon the governor of the city and to Joash the king's son;

26 "and say, 'Thus says the king: [a]"Put this *fellow* in prison, and feed him with bread of affliction and water of affliction, until I return in peace." ' "

27 But Micaiah said, "If you ever return in peace, the LORD has not spoken by [a]me." And he said, "Take heed, all you people!"

Ahab Dies in Battle
(1 Kin. 22:29–40)

28 So the king of Israel and Jehoshaphat the king of Judah went up to Ramoth Gilead.

29 And the king of Israel said to Jehoshaphat, "I will [a]disguise myself and go into battle; but you put on your robes." So the king of Israel disguised himself, and they went into battle.

30 Now the king of Syria had commanded the captains of the chariots who *were* with him, saying, "Fight with no one small or great, but only with the king of Israel."

31 So it was, when the captains of the chariots saw Jehoshaphat, that they said, "It *is* the king of Israel!" Therefore they surrounded him to attack; but Jehoshaphat [a]cried out, and the LORD helped him, and God diverted them from him.

32 For so it was, when the captains of the chariots saw that it was not the king of Israel, that they turned back from pursuing him.

33 Now a certain man drew a bow at random, and struck the king of Israel between the joints of his armor. So he said to the driver of his chariot,

KJV

iot man, Turn thine hand, that thou mayest carry me out of the host; for I am wounded.

34 And the battle increased that day: howbeit the king of Israel stayed *himself* up in *his* chariot against the Syrians until the even: and about the time of the sun going down he died.

19 And Jehoshaphat the king of Judah returned to his house in peace to Jerusalem.

2 And Jehu the son of Hanani [a]the seer went out to meet him, and said to king Jehoshaphat, Shouldest thou help the ungodly, and [b]love them that hate the LORD? therefore *is* [c]wrath upon thee from before the LORD.

3 Nevertheless there are [a]good things found in thee, in that thou hast taken away the groves out of the land, and hast [b]prepared thine heart to seek God.

The Reforms of Jehoshaphat

4 And Jehoshaphat dwelt at Jerusalem: and he went out again through the people from Beer–sheba to mount Ephraim, and brought them back unto the LORD God of their [a]fathers.

5 And he set [a]judges in the land throughout all the fenced cities of Judah, city by city,

6 And said to the judges, Take heed what ye do: for [a]ye judge not for man, but for the LORD, [b]who *is* with you in the judgment.

7 Wherefore now let the fear of the LORD be upon you; take heed and do *it:* for [a]*there is* no iniquity with the LORD our God, nor [b]respect of persons, nor taking of gifts.

8 Moreover in Jerusalem did Jehoshaphat [a]set of the Levites, and *of* the priests, and of the chief of the fathers of Israel, for the judgment of the LORD, and for controversies, when they returned to Jerusalem.

9 And he charged them, saying, Thus shall ye do [a]in the fear of the LORD, faithfully, and with a perfect heart.

10 [a]And what cause soever shall come to you of your brethren that dwell in their cities, between blood and blood, between law and commandment, statutes and judgments, ye shall even warn them that they trespass not against the LORD, and *so* [b]wrath come upon [c]you, and upon your brethren: this do, and ye shall not trespass.

11 And, behold, [a]Amariah the chief priest *is* over you [b]in all matters of the LORD; and Zebadiah the son of Ishmael, the ruler of the house of Judah, for all the king's matters: also the Levites *shall be* officers before you. Deal courageously, and the LORD shall be [c]with the good.

Ammon, Moab, and Mount Seir Defeated

20 It came to pass after this also, *that* the children of [a]Moab, and the children of [b]Ammon, and with them *other* beside the [c]Ammonites, came against Jehoshaphat to battle.

2 Then there came some that told Jehoshaphat, saying, There cometh a great multitude against thee from beyond the sea on this side Syria; and, behold, they *be* [a]in Hazazon–tamar, which *is* [b]En–gedi.

3 And Jehoshaphat feared, and set himself to [a]seek the LORD, and [b]proclaimed a fast throughout all Judah.

4 And Judah gathered themselves together, to ask [a]*help* of the LORD: even out of all the cities of Judah they came to seek the LORD.

5 And Jehoshaphat stood in the congregation of Judah and Jerusalem, in the house of the LORD, before the new court,

6 And said, O LORD God of our fathers, *art* not thou [a]God in heaven? and [b]rulest *not* thou over all the kingdoms of the heathen? and [c]in thine hand *is there not* power and might, so that none is able to withstand thee?

7 *Art* not thou [a]our God, *who* [b]didst drive

CHAPTER 19

2 [a]1 Sam. 9:9; 1 Kin. 16:1; 2 Chr. 20:34 [b]Ps. 139:21 [c]2 Chr. 32:25
3 [a]2 Chr. 17:4, 6 [b]2 Chr. 30:19
4 [a]2 Chr. 15:8–13
5 [a][Deut. 16:18–20]
6 [a][Lev. 19:15; Deut. 1:17]; Ps. 58:1 [b]Ps. 82:1; [Eccl. 5:8]
7 [a][Gen. 18:25; Deut. 32:4]; Rom. 9:17 [b][Deut. 10:17, 18; Job 34:19]; Acts 10:34; Rom. 2:11; Gal. 2:6; [Eph. 6:9; Col. 3:25]
8 [a]Deut. 16:18; 2 Chr. 17:8
9 [a][2 Sam. 23:3]
10 [a]Deut. 17:8 [b]Num. 16:46 [c][Ezek. 3:18]
11 [a]Ezra 7:3 [b]1 Chr. 26:30 [c][2 Chr. 15:2; 20:17]

CHAPTER 20

1 [a]1 Chr. 18:2 [b]1 Chr. 19:15 [c]2 Chr. 26:7
2 [a]Gen. 14:7 [b]Josh. 15:62
3 [a]2 Chr. 19:3 [b]1 Sam. 7:6; Ezra 8:21; Jer. 36:9; Jon. 3:5
4 [a]2 Chr. 14:11
6 [a]Deut. 4:39; Josh. 2:11; [1 Kin. 8:23]; Matt. 6:9 [b]Ps. 22:28; 47:2, 8; Dan. 4:17, 25, 32 [c]1 Chr. 29:12; 2 Chr. 25:8; Ps. 62:11; Matt. 6:13
7 [a]Gen. 13:14–17; 17:7; Ex. 6:7 [b]Ps. 44:2

*

19:8 LXX, Vg. *for the inhabitants of Jerusalem*
20:1 So with MT, Vg.; LXX *Meunites* (cf. 2 Chr. 26:7)
20:2 So with MT, LXX, Vg.; Heb. mss., Old Lat. *Edom*

NKJV

"Turn around and take me out of the battle, for I am wounded."

34 The battle increased that day, and the king of Israel propped *himself* up in *his* chariot facing the Syrians until evening; and about the time of sunset he died.

19 Then Jehoshaphat the king of Judah returned safely to his house in Jerusalem.

2 And Jehu the son of Hanani [a]the seer went out to meet him, and said to King Jehoshaphat, "Should you help the wicked and [b]love those who hate the LORD? Therefore the [c]wrath of the LORD *is* upon you.

3 "Nevertheless [a]good things are found in you, in that you have removed the wooden images from the land, and have [b]prepared your heart to seek God."

The Reforms of Jehoshaphat

4 So Jehoshaphat dwelt at Jerusalem; and he went out again among the people from Beersheba to the mountains of Ephraim, and brought them back to the LORD God of their [a]fathers.

5 Then he set [a]judges in the land throughout all the fortified cities of Judah, city by city,

6 and said to the judges, "Take heed to what you are doing, for [a]you do not judge for man but for the LORD, [b]who *is* with you in the judgment.

7 "Now therefore, let the fear of the LORD be upon you; take care and do *it,* for [a]*there is* no iniquity with the LORD our God, no [b]partiality, nor taking of bribes."

8 Moreover in Jerusalem, for the judgment of the LORD and for controversies, Jehoshaphat [a]appointed some of the Levites and priests, and some of the chief fathers of Israel, *when they returned to Jerusalem.

9 And he commanded them, saying, "Thus you shall act [a]in the fear of the LORD, faithfully and with a loyal heart:

10 [a]"Whatever case comes to you from your brethren who dwell in their cities, whether of bloodshed or offenses against law or commandment, against statutes or ordinances, you shall warn them, lest they trespass against the LORD and [b]wrath come upon [c]you and your brethren. Do this, and you will not be guilty.

11 "And take notice: [a]Amariah the chief priest *is* over you [b]in all matters of the LORD; and Zebadiah the son of Ishmael, the ruler of the house of Judah, for all the king's matters; also the Levites *will be* officials before you. Behave courageously, and the LORD will be [c]with the good."

Ammon, Moab, and Mount Seir Defeated

20 It happened after this *that* the people of [a]Moab with the people of [b]Ammon, and *others* with them besides the [c]Ammonites,* came to battle against Jehoshaphat.

2 Then some came and told Jehoshaphat, saying, "A great multitude is coming against you from beyond the sea, from *Syria; and they are [a]in Hazazon Tamar" (which *is* [b]En Gedi).

3 And Jehoshaphat feared, and set himself to [a]seek the LORD, and [b]proclaimed a fast throughout all Judah.

4 So Judah gathered together to ask [a]*help* from the LORD; and from all the cities of Judah they came to seek the LORD.

5 Then Jehoshaphat stood in the assembly of Judah and Jerusalem, in the house of the LORD, before the new court,

6 and said: "O LORD God of our fathers, *are* You not [a]God in heaven, and [b]do You *not* rule over all the kingdoms of the nations, and [c]in Your hand *is there not* power and might, so that no one is able to withstand You?

7 "*Are* You not [a]our God, *who* [b]drove out

KJV

out the inhabitants of this land before thy people
Israel, and gavest it to the seed of Abraham [c]thy
friend for ever?
8 And they dwelt therein, and have built
thee a sanctuary therein for thy name, saying,
9 [a]If, *when* evil cometh upon us, *as* the
sword, judgment, or pestilence, or famine, we
stand before this house, and in thy presence, (for
thy [b]name *is* in this house,) and cry unto thee in
our affliction, then thou wilt hear and help.
10 And now, behold, the children of Ammon
and Moab and mount Seir, whom thou [a]wouldest
not let Israel invade, when they came out of the
land of Egypt, but [b]they turned from them, and
destroyed them not;
11 Behold, *I say, how* they reward us, [a]to
come to cast us out of thy possession, which thou
hast given us to inherit.
12 O our God, wilt thou not [a]judge them? for
we have no might against this great company that
cometh against us; neither know we what to do:
but [b]our eyes *are* upon thee.
13 And all Judah stood before the LORD, with
their little ones, their wives, and their children.
14 Then upon Jahaziel the son of Zechariah,
the son of Benaiah, the son of Jeiel, the son of
Mattaniah, a Levite of the sons of Asaph, [a]came
the Spirit of the LORD in the midst of the
congregation;
15 And he said, Hearken ye, all Judah, and
ye inhabitants of Jerusalem, and thou king Jehoshaphat, Thus saith the LORD unto you, [a]Be not
afraid nor dismayed by reason of this great multitude; [b]for the battle *is* not your's, but God's.
16 To morrow go ye down against them: behold, they come up by the cliff of Ziz; and ye shall
find them at the end of the brook, before the wilderness of Jeruel.
17 [a]Ye shall not *need* to fight in this *battle:*
set yourselves, stand ye *still,* and see the salvation
of the LORD with you, O Judah and Jerusalem:
fear not, nor be dismayed; to morrow go out
against them: [b]for the LORD *will be* with you.
18 And Jehoshaphat [a]bowed his head with
his face to the ground: and all Judah and the inhabitants of Jerusalem fell before the LORD, worshipping the LORD.
19 And the Levites, of the children of the Kohathites, and of the children of the Korhites, stood
up to praise the LORD God of Israel with a loud
voice on high.
20 And they rose early in the morning, and
went forth into the wilderness of Tekoa: and as
they went forth, Jehoshaphat stood and said, Hear
me, O Judah, and ye inhabitants of Jerusalem;
[a]Believe in the LORD your God, so shall ye be
established; believe his prophets, so shall ye
prosper.
21 And when he had consulted with the people, he appointed singers unto the LORD, [a]and that
should praise the beauty of holiness, as they went
out before the army, and to say, [b]Praise the LORD;
[c]for his mercy *endureth* for ever.
22 And when they began to sing and to
praise, [a]the LORD set ambushments against the
children of Ammon, Moab, and mount Seir, which
were come against Judah; and they were smitten.
23 For the children of Ammon and Moab
stood up against the inhabitants of mount Seir,
utterly to slay and destroy *them:* and when they
had made an end of the inhabitants of Seir, [a]every
one helped to destroy another.
24 And when Judah came toward the watch
tower in the wilderness, they looked unto the multitude, and, behold, they *were* dead bodies fallen
to the earth, and none escaped.
25 And when Jehoshaphat and his people
came to take away the spoil of them, they found
among them in abundance both riches with the

7 [c]Is. 41:8; James 2:23
9 [a]1 Kin. 8:33, 37; 2 Chr. 6:28–30 [b]2 Chr. 6:20
10 [a]Deut. 2:4, 9, 19 [b]Num. 20:21
11 [a]Ps. 83:1–18
12 [a]Judg. 11:27; [1 Sam. 3:13] [b]Ps. 25:15; 121:1, 2; 123:1, 2; 141:8
14 [a]Num. 11:25, 26; 24:2; 2 Chr. 15:1; 24:20
15 [a]Ex. 14:13, 14; [Deut. 1:29, 30; 31:6, 8]; 2 Chr. 32:7 [b]1 Sam. 17:47; Zech. 14:3
17 [a]Ex. 14:13, 14 [b]Num. 14:9; [2 Chr. 15:2; 32:8]
18 [a]Ex. 4:31; 2 Chr. 7:3; 29:28
20 [a]Is. 7:9
21 [a]1 Chr. 16:29; Ps. 29:2; 90:17; 96:9; 110:3 [b]1 Chr. 16:34; Ps. 106:1; 136:1 [c]1 Chr. 16:41; 2 Chr. 5:13
22 [a]Judg. 7:22; 1 Sam. 14:20
23 [a]Judg. 7:22; 1 Sam. 14:20

NKJV

the inhabitants of this land before Your people
Israel, and gave it to the descendants of Abraham
[c]Your friend forever?
8 "And they dwell in it, and have built You
a sanctuary in it for Your name, saying,
9 [a]'If disaster comes upon us—sword, judgment, pestilence, or famine—we will stand before
this temple and in Your presence (for Your [b]name
is in this temple), and cry out to You in our affliction, and You will hear and save.'
10 "And now, here are the people of Ammon,
Moab, and Mount Seir—whom You [a]would not
let Israel invade when they came out of the land
of Egypt, but [b]they turned from them and did not
destroy them—
11 "here they are, rewarding us [a]by coming
to throw us out of Your possession which You
have given us to inherit.
12 "O our God, will You not [a]judge them?
For we have no power against this great multitude
that is coming against us; nor do we know what
to do, but [b]our eyes *are* upon You."
13 Now all Judah, with their little ones, their
wives, and their children, stood before the LORD.
14 Then [a]the Spirit of the LORD came upon
Jahaziel the son of Zechariah, the son of Benaiah,
the son of Jeiel, the son of Mattaniah, a Levite
of the sons of Asaph, in the midst of the assembly.
15 And he said, "Listen, all you of Judah and
you inhabitants of Jerusalem, and you, King Jehoshaphat! Thus says the LORD to you: [a]'Do not
be afraid nor dismayed because of this great multitude, [b]for the battle *is* not yours, but God's.
16 'Tomorrow go down against them. They
will surely come up by the Ascent of Ziz, and you
will find them at the end of the brook before the
Wilderness of Jeruel.
17 [a]'You will not *need* to fight in this *battle.*
Position yourselves, stand still and see the salvation of the LORD, who is with you, O Judah and
Jerusalem!' Do not fear or be dismayed; tomorrow
go out against them, [b]for the LORD *is* with you."
18 And Jehoshaphat [a]bowed his head with
his face to the ground, and all Judah and the inhabitants of Jerusalem bowed before the LORD,
worshiping the LORD.
19 Then the Levites of the children of the Kohathites and of the children of the Korahites stood
up to praise the LORD God of Israel with voices
loud and high.
20 So they rose early in the morning and
went out into the Wilderness of Tekoa; and as
they went out, Jehoshaphat stood and said, "Hear
me, O Judah and you inhabitants of Jerusalem:
[a]Believe in the LORD your God, and you shall be
established; believe His prophets, and you shall
prosper."
21 And when he had consulted with the people, he appointed those who should sing to the
LORD, [a]and who should praise the beauty of holiness, as they went out before the army and were
saying:

[b]"Praise the LORD,
[c]For His mercy *endures* forever."

22 Now when they began to sing and to
praise, [a]the LORD set ambushes against the people
of Ammon, Moab, and Mount Seir, who had come
against Judah; and they were defeated.
23 For the people of Ammon and Moab stood
up against the inhabitants of Mount Seir to utterly
kill and destroy *them.* And when they had made
an end of the inhabitants of Seir, [a]they helped to
destroy one another.
24 So when Judah came to a place overlook-
ing the wilderness, they looked toward the multitude; and there *were* their dead bodies, fallen on
the earth. No one had escaped.
25 When Jehoshaphat and his people came
to take away their spoil, they found among them
an abundance of valuables on the *dead bodies,

*———
20:25 A few Heb. mss., Old Lat., Vg. *garments;* LXX *armor*

KJV

dead bodies, and precious jewels, which they
stripped off for themselves, more than they could
carry away: and they were three days in gathering
of the spoil, it was so much.
26 And on the fourth day they assembled
themselves in the valley of Berachah; for there
they blessed the LORD: therefore the name of the
same place was called, The valley of Berachah,
unto this day.
27 Then they returned, every man of Judah
and Jerusalem, and Jehoshaphat in the forefront
of them, to go again to Jerusalem with joy; for
the LORD had [a]made them to rejoice over their
enemies.
28 And they came to Jerusalem with psalteries and harps and trumpets unto the house of the
LORD.
29 And [a]the fear of God was on all the kingdoms of *those* countries, when they had heard
that the LORD fought against the enemies of Israel.
30 So the realm of Jehoshaphat was quiet:
for his [a]God gave him rest round about.

The End of Jehoshaphat's Reign
(1 Kin. 22:41–50)

31 [a]And Jehoshaphat reigned over Judah: *he*
was thirty and five years old when he began to
reign, and he reigned twenty and five years in
Jerusalem. And his mother's name *was* Azubah
the daughter of Shilhi.
32 And he walked in the way of [a]Asa his father, and departed not from it, doing *that which*
was right in the sight of the LORD.
33 Howbeit [a]the high places were not taken
away: for as yet the people had not [b]prepared
their hearts unto the God of their fathers.
34 Now the rest of the acts of Jehoshaphat,
first and last, behold, they *are* written in the book
of Jehu the son of Hanani, [a]who *is* mentioned in
the book of the kings of Israel.
35 And after this [a]did Jehoshaphat king of
Judah join himself with Ahaziah king of Israel,
[b]who did very [c]wickedly:
36 And he joined himself with him [a]to make
ships to go to Tarshish: and they made the ships
in Ezion–gaber.
37 Then Eliezer the son of Dodavah of Mareshah prophesied against Jehoshaphat, saying,
Because thou hast joined thyself with Ahaziah,
the LORD hath broken thy works. [a]And the ships
were broken, that they were not able to go [b]to
Tarshish.

Jehoram Reigns in Judah
(1 Kin. 22:50; 2 Kin. 8:16–24)

21 Now [a]Jehoshaphat slept with his fathers,
and was buried with his fathers in the city
of David. And Jehoram his son reigned in his
stead.
2 And he had brethren the sons of Jehoshaphat, Azariah, and Jehiel, and Zechariah,
and Azariah, and Michael, and Shephatiah: all
these *were* the sons of Jehoshaphat king of
Israel.
3 And their father gave them great gifts of
silver, and of gold, and of precious things, with
fenced cities in Judah: but the kingdom gave he
to Jehoram; because he *was* the firstborn.
4 Now when Jehoram was risen up to the
kingdom of his father, he strengthened himself,
and slew all his brethren with the sword, and *di-*
vers also of the princes of Israel.
5 [a]Jehoram *was* thirty and two years old
when he began to reign, and he reigned eight
years in Jerusalem.
6 And he walked in the way of the kings
of Israel, like as did the house of Ahab: for he
had the daughter of [a]Ahab to wife: and he
wrought *that which was* evil in the eyes of the
LORD.
7 Howbeit the LORD would not destroy the
house of David, because of the [a]covenant that he

27 [a]Neh. 12:43
29 [a]2 Chr. 14:14; 17:10
30 [a]1 Kin. 22:41–43; 2 Chr. 14:6, 7; 15:15; Job 34:29
31 [a][1 Kin. 22:41–43]
32 [a]2 Chr. 14:2
33 [a]2 Chr. 15:17; 17:6 [b]2 Chr. 12:14; 19:3
34 [a]1 Kin. 16:1, 7
35 [a]2 Chr. 18:1 [b]1 Kin. 22:48–53 [c][2 Chr. 19:2]
36 [a]1 Kin. 9:26; 10:22
37 [a]1 Kin. 22:48 [b]2 Chr. 9:21

CHAPTER 21

1 [a]1 Kin. 22:50
5 [a]2 Kin. 8:17–22
6 [a]2 Chr. 18:1
7 [a]2 Sam. 7:8–17

*

20:26 Lit. *Blessing*

NKJV

and precious jewelry, which they stripped off for
themselves, more than they could carry away; and
they were three days gathering the spoil because
there was so much.
26 And on the fourth day they assembled in
the Valley of *Berachah, for there they blessed
the LORD; therefore the name of that place was
called The Valley of Berachah until this day.
27 Then they returned, every man of Judah
and Jerusalem, with Jehoshaphat in front of them,
to go back to Jerusalem with joy, for the LORD
had [a]made them rejoice over their enemies.
28 So they came to Jerusalem, with stringed
instruments and harps and trumpets, to the house
of the LORD.
29 And [a]the fear of God was on all the kingdoms of *those* countries when they heard that the
LORD had fought against the enemies of Israel.
30 Then the realm of Jehoshaphat was quiet,
for his [a]God gave him rest all around.

The End of Jehoshaphat's Reign
(1 Kin. 22:41–50)

31 [a]So Jehoshaphat was king over Judah. *He*
was thirty-five years old when he became king,
and he reigned twenty-five years in Jerusalem.
His mother's name *was* Azubah the daughter of
Shilhi.
32 And he walked in the way of his father
[a]Asa, and did not turn aside from it, doing *what*
was right in the sight of the LORD.
33 Nevertheless [a]the high places were not
taken away, for as yet the people had not [b]di-
rected their hearts to the God of their fathers.
34 Now the rest of the acts of Jehoshaphat,
first and last, indeed they *are* written in the book
of Jehu the son of Hanani, [a]which *is* mentioned
in the book of the kings of Israel.
35 After this [a]Jehoshaphat king of Judah allied himself with Ahaziah king of Israel, [b]who
acted very [c]wickedly.
36 And he allied himself with him [a]to make
ships to go to Tarshish, and they made the ships
in Ezion Geber.
37 But Eliezer the son of Dodavah of Mareshah prophesied against Jehoshaphat, saying,
"Because you have allied yourself with Ahaziah,
the LORD has destroyed your works." [a]Then the
ships were wrecked, so that they were not able
to go [b]to Tarshish.

Jehoram Reigns in Judah
(1 Kin. 22:50; 2 Kin. 8:16–24)

21 And [a]Jehoshaphat rested with his fathers,
and was buried with his fathers in the City
of David. Then Jehoram his son reigned in his
place.
2 He had brothers, the sons of Jehoshaphat:
Azariah, Jehiel, Zechariah, Azaryahu, Michael,
and Shephatiah; all these *were* the sons of Jehoshaphat king of Israel.
3 Their father gave them great gifts of silver
and gold and precious things, with fortified cities
in Judah; but he gave the kingdom to Jehoram,
because he *was* the firstborn.
4 Now when Jehoram was established over
the kingdom of his father, he strengthened himself and killed all his brothers with the sword,
and also *others* of the princes of Israel.
5 [a]Jehoram *was* thirty-two years old when
he became king, and he reigned eight years in
Jerusalem.
6 And he walked in the way of the kings
of Israel, just as the house of Ahab had done, for
he had the daughter of [a]Ahab as a wife; and he
did evil in the sight of the LORD.
7 Yet the LORD would not destroy the house
of David, because of the [a]covenant that He had

KJV

had made with David, and as he promised to give a light to him and to his [b]sons for ever.

8 [a]In his days the Edomites revolted from under the dominion of Judah, and made themselves a king.

9 Then Jehoram went forth with his princes, and all his chariots with him: and he rose up by night, and smote the Edomites which compassed him in, and the captains of the chariots.

10 So the Edomites revolted from under the hand of Judah unto this day. The same time *also* did Libnah revolt from under his hand; because he had forsaken the LORD God of his fathers.

11 Moreover he made high places in the mountains of Judah, and caused the inhabitants of Jerusalem to [a]commit fornication, and compelled Judah *thereto.*

12 And there came a writing to him from Elijah the prophet, saying, Thus saith the LORD God of David thy father, Because thou hast not walked in the ways of Jehoshaphat thy father, nor in the ways of Asa king of Judah,

13 But hast walked in the way of the kings of Israel, and hast [a]made Judah and the inhabitants of Jerusalem to [b]go a whoring, like to the [c]whoredoms of the house of Ahab, and also hast [d]slain thy brethren of thy father's house, *which were* better than thyself:

14 Behold, with a great plague will the LORD smite thy people, and thy children, and thy wives, and all thy goods:

15 And thou *shalt have* great sickness by [a]disease of thy bowels, until thy bowels fall out by reason of the sickness day by day.

16 Moreover the [a]LORD [b]stirred up against Jehoram the spirit of the Philistines, and of the [c]Arabians, that *were* near the Ethiopians:

17 And they came up into Judah, and brake into it, and carried away all the substance that was found in the king's house, and [a]his sons also, and his wives; so that there was never a son left him, save Jehoahaz, the youngest of his sons.

18 And after all this the LORD smote him [a]in his bowels with an incurable disease.

19 And it came to pass, that in process of time, after the end of two years, his bowels fell out by reason of his sickness: so he died of sore diseases. And his people made no burning for him, like [a]the burning of his fathers.

20 Thirty and two years old was he when he began to reign, and he reigned in Jerusalem eight years, and departed without being desired. Howbeit they buried him in the city of David, but not in the sepulchres of the kings.

Ahaziah Reigns in Judah
(2 Kin. 8:25–29; 9:14–16, 27–29)

22 And the inhabitants of Jerusalem made [a]Ahaziah his youngest son king in his stead: for the band of men that came with the [b]Arabians to the camp had slain all the [c]eldest. So Ahaziah the son of Jehoram king of Judah reigned.

2 Forty and two years old *was* Ahaziah when he began to reign, and he reigned one year in Jerusalem. His mother's name also *was* [a]Athaliah the daughter of Omri.

3 He also walked in the ways of the house of Ahab: for his mother was his counsellor to do wickedly.

4 Wherefore he did evil in the sight of the LORD like the house of Ahab: for they were his counsellors after the death of his father to his destruction.

5 He walked also after their counsel, and went with Jehoram the son of Ahab king of Israel

---

7 [b]1 Kin. 11:36; 2 Kin. 8:19; Ps. 132:11
8 [a]2 Kin. 8:20; 14:7, 10; 2 Chr. 25:14, 19
11 [a][Lev. 20:5]
13 [a]2 Chr. 21:11 [b][Ex. 34:15]; Deut. 31:16 [c]1 Kin. 16:31–33; 2 Kin. 9:22 [d]1 Kin. 2:32; 2 Chr. 21:4
15 [a]2 Chr. 21:18, 19
16 [a]2 Chr. 33:11; [Jer. 51:11] [b]1 Kin. 11:14, 23 [c]2 Chr. 17:11
17 [a]2 Chr. 24:7
18 [a]2 Chr. 13:20; 21:15; Acts 12:23
19 [a]2 Chr. 16:14

CHAPTER 22

1 [a]2 Chr. 21:17; 22:6 [b]2 Chr. 21:16 [c]2 Chr. 21:17
2 [a]2 Chr. 21:6

*

21:17 *Ahaziah* or *Azariah,* 2 Chr. 22:1
22:2 *twenty-two,* 2 Kin. 8:26
22:5 *Joram,* v. 7; 2 Kin. 8:28

NKJV

made with David, and since He had promised to give a lamp to him and to his [b]sons forever.

8 [a]In his days Edom revolted against Judah's authority, and made a king over themselves.

9 So Jehoram went out with his officers, and all his chariots with him. And he rose by night and attacked the Edomites who had surrounded him and the captains of the chariots.

10 Thus Edom has been in revolt against Judah's authority to this day. At that time Libnah revolted against his rule, because he had forsaken the LORD God of his fathers.

11 Moreover he made high places in the mountains of Judah, and caused the inhabitants of Jerusalem to [a]commit harlotry, and led Judah astray.

12 And a letter came to him from Elijah the prophet, saying,

Thus says the LORD God of your father David:
Because you have not walked in the ways of Jehoshaphat your father, or in the ways of Asa king of Judah,
13 but have walked in the way of the kings of Israel, and have [a]made Judah and the inhabitants of Jerusalem to [b]play the harlot like the [c]harlotry of the house of Ahab, and also have [d]killed your brothers, those of your father's household, *who were* better than yourself,
14 behold, the LORD will strike your people with a serious affliction—your children, your wives, and all your possessions;
15 and you *will become* very sick with a [a]disease of your intestines, until your intestines come out by reason of the sickness, day by day.

16 Moreover the [a]LORD [b]stirred up against Jehoram the spirit of the Philistines and the [c]Arabians who *were* near the Ethiopians.

17 And they came up into Judah and invaded it, and carried away all the possessions that were found in the king's house, and also [a]his sons and his wives, so that there was not a son left to him except *Jehoahaz, the youngest of his sons.

18 After all this the LORD struck him [a]in his intestines with an incurable disease.

19 Then it happened in the course of time, after the end of two years, that his intestines came out because of his sickness; so he died in severe pain. And his people made no burning for him, like [a]the burning for his fathers.

20 He was thirty-two years old when he became king. He reigned in Jerusalem eight years and, to no one's sorrow, departed. However they buried him in the City of David, but not in the tombs of the kings.

Ahaziah Reigns in Judah
(2 Kin. 8:25–29; 9:14–16, 27–29)

22 Then the inhabitants of Jerusalem made [a]Ahaziah his youngest son king in his place, for the raiders who came with the [b]Arabians into the camp had killed all the [c]older *sons.* So Ahaziah the son of Jehoram, king of Judah, reigned.

2 Ahaziah *was* *forty-two years old when he became king, and he reigned one year in Jerusalem. His mother's name *was* [a]Athaliah the granddaughter of Omri.

3 He also walked in the ways of the house of Ahab, for his mother advised him to do wickedly.

4 Therefore he did evil in the sight of the LORD, like the house of Ahab; for they were his counselors after the death of his father, to his destruction.

5 He also followed their advice, and went with *Jehoram the son of Ahab king of Israel to

KJV

to war against Hazael king of Syria at Ramoth–
gilead: and the Syrians smote Joram.
6 [a]And he returned to be healed in Jezreel
because of the wounds which were given him at
Ramah, when he fought with Hazael king of Syria.
And Azariah the son of Jehoram king of Judah
went down to see Jehoram the son of Ahab at
Jezreel, because he was sick.
7 And the destruction of Ahaziah [a]was of
God by coming to Joram: for when he was come,
he [b]went out with Jehoram against Jehu the son
of Nimshi, [c]whom the LORD had anointed to cut
off the house of Ahab.
8 And it came to pass, that, when Jehu was
[a]executing judgment upon the house of Ahab, and
[b]found the princes of Judah, and the sons of the
brethren of Ahaziah, that ministered to Ahaziah,
he slew them.
9 [a]And he sought Ahaziah: and they caught
him, (for he was hid in Samaria,) and brought
him to Jehu: and when they had slain him, they
buried him: Because, said they, he *is* the son of
[b]Jehoshaphat, who [c]sought the LORD with all his
heart. So the house of Ahaziah had no power to
keep still the kingdom.

Athaliah Reigns in Judah
(*2 Kin. 11:1–3*)

10 [a]But when Athaliah the mother of Ahaziah saw that her son was dead, she arose and
destroyed all the seed royal of the house of Judah.
11 But Jehoshabeath, the daughter of the
king, took [a]Joash the son of Ahaziah, and stole
him from among the king's sons that were slain,
and put him and his nurse in a bedchamber. So
Jehoshabeath, the daughter of king Jehoram, the
wife of Jehoiada the priest, (for she was the sister
of Ahaziah,) hid him from Athaliah, so that she
slew him not.
12 And he was with them hid in the house
of God six years: and Athaliah reigned over the
land.

Joash Crowned King of Judah
(*2 Kin. 11:4–12*)

23 And [a]in the seventh year [b]Jehoiada
strengthened himself, and took the captains
of hundreds, Azariah the son of Jeroham, and Ishmael the son of Jehohanan, and Azariah the son
of [c]Obed, and Maaseiah the son of Adaiah, and
Elishaphat the son of Zichri, into covenant with
him.
2 And they went about in Judah, and gathered the Levites out of all the cities of Judah, and
the [a]chief of the fathers of Israel, and they came
to Jerusalem.
3 And all the congregation made a covenant
with the king in the house of God. And he said
unto them, Behold, the king's son shall reign, as
the LORD hath [a]said of the sons of David.
4 This *is* the thing that ye shall do; A third
part of you [a]entering on the sabbath, of the priests
and of the Levites, *shall be* porters of the
doors;
5 And a third part *shall be* at the king's
house; and a third part at the gate of the foundation: and all the people *shall be* in the courts of
the house of the LORD.
6 But let none come into the house of the
LORD, save the priests, and [a]they that minister of
the Levites; they shall go in, for they *are* holy:
but all the people shall keep the watch of the
LORD.
7 And the Levites shall compass the king
round about, every man with his weapons in his
hand; and whosoever *else* cometh into the house,
he shall be put to death: but be ye with the king
when he cometh in, and when he goeth out.
8 So the Levites and all Judah did according
to all things that Jehoiada the priest had commanded, and took every man his men that were
to come in on the sabbath, with them that were

---

6 [a]2 Kin. 9:15
7 [a]Judg. 14:4; 1 Kin. 12:15; 2 Chr. 10:15 [b]2 Kin. 9:21–24 [c]2 Kin. 9:6, 7
8 [a]2 Kin. 9:22–24 [b]2 Kin. 10:10–14; Hos. 1:4
9 [a][2 Kin. 9:27] [b]1 Kin. 15:24 [c]2 Chr. 17:4; 20:3, 4
10 [a]2 Kin. 11:1–3
11 [a]2 Kin. 12:18

CHAPTER 23
1 [a]2 Kin. 11:4 [b]2 Kin. 12:2 [c]1 Chr. 2:37, 38
2 [a]Ezra 1:5
3 [a]2 Sam. 7:12; 1 Kin. 2:4; 9:5; 2 Chr. 6:16; 7:18; 21:7
4 [a]1 Chr. 9:25
6 [a]1 Chr. 23:28–32

NKJV

war against Hazael king of Syria at Ramoth Gilead; and the Syrians wounded Joram.
6 [a]Then he returned to Jezreel to recover
from the wounds which he had received at Ramah, when he fought against Hazael king of
Syria. And *Azariah the son of Jehoram, king of
Judah, went down to see Jehoram the son of Ahab
in Jezreel, because he was sick.
7 His going to Joram [a]was God's occasion
for Ahaziah's downfall; for when he arrived, [b]he
went out with Jehoram against Jehu the son of
Nimshi, [c]whom the LORD had anointed to cut off
the house of Ahab.
8 And it happened, when Jehu was [a]execut-
ing judgment on the house of Ahab, and [b]found
the princes of Judah and the sons of Ahaziah's
brothers who served Ahaziah, that he killed them.
9 [a]Then he searched for Ahaziah; and they
caught him (he was hiding in Samaria), and
brought him to Jehu. When they had killed him,
they buried him, "because," they said, "he is the
son of [b]Jehoshaphat, who [c]sought the LORD with
all his heart." So the house of Ahaziah had no
one to assume power over the kingdom.

Athaliah Reigns in Judah
(*2 Kin. 11:1–3*)

10 [a]Now when Athaliah the mother of Ahaziah saw that her son was dead, she arose and
destroyed all the royal heirs of the house of Judah.
11 But *Jehoshabeath, the daughter of the
king, took [a]Joash the son of Ahaziah, and stole
him away from among the king's sons who were
being murdered, and put him and his nurse in a
bedroom. So Jehoshabeath, the daughter of King
Jehoram, the wife of Jehoiada the priest (for she
was the sister of Ahaziah), hid him from Athaliah
so that she did not kill him.
12 And he was hidden with them in the house
of God for six years, while Athaliah reigned over
the land.

Joash Crowned King of Judah
(*2 Kin. 11:4–12*)

23 In [a]the seventh year [b]Jehoiada strengthened himself, *and made a* covenant with
the captains of hundreds: Azariah the son of Jeroham, Ishmael the son of Jehohanan, Azariah the
son of [c]Obed, Maaseiah the son of Adaiah, and
Elishaphat the son of Zichri.
2 And they went throughout Judah and
gathered the Levites from all the cities of Judah,
and the [a]chief fathers of Israel, and they came to
Jerusalem.
3 Then all the assembly made a covenant
with the king in the house of God. And he said
to them, "Behold, the king's son shall reign, as
the LORD has [a]said of the sons of David.
4 "This *is* what you shall do: One-third of
you [a]entering on the Sabbath, of the priests and
the Levites, *shall be* keeping watch over the doors;
5 "one-third *shall be* at the king's house;
and one-third at the Gate of the Foundation. All
the people *shall be* in the courts of the house of
the LORD.
6 "But let no one come into the house of
the LORD except the priests and [a]those of the Levites who serve. They may go in, for they *are* holy;
but all the people shall keep the watch of the
LORD.
7 "And the Levites shall surround the king
on all sides, every man with his weapons in his
hand; and whoever comes into the house, let him
be put to death. You are to be with the king when
he comes in and when he goes out."
8 So the Levites and all Judah did according
to all that Jehoiada the priest commanded. And
each man took his men who were to be on duty
on the Sabbath, with those who were going *off*

---

*22:6 Heb. mss., LXX, Syr., Vg. *Ahaziah* and 2 Kin. 8:29
22:11 *Jehosheba*, 2 Kin. 11:2

KJV

to go *out* on the sabbath: for Jehoiada the priest
dismissed not [a]the courses.
9 Moreover Jehoiada the priest delivered to
the captains of hundreds spears, and bucklers,
and [a]shields, that *had been* king David's, which
were in the house of God.
10 And he set all the people, every man having his weapon in his hand, from the right side
of the temple to the left side of the temple, along
by the altar and the temple, by the king round
about.
11 Then they brought out the king's son, and
put upon him the crown, and [a]*gave him* the testimony, and made him king. And Jehoiada and his
sons anointed him, and said, God save the king.

Death of Athaliah
(2 Kin. 11:13–20)

12 Now when [a]Athaliah heard the noise of
the people running and praising the king, she
came to the people into the house of the LORD:
13 And she looked, and, behold, the king
stood at his pillar at the entering in, and the
princes and the trumpets by the king: and all the
people of the land rejoiced, and sounded with
trumpets, also the singers with instruments of musick, and [a]such as taught to sing praise. Then
Athaliah rent her clothes, and said, [b]Treason,
Treason.
14 Then Jehoiada the priest brought out the
captains of hundreds that were set over the host,
and said unto them, Have her forth of the ranges:
and whoso followeth her, let him be slain with
the sword. For the priest said, Slay her not in the
house of the LORD.
15 So they laid hands on her; and when she
was come to the entering [a]of the horse gate by
the king's house, they slew her there.
16 And Jehoiada made a [a]covenant between
him, and between all the people, and between the
king, that they should be the LORD's people.
17 Then all the people went to the house of
Baal, and brake it down, and brake his altars and
his images in pieces, and [a]slew Mattan the priest
of Baal before the altars.
18 Also Jehoiada appointed the offices of the
house of the LORD by the hand of the priests the
Levites, whom David had [a]distributed in the
house of the LORD, to offer the burnt offerings of
the LORD, as *it is* written in the [b]law of Moses,
with rejoicing and with singing, *as it was ordained*
by David.
19 And he set the [a]porters at the gates of the
house of the LORD, that none *which was* unclean
in any thing should enter in.
20 [a]And he took the captains of hundreds,
and the nobles, and the governors of the people,
and all the people of the land, and brought down
the king from the house of the LORD: and they
came through the high gate into the king's house,
and set the king upon the throne of the kingdom.
21 And all the people of the land rejoiced:
and the city was quiet, after that they had slain
Athaliah with the sword.

Joash Repairs the Temple
(2 Kin. 11:21—12:16)

24 Joash [a]*was* seven years old when he began
to reign, and he reigned forty years in Jerusalem. His mother's name also *was* Zibiah of
Beer-sheba.
2 And Joash [a]did *that which was* right in
the sight of the LORD all the days of Jehoiada the
priest.
3 And Jehoiada took for him two wives; and
he begat sons and daughters.
4 And it came to pass after this, *that* Joash
was minded to repair the house of the LORD.
5 And he gathered together the priests and
the Levites, and said to them, Go out unto the
cities of Judah, and [a]gather of all Israel money
to repair the house of your God from year to year,

---

8 [a]1 Chr. 24:1–31
9 [a]2 Sam. 8:7
11 [a]Deut. 17:18
12 [a]2 Chr. 22:10
13 [a]1 Chr. 25:8 [b]2 Kin. 9:23
15 [a]Neh. 3:28; Jer. 31:40
16 [a]Josh. 24:24, 25; 2 Chr. 15:12–15
17 [a]Deut. 13:6–9; 1 Kin. 18:40
18 [a]1 Chr. 23:6, 30, 31; 24:1 [b]Num. 28:2
19 [a]1 Chr. 26:1–19
20 [a]1 Kin. 9:22; 2 Kin. 11:19

CHAPTER 24
1 [a]2 Kin. 11:21; 12:1–15
2 [a]2 Chr. 26:4, 5
5 [a]2 Kin. 12:4

*
23:11 Law, Ex. 25:16, 21; 31:18
23:17 Lit. *house*

NKJV

duty on the Sabbath; for Jehoiada the priest had
not dismissed [a]the divisions.
9 And Jehoiada the priest gave to the captains of hundreds the spears and the large and
small [a]shields which *had belonged* to King David,
that *were* in the temple of God.
10 Then he set all the people, every man with
his weapon in his hand, from the right side of
the temple to the left side of the temple, along
by the altar and by the temple, all around the king.
11 And they brought out the king's son, put
the crown on him, [a]*gave him* the *Testimony, and
made him king. Then Jehoiada and his sons
anointed him, and said, "*Long* live the king!"

Death of Athaliah
(2 Kin. 11:13–20)

12 Now when [a]Athaliah heard the noise of
the people running and praising the king, she
came to the people *in* the temple of the LORD.
13 When she looked, there was the king
standing by his pillar at the entrance; and the
leaders and the trumpeters *were* by the king. All
the people of the land were rejoicing and blowing
trumpets, also the singers with musical instruments, and [a]those who led in praise. So Athaliah
tore her clothes and said, [b]"Treason! Treason!"
14 And Jehoiada the priest brought out the
captains of hundreds who were set over the army,
and said to them, "Take her outside under guard,
and slay with the sword whoever follows her."
For the priest had said, "Do not kill her in the
house of the LORD."
15 So they seized her; and she went by way
of the entrance [a]of the Horse Gate *into* the king's
house, and they killed her there.
16 Then Jehoiada made a [a]covenant between
himself, the people, and the king, that they should
be the LORD's people.
17 And all the people went to the *temple of
Baal, and tore it down. They broke in pieces its
altars and images, and [a]killed Mattan the priest
of Baal before the altars.
18 Also Jehoiada appointed the oversight of
the house of the LORD to the hand of the priests,
the Levites, whom David had [a]assigned in the
house of the LORD, to offer the burnt offerings of
the LORD, as *it is* written in the [b]Law of Moses,
with rejoicing and with singing, *as it was established* by David.
19 And he set the [a]gatekeepers at the gates
of the house of the LORD, so that no one *who was*
in any way unclean should enter.
20 [a]Then he took the captains of hundreds,
the nobles, the governors of the people, and all
the people of the land, and brought the king down
from the house of the LORD; and they went
through the Upper Gate to the king's house, and
set the king on the throne of the kingdom.
21 So all the people of the land rejoiced; and
the city was quiet, for they had slain Athaliah with
the sword.

Joash Repairs the Temple
(2 Kin. 11:21—12:16)

24 Joash [a]*was* seven years old when he became king, and he reigned forty years in
Jerusalem. His mother's name *was* Zibiah of
Beersheba.
2 Joash [a]did *what was* right in the sight of
the LORD all the days of Jehoiada the priest.
3 And Jehoiada took two wives for him, and
he had sons and daughters.
4 Now it happened after this *that* Joash set
his heart on repairing the house of the LORD.
5 Then he gathered the priests and the Levites, and said to them, "Go out to the cities of
Judah, and [a]gather from all Israel money to repair
the house of your God from year to year, and see

KJV

and see that ye hasten the matter. Howbeit the Levites hastened *it* not.

6 [a]And the king called for Jehoiada the chief, and said unto him, Why hast thou not required of the Levites to bring in out of Judah and out of Jerusalem the collection, *according to the commandment* of [b]Moses the servant of the LORD, and of the congregation of Israel, for the [c]tabernacle of witness?

7 For [a]the sons of Athaliah, that wicked woman, had broken up the house of God; and also all the [b]dedicated things of the house of the LORD did they bestow upon Baalim.

8 And at the king's commandment [a]they made a chest, and set it without at the gate of the house of the LORD.

9 And they made a proclamation through Judah and Jerusalem, to bring in to the LORD [a]the collection *that* Moses the servant of God *laid* upon Israel in the wilderness.

10 And all the princes and all the people rejoiced, and brought in, and cast into the chest, until they had made an end.

11 Now it came to pass, that at what time the chest was brought unto the king's office by the hand of the Levites, and [a]when they saw that *there was* much money, the king's scribe and the high priest's officer came and emptied the chest, and took it, and carried it to his place again. Thus they did day by day, and gathered money in abundance.

12 And the king and Jehoiada gave it to such as did the work of the service of the house of the LORD, and hired masons and carpenters to [a]repair the house of the LORD, and also such as wrought iron and brass to mend the house of the LORD.

13 So the workmen wrought, and the work was perfected by them, and they set the house of God in his state, and strengthened it.

14 And when they had finished *it*, they brought the rest of the money before the king and Jehoiada, [a]whereof were made vessels for the house of the LORD, *even* vessels to minister, and to offer *withal*, and spoons, and vessels of gold and silver. And they offered burnt offerings in the house of the LORD continually all the days of Jehoiada.

Apostasy of Joash

15 But Jehoiada waxed old, and was full of days when he died; an hundred and thirty years old *was he* when he died.

16 And they buried him in the city of David among the kings, because he had done good in Israel, both toward God, and toward his house.

17 Now after the death of Jehoiada came the princes of Judah, and made obeisance to the king. Then the king hearkened unto them.

18 And they left the house of the LORD God of their fathers, and served [a]groves and idols: and [b]wrath came upon Judah and Jerusalem for this their trespass.

19 Yet he [a]sent prophets to them, to bring them again unto the LORD; and they testified against them: but they would not give ear.

20 And the Spirit of God came upon [a]Zechariah the son of Jehoiada the priest, which stood above the people, and said unto them, Thus saith God, [b]Why transgress ye the commandments of the LORD, that ye cannot prosper? [c]because ye have forsaken the LORD, he hath also forsaken you.

21 And they conspired against him, and [a]stoned him with stones at the commandment of the king in the court of the house of the LORD.

22 Thus Joash the king remembered not the kindness which Jehoiada his father had done to him, but slew his son. And when he died, he said, The LORD look upon *it*, and [a]require *it*.

6 [a]2 Kin. 12:7 [b]Ex. 30:12–16 [c]Num. 1:50; Acts 7:44
7 [a]2 Chr. 21:17 [b]2 Kin. 12:4
8 [a]2 Kin. 12:9
9 [a]2 Chr. 24:6
11 [a]2 Kin. 12:10
12 [a]2 Chr. 30:12
14 [a]2 Kin. 12:13
18 [a]1 Kin. 14:23 [b][Ex. 34:12–14]; Judg. 5:8; 2 Chr. 19:2; 28:13; 29:8; 32:25
19 [a]2 Kin. 17:13; 21:10–15; 2 Chr. 36:15, 16; Jer. 7:25, 26; 25:4
20 [a]Judg. 6:34; Matt. 23:35 [b]Num. 14:41; [Prov. 28:13] [c][2 Chr. 15:2]
21 [a][Neh. 9:26]; Matt. 23:35; Acts 7:58, 59
22 [a][Gen. 9:5]

NKJV

that you do it quickly." However the Levites did not do it quickly.

6 [a]So the king called Jehoiada the chief *priest*, and said to him, "Why have you not required the Levites to bring in from Judah and from Jerusalem the collection, *according to the commandment* of [b]Moses the servant of the LORD and of the assembly of Israel, for the [c]tabernacle of witness?"

7 For [a]the sons of Athaliah, that wicked woman, had broken into the house of God, and had also presented all the [b]dedicated things of the house of the LORD to the Baals.

8 Then at the king's command [a]they made a chest, and set it outside at the gate of the house of the LORD.

9 And they made a proclamation throughout Judah and Jerusalem to bring to the LORD [a]the collection *that* Moses the servant of God *had imposed* on Israel in the wilderness.

10 Then all the leaders and all the people rejoiced, brought their contributions, and put *them* into the chest until all had given.

11 So it was, at that time, when the chest was brought to the king's official by the hand of the Levites, and [a]when they saw that *there was* much money, that the king's scribe and the high priest's officer came and emptied the chest, and took it and returned it to its place. Thus they did day by day, and gathered money in abundance.

12 The king and Jehoiada gave it to those who did the work of the service of the house of the LORD; and they hired masons and carpenters to [a]repair the house of the LORD, and also those who worked in iron and bronze to restore the house of the LORD.

13 So the workmen labored, and the work was completed by them; they restored the house of God to its original condition and reinforced it.

14 When they had finished, they brought the rest of the money before the king and Jehoiada; [a]they made from it articles for the house of the LORD, articles for serving and offering, spoons and vessels of gold and silver. And they offered burnt offerings in the house of the LORD continually all the days of Jehoiada.

Apostasy of Joash

15 But Jehoiada grew old and was full of days, and he died; *he was* one hundred and thirty years old when he died.

16 And they buried him in the City of David among the kings, because he had done good in Israel, both toward God and His house.

17 Now after the death of Jehoiada the leaders of Judah came and bowed down to the king. And the king listened to them.

18 Therefore they left the house of the LORD God of their fathers, and served [a]wooden images and idols; and [b]wrath came upon Judah and Jerusalem because of their trespass.

19 Yet He [a]sent prophets to them, to bring them back to the LORD; and they testified against them, but they would not listen.

20 Then the Spirit of God came upon [a]Zechariah the son of Jehoiada the priest, who stood above the people, and said to them, "Thus says God: [b]'Why do you transgress the commandments of the LORD, so that you cannot prosper? [c]Because you have forsaken the LORD, He also has forsaken you.'"

21 So they conspired against him, and at the command of the king they [a]stoned him with stones in the court of the house of the LORD.

22 Thus Joash the king did not remember the kindness which Jehoiada his father had done to him, but killed his son; and as he died, he said, "The LORD look on *it*, and [a]repay!"

KJV

Death of Joash
(2 Kin. 12:19–21)

23 And it came to pass at the end of the year,
that [a]the host of Syria came up against him: and
they came to Judah and Jerusalem, and destroyed
all the princes of the people from among the people, and sent all the spoil of them unto the king
of Damascus.
24 For the army of the Syrians [a]came with
a small company of men, and the LORD [b]delivered
a very great host into their hand, because they
had forsaken the LORD God of their fathers. So
they [c]executed judgment against Joash.
25 And when they were departed from him,
(for they left him in great diseases,) [a]his own servants conspired against him for the blood of the
sons of Jehoiada the priest, and slew him on his
bed, and he died: and they buried him in the city
of David, but they buried him not in the sepulchres of the kings.
26 And these are they that conspired against
him; Zabad the son of Shimeath an Ammonitess,
and Jehozabad the son of Shimrith a Moabitess.
27 Now *concerning* his sons, and the greatness of [a]the burdens *laid* upon him, and the repairing of the house of God, behold, they *are* written in the story of the book of the kings. [b]And
Amaziah his son reigned in his stead.

Amaziah Reigns in Judah
(2 Kin. 14:1–6)

25 Amaziah [a]*was* twenty and five years old
when he began to reign, and he reigned
twenty and nine years in Jerusalem. And his
mother's name *was* Jehoaddan of Jerusalem.
2 And he did *that which was* right in the
sight of the LORD, [a]but not with a perfect heart.
3 [a]Now it came to pass, when the kingdom
was established to him, that he slew his servants
that had killed the king his father.
4 But he slew not their children, but *did* as
it is written in the law in the book of Moses, where
the LORD commanded, saying, [a]The fathers shall
not die for the children, neither shall the children
die for the fathers, but every man shall die for
his own sin.

The War Against Edom
(2 Kin. 14:7)

5 Moreover Amaziah gathered Judah together, and made them captains over thousands,
and captains over hundreds, according to the
houses of *their* fathers, throughout all Judah and
Benjamin: and he numbered them [a]from twenty
years old and above, and found them three hundred thousand choice *men, able* to go forth to war,
that could handle spear and shield.
6 He hired also an hundred thousand
mighty men of valour out of Israel for an hundred
talents of silver.
7 But there came a [a]man of God to him, saying, O king, let not the army of Israel go with
thee; for the LORD *is* not with Israel, *to wit, with*
all the children of Ephraim.
8 But if thou wilt go, do *it,* be strong for
the battle: God shall make thee fall before the enemy: for God hath [a]power to help, and to cast
down.
9 And Amaziah said to the man of God, But
what shall we do for the hundred talents which I
have given to the army of Israel? And the man
of God answered, [a]The LORD is able to give thee
much more than this.
10 Then Amaziah separated them, *to wit,* the
army that was come to him out of Ephraim, to
go home again: wherefore their anger was greatly
kindled against Judah, and they returned home
in great anger.
11 And Amaziah strengthened himself, and

23 [a]2 Kin. 12:17; Is. 7:2
24 [a]Lev. 26:8; [Deut. 32:30]; Is. 30:17 [b]Lev. 26:25; [Deut. 28:25] [c]2 Chr. 22:8; Is. 10:5
25 [a]2 Kin. 12:20, 21; 2 Chr. 25:3
27 [a]2 Kin. 12:18 [b]2 Kin. 12:21

CHAPTER 25

1 [a]2 Kin. 14:1–6
2 [a]2 Kin. 14:4; 2 Chr. 25:14
3 [a]2 Kin. 14:5; 2 Chr. 24:25
4 [a]Deut. 24:16; 2 Kin. 14:6; Jer. 31:30; [Ezek. 18:20]
5 [a]Num. 1:3
7 [a]2 Chr. 11:2
8 [a]2 Chr. 14:11; 20:6
9 [a][Deut. 8:18]; Prov. 10:22

*

24:25 LXX, Vg. *son* and vv. 20–22
24:26 *Jozachar,* 2 Kin. 12:21
• *Shomer,* 2 Kin. 12:21

NKJV

Death of Joash
(2 Kin. 12:19–21)

23 So it happened in the spring of the year
that [a]the army of Syria came up against him; and
they came to Judah and Jerusalem, and destroyed
all the leaders of the people from among the people, and sent all their spoil to the king of
Damascus.
24 For the army of the Syrians [a]came with
a small company of men; but the LORD [b]delivered
a very great army into their hand, because they
had forsaken the LORD God of their fathers. So
they [c]executed judgment against Joash.
25 And when they had withdrawn from him
(for they left him severely wounded), [a]his own
servants conspired against him because of the
blood of the *sons of Jehoiada the priest, and
killed him on his bed. So he died. And they buried
him in the City of David, but they did not bury
him in the tombs of the kings.
26 These are the ones who conspired against
him: *Zabad the son of Shimeath the Ammonitess,
and Jehozabad the son of *Shimrith the Moabitess.
27 Now *concerning* his sons, and [a]the many
oracles about him, and the repairing of the house
of God, indeed they *are* written in the annals of
the book of the kings. [b]Then Amaziah his son
reigned in his place.

Amaziah Reigns in Judah
(2 Kin. 14:1–6)

25 Amaziah [a]*was* twenty-five years old *when*
he became king, and he reigned twenty-
nine years in Jerusalem. His mother's name *was*
Jehoaddan of Jerusalem.
2 And he did *what was* right in the sight
of the LORD, [a]but not with a loyal heart.
3 [a]Now it happened, as soon as the kingdom
was established for him, that he executed his servants who had murdered his father the king.
4 However he did not execute their children,
but *did* as *it is* written in the Law in the Book of
Moses, where the LORD commanded, saying,
[a]"The fathers shall not be put to death for their
children, nor shall the children be put to death
for their fathers; but a person shall die for his
own sin."

The War Against Edom
(2 Kin. 14:7)

5 Moreover Amaziah gathered Judah together and set over them captains of thousands
and captains of hundreds, according to *their* fathers' houses, throughout all Judah and Benjamin;
and he numbered them [a]from twenty years old
and above, and found them to be three hundred
thousand choice *men, able* to go to war, who could
handle spear and shield.
6 He also hired one hundred thousand
mighty men of valor from Israel for one hundred
talents of silver.
7 But a [a]man of God came to him, saying,
"O king, do not let the army of Israel go with
you, for the LORD *is* not with Israel—*not with* any
of the children of Ephraim.
8 "But if you go, be gone! Be strong in battle! *Even so,* God shall make you fall before the
enemy; for God has [a]power to help and to
overthrow."
9 Then Amaziah said to the man of God,
"But what *shall we* do about the hundred talents
which I have given to the troops of Israel?" And
the man of God answered, [a]"The LORD is able to
give you much more than this."
10 So Amaziah discharged the troops that
had come to him from Ephraim, to go back
home. Therefore their anger was greatly aroused
against Judah, and they returned home in great
anger.
11 Then Amaziah strengthened himself, and

KJV

led forth his people, and went to [a]the valley of
salt, and smote of the children of Seir ten
thousand.
12 And *other* ten thousand *left* alive did the
children of Judah carry away captive, and
brought them unto the top of the rock, and cast
them down from the top of the rock, that they
all were broken in pieces.
13 But the soldiers of the army which Amaziah sent back, that they should not go with him
to battle, fell upon the cities of Judah, from Samaria even unto Beth–horon, and smote three
thousand of them, and took much spoil.
14 Now it came to pass, after that Amaziah
was come from the slaughter of the Edomites, that
[a]he brought the gods of the children of Seir, and
set them up *to be* [b]his gods, and bowed down
himself before them, and burned incense unto
them.
15 Wherefore the anger of the LORD was kindled against Amaziah, and he sent unto him a
prophet, which said unto him, Why hast thou
sought after [a]the gods of the people, which [b]could
not deliver their own people out of thine hand?
16 And it came to pass, as he talked with him,
that *the king* said unto him, Art thou made of
the king's counsel? forbear; why shouldest thou
be smitten? Then the prophet forbare, and said, I
know that God hath [a]determined to destroy thee,
because thou hast done this, and hast not hearkened unto my counsel.

Israel Defeats Judah
(*2 Kin. 14:8–14*)

17 Then [a]Amaziah king of Judah took advice, and sent to Joash, the son of Jehoahaz, the
son of Jehu, king of Israel, saying, Come, let us
see one another in the face.
18 And Joash king of Israel sent to Amaziah
king of Judah, saying, The thistle that *was* in
Lebanon sent to the cedar that *was* in Lebanon,
saying, Give thy daughter to my son to wife: and
there passed by a wild beast that *was* in Lebanon,
and trode down the thistle.
19 Thou sayest, Lo, thou hast smitten the
Edomites; and thine heart lifteth thee up to [a]boast:
abide now at home; why shouldest thou meddle
to *thine* hurt, that thou shouldest fall, *even* thou,
and Judah with thee?
20 But Amaziah would not hear; for [a]it *came*
of God, that he might deliver them into the hand
of their enemies, because they [b]sought after the
gods of Edom.
21 So Joash the king of Israel went up; and
they saw one another in the face, *both* he and
Amaziah king of Judah, at [a]Beth–shemesh, which
belongeth to Judah.
22 And Judah was put to the worse before
Israel, and they fled every man to his tent.
23 And Joash the king of Israel took Amaziah king of Judah, the son of Joash, the son of
[a]Jehoahaz, at Beth–shemesh, and brought him to
Jerusalem, and brake down the wall of Jerusalem
from the gate of Ephraim to the corner gate, four
hundred cubits.
24 And *he took* all the gold and the silver,
and all the vessels that were found in the house
of God with [a]Obed–edom, and the treasures of
the king's house, the hostages also, and returned
to Samaria.

Death of Amaziah
(*2 Kin. 14:17–20*)

25 [a]And Amaziah the son of Joash king of
Judah lived after the death of Joash son of Jehoahaz king of Israel fifteen years.
26 Now the rest of the acts of Amaziah, first
and last, behold, *are* they not written in the book
of the kings of Judah and Israel?
27 Now after the time that Amaziah did turn
away from following the LORD they made a conspiracy against him in Jerusalem; and he fled to

11 [a]2 Kin. 14:7
14 [a]2 Chr. 28:23 [b][Ex. 20:3, 5]
15 [a][Ps. 96:5] [b]2 Chr. 25:11
16 [a][1 Sam. 2:25]
17 [a]2 Kin. 14:8–14
19 [a]2 Chr. 26:16; 32:25; [Prov. 16:18]
20 [a]1 Kin. 12:15; 2 Chr. 22:7 [b]2 Chr. 25:14
21 [a]Josh. 19:38
23 [a]2 Chr. 21:17; 22:1, 6
24 [a]1 Chr. 26:15
25 [a]2 Kin. 14:17–22

NKJV

leading his people, he went to [a]the Valley of Salt
and killed ten thousand of the people of Seir.
12 Also the children of Judah took captive
ten thousand alive, brought them to the top of
the rock, and cast them down from the top of the
rock, so that they all were dashed in pieces.
13 But as for the soldiers of the army which
Amaziah had discharged, so that they would not
go with him to battle, they raided the cities of
Judah from Samaria to Beth Horon, killed three
thousand in them, and took much spoil.
14 Now it was so, after Amaziah came from
the slaughter of the Edomites, that [a]he brought
the gods of the people of Seir, set them up *to be*
[b]his gods, and bowed down before them and
burned incense to them.
15 Therefore the anger of the LORD was
aroused against Amaziah, and He sent him a
prophet who said to him, "Why have you sought
[a]the gods of the people, which [b]could not rescue
their own people from your hand?"
16 So it was, as he talked with him, that *the
king* said to him, "Have we made you the king's
counselor? Cease! Why should you be killed?"
Then the prophet ceased, and said, "I know that
God has [a]determined to destroy you, because you
have done this and have not heeded my advice."

Israel Defeats Judah
(*2 Kin. 14:8–14*)

17 Now [a]Amaziah king of Judah asked advice and sent to *Joash the son of Jehoahaz, the
son of Jehu, king of Israel, saying, "Come, let us
face one another *in battle.*"
18 And Joash king of Israel sent to Amaziah
king of Judah, saying, "The thistle that *was* in
Lebanon sent to the cedar that was in Lebanon,
saying, 'Give your daughter to my son as wife';
and a wild beast that *was* in Lebanon passed by
and trampled the thistle.
19 "Indeed you say that you have defeated
the Edomites, and your heart is lifted up to [a]boast.
Stay at home now; why should you meddle with
trouble, that you should fall—you and Judah with
you?"
20 But Amaziah would not heed, for [a]it *came*
from God, that He might give them into the hand
of their enemies, because they [b]sought the gods
of Edom.
21 So Joash king of Israel went out; and he
and Amaziah king of Judah faced one another at
[a]Beth Shemesh, which *belongs* to Judah.
22 And Judah was defeated by Israel, and every man fled to his tent.
23 Then Joash the king of Israel captured
Amaziah king of Judah, the son of Joash, the son
of [a]Jehoahaz, at Beth Shemesh; and he brought
him to Jerusalem, and broke down the wall of
Jerusalem from the Gate of Ephraim to the Corner
Gate—four hundred cubits.
24 And *he took* all the gold and silver, all
the articles that were found in the house of God
with [a]Obed-Edom, the treasures of the king's
house, and hostages, and returned to Samaria.

Death of Amaziah
(*2 Kin. 14:17–20*)

25 [a]Amaziah the son of Joash, king of Judah,
lived fifteen years after the death of Joash the
son of Jehoahaz, king of Israel.
26 Now the rest of the acts of Amaziah, from
first to last, indeed *are* they not written in the book
of the kings of Judah and Israel?
27 After the time that Amaziah turned away
from following the LORD, they made a conspiracy
against him in Jerusalem, and he fled to Lachish;

*________

25:17 *Jehoash,* 2 Kin. 14:8ff.

KJV

Lachish: but they sent to Lachish after him, and slew him there.

28 And they brought him upon horses, and buried him with his fathers in the city of Judah.

Uzziah Reigns in Judah
(*2 Kin. 14:21, 22; 15:1–3*)

26 Then all the people of Judah took Uzziah, who *was* sixteen years old, and made him king in the room of his father Amaziah.

2 He built Eloth, and restored it to Judah, after that the king slept with his fathers.

3 Sixteen years old *was* Uzziah when he began to reign, and he reigned fifty and two years in Jerusalem. His mother's name also *was* Jecoliah of Jerusalem.

4 And he did *that which was* [a]right in the sight of the LORD, according to all that his father Amaziah did.

5 And [a]he sought God in the days of Zechariah, who [b]had understanding in the visions of God: and as long as he sought the LORD, God made him to [c]prosper.

6 And he went forth and [a]warred against the Philistines, and brake down the wall of Gath, and the wall of Jabneh, and the wall of Ashdod, and built cities about Ashdod, and among the Philistines.

7 And God helped him against [a]the Philistines, and against the Arabians that dwelt in Gurbaal, and the Mehunims.

8 And the Ammonites [a]gave gifts to Uzziah: and his name spread abroad *even* to the entering in of Egypt; for he strengthened *himself* exceedingly.

9 Moreover Uzziah built towers in Jerusalem at the [a]corner gate, and at the valley gate, and at the turning *of the wall*, and fortified them.

10 Also he built towers in the desert, and digged many wells: for he had much cattle, both in the low country, and in the plains: husbandmen *also*, and vine dressers in the mountains, and in Carmel: for he loved husbandry.

11 Moreover Uzziah had an host of fighting men, that went out to war by bands, according to the number of their account by the hand of Jeiel the scribe and Maaseiah the ruler, under the hand of Hananiah, *one* of the king's captains.

12 The whole number of the chief of the fathers of the mighty men of valour *were* two thousand and six hundred.

13 And under their hand *was* an army, three hundred thousand and seven thousand and five hundred, that made war with mighty power, to help the king against the enemy.

14 And Uzziah prepared for them throughout all the host shields, and spears, and helmets, and habergeons, and bows, and slings *to cast* stones.

15 And he made in Jerusalem engines, invented by [a]cunning men, to be on the towers and upon the bulwarks, to shoot arrows and great stones withal. And his name spread far abroad; for he was marvellously helped, till he was strong.

The Penalty for Uzziah's Pride
(*2 Kin. 15:4–7*)

16 But [a]when he was strong, his heart was [b]lifted up to *his* destruction: for he transgressed against the LORD his God, and [c]went into the temple of the LORD to burn incense upon the altar of incense.

17 And [a]Azariah the priest went in after him, and with him fourscore priests of the LORD, *that were* valiant men:

18 And they withstood Uzziah the king, and said unto him, *It* [a]*appertaineth* not unto thee, Uzziah, to burn incense unto the LORD, but to the [b]priests the sons of Aaron, that are consecrated to burn incense: go out of the sanctuary; for thou hast trespassed; neither *shall it be* for thine honour from the LORD God.

19 Then Uzziah was wroth, and *had* a censer

CHAPTER 26
4 [a]2 Chr. 24:2
5 [a]2 Chr. 24:2 [b]Gen. 41:15; Dan. 1:17; 10:1 [c][2 Chr. 15:2; 20:20; 31:21]
6 [a]Is. 14:29
7 [a]2 Chr. 21:16
8 [a]2 Sam. 8:2; 2 Chr. 17:11
9 [a]2 Kin. 14:13; 2 Chr. 25:23; Neh. 3:13, 19, 32; Zech. 14:10
15 [a]Ex. 39:3, 8
16 [a][Deut. 32:15] [b]Deut. 8:14; 2 Chr. 25:19 [c]1 Kin. 13:1–4; 2 Kin. 16:12, 13
17 [a]1 Chr. 6:10
18 [a][Num. 3:10; 16:39, 40; 18:7] [b]Ex. 30:7, 8; Heb. 7:14

NKJV

but they sent after him to Lachish and killed him there.

28 Then they brought him on horses and buried him with his fathers in the City of Judah.

Uzziah Reigns in Judah
(*2 Kin. 14:21, 22; 15:1–3*)

26 Now all the people of Judah took *Uzziah, who *was* sixteen years old, and made him king instead of his father Amaziah.

2 He built *Elath and restored it to Judah, after the king rested with his fathers.

3 Uzziah *was* sixteen years old when he became king, and he reigned fifty-two years in Jerusalem. His mother's name was Jecholiah of Jerusalem.

4 And he did *what was* [a]right in the sight of the LORD, according to all that his father Amaziah had done.

5 [a]He sought God in the days of Zechariah, who [b]had understanding in the *visions of God; and as long as he sought the LORD, God made him [c]prosper.

6 Now he went out and [a]made war against the Philistines, and broke down the wall of Gath, the wall of Jabneh, and the wall of Ashdod; and he built cities *around* Ashdod and among the Philistines.

7 God helped him against [a]the Philistines, against the Arabians who lived in Gur Baal, and against the Meunites.

8 Also the Ammonites [a]brought tribute to Uzziah. His fame spread as far as the entrance of Egypt, for he became exceedingly strong.

9 And Uzziah built towers in Jerusalem at the [a]Corner Gate, at the Valley Gate, and at the corner buttress of the wall; then he fortified them.

10 Also he built towers in the desert. He dug many wells, for he had much livestock, both in the lowlands and in the plains; *he also had* farmers and vinedressers in the mountains and in Carmel, for he loved the soil.

11 Moreover Uzziah had an army of fighting men who went out to war by companies, according to the number on their roll as prepared by Jeiel the scribe and Maaseiah the officer, under the hand of Hananiah, *one* of the king's captains.

12 The total number of *chief officers of the mighty men of valor *was* two thousand six hundred.

13 And under their authority *was* an army of three hundred and seven thousand five hundred, that made war with mighty power, to help the king against the enemy.

14 Then Uzziah prepared for them, for the entire army, shields, spears, helmets, body armor, bows, and slings *to cast* stones.

15 And he made devices in Jerusalem, invented by [a]skillful men, to be on the towers and the corners, to shoot arrows and large stones. So his fame spread far and wide, for he was marvelously helped till he became strong.

The Penalty for Uzziah's Pride
(*2 Kin. 15:4–7*)

16 But [a]when he was strong his heart was [b]lifted up, to *his* destruction, for he transgressed against the LORD his God [c]by entering the temple of the LORD to burn incense on the altar of incense.

17 So [a]Azariah the priest went in after him, and with him were eighty priests of the LORD—valiant men.

18 And they withstood King Uzziah, and said to him, "*It* [a]*is* not for you, Uzziah, to burn incense to the LORD, but for the [b]priests, the sons of Aaron, who are consecrated to burn incense. Get out of the sanctuary, for you have trespassed! You *shall have* no honor from the LORD God."

19 Then Uzziah became furious; and he *had*

*

26:1 *Azariah*, 2 Kin. 14:21ff.
26:2 Heb. *Eloth*
26:5 Heb. mss., LXX, Syr., Tg., Arab. *fear*
26:12 Lit. *chief fathers*

KJV

in his hand to burn incense: and while he was wroth with the priests, [a]the leprosy even rose up in his forehead before the priests in the house of the LORD, from beside the incense altar.

20 And Azariah the chief priest, and all the priests, looked upon him, and, behold, he *was* leprous in his forehead, and they thrust him out from thence; yea, himself [a]hasted also to go out, because the LORD had smitten him.

21 [a]And Uzziah the king was a leper unto the day of his death, and dwelt in a [b]several house, *being* a leper; for he was cut off from the house of the LORD: and Jotham his son *was* over the king's house, judging the people of the land.

22 Now the rest of the acts of Uzziah, first and last, did [a]Isaiah the prophet, the son of Amoz, write.

23 [a]So Uzziah slept with his fathers, and they buried him with his fathers in the field of the burial which *belonged* to the kings; for they said, He *is* a leper: and Jotham his son reigned in his stead.

Jotham Reigns in Judah
(2 Kin. 15:32–38)

27 Jotham [a]*was* twenty and five years old when he began to reign, and he reigned sixteen years in Jerusalem. His mother's name also *was* Jerushah, the daughter of Zadok.

2 And he did *that which was* right in the sight of the LORD, according to all that his father Uzziah did: howbeit he entered not into the temple of the LORD. And [a]the people did yet corruptly.

3 He built the high gate of the house of the LORD, and on the wall of [a]Ophel he built much.

4 Moreover he built cities in the mountains of Judah, and in the forests he built castles and towers.

5 He fought also with the king of the [a]Ammonites, and prevailed against them. And the children of Ammon gave him the same year an hundred talents of silver, and ten thousand measures of wheat, and ten thousand of barley. So much did the children of Ammon pay unto him, both the second year, and the third.

6 So Jotham became mighty, [a]because he prepared his ways before the LORD his God.

7 Now the rest of the acts of Jotham, and all his wars, and his ways, lo, they *are* written in the book of the kings of Israel and Judah.

8 He was five and twenty years old when he began to reign, and reigned sixteen years in Jerusalem.

9 [a]And Jotham slept with his fathers, and they buried him in the city of David: and [b]Ahaz his son reigned in his stead.

Ahaz Reigns in Judah
(2 Kin. 16:1–4)

28 Ahaz [a]*was* twenty years old when he began to reign, and he reigned sixteen years in Jerusalem: but he did not *that which was* right in the sight of the LORD, like David his father:

2 For he walked in the ways of the kings of Israel, and made also [a]molten images for [b]Baalim.

3 Moreover he burnt incense in [a]the valley of the son of Hinnom, and burnt [b]his children in the [c]fire, after the abominations of the heathen whom the LORD had [d]cast out before the children of Israel.

4 He sacrificed also and burnt incense in the high places, and on the hills, and under every green tree.

Syria and Israel Defeat Judah
(2 Kin. 16:5, 6; Is. 7:1)

5 Wherefore [a]the LORD his God delivered him into the hand of the king of Syria; and they [b]smote him, and carried away a great multitude of them captives, and brought *them* to Damascus.

19 [a]Lev. 13:42; Num. 12:10; 2 Kin. 5:25–27
20 [a]Esth. 6:12
21 [a]2 Kin. 15:5 [b][Lev. 13:46; Num. 5:2]
22 [a]2 Kin. 20:1; 2 Chr. 32:20, 32; Is. 1:1
23 [a]2 Kin. 15:7; 2 Chr. 21:20; 28:27; Is. 6:1

CHAPTER 27

1 [a]2 Kin. 15:32–35
2 [a]2 Kin. 15:35; Ezek. 20:44; 30:13
3 [a]2 Chr. 33:14; Neh. 3:26
5 [a]2 Chr. 26:8
6 [a]2 Chr. 26:5
9 [a]2 Kin. 15:38 [b]Is. 1:1; Hos. 1:1; Mic. 1:1

CHAPTER 28

1 [a]2 Kin. 16:2–4
2 [a]Ex. 34:17; Lev. 19:4 [b]Judg. 2:11
3 [a]Josh. 15:8 [b]2 Kin. 23:10 [c][Lev. 18:21]; 2 Kin. 16:3; 2 Chr. 33:6 [d][Lev. 18:24–30]
5 [a][Is. 10:5] [b]2 Kin. 16:5, 6; [2 Chr. 24:24]; Is. 7:1, 17

*———

27:1 *Jerusha,* 2 Kin. 15:33

NKJV

a censer in his hand to burn incense. And while he was angry with the priests, [a]leprosy broke out on his forehead, before the priests in the house of the LORD, beside the incense altar.

20 And Azariah the chief priest and all the priests looked at him, and there, on his forehead, he *was* leprous; so they thrust him out of that place. Indeed he also [a]hurried to get out, because the LORD had struck him.

21 [a]King Uzziah was a leper until the day of his death. He dwelt in an [b]isolated house, because he was a leper; for he was cut off from the house of the LORD. Then Jotham his son *was* over the king's house, judging the people of the land.

22 Now the rest of the acts of Uzziah, from first to last, the prophet [a]Isaiah the son of Amoz wrote.

23 [a]So Uzziah rested with his fathers, and they buried him with his fathers in the field of burial which *belonged* to the kings, for they said, "He is a leper." Then Jotham his son reigned in his place.

Jotham Reigns in Judah
(2 Kin. 15:32–38)

27 Jotham [a]*was* twenty-five years old when he became king, and he reigned sixteen years in Jerusalem. His mother's name *was* *Jerushah the daughter of Zadok.

2 And he did *what was* right in the sight of the LORD, according to all that his father Uzziah had done (although he did not enter the temple of the LORD). But still [a]the people acted corruptly.

3 He built the Upper Gate of the house of the LORD, and he built extensively on the wall of [a]Ophel.

4 Moreover he built cities in the mountains of Judah, and in the forests he built fortresses and towers.

5 He also fought with the king of the [a]Ammonites and defeated them. And the people of Ammon gave him in that year one hundred talents of silver, ten thousand kors of wheat, and ten thousand of barley. The people of Ammon paid this to him in the second and third years also.

6 So Jotham became mighty, [a]because he prepared his ways before the LORD his God.

7 Now the rest of the acts of Jotham, and all his wars and his ways, indeed they *are* written in the book of the kings of Israel and Judah.

8 He was twenty-five years old when he became king, and he reigned sixteen years in Jerusalem.

9 [a]So Jotham rested with his fathers, and they buried him in the City of David. Then [b]Ahaz his son reigned in his place.

Ahaz Reigns in Judah
(2 Kin. 16:1–4)

28 Ahaz [a]*was* twenty years old when he became king, and he reigned sixteen years in Jerusalem; and he did not do *what was* right in the sight of the LORD, as his father David *had done.*

2 For he walked in the ways of the kings of Israel, and made [a]molded images for [b]the Baals.

3 He burned incense in [a]the Valley of the Son of Hinnom, and burned [b]his children in the [c]fire, according to the abominations of the nations whom the LORD had [d]cast out before the children of Israel.

4 And he sacrificed and burned incense on the high places, on the hills, and under every green tree.

Syria and Israel Defeat Judah
(2 Kin. 16:5, 6; Is. 7:1)

5 Therefore [a]the LORD his God delivered him into the hand of the king of Syria. They [b]defeated him, and carried away a great multitude of them as captives, and brought *them* to Damas-

KJV

And he was also delivered into the hand of the
king of Israel, who smote him with a great
slaughter.
6 For [a]Pekah the son of Remaliah slew in
Judah an hundred and twenty thousand in one
day, *which were* all valiant men; [b]because they
had forsaken the LORD God of their fathers.
7 And Zichri, a mighty man of Ephraim,
slew Maaseiah the king's son, and Azrikam the
governor of the house, and Elkanah *that was* next
to the king.
8 And the children of Israel carried away
captive of their [a]brethren two hundred thousand,
women, sons, and daughters, and took also away
much spoil from them, and brought the spoil to
Samaria.

Israel Returns the Captives

9 But a [a]prophet of the LORD was there,
whose name *was* Oded: and he went out before
the host that came to Samaria, and said unto
them, Behold, [b]because the LORD God of your fathers was wroth with Judah, he hath delivered
them into your hand, and ye have slain them in
a rage *that* [c]reacheth up unto heaven.
10 And now ye purpose to keep under the
children of Judah and Jerusalem for [a]bondmen
and bondwomen unto you: *but are there* not with
you, even with you, sins against the LORD your
God?
11 Now hear me therefore, and deliver the
captives again, which ye have taken captive of
your brethren: [a]for the fierce wrath of the LORD
is upon you.
12 Then certain of the heads of the children
of Ephraim, Azariah the son of Johanan, Berechiah the son of Meshillemoth, and Jehizkiah
the son of Shallum, and Amasa the son of
Hadlai, stood up against them that came from the
war,
13 And said unto them, Ye shall not bring
in the captives hither: for whereas we have offended against the LORD *already*, ye intend to add
more to our sins and to our trespass: for our trespass is great, and *there is* fierce wrath against
Israel.
14 So the armed men left the captives and
the spoil before the princes and all the congregation.
15 And the men [a]which were expressed by
name rose up, and took the captives, and with
the spoil clothed all that were naked among them,
and arrayed them, and shod them, and [b]gave them
to eat and to drink, and anointed them, and carried all the feeble of them upon asses, and brought
them to Jericho, [c]the city of palm trees, to their
brethren: then they returned to Samaria.

Assyria Refuses to Help Judah
(2 Kin. 16:7–9)

16 [a]At that time did king Ahaz send unto the
kings of Assyria to help him.
17 For again the [a]Edomites had come and
smitten Judah, and carried away captives.
18 [a]The Philistines also had invaded the cities of the low country, and of the south of Judah,
and had taken Beth–shemesh, and Ajalon, and
Gederoth, and Shocho with the villages thereof,
and Timnah with the villages thereof, Gimzo
also and the villages thereof: and they dwelt
there.
19 For the LORD brought Judah low because
of Ahaz king of [a]Israel; for he [b]made Judah
naked, and transgressed sore against the
LORD.
20 And [a]Tilgath–pilneser king of Assyria
came unto him, and distressed him, but strengthened him not.
21 For Ahaz took away a portion *out* of the
house of the LORD, and *out* of the house of the
king, and of the princes, and gave *it* unto the king
of Assyria: but he helped him not.

6 [a]2 Kin. 15:27 [b][2 Chr. 29:8]
8 [a]Deut. 28:25, 41; 2 Chr. 11:4
9 [a]2 Chr. 25:15 [b]Ps. 69:26; [Is. 10:5; 47:6]; Ezek. 25:12, 15; 26:2; Obad. 10; [Zech. 1:15] [c]Ezra 9:6; Rev. 18:5
10 [a][Lev. 25:39, 42, 43, 46]
11 [a]Ps. 78:49; James 2:13
15 [a]2 Chr. 28:12 [b][Prov. 25:21, 22; Luke 6:27; Rom. 12:20] [c]Deut. 34:3; Judg. 1:16
16 [a]2 Kin. 16:7
17 [a]2 Chr. 21:10; Obad. 10–14
18 [a]2 Chr. 21:16, 17; Ezek. 16:27, 57
19 [a]2 Kin. 16:2; 2 Chr. 21:2 [b]Ex. 32:25
20 [a]2 Kin. 15:29; 16:7–9; 1 Chr. 5:26

NKJV

cus. Then he was also delivered into the hand of
the king of Israel, who defeated him with a great
slaughter.
6 For [a]Pekah the son of Remaliah killed one
hundred and twenty thousand in Judah in one
day, all valiant men, [b]because they had forsaken
the LORD God of their fathers.
7 Zichri, a mighty man of Ephraim, killed
Maaseiah the king's son, Azrikam the officer over
the house, and Elkanah *who was* second to the
king.
8 And the children of Israel carried away
captive of their [a]brethren two hundred thousand
women, sons, and daughters; and they also took
away much spoil from them, and brought the spoil
to Samaria.

Israel Returns the Captives

9 But a [a]prophet of the LORD was there,
whose name *was* Oded; and he went out before
the army that came to Samaria, and said to them:
"Look, [b]because the LORD God of your fathers was
angry with Judah, He has delivered them into
your hand; but you have killed them in a rage
that [c]reaches up to heaven.
10 "And now you propose to force the children of Judah and Jerusalem to be your [a]male
and female slaves; *but are* you not also guilty before the LORD your God?
11 "Now hear me, therefore, and return the
captives, whom you have taken captive from your
brethren, [a]for the fierce wrath of the LORD *is* upon
you."
12 Then some of the heads of the children
of Ephraim, Azariah the son of Johanan, Berechiah the son of Meshillemoth, Jehizkiah the son
of Shallum, and Amasa the son of Hadlai, stood
up against those who came from the war,
13 and said to them, "You shall not bring the
captives here, for we *already* have offended the
LORD. You intend to add to our sins and to our
guilt; for our guilt is great, and *there is* fierce
wrath against Israel."
14 So the armed men left the captives and
the spoil before the leaders and all the assembly.
15 Then the men [a]who were designated by
name rose up and took the captives, and from
the spoil they clothed all who were naked among
them, dressed them and gave them sandals, [b]gave
them food and drink, and anointed them; and they
let all the feeble ones ride on donkeys. So they
brought them to their brethren at Jericho, [c]the
city of palm trees. Then they returned to Samaria.

Assyria Refuses to Help Judah
(2 Kin. 16:7–9)

16 [a]At the same time King Ahaz sent to the
*kings of Assyria to help him.
17 For again the [a]Edomites had come, attacked Judah, and carried away captives.
18 [a]The Philistines also had invaded the cities of the lowland and of the South of Judah, and
had taken Beth Shemesh, Aijalon, Gederoth, Sochoh with its villages, Timnah with its villages,
and Gimzo with its villages; and they dwelt there.
19 For the LORD brought Judah low because
of Ahaz king of [a]Israel, for he had [b]encouraged
moral decline in Judah and had been continually
unfaithful to the LORD.
20 Also [a]Tiglath-Pileser* king of Assyria
came to him and distressed him, and did not assist
him.
21 For Ahaz took part *of the treasures* from
the house of the LORD, from the house of the king,
and from the leaders, and he gave *it* to the king
of Assyria; but he did not help him.

*———

28:16 LXX, Syr., Vg. *king* (cf. v. 20) **28:20** Heb. *Tilgath-Pilneser*

KJV

Apostasy and Death of Ahaz
(2 Kin. 16:12–20)

22 And in the time of his distress did he trespass yet more against the LORD: this *is that* king Ahaz.

23 For [a]he sacrificed unto the gods of Damascus, which smote him: and he said, Because the gods of the kings of Syria help them, *therefore* will I sacrifice to them, that [b]they may help me. But they were the ruin of him, and of all Israel.

24 And Ahaz gathered together the vessels of the house of God, and cut in pieces the vessels of the house of God, [a]and shut up the doors of the house of the LORD, and he made him altars in every corner of Jerusalem.

25 And in every several city of Judah he made high places to burn incense unto other gods, and provoked to anger the LORD God of his fathers.

26 [a]Now the rest of his acts and of all his ways, first and last, behold, they *are* written in the book of the kings of Judah and Israel.

27 And Ahaz slept with his fathers, and they buried him in the city, *even* in Jerusalem: but they brought him [a]not into the sepulchres of the kings of Israel: and Hezekiah his son reigned in his stead.

Hezekiah Reigns in Judah
(2 Kin. 18:1–3)

29 Hezekiah [a]began to reign *when he was* five and twenty years old, and he reigned nine and twenty years in Jerusalem. And his mother's name *was* Abijah, the daughter [b]of Zechariah.

2 And he did *that which was* right in the sight of the LORD, according to all that David his father had done.

Hezekiah Cleanses the Temple

3 He in the first year of his reign, in the first month, [a]opened the doors of the house of the LORD, and repaired them.

4 And he brought in the priests and the Levites, and gathered them together into the east street,

5 And said unto them, Hear me, ye Levites, sanctify now yourselves, and [a]sanctify the house of the LORD God of your fathers, and carry forth the filthiness out of the holy *place*.

6 For our fathers have trespassed, and done *that which was* evil in the eyes of the LORD our God, and have forsaken him, and have [a]turned away their faces from the habitation of the LORD, and turned *their* backs.

7 [a]Also they have shut up the doors of the porch, and put out the lamps, and have not burned incense nor offered burnt offerings in the holy *place* unto the God of Israel.

8 Wherefore the [a]wrath of the LORD was upon Judah and Jerusalem, and he hath [b]delivered them to trouble, to astonishment, and to [c]hissing, as ye see with your [d]eyes.

9 For, lo, [a]our fathers have fallen by the sword, and our sons and our daughters and our wives *are* in captivity for this.

10 Now *it is* in mine heart to make [a]a covenant with the LORD God of Israel, that his fierce wrath may turn away from us.

11 My sons, be not now negligent: for the LORD hath [a]chosen you to stand before him, to serve him, and that ye should minister unto him, and burn incense.

12 Then the Levites arose, [a]Mahath the son of Amasai, and Joel the son of Azariah, of the sons of the [b]Kohathites: and of the sons of Merari, Kish the son of Abdi, and Azariah the son of Jehalelel: and of the Gershonites; Joah the son of Zimmah, and Eden the son of Joah:

13 And of the sons of Elizaphan; Shimri, and Jeiel: and of the sons of Asaph; Zechariah, and Mattaniah:

23 [a]2 Chr. 25:14 [b]Jer. 44:17, 18
24 [a]2 Chr. 29:3, 7
26 [a]2 Kin. 16:19, 20
27 [a]2 Chr. 21:20; 24:25

CHAPTER 29

1 [a]2 Kin. 18:1; 2 Chr. 32:22, 33 [b]2 Chr. 26:5
3 [a]2 Chr. 28:24; 29:7
5 [a]1 Chr. 15:12; 2 Chr. 29:15, 34; 35:6
6 [a][Is. 1:4]; Jer. 2:27; Ezek. 8:16
7 [a]2 Chr. 28:24
8 [a]2 Chr. 24:18 [b]2 Chr. 28:5 [c]1 Kin. 9:8; Jer. 18:16; 19:8; 25:9, 18; 29:18 [d]Deut. 28:32
9 [a]Deut. 28:25; 2 Chr. 28:5–8, 17
10 [a]2 Chr. 15:12; 23:16
11 [a]Num. 3:6; 8:14; 18:2, 6; 2 Chr. 30:16, 17
12 [a]2 Chr. 31:13 [b]Num. 3:19, 20

*———

29:1 *Abi,* 2 Kin. 18:2

NKJV

Apostasy and Death of Ahaz
(2 Kin. 16:12–20)

22 Now in the time of his distress King Ahaz became increasingly unfaithful to the LORD. This *is that* King Ahaz.

23 For [a]he sacrificed to the gods of Damascus which had defeated him, saying, "Because the gods of the kings of Syria help them, I will sacrifice to them [b]that they may help me." But they were the ruin of him and of all Israel.

24 So Ahaz gathered the articles of the house of God, cut in pieces the articles of the house of God, [a]shut up the doors of the house of the LORD, and made for himself altars in every corner of Jerusalem.

25 And in every single city of Judah he made high places to burn incense to other gods, and provoked to anger the LORD God of his fathers.

26 [a]Now the rest of his acts and all his ways, from first to last, indeed they *are* written in the book of the kings of Judah and Israel.

27 So Ahaz rested with his fathers, and they buried him in the city, in Jerusalem; but they [a]did not bring him into the tombs of the kings of Israel. Then Hezekiah his son reigned in his place.

Hezekiah Reigns in Judah
(2 Kin. 18:1–3)

29 Hezekiah [a]became king *when he was* twenty-five years old, and he reigned twenty-nine years in Jerusalem. His mother's name *was* *Abijah the daughter [b]of Zechariah.

2 And he did *what was* right in the sight of the LORD, according to all that his father David had done.

Hezekiah Cleanses the Temple

3 In the first year of his reign, in the first month, he [a]opened the doors of the house of the LORD and repaired them.

4 Then he brought in the priests and the Levites, and gathered them in the East Square,

5 and said to them: "Hear me, Levites! Now sanctify yourselves, [a]sanctify the house of the LORD God of your fathers, and carry out the rubbish from the holy *place*.

6 "For our fathers have trespassed and done evil in the eyes of the LORD our God; they have forsaken Him, have [a]turned their faces away from the dwelling place of the LORD, and turned *their* backs *on Him*.

7 [a]"They have also shut up the doors of the vestibule, put out the lamps, and have not burned incense or offered burnt offerings in the holy *place* to the God of Israel.

8 "Therefore the [a]wrath of the LORD fell upon Judah and Jerusalem, and He has [b]given them up to trouble, to desolation, and to [c]jeering, as you see with your [d]eyes.

9 "For indeed, because of this [a]our fathers have fallen by the sword; and our sons, our daughters, and our wives *are* in captivity.

10 "Now *it is* in my heart to make [a]a covenant with the LORD God of Israel, that His fierce wrath may turn away from us.

11 "My sons, do not be negligent now, for the LORD has [a]chosen you to stand before Him, to serve Him, and that you should minister to Him and burn incense."

12 Then these Levites arose: [a]Mahath the son of Amasai and Joel the son of Azariah, of the sons of the [b]Kohathites; of the sons of Merari, Kish the son of Abdi and Azariah the son of Jehallelel; of the Gershonites, Joah the son of Zimmah and Eden the son of Joah;

13 of the sons of Elizaphan, Shimri and Jeiel; of the sons of Asaph, Zechariah and Mattaniah;

KJV

14 And of the sons of Heman; Jehiel, and Shimei: and of the sons of Jeduthun; Shemaiah, and Uzziel.

15 And they gathered their brethren, and [a]sanctified themselves, and came, according to the commandment of the king, by the words of the LORD, [b]to cleanse the house of the LORD.

16 And the priests went into the inner part of the house of the LORD, to cleanse *it*, and brought out all the uncleanness that they found in the temple of the LORD into the court of the house of the LORD. And the Levites took *it*, to carry *it* out abroad into the brook [a]Kidron.

17 Now they began on the first *day* of the first month to sanctify, and on the eighth day of the month came they to the porch of the LORD: so they sanctified the house of the LORD in eight days; and in the sixteenth day of the first month they made an end.

18 Then they went in to Hezekiah the king, and said, We have cleansed all the house of the LORD, and the altar of burnt offering, with all the vessels thereof, and the shewbread table, with all the vessels thereof.

19 Moreover all the vessels, which king Ahaz in his reign did [a]cast away in his transgression, have we prepared and sanctified, and, behold, they *are* before the altar of the LORD.

Hezekiah Restores Temple Worship

20 Then Hezekiah the king rose early, and gathered the rulers of the city, and went up to the house of the LORD.

21 And they brought seven bullocks, and seven rams, and seven lambs, and seven he goats, for a [a]sin offering for the kingdom, and for the sanctuary, and for Judah. And he commanded the priests the sons of Aaron to offer *them* on the altar of the LORD.

22 So they killed the bullocks, and the priests received the blood, and [a]sprinkled *it* on the altar: likewise, when they had killed the rams, they sprinkled the blood upon the altar: they killed also the lambs, and they sprinkled the blood upon the altar.

23 And they brought forth the he goats *for* the sin offering before the king and the congregation; and they laid their [a]hands upon them:

24 And the priests killed them, and they made reconciliation with their blood upon the altar, [a]to make an atonement for all Israel: for the king commanded *that* the burnt offering and the sin offering *should be made* for all Israel.

25 [a]And he set the Levites in the house of the LORD with cymbals, with psalteries, and with harps, [b]according to the commandment of David, and of [c]Gad the king's seer, and Nathan the prophet: [d]for *so was* the commandment of the LORD by his prophets.

26 And the Levites stood with the instruments [a]of David, and the priests with [b]the trumpets.

27 And Hezekiah commanded to offer the burnt offering upon the altar. And when the burnt offering began, [a]the song of the LORD began *also* with the trumpets, and with the instruments *ordained* by David king of Israel.

28 And all the congregation worshipped, and the singers sang, and the trumpeters sounded: *and* all *this continued* until the burnt offering was finished.

29 And when they had made an end of offering, [a]the king and all that were present with him bowed themselves, and worshipped.

30 Moreover Hezekiah the king and the princes commanded the Levites to sing praise unto the LORD with the words of David, and of Asaph the seer. And they sang praises with gladness, and they bowed their heads and worshipped.

31 Then Hezekiah answered and said, Now ye have consecrated yourselves unto the LORD, come near and bring sacrifices and [a]thank offer-

15 [a]2 Chr. 29:5 [b]1 Chr. 23:28
16 [a]2 Chr. 15:16; 30:14
19 [a]2 Chr. 28:24
21 [a]Lev. 4:3–14
22 [a]Lev. 8:14, 15, 19, 24; Heb. 9:21
23 [a]Lev. 4:15, 24; 8:14
24 [a]Lev. 14:20
25 [a]1 Chr. 16:4; 25:6 [b]1 Chr. 23:5; 25:1; 2 Chr. 8:14 [c]2 Sam. 24:11 [d]2 Chr. 30:12
26 [a]1 Chr. 23:5; Amos 6:5 [b]Num. 10:8, 10; 1 Chr. 15:24; 16:6; 2 Chr. 5:12
27 [a]2 Chr. 23:18
29 [a]2 Chr. 20:18
31 [a]Lev. 7:12

NKJV

14 of the sons of Heman, Jehiel and Shimei; and of the sons of Jeduthun, Shemaiah and Uzziel.

15 And they gathered their brethren, [a]sanctified themselves, and went according to the commandment of the king, at the words of the LORD, [b]to cleanse the house of the LORD.

16 Then the priests went into the inner part of the house of the LORD to cleanse *it*, and brought out all the debris that they found in the temple of the LORD to the court of the house of the LORD. And the Levites took *it* out and carried *it* to the Brook [a]Kidron.

17 Now they began to sanctify on the first *day* of the first month, and on the eighth day of the month they came to the vestibule of the LORD. So they sanctified the house of the LORD in eight days, and on the sixteenth day of the first month they finished.

18 Then they went in to King Hezekiah and said, "We have cleansed all the house of the LORD, the altar of burnt offerings with all its articles, and the table of the showbread with all its articles.

19 "Moreover all the articles which King Ahaz in his reign had [a]cast aside in his transgression we have prepared and sanctified; and there they *are*, before the altar of the LORD."

Hezekiah Restores Temple Worship

20 Then King Hezekiah rose early, gathered the rulers of the city, and went up to the house of the LORD.

21 And they brought seven bulls, seven rams, seven lambs, and seven male goats for a [a]sin offering for the kingdom, for the sanctuary, and for Judah. Then he commanded the priests, the sons of Aaron, to offer *them* on the altar of the LORD.

22 So they killed the bulls, and the priests received the blood and [a]sprinkled *it* on the altar. Likewise they killed the rams and sprinkled the blood on the altar. They also killed the lambs and sprinkled the blood on the altar.

23 Then they brought out the male goats *for* the sin offering before the king and the assembly, and they laid their [a]hands on them.

24 And the priests killed them; and they presented their blood on the altar as a sin offering [a]to make an atonement for all Israel, for the king commanded *that* the burnt offering and the sin offering *be made* for all Israel.

25 [a]And he stationed the Levites in the house of the LORD with cymbals, with stringed instruments, and with harps, [b]according to the commandment of David, of [c]Gad the king's seer, and of Nathan the prophet; [d]for thus *was* the commandment of the LORD by his prophets.

26 The Levites stood with the instruments [a]of David, and the priests with [b]the trumpets.

27 Then Hezekiah commanded *them* to offer the burnt offering on the altar. And when the burnt offering began, [a]the song of the LORD *also* began, with the trumpets and with the instruments of David king of Israel.

28 So all the assembly worshiped, the singers sang, and the trumpeters sounded; all *this continued* until the burnt offering was finished.

29 And when they had finished offering, [a]the king and all who were present with him bowed and worshiped.

30 Moreover King Hezekiah and the leaders commanded the Levites to sing praise to the LORD with the words of David and of Asaph the seer. So they sang praises with gladness, and they bowed their heads and worshiped.

31 Then Hezekiah answered and said, "Now *that* you have consecrated yourselves to the LORD, come near, and bring sacrifices and [a]thank offer-

KJV

ings into the house of the LORD. And the congregation brought in sacrifices and thank offerings; and
as many as were of a [b]free heart burnt offerings.
32 And the number of the burnt offerings,
which the congregation brought, was threescore
and ten bullocks, an hundred rams, *and* two hundred lambs: all these *were* for a burnt offering to
the LORD.
33 And the consecrated things *were* six hundred oxen and three thousand sheep.
34 But the priests were too few, so that they
could not flay all the burnt offerings: wherefore
[a]their brethren the Levites did help them, till the
work was ended, and until the *other* priests had
sanctified themselves: [b]for the Levites *were* more
[c]upright in heart to [d]sanctify themselves than the
priests.
35 And also the burnt offerings *were* in abundance, with [a]the fat of the peace offerings, and
[b]the drink offerings for *every* burnt offering. So
the service of the house of the LORD was set in
order.
36 And Hezekiah rejoiced, and all the people,
that God had prepared the people: for the thing
was *done* suddenly.

Hezekiah Keeps the Passover

30 And Hezekiah sent to all Israel and Judah,
and wrote letters also to Ephraim and Manasseh, that they should come to the house of the
LORD at Jerusalem, to keep the passover unto the
LORD God of Israel.
2 For the king had taken counsel, and his
princes, and all the congregation in Jerusalem,
to keep the passover in the second [a]month.
3 For they could not keep it [a]at that time,
[b]because the priests had not sanctified themselves
sufficiently, neither had the people gathered
themselves together to Jerusalem.
4 And the thing pleased the king and all the
congregation.
5 So they established a decree to make proclamation throughout all Israel, from Beer–sheba
even to Dan, that they should come to keep the
passover unto the LORD God of Israel at Jerusalem: for they had not done *it* of a long *time in
such sort* as it was written.
6 So the [a]posts went with the letters from
the king and his princes throughout all Israel and
Judah, and according to the commandment of the
king, saying, Ye children of Israel, [b]turn again
unto the LORD God of Abraham, Isaac, and Israel,
and he will return to the remnant of you, that are
escaped out of the hand of [c]the kings of [d]Assyria.
7 And be not ye [a]like your fathers, and like
your brethren, which trespassed against the LORD
God of their fathers, *who* therefore [b]gave them
up to [c]desolation, as ye see.
8 Now be ye not [a]stiffnecked, as your fathers *were, but* yield yourselves unto the LORD,
and enter into his sanctuary, which he hath sanctified for ever: and serve the LORD your God, [b]that
the fierceness of his wrath may turn away from
you.
9 For if ye turn again unto the LORD, your
brethren and your children *shall find* [a]compassion
before them that lead them captive, so that they
shall come again into this land: for the LORD your
God *is* [b]gracious and merciful, and will not turn
away *his* face from you, if ye [c]return unto him.
10 So the posts passed from city to city
through the country of Ephraim and Manasseh
even unto Zebulun: but [a]they laughed them to
scorn, and mocked them.
11 Nevertheless [a]divers of Asher and Manasseh and of Zebulun humbled themselves, and
came to Jerusalem.
12 Also in Judah [a]the hand of God was to
give them one heart to do the commandment of
the king and of the princes, [b]by the word of the
LORD.
13 And there assembled at Jerusalem much

31 [b]Ex. 35:5, 22
34 [a]2 Chr. 35:11 [b]2 Chr. 30:3 [c]Ps. 7:10 [d]2 Chr. 29:5
35 [a]Lev. 3:16 [b]Num. 15:5–10

CHAPTER 30

2 [a]Num. 9:10, 11; 2 Chr. 30:13, 15
3 [a]Ex. 12:6, 18 [b]2 Chr. 19:17, 34
6 [a]Esth. 8:14; Job 9:25; Jer. 51:31 [b][Jer. 4:1; Joel 2:13] [c]2 Kin. 15:19, 29 [d]2 Chr. 28:20
7 [a]Ezek. 20:18 [b]Is. 1:9 [c]2 Chr. 29:8
8 [a]Ex. 32:9; Deut. 10:16; Acts 7:51 [b]2 Chr. 29:10
9 [a]Ps. 106:46 [b][Ex. 34:6; Mic. 7:18] [c][Is. 55:7]
10 [a]2 Chr. 36:16
11 [a]2 Chr. 11:16; 30:18, 21
12 [a][2 Cor. 3:5; Phil. 2:13; Heb. 13:20, 21] [b]2 Chr. 29:25

*30:3 The first month, Lev. 23:5; lit. *that time*

NKJV

ings into the house of the LORD." So the assembly
brought in sacrifices and thank offerings, and as
many as were of a [b]willing heart *brought* burnt
offerings.
32 And the number of the burnt offerings
which the assembly brought was seventy bulls,
one hundred rams, *and* two hundred lambs; all
these *were* for a burnt offering to the LORD.
33 The consecrated things *were* six hundred
bulls and three thousand sheep.
34 But the priests were too few, so that they
could not skin all the burnt offerings; therefore
[a]their brethren the Levites helped them until the
work was ended and until the *other* priests had
sanctified themselves, [b]for the Levites were [c]more
diligent in [d]sanctifying themselves than the
priests.
35 Also the burnt offerings *were* in abundance, with [a]the fat of the peace offerings and
with [b]the drink offerings for *every* burnt offering.
So the service of the house of the LORD was set
in order.
36 Then Hezekiah and all the people rejoiced
that God had prepared the people, since the events
took place so suddenly.

Hezekiah Keeps the Passover

30 And Hezekiah sent to all Israel and Judah,
and also wrote letters to Ephraim and Manasseh, that they should come to the house of the
LORD at Jerusalem, to keep the Passover to the
LORD God of Israel.
2 For the king and his leaders and all the
assembly in Jerusalem had agreed to keep the
Passover in the second [a]month.
3 For they could not keep it [a]at *the regular
time, [b]because a sufficient number of priests had
not consecrated themselves, nor had the people
gathered together at Jerusalem.
4 And the matter pleased the king and all
the assembly.
5 So they resolved to make a proclamation
throughout all Israel, from Beersheba to Dan, that
they should come to keep the Passover to the LORD
God of Israel at Jerusalem, since they had not
done *it* for a long *time* in the *prescribed* manner.
6 Then the [a]runners went throughout all Israel and Judah with the letters from the king and
his leaders, and spoke according to the command
of the king: "Children of Israel, [b]return to the
LORD God of Abraham, Isaac, and Israel; then He
will return to the remnant of you who have escaped from the hand of [c]the kings of [d]Assyria.
7 "And do not be [a]like your fathers and
your brethren, who trespassed against the LORD
God of their fathers, so that He [b]gave them up
to [c]desolation, as you see.
8 "Now do not be [a]stiff-necked, as your fathers *were, but* yield yourselves to the LORD; and
enter His sanctuary, which He has sanctified forever, and serve the LORD your God, [b]that the
fierceness of His wrath may turn away from you.
9 "For if you return to the LORD, your brethren and your children *will be treated* with [a]com-
passion by those who lead them captive, so that
they may come back to this land; for the LORD
your God *is* [b]gracious and merciful, and will not
turn *His* face from you if you [c]return to Him."
10 So the runners passed from city to city
through the country of Ephraim and Manasseh,
as far as Zebulun; but [a]they laughed at them and
mocked them.
11 Nevertheless [a]some from Asher, Manasseh, and Zebulun humbled themselves and came
to Jerusalem.
12 Also [a]the hand of God was on Judah to
give them singleness of heart to obey the command of the king and the leaders, [b]at the word
of the LORD.
13 Now many people, a very great assembly,

KJV

people to keep the feast of [a]unleavened bread in
the second month, a very great congregation.
14 And they arose and took away the [a]altars
that *were* in Jerusalem, and all the altars for incense took they away, and cast *them* into the
brook [b]Kidron.
15 Then they killed the passover on the fourteenth *day* of the second month: and the priests
and the Levites were [a]ashamed, and sanctified
themselves, and brought in the burnt offerings
into the house of the LORD.
16 And they stood in their [a]place after their
manner, according to the law of Moses the man
of God: the priests sprinkled the blood, *which they*
received of the hand of the Levites.
17 For *there were* many in the congregation
that were not sanctified: [a]therefore the Levites
had the charge of the killing of the passovers for
every one *that was* not clean, to sanctify *them*
unto the LORD.
18 For a multitude of the people, *even* [a]many
of Ephraim, and Manasseh, Issachar, and Zebulun, had not cleansed themselves, [b]yet did they
eat the passover otherwise than it was written.
But Hezekiah prayed for them, saying, The good
LORD pardon every one
19 *That* [a]prepareth his heart to seek God, the
LORD God of his fathers, though *he be* not *cleansed*
according to the purification of the sanctuary.
20 And the LORD hearkened to Hezekiah, and
healed the people.
21 And the children of Israel that were present at Jerusalem kept [a]the feast of unleavened
bread seven days with great gladness: and the
Levites and the priests praised the LORD day by
day, *singing* with loud instruments unto the LORD.
22 And Hezekiah spake comfortably unto all
the Levites [a]that taught the good knowledge of
the LORD: and they did eat throughout the feast
seven days, offering peace offerings, and [b]making
confession to the LORD God of their fathers.
23 And the whole assembly took counsel to
keep [a]other seven days: and they kept *other* seven
days with gladness.
24 For Hezekiah king of Judah [a]did give to
the congregation a thousand bullocks and seven
thousand sheep; and the princes gave to the congregation a thousand bullocks and ten thousand
sheep: and a great number of priests [b]sanctified
themselves.
25 And all the congregation of Judah, with
the priests and the Levites, and all the congregation that came out of Israel, and the strangers
[a]that came out of the land of Israel, and that dwelt
in Judah, rejoiced.
26 So there was great joy in Jerusalem: for
since the time of [a]Solomon the son of David king
of Israel *there was* not the like in Jerusalem.
27 Then the priests the Levites arose and
[a]blessed the people: and their voice was heard,
and their prayer came *up* to [b]his holy dwelling
place, *even* unto heaven.

The Reforms of Hezekiah
(2 Kin. 18:4)

31 Now when all this was finished, all Israel
that were present went out to the cities of
Judah, and [a]brake the images in pieces, and cut
down the groves, and threw down the high places
and the altars out of all Judah and Benjamin, in
Ephraim also and Manasseh, until they had utterly destroyed them all. Then all the children of
Israel returned, every man to his possession, into
their own cities.
2 And Hezekiah appointed [a]the courses of
the priests and the Levites after their courses, every man according to his service, the priests and
Levites [b]for burnt offerings and for peace offerings, to minister, and to give thanks, and to praise
in the gates of the tents of the LORD.
3 *He appointed* also the king's portion of
his [a]substance for the burnt offerings, *to wit*, for

13 [a]Lev. 23:6; Num. 9:11
14 [a]2 Chr. 28:24 [b]2 Chr. 29:16
15 [a]2 Chr. 29:34
16 [a]2 Chr. 35:10, 15
17 [a]2 Chr. 29:34
18 [a]2 Chr. 30:1, 11, 25 [b]Ex. 12:43–49; [Num. 9:10]
19 [a]2 Chr. 19:3
21 [a]Ex. 12:15; 13:6; 1 Kin. 8:65
22 [a][Deut. 33:10]; 2 Chr. 17:9; 35:3 [b]Ezra 10:11
23 [a]1 Kin. 8:65; 2 Chr. 35:17, 18
24 [a]2 Chr. 35:7, 8 [b]2 Chr. 29:34
25 [a]2 Chr. 30:11, 18
26 [a]2 Chr. 7:8–10
27 [a]Num. 6:23 [b]Deut. 26:15; Ps. 68:5

CHAPTER 31

1 [a]2 Kin. 18:4
2 [a]1 Chr. 23:6; 24:1 [b]1 Chr. 23:30, 31
3 [a]2 Chr. 35:7

NKJV

gathered at Jerusalem to keep the Feast of [a]Un-
leavened Bread in the second month.
14 They arose and took away the [a]altars that
were in Jerusalem, and they took away all the
incense altars and cast *them* into the Brook
[b]Kidron.
15 Then they slaughtered the Passover *lambs*
on the fourteenth *day* of the second month. The
priests and the Levites were [a]ashamed, and sanctified themselves, and brought the burnt offerings
to the house of the LORD.
16 They stood in their [a]place according to
their custom, according to the Law of Moses the
man of God; the priests sprinkled the blood *re-*
ceived from the hand of the Levites.
17 For *there were* many in the assembly who
had not sanctified themselves; [a]therefore the Levites had charge of the slaughter of the Passover
lambs for everyone *who was* not clean, to sanctify
them to the LORD.
18 For a multitude of the people, [a]many from
Ephraim, Manasseh, Issachar, and Zebulun, had
not cleansed themselves, [b]yet they ate the Passover contrary to what was written. But Hezekiah
prayed for them, saying, "May the good LORD provide atonement for everyone
19 "*who* [a]prepares his heart to seek God, the
LORD God of his fathers, though *he is* not *cleansed*
according to the purification of the sanctuary."
20 And the LORD listened to Hezekiah and
healed the people.
21 So the children of Israel who were present
at Jerusalem kept [a]the Feast of Unleavened Bread
seven days with great gladness; and the Levites
and the priests praised the LORD day by day, *sing-*
ing to the LORD, accompanied by loud instruments.
22 And Hezekiah gave encouragement to all
the Levites [a]who taught the good knowledge of
the LORD; and they ate throughout the feast seven
days, offering peace offerings and [b]making confession to the LORD God of their fathers.
23 Then the whole assembly agreed to keep
the feast [a]another seven days, and they kept it
another seven days with gladness.
24 For Hezekiah king of Judah [a]gave to the
assembly a thousand bulls and seven thousand
sheep, and the leaders gave to the assembly a
thousand bulls and ten thousand sheep; and a
great number of priests [b]sanctified themselves.
25 The whole assembly of Judah rejoiced,
also the priests and Levites, all the assembly that
came from Israel, the sojourners [a]who came from
the land of Israel, and those who dwelt in Judah.
26 So there was great joy in Jerusalem, for
since the time of [a]Solomon the son of David, king
of Israel, *there had* been nothing like this in
Jerusalem.
27 Then the priests, the Levites, arose and
[a]blessed the people, and their voice was heard;
and their prayer came *up* to [b]His holy dwelling
place, to heaven.

The Reforms of Hezekiah
(2 Kin. 18:4)

31 Now when all this was finished, all Israel
who were present went out to the cities of
Judah and [a]broke the sacred pillars in pieces, cut
down the wooden images, and threw down the
high places and the altars—from all Judah, Benjamin, Ephraim, and Manasseh—until they had utterly destroyed them all. Then all the children of
Israel returned to their own cities, every man to
his possession.
2 And Hezekiah appointed [a]the divisions of
the priests and the Levites according to their divisions, each man according to his service, the
priests and Levites [b]for burnt offerings and peace
offerings, to serve, to give thanks, and to praise
in the gates of the *camp of the LORD.
3 The king also *appointed* a portion of his
[a]possessions for the burnt offerings: for the morn-

*31:2 Temple

KJV

the morning and evening burnt offerings, and the burnt offerings for the sabbaths, and for the new moons, and for the set feasts, as *it is* written in the [b]law of the LORD.

4 Moreover he commanded the people that dwelt in Jerusalem to give the [a]portion of the priests and the Levites, that they might be encouraged in [b]the law of the LORD.

5 And as soon as the commandment came abroad, the children of Israel brought in abundance [a]the firstfruits of corn, wine, and oil, and honey, and of all the increase of the field; and the [b]tithe of all *things* brought they in abundantly.

6 And *concerning* the children of Israel and Judah, that dwelt in the cities of Judah, they also brought in the tithe of oxen and sheep, and the [a]tithe of holy things which were consecrated unto the LORD their God, and laid *them* by heaps.

7 In the third month they began to lay the foundation of the heaps, and finished *them* in the seventh month.

8 And when Hezekiah and the princes came and saw the heaps, they blessed the LORD, and his people Israel.

9 Then Hezekiah questioned with the priests and the Levites concerning the heaps.

10 And Azariah the chief priest of the [a]house of Zadok answered him, and said, [b]Since *the people* began to bring the offerings into the house of the LORD, we have had enough to eat, and have left plenty: for the LORD hath blessed his people; and that which is left *is* this great [c]store.

11 Then Hezekiah commanded to prepare [a]chambers in the house of the LORD; and they prepared *them,*

12 And brought in the offerings and the tithes and the dedicated *things* faithfully: [a]over which Cononiah the Levite *was* ruler, and Shimei his brother *was* the next.

13 And Jehiel, and Azaziah, and Nahath, and Asahel, and Jerimoth, and Jozabad, and Eliel, and Ismachiah, and Mahath, and Benaiah, *were* overseers under the hand of Cononiah and Shimei his brother, at the commandment of Hezekiah the king, and Azariah the [a]ruler of the house of God.

14 And Kore the son of Imnah the Levite, the porter toward the east, *was* over the [a]freewill offerings of God, to distribute the oblations of the LORD, and the most holy things.

15 And next him *were* [a]Eden, and Miniamin, and Jeshua, and Shemaiah, Amariah, and Shecaniah, in [b]the cities of the priests, in *their* [c]set office, to give to their brethren by courses, as well to the great as to the small:

16 Beside their genealogy of males, from three years old and upward, *even* unto every one that entereth into the house of the LORD, his daily portion for their service in their charges according to their courses;

17 Both to the genealogy of the priests by the house of their fathers, and the Levites [a]from twenty years old and upward, in their charges by their courses;

18 And to the genealogy of all their little ones, their wives, and their sons, and their daughters, through all the congregation: for in their set office they sanctified themselves in holiness:

19 Also of the sons of Aaron the priests, *which were* in [a]the fields of the suburbs of their cities, in every several city, the men that were [b]expressed by name, to give portions to all the males among the priests, and to all that were reckoned by genealogies among the Levites.

20 And thus did Hezekiah throughout all Judah, and [a]wrought *that which was* good and right and truth before the LORD his God.

21 And in every work that he began in the service of the house of God, and in the law, and in the commandments, to seek his God, he did *it* with all his heart, and [a]prospered.

3 [b]Num. 28:1—29:40
4 [a]Num. 18:8; 2 Kin. 12:16; Neh. 13:10; Ezek. 44:29 [b]Mal. 2:7
5 [a]Ex. 22:29; Neh. 13:12 [b][Lev. 27:30]; Deut. 14:28; 26:12, 13
6 [a][Lev. 27:30]; Deut. 14:28
10 [a]1 Chr. 6:8, 9 [b][Mal. 3:10] [c]Ex. 36:5
11 [a]1 Kin. 6:5–8
12 [a]2 Chr. 35:9; Neh. 13:13
13 [a]1 Chr. 9:11; Jer. 20:1
14 [a]Deut. 23:23; 2 Chr. 35:8
15 [a]2 Chr. 29:12 [b]Josh. 21:1–3, 9 [c]1 Chr. 9:26
17 [a]1 Chr. 23:24, 27
19 [a]Lev. 25:34; Num. 35:1–4 [b]2 Chr. 31:12–15
20 [a]2 Kin. 20:3; 22:2
21 [a]2 Chr. 26:5; 32:30; Ps. 1:3

NKJV

ing and evening burnt offerings, the burnt offerings for the Sabbaths and the New Moons and the set feasts, as *it is* written in the [b]Law of the LORD.

4 Moreover he commanded the people who dwelt in Jerusalem to contribute [a]support for the priests and the Levites, that they might devote themselves to [b]the Law of the LORD.

5 As soon as the commandment was circulated, the children of Israel brought in abundance [a]the firstfruits of grain and wine, oil and honey, and of all the produce of the field; and they brought in abundantly the [b]tithe of everything.

6 And the children of Israel and Judah, who dwelt in the cities of Judah, brought the tithe of oxen and sheep; also the [a]tithe of holy things which were consecrated to the LORD their God they laid in heaps.

7 In the third month they began laying them in heaps, and they finished in the seventh month.

8 And when Hezekiah and the leaders came and saw the heaps, they blessed the LORD and His people Israel.

9 Then Hezekiah questioned the priests and the Levites concerning the heaps.

10 And Azariah the chief priest, from the [a]house of Zadok, answered him and said, [b]"Since *the people* began to bring the offerings into the house of the LORD, we have had enough to eat and have plenty left, for the LORD has blessed His people; and what is left *is* this great [c]abundance."

11 Now Hezekiah commanded *them* to prepare [a]rooms in the house of the LORD, and they prepared them.

12 Then they faithfully brought in the offerings, the tithes, and the dedicated things; [a]Cononiah the Levite had charge of them, and Shimei his brother *was* the next.

13 Jehiel, Azaziah, Nahath, Asahel, Jerimoth, Jozabad, Eliel, Ismachiah, Mahath, and Benaiah *were* overseers under the hand of Cononiah and Shimei his brother, at the commandment of Hezekiah the king and Azariah the [a]ruler of the house of God.

14 Kore the son of Imnah the Levite, the keeper of the East Gate, *was* over the [a]freewill offerings to God, to distribute the offerings of the LORD and the most holy things.

15 And under him *were* [a]Eden, Miniamin, Jeshua, Shemaiah, Amariah, and Shecaniah, *his* faithful assistants in [b]the cities of the priests, to distribute [c]allotments to their brethren by divisions, to the great as well as the small.

16 Besides those males from three years old and up who were written in the genealogy, they distributed to everyone who entered the house of the LORD his daily portion for the work of his service, by his division,

17 and to the priests who were written in the genealogy according to their father's house, and to the Levites [a]from twenty years old and up according to their work, by their divisions,

18 and to all who were written in the genealogy—their little ones and their wives, their sons and daughters, the whole company of them—for in their faithfulness they sanctified themselves in holiness.

19 Also for the sons of Aaron the priests, *who were* in [a]the fields of the common-lands of their cities, in every single city, *there were* men who were [b]designated by name to distribute portions to all the males among the priests and to all who were listed by genealogies among the Levites.

20 Thus Hezekiah did throughout all Judah, and he [a]did what *was* good and right and true before the LORD his God.

21 And in every work that he began in the service of the house of God, in the law and in the commandment, to seek his God, he did *it* with all his heart. So he [a]prospered.

KJV

Sennacherib Boasts Against the LORD
(2 Kin. 18:13—19:34; Is. 36:1–22)

32 After [a]these things, and the establishment
thereof, Sennacherib king of Assyria came,
and entered into Judah, and encamped against
the fenced cities, and thought to win them for
himself.
2 And when Hezekiah saw that Sennacherib was come, and that he was purposed to
fight against Jerusalem,
3 He took counsel with his princes and his
mighty men to stop the waters of the fountains
which *were* without the city: and they did help
him.
4 So there was gathered much people together, who stopped all the [a]fountains, and the
brook that ran through the midst of the land, saying, Why should the kings of Assyria come, and
find much water?
5 Also [a]he strengthened himself, [b]and built
up all the wall that was broken, and raised *it* up
to the towers, and another wall without, and repaired [c]Millo *in* the city of David, and made darts
and shields in abundance.
6 And he set captains of war over the people, and gathered them together to him in the
street of the gate of the city, and spake [a]comfort-
ably to them, saying,
7 [a]Be strong and courageous, [b]be not afraid
nor dismayed for the king of Assyria, nor for all
the multitude that *is* with him: for [c]*there be* more
with us than with him:
8 With him *is* an [a]arm of flesh; but [b]with
us *is* the LORD our God to help us, and to fight
our battles. And the people rested themselves
upon the words of Hezekiah king of Judah.
9 [a]After this did Sennacherib king of Assyria send his servants to Jerusalem, (but he *himself laid siege* against Lachish, and all his power
with him,) unto Hezekiah king of Judah, and unto
all Judah that *were* at Jerusalem, saying,
10 [a]Thus saith Sennacherib king of Assyria,
Whereon do ye trust, that ye abide in the siege
in Jerusalem?
11 Doth not Hezekiah persuade you to give
over yourselves to die by famine and by thirst,
saying, [a]The LORD our God shall deliver us out
of the hand of the king of Assyria?
12 [a]Hath not the same Hezekiah taken away
his high places and his altars, and commanded
Judah and Jerusalem, saying, Ye shall worship
before one altar, and burn incense upon [b]it?
13 Know ye not what I and my fathers have
done unto all the people of *other* lands? [a]were
the gods of the nations of those lands any ways
able to deliver their lands out of mine hand?
14 Who *was there* among all the gods of
those nations that my fathers utterly destroyed,
that could deliver his people out of mine hand,
that your God should be able to deliver you out
of mine [a]hand?
15 Now therefore [a]let not Hezekiah deceive
you, nor persuade you on this manner, neither
yet believe him: for no god of any nation or kingdom was able to deliver his people out of mine
hand, and out of the hand of my fathers: how
much less shall your God deliver you out of mine
hand?
16 And his servants spake yet *more* against
the LORD God, and against his servant Hezekiah.
17 He wrote also letters to rail on the LORD
God of Israel, and to speak against him, saying,
[a]As the gods of the nations of *other* lands have
not delivered their people out of mine hand, so
shall not the God of Hezekiah deliver his people
out of mine [b]hand.
18 [a]Then they cried with a loud voice in the
Jews' speech unto the people of Jerusalem that
were on the wall, to affright them, and to trouble
them; that they might take the city.
19 And they spake against the God of Jerusa-

CHAPTER 32
1 [a]2 Kin. 18:13—19:37; Is. 36:1—37:38
4 [a]2 Kin. 20:20
5 [a]Is. 22:9, 10 [b]2 Kin. 25:4; 2 Chr. 25:23 [c]2 Sam. 5:9; 1 Kin. 9:15, 24; 11:27; 2 Kin. 12:20; 1 Chr. 11:8
6 [a]2 Chr. 30:22; Is. 40:2
7 [a][Deut. 31:6] [b]2 Chr. 20:15 [c]2 Kin. 6:16; [Rom. 8:31]
8 [a][Jer. 17:5; 1 John 4:4] [b]Ex. 14:13; [1 Sam. 17:45–47]; 2 Chr. 13:12; 20:17; [Rom. 8:31]
9 [a]2 Kin. 18:17
10 [a]2 Kin. 18:19
11 [a]2 Kin. 18:30
12 [a]2 Kin. 18:22 [b]2 Chr. 31:1, 2
13 [a]2 Kin. 18:33–35
14 [a][Is. 10:5–12]
15 [a]2 Kin. 18:29
17 [a]2 Kin. 19:9; [1 Cor. 8:5, 6] [b]2 Kin. 19:12; Dan. 3:15
18 [a]2 Kin. 18:28; Ps. 59:6

*
32:3 Lit. *mighty men*
32:4 So with MT, Vg.; Arab., LXX, Syr. *king*
32:5 Lit. *The Landfill*
32:18 Lit. *Judean*

NKJV

Sennacherib Boasts Against the LORD
(2 Kin. 18:13—19:34; Is. 36:1–22)

32 After [a]these deeds of faithfulness, Sennacherib king of Assyria came and entered
Judah; he encamped against the fortified cities,
thinking to win them over to himself.
2 And when Hezekiah saw that Sennacherib had come, and that his purpose was to make
war against Jerusalem,
3 he consulted with his leaders and *commanders to stop the water from the springs which
were outside the city; and they helped him.
4 Thus many people gathered together who
stopped all the [a]springs and the brook that ran
through the land, saying, "Why should the *kings
of Assyria come and find much water?"
5 And [a]he strengthened himself, [b]built up
all the wall that was broken, raised *it* up to the
towers, and *built* another wall outside; also he
repaired *the [c]Millo *in* the City of David, and
made weapons and shields in abundance.
6 Then he set military captains over the people, gathered them together to him in the open
square of the city gate, and [a]gave them encouragement, saying,
7 [a]"Be strong and courageous; [b]do not be
afraid nor dismayed before the king of Assyria,
nor before all the multitude that *is* with him; for
[c]*there are* more with us than with him.
8 "With him *is* an [a]arm of flesh; but [b]with
us *is* the LORD our God, to help us and to fight
our battles." And the people were strengthened
by the words of Hezekiah king of Judah.
9 [a]After this Sennacherib king of Assyria
sent his servants to Jerusalem (but he and all the
forces with him *laid siege* against Lachish), to
Hezekiah king of Judah, and to all Judah who
were in Jerusalem, saying,
10 [a]"Thus says Sennacherib king of Assyria:
'In what do you trust, that you remain under siege
in Jerusalem?
11 'Does not Hezekiah persuade you to give
yourselves over to die by famine and by thirst,
saying, [a]"The LORD our God will deliver us from
the hand of the king of Assyria"?
12 [a]'Has not the same Hezekiah taken away
His high places and His altars, and commanded
Judah and Jerusalem, saying, "You shall worship
before one altar and burn incense on [b]it"?
13 'Do you not know what I and my fathers
have done to all the peoples of *other* lands? [a]Were
the gods of the nations of those lands in any way
able to deliver their lands out of my hand?
14 'Who *was there* among all the gods of
those nations that my fathers utterly destroyed
that could deliver his people from my hand, that
your God should be able to deliver you from my
[a]hand?
15 'Now therefore, [a]do not let Hezekiah deceive you or persuade you like this, and do not
believe him; for no god of any nation or kingdom
was able to deliver his people from my hand or
the hand of my fathers. How much less will your
God deliver you from my hand?' "
16 Furthermore, his servants spoke against
the LORD God and against His servant Hezekiah.
17 He also wrote letters to revile the LORD
God of Israel, and to speak against Him, saying,
[a]"As the gods of the nations of *other* lands have
not delivered their people from my hand, so the
God of Hezekiah will not deliver His people from
my [b]hand."
18 [a]Then they called out with a loud voice
in *Hebrew to the people of Jerusalem who *were*
on the wall, to frighten them and trouble them,
that they might take the city.
19 And they spoke against the God of Jerusa-

KJV

lem, as against the gods of the people of the earth,
which were [a]the work of the hands of man.

Sennacherib's Defeat and Death
(2 Kin. 19:35–37)

20 [a]And for this *cause* Hezekiah the king,
and [b]the prophet Isaiah the son of Amoz, prayed
and cried to heaven.
21 [a]And the LORD sent an angel, which cut
off all the mighty men of valour, and the leaders
and captains in the camp of the king of Assyria.
So he returned with [b]shame of face to his own
land. And when he was come into the house of
his god, they that came forth of his own bowels
slew him there with the sword.
22 Thus the LORD saved Hezekiah and the inhabitants of Jerusalem from the hand of Sennacherib the king of Assyria, and from the hand
of all *other,* and guided them on every side.
23 And many brought gifts unto the LORD to
Jerusalem, and [a]presents to Hezekiah king of Judah: so that he was [b]magnified in the sight of all
nations from thenceforth.

Hezekiah Humbles Himself
(2 Kin. 20:1–11; Is. 38:1–8)

24 [a]In those days Hezekiah was sick to the
death, and prayed unto the LORD: and he spake
unto him, and he gave him a sign.
25 But Hezekiah [a]rendered not again according to the benefit *done* unto him; for [b]his heart
was lifted up: [c]therefore there was wrath upon
him, and upon Judah and Jerusalem.
26 [a]Notwithstanding Hezekiah humbled
himself for the pride of his heart, *both* he and
the inhabitants of Jerusalem, so that the wrath
of the LORD came not upon them [b]in the days of
Hezekiah.

Hezekiah's Wealth and Honor
(2 Kin. 20:12–21; Is. 39:1–8)

27 And Hezekiah had exceeding much riches
and honour: and he made himself treasuries for
silver, and for gold, and for precious stones, and
for spices, and for shields, and for all manner of
pleasant jewels;
28 Storehouses also for the increase of corn,
and wine, and oil; and stalls for all manner of
beasts, and cotes for flocks.
29 Moreover he provided him cities, and possessions of flocks and herds in abundance: for
[a]God had given him substance very much.
30 [a]This same Hezekiah also stopped the upper watercourse of Gihon, and brought it straight
down to the west side of the city of David. And
Hezekiah [b]prospered in all his works.
31 Howbeit in *the business of* the ambassadors of the princes of Babylon, who [a]sent unto
him to enquire of the wonder that was *done* in
the land, God left him, to [b]try him, that he might
know all *that was* in his heart.

Death of Hezekiah

32 Now the rest of the acts of Hezekiah, and
his goodness, behold, they *are* written in [a]the vision of Isaiah the prophet, the son of Amoz, *and*
in the [b]book of the kings of Judah and Israel.
33 [a]And Hezekiah slept with his fathers, and
they buried him in the chiefest of the sepulchres
of the sons of David: and all Judah and the inhabitants of Jerusalem did him [b]honour at his death.
And Manasseh his son reigned in his stead.

Manasseh Reigns in Judah
(2 Kin. 21:1–9)

33 Manasseh [a]*was* twelve years old when he
began to reign, and he reigned fifty and five
years in Jerusalem:
2 But did *that which was* evil in the sight
of the LORD, like unto the [a]abominations of the
heathen, whom the LORD had cast out before the
children of Israel.

19 [a]2 Kin. 19:18; [Ps. 96:5; 115:4–8]
20 [a]2 Kin. 19:15 [b]2 Kin. 19:2
21 [a]2 Kin. 19:35; Is. 10:12–19; Zech. 14:3 [b]Ps. 44:7
23 [a]2 Sam. 8:10; 2 Chr. 17:5; 26:8; Ps. 45:12 [b]2 Chr. 1:1
24 [a]2 Kin. 20:1–11; Is. 38:1–8
25 [a]Ps. 116:12 [b]2 Chr. 26:16; [Hab. 2:4] [c]2 Chr. 24:18
26 [a]Jer. 26:18, 19 [b]2 Kin. 20:19
29 [a]1 Chr. 29:12
30 [a]Is. 22:9–11 [b]2 Chr. 31:21
31 [a]2 Kin. 20:12; Is. 39:1 [b][Deut. 8:2, 16]
32 [a]Is. 36—39 [b]2 Kin. 18—20
33 [a]1 Kin. 1:21; 2 Kin. 20:21 [b]Ps. 112:6; Prov. 10:7

CHAPTER 33

1 [a]2 Kin. 21:1–9
2 [a][Deut. 18:9–12]; 2 Chr. 28:3; [Jer. 15:4]

*

32:22 LXX *gave them rest;* Vg. *gave them treasures*
32:28 So with LXX, Vg.; Arab., Syr. omit *folds for flocks;* MT *flocks for sheepfolds*
32:30 Lit. *brought it straight to* (cf. 2 Kin. 20:20)

NKJV

lem, as against the gods of the people of the
earth—[a]the work of men's hands.

Sennacherib's Defeat and Death
(2 Kin. 19:35–37)

20 [a]Now because of this King Hezekiah and
[b]the prophet Isaiah, the son of Amoz, prayed and
cried out to heaven.
21 [a]Then the LORD sent an angel who cut
down every mighty man of valor, leader, and captain in the camp of the king of Assyria. So he
returned [b]shamefaced to his own land. And when
he had gone into the temple of his god, some of
his own offspring struck him down with the sword
there.
22 Thus the LORD saved Hezekiah and the inhabitants of Jerusalem from the hand of Sennacherib the king of Assyria, and from the hand
of all *others,* and *guided them on every side.
23 And many brought gifts to the LORD at Jerusalem, and [a]presents to Hezekiah king of Judah,
so that he was [b]exalted in the sight of all nations
thereafter.

Hezekiah Humbles Himself
(2 Kin. 20:1–11; Is. 38:1–8)

24 [a]In those days Hezekiah was sick and
near death, and he prayed to the LORD; and He
spoke to him and gave him a sign.
25 But Hezekiah [a]did not repay according to
the favor *shown* him, for [b]his heart was lifted up;
[c]therefore wrath was looming over him and over
Judah and Jerusalem.
26 [a]Then Hezekiah humbled himself for the
pride of his heart, he and the inhabitants of Jerusalem, so that the wrath of the LORD did not come
upon them [b]in the days of Hezekiah.

Hezekiah's Wealth and Honor
(2 Kin. 20:12–21; Is. 39:1–8)

27 Hezekiah had very great riches and
honor. And he made himself treasuries for silver,
for gold, for precious stones, for spices, for
shields, and for all kinds of desirable items;
28 storehouses for the harvest of grain, wine,
and oil; and stalls for all kinds of livestock, and
*folds for flocks.
29 Moreover he provided cities for himself,
and possessions of flocks and herds in abundance;
for [a]God had given him very much property.
30 [a]This same Hezekiah also stopped the water outlet of Upper Gihon, and *brought the water
by tunnel to the west side of the City of David.
Hezekiah [b]prospered in all his works.
31 However, *regarding* the ambassadors of
the princes of Babylon, whom they [a]sent to him
to inquire about the wonder that was *done* in the
land, God withdrew from him, in order to [b]test
him, that He might know all *that was* in his heart.

Death of Hezekiah

32 Now the rest of the acts of Hezekiah, and
his goodness, indeed they *are* written in [a]the vision of Isaiah the prophet, the son of Amoz, *and*
in the [b]book of the kings of Judah and Israel.
33 [a]So Hezekiah rested with his fathers, and
they buried him in the upper tombs of the sons
of David; and all Judah and the inhabitants of
Jerusalem [b]honored him at his death. Then Manasseh his son reigned in his place.

Manasseh Reigns in Judah
(2 Kin. 21:1–9)

33 Manasseh [a]*was* twelve years old when he
became king, and he reigned fifty-five
years in Jerusalem.
2 But he did evil in the sight of the LORD,
according to the [a]abominations of the nations
whom the LORD had cast out before the children
of Israel.

KJV

3 For he built again the high places which Hezekiah his father had [a]broken down, and he reared up altars for Baalim, and [b]made groves, and worshipped [c]all the host of heaven, and served them.

4 Also he built altars in the house of the LORD, whereof the LORD had said, [a]In Jerusalem shall my name be for ever.

5 And he built altars for all the host of heaven [a]in the two courts of the house of the LORD.

6 [a]And he caused his children to pass through the fire in the valley of the son of Hinnom: also he observed times, and used [b]enchantments, and used witchcraft, and [c]dealt with a familiar spirit, and with wizards: he wrought much evil in the sight of the LORD, to provoke him to anger.

7 And [a]he set a carved image, the idol which he had made, in the house of God, of which God had said to David and to Solomon his son, In [b]this house, and in Jerusalem, which I have chosen before all the tribes of Israel, will I put my name for ever:

8 [a]Neither will I any more remove the foot of Israel from out of the land which I have appointed for your fathers; so that they will take heed to do all that I have commanded them, according to the whole law and the statutes and the ordinances by the hand of Moses.

9 So Manasseh made Judah and the inhabitants of Jerusalem to err, *and* to do worse than the heathen, whom the LORD had destroyed before the children of Israel.

Manasseh Restored After Repentance

10 And the LORD spake to Manasseh, and to his people: but they would not hearken.

11 [a]Wherefore the LORD brought upon them the captains of the host of the king of Assyria, which took Manasseh among the thorns, and [b]bound him with fetters, and carried him to Babylon.

12 And when he was in affliction, he besought the LORD his God, and [a]humbled himself greatly before the God of his fathers,

13 And prayed unto him: and he was [a]intreated of him, and heard his supplication, and brought him again to Jerusalem into his kingdom. Then Manasseh [b]knew that the LORD he *was* God.

14 Now after this he built a wall without the city of David, on the west side of [a]Gihon, in the valley, even to the entering in at the fish gate, and compassed [b]about Ophel, and raised it up a very great height, and put captains of war in all the fenced cities of Judah.

15 And he took away [a]the strange gods, and the idol out of the house of the LORD, and all the altars that he had built in the mount of the house of the LORD, and in Jerusalem, and cast *them* out of the city.

16 And he repaired the altar of the LORD, and sacrificed thereon peace offerings and [a]thank offerings, and commanded Judah to serve the LORD God of Israel.

17 [a]Nevertheless the people did sacrifice still in the high places, *yet* unto the LORD their God only.

Death of Manasseh
(2 Kin. 21:17, 18)

18 Now the rest of the acts of Manasseh, and his prayer unto his God, and the words of [a]the seers that spake to him in the name of the LORD God of Israel, behold, they *are written* in the book of the kings of Israel.

19 His prayer also, and *how God* was intreated of him, and all his sin, and his trespass, and the places wherein he built high places, and set up groves and graven images, before he was humbled: behold, they *are* written among the sayings of the seers.

20 [a]So Manasseh slept with his fathers, and

---

3 [a]2 Kin. 18:4; 2 Chr. 30:14; 31:1 [b]Deut. 16:21; 2 Kin. 23:5, 6 [c]Deut. 17:3
4 [a]Deut. 12:11; 1 Kin. 8:29; 9:3; 2 Chr. 6:6; 7:16
5 [a]2 Chr. 4:9
6 [a][Lev. 18:21]; Deut. 18:10; 2 Kin. 23:10; 2 Chr. 28:3; Ezek. 23:37, 39 [b]Deut. 18:11; 2 Kin. 17:17 [c][Lev. 19:31; 20:27]; 2 Kin. 21:6
7 [a]2 Kin. 21:7; 2 Chr. 25:14 [b]Ps. 132:14
8 [a]2 Sam. 7:10
11 [a]Deut. 28:36 [b]2 Chr. 36:6; Job 36:8; Ps. 107:10, 11
12 [a]2 Chr. 7:14; 32:26; [1 Pet. 5:6]
13 [a]1 Chr. 5:20; Ezra 8:23 [b]1 Kin. 20:13; Ps. 9:16; Dan. 4:25
14 [a]1 Kin. 1:33 [b]2 Chr. 27:3
15 [a]2 Chr. 33:3, 5, 7
16 [a]Lev. 7:12
17 [a]2 Chr. 32:12
18 [a]1 Sam. 9:9
20 [a]1 Kin. 1:21; 2 Kin. 21:18

*

33:3 The gods of the Assyrians
33:11 Nose hooks, 2 Kin. 19:28
33:18 Lit. *words*
33:19 LXX *the seers*

NKJV

3 For he rebuilt the high places which Hezekiah his father had [a]broken down; he raised up altars for the Baals, and [b]made wooden images; and he worshiped [c]all *the host of heaven and served them.

4 He also built altars in the house of the LORD, of which the LORD had said, [a]"In Jerusalem shall My name be forever."

5 And he built altars for all the host of heaven [a]in the two courts of the house of the LORD.

6 [a]Also he caused his sons to pass through the fire in the Valley of the Son of Hinnom; he practiced [b]soothsaying, used witchcraft and sorcery, and [c]consulted mediums and spiritists. He did much evil in the sight of the LORD, to provoke Him to anger.

7 [a]He even set a carved image, the idol which he had made, in the house of God, of which God had said to David and to Solomon his son, [b]"In this house and in Jerusalem, which I have chosen out of all the tribes of Israel, I will put My name forever;

8 [a]"and I will not again remove the foot of Israel from the land which I have appointed for your fathers—only if they are careful to do all that I have commanded them, according to the whole law and the statutes and the ordinances by the hand of Moses."

9 So Manasseh seduced Judah and the inhabitants of Jerusalem to do more evil than the nations whom the LORD had destroyed before the children of Israel.

Manasseh Restored After Repentance

10 And the LORD spoke to Manasseh and his people, but they would not listen.

11 [a]Therefore the LORD brought upon them the captains of the army of the king of Assyria, who took Manasseh with *hooks, [b]bound him with bronze *fetters,* and carried him off to Babylon.

12 Now when he was in affliction, he implored the LORD his God, and [a]humbled himself greatly before the God of his fathers,

13 and prayed to Him; and He [a]received his entreaty, heard his supplication, and brought him back to Jerusalem into his kingdom. Then Manasseh [b]knew that the LORD *was* God.

14 After this he built a wall outside the City of David on the west side of [a]Gihon, in the valley, as far as the entrance of the Fish Gate; and *it* [b]enclosed Ophel, and he raised it to a very great height. Then he put military captains in all the fortified cities of Judah.

15 He took away [a]the foreign gods and the idol from the house of the LORD, and all the altars that he had built in the mount of the house of the LORD and in Jerusalem; and he cast *them* out of the city.

16 He also repaired the altar of the LORD, sacrificed peace offerings and [a]thank offerings on it, and commanded Judah to serve the LORD God of Israel.

17 [a]Nevertheless the people still sacrificed on the high places, *but* only to the LORD their God.

Death of Manasseh
(2 Kin. 21:17, 18)

18 Now the rest of the acts of Manasseh, his prayer to his God, and the words of [a]the seers who spoke to him in the name of the LORD God of Israel, indeed they *are written* in the *book of the kings of Israel.

19 Also his prayer and *how God* received his entreaty, and all his sin and trespass, and the sites where he built high places and set up wooden images and carved images, before he was humbled, indeed they *are* written among the sayings of *Hozai.

20 [a]So Manasseh rested with his fathers, and

KJV

they buried him in his own house: and Amon his
son reigned in his stead.

Amon's Reign and Death
(2 Kin. 21:19–26)

21 [a]Amon *was* two and twenty years old
when he began to reign, and reigned two years
in Jerusalem.
22 But he did *that which was* evil in the sight
of the LORD, as did Manasseh his father: for Amon
sacrificed unto all the carved images which Manasseh his father had made, and served them;
23 And humbled not himself before the LORD,
[a]as Manasseh his father had humbled himself; but
Amon trespassed more and more.
24 [a]And his servants conspired against him,
and [b]slew him in his own house.
25 But the people of the land slew all them
that had conspired against king Amon; and the
people of the land made Josiah his son king in
his stead.

Josiah Reigns in Judah
(2 Kin. 22:1, 2)

34 Josiah [a]*was* eight years old when he began
to reign, and he reigned in Jerusalem one
and thirty years.
2 And he did *that which was* right in the
sight of the LORD, and walked in the ways of David
his father, and declined *neither* to the right hand,
nor to the left.
3 For in the eighth year of his reign, while
he was yet [a]young, he began to [b]seek after the
God of David his father: and in the twelfth year
he began [c]to purge Judah and Jerusalem [d]from
the high places, and the groves, and the carved
images, and the molten images.
4 [a]And they brake down the altars of Baalim in his presence; and the images, that *were*
on high above them, he cut down; and the groves,
and the carved images, and the molten images,
he brake in pieces, and made dust *of them*, [b]and
strowed *it* upon the graves of them that had sacrificed unto them.
5 And he [a]burnt the bones of the priests
upon their [b]altars, and cleansed Judah and
Jerusalem.
6 And *so did he* in the cities of Manasseh,
and Ephraim, and Simeon, even unto Naphtali,
with their mattocks round about.
7 And when he had broken down the altars
and the groves, and had [a]beaten the graven images into powder, and cut down all the idols
throughout all the land of Israel, he returned to
Jerusalem.

Hilkiah Finds the Book of the Law
(2 Kin. 22:3–20)

8 Now [a]in the eighteenth year of his reign,
when he had purged the land, and the house, he
sent [b]Shaphan the son of Azaliah, and Maaseiah
the [c]governor of the city, and Joah the son of Joahaz the recorder, to repair the house of the LORD
his God.
9 And when they came to Hilkiah the high
priest, they delivered [a]the money that was
brought into the house of God, which the Levites
that kept the doors had gathered of the hand of
Manasseh and Ephraim, and of all the [b]remnant
of Israel, and of all Judah and Benjamin; and they
returned to Jerusalem.
10 And they put *it* in the hand of the workmen that had the oversight of the house of the
LORD, and they gave it to the workmen that
wrought in the house of the LORD, to repair and
amend the house:
11 Even to the artificers and builders gave
they *it*, to buy hewn stone, and timber for cou-
plings, and to floor the houses which the kings
of Judah had destroyed.
12 And the men did the work faithfully: and
the overseers of them *were* Jahath and Obadiah,

21 [a]2 Kin. 21:19–24; 1 Chr. 3:14
23 [a]2 Chr. 33:12, 19
24 [a]2 Kin. 21:23, 24; 2 Chr. 24:25 [b]2 Chr. 25:27

CHAPTER 34

1 [a]2 Kin. 22:1, 2; Jer. 1:2; 3:6
3 [a]Eccl. 12:1 [b]2 Chr. 15:2; [Prov. 8:17] [c]1 Kin. 13:2 [d]2 Chr. 33:17–19, 22
4 [a]Lev. 26:30; 2 Kin. 23:4 [b]2 Kin. 23:6
5 [a]1 Kin. 13:2 [b]2 Kin. 23:20
7 [a]Deut. 9:21
8 [a]2 Kin. 22:3–20 [b]2 Kin. 25:22 [c]2 Chr. 18:25
9 [a]2 Kin. 12:4 [b]2 Chr. 30:6

*

34:6 Lit. *swords*
34:8 Lit. *house*

NKJV

they buried him in his own house. Then his son
Amon reigned in his place.

Amon's Reign and Death
(2 Kin. 21:19–26)

21 [a]Amon *was* twenty-two years old when
he became king, and he reigned two years in
Jerusalem.
22 But he did evil in the sight of the LORD,
as his father Manasseh had done; for Amon sacrificed to all the carved images which his father
Manasseh had made, and served them.
23 And he did not humble himself before the
LORD, [a]as his father Manasseh had humbled himself; but Amon trespassed more and more.
24 [a]Then his servants conspired against him,
and [b]killed him in his own house.
25 But the people of the land executed all
those who had conspired against King Amon.
Then the people of the land made his son Josiah
king in his place.

Josiah Reigns in Judah
(2 Kin. 22:1, 2)

34 Josiah [a]*was* eight years old when he became king, and he reigned thirty-one years
in Jerusalem.
2 And he did *what was* right in the sight
of the LORD, and walked in the ways of his father
David; *he* did *not* turn aside to the right hand or
to the left.
3 For in the eighth year of his reign, while
he was still [a]young, he began to [b]seek the God
of his father David; and in the twelfth year he
began [c]to purge Judah and Jerusalem [d]of the high
places, the wooden images, the carved images,
and the molded images.
4 [a]They broke down the altars of the Baals
in his presence, and the incense altars which *were*
above them he cut down; and the wooden images,
the carved images, and the molded images he
broke in pieces, and made dust of them [b]and scattered *it* on the graves of those who had sacrificed
to them.
5 He also [a]burned the bones of the priests
on their [b]altars, and cleansed Judah and Jerusalem.
6 And *so he did* in the cities of Manasseh,
Ephraim, and Simeon, as far as Naphtali and all
around, with *axes.
7 When he had broken down the altars and
the wooden images, had [a]beaten the carved images into powder, and cut down all the incense
altars throughout all the land of Israel, he returned to Jerusalem.

Hilkiah Finds the Book of the Law
(2 Kin. 22:3–20)

8 [a]In the eighteenth year of his reign, when
he had purged the land and the *temple, he sent
[b]Shaphan the son of Azaliah, Maaseiah the
[c]governor of the city, and Joah the son of Joahaz
the recorder, to repair the house of the LORD his
God.
9 When they came to Hilkiah the high
priest, they delivered [a]the money that was
brought into the house of God, which the Levites
who kept the doors had gathered from the hand
of Manasseh and Ephraim, from all the [b]remnant
of Israel, from all Judah and Benjamin, and *which*
they had brought back to Jerusalem.
10 Then they put *it* in the hand of the fore-
men who had the oversight of the house of the
LORD; and they gave it to the workmen who
worked in the house of the LORD, to repair and
restore the house.
11 They gave *it* to the craftsmen and builders
to buy hewn stone and timber for beams, and to
floor the houses which the kings of Judah had
destroyed.
12 And the men did the work faithfully. Their
overseers *were* Jahath and Obadiah the Levites,

KJV

the Levites, of the sons of Merari; and Zechariah
and Meshullam, of the sons of the Kohathites, to
set *it* forward; and *other of* the Levites, all that
could skill of instruments of musick.
13 Also *they were* [a]over the bearers of burdens, and *were* overseers of all that wrought the
work in any manner of service: [b]and of the Levites
there were scribes, and officers, and porters.
14 And when they brought out the money that
was brought into the house of the LORD, Hilkiah the priest [a]found a book of the law of the
LORD *given* by Moses.
15 And Hilkiah answered and said to Shaphan the scribe, I have found the book of the law
in the house of the LORD. And Hilkiah delivered
the [a]book to Shaphan.
16 And Shaphan carried the book to the king,
and brought the king word back again, saying,
All that was committed to thy servants, they do
it.
17 And they have gathered together the
money that was found in the house of the LORD,
and have delivered it into the hand of the overseers, and to the hand of the workmen.
18 Then Shaphan the scribe told the king,
saying, Hilkiah the priest hath given me a book.
And Shaphan read it before the king.
19 And it came to pass, when the king had
heard the words of the law, that he rent his
clothes.
20 And the king commanded Hilkiah, and
[a]Ahikam the son of Shaphan, and Abdon the son
of Micah, and Shaphan the scribe, and Asaiah a
servant of the king's, saying,
21 Go, enquire of the LORD for me, and for
them that are left in Israel and in Judah, concerning the words of the book that is found: for great
is the wrath of the LORD that is poured out upon
us, because our fathers have not [a]kept the word
of the LORD, to do after all that is written in this
book.
22 And Hilkiah, and *they* that the king *had
appointed,* went to Huldah the prophetess, the
wife of Shallum the son of Tikvath, the son of
Hasrah, keeper of the wardrobe; (now she dwelt
in Jerusalem in the college:) and they spake to
her to that *effect.*
23 And she answered them, Thus saith the
LORD God of Israel, Tell ye the man that sent you
to me,
24 Thus saith the LORD, Behold, I will [a]bring
evil upon this place, and upon the inhabitants
thereof, *even* all the curses that are written in the
[b]book which they have read before the king of
Judah:
25 Because they have forsaken me, and have
burned incense unto other gods, that they might
provoke me to anger with all the works of their
hands; therefore my wrath shall be poured out
upon this place, and shall not be quenched.
26 And as for the king of Judah, who sent
you to enquire of the LORD, so shall ye say unto
him, Thus saith the LORD God of Israel *concerning*
the words which thou hast heard;
27 Because thine heart was tender, and thou
didst humble thyself before God, when thou
heardest his words against this place, and against
the inhabitants thereof, and humbledst thyself
before me, and didst rend thy clothes, and weep
before me; I have even heard *thee* also, saith the
[a]LORD.
28 Behold, I will gather thee to thy fathers,
and thou shalt be gathered to thy grave in peace,
neither shall thine eyes see all the evil that I will
bring upon this place, and upon the inhabitants
of the same. So they brought the king word again.

Josiah Restores True Worship
(2 Kin. 23:1–20)

29 [a]Then the king sent and gathered together
all the elders of Judah and Jerusalem.
30 And the king went up into the house of

13 [a]2 Chr. 8:10 [b]1 Chr. 23:4, 5
14 [a]2 Kin. 22:8
15 [a]Deut. 31:24, 26
20 [a]Jer. 26:24
21 [a]2 Kin. 17:15–19
24 [a]2 Chr. 36:14–20 [b]Deut. 28:15–68
27 [a]2 Kin. 22:19; 2 Chr. 12:7; 30:6; 33:12, 13
29 [a]2 Kin. 23:1–3

NKJV

of the sons of Merari, and Zechariah and Meshullam, of the sons of the Kohathites, to super-
vise. *Others of* the Levites, all of whom were skillful with instruments of music,
13 *were* [a]over the burden bearers and *were*
overseers of all who did work in any kind of service. [b]And *some* of the Levites *were* scribes, officers, and gatekeepers.
14 Now when they brought out the money
that was brought into the house of the LORD, Hilkiah the priest [a]found the Book of the Law of the
LORD *given* by Moses.
15 Then Hilkiah answered and said to Shaphan the scribe, "I have found the Book of the
Law in the house of the LORD." And Hilkiah gave
the [a]book to Shaphan.
16 So Shaphan carried the book to the king,
bringing the king word, saying, "All that was
committed to your servants they are doing.
17 "And they have gathered the money that
was found in the house of the LORD, and have
delivered it into the hand of the overseers and
the workmen."
18 Then Shaphan the scribe told the king,
saying, "Hilkiah the priest has given me a book."
And Shaphan read it before the king.
19 Thus it happened, when the king heard
the words of the Law, that he tore his clothes.
20 Then the king commanded Hilkiah, [a]Ahi-
kam the son of Shaphan, *Abdon the son of Micah,
Shaphan the scribe, and Asaiah a servant of the
king, saying,
21 "Go, inquire of the LORD for me, and for
those who are left in Israel and Judah, concerning
the words of the book that is found; for great *is*
the wrath of the LORD that is poured out on us,
because our fathers have not [a]kept the word of
the LORD, to do according to all that is written in
this book."
22 So Hilkiah and those the king *had appointed* went to Huldah the prophetess, the wife
of Shallum the son of *Tokhath, the son of *Hasrah, keeper of the wardrobe. (She dwelt in Jerusalem in the Second Quarter.) And they spoke to
her to that *effect.*
23 Then she answered them, "Thus says the
LORD God of Israel, 'Tell the man who sent you
to Me,
24 "Thus says the LORD: 'Behold, I will [a]bring
calamity on this place and on its inhabitants, all
the curses that are written in the [b]book which
they have read before the king of Judah,
25 'because they have forsaken Me and
burned incense to other gods, that they might provoke Me to anger with all the works of their
hands. Therefore My wrath will be poured out on
this place, and not be quenched.' " '
26 "But as for the king of Judah, who sent
you to inquire of the LORD, in this manner you
shall speak to him, 'Thus says the LORD God of
Israel: "*Concerning* the words which you have
heard—
27 "because your heart was tender, and you
humbled yourself before God when you heard His
words against this place and against its inhabitants, and you humbled yourself before Me, and
you tore your clothes and wept before Me, I also
have heard *you,*" says the [a]LORD.
28 "Surely I will gather you to your fathers,
and you shall be gathered to your grave in peace;
and your eyes shall not see all the calamity which
I will bring on this place and its inhabitants." ' "
So they brought back word to the king.

Josiah Restores True Worship
(2 Kin. 23:1–20)

29 [a]Then the king sent and gathered all the
elders of Judah and Jerusalem.
30 The king went up to the house of the LORD,

*
34:20 *Achbor the son of Michaiah,* 2 Kin. 22:12
34:22 *Tikvah,* 2 Kin. 22:14 • *Harhas,* 2 Kin. 22:14

KJV

the LORD, and all the men of Judah, and the inhabitants of Jerusalem, and the priests, and the Levites, and all the people, great and small: and he [a]read in their ears all the words of the book of the covenant that was found in the house of the LORD.

31 And the king [a]stood in [b]his place, and made a [c]covenant before the LORD, to walk after the LORD, and to keep his commandments, and his testimonies, and his statutes, with all his heart, and with all his soul, to perform the words of the covenant which are written in this book.

32 And he caused all that were present in Jerusalem and Benjamin to stand *to it*. And the inhabitants of Jerusalem did according to the covenant of God, the God of their fathers.

33 And Josiah took away all the [a]abominations out of all the countries that *pertained* to the children of Israel, and made all that were present in Israel to serve, *even* to serve the LORD their God. [b]*And* all his days they departed not from following the LORD, the God of their fathers.

Josiah Keeps the Passover
(2 Kin. 23:21–23)

35 Moreover [a]Josiah kept a passover unto the LORD in Jerusalem: and they killed the passover on the [b]fourteenth *day* of the first month.

2 And he set the priests in their [a]charges, and [b]encouraged them to the service of the house of the LORD,

3 And said unto the Levites [a]that taught all Israel, which were holy unto the LORD, [b]Put the holy ark [c]in the house which Solomon the son of David king of Israel did build; [d]*it shall* not *be* a burden upon *your* shoulders: serve now the LORD your God, and his people Israel,

4 And prepare *yourselves* [a]by the houses of your fathers, after your courses, according to the [b]writing of David king of Israel, and according to the [c]writing of Solomon his son.

5 And [a]stand in the holy *place* according to the divisions of the families of the fathers of your brethren the people, and *after* the division of the families of the Levites.

6 So kill the passover, and [a]sanctify yourselves, and prepare your brethren, that *they* may do according to the word of the LORD by the hand of Moses.

7 And Josiah [a]gave to the people, of the flock, lambs and kids, all for the passover offerings, for all that were present, to the number of thirty thousand, and three thousand bullocks: these *were* of the king's [b]substance.

8 And his [a]princes gave willingly unto the people, to the priests, and to the Levites: Hilkiah and Zechariah and Jehiel, rulers of the house of God, gave unto the priests for the passover offerings two thousand and six hundred *small cattle*, and three hundred oxen.

9 [a]Conaniah also, and Shemaiah and Nethaneel, his brethren, and Hashabiah and Jeiel and Jozabad, chief of the Levites, gave unto the Levites for passover offerings five thousand *small cattle*, and five hundred oxen.

10 So the service was prepared, and the priests [a]stood in their place, and the [b]Levites in their courses, according to the king's commandment.

11 And they killed the passover, and the priests [a]sprinkled *the blood* from their hands, and the Levites [b]flayed *them*.

12 And they removed the burnt offerings, that they might give according to the divisions of the families of the people, to offer unto the LORD, as *it is* written [a]in the book of Moses. And so *did they* with the oxen.

13 And they [a]roasted the passover with fire according to the ordinance: but the *other* holy *offerings* [b]sod they in pots, and in caldrons, and in

30 [a]Neh. 8:1–3
31 [a]2 Chr. 6:13 [b]2 Kin. 11:14; 23:3; 2 Chr. 30:16 [c]2 Chr. 23:16; 29:10
33 [a]1 Kin. 11:5; 2 Chr. 33:2 [b]Jer. 3:10

CHAPTER 35

1 [a]2 Kin. 23:21, 22 [b]Ex. 12:6; Num. 9:3; Ezra 6:19
2 [a]2 Chr. 23:18; Ezra 6:18 [b]2 Chr. 29:5–15
3 [a]Deut. 33:10; 2 Chr. 17:8, 9; Neh. 8:7 [b]2 Chr. 34:14 [c]Ex. 40:21; 2 Chr. 5:7 [d]1 Chr. 23:26
4 [a]1 Chr. 9:10–13 [b]1 Chr. 23—26 [c]2 Chr. 8:14
5 [a]Ps. 134:1
6 [a]2 Chr. 29:5, 15
7 [a]2 Chr. 30:24 [b]2 Chr. 31:3
8 [a]Num. 7:2
9 [a]2 Chr. 31:12
10 [a]Ezra 6:18; Heb. 9:6 [b]2 Chr. 5:12; 7:6; 8:14, 15; 13:10; 29:25–34
11 [a]Ex. 12:22; 2 Chr. 29:22 [b]2 Chr. 29:34
12 [a]Lev. 3:3; Ezra 6:18
13 [a]Ex. 12:8, 9; Deut. 16:7 [b]1 Sam. 2:13–15

NKJV

with all the men of Judah and the inhabitants of Jerusalem—the priests and the Levites, and all the people, great and small. And he [a]read in their hearing all the words of the Book of the Covenant which had been found in the house of the LORD.

31 Then the king [a]stood in [b]his place and made a [c]covenant before the LORD, to follow the LORD, and to keep His commandments and His testimonies and His statutes with all his heart and all his soul, to perform the words of the covenant that were written in this book.

32 And he made all who were present in Jerusalem and Benjamin take a stand. So the inhabitants of Jerusalem did according to the covenant of God, the God of their fathers.

33 Thus Josiah removed all the [a]abominations from all the country that *belonged* to the children of Israel, and made all who were present in Israel diligently serve the LORD their God. [b]All his days they did not depart from following the LORD God of their fathers.

Josiah Keeps the Passover
(2 Kin. 23:21–23)

35 Now [a]Josiah kept a Passover to the LORD in Jerusalem, and they slaughtered the Passover *lambs* on the [b]fourteenth *day* of the first month.

2 And he set the priests in their [a]duties and [b]encouraged them for the service of the house of the LORD.

3 Then he said to the Levites [a]who taught all Israel, who were holy to the LORD: [b]"Put the holy ark [c]in the house which Solomon the son of David, king of Israel, built. [d]*It shall* no longer *be* a burden on *your* shoulders. Now serve the LORD your God and His people Israel.

4 "Prepare *yourselves* [a]according to your fathers' houses, according to your divisions, following the [b]written instruction of David king of Israel and the [c]written instruction of Solomon his son.

5 "And [a]stand in the holy *place* according to the divisions of the fathers' houses of your brethren the *lay* people, and *according to* the division of the father's house of the Levites.

6 "So slaughter the Passover *offerings*, [a]consecrate yourselves, and prepare *them* for your brethren, that *they* may do according to the word of the LORD by the hand of Moses."

7 Then Josiah [a]gave the *lay* people lambs and young goats from the flock, all for Passover *offerings* for all who were present, to the number of thirty thousand, as well as three thousand cattle; these *were* from the king's [b]possessions.

8 And his [a]leaders gave willingly to the people, to the priests, and to the Levites. Hilkiah, Zechariah, and Jehiel, rulers of the house of God, gave to the priests for the Passover *offerings* two thousand six hundred *from the flock*, and three hundred cattle.

9 Also [a]Conaniah, his brothers Shemaiah and Nethanel, and Hashabiah and Jeiel and Jozabad, chief of the Levites, gave to the Levites for Passover *offerings* five thousand *from the flock* and five hundred cattle.

10 So the service was prepared, and the priests [a]stood in their places, and the [b]Levites in their divisions, according to the king's command.

11 And they slaughtered the Passover *offerings;* and the priests [a]sprinkled *the blood* with their hands, while the Levites [b]skinned *the animals*.

12 Then they removed the burnt offerings that *they* might give them to the divisions of the fathers' houses of the *lay* people, to offer to the LORD, as *it is* written [a]in the Book of Moses. And so *they did* with the cattle.

13 Also they [a]roasted the Passover *offerings* with fire according to the ordinance; but the *other* holy *offerings* they [b]boiled in pots, in caldrons,

KJV

pans, and divided *them* speedily among all the people.

14 And afterward they made ready for themselves, and for the priests: because the priests the sons of Aaron *were busied* in offering of burnt offerings and the fat until night; therefore the Levites prepared for themselves, and for the priests the sons of Aaron.

15 And the singers the sons of Asaph *were* in their place, according to the [a]commandment of David, and Asaph, and Heman, and Jeduthun the king's seer; and the porters [b]*waited* at every gate; they might not depart from their service; for their brethren the Levites prepared for them.

16 So all the service of the LORD was prepared the same day, to keep the passover, and to offer burnt offerings upon the altar of the LORD, according to the commandment of king Josiah.

17 And the children of Israel that were present kept the passover at that time, and the feast of [a]unleavened bread seven days.

18 And [a]there was no passover like to that kept in Israel from the days of Samuel the prophet; neither did all the kings of Israel keep such a passover as Josiah kept, and the priests, and the Levites, and all Judah and Israel that were present, and the inhabitants of Jerusalem.

19 In the eighteenth year of the reign of Josiah was this passover kept.

Josiah Dies in Battle
(2 Kin. 23:28–30)

20 [a]After all this, when Josiah had prepared the temple, Necho king of Egypt came up to fight against [b]Charchemish by Euphrates: and Josiah went out against him.

21 But he sent ambassadors to him, saying, What have I to do with thee, thou king of Judah? *I come* not against thee this day, but against the house wherewith I have war: for God commanded me to make haste: forbear thee from *meddling with* God, who *is* with me, that he destroy thee not.

22 Nevertheless Josiah would not turn his face from him, but [a]disguised himself, that he might fight with him, and hearkened not unto the words of Necho from the mouth of God, and came to fight in the valley of Megiddo.

23 And the archers shot at king Josiah; and the king said to his servants, Have me away; for I am sore wounded.

24 [a]His servants therefore took him out of that chariot, and put him in the second chariot that he had; and they brought him to Jerusalem, and he died, and was buried in *one of* the sepulchres of his fathers. And [b]all Judah and Jerusalem mourned for Josiah.

25 And Jeremiah [a]lamented for [b]Josiah: and [c]all the singing men and the singing women spake of Josiah in their lamentations to this day, [d]and made them an ordinance in Israel: and, behold, they *are* written in the lamentations.

26 Now the rest of the acts of Josiah, and his goodness, according to *that which was* written in the law of the LORD,

27 And his deeds, first and last, behold, they *are* written in the book of the kings of Israel and Judah.

The Reign and Captivity of Jehoahaz
(2 Kin. 23:31–33)

36 Then [a]the people of the land took Jehoahaz the son of Josiah, and made him king in his father's stead in Jerusalem.

2 Jehoahaz *was* twenty and three years old when he began to reign, and he reigned three months in Jerusalem.

3 And the king of Egypt put him down at Jerusalem, and condemned the land in an hundred talents of silver and a talent of gold.

4 And the king of Egypt made Eliakim his brother king over Judah and Jerusalem, and

15 [a]1 Chr. 25:1–6 [b]1 Chr. 9:17, 18
17 [a]Ex. 12:15; 13:6; 2 Chr. 30:21
18 [a]2 Kin. 23:22, 23
20 [a]2 Kin. 23:29 [b]Is. 10:9; Jer. 46:2
22 [a]1 Kin. 22:30; 2 Chr. 18:29
24 [a]2 Kin. 23:30 [b]1 Kin. 14:18; Zech. 12:11
25 [a]Lam. 4:20 [b]Jer. 22:10, 11 [c]Matt. 9:23 [d]Jer. 22:20

CHAPTER 36

1 [a]2 Kin. 23:30–34

NKJV

and in pans, and divided *them* quickly among all the *lay* people.

14 Then afterward they prepared portions for themselves and for the priests, because the priests, the sons of Aaron, *were busy* in offering burnt offerings and fat until night; therefore the Levites prepared portions for themselves and for the priests, the sons of Aaron.

15 And the singers, the sons of Asaph, *were* in their places, according to the [a]command of David, Asaph, Heman, and Jeduthun the king's seer. Also the gatekeepers [b]were at each gate; they did not have to leave their position, because their brethren the Levites prepared portions for them.

16 So all the service of the LORD was prepared the same day, to keep the Passover and to offer burnt offerings on the altar of the LORD, according to the command of King Josiah.

17 And the children of Israel who were present kept the Passover at that time, and the Feast of [a]Unleavened Bread for seven days.

18 [a]There had been no Passover kept in Israel like that since the days of Samuel the prophet; and none of the kings of Israel had kept such a Passover as Josiah kept, with the priests and the Levites, all Judah and Israel who were present, and the inhabitants of Jerusalem.

19 In the eighteenth year of the reign of Josiah this Passover was kept.

Josiah Dies in Battle
(2 Kin. 23:28–30)

20 [a]After all this, when Josiah had prepared the temple, Necho king of Egypt came up to fight against [b]Carchemish by the Euphrates; and Josiah went out against him.

21 But he sent messengers to him, saying, "What have I to do with you, king of Judah? *I have* not *come* against you this day, but against the house with which I have war; for God commanded me to make haste. Refrain *from meddling with* God, who *is* with me, lest He destroy you."

22 Nevertheless Josiah would not turn his face from him, but [a]disguised himself so that he might fight with him, and did not heed the words of Necho from the mouth of God. So he came to fight in the Valley of Megiddo.

23 And the archers shot King Josiah; and the king said to his servants, "Take me away, for I am severely wounded."

24 [a]His servants therefore took him out of that chariot and put him in the second chariot that he had, and they brought him to Jerusalem. So he died, and was buried in *one of* the tombs of his fathers. And [b]all Judah and Jerusalem mourned for Josiah.

25 Jeremiah also [a]lamented for [b]Josiah. And to this day [c]all the singing men and the singing women speak of Josiah in their lamentations. [d]They made it a custom in Israel; and indeed they *are* written in the Laments.

26 Now the rest of the acts of Josiah and his goodness, according to *what was* written in the Law of the LORD,

27 and his deeds from first to last, indeed they *are* written in the book of the kings of Israel and Judah.

The Reign and Captivity of Jehoahaz
(2 Kin. 23:31–33)

36 Then [a]the people of the land took Jehoahaz the son of Josiah, and made him king in his father's place in Jerusalem.

2 *Jehoahaz *was* twenty-three years old when he became king, and he reigned three months in Jerusalem.

3 Now the king of Egypt deposed him at Jerusalem; and he imposed on the land a tribute of one hundred talents of silver and a talent of gold.

4 Then the king of Egypt made **Jehoahaz's* brother Eliakim king over Judah and Jerusalem,

*———

36:2 MT *Joahaz*
36:4 Lit. *his*

KJV

turned his name to Jehoiakim. And Necho took Jehoahaz his brother, and carried him to Egypt.

The Reign and Captivity of Jehoiakim
(2 Kin. 23:34—24:7)

5 [a]Jehoiakim *was* twenty and five years old when he began to reign, and he reigned eleven years in Jerusalem: and he did *that which was* [b]evil in the sight of the LORD his God.

6 [a]Against him came up Nebuchadnezzar king of Babylon, and bound him in fetters, to [b]carry him to Babylon.

7 [a]Nebuchadnezzar also carried of the vessels of the house of the LORD to Babylon, and put them in his temple at Babylon.

8 Now the rest of the acts of Jehoiakim, and his abominations which he did, and that which was found in him, behold, they *are* written in the book of the kings of Israel and Judah: and Jehoiachin his son reigned in his stead.

The Reign and Captivity of Jehoiachin
(2 Kin. 24:8–17)

9 [a]Jehoiachin *was* eight years old when he began to reign, and he reigned three months and ten days in Jerusalem: and he did *that which was* evil in the sight of the LORD.

10 And when the year was expired, [a]king Nebuchadnezzar sent, and brought him to Babylon, [b]with the goodly vessels of the house of the LORD, and made [c]Zedekiah his brother king over Judah and Jerusalem.

Zedekiah Reigns in Judah
(2 Kin. 24:18–20; Jer. 52:1–3)

11 [a]Zedekiah *was* one and twenty years old when he began to reign, and reigned eleven years in Jerusalem.

12 And he did *that which was* evil in the sight of the LORD his God, *and* humbled [a]not himself before Jeremiah the prophet *speaking* from the mouth of the LORD.

13 And he also [a]rebelled against king Nebuchadnezzar, who had made him swear by God: but he [b]stiffened his neck, and hardened his heart from turning unto the LORD God of Israel.

14 Moreover all the chief of the priests, and the people, transgressed very much after all the abominations of the heathen; and polluted the house of the LORD which he had hallowed in Jerusalem.

The Fall of Jerusalem
(2 Kin. 25:1–21; Jer. 52:4 –30)

15 [a]And the LORD God of their fathers sent to them by his messengers, rising up betimes, and sending; because he had compassion on his people, and on his dwelling place:

16 But [a]they mocked the messengers of God, and [b]despised his words, and [c]misused his prophets, until the [d]wrath of the LORD arose against his people, till *there was* no remedy.

17 [a]Therefore he brought upon them the king of the Chaldees, who [b]slew their young men with the sword in the house of their sanctuary, and had no compassion upon young man or maiden, old man, or him that stooped for age: he gave *them* all into his hand.

18 [a]And all the vessels of the house of God, great and small, and the treasures of the house of the LORD, and the treasures of the king, and of his princes; all *these* he brought to Babylon.

19 [a]And they burnt the house of God, and brake down the wall of Jerusalem, and burnt all the palaces thereof with fire, and destroyed all the goodly vessels thereof.

20 And [a]them that had escaped from the sword carried he away to Babylon; [b]where they were servants to him and his sons until the reign of the kingdom of Persia:

21 To fulfil the word of the LORD by the

5 [a]2 Kin. 23:36, 37; 1 Chr. 3:15 [b][Jer. 22:13–19]
6 [a]2 Kin. 24:1; Hab. 1:6 [b][Deut. 29:22–29]; 2 Chr. 33:11; Jer. 36:30
7 [a]2 Kin. 24:13; Dan. 1:1, 2
9 [a]2 Kin. 24:8–17
10 [a]2 Kin. 24:10–17 [b]Dan. 1:1, 2 [c]Jer. 37:1
11 [a]2 Kin. 24:18–20; Jer. 52:1
12 [a]Jer. 21:3–7; 44:10
13 [a]Jer. 52:3; Ezek. 17:15 [b]2 Kin. 17:14; [2 Chr. 30:8]
15 [a]Jer. 7:13; 25:3, 4
16 [a]2 Chr. 30:10; Jer. 5:12, 13 [b][Prov. 1:24–32] [c]Jer. 38:6; Matt. 23:34 [d]2 Chr. 34:25; Ps. 79:5
17 [a]Num. 33:56; Deut. 4:26; 28:49; 2 Kin. 25:1; Ezra 9:7; Is. 3:8 [b]Ps. 74:20
18 [a]2 Kin. 25:13–15; 2 Chr. 36:7, 10
19 [a]2 Kin. 25:9; Ps. 79:1, 7; Is. 1:7, 8; Jer. 52:13
20 [a]2 Kin. 25:11; Jer. 5:19; Mic. 4:10 [b]Jer. 17:4; 27:7

NKJV

and changed his name to Jehoiakim. And Necho took *Jehoahaz his brother and carried him off to Egypt.

The Reign and Captivity of Jehoiakim
(2 Kin. 23:34—24:7)

5 [a]Jehoiakim *was* twenty-five years old when he became king, and he reigned eleven years in Jerusalem. And he did [b]evil in the sight of the LORD his God.

6 [a]Nebuchadnezzar king of Babylon came up against him, and bound him in bronze *fetters* to [b]carry him off to Babylon.

7 [a]Nebuchadnezzar also carried off *some* of the articles from the house of the LORD to Babylon, and put them in his temple at Babylon.

8 Now the rest of the acts of Jehoiakim, the abominations which he did, and what was found against him, indeed they *are* written in the book of the kings of Israel and Judah. Then Jehoiachin his son reigned in his place.

The Reign and Captivity of Jehoiachin
(2 Kin. 24:8–17)

9 [a]Jehoiachin *was* *eight years old when he became king, and he reigned in Jerusalem three months and ten days. And he did evil in the sight of the LORD.

10 At the turn of the year [a]King Nebuchadnezzar summoned *him* and took him to Babylon, [b]with the costly articles from the house of the LORD, and made [c]Zedekiah, **Jehoiakim's* brother, king over Judah and Jerusalem.

Zedekiah Reigns in Judah
(2 Kin. 24:18–20; Jer. 52:1–3)

11 [a]Zedekiah *was* twenty-one years old when he became king, and he reigned eleven years in Jerusalem.

12 He did evil in the sight of the LORD his God, *and* [a]did not humble himself before Jeremiah the prophet, *who spoke* from the mouth of the LORD.

13 And he also [a]rebelled against King Nebuchadnezzar, who had made him swear *an oath* by God; but he [b]stiffened his neck and hardened his heart against turning to the LORD God of Israel.

14 Moreover all the leaders of the priests and the people transgressed more and more, *according* to all the abominations of the nations, and defiled the house of the LORD which He had consecrated in Jerusalem.

The Fall of Jerusalem
(2 Kin. 25:1–21; Jer. 52:4–30)

15 [a]And the LORD God of their fathers sent *warnings* to them by His messengers, rising up early and sending *them,* because He had compassion on His people and on His dwelling place.

16 But [a]they mocked the messengers of God, [b]despised His words, and [c]scoffed at His prophets, until the [d]wrath of the LORD arose against His people, till *there was* no remedy.

17 [a]Therefore He brought against them the king of the Chaldeans, who [b]killed their young men with the sword in the house of their sanctuary, and had no compassion on young man or virgin, on the aged or the weak; He gave *them* all into his hand.

18 [a]And all the articles from the house of God, great and small, the treasures of the house of the LORD, and the treasures of the king and of his leaders, all *these* he took to Babylon.

19 [a]Then they burned the house of God, broke down the wall of Jerusalem, burned all its palaces with fire, and destroyed all its precious possessions.

20 And [a]those who escaped from the sword he carried away to Babylon, [b]where they became servants to him and his sons until the rule of the kingdom of Persia,

21 to fulfill the word of the LORD by the

*

36:4 MT *Joahaz*
36:9 Heb. mss., LXX, Syr., *eighteen* and 2 Kin. 24:8
36:10 Lit. *his brother,* 2 Kin. 24:17

KJV

mouth of [a]Jeremiah, until the land [b]had enjoyed
her sabbaths: *for* as long as she lay desolate [c]she
kept sabbath, to fulfil threescore and ten years.

The Proclamation of Cyrus
(Ezra 1:1–4)

22 [a]Now in the first year of Cyrus king of
Persia, that the word of the LORD *spoken* by the
mouth of [b]Jeremiah might be accomplished, the
LORD stirred up the spirit of [c]Cyrus king of Persia,
that he made a proclamation throughout all his
kingdom, and *put it* also in writing, saying,
23 [a]Thus saith Cyrus king of Persia, All the
kingdoms of the earth hath the LORD God of
heaven given me; and he hath charged me to build
him an house in Jerusalem, which *is* in Judah.
Who *is there* among you of all his people? The
LORD his God *be* with him, and let him go up.

21 [a]Jer. 25:9–12; 27:6–8; 29:10 [b]Lev. 26:34–43; Dan. 9:2 [c]Lev. 25:4, 5
22 [a]Ezra 1:1–3 [b]Jer. 29:10 [c]Is. 44:28; 45:1
23 [a]Ezra 1:2, 3

NKJV

mouth of [a]Jeremiah, until the land [b]had enjoyed
her Sabbaths. As long as she lay desolate [c]she
kept Sabbath, to fulfill seventy years.

The Proclamation of Cyrus
(Ezra 1:1–4)

22 [a]Now in the first year of Cyrus king of
Persia, that the word of the LORD by the mouth
of [b]Jeremiah might be fulfilled, the LORD stirred
up the spirit of [c]Cyrus king of Persia, so that he
made a proclamation throughout all his kingdom,
and also *put it* in writing, saying,

23 [a]Thus says Cyrus king of Persia: All the
kingdoms of the earth the LORD God of
heaven has given me. And He has
commanded me to build Him a house at
Jerusalem which is in Judah. Who *is*
among you of all His people? May the
LORD his God *be* with him, and let him
go up!

KJV

THE BOOK OF

EZRA

End of the Babylonian Captivity
(2 Chr. 36:22, 23)

1 Now in the first year of Cyrus king of Persia, that the word of the LORD [a]by the mouth of Jeremiah might be fulfilled, the LORD stirred up the spirit of Cyrus king of Persia, [b]that he made a proclamation throughout all his kingdom, and *put it* also in writing, saying,

2 Thus saith Cyrus king of Persia, The LORD God of heaven hath given me all the kingdoms of the earth; and he hath [a]charged me to build him an house at Jerusalem, which *is* in Judah.

3 Who *is there* among you of all his people? his God be with him, and let him go up to Jerusalem, which *is* in Judah, and build the house of the LORD God of Israel, ([a]he *is* the God,) which *is* in Jerusalem.

4 And whosoever remaineth in any place where he sojourneth, let the men of his place help him with silver, and with gold, and with goods, and with beasts, beside the freewill offering for the house of God that *is* in Jerusalem.

5 Then rose up the chief of the fathers of Judah and Benjamin, and the priests, and the Levites, with all *them* whose spirit [a]God had raised, to go up to build the house of the LORD which *is* in Jerusalem.

6 And all they that *were* about them strengthened their hands with vessels of silver, with gold, with goods, and with beasts, and with precious things, beside all *that* was [a]willingly offered.

7 [a]Also Cyrus the king brought forth the vessels of the house of the LORD, [b]which Nebuchadnezzar had brought forth out of Jerusalem, and had put them in the house of his gods;

8 Even those did Cyrus king of Persia bring forth by the hand of Mithredath the treasurer, and numbered them unto [a]Sheshbazzar, the prince of Judah.

9 And this *is* the number of them: thirty chargers of gold, a thousand chargers of silver, nine and twenty knives,

10 Thirty basons of gold, silver basons of a second *sort* four hundred and ten, *and* other vessels a thousand.

11 All the vessels of gold and of silver *were* five thousand and four hundred. All *these* did Sheshbazzar bring up with *them of* the captivity that were brought up from Babylon unto Jerusalem.

The Captives Who Returned to Jerusalem
(Neh. 7:6–73)

2 Now [a]these *are* the children of the province that went up out of the captivity, of those which had been carried away, [b]whom Nebuchadnezzar the king of Babylon had carried away unto Babylon, and came again unto Jerusalem and Judah, every one unto his city;

2 Which came with Zerubbabel: Jeshua, Nehemiah, Seraiah, Reelaiah, Mordecai, Bilshan, Mizpar, Bigvai, Rehum, Baanah. The number of the men of the people of Israel:

CHAPTER 1

1 [a]2 Chr. 36:22, 23; Jer. 25:12; 29:10 [b]Ezra 5:13, 14; Is. 44:28—45:13
2 [a]Is. 44:28; 45:1, 13
3 [a]1 Kin. 8:23; 18:39; Is. 37:16; Dan. 6:26
5 [a][Phil. 2:13]
6 [a]Ezra 2:68
7 [a]Ezra 5:14; 6:5; Dan. 1:2; 5:2, 3 [b]2 Kin. 24:13; 2 Chr. 36:7, 18
8 [a]Ezra 5:14, 16

CHAPTER 2

1 [a]Neh. 7:6–73; Jer. 32:15; 50:5; Ezek. 14:22 [b]2 Kin. 24:14–16; 25:11; 2 Chr. 36:20

*

2:2 *Mispereth,* Neh. 7:7
• *Nehum,* Neh. 7:7

NKJV

THE BOOK OF

EZRA

End of The Babylonian Captivity
(2 Chr. 36:22, 23)

1 Now in the first year of Cyrus king of Persia, that the word of the LORD [a]by the mouth of Jeremiah might be fulfilled, the LORD stirred up the spirit of Cyrus king of Persia, [b]so that he made a proclamation throughout all his kingdom, and also *put it* in writing, saying,

2 Thus says Cyrus king of Persia: All the
kingdoms of the earth the LORD God of
heaven has given me. And He has
[a]commanded me to build Him a house at
Jerusalem which *is* in Judah.
3 Who *is* among you of all His people? May
his God be with him, and let him go up
to Jerusalem which *is* in Judah, and build
the house of the LORD God of Israel [a](He
is God), which *is* in Jerusalem.
4 And whoever is left in any place where
he dwells, let the men of his place help
him with silver and gold, with goods and
livestock, besides the freewill offerings for
the house of God which *is* in Jerusalem.

5 Then the heads of the fathers' *houses* of Judah and Benjamin, and the priests and the Levites, with all whose spirits [a]God had moved, arose to go up and build the house of the LORD which *is* in Jerusalem.

6 And all those who *were* around them encouraged them with articles of silver and gold, with goods and livestock, and with precious things, besides all *that* was [a]willingly offered.

7 [a]King Cyrus also brought out the articles of the house of the LORD, [b]which Nebuchadnezzar had taken from Jerusalem and put in the temple of his gods;

8 and Cyrus king of Persia brought them out by the hand of Mithredath the treasurer, and counted them out to [a]Sheshbazzar the prince of Judah.

9 This *is* the number of them: thirty gold platters, one thousand silver platters, twenty-nine knives,

10 thirty gold basins, four hundred and ten silver basins of a similar *kind, and* one thousand other articles.

11 All the articles of gold and silver *were* five thousand four hundred. All *these* Sheshbazzar took with the captives who were brought from Babylon to Jerusalem.

The Captives Who Returned to Jerusalem
(Neh. 7:6–73)

2 Now [a]these *are* the people of the province who came back from the captivity, of those who had been carried away, [b]whom Nebuchadnezzar the king of Babylon had carried away to Babylon, and who returned to Jerusalem and Judah, everyone to his *own* city.

2 *Those* who came with Zerubbabel *were* Jeshua, Nehemiah, Seraiah, Reelaiah, Mordecai, Bilshan, *Mispar, Bigvai, *Rehum, *and* Baanah. The number of the men of the people of Israel:

KJV

3 The children of Parosh, two thousand an hundred seventy and two.
4 The children of Shephatiah, three hundred seventy and two.
5 The children of Arah, [a]seven hundred seventy and five.
6 The children of [a]Pahath–moab, of the children of Jeshua *and* Joab, two thousand eight hundred and twelve.
7 The children of Elam, a thousand two hundred fifty and four.
8 The children of Zattu, nine hundred forty and five.
9 The children of Zaccai, seven hundred and threescore.
10 The children of Bani, six hundred forty and two.
11 The children of Bebai, six hundred twenty and three.
12 The children of Azgad, a thousand two hundred twenty and two.
13 The children of Adonikam, six hundred sixty and six.
14 The children of Bigvai, two thousand fifty and six.
15 The children of Adin, four hundred fifty and four.
16 The children of Ater of Hezekiah, ninety and eight.
17 The children of Bezai, three hundred twenty and three.
18 The children of Jorah, an hundred and twelve.
19 The children of Hashum, two hundred twenty and three.
20 The children of Gibbar, ninety and five.
21 The children of Beth–lehem, an hundred twenty and three.
22 The men of Netophah, fifty and six.
23 The men of Anathoth, an hundred twenty and eight.
24 The children of Azmaveth, forty and two.
25 The children of Kirjath–arim, Chephirah, and Beeroth, seven hundred and forty and three.
26 The children of Ramah and Gaba, six hundred twenty and one.
27 The men of Michmas, an hundred twenty and two.
28 The men of Beth–el and Ai, two hundred twenty and three.
29 The children of Nebo, fifty and two.
30 The children of Magbish, an hundred fifty and six.
31 The children of the other [a]Elam, a thousand two hundred fifty and four.
32 The children of Harim, three hundred and twenty.
33 The children of Lod, Hadid, and Ono, seven hundred twenty and five.
34 The children of Jericho, three hundred forty and five.
35 The children of Senaah, three thousand and six hundred and thirty.
36 The priests: the children of [a]Jedaiah, of the house of Jeshua, nine hundred seventy and three.
37 The children of [a]Immer, a thousand fifty and two.
38 The children of [a]Pashur, a thousand two hundred forty and seven.
39 The children of [a]Harim, a thousand and seventeen.
40 The Levites: the children of Jeshua and Kadmiel, of the children of Hodaviah, seventy and four.
41 The singers: the children of Asaph, an hundred twenty and eight.
42 The children of the porters: the children of Shallum, the children of Ater, the children of Talmon, the children of Akkub, the children of Hatita, the children of Shobai, *in* all an hundred thirty and nine.

5 [a]Neh. 7:10
6 [a]Neh. 7:11
31 [a]Ezra 2:7
36 [a]1 Chr. 24:7–18
37 [a]1 Chr. 24:14
38 [a]1 Chr. 9:12
39 [a]1 Chr. 24:8

NKJV

3 the people of Parosh, two thousand one hundred and seventy-two;
4 the people of Shephatiah, three hundred and seventy-two;
5 the people of Arah, [a]seven hundred and seventy-five;
6 the people of [a]Pahath-Moab, of the people of Jeshua *and* Joab, two thousand eight hundred and twelve;
7 the people of Elam, one thousand two hundred and fifty-four;
8 the people of Zattu, nine hundred and forty-five;
9 the people of Zaccai, seven hundred and sixty;
10 the people of *Bani, six hundred and forty-two;
11 the people of Bebai, six hundred and twenty-three;
12 the people of Azgad, one thousand two hundred and twenty-two;
13 the people of Adonikam, six hundred and sixty-six;
14 the people of Bigvai, two thousand and fifty-six;
15 the people of Adin, four hundred and fifty-four;
16 the people of Ater of Hezekiah, ninety-eight;
17 the people of Bezai, three hundred and twenty-three;
18 the people of *Jorah, one hundred and twelve;
19 the people of Hashum, two hundred and twenty-three;
20 the people of *Gibbar, ninety-five;
21 the people of Bethlehem, one hundred and twenty-three;
22 the men of Netophah, fifty-six;
23 the men of Anathoth, one hundred and twenty-eight;
24 the people of *Azmaveth, forty-two;
25 the people of *Kirjath Arim, Chephirah, and Beeroth, seven hundred and forty-three;
26 the people of Ramah and Geba, six hundred and twenty-one;
27 the men of Michmas, one hundred and twenty-two;
28 the men of Bethel and Ai, two hundred and twenty-three;
29 the people of Nebo, fifty-two;
30 the people of Magbish, one hundred and fifty-six;
31 the people of the other [a]Elam, one thousand two hundred and fifty-four;
32 the people of Harim, three hundred and twenty;
33 the people of Lod, Hadid, and Ono, seven hundred and twenty-five;
34 the people of Jericho, three hundred and forty-five;
35 the people of Senaah, three thousand six hundred and thirty.
36 The priests: the sons of [a]Jedaiah, of the house of Jeshua, nine hundred and seventy-three;
37 the sons of [a]Immer, one thousand and fifty-two;
38 the sons of [a]Pashhur, one thousand two hundred and forty-seven;
39 the sons of [a]Harim, one thousand and seventeen.
40 The Levites: the sons of Jeshua and Kadmiel, of the sons of *Hodaviah, seventy-four.
41 The singers: the sons of Asaph, one hundred and twenty-eight.
42 The sons of the gatekeepers: the sons of Shallum, the sons of Ater, the sons of Talmon, the sons of Akkub, the sons of Hatita, and the sons of Shobai, one hundred and thirty-nine *in* all.

*———

2:10 *Binnui,* Neh. 7:15
2:18 *Hariph,* Neh. 7:24
2:20 *Gibeon,* Neh. 7:25
2:24 *Beth Azmaveth,* Neh. 7:28
2:25 *Kirjath Jearim,* Neh. 7:29
2:40 *Judah,* Ezra 3:9, or *Hodevah,* Neh. 7:43

KJV

43 [a]The Nethinims: the children of Ziha, the children of Hasupha, the children of Tabbaoth,
44 The children of Keros, the children of Siaha, the children of Padon,
45 The children of Lebanah, the children of Hagabah, the children of Akkub,
46 The children of Hagab, the children of Shalmai, the children of Hanan,
47 The children of Giddel, the children of Gahar, the children of Reaiah,
48 The children of Rezin, the children of Nekoda, the children of Gazzam,
49 The children of Uzza, the children of Paseah, the children of Besai,
50 The children of Asnah, the children of Mehunim, the children of Nephusim,
51 The children of Bakbuk, the children of Hakupha, the children of Harhur,
52 The children of Bazluth, the children of Mehida, the children of Harsha,
53 The children of Barkos, the children of Sisera, the children of Thamah,
54 The children of Neziah, the children of Hatipha.
55 The children of [a]Solomon's servants: the children of Sotai, the children of [b]Sophereth, the children of Peruda,
56 The children of Jaalah, the children of Darkon, the children of Giddel,
57 The children of Shephatiah, the children of Hattil, the children of Pochereth of Zebaim, the children of Ami.
58 All the [a]Nethinims, and the children of [b]Solomon's servants, *were* three hundred ninety and two.
59 And these *were* they which went up from Tel–melah, Tel–harsa, Cherub, Addan, *and* Immer: but they could not shew their father's house, and their seed, whether they *were* of Israel:
60 The children of Delaiah, the children of Tobiah, the children of Nekoda, six hundred fifty and two.
61 And of the children of the priests: the children of [a]Habaiah, the children of Koz, the children of [b]Barzillai; which took a wife of the daughters of Barzillai the Gileadite, and was called after their name:
62 These sought their register *among* those that were reckoned by genealogy, but they were not found: [a]therefore were they, as polluted, put from the priesthood.
63 And the Tirshatha said unto them, that they [a]should not eat of the most holy things, till there stood up a priest with [b]Urim and with Thummim.
64 [a]The whole congregation together *was* forty and two thousand three hundred *and* threescore,
65 Beside their servants and their maids, of whom *there were* seven thousand three hundred thirty and seven: and *there were* among them two hundred singing men and singing women.
66 Their horses *were* seven hundred thirty and six; their mules, two hundred forty and five;
67 Their camels, four hundred thirty and five; *their* asses, six thousand seven hundred and twenty.
68 [a]And *some* of the chief of the fathers, when they came to the house of the LORD which *is* at Jerusalem, offered freely for the house of God to set it up in his place:
69 They gave after their ability unto the [a]treasure of the work threescore and one thousand drams of gold, and five thousand pound of silver, and one hundred priests' garments.
70 [a]So the priests, and the Levites, and *some* of the people, and the singers, and the porters, and the Nethinims, dwelt in their cities, and all Israel in their cities.

43 [a]1 Chr. 9:2; Ezra 7:7
55 [a]1 Kin. 9:21 [b]Neh. 7:57–60
58 [a]Josh. 9:21, 27; 1 Chr. 9:2 [b]1 Kin. 9:21
61 [a]Neh. 7:63 [b]2 Sam. 17:27; 1 Kin. 2:7
62 [a]Num. 3:10
63 [a]Lev. 22:2, 10, 15, 16 [b]Ex. 28:30; Num. 27:21
64 [a]Neh. 7:66; Is. 10:22
68 [a]Ezra 1:6; 3:5; Neh. 7:70
69 [a]1 Chr. 26:20; Ezra 8:25–35
70 [a]Ezra 6:16, 17; Neh. 7:73

NKJV

43 [a]The Nethinim: the sons of Ziha, the sons of Hasupha, the sons of Tabbaoth,
44 the sons of Keros, the sons of *Siaha, the sons of Padon,
45 the sons of Lebanah, the sons of Hagabah, the sons of Akkub,
46 the sons of Hagab, the sons of Shalmai, the sons of Hanan,
47 the sons of Giddel, the sons of Gahar, the sons of Reaiah,
48 the sons of Rezin, the sons of Nekoda, the sons of Gazzam,
49 the sons of Uzza, the sons of Paseah, the sons of Besai,
50 the sons of Asnah, the sons of Meunim, the sons of *Nephusim,
51 the sons of Bakbuk, the sons of Hakupha, the sons of Harhur,
52 the sons of *Bazluth, the sons of Mehida, the sons of Harsha,
53 the sons of Barkos, the sons of Sisera, the sons of Tamah,
54 the sons of Neziah, and the sons of Hatipha.
55 The sons of [a]Solomon's servants: the sons of Sotai, the sons of [b]Sophereth, the sons of *Peruda,
56 the sons of Jaala, the sons of Darkon, the sons of Giddel,
57 the sons of Shephatiah, the sons of Hattil, the sons of Pochereth of Zebaim, and the sons of *Ami.
58 All the [a]Nethinim and the children of [b]Solomon's servants were three hundred and ninety-two.
59 And these *were* the ones who came up from Tel Melah, Tel Harsha, Cherub, *Addan, and Immer; but they could not identify their father's house or their *genealogy, whether they *were* of Israel:
60 the sons of Delaiah, the sons of Tobiah, and the sons of Nekoda, six hundred and fifty-two;
61 and of the sons of the priests: the sons of [a]Habaiah, the sons of *Koz, and the sons of [b]Barzillai, who took a wife of the daughters of Barzillai the Gileadite, and was called by their name.
62 These sought their listing *among* those who were registered by genealogy, but they were not found; [a]therefore they *were excluded* from the priesthood as defiled.
63 And the *governor said to them that they [a]should not eat of the most holy things till a priest could consult with the [b]Urim and Thummim.
64 [a]The whole assembly together *was* forty-two thousand three hundred *and* sixty,
65 besides their male and female servants, of whom *there were* seven thousand three hundred and thirty-seven; and they had two hundred men and women singers.
66 Their horses *were* seven hundred and thirty-six, their mules two hundred and forty-five,
67 their camels four hundred and thirty-five, and *their* donkeys six thousand seven hundred and twenty.
68 [a]*Some* of the heads of the fathers' *houses,* when they came to the house of the LORD which *is* in Jerusalem, offered freely for the house of God, to erect it in its place:
69 According to their ability, they gave to the [a]treasury for the work sixty-one thousand gold drachmas, five thousand minas of silver, and one hundred priestly garments.
70 [a]So the priests and the Levites, *some* of the people, the singers, the gatekeepers, and the Nethinim, dwelt in their cities, and all Israel in their cities.

*

2:44 *Sia,* Neh. 7:47
2:50 *Nephishesim,* Neh. 7:52
2:52 *Bazlith,* Neh. 7:54
2:55 *Perida,* Neh. 7:57
2:57 *Amon,* Neh. 7:59
2:59 *Addon,* Neh. 7:61 • Lit. *seed*
2:61 Or *Hakkoz*
2:63 Heb. *Tirshatha*

KJV

Worship Restored at Jerusalem

3 And when the [a]seventh month was come, and the children of Israel *were* in the cities, the people gathered themselves together as one man to Jerusalem.

2 Then stood up Jeshua the son of [a]Jozadak, and his brethren the priests, and [b]Zerubbabel the son of [c]Shealtiel, and his brethren, and builded the altar of the God of Israel, to offer burnt offerings thereon, as *it is* [d]written in the law of Moses the man of God.

3 And they set the altar upon his bases; for fear *was* upon them because of the people of those countries: and they offered burnt offerings thereon unto the LORD, *even* [a]burnt offerings morning and evening.

4 [a]They kept also the feast of tabernacles, [b]as *it is* written, and [c]*offered* the daily burnt offerings by number, according to the custom, as the duty of every day required;

5 And afterward *offered* the [a]continual burnt offering, both of the new moons, and of all the set feasts of the LORD that were consecrated, and of every one that willingly offered a freewill offering unto the LORD.

6 From the first day of the seventh month began they to offer burnt offerings unto the LORD. But the foundation of the temple of the LORD was not *yet* laid.

7 They gave money also unto the masons, and to the carpenters; and [a]meat, and drink, and oil, unto them of Zidon, and to them of Tyre, to bring cedar trees from Lebanon to the sea of [b]Joppa, [c]according to the grant that they had of Cyrus king of Persia.

Restoration of the Temple Begins

8 Now in the second year of their coming unto the house of God at Jerusalem, in the second month, began [a]Zerubbabel the son of Shealtiel, and Jeshua the son of Jozadak, and the remnant of their brethren the priests and the Levites, and all they that were come out of the captivity unto Jerusalem; [b]and appointed the Levites, from twenty years old and upward, to set forward the work of the house of the LORD.

9 Then stood Jeshua *with* his sons and his brethren, Kadmiel and his sons, the sons of Judah, together, to set forward the workmen in the house of God: the sons of Henadad, *with* their sons and their brethren the Levites.

10 And when the builders laid the foundation of the temple of the LORD, [a]they set the priests in their apparel with trumpets, and the Levites the sons of Asaph with cymbals, to praise the LORD, after the [b]ordinance of David king of Israel.

11 [a]And they sang together by course in praising and giving thanks unto the LORD; [b]because *he is* good, [c]for his mercy *endureth* for ever toward Israel. And all the people shouted with a great shout, when they praised the LORD, because the foundation of the house of the LORD was laid.

12 But many of the priests and Levites and [a]chief of the fathers, *who were* ancient men, that had seen the first house, when the foundation of this house was laid before their eyes, wept with a loud voice; and many shouted aloud for joy:

13 So that the people could not discern the noise of the shout of joy from the noise of the weeping of the people: for the people shouted with a loud shout, and the noise was heard afar off.

Resistance to Rebuilding the Temple

4 Now when [a]the adversaries of Judah and Benjamin heard that the children of the captivity builded the temple unto the LORD God of Israel;

CHAPTER 3

1 [a]Neh. 7:73; 8:1, 2
2 [a]1 Chr. 6:14, 15; Ezra 4:3; Neh. 12:1, 8; Hag. 1:1; 2:2 [b]Ezra 2:2; 4:2, 3; 5:2 [c]1 Chr. 3:17 [d]Deut. 12:5, 6
3 [a]Num. 28:3
4 [a]Lev. 23:33–43; Neh. 8:14–18; Zech. 14:16 [b]Ex. 23:16 [c]Num. 29:12, 13
5 [a]Ex. 29:38; Num. 28:3, 11, 19, 26; Ezra 1:4; 2:68; 7:15, 16; 8:28
7 [a]1 Kin. 5:6, 9; 2 Chr. 2:10; Acts 12:20 [b]2 Chr. 2:16; Acts 9:36 [c]Ezra 1:2; 6:3
8 [a]Ezra 3:2; 4:3 [b]1 Chr. 23:4, 24
10 [a]1 Chr. 16:5, 6 [b]1 Chr. 6:31; 16:4; 25:1
11 [a]Ex. 15:21; 2 Chr. 7:3; Neh. 12:24 [b]1 Chr. 16:34; Ps. 136:1 [c]1 Chr. 16:41; Jer. 33:11
12 [a]Ezra 2:68

CHAPTER 4

1 [a]Ezra 4:7–9

*______________

3:2 *Jehozadak,* 1 Chr. 6:14
3:8 *Jehozadak,* 1 Chr. 6:14
3:9 *Hodaviah,* Ezra 2:40
3:10 So with LXX, Syr., Vg.; MT *they stationed the priests*

NKJV

Worship Restored at Jerusalem

3 And when the [a]seventh month had come, and the children of Israel *were* in the cities, the people gathered together as one man to Jerusalem.

2 Then Jeshua the son of [a]Jozadak* and his brethren the priests, [b]and Zerubbabel the son of [c]Shealtiel and his brethren, arose and built the altar of the God of Israel, to offer burnt offerings on it, as *it is* [d]written in the Law of Moses the man of God.

3 Though fear *had come* upon them because of the people of those countries, they set the altar on its bases; and they offered [a]burnt offerings on it to the LORD, *both* the morning and evening burnt offerings.

4 [a]They also kept the Feast of Tabernacles, [b]as *it is* written, and [c]*offered* the daily burnt offerings in the number required by ordinance for each day.

5 Afterwards *they offered* the [a]regular burnt offering, and *those* for New Moons and for all the appointed feasts of the LORD that were consecrated, and *those* of everyone who willingly offered a freewill offering to the LORD.

6 From the first day of the seventh month they began to offer burnt offerings to the LORD, although the foundation of the temple of the LORD had not been laid.

7 They also gave money to the masons and the carpenters, and [a]food, drink, and oil to the people of Sidon and Tyre to bring cedar logs from Lebanon to the sea, to [b]Joppa, [c]according to the permission which they had from Cyrus king of Persia.

Restoration of the Temple Begins

8 Now in the second month of the second year of their coming to the house of God at Jerusalem, [a]Zerubbabel the son of Shealtiel, Jeshua the son of *Jozadak, and the rest of their brethren the priests and the Levites, and all those who had come out of the captivity to Jerusalem, began *work* [b]and appointed the Levites from twenty years old and above to oversee the work of the house of the LORD.

9 Then Jeshua *with* his sons and brothers, Kadmiel *with* his sons, and the sons of *Judah, arose as one to oversee those working on the house of God: the sons of Henadad *with* their sons and their brethren the Levites.

10 When the builders laid the foundation of the temple of the LORD, [a]the* priests stood in their apparel with trumpets, and the Levites, the sons of Asaph, with cymbals, to praise the LORD, according to the [b]ordinance of David king of Israel.

11 [a]And they sang responsively, praising and giving thanks to the LORD:

[b]"For He *is* good,
[c]For His mercy *endures* forever toward Israel."

Then all the people shouted with a great shout, when they praised the LORD, because the foundation of the house of the LORD was laid.

12 But many of the priests and Levites and [a]heads of the fathers' *houses,* old men who had seen the first temple, wept with a loud voice when the foundation of this temple was laid before their eyes. Yet many shouted aloud for joy,

13 so that the people could not discern the noise of the shout of joy from the noise of the weeping of the people, for the people shouted with a loud shout, and the sound was heard afar off.

Resistance to Rebuilding the Temple

4 Now when [a]the adversaries of Judah and Benjamin heard that the descendants of the captivity were building the temple of the LORD God of Israel,

KJV

2 Then they came to Zerubbabel, and to the chief of the fathers, and said unto them, Let us build with you: for we seek your God, as ye *do;* and we do sacrifice unto him [a]since the days of Esar–haddon king of Assur, which brought us up hither.

3 But Zerubbabel, and Jeshua, and the rest of the chief of the fathers of Israel, said unto them, [a]Ye have nothing to do with us to build an house unto our God; but we ourselves together will build unto the LORD God of Israel, as [b]king Cyrus the king of Persia hath commanded us.

4 Then [a]the people of the land weakened the hands of the people of Judah, and troubled them in building,

5 And hired counsellors against them, to frustrate their purpose, all the days of Cyrus king of Persia, even until the reign of [a]Darius king of Persia.

Rebuilding of Jerusalem Opposed

6 And in the reign of Ahasuerus, in the beginning of his reign, wrote they *unto him* an accusation against the inhabitants of Judah and Jerusalem.

7 And in the days of [a]Artaxerxes wrote Bishlam, Mithredath, Tabeel, and the rest of their companions, unto Artaxerxes king of Persia; and the writing of the letter *was* written in the [b]Syrian tongue, and interpreted in the Syrian tongue.

8 Rehum the chancellor and Shimshai the scribe wrote a letter against Jerusalem to Artaxerxes the king in this sort:

9 Then *wrote* Rehum the chancellor, and Shimshai the scribe, and the rest of their companions; [a]the Dinaites, the Apharsathchites, the Tarpelites, the Apharsites, the Archevites, the Babylonians, the Susanchites, the Dehavites, *and* the Elamites,

10 [a]And the rest of the nations whom the great and noble Asnapper brought over, and set in the cities of Samaria, and the rest *that are* on this side the river, [b]and at such a time.

11 This *is* the copy of the letter that they sent unto him, *even* unto Artaxerxes the king; Thy servants the men on this side the river, and at such a time.

12 Be it known unto the king, that the Jews which came up from thee to us are come unto Jerusalem, building the [a]rebellious and the bad city, and have set up the [b]walls *thereof,* and joined the foundations.

13 Be it known now unto the king, that, if this city be builded, and the walls set up *again, then* will they not pay [a]toll, tribute, and custom, and *so* thou shalt endamage the revenue of the kings.

14 Now because we have maintenance from *the king's* palace, and it was not meet for us to see the king's dishonour, therefore have we sent and certified the king;

15 That search may be made in the book of the records of thy fathers: so shalt thou find in the book of the records, and know that this city *is* a rebellious city, and hurtful unto kings and provinces, and that they have moved sedition within the same of old time: for which cause was this city destroyed.

16 We certify the king that, if this city be builded *again,* and the walls thereof set up, by this means thou shalt have no portion on this side the river.

17 *Then* sent the king an answer unto Rehum the chancellor, and *to* Shimshai the scribe, and *to* the rest of their companions that dwell in

2 [a]2 Kin. 17:24; 19:37; Ezra 4:10
3 [a]Neh. 2:20 [b]Ezra 1:1–4
4 [a]Ezra 3:3
5 [a]Ezra 5:5; 6:1
7 [a]Ezra 7:1, 7, 21 [b]2 Kin. 18:26
9 [a]2 Kin. 17:30, 31
10 [a]2 Kin. 17:24; Ezra 4:1 [b]Ezra 4:11, 17; 7:12
12 [a]2 Chr. 36:13 [b]Ezra 5:3, 9
13 [a]Ezra 4:20; 7:24

NKJV

2 they came to Zerubbabel and the heads of the fathers' *houses,* and said to them, "Let us build with you, for we seek your God as you *do;* and we have sacrificed to Him [a]since the days of Esarhaddon king of Assyria, who brought us here."

3 But Zerubbabel and Jeshua and the rest of the heads of the fathers' *houses* of Israel said to them, [a]"You may do nothing with us to build a house for our God; but we alone will build to the LORD God of Israel, as [b]King Cyrus the king of Persia has commanded us."

4 Then [a]the people of the land tried to discourage the people of Judah. They troubled them in building,

5 and hired counselors against them to frustrate their purpose all the days of Cyrus king of Persia, even until the reign of [a]Darius king of Persia.

Rebuilding of Jerusalem Opposed

6 In the reign of Ahasuerus, in the beginning of his reign, they wrote an accusation against the inhabitants of Judah and Jerusalem.

7 In the days of [a]Artaxerxes also, Bishlam, Mithredath, Tabel, and the rest of their companions wrote to Artaxerxes king of Persia; and the letter *was* written in [b]Aramaic script, and translated into the Aramaic language.

8 *Rehum the commander and Shimshai the scribe wrote a letter against Jerusalem to King Artaxerxes in this fashion:

9 *From Rehum the commander, Shimshai the scribe, and the rest of their companions—*representatives* of [a]the Dinaites, the Apharsathchites, the Tarpelites, the people of Persia and Erech and Babylon and *Shushan, the Dehavites, the Elamites,

10 [a]and the rest of the nations whom the great and noble Osnapper took captive and settled in the cities of Samaria and the remainder beyond *the River—[b]and* so forth.

11 (This *is* a copy of the letter that they sent him)

To King Artaxerxes from your servants, the men *of the region* beyond the River, *and so forth:

12 Let it be known to the king that the Jews who came up from you have come to us at Jerusalem, and are building the [a]rebellious and evil city, and are finishing *its* [b]walls and repairing the foundations.

13 Let it now be known to the king that, if this city is built and the walls completed, they will not pay [a]tax, tribute, or custom, and the king's treasury will be diminished.

14 Now because we receive support from the palace, it was not proper for us to see the king's dishonor; therefore we have sent and informed the king,

15 that search may be made in the book of the records of your fathers. And you will find in the book of the records and know that this city *is* a rebellious city, harmful to kings and provinces, and that they have incited sedition within the city in former times, for which cause this city was destroyed.

16 We inform the king that if this city is rebuilt and its walls are completed, the result will be that you will have no dominion beyond the River.

17 The king sent an answer:

To Rehum the commander, *to* Shimshai the scribe, *to* the rest of their companions

---

4:8 The original language of Ezra 4:8 through 6:18 is Aramaic.
4:9 Lit. *Then* • Or *Susa*
4:10 The Euphrates • Lit. *and now*
4:11 Lit. *and now*

KJV

Samaria, and *unto* the rest beyond the river, Peace, and at such a time.

18 The letter which ye sent unto us hath been plainly read before me.

19 And I commanded, and search hath been made, and it is found that this city of old time hath made insurrection against kings, and *that* rebellion and sedition have been made therein.

20 There have been mighty kings also over Jerusalem, which have [a]ruled over all *countries* [b]beyond the river; and toll, tribute, and custom, was paid unto them.

21 Give ye now commandment to cause these men to cease, and that this city be not builded, until *another* commandment shall be given from me.

22 Take heed now that ye fail not to do this: why should damage grow to the hurt of the kings?

23 Now when the copy of king Artaxerxes' letter *was* read before Rehum, and Shimshai the scribe, and their companions, they went up in haste to Jerusalem unto the Jews, and made them to cease by force and power.

24 Then ceased the work of the house of God which *is* at Jerusalem. So it ceased unto the second year of the reign of Darius king of Persia.

Restoration of the Temple Resumed
(*Hab. 1:1; Zech. 1:1*)

5 Then the prophets, [a]Haggai the prophet, and [b]Zechariah the son of Iddo, prophesied unto the Jews that *were* in Judah and Jerusalem in the name of the God of Israel, *even* unto them.

2 Then rose up [a]Zerubbabel the son of Shealtiel, and Jeshua the son of Jozadak, and began to build the house of God which *is* at Jerusalem: and [b]with them *were* the prophets of God helping them.

3 At the same time came to them [a]Tatnai, governor on this side the river, and Shethar–boznai, and their companions, and said thus unto them, [b]Who hath commanded you to build this house, and to make up this wall?

4 [a]Then said we unto them after this manner, What are the names of the men that make this building?

5 But [a]the eye of their God was upon the elders of the Jews, that they could not cause them to cease, till the matter came to Darius: and then they returned [b]answer by letter concerning this *matter*.

6 The copy of the letter that Tatnai, governor on this side the river, and Shethar–boznai, [a]and his companions the Apharsachites, which *were* on this side the river, sent unto Darius the king:

7 They sent a letter unto him, wherein was written thus; Unto Darius the king, all peace.

8 Be it known unto the king, that we went into the province of Judea, to the house of the great God, which is builded with great stones, and timber is laid in the walls, and this work goeth fast on, and prospereth in their hands.

9 Then asked we those elders, *and* said unto them thus, [a]Who commanded you to build this house, and to make up these walls?

20 [a]1 Kin. 4:21; 1 Chr. 18:3; Ps. 72:8 [b]Gen. 15:18; Josh. 1:4

CHAPTER 5

1 [a]Hag. 1:1 [b]Zech. 1:1
2 [a]Ezra 3:2; Hag. 1:12 [b]Ezra 6:14; Hag. 2:4
3 [a]Ezra 5:6; 6:6 [b]Ezra 1:3; 5:9
4 [a]Ezra 5:10
5 [a]2 Chr. 16:9; Ezra 7:6, 28; Ps. 33:18 [b]Ezra 6:6
6 [a]Ezra 4:7–10
9 [a]Ezra 5:3, 4

*

4:17 Lit. *and now*
5:2 *Jehozadak*, 1 Chr. 6:14
5:3 The Euphrates

NKJV

who dwell in Samaria, and *to* the remainder beyond the River:

Peace, *and so forth.

18 The letter which you sent to us has been clearly read before me.

19 And I gave the command, and a search has been made, and it was found that this city in former times has revolted against kings, and rebellion and sedition have been fostered in it.

20 There have also been mighty kings over Jerusalem, who have [a]ruled over all *the region* [b]beyond the River; and tax, tribute, and custom were paid to them.

21 Now give the command to make these men cease, that this city may not be built until the command is given by me.

22 Take heed now that you do not fail to do this. Why should damage increase to the hurt of the kings?

23 Now when the copy of King Artaxerxes' letter *was* read before Rehum, Shimshai the scribe, and their companions, they went up in haste to Jerusalem against the Jews, and by force of arms made them cease.

24 Thus the work of the house of God which *is* at Jerusalem ceased, and it was discontinued until the second year of the reign of Darius king of Persia.

Restoration of the Temple Resumed
(*Hab. 1:1; Zech. 1:1*)

5 Then the prophet [a]Haggai and [b]Zechariah the son of Iddo, prophets, prophesied to the Jews who *were* in Judah and Jerusalem, in the name of the God of Israel, *who was* over them.

2 So [a]Zerubbabel the son of Shealtiel and Jeshua the son of *Jozadak rose up and began to build the house of God which *is* in Jerusalem; and [b]the prophets of God *were* with them, helping them.

3 At the same time [a]Tattenai the governor of *the region* beyond *the River and Shethar-Boznai and their companions came to them and spoke thus to them: [b]"Who has commanded you to build this temple and finish this wall?"

4 [a]Then, accordingly, we told them the names of the men who were constructing this building.

5 But [a]the eye of their God was upon the elders of the Jews, so that they could not make them cease till a report could go to Darius. Then a [b]written answer was returned concerning this *matter*.

6 This is a copy of the letter that Tattenai sent:

The governor of *the region* beyond the River, and Shethar-Boznai, [a]and his companions, the Persians who *were in the region* beyond the River, to Darius the king.

7 (They sent a letter to him, in which was written thus)

To Darius the king:

All peace.

8 Let it be known to the king that we went into the province of Judea, to the temple of the great God, which is being built with heavy stones, and timber is being laid in the walls; and this work goes on diligently and prospers in their hands.

9 Then we asked those elders, *and* spoke thus to them: [a]"Who commanded you to build this temple and to finish these walls?"

KJV

10 We asked their names also, to certify thee,
that we might write the names of the men that
were the chief of them.
11 And thus they returned us answer, saying,
We are the servants of the God of heaven and
earth, and build the house that was builded these
many years ago, which a great king of Israel
builded [a]and set up.
12 But [a]after that our fathers had provoked
the God of heaven unto wrath, he gave them into
the hand of [b]Nebuchadnezzar the king of Babylon, the Chaldean, who destroyed this house, and
[c]carried the people away into Babylon.
13 But in the first year of [a]Cyrus the king of
Babylon *the same* king Cyrus made a decree to
build this house of God.
14 And [a]the vessels also of gold and silver
of the house of God, which Nebuchadnezzar took
out of the temple that *was* in Jerusalem, and
brought them into the temple of Babylon, those
did Cyrus the king take out of the temple of Babylon, and they were delivered unto *one,* [b]whose
name *was* Sheshbazzar, whom he had made
governor;
15 And said unto him, Take these vessels, go,
carry them into the temple that *is* in Jerusalem,
and let the house of God be builded in his place.
16 Then came the same Sheshbazzar, *and*
[a]laid the foundation of the house of God which
is in Jerusalem: and since that time even until now
hath it been in building, and [b]*yet* it is not finished.
17 Now therefore, if *it seem* good to the king,
[a]let there be search made in the king's treasure
house, which *is* there at Babylon, whether it be
so, that a decree was made of Cyrus the king to
build this house of God at Jerusalem, and let the
king send his pleasure to us concerning this matter.

The Decree of Darius

6 Then Darius the king made a decree, [a]and
search was made in the house of the rolls,
where the treasures were laid up in Babylon.
2 And there was found at Achmetha, in the
palace that *is* in the province of the [a]Medes, a
roll, and therein *was* a record thus written:
3 In the first year of Cyrus the king *the same*
Cyrus the king made a [a]decree *concerning* the
house of God at Jerusalem, Let the house be
builded, the place where they offered sacrifices,
and let the foundations thereof be strongly laid;
the height thereof threescore cubits, *and* the
breadth thereof threescore cubits;
4 [a]*With* three rows of great stones, and a
row of new timber: and let the [b]expences be given
out of the king's house:
5 And also let [a]the golden and silver vessels
of the house of God, which Nebuchadnezzar took
forth out of the temple which *is* at Jerusalem, and
brought unto Babylon, be restored, and brought
again unto the temple which *is* at Jerusalem, *every
one* to his place, and place *them* in the house of
God.
6 [a]Now *therefore,* Tatnai, governor beyond
the river, Shethar–boznai, and your companions
the Apharsachites, which *are* beyond the river,
be ye far from thence:
7 Let the work of this house of God alone;
let the governor of the Jews and the elders of the
Jews build this house of God in his place.
8 Moreover I make a decree what ye shall
do to the elders of these Jews for the building of
this house of God: that of the king's goods, *even*
of the tribute beyond the river, forthwith expences

11 [a]1 Kin. 6:1, 38
12 [a]2 Chr. 34:25; 36:16, 17 [b]2 Kin. 24:2; 25:8–11; 2 Chr. 36:17; Jer. 52:12–15 [c]Jer. 13:19
13 [a]Ezra 1:1
14 [a]Ezra 1:7, 8; 6:5; Dan. 5:2 [b]Hag. 1:14; 2:2, 21
16 [a]Ezra 3:8–10; Hag. 2:18 [b]Ezra 6:15
17 [a]Ezra 6:1, 2

CHAPTER 6

1 [a]Ezra 5:17
2 [a]2 Kin. 17:6
3 [a]Ezra 1:1; 5:13
4 [a]1 Kin. 6:36 [b]Ezra 3:7
5 [a]Ezra 1:7, 8; 5:14
6 [a]Ezra 5:3, 6

*

6:1 Lit. *house of the scrolls*
6:2 Probably *Ecbatana,* the ancient capital of Media

NKJV

10 We also asked them their names to inform you, that we might write the names of the men who *were* chief among them.
11 And thus they returned us an answer, saying: "We are the servants of the God of heaven and earth, and we are rebuilding the temple that was built many years ago, which a great king of Israel built [a]and completed.
12 "But [a]because our fathers provoked the God of heaven to wrath, He gave them into the hand of [b]Nebuchadnezzar king of Babylon, the Chaldean, *who* destroyed this temple and [c]carried the people away to Babylon.
13 "However, in the first year of [a]Cyrus king of Babylon, King Cyrus issued a decree to build this house of God.
14 "Also, [a]the gold and silver articles of the house of God, which Nebuchadnezzar had taken from the temple that *was* in Jerusalem and carried into the temple of Babylon—those King Cyrus took from the temple of Babylon, and they were given to [b]one named Sheshbazzar, whom he had made governor.
15 "And he said to him, 'Take these articles; go, carry them to the temple *site* that *is* in Jerusalem, and let the house of God be rebuilt on its former site.'
16 "Then the same Sheshbazzar came *and* [a]laid the foundation of the house of God which *is* in Jerusalem; but from that time even until now it has been under construction, and [b]it is not finished."
17 Now therefore, if *it seems* good to the king, [a]let a search be made in the king's treasure house, which *is* there in Babylon, whether it is *so* that a decree was issued by King Cyrus to build this house of God at Jerusalem, and let the king send us his pleasure concerning this *matter.*

The Decree of Darius

6 Then King Darius issued a decree, [a]and a
search was made in the *archives, where the
treasures were stored in Babylon.
2 And at *Achmetha, in the palace that *is*
in the province of [a]Media, a scroll was found, and
in it a record *was* written thus:

3 In the first year of King Cyrus, King Cyrus issued a [a]decree *concerning* the house of God at Jerusalem: "Let the house be rebuilt, the place where they offered sacrifices; and let the foundations of it be firmly laid, its height sixty cubits *and* its width sixty cubits,
4 [a]*with* three rows of heavy stones and one row of new timber. Let the [b]expenses be paid from the king's treasury.
5 Also let [a]the gold and silver articles of the house of God, which Nebuchadnezzar took from the temple which *is* in Jerusalem and brought to Babylon, be restored and taken back to the temple which *is* in Jerusalem, *each* to its place; and deposit *them* in the house of God"—
6 [a]Now *therefore,* Tattenai, governor of *the region* beyond the River, and Shethar-Boznai, and your companions the Persians who *are* beyond the River, keep yourselves far from there.
7 Let the work of this house of God alone; let the governor of the Jews and the elders of the Jews build this house of God on its site.
8 Moreover I issue a decree *as to* what you shall do for the elders of these Jews, for the building of this house of God: Let the cost be paid at the king's expense from

KJV

be given unto these men, that they be not hindered.

9 And that which they have need of, both young bullocks, and rams, and lambs, for the burnt offerings of the God of heaven, wheat, salt, wine, and oil, according to the appointment of the priests which *are* at Jerusalem, let it be given them day by day without fail:

10 [a]That they may offer sacrifices of sweet savours unto the God of heaven, and pray for the life of the king, and of his sons.

11 Also I have made a decree, that whosoever shall alter this word, let timber be pulled down from his house, and being set up, let him be hanged thereon; [a]and let his house be made a dunghill for this.

12 And the God that hath caused his [a]name to dwell there destroy all kings and people, that shall put to their hand to alter *and* to destroy this house of God which *is* at Jerusalem. I Darius have made a decree; let it be done with speed.

The Temple Completed and Dedicated

13 Then Tatnai, governor on this side the river, Shethar–boznai, and their companions, according to that which Darius the king had sent, so they did speedily.

14 [a]And the elders of the Jews builded, and they prospered through the prophesying of Haggai the prophet and Zechariah the son of Iddo. And they builded, and finished *it*, according to the commandment of the God of Israel, and according to the commandment of [b]Cyrus, and [c]Darius, and [d]Artaxerxes king of Persia.

15 And this house was finished on the third day of the month Adar, which was in the sixth year of the reign of Darius the king.

16 And the children of Israel, the priests, and the Levites, and the rest of the children of the captivity, kept [a]the dedication of this house of God with joy,

17 And [a]offered at the dedication of this house of God an hundred bullocks, two hundred rams, four hundred lambs; and for a sin offering for all Israel, twelve he goats, according to the number of the tribes of Israel.

18 And they set the priests in their [a]divisions, and the Levites in their [b]courses, for the service of God, which *is* at Jerusalem; [c]as it is written in the book of Moses.

The Passover Celebrated
(cf. Deut. 16:1–8)

19 And the children of the captivity kept the passover [a]upon the fourteenth *day* of the first month.

20 For the priests and the Levites were [a]purified together, all of them *were* pure, and [b]killed the passover for all the children of the captivity, and for their brethren the priests, and for themselves.

21 And the children of Israel, which were come again out of captivity, and all such as had separated themselves unto them from the [a]filthiness of the heathen of the land, to seek the LORD God of Israel, did eat,

22 And kept the [a]feast of unleavened bread seven days with joy: for the LORD had made them joyful, and [b]turned the heart [c]of the king of Assyria unto them, to strengthen their hands in the work of the house of God, the God of Israel.

The Arrival of Ezra

7 Now after these things, in the reign of [a]Artaxerxes king of Persia, Ezra the [b]son of Seraiah, [c]the son of Azariah, the son of [d]Hilkiah,

2 The son of Shallum, the son of Zadok, the son of Ahitub,

3 The son of Amariah, the son of Azariah, the son of Meraioth,

10 [a]Ezra 7:23; [Jer. 29:7; 1 Tim. 2:1, 2] **11** [a]Dan. 2:5; 3:29 **12** [a]Deut. 12:5, 11; 1 Kin. 9:3 **14** [a]Ezra 5:1, 2 [b]Ezra 1:1; 5:13; 6:3 [c]Ezra 4:24; 6:12 [d]Ezra 7:1, 11; Neh. 2:1 **16** [a]1 Kin. 8:63; 2 Chr. 7:5 **17** [a]Ezra 8:35 **18** [a]1 Chr. 24:1; 2 Chr. 35:5 [b]1 Chr. 23:6 [c]Num. 3:6; 8:9 **19** [a]Ex. 12:6 **20** [a]2 Chr. 29:34; 30:15 [b]2 Chr. 35:11 **21** [a]Ezra 9:11 **22** [a]Ex. 12:15; 13:6, 7; 2 Chr. 30:21; 35:17 [b]Ezra 7:27; [Prov. 21:1] [c]2 Kin. 23:29; 2 Chr. 33:11; Ezra 1:1; 6:1

CHAPTER 7

1 [a]Neh. 2:1 [b]1 Chr. 6:14 [c]Jer. 52:24 [d]2 Chr. 35:8

NKJV

taxes *on the region* beyond the River; this
is to be given immediately to these men,
so that they are not hindered.

9 And whatever they need—young bulls,
rams, and lambs for the burnt offerings
of the God of heaven, wheat, salt, wine,
and oil, according to the request of the
priests who *are* in Jerusalem—let it be
given them day by day without fail,

10 [a]that they may offer sacrifices of sweet
aroma to the God of heaven, and pray for
the life of the king and his sons.

11 Also I issue a decree that whoever alters
this edict, let a timber be pulled from his
house and erected, and let him be hanged
on it; [a]and let his house be made a refuse
heap because of this.

12 And may the God who causes His [a]name
to dwell there destroy any king or people
who put their hand to alter it, or to destroy
this house of God which is in Jerusalem.
I Darius issue a decree; let it be done
diligently.

The Temple Completed and Dedicated

13 Then Tattenai, governor of *the region* beyond the River, Shethar-Boznai, and their companions diligently did according to what King Darius had sent.

14 [a]So the elders of the Jews built, and they prospered through the prophesying of Haggai the prophet and Zechariah the son of Iddo. And they built and finished *it*, according to the commandment of the God of Israel, and according to the command of [b]Cyrus, [c]Darius, and [d]Artaxerxes king of Persia.

15 Now the temple was finished on the third day of the month of Adar, which was in the sixth year of the reign of King Darius.

16 Then the children of Israel, the priests and the Levites and the rest of the descendants of the captivity, celebrated [a]the dedication of this house of God with joy.

17 And they [a]offered sacrifices at the dedication of this house of God, one hundred bulls, two hundred rams, four hundred lambs, and as a sin offering for all Israel twelve male goats, according to the number of the tribes of Israel.

18 They assigned the priests to their [a]divisions and the Levites to their [b]divisions, over the service of God in Jerusalem, [c]as it is written in the Book of Moses.

The Passover Celebrated
(cf. Deut. 16:1–8)

19 And the descendants of the captivity kept the Passover [a]on the fourteenth *day* of the first month.

20 For the priests and the Levites had [a]purified themselves; all of them *were ritually* clean. And they [b]slaughtered the Passover *lambs* for all the descendants of the captivity, for their brethren the priests, and for themselves.

21 Then the children of Israel who had returned from the captivity ate together with all who had separated themselves from the [a]filth of the nations of the land in order to seek the LORD God of Israel.

22 And they kept the [a]Feast of Unleavened Bread seven days with joy; for the LORD made them joyful, and [b]turned the heart [c]of the king of Assyria toward them, to strengthen their hands in the work of the house of God, the God of Israel.

The Arrival of Ezra

7 Now after these things, in the reign of [a]Artaxerxes king of Persia, Ezra the [b]son of Seraiah, [c]the son of Azariah, the son of [d]Hilkiah,

2 the son of Shallum, the son of Zadok, the son of Ahitub,

3 the son of Amariah, the son of Azariah, the son of Meraioth,

KJV

4 The son of Zerahiah, the son of Uzzi, the son of Bukki,

5 The son of Abishua, the son of Phinehas, the son of Eleazar, the son of Aaron the chief priest:

6 This Ezra went up from Babylon; and he *was* [a]a ready scribe in the law of Moses, which the LORD God of Israel had given: and the king granted him all his request, [b]according to the hand of the LORD his God upon him.

7 [a]And there went up *some* of the children of Israel, and of the priests, and [b]the Levites, and the singers, and the porters, and [c]the Nethinims, unto Jerusalem, in the seventh year of Artaxerxes the king.

8 And he came to Jerusalem in the fifth month, which *was* in the seventh year of the king.

9 For upon the first *day* of the first month began he to go up from Babylon, and on the first *day* of the fifth month came he to Jerusalem, [a]according to the good hand of his God upon him.

10 For Ezra had prepared his heart to [a]seek the law of the LORD, and to do *it*, and to [b]teach in Israel statutes and judgments.

The Letter of Artaxerxes to Ezra

11 Now this *is* the copy of the letter that the king Artaxerxes gave unto Ezra the priest, the scribe, *even* a scribe of the words of the commandments of the LORD, and of his statutes to Israel.

12 Artaxerxes, [a]king of kings, unto Ezra the priest, a scribe of the law of the God of heaven, perfect *peace,* [b]and at such a time.

13 I make a decree, that all they of the people of Israel, and *of* his priests and Levites, in my realm, which are minded of their own freewill to go up to Jerusalem, go with thee.

14 Forasmuch as thou art sent of the king, and of his [a]seven counsellors, to enquire concerning Judah and Jerusalem, according to the law of thy God which *is* in thine hand;

15 And to carry the silver and gold, which the king and his counsellors have freely offered unto the God of Israel, [a]whose habitation *is* in Jerusalem,

16 [a]And all the silver and gold that thou canst find in all the province of Babylon, with the freewill offering of the people, and of the priests, [b]offering willingly for the house of their God which *is* in Jerusalem:

17 That thou mayest buy speedily with this money bullocks, rams, lambs, with their [a]meat offerings and their drink offerings, and [b]offer them upon the altar of the house of your God which *is* in Jerusalem.

18 And whatsoever shall seem good to thee, and to thy brethren, to do with the rest of the silver and the gold, that do after the will of your God.

19 The vessels also that are given thee for the service of the house of thy God, *those* deliver thou before the God of Jerusalem.

20 And whatsoever more shall be needful for the house of thy God, which thou shalt have occasion to bestow, bestow *it* out of the king's treasure house.

21 And I, *even* I Artaxerxes the king, do make a decree to all the treasurers which *are* beyond the river, that whatsoever Ezra the priest, the scribe of the law of the God of heaven, shall require of you, it be done speedily,

22 Unto an hundred talents of silver, and to an hundred measures of wheat, and to an hundred baths of wine, and to an hundred baths of oil, and salt without prescribing *how much.*

6 [a]Ezra 7:11, 12, 21 [b]Ezra 7:9, 28; 8:22
7 [a]Ezra 8:1–14 [b]Ezra 8:15 [c]Ezra 2:43; 8:20
9 [a]Ezra 7:6; Neh. 2:8, 18
10 [a]Ps. 119:45 [b]Deut. 33:10; Ezra 7:6, 25; Neh. 8:1–8; [Mal. 2:7]
12 [a]Ezek. 26:7; Dan. 2:37 [b]Ezra 4:10
14 [a]Esth. 1:14
15 [a]2 Chr. 6:2; Ezra 6:12; Ps. 135:21
16 [a]Ezra 8:25 [b]1 Chr. 29:6, 9
17 [a]Num. 15:4–13 [b]Deut. 12:5–11

NKJV

4 the son of Zerahiah, the son of Uzzi, the son of Bukki,

5 the son of Abishua, the son of Phinehas, the son of Eleazar, the son of Aaron the chief priest—

6 this Ezra came up from Babylon; and he *was* [a]a skilled scribe in the Law of Moses, which the LORD God of Israel had given. The king granted him all his request, [b]according to the hand of the LORD his God upon him.

7 [a]*Some* of the children of Israel, the priests, [b]the Levites, the singers, the gatekeepers, and [c]the Nethinim came up to Jerusalem in the seventh year of King Artaxerxes.

8 And Ezra came to Jerusalem in the fifth month, which *was* in the seventh year of the king.

9 On the first *day* of the first month he began *his* journey from Babylon, and on the first *day* of the fifth month he came to Jerusalem, [a]according to the good hand of his God upon him.

10 For Ezra had prepared his heart to [a]seek the Law of the LORD, and to do *it*, and to [b]teach statutes and ordinances in Israel.

The Letter of Artaxerxes to Ezra

11 This *is* a copy of the letter that King Artaxerxes gave Ezra the priest, the scribe, expert in the words of the commandments of the LORD, and of His statutes to Israel:

12 *Artaxerxes, [a]king of kings,

To Ezra the priest, a scribe of the Law of the God of heaven:

Perfect *peace,* [b]and* so forth.

13 I issue a decree that all those of the people of Israel and the priests and Levites in my realm, who volunteer to go up to Jerusalem, may go with you.

14 And whereas you are being sent by the king and his [a]seven counselors to inquire concerning Judah and Jerusalem, with regard to the Law of your God which *is* in your hand;

15 and *whereas you are* to carry the silver and gold which the king and his counselors have freely offered to the God of Israel, [a]whose dwelling *is* in Jerusalem;

16 [a]and *whereas* all the silver and gold that you may find in all the province of Babylon, along with the freewill offering of the people and the priests, *are to be* [b]freely offered for the house of their God in Jerusalem—

17 now therefore, be careful to buy with this money bulls, rams, and lambs, with their [a]grain offerings and their drink offerings, and [b]offer them on the altar of the house of your God in Jerusalem.

18 And whatever seems good to you and your brethren to do with the rest of the silver and the gold, do it according to the will of your God.

19 Also the articles that are given to you for the service of the house of your God, deliver in full before the God of Jerusalem.

20 And whatever more may be needed for the house of your God, which you may have occasion to provide, pay *for it* from the king's treasury.

21 And I, *even* I, Artaxerxes the king, issue a decree to all the treasurers who *are in the region* beyond the River, that whatever Ezra the priest, the scribe of the Law of the God of heaven, may require of you, let it be done diligently,

22 up to one hundred talents of silver, one hundred kors of wheat, one hundred baths of wine, one hundred baths of oil, and salt without prescribed limit.

***7:12** The original language of Ezra 7:12–26 is Aramaic. • Lit. *and now*

KJV

23 Whatsoever is commanded by the God of heaven, let it be diligently done for the house of the God of heaven: for why should there be wrath against the realm of the king and his sons?

24 Also we certify you, that touching any of the priests and Levites, singers, porters, Nethinims, or ministers of this house of God, it shall not be lawful to impose toll, tribute, or custom, upon them.

25 And thou, Ezra, after the wisdom of thy God, that *is* in thine hand, [a]set magistrates and judges, which may judge all the people that *are* beyond the river, all such as know the laws of thy God; and [b]teach ye them that know *them* not.

26 And whosoever will not do the law of thy God, and the law of the king, let judgment be executed speedily upon him, whether *it be* unto death, or to banishment, or to confiscation of goods, or to imprisonment.

27 [a]Blessed *be* the LORD God of our fathers, [b]which hath put *such a thing* as this in the king's heart, to beautify the house of the LORD which *is* in Jerusalem:

28 And [a]hath extended mercy unto me before the king, and his counsellors, and before all the king's mighty princes. And I was strengthened as [b]the hand of the LORD my God *was* upon me, and I gathered together out of Israel chief men to go up with me.

Heads of Families Who Returned with Ezra

8 These *are* now the chief of their fathers, and *this is* the genealogy of them that went up with me from Babylon, in the reign of Artaxerxes the king.

2 Of the sons of Phinehas; Gershom: of the sons of Ithamar; Daniel: of the sons of David; [a]Hattush.

3 Of the sons of Shechaniah, of the sons of [a]Pharosh; Zechariah: and with him were reckoned by genealogy of the males an hundred and fifty.

4 Of the sons of [a]Pahath–moab; Elihoenai the son of Zerahiah, and with him two hundred males.

5 Of the sons of Shechaniah; the son of Jahaziel, and with him three hundred males.

6 Of the sons also of Adin; Ebed the son of Jonathan, and with him fifty males.

7 And of the sons of Elam; Jeshaiah the son of Athaliah, and with him seventy males.

8 And of the sons of Shephatiah; Zebadiah the son of Michael, and with him fourscore males.

9 Of the sons of Joab; Obadiah the son of Jehiel, and with him two hundred and eighteen males.

10 And of the sons of Shelomith; the son of Josiphiah, and with him an hundred and threescore males.

11 And of the sons of [a]Bebai; Zechariah the son of Bebai, and with him twenty and eight males.

12 And of the sons of Azgad; Johanan the son of Hakkatan, and with him an hundred and ten males.

13 And of the last sons of Adonikam, whose names *are* these, Eliphelet, Jeiel, and Shemaiah, and with them threescore males.

14 Of the sons also of Bigvai; Uthai, and Zabbud, and with them seventy males.

Servants for the Temple

15 And I gathered them together to the river that runneth to Ahava; and there abode we in tents three days: and I viewed the people, and the priests, and found there none of the [a]sons of Levi.

16 Then sent I for Eliezer, for Ariel, for Shemaiah, and for Elnathan, and for Jarib, and

25 [a]Ex. 18:21, 22; Deut. 16:18 [b]2 Chr. 17:7; Ezra 7:10; [Mal. 2:7; Col. 1:28]
27 [a]1 Chr. 29:10 [b]Ezra 6:22; [Prov. 21:1]
28 [a]Ezra 9:9 [b]Ezra 5:5; 7:6, 9; 8:18

CHAPTER 8

2 [a]1 Chr. 3:22; Ezra 2:68
3 [a]Ezra 2:3
4 [a]Ezra 10:30
11 [a]Ezra 10:28
15 [a]Ezra 7:7; 8:2

*

8:5 So with MT, Vg.; LXX *the sons of Zatho, Shechaniah*
8:10 So with MT, Vg.; LXX *the sons of Banni, Shelomith*

NKJV

23 Whatever is commanded by the God of heaven, let it diligently be done for the house of the God of heaven. For why should there be wrath against the realm of the king and his sons?

24 Also we inform you that it shall not be lawful to impose tax, tribute, or custom *on* any of the priests, Levites, singers, gatekeepers, Nethinim, or servants of this house of God.

25 And you, Ezra, according to your God-given wisdom, [a]set magistrates and judges who may judge all the people who *are in the region* beyond the River, all such as know the laws of your God; and [b]teach those who do not know *them.*

26 Whoever will not observe the law of your God and the law of the king, let judgment be executed speedily on him, whether *it be* death, or banishment, or confiscation of goods, or imprisonment.

27 [a]Blessed *be* the LORD God of our fathers, [b]who has put *such a thing* as this in the king's heart, to beautify the house of the LORD which *is* in Jerusalem,

28 and [a]has extended mercy to me before the king and his counselors, and before all the king's mighty princes.

So I was encouraged, as [b]the hand of the LORD my God *was* upon me; and I gathered leading men of Israel to go up with me.

Heads of Families Who Returned with Ezra

8 These *are* the heads of their fathers' *houses,* and *this is* the genealogy of those who went up with me from Babylon, in the reign of King Artaxerxes:

2 of the sons of Phinehas, Gershom; of the sons of Ithamar, Daniel; of the sons of David, [a]Hattush;

3 of the sons of Shecaniah, of the sons of [a]Parosh, Zechariah; and registered with him *were* one hundred and fifty males;

4 of the sons of [a]Pahath-Moab, Eliehoenai the son of Zerahiah, and with him two hundred males;

5 of *the sons of Shechaniah, Ben-Jahaziel, and with him three hundred males;

6 of the sons of Adin, Ebed the son of Jonathan, and with him fifty males;

7 of the sons of Elam, Jeshaiah the son of Athaliah, and with him seventy males;

8 of the sons of Shephatiah, Zebadiah the son of Michael, and with him eighty males;

9 of the sons of Joab, Obadiah the son of Jehiel, and with him two hundred and eighteen males;

10 of *the sons of Shelomith, Ben-Josiphiah, and with him one hundred and sixty males;

11 of the sons of [a]Bebai, Zechariah the son of Bebai, and with him twenty-eight males;

12 of the sons of Azgad, Johanan the son of Hakkatan, and with him one hundred and ten males;

13 of the last sons of Adonikam, whose names *are* these—Eliphelet, Jeiel, and Shemaiah—and with them sixty males;

14 also of the sons of Bigvai, Uthai and Zabbud, and with them seventy males.

Servants for the Temple

15 Now I gathered them by the river that flows to Ahava, and we camped there three days. And I looked among the people and the priests, and found none of the [a]sons of Levi there.

16 Then I sent for Eliezer, Ariel, Shemaiah, Elnathan, Jarib, Elnathan, Nathan, Zechariah,

KJV

for Elnathan, and for Nathan, and for Zechariah, and for [a]Meshullam, chief men; also for Joiarib, and for Elnathan, men of understanding.

17 And I sent them with commandment unto Iddo the chief at the place Casiphia, and I told them what they should say unto Iddo, *and* to his brethren the Nethinims, at the place Casiphia, that they should bring unto us ministers for the house of our God.

18 And by the good hand of our God upon us they [a]brought us a man of understanding, of the sons of Mahli, the son of Levi, the son of Israel; and Sherebiah, with his sons and his brethren, eighteen;

19 And [a]Hashabiah, and with him Jeshaiah of the sons of Merari, his brethren and their sons, twenty;

20 [a]Also of the Nethinims, whom David and the princes had appointed for the service of the Levites, two hundred and twenty Nethinims: all of them were expressed by name.

Fasting and Prayer for Protection

21 Then I [a]proclaimed a fast there, at the river of Ahava, that we might [b]afflict ourselves before our God, to seek of him a [c]right way for us, and for our little ones, and for all our substance.

22 For [a]I was ashamed to require of the king a band of soldiers and horsemen to help us against the enemy in the way: because we had spoken unto the king, saying, [b]The hand of our God *is* upon all them for [c]good that seek him; but his power and his wrath *is* [d]against all them that [e]forsake him.

23 So we fasted and besought our God for this: and he was [a]intreated of us.

Gifts for the Temple

24 Then I separated twelve of the chief of the priests, Sherebiah, Hashabiah, and ten of their brethren with them,

25 And weighed unto them [a]the silver, and the gold, and the vessels, *even* the offering of the house of our God, which the king, and his counsellors, and his lords, and all Israel *there* present, had offered:

26 I even weighed unto their hand six hundred and fifty talents of silver, and silver vessels an hundred talents, *and* of gold an hundred talents;

27 Also twenty basons of gold, of a thousand drams; and two vessels of fine copper, precious as gold.

28 And I said unto them, Ye *are* [a]holy unto the LORD; the vessels *are* [b]holy also; and the silver and the gold *are* a freewill offering unto the LORD God of your fathers.

29 Watch ye, and keep *them,* until ye weigh *them* before the chief of the priests and the Levites, and [a]chief of the fathers of Israel, at Jerusalem, in the chambers of the house of the LORD.

30 So took the priests and the Levites the weight of the silver, and the gold, and the vessels, to bring *them* to Jerusalem unto the house of our God.

The Return to Jerusalem

31 Then we departed from the river of Ahava on the twelfth *day* of the first month, to go unto Jerusalem: and [a]the hand of our God was upon us, and he delivered us from the hand of the enemy, and of such as lay in wait by the way.

32 And we [a]came to Jerusalem, and abode there three days.

33 Now on the fourth day was the silver and the gold and the vessels [a]weighed in the house of our God by the hand of Meremoth the son of Uriah the priest; and with him *was* Eleazar the son of Phinehas; and with them *was* [b]Jozabad the son of Jeshua, and Noadiah the son of Binnui, Levites;

16 [a]Ezra 10:15
18 [a]2 Chr. 30:22; Neh. 8:7
19 [a]Neh. 12:24
20 [a]Ezra 2:43; 7:7
21 [a]1 Sam. 7:6; 2 Chr. 20:3 [b]Lev. 16:29; 23:29; Is. 58:3, 5 [c]Ps. 5:8
22 [a]1 Cor. 9:15 [b]Ezra 7:6, 9, 28 [c][Ps. 33:18, 19; 34:15, 22; Rom. 8:28] [d][Ps. 34:16] [e][2 Chr. 15:2]
23 [a][1 Chr. 5:20]; 2 Chr. 33:13; Is. 19:22
25 [a]Ezra 7:15, 16
28 [a]Lev. 21:6–9; Deut. 33:8 [b]Lev. 22:2, 3; Num. 4:4, 15, 19, 20
29 [a]Ezra 4:3
31 [a]Ezra 7:6, 9, 28
32 [a]Neh. 2:11
33 [a]Ezra 8:26, 30 [b]Neh. 11:16

NKJV

and [a]Meshullam, leaders; also for Joiarib and Elnathan, men of understanding.

17 And I gave them a command for Iddo the chief man at the place Casiphia, and I told them what they should say to *Iddo *and* his brethren the Nethinim at the place Casiphia—that they should bring us servants for the house of our God.

18 Then, by the good hand of our God upon us, they [a]brought us a man of understanding, of the sons of Mahli the son of Levi, the son of Israel, namely Sherebiah, with his sons and brothers, eighteen men;

19 and [a]Hashabiah, and with him Jeshaiah of the sons of Merari, his brothers and their sons, twenty men;

20 [a]also of the Nethinim, whom David and the leaders had appointed for the service of the Levites, two hundred and twenty Nethinim. All of them were designated by name.

Fasting and Prayer for Protection

21 Then I [a]proclaimed a fast there at the river of Ahava, that we might [b]humble ourselves before our God, to seek from Him the [c]right way for us and our little ones and all our possessions.

22 For [a]I was ashamed to request of the king an escort of soldiers and horsemen to help us against the enemy on the road, because we had spoken to the king, saying, [b]"The hand of our God *is* upon all those for [c]good who seek Him, but His power and His wrath *are* [d]against all those who [e]forsake Him."

23 So we fasted and entreated our God for this, and He [a]answered our prayer.

Gifts for the Temple

24 And I separated twelve of the leaders of the priests—Sherebiah, Hashabiah, and ten of their brethren with them—

25 and weighed out to them [a]the silver, the gold, and the articles, the offering for the house of our God which the king and his counselors and his princes, and all Israel *who were* present, had offered.

26 I weighed into their hand six hundred and fifty talents of silver, silver articles *weighing* one hundred talents, one hundred talents of gold,

27 twenty gold basins *worth* a thousand drachmas, and two vessels of fine polished bronze, precious as gold.

28 And I said to them, "You *are* [a]holy to the LORD; the articles *are* [b]holy also; and the silver and the gold *are* a freewill offering to the LORD God of your fathers.

29 "Watch and keep *them* until you weigh *them* before the leaders of the priests and the Levites and [a]heads of the fathers' *houses* of Israel in Jerusalem, *in* the chambers of the house of the LORD."

30 So the priests and the Levites received the silver and the gold and the articles by weight, to bring *them* to Jerusalem to the house of our God.

The Return to Jerusalem

31 Then we departed from the river of Ahava on the twelfth *day* of the first month, to go to Jerusalem. And [a]the hand of our God was upon us, and He delivered us from the hand of the enemy and from ambush along the road.

32 So we [a]came to Jerusalem, and stayed there three days.

33 Now on the fourth day the silver and the gold and the articles were [a]weighed in the house of our God by the hand of Meremoth the son of Uriah the priest, and with him *was* Eleazar the son of Phinehas; with them *were* the Levites, [b]Jozabad the son of Jeshua and Noadiah the son of Binnui,

*———

8:17 So with Vg.; MT to *Iddo his brother;* LXX *to their brethren*

KJV

34 By number *and* by weight of every one:
and all the weight was written at that time.
35 *Also* the children of those that had been
[a]carried away, which were come out of the captivity, [b]offered burnt offerings unto the God of Israel,
twelve bullocks for all Israel, ninety and six rams,
seventy and seven lambs, twelve he goats *for* a
sin offering: all *this was* a burnt offering unto the
LORD.
36 And they delivered the king's [a]commis-
sions unto the king's lieutenants, and to the governors on this side the river: and they furthered the
people, and the house of God.

Intermarriage with Pagans

9 Now when these things were done, the princes
came to me, saying, The people of Israel, and
the priests, and the Levites, have not [a]separated
themselves from the people of the lands, [b]*doing*
according to their abominations, *even* of the Canaanites, the Hittites, the Perizzites, the Jebusites,
the Ammonites, the Moabites, the Egyptians, and
the Amorites.
2 For they have [a]taken of their daughters
for themselves, and for their sons: so that the
[b]holy seed have [c]mingled themselves with the
people of *those* lands: yea, the hand of the princes
and rulers hath been chief in this trespass.
3 And when I heard this thing, [a]I rent my
garment and my mantle, and plucked off the hair
of my head and of my beard, and sat down
[b]astonied.
4 Then were assembled unto me every one
that [a]trembled at the words of the God of Israel,
because of the transgression of those that had
been carried away; and I sat astonied until the
[b]evening sacrifice.
5 And at the evening sacrifice I arose up
from my heaviness; and having rent my garment
and my mantle, I fell upon my knees, and [a]spread
out my hands unto the LORD my God,
6 And said, O my God, I am [a]ashamed and
blush to lift up my face to thee, my God: for [b]our
iniquities are increased over *our* head, and our
trespass is [c]grown up unto the heavens.
7 Since the days of our fathers *have* [a]we
been in a great trespass unto this day; and for
our iniquities [b]have we, our kings, *and* our priests,
been delivered into the hand of the kings of the
lands, to the [c]sword, to captivity, and to a spoil,
and to [d]confusion of face, as *it is* this day.
8 And now for a little space grace hath been
shewed from the LORD our God, to leave us a remnant to escape, and to give us a nail in his holy
place, that our God may [a]lighten our eyes, and
give us a little reviving in our bondage.
9 [a]For we *were* bondmen; [b]yet our God hath
not forsaken us in our bondage, but [c]hath extended mercy unto us in the sight of the kings of
Persia, to give us a reviving, to set up the house
of our God, and to repair the desolations thereof,
and to give us [d]a wall in Judah and in Jerusalem.
10 And now, O our God, what shall we say
after this? for we have forsaken thy commandments,
11 Which thou hast commanded by thy servants the prophets, saying, The land, unto which
ye go to possess it, is an unclean land with the
[a]filthiness of the people of the lands, with their
abominations, which have filled it from one end
to another with their uncleanness.
12 Now therefore [a]give not your daughters
unto their sons, neither take their daughters unto
your sons, [b]nor seek their peace or their wealth
for ever: that ye may be strong, and eat the good
of the land, and [c]leave *it* for an inheritance to
your children for ever.
13 And after all that is come upon us for our
evil deeds, and for our great trespass, seeing that
thou our God [a]hast punished us less than our iniquities *deserve,* and hast given us *such* deliverance as this;

NKJV

34 with the number *and* weight of everything.
All the weight was written down at that time.
35 The children of those who had been [a]car-
ried away captive, who had come from the captivity, [b]offered burnt offerings to the God of Israel:
twelve bulls for all Israel, ninety-six rams, seventy-seven lambs, and twelve male goats *as* a sin
offering. All *this was* a burnt offering to the LORD.
36 And they delivered the king's [a]orders to
the king's satraps and the governors *in the region*
beyond the River. So they gave support to the people and the house of God.

Intermarriage with Pagans

9 When these things were done, the leaders
came to me, saying, "The people of Israel and
the priests and the Levites have not [a]separated
themselves from the peoples of the lands, [b]with
respect to the abominations of the Canaanites, the
Hittites, the Perizzites, the Jebusites, the Ammonites, the Moabites, the Egyptians, and the Amorites.
2 "For they have [a]taken some of their
daughters *as wives* for themselves and their sons,
so that the [b]holy seed is [c]mixed with the peoples
of *those* lands. Indeed, the hand of the leaders
and rulers has been foremost in this trespass."
3 So when I heard this thing, [a]I tore my garment and my robe, and plucked out some of the
hair of my head and beard, and sat down
[b]astonished.
4 Then everyone who [a]trembled at the
words of the God of Israel assembled to me, because of the transgression of those who had been
carried away captive, and I sat astonished until
the [b]evening sacrifice.
5 At the evening sacrifice I arose from my
fasting; and having torn my garment and my robe,
I fell on my knees and [a]spread out my hands to
the LORD my God.
6 And I said: "O my God, I am too [a]ashamed
and humiliated to lift up my face to You, my God;
for [b]our iniquities have risen higher than *our*
heads, and our guilt has [c]grown up to the heavens.
7 "Since the days of our fathers to this day
[a]we *have been* very guilty, and for our iniquities
[b]we, our kings, *and* our priests have been delivered into the hand of the kings of the lands, to
the [c]sword, to captivity, to plunder, and to [d]humili-
ation, as *it is* this day.
8 "And now for a little while grace has been
shown from the LORD our God, to leave us a remnant to escape, and to give us a peg in His holy
place, that our God may [a]enlighten our eyes and
give us a measure of revival in our bondage.
9 [a]"For we *were* slaves. [b]Yet our God did
not forsake us in our bondage; but [c]He extended
mercy to us in the sight of the kings of Persia, to
revive us, to repair the house of our God, to rebuild its ruins, and to give us [d]a wall in Judah
and Jerusalem.
10 "And now, O our God, what shall we say
after this? For we have forsaken Your commandments,
11 "which You commanded by Your servants
the prophets, saying, 'The land which you are entering to possess is an unclean land, with the [a]un-
cleanness of the peoples of the lands, with their
abominations which have filled it from one end
to another with their impurity.
12 'Now therefore, [a]do not give your daughters as wives for their sons, nor take their
daughters to your sons; and [b]never seek their
peace or prosperity, that you may be strong and
eat the good of the land, and [c]leave *it* as an inheritance to your children forever.'
13 "And after all that has come upon us for
our evil deeds and for our great guilt, since You
our God [a]have punished us less than our iniquities
deserve, and have given us *such* deliverance as
this,

---

35 [a]Ezra 2:1 [b]Ezra 6:17
36 [a]Ezra 7:21–24

CHAPTER 9

1 [a]Ezra 6:21; Neh. 9:2 [b]Deut. 12:30, 31
2 [a]Ex. 34:16; [Deut. 7:3]; Ezra 10:2; Neh. 13:23 [b]Ex. 22:31; [Deut. 7:6] [c][2 Cor. 6:14]
3 [a]Job 1:20 [b]Ps. 143:4
4 [a]Ezra 10:3; Is. 66:2 [b]Ex. 29:39
5 [a]Ex. 9:29
6 [a]Dan. 9:7, 8 [b]Ps. 38:4 [c]2 Chr. 28:9; [Ezra 9:13, 15]; Rev. 18:5
7 [a]2 Chr. 36:14–17; Ps. 106:6; Dan. 9:5, 6 [b]Deut. 28:36; Neh. 9:30 [c]Deut. 32:25 [d]Dan. 9:7, 8
8 [a]Ps. 34:5
9 [a]Neh. 9:36; Esth. 7:4 [b]Neh. 9:17; Ps. 136:23 [c]Ezra 7:28 [d]Is. 5:2
11 [a]Ezra 6:21
12 [a][Ex. 23:32; 34:15, 16; Deut. 7:3, 4]; Ezra 9:2 [b]Deut. 23:6 [c][Prov. 13:22; 20:7]
13 [a][Ps. 103:10]

KJV

14 Should we [a]again break thy commandments, and [b]join in affinity with the people of these abominations? wouldest not thou be [c]angry with us till thou hadst consumed *us*, so that *there should be* no remnant nor escaping?

15 O LORD God of Israel, [a]thou *art* righteous: for we remain yet escaped, as *it is* this day: [b]behold, we *are* before thee [c]in our trespasses: for we cannot stand before thee because of this.

Confession of Improper Marriages

10 Now [a]when Ezra had prayed, and when he had confessed, weeping and casting himself down [b]before the house of God, there assembled unto him out of Israel a very great congregation of men and women and children: for the people wept very [c]sore.

2 And Shechaniah the son of Jehiel, *one* of the sons of Elam, answered and said unto Ezra, We have [a]trespassed against our God, and have taken strange wives of the people of the land: yet now there is hope in Israel concerning this thing.

3 Now therefore let us make [a]a covenant with our God to put away all the wives, and such as are born of them, according to the counsel of my lord, and of those that [b]tremble at [c]the commandment of our God; and let it be done according to the [d]law.

4 Arise; for *this* matter *belongeth* unto thee: we also *will be* with thee: [a]be of good courage, and do *it*.

5 Then arose Ezra, and made the chief priests, the Levites, and all Israel, [a]to swear that they should do according to this word. And they sware.

6 Then Ezra rose up from before the house of God, and went into the chamber of Johanan the son of Eliashib: and *when* he came thither, he [a]did eat no bread, nor drink water: for he mourned because of the transgression of them that had been carried away.

7 And they made proclamation throughout Judah and Jerusalem unto all the children of the captivity, that they should gather themselves together unto Jerusalem;

8 And that whosoever would not come within three days, according to the counsel of the princes and the elders, all his substance should be forfeited, and himself separated from the congregation of those that had been carried away.

9 Then all the men of Judah and Benjamin gathered themselves together unto Jerusalem within three days. It *was* the ninth month, on the twentieth *day* of the month; and [a]all the people sat in the street of the house of God, trembling because of *this* matter, and for the great rain.

10 And Ezra the priest stood up, and said unto them, Ye have transgressed, and have taken strange wives, to increase the trespass of Israel.

11 Now therefore [a]make confession unto the LORD God of your fathers, and do his pleasure: and [b]separate yourselves from the people of the land, and from the strange wives.

12 Then all the congregation answered and said with a loud voice, As thou hast said, so must we do.

13 But the people *are* many, and *it is* a time of much rain, and we are not able to stand without, neither *is this* a work of one day or two: for we are many that have transgressed in this thing.

14 Let now our rulers of all the congregation stand, and let all them which have taken strange wives in our cities come at appointed times, and with them the elders of every city, and the judges thereof, until [a]the fierce wrath of our God for this matter be turned from us.

15 Only Jonathan the son of Asahel and Jahaziah the son of Tikvah were employed about this *matter*: and [a]Meshullam and Shabbethai the Levite helped them.

16 And the children of the captivity did so. And Ezra the priest, *with* certain [a]chief of the

---

14 [a][John 5:14; 2 Pet. 2:20] [b]Neh. 13:23 [c]Deut. 9:8
15 [a]Neh. 9:33; Dan. 9:14 [b][Rom. 3:19] [c]1 Cor. 15:17

CHAPTER 10

1 [a]Dan. 9:4, 20 [b]2 Chr. 20:9 [c]Neh. 8:1–9
2 [a]Ezra 10:10, 13, 14, 17, 18; Neh. 13:23–27
3 [a]2 Chr. 34:31 [b]Ezra 9:4 [c]Deut. 7:2, 3 [d]Deut. 24:1, 2
4 [a]1 Chr. 28:10
5 [a]Ezra 10:12, 19; Neh. 5:12; 13:25
6 [a]Deut. 9:18
9 [a]1 Sam. 12:18; Ezra 9:4; 10:3
11 [a][Lev. 26:40–42]; Josh. 7:19; [Prov. 28:13] [b]Ezra 10:3
14 [a]2 Kin. 23:26; 2 Chr. 28:11–13; 29:10; 30:8
15 [a]Ezra 8:16; Neh. 3:4
16 [a]Ezra 4:3

NKJV

14 "should we [a]again break Your commandments, and [b]join in marriage with the people *committing* these abominations? Would You not be [c]angry with us until You had consumed *us*, so that *there would be* no remnant or survivor?

15 "O LORD God of Israel, [a]You *are* righteous, for we are left as a remnant, as *it is* this day. [b]Here we *are* before You, [c]in our guilt, though no one can stand before You because of this!"

Confession of Improper Marriages

10 Now [a]while Ezra was praying, and while he was confessing, weeping, and bowing down [b]before the house of God, a very large assembly of men, women, and children gathered to him from Israel; for the people wept very [c]bitterly.

2 And Shechaniah the son of Jehiel, *one* of the sons of Elam, spoke up and said to Ezra, "We have [a]trespassed against our God, and have taken pagan wives from the peoples of the land; yet now there is hope in Israel in spite of this.

3 "Now therefore, let us make [a]a covenant with our God to put away all these wives and those who have been born to them, according to the advice of my master and of those who [b]tremble at [c]the commandment of our God; and let it be done according to the [d]law.

4 "Arise, for *this* matter *is* your *responsibility*. We also *are* with you. [a]Be of good courage, and do *it*."

5 Then Ezra arose, and made the leaders of the priests, the Levites, and all Israel [a]swear an oath that they would do according to this word. So they swore an oath.

6 Then Ezra rose up from before the house of God, and went into the chamber of Jehohanan the son of Eliashib; and *when* he came there, he [a]ate no bread and drank no water, for he mourned because of the guilt of those from the captivity.

7 And they issued a proclamation throughout Judah and Jerusalem to all the descendants of the captivity, that they must gather at Jerusalem,

8 and that whoever would not come within three days, according to the instructions of the leaders and elders, all his property would be confiscated, and he himself would be separated from the assembly of those from the captivity.

9 So all the men of Judah and Benjamin gathered at Jerusalem within three days. It *was* the ninth month, on the twentieth of the month; and [a]all the people sat in the open square of the house of God, trembling because of *this* matter and because of heavy rain.

10 Then Ezra the priest stood up and said to them, "You have transgressed and have taken pagan wives, adding to the guilt of Israel.

11 "Now therefore, [a]make confession to the LORD God of your fathers, and do His will; [b]separate yourselves from the peoples of the land, and from the pagan wives."

12 Then all the assembly answered and said with a loud voice, "Yes! As you have said, so we must do.

13 "But *there are* many people; *it is* the season for heavy rain, and we are not able to stand outside. Nor *is this* the work of one or two days, for *there are* many of us who have transgressed in this matter.

14 "Please, let the leaders of our entire assembly stand; and let all those in our cities who have taken pagan wives come at appointed times, together with the elders and judges of their cities, until [a]the fierce wrath of our God is turned away from us in this matter."

15 Only Jonathan the son of Asahel and Jahaziah the son of Tikvah opposed this, and [a]Meshullam and Shabbethai the Levite gave them support.

16 Then the descendants of the captivity did so. And Ezra the priest, *with* certain [a]heads of

KJV

fathers, after the house of their fathers, and all of them by *their* names, were separated, and sat down in the first day of the tenth month to examine the matter.

17 And they made an end with all the men that had taken strange wives by the first day of the first month.

Pagan Wives Put Away

18 And among the sons of the priests there were found that had taken strange wives: *namely*, of the sons of [a]Jeshua the son of Jozadak, and his brethren; Maaseiah, and Eliezer, and Jarib, and Gedaliah.

19 And they [a]gave their hands that they would put away their wives; and *being* [b]guilty, *they offered* a ram of the flock for their [c]trespass.

20 And of the sons of Immer; Hanani, and Zebadiah.

21 And of the sons of Harim; Maaseiah, and Elijah, and Shemaiah, and Jehiel, and Uzziah.

22 And of the sons of Pashur; Elioenai, Maaseiah, Ishmael, Nethaneel, Jozabad, and Elasah.

23 Also of the Levites; Jozabad, and Shimei, and Kelaiah, (the same *is* Kelita,) Pethahiah, Judah, and Eliezer.

24 Of the singers also; Eliashib: and of the porters; Shallum, and Telem, and Uri.

25 Moreover of Israel: of the [a]sons of Parosh; Ramiah, and Jeziah, and Malchiah, and Miamin, and Eleazar, and Malchijah, and Benaiah.

26 And of the sons of Elam; Mattaniah, Zechariah, and Jehiel, and Abdi, and Jeremoth, and Eliah.

27 And of the sons of Zattu; Elioenai, Eliashib, Mattaniah, and Jeremoth, and Zabad, and Aziza.

28 Of the [a]sons also of Bebai; Jehohanan, Hananiah, Zabbai, *and* Athlai.

29 And of the sons of Bani; Meshullam, Malluch, and Adaiah, Jashub, and Sheal, and Ramoth.

30 And of the [a]sons of Pahath–moab; Adna, and Chelal, Benaiah, Maaseiah, Mattaniah, Bezaleel, and Binnui, and Manasseh.

31 And *of* the sons of Harim; Eliezer, Ishijah, Malchiah, Shemaiah, Shimeon,

32 Benjamin, Malluch, *and* Shemariah.

33 Of the sons of Hashum; Mattenai, Mattathah, Zabad, Eliphelet, Jeremai, Manasseh, *and* Shimei.

34 Of the sons of Bani; Maadai, Amram, and Uel,

35 Benaiah, Bedeiah, Chelluh,

36 Vaniah, Meremoth, Eliashib,

37 Mattaniah, Mattenai, and Jaasau,

38 And Bani, and Binnui, Shimei,

39 And Shelemiah, and Nathan, and Adaiah,

40 Machnadebai, Shashai, Sharai,

41 Azareel, and Shelemiah, Shemariah,

42 Shallum, Amariah, *and* Joseph.

43 Of the sons of Nebo; Jeiel, Mattithiah, Zabad, Zebina, Jadau, and Joel, Benaiah.

44 All these had taken strange wives: and *some* of them had wives by whom they had children.

18 [a]Ezra 5:2; Hag. 1:1, 12; 2:4; Zech. 3:1; 6:11
19 [a]2 Kin. 10:15 [b]Lev. 6:4, 6 [c]Lev. 5:6, 15
25 [a]Ezra 2:3; 8:3; Neh. 7:8
28 [a]Ezra 8:11
30 [a]Ezra 8:4

*

10:18 *Jehozadak*, 1 Chr. 6:14
10:29 Or *Jeremoth*
10:35 Or *Cheluhi*, or *Cheluhu*
10:37 Or *Jaasu*
10:43 Or *Jaddu*

NKJV

the fathers' *households*, were set apart by the fathers' *households*, each of them by name; and they sat down on the first day of the tenth month to examine the matter.

17 By the first day of the first month they finished *questioning* all the men who had taken pagan wives.

Pagan Wives Put Away

18 And among the sons of the priests who had taken pagan wives *the following* were found of the sons of [a]Jeshua the son of *Jozadak, and his brothers: Maaseiah, Eliezer, Jarib, and Gedaliah.

19 And they [a]gave their promise that they would put away their wives; and *being* [b]guilty, *they presented* a ram of the flock as their [c]trespass offering.

20 Also of the sons of Immer: Hanani and Zebadiah;

21 of the sons of Harim: Maaseiah, Elijah, Shemaiah, Jehiel, and Uzziah;

22 of the sons of Pashhur: Elioenai, Maaseiah, Ishmael, Nethanel, Jozabad, and Elasah.

23 Also of the Levites: Jozabad, Shimei, Kelaiah (the same *is* Kelita), Pethahiah, Judah, and Eliezer.

24 Also of the singers: Eliashib; and of the gatekeepers: Shallum, Telem, and Uri.

25 And others of Israel: of the [a]sons of Parosh: Ramiah, Jeziah, Malchiah, Mijamin, Eleazar, Malchijah, and Benaiah;

26 of the sons of Elam: Mattaniah, Zechariah, Jehiel, Abdi, Jeremoth, and Eliah;

27 of the sons of Zattu: Elioenai, Eliashib, Mattaniah, Jeremoth, Zabad, and Aziza;

28 of the [a]sons of Bebai: Jehohanan, Hananiah, Zabbai, *and* Athlai;

29 of the sons of Bani: Meshullam, Malluch, Adaiah, Jashub, Sheal, *and* *Ramoth;

30 of the [a]sons of Pahath-Moab: Adna, Chelal, Benaiah, Maaseiah, Mattaniah, Bezalel, Binnui, and Manasseh;

31 *of* the sons of Harim: Eliezer, Ishijah, Malchijah, Shemaiah, Shimeon,

32 Benjamin, Malluch, *and* Shemariah;

33 of the sons of Hashum: Mattenai, Mattattah, Zabad, Eliphelet, Jeremai, Manasseh, *and* Shimei;

34 of the sons of Bani: Maadai, Amram, Uel,

35 Benaiah, Bedeiah, *Cheluh,

36 Vaniah, Meremoth, Eliashib,

37 Mattaniah, Mattenai, *Jaasai,

38 Bani, Binnui, Shimei,

39 Shelemiah, Nathan, Adaiah,

40 Machnadebai, Shashai, Sharai,

41 Azarel, Shelemiah, Shemariah,

42 Shallum, Amariah, *and* Joseph;

43 of the sons of Nebo: Jeiel, Mattithiah, Zabad, Zebina, *Jaddai, Joel, *and* Benaiah.

44 All these had taken pagan wives, and *some* of them had wives *by whom* they had children.

KJV

THE BOOK OF

NEHEMIAH

Nehemiah Prays for His People

1 The words of [a]Nehemiah the son of Hachaliah. And it came to pass in the month Chisleu, in the [b]twentieth year, as I was in [c]Shushan the palace,

2 That [a]Hanani, one of my brethren, came, he and *certain* men of Judah; and I asked them concerning the Jews that had escaped, which were left of the captivity, and concerning Jerusalem.

3 And they said unto me, The remnant that are left of the captivity there in the [a]province *are* in great affliction and [b]reproach: [c]the wall of Jerusalem also [d]*is* broken down, and the gates thereof are burned with fire.

4 And it came to pass, when I heard these words, that I sat down and wept, and mourned *certain* days, and fasted, and prayed before the God of heaven,

5 And said, I beseech thee, [a]O LORD God of heaven, the great and [b]terrible God, [c]that keepeth covenant and mercy for them that love him and observe his commandments:

6 Let thine ear now be attentive, and [a]thine eyes open, that thou mayest hear the prayer of thy servant, which I pray before thee now, day and night, for the children of Israel thy servants, and [b]confess the sins of the children of Israel, which we have sinned against thee: both I and my father's house have sinned.

7 [a]We have dealt very corruptly against thee, and have [b]not kept the commandments, nor the statutes, nor the judgments, which thou commandedst thy servant Moses.

8 Remember, I beseech thee, the word that thou commandedst thy servant Moses, saying, [a]*If* ye transgress, I will scatter you abroad among the nations:

9 [a]But *if* ye turn unto me, and keep my commandments, and do them; [b]though there were of you cast out unto the uttermost part of the heaven, *yet* will I gather them from thence, and will bring them unto the place that I have chosen to set my name there.

10 [a]Now these *are* thy servants and thy people, whom thou hast redeemed by thy great power, and by thy strong hand.

11 O Lord, I beseech thee, [a]let now thine ear be attentive to the prayer of thy servant, and to the prayer of thy servants, who [b]desire to fear thy name: and prosper, I pray thee, thy servant this day, and grant him mercy in the sight of this man. For I was the king's [c]cupbearer.

Nehemiah Sent to Judah

2 And it came to pass in the month Nisan, in the twentieth year of [a]Artaxerxes the king, *that* wine *was* before him: and [b]I took up the wine, and gave *it* unto the king. Now I had not been *beforetime* sad in his presence.

2 Wherefore the king said unto me, Why *is* thy countenance sad, seeing thou *art* not sick? this *is* nothing *else* but [a]sorrow of heart. Then I was very sore afraid,

3 And said unto the king, [a]Let the king live for ever: why should not my countenance be sad,

CHAPTER 1

1 [a]Neh. 10:1 [b]Neh. 2:1 [c]Esth. 1:1, 2, 5; Dan. 8:2
2 [a]Neh. 7:2
3 [a]Neh. 7:6 [b]Neh. 2:17 [c]Neh. 2:17 [d]2 Kin. 25:10
5 [a]Dan. 9:4 [b]Neh. 4:14 [c][Ex. 20:6; 34:6, 7]; Ps. 89:2, 3
6 [a]1 Kin. 8:28, 29; 2 Chr. 6:40; Dan. 9:17, 18 [b]Ezra 10:1; Neh. 9:2; Dan. 9:20
7 [a]Ps. 106:6; Dan. 9:5 [b]Deut. 28:15
8 [a]Lev. 26:33; Deut. 4:25–27; 28:63–67
9 [a]Lev. 26:39; [Deut. 4:29–31; 30:2–5] [b]Deut. 30:4
10 [a]Ex. 32:11; Deut. 9:29; Dan. 9:15
11 [a]Neh. 1:6 [b]Is. 26:8; [Heb. 13:18] [c]Gen. 40:21; Neh. 2:1

CHAPTER 2

1 [a]Ezra 7:1 [b]Neh. 1:11
2 [a]Prov. 15:13
3 [a]1 Kin. 1:31; Dan. 2:4; 5:10; 6:6, 21

NKJV

THE BOOK OF

NEHEMIAH

Nehemiah Prays for His People

1 The words of [a]Nehemiah the son of Hachaliah.

It came to pass in the month of Chislev, *in* the [b]twentieth year, as I was in [c]Shushan* the citadel,

2 that [a]Hanani one of my brethren came with men from Judah; and I asked them concerning the Jews who had escaped, who had survived the captivity, and concerning Jerusalem.

3 And they said to me, "The survivors who are left from the captivity in the [a]province *are* there in great distress and [b]reproach. [c]The wall of Jerusalem [d]*is* also broken down, and its gates *are* burned with fire."

4 So it was, when I heard these words, that I sat down and wept, and mourned *for many* days; I was fasting and praying before the God of heaven.

5 And I said: "I pray, [a]LORD God of heaven, O great and [b]awesome God, [c]*You* who keep *Your* covenant and mercy with those who love *You and observe *Your commandments,

6 "please let Your ear be attentive and [a]Your eyes open, that You may hear the prayer of Your servant which I pray before You now, day and night, for the children of Israel Your servants, and [b]confess the sins of the children of Israel which we have sinned against You. Both my father's house and I have sinned.

7 [a]"We have acted very corruptly against You, and have [b]not kept the commandments, the statutes, nor the ordinances which You commanded Your servant Moses.

8 "Remember, I pray, the word that You commanded Your servant Moses, saying, [a]'*If* you are unfaithful, I will scatter you among the nations;

9 [a]'but *if* you return to Me, and keep My commandments and do them, [b]though some of you were cast out to the farthest part of the heavens, *yet* I will gather them from there, and bring them to the place which I have chosen as a dwelling for My name.'

10 [a]"Now these *are* Your servants and Your people, whom You have redeemed by Your great power, and by Your strong hand.

11 "O Lord, I pray, please [a]let Your ear be attentive to the prayer of Your servant, and to the prayer of Your servants who [b]desire to fear Your name; and let Your servant prosper this day, I pray, and grant him mercy in the sight of this man." For I was the king's [c]cupbearer.

Nehemiah Sent to Judah

2 And it came to pass in the month of Nisan, in the twentieth year of [a]King Artaxerxes, *when* wine *was* before him, that [b]I took the wine and gave it to the king. Now I had never been sad in his presence before.

2 Therefore the king said to me, "Why *is* your face sad, since you *are* not sick? This *is* nothing but [a]sorrow of heart." So I became dreadfully afraid,

3 and said to the king, [a]"May the king live forever! Why should my face not be sad, when

*

1:1 Or *Susa*
1:5 Lit. *Him*
• Lit. *His*

KJV

when [b]the city, the place of my fathers' sepulchres, *lieth* waste, and the gates thereof are consumed with [c]fire?

4 Then the king said unto me, For what dost thou make request? So I [a]prayed to the God of heaven.

5 And I said unto the king, If it please the king, and if thy servant have found favour in thy sight, that thou wouldest send me unto Judah, unto the city of my fathers' sepulchres, that I may build it.

6 And the king said unto me, (the queen also sitting by him,) For how long shall thy journey be? and when wilt thou return? So it pleased the king to send me; and I set him [a]a time.

7 Moreover I said unto the king, If it please the king, let letters be given me to the [a]governors beyond the river, that they may convey me over till I come into Judah;

8 And a letter unto Asaph the keeper of the king's forest, that he may give me timber to make beams for the gates of the palace which *appertained* [a]to the house, and for the wall of the city, and for the house that I shall enter into. And the king granted me, [b]according to the good hand of my God upon me.

9 Then I came to the governors beyond the river, and gave them the king's letters. Now the king had sent captains of the army and horsemen with me.

10 When [a]Sanballat the Horonite, and Tobiah the servant, the Ammonite, heard *of it,* it grieved them exceedingly that there was come a man to seek the welfare of the children of Israel.

Nehemiah Views the Wall of Jerusalem

11 So I [a]came to Jerusalem, and was there three days.

12 And I arose in the night, I and some few men with me; neither told I *any* man what my God had put in my heart to do at Jerusalem: neither *was there any* beast with me, save the beast that I rode upon.

13 And I went out by night [a]by the gate of the valley, even before the dragon well, and to the dung port, and viewed the walls of Jerusalem, which were [b]broken down, and the gates thereof were consumed with fire.

14 Then I went on to the [a]gate of the fountain, and to the [b]king's pool: but *there was* no place for the beast *that was* under me to pass.

15 Then went I up in the night by the [a]brook, and viewed the wall, and turned back, and entered by the gate of the valley, and *so* returned.

16 And the rulers knew not whither I went, or what I did; neither had I as yet told *it* to the Jews, nor to the priests, nor to the nobles, nor to the rulers, nor to the rest that did the work.

17 Then said I unto them, Ye see the distress that we *are* in, how Jerusalem *lieth* waste, and the gates thereof are burned with fire: come, and let us build up the wall of Jerusalem, that we be no more [a]a reproach.

18 Then I told them of [a]the hand of my God which was good upon me; as also the king's words that he had spoken unto me. And they said, Let us rise up and build. So they [b]strengthened their hands for *this* good *work.*

19 But when Sanballat the Horonite, and Tobiah the servant, the Ammonite, and Geshem the Arabian, heard *it,* they laughed us to scorn, and despised us, and said, What *is* this thing that ye do? [a]will ye rebel against the king?

20 Then answered I them, and said unto them, The God of heaven, he will prosper us; therefore we his servants will arise and build: [a]but ye have no portion, nor right, nor memorial, in Jerusalem.

Rebuilding the Wall

3 Then [a]Eliashib the high priest rose up with his brethren the priests, [b]and they builded the

---

3 [b]2 Kin. 25:8–10; 2 Chr. 36:19; Jer. 52:12–14 [c]2 Kin. 24:10; Neh. 1:3
4 [a]Neh. 1:4
6 [a]Neh. 5:14; 13:6
7 [a]Ezra 7:21; 8:36
8 [a]Neh. 3:7 [b]Ezra 5:5; 7:6, 9, 28; Neh. 2:18
10 [a]Neh. 2:19; 4:1
11 [a]Ezra 8:32
13 [a]2 Chr. 26:9; Neh. 3:13 [b]Neh. 1:3; 2:17
14 [a]Neh. 3:15 [b]2 Kin. 20:20
15 [a]2 Sam. 15:23; Jer. 31:40
17 [a]Neh. 1:3; Ps. 44:13; 79:4; Jer. 24:9; Ezek. 5:14, 15; 22:4
18 [a]Neh. 2:8 [b]2 Sam. 2:7
19 [a]Neh. 6:6
20 [a]Ezra 4:3; Neh. 6:16

CHAPTER 3

1 [a]Neh. 3:20; 12:10; 13:4, 7, 28 [b]John 5:2

NKJV

[b]the city, the place of my fathers' tombs, *lies* waste, and its gates are burned with [c]fire?"

4 Then the king said to me, "What do you request?" So I [a]prayed to the God of heaven.

5 And I said to the king, "If it pleases the king, and if your servant has found favor in your sight, I ask that you send me to Judah, to the city of my fathers' tombs, that I may rebuild it."

6 Then the king said to me (the queen also sitting beside him), "How long will your journey be? And when will you return?" So it pleased the king to send me; and I set him [a]a time.

7 Furthermore I said to the king, "If it pleases the king, let letters be given to me for the [a]governors *of the region* beyond *the River, that they must permit me to pass through till I come to Judah,

8 "and a letter to Asaph the keeper of the king's forest, that he must give me timber to make beams for the gates of the citadel which *pertains* [a]to the *temple, for the city wall, and for the house that I will occupy." And the king granted *them* to me [b]according to the good hand of my God upon me.

9 Then I went to the governors *in the region* beyond the River, and gave them the king's letters. Now the king had sent captains of the army and horsemen with me.

10 When [a]Sanballat the Horonite and Tobiah the Ammonite *official heard *of it,* they were deeply disturbed that a man had come to seek the well-being of the children of Israel.

Nehemiah Views the Wall of Jerusalem

11 So I [a]came to Jerusalem and was there three days.

12 Then I arose in the night, I and a few men with me; I told no one what my God had put in my heart to do at Jerusalem; nor was there any animal with me, except the one on which I rode.

13 And I went out by night [a]through the Valley Gate to the Serpent Well and the Refuse Gate, and viewed the walls of Jerusalem which were [b]broken down and its gates which were burned with fire.

14 Then I went on to the [a]Fountain Gate and to the [b]King's Pool, but *there was* no room for the animal under me to pass.

15 So I went up in the night by the [a]valley, and viewed the wall; then I turned back and entered by the Valley Gate, and so returned.

16 And the officials did not know where I had gone or what I had done; I had not yet told the Jews, the priests, the nobles, the officials, or the others who did the work.

17 Then I said to them, "You see the distress that we *are* in, how Jerusalem *lies* waste, and its gates are burned with fire. Come and let us build the wall of Jerusalem, that we may no longer be [a]a reproach."

18 And I told them of [a]the hand of my God which had been good upon me, and also of the king's words that he had spoken to me. So they said, "Let us rise up and build." Then they [b]set their hands to *this* good *work.*

19 But when Sanballat the Horonite, Tobiah the Ammonite official, and Geshem the Arab heard *of it,* they laughed at us and despised us, and said, "What *is* this thing that you are doing? [a]Will you rebel against the king?"

20 So I answered them, and said to them, "The God of heaven Himself will prosper us; therefore we His servants will arise and build, [a]but you have no heritage or right or memorial in Jerusalem."

Rebuilding the Wall

3 Then [a]Eliashib the high priest rose up with his brethren the priests [b]and built the Sheep

---

*

2:7 The Euphrates
2:8 Lit. *house*
2:10 Lit. *servant*

KJV

sheep gate; they sanctified it, and set up the doors of it; [c]even unto the tower of Meah they sanctified it, unto the tower of [d]Hananeel.

2 And next unto him builded [a]the men of Jericho. And next to them builded Zaccur the son of Imri.

3 [a]But the fish gate did the sons of Hassenaah build, who *also* laid the beams thereof, and [b]set up the doors thereof, the locks thereof, and the bars thereof.

4 And next unto them repaired [a]Meremoth the son of Urijah, the son of Koz. And next unto them repaired [b]Meshullam the son of Berechiah, the son of Meshezabeel. And next unto them repaired Zadok the son of Baana.

5 And next unto them the Tekoites repaired; but their nobles put not their necks to [a]the work of their Lord.

6 Moreover [a]the old gate repaired Jehoiada the son of Paseah, and Meshullam the son of Besodeiah; they laid the beams thereof, and set up the doors thereof, and the locks thereof, and the bars thereof.

7 And next unto them repaired Melatiah the Gibeonite, and Jadon the Meronothite, the [a]men of Gibeon, and of Mizpah, unto the [b]throne of the governor on this side the river.

8 Next unto him repaired Uzziel the son of Harhaiah, of the goldsmiths. Next unto him also repaired Hananiah the son of *one of* the apothecaries, and they fortified Jerusalem unto the [a]broad wall.

9 And next unto them repaired Rephaiah the son of Hur, the ruler of the half part of Jerusalem.

10 And next unto them repaired Jedaiah the son of Harumaph, even over against his house. And next unto him repaired Hattush the son of Hashabniah.

11 Malchijah the son of Harim, and Hashub the son of Pahath–moab, repaired the other piece, [a]and the tower of the furnaces.

12 And next unto him repaired Shallum the son of Halohesh, the ruler of the half part of Jerusalem, he and his daughters.

13 [a]The valley gate repaired Hanun, and the inhabitants of Zanoah; they built it, and set up the doors thereof, the locks thereof, and the bars thereof, and a thousand cubits on the wall unto [b]the dung gate.

14 But the dung gate repaired Malchiah the son of Rechab, the ruler of part of [a]Beth–haccerem; he build it, and set up the doors thereof, the locks thereof, and the bars thereof.

15 But [a]the gate of the fountain repaired Shallun the son of Colhozeh, the ruler of part of Mizpah; he built it, and covered it, and set up the doors thereof, the locks thereof, and the bars thereof, and the wall of the pool of [b]Siloah by the [c]king's garden, and unto the stairs that go down from the city of David.

16 After him repaired Nehemiah the son of Azbuk, the ruler of the half part of Beth–zur, unto *the place* over against the sepulchres of David, and to the [a]pool that was made, and unto the house of the mighty.

17 After him repaired the Levites, Rehum the son of Bani. Next unto him repaired Hashabiah, the ruler of the half part of Keilah, in his part.

18 After him repaired their brethren, Bavai the son of Henadad, the ruler of the half part of Keilah.

19 And next to him repaired Ezer the son of Jeshua, the ruler of Mizpah, another piece over against the going up to the armoury at the [a]turning *of the wall.*

20 After him Baruch the son of Zabbai earnestly repaired the other piece, from the turning *of the wall* unto the door of the house of Eliashib the high priest.

21 After him repaired Meremoth the son of Urijah the son of Koz another piece, from the door

1 [c]Neh. 12:39 [d]Jer. 31:38; Zech. 14:10
2 [a]Ezra 2:34; Neh. 7:36
3 [a]2 Chr. 33:14; Neh. 12:39; Zeph. 1:10 [b]Neh. 6:1; 7:1
4 [a]Ezra 8:33 [b]Ezra 10:15
5 [a][Judg. 5:23]
6 [a]Neh. 12:39
7 [a]Neh. 7:25 [b]Ezra 8:36; Neh. 2:7–9
8 [a]Neh. 12:38
11 [a]Neh. 12:38
13 [a]Neh. 2:13, 15 [b]Neh. 2:13
14 [a]Jer. 6:1
15 [a]Neh. 2:14 [b]Is. 8:6; John 9:7 [c]2 Kin. 25:4
16 [a]2 Kin. 20:20; Is. 7:3; 22:11
19 [a]2 Chr. 26:9

NKJV

Gate; they consecrated it and hung its doors. They built [c]as far as the Tower of *the Hundred, *and* consecrated it, then as far as the Tower of [d]Hananel.

2 *Next to *Eliashib* [a]the men of Jericho built. And next to them Zaccur the son of Imri built.

3 Also the sons of Hassenaah built [a]the Fish Gate; they laid its beams and [b]hung its doors with its bolts and bars.

4 And next to them [a]Meremoth the son of Urijah, the son of *Koz, made repairs. Next to them [b]Meshullam the son of Berechiah, the son of Meshezabel, made repairs. Next to them Zadok the son of Baana made repairs.

5 Next to them the Tekoites made repairs; but their nobles did not put their *shoulders to [a]the work of their Lord.

6 Moreover Jehoiada the son of Paseah and Meshullam the son of Besodeiah repaired [a]the Old Gate; they laid its beams and hung its doors, with its bolts and bars.

7 And next to them Melatiah the Gibeonite, Jadon the Meronothite, the [a]men of Gibeon and Mizpah, repaired the [b]residence* of the governor *of the region* beyond the River.

8 Next to him Uzziel the son of Harhaiah, one of the goldsmiths, made repairs. Also next to him Hananiah, *one of the perfumers, made repairs; and they fortified Jerusalem as far as the [a]Broad Wall.

9 And next to them Rephaiah the son of Hur, leader of half the district of Jerusalem, made repairs.

10 Next to them Jedaiah the son of Harumaph made repairs in front of his house. And next to him Hattush the son of Hashabniah made repairs.

11 Malchijah the son of Harim and Hashub the son of Pahath-Moab repaired another section, [a]as well as the Tower of the Ovens.

12 And next to him was Shallum the son of Hallohesh, leader of half the district of Jerusalem; he and his daughters made repairs.

13 Hanun and the inhabitants of Zanoah repaired [a]the Valley Gate. They built it, hung its doors with its bolts and bars, and *repaired* a thousand cubits of the wall as far as [b]the Refuse Gate.

14 Malchijah the son of Rechab, leader of the district of [a]Beth Haccerem, repaired the Refuse Gate; he built it and hung its doors with its bolts and bars.

15 Shallun the son of Col-Hozeh, leader of the district of Mizpah, repaired [a]the Fountain Gate; he built it, covered it, hung its doors with its bolts and bars, and repaired the wall of the Pool of [b]Shelah by the [c]King's Garden, as far as the stairs that go down from the City of David.

16 After him Nehemiah the son of Azbuk, leader of half the district of Beth Zur, made repairs as far as *the place* in front of the *tombs of David, to the [a]man-made pool, and as far as the House of the Mighty.

17 After him the Levites, *under* Rehum the son of Bani, made repairs. Next to him Hashabiah, leader of half the district of Keilah, made repairs for his district.

18 After him their brethren, *under* *Bavai the son of Henadad, leader of the *other* half of the district of Keilah, made repairs.

19 And next to him Ezer the son of Jeshua, the leader of Mizpah, repaired another section in front of the Ascent to the Armory at the [a]buttress.

20 After him Baruch the son of *Zabbai carefully repaired the other section, from the buttress to the door of the house of Eliashib the high priest.

21 After him Meremoth the son of Urijah, the son of *Koz, repaired another section, from the

*

3:1 Heb. *Hammeah*
3:2 Lit. *On his hand*
3:4 Or *Hakkoz*
3:5 Lit. *necks*
3:7 Lit. *throne*
3:8 Lit. *the son*
3:16 LXX, Syr., Vg. *tomb*
3:18 So with MT, Vg.; some Heb. mss., LXX, Syr. *Binnui* (cf. v. 24)
3:20 A few Heb. mss., Syr., Vg. *Zaccai*
3:21 Or *Hakkoz*

KJV

of the house of Eliashib even to the end of the house of Eliashib.

22 And after him repaired the priests, the men of the plain.

23 After him repaired Benjamin and Hashub over against their house. After him repaired Azariah the son of Maaseiah the son of Ananiah by his house.

24 After him repaired [a]Binnui the son of Henadad another piece, from the house of Azariah unto [b]the turning *of the wall,* even unto the corner.

25 Palal the son of Uzai, over against the turning *of the wall,* and the tower which lieth out from the king's high house, that *was* by the [a]court of the prison. After him Pedaiah the son of Parosh.

26 Moreover [a]the Nethinims dwelt in [b]Ophel, unto *the place* over against [c]the water gate toward the east, and the tower that lieth out.

27 After them the Tekoites repaired another piece, over against the great tower that lieth out, even unto the wall of Ophel.

28 From above the [a]horse gate repaired the priests, every one over against his house.

29 After them repaired Zadok the son of Immer over against his house. After him repaired also Shemaiah the son of Shechaniah, the keeper of the east gate.

30 After him repaired Hananiah the son of Shelemiah, and Hanun the sixth son of Zalaph, another piece. After him repaired Meshullam the son of Berechiah over against his chamber.

31 After him repaired Malchiah the goldsmith's son unto the place of the Nethinims, and of the merchants, over against the gate Miphkad, and to the going up of the corner.

32 And between the going up of the corner unto the [a]sheep gate repaired the goldsmiths and the merchants.

The Wall Defended Against Enemies

4 But it came to pass, [a]that when Sanballat heard that we builded the wall, he was wroth, and took great indignation, and mocked the Jews.

2 And he spake before his brethren and the army of Samaria, and said, What do these feeble Jews? will they fortify themselves? will they sacrifice? will they make an end in a day? will they revive the stones out of the heaps of the rubbish which are burned?

3 Now [a]Tobiah the Ammonite *was* by him, and he said, Even that which they build, if a fox go up, he shall even break down their stone wall.

4 [a]Hear, O our God; for we are despised: and [b]turn their reproach upon their own head, and give them for a prey in the land of captivity:

5 And [a]cover not their iniquity, and let not their sin be blotted out from before thee: for they have provoked *thee* to anger before the builders.

6 So built we the wall; and all the wall was joined together unto the half thereof: for the people had a mind to work.

7 But it came to pass, *that* [a]when Sanballat, and Tobiah, and [b]the Arabians, and the Ammonites, and the Ashdodites, heard that the walls of Jerusalem were made up, *and* that the breaches began to be stopped, then they were very wroth,

8 And [a]conspired all of them together to come *and* to fight against Jerusalem, and to hinder it.

9 Nevertheless [a]we made our prayer unto our God, and set a watch against them day and night, because of them.

10 And Judah said, The strength of the bearers of burdens is decayed, and *there is* much rubbish; so that we are not able to build the wall.

11 And our adversaries said, They shall not know, neither see, till we come in the midst among them, and slay them, and cause the work to cease.

24 [a]Ezra 8:33 [b]Neh. 3:19
25 [a]Jer. 32:2; 33:1; 37:21
26 [a]Ezra 2:43; Neh. 11:21 [b]2 Chr. 27:3 [c]Neh. 8:1, 3; 12:37
28 [a]2 Kin. 11:16; 2 Chr. 23:15; Jer. 31:40
32 [a]Neh. 3:1; 12:39

CHAPTER 4

1 [a]Neh. 2:10, 19
3 [a]Neh. 2:10, 19
4 [a]Ps. 123:3, 4 [b]Ps. 79:12; Prov. 3:34
5 [a]Ps. 69:27, 28; 109:14, 15; Jer. 18:23
7 [a]Neh. 4:1 [b]Neh. 2:19
8 [a]Ps. 83:3–5
9 [a][Ps. 50:15]

*———

3:31 Lit. *Inspection* or *Recruiting*

NKJV

door of the house of Eliashib to the end of the house of Eliashib.

22 And after him the priests, the men of the plain, made repairs.

23 After him Benjamin and Hasshub made repairs opposite their house. After them Azariah the son of Maaseiah, the son of Ananiah, made repairs by his house.

24 After him [a]Binnui the son of Henadad repaired another section, from the house of Azariah to [b]the buttress, even as far as the corner.

25 Palal the son of Uzai *made repairs* opposite the buttress, and on the tower which projects from the king's upper house that *was* by the [a]court of the prison. After him Pedaiah the son of Parosh *made repairs.*

26 Moreover [a]the Nethinim who dwelt in [b]Ophel *made repairs* as far as *the place* in front of [c]the Water Gate toward the east, and on the projecting tower.

27 After them the Tekoites repaired another section, next to the great projecting tower, and as far as the wall of Ophel.

28 Beyond the [a]Horse Gate the priests made repairs, each in front of his *own* house.

29 After them Zadok the son of Immer made repairs in front of his *own* house. After him Shemaiah the son of Shechaniah, the keeper of the East Gate, made repairs.

30 After him Hananiah the son of Shelemiah, and Hanun, the sixth son of Zalaph, repaired another section. After him Meshullam the son of Berechiah made repairs in front of his dwelling.

31 After him Malchijah, one of the goldsmiths, made repairs as far as the house of the Nethinim and of the merchants, in front of the *Miphkad Gate, and as far as the upper room at the corner.

32 And between the upper room at the corner, as far as the [a]Sheep Gate, the goldsmiths and the merchants made repairs.

The Wall Defended Against Enemies

4 But it so happened, [a]when Sanballat heard that we were rebuilding the wall, that he was furious and very indignant, and mocked the Jews.

2 And he spoke before his brethren and the army of Samaria, and said, "What are these feeble Jews doing? Will they fortify themselves? Will they offer sacrifices? Will they complete it in a day? Will they revive the stones from the heaps of rubbish—*stones* that are burned?"

3 Now [a]Tobiah the Ammonite *was* beside him, and he said, "Whatever they build, if even a fox goes up *on it,* he will break down their stone wall."

4 [a]Hear, O our God, for we are despised; [b]turn their reproach on their own heads, and give them as plunder to a land of captivity!

5 [a]Do not cover their iniquity, and do not let their sin be blotted out from before You; for they have provoked *You* to anger before the builders.

6 So we built the wall, and the entire wall was joined together up to half its *height,* for the people had a mind to work.

7 Now it happened, [a]when Sanballat, Tobiah, [b]the Arabs, the Ammonites, and the Ashdodites heard that the walls of Jerusalem were being restored and the gaps were beginning to be closed, that they became very angry,

8 and all of them [a]conspired together to come *and* attack Jerusalem and create confusion.

9 Nevertheless [a]we made our prayer to our God, and because of them we set a watch against them day and night.

10 Then Judah said, "The strength of the laborers is failing, and *there is* so much rubbish that we are not able to build the wall."

11 And our adversaries said, "They will neither know nor see anything, till we come into their midst and kill them and cause the work to cease."

KJV

12 And it came to pass, that when the Jews which dwelt by them came, they said unto us ten times, From all places whence ye shall return unto us *they will be upon you.*

13 Therefore set I in the lower places behind the wall, *and* on the higher places, I even set the people after their families with their swords, their spears, and their bows.

14 And I looked, and rose up, and said unto the nobles, and to the rulers, and to the rest of the people, [a]Be not ye afraid of them: remember the Lord, *which is* [b]great and terrible, and [c]fight for your brethren, your sons, and your daughters, your wives, and your houses.

15 And it came to pass, when our enemies heard that it was known unto us, [a]and God had brought their counsel to nought, that we returned all of us to the wall, every one unto his work.

16 And it came to pass from that time forth, *that* the half of my servants wrought in the work, and the other half of them held both the spears, the shields, and the bows, and the habergeons; and the rulers *were* behind all the house of Judah.

17 They which builded on the wall, and they that bare burdens, with those that laded, *every one* with one of his hands wrought in the work, and with the other *hand* held a weapon.

18 For the builders, every one had his sword girded by his side, and *so* builded. And he that sounded the trumpet *was* by me.

19 And I said unto the nobles, and to the rulers, and to the rest of the people, The work *is* great and large, and we are separated upon the wall, one far from another.

20 In what place *therefore* ye hear the sound of the trumpet, resort ye thither unto us: [a]our God shall fight for us.

21 So we laboured in the work: and half of them held the spears from the rising of the morning till the stars appeared.

22 Likewise at the same time said I unto the people, Let every one with his servant lodge within Jerusalem, that in the night they may be a guard to us, and labour on the day.

23 So neither I, nor my brethren, nor my servants, nor the men of the guard which followed me, none of us put off our clothes, *saving that* every one put them off for washing.

Nehemiah Deals with Oppression

5 And there was a great [a]cry of the people and of their wives against their [b]brethren the Jews.

2 For there were that said, We, our sons, and our daughters, *are* many: therefore we take up corn *for them,* that we may eat, and live.

3 *Some* also there were that said, We have mortgaged our lands, vineyards, and houses, that we might buy corn, because of the dearth.

4 There were also that said, We have borrowed money for the king's tribute, *and that upon* our lands and vineyards.

5 Yet now [a]our flesh *is* as the flesh of our brethren, our children as their children: and, lo, we [b]bring into bondage our sons and our daughters to be servants, and *some* of our daughters are brought unto bondage *already:* neither *is it* in our power *to redeem them;* for other men have our lands and vineyards.

6 And I was very angry when I heard their cry and these words.

7 Then I consulted with myself, and I rebuked the nobles, and the rulers, and said unto them, [a]Ye exact usury, every one of his brother. And I set a great assembly against them.

8 And I said unto them, We after our ability have [a]redeemed our brethren the Jews, which were sold unto the heathen; and will ye even sell your brethren? or shall they be sold unto us? Then held they their peace, and found nothing *to answer.*

9 Also I said, It *is* not good that ye do: ought

14 [a][Num. 14:9]; Deut. 1:29 [b][Deut. 10:17] [c]2 Sam. 10:12
15 [a]Job 5:12
20 [a]Ex. 14:14, 25; Deut. 1:30; 3:22; 20:4; Josh. 23:10; 2 Chr. 20:29

CHAPTER 5

1 [a]Lev. 25:35–37; Neh. 5:7, 8 [b]Deut. 15:7
5 [a]Is. 58:7 [b]Ex. 21:7; [Lev. 25:39]
7 [a][Ex. 22:25; Lev. 25:36; Deut. 23:19, 20]; Ezek. 22:12
8 [a]Lev. 25:48

* **4:21** Lit. *them*

NKJV

12 So it was, when the Jews who dwelt near them came, that they told us ten times, "From whatever place you turn, *they will be* upon us."

13 Therefore I positioned *men* behind the lower parts of the wall, at the openings; and I set the people according to their families, with their swords, their spears, and their bows.

14 And I looked, and arose and said to the nobles, to the leaders, and to the rest of the people, [a]"Do not be afraid of them. Remember the Lord, [b]great and awesome, and [c]fight for your brethren, your sons, your daughters, your wives, and your houses."

15 And it happened, when our enemies heard that it was known to us, and [a]*that* God had brought their plot to nothing, that all of us returned to the wall, everyone to his work.

16 So it was, from that time on, *that* half of my servants worked at construction, while the other half held the spears, the shields, the bows, and *wore* armor; and the leaders *were* behind all the house of Judah.

17 Those who built on the wall, and those who carried burdens, loaded themselves so that with one hand they worked at construction, and with the other held a weapon.

18 Every one of the builders had his sword girded at his side as he built. And the one who sounded the trumpet *was* beside me.

19 Then I said to the nobles, the rulers, and the rest of the people, "The work *is* great and extensive, and we are separated far from one another on the wall.

20 "Wherever you hear the sound of the trumpet, rally to us there. [a]Our God will fight for us."

21 So we labored in the work, and half of **the men* held the spears from daybreak until the stars appeared.

22 At the same time I also said to the people, "Let each man and his servant stay at night in Jerusalem, that they may be our guard by night and a working party by day."

23 So neither I, my brethren, my servants, nor the men of the guard who followed me took off our clothes, *except* that everyone took them off for washing.

Nehemiah Deals with Oppression

5 And there was a great [a]outcry of the people and their wives against their [b]Jewish brethren.

2 For there were those who said, "We, our sons, and our daughters *are* many; therefore let us get grain, that we may eat and live."

3 There were also *some* who said, "We have mortgaged our lands and vineyards and houses, that we might buy grain because of the famine."

4 There were also those who said, "We have borrowed money for the king's tax *on* our lands and vineyards.

5 "Yet now [a]our flesh *is* as the flesh of our brethren, our children as their children; and indeed we [b]are forcing our sons and our daughters to be slaves, and *some* of our daughters have been brought into slavery. *It is* not in our power *to redeem them,* for other men have our lands and vineyards."

6 And I became very angry when I heard their outcry and these words.

7 After serious thought, I rebuked the nobles and rulers, and said to them, [a]"Each of you is exacting usury from his brother." So I called a great assembly against them.

8 And I said to them, "According to our ability we have [a]redeemed our Jewish brethren who were sold to the nations. Now indeed, will you even sell your brethren? Or should they be sold to us?" Then they were silenced and found nothing *to say.*

9 Then I said, "What you are doing *is* not

KJV

ye not to walk [a]in the fear of our God [b]because
of the reproach of the heathen our enemies?
10 I likewise, *and* my brethren, and my servants, might exact of them money and corn: I pray
you, let us leave off this usury.
11 Restore, I pray you, to them, even this day,
their lands, their vineyards, their oliveyards, and
their houses, also the hundredth *part* of the
money, and of the corn, the wine, and the oil, that
ye exact of them.
12 Then said they, We will restore *them,* and
will require nothing of them; so will we do as thou
sayest. Then I called the priests, [a]and took an oath
of them, that they should do according to this
promise.
13 Also [a]I shook my lap, and said, So God
shake out every man from his house, and from
his labour, that performeth not this promise, even
thus be he shaken out, and emptied. And all the
congregation said, Amen, and praised the LORD.
[b]And the people did according to this promise.

The Generosity of Nehemiah

14 Moreover from the time that I was appointed to be their governor in the land of Judah,
from the twentieth year [a]even unto the two and
thirtieth year of Artaxerxes the king, *that is,*
twelve years, I and my brethren have not [b]eaten
the bread of the governor.
15 But the former governors that *had been*
before me were chargeable unto the people, and
had taken of them bread and wine, beside forty
shekels of silver; yea, even their servants bare
rule over the people: but [a]so did not I, because
of the [b]fear of God.
16 Yea, also I continued in the [a]work of this
wall, neither bought we any land: and all my servants *were* gathered thither unto the work.
17 Moreover *there were* [a]at my table an hundred and fifty of the Jews and rulers, beside those
that came unto us from among the heathen that
are about us.
18 Now *that* [a]which was prepared *for me*
daily *was* one ox *and* six choice sheep; also fowls
were prepared for me, and once in ten days store
of all sorts of wine: yet for all this [b]required not
I the bread of the governor, because the bondage
was heavy upon this people.
19 [a]Think upon me, my God, for good, *according* to all that I have done for this people.

Conspiracy Against Nehemiah

6 Now it came to pass, [a]when Sanballat, and
Tobiah, and Geshem the Arabian, and the rest
of our enemies, heard that I had builded the wall,
and *that* there was no breach left therein;
[b](though at that time I had not set up the doors
upon the gates;)
2 That Sanballat and Geshem [a]sent unto
me, saying, Come, let us meet together in *some
one of* the villages in the plain of [b]Ono. But they
[c]thought to do me mischief.
3 And I sent messengers unto them, saying,
I *am* doing a great work, so that I cannot come
down: why should the work cease, whilst I leave
it, and come down to you?
4 Yet they sent unto me four times after this
sort; and I answered them after the same manner.
5 Then sent Sanballat his servant unto me
in like manner the fifth time with an open letter
in his hand;
6 Wherein *was* written, It is reported among
the heathen, and Gashmu saith *it, that* thou and
the Jews think to rebel: for which cause thou
buildest the wall, [a]that thou mayest be their king,
according to these words.
7 And thou hast also appointed prophets to
preach of thee at Jerusalem, saying, *There is* a
king in Judah: and now shall it be reported to

9 [a]Lev. 25:36 [b]2 Sam. 12:14; Rom. 2:24; [1 Pet. 2:12]
12 [a]Ezra 10:5; Jer. 34:8, 9
13 [a]Matt. 10:14; Acts 13:51; 18:6 [b]2 Kin. 23:3
14 [a]Neh. 2:1; 13:6 [b][1 Cor. 9:4–15]
15 [a]2 Cor. 11:9; 12:13 [b]Neh. 5:9
16 [a]Neh. 4:1; 6:1
17 [a]2 Sam. 9:7; 1 Kin. 18:19
18 [a]1 Kin. 4:22 [b]Neh. 5:14, 15
19 [a]2 Kin. 20:3; Neh. 13:14, 22, 31

CHAPTER 6

1 [a]Neh. 2:10, 19; 4:1, 7; 13:28 [b]Neh. 3:1, 3
2 [a]Prov. 26:24, 25 [b]1 Chr. 8:12; Neh. 11:35 [c]Ps. 37:12, 32
6 [a]Neh. 2:19

*———

5:13 Lit. *my lap*
5:16 So with MT; LXX, Syr., Vg. *I*
6:6 Heb. *Gashmu*

NKJV

good. Should you not walk [a]in the fear of our God
[b]because of the reproach of the nations, our
enemies?
10 "I also, *with* my brethren and my servants, am lending them money and grain. Please,
let us stop this usury!
11 "Restore now to them, even this day, their
lands, their vineyards, their olive groves, and their
houses, also a hundredth of the money and the
grain, the new wine and the oil, that you have
charged them."
12 So they said, "We will restore *it,* and will
require nothing from them; we will do as you
say." Then I called the priests, [a]and required an
oath from them that they would do according to
this promise.
13 Then [a]I shook out *the fold of my garment
and said, "So may God shake out each man from
his house, and from his property, who does not
perform this promise. Even thus may he be
shaken out and emptied." And all the assembly
said, "Amen!" and praised the LORD. [b]Then the
people did according to this promise.

The Generosity of Nehemiah

14 Moreover, from the time that I was
appointed to be their governor in the land of
Judah, from the twentieth year [a]until the thirty-
second year of King Artaxerxes, twelve years,
neither I nor my brothers [b]ate the governor's
provisions.
15 But the former governors who *were* before
me laid burdens on the people, and took from
them bread and wine, besides forty shekels of silver. Yes, even their servants bore rule over the
people, but [a]I did not do so, because of the [b]fear
of God.
16 Indeed, I also continued the [a]work on this
wall, and *we did not buy any land. All my servants *were* gathered there for the work.
17 And [a]at my table *were* one hundred and
fifty Jews and rulers, besides those who came to
us from the nations around us.
18 Now *that* [a]which was prepared daily
was one ox *and* six choice sheep. Also fowl
were prepared for me, and once every ten days
an abundance of all kinds of wine. Yet in spite
of this [b]I did not demand the governor's provisions, because the bondage was heavy on this
people.
19 [a]Remember me, my God, for good, *according to* all that I have done for this people.

Conspiracy Against Nehemiah

6 Now it happened [a]when Sanballat, Tobiah,
Geshem the Arab, and the rest of our enemies
heard that I had rebuilt the wall, and *that* there
were no breaks left in it [b](though at that time I
had not hung the doors in the gates),
2 that Sanballat and Geshem [a]sent to me,
saying, "Come, let us meet together among the
villages in the plain of [b]Ono." But they [c]thought
to do me harm.
3 So I sent messengers to them, saying, "I
am doing a great work, so that I cannot come
down. Why should the work cease while I leave
it and go down to you?"
4 But they sent me this message four times,
and I answered them in the same manner.
5 Then Sanballat sent his servant to me as
before, the fifth time, with an open letter in his
hand.
6 In it *was* written:

It is reported among the nations, and
*Geshem says, *that* you and the Jews plan
to rebel; therefore, according to these
rumors, you are rebuilding the wall, [a]that
you may be their king.
7 And you have also appointed prophets to
proclaim concerning you at Jerusalem,
saying, "*There is* a king in Judah!" Now

KJV

the king according to these words. Come now
therefore, and let us take counsel together.
8 Then I sent unto him, saying, There are
no such things done as thou sayest, but thou
feignest them out of thine own heart.
9 For they all made us afraid, saying, Their
hands shall be weakened from the work, that it
be not done. Now therefore, *O God,* strengthen
my hands.
10 Afterward I came unto the house of Shemaiah the son of Delaiah the son of Mehetabeel,
who *was* shut up; and he said, Let us meet together in the house of God, within the temple,
and let us shut the doors of the temple: for they
will come to slay thee; yea, in the night will they
come to slay thee.
11 And I said, Should such a man as I flee?
and who *is there,* that, *being* as I *am,* would go
into the temple to save his life? I will not go in.
12 And, lo, I perceived that God had not sent
him; but that [a]he pronounced this prophecy
against me: for Tobiah and Sanballat had hired
him.
13 Therefore *was* he hired, that I should be
afraid, and do so, and sin, and *that* they might
have *matter* for an evil report, that they might
reproach me.
14 [a]My God, think thou upon Tobiah and
Sanballat according to these their works, and on
the [b]prophetess Noadiah, and the rest of the
prophets, that would have put me in fear.

The Wall Completed

15 So the wall was finished in the twenty and
fifth *day* of *the month* Elul, in fifty and two days.
16 And it came to pass, that [a]when all our
enemies heard *thereof,* and all the heathen that
were about us saw *these things,* they were much
cast down in their own eyes: for [b]they perceived
that this work was wrought of our God.
17 Moreover in those days the nobles of Judah sent many letters unto Tobiah, and *the letters*
of Tobiah came unto them.
18 For *there were* many in Judah sworn unto
him, because he *was* the [a]son in law of Shechaniah the son of Arah; and his son Johanan had
taken the daughter of [b]Meshullam the son of
Berechiah.
19 Also they reported his good deeds before
me, and uttered my words to him. *And* Tobiah
sent letters to put me in fear.

7 Now it came to pass, when the wall was built,
and I had [a]set up the doors, and the porters
and the singers and the Levites were appointed,
2 That I gave my brother [a]Hanani, and
Hananiah the ruler [b]of the palace, charge over
Jerusalem: for he *was* a faithful man, and [c]feared
God above many.
3 And I said unto them, Let not the gates
of Jerusalem be opened until the sun be hot; and
while they stand by, let them shut the doors, and
bar *them:* and appoint watches of the inhabitants
of Jerusalem, every one in his watch, and every
one *to be* over against his house.

The Captives Who Returned to Jerusalem
(Ezra 2:1–70)

4 Now the city *was* large and great: but the
people *were* [a]few therein, and the houses *were*
not builded.
5 And my God put into mine heart to gather
together the nobles, and the rulers, and the people, that they might be reckoned by genealogy.
And I found a register of the genealogy of them
which came up at the first, and found written
therein,
6 [a]These *are* the children of the province,
that went up out of the captivity, of those that
had been carried away, whom Nebuchadnezzar
the king of Babylon had carried away, and came

12 [a]Ezek. 13:22
14 [a]Neh. 13:29 [b]Ezek. 13:17
16 [a]Neh. 2:10, 20; 4:1, 7; 6:1 [b]Ps. 126:2
18 [a]Neh. 13:4, 28 [b]Ezra 10:15; Neh. 3:4

CHAPTER 7
1 [a]Neh. 6:1, 15
2 [a]Neh. 1:2 [b]Neh. 2:8; 10:23 [c]Ex. 18:21
4 [a]Deut. 4:27
6 [a]Ezra 2:1–70

NKJV

these matters will be reported to the king.
So come, therefore, and let us consult
together.

8 Then I sent to him, saying, "No such
things as you say are being done, but you invent
them in your own heart."
9 For they all *were trying to* make us afraid,
saying, "Their hands will be weakened in the
work, and it will not be done."
Now therefore, *O God,* strengthen my hands.
10 Afterward I came to the house of Shemaiah the son of Delaiah, the son of Mehetabel,
who *was* a secret informer; and he said, "Let us
meet together in the house of God, within the temple, and let us close the doors of the temple, for
they are coming to kill you; indeed, at night they
will come to kill you."
11 And I said, "Should such a man as I flee?
And who *is there* such as I who would go into
the temple to save his life? I will not go in!"
12 Then I perceived that God had not sent
him at all, but that [a]he pronounced *this* prophecy
against me because Tobiah and Sanballat had
hired him.
13 For this reason he *was* hired, that I should
be afraid and act that way and sin, so *that* they
might have *cause* for an evil report, that they
might reproach me.
14 [a]My God, remember Tobiah and Sanballat, according to these their works, and the
[b]prophetess Noadiah and the rest of the prophets
who would have made me afraid.

The Wall Completed

15 So the wall was finished on the twenty-
fifth *day* of Elul, in fifty-two days.
16 And it happened, [a]when all our enemies
heard *of it,* and all the nations around us saw
these things, that they were very disheartened in
their own eyes; for [b]they perceived that this work
was done by our God.
17 Also in those days the nobles of Judah
sent many letters to Tobiah, and *the letters of*
Tobiah came to them.
18 For many in Judah were pledged to him,
because he was the [a]son-in-law of Shechaniah the
son of Arah, and his son Jehohanan had married
the daughter of [b]Meshullam the son of Berechiah.
19 Also they reported his good deeds before
me, and reported my words to him. Tobiah sent
letters to frighten me.

7 Then it was, when the wall was built and I
had [a]hung the doors, when the gatekeepers,
the singers, and the Levites had been appointed,
2 that I gave the charge of Jerusalem to my
brother [a]Hanani, and Hananiah the leader [b]of the
citadel, for he *was* a faithful man and [c]feared God
more than many.
3 And I said to them, "Do not let the gates
of Jerusalem be opened until the sun is hot; and
while they stand *guard,* let them shut and bar the
doors; and appoint guards from among the inhabitants of Jerusalem, one at his watch station and
another in front of his own house."

The Captives Who Returned to Jerusalem
(Ezra 2:1–70)

4 Now the city *was* large and spacious, but
the people in it *were* [a]few, and the houses *were*
not rebuilt.
5 Then my God put it into my heart to gather
the nobles, the rulers, and the people, that they
might be registered by genealogy. And I found a
register of the genealogy of those who had come
up in the first *return,* and found written in it:

6 [a]These *are* the people of the province who
came back from the captivity, of those
who had been carried away, whom
Nebuchadnezzar the king of Babylon had

KJV

again to Jerusalem and to Judah, every one unto
his city;
7 Who came with [a]Zerubbabel, Jeshua,
Nehemiah, Azariah, Raamiah, Nahamani, Mordecai, Bilshan, Mispereth, Bigvai, Nehum, Baanah.
The number, *I say,* of the men of the people of
Israel *was this;*
8 The children of Parosh, two thousand an
hundred seventy and two.
9 The children of Shephatiah, three hundred seventy and two.
10 The children of Arah, six hundred fifty
and two.
11 The children of Pahath–moab, of the children of Jeshua and Joab, two thousand and eight
hundred *and* eighteen.
12 The children of Elam, a thousand two hundred fifty and four.
13 The children of Zattu, eight hundred forty
and five.
14 The children of Zaccai, seven hundred
and threescore.
15 The children of Binnui, six hundred forty
and eight.
16 The children of Bebai, six hundred twenty
and eight.
17 The children of Azgad, two thousand
three hundred twenty and two.
18 The children of Adonikam, six hundred
threescore and seven.
19 The children of Bigvai, two thousand
threescore and seven.
20 The children of Adin, six hundred fifty
and five.
21 The children of Ater of Hezekiah, ninety
and eight.
22 The children of Hashum, three hundred
twenty and eight.
23 The children of Bezai, three hundred
twenty and four.
24 The children of Hariph, an hundred and
twelve.
25 The children of Gibeon, ninety and five.
26 The men of Beth–lehem and Netophah, an
hundred fourscore and eight.
27 The men of Anathoth, an hundred twenty
and eight.
28 The men of Beth–azmaveth, forty and two.
29 The men of Kirjath–jearim, Chephirah,
and Beeroth, seven hundred forty and three.
30 The men of Ramah and Gaba, six hundred
twenty and one.
31 The men of Michmas, an hundred and
twenty and two.
32 The men of Beth–el and Ai, an hundred
twenty and three.
33 The men of the other Nebo, fifty and two.
34 The children of the other [a]Elam, a thousand two hundred fifty and four.
35 The children of Harim, three hundred and
twenty.
36 The children of Jericho, three hundred
forty and five.
37 The children of Lod, Hadid, and Ono,
seven hundred twenty and one.
38 The children of Senaah, three thousand
nine hundred and thirty.
39 The priests: the children of [a]Jedaiah, of
the house of Jeshua, nine hundred seventy and
three.
40 The children of [a]Immer, a thousand fifty
and two.
41 The children of [a]Pashur, a thousand two
hundred forty and seven.
42 The children of [a]Harim, a thousand and
seventeen.
43 The Levites: the children of Jeshua, of
Kadmiel, *and* of the children of Hodevah, seventy
and four.
44 The singers: the children of Asaph, an
hundred forty and eight.
45 The porters: the children of Shallum, the

7 [a]Ezra 5:2; Neh. 12:1, 47; Matt. 1:12, 13
34 [a]Neh. 7:12
39 [a]1 Chr. 24:7
40 [a]1 Chr. 9:12
41 [a]1 Chr. 9:12; 24:9
42 [a]1 Chr. 24:8

*

7:7 *Mispar,* Ezra 2:2
7:15 *Bani,* Ezra 2:10
7:24 *Jorah,* Ezra 2:18
7:25 *Gibbar,* Ezra 2:20
7:28 *Azmaveth,* Ezra 2:24
7:43 *Hodaviah,* Ezra 2:40; or *Judah,* Ezra 3:9

NKJV

carried away, and who returned to
Jerusalem and Judah, everyone to his city.
7 Those who came with [a]Zerubbabel *were*
Jeshua, Nehemiah, Azariah, Raamiah,
Nahamani, Mordecai, Bilshan,
*Mispereth, Bigvai, Nehum, and Baanah.
The number of the men of the people
of Israel:
8 the sons of Parosh, two thousand one
hundred and seventy-two;
9 the sons of Shephatiah, three hundred and
seventy-two;
10 the sons of Arah, six hundred and fifty-
two;
11 the sons of Pahath-Moab, of the sons of
Jeshua and Joab, two thousand eight
hundred and eighteen;
12 the sons of Elam, one thousand two
hundred and fifty-four;
13 the sons of Zattu, eight hundred and forty-
five;
14 the sons of Zaccai, seven hundred and
sixty;
15 the sons of *Binnui, six hundred and forty-
eight;
16 the sons of Bebai, six hundred and twenty-
eight;
17 the sons of Azgad, two thousand three
hundred and twenty-two;
18 the sons of Adonikam, six hundred and
sixty-seven;
19 the sons of Bigvai, two thousand and
sixty-seven;
20 the sons of Adin, six hundred and fifty-
five;
21 the sons of Ater of Hezekiah, ninety-eight;
22 the sons of Hashum, three hundred and
twenty-eight;
23 the sons of Bezai, three hundred and
twenty-four;
24 the sons of *Hariph, one hundred and
twelve;
25 the sons of *Gibeon, ninety-five;
26 the men of Bethlehem and Netophah, one
hundred and eighty-eight;
27 the men of Anathoth, one hundred and
twenty-eight;
28 the men of *Beth Azmaveth, forty-two;
29 the men of Kirjath Jearim, Chephirah, and
Beeroth, seven hundred and forty-three;
30 the men of Ramah and Geba, six hundred
and twenty-one;
31 the men of Michmas, one hundred and
twenty-two;
32 the men of Bethel and Ai, one hundred
and twenty-three;
33 the men of the other Nebo, fifty-two;
34 the sons of the other [a]Elam, one thousand
two hundred and fifty-four;
35 the sons of Harim, three hundred and
twenty;
36 the sons of Jericho, three hundred and
forty-five;
37 the sons of Lod, Hadid, and Ono, seven
hundred and twenty-one;
38 the sons of Senaah, three thousand nine
hundred and thirty.
39 The priests: the sons of [a]Jedaiah, of the
house of Jeshua, nine hundred and
seventy-three;
40 the sons of [a]Immer, one thousand and
fifty-two;
41 the sons of [a]Pashhur, one thousand two
hundred and forty-seven;
42 the sons of [a]Harim, one thousand and
seventeen.
43 The Levites: the sons of Jeshua, of
Kadmiel, *and* of the sons of *Hodevah,
seventy-four.
44 The singers: the sons of Asaph, one
hundred and forty-eight.
45 The gatekeepers: the sons of Shallum, the

KJV

children of Ater, the children of Talmon, the children of Akkub, the children of Hatita, the children
of Shobai, an hundred thirty and eight.
46 The Nethinims: the children of Ziha, the
children of Hashupha, the children of Tabbaoth,
47 The children of Keros, the children of Sia,
the children of Padon,
48 The children of Lebana, the children of
Hagaba, the children of Shalmai,
49 The children of Hanan, the children of
Giddel, the children of Gahar,
50 The children of Reaiah, the children of
Rezin, the children of Nekoda,
51 The children of Gazzam, the children of
Uzza, the children of Phaseah,
52 The children of Besai, the children of Meunim, the children of Nephishesim,
53 The children of Bakbuk, the children of
Hakupha, the children of Harhur,
54 The children of Bazlith, the children of
Mehida, the children of Harsha,
55 The children of Barkos, the children of
Sisera, the children of Tamah,
56 The children of Neziah, the children of
Hatipha.
57 The children of Solomon's servants: the
children of Sotai, the children of Sophereth, the
children of Perida,
58 The children of Jaala, the children of Darkon, the children of Giddel,
59 The children of Shephatiah, the children
of Hattil, the children of Pochereth of Zebaim, the
children of Amon.
60 All the Nethinims, and the children of Solomon's servants, *were* three hundred ninety and
two.
61 And these *were* they which went up *also*
from Tel–melah, Tel–haresha, Cherub, Addon,
and Immer: but they could not shew their father's
house, nor their seed, whether they *were* of Israel.
62 The children of Delaiah, the children of
Tobiah, the children of Nekoda, six hundred forty
and two.
63 And of the priests: the children of Habaiah, the children of Koz, the children of Barzillai,
which took *one* of the daughters of Barzillai the
Gileadite to wife, and was called after their name.
64 These sought their register *among* those
that were reckoned by genealogy, but it was not
found: therefore were they, as polluted, put from
the priesthood.
65 And the Tirshatha said unto them, that
they should not eat of the most holy things, till
there stood *up* a priest with Urim and Thummim.
66 The whole congregation together *was*
forty and two thousand three hundred and
threescore,
67 Beside their manservants and their maidservants, of whom *there were* seven thousand
three hundred thirty and seven: and they had two
hundred forty and five singing men and singing
women.
68 Their horses, seven hundred thirty and
six: their mules, two hundred forty and five:
69 *Their* camels, four hundred thirty and five:
six thousand seven hundred and twenty asses.
70 And some of the chief of the fathers gave
unto the work. ᵃThe Tirshatha gave to the treasure a thousand drams of gold, fifty basons, five
hundred and thirty priests' garments.
71 And *some* of the chief of the fathers gave
to the treasure of the work ᵃtwenty thousand
drams of gold, and two thousand and two hundred
pounds of silver.
72 And *that* which the rest of the people gave
was twenty thousand drams of gold, and two

70 ᵃNeh. 8:9
71 ᵃEzra 2:69

*

7:47 *Siaha,* Ezra 2:44
7:48 MT *Lebanah* • MT *Hogabah* • *Shalmai,* Ezra 2:46; or *Shamlai*
7:52 *Nephusim,* Ezra 2:50
7:54 *Bazluth,* Ezra 2:52
7:57 *Peruda,* Ezra 2:55
7:59 *Ami,* Ezra 2:57
7:61 *Addan,* Ezra 2:59
7:63 Or *Hakkoz*
7:65 Heb. *Tirshatha*
7:70 Heb. *Tirshatha*

NKJV

sons of Ater, the sons of Talmon, the sons
of Akkub, the sons of Hatita, the sons of
Shobai, one hundred and thirty-eight.
46 The Nethinim: the sons of Ziha, the sons
of Hasupha, the sons of Tabbaoth,
47 the sons of Keros, the sons of *Sia, the
sons of Padon,
48 the sons of *Lebana, the sons of *Hagaba,
the sons of *Salmai,
49 the sons of Hanan, the sons of Giddel, the
sons of Gahar,
50 the sons of Reaiah, the sons of Rezin, the
sons of Nekoda,
51 the sons of Gazzam, the sons of Uzza, the
sons of Paseah,
52 the sons of Besai, the sons of Meunim, the
sons of *Nephishesim,
53 the sons of Bakbuk, the sons of Hakupha,
the sons of Harhur,
54 the sons of *Bazlith, the sons of Mehida,
the sons of Harsha,
55 the sons of Barkos, the sons of Sisera, the
sons of Tamah,
56 the sons of Neziah, and the sons of
Hatipha.
57 The sons of Solomon's servants: the sons
of Sotai, the sons of Sophereth, the sons
of *Perida,
58 the sons of Jaala, the sons of Darkon, the
sons of Giddel,
59 the sons of Shephatiah, the sons of Hattil,
the sons of Pochereth of Zebaim, and the
sons of *Amon.
60 All the Nethinim, and the sons of
Solomon's servants, *were* three hundred
and ninety-two.
61 And these *were* the ones who came up
from Tel Melah, Tel Harsha, Cherub,
*Addon, and Immer, but they could not
identify their father's house nor their
lineage, whether they *were* of Israel:
62 the sons of Delaiah, the sons of Tobiah,
the sons of Nekoda, six hundred and forty-
two;
63 and of the priests: the sons of Habaiah,
the sons of *Koz, the sons of Barzillai, who
took a wife of the daughters of Barzillai
the Gileadite, and was called by their
name.
64 These sought their listing *among* those
who were registered by genealogy, but it
was not found; therefore they were
excluded from the priesthood as defiled.
65 And the *governor said to them that they
should not eat of the most holy things till
a priest could consult with the Urim and
Thummim.
66 Altogether the whole assembly *was*
forty-two thousand three hundred and
sixty,
67 besides their male and female servants,
of whom *there were* seven thousand three
hundred and thirty-seven; and they had
two hundred and forty-five men and
women singers.
68 Their horses were seven hundred and
thirty-six, their mules two hundred and
forty-five,
69 *their* camels four hundred and thirty-five,
and donkeys six thousand seven hundred
and twenty.
70 And some of the heads of the fathers'
houses gave to the work. ᵃThe *governor
gave to the treasury one thousand gold
drachmas, fifty basins, and five hundred
and thirty priestly garments.
71 Some of the heads of the fathers' *houses*
gave to the treasury of the work ᵃtwenty
thousand gold drachmas, and two
thousand two hundred silver minas.
72 And that which the rest of the people gave
was twenty thousand gold drachmas, two

KJV

thousand pounds of silver, and threescore and seven priests' garments.

73 So the priests, and the Levites, and the porters, and the singers, and *some* of the people, and the Nethinims, and all Israel, dwelt in their cities; [a]and when the seventh month came, the children of Israel *were* in their cities.

Ezra Reads the Law

8 And all [a]the people gathered themselves together as one man into the street that *was* [b]before the water gate; and they spake unto Ezra the [c]scribe to bring the book of the law of Moses, which the LORD had commanded to Israel.

2 And Ezra the priest brought [a]the law before the congregation both of men and women, and all that could hear with understanding, [b]upon the first day of the seventh month.

3 And he [a]read therein before the street that *was* before the water gate from the morning until midday, before the men and the women, and those that could understand; and the ears of all the people *were attentive* unto the book of the law.

4 And Ezra the scribe stood upon a pulpit of wood, which they had made for the purpose; and beside him stood Mattithiah, and Shema, and Anaiah, and Urijah, and Hilkiah, and Maaseiah, on his right hand; and on his left hand, Pedaiah, and Mishael, and Malchiah, and Hashum, and Hashbadana, Zechariah, *and* Meshullam.

5 And Ezra opened the book in the sight of all people; (for he was above all the people;) and when he opened it, all the people [a]stood up:

6 And Ezra blessed the LORD, the great God. And all the people [a]answered, Amen, Amen, with [b]lifting up their hands: and they [c]bowed their heads, and worshipped the LORD with *their* faces to the ground.

7 Also Jeshua, and Bani, and Sherebiah, Jamin, Akkub, Shabbethai, Hodijah, Maaseiah, Kelita, Azariah, Jozabad, Hanan, Pelaiah, and the Levites, [a]caused the people to understand the law: and the people [b]*stood* in their place.

8 So they read in the book in the law of God distinctly, and gave the sense, and caused *them* to understand the reading.

9 [a]And Nehemiah, which *is* the Tirshatha, and Ezra the priest the scribe, and the Levites that taught the people, said unto all the people, [b]This day *is* holy unto the LORD your God; [c]mourn not, nor weep. For all the people wept, when they heard the words of the law.

10 Then he said unto them, Go your way, eat the fat, and drink the sweet, [a]and send portions unto them for whom nothing is prepared: for *this* day *is* holy unto our Lord: neither be ye sorry; for the joy of the LORD is your strength.

11 So the Levites stilled all the people, saying, Hold your peace, for the day *is* holy; neither be ye grieved.

12 And all the people went their way to eat, and to drink, and to [a]send portions, and to make great mirth, because they had [b]understood the words that were declared unto them.

The Feast of Tabernacles
(cf. Lev. 23:33–43)

13 And on the second day were gathered together the chief of the fathers of all the people, the priests, and the Levites, unto Ezra the scribe, even to understand the words of the law.

14 And they found written in the law which the LORD had commanded by Moses, that the children of Israel should dwell in [a]booths in the feast of the seventh month:

15 And [a]that they should publish and proclaim in all their cities, and [b]in Jerusalem, saying, Go forth unto the mount, and [c]fetch olive branches, and pine branches, and myrtle

---

73 [a]Ezra 3:1

CHAPTER 8

1 [a]Ezra 3:1 [b]Neh. 3:26 [c]Ezra 7:6
2 [a][Deut. 31:11, 12]; Neh. 8:9 [b]Lev. 23:24; Num. 29:1–6
3 [a]Deut. 31:9–11; 2 Kin. 23:2
5 [a]Judg. 3:20; 1 Kin. 8:12–14
6 [a]Neh. 5:13; [1 Cor. 14:16] [b]Ps. 28:2; Lam. 3:41; 1 Tim. 2:8 [c]Ex. 4:31; 12:27; 2 Chr. 20:18
7 [a]Lev. 10:11; Deut. 33:10; 2 Chr. 17:7; [Mal. 2:7] [b]Neh. 9:3
9 [a]Ezra 2:63; Neh. 7:65, 70; 10:1 [b]Lev. 23:24; Num. 29:1 [c]Deut. 16:14; Eccl. 3:4
10 [a][Deut. 26:11–13]; Esth. 9:19, 22; Rev. 11:10
12 [a]Neh. 8:10 [b]Neh. 8:7, 8
14 [a]Lev. 23:34, 40, 42; Deut. 16:13
15 [a]Lev. 23:4 [b]Deut. 16:16 [c]Lev. 23:40

*8:9 Heb. *Tirshatha*

NKJV

thousand silver minas, and sixty-seven priestly garments.

73 So the priests, the Levites, the gatekeepers, the singers, *some* of the people, the Nethinim, and all Israel dwelt in their cities.

Ezra Reads the Law

[a]When the seventh month came, the children of Israel *were* in their cities.

8 Now all [a]the people gathered together as one man in the open square that *was* [b]in front of the Water Gate; and they told Ezra the [c]scribe to bring the Book of the Law of Moses, which the LORD had commanded Israel.

2 So Ezra the priest brought [a]the Law before the assembly of men and women and all who *could* hear with understanding [b]on the first day of the seventh month.

3 Then he [a]read from it in the open square that *was* in front of the Water Gate from morning until midday, before the men and women and those who could understand; and the ears of all the people *were attentive* to the Book of the Law.

4 So Ezra the scribe stood on a platform of wood which they had made for the purpose; and beside him, at his right hand, stood Mattithiah, Shema, Anaiah, Urijah, Hilkiah, and Maaseiah; and at his left hand Pedaiah, Mishael, Malchijah, Hashum, Hashbadana, Zechariah, *and* Meshullam.

5 And Ezra opened the book in the sight of all the people, for he was *standing* above all the people; and when he opened it, all the people [a]stood up.

6 And Ezra blessed the LORD, the great God. Then all the people [a]answered, "Amen, Amen!" while [b]lifting up their hands. And they [c]bowed their heads and worshiped the LORD with *their* faces to the ground.

7 Also Jeshua, Bani, Sherebiah, Jamin, Akkub, Shabbethai, Hodijah, Maaseiah, Kelita, Azariah, Jozabad, Hanan, Pelaiah, and the Levites, [a]helped the people to understand the Law; and the people [b]*stood* in their place.

8 So they read distinctly from the book, in the Law of God; and they gave the sense, and helped *them* to understand the reading.

9 [a]And Nehemiah, who *was* the *governor, Ezra the priest *and* scribe, and the Levites who taught the people said to all the people, [b]"This day *is* holy to the LORD your God; [c]do not mourn nor weep." For all the people wept, when they heard the words of the Law.

10 Then he said to them, "Go your way, eat the fat, drink the sweet, [a]and send portions to those for whom nothing is prepared; for *this* day *is* holy to our Lord. Do not sorrow, for the joy of the LORD is your strength."

11 So the Levites quieted all the people, saying, "Be still, for the day *is* holy; do not be grieved."

12 And all the people went their way to eat and drink, to [a]send portions and rejoice greatly, because they [b]understood the words that were declared to them.

The Feast of Tabernacles
(cf. Lev. 23:33–43)

13 Now on the second day the heads of the fathers' *houses* of all the people, with the priests and Levites, were gathered to Ezra the scribe, in order to understand the words of the Law.

14 And they found written in the Law, which the LORD had commanded by Moses, that the children of Israel should dwell in [a]booths during the feast of the seventh month,

15 and [a]that they should announce and proclaim in all their cities and [b]in Jerusalem, saying, "Go out to the mountain, and [c]bring olive branches, branches of oil trees, myrtle branches,

KJV

branches, and palm branches, and branches of thick trees, to make booths, as *it is* written.

16 So the people went forth, and brought *them,* and made themselves booths, every one upon the [a]roof of his house, and in their courts, and in the courts of the house of God, and in the street of the [b]water gate, [c]and in the street of the gate of Ephraim.

17 And all the congregation of them that were come again out of the captivity made booths, and sat under the booths: for since the days of Jeshua the son of Nun unto that day had not the children of Israel done so. And there was very [a]great gladness.

18 Also [a]day by day, from the first day unto the last day, he read in the book of the law of God. And they kept the feast [b]seven days; and on the [c]eighth day *was* a solemn assembly, according unto the manner.

The People Confess Their Sins

9 Now in the twenty and fourth day of [a]this month the children of Israel were assembled with fasting, and with sackclothes, [b]and earth upon them.

2 And [a]the seed of Israel separated themselves from all strangers, and stood and [b]confessed their sins, and the iniquities of their fathers.

3 And they stood up in their place, and [a]read in the book of the law of the LORD their God *one* fourth part of the day; and *another* fourth part they confessed, and worshipped the LORD their God.

4 Then stood up upon the stairs, of the Levites, Jeshua, and Bani, Kadmiel, Shebaniah, Bunni, Sherebiah, Bani, *and* Chenani, and cried with a loud voice unto the LORD their God.

5 Then the Levites, Jeshua, and Kadmiel, Bani, Hashabniah, Sherebiah, Hodijah, Shebaniah, *and* Pethahiah, said, Stand up *and* bless the LORD your God for ever and ever: and blessed be [a]thy glorious name, which is exalted above all blessing and praise.

6 [a]Thou, *even* thou, *art* LORD alone; [b]thou hast made heaven, [c]the heaven of heavens, with [d]all their host, the earth, and all *things* that *are* therein, the seas, and all that *is* therein, and thou [e]preservest them all; and the host of heaven worshippeth thee.

7 Thou *art* the LORD the God, who didst choose [a]Abram, and broughtest him forth out of Ur of the Chaldees, and gavest him the name of [b]Abraham;

8 And foundest his heart [a]faithful before thee, and madest a [b]covenant with him to give the land of the Canaanites, the Hittites, the Amorites, and the Perizzites, and the Jebusites, and the Girgashites, to give *it, I say,* to his seed, and [c]hast performed thy words; for thou *art* righteous:

9 [a]And didst see the affliction of our fathers in Egypt, and [b]heardest their cry by the Red sea;

10 And [a]shewedst signs and wonders upon Pharaoh, and on all his servants, and on all the people of his land: for thou knewest that they [b]dealt proudly against them. So didst thou [c]get thee a name, as *it is* this day.

16 [a]Deut. 22:8 [b]Neh. 12:37 [c]2 Kin. 14:13; Neh. 12:39
17 [a]2 Chr. 30:21
18 [a]Deut. 31:11 [b]Lev. 23:36 [c]Num. 29:35

CHAPTER 9

1 [a]Neh. 8:2 [b]Josh. 7:6; 1 Sam. 4:12; 2 Sam. 1:2; Job 2:12
2 [a]Ezra 10:11; Neh. 13:3, 30 [b]Neh. 1:6
3 [a]Neh. 8:7, 8
5 [a]1 Chr. 29:13
6 [a]Deut. 6:4; 2 Kin. 19:15, 19; [Ps. 86:10]; Is. 37:16, 20 [b]Gen. 1:1; Ex. 20:11; Rev. 14:7 [c][Deut. 10:14]; 1 Kin. 8:27 [d]Gen. 2:1 [e][Ps. 36:6]
7 [a]Gen. 11:31 [b]Gen. 17:5
8 [a]Gen. 15:6; 22:1–3; [James 2:21–23] [b]Gen. 15:18 [c]Josh. 23:14
9 [a]Ex. 2:25; 3:7 [b]Ex. 14:10
10 [a]Ex. 7—14 [b]Ex. 18:11 [c]Jer. 32:20

NKJV

palm branches, and branches of leafy trees, to make booths, as *it is* written."

16 Then the people went out and brought *them* and made themselves booths, each one on the [a]roof of his house, or in their courtyards or the courts of the house of God, and in the open square of the [b]Water Gate [c]and in the open square of the Gate of Ephraim.

17 So the whole assembly of those who had returned from the captivity made booths and sat under the booths; for since the days of Joshua the son of Nun until that day the children of Israel had not done so. And there was very [a]great gladness.

18 Also [a]day by day, from the first day until the last day, he read from the Book of the Law of God. And they kept the feast [b]seven days; and on the [c]eighth day *there was* a sacred assembly, according to the *prescribed* manner.

The People Confess Their Sins

9 Now on the twenty-fourth day of [a]this month the children of Israel were assembled with fasting, in sackcloth, [b]and with *dust on their heads.

2 Then [a]those of Israelite lineage separated themselves from all foreigners; and they stood and [b]confessed their sins and the iniquities of their fathers.

3 And they stood up in their place and [a]read from the Book of the Law of the LORD their God *for one*-fourth of the day; and *for another* fourth they confessed and worshiped the LORD their God.

4 Then Jeshua, Bani, Kadmiel, Shebaniah, Bunni, Sherebiah, Bani, *and* Chenani stood on the stairs of the Levites and cried out with a loud voice to the LORD their God.

5 And the Levites, Jeshua, Kadmiel, Bani, Hashabniah, Sherebiah, Hodijah, Shebaniah, *and* Pethahiah, said:

"Stand up *and* bless the LORD your God
Forever and ever!

"Blessed be [a]Your glorious name,
Which is exalted above all blessing and
praise!

6 [a]You alone *are* the LORD;
[b]You have made heaven,
[c]The heaven of heavens, with [d]all their
host,
The earth and everything on it,
The seas and all that is in them,
And You [e]preserve them all.
The host of heaven worships You.

7 "You *are* the LORD God,
Who chose [a]Abram,
And brought him out of Ur of the
Chaldeans,
And gave him the name [b]Abraham;
8 You found his heart [a]faithful before You,
And made a [b]covenant with him
To give the land of the Canaanites,
The Hittites, the Amorites,
The Perizzites, the Jebusites,
And the Girgashites—
To give *it* to his descendants.
You [c]have performed Your words,
For You *are* righteous.

9 "You[a] saw the affliction of our fathers in
Egypt,
And [b]heard their cry by the Red Sea.
10 You [a]showed signs and wonders against
Pharaoh,
Against all his servants,
And against all the people of his land.
For You knew that they [b]acted proudly
against them.
So You [c]made a name for Yourself, as *it
is* this day.

*9:1 Lit. *earth on them*

KJV

11 [a]And thou didst divide the sea before them, so that they went through the midst of the sea on the dry land; and their persecutors thou threwest into the deeps, [b]as a stone into the mighty waters.

12 Moreover thou [a]leddest them in the day by a cloudy pillar; and in the night by a pillar of fire, to give them light in the way wherein they should go.

13 [a]Thou camest down also upon mount Sinai, and spakest with them from heaven, and gavest them [b]right judgments, and true laws, good statutes and commandments:

14 And madest known unto them thy [a]holy sabbath, and commandedst them precepts, statutes, and laws, by the hand of Moses thy servant:

15 And [a]gavest them bread from heaven for their hunger, and [b]broughtest forth water for them out of the rock for their thirst, and promisedst them that they should [c]go in to possess the land which thou hadst sworn to give them.

16 [a]But they and our fathers dealt proudly, and [b]hardened their necks, and hearkened not to thy commandments,

17 And refused to obey, [a]neither were mindful of thy wonders that thou didst among them; but hardened their necks, and in their rebellion appointed [b]a captain to return to their bondage: but thou *art* a God ready to pardon, [c]gracious and merciful, slow to anger, and of great kindness, and forsookest them not.

18 Yea, [a]when they had made them a molten calf, and said, This *is* thy God that brought thee up out of Egypt, and had wrought great provocations;

19 Yet thou in thy [a]manifold mercies forsookest them not in the wilderness: the [b]pillar of the cloud departed not from them by day, to lead them in the way; neither the pillar of fire by night, to shew them light, and the way wherein they should go.

20 Thou gavest also thy [a]good spirit to instruct them, and withheldest not thy [b]manna from their mouth, and gavest them [c]water for their thirst.

21 Yea, [a]forty years didst thou sustain them in the wilderness, *so that* they lacked nothing; their [b]clothes waxed not old, and their feet swelled not.

22 Moreover thou gavest them kingdoms and nations, and didst divide them into corners: so they possessed the land of [a]Sihon, and the land of the king of Heshbon, and the land of Og king of Bashan.

23 [a]Their children also multipliedst thou as the stars of heaven, and broughtest them into the

11 [a]Ex. 14:20–28 [b]Ex. 15:1, 5
12 [a]Ex. 13:21, 22
13 [a]Ex. 20:1–18 [b][Rom. 7:12]
14 [a]Gen. 2:3; Ex. 16:23; 20:8; 23:12
15 [a]Ex. 16:14–17; John 6:31 [b]Ex. 17:6; Num. 20:8; [1 Cor. 10:4] [c]Deut. 1:8
16 [a]Ps. 106:6 [b]Deut. 1:26–33; 31:27; Neh. 9:29
17 [a]Ps. 78:11, 42–45 [b]Num. 14:4; Acts 7:39 [c]Joel 2:13
18 [a]Ex. 32:4–8, 31
19 [a]Ps. 106:45 [b]Ex. 13:20–22; 1 Cor. 10:1
20 [a]Num. 11:17 [b]Ex. 16:14–16 [c]Ex. 17:6
21 [a]Deut. 2:7 [b]Deut. 8:4; 29:5
22 [a]Num. 21:21–35
23 [a]Gen. 15:5; 22:17; Heb. 11:12

NKJV

11 [a]And You divided the sea before them,
So that they went through the midst of the sea on the dry land;
And their persecutors You threw into the deep,
[b]As a stone into the mighty waters.
12 Moreover You [a]led them by day with a cloudy pillar,
And by night with a pillar of fire,
To give them light on the road
Which they should travel.

13 "You[a] came down also on Mount Sinai,
And spoke with them from heaven,
And gave them [b]just ordinances and true laws,
Good statutes and commandments.
14 You made known to them Your [a]holy Sabbath,
And commanded them precepts, statutes and laws,
By the hand of Moses Your servant.
15 You [a]gave them bread from heaven for their hunger,
And [b]brought them water out of the rock for their thirst,
And told them to [c]go in to possess the land
Which You had sworn to give them.

16 "But[a] they and our fathers acted proudly,
[b]Hardened their necks,
And did not heed Your commandments.
17 They refused to obey,
And [a]they were not mindful of Your wonders
That You did among them.
But they hardened their necks,
And *in their rebellion
They appointed [b]a leader
To return to their bondage.
But You *are* God,
Ready to pardon,
[c]Gracious and merciful,
Slow to anger,
Abundant in kindness,
And did not forsake them.

18 "Even [a]when they made a molded calf for themselves,
And said, 'This *is* your god
That brought you up out of Egypt,'
And worked great provocations,
19 Yet in Your [a]manifold mercies
You did not forsake them in the wilderness.
The [b]pillar of the cloud did not depart from them by day,
To lead them on the road;
Nor the pillar of fire by night,
To show them light,
And the way they should go.
20 You also gave Your [a]good Spirit to instruct them,
And did not withhold Your [b]manna from their mouth,
And gave them [c]water for their thirst.
21 [a]Forty years You sustained them in the wilderness;
They lacked nothing;
Their [b]clothes did not wear out
And their feet did not swell.

22 "Moreover You gave them kingdoms and nations,
And divided them into *districts.
So they took possession of the land of [a]Sihon,
*The land of the king of Heshbon,
And the land of Og king of Bashan.
23 You also multiplied [a]their children as the stars of heaven,

---

9:17 So with MT, Vg.; LXX *in Egypt*
9:22 Lit. *corners* • So with MT, Vg.; LXX omits *The land of*

KJV

land, concerning which thou hadst promised to
their fathers, that they should go in to possess *it*.
24 So [a]the children went in and possessed
the land, and [b]thou subduedst before them the
inhabitants of the land, the Canaanites, and gavest them into their hands, with their kings, and
the people of the land, that they might do with
them as they would.
25 And they took strong cities, and a [a]fat
land, and possessed [b]houses full of all goods,
wells digged, vineyards, and oliveyards, and fruit
trees in abundance: so they did eat, and were
filled, and [c]became fat, and delighted themselves
in thy great [d]goodness.
26 Nevertheless they [a]were disobedient, and
rebelled against thee, and [b]cast thy law behind
their backs, and slew thy [c]prophets which testified against them to turn them to thee, and they
wrought great provocations.
27 [a]Therefore thou deliveredst them into the
hand of their enemies, who vexed them: and in
the time of their trouble, when they cried unto
thee, thou [b]heardest *them* from heaven; and according to thy manifold mercies [c]thou gavest
them saviours, who saved them out of the hand
of their enemies.
28 But after they had rest, [a]they did evil
again before thee: therefore leftest thou them in
the hand of their enemies, so that they had the
dominion over them: yet when they returned, and
cried unto thee, thou heardest *them* from heaven;
and [b]many times didst thou deliver them according to thy mercies;
29 And testifiedst against them, that thou
mightest bring them again unto thy law: yet they
dealt proudly, and hearkened not unto thy commandments, but sinned against thy judgments,
([a]which if a man do, he shall live in them;) and
withdrew the shoulder, and hardened their neck,
and would not hear.
30 Yet many years didst thou forbear them,
and testifiedst [a]against them by thy spirit [b]in thy
prophets: yet would they not give ear: [c]therefore
gavest thou them into the hand of the people of
the lands.
31 Nevertheless for thy great mercies' sake
[a]thou didst not utterly consume them, nor forsake
them; for thou *art* a gracious and merciful God.
32 Now therefore, our God, the great, the
[a]mighty, and the terrible God, who keepest covenant and mercy, let not all the trouble seem little
before thee, that hath come upon us, on our kings,
on our princes, and on our priests, and on our
prophets, and on our fathers, and on all thy peo-

24 [a]Josh. 1:2–4 [b]Josh. 18:1; [Ps. 44:2, 3]
25 [a]Num. 13:27 [b]Deut. 6:11; Josh. 24:13 [c][Deut. 32:15] [d]Hos. 3:5
26 [a]Judg. 2:11 [b]1 Kin. 14:9; Ps. 50:17 [c]1 Kin. 18:4; 19:10; Matt. 23:37; Acts 7:52
27 [a]Judg. 2:14; Ps. 106:41 [b]Ps. 106:44 [c]Judg. 2:18
28 [a]Judg. 3:12 [b]Ps. 106:43
29 [a]Lev. 18:5; Rom. 10:5; [Gal. 3:12]
30 [a]2 Kin. 17:13–18; 2 Chr. 36:11–20; Jer. 7:25 [b][Acts 7:51]; 1 Pet. 1:11 [c]Is. 5:5
31 [a]Jer. 4:27; [Rom. 11:2–5]
32 [a][Ex. 34:6, 7]

NKJV

And brought them into the land
Which You had told their fathers
To go in and possess.
24 So [a]the people went in
And possessed the land;
[b]You subdued before them the inhabitants of the land,
The Canaanites,
And gave them into their hands,
With their kings
And the people of the land,
That they might do with them as they wished.
25 And they took strong cities and a [a]rich land,
And possessed [b]houses full of all goods,
Cisterns *already* dug, vineyards, olive groves,
And fruit trees in abundance.
So they ate and were filled and [c]grew fat,
And delighted themselves in Your great [d]goodness.

26 "Nevertheless they [a]were disobedient
And rebelled against You,
[b]Cast Your law behind their backs
And killed Your [c]prophets, who testified against them
To turn them to Yourself;
And they worked great provocations.
27 [a]Therefore You delivered them into the hand of their enemies,
Who oppressed them;
And in the time of their trouble,
When they cried to You,
You [b]heard from heaven;
And according to Your abundant mercies
[c]You gave them deliverers who saved them
From the hand of their enemies.

28 "But after they had rest,
[a]They again did evil before You.
Therefore You left them in the hand of their enemies,
So that they had dominion over them;
Yet when they returned and cried out to You,
You heard from heaven;
And [b]many times You delivered them according to Your mercies,
29 And testified against them,
That You might bring them back to Your law.
Yet they acted proudly,
And did not heed Your commandments,
But sinned against Your judgments,
[a]'Which if a man does, he shall live by them.'
And they shrugged their shoulders,
Stiffened their necks,
And would not hear.
30 Yet for many years You had patience with them,
And testified [a]against them by Your Spirit [b]in Your prophets.
Yet they would not listen;
[c]Therefore You gave them into the hand of the peoples of the lands.
31 Nevertheless in Your great mercy
[a]You did not utterly consume them nor forsake them;
For You *are* God, gracious and merciful.

32 "Now therefore, our God,
The great, the [a]mighty, and awesome God,
Who keeps covenant and mercy:
Do not let all the trouble seem small before You
That has come upon us,
Our kings and our princes,
Our priests and our prophets,
Our fathers and on all Your people,

KJV

ple, [b]since the time of the kings of Assyria unto
this day.
33 Howbeit [a]thou *art* just in all that is
brought upon us; for thou hast done right, but
[b]we have done wickedly:
34 Neither have our kings, our princes, our
priests, nor our fathers, kept thy law, nor hearkened unto thy commandments and thy testimonies, wherewith thou didst testify against them.
35 For they have [a]not served thee in their
kingdom, and in thy great goodness that thou
gavest them, and in the large and fat land which
thou gavest before them, neither turned they from
their wicked works.
36 Behold, [a]we *are* servants this day, and *for*
the land that thou gavest unto our fathers to eat
the fruit thereof and the good thereof, behold, we
are servants in it:
37 And [a]it yieldeth much increase unto the
kings whom thou hast set over us because of our
sins: also they have [b]dominion over our bodies,
and over our cattle, at their pleasure, and we *are*
in great distress.
38 And because of all this we [a]make a sure
covenant, and write *it;* and our princes, Levites,
and priests, [b]seal *unto it*.

The People Who Sealed the Covenant

10 Now those that sealed *were*, Nehemiah, the
Tirshatha, [a]the son of Hachaliah, and
Zidkijah,
2 [a]Seraiah, Azariah, Jeremiah,
3 Pashur, Amariah, Malchijah,
4 Hattush, Shebaniah, Malluch,
5 Harim, Meremoth, Obadiah,
6 Daniel, Ginnethon, Baruch,
7 Meshullam, Abijah, Mijamin,
8 Maaziah, Bilgai, Shemaiah: these *were* the
priests.
9 And the Levites: both Jeshua the son of
Azaniah, Binnui of the sons of Henadad, Kadmiel;
10 And their brethren, Shebaniah, Hodijah,
Kelita, Pelaiah, Hanan,
11 Micha, Rehob, Hashabiah,
12 Zaccur, Sherebiah, Shebaniah,
13 Hodijah, Bani, Beninu.
14 The chief of the people; [a]Parosh, Pahath-
moab, Elam, Zatthu, Bani,
15 Bunni, Azgad, Bebai,
16 Adonijah, Bigvai, Adin,
17 Ater, Hizkijah, Azzur,
18 Hodijah, Hashum, Bezai,
19 Hariph, Anathoth, Nebai,
20 Magpiash, Meshullam, Hezir,
21 Meshezabeel, Zadok, Jaddua,
22 Pelatiah, Hanan, Anaiah,
23 Hoshea, Hananiah, Hashub,
24 Hallohesh, Pileha, Shobek,
25 Rehum, Hashabnah, Maaseiah,
26 And Ahijah, Hanan, Anan,
27 Malluch, Harim, Baanah.

The Covenant That Was Sealed

28 [a]And the rest of the people, the priests,
the Levites, the porters, the singers, the Nethinims, [b]and all they that had separated themselves
from the people of the lands unto the law of God,
their wives, their sons, and their daughters, every

32 [b]2 Kin. 15:19; 17:3–6; Ezra 4:2, 10
33 [a]Ps. 119:137; [Dan. 9:14] [b]Ps. 106:6; [Dan. 9:5, 6, 8]
35 [a]Deut. 28:47
36 [a]Deut. 28:48; Ezra 9:9
37 [a]Deut. 28:33, 51 [b]Deut. 28:48
38 [a]2 Kin. 23:3; 2 Chr. 29:10; Ezra 10:3 [b]Neh. 10:1

CHAPTER 10
1 [a]Neh. 1:1
2 [a]Neh. 12:1–21
14 [a]Ezra 2:3
28 [a]Ezra 2:36–43 [b]Ezra 9:1; Neh. 13:3

NKJV

[b]From the days of the kings of Assyria until
this day.
33 However [a]You *are* just in all that has
befallen us;
For You have dealt faithfully,
But [b]we have done wickedly.
34 Neither our kings nor our princes,
Our priests nor our fathers,
Have kept Your law,
Nor heeded Your commandments and
Your testimonies,
With which You testified against them.
35 For they have [a]not served You in their
kingdom,
Or in the many good *things* that You gave
them,
Or in the large and rich land which You
set before them;
Nor did they turn from their wicked
works.

36 "Here [a]we *are*, servants today!
And the land that You gave to our
fathers,
To eat its fruit and its bounty,
Here we *are*, servants in it!
37 And [a]it yields much increase to the kings
You have set over us,
Because of our sins;
Also they have [b]dominion over our bodies
and our cattle
At their pleasure;
And we *are* in great distress.

38 "And because of all this,
We [a]make a sure *covenant* and write *it;*
Our leaders, our Levites, *and* our priests
[b]seal *it*."

The People Who Sealed the Covenant

10 Now those who placed *their* seal on *the
document were:*
Nehemiah the governor, [a]the son of Haca-
liah, and Zedekiah,
2 [a]Seraiah, Azariah, Jeremiah,
3 Pashhur, Amariah, Malchijah,
4 Hattush, Shebaniah, Malluch,
5 Harim, Meremoth, Obadiah,
6 Daniel, Ginnethon, Baruch,
7 Meshullam, Abijah, Mijamin,
8 Maaziah, Bilgai, *and* Shemaiah. These
were the priests.
9 The Levites: Jeshua the son of Azaniah,
Binnui of the sons of Henadad, *and* Kadmiel.
10 Their brethren: Shebaniah, Hodijah,
Kelita, Pelaiah, Hanan,
11 Micha, Rehob, Hashabiah,
12 Zaccur, Sherebiah, Shebaniah,
13 Hodijah, Bani, *and* Beninu.
14 The leaders of the people: [a]Parosh,
Pahath-Moab, Elam, Zattu, Bani,
15 Bunni, Azgad, Bebai,
16 Adonijah, Bigvai, Adin,
17 Ater, Hezekiah, Azzur,
18 Hodijah, Hashum, Bezai,
19 Hariph, Anathoth, Nebai,
20 Magpiash, Meshullam, Hezir,
21 Meshezabel, Zadok, Jaddua,
22 Pelatiah, Hanan, Anaiah,
23 Hoshea, Hananiah, Hasshub,
24 Hallohesh, Pilha, Shobek,
25 Rehum, Hashabnah, Maaseiah,
26 Ahijah, Hanan, Anan,
27 Malluch, Harim, *and* Baanah.

The Covenant That Was Sealed

28 [a]Now the rest of the people—the priests,
the Levites, the gatekeepers, the singers, the Nethinim, [b]and all those who had separated themselves from the peoples of the lands to the Law
of God, their wives, their sons, and their daugh-

KJV

one having knowledge, and having understanding;
29 They clave to their brethren, their nobles,
[a]and entered into a curse, and into an oath, [b]to
walk in God's law, which was given by Moses
the servant of God, and to observe and do all the
commandments of the LORD our Lord, and his
judgments and his statutes;
30 And that we would not give [a]our daughters unto the people of the land, nor take their
daughters for our sons:
31 [a]And *if* the people of the land bring ware
or any victuals on the sabbath day to sell, *that*
we would not buy it of them on the sabbath,
or on the holy day: and *that* we would leave
the [b]seventh year, and the [c]exaction of every
debt.
32 Also we made ordinances for us, to charge
ourselves yearly with the third [a]part of a shekel
for the service of the house of our God;
33 For [a]the shewbread, and for the [b]con-
tinual meat offering, and for the continual burnt
offering, of the sabbaths, of the new moons, for
the set feasts, and for the holy *things,* and for
the sin offerings to make an atonement for Israel,
and *for* all the work of the house of our God.
34 And we cast the lots among the priests,
the Levites, and the people, [a]for the wood offering, to bring *it* into the house of our God, after
the houses of our fathers, at times appointed year
by year, to burn upon the altar of the LORD our
God, [b]as *it is* written in the law:
35 And [a]to bring the firstfruits of our ground,
and the firstfruits of all fruit of all trees, year by
year, unto the house of the LORD:
36 Also the [a]firstborn of our sons, and of our
cattle, as *it is* written in the law, and the firstlings
of our herds and of our flocks, to bring to the
house of our God, unto the priests that minister
in the house of our God:
37 [a]And *that* we should bring the firstfruits
of our dough, and our offerings, and the fruit of
all manner of trees, of wine and of oil, unto the
priests, to the chambers of the house of our God;
and [b]the tithes of our ground unto the Levites,
that the same Levites might have the tithes in all
the cities of our tillage.
38 And the priest the son of Aaron shall be
with the Levites, [a]when the Levites take tithes:
and the Levites shall bring up the tithe of the
tithes unto the house of our God, to [b]the chambers, into the treasure house.
39 For the children of Israel and the children
of Levi [a]shall bring the offering of the corn, of
the new wine, and the oil, unto the chambers,
where *are* the vessels of the sanctuary, and the
priests that minister, and the porters, [b]and the
singers: and we will not [c]forsake the house of our
God.

The People Dwelling in Jerusalem

11 And the rulers of the people dwelt at Jerusalem: the rest of the people also cast lots,
to bring one of ten to dwell in Jerusalem [a]the holy
city, and nine parts *to dwell* in *other* cities.
2 And the people blessed all the men, that
[a]willingly offered themselves to dwell at Jerusalem.
3 [a]Now these *are* the chief of the province
that dwelt in Jerusalem: but in the cities of Judah
dwelt every one in his possession in their cities,
to wit, Israel, the priests, and the Levites, and
[b]the Nethinims, and the [c]children of Solomon's
servants.
4 And [a]at Jerusalem dwelt *certain* of the
children of Judah, and of the children of Benjamin. Of the children of Judah; Athaiah the son
of Uzziah, the son of Zechariah, the son of Amariah, the son of Shephatiah, the son of Mahalaleel,
of the children of [b]Perez;
5 And Maaseiah the son of Baruch, the son
of Colhozeh, the son of Hazaiah, the son of

29 [a]Deut. 29:12; Neh. 5:12; Ps. 119:106 [b]2 Kin. 23:3; 2 Chr. 34:31
30 [a]Ex. 34:16; Deut. 7:3; [Ezra 9:12]
31 [a]Ex. 20:10; Lev. 23:3; Deut. 5:12 [b]Ex. 23:10, 11; Lev. 25:4; Jer. 34:14 [c][Deut. 15:1, 2]; Neh. 5:12
32 [a]Ex. 30:11–16; 38:25, 26; 2 Chr. 24:6, 9; Matt. 17:24
33 [a]Lev. 24:5; 2 Chr. 2:4 [b]Num. 28; 29
34 [a]Neh. 13:31; [Is. 40:16] [b]Lev. 6:12
35 [a]Ex. 23:19; 34:26; Lev. 19:23; Num. 18:12; Deut. 26:1, 2
36 [a]Ex. 13:2, 12, 13; Lev. 27:26, 27; Num. 18:15, 16
37 [a]Lev. 23:17; Num. 15:19; 18:12; Deut. 18:4; 26:2 [b]Lev. 27:30; Num. 18:21; Mal. 3:10
38 [a]Num. 18:26 [b]1 Chr. 9:26; 2 Chr. 31:11
39 [a]Deut. 12:6, 11; 2 Chr. 31:12; Neh. 13:12 [b]Neh. 13:10, 11 [c][Heb. 10:25]

CHAPTER 11
1 [a]Neh. 10:18; Matt. 4:5; 5:35; 27:53
2 [a]Judg. 5:9; 2 Chr. 17:16
3 [a]1 Chr. 9:2, 3 [b]Ezra 2:43 [c]Ezra 2:55
4 [a]1 Chr. 9:3 [b]Gen. 38:29

NKJV

ters, everyone who had knowledge and understanding—
29 these joined with their brethren, their nobles, [a]and entered into a curse and an oath [b]to
walk in God's Law, which was given by Moses
the servant of God, and to observe and do all the
commandments of the LORD our Lord, and His
ordinances and His statutes:
30 We would not give [a]our daughters as
wives to the peoples of the land, nor take their
daughters for our sons;
31 [a]*if* the peoples of the land brought wares
or any grain to sell on the Sabbath day, we would
not buy it from them on the Sabbath, or on a holy
day; and we would forego the [b]seventh year's *produce* and the [c]exacting of every debt.
32 Also we made ordinances for ourselves,
to exact from ourselves yearly [a]one-third of a
shekel for the service of the house of our God:
33 for [a]the showbread, for the regular grain
offering, for the [b]regular burnt offering of the Sabbaths, the New Moons, and the set feasts; for the
holy things, for the sin offerings to make atonement for Israel, and all the work of the house of
our God.
34 We cast lots among the priests, the Levites, and the people, [a]for *bringing* the wood offering into the house of our God, according to our
fathers' houses, at the appointed times year by
year, to burn on the altar of the LORD our God
[b]as *it is* written in the Law.
35 And *we made ordinances* [a]to bring the
firstfruits of our ground and the firstfruits of all
fruit of all trees, year by year, to the house of
the LORD;
36 to bring the [a]firstborn of our sons and our
cattle, as *it is* written in the Law, and the firstborn
of our herds and our flocks, to the house of our
God, to the priests who minister in the house of
our God;
37 [a]to bring the firstfruits of our dough, our
offerings, the fruit from all kinds of trees, *the* new
wine and oil, to the priests, to the storerooms of
the house of our God; and to bring [b]the tithes of
our land to the Levites, for the Levites should receive the tithes in all our farming communities.
38 And the priest, the descendant of Aaron,
shall be with the Levites [a]when the Levites receive
tithes; and the Levites shall bring up a tenth of
the tithes to the house of our God, to [b]the rooms
of the storehouse.
39 For the children of Israel and the children
of Levi [a]shall bring the offering of the grain, of
the new wine and the oil, to the storerooms where
the articles of the sanctuary *are, where* the priests
who minister and the gatekeepers [b]and the singers *are;* and we will not [c]neglect the house of our
God.

The People Dwelling in Jerusalem

11 Now the leaders of the people dwelt at Jerusalem; the rest of the people cast lots to
bring one out of ten to dwell in Jerusalem, [a]the
holy city, and nine-tenths *were to dwell* in *other*
cities.
2 And the people blessed all the men who
[a]willingly offered themselves to dwell at Jerusalem.
3 [a]These *are* the heads of the province who
dwelt in Jerusalem. (But in the cities of Judah
everyone dwelt in his own possession in their cities—Israelites, priests, Levites, [b]Nethinim, and
[c]descendants of Solomon's servants.)
4 Also [a]in Jerusalem dwelt *some* of the children of Judah and of the children of Benjamin.
The children of Judah: Athaiah the son of Uzziah,
the son of Zechariah, the son of Amariah, the son
of Shephatiah, the son of Mahalalel, of the children of [b]Perez;
5 and Maaseiah the son of Baruch, the son
of Col-Hozeh, the son of Hazaiah, the son of

KJV

Adaiah, the son of Joiarib, the son of Zechariah,
the son of Shiloni.
6 All the sons of Perez that dwelt at Jerusalem *were* four hundred threescore and eight valiant men.
7 And these *are* the sons of Benjamin; Sallu
the son of Meshullam, the son of Joed, the son
of Pedaiah, the son of Kolaiah, the son of Maaseiah, the son of Ithiel, the son of Jesaiah.
8 And after him Gabbai, Sallai, nine hundred twenty and eight.
9 And Joel the son of Zichri *was* their overseer: and Judah the son of Senuah *was* second
over the city.
10 [a]Of the priests: Jedaiah the son of Joiarib,
Jachin.
11 Seraiah the son of Hilkiah, the son of
Meshullam, the son of Zadok, the son of Meraioth,
the son of Ahitub, *was* the ruler of the house of
God.
12 And their brethren that did the work of
the house *were* eight hundred twenty and two:
and Adaiah the son of Jeroham, the son of Pelaliah, the son of Amzi, the son of Zechariah, the
son of Pashur, the son of Malchiah,
13 And his brethren, chief of the fathers, two
hundred forty and two: and Amashai the son of
Azareel, the son of Ahasai, the son of Meshillemoth, the son of Immer,
14 And their brethren, mighty men of valour,
an hundred twenty and eight: and their overseer
was Zabdiel, the son of *one of* the great men.
15 Also of the Levites: Shemaiah the son of
Hashub, the son of Azrikam, the son of Hashabiah, the son of Bunni;
16 And [a]Shabbethai and [b]Jozabad, of the
chief of the Levites, *had* the oversight of [c]the outward business of the house of God.
17 And Mattaniah the son of Micha, the son
of Zabdi, the son of Asaph, *was* the principal to
begin the thanksgiving in prayer: and Bakbukiah
the second among his brethren, and Abda the son
of Shammua, the son of Galal, the son of
Jeduthun.
18 All the Levites in [a]the holy city *were* two
hundred fourscore and four.
19 Moreover the porters, Akkub, Talmon,
and their brethren that kept the gates, *were* an
hundred seventy and two.
20 And the residue of Israel, of the priests,
and the Levites, *were* in all the cities of Judah,
every one in his inheritance.
21 [a]But the Nethinims dwelt in Ophel: and
Ziha and Gispa *were* over the Nethinims.
22 The overseer also of the Levites at Jerusalem *was* Uzzi the son of Bani, the son of Hashabiah, the son of Mattaniah, the son of Micha. Of
the sons of Asaph, the singers *were* over the business of the house of God.
23 For [a]*it was* the king's commandment concerning them, that a certain portion should be for
the singers, due for every day.
24 And Pethahiah the son of Meshezabeel,
of the children of [a]Zerah the son of Judah, *was*
[b]at the king's hand in all matters concerning the
people.

The People Dwelling Outside Jerusalem

25 And for the villages, with their fields,
some of the children of Judah dwelt at [a]Kirjath–
arba, and *in* the villages thereof, and at Dibon,
and *in* the villages thereof, and at Jekabzeel, and
in the villages thereof,
26 And at Jeshua, and at Moladah, and at
Beth–phelet,
27 And at Hazar–shual, and at Beer–sheba,
and *in* the villages thereof,
28 And at Ziklag, and at Mekonah, and in
the villages thereof,
29 And at En–rimmon, and at Zareah, and
at Jarmuth,
30 Zanoah, Adullam, and *in* their villages, at

10 [a]1 Chr. 9:10
16 [a]Ezra 10:15 [b]Ezra 8:33 [c]1 Chr. 26:29
18 [a]Neh. 11:1
21 [a]2 Chr. 27:3; Neh. 3:26
23 [a]Ezra 6:8, 9; 7:20
24 [a]Gen. 38:30 [b]1 Chr. 18:17
25 [a]Josh. 14:15

*

11:9 Or *Hassenuah*
11:14 Or *the son of Haggedolim*
11:17 Or *Michah*
11:24 Lit. *at the king's hand*

NKJV

Adaiah, the son of Joiarib, the son of Zechariah,
the son of Shiloni.
6 All the sons of Perez who dwelt at Jerusalem *were* four hundred and sixty-eight valiant
men.
7 And these are the sons of Benjamin: Sallu
the son of Meshullam, the son of Joed, the son
of Pedaiah, the son of Kolaiah, the son of Maaseiah, the son of Ithiel, the son of Jeshaiah;
8 and after him Gabbai *and* Sallai, nine hundred and twenty-eight.
9 Joel the son of Zichri *was* their overseer,
and Judah the son of *Senuah *was* second over
the city.
10 [a]Of the priests: Jedaiah the son of Joiarib,
and Jachin;
11 Seraiah the son of Hilkiah, the son of
Meshullam, the son of Zadok, the son of Meraioth,
the son of Ahitub, *was* the leader of the house of
God.
12 Their brethren who did the work of the
house *were* eight hundred and twenty-two; and
Adaiah the son of Jeroham, the son of Pelaliah,
the son of Amzi, the son of Zechariah, the son of
Pashhur, the son of Malchijah,
13 and his brethren, heads of the fathers'
houses, were two hundred and forty-two; and
Amashai the son of Azarel, the son of Ahzai, the
son of Meshillemoth, the son of Immer,
14 and their brethren, mighty men of valor,
were one hundred and twenty-eight. Their overseer *was* Zabdiel *the son of *one of* the great men.
15 Also of the Levites: Shemaiah the son of
Hasshub, the son of Azrikam, the son of Hashabiah, the son of Bunni;
16 [a]Shabbethai and [b]Jozabad, of the heads
of the Levites, *had* the oversight of [c]the business
outside of the house of God;
17 Mattaniah the son of *Micha, the son of
Zabdi, the son of Asaph, the leader *who* began
the thanksgiving with prayer; Bakbukiah, the second among his brethren; and Abda the son of
Shammua, the son of Galal, the son of Jeduthun.
18 All the Levites in [a]the holy city *were* two
hundred and eighty-four.
19 Moreover the gatekeepers, Akkub, Talmon, and their brethren who kept the gates, *were*
one hundred and seventy-two.
20 And the rest of Israel, of the priests *and*
Levites, *were* in all the cities of Judah, everyone
in his inheritance.
21 [a]But the Nethinim dwelt in Ophel. And
Ziha and Gishpa *were* over the Nethinim.
22 Also the overseer of the Levites at Jerusalem *was* Uzzi the son of Bani, the son of Hashabiah, the son of Mattaniah, the son of Micha, of
the sons of Asaph, the singers in charge of the
service of the house of God.
23 For [a]*it was* the king's command concerning them that a certain portion should be for the
singers, a quota day by day.
24 Pethahiah the son of Meshezabel, of the
children of [a]Zerah the son of Judah, *was* [b]the*
king's deputy in all matters concerning the people.

The People Dwelling Outside Jerusalem

25 And as for the villages with their fields,
some of the children of Judah dwelt in [a]Kirjath
Arba and its villages, Dibon and its villages, Jekabzeel and its villages;
26 in Jeshua, Moladah, Beth Pelet,
27 Hazar Shual, and Beersheba and its
villages;
28 in Ziklag and Meconah and its villages;
29 in En Rimmon, Zorah, Jarmuth,
30 Zanoah, Adullam, and their villages; in

KJV

Lachish, and the fields thereof, at Azekah, and
in the villages thereof. And they dwelt from Beer–
sheba unto the valley of Hinnom.
31 The children also of Benjamin from Geba
dwelt at Michmash, and Aija, and Beth–el, and
in their villages,
32 *And* at Anathoth, Nob, Ananiah,
33 Hazor, Ramah, Gittaim,
34 Hadid, Zeboim, Neballat,
35 Lod, and Ono, [a]the valley of craftsmen.
36 And of the Levites *were* divisions *in* Judah, *and* in Benjamin.

The Priests and Levites
(*cf. Ezra 2:36–40*)

12 Now these *are* the [a]priests and the Levites
that went up with [b]Zerubbabel the son of
Shealtiel, and Jeshua: [c]Seraiah, Jeremiah, Ezra,
2 Amariah, Malluch, Hattush,
3 Shechaniah, Rehum, Meremoth,
4 Iddo, Ginnetho, [a]Abijah,
5 Miamin, Maadiah, Bilgah,
6 Shemaiah, and Joiarib, Jedaiah,
7 Sallu, Amok, Hilkiah, Jedaiah. These *were*
the chief of the priests and of their brethren in
the days of [a]Jeshua.
8 Moreover the Levites: Jeshua, Binnui,
Kadmiel, Sherebiah, Judah, *and* Mattaniah,
[a]*which was* over the thanksgiving, he and his
brethren.
9 Also Bakbukiah and Unni, their brethren,
were over against them in the watches.
10 And Jeshua begat Joiakim, Joiakim also
begat Eliashib, and Eliashib begat Joiada,
11 And Joiada begat Jonathan, and Jonathan
begat Jaddua.
12 And in the days of Joiakim were priests,
the [a]chief of the fathers: of Seraiah, Meraiah; of
Jeremiah, Hananiah;
13 Of Ezra, Meshullam; of Amariah, Jehohanan;
14 Of Melicu, Jonathan; of Shebaniah, Joseph;
15 Of Harim, Adna; of Meraioth, Helkai;
16 Of Iddo, Zechariah; of Ginnethon, Meshullam;
17 Of Abijah, Zichri; of Miniamin, of Moadiah, Piltai;
18 Of Bilgah, Shammua; of Shemaiah, Jehonathan;
19 And of Joiarib, Mattenai; of Jedaiah, Uzzi;
20 Of Sallai, Kallai; of Amok, Eber;
21 Of Hilkiah, Hashabiah; of Jedaiah,
Nethaneel.
22 The Levites in the days of Eliashib, Joiada,
and Johanan, and Jaddua, *were* [a]recorded chief
of the fathers: also the priests, to the reign of Darius the Persian.
23 The sons of Levi, the chief of the fathers,
were written in the book of the [a]chronicles, even
until the days of Johanan the son of Eliashib.
24 And the chief of the Levites: Hashabiah,
Sherebiah, and Jeshua the son of Kadmiel, with
their brethren over against them, to [a]praise *and*
to give thanks, [c]according to the commandment
of David the man of God, [b]ward over against
ward.
25 Mattaniah, and Bakbukiah, Obadiah,
Meshullam, Talmon, Akkub, *were* porters keeping
the ward at the thresholds of the gates.
26 These *were* in the days of Joiakim the son
of Jeshua, the son of Jozadak, and in the days of
Nehemiah [a]the governor, and of Ezra the priest,
[b]the scribe.

Nehemiah Dedicates the Wall

27 And at [a]the dedication of the wall of Jerusalem they sought the Levites out of all their
places, to bring them to Jerusalem, to keep the
dedication with gladness, [b]both with thanksgivings, and with singing, *with* cymbals, psalteries, and with harps.

35 [a]1 Chr. 4:14

CHAPTER 12

1 [a]Ezra 2:1, 2; 7:7 [b]Neh. 7:7; Matt. 1:12, 13 [c]Neh. 10:2–8
4 [a]Luke 1:5
7 [a]Ezra 3:2; Hag. 1:1; Zech. 3:1
8 [a]Neh. 11:17
12 [a]Neh. 7:70, 71; 8:13; 11:13
22 [a]1 Chr. 24:6
23 [a]1 Chr. 9:14–22
24 [a]Neh. 11:17 [b]Ezra 3:11 [c]1 Chr. 23—26
26 [a]Neh. 8:9 [b]Ezra 7:6, 11
27 [a]Deut. 20:5; Neh. 7:1; Ps. 30:title [b]1 Chr. 25:6; 2 Chr. 5:13; 7:6

*

12:4 *Ginnethon,* v. 16
12:14 *Malluch,* v. 2 • *Shechaniah,* v. 3
12:15 *Rehum,* v. 3 • *Meremoth,* v. 3
12:17 *Mijamin,* v. 5 • *Maadiah,* v. 5
12:20 *Sallu,* v. 7
12:26 *Jehozadak,* 1 Chr. 6:14

NKJV

Lachish and its fields; in Azekah and its villages.
They dwelt from Beersheba to the Valley of
Hinnom.
31 Also the children of Benjamin from Geba
dwelt in Michmash, Aija, and Bethel, and their
villages;
32 in Anathoth, Nob, Ananiah;
33 in Hazor, Ramah, Gittaim;
34 in Hadid, Zeboim, Neballat;
35 in Lod, Ono, *and* [a]the Valley of Craftsmen.
36 Some of the Judean divisions of Levites
were in Benjamin.

The Priests and Levites
(*cf. Ezra 2:36–40*)

12 Now these *are* the [a]priests and the Levites
who came up with [b]Zerubbabel the son of
Shealtiel, and Jeshua: [c]Seraiah, Jeremiah, Ezra,
2 Amariah, Malluch, Hattush,
3 Shechaniah, Rehum, Meremoth,
4 Iddo, *Ginnethoi, [a]Abijah,
5 Mijamin, Maadiah, Bilgah,
6 Shemaiah, Joiarib, Jedaiah,
7 Sallu, Amok, Hilkiah, *and* Jedaiah.
These *were* the heads of the priests and their
brethren in the days of [a]Jeshua.
8 Moreover the Levites *were* Jeshua, Binnui, Kadmiel, Sherebiah, Judah, *and* Mattaniah
[a]*who led* the thanksgiving *psalms,* he and his
brethren.
9 Also Bakbukiah and Unni, their brethren,
stood across from them in *their* duties.
10 Jeshua begot Joiakim, Joiakim begot Eliashib, Eliashib begot Joiada,
11 Joiada begot Jonathan, and Jonathan begot Jaddua.
12 Now in the days of Joiakim, the priests,
the [a]heads of the fathers' *houses were:* of Seraiah,
Meraiah; of Jeremiah, Hananiah;
13 of Ezra, Meshullam; of Amariah, Jehohanan;
14 of *Melichu, Jonathan; of *Shebaniah, Joseph;
15 of *Harim, Adna; of *Meraioth, Helkai;
16 of Iddo, Zechariah; of Ginnethon, Meshullam;
17 of Abijah, Zichri; *the son* of *Minjamin;
of *Moadiah, Piltai;
18 of Bilgah, Shammua; of Shemaiah, Jehonathan;
19 of Joiarib, Mattenai; of Jedaiah, Uzzi;
20 of *Sallai, Kallai; of Amok, Eber;
21 of Hilkiah, Hashabiah; *and* of Jedaiah,
Nethanel.
22 During the reign of Darius the Persian, a
record *was also kept* of the Levites and priests
who had been [a]heads of their fathers' *houses* in
the days of Eliashib, Joiada, Johanan, and Jaddua.
23 The sons of Levi, the heads of the fathers'
houses until the days of Johanan the son of Eliashib, *were* written in the book of the [a]chronicles.
24 And the heads of the Levites *were* Hashabiah, Sherebiah, and Jeshua the son of Kadmiel,
with their brothers across from them, to [a]praise
and give thanks, [b]group alternating with group,
[c]according to the command of David the man of
God.
25 Mattaniah, Bakbukiah, Obadiah, Meshullam, Talmon, and Akkub *were* gatekeepers keeping the watch at the storerooms of the gates.
26 These *lived* in the days of Joiakim the son
of Jeshua, the son of *Jozadak, and in the days
of Nehemiah [a]the governor, and of Ezra the priest,
[b]the scribe.

Nehemiah Dedicates the Wall

27 Now at [a]the dedication of the wall of Jerusalem they sought out the Levites in all their
places, to bring them to Jerusalem to celebrate
the dedication with gladness, [b]both with thanksgivings and singing, *with* cymbals and stringed
instruments and harps.

KJV

28 And the sons of the singers gathered
themselves together, both out of the plain country
round about Jerusalem, and from the [a]villages of
Netophathi;
29 Also from the house of Gilgal, and out
of the fields of Geba and Azmaveth: for the
singers had builded them villages round about
Jerusalem.
30 And the priests and the Levites [a]purified
themselves, and purified the people, and the gates,
and the wall.
31 Then I brought up the princes of Judah
upon the wall, and appointed two great *companies
of them that gave* thanks, *whereof* [a]*one* went on
the right hand upon the wall [b]toward the dung
gate:
32 And after them went Hoshaiah, and half
of the princes of Judah,
33 And Azariah, Ezra, and Meshullam,
34 Judah, and Benjamin, and Shemaiah, and
Jeremiah,
35 And *certain* of the priests' sons [a]with
trumpets; *namely,* Zechariah the son of Jonathan,
the son of Shemaiah, the son of Mattaniah, the
son of Michaiah, the son of Zaccur, the son of
Asaph:
36 And his brethren, Shemaiah, and Azarael,
Milalai, Gilalai, Maai, Nethaneel, and Judah, Hanani, with [a]the musical [b]instruments of David the
man of God, and Ezra the scribe before them.
37 [a]And at the fountain gate, which was over
against them, they went up by [b]the stairs of the
[c]city of David, at the going up of the wall, above
the house of David, even unto [d]the water gate
eastward.
38 [a]And the other *company of them that
gave* thanks went over against *them,* and I after
them, and the half of the people upon the wall,
from beyond [b]the tower of the furnaces even unto
[c]the broad wall;
39 [a]And from above the gate of Ephraim, and
above [b]the old gate, and above [c]the fish gate, [d]and
the tower of Hananeel, and the tower of Meah,
even unto [e]the sheep gate: and they stood still in
[f]the prison gate.
40 So stood the two *companies of them that
gave* thanks in the house of God, and I, and the
half of the rulers with me:
41 And the priests; Eliakim, Maaseiah,
Miniamin, Michaiah, Elioenai, Zechariah, *and*
Hananiah, with trumpets;
42 And Maaseiah, and Shemaiah, and Eleazar, and Uzzi, and Jehohanan, and Malchijah, and
Elam, and Ezer. And the singers sang loud, with
Jezrahiah *their* overseer.
43 Also that day they offered great sacrifices,
and rejoiced: for God had made them rejoice with
great joy: the wives also and the children rejoiced:
so that the joy of Jerusalem was heard even [a]afar
off.

Temple Responsibilities

44 [a]And at that time were some appointed
over the chambers for the treasures, for the offerings, for the firstfruits, and for the [b]tithes, to
gather into them out of the fields of the cities the
portions of the law for the priests and Levites:
for Judah rejoiced for the priests and for the Levites that waited.
45 And both the singers and the porters kept
the ward of their God, and the ward of the purification, [a]according to the commandment of David,
and of Solomon his son.
46 For in the days of David [a]and Asaph of
old *there were* chief of the singers, and songs of
praise and thanskgiving unto God.
47 And all Israel in the days of Zerubbabel,
and in the days of Nehemiah, gave the portions
of the singers and the porters, [a]every day his portion: [b]and they sanctified *holy things* unto the
Levites; [c]and the Levites sanctified *them* unto the
children of Aaron.

28 [a]1 Chr. 9:16
30 [a]Ezra 6:20; Neh. 13:22, 30
31 [a]Neh. 12:38 [b]Neh. 2:13; 3:13
35 [a]Num. 10:2, 8
36 [a]1 Chr. 23:5 [b]2 Chr. 29:26, 27
37 [a]Neh. 2:14; 3:15 [b]Neh. 3:15 [c]2 Sam. 5:7–9 [d]Neh. 3:26; 8:1, 3, 16
38 [a]Neh. 12:31 [b]Neh. 3:11 [c]Neh. 3:8
39 [a]2 Kin. 14:13; Neh. 8:16 [b]Neh. 3:6 [c]Neh. 3:3 [d]Neh. 3:1 [e]Neh. 3:32 [f]Jer. 32:2
43 [a]Ezra 3:13
44 [a]2 Chr. 31:11, 12; Neh. 13:5, 12, 13 [b]Neh. 10:37–39
45 [a]1 Chr. 25; 26
46 [a]1 Chr. 25:1; 2 Chr. 29:30
47 [a]Neh. 11:23 [b]Num. 18:21, 24 [c]Num. 18:26

NKJV

28 And the sons of the singers gathered together from the countryside around Jerusalem,
from the [a]villages of the Netophathites,
29 from the house of Gilgal, and from the
fields of Geba and Azmaveth; for the singers had
built themselves villages all around Jerusalem.
30 Then the priests and Levites [a]purified
themselves, and purified the people, the gates, and
the wall.
31 So I brought the leaders of Judah up on
the wall, and appointed two large thanksgiving
choirs. [a]*One* went to the right hand on the wall
[b]toward the Refuse Gate.
32 After them went Hoshaiah and half of the
leaders of Judah,
33 and Azariah, Ezra, Meshullam,
34 Judah, Benjamin, Shemaiah, Jeremiah,
35 and some of the priests' sons [a]with trumpets—Zechariah the son of Jonathan, the son of
Shemaiah, the son of Mattaniah, the son of Michaiah, the son of Zaccur, the son of Asaph,
36 and his brethren, Shemaiah, Azarel, Milalai, Gilalai, Maai, Nethanel, Judah, *and* Hanani,
with [a]the musical [b]instruments of David the man
of God. Ezra the scribe *went* before them.
37 [a]By the Fountain Gate, in front of them,
they went up [b]the stairs of the [c]City of David,
on the stairway of the wall, beyond the house of
David, as far as [d]the Water Gate eastward.
38 [a]The other thanksgiving choir went the
opposite *way,* and I *was* behind them with half
of the people on the wall, going past the [b]Tower
of the Ovens as far as [c]the Broad Wall,
39 [a]and above the Gate of Ephraim, above
[b]the Old Gate, above [c]the Fish Gate, [d]the Tower
of Hananel, the Tower of the Hundred, as far as
[e]the Sheep Gate; and they stopped by [f]the Gate
of the Prison.
40 So the two thanksgiving choirs stood in
the house of God, likewise I and the half of the
rulers with me;
41 and the priests, Eliakim, Maaseiah, *Minjamin, Michaiah, Elioenai, Zechariah, *and* Hananiah, with trumpets;
42 also Maaseiah, Shemaiah, Eleazar, Uzzi,
Jehohanan, Malchijah, Elam, and Ezer. The singers sang loudly with Jezrahiah the director.
43 Also that day they offered great sacrifices,
and rejoiced, for God had made them rejoice with
great joy; the women and the children also rejoiced, so that the joy of Jerusalem was heard
[a]afar off.

Temple Responsibilities

44 [a]And at the same time some were appointed over the rooms of the storehouse for the
offerings, the firstfruits, and the [b]tithes, to gather
into them from the fields of the cities the portions
specified by the Law for the priests and Levites;
for Judah rejoiced over the priests and Levites
who ministered.
45 Both the singers and the gatekeepers kept
the charge of their God and the charge of the purification, [a]according to the command of David *and*
Solomon his son.
46 For in the days of David [a]and Asaph of
old *there were* chiefs of the singers, and songs
of praise and thanksgiving to God.
47 In the days of Zerubbabel and in the days
of Nehemiah all Israel gave the portions for the
singers and the gatekeepers, a portion for [a]each
day. [b]They also consecrated *holy things* for the
Levites, [c]and the Levites consecrated *them* for the
children of Aaron.

*———
12:41 *Mijamin,* v. 5

KJV

Principles of Separation
(Num. 22:1—24:25)

13 On that day [a]they read in the book of Moses
in the audience of the people; and therein
was found written, [b]that the Ammonite and the
Moabite should not come into the congregation
of God for ever;
2 Because they met not the children of Israel
with bread and with water, but [a]hired Balaam
against them, that he should curse them: [b]howbeit
our God turned the curse into a blessing.
3 Now it came to pass, when they had heard
the law, [a]that they separated from Israel all the
mixed multitude.

The Reforms of Nehemiah

4 And before this, [a]Eliashib the priest, having the oversight of the chamber of the house of
our God, *was* allied unto [b]Tobiah:
5 And he had prepared for him a great
chamber, [a]where aforetime they laid the meat offerings, the frankincense, and the vessels, and the
tithes of the corn, the new wine, and the oil,
[b]which was commanded *to be given* to the Levites, and the singers, and the porters; and the
offerings of the priests.
6 But in all this *time* was not I at Jerusalem:
[a]for in the two and thirtieth year of Artaxerxes
king of Babylon came I unto the king, and after
certain days obtained I leave of the king:
7 And I came to Jerusalem, and understood
of the evil that Eliashib did for Tobiah, in [a]prepar-
ing him a chamber in the courts of the house of
God.
8 And it grieved me sore: therefore I cast
forth all the household stuff of Tobiah out of the
chamber.
9 Then I commanded, and they [a]cleansed
the chambers: and thither brought I again the vessels of the house of God, with the meat offering
and the frankincense.
10 And I perceived that the portions of the
Levites had [a]not been given *them:* for the Levites
and the singers, that did the work, were fled every
one to [b]his field.
11 Then [a]contended I with the rulers, and
said, [b]Why is the house of God forsaken? And I
gathered them together, and set them in their
place.
12 [a]Then brought all Judah the tithe of the
corn and the new wine and the oil unto the
treasuries.
13 [a]And I made treasurers over the treasuries, Shelemiah the priest, and Zadok the scribe,
and of the Levites, Pedaiah: and next to them *was*
Hanan the son of Zaccur, the son of Mattaniah:
for they were counted [b]faithful, and their office
was to distribute unto their brethren.
14 [a]Remember me, O my God, concerning
this, and wipe not out my good deeds that I have
done for the house of my God, and for the offices
thereof.
15 In those days saw I in Judah *some* treading winepresses [a]on the sabbath, and bringing in
sheaves, and lading asses; as also wine, grapes,
and figs, and all *manner of* burdens, [b]which they
brought into Jerusalem on the sabbath day: and
I testified *against them* in the day wherein they
sold victuals.
16 There dwelt men of Tyre also therein,
which brought fish, and all manner of ware, and
sold on the sabbath unto the children of Judah,
and in Jerusalem.
17 Then I contended with the nobles of Judah, and said unto them, What evil thing *is* this
that ye do, and profane the sabbath day?
18 [a]Did not your fathers thus, and did not
our God bring all this evil upon us, and upon this
city? yet ye bring more wrath upon Israel by profaning the sabbath.
19 And it came to pass, that when the gates

CHAPTER 13
1 [a][Deut. 31:11, 12]; 2 Kin. 23:2; Neh. 8:3, 8; 9:3; Is. 34:16 [b]Deut. 23:3, 4
2 [a]Num. 22:5; Josh. 24:9, 10 [b]Num. 23:1; 24:10; Deut. 23:5
3 [a]Neh. 9:2; 10:28
4 [a]Neh. 12:10 [b]Neh. 2:10; 4:3; 6:1
5 [a]Neh. 12:44 [b]Num. 18:21, 24
6 [a]Neh. 5:14–16
7 [a]Neh. 13:1, 5
9 [a]2 Chr. 29:5, 15, 16
10 [a]Neh. 10:37; Mal. 3:8 [b]Num. 35:2
11 [a]Neh. 13:17, 25 [b]Neh. 10:39
12 [a]Neh. 10:38; 12:44
13 [a]2 Chr. 31:12 [b]1 Cor. 4:2
14 [a]Neh. 5:19; 13:22, 31
15 [a][Ex. 20:10] [b]Neh. 10:31; [Jer. 17:21]
18 [a]Ezra 9:13; [Jer. 17:21]

NKJV

Principles of Separation
(Num. 22:1—24:25)

13 On that day [a]they read from the Book of
Moses in the hearing of the people, and in
it was found written [b]that no Ammonite or Moabite should ever come into the assembly of God,
2 because they had not met the children of
Israel with bread and water, but [a]hired Balaam
against them to curse them. [b]However, our God
turned the curse into a blessing.
3 So it was, when they had heard the Law,
[a]that they separated all the mixed multitude from
Israel.

The Reforms of Nehemiah

4 Now before this, [a]Eliashib the priest, having authority over the storerooms of the house
of our God, *was* allied with [b]Tobiah.
5 And he had prepared for him a large
room, [a]where previously they had stored the grain
offerings, the frankincense, the articles, the tithes
of grain, the new wine and oil, [b]which were commanded *to be given* to the Levites and singers
and gatekeepers, and the offerings for the priests.
6 But during all this I was not in Jerusalem,
[a]for in the thirty-second year of Artaxerxes king
of Babylon I had returned to the king. Then after
certain days I obtained leave from the king,
7 and I came to Jerusalem and discovered
the evil that Eliashib had done for Tobiah, in [a]pre-
paring a room for him in the courts of the house
of God.
8 And it grieved me bitterly; therefore I
threw all the household goods of Tobiah out of
the room.
9 Then I commanded them to [a]cleanse the
rooms; and I brought back into them the articles
of the house of God, with the grain offering and
the frankincense.
10 I also realized that the portions for the
Levites had [a]not been given *them;* for each of the
Levites and the singers who did the work had
gone back to [b]his field.
11 So [a]I contended with the rulers, and said,
[b]"Why is the house of God forsaken?" And I gathered them together and set them in their place.
12 [a]Then all Judah brought the tithe of the
grain and the new wine and the oil to the
storehouse.
13 [a]And I appointed as treasurers over the
storehouse Shelemiah the priest and Zadok the
scribe, and of the Levites, Pedaiah; and next to
them *was* Hanan the son of Zaccur, the son of
Mattaniah; for they were considered [b]faithful, and
their task *was* to distribute to their brethren.
14 [a]Remember me, O my God, concerning
this, and do not wipe out my good deeds that I
have done for the house of my God, and for its
services!
15 In those days I saw *people* in Judah treading wine presses [a]on the Sabbath, and bringing
in sheaves, and loading donkeys with wine,
grapes, figs, and all *kinds of* burdens, [b]which they
brought into Jerusalem on the Sabbath day. And
I warned *them* about the day on which they were
selling provisions.
16 Men of Tyre dwelt there also, who brought
in fish and all kinds of goods, and sold *them* on
the Sabbath to the children of Judah, and in
Jerusalem.
17 Then I contended with the nobles of Judah, and said to them, "What evil thing *is* this
that you do, by which you profane the Sabbath
day?
18 [a]"Did not your fathers do thus, and did
not our God bring all this disaster on us and on
this city? Yet you bring added wrath on Israel
by profaning the Sabbath."
19 So it was, at the gates of Jerusalem, as it

KJV

of Jerusalem [a]began to be dark before the sabbath, I commanded that the gates should be shut,
and charged that they should not be opened till
after the sabbath: [b]and *some* of my servants set
I at the gates, *that* there should no burden be
brought in on the sabbath day.
20 So the merchants and sellers of all kind
of ware lodged without Jerusalem once or twice.
21 Then I testified against them, and said
unto them, Why lodge ye about the wall? if ye
do *so* again, I will lay hands on you. From that
time forth came they no *more* on the sabbath.
22 And I commanded the Levites that [a]they
should cleanse themselves, and *that* they should
come *and* keep the gates, to sanctify the sabbath
day. Remember me, O my God, *concerning* this
also, and spare me according to the greatness of
thy mercy.
23 In those days also saw I Jews *that* [a]had
married wives of [b]Ashdod, of Ammon, *and* of
Moab:
24 And their children spake half in the
speech of Ashdod, and could not speak in the
Jews' language, but according to the language of
each people.
25 And I [a]contended with them, and cursed
them, and smote certain of them, and plucked off
their hair, and made them [b]swear by God, *saying,*
Ye shall not give your daughters unto their sons,
nor take their daughters unto your sons, or for
yourselves.
26 [a]Did not Solomon king of Israel sin by
these things? yet among many nations was there
no king like him, [b]who was beloved of his God,
and God made him king over all Israel: [c]neverthe-
less even him did outlandish women cause to sin.
27 Shall we then hearken unto you to do all
this great evil, to [a]transgress against our God in
marrying strange wives?
28 And *one* of the sons [a]of Joiada, the son
of Eliashib the high priest, *was* son in law to [b]San-
bal lat the Horonite: therefore I chased him from
me.
29 [a]Remember them, O my God, because
they have defiled the priesthood, and [b]the covenant of the priesthood, and of the Levites.
30 [a]Thus cleansed I them from all strangers,
and [b]appointed the wards of the priests and the
Levites, every one in his business;
31 And for [a]the wood offering, at times appointed, and for the firstfruits. [b]Remember me,
O my God, for good.

19 [a]Lev. 23:32 [b]Jer. 17:21, 22
22 [a]1 Chr. 15:12; Neh. 12:30
23 [a][Ex. 34:16; Deut. 7:3, 4]; Ezra 9:2; Neh. 10:30 [b]Neh. 4:7
25 [a]Prov. 28:4 [b]Ezra 10:5; Neh. 10:29, 30
26 [a]1 Kin. 11:1, 2 [b]2 Sam. 12:24, 25 [c]1 Kin. 11:4–8
27 [a][Ezra 10:2]; Neh. 13:23
28 [a]Neh. 12:10, 12 [b]Neh. 4:1, 7; 6:1, 2
29 [a]Neh. 6:14 [b]Mal. 2:4, 11, 12
30 [a]Neh. 10:30 [b]Neh. 12:1
31 [a]Neh. 10:34 [b]Neh. 13:14, 22

NKJV

[a]began to be dark before the Sabbath, that I commanded the gates to be shut, and charged that
they must not be opened till after the Sabbath.
[b]Then I posted *some* of my servants at the gates,
so that no burdens would be brought in on the
Sabbath day.
20 Now the merchants and sellers of all kinds
of wares lodged outside Jerusalem once or twice.
21 Then I warned them, and said to them,
"Why do you spend the night around the wall?
If you do *so* again, I will lay hands on you!" From
that time on they came no *more* on the Sabbath.
22 And I commanded the Levites that [a]they
should cleanse themselves, and that they should
go and guard the gates, to sanctify the Sabbath
day.

Remember me, O my God, *concerning* this
also, and spare me according to the greatness of
Your mercy!
23 In those days I also saw Jews *who* [a]had
married women of [b]Ashdod, Ammon, *and* Moab.
24 And half of their children spoke the language of Ashdod, and could not speak the
language of Judah, but spoke according to the language of one or the other people.
25 So I [a]contended with them and cursed
them, struck some of them and pulled out their
hair, and made them [b]swear by God, *saying,* "You
shall not give your daughters as wives to their
sons, nor take their daughters for your sons or
yourselves.
26 [a]"Did not Solomon king of Israel sin by
these things? Yet among many nations there was
no king like him, [b]who was beloved of his God;
and God made him king over all Israel. [c]Neverthe-
less pagan women caused even him to sin.
27 "Should we then hear of your doing all
this great evil, [a]transgressing against our God by
marrying pagan women?"
28 And *one* of the sons [a]of Joiada, the son
of Eliashib the high priest, *was* a son-in-law of
[b]Sanballat the Horonite; therefore I drove him
from me.
29 [a]Remember them, O my God, because
they have defiled the priesthood and [b]the covenant of the priesthood and the Levites.
30 [a]Thus I cleansed them of everything pagan. I also [b]assigned duties to the priests and the
Levites, each to his service,
31 and *to bringing* [a]the wood offering and
the firstfruits at appointed times.

[b]Remember me, O my God, for good!

KJV

THE BOOK OF

ESTHER

The King Dethrones Queen Vashti

1 Now it came to pass in the days of [a]Ahasuerus, (this *is* Ahasuerus which reigned, [c]from India even unto Ethiopia, [b]*over* an hundred and seven and twenty provinces:)

2 *That* in those days, when the king Ahasuerus [a]sat on the throne of his kingdom, which *was* in [b]Shushan the palace,

3 In the third year of his reign, he [a]made a feast unto all his princes and his servants; the power of Persia and Media, the nobles and princes of the provinces, *being* before him:

4 When he shewed the riches of his glorious kingdom and the honour of his excellent majesty many days, *even* an hundred and fourscore days.

5 And when these days were expired, the king made a feast unto all the people that were present in Shushan the palace, both unto great and small, seven days, in the court of the garden of the king's palace;

6 *Where were* white, green, and blue, *hangings,* fastened with cords of fine linen and purple to silver rings and pillars of marble: [a]the beds *were of* gold and silver, upon a pavement of red, and blue, and white, and black, marble.

7 And they gave *them* drink in vessels of gold, (the vessels being diverse one from another,) and royal wine in abundance, [a]according to the state of the king.

8 And the drinking *was* according to the law; none did compel: for so the king had appointed to all the officers of his house, that they should do according to every man's pleasure.

9 Also Vashti the queen made a feast for the women *in* the royal house which *belonged* to king Ahasuerus.

10 On the seventh day, when the heart of the king was merry with wine, he commanded Mehuman, Biztha, [a]Harbona, Bigtha, and Abagtha, Zethar, and Carcas, the seven chamberlains that served in the presence of Ahasuerus the king,

11 To bring Vashti the queen before the king with the crown royal, to shew the people and the princes her beauty: for she *was* fair to look on.

12 But the queen Vashti refused to come at the king's commandment by *his* chamberlains: therefore was the king very wroth, and his anger burned in him.

13 Then the king said to the [a]wise men, [b]which knew the times, (for so *was* the king's manner toward all that knew law and judgment:

14 And the next unto him *was* Carshena, Shethar, Admatha, Tarshish, Meres, Marsena, *and* Memucan, the [a]seven princes of Persia and Media, [b]which saw the king's face, *and* which sat the first in the kingdom;)

15 What shall we do unto the queen Vashti according to law, because she hath not performed the commandment of the king Ahasuerus by the chamberlains?

16 And Memucan answered before the king and the princes, Vashti the queen hath not done wrong to the king only, but also to all the princes,

CHAPTER 1

1 [a]Ezra 4:6; Dan. 9:1
[b]Esth. 8:9
[c]Dan. 6:1
2 [a]1 Kin. 1:46
[b]Neh. 1:1; Dan. 8:2
3 [a]Gen. 40:20; Esth. 2:18
6 [a]Esth. 7:8; Ezek. 23:41; Amos 2:8; 6:4
7 [a]Esth. 2:18
10 [a]Esth. 7:9
13 [a]Jer. 10:7; Dan. 2:12; Matt. 2:1
[b]1 Chr. 12:32
14 [a]Ezra 7:14
[b]2 Kin. 25:19; [Matt. 18:10]

*________

1:1 Generally identified with Xerxes I (485–464 B.C.)
1:2 Or *Susa*

NKJV

THE BOOK OF

ESTHER

The King Dethrones Queen Vashti

1 Now it came to pass in the days of [a]Ahasuerus* (this *was* the Ahasuerus who reigned [b]over one hundred and twenty-seven provinces, [c]from India to Ethiopia),

2 in those days when King Ahasuerus [a]sat on the throne of his kingdom, which *was* in [b]Shushan* the citadel,

3 *that* in the third year of his reign he [a]made a feast for all his officials and servants—the powers of Persia and Media, the nobles, and the princes of the provinces *being* before him—

4 when he showed the riches of his glorious kingdom and the splendor of his excellent majesty for many days, one hundred and eighty days *in all.*

5 And when these days were completed, the king made a feast lasting seven days for all the people who were present in Shushan the citadel, from great to small, in the court of the garden of the king's palace.

6 *There were* white and blue linen *curtains* fastened with cords of fine linen and purple on silver rods and marble pillars; *and the* [a]couches *were* of gold and silver on a *mosaic* pavement of alabaster, turquoise, and white and black marble.

7 And they served drinks in golden vessels, each vessel being different from the other, with royal wine in abundance, [a]according to the generosity of the king.

8 In accordance with the law, the drinking was not compulsory; for so the king had ordered all the officers of his household, that they should do according to each man's pleasure.

9 Queen Vashti also made a feast for the women *in* the royal palace which *belonged* to King Ahasuerus.

10 On the seventh day, when the heart of the king was merry with wine, he commanded Mehuman, Biztha, [a]Harbona, Bigtha, Abagtha, Zethar, and Carcas, seven eunuchs who served in the presence of King Ahasuerus,

11 to bring Queen Vashti before the king, *wearing* her royal crown, in order to show her beauty to the people and the officials, for she *was* beautiful to behold.

12 But Queen Vashti refused to come at the king's command *brought* by *his* eunuchs; therefore the king was furious, and his anger burned within him.

13 Then the king said to the [a]wise men [b]who understood the times (for this *was* the king's manner toward all who knew law and justice,

14 those closest to him *being* Carshena, Shethar, Admatha, Tarshish, Meres, Marsena, and Memucan, the [a]seven princes of Persia and Media, [b]who had access to the king's presence, *and* who ranked highest in the kingdom):

15 "What *shall we* do to Queen Vashti, according to law, because she did not obey the command of King Ahasuerus *brought to her* by the eunuchs?"

16 And Memucan answered before the king and the princes: "Queen Vashti has not only wronged the king, but also all the princes, and

KJV

and to all the people that *are* in all the provinces of the king Ahasuerus.

17 For *this* deed of the queen shall come abroad unto all women, so that they shall [a]despise their husbands in their eyes, when it shall be reported, The king Ahasuerus commanded Vashti the queen to be brought in before him, but she came not.

18 *Likewise* shall the ladies of Persia and Media say this day unto all the king's princes, which have heard of the deed of the queen. Thus *shall there arise* too much contempt and wrath.

19 If it please the king, let there go a royal commandment from him, and let it be written among the laws of the Persians and the Medes, that it be [a]not altered, That Vashti come no more before king Ahasuerus; and let the king give her royal estate unto another that is better than she.

20 And when the king's decree which he shall make shall be published throughout all his empire, (for it is great,) all the wives shall [a]give to their husbands honour, both to great and small.

21 And the saying pleased the king and the princes; and the king did according to the word of Memucan:

22 For he sent letters into all the king's provinces, [a]into every province according to the writing thereof, and to every people after their language, that every man should [b]bear rule in his own house, and that *it* should be published according to the language of every people.

Esther Becomes Queen

2 After these things, when the wrath of king Ahasuerus was appeased, he remembered Vashti, and [a]what she had done, and what was decreed against her.

2 Then said the king's servants that ministered unto him, Let there be fair young virgins sought for the king:

3 And let the king appoint officers in all the provinces of his kingdom, that they may gather together all the fair young virgins unto Shushan the palace, to the house of the women, unto the custody of Hege the king's chamberlain, keeper of the women; and let their things for purification be given *them:*

4 And let the maiden which pleaseth the king be queen instead of Vashti. And the thing pleased the king; and he did so.

5 *Now* in Shushan the palace there was a certain Jew, whose name *was* Mordecai, the son of Jair, the son of Shimei, the son of [a]Kish, a Benjamite;

6 [a]Who had been carried away from Jerusalem with the captivity which had been carried away with Jeconiah king of Judah, whom Nebuchadnezzar the king of Babylon had carried away.

7 And he brought up Hadassah, that *is,* Esther, [a]his uncle's daughter: for she had neither father nor mother, and the maid *was* fair and beautiful; whom Mordecai, when her father and mother were dead, took for his own daughter.

8 So it came to pass, when the king's commandment and his decree was heard, and when many maidens were [a]gathered together unto Shushan the palace, to the custody of Hegai, that Esther was brought also unto the king's house, to the custody of Hegai, keeper of the women.

9 And the maiden pleased him, and she obtained kindness of him; and he speedily gave her her [a]things for purification, with such things as belonged to her, and seven maidens, *which were* meet to be given her, out of the king's house: and he preferred her and her maids unto the best *place* of the house of the women.

10 [a]Esther had not shewed her people nor her kindred: for Mordecai had charged her that she should not shew *it.*

11 And Mordecai walked every day before the court of the women's house, to know how Esther did, and what should become of her.

17 [a][Eph. 5:33]
19 [a]Esth. 8:8; Dan. 6:8
20 [a][Eph. 5:33; Col. 3:18; 1 Pet. 3:1]
22 [a]Esth. 3:12; 8:9
[b][Eph. 5:22–24; 1 Tim. 2:12]

CHAPTER 2

1 [a]Esth. 1:19, 20
5 [a]1 Sam. 9:1
6 [a]2 Kin. 24:14, 15; 2 Chr. 36:10, 20; Jer. 24:1
7 [a]Esth. 2:15
8 [a]Esth. 2:3
9 [a]Esth. 2:3, 12
10 [a]Esth. 2:20

NKJV

all the people who *are* in all the provinces of King Ahasuerus.

17 "For the queen's behavior will become known to all women, so that they will [a]despise their husbands in their eyes, when they report, 'King Ahasuerus commanded Queen Vashti to be brought in before him, but she did not come.'

18 "This very day the *noble* ladies of Persia and Media will say to all the king's officials that they have heard of the behavior of the queen. Thus *there will be* excessive contempt and wrath.

19 "If it pleases the king, let a royal decree go out from him, and let it be recorded in the laws of the Persians and the Medes, so that it will [a]not be altered, that Vashti shall come no more before King Ahasuerus; and let the king give her royal position to another who is better than she.

20 "When the king's decree which he will make is proclaimed throughout all his empire (for it is great), all wives will [a]honor their husbands, both great and small."

21 And the reply pleased the king and the princes, and the king did according to the word of Memucan.

22 Then he sent letters to all the king's provinces, [a]to each province in its own script, and to every people in their own language, that each man should [b]be master in his own house, and speak in the language of his own people.

Esther Becomes Queen

2 After these things, when the wrath of King Ahasuerus subsided, he remembered Vashti, [a]what she had done, and what had been decreed against her.

2 Then the king's servants who attended him said: "Let beautiful young virgins be sought for the king;

3 "and let the king appoint officers in all the provinces of his kingdom, that they may gather all the beautiful young virgins to Shushan the citadel, into the women's quarters, under the custody of *Hegai the king's eunuch, custodian of the women. And let beauty preparations be given *them.*

4 "Then let the young woman who pleases the king be queen instead of Vashti." This thing pleased the king, and he did so.

5 In Shushan the citadel there was a certain Jew whose name *was* Mordecai the son of Jair, the son of Shimei, the son of [a]Kish, a Benjamite.

6 [a]*Kish** had been carried away from Jerusalem with the captives who had been captured with *Jeconiah king of Judah, whom Nebuchadnezzar the king of Babylon had carried away.

7 And *Mordecai* had brought up Hadassah, that *is,* Esther, [a]his uncle's daughter, for she had neither father nor mother. The young woman *was* lovely and beautiful. When her father and mother died, Mordecai took her as his own daughter.

8 So it was, when the king's command and decree were heard, and when many young women were [a]gathered at Shushan the citadel, *under* the custody of Hegai, that Esther also was taken to the king's palace, into the care of Hegai the custodian of the women.

9 Now the young woman pleased him, and she obtained his favor; so he readily gave [a]beauty preparations to her, besides her allowance. Then seven choice maidservants were provided for her from the king's palace, and he moved her and her maidservants to the best *place* in the house of the women.

10 [a]Esther had not revealed her people or family, for Mordecai had charged her not to reveal *it.*

11 And every day Mordecai paced in front of the court of the women's quarters, to learn of Esther's welfare and what was happening to her.

2:3 Heb. *Hege*
2:6 Lit. *Who* • *Jehoiachin,* 2 Kin. 24:6

KJV

12 Now when every maid's turn was come
to go in to king Ahasuerus, after that she had been
twelve months, according to the manner of the
women, (for so were the days of their purifications
accomplished, *to wit*, six months with oil of
myrrh, and six months with sweet odours, and
with *other* things for the purifying of the women;)
13 Then thus came *every* maiden unto the
king; whatsoever she desired was given her to
go with her out of the house of the women unto
the king's house.
14 In the evening she went, and on the morrow she returned into the second house of the
women, to the custody of Shaashgaz, the king's
chamberlain, which kept the concubines: she
came in unto the king no more, except the king
delighted in her, and that she were called by
name.
15 Now when the turn of Esther, [a]the daughter of Abihail the uncle of Mordecai, who had
taken her for his daughter, was come to go in
unto the king, she required nothing but what Hegai the king's chamberlain, the keeper of the
women, appointed. And Esther [b]obtained favour
in the sight of all them that looked upon her.
16 So Esther was taken unto king Ahasuerus
into his house royal in the tenth month, which *is*
the month Tebeth, in the seventh year of his reign.
17 And the king loved Esther above all the
women, and she obtained grace and favour in his
sight more than all the virgins; so that he set the
royal [a]crown upon her head, and made her queen
instead of Vashti.
18 Then the king [a]made a great feast unto
all his princes and his servants, *even* Esther's
feast; and he made a release to the provinces, and
gave gifts, according to the state of the king.

Mordecai Discovers a Plot

19 And when the virgins were gathered together the second time, then Mordecai sat in the
king's gate.
20 [a]Esther had not *yet* shewed her kindred
nor her people; as Mordecai had charged her: for
Esther did the commandment of Mordecai, like
as when she was brought up with him.
21 In those days, while Mordecai sat in the
king's gate, two of the king's chamberlains,
Bigthan and Teresh, of those which kept the door,
were wroth, and sought to lay hand on the king
Ahasuerus.
22 And the thing was known to Mordecai,
[a]who told *it* unto Esther the queen; and Esther
certified the king *thereof* in Mordecai's name.
23 And when inquisition was made of the
matter, it was found out; therefore they were both
hanged on a tree: and it was written in [a]the book
of the chronicles before the king.

Haman's Conspiracy Against the Jews

3 After these things did king Ahasuerus promote Haman the son of Hammedatha the
[a]Agagite, and [b]advanced him, and set his seat
above all the princes that *were* with him.
2 And all the king's servants, that *were* [a]in
the king's gate, bowed, and reverenced Haman:
for the king had so commanded concerning him.
But Mordecai [b]bowed not, nor did *him* reverence.
3 Then the king's servants, which *were* in
the king's gate, said unto Mordecai, Why trans-
gressest thou the [a]king's commandment?
4 Now it came to pass, when they spake
daily unto him, and he hearkened not unto them,
that they told Haman, to see whether Mordecai's
matters would stand: for he had told them that
he *was* a Jew.
5 And when Haman saw that Mordecai
[a]bowed not, nor did him reverence, then was Haman [b]full of wrath.
6 And he thought scorn to lay hands on
Mordecai alone; for they had shewed him the peo-

15 [a]Esth. 2:7; 9:29 [b]Esth. 5:2, 8
17 [a]Esth. 1:11
18 [a]Esth. 1:3
20 [a]Esth. 2:10; [Prov. 22:6]
22 [a]Esth. 6:1, 2
23 [a]Esth. 6:1

CHAPTER 3
1 [a]Num. 24:7; 1 Sam. 15:8 [b]Esth. 5:11
2 [a]Esth. 2:19, 21; 5:9 [b]Esth. 3:5; Ps. 15:4
3 [a]Esth. 3:2
5 [a]Esth. 3:2; 5:9 [b]Dan. 3:19

NKJV

12 Each young woman's turn came to go in
to King Ahasuerus after she had completed twelve
months' preparation, according to the regulations
for the women, for thus were the days of their
preparation apportioned: six months with oil of
myrrh, and six months with perfumes and preparations for beautifying women.
13 Thus *prepared, each* young woman went
to the king, and she was given whatever she desired to take with her from the women's quarters
to the king's palace.
14 In the evening she went, and in the morning she returned to the second house of the
women, to the custody of Shaashgaz, the king's
eunuch who kept the concubines. She would not
go in to the king again unless the king delighted
in her and called for her by name.
15 Now when the turn came for Esther [a]the
daughter of Abihail the uncle of Mordecai, who
had taken her as his daughter, to go in to the king,
she requested nothing but what Hegai the king's
eunuch, the custodian of the women, advised. And
Esther [b]obtained favor in the sight of all who saw
her.
16 So Esther was taken to King Ahasuerus,
into his royal palace, in the tenth month, which
is the month of Tebeth, in the seventh year of
his reign.
17 The king loved Esther more than all the
other women, and she obtained grace and favor
in his sight more than all the virgins; so he set
the royal [a]crown upon her head and made her
queen instead of Vashti.
18 Then the king [a]made a great feast, the
Feast of Esther, for all his officials and servants;
and he proclaimed a holiday in the provinces and
gave gifts according to the generosity of a king.

Mordecai Discovers a Plot

19 When virgins were gathered together a
second time, Mordecai sat within the king's gate.
20 [a]*Now* Esther had not revealed her family
and her people, just as Mordecai had charged her,
for Esther obeyed the command of Mordecai as
when she was brought up by him.
21 In those days, while Mordecai sat within
the king's gate, two of the king's eunuchs, Bigthan
and Teresh, doorkeepers, became furious and
sought to lay hands on King Ahasuerus.
22 So the matter became known to Mordecai,
[a]who told Queen Esther, and Esther informed the
king in Mordecai's name.
23 And when an inquiry was made into the
matter, it was confirmed, and both were hanged
on a gallows; and it was written in [a]the book of
the chronicles in the presence of the king.

Haman's Conspiracy Against the Jews

3 After these things King Ahasuerus promoted
Haman, the son of Hammedatha the [a]Agagite,
and [b]advanced him and set his seat above all the
princes who *were* with him.
2 And all the king's servants who *were*
[a]within the king's gate bowed and paid homage
to Haman, for so the king had commanded concerning him. But Mordecai [b]would not bow or pay
homage.
3 Then the king's servants who *were* within
the king's gate said to Mordecai, "Why do you
transgress the [a]king's command?"
4 Now it happened, when they spoke to him
daily and he would not listen to them, that they
told *it* to Haman, to see whether Mordecai's words
would stand; for *Mordecai* had told them that he
was a Jew.
5 When Haman saw that Mordecai [a]did not
bow or pay him homage, Haman was [b]filled with
wrath.
6 But he disdained to lay hands on Mordecai
alone, for they had told him of the people of Mor-

KJV

ple of Mordecai: wherefore Haman [a]sought to destroy all the Jews that *were* throughout the whole kingdom of Ahasuerus, *even* the people of Mordecai.

7 In the first month, that *is*, the month Nisan, in the twelfth year of king Ahasuerus, [a]they cast Pur, that *is*, the lot, before Haman from day to day, and from month to month, *to* the twelfth *month*, that *is*, the month Adar.

8 And Haman said unto king Ahasuerus, There is a certain people scattered abroad and dispersed among the people in all the provinces of thy kingdom; and [a]their laws *are* diverse from all people; neither keep they the king's laws: therefore it *is* not for the king's profit to suffer them.

9 If it please the king, let it be written that they may be destroyed: and I will pay ten thousand talents of silver to the hands of those that have the charge of the business, to bring *it* into the king's treasuries.

10 And the king [a]took [b]his ring from his hand, and gave it unto Haman the son of Hammedatha the Agagite, the Jews' [c]enemy.

11 And the king said unto Haman, The silver *is* given to thee, the people also, to do with them as it seemeth good to thee.

12 [a]Then were the king's scribes called on the thirteenth day of the first month, and there was written according to all that Haman had commanded unto the king's lieutenants, and to the governors that *were* over every province, and to the rulers of every people of every province [b]according to the writing thereof, and *to* every people after their language; [c]in the name of king Ahasuerus was it written, and sealed with the king's ring.

13 And the letters were [a]sent by posts into all the king's provinces, to destroy, to kill, and to cause to perish, all Jews, both young and old, little children and women, [b]in one day, *even* upon the thirteenth *day* of the twelfth month, which *is* the month Adar, and [c]*to take* the spoil of them for a prey.

14 [a]The copy of the writing for a commandment to be given in every province was published unto all people, that they should be ready against that day.

15 The posts went out, being hastened by the king's commandment, and the decree was given in Shushan the palace. And the king and Haman sat down to drink; but [a]the city Shushan was perplexed.

Esther Agrees to Help the Jews

4 When Mordecai perceived all that was done, Mordecai [a]rent his clothes, and put on sackcloth [b]with ashes, and went out into the midst of the city, and [c]cried with a loud and a bitter cry;

2 And came even before the king's gate: for none *might* enter into the king's gate clothed with sackcloth.

3 And in every province, whithersoever the king's commandment and his decree came, *there was* great mourning among the Jews, and fasting, and weeping, and wailing; and many lay in sackcloth and ashes.

4 So Esther's maids and her chamberlains came and told *it* her. Then was the queen exceedingly grieved; and she sent raiment to clothe Mordecai, and to take away his sackcloth from him: but he received *it* not.

5 Then called Esther for Hatach, *one* of the king's chamberlains, whom he had appointed to attend upon her, and gave him a commandment to Mordecai, to know what it *was*, and why it *was*.

6 So Hatach went forth to Mordecai unto the street of the city, which *was* before the king's gate.

7 And Mordecai told him of all that had happened unto him, and of [a]the sum of the money

NKJV

decai. Instead, Haman [a]sought to destroy all the Jews who *were* throughout the whole kingdom of Ahasuerus—the people of Mordecai.

7 In the first month, which is the month of Nisan, in the twelfth year of King Ahasuerus, [a]they cast Pur (that *is*, the lot), before Haman to determine the day and the *month, *until *it fell on the* twelfth *month*, which *is* the month of Adar.

8 Then Haman said to King Ahasuerus, "There is a certain people scattered and dispersed among the people in all the provinces of your kingdom; [a]their laws *are* different from all *other* people's, and they do not keep the king's laws. Therefore it *is* not fitting for the king to let them remain.

9 "If it pleases the king, let *a decree* be written that they be destroyed, and I will pay ten thousand talents of silver into the hands of those who do the work, to bring *it* into the king's treasuries."

10 So the king [a]took [b]his signet ring from his hand and gave it to Haman, the son of Hammedatha the Agagite, the [c]enemy of the Jews.

11 And the king said to Haman, "The money and the people *are* given to you, to do with them as seems good to you."

12 [a]Then the king's scribes were called on the thirteenth day of the first month, and *a decree* was written according to all that Haman commanded—to the king's satraps, to the governors who *were* over each province, to the officials of all people, to every province [b]according to its script, and to every people in their language. [c]In the name of King Ahasuerus it was written, and sealed with the king's signet ring.

13 And the letters were [a]sent by couriers into all the king's provinces, to destroy, to kill, and to annihilate all the Jews, both young and old, little children and women, [b]in one day, on the thirteenth *day* of the twelfth *month*, which *is* the month of Adar, and [c]to plunder their *possessions.

14 [a]A copy of the document was to be issued as law in every province, being published for all people, that they should be ready for that day.

15 The couriers went out, hastened by the king's command; and the decree was proclaimed in Shushan the citadel. So the king and Haman sat down to drink, but [a]the city of Shushan was perplexed.

Esther Agrees to Help the Jews

4 When Mordecai learned all that had happened, he [a]tore his clothes and put on sackcloth [b]and ashes, and went out into the midst of the city. He [c]cried out with a loud and bitter cry.

2 He went as far as the front of the king's gate, for no one *might* enter the king's gate clothed with sackcloth.

3 And in every province where the king's command and decree arrived, *there was* great mourning among the Jews, with fasting, weeping, and wailing; and many lay in sackcloth and ashes.

4 So Esther's maids and eunuchs came and told her, and the queen was deeply distressed. Then she sent garments to clothe Mordecai and take his sackcloth away from him, but he would not accept *them*.

5 Then Esther called Hathach, *one* of the king's eunuchs whom he had appointed to attend her, and she gave him a command concerning Mordecai, to learn what and why this *was*.

6 So Hathach went out to Mordecai in the city square that *was* in front of the king's gate.

7 And Mordecai told him all that had happened to him, and [a]the sum of money that Haman

---

6 [a]Ps. 83:4; [Rev. 12:1–17] **7** [a]Esth. 9:24–26 **8** [a]Ezra 4:12–15; Acts 16:20, 21 **10** [a]Gen. 41:42 [b]Esth. 8:2, 8 [c]Esth. 7:6 **12** [a]Esth. 8:9 [b]Esth. 1:22 [c]1 Kin. 21:8; Esth. 8:8–10 **13** [a]2 Chr. 30:6; Esth. 8:10, 14 [b]Esth. 8:12 [c]Esth. 8:11; 9:10 **14** [a]Esth. 8:13, 14 **15** [a]Esth. 8:15; [Prov. 29:2]

CHAPTER 4

1 [a]2 Sam. 1:11; Esth. 3:8–10; Jon. 3:5, 6 [b]Josh. 7:6; Ezek. 27:30 [c]Gen. 27:34 **7** [a]Esth. 3:9

*

3:7 LXX adds *to destroy the people of Mordecai in one day;* Vg. adds *the nation of the Jews should be destroyed* • So with MT, Vg.; LXX *and the lot fell on the fourteenth of the month* **3:13** LXX adds the text of the letter here

KJV

that Haman had promised to pay to the king's treasuries for the Jews, to destroy them.

8 Also he gave him [a]the copy of the writing of the decree that was given at Shushan to destroy them, to shew *it* unto Esther, and to declare *it* unto her, and to charge her that she should go in unto the king, to make supplication unto him, and to make request before him for her people.

9 And Hatach came and told Esther the words of Mordecai.

10 Again Esther spake unto Hatach, and gave him commandment unto Mordecai;

11 All the king's servants, and the people of the king's provinces, do know, that whosoever, whether man or woman, shall come unto the king into [a]the inner court, who is not called, [b]*there is* one law of his to put *him* to death, except such [c]to whom the king shall hold out the golden sceptre, that he may live: but I have not been [d]called to come in unto the king these thirty days.

12 And they told to Mordecai Esther's words.

13 Then Mordecai commanded to answer Esther, Think not with thyself that thou shalt escape in the king's house, more than all the Jews.

14 For if thou altogether holdest thy peace at this time, *then* shall there enlargement and deliverance arise to the Jews from another place; but thou and thy father's house shall be destroyed: and who knoweth whether thou art come to the kingdom for *such* a time as this?

15 Then Esther bade *them* return Mordecai *this answer,*

16 Go, gather together all the Jews that are present in Shushan, and fast ye for me, and neither eat nor drink [a]three days, night or day: I also and my maidens will fast likewise; and so will I go in unto the king, which *is* not according to the law: [b]and if I perish, I perish.

17 So Mordecai went his way, and did according to all that Esther had commanded him.

Esther's Banquet

5 Now it came to pass [a]on the third day, that Esther put on *her* royal *apparel,* and stood in [b]the inner court of the king's house, over against the king's house: and the king sat upon his royal throne in the royal house, over against the gate of the house.

2 And it was so, when the king saw Esther the queen standing in the court, *that* [a]she obtained favour in his sight: and [b]the king held out to Esther the golden sceptre that *was* in his hand. So Esther drew near, and touched the top of the sceptre.

3 Then said the king unto her, What wilt thou, queen Esther? and what *is* thy request? [a]it shall be even given thee to the half of the kingdom.

4 And Esther answered, If *it seem* good unto the king, let the king and Haman come this day unto the banquet that I have prepared for him.

5 Then the king said, Cause Haman to make haste, that he may do as Esther hath said. So the king and Haman came to the banquet that Esther had prepared.

6 [a]And the king said unto Esther at the banquet of wine, [b]What *is* thy petition? and it shall be granted thee: and what *is* thy request? even to the half of the kingdom it shall be performed.

7 Then answered Esther, and said, My petition and my request *is;*

8 If I have found favour in the sight of the king, and if it please the king to grant my petition, and to perform my request, let the king and Haman come to the [a]banquet that I shall prepare for them, and I will do to morrow as the king hath said.

Haman's Plot Against Mordecai

9 Then went Haman forth that day [a]joyful and with a glad heart: but when Haman saw Mordecai in the king's gate, [b]that he stood not up,

8 [a]Esth. 3:14, 15
11 [a]Esth. 5:1; 6:4 [b]Dan. 2:9 [c]Esth. 5:2; 8:4 [d]Esth. 2:14
16 [a]Esth. 5:1 [b]Gen. 43:14

CHAPTER 5

1 [a]Esth. 4:16 [b]Esth. 4:11; 6:4
2 [a][Prov. 21:1] [b]Esth. 4:11; 8:4
3 [a]Esth. 7:2; Mark 6:23
6 [a]Esth. 7:2 [b]Esth. 9:12
8 [a]Esth. 6:14
9 [a][Job 20:5; Luke 6:25] [b]Esth. 3:5

*

4:17 LXX adds a prayer of Mordecai here
5:1 LXX adds many extra details in vv. 1, 2

NKJV

had promised to pay into the king's treasuries to destroy the Jews.

8 He also gave him [a]a copy of the written decree for their destruction, which was given at Shushan, that he might show it to Esther and explain it to her, and that he might command her to go in to the king to make supplication to him and plead before him for her people.

9 So Hathach returned and told Esther the words of Mordecai.

10 Then Esther spoke to Hathach, and gave him a command for Mordecai:

11 "All the king's servants and the people of the king's provinces know that any man or woman who goes into [a]the inner court to the king, who has not been called, [b]*he has* but one law: put *all* to death, except the one [c]to whom the king holds out the golden scepter, that he may live. Yet I myself have not been [d]called to go in to the king these thirty days."

12 So they told Mordecai Esther's words.

13 And Mordecai told *them* to answer Esther: "Do not think in your heart that you will escape in the king's palace any more than all the other Jews.

14 "For if you remain completely silent at this time, relief and deliverance will arise for the Jews from another place, but you and your father's house will perish. Yet who knows whether you have come to the kingdom for *such* a time as this?"

15 Then Esther told *them* to reply to Mordecai:

16 "Go, gather all the Jews who are present in Shushan, and fast for me; neither eat nor drink for [a]three days, night or day. My maids and I will fast likewise. And so I will go to the king, which *is* against the law; [b]and if I perish, I perish!"

17 So Mordecai went his way and did according to all that Esther commanded *him.

Esther's Banquet

5 Now it happened [a]on the third day that Esther put on *her* royal *robes* and stood in [b]the inner court of the king's palace, across from the king's house, while the king sat on his royal throne in the royal house, facing the entrance of the *house.

2 So it was, when the king saw Queen Esther standing in the court, *that* [a]she found favor in his sight, and [b]the king held out to Esther the golden scepter that *was* in his hand. Then Esther went near and touched the top of the scepter.

3 And the king said to her, "What do you wish, Queen Esther? What *is* your request? [a]It shall be given to you—up to half the kingdom!"

4 So Esther answered, "If it pleases the king, let the king and Haman come today to the banquet that I have prepared for him."

5 Then the king said, "Bring Haman quickly, that he may do as Esther has said." So the king and Haman went to the banquet that Esther had prepared.

6 At the banquet of wine [a]the king said to Esther, [b]"What *is* your petition? It shall be granted you. What *is* your request, up to half the kingdom? It shall be done!"

7 Then Esther answered and said, "My petition and request *is this:*

8 "If I have found favor in the sight of the king, and if it pleases the king to grant my petition and fulfill my request, then let the king and Haman come to the [a]banquet which I will prepare for them, and tomorrow I will do as the king has said."

Haman's Plot Against Mordecai

9 So Haman went out that day [a]joyful and with a glad heart; but when Haman saw Mordecai in the king's gate, and [b]that he did not stand or

KJV

nor moved for him, he was full of indignation
against Mordecai.
10 Nevertheless Haman [a]refrained himself:
and when he came home, he sent and called for
his friends, and Zeresh his wife.
11 And Haman told them of the glory of his
riches, and [a]the multitude of his children, and all
the things wherein the king had promoted him,
and how he had [b]advanced him above the princes
and servants of the king.
12 Haman said moreover, Yea, Esther the
queen did let no man come in with the king unto
the banquet that she had prepared but myself; and
to morrow am I invited unto her also with the
king.
13 Yet all this availeth me nothing, so long
as I see Mordecai the Jew sitting at the king's
gate.
14 Then said Zeresh his wife and all his
friends unto him, Let a [a]gallows be made of fifty
cubits high, and to morrow [b]speak thou unto the
king that Mordecai may be hanged thereon: then
go thou in merrily with the king unto the banquet.
And the thing pleased Haman; and he caused [c]the
gallows to be made.

The King Honors Mordecai

6 On that night could not the king sleep, and
he commanded to bring [a]the book of records
of the chronicles; and they were read before the
king.
2 And it was found written, that Mordecai
had told of Bigthana and Teresh, two of the king's
chamberlains, the keepers of the door, who
sought to lay hand on the king Ahasuerus.
3 And the king said, What honour and dignity hath been done to Mordecai for this? Then
said the king's servants that ministered unto
him,There is nothing done for him.
4 And the king said, Who *is* in the court?
Now Haman was come into [a]the outward court
of the king's house, [b]to speak unto the king to
hang Mordecai on the gallows that he had prepared for him.
5 And the king's servants said unto him, Behold, Haman standeth in the court. And the king
said, Let him come in.
6 So Haman came in. And the king said unto
him, What shall be done unto the man whom the
king delighteth to honour? Now Haman thought
in his heart, To whom would the king delight to
do honour more than to [a]myself?
7 And Haman answered the king, For the
man whom the king delighteth to honour,
8 Let the royal apparel be brought which
the king *useth* to wear, and [a]the horse that the
king rideth upon, and the crown royal which is
set upon his head:
9 And let this apparel and horse be delivered to the hand of one of the king's most noble
princes, that they may array the man *withal*
whom the king delighteth to honour, and bring
him on horseback through the street of the city,
[a]and proclaim before him, Thus shall it be done
to the man whom the king delighteth to honour.
10 Then the king said to Haman, Make haste,
and take the apparel and the horse, as thou hast
said, and do even so to Mordecai the Jew, that
sitteth at the king's gate: let nothing fail of all
that thou hast spoken.
11 Then took Haman the apparel and the
horse, and arrayed Mordecai, and brought him
on horseback through the street of the city, and
proclaimed before him, Thus shall it be done unto
the man whom the king delighteth to honour.
12 And Mordecai came again to the king's
gate. But Haman [a]hasted to his house mourning,
[b]and having his head covered.
13 And Haman told Zeresh his wife and all
his friends every *thing* that had befallen him.
Then said his wise men and Zeresh his wife unto
him, If Mordecai *be* of the seed of the Jews, before

10 [a]2 Sam. 13:22
11 [a]Esth. 9:7–10 [b]Esth. 3:1
14 [a]Esth. 7:9 [b]Esth. 6:4 [c]Esth. 7:10

CHAPTER 6

1 [a]Esth. 2:23; 10:2
4 [a]Esth. 5:1 [b]Esth. 5:14
6 [a][Prov. 16:18; 18:12]
8 [a]1 Kin. 1:33
9 [a]Gen. 41:43
12 [a]2 Chr. 26:20 [b]2 Sam. 15:30; Jer. 14:3, 4

NKJV

tremble before him, he was filled with indignation
against Mordecai.
10 Nevertheless Haman [a]restrained himself
and went home, and he sent and called for his
friends and his wife Zeresh.
11 Then Haman told them of his great riches,
[a]the multitude of his children, everything in which
the king had promoted him, and how he had [b]ad-
vanced him above the officials and servants of the
king.
12 Moreover Haman said, "Besides, Queen
Esther invited no one but me to come in with the
king to the banquet that she prepared; and tomorrow I am again invited by her, along with the king.
13 "Yet all this avails me nothing, so long
as I see Mordecai the Jew sitting at the king's
gate."
14 Then his wife Zeresh and all his friends
said to him, "Let a [a]gallows be made, fifty cubits
high, and in the morning [b]suggest to the king that
Mordecai be hanged on it; then go merrily with
the king to the banquet." And the thing pleased
Haman; so he had [c]the gallows made.

The King Honors Mordecai

6 That night the king could not sleep. So one
was commanded to bring [a]the book of the records of the chronicles; and they were read before
the king.
2 And it was found written that Mordecai
had told of Bigthana and Teresh, two of the king's
eunuchs, the doorkeepers who had sought to lay
hands on King Ahasuerus.
3 Then the king said, "What honor or dignity has been bestowed on Mordecai for this?"
And the king's servants who attended him said,
"Nothing has been done for him."
4 So the king said, "Who *is* in the court?"
Now Haman had *just* entered [a]the outer court of
the king's palace [b]to suggest that the king hang
Mordecai on the gallows that he had prepared for
him.
5 The king's servants said to him, "Haman
is there, standing in the court." And the king said,
"Let him come in."
6 So Haman came in, and the king asked
him, "What shall be done for the man whom the
king delights to honor?" Now Haman thought in
his heart, "Whom would the king delight to honor
more than [a]me?"
7 And Haman answered the king, "*For* the
man whom the king delights to honor,
8 "let a royal robe be brought which the
king has worn, and [a]a horse on which the king
has ridden, which has a royal crest placed on its
head.
9 "Then let this robe and horse be delivered
to the hand of one of the king's most noble
princes, that he may array the man whom the king
delights to honor. Then parade him on horseback
through the city square, [a]and proclaim before
him: 'Thus shall it be done to the man whom the
king delights to honor!' "
10 Then the king said to Haman, "Hurry,
take the robe and the horse, as you have suggested, and do so for Mordecai the Jew who sits
within the king's gate! Leave nothing undone of
all that you have spoken."
11 So Haman took the robe and the horse,
arrayed Mordecai and led him on horseback
through the city square, and proclaimed before
him, "Thus shall it be done to the man whom the
king delights to honor!"
12 Afterward Mordecai went back to the
king's gate. But Haman [a]hurried to his house,
mourning [b]and with his head covered.
13 When Haman told his wife Zeresh and all
his friends everything that had happened to him,
his wise men and his wife Zeresh said to him,
"If Mordecai, before whom you have begun to fall,

KJV

whom thou hast begun to fall, thou shalt not prevail against [a]him, but shalt surely fall before him.
14 And while they *were* yet talking with him,
came the king's chamberlains, and hasted to bring
Haman unto [a]the banquet that Esther had prepared.

Haman Hanged Instead of Mordecai

7 So the king and Haman came to banquet with
Esther the queen.
2 And the king said again unto Esther on
the second day [a]at the banquet of wine, What *is*
thy petition, queen Esther? and it shall be granted
thee: and what *is* thy request? and it shall be performed, *even* to the half of the kingdom.
3 Then Esther the queen answered and said,
If I have found favour in thy sight, O king, and
if it please the king, let my life be given me at
my petition, and my people at my request:
4 For we are [a]sold, I and my people, to be
destroyed, to be slain, and to perish. But if we
had been sold for [b]bondmen and bondwomen, I
had held my tongue, although the enemy could
not countervail the king's damage.
5 Then the king Ahasuerus answered and
said unto Esther the queen, Who is he, and where
is he, that durst presume in his heart to do so?
6 And Esther said, The adversary and
[a]enemy *is* this wicked Haman. Then Haman was
afraid before the king and the queen.
7 And the king arising from the banquet of
wine in his wrath *went* into the palace garden:
and Haman stood up to make request for his life
to Esther the queen; for he saw that there was
evil determined against him by the king.
8 Then the king returned out of the palace
garden into the place of the banquet of wine; and
Haman was fallen upon [a]the bed whereon Esther
was. Then said the king, Will he force the queen
also before me in the house? As the word went
out of the king's mouth, they [b]covered Haman's
face.
9 And [a]Harbonah, one of the chamberlains,
said before the king, Behold also, [b]the gallows
fifty cubits high, which Haman had made for Mordecai, who had spoken [c]good for the king, standeth in the house of Haman. Then the king said,
Hang him thereon.
10 So [a]they [b]hanged Haman on the gallows
that he had prepared for Mordecai. Then was the
king's wrath pacified.

Esther Saves the Jews

8 On that day did the king Ahasuerus give the
house of Haman the Jews' [a]enemy unto
Esther the queen. And Mordecai came before the
king; for Esther had told [b]what he *was* unto her.
2 And the king took off [a]his ring, which he
had taken from Haman, and gave it unto Mordecai. And Esther set Mordecai over the house of
Haman.
3 And Esther spake yet again before the
king, and fell down at his feet, and besought him
with tears to put away the mischief of Haman the
Agagite, and his device that he had devised
against the Jews.
4 Then [a]the king held out the golden sceptre
toward Esther. So Esther arose, and stood before
the king,
5 And said, If it please the king, and if I have
found favour in his sight, and the thing *seem* right
before the king, and I *be* pleasing in his eyes, let
it be written to reverse the [a]letters devised by Haman the son of Hammedatha the Agagite, which
he wrote to destroy the Jews which *are* in all the
king's provinces:
6 For how can I endure to see [a]the evil that
shall come unto my people? or how can I endure
to see the destruction of my kindred?
7 Then the king Ahasuerus said unto Esther
the queen and to Mordecai the Jew, Behold, [a]I

---

13 [a][Gen. 12:3]; Zech. 2:8
14 [a]Esth. 5:8

CHAPTER 7

2 [a]Esth. 5:6
4 [a]Esth. 3:9; 4:7 [b]Deut. 28:68
6 [a]Esth. 3:10
8 [a]Esth. 1:6 [b]Job 9:24
9 [a]Esth. 1:10 [b]Esth. 5:14; [Ps. 7:16; Prov. 11:5, 6] [c]Esth. 6:2
10 [a][Ps. 7:16; 94:23; Prov. 11:5, 6] [b]Ps. 37:35, 36; Dan. 6:24

CHAPTER 8

1 [a]Esth. 7:6 [b]Esth. 2:7, 15
2 [a]Esth. 3:10
4 [a]Esth. 4:11; 5:2
5 [a]Esth. 3:13
6 [a]Neh. 2:3; Esth. 7:4; 9:1
7 [a]Esth. 8:1; Prov. 13:22

NKJV

is of Jewish descent, you will not prevail against
[a]him but will surely fall before him."
14 While they *were* still talking with him, the
king's eunuchs came, and hastened to bring
Haman to [a]the banquet which Esther had prepared.

Haman Hanged Instead of Mordecai

7 So the king and Haman went to dine with
Queen Esther.
2 And on the second day, [a]at the banquet
of wine, the king again said to Esther, "What *is*
your petition, Queen Esther? It shall be granted
you. And what *is* your request, up to half the kingdom? It shall be done!"
3 Then Queen Esther answered and said, "If
I have found favor in your sight, O king, and if it
pleases the king, let my life be given me at my
petition, and my people at my request.
4 "For we have been [a]sold, my people and
I, to be destroyed, to be killed, and to be annihi-
lated. Had we been sold as [b]male and female
slaves, I would have held my tongue, although
the enemy could never compensate for the king's
loss."
5 So King Ahasuerus answered and said to
Queen Esther, "Who is he, and where is he, who
would dare presume in his heart to do such a
thing?"
6 And Esther said, "The adversary and
[a]enemy *is* this wicked Haman!" So Haman was
terrified before the king and queen.
7 Then the king arose in his wrath from the
banquet of wine *and went* into the palace garden;
but Haman stood before Queen Esther, pleading
for his life, for he saw that evil was determined
against him by the king.
8 When the king returned from the palace
garden to the place of the banquet of wine, Haman
had fallen across [a]the couch where Esther *was*.
Then the king said, "Will he also assault the queen
while I *am* in the house?" As the word left the
king's mouth, they [b]covered Haman's face.
9 Now [a]Harbonah, one of the eunuchs, said
to the king, "Look! [b]The gallows, fifty cubits high,
which Haman made for Mordecai, who spoke
[c]good on the king's behalf, is standing at the
house of Haman." Then the king said, "Hang him
on it!"
10 So [a]they [b]hanged Haman on the gallows
that he had prepared for Mordecai. Then the
king's wrath subsided.

Esther Saves the Jews

8 On that day King Ahasuerus gave Queen
Esther the house of Haman, the [a]enemy of
the Jews. And Mordecai came before the king,
for Esther had told [b]how he *was related* to her.
2 So the king took off [a]his signet ring, which
he had taken from Haman, and gave it to Mordecai; and Esther appointed Mordecai over the
house of Haman.
3 Now Esther spoke again to the king, fell
down at his feet, and implored him with tears to
counteract the evil of Haman the Agagite, and the
scheme which he had devised against the Jews.
4 And [a]the king held out the golden scepter
toward Esther. So Esther arose and stood before
the king,
5 and said, "If it pleases the king, and if I
have found favor in his sight and the thing *seems*
right to the king and I am pleasing in his eyes,
let it be written to revoke the [a]letters devised by
Haman, the son of Hammedatha the Agagite,
which he wrote to annihilate the Jews who *are*
in all the king's provinces.
6 "For how can I endure to see [a]the evil that
will come to my people? Or how can I endure to
see the destruction of my countrymen?"
7 Then King Ahasuerus said to Queen
Esther and Mordecai the Jew, "Indeed, [a]I have

KJV

have given Esther the house of Haman, and him they have hanged upon the gallows, because he laid his hand upon the Jews.

8 Write ye also for the Jews, as it liketh you, in the king's name, and seal *it* with the king's ring: for the writing which is written in the king's name, and sealed with the king's ring, [a]may no man reverse.

9 [a]Then were the king's scribes called at that time in the third month, that *is*, the month Sivan, on the three and twentieth *day* thereof; and it was written according to all that Mordecai commanded unto the Jews, and to the lieutenants, and the deputies and rulers of the provinces which *are* [b]from India unto Ethiopia, an hundred twenty and seven provinces, unto every province [c]according to the writing thereof, and unto every people after their language, and to the Jews according to their writing, and according to their language.

10 [a]And he wrote in the king Ahasuerus' name, and sealed *it* with the king's ring, and sent letters by posts on horseback, *and* riders on mules, camels, *and* young dromedaries:

11 Wherein the king granted the Jews which *were* in every city to [a]gather themselves together, and to stand for their life, to [b]destroy, to slay, and to cause to perish, all the power of the people and province that would assault them, *both* little ones and women, and *to take* the spoil of them for a prey,

12 [a]Upon one day in all the provinces of king Ahasuerus, *namely*, upon the thirteenth *day* of the twelfth month, which *is* the month Adar.

13 [a]The copy of the writing for a commandment to be given in every province *was* published unto all people, and that the Jews should be ready against that day to avenge themselves on their enemies.

14 *So* the posts that rode upon mules *and* camels went out, being hastened and pressed on by the king's commandment. And the decree was given at Shushan the palace.

15 And Mordecai went out from the presence of the king in royal apparel of blue and white, and with a great crown of gold, and with a garment of fine linen and purple: and [a]the city of Shushan rejoiced and was glad.

16 The Jews had [a]light, and gladness, and joy, and honour.

17 And in every province, and in every city, whithersoever the king's commandment and his decree came, the Jews had joy and gladness, a feast [a]and a good day. And many of the people of the land [b]became Jews; for [c]the fear of the Jews fell upon them.

The Jews Destroy Their Tormentors

9 Now[a] in the twelfth month, that *is*, the month Adar, on the thirteenth day of the same, [b]when the king's commandment and his decree drew near to be put in execution, in the day that the enemies of the Jews hoped to have power over them, (though it was turned to the contrary, that the Jews [c]had rule over them that hated them;)

2 The Jews [a]gathered themselves together in their cities throughout all the provinces of the king Ahasuerus, to lay hand on such as [b]sought their hurt: and no man could withstand them; for [c]the fear of them fell upon all people.

3 And all the rulers of the provinces, and the lieutenants, and the deputies, and officers of the king, helped the Jews; because the fear of Mordecai fell upon them.

4 For Mordecai *was* great in the king's house, and his fame went out throughout all the provinces: for this man Mordecai [a]waxed greater and greater.

5 Thus the Jews smote all their enemies with the stroke of the sword, and slaughter, and destruction, and did what they would unto those that hated them.

8 [a]Esth. 1:19; Dan. 6:8, 12, 15
9 [a]Esth. 3:12 [b]Esth. 1:1 [c]Esth. 1:22; 3:12
10 [a]1 Kin. 21:8; Esth. 3:12, 13
11 [a]Esth. 9:2 [b]Esth. 9:10, 15, 16
12 [a]Esth. 3:13; 9:1
13 [a]Esth. 3:14, 15
15 [a]Esth. 3:15; Prov. 29:2
16 [a]Ps. 97:11; 112:4
17 [a]1 Sam. 25:8; Esth. 9:19 [b]Ps. 18:43 [c]Gen. 35:5; Ex. 15:16; Deut. 2:25; 11:25; 1 Chr. 14:17; Esth. 9:2

CHAPTER 9

1 [a]Esth. 8:12 [b]Esth. 3:13 [c]2 Sam. 22:41
2 [a]Esth. 8:11; 9:15–18 [b]Ps. 71:13, 14 [c]Esth. 8:17
4 [a]2 Sam. 3:1; 1 Chr. 11:9; [Prov. 4:18]

*

8:10 Lit. *sons of the swift horses*
8:12 LXX adds the text of the letter here

NKJV

given Esther the house of Haman, and they have hanged him on the gallows because he *tried to* lay his hand on the Jews.

8 "You yourselves write *a decree* concerning the Jews, as you please, in the king's name, and seal *it* with the king's signet ring; for whatever is written in the king's name and sealed with the king's signet ring [a]no one can revoke."

9 [a]So the king's scribes were called at that time, in the third month, which *is* the month of Sivan, on the twenty-third *day;* and it was written, according to all that Mordecai commanded, to the Jews, the satraps, the governors, and the princes of the provinces [b]from India to Ethiopia, one hundred and twenty-seven provinces *in all*, to every province [c]in its own script, to every people in their own language, and to the Jews in their own script and language.

10 [a]And he wrote in the name of King Ahasuerus, sealed *it* with the king's signet ring, and sent letters by couriers on horseback, riding on royal horses *bred from swift steeds.

11 By these letters the king permitted the Jews who *were* in every city to [a]gather together and protect their lives—to [b]destroy, kill, and annihilate all the forces of any people or province that would assault them, *both* little children and women, and to plunder their possessions,

12 [a]on one day in all the provinces of King Ahasuerus, on the thirteenth *day* of the twelfth month, which *is* the month of *Adar.

13 [a]A copy of the document was to be issued as a decree in every province and published for all people, so that the Jews would be ready on that day to avenge themselves on their enemies.

14 The couriers who rode on royal horses went out, hastened and pressed on by the king's command. And the decree was issued in Shushan the citadel.

15 So Mordecai went out from the presence of the king in royal apparel of blue and white, with a great crown of gold and a garment of fine linen and purple; and [a]the city of Shushan rejoiced and was glad.

16 The Jews had [a]light and gladness, joy and honor.

17 And in every province and city, wherever the king's command and decree came, the Jews had joy and gladness, a feast [a]and a holiday. Then many of the people of the land [b]became Jews, because [c]fear of the Jews fell upon them.

The Jews Destroy Their Tormentors

9 Now [a]in the twelfth month, that *is*, the month of Adar, on the thirteenth day, [b]*the time* came for the king's command and his decree to be executed. On the day that the enemies of the Jews had hoped to overpower them, the opposite occurred, in that the Jews themselves [c]overpowered those who hated them.

2 The Jews [a]gathered together in their cities throughout all the provinces of King Ahasuerus to lay hands on those who [b]sought their harm. And no one could withstand them, [c]because fear of them fell upon all people.

3 And all the officials of the provinces, the satraps, the governors, and all those doing the king's work, helped the Jews, because the fear of Mordecai fell upon them.

4 For Mordecai *was* great in the king's palace, and his fame spread throughout all the provinces; for this man Mordecai [a]became increasingly prominent.

5 Thus the Jews defeated all their enemies with the stroke of the sword, with slaughter and destruction, and did what they pleased with those who hated them.

KJV

6 And in [a]Shushan the palace the Jews slew
and destroyed five hundred men.
7 And Parshandatha, and Dalphon, and
Aspatha,
8 And Poratha, and Adalia, and Aridatha,
9 And Parmashta, and Arisai, and Aridai,
and Vajezatha,
10 [a]The ten sons of Haman the son of Hammedatha, the enemy of the Jews, slew they; [b]but
on the spoil laid they not their hand.
11 On that day the number of those that were
slain in Shushan the palace was brought before
the king.
12 And the king said unto Esther the queen,
The Jews have slain and destroyed five hundred
men in Shushan the palace, and the ten sons of
Haman; what have they done in the rest of the
king's provinces? now [a]what *is* thy petition? and
it shall be granted thee: or what *is* thy request
further? and it shall be done.
13 Then said Esther, If it please the king, let
it be granted to the Jews which *are* in Shushan
to do to morrow also [a]according unto this day's
decree, and let Haman's ten sons [b]be hanged upon
the gallows.
14 And the king commanded it so to be done:
and the decree was given at Shushan; and they
hanged Haman's ten sons.
15 For the Jews that *were* in Shushan [a]gath-
ered themselves together on the fourteenth day
also of the month Adar, and slew three hundred
men at Shushan; [b]but on the prey they laid not
their hand.
16 But the other Jews that *were* in the king's
provinces [a]gathered themselves together, and
stood for their lives, and had rest from their enemies, and slew of their foes seventy and five
thousand, [b]but they laid not their hands on the
prey,
17 On the thirteenth day of the month Adar;
and on the fourteenth day of the same rested they,
and made it a day of feasting and gladness.

The Feast of Purim

18 But the Jews that *were* at Shushan assembled together [a]on the thirteenth *day* thereof, and
on the fourteenth thereof; and on the fifteenth *day*
of the same they rested, and made it a day of feasting and gladness.
19 Therefore the Jews of the villages, that
dwelt in the unwalled towns, made the fourteenth
day of the month Adar [a]*a day of* gladness and
feasting, [b]and a good day, and of [c]sending portions one to another.
20 And Mordecai wrote these things, and
sent letters unto all the Jews that *were* in all the
provinces of the king Ahasuerus, *both* nigh and
far,
21 To stablish *this* among them, that they
should keep the fourteenth day of the month
Adar, and the fifteenth day of the same,
yearly,
22 As the days wherein the Jews rested from
their enemies, and the month which was turned
unto them from sorrow to joy, and from mourning
into a good day: that they should make them days
of feasting and joy, and of [a]sending portions one
to another, and gifts to the [b]poor.
23 And the Jews undertook to do as they had
begun, and as Mordecai had written unto them;
24 Because Haman the son of Hammedatha,
the Agagite, the enemy of all the Jews, [a]had devised against the Jews to destroy them, and had
cast Pur, that *is,* the lot, to consume them, and
to destroy them;
25 But [a]when *Esther* came before the king,
he commanded by letters that his wicked device,
which he devised against the Jews, should [b]return
upon his own head, and that he and his sons
should be hanged on the gallows.
26 Wherefore they called these days Purim
after the name of Pur. Therefore for all the words

6 [a]Esth. 1:2; 3:15; 4:16
10 [a]Esth. 5:11; 9:7–10; Job 18:19; 27:13–15; Ps. 21:10 [b]Esth. 8:11
12 [a]Esth. 5:6; 7:2
13 [a]Esth. 8:11; 9:15 [b]2 Sam. 21:6, 9
15 [a]Esth. 8:11; 9:2 [b]Esth. 9:10
16 [a]Esth. 9:2 [b]Esth. 8:11
18 [a]Esth. 9:11, 15
19 [a]Deut. 16:11, 14 [b]Esth. 8:16, 17 [c]Neh. 8:10, 12; Esth. 9:22
22 [a]Neh. 8:10; Esth. 9:19 [b][Deut. 15:7–11]; Job 29:16
24 [a]Esth. 3:6, 7; 9:26
25 [a]Esth. 7:4–10; 8:3; 9:13, 14 [b]Esth. 7:10

NKJV

6 And in [a]Shushan the citadel the Jews
killed and destroyed five hundred men.
7 Also Parshandatha, Dalphon, Aspatha,
8 Poratha, Adalia, Aridatha,
9 Parmashta, Arisai, Aridai, and Vajezatha—
10 [a]the ten sons of Haman the son of Hammedatha, the enemy of the Jews—they killed; [b]but
they did not lay a hand on the plunder.
11 On that day the number of those who were
killed in Shushan the citadel was brought to the
king.
12 And the king said to Queen Esther, "The
Jews have killed and destroyed five hundred men
in Shushan the citadel, and the ten sons of Haman.
What have they done in the rest of the king's provinces? Now [a]what *is* your petition? It shall be
granted to you. Or what *is* your further request?
It shall be done."
13 Then Esther said, "If it pleases the king,
let it be granted to the Jews who *are* in Shushan
to do again tomorrow [a]according to today's decree, and let Haman's ten sons [b]be hanged on the
gallows."
14 So the king commanded this to be done;
the decree was issued in Shushan, and they
hanged Haman's ten sons.
15 And the Jews who *were* in Shushan [a]gath-
ered together again on the fourteenth day of the
month of Adar and killed three hundred men at
Shushan; [b]but they did not lay a hand on the
plunder.
16 The remainder of the Jews in the king's
provinces [a]gathered together and protected their
lives, had rest from their enemies, and killed
seventy-five thousand of their enemies; [b]but they
did not lay a hand on the plunder.
17 *This was* on the thirteenth day of the
month of Adar. And on the fourteenth of **the
month* they rested and made it a day of feasting
and gladness.

The Feast of Purim

18 But the Jews who *were* at Shushan assembled together [a]on the thirteenth *day*, as well as
on the fourteenth; and on the fifteenth of **the
month* they rested, and made it a day of feasting
and gladness.
19 Therefore the Jews of the villages who
dwelt in the unwalled towns celebrated the fourteenth day of the month of Adar [a]*with* gladness
and feasting, [b]as a holiday, and for [c]sending presents to one another.
20 And Mordecai wrote these things and sent
letters to all the Jews, near and far, who *were* in
all the provinces of King Ahasuerus,
21 to establish among them that they should
celebrate yearly the fourteenth and fifteenth days
of the month of Adar,
22 as the days on which the Jews had rest
from their enemies, as the month which was
turned from sorrow to joy for them, and from
mourning to a holiday; that they should make
them days of feasting and joy, of [a]sending presents to one another and gifts to the [b]poor.
23 So the Jews accepted the custom which
they had begun, as Mordecai had written to them,
24 because Haman, the son of Hammedatha
the Agagite, the enemy of all the Jews, [a]had plotted against the Jews to annihilate them, and had
cast Pur (that *is,* the lot), to consume them and
destroy them;
25 but [a]when **Esther* came before the king,
he commanded by letter that *this wicked plot
which *Haman* had devised against the Jews
should [b]return on his own head, and that he and
his sons should be hanged on the gallows.
26 So they called these days Purim, after the
name Pur. Therefore, because of all the words of

*———
9:17 Lit. *it*
9:18 Lit. *it*
9:25 Lit. *she* or *it* • Lit. *his*

KJV

of [a]this letter, and *of that* which they had seen
concerning this matter, and which had come unto
them,
27 The Jews ordained, and took upon them,
and upon their seed, and upon all such as [a]joined
themselves unto them, so as it should not fail, that
they would keep these two days according to their
writing, and according to their *appointed* time
every year;
28 And *that* these days *should be* remembered and kept throughout every generation,
every family, every province, and every city; and
that these days of Purim should not fail from
among the Jews, nor the memorial of them perish
from their seed.
29 Then Esther the queen, [a]the daughter of
Abihail, and Mordecai the Jew, wrote with all authority, to confirm this [b]second letter of Purim.
30 And he sent the letters unto all the Jews,
to [a]the hundred twenty and seven provinces of
the kingdom of Ahasuerus, *with* words of peace
and truth,
31 To confirm these days of Purim in their
times *appointed*, according as Mordecai the Jew
and Esther the queen had enjoined them, and as
they had decreed for themselves and for their
seed, the matters of [a]the fastings and their cry.
32 And the decree of Esther confirmed these
matters of Purim; and it was written in the book.

Mordecai's Advancement

10 And the king Ahasuerus laid a tribute upon
the land, and *upon* [a]the isles of the sea.
2 And all the acts of his power and of his
might, and the declaration of the greatness of
Mordecai, [a]whereunto the king advanced him, *are*
they not written in the book of the [b]chronicles of
the kings of Media and Persia?
3 For Mordecai the Jew *was* [a]next unto king
Ahasuerus, and great among the Jews, and accepted of the multitude of his brethren, [b]seeking
the wealth of his people, and speaking peace to
all his seed.

26 [a]Esth. 9:20
27 [a]Esth. 8:17; [Is. 56:3, 6]; Zech. 2:11
29 [a]Esth. 2:15 [b]Esth. 8:10; 9:20, 21
30 [a]Esth. 1:1
31 [a]Esth. 4:3, 16

CHAPTER 10

1 [a]Gen. 10:5; Ps. 72:10; Is. 11:11; 24:15
2 [a]Esth. 8:15; 9:4 [b]Esth. 6:1
3 [a]Gen. 41:40, 43, 44; 2 Chr. 28:7 [b]Neh. 2:10; Ps. 122:8, 9

*

10:3 Lit. *seed.* LXX, Vg. add a dream of Mordecai here; Vg. adds six more chapters

NKJV

[a]this letter, what they had seen concerning this
matter, and what had happened to them,
27 the Jews established and imposed it upon
themselves and their descendants and all who
would [a]join them, that without fail they should
celebrate these two days every year, according
to the written *instructions* and according to the
prescribed time,
28 *that* these days *should be* remembered
and kept throughout every generation, every family, every province, and every city, that these days
of Purim should not fail *to be observed* among
the Jews, and *that* the memory of them should
not perish among their descendants.
29 Then Queen Esther, [a]the daughter of Abihail, with Mordecai the Jew, wrote with full authority to confirm this [b]second letter about Purim.
30 And *Mordecai* sent letters to all the Jews,
to [a]the one hundred and twenty-seven provinces
of the kingdom of Ahasuerus, *with* words of peace
and truth,
31 to confirm these days of Purim at their
appointed time, as Mordecai the Jew and Queen
Esther had prescribed for them, and as they had
decreed for themselves and their descendants
concerning matters of their [a]fasting and lamenting.
32 So the decree of Esther confirmed these
matters of Purim, and it was written in the book.

Mordecai's Advancement

10 And King Ahasuerus imposed tribute on
the land and *on* [a]the islands of the sea.
2 Now all the acts of his power and his
might, and the account of the greatness of Mordecai, [a]to which the king advanced him, *are* they
not written in the book of the [b]chronicles of the
kings of Media and Persia?
3 For Mordecai the Jew *was* [a]second to King
Ahasuerus, and was great among the Jews and
well received by the multitude of his brethren,
[b]seeking the good of his people and speaking
peace to all his *countrymen.

KJV

THE BOOK OF

JOB

Job and His Family in Uz

1 There was a man [a]in the land of Uz, whose
name *was* [b]Job; and that man was [c]perfect
and upright, and one that [d]feared God, and es-
chewed evil.
2 And there were born unto him seven sons
and three daughters.
3 His substance also was seven thousand
sheep, and three thousand camels, and five hundred yoke of oxen, and five hundred she asses,
and a very great household; so that this man was
the greatest of all the men of the east.
4 And his sons went and feasted *in their*
houses, every one his day; and sent and called
for their three sisters to eat and to drink with
them.
5 And it was so, when the days of *their*
feasting were gone about, that Job sent and sanctified them, and rose up early in the morning, [a]and
offered burnt offerings *according* to the number
of them all: for Job said, It may be that my sons
have sinned, and [b]cursed God in their hearts.
Thus did Job continually.

Satan Attacks Job's Character

6 Now [a]there was a day when the sons of
God came to present themselves before the LORD,
and Satan came also among them.
7 And the LORD said unto Satan, Whence
comest thou? Then Satan answered the LORD, and
said, From [a]going to and fro in the earth, and from
walking up and down in it.
8 And the LORD said unto Satan, Hast thou
considered my servant Job, that *there is* none like
him in the earth, a perfect and an upright man,
one that feareth God, and escheweth evil?
9 Then Satan answered the LORD, and said,
Doth Job fear God for nought?
10 [a]Hast not thou made an hedge about him,
and about his house, and about all that he hath
on every side? [b]thou hast blessed the work of his
hands, and his substance is increased in the land.
11 [a]But put forth thine hand now, and touch
all that he hath, and he will [b]curse thee to thy
face.
12 And the LORD said unto Satan, Behold, all
that he hath *is* in thy power; only upon himself
put not forth thine hand. So Satan went forth from
the presence of the LORD.

Job Loses His Property and Children

13 And there was a day [a]when his sons and
his daughters *were* eating and drinking wine in
their eldest brother's house:
14 And there came a messenger unto Job,
and said, The oxen were plowing, and the asses
feeding beside them:
15 And the Sabeans fell *upon them*, and took
them away; yea, they have slain the servants with
the edge of the sword; and I only am escaped
alone to tell thee.
16 While he *was* yet speaking, there came
also another, and said, The fire of God is fallen
from heaven, and hath burned up the sheep, and

CHAPTER 1

1 [a]1 Chr. 1:17 [b]Ezek. 14:14, 20; James 5:11 [c]Gen. 6:9; 17:1; [Deut. 18:13] [d][Prov. 16:6]
5 [a]Gen. 8:20; [Job 42:8] [b]1 Kin. 21:10, 13
6 [a]Job 2:1
7 [a][1 Pet. 5:8]
10 [a]Job 29:2–6; Ps. 34:7; Is. 5:2 [b][Ps. 128:1, 2; Prov. 10:22]
11 [a]Job 2:5; 19:21 [b]Is. 8:21; Mal. 3:13, 14
13 [a][Eccl. 9:12]

NKJV

THE BOOK OF

JOB

Job and His Family in Uz

1 There was a man [a]in the land of Uz, whose
name *was* [b]Job; and that man was [c]blame-
less and upright, and one who [d]feared God and
shunned evil.
2 And seven sons and three daughters were
born to him.
3 Also, his possessions were seven thousand sheep, three thousand camels, five hundred
yoke of oxen, five hundred female donkeys, and
a very large household, so that this man was the
greatest of all the people of the East.
4 And his sons would go and feast *in their*
houses, each on his *appointed* day, and would
send and invite their three sisters to eat and drink
with them.
5 So it was, when the days of feasting had
run their course, that Job would send and sanctify
them, and he would rise early in the morning [a]and
offer burnt offerings *according to* the number of
them all. For Job said, "It may be that my sons
have sinned and [b]cursed* God in their hearts."
Thus Job did regularly.

Satan Attacks Job's Character

6 Now [a]there was a day when the sons of
God came to present themselves before the LORD,
and *Satan also came among them.
7 And the LORD said to Satan, "From where
do you come?" So Satan answered the LORD and
said, "From [a]going to and fro on the earth, and
from walking back and forth on it."
8 Then the LORD said to Satan, "Have you
considered My servant Job, that *there is* none like
him on the earth, a blameless and upright man,
one who fears God and shuns evil?"
9 So Satan answered the LORD and said,
"Does Job fear God for nothing?
10 [a]"Have You not made a hedge around
him, around his household, and around all that
he has on every side? [b]You have blessed the work
of his hands, and his possessions have increased
in the land.
11 [a]"But now, stretch out Your hand and
touch all that he has, and he will surely [b]curse
You to Your face!"
12 And the LORD said to Satan, "Behold, all
that he has *is* in your power; only do not lay a
hand on his *person*." So Satan went out from the
presence of the LORD.

Job Loses His Property and Children

13 Now there was a day [a]when his sons and
daughters *were* eating and drinking wine in their
oldest brother's house;
14 and a messenger came to Job and said,
"The oxen were plowing and the donkeys feeding
beside them,
15 "when the *Sabeans raided *them* and took
them away—indeed they have killed the servants
with the edge of the sword; and I alone have escaped to tell you!"
16 While he *was* still speaking, another also
came and said, "The fire of God fell from heaven
and burned up the sheep and the servants, and

*

1:5 Lit. *blessed*, but in an evil sense; cf. Job 1:11; 2:5, 9
1:6 Lit. *the Adversary*
1:15 Lit. *Sheba;* cf. Job 6:19

KJV

the servants, and consumed them; and I only am escaped alone to tell thee.

17 While he *was* yet speaking, there came also another, and said, The Chaldeans made out three bands, and fell upon the camels, and have carried them away, yea, and slain the servants with the edge of the sword; and I only am escaped alone to tell thee.

18 While he *was* yet speaking, there came also another, and said, [a]Thy sons and thy daughters *were* eating and drinking wine in their eldest brother's house:

19 And, behold, there came a great wind from the wilderness, and smote the four corners of the house, and it fell upon the young men, and they are dead; and I only am escaped alone to tell thee.

20 Then Job arose, [a]and rent his mantle, and shaved his head, and [b]fell down upon the ground, and worshipped,

21 And said, [a]Naked came I out of my mother's womb, and naked shall I return thither: the LORD [b]gave, and the LORD hath [c]taken away; [d]blessed be the name of the LORD.

22 [a]In all this Job sinned not, nor charged God foolishly.

Satan Attacks Job's Health

2 Again [a]there was a day when the sons of God came to present themselves before the LORD, and Satan came also among them to present himself before the LORD.

2 And the LORD said unto Satan, From whence comest thou? And [a]Satan answered the LORD, and said, From going to and fro in the earth, and from walking up and down in it.

3 And the LORD said unto Satan, Hast thou considered my servant Job, that *there is* none like him in the earth, [a]a perfect and an upright man, one that feareth God, and escheweth evil? and still he [b]holdeth fast his integrity, although thou movedst me against him, [c]to destroy him without cause.

4 And Satan answered the LORD, and said, Skin for skin, yea, all that a man hath will he give for his life.

5 [a]But put forth thine hand now, and touch his [b]bone and his flesh, and he will curse thee to thy face.

6 [a]And the LORD said unto Satan, Behold, he *is* in thine hand; but save his life.

7 So went Satan forth from the presence of the LORD, and smote Job with sore boils [a]from the sole of his foot unto his crown.

8 And he took him a potsherd to scrape himself withal; [a]and he sat down among the ashes.

9 Then said his wife unto him, Dost thou still retain thine integrity? curse God, and die.

10 But he said unto her, Thou speakest as one of the foolish women speaketh. What? [a]shall we receive good at the hand of God, and shall we not receive evil? [b]In all this did not Job [c]sin with his lips.

Job's Three Friends

11 Now when Job's three friends heard of all this evil that was come upon him, they came every one from his own place; Eliphaz the [a]Temanite, and Bildad the [b]Shuhite, and Zophar the Naamathite: for they had made an appointment together to come [c]to mourn with him and to comfort him.

12 And when they lifted up their eyes afar off, and knew him not, they lifted up their voice, and wept; and they rent every one his mantle, and [a]sprinkled dust upon their heads toward heaven.

13 So they sat down with him upon the ground [a]seven days and seven nights, and none

---

18 [a]Job 1:4, 13
20 [a]Gen. 37:29, 34; Josh. 7:6; Ezra 9:3 [b][1 Pet. 5:6]
21 [a][Ps. 49:17; Eccl. 5:15]; 1 Tim. 6:7 [b]Eccl. 5:19; [James 1:17] [c]Gen. 31:16; [1 Sam. 2:6] [d]Eph. 5:20; [1 Thess. 5:18]
22 [a]Job 2:10

CHAPTER 2

1 [a]Job 1:6–8
2 [a]Job 1:7
3 [a]Job 1:1, 8 [b]Job 27:5, 6 [c]Job 9:17
5 [a]Job 1:11 [b]Job 19:20
6 [a]Job 1:12
7 [a]Is. 1:6
8 [a]Job 42:6; Jer. 6:26; Ezek. 27:30; Jon. 3:6; Matt. 11:21
10 [a]Job 1:21, 22; [Heb. 12:6; James 5:10, 11] [b]Job 1:22; [James 1:12] [c]Ps. 39:1
11 [a]Gen. 36:11; 1 Chr. 1:36; Job 6:19; Jer. 49:7; Obad. 9 [b]Gen. 25:2; 1 Chr. 1:32 [c]Job 42:11; Rom. 12:15
12 [a]Josh. 7:6; Neh. 9:1; Lam. 2:10; Ezek. 27:30
13 [a]Gen. 50:10; Ezek. 3:15

NKJV

consumed them; and I alone have escaped to tell you!"

17 While he *was* still speaking, another also came and said, "The Chaldeans formed three bands, raided the camels and took them away, yes, and killed the servants with the edge of the sword; and I alone have escaped to tell you!"

18 While he *was* still speaking, another also came and said, [a]"Your sons and daughters *were* eating and drinking wine in their oldest brother's house,

19 "and suddenly a great wind came from *across the wilderness and struck the four corners of the house, and it fell on the young people, and they are dead; and I alone have escaped to tell you!"

20 Then Job arose, [a]tore his robe, and shaved his head; and he [b]fell to the ground and worshiped.

21 And he said:

[a]"Naked I came from my mother's womb,
And naked shall I return there.
The LORD [b]gave, and the LORD has [c]taken away;
[d]Blessed be the name of the LORD."

22 [a]In all this Job did not sin nor charge God with wrong.

Satan Attacks Job's Health

2 Again [a]there was a day when the sons of God came to present themselves before the LORD, and Satan came also among them to present himself before the LORD.

2 And the LORD said to Satan, "From where do you come?" So [a]Satan answered the LORD and said, "From going to and fro on the earth, and from walking back and forth on it."

3 Then the LORD said to Satan, "Have you considered My servant Job, that *there is* none like him on the earth, [a]a blameless and upright man, one who fears God and shuns evil? And still he [b]holds fast to his integrity, although you incited Me against him, [c]to destroy him without cause."

4 So Satan answered the LORD and said, "Skin for skin! Yes, all that a man has he will give for his life.

5 [a]"But stretch out Your hand now, and touch his [b]bone and his flesh, and he will surely curse You to Your face!"

6 [a]And the LORD said to Satan, "Behold, he *is* in your hand, but spare his life."

7 So Satan went out from the presence of the LORD, and struck Job with painful boils [a]from the sole of his foot to the crown of his head.

8 And he took for himself a potsherd with which to scrape himself [a]while he sat in the midst of the ashes.

9 Then his wife said to him, "Do you still hold fast to your integrity? Curse God and die!"

10 But he said to her, "You speak as one of the foolish women speaks. [a]Shall we indeed accept good from God, and shall we not accept adversity?" [b]In all this Job did not [c]sin with his lips.

Job's Three Friends

11 Now when Job's three friends heard of all this adversity that had come upon him, each one came from his own place—Eliphaz the [a]Temanite, Bildad the [b]Shuhite, and Zophar the Naamathite. For they had made an appointment together to come [c]and mourn with him, and to comfort him.

12 And when they raised their eyes from afar, and did not recognize him, they lifted their voices and wept; and each one tore his robe and [a]sprinkled dust on his head toward heaven.

13 So they sat down with him on the ground [a]seven days and seven nights, and no one spoke

---

*1:19 LXX omits *across*

KJV

spake a word unto him: for they saw that *his* grief was very great.

Job Deplores His Birth

3 After this opened Job his mouth, and cursed his day.

2 And Job spake, and said,

3 [a]Let the day perish wherein I was born, and the night *in which* it was said, There is a man child conceived.

4 Let that day be darkness; let not God regard it from above, neither let the light shine upon it.

5 Let darkness and [a]the shadow of death stain it; let a cloud dwell upon it; let the blackness of the day terrify it.

6 *As for* that night, let darkness seize upon it; let it not be joined unto the days of the year, let it not come into the number of the months.

7 Lo, let that night be solitary, let no joyful voice come therein.

8 Let them curse it that curse the day, [a]who are ready to raise up their mourning.

9 Let the stars of the twilight thereof be dark; let it look for light, but *have* none; neither let it see the dawning of the day:

10 Because it shut not up the doors of my *mother's* womb, nor hid sorrow from mine eyes.

11 [a]Why died I not from the womb? *why* did I *not* give up the ghost when I came out of the belly?

12 [a]Why did the knees prevent me? or why the breasts that I should suck?

13 For now should I have lain still and been quiet, I should have slept: then had I been at rest,

14 With kings and counsellors of the earth, which [a]built desolate places for themselves;

15 Or with princes that had gold, who filled their houses with silver:

16 Or [a]as an hidden untimely birth I had not been; as infants *which* never saw light.

17 There the wicked cease *from* troubling; and there the weary be at [a]rest.

18 *There* the prisoners rest together; [a]they hear not the voice of the oppressor.

19 The small and great are there; and the servant *is* free from his master.

20 [a]Wherefore is light given to him that is in misery, and life unto the [b]bitter *in* soul;

21 Which [a]long for death, but it *cometh* not; and dig for it more than [b]for hid treasures;

22 Which rejoice exceedingly, *and* are glad, when they can find the [a]grave?

23 *Why is light given* to a man whose way is hid, [a]and whom God hath hedged in?

24 For my sighing cometh before I eat, and my roarings are poured out like the waters.

25 For the thing which I greatly [a]feared is come upon me, and that which I was afraid of is come unto me.

26 I was not in safety, neither had I rest, neither was I quiet; yet trouble came.

Eliphaz: Job Has Sinned

4 Then Eliphaz the Temanite answered and said,

CHAPTER 3

3 [a]Job 10:18, 19; Jer. 20:14–18
5 [a]Job 10:21, 22; Jer. 13:16; Amos 5:8
8 [a]Jer. 9:17
11 [a]Job 10:18, 19
12 [a]Gen. 30:3
14 [a]Job 15:28; Is. 58:12
16 [a]Ps. 58:8
17 [a]Job 17:16
18 [a]Job 39:7
20 [a]Jer. 20:18 [b]2 Kin. 4:27
21 [a]Rev. 9:6 [b]Prov. 2:4
22 [a]Job 7:15, 16
23 [a]Job 19:8; Ps. 88:8; Lam. 3:7
25 [a][Job 9:28; 30:15]

*
3:6 LXX, Syr., Tg., Vg. *be joined*
3:24 Lit. *my bread*

NKJV

a word to him, for they saw that *his* grief was very great.

Job Deplores His Birth

3 After this Job opened his mouth and cursed the day of his *birth.*

2 And Job spoke, and said:

3 "May[a] the day perish on which I was born,
And the night *in which* it was said,
'A male child is conceived.'
4 May that day be darkness;
May God above not seek it,
Nor the light shine upon it.
5 May darkness and [a]the shadow of death claim it;
May a cloud settle on it;
May the blackness of the day terrify it.
6 *As for* that night, may darkness seize it;
May it not *rejoice among the days of the year,
May it not come into the number of the months.
7 Oh, may that night be barren!
May no joyful shout come into it!
8 May those curse it who curse the day,
Those [a]who are ready to arouse Leviathan.
9 May the stars of its morning be dark;
May it look for light, but *have* none,
And not see the dawning of the day;
10 Because it did not shut up the doors of my *mother's* womb,
Nor hide sorrow from my eyes.

11 "Why[a] did I not die at birth?
Why did I *not* perish when I came from the womb?
12 [a]Why did the knees receive me?
Or why the breasts, that I should nurse?
13 For now I would have lain still and been quiet,
I would have been asleep;
Then I would have been at rest
14 With kings and counselors of the earth,
Who [a]built ruins for themselves,
15 Or with princes who had gold,
Who filled their houses *with* silver;
16 Or *why* was I not hidden [a]like a stillborn child,
Like infants who never saw light?
17 There the wicked cease *from* troubling,
And there the weary are at [a]rest.
18 *There* the prisoners rest together;
[a]They do not hear the voice of the oppressor.
19 The small and great are there,
And the servant *is* free from his master.

20 "Why[a] is light given to him who is in misery,
And life to the [b]bitter of soul,
21 Who [a]long for death, but it does not *come,*
And search for it more than [b]hidden treasures;
22 Who rejoice exceedingly,
And are glad when they can find the [a]grave?
23 *Why is light given* to a man whose way is hidden,
[a]And whom God has hedged in?
24 For my sighing comes before *I eat,
And my groanings pour out like water.
25 For the thing I greatly [a]feared has come upon me,
And what I dreaded has happened to me.
26 I am not at ease, nor am I quiet;
I have no rest, for trouble comes."

Eliphaz: Job Has Sinned

4 Then Eliphaz the Temanite answered and said:

KJV

2 *If* we assay to commune with thee, wilt
thou be grieved? but who can withhold himself
from speaking?
3 Behold, thou hast instructed many, and
thou [a]hast strengthened the weak hands.
4 Thy words have upholden him that was
falling, and thou [a]hast strengthened the feeble
knees.
5 But now it is come upon thee, and thou
faintest; it toucheth thee, and thou art troubled.
6 *Is* not *this* [a]thy fear, [b]thy confidence, thy
hope, and the uprightness of thy ways?
7 Remember, I pray thee, [a]who *ever* perished, being innocent? or where were the righteous cut off?
8 Even as I have seen, [a]they that plow iniquity, and sow wickedness, reap the same.
9 By the blast of God they perish, and by
the breath of his nostrils are they consumed.
10 The roaring of the lion, and the voice of
the fierce lion, and [a]the teeth of the young lions,
are broken.
11 [a]The old lion perisheth for lack of prey,
and the stout lion's whelps are scattered abroad.
12 Now a thing was secretly brought to me,
and mine ear received a little thereof.
13 [a]In thoughts from the visions of the night,
when deep sleep falleth on men,
14 Fear came upon me, and [a]trembling,
which made all my bones to shake.
15 Then a spirit passed before my face; the
hair of my flesh stood up:
16 It stood still, but I could not discern the
form thereof: an image *was* before mine eyes,
there was silence, and I heard a voice, *saying*,
17 Shall mortal man be more just than God?
shall a man be more pure than his maker?
18 Behold, he [a]put no trust in his servants;
and his angels he charged with folly:
19 How much less *in* them that dwell in
houses of clay, whose foundation *is* in the dust,
which are crushed before the moth?
20 [a]They are destroyed from morning to evening: they perish for ever without any regarding
it.
21 Doth not their excellency *which is* in them
go away? they die, even without wisdom.

Job Is Chastened by God

5 Call now, if there be any that will answer thee;
and to which of the saints wilt thou turn?
2 For wrath killeth the foolish man, and
envy slayeth the silly one.
3 [a]I have seen the foolish taking root: but
suddenly I cursed his habitation.
4 His children are [a]far from safety, and they
are crushed in the gate, [b]neither *is there* any to
deliver *them*.
5 Whose harvest the hungry eateth up, and
taketh it even out of the thorns, and the robber
swalloweth up their substance.
6 Although affliction cometh not forth of the
dust, neither doth trouble spring out of the
ground;
7 Yet man is [a]born unto trouble, as the
sparks fly upward.

CHAPTER 4

3 [a]Is. 35:3
4 [a]Is. 35:3
6 [a]Job 1:1
[b]Prov. 3:26
7 [a][Job 8:20; 36:6, 7; Ps. 37:25]
8 [a][Job 15:31, 35; Prov. 22:8; Hos. 10:13; Gal. 6:7]
10 [a]Job 5:15; Ps. 58:6
11 [a]Job 29:17; Ps. 34:10
13 [a]Job 33:15
14 [a]Hab. 3:16
18 [a]Job 15:15
20 [a]Ps. 90:5, 6

CHAPTER 5

3 [a][Ps. 37:35, 36]; Jer. 12:1–3
4 [a]Ps. 119:155
[b]Ps. 109:12
7 [a]Job 14:1

*5:5 LXX *They shall not be taken from evil men;* Vg. *And the armed man shall take him by violence* • LXX *The might shall draw them off;* Vg. *And the thirsty shall drink up their riches*

NKJV

2 "*If* one attempts a word with you, will you
become weary?
But who can withhold himself from
speaking?
3 Surely you have instructed many,
And you [a]have strengthened weak
hands.
4 Your words have upheld him who was
stumbling,
And you [a]have strengthened the feeble
knees;
5 But now it comes upon you, and you are
weary;
It touches you, and you are troubled.
6 *Is* not [a]your reverence [b]your confidence?
And the integrity of your ways your hope?

7 "Remember now, [a]who *ever* perished being
innocent?
Or where were the upright *ever* cut off?
8 Even as I have seen,
[a]Those who plow iniquity
And sow trouble reap the same.
9 By the blast of God they perish,
And by the breath of His anger they are
consumed.
10 The roaring of the lion,
The voice of the fierce lion,
And [a]the teeth of the young lions are
broken.
11 [a]The old lion perishes for lack of prey,
And the cubs of the lioness are scattered.

12 "Now a word was secretly brought to me,
And my ear received a whisper of it.
13 [a]In disquieting thoughts from the visions
of the night,
When deep sleep falls on men,
14 Fear came upon me, and [a]trembling,
Which made all my bones shake.
15 Then a spirit passed before my face;
The hair on my body stood up.
16 It stood still,
But I could not discern its appearance.
A form *was* before my eyes;
There was silence;
Then I heard a voice *saying*:
17 'Can a mortal be more righteous than
God?
Can a man be more pure than his Maker?
18 If He [a]puts no trust in His servants,
If He charges His angels with error,
19 How much more those who dwell in
houses of clay,
Whose foundation is in the dust,
Who are crushed before a moth?
20 [a]They are broken in pieces from morning
till evening;
They perish forever, with no one
regarding.
21 Does not their own excellence go away?
They die, even without wisdom.'

Job Is Chastened by God

5 "Call out now;
Is there anyone who will answer you?
And to which of the holy ones will you
turn?
2 For wrath kills a foolish man,
And envy slays a simple one.
3 [a]I have seen the foolish taking root,
But suddenly I cursed his dwelling place.
4 His sons are [a]far from safety,
They are crushed in the gate,
And [b]*there is* no deliverer.
5 Because the hungry eat up his harvest,
*Taking it even from the thorns,
*And a snare snatches their substance.
6 For affliction does not come from the dust,
Nor does trouble spring from the ground;
7 Yet man is [a]born to trouble,
As the sparks fly upward.

KJV

8 I would seek unto God, and unto God
would I commit my cause:
9 Which doeth great things and unsearchable; marvellous things without number:
10 [a]Who giveth rain upon the earth, and
sendeth waters upon the fields:
11 [a]To set up on high those that be low; that
those which mourn may be exalted to safety.
12 [a]He disappointeth the devices of the
crafty, so that their hands cannot perform *their*
enterprise.
13 He taketh the [a]wise in their own craftiness: and the counsel of the froward is carried
headlong.
14 They meet with darkness in the daytime,
and grope in the noonday as in the night.
15 But [a]he saveth the poor from the sword,
from their mouth, and from the hand of the
mighty.
16 [a]So the poor hath hope, and iniquity stoppeth her mouth.
17 [a]Behold, happy *is* the man whom God correcteth: therefore despise not thou the chastening
of the Almighty:
18 [a]For he maketh sore, and bindeth up: he
woundeth, and his hands make whole.
19 [a]He shall deliver thee in six troubles: yea,
in seven [b]there shall no evil touch thee.
20 [a]In famine he shall redeem thee from
death: and in war from the power of the sword.
21 [a]Thou shalt be hid from the scourge of
the tongue: neither shalt thou be afraid of destruction when it cometh.
22 At destruction and famine thou shalt
laugh: [a]neither shalt thou be afraid of the [b]beasts
of the earth.
23 [a]For thou shalt be in league with the
stones of the field: and the beasts of the field shall
be at peace with thee.
24 And thou shalt know that thy tabernacle
shall be in peace; and thou shalt visit thy habitation, and shalt not sin.
25 Thou shalt know also that [a]thy seed *shall
be* great, and thine offspring [b]as the grass of the
earth.
26 [a]Thou shalt come to *thy* grave in a full
age, like as a shock of corn cometh in in his
season.
27 Lo this, we have [a]searched it, so it *is;* hear
it, and know thou *it* for thy good.

Job: My Complaint Is Just

6 But Job answered and said,
2 O that my grief were throughly weighed,
and my calamity laid in the balances together!
3 For now it would be heavier than the sand
of the sea: therefore my words are swallowed up.
4 [a]For the arrows of the Almighty *are* within
me, the poison whereof drinketh up my spirit: [b]the
terrors of God do set themselves in array [c]against
me.
5 Doth the [a]wild ass bray when he hath
grass? or loweth the ox over his fodder?
6 Can that which is unsavoury be eaten
without salt? or is there *any* taste in the white of
an egg?
7 The things *that* my soul refused to touch
are as my sorrowful meat.

10 [a][Job 36:27–29; 37:6–11; 38:26]
11 [a]Ps. 113:7
12 [a]Neh. 4:15
13 [a][Job 37:24; 1 Cor. 3:19]
15 [a]Job 4:10, 11; Ps. 35:10
16 [a]1 Sam. 2:8; Ps. 107:41, 42
17 [a]Ps. 94:12; [Prov. 3:11, 12; Heb. 12:5, 6; Rev. 3:19]
18 [a][Deut. 32:39; 1 Sam. 2:6, 7]; Is. 30:26; Hos. 6:1
19 [a]Ps. 34:19; 91:3; [1 Cor. 10:13] [b]Ps. 91:10; [Prov. 24:16]
20 [a]Ps. 33:19, 20; 37:19
21 [a]Job 5:15; Ps. 31:20
22 [a]Ps. 91:13; Is. 11:9; 35:9; 65:25; Ezek. 34:25 [b]Hos. 2:18
23 [a]Ps. 91:12
25 [a]Ps. 112:2 [b]Ps. 72:16
26 [a][Prov. 9:11; 10:27]
27 [a]Ps. 111:2

CHAPTER 6
4 [a]Job 16:13; Ps. 38:2 [b]Ps. 88:15, 16 [c]Job 30:15
5 [a]Job 39:5–8

NKJV

8 "But as for me, I would seek God,
And to God I would commit my cause—
9 Who does great things, and unsearchable,
Marvelous things without number.
10 [a]He gives rain on the earth,
And sends waters on the fields.
11 [a]He sets on high those who are lowly,
And those who mourn are lifted to
safety.
12 [a]He frustrates the devices of the crafty,
So that their hands cannot carry out their
plans.
13 He catches the [a]wise in their own
craftiness,
And the counsel of the cunning comes
quickly upon them.
14 They meet with darkness in the daytime,
And grope at noontime as in the night.
15 But [a]He saves the needy from the sword,
From the mouth of the mighty,
And from their hand.
16 [a]So the poor have hope,
And injustice shuts her mouth.

17 "Behold,[a] happy *is* the man whom God
corrects;
Therefore do not despise the chastening
of the Almighty.
18 [a]For He bruises, but He binds up;
He wounds, but His hands make whole.
19 [a]He shall deliver you in six troubles,
Yes, in seven [b]no evil shall touch you.
20 [a]In famine He shall redeem you from
death,
And in war from the power of the
sword.
21 [a]You shall be hidden from the scourge of
the tongue,
And you shall not be afraid of destruction
when it comes.
22 You shall laugh at destruction and famine,
And [a]you shall not be afraid of the [b]beasts
of the earth.
23 [a]For you shall have a covenant with the
stones of the field,
And the beasts of the field shall be at
peace with you.
24 You shall know that your tent *is* in peace;
You shall visit your dwelling and find
nothing amiss.
25 You shall also know that [a]your
descendants *shall be* many,
And your offspring [b]like the grass of the
earth.
26 [a]You shall come to the grave at a full age,
As a sheaf of grain ripens in its season.
27 Behold, this we have [a]searched out;
It *is* true.
Hear it, and know for yourself."

Job: My Complaint Is Just

6 Then Job answered and said:

2 "Oh, that my grief were fully weighed,
And my calamity laid with it on the
scales!
3 For then it would be heavier than the sand
of the sea—
Therefore my words have been rash.
4 [a]For the arrows of the Almighty *are* within
me;
My spirit drinks in their poison;
[b]The terrors of God are arrayed [c]against
me.
5 Does the [a]wild donkey bray when it has
grass,
Or does the ox low over its fodder?
6 Can flavorless food be eaten without salt?
Or is there *any* taste in the white of an
egg?
7 My soul refuses to touch them;
They *are* as loathsome food to me.

KJV

8 Oh that I might have my request; and that
God would grant *me* the thing that I long for!
9 Even that it would please God to destroy
me; that he would let loose his hand, and [a]cut
me off!
10 Then should I yet have comfort; yea, I
would harden myself in sorrow: let him not spare;
for [a]I have not concealed the words of [b]the Holy
One.
11 What *is* my strength, that I should hope?
and what *is* mine end, that I should prolong my
life?
12 *Is* my strength the strength of stones? or
is my flesh of brass?
13 *Is* not my help in me? and is wisdom
driven quite from me?
14 [a]To him that is afflicted pity *should be*
shewed from his friend; but he forsaketh the fear
of the Almighty.
15 [a]My brethren have dealt deceitfully as a
brook, *and* [b]as the stream of brooks they pass
away;
16 Which are blackish by reason of the ice,
and wherein the snow is hid:
17 What time they wax warm, they vanish:
when it is hot, they are consumed out of their
place.
18 The paths of their way are turned aside;
they go to nothing, and perish.
19 The troops of [a]Tema looked, the companies of [b]Sheba waited for them.
20 They were [a]confounded because they had
hoped; they came thither, and were ashamed.
21 For now [a]ye are no thing; ye see *my* casting down, and [b]are afraid.
22 Did I say, Bring unto me? or, Give a reward for me of your substance?
23 Or, Deliver me from the enemy's hand?
or, Redeem me from the hand of the mighty?
24 Teach me, and I will hold my tongue: and
cause me to understand wherein I have erred.
25 How forcible are right words! but what
doth your arguing reprove?
26 Do ye imagine to reprove words, and the
speeches of one that is desperate, *which are* as
wind?
27 Yea, ye overwhelm the fatherless, and ye
[a]dig *a pit* for your friend.
28 Now therefore be content, look upon me;
for *it is* evident unto you if I lie.
29 [a]Return, I pray you, let it not be iniquity;
yea, return again, my [b]righteousness *is* in it.
30 Is there iniquity in my tongue? cannot my
taste discern perverse things?

Job: My Suffering Is Comfortless

7 *Is there* not [a]an appointed time to man upon
earth? *are not* his days also like the days of
an hireling?
2 As a servant earnestly desireth the
shadow, and as an hireling looketh for *the reward*
of his work;
3 So am I made to possess [a]months of vanity, and wearisome nights are appointed to me.
4 [a]When I lie down, I say, When shall I

9 [a]Num. 11:15; 1 Kin. 19:4; Job 7:16; 9:21; 10:1
10 [a]Acts 20:20 [b][Lev. 19:2; Is. 57:15]
14 [a][Prov. 17:17]
15 [a]Ps. 38:11 [b]Jer. 15:18
19 [a]Gen. 25:15; Is. 21:14; Jer. 25:23 [b]1 Kin. 10:1; Ps. 72:10; Ezek. 27:22, 23
20 [a]Jer. 14:3
21 [a]Job 13:4 [b]Ps. 38:11
27 [a]Ps. 57:6
29 [a]Job 17:10 [b]Job 27:5, 6; 34:5

CHAPTER 7
1 [a][Job 14:5, 13, 14]; Ps. 39:4
3 [a][Job 15:31]
4 [a]Deut. 28:67; Job 7:13, 14

NKJV

8 "Oh, that I might have my request,
That God would grant *me* the thing that I long for!
9 That it would please God to crush me,
That He would loose His hand and [a]cut me off!
10 Then I would still have comfort;
Though in anguish I would exult,
He will not spare;
For [a]I have not concealed the words of [b]the Holy One.

11 "What strength do I have, that I should hope?
And what *is* my end, that I should prolong my life?
12 *Is* my strength the strength of stones?
Or is my flesh bronze?
13 *Is* my help not within me?
And is success driven from me?

14 "To[a] him who is afflicted, kindness *should be shown* by his friend,
Even though he forsakes the fear of the Almighty.
15 [a]My brothers have dealt deceitfully like a brook,
[b]Like the streams of the brooks that pass away,
16 Which are dark because of the ice,
And into which the snow vanishes.
17 When it is warm, they cease to flow;
When it is hot, they vanish from their place.
18 The paths of their way turn aside,
They go nowhere and perish.
19 The caravans of [a]Tema look,
The travelers of [b]Sheba hope for them.
20 They are [a]disappointed because they were confident;
They come there and are confused.
21 For now [a]you are nothing,
You see terror and [b]are afraid.
22 Did I ever say, 'Bring *something* to me'?
Or, 'Offer a bribe for me from your wealth'?
23 Or, 'Deliver me from the enemy's hand'?
Or, 'Redeem me from the hand of oppressors'?

24 "Teach me, and I will hold my tongue;
Cause me to understand wherein I have erred.
25 How forceful are right words!
But what does your arguing prove?
26 Do you intend to rebuke *my* words,
And the speeches of a desperate one, *which are* as wind?
27 Yes, you overwhelm the fatherless,
And you [a]undermine your friend.
28 Now therefore, be pleased to look at me;
For I would never lie to your face.
29 [a]Yield now, let there be no injustice!
Yes, concede, my [b]righteousness still stands!
30 Is there injustice on my tongue?
Cannot my taste discern the unsavory?

Job: My Suffering Is Comfortless

7 "*Is there* not [a]a time of hard service for man on earth?
Are not his days also like the days of a hired man?
2 Like a servant who earnestly desires the shade,
And like a hired man who eagerly looks for his wages,
3 So I have been allotted [a]months of futility,
And wearisome nights have been appointed to me.
4 [a]When I lie down, I say, 'When shall I arise,

KJV

arise, and the night be gone? and I am full of toss-
ings to and fro unto the dawning of the day.
5 My flesh is [a]clothed with worms and clods
of dust; my skin is broken, and become loathsome.
6 [a]My days are swifter than a weaver's shuttle, and are spent without hope.
7 O remember that [a]my life *is* wind: mine
eye shall no more see good.
8 [a]The eye of him that hath seen me shall
see me no *more:* thine eyes *are* upon me, and I
am not.
9 *As* the cloud is consumed and vanisheth
away; so [a]he that goeth down to the grave shall
come up no *more.*
10 He shall return no more to his house,
[a]neither shall his place know him any more.
11 Therefore I will [a]not refrain my mouth; I
will speak in the anguish of my spirit; I will [b]com-
plain in the bitterness of my soul.
12 *Am* I a sea, or a whale, that thou settest
a watch over me?
13 [a]When I say, My bed shall comfort me,
my couch shall ease my complaint;
14 Then thou scarest me with dreams, and
terrifiest me through visions:
15 So that my soul chooseth strangling, *and*
death rather than my life.
16 [a]I loathe *it;* I would not live alway: [b]let
me alone; for [c]my days *are* vanity.
17 [a]What *is* man, that thou shouldest magnify him? and that thou shouldest set thine heart
upon him?
18 And *that* thou shouldest visit him every
morning, *and* try him every moment?
19 How long wilt thou not depart from me,
nor let me alone till I swallow down my spittle?
20 I have sinned; what shall I do unto thee,
[a]O thou preserver of men? why [b]hast thou set me
as a mark against thee, so that I am a burden to
myself?
21 And why dost thou not pardon my transgression, and take away mine iniquity? for now
shall I sleep in the dust; and thou shalt seek me
in the morning, but I *shall* not *be.*

Bildad: Job Should Repent

8 Then answered Bildad the Shuhite, and said,
2 How long wilt thou speak these *things?*
and *how long shall* the words of thy mouth *be*
like a strong wind?
3 [a]Doth God pervert judgment? or doth the
Almighty pervert justice?
4 If [a]thy children have sinned against him,
and he have cast them away for their transgression;
5 [a]If thou wouldest seek unto God betimes,
and make thy supplication to the Almighty;
6 If thou *wert* pure and upright; surely now
he would awake for thee, and make the habitation
of thy righteousness prosperous.
7 Though thy beginning was small, yet thy
latter end should greatly [a]increase.
8 [a]For enquire, I pray thee, of the former
age, and prepare thyself to the search of their
fathers:

5 [a]Is. 14:11
6 [a]Job 9:25; 16:22; 17:11; Is. 38:12; [James 4:14]
7 [a]Job 7:16; Ps. 78:39; 89:47
8 [a]Job 8:18; 20:9
9 [a]2 Sam. 12:23
10 [a]Ps. 103:16
11 [a]Ps. 39:1, 9 [b]1 Sam. 1:10
13 [a]Job 9:27
16 [a]Job 10:1 [b]Job 14:6 [c]Ps. 62:9
17 [a]Job 22:2; Ps. 8:4; 144:3; Heb. 2:6
20 [a]Ps. 36:6 [b]Ps. 21:12

CHAPTER 8
3 [a]Gen. 18:25; [Deut. 32:4; 2 Chr. 19:7; Job 34:10, 12; 36:23; 37:23]; Rom. 3:5
4 [a]Job 1:5, 18, 19
5 [a][Job 5:17–27; 11:13]
7 [a]Job 42:12
8 [a]Deut. 4:32; 32:7; Job 15:18; 20:4

*______

7:15 Lit. *my bones*
7:20 So with MT, Tg., Vg.; LXX, Jewish tradition *to You*

NKJV

And the night be ended?'
For I have had my fill of tossing till dawn.
5 My flesh is [a]caked with worms and dust,
My skin is cracked and breaks out afresh.

6 "My[a] days are swifter than a weaver's shuttle,
And are spent without hope.
7 Oh, remember that [a]my life *is* a breath!
My eye will never again see good.
8 [a]The eye of him who sees me will see me no *more;*
While your *eyes* are upon me, I shall no longer *be.*
9 *As* the cloud disappears and vanishes away,
So [a]he who goes down to the grave does not come up.
10 He shall never return to his house,
[a]Nor shall his place know him anymore.

11 "Therefore I will [a]not restrain my mouth;
I will speak in the anguish of my spirit;
I will [b]complain in the bitterness of my soul.
12 *Am* I a sea, or a sea serpent,
That You set a guard over me?
13 [a]When I say, 'My bed will comfort me,
My couch will ease my complaint,'
14 Then You scare me with dreams
And terrify me with visions,
15 So that my soul chooses strangling
And death rather than *my body.
16 [a]I loathe *my life;*
I would not live forever.
[b]Let me alone,
For [c]my days *are but* a breath.

17 "What[a] *is* man, that You should exalt him,
That You should set Your heart on him,
18 That You should visit him every morning,
And test him every moment?
19 How long?
Will You not look away from me,
And let me alone till I swallow my saliva?
20 Have I sinned?
What have I done to You, [a]O watcher of men?
Why [b]have You set me as Your target,
So that I am a burden *to myself?
21 Why then do You not pardon my transgression,
And take away my iniquity?
For now I will lie down in the dust,
And You will seek me diligently,
But I *will* no longer *be.*"

Bildad: Job Should Repent

8 Then Bildad the Shuhite answered and said:
2 "How long will you speak these *things,*
And the words of your mouth *be like* a strong wind?
3 [a]Does God subvert judgment?
Or does the Almighty pervert justice?
4 If [a]your sons have sinned against Him,
He has cast them away for their transgression.
5 [a]If you would earnestly seek God
And make your supplication to the Almighty,
6 If you *were* pure and upright,
Surely now He would awake for you,
And prosper your rightful dwelling place.
7 Though your beginning was small,
Yet your latter end would [a]increase abundantly.

8 "For[a] inquire, please, of the former age,
And consider the things discovered by their fathers;

KJV

9 (For [a]we *are but of* yesterday, and know
nothing, because our days upon earth *are* a
shadow:)
10 Shall not they teach thee, *and* tell thee,
and utter words out of their heart?
11 Can the rush grow up without mire? can
the flag grow without water?
12 [a]Whilst it *is* yet in his greenness, *and* not
cut down, it withereth before any *other* herb.
13 So *are* the paths of all that [a]forget God;
and the [b]hypocrite's hope shall perish:
14 Whose hope shall be cut off, and whose
trust *shall be* a spider's web.
15 [a]He shall lean upon his house, but it shall
not stand: he shall hold it fast, but it shall not
endure.
16 He *is* green before the sun, and his branch
shooteth forth in his garden.
17 His roots are wrapped about the heap, *and*
seeth the place of stones.
18 [a]If he destroy him from his place, then *it*
shall deny him, *saying,* I have not seen thee.
19 Behold, this *is* the joy of his way, and [a]out
of the earth shall others grow.
20 Behold, [a]God will not cast away a perfect
man, neither will he help the evil doers:
21 Till he fill thy mouth with laughing, and
thy lips with rejoicing.
22 They that hate thee shall be [a]clothed with
shame; and the dwelling place of the wicked shall
come to nought.

Job: There Is No Mediator

9 Then Job answered and said,
2 I know *it is* so of a truth: but how should
[a]man be [b]just with God?
3 If he will contend with him, he cannot answer him one of a thousand.
4 [a]*He is* wise in heart, and mighty in
strength: who hath hardened *himself* against him,
and hath prospered?
5 Which removeth the mountains, and they
know not; which overturneth them in his anger.
6 Which [a]shaketh the earth out of her place,
and the [b]pillars thereof tremble.
7 Which commandeth the sun, and it riseth
not; and sealeth up the stars.
8 [a]Which alone spreadeth out the heavens,
and treadeth upon the waves of the sea.
9 [a]Which maketh Arcturus, Orion, and
Pleiades, and the chambers of the south.
10 [a]Which doeth great things past finding
out; yea, and wonders without number.
11 [a]Lo, he goeth by me, and I see *him* not:
he passeth on also, but I perceive him not.
12 [a]Behold, he taketh away, who can hinder
him? who will say unto him, What doest thou?
13 *If* God will not withdraw his anger, [a]the
proud helpers do stoop under him.
14 How much less shall I answer him, *and*
choose out my words *to reason* with him?

9 [a]Gen. 47:9; [1 Chr. 29:15]; Job 7:6; [Ps. 39:5; 102:11; 144:4]
12 [a]Ps. 129:6
13 [a]Ps. 9:17 [b]Job 11:20; 18:14; 27:8; Ps. 112:10; [Prov. 10:28]
15 [a]Job 8:22; 27:18; Ps. 49:11
18 [a]Job 7:10
19 [a]Ps. 113:7
20 [a]Job 4:7
22 [a]Ps. 35:26; 109:29

CHAPTER 9

2 [a][Job 4:17; 15:14–16; Ps. 143:2; Rom. 3:20] [b][Hab. 2:4; Rom. 1:17; Gal. 3:11; Heb. 10:38]
4 [a]Job 36:5
6 [a]Is. 2:19, 21; Hag. 2:6; Heb. 12:26 [b]Job 26:11
8 [a]Gen. 1:6; Job 37:18; Ps. 104:2, 3; Is. 40:22
9 [a]Gen. 1:16; Job 38:31; Amos 5:8
10 [a]Job 5:9
11 [a][Job 23:8, 9; 35:14]
12 [a][Is. 45:9; Dan. 4:35; Rom. 9:20]
13 [a]Job 26:12

NKJV

9 For [a]we *were born* yesterday, and know nothing,
Because our days on earth *are* a shadow.
10 Will they not teach you and tell you,
And utter words from their heart?

11 "Can the papyrus grow up without a marsh?
Can the reeds flourish without water?
12 [a]While it *is* yet green *and* not cut down,
It withers before any *other* plant.
13 So *are* the paths of all who [a]forget God;
And the hope of the [b]hypocrite shall perish,
14 Whose confidence shall be cut off,
And whose trust *is* a spider's web.
15 [a]He leans on his house, but it does not stand.
He holds it fast, but it does not endure.
16 He grows green in the sun,
And his branches spread out in his garden.
17 His roots wrap around the rock heap,
And look for a place in the stones.
18 [a]If he is destroyed from his place,
Then *it* will deny him, *saying,* 'I have not seen you.'

19 "Behold, this is the joy of His way,
And [a]out of the earth others will grow.
20 Behold, [a]God will not cast away the blameless,
Nor will He uphold the evildoers.
21 He will yet fill your mouth with laughing,
And your lips with rejoicing.
22 Those who hate you will be [a]clothed with shame,
And the dwelling place of the wicked *will come to nothing."

Job: There Is No Mediator

9 Then Job answered and said:

2 "Truly I know *it is* so,
But how can a [a]man be [b]righteous before God?
3 If one wished to contend with Him,
He could not answer Him one time out of a thousand.
4 [a]*God is* wise in heart and mighty in strength.
Who has hardened *himself* against Him and prospered?
5 He removes the mountains, and they do not know
When He overturns them in His anger;
6 He [a]shakes the earth out of its place,
And its [b]pillars tremble;
7 He commands the sun, and it does not rise;
He seals off the stars;
8 [a]He alone spreads out the heavens,
And treads on the waves of the sea;
9 [a]He made the Bear, Orion, and the Pleiades,
And the chambers of the south;
10 [a]He does great things past finding out,
Yes, wonders without number.
11 [a]If He goes by me, I do not see *Him;*
If He moves past, I do not perceive Him;
12 [a]If He takes away, who can hinder Him?
Who can say to Him, 'What are You doing?'
13 God will not withdraw His anger,
[a]The allies of *the proud lie prostrate beneath Him.

14 "How then can I answer Him,
And choose my words *to reason* with Him?

8:22 Lit. *will not be*
9:13 Heb. *rahab*

KJV

15 [a]Whom, though I were righteous, *yet* would I not answer, *but* I would make supplication to my judge.
16 If I had called, and he had answered me; *yet* would I not believe that he had hearkened unto my voice.
17 For he breaketh me with a tempest, and multiplieth my wounds [a]without cause.
18 He will not suffer me to take my breath, but filleth me with bitterness.
19 If *I speak* of strength, lo, *he is* strong: and if of judgment, who shall set me a time *to plead?*
20 If I justify myself, mine own mouth shall condemn me: *if I say,* I *am* perfect, it shall also prove me perverse.
21 *Though* I *were* perfect, *yet* would I not know my soul: I would despise my life.
22 This *is* one *thing,* therefore I said *it,* [a]He destroyeth the perfect and the wicked.
23 If the scourge slay suddenly, he will laugh at the trial of the innocent.
24 The earth is given into the hand of the wicked: he covereth the faces of the judges thereof; if not, where, *and* who *is* he?
25 Now [a]my days are swifter than a post: they flee away, they see no good.
26 They are passed away as the swift ships: [a]as the eagle *that* hasteth to the prey.
27 [a]If I say, I will forget my complaint, I will leave off my heaviness, and comfort *myself;*
28 [a]I am afraid of all my sorrows, I know that thou [b]wilt not hold me innocent.
29 *If* I be wicked, why then labour I in vain?
30 [a]If I wash myself with snow water, and make my hands never so clean;
31 Yet shalt thou plunge me in the ditch, and mine own clothes shall abhor me.
32 For [a]*he is* not a man, as I *am, that* I should answer him, *and* we should come together in judgment.
33 [a]Neither is there any daysman betwixt us, *that* might lay his hand upon us both.
34 [a]Let him take his rod away from me, and let not his fear terrify me:
35 *Then* would I speak, and not fear him; *but it is* not so with me.

Job: I Would Plead with God

10 My [a]soul is weary of my life; I will leave my complaint upon myself; [b]I will speak in the bitterness of my soul.
2 I will say unto God, Do not condemn me; shew me wherefore thou contendest with me.
3 *Is it* good unto thee that thou shouldest oppress, that thou shouldest despise the work of thine hands, and shine upon the counsel of the wicked?
4 Hast thou eyes of flesh? or [a]seest thou as man seeth?
5 *Are* thy days as the days of man? *are* thy years as man's days,
6 That thou enquirest after mine iniquity, and searchest after my sin?
7 Thou knowest that I am not wicked; and *there is* none that can deliver out of thine hand.

15 [a]Job 10:15; 23:1–7
17 [a]Job 2:3
22 [a][Eccl. 9:2, 3]; Ezek. 21:3
25 [a]Job 7:6, 7
26 [a]Job 39:29; Hab. 1:8
27 [a]Job 7:13
28 [a]Ps. 119:120 [b]Ex. 20:7
30 [a][Jer. 2:22]
32 [a]Eccl. 6:10; [Is. 45:9; Jer. 49:19; Rom. 9:20]
33 [a][1 Sam. 2:25]; Job 9:19; Is. 1:18
34 [a]Job 13:20, 21; Ps. 39:10

CHAPTER 10
1 [a]1 Kin. 19:4; Job 7:16; Jon. 4:3 [b]Job 7:11
4 [a][1 Sam. 16:7; Job 28:24; 34:21]

NKJV

15 [a]For though I were righteous, I could not answer Him;
I would beg mercy of my Judge.
16 If I called and He answered me,
I would not believe that He was listening to my voice.
17 For He crushes me with a tempest,
And multiplies my wounds [a]without cause.
18 He will not allow me to catch my breath,
But fills me with bitterness.
19 If *it is a matter* of strength, indeed *He is* strong;
And if of justice, who will appoint my day *in court?*
20 Though I were righteous, my own mouth would condemn me;
Though I *were* blameless, it would prove me perverse.

21 "I am blameless, yet I do not know myself;
I despise my life.
22 It *is* all one *thing;*
Therefore I say, [a]'He destroys the blameless and the wicked.'
23 If the scourge slays suddenly,
He laughs at the plight of the innocent.
24 The earth is given into the hand of the wicked.
He covers the faces of its judges.
If it is not *He,* who else could it be?

25 "Now [a]my days are swifter than a runner;
They flee away, they see no good.
26 They pass by like swift ships,
[a]Like an eagle swooping on its prey.
27 [a]If I say, 'I will forget my complaint,
I will put off my sad face and wear a smile,'
28 [a]I am afraid of all my sufferings;
I know that You [b]will not hold me innocent.
29 *If* I am condemned,
Why then do I labor in vain?
30 [a]If I wash myself with snow water,
And cleanse my hands with soap,
31 Yet You will plunge me into the pit,
And my own clothes will abhor me.

32 "For [a]*He is* not a man, as I *am,*
That I may answer Him,
And that we should go to court together.
33 [a]Nor is there any mediator between us,
Who may lay his hand on us both.
34 [a]Let Him take His rod away from me,
And do not let dread of Him terrify me.
35 *Then* I would speak and not fear Him,
But it is not so with me.

Job: I Would Plead with God

10 "My [a]soul loathes my life;
I will give free course to my complaint,
[b]I will speak in the bitterness of my soul.
2 I will say to God, 'Do not condemn me;
Show me why You contend with me.
3 *Does it* seem good to You that You should oppress,
That You should despise the work of Your hands,
And smile on the counsel of the wicked?
4 Do You have eyes of flesh?
Or [a]do You see as man sees?
5 *Are* Your days like the days of a mortal man?
Are Your years like the days of a mighty man,
6 That You should seek for my iniquity
And search out my sin,
7 Although You know that I am not wicked,
And *there is* no one who can deliver from Your hand?

KJV

8 [a]Thine hands have made me and fashioned me together round about; yet thou dost
[b]destroy me.
9 Remember, I beseech thee, [a]that thou hast
made me as the clay; and wilt thou bring me into
dust again?
10 [a]Hast thou not poured me out as milk, and
curdled me like cheese?
11 Thou hast clothed me with skin and flesh,
and hast fenced me with bones and sinews.
12 Thou hast granted me life and favour, and
thy visitation hath preserved my spirit.
13 And these *things* hast thou hid in thine
heart: I know that this *is* with thee.
14 If I sin, then [a]thou markest me, and thou
wilt not acquit me from mine iniquity.
15 If I be wicked, [a]woe unto me; [b]and *if* I be
righteous, *yet* will I not lift up my head. *I am* full
of confusion; therefore [c]see thou mine affliction;
16 For it increaseth. [a]Thou huntest me as a
fierce lion: and again thou shewest thyself marvellous upon me.
17 Thou renewest thy witnesses against me,
and increasest thine indignation upon me;
changes and war *are* against me.
18 [a]Wherefore then hast thou brought me
forth out of the womb? Oh that I had given up
the ghost, and no eye had seen me!
19 I should have been as though I had not
been; I should have been carried from the womb
to the grave.
20 [a]*Are* not my days few? cease *then, and*
[b]let me alone, that I may take comfort a little,
21 Before I go *whence* I shall not return,
[a]*even* to the land of darkness [b]and the shadow
of death;
22 A land of darkness, as darkness *itself; and*
of the shadow of death, without any order, and
where the light *is* as darkness.

Zophar Urges Job to Repent

11 Then answered Zophar the Naamathite,
and said,
2 Should not the multitude of words be answered? and should a man full of talk be justified?
3 Should thy lies make men hold their
peace? and when thou mockest, shall no man
make thee ashamed?
4 For [a]thou hast said, My doctrine *is* pure,
and I am clean in thine eyes.
5 But oh that God would speak, and open
his lips against thee;
6 And that he would shew thee the secrets
of wisdom, that *they are* double to that which is!
Know therefore that [a]God exacteth of thee *less*
than thine iniquity *deserveth*.
7 [a]Canst thou by searching find out God?
canst thou find out the Almighty unto perfection?

8 [a]Job 10:3; Ps. 119:73 [b][Job 9:22] **9** [a]Gen. 2:7; Job 33:6 **10** [a][Ps. 139:14–16] **14** [a]Job 7:20; Ps. 139:1 **15** [a]Job 10:7; Is. 3:11 [b][Job 9:12, 15] [c]Ps. 25:18 **16** [a]Is. 38:13; Lam. 3:10; Hos. 13:7 **18** [a]Job 3:11–13 **20** [a]Ps. 39:5 [b]Job 7:16, 19 **21** [a]Ps. 88:12 [b]Ps. 23:4

CHAPTER 11

4 [a]Job 6:30 **6** [a][Ezra 9:13] **7** [a]Job 33:12, 13; 36:26; [Eccl. 3:11; Rom. 11:33]

NKJV

8 'Your[a] hands have made me and fashioned
me,
An intricate unity;
Yet You would [b]destroy me.
9 Remember, I pray, [a]that You have made
me like clay.
And will You turn me into dust again?
10 [a]Did You not pour me out like milk,
And curdle me like cheese,
11 Clothe me with skin and flesh,
And knit me together with bones and
sinews?
12 You have granted me life and favor,
And Your care has preserved my spirit.

13 'And these *things* You have hidden in Your
heart;
I know that this *was* with You:
14 If I sin, then [a]You mark me,
And will not acquit me of my iniquity.
15 If I am wicked, [a]woe to me;
[b]Even *if* I am righteous, I cannot lift up my
head.
I am full of disgrace;
[c]See my misery!
16 If *my head* is exalted,
[a]You hunt me like a fierce lion,
And again You show Yourself awesome
against me.
17 You renew Your witnesses against me,
And increase Your indignation toward
me;
Changes and war are *ever* with me.

18 'Why[a] then have You brought me out of
the womb?
Oh, that I had perished and no eye had
seen me!
19 I would have been as though I had not
been.
I would have been carried from the womb
to the grave.
20 [a]Are not my days few?
Cease! [b]Leave me alone, that I may take
a little comfort,
21 Before I go *to the place from which* I shall
not return,
[a]To the land of darkness [b]and the shadow
of death,
22 A land as dark as darkness *itself*,
As the shadow of death, without any
order,
Where even the light *is* like darkness.' "

Zophar Urges Job to Repent

11 Then Zophar the Naamathite answered and
said:

2 "Should not the multitude of words be
answered?
And should a man full of talk be
vindicated?
3 Should your empty talk make men hold
their peace?
And when you mock, should no one
rebuke you?
4 For you have said,
[a]'My doctrine *is* pure,
And I am clean in your eyes.'
5 But oh, that God would speak,
And open His lips against you,
6 That He would show you the secrets of
wisdom!
For *they would* double *your* prudence.
Know therefore that [a]God exacts from you
Less than your iniquity *deserves*.

7 "Can[a] you search out the deep things of
God?
Can you find out the limits of the
Almighty?

KJV

8 *It is* as high as heaven; what canst thou do? deeper than hell; what canst thou know?

9 The measure thereof *is* longer than the earth, and broader than the sea.

10 [a]If he cut off, and shut up, or gather together, then who can hinder him?

11 For [a]he knoweth vain men: he seeth wickedness also; will he not then consider *it?*

12 For [a]vain man would be wise, though man be born *like* a wild ass's colt.

13 If thou [a]prepare thine heart, and [b]stretch out thine hands toward him;

14 If iniquity *be* in thine hand, put it far away, and [a]let not wickedness dwell in thy tabernacles.

15 [a]For then shalt thou lift up thy face without spot; yea, thou shalt be stedfast, and shalt not fear:

16 Because thou shalt [a]forget *thy* misery, *and* remember *it* as waters *that* pass away:

17 And *thine* age [a]shall be clearer than the noonday; thou shalt shine forth, thou shalt be as the morning.

18 And thou shalt be secure, because there is hope; yea, thou shalt dig *about thee, and* [a]thou shalt take thy rest in safety.

19 Also thou shalt lie down, and none shall make *thee* afraid; yea, many shall make suit unto thee.

20 But [a]the eyes of the wicked shall fail, and they shall not escape, and [b]their hope *shall be as* the giving up of the ghost.

Job Answers His Critics

12 And Job answered and said,

2 No doubt but ye *are* the people, and wisdom shall die with you.

3 But I have understanding as well as you; I *am* not [a]inferior to you: yea, who knoweth not such things as these?

4 [a]I am *as* one mocked of his neighbour, who [b]calleth upon God, and he answereth him: the just upright *man is* laughed to scorn.

5 [a]He that is ready to slip with *his* feet *is as* a lamp despised in the thought of him that is at ease.

6 [a]The tabernacles of robbers prosper, and they that provoke God are secure; into whose hand God bringeth *abundantly.*

7 But ask now the beasts, and they shall teach thee; and the fowls of the air, and they shall tell thee:

8 Or speak to the earth, and it shall teach thee; and the fishes of the sea shall declare unto thee:

9 Who knoweth not in all these that the hand of the LORD hath wrought this?

10 [a]In whose hand *is* the soul of every living thing, and the [b]breath of all mankind.

11 Doth not the ear try words? and the mouth taste his meat?

12 With the ancient *is* wisdom; and in length of days understanding.

13 With him *is* [a]wisdom and strength, he hath counsel and understanding.

---

10 [a]Job 9:12; [Rev. 3:7]
11 [a][Ps. 10:14]
12 [a][Ps. 39:5]; Rom. 1:22
13 [a][1 Sam. 7:3] [b]Ps. 88:9
14 [a]Ps. 101:3
15 [a]Job 22:26; Ps. 119:6; [1 John 3:21]
16 [a]Is. 65:16
17 [a]Ps. 37:6; Prov. 4:18; Is. 58:8, 10
18 [a]Lev. 26:5, 6; Ps. 3:5; Prov. 3:24
20 [a]Lev. 26:16; Deut. 28:65; Job 17:5 [b]Job 18:14; [Prov. 11:7]

CHAPTER 12

3 [a]Job 13:2
4 [a]Job 21:3 [b]Ps. 91:15
5 [a]Prov. 14:2
6 [a][Job 9:24; 21:6–16; Ps. 73:12; Jer. 12:1; Mal. 3:15]
10 [a][Acts 17:28] [b]Job 27:3; 33:4
13 [a]Job 9:4; 36:5

*

12:5 Or *disaster*

NKJV

8 *They are* higher than heaven— what can you do?
Deeper than Sheol— what can you know?
9 Their measure *is* longer than the earth
And broader than the sea.

10 "If[a] He passes by, imprisons, and gathers *to judgment,*
Then who can hinder Him?
11 For [a]He knows deceitful men;
He sees wickedness also.
Will He not then consider *it?*
12 For an [a]empty-headed man will be wise,
When a wild donkey's colt is born a man.

13 "If you would [a]prepare your heart,
And [b]stretch out your hands toward Him;
14 If iniquity *were* in your hand, *and you* put it far away,
And [a]would not let wickedness dwell in your tents;
15 [a]Then surely you could lift up your face without spot;
Yes, you could be steadfast, and not fear;
16 Because you would [a]forget *your* misery,
And remember *it* as waters *that have* passed away,
17 And *your* life [a]would be brighter than noonday.
Though you were dark, you would be like the morning.
18 And you would be secure, because there is hope;
Yes, you would dig *around you, and* [a]take your rest in safety.
19 You would also lie down, and no one would make *you* afraid;
Yes, many would court your favor.
20 But [a]the eyes of the wicked will fail,
And they shall not escape,
And [b]their hope—loss of life!"

Job Answers His Critics

12 Then Job answered and said:

2 "No doubt you *are* the people,
And wisdom will die with you!
3 But I have understanding as well as you;
I *am* not [a]inferior to you.
Indeed, who does not *know* such things as these?

4 "I[a] am one mocked by his friends,
Who [b]called on God, and He answered him,
The just and blameless *who is* ridiculed.
5 A *lamp is despised in the thought of one who is at ease;
It is made ready for [a]those whose feet slip.
6 [a]The tents of robbers prosper,
And those who provoke God are secure—
In what God provides by His hand.

7 "But now ask the beasts, and they will teach you;
And the birds of the air, and they will tell you;
8 Or speak to the earth, and it will teach you;
And the fish of the sea will explain to you.
9 Who among all these does not know
That the hand of the LORD has done this,
10 [a]In whose hand *is* the life of every living thing,
And the [b]breath of all mankind?
11 Does not the ear test words
And the mouth taste its food?
12 Wisdom *is* with aged men,
And with length of days, understanding.

13 "With Him *are* [a]wisdom and strength,
He has counsel and understanding.

KJV

14 Behold, [a]he breaketh down, and it cannot be built again: he shutteth up a man, and there can be no opening.

15 Behold, he [a]withholdeth the waters, and they dry up: also he [b]sendeth them out, and they overturn the earth.

16 With him *is* strength and wisdom: the deceived and the deceiver *are* his.

17 He leadeth counsellors away spoiled, and maketh the judges fools.

18 He looseth the bond of kings, and girdeth their loins with a girdle.

19 He leadeth princes away spoiled, and overthroweth the mighty.

20 [a]He removeth away the speech of the trusty, and taketh away the understanding of the aged.

21 [a]He poureth contempt upon princes, and weakeneth the strength of the mighty.

22 He [a]discovereth deep things out of darkness, and bringeth out to light the shadow of death.

23 [a]He increaseth the nations, and destroyeth them: he enlargeth the nations, and straiteneth them *again*.

24 He taketh away the heart of the chief of the people of the earth, and [a]causeth them to wander in a wilderness *where there is* no way.

25 [a]They grope in the dark without light, and he maketh them to [b]stagger like *a* drunken *man*.

13 Lo, mine eye hath seen all *this*, mine ear hath heard and understood it.

2 [a]What ye know, *the same* do I know also: I *am* not inferior unto you.

3 [a]Surely I would speak to the Almighty, and I desire to reason with God.

4 But ye *are* forgers of lies, [a]ye *are* all physicians of no value.

5 O that ye would altogether hold your peace! and [a]it should be your wisdom.

6 Hear now my reasoning, and hearken to the pleadings of my lips.

7 [a]Will ye speak wickedly for God? and talk deceitfully for him?

8 Will ye accept his person? will ye contend for God?

9 Is it good that he should search you out? or as one man mocketh another, do ye *so* mock him?

10 He will surely reprove you, if ye do secretly accept persons.

11 Shall not his excellency make you afraid? and his dread fall upon you?

12 Your remembrances *are* like unto ashes, your bodies to bodies of clay.

13 Hold your peace, let me alone, that I may speak, and let come on me what *will*.

14 Wherefore [a]do I take my flesh in my teeth, and put my life in mine hand?

15 [a]Though he slay me, yet will I trust in him: [b]but I will maintain mine own ways before him.

16 He also *shall be* my salvation: for an [a]hypocrite shall not come before him.

17 Hear diligently my speech, and my declaration with your ears.

18 Behold now, I have ordered *my* cause; I know that I shall be [a]justified.

19 [a]Who *is* he *that* will plead with me? for now, if I hold my tongue, I shall give up the ghost.

Job's Despondent Prayer

20 [a]Only do not two *things* unto me: then I will not hide myself from thee.

14 [a]Job 11:10; Is. 25:2
15 [a]Deut. 11:17; [1 Kin. 8:35, 36] [b]Gen. 7:11–24
20 [a]Job 32:9
21 [a][Job 34:19]; Ps. 107:40; [Dan. 2:21]
22 [a]Dan. 2:22; [1 Cor. 4:5]
23 [a]Is. 9:3; 26:15
24 [a]Ps. 107:4
25 [a]Job 5:14; 15:30; 18:18 [b]Ps. 107:27

CHAPTER 13

2 [a]Job 12:3
3 [a]Job 23:3; 31:35
4 [a]Job 6:21; [Jer. 23:32]
5 [a]Job 13:13; 21:5; Prov. 17:28
7 [a]Job 27:4; 36:4
14 [a]Job 18:4
15 [a]Ps. 23:4; [Prov. 14:32] [b]Job 27:5
16 [a]Job 8:13
18 [a][Rom. 8:34]
19 [a]Job 7:21; 10:8; Is. 50:8
20 [a]Job 9:34

*

12:19 Lit. *priests*, but not in a technical sense
12:24 Lit. *heart*

NKJV

14 If [a]He breaks *a thing* down, it cannot be rebuilt;
If He imprisons a man, there can be no release.
15 If He [a]withholds the waters, they dry up;
If He [b]sends them out, they overwhelm the earth.
16 With Him *are* strength and prudence.
The deceived and the deceiver *are* His.
17 He leads counselors away plundered,
And makes fools of the judges.
18 He loosens the bonds of kings,
And binds their waist with a belt.
19 He leads *princes away plundered,
And overthrows the mighty.
20 [a]He deprives the trusted ones of speech,
And takes away the discernment of the elders.
21 [a]He pours contempt on princes,
And disarms the mighty.
22 He [a]uncovers deep things out of darkness,
And brings the shadow of death to light.
23 [a]He makes nations great, and destroys them;
He enlarges nations, and guides them.
24 He takes away the *understanding of the chiefs of the people of the earth,
And [a]makes them wander in a pathless wilderness.
25 [a]They grope in the dark without light,
And He makes them [b]stagger like a drunken *man*.

13 "Behold, my eye has seen all *this*,
My ear has heard and understood it.
2 [a]What you know, I also know;
I *am* not inferior to you.
3 [a]But I would speak to the Almighty,
And I desire to reason with God.
4 But you forgers of lies,
[a]You *are* all worthless physicians.
5 Oh, that you would be silent,
And [a]it would be your wisdom!
6 Now hear my reasoning,
And heed the pleadings of my lips.
7 [a]Will you speak wickedly for God,
And talk deceitfully for Him?
8 Will you show partiality for Him?
Will you contend for God?
9 Will it be well when He searches you out?
Or can you mock Him as one mocks a man?
10 He will surely rebuke you
If you secretly show partiality.
11 Will not His excellence make you afraid,
And the dread of Him fall upon you?
12 Your platitudes *are* proverbs of ashes,
Your defenses are defenses of clay.

13 "Hold your peace with me, and let me speak,
Then let come on me what *may!*
14 Why [a]do I take my flesh in my teeth,
And put my life in my hands?
15 [a]Though He slay me, yet will I trust Him.
[b]Even so, I will defend my own ways before Him.
16 He also *shall* be my salvation,
For a [a]hypocrite could not come before Him.
17 Listen carefully to my speech,
And to my declaration with your ears.
18 See now, I have prepared *my* case,
I know that I shall be [a]vindicated.
19 [a]Who *is* he *who* will contend with me?
If now I hold my tongue, I perish.

Job's Despondent Prayer

20 "Only[a] two *things* do not do to me,
Then I will not hide myself from You:

KJV

21 [a]Withdraw thine hand far from me: and
let not thy dread make me afraid.
22 Then call thou, and I will [a]answer: or let
me speak, and answer thou me.
23 How many *are* mine iniquities and sins?
make me to know my transgression and my sin.
24 [a]Wherefore hidest thou thy face, and
[b]holdest me for thine enemy?
25 [a]Wilt thou break a leaf driven to and fro?
and wilt thou pursue the dry stubble?
26 For thou writest bitter things against me,
and [a]makest me to possess the iniquities of my
youth.
27 [a]Thou puttest my feet also in the stocks,
and lookest narrowly unto all my paths; thou settest a print upon the heels of my feet.
28 And he, as a rotten thing, consumeth, as
a garment that is moth eaten.

14 Man *that is* born of a woman *is* of few days,
and [a]full of trouble.
2 [a]He cometh forth like a flower, and is cut
down: he fleeth also as a shadow, and continueth
not.
3 And [a]dost thou open thine eyes upon such
an one, and [b]bringest me into judgment with thee?
4 Who [a]can bring a clean *thing* out of an
unclean? not one.
5 [a]Seeing his days *are* determined, the number of his months *are* with thee, thou hast appointed his bounds that he cannot pass;
6 [a]Turn from him, that he may rest, till he
shall accomplish, [b]as an hireling, his day.
7 For there is hope of a tree, if it be cut
down, that it will sprout again, and that the tender
branch thereof will not cease.
8 Though the root thereof wax old in the
earth, and the stock thereof die in the ground;
9 *Yet* through the scent of water it will bud,
and bring forth boughs like a plant.
10 But man dieth, and wasteth away: yea,
man giveth up the ghost, and where *is* [a]he?
11 *As* the waters fail from the sea, and the
flood decayeth and drieth up:
12 So man lieth down, and riseth not: [a]till
the heavens *be* no more, they shall not awake,
nor be raised out of their sleep.
13 O that thou wouldest hide me in the grave,
that thou wouldest keep me secret, until thy wrath
be past, that thou wouldest appoint me a set time,
and remember me!
14 If a man die, shall he live *again?* all the
days of my appointed time [a]will I wait, till my
change come.
15 [a]Thou shalt call, and I will answer thee:
thou wilt have a desire to the work of thine hands.
16 [a]For now thou numberest my steps: dost
thou not watch over my sin?
17 [a]My transgression *is* sealed up in a bag,
and thou sewest up mine iniquity.
18 And surely the mountain falling cometh
to nought, and the rock is removed out of his
place.
19 The waters wear the stones: thou washest
away the things which grow *out* of the dust of
the earth; and thou destroyest the hope of man.

21 [a]Job 9:34; Ps. 39:10
22 [a]Job 9:16; 14:15
24 [a][Deut. 32:20]; Ps. 13:1 [b]Lam. 2:5
25 [a]Is. 42:3
26 [a]Job 20:11
27 [a]Job 33:11

CHAPTER 14
1 [a]Job 5:7; Eccl. 2:23
2 [a]Job 8:9; Ps. 90:5, 6, 9; 102:11; 103:15; 144:4; Is. 40:6; James 1:10, 11; 1 Pet. 1:24
3 [a]Ps. 8:4; 144:3 [b][Ps. 143:2]
4 [a][Job 15:14; 25:4; Ps. 51:2, 5, 10; John 3:6; Rom. 5:12; Eph. 2:3]
5 [a]Job 7:1; 21:21; Heb. 9:27
6 [a]Job 7:16, 19; Ps. 39:13 [b]Job 7:1
10 [a]Job 10:21, 22
12 [a]Ps. 102:25, 26; [Is. 51:6; 65:17; 66:22]; Acts 3:21; [2 Pet. 3:7, 10, 11; Rev. 20:11; 21:1]
14 [a]Job 13:15
15 [a]Job 13:22
16 [a]Job 10:6, 14; 13:27; 31:4; 34:21; Ps. 56:8; 139:1–3; Prov. 5:21; [Jer. 32:19]
17 [a]Deut. 32:32–34

*
13:27 Lit. *inscribe a print*
13:28 Lit. *He*
14:3 LXX, Syr., Vg. *him*
14:17 Lit. *plaster over*

NKJV

21 [a]Withdraw Your hand far from me,
And let not the dread of You make me afraid.
22 Then call, and I will [a]answer;
Or let me speak, then You respond to me.
23 How many *are* my iniquities and sins?
Make me know my transgression and my sin.
24 [a]Why do You hide Your face,
And [b]regard me as Your enemy?
25 [a]Will You frighten a leaf driven to and fro?
And will You pursue dry stubble?
26 For You write bitter things against me,
And [a]make me inherit the iniquities of my youth.
27 [a]You put my feet in the stocks,
And watch closely all my paths.
You *set a limit for the soles of my feet.

28 "*Man** decays like a rotten thing,
Like a garment that is moth-eaten.

14 "Man *who is* born of woman
Is of few days and [a]full of trouble.
2 [a]He comes forth like a flower and fades away;
He flees like a shadow and does not continue.
3 And [a]do You open Your eyes on *such a one,
And [b]bring me to judgment with Yourself?
4 Who [a]can bring a clean *thing* out of an unclean?
No one!
5 [a]Since his days *are* determined,
The number of his months *is* with You;
You have appointed his limits, so that he cannot pass.
6 [a]Look away from him that he may rest,
Till [b]like a hired man he finishes his day.

7 "For there is hope for a tree,
If it is cut down, that it will sprout again,
And that its tender shoots will not cease.
8 Though its root may grow old in the earth,
And its stump may die in the ground,
9 *Yet* at the scent of water it will bud
And bring forth branches like a plant.
10 But man dies and is laid away;
Indeed he breathes his last
And where *is* [a]he?
11 *As* water disappears from the sea,
And a river becomes parched and dries up,
12 So man lies down and does not rise.
[a]Till the heavens *are* no more,
They will not awake
Nor be roused from their sleep.

13 "Oh, that You would hide me in the grave,
That You would conceal me until Your wrath is past,
That You would appoint me a set time, and remember me!
14 If a man dies, shall he live *again?*
All the days of my hard service [a]I will wait,
Till my change comes.
15 [a]You shall call, and I will answer You;
You shall desire the work of Your hands.
16 For now [a]You number my steps,
But do not watch over my sin.
17 [a]My transgression *is* sealed up in a bag,
And You *cover my iniquity.

18 "But *as* a mountain falls *and* crumbles away,
And *as* a rock is moved from its place;
19 *As* water wears away stones,
And as torrents wash away the soil of the earth;
So You destroy the hope of man.

KJV

20 Thou prevailest for ever against him, and he passeth: thou changest his countenance, and sendest him away.
21 His sons come to honour, and [a]he knoweth *it* not; and they are brought low, but he perceiveth *it* not of them.
22 But his flesh upon him shall have pain, and his soul within him shall mourn.

Eliphaz Accuses Job of Folly

15 Then answered [a]Eliphaz the Temanite, and said,
2 Should a wise man utter vain knowledge, and fill his belly with the east wind?
3 Should he reason with unprofitable talk? or with speeches wherewith he can do no good?
4 Yea, thou castest off fear, and restrainest prayer before God.
5 For thy mouth uttereth thine iniquity, and thou choosest the tongue of the crafty.
6 [a]Thine own mouth condemneth thee, and not I: yea, thine own lips testify against thee.
7 *Art* thou the first man *that* was born? [a]or wast thou made before the hills?
8 [a]Hast thou heard the secret of God? and dost thou restrain wisdom to thyself?
9 [a]What knowest thou, that we know not? *what* understandest thou, which *is* not in us?
10 [a]With us *are* both the grayheaded and very aged men, much elder than thy father.
11 *Are* the consolations of God small with thee? is there any secret thing with thee?
12 Why doth thine heart carry thee away? and what do thy eyes wink at,
13 That thou turnest thy spirit against God, and lettest *such* words go out of thy mouth?
14 [a]What *is* man, that he should be clean? and *he which is* born of a woman, that he should be righteous?
15 [a]Behold, he putteth no trust in his saints; yea, the heavens are not clean in his sight.
16 [a]How much more abominable and filthy *is* man, [b]which drinketh iniquity like water?
17 I will shew thee, hear me; and that *which* I have seen I will declare;
18 Which wise men have told [a]from their fathers, and have not hid *it:*
19 Unto whom alone the earth was given, and [a]no stranger passed among them.
20 The wicked man travaileth with pain all *his* days, [a]and the number of years is hidden to the oppressor.
21 A dreadful sound *is* in his ears: [a]in prosperity the destroyer shall come upon him.
22 He believeth not that he shall [a]return out of darkness, and he is waited for of the sword.
23 He [a]wandereth abroad for bread, *saying,* Where *is it?* he knoweth [b]that the day of darkness is ready at his hand.
24 Trouble and anguish shall make him afraid; they shall prevail against him, as a king ready to the battle.
25 For he stretcheth out his hand against God, and strengtheneth himself against the Almighty.

21 [a]Eccl. 9:5; Is. 63:16

CHAPTER 15

1 [a]Job 4:1
6 [a]Job 9:20; [Luke 19:22]
7 [a]Job 38:4, 21; Ps. 90:2; Prov. 8:25
8 [a]Job 29:4; Rom. 11:34; [1 Cor. 2:11]
9 [a]Job 12:3; 13:2
10 [a]Job 8:8–10; 12:12; 32:6, 7
14 [a]Job 14:4; Prov. 20:9; [Eccl. 7:20; 1 John 1:8, 10]
15 [a]Job 4:18; 25:5
16 [a]Job 4:19; Ps. 14:3; 53:3 [b]Job 34:7; Prov. 19:28
18 [a]Job 8:8; 20:4
19 [a]Joel 3:17
20 [a]Ps. 90:12
21 [a]Job 20:21; 1 Thess. 5:3
22 [a]Job 14:10–12
23 [a]Ps. 59:15; 109:10 [b]Job 18:12

***15:11** Or *a secret thing*

NKJV

20 You prevail forever against him, and he passes on;
You change his countenance and send him away.
21 His sons come to honor, and [a]he does not know *it;*
They are brought low, and he does not perceive *it.*
22 But his flesh will be in pain over it,
And his soul will mourn over it."

Eliphaz Accuses Job of Folly

15 Then [a]Eliphaz the Temanite answered and said:

2 "Should a wise man answer with empty knowledge,
And fill himself with the east wind?
3 Should he reason with unprofitable talk,
Or by speeches with which he can do no good?
4 Yes, you cast off fear,
And restrain prayer before God.
5 For your iniquity teaches your mouth,
And you choose the tongue of the crafty.
6 [a]Your own mouth condemns you, and not I;
Yes, your own lips testify against you.

7 "*Are* you the first man *who* was born?
[a]Or were you made before the hills?
8 [a]Have you heard the counsel of God?
Do you limit wisdom to yourself?
9 [a]What do you know that we do not know?
What do you understand that *is* not in us?
10 [a]Both the gray-haired and the aged *are* among us,
Much older than your father.
11 *Are* the consolations of God too small for you,
And the word *spoken* *gently with you?
12 Why does your heart carry you away,
And what do your eyes wink at,
13 That you turn your spirit against God,
And let *such* words go out of your mouth?

14 "What[a] *is* man, that he could be pure?
And *he who is* born of a woman, that he could be righteous?
15 [a]If *God* puts no trust in His saints,
And the heavens are not pure in His sight,
16 [a]How much less man, *who is* abominable and filthy,
[b]Who drinks iniquity like water!

17 "I will tell you, hear me;
What I have seen I will declare,
18 What wise men have told,
Not hiding *anything received* [a]from their fathers,
19 To whom alone the land was given,
And [a]no alien passed among them:
20 The wicked man writhes with pain all *his* days,
[a]And the number of years is hidden from the oppressor.
21 Dreadful sounds *are* in his ears;
[a]In prosperity the destroyer comes upon him.
22 He does not believe that he will [a]return from darkness,
For a sword is waiting for him.
23 He [a]wanders about for bread, *saying,* 'Where *is it?*'
He knows [b]that a day of darkness is ready at his hand.
24 Trouble and anguish make him afraid;
They overpower him, like a king ready for battle.
25 For he stretches out his hand against God,
And acts defiantly against the Almighty,

KJV

26 He runneth upon him, *even* on *his* neck, upon the thick bosses of his bucklers:

27 [a]Because he covereth his face with his fatness, and maketh collops of fat on *his* flanks.

28 And he dwelleth in desolate cities, *and* in houses which no man inhabiteth, which are ready to become heaps.

29 He shall not be rich, neither shall his substance [a]continue, neither shall he prolong the perfection thereof upon the earth.

30 He shall not depart out of darkness; the flame shall dry up his branches, and [a]by the breath of his mouth shall he go away.

31 Let not him that is deceived [a]trust in vanity: for vanity shall be his recompence.

32 It shall be accomplished [a]before his time, and his branch shall not be green.

33 He shall shake off his unripe grape as the vine, and shall cast off his flower as the olive.

34 For the congregation of hypocrites *shall be* desolate, and fire shall consume the tabernacles of bribery.

35 [a]They conceive mischief, and bring forth vanity, and their belly prepareth deceit.

Job Reproaches His Pitiless Friends

16 Then Job answered and said,

2 I have heard many such things: [a]miserable comforters *are* ye all.

3 Shall vain words have an end? or what emboldeneth thee that thou answerest?

4 I also could speak as ye *do:* if your soul were in my soul's stead, I could heap up words against you, and [a]shake mine head at you.

5 *But* I would strengthen you with my mouth, and the moving of my lips should asswage *your grief.*

6 Though I speak, my grief is not asswaged: and *though* I forbear, what am I eased?

7 But now he hath made me [a]weary: thou [b]hast made desolate all my company.

8 And thou hast filled me with wrinkles, *which* is a [a]witness *against me:* and my leanness rising up in me beareth witness to my face.

9 [a]He teareth *me* in his wrath, who hateth me: he gnasheth upon me with his teeth; [b]mine enemy sharpeneth his eyes upon me.

10 They have [a]gaped upon me with their mouth; they [b]have smitten me upon the cheek reproachfully; they have gathered themselves together against me.

11 God [a]hath delivered me to the ungodly, and turned me over into the hands of the wicked.

12 I was at ease, but he hath broken me [a]asunder: he hath also taken *me* by my neck, and shaken me to pieces, and [b]set me up for his mark.

13 His archers compass me round about, he cleaveth my reins asunder, and doth not spare; he poureth out my gall upon the ground.

14 He breaketh me with breach upon breach, he runneth upon me like a giant.

15 I have sewed sackcloth upon my skin, and [a]defiled my horn in the dust.

16 My face is foul with weeping, and on my eyelids *is* the shadow of death;

17 Not for *any* injustice in mine hands: also my prayer *is* pure.

---

27 [a]Ps. 17:10; 73:7; 119:70
29 [a]Job 20:28; 27:16, 17
30 [a]Job 4:9
31 [a]Job 35:13; Is. 59:4
32 [a]Job 22:16; Ps. 55:23; Eccl. 7:17
35 [a]Ps. 7:14; Is. 59:4; [Hos. 10:13]

CHAPTER 16

2 [a]Job 13:4; 21:34
4 [a]Ps. 22:7; 109:25; Lam. 2:15; Zeph. 2:15; Matt. 27:39
7 [a]Job 7:3 [b]Job 16:20; 19:13–15
8 [a]Job 10:17
9 [a]Job 10:16, 17; 19:11; Hos. 6:1 [b]Job 13:24; 33:10
10 [a]Ps. 22:13; 35:21 [b]Is. 50:6; Lam. 3:30; Mic. 5:1; Matt. 26:67; Mark 14:65; Luke 22:63; Acts 23:2
11 [a]Job 1:15, 17
12 [a]Job 9:17 [b]Job 7:20; Lam. 3:12
15 [a]Job 30:19; Ps. 7:5

NKJV

26 Running stubbornly against Him
With his strong, embossed shield.

27 "Though[a] he has covered his face with his fatness,
And made *his* waist heavy with fat,
28 He dwells in desolate cities,
In houses which no one inhabits,
Which are destined to become ruins.
29 He will not be rich,
Nor will his wealth [a]continue,
Nor will his possessions overspread the earth.
30 He will not depart from darkness;
The flame will dry out his branches,
And [a]by the breath of His mouth he will go away.
31 Let him not [a]trust in futile *things,*
deceiving himself,
For futility will be his reward.
32 It will be accomplished [a]before his time,
And his branch will not be green.
33 He will shake off his unripe grape like a vine,
And cast off his blossom like an olive tree.
34 For the company of hypocrites *will be* barren,
And fire will consume the tents of bribery.
35 [a]They conceive trouble and bring forth futility;
Their womb prepares deceit."

Job Reproaches His Pitiless Friends

16 Then Job answered and said:

2 "I have heard many such things;
[a]Miserable comforters *are* you all!
3 Shall words of wind have an end?
Or what provokes you that you answer?
4 I also could speak as you *do,*
If your soul were in my soul's place.
I could heap up words against you,
And [a]shake my head at you;
5 *But* I would strengthen you with my mouth,
And the comfort of my lips would relieve *your grief.*

6 "Though I speak, my grief is not relieved;
And *if* I remain silent, how am I eased?
7 But now He has [a]worn me out;
You [b]have made desolate all my company.
8 You have shriveled me up,
And it is a [a]witness *against me;*
My leanness rises up against me
And bears witness to my face.
9 [a]He tears *me* in His wrath, and hates me;
He gnashes at me with His teeth;
[b]My adversary sharpens His gaze on me.
10 They [a]gape at me with their mouth,
They [b]strike me reproachfully on the cheek,
They gather together against me.
11 God [a]has delivered me to the ungodly,
And turned me over to the hands of the wicked.
12 I was at ease, but He has [a]shattered me;
He also has taken *me* by my neck, and shaken me to pieces;
He has [b]set me up for His target,
13 His archers surround me.
He pierces my *heart and does not pity;
He pours out my gall on the ground.
14 He breaks me with wound upon wound;
He runs at me like a *warrior.

15 "I have sewn sackcloth over my skin,
And [a]laid my *head in the dust.
16 My face is flushed from weeping,
And on my eyelids *is* the shadow of death;
17 Although no violence *is* in my hands,
And my prayer *is* pure.

---

*

16:13 Lit. *kidneys*
16:14 Vg. *giant*
16:15 Lit. *horn*

KJV

18 O earth, cover not thou my blood, and [a]let
my cry have no place.
19 Also now, behold, [a]my witness *is* in
heaven, and my record *is* on high.
20 My friends scorn me: *but* mine eye poureth out *tears* unto God.
21 [a]O that one might plead for a man with
God, as a man *pleadeth* for his neighbour!
22 When a few years are come, then I shall
[a]go the way *whence* I shall not return.

Job Prays for Relief

17 My breath is corrupt, my days are extinct,
[a]the graves *are ready* for me.
2 *Are there* not mockers with me? and doth
not mine eye continue in their [a]provocation?
3 Lay down now, put me in a surety with
thee; who *is* he *that* [a]will strike hands with me?
4 For thou hast hid their heart from [a]under-
standing: therefore shalt thou not exalt *them*.
5 He that speaketh flattery to *his* friends,
even the eyes of his children shall [a]fail.
6 He hath made me also [a]a byword of the
people; and aforetime I was as a tabret.
7 [a]Mine eye also is dim by reason of sorrow,
and all my members *are* as a shadow.
8 Upright *men* shall be astonied at this, and
the innocent shall stir up himself against the
hypocrite.
9 The righteous also shall hold on his [a]way,
and he that hath [b]clean hands shall be stronger
and stronger.
10 But as for you all, [a]do ye return, and come
now: for I cannot find *one* wise *man* among you.
11 [a]My days are past, my purposes are broken off, *even* the thoughts of my heart.
12 They change the night into day: the light
is short because of darkness.
13 If I wait, the grave *is* mine house: I have
made my bed in the darkness.
14 I have said to corruption, Thou *art* my father: to the worm, *Thou art* my mother, and my
sister.
15 And where *is* now my [a]hope? as for my
hope, who shall see it?
16 They shall go down [a]to the bars of the
pit, when *our* [b]rest together *is* in the dust.

Bildad: The Wicked Are Punished

18 Then answered [a]Bildad the Shuhite, and
said,
2 How long *will it be ere* ye make an end
of words? mark, and afterwards we will speak.
3 Wherefore are we counted [a]as beasts, *and*
reputed vile in your sight?
4 [a]He teareth himself in his anger: shall the
earth be forsaken for thee? and shall the rock be
removed out of his place?
5 Yea, [a]the light of the wicked shall be put
out, and the spark of his fire shall not shine.
6 The light shall be dark in his tabernacle,
[a]and his candle shall be put out with him.
7 The steps of his strength shall be straitened, and [a]his own counsel shall cast him down.

18 [a]Job 27:9; [Ps. 66:18]
19 [a]Gen. 31:50; Rom. 1:9; Phil. 1:8; 1 Thess. 2:5
21 [a]Job 31:35; Eccl. 6:10; [Is. 45:9; Rom. 9:20]
22 [a]Job 10:21; Eccl. 12:5

CHAPTER 17

1 [a]Ps. 88:3, 4
2 [a]1 Sam. 1:6; Job 12:4; 17:6; 30:1, 9; 34:7
3 [a]Prov. 6:1; 17:18; 22:26
4 [a]Job 12:20; 32:9
5 [a]Job 11:20
6 [a]Job 30:9
7 [a]Ps. 6:7; 31:9
9 [a]Prov. 4:18 [b]Ps. 24:4
10 [a]Job 6:29
11 [a]Job 7:6
15 [a]Job 7:6; 13:15; 14:19; 19:10
16 [a]Jon. 2:6 [b]Job 3:17–19; 21:33

CHAPTER 18

1 [a]Job 8:1
3 [a]Ps. 73:22
4 [a]Job 13:14
5 [a]Job 21:17; Prov. 13:9; 20:20; 24:20
6 [a]Job 21:17; Ps. 18:28
7 [a]Job 5:12, 13; 15:6

***17:10** So with some Heb. mss., LXX, Syr., Vg.; MT, Tg. *all of them*

NKJV

18 "O earth, do not cover my blood,
And [a]let my cry have no *resting* place!
19 Surely even now [a]my witness *is* in heaven,
And my evidence *is* on high.
20 My friends scorn me;
My eyes pour out *tears* to God.
21 [a]Oh, that one might plead for a man with God,
As a man *pleads* for his neighbor!
22 For when a few years are finished,
I shall [a]go the way of no return.

Job Prays for Relief

17 "My spirit is broken,
My days are extinguished,
[a]The grave *is ready* for me.
2 *Are* not mockers with me?
And does not my eye dwell on their [a]provocation?

3 "Now put down a pledge for me with Yourself.
Who *is* he *who* [a]will shake hands with me?
4 For You have hidden their heart from [a]understanding;
Therefore You will not exalt *them*.
5 He who speaks flattery to *his* friends,
Even the eyes of his children will [a]fail.

6 "But He has made me [a]a byword of the people,
And I have become one in whose face men spit.
7 [a]My eye has also grown dim because of sorrow,
And all my members *are* like shadows.
8 Upright *men* are astonished at this,
And the innocent stirs himself up against the hypocrite.
9 Yet the righteous will hold to his [a]way,
And he who has [b]clean hands will be stronger and stronger.

10 "But please, [a]come back again, *all of you,
For I shall not find *one* wise *man* among you.
11 [a]My days are past,
My purposes are broken off,
Even the thoughts of my heart.
12 They change the night into day;
'The light *is* near,' *they say*, in the face of darkness.
13 If I wait *for* the grave *as* my house,
If I make my bed in the darkness,
14 If I say to corruption, 'You *are* my father,'
And to the worm, 'You *are* my mother and my sister,'
15 Where then *is* my [a]hope?
As for my hope, who can see it?
16 *Will* they go down [a]to the gates of Sheol?
Shall *we have* [b]rest together in the dust?"

Bildad: The Wicked Are Punished

18 Then [a]Bildad the Shuhite answered and said:

2 "How long *till* you put an end to words?
Gain understanding, and afterward we will speak.
3 Why are we counted [a]as beasts,
And regarded as stupid in your sight?
4 [a]You who tear yourself in anger,
Shall the earth be forsaken for you?
Or shall the rock be removed from its place?

5 "The[a] light of the wicked indeed goes out,
And the flame of his fire does not shine.
6 The light is dark in his tent,
[a]And his lamp beside him is put out.
7 The steps of his strength are shortened,
And [a]his own counsel casts him down.

KJV

8 For [a]he is cast into a net by his own feet,
and he walketh upon a snare.
9 The gin shall take *him* by the heel, *and*
[a]the robber shall prevail against him.
10 The snare *is* laid for him in the ground,
and a trap for him in the way.
11 [a]Terrors shall make him afraid on every
side, and shall drive him to his feet.
12 His strength shall be hungerbitten, and
[a]destruction *shall be* ready at his side.
13 It shall devour the strength of his skin:
even the firstborn of death shall devour his
strength.
14 [a]His confidence shall be rooted out of his
tabernacle, and it shall bring him to the king of
terrors.
15 It shall dwell in his tabernacle, because
it is none of his: brimstone shall be scattered upon
his habitation.
16 [a]His roots shall be dried up beneath, and
above shall his branch be cut off.
17 [a]His remembrance shall perish from the
earth, and he shall have no name in the street.
18 He shall be driven from light into darkness, and chased out of the world.
19 [a]He shall neither have son nor nephew
among his people, nor any remaining in his
dwellings.
20 They that come after *him* shall be astonied
[a]at his day, as they that went before were
affrighted.
21 Surely such *are* the dwellings of the
wicked, and this *is* the place *of him that* [a]knoweth
not God.

Job Trusts in His Redeemer

19 Then Job answered and said,
2 How long will ye vex my soul, and
break me in pieces with words?
3 These ten times have ye reproached me:
ye are not ashamed *that* ye make yourselves
strange to me.
4 And be it indeed *that* I have erred, mine
error remaineth with myself.
5 If indeed ye will [a]magnify *yourselves* a-
gainst me, and plead against me my reproach:
6 Know now that [a]God hath overthrown me,
and hath compassed me with his net.
7 Behold, I cry out of wrong, but I am not
heard: I cry aloud, but *there is* no judgment.
8 [a]He hath fenced up my way that I cannot
pass, and he hath set darkness in my paths.
9 [a]He hath stripped me of my glory, and
taken the crown *from* my head.
10 He hath destroyed me on every side, and
I am gone: and mine [a]hope hath he removed like
a tree.
11 He hath also kindled his wrath against me,
and [a]he counteth me unto him as *one of* his
enemies.
12 His troops come together, and raise up
their way against me, and encamp round about
my tabernacle.
13 [a]He hath put my brethren far from me,
and mine acquaintance are verily estranged from
me.
14 My kinsfolk have failed, and my familiar
friends have forgotten me.
15 They that dwell in mine house, and my
maids, count me for a stranger: I am an alien in
their sight.

8 [a]Job 22:10; Ps. 9:15; 35:8; Is. 24:17, 18
9 [a]Job 5:5
11 [a]Job 20:25; Jer. 6:25
12 [a]Job 15:23
14 [a]Job 11:20
16 [a]Job 29:19
17 [a]Job 24:20; [Ps. 34:16]; Prov. 10:7
19 [a]Job 27:14, 15; Is. 14:22
20 [a]Ps. 37:13; Jer. 50:27; Obad. 12
21 [a]Jer. 9:3; 1 Thess. 4:5

CHAPTER 19

5 [a]Ps. 35:26; 38:16; 55:12, 13
6 [a]Job 16:11
8 [a]Job 3:23; Ps. 88:8; Lam. 3:7, 9
9 [a]Job 12:17, 19; Ps. 89:44
10 [a]Job 17:14, 16
11 [a]Job 13:24; 33:10
13 [a]Job 16:20; Ps. 31:11; 38:11; 69:8; 88:8, 18

*
18:17 Lit. *before the outside,* i.e., the distinguished or famous
19:3 A Jewish tradition *make yourselves strange to me*

NKJV

8 For [a]he is cast into a net by his own feet,
And he walks into a snare.
9 The net takes *him* by the heel,
And [a]a snare lays hold of him.
10 A noose *is* hidden for him on the ground,
And a trap for him in the road.
11 [a]Terrors frighten him on every side,
And drive him to his feet.
12 His strength is starved,
And [a]destruction *is* ready at his side.
13 It devours patches of his skin;
The firstborn of death devours his limbs.
14 He is uprooted from [a]the shelter of his tent,
And they parade him before the king of terrors.
15 They dwell in his tent *who are* none of his;
Brimstone is scattered on his dwelling.
16 [a]His roots are dried out below,
And his branch withers above.
17 [a]The memory of him perishes from the earth,
And he has no name *among the renowned.
18 He is driven from light into darkness,
And chased out of the world.
19 [a]He has neither son nor posterity among his people,
Nor any remaining in his dwellings.
20 Those in the west are astonished [a]at his day,
As those in the east are frightened.
21 Surely such *are* the dwellings of the wicked,
And this *is* the place *of him who* [a]does not know God."

Job Trusts in His Redeemer

19 Then Job answered and said:

2 "How long will you torment my soul,
And break me in pieces with words?
3 These ten times you have reproached me;
You are not ashamed *that* you *have wronged me.
4 And if indeed I have erred,
My error remains with me.
5 If indeed you [a]exalt *yourselves* against me,
And plead my disgrace against me,
6 Know then that [a]God has wronged me,
And has surrounded me with His net.

7 "If I cry out concerning wrong, I am not heard.
If I cry aloud, *there is* no justice.
8 [a]He has fenced up my way, so that I cannot pass;
And He has set darkness in my paths.
9 [a]He has stripped me of my glory,
And taken the crown *from* my head.
10 He breaks me down on every side,
And I am gone;
My [a]hope He has uprooted like a tree.
11 He has also kindled His wrath against me,
And [a]He counts me as *one of* His enemies.
12 His troops come together
And build up their road against me;
They encamp all around my tent.

13 "He[a] has removed my brothers far from me,
And my acquaintances are completely estranged from me.
14 My relatives have failed,
And my close friends have forgotten me.
15 Those who dwell in my house, and my maidservants,
Count me as a stranger;
I am an alien in their sight.

KJV

16 I called my servant, and he gave *me* no
answer; I intreated him with my mouth.
17 My breath is strange to my wife, though
I intreated for the children's *sake* of mine own
body.
18 Yea, [a]young children despised me; I arose,
and they spake against me.
19 [a]All my inward friends abhorred me: and
they whom I loved are turned against me.
20 [a]My bone cleaveth to my skin and to my
flesh, and I am escaped with the skin of my teeth.
21 Have pity upon me, have pity upon me,
O ye my friends; for the hand of God hath touched
me.
22 Why do ye [a]persecute me as God, and are
not satisfied with my flesh?
23 Oh that my words were now written! oh
that they were printed in a book!
24 That they were graven with an iron pen
and lead in the rock for ever!
25 For I know *that* my redeemer liveth, and
that he shall stand at the latter *day* upon the
earth:
26 And *though* after my skin *worms* destroy
this *body*, yet [a]in my flesh shall I see God:
27 Whom I shall see for myself, and mine
eyes shall behold, and not another; *though* my
reins be consumed within me.
28 But ye should say, Why persecute we him,
seeing the root of the matter is found in me?
29 Be ye afraid of the sword: for wrath *bringeth* the punishments of the sword, that ye may
know *there is* a judgment.

18 [a]2 Kin. 2:23; Job 17:6
19 [a]Ps. 38:11; 55:12, 13
20 [a]Job 16:8; 33:21; Ps. 102:5; Lam. 4:8
22 [a]Job 13:24, 25; 16:11; 19:6; Ps. 69:26
26 [a][Ps. 17:15]; Matt. 5:8; 1 Cor. 13:12; [1 John 3:2]

NKJV

16 I call my servant, but he gives no answer;
I beg him with my mouth.
17 My breath is offensive to my wife,
And I am repulsive to the children of my own body.
18 Even [a]young children despise me;
I arise, and they speak against me.
19 [a]All my close friends abhor me,
And those whom I love have turned against me.
20 [a]My bone clings to my skin and to my flesh,
And I have escaped by the skin of my teeth.

21 "Have pity on me, have pity on me, O you my friends,
For the hand of God has struck me!
22 Why do you [a]persecute me as God *does*,
And are not satisfied with my flesh?

23 "Oh, that my words were written!
Oh, that they were inscribed in a book!
24 That they were engraved on a rock
With an iron pen and lead, forever!
25 For I know *that* my Redeemer lives,
And He shall stand at last on the earth;
26 And after my skin is destroyed, this *I know*,
That [a]in my flesh I shall see God,
27 Whom I shall see for myself,
And my eyes shall behold, and not another.
How my heart yearns within me!
28 If you should say, 'How shall we persecute him?'—
Since the root of the matter is found in me,
29 Be afraid of the sword for yourselves;
For wrath *brings* the punishment of the sword,
That you may know *there is* a judgment."

Zophar's Sermon on the Wicked Man

20 Then answered [a]Zophar the Naamathite,
and said,
2 Therefore do my thoughts cause me to answer, and for *this* I make haste.
3 I have heard the check of my reproach,
and the spirit of my understanding causeth me
to answer.
4 Knowest thou *not* this of [a]old, since man
was placed upon earth,
5 [a]That the triumphing of the wicked *is*
short, and the joy of the hypocrite *but* for a
[b]moment?
6 [a]Though his excellency mount up to the
heavens, and his head reach unto the clouds;
7 *Yet* he shall perish for ever like his own
dung: they which have seen him shall say, Where
is he?
8 He shall fly away [a]as a dream, and shall
not be found: yea, he [b]shall be chased away as a
vision of the night.
9 The eye also *which* saw him shall *see him*
no more; neither shall his place any more behold
him.
10 His children shall seek to please the poor,
and his hands shall restore their goods.
11 His bones are full *of* [a]*the sin* of his youth,
[b]which shall lie down with him in the dust.
12 Though wickedness be sweet in his
mouth, *though* he hide it under his tongue;

CHAPTER 20
1 [a]Job 11:1
4 [a]Job 8:8; 15:10
5 [a]Ps. 37:35, 36 [b][Job 8:13; 13:16; 15:34; 27:8]
6 [a]Is. 14:13, 14
8 [a]Ps. 73:20; 90:5 [b]Job 18:18; 27:21–23
11 [a]Job 13:26 [b]Job 21:26

Zophar's Sermon on the Wicked Man

20 Then [a]Zophar the Naamathite answered and said:

2 "Therefore my anxious thoughts make me answer,
Because of the turmoil within me.
3 I have heard the rebuke that reproaches me,
And the spirit of my understanding causes me to answer.

4 "Do you *not* know this of [a]old,
Since man was placed on earth,
5 [a]That the triumphing of the wicked is short,
And the joy of the hypocrite is *but* for a [b]moment?
6 [a]Though his haughtiness mounts up to the heavens,
And his head reaches to the clouds,
7 *Yet* he will perish forever like his own refuse;
Those who have seen him will say, 'Where is he?'
8 He will fly away [a]like a dream, and not be found;
Yes, he [b]will be chased away like a vision of the night.
9 The eye *that* saw him will *see him* no more,
Nor will his place behold him anymore.
10 His children will seek the favor of the poor,
And his hands will restore his wealth.
11 His bones are full of [a]his youthful vigor,
[b]But it will lie down with him in the dust.
12 "Though evil is sweet in his mouth,
And he hides it under his tongue,

KJV

13 *Though* he spare it, and forsake it not; but keep it still within his mouth:

14 *Yet* his meat in his bowels is turned, *it is* the gall of asps within him.

15 He hath swallowed down riches, and he shall vomit them up again: God shall cast them out of his belly.

16 He shall suck the poison of asps: the viper's tongue shall slay him.

17 He shall not see [a]the rivers, the floods, the brooks of honey and butter.

18 That which he laboured for shall he restore, and shall not swallow *it* down: according to *his* substance *shall* the restitution *be,* and he shall not rejoice *therein.*

19 Because he hath oppressed *and* hath forsaken the poor; *because* he hath violently taken away an house which he builded not;

20 [a]Surely he shall not feel quietness in his belly, he shall not save of that which he desired.

21 There shall none of his meat be left; therefore shall no man look for his goods.

22 In the fulness of his sufficiency he shall be in straits: every hand of the wicked shall come upon him.

23 *When* he is about to fill his belly, *God* shall cast the fury of his wrath upon him, and shall rain *it* upon him while he is eating.

24 [a]He shall flee from the iron weapon, *and* the bow of steel shall strike him through.

25 It is drawn, and cometh out of the body; yea, [a]the glittering sword cometh out of his gall: [b]terrors *are* upon him.

26 All darkness *shall be* hid in his secret places: [a]a fire not blown shall consume him; it shall go ill with him that is left in his tabernacle.

27 The heaven shall reveal his iniquity; and the earth shall rise up against him.

28 The increase of his house shall depart, *and his goods* shall flow away in the day of his [a]wrath.

29 [a]This *is* the portion of a wicked man from God, and the heritage appointed unto him by God.

Job's Discourse on the Wicked

21 But Job answered and said,

2 Hear diligently my speech, and let this be your consolations.

3 Suffer me that I may speak; and after that I have spoken, [a]mock on.

4 As for me, *is* my complaint to man? and if *it were so,* why should not my spirit be troubled?

5 Mark me, and be astonished, [a]and lay *your* hand upon *your* mouth.

6 Even when I remember I am afraid, and trembling taketh hold on my flesh.

7 [a]Wherefore do the wicked live, become old, yea, are mighty in power?

8 Their seed is established in their sight with them, and their offspring before their eyes.

9 Their houses *are* safe from fear, [a]neither *is* the rod of God upon them.

10 Their bull gendereth, and faileth not; their cow calveth, and [a]casteth not her calf.

11 They send forth their little ones like a flock, and their children dance.

12 They take the timbrel and harp, and rejoice at the sound of the organ.

---

17 [a]Ps. 36:8; Jer. 17:8
20 [a]Eccl. 5:13–15
24 [a]Is. 24:18; Amos 5:19
25 [a]Job 16:13 [b]Job 18:11, 14
26 [a]Ps. 21:9
28 [a]Job 20:15; 21:30
29 [a]Job 27:13; 31:2, 3

CHAPTER 21

3 [a]Job 16:10
5 [a]Judg. 18:19; Job 13:5; 29:9; 40:4
7 [a]Job 12:6; Ps. 17:10, 14; 73:3, 12; [Jer. 12:1]; Hab. 1:13, 16
9 [a]Ps. 73:5
10 [a]Ex. 23:26

*———

20:20 Lit. *belly*

NKJV

13 *Though* he spares it and does not forsake it,
But still keeps it in his mouth,
14 *Yet* his food in his stomach turns sour;
It becomes cobra venom within him.
15 He swallows down riches
And vomits them up again;
God casts them out of his belly.
16 He will suck the poison of cobras;
The viper's tongue will slay him.
17 He will not see [a]the streams,
The rivers flowing with honey and cream.
18 He will restore that for which he labored,
And will not swallow *it* down;
From the proceeds of business
He will get no enjoyment.
19 For he has oppressed *and* forsaken the poor,
He has violently seized a house which he did not build.

20 "Because[a] he knows no quietness in his *heart,
He will not save anything he desires.
21 Nothing is left for him to eat;
Therefore his well-being will not last.
22 In his self-sufficiency he will be in distress;
Every hand of misery will come against him.
23 *When* he is about to fill his stomach,
God will cast on him the fury of His wrath,
And will rain *it* on him while he is eating.
24 [a]He will flee from the iron weapon;
A bronze bow will pierce him through.
25 It is drawn, and comes out of the body;
Yes, [a]the glittering *point comes* out of his gall.
[b]Terrors *come* upon him;
26 Total darkness *is* reserved for his treasures.
[a]An unfanned fire will consume him;
It shall go ill with him who is left in his tent.
27 The heavens will reveal his iniquity,
And the earth will rise up against him.
28 The increase of his house will depart,
And his goods will flow away in the day of His [a]wrath.
29 [a]This *is* the portion from God for a wicked man,
The heritage appointed to him by God."

Job's Discourse on the Wicked

21 Then Job answered and said:

2 "Listen carefully to my speech,
And let this be your consolation.
3 Bear with me that I may speak,
And after I have spoken, keep [a]mocking.

4 "As for me, *is* my complaint against man?
And if *it were,* why should I not be impatient?
5 Look at me and be astonished;
[a]Put *your* hand over *your* mouth.
6 Even when I remember I am terrified,
And trembling takes hold of my flesh.
7 [a]Why do the wicked live *and* become old,
Yes, become mighty in power?
8 Their descendants are established with them in their sight,
And their offspring before their eyes.
9 Their houses *are* safe from fear,
[a]Neither *is* the rod of God upon them.
10 Their bull breeds without failure;
Their cow calves [a]without miscarriage.
11 They send forth their little ones like a flock,
And their children dance.
12 They sing to the tambourine and harp,
And rejoice to the sound of the flute.

KJV

13 They [a]spend their days in wealth, and in
a moment go down to the grave.
14 [a]Therefore they say unto God, Depart
from us; for we desire not the knowledge of thy
ways.
15 [a]What *is* the Almighty, that we should
serve him? and [b]what profit should we have, if
we pray unto him?
16 Lo, their good *is* not in their hand: [a]the
counsel of the wicked is far from me.
17 How oft is the candle of the wicked put
out! and *how oft* cometh their destruction upon
them! *God* [a]distributeth sorrows in his anger.
18 [a]They are as stubble before the wind, and
as chaff that the storm carrieth away.
19 God layeth up his iniquity [a]for his children: he rewardeth him, and he shall know *it*.
20 His eyes shall see his destruction, and [a]he
shall drink of the wrath of the Almighty.
21 For what pleasure *hath* he in his house
after him, when the number of his months is cut
off in the midst?
22 [a]Shall *any* teach God knowledge? seeing
he judgeth those that are high.
23 One dieth in his full strength, being wholly
at ease and quiet.
24 His breasts are full of milk, and his bones
are moistened with marrow.
25 And another dieth in the bitterness of his
soul, and never eateth with pleasure.
26 They shall [a]lie down alike in the dust, and
the worms shall cover them.
27 Behold, I know your thoughts, and the devices *which* ye wrongfully imagine against me.
28 For ye say, Where *is* the house of the
prince? and where *are* the dwelling places of the
wicked?
29 Have ye not asked them that go by the
way? and do ye not know their tokens,
30 [a]That the wicked is reserved to the day
of destruction? they shall be brought forth to the
day of wrath.
31 Who shall declare his way to his face? and
who shall repay him *what* he hath done?
32 Yet shall he be brought to the grave, and
shall remain in the tomb.
33 The clods of the valley shall be sweet unto
him, and [a]every man shall draw after him, as
there are innumerable before him.
34 How then comfort ye me in vain, seeing
in your answers there remaineth falsehood?

Eliphaz Accuses Job of Wickedness

22 Then [a]Eliphaz the Temanite answered and
said,
2 [a]Can a man be profitable unto God, as he
that is wise may be profitable unto himself?

13 [a]Job 21:23; 36:11
14 [a]Job 22:17
15 [a]Ex. 5:2; Job 22:17; 34:9 [b]Job 35:3; Mal. 3:14
16 [a]Job 22:18; Ps. 1:1; Prov. 1:10
17 [a][Job 31:2, 3; Luke 12:46]
18 [a]Ps. 1:4; 35:5; Is. 17:13; Hos. 13:3
19 [a][Ex. 20:5]; Jer. 31:29; Ezek. 18:2
20 [a]Ps. 75:8; Is. 51:17; Jer. 25:15; Rev. 14:10; 19:15
22 [a]Job 35:11; 36:22; [Is. 40:13; 45:9; Rom. 11:34; 1 Cor. 2:16]
26 [a]Job 3:13; 20:11; Eccl. 9:2
30 [a]Job 20:29; [Prov. 16:4; 2 Pet. 2:9]
33 [a]Heb. 9:27

CHAPTER 22

1 [a]Job 4:1; 15:1; 42:9
2 [a]Job 35:7; [Ps. 16:2; Luke 17:10]

**

21:13 Or *Sheol*
21:19 Lit. *his*
21:24 LXX, Vg. *bowels;* Syr. *sides;* Tg. *breasts*
21:28 Vg. omits *the tent*

NKJV

13 They [a]spend their days in wealth,
And in a moment go down to the *grave.
14 [a]Yet they say to God, 'Depart from us,
For we do not desire the knowledge of
Your ways.
15 [a]Who *is* the Almighty, that we should serve
Him?
And [b]what profit do we have if we pray
to Him?'
16 Indeed their prosperity *is* not in their
hand;
[a]The counsel of the wicked is far from
me.

17 "How often is the lamp of the wicked put
out?
How often does their destruction come
upon them,
The sorrows *God* [a]distributes in His
anger?
18 [a]They are like straw before the wind,
And like chaff that a storm carries
away.
19 *They say,* 'God lays up *one's iniquity [a]for
his children';
Let Him recompense him, that he may
know *it*.
20 Let his eyes see his destruction,
And [a]let him drink of the wrath of the
Almighty.
21 For what does he care about his household
after him,
When the number of his months is cut in
half?

22 "Can[a] *anyone* teach God knowledge,
Since He judges those on high?
23 One dies in his full strength,
Being wholly at ease and secure;
24 His *pails are full of milk,
And the marrow of his bones is moist.
25 Another man dies in the bitterness of his
soul,
Never having eaten with pleasure.
26 They [a]lie down alike in the dust,
And worms cover them.

27 "Look, I know your thoughts,
And the schemes *with which* you would
wrong me.
28 For you say,
'Where *is* the house of the prince?
And where *is* *the tent,
The dwelling place of the wicked?'
29 Have you not asked those who travel the
road?
And do you not know their signs?
30 [a]For the wicked are reserved for the day
of doom;
They shall be brought out on the day of
wrath.
31 Who condemns his way to his face?
And who repays him *for what* he has
done?
32 Yet he shall be brought to the grave,
And a vigil kept over the tomb.
33 The clods of the valley shall be sweet to
him;
[a]Everyone shall follow him,
As countless *have gone* before him.
34 How then can you comfort me with empty
words,
Since falsehood remains in your
answers?"

Eliphaz Accuses Job of Wickedness

22 Then [a]Eliphaz the Temanite answered and
said:

2 "Can[a] a man be profitable to God,
Though he who is wise may be profitable
to himself?

KJV

3 *Is it* any pleasure to the Almighty, that thou art righteous? or *is it* gain *to him*, that thou makest thy ways perfect?

4 Will he reprove thee for fear of thee? will he enter with thee into judgment?

5 *Is* not thy wickedness great? and thine iniquities infinite?

6 For thou hast [a]taken a pledge from thy brother for nought, and stripped the naked of their clothing.

7 Thou hast not given water to the weary to drink, and thou [a]hast withholden bread from the hungry.

8 But *as for* the mighty man, he had the earth; and the honourable man dwelt in it.

9 Thou hast sent widows away empty, and the arms of the fatherless have been broken.

10 Therefore snares *are* round about thee, and sudden fear troubleth thee;

11 Or darkness, *that* thou canst not see; and abundance of [a]waters cover thee.

12 *Is* not God in the height of heaven? and behold the height of the stars, how high they are!

13 And thou sayest, [a]How doth God know? can he judge through the dark cloud?

14 [a]Thick clouds *are* a covering to him, that he seeth not; and he walketh in the circuit of heaven.

15 Hast thou marked the old way which wicked men have trodden?

16 Which [a]were cut down out of time, whose foundation was overflown with a flood:

17 [a]Which said unto God, Depart from us: and what can the Almighty do for them?

18 Yet he filled their houses with good *things:* but the counsel of the wicked is far from me.

19 [a]The righteous see *it*, and are glad: and the innocent laugh them to scorn.

20 Whereas our substance is not cut down, but the remnant of them the fire consumeth.

21 Acquaint now thyself with him, and [a]be at peace: thereby good shall come unto thee.

22 Receive, I pray thee, the [a]law from his mouth, and [b]lay up his words in thine heart.

23 If thou return to the Almighty, thou shalt be built up, thou shalt put away iniquity far from thy tabernacles.

24 Then shalt thou [a]lay up gold as dust, and the *gold* of Ophir as the stones of the brooks.

25 Yea, the Almighty shall be thy defence, and thou shalt have plenty of silver.

26 For then shalt thou have thy [a]delight in the Almighty, and shalt lift up thy face unto God.

27 [a]Thou shalt make thy prayer unto him, and he shall hear thee, and thou shalt pay thy vows.

28 Thou shalt also decree a thing, and it shall be established unto thee: and the light shall shine upon thy ways.

29 When *men* are cast down, then thou shalt say, *There is* lifting up; and [a]he shall save the humble person.

6 [a][Ex. 22:26, 27]; Deut. 24:6, 10, 17; Job 24:3, 9; Ezek. 18:16 **7** [a]Deut. 15:7; Job 31:17; Is. 58:7; Ezek. 18:7; Matt. 25:42 **11** [a]Job 38:34; Ps. 69:1, 2; 124:5; Lam. 3:54 **13** [a]Ps. 73:11 **14** [a]Ps. 139:11, 12 **16** [a]Job 14:19; 15:32; Ps. 90:5; Is. 28:2; Matt. 7:26, 27 **17** [a]Job 21:14, 15 **19** [a]Ps. 52:6; 58:10; 107:42 **21** [a][Ps. 34:10]; Is. 27:5 **22** [a]Job 6:10; 23:12; Prov. 2:6 [b][Ps. 119:11] **24** [a]2 Chr. 1:15 **26** [a]Job 27:10; Ps. 37:4; Is. 58:14 **27** [a]Job 11:13; 33:26; [Is. 58:9–11] **29** [a]Job 5:11; [Matt. 23:12; James 4:6; 1 Pet. 5:5]

NKJV

3 *Is it* any pleasure to the Almighty that you are righteous?
Or *is it* gain *to Him* that you make your ways blameless?

4 "Is it because of your fear of Him that He corrects you,
And enters into judgment with you?
5 *Is* not your wickedness great,
And your iniquity without end?
6 For you have [a]taken pledges from your brother for no reason,
And stripped the naked of their clothing.
7 You have not given the weary water to drink,
And you [a]have withheld bread from the hungry.
8 But the mighty man possessed the land,
And the honorable man dwelt in it.
9 You have sent widows away empty,
And the strength of the fatherless was crushed.
10 Therefore snares *are* all around you,
And sudden fear troubles you,
11 Or darkness *so that* you cannot see;
And an abundance of [a]water covers you.

12 "Is not God in the height of heaven?
And see the highest stars, how lofty they are!
13 And you say, [a]'What does God know?
Can He judge through the deep darkness?
14 [a]Thick clouds cover Him, so that He cannot see,
And He walks above the circle of heaven.'
15 Will you keep to the old way
Which wicked men have trod,
16 Who [a]were cut down before their time,
Whose foundations were swept away by a flood?
17 [a]They said to God, 'Depart from us!
What can the Almighty do to *them?'
18 Yet He filled their houses with good *things;*
But the counsel of the wicked is far from me.

19 "The[a] righteous see *it* and are glad,
And the innocent laugh at them:
20 'Surely our *adversaries are cut down,
And the fire consumes their remnant.'

21 "Now acquaint yourself with Him, and [a]be at peace;
Thereby good will come to you.
22 Receive, please, [a]instruction from His mouth,
And [b]lay up His words in your heart.
23 If you return to the Almighty, you will be built up;
You will remove iniquity far from your tents.
24 Then you will [a]lay your gold in the dust,
And the *gold* of Ophir among the stones of the brooks.
25 Yes, the Almighty will be your *gold
And your precious silver;
26 For then you will have your [a]delight in the Almighty,
And lift up your face to God.
27 [a]You will make your prayer to Him,
He will hear you,
And you will pay your vows.
28 You will also declare a thing,
And it will be established for you;
So light will shine on your ways.
29 When they cast *you* down, and you say,
'Exaltation *will come!*'
Then [a]He will save the humble *person*.

*

22:17 LXX, Syr. *us* **22:20** LXX *substance is* **22:25** Ancient vss. suggest *defense;* MT *gold,* as in v. 24

KJV

30 He shall deliver the island of the innocent:
and it is delivered by the pureness of thine hands.

Job Proclaims God's Righteous Judgments

23 Then Job answered and said,
2 Even to day *is* my [a]complaint bitter:
my stroke is heavier than my groaning.
3 [a]Oh that I knew where I might find him!
that I might come *even* to his seat!
4 I would order *my* cause before him, and
fill my mouth with arguments.
5 I would know the words *which* he would
answer me, and understand what he would say
unto me.
6 [a]Will he plead against me with *his* great
power? No; but he would put *strength* in me.
7 There the righteous might dispute with
him; so should I be delivered for ever from my
judge.
8 [a]Behold, I go forward, but he *is* not *there;*
and backward, but I cannot perceive him:
9 On the left hand, where he doth work, but
I cannot behold *him:* he hideth himself on the right
hand, that I cannot see *him:*
10 But [a]he knoweth the way that I take: *when*
[b]he hath tried me, I shall come forth as gold.
11 [a]My foot hath held his steps, his way have
I kept, and not declined.
12 Neither have I gone back from the [a]com-
mandment of his lips; [b]I have esteemed the words
of his mouth more than my necessary *food.*
13 But he *is* in one *mind,* and who can turn
him? and *what* [a]his soul desireth, even *that* he
doeth.
14 For he performeth *the thing that is* [a]ap-
pointed for me: and many such *things are* with
him.
15 Therefore am I troubled at his presence:
when I consider, I am afraid of him.
16 For God [a]maketh my heart soft, and the
Almighty troubleth me:
17 Because I was not [a]cut off before the darkness, *neither* hath he covered the darkness from
my face.

Job Complains of Violence on the Earth

24 Why, seeing [a]times are not hidden from the
Almighty, do they that know him not see
his [b]days?
2 *Some* remove the [a]landmarks; they violently take away flocks, and feed *thereof.*
3 They drive away the ass of the fatherless,
they [a]take the widow's ox for a pledge.
4 They turn the needy out of the way: the
[a]poor of the earth hide themselves together.
5 Behold, *as* wild asses in the desert, go they
forth to their work; rising betimes for a prey: the
wilderness *yieldeth* food for them *and* for *their*
children.
6 They reap *every one* his corn in the field:
and they gather the vintage of the wicked.
7 They [a]cause the naked to lodge without
clothing, that *they have* no covering in the cold.

CHAPTER 23

2 [a]Job 7:11
3 [a]Job 13:3, 18; 16:21; 31:35
6 [a]Is. 57:16
8 [a]Job 9:11; 35:14
10 [a][Ps. 1:6; 139:1–3] [b][Ps. 17:3; 66:10; James 1:12]
11 [a]Job 31:7; Ps. 17:5
12 [a]Job 6:10; 22:22 [b]Ps. 44:18
13 [a][Ps. 115:3]
14 [a][1 Thess. 3:2–4]
16 [a]Ps. 22:14
17 [a]Job 10:18, 19

CHAPTER 24

1 [a][Acts 1:7] [b][Is. 2:12]; Jer. 46:10; [Obad. 15]; Zeph. 1:7
2 [a][Deut. 19:14; 27:17]; Prov. 22:28; 23:10; Hos. 5:10
3 [a][Deut. 24:6, 10, 12, 17]; Job 22:6, 9
4 [a]Job 29:16; Prov. 28:28
7 [a]Ex. 22:26, 27; [Deut. 24:12, 13]; Job 22:6; [James 2:15, 16]

*

23:2 So with MT, Tg., Vg.; LXX, Syr. *His*

NKJV

30 He will *even* deliver one who is not
innocent;
Yes, he will be delivered by the purity of
your hands."

Job Proclaims God's Righteous Judgments

23 Then Job answered and said:
2 "Even today my [a]complaint is bitter;
*My hand is listless because of my
groaning.
3 [a]Oh, that I knew where I might find Him,
That I might come to His seat!
4 I would present *my* case before Him,
And fill my mouth with arguments.
5 I would know the words *which* He would
answer me,
And understand what He would say to me.
6 [a]Would He contend with me in His great
power?
No! But He would take *note* of me.
7 There the upright could reason with Him,
And I would be delivered forever from my
Judge.

8 "Look,[a] I go forward, but He is not *there,*
And backward, but I cannot perceive Him;
9 When He works on the left hand, I cannot
behold *Him;*
When He turns to the right hand, I cannot
see *Him.*
10 But [a]He knows the way that I take;
When [b]He has tested me, I shall come
forth as gold.
11 [a]My foot has held fast to His steps;
I have kept His way and not turned aside.
12 I have not departed from the
[a]commandment of His lips;
[b]I have treasured the words of His mouth
More than my necessary *food.*

13 "But He *is* unique, and who can make Him
change?
And *whatever* [a]His soul desires, *that* He
does.
14 For He performs *what is* [a]appointed for
me,
And many such *things are* with Him.
15 Therefore I am terrified at His presence;
When I consider *this,* I am afraid of Him.
16 For God [a]made my heart weak,
And the Almighty terrifies me;
17 Because I was not [a]cut off from the
presence of darkness,
And He did *not* hide deep darkness from
my face.

Job Complains of Violence on the Earth

24 "*Since* [a]times are not hidden from the
Almighty,
Why do those who know Him see not His
[b]days?

2 "*Some* remove [a]landmarks;
They seize flocks violently and feed *on
them;*
3 They drive away the donkey of the
fatherless;
They [a]take the widow's ox as a pledge.
4 They push the needy off the road;
All the [a]poor of the land are forced to
hide.
5 Indeed, *like* wild donkeys in the desert,
They go out to their work, searching for
food.
The wilderness *yields* food for them *and*
for *their* children.
6 They gather their fodder in the field
And glean in the vineyard of the wicked.
7 They [a]spend the night naked, without
clothing,
And have no covering in the cold.

KJV

8 They are wet with the showers of the
mountains, and [a]embrace the rock for want of a
shelter.
9 They pluck the fatherless from the breast,
and take a pledge of the poor.
10 They cause *him* to go naked without
[a]clothing, and they take away the sheaf *from* the
hungry;
11 *Which* make oil within their walls, *and*
tread *their* winepresses, and suffer thirst.
12 Men groan from out of the city, and the
soul of the wounded crieth out: yet God layeth
not folly *to them.*
13 They are of those that rebel against the
light; they know not the ways thereof, nor abide
in the paths thereof.
14 [a]The murderer rising with the light killeth
the poor and needy, and in the night is as a thief.
15 [a]The eye also of the adulterer waiteth for
the twilight, [b]saying, No eye shall see me: and
disguiseth *his* face.
16 In the dark they dig through houses,
which they had marked for themselves in the daytime: [a]they know not the light.
17 For the morning *is* to them even as the
shadow of death: if *one* know *them, they are in*
the terrors of the shadow of death.
18 He *is* swift as the waters; their portion is
cursed in the earth: he beholdeth not the way of
the vineyards.
19 Drought and heat consume the snow waters: *so doth* the grave *those which* have sinned.
20 The womb shall forget him; the worm
shall feed sweetly on him; [a]he shall be no more
remembered; and wickedness shall be broken as
a tree.
21 He evil entreateth the barren *that* beareth
not: and doeth not good to the widow.
22 He draweth also the mighty with his
power: he riseth up, and no *man* is sure of life.
23 *Though* it be given him *to be* in safety,
whereon he resteth; yet [a]his eyes *are* upon their
ways.
24 They are exalted for a little while, but are
gone and brought low; they are taken out of the
way as all *other,* and cut off as the tops of the
ears of corn.
25 And if *it be* not so now, who will make
me a liar, and make my speech nothing worth?

Bildad: How Can Man Be Righteous?

25 Then answered [a]Bildad the Shuhite, and
said,
2 Dominion and fear *are* with him; he maketh peace in his high places.

NKJV

8 They are wet with the showers of the mountains,
And [a]huddle around the rock for want of shelter.

9 "*Some* snatch the fatherless from the breast,
And take a pledge from the poor.
10 They cause *the poor* to go naked, without [a]clothing;
And they take away the sheaves from the hungry.
11 They press out oil within their walls,
And tread winepresses, yet suffer thirst.
12 The dying groan in the city,
And the souls of the wounded cry out;
Yet God does not charge *them* with wrong.

13 "There are those who rebel against the light;
They do not know its ways
Nor abide in its paths.
14 [a]The murderer rises with the light;
He kills the poor and needy;
And in the night he is like a thief.
15 [a]The eye of the adulterer waits for the twilight,
[b]Saying, 'No eye will see me';
And he disguises *his* face.
16 In the dark they break into houses
Which they marked for themselves in the daytime;
[a]They do not know the light.
17 For the morning is the same to them as the shadow of death;
If *someone* recognizes *them,*
They are in the terrors of the shadow of death.

18 "They *should be* swift on the face of the waters,
Their portion *should be* cursed in the earth,
So that no *one would* turn into the way of their vineyards.
19 As drought and heat consume the snow waters,
So *the grave *consumes those who* have sinned.
20 The womb *should* forget him,
The worm *should* feed sweetly on him;
[a]He *should* be remembered no more,
And wickedness *should* be broken like a tree.
21 For he preys on the barren *who* do not bear,
And does no good for the widow.

22 "But *God* draws the mighty away with His power;
He rises up, but no *man* is sure of life.
23 He gives them security, and they rely *on it;*
Yet [a]His eyes *are* on their ways.
24 They are exalted for a little while,
Then they are gone.
They are brought low;
They are taken out of the way like all *others;*
They dry out like the heads of grain.

25 "Now if *it is* not *so,* who will prove me a liar,
And make my speech worth nothing?"

Bildad: How Can Man Be Righteous?

25 Then [a]Bildad the Shuhite answered and said:

2 "Dominion and fear *belong* to Him;
He makes peace in His high places.

---

8 [a]Lam. 4:5
10 [a]Job 31:19
14 [a]Ps. 10:8
15 [a]Prov. 7:7–10 [b]Ps. 10:11
16 [a][John 3:20]
20 [a]Job 18:17; Ps. 34:16; Prov. 10:7
23 [a]Ps. 11:4; [Prov. 15:3]

CHAPTER 25

1 [a]Job 8:1; 18:1

*

24:19 Or *Sheol*

KJV

3 Is there any number of his armies? and
upon whom doth not [a]his light arise?
4 [a]How then can man be justified with God?
or how can he be [b]clean *that is* born of a woman?
5 Behold even to the moon, and it shineth
not; yea, the stars are not pure in his [a]sight.
6 How much less man, *that is* [a]a worm? and
the son of man, *which is* a worm?

Job: Man's Frailty and God's Majesty

26 But Job answered and said,
2 How hast thou helped *him that is* without power? *how* savest thou the arm *that hath*
no strength?
3 How hast thou counseled *him that hath*
no wisdom? and *how* hast thou plentifully declared the thing as it is?
4 To whom hast thou uttered words? and
whose spirit came from thee?
5 Dead *things* are formed from under the
waters, and the inhabitants thereof.
6 [a]Hell *is* naked before him, and destruction
hath no covering.
7 [a]He stretcheth out the north over the
empty place, *and* hangeth the earth upon nothing.
8 [a]He bindeth up the waters in his thick
clouds; and the cloud is not rent under them.
9 He holdeth back the face of his throne,
and spreadeth his cloud upon it.
10 [a]He hath compassed the waters with
bounds, until the day and night come to an end.
11 The pillars of heaven tremble and are astonished at his reproof.
12 [a]He divideth the sea with his power, and
by his understanding he smiteth through the
proud.
13 [a]By his spirit he hath garnished the heavens; his hand hath formed [b]the crooked serpent.
14 Lo, these *are* parts of his ways: but how
little a portion is heard of him? but the thunder
of his power who can understand?

Job Maintains His Integrity

27 Moreover Job continued his parable, and
said,
2 *As* God liveth, [a]*who* hath taken away my
judgment; and the Almighty, *who* hath vexed my
soul;
3 All the while my breath *is* in me, and the
spirit of God *is* in my nostrils;
4 My lips shall not speak wickedness, nor
my tongue utter deceit.
5 God forbid that I should justify you: till I
die [a]I will not remove mine integrity from me.
6 My righteousness I [a]hold fast, and will not
let it go: [b]my heart shall not reproach *me* so long
as I live.
7 Let mine enemy be as the wicked, and he
that riseth up against me as the unrighteous.
8 [a]For what *is* the hope of the hypocrite,
though he hath gained, when God taketh away
his soul?
9 [a]Will God hear his cry when trouble cometh upon him?

3 [a]James 1:17
4 [a]Job 4:17; 15:14; Ps. 130:3; 143:2 [b][Job 14:4]
5 [a]Job 15:15
6 [a]Ps. 22:6

CHAPTER 26

6 [a][Ps. 139:8]; Prov. 15:11; [Heb. 4:13]
7 [a]Job 9:8; Ps. 24:2; 104:2
8 [a]Job 37:11; Prov. 30:4
10 [a][Job 38:1–11]; Ps. 33:7; 104:9; Prov. 8:29; Jer. 5:22
12 [a]Ex. 14:21; Job 9:13; Is. 51:15; [Jer. 31:35]
13 [a][Job 9:8]; Ps. 33:6 [b]Is. 27:1

CHAPTER 27

2 [a]Job 34:5
5 [a]Job 2:9; 13:15
6 [a]Job 2:3; 33:9 [b]Acts 24:16
8 [a]Matt. 16:26; Luke 12:20
9 [a]Job 35:12, 13; Ps. 18:41; Prov. 1:28; 28:9; [Is. 1:15]; Jer. 14:12; Ezek. 8:18; [Mic. 3:4; John 9:31; James 4:3]

NKJV

3 Is there any number to His armies?
Upon whom does [a]His light not rise?
4 [a]How then can man be righteous before God?
Or how can he be [b]pure *who is* born of a woman?
5 If even the moon does not shine,
And the stars are not pure in His [a]sight,
6 How much less man, *who is* [a]a maggot,
And a son of man, *who is* a worm?"

Job: Man's Frailty and God's Majesty

26 But Job answered and said:

2 "How have you helped *him who is* without power?
How have you saved the arm *that has* no strength?
3 How have you counseled *one who has* no wisdom?
And *how* have you declared sound advice to many?
4 To whom have you uttered words?
And whose spirit came from you?

5 "The dead tremble,
Those under the waters and those inhabiting them.
6 [a]Sheol *is* naked before Him,
And Destruction has no covering.
7 [a]He stretches out the north over empty space;
He hangs the earth on nothing.
8 [a]He binds up the water in His thick clouds,
Yet the clouds are not broken under it.
9 He covers the face of *His* throne,
And spreads His cloud over it.
10 [a]He drew a circular horizon on the face of the waters,
At the boundary of light and darkness.
11 The pillars of heaven tremble,
And are astonished at His rebuke.
12 [a]He stirs up the sea with His power,
And by His understanding He breaks up the storm.
13 [a]By His Spirit He adorned the heavens;
His hand pierced [b]the fleeing serpent.
14 Indeed these *are* the mere edges of His ways,
And how small a whisper we hear of Him!
But the thunder of His power who can understand?"

Job Maintains His Integrity

27 Moreover Job continued his discourse, and said:

2 "*As* God lives, [a]*who* has taken away my justice,
And the Almighty, *who* has made my soul bitter,
3 As long as my breath *is* in me,
And the breath of God in my nostrils,
4 My lips will not speak wickedness,
Nor my tongue utter deceit.
5 Far be it from me
That I should say you are right;
Till I die [a]I will not put away my integrity from me.
6 My righteousness I [a]hold fast, and will not let it go;
[b]My heart shall not reproach *me* as long as I live.

7 "May my enemy be like the wicked,
And he who rises up against me like the unrighteous.
8 [a]For what is the hope of the hypocrite,
Though he may gain *much*,
If God takes away his life?
9 [a]Will God hear his cry
When trouble comes upon him?

KJV

10 [a]Will he delight himself in the Almighty? will he always call upon God?

11 I will teach you by the hand of God: *that* which *is* with the Almighty will I not conceal.

12 Behold, all ye yourselves have seen *it;* why then are ye thus altogether vain?

13 [a]This *is* the portion of a wicked man with God, and the heritage of oppressors, *which* they shall receive of the Almighty.

14 [a]If his children be multiplied, *it is* for the sword: and his offspring shall not be satisfied with bread.

15 Those that remain of him shall be buried in death: and [a]his widows shall not weep.

16 Though he heap up silver as the dust, and prepare raiment as the clay;

17 He may prepare *it,* but [a]the just shall put *it* on, and the innocent shall divide the silver.

18 He buildeth his house as a moth, and [a]as a booth *that* the keeper maketh.

19 The rich man shall lie down, but he shall not be gathered: he openeth his eyes, and he *is* [a]not.

20 [a]Terrors take hold on him as waters, a tempest stealeth him away in the night.

21 The east wind carrieth him away, and he departeth: and as a storm hurleth him out of his place.

22 For *God* shall cast upon him, and not [a]spare: he would fain flee out of his hand.

23 *Men* shall clap their hands at him, and shall hiss him out of his place.

10 [a]Job 22:26, 27; [Ps. 37:4; Is. 58:14]
13 [a]Job 20:29
14 [a]Deut. 28:41; Esth. 9:10; Hos. 9:13
15 [a]Ps. 78:64
17 [a]Prov. 28:8; [Eccl. 2:26]
18 [a]Is. 1:8; Lam. 2:6
19 [a]Job 7:8, 21; 20:7
20 [a]Job 18:11
22 [a]Jer. 13:14; Ezek. 5:11; 24:14

NKJV

10 [a]Will he delight himself in the Almighty?
Will he always call on God?

11 "I will teach you about the hand of God;
What *is* with the Almighty I will not conceal.
12 Surely all of you have seen *it;*
Why then do you behave with complete nonsense?

13 "This[a] is the portion of a wicked man with God,
And the heritage of oppressors, received from the Almighty:
14 [a]If his children are multiplied, *it is* for the sword;
And his offspring shall not be satisfied with bread.
15 Those who survive him shall be buried in death,
And [a]their* widows shall not weep,
16 Though he heaps up silver like dust,
And piles up clothing like clay—
17 He may pile *it* up, but [a]the just will wear *it,*
And the innocent will divide the silver.
18 He builds his house like a *moth,
[a]Like a booth *which* a watchman makes.
19 The rich man will lie down,
*But not be gathered *up;*
He opens his eyes,
And he *is* [a]no more.
20 [a]Terrors overtake him like a flood;
A tempest steals him away in the night.
21 The east wind carries him away, and he is gone;
It sweeps him out of his place.
22 It hurls against him and does not [a]spare;
He flees desperately from its power.
23 *Men* shall clap their hands at him,
And shall hiss him out of his place.

Job's Discourse on Wisdom (KJV)

28 Surely there is a vein for the silver, and a place for gold *where* they fine *it.*

2 Iron is taken out of the earth, and brass *is* molten *out of* the stone.

3 He setteth an end to darkness, and searcheth out all perfection: the stones of darkness, and the shadow of death.

4 The flood breaketh out from the inhabitant; *even the waters* forgotten of the foot: they are dried up, they are gone away from men.

5 *As for* the earth, out of it cometh bread: and under it is turned up as it were fire.

6 The stones of it *are* the place of sapphires: and it hath dust of gold.

7 *There is* a path which no fowl knoweth, and which the vulture's eye hath not seen:

8 The lion's whelps have not trodden it, nor the fierce lion passed by it.

9 He putteth forth his hand upon the rock; he overturneth the mountains by the roots.

10 He cutteth out rivers among the rocks; and his eye seeth every precious thing.

11 He bindeth the floods from overflowing; and *the thing that is* hid bringeth he forth to light.

12 [a]But where shall wisdom be found? and where *is* the place of understanding?

13 Man knoweth not the [a]price thereof; neither is it found in the land of the living.

14 [a]The depth saith, It *is* not in me: and the sea saith, *It is* not with me.

15 It [a]cannot be gotten for gold, neither shall silver be weighed *for* the price thereof.

16 It cannot be valued with the gold of Ophir, with the precious onyx, or the sapphire.

17 The [a]gold and the crystal cannot equal it:

CHAPTER 28
12 [a]Eccl. 7:24
13 [a]Prov. 3:15
14 [a]Job 28:22
15 [a]Prov. 3:13–15; 8:10, 11, 19
17 [a]Prov. 8:10; 16:16

*

27:15 Lit. *his*
27:18 So with MT, Vg.; LXX, Syr. *spider* (cf. Job 8:14); Tg. *decay*
27:19 So with MT, Tg.; LXX, Syr. *But shall not add* (i.e., do it again); Vg. *But take away nothing*
28:8 Lit. *sons of pride,* figurative of the great lions

Job's Discourse on Wisdom (NKJV)

28 "Surely there is a mine for silver,
And a place *where* gold is refined.
2 Iron is taken from the earth,
And copper *is* smelted *from* ore.
3 *Man* puts an end to darkness,
And searches every recess
For ore in the darkness and the shadow of death.
4 He breaks open a shaft away from people;
In places forgotten by feet
They hang far away from men;
They swing to and fro.
5 *As for* the earth, from it comes bread,
But underneath it is turned up as by fire;
6 Its stones *are* the source of sapphires,
And it contains gold dust.
7 *That* path no bird knows,
Nor has the falcon's eye seen it.
8 The *proud lions have not trodden it,
Nor has the fierce lion passed over it.
9 He puts his hand on the flint;
He overturns the mountains at the roots.
10 He cuts out channels in the rocks,
And his eye sees every precious thing.
11 He dams up the streams from trickling;
What is hidden he brings forth to light.

12 "But[a] where can wisdom be found?
And where *is* the place of understanding?
13 Man does not know its [a]value,
Nor is it found in the land of the living.
14 [a]The deep says, *'It is* not in me';
And the sea says, *'It is* not with me.'
15 It [a]cannot be purchased for gold,
Nor can silver be weighed *for* its price.
16 It cannot be valued in the gold of Ophir,
In precious onyx or sapphire.
17 Neither [a]gold nor crystal can equal it,

KJV

and the exchange of it *shall not be for* jewels of
fine gold.
18 No mention shall be made of coral, or of
pearls: for the price of wisdom *is* above [a]rubies.
19 The topaz of Ethiopia shall not equal it,
neither shall it be valued with pure [a]gold.
20 [a]Whence then cometh wisdom? and
where *is* the place of understanding?
21 Seeing it is hid from the eyes of all living,
and kept close from the fowls of the air.
22 [a]Destruction and death say, We have
heard the fame thereof with our ears.
23 God understandeth the way thereof, and
he knoweth the place thereof.
24 For he looketh to the ends of the earth,
and [a]seeth under the whole heaven;
25 [a]To make the weight for the winds; and
he weigheth the waters by measure.
26 When he [a]made a decree for the rain, and
a way for the lightning of the thunder;
27 Then did he see it, and declare it; he prepared it, yea, and searched it out.
28 And unto man he said, Behold, [a]the fear
of the Lord, that *is* wisdom; and to depart from
evil *is* understanding.

Job's Summary Defense

29 Moreover Job continued his parable, and
said,
2 Oh that I were as *in* months [a]past, as *in*
the days *when* God [b]preserved me;
3 [a]When his candle shined upon my head,
and when by his light I walked *through* darkness;
4 As I was in the days of my youth, when
[a]the secret of God *was* upon my tabernacle;
5 When the Almighty *was* yet with me,
when my children *were* about me;
6 When [a]I washed my steps with butter, and
[b]the rock poured me out rivers of oil;
7 When I went out to the gate through the
city, *when* I prepared my seat in the street!
8 The young men saw me, and hid themselves: and the aged arose, *and* stood up.
9 The princes refrained talking, and [a]laid
their hand on their mouth.
10 The nobles held their peace, and their
[a]tongue cleaved to the roof of their mouth.
11 When the ear heard *me*, then it blessed
me; and when the eye saw *me*, it gave witness to
me:
12 Because [a]I delivered the poor that cried,
and the fatherless, and *him that had* none to help
him.
13 The blessing of him that was ready to perish came upon me: and I caused the widow's heart
to sing for joy.
14 [a]I put on righteousness, and it clothed me:
my judgment *was* as a robe and a diadem.
15 I was [a]eyes to the blind, and feet *was* I
to the lame.
16 I *was* a father to the poor: and [a]the cause
which I knew not I searched out.
17 And I brake [a]the jaws of the wicked, and
plucked the spoil out of his teeth.
18 Then I said, [a]I shall die in my nest, and I
shall multiply *my* days as the sand.

18 [a]Prov. 3:15; 8:11
19 [a]Prov. 8:19
20 [a]Job 28:12; [Ps. 111:10; Prov. 1:7; 9:10]
22 [a]Job 28:14
24 [a][Ps. 11:4; 33:13, 14; 66:7; Prov. 15:3]
25 [a]Ps. 135:7
26 [a]Job 37:3; 38:25
28 [a][Deut. 4:6; Ps. 111:10; Prov. 1:7; 9:10; Eccl. 12:13]

CHAPTER 29

2 [a]Job 1:1–5 [b]Job 1:10
3 [a]Job 18:6
4 [a]Job 15:8; [Ps. 25:14; Prov. 3:32]
6 [a]Gen. 49:11; Deut. 32:14; Job 20:17 [b]Deut. 32:13; Ps. 81:16
9 [a]Job 21:5
10 [a]Ps. 137:6
12 [a]Job 31:16–23; [Ps. 72:12; Prov. 21:13; 24:11]
14 [a]Deut. 24:13; Job 27:5, 6; Ps. 132:9; [Is. 59:17; 61:10; Eph. 6:14]
15 [a]Num. 10:31
16 [a]Prov. 29:7
17 [a]Ps. 58:6; Prov. 30:14
18 [a]Ps. 30:6

*
28:27 Lit. *it*
29:6 So with ancient vss. and a few Heb. mss. (cf. Job 20:17); MT *wrath*

NKJV

Nor can it be exchanged for jewelry of fine
gold.
18 No mention shall be made of coral or
quartz,
For the price of wisdom *is* above [a]rubies.
19 The topaz of Ethiopia cannot equal it,
Nor can it be valued in pure [a]gold.

20 "From[a] where then does wisdom come?
And where *is* the place of understanding?
21 It is hidden from the eyes of all living,
And concealed from the birds of the air.
22 [a]Destruction and Death say,
'We have heard a report about it with our
ears.'
23 God understands its way,
And He knows its place.
24 For He looks to the ends of the earth,
And [a]sees under the whole heavens,
25 [a]To establish a weight for the wind,
And apportion the waters by measure.
26 When He [a]made a law for the rain,
And a path for the thunderbolt,
27 Then He saw **wisdom* and declared it;
He prepared it, indeed, He searched it out.
28 And to man He said,
'Behold, [a]the fear of the Lord, that *is*
wisdom,
And to depart from evil *is*
understanding.' "

Job's Summary Defense

29 Job further continued his discourse, and
said:

2 "Oh, that I were as *in* months [a]past,
As *in* the days *when* God [b]watched over
me;
3 [a]When His lamp shone upon my head,
And when by His light I walked *through*
darkness;
4 Just as I was in the days of my prime,
When [a]the friendly counsel of God *was*
over my tent;
5 When the Almighty *was* yet with me,
When my children *were* around me;
6 When [a]my steps were bathed with *cream,
And [b]the rock poured out rivers of oil for
me!

7 "When I went out to the gate by the city,
When I took my seat in the open square,
8 The young men saw me and hid,
And the aged arose *and* stood;
9 The princes refrained from talking,
And [a]put *their* hand on their mouth;
10 The voice of nobles was hushed,
And their [a]tongue stuck to the roof of their
mouth.
11 When the ear heard, then it blessed me,
And when the eye saw, then it approved
me;
12 Because [a]I delivered the poor who cried
out,
The fatherless and *the one who* had no
helper.
13 The blessing of a perishing *man* came
upon me,
And I caused the widow's heart to sing
for joy.
14 [a]I put on righteousness, and it clothed me;
My justice *was* like a robe and a turban.
15 I *was* [a]eyes to the blind,
And I *was* feet to the lame.
16 I *was* a father to the poor,
And [a]I searched out the case *that* I did
not know.
17 I broke [a]the fangs of the wicked,
And plucked the victim from his teeth.

18 "Then I said, [a]'I shall die in my nest,
And multiply *my* days as the sand.

KJV

19 [a]My root *was* spread out [b]by the waters,
and the dew lay all night upon my branch.
20 My glory *was* fresh in me, and my [a]bow
was renewed in my hand.
21 Unto me *men* gave ear, and waited, and
kept silence at my counsel.
22 After my words they spake not again; and
my speech dropped upon them.
23 And they waited for me as for the rain;
and they opened their mouth wide *as* for [a]the latter rain.
24 *If* I laughed on them, they believed *it* not;
and the light of my countenance they cast not
down.
25 I chose out their way, and sat chief, and
dwelt as a king in the army, as one *that* comforteth the mourners.

30 But now *they that are* younger than I have
me in derision, whose fathers I would have
disdained to have set with the dogs of my flock.
2 Yea, whereto *might* the strength of their
hands *profit* me, in whom old age was perished?
3 For want and famine *they were* solitary;
fleeing into the wilderness in former time desolate
and waste.
4 Who cut up mallows by the bushes, and
juniper roots *for* their meat.
5 They were driven forth from among *men*,
(they cried after them as *after* a thief;)
6 To dwell in the cliffs of the valleys, *in*
caves of the earth, and *in* the rocks.
7 Among the bushes they brayed; under the
nettles they were gathered together.
8 *They were* children of fools, yea, children
of base men: they were viler than the earth.
9 [a]And now am I their song, yea, I am their
byword.
10 They abhor me, they flee far from me, and
spare not [a]to spit in my face.
11 Because he [a]hath loosed my cord, and afflicted me, they have also let loose the bridle before me.
12 Upon *my* right *hand* rise the youth; they
push away my feet, and [a]they raise up against
me the ways of their destruction.
13 They mar my path, they set forward my
calamity, they have no helper.
14 They came *upon me* as a wide breaking
in *of waters:* in the desolation they rolled themselves *upon me.*
15 Terrors are turned upon me: they pursue
my soul as the wind: and my welfare passeth
away as a cloud.
16 [a]And now my soul is [b]poured out upon
me; the days of affliction have taken hold upon
me.
17 My bones are pierced in me in the night
season: and my sinews take no rest.
18 By the great force *of my disease* is my garment changed: it bindeth me about as the collar
of my coat.
19 He hath cast me into the mire, and I am
become like dust and ashes.
20 I [a]cry unto thee, and thou dost not hear
me: I stand up, and thou regardest me *not*.
21 Thou art become cruel to me: with thy
strong hand thou [a]opposest thyself against me.
22 Thou liftest me up to the wind; thou causest me to ride *upon it,* and dissolvest my substance.

19 [a]Job 18:16 [b]Ps. 1:3; [Jer. 17:7, 8]
20 [a]Gen. 49:24; Ps. 18:34
23 [a][Zech. 10:1]

CHAPTER 30
9 [a]Job 17:6; Ps. 69:12; Lam. 3:14, 63
10 [a]Num. 12:14; Deut. 25:9; Job 17:6; Is. 50:6; Matt. 26:67; 27:30
11 [a]Job 12:18
12 [a]Job 19:12
16 [a]Ps. 42:4 [b]Ps. 22:14; Is. 53:12
20 [a]Job 19:7
21 [a]Job 10:3; 16:9, 14; 19:6, 22

*____
30:11 So with MT, Syr., Tg.; LXX, Vg. *His*

NKJV

19 [a]My root *is* spread out [b]to the waters,
And the dew lies all night on my branch.
20 My glory *is* fresh within me,
And my [a]bow is renewed in my hand.'
21 "*Men* listened to me and waited,
And kept silence for my counsel.
22 After my words they did not speak again,
And my speech settled on them *as dew.*
23 They waited for me *as* for the rain,
And they opened their mouth wide *as* for
[a]the spring rain.
24 *If* I mocked at them, they did not believe
it,
And the light of my countenance they did
not cast down.
25 I chose the way for them, and sat as chief;
So I dwelt as a king in the army,
As one *who* comforts mourners.

30 "But now they mock at me, *men* younger
than I,
Whose fathers I disdained to put with the
dogs of my flock.
2 Indeed, what *profit* is the strength of their
hands to me?
Their vigor has perished.
3 *They are* gaunt from want and famine,
Fleeing late to the wilderness, desolate
and waste,
4 Who pluck mallow by the bushes,
And broom tree roots *for* their food.
5 They were driven out from among *men,*
They shouted at them as *at* a thief.
6 *They had* to live in the clefts of the valleys,
In caves of the earth and the rocks.
7 Among the bushes they brayed,
Under the nettles they nestled.
8 *They were* sons of fools,
Yes, sons of vile men;
They were scourged from the land.

9 "And[a] now I am their taunting song;
Yes, I am their byword.
10 They abhor me, they keep far from me;
They do not hesitate [a]to spit in my face.
11 Because [a]He has loosed *my bowstring
and afflicted me,
They have cast off restraint before me.
12 At *my* right *hand* the rabble arises;
They push away my feet,
And [a]they raise against me their ways of
destruction.
13 They break up my path,
They promote my calamity;
They have no helper.
14 They come as broad breakers;
Under the ruinous storm they roll along.
15 Terrors are turned upon me;
They pursue my honor as the wind,
And my prosperity has passed like a
cloud.

16 "And[a] now my soul is [b]poured out because
of my *plight;*
The days of affliction take hold of me.
17 My bones are pierced in me at night,
And my gnawing pains take no rest.
18 By great force my garment is disfigured;
It binds me about as the collar of my coat.
19 He has cast me into the mire,
And I have become like dust and ashes.

20 "I [a]cry out to You, but You do not answer
me;
I stand up, and You regard me.
21 *But* You have become cruel to me;
With the strength of Your hand You
[a]oppose me.
22 You lift me up to the wind and cause me
to ride *on it;*
You spoil my success.

KJV

23 For I know *that* thou wilt bring me *to*
death, and *to* the house [a]appointed for all living.
24 Howbeit he will not stretch out *his* hand
to the grave, though they cry in his destruction.
25 [a]Did not I weep for him that was in trouble? was *not* my soul grieved for the poor?
26 [a]When I looked for good, then evil came
unto me: and when I waited for light, there came
darkness.
27 My bowels boiled, and rested not: the days
of affliction prevented me.
28 [a]I went mourning without the sun: I stood
up, *and* I cried in the congregation.
29 [a]I am a brother to dragons, and a companion to owls.
30 [a]My skin is black upon me, and [b]my bones
are burned with heat.
31 My harp also is *turned* to mourning, and
my organ into the voice of them that weep.

31 I made a covenant with mine eyes; why
then should I think upon a [a]maid?
2 For what [a]portion of God *is there* from
above? and *what* inheritance of the Almighty
from on high?
3 *Is* not destruction to the wicked? and a
strange *punishment* to the workers of iniquity?
4 [a]Doth not he see my ways, and count all
my steps?
5 If I have walked with vanity, or if my foot
hath hasted to deceit;
6 Let me be weighed in an even balance,
that God may know mine [a]integrity.
7 If my step hath turned out of the way, and
[a]mine heart walked after mine eyes, and if any
blot hath cleaved to mine hands;
8 *Then* [a]let me sow, and let another eat; yea,
let my offspring be rooted out.
9 If mine heart have been deceived by a
woman, or *if* I have laid wait at my neighbour's
door;
10 *Then* let my wife grind unto [a]another, and
let others bow down upon her.
11 For this *is* an heinous crime; yea, [a]it *is*
an iniquity *to be punished by* the judges.
12 For it *is* a fire *that* consumeth to destruction, and would root out all mine increase.
13 If I did [a]despise the cause of my manservant or of my maidservant, when they contended with me;
14 What then shall I do when [a]God riseth up?
and when he visiteth, what shall I answer him?
15 [a]Did not he that made me in the womb
make him? and did not one fashion us in the
womb?
16 If I have withheld the poor from *their* desire, or have caused the eyes of the widow to [a]fail;
17 Or have eaten my morsel myself alone,
and the fatherless hath not eaten thereof;
18 (For from my youth he was brought up
with me, as *with* a father, and I have guided her
from my mother's womb;)
19 If I have seen any perish for want of clothing, or any poor without covering;

23 [a][Heb. 9:27] **25** [a]Ps. 35:13, 14; Rom. 12:15 **26** [a]Job 3:25, 26; Jer. 8:15 **28** [a]Job 30:31; Ps. 38:6; 42:9; 43:2 **29** [a]Ps. 44:19; 102:6; Mic. 1:8 **30** [a]Ps. 119:83; Lam. 4:8; 5:10 [b]Ps. 102:3

CHAPTER 31

1 [a][Matt. 5:28] **2** [a]Job 20:29 **4** [a][2 Chr. 16:9]; Job 24:23; 28:24; 34:21; 36:7; [Prov. 5:21; 15:3; Jer. 32:19] **6** [a]Job 23:10; 27:5, 6 **7** [a]Num. 15:39; [Eccl. 11:9]; Ezek. 6:9; [Matt. 5:29] **8** [a]Lev. 26:16; Deut. 28:30, 38; Job 20:18; Mic. 6:15 **10** [a]Deut. 28:30; 2 Sam. 12:11; Jer. 8:10 **11** [a]Gen. 38:24; [Lev. 20:10; Deut. 22:22]; Job 31:28 **13** [a][Deut. 24:14, 15] **14** [a][Ps. 44:21] **15** [a]Job 34:19; Prov. 14:31; 22:2; [Mal. 2:10] **16** [a]Job 29:12

*31:18 Lit. *her*

NKJV

23 For I know *that* You will bring me *to*
death,
And *to* the house [a]appointed for all living.

24 "Surely He would not stretch out *His* hand
against a heap of ruins,
If they cry out when He destroys *it.*
25 [a]Have I not wept for him who was in
trouble?
Has *not* my soul grieved for the poor?
26 [a]But when I looked for good, evil came *to*
me;
And when I waited for light, then came
darkness.
27 My heart is in turmoil and cannot rest;
Days of affliction confront me.
28 [a]I go about mourning, but not in the sun;
I stand up in the assembly *and* cry out
for help.
29 [a]I am a brother of jackals,
And a companion of ostriches.
30 [a]My skin grows black and falls from me;
[b]My bones burn with fever.
31 My harp is *turned* to mourning,
And my flute to the voice of those who
weep.

31 "I have made a covenant with my eyes;
Why then should I look upon a [a]young
woman?
2 For what *is* the [a]allotment of God from
above,
And the inheritance of the Almighty from
on high?
3 *Is* it not destruction for the wicked,
And disaster for the workers of iniquity?
4 [a]Does He not see my ways,
And count all my steps?

5 "If I have walked with falsehood,
Or if my foot has hastened to deceit,
6 Let me be weighed on honest scales,
That God may know my [a]integrity.
7 If my step has turned from the way,
Or [a]my heart walked after my eyes,
Or if any spot adheres to my hands,
8 *Then* [a]let me sow, and another eat;
Yes, let my harvest be rooted out.

9 "If my heart has been enticed by a woman,
Or *if* I have lurked at my neighbor's door,
10 *Then* let my wife grind for [a]another,
And let others bow down over her.
11 For that *would be* wickedness;
Yes, [a]it *would be* iniquity *deserving of*
judgment.
12 For that *would be* a fire *that* consumes
to destruction,
And would root out all my increase.

13 "If I have [a]despised the cause of my male
or female servant
When they complained against me,
14 What then shall I do when [a]God rises up?
When He punishes, how shall I answer
Him?
15 [a]Did not He who made me in the womb
make them?
Did not the same One fashion us in the
womb?

16 "If I have kept the poor from *their* desire,
Or caused the eyes of the widow to [a]fail,
17 Or eaten my morsel by myself,
So that the fatherless could not eat of it
18 (But from my youth I reared him as a
father,
And from my mother's womb I guided
**the widow*);
19 If I have seen anyone perish for lack of
clothing,
Or any poor *man* without covering;

KJV

20 If his loins have not [a]blessed me, and *if*
he were *not* warmed with the fleece of my sheep;
21 If I have lifted up my hand [a]against the
fatherless, when I saw my help in the gate:
22 *Then* let mine arm fall from my shoulder
blade, and mine arm be broken from the bone.
23 For [a]destruction *from* God *was* a terror
to me, and by reason of his highness I could not
endure.
24 [a]If I have made gold my hope, or have
said to the fine gold, *Thou art* my confidence;
25 [a]If I rejoiced because my wealth *was*
great, and because mine hand had gotten much;
26 [a]If I beheld the sun when it shined, or the
moon walking *in* brightness;
27 And my heart hath been secretly enticed,
or my mouth hath kissed my hand:
28 This also *were* an iniquity *to be punished
by* the judge: for I should have denied the God
that is above.
29 [a]If I rejoiced at the destruction of him that
hated me, or lifted up myself when evil found him;
30 [a]Neither have I suffered my mouth to sin
by wishing a curse to his soul.
31 If the men of my tabernacle said not, Oh
that we had of his flesh! we cannot be satisfied.
32 [a]The stranger did not lodge in the street:
but I opened my doors to the traveller.
33 If I covered my transgressions [a]as Adam,
by hiding mine iniquity in my bosom:
34 Did I fear a great [a]multitude, or did the
contempt of families terrify me, that I kept silence,
and went not out of the door?
35 [a]Oh that one would hear me! behold, my
desire *is*, [b]*that* the Almighty would answer me,
and *that* mine adversary had written a book.
36 Surely I would take it upon my shoulder,
and bind it *as* a crown to me.
37 I would declare unto him the number of
my steps; as a prince would I go near unto him.
38 If my land cry against me, or that the furrows likewise thereof complain;
39 If [a]I have eaten the fruits thereof without
money, or [b]have caused the owners thereof to lose
their life:
40 Let [a]thistles grow instead of wheat, and
cockle instead of barley. The words of Job are
ended.

Elihu Contradicts Job's Friends

32 So these three men ceased to answer Job,
because he *was* [a]righteous in his own eyes.
2 Then was kindled the wrath of Elihu the
son of Barachel the [a]Buzite, of the kindred of
Ram: against Job was his wrath kindled, because
he [b]justified himself rather than God.
3 Also against his three friends was his
wrath kindled, because they had found no answer,
and *yet* had condemned Job.
4 Now Elihu had waited till Job had spoken,
because they *were* elder than he.
5 When Elihu saw that *there was* no answer

20 [a][Deut. 24:13]
21 [a]Job 22:9
23 [a]Is. 13:6
24 [a][Matt. 6:19, 20; Mark 10:23–25]
25 [a]Job 1:3, 10; Ps. 62:10
26 [a][Deut. 4:19; 17:3]; Ezek. 8:16
29 [a][Prov. 17:5; 24:17]; Obad. 12
30 [a][Matt. 5:44]
32 [a]Gen. 19:2, 3
33 [a]Gen. 3:10; [Prov. 28:13]
34 [a]Ex. 23:2
35 [a]Job 19:7; 30:20, 24, 28 [b]Job 13:22, 24; 33:10
39 [a]Job 24:6, 10–12; [James 5:4] [b]1 Kin. 21:19
40 [a]Gen. 3:18

CHAPTER 32

1 [a]Job 6:29; 31:6; 33:9
2 [a]Gen. 22:21 [b]Job 27:5, 6

*

31:20 Lit. *loins*
31:26 Lit. *light*
31:32 So with LXX, Syr., Tg., Vg.; MT *road*
31:39 Lit. *strength*
32:4 Vg. *till Job had spoken*

NKJV

20 If his *heart has not [a]blessed me,
And *if* he was *not* warmed with the fleece
of my sheep;
21 If I have raised my hand [a]against the
fatherless,
When I saw I had help in the gate;
22 *Then* let my arm fall from my shoulder,
Let my arm be torn from the socket.
23 For [a]destruction *from* God *is* a terror to
me,
And because of His magnificence I cannot
endure.

24 "If[a] I have made gold my hope,
Or said to fine gold, '*You are* my
confidence';
25 [a]If I have rejoiced because my wealth *was*
great,
And because my hand had gained much;
26 [a]If I have observed the *sun when it shines,
Or the moon moving *in* brightness,
27 So that my heart has been secretly
enticed,
And my mouth has kissed my hand;
28 This also *would be* an iniquity *deserving
of* judgment,
For I would have denied God *who is*
above.

29 "If[a] I have rejoiced at the destruction of
him who hated me,
Or lifted myself up when evil found him
30 [a](Indeed I have not allowed my mouth to
sin
By asking for a curse on his soul);
31 If the men of my tent have not said,
'Who is there that has not been satisfied
with his meat?'
32 [a](*But* no sojourner had to lodge in the
street,
For I have opened my doors to the
*traveler);
33 If I have covered my transgressions [a]as
Adam,
By hiding my iniquity in my bosom,
34 Because I feared the great [a]multitude,
And dreaded the contempt of families,
So that I kept silence
And did not go out of the door—
35 [a]Oh, that I had one to hear me!
Here is my mark.
Oh, [b]*that* the Almighty would answer me,
That my Prosecutor had written a book!
36 Surely I would carry it on my shoulder,
And bind it on me *like* a crown;
37 I would declare to Him the number of my
steps;
Like a prince I would approach Him.

38 "If my land cries out against me,
And its furrows weep together;
39 If [a]I have eaten its *fruit without money,
Or [b]caused its owners to lose their lives;
40 *Then* let [a]thistles grow instead of wheat,
And weeds instead of barley."

The words of Job are ended.

Elihu Contradicts Job's Friends

32 So these three men ceased answering Job,
because he *was* [a]righteous in his own
eyes.
2 Then the wrath of Elihu, the son of Barachel the [a]Buzite, of the family of Ram, was
aroused against Job; his wrath was aroused because he [b]justified himself rather than God.
3 Also against his three friends his wrath
was aroused, because they had found no answer,
and *yet* had condemned Job.
4 Now because they *were* years older than
he, Elihu had waited *to speak to Job.
5 When Elihu saw that *there was* no answer

KJV

in the mouth of *these* three men, then his wrath was kindled.

6 And Elihu the son of Barachel the Buzite answered and said, I *am* [a]young, and ye *are* very old; wherefore I was afraid, and durst not shew you mine opinion.

7 I said, Days should speak, and multitude of years should teach wisdom.

8 But *there is* a spirit in man: and [a]the inspiration of the Almighty giveth them understanding.

9 [a]Great men are not *always* wise: neither do the aged understand judgment.

10 Therefore I said, Hearken to me; I also will shew mine opinion.

11 Behold, I waited for your words; I gave ear to your reasons, whilst ye searched out what to say.

12 Yea, I attended unto you, and, behold, *there was* none of you that convinced Job, *or* that answered his words:

13 [a]Lest ye should say, We have found out wisdom: God thrusteth him down, not man.

14 Now he hath not directed *his* words against me: neither will I answer him with your speeches.

15 They were amazed, they answered no more: they left off speaking.

16 When I had waited, (for they spake not, but stood still, *and* answered no more;)

17 *I said,* I will answer also my part, I also will shew mine opinion.

18 For I am full of matter, the spirit within me constraineth me.

19 Behold, my belly *is* as wine *which* hath no vent; it is ready to burst like new bottles.

20 I will speak, that I may be refreshed: I will open my lips and answer.

21 Let me not, I pray you, accept any man's person, neither let me give flattering titles unto man.

22 For I know not to give flattering titles; *in so doing* my maker would soon take me [a]away.

Elihu Contradicts Job

33 Wherefore, Job, I pray thee, hear my speeches, and hearken to all my words.

2 Behold, now I have opened my mouth, my tongue hath spoken in my mouth.

3 My words *shall be of* the uprightness of my heart: and my lips shall utter knowledge clearly.

4 [a]The spirit of God hath made me, and the breath of the Almighty hath given me life.

5 If thou canst answer me, set *thy words* in order before me, stand up.

6 [a]Behold, I *am* according to thy wish in God's stead: I also am formed out of the clay.

7 [a]Behold, my terror shall not make thee afraid, neither shall my hand be heavy upon thee.

8 Surely thou hast spoken in mine hearing, and I have heard the voice of *thy* words, *saying,*

9 [a]I am clean without transgression, I *am* innocent; neither *is there* iniquity in me.

---

6 [a]Lev. 19:32
8 [a]1 Kin. 3:12; 4:29; [Job 35:11; 38:36; Prov. 2:6; Eccl. 2:26; Dan. 1:17; 2:21; Matt. 11:25; James 1:5]
9 [a][1 Cor. 1:26]
13 [a][Jer. 9:23; 1 Cor. 1:29]
22 [a]Job 27:8

CHAPTER 33
4 [a][Gen. 2:7]; Job 32:8
6 [a]Job 4:19
7 [a]Job 9:34
9 [a]Job 10:7

*
32:7 Lit. *Days,* i.e., years
32:9 Or *Men of many years*
33:6 Lit. *as your mouth*

NKJV

in the mouth of these three men, his wrath was aroused.

6 So Elihu, the son of Barachel the Buzite, answered and said:

"I *am* [a]young in years, and you *are* very old;
Therefore I was afraid,
And dared not declare my opinion to you.
7 I said, *'Age should speak,
And multitude of years should teach wisdom.'
8 But *there is* a spirit in man,
And [a]the breath of the Almighty gives him understanding.
9 [a]Great* men are not *always* wise,
Nor do the aged *always* understand justice.

10 "Therefore I say, 'Listen to me,
I also will declare my opinion.'
11 Indeed I waited for your words,
I listened to your reasonings, while you searched out what to say.
12 I paid close attention to you;
And surely not one of you convinced Job,
Or answered his words—
13 [a]Lest you say,
'We have found wisdom';
God will vanquish him, not man.
14 Now he has not directed *his* words against me;
So I will not answer him with your words.

15 "They are dismayed and answer no more;
Words escape them.
16 And I have waited, because they did not speak,
Because they stood still *and* answered no more.
17 I also will answer my part,
I too will declare my opinion.
18 For I am full of words;
The spirit within me compels me.
19 Indeed my belly *is* like wine *that* has no vent;
It is ready to burst like new wineskins.
20 I will speak, that I may find relief;
I must open my lips and answer.
21 Let me not, I pray, show partiality to anyone;
Nor let me flatter any man.
22 For I do not know how to flatter,
Else my Maker would soon take me [a]away.

Elihu Contradicts Job

33 "But please, Job, hear my speech,
And listen to all my words.
2 Now, I open my mouth;
My tongue speaks in my mouth.
3 My words *come* from my upright heart;
My lips utter pure knowledge.
4 [a]The Spirit of God has made me,
And the breath of the Almighty gives me life.
5 If you can answer me,
Set *your words* in order before me;
Take your stand.
6 [a]Truly I *am* *as your spokesman before God;
I also have been formed out of clay.
7 [a]Surely no fear of me will terrify you,
Nor will my hand be heavy on you.

8 "Surely you have spoken in my hearing,
And I have heard the sound of *your* words, *saying,*
9 'I[a] *am* pure, without transgression;
I *am* innocent, and *there is* no iniquity in me.

KJV

10 Behold, he findeth occasions against me,
[a]he counteth me for his enemy,
11 [a]He putteth my feet in the stocks, he
marketh all my paths.
12 Behold, *in* this thou art not just: I will answer thee, that God is greater than man.
13 Why dost thou [a]strive against him? for he
giveth not account of any of his matters.
14 [a]For God speaketh once, yea twice, *yet
man* perceiveth it not.
15 [a]In a dream, in a vision of the night, when
deep sleep falleth upon men, in slumberings upon
the bed;
16 [a]Then he openeth the ears of men, and
sealeth their instruction,
17 That he may withdraw man *from his* purpose, and hide pride from man.
18 He keepeth back his soul from the pit, and
his life from perishing by the sword.
19 He is chastened also with pain upon his
[a]bed, and the multitude of his bones with strong
pain:
20 [a]So that his life abhorreth [b]bread, and his
soul dainty meat.
21 His flesh is consumed away, that it cannot
be seen; and his bones *that* were not seen stick
out.
22 Yea, his soul draweth near unto the grave,
and his life to the destroyers.
23 If there be a messenger with him, an interpreter, one among a thousand, to shew unto man
his uprightness;
24 Then he is gracious unto him, and saith,
Deliver him from going down to the pit: I have
found a ransom.
25 His flesh shall be fresher than a child's:
he shall return to the days of his youth:
26 He shall pray unto God, and he will be
favourable unto him: and he shall see his face
with joy: for he will render unto man his
righteousness.
27 He looketh upon men, and *if any* [a]say, I
have sinned, and perverted *that which was* right,
and it [b]profited me not;
28 He will [a]deliver his soul from going into
the pit, and his life shall see the light.
29 Lo, all these *things* worketh God oftentimes with man,
30 [a]To bring back his soul from the pit, to
be enlightened with the light of the living.
31 Mark well, O Job, hearken unto me: hold
thy peace, and I will speak.
32 If thou hast any thing to say, answer me:
speak, for I desire to justify thee.
33 If not, [a]hearken unto me: hold thy peace,
and I shall teach thee wisdom.

Elihu Proclaims God's Justice

34 Furthermore Elihu answered and said,
2 Hear my words, O ye wise *men;* and
give ear unto me, ye that have knowledge.
3 [a]For the ear trieth words, as the mouth
tasteth meat.
4 Let us choose to us judgment: let us know
among ourselves what *is* good.

---

10 [a]Job 13:24; 16:9
11 [a]Job 13:27; 19:8
13 [a]Job 40:2; [Is. 45:9]
14 [a]Job 33:29; 40:5; Ps. 62:11
15 [a][Num. 12:6]
16 [a][Job 36:10, 15]
19 [a]Job 30:17
20 [a]Ps. 107:18 [b]Job 3:24; 6:7
27 [a][2 Sam. 12:13; Prov. 28:13; Luke 15:21; 1 John 1:9] [b][Rom. 6:21]
28 [a]Is. 38:17
30 [a]Ps. 56:13
33 [a]Ps. 34:11

CHAPTER 34
3 [a]Job 6:30; 12:11

*
33:28 Kt. *my*
• Kt. *my*

NKJV

10 Yet He finds occasions against me,
[a]He counts me as His enemy;
11 [a]He puts my feet in the stocks,
He watches all my paths.'

12 "Look, *in* this you are not righteous.
I will answer you,
For God is greater than man.
13 Why do you [a]contend with Him?
For He does not give an accounting of any
of His words.
14 [a]For God may speak in one way, or in
another,
Yet man does not perceive it.
15 [a]In a dream, in a vision of the night,
When deep sleep falls upon men,
While slumbering on their beds,
16 [a]Then He opens the ears of men,
And seals their instruction.
17 In order to turn man *from his* deed,
And conceal pride from man,
18 He keeps back his soul from the Pit,
And his life from perishing by the
sword.

19 "*Man* is also chastened with pain on his
[a]bed,
And with strong *pain* in many of his
bones,
20 [a]So that his life abhors [b]bread,
And his soul succulent food.
21 His flesh wastes away from sight,
And his bones stick out *which once* were
not seen.
22 Yes, his soul draws near the Pit,
And his life to the executioners.

23 "If there is a messenger for him,
A mediator, one among a thousand,
To show man His uprightness,
24 Then He is gracious to him, and says,
'Deliver him from going down to the
Pit;
I have found a ransom';
25 His flesh shall be young like a child's,
He shall return to the days of his youth.
26 He shall pray to God, and He will delight
in him,
He shall see His face with joy,
For He restores to man His righteousness.
27 Then he looks at men and [a]says,
'I have sinned, and perverted *what was*
right,
And it [b]did not profit me.'
28 He will [a]redeem *his soul from going
down to the Pit,
And *his life shall see the light.

29 "Behold, God works all these *things,*
Twice, *in fact,* three *times* with a man,
30 [a]To bring back his soul from the Pit,
That he may be enlightened with the light
of life.

31 "Give ear, Job, listen to me;
Hold your peace, and I will speak.
32 If you have anything to say, answer me;
Speak, for I desire to justify you.
33 If not, [a]listen to me;
Hold your peace, and I will teach you
wisdom."

Elihu Proclaims God's Justice

34 Elihu further answered and said:

2 "Hear my words, you wise *men;*
Give ear to me, you who have knowledge.
3 [a]For the ear tests words
As the palate tastes food.
4 Let us choose justice for ourselves;
Let us know among ourselves what *is*
good.

KJV

5 For Job hath said, [a]I am righteous: and
[b]God hath taken away my judgment.
6 [a]Should I lie against my right? my wound
is incurable without transgression.
7 What man *is* like Job, [a]*who* drinketh up
scorning like water?
8 Which goeth in company with the workers
of iniquity, and walketh with wicked men.
9 For [a]he hath said, It profiteth a man nothing that he should delight himself with God.
10 Therefore hearken unto me, ye men of understanding: [a]far be it from God, *that he should*
do wickedness; and *from* the Almighty, *that he*
should commit iniquity.
11 [a]For the work of a man shall he render
unto him, and cause every man to find according
to *his* ways.
12 Yea, surely God will not do wickedly, neither will the Almighty [a]pervert judgment.
13 Who hath given him a charge over the
earth? or who hath disposed the whole world?
14 If he set his heart upon man, *if* he [a]gather
unto himself his spirit and his breath;
15 [a]All flesh shall perish together, and man
shall turn again unto dust.
16 If now *thou hast* understanding, hear this:
hearken to the voice of my words.
17 [a]Shall even he that hateth right govern?
and wilt thou [b]condemn him that is most just?
18 [a]*Is it fit* to say to a king, *Thou art* wicked?
and to princes, *Ye are* ungodly?
19 *How much less to him* that [a]accepteth not
the persons of princes, nor regardeth the rich
more than the poor? for [b]they all *are* the work
of his hands.
20 In a moment shall they die, and the people
shall be troubled [a]at midnight, and pass away:
and the mighty shall be taken away without hand.
21 [a]For his eyes *are* upon the ways of man,
and he seeth all his goings.
22 [a]*There is* no darkness, nor shadow of
death, where the workers of iniquity may hide
themselves.
23 For he will not lay upon man more *than*
right; that he should enter into judgment with
God.
24 [a]He shall break in pieces mighty men
without number, and set others in their stead.
25 Therefore he knoweth their works, and he
overturneth *them* in the night, so that they are
destroyed.
26 He striketh them as wicked men in the
open sight of others;
27 Because they [a]turned back from him, and
[b]would not consider any of his ways:
28 So that they [a]cause the cry of the poor to
come unto him, and he [b]heareth the cry of the
afflicted.
29 When he giveth quietness, who then can
make trouble? and when he hideth *his* face, who
then can behold him? whether *it be done* against
a nation, or against a man only:
30 That the hypocrite reign not, lest the people be ensnared.
31 Surely it is meet to be said unto God, I
have borne *chastisement,* I will not offend *any*
more:

5 [a]Job 13:18; 33:9 [b]Job 27:2
6 [a]Job 6:4; 9:17
7 [a]Job 15:16
9 [a]Mal. 3:14
10 [a][Gen. 18:25; Deut. 32:4; 2 Chr. 19:7]; Job 8:3; 36:23; Ps. 92:15; Rom. 9:14
11 [a]Job 34:25; Ps. 62:12; [Prov. 24:12; Jer. 32:19]; Ezek. 33:20; [Matt. 16:27]; Rom. 2:6; [2 Cor. 5:10; Rev. 22:12]
12 [a]Job 8:3
14 [a]Job 12:10; Ps. 104:29; [Eccl. 12:7]
15 [a][Gen. 3:19]; Job 10:9; [Eccl. 12:7]
17 [a]2 Sam. 23:3; Job 34:30 [b]Job 40:8
18 [a]Ex. 22:28
19 [a][Deut. 10:17; Acts 10:34; Rom. 2:11, 12] [b]Job 31:15
20 [a]Ex. 12:29; Job 34:25; 36:20
21 [a][2 Chr. 16:9]; Job 31:4; Ps. 34:15; [Prov. 5:21; 15:3; Jer. 16:17; 32:19]
22 [a][Ps. 139:11, 12; Amos 9:2, 3]
24 [a]Job 12:19; [Dan. 2:21]
27 [a]1 Sam. 15:11 [b]Ps. 28:5; Is. 5:12
28 [a]Job 35:9; James 5:4 [b][Ex. 22:23]; Job 22:27

NKJV

5 "For Job has said, [a]'I am righteous,
But [b]God has taken away my justice;
6 [a]Should I lie concerning my right?
My wound *is* incurable, *though I am*
without transgression.'
7 What man *is* like Job,
[a]*Who* drinks scorn like water,
8 Who goes in company with the workers
of iniquity,
And walks with wicked men?
9 For [a]he has said, 'It profits a man nothing
That he should delight in God.'

10 "Therefore listen to me, you men of
understanding:
[a]Far be it from God *to do* wickedness,
And *from* the Almighty to *commit*
iniquity.
11 [a]For He repays man *according to* his work,
And makes man to find a reward
according to *his* way.
12 Surely God will never do wickedly,
Nor will the Almighty [a]pervert justice.
13 Who gave Him charge over the earth?
Or who appointed *Him over* the whole
world?
14 If He should set His heart on it,
If He should [a]gather to Himself His Spirit
and His breath,
15 [a]All flesh would perish together,
And man would return to dust.

16 "If *you have* understanding, hear this;
Listen to the sound of my words:
17 [a]Should one who hates justice govern?
Will you [b]condemn *Him who is* most just?
18 [a]*Is it fitting* to say to a king, '*You are*
worthless,'
And to nobles, '*You are* wicked'?
19 Yet He [a]is not partial to princes,
Nor does He regard the rich more than
the poor;
For [b]they *are* all the work of His hands.
20 In a moment they die, [a]in the middle of
the night;
The people are shaken and pass away;
The mighty are taken away without a
hand.

21 "For[a] His eyes *are* on the ways of man,
And He sees all his steps.
22 [a]There is no darkness nor shadow of death
Where the workers of iniquity may hide
themselves.
23 For He need not further consider a man,
That he should go before God in
judgment.
24 [a]He breaks in pieces mighty men without
inquiry,
And sets others in their place.
25 Therefore He knows their works;
He overthrows *them* in the night,
And they are crushed.
26 He strikes them as wicked *men*
In the open sight of others,
27 Because they [a]turned back from Him,
And [b]would not consider any of His ways,
28 So that they [a]caused the cry of the poor
to come to Him;
For He [b]hears the cry of the afflicted.
29 When He gives quietness, who then can
make trouble?
And when He hides *His* face, who then
can see Him,
Whether *it is* against a nation or a man
alone?—
30 That the hypocrite should not reign,
Lest the people be ensnared.

31 "For has *anyone* said to God,
'I have borne *chastening;*
I will offend no more;

KJV

32 *That which* I see not teach thou me: if I
have done iniquity, I will do no more.
33 *Should it be* according to thy mind? he
will recompense it, whether thou refuse, or
whether thou choose; and not I: therefore speak
what thou knowest.
34 Let men of understanding tell me, and let
a wise man hearken unto me.
35 [a]Job hath spoken without knowledge, and
his words *were* without wisdom.
36 My desire *is that* Job may be tried unto
the end because of *his* answers for wicked men.
37 For he addeth [a]rebellion unto his sin, he
clappeth *his hands* among us, and multiplieth his
words against God.

Elihu Condemns Self-Righteousness

35 Elihu spake moreover, and said,
2 Thinkest thou this to be right, *that* thou
saidst, My righteousness *is* more than God's?
3 For [a]thou saidst, What advantage will it
be unto thee? *and,* What profit shall I have, *if I
be cleansed* from my sin?
4 I will answer thee, and [a]thy companions
with thee.
5 [a]Look unto the heavens, and see; and behold the clouds *which* are higher than thou.
6 If thou sinnest, what doest thou [a]against
him? or *if* thy transgressions be multiplied, what
doest thou unto him?
7 [a]If thou be righteous, what givest thou
him? or what receiveth he of thine hand?
8 Thy wickedness *may hurt* a man as thou
art; and thy righteousness *may profit* the son of
man.
9 [a]By reason of the multitude of oppressions
they make *the oppressed* to cry: they cry out by
reason of the arm of the mighty.
10 But none saith, [a]Where *is* God my maker,
[b]who giveth songs in the night;
11 Who [a]teacheth us more than the beasts
of the earth, and maketh us wiser than the fowls
of heaven?
12 [a]There they cry, but none giveth answer,
because of the pride of evil men.
13 [a]Surely God will not hear vanity, neither
will the Almighty regard it.
14 [a]Although thou sayest thou shalt not see
him, *yet* judgment *is* before him; therefore [b]trust
thou in him.
15 But now, because *it is* not *so,* he hath
[a]visited in his anger; yet he knoweth *it* not in great
extremity:
16 [a]Therefore doth Job open his mouth in
vain; he multiplieth words without knowledge.

Elihu Proclaims God's Goodness

36 Elihu also proceeded, and said,
2 Suffer me a little, and I will shew thee
that *I have* yet to speak on God's behalf.
3 I will fetch my knowledge from afar, and
will ascribe righteousness to my Maker.
4 For truly my words *shall* not *be* false: he
that is perfect in knowledge *is* with thee.

---

35 [a]Job 35:16; 38:2
37 [a]Job 7:11; 10:1

CHAPTER 35

3 [a]Job 21:15; 34:9
4 [a]Job 34:8
5 [a]Gen. 15:5; [Job 22:12; Ps. 8:3]
6 [a]Job 7:20; [Prov. 8:36; Jer. 7:19]
7 [a]Job 22:2; Ps. 16:2; Prov. 9:12; [Luke 17:10]; Rom. 11:35
9 [a]Job 34:28
10 [a]Is. 51:13 [b]Job 8:21; Ps. 42:8; 77:6; 149:5; Acts 16:25
11 [a]Job 36:22; Ps. 94:12; [Is. 48:17]; Jer. 32:33; [1 Cor. 2:13]
12 [a]Prov. 1:28
13 [a]Job 27:9; [Prov. 15:29; Is. 1:15]; Jer. 11:11; [Mic. 3:4]
14 [a]Job 9:11 [b][Ps. 37:5, 6]
15 [a]Ps. 89:32
16 [a]Job 34:35; 38:2

NKJV

32 Teach me *what* I do not see;
If I have done iniquity, I will do no more'?
33 Should He repay *it* according to your
terms,
Just because you disavow it?
You must choose, and not I;
Therefore speak what you know.

34 "Men of understanding say to me,
Wise men who listen to me:
35 'Job[a] speaks without knowledge,
His words *are* without wisdom.'
36 Oh, that Job were tried to the utmost,
Because *his* answers *are like* those of
wicked men!
37 For he adds [a]rebellion to his sin;
He claps *his hands* among us,
And multiplies his words against God."

Elihu Condemns Self-Righteousness

35 Moreover Elihu answered and said:

2 "Do you think this is right?
Do you say,
'My righteousness is more than God's'?
3 For [a]you say,
'What advantage will it be to You?
What profit shall I have, more than *if* I
had sinned?'

4 "I will answer you,
And [a]your companions with you.
5 [a]Look to the heavens and see;
And behold the clouds—
They are higher than you.
6 If you sin, what do you accomplish
[a]against Him?
Or, *if* your transgressions are multiplied,
what do you do to Him?
7 [a]If you are righteous, what do you give
Him?
Or what does He receive from your hand?
8 Your wickedness affects a man such as
you,
And your righteousness a son of man.

9 "Because[a] of the multitude of oppressions
they cry out;
They cry out for help because of the arm
of the mighty.
10 But no one says, [a]'Where *is* God my
Maker,
[b]Who gives songs in the night,
11 Who [a]teaches us more than the beasts of
the earth,
And makes us wiser than the birds of
heaven?'
12 [a]There they cry out, but He does not
answer,
Because of the pride of evil men.
13 [a]Surely God will not listen to empty *talk,*
Nor will the Almighty regard it.
14 [a]Although you say you do not see Him,
Yet justice *is* before Him, and [b]you must
wait for Him.
15 And now, because He has not [a]punished
in His anger,
Nor taken much notice of folly,
16 [a]Therefore Job opens his mouth in vain;
He multiplies words without knowledge."

Elihu Proclaims God's Goodness

36 Elihu also proceeded and said:

2 "Bear with me a little, and I will show you
That *there are* yet words to speak on
God's behalf.
3 I will fetch my knowledge from afar;
I will ascribe righteousness to my Maker.
4 For truly my words *are* not false;
One who is perfect in knowledge *is* with
you.

KJV

5 Behold, God *is* mighty, and despiseth not
any: [a]*he is* mighty in strength *and* wisdom.
6 He preserveth not the life of the wicked:
but giveth right to the [a]poor.
7 [a]He withdraweth not his eyes from the
righteous: but [b]with kings *are they* on the throne;
yea, he doth establish them for ever, and they are
exalted.
8 And [a]if *they be* bound in fetters, *and* be
holden in cords of affliction;
9 Then he sheweth them their work, and
their transgressions that they have exceeded.
10 [a]He openeth also their ear to discipline,
and commandeth that they return from iniquity.
11 If they obey and serve *him,* they shall
[a]spend their days in prosperity, and their years
in pleasures.
12 But if they obey not, they shall perish by
the sword, and they shall die without [a]knowledge.
13 But the hypocrites in heart [a]heap up
wrath: they cry not when he bindeth them.
14 [a]They die in youth, and their life *is* among
the unclean.
15 He delivereth the poor in his affliction,
and openeth their ears in oppression.
16 Even so would he have removed thee out
of the strait [a]*into* a broad place, where *there is*
no straitness; and [b]that which should be set on
thy table *should be* full of [c]fatness.
17 But thou hast fulfilled the judgment of the
[a]wicked: judgment and justice take hold *on thee.*
18 Because *there is* wrath, *beware* lest he
take thee away with *his* stroke: then [a]a great ransom cannot deliver thee.
19 [a]Will he esteem thy riches? *no,* not gold,
nor all the forces of strength.
20 Desire not the night, when people are cut
off in their place.
21 Take heed, [a]regard not iniquity: for [b]this
hast thou chosen rather than affliction.
22 Behold, God exalteth by his power: who
teacheth like him?
23 [a]Who hath enjoined him his way? or who
can say, Thou hast wrought [b]iniquity?

Elihu Proclaims God's Majesty

24 Remember that thou [a]magnify his work,
which men behold.
25 Every man may see it; man may behold
it afar off.
26 Behold, God *is* great, and we [a]know *him*
not, [b]neither can the number of his years be
searched out.
27 For he [a]maketh small the drops of water:
they pour down rain according to the vapour
thereof;
28 [a]Which the clouds do drop *and* distil upon
man abundantly.
29 Also can *any* understand the spreadings
of the clouds, *or* the noise of his tabernacle?
30 Behold, he [a]spreadeth his light upon it,
and covereth the bottom of the sea.

CHAPTER 36

5 [a]Job 12:13, 16; 37:23; [Ps. 99:2–5]
6 [a]Job 5:15
7 [a][Ps. 33:18; 34:15] [b]Job 5:11; Ps. 113:8
8 [a]Ps. 107:10
10 [a]Job 33:16; 36:15
11 [a]Job 21:13; [Is. 1:19, 20]
12 [a]Job 4:21
13 [a][Rom. 2:5]
14 [a]Ps. 55:23
16 [a]Ps. 18:19; 31:8; 118:5 [b]Ps. 23:5 [c]Ps. 36:8
17 [a]Job 22:5, 10, 11
18 [a]Ps. 49:7
19 [a][Prov. 11:4]
21 [a]Job 36:10; [Ps. 31:6; 66:18] [b]Job 36:8, 15; [Heb. 11:25]
23 [a]Job 34:13; [Is. 40:13, 14] [b][Deut. 32:4]; Job 8:3
24 [a][Ps. 92:5; Rev. 15:3]
26 [a]Job 11:7–9; 37:23; [1 Cor. 13:12] [b]Job 10:5; [Ps. 90:2; 102:24, 27]; Heb. 1:12
27 [a]Job 5:10; 37:6, 11; 38:28; Ps. 147:8
28 [a][Prov. 3:20]
30 [a]Job 37:3

NKJV

5 "Behold, God *is* mighty, but despises *no one;*
[a]*He is* mighty in strength of understanding.
6 He does not preserve the life of the wicked,
But gives justice to the [a]oppressed.
7 [a]He does not withdraw His eyes from the righteous;
But [b]*they are* on the throne with kings,
For He has seated them forever,
And they are exalted.
8 And [a]if *they are* bound in fetters,
Held in the cords of affliction,
9 Then He tells them their work and their transgressions—
That they have acted defiantly.
10 [a]He also opens their ear to instruction,
And commands that they turn from iniquity.
11 If they obey and serve *Him,*
They shall [a]spend their days in prosperity,
And their years in pleasures.
12 But if they do not obey,
They shall perish by the sword,
And they shall die *without [a]knowledge.

13 "But the hypocrites in heart [a]store up wrath;
They do not cry for help when He binds them.
14 [a]They die in youth,
And their life *ends* among the *perverted persons.
15 He delivers the poor in their affliction,
And opens their ears in oppression.

16 "Indeed He would have brought you out of dire distress,
[a]*Into* a broad place where *there is* no restraint;
And [b]what is set on your table *would be* full of [c]richness.
17 But you are filled with the judgment due the [a]wicked;
Judgment and justice take hold *of you.*
18 Because *there is* wrath, *beware* lest He take you away with *one* blow;
For [a]a large ransom would not help you avoid *it.*
19 [a]Will your riches,
Or all the mighty forces,
Keep you from distress?
20 Do not desire the night,
When people are cut off in their place.
21 Take heed, [a]do not turn to iniquity,
For [b]you have chosen this rather than affliction.

22 "Behold, God is exalted by His power;
Who teaches like Him?
23 [a]Who has assigned Him His way,
Or who has said, 'You have done [b]wrong'?

Elihu Proclaims God's Majesty

24 "Remember to [a]magnify His work,
Of which men have sung.
25 Everyone has seen it;
Man looks on *it* from afar.

26 "Behold, God *is* great, and we [a]do not know *Him;*
[b]Nor can the number of His years *be* discovered.
27 For He [a]draws up drops of water,
Which distill as rain from the mist,
28 [a]Which the clouds drop down
And pour abundantly on man.
29 Indeed, can *anyone* understand the spreading of clouds,
The thunder from His canopy?
30 Look, He [a]scatters His light upon it,
And covers the depths of the sea.

*
36:12 MT *as one without knowledge*
36:14 Heb. *qedeshim,* those practicing sodomy or prostitution in religious rituals

KJV

31 For [a]by them judgeth he the people; he [b]giveth meat in abundance.

32 [a]With clouds he covereth the light; and commandeth it *not to shine* by *the cloud* that cometh betwixt.

33 [a]The noise thereof sheweth concerning it, the cattle also concerning the vapour.

37 At this also my heart trembleth, and is moved out of his place.

2 Hear attentively the noise of his voice, and the sound *that* goeth out of his mouth.

3 He directeth it under the whole heaven, and his lightning unto the ends of the earth.

4 After it [a]a voice roareth: he thundereth with the voice of his excellency; and he will not stay them when his voice is heard.

5 God thundereth marvellously with his voice; [a]great things doeth he, which we cannot comprehend.

6 For [a]he saith to the snow, Be thou *on* the earth; likewise to the small rain, and to the great rain of his strength.

7 He sealeth up the hand of every man; [a]that [b]all men may know his work.

8 Then the beasts [a]go into dens, and remain in their places.

9 Out of the south cometh the whirlwind: and cold out of the north.

10 [a]By the breath of God frost is given: and the breadth of the waters is straitened.

11 Also by watering he wearieth the thick cloud: he scattereth his bright cloud:

12 And it is turned round about by his counsels: that they may [a]do whatsoever he commandeth them upon the face of the world in the earth.

13 [a]He causeth it to come, whether for correction, or [b]for his land, or [c]for mercy.

14 Hearken unto this, O Job: stand still, and [a]consider the wondrous works of God.

15 Dost thou know when God disposed them, and caused the light of his cloud to shine?

16 [a]Dost thou know the balancings of the clouds, the wondrous works of [b]him which is perfect in knowledge?

17 How thy garments *are* warm, when he quieteth the earth by the south *wind?*

18 Hast thou with him [a]spread out the [b]sky, *which is* strong, *and* as a molten looking glass?

19 Teach us what we shall say unto him; *for* we cannot order *our speech* by reason of darkness.

20 Shall it be told him that I speak? If a man speak, surely he shall be swallowed up.

21 And now *men* see not the bright light which *is* in the clouds: but the wind passeth, and cleanseth them.

22 Fair weather cometh out of the north: with God *is* terrible majesty.

23 *Touching* the Almighty, [a]we cannot find him out: [b]*he is* excellent in power, and in judgment, and in plenty of justice: he will not afflict.

31 [a][Acts 14:17] [b]Gen. 9:3; Ps. 104:14, 15
32 [a]Ps. 147:8
33 [a]1 Kin. 18:41; Job 37:2

CHAPTER 37

4 [a]Ps. 29:3
5 [a]Job 5:9; 9:10; 36:26; Rev. 15:3
6 [a]Ps. 147:16, 17
7 [a]Ps. 109:27 [b]Ps. 19:3, 4
8 [a]Job 38:40; Ps. 104:21, 22
10 [a]Job 38:29, 30; Ps. 147:17, 18
12 [a]Job 36:32; Ps. 148:8
13 [a]Ex. 9:18, 23; 1 Sam. 12:18, 19 [b]Job 38:26, 27 [c]1 Kin. 18:41–46
14 [a]Ps. 111:2
16 [a]Job 36:29 [b]Job 36:4
18 [a]Gen. 1:6; [Is. 44:24] [b]Job 9:8; Ps. 104:2; [Is. 45:12; Jer. 10:12; Zech. 12:1]
23 [a][Job 11:7, 8; Rom. 11:33, 34; 1 Tim. 6:16] [b][Job 9:4; 36:5]

*

37:12 Lit. *the world of the earth*

NKJV

31 For [a]by these He judges the peoples;
He [b]gives food in abundance.
32 [a]He covers *His* hands with lightning,
And commands it to strike.
33 [a]His thunder declares it,
The cattle also, concerning the rising *storm.*

37 "At this also my heart trembles,
And leaps from its place.
2 Hear attentively the thunder of His voice,
And the rumbling *that* comes from His mouth.
3 He sends it forth under the whole heaven,
His lightning to the ends of the earth.
4 After it [a]a voice roars;
He thunders with His majestic voice,
And He does not restrain them when His voice is heard.
5 God thunders marvelously with His voice;
[a]He does great things which we cannot comprehend.
6 For [a]He says to the snow, 'Fall *on* the earth';
Likewise to the gentle rain and the heavy rain of His strength.
7 He seals the hand of every man,
[a]That [b]all men may know His work.
8 The beasts [a]go into dens,
And remain in their lairs.
9 From the chamber *of the south* comes the whirlwind,
And cold from the scattering winds *of the north.*
10 [a]By the breath of God ice is given,
And the broad waters are frozen.
11 Also with moisture He saturates the thick clouds;
He scatters His bright clouds.
12 And they swirl about, being turned by His guidance,
That they may [a]do whatever He commands them
On the face of *the whole earth.
13 [a]He causes it to come,
Whether for correction,
Or [b]for His land,
Or [c]for mercy.

14 "Listen to this, O Job;
Stand still and [a]consider the wondrous works of God.
15 Do you know when God dispatches them,
And causes the light of His cloud to shine?
16 [a]Do you know how the clouds are balanced,
Those wondrous works of [b]Him who is perfect in knowledge?
17 Why *are* your garments hot,
When He quiets the earth by the south *wind?*
18 With Him, have you [a]spread out the [b]skies,
Strong as a cast metal mirror?

19 "Teach us what we should say to Him,
For we can prepare nothing because of the darkness.
20 Should He be told that I *wish to* speak?
If a man were to speak, surely he would be swallowed up.
21 Even now *men* cannot look at the light
when it is bright in the skies,
When the wind has passed and cleared them.
22 He comes from the north *as* golden *splendor;*
With God *is* awesome majesty.
23 *As for* the Almighty, [a]we cannot find Him;
[b]*He is* excellent in power,
In judgment and abundant justice;
He does not oppress.

KJV

24 Men do therefore [a]fear him: he respecteth
not any *that are* [b]wise of heart.

The LORD *Reveals His Omnipotence to Job*
(Gen. 1:1–10)

38 Then the LORD answered Job [a]out of the
whirlwind, and said,
2 [a]Who *is* this that darkeneth counsel by
[b]words without knowledge?
3 [a]Gird up now thy loins like a man; for I
will demand of thee, and answer thou me.
4 [a]Where wast thou when I laid the foundations of the earth? declare, if thou hast understanding.
5 Who hath laid the measures thereof, if
thou knowest? or who hath stretched the line
upon it?
6 Whereupon are the foundations thereof
fastened? or who laid the corner stone thereof;
7 When the morning stars sang together,
and all [a]the sons of God shouted for joy?
8 [a]Or *who* shut up the sea with doors, when
it brake forth, *as if* it had issued out of the womb?
9 When I made the cloud the garment
thereof, and thick darkness a swaddlingband for
it,
10 And [a]brake up for it my decreed *place,*
and set bars and doors,
11 And said, Hitherto shalt thou come, but
no further: and here shall thy proud waves [a]be
stayed?
12 Hast thou [a]commanded the morning since
thy days; *and* caused the dayspring to know his
place;
13 That it might take hold of the ends of the
earth, that [a]the wicked might be shaken out of
it?
14 It is turned as clay *to* the seal; and they
stand as a garment.
15 And from the wicked their [a]light is withholden, and [b]the high arm shall be broken.
16 Hast thou [a]entered into the springs of the
sea? or hast thou walked in the search of the
depth?
17 Have [a]the gates of death been opened
unto thee? or hast thou seen the doors of the
shadow of death?
18 Hast thou perceived the breadth of the
earth? declare if thou knowest it all.
19 Where *is* the way *where* light dwelleth?
and *as for* darkness, where *is* the place thereof,
20 That thou shouldest take it to the bound
thereof, and that thou shouldest know the paths
to the house thereof?
21 Knowest thou *it,* because thou wast then
born? or *because* the number of thy days *is* great?
22 Hast thou entered into [a]the treasures of
the snow? or hast thou seen the treasures of the
hail,
23 [a]Which I have reserved against the time
of trouble, against the day of battle and war?
24 By what way is the light parted, *which*
scattereth the east wind upon the earth?
25 Who [a]hath divided a watercourse for the
overflowing of waters, or a way for the lightning
of thunder;
26 To cause it to rain on the earth, *where* no
man *is; on* the wilderness, wherein *there is* no
man;

---

24 [a][Matt. 10:28] [b][Job 5:13; Matt. 11:25]; 1 Cor. 1:26

CHAPTER 38

1 [a]Ex. 19:16; Job 40:6
2 [a]Job 34:35; 42:3 [b]1 Tim. 1:7
3 [a]Job 40:7
4 [a]Job 15:7; Ps. 104:5
7 [a]Job 1:6
8 [a]Gen. 1:9; Ps. 33:7; 104:9; Prov. 8:29; [Jer. 5:22]
10 [a]Job 26:10
11 [a][Ps. 89:9; 93:4]
12 [a][Ps. 74:16; 148:5]
13 [a]Job 34:25; Ps. 104:35
15 [a]Job 18:5; [Prov. 13:9] [b][Num. 15:30]; Ps. 10:15; 37:17
16 [a][Ps. 77:19]; Prov. 8:24
17 [a]Ps. 9:13
22 [a]Ps. 135:7
23 [a]Ex. 9:18; Josh. 10:11; Is. 30:30; Ezek. 13:11, 13; Rev. 16:21
25 [a]Job 28:26

NKJV

24 Therefore men [a]fear Him;
He shows no partiality to any *who are*
[b]wise of heart."

The LORD *Reveals His Omnipotence to Job*
(Gen. 1:1–10)

38 Then the LORD answered Job [a]out of the
whirlwind, and said:

2 "Who[a] *is* this who darkens counsel
By [b]words without knowledge?
3 [a]Now prepare yourself like a man;
I will question you, and you shall answer
Me.

4 "Where[a] were you when I laid the
foundations of the earth?
Tell *Me,* if you have understanding.
5 Who determined its measurements?
Surely you know!
Or who stretched the line upon it?
6 To what were its foundations fastened?
Or who laid its cornerstone,
7 When the morning stars sang together,
And all [a]the sons of God shouted for joy?

8 "Or[a] *who* shut in the sea with doors,
When it burst forth *and* issued from the
womb;
9 When I made the clouds its garment,
And thick darkness its swaddling band;
10 When [a]I fixed My limit for it,
And set bars and doors;
11 When I said,
'This far you may come, but no farther,
And here your proud waves [a]must stop!'

12 "Have you [a]commanded the morning since
your days *began,*
And caused the dawn to know its place,
13 That it might take hold of the ends of the
earth,
And [a]the wicked be shaken out of it?
14 It takes on form like clay *under* a seal,
And stands out like a garment.
15 From the wicked their [a]light is withheld,
And [b]the upraised arm is broken.

16 "Have you [a]entered the springs of the sea?
Or have you walked in search of the
depths?
17 Have [a]the gates of death been revealed
to you?
Or have you seen the doors of the shadow
of death?
18 Have you comprehended the breadth of
the earth?
Tell *Me,* if you know all this.

19 "Where *is* the way *to* the dwelling of light?
And darkness, where *is* its place,
20 That you may take it to its territory,
That you may know the paths *to* its home?
21 Do you know *it,* because you were born
then,
Or *because* the number of your days *is*
great?

22 "Have you entered [a]the treasury of snow,
Or have you seen the treasury of hail,
23 [a]Which I have reserved for the time of
trouble,
For the day of battle and war?
24 By what way is light diffused,
Or the east wind scattered over the earth?

25 "Who [a]has divided a channel for the
overflowing *water,*
Or a path for the thunderbolt,
26 To cause it to rain on a land *where there*
is no one,
A wilderness in which *there is* no man;

KJV

27 [a]To satisfy the desolate and waste *ground;* and to cause the bud of the tender herb to spring forth?
28 [a]Hath the rain a father? or who hath begotten the drops of dew?
29 Out of whose womb came the ice? and the [a]hoary frost of heaven, who hath gendered it?
30 The waters are hid as *with* a stone, and the face of the deep is [a]frozen.
31 Canst thou bind the sweet influences of [a]Pleiades, or loose the bands of Orion?
32 Canst thou bring forth Mazzaroth in his season? or canst thou guide Arcturus with his sons?
33 Knowest thou [a]the ordinances of heaven? canst thou set the dominion thereof in the earth?
34 Canst thou lift up thy voice to the clouds, that abundance of waters may cover thee?
35 Canst thou send lightnings, that they may go, and say unto thee, Here we *are?*
36 [a]Who hath put wisdom in the inward parts? or who hath given understanding to the heart?
37 Who can number the clouds in wisdom? or who can stay the bottles of heaven,
38 When the dust groweth into hardness, and the clods cleave fast together?
39 [a]Wilt thou hunt the prey for the lion? or fill the appetite of the young lions,
40 When they couch in *their* dens, *and* abide in the covert to lie in wait?
41 [a]Who provideth for the raven his food? when his young ones cry unto God, they wander for lack of meat.

27 [a]Ps. 104:13, 14; 107:35
28 [a]Job 36:27, 28; [Ps. 147:8; Jer. 14:22]
29 [a][Job 37:10]; Ps. 147:16, 17
30 [a][Job 37:10]
31 [a]Job 9:9; Amos 5:8
33 [a][Ps. 148:6]; Jer. 31:35, 36
36 [a][Job 9:4; 32:8; Ps. 51:6; Eccl. 2:26; James 1:5]
39 [a]Ps. 104:21
41 [a]Ps. 147:9; [Matt. 6:26; Luke 12:24]

NKJV

27 [a]To satisfy the desolate waste,
And cause to spring forth the growth of tender grass?
28 [a]Has the rain a father?
Or who has begotten the drops of dew?
29 From whose womb comes the ice?
And the [a]frost of heaven, who gives it birth?
30 The waters harden like stone,
And the surface of the deep is [a]frozen.

31 "Can you bind the cluster of the [a]Pleiades,
Or loose the belt of Orion?
32 Can you bring out *Mazzaroth in its season?
Or can you guide the Great Bear with its cubs?
33 Do you know [a]the ordinances of the heavens?
Can you set their dominion over the earth?

34 "Can you lift up your voice to the clouds,
That an abundance of water may cover you?
35 Can you send out lightnings, that they may go,
And say to you, 'Here we *are!*'?
36 [a]Who has put wisdom in *the mind?
Or who has given understanding to the heart?
37 Who can number the clouds by wisdom?
Or who can pour out the bottles of heaven,
38 When the dust hardens in clumps,
And the clods cling together?

39 "Can[a] you hunt the prey for the lion,
Or satisfy the appetite of the young lions,
40 When they crouch in *their* dens,
Or lurk in their lairs to lie in wait?
41 [a]Who provides food for the raven,
When its young ones cry to God,
And wander about for lack of food?

39 Knowest thou the time when the wild [a]goats of the rock bring forth? *or* canst thou mark when [b]the hinds do calve?
2 Canst thou number the months *that* they fulfil? or knowest thou the time when they bring forth?
3 They bow themselves, they bring forth their young ones, they cast out their sorrows.
4 Their young ones are in good liking, they grow up with corn; they go forth, and return not unto them.
5 Who hath sent out the wild ass free? or who hath loosed the bands of the wild ass?
6 [a]Whose house I have made the wilderness, and the barren land his dwellings.
7 He scorneth the multitude of the city, neither regardeth he the crying of the driver.
8 The range of the mountains *is* his pasture, and he searcheth after [a]every green thing.
9 Will the [a]unicorn be willing to serve thee, or abide by thy crib?
10 Canst thou bind the unicorn with his band in the furrow? or will he harrow the valleys after thee?
11 Wilt thou trust him, because his strength *is* great? or wilt thou leave thy labour to him?
12 Wilt thou believe him, that he will bring home thy seed, and gather *it into* thy barn?
13 *Gavest thou* the goodly wings unto the peacocks? or wings and feathers unto the ostrich?

CHAPTER 39

1 [a]Deut. 14:5; 1 Sam. 24:2; Ps. 104:18 [b]Ps. 29:9
6 [a]Job 24:5; Jer. 2:24; Hos. 8:9
8 [a]Gen. 1:29
9 [a]Num. 23:22; Deut. 33:17; Ps. 22:21; 29:6; 92:10; Is. 34:7

39 "Do you know the time when the wild [a]mountain goats bear young?
Or can you mark when [b]the deer gives birth?
2 Can you number the months *that* they fulfill?
Or do you know the time when they bear young?
3 They bow down,
They bring forth their young,
They deliver their *offspring.
4 Their young ones are healthy,
They grow strong with grain;
They depart and do not return to them.

5 "Who set the wild donkey free?
Who loosed the bonds of the onager,
6 [a]Whose home I have made the wilderness,
And the barren land his dwelling?
7 He scorns the tumult of the city;
He does not heed the shouts of the driver.
8 The range of the mountains *is* his pasture,
And he searches after [a]every green thing.

9 "Will the [a]wild ox be willing to serve you?
Will he bed by your manger?
10 Can you bind the wild ox in the furrow with ropes?
Or will he plow the valleys behind you?
11 Will you trust him because his strength *is* great?
Or will you leave your labor to him?
12 Will you trust him to bring home your grain,
And gather it to your threshing floor?

13 "The wings of the ostrich wave proudly,
But are her wings and pinions *like the* kindly stork's?

*
38:32 Lit. *Constellations*
38:36 Lit. *the inward parts*
39:3 Lit. *pangs*

KJV

14 Which leaveth her eggs in the earth, and warmeth them in dust,

15 And forgetteth that the foot may crush them, or that the wild beast may break them.

16 She is [a]hardened against her young ones, as though *they were* not her's: her labour is in vain without fear;

17 Because God hath deprived her of wisdom, neither hath he [a]imparted to her understanding.

18 What time she lifteth up herself on high, she scorneth the horse and his rider.

19 Hast thou given the horse strength? hast thou clothed his neck with thunder?

20 Canst thou make him afraid as a grasshopper? the glory of his nostrils *is* terrible.

21 He paweth in the valley, and rejoiceth in *his* strength: [a]he goeth on to meet the armed men.

22 He mocketh at fear, and is not affrighted; neither turneth he back from the sword.

23 The quiver rattleth against him, the glittering spear and the shield.

24 He swalloweth the ground with fierceness and rage: neither believeth he that *it is* the sound of the trumpet.

25 He saith among the trumpets, Ha, ha; and he smelleth the battle afar off, the thunder of the captains, and the shouting.

26 Doth the hawk fly by thy wisdom, *and* stretch her wings toward the south?

27 Doth the [a]eagle mount up at thy command, and [b]make her nest on high?

28 She dwelleth and abideth on the rock, upon the crag of the rock, and the strong place.

29 From thence she seeketh the prey, *and* her eyes behold afar off.

30 Her young ones also suck up blood: and [a]where the slain *are*, there *is* she.

16 [a]Lam. 4:3
17 [a]Job 35:11
21 [a]Jer. 8:6
27 [a]Prov. 30:18, 19 [b]Jer. 49:16; Obad. 4
30 [a]Matt. 24:28; Luke 17:37

NKJV

14 For she leaves her eggs on the ground,
And warms them in the dust;
15 She forgets that a foot may crush them,
Or that a wild beast may break them.
16 She [a]treats her young harshly, as though *they were* not hers;
Her labor is in vain, without concern,
17 Because God deprived her of wisdom,
And did not [a]endow her with understanding.
18 When she lifts herself on high,
She scorns the horse and its rider.

19 "Have you given the horse strength?
Have you clothed his neck with *thunder?
20 Can you frighten him like a locust?
His majestic snorting strikes terror.
21 He paws in the valley, and rejoices in *his* strength;
[a]He gallops into the clash of arms.
22 He mocks at fear, and is not frightened;
Nor does he turn back from the sword.
23 The quiver rattles against him,
The glittering spear and javelin.
24 He devours the distance with fierceness and rage;
Nor does he come to a halt because the trumpet *has* sounded.
25 At *the blast of* the trumpet he says, 'Aha!'
He smells the battle from afar,
The thunder of captains and shouting.

26 "Does the hawk fly by your wisdom,
And spread its wings toward the south?
27 Does the [a]eagle mount up at your command,
And [b]make its nest on high?
28 On the rock it dwells and resides,
On the crag of the rock and the stronghold.
29 From there it spies out the prey;
Its eyes observe from afar.
30 Its young ones suck up blood;
And [a]where the slain *are*, there it *is*."

KJV

40 Moreover the LORD [a]answered Job, and said,

2 Shall he that [a]contendeth with the Almighty instruct *him?* he that [b]reproveth God, let him answer it.

Job's Response to God

3 Then Job answered the LORD, and said,

4 [a]Behold, I am vile; what shall I answer thee? [b]I will lay mine hand upon my mouth.

5 Once have I spoken; but I will not answer: yea, twice; but I will proceed no further.

God's Challenge to Job

6 [a]Then answered the LORD unto Job out of the whirlwind, and said,

7 [a]Gird up thy loins now like a man: [b]I will demand of thee, and declare thou unto me.

8 [a]Wilt thou also disannul my judgment? wilt thou condemn me, that thou mayest be righteous?

9 Hast thou an arm like God? or canst thou thunder with [a]a voice like him?

10 [a]Deck thyself now *with* majesty and excellency; and array thyself with glory and beauty.

11 Cast abroad the rage of thy wrath: and behold every one *that is* proud, and abase him.

CHAPTER 40

1 [a]Job 38:1
2 [a]Job 9:3; 10:2; 33:13 [b]Job 13:3; 23:4
4 [a]Ezra 9:6; Job 42:6 [b]Job 29:9; Ps. 39:9
6 [a]Job 38:1
7 [a]Job 38:3 [b]Job 42:4
8 [a]Job 16:11; 19:6; [Ps. 51:4; Rom. 3:4]
9 [a]Job 37:4; [Ps. 29:3, 4]
10 [a]Ps. 93:1; 104:1

NKJV

40 Moreover the LORD [a]answered Job, and said:

2 "Shall [a]the one who contends with the Almighty correct *Him?*
He who [b]rebukes God, let him answer it."

Job's Response to God

3 Then Job answered the LORD and said:

4 "Behold,[a] I am vile;
What shall I answer You?
[b]I lay my hand over my mouth.
5 Once I have spoken, but I will not answer;
Yes, twice, but I will proceed no further."

God's Challenge to Job

6 [a]Then the LORD answered Job out of the whirlwind, and said:

7 "Now[a] prepare yourself like a man;
[b]I will question you, and you shall answer Me:

8 "Would[a] you indeed annul My judgment?
Would you condemn Me that you may be justified?
9 Have you an arm like God?
Or can you thunder with [a]a voice like His?
10 [a]Then adorn yourself *with* majesty and splendor,
And array yourself with glory and beauty.
11 Disperse the rage of your wrath;
Look on everyone *who is* proud, and humble him.

*________

39:19 Or *a mane*

KJV

12 Look on every one *that is* [a]proud, *and* bring him low; and tread down the wicked in their place.
13 Hide them in the dust together; *and* bind their faces in secret.
14 Then will I also confess unto thee that thine own right hand can save thee.
15 Behold now behemoth, which I made with thee; he eateth grass as an ox.
16 Lo now, his strength *is* in his loins, and his force *is* in the navel of his belly.
17 He moveth his tail like a cedar: the sinews of his stones are wrapped together.
18 His bones *are as* strong pieces of brass; his bones *are* like bars of iron.
19 He *is* the chief of the [a]ways of God: he that made him can make his sword to approach *unto him.*
20 Surely the mountains [a]bring him forth food, where all the beasts of the field play.
21 He lieth under the shady trees, in the covert of the reed, and fens.
22 The shady trees cover him *with* their shadow; the willows of the brook compass him about.
23 Behold, he drinketh up a river, *and* hasteth not: he trusteth that he can draw up Jordan into his mouth.
24 He taketh it with his eyes: *his* nose pierceth through snares.

41 Canst thou draw out [a]leviathan with an hook? or his tongue with a cord *which* thou lettest down?
2 Canst thou [a]put an hook into his nose? or bore his jaw through with a thorn?
3 Will he make many supplications unto thee? will he speak soft *words* unto thee?
4 Will he make a covenant with thee? wilt thou take him for a servant for ever?
5 Wilt thou play with him as *with* a bird? or wilt thou bind him for thy maidens?
6 Shall the companions make a banquet of him? shall they part him among the merchants?
7 Canst thou fill his skin with barbed irons? or his head with fish spears?
8 Lay thine hand upon him, remember the battle, do no more.
9 Behold, the hope of him is in vain: shall not *one* be cast down even at the sight of him?
10 None *is so* fierce that dare stir him up: who then is able to stand before me?
11 [a]Who hath prevented me, that I should repay *him?* [b]*whatsoever is* under the whole heaven is mine.
12 I will not conceal his parts, nor his power, nor his comely proportion.
13 Who can discover the face of his garment? *or* who can come *to him* with his double bridle?
14 Who can open the doors of his face? his teeth *are* terrible round about.
15 *His* scales *are his* pride, shut up together *as with* a close seal.
16 One is so near to another, that no air can come between them.
17 They are joined one to another, they stick together, that they cannot be sundered.
18 By his neesings a light doth shine, and his eyes *are* like the eyelids of the morning.

12 [a]1 Sam. 2:7; [Is. 2:12; 13:11]; Dan. 4:37
19 [a]Job 26:14
20 [a]Ps. 104:14

CHAPTER 41
1 [a]Ps. 74:14; 104:26; Is. 27:1
2 [a]2 Kin. 19:38; Is. 37:29
11 [a][Rom. 11:35] [b]Ex. 19:5; [Deut. 10:14; Job 9:5–10; 26:6–14]; Ps. 24:1; 50:12; 1 Cor. 10:26, 28

NKJV

12 Look on everyone *who is* [a]proud, *and* bring him low;
Tread down the wicked in their place.
13 Hide them in the dust together,
Bind their faces in hidden *darkness.*
14 Then I will also confess to you
That your own right hand can save you.

15 "Look now at the *behemoth, which I made *along* with you;
He eats grass like an ox.
16 See now, his strength *is* in his hips,
And his power *is* in his stomach muscles.
17 He moves his tail like a cedar;
The sinews of his thighs are tightly knit.
18 His bones *are like* beams of bronze,
His ribs like bars of iron.
19 He *is* the first of the [a]ways of God;
Only He who made him can bring near His sword.
20 Surely the mountains [a]yield food for him,
And all the beasts of the field play there.
21 He lies under the lotus trees,
In a covert of reeds and marsh.
22 The lotus trees cover him *with* their shade;
The willows by the brook surround him.
23 Indeed the river may rage,
Yet he is not disturbed;
He is confident, though the Jordan gushes into his mouth,
24 *Though* he takes it in his eyes,
Or one pierces *his* nose with a snare.

41 "Can you draw out [a]Leviathan* with a hook,
Or *snare* his tongue with a line *which* you lower?
2 Can you [a]put a reed through his nose,
Or pierce his jaw with a hook?
3 Will he make many supplications to you?
Will he speak softly to you?
4 Will he make a covenant with you?
Will you take him as a servant forever?
5 Will you play with him as *with* a bird,
Or will you leash him for your maidens?
6 Will *your* companions *make a banquet of him?
Will they apportion him among the merchants?
7 Can you fill his skin with harpoons,
Or his head with fishing spears?
8 Lay your hand on him;
Remember the battle—
Never do it again!
9 Indeed, *any* hope of *overcoming* him is false;
Shall *one not* be overwhelmed at the sight of him?
10 No one *is so* fierce that he would dare stir him up.
Who then is able to stand against Me?
11 [a]Who has preceded Me, that I should pay *him?*
[b]Everything under heaven is Mine.

12 "I will not *conceal his limbs,
His mighty power, or his graceful proportions.
13 Who can remove his outer coat?
Who can approach *him* with a double bridle?
14 Who can open the doors of his face,
With his terrible teeth all around?
15 *His* rows of scales are *his* pride,
Shut up tightly *as with* a seal;
16 One is so near another
That no air can come between them;
17 They are joined one to another,
They stick together and cannot be parted.
18 His sneezings flash forth light,
And his eyes *are* like the eyelids of the morning.

*
40:15 A large animal, exact identity unknown
41:1 A large sea creature, exact identity unknown
41:6 Or *bargain over him*
41:12 Lit. *keep silent about*

KJV

19 Out of his mouth go burning lamps, *and* sparks of fire leap out.

20 Out of his nostrils goeth smoke, as *out* of a seething pot or caldron.

21 His breath kindleth coals, and a flame goeth out of his mouth.

22 In his neck remaineth strength, and sorrow is turned into joy before him.

23 The flakes of his flesh are joined together: they are firm in themselves; they cannot be moved.

24 His heart is as firm as a stone; yea, as hard as a piece of the nether *millstone.*

25 When he raiseth up himself, the mighty are afraid: by reason of breakings they purify themselves.

26 The sword of him that layeth at him cannot hold: the spear, the dart, nor the habergeon.

27 He esteemeth iron as straw, *and* brass as rotten wood.

28 The arrow cannot make him flee: slingstones are turned with him into stubble.

29 Darts are counted as stubble: he laugheth at the shaking of a spear.

30 Sharp stones *are* under him: he spreadeth sharp pointed things upon the mire.

31 He maketh the deep to boil like a pot: he maketh the sea like a pot of ointment.

32 He maketh a path to shine after him; *one* would think the deep *to be* hoary.

33 Upon earth there is not his like, who is made without fear.

34 He beholdeth all high *things:* he *is* a king over all the children of pride.

Job's Repentance and Restoration

42 Then Job answered the LORD, and said,

2 I know that thou [a]canst do every *thing,* and *that* no thought can be withholden from thee.

3 [a]Who *is* he that hideth counsel without knowledge? therefore have I uttered that I understood not; [b]things too wonderful for me, which I knew not.

4 Hear, I beseech thee, and I will speak: [a]I will demand of thee, and declare thou unto me.

5 I have [a]heard of thee by the hearing of the ear: but now mine eye seeth thee.

6 Wherefore I [a]abhor *myself,* and repent in dust and ashes.

7 And it was *so,* that after the LORD had spoken these words unto Job, the LORD said to Eliphaz the Temanite, My wrath is kindled against thee, and against thy two friends: for ye have not spoken of me *the thing that is* right, as my servant Job *hath.*

8 Therefore take unto you now [a]seven bullocks and seven rams, and [b]go to my servant Job, and offer up for yourselves a burnt offering; and my servant Job shall [c]pray for you: for him will I accept: lest I deal with you *after your* folly, in that ye have not spoken of me *the thing which is* right, like my servant Job.

9 So Eliphaz the Temanite and Bildad the Shuhite *and* Zophar the Naamathite went, and did according as the LORD commanded them: the LORD also accepted Job.

10 [a]And the LORD turned the captivity of Job, when he prayed for his friends: also the LORD gave Job [b]twice as much as he had before.

11 Then came there unto him [a]all his brethren, and all his sisters, and all they that had been of his acquaintance before, and did eat bread with him in his house: and they bemoaned him, and

NKJV

19 Out of his mouth go burning lights;
Sparks of fire shoot out.
20 Smoke goes out of his nostrils,
As *from* a boiling pot and burning rushes.
21 His breath kindles coals,
And a flame goes out of his mouth.
22 Strength dwells in his neck,
And sorrow dances before him.
23 The folds of his flesh are joined together;
They are firm on him and cannot be moved.
24 His heart is as hard as stone,
Even as hard as the lower *millstone.*
25 When he raises himself up, the mighty are afraid;
Because of his crashings they *are beside themselves.
26 *Though* the sword reaches him, it cannot avail;
Nor does spear, dart, or javelin.
27 He regards iron as straw,
And bronze as rotten wood.
28 The arrow cannot make him flee;
Slingstones become like stubble to him.
29 Darts are regarded as straw;
He laughs at the threat of javelins.
30 His undersides *are* like sharp potsherds;
He spreads pointed *marks* in the mire.
31 He makes the deep boil like a pot;
He makes the sea like a pot of ointment.
32 He leaves a shining wake behind him;
One would think the deep had white hair.
33 On earth there is nothing like him,
Which is made without fear.
34 He beholds every high *thing;*
He *is* king over all the children of pride."

Job's Repentance and Restoration

42 Then Job answered the LORD and said:

2 "I know that You [a]can do everything,
And that no purpose *of Yours* can be withheld from You.
3 *You asked,* [a]'Who *is* this who hides counsel without knowledge?'
Therefore I have uttered what I did not understand,
[b]Things too wonderful for me, which I did not know.
4 Listen, please, and let me speak;
You said, [a]'I will question you, and you shall answer Me.'

5 "I have [a]heard of You by the hearing of the ear,
But now my eye sees You.
6 Therefore I [a]abhor *myself,*
And repent in dust and ashes."

7 And so it was, after the LORD had spoken these words to Job, that the LORD said to Eliphaz the Temanite, "My wrath is aroused against you and your two friends, for you have not spoken of Me *what is* right, as My servant Job *has.*

8 "Now therefore, take for yourselves [a]seven bulls and seven rams, [b]go to My servant Job, and offer up for yourselves a burnt offering; and My servant Job shall [c]pray for you. For I will accept him, lest I deal with you *according to your* folly; because you have not spoken of Me *what is* right, as My servant Job *has.*"

9 So Eliphaz the Temanite and Bildad the Shuhite *and* Zophar the Naamathite went and did as the LORD commanded them; for the LORD had accepted Job.

10 [a]And the LORD *restored Job's losses when he prayed for his friends. Indeed the LORD gave Job [b]twice as much as he had before.

11 Then [a]all his brothers, all his sisters, and all those who had been his acquaintances before, came to him and ate food with him in his house; and they consoled him and comforted him for all

CHAPTER 42

2 [a]Gen. 18:14; [Matt. 19:26; Mark 10:27; 14:36; Luke 18:27]
3 [a]Job 38:2 [b]Ps. 40:5; 131:1; 139:6
4 [a]Job 38:3; 40:7
5 [a]Job 26:14; [Rom. 10:17]
6 [a]Ezra 9:6; Job 40:4
8 [a]Num. 23:1 [b][Matt. 5:24] [c]Gen. 20:17; [James 5:15, 16; 1 John 5:16]
10 [a]Deut. 30:3; Ps. 14:7; 85:1–3; 126:1 [b]Is. 40:2
11 [a]Job 19:13

*

41:25 Or *purify themselves*
42:10 Lit. *turned the captivity of Job,* what was captured from Job

KJV

comforted him over all the evil that the LORD had
brought upon him: every man also gave him a
piece of money, and every one an earring of gold.
12 So the LORD blessed [a]the latter end of Job
more than his beginning: for he had [b]fourteen
thousand sheep, and six thousand camels, and a
thousand yoke of oxen, and a thousand she asses.
13 [a]He had also seven sons and three
daughters.
14 And he called the name of the first, Jemima; and the name of the second, Kezia; and the
name of the third, Keren–happuch.
15 And in all the land were no women found
so fair as the daughters of Job: and their father
gave them inheritance among their brethren.
16 After this [a]lived Job an hundred and forty
years, and saw his sons, and his sons' sons, *even*
four generations.
17 So Job died, *being* old and [a]full of days.

12 [a]Job 1:10; 8:7; James 5:11 [b]Job 1:3
13 [a]Job 1:2
16 [a]Job 5:26; Prov. 3:16
17 [a]Gen. 15:15; 25:8; Job 5:26

NKJV

the adversity that the LORD had brought upon him.
Each one gave him a piece of silver and each a
ring of gold.
12 Now the LORD blessed [a]the latter *days* of
Job more than his beginning; for he had [b]fourteen
thousand sheep, six thousand camels, one thousand yoke of oxen, and one thousand female
donkeys.
13 [a]He also had seven sons and three daughters.
14 And he called the name of the first Jemimah, the name of the second Keziah, and the
name of the third Keren-Happuch.
15 In all the land were found no women *so*
beautiful as the daughters of Job; and their father
gave them an inheritance among their brothers.
16 After this Job [a]lived one hundred and
forty years, and saw his children and grandchildren *for* four generations.
17 So Job died, old and [a]full of days.

KJV

THE BOOK OF

PSALMS

BOOK I

PSALM 1

The Way of the Righteous and the End of the Ungodly

BLESSED [a]*is* the man that walketh not in the
counsel of the ungodly, nor standeth in the
way of sinners, [b]nor sitteth in the seat of the
scornful.
2 But [a]his delight *is* in the law of the LORD;
[b]and in his law doth he meditate day and night.
3 And he shall be like a tree [a]planted by
the rivers of water, that bringeth forth his fruit
in his season; his leaf also shall not wither; and
whatsoever he doeth shall [b]prosper.
4 The ungodly *are* not so: but *are* [a]like the
chaff which the wind driveth away.
5 Therefore the ungodly shall not stand in
the judgment, nor sinners in the congregation of
the righteous.
6 For [a]the LORD knoweth the way of the
righteous: but the way of the ungodly shall perish.

PSALM 2

The Messiah's Triumph and Kingdom (Acts 4:23–31)

WHY [a]do the heathen rage, and the people
imagine a vain thing?
2 The kings of the earth set themselves, and
the [a]rulers take counsel together, against the
LORD, and against his [b]anointed, *saying,*
3 [a]Let us break their bands asunder, and
cast away their cords from us.
4 He that sitteth in the heavens [a]shall laugh:
the Lord shall have them in derision.
5 Then shall he speak unto them in his
wrath, and vex them in his sore displeasure.
6 Yet have I set my king upon my holy hill
of Zion.
7 I will declare the decree: the LORD hath
said unto me, [a]Thou *art* my Son; this day have I
begotten thee.
8 Ask of me, and I shall give *thee* the
heathen *for* thine inheritance, and the uttermost
parts of the earth *for* thy possession.
9 [a]Thou shalt break them with a rod of iron;
thou shalt dash them in pieces like a potter's
vessel.

PSALM 1

1 [a]Prov. 4:14 [b]Ps. 26:4, 5; Jer. 15:17
2 [a]Ps. 119:14, 16, 35 [b][Josh. 1:8]
3 [a][Ps. 92:12–14]; Jer. 17:8; Ezek. 19:10 [b]Gen. 39:2, 3, 23; Ps. 128:2
4 [a]Job 21:18; Ps. 35:5; Is. 17:13
6 [a]Ps. 37:18; [Nah. 1:7; John 10:14; 2 Tim. 2:19]

PSALM 2

1 [a]Acts 4:25, 26
2 [a][Matt. 12:14; 26:3, 4, 59–66; 27:1, 2; Mark 3:6; 11:18] [b][John 1:41]
3 [a]Luke 19:14
4 [a]Ps. 37:13
7 [a]Matt. 3:17; Mark 1:1, 11; Luke 3:22; John 1:18; Acts 13:33; [Heb. 1:5; 5:5]
9 [a]Ps. 89:23; 110:5, 6; [Rev. 2:26, 27; 12:5; 19:15]

*——————

2:9 So with MT, Tg.; LXX, Syr., Vg. *rule* (cf. Rev. 2:27)

NKJV

THE BOOK OF

PSALMS

BOOK ONE

Psalms 1–41

PSALM 1

The Way of the Righteous and the End of the Ungodly

BLESSED [a]*is* the man
Who walks not in the counsel of the ungodly,
Nor stands in the path of sinners,
[b]Nor sits in the seat of the scornful;
2 But [a]his delight *is* in the law of the LORD,
[b]And in His law he meditates day and night.
3 He shall be like a tree
[a]Planted by the rivers of water,
That brings forth its fruit in its season,
Whose leaf also shall not wither;
And whatever he does shall [b]prosper.

4 The ungodly *are* not so,
But *are* [a]like the chaff which the wind drives away.
5 Therefore the ungodly shall not stand in the judgment,
Nor sinners in the congregation of the righteous.

6 For [a]the LORD knows the way of the righteous,
But the way of the ungodly shall perish.

PSALM 2

The Messiah's Triumph and Kingdom (Acts 4:23–31)

WHY [a]do the nations rage,
And the people plot a vain thing?
2 The kings of the earth set themselves,
And the [a]rulers take counsel together,
Against the LORD and against His
[b]Anointed, *saying,*
3 "Let [a]us break Their bonds in pieces
And cast away Their cords from us."

4 He who sits in the heavens [a]shall laugh;
The LORD shall hold them in derision.
5 Then He shall speak to them in His wrath,
And distress them in His deep displeasure:
6 "Yet I have set My King
On My holy hill of Zion."

7 "I will declare the decree:
The LORD has said to Me,
[a]'You *are* My Son,
Today I have begotten You.
8 Ask of Me, and I will give *You*
The nations *for* Your inheritance,
And the ends of the earth *for* Your possession.
9 [a]You shall *break them with a rod of iron;
You shall dash them to pieces like a potter's vessel.' "

KJV

10 Be wise now therefore, O ye kings: be instructed, ye judges of the earth.

11 Serve the LORD with fear, and rejoice with trembling.

12 Kiss the Son, lest he be angry, and ye perish *from* the way, when [a]his wrath is kindled but a little. [b]Blessed *are* all they that put their trust in him.

PSALM 3

The LORD Helps His Troubled People

A Psalm of David, [a]when he fled from Absalom his son.

LORD, how are they increased that trouble me! many *are* they that rise up against me.

2 Many *there be* which say of my soul, *There is* no help for him in God. Selah.

3 But thou, O LORD, *art* [a]a shield for me; my glory, and [b]the lifter up of mine head.

4 I cried unto the LORD with my voice, and [a]he heard me out of his [b]holy hill. Selah.

5 [a]I laid me down and slept; I awaked; for the LORD sustained me.

6 [a]I will not be afraid of ten thousands of people, that have set *themselves* against me round about.

7 Arise, O LORD; save me, O my God: [a]for thou hast smitten all mine enemies *upon* the cheek bone; thou hast broken the teeth of the ungodly.

8 [a]Salvation *belongeth* unto the LORD: thy blessing *is* upon thy people. Selah.

PSALM 4

The Safety of the Faithful

To the chief Musician on Neginoth, A Psalm of David.

HEAR me when I call, O God of my righteousness: thou hast enlarged me *when I was* in distress; have mercy upon me, and hear my prayer.

2 O ye sons of men, how long *will ye turn* my glory into shame? *how long* will ye love vanity, *and* seek after leasing? Selah.

3 But know that [a]the LORD hath set apart him that is godly for himself: the LORD will hear when I call unto him.

4 [a]Stand in awe, and sin not: [b]commune with your own heart upon your bed, and be still. Selah.

5 Offer [a]the sacrifices of righteousness, and [b]put your trust in the LORD.

6 *There be* many that say, Who will shew us *any* good? [a]LORD, lift thou up the light of thy countenance upon us.

7 Thou hast put [a]gladness in my heart, more than in the time *that* their corn and their wine increased.

8 [a]I will both lay me down in peace, and sleep: [b]for thou, LORD, only makest me dwell in safety.

12 [a][Rev. 6:16, 17] [b][Ps. 5:11; 34:22]

PSALM 3

title [a]2 Sam. 15:13–17
3 [a]Ps. 5:12; 28:7 [b]Ps. 9:13; 27:6
4 [a]Ps. 4:3; 34:4 [b]Ps. 2:6; 15:1; 43:3
5 [a]Lev. 26:6; Ps. 4:8; Prov. 3:24
6 [a]Ps. 23:4; 27:3
7 [a]Job 16:10
8 [a]Ps. 28:8; 35:3; [Is. 43:11]

PSALM 4

3 [a][2 Tim. 2:19]
4 [a][Ps. 119:11; Eph. 4:26] [b]Ps. 77:6
5 [a]Deut. 33:19; Ps. 51:19 [b]Ps. 37:3, 5; 62:8
6 [a]Num. 6:26; Ps. 80:3, 7, 19
7 [a]Ps. 97:11, 12; Is. 9:3; Acts 14:17
8 [a]Job 11:19; Ps. 3:5 [b][Lev. 25:18]; Deut. 12:10

*

2:12 LXX, Vg. *Embrace discipline;* Tg. *Receive instruction* • LXX *the* LORD
4:3 Many Heb. mss., LXX, Tg., Vg. *made wonderful*

NKJV

10 Now therefore, be wise, O kings;
Be instructed, you judges of the earth.
11 Serve the LORD with fear,
And rejoice with trembling.
12 *Kiss the Son, lest *He be angry,
And you perish *in* the way,
When [a]His wrath is kindled but a little.
[b]Blessed *are* all those who put their trust in Him.

PSALM 3

The LORD Helps His Troubled People

A Psalm of David [a]when he fled from Absalom his son.

LORD, how they have increased who trouble me!
Many *are* they who rise up against me.
2 Many *are* they who say of me,
"There is no help for him in God." Selah

3 But You, O LORD, *are* [a]a shield for me,
My glory and [b]the One who lifts up my head.
4 I cried to the LORD with my voice,
And [a]He heard me from His [b]holy hill. Selah

5 [a]I lay down and slept;
I awoke, for the LORD sustained me.
6 [a]I will not be afraid of ten thousands of people
Who have set *themselves* against me all around.

7 Arise, O LORD;
Save me, O my God!
[a]For You have struck all my enemies on the cheekbone;
You have broken the teeth of the ungodly.
8 [a]Salvation *belongs* to the LORD.
Your blessing *is* upon Your people. Selah

PSALM 4

The Safety of the Faithful

To the Chief Musician. With stringed instruments. A Psalm of David.

HEAR me when I call, O God of my righteousness!
You have relieved me in *my* distress;
Have mercy on me, and hear my prayer.

2 How long, O you sons of men,
Will you turn my glory to shame?
How long will you love worthlessness
And seek falsehood? Selah
3 But know that [a]the LORD has *set apart for Himself him who is godly;
The LORD will hear when I call to Him.

4 [a]Be angry, and do not sin.
[b]Meditate within your heart on your bed, and be still. Selah
5 Offer [a]the sacrifices of righteousness,
And [b]put your trust in the LORD.

6 *There are* many who say,
"Who will show us *any* good?"
[a]LORD, lift up the light of Your countenance upon us.
7 You have put [a]gladness in my heart,
More than in the season that their grain and wine increased.
8 [a]I will both lie down in peace, and sleep;
[b]For You alone, O LORD, make me dwell in safety.

KJV

PSALM 5

A Prayer for Guidance

To the Chief Musician upon Nehiloth, A Psalm of David.

GIVE [a]ear to my words, O LORD, consider my
meditation.
2 Hearken unto the voice of my cry, my
King, and my God: for unto thee will I pray.
3 My voice shalt thou hear in the morning,
O LORD; [a]in the morning will I direct *my prayer*
unto thee, and will look up.
4 For thou *art* not a God that hath pleasure
in wickedness: neither shall evil dwell with thee.
5 The [a]foolish shall not [b]stand in thy sight:
thou hatest all workers of iniquity.
6 Thou shalt destroy them that speak leasing: the LORD will abhor the [a]bloody and deceitful
man.
7 But as for me, I will come *into* thy house
in the multitude of thy mercy: *and* in thy fear will
I worship toward thy holy temple.
8 [a]Lead me, O LORD, in thy righteousness
because of mine enemies; make thy way straight
before my face.
9 For *there is* no faithfulness in their mouth;
their inward part *is* very wickedness; [a]their throat
is an open sepulchre; they flatter with their
tongue.
10 Destroy thou them, O God; let them fall
by their own counsels; cast them out in the multitude of their transgressions; for they have rebelled
against thee.
11 But let all those that put their trust in thee
rejoice: let them ever shout for joy, because thou
defendest them: let them also that love thy name
be joyful in thee.
12 For thou, LORD, wilt bless the righteous;
with favour wilt thou compass him as *with* a
shield.

PSALM 6

A Prayer of Faith in Time of Distress

To the chief Musician on Neginoth [a]upon Sheminith, A Psalm of David.

O LORD, [a]rebuke me not in thine anger, neither
chasten me in thy hot displeasure.
2 Have mercy upon me, O LORD; for I *am*
weak: O LORD, [a]heal me; for my bones are vexed.
3 My soul is also sore [a]vexed: but thou, O
LORD, how long?
4 Return, O LORD, deliver my soul: oh save
me for thy mercies' sake.
5 [a]For in death *there is* no remembrance of
thee: in the grave who shall give thee thanks?
6 I am weary with my groaning; all the night
make I my bed to swim; I water my couch with
my tears.
7 [a]Mine eye is consumed because of grief;
it waxeth old because of all mine enemies.

PSALM 5

1 [a]Ps. 4:1
3 [a]Ps. 55:17; 88:13
5 [a][Hab. 1:13] [b]Ps. 1:5
6 [a]Ps. 55:23
8 [a]Ps. 25:4, 5; 27:11; 31:3
9 [a]Rom. 3:13

PSALM 6

title [a]Ps. 12:title
1 [a]Ps. 38:1; 118:18; [Jer. 10:24]
2 [a]Ps. 41:4; 147:3; [Hos. 6:1]
3 [a]Ps. 88:3; John 12:27
5 [a]Ps. 30:9; 88:10–12; 115:17; [Eccl. 9:10]; Is. 38:18
7 [a]Job 17:7; Ps. 31:9

*———

5:title Heb. *nehiloth*
6:title Heb. *sheminith*

NKJV

PSALM 5

A Prayer for Guidance

To the Chief Musician. With *flutes. A Psalm of David.

GIVE [a]ear to my words, O LORD,
Consider my meditation.
2 Give heed to the voice of my cry,
My King and my God,
For to You I will pray.
3 My voice You shall hear in the morning, O LORD;
[a]In the morning I will direct *it* to You,
And I will look up.

4 For You *are* not a God who takes pleasure in wickedness,
Nor shall evil dwell with You.
5 The [a]boastful shall not [b]stand in Your sight;
You hate all workers of iniquity.
6 You shall destroy those who speak falsehood;
The LORD abhors the [a]bloodthirsty and deceitful man.

7 But as for me, I will come into Your house in the multitude of Your mercy;
In fear of You I will worship toward Your holy temple.
8 [a]Lead me, O LORD, in Your righteousness because of my enemies;
Make Your way straight before my face.

9 For *there is* no faithfulness in their mouth;
Their inward part *is* destruction;
[a]Their throat *is* an open tomb;
They flatter with their tongue.
10 Pronounce them guilty, O God!
Let them fall by their own counsels;
Cast them out in the multitude of their transgressions,
For they have rebelled against You.

11 But let all those rejoice who put their trust in You;
Let them ever shout for joy, because You defend them;
Let those also who love Your name
Be joyful in You.
12 For You, O LORD, will bless the righteous;
With favor You will surround him as *with* a shield.

PSALM 6

A Prayer of Faith in Time of Distress

To the Chief Musician. With stringed instruments. [a]On *an eight-stringed harp. A Psalm of David.

O LORD, [a]do not rebuke me in Your anger,
Nor chasten me in Your hot displeasure.
2 Have mercy on me, O LORD, for I *am* weak;
O LORD, [a]heal me, for my bones are troubled.
3 My soul also is greatly [a]troubled;
But You, O LORD—how long?

4 Return, O LORD, deliver me!
Oh, save me for Your mercies' sake!
5 [a]For in death *there is* no remembrance of You;
In the grave who will give You thanks?

6 I am weary with my groaning;
All night I make my bed swim;
I drench my couch with my tears.
7 [a]My eye wastes away because of grief;
It grows old because of all my enemies.

KJV

8 [a]Depart from me, all ye workers of iniquity; for the LORD hath [b]heard the voice of my
weeping.
9 The LORD hath heard my supplication; the
LORD will receive my prayer.
10 Let all mine enemies be ashamed and sore
vexed: let them return *and* be ashamed suddenly.

PSALM 7

Prayer and Praise for Deliverance from Enemies

[a]Shiggaion of David, which he sang unto the LORD, [b]concerning the words of Cush the Benjamite.

O LORD my God, in thee do I put my trust:
[a]save me from all them that persecute me,
and deliver me:
2 [a]Lest he tear my soul like a lion, [b]rending
it in pieces, while *there is* none to deliver.
3 O LORD my God, [a]if I have done this; if
there be [b]iniquity in my hands;
4 If I have rewarded evil unto him that was
at peace with me; (yea, [a]I have delivered him that
without cause is mine enemy:)
5 Let the enemy persecute my soul, and take
it; yea, let him tread down my life upon the earth,
and lay mine honour in the dust. Selah.
6 Arise, O LORD, in thine anger, [a]lift up thyself because of the rage of mine enemies: and
[b]awake for me *to* the judgment *that* thou hast
commanded.
7 So shall the congregation of the people
compass thee about: for their sakes therefore return thou on high.
8 The LORD shall judge the people: [a]judge
me, O LORD, [b]according to my righteousness, and
according to mine integrity *that is* in me.
9 Oh let the wickedness of the wicked come
to an end; but establish the just: [a]for the righteous
God trieth the hearts and reins.
10 My defence *is* of God, which saveth the
[a]upright in heart.
11 God judgeth the righteous, and God is angry *with the wicked* every day.
12 If he turn not, he will [a]whet his sword;
he hath bent his bow, and made it ready.
13 He hath also prepared for him the instruments of death; he ordaineth his arrows against
the persecutors.
14 [a]Behold, he travaileth with iniquity, and
hath conceived mischief, and brought forth
falsehood.
15 He made a pit, and digged it, [a]and is fallen
into the ditch *which* he made.
16 [a]His mischief shall return upon his own
head, and his violent dealing shall come down
upon his own pate.
17 I will praise the LORD according to his
righteousness: and will sing praise to the name
of the LORD most high.

---

8 [a][Matt. 25:41] [b]Ps. 3:4; 28:6

PSALM 7

title [a]Hab. 3:1 [b]2 Sam. 16
1 [a]Ps. 31:15
2 [a]Ps. 57:4; Is. 38:13 [b]Ps. 50:22
3 [a]2 Sam. 16:7 [b]1 Sam. 24:11
4 [a]1 Sam. 24:7; 26:9
6 [a]Ps. 94:2 [b]Ps. 35:23; 44:23
8 [a]Ps. 26:1; 35:24; 43:1 [b]Ps. 18:20; 35:24
9 [a][1 Sam. 16:7]
10 [a]Ps. 97:10, 11; 125:4
12 [a]Deut. 32:41
14 [a]Job 15:35; Is. 59:4; [James 1:15]
15 [a][Job 4:8]; Ps. 57:6
16 [a]Esth. 9:25; Ps. 140:9

NKJV

8 [a]Depart from me, all you workers of iniquity;
For the LORD has [b]heard the voice of my weeping.
9 The LORD has heard my supplication;
The LORD will receive my prayer.
10 Let all my enemies be ashamed and greatly troubled;
Let them turn back *and* be ashamed suddenly.

PSALM 7

Prayer and Praise for Deliverance from Enemies

A [a]Meditation* of David, which he sang to the LORD [b]concerning the words of Cush, a Benjamite.

O LORD my God, in You I put my trust;
[a]Save me from all those who persecute me;
And deliver me,
2 [a]Lest they tear me like a lion,
[b]Rending *me* in pieces, while *there is* none to deliver.

3 O LORD my God, [a]if I have done this:
If there is [b]iniquity in my hands,
4 If I have repaid evil to him who was at peace with me,
Or [a]have plundered my enemy without cause,
5 Let the enemy pursue me and overtake *me;*
Yes, let him trample my life to the earth,
And lay my honor in the dust. Selah

6 Arise, O LORD, in Your anger;
[a]Lift Yourself up because of the rage of my enemies;
[b]Rise up *for me *to* the judgment You have commanded!
7 So the congregation of the peoples shall surround You;
For their sakes, therefore, return on high.
8 The LORD shall judge the peoples;
[a]Judge me, O LORD, [b]according to my righteousness,
And according to my integrity within me.

9 Oh, let the wickedness of the wicked come to an end,
But establish the just;
[a]For the righteous God tests the hearts and minds.
10 My defense *is* of God,
Who saves the [a]upright in heart.

11 God *is* a just judge,
And God is angry *with the wicked* every day.
12 If he does not turn back,
He will [a]sharpen His sword;
He bends His bow and makes it ready.
13 He also prepares for Himself instruments of death;
He makes His arrows into fiery shafts.

14 [a]Behold, *the wicked* brings forth iniquity;
Yes, he conceives trouble and brings forth falsehood.
15 He made a pit and dug it out,
[a]And has fallen into the ditch *which* he made.
16 [a]His trouble shall return upon his own head,
And his violent dealing shall come down on his own crown.

17 I will praise the LORD according to His righteousness,
And will sing praise to the name of the LORD Most High.

7:title Heb. *Shiggaion*
7:6 So with MT, Tg., Vg.; LXX O *LORD my God*

KJV

PSALM 8

The Glory of the LORD in Creation

To the chief Musician upon Gittith, A Psalm of David.

O LORD our Lord, how [a]excellent *is* thy name
in all the earth! who [b]hast set thy glory above
the heavens.
2 [a]Out of the mouth of babes and sucklings
hast thou ordained strength because of thine enemies, that thou mightest still [b]the enemy and the
avenger.
3 When I [a]consider thy heavens, the work
of thy fingers, the moon and the stars, which thou
hast ordained;
4 [a]What is man, that thou art mindful of
him? and the son of man, that thou [b]visitest him?
5 For thou hast made him a little lower than
the angels, and hast crowned him with glory and
honour.
6 [a]Thou madest him to have dominion over
the works of thy hands; [b]thou hast put all *things*
under his feet:
7 All sheep and oxen, yea, and the beasts
of the field;
8 The fowl of the air, and the fish of the
sea, *and whatsoever* passeth through the paths
of the seas.
9 [a]O LORD our Lord, how excellent *is* thy
name in all the earth!

PSALM 9

Prayer and Thanksgiving for the LORD's Righteous Judgments

To the chief Musician upon Muth-labben, A Psalm of David.

I WILL praise *thee,* O LORD, with my whole
heart; I will shew forth all thy marvellous
works.
2 I will be glad and [a]rejoice in thee: I will
sing praise to thy name, O [b]thou most High.
3 When mine enemies are turned back, they
shall fall and perish at thy presence.
4 For thou hast maintained my right and my
cause; thou satest in the throne judging right.
5 Thou hast rebuked the heathen, thou hast
destroyed the wicked, thou hast [a]put out their
name for ever and ever.
6 O thou enemy, destructions are come to
a perpetual end: and thou hast destroyed cities;
their memorial is [a]perished with them.
7 [a]But the LORD shall endure for ever: he
hath prepared his throne for judgment.
8 And [a]he shall judge the world in righteousness, he shall minister judgment to the people in uprightness.
9 The LORD also will be a [a]refuge for the
oppressed, a refuge in times of trouble.

PSALM 8

1 [a]Ps. 148:13 [b]Ps. 113:4
2 [a]Matt. 21:16; [1 Cor. 1:27] [b]Ps. 44:16
3 [a]Ps. 111:2
4 [a]Job 7:17, 18; [Heb. 2:6–8] [b][Job 10:12]
6 [a][Gen. 1:26, 28] [b][1 Cor. 15:27; Eph. 1:22; Heb. 2:8]
9 [a]Ps. 8:1

PSALM 9

2 [a]Ps. 5:11; 104:34 [b][Ps. 83:18; 92:1]
5 [a]Prov. 10:7
6 [a][Ps. 34:16]
7 [a]Ps. 102:12, 26; Heb. 1:11
8 [a][Ps. 96:13; 98:9; Acts 17:31]
9 [a]Ps. 32:7; 46:1; 91:2

*

8:title Heb. *Al Gittith*
8:5 Heb. *Elohim, God;* LXX, Syr., Tg., Jewish tradition *angels*
9:title Heb. *Muth Labben*

NKJV

PSALM 8

The Glory of the LORD in Creation

To the Chief Musician. *On the instrument of Gath. A Psalm of David.

O LORD, our Lord,
How [a]excellent *is* Your name in all the earth,
Who have [b]set Your glory above the heavens!

2 [a]Out of the mouth of babes and nursing infants
You have ordained strength,
Because of Your enemies,
That You may silence [b]the enemy and the avenger.

3 When I [a]consider Your heavens, the work of Your fingers,
The moon and the stars, which You have ordained,
4 [a]What is man that You are mindful of him,
And the son of man that You [b]visit him?
5 For You have made him a little lower than *the angels,
And You have crowned him with glory and honor.

6 [a]You have made him to have dominion over the works of Your hands;
[b]You have put all *things* under his feet,
7 All sheep and oxen—
Even the beasts of the field,
8 The birds of the air,
And the fish of the sea
That pass through the paths of the seas.

9 [a]O LORD, our Lord,
How excellent *is* Your name in all the earth!

PSALM 9

Prayer and Thanksgiving for the LORD's Righteous Judgments

To the Chief Musician. To *the tune of* *"Death of the Son." A Psalm of David.

I WILL praise *You,* O LORD, with my whole heart;
I will tell of all Your marvelous works.
2 I will be glad and [a]rejoice in You;
I will sing praise to Your name, [b]O Most High.

3 When my enemies turn back,
They shall fall and perish at Your presence.
4 For You have maintained my right and my cause;
You sat on the throne judging in righteousness.
5 You have rebuked the nations,
You have destroyed the wicked;
You have [a]blotted out their name forever and ever.

6 O enemy, destructions are finished forever!
And you have destroyed cities;
Even their memory has [a]perished.
7 [a]But the LORD shall endure forever;
He has prepared His throne for judgment.
8 [a]He shall judge the world in righteousness,
And He shall administer judgment for the peoples in uprightness.

9 The LORD also will be a [a]refuge for the oppressed,
A refuge in times of trouble.

KJV

10 And they that [a]know thy name will put
their trust in thee: for thou, LORD, hast not forsaken them that seek thee.
11 Sing praises to the LORD, which dwelleth
in Zion: [a]declare among the people his doings.
12 [a]When he maketh inquisition for blood,
he remembereth them: he forgetteth not the cry
of the humble.
13 Have mercy upon me, O LORD; consider
my trouble *which I suffer* of them that hate me,
thou that liftest me up from the gates of death:
14 That I may shew forth all thy praise in
the gates of the daughter of Zion: I will [a]rejoice
in thy salvation.
15 [a]The heathen are sunk down in the pit
that they made: in the net which they hid is their
own foot taken.
16 The LORD is [a]known *by* the judgment
which he executeth: the wicked is snared in the
work of his own hands. [b]Higgaion. Selah.
17 The wicked shall be turned into hell, *and*
all the nations [a]that forget God.
18 [a]For the needy shall not alway be forgotten: [b]the expectation of the poor shall *not* perish
for ever.
19 Arise, O LORD; let not man prevail: let the
heathen be judged in thy sight.
20 Put them in fear, O LORD: *that* the nations
may know themselves *to be but* men. Selah.

PSALM 10

A Song of Confidence in God's Triumph over Evil

WHY standest thou afar off, O LORD? *why* hidest thou *thyself* in times of trouble?
2 The wicked in *his* pride doth persecute the
poor: [a]let them be taken in the devices that they
have imagined.
3 For the wicked [a]boasteth of his heart's desire, and [b]blesseth the covetous, *whom* the LORD
abhorreth.
4 The wicked, through the pride of his countenance, will not seek *after God:* God *is* not in
all his [a]thoughts.
5 His ways are always grievous; thy judgments *are* far above out of his sight: *as for* all
his enemies, he puffeth at them.
6 [a]He hath said in his heart, I shall not be
moved: for [b]*I shall* never *be* in adversity.
7 [a]His mouth is full of cursing and [b]deceit
and fraud: under his tongue *is* mischief and
vanity.
8 He sitteth in the lurking places of the villages: in the secret places doth he murder the innocent: his eyes are privily set against the poor.
9 He lieth in wait secretly as a lion in his
den: he lieth in wait to catch the poor: he doth
catch the poor, when he draweth him into his net.

10 [a]Ps. 91:14
11 [a]Ps. 66:16; 107:22
12 [a][Gen. 9:5; Ps. 72:14]
14 [a]Ps. 13:5; 20:5; 35:9
15 [a]Ps. 7:15, 16
16 [a]Ex. 7:5 [b]Ps. 92:3
17 [a]Job 8:13; Ps. 50:22
18 [a]Ps. 9:12; 12:5 [b][Ps. 62:5; 71:5]; Prov. 23:18

PSALM 10

2 [a]Ps. 7:16; 9:16
3 [a]Ps. 49:6; 94:3, 4 [b]Prov. 28:4
4 [a]Ps. 14:1; 36:1
6 [a]Ps. 49:11; [Eccl. 8:11] [b]Rev. 18:7
7 [a][Rom. 3:14] [b]Ps. 55:10, 11

*
9:16 Heb. *Higgaion*

NKJV

10 And those who [a]know Your name will put
their trust in You;
For You, LORD, have not forsaken those
who seek You.

11 Sing praises to the LORD, who dwells in
Zion!
[a]Declare His deeds among the people.
12 [a]When He avenges blood, He remembers
them;
He does not forget the cry of the humble.

13 Have mercy on me, O LORD!
Consider my trouble from those who hate
me,
You who lift me up from the gates of
death,
14 That I may tell of all Your praise
In the gates of the daughter of Zion.
I will [a]rejoice in Your salvation.

15 [a]The nations have sunk down in the pit
which they made;
In the net which they hid, their own foot
is caught.
16 The LORD is [a]known *by* the judgment He
executes;
The wicked is snared in the work of his
own hands.
[b]Meditation.* Selah

17 The wicked shall be turned into hell,
And all the nations [a]that forget God.
18 [a]For the needy shall not always be
forgotten;
[b]The expectation of the poor shall *not*
perish forever.

19 Arise, O LORD,
Do not let man prevail;
Let the nations be judged in Your sight.
20 Put them in fear, O LORD,
That the nations may know themselves *to
be but* men. Selah

PSALM 10

A Song of Confidence in God's Triumph over Evil

WHY do You stand afar off, O LORD?
Why do You hide in times of trouble?
2 The wicked in *his* pride persecutes the
poor;
[a]Let them be caught in the plots which they
have devised.

3 For the wicked [a]boasts of his heart's
desire;
He [b]blesses the greedy *and* renounces the
LORD.
4 The wicked in his proud countenance does
not seek *God;*
God *is* in none of his [a]thoughts.

5 His ways are always prospering;
Your judgments *are* far above, out of his
sight;
As for all his enemies, he sneers at them.
6 [a]He has said in his heart,
"I shall not be moved;
[b]I shall never be in adversity."
7 [a]His mouth is full of cursing and [b]deceit
and oppression;
Under his tongue *is* trouble and iniquity.

8 He sits in the lurking places of the
villages;
In the secret places he murders the
innocent;
His eyes are secretly fixed on the helpless.
9 He lies in wait secretly, as a lion in his
den;
He lies in wait to catch the poor;
He catches the poor when he draws him
into his net.

KJV

10 He croucheth, *and* humbleth himself, that
the poor may fall by his strong ones.
11 He hath said in his heart, God hath forgotten: he hideth his face; he will never see *it*.
12 Arise, O LORD; O God, [a]lift up thine hand:
forget not the [b]humble.
13 Wherefore doth the wicked contemn God?
he hath said in his heart, Thou wilt not require
it.
14 Thou hast [a]seen *it;* for thou beholdest mischief and spite, to requite *it* with thy hand: the
poor [b]committeth himself unto thee; [c]thou art the
helper of the fatherless.
15 Break thou the arm of the wicked and the
evil *man:* seek out his wickedness *till* thou find
none.
16 [a]The LORD *is* King for ever and ever: the
heathen are perished out of his land.
17 LORD, thou hast heard the desire of the
humble: thou wilt prepare their heart, thou wilt
cause thine ear to hear:
18 To judge the fatherless and the oppressed,
that the man of the earth may no more oppress.

PSALM 11

Faith in the LORD's Righteousness

To the chief Musician, *A Psalm* of David.

IN [a]the LORD put I my trust: how say ye to my
soul, Flee *as* a bird to your mountain?
2 For, lo, [a]the wicked bend *their* bow, they
make ready their arrow upon the string, that they
may privily shoot at the upright in heart.
3 [a]If the foundations be destroyed, what can
the righteous do?
4 The LORD *is* in his holy temple, the LORD's
[a]throne *is* in heaven: [b]his eyes behold, his eyelids
try, the children of men.
5 The LORD [a]trieth the righteous: but the
wicked and him that loveth violence his soul
hateth.
6 Upon the wicked he shall rain snares, fire
and brimstone, and an horrible tempest: [a]*this
shall be* the portion of their cup.
7 For the righteous LORD [a]loveth righteousness; his countenance doth behold the upright.

PSALM 12

Man's Treachery and God's Constancy

To the chief Musician [a]upon Sheminith, A Psalm
of David.

HELP, LORD; for the godly man [a]ceaseth; for
the faithful fail from among the children of
men.
2 [a]They speak vanity every one with his
neighbour: *with* flattering lips *and* with a double
heart do they speak.

---

12 [a]Ps. 17:7; 94:2; Mic. 5:9 [b]Ps. 9:12
14 [a][Ps. 11:4] [b][2 Tim. 1:12] [c]Ps. 68:5; Hos. 14:3
16 [a]Ps. 29:10

PSALM 11

1 [a]Ps. 56:11
2 [a]Ps. 64:3, 4
3 [a]Ps. 82:5; 87:1; 119:152
4 [a]Ps. 2:4; [Is. 66:1]; Matt. 5:34; 23:22; [Acts 7:49]; Rev. 4:2 [b][Ps. 33:18; 34:15, 16]
5 [a]Gen. 22:1; [James 1:12]
6 [a]1 Sam. 1:4; Ps. 75:8; Ezek. 38:22
7 [a]Ps. 33:5; 45:7

PSALM 12

title [a]Ps. 6:title
1 [a][Is. 57:1]; Mic. 7:2
2 [a]Ps. 10:7; 41:6

11:7 Or *The upright beholds His countenance*
12:title Heb. *sheminith*

NKJV

10 So he crouches, he lies low,
That the helpless may fall by his
strength.
11 He has said in his heart,
"God has forgotten;
He hides His face;
He will never see."

12 Arise, O LORD!
O God, [a]lift up Your hand!
Do not forget the [b]humble.
13 Why do the wicked renounce God?
He has said in his heart,
"You will not require *an account.*"

14 But You have [a]seen, for You observe
trouble and grief,
To repay *it* by Your hand.
The helpless [b]commits himself to You;
[c]You are the helper of the fatherless.
15 Break the arm of the wicked and the evil
man;
Seek out his wickedness *until* You find
none.

16 [a]The LORD *is* King forever and ever;
The nations have perished out of His
land.
17 LORD, You have heard the desire of the
humble;
You will prepare their heart;
You will cause Your ear to hear,
18 To do justice to the fatherless and the
oppressed,
That the man of the earth may oppress
no more.

PSALM 11

Faith in the LORD's Righteousness

To the Chief Musician. A Psalm of David.

IN [a]the LORD I put my trust; How can you say
to my soul,
"Flee *as* a bird to your mountain"?
2 For look! [a]The wicked bend *their* bow,
They make ready their arrow on the
string,
That they may shoot secretly at the
upright in heart.
3 [a]If the foundations are destroyed,
What can the righteous do?

4 The LORD *is* in His holy temple,
The LORD's [a]throne *is* in heaven;
[b]His eyes behold,
His eyelids test the sons of men.
5 The LORD [a]tests the righteous,
But the wicked and the one who loves
violence His soul hates.
6 Upon the wicked He will rain coals;
Fire and brimstone and a burning
wind
[a]*Shall be* the portion of their cup.

7 For the LORD *is* righteous,
He [a]loves righteousness;
*His countenance beholds the upright.

PSALM 12

Man's Treachery and God's Constancy

To the Chief Musician. [a]On *an eight-stringed
harp. A Psalm of David.

HELP, LORD, for the godly man [a]ceases!
For the faithful disappear from among the
sons of men.
2 [a]They speak idly everyone with his
neighbor;
With flattering lips *and* a double heart
they speak.

KJV

3 The LORD shall cut off all flattering lips,
and the tongue that speaketh proud things:
4 Who have said, With our tongue will we
prevail; our lips *are* our own: who *is* lord over
us?
5 For the oppression of the poor, for the
sighing of the needy, now will I arise, saith the
LORD; I will set *him* in safety *from him that* puffeth
at him.
6 The words of the LORD *are* [a]pure words:
as silver tried in a furnace of earth, purified seven
times.
7 Thou shalt keep them, O LORD, thou shalt
preserve them from this generation for ever.
8 The wicked walk on every side, when the
vilest men are exalted.

6 [a]2 Sam. 22:31; Ps. 18:30; 119:140; Prov. 30:5

NKJV

3 May the LORD cut off all flattering lips,
And the tongue that speaks proud things,
4 Who have said,
"With our tongue we will prevail;
Our lips *are* our own;
Who *is* lord over us?"

5 "For the oppression of the poor, for the sighing of the needy,
Now I will arise," says the LORD;
"I will set *him* in the safety for which he yearns."

6 The words of the LORD *are* [a]pure words,
Like silver tried in a furnace of earth,
Purified seven times.
7 You shall keep them, O LORD,
You shall preserve them from this generation forever.

8 The wicked prowl on every side,
When vileness is exalted among the sons of men.

PSALM 13

Trust in the Salvation of the LORD

To the chief Musician, A Psalm of David.

HOW long wilt thou forget me, O LORD? for
ever? [a]how long wilt thou hide thy face from
me?
2 How long shall I take counsel in my soul,
having sorrow in my heart daily? how long shall
mine enemy be exalted over me?
3 Consider *and* hear me, O LORD my God:
[a]lighten mine eyes, [b]lest I sleep the *sleep of* death;
4 Lest mine enemy say, I have prevailed
against him; *and* those that trouble me rejoice
when I am moved.
5 But I have trusted in thy mercy; my heart
shall rejoice in thy salvation.
6 I will sing unto the LORD, because he hath
dealt bountifully with me.

PSALM 13

1 [a]Job 13:24; Ps. 89:46
3 [a]1 Sam. 14:29; Ezra 9:8; Job 33:30; Ps. 18:28 [b]Jer. 51:39

PSALM 13

Trust in the Salvation of the LORD

To the Chief Musician. A Psalm of David.

HOW long, O LORD? Will You forget me forever?
[a]How long will You hide Your face from me?
2 How long shall I take counsel in my soul,
Having sorrow in my heart daily?
How long will my enemy be exalted over me?

3 Consider *and* hear me, O LORD my God;
[a]Enlighten my eyes,
[b]Lest I sleep the *sleep of* death;
4 Lest my enemy say,
"I have prevailed against him";
Lest those who trouble me rejoice when I am moved.

5 But I have trusted in Your mercy;
My heart shall rejoice in Your salvation.
6 I will sing to the LORD,
Because He has dealt bountifully with me.

PSALM 14

Folly of the Godless, and God's Final Triumph
(Ps. 53:1–6)

To the chief Musician, *A Psalm* of David.

THE [a]fool hath said in his heart, *There is* no
God. They are corrupt, they have done abominable works, *there is* none that doeth good.
2 [a]The LORD looked down from heaven
upon the children of men, to see if there were
any that did understand, *and* seek God.
3 [a]They are all gone aside, they are *all* together become filthy: *there is* none that doeth
good, no, not one.
4 Have all the workers of iniquity no knowledge? who eat up my people *as* they eat bread,
and [a]call not upon the LORD.
5 There were they in great fear: for God *is*
in the generation of the righteous.
6 Ye have shamed the counsel of the poor,
because the LORD *is* his [a]refuge.

PSALM 14

1 [a]Ps. 10:4; 53:1
2 [a]Ps. 33:13, 14; 102:19; Rom. 3:11
3 [a]Rom. 3:12
4 [a]Ps. 79:6; Is. 64:7; Jer. 10:25; Amos 8:4; Mic. 3:3
6 [a]Ps. 9:9; 40:17; 46:1; 142:5

PSALM 14

Folly of the Godless, and God's Final Triumph
(Ps. 53:1–6)

To the Chief Musician. A Psalm of David.

THE [a]fool has said in his heart,
"*There is* no God."
They are corrupt,
They have done abominable works,
There is none who does good.

2 [a]The LORD looks down from heaven upon the children of men,
To see if there are any who understand, who seek God.
3 [a]They have all turned aside,
They have together become corrupt;
There is none who does good,
No, not one.

4 Have all the workers of iniquity no knowledge,
Who eat up my people *as* they eat bread,
And [a]do not call on the LORD?
5 There they are in great fear,
For God *is* with the generation of the righteous.
6 You shame the counsel of the poor,
But the LORD *is* his [a]refuge.

KJV

7 [a]Oh that the salvation of Israel *were come*
out of Zion! [b]when the LORD bringeth back the
captivity of his people, Jacob shall rejoice, *and*
Israel shall be glad.

PSALM 15

The Character of Those Who May Dwell with the LORD

A Psalm of David.

LORD, [a]who shall abide in thy tabernacle? who
shall dwell in thy holy hill?
2 He that walketh uprightly, and worketh
righteousness, and speaketh the [a]truth in his
heart.
3 *He that* [a]backbiteth not with his tongue,
nor doeth evil to his neighbour, [b]nor taketh up a
reproach against his neighbour.
4 [a]In whose eyes a vile person is contemned; but he honoureth them that fear the LORD.
He that [b]sweareth to *his own* hurt, and changeth
not.
5 *He that* putteth not out his money to
usury, nor taketh reward against the innocent. He
that doeth these *things* [a]shall never be moved.

PSALM 16

The Hope of the Faithful, and the Messiah's Victory

[a]Michtam of David.

PRESERVE me, O God: for in thee do I put my
trust.
2 O *my soul,* thou hast said unto the LORD,
Thou *art* my Lord: [a]my goodness *extendeth* not
to thee:
3 *But* to the saints that *are* in the earth, and
to the excellent, in [a]whom *is* all my delight.
4 Their sorrows shall be multiplied *that*
hasten *after* another *god:* their drink offerings of
[a]blood will I not offer, [b]nor take up their names
into my lips.
5 The LORD *is* the portion of mine inheritance and of my cup: thou maintainest my lot.
6 The lines are fallen unto me in pleasant
places; yea, I have a goodly heritage.
7 I will bless the LORD, who hath given me
counsel: my reins also instruct me in the night
seasons.
8 [a]I have set the LORD always before me:
because *he is* at my right hand, I shall not be
moved.
9 Therefore my heart is glad, and my glory
rejoiceth: my flesh also shall rest in hope.
10 [a]For thou wilt not leave my soul in hell;
neither wilt thou suffer thine Holy One to see
corruption.
11 Thou wilt shew me the [a]path of life: in
thy presence *is* fulness of joy; at thy right hand
there are pleasures for evermore.

---

7 [a]Ps. 53:6; [Rom. 11:25–27] [b]Deut. 30:3; Job 42:10

PSALM 15

1 [a]Ps. 24:3–5
2 [a]Zech. 8:16; [Eph. 4:25]
3 [a][Lev. 19:16–18] [b]Ex. 23:1
4 [a]Esth. 3:2 [b]Lev. 5:4
5 [a]2 Pet. 1:10

PSALM 16

title [a]Ps. 56—60
2 [a]Job 35:7
3 [a]Ps. 119:63
4 [a]Ps. 106:37, 38 [b][Ex. 23:13]; Josh. 23:7
8 [a][Acts 2:25–28]
10 [a]Ps. 49:15; 86:13; Acts 2:31, 32; Heb. 13:20
11 [a]Ps. 139:24; [Matt. 7:14]

NKJV

7 [a]Oh, that the salvation of Israel *would*
come out of Zion!
[b]When the LORD brings back the captivity
of His people,
Let Jacob rejoice *and* Israel be glad.

PSALM 15

The Character of Those Who May Dwell with the LORD

A Psalm of David.

LORD, [a]who may abide in Your tabernacle?
Who may dwell in Your holy hill?

2 He who walks uprightly,
And works righteousness,
And speaks the [a]truth in his heart;
3 He *who* [a]does not backbite with his
tongue,
Nor does evil to his neighbor,
[b]Nor does he take up a reproach against
his friend;
4 [a]In whose eyes a vile person is despised,
But he honors those who fear the
LORD;
He *who* [b]swears to his own hurt and does
not change;
5 He *who* does not put out his money at
usury,
Nor does he take a bribe against the
innocent.

He who does these *things* [a]shall never be
moved.

PSALM 16

The Hope of the Faithful, and the Messiah's Victory

A [a]Michtam of David.

PRESERVE me, O God, for in You I put my
trust.

2 *O my soul,* you have said to the LORD,
"You *are* my Lord,
[a]My goodness is nothing apart from You."
3 As for the saints who *are* on the earth,
"They are the excellent ones, in [a]whom is
all my delight."

4 Their sorrows shall be multiplied who
hasten *after* another *god;*
Their drink offerings of [a]blood I will not
offer,
[b]Nor take up their names on my lips.

5 O LORD, *You are* the portion of my
inheritance and my cup;
You maintain my lot.
6 The lines have fallen to me in pleasant
places;
Yes, I have a good inheritance.

7 I will bless the LORD who has given me
counsel;
My heart also instructs me in the night
seasons.
8 [a]I have set the LORD always before me;
Because *He is* at my right hand I shall not
be moved.

9 Therefore my heart is glad, and my glory
rejoices;
My flesh also will rest in hope.
10 [a]For You will not leave my soul in Sheol,
Nor will You allow Your Holy One to see
corruption.
11 You will show me the [a]path of life;
In Your presence *is* fullness of joy;
At Your right hand *are* pleasures
forevermore.

KJV

PSALM 17

Prayer with Confidence in Final Salvation

A Prayer of David.

HEAR the right, O LORD, attend unto my cry,
give ear unto my prayer, *that goeth* not out
of feigned lips.
2 Let my sentence come forth from thy presence; let thine eyes behold the things that are
equal.
3 Thou hast proved mine heart; thou hast
visited *me* in the night; [a]thou hast tried me, *and*
shalt find nothing; I am purposed *that* my mouth
shall not [b]transgress.
4 Concerning the works of men, by the word
of thy lips I have kept *me from* the paths of the
destroyer.
5 [a]Hold up my goings in thy paths, *that* my
footsteps slip not.
6 [a]I have called upon thee, for thou wilt hear
me, O God: incline thine ear unto me, *and hear*
my speech.
7 Shew thy marvellous lovingkindness, O
thou that savest by thy right hand them which
put their trust *in thee* from those that rise up
against them.
8 Keep me as the apple of the eye, hide me
under the shadow of thy wings,
9 From the wicked that oppress me, *from*
my deadly enemies, *who* compass me about.
10 They are inclosed in their own [a]fat: with
their mouth they [b]speak proudly.
11 They have now compassed us in our steps:
they have set their eyes bowing down to the earth;
12 Like as a lion *that* is greedy of his prey,
and as it were a young lion lurking in secret
places.
13 Arise, O LORD, disappoint him, cast him
down: deliver my soul from the wicked, *which is*
thy sword:
14 From men *which are* thy hand, O LORD,
from men of the world, *which have* their portion
in *this* life, and whose belly thou fillest with thy
hid *treasure:* they are full of children, and leave
the rest of their *substance* to their babes.
15 As for me, [a]I will behold thy face in righteousness: [b]I shall be satisfied, when I [c]awake,
with thy likeness.

PSALM 18

God the Sovereign Savior
(2 Sam. 22:1–51)

To the chief Musician, *A Psalm* of David, [a]the servant of the LORD, who spake unto the LORD the words of [b]this song in the day *that* the LORD delivered him from the hand of all his enemies, and from the hand of Saul: And he said,

I [a]WILL love thee, O LORD, my strength.
2 The LORD *is* my rock, and my fortress, and
my deliverer; my God, my strength, [a]in whom I

PSALM 17
3 [a]Job 23:10; Ps. 66:10; Zech. 13:9; [1 Pet. 1:7] [b]Ps. 39:1
5 [a]Job 23:11; Ps. 44:18; 119:133
6 [a]Ps. 86:7; 116:2
10 [a]Ezek. 16:49 [b][1 Sam. 2:3]
15 [a][1 John 3:2] [b]Ps. 4:6, 7; 16:11 [c][Is. 26:19]

PSALM 18
title [a]Ps. 36:title [b]2 Sam. 22
1 [a]Ps. 144:1
2 [a]Heb. 2:13

NKJV

PSALM 17

Prayer with Confidence in Final Salvation

A Prayer of David.

HEAR a just cause, O LORD,
Attend to my cry;
Give ear to my prayer *which is* not from deceitful lips.
2 Let my vindication come from Your presence;
Let Your eyes look on the things that are upright.

3 You have tested my heart;
You have visited *me* in the night;
[a]You have tried me and have found nothing;
I have purposed that my mouth shall not [b]transgress.
4 Concerning the works of men,
By the word of Your lips,
I have kept away from the paths of the destroyer.
5 [a]Uphold my steps in Your paths,
That my footsteps may not slip.

6 [a]I have called upon You, for You will hear me, O God;
Incline Your ear to me, *and* hear my speech.
7 Show Your marvelous lovingkindness by Your right hand,
O You who save those who trust *in You*
From those who rise up *against them.*
8 Keep me as the apple of Your eye;
Hide me under the shadow of Your wings,
9 From the wicked who oppress me,
From my deadly enemies who surround me.

10 They have closed up their [a]fat *hearts;*
With their mouths they [b]speak proudly.
11 They have now surrounded us in our steps;
They have set their eyes, crouching down to the earth,
12 As a lion is eager to tear his prey,
And like a young lion lurking in secret places.

13 Arise, O LORD,
Confront him, cast him down;
Deliver my life from the wicked with Your sword,
14 With Your hand from men, O LORD,
From men of the world *who have* their portion in *this* life,
And whose belly You fill with Your hidden treasure.
They are satisfied with children,
And leave the rest of their *possession* for their babes.

15 As for me, [a]I will see Your face in righteousness;
[b]I shall be satisfied when I [c]awake in Your likeness.

PSALM 18

God the Sovereign Savior
(2 Sam. 22:1–51)

To the Chief Musician. A Psalm of David [a]the servant of the LORD, who spoke to the LORD the words of [b]this song on the day that the LORD delivered him from the hand of all his enemies and from the hand of Saul. And he said:

I [a]WILL love You, O LORD, my strength.
2 The LORD is my rock and my fortress and my deliverer;
My God, my strength, [a]in whom I will trust;

KJV

will trust; my buckler, and the horn of my salvation, *and* my high tower.
3 I will call upon the LORD, [a]*who is worthy*
to be praised: so shall I be saved from mine
enemies.
4 [a]The sorrows of death compassed me, and
the floods of ungodly men made me afraid.
5 The sorrows of hell compassed me about:
the snares of death prevented me.
6 In my distress I called upon the LORD, and
cried unto my God: he heard my voice out of his
temple, and my cry came before him, *even* into
his ears.
7 [a]Then the earth shook and trembled; the
foundations also of the hills moved and were
shaken, because he was wroth.
8 There went up a smoke out of his nostrils,
and fire out of his mouth devoured: coals were
kindled by it.
9 [a]He bowed the heavens also, and came
down: and darkness *was* under his feet.
10 [a]And he rode upon a cherub, and did fly:
yea, [b]he did fly upon the wings of the wind.
11 He made darkness his secret place; [a]his
pavilion round about him *were* dark waters *and*
thick clouds of the skies.
12 [a]At the brightness *that was* before him
his thick clouds passed, hail *stones* and coals of
fire.
13 The LORD also thundered in the heavens,
and the Highest gave [a]his voice; hail *stones* and
coals of fire.
14 [a]Yea, he sent out his arrows, and scattered
them; and he shot out lightnings, and discomfited
them.
15 Then the channels of waters were seen,
and the foundations of the world were discovered
at thy rebuke, O LORD, at the blast of the breath
of thy nostrils.
16 [a]He sent from above, he took me, he drew
me out of many waters.
17 He delivered me from my strong enemy,
and from them which hated me: for they were
too strong for me.
18 They prevented me in the day of my calamity: but the LORD was my stay.
19 [a]He brought me forth also into a large
place; he delivered me, because he delighted in
me.
20 [a]The LORD rewarded me according to my
righteousness; according to the cleanness of my
hands hath he recompensed me.
21 For I have kept the ways of the LORD, and
have not wickedly departed from my God.
22 For all his judgments *were* before me, and
I did not put away his statutes from me.
23 I was also upright before him, and I kept
myself from mine iniquity.
24 [a]Therefore hath the LORD recompensed
me according to my righteousness, according to
the cleanness of my hands in his eyesight.
25 [a]With the merciful thou wilt shew thyself
merciful; with an upright man thou wilt shew thyself upright;

3 [a]Ps. 76:4; Rev. 5:12
4 [a]Ps. 116:3
7 [a]Acts 4:31
9 [a]Ps. 144:5
10 [a]Ps. 80:1; 99:1 [b][Ps. 104:3]
11 [a]Ps. 97:2
12 [a]Ps. 97:3; 140:10; Hab. 3:11
13 [a][Ps. 29:3–9; 104:7]
14 [a]Josh. 10:10; Ps. 144:6; Is. 30:30; Hab. 3:11
16 [a]Ps. 144:7
19 [a]Ps. 4:1; 31:8; 118:5
20 [a]1 Sam. 24:19; [Job 33:26]; Ps. 7:8
24 [a]1 Sam. 26:23; Ps. 18:20
25 [a][1 Kin. 8:32; Ps. 62:12]; Matt. 5:7

NKJV

My shield and the horn of my salvation,
my stronghold.
3 I will call upon the LORD, [a]*who is worthy*
to be praised;
So shall I be saved from my enemies.

4 [a]The pangs of death surrounded me,
And the floods of ungodliness made me
afraid.
5 The sorrows of Sheol surrounded me;
The snares of death confronted me.
6 In my distress I called upon the LORD,
And cried out to my God;
He heard my voice from His temple,
And my cry came before Him, *even* to His
ears.

7 [a]Then the earth shook and trembled;
The foundations of the hills also quaked
and were shaken,
Because He was angry.
8 Smoke went up from His nostrils,
And devouring fire from His mouth;
Coals were kindled by it.
9 [a]He bowed the heavens also, and came
down
With darkness under His feet.
10 [a]And He rode upon a cherub, and flew;
[b]He flew upon the wings of the wind.
11 He made darkness His secret place;
[a]His canopy around Him *was* dark waters
And thick clouds of the skies.
12 [a]From the brightness before Him,
His thick clouds passed with hailstones
and coals of fire.

13 The LORD thundered from heaven,
And the Most High uttered [a]His voice,
*Hailstones and coals of fire.
14 [a]He sent out His arrows and scattered the
foe,
Lightnings in abundance, and He
vanquished them.
15 Then the channels of the sea were seen,
The foundations of the world were
uncovered
At Your rebuke, O LORD,
At the blast of the breath of Your nostrils.

16 [a]He sent from above, He took me;
He drew me out of many waters.
17 He delivered me from my strong enemy,
From those who hated me,
For they were too strong for me.
18 They confronted me in the day of my
calamity,
But the LORD was my support.
19 [a]He also brought me out into a broad place;
He delivered me because He delighted in
me.

20 [a]The LORD rewarded me according to my
righteousness;
According to the cleanness of my hands
He has recompensed me.
21 For I have kept the ways of the LORD,
And have not wickedly departed from my
God.
22 For all His judgments *were* before me,
And I did not put away His statutes from
me.
23 I was also blameless before Him,
And I kept myself from my iniquity.
24 [a]Therefore the LORD has recompensed me
according to my righteousness,
According to the cleanness of my hands
in His sight.

25 [a]With the merciful You will show Yourself
merciful;
With a blameless man You will show
Yourself blameless;

*18:13 So with MT, Tg., Vg.; a few Heb. mss., LXX omit *Hailstones and coals of fire*

KJV

26 With the pure thou wilt shew thyself pure;
and [a]with the froward thou wilt shew thyself
froward.
27 For thou wilt save the afflicted people; but
wilt bring down [a]high looks.
28 [a]For thou wilt light my candle: the LORD
my God will enlighten my darkness.
29 For by thee I have run through a troop;
and by my God have I leaped over a wall.
30 *As for* God, [a]his way *is* perfect: [b]the word
of the LORD is tried: he *is* a buckler [c]to all those
that trust in him.
31 [a]For who *is* God save the LORD? or who
is a rock save our God?
32 *It is* God that [a]girdeth me with strength,
and maketh my way perfect.
33 [a]He maketh my feet like hinds' *feet,* and
[b]setteth me upon my high places.
34 [a]He teacheth my hands to war, so that a
bow of steel is broken by mine arms.
35 Thou hast also given me the shield of thy
salvation: and thy right hand hath holden me up,
and thy gentleness hath made me great.
36 Thou hast enlarged my steps under me,
[a]that my feet did not slip.
37 I have pursued mine enemies, and overtaken them: neither did I turn again till they were
consumed.
38 I have wounded them that they were not
able to rise: they are fallen under my feet.
39 For thou hast girded me with strength
unto the battle: thou hast subdued under me those
that rose up against me.
40 Thou hast also given me the necks of mine
enemies; that I might destroy them that hate me.
41 They cried, but *there was* none to save
them: [a]*even* unto the LORD, but he answered them
not.
42 Then did I beat them small as the dust
before the wind: I did [a]cast them out as the dirt
in the streets.
43 Thou hast delivered me from the strivings
of the people; *and* [a]thou hast made me the head
of the heathen: [b]a people *whom* I have not known
shall serve me.
44 As soon as they hear of me, they shall
obey me: the strangers shall submit themselves
unto me.
45 [a]The strangers shall fade away, and be
afraid out of their close places.
46 The LORD liveth; and blessed *be* my rock;
and let the God of my salvation be exalted.
47 *It is* God that avengeth me, [a]and subdueth
the people under me.
48 He delivereth me from mine enemies: yea,
[a]thou liftest me up above those that rise up against
me: thou hast delivered me from the violent man.
49 [a]Therefore will I give thanks unto thee,
O LORD, among the heathen, and sing praises unto
thy name.

26 [a][Lev. 26:23–28]; Prov. 3:34
27 [a][Ps. 101:5]; Prov. 6:17
28 [a]1 Kin. 15:4; Job 18:6; [Ps. 119:105]
30 [a][Deut. 32:4]; Rev. 15:3 [b]Ps. 12:6; 119:140; [Prov. 30:5] [c][Ps. 17:7]
31 [a][Deut. 32:31, 39; 1 Sam. 2:2; Ps. 86:8–10; Is. 45:5]
32 [a][Ps. 91:2]
33 [a]2 Sam. 2:18; Hab. 3:19 [b]Deut. 32:13; 33:29
34 [a]Ps. 144:1
36 [a]Ps. 66:9; Prov. 4:12
41 [a]Job 27:9; Prov. 1:28; Is. 1:15; Ezek. 8:18; Zech. 7:13
42 [a]Zech. 10:5
43 [a]2 Sam. 8; Ps. 89:27 [b]Is. 52:15
45 [a]Mic. 7:17
47 [a]Ps. 47:3
48 [a]Ps. 27:6; 59:1
49 [a]2 Sam. 22:50; Rom. 15:9

NKJV

26 With the pure You will show Yourself
pure;
And [a]with the devious You will show
Yourself shrewd.
27 For You will save the humble people,
But will bring down [a]haughty looks.

28 [a]For You will light my lamp;
The LORD my God will enlighten my
darkness.
29 For by You I can run against a troop,
By my God I can leap over a wall.
30 *As for* God, [a]His way *is* perfect;
[b]The word of the LORD is proven;
He *is* a shield [c]to all who trust in Him.

31 [a]For who *is* God, except the LORD?
And who *is* a rock, except our God?
32 *It is* God who [a]arms me with strength,
And makes my way perfect.
33 [a]He makes my feet like the *feet of* deer,
And [b]sets me on my high places.
34 [a]He teaches my hands to make war,
So that my arms can bend a bow of
bronze.

35 You have also given me the shield of Your
salvation;
Your right hand has held me up,
Your gentleness has made me great.
36 You enlarged my path under me,
[a]So my feet did not slip.

37 I have pursued my enemies and overtaken
them;
Neither did I turn back again till they were
destroyed.
38 I have wounded them,
So that they could not rise;
They have fallen under my feet.
39 For You have armed me with strength for
the battle;
You have subdued under me those who
rose up against me.
40 You have also given me the necks of my
enemies,
So that I destroyed those who hated me.
41 They cried out, but *there was* none to
save;
[a]*Even* to the LORD, but He did not answer
them.
42 Then I beat them as fine as the dust before
the wind;
I [a]cast them out like dirt in the streets.

43 You have delivered me from the strivings
of the people;
[a]You have made me the head of the
nations;
[b]A people I have not known shall serve
me.
44 As soon as they hear of me they obey
me;
The foreigners submit to me.
45 [a]The foreigners fade away,
And come frightened from their
hideouts.

46 The LORD lives!
Blessed *be* my Rock!
Let the God of my salvation be exalted.
47 *It is* God who avenges me,
[a]And subdues the peoples under me;
48 He delivers me from my enemies.
[a]You also lift me up above those who rise
against me;
You have delivered me from the violent
man.
49 [a]Therefore I will give thanks to You, O
LORD, among the Gentiles,
And sing praises to Your name.

KJV

50 [a]Great deliverance giveth he to his king;
and sheweth mercy to his anointed, to David, and
to his seed for evermore.

PSALM 19

The Perfect Revelation of the L**ORD**

To the chief Musician, A Psalm of David.

THE [a]heavens declare the glory of God; and
the [b]firmament sheweth his handywork.
2 Day unto day uttereth speech, and night
unto night sheweth knowledge.
3 *There is* no speech nor language, *where*
their voice is not heard.
4 [a]Their line is gone out through all the
earth, and their words to the end of the world.
In them hath he set a tabernacle for the sun,
5 Which *is* as a bridegroom coming out of
his chamber, [a]*and* rejoiceth as a strong man to
run a race.
6 His going forth *is* from the end of the
heaven, and his circuit unto the ends of it: and
there is nothing hid from the heat thereof.
7 [a]The law of the LORD *is* perfect, converting
the soul: the testimony of the LORD *is* sure, making
[b]wise the simple.
8 The statutes of the LORD *are* right, rejoicing the heart: the commandment of the LORD *is*
pure, enlightening the eyes.
9 The fear of the LORD *is* clean, enduring
for ever: the judgments of the LORD *are* true *and*
righteous altogether.
10 More to be desired *are they* than [a]gold,
yea, than much fine gold: sweeter also than honey
and the honeycomb.
11 Moreover by them is thy servant warned:
and in keeping of them *there is* great reward.
12 Who can understand *his* errors? [a]cleanse
thou me from secret *faults.*
13 Keep back thy servant also from [a]pre-
sumptuous *sins;* let them not have [b]dominion over
me: then shall I be upright, and I shall be innocent
from the great transgression.
14 [a]Let the words of my mouth, and the
meditation of my heart, be acceptable in thy sight,
O LORD, my strength, and my [b]redeemer.

PSALM 20

The Assurance of God's Saving Work

To the chief Musician, A Psalm of David.

THE LORD hear thee in the day of trouble; the
name of the God of Jacob defend thee;
2 Send thee help from the sanctuary, and
strengthen thee out of Zion;
3 Remember all thy offerings, and accept
thy burnt sacrifice; Selah.
4 Grant thee according to thine own heart,
and [a]fulfil all thy counsel.

---

50 [a]2 Sam. 7:12; Ps. 21:1; 144:10

PSALM 19

1 [a]Is. 40:22; [Rom. 1:19, 20] [b]Gen. 1:6, 7
4 [a]Rom. 10:18
5 [a]Eccl. 1:5
7 [a]Ps. 111:7; [Rom. 7:12] [b]Ps. 119:130
10 [a]Ps. 119:72, 127; Prov. 8:10, 11, 19
12 [a][Ps. 51:1, 2]
13 [a]Num. 15:30 [b]Ps. 119:133; [Rom. 6:12–14]
14 [a]Ps. 51:15 [b]Ps. 31:5; Is. 47:4

PSALM 20

4 [a]Ps. 21:2

*______

19:4 LXX, Syr., Vg. *sound;* Tg. *business*

NKJV

50 [a]Great deliverance He gives to His king,
And shows mercy to His anointed,
To David and his descendants
forevermore.

PSALM 19

The Perfect Revelation of the L**ORD**

To the Chief Musician. A Psalm of David.

THE [a]heavens declare the glory of God;
And the [b]firmament shows His
handiwork.
2 Day unto day utters speech,
And night unto night reveals knowledge.
3 *There is* no speech nor language
Where their voice is not heard.
4 [a]Their *line has gone out through all the
earth,
And their words to the end of the world.

In them He has set a tabernacle for the
sun,
5 Which *is* like a bridegroom coming out
of his chamber,
[a]*And* rejoices like a strong man to run its
race.
6 Its rising *is* from one end of heaven,
And its circuit to the other end;
And there is nothing hidden from its heat.

7 [a]The law of the LORD *is* perfect, converting
the soul;
The testimony of the LORD *is* sure, making
[b]wise the simple;
8 The statutes of the LORD *are* right,
rejoicing the heart;
The commandment of the LORD *is* pure,
enlightening the eyes;
9 The fear of the LORD *is* clean, enduring
forever;
The judgments of the LORD *are* true *and*
righteous altogether.
10 More to be desired *are they* than [a]gold,
Yea, than much fine gold;
Sweeter also than honey and the
honeycomb.
11 Moreover by them Your servant is
warned,
And in keeping them *there is* great
reward.

12 Who can understand *his* errors?
[a]Cleanse me from secret *faults.*
13 Keep back Your servant also from
[a]presumptuous *sins;*
Let them not have [b]dominion over me.
Then I shall be blameless,
And I shall be innocent of great
transgression.

14 [a]Let the words of my mouth and the
meditation of my heart
Be acceptable in Your sight,
O LORD, my strength and my [b]Redeemer.

PSALM 20

The Assurance of God's Saving Work

To the Chief Musician. A Psalm of David.

MAY the LORD answer you in the day of
trouble;
May the name of the God of Jacob defend
you;
2 May He send you help from the sanctuary,
And strengthen you out of Zion;
3 May He remember all your offerings,
And accept your burnt sacrifice. Selah

4 May He grant you according to your
heart's *desire,*
And [a]fulfill all your purpose.

KJV

5 We will rejoice in thy salvation, and in the name of our God we will set up *our* banners: the LORD fulfil all thy petitions.
6 Now know I that the LORD saveth his anointed; he will hear him from his holy heaven with the saving strength of his right hand.
7 Some *trust* in chariots, and some in [a]horses: but we will remember the name of the LORD our God.
8 They are brought down and fallen: but we are risen, and stand upright.
9 Save, LORD: let the king hear us when we call.

PSALM 21

Joy in the Salvation of the LORD

To the chief Musician, A Psalm of David.

THE king shall joy in thy strength, O LORD; and in thy salvation how greatly shall he rejoice!
2 Thou hast given him his heart's desire, and hast not withholden the [a]request of his lips. Selah.
3 For thou preventest him with the blessings of goodness: thou settest a crown of pure gold on his head.
4 [a]He asked life of thee, *and* thou gavest *it* him, *even* length of days for ever and ever.
5 His glory *is* great in thy salvation: honour and majesty hast thou laid upon him.
6 For thou hast made him most blessed for ever: [a]thou hast made him exceeding glad with thy countenance.
7 For the king trusteth in the LORD, and through the mercy of the most High he shall not be moved.
8 Thine hand shall find out all thine enemies: thy right hand shall find out those that hate thee.
9 Thou shalt make them as a fiery oven in the time of thine anger: the LORD shall swallow them up in his wrath, and the fire shall devour them.
10 Their fruit shalt thou destroy from the earth, and their seed from among the children of men.
11 For they intended evil against thee: they imagined a mischievous device, *which* they are not able *to* [a]*perform.*
12 Therefore shalt thou make them turn their back, *when* thou shalt make ready *thine arrows* upon thy strings against the face of them.
13 Be thou exalted, LORD, in thine own strength: *so* will we sing and praise thy power.

PSALM 22

The Suffering, Praise, and Posterity of the Messiah

To the chief Musician upon Aijeleth Shahar, A Psalm of David.

MY [a]God, my God, why hast thou forsaken me? *why art thou so* far from helping me, *and from* the words of my roaring?

---

7 [a]Deut. 20:1; Ps. 33:16, 17; Prov. 21:31; Is. 31:1

PSALM 21

2 [a]2 Sam. 7:26–29
4 [a]Ps. 61:5, 6; 133:3
6 [a]Ps. 16:11; 45:7
11 [a]Ps. 2:1–4

PSALM 22

1 [a][Matt. 27:46; Mark 15:34]

*22:title Heb. *Aijeleth Hashahar*

NKJV

5 We will rejoice in your salvation,
And in the name of our God we will set up *our* banners!
May the LORD fulfill all your petitions.

6 Now I know that the LORD saves His anointed;
He will answer him from His holy heaven
With the saving strength of His right hand.

7 Some *trust* in chariots, and some in [a]horses;
But we will remember the name of the LORD our God.
8 They have bowed down and fallen;
But we have risen and stand upright.
9 Save, LORD!
May the King answer us when we call.

PSALM 21

Joy in the Salvation of the LORD

To the Chief Musician. A Psalm of David.

THE king shall have joy in Your strength, O LORD;
And in Your salvation how greatly shall he rejoice!
2 You have given him his heart's desire,
And have not withheld the [a]request of his lips. Selah

3 For You meet him with the blessings of goodness;
You set a crown of pure gold upon his head.
4 [a]He asked life from You, *and* You gave *it* to him—
Length of days forever and ever.
5 His glory *is* great in Your salvation;
Honor and majesty You have placed upon him.
6 For You have made him most blessed forever;
[a]You have made him exceedingly glad with Your presence.
7 For the king trusts in the LORD,
And through the mercy of the Most High he shall not be moved.

8 Your hand will find all Your enemies;
Your right hand will find those who hate You.
9 You shall make them as a fiery oven in the time of Your anger;
The LORD shall swallow them up in His wrath,
And the fire shall devour them.
10 Their offspring You shall destroy from the earth,
And their descendants from among the sons of men.
11 For they intended evil against You;
They devised a plot *which* they are not able *to* [a]*perform.*
12 Therefore You will make them turn their back;
You will make ready *Your arrows* on Your string toward their faces.

13 Be exalted, O LORD, in Your own strength!
We will sing and praise Your power.

PSALM 22

The Suffering, Praise, and Posterity of the Messiah

To the Chief Musician. Set to *"The Deer of the Dawn." A Psalm of David.

MY [a]God, My God, why have You forsaken Me?
Why are You so far from helping Me,
And from the words of My groaning?

KJV

2 O my God, I cry in the daytime, but thou
hearest not; and in the night season, and am not
silent.
3 But thou *art* holy, O *thou* that inhabitest
the [a]praises of Israel.
4 Our fathers trusted in thee: they trusted,
and thou didst deliver them.
5 They cried unto thee, and were delivered:
[a]they trusted in thee, and were not confounded.
6 But I *am* [a]a worm, and no man; [b]a reproach of men, and despised of the people.
7 [a]All they that see me laugh me to scorn:
they shoot out the lip, they shake the head, *saying*,
8 [a]He trusted on the LORD *that* he would
deliver him: [b]let him deliver him, seeing he delighted in him.
9 [a]But thou *art* he that took me out of the
womb: thou didst make me hope *when I was* upon
my mother's breasts.
10 I was cast upon thee from the womb:
[a]thou *art* my God from my mother's belly.
11 Be not far from me; for trouble *is* near;
for *there is* none to help.
12 [a]Many bulls have compassed me: strong
bulls of [b]Bashan have beset me round.
13 [a]They gaped upon me *with* their mouths,
as a ravening and a roaring lion.
14 I am poured out like water, [a]and all my
bones are out of joint: my heart is like wax; it is
melted in the midst of my bowels.
15 [a]My strength is dried up like a potsherd;
and [b]my tongue cleaveth to my jaws; and thou
hast brought me into the dust of death.
16 For dogs have compassed me: the assembly of the wicked have inclosed me: [a]they pierced
my hands and my feet.
17 I may tell all my bones: [a]they look *and*
stare upon me.
18 [a]They part my garments among them, and
cast lots upon my vesture.
19 But be not thou far from me, O LORD: O
my strength, haste thee to help me.
20 Deliver my soul from the sword; [a]my darling from the power of the dog.
21 [a]Save me from the lion's mouth: [b]for thou
hast heard me from the horns of the unicorns.
22 [a]I will declare thy name unto [b]my brethren: in the midst of the congregation will I praise
thee.
23 [a]Ye that fear the LORD, praise him; all ye
the seed of Jacob, glorify him; and fear him, all
ye the seed of Israel.
24 For he hath not despised nor abhorred the
affliction of the afflicted; neither hath he hid his
face from him; but [a]when he cried unto him, he
heard.
25 [a]My praise *shall be* of thee in the great
congregation: [b]I will pay my vows before them
that fear him.

3 [a]Deut. 10:21; Ps. 148:14
5 [a]Is. 49:23
6 [a]Job 25:6; Is. 41:14 [b]Ps. 109:25; [Is. 53:3]; Matt. 27:39–44
7 [a]Matt. 27:39; Mark 15:29
8 [a]Matt. 27:43; Luke 23:35 [b]Ps. 91:14
9 [a][Ps. 71:5, 6]
10 [a][Is. 46:3; 49:1]; Luke 1:35
12 [a]Ps. 22:21; 68:30 [b]Deut. 32:14
13 [a]Job 16:10; Ps. 35:21; Lam. 2:16; 3:46
14 [a]Ps. 31:10; Dan. 5:6
15 [a]Prov. 17:22 [b]John 19:28
16 [a]Is. 53:7; Matt. 27:35; John 20:25
17 [a]Luke 23:27, 35
18 [a]Matt. 27:35; Mark 15:24; Luke 23:34; John 19:24
20 [a]Ps. 35:17
21 [a]2 Tim. 4:17 [b]Is. 34:7
22 [a]Matt. 4:23; Mark 1:21, 39; Heb. 2:12 [b][Rom. 8:29]
23 [a]Ps. 135:19, 20
24 [a]Ps. 31:22; Heb. 5:7
25 [a]Ps. 35:18; 40:9, 10 [b]Ps. 61:8; Eccl. 5:4

NKJV

2 O My God, I cry in the daytime, but You
do not hear;
And in the night season, and am not
silent.

3 But You *are* holy,
Enthroned in the [a]praises of Israel.
4 Our fathers trusted in You;
They trusted, and You delivered them.
5 They cried to You, and were delivered;
[a]They trusted in You, and were not
ashamed.

6 But I *am* [a]a worm, and no man;
[b]A reproach of men, and despised by the
people.
7 [a]All those who see Me ridicule Me;
They shoot out the lip, they shake the
head, *saying*,
8 "He[a] *trusted in the LORD, let Him rescue
Him;
[b]Let Him deliver Him, since He delights in
Him!"

9 [a]But You *are* He who took Me out of the
womb;
You made Me trust *while* on My mother's
breasts.
10 I was cast upon You from birth.
From My mother's womb
[a]You *have been* My God.
11 Be not far from Me,
For trouble *is* near;
For *there is* none to help.

12 [a]Many bulls have surrounded Me;
Strong *bulls* of [b]Bashan have encircled
Me.
13 [a]They gape at Me *with* their mouths,
Like a raging and roaring lion.

14 I am poured out like water,
[a]And all My bones are out of joint;
My heart is like wax;
It has melted within Me.
15 [a]My strength is dried up like a potsherd,
And [b]My tongue clings to My jaws;
You have brought Me to the dust of death.

16 For dogs have surrounded Me;
The congregation of the wicked has
enclosed Me.
[a]They* pierced My hands and My feet;
17 I can count all My bones.
[a]They look *and* stare at Me.
18 [a]They divide My garments among them,
And for My clothing they cast lots.

19 But You, O LORD, do not be far from Me;
O My Strength, hasten to help Me!
20 Deliver Me from the sword,
[a]My precious *life* from the power of the
dog.
21 [a]Save Me from the lion's mouth
And from the horns of the wild oxen!

[b]You have answered Me.

22 [a]I will declare Your name to [b]My brethren;
In the midst of the assembly I will praise
You.
23 [a]You who fear the LORD, praise Him!
All you descendants of Jacob, glorify Him,
And fear Him, all you offspring of Israel!
24 For He has not despised nor abhorred the
affliction of the afflicted;
Nor has He hidden His face from Him;
But [a]when He cried to Him, He heard.

25 [a]My praise *shall be* of You in the great
assembly;
[b]I will pay My vows before those who fear
Him.

*

22:8 LXX, Syr., Vg. *hoped;* Tg. *praised*
22:16 So with some Heb. mss., LXX, Syr., Vg.; MT *Like a lion* instead of *They pierced*

KJV

26 The meek shall eat and be satisfied: they shall praise the LORD that seek him: your heart shall live for ever.

27 All the ends of the world shall remember and turn unto the LORD: and all the kindreds of the nations shall worship before thee.

28 [a]For the kingdom *is* the LORD's: and he *is* the governor among the nations.

29 [a]All *they that be* fat upon earth shall eat and worship: [b]all they that go down to the dust shall bow before him: and none can keep alive his own soul.

30 A seed shall serve him; it shall be accounted to the Lord for a generation.

31 They shall come, and shall declare his righteousness unto a people that shall be born, that he hath done *this*.

PSALM 23

The LORD the Shepherd of His People

A Psalm of David.

THE LORD *is* [a]my shepherd; [b]I shall not want.

2 [a]He maketh me to lie down in green pastures: [b]he leadeth me beside the still waters.

3 He restoreth my soul: [a]he leadeth me in the paths of righteousness for his name's sake.

4 Yea, though I walk through the valley of [a]the shadow of death, [b]I will fear no evil: [c]for thou *art* with me; thy rod and thy staff they comfort me.

5 Thou [a]preparest a table before me in the presence of mine enemies: thou [b]anointest my head with oil; my cup runneth over.

6 Surely goodness and mercy shall follow me all the days of my life: and I will dwell in the house of the LORD for ever.

PSALM 24

The King of Glory and His Kingdom

A Psalm of David.

THE [a]earth *is* the LORD's, and the fulness thereof; the world, and they that dwell therein.

2 For he hath [a]founded it upon the seas, and established it upon the floods.

3 [a]Who shall ascend into the hill of the LORD? or who shall stand in his holy place?

4 He that hath [a]clean hands, and [b]a pure heart; who hath not lifted up his soul unto vanity, nor [c]sworn deceitfully.

5 He shall receive the blessing from the LORD, and righteousness from the God of his salvation.

6 This *is* the generation of them that [a]seek him, that seek thy face, O Jacob. Selah.

7 [a]Lift up your heads, O ye gates; and be ye lift up, ye everlasting doors; [b]and the King of glory shall come in.

---

28 [a][Ps. 47:7]; Obad. 21; [Zech. 14:9]; Matt. 6:13
29 [a]Ps. 17:10; 45:12; Hab. 1:16 [b]Ps. 28:1; [Is. 26:19]

PSALM 23

1 [a]Ps. 78:52; 80:1; [Is. 40:11]; Ezek. 34:11, 12; [John 10:11; 1 Pet. 2:25; Rev. 7:16, 17] [b][Ps. 34:9, 10; Phil. 4:19]
2 [a]Ps. 65:11–13; Ezek. 34:14 [b][Rev. 7:17]
3 [a]Ps. 5:8; 31:3; Prov. 8:20
4 [a]Job 3:5; 10:21, 22; 24:17; Ps. 44:19 [b][Ps. 3:6; 27:1] [c]Ps. 16:8; [Is. 43:2]
5 [a]Ps. 104:15 [b]Ps. 92:10; Luke 7:46

PSALM 24

1 [a]1 Cor. 10:26, 28
2 [a]Ps. 89:11
3 [a]Ps. 15:1–5
4 [a][Job 17:9]; Ps. 26:6 [b]Ps. 51:10; 73:1; [Matt. 5:8] [c]Ps. 15:4
6 [a]Ps. 27:4, 8
7 [a]Ps. 118:20; Is. 26:2 [b]Ps. 29:2, 9; 97:6; Hag. 2:7; Acts 7:2; [1 Cor. 2:8]

*

22:27 So with MT, LXX, Tg.; Arab., Syr., Vg. *Him*
23:6 So with LXX, Syr., Tg., Vg.; MT *return*

NKJV

26 The poor shall eat and be satisfied;
Those who seek Him will praise the LORD.
Let your heart live forever!

27 All the ends of the world
Shall remember and turn to the LORD,
And all the families of the nations
Shall worship before *You.

28 [a]For the kingdom *is* the LORD's,
And He rules over the nations.

29 [a]All the prosperous of the earth
Shall eat and worship;
[b]All those who go down to the dust
Shall bow before Him,
Even he who cannot keep himself alive.

30 A posterity shall serve Him.
It will be recounted of the Lord to the *next*
generation,

31 They will come and declare His
righteousness to a people who will be
born,
That He has done *this*.

PSALM 23

The LORD the Shepherd of His People

A Psalm of David.

THE LORD *is* [a]my shepherd;
[b]I shall not want.

2 [a]He makes me to lie down in green
pastures;
[b]He leads me beside the still waters.

3 He restores my soul;
[a]He leads me in the paths of righteousness
For His name's sake.

4 Yea, though I walk through the valley of
[a]the shadow of death,
[b]I will fear no evil;
[c]For You *are* with me;
Your rod and Your staff, they comfort
me.

5 You [a]prepare a table before me in the
presence of my enemies;
You [b]anoint my head with oil;
My cup runs over.

6 Surely goodness and mercy shall follow
me
All the days of my life;
And I will *dwell in the house of the LORD
Forever.

PSALM 24

The King of Glory and His Kingdom

A Psalm of David.

THE [a]earth *is* the LORD's, and all its fullness,
The world and those who dwell therein.

2 For He has [a]founded it upon the seas,
And established it upon the waters.

3 [a]Who may ascend into the hill of the
LORD?
Or who may stand in His holy place?

4 He who has [a]clean hands and [b]a pure
heart,
Who has not lifted up his soul to an idol,
Nor [c]sworn deceitfully.

5 He shall receive blessing from the LORD,
And righteousness from the God of his
salvation.

6 This *is* Jacob, the generation of those who
[a]seek Him,
Who seek Your face. Selah

7 [a]Lift up your heads, O you gates!
And be lifted up, you everlasting doors!
[b]And the King of glory shall come in.

KJV

8 Who *is* this King of glory? The LORD
strong and mighty, the LORD mighty in [a]battle.
9 Lift up your heads, O ye gates; even lift
them up, ye everlasting doors; and the King of
glory shall come in.
10 Who is this King of glory? The LORD of
hosts, he *is* the King of glory. Selah.

PSALM 25

A Plea for Deliverance and Forgiveness

A Psalm of David.

UNTO [a]thee, O LORD, do I lift up my soul.
2 O my God, I [a]trust in thee: let me not be
ashamed, [b]let not mine enemies triumph over me.
3 Yea, let none that wait on thee be
ashamed: let them be ashamed which transgress
without cause.
4 [a]Shew me thy ways, O LORD; teach me
thy paths.
5 Lead me in thy truth, and teach me: for
thou *art* the God of my salvation; on thee do I
wait all the day.
6 Remember, O LORD, [a]thy tender mercies
and thy lovingkindnesses; for they *have been* ever
of old.
7 Remember not [a]the sins of my youth, nor
my transgressions: [b]according to thy mercy remember thou me for thy goodness' sake, O LORD.
8 Good and upright *is* the LORD: therefore
will he teach sinners in the way.
9 The meek will he guide in judgment: and
the meek will he teach his way.
10 All the paths of the LORD *are* mercy and
truth unto such as keep his covenant and his
testimonies.
11 [a]For thy name's sake, O LORD, pardon
mine iniquity; for it *is* great.
12 What man *is* he that feareth the LORD?
[a]him shall he teach in the way *that* he shall
choose.
13 [a]His soul shall dwell at ease; and [b]his seed
shall inherit the earth.
14 [a]The secret of the LORD *is* with them that
fear him; and he will shew them his covenant.
15 [a]Mine eyes *are* ever toward the LORD; for
he shall pluck my feet out of the net.
16 [a]Turn thee unto me, and have mercy upon
me; for I *am* desolate and afflicted.
17 The troubles of my heart are enlarged: O
bring thou me out of my distresses.
18 [a]Look upon mine affliction and my pain;
and forgive all my sins.
19 Consider mine enemies; for they are
many; and they hate me with cruel hatred.
20 O keep my soul, and deliver me: let me
not be ashamed; for I put my trust in thee.
21 Let integrity and uprightness preserve me;
for I wait on thee.
22 [a]Redeem Israel, O God, out of all his
troubles.

8 [a]Rev. 19:13–16

PSALM 25

1 [a]Ps. 86:4; 143:8
2 [a]Ps. 34:8 [b]Ps. 13:4; 41:11
4 [a]Ex. 33:13; Ps. 5:8; 27:11; 86:11; 119:27; 143:8
6 [a]Ps. 103:17; 106:1
7 [a]Job 13:26; [Jer. 3:25] [b]Ps. 51:1
11 [a]Ps. 31:3; 79:9; 109:21; 143:11
12 [a][Ps. 25:8; 37:23]
13 [a][Prov. 19:23] [b]Ps. 37:11; 69:36; Matt. 5:5
14 [a][Prov. 3:32; John 7:17]
15 [a][Ps. 123:2; 141:8]
16 [a]Ps. 69:16
18 [a]2 Sam. 16:12; Ps. 31:7
22 [a][Ps. 130:8]

*______

25:12 Or *he* • Or *he*

NKJV

8 Who *is* this King of glory?
The LORD strong and mighty,
The LORD mighty in [a]battle.
9 Lift up your heads, O you gates!
Lift up, you everlasting doors!
And the King of glory shall come in.
10 Who is this King of glory?
The LORD of hosts,
He *is* the King of glory. Selah

PSALM 25

A Plea for Deliverance and Forgiveness

A Psalm of David.

TO [a]You, O LORD, I lift up my soul.
2 O my God, I [a]trust in You;
Let me not be ashamed;
[b]Let not my enemies triumph over me.
3 Indeed, let no one who waits on You be ashamed;
Let those be ashamed who deal treacherously without cause.

4 [a]Show me Your ways, O LORD;
Teach me Your paths.
5 Lead me in Your truth and teach me,
For You *are* the God of my salvation;
On You I wait all the day.

6 Remember, O LORD, [a]Your tender mercies and Your lovingkindnesses,
For they *are* from of old.
7 Do not remember [a]the sins of my youth, nor my transgressions;
[b]According to Your mercy remember me,
For Your goodness' sake, O LORD.

8 Good and upright *is* the LORD;
Therefore He teaches sinners in the way.
9 The humble He guides in justice,
And the humble He teaches His way.
10 All the paths of the LORD *are* mercy and truth,
To such as keep His covenant and His testimonies.
11 [a]For Your name's sake, O LORD,
Pardon my iniquity, for it *is* great.

12 Who *is* the man that fears the LORD?
[a]Him shall *He teach in the way *He chooses.
13 [a]He himself shall dwell in prosperity,
And [b]his descendants shall inherit the earth.
14 [a]The secret of the LORD *is* with those who fear Him,
And He will show them His covenant.
15 [a]My eyes *are* ever toward the LORD,
For He shall pluck my feet out of the net.

16 [a]Turn Yourself to me, and have mercy on me,
For I *am* desolate and afflicted.
17 The troubles of my heart have enlarged;
Bring me out of my distresses!
18 [a]Look on my affliction and my pain,
And forgive all my sins.
19 Consider my enemies, for they are many;
And they hate me with cruel hatred.
20 Keep my soul, and deliver me;
Let me not be ashamed, for I put my trust in You.
21 Let integrity and uprightness preserve me,
For I wait for You.

22 [a]Redeem Israel, O God,
Out of all their troubles!

KJV

NKJV

PSALM 26 (KJV)

A Prayer for Divine Scrutiny and Redemption

A Psalm of David.

JUDGE [a]me, O LORD; for I have [b]walked in mine integrity: [c]I have trusted also in the LORD; *therefore* I shall not slide.
2 [a]Examine me, O LORD, and prove me: try my reins and my heart.
3 For thy lovingkindness *is* before mine eyes: and [a]I have walked in thy truth.
4 I have not [a]sat with vain persons, neither will I go in with dissemblers.
5 I have [a]hated the congregation of evildoers; and will not sit with the wicked.
6 I will wash mine hands in innocency: so will I compass thine altar, O LORD:
7 That I may publish with the voice of thanksgiving, and tell of all thy wondrous works.
8 LORD, [a]I have loved the habitation of thy house, and the place where thine honour dwelleth.
9 [a]Gather not my soul with sinners, nor my life with bloody men:
10 In whose hands *is* mischief, and their right hand is full of [a]bribes.
11 But as for me, I will walk in mine integrity: redeem me, and be merciful unto me.
12 [a]My foot standeth in an even place: in the congregations will I bless the LORD.

PSALM 26

1 [a]Ps. 7:8 [b]2 Kin. 20:3; [Prov. 20:7] [c][Ps. 13:5; 28:7] **2** [a]Ps. 17:3; 139:23 **3** [a]2 Kin. 20:3; Ps. 86:11 **4** [a]Ps. 1:1; Jer. 15:17 **5** [a]Ps. 31:6; 139:21 **8** [a]Ps. 27:4; 84:1–4, 10 **9** [a]Ps. 28:3 **10** [a]1 Sam. 8:3 **12** [a]Ps. 40:2

PSALM 26 (NKJV)

A Prayer for Divine Scrutiny and Redemption

A Psalm of David.

VINDICATE [a]me, O LORD,
For I have [b]walked in my integrity.
[c]I have also trusted in the LORD;
I shall not slip.
2 [a]Examine me, O LORD, and prove me;
Try my mind and my heart.
3 For Your lovingkindness *is* before my eyes,
And [a]I have walked in Your truth.
4 I have not [a]sat with idolatrous mortals,
Nor will I go in with hypocrites.
5 I have [a]hated the assembly of evildoers,
And will not sit with the wicked.

6 I will wash my hands in innocence;
So I will go about Your altar, O LORD,
7 That I may proclaim with the voice of thanksgiving,
And tell of all Your wondrous works.
8 LORD, [a]I have loved the habitation of Your house,
And the place where Your glory dwells.

9 [a]Do not gather my soul with sinners,
Nor my life with bloodthirsty men,
10 In whose hands *is* a sinister scheme,
And whose right hand is full of [a]bribes.

11 But as for me, I will walk in my integrity;
Redeem me and be merciful to me.
12 [a]My foot stands in an even place;
In the congregations I will bless the LORD.

PSALM 27 (KJV)

An Exuberant Declaration of Faith

A *Psalm* of David.

THE LORD *is* my [a]light and my salvation; whom shall I fear? the [b]LORD *is* the strength of my life; of whom shall I be afraid?
2 When the wicked, *even* mine enemies and my foes, came upon me to [a]eat up my flesh, they stumbled and fell.
3 [a]Though an host should encamp against me, my heart shall not fear: though war should rise against me, in this *will* I *be* confident.
4 [a]One *thing* have I desired of the LORD, that will I seek after; that I may [b]dwell in the house of the LORD all the days of my life, to behold the beauty of the LORD, and to enquire in his temple.
5 For [a]in the time of trouble he shall hide me in his pavilion: in the secret of his tabernacle shall he hide me; he shall [b]set me up upon a rock.
6 And now shall [a]mine head be lifted up above mine enemies round about me: therefore will I offer in his tabernacle sacrifices of joy; I will sing, yea, I will sing praises unto the LORD.
7 Hear, O LORD, *when* I cry with my voice: have mercy also upon me, and answer me.
8 *When thou saidst,* Seek ye my face; my heart said unto thee, Thy face, LORD, will I seek.
9 [a]Hide not thy face *far* from me; put not thy servant away in anger: thou hast been my

PSALM 27

1 [a]Ps. 18:28; 84:11; [Is. 60:19, 20; Mic. 7:8] [b]Ex. 15:2; Ps. 62:7; 118:14; Is. 12:2; 33:2 **2** [a]Ps. 14:4 **3** [a]Ps. 3:6 **4** [a]Ps. 26:8; 65:4 [b]Luke 2:37 **5** [a]Ps. 31:20; 91:1 [b]Ps. 40:2 **6** [a]Ps. 3:3 **9** [a]Ps. 69:17; 143:7

PSALM 27 (NKJV)

An Exuberant Declaration of Faith

A Psalm of David.

THE LORD *is* my [a]light and my salvation;
Whom shall I fear?
The [b]LORD *is* the strength of my life;
Of whom shall I be afraid?
2 When the wicked came against me
To [a]eat up my flesh,
My enemies and foes,
They stumbled and fell.
3 [a]Though an army may encamp against me,
My heart shall not fear;
Though war may rise against me,
In this I *will be* confident.

4 [a]One *thing* I have desired of the LORD,
That will I seek:
That I may [b]dwell in the house of the LORD
All the days of my life,
To behold the beauty of the LORD,
And to inquire in His temple.
5 For [a]in the time of trouble
He shall hide me in His pavilion;
In the secret place of His tabernacle
He shall hide me;
He shall [b]set me high upon a rock.

6 And now [a]my head shall be lifted up above my enemies all around me;
Therefore I will offer sacrifices of joy in His tabernacle;
I will sing, yes, I will sing praises to the LORD.

7 Hear, O LORD, *when* I cry with my voice!
Have mercy also upon me, and answer me.
8 *When You said,* "Seek My face,"
My heart said to You, "Your face, LORD, I will seek."
9 [a]Do not hide Your face from me;
Do not turn Your servant away in anger;

KJV

help; leave me not, neither forsake me, O God of
my salvation.
10 [a]When my father and my mother forsake
me, then the LORD will take me up.
11 [a]Teach me thy way, O LORD, and lead me
in a plain path, because of mine enemies.
12 Deliver me not over unto the will of mine
enemies: for [a]false witnesses are risen up against
me, and such as breathe out cruelty.
13 *I had fainted,* unless I had believed to see
the goodness of the LORD [a]in the land of the living.
14 [a]Wait on the LORD: be of good courage,
and he shall strengthen thine heart: wait, I say,
on the LORD.

PSALM 28

Rejoicing in Answered Prayer

A Psalm of David.

UNTO thee will I cry, O LORD my rock; [a]be not
silent to me: [b]lest, *if* thou be silent to me, I
become like them that go down into the pit.
2 Hear the voice of my supplications, when
I cry unto thee, [a]when I lift up my hands [b]toward
thy holy oracle.
3 Draw me not away with the wicked, and
with the workers of iniquity, [a]which speak peace
to their neighbours, but mischief *is* in their hearts.
4 [a]Give them according to their deeds, and
according to the wickedness of their endeavours:
give them after the work of their hands; render
to them their desert.
5 Because [a]they regard not the works of the
LORD, nor the operation of his hands, he shall destroy them, and not build them up.
6 Blessed *be* the LORD, because he hath
heard the voice of my supplications.
7 The LORD *is* [a]my strength and my shield;
my heart [b]trusted in him, and I am helped: therefore my heart greatly rejoiceth; and with my song
will I praise him.
8 The LORD *is* their strength, and he *is* the
[a]saving strength of his anointed.
9 Save thy people, and bless [a]thine inheritance: feed them also, [b]and lift them up for ever.

PSALM 29

Praise to God in His Holiness and Majesty

A Psalm of David.

GIVE [a]unto the LORD, O ye mighty, give unto
the LORD glory and strength.
2 Give unto the LORD the glory due unto his
name; worship the LORD in [a]the beauty of
holiness.

---

10 [a]Is. 49:15
11 [a]Ps. 25:4; 86:11; 119:33
12 [a]Deut. 19:18; Ps. 35:11; Matt. 26:60; Mark 14:56; John 19:33
13 [a]Job 28:13; Ps. 52:5; 116:9; 142:5; Is. 38:11; Jer. 11:19; Ezek. 26:20
14 [a]Ps. 25:3; 37:34; 40:1; 62:5; 130:5; Prov. 20:22; Is. 25:9; [Hab. 2:3]

PSALM 28

1 [a]Ps. 35:22; 39:12; 83:1 [b]Ps. 88:4; 143:7; Prov. 1:12
2 [a]Ps. 5:7 [b]Ps. 138:2
3 [a]Ps. 12:2; 52:21; 62:4; Jer. 9:8
4 [a][Ps. 62:12]; 2 Tim. 4:14; [Rev. 18:6; 22:12]
5 [a]Is. 5:12
7 [a]Ps. 18:2; 59:17 [b]Ps. 13:5; 112:7
8 [a]Ps. 20:6
9 [a][Deut. 9:29; 32:9; 1 Kin. 8:51; Ps. 33:12]; 106:40 [b]Deut. 1:31; Is. 63:9

PSALM 29

1 [a]1 Chr. 16:28, 29
2 [a]2 Chr. 20:21; Ps. 110:3

*———

28:8 So with MT, Tg.; LXX, Syr., Vg. *the strength of His people*

NKJV

You have been my help;
Do not leave me nor forsake me,
O God of my salvation.
10 [a]When my father and my mother forsake me,
Then the LORD will take care of me.

11 [a]Teach me Your way, O LORD,
And lead me in a smooth path, because of my enemies.
12 Do not deliver me to the will of my adversaries;
For [a]false witnesses have risen against me,
And such as breathe out violence.
13 *I would have lost heart,* unless I had believed
That I would see the goodness of the LORD
[a]In the land of the living.

14 [a]Wait on the LORD;
Be of good courage,
And He shall strengthen your heart;
Wait, I say, on the LORD!

PSALM 28

Rejoicing in Answered Prayer

A Psalm of David.

TO You I will cry, O LORD my Rock:
[a]Do not be silent to me,
[b]Lest, if You *are* silent to me,
I become like those who go down to the pit.
2 Hear the voice of my supplications
When I cry to You,
[a]When I lift up my hands [b]toward Your holy sanctuary.

3 Do not take me away with the wicked
And with the workers of iniquity,
[a]Who speak peace to their neighbors,
But evil *is* in their hearts.
4 [a]Give them according to their deeds,
And according to the wickedness of their endeavors;
Give them according to the work of their hands;
Render to them what they deserve.
5 Because [a]they do not regard the works of the LORD,
Nor the operation of His hands,
He shall destroy them
And not build them up.

6 Blessed *be* the LORD,
Because He has heard the voice of my supplications!
7 The LORD *is* [a]my strength and my shield;
My heart [b]trusted in Him, and I am helped;
Therefore my heart greatly rejoices,
And with my song I will praise Him.

8 The LORD *is* *their strength,
And He *is* the [a]saving refuge of His anointed.
9 Save Your people,
And bless [a]Your inheritance;
Shepherd them also,
[b]And bear them up forever.

PSALM 29

Praise to God in His Holiness and Majesty

A Psalm of David.

GIVE [a]unto the LORD, O you mighty ones,
Give unto the LORD glory and strength.
2 Give unto the LORD the glory due to His name;
Worship the LORD in [a]the beauty of holiness.

KJV

3 The voice of the LORD *is* upon the waters:
[a]the God of glory thundereth: the LORD *is* upon
many waters.
4 The voice of the LORD *is* powerful; the
voice of the LORD *is* full of majesty.
5 The voice of the LORD breaketh [a]the cedars; yea, the LORD breaketh the cedars of Lebanon.
6 [a]He maketh them also to skip like a calf;
Lebanon and [b]Sirion like a young unicorn.
7 The voice of the LORD divideth the flames
of fire.
8 The voice of the LORD shaketh the wilderness; the LORD shaketh the wilderness of [a]Kadesh.
9 The voice of the LORD maketh the [a]hinds
to calve, and discovereth the forests: and in his
temple doth every one speak of *his* glory.
10 The [a]LORD sitteth upon the flood; yea, [b]the
LORD sitteth King for ever.
11 [a]The LORD will give strength unto his people; the LORD will bless his people with peace.

PSALM 30

The Blessedness of Answered Prayer

A Psalm *and* Song [a]*at* the dedication of the house of David.

I WILL extol thee, O LORD; for thou hast [a]lifted
me up, and hast not made my foes to [b]rejoice
over me.
2 O LORD my God, I cried unto thee, and
thou hast [a]healed me.
3 O LORD, [a]thou hast brought up my soul
from the grave: thou hast kept me alive, that I
should not go down to the pit.
4 [a]Sing unto the LORD, O ye saints of his,
and give thanks at the remembrance of his
holiness.
5 For [a]his anger *endureth but* a moment;
[b]in his favour *is* life: weeping may endure for a
night, but joy *cometh* in the morning.
6 And in my prosperity I said, I shall never
be moved.
7 LORD, by thy favour thou hast made my
mountain to stand strong: [a]thou didst hide thy
face, *and* I was troubled.
8 I cried to thee, O LORD; and unto the LORD
I made supplication.
9 What profit *is there* in my blood, when I
go down to the pit? [a]Shall the dust praise thee?
shall it declare thy truth?
10 Hear, O LORD, and have mercy upon me:
LORD, be thou my helper.
11 [a]Thou hast turned for me my mourning
into dancing: thou hast put off my sackcloth, and
girded me with gladness;
12 To the end that *my* glory may sing praise
to thee, and not be silent. O LORD my God, I will
give thanks unto thee for ever.

3 [a][Job 37:4, 5]; Ps. 18:13; Acts 7:2
5 [a]Judg. 9:15; 1 Kin. 5:6; Ps. 104:16; Is. 2:13; 14:8
6 [a]Ps. 114:4 [b]Deut. 3:9
8 [a]Num. 13:26
9 [a]Job 39:1
10 [a]Gen. 6:17; Job 38:8, 25 [b]Ps. 10:16
11 [a]Ps. 28:8; 68:35; [Is. 40:29]

PSALM 30

title [a]Deut. 20:5
1 [a]Ps. 28:9 [b]Ps. 25:2
2 [a]Ps. 6:2; 103:3; [Is. 53:5]
3 [a]Ps. 86:13
4 [a]Ps. 97:12
5 [a]Ps. 103:9; Is. 26:20; 54:7, 8 [b]Ps. 63:3
7 [a][Deut. 31:17; Ps. 104:29; 143:7]
9 [a][Ps. 6:5]
11 [a]Eccl. 3:4; Is. 61:3; Jer. 31:4

NKJV

3 The voice of the LORD *is* over the
waters;
[a]The God of glory thunders;
The LORD *is* over many waters.
4 The voice of the LORD *is* powerful;
The voice of the LORD *is* full of majesty.

5 The voice of the LORD breaks [a]the cedars,
Yes, the LORD splinters the cedars of
Lebanon.
6 [a]He makes them also skip like a calf,
Lebanon and [b]Sirion like a young wild
ox.
7 The voice of the LORD divides the flames
of fire.

8 The voice of the LORD shakes the
wilderness;
The LORD shakes the Wilderness of
[a]Kadesh.
9 The voice of the LORD makes the [a]deer
give birth,
And strips the forests bare;
And in His temple everyone says,
"Glory!"

10 The [a]LORD sat *enthroned* at the Flood,
And [b]the LORD sits as King forever.
11 [a]The LORD will give strength to His
people;
The LORD will bless His people with
peace.

PSALM 30

The Blessedness of Answered Prayer

A Psalm. A Song [a]at the dedication of the house of David.

I WILL extol You, O LORD, for You have [a]lifted
me up,
And have not let my foes [b]rejoice over
me.
2 O LORD my God, I cried out to You,
And You [a]healed me.
3 O LORD, [a]You brought my soul up from
the grave;
You have kept me alive, *that I should not
go down to the pit.

4 [a]Sing praise to the LORD, you saints of
His,
And give thanks at the remembrance of
*His holy name.
5 For [a]His anger *is but for* a moment,
[b]His favor *is for* life;
Weeping may endure for a night,
But joy *comes* in the morning.

6 Now in my prosperity I said,
"I shall never be moved."
7 LORD, by Your favor You have made my
mountain stand strong;
[a]You hid Your face, *and* I was troubled.

8 I cried out to You, O LORD;
And to the LORD I made supplication:
9 "What profit *is there* in my blood,
When I go down to the pit?
[a]Will the dust praise You?
Will it declare Your truth?
10 Hear, O LORD, and have mercy on me;
LORD, be my helper!"

11 [a]You have turned for me my mourning into
dancing;
You have put off my sackcloth and clothed
me with gladness,
12 To the end that *my* glory may sing praise
to You and not be silent.
O LORD my God, I will give thanks to You
forever.

30:3 So with Qr., Tg.; Kt., LXX, Syr., Vg. *from those who descend to the pit*
30:4 Or *His holiness*

KJV

PSALM 31

The LORD a Fortress in Adversity

To the chief Musician, A Psalm of David.

IN [a]thee, O LORD, do I put my trust; let me never be ashamed: deliver me in thy righteousness.

2 [a]Bow down thine ear to me; deliver me speedily: be thou my strong rock, for an house of defence to save me.

3 [a]For thou *art* my rock and my fortress; therefore [b]for thy name's sake lead me, and guide me.

4 Pull me out of the net that they have laid privily for me: for thou *art* my strength.

5 [a]Into thine hand I commit my spirit: thou hast redeemed me, O LORD God of [b]truth.

6 I have hated them [a]that regard lying vanities: but I trust in the LORD.

7 I will be glad and rejoice in thy mercy: for thou hast considered my trouble; thou hast [a]known my soul in adversities;

8 And hast not [a]shut me up into the hand of the enemy: [b]thou hast set my feet in a large room.

9 Have mercy upon me, O LORD, for I am in trouble: [a]mine eye is consumed with grief, *yea,* my soul and my belly.

10 For my life is spent with grief, and my years with sighing: my strength faileth because of mine iniquity, and my bones are consumed.

11 [a]I was a reproach among all mine enemies, but [b]especially among my neighbours, and a fear to mine acquaintance: [c]they that did see me without fled from me.

12 [a]I am forgotten as a dead man out of mind: I am like a broken vessel.

13 [a]For I have heard the slander of many: [b]fear *was* on every side: while they [c]took counsel together against me, they devised to take away my life.

14 But I trusted in thee, O LORD: I said, Thou *art* my God.

15 My times *are* in thy [a]hand: deliver me from the hand of mine enemies, and from them that persecute me.

16 [a]Make thy face to shine upon thy servant: save me for thy mercies' sake.

17 [a]Let me not be ashamed, O LORD; for I have called upon thee: let the wicked be ashamed, *and* [b]let them be silent in the grave.

18 [a]Let the lying lips be put to silence; which [b]speak grievous things proudly and contemptuously against the righteous.

19 [a]*Oh* how great *is* thy goodness, which thou hast laid up for them that fear thee; *which* thou hast wrought for them that trust in thee before the sons of men!

20 [a]Thou shalt hide them in the secret of thy presence from the pride of man: [b]thou shalt keep them secretly in a pavilion from the strife of tongues.

PSALM 31

1 [a]Ps. 22:5
2 [a]Ps. 17:6; 71:2; 86:1; 102:2
3 [a][Ps. 18:2] [b]Ps. 23:3; 25:11
5 [a]Luke 23:46 [b][Deut. 32:4]; Ps. 71:22
6 [a]Jon. 2:8
7 [a][John 10:27]
8 [a][Deut. 32:30]; Ps. 37:33 [b][Ps. 4:1; 18:19]
9 [a]Ps. 6:7
11 [a][Is. 53:4] [b]Job 19:13; Ps. 38:11; 88:8, 18 [c]Ps. 64:8
12 [a]Ps. 88:4, 5
13 [a]Ps. 50:20; Jer. 20:10 [b]Lam. 2:22 [c]Ps. 62:4; Matt. 27:1
15 [a][Job 14:5; 24:1]
16 [a]Ps. 4:6; 80:3
17 [a]Ps. 25:2, 20 [b][1 Sam. 2:9]; Ps. 94:17; 115:17
18 [a]Ps. 109:2; 120:2 [b][1 Sam. 2:3]; Ps. 94:4; [Jude 15]
19 [a]Ps. 145:7; [Rom. 2:4; 11:22]
20 [a][Ps. 27:5; 32:7] [b]Job 5:21

NKJV

PSALM 31

The LORD a Fortress in Adversity

To the Chief Musician. A Psalm of David.

IN [a]You, O LORD, I put my trust;
Let me never be ashamed;
Deliver me in Your righteousness.
2 [a]Bow down Your ear to me,
Deliver me speedily;
Be my rock of refuge,
A fortress of defense to save me.

3 [a]For You *are* my rock and my fortress;
Therefore, [b]for Your name's sake,
Lead me and guide me.
4 Pull me out of the net which they have secretly laid for me,
For You *are* my strength.
5 [a]Into Your hand I commit my spirit;
You have redeemed me, O LORD God of [b]truth.

6 I have hated those [a]who regard useless idols;
But I trust in the LORD.
7 I will be glad and rejoice in Your mercy,
For You have considered my trouble;
You have [a]known my soul in adversities,
8 And have not [a]shut me up into the hand of the enemy;
[b]You have set my feet in a wide place.

9 Have mercy on me, O LORD, for I am in trouble;
[a]My eye wastes away with grief,
Yes, my soul and my body!
10 For my life is spent with grief,
And my years with sighing;
My strength fails because of my iniquity,
And my bones waste away.
11 [a]I am a reproach among all my enemies,
But [b]especially among my neighbors,
And *am* repulsive to my acquaintances;
[c]Those who see me outside flee from me.
12 [a]I am forgotten like a dead man, out of mind;
I am like a broken vessel.
13 [a]For I hear the slander of many;
[b]Fear *is* on every side;
While they [c]take counsel together against me,
They scheme to take away my life.

14 But as for me, I trust in You, O LORD;
I say, "You *are* my God."
15 My times *are* in Your [a]hand;
Deliver me from the hand of my enemies,
And from those who persecute me.
16 [a]Make Your face shine upon Your servant;
Save me for Your mercies' sake.
17 [a]Do not let me be ashamed, O LORD, for I have called upon You;
Let the wicked be ashamed;
[b]Let them be silent in the grave.
18 [a]Let the lying lips be put to silence,
Which [b]speak insolent things proudly and contemptuously against the righteous.

19 [a]Oh, how great *is* Your goodness,
Which You have laid up for those who fear You,
Which You have prepared for those who trust in You
In the presence of the sons of men!
20 [a]You shall hide them in the secret place of Your presence
From the plots of man;
[b]You shall keep them secretly in a pavilion
From the strife of tongues.

KJV

21 Blessed *be* the LORD: for [a]he hath shewed me his marvellous kindness in a strong city.
22 For I said in my haste, I am cut off from before thine eyes: nevertheless thou heardest the voice of my supplications when I cried unto thee.
23 O love the LORD, all ye his saints: *for* the LORD preserveth the faithful, and plentifully rewardeth the proud doer.
24 [a]Be of good courage, and he shall strengthen your heart, all ye that hope in the LORD.

PSALM 32

The Joy of Forgiveness

A *Psalm* of David, Maschil.

BLESSED *is he whose* [a]transgression *is* forgiven, *whose* sin *is* covered.
2 Blessed *is* the man unto whom the LORD [a]imputeth not iniquity, and [b]in whose spirit *there is* no guile.
3 When I kept silence, my bones waxed old through my roaring all the day long.
4 For day and night thy [a]hand was heavy upon me: my moisture is turned into the drought of summer. Selah.
5 I acknowledged my sin unto thee, and mine iniquity have I not hid. [a]I said, I will confess my transgressions unto the LORD; and thou forgavest the iniquity of my sin. Selah.
6 [a]For this shall every one that is godly [b]pray unto thee in a time when thou mayest be found: surely in the floods of great waters they shall not come nigh unto him.
7 [a]Thou *art* my hiding place; thou shalt preserve me from trouble; thou shalt compass me about with [b]songs of deliverance. Selah.
8 I will instruct thee and teach thee in the way which thou shalt go: I will guide thee with mine eye.
9 Be ye not as the [a]horse, *or* as the mule, *which* have no understanding: whose mouth must be held in with bit and bridle, lest they come near unto thee.
10 [a]Many sorrows *shall be* to the wicked: but [b]he that trusteth in the LORD, mercy shall compass him about.
11 [a]Be glad in the LORD, and rejoice, ye righteous: and shout for joy, all *ye that are* upright in heart.

PSALM 33

The Sovereignty of the LORD in Creation and History

REJOICE [a]in the LORD, O ye righteous: *for* praise is comely for the upright.
2 Praise the LORD with harp: sing unto him with the psaltery *and* an instrument of ten strings.
3 Sing unto him a new song; play skilfully with a loud noise.
4 For the word of the LORD *is* right; and all his works *are done* in truth.

---

21 [a][Ps. 17:7] **24** [a][Ps. 27:14]

PSALM 32

1 [a][Ps. 85:2; 103:3]; Rom. 4:7, 8 **2** [a][2 Cor. 5:19] [b]John 1:47 **4** [a]1 Sam. 5:6; Ps. 38:2; 39:10 **5** [a]2 Sam. 12:13; Ps. 38:18; [Prov. 28:13; 1 John 1:9] **6** [a][1 Tim. 1:16] [b]Ps. 69:13; Is. 55:6 **7** [a]Ps. 9:9 [b]Ex. 15:1; Judg. 5:1; [Ps. 40:3] **9** [a]Prov. 26:3 **10** [a]Ps. 16:4; [Prov. 13:21; Rom. 2:9] [b][Ps. 5:11, 12]; Prov. 16:20 **11** [a]Ps. 64:10; 68:3; 97:12

PSALM 33

1 [a]Ps. 32:11; 97:12; Phil. 3:1; 4:4

*

32:title Heb. *Maschil*

NKJV

21 Blessed *be* the LORD,
For [a]He has shown me His marvelous kindness in a strong city!
22 For I said in my haste,
"I am cut off from before Your eyes";
Nevertheless You heard the voice of my supplications
When I cried out to You.

23 Oh, love the LORD, all you His saints!
For the LORD preserves the faithful,
And fully repays the proud person.
24 [a]Be of good courage,
And He shall strengthen your heart,
All you who hope in the LORD.

PSALM 32

The Joy of Forgiveness

A Psalm of David. A *Contemplation.

BLESSED *is he whose* [a]transgression *is* forgiven,
Whose sin *is* covered.
2 Blessed *is* the man to whom the LORD [a]does not impute iniquity,
And [b]in whose spirit *there is* no deceit.

3 When I kept silent, my bones grew old
Through my groaning all the day long.
4 For day and night Your [a]hand was heavy upon me;
My vitality was turned into the drought of summer. Selah
5 I acknowledged my sin to You,
And my iniquity I have not hidden.
[a]I said, "I will confess my transgressions to the LORD,"
And You forgave the iniquity of my sin. Selah

6 [a]For this cause everyone who is godly shall [b]pray to You
In a time when You may be found;
Surely in a flood of great waters
They shall not come near him.
7 [a]You *are* my hiding place;
You shall preserve me from trouble;
You shall surround me with [b]songs of deliverance. Selah

8 I will instruct you and teach you in the way you should go;
I will guide you with My eye.
9 Do not be like the [a]horse *or* like the mule,
Which have no understanding,
Which must be harnessed with bit and bridle,
Else they will not come near you.

10 [a]Many sorrows *shall be* to the wicked;
But [b]he who trusts in the LORD, mercy shall surround him.
11 [a]Be glad in the LORD and rejoice, you righteous;
And shout for joy, all *you* upright in heart!

PSALM 33

The Sovereignty of the LORD in Creation and History

REJOICE [a]in the LORD, O you righteous!
For praise from the upright is beautiful.
2 Praise the LORD with the harp;
Make melody to Him with an instrument of ten strings.
3 Sing to Him a new song;
Play skillfully with a shout of joy.

4 For the word of the LORD *is* right,
And all His work *is done* in truth.

KJV

5 He loveth righteousness and judgment:
the earth is full of the goodness of the LORD.
6 [a]By the word of the LORD were the heavens made; and all the [b]host of them [c]by the breath
of his mouth.
7 [a]He gathereth the waters of the sea together as an heap: he layeth up the depth in
storehouses.
8 Let all the earth fear the LORD: let all the
inhabitants of the world stand in awe of him.
9 For [a]he spake, and it was *done;* he commanded, and it stood fast.
10 [a]The LORD bringeth the counsel of the
heathen to nought: he maketh the devices of the
people of none effect.
11 [a]The counsel of the LORD standeth for
ever, the thoughts of his heart to all generations.
12 Blessed *is* the nation whose God *is* the
LORD; *and* the people *whom* he hath [a]chosen for
his own inheritance.
13 [a]The LORD looketh from heaven; he beholdeth all the sons of men.
14 From the place of his habitation he looketh upon all the inhabitants of the earth.
15 He fashioneth their hearts alike; [a]he considereth all their works.
16 [a]There is no king saved by the multitude
of an host: a mighty man is not delivered by much
strength.
17 [a]An horse *is* a vain thing for safety: neither shall he deliver *any* by his great strength.
18 [a]Behold, the eye of the LORD *is* upon them
that fear him, upon them that hope in his mercy;
19 To deliver their soul from death, and [a]to
keep them alive in famine.
20 Our soul waiteth for the LORD: he *is* our
help and our shield.
21 For our heart shall rejoice in him, because
we have trusted in his holy name.
22 Let thy mercy, O LORD, be upon us, according as we hope in thee.

PSALM 34

The Happiness of Those Who Trust in God

A *Psalm* of David, [a]when he changed his behaviour before Abimelech; who drove him away, and he departed.

I WILL [a]bless the LORD at all times: his praise
shall continually *be* in my mouth.
2 My soul shall make her boast in the LORD:
the humble shall hear *thereof,* and be glad.
3 O magnify the LORD with me, and let us
exalt his name together.
4 I [a]sought the LORD, and he heard me, and
delivered me from all my fears.
5 They looked unto him, and were lightened: and their faces were not ashamed.
6 This poor man cried, and the LORD heard
him, and saved him out of all his troubles.
7 [a]The angel of the LORD [b]encampeth round
about them that fear him, and delivereth them.

---

6 [a]Gen. 1:6, 7; Ps. 148:5; [Heb. 11:3; 2 Pet. 3:5] [b]Gen. 2:1 [c][Job 26:13]
7 [a]Gen. 1:9; Job 26:10; 38:8
9 [a]Gen. 1:3; Ps. 148:5
10 [a][Ps. 2:1–3]; Is. 8:10; 19:3
11 [a][Job 23:13; Prov. 19:21]
12 [a][Ex. 19:5; Deut. 7:6]; Ps. 28:9
13 [a]Job 28:24; [Ps. 14:2]
15 [a][2 Chr. 16:9]; Job 34:21; [Jer. 32:19]
16 [a]Ps. 44:6; 60:11; [Jer. 9:23, 24]
17 [a][Ps. 20:7; 147:10; Prov. 21:31]
18 [a][Job 36:7]; Ps. 32:8; 34:15; [1 Pet. 3:12]
19 [a]Job 5:20; Ps. 37:19

PSALM 34

title [a]1 Sam. 21:10–15
1 [a][Eph. 5:20; 1 Thess. 5:18]
4 [a][2 Chr. 15:2; Ps. 9:10; Matt. 7:7; Luke 11:9]
7 [a][Ps. 91:11]; Dan. 6:22 [b]2 Kin. 6:17

---

*

33:7 LXX, Tg., Vg. *in a vessel*
34:7 Or *Angel*

NKJV

5 He loves righteousness and justice;
The earth is full of the goodness of the
LORD.

6 [a]By the word of the LORD the heavens were
made,
And all the [b]host of them [c]by the breath
of His mouth.
7 [a]He gathers the waters of the sea together
*as a heap;
He lays up the deep in storehouses.

8 Let all the earth fear the LORD;
Let all the inhabitants of the world stand
in awe of Him.
9 For [a]He spoke, and it was *done;*
He commanded, and it stood fast.

10 [a]The LORD brings the counsel of the nations
to nothing;
He makes the plans of the peoples of no
effect.
11 [a]The counsel of the LORD stands forever,
The plans of His heart to all generations.
12 Blessed *is* the nation whose God *is* the
LORD,
The people He has [a]chosen as His own
inheritance.

13 [a]The LORD looks from heaven;
He sees all the sons of men.
14 From the place of His dwelling He looks
On all the inhabitants of the earth;
15 He fashions their hearts individually;
[a]He considers all their works.

16 [a]No king *is* saved by the multitude of an
army;
A mighty man is not delivered by great
strength.
17 [a]A horse *is* a vain hope for safety;
Neither shall it deliver *any* by its great
strength.

18 [a]Behold, the eye of the LORD *is* on those
who fear Him,
On those who hope in His mercy,
19 To deliver their soul from death,
And [a]to keep them alive in famine.

20 Our soul waits for the LORD;
He *is* our help and our shield.
21 For our heart shall rejoice in Him,
Because we have trusted in His holy name.
22 Let Your mercy, O LORD, be upon us,
Just as we hope in You.

PSALM 34

The Happiness of Those Who Trust in God

A Psalm of David [a]when he pretended madness before Abimelech, who drove him away, and he departed.

I WILL [a]bless the LORD at all times;
His praise *shall* continually *be* in my
mouth.
2 My soul shall make its boast in the LORD;
The humble shall hear *of it* and be glad.
3 Oh, magnify the LORD with me,
And let us exalt His name together.

4 I [a]sought the LORD, and He heard me,
And delivered me from all my fears.
5 They looked to Him and were radiant,
And their faces were not ashamed.
6 This poor man cried out, and the LORD
heard *him,*
And saved him out of all his troubles.
7 [a]The *angel of the LORD [b]encamps all
around those who fear Him,
And delivers them.

KJV

8 O [a]taste and see that the LORD *is* good: [b]blessed *is* the man *that* trusteth in him.
9 O fear the LORD, ye his saints: for *there is* no want to them that fear him.
10 The young lions do lack, and suffer hunger: [a]but they that seek the LORD shall not want any good *thing*.
11 Come, ye children, hearken unto me: [a]I will teach you the fear of the LORD.
12 [a]What man *is he that* desireth life, *and* loveth *many* days, that he may see good?
13 Keep thy tongue from evil, and thy lips from speaking [a]guile.
14 [a]Depart from evil, and do good; [b]seek peace, and pursue it.
15 [a]The eyes of the LORD *are* upon the righteous, and his ears *are open* unto their cry.
16 [a]The face of the LORD *is* against them that do evil, [b]to cut off the remembrance of them from the earth.
17 *The righteous* cry, and [a]the LORD heareth, and delivereth them out of all their troubles.
18 [a]The LORD *is* nigh [b]unto them that are of a broken heart; and saveth such as be of a contrite spirit.
19 [a]Many *are* the afflictions of the righteous: [b]but the LORD delivereth him out of them all.
20 He keepeth all his bones: [a]not one of them is broken.
21 [a]Evil shall slay the wicked: and they that hate the righteous shall be desolate.
22 The LORD [a]redeemeth the soul of his servants: and none of them that trust in him shall be desolate.

8 [a]Ps. 119:103; [Heb. 6:5]; 1 Pet. 2:3 [b]Ps. 2:12
10 [a][Ps. 84:11]
11 [a]Ps. 32:8
12 [a][1 Pet. 3:10–12]
13 [a][Eph. 4:25]
14 [a]Ps. 37:27; Is. 1:16, 17 [b][Rom. 14:19; Heb. 12:14]
15 [a]Job 36:7; [Ps. 33:18]
16 [a]Lev. 17:10; Jer. 44:11; Amos 9:4 [b]Job 18:17; Ps. 9:6; 109:15; [Prov. 10:7]
17 [a]Ps. 34:6; 145:19
18 [a][Ps. 145:18] [b]Ps. 51:17; [Is. 57:15]
19 [a]Prov. 24:16 [b]Ps. 34:4, 6, 17
20 [a]John 19:33, 36
21 [a]Ps. 94:23; 140:11; Prov. 24:16
22 [a]1 Kin. 1:29

NKJV

8 Oh, [a]taste and see that the LORD *is* good;
[b]Blessed *is* the man *who* trusts in Him!
9 Oh, fear the LORD, you His saints!
There is no want to those who fear Him.
10 The young lions lack and suffer hunger;
[a]But those who seek the LORD shall not lack any good *thing*.

11 Come, you children, listen to me;
[a]I will teach you the fear of the LORD.
12 [a]Who *is* the man *who* desires life,
And loves *many* days, that he may see good?
13 Keep your tongue from evil,
And your lips from speaking [a]deceit.
14 [a]Depart from evil and do good;
[b]Seek peace and pursue it.

15 [a]The eyes of the LORD *are* on the righteous,
And His ears *are open* to their cry.
16 [a]The face of the LORD *is* against those who do evil,
[b]To cut off the remembrance of them from the earth.

17 *The righteous* cry out, and [a]the LORD hears,
And delivers them out of all their troubles.
18 [a]The LORD *is* near [b]to those who have a broken heart,
And saves such as have a contrite spirit.

19 [a]Many *are* the afflictions of the righteous,
[b]But the LORD delivers him out of them all.
20 He guards all his bones;
[a]Not one of them is broken.
21 [a]Evil shall slay the wicked,
And those who hate the righteous shall be condemned.
22 The LORD [a]redeems the soul of His servants,
And none of those who trust in Him shall be condemned.

PSALM 35

The LORD *the Avenger of His People*

A Psalm of David.

PLEAD *my cause,* O LORD, with them that strive with me: fight against them that fight against me.
2 Take hold of shield and buckler, and stand up for mine help.
3 Draw out also the spear, and stop *the way* against them that persecute me: say unto my soul, I *am* thy salvation.
4 [a]Let them be confounded and put to shame that seek after my soul: let them be [b]turned back and brought to confusion that devise my hurt.
5 [a]Let them be as chaff before the wind: and let the angel of the LORD chase *them*.
6 Let their way be [a]dark and slippery: and let the angel of the LORD persecute them.
7 For without cause have they [a]hid for me their net *in* a pit, *which* without cause they have digged for my soul.
8 Let [a]destruction come upon him at unawares; and let his net that he hath hid catch himself: into that very destruction let him fall.
9 And my soul shall be joyful in the LORD: it shall rejoice in his salvation.

PSALM 35

4 [a]Ps. 40:14, 15; 70:2, 3 [b]Ps. 129:5
5 [a]Job 21:18; Ps. 83:13; Is. 29:5
6 [a]Ps. 73:18; Jer. 23:12
7 [a]Ps. 9:15
8 [a][Ps. 55:23]; Is. 47:11; [1 Thess. 5:3]

PSALM 35

The LORD *the Avenger of His People*

A Psalm of David.

PLEAD *my cause,* O LORD, with those who strive with me;
Fight against those who fight against me.
2 Take hold of shield and buckler,
And stand up for my help.
3 Also draw out the spear,
And stop those who pursue me.
Say to my soul,
"I *am* your salvation."

4 [a]Let those be put to shame and brought to dishonor
Who seek after my life;
Let those be [b]turned back and brought to confusion
Who plot my hurt.
5 [a]Let them be like chaff before the wind,
And let the *angel of the LORD chase *them*.
6 Let their way be [a]dark and slippery,
And let the angel of the LORD pursue them.
7 For without cause they have [a]hidden their net for me *in* a pit,
Which they have dug without cause for my life.
8 Let [a]destruction come upon him unexpectedly,
And let his net that he has hidden catch himself;
Into that very destruction let him fall.

9 And my soul shall be joyful in the LORD;
It shall rejoice in His salvation.

*———
35:5 Or *Angel*

KJV

10 [a]All my bones shall say, LORD, [b]who *is* like unto thee, which deliverest the poor from him that is too strong for him, yea, the poor and the needy from him that spoileth him?

11 False witnesses did rise up; they laid to my charge *things* that I knew not.

12 [a]They rewarded me evil for good *to* the spoiling of my soul.

13 But as for me, [a]when they were sick, my clothing *was* sackcloth: I humbled my soul with fasting; and my prayer returned into mine own bosom.

14 I behaved myself as though *he had been* my friend *or* brother: I bowed down heavily, as one that mourneth *for his* mother.

15 But in mine adversity they rejoiced, and gathered themselves together: *yea,* the abjects gathered themselves together against me, and I knew *it* not; they did tear *me,* and ceased not:

16 With hypocritical mockers in feasts, they gnashed upon me with their teeth.

17 LORD, how long wilt thou [a]look on? rescue my soul from their destructions, my darling from the lions.

18 I will give thee thanks in the great congregation: I will praise thee among much people.

19 [a]Let not them that are mine enemies wrongfully rejoice over me: *neither* let them wink with the eye that hate me without a cause.

20 For they speak not peace: but they devise deceitful matters against *them that are* quiet in the land.

21 Yea, they opened their mouth wide against me, *and* said, Aha, aha, our eye hath seen *it.*

22 *This* thou hast seen, O LORD: keep not silence: O Lord, be not far from me.

23 Stir up thyself, and awake to my judgment, *even* unto my cause, my God and my Lord.

24 Judge me, O LORD my God, according to thy righteousness; and let them not rejoice over me.

25 Let them not say in their hearts, Ah, so would we have it: let them not say, We have swallowed him up.

26 Let them be ashamed and brought to confusion together that rejoice at mine hurt: let them be [a]clothed with shame and dishonour that magnify *themselves* against me.

27 [a]Let them shout for joy, and be glad, that favour my righteous cause: yea, let them say continually, Let the LORD be magnified, which hath pleasure in the prosperity of his servant.

28 And my tongue shall speak of thy righteousness *and* of thy praise all the day long.

10 [a]Ps. 51:8 [b][Ex. 15:11]; Ps. 71:19; 86:8; [Mic. 7:18]
12 [a]Ps. 38:20; 109:5; Jer. 18:20; John 10:32
13 [a]Job 30:25
17 [a]Ps. 13:1; [Hab. 1:13]
19 [a]Ps. 69:4; 109:3; Lam. 3:52; [John 15:25]
26 [a]Ps. 109:29
27 [a]Rom. 12:15

NKJV

10 [a]All my bones shall say,
"LORD, [b]who *is* like You,
Delivering the poor from him who is too strong for him,
Yes, the poor and the needy from him who plunders him?"

11 Fierce witnesses rise up;
They ask me *things* that I do not know.
12 [a]They reward me evil for good,
To the sorrow of my soul.
13 But as for me, [a]when they were sick,
My clothing *was* sackcloth;
I humbled myself with fasting;
And my prayer would return to my own heart.
14 I paced about as though *he were* my friend *or* brother;
I bowed down heavily, as one who mourns *for his* mother.

15 But in my adversity they rejoiced
And gathered together;
Attackers gathered against me,
And I did not know *it;*
They tore *at me* and did not cease;
16 With ungodly mockers at feasts
They gnashed at me with their teeth.

17 Lord, how long will You [a]look on?
Rescue me from their destructions,
My precious *life* from the lions.
18 I will give You thanks in the great assembly;
I will praise You among many people.

19 [a]Let them not rejoice over me who are wrongfully my enemies;
Nor let them wink with the eye who hate me without a cause.
20 For they do not speak peace,
But they devise deceitful matters
Against *the* quiet ones in the land.
21 They also opened their mouth wide against me,
And said, "Aha, aha!
Our eyes have seen *it.*"

22 *This* You have seen, O LORD;
Do not keep silence.
O Lord, do not be far from me.
23 Stir up Yourself, and awake to my vindication,
To my cause, my God and my Lord.
24 Vindicate me, O LORD my God, according to Your righteousness;
And let them not rejoice over me.
25 Let them not say in their hearts, "Ah, so we would have it!"
Let them not say, "We have swallowed him up."

26 Let them be ashamed and brought to mutual confusion
Who rejoice at my hurt;
Let them be [a]clothed with shame and dishonor
Who exalt themselves against me.

27 [a]Let them shout for joy and be glad,
Who favor my righteous cause;
And let them say continually,
"Let the LORD be magnified,
Who has pleasure in the prosperity of His servant."
28 And my tongue shall speak of Your righteousness
And of Your praise all the day long.

KJV

PSALM 36

Man's Wickedness and God's Perfections

To the chief Musician, *A Psalm* of David, the servant of the LORD.

THE transgression of the wicked saith within my heart, *that* [a]*there is* no fear of God before his eyes.

2 For he flattereth himself in his own eyes, until his iniquity be found to be hateful.

3 The words of his mouth *are* iniquity and deceit: [a]he hath left off to be wise, *and* to do good.

4 [a]He deviseth mischief upon his bed; he setteth himself [b]in a way *that is* not good; he abhorreth not [c]evil.

5 Thy mercy, O LORD, *is* in the heavens; *and* thy faithfulness *reacheth* unto the clouds.

6 Thy righteousness *is* like the great mountains; [a]thy judgments *are* a great deep: O LORD, thou preservest man and beast.

7 How excellent *is* thy lovingkindness, O God! therefore the children of men [a]put their trust under the shadow of thy wings.

8 [a]They shall be abundantly satisfied with the fatness of thy house; and thou shalt make them drink of [b]the river of thy pleasures.

9 [a]For with thee *is* the fountain of life: [b]in thy light shall we see light.

10 O continue thy lovingkindness unto them that know thee; and thy righteousness to the upright in heart.

11 Let not the foot of pride come against me, and let not the hand of the wicked remove me.

12 There are the workers of iniquity fallen: they are cast down, and shall not be able to rise.

PSALM 36

1 [a]Rom. 3:18
3 [a]Ps. 94:8; Jer. 4:22
4 [a]Prov. 4:16; [Mic. 2:1] [b]Is. 65:2 [c][Ps. 52:3; Rom. 12:9]
6 [a]Job 11:8; Ps. 77:19; [Rom. 11:33]
7 [a]Ruth 2:12; Ps. 17:8; 57:1; 91:4
8 [a]Ps. 63:5; 65:4; Is. 25:6; Jer. 31:12–14 [b]Ps. 46:4; Rev. 22:1
9 [a][Jer. 2:13; John 4:10, 14] [b][1 Pet. 2:9]

NKJV

PSALM 36

Man's Wickedness and God's Perfections

To the Chief Musician. A Psalm of David the servant of the LORD.

AN oracle within my heart concerning the
transgression of the wicked:
[a]*There is* no fear of God before his eyes.
2 For he flatters himself in his own eyes,
When he finds out his iniquity *and* when
he hates.
3 The words of his mouth *are* wickedness
and deceit;
[a]He has ceased to be wise *and* to do good.
4 [a]He devises wickedness on his bed;
He sets himself [b]in a way *that is* not good;
He does not abhor [c]evil.

5 Your mercy, O LORD, *is* in the heavens;
Your faithfulness *reaches* to the clouds.
6 Your righteousness *is* like the great
mountains;
[a]Your judgments *are* a great deep;
O LORD, You preserve man and beast.

7 How precious *is* Your lovingkindness, O
God!
Therefore the children of men [a]put their
trust under the shadow of Your wings.
8 [a]They are abundantly satisfied with the
fullness of Your house,
And You give them drink from [b]the river
of Your pleasures.
9 [a]For with You *is* the fountain of life;
[b]In Your light we see light.

10 Oh, continue Your lovingkindness to
those who know You,
And Your righteousness to the upright in
heart.
11 Let not the foot of pride come against
me,
And let not the hand of the wicked drive
me away.
12 There the workers of iniquity have fallen;
They have been cast down and are not
able to rise.

PSALM 37

The Heritage of the Righteous and the Calamity of the Wicked

A Psalm of David.

FRET[a] not thyself because of evildoers, neither be thou envious against the workers of iniquity.

2 For they shall soon be cut down [a]like the grass, and wither as the green herb.

3 Trust in the LORD, and do good; *so* shalt thou dwell in the land, and verily thou shalt be fed.

4 [a]Delight thyself also in the LORD; and he shall give thee the desires of thine [b]heart.

5 [a]Commit thy way unto the LORD; trust also in him; and he shall bring *it* to pass.

6 [a]And he shall bring forth thy righteousness as the light, and thy judgment as the noonday.

7 Rest in the LORD, [a]and wait patiently for him: fret not thyself because of him who [b]prospereth in his way, because of the man who bringeth wicked devices to pass.

8 [a]Cease from anger, and forsake wrath: [b]fret not thyself in any wise to do evil.

PSALM 37

1 [a]Ps. 73:3; [Prov. 23:17; 24:19]
2 [a]Job 14:2; Ps. 90:5, 6; 92:7; James 1:11
4 [a]Job 22:26; Ps. 94:19; Is. 58:14 [b]Ps. 21:2; 145:19; [Matt. 7:7, 8]
5 [a][Ps. 55:22; Prov. 16:3; 1 Pet. 5:7]
6 [a]Job 11:17; [Is. 58:8, 10]
7 [a]Ps. 40:1; 62:5; [Lam. 3:26] [b][Ps. 73:3–12]
8 [a][Eph. 4:26] [b]Ps. 73:3

PSALM 37

The Heritage of the Righteous and the Calamity of the Wicked

A Psalm of David.

DO[a] not fret because of evildoers,
Nor be envious of the workers of iniquity.
2 For they shall soon be cut down [a]like the
grass,
And wither as the green herb.

3 Trust in the LORD, and do good;
Dwell in the land, and feed on His
faithfulness.
4 [a]Delight yourself also in the LORD,
And He shall give you the desires of your
[b]heart.

5 [a]Commit your way to the LORD,
Trust also in Him,
And He shall bring *it* to pass.
6 [a]He shall bring forth your righteousness as
the light,
And your justice as the noonday.

7 Rest in the LORD, [a]and wait patiently for
Him;
Do not fret because of him who [b]prospers
in his way,
Because of the man who brings wicked
schemes to pass.
8 [a]Cease from anger, and forsake wrath;
[b]Do not fret—*it* only *causes* harm.

KJV

9 For evildoers shall be cut off: but those
that wait upon the LORD, they shall [a]inherit the
earth.
10 For [a]yet a little while, and the wicked *shall*
not *be*: yea, [b]thou shalt diligently consider his
place, and it *shall* not *be*.
11 [a]But the meek shall inherit the earth; and
shall delight themselves in the abundance of
peace.
12 The wicked plotteth against the just, [a]and
gnasheth upon him with his teeth.
13 [a]The Lord shall laugh at him: for he seeth
that [b]his day is coming.
14 The wicked have drawn out the sword,
and have bent their bow, to cast down the poor
and needy, *and* to slay such as be of upright
conversation.
15 Their sword shall enter into their own
heart, and their bows shall be broken.
16 [a]A little that a righteous man hath *is* better
than the riches of many wicked.
17 For the arms of the wicked shall be broken: but the LORD upholdeth the righteous.
18 The LORD knoweth the days of the upright:
and their inheritance shall be for ever.
19 They shall not be ashamed in the evil time:
and in the days of famine they shall be satisfied.
20 But the wicked shall perish, and the enemies of the LORD *shall be* as the fat of lambs: they
shall consume; into smoke shall they consume
away.
21 The wicked borroweth, and payeth not
again: but [a]the righteous sheweth mercy, and
giveth.
22 [a]For *such as be* blessed of him shall inherit the earth; and *they that be* cursed of him
shall be cut off.
23 [a]The steps of a *good* man are ordered by
the LORD: and he delighteth in his way.
24 [a]Though he fall, he shall not be utterly
cast down: for the LORD upholdeth *him with* his
hand.
25 I have been young, and *now* am old; yet
have I not seen the righteous forsaken, nor his
seed begging bread.
26 [a]*He is* ever merciful, and lendeth; and his
seed *is* blessed.
27 Depart from evil, and do good; and dwell
for evermore.
28 For the LORD loveth judgment, and forsaketh not his saints; they are preserved for ever:
but the seed of the wicked shall be cut off.
29 [a]The righteous shall inherit the land, and
dwell therein for ever.
30 [a]The mouth of the righteous speaketh wisdom, and his tongue talketh of judgment.
31 The law of his God *is* in his heart; none
of his steps shall slide.
32 The wicked [a]watcheth the righteous, and
seeketh to slay him.
33 The LORD [a]will not leave him in his hand,
nor condemn him when he is judged.

9 [a]Ps. 25:13; Prov. 2:21; [Is. 57:13; 60:21; Matt. 5:5]
10 [a][Heb. 10:36] [b]Job 7:10; Ps. 37:35, 36
11 [a][Matt. 5:5]
12 [a]Ps. 35:16
13 [a]Ps. 2:4; 59:8 [b]1 Sam. 26:10; Job 18:20
16 [a]Prov. 15:16; 16:8; [1 Tim. 6:6]
21 [a]Ps. 112:5, 9
22 [a][Prov. 3:33]
23 [a][1 Sam. 2:9]; Ps. 40:2; 66:9; 119:5
24 [a]Prov. 24:16
26 [a][Deut. 15:8]; Ps. 37:21
29 [a]Ps. 37:9; Prov. 2:21
30 [a][Matt. 12:35]
32 [a]Ps. 10:8; 17:11
33 [a]Ps. 31:8; [2 Pet. 2:9]

NKJV

9 For evildoers shall be cut off;
But those who wait on the LORD,
They shall [a]inherit the earth.
10 For [a]yet a little while and the wicked *shall be* no *more;*
Indeed, [b]you will look carefully for his place,
But it *shall be* no *more.*
11 [a]But the meek shall inherit the earth,
And shall delight themselves in the abundance of peace.

12 The wicked plots against the just,
[a]And gnashes at him with his teeth.
13 [a]The Lord laughs at him,
For He sees that [b]his day is coming.
14 The wicked have drawn the sword
And have bent their bow,
To cast down the poor and needy,
To slay those who are of upright conduct.
15 Their sword shall enter their own heart,
And their bows shall be broken.

16 [a]A little that a righteous man has
Is better than the riches of many wicked.
17 For the arms of the wicked shall be broken,
But the LORD upholds the righteous.

18 The LORD knows the days of the upright,
And their inheritance shall be forever.
19 They shall not be ashamed in the evil time,
And in the days of famine they shall be satisfied.
20 But the wicked shall perish;
And the enemies of the LORD,
Like the splendor of the meadows, shall vanish.
Into smoke they shall vanish away.

21 The wicked borrows and does not repay,
But [a]the righteous shows mercy and gives.
22 [a]For *those* blessed by Him shall inherit the earth,
But *those* cursed by Him shall be cut off.

23 [a]The steps of a *good* man are ordered by the LORD,
And He delights in his way.
24 [a]Though he fall, he shall not be utterly cast down;
For the LORD upholds *him with* His hand.

25 I have been young, and *now* am old;
Yet I have not seen the righteous forsaken,
Nor his descendants begging bread.
26 [a]*He is* ever merciful, and lends;
And his descendants *are* blessed.

27 Depart from evil, and do good;
And dwell forevermore.
28 For the LORD loves justice,
And does not forsake His saints;
They are preserved forever,
But the descendants of the wicked shall be cut off.
29 [a]The righteous shall inherit the land,
And dwell in it forever.

30 [a]The mouth of the righteous speaks wisdom,
And his tongue talks of justice.
31 The law of his God *is* in his heart;
None of his steps shall slide.

32 The wicked [a]watches the righteous,
And seeks to slay him.
33 The LORD [a]will not leave him in his hand,
Nor condemn him when he is judged.

KJV

34 [a]Wait on the LORD, and keep his way, and he shall exalt thee to inherit the land: when the wicked are cut off, thou shalt see *it.*

35 I have seen the wicked in great power, and spreading himself like a green bay tree.

36 Yet he passed away, and, lo, he *was* not: yea, I sought him, but he could not be found.

37 Mark the perfect *man,* and behold the upright: for the end of *that* man *is* peace.

38 [a]But the transgressors shall be destroyed together: the end of the wicked shall be cut off.

39 But the salvation of the righteous *is* of the LORD: *he is* their strength [a]in the time of trouble.

40 And [a]the LORD shall help them, and deliver them: he shall deliver them from the wicked, and save them, [b]because they trust in him.

34 [a]Ps. 27:14; 37:9
38 [a][Ps. 1:4–6; 37:20, 28]
39 [a]Ps. 9:9; 37:19
40 [a]Ps. 22:4; Is. 31:5; Dan. 3:17; 6:23 [b]1 Chr. 5:20; Ps. 34:22

NKJV

34 [a]Wait on the LORD,
And keep His way,
And He shall exalt you to inherit the land;
When the wicked are cut off, you shall see *it.*

35 I have seen the wicked in great power,
And spreading himself like a native green tree.

36 Yet *he passed away, and behold, he *was* no *more;*
Indeed I sought him, but he could not be found.

37 Mark the blameless *man,* and observe the upright;
For the future of *that* man *is* peace.

38 [a]But the transgressors shall be destroyed together;
The future of the wicked shall be cut off.

39 But the salvation of the righteous *is* from the LORD;
He is their strength [a]in the time of trouble.

40 And [a]the LORD shall help them and deliver them;
He shall deliver them from the wicked,
And save them,
[b]Because they trust in Him.

PSALM 38

Prayer in Time of Chastening

A Psalm of David, [a]to bring to remembrance.

O LORD, [a]rebuke me not in thy wrath: neither chasten me in thy hot displeasure.

2 For thine arrows stick fast in me, and thy hand presseth me sore.

3 *There is* no soundness in my flesh because of thine anger; neither *is there any* rest in my bones because of my sin.

4 For mine iniquities are gone over mine head: as an heavy burden they are too heavy for me.

5 My wounds stink *and* are corrupt because of my foolishness.

6 I am troubled; I am bowed down greatly; I go mourning all the day long.

7 For my loins are filled with a loathsome *disease:* and *there is* no soundness in my flesh.

8 I am feeble and sore broken: I have roared by reason of the disquietness of my heart.

9 LORD, all my desire *is* before thee; and my groaning is not hid from thee.

10 My heart panteth, my strength faileth me: as for the light of mine eyes, it also is gone from me.

11 My lovers and my friends [a]stand aloof from my sore; and my kinsmen stand afar off.

12 They also that seek after my life lay snares *for me:* and they that seek my hurt speak mischievous things, and imagine deceits all the day long.

13 But I, as a deaf *man,* heard not; and *I was* as a dumb man *that* openeth not his mouth.

14 Thus I was as a man that heareth not, and in whose mouth *are* no reproofs.

15 For in thee, O LORD, [a]do I hope: thou wilt hear, O Lord my God.

16 For I said, *Hear me,* lest *otherwise* they should rejoice over me: when my foot slippeth, they magnify *themselves* against me.

PSALM 38

title [a]Ps. 70:title
1 [a]Ps. 6:1
11 [a]Ps. 31:11; 88:18
15 [a][Ps. 39:7]

PSALM 38

Prayer in Time of Chastening

A Psalm of David. [a]To bring to remembrance.

O LORD, do not [a]rebuke me in Your wrath,
Nor chasten me in Your hot displeasure!

2 For Your arrows pierce me deeply,
And Your hand presses me down.

3 *There is* no soundness in my flesh
Because of Your anger,
Nor *any* health in my bones
Because of my sin.

4 For my iniquities have gone over my head;
Like a heavy burden they are too heavy for me.

5 My wounds are foul *and* festering
Because of my foolishness.

6 I am troubled, I am bowed down greatly;
I go mourning all the day long.

7 For my loins are full of inflammation,
And *there is* no soundness in my flesh.

8 I am feeble and severely broken;
I groan because of the turmoil of my heart.

9 Lord, all my desire *is* before You;
And my sighing is not hidden from You.

10 My heart pants, my strength fails me;
As for the light of my eyes, it also has gone from me.

11 My loved ones and my friends [a]stand aloof from my plague,
And my relatives stand afar off.

12 Those also who seek my life lay snares *for me;*
Those who seek my hurt speak of destruction,
And plan deception all the day long.

13 But I, like a deaf *man,* do not hear;
And *I am* like a mute *who* does not open his mouth.

14 Thus I am like a man who does not hear,
And in whose mouth *is* no response.

15 For in You, O LORD, [a]I hope;
You will hear, O Lord my God.

16 For I said, "*Hear me,* lest they rejoice over me,
Lest, when my foot slips, they exalt *themselves* against me."

*———
37:36 So with MT, LXX, Tg.; Syr., Vg. *I passed by*

KJV

17 [a]For I *am* ready to halt, and my sorrow *is* continually before me.
18 For I will [a]declare mine iniquity; I will be [b]sorry for my sin.
19 But mine enemies *are* lively, *and* they are strong: and they that hate me wrongfully are multiplied.
20 They also [a]that render evil for good are mine adversaries; because I follow *the thing that* good *is*.
21 Forsake me not, O LORD: O my God, [a]be not far from me.
22 Make haste to help me, O Lord my salvation.

PSALM 39

Prayer for Wisdom and Forgiveness

To the chief Musician, even to Jeduthun, A Psalm of David.

I SAID, I will take heed to my ways, that I sin not with my [a]tongue: I will keep my mouth with a bridle, while the wicked is before me.
2 [a]I was dumb with silence, I held my peace, *even* from good; and my sorrow was stirred.
3 My heart was hot within me, while I was musing the fire burned: *then* spake I with my tongue,
4 LORD, [a]make me to know mine end, and the measure of my days, what it *is; that* I may know how frail I *am*.
5 Behold, thou hast made my days *as* an handbreadth; and mine age *is* as nothing before thee: verily every man at his best state *is* altogether [a]vanity. Selah.
6 Surely every man walketh in a vain shew: surely they are disquieted in vain: he heapeth up *riches*, and knoweth not who shall gather them.
7 And now, Lord, what wait I for? my [a]hope *is* in thee.
8 Deliver me from all my transgressions: make me not [a]the reproach of the foolish.
9 [a]I was dumb, I opened not my mouth; because [b]thou didst *it*.
10 [a]Remove thy stroke away from me: I am consumed by the blow of thine hand.
11 When thou with rebukes dost correct man for iniquity, thou makest his beauty [a]to consume away like a moth: surely every man *is* vanity. Selah.
12 Hear my prayer, O LORD, and give ear unto my cry; hold not thy peace at my tears: for I *am* a stranger with thee, *and* a sojourner, [a]as all my fathers *were*.
13 [a]O spare me, that I may recover strength, before I go hence, and [b]be no more.

PSALM 40

Faith Persevering in Trial
(*Ps. 70:1–5*)

To the chief Musician, A Psalm of David.

I [a]WAITED patiently for the LORD; and he inclined unto me, and heard my cry.

---

17 [a]Ps. 51:3
18 [a]Ps. 32:5 [b][2 Cor. 7:9, 10]
20 [a]Ps. 35:12
21 [a]Ps. 22:19; 35:22

PSALM 39

1 [a]Job 2:10; Ps. 34:13; [James 3:5–12]
2 [a]Ps. 38:13
4 [a]Ps. 90:12; 119:84
5 [a]Ps. 62:9; [Eccl. 6:12]
7 [a]Ps. 38:15
8 [a]Ps. 44:13; 79:4; 119:22
9 [a]Ps. 39:2 [b]2 Sam. 16:10; Job 2:10
10 [a]Job 9:34; 13:21
11 [a]Job 13:28; [Ps. 90:7]; Is. 50:9
12 [a]Gen. 47:9; Lev. 25:23; 1 Chr. 29:15; Ps. 119:19; Heb. 11:13; 1 Pet. 2:11
13 [a]Job 7:19; 10:20, 21; 14:6; Ps. 102:24 [b][Job 14:10]

PSALM 40

1 [a]Ps. 25:5; 27:14; 37:7

NKJV

17 [a]For I *am* ready to fall,
And my sorrow *is* continually before me.
18 For I will [a]declare my iniquity;
I will be [b]in anguish over my sin.
19 But my enemies *are* vigorous, *and* they are strong;
And those who hate me wrongfully have multiplied.
20 Those also [a]who render evil for good,
They are my adversaries, because I follow *what is* good.

21 Do not forsake me, O LORD;
O my God, [a]be not far from me!
22 Make haste to help me,
O Lord, my salvation!

PSALM 39

Prayer for Wisdom and Forgiveness

To the Chief Musician. To Jeduthun. A Psalm of David.

I SAID, "I will guard my ways,
Lest I sin with my [a]tongue;
I will restrain my mouth with a muzzle,
While the wicked are before me."
2 [a]I was mute with silence,
I held my peace *even* from good;
And my sorrow was stirred up.
3 My heart was hot within me;
While I was musing, the fire burned.
Then I spoke with my tongue:

4 "LORD, [a]make me to know my end,
And what *is* the measure of my days,
That I may know how frail I *am*.
5 Indeed, You have made my days *as* handbreadths,
And my age *is* as nothing before You;
Certainly every man at his best state *is* but [a]vapor. Selah
6 Surely every man walks about like a shadow;
Surely they busy themselves in vain;
He heaps up *riches*,
And does not know who will gather them.

7 "And now, Lord, what do I wait for?
My [a]hope *is* in You.
8 Deliver me from all my transgressions;
Do not make me [a]the reproach of the foolish.
9 [a]I was mute, I did not open my mouth,
Because it was [b]You who did *it*.
10 [a]Remove Your plague from me;
I am consumed by the blow of Your hand.
11 When with rebukes You correct man for iniquity,
You make his beauty [a]melt away like a moth;
Surely every man *is* vapor. Selah

12 "Hear my prayer, O LORD,
And give ear to my cry;
Do not be silent at my tears;
For I *am* a stranger with You,
A sojourner, [a]as all my fathers *were*.
13 [a]Remove Your gaze from me, that I may regain strength,
Before I go away and [b]am no more."

PSALM 40

Faith Persevering in Trial
(*Ps. 70:1–5*)

To the Chief Musician. A Psalm of David.

I [a]WAITED patiently for the LORD;
And He inclined to me,
And heard my cry.

KJV

2 He brought me up also out of an horrible pit, out of [a]the miry clay, and [b]set my feet upon a rock, *and* established my goings.

3 [a]And he hath put a new song in my mouth, *even* praise unto our God: many shall see *it*, and fear, and shall trust in the LORD.

4 [a]Blessed *is* that man that maketh the LORD his trust, and respecteth not the proud, nor such as turn aside to lies.

5 [a]Many, O LORD my God, *are* thy wonderful works *which* thou hast done, [b]and thy thoughts *which are* to us-ward: they cannot be reckoned up in order unto thee: *if* I would declare and speak *of them*, they are more than can be numbered.

6 [a]Sacrifice and offering thou didst not desire; mine ears hast thou opened: burnt offering and sin offering hast thou not required.

7 Then said I, Lo, I come: in the volume of the book *it is* written of me,

8 [a]I delight to do thy will, O my God: yea, thy law *is* [b]within my heart.

9 [a]I have preached righteousness in the great congregation: lo, [b]I have not refrained my lips, O LORD, thou knowest.

10 [a]I have not hid thy righteousness within my heart; I have declared thy faithfulness and thy salvation: I have not concealed thy lovingkindness and thy truth from the great congregation.

11 Withhold not thou thy tender mercies from me, O LORD: [a]let thy lovingkindness and thy truth continually preserve me.

12 For innumerable evils have compassed me about: [a]mine iniquities have taken hold upon me, so that I am not able to look up; they are more than the hairs of mine head: therefore my heart faileth me.

13 [a]Be pleased, O LORD, to deliver me: O LORD, make haste to help me.

14 [a]Let them be ashamed and confounded together that seek after my soul to destroy it; let them be driven backward and put to shame that wish me evil.

15 Let them be [a]desolate for a reward of their shame that say unto me, Aha, aha.

16 [a]Let all those that seek thee rejoice and be glad in thee: let such as love thy salvation [b]say continually, The LORD be magnified.

17 [a]But I *am* poor and needy; [b]*yet* the Lord thinketh upon me: thou *art* my help and my deliverer; make no tarrying, O my God.

2 [a]Ps. 69:2, 14; Jer. 38:6 [b]Ps. 27:5
3 [a]Ps. 32:7; 33:3
4 [a]Ps. 34:8; 84:12
5 [a]Job 9:10 [b]Ps. 139:17; [Is. 55:8]
6 [a][1 Sam. 15:22]; Ps. 51:16; Is. 1:11; [Jer. 6:20; 7:22, 23]; Amos 5:22; [Mic. 6:6–8; Heb. 10:5–9]
8 [a][Matt. 26:39; John 4:34; 6:38]; Heb. 10:7 [b][Ps. 37:31; Jer. 31:33; 2 Cor. 3:3]
9 [a]Ps. 22:22, 25 [b]Ps. 119:13
10 [a]Acts 20:20, 27
11 [a]Ps. 61:7; Prov. 20:28
12 [a]Ps. 38:4; 65:3
13 [a]Ps. 70:1
14 [a]Ps. 35:4, 26; 70:2; 71:13
15 [a]Ps. 73:19
16 [a]Ps. 70:4 [b]Ps. 35:27
17 [a]Ps. 70:5; 86:1; 109:22 [b]Ps. 40:5; 1 Pet. 5:7

NKJV

2 He also brought me up out of a horrible pit,
Out of [a]the miry clay,
And [b]set my feet upon a rock,
And established my steps.
3 [a]He has put a new song in my mouth—
Praise to our God;
Many will see *it* and fear,
And will trust in the LORD.

4 [a]Blessed *is* that man who makes the LORD his trust,
And does not respect the proud, nor such as turn aside to lies.
5 [a]Many, O LORD my God, *are* Your wonderful works
Which You have done;
[b]And Your thoughts toward us
Cannot be recounted to You in order;
If I would declare and speak *of them*,
They are more than can be numbered.

6 [a]Sacrifice and offering You did not desire;
My ears You have opened.
Burnt offering and sin offering You did not require.
7 Then I said, "Behold, I come;
In the scroll of the book *it is* written of me.
8 [a]I delight to do Your will, O my God,
And Your law *is* [b]within my heart."

9 [a]I have proclaimed the good news of righteousness
In the great assembly;
Indeed, [b]I do not restrain my lips,
O LORD, You Yourself know.
10 [a]I have not hidden Your righteousness within my heart;
I have declared Your faithfulness and Your salvation;
I have not concealed Your lovingkindness and Your truth
From the great assembly.

11 Do not withhold Your tender mercies from me, O LORD;
[a]Let Your lovingkindness and Your truth continually preserve me.
12 For innumerable evils have surrounded me;
[a]My iniquities have overtaken me, so that I am not able to look up;
They are more than the hairs of my head;
Therefore my heart fails me.

13 [a]Be pleased, O LORD, to deliver me;
O LORD, make haste to help me!
14 [a]Let them be ashamed and brought to mutual confusion
Who seek to destroy my life;
Let them be driven backward and brought to dishonor
Who wish me evil.
15 Let them be [a]confounded because of their shame,
Who say to me, "Aha, aha!"

16 [a]Let all those who seek You rejoice and be glad in You;
Let such as love Your salvation [b]say continually,
"The LORD be magnified!"
17 [a]But I *am* poor and needy;
[b]*Yet* the LORD thinks upon me.
You *are* my help and my deliverer;
Do not delay, O my God.

KJV

PSALM 41

The Blessing and Suffering of the Godly

To the chief Musician, A Psalm of David.

BLESSED *is* he that considereth the poor: the
LORD will deliver him in time of trouble.
2 The LORD will preserve him, and keep him
alive; *and* he shall be blessed upon the earth: [a]and
thou wilt not deliver him unto the will of his
enemies.
3 The LORD will strengthen him upon the
bed of languishing: thou wilt make all his bed in
his sickness.
4 I said, LORD, be merciful unto me: [a]heal
my soul; for I have sinned against thee.
5 Mine enemies speak evil of me, When
shall he die, and his name perish?
6 And if he come to see *me*, he speaketh
vanity: his heart gathereth iniquity to itself; *when*
he goeth abroad, he telleth *it*.
7 All that hate me whisper together against
me: against me do they devise my hurt.
8 An evil disease, *say they*, cleaveth fast
unto him: and *now* that he lieth he shall rise up
no more.
9 [a]Yea, mine own familiar friend, in whom
I trusted, [b]which did eat of my bread, hath lifted
up *his* heel against me.
10 But thou, O LORD, be merciful unto me,
and raise me up, that I may requite them.
11 By this I know that thou favourest me, because mine enemy doth not triumph over me.
12 And as for me, thou upholdest me in mine
integrity, and [a]settest me before thy face for ever.
13 [a]Blessed *be* the LORD God of Israel from
everlasting, and to everlasting. Amen, and Amen.

BOOK II

PSALM 42

Yearning for God in the Midst of Distresses

To the chief Musician, Maschil, for the sons of Korah.

AS the hart panteth after the water brooks, so
panteth my soul after thee, O God.
2 [a]My soul thirsteth for God, for the [b]living
God: when shall I come and appear before God?
3 [a]My tears have been my meat day and
night, while they continually say unto me, [b]Where
is thy God?
4 When I remember these *things*, [a]I pour
out my soul in me: for I had gone with the multitude, [b]I went with them to the house of God, with
the voice of joy and praise, with a multitude that
kept holyday.
5 [a]Why art thou cast down, O my soul? and
why art thou disquieted in me? [b]hope thou in God:
for I shall yet praise him *for* the help of his
countenance.

PSALM 41

2 [a]Ps. 27:12
4 [a]Ps. 6:2; 103:3; 147:3
9 [a]2 Sam. 15:12; Job 19:13, 19 [b]Ps. 55:12–14, 20; Jer. 20:10; Obad. 7; [Mic. 7:5]; Matt. 26:14–16, 21–25, 47–50; John 13:18, 21–30; Acts 1:16, 17
12 [a][Job 36:7; Ps. 21:6; 34:15]
13 [a]Ps. 72:18, 19; 89:52; 106:48; 150:6

PSALM 42

2 [a]Ps. 63:1; 84:2; 143:6; [Jer. 10:10] [b]Rom. 9:26; 1 Thess. 1:9
3 [a]Ps. 80:5; 102:9 [b]Ps. 79:10; 115:2; Joel 2:17; Mic. 7:10
4 [a]1 Sam. 1:15; Job 30:16 [b]Ps. 55:14; 122:1; Is. 30:29
5 [a]Ps. 42:11; 43:5 [b]Ps. 71:14; Lam. 3:24

42:title Heb. *Maschil*
42:2 So with MT, Vg.; some Heb. mss., LXX, Syr., Tg. *I see the face of God*
42:5 So with MT, Tg.; a few Heb. mss., LXX, Syr., Vg. *The help of my countenance, my God*

NKJV

PSALM 41

The Blessing and Suffering of the Godly

To the Chief Musician. A Psalm of David.

BLESSED *is* he who considers the poor;
The LORD will deliver him in time of trouble.
2 The LORD will preserve him and keep him alive,
And he will be blessed on the earth;
[a]You will not deliver him to the will of his enemies.
3 The LORD will strengthen him on his bed of illness;
You will sustain him on his sickbed.

4 I said, "LORD, be merciful to me;
[a]Heal my soul, for I have sinned against You."
5 My enemies speak evil of me:
"When will he die, and his name perish?"
6 And if he comes to see *me*, he speaks lies;
His heart gathers iniquity to itself;
When he goes out, he tells *it*.

7 All who hate me whisper together against me;
Against me they devise my hurt.
8 "An evil disease," *they say*, "clings to him.
And *now* that he lies down, he will rise up no more."
9 [a]Even my own familiar friend in whom I trusted,
[b]Who ate my bread,
Has lifted up *his* heel against me.

10 But You, O LORD, be merciful to me, and raise me up,
That I may repay them.
11 By this I know that You are well pleased with me,
Because my enemy does not triumph over me.
12 As for me, You uphold me in my integrity,
And [a]set me before Your face forever.

13 [a]Blessed *be* the LORD God of Israel
From everlasting to everlasting!
Amen and Amen.

BOOK TWO

Psalms 42–72

PSALM 42

Yearning for God in the Midst of Distresses

To the Chief Musician. A *Contemplation of the sons of Korah.

AS the deer pants for the water brooks,
So pants my soul for You, O God.
2 [a]My soul thirsts for God, for the [b]living God.
When shall I come and *appear before God?
3 [a]My tears have been my food day and night,
While they continually say to me,
[b]"Where *is* your God?"

4 When I remember these *things*,
[a]I pour out my soul within me.
For I used to go with the multitude;
[b]I went with them to the house of God,
With the voice of joy and praise,
With a multitude that kept a pilgrim feast.

5 [a]Why are you cast down, O my soul?
And *why* are you disquieted within me?
[b]Hope in God, for I shall yet praise Him
**For* the help of His countenance.

KJV

6 O my God, my soul is cast down within
me: therefore will I remember thee from the land
of Jordan, and of the Hermonites, from the hill
Mizar.
7 Deep calleth unto deep at the noise of thy
waterspouts: [a]all thy waves and thy billows are
gone over me.
8 *Yet* the LORD will [a]command his lovingkindness in the daytime, and [b]in the night his song
shall be with me, *and* my prayer unto the God of
my life.
9 I will say unto God my rock, [a]Why hast
thou forgotten me? why go I mourning because
of the oppression of the enemy?
10 *As* with a sword in my bones, mine enemies reproach me; [a]while they say daily unto me,
Where *is* thy God?
11 [a]Why art thou cast down, O my soul? and
why art thou disquieted within me? hope thou in
God: for I shall yet praise him, *who is* the health
of my countenance, and my God.

PSALM 43

Prayer to God in Time of Trouble

JUDGE [a]me, O God, and [b]plead my cause
against an ungodly nation: O deliver me from
the deceitful and unjust man.
2 For thou *art* the God of my strength: why
dost thou cast me off? [a]why go I mourning because of the oppression of the enemy?
3 [a]O send out thy light and thy truth: let
them lead me; let them bring me unto [b]thy holy
hill, and to thy tabernacles.
4 Then will I go unto the altar of God, unto
God my exceeding joy: yea, upon the harp will I
praise thee, O God my God.
5 [a]Why art thou cast down, O my soul? and
why art thou disquieted within me? hope in God:
for I shall yet praise him, *who is* the health of
my countenance, and my God.

PSALM 44

Redemption Remembered in Present Dishonor

To the Chief Musician for the sons of Korah,
[a]Maschil.

WE have heard with our ears, O God, [a]our fathers have told us, *what* work thou didst in
their days, in the times of old.
2 *How* [a]thou didst drive out the heathen
with thy hand, and plantedst them; *how* thou didst
afflict the people, and cast them out.
3 For [a]they got not the land in possession
by their own sword, neither did their own arm
save them: but thy right hand, and thine arm, and
the light of thy countenance, [b]because thou hadst
a favour unto them.
4 [a]Thou art my King, O God: command de-
liverances for Jacob.

---

7 [a]Ps. 69:1, 2; 88:7; Jon. 2:3
8 [a]Deut. 28:8 [b]Job 35:10; Ps. 149:5
9 [a]Ps. 38:6
10 [a]Ps. 42:3; Joel 2:17; Mic. 7:10
11 [a]Ps. 43:5

PSALM 43

1 [a][Ps. 26:1; 35:24] [b]1 Sam. 24:15; Ps. 35:1
2 [a]Ps. 42:9
3 [a][Ps. 40:11] [b]Ps. 3:4
5 [a]Ps. 42:5, 11

PSALM 44

title [a]Ps. 42:title
1 [a][Ex. 12:26, 27; Deut. 6:20]; Judg. 6:13; Ps. 78:3
2 [a]Ex. 15:17; 2 Sam. 7:10; Jer. 24:6; Amos 9:15
3 [a][Deut. 8:17, 18]; Josh. 24:12 [b][Deut. 4:37; 7:7, 8]
4 [a][Ps. 74:12]

*

42:6 So with MT, Tg.; a few Heb. mss., LXX, Syr., Vg. put *my God* at the end of v. 5
44:title Heb. *Maschil*
44:4 So with MT, Tg.; LXX, Vg. *and my God* • So with MT, Tg.; LXX, Syr., Vg. *who commands*

NKJV

6 *O my God, my soul is cast down within
me;
Therefore I will remember You from the
land of the Jordan,
And from the heights of Hermon,
From the Hill Mizar.
7 Deep calls unto deep at the noise of Your
waterfalls;
[a]All Your waves and billows have gone
over me.
8 The LORD will [a]command His
lovingkindness in the daytime,
And [b]in the night His song *shall be* with
me—
A prayer to the God of my life.

9 I will say to God my Rock,
[a]"Why have You forgotten me?
Why do I go mourning because of the
oppression of the enemy?"
10 *As* with a breaking of my bones,
My enemies reproach me,
[a]While they say to me all day long,
"Where *is* your God?"

11 [a]Why are you cast down, O my soul?
And why are you disquieted within me?
Hope in God;
For I shall yet praise Him,
The help of my countenance and my
God.

PSALM 43

Prayer to God in Time of Trouble

VINDICATE [a]me, O God,
And [b]plead my cause against an ungodly
nation;
Oh, deliver me from the deceitful and
unjust man!
2 For You *are* the God of my strength;
Why do You cast me off?
[a]Why do I go mourning because of the
oppression of the enemy?

3 [a]Oh, send out Your light and Your truth!
Let them lead me;
Let them bring me to [b]Your holy hill
And to Your tabernacle.
4 Then I will go to the altar of God,
To God my exceeding joy;
And on the harp I will praise You,
O God, my God.

5 [a]Why are you cast down, O my soul?
And why are you disquieted within me?
Hope in God;
For I shall yet praise Him,
The help of my countenance and my God.

PSALM 44

Redemption Remembered in Present Dishonor

To the Chief Musician. A [a]Contemplation* of the
sons of Korah.

WE have heard with our ears, O God,
[a]Our fathers have told us,
The deeds You did in their days,
In days of old:
2 [a]You drove out the nations with Your hand,
But them You planted;
You afflicted the peoples, and cast them
out.
3 For [a]they did not gain possession of the
land by their own sword,
Nor did their own arm save them;
But it was Your right hand, Your arm, and
the light of Your countenance,
[b]Because You favored them.

4 [a]You are my King, *O God;
*Command victories for Jacob.

KJV

5 Through thee [a]will we push down our enemies: through thy name will we tread them under
that rise up against us.
6 For [a]I will not trust in my bow, neither
shall my sword save me.
7 But thou hast saved us from our enemies,
and hast put them to shame that hated us.
8 [a]In God we boast all the day long, and
praise thy name for ever. Selah.
9 But [a]thou hast cast off, and put us to
shame; and goest not forth with our armies.
10 Thou makest us to [a]turn back from the
enemy: and they which hate us spoil for themselves.
11 [a]Thou hast given us like sheep *appointed*
for meat; and hast [b]scattered us among the
heathen.
12 [a]Thou sellest thy people for nought, and
dost not increase *thy wealth* by their price.
13 [a]Thou makest us a reproach to our neighbours, a scorn and a derision to them that are
round about us.
14 [a]Thou makest us a byword among the
heathen, [b]a shaking of the head among the
people.
15 My confusion *is* continually before me,
and the shame of my face hath covered me,
16 For the voice of him that reproacheth and
blasphemeth; [a]by reason of the enemy and
avenger.
17 [a]All this is come upon us; yet have we
not forgotten thee, neither have we dealt falsely
in thy covenant.
18 Our heart is not turned back, [a]neither
have our steps declined from thy way;
19 Though thou hast sore broken us in [a]the
place of dragons, and covered us [b]with the
shadow of death.
20 If we have forgotten the name of our God,
or [a]stretched out our hands to a strange god;
21 [a]Shall not God search this out? for he
knoweth the secrets of the heart.
22 [a]Yea, for thy sake are we killed all the
day long; we are counted as sheep for the
slaughter.
23 [a]Awake, why sleepest thou, O Lord?
arise, cast *us* not off for ever.
24 [a]Wherefore hidest thou thy face, *and* for-
gettest our affliction and our oppression?
25 For [a]our soul is bowed down to the dust:
our belly cleaveth unto the earth.
26 Arise for our help, and redeem us for thy
mercies' sake.

PSALM 45

The Glories of the Messiah and His Bride

To the chief Musician [a]upon Shoshannim, for the sons of Korah, Maschil, A Song of loves.

MY heart is inditing a good matter: I speak
of the things which I have made touching
the king: my tongue *is* the pen of a ready writer.

5 [a]Deut. 33:17; [Dan. 8:4]
6 [a][1 Sam. 17:47]; Ps. 33:16; [Hos. 1:7]
8 [a]Ps. 34:2; [Jer. 9:24]
9 [a]Ps. 60:1
10 [a]Lev. 26:17; Josh. 7:8, 12; Ps. 89:43
11 [a]Ps. 44:22; Rom. 8:36 [b]Lev. 26:33; Deut. 4:27; 28:64; Ps. 106:27; Ezek. 20:23
12 [a]Is. 52:3, 4; Jer. 15:13
13 [a]Deut. 28:37; Ps. 79:4; 80:6
14 [a]Jer. 24:9 [b]Job 16:4
16 [a]Ps. 8:2
17 [a]Dan. 9:13
18 [a]Job 23:11
19 [a]Is. 34:13 [b][Ps. 23:4]
20 [a][Deut. 6:14]
21 [a]Job 31:14; [Ps. 139:1, 2; Jer. 17:10]
22 [a]Rom. 8:36
23 [a]Ps. 7:6
24 [a]Job 13:24
25 [a]Ps. 119:25

PSALM 45
title [a]Ps. 69:title

*45:title Heb. *Shoshannim* • Heb. *Maschil*

NKJV

5 Through You [a]we will push down our enemies;
Through Your name we will trample those who rise up against us.
6 For [a]I will not trust in my bow,
Nor shall my sword save me.
7 But You have saved us from our enemies,
And have put to shame those who hated us.
8 [a]In God we boast all day long,
And praise Your name forever. Selah
9 But [a]You have cast *us* off and put us to shame,
And You do not go out with our armies.
10 You make us [a]turn back from the enemy,
And those who hate us have taken spoil for themselves.
11 [a]You have given us up like sheep *intended* for food,
And have [b]scattered us among the nations.
12 [a]You sell Your people for *next to* nothing,
And are not enriched by selling them.

13 [a]You make us a reproach to our neighbors,
A scorn and a derision to those all around us.
14 [a]You make us a byword among the nations,
[b]A shaking of the head among the peoples.
15 My dishonor *is* continually before me,
And the shame of my face has covered me,
16 Because of the voice of him who reproaches and reviles,
[a]Because of the enemy and the avenger.

17 [a]All this has come upon us;
But we have not forgotten You,
Nor have we dealt falsely with Your covenant.
18 Our heart has not turned back,
[a]Nor have our steps departed from Your way;
19 But You have severely broken us in [a]the place of jackals,
And covered us [b]with the shadow of death.

20 If we had forgotten the name of our God,
Or [a]stretched out our hands to a foreign god,
21 [a]Would not God search this out?
For He knows the secrets of the heart.
22 [a]Yet for Your sake we are killed all day long;
We are accounted as sheep for the slaughter.

23 [a]Awake! Why do You sleep, O Lord?
Arise! Do not cast *us* off forever.
24 [a]Why do You hide Your face,
And forget our affliction and our oppression?
25 For [a]our soul is bowed down to the dust;
Our body clings to the ground.
26 Arise for our help,
And redeem us for Your mercies' sake.

PSALM 45

The Glories of the Messiah and His Bride

To the Chief Musician. [a]Set to *"The Lilies." A •Contemplation of the sons of Korah. A Song of Love.

MY heart is overflowing with a good theme;
I recite my composition concerning the King;
My tongue *is* the pen of a ready writer.

KJV

2 Thou art fairer than the children of men: [a]grace is poured into thy lips: therefore God hath blessed thee for ever.

3 Gird thy [a]sword upon *thy* thigh, [b]O *most* mighty, with thy [c]glory and thy majesty.

4 [a]And in thy majesty ride prosperously because of truth and meekness *and* righteousness; and thy right hand shall teach thee terrible things.

5 Thine arrows *are* sharp in the heart of the king's enemies; *whereby* the people fall under thee.

6 [a]Thy throne, O God, *is* for ever and ever: the [b]sceptre of thy kingdom *is* a right sceptre.

7 Thou lovest righteousness, and hatest wickedness: therefore God, thy God, hath [a]anointed thee with the oil of [b]gladness above thy fellows.

8 All thy garments [a]*smell* of myrrh, and aloes, *and* cassia, out of the ivory palaces, whereby they have made thee glad.

9 [a]Kings' daughters *were* among thy honourable women: [b]upon thy right hand did stand the queen in gold of Ophir.

10 Hearken, O daughter, and consider, and incline thine ear; [a]forget also thine own people, and thy father's house;

11 So shall the king greatly desire thy beauty: [a]for he *is* thy Lord; and worship thou him.

12 And the daughter of Tyre *shall be there* with a gift; *even* [a]the rich among the people shall intreat thy favour.

13 The king's daughter *is* all glorious within: her clothing *is* of wrought gold.

14 [a]She shall be brought unto the king in raiment of needlework: the virgins her companions that follow her shall be brought unto thee.

15 With gladness and rejoicing shall they be brought: they shall enter into the king's palace.

16 Instead of thy fathers shall be thy children, [a]whom thou mayest make princes in all the earth.

17 [a]I will make thy name to be remembered in all generations: therefore shall the people praise thee for ever and ever.

2 [a]Luke 4:22
3 [a][Is. 49:2; Heb. 4:12]; Rev. 1:16 [b][Is. 9:6] [c]Jude 25
4 [a]Rev. 6:2
6 [a][Ps. 93:2]; Heb. 1:8, 9 [b][Num. 24:17]
7 [a]Ps. 2:2 [b]Ps. 21:6; Heb. 1:8, 9
8 [a]Song 1:12, 13
9 [a]Song 6:8 [b]1 Kin. 2:19
10 [a]Deut. 21:13; Ruth 1:16, 17
11 [a]Ps. 95:6; [Is. 54:5]
12 [a]Is. 49:23
14 [a]Song 1:4
16 [a][1 Pet. 2:9; Rev. 1:6; 20:6]
17 [a]Mal. 1:11

NKJV

2 You are fairer than the sons of men;
[a]Grace is poured upon Your lips;
Therefore God has blessed You forever.
3 Gird Your [a]sword upon *Your* thigh, [b]O Mighty One,
With Your [c]glory and Your majesty.
4 [a]And in Your majesty ride prosperously because of truth, humility, *and* righteousness;
And Your right hand shall teach You awesome things.
5 Your arrows *are* sharp in the heart of the King's enemies;
The peoples fall under You.

6 [a]Your throne, O God, *is* forever and ever;
A [b]scepter of righteousness *is* the scepter of Your kingdom.
7 You love righteousness and hate wickedness;
Therefore God, Your God, has [a]anointed You
With the oil of [b]gladness more than Your companions.
8 All Your garments are [a]scented with myrrh and aloes *and* cassia,
Out of the ivory palaces, by which they have made You glad.
9 [a]Kings' daughters *are* among Your honorable women;
[b]At Your right hand stands the queen in gold from Ophir.

10 Listen, O daughter,
Consider and incline your ear;
[a]Forget your own people also, and your father's house;
11 So the King will greatly desire your beauty;
[a]Because He *is* your Lord, worship Him.
12 And the daughter of Tyre *will come* with a gift;
[a]The rich among the people will seek your favor.

13 The royal daughter *is* all glorious within *the palace;*
Her clothing *is* woven with gold.
14 [a]She shall be brought to the King in robes of many colors;
The virgins, her companions who follow her, shall be brought to You.
15 With gladness and rejoicing they shall be brought;
They shall enter the King's palace.

16 Instead of Your fathers shall be Your sons,
[a]Whom You shall make princes in all the earth.
17 [a]I will make Your name to be remembered in all generations;
Therefore the people shall praise You forever and ever.

PSALM 46

God the Refuge of His People and Conqueror of the Nations

To the chief Musician for the sons of Korah, A Song [a]upon Alamoth.

GOD *is* our [a]refuge and strength, [b]a very present help in trouble.

2 Therefore will not we fear, though the earth be removed, and though the mountains be carried into the midst of the sea;

3 [a]*Though* the waters thereof roar *and* be troubled, *though* the mountains shake with the swelling thereof. Selah.

PSALM 46
title [a]1 Chr. 15:20
1 [a]Ps. 62:7, 8 [b][Deut. 4:7; Ps. 145:18]
3 [a][Ps. 93:3, 4]

PSALM 46

God the Refuge of His People and Conqueror of the Nations

To the Chief Musician. A Psalm of the sons of Korah. A Song [a]for Alamoth.

GOD *is* our [a]refuge and strength,
[b]A very present help in trouble.
2 Therefore we will not fear,
Even though the earth be removed,
And though the mountains be carried into the midst of the sea;
3 [a]*Though* its waters roar *and* be troubled,
Though the mountains shake with its swelling. Selah

KJV

4 *There is* a [a]river, the streams whereof
shall make glad the [b]city of God, the holy *place*
of the tabernacles of the most High.
5 God *is* [a]in the midst of her; she shall not
be moved: God shall help her, *and that* right early.
6 [a]The heathen raged, the kingdoms were
moved: he uttered his voice, the earth melted.
7 The [a]LORD of hosts *is* with us; the God of
Jacob *is* our refuge. Selah.
8 Come, behold the works of the LORD, what
desolations he hath made in the earth.
9 [a]He maketh wars to cease unto the end
of the earth; [b]he breaketh the bow, and cutteth
the spear in sunder; [c]he burneth the chariot in
the fire.
10 Be still, and know that I *am* God: [a]I will
be exalted among the heathen, I will be exalted
in the earth.
11 The LORD of hosts *is* with us; the God of
Jacob *is* our refuge. Selah.

PSALM 47

Praise to God, the Ruler of the Earth

To the chief Musician, A Psalm for the sons of Korah.

O CLAP your hands, all ye people; shout unto
God with the voice of triumph.
2 For the LORD most high *is* terrible; *he is*
a great [a]King over all the earth.
3 [a]He shall subdue the people under us, and
the nations under our feet.
4 He shall choose our [a]inheritance for us,
the excellency of Jacob whom he loved. Selah.
5 [a]God is gone up with a shout, the LORD
with the sound of a trumpet.
6 Sing praises to God, sing praises: sing
praises unto our King, sing praises.
7 [a]For God *is* the King of all the earth: [b]sing
ye praises with understanding.
8 [a]God reigneth over the heathen: God [b]sit-
teth upon the throne of his [c]holiness.
9 The princes of the people are gathered together, [a]*even* the people of the God of Abraham:
[b]for the shields of the earth *belong* unto God: he
is greatly exalted.

PSALM 48

The Glory of God in Zion

A Song *and* Psalm for the sons of Korah.

GREAT *is* the LORD, and greatly to be praised
in the [a]city of our God, *in* the mountain of
his holiness.
2 [a]Beautiful for situation, the joy of the
whole earth, *is* mount Zion, *on* the sides of the
north, the city of the great King.
3 God is known in her palaces for a refuge.
4 For, lo, [a]the kings were assembled, they
passed by together.
5 They saw *it, and* so they marvelled; they
were troubled, *and* hasted away.
6 Fear [a]took hold upon them there, *and*
pain, as of a woman in travail.
7 Thou breakest the [a]ships of Tarshish with
an east wind.

4 [a][Ezek. 47:1–12] [b]Ps. 48:1, 8; Is. 60:14
5 [a][Deut. 23:14; Is. 12:6]; Ezek. 43:7; Hos. 11:9; [Joel 2:27; Zeph. 3:15; Zech. 2:5, 10, 11; 8:3]
6 [a]Ps. 2:1, 2
7 [a]Num. 14:9; 2 Chr. 13:12
9 [a]Is. 2:4 [b]Ps. 76:3 [c]Ezek. 39:9
10 [a][Is. 2:11, 17]

PSALM 47

2 [a]Deut. 7:21; Neh. 1:5; Ps. 76:12
3 [a]Ps. 18:47
4 [a][1 Pet. 1:4]
5 [a]Ps. 68:24, 25
7 [a]Zech. 14:9 [b]1 Cor. 14:15
8 [a]1 Chr. 16:31 [b]Ps. 97:2 [c]Ps. 48:1
9 [a][Rom. 4:11, 12] [b][Ps. 89:18]

PSALM 48

1 [a]Ps. 46:4; 87:3; Matt. 5:35
2 [a]Ps. 50:2
4 [a]2 Sam. 10:6, 14
6 [a]Ex. 15:15
7 [a]1 Kin. 10:22; Ezek. 27:25

NKJV

4 *There is* a [a]river whose streams shall
make glad the [b]city of God,
The holy *place* of the tabernacle of the
Most High.
5 God *is* [a]in the midst of her, she shall not
be moved;
God shall help her, just at the break of
dawn.
6 [a]The nations raged, the kingdoms were
moved;
He uttered His voice, the earth melted.

7 The [a]LORD of hosts *is* with us;
The God of Jacob *is* our refuge. Selah

8 Come, behold the works of the LORD,
Who has made desolations in the earth.
9 [a]He makes wars cease to the end of the
earth;
[b]He breaks the bow and cuts the spear in
two;
[c]He burns the chariot in the fire.

10 Be still, and know that I *am* God;
[a]I will be exalted among the nations,
I will be exalted in the earth!

11 The LORD of hosts *is* with us;
The God of Jacob *is* our refuge. Selah

PSALM 47

Praise to God, the Ruler of the Earth

To the Chief Musician. A Psalm of the sons of Korah.

OH, clap your hands, all you peoples!
Shout to God with the voice of triumph!
2 For the LORD Most High *is* awesome;
He is a great [a]King over all the earth.
3 [a]He will subdue the peoples under us,
And the nations under our feet.
4 He will choose our [a]inheritance for us,
The excellence of Jacob whom He loves.
Selah

5 [a]God has gone up with a shout,
The LORD with the sound of a trumpet.
6 Sing praises to God, sing praises!
Sing praises to our King, sing praises!
7 [a]For God *is* the King of all the earth;
[b]Sing praises with understanding.

8 [a]God reigns over the nations;
God [b]sits on His [c]holy throne.
9 The princes of the people have gathered
together,
[a]The people of the God of Abraham.
[b]For the shields of the earth *belong* to God;
He is greatly exalted.

PSALM 48

The Glory of God in Zion

A Song. A Psalm of the sons of Korah.

GREAT *is* the LORD, and greatly to be praised
In the [a]city of our God,
In His holy mountain.
2 [a]Beautiful in elevation,
The joy of the whole earth,
Is Mount Zion *on* the sides of the north,
The city of the great King.
3 God *is* in her palaces;
He is known as her refuge.

4 For behold, [a]the kings assembled,
They passed by together.
5 They saw *it, and* so they marveled;
They were troubled, they hastened away.
6 Fear [a]took hold of them there,
And pain, as of a woman in birth pangs,
7 *As when* You break the [a]ships of Tarshish
With an east wind.

KJV

8 As we have heard, so have we seen in the
city of the LORD of hosts, in the city of our God:
God will [a]establish it for ever. Selah.
9 We have thought of [a]thy lovingkindness,
O God, in the midst of thy temple.
10 According to [a]thy name, O God, so *is* thy
praise unto the ends of the earth: thy right hand
is full of righteousness.
11 Let mount Zion rejoice, let the daughters
of Judah be glad, because of thy judgments.
12 Walk about Zion, and go round about her:
tell the towers thereof.
13 Mark ye well her bulwarks, consider her
palaces; that ye may [a]tell *it* to the generation
following.
14 For this God *is* our God for ever and ever:
[a]he will be our guide *even* unto death.

8 [a][Ps. 87:5; Is. 2:2]; Mic. 4:1
9 [a]Ps. 26:3
10 [a][Deut. 28:58]; Josh. 7:9; Mal. 1:11
13 [a][Ps. 78:5–7]
14 [a]Is. 58:11

NKJV

8 As we have heard,
So we have seen
In the city of the LORD of hosts,
In the city of our God:
God will [a]establish it forever. Selah

9 We have thought, O God, on [a]Your
lovingkindness,
In the midst of Your temple.
10 According to [a]Your name, O God,
So *is* Your praise to the ends of the
earth;
Your right hand is full of righteousness.
11 Let Mount Zion rejoice,
Let the daughters of Judah be glad,
Because of Your judgments.

12 Walk about Zion,
And go all around her.
Count her towers;
13 Mark well her bulwarks;
Consider her palaces;
That you may [a]tell *it* to the generation
following.
14 For this *is* God,
Our God forever and ever;
[a]He will be our guide
*Even to death.

PSALM 49

The Confidence of the Foolish

To the chief Musician, A Psalm for the sons of Korah.

HEAR this, all *ye* people; give ear, all *ye* inhabitants of the world:
2 Both low and high, rich and poor, together.
3 My mouth shall speak of wisdom; and the
meditation of my heart *shall be* of understanding.
4 I will incline mine ear to a parable: I will
open my dark saying upon the harp.
5 Wherefore should I fear in the days of evil,
when the iniquity of my heels shall compass me
about?
6 They that [a]trust in their wealth, and boast
themselves in the multitude of their riches;
7 None *of them* can by any means redeem
his brother, nor [a]give to God a ransom for him:
8 (For [a]the redemption of their soul *is* precious, and it ceaseth for ever:)
9 That he should still live for ever, *and* [a]not
see corruption.
10 For he seeth *that* wise men die, likewise
the fool and the brutish person perish, and leave
their wealth to others.
11 Their inward thought *is, that* their houses
shall continue for ever, *and* their dwelling places
to all generations; they [a]call *their* lands after their
own names.
12 Nevertheless man *being* in honour abideth
not: he is like the beasts *that* perish.
13 This their way *is* their [a]folly: yet their posterity approve their sayings. Selah.
14 Like sheep they are laid in the grave;
death shall feed on them; and [a]the upright shall
have dominion over them in the morning; [b]and
their beauty shall consume in the grave from their
dwelling.

PSALM 49

6 [a]Job 31:24; Ps. 52:7; [Prov. 11:28; Mark 10:24]
7 [a]Job 36:18, 19
8 [a][Matt. 16:26]
9 [a]Ps. 89:48
11 [a]Gen. 4:17; Deut. 3:14
13 [a][Luke 12:20]
14 [a]Ps. 47:3; [Dan. 7:18; 1 Cor. 6:2; Rev. 2:26] [b]Job 4:21

PSALM 49

The Confidence of the Foolish

To the Chief Musician. A Psalm of the sons of Korah.

HEAR this, all peoples;
Give ear, all inhabitants of the world,
2 Both low and high,
Rich and poor together.
3 My mouth shall speak wisdom,
And the meditation of my heart *shall give*
understanding.
4 I will incline my ear to a proverb;
I will disclose my dark saying on the
harp.

5 Why should I fear in the days of evil,
When the iniquity at my heels surrounds
me?
6 Those who [a]trust in their wealth
And boast in the multitude of their riches,
7 None *of them* can by any means redeem
his brother,
Nor [a]give to God a ransom for him—
8 For [a]the redemption of their souls *is*
costly,
And it shall cease forever—
9 That he should continue to live eternally,
And [a]not see the Pit.

10 For he sees wise men die;
Likewise the fool and the senseless person
perish,
And leave their wealth to others.
11 *Their inner thought *is that* their houses
will last forever,
Their dwelling places to all generations;
They [a]call *their* lands after their own
names.
12 Nevertheless man, *though* in honor, does
not *remain;
He is like the beasts *that* perish.

13 This is the way of those who *are*
[a]foolish,
And of their posterity who approve their
sayings. Selah
14 Like sheep they are laid in the grave;
Death shall feed on them;
[a]The upright shall have dominion over
them in the morning;
[b]And their beauty shall be consumed in the
grave, far from their dwelling.

48:14 So with MT, Syr.; LXX, Vg. *Forever*
49:11 LXX, Syr., Tg., Vg. *Their graves shall be their houses forever*
49:12 So with MT, Tg.; LXX, Syr., Vg. *understand* (cf. v. 20)

KJV

15 But God [a]will redeem my soul from the power of the grave: for he shall [b]receive me. Selah.

16 Be not thou afraid when one is made rich, when the glory of his house is increased;

17 For when he dieth he shall carry nothing away: his glory shall not descend after him.

18 Though while he lived [a]he blessed his soul: and *men* will praise thee, when thou doest well to thyself.

19 He shall go to the generation of his fathers; they shall never see [a]light.

20 Man *that is* in honour, and understandeth not, [a]is like the beasts *that* perish.

PSALM 50

God the Righteous Judge

A Psalm of Asaph.

THE [a]mighty God, *even* the LORD, hath spoken, and called the earth from the rising of the sun unto the going down thereof.

2 Out of Zion, the perfection of beauty, [a]God hath shined.

3 Our God shall come, and shall not keep silence: [a]a fire shall devour before him, and it shall be very tempestuous round about him.

4 [a]He shall call to the heavens from above, and to the earth, that he may judge his people.

5 Gather [a]my saints together unto me; [b]those that have made a covenant with me by sacrifice.

6 And the [a]heavens shall declare his righteousness: for [b]God *is* judge himself. Selah.

7 Hear, O my people, and I will speak; O Israel, and I will testify against thee: [a]I *am* God, *even* thy God.

8 [a]I will not reprove thee [b]for thy sacrifices or thy burnt offerings, *to have been* continually before me.

9 [a]I will take no bullock out of thy house, *nor* he goats out of thy folds.

10 For every beast of the forest *is* mine, *and* the cattle upon a thousand hills.

11 I know all the fowls of the mountains: and the wild beasts of the field *are* mine.

12 If I were hungry, I would not tell thee: [a]for the world *is* mine, and the fulness thereof.

13 [a]Will I eat the flesh of bulls, or drink the blood of goats?

14 [a]Offer unto God thanksgiving; and [b]pay thy vows unto the most High:

15 And [a]call upon me in the day of trouble: I will deliver thee, and thou shalt glorify me.

16 But unto the wicked God saith, What hast thou to do to declare my statutes, or *that* thou shouldest take my covenant in thy mouth?

17 [a]Seeing thou hatest instruction, and castest my words behind thee.

18 When thou sawest a thief, then thou [a]consentedst with him, and hast been [b]partaker with adulterers.

19 Thou givest thy mouth to evil, and [a]thy tongue frameth deceit.

15 [a][Hos. 13:4]; Mark 16:6, 7; Acts 2:31, 32 [b]Ps. 73:24
18 [a]Deut. 29:19; Luke 12:19
19 [a]Job 33:30
20 [a]Eccl. 3:19

PSALM 50

1 [a]Is. 9:6
2 [a]Deut. 33:2; Ps. 80:1
3 [a]Lev. 10:2; Num. 16:35; [Ps. 97:3]
4 [a]Deut. 4:26; 31:28; 32:1; Is. 1:2
5 [a]Deut. 33:3 [b]Ex. 24:7
6 [a][Ps. 97:6] [b]Ps. 75:7
7 [a]Ex. 20:2
8 [a]Jer. 7:22 [b]Is. 1:11; [Hos. 6:6]
9 [a]Ps. 69:31
12 [a]Ex. 19:5; [Deut. 10:14; Job 41:11]; 1 Cor. 10:26
13 [a][Ps. 51:15–17]
14 [a]Hos. 14:2; Heb. 13:15 [b]Num. 30:2; Deut. 23:21
15 [a]Job 22:27; [Zech. 13:9]
17 [a]Neh. 9:26; Rom. 2:21
18 [a][Rom. 1:32] [b]1 Tim. 5:22
19 [a]Ps. 52:2

*

50:18 LXX, Syr., Tg., Vg. *run*

NKJV

15 But God [a]will redeem my soul from the power of the grave,
For He shall [b]receive me. Selah

16 Do not be afraid when one becomes rich,
When the glory of his house is increased;
17 For when he dies he shall carry nothing away;
His glory shall not descend after him.
18 Though while he lives [a]he blesses himself
(For *men* will praise you when you do well for yourself),
19 He shall go to the generation of his fathers;
They shall never see [a]light.
20 A man *who is* in honor, yet does not understand,
[a]Is like the beasts *that* perish.

PSALM 50

God the Righteous Judge

A Psalm of Asaph.

THE [a]Mighty One, God the LORD,
Has spoken and called the earth
From the rising of the sun to its going down.
2 Out of Zion, the perfection of beauty,
[a]God will shine forth.
3 Our God shall come, and shall not keep silent;
[a]A fire shall devour before Him,
And it shall be very tempestuous all around Him.

4 [a]He shall call to the heavens from above,
And to the earth, that He may judge His people:
5 "Gather [a]My saints together to Me,
[b]Those who have made a covenant with Me by sacrifice."
6 Let the [a]heavens declare His righteousness,
For [b]God Himself *is* Judge. Selah

7 "Hear, O My people, and I will speak,
O Israel, and I will testify against you;
[a]I *am* God, your God!
8 [a]I will not rebuke you [b]for your sacrifices
Or your burnt offerings,
Which are continually before Me.
9 [a]I will not take a bull from your house,
Nor goats out of your folds.
10 For every beast of the forest *is* Mine,
And the cattle on a thousand hills.
11 I know all the birds of the mountains,
And the wild beasts of the field *are* Mine.

12 "If I were hungry, I would not tell you;
[a]For the world *is* Mine, and all its fullness.
13 [a]Will I eat the flesh of bulls,
Or drink the blood of goats?
14 [a]Offer to God thanksgiving,
And [b]pay your vows to the Most High.
15 [a]Call upon Me in the day of trouble;
I will deliver you, and you shall glorify Me."

16 But to the wicked God says:
"What *right* have you to declare My statutes,
Or take My covenant in your mouth,
17 [a]Seeing you hate instruction
And cast My words behind you?
18 When you saw a thief, you [a]consented* with him,
And have been a [b]partaker with adulterers.
19 You give your mouth to evil,
And [a]your tongue frames deceit.

KJV

20 Thou sittest *and* speakest against thy brother; thou slanderest thine own mother's son.

21 These *things* hast thou done, and I kept silence; [a]thou thoughtest that I was altogether *such an one* as thyself: *but* I will reprove thee, and [b]set *them* in order before thine eyes.

22 Now consider this, ye that [a]forget God, lest I tear *you* in pieces, and *there be* none to deliver.

23 Whoso offereth praise glorifieth me: and [a]to him that ordereth *his* conversation *aright* will I shew the salvation of God.

PSALM 51

A Prayer of Repentance

To the chief Musician, A Psalm of David, [a]when Nathan the prophet come unto him, after he had gone in to Bath–sheba.

HAVE mercy upon me, O God, according to thy lovingkindness: according unto the multitude of thy tender mercies [a]blot out my transgressions.

2 [a]Wash me throughly from mine iniquity, and cleanse me from my sin.

3 For I acknowledge my transgressions: and my sin *is* ever before me.

4 [a]Against thee, thee only, have I sinned, and done *this* evil [b]in thy sight: [c]that thou mightest be justified when thou speakest, *and* be clear when thou judgest.

5 [a]Behold, I was shapen in iniquity; and in sin did my mother conceive me.

6 Behold, thou desirest truth in the inward parts: and in the hidden *part* thou shalt make me to know wisdom.

7 [a]Purge me with hyssop, and I shall be clean: wash me, and I shall be [b]whiter than snow.

8 Make me to hear joy and gladness; *that* the bones *which* thou hast broken [a]may rejoice.

9 Hide thy face from my sins, and blot out all mine iniquities.

10 [a]Create in me a clean heart, O God; and renew a right spirit within me.

11 Cast me not away from thy presence; and take not thy [a]holy spirit from me.

12 Restore unto me the joy of thy salvation; and uphold me *with thy* [a]free spirit.

13 *Then* will I teach transgressors thy ways; and sinners shall be converted unto thee.

14 Deliver me from bloodguiltiness, O God, thou God of my salvation: *and* my tongue shall sing aloud of thy righteousness.

15 O Lord, open thou my lips; and my mouth shall shew forth thy praise.

16 For [a]thou desirest not sacrifice; else would I give *it:* thou delightest not in burnt offering.

17 [a]The sacrifices of God *are* a broken spirit: a broken and a contrite heart, O God, thou wilt not despise.

21 [a][Rom. 2:4] [b][Ps. 90:8]
22 [a][Job 8:13]
23 [a]Gal. 6:16

PSALM 51

title [a]2 Sam. 12:1
1 [a][Is. 43:25; 44:22; Acts 3:19; Col. 2:14]
2 [a]Jer. 33:8; Ezek. 36:33; [Heb. 9:14; 1 John 1:7, 9]
4 [a]2 Sam. 12:13 [b][Luke 5:21] [c]Rom. 3:4
5 [a][Job 14:4; Ps. 58:3; John 3:6; Rom. 5:12]
7 [a]Ex. 12:22; Lev. 14:4; Num. 19:18; Heb. 9:19 [b][Is. 1:18]
8 [a][Matt. 5:4]
10 [a][Ezek. 18:31; Eph. 2:10]
11 [a][Luke 11:13]
12 [a][2 Cor. 3:17]
16 [a][1 Sam. 15:22]; Ps. 50:8–14; [Mic. 6:6–8]
17 [a]Ps. 34:18; [Is. 57:15]; 66:2

NKJV

20 You sit *and* speak against your brother;
You slander your own mother's son.
21 These *things* you have done, and I kept silent;
[a]You thought that I was altogether like you;
But I will rebuke you,
And [b]set *them* in order before your eyes.

22 "Now consider this, you who [a]forget God,
Lest I tear *you* in pieces,
And *there be* none to deliver:
23 Whoever offers praise glorifies Me;
And [a]to him who orders *his* conduct *aright*
I will show the salvation of God."

PSALM 51

A Prayer of Repentance

To the Chief Musician. A Psalm of David [a]when Nathan the prophet went to him, after he had gone in to Bathsheba.

HAVE mercy upon me, O God,
According to Your lovingkindness;
According to the multitude of Your tender mercies,
[a]Blot out my transgressions.
2 [a]Wash me thoroughly from my iniquity,
And cleanse me from my sin.

3 For I acknowledge my transgressions,
And my sin *is* always before me.
4 [a]Against You, You only, have I sinned,
And done *this* evil [b]in Your sight—
[c]That You may be found just *when You speak,
And blameless when You judge.

5 [a]Behold, I was brought forth in iniquity,
And in sin my mother conceived me.
6 Behold, You desire truth in the inward parts,
And in the hidden *part* You will make me to know wisdom.

7 [a]Purge me with hyssop, and I shall be clean;
Wash me, and I shall be [b]whiter than snow.
8 Make me hear joy and gladness,
That the bones You have broken [a]may rejoice.
9 Hide Your face from my sins,
And blot out all my iniquities.

10 [a]Create in me a clean heart, O God,
And renew a steadfast spirit within me.
11 Do not cast me away from Your presence,
And do not take Your [a]Holy Spirit from me.

12 Restore to me the joy of Your salvation,
And uphold me *by Your* [a]generous Spirit.
13 *Then* I will teach transgressors Your ways,
And sinners shall be converted to You.

14 Deliver me from the guilt of bloodshed, O God,
The God of my salvation,
And my tongue shall sing aloud of Your righteousness.
15 O Lord, open my lips,
And my mouth shall show forth Your praise.
16 For [a]You do not desire sacrifice, or else I would give *it;*
You do not delight in burnt offering.
17 [a]The sacrifices of God *are* a broken spirit,
A broken and a contrite heart—
These, O God, You will not despise.

*———
51:4 LXX, Tg., Vg. *in Your words*

KJV

18 Do good in thy good pleasure unto Zion: build thou the walls of Jerusalem.
19 Then shalt thou be pleased with [a]the sacrifices of righteousness, with burnt offering and whole burnt offering: then shall they offer bullocks upon thine altar.

PSALM 52

The End of the Wicked and the Peace of the Godly

To the chief Musician, Maschil, A Psalm of David, [a]when Doeg the Edomite came and [b]told Saul, and said unto him, David is come to the house of Ahimelech.

WHY boastest thou thyself in mischief, O mighty man? the goodness of God *endureth* continually.
2 Thy tongue deviseth mischiefs; like a sharp rasor, working deceitfully.
3 Thou lovest evil more than good; *and* lying rather than to speak righteousness. Selah.
4 Thou lovest all devouring words, O *thou* deceitful tongue.
5 God shall likewise destroy thee for ever, he shall take thee away, and pluck thee out of *thy* dwelling place, and root thee out of the land of the living. Selah.
6 The righteous also shall see, and fear, and shall laugh at him:
7 Lo, *this is* the man *that* made not God his strength; but trusted in the abundance of his riches, *and* strengthened himself in his wickedness.
8 But I *am* [a]like a green olive tree in the house of God: I trust in the mercy of God for ever and ever.
9 I will praise thee for ever, because thou hast done *it:* and I will wait on thy name; for *it is* good before thy saints.

PSALM 53

Folly of the Godless, and the Restoration of Israel
(Ps. 14:1–7)

To the chief Musician upon Mahalath, Maschil, A Psalm of David.

THE [a]fool hath said in his heart, *There is* no God. Corrupt are they, and have done abominable iniquity: [b]*there is* none that doeth good.
2 God looked down from heaven upon the children of men, to see if there were *any* that did understand, that did [a]seek God.
3 Every one of them is gone back: they are altogether become filthy; *there is* none that doeth good, no, not one.
4 Have the workers of iniquity [a]no knowledge? who eat up my people *as* they eat bread: they have not called upon God.
5 [a]There were they in great fear, *where* no fear was: for God hath scattered the bones of him that encampeth *against* thee: thou hast put *them* to shame, because God hath despised them.
6 [a]Oh that the salvation of Israel *were come* out of Zion! When God bringeth back the captivity

19 [a]Ps. 4:5

PSALM 52

title [a]1 Sam. 22:9 [b]Ezek. 22:9
8 [a]Jer. 11:16

PSALM 53

1 [a]Ps. 10:4 [b]Rom. 3:10–12
2 [a][2 Chr. 15:2]
4 [a]Jer. 4:22
5 [a]Lev. 26:17, 36; Prov. 28:1
6 [a]Ps. 14:7

*

52:title Heb. *Maschil*
53:title Heb. *Maschil*

NKJV

18 Do good in Your good pleasure to Zion;
Build the walls of Jerusalem.
19 Then You shall be pleased with [a]the sacrifices of righteousness,
With burnt offering and whole burnt offering;
Then they shall offer bulls on Your altar.

PSALM 52

The End of the Wicked and the Peace of the Godly

To the Chief Musician. A *Contemplation of David [a]when Doeg the Edomite went and [b]told Saul, and said to him, "David has gone to the house of Ahimelech."

WHY do you boast in evil, O mighty man?
The goodness of God *endures* continually.
2 Your tongue devises destruction,
Like a sharp razor, working deceitfully.
3 You love evil more than good,
Lying rather than speaking righteousness. Selah
4 You love all devouring words,
You deceitful tongue.

5 God shall likewise destroy you forever;
He shall take you away, and pluck you out of *your* dwelling place,
And uproot you from the land of the living. Selah
6 The righteous also shall see and fear,
And shall laugh at him, *saying,*
7 "Here is the man *who* did not make God his strength,
But trusted in the abundance of his riches,
And strengthened himself in his wickedness."

8 But I *am* [a]like a green olive tree in the house of God;
I trust in the mercy of God forever and ever.
9 I will praise You forever,
Because You have done *it;*
And in the presence of Your saints
I will wait on Your name, for *it is* good.

PSALM 53

Folly of the Godless, and the Restoration of Israel
(Ps. 14:1–7)

To the Chief Musician. Set to "Mahalath." A *Contemplation of David.

THE [a]fool has said in his heart,
"*There is* no God."
They are corrupt, and have done abominable iniquity;
[b]*There is* none who does good.

2 God looks down from heaven upon the children of men,
To see if there are *any* who understand, who [a]seek God.
3 Every one of them has turned aside;
They have together become corrupt;
There is none who does good,
No, not one.

4 Have the workers of iniquity [a]no knowledge,
Who eat up my people *as* they eat bread,
And do not call upon God?
5 [a]There they are in great fear
Where no fear was,
For God has scattered the bones of him who encamps against you;
You have put *them* to shame,
Because God has despised them.

6 [a]Oh, that the salvation of Israel would come out of Zion!

KJV

of his people, Jacob shall rejoice, *and* Israel shall
be glad.

PSALM 54

Answered Prayer for Deliverance from Adversaries

To the chief Musician on Neginoth, Maschil, A Psalm of David, [a]when the Ziphims came and said to Saul, Doth not David hide himself with us?

SAVE me, O God, by thy name, and judge me by thy strength.
2 Hear my prayer, O God; give ear to the
words of my mouth.
3 For strangers are risen up against me, and
oppressors seek after my soul: they have not set
God before them. Selah.
4 Behold, God *is* mine helper: the Lord *is*
with them that uphold my soul.
5 He shall reward evil unto mine enemies:
cut them off in thy truth.
6 I will freely sacrifice unto thee: I will
praise thy name, O LORD; for *it is* good.
7 For he hath delivered me out of all trouble:
[a]and mine eye hath seen *his desire* upon mine
enemies.

PSALM 55

Trust in God Concerning the Treachery of Friends

To the chief Musician on Neginoth, Maschil, A Psalm of David.

GIVE ear to my prayer, O God; and hide not thyself from my supplication.
2 Attend unto me, and hear me: I [a]mourn
in my complaint, and make a noise;
3 Because of the voice of the enemy, because of the oppression of the wicked: [a]for they
cast iniquity upon me, and in wrath they hate me.
4 [a]My heart is sore pained within me: and
the terrors of death are fallen upon me.
5 Fearfulness and trembling are come upon
me, and horror hath overwhelmed me.
6 And I said, Oh that I had wings like a
dove! *for then* would I fly away, and be at rest.
7 Lo, *then* would I wander far off, *and* remain in the wilderness. Selah.
8 I would hasten my escape from the windy
storm *and* tempest.
9 Destroy, O Lord, *and* divide their tongues:
for I have seen [a]violence and strife in the city.
10 Day and night they go about it upon the
walls thereof: [a]mischief also and sorrow *are* in
the midst of it.
11 Wickedness *is* in the midst thereof: [a]deceit
and guile depart not from her streets.
12 [a]For *it was* not an enemy *that* reproached
me; then I could have borne *it:* neither *was it* he
that hated me *that* did [b]magnify *himself* against
me; then I would have hid myself from him:

PSALM 54
title [a]1 Sam. 23:19
7 [a]Ps. 59:10

PSALM 55
2 [a]Is. 38:14; 59:11; Ezek. 7:16
3 [a]2 Sam. 16:7, 8
4 [a]Ps. 116:3
9 [a]Jer. 6:7
10 [a]Ps. 10:7
11 [a]Ps. 10:7
12 [a]Ps. 41:9 [b]Ps. 35:26; 38:16

NKJV

When God brings back the captivity of His people,
Let Jacob rejoice *and* Israel be glad.

PSALM 54

Answered Prayer for Deliverance from Adversaries

To the Chief Musician. With *stringed instruments. A *Contemplation of David [a]when the Ziphites went and said to Saul, "Is David not hiding with us?"

SAVE me, O God, by Your name,
And vindicate me by Your strength.
2 Hear my prayer, O God;
Give ear to the words of my mouth.
3 For strangers have risen up against me,
And oppressors have sought after my life;
They have not set God before them. Selah

4 Behold, God *is* my helper;
The Lord *is* with those who uphold my life.
5 He will repay my enemies for their evil.
Cut them off in Your truth.

6 I will freely sacrifice to You;
I will praise Your name, O LORD, for *it is* good.
7 For He has delivered me out of all trouble;
[a]And my eye has seen *its desire* upon my enemies.

PSALM 55

Trust in God Concerning the Treachery of Friends

To the Chief Musician. With *stringed instruments. A *Contemplation of David.

GIVE ear to my prayer, O God,
And do not hide Yourself from my supplication.
2 Attend to me, and hear me;
I [a]am restless in my complaint, and moan noisily,
3 Because of the voice of the enemy,
Because of the oppression of the wicked;
[a]For they bring down trouble upon me,
And in wrath they hate me.

4 [a]My heart is severely pained within me,
And the terrors of death have fallen upon me.
5 Fearfulness and trembling have come upon me,
And horror has overwhelmed me.
6 So I said, "Oh, that I had wings like a dove!
I would fly away and be at rest.
7 Indeed, I would wander far off,
And remain in the wilderness. Selah
8 I would hasten my escape
From the windy storm *and* tempest."

9 Destroy, O Lord, *and* divide their tongues,
For I have seen [a]violence and strife in the city.
10 Day and night they go around it on its walls;
[a]Iniquity and trouble *are* also in the midst of it.
11 Destruction *is* in its midst;
[a]Oppression and deceit do not depart from its streets.

12 [a]For *it is* not an enemy *who* reproaches me;
Then I could bear *it*.
Nor *is it* one *who* hates me who has [b]exalted *himself* against me;
Then I could hide from him.

*
54:title Heb. *neginoth* • Heb. *Maschil*
55:title Heb. *neginoth* • Heb. *Maschil*

KJV

13 But *it was* thou, a man mine equal, [a]my guide, and mine acquaintance.

14 We took sweet counsel together, *and* [a]walked unto the house of God in company.

15 Let death seize upon them, *and* let them [a]go down quick into hell: for wickedness *is* in their dwellings, *and* among them.

16 As for me, I will call upon God; and the LORD shall save me.

17 [a]Evening, and morning, and at noon, will I pray, and cry aloud: and he shall hear my voice.

18 He hath delivered my soul in peace from the battle *that was* against me: for [a]there were many with me.

19 God shall hear, and afflict them, [a]even he that abideth of old. Selah. Because they have no changes, therefore they fear not God.

20 He hath [a]put forth his hands against such as [b]be at peace with him: he hath broken his covenant.

21 [a]*The words* of his mouth were smoother than butter, but war *was* in his heart: his words were softer than oil, yet *were* they drawn swords.

22 [a]Cast thy burden upon the LORD, and [b]he shall sustain thee: he shall never suffer the righteous to be moved.

23 But thou, O God, shalt bring them down into the pit of destruction: [a]bloody and deceitful men [b]shall not live out half their days; but I will trust in thee.

13 [a]2 Sam. 15:12
14 [a]Ps. 42:4
15 [a]Num. 16:30, 33
17 [a]Dan. 6:10; Luke 18:1; Acts 3:1; 10:3, 30
18 [a]2 Chr. 32:7, 8
19 [a][Deut. 33:27]
20 [a]Acts 12:1 [b]Ps. 7:4
21 [a]Ps. 28:3; 57:4; [Prov. 5:3, 4; 12:18]
22 [a][Ps. 37:5; Matt. 6:25–34; Luke 12:22–31; 1 Pet. 5:7] [b]Ps. 37:24
23 [a]Ps. 5:6 [b]Prov. 10:27

NKJV

13 But *it was* you, a man my equal,
[a]My companion and my acquaintance.
14 We took sweet counsel together,
And [a]walked to the house of God in the throng.

15 Let death seize them;
Let them [a]go down alive into hell,
For wickedness *is* in their dwellings *and* among them.

16 As for me, I will call upon God,
And the LORD shall save me.
17 [a]Evening and morning and at noon
I will pray, and cry aloud,
And He shall hear my voice.
18 He has redeemed my soul in peace from the battle *that was* against me,
For [a]there were many against me.
19 God will hear, and afflict them,
[a]Even He who abides from of old. Selah
Because they do not change,
Therefore they do not fear God.

20 He has [a]put forth his hands against those who [b]were at peace with him;
He has broken his covenant.
21 [a]*The words* of his mouth were smoother than butter,
But war *was* in his heart;
His words were softer than oil,
Yet they *were* drawn swords.

22 [a]Cast your burden on the LORD,
And [b]He shall sustain you;
He shall never permit the righteous to be moved.

23 But You, O God, shall bring them down to the pit of destruction;
[a]Bloodthirsty and deceitful men [b]shall not live out half their days;

But I will trust in You.

PSALM 56

Prayer for Relief from Tormentors

To the chief Musician upon Jonath–elem–rechokim, Michtam of David, when the [a]Philistines took him in Gath.

BE [a]merciful unto me, O God: for man would swallow me up; he fighting daily oppresseth me.

2 Mine enemies would daily [a]swallow *me* up: for *they be* many that fight against me, O thou most High.

3 What time I am afraid, I will trust in thee.

4 In God I will praise his word, in God I have put my trust; [a]I will not fear what flesh can do unto me.

5 Every day they wrest my words: all their thoughts *are* against me for evil.

6 They gather themselves together, they hide themselves, they mark my steps, when they wait for my soul.

7 Shall they escape by iniquity? in *thine* anger cast down the people, O God.

8 Thou tellest my wanderings: put thou my tears into thy bottle: [a]*are they* not in thy book?

9 When I cry *unto thee*, then shall mine enemies turn back: this I know; for [a]God *is* for me.

10 In God will I praise *his* word: in the LORD will I praise *his* word.

PSALM 56

title [a]1 Sam. 21:11
1 [a]Ps. 57:1
2 [a]Ps. 57:3
4 [a]Ps. 118:6; Is. 31:3; [Heb. 13:6]
8 [a][Mal. 3:16]
9 [a][Ps. 118:6; Rom. 8:31]

PSALM 56

Prayer for Relief from Tormentors

To the Chief Musician. Set to *"The Silent Dove in Distant Lands." A Michtam of David when the [a]Philistines captured him in Gath.

BE [a]merciful to me, O God, for man would swallow me up;
Fighting all day he oppresses me.
2 My enemies would [a]hound *me* all day,
For *there are* many who fight against me, O Most High.

3 Whenever I am afraid,
I will trust in You.
4 In God (I will praise His word),
In God I have put my trust;
[a]I will not fear.
What can flesh do to me?

5 All day they twist my words;
All their thoughts *are* against me for evil.
6 They gather together,
They hide, they mark my steps,
When they lie in wait for my life.
7 Shall they escape by iniquity?
In anger cast down the peoples, O God!

8 You number my wanderings;
Put my tears into Your bottle;
[a]*Are they* not in Your book?
9 When I cry out *to You*,
Then my enemies will turn back;
This I know, because [a]God *is* for me.
10 In God (I will praise *His* word),
In the LORD (I will praise *His* word),

*56:title Heb. *Jonath Elem Rechokim*

KJV

11 In God have I put my trust: I will not be
afraid what man can do unto me.
12 Thy vows *are* upon me, O God: I will render praises unto thee.
13 [a]For thou hast delivered my soul from
death: *wilt* not *thou deliver* my feet from falling,
that I may walk before God in the [b]light of the
living?

PSALM 57

Prayer for Safety from Enemies
(*cf. Ps. 108:1–5*)

To the chief Musician, Altaschith, Michtam of
David, [a]when he fled from Saul in the cave.

BE merciful unto me, O God, be merciful unto
me: for my soul trusteth in thee: [a]yea, in the
shadow of thy wings will I make my refuge, [b]until
these calamities be overpast.
2 I will cry unto God most high; unto God
[a]that performeth *all things* for me.
3 [a]He shall send from heaven, and save me
from the reproach of him that would swallow me
up. Selah. God [b]shall send forth his mercy and
his truth.
4 My soul *is* among lions: *and* I lie *even*
among them that are set on fire, *even* the sons of
men, [a]whose teeth *are* spears and arrows, and
their tongue a sharp sword.
5 [a]Be thou exalted, O God, above the heavens; *let* thy glory *be* above all the earth.
6 [a]They have prepared a net for my steps;
my soul is bowed down: they have digged a pit
before me, into the midst whereof they are fallen
themselves. Selah.
7 [a]My heart is fixed, O God, my heart is
fixed: I will sing and give praise.
8 Awake up, [a]my glory; awake, psaltery and
harp: I *myself* will awake early.
9 [a]I will praise thee, O Lord, among the people: I will sing unto thee among the nations.
10 [a]For thy mercy *is* great unto the heavens,
and thy truth unto the clouds.
11 [a]Be thou exalted, O God, above the heavens: *let* thy glory *be* above all the earth.

PSALM 58

The Just Judgment of the Wicked

To the chief Musician, Altaschith, Michtam of
David.

DO ye indeed speak righteousness, O congregation? do ye judge uprightly, O ye sons of
men?
2 Yea, in heart ye work wickedness; ye
weigh the violence of your hands in the earth.
3 [a]The wicked are estranged from the
womb: they go astray as soon as they be born,
speaking lies.

13 [a]Ps. 116:8, 9 [b]Job 33:30

PSALM 57

title [a]1 Sam. 22:1
1 [a]Ruth 2:12; Ps. 17:8; 63:7 [b]Is. 26:20
2 [a][Ps. 138:8]
3 [a]Ps. 144:5, 7 [b]Ps. 43:3
4 [a]Prov. 30:14
5 [a]Ps. 108:5
6 [a]Ps. 9:15
7 [a]Ps. 108:1–5
8 [a]Ps. 16:9
9 [a]Ps. 108:3
10 [a]Ps. 103:11
11 [a]Ps. 57:5

PSALM 58

3 [a][Ps. 53:3; Is. 48:8]

*

57:title Heb. *Al Tashcheth*
58:title Heb. *Al Tashcheth*

NKJV

11 In God I have put my trust;
I will not be afraid.
What can man do to me?

12 Vows *made* to You *are binding* upon me,
O God;
I will render praises to You,
13 [a]For You have delivered my soul from
death.
Have You not *kept* my feet from falling,
That I may walk before God
In the [b]light of the living?

PSALM 57

Prayer for Safety from Enemies
(*cf. Ps. 108:1–5*)

To the Chief Musician. Set to *"Do Not Destroy."
A Michtam of David [a]when he fled from Saul into
the cave.

BE merciful to me, O God, be merciful to me!
For my soul trusts in You;
[a]And in the shadow of Your wings I will
make my refuge,
[b]Until *these* calamities have passed by.

2 I will cry out to God Most High,
To God [a]who performs *all things* for me.
3 [a]He shall send from heaven and save me;
He reproaches the one who would
swallow me up. Selah
God [b]shall send forth His mercy and His
truth.

4 My soul *is* among lions;
I lie *among* the sons of men
Who are set on fire,
[a]Whose teeth *are* spears and arrows,
And their tongue a sharp sword.
5 [a]Be exalted, O God, above the heavens;
Let Your glory *be* above all the earth.

6 [a]They have prepared a net for my steps;
My soul is bowed down;
They have dug a pit before me;
Into the midst of it they *themselves* have
fallen. Selah

7 [a]My heart is steadfast, O God, my heart is
steadfast;
I will sing and give praise.
8 Awake, [a]my glory!
Awake, lute and harp!
I will awaken the dawn.

9 [a]I will praise You, O Lord, among the
peoples;
I will sing to You among the nations.
10 [a]For Your mercy reaches unto the
heavens,
And Your truth unto the clouds.

11 [a]Be exalted, O God, above the heavens;
Let Your glory *be* above all the earth.

PSALM 58

The Just Judgment of the Wicked

To the Chief Musician. Set to *"Do Not Destroy."
A Michtam of David.

DO you indeed speak righteousness, you silent
ones?
Do you judge uprightly, you sons of
men?
2 No, in heart you work wickedness;
You weigh out the violence of your hands
in the earth.

3 [a]The wicked are estranged from the womb;
They go astray as soon as they are born,
speaking lies.

KJV

4 [a]Their poison *is* like the poison of a serpent: *they are* like the deaf adder *that* stoppeth
her ear;
5 Which will not [a]hearken to the voice of
charmers, charming never so wisely.
6 [a]Break their teeth, O God, in their mouth:
break out the great teeth of the young lions, O
LORD.
7 [a]Let them melt away as waters *which* run
continually: *when* he bendeth *his bow to shoot*
his arrows, let them be as cut in pieces.
8 As a snail *which* melteth, let *every one of*
them pass away: [a]*like* the untimely birth of a
woman, *that* they may not see the sun.
9 Before your [a]pots can feel the thorns, he
shall take them away [b]as with a whirlwind, both
living, and in *his* wrath.
10 The righteous shall rejoice when he seeth
the [a]vengeance: [b]he shall wash his feet in the
blood of the wicked.
11 [a]So that a man shall say, Verily *there is*
a reward for the righteous: verily he is a God that
[b]judgeth in the earth.

4 [a]Eccl. 10:11
5 [a]Jer. 8:17
6 [a]Job 4:10
7 [a]Josh. 2:11; 7:5; Ps. 112:10; Is. 13:7; Ezek. 21:7
8 [a]Job 3:16
9 [a]Ps. 118:12; Eccl. 7:6 [b]Job 27:21; Prov. 10:25
10 [a][Deut. 32:43]; Jer. 11:20 [b]Ps. 68:23
11 [a]Ps. 92:15; Prov. 11:18; [2 Cor. 5:10] [b]Ps. 50:6; 75:7

NKJV

4 [a]Their poison *is* like the poison of a serpent;
They are like the deaf cobra *that* stops its ear,
5 Which will not [a]heed the voice of charmers,
Charming ever so skillfully.

6 [a]Break their teeth in their mouth, O God!
Break out the fangs of the young lions, O LORD!
7 [a]Let them flow away as waters *which* run continually;
When he bends *his bow,*
Let his arrows be as if cut in pieces.
8 *Let them be* like a snail which melts away as it goes,
[a]*Like* a stillborn child of a woman, that they may not see the sun.

9 Before your [a]pots can feel *the burning* thorns,
He shall take them away [b]as with a whirlwind,
As in His living and burning wrath.
10 The righteous shall rejoice when he sees the [a]vengeance;
[b]He shall wash his feet in the blood of the wicked,
11 [a]So that men will say,
"Surely *there is* a reward for the righteous;
Surely He is God who [b]judges in the earth."

PSALM 59

The Assured Judgment of the Wicked

To the chief Musician, Altaschith, Michtam of David; [a]when Saul sent, and they watched the house to kill him.

DELIVER me from mine enemies, O my God:
defend me from them that rise up against me.
2 Deliver me from the workers of iniquity,
and save me from bloody men.
3 For, lo, they lie in wait for my soul: [a]the
mighty are gathered against me; not *for* my transgression, nor *for* my sin, O LORD.
4 They run and prepare themselves without
my fault: [a]awake to help me, and behold.
5 Thou therefore, O LORD God of hosts, the
God of Israel, awake to visit all the heathen: be
not merciful to any wicked transgressors. Selah.
6 [a]They return at evening: they make a
noise like a dog, and go round about the city.
7 Behold, they belch out with their mouth:
[a]swords *are* in their lips: for [b]who, *say they,* doth
hear?
8 But [a]thou, O LORD, shalt laugh at them;
thou shalt have all the heathen in derision.
9 *Because of* his strength will I wait upon
thee: [a]for God *is* my defence.
10 The God of my mercy shall [a]prevent me:
God shall let [b]me see *my desire* upon mine
enemies.
11 Slay them not, lest my people forget: scatter them by thy power; and bring them down, O
Lord our shield.

PSALM 59

title [a]1 Sam. 19:11
3 [a]Ps. 56:6
4 [a]Ps. 35:23
6 [a]Ps. 59:14
7 [a]Ps. 57:4; Prov. 12:18 [b]Job 22:13; Ps. 10:11
8 [a]Prov. 1:26
9 [a][Ps. 62:2]
10 [a]Ps. 21:3 [b]Ps. 54:7

PSALM 59

The Assured Judgment of the Wicked

To the Chief Musician. Set to *"Do Not Destroy." A Michtam of David [a]when Saul sent men, and they watched the house in order to kill him.

DELIVER me from my enemies, O my God;
Defend me from those who rise up against me.
2 Deliver me from the workers of iniquity,
And save me from bloodthirsty men.

3 For look, they lie in wait for my life;
[a]The mighty gather against me,
Not *for* my transgression nor *for* my sin, O LORD.
4 They run and prepare themselves through no fault *of mine.*

[a]Awake to help me, and behold!
5 You therefore, O LORD God of hosts, the God of Israel,
Awake to punish all the nations;
Do not be merciful to any wicked transgressors. Selah

6 [a]At evening they return,
They growl like a dog,
And go all around the city.
7 Indeed, they belch with their mouth;
[a]Swords *are* in their lips;
For *they say,* [b]"Who hears?"

8 But [a]You, O LORD, shall laugh at them;
You shall have all the nations in derision.
9 I will wait for You, O You *his Strength;
[a]For God *is* my defense.
10 *My God of mercy shall [a]come to meet me;
God shall let [b]me see *my desire* on my enemies.

11 Do not slay them, lest my people forget;
Scatter them by Your power,
And bring them down,
O Lord our shield.

59:title Heb. *Al Tashcheth*
59:9 So with MT, Syr.; some Heb. mss., LXX, Tg., Vg. *my Strength*
59:10 So with Qr.; some Heb. mss., LXX, Vg. *My God, His mercy;* Kt., some Heb. mss., Tg. *O God, my mercy;* Syr. *O God, Your mercy*

KJV

12 [a]*For* the sin of their mouth *and* the words of their lips let them even be taken in their pride: and for cursing and lying *which* they speak.

13 [a]Consume *them* in wrath, consume *them,* that they *may* not *be:* and [b]let them know that God ruleth in Jacob unto the ends of the earth. Selah.

14 And [a]at evening let them return; *and* let them make a noise like a dog, and go round about the city.

15 Let them [a]wander up and down for meat, and grudge if they be not satisfied.

16 But I will sing of thy power; yea, I will sing aloud of thy mercy in the morning: for thou hast been my defence and refuge in the day of my trouble.

17 Unto thee, [a]O my strength, will I sing: for God *is* my defence, *and* the God of my mercy.

12 [a]Prov. 12:13
13 [a]Ps. 104:35 [b]Ps. 83:18
14 [a]Ps. 59:6
15 [a]Job 15:23
17 [a]Ps. 18:1

NKJV

12 [a]*For* the sin of their mouth *and* the words of their lips,
Let them even be taken in their pride,
And for the cursing and lying *which* they speak.
13 [a]Consume *them* in wrath, consume *them,*
That they *may* not *be;*
And [b]let them know that God rules in Jacob
To the ends of the earth. Selah

14 And [a]at evening they return,
They growl like a dog,
And go all around the city.
15 They [a]wander up and down for food,
And *howl if they are not satisfied.

16 But I will sing of Your power;
Yes, I will sing aloud of Your mercy in the morning;
For You have been my defense
And refuge in the day of my trouble.
17 To You, [a]O my Strength, I will sing praises;
For God *is* my defense,
My God of mercy.

PSALM 60

Urgent Prayer for the Restored Favor of God
(*cf. Ps.* 108:6–13)

To the chief Musician [a]upon Shushan–eduth, Michtam of David, to teach; [b]when he strove with Aram–naharaim and with Aram–zobah, when Joab returned, and smote of Edom in the valley of salt twelve thousand.

O GOD, [a]thou hast cast us off, thou hast scattered us, thou hast been displeased; O turn thyself to us again.

2 Thou hast made the earth to tremble; thou hast broken it: [a]heal the breaches thereof; for it shaketh.

3 [a]Thou hast shewed thy people hard things: [b]thou hast made us to drink the wine of astonishment.

4 [a]Thou hast given a banner to them that fear thee, that it may be displayed because of the truth. Selah.

5 [a]That thy beloved may be delivered; save *with* thy right hand, and hear me.

6 God hath [a]spoken in his holiness; I will rejoice, I will [b]divide [c]Shechem, and mete out [d]the valley of Succoth.

7 Gilead *is* mine, and Manasseh *is* mine; [a]Ephraim also *is* the strength of mine head; [b]Judah *is* my lawgiver;

8 [a]Moab *is* my washpot; [b]over Edom will I cast out my shoe: [c]Philistia, triumph thou because of me.

9 Who will bring me *into* the strong city? who will lead me into Edom?

10 *Wilt* not thou, O God, [a]*which* hadst cast us off? and *thou,* O God, *which* didst [b]not go out with our armies?

11 Give us help from trouble: [a]for vain *is* the help of man.

12 Through God [a]we shall do valiantly: for he *it is that* shall tread down our enemies.

PSALM 60

title [a]Ps. 80 [b]2 Sam. 8:3, 13; 1 Chr. 18:3
1 [a]Ps. 44:9
2 [a][2 Chr. 7:14]; Is. 30:26
3 [a]Ps. 71:20 [b]Is. 51:17, 22; Jer. 25:15
4 [a]Ps. 20:5; Is. 5:26; 11:12; 13:2
5 [a]Ps. 108:6–13
6 [a]Ps. 89:35 [b]Josh. 1:6 [c]Gen. 12:6 [d]Josh. 13:27
7 [a]Deut. 33:17 [b][Gen. 49:10]
8 [a]2 Sam. 8:2 [b]2 Sam. 8:14; Ps. 108:9 [c]2 Sam. 8:1
10 [a]Ps. 108:11 [b]Josh. 7:12
11 [a]Ps. 118:8; 146:3
12 [a]Num. 24:18

PSALM 60

Urgent Prayer for the Restored Favor of God
(*cf. Ps.* 108:6–13)

To the Chief Musician. [a]Set to *"Lily of the Testimony." A Michtam of David. For teaching. [b]When he fought against Mesopotamia and Syria of Zobah, and Joab returned and killed twelve thousand Edomites in the Valley of Salt.

O GOD, [a]You have cast us off;
You have broken us down;
You have been displeased;
Oh, restore us again!
2 You have made the earth tremble;
You have broken it;
[a]Heal its breaches, for it is shaking.
3 [a]You have shown Your people hard things;
[b]You have made us drink the wine of confusion.

4 [a]You have given a banner to those who fear You,
That it may be displayed because of the truth. Selah
5 [a]That Your beloved may be delivered,
Save *with* Your right hand, and hear me.

6 God has [a]spoken in His holiness:
"I will rejoice;
I will [b]divide [c]Shechem
And measure out [d]the Valley of Succoth.
7 Gilead *is* Mine, and Manasseh *is* Mine;
[a]Ephraim also *is* the helmet for My head;
[b]Judah *is* My lawgiver.
8 [a]Moab *is* My washpot;
[b]Over Edom I will cast My shoe;
[c]Philistia, shout in triumph because of Me."

9 Who will bring me *to* the strong city?
Who will lead me to Edom?
10 *Is it* not You, O God, [a]*who* cast us off?
And You, O God, *who* did [b]not go out with our armies?
11 Give us help from trouble,
[a]For the help of man *is* useless.
12 Through God [a]we will do valiantly,
For *it is* He *who* shall tread down our enemies.

*

59:15 So with LXX, Vg.; MT, Syr., Tg. *spend the night*
60:title Heb. *Shushan Eduth*

KJV

PSALM 61

Assurance of God's Eternal Protection

To the chief Musician upon Neginah, A Psalm of David.

HEAR my cry, O God; attend unto my prayer.
2 From the end of the earth will I cry unto
thee, when my heart is overwhelmed: lead me to
the rock *that* is higher than I.
3 For thou hast been a shelter for me, *and*
[a]a strong tower from the enemy.
4 I will abide in thy tabernacle for ever: [a]I
will trust in the covert of thy wings. Selah.
5 For thou, O God, hast heard my vows:
thou hast given *me* the heritage of those that fear
thy name.
6 Thou wilt prolong the king's life: *and* his
years as many generations.
7 He shall abide before God for ever: O prepare mercy [a]and truth, *which* may preserve him.
8 So will I sing praise unto thy name for
ever, that I may daily perform my vows.

PSALM 62

A Calm Resolve to Wait for the Salvation of God

To the chief Musician, to [a]Jeduthun, A Psalm of David.

TRULY [a]my soul waiteth upon God: from him
cometh my salvation.
2 He only *is* my rock and my salvation; *he*
is my defence; I shall not be greatly [a]moved.
3 How long will ye imagine mischief against
a man? ye shall be slain all of you: [a]as a bowing
wall *shall ye be, and as* a tottering fence.
4 They only consult to cast *him* down from
his excellency: they [a]delight in lies: they bless
with their mouth, but they curse inwardly. Selah.
5 My soul, wait thou only upon God; for my
expectation *is* from him.
6 He only *is* my rock and my salvation: *he*
is my defence; I shall not be moved.
7 [a]In God *is* my salvation and my glory: the
rock of my strength, *and* my refuge, *is* in God.
8 Trust in him at all times; ye people, [a]pour
out your heart before him: God *is* a refuge for
us. Selah.
9 [a]Surely men of low degree *are* vanity, *and*
men of high degree *are* a lie: to be laid in the
balance, they *are* altogether *lighter* than vanity.
10 Trust not in oppression, and become not
vain in robbery: [a]if riches increase, set not your
heart *upon them.*
11 God hath spoken once; twice have I heard
this; that power *belongeth* unto God.
12 Also unto thee, O Lord, *belongeth* mercy:
for [a]thou renderest to every man according to his
work.

PSALM 61

3 [a]Prov. 18:10
4 [a]Ps. 91:4
7 [a]Ps. 40:11

PSALM 62

title [a]1 Chr. 25:1
1 [a]Ps. 33:20
2 [a]Ps. 55:22
3 [a]Is. 30:13
4 [a]Ps. 28:3
7 [a][Jer. 3:23]
8 [a]1 Sam. 1:15; Ps. 42:4; Lam. 2:19
9 [a]Job 7:16; Ps. 39:5; Is. 40:17
10 [a]Job 31:25; [Mark 10:24; Luke 12:15; 1 Tim. 6:10]
12 [a][Matt. 16:27]; Rom. 2:6; 1 Cor. 3:8

NKJV

PSALM 61

Assurance of God's Eternal Protection

To the Chief Musician. On *[a] stringed instrument. A Psalm of David.

HEAR my cry, O God;
Attend to my prayer.
2 From the end of the earth I will cry to You,
When my heart is overwhelmed;
Lead me to the rock that is higher than I.

3 For You have been a shelter for me,
[a]A strong tower from the enemy.
4 I will abide in Your tabernacle forever;
[a]I will trust in the shelter of Your wings. Selah

5 For You, O God, have heard my vows;
You have given *me* the heritage of those who fear Your name.
6 You will prolong the king's life,
His years as many generations.
7 He shall abide before God forever.
Oh, prepare mercy [a]and truth, *which* may preserve him!

8 So I will sing praise to Your name forever,
That I may daily perform my vows.

PSALM 62

A Calm Resolve to Wait for the Salvation of God

To the Chief Musician. To [a]Jeduthun. A Psalm of David.

TRULY [a]my soul silently *waits* for God;
From Him *comes* my salvation.
2 He only *is* my rock and my salvation;
He is my defense;
I shall not be greatly [a]moved.

3 How long will you attack a man?
You shall be slain, all of you,
[a]Like a leaning wall and a tottering fence.
4 They only consult to cast *him* down from his high position;
They [a]delight in lies;
They bless with their mouth,
But they curse inwardly. Selah

5 My soul, wait silently for God alone,
For my expectation *is* from Him.
6 He only *is* my rock and my salvation;
He is my defense;
I shall not be moved.
7 [a]In God *is* my salvation and my glory;
The rock of my strength,
And my refuge, *is* in God.

8 Trust in Him at all times, you people;
[a]Pour out your heart before Him;
God *is* a refuge for us. Selah

9 [a]Surely men of low degree *are* a vapor,
Men of high degree *are* a lie;
If they are weighed on the scales,
They *are* altogether *lighter* than vapor.
10 Do not trust in oppression,
Nor vainly hope in robbery;
[a]If riches increase,
Do not set *your* heart *on them.*

11 God has spoken once,
Twice I have heard this:
That power *belongs* to God.
12 Also to You, O Lord, *belongs* mercy;
For [a]You render to each one according to his work.

*
61:title Heb. *neginah*

KJV

PSALM 63

Joy in the Fellowship of God

A Psalm of David, [a]when he was in the wilderness of Judah.

O GOD, thou *art* my God; early will I seek thee: [a]my soul thirsteth for thee, my flesh longeth for thee in a dry and thirsty land, where no water is;

2 To see [a]thy power and thy glory, so *as* I have seen thee in the sanctuary.

3 [a]Because thy lovingkindness *is* better than life, my lips shall praise thee.

4 Thus will I bless thee while I live: I will [a]lift up my hands in thy name.

5 My soul shall be satisfied as *with* marrow and fatness; and my mouth shall praise *thee* with joyful lips:

6 When [a]I remember thee upon my bed, *and* meditate on thee in the *night* watches.

7 Because thou hast been my help, therefore in the shadow of thy wings will I rejoice.

8 My soul followeth hard after thee: thy right hand upholdeth me.

9 But those *that* seek my soul, to destroy *it*, shall go into the lower parts of the earth.

10 They shall fall by the sword: they shall be a portion for foxes.

11 But the king shall rejoice in God; [a]every one that sweareth by him shall glory: but the mouth of them that speak lies shall be stopped.

PSALM 64

Oppressed by the Wicked but Rejoicing in the LORD

To the chief Musician, A Psalm of David.

HEAR my voice, O God, in my prayer: preserve my life from fear of the enemy.

2 Hide me from the secret counsel of the wicked; from the insurrection of the workers of iniquity:

3 Who whet their tongue like a sword, [a]*and* bend *their bows to shoot* their arrows, *even* bitter words:

4 That they may shoot in secret at the perfect: suddenly do they shoot at him, and fear not.

5 They encourage themselves *in* an evil matter: they commune of laying snares privily; [a]they say, Who shall see them?

6 They search out iniquities; they accomplish a diligent search: both the inward *thought* of every one *of them*, and the heart, *is* deep.

7 But God shall shoot at them *with* an arrow; suddenly shall they be wounded.

8 So they shall make their own tongue to fall upon themselves: [a]all that see them shall flee away.

9 And all men shall fear, and shall [a]declare the work of God; for they shall wisely consider of his doing.

PSALM 63

title [a]1 Sam. 22:5
1 [a]Ps. 42:2; [Matt. 5:6]
2 [a]Ps. 27:4
3 [a]Ps. 138:2
4 [a]Ps. 28:2; 143:6
6 [a]Ps. 42:8
11 [a]Deut. 6:13; [Is. 45:23; 65:16]

PSALM 64

3 [a]Ps. 58:7
5 [a]Ps. 10:11; 59:7
8 [a]Ps. 31:11
9 [a]Jer. 50:28; 51:10

NKJV

PSALM 63

Joy in the Fellowship of God

A Psalm of David [a]when he was in the wilderness of Judah.

O GOD, You *are* my God;
Early will I seek You;
[a]My soul thirsts for You;
My flesh longs for You
In a dry and thirsty land
Where there is no water.
2 So I have looked for You in the sanctuary,
To see [a]Your power and Your glory.

3 [a]Because Your lovingkindness *is* better than life,
My lips shall praise You.
4 Thus I will bless You while I live;
I will [a]lift up my hands in Your name.
5 My soul shall be satisfied as with marrow and fatness,
And my mouth shall praise You with joyful lips.

6 When [a]I remember You on my bed,
I meditate on You in the *night* watches.
7 Because You have been my help,
Therefore in the shadow of Your wings I will rejoice.
8 My soul follows close behind You;
Your right hand upholds me.

9 But those *who* seek my life, to destroy *it*,
Shall go into the lower parts of the earth.
10 They shall fall by the sword;
They shall be a portion for jackals.

11 But the king shall rejoice in God;
[a]Everyone who swears by Him shall glory;
But the mouth of those who speak lies shall be stopped.

PSALM 64

Oppressed by the Wicked but Rejoicing in the LORD

To the Chief Musician. A Psalm of David.

HEAR my voice, O God, in my meditation;
Preserve my life from fear of the enemy.
2 Hide me from the secret plots of the wicked,
From the rebellion of the workers of iniquity,
3 Who sharpen their tongue like a sword,
[a]And bend *their bows to shoot* their arrows—bitter words,
4 That they may shoot in secret at the blameless;
Suddenly they shoot at him and do not fear.

5 They encourage themselves *in* an evil matter;
They talk of laying snares secretly;
[a]They say, "Who will see them?"
6 They devise iniquities:
"We have perfected a shrewd scheme."
Both the inward thought and the heart of man are deep.

7 But God shall shoot at them *with* an arrow;
Suddenly they shall be wounded.
8 So He will make them stumble over their own tongue;
[a]All who see them shall flee away.
9 All men shall fear,
And shall [a]declare the work of God;
For they shall wisely consider His doing.

KJV

10 [a]The righteous shall be glad in the LORD,
and shall trust in him; and all the upright in heart
shall glory.

PSALM 65

Praise to God for His Salvation and Providence

To the chief Musician, A Psalm *and* Song of David.

PRAISE waiteth for thee, O God in Sion: and
unto thee shall the vow be performed.
2 O thou that hearest prayer, [a]unto thee
shall all flesh come.
3 Iniquities prevail against me: *as for* our
transgressions, thou shalt [a]purge them away.
4 [a]Blessed *is the man whom* thou [b]choosest,
and causest to approach *unto thee, that* he may
dwell in thy courts: [c]we shall be satisfied with
the goodness of thy house, *even* of thy holy
temple.
5 *By* terrible things in righteousness wilt
thou answer us, O God of our salvation; *who art*
the confidence of all the ends of the earth, and
of them that are afar off *upon* the sea:
6 Which by his strength setteth fast the
mountains; [a]*being* girded with power:
7 [a]Which stilleth the noise of the seas, the
noise of their waves, [b]and the tumult of the
people.
8 They also that dwell in the uttermost parts
are afraid at thy tokens: thou makest the outgoings of the morning and evening to rejoice.
9 Thou visitest the earth, and [a]waterest it:
thou greatly enrichest it [b]with the river of God,
which is full of water: thou preparest them corn,
when thou hast so provided for it.
10 Thou waterest the ridges thereof abundantly: thou settlest the furrows thereof: thou
makest it soft with showers: thou blessest the
springing thereof.
11 Thou crownest the year with thy goodness; and thy paths drop fatness.
12 They drop *upon* the pastures of the wilderness: and the little hills rejoice on every side.
13 The pastures are clothed with flocks; [a]the
valleys also are covered over with corn; they
shout for joy, they also sing.

PSALM 66

Praise to God for His Awesome Works

To the chief Musician, A Song *or* Psalm.

MAKE [a]a joyful noise unto God, all ye lands:
2 Sing forth the honour of his name: make
his praise glorious.
3 Say unto God, How [a]terrible *art thou in*
thy works! [b]through the greatness of thy power
shall thine enemies submit themselves unto thee.
4 [a]All the earth shall worship thee, and shall
sing unto thee; they shall sing *to* thy name.
Selah.
5 Come and see the works of God: *he is* terrible *in his* doing toward the children of men.

10 [a]Job 22:19; Ps. 32:11

PSALM 65

2 [a][Is. 66:23]
3 [a]Ps. 51:2; 79:9; Is. 6:7; [Heb. 9:14; 1 John 1:7, 9]
4 [a]Ps. 33:12 [b]Ps. 4:3 [c]Ps. 36:8
6 [a]Ps. 93:1
7 [a]Matt. 8:26 [b]Is. 17:12, 13
9 [a][Deut. 11:12]; Jer. 5:24 [b]Ps. 46:4; 104:13; 147:8
13 [a]Is. 44:23; 55:12

PSALM 66

1 [a]Ps. 100:1
3 [a]Ps. 65:5 [b]Ps. 18:44
4 [a]Ps. 117:1; Zech. 14:16

NKJV

10 [a]The righteous shall be glad in the LORD,
and trust in Him.
And all the upright in heart shall glory.

PSALM 65

Praise to God for His Salvation and Providence

To the Chief Musician. A Psalm of David. A Song.

PRAISE is awaiting You, O God, in Zion;
And to You the vow shall be performed.
2 O You who hear prayer,
[a]To You all flesh will come.
3 Iniquities prevail against me;
As for our transgressions,
You will [a]provide atonement for them.

4 [a]Blessed *is the man* You [b]choose,
And cause to approach *You,*
That he may dwell in Your courts.
[c]We shall be satisfied with the goodness
of Your house,
Of Your holy temple.

5 *By* awesome deeds in righteousness You
will answer us,
O God of our salvation,
You who are the confidence of all the ends
of the earth,
And of the far-off seas;
6 Who established the mountains by His
strength,
[a]*Being* clothed with power;
7 [a]You who still the noise of the seas,
The noise of their waves,
[b]And the tumult of the peoples.
8 They also who dwell in the farthest parts
are afraid of Your signs;
You make the outgoings of the morning
and evening rejoice.

9 You visit the earth and [a]water it,
You greatly enrich it;
[b]The river of God is full of water;
You provide their grain,
For so You have prepared it.
10 You water its ridges abundantly,
You settle its furrows;
You make it soft with showers,
You bless its growth.

11 You crown the year with Your
goodness,
And Your paths drip *with* abundance.
12 They drop *on* the pastures of the
wilderness,
And the little hills rejoice on every side.
13 The pastures are clothed with flocks;
[a]The valleys also are covered with grain;
They shout for joy, they also sing.

PSALM 66

Praise to God for His Awesome Works

To the Chief Musician. A Song. A Psalm.

MAKE [a]a joyful shout to God, all the
earth!
2 Sing out the honor of His name;
Make His praise glorious.
3 Say to God,
"How [a]awesome are Your works!
[b]Through the greatness of Your power
Your enemies shall submit themselves to
You.
4 [a]All the earth shall worship You
And sing praises to You;
They shall sing praises *to* Your name."
Selah

5 Come and see the works of God;
He is awesome *in His* doing toward the
sons of men.

KJV

6 [a]He turned the sea into dry *land:* [b]they
went through the flood on foot: there did we rejoice in him.
7 He ruleth by his power for ever; his eyes
behold the nations: let not the rebellious exalt
themselves. Selah.
8 O bless our God, ye people, and make the
voice of his praise to be heard:
9 Which holdeth our soul in life, and suffereth not our feet to be moved.
10 For [a]thou, O God, hast proved us: [b]thou
hast tried us, as silver is tried.
11 [a]Thou broughtest us into the net; thou
laidst affliction upon our loins.
12 [a]Thou hast caused men to ride over our
heads; [b]we went through fire and through water:
but thou broughtest us out into a wealthy *place.*
13 [a]I will go into thy house with burnt offerings: [b]I will pay thee my vows,
14 Which my lips have uttered, and my
mouth hath spoken, when I was in trouble.
15 I will offer unto thee burnt sacrifices of
fatlings, with the incense of rams: I will offer bullocks with goats. Selah.
16 Come *and* hear, all ye that fear God, and
I will declare what he hath done for my soul.
17 I cried unto him with my mouth, and he
was extolled with my tongue.
18 [a]If I regard iniquity in my heart, the Lord
will not hear *me:*
19 *But* verily God [a]hath heard *me;* he hath
attended to the voice of my prayer.
20 Blessed *be* God, which hath not turned
away my prayer, nor his mercy from me.

6 [a]Ex. 14:21 [b]Josh. 3:14–16
10 [a]Job 23:10; Ps. 17:3 [b][Is. 48:10; Zech. 13:9; Mal. 3:3; 1 Pet. 1:7]
11 [a]Lam. 1:13; Ezek. 12:13
12 [a]Is. 51:23 [b]Is. 43:2
13 [a]Ps. 100:4; 116:14, 17–19 [b][Eccl. 5:4]
18 [a]Job 27:9; [Prov. 15:29; 28:9]; Is. 1:15; [John 9:31; James 4:3]
19 [a]Ps. 116:1, 2

NKJV

6 [a]He turned the sea into dry *land;*
[b]They went through the river on foot.
There we will rejoice in Him.
7 He rules by His power forever;
His eyes observe the nations;
Do not let the rebellious exalt themselves.
Selah

8 Oh, bless our God, you peoples!
And make the voice of His praise to be heard,
9 Who keeps our soul among the living,
And does not allow our feet to be moved.
10 For [a]You, O God, have tested us;
[b]You have refined us as silver is refined.
11 [a]You brought us into the net;
You laid affliction on our backs.
12 [a]You have caused men to ride over our heads;
[b]We went through fire and through water;
But You brought us out to rich *fulfillment.*

13 [a]I will go into Your house with burnt offerings;
[b]I will pay You my vows,
14 Which my lips have uttered
And my mouth has spoken when I was in trouble.
15 I will offer You burnt sacrifices of fat animals,
With the sweet aroma of rams;
I will offer bulls with goats. Selah

16 Come *and* hear, all you who fear God,
And I will declare what He has done for my soul.
17 I cried to Him with my mouth,
And He was extolled with my tongue.
18 [a]If I regard iniquity in my heart,
The Lord will not hear.
19 *But* certainly God [a]has heard *me;*
He has attended to the voice of my prayer.

20 Blessed *be* God,
Who has not turned away my prayer,
Nor His mercy from me!

PSALM 67

An Invocation and a Doxology

To the chief Musician on Neginoth, A Psalm *or* Song.

GOD be merciful unto us, and bless us; *and*
[a]cause his face to shine upon us; Selah.
2 That [a]thy way may be known upon earth,
[b]thy saving health among all nations.
3 Let the people praise thee, O God; let all
the people praise thee.
4 O let the nations be glad and sing for joy:
for [a]thou shalt judge the people righteously, and
govern the nations upon earth. Selah.
5 Let the people praise thee, O God; let all
the people praise thee.
6 [a]*Then* shall the earth yield her increase;
and God, *even* our own God, shall bless us.
7 God shall bless us; and all the ends of the
earth shall fear him.

PSALM 67

1 [a]Num. 6:25
2 [a]Acts 18:25 [b]Is. 52:10; Titus 2:11
4 [a][Ps. 96:10, 13; 98:9]
6 [a]Lev. 26:4; Ps. 85:12; [Ezek. 34:27]; Zech. 8:12

PSALM 67

An Invocation and a Doxology

To the Chief Musician. On *stringed instruments. A Psalm. A Song.

GOD be merciful to us and bless us,
And [a]cause His face to shine upon us,
Selah
2 That [a]Your way may be known on earth,
[b]Your salvation among all nations.

3 Let the peoples praise You, O God;
Let all the peoples praise You.
4 Oh, let the nations be glad and sing for joy!
For [a]You shall judge the people righteously,
And govern the nations on earth. Selah

5 Let the peoples praise You, O God;
Let all the peoples praise You.
6 [a]*Then* the earth shall yield her increase;
God, our own God, shall bless us.
7 God shall bless us,
And all the ends of the earth shall fear Him.

PSALM 68

The Glory of God in His Goodness to Israel

To the chief Musician, A Psalm *or* Song of David.

LET [a]God arise, let his enemies be scattered:
let them also that hate him flee before him.

PSALM 68

1 [a]Num. 10:35

*—————

67:title Heb. *neginoth*

PSALM 68

The Glory of God in His Goodness to Israel

To the Chief Musician. A Psalm of David. A Song.

LET [a]God arise,
Let His enemies be scattered;
Let those also who hate Him flee before Him.

KJV

2 [a]As smoke is driven away, so drive *them* away: [b]as wax melteth before the fire, *so* let the wicked perish at the presence of God.

3 But [a]let the righteous be glad; let them rejoice before God: yea, let them exceedingly rejoice.

4 Sing unto God, sing praises to his name: [a]extol him that rideth upon the heavens [b]by his name JAH, and rejoice before him.

5 [a]A father of the fatherless, and a judge of the widows, *is* God in his holy habitation.

6 [a]God setteth the solitary in families: [b]he bringeth out those which are bound with chains: but [c]the rebellious dwell in a dry *land.*

7 O God, [a]when thou wentest forth before thy people, when thou didst march through the wilderness; Selah:

8 The earth shook, the heavens also dropped at the presence of God: *even* Sinai itself *was moved* at the presence of God, the God of Israel.

9 [a]Thou, O God, didst send a plentiful rain, whereby thou didst confirm thine inheritance, when it was weary.

10 Thy congregation hath dwelt therein: [a]thou, O God, hast prepared of thy goodness for the poor.

11 The Lord gave the word: great *was* the company of those that published *it.*

12 [a]Kings of armies did flee apace: and she that tarried at home divided the spoil.

13 [a]Though ye have lien among the pots, [b]*yet shall ye be as* the wings of a dove covered with silver, and her feathers with yellow gold.

14 [a]When the Almighty scattered kings in it, it was *white* as snow in Salmon.

15 The hill of God *is as* the hill of Bashan; an high hill *as* the hill of Bashan.

16 Why leap ye, ye high hills? [a]*this is* the hill *which* God desireth to dwell in; yea, the LORD will dwell *in it* for ever.

17 [a]The chariots of God *are* twenty thousand, *even* thousands of angels: the Lord *is* among them, *as in* Sinai, in the holy *place.*

18 [a]Thou hast ascended on high, [b]thou hast led captivity captive: [c]thou hast received gifts for men; yea, *for* [d]the rebellious also, [e]that the LORD God might dwell *among them.*

19 Blessed *be* the Lord, *who* daily loadeth us *with benefits, even* the God of our salvation. Selah.

20 *He that is* our God *is* the God of salvation; and [a]unto GOD the Lord *belong* the issues from death.

2 [a][Is. 9:18]; Hos. 13:3 [b]Ps. 97:5; Mic. 1:4
3 [a]Ps. 32:11
4 [a]Deut. 33:26 [b][Ex. 6:3]
5 [a][Ps. 10:14, 18; 146:9]
6 [a]Ps. 107:4–7 [b]Acts 12:6 [c]Ps. 107:34
7 [a]Ex. 13:21; [Hab. 3:13]
9 [a]Lev. 26:4; Deut. 11:11; Job 5:10; Ezek. 34:26
10 [a]Deut. 26:5; Ps. 74:19
12 [a]Num. 31:8; Josh. 10:16; Judg. 5:19
13 [a]Ps. 81:6 [b]Ps. 105:37
14 [a]Josh. 10:10
16 [a][Deut. 12:5]; 1 Kin. 9:3
17 [a]Deut. 33:2; Dan. 7:10
18 [a]Mark 16:19; Acts 1:9; Eph. 4:8; Phil. 2:9; Col. 3:1; Heb. 1:3 [b]Judg. 5:12 [c]Acts 2:4, 33; 10:44–46; [1 Cor. 12:4–11; Eph. 4:7–12] [d][1 Tim. 1:13] [e]Ps. 78:60
20 [a][Deut. 32:39]

NKJV

2 [a]As smoke is driven away,
So drive *them* away;
[b]As wax melts before the fire,
So let the wicked perish at the presence of God.
3 But [a]let the righteous be glad;
Let them rejoice before God;
Yes, let them rejoice exceedingly.

4 Sing to God, sing praises to His name;
[a]Extol Him who rides on the *clouds,
[b]By His name YAH,
And rejoice before Him.

5 [a]A father of the fatherless, a defender of widows,
Is God in His holy habitation.
6 [a]God sets the solitary in families;
[b]He brings out those who are bound into prosperity;
But [c]the rebellious dwell in a dry *land.*

7 O God, [a]when You went out before Your people,
When You marched through the wilderness, Selah
8 The earth shook;
The heavens also dropped *rain* at the presence of God;
Sinai itself *was moved* at the presence of God, the God of Israel.
9 [a]You, O God, sent a plentiful rain,
Whereby You confirmed Your inheritance,
When it was weary.
10 Your congregation dwelt in it;
[a]You, O God, provided from Your goodness for the poor.

11 The Lord gave the word;
Great *was* the company of those who proclaimed *it:*
12 "Kings[a] of armies flee, they flee,
And she who remains at home divides the spoil.
13 [a]Though you lie down among the sheepfolds,
[b]*You will be* like the wings of a dove covered with silver,
And her feathers with yellow gold."
14 [a]When the Almighty scattered kings in it,
It was *white* as snow in Zalmon.

15 A mountain of God *is* the mountain of Bashan;
A mountain *of many* peaks *is* the mountain of Bashan.
16 Why do you fume with envy, you mountains of *many* peaks?
[a]*This is* the mountain *which* God desires to dwell in;
Yes, the LORD will dwell *in it* forever.

17 [a]The chariots of God *are* twenty thousand,
Even thousands of thousands;
The Lord is among them *as in* Sinai, in the Holy *Place.*
18 [a]You have ascended on high,
[b]You have led captivity captive;
[c]You have received gifts among men,
Even *from* [d]the rebellious,
[e]That the LORD God might dwell *there.*

19 Blessed *be* the Lord,
Who daily loads us *with benefits,*
The God of our salvation! Selah
20 Our God *is* the God of salvation;
And [a]to GOD the Lord *belong* escapes from death.

*68:4 MT *deserts;* Tg. *heavens* (cf. v. 34 and Is. 19:1)

KJV

21 But [a]God shall wound the head of his enemies, [b]*and* the hairy scalp of such an one as goeth
on still in his trespasses.
22 The Lord said, I will bring [a]again from
Bashan, I will bring *my people* again [b]from the
depths of the sea:
23 [a]That thy foot may be dipped in the blood
of *thine* enemies, [b]*and* the tongue of thy dogs in
the same.
24 They have seen thy goings, O God; *even*
the goings of my God, my King, in the sanctuary.
25 [a]The singers went before, the players on
instruments *followed* after; among *them were* the
damsels playing with timbrels.
26 Bless ye God in the congregations, *even*
the Lord, from [a]the fountain of Israel.
27 There *is* [a]little Benjamin *with* their ruler,
the princes of Judah *and* their council, the princes
of Zebulun, *and* the princes of Naphtali.
28 Thy God hath [a]commanded thy strength:
strengthen, O God, that which thou hast wrought
for us.
29 Because of thy temple at Jerusalem [a]shall
kings bring presents unto thee.
30 Rebuke the company of spearmen, [a]the
multitude of the bulls, with the calves of the people, *till every one* [b]submit himself with pieces of
silver: scatter thou the people *that* delight in war.
31 [a]Princes shall come out of Egypt; [b]Ethio-
pia shall soon [c]stretch out her hands unto God.
32 Sing unto God, ye [a]kingdoms of the earth;
O sing praises unto the Lord. Selah:
33 To him [a]that rideth upon the heavens of
heavens, *which were* of old; lo, he doth send out
his voice, *and that* a [b]mighty voice.
34 [a]Ascribe ye strength unto God: his excellency *is* over Israel, and his strength *is* in the
clouds.
35 O God, [a]*thou art* terrible out of thy holy
places: the God of Israel *is* he that giveth strength
and power unto *his* people. Blessed *be* God.

PSALM 69

An Urgent Plea for Help in Trouble

To the chief Musician upon Shoshannim, *A Psalm* of David.

SAVE me, O God; for [a]the waters are come in
unto *my* soul.
2 [a]I sink in deep mire, where *there is* no
standing: I am come into deep waters, where the
floods overflow me.
3 [a]I am weary of my crying: my throat is
dried: [b]mine eyes fail while I wait for my God.
4 They that [a]hate me without a cause are
more than the hairs of mine head: they that would
destroy me, *being* mine enemies wrongfully, are
mighty: then I restored *that* which I took not
away.

21 [a]Hab. 3:13 [b]Ps. 55:23 **22** [a]Num. 21:33; Deut. 30:1–9; Amos 9:1–3 [b]Ex. 14:22 **23** [a]Ps. 58:10 [b]1 Kin. 21:19; Jer. 15:3 **25** [a]1 Chr. 13:8 **26** [a]Deut. 33:28; Is. 48:1 **27** [a]Judg. 5:14; 1 Sam. 9:21 **28** [a]Ps. 42:8; Is. 26:12 **29** [a]1 Kin. 10:10, 25; 2 Chr. 32:23; Ps. 45:12; 72:10; Is. 18:7 **30** [a]Ps. 22:12 [b]2 Sam. 8:2 **31** [a]Is. 19:19–23 [b]Is. 45:14; Zeph. 3:10 [c]Ps. 44:20 **32** [a][Ps. 67:3, 4] **33** [a]Deut. 33:26; Ps. 18:10 [b]Ps. 46:6; Is. 30:30 **34** [a]Ps. 29:1 **35** [a]Ps. 76:12

PSALM 69

1 [a]Job 22:11; Jon. 2:5 **2** [a]Ps. 40:2 **3** [a]Ps. 6:6 [b]Deut. 28:32; Ps. 119:82, 123; Is. 38:14 **4** [a]Ps. 35:19; John 15:25

*______

68:23 LXX, [Syr.], Tg., Vg. *you may dip your foot* **68:28** LXX, [Syr.], Tg., Vg. *Command, O God* **69:title** Heb. *Shoshannim*

NKJV

21 But [a]God will wound the head of His enemies,
[b]The hairy scalp of the one who still goes on in his trespasses.
22 The Lord said, "I will bring [a]back from Bashan,
I will bring *them* back [b]from the depths of the sea,
23 [a]That *your foot may crush *them* in blood,
[b]And the tongues of your dogs *may have* their portion from *your* enemies."

24 They have seen Your procession, O God,
The procession of my God, my King, into the sanctuary.
25 [a]The singers went before, the players on instruments *followed* after;
Among *them were* the maidens playing timbrels.
26 Bless God in the congregations,
The Lord, from [a]the fountain of Israel.
27 [a]There *is* little Benjamin, their leader,
The princes of Judah *and* their company,
The princes of Zebulun *and* the princes of Naphtali.

28 *Your God has [a]commanded your strength;
Strengthen, O God, what You have done for us.
29 Because of Your temple at Jerusalem,
[a]Kings will bring presents to You.
30 Rebuke the beasts of the reeds,
[a]The herd of bulls with the calves of the peoples,
Till everyone [b]submits himself with pieces of silver.
Scatter the peoples *who* delight in war.
31 [a]Envoys will come out of Egypt;
[b]Ethiopia will quickly [c]stretch out her hands to God.

32 Sing to God, you [a]kingdoms of the earth;
Oh, sing praises to the Lord, Selah
33 To Him [a]who rides on the heaven of heavens, *which were* of old!
Indeed, He sends out His voice, a [b]mighty voice.
34 [a]Ascribe strength to God;
His excellence *is* over Israel,
And His strength *is* in the clouds.
35 O God, [a]*You are* more awesome than Your holy places.
The God of Israel *is* He who gives strength and power to *His* people.

Blessed *be* God!

PSALM 69

An Urgent Plea for Help in Trouble

To the Chief Musician. Set to *"The Lilies." A Psalm of David.

SAVE me, O God!
For [a]the waters have come up to *my* neck.
2 [a]I sink in deep mire,
Where *there is* no standing;
I have come into deep waters,
Where the floods overflow me.
3 [a]I am weary with my crying;
My throat is dry;
[b]My eyes fail while I wait for my God.

4 Those who [a]hate me without a cause
Are more than the hairs of my head;
They are mighty who would destroy me,
Being my enemies wrongfully;
Though I have stolen nothing,
I *still* must restore *it*.

KJV

5 O God, thou knowest my foolishness; and
my sins are not hid from thee.
6 Let not them that wait on thee, O Lord
GOD of hosts, be ashamed for my sake: let not
those that seek thee be confounded for my sake,
O God of Israel.
7 Because for thy sake I have borne reproach; shame hath covered my face.
8 [a]I am become a stranger unto my brethren, and an alien unto my mother's children.
9 [a]For the zeal of thine house hath eaten
me up; [b]and the reproaches of them that reproached thee are fallen upon me.
10 When I wept, *and chastened* my soul with
fasting, that was to my reproach.
11 I made sackcloth also my garment; and I
became a proverb to them.
12 They that sit in the gate speak against me;
and I *was* the song of the [a]drunkards.
13 But as for me, my prayer *is* unto thee, O
LORD, *in* an acceptable time: O God, in the multitude of thy mercy hear me, in the truth of thy
salvation.
14 Deliver me out of the mire, and let me not
sink: let me be delivered from them that hate me,
and out of the deep waters.
15 Let not the waterflood overflow me, neither let the deep swallow me up, and let not the
pit shut her mouth upon me.
16 Hear me, O LORD; for thy lovingkindness
is good: turn unto me according to the multitude
of thy tender mercies.
17 And hide not thy face from thy servant;
for I am in trouble: hear me speedily.
18 Draw nigh unto my soul, *and* redeem it:
deliver me because of mine enemies.
19 Thou hast known [a]my reproach, and my
shame, and my dishonour: mine adversaries *are*
all before thee.
20 Reproach hath broken my heart; and I am
full of heaviness: and [a]I looked *for some* to take
pity, but *there was* none; and for [b]comforters, but
I found none.
21 They gave me also gall for my meat; [a]and
in my thirst they gave me vinegar to drink.
22 [a]Let their table become a snare before
them: and *that which should have been* for *their*
welfare, *let it become* a trap.
23 [a]Let their eyes be darkened, that they see
not; and make their loins continually to shake.
24 [a]Pour out thine indignation upon them,
and let thy wrathful anger take hold of them.
25 [a]Let their habitation be desolate; *and* let
none dwell in their tents.
26 For they persecute [a]*him* whom thou hast
smitten; and they talk to the grief of those whom
thou hast wounded.
27 [a]Add iniquity unto their iniquity: [b]and let
them not come into thy righteousness.

8 [a]Is. 53:3; Mark 3:21; Luke 8:19; John 7:3–5
9 [a]John 2:17 [b]Rom. 15:3
12 [a]Job 30:9
19 [a]Ps. 22:6, 7; Heb. 12:2
20 [a]Is. 63:5 [b]Job 16:2
21 [a]Matt. 27:34, 48; Mark 15:23, 36; Luke 23:36; John 19:28–30
22 [a]Rom. 11:9, 10
23 [a]Is. 6:9, 10
24 [a][1 Thess. 2:16; Jer. 10:25]
25 [a]Matt. 23:38; Luke 13:35; Acts 1:20
26 [a][Is. 53:4; 1 Pet. 2:24]
27 [a]Neh. 4:5; [Rom. 1:28] [b][Is. 26:10]

NKJV

5 O God, You know my foolishness;
And my sins are not hidden from You.
6 Let not those who wait for You, O Lord GOD of hosts, be ashamed because of me;
Let not those who seek You be confounded because of me, O God of Israel.
7 Because for Your sake I have borne reproach;
Shame has covered my face.
8 [a]I have become a stranger to my brothers,
And an alien to my mother's children;
9 [a]Because zeal for Your house has eaten me up,
[b]And the reproaches of those who reproach You have fallen on me.
10 When I wept *and chastened* my soul with fasting,
That became my reproach.
11 I also made sackcloth my garment;
I became a byword to them.
12 Those who sit in the gate speak against me,
And I *am* the song of the [a]drunkards.

13 But as for me, my prayer *is* to You,
O LORD, *in* the acceptable time;
O God, in the multitude of Your mercy,
Hear me in the truth of Your salvation.
14 Deliver me out of the mire,
And let me not sink;
Let me be delivered from those who hate me,
And out of the deep waters.
15 Let not the floodwater overflow me,
Nor let the deep swallow me up;
And let not the pit shut its mouth on me.

16 Hear me, O LORD, for Your lovingkindness *is* good;
Turn to me according to the multitude of Your tender mercies.
17 And do not hide Your face from Your servant,
For I am in trouble;
Hear me speedily.
18 Draw near to my soul, *and* redeem it;
Deliver me because of my enemies.

19 You know [a]my reproach, my shame, and my dishonor;
My adversaries *are* all before You.
20 Reproach has broken my heart,
And I am full of heaviness;
[a]I looked *for someone* to take pity, but *there was* none;
And for [b]comforters, but I found none.
21 They also gave me gall for my food,
[a]And for my thirst they gave me vinegar to drink.

22 [a]Let their table become a snare before them,
And their well-being a trap.
23 [a]Let their eyes be darkened, so that they do not see;
And make their loins shake continually.
24 [a]Pour out Your indignation upon them,
And let Your wrathful anger take hold of them.
25 [a]Let their dwelling place be desolate;
Let no one live in their tents.
26 For they persecute the *ones* [a]You have struck,
And talk of the grief of those You have wounded.
27 [a]Add iniquity to their iniquity,
[b]And let them not come into Your righteousness.

KJV

28 Let them [a]be blotted out of the book of
the living, [b]and not be written with the righteous.
29 But I *am* poor and sorrowful: let thy salvation, O God, set me up on high.
30 [a]I will praise the name of God with a song,
and will magnify him with thanksgiving.
31 [a]*This* also shall please the LORD better
than an ox *or* bullock that hath horns and hoofs.
32 [a]The humble shall see *this, and* be glad:
and [b]your heart shall live that seek God.
33 For the LORD heareth the poor, and despiseth not [a]his prisoners.
34 [a]Let the heaven and earth praise him, the
seas, [b]and every thing that moveth therein.
35 [a]For God will save Zion, and will build
the cities of Judah: that they may dwell there, and
have it in possession.
36 [a]The seed also of his servants shall inherit
it: and they that love his name shall dwell therein.

28 [a][Ex. 32:32]; Phil. 4:3; [Rev. 3:5; 13:8] [b]Ezek. 13:9; Luke 10:20; Heb. 12:23
30 [a][Ps. 28:7]
31 [a]Ps. 50:13, 14, 23; 51:16
32 [a]Ps. 34:2 [b]Ps. 22:26
33 [a][Ps. 68:6]; Eph. 3:1
34 [a]Ps. 96:11; Is. 44:23; 49:13 [b]Is. 55:12
35 [a]Ps. 51:18; Is. 44:26
36 [a]Ps. 102:28

NKJV

28 Let them [a]be blotted out of the book of the living,
[b]And not be written with the righteous.

29 But I *am* poor and sorrowful;
Let Your salvation, O God, set me up on high.
30 [a]I will praise the name of God with a song,
And will magnify Him with thanksgiving.
31 [a]*This* also shall please the LORD better than an ox *or* bull,
Which has horns and hooves.
32 [a]The humble shall see *this and* be glad;
And you who seek God, [b]your hearts shall live.
33 For the LORD hears the poor,
And does not despise [a]His prisoners.

34 [a]Let heaven and earth praise Him,
The seas [b]and everything that moves in them.
35 [a]For God will save Zion
And build the cities of Judah,
That they may dwell there and possess it.
36 Also, [a]the descendants of His servants shall inherit it,
And those who love His name shall dwell in it.

PSALM 70 (KJV)

Prayer for Relief from Adversaries
(Ps. 40:13–17)

To the chief Musician, *A Psalm* of David, [a]to bring to remembrance.

MAKE *haste,* [a]O God, to deliver me; make
haste to help me, O LORD.
2 [a]Let them be ashamed and confounded
that seek after my soul: let them be turned backward, and put to confusion, that desire my hurt.
3 [a]Let them be turned back for a reward of
their shame that say, Aha, aha.
4 Let all those that seek thee rejoice and be
glad in thee: and let such as love thy salvation
say continually, Let God be magnified.
5 [a]But I *am* poor and needy: [b]make haste
unto me, O God: thou *art* my help and my deliverer; O LORD, make no tarrying.

PSALM 70

title [a]Ps. 38:title
1 [a]Ps. 40:13–17
2 [a]Ps. 35:4, 26
3 [a]Ps. 40:15
5 [a]Ps. 72:12, 13 [b]Ps. 141:1

PSALM 70 (NKJV)

Prayer for Relief from Adversaries
(Ps. 40:13–17)

To the Chief Musician. *A Psalm* of David. [a]To bring to remembrance.

MAKE *haste,* [a]O God, to deliver me!
Make haste to help me, O LORD!

2 [a]Let them be ashamed and confounded
Who seek my life;
Let them be *turned back and confused
Who desire my hurt.
3 [a]Let them be turned back because of their shame,
Who say, "Aha, aha!"

4 Let all those who seek You rejoice and be glad in You;
And let those who love Your salvation say continually,
"Let God be magnified!"

5 [a]But I *am* poor and needy;
[b]Make haste to me, O God!
You *are* my help and my deliverer;
O LORD, do not delay.

PSALM 71 (KJV)

God the Rock of Salvation

IN [a]thee, O LORD, do I put my trust: let me never
be put to confusion.
2 [a]Deliver me in thy righteousness, and
cause me to escape: [b]incline thine ear unto me,
and save me.
3 [a]Be thou my strong habitation, whereunto
I may continually resort: thou hast given [b]com-
mandment to save me, for thou *art* my rock and
my fortress.
4 [a]Deliver me, O my God, out of the hand
of the wicked, out of the hand of the unrighteous
and cruel man.
5 For thou *art* [a]my hope, O Lord GOD: *thou*
art my trust from my youth.
6 [a]By thee have I been holden up from the
womb: thou art he that took me out of my
mother's bowels: my praise *shall be* continually
of thee.

PSALM 71

1 [a]Ps. 25:2, 3
2 [a]Ps. 31:1 [b]Ps. 17:6
3 [a]Ps. 31:2, 3 [b]Ps. 44:4
4 [a]Ps. 140:1, 3
5 [a]Jer. 14:8; 17:7, 13, 17; 50:7
6 [a]Ps. 22:9, 10; Is. 46:3

PSALM 71 (NKJV)

God the Rock of Salvation

IN [a]You, O LORD, I put my trust;
Let me never be put to shame.
2 [a]Deliver me in Your righteousness, and cause me to escape;
[b]Incline Your ear to me, and save me.
3 [a]Be my strong refuge,
To which I may resort continually;
You have given the [b]commandment to save me,
For You *are* my rock and my fortress.

4 [a]Deliver me, O my God, out of the hand of the wicked,
Out of the hand of the unrighteous and cruel man.
5 For You are [a]my hope, O Lord GOD;
You are my trust from my youth.
6 [a]By You I have been upheld from birth;
You are He who took me out of my mother's womb.
My praise *shall be* continually of You.

---

* **70:2** So with MT, LXX, Tg., Vg.; some Heb. mss., Syr. *appalled* (cf. 40:15)

KJV

7 [a]I am as a wonder unto many; but thou *art* my strong refuge.

8 Let [a]my mouth be filled *with* thy praise *and with* thy honour all the day.

9 Cast me not off in the time of old age; forsake me not when my strength faileth.

10 For mine enemies speak against me; and they that lay wait for my soul [a]take counsel together,

11 Saying, God hath forsaken him: persecute and take him; for *there is* none to deliver *him.*

12 [a]O God, be not far from me: O my God, [b]make haste for my help.

13 Let them be confounded *and* consumed that are adversaries to my soul; let them be covered *with* reproach and dishonour that seek my hurt.

14 But I will hope continually, and will yet praise thee more and more.

15 My mouth shall shew forth thy righteousness *and* thy salvation all the day; for I know not the numbers *thereof.*

16 I will go in the strength of the Lord GOD: I will make mention of thy righteousness, *even* of thine only.

17 O God, thou hast taught me from my [a]youth: and hitherto have I declared thy wondrous works.

18 Now also [a]when I am old and greyheaded, O God, forsake me not; until I have shewed thy strength unto *this* generation, *and* thy power to every one *that* is to come.

19 [a]Thy righteousness also, O God, *is* very high, who hast done great things: [b]O God, who *is* like unto thee!

20 [a]*Thou,* which hast shewed me great and sore troubles, [b]shalt quicken me again, and shalt bring me up again from the depths of the earth.

21 Thou shalt increase my greatness, and comfort me on every side.

22 I will also praise thee [a]with the psaltery, *even* thy truth, O my God: unto thee will I sing with the harp, O thou [b]Holy One of Israel.

23 My lips shall greatly rejoice when I sing unto thee; and [a]my soul, which thou hast redeemed.

24 My tongue also shall talk of thy righteousness all the day long: for they are confounded, for they are brought unto shame, that seek my hurt.

7 [a]Is. 8:18; Zech. 3:8; 1 Cor. 4:9
8 [a]Ps. 35:28
10 [a]2 Sam. 17:1
12 [a]Ps. 35:22 [b]Ps. 70:1
17 [a]Deut. 4:5; 6:7
18 [a][Is. 46:4]
19 [a]Deut. 3:24; Ps. 57:10 [b]Ps. 35:10
20 [a]Ps. 60:3 [b]Hos. 6:1, 2
22 [a]Ps. 92:1–3 [b]2 Kin. 19:22; Is. 1:4
23 [a]Ps. 103:4

NKJV

7 [a]I have become as a wonder to many,
But You *are* my strong refuge.
8 Let [a]my mouth be filled *with* Your praise
And with Your glory all the day.

9 Do not cast me off in the time of old age;
Do not forsake me when my strength fails.
10 For my enemies speak against me;
And those who lie in wait for my life [a]take counsel together,
11 Saying, "God has forsaken him;
Pursue and take him, for *there is* none to deliver *him.*"

12 [a]O God, do not be far from me;
O my God, [b]make haste to help me!
13 Let them be confounded *and* consumed
Who are adversaries of my life;
Let them be covered *with* reproach and dishonor
Who seek my hurt.

14 But I will hope continually,
And will praise You yet more and more.
15 My mouth shall tell of Your righteousness
And Your salvation all the day,
For I do not know *their* limits.
16 I will go in the strength of the Lord GOD;
I will make mention of Your righteousness, of Yours only.

17 O God, You have taught me from my [a]youth;
And to this *day* I declare Your wondrous works.
18 Now also [a]when *I am* old and grayheaded,
O God, do not forsake me,
Until I declare Your strength to *this* generation,
Your power to everyone *who* is to come.

19 Also [a]Your righteousness, O God, *is* very high,
You who have done great things;
[b]O God, who *is* like You?
20 [a]*You,* who have shown me great and severe troubles,
[b]Shall revive me again,
And bring me up again from the depths of the earth.
21 You shall increase my greatness,
And comfort me on every side.

22 Also [a]with the lute I will praise You—
And Your faithfulness, O my God!
To You I will sing with the harp,
O [b]Holy One of Israel.
23 My lips shall greatly rejoice when I sing to You,
And [a]my soul, which You have redeemed.
24 My tongue also shall talk of Your righteousness all the day long;
For they are confounded,
For they are brought to shame
Who seek my hurt.

PSALM 72

Glory and Universality of the Messiah's Reign

A Psalm [a]for Solomon.

GIVE the king thy judgments, O God, and thy righteousness unto the king's son.

2 [a]He shall judge thy people with righteousness, and thy poor with judgment.

3 [a]The mountains shall bring peace to the people, and the little hills, by righteousness.

4 [a]He shall judge the poor of the people, he shall save the children of the needy, and shall break in pieces the oppressor.

PSALM 72

title [a]Ps. 127:title
2 [a][Is. 9:7; 11:2–5; 32:1]
3 [a]Ps. 85:10
4 [a]Is. 11:4

PSALM 72

Glory and Universality of the Messiah's Reign

A Psalm [a]of Solomon.

GIVE the king Your judgments, O God,
And Your righteousness to the king's Son.
2 [a]He will judge Your people with righteousness,
And Your poor with justice.
3 [a]The mountains will bring peace to the people,
And the little hills, by righteousness.
4 [a]He will bring justice to the poor of the people;
He will save the children of the needy,
And will break in pieces the oppressor.

KJV

5 They shall fear thee [a]as long as the sun and moon endure, throughout all generations.

6 [a]He shall come down like rain upon the mown grass: as showers *that* water the earth.

7 In his days shall the righteous flourish; [a]and abundance of peace so long as the moon endureth.

8 [a]He shall have dominion also from sea to sea, and from the river unto the ends of the earth.

9 [a]They that dwell in the wilderness shall bow before him; [b]and his enemies shall lick the dust.

10 [a]The kings of Tarshish and of the isles shall bring presents: the kings of Sheba and Seba shall offer gifts.

11 [a]Yea, all kings shall fall down before him: all nations shall serve him.

12 For he [a]shall deliver the needy when he crieth; the poor also, and *him* that hath no helper.

13 He shall spare the poor and needy, and shall save the souls of the needy.

14 He shall redeem their soul from deceit and violence: and [a]precious shall their blood be in his sight.

15 And he shall live, and to him shall be given of the gold of [a]Sheba: prayer also shall be made for him continually; *and* daily shall he be praised.

16 There shall be an handful of corn in the earth upon the top of the mountains; the fruit thereof shall shake like Lebanon: [a]and *they* of the city shall flourish like grass of the earth.

17 [a]His name shall endure for ever: his name shall be continued as long as the sun: and [b]*men* shall be blessed in him: [c]all nations shall call him blessed.

18 [a]Blessed *be* the LORD God, the God of Israel, [b]who only doeth wondrous things.

19 And [a]blessed *be* his glorious name for ever: [b]and let the whole earth be filled *with* his glory; Amen, and Amen.

20 The prayers of David the son of Jesse are ended.

BOOK III

PSALM 73

The Tragedy of the Wicked, and the Blessedness of Trust in God

A Psalm of [a]Asaph.

TRULY God *is* good to Israel, *even* to such as are of a clean heart.

2 But as for me, my feet were almost gone; my steps had well nigh [a]slipped.

3 [a]For I was envious at the foolish, *when* I saw the prosperity of the [b]wicked.

5 [a]Ps. 72:7, 17; 89:36
6 [a]Deut. 32:2; 2 Sam. 23:4; Hos. 6:3
7 [a]Is. 2:4
8 [a]Ex. 23:31; [Is. 9:6; Zech. 9:10]
9 [a]Ps. 74:14; Is. 23:13 [b]Is. 49:23; Mic. 7:17
10 [a]1 Kin. 10:2; 2 Chr. 9:21
11 [a]Is. 49:23
12 [a]Job 29:12
14 [a]1 Sam. 26:21; [Ps. 116:15]
15 [a]Is. 60:6
16 [a]1 Kin. 4:20
17 [a][Ps. 89:36] [b][Gen. 12:3] [c]Luke 1:48
18 [a]1 Chr. 29:10 [b]Ex. 15:11; Job 5:9
19 [a][Neh. 9:5] [b]Num. 14:21; Hab. 2:14

PSALM 73

title [a]Ps. 50:title
2 [a]Job 12:5
3 [a]Ps. 37:1, 7; [Prov. 23:17] [b]Job 21:5–16; Jer. 12:1

*72:5 So with MT, Tg.; LXX, Vg. *They shall continue*

NKJV

5 *They shall fear You
[a]As long as the sun and moon endure,
Throughout all generations.
6 [a]He shall come down like rain upon the grass before mowing,
Like showers *that* water the earth.
7 In His days the righteous shall flourish,
[a]And abundance of peace,
Until the moon is no more.

8 [a]He shall have dominion also from sea to sea,
And from the River to the ends of the earth.
9 [a]Those who dwell in the wilderness will bow before Him,
[b]And His enemies will lick the dust.
10 [a]The kings of Tarshish and of the isles
Will bring presents;
The kings of Sheba and Seba
Will offer gifts.
11 [a]Yes, all kings shall fall down before Him;
All nations shall serve Him.

12 For He [a]will deliver the needy when he cries,
The poor also, and *him* who has no helper.
13 He will spare the poor and needy,
And will save the souls of the needy.
14 He will redeem their life from oppression and violence;
And [a]precious shall be their blood in His sight.

15 And He shall live;
And the gold of [a]Sheba will be given to Him;
Prayer also will be made for Him continually,
And daily He shall be praised.

16 There will be an abundance of grain in the earth,
On the top of the mountains;
Its fruit shall wave like Lebanon;
[a]And *those* of the city shall flourish like grass of the earth.

17 [a]His name shall endure forever;
His name shall continue as long as the sun.
And [b]*men* shall be blessed in Him;
[c]All nations shall call Him blessed.

18 [a]Blessed *be* the LORD God, the God of Israel,
[b]Who only does wondrous things!
19 And [a]blessed *be* His glorious name forever!
[b]And let the whole earth be filled *with* His glory.
Amen and Amen.

20 The prayers of David the son of Jesse are ended.

BOOK THREE

Psalms 73–89

PSALM 73

The Tragedy of the Wicked, and the Blessedness of Trust in God

A Psalm of [a]Asaph.

TRULY God *is* good to Israel,
To such as are pure in heart.
2 But as for me, my feet had almost stumbled;
My steps had nearly [a]slipped.
3 [a]For I *was* envious of the boastful,
When I saw the prosperity of the [b]wicked.

KJV

4 For *there are* no bands in their death: but
their strength *is* firm.
5 [a]They *are* not in trouble *as other* men; neither are they plagued like *other* men.
6 Therefore pride compasseth them about
as a chain; violence covereth them [a]*as* a garment.
7 [a]Their eyes stand out with fatness: they
have more than heart could wish.
8 [a]They are corrupt, and speak wickedly
concerning oppression: they [b]speak loftily.
9 They set their mouth [a]against the heavens, and their tongue walketh through the earth.
10 Therefore his people return hither: [a]and
waters of a full *cup* are wrung out to them.
11 And they say, [a]How doth God know? and
is there knowledge in the most High?
12 Behold, these *are* the ungodly, who prosper in the world; they increase *in* riches.
13 Verily I have cleansed my heart *in* [a]vain,
and washed my hands in innocency.
14 For all the day long have I been plagued,
and chastened every morning.
15 If I say, I will speak thus; behold, I should
offend *against* the generation of thy children.
16 When I thought to know this, it *was* too
painful for me;
17 Until I went into the sanctuary of God;
then understood I their [a]end.
18 Surely [a]thou didst set them in slippery
places: thou castedst them down into destruction.
19 How are they *brought* into desolation, as
in a moment! they are utterly consumed with
terrors.
20 As a dream when *one* awaketh; *so,* O
Lord, when thou awakest, thou shalt despise their
image.
21 Thus my heart was grieved, and I was
pricked in my reins.
22 [a]So foolish *was* I, and ignorant: I was *as*
a beast before thee.
23 Nevertheless I *am* continually with thee:
thou hast holden *me* by my right hand.
24 [a]Thou shalt guide me with thy counsel,
and afterward receive me *to* glory.
25 [a]Whom have I in heaven *but thee?* and
there is none upon earth *that* I desire beside thee.
26 [a]My flesh and my heart faileth: *but* God
is the strength of my heart, and my [b]portion for
ever.
27 For, lo, [a]they that are far from thee shall
perish: thou hast destroyed all them that go a
whoring from thee.
28 But *it is* good for me to [a]draw near to God:
I have put my trust in the Lord GOD, that I may
[b]declare all thy works.

5 [a]Job 21:9
6 [a]Ps. 109:18
7 [a]Job 15:27; Jer. 5:28
8 [a]Ps. 53:1 [b]2 Pet. 2:18; Jude 16
9 [a]Rev. 13:6
10 [a][Ps. 75:8]
11 [a]Job 22:13
13 [a]Job 21:15; 35:3; Mal. 3:14
17 [a][Ps. 37:38; 55:23]
18 [a]Ps. 35:6
22 [a]Ps. 92:6
24 [a]Ps. 32:8; 48:14; Is. 58:11
25 [a][Phil. 3:8]
26 [a]Ps. 84:2 [b]Ps. 16:5
27 [a][Ps. 119:155]
28 [a][Heb. 10:22; James 4:8] [b]Ps. 116:10; 2 Cor. 4:13

NKJV

4 For *there are* no pangs in their death,
But their strength *is* firm.
5 [a]They *are* not in trouble *as other* men,
Nor are they plagued like *other* men.
6 Therefore pride serves as their
necklace;
Violence covers them [a]*like* a garment.
7 [a]Their *eyes bulge with abundance;
They have more than heart could wish.
8 [a]They scoff and speak wickedly *concerning*
oppression;
They [b]speak loftily.
9 They set their mouth [a]against the
heavens,
And their tongue walks through the earth.

10 Therefore his people return here,
[a]And waters of a full *cup* are drained by
them.
11 And they say, [a]"How does God know?
And is there knowledge in the Most
High?"
12 Behold, these *are* the ungodly,
Who are always at ease;
They increase *in* riches.
13 Surely I have cleansed my heart *in*
[a]vain,
And washed my hands in innocence.
14 For all day long I have been plagued,
And chastened every morning.

15 If I had said, "I will speak thus,"
Behold, I would have been untrue to the
generation of Your children.
16 When I thought *how* to understand this,
It *was* too painful for me—
17 Until I went into the sanctuary of God;
Then I understood their [a]end.

18 Surely [a]You set them in slippery places;
You cast them down to destruction.
19 Oh, how they are *brought* to desolation,
as in a moment!
They are utterly consumed with terrors.
20 As a dream when *one* awakes,
So, Lord, when You awake,
You shall despise their image.

21 Thus my heart was grieved,
And I was vexed in my mind.
22 [a]I *was* so foolish and ignorant;
I was *like* a beast before You.
23 Nevertheless I *am* continually with You;
You hold *me* by my right hand.
24 [a]You will guide me with Your counsel,
And afterward receive me *to* glory.

25 [a]Whom have I in heaven *but You?*
And *there is* none upon earth *that* I desire
besides You.
26 [a]My flesh and my heart fail;
But God *is* the strength of my heart and
my [b]portion forever.

27 For indeed, [a]those who are far from You
shall perish;
You have destroyed all those who desert
You for harlotry.
28 But *it is* good for me to [a]draw near to God;
I have put my trust in the Lord GOD,
That I may [b]declare all Your works.

PSALM 74

A Plea for Relief from Oppressors

Maschil of Asaph.

O GOD, why hast thou cast *us* off for ever? *why*
doth thine anger smoke against the sheep of
thy pasture?
2 Remember thy congregation, *which* thou
hast purchased of old; the rod of thine inheritance,

*
73:7 Tg. *face bulges;* LXX, Syr., Vg. *iniquity bulges*
74:title Heb. *Maschil*

PSALM 74

A Plea for Relief from Oppressors

A *Contemplation of Asaph.

O GOD, why have You cast *us* off forever?
Why does Your anger smoke against the
sheep of Your pasture?
2 Remember Your congregation, *which* You
have purchased of old,

KJV

which thou hast redeemed; this mount Zion,
wherein thou hast dwelt.
3 Lift up thy feet unto the perpetual desolations; *even* all *that* the enemy hath done wickedly
in the sanctuary.
4 [a]Thine enemies roar in the midst of thy
congregations; [b]they set up their ensigns *for*
signs.
5 *A man* was famous according as he had
lifted up axes upon the thick trees.
6 But now they break down the carved work
thereof at once with axes and hammers.
7 They have cast fire into thy sanctuary,
they have defiled *by casting down* the dwelling
place of thy name to the ground.
8 [a]They said in their hearts, Let us destroy
them together: they have burned up all the synagogues of God in the land.
9 We see not our signs: [a]*there is* no more
any prophet: neither *is there* among us any that
knoweth how long.
10 O God, how long shall the adversary reproach? shall the enemy blaspheme thy name for
ever?
11 [a]Why withdrawest thou thy hand, even
thy right hand? pluck *it* out of thy bosom.
12 For [a]God *is* my King of old, working salvation in the midst of the earth.
13 [a]Thou didst divide the sea by thy strength:
thou brakest the heads of the dragons in the
waters.
14 Thou brakest the heads of leviathan in
pieces, *and* gavest him *to be* meat to the people
inhabiting the wilderness.
15 [a]Thou didst cleave the fountain and the
flood: [b]thou driedst up mighty rivers.
16 The day *is* thine, the night also *is* [a]thine:
[b]thou hast prepared the light and the sun.
17 Thou hast [a]set all the borders of the earth:
[b]thou hast made summer and winter.
18 Remember this, *that* the enemy hath reproached, O LORD, and *that* the foolish people
have blasphemed thy name.
19 O deliver not the soul of thy turtledove
unto the multitude *of the wicked:* forget not the
congregation of thy poor for ever.
20 [a]Have respect unto the covenant: for the
dark places of the earth are full of the habitations
of cruelty.
21 O let not the oppressed return ashamed:
let the poor and needy praise thy name.
22 Arise, O God, plead thine own cause: remember how the foolish man reproacheth thee
daily.
23 Forget not the voice of thine enemies: the
tumult of those that rise up against thee increaseth
continually.

PSALM 75

Thanksgiving for God's Righteous Judgment

To the chief Musician, [a]Altaschith, A Psalm *or* Song of Asaph.

UNTO thee, O God, do we give thanks, *unto*
thee do we give thanks: for *that* thy name is
near thy wondrous works declare.

PSALM 74

4 [a]Lam. 2:7 [b]Num. 2:2
8 [a]Ps. 83:4
9 [a]1 Sam. 3:1; Lam. 2:9; Ezek. 7:26; Amos 8:11
11 [a]Lam. 2:3
12 [a]Ps. 44:4
13 [a]Ex. 14:21
15 [a]Ex. 17:5, 6; Num. 20:11; Ps. 105:41; Is. 48:21 [b]Ex. 14:21, 22; Josh. 2:10; 3:13
16 [a]Job 38:12 [b]Gen. 1:14–18
17 [a]Deut. 32:8; Acts 17:26 [b]Gen. 8:22
20 [a]Gen. 17:7, 8; Lev. 26:44, 45

PSALM 75

title [a]Ps. 57:title

*75:title Heb. *Al Tashcheth*

NKJV

The tribe of Your inheritance, *which* You have redeemed—
This Mount Zion where You have dwelt.
3 Lift up Your feet to the perpetual desolations.
The enemy has damaged everything in the sanctuary.
4 [a]Your enemies roar in the midst of Your meeting place;
[b]They set up their banners *for* signs.
5 They seem like men who lift up
Axes among the thick trees.
6 And now they break down its carved work, all at once,
With axes and hammers.
7 They have set fire to Your sanctuary;
They have defiled the dwelling place of Your name to the ground.
8 [a]They said in their hearts,
"Let us destroy them altogether."
They have burned up all the meeting places of God in the land.

9 We do not see our signs;
[a]*There is* no longer any prophet;
Nor *is there* any among us who knows how long.
10 O God, how long will the adversary reproach?
Will the enemy blaspheme Your name forever?
11 [a]Why do You withdraw Your hand, even Your right hand?
Take it out of Your bosom and destroy *them.*
12 For [a]God *is* my King from of old,
Working salvation in the midst of the earth.
13 [a]You divided the sea by Your strength;
You broke the heads of the sea serpents in the waters.
14 You broke the heads of Leviathan in pieces,
And gave him *as* food to the people inhabiting the wilderness.
15 [a]You broke open the fountain and the flood;
[b]You dried up mighty rivers.
16 The day *is* Yours, the night also *is* [a]Yours;
[b]You have prepared the light and the sun.
17 You have [a]set all the borders of the earth;
[b]You have made summer and winter.

18 Remember this, *that* the enemy has reproached, O LORD,
And *that* a foolish people has blasphemed Your name.
19 Oh, do not deliver the life of Your turtledove to the wild beast!
Do not forget the life of Your poor forever.
20 [a]Have respect to the covenant;
For the dark places of the earth are full of the haunts of cruelty.
21 Oh, do not let the oppressed return ashamed!
Let the poor and needy praise Your name.

22 Arise, O God, plead Your own cause;
Remember how the foolish man reproaches You daily.
23 Do not forget the voice of Your enemies;
The tumult of those who rise up against You increases continually.

PSALM 75

Thanksgiving for God's Righteous Judgment

To the Chief Musician. Set to [a]"Do* Not Destroy." A Psalm of Asaph. A Song.

WE give thanks to You, O God, we give thanks!
For Your wondrous works declare *that* Your name is near.

KJV

2 When I shall receive the congregation I will judge uprightly.
3 The earth and all the inhabitants thereof are dissolved: I bear up the pillars of it. Selah.
4 I said unto the fools, Deal not foolishly: and to the wicked, [a]Lift not up the horn:
5 Lift not up your horn on high: speak *not with* a stiff neck.
6 For promotion *cometh* neither from the east, nor from the west, nor from the south.
7 But [a]God *is* the judge: [b]he putteth down one, and setteth up another.
8 For [a]in the hand of the LORD *there is* a cup, and the wine is red; it is full of mixture; and he poureth out of the same: but the dregs thereof, all the wicked of the earth shall wring *them* out, *and* drink *them*.
9 But I will declare for ever; I will sing praises to the God of Jacob.
10 [a]All the horns of the wicked also will I cut off; *but* [b]the horns of the righteous shall be [c]exalted.

4 [a][1 Sam. 2:3]; Ps. 94:4 **7** [a]Ps. 50:6 [b]1 Sam. 2:7; Ps. 147:6; Dan. 2:21 **8** [a]Job 21:20; Ps. 60:3; Jer. 25:15; Rev. 14:10; 16:19 **10** [a]Ps. 101:8; Jer. 48:25 [b]Ps. 89:17; 148:14 [c]1 Sam. 2:1

NKJV

2 "When I choose the proper time,
I will judge uprightly.
3 The earth and all its inhabitants are dissolved;
I set up its pillars firmly. Selah

4 "I said to the boastful, 'Do not deal boastfully,'
And to the wicked, [a]'Do not lift up the horn.
5 Do not lift up your horn on high;
Do *not* speak with a stiff neck.' "

6 For exaltation *comes* neither from the east
Nor from the west nor from the south.
7 But [a]God *is* the Judge:
[b]He puts down one,
And exalts another.
8 For [a]in the hand of the LORD *there is* a cup,
And the wine is red;
It is fully mixed, and He pours it out;
Surely its dregs shall all the wicked of the earth
Drain *and* drink down.

9 But I will declare forever,
I will sing praises to the God of Jacob.

10 "All[a] the horns of the wicked I will also cut off,
But [b]the horns of the righteous shall be [c]exalted."

PSALM 76

The Majesty of God in Judgment

To the chief Musician on Neginoth, A Psalm *or* Song of Asaph.

IN [a]Judah *is* God known: his name *is* great in Israel.
2 In Salem also is his tabernacle, and his dwelling place in Zion.
3 There brake he the arrows of the bow, the shield, and the sword, and the battle. Selah.
4 Thou *art* more glorious *and* excellent [a]than the mountains of prey.
5 [a]The stouthearted are spoiled, [b]they have slept their sleep: and none of the men of might have found their hands.
6 [a]At thy rebuke, O God of Jacob, both the chariot and horse are cast into a dead sleep.
7 Thou, *even* thou, *art* to be feared: and [a]who may stand in thy sight when once thou art angry?
8 [a]Thou didst cause judgment to be heard from heaven; [b]the earth feared, and was still,
9 When God [a]arose to judgment, to save all the meek of the earth. Selah.
10 [a]Surely the wrath of man shall praise thee: the remainder of wrath shalt thou restrain.
11 [a]Vow, and pay unto the LORD your God: [b]let all that be round about him bring presents unto him that ought to be feared.
12 He shall cut off the spirit of princes: [a]*he is* terrible to the kings of the earth.

PSALM 76

1 [a]Ps. 48:1, 3 **4** [a]Ezek. 38:12 **5** [a]Is. 10:12; 46:12 [b]Ps. 13:3 **6** [a]Ex. 15:1–21; Ezek. 39:20; Nah. 2:13; Zech. 12:4 **7** [a][Ezra 9:15; Nah. 1:6; Mal. 3:2; Rev. 6:17] **8** [a]Ex. 19:9 [b]1 Chr. 16:30; 2 Chr. 20:29 **9** [a][Ps. 9:7–9] **10** [a]Ex. 9:16; Rom. 9:17 **11** [a][Eccl. 5:4–6] [b]2 Chr. 32:22, 23 **12** [a]Ps. 68:35

PSALM 76

The Majesty of God in Judgment

To the Chief Musician. On *stringed instruments. A Psalm of Asaph. A Song.

IN [a]Judah God *is* known;
His name *is* great in Israel.
2 In *Salem also is His tabernacle,
And His dwelling place in Zion.
3 There He broke the arrows of the bow,
The shield and sword of battle. Selah

4 You *are* more glorious and excellent
[a]*Than* the mountains of prey.
5 [a]The stouthearted were plundered;
[b]They have sunk into their sleep;
And none of the mighty men have found the use of their hands.
6 [a]At Your rebuke, O God of Jacob,
Both the chariot and horse were cast into a dead sleep.

7 You, Yourself, *are* to be feared;
And [a]who may stand in Your presence
When once You are angry?
8 [a]You caused judgment to be heard from heaven;
[b]The earth feared and was still,
9 When God [a]arose to judgment,
To deliver all the oppressed of the earth. Selah

10 [a]Surely the wrath of man shall praise You;
With the remainder of wrath You shall gird Yourself.

11 [a]Make vows to the LORD your God, and pay *them;*
[b]Let all who are around Him bring presents
to Him who ought to be feared.
12 He shall cut off the spirit of princes;
[a]*He is* awesome to the kings of the earth.

76:title Heb. *neginoth* **76:2** Jerusalem

KJV

PSALM 77

The Consoling Memory of God's Redemptive Works

To the chief Musician, [a]to Jeduthun, A Psalm of Asaph.

I CRIED unto God with my voice, *even* unto God
with my voice; and he gave ear unto me.
2 In the day of my trouble I sought the Lord:
my sore ran in the night, and ceased not: my soul
refused to be comforted.
3 I remembered God, and was troubled: I
complained, and my spirit was overwhelmed.
Selah.
4 Thou holdest mine eyes waking: I am so
troubled that I cannot speak.
5 I have considered the days of old, the
years of ancient times.
6 I call to remembrance my song in the
night: I commune with mine own heart: and my
spirit made diligent search.
7 Will the Lord cast off for ever? and will
he be favourable no more?
8 Is his mercy clean gone for ever? doth *his*
[a]promise fail for evermore?
9 Hath God forgotten to be gracious? hath
he in anger shut up his tender mercies? Selah.
10 And I said, This *is* my infirmity: *but I will*
remember the years of the right hand of the most
High.
11 I will remember the works of the LORD:
surely I will remember thy wonders of old.
12 I will meditate also of all thy work, and
talk of thy doings.
13 Thy way, O God, *is* in the [a]sanctuary: who
is so great a God as *our* God?
14 Thou *art* the God that doest wonders: thou
hast declared thy strength among the people.
15 Thou hast with *thine* arm redeemed thy
people, the sons of Jacob and Joseph. Selah.
16 The waters saw thee, O God, the waters
saw thee; they were [a]afraid: the depths also were
troubled.
17 The clouds poured out water: the skies
sent out a sound: thine arrows also went abroad.
18 The voice of thy thunder *was* in the
heaven: the lightnings lightened the world: the
earth trembled and shook.
19 Thy way *is* in the sea, and thy path in the
great waters, and thy footsteps are not known.
20 Thou leddest thy people like a flock by
the hand of Moses and Aaron.

PSALM 77

title [a]Ps. 39:title
8 [a][2 Pet. 2:8, 9]
13 [a]Ps. 73:17
16 [a]Ex. 14:21; Hab. 3:8, 10

NKJV

PSALM 77

The Consoling Memory of God's Redemptive Works

To the Chief Musician. [a]To Jeduthun. A Psalm of Asaph.

I CRIED out to God with my voice—
To God with my voice;
And He gave ear to me.
2 In the day of my trouble I sought the Lord;
My hand was stretched out in the night without ceasing;
My soul refused to be comforted.
3 I remembered God, and was troubled;
I complained, and my spirit was overwhelmed. Selah

4 You hold my eyelids *open;*
I am so troubled that I cannot speak.
5 I have considered the days of old,
The years of ancient times.
6 I call to remembrance my song in the night;
I meditate within my heart,
And my spirit makes diligent search.

7 Will the Lord cast off forever?
And will He be favorable no more?
8 Has His mercy ceased forever?
Has *His* [a]promise failed forevermore?
9 Has God forgotten to be gracious?
Has He in anger shut up His tender mercies? Selah

10 And I said, "This *is* my anguish;
But I will remember the years of the right hand of the Most High."
11 I will remember the works of the LORD;
Surely I will remember Your wonders of old.
12 I will also meditate on all Your work,
And talk of Your deeds.
13 Your way, O God, *is* in the [a]sanctuary;
Who *is* so great a God as *our* God?
14 You *are* the God who does wonders;
You have declared Your strength among the peoples.
15 You have with *Your* arm redeemed Your people,
The sons of Jacob and Joseph. Selah

16 The waters saw You, O God;
The waters saw You, they were [a]afraid;
The depths also trembled.
17 The clouds poured out water;
The skies sent out a sound;
Your arrows also flashed about.
18 The voice of Your thunder *was* in the whirlwind;
The lightnings lit up the world;
The earth trembled and shook.
19 Your way *was* in the sea,
Your path in the great waters,
And Your footsteps were not known.
20 You led Your people like a flock
By the hand of Moses and Aaron.

KJV

PSALM 78

God's Kindness to Rebellious Israel

[a]Maschil of Asaph.

GIVE ear, O my people, *to* my law: incline your
ears to the words of my mouth.
2 I will open my mouth in a [a]parable: I will
utter dark sayings of old:
3 Which we have heard and known, and our
fathers have told us.
4 [a]We will not hide *them* from their chil-

PSALM 78

title [a]Ps. 74:title
2 [a]Matt. 13:34, 35
4 [a]Ex. 12:26, 27; Deut. 4:9; 6:7; Job 15:18; Is. 38:19; Joel 1:3

*———————

78:title Heb. *Maschil*

NKJV

PSALM 78

God's Kindness to Rebellious Israel

A [a]Contemplation* of Asaph.

GIVE ear, O my people, *to* my law;
Incline your ears to the words of my mouth.
2 I will open my mouth in a [a]parable;
I will utter dark sayings of old,
3 Which we have heard and known,
And our fathers have told us.
4 [a]We will not hide *them* from their children,

KJV

dren, [b]shewing to the generation to come the praises of the LORD, and his strength, and his wonderful works that he hath done.

5 For [a]he established a testimony in Jacob, and appointed a law in Israel, which he commanded our fathers, that [b]they should make them known to their children:

6 [a]That the generation to come might know *them, even* the children *which* should be born; *who* should arise and declare *them* to their children:

7 That they might set their hope in God, and not forget the works of God, but keep his commandments:

8 And [a]might not be as their fathers, [b]a stubborn and rebellious generation; a generation [c]*that* set not their heart aright, and whose spirit was not stedfast with God.

9 The children of Ephraim, *being* armed, *and* carrying bows, turned back in the day of battle.

10 [a]They kept not the covenant of God, and refused to walk in his law;

11 And [a]forgat his works, and his wonders that he had shewed them.

12 [a]Marvellous things did he in the sight of their fathers, in the land of Egypt, [b]*in* the field of Zoan.

13 [a]He divided the sea, and caused them to pass through; and [b]he made the waters to stand as an heap.

14 [a]In the daytime also he led them with a cloud, and all the night with a light of fire.

15 [a]He clave the rocks in the wilderness, and gave *them* drink as *out of* the great depths.

16 He brought [a]streams also out of the rock, and caused waters to run down like rivers.

17 And they sinned yet more against him by [a]provoking the most High in the wilderness.

18 And [a]they tempted God in their heart by asking meat for their lust.

19 [a]Yea, they spake against God; they said, Can God furnish a table in the wilderness?

20 [a]Behold, he smote the rock, that the waters gushed out, and the streams overflowed; can he give bread also? can he provide flesh for his people?

21 Therefore the LORD heard *this*, and [a]was wroth: so a fire was kindled against Jacob, and anger also came up against Israel;

22 Because they [a]believed not in God, and trusted not in his salvation:

23 Though he had commanded the clouds from above, [a]and opened the doors of heaven,

24 [a]And had rained down manna upon them to eat, and had given them of the corn of [b]heaven.

25 Man did eat angels' food: he sent them meat to the full.

26 [a]He caused an east wind to blow in the heaven: and by his power he brought in the south wind.

4 [b]Ex. 13:8, 14
5 [a]Ps. 147:19 [b]Deut. 4:9; 11:19
6 [a]Ps. 102:18
8 [a]2 Kin. 17:14; 2 Chr. 30:7; Ezek. 20:18 [b]Ex. 32:9; Deut. 9:7, 24; 31:27; Judg. 2:19; Is. 30:9 [c]Job 11:13; Ps. 78:37
10 [a]2 Kin. 17:15
11 [a]Ps. 106:13
12 [a]Ex. 7—12 [b]Num. 13:22; Is. 19:11; 30:4; Ezek. 30:14
13 [a]Ex. 14:21 [b]Ex. 15:8
14 [a]Ex. 13:21
15 [a]Ex. 17:6; Num. 20:11; Is. 48:21; [1 Cor. 10:4]
16 [a]Num. 20:8, 10, 11
17 [a]Deut. 9:22; Is. 63:10; Heb. 3:16
18 [a]Ex. 16:2
19 [a]Ex. 16:3; Num. 11:4; 20:3; 21:5
20 [a]Num. 20:11
21 [a]Num. 11:1
22 [a]Deut. 1:32; 9:23; [Heb. 3:18]
23 [a]Gen. 7:11; [Mal. 3:10]
24 [a]Ex. 16:4 [b]John 6:31
26 [a]Num. 11:31

NKJV

[b]Telling to the generation to come the praises of the LORD,
And His strength and His wonderful works that He has done.

5 For [a]He established a testimony in Jacob,
And appointed a law in Israel,
Which He commanded our fathers,
That [b]they should make them known to their children;
6 [a]That the generation to come might know *them*,
The children *who* would be born,
That they may arise and declare *them* to their children,
7 That they may set their hope in God,
And not forget the works of God,
But keep His commandments;
8 And [a]may not be like their fathers,
[b]A stubborn and rebellious generation,
A generation [c]*that* did not set its heart aright,
And whose spirit was not faithful to God.

9 The children of Ephraim, *being* armed *and* carrying bows,
Turned back in the day of battle.
10 [a]They did not keep the covenant of God;
They refused to walk in His law,
11 And [a]forgot His works
And His wonders that He had shown them.

12 [a]Marvelous things He did in the sight of their fathers,
In the land of Egypt, [b]*in* the field of Zoan.
13 [a]He divided the sea and caused them to pass through;
And [b]He made the waters stand up like a heap.
14 [a]In the daytime also He led them with the cloud,
And all the night with a light of fire.
15 [a]He split the rocks in the wilderness,
And gave *them* drink in abundance like the depths.
16 He also brought [a]streams out of the rock,
And caused waters to run down like rivers.

17 But they sinned even more against Him
By [a]rebelling against the Most High in the wilderness.
18 And [a]they tested God in their heart
By asking for the food of their fancy.
19 [a]Yes, they spoke against God:
They said, "Can God prepare a table in the wilderness?
20 [a]Behold, He struck the rock,
So that the waters gushed out,
And the streams overflowed.
Can He give bread also?
Can He provide meat for His people?"

21 Therefore the LORD heard *this* and [a]was furious;
So a fire was kindled against Jacob,
And anger also came up against Israel,
22 Because they [a]did not believe in God,
And did not trust in His salvation.
23 Yet He had commanded the clouds above,
[a]And opened the doors of heaven,
24 [a]Had rained down manna on them to eat,
And given them of the bread of [b]heaven.
25 Men ate angels' food;
He sent them food to the full.

26 [a]He caused an east wind to blow in the heavens;
And by His power He brought in the south wind.

KJV

27 He rained flesh also upon them as dust,
and feathered fowls like as the sand of the sea:
28 And he let *it* fall in the midst of their camp,
round about their habitations.
29 [a]So they did eat, and were well filled: for
he gave them their own desire;
30 They were not estranged from their lust.
But [a]while their meat *was* yet in their mouths,
31 The wrath of God came upon them, and
slew the fattest of them, and smote down the chosen *men* of Israel.
32 For all this [a]they sinned still, and [b]be-
lieved not for his wondrous works.
33 [a]Therefore their days did he consume in
vanity, and their years in trouble.
34 [a]When he slew them, then they sought
him: and they returned and enquired early after
God.
35 And they remembered that [a]God *was* their
rock, and the high God [b]their redeemer.
36 Nevertheless they did [a]flatter him with
their mouth, and they lied unto him with their
tongues.
37 For their heart was not right with him, neither were they stedfast in his covenant.
38 [a]But he, *being* full of [b]compassion, forgave *their* iniquity, and destroyed *them* not: yea,
many a time [c]turned he his anger away, and [d]did
not stir up all his wrath.
39 For [a]he remembered [b]that they *were but*
flesh; [c]a wind that passeth away, and cometh not
again.
40 How oft did they [a]provoke him in the wilderness, *and* grieve him in the desert!
41 Yea, [a]they turned back and tempted God,
and limited the Holy One of Israel.
42 They remembered not his hand, *nor* the
day when he delivered them from the enemy.
43 How he had wrought his signs in Egypt,
and his wonders in the field of Zoan:
44 [a]And had turned their rivers into blood;
and their floods, that they could not drink.
45 [a]He sent divers sorts of flies among them,
which devoured them; and [b]frogs, which destroyed them.
46 He gave also their increase unto the caterpiller, and their labour unto the [a]locust.
47 [a]He destroyed their vines with hail, and
their sycomore trees with frost.
48 He gave up their [a]cattle also to the hail,
and their flocks to hot thunderbolts.
49 He cast upon them the fierceness of his
anger, wrath, and indignation, and trouble, by
sending evil angels *among them*.
50 He made a way to his anger; he spared
not their soul from death, but gave their life over
to the pestilence;
51 And smote all the [a]firstborn in Egypt; the
chief of *their* strength in the tabernacles of Ham:
52 But [a]made his own people to go forth like
sheep, and guided them in the wilderness like a
flock.

29 [a]Num. 11:19, 20
30 [a]Num. 11:33
32 [a]Num. 14:16, 17 [b]Num. 14:11; Ps. 78:11, 22
33 [a]Num. 14:29, 35
34 [a]Num. 21:7; [Hos. 5:15]
35 [a][Deut. 32:4, 15] [b][Ex. 15:13]; Deut. 7:8; Is. 41:14; 44:6; 63:9
36 [a]Ex. 24:7, 8; Ezek. 33:31
38 [a][Num. 14:18–20] [b]Ex. 34:6 [c][Is. 48:9] [d]1 Kin. 21:29
39 [a]Job 10:9; Ps. 103:14–16 [b]John 3:6 [c][Job 7:7, 16; James 4:14]
40 [a]Ps. 95:8–10; [Eph. 4:30]; Heb. 3:16
41 [a]Num. 14:22; Deut. 6:16
44 [a]Ex. 7:20
45 [a]Ex. 8:24 [b]Ex. 8:6
46 [a]Ex. 10:14
47 [a]Ex. 9:23–25
48 [a]Ex. 9:19
51 [a]Ex. 12:29, 30
52 [a]Ps. 77:20

NKJV

27 He also rained meat on them like the dust,
Feathered fowl like the sand of the seas;
28 And He let *them* fall in the midst of their
camp,
All around their dwellings.
29 [a]So they ate and were well filled,
For He gave them their own desire.
30 They were not deprived of their craving;
But [a]while their food *was* still in their
mouths,
31 The wrath of God came against them,
And slew the stoutest of them,
And struck down the choice *men* of Israel.

32 In spite of this [a]they still sinned,
And [b]did not believe in His wondrous
works.
33 [a]Therefore their days He consumed in
futility,
And their years in fear.

34 [a]When He slew them, then they sought
Him;
And they returned and sought earnestly
for God.
35 Then they remembered that [a]God *was*
their rock,
And the Most High God [b]their Redeemer.
36 Nevertheless they [a]flattered Him with
their mouth,
And they lied to Him with their tongue;
37 For their heart was not steadfast with
Him,
Nor were they faithful in His covenant.
38 [a]But He, *being* full of [b]compassion, forgave
their iniquity,
And did not destroy *them*.
Yes, many a time [c]He turned His anger
away,
And [d]did not stir up all His wrath;
39 For [a]He remembered [b]that they *were but*
flesh,
[c]A breath that passes away and does not
come again.

40 How often they [a]provoked Him in the
wilderness,
And grieved Him in the desert!
41 Yes, [a]again and again they tempted God,
And limited the Holy One of Israel.
42 They did not remember His power:
The day when He redeemed them from
the enemy,
43 When He worked His signs in Egypt,
And His wonders in the field of Zoan;
44 [a]Turned their rivers into blood,
And their streams, that they could not
drink.
45 [a]He sent swarms of flies among them,
which devoured them,
And [b]frogs, which destroyed them.
46 He also gave their crops to the caterpillar,
And their labor to the [a]locust.
47 [a]He destroyed their vines with hail,
And their sycamore trees with frost.
48 He also gave up their [a]cattle to the hail,
And their flocks to fiery lightning.
49 He cast on them the fierceness of His
anger,
Wrath, indignation, and trouble,
By sending angels of destruction *among
them*.
50 He made a path for His anger;
He did not spare their soul from death,
But gave their life over to the plague,
51 And destroyed all the [a]firstborn in Egypt,
The first of *their* strength in the tents of
Ham.
52 But He [a]made His own people go forth
like sheep,
And guided them in the wilderness like a
flock;

KJV

53 And he [a]led them on safely, so that they
feared not: but the sea [b]overwhelmed their
enemies.
54 And he brought them to the border of his
[a]sanctuary, *even to* this mountain, [b]*which* his
right hand had purchased.
55 [a]He cast out the heathen also before them,
and [b]divided them an inheritance by line, and
made the tribes of Israel to dwell in their tents.
56 [a]Yet they tempted and provoked the most
high God, and kept not his testimonies:
57 But [a]turned back, and dealt unfaithfully
like their fathers: they were turned aside [b]like a
deceitful bow.
58 [a]For they provoked him to anger with
their [b]high places, and moved him to jealousy
with their graven images.
59 When God heard *this,* he was wroth, and
greatly abhorred Israel:
60 [a]So that he forsook the tabernacle of Shiloh, the tent *which* he placed among men;
61 [a]And delivered his strength into captivity,
and his glory into the enemy's hand.
62 [a]He gave his people over also unto the
sword; and was wroth with his inheritance.
63 The fire consumed their young men; and
[a]their maidens were not given to marriage.
64 [a]Their priests fell by the sword; and [b]their
widows made no lamentation.
65 Then the Lord awaked as one out of sleep,
and [a]like a mighty man that shouteth by reason
of wine.
66 And [a]he smote his enemies in the hinder
parts: he put them to a perpetual reproach.
67 Moreover he refused the tabernacle of Joseph, and chose not the tribe of Ephraim:
68 But chose the tribe of Judah, the mount
Zion [a]which he loved.
69 And he built his [a]sanctuary like high *palaces,* like the earth which he hath established for
ever.
70 [a]He chose David also his servant, and
took him from the sheepfolds:
71 From following [a]the ewes great with
young he brought him [b]to feed Jacob his people,
and Israel his inheritance.
72 So he fed them according to the [a]integrity
of his heart; and guided them by the skilfulness
of his hands.

53 [a]Ex. 14:19, 20 [b]Ex. 14:27, 28
54 [a]Ex. 15:17 [b]Ps. 44:3
55 [a]Josh. 11:16–23; Ps. 44:2 [b]Josh. 13:7; 19:51; 23:4
56 [a]Judg. 2:11–13
57 [a]Ezek. 20:27, 28 [b]Hos. 7:16
58 [a]Deut. 32:16, 21; Judg. 2:12; 1 Kin. 14:9; Is. 65:3 [b]Deut. 12:2
60 [a]1 Sam. 4:11; Jer. 7:12–14; 26:6–9
61 [a]Judg. 18:30
62 [a]Judg. 20:21; 1 Sam. 4:10
63 [a]Jer. 7:34; 16:9; 25:10
64 [a]1 Sam. 4:17; 22:18 [b]Job 27:15; Ezek. 24:23
65 [a]Is. 42:13
66 [a]1 Sam. 5:6
68 [a][Ps. 87:2]
69 [a]1 Kin. 6:1–38
70 [a]1 Sam. 16:11, 12; 2 Sam. 7:8
71 [a]2 Sam. 7:8; [Is. 40:11] [b]2 Sam. 5:2; 1 Chr. 11:2
72 [a]1 Kin. 9:4

NKJV

53 And He [a]led them on safely, so that they
did not fear;
But the sea [b]overwhelmed their enemies.
54 And He brought them to His [a]holy border,
This mountain [b]*which* His right hand had
acquired.
55 [a]He also drove out the nations before
them,
[b]Allotted them an inheritance by survey,
And made the tribes of Israel dwell in their
tents.

56 [a]Yet they tested and provoked the Most
High God,
And did not keep His testimonies,
57 But [a]turned back and acted unfaithfully
like their fathers;
They were turned aside [b]like a deceitful
bow.
58 [a]For they provoked Him to anger with their
[b]high places,
And moved Him to jealousy with their
carved images.
59 When God heard *this,* He was furious,
And greatly abhorred Israel,
60 [a]So that He forsook the tabernacle of
Shiloh,
The tent He had placed among men,
61 [a]And delivered His strength into captivity,
And His glory into the enemy's hand.
62 [a]He also gave His people over to the
sword,
And was furious with His inheritance.
63 The fire consumed their young men,
And [a]their maidens were not given in
marriage.
64 [a]Their priests fell by the sword,
And [b]their widows made no lamentation.

65 Then the Lord awoke as *from* sleep,
[a]Like a mighty man who shouts because
of wine.
66 And [a]He beat back His enemies;
He put them to a perpetual reproach.

67 Moreover He rejected the tent of Joseph,
And did not choose the tribe of Ephraim,
68 But chose the tribe of Judah,
Mount Zion [a]which He loved.
69 And He built His [a]sanctuary like the
heights,
Like the earth which He has established
forever.
70 [a]He also chose David His servant,
And took him from the sheepfolds;
71 From following [a]the ewes that had young
He brought him,
[b]To shepherd Jacob His people,
And Israel His inheritance.
72 So he shepherded them according to the
[a]integrity of his heart,
And guided them by the skillfulness of his
hands.

PSALM 79

A Dirge and a Prayer for Israel, Destroyed by Enemies

A Psalm of Asaph.

O GOD, the heathen are come into [a]thine inheritance; thy holy temple have they defiled;
[b]they have laid Jerusalem on heaps.
2 [a]The dead bodies of thy servants have
they given *to be* meat unto the fowls of the
heaven, the flesh of thy saints unto the beasts of
the earth.
3 Their blood have they shed like water
round about Jerusalem; and *there was* none to
bury *them.*

PSALM 79

1 [a]Ps. 74:2 [b]2 Kin. 25:9, 10; 2 Chr. 36:17–19; Jer. 26:18; 52:12–14; Mic. 3:12
2 [a]Deut. 28:26; Jer. 7:33; 19:7; 34:20

PSALM 79

A Dirge and a Prayer for Israel, Destroyed by Enemies

A Psalm of Asaph.

O GOD, the nations have come into [a]Your
inheritance;
Your holy temple they have defiled;
[b]They have laid Jerusalem in heaps.
2 [a]The dead bodies of Your servants
They have given *as* food for the birds of
the heavens,
The flesh of Your saints to the beasts of
the earth.
3 Their blood they have shed like water all
around Jerusalem,
And *there was* no one to bury *them.*

KJV

4 We are become a reproach to our [a]neighbours, a scorn and derision to them that are round about us.
5 [a]How long, LORD? wilt thou be angry for ever? shall thy [b]jealousy burn like fire?
6 [a]Pour out thy wrath upon the heathen that have [b]not known thee, and upon the kingdoms that have [c]not called upon thy name.
7 For they have devoured Jacob, and laid waste his dwelling place.
8 [a]O remember not against us former iniquities: let thy tender mercies speedily prevent us: for we are brought very low.
9 Help us, O God of our salvation, for the glory of thy name: and deliver us, and purge away our sins, [a]for thy name's sake.
10 [a]Wherefore should the heathen say, Where *is* their God? let him be known among the heathen in our sight *by* the revenging of the blood of thy servants *which is* shed.
11 Let [a]the sighing of the prisoner come before thee; according to the greatness of thy power preserve thou those that are appointed to die;
12 And render unto our neighbours [a]sevenfold into their bosom [b]their reproach, wherewith they have reproached thee, O Lord.
13 So [a]we thy people and sheep of thy pasture will give thee thanks for ever: [b]we will shew forth thy praise to all generations.

4 [a]Ps. 44:13; [Dan. 9:16] **5** [a]Ps. 74:1, 9 [b][Zeph. 3:8] **6** [a]Jer. 10:25; [Zeph. 3:8] [b]Is. 45:4, 5; 1 Thess. 4:5; [2 Thess. 1:8] [c]Ps. 53:4 **8** [a]Is. 64:9 **9** [a]Jer. 14:7, 21 **10** [a]Ps. 42:10 **11** [a]Ps. 102:20 **12** [a]Gen. 4:15; Lev. 26:21; Prov. 6:31; Is. 30:26 [b]Ps. 74:10, 18, 22 **13** [a]Ps. 74:1; 95:7 [b]Is. 43:21

NKJV

4 We have become a reproach to our
[a]neighbors,
A scorn and derision to those who are
around us.
5 [a]How long, LORD?
Will You be angry forever?
Will Your [b]jealousy burn like fire?
6 [a]Pour out Your wrath on the nations that
[b]do not know You,
And on the kingdoms that [c]do not call on
Your name.
7 For they have devoured Jacob,
And laid waste his dwelling place.

8 [a]Oh, do not remember former iniquities
against us!
Let Your tender mercies come speedily to
meet us,
For we have been brought very low.
9 Help us, O God of our salvation,
For the glory of Your name;
And deliver us, and provide atonement for
our sins,
[a]For Your name's sake!
10 [a]Why should the nations say,
"Where *is* their God?"
Let there be known among the nations in
our sight
The avenging of the blood of Your
servants *which has been* shed.

11 Let [a]the groaning of the prisoner come
before You;
According to the greatness of Your
power
Preserve those who are appointed to die;
12 And return to our neighbors [a]sevenfold
into their bosom
[b]Their reproach with which they have
reproached You, O Lord.

13 So [a]we, Your people and sheep of Your
pasture,
Will give You thanks forever;
[b]We will show forth Your praise to all
generations.

PSALM 80

Prayer for Israel's Restoration

To the chief Musician [a]upon Shoshannim–Eduth, A Psalm of Asaph.

GIVE ear, O Shepherd of Israel, [a]thou that leadest Joseph [b]like a flock; thou that dwellest *between* the cherubims, [c]shine forth.
2 Before [a]Ephraim and Benjamin and Manasseh stir up thy strength, and come *and* save us.
3 [a]Turn us again, O God, [b]and cause thy face to shine; and we shall be saved.
4 O LORD God of hosts, [a]how long wilt thou be angry against the prayer of thy people?
5 [a]Thou feedest them with the bread of tears; and givest them tears to drink in great measure.
6 Thou makest us a strife unto our neighbours: and our enemies laugh among themselves.
7 Turn us again, O God of hosts, and cause thy face to shine; and we shall be saved.

PSALM 80

title [a]Ps. 45:title **1** [a][Ex. 25:20–22]; 1 Sam. 4:4; 2 Sam. 6:2 [b]Ps. 77:20 [c]Deut. 33:2 **2** [a]Ps. 78:9, 67 **3** [a]Lam. 5:21 [b]Num. 6:25; Ps. 4:6 **4** [a]Ps. 79:5 **5** [a]Ps. 42:3; Is. 30:20

PSALM 80

Prayer for Israel's Restoration

To the Chief Musician. [a]Set to *"The Lilies." A *Testimony of Asaph. A Psalm.

GIVE ear, O Shepherd of Israel,
[a]You who lead Joseph [b]like a flock;
You who dwell *between* the cherubim,
[c]shine forth!
2 Before [a]Ephraim, Benjamin, and
Manasseh,
Stir up Your strength,
And come *and* save us!

3 [a]Restore us, O God;
[b]Cause Your face to shine,
And we shall be saved!

4 O LORD God of hosts,
[a]How long will You be angry
Against the prayer of Your people?
5 [a]You have fed them with the bread of
tears,
And given them tears to drink in great
measure.
6 You have made us a strife to our
neighbors,
And our enemies laugh among
themselves.

7 Restore us, O God of hosts;
Cause Your face to shine,
And we shall be saved!

---

*

80:title Heb. *Shoshannim* • Heb. *Eduth*

8 Thou hast brought [a]a vine out of Egypt: [b]thou hast cast out the heathen, and planted it.

9 Thou preparedst *room* before it, and didst cause it to take deep root, and it filled the land.

10 The hills were covered with the shadow of it, and the [a]boughs thereof *were like* the goodly cedars.

11 She sent out her boughs unto the sea, and her branches unto the river.

12 Why hast thou *then* [a]broken down her hedges, so that all they which pass by the way do pluck her?

13 The boar out of the wood doth waste it, and the wild beast of the field doth devour it.

14 Return, we beseech thee, O God of hosts: [a]look down from heaven, and behold, and visit this vine;

15 And the vineyard which thy right hand hath planted, and the branch *that* thou madest strong [a]for thyself.

16 *It is* burned with fire, *it is* cut down: [a]they perish at the rebuke of thy countenance.

17 [a]Let thy hand be upon the man of thy right hand, upon the son of man *whom* thou madest strong for thyself.

18 So will not we go back from thee: quicken us, and we will call upon thy name.

19 Turn us again, O LORD God of hosts, cause thy face to shine; and we shall be saved.

8 [a][Is. 5:1, 7]; Jer. 2:21; Ezek. 15:6; 17:6; 19:10 [b]Ps. 44:2; Acts 7:45
10 [a]Lev. 23:40
12 [a]Is. 5:5; Nah. 2:2
14 [a]Is. 63:15
15 [a][Is. 49:5]
16 [a][Ps. 39:11]
17 [a]Ps. 89:21

8 You have brought [a]a vine out of Egypt;
[b]You have cast out the nations, and planted it.
9 You prepared *room* for it,
And caused it to take deep root,
And it filled the land.
10 The hills were covered with its shadow,
And the mighty cedars with its [a]boughs.
11 She sent out her boughs to *the Sea,
And her branches to *the River.
12 Why have You [a]broken down her hedges,
So that all who pass by the way pluck her *fruit?*
13 The boar out of the woods uproots it,
And the wild beast of the field devours it.

14 Return, we beseech You, O God of hosts;
[a]Look down from heaven and see,
And visit this vine
15 And the vineyard which Your right hand has planted,
And the branch *that* You made strong [a]for Yourself.
16 *It is* burned with fire, *it is* cut down;
[a]They perish at the rebuke of Your countenance.
17 [a]Let Your hand be upon the man of Your right hand,
Upon the son of man *whom* You made strong for Yourself.
18 Then we will not turn back from You;
Revive us, and we will call upon Your name.

19 Restore us, O LORD God of hosts;
Cause Your face to shine,
And we shall be saved!

PSALM 81

An Appeal for Israel's Repentance

To the chief Musician [a]upon Gittith, *A Psalm* of Asaph.

SING aloud unto God our strength: make a joyful noise unto the God of Jacob.

2 Take a psalm, and bring hither the timbrel, the pleasant harp with the psaltery.

3 Blow up the trumpet in the new moon, in the time appointed, on our solemn feast day.

4 For [a]this *was* a statute for Israel, *and* a law of the God of Jacob.

5 This he ordained in Joseph *for* a testimony, when he went out through the land of Egypt: [a]*where* I heard a language *that* I understood not.

6 I removed his shoulder from the burden: his hands were delivered from the pots.

7 [a]Thou calledst in trouble, and I delivered thee; [b]I answered thee in the secret place of thunder: I [c]proved thee at the waters of Meribah. Selah.

8 [a]Hear, O my people, and I will testify unto thee: O Israel, if thou wilt hearken unto me;

9 There shall no [a]strange god be in thee; neither shalt thou worship any strange god.

10 [a]I *am* the LORD thy God, which brought thee out of the land of Egypt: [b]open thy mouth wide, and I will fill it.

11 But my people would not hearken to my voice; and Israel would [a]none of me.

PSALM 81
title [a]Ps. 8:title
4 [a]Lev. 23:24; Num. 10:10
5 [a]Deut. 28:49; Ps. 114:1; Jer. 5:15
7 [a]Ex. 2:23; 14:10; Ps. 50:15 [b]Ex. 19:19; 20:18 [c]Ex. 17:6, 7; Num. 20:13
8 [a][Ps. 50:7]
9 [a][Ex. 20:3; Deut. 5:7; 32:12]; Ps. 44:20; [Is. 43:12]
10 [a]Ex. 20:2; Deut. 5:6 [b]Ps. 103:5
11 [a]Ex. 32:1; Deut. 32:15

PSALM 81

An Appeal for Israel's Repentance

To the Chief Musician. [a]On* an instrument of Gath. A Psalm of Asaph.

SING aloud to God our strength;
Make a joyful shout to the God of Jacob.
2 Raise a song and strike the timbrel,
The pleasant harp with the lute.

3 Blow the trumpet at the time of the New Moon,
At the full moon, on our solemn feast day.
4 For [a]this *is* a statute for Israel,
A law of the God of Jacob.
5 This He established in Joseph *as* a testimony,
When He went throughout the land of Egypt,
[a]*Where* I heard a language I did not understand.

6 "I removed his shoulder from the burden;
His hands were freed from the baskets.
7 [a]You called in trouble, and I delivered you;
[b]I answered you in the secret place of thunder;
I [c]tested you at the waters of Meribah.
Selah

8 "Hear,[a] O My people, and I will admonish you!
O Israel, if you will listen to Me!
9 There shall be no [a]foreign god among you;
Nor shall you worship any foreign god.
10 [a]I *am* the LORD your God,
Who brought you out of the land of Egypt;
[b]Open your mouth wide, and I will fill it.

11 "But My people would not heed My voice,
And Israel would *have* [a]none of Me.

*
80:11 The Mediterranean • The Euphrates
81:title Heb. *Al Gittith*

KJV

12 [a]So I gave them up unto their own hearts' lust: *and* they walked in their own counsels.

13 [a]Oh that my people had hearkened unto me, *and* Israel had walked in my ways!

14 I should soon have subdued their enemies, and turned my hand against their adversaries.

15 [a]The haters of the LORD should have submitted themselves unto him: but their time should have endured for ever.

16 He should [a]have fed them also with the finest of the wheat: and with honey [b]out of the rock should I have satisfied thee.

12 [a][Job 8:4; Acts 7:42; Rom. 1:24, 26] **13** [a][Deut. 5:29; Is. 48:18] **15** [a]Rom. 1:30 **16** [a]Deut. 32:14 [b]Job 29:6

NKJV

12 [a]So I gave them over to their own stubborn heart,
To walk in their own counsels.

13 "Oh,[a] that My people would listen to Me,
That Israel would walk in My ways!
14 I would soon subdue their enemies,
And turn My hand against their adversaries.
15 [a]The haters of the LORD would pretend submission to Him,
But their fate would endure forever.
16 He would [a]have fed them also with the finest of wheat;
And with honey [b]from the rock I would have satisfied you."

PSALM 82

A Plea for Justice

A Psalm of Asaph.

GOD [a]standeth in the congregation of the mighty; he judgeth among [b]the gods.

2 How long will ye judge unjustly, and [a]accept the persons of the wicked? Selah.

3 Defend the poor and fatherless: do justice to the afflicted and [a]needy.

4 Deliver the poor and needy: rid *them* out of the hand of the wicked.

5 They know not, neither will they understand; they walk on in darkness: all the [a]foundations of the earth are out of course.

6 I have said, [a]Ye *are* gods; and all of you *are* children of the most High.

7 But ye shall die like men, and fall like one of the princes.

8 Arise, O God, judge the earth: [a]for thou shalt inherit all nations.

PSALM 82

1 [a][2 Chr. 19:6; Eccl. 5:8] [b]Ps. 82:6 **2** [a][Deut. 1:17]; Prov. 18:5 **3** [a][Deut. 24:17; Is. 11:4; Jer. 22:16] **5** [a]Ps. 11:3 **6** [a]John 10:34 **8** [a]Ps. 2:8; [Rev. 11:15]

PSALM 82

A Plea for Justice

A Psalm of Asaph.

GOD [a]stands in the congregation of the mighty;
He judges among [b]the *gods.
2 How long will you judge unjustly,
And [a]show partiality to the wicked? Selah
3 Defend the poor and fatherless;
Do justice to the afflicted and [a]needy.
4 Deliver the poor and needy;
Free *them* from the hand of the wicked.

5 They do not know, nor do they understand;
They walk about in darkness;
All the [a]foundations of the earth are unstable.

6 I said, [a]"You *are* *gods,
And all of you *are* children of the Most High.
7 But you shall die like men,
And fall like one of the princes."

8 Arise, O God, judge the earth;
[a]For You shall inherit all nations.

PSALM 83

Prayer to Frustrate Conspiracy Against Israel

A Song or Psalm of Asaph.

KEEP [a]not thou silence, O God: hold not thy peace, and be not still, O God.

2 For, lo, [a]thine enemies make a tumult: and they that hate thee have lifted up the head.

3 They have taken crafty counsel against thy people, and consulted [a]against thy hidden ones.

4 They have said, Come, and [a]let us cut them off from *being* a nation; that the name of Israel may be no more in remembrance.

5 For they have consulted together with one consent: they are confederate against thee:

6 [a]The tabernacles of Edom, and the Ishmaelites; of Moab, and the Hagarenes;

7 Gebal, and Ammon, and Amalek; the Philistines with the inhabitants of Tyre;

8 Assur also is joined with them: they have holpen the children of Lot. Selah.

9 Do unto them as *unto* the [a]Midianites; as *to* [b]Sisera, as *to* Jabin, at the brook of Kison:

10 *Which* perished at En–dor: [a]they became *as* dung for the earth.

PSALM 83

1 [a]Ps. 28:1 **2** [a]Ps. 81:15; Is. 17:12; Acts 4:25 **3** [a][Ps. 27:5] **4** [a]Esth. 3:6, 9; Jer. 11:19; 31:36 **6** [a]2 Chr. 20:1, 10, 11 **9** [a]Num. 31:7; Judg. 7:22 [b]Judg. 4:15–24; 5:20, 21 **10** [a]Zeph. 1:17

PSALM 83

Prayer to Frustrate Conspiracy Against Israel

A Song. A Psalm of Asaph.

DO[a] not keep silent, O God!
Do not hold Your peace,
And do not be still, O God!
2 For behold, [a]Your enemies make a tumult;
And those who hate You have lifted up their head.
3 They have taken crafty counsel against Your people,
And consulted together [a]against Your sheltered ones.
4 They have said, "Come, and [a]let us cut them off from *being* a nation,
That the name of Israel may be remembered no more."

5 For they have consulted together with one consent;
They form a confederacy against You:
6 [a]The tents of Edom and the Ishmaelites;
Moab and the Hagrites;
7 Gebal, Ammon, and Amalek;
Philistia with the inhabitants of Tyre;
8 Assyria also has joined with them;
They have helped the children of Lot. Selah

9 Deal with them as *with* [a]Midian,
As *with* [b]Sisera,
As *with* Jabin at the Brook Kishon,
10 Who perished at En Dor,
[a]*Who* became *as* refuse on the earth.

*

82:1 Judges; Heb. *elohim,* lit. *mighty ones* or *gods*
82:6 Judges; Heb. *elohim,* lit. *mighty ones* or *gods*

KJV

11 Make their nobles like Oreb, and like
[a]Zeeb: yea, all their princes as [b]Zebah, and as
Zalmunna:
12 Who said, Let us take to ourselves the
houses of God in possession.
13 [a]O my God, make them like a wheel; [b]as
the stubble before the wind.
14 As the fire burneth a wood, and as the
flame [a]setteth the mountains on fire;
15 So persecute them with thy tempest, and
make them afraid with thy storm.
16 Fill their faces with shame; that they may
seek thy name, O LORD.
17 Let them be confounded and troubled for
ever; yea, let them be put to shame, and perish:
18 [a]That *men* may know that thou, whose
[b]name alone *is* JEHOVAH, *art* [c]the most high
over all the earth.

PSALM 84

The Blessedness of Dwelling in the House of God

To the chief Musician [a]upon Gittith, A Psalm for the sons of Korah.

HOW [a]amiable *are* thy tabernacles, O LORD of
hosts!
2 [a]My soul longeth, yea, even fainteth for
the courts of the LORD: my heart and my flesh
crieth out for the living God.
3 Yea, the sparrow hath found an house,
and the swallow a nest for herself, where she may
lay her young, *even* thine altars, O LORD of hosts,
my King, and my God.
4 Blessed *are* they that dwell in thy [a]house:
they will be still praising thee. Selah.
5 Blessed *is* the man whose strength *is* in
thee; in whose heart *are* the ways *of them*.
6 *Who* passing through the valley [a]of Baca
make it a well; the rain also filleth the pools.
7 They go [a]from strength to strength, *every*
one of them in Zion [b]appeareth before God.
8 O LORD God of hosts, hear my prayer: give
ear, O God of Jacob. Selah.
9 Behold, [a]O God our shield, and look upon
the face of thine anointed.
10 For a day in thy courts *is* better than a
thousand. I had rather be a doorkeeper in the
house of my God, than to dwell in the tents of
wickedness.
11 For the LORD God *is* [a]a sun and [b]shield:
the LORD will give grace and glory: [c]no good *thing*
will he withhold from them that walk uprightly.
12 O LORD of hosts, [a]blessed *is* the man that
trusteth in thee.

PSALM 85

Prayer that the LORD Will Restore Favor to the Land

To the chief Musician, A Psalm [a]for the sons of Korah.

LORD, thou hast been favourable unto thy land:
thou hast [a]brought back the captivity of Jacob.

---

11 [a]Judg. 7:25 [b]Judg. 8:12–21
13 [a]Is. 17:13 [b]Job 21:18; Ps. 35:5; Is. 40:24; Jer. 13:24
14 [a]Ex. 19:18; Deut. 32:22
18 [a]Ps. 59:13 [b]Ex. 6:3 [c][Ps. 92:8]

PSALM 84
title [a]Ps. 8:title
1 [a]Ps. 27:4; 46:4, 5
2 [a]Ps. 42:1, 2
4 [a][Ps. 65:4]
6 [a]2 Sam. 5:22–25
7 [a]Prov. 4:18; Is. 40:31; John 1:16; 2 Cor. 3:18 [b]Ex. 34:23; Deut. 16:16
9 [a]Gen. 15:1
11 [a]Is. 60:19, 20; Mal. 4:2; Rev. 21:23 [b]Gen. 15:1 [c]Ps. 34:9, 10
12 [a][Ps. 2:12; 40:4]

PSALM 85
title [a]Ps. 42:title
1 [a]Ezra 1:11—2:1; Ps. 14:7; Jer. 30:18; 31:23; Ezek. 39:25; Hos. 6:11; Joel 3:1

*———

84:title Heb. *Al Gittith*
84:7 LXX, Syr., Vg. *The God of gods shall be seen*

NKJV

11 Make their nobles like Oreb and like
[a]Zeeb,
Yes, all their princes like [b]Zebah and
Zalmunna,
12 Who said, "Let us take for ourselves
The pastures of God for a possession."

13 [a]O my God, make them like the whirling
dust,
[b]Like the chaff before the wind!
14 As the fire burns the woods,
And as the flame [a]sets the mountains on
fire,
15 So pursue them with Your tempest,
And frighten them with Your storm.
16 Fill their faces with shame,
That they may seek Your name, O LORD.
17 Let them be confounded and dismayed
forever;
Yes, let them be put to shame and perish,
18 [a]That they may know that You, whose
[b]name alone *is* the LORD,
Are [c]the Most High over all the earth.

PSALM 84

The Blessedness of Dwelling in the House of God

To the Chief Musician. [a]On* an instrument of Gath. A Psalm of the sons of Korah.

HOW [a]lovely *is* Your tabernacle,
O LORD of hosts!
2 [a]My soul longs, yes, even faints
For the courts of the LORD;
My heart and my flesh cry out for the
living God.

3 Even the sparrow has found a home,
And the swallow a nest for herself,
Where she may lay her young—
Even Your altars, O LORD of hosts,
My King and my God.
4 Blessed *are* those who dwell in Your
[a]house;
They will still be praising You. Selah

5 Blessed *is* the man whose strength *is* in
You,
Whose heart *is* set on pilgrimage.
6 *As they* pass through the Valley [a]of Baca,
They make it a spring;
The rain also covers it with pools.
7 They go [a]from strength to strength;
**Each one* [b]appears before God in Zion.

8 O LORD God of hosts, hear my prayer;
Give ear, O God of Jacob! Selah
9 [a]O God, behold our shield,
And look upon the face of Your anointed.

10 For a day in Your courts *is* better than a
thousand.
I would rather be a doorkeeper in the
house of my God
Than dwell in the tents of wickedness.
11 For the LORD God *is* [a]a sun and [b]shield;
The LORD will give grace and glory;
[c]No good *thing* will He withhold
From those who walk uprightly.

12 O LORD of hosts,
[a]Blessed *is* the man who trusts in You!

PSALM 85

Prayer that the LORD Will Restore Favor to the Land

To the Chief Musician. A Psalm [a]of the sons of Korah.

LORD, You have been favorable to Your land;
You have [a]brought back the captivity of
Jacob.

KJV

2 Thou hast forgiven the iniquity of thy people; thou hast covered all their sin. Selah.
3 Thou hast taken away all thy wrath: thou
hast turned *thyself* from the fierceness of thine
anger.
4 [a]Turn us, O God of our salvation, and
cause thine anger toward us to cease.
5 [a]Wilt thou be angry with us for ever? wilt
thou draw out thine anger to all generations?
6 Wilt thou not [a]revive us again: that thy
people may rejoice in thee?
7 Shew us thy mercy, O LORD, and grant us
thy salvation.
8 I will hear what God the LORD will speak:
for he will speak peace unto his people, and to
his saints: but let them not turn again to folly.
9 Surely [a]his salvation *is* nigh them that fear
him; [b]that glory may dwell in our land.
10 Mercy and truth are met together; [a]righ-
teousness and peace have kissed *each other*.
11 Truth shall spring out of the earth; and
righteousness shall look down from heaven.
12 [a]Yea, the LORD shall give *that which is*
good; and our land shall yield her increase.
13 Righteousness shall go before him; and
shall set *us* in the way of his steps.

PSALM 86

Prayer for Mercy, with Meditation on the Excellencies of the LORD

A Prayer of David.

BOW down thine ear, O LORD, hear me: for I
am poor and needy.
2 Preserve my soul; for I *am* holy: O thou
my God, save thy servant that trusteth in thee.
3 Be merciful unto me, O Lord: for I cry
unto thee daily.
4 Rejoice the soul of thy servant: [a]for unto
thee, O Lord, do I lift up my soul.
5 For [a]thou, Lord, *art* good, and ready to
forgive; and plenteous in mercy unto all them that
call upon thee.
6 Give ear, O LORD, unto my prayer; and
attend to the voice of my supplications.
7 In the day of my trouble I will call upon
thee: for thou wilt answer me.
8 [a]Among the gods *there is* none like unto
thee, O Lord; neither *are there any works* like
unto thy works.
9 All nations whom thou hast made shall
come and worship before thee, O Lord; and shall
glorify thy name.
10 For thou *art* great, and [a]doest wondrous
things: [b]thou *art* God alone.
11 [a]Teach me thy way, O LORD; I will walk
in thy truth: unite my heart to fear thy name.
12 I will praise thee, O Lord my God, with
all my heart: and I will glorify thy name for
evermore.

4 [a]Ps. 80:3, 7
5 [a]Ps. 79:5
6 [a]Hab. 3:2
9 [a]Is. 46:13 [b]Hag. 2:7; Zech. 2:5; [John 1:14]
10 [a]Ps. 72:3; [Is. 32:17]; Luke 2:14
12 [a][Ps. 84:11; James 1:17]

PSALM 86

4 [a]Ps. 25:1; 143:8
5 [a]Ps. 130:7; 145:9; [Joel 2:13]
8 [a][Ex. 15:11]; 2 Sam. 7:22; 1 Kin. 8:23; Ps. 89:6; Jer. 10:6
10 [a][Ex. 15:11] [b]Deut. 6:4; Is. 37:16; Mark 12:29; 1 Cor. 8:4
11 [a]Ps. 27:11; 143:8

NKJV

2 You have forgiven the iniquity of Your
people;
You have covered all their sin. Selah
3 You have taken away all Your wrath;
You have turned from the fierceness of
Your anger.

4 [a]Restore us, O God of our salvation,
And cause Your anger toward us to cease.
5 [a]Will You be angry with us forever?
Will You prolong Your anger to all
generations?
6 Will You not [a]revive us again,
That Your people may rejoice in You?
7 Show us Your mercy, LORD,
And grant us Your salvation.

8 I will hear what God the LORD will
speak,
For He will speak peace
To His people and to His saints;
But let them not turn back to folly.
9 Surely [a]His salvation *is* near to those who
fear Him,
[b]That glory may dwell in our land.

10 Mercy and truth have met together;
[a]Righteousness and peace have kissed.
11 Truth shall spring out of the earth,
And righteousness shall look down from
heaven.
12 [a]Yes, the LORD will give *what is* good;
And our land will yield its increase.
13 Righteousness will go before Him,
And shall make His footsteps *our*
pathway.

PSALM 86

Prayer for Mercy, with Meditation on the Excellencies of the LORD

A Prayer of David.

BOW down Your ear, O LORD, hear me;
For I *am* poor and needy.
2 Preserve my life, for I *am* holy;
You are my God;
Save Your servant who trusts in You!
3 Be merciful to me, O Lord,
For I cry to You all day long.
4 Rejoice the soul of Your servant,
[a]For to You, O Lord, I lift up my soul.
5 For [a]You, Lord, *are* good, and ready to
forgive,
And abundant in mercy to all those who
call upon You.

6 Give ear, O LORD, to my prayer;
And attend to the voice of my
supplications.
7 In the day of my trouble I will call upon
You,
For You will answer me.

8 [a]Among the gods *there is* none like You,
O Lord;
Nor *are there any works* like Your
works.
9 All nations whom You have made
Shall come and worship before You, O
Lord,
And shall glorify Your name.
10 For You *are* great, and [a]do wondrous
things;
[b]You alone *are* God.

11 [a]Teach me Your way, O LORD;
I will walk in Your truth;
Unite my heart to fear Your name.
12 I will praise You, O Lord my God, with
all my heart,
And I will glorify Your name forevermore.

KJV

13 For great *is* thy mercy toward me: and
thou hast delivered my soul from the lowest hell.
14 O God, the proud are risen against me,
and the assemblies of violent *men* have sought
after my soul; and have not set thee before them.
15 But [a]thou, O Lord, *art* a God full of compassion, and gracious, longsuffering, and plenteous in mercy and truth.
16 O turn unto me, and have mercy upon me;
give thy strength unto thy servant, and save the
son of thine handmaid.
17 Shew me a token for good; that they
which hate me may see *it*, and be ashamed: because thou, LORD, hast holpen me, and comforted
me.

PSALM 87

The Glories of the City of God

A Psalm *or* Song for the sons of Korah.

HIS foundation *is* in the holy mountains.
2 [a]The LORD loveth the gates of Zion more
than all the dwellings of Jacob.
3 [a]Glorious things are spoken of thee, O city
of God. Selah.
4 I will make mention of Rahab and Babylon to them that know me: behold Philistia, and
Tyre, with Ethiopia; this *man* was born there.
5 And of Zion it shall be said, This and that
man was born in her: and the highest himself shall
establish her.
6 The LORD shall count, when he [a]writeth
up the people, *that* this *man* was born there.
Selah.
7 As well the singers as the players on instruments *shall be there:* all my springs *are* in
thee.

PSALM 88

A Prayer for Help in Despondency

A Song *or* Psalm for the sons of Korah, to the chief Musician upon Mahalath Leannoth, Maschil of [a]Heman the Ezrahite.

O LORD [a]God of my salvation, I have cried day
and night before thee:
2 Let my prayer come before thee: incline
thine ear unto my cry;
3 For my soul is full of troubles: and my
life [a]draweth nigh unto the grave.
4 I am counted with them that [a]go down into
the pit: [b]I am as a man *that hath* no strength:
5 Free among the dead, like the slain that
lie in the grave, whom thou rememberest no more:
and they are cut off from thy hand.
6 Thou hast laid me in the lowest pit, in
darkness, in the deeps.
7 Thy wrath lieth hard upon me, and thou
hast afflicted *me* with all [a]thy waves. Selah.
8 [a]Thou hast put away mine acquaintance
far from me; thou hast made me an abomination
unto them: [b]*I am* shut up, and I cannot come forth.

15 [a]Ex. 34:6; [Ps. 86:5]

PSALM 87

2 [a]Ps. 78:67, 68
3 [a]Is. 60:1
6 [a]Is. 4:3

PSALM 88

title [a]1 Kin. 4:31; 1 Chr. 2:6
1 [a]Ps. 27:9; [Luke 18:7]
3 [a]Ps. 107:18
4 [a][Ps. 28:1] [b]Ps. 31:12
7 [a]Ps. 42:7
8 [a]Job 19:13, 19; Ps. 31:11; 142:4 [b]Lam. 3:7

*———

88:title Heb. *Maschil*

NKJV

13 For great *is* Your mercy toward me,
And You have delivered my soul from the depths of Sheol.

14 O God, the proud have risen against me,
And a mob of violent *men* have sought my life,
And have not set You before them.
15 But [a]You, O Lord, *are* a God full of compassion, and gracious,
Longsuffering and abundant in mercy and truth.

16 Oh, turn to me, and have mercy on me!
Give Your strength to Your servant,
And save the son of Your maidservant.
17 Show me a sign for good,
That those who hate me may see *it* and be ashamed,
Because You, LORD, have helped me and comforted me.

PSALM 87

The Glories of the City of God

A Psalm of the sons of Korah. A Song.

HIS foundation *is* in the holy mountains.
2 [a]The LORD loves the gates of Zion
More than all the dwellings of Jacob.
3 [a]Glorious things are spoken of you,
O city of God! Selah

4 "I will make mention of Rahab and Babylon to those who know Me;
Behold, O Philistia and Tyre, with Ethiopia:
'This *one* was born there.' "

5 And of Zion it will be said,
"This *one* and that *one* were born in her;
And the Most High Himself shall establish her."
6 The LORD will record,
When He [a]registers the peoples:
"This *one* was born there." Selah

7 Both the singers and the players on instruments *say*,
"All my springs *are* in you."

PSALM 88

A Prayer for Help in Despondency

A Song. A Psalm of the sons of Korah. To the Chief Musician. Set to "Mahalath Leannoth." A *Contemplation of [a]Heman the Ezrahite.

O LORD, [a]God of my salvation,
I have cried out day and night before You.
2 Let my prayer come before You;
Incline Your ear to my cry.

3 For my soul is full of troubles,
And my life [a]draws near to the grave.
4 I am counted with those who [a]go down to the pit;
[b]I am like a man *who has* no strength,
5 Adrift among the dead,
Like the slain who lie in the grave,
Whom You remember no more,
And who are cut off from Your hand.

6 You have laid me in the lowest pit,
In darkness, in the depths.
7 Your wrath lies heavy upon me,
And You have afflicted *me* with all [a]Your waves. Selah
8 [a]You have put away my acquaintances far from me;
You have made me an abomination to them;
[b]*I am* shut up, and I cannot get out;

KJV

9 Mine eye mourneth by reason of affliction:
[a]LORD, I have called daily upon thee, I have stretched out my hands unto thee.
10 Wilt thou shew wonders to the dead? shall the dead arise *and* praise thee? Selah.
11 Shall thy lovingkindness be declared in the grave? *or* thy faithfulness in destruction?
12 Shall thy wonders be known in the dark? and thy righteousness in the land of forgetfulness?
13 But unto thee have I cried, O LORD; and in the morning shall my prayer prevent thee.
14 LORD, why castest thou off my soul? *why* hidest thou thy face from me?
15 I *am* afflicted and ready to die from *my* youth up: *while* I suffer thy terrors I am distracted.
16 Thy fierce wrath goeth over me; thy terrors have cut me off.
17 They came round about me daily like water; they compassed me about together.
18 [a]Lover and friend hast thou put far from me, *and* mine acquaintance into darkness.

PSALM 89

Remembering the Covenant with David, and Sorrow for Lost Blessings

Maschil of [a]Ethan the Ezrahite.

I WILL sing of the mercies of the LORD for ever: with my mouth will I make known thy faithfulness to all generations.
2 For I have said, Mercy shall be built up for ever: [a]thy faithfulness shalt thou establish in the very heavens.
3 [a]I have made a covenant with my chosen, I have [b]sworn unto David my servant,
4 Thy seed will I establish for ever, and build up thy throne [a]to all generations. Selah.
5 And [a]the heavens shall praise thy wonders, O LORD: thy faithfulness also in the congregation of the saints.
6 [a]For who in the heaven can be compared unto the LORD? *who* among the sons of the mighty can be likened unto the LORD?
7 [a]God is greatly to be feared in the assembly of the saints, and to be had in reverence of all *them that are* about him.
8 O LORD God of hosts, who *is* a strong LORD like unto thee? or to thy faithfulness round about thee?
9 [a]Thou rulest the raging of the sea: when the waves thereof arise, thou stillest them.
10 [a]Thou hast broken Rahab in pieces, as one that is slain; thou hast scattered thine enemies with thy strong arm.
11 [a]The heavens *are* thine, the earth also *is* thine: *as for* the world and the fulness thereof, thou hast founded them.
12 The north and the south thou hast created them: [a]Tabor and [b]Hermon shall rejoice in thy name.

9 [a]Ps. 86:3
18 [a]Job 19:13; Ps. 31:11; 38:11

PSALM 89

title [a]1 Kin. 4:31
2 [a][Ps. 119:89, 90]
3 [a]1 Kin. 8:16 [b]2 Sam. 7:11; 1 Chr. 17:10–12
4 [a][2 Sam. 7:13; Is. 9:7; Luke 1:33]
5 [a][Ps. 19:1]
6 [a]Ps. 86:8; 113:5
7 [a]Ps. 76:7, 11
9 [a]Ps. 65:7; 93:3, 4; 107:29
10 [a]Ex. 14:26–28; Ps. 87:4; Is. 30:7; 51:9
11 [a][Gen. 1:1; 1 Chr. 29:11]
12 [a]Josh. 19:22; Judg. 4:6; Jer. 46:18 [b]Deut. 3:8; Josh. 11:17; 12:1; Song 4:8

*

89:title Heb. *Maschil*

NKJV

9 My eye wastes away because of affliction.
[a]LORD, I have called daily upon You;
I have stretched out my hands to You.
10 Will You work wonders for the dead?
Shall the dead arise *and* praise You? Selah
11 Shall Your lovingkindness be declared in the grave?
Or Your faithfulness in the place of destruction?
12 Shall Your wonders be known in the dark?
And Your righteousness in the land of forgetfulness?

13 But to You I have cried out, O LORD,
And in the morning my prayer comes before You.
14 LORD, why do You cast off my soul?
Why do You hide Your face from me?
15 I *have been* afflicted and ready to die from *my* youth;
I suffer Your terrors;
I am distraught.
16 Your fierce wrath has gone over me;
Your terrors have cut me off.
17 They came around me all day long like water;
They engulfed me altogether.
18 [a]Loved one and friend You have put far from me,
And my acquaintances into darkness.

PSALM 89

Remembering the Covenant with David, and Sorrow for Lost Blessings

A *Contemplation of [a]Ethan the Ezrahite.

I WILL sing of the mercies of the LORD forever;
With my mouth will I make known Your faithfulness to all generations.
2 For I have said, "Mercy shall be built up forever;
[a]Your faithfulness You shall establish in the very heavens."

3 "I[a] have made a covenant with My chosen,
I have [b]sworn to My servant David:
4 'Your seed I will establish forever,
And build up your throne [a]to all generations.' " Selah

5 And [a]the heavens will praise Your wonders, O LORD;
Your faithfulness also in the assembly of the saints.
6 [a]For who in the heavens can be compared to the LORD?
Who among the sons of the mighty can be likened to the LORD?
7 [a]God is greatly to be feared in the assembly of the saints,
And to be held in reverence by all *those* around Him.
8 O LORD God of hosts,
Who *is* mighty like You, O LORD?
Your faithfulness also surrounds You.
9 [a]You rule the raging of the sea;
When its waves rise, You still them.
10 [a]You have broken Rahab in pieces, as one who is slain;
You have scattered Your enemies with Your mighty arm.

11 [a]The heavens *are* Yours, the earth also *is* Yours;
The world and all its fullness, You have founded them.
12 The north and the south, You have created them;
[a]Tabor and [b]Hermon rejoice in Your name.

KJV

13 Thou hast a mighty arm: strong is thy hand, *and* high is thy right hand.

14 Justice and judgment *are* the habitation of thy throne: mercy and truth shall go before thy face.

15 Blessed *is* the people that know the [a]joyful sound: they shall walk, O LORD, in the light of thy countenance.

16 In thy name shall they rejoice all the day: and in thy righteousness shall they be exalted.

17 For thou *art* the glory of their strength: and in thy favour our horn shall be [a]exalted.

18 For the LORD *is* our defence; and the Holy One of Israel *is* our king.

19 Then thou spakest in vision to thy holy one, and saidst, I have laid help upon *one that is* mighty; I have exalted *one* [a]chosen out of the people.

20 [a]I have found David my servant; with my holy oil have I anointed him:

21 [a]With whom my hand shall be established: mine arm also shall strengthen him.

22 The enemy shall not exact upon him; nor the son of wickedness afflict him.

23 And I will beat down his foes before his face, and plague them that hate him.

24 But my faithfulness and my mercy *shall be* with him: and in my name shall his horn be exalted.

25 I will [a]set his hand also in the sea, and his right hand in the rivers.

26 He shall cry unto me, Thou *art* [a]my father, my God, and [b]the rock of my salvation.

27 Also I will make him [a]*my* firstborn, [b]higher than the kings of the earth.

28 [a]My mercy will I keep for him for evermore, and my covenant shall stand fast with him.

29 His seed also will I make *to endure* for ever, [a]and his throne [b]as the days of heaven.

30 [a]If his children [b]forsake my law, and walk not in my judgments;

31 If they break my statutes, and keep not my commandments;

32 Then will I visit their transgression with the rod, and their iniquity with stripes.

33 [a]Nevertheless my lovingkindness will I not utterly take from him, nor suffer my faithfulness to fail.

34 My covenant will I not break, nor [a]alter the thing that is gone out of my lips.

35 Once have I sworn [a]by my holiness that I will not lie unto David.

36 [a]His seed shall endure for ever, and his throne [b]as the sun before me.

37 It shall be established for ever as the moon, and *as* a faithful witness in heaven. Selah.

38 But thou hast [a]cast off and [b]abhorred, thou hast been wroth with thine anointed.

39 Thou hast made void the covenant of thy servant: [a]thou hast profaned his crown *by casting it* to the ground.

40 Thou hast broken down all his hedges; thou hast brought his strong holds to ruin.

41 All that pass by the way [a]spoil him: he is a reproach to his neighbours.

15 [a]Lev. 23:24; Num. 10:10; Ps. 98:6
17 [a]Ps. 75:10; 92:10; 132:17
19 [a]1 Kin. 11:34
20 [a]1 Sam. 13:14; 16:1–12; Acts 13:22
21 [a]Ps. 80:17
25 [a]Ps. 72:8
26 [a]2 Sam. 7:14; [1 Chr. 22:10]; Jer. 3:19 [b]2 Sam. 22:47
27 [a]Ex. 4:22; Ps. 2:7; Jer. 31:9; [Col. 1:15, 18] [b]Num. 24:7; [Ps. 72:11]; Rev. 19:16
28 [a]Is. 55:3
29 [a][1 Kin. 2:4; Is. 9:7]; Jer. 33:17 [b]Deut. 11:21
30 [a][2 Sam. 7:14] [b]Ps. 119:53
33 [a]2 Sam. 7:14, 15
34 [a][Num. 23:19]; Jer. 33:20–22
35 [a][1 Sam. 15:29]; Amos 4:2; [Titus 1:2]
36 [a][Luke 1:33] [b]Ps. 72:17
38 [a][1 Chr. 28:9] [b]Deut. 32:19
39 [a]Ps. 74:7; Lam. 5:16
41 [a]Ps. 80:12

NKJV

13 You have a mighty arm;
Strong is Your hand, *and* high is Your right hand.
14 Righteousness and justice *are* the foundation of Your throne;
Mercy and truth go before Your face.
15 Blessed *are* the people who know the [a]joyful sound!
They walk, O LORD, in the light of Your countenance.
16 In Your name they rejoice all day long,
And in Your righteousness they are exalted.
17 For You *are* the glory of their strength,
And in Your favor our horn is [a]exalted.
18 For our shield *belongs* to the LORD,
And our king to the Holy One of Israel.

19 Then You spoke in a vision to Your *holy one,
And said: "I have given help to *one who is* mighty;
I have exalted one [a]chosen from the people.
20 [a]I have found My servant David;
With My holy oil I have anointed him,
21 [a]With whom My hand shall be established;
Also My arm shall strengthen him.
22 The enemy shall not outwit him,
Nor the son of wickedness afflict him.
23 I will beat down his foes before his face,
And plague those who hate him.

24 "But My faithfulness and My mercy *shall be* with him,
And in My name his horn shall be exalted.
25 Also I will [a]set his hand over the sea,
And his right hand over the rivers.
26 He shall cry to Me, 'You *are* [a]my Father,
My God, and [b]the rock of my salvation.'
27 Also I will make him [a]*My* firstborn,
[b]The highest of the kings of the earth.
28 [a]My mercy I will keep for him forever,
And My covenant shall stand firm with him.
29 His seed also I will make *to endure* forever,
[a]And his throne [b]as the days of heaven.

30 "If[a] his sons [b]forsake My law
And do not walk in My judgments,
31 If they break My statutes
And do not keep My commandments,
32 Then I will punish their transgression with the rod,
And their iniquity with stripes.
33 [a]Nevertheless My lovingkindness I will not utterly take from him,
Nor allow My faithfulness to fail.
34 My covenant I will not break,
Nor [a]alter the word that has gone out of My lips.
35 Once I have sworn [a]by My holiness;
I will not lie to David:
36 [a]His seed shall endure forever,
And his throne [b]as the sun before Me;
37 It shall be established forever like the moon,
Even *like* the faithful witness in the sky."
Selah

38 But You have [a]cast off and [b]abhorred,
You have been furious with Your anointed.
39 You have renounced the covenant of Your servant;
[a]You have profaned his crown *by casting it* to the ground.
40 You have broken down all his hedges;
You have brought his strongholds to ruin.
41 All who pass by the way [a]plunder him;
He is a reproach to his neighbors.

*———
89:19 So with many Heb. mss.; MT, LXX, Tg., Vg. *holy ones*

KJV

42 Thou hast set up the right hand of his adversaries; thou hast made all his enemies to rejoice.
43 Thou hast also turned the edge of his sword, and hast not made him to stand in the battle.
44 Thou hast made his glory to cease, and cast his throne down to the ground.
45 The days of his youth hast thou shortened: thou hast covered him with shame. Selah.
46 How long, LORD? wilt thou hide thyself for ever? shall thy wrath burn like fire?
47 Remember how short my time [a]is: wherefore hast thou made all men in [b]vain?
48 What man *is he that* liveth, and shall not see [a]death? shall he deliver his soul from the hand of the grave? Selah.
49 Lord, where *are* thy former lovingkindnesses, *which* thou [a]swarest unto David [b]in thy truth?
50 Remember, Lord, the reproach of thy servants; [a]*how* I do bear in my bosom *the reproach of* all the mighty people;
51 [a]Wherewith thine enemies have reproached, O LORD; wherewith they have reproached the footsteps of thine anointed.
52 [a]Blessed *be* the LORD for evermore. Amen, and Amen.

BOOK IV

PSALM 90

The Eternity of God, and Man's Frailty

A Prayer [a]of Moses the man of God.

LORD, [a]thou hast been our dwelling place in all generations.
2 [a]Before the mountains were brought forth, or ever thou hadst formed the earth and the world, even from everlasting to everlasting, thou *art* God.
3 Thou turnest man to destruction; and sayest, [a]Return, ye children of men.
4 [a]For a thousand years in thy sight *are but* as yesterday when it is past, and *as* a watch in the night.
5 Thou carriest them away as with a flood; [a]they are *as* a sleep: in the morning [b]*they are* like grass *which* groweth up.
6 In the morning it flourisheth, and groweth up; in the evening it is cut down, and withereth.
7 For we are consumed by thine anger, and by thy wrath are we troubled.
8 [a]Thou hast set our iniquities before thee, our [b]secret *sins* in the light of thy countenance.
9 For all our days are passed away in thy wrath: we spend our years as a tale *that is told*.
10 The days of our years *are* threescore years and ten; and if by reason of strength *they be* fourscore years, yet *is* their strength labour and sorrow; for it is soon cut off, and we fly away.
11 Who knoweth the power of thine anger? even according to thy fear, *so is* thy wrath.

47 [a]Ps. 90:9 [b]Ps. 62:9
48 [a][Eccl. 3:19]
49 [a][2 Sam. 7:15]; Jer. 30:9; Ezek. 34:23 [b]Ps. 54:5
50 [a]Ps. 69:9, 19
51 [a]Ps. 74:10, 18, 22
52 [a]Ps. 41:13

PSALM 90

title [a]Deut. 33:1
1 [a][Deut. 33:27; Ezek. 11:16]
2 [a]Job 15:7; [Prov. 8:25, 26]
3 [a]Gen. 3:19; Job 34:14, 15
4 [a]2 Pet. 3:8
5 [a]Ps. 73:20 [b]Is. 40:6
8 [a]Ps. 50:21; [Jer. 16:17] [b]Ps. 19:12; [Eccl. 12:14]

NKJV

42 You have exalted the right hand of his adversaries;
You have made all his enemies rejoice.
43 You have also turned back the edge of his sword,
And have not sustained him in the battle.
44 You have made his glory cease,
And cast his throne down to the ground.
45 The days of his youth You have shortened;
You have covered him with shame. Selah

46 How long, LORD?
Will You hide Yourself forever?
Will Your wrath burn like fire?
47 Remember how short my time [a]is;
For what [b]futility have You created all the children of men?
48 What man can live and not see [a]death?
Can he deliver his life from the power of the grave? Selah

49 Lord, where *are* Your former lovingkindnesses,
Which You [a]swore to David [b]in Your truth?
50 Remember, Lord, the reproach of Your servants—
[a]*How* I bear in my bosom *the reproach of* all the many peoples,
51 [a]With which Your enemies have reproached, O LORD,
With which they have reproached the footsteps of Your anointed.

52 [a]Blessed *be* the LORD forevermore!
Amen and Amen.

BOOK FOUR

Psalms 90–106

PSALM 90

The Eternity of God, and Man's Frailty

A Prayer [a]of Moses the man of God.

LORD, [a]You have been our *dwelling place in all generations.
2 [a]Before the mountains were brought forth,
Or ever You had formed the earth and the world,
Even from everlasting to everlasting, You *are* God.

3 You turn man to destruction,
And say, [a]"Return, O children of men."
4 [a]For a thousand years in Your sight
Are like yesterday when it is past,
And *like* a watch in the night.
5 You carry them away *like* a flood;
[a]*They are* like a sleep.
In the morning [b]they are like grass *which* grows up:
6 In the morning it flourishes and grows up;
In the evening it is cut down and withers.

7 For we have been consumed by Your anger,
And by Your wrath we are terrified.
8 [a]You have set our iniquities before You,
Our [b]secret *sins* in the light of Your countenance.
9 For all our days have passed away in Your wrath;
We finish our years like a sigh.
10 The days of our lives *are* seventy years;
And if by reason of strength *they are* eighty years,
Yet their boast *is* only labor and sorrow;
For it is soon cut off, and we fly away.
11 Who knows the power of Your anger?
For as the fear of You, *so is* Your wrath.

90:1 LXX, Tg., Vg. *refuge*

KJV

12 [a]So teach *us* to number our days, that we
may apply *our* hearts unto wisdom.
13 Return, O LORD, how long? and let it [a]re-
pent thee concerning thy servants.
14 O satisfy us early with thy mercy; [a]that
we may rejoice and be glad all our days.
15 Make us glad according to the days
wherein thou hast afflicted us, *and* the years
wherein we have seen evil.
16 Let [a]thy work appear unto thy servants,
and thy glory unto their children.
17 [a]And let the beauty of the LORD our God
be upon us: and [b]establish thou the work of our
hands upon us; yea, the work of our hands establish thou it.

PSALM 91

Safety of Abiding in the Presence of God

HE [a]that dwelleth in the secret place of the
most High shall abide [b]under the shadow of
the Almighty.
2 [a]I will say of the LORD, *He is* my refuge
and my fortress: my God; in him will I trust.
3 Surely [a]he shall deliver thee from the
snare of the fowler, *and* from the noisome
pestilence.
4 [a]He shall cover thee with his feathers, and
under his wings shalt thou trust: his truth *shall
be thy* shield and buckler.
5 [a]Thou shalt not be afraid for the terror
by night; *nor* for the arrow *that* flieth by day;
6 *Nor* for the pestilence *that* walketh in
darkness; *nor* for the destruction *that* wasteth at
noonday.
7 A thousand shall fall at thy side, and ten
thousand at thy right hand; *but* it shall not come
nigh thee.
8 Only [a]with thine eyes shalt thou behold
and see the reward of the wicked.
9 Because thou hast made the LORD, *which
is* [a]my refuge, *even* the most High, [b]thy habitation;
10 [a]There shall no evil befall thee, neither
shall any plague come nigh thy dwelling.
11 [a]For he shall give his angels charge over
thee, to keep thee in all thy ways.
12 They shall bear thee up in *their* hands,
[a]lest thou dash thy foot against a stone.
13 Thou shalt tread upon the lion and adder:
the young lion and the dragon shalt thou trample
under feet.
14 Because he hath set his love upon me,
therefore will I deliver him: I will set him on high,
because he hath [a]known my name.
15 He shall [a]call upon me, and I will answer
him: I *will be* [b]with him in trouble; I will deliver
him, and honour him.
16 With long life will I satisfy him, and shew
him my salvation.

12 [a]Deut. 32:29; Ps. 39:4
13 [a]Ex. 32:12; Deut. 32:36
14 [a]Ps. 85:6
16 [a][Deut. 32:4]; Hab. 3:2
17 [a]Ps. 27:4 [b]Is. 26:12

PSALM 91

1 [a]Ps. 27:5; 31:20; 32:7 [b]Ps. 17:8; Is. 25:4; 32:2
2 [a]Ps. 142:5
3 [a]Ps. 124:7; Prov. 6:5
4 [a]Ps. 17:8
5 [a][Job 5:19; Ps. 112:7; Is. 43:2]
8 [a]Ps. 37:34; Mal. 1:5
9 [a]Ps. 91:2 [b]Ps. 90:1
10 [a][Prov. 12:21]
11 [a]Ps. 34:7; Matt. 4:6; Luke 4:10; [Heb. 1:14]
12 [a]Matt. 4:6; Luke 4:11
14 [a][Ps. 9:10]
15 [a]Job 12:4; Ps. 50:15 [b]Is. 43:2

NKJV

12 [a]So teach *us* to number our days,
That we may gain a heart of wisdom.

13 Return, O LORD!
How long?
And [a]have compassion on Your
servants.
14 Oh, satisfy us early with Your mercy,
[a]That we may rejoice and be glad all our
days!
15 Make us glad according to the days *in
which* You have afflicted us,
The years *in which* we have seen evil.
16 Let [a]Your work appear to Your
servants,
And Your glory to their children.
17 [a]And let the beauty of the LORD our God
be upon us,
And [b]establish the work of our hands for
us;
Yes, establish the work of our hands.

PSALM 91

Safety of Abiding in the Presence of God

HE [a]who dwells in the secret place of the Most
High
Shall abide [b]under the shadow of the
Almighty.
2 [a]I will say of the LORD, "*He is* my refuge
and my fortress;
My God, in Him I will trust."

3 Surely [a]He shall deliver you from the
snare of the *fowler
And from the perilous pestilence.
4 [a]He shall cover you with His feathers,
And under His wings you shall take
refuge;
His truth *shall be your* shield and
buckler.
5 [a]You shall not be afraid of the terror by
night,
Nor of the arrow *that* flies by day,
6 *Nor* of the pestilence *that* walks in
darkness,
Nor of the destruction *that* lays waste at
noonday.

7 A thousand may fall at your side,
And ten thousand at your right hand;
But it shall not come near you.
8 Only [a]with your eyes shall you look,
And see the reward of the wicked.

9 Because you have made the LORD, *who is*
[a]my refuge,
Even the Most High, [b]your dwelling
place,
10 [a]No evil shall befall you,
Nor shall any plague come near your
dwelling;
11 [a]For He shall give His angels charge over
you,
To keep you in all your ways.
12 In *their* hands they shall bear you up,
[a]Lest you dash your foot against a stone.
13 You shall tread upon the lion and the
cobra,
The young lion and the serpent you shall
trample underfoot.

14 "Because he has set his love upon Me,
therefore I will deliver him;
I will set him on high, because he has
[a]known My name.
15 He shall [a]call upon Me, and I will answer
him;
I *will be* [b]with him in trouble;
I will deliver him and honor him.
16 With long life I will satisfy him,
And show him My salvation."

*

91:3 One who catches birds in a trap or snare

KJV

PSALM 92

Praise to the L*ORD for His Love and Faithfulness*

A Psalm *or* Song for the sabbath day.

IT *is a* [a]good *thing* to give thanks unto the LORD, and to sing praises unto thy name, O most High:

2 To [a]shew forth thy lovingkindness in the morning, and thy faithfulness every night,

3 [a]Upon an instrument of ten strings, and upon the psaltery; upon the harp with a solemn sound.

4 For thou, LORD, hast made me glad through thy work: I will triumph in the works of thy hands.

5 [a]O LORD, how great are thy works! *and* [b]thy thoughts are very deep.

6 [a]A brutish man knoweth not; neither doth a fool understand this.

7 When [a]the wicked spring as the grass, and when all the workers of iniquity do flourish; *it is* that they shall be destroyed for ever:

8 [a]But thou, LORD, *art most* high for evermore.

9 For, lo, thine enemies, O LORD, for, lo, thine enemies shall perish; all the workers of iniquity shall [a]be scattered.

10 But [a]my horn shalt thou exalt like *the horn of* an unicorn: I shall be [b]anointed with fresh oil.

11 [a]Mine eye also shall see *my desire* on mine enemies, *and* mine ears shall hear *my desire* of the wicked that rise up against me.

12 [a]The righteous shall flourish like the palm tree: he shall grow like a cedar in Lebanon.

13 Those that be planted in the house of the LORD shall flourish in the courts of our God.

14 They shall still bring forth fruit in old age; they shall be fat and flourishing;

15 To shew that the LORD *is* upright: [a]*he is* my rock, and [b]*there is* no unrighteousness in him.

PSALM 93

The Eternal Reign of the L*ORD*

THE [a]LORD reigneth, he is clothed with majesty; the LORD is clothed with strength, [b]*wherewith* he hath girded himself: the world also is stablished, that it cannot be moved.

2 [a]Thy throne *is* established of old: thou *art* from everlasting.

3 The floods have lifted up, O LORD, the floods have lifted up their voice; the floods lift up their waves.

4 [a]The LORD on high *is* mightier than the noise of many waters, *yea, than* the mighty waves of the sea.

5 Thy testimonies are very sure: holiness becometh thine house, O LORD, for ever.

PSALM 94

God the Refuge of the Righteous

O LORD God, [a]to whom vengeance belongeth; O God, to whom vengeance belongeth, shew thyself.

PSALM 92

1 [a]Ps. 147:1
2 [a]Ps. 89:1
3 [a]1 Chr. 23:5
5 [a]Ps. 40:5; [Rev. 15:3] [b]Ps. 139:17, 18; [Is. 28:29; Rom. 11:33, 34]
6 [a]Ps. 73:22
7 [a]Job 12:6; Ps. 37:1, 2; Jer. 12:1, 2; [Mal. 3:15]
8 [a][Ps. 83:18]
9 [a]Ps. 68:1
10 [a]Ps. 89:17 [b]Ps. 23:5
11 [a]Ps. 54:7
12 [a]Num. 24:6; Ps. 52:8; Jer. 17:8; Hos. 14:5, 6
15 [a][Deut. 32:4] [b][Rom. 9:14]

PSALM 93

1 [a]Ps. 96:10 [b]Ps. 65:6
2 [a]Ps. 45:6; [Lam. 5:19]
4 [a]Ps. 65:7

PSALM 94

1 [a]Deut. 32:35; [Is. 35:4; Nah. 1:2; Rom. 12:19]

NKJV

PSALM 92

Praise to the L*ORD for His Love and Faithfulness*

A Psalm. A Song for the Sabbath day.

IT *is* [a]good to give thanks to the LORD,
And to sing praises to Your name, O Most High;
2 To [a]declare Your lovingkindness in the morning,
And Your faithfulness every night,
3 [a]On an instrument of ten strings,
On the lute,
And on the harp,
With harmonious sound.
4 For You, LORD, have made me glad through Your work;
I will triumph in the works of Your hands.

5 [a]O LORD, how great are Your works!
[b]Your thoughts are very deep.
6 [a]A senseless man does not know,
Nor does a fool understand this.
7 When [a]the wicked spring up like grass,
And when all the workers of iniquity flourish,
It is that they may be destroyed forever.

8 [a]But You, LORD, *are* on high forevermore.
9 For behold, Your enemies, O LORD,
For behold, Your enemies shall perish;
All the workers of iniquity shall [a]be scattered.

10 But [a]my horn You have exalted like a wild ox;
I have been [b]anointed with fresh oil.
11 [a]My eye also has seen *my desire* on my enemies;
My ears hear *my desire* on the wicked
Who rise up against me.

12 [a]The righteous shall flourish like a palm tree,
He shall grow like a cedar in Lebanon.
13 Those who are planted in the house of the LORD
Shall flourish in the courts of our God.
14 They shall still bear fruit in old age;
They shall be fresh and flourishing,
15 To declare that the LORD is upright;
[a]*He is* my rock, and [b]*there is* no unrighteousness in Him.

PSALM 93

The Eternal Reign of the L*ORD*

THE [a]LORD reigns, He is clothed with majesty;
The LORD is clothed,
[b]He has girded Himself with strength.
Surely the world is established, so that it cannot be moved.
2 [a]Your throne *is* established from of old;
You *are* from everlasting.

3 The floods have lifted up, O LORD,
The floods have lifted up their voice;
The floods lift up their waves.
4 [a]The LORD on high *is* mightier
Than the noise of many waters,
Than the mighty waves of the sea.

5 Your testimonies are very sure;
Holiness adorns Your house,
O LORD, forever.

PSALM 94

God the Refuge of the Righteous

O LORD God, [a]to whom vengeance belongs—
O God, to whom vengeance belongs, shine forth!

KJV

2 Lift up thyself, thou [a]judge of the earth:
render a reward to the proud.
3 LORD, [a]how long shall the wicked, how
long shall the wicked triumph?
4 *How long* shall they [a]utter *and* speak hard
things? *and* all the workers of iniquity boast
themselves?
5 They break in pieces thy people, O LORD,
and afflict thine heritage.
6 They slay the widow and the stranger, and
murder the fatherless.
7 [a]Yet they say, The LORD shall not see, neither shall the God of Jacob regard *it*.
8 Understand, ye brutish among the people:
and *ye* fools, when will ye be wise?
9 [a]He that planted the ear, shall he not hear?
he that formed the eye, shall he not see?
10 He that chastiseth the heathen, shall not
he correct? he that teacheth man knowledge, *shall*
not he know?
11 The LORD [a]knoweth the thoughts of man,
that they *are* vanity.
12 Blessed *is* the man whom thou [a]chasten-
est, O LORD, and teachest him out of thy law;
13 That thou mayest give him rest from the
days of adversity, until the pit be digged for the
wicked.
14 For the LORD will not cast off his people,
neither will he forsake his inheritance.
15 But judgment shall return unto righteousness: and all the upright in heart shall follow it.
16 Who will rise up for me against the evildoers? *or* who will stand up for me against the
workers of iniquity?
17 Unless the LORD *had been* my help, my
soul had almost dwelt in silence.
18 When I said, My foot slippeth; thy mercy,
O LORD, held me up.
19 In the multitude of my thoughts within me
thy comforts delight my soul.
20 Shall [a]the throne of iniquity have fellowship with thee, which frameth mischief by a law?
21 They gather themselves together against
the soul of the righteous, and condemn the [a]inno-
cent blood.
22 But the LORD is my defence; and my God
is the rock of my refuge.
23 And he shall bring upon them their own
iniquity, and shall cut them off in their own wickedness; *yea*, the LORD our God shall cut them off.

2 [a][Gen. 18:25]
3 [a][Job 20:5]
4 [a]Ps. 31:18; Jude 15
7 [a]Job 22:13; Ps. 10:11
9 [a][Ex. 4:11; Prov. 20:12]
11 [a]Job 11:11; 1 Cor. 3:20
12 [a][Deut. 8:5; Job 5:17; Ps. 119:71; Prov. 3:11, 12; Heb. 12:5, 6]
20 [a]Amos 6:3
21 [a][Ex. 23:7]; Ps. 106:38; [Prov. 17:15]; Matt. 27:4

NKJV

2 Rise up, O [a]Judge of the earth;
Render punishment to the proud.
3 LORD, [a]how long will the wicked,
How long will the wicked triumph?

4 They [a]utter speech, *and* speak insolent
things;
All the workers of iniquity boast in
themselves.
5 They break in pieces Your people, O LORD,
And afflict Your heritage.
6 They slay the widow and the stranger,
And murder the fatherless.
7 [a]Yet they say, "The LORD does not see,
Nor does the God of Jacob understand."

8 Understand, you senseless among the
people;
And *you* fools, when will you be wise?
9 [a]He who planted the ear, shall He not hear?
He who formed the eye, shall He not see?
10 He who instructs the nations, shall He not
correct,
He who teaches man knowledge?
11 The LORD [a]knows the thoughts of man,
That they *are* futile.

12 Blessed *is* the man whom You [a]instruct,
O LORD,
And teach out of Your law,
13 That You may give him rest from the days
of adversity,
Until the pit is dug for the wicked.
14 For the LORD will not cast off His people,
Nor will He forsake His inheritance.
15 But judgment will return to righteousness,
And all the upright in heart will follow it.

16 Who will rise up for me against the
evildoers?
Who will stand up for me against the
workers of iniquity?
17 Unless the LORD *had been* my help,
My soul would soon have settled in
silence.
18 If I say, "My foot slips,"
Your mercy, O LORD, will hold me up.
19 In the multitude of my anxieties within
me,
Your comforts delight my soul.

20 Shall [a]the throne of iniquity, which
devises evil by law,
Have fellowship with You?
21 They gather together against the life of
the righteous,
And condemn [a]innocent blood.
22 But the LORD has been my defense,
And my God the rock of my refuge.
23 He has brought on them their own
iniquity,
And shall cut them off in their own
wickedness;
The LORD our God shall cut them off.

PSALM 95

A Call to Worship and Obedience

O COME, let us sing unto the LORD: let us make
a joyful noise to the rock of our salvation.
2 Let us come before his presence with
thanksgiving, and make a joyful noise unto him
with [a]psalms.
3 For [a]the LORD *is* a great God, and a great
King above all gods.
4 In his hand *are* the deep places of the
earth: the strength of the hills *is* his also.
5 [a]The sea *is* his, and he made it: and his
hands formed the dry *land*.

PSALM 95

2 [a]Eph. 5:19; James 5:13
3 [a][Ps. 96:4; 1 Cor. 8:5, 6]
5 [a]Gen. 1:9, 10; Jon. 1:9

PSALM 95

A Call to Worship and Obedience

OH come, let us sing to the LORD!
Let us shout joyfully to the Rock of our
salvation.
2 Let us come before His presence with
thanksgiving;
Let us shout joyfully to Him with [a]psalms.
3 For [a]the LORD *is* the great God,
And the great King above all gods.
4 In His hand *are* the deep places of the
earth;
The heights of the hills *are* His also.
5 [a]The sea *is* His, for He made it;
And His hands formed the dry *land*.

KJV

6 O come, let us worship and bow down:
let [a]us kneel before the LORD our maker.
7 For he *is* our God; and [a]we *are* the people
of his pasture, and the sheep of his hand. [b]To day
if ye will hear his voice,
8 Harden not your heart, as in the provocation,
and [a]as *in* the day of temptation in the
wilderness:
9 When [a]your fathers tempted me, proved
me, and [b]saw my work.
10 [a]Forty years long was I grieved with *this*
generation, and said, It *is* a people that do err in
their heart, and they have not known my ways:
11 Unto whom [a]I sware in my wrath that they
should not enter into my rest.

PSALM 96

A Song of Praise to God Coming in Judgment
(*1 Chr. 16:23–33*)

O [a]SING unto the LORD a new song: sing unto
the LORD, all the earth.
2 Sing unto the LORD, bless his name; shew
forth his salvation from day to day.
3 Declare his glory among the heathen, his
wonders among all people.
4 For [a]the LORD *is* great, and [b]greatly to be
praised: [c]he *is* to be feared above all gods.
5 For [a]all the gods of the nations *are* idols:
[b]but the LORD made the heavens.
6 Honour and majesty *are* before him:
strength and [a]beauty *are* in his sanctuary.
7 [a]Give unto the LORD, O ye kindreds of the
people, give unto the LORD glory and strength.
8 Give unto the LORD the glory *due unto* his
name: bring an offering, and come into his courts.
9 O worship the LORD [a]in the beauty of holiness:
fear before him, all the earth.
10 Say among the heathen *that* [a]the LORD
reigneth: the world also shall be established that
it shall not be moved: [b]he shall judge the people
righteously.
11 [a]Let the heavens rejoice, and let the earth
be glad; [b]let the sea roar, and the fulness thereof.
12 Let the field be joyful, and all that *is*
therein: then shall all the trees of the wood rejoice
13 Before the LORD: for he cometh, for he
cometh to judge the earth: [a]he shall judge the
world with righteousness, and the people with his
truth.

PSALM 97

A Song of Praise to the Sovereign LORD

THE LORD [a]reigneth; let the earth rejoice; let
the multitude of isles be glad *thereof*.
2 [a]Clouds and darkness *are* round about
him: [b]righteousness and judgment *are* the habitation
of his throne.

---

6 [a]2 Chr. 6:13; Dan. 6:10; [Phil. 2:10]
7 [a]Ps. 79:13 [b]Heb. 3:7–11, 15; 4:7
8 [a]Ex. 17:2–7; Num. 20:13
9 [a]Ps. 78:18; [1 Cor. 10:9] [b]Num. 14:22
10 [a]Acts 7:36; 13:18; Heb. 3:10, 17
11 [a]Num. 14:23, 28–30; Deut. 1:35; Heb. 4:3, 5

PSALM 96

1 [a]1 Chr. 16:23–33
4 [a]Ps. 145:3 [b]Ps. 18:3 [c]Ps. 95:3
5 [a]1 Chr. 16:26; [Jer. 10:11] [b]Ps. 115:15; Is. 42:5
6 [a]Ps. 29:2
7 [a]1 Chr. 16:28, 29; Ps. 29:1, 2
9 [a]1 Chr. 16:29; 2 Chr. 20:21; Ps. 29:2
10 [a]Ps. 93:1; 97:1; [Rev. 11:15; 19:6] [b]Ps. 67:4
11 [a]Ps. 69:34; Is. 49:13 [b]Ps. 98:7
13 [a][Rev. 19:11]

PSALM 97

1 [a][Ps. 96:10]
2 [a]Ex. 19:9; Deut. 4:11; 1 Kin. 8:12; Ps. 18:11 [b][Ps. 89:14]

*

95:8 Or *Meribah*, lit. *Strife, Contention* • Or *Massah*, lit. *Trial, Testing*

NKJV

6 Oh come, let us worship and bow down;
Let [a]us kneel before the LORD our Maker.
7 For He *is* our God,
And [a]we *are* the people of His pasture,
And the sheep of His hand.
[b]Today, if you will hear His voice:
8 "Do not harden your hearts, as in the
*rebellion,
[a]As *in* the day of *trial in the wilderness,
9 When [a]your fathers tested Me;
They tried Me, though they [b]saw My
work.
10 For [a]forty years I was grieved with *that*
generation,
And said, 'It *is* a people who go astray in
their hearts,
And they do not know My ways.'
11 So [a]I swore in My wrath,
'They shall not enter My rest.'"

PSALM 96

A Song of Praise to God Coming in Judgment
(*1 Chr. 16:23–33*)

OH, [a]sing to the LORD a new song!
Sing to the LORD, all the earth.
2 Sing to the LORD, bless His name;
Proclaim the good news of His salvation
from day to day.
3 Declare His glory among the nations,
His wonders among all peoples.

4 For [a]the LORD *is* great and [b]greatly to be
praised;
[c]He *is* to be feared above all gods.
5 For [a]all the gods of the peoples *are* idols,
[b]But the LORD made the heavens.
6 Honor and majesty *are* before Him;
Strength and [a]beauty *are* in His
sanctuary.

7 [a]Give to the LORD, O families of the
peoples,
Give to the LORD glory and strength.
8 Give to the LORD the glory *due* His
name;
Bring an offering, and come into His
courts.
9 Oh, worship the LORD [a]in the beauty of
holiness!
Tremble before Him, all the earth.

10 Say among the nations, [a]"The LORD
reigns;
The world also is firmly established,
It shall not be moved;
[b]He shall judge the peoples righteously."

11 [a]Let the heavens rejoice, and let the earth
be glad;
[b]Let the sea roar, and all its fullness;
12 Let the field be joyful, and all that *is* in
it.
Then all the trees of the woods will rejoice
before the LORD.
13 For He is coming, for He is coming to
judge the earth.
[a]He shall judge the world with
righteousness,
And the peoples with His truth.

PSALM 97

A Song of Praise to the Sovereign LORD

THE LORD [a]reigns;
Let the earth rejoice;
Let the multitude of isles be glad!

2 [a]Clouds and darkness surround Him;
[b]Righteousness and justice *are* the
foundation of His throne.

KJV

3 [a]A fire goeth before him, and burneth up
his enemies round about.
4 [a]His lightnings enlightened the world: the
earth saw, and trembled.
5 [a]The hills melted like wax at the presence
of the LORD, at the presence of the Lord of the
whole earth.
6 [a]The heavens declare his righteousness,
and all the people see his glory.
7 [a]Confounded be all they that serve graven
images, that boast themselves of idols: [b]worship
him, all *ye* gods.
8 Zion heard, and was glad; and the daughters of Judah rejoiced because of thy judgments,
O LORD.
9 For thou, LORD, *art* [a]high above all the
earth: [b]thou art exalted far above all gods.
10 Ye that love the LORD, [a]hate evil: [b]*he* preserveth the souls of his saints; [c]he delivereth them
out of the hand of the wicked.
11 [a]Light is sown for the righteous, and gladness for the upright in heart.
12 [a]Rejoice in the LORD, ye righteous; [b]and
give thanks at the remembrance of his holiness.

3 [a]Ps. 18:8; Dan. 7:10; Hab. 3:5 **4** [a]Ex. 19:18 **5** [a]Ps. 46:6; Amos 9:5; Mic. 1:4; Nah. 1:5 **6** [a]Ps. 19:1 **7** [a][Ex. 20:4] [b][Heb. 1:6] **9** [a]Ps. 83:18 [b]Ex. 18:11; Ps. 95:3; 96:4 **10** [a][Ps. 34:14; Prov. 8:13; Amos 5:15; Rom. 12:9] [b]Ps. 31:23; *145:20; Prov.* 2:8 [c]Ps. 37:40; Jer. 15:21; Dan. 3:28 **11** [a]Job 22:28; Ps. 112:4; Prov. 4:18 **12** [a]Ps. 33:1 [b]Ps. 30:4

NKJV

3 [a]A fire goes before Him,
And burns up His enemies round about.
4 [a]His lightnings light the world;
The earth sees and trembles.
5 [a]The mountains melt like wax at the
presence of the LORD,
At the presence of the Lord of the whole
earth.
6 [a]The heavens declare His righteousness,
And all the peoples see His glory.

7 [a]Let all be put to shame who serve carved
images,
Who boast of idols.
[b]Worship Him, all *you* gods.
8 Zion hears and is glad,
And the daughters of Judah rejoice
Because of Your judgments, O LORD.
9 For You, LORD, *are* [a]most high above all
the earth;
[b]You are exalted far above all gods.

10 You who love the LORD, [a]hate evil!
[b]He preserves the souls of His saints;
[c]He delivers them out of the hand of the
wicked.
11 [a]Light is sown for the righteous,
And gladness for the upright in heart.
12 [a]Rejoice in the LORD, you righteous,
[b]And give thanks at the remembrance of
*His holy name.

PSALM 98

A Song of Praise to the LORD for His Salvation and Judgment

A Psalm.

O [a]SING unto the LORD a new song; for he hath
[b]done marvellous things: his right hand, and
his holy arm, hath gotten him the victory.
2 [a]The LORD hath made known his salvation: [b]his righteousness hath he openly shewed
in the sight of the heathen.
3 He hath remembered his mercy and his
truth toward the house of Israel: [a]all the ends of
the earth have seen the salvation of our God.
4 Make a joyful noise unto the LORD, all the
earth: make a loud noise, and rejoice, and sing
praise.
5 Sing unto the LORD with the harp; with
the harp, and the voice of a psalm.
6 With trumpets and sound of cornet make
a joyful noise before the LORD, the King.
7 Let the sea roar, and the fulness thereof;
the world, and they that dwell therein.
8 Let the floods clap *their* hands: let the hills
be joyful together
9 Before the LORD; [a]for he cometh to judge
the earth: with righteousness shall he judge the
world, and the people with equity.

PSALM 98

1 [a]Ps. 33:3; Is. 42:10 [b]Ex. 15:11; Ps. 77:14 **2** [a]Is. 52:10; [Luke 1:77; 2:30, 31] [b]Is. 62:2; Rom. 3:25 **3** [a][Is. 49:6]; Luke 3:6; [Acts 13:47; 28:28] **9** [a][Ps. 96:10, 13]

PSALM 98

A Song of Praise to the LORD for His Salvation and Judgment

A Psalm.

OH, [a]sing to the LORD a new song!
For He has [b]done marvelous things;
His right hand and His holy arm have
gained Him the victory.
2 [a]The LORD has made known His
salvation;
[b]His righteousness He has revealed in the
sight of the nations.
3 He has remembered His mercy and His
faithfulness to the house of Israel;
[a]All the ends of the earth have seen the
salvation of our God.

4 Shout joyfully to the LORD, all the earth;
Break forth in song, rejoice, and sing
praises.
5 Sing to the LORD with the harp,
With the harp and the sound of a psalm,
6 With trumpets and the sound of a horn;
Shout joyfully before the LORD, the
King.

7 Let the sea roar, and all its fullness,
The world and those who dwell in it;
8 Let the rivers clap *their* hands;
Let the hills be joyful together before the
LORD,
9 [a]For He is coming to judge the earth.
With righteousness He shall judge the
world,
And the peoples with equity.

PSALM 99

Praise to the LORD for His Holiness

THE LORD reigneth; let the people tremble: [a]he
sitteth *between* the cherubims; let the earth
be moved.
2 The LORD *is* great in Zion; and he *is* high
above all the people.
3 Let them praise thy great and terrible
name; *for* it *is* holy.

PSALM 99

1 [a]Ex. 25:22; 1 Sam. 4:4; Ps. 80:1

*97:12 Or *His holiness*

PSALM 99

Praise to the LORD for His Holiness

THE LORD reigns;
Let the peoples tremble!
[a]He dwells *between* the cherubim;
Let the earth be moved!
2 The LORD *is* great in Zion,
And He *is* high above all the peoples.
3 Let them praise Your great and awesome
name—
He *is* holy.

KJV

4 The king's strength also loveth judgment;
thou dost establish equity, thou executest judgment and righteousness in Jacob.
5 Exalt ye the LORD our God, and worship
at his footstool; *for* he *is* holy.
6 Moses and Aaron among his priests, and
Samuel among them that [a]call upon his name;
they called upon the LORD, and he answered them.
7 He spake unto them in the cloudy pillar:
they kept his testimonies, and the ordinance *that*
he gave them.
8 Thou answeredst them, O LORD our God:
thou wast a God that forgavest them, though thou
tookest vengeance of their inventions.
9 Exalt the LORD our God, and worship at
his holy hill; for the LORD our God *is* holy.

PSALM 100

A Song of Praise for the LORD's Faithfulness to His People

[a]A Psalm of praise.

MAKE [a]a joyful noise unto the LORD, all ye
lands.
2 Serve the LORD with gladness: come before his presence with singing.
3 Know ye that the LORD he *is* God: [a]*it is*
he *that* hath made us, and not we ourselves; [b]*we*
are his people, and the sheep of his pasture.
4 [a]Enter into his gates with thanksgiving,
and into his courts with praise: be thankful unto
him, *and* bless his name.
5 For the LORD *is* good; [a]his mercy *is* everlasting; and his truth *endureth* to all generations.

PSALM 101

Promised Faithfulness to the LORD

A Psalm of David.

I WILL sing of mercy and judgment: unto thee,
O LORD, will I sing.
2 I will behave myself wisely in a perfect
way. O when wilt thou come unto me? I will [a]walk
within my house with a perfect heart.
3 I will set no wicked thing before mine
eyes: [a]I hate the work of them [b]that turn aside;
it shall not cleave to me.
4 A froward heart shall depart from me: I
will not [a]know a wicked *person*.
5 Whoso privily slandereth his neighbour,
him will I cut off: [a]him that hath an high look
and a proud heart will not I suffer.
6 Mine eyes *shall be* upon the faithful of the
land, that they may dwell with me: he that walketh in a perfect way, he shall serve me.
7 He that worketh deceit shall not dwell
within my house: he that telleth lies shall not tarry
in my sight.

---

6 [a]1 Sam. 7:9; 12:18

PSALM 100

title [a]Ps. 145:title
1 [a]Ps. 95:1
3 [a]Job 10:3, 8; Ps. 119:73; 139:13, 14; [Eph. 2:10] [b]Ps. 95:7; [Is. 40:11]; Ezek. 34:30, 31
4 [a]Ps. 66:13; 116:17–19
5 [a]Ps. 136:1

PSALM 101

2 [a]1 Kin. 11:4
3 [a]Ps. 97:10 [b]Josh. 23:6
4 [a][Ps. 119:115]
5 [a]Prov. 6:17

NKJV

4 The King's strength also loves justice;
You have established equity;
You have executed justice and
righteousness in Jacob.
5 Exalt the LORD our God,
And worship at His footstool—
He *is* holy.

6 Moses and Aaron were among His priests,
And Samuel was among those who [a]called
upon His name;
They called upon the LORD, and He
answered them.
7 He spoke to them in the cloudy pillar;
They kept His testimonies and the
ordinance He gave them.

8 You answered them, O LORD our God;
You were to them God-Who-Forgives,
Though You took vengeance on their
deeds.
9 Exalt the LORD our God,
And worship at His holy hill;
For the LORD our God *is* holy.

PSALM 100

A Song of Praise for the LORD's Faithfulness to His People

[a]A Psalm of Thanksgiving.

MAKE [a]a joyful shout to the LORD, all you
lands!
2 Serve the LORD with gladness;
Come before His presence with singing.
3 Know that the LORD, He *is* God;
[a]*It is* He *who* has made us, and *not we
ourselves;
[b]*We are* His people and the sheep of His
pasture.

4 [a]Enter into His gates with thanksgiving,
And into His courts with praise.
Be thankful to Him, *and* bless His
name.
5 For the LORD *is* good;
[a]His mercy *is* everlasting,
And His truth *endures* to all generations.

PSALM 101

Promised Faithfulness to the LORD

A Psalm of David.

I WILL sing of mercy and justice;
To You, O LORD, I will sing praises.

2 I will behave wisely in a perfect way.
Oh, when will You come to me?
I will [a]walk within my house with a
perfect heart.

3 I will set nothing wicked before my eyes;
[a]I hate the work of those [b]who fall away;
It shall not cling to me.
4 A perverse heart shall depart from me;
I will not [a]know wickedness.

5 Whoever secretly slanders his neighbor,
Him I will destroy;
[a]The one who has a haughty look and a
proud heart,
Him I will not endure.

6 My eyes *shall be* on the faithful of the
land,
That they may dwell with me;
He who walks in a perfect way,
He shall serve me.
7 He who works deceit shall not dwell
within my house;
He who tells lies shall not continue in my
presence.

100:3 So with Kt., LXX, Vg.; Qr., many Heb. mss., Tg. *we are His*

KJV

8 I will [a]early destroy all the wicked of the
land; that I may cut off all wicked doers [b]from
the city of the LORD.

PSALM 102

The LORD's Eternal Love

A Prayer of the afflicted, [a]when he is overwhelmed, and poureth out his complaint before the LORD.

HEAR my prayer, O LORD, and let my cry come
unto thee.
2 [a]Hide not thy face from me in the day
when I am in trouble; incline thine ear unto me:
in the day *when* I call answer me speedily.
3 For my days are [a]consumed like smoke,
and my bones are burned as an hearth.
4 My heart is smitten, and withered like
grass; so that I forget to eat my bread.
5 By reason of the voice of my groaning my
bones cleave to my skin.
6 I am like a pelican of the wilderness: I am
like an owl of the desert.
7 I watch, and am as a sparrow alone upon
the house top.
8 Mine enemies reproach me all the day;
and they that are mad against me are sworn
against me.
9 For I have eaten ashes like bread, and
mingled my drink with weeping,
10 Because of thine indignation and thy
wrath: for thou hast lifted me up, and cast me
down.
11 My days *are* like a shadow that declineth;
and I am withered like grass.
12 But thou, O LORD, shalt endure for ever;
and thy remembrance unto all generations.
13 Thou shalt arise, *and* have mercy upon
Zion: for the time to favour her, yea, the set time,
is come.
14 For thy servants take pleasure in her
stones, and favour the dust thereof.
15 So the heathen shall [a]fear the name of the
LORD, and all the kings of the earth thy glory.
16 When the LORD shall build up Zion, [a]he
shall appear in his glory.
17 [a]He will regard the prayer of the destitute,
and not despise their prayer.
18 This shall be [a]written for the generation
to come: and [b]the people which shall be created
shall praise the LORD.
19 For he hath [a]looked down from the height
of his sanctuary; from heaven did the LORD behold
the earth;
20 [a]To hear the groaning of the prisoner; to
loose those that are appointed to death;
21 To [a]declare the name of the LORD in Zion,
and his praise in Jerusalem;
22 [a]When the people are gathered together,
and the kingdoms, to serve the LORD.
23 He weakened my strength in the way; he
[a]shortened my days.
24 [a]I said, O my God, take me not away in
the midst of my days: [b]thy years *are* throughout
all generations.

8 [a][Ps. 75:10]; Jer. 21:12 [b]Ps. 48:2, 8

PSALM 102

title [a]Ps. 61:2
2 [a]Ps. 27:9; 69:17
3 [a]James 4:14
15 [a]1 Kin. 8:43
16 [a][Is. 60:1, 2]
17 [a]Neh. 1:6; Ps. 22:24
18 [a]Deut. 31:19; [Rom. 15:4; 1 Cor. 10:11] [b]Ps. 22:31
19 [a]Deut. 26:15; Ps. 14:2
20 [a]Ps. 79:11
21 [a]Ps. 22:22
22 [a][Is. 2:2, 3; 49:22, 23; 60:3]; Zech. 8:20–23
23 [a]Job 21:21
24 [a][Ps. 39:13]; Is. 38:10 [b]Job 36:26; [Ps. 90:2]; Hab. 1:12

NKJV

8 [a]Early I will destroy all the wicked of the land,
That I may cut off all the evildoers [b]from the city of the LORD.

PSALM 102

The LORD's Eternal Love

A Prayer of the afflicted, [a]when he is overwhelmed and pours out his complaint before the LORD.

HEAR my prayer, O LORD,
And let my cry come to You.
2 [a]Do not hide Your face from me in the day of my trouble;
Incline Your ear to me;
In the day that I call, answer me speedily.

3 For my days are [a]consumed like smoke,
And my bones are burned like a hearth.
4 My heart is stricken and withered like grass,
So that I forget to eat my bread.
5 Because of the sound of my groaning
My bones cling to my skin.
6 I am like a pelican of the wilderness;
I am like an owl of the desert.
7 I lie awake,
And am like a sparrow alone on the housetop.

8 My enemies reproach me all day long;
Those who deride me swear an oath against me.
9 For I have eaten ashes like bread,
And mingled my drink with weeping,
10 Because of Your indignation and Your wrath;
For You have lifted me up and cast me away.
11 My days *are* like a shadow that lengthens,
And I wither away like grass.

12 But You, O LORD, shall endure forever,
And the remembrance of Your name to all generations.
13 You will arise *and* have mercy on Zion;
For the time to favor her,
Yes, the set time, has come.
14 For Your servants take pleasure in her stones,
And show favor to her dust.
15 So the nations shall [a]fear the name of the LORD,
And all the kings of the earth Your glory.
16 For the LORD shall build up Zion;
[a]He shall appear in His glory.
17 [a]He shall regard the prayer of the destitute,
And shall not despise their prayer.

18 This will be [a]written for the generation to come,
That [b]a people yet to be created may praise the LORD.
19 For He [a]looked down from the height of His sanctuary;
From heaven the LORD viewed the earth,
20 [a]To hear the groaning of the prisoner,
To release those appointed to death,
21 To [a]declare the name of the LORD in Zion,
And His praise in Jerusalem,
22 [a]When the peoples are gathered together,
And the kingdoms, to serve the LORD.

23 He weakened my strength in the way;
He [a]shortened my days.
24 [a]I said, "O my God,
Do not take me away in the midst of my days;
[b]Your years *are* throughout all generations.

KJV

25 [a]Of old hast thou laid the foundation of
the earth: and the heavens *are* the work of thy
hands.
26 [a]They shall perish, but thou shalt endure:
yea, all of them shall wax old like a garment; as
a vesture shalt thou change them, and they shall
be changed:
27 But [a]thou *art* the same, and thy years shall
have no end.
28 [a]The children of thy servants shall continue, and their seed shall be established before
thee.

PSALM 103

Praise for the LORD's Mercies

A Psalm of David.

BLESS [a]the LORD, O my soul: and all that is
within me, *bless* his holy name.
2 Bless the LORD, O my soul, and forget not
all his benefits:
3 [a]Who forgiveth all thine iniquities; who
[b]healeth all thy diseases;
4 Who redeemeth thy life from destruction;
[a]who crowneth thee with lovingkindness and
tender mercies;
5 Who satisfieth thy mouth with good
things; so that [a]thy youth is renewed like the
eagle's.
6 The LORD executeth righteousness and
judgment for all that are oppressed.
7 [a]He made known his ways unto Moses,
his acts unto the children of Israel.
8 [a]The LORD *is* merciful and gracious, slow
to anger, and plenteous in mercy.
9 [a]He will not always chide: neither will he
keep *his anger* for ever.
10 [a]He hath not dealt with us after our sins;
nor rewarded us according to our iniquities.
11 For as the heaven is high above the earth,
so great is his mercy toward them that fear him.
12 As far as the east is from the west, *so* far
hath he [a]removed our transgressions from us.
13 [a]Like as a father pitieth *his* children, *so*
the LORD pitieth them that fear him.
14 For he knoweth our frame; he remembereth that we *are* dust.
15 *As for* man, [a]his days *are* as grass: as a
flower of the field, so he flourisheth.
16 [a]For the wind passeth over it, and it is
gone; and [b]the place thereof shall know it no
more.
17 But the mercy of the LORD *is* from everlasting to everlasting upon them that fear him, and
his righteousness unto children's children;
18 [a]To such as keep his covenant, and to
those that remember his commandments to do
them.
19 The LORD hath prepared his throne in the
heavens; and [a]his kingdom ruleth over all.
20 [a]Bless the LORD, ye his angels, that excel
in strength, that [b]do his commandments, hearken-
ing unto the voice of his word.
21 Bless ye the LORD, all *ye* his hosts; [a]*ye*
ministers of his, that do his pleasure.

25 [a][Gen. 1:1; Neh. 9:6; Heb. 1:10–12]
26 [a]Is. 34:4; 51:6; Matt. 24:35; [2 Pet. 3:7, 10–12]; Rev. 20:11
27 [a][Is. 41:4; 43:10; Mal. 3:6; Heb. 13:8]; James 1:17
28 [a]Ps. 69:36

PSALM 103

1 [a]Ps. 104:1, 35
3 [a]Ps. 130:8; Is. 33:24 [b][Ex. 15:26]; Ps. 147:3; [Is. 53:5]; Jer. 17:14
4 [a][Ps. 5:12]
5 [a][Is. 40:31]
7 [a]Ex. 33:12–17; Ps. 147:19
8 [a][Ex. 34:6, 7; Num. 14:18]; Deut. 5:10; Neh. 9:17; Ps. 86:15; Jer. 32:18; Jon. 4:2; James 5:11
9 [a][Ps. 30:5; Is. 57:16]; Jer. 3:5; [Mic. 7:18]
10 [a][Ezra 9:13; Lam. 3:22]
12 [a][2 Sam. 12:13; Is. 38:17; 43:25; Zech. 3:9; Heb. 9:26]
13 [a]Mal. 3:17
15 [a]Is. 40:6–8; James 1:10, 11; 1 Pet. 1:24
16 [a][Is. 40:7] [b]Job 7:10
18 [a][Deut. 7:9]; Ps. 25:10
19 [a][Ps. 47:2; Dan. 4:17, 25]
20 [a]Ps. 148:2 [b][Matt. 6:10]
21 [a][Heb. 1:14]

NKJV

25 [a]Of old You laid the foundation of the
earth,
And the heavens *are* the work of Your
hands.
26 [a]They will perish, but You will endure;
Yes, they will all grow old like a garment;
Like a cloak You will change them,
And they will be changed.
27 But [a]You *are* the same,
And Your years will have no end.
28 [a]The children of Your servants will
continue,
And their descendants will be established
before You."

PSALM 103

Praise for the LORD's Mercies

A Psalm of David.

BLESS [a]the LORD, O my soul;
And all that is within me, *bless* His holy
name!
2 Bless the LORD, O my soul,
And forget not all His benefits:
3 [a]Who forgives all your iniquities,
Who [b]heals all your diseases,
4 Who redeems your life from destruction,
[a]Who crowns you with lovingkindness and
tender mercies,
5 Who satisfies your mouth with good
things,
So that [a]your youth is renewed like the
eagle's.

6 The LORD executes righteousness
And justice for all who are oppressed.
7 [a]He made known His ways to Moses,
His acts to the children of Israel.
8 [a]The LORD *is* merciful and gracious,
Slow to anger, and abounding in mercy.
9 [a]He will not always strive *with us,*
Nor will He keep *His anger* forever.
10 [a]He has not dealt with us according to our
sins,
Nor punished us according to our
iniquities.

11 For as the heavens are high above the
earth,
So great is His mercy toward those who
fear Him;
12 As far as the east is from the west,
So far has He [a]removed our
transgressions from us.
13 [a]As a father pities *his* children,
So the LORD pities those who fear Him.
14 For He knows our frame;
He remembers that we *are* dust.

15 *As for* man, [a]his days *are* like grass;
As a flower of the field, so he flourishes.
16 [a]For the wind passes over it, and it is gone,
And [b]its place remembers it no more.
17 But the mercy of the LORD *is* from
everlasting to everlasting
On those who fear Him,
And His righteousness to children's
children,
18 [a]To such as keep His covenant,
And to those who remember His
commandments to do them.

19 The LORD has established His throne in
heaven,
And [a]His kingdom rules over all.

20 [a]Bless the LORD, you His angels,
Who excel in strength, who [b]do His word,
Heeding the voice of His word.
21 Bless the LORD, all *you* His hosts,
[a]*You* ministers of His, who do His pleasure.

KJV

22 Bless the LORD, all his works in all places
of his dominion: bless the LORD, O my soul.

PSALM 104

Praise to the Sovereign LORD for His Creation and Providence
(cf. Gen. 1:1–31)

BLESS [a]the LORD, O my soul. O LORD my God,
thou art very great; thou art clothed with honour and majesty.
2 Who coverest *thyself* with light as *with* a
garment: who stretchest out the heavens like a
curtain:
3 [a]Who layeth the beams of his chambers
in the waters: who maketh the clouds his chariot:
who walketh upon the wings of the wind:
4 Who maketh his angels spirits; his ministers a flaming fire:
5 *Who* laid the foundations of the earth,
that it should not be removed for ever.
6 Thou [a]coveredst it with the deep as *with*
a garment: the waters stood above the mountains.
7 At thy rebuke they fled; at the voice of
thy thunder they hasted away.
8 They go up by the mountains; they go
down by the valleys unto the place which thou
hast founded for them.
9 Thou hast [a]set a bound that they may not
pass over; [b]that they turn not again to cover the
earth.
10 He sendeth the springs into the valleys,
which run among the hills.
11 They give drink to every beast of the field:
the wild asses quench their thirst.
12 By them shall the fowls of the heaven have
their habitation, *which* sing among the branches.
13 [a]He watereth the hills from his chambers:
the earth is satisfied with [b]the fruit of thy works.
14 [a]He causeth the grass to grow for the cattle, and herb for the service of man: that he may
bring forth [b]food out of the earth;
15 And [a]wine *that* maketh glad the heart of
man, *and* oil to make *his* face to shine, and bread
which strengtheneth man's heart.
16 The trees of the LORD are full *of sap;* the
cedars of Lebanon, which he hath planted;
17 Where the birds make their nests: *as for*
the stork, the fir trees *are* her house.
18 The high hills *are* a refuge for the wild
goats; *and* the rocks for the [a]conies.
19 [a]He appointed the moon for seasons: the
[b]sun knoweth his going down.
20 [a]Thou makest darkness, and it is night:
wherein all the beasts of the forest do creep *forth.*
21 [a]The young lions roar after their prey, and
seek their meat from God.
22 The sun ariseth, they gather themselves
together, and lay them down in their dens.
23 Man goeth forth unto [a]his work and to
his labour until the evening.

PSALM 104

1 [a]Ps. 103:1
3 [a][Amos 9:6]
6 [a]Gen. 1:6
9 [a]Job 26:10; Ps. 33:7; [Jer. 5:22] [b]Gen. 9:11–15
13 [a]Ps. 147:8 [b]Jer. 10:13
14 [a]Gen. 1:29 [b]Job 28:5
15 [a]Judg. 9:13; Ps. 23:5; Prov. 31:6; Eccl. 10:19
18 [a]Lev. 11:5
19 [a]Gen. 1:14 [b]Job 38:12; Ps. 19:6
20 [a][Ps. 74:16; Is. 45:7]
21 [a]Job 38:39
23 [a]Gen. 3:19

*———

104:18 *rock hyraxes*

NKJV

22 Bless the LORD, all His works,
In all places of His dominion.

Bless the LORD, O my soul!

PSALM 104

Praise to the Sovereign LORD for His Creation and Providence
(cf. Gen. 1:1–31)

BLESS [a]the LORD, O my soul!

O LORD my God, You are very great:
You are clothed with honor and majesty,
2 Who cover *Yourself* with light as *with* a
garment,
Who stretch out the heavens like a
curtain.

3 [a]He lays the beams of His upper chambers
in the waters,
Who makes the clouds His chariot,
Who walks on the wings of the wind,
4 Who makes His angels spirits,
His ministers a flame of fire.

5 *You who* laid the foundations of the earth,
So *that* it should not be moved forever,
6 You [a]covered it with the deep as *with* a
garment;
The waters stood above the mountains.
7 At Your rebuke they fled;
At the voice of Your thunder they
hastened away.
8 They went up over the mountains;
They went down into the valleys,
To the place which You founded for them.
9 You have [a]set a boundary that they may
not pass over,
[b]That they may not return to cover the
earth.

10 He sends the springs into the valleys;
They flow among the hills.
11 They give drink to every beast of the field;
The wild donkeys quench their thirst.
12 By them the birds of the heavens have
their home;
They sing among the branches.
13 [a]He waters the hills from His upper
chambers;
The earth is satisfied with [b]the fruit of
Your works.

14 [a]He causes the grass to grow for the cattle,
And vegetation for the service of man,
That he may bring forth [b]food from the
earth,
15 And [a]wine *that* makes glad the heart of
man,
Oil to make *his* face shine,
And bread *which* strengthens man's heart.
16 The trees of the LORD are full *of sap,*
The cedars of Lebanon which He planted,
17 Where the birds make their nests;
The stork has her home in the fir trees.
18 The high hills *are* for the wild goats;
The cliffs are a refuge for the [a]rock*
badgers.

19 [a]He appointed the moon for seasons;
The [b]sun knows its going down.
20 [a]You make darkness, and it is night,
In which all the beasts of the forest creep
about.
21 [a]The young lions roar after their prey,
And seek their food from God.
22 *When* the sun rises, they gather together
And lie down in their dens.
23 Man goes out to [a]his work
And to his labor until the evening.

KJV

24 [a]O LORD, how manifold are thy works! in
wisdom hast thou made them all: the earth is full
of thy [b]riches.
25 *So is* this great and wide sea, wherein *are*
things creeping innumerable, both small and
great beasts.
26 There go the ships: *there is* that [a]levia-
than, *whom* thou hast made to play therein.
27 [a]These wait all upon thee; that thou mayest give *them* their meat in due season.
28 *That* thou givest them they gather: thou
openest thine hand, they are filled with good.
29 Thou hidest thy face, they are troubled:
[a]thou takest away their breath, they die, and return to their dust.
30 [a]Thou sendest forth thy spirit, they are
created: and thou renewest the face of the earth.
31 The glory of the LORD shall endure for
ever: the LORD [a]shall rejoice in his works.
32 He looketh on the earth, and it [a]trembleth:
[b]he toucheth the hills, and they smoke.
33 [a]I will sing unto the LORD as long as I live:
I will sing praise to my God while I have my being.
34 My [a]meditation of him shall be sweet: I
will be glad in the LORD.
35 Let [a]the sinners be consumed out of the
earth, and let the wicked be no more. Bless thou
the LORD, O my soul. Praise ye the LORD.

PSALM 105

The Eternal Faithfulness of the LORD
(Ex. 7:8—11:10; 1 Chr. 16:8–22)

1 O [a]GIVE thanks unto the LORD; call upon his
name: [b]make known his deeds among the
people.
2 Sing unto him, sing psalms unto him: [a]talk
ye of all his wondrous works.
3 Glory ye in his holy name: let the heart
of them rejoice that seek the LORD.
4 Seek the LORD, and his strength: [a]seek his
face evermore.
5 [a]Remember his marvellous works that he
hath done; his wonders, and the judgments of his
mouth;
6 O ye seed of Abraham his servant, ye children of Jacob his chosen.
7 He *is* the LORD our God: [a]his judgments
are in all the earth.
8 He hath [a]remembered his covenant for
ever, the word *which* he commanded to a thousand generations.
9 [a]Which *covenant* he made with Abraham,
and his oath unto Isaac;
10 And confirmed the same unto Jacob for
a law, *and* to Israel *for* an everlasting covenant:
11 Saying, [a]Unto thee will I give the land of
Canaan, the lot of your inheritance:
12 [a]When they were *but* a few men in number; yea, very few, [b]and strangers in it.
13 When they went from one nation to another, from *one* kingdom to another people;
14 [a]He suffered no man to do them wrong:
yea, [b]he reproved kings for their sakes;

24 [a]Ps. 40:5; Prov. 3:19; [Jer. 10:12]; 51:15 [b]Ps. 65:9 **26** [a]Job 41:1; Is. 27:1 **27** [a]Job 36:31; Ps. 136:25 **29** [a]Job 34:15; [Eccl. 12:7] **30** [a]Is. 32:15 **31** [a]Gen. 1:31; Prov. 8:31 **32** [a]Hab. 3:10 [b]Ex. 19:18; Ps. 144:5 **33** [a]Ps. 63:4 **34** [a]Ps. 19:14 **35** [a]Ps. 37:38

PSALM 105

1 [a]1 Chr. 16:8–22, 34; Ps. 106:1; Is. 12:4 [b]Ps. 145:12 **2** [a]Ps. 119:27 **4** [a]Ps. 27:8 **5** [a]Ps. 77:11 **7** [a][Is. 26:9] **8** [a]Luke 1:72 **9** [a]Gen. 17:2; Luke 1:73; [Gal. 3:17]; Heb. 6:17 **11** [a]Gen. 13:15; 15:18 **12** [a]Gen. 34:30; [Deut. 7:7] [b]Gen. 23:4; Heb. 11:9 **14** [a]Gen. 35:5 [b]Gen. 12:17

NKJV

24 [a]O LORD, how manifold are Your works!
In wisdom You have made them all.
The earth is full of Your [b]possessions—
25 This great and wide sea,
In which *are* innumerable teeming things,
Living things both small and great.
26 There the ships sail about;
There is that [a]Leviathan
Which You have made to play there.

27 [a]These all wait for You,
That You may give *them* their food in due season.
28 *What* You give them they gather in;
You open Your hand, they are filled with good.
29 You hide Your face, they are troubled;
[a]You take away their breath, they die and return to their dust.
30 [a]You send forth Your Spirit, they are created;
And You renew the face of the earth.

31 May the glory of the LORD endure forever;
May the LORD [a]rejoice in His works.
32 He looks on the earth, and it [a]trembles;
[b]He touches the hills, and they smoke.

33 [a]I will sing to the LORD as long as I live;
I will sing praise to my God while I have my being.
34 May my [a]meditation be sweet to Him;
I will be glad in the LORD.
35 May [a]sinners be consumed from the earth,
And the wicked be no more.

Bless the LORD, O my soul!
Praise the LORD!

PSALM 105

The Eternal Faithfulness of the LORD
(Ex. 7:8—11:10; 1 Chr. 16:8–22)

1 OH, [a]give thanks to the LORD!
Call upon His name;
[b]Make known His deeds among the peoples!
2 Sing to Him, sing psalms to Him;
[a]Talk of all His wondrous works!
3 Glory in His holy name;
Let the hearts of those rejoice who seek the LORD!
4 Seek the LORD and His strength;
[a]Seek His face evermore!
5 [a]Remember His marvelous works which He has done,
His wonders, and the judgments of His mouth,
6 O seed of Abraham His servant,
You children of Jacob, His chosen ones!

7 He *is* the LORD our God;
[a]His judgments *are* in all the earth.
8 He [a]remembers His covenant forever,
The word *which* He commanded, for a thousand generations,
9 [a]*The covenant* which He made with Abraham,
And His oath to Isaac,
10 And confirmed it to Jacob for a statute,
To Israel *as* an everlasting covenant,
11 Saying, [a]"To you I will give the land of Canaan
As the allotment of your inheritance,"
12 [a]When they were few in number,
Indeed very few, [b]and strangers in it.

13 When they went from one nation to another,
From *one* kingdom to another people,
14 [a]He permitted no one to do them wrong;
Yes, [b]He rebuked kings for their sakes,

KJV

15 *Saying,* Touch not mine anointed, and do
my prophets no harm.
16 Moreover [a]he called for a famine upon the
land: he brake the whole [b]staff of bread.
17 [a]He sent a man before them, *even* Joseph,
who [b]was sold for a servant:
18 [a]Whose feet they hurt with fetters: he was
laid in iron:
19 Until the time that his word came: [a]the
word of the LORD tried him.
20 [a]The king sent and loosed him; *even* the
ruler of the people, and let him go free.
21 [a]He made him lord of his house, and ruler
of all his substance:
22 To bind his princes at his pleasure; and
teach his senators wisdom.
23 [a]Israel also came into Egypt; and Jacob
sojourned [b]in the land of Ham.
24 And [a]he increased his people greatly; and
made them stronger than their enemies.
25 [a]He turned their heart to hate his people,
to deal subtilly with his servants.
26 [a]He sent Moses his servant; *and* Aaron
whom he had chosen.
27 They [a]shewed his signs among them, and
wonders in the land of Ham.
28 He sent darkness, and made it dark; and
they rebelled not against his word.
29 [a]He turned their waters into blood, and
slew their fish.
30 [a]Their land brought forth frogs in abundance, in the chambers of their kings.
31 [a]He spake, and there came divers sorts
of flies, *and* lice in all their coasts.
32 [a]He gave them hail for rain, *and* flaming
fire in their land.
33 [a]He smote their vines also and their fig
trees; and brake the trees of their coasts.
34 [a]He spake, and the locusts came, and caterpillers, and that without number,
35 And did eat up all the herbs in their land,
and devoured the fruit of their ground.
36 [a]He smote also all the firstborn in their
land, [b]the chief of all their strength.
37 [a]He brought them forth also with silver
and gold: and *there was* not one feeble *person*
among their tribes.
38 [a]Egypt was glad when they departed: for
the fear of them fell upon them.
39 [a]He spread a cloud for a covering; and
fire to give light in the night.
40 [a]*The people* asked, and he brought quails,
and [b]satisfied them with the bread of heaven.
41 [a]He opened the rock, and the waters
gushed out; they ran in the dry places *like* a river.
42 For he remembered [a]his holy promise,
and Abraham his servant.
43 And he brought forth his people with joy,
and his chosen with gladness:
44 [a]And gave them the lands of the heathen:
and they inherited the labour of the people;
45 [a]That they might observe his statutes, and
keep his laws. Praise ye the LORD.

16 [a]Gen. 41:54 [b]Lev. 26:26; Is. 3:1; Ezek. 4:16
17 [a][Gen. 45:5] [b]Gen. 37:28, 36; Acts 7:9
18 [a]Gen. 40:15
19 [a]Gen. 39:11–21; 41:25, 42, 43
20 [a]Gen. 41:14
21 [a]Gen. 41:40–44
23 [a]Gen. 46:6; Acts 7:15 [b]Ps. 78:51
24 [a]Ex. 1:7, 9
25 [a]Ex. 1:8–10; 4:21
26 [a]Ex. 3:10; 4:12–15
27 [a]Ex. 7—12; Ps. 78:43
29 [a]Ex. 7:20, 21; Ps. 78:44
30 [a]Ex. 8:6
31 [a]Ex. 8:16, 17
32 [a]Ex. 9:23–25
33 [a]Ps. 78:47
34 [a]Ex. 10:4
36 [a]Ex. 12:29; 13:15; Ps. 135:8; 136:10 [b]Gen. 49:3
37 [a]Ex. 12:35, 36
38 [a]Ex. 12:33
39 [a]Ex. 13:21; Neh. 9:12; Ps. 78:14; Is. 4:5
40 [a]Ex. 16:12 [b]Ps. 78:24
41 [a]Ex. 17:6; Num. 20:11; Ps. 78:15; 114:8; Is. 48:21; [1 Cor. 10:4]
42 [a]Gen. 15:13, 14; Ps. 105:8
44 [a]Josh. 11:16–23; 13:7; Ps. 78:55
45 [a][Deut. 4:1, 40]

NKJV

15 *Saying,* "Do not touch My anointed ones,
And do My prophets no harm."

16 Moreover [a]He called for a famine in the
land;
He destroyed all the [b]provision of bread.
17 [a]He sent a man before them—
Joseph—*who* [b]was sold as a slave.
18 [a]They hurt his feet with fetters,
He was laid in irons.
19 Until the time that his word came to
pass,
[a]The word of the LORD tested him.
20 [a]The king sent and released him,
The ruler of the people let him go free.
21 [a]He made him lord of his house,
And ruler of all his possessions,
22 To bind his princes at his pleasure,
And teach his elders wisdom.

23 [a]Israel also came into Egypt,
And Jacob dwelt [b]in the land of Ham.
24 [a]He increased His people greatly,
And made them stronger than their
enemies.
25 [a]He turned their heart to hate His people,
To deal craftily with His servants.

26 [a]He sent Moses His servant,
And Aaron whom He had chosen.
27 They [a]performed His signs among them,
And wonders in the land of Ham.
28 He sent darkness, and made *it* dark;
And they did not rebel against His word.
29 [a]He turned their waters into blood,
And killed their fish.
30 [a]Their land abounded with frogs,
Even in the chambers of their kings.
31 [a]He spoke, and there came swarms of
flies,
And lice in all their territory.
32 [a]He gave them hail for rain,
And flaming fire in their land.
33 [a]He struck their vines also, and their fig
trees,
And splintered the trees of their territory.
34 [a]He spoke, and locusts came,
Young locusts without number,
35 And ate up all the vegetation in their
land,
And devoured the fruit of their ground.
36 [a]He also destroyed all the firstborn in their
land,
[b]The first of all their strength.

37 [a]He also brought them out with silver and
gold,
And *there was* none feeble among His
tribes.
38 [a]Egypt was glad when they departed,
For the fear of them had fallen upon
them.
39 [a]He spread a cloud for a covering,
And fire to give light in the night.
40 [a]*The people* asked, and He brought quail,
And [b]satisfied them with the bread of
heaven.
41 [a]He opened the rock, and water gushed
out;
It ran in the dry places *like* a river.

42 For He remembered [a]His holy promise,
And Abraham His servant.
43 He brought out His people with joy,
His chosen ones with gladness.
44 [a]He gave them the lands of the Gentiles,
And they inherited the labor of the
nations,
45 [a]That they might observe His statutes
And keep His laws.

Praise the LORD!

KJV

PSALM 106

Joy in Forgiveness of Israel's Sins

PRAISE ye the LORD. [a]O give thanks unto the LORD; for *he is* good: for his mercy *endureth* for ever.

2 Who can utter the mighty acts of the LORD? *who* can shew forth all his praise?

3 Blessed *are* they that keep judgment, *and* he that [a]doeth righteousness at [b]all times.

4 [a]Remember me, O LORD, with the favour *that thou bearest unto* thy people: O visit me with thy salvation;

5 That I may see the good of thy chosen, that I may rejoice in the gladness of thy nation, that I may glory with thine inheritance.

6 [a]We have sinned with our fathers, we have committed iniquity, we have done wickedly.

7 Our fathers understood not thy wonders in Egypt; they remembered not the multitude of thy mercies; [a]but provoked *him* at the sea, *even* at the Red sea.

8 Nevertheless he saved them for his name's sake, [a]that he might make his mighty power to be known.

9 [a]He rebuked the Red sea also, and it was dried up: so [b]he led them through the depths, as through the wilderness.

10 And he [a]saved them from the hand of him that hated *them*, and redeemed them from the hand of the enemy.

11 [a]And the waters covered their enemies: there was not one of them left.

12 [a]Then believed they his words; they sang his praise.

13 [a]They soon forgat his works; they waited not for his counsel:

14 [a]But lusted exceedingly in the wilderness, and tempted God in the desert.

15 [a]And he gave them their request; but [b]sent leanness into their soul.

16 [a]They envied Moses also in the camp, *and* Aaron the saint of the LORD.

17 [a]The earth opened and swallowed up Dathan, and covered the company of Abiram.

18 [a]And a fire was kindled in their company; the flame burned up the wicked.

19 [a]They made a calf in Horeb, and worshipped the molten image.

20 Thus [a]they changed their glory into the similitude of an ox that eateth grass.

21 They forgat God their saviour, which had done great things in Egypt;

22 Wondrous works in the land of Ham, *and* terrible things by the Red sea.

23 [a]Therefore he said that he would destroy them, had not Moses his chosen [b]stood before him in the breach, to turn away his wrath, lest he should destroy *them*.

PSALM 106

1 [a]1 Chr. 16:34, 41
3 [a]Ps. 15:2 [b][Gal. 6:9]
4 [a]Ps. 119:132
6 [a]1 Kin. 8:47; [Ezra 9:7; Neh. 1:7; Jer. 3:25; Dan. 9:5]
7 [a]Ex. 14:11, 12
8 [a]Ex. 9:16
9 [a]Ex. 14:21; Ps. 18:15; Is. 51:10; Nah. 1:4 [b]Is. 63:11–13
10 [a]Ex. 14:30
11 [a]Ex. 14:27, 28; 15:5
12 [a]Ex. 15:1–21
13 [a]Ex. 15:24; 16:2; 17:2
14 [a]Num. 11:4; 1 Cor. 10:6
15 [a]Num. 11:31 [b]Is. 10:16
16 [a]Num. 16:1–3
17 [a]Num. 16:31, 32; Deut. 11:6
18 [a]Num. 16:35, 46
19 [a]Ex. 32:1–4; Deut. 9:8; Acts 7:41
20 [a]Jer. 2:11; Rom. 1:23
23 [a]Ex. 32:10; Deut. 9:19 [b]Ezek. 22:30

*———

106:3 LXX, Syr., Tg., Vg. *those who do*

NKJV

PSALM 106

Joy in Forgiveness of Israel's Sins

PRAISE the LORD!

[a]Oh, give thanks to the LORD, for *He is* good!
For His mercy *endures* forever.

2 Who can utter the mighty acts of the LORD?
Who can declare all His praise?
3 Blessed *are* those who keep justice,
And *he who [a]does righteousness at [b]all times!

4 [a]Remember me, O LORD, with the favor *You have toward* Your people.
Oh, visit me with Your salvation,
5 That I may see the benefit of Your chosen ones,
That I may rejoice in the gladness of Your nation,
That I may glory with Your inheritance.

6 [a]We have sinned with our fathers,
We have committed iniquity,
We have done wickedly.
7 Our fathers in Egypt did not understand Your wonders;
They did not remember the multitude of Your mercies,
[a]But rebelled by the sea—the Red Sea.

8 Nevertheless He saved them for His name's sake,
[a]That He might make His mighty power known.
9 [a]He rebuked the Red Sea also, and it dried up;
So [b]He led them through the depths,
As through the wilderness.
10 He [a]saved them from the hand of him who hated *them*,
And redeemed them from the hand of the enemy.
11 [a]The waters covered their enemies;
There was not one of them left.
12 [a]Then they believed His words;
They sang His praise.

13 [a]They soon forgot His works;
They did not wait for His counsel,
14 [a]But lusted exceedingly in the wilderness,
And tested God in the desert.
15 [a]And He gave them their request,
But [b]sent leanness into their soul.

16 When [a]they envied Moses in the camp,
And Aaron the saint of the LORD,
17 [a]The earth opened up and swallowed Dathan,
And covered the faction of Abiram.
18 [a]A fire was kindled in their company;
The flame burned up the wicked.

19 [a]They made a calf in Horeb,
And worshiped the molded image.
20 Thus [a]they changed their glory
Into the image of an ox that eats grass.
21 They forgot God their Savior,
Who had done great things in Egypt,
22 Wondrous works in the land of Ham,
Awesome things by the Red Sea.
23 [a]Therefore He said that He would destroy them,
Had not Moses His chosen one [b]stood before Him in the breach,
To turn away His wrath, lest He destroy *them*.

KJV

24 Yea, they despised [a]the pleasant land, they [b]believed not his word:

25 [a]But murmured in their tents, *and* hearkened not unto the voice of the LORD.

26 [a]Therefore he lifted up his hand against them, [b]to overthrow them in the wilderness:

27 [a]To overthrow their seed also among the nations, and to scatter them in the lands.

28 [a]They joined themselves also unto Baalpeor, and ate the sacrifices of the dead.

29 Thus they provoked *him* to anger with their inventions: and the plague brake in upon them.

30 [a]Then stood up Phinehas, and executed judgment: and *so* the plague was stayed.

31 And that was counted unto him [a]for righteousness unto all generations for evermore.

32 [a]They angered *him* also at the waters of strife, [b]so that it went ill with Moses for their sakes:

33 [a]Because they provoked his spirit, so that he spake unadvisedly with his lips.

34 [a]They did not destroy the nations, [b]concerning whom the LORD commanded them:

35 [a]But were mingled among the heathen, and learned their works.

36 And [a]they served their idols: [b]which were a snare unto them.

37 Yea, [a]they sacrificed their sons and their daughters unto [b]devils,

38 And shed innocent blood, *even* the blood of their sons and of their daughters, whom they sacrificed unto the idols of Canaan: and [a]the land was polluted with blood.

39 Thus were they [a]defiled with their own works, and [b]went a whoring with their own inventions.

40 Therefore [a]was the wrath of the LORD kindled against his people, insomuch that he abhorred [b]his own inheritance.

41 And [a]he gave them into the hand of the heathen; and they that hated them ruled over them.

42 Their enemies also oppressed them, and they were brought into subjection under their hand.

43 [a]Many times did he deliver them; but they provoked *him* with their counsel, and were brought low for their iniquity.

44 Nevertheless he regarded their affliction, when [a]he heard their cry:

45 [a]And he remembered for them his covenant, and [b]repented [c]according to the multitude of his mercies.

46 [a]He made them also to be pitied of all those that carried them captives.

47 [a]Save us, O LORD our God, and gather us from among the heathen, to give thanks unto thy holy name, *and* to triumph in thy praise.

24 [a]Deut. 8:7; Jer. 3:19; Ezek. 20:6 [b]Deut. 1:32; 9:23; [Heb. 3:18, 19]
25 [a]Num. 14:2, 27; Deut. 1:27
26 [a]Ezek. 20:15, 16; [Heb. 3:11, 18] [b]Num. 14:28–30
27 [a]Lev. 26:33; Ezek. 20:23
28 [a]Num. 25:3; Deut. 4:3; Hos. 9:10
30 [a]Num. 25:7, 8
31 [a]Gen. 15:6; Num. 25:11–13
32 [a]Num. 20:3–13; Ps. 81:7 [b]Deut. 1:37; 3:26
33 [a]Num. 20:3, 10
34 [a]Judg. 1:21 [b][Deut. 7:2, 16]; Judg. 2:2
35 [a]Judg. 3:5, 6
36 [a]Judg. 2:12 [b]Deut. 7:16
37 [a][Deut. 12:31; 32:17, 18]; 2 Kin. 16:3; 17:17; Ezek. 16:20, 21; [1 Cor. 10:20] [b][Lev. 17:7]
38 [a][Num. 35:33; Is. 24:5; Jer. 3:1, 2]
39 [a][Lev. 18:24]; Ezek. 20:18 [b][Lev. 17:7; Num. 15:39]; Judg. 2:17; Hos. 4:12
40 [a]Judg. 2:14; Ps. 78:59 [b][Deut. 9:29; 32:9]
41 [a]Judg. 2:14; [Neh. 9:27]
43 [a]Judg. 2:16; [Neh. 9:27]
44 [a]Judg. 3:9; 6:7; 10:10
45 [a][Lev. 26:41, 42] [b]Judg. 2:18 [c]Ps. 69:16
46 [a]1 Kin. 8:50; [2 Chr. 30:9]; Ezra 9:9; Neh. 1:11; Jer. 42:12
47 [a]1 Chr. 16:35, 36

NKJV

24 Then they despised [a]the pleasant land;
They [b]did not believe His word,
25 [a]But complained in their tents,
And did not heed the voice of the LORD.
26 [a]Therefore He raised up His hand *in an oath* against them,
[b]To overthrow them in the wilderness,
27 [a]To overthrow their descendants among the nations,
And to scatter them in the lands.

28 [a]They joined themselves also to Baal of Peor,
And ate sacrifices made to the dead.
29 Thus they provoked *Him* to anger with their deeds,
And the plague broke out among them.
30 [a]Then Phinehas stood up and intervened,
And the plague was stopped.
31 And that was accounted to him [a]for righteousness
To all generations forevermore.

32 [a]They angered *Him* also at the waters of *strife,
[b]So that it went ill with Moses on account of them;
33 [a]Because they rebelled against His Spirit,
So that he spoke rashly with his lips.

34 [a]They did not destroy the peoples,
[b]Concerning whom the LORD had commanded them,
35 [a]But they mingled with the Gentiles
And learned their works;
36 [a]They served their idols,
[b]Which became a snare to them.
37 [a]They even sacrificed their sons
And their daughters to [b]demons,
38 And shed innocent blood,
The blood of their sons and daughters,
Whom they sacrificed to the idols of Canaan;
And [a]the land was polluted with blood.
39 Thus they were [a]defiled by their own works,
And [b]played the harlot by their own deeds.

40 Therefore [a]the wrath of the LORD was kindled against His people,
So that He abhorred [b]His own inheritance.
41 And [a]He gave them into the hand of the Gentiles,
And those who hated them ruled over them.
42 Their enemies also oppressed them,
And they were brought into subjection under their hand.
43 [a]Many times He delivered them;
But they rebelled in their counsel,
And were brought low for their iniquity.

44 Nevertheless He regarded their affliction,
When [a]He heard their cry;
45 [a]And for their sake He remembered His covenant,
And [b]relented [c]according to the multitude of His mercies.
46 [a]He also made them to be pitied
By all those who carried them away captive.

47 [a]Save us, O LORD our God,
And gather us from among the Gentiles,
To give thanks to Your holy name,
To triumph in Your praise.

---

*106:32 Or *Meribah*

KJV

48 [a]Blessed *be* the LORD God of Israel from everlasting to everlasting: and let all the people say, Amen. Praise ye the LORD.

BOOK V

PSALM 107

Thanksgiving to the LORD for His Great Works of Deliverance

O [a]GIVE thanks unto the LORD, for *he is* good: for his mercy *endureth* for ever.
2 Let the redeemed of the LORD say *so,* whom he hath redeemed from the hand of the enemy;
3 And [a]gathered them out of the lands, from the east, and from the west, from the north, and from the south.
4 They wandered in [a]the wilderness in a solitary way; they found no city to dwell in.
5 Hungry and thirsty, their soul fainted in them.
6 [a]Then they cried unto the LORD in their trouble, *and* he delivered them out of their distresses.
7 And he led them forth by the [a]right way, that they might go to a city of habitation.
8 [a]Oh that *men* would praise the LORD *for* his goodness, and *for* his wonderful works to the children of men!
9 For [a]he satisfieth the longing soul, and filleth the hungry soul with goodness.
10 Such as [a]sit in darkness and in the shadow of death, *being* [b]bound in affliction and iron;
11 Because they [a]rebelled against the words of God, and contemned [b]the counsel of the most High:
12 Therefore he brought down their heart with labour; they fell down, and *there was* [a]none to help.
13 Then they cried unto the LORD in their trouble, *and* he saved them out of their distresses.
14 [a]He brought them out of darkness and the shadow of death, and brake their bands in sunder.
15 Oh that *men* would praise the LORD *for* his goodness, and *for* his wonderful works to the children of men!
16 For he hath [a]broken the gates of brass, and cut the bars of iron in sunder.
17 Fools [a]because of their transgression, and because of their iniquities, are afflicted.
18 [a]Their soul abhorreth all manner of meat; and they [b]draw near unto the gates of death.
19 Then they cry unto the LORD in their trouble, *and* he saveth them out of their distresses.
20 [a]He sent his word, and [b]healed them, and [c]delivered *them* from their destructions.
21 Oh that *men* would praise the LORD *for* his goodness, and *for* his wonderful works to the children of men!

48 [a]Ps. 41:13

PSALM 107

1 [a]1 Chr. 16:34; Ps. 106:1; Jer. 33:11
3 [a]Is. 43:5, 6; Jer. 29:14; 31:8–10; [Ezek. 39:27, 28]
4 [a]Num. 14:33; 32:13; [Deut. 2:7; 32:10]; Josh. 5:6; 14:10
6 [a]Ps. 50:15; [Hos. 5:15]
7 [a]Ezra 8:21; Ps. 5:8; Jer. 31:9
8 [a]Ps. 107:15, 21
9 [a][Ps. 34:10; Luke 1:53]
10 [a][Is. 42:7; Mic. 7:8; Luke 1:79] [b]Job 36:8
11 [a]Lam. 3:42 [b][Ps. 73:24]
12 [a]Ps. 22:11
14 [a]Ps. 68:6
16 [a]Is. 45:1, 2
17 [a][Is. 65:6, 7; Jer. 30:14, 15]; Lam. 3:39; Ezek. 24:23
18 [a]Job 33:20 [b]Job 33:22
20 [a]Matt. 8:8 [b]2 Kin. 20:5; Ps. 30:2 [c]Job 33:28, 30

NKJV

48 [a]Blessed *be* the LORD God of Israel
From everlasting to everlasting!
And let all the people say, "Amen!"

Praise the LORD!

BOOK FIVE

Psalms 107–150

PSALM 107

Thanksgiving to the LORD for His Great Works of Deliverance

OH, [a]give thanks to the LORD, for *He is* good!
For His mercy *endures* forever.
2 Let the redeemed of the LORD say *so,*
Whom He has redeemed from the hand of the enemy,
3 And [a]gathered out of the lands,
From the east and from the west,
From the north and from the south.

4 They wandered in [a]the wilderness in a desolate way;
They found no city to dwell in.
5 Hungry and thirsty,
Their soul fainted in them.
6 [a]Then they cried out to the LORD in their trouble,
And He delivered them out of their distresses.
7 And He led them forth by the [a]right way,
That they might go to a city for a dwelling place.
8 [a]Oh, that *men* would give thanks to the LORD *for* His goodness,
And *for* His wonderful works to the children of men!
9 For [a]He satisfies the longing soul,
And fills the hungry soul with goodness.

10 Those who [a]sat in darkness and in the shadow of death,
[b]Bound in affliction and irons—
11 Because they [a]rebelled against the words of God,
And despised [b]the counsel of the Most High,
12 Therefore He brought down their heart with labor;
They fell down, and *there was* [a]none to help.
13 Then they cried out to the LORD in their trouble,
And He saved them out of their distresses.
14 [a]He brought them out of darkness and the shadow of death,
And broke their chains in pieces.
15 Oh, that *men* would give thanks to the LORD *for* His goodness,
And *for* His wonderful works to the children of men!
16 For He has [a]broken the gates of bronze,
And cut the bars of iron in two.

17 Fools, [a]because of their transgression,
And because of their iniquities, were afflicted.
18 [a]Their soul abhorred all manner of food,
And they [b]drew near to the gates of death.
19 Then they cried out to the LORD in their trouble,
And He saved them out of their distresses.
20 [a]He sent His word and [b]healed them,
And [c]delivered *them* from their destructions.
21 Oh, that *men* would give thanks to the LORD *for* His goodness,
And *for* His wonderful works to the children of men!

KJV

22 And [a]let them sacrifice the sacrifices of
thanksgiving, and [b]declare his works with
rejoicing.
23 They that go down to the sea in ships, that
do business in great waters;
24 These see the works of the LORD, and his
wonders in the deep.
25 For he commandeth, and [a]raiseth the
stormy wind, which lifteth up the waves thereof.
26 They mount up to the heaven, they go
down again to the depths: [a]their soul is melted
because of trouble.
27 They reel to and fro, and stagger like a
drunken man, and are at their wit's end.
28 Then they cry unto the LORD in their trouble, and he bringeth them out of their distresses.
29 [a]He maketh the storm a calm, so that the
waves thereof are still.
30 Then are they glad because they be quiet;
so he bringeth them unto their desired haven.
31 [a]Oh that *men* would praise the LORD *for*
his goodness, and *for* his wonderful works to the
children of men!
32 Let them exalt him also [a]in the congregation of the people, and praise him in the assembly
of the elders.
33 He [a]turneth rivers into a wilderness, and
the watersprings into dry ground;
34 A [a]fruitful land into barrenness, for the
wickedness of them that dwell therein.
35 [a]He turneth the wilderness into a standing
water, and dry ground into watersprings.
36 And there he maketh the hungry to dwell,
that they may prepare a city for habitation;
37 And sow the fields, and plant vineyards,
which may yield fruits of increase.
38 [a]He blesseth them also, so that they are
multiplied greatly; and suffereth not their cattle
to [b]decrease.
39 Again, they are [a]minished and brought
low through oppression, affliction, and sorrow.
40 [a]He poureth contempt upon princes, and
causeth them to wander in the wilderness, *where
there is* no way.
41 [a]Yet setteth he the poor on high from affliction, and [b]maketh *him* families like a flock.
42 [a]The righteous shall see *it*, and rejoice:
and all [b]iniquity shall stop her mouth.
43 [a]Whoso *is* wise, and will observe these
things, even they shall understand the lovingkindness of the LORD.

PSALM 108

Assurance of God's Victory over Enemies
(Ps. 57:7–11; 60:5–12)

A Song *or* Psalm of David.

O [a]GOD, my heart is fixed; I will sing and give
praise, even with my glory.
2 [a]Awake, psaltery and harp: I *myself* will
awake early.
3 I will praise thee, O LORD, among the people: and I will sing praises unto thee among the
nations.

22 [a]Lev. 7:12; Ps. 50:14; Heb. 13:15 [b]Ps. 9:11
25 [a]Jon. 1:4
26 [a]Ps. 22:14
29 [a]Ps. 89:9; Matt. 8:26; Luke 8:24
31 [a]Ps. 107:8, 15, 21
32 [a]Ps. 22:22, 25
33 [a]1 Kin. 17:1, 7; Is. 50:2
34 [a]Gen. 13:10; Deut. 29:23
35 [a]Ps. 114:8; [Is. 41:17, 18]
38 [a]Gen. 12:2; 17:16, 20 [b]Ex. 1:7; [Deut. 7:14]
39 [a]2 Kin. 10:32
40 [a]Job 12:21, 24
41 [a]1 Sam. 2:8; [Ps. 113:7, 8] [b]Ps. 78:52
42 [a]Job 5:15, 16 [b]Job 5:16; Ps. 63:11; [Rom. 3:19]
43 [a]Ps. 64:9; Jer. 9:12; [Hos. 14:9]

PSALM 108

1 [a]Ps. 57:7–11
2 [a]Ps. 57:8–11

NKJV

22 [a]Let them sacrifice the sacrifices of
thanksgiving,
And [b]declare His works with rejoicing.

23 Those who go down to the sea in ships,
Who do business on great waters,
24 They see the works of the LORD,
And His wonders in the deep.
25 For He commands and [a]raises the stormy
wind,
Which lifts up the waves of the sea.
26 They mount up to the heavens,
They go down again to the depths;
[a]Their soul melts because of trouble.
27 They reel to and fro, and stagger like a
drunken man,
And are at their wits' end.
28 Then they cry out to the LORD in their
trouble,
And He brings them out of their
distresses.
29 [a]He calms the storm,
So that its waves are still.
30 Then they are glad because they are quiet;
So He guides them to their desired haven.
31 [a]Oh, that *men* would give thanks to the
LORD *for* His goodness,
And *for* His wonderful works to the
children of men!
32 Let them exalt Him also [a]in the assembly
of the people,
And praise Him in the company of the
elders.

33 He [a]turns rivers into a wilderness,
And the watersprings into dry ground;
34 A [a]fruitful land into barrenness,
For the wickedness of those who dwell in
it.
35 [a]He turns a wilderness into pools of water,
And dry land into watersprings.
36 There He makes the hungry dwell,
That they may establish a city for a
dwelling place,
37 And sow fields and plant vineyards,
That they may yield a fruitful harvest.
38 [a]He also blesses them, and they multiply
greatly;
And He does not let their cattle [b]decrease.

39 When they are [a]diminished and brought
low
Through oppression, affliction and
sorrow,
40 [a]He pours contempt on princes,
And causes them to wander in the
wilderness *where there is* no way;
41 [a]Yet He sets the poor on high, far from
affliction,
And [b]makes *their* families like a flock.
42 [a]The righteous see *it* and rejoice,
And all [b]iniquity stops its mouth.

43 [a]Whoever *is* wise will observe these *things*,
And they will understand the
lovingkindness of the LORD.

PSALM 108

Assurance of God's Victory over Enemies
(Ps. 57:7–11; 60:5–12)

A Song. A Psalm of David.

O [a]GOD, my heart is steadfast;
I will sing and give praise, even with my
glory.
2 [a]Awake, lute and harp!
I will awaken the dawn.
3 I will praise You, O LORD, among the
peoples,
And I will sing praises to You among the
nations.

KJV

4 For thy mercy *is* great above the heavens:
and thy truth *reacheth* unto the clouds.
5 [a]Be thou exalted, O God, above the heavens: and thy glory above all the earth;
6 [a]That thy beloved may be delivered: save
with thy right hand, and answer me.
7 God hath spoken in his holiness; I will rejoice, I will divide Shechem, and mete out the valley of Succoth.
8 Gilead *is* mine; Manasseh *is* mine;
Ephraim also *is* the strength of mine head; [a]Judah
is my lawgiver;
9 Moab *is* my washpot; over Edom will I
cast out my shoe; over Philistia will I triumph.
10 [a]Who will bring me into the strong city?
who will lead me into Edom?
11 *Wilt* not *thou,* O God, *who* hast cast us
off? and wilt not thou, O God, go forth with our
hosts?
12 Give us help from trouble: for vain *is* the
help of man.
13 [a]Through God we shall do valiantly: for
he *it is that* shall tread down our enemies.

PSALM 109

Plea for Judgment of False Accusers

To the chief Musician, A Psalm of David.

HOLD [a]not thy peace, O God of my praise;
2 For the mouth of the wicked and the
mouth of the deceitful are opened against me:
they have spoken against me with a [a]lying tongue.
3 They compassed me about also with
words of hatred; and fought against me [a]without
a cause.
4 For my love they are my adversaries: but
I *give myself unto* prayer.
5 And [a]they have rewarded me evil for
good, and hatred for my love.
6 Set thou a wicked man over him: and let
[a]Satan stand at his right hand.
7 When he shall be judged, let him be condemned: and [a]let his prayer become sin.
8 Let his days be [a]few; *and* [b]let another take
his office.
9 [a]Let his children be fatherless, and his
wife a widow.
10 Let his children be continually vagabonds,
and beg: let them seek *their bread* also out of their
desolate places.
11 [a]Let the extortioner catch all that he hath;
and let the strangers spoil his labour.
12 Let there be none to extend mercy unto
him: neither let there be any to favour his fatherless children.
13 [a]Let his posterity be cut off; *and* in the
generation following let their [b]name be blotted
out.
14 [a]Let the iniquity of his fathers be remembered with the LORD; and let not the sin of his
mother [b]be blotted out.
15 Let them be before the LORD continually,
that he may [a]cut off the memory of them from
the earth.

5 [a]Ps. 57:5, 11
6 [a]Ps. 60:5–12
8 [a][Gen. 49:10]
10 [a]Ps. 60:9
13 [a]Ps. 60:12

PSALM 109

1 [a]Ps. 83:1
2 [a]Ps. 27:12
3 [a]Ps. 35:7; 69:4; John 15:25
5 [a]Ps. 35:7, 12; 38:20; Prov. 17:13
6 [a]Zech. 3:1
7 [a][Prov. 28:9]
8 [a][Ps. 55:23]; John 17:12 [b]Ps. 69:25; Acts 1:20
9 [a]Ex. 22:24
11 [a]Neh. 5:7; Job 5:5; 18:9
13 [a]Job 18:19; Ps. 37:28 [b]Prov. 10:7
14 [a][Ex. 20:5; Num. 14:18]; Is. 65:6; [Jer. 32:18] [b]Neh. 4:5; Jer. 18:23
15 [a]Job 18:17; [Ps. 34:16]

*
109:6 Heb. *satan*
109:10 So with MT, Tg.; LXX, Vg. *be cast out*

NKJV

4 For Your mercy *is* great above the
heavens,
And Your truth *reaches* to the clouds.

5 [a]Be exalted, O God, above the heavens,
And Your glory above all the earth;
6 [a]That Your beloved may be delivered,
Save *with* Your right hand, and hear me.

7 God has spoken in His holiness:
"I will rejoice;
I will divide Shechem
And measure out the Valley of Succoth.
8 Gilead *is* Mine; Manasseh *is* Mine;
Ephraim also *is* the helmet for My head;
[a]Judah *is* My lawgiver.
9 Moab *is* My washpot;
Over Edom I will cast My shoe;
Over Philistia I will triumph."

10 [a]Who will bring me *into* the strong city?
Who will lead me to Edom?
11 *Is it* not *You,* O God, *who* cast us off?
And *You,* O God, *who* did not go out with
our armies?
12 Give us help from trouble,
For the help of man is useless.
13 [a]Through God we will do valiantly,
For *it is* He *who* shall tread down our
enemies.

PSALM 109

Plea for Judgment of False Accusers

To the Chief Musician. A Psalm of David.

DO[a] not keep silent,
O God of my praise!
2 For the mouth of the wicked and the
mouth of the deceitful
Have opened against me;
They have spoken against me with a
[a]lying tongue.
3 They have also surrounded me with words
of hatred,
And fought against me [a]without a cause.
4 In return for my love they are my
accusers,
But I *give myself to* prayer.
5 Thus [a]they have rewarded me evil for
good,
And hatred for my love.

6 Set a wicked man over him,
And let [a]an *accuser stand at his right
hand.
7 When he is judged, let him be found guilty,
And [a]let his prayer become sin.
8 Let his days be [a]few,
And [b]let another take his office.
9 [a]Let his children be fatherless,
And his wife a widow.
10 Let his children continually be vagabonds,
and beg;
Let them *seek *their bread* also from their
desolate places.
11 [a]Let the creditor seize all that he has,
And let strangers plunder his labor.
12 Let there be none to extend mercy to him,
Nor let there be any to favor his fatherless
children.
13 [a]Let his posterity be cut off,
And in the generation following let their
[b]name be blotted out.

14 [a]Let the iniquity of his fathers be
remembered before the LORD,
And let not the sin of his mother [b]be
blotted out.
15 Let them be continually before the LORD,
That He may [a]cut off the memory of them
from the earth;

KJV

16 Because that he remembered not to shew mercy, but persecuted the poor and needy man, that he might even slay the [a]broken in heart.

17 [a]As he loved cursing, so let it come unto him: as he delighted not in blessing, so let it be far from him.

18 As he clothed himself with cursing like as with his garment, so let it [a]come into his bowels like water, and like oil into his bones.

19 Let it be unto him as the garment *which* covereth him, and for a girdle wherewith he is girded continually.

20 *Let* this *be* the reward of mine adversaries from the LORD, and of them that speak evil against my soul.

21 But do thou for me, O GOD the Lord, for thy name's sake: because thy mercy *is* good, deliver thou me.

22 For I *am* poor and needy, and my heart is wounded within me.

23 I am gone [a]like the shadow when it declineth: I am tossed up and down as the locust.

24 My [a]knees are weak through fasting; and my flesh faileth of fatness.

25 I became also [a]a reproach unto them: *when* they looked upon me [b]they shaked their heads.

26 Help me, O LORD my God: O save me according to thy mercy:

27 [a]That they may know that this *is* thy hand; *that* thou, LORD, hast done it.

28 [a]Let them curse, but bless thou: when they arise, let them be ashamed; but let [b]thy servant rejoice.

29 [a]Let mine adversaries be clothed with shame, and let them cover themselves with their own confusion, as with a mantle.

30 I will greatly praise the LORD with my mouth; yea, [a]I will praise him among the multitude.

31 For [a]he shall stand at the right hand of the poor, to save *him* from those that condemn his soul.

16 [a][Ps. 34:18] **17** [a]Prov. 14:14; [Matt. 7:2] **18** [a]Num. 5:22 **23** [a]Ps. 102:11 **24** [a]Heb. 12:12 **25** [a]Ps. 22:7; Jer. 18:16; Lam. 2:15 [b]Matt. 27:39; Mark 15:29 **27** [a]Job 37:7 **28** [a]2 Sam. 6:11, 12 [b]Is. 65:14 **29** [a]Job 8:22; Ps. 35:26 **30** [a]Ps. 35:18; 111:1 **31** [a][Ps. 16:8]

NKJV

16 Because he did not remember to show
mercy,
But persecuted the poor and needy man,
That he might even slay the [a]broken in
heart.
17 [a]As he loved cursing, so let it come to
him;
As he did not delight in blessing, so let it
be far from him.
18 As he clothed himself with cursing as with
his garment,
So let it [a]enter his body like water,
And like oil into his bones.
19 Let it be to him like the garment which
covers him,
And for a belt with which he girds himself
continually.
20 *Let* this *be* the LORD's reward to my
accusers,
And to those who speak evil against my
person.

21 But You, O GOD the Lord,
Deal with me for Your name's sake;
Because Your mercy *is* good, deliver
me.
22 For I *am* poor and needy,
And my heart is wounded within me.
23 I am gone [a]like a shadow when it
lengthens;
I am shaken off like a locust.
24 My [a]knees are weak through fasting,
And my flesh is feeble from lack of
fatness.
25 I also have become [a]a reproach to them;
When they look at me, [b]they shake their
heads.

26 Help me, O LORD my God!
Oh, save me according to Your mercy,
27 [a]That they may know that this *is* Your
hand—
That You, LORD, have done it!
28 [a]Let them curse, but You bless;
When they arise, let them be ashamed,
But let [b]Your servant rejoice.
29 [a]Let my accusers be clothed with shame,
And let them cover themselves with their
own disgrace as with a mantle.

30 I will greatly praise the LORD with my
mouth;
Yes, [a]I will praise Him among the
multitude.
31 For [a]He shall stand at the right hand of
the poor,
To save *him* from those who condemn
him.

PSALM 110

Announcement of the Messiah's Reign
(*Matt. 22:44; Acts 2:34, 35*)

A Psalm of David.

THE [a]LORD said unto my Lord, Sit thou at my right hand, until I make thine enemies thy [b]footstool.

2 The LORD shall send the rod of thy strength [a]out of Zion: [b]rule thou in the midst of thine enemies.

3 [a]Thy people *shall be* willing in the day of thy power, [b]in the beauties of holiness from the womb of the morning: thou hast the dew of thy youth.

4 The LORD hath sworn, and [a]will not repent, Thou *art* a [b]priest for ever after the order of [c]Melchizedek.

PSALM 110

1 [a]Matt. 22:44; Mark 12:36; 16:19; Luke 20:42, 43; Acts 2:34, 35; Col. 3:1; Heb. 1:13 [b][1 Cor. 15:25; Eph. 1:22] **2** [a][Rom. 11:26, 27] [b][Ps. 2:9; Dan. 7:13, 14] **3** [a]Judg. 5:2; Neh. 11:2 [b]1 Chr. 16:29; Ps. 96:9 **4** [a][Num. 23:19] [b][Zech. 6:13] [c][Heb. 5:6, 10; 6:20]

PSALM 110

Announcement of the Messiah's Reign
(*Matt. 22:44; Acts 2:34, 35*)

A Psalm of David.

THE [a]LORD said to my Lord,
"Sit at My right hand,
Till I make Your enemies Your
[b]footstool."
2 The LORD shall send the rod of Your
strength [a]out of Zion.
[b]Rule in the midst of Your enemies!

3 [a]Your people *shall be* volunteers
In the day of Your power;
[b]In the beauties of holiness, from the womb
of the morning,
You have the dew of Your youth.
4 The LORD has sworn
And [a]will not relent,
"You *are* a [b]priest forever
According to the order of [c]Melchizedek."

KJV

5 The Lord [a]at thy right hand shall strike
through kings [b]in the day of his wrath.
6 He shall judge among the heathen, he
shall fill *the places* with the dead bodies; [a]he shall
wound the heads over many countries.
7 He shall drink of the brook in the way:
[a]therefore shall he lift up the head.

5 [a][Ps. 16:8] [b]Ps. 2:5, 12; [Rom. 2:5; Rev. 6:17] 6 [a]Ps. 68:21 7 [a][Is. 53:12]

PSALM 111

Praise to God for His Faithfulness and Justice

PRAISE ye the LORD. [a]I will praise the LORD
with *my* whole heart, in the assembly of the
upright, and *in* the congregation.
2 [a]The works of the LORD *are* great, [b]sought
out of all them that have pleasure therein.
3 His work *is* [a]honourable and glorious: and
his righteousness endureth for ever.
4 He hath made his wonderful works to be
remembered: [a]the LORD *is* gracious and full of
compassion.
5 He hath given meat unto them that fear
him: he will ever be mindful of his covenant.
6 He hath shewed his people the power of
his works, that he may give them the heritage of
the heathen.
7 The works of his hands *are* [a]verity and
judgment; all his commandments *are* sure.
8 [a]They stand fast for ever and ever, *and
are* [b]done in truth and uprightness.
9 [a]He sent redemption unto his people: he
hath commanded his covenant for ever: [b]holy and
reverend *is* his name.
10 [a]The fear of the LORD *is* the beginning of
wisdom: a good understanding have all they that
do *his commandments:* his praise endureth for
ever.

PSALM 111

1 [a]Ps. 35:18 2 [a]Ps. 92:5 [b]Ps. 143:5 3 [a]Ps. 145:4, 5 4 [a][Ps. 86:5] 7 [a][Rev. 15:3] 8 [a]Is. 40:8; Matt. 5:18 [b][Rev. 15:3] 9 [a]Luke 1:68 [b]Luke 1:49 10 [a]Job 28:28; [Prov. 1:7; 9:10]; Eccl. 12:13

PSALM 112

The Blessed State of the Righteous

PRAISE ye the LORD. Blessed *is* the man *that*
feareth the LORD, *that* [a]delighteth greatly in
his commandments.
2 [a]His seed shall be mighty upon earth: the
generation of the upright shall be blessed.
3 [a]Wealth and riches *shall be* in his house:
and his righteousness endureth for ever.
4 [a]Unto the upright there ariseth light in the
darkness: *he is* gracious, and full of compassion,
and righteous.
5 [a]A good man sheweth favour, and lendeth: he will guide his affairs [b]with discretion.
6 Surely he shall not be moved for ever: [a]the
righteous shall be in everlasting remembrance.
7 [a]He shall not be afraid of evil tidings: his
heart is fixed, trusting in the LORD.
8 His [a]heart *is* established, [b]he shall not be
afraid, until he [c]see *his desire* upon his enemies.
9 He hath dispersed, he hath given to the
poor; his righteousness endureth for ever; his
horn shall be exalted with honour.

PSALM 112

1 [a]Ps. 128:1 2 [a][Ps. 102:28] 3 [a]Prov. 3:16; 8:18; [Matt. 6:33] 4 [a]Job 11:17; Ps. 97:11 5 [a]Ps. 37:26; [Luke 6:35] [b][Eph. 5:15; Col. 4:5] 6 [a]Prov. 10:7 7 [a][Prov. 1:33] 8 [a]Heb. 13:9 [b][Ps. 27:1; 56:11]; Prov. 1:33; 3:24; [Is. 12:2] [c]Ps. 59:10

NKJV

5 The Lord *is* [a]at Your right hand;
He shall execute kings [b]in the day of His
wrath.
6 He shall judge among the nations,
He shall fill *the places* with dead bodies,
[a]He shall execute the heads of many
countries.
7 He shall drink of the brook by the
wayside;
[a]Therefore He shall lift up the head.

PSALM 111

Praise to God for His Faithfulness and Justice

PRAISE the LORD!

[a]I will praise the LORD with *my* whole heart,
In the assembly of the upright and *in* the
congregation.

2 [a]The works of the LORD *are* great,
[b]Studied by all who have pleasure in them.
3 His work *is* [a]honorable and glorious,
And His righteousness endures forever.
4 He has made His wonderful works to be
remembered;
[a]The LORD *is* gracious and full of
compassion.
5 He has given food to those who fear Him;
He will ever be mindful of His covenant.
6 He has declared to His people the power
of His works,
In giving them the heritage of the nations.

7 The works of His hands *are* [a]verity and
justice;
All His precepts *are* sure.
8 [a]They stand fast forever and ever,
And are [b]done in truth and uprightness.
9 [a]He has sent redemption to His people;
He has commanded His covenant forever:
[b]Holy and awesome *is* His name.

10 [a]The fear of the LORD *is* the beginning of
wisdom;
A good understanding have all those who
do *His commandments.*
His praise endures forever.

PSALM 112

The Blessed State of the Righteous

PRAISE the LORD!

Blessed *is* the man *who* fears the LORD,
Who [a]delights greatly in His
commandments.

2 [a]His descendants will be mighty on earth;
The generation of the upright will be
blessed.
3 [a]Wealth and riches *will be* in his house,
And his righteousness endures forever.
4 [a]Unto the upright there arises light in the
darkness;
He is gracious, and full of compassion,
and righteous.
5 [a]A good man deals graciously and lends;
He will guide his affairs [b]with discretion.
6 Surely he will never be shaken;
[a]The righteous will be in everlasting
remembrance.
7 [a]He will not be afraid of evil tidings;
His heart is steadfast, trusting in the LORD.
8 His [a]heart *is* established;
[b]He will not be afraid,
Until he [c]sees *his desire* upon his enemies.

9 He has dispersed abroad,
He has given to the poor;
His righteousness endures forever;
His horn will be exalted with honor.

KJV

10 The wicked shall see *it*, and be grieved;
he shall gnash with his teeth, and melt away: the
desire of the wicked shall perish.

PSALM 113

The Majesty and Condescension of God

PRAISE ye the LORD. [a]Praise, O ye servants of
the LORD, praise the name of the LORD.
2 [a]Blessed be the name of the LORD from
this time forth and for evermore.
3 [a]From the rising of the sun unto the going
down of the same the LORD's name *is* to be
praised.
4 The LORD *is* [a]high above all nations, *and*
[b]his glory above the heavens.
5 [a]Who *is* like unto the LORD our God, who
dwelleth on high,
6 [a]Who humbleth *himself* to behold *the*
things that are in heaven, and in the earth!
7 [a]He raiseth up the poor out of the dust,
and lifteth the [b]needy out of the dunghill;
8 That he may [a]set *him* with princes, *even*
with the princes of his people.
9 [a]He maketh the barren woman to keep
house, *and to be* a joyful mother of children.
Praise ye the LORD.

PSALM 114

The Power of God in His Deliverance of Israel
(cf. Ex. 14:1–31)

WHEN [a]Israel went out of Egypt, the house
of Jacob [b]from a people of strange language;
2 [a]Judah was his sanctuary, *and* Israel his
dominion.
3 [a]The sea saw *it*, and fled: [b]Jordan was
driven back.
4 [a]The mountains skipped like rams, *and*
the little hills like lambs.
5 [a]What *ailed* thee, O thou sea, that thou
fleddest? thou Jordan, *that* thou wast driven
back?
6 Ye mountains, *that* ye skipped like rams;
and ye little hills, like lambs?
7 Tremble, thou earth, at the presence of the
Lord, at the presence of the God of Jacob;
8 [a]Which turned the rock *into* a standing
water, the flint into a fountain of waters.

PSALM 115

The Futility of Idols and the Trustworthiness of God

NOT [a]unto us, O LORD, not unto us, but unto
thy name give glory, for thy mercy, *and* for
thy truth's sake.
2 Wherefore should the heathen say,
[a]Where *is* now their God?
3 [a]But our God *is* in the heavens: he hath
done whatsoever he hath pleased.
4 [a]Their idols *are* silver and gold, the work
of men's hands.
5 They have mouths, but they speak not:
eyes have they, but they see not:
6 They have ears, but they hear not: noses
have they, but they smell not:
7 They have hands, but they handle not: feet
have they, but they walk not: neither speak they
through their throat.

PSALM 113
1 [a]Ps. 135:1
2 [a][Dan. 2:20]
3 [a]Is. 59:19; Mal. 1:11
4 [a]Ps. 97:9; 99:2 [b][Ps. 8:1]
5 [a]Ps. 89:6; [Is. 57:15]
6 [a][Ps. 11:4; Is. 57:15]
7 [a]1 Sam. 2:8; Ps. 107:41 [b]Ps. 72:12
8 [a][Job 36:7]
9 [a]1 Sam. 2:5; Is. 54:1

PSALM 114
1 [a]Ex. 12:51; 13:3 [b]Ps. 81:5
2 [a]Ex. 6:7; 19:6; 25:8; 29:45, 46; Deut. 27:9
3 [a]Ex. 14:21; Ps. 77:16 [b]Josh. 3:13–16
4 [a]Ex. 19:18; Judg. 5:5; Ps. 29:6; Hab. 3:6
5 [a]Hab. 3:8
8 [a]Ex. 17:6; Num. 20:11; Ps. 107:35

PSALM 115
1 [a][Is. 48:11]; Ezek. 36:32
2 [a]Ps. 42:3, 10
3 [a][1 Chr. 16:26]
4 [a]Deut. 4:28; 2 Kin. 19:18; Is. 37:19; 44:10, 20; Jer. 10:3

NKJV

10 The wicked will see *it* and be grieved;
He will gnash his teeth and melt away;
The desire of the wicked shall perish.

PSALM 113

The Majesty and Condescension of God

PRAISE the LORD!

[a]Praise, O servants of the LORD,
Praise the name of the LORD!
2 [a]Blessed be the name of the LORD
From this time forth and forevermore!
3 [a]From the rising of the sun to its going
down
The LORD's name *is* to be praised.

4 The LORD *is* [a]high above all nations,
[b]His glory above the heavens.
5 [a]Who *is* like the LORD our God,
Who dwells on high,
6 [a]Who humbles Himself to behold
The things that are in the heavens and
in the earth?

7 [a]He raises the poor out of the dust,
And lifts the [b]needy out of the ash heap,
8 That He may [a]seat *him* with princes—
With the princes of His people.
9 [a]He grants the barren woman a home,
Like a joyful mother of children.

Praise the LORD!

PSALM 114

The Power of God in His Deliverance of Israel
(cf. Ex. 14:1–31)

WHEN [a]Israel went out of Egypt,
The house of Jacob [b]from a people of
strange language,
2 [a]Judah became His sanctuary,
And Israel His dominion.

3 [a]The sea saw *it* and fled;
[b]Jordan turned back.
4 [a]The mountains skipped like rams,
The little hills like lambs.
5 [a]What ails you, O sea, that you fled?
O Jordan, *that* you turned back?
6 O mountains, *that* you skipped like rams?
O little hills, like lambs?

7 Tremble, O earth, at the presence of the
Lord,
At the presence of the God of Jacob,
8 [a]Who turned the rock *into* a pool of water,
The flint into a fountain of waters.

PSALM 115

The Futility of Idols and the Trustworthiness of God

NOT [a]unto us, O LORD, not unto us,
But to Your name give glory,
Because of Your mercy,
Because of Your truth.
2 Why should the Gentiles say,
[a]"So where *is* their God?"

3 [a]But our God *is* in heaven;
He does whatever He pleases.
4 [a]Their idols *are* silver and gold,
The work of men's hands.
5 They have mouths, but they do not
speak;
Eyes they have, but they do not see;
6 They have ears, but they do not hear;
Noses they have, but they do not smell;
7 They have hands, but they do not handle;
Feet they have, but they do not walk;
Nor do they mutter through their throat.

KJV

8 [a]They that make them are like unto them;
so *is* every one that trusteth in them.
9 [a]O Israel, trust thou in the LORD: [b]he *is*
their help and their shield.
10 O house of Aaron, trust in the LORD: he
is their help and their shield.
11 Ye that fear the LORD, trust in the LORD:
he *is* their help and their shield.
12 The LORD hath been mindful of us: he will
bless *us;* he will bless the house of Israel; he will
bless the house of Aaron.
13 [a]He will bless them that fear the LORD,
both small and great.
14 The LORD shall increase you more and
more, you and your children.
15 Ye *are* [a]blessed of the LORD [b]which made
heaven and earth.
16 The heaven, *even* the heavens, *are* the
LORD's: but the earth hath he given to the children
of men.
17 [a]The dead praise not the LORD, neither any
that go down into silence.
18 [a]But we will bless the LORD from this time
forth and for evermore. Praise the LORD.

8 [a]Ps. 135:18; Is. 44:9–11
9 [a]Ps. 118:2, 3 [b]Ps. 33:20
13 [a]Ps. 128:1, 4
15 [a][Gen. 14:19] [b]Gen. 1:1; Acts 14:15; Rev. 14:7
17 [a]Ps. 6:5; 88:10–12; [Is. 38:18]
18 [a]Ps. 113:2; Dan. 2:20

NKJV

8 [a]Those who make them are like them;
So is everyone who trusts in them.

9 [a]O Israel, trust in the LORD;
[b]He *is* their help and their shield.
10 O house of Aaron, trust in the LORD;
He *is* their help and their shield.
11 You who fear the LORD, trust in the LORD;
He *is* their help and their shield.

12 The LORD has been mindful of *us;*
He will bless us;
He will bless the house of Israel;
He will bless the house of Aaron.
13 [a]He will bless those who fear the LORD,
Both small and great.

14 May the LORD give you increase more and more,
You and your children.
15 *May* you *be* [a]blessed by the LORD,
[b]Who made heaven and earth.

16 The heaven, *even* the heavens, *are* the LORD's;
But the earth He has given to the children of men.
17 [a]The dead do not praise the LORD,
Nor any who go down into silence.
18 [a]But we will bless the LORD
From this time forth and forevermore.

Praise the LORD!

PSALM 116

Thanksgiving for Deliverance from Death

I [a]LOVE the LORD, because he hath heard my
voice *and* my supplications.
2 Because he hath inclined his ear unto me,
therefore will I call upon *him* as long as I live.
3 [a]The sorrows of death compassed me, and
the pains of hell gat hold upon me: I found trouble
and sorrow.
4 Then called I upon the name of the LORD;
O LORD, I beseech thee, deliver my soul.
5 [a]Gracious *is* the LORD, and [b]righteous;
yea, our God *is* merciful.
6 The LORD preserveth the simple: I was
brought low, and he helped me.
7 Return unto thy [a]rest, O my soul; for [b]the
LORD hath dealt bountifully with thee.
8 [a]For thou hast delivered my soul from
death, mine eyes from tears, *and* my feet from
falling.
9 I will walk before the LORD [a]in the land
of the living.
10 [a]I believed, therefore have I spoken: I was
greatly afflicted:
11 [a]I said in my haste, [b]All men *are* liars.
12 What shall I render unto the LORD *for* all
his benefits toward me?
13 I will take the cup of salvation, and call
upon the name of the LORD.
14 [a]I will pay my vows unto the LORD now
in the presence of all his people.
15 [a]Precious in the sight of the LORD *is* the
death of his saints.
16 O LORD, truly [a]I *am* thy servant; I *am* thy
servant, *and* [b]the son of thine handmaid: thou
hast loosed my bonds.

PSALM 116

1 [a]Ps. 18:1
3 [a]Ps. 18:4–6
5 [a][Ps. 103:8] [b][Ezra 9:15]; Neh. 9:8; [Ps. 119:137; 145:17; Jer. 12:1; Dan. 9:14]
7 [a][Jer. 6:16; Matt. 11:29] [b]Ps. 13:6
8 [a]Ps. 56:13
9 [a]Ps. 27:13
10 [a]2 Cor. 4:13
11 [a]Ps. 31:22 [b]Rom. 3:4
14 [a]Ps. 116:18
15 [a]Ps. 72:14; [Rev. 14:13]
16 [a]Ps. 119:125; 143:12 [b]Ps. 86:16

PSALM 116

Thanksgiving for Deliverance from Death

I [a]LOVE the LORD, because He has heard
My voice *and* my supplications.
2 Because He has inclined His ear to me,
Therefore I will call *upon Him* as long as I live.

3 [a]The pains of death surrounded me,
And the pangs of Sheol laid hold of me;
I found trouble and sorrow.
4 Then I called upon the name of the LORD:
"O LORD, I implore You, deliver my soul!"

5 [a]Gracious *is* the LORD, and [b]righteous;
Yes, our God *is* merciful.
6 The LORD preserves the simple;
I was brought low, and He saved me.
7 Return to your [a]rest, O my soul,
For [b]the LORD has dealt bountifully with you.

8 [a]For You have delivered my soul from death,
My eyes from tears,
And my feet from falling.
9 I will walk before the LORD
[a]In the land of the living.
10 [a]I believed, therefore I spoke,
"I am greatly afflicted."
11 [a]I said in my haste,
[b]"All men *are* liars."

12 What shall I render to the LORD
For all His benefits toward me?
13 I will take up the cup of salvation,
And call upon the name of the LORD.
14 [a]I will pay my vows to the LORD
Now in the presence of all His people.

15 [a]Precious in the sight of the LORD
Is the death of His saints.

16 O LORD, truly [a]I *am* Your servant;
I *am* Your servant, [b]the son of Your maidservant;
You have loosed my bonds.

KJV

17 I will offer to thee [a]the sacrifice of thanksgiving, and will call upon the name of the LORD.
18 I will pay my vows unto the LORD now in the presence of all his people,
19 In the [a]courts of the LORD's house, in the midst of thee, O Jerusalem. Praise ye the LORD.

PSALM 117

Let All Peoples Praise the LORD

O [a]PRAISE the LORD, all ye nations: praise him, all ye people.
2 For his merciful kindness is great toward us: and [a]the truth of the LORD *endureth* for ever. Praise ye the LORD.

PSALM 118

Praise to God for His Everlasting Mercy

O [a]GIVE thanks unto the LORD; for *he is* good: [b]because his mercy *endureth* for ever.
2 [a]Let Israel now say, that his mercy *endureth* for ever.
3 Let the house of Aaron now say, that his mercy *endureth* for ever.
4 Let them now that fear the LORD say, that his mercy *endureth* for ever.
5 [a]I called upon the LORD in distress: the LORD answered me, *and* [b]*set me* in a large place.
6 [a]The LORD *is* on my side; I will not fear: what can man do unto me?
7 [a]The LORD taketh my part with them that help me: therefore shall [b]I see *my desire* upon them that hate me.
8 [a]*It is* better to trust in the LORD than to put confidence in man.
9 [a]*It is* better to trust in the LORD than to put confidence in princes.
10 All nations compassed me about: but in the name of the LORD will I destroy them.
11 They [a]compassed me about; yea, they compassed me about: but in the name of the LORD I will destroy them.
12 They compassed me about [a]like bees; they are quenched [b]as the fire of thorns: for in the name of the LORD I will destroy them.
13 Thou hast thrust sore at me that I might fall: but the LORD helped me.
14 [a]The LORD *is* my strength and song, and is become my salvation.
15 The voice of rejoicing and salvation *is* in the tabernacles of the righteous: the right hand of the LORD doeth valiantly.
16 [a]The right hand of the LORD is exalted: the right hand of the LORD doeth valiantly.
17 [a]I shall not die, but live, and [b]declare the works of the LORD.
18 The LORD hath [a]chastened me sore: but he hath not given me over unto death.
19 [a]Open to me the gates of righteousness: I will go into them, *and* I will praise the LORD:
20 [a]This gate of the LORD, [b]into which the righteous shall enter.

17 [a]Lev. 7:12; Ps. 50:14; 107:22
19 [a]Ps. 96:8

PSALM 117

1 [a]Rom. 15:11
2 [a][Ps. 100:5]

PSALM 118

1 [a]1 Chr. 16:8, 34; Jer. 33:11 [b]2 Chr. 5:13; 7:3; Ezra 3:11; [Ps. 136:1–26]
2 [a][Ps. 115:9]
5 [a]Ps. 120:1 [b]Ps. 18:19
6 [a]Ps. 27:1; 56:9; [Rom. 8:31; Heb. 13:6]
7 [a]Ps. 54:4 [b]Ps. 59:10
8 [a]2 Chr. 32:7, 8; Ps. 40:4; Is. 31:1, 3; 57:13; Jer. 17:5
9 [a]Ps. 146:3
11 [a]Ps. 88:17
12 [a]Deut. 1:44 [b]Eccl. 7:6; Nah. 1:10
14 [a]Ex. 15:2; Is. 12:2
16 [a]Ex. 15:6
17 [a][Ps. 6:5]; Hab. 1:12 [b]Ps. 73:28
18 [a]Ps. 73:14; Jer. 31:18; [1 Cor. 11:32]; 2 Cor. 6:9
19 [a]Is. 26:2
20 [a]Ps. 24:7 [b]Is. 35:8; [Rev. 21:27; 22:14, 15]

NKJV

17 I will offer to You [a]the sacrifice of
thanksgiving,
And will call upon the name of the LORD.

18 I will pay my vows to the LORD
Now in the presence of all His people,
19 In the [a]courts of the LORD's house,
In the midst of you, O Jerusalem.

Praise the LORD!

PSALM 117

Let All Peoples Praise the LORD

PRAISE, [a]the LORD, all you Gentiles!
Laud Him, all you peoples!
2 For His merciful kindness is great toward
us,
And [a]the truth of the LORD *endures*
forever.

Praise the LORD!

PSALM 118

Praise to God for His Everlasting Mercy

OH, [a]give thanks to the LORD, for *He is* good!
[b]For His mercy *endures* forever.

2 [a]Let Israel now say,
"His mercy *endures* forever."
3 Let the house of Aaron now say,
"His mercy *endures* forever."
4 Let those who fear the LORD now say,
"His mercy *endures* forever."

5 [a]I called on the LORD in distress;
The LORD answered me *and* [b]*set me* in a
broad place.
6 [a]The LORD *is* on my side;
I will not fear.
What can man do to me?
7 [a]The LORD is for me among those who help
me;
Therefore [b]I shall see *my desire* on those
who hate me.
8 [a]*It is* better to trust in the LORD
Than to put confidence in man.
9 [a]*It is* better to trust in the LORD
Than to put confidence in princes.

10 All nations surrounded me,
But in the name of the LORD I will destroy
them.
11 They [a]surrounded me,
Yes, they surrounded me;
But in the name of the LORD I will destroy
them.
12 They surrounded me [a]like bees;
They were quenched [b]like a fire of thorns;
For in the name of the LORD I will destroy
them.
13 You pushed me violently, that I might fall,
But the LORD helped me.
14 [a]The LORD *is* my strength and song,
And He has become my salvation.

15 The voice of rejoicing and salvation
Is in the tents of the righteous;
The right hand of the LORD does valiantly.
16 [a]The right hand of the LORD is exalted;
The right hand of the LORD does valiantly.
17 [a]I shall not die, but live,
And [b]declare the works of the LORD.
18 The LORD has [a]chastened me severely,
But He has not given me over to death.

19 [a]Open to me the gates of righteousness;
I will go through them,
And I will praise the LORD.
20 [a]This is the gate of the LORD,
[b]Through which the righteous shall enter.

KJV

21 I will praise thee: for thou hast [a]heard me,
and art become my salvation.
22 [a]The stone *which* the builders refused is
become the head *stone* of the corner.
23 This is the LORD's doing; it *is* marvellous
in our eyes.
24 This *is* the day *which* the LORD hath made;
we will rejoice and be glad in it.
25 Save now, I beseech thee, O LORD: O LORD,
I beseech thee, send now prosperity.
26 [a]Blessed *be* he that cometh in the name
of the LORD: we have blessed you out of the house
of the LORD.
27 God *is* the LORD, which hath shewed us
[a]light: bind the sacrifice with cords, *even* unto the
horns of the altar.
28 Thou *art* my God, and I will praise thee:
[a]*thou art* my God, I will exalt thee.
29 O give thanks unto the LORD; for *he is*
good: for his mercy *endureth* for ever.

PSALM 119

Meditations on the Excellencies of the Word of God

ℵ ALEPH

1 BLESSED *are* the undefiled in the way, [a]who
walk in the law of the LORD.
2 Blessed *are* they that keep his testimonies,
and that seek him with the [a]whole heart.
3 [a]They also do no iniquity: they walk in
his ways.
4 Thou hast commanded *us* to keep thy precepts diligently.
5 O that my ways were directed to keep thy
statutes!
6 [a]Then shall I not be ashamed, when I have
respect unto all thy commandments.
7 I will praise thee with uprightness of
heart, when I shall have learned thy righteous
judgments.
8 I will keep thy statutes: O forsake me not
utterly.

ב BETH

9 Wherewithal shall a young man cleanse
his way? by taking heed *thereto* according to thy
word.
10 With my whole heart have I [a]sought thee:
O let me not wander from thy commandments.
11 [a]Thy word have I hid in mine heart, that
I might not sin against thee.
12 Blessed *art* thou, O LORD: teach me thy
statutes.
13 With my lips have I [a]declared all the judgments of thy mouth.
14 I have rejoiced in the way of thy testimonies, as *much as* in all riches.
15 I will meditate in thy precepts, and have
respect unto thy ways.
16 I will [a]delight myself in thy statutes: I will
not forget thy word.

ג GIMEL

17 [a]Deal bountifully with thy servant, *that* I
may live, and keep thy word.
18 Open thou mine eyes, that I may behold
wondrous things out of thy law.
19 [a]I *am* a stranger in the earth: hide not thy
commandments from me.
20 [a]My soul breaketh for the longing *that it*
hath unto thy judgments at all times.

21 [a]Ps. 116:1
22 [a]Matt. 21:42; Mark 12:10, 11; Luke 20:17; Acts 4:11; [Eph. 2:20; 1 Pet. 2:7, 8]
26 [a]Matt. 21:9; 23:39; Mark 11:9; Luke 13:35; 19:38
27 [a]Esth. 8:16; [1 Pet. 2:9]
28 [a]Ex. 15:2; Is. 25:1

PSALM 119

1 [a]Ps. 128:1; [Ezek. 11:20; 18:17]; Mic. 4:2
2 [a]Deut. 6:5; 10:12; 11:13; 13:3
3 [a][1 John 3:9; 5:18]
6 [a]Job 22:26
10 [a]2 Chr. 15:15
11 [a]Ps. 37:31; Luke 2:19
13 [a]Ps. 34:11
16 [a]Ps. 1:2
17 [a]Ps. 116:7
19 [a]Gen. 47:9; Lev. 25:23; 1 Chr. 29:15; Ps. 39:12; Heb. 11:13
20 [a]Ps. 42:1, 2; 63:1; 84:2

NKJV

21 I will praise You,
For You have [a]answered me,
And have become my salvation.

22 [a]The stone *which* the builders rejected
Has become the chief cornerstone.
23 This was the LORD's doing;
It *is* marvelous in our eyes.
24 This *is* the day the LORD has made;
We will rejoice and be glad in it.

25 Save now, I pray, O LORD;
O LORD, I pray, send now prosperity.
26 [a]Blessed *is* he who comes in the name of
the LORD!
We have blessed you from the house of
the LORD.
27 God *is* the LORD,
And He has given us [a]light;
Bind the sacrifice with cords to the horns
of the altar.
28 You *are* my God, and I will praise You;
[a]*You are* my God, I will exalt You.

29 Oh, give thanks to the LORD, for *He is*
good!
For His mercy *endures* forever.

PSALM 119

Meditations on the Excellencies of the Word of God

ℵ ALEPH

1 BLESSED *are* the undefiled in the way,
[a]Who walk in the law of the LORD!
2 Blessed *are* those who keep His
testimonies,
Who seek Him with the [a]whole heart!
3 [a]They also do no iniquity;
They walk in His ways.
4 You have commanded *us*
To keep Your precepts diligently.
5 Oh, that my ways were directed
To keep Your statutes!
6 [a]Then I would not be ashamed,
When I look into all Your commandments.
7 I will praise You with uprightness of
heart,
When I learn Your righteous judgments.
8 I will keep Your statutes;
Oh, do not forsake me utterly!

ב BETH

9 How can a young man cleanse his way?
By taking heed according to Your word.
10 With my whole heart I have [a]sought You;
Oh, let me not wander from Your
commandments!
11 [a]Your word I have hidden in my heart,
That I might not sin against You.
12 Blessed *are* You, O LORD!
Teach me Your statutes.
13 With my lips I have [a]declared
All the judgments of Your mouth.
14 I have rejoiced in the way of Your
testimonies,
As *much as* in all riches.
15 I will meditate on Your precepts,
And contemplate Your ways.
16 I will [a]delight myself in Your statutes;
I will not forget Your word.

ג GIMEL

17 [a]Deal bountifully with Your servant,
That I may live and keep Your word.
18 Open my eyes, that I may see
Wondrous things from Your law.
19 [a]I *am* a stranger in the earth;
Do not hide Your commandments from
me.
20 [a]My soul breaks with longing
For Your judgments at all times.

KJV

21 Thou hast rebuked the proud *that are*
cursed, which do err from thy commandments.
22 [a]Remove from me reproach and contempt; for I have kept thy testimonies.
23 Princes also did sit *and* speak against me:
but thy servant did meditate in thy statutes.
24 Thy testimonies also *are* my delight *and*
my counsellors.

ד DALETH

25 [a]My soul cleaveth unto the dust: [b]quicken
thou me according to thy word.
26 I have declared my ways, and thou heardest me: [a]teach me thy statutes.
27 Make me to understand the way of thy
precepts: so [a]shall I talk of thy wondrous works.
28 [a]My soul melteth for heaviness:
strengthen thou me according unto thy word.
29 Remove from me the way of lying: and
grant me thy law graciously.
30 I have chosen the way of truth: thy judgments have I laid *before me.*
31 I have stuck unto thy testimonies: O LORD,
put me not to shame.
32 I will run the way of thy commandments,
when thou shalt [a]enlarge my heart.

ה HE

33 [a]Teach me, O LORD, the way of thy statutes; and I shall keep it *unto* the end.
34 [a]Give me understanding, and I shall keep
thy law; yea, I shall observe it with *my* whole
heart.
35 Make me to go in the path of thy commandments; for therein do I delight.
36 Incline my heart unto thy testimonies, and
not to [a]covetousness.
37 [a]Turn away mine eyes from [b]beholding
vanity; *and* quicken thou me in thy way.
38 [a]Stablish thy word unto thy servant, who
is devoted to thy fear.
39 Turn away my reproach which I fear: for
thy judgments *are* good.
40 Behold, I have longed after thy precepts:
quicken me in thy righteousness.

ו VAU

41 Let thy mercies come also unto me, O
LORD, *even* thy salvation, according to thy word.
42 So shall I have wherewith to answer him
that reproacheth me: for I trust in thy word.
43 And take not the word of truth utterly out
of my mouth; for I have hoped in thy judgments.
44 So shall I keep thy law continually for
ever and ever.
45 And I will walk at [a]liberty: for I seek thy
precepts.
46 [a]I will speak of thy testimonies also before
kings, and will not be ashamed.
47 And I will delight myself in thy commandments, which I have loved.
48 My hands also will I lift up unto thy commandments, which I have loved; and I will meditate in thy statutes.

ז ZAIN

49 Remember the word unto thy servant,
upon which thou hast caused me to hope.

22 [a]Ps. 39:8
25 [a]Ps. 44:25
[b]Ps. 143:11
26 [a]Ps. 25:4; 27:11; 86:11
27 [a]Ps. 145:5, 6
28 [a]Ps. 107:26
32 [a]1 Kin. 4:29; Is. 60:5; 2 Cor. 6:11, 13
33 [a][Matt. 10:22; Rev. 2:26]
34 [a][Prov. 2:6; James 1:5]
36 [a]Ezek. 33:31; [Mark 7:20–23]; Luke 12:15; [Heb. 13:5]
37 [a]Is. 33:15
[b]Prov. 23:5
38 [a]2 Sam. 7:25
45 [a]Prov. 4:12
46 [a]Ps. 138:1; Matt. 10:18; Acts 26

NKJV

21 You rebuke the proud—the cursed,
Who stray from Your commandments.
22 [a]Remove from me reproach and contempt,
For I have kept Your testimonies.
23 Princes also sit *and* speak against me,
But Your servant meditates on Your statutes.
24 Your testimonies also *are* my delight
And my counselors.

ד DALETH

25 [a]My soul clings to the dust;
[b]Revive me according to Your word.
26 I have declared my ways, and You answered me;
[a]Teach me Your statutes.
27 Make me understand the way of Your precepts;
So [a]shall I meditate on Your wonderful works.
28 [a]My soul melts from heaviness;
Strengthen me according to Your word.
29 Remove from me the way of lying,
And grant me Your law graciously.
30 I have chosen the way of truth;
Your judgments I have laid *before me.*
31 I cling to Your testimonies;
O LORD, do not put me to shame!
32 I will run the course of Your commandments,
For You shall [a]enlarge my heart.

ה HE

33 [a]Teach me, O LORD, the way of Your statutes,
And I shall keep it *to* the end.
34 [a]Give me understanding, and I shall keep Your law;
Indeed, I shall observe it with *my* whole heart.
35 Make me walk in the path of Your commandments,
For I delight in it.
36 Incline my heart to Your testimonies,
And not to [a]covetousness.
37 [a]Turn away my eyes from [b]looking at worthless things,
And revive me in *Your way.
38 [a]Establish Your word to Your servant,
Who *is devoted* to fearing You.
39 Turn away my reproach which I dread,
For Your judgments *are* good.
40 Behold, I long for Your precepts;
Revive me in Your righteousness.

ו WAW

41 Let Your mercies come also to me,
O LORD—
Your salvation according to Your word.
42 So shall I have an answer for him who reproaches me,
For I trust in Your word.
43 And take not the word of truth utterly out of my mouth,
For I have hoped in Your ordinances.
44 So shall I keep Your law continually,
Forever and ever.
45 And I will walk at [a]liberty,
For I seek Your precepts.
46 [a]I will speak of Your testimonies also before kings,
And will not be ashamed.
47 And I will delight myself in Your commandments,
Which I love.
48 My hands also I will lift up to Your commandments,
Which I love,
And I will meditate on Your statutes.

ז ZAIN

49 Remember the word to Your servant,
Upon which You have caused me to hope.

*————

119:37 So with MT, LXX, Vg.; Tg. *Your words*

KJV

50 This *is* my [a]comfort in my affliction: for
thy word hath quickened me.
51 The proud have had me greatly in derision: *yet* have I not declined from thy law.
52 I remembered thy judgments of old, O
LORD; and have comforted myself.
53 [a]Horror hath taken hold upon me because
of the wicked that forsake thy law.
54 Thy statutes have been my songs in the
house of my pilgrimage.
55 [a]I have remembered thy name, O LORD,
in the night, and have kept thy law.
56 This I had, because I kept thy precepts.

ח CHETH
57 [a]*Thou art* my portion, O LORD: I have said
that I would keep thy words.
58 I entreated thy favour with *my* whole
heart: be merciful unto me according to thy word.
59 I [a]thought on my ways, and turned my
feet unto thy testimonies.
60 I made haste, and delayed not to keep thy
commandments.
61 The bands of the wicked have robbed me:
but I have not forgotten thy law.
62 [a]At midnight I will rise to give thanks unto
thee because of thy righteous judgments.
63 I *am* a companion of all *them* that fear
thee, and of them that keep thy precepts.
64 [a]The earth, O LORD, is full of thy mercy:
teach me thy statutes.

ט TETH
65 Thou hast dealt well with thy servant, O
LORD, according unto thy word.
66 Teach me good judgment and [a]knowl-
edge: for I have believed thy commandments.
67 Before I was [a]afflicted I went astray: but
now have I kept thy word.
68 Thou *art* [a]good, and doest good; teach me
thy statutes.
69 The proud have [a]forged a lie against me:
but I will keep thy precepts with *my* whole heart.
70 [a]Their heart is as fat as grease; *but* I delight in thy law.
71 *It is* good for me that I have been afflicted;
that I might learn thy statutes.
72 [a]The law of thy mouth *is* better unto me
than thousands of gold and silver.

י JOD
73 [a]Thy hands have made me and fashioned
me: give me understanding, that I may learn thy
commandments.
74 [a]They that fear thee will be glad when
they see me; because I have hoped in thy word.
75 I know, O LORD, [a]that thy judgments *are*
right, and *that* thou in faithfulness hast afflicted
me.
76 Let, I pray thee, thy merciful kindness be
for my comfort, according to thy word unto thy
servant.
77 Let thy tender mercies come unto me, that
I may live: for thy law *is* my delight.
78 Let the proud [a]be ashamed; for they dealt
perversely with me without a cause: *but* I will
meditate in thy precepts.
79 Let those that fear thee turn unto me, and
those that have known thy testimonies.

50 [a]Job 6:10; [Rom. 15:4]
53 [a]Ex. 32:19; Ezra 9:3; Neh. 13:25
55 [a]Ps. 63:6
57 [a]Num. 18:20; Ps. 16:5; Jer. 10:16; Lam. 3:24
59 [a]Mark 14:72; Luke 15:17
62 [a]Acts 16:25
64 [a]Ps. 33:5
66 [a]Phil. 1:9
67 [a]Prov. 3:11; Jer. 31:18, 19; [Heb. 12:5–11]
68 [a]Ps. 106:1; 107:1; [Matt. 19:17]
69 [a]Job 13:4; Ps. 109:2
70 [a]Deut. 32:15; Job 15:27; Ps. 17:10; Is. 6:10; Jer. 5:28; Acts 28:27
72 [a]Ps. 19:10; Prov. 8:10, 11, 19
73 [a]Job 10:8; 31:15; [Ps. 139:15, 16]
74 [a]Ps. 34:2
75 [a][Heb. 12:10]
78 [a]Ps. 25:3

NKJV

50 This *is* my [a]comfort in my affliction,
For Your word has given me life.
51 The proud have me in great derision,
Yet I do not turn aside from Your law.
52 I remembered Your judgments of old,
O LORD,
And have comforted myself.
53 [a]Indignation has taken hold of me
Because of the wicked, who forsake Your
law.
54 Your statutes have been my songs
In the house of my pilgrimage.
55 [a]I remember Your name in the night,
O LORD,
And I keep Your law.
56 This has become mine,
Because I kept Your precepts.

ח HETH
57 [a]*You are* my portion, O LORD;
I have said that I would keep Your words.
58 I entreated Your favor with *my* whole
heart;
Be merciful to me according to Your word.
59 I [a]thought about my ways,
And turned my feet to Your testimonies.
60 I made haste, and did not delay
To keep Your commandments.
61 The cords of the wicked have bound me,
But I have not forgotten Your law.
62 [a]At midnight I will rise to give thanks to
You,
Because of Your righteous judgments.
63 I *am* a companion of all who fear You,
And of those who keep Your precepts.
64 [a]The earth, O LORD, is full of Your mercy;
Teach me Your statutes.

ט TETH
65 You have dealt well with Your servant,
O LORD, according to Your word.
66 Teach me good judgment and
[a]knowledge,
For I believe Your commandments.
67 Before I was [a]afflicted I went astray,
But now I keep Your word.
68 You *are* [a]good, and do good;
Teach me Your statutes.
69 The proud have [a]forged a lie against me,
But I will keep Your precepts with *my*
whole heart.
70 [a]Their heart is as fat as grease,
But I delight in Your law.
71 *It is* good for me that I have been afflicted,
That I may learn Your statutes.
72 [a]The law of Your mouth *is* better to me
Than thousands of *coins of* gold and
silver.

י YOD
73 [a]Your hands have made me and fashioned
me;
Give me understanding, that I may learn
Your commandments.
74 [a]Those who fear You will be glad when
they see me,
Because I have hoped in Your word.
75 I know, O LORD, [a]that Your judgments *are*
right,
And *that* in faithfulness You have
afflicted me.
76 Let, I pray, Your merciful kindness be for
my comfort,
According to Your word to Your servant.
77 Let Your tender mercies come to me, that
I may live;
For Your law *is* my delight.
78 Let the proud [a]be ashamed,
For they treated me wrongfully with
falsehood;
But I will meditate on Your precepts.
79 Let those who fear You turn to me,
Those who know Your testimonies.

KJV

80 Let my heart be sound in thy statutes; that
I be not ashamed.

כ CAPH

81 [a]My soul fainteth for thy salvation: *but* I
hope in thy word.
82 Mine eyes fail for thy word, saying, When
wilt thou comfort me?
83 For [a]I am become like a bottle in the
smoke; *yet* do I not forget thy statutes.
84 [a]How many *are* the days of thy servant?
[b]when wilt thou execute judgment on them that
persecute me?
85 [a]The proud have digged pits for me, which
are not after thy law.
86 All thy commandments *are* faithful: they
persecute me [a]wrongfully; help thou me.
87 They had almost consumed me upon
earth; but I forsook not thy precepts.
88 Quicken me after thy lovingkindness; so
shall I keep the testimony of thy mouth.

ל LAMED

89 [a]For ever, O LORD, thy word is settled in
heaven.
90 Thy faithfulness *is* unto all generations:
thou hast established the earth, and it abideth.
91 They continue this day according to [a]thine
ordinances: for all *are* thy servants.
92 Unless thy law *had been* my delights, I
should then have perished in mine affliction.
93 I will never forget thy precepts: for with
them thou hast quickened me.
94 I *am* thine, save me; for I have sought thy
precepts.
95 The wicked have waited for me to destroy
me: *but* I will consider thy testimonies.
96 [a]I have seen an end of all perfection: *but*
thy commandment *is* exceeding broad.

מ MEM

97 O how love I thy law! [a]it *is* my meditation
all the day.
98 Thou through thy commandments hast
made me [a]wiser than mine enemies: for they *are*
ever with me.
99 I have more understanding than all my
teachers: [a]for thy testimonies *are* my meditation.
100 [a]I understand more than the ancients, because I keep thy precepts.
101 I have refrained my feet from every evil
way, that I might keep thy word.
102 I have not departed from thy judgments:
for thou hast taught me.
103 [a]How sweet are thy words unto my taste!
yea, sweeter than honey to my mouth.
104 Through thy precepts I get understanding:
therefore I hate every false way.

נ NUN

105 [a]Thy word *is* a lamp unto my feet, and a
light unto my path.
106 [a]I have sworn, and I will perform *it*, that
I will keep thy righteous judgments.
107 I am afflicted very much: quicken me, O
LORD, according unto thy word.

81 [a]Ps. 73:26; 84:2
83 [a]Job 30:30
84 [a]Ps. 39:4 [b]Rev. 6:10
85 [a]Ps. 35:7; Prov. 16:27; Jer. 18:22
86 [a]Ps. 35:19
89 [a]Ps. 89:2; Is. 40:8; Matt. 24:35; [1 Pet. 1:25]
91 [a]Jer. 33:25
96 [a]Matt. 5:18
97 [a]Ps. 1:2
98 [a]Deut. 4:6
99 [a][2 Tim. 3:15]
100 [a][Job 32:7–9]
103 [a]Ps. 19:10; Prov. 8:11
105 [a]Prov. 6:23
106 [a]Neh. 10:29

NKJV

80 Let my heart be blameless regarding Your
statutes,
That I may not be ashamed.

כ KAPH

81 [a]My soul faints for Your salvation,
But I hope in Your word.
82 My eyes fail *from searching* Your
word,
Saying, "When will You comfort me?"
83 For [a]I have become like a wineskin in
smoke,
Yet I do not forget Your statutes.
84 [a]How many *are* the days of Your servant?
[b]When will You execute judgment on those
who persecute me?
85 [a]The proud have dug pits for me,
Which *is* not according to Your law.
86 All Your commandments *are* faithful;
They persecute me [a]wrongfully;
Help me!
87 They almost made an end of me on earth,
But I did not forsake Your precepts.
88 Revive me according to Your
lovingkindness,
So that I may keep the testimony of Your
mouth.

ל LAMED

89 [a]Forever, O LORD,
Your word is settled in heaven.
90 Your faithfulness *endures* to all
generations;
You established the earth, and it abides.
91 They continue this day according to [a]Your
ordinances,
For all *are* Your servants.
92 Unless Your law *had been* my delight,
I would then have perished in my
affliction.
93 I will never forget Your precepts,
For by them You have given me life.
94 I *am* Yours, save me;
For I have sought Your precepts.
95 The wicked wait for me to destroy me,
But I will consider Your testimonies.
96 [a]I have seen the consummation of all
perfection,
But Your commandment *is* exceedingly
broad.

מ MEM

97 Oh, how I love Your law!
[a]It *is* my meditation all the day.
98 You, through Your commandments, make
me [a]wiser than my enemies;
For they *are* ever with me.
99 I have more understanding than all my
teachers,
[a]For Your testimonies *are* my meditation.
100 [a]I understand more than the ancients,
Because I keep Your precepts.
101 I have restrained my feet from every evil
way,
That I may keep Your word.
102 I have not departed from Your judgments,
For You Yourself have taught me.
103 [a]How sweet are Your words to my taste,
Sweeter than honey to my mouth!
104 Through Your precepts I get
understanding;
Therefore I hate every false way.

נ NUN

105 [a]Your word *is* a lamp to my feet
And a light to my path.
106 [a]I have sworn and confirmed
That I will keep Your righteous
judgments.
107 I am afflicted very much;
Revive me, O LORD, according to Your
word.

KJV

108 Accept, I beseech thee, [a]the freewill offerings of my mouth, O LORD, and teach me thy
judgments.
109 [a]My soul *is* continually in my hand: yet
do I not forget thy law.
110 [a]The wicked have laid a snare for me: yet
I erred not from thy precepts.
111 [a]Thy testimonies have I taken as an heritage for ever: for they *are* the rejoicing of my
heart.
112 I have inclined mine heart to perform thy
statutes alway, *even unto* the end.

ס SAMECH
113 I hate *vain* thoughts: but thy law do I love.
114 [a]Thou *art* my hiding place and my shield:
I hope in thy word.
115 [a]Depart from me, ye evildoers: for I will
keep the commandments of my God.
116 Uphold me according unto thy word, that
I may live: and let me not [a]be ashamed of my
hope.
117 Hold thou me up, and I shall be safe: and
I will have respect unto thy statutes continually.
118 Thou hast trodden down all them that err
from thy statutes: for their deceit *is* falsehood.
119 Thou puttest away all the wicked of the
earth [a]*like* dross: therefore I love thy testimonies.
120 [a]My flesh trembleth for fear of thee; and
I am afraid of thy judgments.

ע AIN
121 I have done judgment and justice: leave
me not to mine oppressors.
122 Be [a]surety for thy servant for good: let
not the proud oppress me.
123 Mine eyes fail for thy salvation, and for
the word of thy righteousness.
124 Deal with thy servant according unto thy
mercy, and teach me thy statutes.
125 [a]I *am* thy servant; give me understanding,
that I may know thy testimonies.
126 *It is* time for *thee*, LORD, to work: *for* they
have made void thy law.
127 [a]Therefore I love thy commandments
above gold; yea, above fine gold.
128 Therefore I esteem all *thy* precepts *concerning* all *things to be* right; *and* I hate every
false way.

פ PE
129 Thy testimonies *are* wonderful: therefore
doth my soul keep them.
130 The entrance of thy words giveth light; [a]it
giveth understanding unto the [b]simple.
131 I opened my mouth, and [a]panted: for I
longed for thy commandments.
132 [a]Look thou upon me, and be merciful unto
me, [b]as thou usest to do unto those that love thy
name.
133 [a]Order my steps in thy word: and [b]let not
any iniquity have dominion over me.
134 [a]Deliver me from the oppression of man:
so will I keep thy precepts.
135 [a]Make thy face to shine upon thy servant;
and teach me thy statutes.
136 [a]Rivers of waters run down mine eyes, because they keep not thy law.

צ TZADDI
137 [a]Righteous *art* thou, O LORD, and upright
are thy judgments.

108 [a]Hos. 14:2; Heb. 13:15
109 [a]Judg. 12:3; Job 13:14
110 [a]Ps. 140:5
111 [a]Deut. 33:4
114 [a][Ps. 32:7]
115 [a]Ps. 6:8; Matt. 7:23
116 [a]Ps. 25:2; [Rom. 5:5; 9:33; 10:11; Phil. 1:20]
119 [a]Is. 1:22, 25; Ezek. 22:18, 19
120 [a]Job 4:14; Hab. 3:16
122 [a]Job 17:3; Heb. 7:22
125 [a]Ps. 116:16
127 [a]Ps. 19:10
130 [a]Prov. 6:23 [b][Ps. 19:7]; Prov. 1:4
131 [a]Ps. 42:1
132 [a]Ps. 106:4 [b]Ps. 51:1; [2 Thess. 1:6]
133 [a]Ps. 17:5 [b][Ps. 19:13; Rom. 6:12]
134 [a]Luke 1:74
135 [a]Num. 6:25; Ps. 4:6
136 [a]Jer. 9:1, 18; 14:17; Lam. 3:48; Ezek. 9:4
137 [a]Ezra 9:15; Neh. 9:33; Jer. 12:1; Lam. 1:18; Dan. 9:7, 14

NKJV

108 Accept, I pray, [a]the freewill offerings of
my mouth, O LORD,
And teach me Your judgments.
109 [a]My life *is* continually in my hand,
Yet I do not forget Your law.
110 [a]The wicked have laid a snare for me,
Yet I have not strayed from Your precepts.
111 [a]Your testimonies I have taken as a
heritage forever,
For they *are* the rejoicing of my heart.
112 I have inclined my heart to perform Your
statutes
Forever, to the very end.

ס SAMEK
113 I hate the double-minded,
But I love Your law.
114 [a]You *are* my hiding place and my shield;
I hope in Your word.
115 [a]Depart from me, you evildoers,
For I will keep the commandments of my
God!
116 Uphold me according to Your word, that
I may live;
And do not let me [a]be ashamed of my
hope.
117 Hold me up, and I shall be safe,
And I shall observe Your statutes
continually.
118 You reject all those who stray from Your
statutes,
For their deceit *is* falsehood.
119 You put away all the wicked of the earth
[a]*like* dross;
Therefore I love Your testimonies.
120 [a]My flesh trembles for fear of You,
And I am afraid of Your judgments.

ע AYIN
121 I have done justice and righteousness;
Do not leave me to my oppressors.
122 Be [a]surety for Your servant for good;
Do not let the proud oppress me.
123 My eyes fail *from seeking* Your salvation
And Your righteous word.
124 Deal with Your servant according to Your
mercy,
And teach me Your statutes.
125 [a]I *am* Your servant;
Give me understanding,
That I may know Your testimonies.
126 *It is* time for *You* to act, O LORD,
For they have regarded Your law as void.
127 [a]Therefore I love Your commandments
More than gold, yes, than fine gold!
128 Therefore all *Your* precepts *concerning* all
things
I consider *to be* right;
I hate every false way.

פ PE
129 Your testimonies are wonderful;
Therefore my soul keeps them.
130 The entrance of Your words gives light;
[a]It gives understanding to the [b]simple.
131 I opened my mouth and [a]panted,
For I longed for Your commandments.
132 [a]Look upon me and be merciful to me,
[b]As Your custom *is* toward those who
love Your name.
133 [a]Direct my steps by Your word,
And [b]let no iniquity have dominion over
me.
134 [a]Redeem me from the oppression of man,
That I may keep Your precepts.
135 [a]Make Your face shine upon Your servant,
And teach me Your statutes.
136 [a]Rivers of water run down from my eyes,
Because *men* do not keep Your law.

צ TSADDE
137 [a]Righteous *are* You, O LORD,
And upright *are* Your judgments.

KJV

138 [a]Thy testimonies *that* thou hast commanded *are* righteous and very faithful.
139 [a]My zeal hath consumed me, because mine enemies have forgotten thy words.
140 [a]Thy word *is* very pure: therefore thy servant loveth it.
141 I *am* small and despised: *yet* do not I forget thy precepts.
142 Thy righteousness *is* an everlasting righteousness, and thy law *is* [a]the truth.
143 Trouble and anguish have taken hold on me: *yet* thy commandments *are* my delights.
144 The righteousness of thy testimonies *is* everlasting: give me understanding, and I shall live.

ק KOPH

145 I cried with *my* whole heart; hear me, O LORD: I will keep thy statutes.
146 I cried unto thee; save me, and I shall keep thy testimonies.
147 [a]I prevented the dawning of the morning, and cried: I hoped in thy word.
148 [a]Mine eyes prevent the *night* watches, that I might meditate in thy word.
149 Hear my voice according unto thy lovingkindness: O LORD, quicken me according to thy judgment.
150 They draw nigh that follow after mischief: they are far from thy law.
151 Thou *art* [a]near, O LORD; and all thy commandments *are* truth.
152 Concerning thy testimonies, I have known of old that thou hast founded them [a]for ever.

ר RESH

153 [a]Consider mine affliction, and deliver me: for I do not forget thy law.
154 [a]Plead my cause, and deliver me: quicken me according to thy word.
155 Salvation *is* far from the wicked: for they seek not thy statutes.
156 Great *are* thy tender mercies, O LORD: quicken me according to thy judgments.
157 Many *are* my persecutors and mine enemies; *yet* do I not [a]decline from thy testimonies.
158 I beheld the transgressors, and was [a]grieved; because they kept not thy word.
159 Consider how I love thy precepts: quicken me, O LORD, according to thy lovingkindness.
160 Thy word *is* true *from* the beginning: and every one of thy righteous judgments *endureth* for ever.

ש SCHIN

161 [a]Princes have persecuted me without a cause: but my heart standeth in awe of thy word.
162 I rejoice at thy word, as one that findeth great spoil.
163 I hate and abhor lying: *but* thy law do I love.
164 Seven times a day do I praise thee because of thy righteous judgments.
165 [a]Great peace have they which love thy law: and nothing shall offend them.
166 [a]LORD, I have hoped for thy salvation, and done thy commandments.
167 My soul hath kept thy testimonies; and I love them exceedingly.

138 [a][Ps. 19:7–9]
139 [a]Ps. 69:9; John 2:17
140 [a]Ps. 12:6
142 [a][Ps. 19:9; John 17:17]
147 [a]Ps. 5:3
148 [a]Ps. 63:1, 6
151 [a][Ps. 145:18]; Is. 50:8
152 [a]Luke 21:33
153 [a]Lam. 5:1
154 [a]1 Sam. 24:15; Mic. 7:9
157 [a]Ps. 44:18
158 [a]Ezek. 9:4
161 [a]1 Sam. 24:11; 26:18
165 [a]Prov. 3:2; [Is. 26:3; 32:17]
166 [a]Gen. 49:18

NKJV

138 [a]Your testimonies, *which* You have commanded,
Are righteous and very faithful.
139 [a]My zeal has consumed me,
Because my enemies have forgotten Your words.
140 [a]Your word *is* very pure;
Therefore Your servant loves it.
141 I *am* small and despised,
Yet I do not forget Your precepts.
142 Your righteousness *is* an everlasting righteousness,
And Your law *is* [a]truth.
143 Trouble and anguish have overtaken me,
Yet Your commandments *are* my delights.
144 The righteousness of Your testimonies *is* everlasting;
Give me understanding, and I shall live.

ק QOPH

145 I cry out with *my* whole heart;
Hear me, O LORD!
I will keep Your statutes.
146 I cry out to You;
Save me, and I will keep Your testimonies.
147 [a]I rise before the dawning of the morning,
And cry for help;
I hope in Your word.
148 [a]My eyes are awake through the *night* watches,
That I may meditate on Your word.
149 Hear my voice according to Your lovingkindness;
O LORD, revive me according to Your justice.
150 They draw near who follow after wickedness;
They are far from Your law.
151 You *are* [a]near, O LORD,
And all Your commandments *are* truth.
152 Concerning Your testimonies,
I have known of old that You have founded them [a]forever.

ר RESH

153 [a]Consider my affliction and deliver me,
For I do not forget Your law.
154 [a]Plead my cause and redeem me;
Revive me according to Your word.
155 Salvation *is* far from the wicked,
For they do not seek Your statutes.
156 Great *are* Your tender mercies, O LORD;
Revive me according to Your judgments.
157 Many *are* my persecutors and my enemies,
Yet I do not [a]turn from Your testimonies.
158 I see the treacherous, and [a]am disgusted,
Because they do not keep Your word.
159 Consider how I love Your precepts;
Revive me, O LORD, according to Your lovingkindness.
160 The entirety of Your word *is* truth,
And every one of Your righteous judgments *endures* forever.

ש SHIN

161 [a]Princes persecute me without a cause,
But my heart stands in awe of Your word.
162 I rejoice at Your word
As one who finds great treasure.
163 I hate and abhor lying,
But I love Your law.
164 Seven times a day I praise You,
Because of Your righteous judgments.
165 [a]Great peace have those who love Your law,
And nothing causes them to stumble.
166 [a]LORD, I hope for Your salvation,
And I do Your commandments.
167 My soul keeps Your testimonies,
And I love them exceedingly.

KJV

168 I have kept thy precepts and thy testimonies: [a]for all my ways *are* before thee.

ת TAU
169 Let my cry come near before thee, O LORD:
[a]give me understanding according to thy word.
170 Let my supplication come before thee: deliver me according to thy word.
171 [a]My lips shall utter praise, when thou hast
taught me thy statutes.
172 My tongue shall speak of thy word: for
all thy commandments *are* righteousness.
173 Let thine hand help me; for [a]I have chosen
thy precepts.
174 [a]I have longed for thy salvation, O LORD;
and [b]thy law *is* my delight.
175 Let my soul live, and it shall praise thee;
and let thy judgments help me.
176 [a]I have gone astray like a lost sheep; seek
thy servant; for I do not forget thy commandments.

PSALM 120

Plea for Relief from Bitter Foes

A Song of degrees.

IN [a]my distress I cried unto the LORD, and he
heard me.
2 Deliver my soul, O LORD, from lying lips,
and from a deceitful tongue.
3 What shall be given unto thee? or what
shall be done unto thee, thou false tongue?
4 Sharp arrows of the mighty, with coals of
juniper.
5 Woe is me, that I sojourn in [a]Mesech,
[b]*that* I dwell in the tents of Kedar!
6 My soul hath long dwelt with him that
hateth peace.
7 I *am for* peace: but when I speak, they
are for war.

PSALM 121

God the Help of Those Who Seek Him

A Song of degrees.

I [a]WILL lift up mine eyes unto the hills, from
whence cometh my help.
2 [a]My help *cometh* from the LORD, which
made heaven and earth.
3 [a]He will not suffer thy foot to be moved:
[b]he that keepeth thee will not slumber.
4 Behold, he that keepeth Israel shall neither slumber nor sleep.
5 The LORD *is* thy keeper: the LORD *is* [a]thy
shade [b]upon thy right hand.
6 [a]The sun shall not smite thee by day, nor
the moon by night.
7 The LORD shall preserve thee from all evil:
he shall [a]preserve thy soul.
8 The LORD shall [a]preserve thy going out
and thy coming in from this time forth, and even
for evermore.

PSALM 122

The Joy of Going to the House of the LORD

A Song of degrees of David.

I WAS glad when they said unto me, [a]Let us go
into the house of the LORD.
2 Our feet shall stand within thy gates, O
Jerusalem.

---

168 [a]Job 24:23; Prov. 5:21
169 [a]Ps. 119:27, 144
171 [a]Ps. 119:7
173 [a]Josh. 24:22; Luke 10:42
174 [a]Ps. 119:166 [b]Ps. 119:16, 24
176 [a][Is. 53:6]; Jer. 50:6; Matt. 18:12; Luke 15:4; [1 Pet. 2:25]

PSALM 120

1 [a]Jon. 2:2
5 [a]Gen. 10:2; 1 Chr. 1:5; Ezek. 27:13; 38:2, 3; 39:1 [b]Gen. 25:13; Is. 21:16; 60:7; Jer. 2:10; 49:28; Ezek. 27:21

PSALM 121

1 [a][Jer. 3:23]
2 [a][Ps. 124:8]
3 [a]1 Sam. 2:9; Prov. 3:23, 26 [b][Ps. 127:1; Prov. 24:12]; Is. 27:3
5 [a]Is. 25:4 [b]Ps. 16:8
6 [a]Ps. 91:5; Is. 49:10; Jon. 4:8; Rev. 7:16
7 [a]Ps. 41:2
8 [a]Deut. 28:6; [Prov. 2:8; 3:6]

PSALM 122

1 [a][Is. 2:3; Mic. 4:2]; Zech. 8:21

NKJV

168 I keep Your precepts and Your
testimonies,
[a]For all my ways *are* before You.

ת TAU
169 Let my cry come before You, O LORD;
[a]Give me understanding according to Your
word.
170 Let my supplication come before You;
Deliver me according to Your word.
171 [a]My lips shall utter praise,
For You teach me Your statutes.
172 My tongue shall speak of Your word,
For all Your commandments *are*
righteousness.
173 Let Your hand become my help,
For [a]I have chosen Your precepts.
174 [a]I long for Your salvation, O LORD,
And [b]Your law *is* my delight.
175 Let my soul live, and it shall praise You;
And let Your judgments help me.
176 [a]I have gone astray like a lost sheep;
Seek Your servant,
For I do not forget Your commandments.

PSALM 120

Plea for Relief from Bitter Foes

A Song of Ascents.

IN [a]my distress I cried to the LORD,
And He heard me.
2 Deliver my soul, O LORD, from lying lips
And from a deceitful tongue.

3 What shall be given to you,
Or what shall be done to you,
You false tongue?
4 Sharp arrows of the warrior,
With coals of the broom tree!

5 Woe is me, that I dwell in [a]Meshech,
[b]*That* I dwell among the tents of Kedar!
6 My soul has dwelt too long
With one who hates peace.
7 I *am for* peace;
But when I speak, they *are* for war.

PSALM 121

God the Help of Those Who Seek Him

A Song of Ascents.

I [a]WILL lift up my eyes to the hills—
From whence comes my help?
2 [a]My help *comes* from the LORD,
Who made heaven and earth.

3 [a]He will not allow your foot to be moved;
[b]He who keeps you will not slumber.
4 Behold, He who keeps Israel
Shall neither slumber nor sleep.

5 The LORD *is* your keeper;
The LORD *is* [a]your shade [b]at your right
hand.
6 [a]The sun shall not strike you by day,
Nor the moon by night.

7 The LORD shall preserve you from all evil;
He shall [a]preserve your soul.
8 The LORD shall [a]preserve your going out
and your coming in
From this time forth, and even
forevermore.

PSALM 122

The Joy of Going to the House of the LORD

A Song of Ascents. Of David.

I WAS glad when they said to me,
[a]"Let us go into the house of the LORD."
2 Our feet have been standing
Within your gates, O Jerusalem!

KJV

3 Jerusalem is builded as a city that is [a]com-
pact together:
4 [a]Whither the tribes go up, the tribes of
the LORD, unto [b]the testimony of Israel, to give
thanks unto the name of the LORD.
5 [a]For there are set thrones of judgment, the
thrones of the house of David.
6 [a]Pray for the peace of Jerusalem: they
shall prosper that love thee.
7 Peace be within thy walls, *and* prosperity
within thy palaces.
8 For my brethren and companions' sakes,
I will now say, Peace *be* within thee.
9 Because of the house of the LORD our God
I will [a]seek thy good.

PSALM 123

Prayer for Relief from Contempt

A Song of degrees.

UNTO thee [a]lift I up mine eyes, O thou [b]that
dwellest in the heavens.
2 Behold, as the eyes of servants *look* unto
the hand of their masters, *and* as the eyes of a
maiden unto the hand of her mistress; [a]so our
eyes *wait* upon the LORD our God, until that he
have mercy upon us.
3 Have mercy upon us, O LORD, have mercy
upon us: for we are exceedingly filled with
contempt.
4 Our soul is exceedingly filled with the
scorning of those that are at ease, *and* with the
contempt of the proud.

PSALM 124

The LORD the Defense of His People

A Song of degrees of David.

IF *it had not been* the LORD who was on our
[a]side, [b]now may Israel say;
2 If *it had not been* the LORD who was on
our side, when men rose up against us:
3 Then they had [a]swallowed us up quick,
when their wrath was kindled against us:
4 Then the waters had overwhelmed us, the
stream had gone over our soul:
5 Then the proud waters had gone over our
soul.
6 Blessed *be* the LORD, who hath not given
us *as* a prey to their teeth.
7 [a]Our soul is escaped [b]as a bird out of the
snare of the fowlers: the snare is broken, and we
are escaped.
8 [a]Our help *is* in the name of the LORD, [b]who
made heaven and earth.

PSALM 125

The LORD the Strength of His People

A Song of degrees.

THEY that trust in the LORD *shall be* as mount
Zion, *which* cannot be removed, *but* abideth
for ever.
2 *As* the mountains *are* round about Jerusalem, so the LORD *is* round about his people from
henceforth even for ever.

3 [a]2 Sam. 5:9 **4** [a]Ex. 23:17; Deut. 16:16 [b]Ex. 16:34 **5** [a]Deut. 17:8; 2 Chr. 19:8 **6** [a]Ps. 51:18 **9** [a]Neh. 2:10; Esth. 10:3

PSALM 123

1 [a]Ps. 121:1; 141:8 [b]Ps. 2:4; 11:4; 115:3 **2** [a]Ps. 25:15

PSALM 124

1 [a]Ps. 118:6; [Rom. 8:31] [b]Ps. 129:1 **3** [a]Num. 16:30; Ps. 56:1, 2; 57:3; Prov. 1:12 **7** [a]Ps. 91:3 [b]Prov. 6:5; Hos. 9:8 **8** [a][Ps. 121:2] [b]Gen. 1:1; Ps. 134:3

*124:7 Persons who catch birds in a trap or snare

NKJV

3 Jerusalem is built
As a city that is [a]compact together,
4 [a]Where the tribes go up,
The tribes of the LORD,
To [b]the Testimony of Israel,
To give thanks to the name of the LORD.
5 [a]For thrones are set there for judgment,
The thrones of the house of David.

6 [a]Pray for the peace of Jerusalem:
"May they prosper who love you.
7 Peace be within your walls,
Prosperity within your palaces."
8 For the sake of my brethren and companions,
I will now say, "Peace *be* within you."
9 Because of the house of the LORD our God
I will [a]seek your good.

PSALM 123

Prayer for Relief from Contempt

A Song of Ascents.

UNTO You [a]I lift up my eyes,
O You [b]who dwell in the heavens.
2 Behold, as the eyes of servants *look* to the hand of their masters,
As the eyes of a maid to the hand of her mistress,
[a]So our eyes *look* to the LORD our God,
Until He has mercy on us.
3 Have mercy on us, O LORD, have mercy on us!
For we are exceedingly filled with contempt.
4 Our soul is exceedingly filled
With the scorn of those who are at ease,
With the contempt of the proud.

PSALM 124

The LORD the Defense of His People

A Song of Ascents. Of David.

"IF it had not been the LORD who was on our [a]side,"
[b]Let Israel now say—
2 "If it had not been the LORD who was on our side,
When men rose up against us,
3 Then they would have [a]swallowed us alive,
When their wrath was kindled against us;
4 Then the waters would have overwhelmed us,
The stream would have gone over our soul;
5 Then the swollen waters
Would have gone over our soul."

6 Blessed *be* the LORD,
Who has not given us *as* prey to their teeth.
7 [a]Our soul has escaped [b]as a bird from the snare of the *fowlers;
The snare is broken, and we have escaped.
8 [a]Our help *is* in the name of the LORD,
[b]Who made heaven and earth.

PSALM 125

The LORD the Strength of His People

A Song of Ascents.

THOSE who trust in the LORD
Are like Mount Zion,
Which cannot be moved, *but* abides forever.
2 As the mountains surround Jerusalem,
So the LORD surrounds His people
From this time forth and forever.

KJV

3 For [a]the rod of the wicked shall not rest
upon the lot of the righteous; lest the righteous
put forth their hands unto iniquity.
4 Do good, O LORD, unto *those that be* good,
and to *them that are* upright in their hearts.
5 As for such as turn aside unto their
[a]crooked ways, the LORD shall lead them forth
with the workers of iniquity: *but* [b]peace *shall be*
upon Israel.

PSALM 125

3 [a]Prov. 22:8; Is. 14:5
5 [a]Prov. 2:15; Is. 59:8 [b]Ps. 128:6; [Gal. 6:16]

NKJV

3 For [a]the scepter of wickedness shall not rest
On the land allotted to the righteous,
Lest the righteous reach out their hands to iniquity.

4 Do good, O LORD, to *those who are* good,
And to *those who are* upright in their hearts.

5 As for such as turn aside to their [a]crooked ways,
The LORD shall lead them away
With the workers of iniquity.

[b]Peace *be* upon Israel!

PSALM 126

A Joyful Return to Zion

A Song of degrees.

WHEN [a]the LORD turned again the captivity
of Zion, [b]we were like them that dream.
2 Then [a]was our mouth filled with laughter,
and our tongue with singing: then said they
among the heathen, The LORD hath done great
things for them.
3 The LORD hath done great things for us;
whereof we are glad.
4 Turn again our captivity, O LORD, as the
streams in the south.
5 [a]They that sow in tears shall reap in joy.
6 He that goeth forth and weepeth, bearing
precious seed, shall doubtless come again with
[a]rejoicing, bringing his sheaves *with him*.

PSALM 126

1 [a]Ps. 85:1; Jer. 29:14; Hos. 6:11; Joel 3:1 [b]Acts 12:9
2 [a]Job 8:21
5 [a]Is. 35:10; 51:11; 61:7; Jer. 31:9; [Gal. 6:9]
6 [a]Is. 61:3

PSALM 126

A Joyful Return to Zion

A Song of Ascents.

WHEN [a]the LORD brought back the captivity of Zion,
[b]We were like those who dream.
2 Then [a]our mouth was filled with laughter,
And our tongue with singing.
Then they said among the nations,
"The LORD has done great things for them."
3 The LORD has done great things for us,
And we are glad.

4 Bring back our captivity, O LORD,
As the streams in the South.

5 [a]Those who sow in tears
Shall reap in joy.
6 He who continually goes forth weeping,
Bearing seed for sowing,
Shall doubtless come again with [a]rejoicing,
Bringing his sheaves *with him*.

PSALM 127

Laboring and Prospering with the LORD

A Song of degrees for Solomon.

EXCEPT the LORD build the house, they labour
in vain that build it: except [a]the LORD keep
the city, the watchman waketh *but* in vain.
2 *It is* vain for you to rise up early, to sit
up late, to [a]eat the bread of sorrows: *for* so he
giveth his beloved sleep.
3 Lo, [a]children *are* an heritage of the LORD:
and [b]the fruit of the womb *is his* [c]reward.
4 As arrows *are* in the hand of a mighty
man; so *are* children of the youth.
5 [a]Happy *is* the man that hath his quiver
full of them: [b]they shall not be ashamed, but they
shall speak with the enemies in the gate.

PSALM 127

1 [a][Ps. 121:3–5]
2 [a][Gen. 3:17, 19]
3 [a][Gen. 33:5; Josh. 24:3, 4; Ps. 113:9] [b]Deut. 7:13; 28:4; Is. 13:18 [c][Ps. 113:9]
5 [a]Ps. 128:2, 3 [b]Job 5:4; Prov. 27:11

PSALM 127

Laboring and Prospering with the LORD

A Song of Ascents. Of Solomon.

UNLESS the LORD builds the house,
They labor in vain who build it;
Unless [a]the LORD guards the city,
The watchman stays awake in vain.
2 *It is* vain for you to rise up early,
To sit up late,
To [a]eat the bread of sorrows;
For so He gives His beloved sleep.

3 Behold, [a]children *are* a heritage from the LORD,
[b]The fruit of the womb *is* a [c]reward.
4 Like arrows in the hand of a warrior,
So *are* the children of one's youth.
5 [a]Happy *is* the man who has his quiver full of them;
[b]They shall not be ashamed,
But shall speak with their enemies in the gate.

PSALM 128

Blessings of Those Who Fear the LORD

A Song of degrees.

BLESSED [a]*is* every one that feareth the LORD;
that walketh in his ways.
2 [a]For thou shalt eat the labour of thine
hands: happy *shalt* thou *be*, and *it shall be* [b]well
with thee.
3 Thy wife *shall be* [a]as a fruitful vine by
the sides of thine house: thy [b]children [c]like olive
plants round about thy table.

PSALM 128

1 [a]Ps. 119:1
2 [a]Is. 3:10 [b]Deut. 4:40
3 [a]Ezek. 19:10 [b]Ps. 127:3–5 [c]Ps. 52:8; 144:12

PSALM 128

Blessings of Those Who Fear the LORD

A Song of Ascents.

BLESSED [a]*is* every one who fears the LORD,
Who walks in His ways.

2 [a]When you eat the labor of your hands,
You *shall be* happy, and *it shall be* [b]well with you.
3 Your wife *shall be* [a]like a fruitful vine
In the very heart of your house,
Your [b]children [c]like olive plants
All around your table.

KJV

4 Behold, that thus shall the man be blessed
that feareth the LORD.
5 [a]The LORD shall bless thee out of Zion:
and thou shalt see the good of Jerusalem all the
days of thy life.
6 Yea, thou shalt [a]see thy children's children, *and* [b]peace upon Israel.

PSALM 129

Song of Victory over Zion's Enemies

A Song of degrees.

MANY a time have they [a]afflicted me from
[b]my youth, [c]may Israel now say:
2 Many a time have they afflicted me from
my youth: yet they have not prevailed against me.
3 The plowers plowed upon my back: they
made long their furrows.
4 The LORD *is* righteous: he hath cut asunder
the cords of the wicked.
5 Let them all be confounded and turned
back that hate Zion.
6 Let them be as [a]the grass *upon* the housetops, which withereth afore it groweth up:
7 Wherewith the mower filleth not his hand;
nor he that bindeth sheaves his bosom.
8 Neither do they which go by say, [a]The
blessing of the LORD *be* upon you: we bless you
in the name of the LORD.

PSALM 130

Waiting for the Redemption of the LORD

A Song of degrees.

OUT [a]of the depths have I cried unto thee, O
LORD.
2 Lord, hear my voice: let thine ears be attentive to the voice of my supplications.
3 [a]If thou, LORD, shouldest mark iniquities,
O Lord, who shall [b]stand?
4 But *there is* [a]forgiveness with thee, that
[b]thou mayest be feared.
5 [a]I wait for the LORD, my soul doth wait,
and [b]in his word do I hope.
6 [a]My soul *waiteth* for the Lord more than
they that watch for the morning: *I say, more than*
they that watch for the morning.
7 [a]Let Israel hope in the LORD: for [b]with the
LORD *there is* mercy, and with him *is* plenteous
redemption.
8 And [a]he shall redeem Israel from all his
iniquities.

PSALM 131

Simple Trust in the LORD

A Song of degrees of David.

LORD, my heart is not haughty, nor mine eyes
lofty: [a]neither do I exercise myself in great
matters, or in things too high for me.
2 Surely I have behaved and quieted myself,
[a]as a child that is weaned of his mother: my soul
is even as a weaned child.

---

5 [a]Ps. 134:3
6 [a]Gen. 48:11; 50:23; Job 42:16; Ps. 103:17; [Prov. 17:6] [b]Ps. 125:5

PSALM 129
1 [a][Jer. 1:19; 15:20]; Matt. 16:18; 2 Cor. 4:8, 9 [b]Ezek. 23:3; Hos. 2:15 [c]Ps. 124:1
6 [a]Ps. 37:2
8 [a]Ruth 2:4

PSALM 130
1 [a]Lam. 3:55
3 [a][Ps. 143:2] [b][Nah. 1:6; Mal. 3:2]; Rev. 6:17
4 [a][Ex. 34:7; Neh. 9:17; Ps. 86:5; Is. 55:7; Dan. 9:9] [b][1 Kin. 8:39, 40; Jer. 33:8, 9]
5 [a][Ps. 27:14] [b]Ps. 119:81
6 [a]Ps. 119:147
7 [a]Ps. 131:3 [b][Ps. 86:5, 15; Is. 55:7]
8 [a][Ps. 103:3, 4]; Luke 1:68; Titus 2:14

PSALM 131
1 [a]Jer. 45:5; [Rom. 12:16]
2 [a][Matt. 18:3; 1 Cor. 14:20]

NKJV

4 Behold, thus shall the man be blessed
Who fears the LORD.

5 [a]The LORD bless you out of Zion,
And may you see the good of Jerusalem
All the days of your life.
6 Yes, may you [a]see your children's
children.

[b]Peace *be* upon Israel!

PSALM 129

Song of Victory over Zion's Enemies

A Song of Ascents.

"MANY a time they have [a]afflicted me from
[b]my youth,"
[c]Let Israel now say—
2 "Many a time they have afflicted me from
my youth;
Yet they have not prevailed against me.
3 The plowers plowed on my back;
They made their furrows long."
4 The LORD *is* righteous;
He has cut in pieces the cords of the
wicked.

5 Let all those who hate Zion
Be put to shame and turned back.
6 Let them be as the [a]grass *on* the
housetops,
Which withers before it grows up,
7 With which the reaper does not fill his
hand,
Nor he who binds sheaves, his arms.
8 Neither let those who pass by them say,
[a]"The blessing of the LORD *be* upon you;
We bless you in the name of the LORD!"

PSALM 130

Waiting for the Redemption of the LORD

A Song of Ascents.

OUT [a]of the depths I have cried to You,
O LORD;
2 Lord, hear my voice!
Let Your ears be attentive
To the voice of my supplications.

3 [a]If You, LORD, should mark iniquities,
O Lord, who could [b]stand?
4 But *there is* [a]forgiveness with You,
That [b]You may be feared.

5 [a]I wait for the LORD, my soul waits,
And [b]in His word I do hope.
6 [a]My soul *waits* for the Lord
More than those who watch for the
morning—
Yes, more than those who watch for the
morning.

7 [a]O Israel, hope in the LORD;
For [b]with the LORD *there is* mercy,
And with Him *is* abundant redemption.
8 And [a]He shall redeem Israel
From all his iniquities.

PSALM 131

Simple Trust in the LORD

A Song of Ascents. Of David.

LORD, my heart is not haughty,
Nor my eyes lofty.
[a]Neither do I concern myself with great
matters,
Nor with things too profound for me.

2 Surely I have calmed and quieted my soul,
[a]Like a weaned child with his mother;
Like a weaned child *is* my soul within me.

KJV

3 [a]Let Israel hope in the LORD from henceforth and for ever.

PSALM 132

The Eternal Dwelling of God in Zion

A Song of degrees.

LORD, remember David, *and* all his afflictions:
2 How he sware unto the LORD, [a]*and* vowed
unto [b]the mighty *God* of Jacob;
3 Surely I will not come into the tabernacle
of my house, nor go up into my bed;
4 I will [a]not give sleep to mine eyes, *or* slumber to mine eyelids,
5 Until I [a]find out a place for the LORD, an
habitation for the mighty *God* of Jacob.
6 Lo, we heard of it [a]at Ephratah: [b]we found
it [c]in the fields of the wood.
7 We will go into his tabernacles: [a]we will
worship at his footstool.
8 [a]Arise, O LORD, into thy rest; thou, and
[b]the ark of thy strength.
9 Let thy priests [a]be clothed with righteousness; and let thy saints shout for joy.
10 For thy servant David's sake turn not
away the face of thine anointed.
11 [a]The LORD hath sworn *in* truth unto David;
he will not turn from it; [b]Of the fruit of thy body
will I set upon thy throne.
12 If thy children will keep my covenant and
my testimony that I shall teach them, their children shall also sit upon thy throne for evermore.
13 [a]For the LORD hath chosen Zion; he hath
desired *it* for his habitation.
14 [a]This *is* my rest for ever: here will I dwell;
for I have desired it.
15 [a]I will abundantly bless her provision: I
will satisfy her poor with bread.
16 [a]I will also clothe her priests with salvation: [b]and her saints shall shout aloud for joy.
17 [a]There will I make the horn of David to
bud: [b]I have ordained a lamp for mine anointed.
18 His enemies will I [a]clothe with shame: but
upon himself shall his crown flourish.

PSALM 133

Blessed Unity of the People of God

A Song of degrees of David.

BEHOLD, how good and how pleasant *it is* for
[a]brethren to dwell together in unity!
2 *It is* like the precious ointment upon the
head, that ran down upon the beard, *even* Aaron's
beard: that went down to the skirts of his
garments;
3 As the dew of [a]Hermon, *and as the dew*
that descended upon the mountains of Zion: for
[b]there the LORD commanded the blessing, *even*
life for evermore.

---

3 [a][Ps. 130:7]

PSALM 132

2 [a]Ps. 65:1 [b]Gen. 49:24; Is. 49:26; 60:16
4 [a]Prov. 6:4
5 [a]1 Kin. 8:17; 1 Chr. 22:7; Ps. 26:8; Acts 7:46
6 [a]1 Sam. 17:12 [b]1 Sam. 7:1 [c]1 Chr. 13:5
7 [a]Ps. 5:7; 99:5
8 [a]Num. 10:35 [b]Ps. 78:61
9 [a]Job 29:14
11 [a][Ps. 89:3, 4, 33; 110:4] [b]2 Sam. 7:12; [1 Kin. 8:25; 2 Chr. 6:16; Luke 1:69; Acts 2:30]
13 [a][Ps. 48:1, 2]
14 [a]Ps. 68:16; Matt. 23:21
15 [a]Ps. 147:14
16 [a]2 Chr. 6:41; Ps. 132:9; 149:4 [b]1 Sam. 4:5; Hos. 11:12
17 [a]Ezek. 29:21; Luke 1:69 [b]1 Kin. 11:36; 15:4; 2 Kin. 8:19; 2 Chr. 21:7; Ps. 18:28
18 [a]Job 8:22; Ps. 35:26

PSALM 133

1 [a]Gen. 13:8; Heb. 13:1
3 [a]Deut. 4:48 [b]Lev. 25:21; Deut. 28:8; Ps. 42:8

---

*132:6 Heb. *Jaar,* lit. *Woods*

NKJV

3 [a]O Israel, hope in the LORD
From this time forth and forever.

PSALM 132

The Eternal Dwelling of God in Zion

A Song of Ascents.

LORD, remember David
And all his afflictions;
2 How he swore to the LORD,
[a]*And* vowed to [b]the Mighty One of
Jacob:
3 "Surely I will not go into the chamber of
my house,
Or go up to the comfort of my bed;
4 I will [a]not give sleep to my eyes
Or slumber to my eyelids,
5 Until I [a]find a place for the LORD,
A dwelling place for the Mighty One of
Jacob."

6 Behold, we heard of it [a]in Ephrathah;
[b]We found it [c]in the fields of *the
woods.
7 Let us go into His tabernacle;
[a]Let us worship at His footstool.
8 [a]Arise, O LORD, to Your resting place,
You and [b]the ark of Your strength.
9 Let Your priests [a]be clothed with
righteousness,
And let Your saints shout for joy.

10 For Your servant David's sake,
Do not turn away the face of Your
Anointed.

11 [a]The LORD has sworn *in* truth to David;
He will not turn from it:
"I will set upon your throne [b]the fruit of
your body.
12 If your sons will keep My covenant
And My testimony which I shall teach
them,
Their sons also shall sit upon your throne
forevermore."

13 [a]For the LORD has chosen Zion;
He has desired *it* for His dwelling
place:
14 "This[a] *is* My resting place forever;
Here I will dwell, for I have desired it.
15 [a]I will abundantly bless her provision;
I will satisfy her poor with bread.
16 [a]I will also clothe her priests with
salvation,
[b]And her saints shall shout aloud for joy.
17 [a]There I will make the horn of David
grow;
[b]I will prepare a lamp for My Anointed.
18 His enemies I will [a]clothe with shame,
But upon Himself His crown shall
flourish."

PSALM 133

Blessed Unity of the People of God

A Song of Ascents. Of David.

BEHOLD, how good and how pleasant *it is*
For [a]brethren to dwell together in unity!

2 *It is* like the precious oil upon the head,
Running down on the beard,
The beard of Aaron,
Running down on the edge of his
garments.
3 *It is* like the dew of [a]Hermon,
Descending upon the mountains of
Zion;
For [b]there the LORD commanded the
blessing—
Life forevermore.

KJV

PSALM 134

Praising the LORD *in His House at Night*

A Song of degrees.

BEHOLD, bless ye the LORD, all *ye* servants of
the LORD, which by night stand in the house
of the LORD.
2 [a]Lift up your hands *in* the sanctuary, and
bless the LORD.
3 The LORD that made heaven and earth
bless thee out of Zion.

PSALM 135

Praise to God in Creation and Redemption

PRAISE ye the LORD. Praise ye the name of the
LORD; [a]praise *him,* O ye servants of the LORD.
2 [a]Ye that stand in the house of the LORD,
in [b]the courts of the house of our God,
3 Praise the LORD; for [a]the LORD *is* good:
sing praises unto his name; [b]for *it is* pleasant.
4 For [a]the LORD hath chosen Jacob unto
himself, *and* Israel for his peculiar treasure.
5 For I know that [a]the LORD *is* great, and
that our Lord *is* above all gods.
6 [a]Whatsoever the LORD pleased, *that* did
he in heaven, and in earth, in the seas, and all
deep places.
7 [a]He causeth the vapours to ascend from
the ends of the earth; [b]he maketh lightnings for
the rain; he bringeth the wind out of his
[c]treasuries.
8 [a]Who smote the firstborn of Egypt, both
of man and beast.
9 [a]*Who* sent tokens and wonders into the
midst of thee, O Egypt, [b]upon Pharaoh, and upon
all his servants.
10 [a]Who smote great nations, and slew
mighty kings;
11 Sihon king of the Amorites, and Og king
of Bashan, and [a]all the kingdoms of Canaan:
12 [a]And gave their land *for* an heritage, an
heritage unto Israel his people.
13 [a]Thy name, O LORD, *endureth* for ever;
and thy memorial, O LORD, throughout all
generations.
14 [a]For the LORD will judge his people, and
he will repent himself concerning his servants.
15 [a]The idols of the heathen *are* silver and
gold, the work of men's hands.
16 They have mouths, but they speak not;
eyes have they, but they see not;
17 They have ears, but they hear not; neither
is there *any* breath in their mouths.
18 They that make them are like unto them:
so is every one that trusteth in them.
19 [a]Bless the LORD, O house of Israel: bless
the LORD, O house of Aaron:
20 Bless the LORD, O house of Levi: ye that
fear the LORD, bless the LORD.
21 Blessed be the LORD [a]out of Zion, which
dwelleth at Jerusalem. Praise ye the LORD.

PSALM 134
2 [a][1 Tim. 2:8]

PSALM 135
1 [a]Ps. 113:1
2 [a]Luke 2:37 [b]Ps. 116:19
3 [a][Ps. 119:68] [b]Ps. 147:1
4 [a][Ex. 19:5]; Mal. 3:17; [Titus 2:14; 1 Pet. 2:9]
5 [a]Ps. 95:3; 97:9
6 [a]Ps. 115:3
7 [a]Jer. 10:13 [b]Job 28:25, 26; 38:24–28 [c]Jer. 51:16
8 [a]Ex. 12:12; Ps. 78:51
9 [a]Ex. 7:10; Deut. 6:22; Ps. 78:43 [b]Ps. 136:15
10 [a]Num. 21:24; Ps. 136:17
11 [a]Josh. 12:7–24
12 [a]Ps. 78:55; 136:21, 22
13 [a][Ex. 3:15; Ps. 102:12]
14 [a]Deut. 32:36
15 [a][Ps. 115:4–8]
19 [a][Ps. 115:9]
21 [a]Ps. 134:3

NKJV

PSALM 134

Praising the LORD *in His House at Night*

A Song of Ascents.

BEHOLD, bless the LORD,
All *you* servants of the LORD,
Who by night stand in the house of the LORD!
2 [a]Lift up your hands *in* the sanctuary,
And bless the LORD.

3 The LORD who made heaven and earth
Bless you from Zion!

PSALM 135

Praise to God in Creation and Redemption

PRAISE the LORD!

Praise the name of the LORD;
[a]Praise *Him,* O you servants of the LORD!
2 [a]You who stand in the house of the LORD,
In [b]the courts of the house of our God,
3 Praise the LORD, for [a]the LORD *is* good;
Sing praises to His name, [b]for *it is* pleasant.
4 For [a]the LORD has chosen Jacob for Himself,
Israel for His special treasure.

5 For I know that [a]the LORD *is* great,
And our Lord *is* above all gods.
6 [a]Whatever the LORD pleases He does,
In heaven and in earth,
In the seas and in all deep places.
7 [a]He causes the vapors to ascend from the ends of the earth;
[b]He makes lightning for the rain;
He brings the wind out of His [c]treasuries.

8 [a]He destroyed the firstborn of Egypt,
Both of man and beast.
9 [a]He sent signs and wonders into the midst of you, O Egypt,
[b]Upon Pharaoh and all his servants.
10 [a]He defeated many nations
And slew mighty kings—
11 Sihon king of the Amorites,
Og king of Bashan,
And [a]all the kingdoms of Canaan—
12 [a]And gave their land *as* a heritage,
A heritage to Israel His people.

13 [a]Your name, O LORD, *endures* forever,
Your fame, O LORD, throughout all generations.
14 [a]For the LORD will judge His people,
And He will have compassion on His servants.

15 [a]The idols of the nations *are* silver and gold,
The work of men's hands.
16 They have mouths, but they do not speak;
Eyes they have, but they do not see;
17 They have ears, but they do not hear;
Nor is there *any* breath in their mouths.
18 Those who make them are like them;
So is everyone who trusts in them.

19 [a]Bless the LORD, O house of Israel!
Bless the LORD, O house of Aaron!
20 Bless the LORD, O house of Levi!
You who fear the LORD, bless the LORD!
21 Blessed be the LORD [a]out of Zion,
Who dwells in Jerusalem!

Praise the LORD!

KJV

PSALM 136

Thanksgiving to God for His Enduring Mercy

O [a]GIVE thanks unto the LORD; for *he is* good:
[b]for his mercy *endureth* for ever.
2 O give thanks unto [a]the God of gods: for
his mercy *endureth* for ever.
3 O give thanks to the Lord of lords: for
his mercy *endureth* for ever.
4 To him [a]who alone doeth great wonders:
for his mercy *endureth* for ever.
5 [a]To him that by wisdom made the heavens: for his mercy *endureth* for ever.
6 [a]To him that stretched out the earth above
the waters: for his mercy *endureth* for ever.
7 [a]To him that made great lights: for his
mercy *endureth* for ever:
8 [a]The sun to rule by day: for his mercy *endureth* for ever:
9 The moon and stars to rule by night: for
his mercy *endureth* for ever.
10 [a]To him that smote Egypt in their firstborn: for his mercy *endureth* for ever:
11 [a]And brought out Israel from among
them: for his mercy *endureth* for ever:
12 [a]With a strong hand, and with a stretched
out arm: for his mercy *endureth* for ever.
13 [a]To him which divided the Red sea into
parts: for his mercy *endureth* for ever:
14 And made Israel to pass through the midst
of it: for his mercy *endureth* for ever:
15 [a]But overthrew Pharaoh and his host in
the Red sea: for his mercy *endureth* for ever.
16 [a]To him which led his people through the
wilderness: for his mercy *endureth* for ever.
17 [a]To him which smote great kings: for his
mercy *endureth* for ever:
18 [a]And slew famous kings: for his mercy *endureth* for ever:
19 [a]Sihon king of the Amorites: for his mercy
endureth for ever:
20 [a]And Og the king of Bashan: for his mercy
endureth for ever:
21 [a]And gave their land for an heritage: for
his mercy *endureth* for ever:
22 *Even* an heritage unto Israel his servant:
for his mercy *endureth* for ever.
23 Who [a]remembered us in our low estate:
for his mercy *endureth* for ever:
24 And hath [a]redeemed us from our enemies:
for his mercy *endureth* for ever.
25 [a]Who giveth food to all flesh: for his
mercy *endureth* for ever.
26 O give thanks unto the God of heaven: for
his mercy *endureth* for ever.

PSALM 137

Longing for Zion in a Foreign Land

BY the rivers of Babylon, there we sat down,
yea, we wept, when we remembered Zion.
2 We hanged our harps upon the willows
in the midst thereof.
3 For there they that carried us away captive required of us a song; and they that [a]wasted
us *required of us* mirth, *saying,* Sing us *one* of
the songs of Zion.

PSALM 136

1 [a]Ps. 106:1 [b]1 Chr. 16:34; Jer. 33:11
2 [a][Deut. 10:17]
4 [a]Deut. 6:22; Job 9:10; Ps. 72:18
5 [a]Gen. 1:1, 6–8; Prov. 3:19; Jer. 51:15
6 [a]Gen. 1:9; Ps. 24:2; [Is. 42:5]; Jer. 10:12
7 [a]Gen. 1:14–18
8 [a]Gen. 1:16
10 [a]Ex. 12:29; Ps. 135:8
11 [a]Ex. 12:51; 13:3, 16
12 [a]Ex. 6:6; Deut. 4:34; 5:15; 7:19; 9:29; 11:2; 2 Kin. 17:36; 2 Chr. 6:32; Jer. 32:17
13 [a]Ex. 14:21
15 [a]Ex. 14:27
16 [a]Ex. 13:18; 15:22; Deut. 8:15
17 [a]Ps. 135:10–12
18 [a]Deut. 29:7
19 [a]Num. 21:21
20 [a]Num. 21:33
21 [a]Josh. 12:1
23 [a]Gen. 8:1; Deut. 32:36; Ps. 113:7
24 [a]Ps. 44:7
25 [a]Ps. 104:27; 145:15

PSALM 137

3 [a]Ps. 79:1

NKJV

PSALM 136

Thanksgiving to God for His Enduring Mercy

OH, [a]give thanks to the LORD, for *He is* good!
[b]For His mercy *endures* forever.
2 Oh, give thanks to [a]the God of gods!
For His mercy *endures* forever.
3 Oh, give thanks to the Lord of lords!
For His mercy *endures* forever:

4 To Him [a]who alone does great wonders,
For His mercy *endures* forever;
5 [a]To Him who by wisdom made the
heavens,
For His mercy *endures* forever;
6 [a]To Him who laid out the earth above the
waters,
For His mercy *endures* forever;
7 [a]To Him who made great lights,
For His mercy *endures* forever—
8 [a]The sun to rule by day,
For His mercy *endures* forever;
9 The moon and stars to rule by night,
For His mercy *endures* forever.

10 [a]To Him who struck Egypt in their
firstborn,
For His mercy *endures* forever;
11 [a]And brought out Israel from among them,
For His mercy *endures* forever;
12 [a]With a strong hand, and with an
outstretched arm,
For His mercy *endures* forever;
13 [a]To Him who divided the Red Sea in two,
For His mercy *endures* forever;
14 And made Israel pass through the midst
of it,
For His mercy *endures* forever;
15 [a]But overthrew Pharaoh and his army in
the Red Sea,
For His mercy *endures* forever;
16 [a]To Him who led His people through the
wilderness,
For His mercy *endures* forever;
17 [a]To Him who struck down great kings,
For His mercy *endures* forever;
18 [a]And slew famous kings,
For His mercy *endures* forever—
19 [a]Sihon king of the Amorites,
For His mercy *endures* forever;
20 [a]And Og king of Bashan,
For His mercy *endures* forever—
21 [a]And gave their land as a heritage,
For His mercy *endures* forever;
22 A heritage to Israel His servant,
For His mercy *endures* forever.

23 Who [a]remembered us in our lowly
state,
For His mercy *endures* forever;
24 And [a]rescued us from our enemies,
For His mercy *endures* forever;
25 [a]Who gives food to all flesh,
For His mercy *endures* forever.

26 Oh, give thanks to the God of heaven!
For His mercy *endures* forever.

PSALM 137

Longing for Zion in a Foreign Land

BY the rivers of Babylon,
There we sat down, yea, we wept
When we remembered Zion.
2 We hung our harps
Upon the willows in the midst of it.
3 For there those who carried us away
captive asked of us a song,
And those who [a]plundered us *requested*
mirth,
Saying, "Sing us *one* of the songs of
Zion!"

KJV

4 How shall we sing the LORD's song in a
strange land?
5 If I forget thee, O Jerusalem, let my right
hand forget *her cunning*.
6 If I do not remember thee, let my [a]tongue
cleave to the roof of my mouth; if I prefer not
Jerusalem above my chief joy.
7 Remember, O LORD, [a]the children of Edom
in the day of Jerusalem; who said, Rase *it*, rase
it, *even* to the foundation thereof.
8 O daughter of Babylon, [a]who art to be destroyed; happy *shall he be*, [b]that rewardeth thee
as thou hast served us.
9 Happy *shall he be*, that taketh and [a]dash-
eth thy little ones against the stones.

PSALM 138

The LORD's Goodness to the Faithful

A Psalm of David.

I WILL praise thee with my whole heart: [a]be-
fore the gods will I sing praise unto thee.
2 [a]I will worship [b]toward thy holy temple,
and praise thy name for thy lovingkindness and
for thy truth: for thou hast [c]magnified thy word
above all thy name.
3 In the day when I cried thou answeredst
me, *and* strengthenedst me *with* strength in my
soul.
4 [a]All the kings of the earth shall praise
thee, O LORD, when they hear the words of thy
mouth.
5 Yea, they shall sing in the ways of the
LORD: for great *is* the glory of the LORD.
6 [a]Though the LORD *be* high, yet [b]hath he
respect unto the lowly: but the proud he knoweth
afar off.
7 [a]Though I walk in the midst of trouble,
thou wilt revive me: thou shalt stretch forth thine
hand against the wrath of mine enemies, and thy
right hand shall save me.
8 [a]The LORD will perfect *that which* concerneth me: thy mercy, O LORD, *endureth* for ever:
[b]forsake not the works of thine own hands.

PSALM 139

God's Perfect Knowledge of Man

To the chief Musician, A Psalm of David.

O LORD, [a]thou hast searched me, and known
me.
2 [a]Thou knowest my downsitting and mine
uprising, thou [b]understandest my thought afar
off.
3 [a]Thou compassest my path and my lying
down, and art acquainted *with* all my ways.
4 For *there is* not a word in my tongue, *but*,
lo, O LORD, [a]thou knowest it altogether.
5 Thou hast beset me behind and before,
and laid thine hand upon me.
6 [a]*Such* knowledge *is* too wonderful for me;
it is high, I cannot *attain* unto it.

---

6 [a]Job 29:10; Ps. 22:15; Ezek. 3:26
7 [a]Jer. 49:7–22; Lam. 4:21; Ezek. 25:12–14; 35:2; Amos 1:11; Obad. 10–14
8 [a]Is. 13:1–6; 47:1 [b]Jer. 50:15; Rev. 18:6
9 [a]2 Kin. 8:12; Is. 13:16; Hos. 13:16; Nah. 3:10

PSALM 138

1 [a]Ps. 119:46
2 [a]Ps. 28:2 [b]1 Kin. 8:29 [c]Is. 42:21
4 [a]Ps. 102:15
6 [a][Ps. 113:4–7] [b]Prov. 3:34; [Is. 57:15]; Luke 1:48; [James 4:6; 1 Pet. 5:5]
7 [a][Ps. 23:3, 4]
8 [a]Ps. 57:2; [Phil. 1:6] [b]Job 10:3, 8

PSALM 139

1 [a]Ps. 17:3; Jer. 12:3
2 [a]2 Kin. 19:27 [b]Is. 66:18; Matt. 9:4
3 [a]Job 14:16; 31:4
4 [a][Heb. 4:13]
6 [a]Job 42:3; Ps. 40:5

NKJV

4 How shall we sing the LORD's song
In a foreign land?
5 If I forget you, O Jerusalem,
Let my right hand forget *its skill!*
6 If I do not remember you,
Let my [a]tongue cling to the roof of my
mouth—
If I do not exalt Jerusalem
Above my chief joy.

7 Remember, O LORD, against [a]the sons of
Edom
The day of Jerusalem,
Who said, "Raze *it*, raze *it*,
To its very foundation!"

8 O daughter of Babylon, [a]who are to be
destroyed,
Happy the one [b]who repays you as you
have served us!
9 Happy the one who takes and [a]dashes
Your little ones against the rock!

PSALM 138

The LORD's Goodness to the Faithful

A Psalm of David.

I WILL praise You with my whole heart;
[a]Before the gods I will sing praises to
You.
2 [a]I will worship [b]toward Your holy temple,
And praise Your name
For Your lovingkindness and Your truth;
For You have [c]magnified Your word
above all Your name.
3 In the day when I cried out, You answered
me,
And made me bold *with* strength in my
soul.

4 [a]All the kings of the earth shall praise You,
O LORD,
When they hear the words of Your mouth.
5 Yes, they shall sing of the ways of the
LORD,
For great *is* the glory of the LORD.
6 [a]Though the LORD *is* on high,
Yet [b]He regards the lowly;
But the proud He knows from afar.

7 [a]Though I walk in the midst of trouble, You
will revive me;
You will stretch out Your hand
Against the wrath of my enemies,
And Your right hand will save me.
8 [a]The LORD will perfect *that which* concerns
me;
Your mercy, O LORD, *endures* forever;
[b]Do not forsake the works of Your hands.

PSALM 139

God's Perfect Knowledge of Man

For the Chief Musician. A Psalm of David.

O LORD, [a]You have searched me and known
me.
2 [a]You know my sitting down and my rising
up;
You [b]understand my thought afar off.
3 [a]You comprehend my path and my lying
down,
And are acquainted with all my ways.
4 For *there is* not a word on my tongue,
But behold, O LORD, [a]You know it
altogether.
5 You have hedged me behind and before,
And laid Your hand upon me.
6 [a]*Such* knowledge *is* too wonderful for
me;
It is high, I cannot *attain* it.

KJV

7 [a]Whither shall I go from thy spirit? or
whither shall I flee from thy presence?
8 [a]If I ascend up into heaven, thou *art* there:
[b]if I make my bed in hell, behold, thou *art there.*
9 *If* I take the wings of the morning, *and*
dwell in the uttermost parts of the sea;
10 Even there shall thy hand lead me, and
thy right hand shall hold me.
11 If I say, Surely the darkness shall cover
me; even the night shall be light about me.
12 Yea, [a]the darkness hideth not from thee;
but the night shineth as the day: the darkness and
the light *are* both alike *to thee.*
13 For thou hast possessed my reins: thou
hast covered me in my mother's womb.
14 I will praise thee; for I am fearfully *and*
wonderfully made: marvellous *are* thy works; and
that my soul knoweth right well.
15 [a]My substance was not hid from thee,
when I was made in secret, *and* curiously wrought
in the lowest parts of the earth.
16 Thine eyes did see my substance, yet being unperfect; and in thy book all *my members*
were written, *which* in continuance were fashioned, when *as yet there was* none of them.
17 [a]How precious also are thy thoughts unto
me, O God! how great is the sum of them!
18 *If* I should count them, they are more in
number than the sand: when I awake, I am still
with thee.
19 Surely thou wilt [a]slay the wicked, O God:
[b]depart from me therefore, ye bloody men.
20 For they [a]speak against thee wickedly,
and thine enemies take *thy name* in vain.
21 [a]Do not I hate them, O LORD, that hate
thee? and am not I grieved with those that rise
up against thee?
22 I hate them with perfect hatred: I count
them mine enemies.
23 [a]Search me, O God, and know my heart:
try me, and know my thoughts:
24 And see if *there be any* wicked way in
me, and [a]lead me in the way everlasting.

PSALM 140

Prayer for Deliverance from Evil Men

To the chief Musician, A Psalm of David.

DELIVER me, O LORD, from the evil man: preserve me from the violent man;
2 Which imagine mischiefs in *their* heart;
[a]continually are they gathered together *for* war.
3 They have sharpened their tongues like a
serpent; [a]adders' poison *is* under their lips.
Selah.
4 [a]Keep me, O LORD, from the hands of the
wicked; preserve me from the violent man; who
have purposed to overthrow my goings.
5 The proud have hid a [a]snare for me, and
cords; they have spread a net by the wayside; they
have set gins for me. Selah.

7 [a][Jer. 23:24; Amos 9:2–4] 8 [a][Amos 9:2–4] [b][Job 26:6; Prov. 15:11] 12 [a]Job 26:6; 34:22; [Dan. 2:22; Heb. 4:13] 15 [a]Job 10:8, 9; Eccl. 11:5 17 [a][Ps. 40:5; Rom. 11:33] 19 [a][Is. 11:4] [b]Ps. 119:115 20 [a]Jude 15 21 [a]2 Chr. 19:2 23 [a]Job 31:6; Ps. 26:2 24 [a]Ps. 5:8; 143:10

PSALM 140

2 [a]Ps. 56:6 3 [a]Ps. 58:4; Rom. 3:13; James 3:8 4 [a]Ps. 71:4 5 [a]Ps. 35:7; Jer. 18:22

*139:11 Vg., Symmachus *cover*
139:14 So with MT, Tg.; LXX, Syr., Vg. *You are fearfully wonderful*
139:20 LXX, Vg. *They take your cities in vain*

NKJV

7 [a]Where can I go from Your Spirit?
Or where can I flee from Your presence?
8 [a]If I ascend into heaven, You *are* there;
[b]If I make my bed in hell, behold, You *are* *there.*
9 *If* I take the wings of the morning,
And dwell in the uttermost parts of the sea,
10 Even there Your hand shall lead me,
And Your right hand shall hold me.
11 If I say, "Surely the darkness shall *fall on me,"
Even the night shall be light about me;
12 Indeed, [a]the darkness shall not hide from You,
But the night shines as the day;
The darkness and the light *are* both alike *to You.*

13 For You formed my inward parts;
You covered me in my mother's womb.
14 I will praise You, for *I am fearfully *and* wonderfully made;
Marvelous are Your works,
And *that* my soul knows very well.
15 [a]My frame was not hidden from You,
When I was made in secret,
And skillfully wrought in the lowest parts of the earth.
16 Your eyes saw my substance, being yet unformed.
And in Your book they all were written,
The days fashioned for me,
When *as yet there were* none of them.

17 [a]How precious also are Your thoughts to me, O God!
How great is the sum of them!
18 *If* I should count them, they would be more in number than the sand;
When I awake, I am still with You.

19 Oh, that You would [a]slay the wicked, O God!
[b]Depart from me, therefore, you bloodthirsty men.
20 For they [a]speak against You wickedly;
*Your enemies take *Your name* in vain.
21 [a]Do I not hate them, O LORD, who hate You?
And do I not loathe those who rise up against You?
22 I hate them with perfect hatred;
I count them my enemies.

23 [a]Search me, O God, and know my heart;
Try me, and know my anxieties;
24 And see if *there is any* wicked way in me,
And [a]lead me in the way everlasting.

PSALM 140

Prayer for Deliverance from Evil Men

To the Chief Musician. A Psalm of David.

DELIVER me, O LORD, from evil men;
Preserve me from violent men,
2 Who plan evil things in *their* hearts;
[a]They continually gather together *for* war.
3 They sharpen their tongues like a serpent;
The [a]poison of asps *is* under their lips. Selah

4 [a]Keep me, O LORD, from the hands of the wicked;
Preserve me from violent men,
Who have purposed to make my steps stumble.
5 The proud have hidden a [a]snare for me, and cords;
They have spread a net by the wayside;
They have set traps for me. Selah

KJV

6 I said unto the LORD, Thou *art* my God: hear the voice of my supplications, O LORD.

7 O GOD the Lord, the strength of my salvation, thou hast covered my head in the day of battle.

8 Grant not, O LORD, the desires of the wicked: further not his wicked device; [a]*lest* they exalt themselves. Selah.

9 *As for* the head of those that compass me about, let the mischief of their own lips cover them.

10 [a]Let burning coals fall upon them: let them be cast into the fire; into deep pits, that they rise not up again.

11 Let not an evil speaker be established in the earth: evil shall hunt the violent man to overthrow *him*.

12 I know that the LORD will [a]maintain the cause of the afflicted, *and* the right of the poor.

13 Surely the righteous shall give thanks unto thy name: the upright shall dwell in thy presence.

PSALM 141

Prayer for Safekeeping from Wickedness

A Psalm of David.

LORD, I cry unto thee: make haste unto me; give ear unto my voice, when I cry unto thee.

2 Let my prayer be set forth before thee [a]*as* incense; *and* [b]the lifting up of my hands *as* [c]the evening sacrifice.

3 Set a watch, O LORD, before my [a]mouth; keep the door of my lips.

4 Incline not my heart to *any* evil thing, to practise wicked works with men that work iniquity: [a]and let me not eat of their dainties.

5 [a]Let the righteous smite me; *it shall be* a kindness: and let him reprove me; *it shall be* an excellent oil, *which* shall not break my head: for yet my prayer also *shall be* in their calamities.

6 When their judges are overthrown in stony places, they shall hear my words; for they are sweet.

7 Our bones are scattered at the grave's mouth, as when one cutteth and cleaveth *wood* upon the earth.

8 But [a]mine eyes *are* unto thee, O GOD the Lord: in thee is my trust; leave not my soul destitute.

9 Keep me from [a]the snares *which* they have laid for me, and the gins of the workers of iniquity.

10 [a]Let the wicked fall into their own nets, whilst that I withal escape.

---

8 [a]Deut. 32:27 **10** [a]Ps. 11:6 **12** [a]1 Kin. 8:45; Ps. 9:4

PSALM 141

2 [a][Ex. 30:8]; Luke 1:10; [Rev. 5:8; 8:3, 4] [b]Ps. 134:2; [1 Tim. 2:8] [c]Ex. 29:39, 41; 1 Kin. 18:29, 36; Dan. 9:21 **3** [a][Prov. 13:3; 21:23] **4** [a]Prov. 23:6 **5** [a][Prov. 9:8; Eccl. 7:5; Gal. 6:1] **8** [a]2 Chr. 20:12; Ps. 25:15 **9** [a]Ps. 119:110 **10** [a]Ps. 35:8

NKJV

6 I said to the LORD: "You *are* my God;
Hear the voice of my supplications,
O LORD.
7 O GOD the Lord, the strength of my
salvation,
You have covered my head in the day of
battle.
8 Do not grant, O LORD, the desires of the
wicked;
Do not further his *wicked* scheme,
[a]*Lest* they be exalted. Selah

9 "*As for* the head of those who surround
me,
Let the evil of their lips cover them;
10 [a]Let burning coals fall upon them;
Let them be cast into the fire,
Into deep pits, that they rise not up
again.
11 Let not a slanderer be established in the
earth;
Let evil hunt the violent man to overthrow
him."

12 I know that the LORD will [a]maintain
The cause of the afflicted,
And justice for the poor.
13 Surely the righteous shall give thanks to
Your name;
The upright shall dwell in Your
presence.

PSALM 141

Prayer for Safekeeping from Wickedness

A Psalm of David.

LORD, I cry out to You;
Make haste to me!
Give ear to my voice when I cry out to
You.
2 Let my prayer be set before You [a]*as*
incense,
[b]The lifting up of my hands *as* [c]the evening
sacrifice.

3 Set a guard, O LORD, over my [a]mouth;
Keep watch over the door of my lips.
4 Do not incline my heart to any evil
thing,
To practice wicked works
With men who work iniquity;
[a]And do not let me eat of their
delicacies.

5 [a]Let the righteous strike me;
It shall be a kindness.
And let him rebuke me;
It shall be as excellent oil;
Let my head not refuse it.

For still my prayer *is* against the deeds
of the wicked.
6 Their judges are overthrown by the sides
of the cliff,
And they hear my words, for they are
sweet.
7 Our bones are scattered at the mouth of
the grave,
As when one plows and breaks up the
earth.

8 But [a]my eyes *are* upon You, O GOD the
Lord;
In You I take refuge;
Do not leave my soul destitute.
9 Keep me from [a]the snares they have laid
for me,
And from the traps of the workers of
iniquity.
10 [a]Let the wicked fall into their own nets,
While I escape safely.

KJV

PSALM 142

A Plea for Relief from Persecutors

[a]Maschil of David; A Prayer [b]when he was in the cave.

I CRIED unto the LORD with my voice; with my voice unto the LORD did I make my supplication.
2 I poured out my complaint before him; I shewed before him my trouble.
3 When my spirit was [a]overwhelmed within me, then thou knewest my path. In the way wherein I walked have they privily [b]laid a snare for me.
4 I looked on *my* right hand, and beheld, but *there was* no man that would know me: refuge failed me; no man cared for my soul.
5 I cried unto thee, O LORD: I said, Thou *art* my refuge *and* my portion in the land of the living.
6 Attend unto my cry; for I am brought very low: deliver me from my persecutors; for they are stronger than I.
7 Bring my soul out of prison, that I may [a]praise thy name: the righteous shall compass me about; for thou shalt deal bountifully with me.

PSALM 143

An Earnest Appeal for Guidance and Deliverance

A Psalm of David.

HEAR my prayer, O LORD, give ear to my supplications: in thy faithfulness answer me, *and* in thy righteousness.
2 And enter not into judgment with thy servant: [a]for in thy sight shall no man living be justified.
3 For the enemy hath persecuted my soul; he hath smitten my life down to the ground; he hath made me to dwell in darkness, as those that have been long dead.
4 [a]Therefore is my spirit overwhelmed within me; my heart within me is desolate.
5 [a]I remember the days of old; I meditate on all thy works; I muse on the work of thy hands.
6 I stretch forth my hands unto thee: [a]my soul *thirsteth* after thee, as a thirsty land. Selah.
7 Hear me speedily, O LORD: my spirit faileth: hide not thy face from me, [a]lest I be like unto them that go down into the pit.
8 Cause me to hear thy lovingkindness [a]in the morning; for in thee do I trust: [b]cause me to know the way wherein I should walk; for I [c]lift up my soul unto thee.
9 Deliver me, O LORD, from mine enemies: I flee unto thee to hide me.
10 [a]Teach me to do thy will; for thou *art* my God: [b]thy spirit *is* good; lead me into [c]the land of uprightness.

PSALM 142

title [a]Ps. 32:title [b]1 Sam. 22:1; Ps. 57:title
3 [a]Ps. 77:3 [b]Ps. 141:9
7 [a]Ps. 34:1, 2

PSALM 143

2 [a][Ex. 34:7]; Job 4:17; 9:2; 25:4; Ps. 130:3; Eccl. 7:20; [Rom. 3:20–23; Gal. 2:16]
4 [a]Ps. 77:3
5 [a]Ps. 77:5, 10, 11
6 [a]Ps. 63:1
7 [a]Ps. 28:1
8 [a]Ps. 46:5 [b]Ps. 5:8 [c]Ps. 25:1
10 [a]Ps. 25:4, 5 [b]Neh. 9:20 [c]Is. 26:10

*

142:title Heb. *Maschil*
143:9 LXX, Vg. *To You I flee*

NKJV

PSALM 142

A Plea for Relief from Persecutors

A [a]Contemplation* of David. A Prayer [b]when he was in the cave.

I CRY out to the LORD with my voice;
With my voice to the LORD I make my supplication.
2 I pour out my complaint before Him;
I declare before Him my trouble.

3 When my spirit was [a]overwhelmed within me,
Then You knew my path.
In the way in which I walk
They have secretly [b]set a snare for me.
4 Look on *my* right hand and see,
For *there is* no one who acknowledges me;
Refuge has failed me;
No one cares for my soul.

5 I cried out to You, O LORD:
I said, "You *are* my refuge,
My portion in the land of the living.
6 Attend to my cry,
For I am brought very low;
Deliver me from my persecutors,
For they are stronger than I.
7 Bring my soul out of prison,
That I may [a]praise Your name;
The righteous shall surround me,
For You shall deal bountifully with me."

PSALM 143

An Earnest Appeal for Guidance and Deliverance

A Psalm of David.

HEAR my prayer, O LORD,
Give ear to my supplications!
In Your faithfulness answer me,
And in Your righteousness.
2 Do not enter into judgment with Your servant,
[a]For in Your sight no one living is righteous.

3 For the enemy has persecuted my soul;
He has crushed my life to the ground;
He has made me dwell in darkness,
Like those who have long been dead.
4 [a]Therefore my spirit is overwhelmed within me;
My heart within me is distressed.

5 [a]I remember the days of old;
I meditate on all Your works;
I muse on the work of Your hands.
6 I spread out my hands to You;
[a]My soul *longs* for You like a thirsty land. Selah

7 Answer me speedily, O LORD;
My spirit fails!
Do not hide Your face from me,
[a]Lest I be like those who go down into the pit.
8 Cause me to hear Your lovingkindness [a]in the morning,
For in You do I trust;
[b]Cause me to know the way in which I should walk,
For [c]I lift up my soul to You.

9 Deliver me, O LORD, from my enemies;
*In You I take shelter.
10 [a]Teach me to do Your will,
For You *are* my God;
[b]Your Spirit *is* good.
Lead me in [c]the land of uprightness.

KJV

11 [a]Quicken me, O LORD, for thy name's
sake: for thy righteousness' sake bring my soul
out of trouble.
12 And of thy mercy [a]cut off mine enemies,
and destroy all them that afflict my soul: for I
am thy servant.

PSALM 144

A Song to the LORD *Who Preserves and Prospers His People*

A Psalm of David.

BLESSED *be* the LORD my strength, [a]which
teacheth my hands to war, *and* my fingers to
fight:
2 My goodness, and my fortress; my high
tower, and my deliverer; my shield, and *he* in
whom I trust; who subdueth my people under me.
3 [a]LORD, what *is* man, that thou takest
knowledge of him! *or* the son of man, that thou
makest account of him!
4 [a]Man is like to vanity: [b]his days *are* as a
shadow that passeth away.
5 [a]Bow thy heavens, O LORD, and come
down: [b]touch the mountains, and they shall
smoke.
6 [a]Cast forth lightning, and scatter them:
shoot out thine arrows, and destroy them.
7 Send thine hand from above; rid me, and
deliver me out of great waters, from the hand of
strange children;
8 Whose mouth [a]speaketh vanity, and their
right hand *is* a right hand of falsehood.
9 I will [a]sing a new song unto thee, O God:
upon a psaltery *and* an instrument of ten strings
will I sing praises unto thee.
10 [a]*It is he* that giveth salvation unto kings:
who delivereth David his servant from the hurtful
sword.
11 Rid me, and deliver me from the hand of
strange children, whose mouth speaketh vanity,
and their right hand *is* a right hand of falsehood:
12 That our sons *may be* [a]as plants grown
up in their youth; *that* our daughters *may be* as
corner stones, polished *after* the similitude of a
palace:
13 *That* our garners *may be* full, affording
all manner of store: *that* our sheep may bring
forth thousands and ten thousands in our streets:
14 *That* our oxen *may be* strong to labour;
that there be no breaking in, nor going out; that
there be no complaining in our streets.
15 [a]Happy *is that* people, that is in such a
case: *yea,* happy *is that* people, whose God *is* the
LORD.

PSALM 145

A Song of God's Majesty and Love

David's [a]*Psalm* of praise.

I WILL extol thee, my God, O king; and I will
bless thy name for ever and ever.
2 Every day will I bless thee; and I will
praise thy name for ever and ever.

11 [a]Ps. 119:25
12 [a]Ps. 54:5

PSALM 144

1 [a]2 Sam. 22:35; Ps. 18:34
3 [a]Job 7:17; Ps. 8:4; Heb. 2:6
4 [a]Ps. 39:11 [b]Job 8:9; 14:2; Ps. 102:11
5 [a]Ps. 18:9; Is. 64:1 [b]Ps. 104:32
6 [a]Ps. 18:13, 14
8 [a]Ps. 12:2
9 [a]Ps. 33:2, 3; 40:3
10 [a]Ps. 18:50
12 [a]Ps. 128:3
15 [a]Deut. 33:29; [Ps. 33:12; Jer. 17:7]

PSALM 145

title [a]Ps. 100:title

*

144:2 So with MT, LXX, Vg.; Syr., Tg. *the peoples* (cf. 18:47)

NKJV

11 [a]Revive me, O LORD, for Your name's sake!
For Your righteousness' sake bring my
soul out of trouble.
12 In Your mercy [a]cut off my enemies,
And destroy all those who afflict my soul;
For I *am* Your servant.

PSALM 144

A Song to the LORD *Who Preserves and Prospers His People*

A Psalm of David.

BLESSED *be* the LORD my Rock,
[a]Who trains my hands for war,
And my fingers for battle—
2 My lovingkindness and my fortress,
My high tower and my deliverer,
My shield and *the One* in whom I take
refuge,
Who subdues *my people under me.

3 [a]LORD, what *is* man, that You take
knowledge of him?
Or the son of man, that You are mindful
of him?
4 [a]Man is like a breath;
[b]His days *are* like a passing shadow.

5 [a]Bow down Your heavens, O LORD, and
come down;
[b]Touch the mountains, and they shall
smoke.
6 [a]Flash forth lightning and scatter them;
Shoot out Your arrows and destroy them.
7 Stretch out Your hand from above;
Rescue me and deliver me out of great
waters,
From the hand of foreigners,
8 Whose mouth [a]speaks lying words,
And whose right hand *is* a right hand of
falsehood.

9 I will [a]sing a new song to You, O God;
On a harp of ten strings I will sing praises
to You,
10 *The One* who gives salvation to kings,
[a]Who delivers David His servant
From the deadly sword.

11 Rescue me and deliver me from the hand
of foreigners,
Whose mouth speaks lying words,
And whose right hand *is* a right hand of
falsehood—
12 That our sons *may be* [a]as plants grown
up in their youth;
That our daughters *may be* as pillars,
Sculptured in palace style;
13 *That* our barns *may be* full,
Supplying all kinds of produce;
That our sheep may bring forth thousands
And ten thousands in our fields;
14 *That* our oxen *may be* well-laden;
That there be no breaking in or going out;
That there be no outcry in our streets.
15 [a]Happy *are* the people who are in such a
state;
Happy *are* the people whose God *is* the
LORD!

PSALM 145

A Song of God's Majesty and Love

[a]A Praise of David.

I WILL extol You, my God, O King;
And I will bless Your name forever and
ever.
2 Every day I will bless You,
And I will praise Your name forever and
ever.

KJV

3 [a]Great *is* the LORD, and greatly to be
praised; and [b]his greatness *is* unsearchable.
4 [a]One generation shall praise thy works to
another, and shall declare thy mighty acts.
5 I will speak of the glorious honour of thy
majesty, and of thy wondrous works.
6 And *men* shall speak of the might of thy
terrible acts: and I will declare thy greatness.
7 They shall abundantly utter the memory
of thy great goodness, and shall sing of thy
righteousness.
8 [a]The LORD *is* gracious, and full of compassion; slow to anger, and of great mercy.
9 [a]The LORD *is* good to all: and his tender
mercies *are* over all his works.
10 [a]All thy works shall praise thee, O LORD;
and thy saints shall bless thee.
11 They shall speak of the glory of thy kingdom, and talk of thy power;
12 To make known to the sons of men his
mighty acts, and the glorious majesty of his
kingdom.
13 [a]Thy kingdom *is* an everlasting kingdom,
and thy dominion *endureth* throughout all generations.
14 The LORD upholdeth all that fall, and
[a]raiseth up all *those that be* bowed down.
15 [a]The eyes of all wait upon thee; and [b]thou
givest them their meat in due season.
16 Thou openest thine hand, [a]and satisfiest
the desire of every living thing.
17 The LORD *is* righteous in all his ways, and
holy in all his works.
18 [a]The LORD *is* nigh unto all them that call
upon him, to all that call upon him [b]in truth.
19 He will fulfil the desire of them that fear
him: he also will hear their cry, and will save
them.
20 [a]The LORD preserveth all them that love
him: but all the wicked will he destroy.
21 My mouth shall speak the praise of the
LORD: and let all flesh bless his holy name for
ever and ever.

PSALM 146

The Happiness of Those Whose Help Is the LORD

PRAISE ye the LORD. [a]Praise the LORD, O my
soul.
2 [a]While I live will I praise the LORD: I will
sing praises unto my God while I have any being.
3 [a]Put not your trust in princes, *nor* in the
son of man, in whom *there is* no help.
4 [a]His breath goeth forth, he returneth to
his earth; in that very day [b]his thoughts perish.
5 [a]Happy *is he* that *hath* the God of Jacob
for his help, whose hope *is* in the LORD his God:
6 [a]Which made heaven, and earth, the sea,
and all that therein *is*: which keepeth truth for
ever:
7 [a]Which executeth judgment for the op-

3 [a][Ps. 147:5] [b]Job 5:9; 9:10; 11:7; Is. 40:28; [Rom. 11:33]
4 [a]Is. 38:19
8 [a][Ex. 34:6, 7; Num. 14:18]; Ps. 86:5, 15
9 [a][Ps. 100:5]; Jer. 33:11; Nah. 1:7; [Matt. 19:17; Mark 10:18]
10 [a]Ps. 19:1
13 [a]Dan. 2:44; 4:3; [1 Tim. 1:17; 2 Pet. 1:11]
14 [a]Ps. 146:8
15 [a]Ps. 104:27 [b]Ps. 136:25
16 [a]Ps. 104:21, 28
18 [a][Deut. 4:7] [b][John 4:24]
20 [a][Ps. 31:23]

PSALM 146

1 [a]Ps. 103:1
2 [a]Ps. 104:33
3 [a][Is. 2:22]
4 [a][Eccl. 12:7] [b][Ps. 33:10; 1 Cor. 2:6]
5 [a]Jer. 17:7
6 [a]Gen. 1:1; Ex. 20:11; Acts 4:24; Rev. 14:7
7 [a]Ps. 103:6

*

145:5 So with MT, Tg.; DSS, LXX, Syr., Vg. *They* • Lit. *on the words of Your wondrous works*
145:13 So with MT, Tg.; DSS, LXX, Syr., Vg. add *The LORD is faithful in all His words, and holy in all His works*

NKJV

3 [a]Great *is* the LORD, and greatly to be praised;
And [b]His greatness *is* unsearchable.

4 [a]One generation shall praise Your works to another,
And shall declare Your mighty acts.
5 *I will meditate on the glorious splendor of Your majesty,
And *on Your wondrous works.
6 *Men* shall speak of the might of Your awesome acts,
And I will declare Your greatness.
7 They shall utter the memory of Your great goodness,
And shall sing of Your righteousness.

8 [a]The LORD *is* gracious and full of compassion,
Slow to anger and great in mercy.
9 [a]The LORD *is* good to all,
And His tender mercies *are* over all His works.

10 [a]All Your works shall praise You, O LORD,
And Your saints shall bless You.
11 They shall speak of the glory of Your kingdom,
And talk of Your power,
12 To make known to the sons of men His mighty acts,
And the glorious majesty of His kingdom.
13 [a]Your kingdom *is* an everlasting kingdom,
And Your dominion *endures* throughout all *generations.

14 The LORD upholds all who fall,
And [a]raises up all *who are* bowed down.
15 [a]The eyes of all look expectantly to You,
And [b]You give them their food in due season.
16 You open Your hand
[a]And satisfy the desire of every living thing.

17 The LORD *is* righteous in all His ways,
Gracious in all His works.
18 [a]The LORD *is* near to all who call upon Him,
To all who call upon Him [b]in truth.
19 He will fulfill the desire of those who fear Him;
He also will hear their cry and save them.
20 [a]The LORD preserves all who love Him,
But all the wicked He will destroy.
21 My mouth shall speak the praise of the LORD,
And all flesh shall bless His holy name
Forever and ever.

PSALM 146

The Happiness of Those Whose Help Is the LORD

PRAISE the LORD!

[a]Praise the LORD, O my soul!
2 [a]While I live I will praise the LORD;
I will sing praises to my God while I have my being.

3 [a]Do not put your trust in princes,
Nor in a son of man, in whom *there is* no help.
4 [a]His spirit departs, he returns to his earth;
In that very day [b]his plans perish.

5 [a]Happy *is he* who *has* the God of Jacob for his help,
Whose hope *is* in the LORD his God,
6 [a]Who made heaven and earth,
The sea, and all that *is* in them;
Who keeps truth forever,
7 [a]Who executes justice for the oppressed,

KJV

pressed: [b]which giveth food to the hungry. [c]The
LORD looseth the prisoners:
8 [a]The LORD openeth *the eyes of* the blind:
[b]the LORD raiseth them that are bowed down: the
LORD loveth the righteous:
9 [a]The LORD preserveth the strangers; he re-
lieveth the fatherless and widow: [b]but the way
of the wicked he turneth upside down.
10 [a]The LORD shall reign for ever, *even* thy
God, O Zion, unto all generations. Praise ye the
LORD.

PSALM 147

Praise to God for His Word and Providence

PRAISE ye the LORD: for [a]*it is* good to sing
praises unto our God; [b]for *it is* pleasant; *and*
[c]praise is comely.
2 The LORD doth [a]build up Jerusalem: [b]he
gathereth together the outcasts of Israel.
3 [a]He healeth the broken in heart, and
bindeth up their wounds.
4 [a]He telleth the number of the stars; he
calleth them all by *their* names.
5 [a]Great *is* our Lord, and of [b]great power:
[c]his understanding *is* infinite.
6 [a]The LORD lifteth up the meek: he casteth
the wicked down to the ground.
7 Sing unto the LORD with thanksgiving;
sing praise upon the harp unto our God:
8 [a]Who covereth the heaven with clouds,
who prepareth rain for the earth, who maketh
grass to grow upon the mountains.
9 [a]He giveth to the beast his food, *and* [b]to
the young ravens which cry.
10 [a]He delighteth not in the strength of the
horse: he taketh not pleasure in the legs of a man.
11 The LORD taketh pleasure in them that fear
him, in those that hope in his mercy.
12 Praise the LORD, O Jerusalem; praise thy
God, O Zion.
13 For he hath strengthened the bars of thy
gates; he hath blessed thy children within thee.
14 [a]He maketh peace *in* thy borders, *and*
[b]filleth thee with the finest of the wheat.
15 [a]He sendeth forth his commandment *upon*
earth: his word runneth very swiftly.
16 [a]He giveth snow like wool: he scattereth
the hoarfrost like ashes.
17 He casteth forth his ice like morsels: who
can stand before his cold?
18 [a]He sendeth out his word, and melteth
them: he causeth his wind to blow, *and* the waters
flow.
19 [a]He sheweth his word unto Jacob, [b]his
statutes and his judgments unto Israel.
20 [a]He hath not dealt so with any nation: and
as for his judgments, they have not known them.
Praise ye the LORD.

7 [b]Ps. 107:9 [c]Ps. 107:10; Is. 61:1
8 [a]Matt. 9:30; [John 9:7, 32, 33] [b]Luke 13:13
9 [a]Deut. 10:18; Ps. 68:5 [b]Ps. 147:6
10 [a]Ex. 15:18; Ps. 10:16; [Rev. 11:15]

PSALM 147

1 [a]Ps. 92:1 [b]Ps. 135:3 [c]Ps. 33:1
2 [a]Ps. 102:16 [b]Deut. 30:3; Is. 11:12; 56:8; Ezek. 39:28
3 [a][Ps. 51:17]; Is. 61:1; Luke 4:18
4 [a]Is. 40:26
5 [a]Ps. 48:1 [b]Nah. 1:3 [c]Is. 40:28
6 [a]Ps. 146:8, 9
8 [a]Job 38:26; Ps. 104:13
9 [a]Job 38:41 [b][Matt. 6:26]
10 [a]Ps. 33:16, 17
14 [a]Is. 54:13; 60:17, 18 [b]Ps. 132:15
15 [a][Ps. 107:20]
16 [a]Job 37:6
18 [a]Job 37:10
19 [a]Deut. 33:4; Ps. 103:7 [b]Mal. 4:4
20 [a]Deut. 4:32–34; [Rom. 3:1, 2]

NKJV

[b]Who gives food to the hungry.
[c]The LORD gives freedom to the prisoners.

8 [a]The LORD opens *the eyes of* the blind;
[b]The LORD raises those who are bowed down;
The LORD loves the righteous.
9 [a]The LORD watches over the strangers;
He relieves the fatherless and widow;
[b]But the way of the wicked He turns upside down.

10 [a]The LORD shall reign forever—
Your God, O Zion, to all generations.

Praise the LORD!

PSALM 147

Praise to God for His Word and Providence

PRAISE the LORD!
For [a]*it is* good to sing praises to our God;
[b]For *it is* pleasant, *and* [c]praise is beautiful.

2 The LORD [a]builds up Jerusalem;
[b]He gathers together the outcasts of Israel.
3 [a]He heals the brokenhearted
And binds up their wounds.
4 [a]He counts the number of the stars;
He calls them all by name.
5 [a]Great *is* our Lord, and [b]mighty in power;
[c]His understanding *is* infinite.
6 [a]The LORD lifts up the humble;
He casts the wicked down to the ground.

7 Sing to the LORD with thanksgiving;
Sing praises on the harp to our God,
8 [a]Who covers the heavens with clouds,
Who prepares rain for the earth,
Who makes grass to grow on the mountains.
9 [a]He gives to the beast its food,
And [b]to the young ravens that cry.

10 [a]He does not delight in the strength of the horse;
He takes no pleasure in the legs of a man.
11 The LORD takes pleasure in those who fear Him,
In those who hope in His mercy.

12 Praise the LORD, O Jerusalem!
Praise your God, O Zion!
13 For He has strengthened the bars of your gates;
He has blessed your children within you.
14 [a]He makes peace *in* your borders,
And [b]fills you with the finest wheat.

15 [a]He sends out His command *to the* earth;
His word runs very swiftly.
16 [a]He gives snow like wool;
He scatters the frost like ashes;
17 He casts out His hail like morsels;
Who can stand before His cold?
18 [a]He sends out His word and melts them;
He causes His wind to blow, *and* the waters flow.

19 [a]He declares His word to Jacob,
[b]His statutes and His judgments to Israel.
20 [a]He has not dealt thus with any nation;
And *as for His* judgments, they have not known them.

Praise the LORD!

KJV

PSALM 148

Praise to the LORD from Creation

PRAISE ye the LORD. Praise ye the LORD from
the heavens: praise him in the heights.
2 Praise ye him, all his angels: praise ye
him, all his hosts.
3 Praise ye him, sun and moon: praise him,
all ye stars of light.
4 Praise him, [a]ye heavens of heavens, and
[b]ye waters that *be* above the heavens.
5 Let them praise the name of the LORD: for
[a]he commanded, and they were created.
6 [a]He hath also stablished them for ever and
ever: he hath made a decree which shall not pass.
7 Praise the LORD from the earth, [a]ye dragons, and all deeps:
8 Fire, and hail; snow, and vapours; stormy
wind fulfilling his word:
9 [a]Mountains, and all hills; fruitful trees,
and all cedars:
10 Beasts, and all cattle; creeping things, and
flying fowl:
11 Kings of the earth, and all people; princes,
and all judges of the earth:
12 Both young men, and maidens; old men,
and children:
13 Let them praise the name of the LORD: for
his [a]name alone is excellent; his glory *is* above
the earth and heaven.
14 He also [a]exalteth the horn of his people,
the praise of [b]all his saints; *even* of the children
of Israel, [c]a people near unto him. Praise ye the
LORD.

PSALM 148

4 [a]Deut. 10:14; 1 Kin. 8:27; [Neh. 9:6] [b]Gen. 1:7
5 [a]Gen. 1:1, 6
6 [a]Ps. 89:37; [Jer. 31:35, 36; 33:20, 25]
7 [a]Is. 43:20
9 [a]Is. 44:23; 49:13
13 [a]Ps. 8:1
14 [a]1 Sam. 2:1; Ps. 75:10 [b]Ps. 149:9 [c]Lev. 10:3; Eph. 2:17

NKJV

PSALM 148

Praise to the LORD from Creation

PRAISE the LORD!

Praise the LORD from the heavens;
Praise Him in the heights!
2 Praise Him, all His angels;
Praise Him, all His hosts!
3 Praise Him, sun and moon;
Praise Him, all you stars of light!
4 Praise Him, [a]you heavens of heavens,
And [b]you waters above the heavens!

5 Let them praise the name of the LORD,
For [a]He commanded and they were
created.
6 [a]He also established them forever and
ever;
He made a decree which shall not pass
away.

7 Praise the LORD from the earth,
[a]You great sea creatures and all the
depths;
8 Fire and hail, snow and clouds;
Stormy wind, fulfilling His word;
9 [a]Mountains and all hills;
Fruitful trees and all cedars;
10 Beasts and all cattle;
Creeping things and flying fowl;
11 Kings of the earth and all peoples;
Princes and all judges of the earth;
12 Both young men and maidens;
Old men and children.

13 Let them praise the name of the LORD,
For His [a]name alone is exalted;
His glory *is* above the earth and heaven.
14 And He [a]has exalted the horn of His
people,
The praise of [b]all His saints—
Of the children of Israel,
[c]A people near to Him.

Praise the LORD!

KJV

PSALM 149

Praise to God for His Salvation and Judgment

PRAISE ye the LORD. [a]Sing unto the LORD a new
song, *and* his praise in the congregation of
saints.
2 Let Israel rejoice in him that made him:
let the children of Zion be joyful in their [a]King.
3 [a]Let them praise his name in the dance:
let them sing praises unto him with the timbrel
and harp.
4 For [a]the LORD taketh pleasure in his people: [b]he will beautify the meek with salvation.
5 Let the saints be joyful in glory: let them
[a]sing aloud upon their beds.
6 *Let* the high *praises* of God *be* in their
mouth, and [a]a twoedged sword in their hand;
7 To execute vengeance upon the heathen,
and punishments upon the people;
8 To bind their kings with chains, and their
nobles with fetters of iron;
9 [a]To execute upon them the judgment written: [b]this honour have all his saints. Praise ye the
LORD.

PSALM 149

1 [a]Ps. 33:3
2 [a]Judg. 8:23; Zech. 9:9; Matt. 21:5
3 [a]Ex. 15:20; Ps. 81:2
4 [a]Ps. 35:27 [b]Ps. 132:16; Is. 61:3
5 [a]Job 35:10
6 [a]Heb. 4:12; Rev. 1:16
9 [a]Deut. 7:1, 2; Ezek. 28:26 [b]Ps. 148:14; 1 Cor. 6:2

NKJV

PSALM 149

Praise to God for His Salvation and Judgment

PRAISE the LORD!

[a]Sing to the LORD a new song,
And His praise in the assembly of saints.

2 Let Israel rejoice in their Maker;
Let the children of Zion be joyful in their
[a]King.
3 [a]Let them praise His name with the
dance;
Let them sing praises to Him with the
timbrel and harp.
4 For [a]the LORD takes pleasure in His
people;
[b]He will beautify the humble with
salvation.

5 Let the saints be joyful in glory;
Let them [a]sing aloud on their beds.
6 *Let* the high praises of God *be* in their
mouth,
And [a]a two-edged sword in their hand,
7 To execute vengeance on the nations,
And punishments on the peoples;
8 To bind their kings with chains,
And their nobles with fetters of iron;
9 [a]To execute on them the written
judgment—
[b]This honor have all His saints.

Praise the LORD!

PSALM 150

Let All Things Praise the LORD

PRAISE [a]ye the LORD. Praise God in his sanctuary: praise him in the firmament of his power.
2 Praise him for his mighty acts: praise him according to his excellent [a]greatness.
3 Praise him with the sound of the trumpet: praise him with the psaltery and harp.
4 Praise him with the timbrel and dance: praise him with stringed instruments and organs.
5 Praise him upon the loud cymbals: praise him upon the high sounding cymbals.
6 Let every thing that hath breath praise the LORD. Praise ye the LORD.

PSALM 150

1 [a]Ps. 145:5, 6
2 [a]Deut. 3:24

NKJV

PSALM 150

Let All Things Praise the LORD

PRAISE[a] the LORD!

Praise God in His sanctuary;
Praise Him in His mighty firmament!

2 Praise Him for His mighty acts;
Praise Him according to His excellent [a]greatness!

3 Praise Him with the sound of the trumpet;
Praise Him with the lute and harp!
4 Praise Him with the timbrel and dance;
Praise Him with stringed instruments and flutes!
5 Praise Him with loud cymbals;
Praise Him with clashing cymbals!

6 Let everything that has breath praise the LORD.

Praise the LORD!

KJV

THE BOOK OF

PROVERBS

The Beginning of Knowledge

1 The [a]Proverbs of Solomon the son of David,
king of Israel;
2 To know wisdom and instruction; to perceive the words of understanding;
3 To receive the instruction of wisdom, justice, and judgment, and equity;
4 To give subtilty to the [a]simple, to the
young man knowledge and discretion.
5 [a]A wise *man* will hear, and will increase
learning; and a man of understanding shall attain
unto wise counsels:
6 To understand a proverb, and the interpretation; the words of the wise, and their [a]dark
sayings.
7 [a]The fear of the LORD *is* the beginning of
knowledge: *but* fools despise wisdom and instruction.

Shun Evil Counsel

8 [a]My son, hear the instruction of thy father,
and forsake not the law of thy mother:
9 For they *shall be* an ornament of [a]grace
unto thy head, and chains about thy neck.
10 My son, if sinners entice thee, [a]consent
thou not.
11 If they say, Come with us, let us [a]lay wait
for blood, let us lurk privily for the innocent without cause:
12 Let us swallow them up alive as the grave;
and whole, [a]as those that go down into the pit:
13 We shall find all precious substance, we
shall fill our houses with spoil:
14 Cast in thy lot among us; let us all have
one purse:
15 My son, [a]walk not thou in the way with
them; [b]refrain thy foot from their path:
16 [a]For their feet run to evil, and make haste
to shed blood.
17 Surely in vain the net is spread in the sight
of any bird.
18 And they lay wait for their *own* blood;
they lurk privily for their *own* lives.
19 [a]So *are* the ways of every one that is
greedy of gain; *which* taketh away the life of the
owners thereof.

The Call of Wisdom

20 [a]Wisdom crieth without; she uttereth her
voice in the streets:
21 She crieth in the chief place of concourse,
in the openings of the gates: in the city she uttereth her words, *saying*,

CHAPTER 1

1 [a]1 Kin. 4:32; Prov. 10:1; 25:1; Eccl. 12:9
4 [a]Prov. 9:4
5 [a]Prov. 9:9
6 [a]Num. 12:8; Ps. 78:2; Dan. 8:23
7 [a]Job 28:28; Ps. 111:10; Prov. 9:10; 15:33; [Eccl. 12:13]
8 [a]Prov. 4:1
9 [a]Prov. 3:22
10 [a]Gen. 39:7–10; Deut. 13:8; Ps. 50:18; [Eph. 5:11]
11 [a]Prov. 12:6; Jer. 5:26
12 [a]Ps. 28:1
15 [a]Ps. 1:1; Prov. 4:14 [b]Ps. 119:101
16 [a]Prov. 6:17, 18; [Is. 59:7]; Rom. 3:15
19 [a]Prov. 15:27; [1 Tim. 6:10]
20 [a]Prov. 8:1; 9:3; [John 7:37]

NKJV

THE BOOK OF

PROVERBS

The Beginning of Knowledge

1 The [a]proverbs of Solomon the son of David,
king of Israel:

2 To know wisdom and instruction,
To perceive the words of understanding,
3 To receive the instruction of wisdom,
Justice, judgment, and equity;
4 To give prudence to the [a]simple,
To the young man knowledge and discretion—
5 [a]A wise *man* will hear and increase learning,
And a man of understanding will attain wise counsel,
6 To understand a proverb and an enigma,
The words of the wise and their [a]riddles.

7 [a]The fear of the LORD *is* the beginning of knowledge,
But fools despise wisdom and instruction.

Shun Evil Counsel

8 [a]My son, hear the instruction of your father,
And do not forsake the law of your mother;
9 For they *will be* a [a]graceful ornament on your head,
And chains about your neck.

10 My son, if sinners entice you,
[a]Do not consent.
11 If they say, "Come with us,
Let us [a]lie in wait to *shed* blood;
Let us lurk secretly for the innocent without cause;
12 Let us swallow them alive like *Sheol,
And whole, [a]like those who go down to the Pit;
13 We shall find all *kinds* of precious possessions,
We shall fill our houses with spoil;
14 Cast in your lot among us,
Let us all have one purse"—
15 My son, [a]do not walk in the way with them,
[b]Keep your foot from their path;
16 [a]For their feet run to evil,
And they make haste to shed blood.
17 Surely, in vain the net is spread
In the sight of any bird;
18 But they lie in wait for their *own* blood,
They lurk secretly for their *own* lives.
19 [a]So *are* the ways of everyone who is greedy for gain;
It takes away the life of its owners.

The Call of Wisdom

20 [a]Wisdom calls aloud outside;
She raises her voice in the open squares.
21 She cries out in the *chief concourses,
At the openings of the gates in the city
She speaks her words:

*

1:12 Or *the grave*
1:21 LXX, Syr., Tg. *top of the walls;* Vg. *the head of multitudes*

KJV

22 How long, ye simple ones, will ye love
simplicity? and the scorners delight in their scorning, and fools hate knowledge?
23 Turn you at my reproof: behold, [a]I will
pour out my spirit unto you, I will make known
my words unto you.
24 [a]Because I have called, and ye refused; I
have stretched out my hand, and no man
regarded;
25 But ye [a]have set at nought all my counsel,
and would none of my reproof:
26 [a]I also will laugh at your calamity; I will
mock when your fear cometh;
27 When [a]your fear cometh as desolation,
and your destruction cometh as a whirlwind;
when distress and anguish cometh upon you.
28 [a]Then shall they call upon me, but I will
not answer; they shall seek me early, but they
shall not find me:
29 For that they [a]hated knowledge, and did
not [b]choose the fear of the LORD:
30 [a]They would none of my counsel: they despised all my reproof.
31 Therefore [a]shall they eat of the fruit of
their own way, and be filled with their own
devices.
32 For the turning away of the simple shall
slay them, and the prosperity of fools shall destroy them.
33 But whoso hearkeneth unto me shall dwell
[a]safely, and [b]shall be quiet from fear of evil.

The Value of Wisdom

2 My son, if thou wilt receive my words, and
[a]hide my commandments with thee;
2 So that thou incline thine ear unto wisdom, *and* apply thine heart to understanding;
3 Yea, if thou criest after knowledge, *and*
liftest up thy voice for understanding;
4 [a]If thou seekest her as silver, and searchest for her as *for* hid treasures;
5 [a]Then shalt thou understand the fear of
the LORD, and find the knowledge of God.
6 [a]For the LORD giveth wisdom: out of his
mouth *cometh* knowledge and understanding.
7 He layeth up sound wisdom for the righteous: [a]*he is* a buckler to them that walk uprightly.
8 He keepeth the paths of judgment, and
[a]preserveth the way of his saints.
9 Then shalt thou understand righteousness, and judgment, and equity; *yea*, every good
path.
10 When wisdom entereth into thine heart,
and knowledge is pleasant unto thy soul;
11 Discretion shall preserve thee, [a]under-
standing shall keep thee:
12 To deliver thee from the way of the evil
man, from the man that speaketh froward things;
13 Who leave the paths of uprightness, to
[a]walk in the ways of darkness;
14 [a]Who rejoice to do evil, *and* delight in the
frowardness of the wicked;
15 [a]Whose ways *are* crooked, and *they* froward in their paths:

23 [a]Is. 32:15; Joel 2:28; [John 7:39]
24 [a]Is. 65:12; 66:4; Jer. 7:13; Zech. 7:11
25 [a]Ps. 107:11; Luke 7:30
26 [a]Ps. 2:4
27 [a][Prov. 10:24, 25]
28 [a]1 Sam. 8:18; Job 27:9; 35:12; Ps. 18:41; Is. 1:15; Jer. 11:11; 14:12; Ezek. 8:18; Mic. 3:4; Zech. 7:13; [James 4:3]
29 [a]Job 21:14; Prov. 1:22 [b]Ps. 119:173
30 [a]Ps. 81:11; Prov. 1:25
31 [a]Job 4:8; Prov. 5:22, 23; 22:8; Is. 3:11; Jer. 6:19
33 [a]Prov. 3:24–26 [b]Ps. 112:7

CHAPTER 2

1 [a][Prov. 4:21]
4 [a][Prov. 3:14]
5 [a][James 1:5, 6]
6 [a]1 Kin. 3:9, 12; [Job 32:8; James 1:5]
7 [a][Ps. 84:11]; Prov. 30:5
8 [a][1 Sam. 2:9]; Ps. 66:9
11 [a]Prov. 4:6; 6:22
13 [a]Ps. 82:5; Prov. 4:19; [John 3:19, 20]
14 [a]Prov. 10:23; Jer. 11:15; [Rom. 1:32]
15 [a]Ps. 125:5; [Prov. 21:8]

NKJV

22 "How long, you simple ones, will you love
simplicity?
For scorners delight in their scorning,
And fools hate knowledge.
23 Turn at my rebuke;
Surely [a]I will pour out my spirit on you;
I will make my words known to you.
24 [a]Because I have called and you refused,
I have stretched out my hand and no one
regarded,
25 Because you [a]disdained all my counsel,
And would have none of my rebuke,
26 [a]I also will laugh at your calamity;
I will mock when your terror comes,
27 When [a]your terror comes like a storm,
And your destruction comes like a
whirlwind,
When distress and anguish come upon
you.

28 "Then[a] they will call on me, but I will not
answer;
They will seek me diligently, but they will
not find me.
29 Because they [a]hated knowledge
And did not [b]choose the fear of the
LORD,
30 [a]They would have none of my counsel
And despised my every rebuke.
31 Therefore [a]they shall eat the fruit of their
own way,
And be filled to the full with their own
fancies.
32 For the turning away of the simple will
slay them,
And the complacency of fools will destroy
them;
33 But whoever listens to me will dwell
[a]safely,
And [b]will be secure, without fear of evil."

The Value of Wisdom

2 My son, if you receive my words,
And [a]treasure my commands within
you,
2 So that you incline your ear to wisdom,
And apply your heart to understanding;
3 Yes, if you cry out for discernment,
And lift up your voice for understanding,
4 [a]If you seek her as silver,
And search for her as *for* hidden
treasures;
5 [a]Then you will understand the fear of the
LORD,
And find the knowledge of God.
6 [a]For the LORD gives wisdom;
From His mouth *come* knowledge and
understanding;
7 He stores up sound wisdom for the
upright;
[a]*He is* a shield to those who walk uprightly;
8 He guards the paths of justice,
And [a]preserves the way of His saints.
9 Then you will understand righteousness
and justice,
Equity *and* every good path.

10 When wisdom enters your heart,
And knowledge is pleasant to your soul,
11 Discretion will preserve you;
[a]Understanding will keep you,
12 To deliver you from the way of evil,
From the man who speaks perverse
things,
13 From those who leave the paths of
uprightness
To [a]walk in the ways of darkness;
14 [a]Who rejoice in doing evil,
And delight in the perversity of the
wicked;
15 [a]Whose ways *are* crooked,
And *who are* devious in their paths;

KJV

16 To deliver thee from [a]the strange woman, [b]*even* from the stranger *which* flattereth with her words;
17 Which forsaketh the guide of her youth, and forgetteth the covenant of her God.
18 For [a]her house inclineth unto death, and her paths unto the dead.
19 None that go unto her return again, neither take they hold of the paths of life.
20 That thou mayest walk in the way of good *men,* and keep the paths of the righteous.
21 For the upright shall dwell in the [a]land, and the perfect shall remain in it.
22 But the wicked shall be cut off from the earth, and the transgressors shall be rooted out of it.

Guidance for the Young

3 My son, forget not my law; [a]but let thine heart keep my commandments:
2 For length of days, and long life, and [a]peace, shall they add to thee.
3 Let not mercy and truth forsake thee: [a]bind them about thy neck; [b]write them upon the table of thine heart:
4 [a]So shalt thou find favour and good understanding in the sight of God and man.
5 [a]Trust in the LORD with all thine heart; [b]and lean not unto thine own understanding.
6 [a]In all thy ways acknowledge him, and he shall direct thy paths.
7 Be not wise in thine own [a]eyes: fear the LORD, and depart from evil.
8 It shall be health to thy navel, and [a]marrow to thy bones.
9 [a]Honour the LORD with thy substance, and with the firstfruits of all thine increase:
10 [a]So shall thy barns be filled with plenty, and thy presses shall burst out with new wine.
11 [a]My son, despise not the chastening of the LORD; neither be weary of his correction:
12 For whom the LORD loveth he correcteth; [a]even as a father the son *in whom* he delighteth.
13 [a]Happy *is* the man *that* findeth wisdom, and the man *that* getteth understanding.
14 [a]For the merchandise of it *is* better than the merchandise of silver, and the gain thereof than fine gold.
15 She *is* more precious than rubies: and [a]all the things thou canst desire are not to be compared unto her.
16 [a]Length of days *is* in her right hand; *and* in her left hand riches and honour.
17 [a]Her ways *are* ways of pleasantness, and all her paths *are* peace.
18 She *is* [a]a tree of life to them that lay hold upon her: and happy *is every one* that retaineth her.
19 [a]The LORD by wisdom hath founded the earth; by understanding hath he established the heavens.
20 By his knowledge the depths are [a]broken up, and the clouds drop down the dew.
21 My son, let not them depart from thine eyes: keep sound wisdom and discretion:

16 [a]Prov. 5:20; 6:24; 7:5 [b]Prov. 5:3
18 [a]Prov. 7:27
21 [a]Ps. 37:3

CHAPTER 3
1 [a]Deut. 8:1
2 [a]Ps. 119:165; Prov. 4:10
3 [a]Ex. 13:9; Deut. 6:8; Prov. 6:21 [b]Prov. 7:3; Jer. 17:1; [2 Cor. 3:3]
4 [a]1 Sam. 2:26; Luke 2:52; Rom. 14:18
5 [a][Ps. 37:3, 5]; Prov. 22:19 [b]Prov. 23:4; [Jer. 9:23, 24]
6 [a][1 Chr. 28:9]; Prov. 16:3; [Phil. 4:6; James 1:5]
7 [a]Rom. 12:16
8 [a]Job 21:24
9 [a]Ex. 22:29; Deut. 26:2; [Mal. 3:10]
10 [a]Deut. 28:8
11 [a]Job 5:17; Ps. 94:12; Heb. 12:5, 6; Rev. 3:19
12 [a]Deut. 8:5; Prov. 13:24
13 [a]Prov. 8:32, 34, 35
14 [a]Job 28:13
15 [a]Matt. 13:44
16 [a]Prov. 8:18; [1 Tim. 4:8]
17 [a][Matt. 11:29]
18 [a]Gen. 2:9; Prov. 11:30; 13:12; 15:4; Rev. 2:7
19 [a]Ps. 104:24; Prov. 8:27
20 [a]Gen. 7:11

NKJV

16 To deliver you from [a]the immoral woman,
[b]From the seductress *who* flatters with her words,
17 Who forsakes the companion of her youth,
And forgets the covenant of her God.
18 For [a]her house leads down to death,
And her paths to the dead;
19 None who go to her return,
Nor do they regain the paths of life—
20 So you may walk in the way of goodness,
And keep *to* the paths of righteousness.
21 For the upright will dwell in the [a]land,
And the blameless will remain in it;
22 But the wicked will be cut off from the earth,
And the unfaithful will be uprooted from it.

Guidance for the Young

3 My son, do not forget my law,
[a]But let your heart keep my commands;
2 For length of days and long life
And [a]peace they will add to you.

3 Let not mercy and truth forsake you;
[a]Bind them around your neck,
[b]Write them on the tablet of your heart,
4 [a]*And* so find favor and high esteem
In the sight of God and man.

5 [a]Trust in the LORD with all your heart,
[b]And lean not on your own understanding;
6 [a]In all your ways acknowledge Him,
And He shall *direct your paths.

7 Do not be wise in your own [a]eyes;
Fear the LORD and depart from evil.
8 It will be health to your *flesh,
And [a]strength* to your bones.

9 [a]Honor the LORD with your possessions,
And with the firstfruits of all your increase;
10 [a]So your barns will be filled with plenty,
And your vats will overflow with new wine.

11 [a]My son, do not despise the chastening of the LORD,
Nor detest His correction;
12 For whom the LORD loves He corrects,
[a]Just as a father the son *in whom* he delights.

13 [a]Happy *is* the man *who* finds wisdom,
And the man *who* gains understanding;
14 [a]For her proceeds *are* better than the profits of silver,
And her gain than fine gold.
15 She *is* more precious than rubies,
And [a]all the things you may desire cannot compare with her.
16 [a]Length of days *is* in her right hand,
In her left hand riches and honor.
17 [a]Her ways *are* ways of pleasantness,
And all her paths *are* peace.
18 She *is* [a]a tree of life to those who take hold of her,
And happy *are all* who retain her.

19 [a]The LORD by wisdom founded the earth;
By understanding He established the heavens;
20 By His knowledge the depths were [a]broken up,
And clouds drop down the dew.

21 My son, let them not depart from your eyes—
Keep sound wisdom and discretion;

3:6 Or *make smooth* or *straight*
3:8 Body, lit. *navel* • Lit. *drink*

KJV

22 So shall they be life unto thy soul, and
grace to thy neck.
23 [a]Then shalt thou walk in thy way safely,
and thy foot shall not stumble.
24 When thou liest down, thou shalt not be
afraid: yea, thou shalt lie down, and thy sleep
shall be sweet.
25 [a]Be not afraid of sudden fear, neither of
the desolation of the wicked, when it cometh.
26 For the LORD shall be thy confidence, and
shall keep thy foot from being taken.
27 [a]Withhold not good from them to whom
it is due, when it is in the power of thine hand to
do *it*.
28 [a]Say not unto thy neighbour, Go, and
come again, and to morrow I will give; when thou
hast it by thee.
29 Devise not evil against thy neighbour, seeing he dwelleth securely by thee.
30 [a]Strive not with a man without cause, if
he have done thee no harm.
31 [a]Envy thou not the oppressor, and choose
none of his ways.
32 For the froward *is* abomination to the
LORD: [a]but his secret *is* with the righteous.
33 [a]The curse of the LORD *is* in the house of
the wicked: but [b]he blesseth the habitation of the
just.
34 [a]Surely he scorneth the scorners: but he
giveth grace unto the lowly.
35 The wise shall inherit glory: but shame
shall be the promotion of fools.

Security in Wisdom

4 Hear, [a]ye children, the instruction of a father,
and attend to know understanding.
2 For I give you good doctrine, forsake ye
not my law.
3 For I was my father's son, [a]tender and
only *beloved* in the sight of my mother.
4 [a]He taught me also, and said unto me, Let
thine heart retain my words: [b]keep my commandments, and live.
5 [a]Get wisdom, get understanding: forget *it*
not; neither decline from the words of my mouth.
6 Forsake her not, and she shall preserve
thee: [a]love her, and she shall keep thee.
7 [a]Wisdom *is* the principal thing; *therefore*
get wisdom: and with all thy getting get understanding.
8 [a]Exalt her, and she shall promote thee:
she shall bring thee to honour, when thou dost
embrace her.
9 She shall give to thine head [a]an ornament
of grace: a crown of glory shall she deliver to thee.
10 Hear, O my son, and receive my sayings;
[a]and the years of thy life shall be many.
11 I have [a]taught thee in the way of wisdom;
I have led thee in right paths.
12 When thou goest, [a]thy steps shall not be
straitened; [b]and when thou runnest, thou shalt not
stumble.
13 Take fast hold of instruction; let *her* not
go: keep her; for she *is* thy life.
14 [a]Enter not into the path of the wicked, and
go not in the way of evil *men*.

23 [a][Ps. 37:24; 91:11, 12]; Prov. 10:9
25 [a]Ps. 91:5; 1 Pet. 3:14
27 [a]Rom. 13:7; [Gal. 6:10]
28 [a]Lev. 19:13; Deut. 24:15
30 [a]Prov. 26:17; [Rom. 12:18]
31 [a]Ps. 37:1; Prov. 24:1
32 [a]Ps. 25:14
33 [a]Lev. 26:14, 16; Deut. 11:28; Zech. 5:3, 4; Mal. 2:2 [b]Job 8:6; Ps. 1:3
34 [a]James 4:6; 1 Pet. 5:5

CHAPTER 4

1 [a]Ps. 34:11; Prov. 1:8
3 [a]1 Chr. 29:1
4 [a]1 Chr. 28:9; Eph. 6:4 [b]Prov. 7:2
5 [a]Prov. 2:2, 3
6 [a]2 Thess. 2:10
7 [a]Prov. 3:13, 14; Matt. 13:44
8 [a]1 Sam. 2:30
9 [a]Prov. 3:22
10 [a]Prov. 3:2
11 [a]1 Sam. 12:23
12 [a]Job 18:7; Ps. 18:36 [b][Ps. 91:11]; Prov. 3:23
14 [a]Ps. 1:1; Prov. 1:15

NKJV

22 So they will be life to your soul
And grace to your neck.
23 [a]Then you will walk safely in your way,
And your foot will not stumble.
24 When you lie down, you will not be afraid;
Yes, you will lie down and your sleep will
be sweet.
25 [a]Do not be afraid of sudden terror,
Nor of trouble from the wicked when it
comes;
26 For the LORD will be your confidence,
And will keep your foot from being
caught.

27 [a]Do not withhold good from those to whom
it is due,
When it is in the power of your hand to
do *so*.
28 [a]Do not say to your neighbor,
"Go, and come back,
And tomorrow I will give *it*,"
When *you have* it with you.
29 Do not devise evil against your neighbor,
For he dwells by you for safety's sake.
30 [a]Do not strive with a man without cause,
If he has done you no harm.

31 [a]Do not envy the oppressor,
And choose none of his ways;
32 For the perverse *person is* an abomination
to the LORD,
[a]But His secret counsel *is* with the upright.
33 [a]The curse of the LORD *is* on the house of
the wicked,
But [b]He blesses the home of the just.
34 [a]Surely He scorns the scornful,
But gives grace to the humble.
35 The wise shall inherit glory,
But shame shall be the legacy of fools.

Security in Wisdom

4 Hear, [a]*my* children, the instruction of a
father,
And give attention to know
understanding;
2 For I give you good doctrine:
Do not forsake my law.
3 When I was my father's son,
[a]Tender and the only one in the sight of
my mother,
4 [a]He also taught me, and said to me:
"Let your heart retain my words;
[b]Keep my commands, and live.
5 [a]Get wisdom! Get understanding!
Do not forget, nor turn away from the
words of my mouth.
6 Do not forsake her, and she will preserve
you;
[a]Love her, and she will keep you.
7 [a]Wisdom *is* the principal thing;
Therefore get wisdom.
And in all your getting, get understanding.
8 [a]Exalt her, and she will promote you;
She will bring you honor, when you
embrace her.
9 She will place on your head [a]an ornament
of grace;
A crown of glory she will deliver to you."

10 Hear, my son, and receive my sayings,
[a]And the years of your life will be many.
11 I have [a]taught you in the way of wisdom;
I have led you in right paths.
12 When you walk, [a]your steps will not be
hindered,
[b]And when you run, you will not stumble.
13 Take firm hold of instruction, do not let
go;
Keep her, for she *is* your life.

14 [a]Do not enter the path of the wicked,
And do not walk in the way of evil.

KJV

15 Avoid it, pass not by it, turn from it, and
pass away.
16 [a]For they sleep not, except they have done
mischief; and their sleep is taken away, unless
they cause *some* to fall.
17 For they eat the bread of wickedness, and
drink the wine of violence.
18 [a]But the path of the just [b]*is* as the shining
light, that shineth more and more unto the perfect
day.
19 [a]The way of the wicked *is* as darkness:
they know not at what they stumble.
20 My son, attend to my words; incline thine
ear unto my sayings.
21 Let them not depart from thine eyes; keep
them in the midst of thine heart.
22 For they *are* life unto those that find them,
and health to all their flesh.
23 Keep thy heart with all diligence; for out
of it *are* the issues of [a]life.
24 Put away from thee a froward mouth, and
perverse lips put far from thee.
25 Let thine eyes look right on, and let thine
eyelids look straight before thee.
26 Ponder the path of thy [a]feet, and let all
thy ways be established.
27 Turn not to the right hand nor to the left:
remove thy foot from evil.

The Peril of Adultery

5 My son, attend unto my wisdom, *and* bow
thine ear to my understanding:
2 That thou mayest regard discretion, and
that thy lips [a]may keep knowledge.
3 [a]For the lips of a strange woman drop *as*
an honeycomb, and her mouth *is* [b]smoother than
oil:
4 But her end is bitter as wormwood, sharp
as a twoedged sword.
5 Her feet go down to death; [a]her steps take
hold on hell.
6 Lest thou shouldest ponder the path of
life, her ways are moveable, *that* thou canst not
know *them*.
7 Hear me now therefore, O ye children, and
depart not from the words of my mouth.
8 Remove thy way far from her, and come
not nigh the door of her house:
9 Lest thou give thine honour unto others,
and thy years unto the cruel:
10 Lest strangers be filled with thy wealth;
and thy labours *be* in the house of a stranger;
11 And thou mourn at the last, when thy flesh
and thy body are consumed,
12 And say, How have I hated instruction,
and my heart despised reproof;
13 And have not obeyed the voice of my
teachers, nor inclined mine ear to them that instructed me!
14 I was almost in all evil in the midst of the
congregation and assembly.
15 Drink waters out of thine own cistern, and
running waters out of thine own well.
16 Let thy fountains be dispersed abroad,
and rivers of waters in the streets.
17 Let them be only thine own, and not
strangers' with thee.

16 [a]Ps. 36:4; Mic. 2:1
18 [a]Is. 26:7; Matt. 5:14, 45; Phil. 2:15
[b]2 Sam. 23:4
19 [a]1 Sam. 2:9; [Job 18:5, 6]; Prov. 2:13; [Is. 59:9, 10; Jer. 23:12]; John 12:35
23 [a][Matt. 12:34; 15:18, 19; Mark 7:21; Luke 6:45]
26 [a]Prov. 5:21; Heb. 12:13

CHAPTER 5
2 [a]Mal. 2:7
3 [a]Prov. 2:16
[b]Ps. 55:21
5 [a]Prov. 7:27

*
4:18 Lit. *light*
5:5 Or *Sheol*

NKJV

15 Avoid it, do not travel on it;
Turn away from it and pass on.
16 [a]For they do not sleep unless they have
done evil;
And their sleep is taken away unless they
make *someone* fall.
17 For they eat the bread of wickedness,
And drink the wine of violence.

18 [a]But the path of the just [b]*is* like the shining
*sun,
That shines ever brighter unto the perfect
day.
19 [a]The way of the wicked *is* like darkness;
They do not know what makes them
stumble.

20 My son, give attention to my words;
Incline your ear to my sayings.
21 Do not let them depart from your eyes;
Keep them in the midst of your heart;
22 For they *are* life to those who find them,
And health to all their flesh.
23 Keep your heart with all diligence,
For out of it *spring* the issues of [a]life.
24 Put away from you a deceitful mouth,
And put perverse lips far from you.
25 Let your eyes look straight ahead,
And your eyelids look right before you.
26 Ponder the path of your [a]feet,
And let all your ways be established.
27 Do not turn to the right or the left;
Remove your foot from evil.

The Peril of Adultery

5 My son, pay attention to my wisdom;
Lend your ear to my understanding,
2 That you may preserve discretion,
And your lips [a]may keep knowledge.
3 [a]For the lips of an immoral woman drip
honey,
And her mouth *is* [b]smoother than oil;
4 But in the end she is bitter as wormwood,
Sharp as a two-edged sword.
5 Her feet go down to death,
[a]Her steps lay hold of *hell.
6 Lest you ponder *her* path of life—
Her ways are unstable;
You do not know *them*.

7 Therefore hear me now, *my* children,
And do not depart from the words of my
mouth.
8 Remove your way far from her,
And do not go near the door of her house,
9 Lest you give your honor to others,
And your years to the cruel *one;*
10 Lest aliens be filled with your wealth,
And your labors *go* to the house of a
foreigner;
11 And you mourn at last,
When your flesh and your body are
consumed,
12 And say:
"How I have hated instruction,
And my heart despised correction!
13 I have not obeyed the voice of my
teachers,
Nor inclined my ear to those who
instructed me!
14 I was on the verge of total ruin,
In the midst of the assembly and
congregation."

15 Drink water from your own cistern,
And running water from your own
well.
16 Should your fountains be dispersed
abroad,
Streams of water in the streets?
17 Let them be only your own,
And not for strangers with you.

KJV

18 Let thy fountain be blessed: and rejoice with [a]the wife of thy youth.

19 [a]*Let her be as* the loving hind and pleasant roe; let her breasts satisfy thee at all times; and be thou ravished always with her love.

20 And why wilt thou, my son, be ravished with [a]a strange woman, and embrace the bosom of a stranger?

21 [a]For the ways of man *are* before the eyes of the LORD, and he pondereth all his goings.

22 [a]His own iniquities shall take the wicked himself, and he shall be holden with the cords of his sins.

23 [a]He shall die without instruction; and in the greatness of his folly he shall go astray.

Dangerous Promises

6 My son, [a]if thou be surety for thy friend, *if* thou hast stricken thy hand with a stranger,

2 Thou art snared with the words of thy mouth, thou art taken with the words of thy mouth.

3 Do this now, my son, and deliver thyself, when thou art come into the hand of thy friend; go, humble thyself, and make sure thy friend.

4 [a]Give not sleep to thine eyes, nor slumber to thine eyelids.

5 Deliver thyself as a roe from the hand *of the hunter,* and as a bird from the hand of the fowler.

The Folly of Indolence

6 [a]Go to the ant, thou sluggard; consider her ways, and be wise:

7 Which having no guide, overseer, or ruler,

8 Provideth her meat in the summer, *and* gathereth her food in the harvest.

9 [a]How long wilt thou sleep, O sluggard? when wilt thou arise out of thy sleep?

10 *Yet* a little sleep, a little slumber, a little folding of the hands to sleep:

11 [a]So shall thy poverty come as one that travelleth, and thy want as an armed man.

The Wicked Man

12 A naughty person, a wicked man, walketh with a froward mouth.

13 [a]He winketh with his eyes, he speaketh with his feet, he teacheth with his fingers;

14 Frowardness *is* in his heart, [a]he deviseth mischief continually; [b]he soweth discord.

15 Therefore shall his calamity come [a]suddenly; suddenly shall he [b]be broken [c]without remedy.

16 These six *things* doth the LORD hate; yea, seven *are* an abomination unto him:

17 [a]A proud look, [b]a lying tongue, and [c]hands that shed innocent blood,

18 [a]An heart that deviseth wicked imaginations, [b]feet that be swift in running to mischief,

19 [a]A false witness *that* speaketh lies, and he that [b]soweth discord among brethren.

---

18 [a]Deut. 24:5; Eccl. 9:9; Mal. 2:14
19 [a]Song 2:9
20 [a]Prov. 2:16
21 [a]2 Chr. 16:9; Job 31:4; 34:21; Prov. 15:3; Jer. 16:17; 32:19; Hos. 7:2; Heb. 4:13
22 [a]Num. 32:23; Ps. 9:5; Prov. 1:31; Is. 3:11
23 [a]Job 4:21

CHAPTER 6

1 [a]Prov. 11:15
4 [a]Ps. 132:4
6 [a]Job 12:7
9 [a]Prov. 24:33, 34
11 [a]Prov. 10:4
13 [a]Job 15:12; Ps. 35:19; Prov. 10:10
14 [a]Prov. 3:29; Mic. 2:1 [b]Prov. 6:19
15 [a]Prov. 24:22; Is. 30:13; 1 Thess. 5:3 [b]Jer. 19:11 [c]2 Chr. 36:16
17 [a]Ps. 101:5; Prov. 21:4 [b]Ps. 120:2; Prov. 12:22 [c]Deut. 19:10; Prov. 28:17; Is. 1:15
18 [a]Gen. 6:5; Ps. 36:4; Prov. 24:2; Jer. 18:18; Mark 14:1, 43–46 [b]2 Kin. 5:20–27; Is. 59:7; Rom. 3:15
19 [a]Ps. 27:12; Prov. 19:5, 9; Matt. 26:59–66 [b]Prov. 6:14; 1 Cor. 1:11–13; [Jude 3, 4, 16–19]

*6:5 One who catches birds in a trap or snare

NKJV

18 Let your fountain be blessed,
And rejoice with [a]the wife of your youth.
19 [a]*As a* loving deer and a graceful doe,
Let her breasts satisfy you at all times;
And always be enraptured with her love.
20 For why should you, my son, be enraptured by [a]an immoral woman,
And be embraced in the arms of a seductress?

21 [a]For the ways of man *are* before the eyes of the LORD,
And He ponders all his paths.
22 [a]His own iniquities entrap the wicked *man,*
And he is caught in the cords of his sin.
23 [a]He shall die for lack of instruction,
And in the greatness of his folly he shall go astray.

Dangerous Promises

6 My son, [a]if you become surety for your friend,
If you have shaken hands in pledge for a stranger,
2 You are snared by the words of your mouth;
You are taken by the words of your mouth.
3 So do this, my son, and deliver yourself;
For you have come into the hand of your friend:
Go and humble yourself;
Plead with your friend.
4 [a]Give no sleep to your eyes,
Nor slumber to your eyelids.
5 Deliver yourself like a gazelle from the hand *of the hunter,*
And like a bird from the hand of the *fowler.

The Folly of Indolence

6 [a]Go to the ant, you sluggard!
Consider her ways and be wise,
7 Which, having no captain,
Overseer or ruler,
8 Provides her supplies in the summer,
And gathers her food in the harvest.
9 [a]How long will you slumber, O sluggard?
When will you rise from your sleep?
10 A little sleep, a little slumber,
A little folding of the hands to sleep—
11 [a]So shall your poverty come on you like a prowler,
And your need like an armed man.

The Wicked Man

12 A worthless person, a wicked man,
Walks with a perverse mouth;
13 [a]He winks with his eyes,
He shuffles his feet,
He points with his fingers;
14 Perversity *is* in his heart,
[a]He devises evil continually,
[b]He sows discord.
15 Therefore his calamity shall come [a]suddenly;
Suddenly he shall [b]be broken [c]without remedy.

16 These six *things* the LORD hates,
Yes, seven *are* an abomination to Him:
17 [a]A proud look,
[b]A lying tongue,
[c]Hands that shed innocent blood,
18 [a]A heart that devises wicked plans,
[b]Feet that are swift in running to evil,
19 [a]A false witness *who* speaks lies,
And one who [b]sows discord among brethren.

KJV

Beware of Adultery

20 [a]My son, keep thy father's commandment,
and forsake not the law of thy mother:
21 [a]Bind them continually upon thine heart,
and tie them about thy neck.
22 [a]When thou goest, it shall lead thee; when
thou sleepest, [b]it shall keep thee; and *when* thou
awakest, it shall talk with thee.
23 [a]For the commandment *is* a lamp; and the
law *is* light; and reproofs of instruction *are* the
way of life:
24 [a]To keep thee from the evil woman, from
the flattery of the tongue of a strange woman.
25 [a]Lust not after her beauty in thine heart;
neither let her take thee with her eyelids.
26 For [a]by means of a whorish woman *a man*
is brought to a piece of bread: [b]and the adulteress
will [c]hunt for the precious life.
27 Can a man take fire in his bosom, and his
clothes not be burned?
28 Can one go upon hot coals, and his feet
not be burned?
29 So he that goeth in to his neighbour's wife;
whosoever toucheth her shall not be innocent.
30 *Men* do not despise a thief, if he steal to
satisfy his soul when he is hungry;
31 But *if* he be found, [a]he shall restore sevenfold; he shall give all the substance of his house.
32 *But* whoso committeth adultery with a
woman [a]lacketh understanding: he *that* doeth it
destroyeth his own soul.
33 A wound and dishonour shall he get; and
his reproach shall not be wiped away.
34 For [a]jealousy *is* the rage of a man: therefore he will not spare in the day of vengeance.
35 He will not regard any ransom; neither
will he rest content, though thou givest many gifts.

7 My son, keep my words, and [a]lay up my commandments with thee.
2 [a]Keep my commandments, and live; [b]and
my law as the apple of thine eye.
3 [a]Bind them upon thy fingers, write them
upon the table of thine heart.
4 Say unto wisdom, Thou *art* my sister; and
call understanding *thy* kinswoman:
5 [a]That they may keep thee from the
strange woman, from the stranger *which* flattereth with her words.

The Crafty Harlot

6 For at the window of my house I looked
through my casement,
7 And beheld among the simple ones, I discerned among the youths, a young man [a]void of
understanding,
8 Passing through the street near her corner; and he went the way to her house,
9 [a]In the twilight, in the evening, in the
black and dark night:
10 And, behold, there met him a woman *with*
the attire of an harlot, and subtil of heart.
11 [a](She *is* loud and stubborn; [b]her feet abide
not in her house:
12 Now *is she* without, now in the streets,
and lieth in wait at every corner.)

20 [a]Eph. 6:1
21 [a]Prov. 3:3
22 [a][Prov. 3:23] [b]Prov. 2:11
23 [a]Ps. 19:8; 2 Pet. 1:19
24 [a]Prov. 2:16
25 [a]Matt. 5:28
26 [a]Prov. 29:3 [b]Gen. 39:14 [c]Ezek. 13:18
31 [a]Ex. 22:1–4
32 [a]Prov. 7:7
34 [a]Prov. 27:4; Song 8:6

CHAPTER 7
1 [a]Prov. 2:1
2 [a]Lev. 18:5; Prov. 4:4; [Is. 55:3] [b]Deut. 32:10; Ps. 17:8; Zech. 2:8
3 [a]Deut. 6:8; Prov. 6:21
5 [a]Prov. 2:16; 5:3
7 [a][Prov. 6:32; 9:4, 16]
9 [a]Job 24:15
11 [a]Prov. 9:13; 1 Tim. 5:13 [b]Titus 2:5

*
6:22 Lit. *it*
6:26 Wife of another, lit. *a man's wife*

NKJV

Beware of Adultery

20 [a]My son, keep your father's command,
And do not forsake the law of your mother.
21 [a]Bind them continually upon your heart;
Tie them around your neck.
22 [a]When you roam, *they will lead you;
When you sleep, [b]they will keep you;
And *when* you awake, they will speak with you.
23 [a]For the commandment *is* a lamp,
And the law a light;
Reproofs of instruction *are* the way of life,
24 [a]To keep you from the evil woman,
From the flattering tongue of a seductress.
25 [a]Do not lust after her beauty in your heart,
Nor let her allure you with her eyelids.
26 For [a]by means of a harlot
A man is reduced to a crust of bread;
[b]And *an adulteress will [c]prey upon his precious life.
27 Can a man take fire to his bosom,
And his clothes not be burned?
28 Can one walk on hot coals,
And his feet not be seared?
29 So *is* he who goes in to his neighbor's wife;
Whoever touches her shall not be innocent.

30 *People* do not despise a thief
If he steals to satisfy himself when he is starving.
31 Yet *when* he is found, [a]he must restore sevenfold;
He may have to give up all the substance of his house.
32 Whoever commits adultery with a woman [a]lacks understanding;
He *who* does so destroys his own soul.
33 Wounds and dishonor he will get,
And his reproach will not be wiped away.
34 For [a]jealousy *is* a husband's fury;
Therefore he will not spare in the day of vengeance.
35 He will accept no recompense,
Nor will he be appeased though you give many gifts.

7 My son, keep my words,
And [a]treasure my commands within you.
2 [a]Keep my commands and live,
[b]And my law as the apple of your eye.
3 [a]Bind them on your fingers;
Write them on the tablet of your heart.
4 Say to wisdom, "You *are* my sister,"
And call understanding *your* nearest kin,
5 [a]That they may keep you from the immoral woman,
From the seductress *who* flatters with her words.

The Crafty Harlot

6 For at the window of my house
I looked through my lattice,
7 And saw among the simple,
I perceived among the youths,
A young man [a]devoid of understanding,
8 Passing along the street near her corner;
And he took the path to her house
9 [a]In the twilight, in the evening,
In the black and dark night.

10 And there a woman met him,
With the attire of a harlot, and a crafty heart.
11 [a]She *was* loud and rebellious,
[b]Her feet would not stay at home.
12 At times *she was* outside, at times in the open square,
Lurking at every corner.

KJV

13 So she caught him, and kissed him, *and* with an impudent face said unto him,

14 *I have* peace offerings with me; this day have I payed my vows.

15 Therefore came I forth to meet thee, diligently to seek thy face, and I have found thee.

16 I have decked my bed with coverings of tapestry, with carved *works,* with [a]fine linen of Egypt.

17 I have perfumed my bed with myrrh, aloes, and cinnamon.

18 Come, let us take our fill of love until the morning: let us solace ourselves with loves.

19 For the goodman *is* not at home, he is gone a long journey:

20 He hath taken a bag of money with him, *and* will come home at the day appointed.

21 With [a]her much fair speech she caused him to yield, [b]with the flattering of her lips she forced him.

22 He goeth after her straightway, as an ox goeth to the slaughter, or as a fool to the correction of the stocks;

23 Till a dart strike through his liver; [a]as a bird hasteth to the snare, and knoweth not that it *is* for his life.

24 Hearken unto me now therefore, O ye children, and attend to the words of my mouth.

25 Let not thine heart decline to her ways, go not astray in her paths.

26 For she hath cast down many wounded: yea, [a]many strong *men* have been slain by her.

27 [a]Her house *is* the way to hell, going down to the chambers of death.

The Excellence of Wisdom

8 Doth not [a]wisdom cry? and understanding put forth her voice?

2 She standeth in the top of high places, by the way in the places of the paths.

3 She crieth at the gates, at the entry of the city, at the coming in at the doors.

4 Unto you, O men, I call; and my voice *is* to the sons of man.

5 O ye simple, understand wisdom: and, ye fools, be ye of an understanding heart.

6 Hear; for I will speak of [a]excellent things; and the opening of my lips *shall be* right things.

7 For my mouth shall speak truth; and wickedness *is* an abomination to my lips.

8 All the words of my mouth *are* in righteousness; *there is* nothing froward or perverse in them.

9 They *are* all plain to him that understandeth, and right to them that find knowledge.

10 Receive my instruction, and not silver; and knowledge rather than choice gold.

11 [a]For wisdom *is* better than rubies; and all the things that may be desired are not to be compared to it.

12 I wisdom dwell with prudence, and find out knowledge of witty inventions.

13 [a]The fear of the LORD *is* to hate evil: [b]pride, and arrogancy, and the evil way, and [c]the froward mouth, do I hate.

14 Counsel *is* mine, and sound wisdom: I *am* understanding; [a]I have strength.

16 [a]Is. 19:9; Ezek. 27:7
21 [a]Prov. 5:3 [b]Ps. 12:2
23 [a]Eccl. 9:12
26 [a]Neh. 13:26
27 [a]Prov. 2:18; 5:5; 9:18; [1 Cor. 6:9, 10; Rev. 22:15]

CHAPTER 8
1 [a]Prov. 1:20, 21; 9:3; [1 Cor. 1:24]
6 [a]Prov. 22:20
11 [a]Job 28:15; Ps. 19:10; 119:127; Prov. 3:14, 15; 4:5, 7; 16:16
13 [a]Prov. 3:7; 16:6 [b]1 Sam. 2:3; [Prov. 16:17, 18; Is. 13:11] [c]Prov. 4:24
14 [a]Eccl. 7:19; 9:16

NKJV

13 So she caught him and kissed him;
With an impudent face she said to him:
14 "*I have* peace offerings with me;
Today I have paid my vows.
15 So I came out to meet you,
Diligently to seek your face,
And I have found you.
16 I have spread my bed with tapestry,
Colored coverings of [a]Egyptian linen.
17 I have perfumed my bed
With myrrh, aloes, and cinnamon.
18 Come, let us take our fill of love until morning;
Let us delight ourselves with love.
19 For my husband *is* not at home;
He has gone on a long journey;
20 He has taken a bag of money with him,
And will come home on the appointed day."

21 With [a]her enticing speech she caused him to yield,
[b]With her flattering lips she seduced him.
22 Immediately he went after her, as an ox goes to the slaughter,
Or *as a fool to the correction of the stocks,
23 Till an arrow struck his liver.
[a]As a bird hastens to the snare,
He did not know it *would cost* his life.

24 Now therefore, listen to me, *my* children;
Pay attention to the words of my mouth:
25 Do not let your heart turn aside to her ways,
Do not stray into her paths;
26 For she has cast down many wounded,
And [a]all who were slain by her were strong *men.*
27 [a]Her house *is* the way to *hell,
Descending to the chambers of death.

The Excellence of Wisdom

8 Does not [a]wisdom cry out,
And understanding lift up her voice?
2 She takes her stand on the top of the high hill,
Beside the way, where the paths meet.
3 She cries out by the gates, at the entry of the city,
At the entrance of the doors:
4 "To you, O men, I call,
And my voice *is* to the sons of men.
5 O you simple ones, understand prudence,
And you fools, be of an understanding heart.
6 Listen, for I will speak of [a]excellent things,
And from the opening of my lips *will come* right things;
7 For my mouth will speak truth;
Wickedness *is* an abomination to my lips.
8 All the words of my mouth *are* with righteousness;
Nothing crooked or perverse *is* in them.
9 They *are* all plain to him who understands,
And right to those who find knowledge.
10 Receive my instruction, and not silver,
And knowledge rather than choice gold;
11 [a]For wisdom *is* better than rubies,
And all the things one may desire cannot be compared with her.

12 "I, wisdom, dwell with prudence,
And find out knowledge *and* discretion.
13 [a]The fear of the LORD *is* to hate evil;
[b]Pride and arrogance and the evil way
And [c]the perverse mouth I hate.
14 Counsel *is* mine, and sound wisdom;
I *am* understanding, [a]I have strength.

*

7:22 LXX, Syr., Tg. *as a dog to bonds;* Vg. *as a lamb . . . to bonds*
7:27 Or *Sheol*

KJV

15 [a]By me kings reign, and princes decree
justice.
16 By me princes rule, and nobles, *even* all
the judges of the earth.
17 [a]I love them that love me; and [b]those that
seek me early shall find me.
18 [a]Riches and honour *are* with me; *yea,* durable riches and righteousness.
19 My fruit *is* better than gold, yea, than fine
gold; and my revenue than choice silver.
20 I lead in the way of righteousness, in the
midst of the paths of judgment:
21 That I may cause those that love me to
inherit substance; and I will fill their treasures.
22 [a]The LORD possessed me in the beginning
of his way, before his works of old.
23 [a]I was set up from everlasting, from the
beginning, or ever the earth was.
24 When *there were* no depths, I was brought
forth; when *there were* no fountains abounding
with water.
25 [a]Before the mountains were settled, before the hills was I brought forth:
26 While as yet he had not made the earth,
nor the fields, nor the highest part of the dust of
the world.
27 When he prepared the heavens, I *was*
there: when he set a compass upon the face of
the depth:
28 When he established the clouds above:
when he strengthened the fountains of the deep:
29 [a]When he gave to the sea his decree, that
the waters should not pass his commandment:
when [b]he appointed the foundations of the earth:
30 [a]Then I was by him, *as* one brought up
with him: [b]and I was daily *his* delight, rejoicing
always before him;
31 Rejoicing in the habitable part of his
earth; and [a]my delights *were* with the sons of
men.
32 Now therefore hearken unto me, O ye children: for [a]blessed *are they that* keep my ways.
33 Hear instruction, and be wise, and refuse
it not.
34 [a]Blessed *is* the man that heareth me,
watching daily at my gates, waiting at the posts
of my doors.
35 For whoso findeth me findeth life, and
shall [a]obtain favour of the LORD.
36 But he that sinneth against me [a]wrongeth
his own soul: all they that hate me love death.

The Way of Wisdom

9 Wisdom hath [a]builded her house, she hath
hewn out her seven pillars:
2 [a]She hath killed her beasts; [b]she hath
mingled her wine; she hath also furnished her
table.
3 She hath sent forth her maidens: she crieth upon the highest places of the city,
4 [a]Whoso *is* simple, let him turn in hither:
as for him that wanteth understanding, she saith
to him,
5 [a]Come, eat of my bread, and drink of the
wine *which* I have mingled.
6 Forsake the foolish, and live; and go in
the way of understanding.

15 [a]2 Chr. 1:10; Prov. 29:4; Dan. 2:21; [Matt. 28:18]; Rom. 13:1
17 [a]1 Sam. 2:30; [Ps. 91:14]; Prov. 4:6; [John 14:21] [b]Prov. 2:4, 5; John 7:37; James 1:5
18 [a]Prov. 3:16; [Matt. 6:33]
22 [a]Job 28:26–28; Ps. 104:24; Prov. 3:19; [John 1:1]
23 [a][Ps. 2:6]
25 [a]Job 15:7, 8
29 [a]Gen. 1:9, 10; Job 38:8–11; Ps. 33:7; 104:9; Jer. 5:22 [b]Job 28:4, 6; Ps. 104:5
30 [a][John 1:1–3, 18] [b][Matt. 3:17]
31 [a]Ps. 16:3; John 13:1
32 [a]Ps. 119:1, 2; 128:1; Prov. 29:18; Luke 11:28
34 [a]Prov. 3:13, 18
35 [a]Prov. 3:4; 12:2; [John 17:3]
36 [a]Prov. 20:2

CHAPTER 9
1 [a][Matt. 16:18; 1 Cor. 3:9, 10; Eph. 2:20–22; 1 Pet. 2:5]
2 [a]Matt. 22:4 [b]Prov. 23:30
4 [a]Ps. 19:7
5 [a]Song 5:1; Is. 55:1; [John 6:27]

*
8:16 MT, Syr., Tg., Vg. *righteousness;* LXX, Bg., some mss. and editions *earth*
8:30 A Jewish tradition *one brought up*

NKJV

15 [a]By me kings reign,
And rulers decree justice.
16 By me princes rule, and nobles,
All the judges of *the earth.
17 [a]I love those who love me,
And [b]those who seek me diligently will find me.
18 [a]Riches and honor *are* with me,
Enduring riches and righteousness.
19 My fruit *is* better than gold, yes, than fine gold,
And my revenue than choice silver.
20 I traverse the way of righteousness,
In the midst of the paths of justice,
21 That I may cause those who love me to inherit wealth,
That I may fill their treasuries.

22 "The[a] LORD possessed me at the beginning of His way,
Before His works of old.
23 [a]I have been established from everlasting,
From the beginning, before there was ever an earth.
24 When *there were* no depths I was brought forth,
When *there were* no fountains abounding with water.
25 [a]Before the mountains were settled,
Before the hills, I was brought forth;
26 While as yet He had not made the earth or the fields,
Or the primal dust of the world.
27 When He prepared the heavens, I *was* there,
When He drew a circle on the face of the deep,
28 When He established the clouds above,
When He strengthened the fountains of the deep,
29 [a]When He assigned to the sea its limit,
So that the waters would not transgress His command,
When [b]He marked out the foundations of the earth,
30 [a]Then I was beside Him *as* *a master craftsman;
[b]And I was daily *His* delight,
Rejoicing always before Him,
31 Rejoicing in His inhabited world,
And [a]my delight *was* with the sons of men.

32 "Now therefore, listen to me, *my* children,
For [a]blessed *are those who* keep my ways.
33 Hear instruction and be wise,
And do not disdain *it.*
34 [a]Blessed is the man who listens to me,
Watching daily at my gates,
Waiting at the posts of my doors.
35 For whoever finds me finds life,
And [a]obtains favor from the LORD;
36 But he who sins against me [a]wrongs his own soul;
All those who hate me love death."

The Way of Wisdom

9 Wisdom has [a]built her house,
She has hewn out her seven pillars;
2 [a]She has slaughtered her meat,
[b]She has mixed her wine,
She has also furnished her table.
3 She has sent out her maidens,
She cries out from the highest places of the city,
4 "Whoever[a] *is* simple, let him turn in here!"
As for him who lacks understanding, she says to him,
5 "Come,[a] eat of my bread
And drink of the wine I have mixed.
6 Forsake foolishness and live,
And go in the way of understanding.

KJV

7 He that reproveth a scorner getteth to
himself shame: and he that rebuketh a wicked
man getteth himself a blot.
8 [a]Reprove not a scorner, lest he hate thee:
[b]rebuke a wise man, and he will love thee.
9 Give *instruction* to a wise *man,* and he
will be yet wiser: teach a just *man,* [a]and he will
increase in learning.
10 [a]The fear of the LORD *is* the beginning
of wisdom: and the knowledge of the holy *is*
understanding.
11 [a]For by me thy days shall be multiplied,
and the years of thy life shall be increased.
12 [a]If thou be wise, thou shalt be wise for
thyself: but *if* thou scornest, thou alone shalt bear
it.

The Way of Folly

13 [a]A foolish woman *is* clamorous: *she is*
simple, and knoweth nothing.
14 For she sitteth at the door of her house,
on a seat [a]in the high places of the city,
15 To call passengers who go right on their
ways:
16 [a]Whoso *is* simple, let him turn in hither:
and *as for* him that wanteth understanding, she
saith to him,
17 [a]Stolen waters are sweet, and bread *eaten*
in secret is pleasant.
18 But he knoweth not that [a]the dead *are*
there; *and that* her guests *are* in the depths of
hell.

Wise Sayings of Solomon

10 The proverbs of [a]Solomon. [b]A wise son
maketh a glad father: but a foolish son *is*
the heaviness of his mother.
2 [a]Treasures of wickedness profit nothing:
[b]but righteousness delivereth from death.
3 [a]The LORD will not suffer the soul of the
righteous to famish: but he casteth away the substance of the wicked.
4 [a]He becometh poor that dealeth *with* a
slack hand: but [b]the hand of the diligent maketh
rich.
5 He that gathereth in [a]summer *is* a wise
son: *but* he that sleepeth in harvest *is* [b]a son that
causeth shame.
6 Blessings *are* upon the head of the just:
but violence covereth the mouth of the wicked.
7 [a]The memory of the just *is* blessed: but
the name of the wicked shall rot.
8 The wise in heart will receive commandments: [a]but a prating fool shall fall.
9 [a]He that walketh uprightly walketh
surely: but he that perverteth his ways shall be
known.
10 He that winketh with the eye causeth sorrow: but a prating fool shall fall.
11 The mouth of a righteous *man is* a well
of life: but violence covereth the mouth of the
wicked.
12 Hatred stirreth up strifes: but [a]love covereth all sins.

8 [a]Prov. 15:12; Matt. 7:6 [b]Ps. 141:5; Prov. 10:8
9 [a][Matt. 13:12]
10 [a]Job 28:28; Ps. 111:10; Prov. 1:7
11 [a]Prov. 3:2, 16
12 [a]Job 35:6, 7; Prov. 16:26
13 [a]Prov. 7:11
14 [a]Prov. 9:3
16 [a]Prov. 7:7, 8
17 [a]Prov. 20:17
18 [a]Prov. 2:18; 7:27

CHAPTER 10
1 [a]Prov. 1:1; 25:1 [b]Prov. 15:20; 17:21, 25; 19:13; 29:3, 15
2 [a]Ps. 49:7; Prov. 11:4; 21:6; Ezek. 7:19; [Luke 12:19, 20] [b]Dan. 4:27
3 [a]Ps. 34:9, 10; 37:25; Prov. 28:25; [Matt. 6:33]
4 [a]Prov. 19:15 [b]Prov. 12:24; 13:4; 21:5
5 [a]Prov. 6:8 [b]Prov. 19:26
7 [a]Ps. 112:6; Eccl. 8:10
8 [a]Prov. 10:10
9 [a][Ps. 23:4; Prov. 3:23; 28:18; Is. 33:15, 16]
12 [a]Prov. 17:9; [1 Cor. 13:4–7; James 5:20]; 1 Pet. 4:8

*
9:18 Or *Sheol*

NKJV

7 "He who corrects a scoffer gets shame for
himself,
And he who rebukes a wicked *man only*
harms himself.
8 [a]Do not correct a scoffer, lest he hate
you;
[b]Rebuke a wise *man,* and he will love you.
9 Give *instruction* to a wise *man,* and he
will be still wiser;
Teach a just *man,* [a]and he will increase
in learning.

10 "The[a] fear of the LORD *is* the beginning of
wisdom,
And the knowledge of the Holy One *is*
understanding.
11 [a]For by me your days will be multiplied,
And years of life will be added to you.
12 [a]If you are wise, you are wise for
yourself,
And *if* you scoff, you will bear *it* alone."

The Way of Folly

13 [a]A foolish woman is clamorous;
She is simple, and knows nothing.
14 For she sits at the door of her house,
On a seat [a]*by* the highest places of the
city,
15 To call to those who pass by,
Who go straight on their way:
16 "Whoever[a] *is* simple, let him turn in here";
And *as for* him who lacks understanding,
she says to him,
17 "Stolen[a] water is sweet,
And bread *eaten* in secret is pleasant."
18 But he does not know that [a]the dead *are*
there,
That her guests *are* in the depths of *hell.

Wise Sayings of Solomon

10 The proverbs of [a]Solomon:

[b]A wise son makes a glad father,
But a foolish son *is* the grief of his mother.

2 [a]Treasures of wickedness profit nothing,
[b]But righteousness delivers from death.
3 [a]The LORD will not allow the righteous soul
to famish,
But He casts away the desire of the
wicked.
4 [a]He who has a slack hand becomes poor,
But [b]the hand of the diligent makes rich.
5 He who gathers in [a]summer *is* a wise
son;
He who sleeps in harvest *is* [b]a son who
causes shame.

6 Blessings *are* on the head of the righteous,
But violence covers the mouth of the
wicked.
7 [a]The memory of the righteous *is* blessed,
But the name of the wicked will rot.

8 The wise in heart will receive commands,
[a]But a prating fool will fall.

9 [a]He who walks with integrity walks
securely,
But he who perverts his ways will become
known.

10 He who winks with the eye causes trouble,
But a prating fool will fall.

11 The mouth of the righteous *is* a well of
life,
But violence covers the mouth of the
wicked.

12 Hatred stirs up strife,
But [a]love covers all sins.

KJV

13 In the lips of him that hath understanding
wisdom is found: but [a]a rod *is* for the back of
him that is void of understanding.
14 Wise *men* lay up knowledge: but [a]the
mouth of the foolish *is* near destruction.
15 The [a]rich man's wealth *is* his strong city:
the destruction of the poor *is* their poverty.
16 The labour of the righteous *tendeth* to
[a]life: the fruit of the wicked to sin.
17 He *is in* the way of life that keepeth instruction: but he that refuseth reproof erreth.
18 He that [a]hideth hatred *with* lying lips, and
[b]he that uttereth a slander, *is* a fool.
19 [a]In the multitude of words there wanteth
not sin: but [b]he that refraineth his lips *is* wise.
20 The tongue of the just *is as* choice silver:
the heart of the wicked *is* little worth.
21 The lips of the righteous feed many: but
fools die for want of wisdom.
22 [a]The blessing of the LORD, it maketh rich,
and he addeth no sorrow with it.
23 [a]*It is* as sport to a fool to do mischief: but
a man of understanding hath wisdom.
24 [a]The fear of the wicked, it shall come upon
him: but [b]the desire of the righteous shall be
granted.
25 As the whirlwind passeth, [a]so *is* the
wicked no *more:* but [b]the righteous *is* an everlasting foundation.
26 As vinegar to the teeth, and as smoke to
the eyes, so *is* the sluggard to them that send him.
27 [a]The fear of the LORD prolongeth days: but
[b]the years of the wicked shall be shortened.
28 The hope of the righteous *shall be* gladness: but the [a]expectation of the wicked shall
perish.
29 The way of the LORD *is* strength to the upright: but [a]destruction *shall be* to the workers of
iniquity.
30 [a]The righteous shall never be removed:
but the wicked shall not inhabit the earth.
31 [a]The mouth of the just bringeth forth wisdom: but the froward tongue shall be cut out.
32 The lips of the righteous know what is acceptable: but the mouth of the wicked *speaketh*
frowardness.

11 A [a]false balance *is* abomination to the
LORD: but a just weight *is* his delight.
2 *When* pride cometh, then cometh [a]shame:
but with the lowly *is* wisdom.
3 The integrity of the upright shall guide
[a]them: but the perverseness of transgressors shall
destroy them.

13 [a]Prov. 26:3
14 [a]Prov. 18:7
15 [a]Job 31:24; Ps. 52:7; Prov. 18:11; [1 Tim. 6:17]
16 [a]Prov. 6:23
18 [a]Prov. 26:24 [b]Ps. 15:3; 101:5
19 [a]Job 11:2; [Prov. 18:21]; Eccl. 5:3 [b]Prov. 17:27; [James 1:19; 3:2]
22 [a]Gen. 24:35; 26:12; Deut. 8:18; Ps. 37:22; Prov. 8:21
23 [a]Prov. 2:14; 15:21
24 [a]Job 15:21; Prov. 1:27; Is. 66:4 [b]Ps. 145:19; Prov. 15:8; Matt. 5:6; [1 John 5:14, 15]
25 [a]Ps. 37:9, 10 [b]Ps. 15:5; Prov. 12:3; Matt. 7:24, 25
27 [a]Prov. 9:11 [b]Job 15:32
28 [a]Job 8:13
29 [a]Ps. 1:6
30 [a]Ps. 37:22; Prov. 2:21
31 [a]Ps. 37:30; Prov. 10:13

CHAPTER 11

1 [a]Lev. 19:35, 36; Deut. 25:13–16; Prov. 20:10, 23; Mic. 6:11
2 [a]Prov. 16:18; 18:12; 29:23
3 [a]Prov. 13:6

*

10:21 Lit. *heart*

NKJV

13 Wisdom is found on the lips of him who
has understanding,
But [a]a rod *is* for the back of him who is
devoid of understanding.

14 Wise *people* store up knowledge,
But [a]the mouth of the foolish *is* near
destruction.

15 The [a]rich man's wealth *is* his strong city;
The destruction of the poor *is* their
poverty.

16 The labor of the righteous *leads* to [a]life,
The wages of the wicked to sin.

17 He who keeps instruction *is in* the way
of life,
But he who refuses correction goes astray.

18 Whoever [a]hides hatred *has* lying lips,
And [b]whoever spreads slander *is* a fool.

19 [a]In the multitude of words sin is not
lacking,
But [b]he who restrains his lips *is* wise.
20 The tongue of the righteous *is* choice
silver;
The heart of the wicked *is worth* little.
21 The lips of the righteous feed many,
But fools die for lack of *wisdom.

22 [a]The blessing of the LORD makes *one* rich,
And He adds no sorrow with it.

23 [a]To do evil *is* like sport to a fool,
But a man of understanding has wisdom.
24 [a]The fear of the wicked will come upon
him,
And [b]the desire of the righteous will be
granted.
25 When the whirlwind passes by, [a]the
wicked *is* no *more,*
But [b]the righteous *has* an everlasting
foundation.

26 As vinegar to the teeth and smoke to the
eyes,
So *is* the lazy *man* to those who send him.

27 [a]The fear of the LORD prolongs days,
But [b]the years of the wicked will be
shortened.
28 The hope of the righteous *will be* gladness,
But the [a]expectation of the wicked will
perish.
29 The way of the LORD *is* strength for the
upright,
But [a]destruction *will come* to the workers
of iniquity.

30 [a]The righteous will never be removed,
But the wicked will not inhabit the earth.
31 [a]The mouth of the righteous brings forth
wisdom,
But the perverse tongue will be cut out.
32 The lips of the righteous know what is
acceptable,
But the mouth of the wicked *what is*
perverse.

11 [a]Dishonest scales *are* an abomination to
the LORD,
But a just weight *is* His delight.

2 When pride comes, then comes [a]shame;
But with the humble *is* wisdom.

3 The integrity of the upright will guide
[a]them,
But the perversity of the unfaithful will
destroy them.

KJV

4 [a]Riches profit not in the day of wrath: but
[b]righteousness delivereth from death.
5 The righteousness of the perfect shall direct his way: but the wicked shall fall by his own
[a]wickedness.
6 The righteousness of the upright shall deliver them: but transgressors shall be taken in
their own naughtiness.
7 When a wicked man dieth, *his* expectation shall [a]perish: and the hope of unjust *men*
perisheth.
8 [a]The righteous is delivered out of trouble,
and the wicked cometh in his stead.
9 An hypocrite with *his* mouth destroyeth
his neighbour: but through knowledge shall the
just be delivered.
10 [a]When it goeth well with the righteous,
the city rejoiceth: and when the wicked perish,
there is shouting.
11 By the blessing of the upright the city is
[a]exalted: but it is overthrown by the mouth of the
wicked.
12 He that is void of wisdom despiseth his
neighbour: but a man of understanding holdeth
his peace.
13 [a]A talebearer revealeth secrets: but he
that is of a faithful spirit [b]concealeth the matter.
14 [a]Where no counsel *is*, the people fall: but
in the multitude of counsellors *there is* safety.
15 He that is [a]surety for a stranger shall
smart *for it:* and he that hateth suretiship is sure.
16 A gracious woman retaineth honour: and
strong *men* retain riches.
17 [a]The merciful man doeth good to his own
soul: but *he that is* cruel troubleth his own flesh.
18 The wicked worketh a deceitful work: but
[a]to him that soweth righteousness *shall be* a sure
reward.
19 As righteousness *tendeth* to [a]life: so he
that pursueth evil *pursueth it* to his own [b]death.
20 They that are of a froward heart *are*
abomination to the LORD: but *such as are* upright
in *their* way *are* his delight.
21 [a]*Though* hand *join* in hand, the wicked
shall not be unpunished: but [b]the seed of the righteous shall be delivered.
22 *As* a jewel of gold in a swine's snout, *so*
is a fair woman which is without discretion.
23 The desire of the righteous *is* only good:
but the expectation of the wicked [a]*is* wrath.
24 There is that [a]scattereth, and yet increaseth; and *there is* that withholdeth more than is
meet, but *it tendeth* to poverty.
25 [a]The liberal soul shall be made fat: [b]and
he that watereth shall be watered also himself.

4 [a]Prov. 10:2; Ezek. 7:19; Zeph. 1:18 [b]Gen. 7:1
5 [a]Prov. 5:22
7 [a]Prov. 10:28
8 [a]Prov. 21:18
10 [a]Prov. 28:12
11 [a]Prov. 14:34
13 [a]Lev. 19:16; Prov. 20:19; 1 Tim. 5:13 [b]Prov. 19:11
14 [a]1 Kin. 12:1
15 [a]Prov. 6:1, 2
17 [a][Matt. 5:7; 25:34–36]
18 [a]Hos. 10:12; [Gal. 6:8, 9]; James 3:18
19 [a]Prov. 10:16; 12:28 [b]Prov. 21:16; [Rom. 6:23; James 1:15]
21 [a]Prov. 16:5 [b]Ps. 112:2; Prov. 14:26
23 [a]Prov. 10:28; Rom. 2:8, 9
24 [a]Ps. 112:9; Prov. 13:7; 19:17
25 [a]Prov. 3:9, 10; [2 Cor. 9:6, 7] [b][Matt. 5:7]

NKJV

4 [a]Riches do not profit in the day of wrath,
But [b]righteousness delivers from death.
5 The righteousness of the blameless will
*direct his way aright,
But the wicked will fall by his own
[a]wickedness.
6 The righteousness of the upright will
deliver them,
But the unfaithful will be caught by *their*
lust.

7 When a wicked man dies, *his* expectation
will [a]perish,
And the hope of the unjust perishes.
8 [a]The righteous is delivered from trouble,
And it comes to the wicked instead.
9 The hypocrite with *his* mouth destroys his
neighbor,
But through knowledge the righteous will
be delivered.
10 [a]When it goes well with the righteous, the
city rejoices;
And when the wicked perish, *there is*
jubilation.
11 By the blessing of the upright the city is
[a]exalted,
But it is overthrown by the mouth of the
wicked.

12 He who is devoid of wisdom despises his
neighbor,
But a man of understanding holds his
peace.
13 [a]A talebearer reveals secrets,
But he who is of a faithful spirit [b]conceals
a matter.
14 [a]Where *there is* no counsel, the people fall;
But in the multitude of counselors *there*
is safety.
15 He who is [a]surety for a stranger will
suffer,
But one who hates being surety is secure.

16 A gracious woman retains honor,
But ruthless *men* retain riches.
17 [a]The merciful man does good for his own
soul,
But *he who is* cruel troubles his own flesh.
18 The wicked *man* does deceptive work,
But [a]he who sows righteousness *will have*
a sure reward.
19 As righteousness *leads* to [a]life,
So he who pursues evil *pursues it* to his
own [b]death.
20 Those who are of a perverse heart *are* an
abomination to the LORD,
But *the* blameless in their ways *are* His
delight.
21 [a]*Though they join* *forces, the wicked will
not go unpunished;
But [b]the posterity of the righteous will be
delivered.

22 *As* a ring of gold in a swine's snout,
So is a lovely woman who lacks
discretion.

23 The desire of the righteous *is* only good,
But the expectation of the wicked [a]*is*
wrath.

24 There is *one* who [a]scatters, yet increases
more;
And there is *one* who withholds more than
is right,
But it *leads* to poverty.
25 [a]The generous soul will be made rich,
[b]And he who waters will also be watered
himself.

*
11:5 Or *make smooth* or *straight*
11:21 Lit. *hand to hand*

KJV

26 [a]He that withholdeth corn, the people shall curse him: but [b]blessing *shall be* upon the head of him that selleth *it*.

27 He that diligently seeketh good procureth favour: but [a]he that seeketh mischief, it shall come unto him.

28 [a]He that trusteth in his riches shall fall: but [b]the righteous shall flourish as a branch.

29 He that troubleth his own house [a]shall inherit the wind: and the fool *shall be* [b]servant to the wise of heart.

30 The fruit of the righteous *is* a tree of life; and [a]he that winneth souls *is* wise.

31 [a]Behold, the righteous shall be recompensed in the earth: much more the wicked and the sinner.

12

Whoso loveth instruction loveth knowledge: but he that hateth reproof *is* brutish.

2 A good *man* obtaineth favour of the LORD: but a man of wicked devices will he condemn.

3 A man shall not be established by wickedness: but the [a]root of the righteous shall not be moved.

4 [a]A virtuous woman *is* a crown to her husband: but she that maketh ashamed *is* [b]as rottenness in his bones.

5 The thoughts of the righteous *are* right: *but* the counsels of the wicked *are* deceit.

6 [a]The words of the wicked *are* to lie in wait for blood: [b]but the mouth of the upright shall deliver them.

7 [a]The wicked are overthrown, and *are* not: but the house of the righteous shall stand.

8 A man shall be commended according to his wisdom: [a]but he that is of a perverse heart shall be despised.

9 [a]*He that is* despised, and hath a servant, *is* better than he that honoureth himself, and lacketh bread.

10 [a]A righteous *man* regardeth the life of his beast: but the tender mercies of the wicked *are* cruel.

11 [a]He that tilleth his land shall be satisfied with [b]bread: but he that followeth vain *persons* [c]*is* void of understanding.

12 The wicked desireth the net of evil *men:* but the root of the righteous yieldeth *fruit*.

13 [a]The wicked is snared by the transgression of *his* lips: [b]but the just shall come out of trouble.

26 [a]Amos 8:5, 6 [b]Job 29:13
27 [a]Esth. 7:10; Ps. 7:15, 16; 57:6
28 [a]Job 31:24 [b]Ps. 1:3; Jer. 17:8
29 [a]Eccl. 5:16 [b]Prov. 14:19
30 [a]Prov. 14:25; [Dan. 12:3; 1 Cor. 9:19–22; James 5:20]
31 [a]Jer. 25:29

CHAPTER 12
3 [a][Prov. 10:25]
4 [a]Prov. 31:23; 1 Cor. 11:7 [b]Prov. 14:30; Hab. 3:16
6 [a]Prov. 1:11, 18 [b]Prov. 14:3
7 [a]Ps. 37:35–37; Prov. 11:21; Matt. 7:24–27
8 [a]1 Sam. 25:17; Prov. 18:3
9 [a]Prov. 13:7
10 [a]Deut. 25:4
11 [a]Gen. 3:19 [b]Prov. 28:19 [c]Prov. 6:32
13 [a]Prov. 18:7 [b][2 Pet. 2:9]

*

12:4 Lit. A *wife of valor*
12:11 Lit. *heart*

NKJV

26 The people will curse [a]him who withholds grain,
But [b]blessing *will be* on the head of him who sells *it*.

27 He who earnestly seeks good finds favor,
[a]But trouble will come to him who seeks *evil*.

28 [a]He who trusts in his riches will fall,
But [b]the righteous will flourish like foliage.

29 He who troubles his own house [a]will inherit the wind,
And the fool *will be* [b]servant to the wise of heart.

30 The fruit of the righteous *is a* tree of life,
And [a]he who wins souls *is* wise.

31 [a]If the righteous will be recompensed on the earth,
How much more the ungodly and the sinner.

12

Whoever loves instruction loves knowledge,
But he who hates correction *is* stupid.

2 A good *man* obtains favor from the LORD,
But a man of wicked intentions He will condemn.

3 A man is not established by wickedness,
But the [a]root of the righteous cannot be moved.

4 [a]An* excellent wife *is* the crown of her husband,
But she who causes shame *is* [b]like rottenness in his bones.

5 The thoughts of the righteous *are* right,
But the counsels of the wicked *are* deceitful.

6 [a]The words of the wicked *are,* "Lie in wait for blood,"
[b]But the mouth of the upright will deliver them.

7 [a]The wicked are overthrown and *are* no more,
But the house of the righteous will stand.

8 A man will be commended according to his wisdom,
[a]But he who is of a perverse heart will be despised.

9 [a]Better *is the one* who is slighted but has a servant,
Than he who honors himself but lacks bread.

10 [a]A righteous *man* regards the life of his animal,
But the tender mercies of the wicked *are* cruel.

11 [a]He who tills his land will be satisfied with [b]bread,
But he who follows frivolity [c]*is* devoid of *understanding.

12 The wicked covet the catch of evil *men,*
But the root of the righteous yields *fruit*.

13 [a]The wicked is ensnared by the transgression of *his* lips,
[b]But the righteous will come through trouble.

KJV

14 [a]A man shall be satisfied with good by the fruit of *his* mouth: [b]and the recompence of a man's hands shall be rendered unto him.
15 [a]The way of a fool *is* right in his own eyes: but he that hearkeneth unto counsel *is* wise.
16 [a]A fool's wrath is presently known: but a prudent *man* covereth shame.
17 [a]*He that* speaketh truth sheweth forth righteousness: but a false witness deceit.
18 [a]There is that speaketh like the piercings of a sword: but the tongue of the wise *is* health.
19 The lip of truth shall be established for ever: [a]but a lying tongue *is* but for a moment.
20 Deceit *is* in the heart of them that imagine evil: but to the counsellors of peace *is* joy.
21 There shall no [a]evil happen to the just: but the wicked shall be filled with mischief.
22 [a]Lying lips *are* abomination to the LORD: but they that deal truly *are* his delight.
23 [a]A prudent man concealeth knowledge: but the heart of fools proclaimeth foolishness.
24 [a]The hand of the diligent shall bear rule: but the slothful shall be under tribute.
25 [a]Heaviness in the heart of man maketh it stoop: but [b]a good word maketh it glad.
26 The righteous *is* more excellent than his neighbour: but the way of the wicked seduceth them.
27 The slothful *man* roasteth not that which he took in hunting: but the substance of a diligent man *is* precious.
28 In the way of righteousness *is* life; and *in* the pathway *thereof there is* no death.

13 A wise son *heareth* his father's instruction: [a]but a scorner heareth not rebuke.
2 [a]A man shall eat good by the fruit of *his* mouth: but the soul of the transgressors *shall eat* violence.
3 [a]He that keepeth his mouth keepeth his life: *but* he that openeth wide his lips shall have destruction.
4 [a]The soul of the sluggard desireth, and *hath* nothing: but the soul of the diligent shall be made fat.
5 A righteous *man* hateth lying: but a wicked *man* is loathsome, and cometh to shame.
6 [a]Righteousness keepeth *him that is* upright in the way: but wickedness overthroweth the sinner.
7 [a]There is that maketh himself rich, yet *hath* nothing: *there is* that maketh himself poor, yet *hath* great riches.

14 [a]Prov. 13:2; 15:23; 18:20 [b]Job 34:11; Prov. 1:31; 24:12; [Is. 3:10, 11]; Hos. 4:9
15 [a]Prov. 3:7; Luke 18:11
16 [a]Prov. 11:13; 29:11
17 [a]Prov. 14:5
18 [a]Ps. 57:4; Prov. 4:22; 15:4
19 [a][Ps. 52:4, 5]; Prov. 19:9
21 [a]Ps. 91:10; Prov. 1:33; 1 Pet. 3:13
22 [a]Prov. 6:17; 11:20; Rev. 22:15
23 [a]Prov. 13:16
24 [a]Prov. 10:4
25 [a]Prov. 15:13 [b]Is. 50:4

CHAPTER 13
1 [a]Is. 28:14, 15
2 [a]Prov. 12:14
3 [a]Ps. 39:1; Prov. 21:23; [James 3:2]
4 [a]Prov. 10:4
6 [a]Prov. 11:3, 5, 6
7 [a][Prov. 11:24; 12:9; Luke 12:20, 21]

NKJV

14 [a]A man will be satisfied with good by the fruit of *his* mouth,
[b]And the recompense of a man's hands will be rendered to him.

15 [a]The way of a fool *is* right in his own eyes,
But he who heeds counsel *is* wise.
16 [a]A fool's wrath is known at once,
But a prudent *man* covers shame.

17 [a]He *who* speaks truth declares righteousness,
But a false witness, deceit.
18 [a]There is one who speaks like the piercings of a sword,
But the tongue of the wise *promotes* health.
19 The truthful lip shall be established forever,
[a]But a lying tongue *is* but for a moment.
20 Deceit is in the heart of those who devise evil,
But counselors of peace have joy.
21 [a]No grave trouble will overtake the righteous,
But the wicked shall be filled with evil.
22 [a]Lying lips *are* an abomination to the LORD,
But those who deal truthfully *are* His delight.

23 [a]A prudent man conceals knowledge,
But the heart of fools proclaims foolishness.

24 [a]The hand of the diligent will rule,
But the lazy *man* will be put to forced labor.

25 [a]Anxiety in the heart of man causes depression,
But [b]a good word makes it glad.

26 The righteous should choose his friends carefully,
For the way of the wicked leads them astray.

27 The lazy *man* does not roast what he took in hunting,
But diligence *is* man's precious possession.

28 In the way of righteousness *is* life,
And in *its* pathway *there is* no death.

13 A wise son *heeds* his father's instruction,
[a]But a scoffer does not listen to rebuke.

2 [a]A man shall eat well by the fruit of *his* mouth,
But the soul of the unfaithful feeds on violence.
3 [a]He who guards his mouth preserves his life,
But he who opens wide his lips shall have destruction.

4 [a]The soul of a lazy *man* desires, and *has* nothing;
But the soul of the diligent shall be made rich.

5 A righteous *man* hates lying,
But a wicked *man* is loathsome and comes to shame.
6 [a]Righteousness guards *him whose* way is blameless,
But wickedness overthrows the sinner.

7 [a]There is one who makes himself rich, yet *has* nothing;
And one who makes himself poor, yet *has* great riches.

KJV

8 The ransom of a man's life *are* his riches:
but the poor heareth not rebuke.
9 The light of the righteous rejoiceth: [a]but
the lamp of the wicked shall be put out.
10 Only by pride cometh [a]contention: but
with the well advised *is* wisdom.
11 [a]Wealth *gotten* by vanity shall be diminished: but he that gathereth by labour shall
increase.
12 Hope deferred maketh the heart sick, but
[a]*when* the desire cometh, *it is* a tree of life.
13 Whoso [a]despiseth the word shall be destroyed: but he that feareth the commandment
shall be rewarded.
14 [a]The law of the wise *is* a fountain of life,
to depart from [b]the snares of death.
15 Good understanding giveth [a]favour: but
the way of transgressors *is* hard.
16 [a]Every prudent *man* dealeth with knowledge: but a fool layeth open *his* folly.
17 A wicked messenger falleth into mischief:
but [a]a faithful ambassador *is* health.
18 Poverty and shame *shall be to* him that
refuseth instruction: but [a]he that regardeth reproof shall be honoured.
19 The desire accomplished is sweet to the
soul: but *it is* abomination to fools to depart from
evil.
20 He that walketh with wise *men* shall be
wise: but a companion of fools shall be destroyed.
21 [a]Evil pursueth sinners: but to the righteous good shall be repaid.
22 A good *man* leaveth an inheritance to his
children's children: and [a]the wealth of the sinner
is laid up for the just.
23 [a]Much food *is in* the tillage of the poor:
but there is *that is* destroyed for want of judgment.
24 [a]He that spareth his rod hateth his son:
but he that loveth him chasteneth him betimes.
25 [a]The righteous eateth to the satisfying of
his soul: but the belly of the wicked shall want.

9 [a]Job 18:5, 6; 21:17; Prov. 24:20
10 [a]Prov. 10:12
11 [a]Prov. 10:2; 20:21
12 [a]Prov. 13:19
13 [a]Num. 15:31; 2 Chr. 36:16; Is. 5:24
14 [a]Prov. 6:22; 10:11; 14:27 [b]2 Sam. 22:6
15 [a]Ps. 111:10; Prov. 3:4
16 [a]Prov. 12:23
17 [a]Prov. 25:13
18 [a]Prov. 15:5, 31, 32
21 [a]Prov. 32:10; Is. 47:11
22 [a]Job 27:16, 17; Prov. 28:8; [Eccl. 2:26]
23 [a]Prov. 12:11
24 [a]Prov. 19:18
25 [a]Ps. 34:10; Prov. 10:3

NKJV

8 The ransom of a man's life *is* his riches,
But the poor does not hear rebuke.

9 The light of the righteous rejoices,
[a]But the lamp of the wicked will be put out.

10 By pride comes nothing but [a]strife,
But with the well-advised *is* wisdom.

11 [a]Wealth *gained by* dishonesty will be diminished,
But he who gathers by labor will increase.

12 Hope deferred makes the heart sick,
But [a]*when* the desire comes, *it is* a tree of life.

13 He who [a]despises the word will be destroyed,
But he who fears the commandment will be rewarded.

14 [a]The law of the wise *is* a fountain of life,
To turn *one* away from [b]the snares of death.

15 Good understanding gains [a]favor,
But the way of the unfaithful *is* hard.

16 [a]Every prudent *man* acts with knowledge,
But a fool lays open *his* folly.

17 A wicked messenger falls into trouble,
But [a]a faithful ambassador *brings* health.

18 Poverty and shame *will come* to him who disdains correction,
But [a]he who regards a rebuke will be honored.

19 A desire accomplished is sweet to the soul,
But *it is* an abomination to fools to depart from evil.

20 He who walks with wise *men* will be wise,
But the companion of fools will be destroyed.

21 [a]Evil pursues sinners,
But to the righteous, good shall be repaid.

22 A good *man* leaves an inheritance to his children's children,
But [a]the wealth of the sinner is stored up for the righteous.

23 [a]Much food *is in* the fallow *ground* of the poor,
And for lack of justice there is *waste.

24 [a]He who spares his rod hates his son,
But he who loves him disciplines him promptly.

25 [a]The righteous eats to the satisfying of his soul,
But the stomach of the wicked shall be in want.

KJV

14 Every wise woman buildeth her house: but
the foolish plucketh it down with her
hands.
2 He that walketh in his uprightness feareth
the LORD: [a]but *he that is* perverse in his ways
despiseth him.
3 In the mouth of the foolish *is* a rod of
pride: [a]but the lips of the wise shall preserve
them.
4 Where no oxen *are*, the crib *is* clean: but
much increase *is* by the strength of the ox.

CHAPTER 14
2 [a][Rom. 2:4]
3 [a]Prov. 12:6

NKJV

14 The wise woman builds her house,
But the foolish pulls it down with her hands.

2 He who walks in his uprightness fears the LORD,
[a]But *he who is* perverse in his ways despises Him.

3 In the mouth of a fool *is* a rod of pride,
[a]But the lips of the wise will preserve them.

4 Where no oxen *are*, the trough *is* clean;
But much increase *comes* by the strength of an ox.

*

13:23 Lit. *what is swept away*

KJV

5 A [a]faithful witness will not lie: but a false witness will utter [b]lies.

6 A scorner seeketh wisdom, and *findeth it* not: but [a]knowledge *is* easy unto him that understandeth.

7 Go from the presence of a foolish man, when thou perceivest not *in him* the lips of [a]knowledge.

8 The wisdom of the prudent *is* to understand his way: but the folly of fools *is* deceit.

9 [a]Fools make a mock at sin: but among the righteous *there is* favour.

10 The heart knoweth his own bitterness; and a stranger doth not intermeddle with his joy.

11 [a]The house of the wicked shall be overthrown: but the tabernacle of the upright shall flourish.

12 [a]There is a way which seemeth right unto a man, but [b]the end thereof *are* the ways of [c]death.

13 Even in laughter the heart is sorrowful; and [a]the end of that mirth *is* heaviness.

14 The backslider in heart shall be [a]filled with his own ways: and a good man *shall be satisfied* from [b]himself.

15 The simple believeth every word: but the prudent *man* looketh well to his going.

16 [a]A wise *man* feareth, and departeth from evil: but the fool rageth, and is confident.

17 *He that is* soon angry dealeth foolishly: and a man of wicked devices is hated.

18 The simple inherit folly: but the prudent are crowned with knowledge.

19 The evil bow before the good; and the wicked at the gates of the righteous.

20 [a]The poor is hated even of his own neighbour: but the rich *hath* many [b]friends.

21 He that despiseth his neighbour sinneth: [a]but he that hath mercy on the poor, happy *is* he.

22 Do they not err that devise evil? but mercy and truth *shall be* to them that devise good.

23 In all labour there is profit: but the talk of the lips *tendeth* only to penury.

24 The crown of the wise *is* their riches: *but* the foolishness of fools *is* folly.

25 A true witness delivereth [a]souls: but a deceitful *witness* speaketh lies.

26 In the fear of the LORD *is* strong confidence: and his children shall have a place of refuge.

27 [a]The fear of the LORD *is* a fountain of life, to depart from the snares of death.

28 In the multitude of people *is* the king's honour: but in the want of people *is* the destruction of the prince.

29 [a]*He that is* slow to wrath *is* of great understanding: but *he that is* hasty of spirit exalteth folly.

NKJV

5 A [a]faithful witness does not lie,
But a false witness will utter [b]lies.

6 A scoffer seeks wisdom and does not *find it*,
But [a]knowledge *is* easy to him who understands.

7 Go from the presence of a foolish man,
When you do not perceive *in him* the lips of [a]knowledge.

8 The wisdom of the prudent *is* to understand his way,
But the folly of fools *is* deceit.

9 [a]Fools mock at sin,
But among the upright *there is* favor.

10 The heart knows its own bitterness,
And a stranger does not share its joy.

11 [a]The house of the wicked will be overthrown,
But the tent of the upright will flourish.

12 [a]There is a way *that seems* right to a man,
But [b]its end *is* the way of [c]death.

13 Even in laughter the heart may sorrow,
And [a]the end of mirth *may be* grief.

14 The backslider in heart will be [a]filled with his own ways,
But a good man *will be satisfied* *from [b]above.

15 The simple believes every word,
But the prudent considers well his steps.

16 [a]A wise *man* fears and departs from evil,
But a fool rages and is self-confident.

17 A quick-tempered *man* acts foolishly,
And a man of wicked intentions is hated.

18 The simple inherit folly,
But the prudent are crowned with knowledge.

19 The evil will bow before the good,
And the wicked at the gates of the righteous.

20 [a]The poor *man* is hated even by his own neighbor,
But the rich *has* many [b]friends.

21 He who despises his neighbor sins;
[a]But he who has mercy on the poor, happy *is* he.

22 Do they not go astray who devise evil?
But mercy and truth *belong* to those who devise good.

23 In all labor there is profit,
But *idle chatter *leads* only to poverty.

24 The crown of the wise is their riches,
But the foolishness of fools *is* folly.

25 A true witness delivers [a]souls,
But a deceitful *witness* speaks lies.

26 In the fear of the LORD *there is* strong confidence,
And His children will have a place of refuge.

27 [a]The fear of the LORD *is* a fountain of life,
To turn *one* away from the snares of death.

28 In a multitude of people *is* a king's honor,
But in the lack of people *is* the downfall of a prince.

29 [a]*He who is* slow to wrath has great understanding,
But *he who is* *impulsive exalts folly.

5 [a]Rev. 1:5; 3:14 [b]Ex. 23:1; Deut. 19:16; Prov. 6:19; 12:17
6 [a]Prov. 8:9; 17:24
7 [a]Prov. 23:9
9 [a]Prov. 10:23
11 [a]Job 8:15
12 [a]Prov. 16:25 [b]Rom. 6:21 [c]Prov. 12:15
13 [a]Prov. 5:4; Eccl. 2:1, 2
14 [a]Prov. 1:31; 12:15 [b]Prov. 13:2; 18:20
16 [a]Job 28:28; Ps. 34:14; Prov. 22:3
20 [a]Prov. 19:7 [b]Prov. 19:4
21 [a]Ps. 112:9; [Prov. 19:17]
25 [a][Ezek. 3:18–21]
27 [a]Prov. 13:14
29 [a]Prov. 16:32; 19:11; Eccl. 7:9; James 1:19

*
14:14 Lit. *from above himself*
14:23 Lit. *talk of the lips*
14:29 Lit. *short of spirit*

KJV

30 A sound heart *is* the life of the flesh: but
[a]envy [b]the rottenness of the bones.
31 [a]He that oppresseth the poor reproacheth
[b]his Maker: but he that honoureth him hath mercy
on the poor.
32 The wicked is driven away in his wickedness: but [a]the righteous hath hope in his death.
33 Wisdom resteth in the heart of him that
hath understanding: but [a]*that which is* in the
midst of fools is made known.
34 Righteousness exalteth a [a]nation: but sin
is a reproach to any people.
35 [a]The king's favour *is* toward a wise servant: but his wrath is *against* him that causeth
shame.

15 A [a]soft answer turneth away wrath: but
[b]grievous words stir up anger.
2 The tongue of the wise useth knowledge
aright: [a]but the mouth of fools poureth out
foolishness.
3 [a]The eyes of the LORD *are* in every place,
beholding the evil and the good.
4 A wholesome tongue *is* a tree of life: but
perverseness therein *is* a breach in the spirit.
5 [a]A fool despiseth his father's instruction:
[b]but he that regardeth reproof is prudent.
6 In the house of the righteous *is* much treasure: but in the revenues of the wicked is trouble.
7 The lips of the wise disperse knowledge:
but the heart of the foolish *doeth* not so.
8 [a]The sacrifice of the wicked *is* an abomination to the LORD: but the prayer of the upright
is his delight.
9 The way of the wicked *is* an abomination
unto the LORD: but he loveth him that [a]followeth
after righteousness.
10 Correction *is* [a]grievous unto him that forsaketh the way: *and* [b]he that hateth reproof shall
die.
11 [a]Hell and destruction *are* before the LORD:
how much more then [b]the hearts of the children
of men?
12 [a]A scorner loveth not one that reproveth
him: neither will he go unto the wise.
13 [a]A merry heart maketh a cheerful countenance: but [b]by sorrow of the heart the spirit is
broken.
14 The heart of him that hath understanding
seeketh knowledge: but the mouth of fools feedeth
on foolishness.
15 All the days of the afflicted *are* evil: [a]but
he that is of a merry heart *hath* a continual feast.

30 [a]Ps. 112:10 [b]Prov. 12:4; Hab. 3:16
31 [a]Prov. 17:5; Matt. 25:40; 1 John 3:17 [b][Job 31:15; Prov. 22:2]
32 [a]Gen. 49:18; Job 13:15; [Ps. 16:11; 73:24]; 2 Cor. 1:9; 5:8; [2 Tim. 4:18]
33 [a]Prov. 12:16
34 [a]Prov. 11:11
35 [a]Matt. 24:45–47

CHAPTER 15

1 [a]Prov. 25:15 [b]1 Sam. 25:10
2 [a]Prov. 12:23
3 [a]2 Chr. 16:9; Job 34:21; Prov. 5:21; Jer. 16:17; 32:19; Zech. 4:10; Heb. 4:13
5 [a]Prov. 10:1 [b]Prov. 13:18
8 [a]Prov. 21:27; Eccl. 5:1; Is. 1:11; Jer. 6:20; Mic. 6:7
9 [a]Prov. 21:21
10 [a]1 Kin. 22:8 [b]Prov. 5:12
11 [a]Job 26:6; Ps. 139:8 [b]1 Sam. 16:7; 2 Chr. 6:30; Ps. 44:21; Acts 1:24
12 [a]Prov. 13:1; Amos 5:10; 2 Tim. 4:3
13 [a]Prov. 12:25 [b]Prov. 17:22
15 [a]Prov. 17:22

NKJV

30 A sound heart *is* life to the body,
But [a]envy *is* [b]rottenness to the bones.

31 [a]He who oppresses the poor reproaches
[b]his Maker,
But he who honors Him has mercy on the
needy.

32 The wicked is banished in his wickedness,
But [a]the righteous has a refuge in his
death.

33 Wisdom rests in the heart of him who has
understanding,
But [a]*what is* in the heart of fools is made
known.

34 Righteousness exalts a [a]nation,
But sin *is* a reproach to *any* people.

35 [a]The king's favor *is* toward a wise servant,
But his wrath *is against* him who causes
shame.

15 A [a]soft answer turns away wrath,
But [b]a harsh word stirs up anger.
2 The tongue of the wise uses knowledge
rightly,
[a]But the mouth of fools pours forth
foolishness.

3 [a]The eyes of the LORD *are* in every place,
Keeping watch on the evil and the
good.

4 A wholesome tongue *is* a tree of life,
But perverseness in it breaks the spirit.

5 [a]A fool despises his father's instruction,
[b]But he who receives correction is prudent.

6 *In* the house of the righteous *there is* much
treasure,
But in the revenue of the wicked is trouble.

7 The lips of the wise disperse knowledge,
But the heart of the fool *does* not *do* so.

8 [a]The sacrifice of the wicked *is* an
abomination to the LORD,
But the prayer of the upright *is* His delight.
9 The way of the wicked *is* an abomination
to the LORD,
But He loves him who [a]follows
righteousness.

10 [a]Harsh discipline *is* for him who forsakes
the way,
And [b]he who hates correction will die.

11 [a]Hell* and *Destruction *are* before the
LORD;
So how much more [b]the hearts of the sons
of men.

12 [a]A scoffer does not love one who corrects
him,
Nor will he go to the wise.

13 [a]A merry heart makes a cheerful
countenance,
But [b]by sorrow of the heart the spirit is
broken.

14 The heart of him who has understanding
seeks knowledge,
But the mouth of fools feeds on
foolishness.

15 All the days of the afflicted *are* evil,
[a]But he who is of a merry heart *has* a
continual feast.

*

15:11 Or *Sheol* • Heb. *Abaddon*

KJV

16 [a]Better *is* little with the fear of the LORD than great treasure and trouble therewith.

17 [a]Better *is* a dinner of herbs where love is, than a stalled ox and hatred therewith.

18 [a]A wrathful man stirreth up strife: but *he that is* slow to anger appeaseth strife.

19 [a]The way of the slothful *man is* as an hedge of thorns: but the way of the righteous *is* made plain.

20 [a]A wise son maketh a glad father: but a foolish man despiseth his mother.

21 [a]Folly *is* joy to *him that is* destitute of wisdom: [b]but a man of understanding walketh uprightly.

22 [a]Without counsel purposes are disappointed: but in the multitude of counsellors they are established.

23 A man hath joy by the answer of his mouth: and [a]a word *spoken* in due season, how good *is it!*

24 [a]The way of life *is* above to the wise, that he may [b]depart from hell beneath.

25 [a]The LORD will destroy the house of the proud: but [b]he will establish the border of the widow.

26 [a]The thoughts of the wicked *are* an abomination to the LORD: [b]but *the words* of the pure *are* pleasant words.

27 [a]He that is greedy of gain troubleth his own house; but he that hateth gifts shall live.

28 The heart of the righteous [a]studieth to answer: but the mouth of the wicked poureth out evil things.

29 [a]The LORD *is* far from the wicked: but [b]he heareth the prayer of the righteous.

30 The light of the eyes rejoiceth the heart: *and* a good report maketh the bones fat.

31 The ear that heareth the reproof of life abideth among the wise.

32 He that refuseth instruction despiseth his own soul: but he that heareth reproof getteth understanding.

33 [a]The fear of the LORD *is* the instruction of wisdom; and [b]before honour *is* humility.

16 The [a]preparations of the heart in man, [b]and the answer of the tongue, *is* from the LORD.

2 All the ways of a man *are* clean in his own [a]eyes; but the LORD weigheth the spirits.

3 [a]Commit thy works unto the LORD, and thy thoughts shall be established.

4 The [a]LORD hath made all *things* for himself: [b]yea, even the wicked for the day of evil.

16 [a]Ps. 37:16; Prov. 16:8; Eccl. 4:6; 1 Tim. 6:6 **17** [a]Prov. 17:1 **18** [a]Prov. 26:21 **19** [a]Prov. 22:5 **20** [a]Prov. 10:1 **21** [a]Prov. 10:23 [b]Eph. 5:15 **22** [a]Prov. 11:14 **23** [a]Prov. 25:11; Is. 50:4 **24** [a]Phil. 3:20; [Col. 3:1, 2] [b]Prov. 14:16 **25** [a]Prov. 12:7; Is. 2:11 [b]Ps. 68:5, 6 **26** [a]Prov. 6:16, 18 [b]Ps. 37:30 **27** [a]Is. 5:8; [Jer. 17:11] **28** [a]1 Pet. 3:15 **29** [a]Ps. 10:1; 34:16 [b]Ps. 145:18; [James 5:16] **33** [a]Prov. 1:7 [b]Prov. 18:12

CHAPTER 16

1 [a]Jer. 10:23 [b]Matt. 10:19 **2** [a]Prov. 21:2 **3** [a]Ps. 37:5; Prov. 3:6; [1 Pet. 5:7] **4** [a]Is. 43:7; Rom. 11:36 [b]Job 21:30; [Rom. 9:22]

*

15:17 Or *vegetables* **15:24** Or *Sheol* **15:30** Lit. *fat*

NKJV

16 [a]Better *is* a little with the fear of the LORD,
Than great treasure with trouble.

17 [a]Better *is* a dinner of *herbs where love is,
Than a fatted calf with hatred.

18 [a]A wrathful man stirs up strife,
But *he who is* slow to anger allays contention.

19 [a]The way of the lazy *man is* like a hedge of thorns,
But the way of the upright *is* a highway.

20 [a]A wise son makes a father glad,
But a foolish man despises his mother.

21 [a]Folly *is* joy *to him who is* destitute of discernment,
[b]But a man of understanding walks uprightly.

22 [a]Without counsel, plans go awry,
But in the multitude of counselors they are established.

23 A man has joy by the answer of his mouth,
And [a]a word *spoken* in due season, how good *it is!*

24 [a]The way of life *winds* upward for the wise,
That he may [b]turn away from *hell below.

25 [a]The LORD will destroy the house of the proud,
But [b]He will establish the boundary of the widow.

26 [a]The thoughts of the wicked *are* an abomination to the LORD,
[b]But *the words* of the pure *are* pleasant.

27 [a]He who is greedy for gain troubles his own house,
But he who hates bribes will live.

28 The heart of the righteous [a]studies how to answer,
But the mouth of the wicked pours forth evil.

29 [a]The LORD *is* far from the wicked,
But [b]He hears the prayer of the righteous.

30 The light of the eyes rejoices the heart,
And a good report makes the bones *healthy.

31 The ear that hears the rebukes of life
Will abide among the wise.

32 He who disdains instruction despises his own soul,
But he who heeds rebuke gets understanding.

33 [a]The fear of the LORD *is* the instruction of wisdom,
And [b]before honor *is* humility.

16 The [a]preparations of the heart *belong* to man,
[b]But the answer of the tongue *is* from the LORD.

2 All the ways of a man *are* pure in his own [a]eyes,
But the LORD weighs the spirits.

3 [a]Commit your works to the LORD,
And your thoughts will be established.

4 The [a]LORD has made all for Himself,
[b]Yes, even the wicked for the day of doom.

KJV

5 [a]Every one *that is* proud in heart *is* an
abomination to the LORD: *though* hand *join* in
hand, he shall not be unpunished.
6 [a]By mercy and truth iniquity is purged:
and [b]by the fear of the LORD *men* depart from
evil.
7 When a man's ways please the LORD, he
maketh even his enemies to be at peace with him.
8 [a]Better *is* a little with righteousness than
great revenues without right.
9 [a]A man's heart deviseth his way: [b]but the
LORD directeth his steps.
10 A divine sentence *is* in the lips of the king:
his mouth transgresseth not in judgment.
11 [a]A just weight and balance *are* the LORD'S:
all the weights of the bag *are* his work.
12 *It is* an abomination to kings to commit
wickedness: for [a]the throne is established by
righteousness.
13 [a]Righteous lips *are* the delight of kings;
and they love him that speaketh right.
14 The wrath of a king *is as* messengers of
death: but a wise man will [a]pacify it.
15 In the light of the king's countenance *is*
life; and his favour *is* as a [a]cloud of the latter
rain.
16 [a]How much better *is it* to get wisdom than
gold! and to get understanding rather to be chosen
than silver!
17 The highway of the upright *is* to depart
from evil: he that keepeth his way preserveth his
soul.
18 Pride *goeth* before destruction, and an
haughty spirit before a fall.
19 Better *it is to be* of an humble spirit with
the lowly, than to divide the spoil with the proud.
20 He that handleth a matter wisely shall find
good: and whoso [a]trusteth in the LORD, happy *is*
he.
21 The wise in heart shall be called prudent:
and the sweetness of the lips increaseth learning.
22 Understanding *is* a wellspring of life unto
him that hath it: but the instruction of fools *is*
folly.
23 The heart of the wise teacheth his mouth,
and addeth learning to his lips.
24 Pleasant words *are as* an honeycomb,
sweet to the soul, and health to the bones.
25 There is a way that seemeth right unto a
man; but the end thereof *are* the ways of [a]death.
26 He that laboureth laboureth for himself;
for his mouth craveth it of [a]him.
27 An ungodly man diggeth up evil: and in
his lips *there is* as a burning [a]fire.

5 [a]Prov. 6:17; 8:13
6 [a]Dan. 4:27; Luke 11:41 [b]Prov. 8:13; 14:16
8 [a]Ps. 37:16; Prov. 15:16
9 [a]Prov. 19:21 [b]Ps. 37:23; Prov. 20:24; Jer. 10:23
11 [a]Lev. 19:36
12 [a]Prov. 25:5
13 [a]Prov. 14:35
14 [a]Prov. 25:15
15 [a]Zech. 10:1
16 [a]Prov. 8:10, 11, 19
20 [a]Ps. 34:8; Jer. 17:7
25 [a]Prov. 14:12
26 [a][Eccl. 6:7; John 6:35]
27 [a][James 3:6]

NKJV

5 [a]Everyone proud in heart *is* an
abomination to the LORD;
Though they join *forces, none will go
unpunished.

6 [a]In mercy and truth
Atonement is provided for iniquity;
And [b]by the fear of the LORD *one* departs
from evil.

7 When a man's ways please the LORD,
He makes even his enemies to be at peace
with him.

8 [a]Better *is* a little with righteousness,
Than vast revenues without justice.

9 [a]A man's heart plans his way,
[b]But the LORD directs his steps.

10 Divination *is* on the lips of the king;
His mouth must not transgress in
judgment.
11 [a]Honest weights and scales *are* the LORD'S;
All the weights in the bag *are* His work.
12 *It is* an abomination for kings to commit
wickedness,
For [a]a throne is established by
righteousness.
13 [a]Righteous lips *are* the delight of kings,
And they love him who speaks *what is*
right.
14 As messengers of death *is* the king's
wrath,
But a wise man will [a]appease it.
15 In the light of the king's face *is* life,
And his favor *is* like a [a]cloud of the latter
rain.

16 [a]How much better to get wisdom than gold!
And to get understanding is to be chosen
rather than silver.

17 The highway of the upright *is* to depart
from evil;
He who keeps his way preserves his soul.

18 Pride *goes* before destruction,
And a haughty spirit before a fall.
19 Better *to be* of a humble spirit with the
lowly,
Than to divide the spoil with the proud.

20 He who heeds the word wisely will find
good,
And whoever [a]trusts in the LORD, happy
is he.

21 The wise in heart will be called prudent,
And sweetness of the lips increases
learning.

22 Understanding *is* a wellspring of life to
him who has it.
But the correction of fools *is* folly.

23 The heart of the wise teaches his mouth,
And adds learning to his lips.

24 Pleasant words *are like* a honeycomb,
Sweetness to the soul and health to the
bones.

25 There is a way *that seems* right to a man,
But its end *is* the way of [a]death.

26 The person who labors, labors for himself,
For his *hungry* mouth drives [a]him *on*.

27 An ungodly man digs up evil,
And *it is* on his lips like a burning [a]fire.

16:5 Lit. *hand to hand*

KJV

28 A froward man soweth strife: and [a]a whisperer separateth chief friends.
29 A violent man enticeth his neighbour, and
leadeth him into the way *that is* not good.
30 He shutteth his eyes to devise froward
things: moving his lips he bringeth evil to pass.
31 [a]The hoary head *is* a crown of glory, *if* it
be found in the way of righteousness.
32 [a]*He that is* slow to anger *is* better than
the mighty; and he that ruleth his spirit than he
that taketh a city.
33 The lot is cast into the lap; but the whole
disposing thereof *is* of the LORD.

17 Better *is* [a]a dry morsel, and quietness therewith, than an house full of sacrifices *with*
strife.
2 A wise servant shall have rule over [a]a son
that causeth shame, and shall have part of the
inheritance among the brethren.
3 The fining pot *is* for silver, and the furnace
for gold: [a]but the LORD trieth the hearts.
4 A wicked doer giveth heed to false lips;
and a liar giveth ear to a naughty tongue.
5 [a]Whoso mocketh the poor reproacheth his
Maker: *and* [b]he that is glad at calamities shall
not be unpunished.
6 [a]Children's children *are* the crown of old
men; and the glory of children *are* their fathers.
7 Excellent speech becometh not a fool:
much less do lying lips a prince.
8 A gift *is as* a precious stone in the eyes
of him that hath it: whithersoever it turneth, it
prospereth.
9 [a]He that covereth a transgression seeketh
love; but [b]he that repeateth a matter separateth
very friends.
10 A [a]reproof entereth more into a wise man
than an hundred stripes into a fool.
11 An evil *man* seeketh only rebellion: therefore a cruel messenger shall be sent against him.
12 Let [a]a bear robbed of her whelps meet a
man, rather than a fool in his folly.
13 Whoso [a]rewardeth evil for good, evil shall
not depart from his house.
14 The beginning of strife *is as* when one letteth out water: therefore [a]leave off contention, before it be meddled with.
15 [a]He that justifieth the wicked, and he that
condemneth the just, even they both *are* abomination to the LORD.
16 Wherefore *is there* a price in the hand of
a fool to get wisdom, seeing *he hath* no heart *to
it*?

28 [a]Prov. 17:9
31 [a]Prov. 20:29
32 [a]Prov. 14:29; 19:11

CHAPTER 17

1 [a]Prov. 15:17
2 [a]Prov. 10:5
3 [a]1 Chr. 29:17; Ps. 26:2; Prov. 15:11; Jer. 17:10; [Mal. 3:3]
5 [a]Prov. 14:31 [b]Job 31:29; Prov. 24:17; Obad. 12; 1 Cor. 13:6
6 [a][Ps. 127:3; 128:3]
9 [a][Prov. 10:12; 1 Cor. 13:5–7; James 5:20] [b]Prov. 16:28
10 [a]Prov. 10:17; [Mic. 7:9]
12 [a]2 Sam. 17:8; Hos. 13:8
13 [a]Ps. 109:4, 5; Jer. 18:20; Rom. 12:17; 1 Thess. 5:15; [1 Pet. 3:9]
14 [a][Prov. 20:3; 1 Thess. 4:11]
15 [a]Ex. 23:7; Prov. 24:24; Is. 5:23

NKJV

28 A perverse man sows strife,
And [a]a whisperer separates the best of friends.
29 A violent man entices his neighbor,
And leads him in a way *that is* not good.
30 He winks his eye to devise perverse things;
He purses his lips *and* brings about evil.

31 [a]The silver-haired head *is* a crown of glory,
If it is found in the way of righteousness.

32 [a]*He who is* slow to anger *is* better than the mighty,
And he who rules his spirit than he who takes a city.

33 The lot is cast into the lap,
But its every decision *is* from the LORD.

17 Better *is* [a]a dry morsel with quietness,
Than a house full of *feasting *with* strife.

2 A wise servant will rule over [a]a son who causes shame,
And will share an inheritance among the brothers.

3 The refining pot *is* for silver and the furnace for gold,
[a]But the LORD tests the hearts.

4 An evildoer gives heed to false lips;
A liar listens eagerly to a spiteful tongue.

5 [a]He who mocks the poor reproaches his Maker;
[b]He who is glad at calamity will not go unpunished.

6 [a]Children's children *are* the crown of old men,
And the glory of children *is* their father.

7 Excellent speech is not becoming to a fool,
Much less lying lips to a prince.

8 A present *is* a precious stone in the eyes of its possessor;
Wherever he turns, he prospers.

9 [a]He who covers a transgression seeks love,
But [b]he who repeats a matter separates friends.

10 [a]Rebuke is more effective for a wise *man*
Than a hundred blows on a fool.

11 An evil *man* seeks only rebellion;
Therefore a cruel messenger will be sent against him.

12 Let a man meet [a]a bear robbed of her cubs,
Rather than a fool in his folly.

13 Whoever [a]rewards evil for good,
Evil will not depart from his house.

14 The beginning of strife *is like* releasing water;
Therefore [a]stop contention before a quarrel starts.

15 [a]He who justifies the wicked, and he who condemns the just,
Both of them alike *are* an abomination to the LORD.

16 Why *is there* in the hand of a fool the purchase price of wisdom,
Since *he has* no heart *for it*?

17:1 Or *sacrificial meals*

KJV

17 [a]A friend loveth at all times, and a brother
is born for adversity.
18 [a]A man void of understanding striketh
hands, *and* becometh surety in the presence of
his friend.
19 He loveth transgression that loveth strife:
and [a]he that exalteth his gate seeketh destruction.
20 He that hath a froward heart findeth no
good: and he that hath [a]a perverse tongue falleth
into mischief.
21 He that begetteth a fool *doeth it* to his sorrow: and the father of a fool hath no joy.
22 A [a]merry heart doeth good *like* a medicine: but a broken spirit drieth the bones.
23 A wicked *man* taketh a gift out of the bosom to pervert the ways of judgment.
24 [a]Wisdom *is* before him that hath understanding; but the eyes of a fool *are* in the ends
of the earth.
25 A [a]foolish son *is* a grief to his father, and
bitterness to her that bare him.
26 Also to punish the just *is* not good, *nor*
to strike princes for equity.
27 [a]He that hath knowledge spareth his
words: *and* a man of understanding is of an excellent spirit.
28 [a]Even a fool, when he holdeth his peace,
is counted wise: *and* he that shutteth his lips *is*
esteemed a man of understanding.

18 Through desire a man, having separated
himself, seeketh *and* intermeddleth with all
wisdom.
2 A fool hath no delight in understanding,
but that his heart may discover [a]itself.
3 When the wicked cometh, *then* cometh
also contempt, and with ignominy reproach.
4 [a]The words of a man's mouth *are as* deep
waters, [b]*and* the wellspring of wisdom *as* a flowing brook.
5 *It is* not good to accept the person of the
wicked, to overthrow the righteous in [a]judgment.
6 A fool's lips enter into contention, and his
mouth calleth for strokes.
7 [a]A fool's mouth *is* his destruction, and his
lips *are* the snare of his [b]soul.
8 [a]The words of a talebearer *are* as wounds,
and they go down into the innermost parts of the
belly.
9 He also that is slothful in his work is
brother to him that is a great waster.
10 The name of the LORD *is* a strong [a]tower:
the righteous runneth into it, and is safe.

17 [a]Ruth 1:16; Prov. 18:24
18 [a]Prov. 6:1
19 [a]Prov. 16:18
20 [a]James 3:8
22 [a]Prov. 12:25; 15:13, 15
24 [a]Eccl. 2:14
25 [a]Prov. 10:1; 15:20; 19:13
27 [a]Prov. 10:19; James 1:19
28 [a]Job 13:5

CHAPTER 18
2 [a]Eccl. 10:3
4 [a]Prov. 10:11 [b][James 3:17]
5 [a]Lev. 19:15; Deut. 1:17; 16:19; Ps. 82:2; Prov. 17:15
7 [a]Ps. 64:8; 140:9; Prov. 10:14 [b]Eccl. 10:12
8 [a]Prov. 12:18
10 [a]2 Sam. 22:2, 3, 33; Ps. 18:2; 61:3; 91:2; 144:2

NKJV

17 [a]A friend loves at all times,
And a brother is born for adversity.

18 [a]A man devoid of understanding shakes
hands in a pledge,
And becomes surety for his friend.

19 He who loves transgression loves strife,
And [a]he who exalts his gate seeks
destruction.

20 He who has a deceitful heart finds no
good,
And he who has [a]a perverse tongue falls
into evil.

21 He who begets a scoffer *does so* to his
sorrow,
And the father of a fool has no joy.

22 A [a]merry heart *does good, *like* medicine,
But a broken spirit dries the bones.

23 A wicked *man* accepts a bribe *behind the
back
To pervert the ways of justice.

24 [a]Wisdom *is* in the sight of him who has
understanding,
But the eyes of a fool *are* on the ends of
the earth.

25 A [a]foolish son *is* a grief to his father,
And bitterness to her who bore him.

26 Also, to punish the righteous *is* not good,
Nor to strike princes for *their* uprightness.

27 [a]He who has knowledge spares his words,
And a man of understanding is of a calm
spirit.

28 [a]Even a fool is counted wise when he holds
his peace;
When he shuts his lips, *he is considered*
perceptive.

18 A man who isolates himself seeks his own
desire;
He rages against all wise judgment.

2 A fool has no delight in understanding,
But in expressing his [a]own heart.

3 When the wicked comes, contempt comes
also;
And with dishonor *comes* reproach.

4 [a]The words of a man's mouth *are* deep
waters;
[b]The wellspring of wisdom *is* a flowing
brook.

5 *It is* not good to show partiality to the
wicked,
Or to overthrow the righteous in
[a]judgment.

6 A fool's lips enter into contention,
And his mouth calls for blows.
7 [a]A fool's mouth *is* his destruction,
And his lips *are* the snare of his [b]soul.
8 [a]The words of a talebearer *are* like *tasty
trifles,
And they go down into the inmost body.

9 He who is slothful in his work
Is a brother to him who is a great
destroyer.

10 The name of the LORD *is* a strong [a]tower;
The righteous run to it and are safe.

17:22 Or *makes medicine even better*
17:23 Under cover, lit. *from the bosom*
18:8 A Jewish tradition *wounds*

KJV

11 The rich man's wealth *is* his strong city,
and as an high wall in his own conceit.
12 [a]Before destruction the heart of man is
haughty; and before honour *is* humility.
13 He that answereth a matter before he
heareth *it*, it *is* folly and shame unto him.
14 The spirit of a man will sustain his infirmity; but a wounded spirit who can bear?
15 The heart of the prudent getteth knowledge; and the ear of the wise seeketh knowledge.
16 [a]A man's gift maketh room for him, and
bringeth him before great men.
17 *He that is* first in his own cause *seemeth*
just; but his neighbour cometh and searcheth him.
18 The [a]lot causeth contentions to cease, and
parteth between the mighty.
19 A brother offended *is harder to be won*
than a strong city: and *their* contentions *are* like
the bars of a castle.
20 [a]A man's belly shall be satisfied with the
fruit of his mouth; *and* with the increase of his
lips shall he be filled.
21 [a]Death and life *are* in the power of the
tongue: and they that love it shall eat the fruit
thereof.
22 [a]*Whoso* findeth a wife findeth a good
thing, and obtaineth favour of the LORD.
23 The poor useth intreaties; but the rich answereth [a]roughly.
24 A man *that hath* friends must shew himself friendly: [a]and there is a friend *that* sticketh
closer than a brother.

12 [a]Prov. 15:33; 16:18
16 [a]Gen. 32:20, 21; 1 Sam. 25:27; Prov. 17:8; 21:14
18 [a][Prov. 16:33]
20 [a]Prov. 12:14; 14:14
21 [a]Prov. 12:13; 13:3; Matt. 12:37
22 [a]Gen. 2:18; [Prov. 12:4; 19:14]
23 [a]James 2:3, 6
24 [a]Prov. 17:17; [John 15:14, 15]

NKJV

11 The rich man's wealth *is* his strong city,
And like a high wall in his own esteem.

12 [a]Before destruction the heart of a man is haughty,
And before honor *is* humility.

13 He who answers a matter before he hears *it*,
It *is* folly and shame to him.

14 The spirit of a man will sustain him in sickness,
But who can bear a broken spirit?

15 The heart of the prudent acquires knowledge,
And the ear of the wise seeks knowledge.

16 [a]A man's gift makes room for him,
And brings him before great men.

17 The first *one* to plead his cause *seems* right,
Until his neighbor comes and examines him.

18 Casting [a]lots causes contentions to cease,
And keeps the mighty apart.

19 A brother offended *is harder to win* than a strong city,
And contentions *are* like the bars of a castle.

20 [a]A man's stomach shall be satisfied from the fruit of his mouth;
From the produce of his lips he shall be filled.

21 [a]Death and life *are* in the power of the tongue,
And those who love it will eat its fruit.

22 [a]*He who* finds a wife finds a good *thing*,
And obtains favor from the LORD.

23 The poor *man* uses entreaties,
But the rich answers [a]roughly.

24 A man *who has* friends *must himself be friendly,
[a]But there is a friend *who* sticks closer than a brother.

19 Better [a]*is* the poor that walketh in his integrity, than *he that is* perverse in his lips,
and is a fool.
2 Also, *that* the soul *be* without knowledge,
it is not good; and he that hasteth with *his* feet
sinneth.
3 The foolishness of man perverteth his
way: and his heart fretteth against the LORD.
4 [a]Wealth maketh many friends; but the
poor is separated from his neighbour.
5 A [a]false witness shall not be unpunished,
and *he that* speaketh lies shall not escape.
6 Many will intreat the favour of the prince:
and every man *is* a friend to him that giveth gifts.
7 [a]All the brethren of the poor do hate him:
how much more do his friends go [b]far from him?
he pursueth *them with* words, *yet* they *are* wanting *to him*.

CHAPTER 19

1 [a]Prov. 28:6
4 [a]Prov. 14:20
5 [a]Ex. 23:1; Deut. 19:16–19; Prov. 6:19; 21:28
7 [a]Prov. 14:20 [b]Ps. 38:11

19 Better [a]*is* the poor who walks in his integrity
Than *one who is* perverse in his lips, and is a fool.

2 Also it is not good *for* a soul *to be* without knowledge,
And he sins who hastens with *his* feet.

3 The foolishness of a man twists his way,
And his heart frets against the LORD.

4 [a]Wealth makes many friends,
But the poor is separated from his friend.

5 A [a]false witness will not go unpunished,
And *he who* speaks lies will not escape.

6 Many entreat the favor of the nobility,
And every man *is* a friend to one who gives gifts.

7 [a]All the brothers of the poor hate him;
How much more do his friends go [b]far from him!
He may pursue *them with* words, *yet* they abandon *him*.

---
*18:24 So with Gr. mss., Syr., Tg., Vg.; MT *may come to ruin*

KJV

8 He that getteth wisdom loveth his own
soul: he that keepeth understanding [a]shall find
good.
9 A false witness shall not be unpunished,
and *he that* speaketh lies shall perish.
10 Delight is not seemly for a fool; much less
[a]for a servant to have rule over princes.
11 [a]The discretion of a man deferreth his
anger; [b]and *it is* his glory to pass over a transgression.
12 [a]The king's wrath *is* as the roaring of a
lion; but his favour *is* [b]as dew upon the grass.
13 [a]A foolish son *is* the calamity of his father:
[b]and the contentions of a wife *are* a continual
dropping.
14 [a]House and riches *are* the inheritance of
fathers: and [b]a prudent wife *is* from the LORD.
15 [a]Slothfulness casteth into a deep sleep;
and an idle soul shall [b]suffer hunger.
16 [a]He that keepeth the commandment keepeth his own soul; *but* he that despiseth his ways
shall die.
17 [a]He that hath pity upon the poor lendeth
unto the LORD; and that which he hath given will
he pay him again.
18 [a]Chasten thy son while there is hope, and
let not thy soul spare for his crying.
19 A man of great wrath shall suffer punishment: for if thou deliver *him,* yet thou must do it
again.
20 Hear counsel, and receive instruction, that
thou mayest be wise [a]in thy latter end.
21 *There are* many devices in a man's heart;
[a]nevertheless the counsel of the LORD, that shall
stand.
22 The desire of a man *is* his kindness: and
a poor man *is* better than a liar.
23 [a]The fear of the LORD *tendeth* to life: and
he that hath it shall abide satisfied; he shall not
be visited with evil.
24 [a]A slothful *man* hideth his hand in *his* bosom, and will not so much as bring it to his mouth
again.
25 Smite a scorner, and the simple [a]will beware: and [b]reprove one that hath understanding,
and he will understand knowledge.
26 He that wasteth *his* father, *and* chaseth
away *his* mother, *is* [a]a son that causeth shame,
and bringeth reproach.
27 Cease, my son, to hear the instruction *that*
causeth to err from the words of knowledge.

8 [a]Prov. 16:20 **10** [a]Prov. 30:21, 22 **11** [a]James 1:19 [b]Prov. 16:32; [Matt. 5:44]; Eph. 4:32; Col. 3:13 **12** [a]Prov. 16:14 [b]Gen. 27:28; Deut. 33:28; Ps. 133:3; Hos. 14:5; Mic. 5:7 **13** [a]Prov. 10:1 [b]Prov. 21:9, 19 **14** [a]2 Cor. 12:14 [b]Prov. 18:22 **15** [a]Prov. 6:9 [b]Prov. 10:4 **16** [a]Prov. 13:13; 16:17; Luke 10:28; 11:28 **17** [a]Deut. 15:7, 8; Job 23:12, 13; Prov. 28:27; Eccl. 11:1; Matt. 10:42; 25:40; [2 Cor. 9:6–8]; Heb. 6:10 **18** [a]Prov. 13:24 **20** [a]Ps. 37:37 **21** [a]Ps. 33:10, 11; Prov. 16:9; Is. 46:10; Heb. 6:17 **23** [a]Prov. 14:27; [1 Tim. 4:8] **24** [a]Prov. 15:19 **25** [a]Deut. 13:11 [b]Prov. 9:8 **26** [a]Prov. 17:2

*

19:16 Is reckless, lit. *despises*
19:18 Lit. *to put him to death;* a Jewish tradition *on his crying*
19:24 LXX, Syr. *bosom;* Tg., Vg. *armpit*

NKJV

8 He who gets wisdom loves his own soul;
He who keeps understanding [a]will find good.

9 A false witness will not go unpunished,
And *he who* speaks lies shall perish.

10 Luxury is not fitting for a fool,
Much less [a]for a servant to rule over princes.

11 [a]The discretion of a man makes him slow to anger,
[b]And his glory *is* to overlook a transgression.

12 [a]The king's wrath *is* like the roaring of a lion,
But his favor *is* [b]like dew on the grass.

13 [a]A foolish son *is* the ruin of his father,
[b]And the contentions of a wife *are* a continual dripping.

14 [a]Houses and riches *are* an inheritance from fathers,
But [b]a prudent wife *is* from the LORD.

15 [a]Laziness casts *one* into a deep sleep,
And an idle person will [b]suffer hunger.

16 [a]He who keeps the commandment keeps his soul,
But he who *is careless of his ways will die.

17 [a]He who has pity on the poor lends to the LORD,
And He will pay back what he has given.

18 [a]Chasten your son while there is hope,
And do not set your heart *on his destruction.

19 *A man of* great wrath will suffer punishment;
For if you rescue *him,* you will have to do it again.

20 Listen to counsel and receive instruction,
That you may be wise [a]in your latter days.

21 There are many plans in a man's heart,
[a]Nevertheless the LORD's counsel—that will stand.

22 What is desired in a man is kindness,
And a poor man is better than a liar.

23 [a]The fear of the LORD *leads* to life,
And *he who has it* will abide in satisfaction;
He will not be visited with evil.

24 [a]A lazy *man* buries his hand in the *bowl,
And will not so much as bring it to his mouth again.

25 Strike a scoffer, and the simple [a]will become wary;
[b]Rebuke one who has understanding, *and* he will discern knowledge.

26 He who mistreats *his* father *and* chases away *his* mother
Is [a]a son who causes shame and brings reproach.

27 Cease listening to instruction, my son,
And you will stray from the words of knowledge.

KJV

28 An ungodly witness scorneth judgment: and [a]the mouth of the wicked devoureth iniquity.
29 Judgments are prepared for scorners, [a]and stripes for the back of fools.

20 Wine [a]*is* a mocker, strong drink *is* raging: and whosoever is deceived thereby is not wise.
2 The fear of a king *is* as the roaring of a lion: *whoso* provoketh him to anger sinneth *against* his own soul.
3 [a]*It is* an honour for a man to cease from strife: but every fool will be meddling.
4 [a]The sluggard will not plow by reason of the cold; [b]*therefore* shall he beg in harvest, and *have* nothing.
5 Counsel in the heart of man *is like* deep water; but a man of understanding will draw it out.
6 Most men will proclaim every one his own goodness: but a faithful man who can find?
7 [a]The just *man* walketh in his integrity: [b]his children *are* blessed after him.
8 A king that sitteth in the throne of judgment scattereth away all evil with his eyes.
9 [a]Who can say, I have made my heart clean, I am pure from my sin?
10 [a]Divers weights, *and* divers measures, both of them *are* alike abomination to the LORD.
11 Even a child is [a]known by his doings, whether his work *be* pure, and whether *it be* right.
12 [a]The hearing ear, and the seeing eye, the LORD hath made even both of them.
13 [a]Love not sleep, lest thou come to poverty; open thine eyes, *and* thou shalt be satisfied with bread.
14 *It is* naught, *it is* naught, saith the buyer: but when he is gone his way, then he boasteth.
15 There is gold, and a multitude of rubies: but [a]the lips of knowledge *are* a precious jewel.
16 [a]Take his garment that is surety *for* a stranger: and take a pledge of him for a strange woman.
17 [a]Bread of deceit *is* sweet to a man; but afterwards his mouth shall be filled with gravel.
18 [a]*Every* purpose is established by counsel: [b]and with good advice make war.
19 [a]He that goeth about *as* a talebearer revealeth secrets: therefore meddle not with him [b]that flattereth with his lips.

28 [a]Job 15:16
29 [a]Prov. 26:3

CHAPTER 20
1 [a]Gen. 9:21; Prov. 23:29–35; Is. 28:7; Hos. 4:11
3 [a]Prov. 17:14
4 [a]Prov. 10:4 [b]Prov. 19:15
7 [a]2 Cor. 1:12 [b]Ps. 37:26
9 [a][1 Kin. 8:46; 2 Chr. 6:36]; Job 9:30, 31; 14:4; [Ps. 51:5; Eccl. 7:20; Rom. 3:9; 1 John 1:8]
10 [a]Deut. 25:13
11 [a]Matt. 7:16
12 [a]Ex. 4:11; Ps. 94:9
13 [a]Rom. 12:11
15 [a][Job 28:12–19; Prov. 3:13–15]
16 [a]Prov. 22:26
17 [a]Prov. 9:17
18 [a]Prov. 24:6 [b]Luke 14:31
19 [a]Prov. 11:13 [b]Rom. 16:18

NKJV

28 A disreputable witness scorns justice,
And [a]the mouth of the wicked devours iniquity.

29 Judgments are prepared for scoffers,
[a]And beatings for the backs of fools.

20 Wine [a]*is* a mocker,
Strong drink *is* a brawler,
And whoever is led astray by it is not wise.

2 The *wrath of a king *is* like the roaring of a lion;
Whoever provokes him to anger sins *against* his own life.

3 [a]*It is* honorable for a man to stop striving,
Since any fool can start a quarrel.

4 [a]The lazy *man* will not plow because of winter;
[b]He will beg during harvest and *have* nothing.

5 Counsel in the heart of man *is like* deep water,
But a man of understanding will draw it out.

6 Most men will proclaim each his own goodness,
But who can find a faithful man?

7 [a]The righteous *man* walks in his integrity;
[b]His children *are* blessed after him.

8 A king who sits on the throne of judgment
Scatters all evil with his eyes.

9 [a]Who can say, "I have made my heart clean,
I am pure from my sin"?

10 [a]Diverse weights *and* diverse measures,
They *are* both alike, an abomination to the LORD.

11 Even a child is [a]known by his deeds,
Whether what he does *is* pure and right.

12 [a]The hearing ear and the seeing eye,
The LORD has made them both.

13 [a]Do not love sleep, lest you come to poverty;
Open your eyes, *and* you will be satisfied with bread.

14 "*It is* *good for nothing," cries the buyer;
But when he has gone his way, then he boasts.

15 There is gold and a multitude of rubies,
But [a]the lips of knowledge *are* a precious jewel.

16 [a]Take the garment of one who is surety *for* a stranger,
And hold it as a pledge *when it* is for a seductress.

17 [a]Bread gained by deceit *is* sweet to a man,
But afterward his mouth will be filled with gravel.

18 [a]Plans are established by counsel;
[b]By wise counsel wage war.

19 [a]He who goes about *as* a talebearer reveals secrets;
Therefore do not associate with one [b]who flatters with his lips.

*

20:2 Lit. *fear* or *terror*, produced by the king's wrath
20:14 Lit. *evil, evil*

KJV

20 [a]Whoso curseth his father or his mother, [b]his lamp shall be put out in obscure darkness.

21 [a]An inheritance *may be* gotten hastily at the beginning; [b]but the end thereof shall not be blessed.

22 [a]Say not thou, I will recompense evil; *but* [b]wait on the LORD, and he shall save thee.

23 Divers weights *are* an abomination unto the LORD; and a false balance *is* not good.

24 Man's goings *are* of the LORD; how can a man then understand his own way?

25 *It is* a snare to the man *who* devoureth *that which is* holy, and after vows to make enquiry.

26 [a]A wise king scattereth the wicked, and bringeth the wheel over them.

27 [a]The spirit of man *is* the candle of the LORD, searching all the inward parts of the belly.

28 [a]Mercy and truth preserve the king: and his throne is upholden by mercy.

29 The glory of young men *is* their strength: and [a]the beauty of old men *is* the grey head.

30 The blueness of a wound cleanseth away evil: so *do* stripes the inward parts of the belly.

21 The king's heart *is* in the hand of the LORD, *as* the rivers of water: he turneth it whithersoever he will.

2 [a]Every way of a man *is* right in his own eyes: [b]but the LORD pondereth the hearts.

3 [a]To do justice and judgment *is* more acceptable to the LORD than sacrifice.

4 [a]An high look, and a proud heart, *and* the plowing of the wicked, *is* sin.

5 [a]The thoughts of the diligent *tend* only to plenteousness; but of every one *that is* hasty only to want.

6 [a]The getting of treasures by a lying tongue *is* a vanity tossed to and fro of them that seek death.

7 The robbery of the wicked shall destroy them; because they refuse to do judgment.

8 The way of man *is* froward and strange: but *as for* the pure, his work *is* right.

9 *It is* better to dwell in a corner of the housetop, than with [a]a brawling woman in a wide house.

10 [a]The soul of the wicked desireth evil: his neighbour findeth no favour in his eyes.

20 [a]Ex. 21:17; Lev. 20:9; Prov. 30:11; Matt. 15:4 [b]Job 18:5, 6; Prov. 24:20
21 [a]Prov. 28:20 [b]Hab. 2:6
22 [a][Deut. 32:35]; Prov. 17:13; 24:29; [Rom. 12:17–19]; 1 Thess. 5:15; [1 Pet. 3:9] [b]2 Sam. 16:12
26 [a]Ps. 101:8
27 [a]1 Cor. 2:11
28 [a]Ps. 101:1; Prov. 21:21
29 [a]Prov. 16:31

CHAPTER 21

2 [a]Prov. 16:2 [b]Prov. 24:12; Luke 16:15
3 [a]1 Sam. 15:22; Prov. 15:8; Is. 1:11, 16, 17; Hos. 6:6; [Mic. 6:7, 8]
4 [a]Prov. 6:17
5 [a]Prov. 10:4
6 [a]2 Pet. 2:3
9 [a]Prov. 19:13
10 [a]James 4:5

*

20:27 Lit. *rooms of the belly*
20:30 Lit. *rooms of the belly*
21:4 Or *lamp*
21:6 LXX *Pursue vanity on the snares of death;* Vg. *Is vain and foolish, and shall stumble on the snares of death;* Tg. *They shall be destroyed, and they shall fall who seek death*
21:7 Lit. *drag them away*
21:8 Or *The way of a man is perverse and strange;*

NKJV

20 [a]Whoever curses his father or his mother,
[b]His lamp will be put out in deep darkness.

21 [a]An inheritance gained hastily at the beginning
[b]Will not be blessed at the end.

22 [a]Do not say, "I will recompense evil";
[b]Wait for the LORD, and He will save you.

23 Diverse weights *are* an abomination to the LORD,
And dishonest scales *are* not good.

24 A man's steps *are* of the LORD;
How then can a man understand his own way?

25 *It is* a snare for a man to devote rashly *something as* holy,
And afterward to reconsider *his* vows.

26 [a]A wise king sifts out the wicked,
And brings the threshing wheel over them.

27 [a]The spirit of a man *is* the lamp of the LORD,
Searching all the *inner depths of his heart.

28 [a]Mercy and truth preserve the king,
And by lovingkindness he upholds his throne.

29 The glory of young men *is* their strength,
And [a]the splendor of old men *is* their gray head.

30 Blows that hurt cleanse away evil,
As *do* stripes the *inner depths of the heart.

21 The king's heart *is* in the hand of the LORD,
Like the rivers of water;
He turns it wherever He wishes.

2 [a]Every way of a man *is* right in his own eyes,
[b]But the LORD weighs the hearts.

3 [a]To do righteousness and justice
Is more acceptable to the LORD than sacrifice.

4 [a]A haughty look, a proud heart,
And the *plowing of the wicked *are* sin.

5 [a]The plans of the diligent *lead* surely to plenty,
But *those of* everyone *who is* hasty, surely to poverty.

6 [a]Getting treasures by a lying tongue
**Is* the fleeting fantasy of those who seek death.

7 The violence of the wicked will *destroy them,
Because they refuse to do justice.

8 The way of *a guilty man *is* perverse;
But *as for* the pure, his work *is* right.

9 Better to dwell in a corner of a housetop,
Than in a house shared with [a]a contentious woman.

10 [a]The soul of the wicked desires evil;
His neighbor finds no favor in his eyes.

KJV

11 When the scorner is punished, the simple is made wise: and when the [a]wise is instructed, he receiveth knowledge.

12 The righteous *man* wisely considereth the house of the wicked: *but God* overthroweth the wicked for *their* wickedness.

13 [a]Whoso stoppeth his ears at the cry of the poor, he also shall cry himself, but shall not be heard.

14 A gift in secret pacifieth anger: and a reward in the bosom strong wrath.

15 *It is* joy to the just to do judgment: but destruction *shall be* to the workers of iniquity.

16 The man that wandereth out of the way of understanding shall remain in the congregation of the [a]dead.

17 He that loveth pleasure *shall be* a poor man: he that loveth wine and oil shall not be rich.

18 The wicked *shall be* a ransom for the righteous, and the transgressor for the upright.

19 *It is* better to dwell in the wilderness, than with a contentious and an angry woman.

20 [a]*There is* treasure to be desired and oil in the dwelling of the wise; but a foolish man spendeth it up.

21 [a]He that followeth after righteousness and mercy findeth life, righteousness, and honour.

22 A [a]wise *man* scaleth the city of the mighty, and casteth down the strength of the confidence thereof.

23 [a]Whoso keepeth his mouth and his tongue keepeth his soul from troubles.

24 Proud *and* haughty scorner *is* his name, who dealeth in proud wrath.

25 The [a]desire of the slothful killeth him; for his hands refuse to labour.

26 He coveteth greedily all the day long: but the righteous [a]giveth and spareth not.

27 [a]The sacrifice of the wicked *is* abomination: how much more, *when* he bringeth it with a wicked mind?

28 A false witness shall perish: but the man that heareth speaketh constantly.

29 A wicked man hardeneth his face: but *as for* the upright, he directeth his way.

30 [a]*There is* no wisdom nor understanding nor counsel against the LORD.

31 The horse *is* prepared against the day of battle: but [a]safety *is* of the LORD.

22 A [a]*good* name *is* rather to be chosen than great riches, *and* loving favour rather than silver and gold.

---

11 [a]Prov. 19:25
13 [a][Matt. 7:2; 18:30–34]; James 2:13; 1 John 3:17
16 [a]Ps. 49:14
20 [a]Ps. 112:3; Prov. 8:21
21 [a]Prov. 15:9; Matt. 5:6; [Rom. 2:7]; 1 Cor. 15:58
22 [a]2 Sam. 5:6–9; Prov. 24:5; Eccl. 7:19; 9:15, 16
23 [a]Prov. 12:13; 13:3; 18:21; [James 3:2]
25 [a]Prov. 13:4
26 [a][Prov. 22:9; Eph. 4:28]
27 [a]Prov. 15:8; Is. 66:3; Jer. 6:20; Amos 5:22
30 [a]Is. 8:9, 10; [Jer. 9:23, 24]; Acts 5:39; 1 Cor. 3:19, 20
31 [a]Ps. 3:8; Jer. 3:23; [1 Cor. 15:57]

CHAPTER 22

1 [a][Prov. 10:7]; Eccl. 7:1

*

21:14 Under cover, lit. *in the bosom*
21:29 Qr., LXX *understands*

NKJV

11 When the scoffer is punished, the simple is made wise;
But when the [a]wise is instructed, he receives knowledge.

12 The righteous *God* wisely considers the house of the wicked,
Overthrowing the wicked for *their* wickedness.

13 [a]Whoever shuts his ears to the cry of the poor
Will also cry himself and not be heard.

14 A gift in secret pacifies anger,
And a bribe *behind the back, strong wrath.

15 *It is* a joy for the just to do justice,
But destruction *will come* to the workers of iniquity.

16 A man who wanders from the way of understanding
Will rest in the assembly of the [a]dead.

17 He who loves pleasure *will be* a poor man;
He who loves wine and oil will not be rich.

18 The wicked *shall be* a ransom for the righteous,
And the unfaithful for the upright.

19 Better to dwell in the wilderness,
Than with a contentious and angry woman.

20 [a]*There is* desirable treasure,
And oil in the dwelling of the wise,
But a foolish man squanders it.

21 [a]He who follows righteousness and mercy
Finds life, righteousness and honor.

22 A [a]wise *man* scales the city of the mighty,
And brings down the trusted stronghold.

23 [a]Whoever guards his mouth and tongue
Keeps his soul from troubles.

24 A proud *and* haughty *man*— "Scoffer" *is* his name;
He acts with arrogant pride.

25 The [a]desire of the lazy *man* kills him,
For his hands refuse to labor.
26 He covets greedily all day long,
But the righteous [a]gives and does not spare.

27 [a]The sacrifice of the wicked *is* an abomination;
How much more *when* he brings it with wicked intent!

28 A false witness shall perish,
But the man who hears *him* will speak endlessly.

29 A wicked man hardens his face,
But *as for* the upright, he *establishes his way.

30 [a]*There is* no wisdom or understanding
Or counsel against the LORD.

31 The horse *is* prepared for the day of battle,
But [a]deliverance *is* of the LORD.

22 A [a]*good* name is to be chosen rather than great riches,
Loving favor rather than silver and gold.

KJV

2 The [a]rich and poor meet together: the [b]LORD *is* the maker of them all.

3 A prudent *man* foreseeth the evil, and hideth himself: but the simple pass on, and are [a]punished.

4 By humility *and* the fear of the LORD *are* riches, and honour, and life.

5 Thorns *and* snares *are* in the way of the froward: he that doth keep his soul shall be far from them.

6 [a]Train up a child in the way he should go: and when he is old, he will not depart from it.

7 The [a]rich ruleth over the poor, and the borrower *is* servant to the lender.

8 He that soweth iniquity shall reap [a]vanity: and the rod of his anger shall fail.

9 [a]He that hath a bountiful eye shall be [b]blessed; for he giveth of his bread to the poor.

10 [a]Cast out the scorner, and contention shall go out; yea, strife and reproach shall cease.

11 [a]He that loveth pureness of heart, *for* the grace of his lips the king *shall be* his friend.

12 The eyes of the LORD preserve knowledge, and he overthroweth the words of the transgressor.

13 [a]The slothful *man* saith, *There is* a lion without, I shall be slain in the streets.

14 [a]The mouth of strange women *is* a deep pit: [b]he that is abhorred of the LORD shall fall therein.

15 Foolishness *is* bound in the heart of a child; *but* [a]the rod of correction shall drive it far from him.

16 He that oppresseth the poor to increase his *riches, and* he that giveth to the rich, *shall* surely *come* to want.

Sayings of the Wise

17 Bow down thine ear, and hear the words of the wise, and apply thine heart unto my knowledge.

18 For *it is* a pleasant thing if thou keep them within thee; they shall withal be fitted in thy lips.

19 That thy trust may be in the LORD, I have made known to thee this day, even to thee.

20 Have not I written to thee excellent things in counsels and knowledge,

21 [a]That I might make thee know the certainty of the words of truth; [b]that thou mightest answer the words of truth to them that send unto thee?

22 Rob not the [a]poor, because he *is* poor: neither oppress the afflicted in the gate:

23 [a]For the LORD will plead their cause, and spoil the soul of those that spoiled them.

2 [a]Prov. 29:13 [b]Job 31:15; [Prov. 14:31]
3 [a]Prov. 27:12; Is. 26:20
6 [a]Eph. 6:4; 2 Tim. 3:15
7 [a]Prov. 18:23; James 2:6
8 [a]Job 4:8
9 [a]2 Cor. 9:6 [b][Prov. 19:17]
10 [a]Ps. 101:5
11 [a]Ps. 101:6
13 [a]Prov. 26:13
14 [a]Prov. 2:16; 5:3; 7:5 [b]Eccl. 7:26
15 [a]Prov. 13:24; 23:13, 14
21 [a]Luke 1:3, 4 [b]Prov. 25:13; 1 Pet. 3:15
22 [a]Ex. 23:6; Job 31:16–21; Zech. 7:10
23 [a]1 Sam. 24:12; Ps. 12:5; 140:12

NKJV

2 The [a]rich and the poor have this in common,
The [b]LORD *is* the maker of them all.

3 A prudent *man* foresees evil and hides himself,
But the simple pass on and are [a]punished.

4 By humility *and* the fear of the LORD
Are riches and honor and life.

5 Thorns *and* snares *are* in the way of the perverse;
He who guards his soul will be far from them.

6 [a]Train up a child in the way he should go,
And when he is old he will not depart from it.

7 The [a]rich rules over the poor,
And the borrower *is* servant to the lender.

8 He who sows iniquity will reap [a]sorrow,
And the rod of his anger will fail.

9 [a]He who has a generous eye will be [b]blessed,
For he gives of his bread to the poor.

10 [a]Cast out the scoffer, and contention will leave;
Yes, strife and reproach will cease.

11 [a]He who loves purity of heart
And has grace on his lips,
The king *will be* his friend.

12 The eyes of the LORD preserve knowledge,
But He overthrows the words of the faithless.

13 [a]The lazy *man* says, "*There is* a lion outside!
I shall be slain in the streets!"

14 [a]The mouth of an immoral woman *is* a deep pit;
[b]He who is abhorred by the LORD will fall there.

15 Foolishness *is* bound up in the heart of a child;
[a]The rod of correction will drive it far from him.

16 He who oppresses the poor to increase his *riches,*
And he who gives to the rich, *will* surely *come* to poverty.

Sayings of the Wise

17 Incline your ear and hear the words of the wise,
And apply your heart to my knowledge;
18 For *it is* a pleasant thing if you keep them within you;
Let them all be fixed upon your lips,
19 So that your trust may be in the LORD;
I have instructed you today, even you.
20 Have I not written to you excellent things
Of counsels and knowledge,
21 [a]That I may make you know the certainty of the words of truth,
[b]That you may answer words of truth
To those who send to you?

22 Do not rob the [a]poor because he *is* poor,
Nor oppress the afflicted at the gate;
23 [a]For the LORD will plead their cause,
And plunder the soul of those who plunder them.

KJV

24 Make no friendship with an angry man; and with a [a]furious man thou shalt not go;
25 Lest thou learn his ways, and get a snare to thy soul.
26 [a]Be not thou *one* of them that strike hands, *or* of them that are sureties for debts.
27 If thou hast nothing to pay, why should he take away thy bed from under thee?
28 [a]Remove not the ancient landmark, which thy fathers have set.
29 Seest thou a man diligent in his business? he shall stand before kings; he shall not stand before mean *men.*

23 When thou sittest to eat with a ruler, consider diligently what *is* before thee:
2 And put a knife to thy throat, if thou *be* a man given to appetite.
3 Be not desirous of his dainties: for they *are* deceitful meat.
4 [a]Labour not to be rich: [b]cease from thine own wisdom.
5 Wilt thou set thine eyes upon that which is not? for *riches* certainly make themselves wings; they fly away as an eagle toward heaven.
6 Eat thou not the bread of *him that hath* [a]an evil eye, neither desire thou his dainty meats:
7 For as he thinketh in his heart, so *is* he: Eat and drink, [a]saith he to thee; but his heart *is* not with thee.
8 The morsel *which* thou hast eaten shalt thou vomit up, and lose thy sweet words.
9 [a]Speak not in the ears of a fool: for he will despise the wisdom of thy words.
10 Remove not the old landmark; and enter not into the fields of the fatherless:
11 [a]For their redeemer *is* mighty; he shall plead their cause with thee.
12 Apply thine heart unto instruction, and thine ears to the words of knowledge.
13 [a]Withhold not correction from the child: for *if* thou beatest him with the rod, he shall not die.
14 Thou shalt beat him with the rod, and shalt deliver his soul from hell.
15 My son, if thine heart be wise, my heart shall rejoice, even mine.
16 Yea, my reins shall rejoice, when thy lips speak right things.
17 [a]Let not thine heart envy sinners: but [b]*be thou* in the fear of the LORD all the day long.
18 [a]For surely there is an end; and thine expectation shall not be cut off.
19 Hear thou, my son, and be wise, and guide thine heart in the way.
20 [a]Be not among winebibbers; among riotous eaters of flesh:

24 [a]Prov. 29:22
26 [a]Prov. 11:15
28 [a]Deut. 19:14; 27:17; Job 24:2; Prov. 23:10

CHAPTER 23
4 [a][Prov. 28:20; Matt. 6:19; 1 Tim. 6:9, 10; Heb. 13:5] [b]Rom. 12:16
6 [a]Deut. 15:9; Prov. 28:22
7 [a]Prov. 12:2
9 [a]Prov. 9:8; Matt. 7:6
11 [a]Prov. 22:23
13 [a]Prov. 13:24
17 [a]Ps. 37:1; Prov. 24:1, 19 [b]Prov. 28:14
18 [a][Ps. 37:37]
20 [a]Prov. 20:1; 23:29, 30; Is. 5:22; Matt. 24:49; [Luke 21:34]; Rom. 13:13; [Eph. 5:18]

NKJV

24 Make no friendship with an angry man,
And with a [a]furious man do not go,
25 Lest you learn his ways
And set a snare for your soul.

26 [a]Do not be one of those who shakes hands in a pledge,
One of those who is surety for debts;
27 If you have nothing *with which* to pay,
Why should he take away your bed from under you?

28 [a]Do not remove the ancient landmark
Which your fathers have set.

29 Do you see a man *who* excels in his work?
He will stand before kings;
He will not stand before unknown *men.*

23 When you sit down to eat with a ruler,
Consider carefully what *is* before you;
2 And put a knife to your throat
If you *are* a man given to appetite.
3 Do not desire his delicacies,
For they *are* deceptive food.

4 [a]Do not overwork to be rich;
[b]Because of your own understanding, cease!
5 Will you set your eyes on that which is not?
For *riches* certainly make themselves wings;
They fly away like an eagle *toward* heaven.

6 Do not eat the bread of [a]a* miser,
Nor desire his delicacies;
7 For as he thinks in his heart, so *is* he.
"Eat and drink!" [a]he says to you,
But his heart is not with you.
8 The morsel you have eaten, you will vomit up,
And waste your pleasant words.

9 [a]Do not speak in the hearing of a fool,
For he will despise the wisdom of your words.

10 Do not remove the ancient landmark,
Nor enter the fields of the fatherless;
11 [a]For their Redeemer *is* mighty;
He will plead their cause against you.

12 Apply your heart to instruction,
And your ears to words of knowledge.

13 [a]Do not withhold correction from a child,
For *if* you beat him with a rod, he will not die.
14 You shall beat him with a rod,
And deliver his soul from *hell.

15 My son, if your heart is wise,
My heart will rejoice—indeed, I myself;
16 Yes, my inmost being will rejoice
When your lips speak right things.

17 [a]Do not let your heart envy sinners,
But [b]*be zealous* for the fear of the LORD all the day;
18 [a]For surely there is a hereafter,
And your hope will not be cut off.

19 Hear, my son, and be wise;
And guide your heart in the way.
20 [a]Do not mix with winebibbers,
Or with gluttonous eaters of meat;

23:6 Lit. *one who has an evil eye*
23:14 Or *Sheol*

KJV

21 For the drunkard and the glutton shall
come to poverty: and drowsiness shall clothe *a*
man with rags.
22 [a]Hearken unto thy father that begat thee,
and despise not thy mother when she is old.
23 [a]Buy the truth, and sell *it* not; *also* wisdom, and instruction, and understanding.
24 [a]The father of the righteous shall greatly
rejoice: and he that begetteth a wise *child* shall
have joy of him.
25 Thy father and thy mother shall be glad,
and she that bare thee shall rejoice.
26 My son, give me thine heart, and let thine
eyes observe my ways.
27 [a]For a whore *is* a deep ditch; and a strange
woman *is* a narrow pit.
28 [a]She also lieth in wait as *for* a prey, and
increaseth the transgressors among men.
29 [a]Who hath woe? who hath sorrow? who
hath contentions? who hath babbling? who hath
wounds without cause? who [b]hath redness of
eyes?
30 [a]They that tarry long at the wine; they that
go to seek [b]mixed wine.
31 Look not thou upon the wine when it is
red, when it giveth his colour in the cup, *when* it
moveth itself aright.
32 At the last it biteth like a serpent, and
stingeth like an adder.
33 Thine eyes shall behold strange women,
and thine heart shall utter perverse things.
34 Yea, thou shalt be as he that lieth down
in the midst of the sea, or as he that lieth upon
the top of a mast.
35 [a]They have stricken me, *shalt thou say,*
and I was not sick; they have beaten me, *and* I
felt *it* not: when shall [b]I awake? I will seek it yet
again.

24 Be not thou [a]envious against evil men, neither desire to be with them.
2 For their heart studieth destruction, and
their lips talk of mischief.
3 Through wisdom is an house builded; and
by understanding it is established:
4 And by knowledge shall the chambers be
filled with all precious and pleasant riches.
5 [a]A wise man *is* strong; yea, a man of
knowledge increaseth strength.
6 [a]For by wise counsel thou shalt make thy
war: and in multitude of counsellors *there is*
safety.
7 [a]Wisdom *is* too high for a fool: he openeth
not his mouth in the gate.
8 He that [a]deviseth to do evil shall be called
a mischievous person.
9 The thought of foolishness *is* sin: and the
scorner *is* an abomination to men.
10 *If* thou [a]faint in the day of adversity, thy
strength *is* small.

22 [a]Prov. 1:8; Eph. 6:1
23 [a]Prov. 4:7; 18:15; [Matt. 13:44]
24 [a]Prov. 10:1
27 [a]Prov. 22:14
28 [a]Prov. 7:12; Eccl. 7:26
29 [a]Is. 5:11, 22 [b]Gen. 49:12
30 [a]1 Sam. 25:36; Prov. 20:1; 21:17; Is. 5:11; 28:7; [Eph. 5:18] [b]Ps. 75:8
35 [a]Prov. 27:22; Jer. 5:3 [b]Eph. 4:19

CHAPTER 24

1 [a]Ps. 1:1; 37:1; Prov. 23:17
5 [a]Prov. 21:22; Eccl. 9:16
6 [a]Luke 14:31
7 [a]Ps. 10:5; Prov. 14:6
8 [a]Prov. 6:14; 14:22; Rom. 1:30
10 [a]Deut. 20:8; Job 4:5; Jer. 51:46; Heb. 12:3

NKJV

21 For the drunkard and the glutton will
come to poverty,
And drowsiness will clothe *a man* with
rags.
22 [a]Listen to your father who begot you,
And do not despise your mother when she
is old.
23 [a]Buy the truth, and do not sell *it*,
Also wisdom and instruction and
understanding.
24 [a]The father of the righteous will greatly
rejoice,
And he who begets a wise *child* will
delight in him.
25 Let your father and your mother be glad,
And let her who bore you rejoice.

26 My son, give me your heart,
And let your eyes observe my ways.
27 [a]For a harlot *is* a deep pit,
And a seductress *is* a narrow well.
28 [a]She also lies in wait as *for* a victim,
And increases the unfaithful among
men.

29 [a]Who has woe?
Who has sorrow?
Who has contentions?
Who has complaints?
Who has wounds without cause?
Who [b]has redness of eyes?
30 [a]Those who linger long at the wine,
Those who go in search of [b]mixed wine.
31 Do not look on the wine when it is red,
When it sparkles in the cup,
When it swirls around smoothly;
32 At the last it bites like a serpent,
And stings like a viper.
33 Your eyes will see strange things,
And your heart will utter perverse things.
34 Yes, you will be like one who lies down
in the midst of the sea,
Or like one who lies at the top of the mast,
saying:
35 "They[a] have struck me, *but* I was not
hurt;
They have beaten me, but I did not feel
it.
When shall [b]I awake, that I may seek
another *drink*?"

24 Do not be [a]envious of evil men,
Nor desire to be with them;
2 For their heart devises violence,
And their lips talk of troublemaking.

3 Through wisdom a house is built,
And by understanding it is established;
4 By knowledge the rooms are filled
With all precious and pleasant riches.

5 [a]A wise man *is* strong,
Yes, a man of knowledge increases
strength;
6 [a]For by wise counsel you will wage your
own war,
And in a multitude of counselors *there is*
safety.

7 [a]Wisdom *is* too lofty for a fool;
He does not open his mouth in the gate.

8 He who [a]plots to do evil
Will be called a schemer.
9 The devising of foolishness *is* sin,
And the scoffer *is* an abomination to men.

10 *If* you [a]faint in the day of adversity,
Your strength *is* small.

KJV

11 [a]If thou forbear to deliver *them that are*
drawn unto death, and *those that are* ready to
be slain;
12 If thou sayest, Behold, we knew it not;
doth not [a]he that pondereth the heart consider
it? and he that keepeth thy soul, doth *not* he know
it? and shall *not* he render to *every* man [b]accord-
ing to his works?
13 My son, [a]eat thou honey, because *it is*
good; and the honeycomb, *which is* sweet to thy
taste:
14 [a]So *shall* the knowledge of wisdom *be*
unto thy soul: when thou hast found *it*, then there
shall be a reward, and thy expectation shall not
be cut off.
15 Lay not wait, O wicked *man*, against the
dwelling of the righteous; spoil not his resting
place:
16 [a]For a just *man* falleth seven times, and
riseth up again: [b]but the wicked shall fall into
mischief.
17 [a]Rejoice not when thine enemy falleth,
and let not thine heart be glad when he stumbleth:
18 Lest the LORD see *it*, and it displease him,
and he turn away his wrath from him.
19 [a]Fret not thyself because of evil *men*, neither be thou envious at the wicked;
20 For there shall be no reward to the evil
man; the candle of the wicked shall be put out.
21 My son, [a]fear thou the LORD and the king:
and meddle not with them that are given to
change:
22 For their calamity shall rise suddenly; and
who knoweth the ruin of them both?

Further Sayings of the Wise

23 These *things* also *belong* to the wise. [a]*It*
is not good to have respect of persons in
judgment.
24 [a]He that saith unto the wicked, Thou *art*
righteous; him shall the people curse, nations
shall abhor him:
25 But to them that rebuke *him* shall be [a]de-
light, and a good blessing shall come upon them.
26 *Every man* shall kiss *his* lips that giveth
a right answer.
27 [a]Prepare thy work without, and make it
fit for thyself in the field; and afterwards build
thine house.
28 [a]Be not a witness against thy neighbour
without cause; and deceive *not* with thy lips.
29 [a]Say not, I will do so to him as he hath
done to me: I will render to the man according
to his work.
30 I went by the field of the slothful, and by
the vineyard of the man void of understanding;
31 And, lo, [a]it was all grown over with
thorns, *and* nettles had covered the face thereof,
and the stone wall thereof was broken down.

11 [a]Ps. 82:4; Is. 58:6, 7; 1 John 3:16
12 [a]1 Sam. 16:7; Prov. 21:2 [b]Job 34:11; Ps. 62:12; Rev. 2:23; 22:12
13 [a]Ps. 19:10; 119:103; Prov. 25:16; Song 5:1
14 [a]Ps. 19:10; 58:11; Prov. 23:18
16 [a]Job 5:19; [Ps. 34:19; 37:24; Mic. 7:8] [b]Esth. 7:10; Amos 5:2
17 [a]Job 31:29; Ps. 35:15, 19; [Prov. 17:5]; Obad. 12
19 [a]Ps. 37:1
21 [a][Rom. 13:7; 1 Pet. 2:17]
23 [a]Lev. 19:15; Deut. 1:17; 16:19; [John 7:24]
24 [a]Prov. 17:15; Is. 5:23
25 [a]Prov. 28:23
27 [a]1 Kin. 5:17; Prov. 27:23–27
28 [a]Lev. 6:2, 3; 19:11; Eph. 4:25
29 [a][Prov. 20:22; Matt. 5:39–44; Rom. 12:17–19]
31 [a]Gen. 3:18

NKJV

11 [a]Deliver *those who* are drawn toward
death,
And hold back *those* stumbling to the
slaughter.
12 If you say, "Surely we did not know this,"
Does not [a]He who weighs the hearts
consider *it?*
He who keeps your soul, does He *not*
know *it?*
And will He *not* render to *each* man
[b]according to his deeds?

13 My son, [a]eat honey because *it is* good,
And the honeycomb *which is* sweet to
your taste;
14 [a]So *shall* the knowledge of wisdom *be* to
your soul;
If you have found *it*, there is a prospect,
And your hope will not be cut off.

15 Do not lie in wait, O wicked *man*, against
the dwelling of the righteous;
Do not plunder his resting place;
16 [a]For a righteous *man* may fall seven times
And rise again,
[b]But the wicked shall fall by calamity.

17 [a]Do not rejoice when your enemy falls,
And do not let your heart be glad when
he stumbles;
18 Lest the LORD see *it*, and it displease
Him,
And He turn away His wrath from him.

19 [a]Do not fret because of evildoers,
Nor be envious of the wicked;
20 For there will be no prospect for the evil
man;
The lamp of the wicked will be put out.

21 My son, [a]fear the LORD and the king;
Do not associate with those given to
change;
22 For their calamity will rise suddenly,
And who knows the ruin those two can
bring?

Further Sayings of the Wise

23 These *things* also *belong* to the wise:

[a]*It is* not good to show partiality in
judgment.
24 [a]He who says to the wicked, "You *are*
righteous,"
Him the people will curse;
Nations will abhor him.
25 But those who rebuke *the wicked* will
have [a]delight,
And a good blessing will come upon them.

26 He who gives a right answer kisses the
lips.

27 [a]Prepare your outside work,
Make it fit for yourself in the field;
And afterward build your house.

28 [a]Do not be a witness against your neighbor
without cause,
*For would you deceive with your lips?
29 [a]Do not say, "I will do to him just as he
has done to me;
I will render to the man according to his
work."

30 I went by the field of the lazy *man*,
And by the vineyard of the man devoid
of understanding;
31 And there it was, [a]all overgrown with
thorns;
Its surface was covered with nettles;
Its stone wall was broken down.

*———

24:28 LXX, Vg. *Do not deceive*

KJV

32 Then I saw, *and* considered *it* well: I
looked upon *it, and* received instruction.
33 [a]*Yet* a little sleep, a little slumber, a little
folding of the hands to sleep:
34 [a]So shall thy poverty come *as* one that
travelleth; and thy want as an armed man.

Further Wise Sayings of Solomon

25 These[a] *are* also proverbs of Solomon,
which the men of Hezekiah king of Judah
copied out.
2 [a]*It is* the glory of God to conceal a thing:
but the honour of kings *is* to search out a matter.
3 The heaven for height, and the earth for
depth, and the heart of kings *is* unsearchable.
4 [a]Take away the dross from the silver, and
there shall come forth a vessel for the finer.
5 Take away the wicked *from* before the
king, and his throne shall be established in
[a]righteousness.
6 Put not forth thyself in the presence of the
king, and stand not in the place of great *men:*
7 [a]For better *it is* that it be said unto thee,
Come up hither; than that thou shouldest be put
lower in the presence of the prince whom thine
eyes have seen.
8 [a]Go not forth hastily to strive, lest *thou
know not* what to do in the end thereof, when
thy neighbour hath put thee to shame.
9 [a]Debate thy cause with thy neighbour
himself; and discover not a secret to another:
10 Lest he that heareth *it* put thee to shame,
and thine infamy turn not away.
11 A word fitly [a]spoken *is like* apples of gold
in pictures of silver.
12 *As* an earring of gold, and an ornament
of fine gold, *so is* a wise reprover upon an obedient ear.
13 [a]As the cold of snow in the time of harvest, *so is* a faithful messenger to them that send
him: for he refresheth the soul of his masters.
14 [a]Whoso boasteth himself of a false gift *is
like* [b]clouds and wind without rain.
15 [a]By long forbearing is a prince persuaded,
and a soft tongue breaketh the bone.
16 Hast thou found honey? eat so much as
is sufficient for thee, lest thou be filled therewith,
and vomit it.
17 Withdraw thy foot from thy neighbour's
house; lest he be weary of thee, and *so* hate thee.
18 [a]A man that beareth false witness against
his neighbour *is* a maul, and a sword, and a sharp
arrow.
19 Confidence in an unfaithful man in time
of trouble *is like* a broken tooth, and a foot out
of joint.
20 *As* he that taketh away a garment in cold
weather, *and as* vinegar upon nitre, so *is* he that
[a]singeth songs to an heavy heart.

33 [a]Prov. 6:9, 10
34 [a]Prov. 6:9–11

CHAPTER 25
1 [a]1 Kin. 4:32
2 [a]Deut. 29:29; Rom. 11:33
4 [a]2 Tim. 2:21
5 [a]Prov. 16:12; 20:8
7 [a]Luke 14:7–11
8 [a]Prov. 17:14; Matt. 5:25
9 [a][Matt. 18:15]
11 [a]Prov. 15:23; Is. 50:4
13 [a]Prov. 13:17
14 [a]Prov. 20:6 [b]Jude 12
15 [a]Prov. 15:1
18 [a]Ps. 57:4; Prov. 12:18
20 [a]Dan. 6:18

NKJV

32 When I saw *it*, I considered *it* well;
I looked on *it and* received instruction:
33 [a]A little sleep, a little slumber,
A little folding of the hands to rest;
34 [a]So shall your poverty come *like* a prowler,
And your need like an armed man.

Further Wise Sayings of Solomon

25 These[a] also *are* proverbs of Solomon which the men of Hezekiah king of Judah copied:

2 [a]*It is* the glory of God to conceal a matter,
But the glory of kings *is* to search out a matter.

3 *As* the heavens for height and the earth for depth,
So the heart of kings *is* unsearchable.

4 [a]Take away the dross from silver,
And it will go to the silversmith *for* jewelry.
5 Take away the wicked from before the king,
And his throne will be established in [a]righteousness.

6 Do not exalt yourself in the presence of the king,
And do not stand in the place of the great;
7 [a]For *it is* better that he say to you,
"Come up here,"
Than that you should be put lower in the presence of the prince,
Whom your eyes have seen.

8 [a]Do not go hastily to court;
For what will you do in the end,
When your neighbor has put you to shame?
9 [a]Debate your case with your neighbor,
And do not disclose the secret to another;
10 Lest he who hears *it* expose your shame,
And your reputation be ruined.

11 A word fitly [a]spoken *is like* apples of gold
In settings of silver.
12 *Like* an earring of gold and an ornament of fine gold
Is a wise rebuker to an obedient ear.

13 [a]Like the cold of snow in time of harvest
Is a faithful messenger to those who send him,
For he refreshes the soul of his masters.

14 [a]Whoever falsely boasts of giving
Is like [b]clouds and wind without rain.

15 [a]By long forbearance a ruler is persuaded,
And a gentle tongue breaks a bone.

16 Have you found honey?
Eat only as much as you need,
Lest you be filled with it and vomit.

17 Seldom set foot in your neighbor's house,
Lest he become weary of you and hate you.

18 [a]A man who bears false witness against his neighbor
Is like a club, a sword, and a sharp arrow.

19 Confidence in an unfaithful *man* in time of trouble
Is like a bad tooth and a foot out of joint.

20 *Like* one who takes away a garment in cold weather,
And like vinegar on soda,
Is one who [a]sings songs to a heavy heart.

KJV

21 [a]If thine enemy be hungry, give him bread
to eat; and if he be thirsty, give him water to drink:
22 For thou shalt heap coals of fire upon his
head, [a]and the LORD shall reward thee.
23 The north wind driveth away rain: so *doth*
an angry countenance [a]a backbiting tongue.
24 [a]*It is* better to dwell in the corner of the
housetop, than with a brawling woman and in a
wide house.
25 *As* cold waters to a thirsty soul, so *is* [a]good
news from a far country.
26 A righteous man falling down before the
wicked *is as* a troubled fountain, and a corrupt
spring.
27 *It is* not good to eat much honey: so *for
men* [a]to search their own glory *is not* glory.
28 [a]He that *hath* no rule over his own spirit
is like a city *that is* broken down, *and* without
walls.

26

1 As snow in summer, [a]and as rain in harvest, so honour is not seemly for a fool.
2 As the bird by wandering, as the swallow
by flying, so [a]the curse causeless shall not come.
3 [a]A whip for the horse, a bridle for the ass,
and a rod for the fool's back.
4 Answer not a fool according to his folly,
lest thou also be like unto him.
5 [a]Answer a fool according to his folly, lest
he be wise in his own conceit.
6 He that sendeth a message by the hand
of a fool cutteth off the feet, *and* drinketh damage.
7 The legs of the lame are not equal: so *is*
a parable in the mouth of fools.
8 As he that bindeth a stone in a sling, so
is he that giveth honour to a fool.
9 *As* a thorn goeth up into the hand of a
drunkard, so *is* a parable in the mouth of fools.
10 The great *God* that formed all *things* both
rewardeth the fool, and rewardeth transgressors.
11 [a]As a dog returneth to his vomit, [b]*so* a
fool returneth to his folly.
12 [a]Seest thou a man wise in his own conceit? *there is* more hope of a fool than of him.
13 The slothful *man* saith, *There is* a lion in
the way; a lion *is* in the streets.
14 *As* the door turneth upon his hinges, so
doth the slothful upon his bed.
15 The [a]slothful hideth his hand in *his* bosom; it grieveth him to bring it again to his mouth.
16 The sluggard *is* wiser in his own conceit
than seven men that can render a reason.
17 He that passeth by, *and* meddleth with
strife *belonging* not to him, *is like* one that taketh
a dog by the ears.
18 As a mad *man* who casteth firebrands, arrows, and death,

21 [a]Ex. 23:4, 5; 2 Kin. 6:22; 2 Chr. 28:15; Matt. 5:44; Rom. 12:20
22 [a]2 Sam. 16:12; [Matt. 6:4, 6]
23 [a]Ps. 101:5
24 [a]Prov. 19:13
25 [a]Prov. 15:30
27 [a]Prov. 27:2; [Luke 14:11]
28 [a]Prov. 16:32

CHAPTER 26

1 [a]1 Sam. 12:17
2 [a]Num. 23:8; Deut. 23:5; 2 Sam. 16:12
3 [a]Ps. 32:9; Prov. 19:29
5 [a]Matt. 16:1–4; Rom. 12:16
11 [a]2 Pet. 2:22 [b]Ex. 8:15
12 [a]Prov. 29:20; Luke 18:11, 12; [Rev. 3:17]
15 [a]Prov. 19:24

NKJV

21 [a]If your enemy is hungry, give him bread
to eat;
And if he is thirsty, give him water to
drink;
22 For *so* you will heap coals of fire on his
head,
[a]And the LORD will reward you.

23 The north wind brings forth rain,
And [a]a backbiting tongue an angry
countenance.

24 [a]*It is* better to dwell in a corner of a
housetop,
Than in a house shared with a contentious
woman.

25 *As* cold water to a weary soul,
So *is* [a]good news from a far country.

26 A righteous *man* who falters before the
wicked
Is like a murky spring and a polluted well.

27 *It is* not good to eat much honey;
So [a]to seek one's own glory *is not* glory.

28 [a]Whoever *has* no rule over his own spirit
Is like a city broken down, without walls.

26

1 As snow in summer [a]and rain in harvest,
So honor is not fitting for a fool.

2 Like a flitting sparrow, like a flying
swallow,
So [a]a curse without cause shall not alight.

3 [a]A whip for the horse,
A bridle for the donkey,
And a rod for the fool's back.
4 Do not answer a fool according to his
folly,
Lest you also be like him.
5 [a]Answer a fool according to his folly,
Lest he be wise in his own eyes.
6 He who sends a message by the hand of
a fool
Cuts off *his own* feet *and* drinks violence.
7 *Like* the legs of the lame that hang limp
Is a proverb in the mouth of fools.
8 Like one who binds a stone in a sling
Is he who gives honor to a fool.
9 *Like* a thorn *that* goes into the hand of a
drunkard
Is a proverb in the mouth of fools.
10 *The great *God* who formed everything
Gives the fool *his* hire and the
transgressor *his* wages.
11 [a]As a dog returns to his own vomit,
[b]*So* a fool repeats his folly.
12 [a]Do you see a man wise in his own eyes?
There is more hope for a fool than for
him.

13 The lazy *man* says, "*There is* a lion in the
road!
A fierce lion *is* in the streets!"
14 *As* a door turns on its hinges,
So *does* the lazy *man* on his bed.
15 The [a]lazy *man* buries his hand in the
bowl;
It wearies him to bring it back to his
mouth.
16 The lazy *man is* wiser in his own eyes
Than seven men who can answer sensibly.

17 He who passes by *and* meddles in a
quarrel not his own
Is like one who takes a dog by the ears.

18 Like a madman who throws firebrands,
arrows, and death,

*______

26:10 Heb. difficult in v. 10; ancient and modern translators differ greatly

KJV

19 So *is* the man *that* deceiveth his neighbour, and saith, [a]Am not I in sport?
20 Where no wood is, *there* the fire goeth out:
so where *there is* no talebearer, the strife ceaseth.
21 [a]*As* coals *are* to burning coals, and wood
to fire; so *is* a contentious man to kindle strife.
22 The words of a talebearer *are* as wounds,
and they go down into the innermost parts of the
belly.
23 Burning lips and a wicked heart *are like*
a potsherd covered with silver dross.
24 He that hateth dissembleth with his lips,
and layeth up deceit within him;
25 [a]When he speaketh fair, believe him not:
for *there are* seven abominations in his heart.
26 *Whose* hatred is covered by deceit, his
wickedness shall be shewed before the *whole*
congregation.
27 [a]Whoso diggeth a pit shall fall therein:
and he that rolleth a stone, it will return upon
him.
28 A lying tongue hateth *those that are* afflicted by it; and a flattering mouth worketh [a]ruin.

27 Boast [a]not thyself of to morrow; for thou
knowest not what a day may bring forth.
2 [a]Let another man praise thee, and not
thine own mouth; a stranger, and not thine own
lips.
3 A stone *is* heavy, and the sand weighty;
but a fool's wrath *is* heavier than them both.
4 Wrath *is* cruel, and anger *is* outrageous;
but [a]who *is* able to stand before envy?
5 [a]Open rebuke *is* better than secret love.
6 Faithful *are* the wounds of a friend; but
the kisses of an enemy *are* [a]deceitful.
7 The full soul loatheth an honeycomb; but
to the hungry soul every bitter thing is sweet.
8 As a bird that wandereth from her nest,
so *is* a man that wandereth from his place.
9 Ointment and perfume rejoice the heart:
so *doth* the sweetness of a man's friend by hearty
counsel.
10 Thine own friend, and thy father's friend,
forsake not; neither go into thy brother's house
in the day of thy calamity: *for* [a]better *is* a neighbour *that is* near than a brother far off.
11 My son, be wise, and make my heart glad,
[a]that I may answer him that reproacheth me.
12 A prudent *man* foreseeth the evil, *and*
hideth himself; *but* the simple pass on, *and* are
[a]punished.

19 [a]Eph. 5:4
21 [a]Prov. 15:18
25 [a]Ps. 28:3; Prov. 26:23; Jer. 9:8
27 [a]Esth. 7:10; Ps. 7:15; Prov. 28:10; Eccl. 10:8
28 [a]Prov. 29:5

CHAPTER 27
1 [a]Luke 12:19–21; James 4:13–16
2 [a]Prov. 25:27; 2 Cor. 10:12, 18; 12:11
4 [a]Prov. 6:34; 1 John 3:12
5 [a][Prov. 28:23]; Gal. 2:14
6 [a]Matt. 26:49
10 [a]Prov. 17:17; 18:24
11 [a]Prov. 10:1; 23:15–26
12 [a]Prov. 22:3

NKJV

19 *Is* the man *who* deceives his neighbor,
And says, [a]"I was only joking!"

20 Where *there is* no wood, the fire goes out;
And where *there is* no talebearer, strife ceases.
21 [a]*As* charcoal *is* to burning coals, and wood to fire,
So *is* a contentious man to kindle strife.
22 The words of a talebearer *are* like tasty trifles,
And they go down into the inmost body.

23 Fervent lips with a wicked heart
Are like earthenware covered with silver dross.

24 He who hates, disguises *it* with his lips,
And lays up deceit within himself;
25 [a]When he speaks kindly, do not believe him,
For *there are* seven abominations in his heart;
26 *Though his* hatred is covered by deceit,
His wickedness will be revealed before the assembly.

27 [a]Whoever digs a pit will fall into it,
And he who rolls a stone will have it roll back on him.

28 A lying tongue hates *those who are* crushed by it,
And a flattering mouth works [a]ruin.

27 Do[a] not boast about tomorrow,
For you do not know what a day may bring forth.

2 [a]Let another man praise you, and not your own mouth;
A stranger, and not your own lips.

3 A stone *is* heavy and sand *is* weighty,
But a fool's wrath *is* heavier than both of them.

4 Wrath *is* cruel and anger a torrent,
But [a]who *is* able to stand before jealousy?

5 [a]Open rebuke *is* better
Than love carefully concealed.

6 Faithful *are* the wounds of a friend,
But the kisses of an enemy *are* [a]deceitful.

7 A satisfied soul loathes the honeycomb,
But to a hungry soul every bitter thing *is* sweet.

8 Like a bird that wanders from its nest
Is a man who wanders from his place.

9 Ointment and perfume delight the heart,
And the sweetness of a man's friend *gives delight* by hearty counsel.

10 Do not forsake your own friend or your father's friend,
Nor go to your brother's house in the day of your calamity;
[a]Better *is* a neighbor nearby than a brother far away.

11 My son, be wise, and make my heart glad,
[a]That I may answer him who reproaches me.

12 A prudent *man* foresees evil *and* hides himself;
The simple pass on *and* are [a]punished.

KJV

13 Take his garment that is surety for a
stranger, and take a pledge of him for a strange
woman.
14 He that blesseth his friend with a loud
voice, rising early in the morning, it shall be
counted a curse to him.
15 A [a]continual dropping in a very rainy day
and a contentious woman are alike.
16 Whosoever hideth her hideth the wind,
and the ointment of his right hand, *which* bewrayeth *itself*.
17 Iron sharpeneth iron; so a man sharpeneth the countenance of his friend.
18 [a]Whoso keepeth the fig tree shall eat the
fruit thereof: so he that waiteth on his master shall
be honoured.
19 As in water face *answereth* to face, so the
heart of man to man.
20 [a]Hell and destruction are never full; so
[b]the eyes of man are never satisfied.
21 [a]*As* the fining pot for silver, and the furnace for gold; so *is* a man to his praise.
22 [a]Though thou shouldest bray a fool in a
mortar among wheat with a pestle, *yet* will not
his foolishness depart from him.
23 Be thou diligent to know the state of thy
[a]flocks, *and* look well to thy herds.
24 For riches *are* not for ever: and doth the
crown *endure* to every generation?
25 [a]The hay appeareth, and the tender grass
sheweth itself, and herbs of the mountains are
gathered.
26 The lambs *are* for thy clothing, and the
goats *are* the price of the field.
27 And *thou shalt have* goats' milk enough
for thy food, for the food of thy household, and
for the maintenance for thy maidens.

28 The [a]wicked flee when no man pursueth:
but the righteous are bold as a lion.
2 For the transgression of a land many *are*
the princes thereof: but by a man of understanding *and* knowledge the state *thereof* shall be
prolonged.
3 [a]A poor man that oppresseth the poor *is*
like a sweeping rain which leaveth no food.
4 [a]They that forsake the law praise the
wicked: [b]but such as keep the law contend with
them.
5 [a]Evil men understand not judgment: but
[b]they that seek the LORD understand all *things*.
6 Better *is* the poor that walketh in his uprightness, than *he that is* perverse *in his* ways,
though he *be* rich.

15 [a]Prov. 19:13
18 [a]2 Kin. 18:31; Song 8:12; Is. 36:16; [1 Cor. 3:8; 9:7–13]; 2 Tim. 2:6
20 [a]Prov. 30:15, 16; Hab. 2:5 [b]Eccl. 1:8; 4:8
21 [a]Prov. 17:3
22 [a]Prov. 23:35; 26:11; Jer. 5:3
23 [a]Prov. 24:27
25 [a]Ps. 104:14

CHAPTER 28
1 [a]Lev. 26:17, 36; Ps. 53:5
3 [a]Matt. 18:28
4 [a]Ps. 49:18; Rom. 1:32 [b]1 Kin. 18:18; Neh. 13:11, 15; Matt. 3:7; 14:4; Eph. 5:11
5 [a]Ps. 92:6; Is. 6:9; 44:18 [b]Ps. 119:100; Prov. 2:9; John 17:17; 1 Cor. 2:15; [1 John 2:20, 27]

*

27:20 Or *Sheol* • Heb. *Abaddon*

NKJV

13 Take the garment of him who is surety
for a stranger,
And hold it in pledge *when* he is surety
for a seductress.

14 He who blesses his friend with a loud
voice, rising early in the morning,
It will be counted a curse to him.

15 A [a]continual dripping on a very rainy day
And a contentious woman are alike;
16 Whoever restrains her restrains the wind,
And grasps oil with his right hand.

17 *As* iron sharpens iron,
So a man sharpens the countenance of his
friend.

18 [a]Whoever keeps the fig tree will eat its
fruit;
So he who waits on his master will be
honored.

19 As in water face *reflects* face,
So a man's heart *reveals* the man.

20 [a]Hell* and *Destruction are never full;
So [b]the eyes of man are never satisfied.

21 [a]The refining pot *is* for silver and the
furnace for gold,
And a man *is valued* by what others say
of him.

22 [a]Though you grind a fool in a mortar with
a pestle along with crushed grain,
Yet his foolishness will not depart from
him.

23 Be diligent to know the state of your
[a]flocks,
And attend to your herds;
24 For riches *are* not forever,
Nor does a crown *endure* to all
generations.
25 [a]*When* the hay is removed, and the tender
grass shows itself,
And the herbs of the mountains are
gathered in,
26 The lambs *will provide* your clothing,
And the goats the price of a field;
27 *You shall have* enough goats' milk for
your food,
For the food of your household,
And the nourishment of your
maidservants.

28 The [a]wicked flee when no one pursues,
But the righteous are bold as a lion.

2 Because of the transgression of a land,
many *are* its princes;
But by a man of understanding *and*
knowledge
Right will be prolonged.

3 [a]A poor man who oppresses the poor
Is like a driving rain which leaves no food.

4 [a]Those who forsake the law praise the
wicked,
[b]But such as keep the law contend with
them.

5 [a]Evil men do not understand justice,
But [b]those who seek the LORD understand
all.

6 Better *is* the poor who walks in his
integrity
Than one perverse *in his* ways, though he
be rich.

KJV

7 Whoso keepeth the law *is* a wise son: but
he that is a companion of riotous *men* shameth
his father.
8 He that by usury and unjust gain increaseth his substance, he shall gather it for him that
will pity the poor.
9 He that turneth away his ear from hearing
the law, [a]even his prayer *shall be* abomination.
10 [a]Whoso causeth the righteous to go astray
in an evil way, he shall fall himself into his own
pit: [b]but the upright shall have good *things* in
possession.
11 The rich man *is* wise in his own conceit;
but the poor that hath understanding searcheth
him out.
12 When righteous *men* do rejoice, *there is*
great [a]glory: but when the wicked rise, a man is
hidden.
13 [a]He that covereth his sins shall not prosper: but whoso confesseth and forsaketh *them*
shall have mercy.
14 Happy *is* the man that feareth alway: but
he that hardeneth his heart shall fall into mischief.
15 [a]*As* a roaring lion, and a ranging bear;
[b]*so is* a wicked ruler over the poor people.
16 The prince that wanteth understanding *is*
also a great [a]oppressor: *but* he that hateth covetousness shall prolong *his* days.
17 [a]A man that doeth violence to the blood
of *any* person shall flee to the pit; let no man stay
him.
18 Whoso walketh uprightly shall be saved:
but *he that is* perverse *in his* ways shall fall at
once.
19 [a]He that tilleth his land shall have plenty
of bread: but he that followeth after vain *persons*
shall have poverty enough.
20 A faithful man shall abound with blessings: [a]but he that maketh haste to be rich shall
not be innocent.
21 [a]To have respect of persons *is* not good:
[b]for for a piece of bread *that* man will transgress.
22 He that hasteth to be rich *hath* an evil eye,
and considereth not that [a]poverty shall come
upon him.
23 [a]He that rebuketh a man afterwards shall
find more favour than he that flattereth with the
tongue.
24 Whoso robbeth his father or his mother,
and saith, *It is* no transgression; the same [a]*is* the
companion of a destroyer.
25 [a]He that is of a proud heart stirreth up
strife: [b]but he that putteth his trust in the LORD
shall be made fat.

9 [a]Ps. 66:18; 109:7; Prov. 15:8
10 [a]Ps. 7:15; Prov. 26:27 [b][Matt. 6:33; Heb. 6:12; 1 Pet. 3:9]
12 [a]Prov. 11:10; 29:2
13 [a]Ps. 32:3–5; 1 John 1:8–10
15 [a]Prov. 19:12; 1 Pet. 5:8 [b]Ex. 1:14; Prov. 29:2; Matt. 2:16
16 [a]Eccl. 10:16; Is. 3:12
17 [a]Gen. 9:6
19 [a]Prov. 12:11; 20:13
20 [a]Prov. 13:11; 20:21; 23:4; 1 Tim. 6:9
21 [a]Prov. 18:5 [b]Ezek. 13:19
22 [a]Prov. 21:5
23 [a]Prov. 27:5, 6
24 [a]Prov. 18:9
25 [a]Prov. 13:10 [b]Prov. 29:25; 1 Tim. 6:6

NKJV

7 Whoever keeps the law *is* a discerning son,
But a companion of gluttons shames his father.

8 One who increases his possessions by usury and extortion
Gathers it for him who will pity the poor.

9 One who turns away his ear from hearing the law,
[a]Even his prayer *is* an abomination.

10 [a]Whoever causes the upright to go astray in an evil way,
He himself will fall into his own pit;
[b]But the blameless will inherit good.

11 The rich man *is* wise in his own eyes,
But the poor who has understanding searches him out.

12 When the righteous rejoice, *there is* great [a]glory;
But when the wicked arise, men hide themselves.

13 [a]He who covers his sins will not prosper,
But whoever confesses and forsakes *them* will have mercy.

14 Happy *is* the man who is always reverent,
But he who hardens his heart will fall into calamity.

15 [a]*Like* a roaring lion and a charging bear
[b]*Is* a wicked ruler over poor people.

16 A ruler who lacks understanding *is* a great [a]oppressor,
But he who hates covetousness will prolong *his* days.

17 [a]A man burdened with bloodshed will flee into a pit;
Let no one help him.

18 Whoever walks blamelessly will be saved,
But *he who is* perverse *in his* ways will suddenly fall.

19 [a]He who tills his land will have plenty of bread,
But he who follows frivolity will have poverty enough!

20 A faithful man will abound with blessings,
[a]But he who hastens to be rich will not go unpunished.

21 [a]To show partiality *is* not good,
[b]Because for a piece of bread a man will transgress.

22 A man with an evil eye hastens after riches,
And does not consider that [a]poverty will come upon him.

23 [a]He who rebukes a man will find more favor afterward
Than he who flatters with the tongue.

24 Whoever robs his father or his mother,
And says, "*It is* no transgression,"
The same [a]*is* companion to a destroyer.

25 [a]He who is of a proud heart stirs up strife,
[b]But he who trusts in the LORD will be prospered.

KJV

26 He that [a]trusteth in his own heart is a fool:
but whoso walketh wisely, he shall be delivered.
27 [a]He that giveth unto the poor shall not
lack: but he that hideth his eyes shall have many
a curse.
28 When the wicked rise, [a]men hide themselves: but when they perish, the righteous
increase.

29 He,[a] that being often reproved hardeneth
his neck, shall suddenly be destroyed, and
that without remedy.
2 When the righteous are in authority, the
[a]people rejoice: but when the wicked beareth rule,
[b]the people mourn.
3 Whoso loveth wisdom rejoiceth his father:
but he that keepeth company with harlots spendeth *his* substance.
4 The king by judgment establisheth the
land: but he that receiveth gifts overthroweth it.
5 A man that [a]flattereth his neighbour
spreadeth a net for his feet.
6 In the transgression of an evil man *there*
is a snare: but the righteous doth sing and rejoice.
7 The righteous [a]considereth the cause of
the poor: *but* the wicked regardeth not to know
it.
8 Scornful men bring a city into a [a]snare:
but wise *men* turn away wrath.
9 *If* a wise man contendeth with a foolish
man, [a]whether he rage or laugh, *there is* no rest.
10 [a]The bloodthirsty hate the upright: but the
just seek his soul.
11 A fool uttereth all his [a]mind: but a wise
man keepeth it in till afterwards.
12 If a ruler hearken to lies, all his servants
are wicked.
13 The poor and the deceitful man meet together: [a]the LORD lighteneth both their eyes.
14 The king that faithfully judgeth the [a]poor,
his throne shall be established for ever.
15 The rod and reproof give [a]wisdom: but a
child left *to himself* bringeth his mother to shame.
16 When the wicked are multiplied, transgression increaseth: but the righteous shall see
their [a]fall.
17 Correct thy son, and he shall give thee
rest; yea, he shall give delight unto thy soul.
18 [a]Where *there is* no vision, the people perish: but [b]he that keepeth the law, happy *is* he.

26 [a]Prov. 3:5
27 [a]Deut. 15:7; Prov. 19:17; 22:9
28 [a]Job 24:4

CHAPTER 29

1 [a]2 Chr. 36:16; Prov. 6:15
2 [a]Esth. 8:15; Prov. 28:12 [b]Esth. 4:3
5 [a]Prov. 26:28
7 [a]Job 29:16; Ps. 41:1; Prov. 31:8, 9
8 [a]Prov. 11:11
9 [a]Matt. 11:17
10 [a]Gen. 4:5–8; 1 John 3:12
11 [a]Prov. 14:33
13 [a][Matt. 5:45]
14 [a]Ps. 72:4; Is. 11:4
15 [a]Prov. 22:15
16 [a]Ps. 37:34; Prov. 21:12
18 [a]1 Sam. 3:1; Ps. 74:9; Amos 8:11, 12 [b]Prov. 8:32; John 13:17

*

29:10 Lit. *soul or life*
29:11 Lit. *spirit*
29:18 *prophetic vision*

NKJV

26 He who [a]trusts in his own heart is a fool,
But whoever walks wisely will be delivered.

27 [a]He who gives to the poor will not lack,
But he who hides his eyes will have many curses.

28 When the wicked arise, [a]men hide themselves;
But when they perish, the righteous increase.

29 He[a] who is often rebuked, *and* hardens *his* neck,
Will suddenly be destroyed, and that without remedy.

2 When the righteous are in authority, the [a]people rejoice;
But when a wicked *man* rules, [b]the people groan.

3 Whoever loves wisdom makes his father rejoice,
But a companion of harlots wastes *his* wealth.

4 The king establishes the land by justice,
But he who receives bribes overthrows it.

5 A man who [a]flatters his neighbor
Spreads a net for his feet.

6 By transgression an evil man is snared,
But the righteous sings and rejoices.

7 The righteous [a]considers the cause of the poor,
But the wicked does not understand *such* knowledge.

8 Scoffers [a]set a city aflame,
But wise *men* turn away wrath.

9 *If* a wise man contends with a foolish man,
[a]Whether *the fool* rages or laughs, *there is* no peace.

10 [a]The bloodthirsty hate the blameless,
But the upright seek his *well-being.

11 A fool vents all his [a]feelings,*
But a wise *man* holds them back.

12 If a ruler pays attention to lies,
All his servants *become* wicked.

13 The poor *man* and the oppressor have this in common:
[a]The LORD gives light to the eyes of both.

14 The king who judges the [a]poor with truth,
His throne will be established forever.

15 The rod and rebuke give [a]wisdom,
But a child left *to himself* brings shame to his mother.

16 When the wicked are multiplied, transgression increases;
But the righteous will see their [a]fall.

17 Correct your son, and he will give you rest;
Yes, he will give delight to your soul.

18 [a]Where *there is* no *revelation, the people cast off restraint;
But [b]happy *is* he who keeps the law.

KJV

19 A servant will not be corrected by words: for though he understand he will not answer.

20 Seest thou a man *that is* hasty in his words? [a]*there is* more hope of a fool than of him.

21 He that delicately bringeth up his servant from a child shall have him become *his* son at the length.

22 [a]An angry man stirreth up strife, and a furious man aboundeth in transgression.

23 [a]A man's pride shall bring him low: but honour shall uphold the humble in spirit.

24 Whoso is partner with a thief hateth his own soul: [a]he heareth cursing, and bewrayeth *it* not.

25 [a]The fear of man bringeth a snare: but whoso putteth his trust in the LORD shall be safe.

26 [a]Many seek the ruler's favour; but *every* man's judgment *cometh* from the LORD.

27 An unjust man *is* an abomination to the just: and *he that is* upright in the way *is* abomination to the wicked.

20 [a]Prov. 26:12 **22** [a]Prov. 26:21 **23** [a]Job 22:29; Prov. 15:33; 18:12; Is. 66:2; Dan. 4:30; Matt. 23:12; Luke 14:11; 18:14; Acts 12:23; [James 4:6–10; 1 Pet. 5:5, 6] **24** [a]Lev. 5:1 **25** [a]Gen. 12:12; 20:2; Luke 12:4; John 12:42, 43 **26** [a]Ps. 20:9

NKJV

19 A servant will not be corrected by mere words;
For though he understands, he will not respond.

20 Do you see a man hasty in his words?
[a]*There is* more hope for a fool than for him.

21 He who pampers his servant from childhood
Will have him as a son in the end.

22 [a]An angry man stirs up strife,
And a furious man abounds in transgression.

23 [a]A man's pride will bring him low,
But the humble in spirit will retain honor.

24 Whoever is a partner with a thief hates his own life;
[a]He *swears to tell the truth, but reveals nothing.

25 [a]The fear of man brings a snare,
But whoever trusts in the LORD shall be safe.

26 [a]Many seek the ruler's favor,
But justice for man *comes* from the LORD.

27 An unjust man *is* an abomination to the righteous,
And *he who is* upright in the way *is* an abomination to the wicked.

The Wisdom of Agur (KJV)

30 The words of Agur the son of Jakeh, *even* the prophecy: the man spake unto Ithiel, even unto Ithiel and Ucal,

2 [a]Surely I *am* more brutish than *any* man, and have not the understanding of a man.

3 I neither learned wisdom, nor have the [a]knowledge of the holy.

4 [a]Who hath ascended up into heaven, or descended? [b]who hath gathered the wind in his fists? who hath bound the waters in a garment? who hath established all the ends of the earth? what *is* his name, and what *is* his son's name, if thou canst tell?

5 [a]Every word of God *is* pure: [b]he *is* a shield unto them that put their trust in him.

6 [a]Add thou not unto his words, lest he reprove thee, and thou be found a liar.

7 Two *things* have I required of thee; deny me *them* not before I die:

8 Remove far from me vanity and lies: give me neither poverty nor riches; [a]feed me with food convenient for me:

9 [a]Lest I be full, and deny *thee*, and say, Who *is* the LORD? or lest I be poor, and steal, and take the name of my God *in vain*.

10 Accuse not a servant unto his master, lest he curse thee, and thou be found guilty.

11 *There is* a generation *that* curseth their [a]father, and doth not bless their mother.

CHAPTER 30

2 [a]Ps. 73:22; Prov. 12:1 **3** [a][Prov. 9:10] **4** [a][Ps. 68:18; John 3:13] [b]Job 38:4; Ps. 104:3; Is. 40:12 **5** [a]Ps. 12:6; 19:8; 119:140 [b]Ps. 18:30; 84:11; 115:9–11 **6** [a]Deut. 4:2; 12:32; Rev. 22:18 **8** [a]Job 23:12; Matt. 6:11; [Phil. 4:19] **9** [a]Deut. 8:12–14; Neh. 9:25, 26; Hos. 13:6 **11** [a]Ex. 21:17; Prov. 20:20

The Wisdom of Agur (NKJV)

30 The words of Agur the son of Jakeh, *his* utterance. This man declared to Ithiel—to Ithiel and Ucal:

2 [a]Surely I *am* more stupid than *any* man,
And do not have the understanding of a man.

3 I neither learned wisdom
Nor have [a]knowledge of the Holy One.

4 [a]Who has ascended into heaven, or descended?
[b]Who has gathered the wind in His fists?
Who has bound the waters in a garment?
Who has established all the ends of the earth?
What *is* His name, and what *is* His Son's name,
If you know?

5 [a]Every word of God *is* pure;
[b]He *is* a shield to those who put their trust in Him.

6 [a]Do not add to His words,
Lest He rebuke you, and you be found a liar.

7 Two *things* I request of You
(Deprive me not before I die):

8 Remove falsehood and lies far from me;
Give me neither poverty nor riches—
[a]Feed me with the food allotted to me;

9 [a]Lest I be full and deny *You*,
And say, "Who *is* the LORD?"
Or lest I be poor and steal,
And profane the name of my God.

10 Do not malign a servant to his master,
Lest he curse you, and you be found guilty.

11 *There is* a generation *that* curses its [a]father,
And does not bless its mother.

*———

29:24 Lit. *hears the adjuration* or *oath*

KJV

12 *There is* a generation [a]*that are* pure in
their own eyes, and *yet* is not washed from their
filthiness.
13 *There is* a generation, O how [a]lofty are
their eyes! and their eyelids are lifted up.
14 [a]*There is* a generation, whose teeth *are*
as swords, and their jaw teeth *as* knives, [b]to devour the poor from off the earth, and the needy
from *among* men.
15 The horseleach hath two daughters, *cry-*
ing, Give, give. There are three *things that* are
never satisfied, *yea,* four *things* say not, *It is*
enough:
16 [a]The grave; and the barren womb; the
earth *that* is not filled with water; and the fire
that saith not, *It is* enough.
17 [a]The eye *that* mocketh at *his* father, and
despiseth to obey *his* mother, the ravens of the
valley shall pick it out, and the young eagles shall
eat it.
18 There be three *things which* are too wonderful for me, yea, four which I know not:
19 The way of an eagle in the air; the way
of a serpent upon a rock; the way of a ship in
the midst of the sea; and the way of a man with
a maid.
20 Such *is* the way of an adulterous woman;
she eateth, and wipeth her mouth, and saith, I
have done no wickedness.
21 For three *things* the earth is disquieted,
and for four *which* it cannot bear:
22 [a]For a servant when he reigneth; and a
fool when he is filled with meat;
23 For an odious *woman* when she is married; and an handmaid that is heir to her mistress.
24 There be four *things which are* little upon
the earth, but they *are* exceeding wise:
25 [a]The ants *are* a people not strong, yet they
prepare their meat in the summer;
26 [a]The conies *are but* a feeble folk, yet make
they their houses in the rocks;
27 The locusts have no king, yet go they forth
all of them by bands;
28 The spider taketh hold with her hands,
and is in kings' palaces.
29 There be three *things* which go well, yea,
four are comely in going:
30 A lion *which is* strongest among beasts,
and turneth not away for any;
31 A greyhound; an he goat also; and a king,
against whom *there is* no rising up.
32 If thou hast done foolishly in lifting up
thyself, or if thou hast thought evil, [a]*lay* thine
hand upon thy mouth.
33 Surely the churning of milk bringeth forth
butter, and the wringing of the nose bringeth forth
blood: so the forcing of wrath bringeth forth strife.

The Words of King Lemuel's Mother

31 The words of king Lemuel, the prophecy
that his mother taught him.

12 [a][Prov. 16:2]; Is. 65:5; Luke 18:11; [Titus 1:15, 16] **13** [a]Ps. 131:1; Prov. 6:17; Is. 2:11; 5:15 **14** [a]Job 29:17; Ps. 52:2 [b]Ps. 14:4; Amos 8:4 **16** [a]Prov. 27:20; Hab. 2:5 **17** [a]Gen. 9:22; Lev. 20:9; Prov. 20:20 **22** [a]Prov. 19:10; Eccl. 10:7 **25** [a]Prov. 6:6 **26** [a]Lev. 11:5; Ps. 104:18 **32** [a]Job 21:5; 40:4; Mic. 7:16

*

30:16 Or *Sheol* **30:26** *rock hyraxes* **30:28** Or *lizard* **30:31** Or perhaps *strutting rooster,* lit., *girded of waist* • A Jewish tradition *a king against whom there is no uprising*

NKJV

12 *There is* a generation [a]*that is* pure in its
own eyes,
Yet is not washed from its filthiness.
13 *There is* a generation— oh, how [a]lofty are
their eyes!
And their eyelids are lifted up.
14 [a]*There is* a generation whose teeth *are like*
swords,
And whose fangs *are like* knives,
[b]To devour the poor from off the earth,
And the needy from *among* men.

15 The leech has two daughters—
Give *and* Give!

There are three *things that* are never
satisfied,
Four never say, "Enough!":
16 [a]The* grave,
The barren womb,
The earth *that* is not satisfied with
water—
And the fire never says, "Enough!"

17 [a]The eye *that* mocks *his* father,
And scorns obedience to *his* mother,
The ravens of the valley will pick it out,
And the young eagles will eat it.

18 There are three *things which* are too
wonderful for me,
Yes, four *which* I do not understand:
19 The way of an eagle in the air,
The way of a serpent on a rock,
The way of a ship in the midst of the sea,
And the way of a man with a virgin.

20 This *is* the way of an adulterous woman:
She eats and wipes her mouth,
And says, "I have done no wickedness."

21 For three *things* the earth is perturbed,
Yes, for four it cannot bear up:
22 [a]For a servant when he reigns,
A fool when he is filled with food,
23 A hateful *woman* when she is married,
And a maidservant who succeeds her
mistress.

24 There are four *things which* are little on
the earth,
But they *are* exceedingly wise:
25 [a]The ants *are* a people not strong,
Yet they prepare their food in the summer;
26 [a]The *rock badgers are a feeble folk,
Yet they make their homes in the crags;
27 The locusts have no king,
Yet they all advance in ranks;
28 The *spider skillfully grasps with its
hands,
And it is in kings' palaces.

29 There are three *things which* are majestic
in pace,
Yes, four *which* are stately in walk:
30 A lion, *which is* mighty among beasts
And does not turn away from any;
31 A *greyhound,
A male goat also,
And *a king *whose* troops *are* with him.

32 If you have been foolish in exalting
yourself,
Or if you have devised evil, [a]*put your*
hand on *your* mouth.
33 For *as* the churning of milk produces
butter,
And wringing the nose produces blood,
So the forcing of wrath produces strife.

The Words of King Lemuel's Mother

31 The words of King Lemuel, the utterance
which his mother taught him:

KJV

2 What, my son? and what, the son of my womb? and what, [a]the son of my vows?

3 [a]Give not thy strength unto women, nor thy ways [b]to that which destroyeth kings.

4 [a]*It is* not for kings, O Lemuel, *it is* not for kings to drink wine; nor for princes strong drink:

5 [a]Lest they drink, and forget the law, and pervert the judgment of any of the afflicted.

6 [a]Give strong drink unto him that is ready to perish, and wine unto those that be of heavy hearts.

7 Let him drink, and forget his poverty, and remember his misery no more.

8 [a]Open thy mouth for the dumb in the cause of all such as are appointed to destruction.

9 Open thy mouth, [a]judge righteously, and [b]plead the cause of the poor and needy.

The Virtuous Wife

10 [a]Who can find a virtuous woman? for her price *is* far above rubies.

11 The heart of her husband doth safely trust in her, so that he shall have no need of spoil.

12 She will do him good and not evil all the days of her life.

13 She seeketh wool, and flax, and worketh willingly with her hands.

14 She is like the merchants' ships; she bringeth her food from afar.

15 [a]She riseth also while it is yet night, and [b]giveth meat to her household, and a portion to her maidens.

16 She considereth a field, and buyeth it: with the fruit of her hands she planteth a vineyard.

17 She girdeth her loins with strength, and strengtheneth her arms.

18 She perceiveth that her merchandise *is* good: her candle goeth not out by night.

19 She layeth her hands to the spindle, and her hands hold the distaff.

20 [a]She stretcheth out her hand to the poor; yea, she reacheth forth her hands to the needy.

21 She is not afraid of the snow for her household: for all her household *are* clothed with scarlet.

22 She maketh herself coverings of tapestry; her clothing *is* silk and purple.

23 [a]Her husband is known in the gates, when he sitteth among the elders of the land.

24 She maketh fine linen, and selleth *it;* and delivereth girdles unto the merchant.

25 Strength and honour *are* her clothing; and she shall rejoice in time to come.

26 She openeth her mouth with wisdom; and in her tongue *is* the law of kindness.

27 She looketh well to the ways of her household, and eateth not the bread of idleness.

28 Her children arise up, and call her blessed; her husband *also,* and he praiseth her.

29 Many daughters have done virtuously, but thou excellest them all.

30 Favour *is* deceitful, and beauty *is* vain: *but* a woman *that* feareth the LORD, she shall be praised.

31 Give her of the fruit of her hands; and let her own works praise her in the gates.

CHAPTER 31

2 [a]Is. 49:15
3 [a]Prov. 5:9 [b]Deut. 17:17; 1 Kin. 11:1; Neh. 13:26; Prov. 7:26; Hos. 4:11
4 [a]Eccl. 10:17
5 [a]Hos. 4:11
6 [a]Ps. 104:15
8 [a]Job 29:15, 16; Ps. 82
9 [a]Lev. 19:15; Deut. 1:16 [b]Job 29:12; Is. 1:17; Jer. 22:16
10 [a]Ruth 3:11; Prov. 12:4; 19:14
15 [a]Prov. 20:13; Rom. 12:11 [b]Luke 12:42
20 [a]Deut. 15:11; Job 31:16–20; Prov. 22:9; Rom. 12:13; Eph. 4:28; Heb. 13:16
23 [a]Prov. 12:4

*

31:8 Lit. *sons of passing away*
31:10 Vv. 10–31 are an alphabetic acrostic in Hebrew; cf. Ps. 119 • Lit. *a wife of valor,* in the sense of all forms of excellence

NKJV

2 What, my son?
And what, son of my womb?
And what, [a]son of my vows?
3 [a]Do not give your strength to women,
Nor your ways [b]to that which destroys kings.

4 [a]*It is* not for kings, O Lemuel,
It is not for kings to drink wine,
Nor for princes intoxicating drink;
5 [a]Lest they drink and forget the law,
And pervert the justice of all the afflicted.
6 [a]Give strong drink to him who is perishing,
And wine to those who are bitter of heart.
7 Let him drink and forget his poverty,
And remember his misery no more.

8 [a]Open your mouth for the speechless,
In the cause of all *who are* *appointed to die.
9 Open your mouth, [a]judge righteously,
And [b]plead the cause of the poor and needy.

The Virtuous Wife

10 [a]Who* can find a *virtuous wife?
For her worth *is* far above rubies.
11 The heart of her husband safely trusts her;
So he will have no lack of gain.
12 She does him good and not evil
All the days of her life.
13 She seeks wool and flax,
And willingly works with her hands.
14 She is like the merchant ships,
She brings her food from afar.
15 [a]She also rises while it is yet night,
And [b]provides food for her household,
And a portion for her maidservants.
16 She considers a field and buys it;
From her profits she plants a vineyard.
17 She girds herself with strength,
And strengthens her arms.
18 She perceives that her merchandise *is* good,
And her lamp does not go out by night.
19 She stretches out her hands to the distaff,
And her hand holds the spindle.
20 [a]She extends her hand to the poor,
Yes, she reaches out her hands to the needy.
21 She is not afraid of snow for her household,
For all her household *is* clothed with scarlet.
22 She makes tapestry for herself;
Her clothing *is* fine linen and purple.
23 [a]Her husband is known in the gates,
When he sits among the elders of the land.
24 She makes linen garments and sells *them,*
And supplies sashes for the merchants.
25 Strength and honor *are* her clothing;
She shall rejoice in time to come.
26 She opens her mouth with wisdom,
And on her tongue *is* the law of kindness.
27 She watches over the ways of her household,
And does not eat the bread of idleness.
28 Her children rise up and call her blessed;
Her husband *also,* and he praises her:
29 "Many daughters have done well,
But you excel them all."
30 Charm *is* deceitful and beauty *is* passing,
But a woman *who* fears the LORD, she shall be praised.
31 Give her of the fruit of her hands,
And let her own works praise her in the gates.

KJV

THE BOOK OF

ECCLESIASTES

The Vanity of Life

1 The words of the Preacher, the son of David, [a]king in Jerusalem.

2 [a]Vanity of vanities, saith the Preacher, vanity of vanities; [b]all *is* vanity.

3 [a]What profit hath a man of all his labour which he taketh under the sun?

4 *One* generation passeth away, and *another* generation cometh: [a]but the earth abideth for ever.

5 [a]The sun also ariseth, and the sun goeth down, and hasteth to his place where he arose.

6 [a]The wind goeth toward the south, and turneth about unto the north; it whirleth about continually, and the wind returneth again according to his circuits.

7 [a]All the rivers run into the sea; yet the sea *is* not full; unto the place from whence the rivers come, thither they return again.

8 All things *are* full of labour; man cannot utter *it:* [a]the eye is not satisfied with seeing, nor the ear filled with hearing.

9 [a]The thing that hath been, it *is that* which shall be; and that which is done *is* that which shall be done: and *there is* no new *thing* under the sun.

10 Is there *any* thing whereof it may be said, See, this *is* new? it hath been already of old time, which was before us.

11 *There is* [a]no remembrance of former *things;* neither shall there be *any* remembrance of *things* that are to come with *those* that shall come after.

The Grief of Wisdom

12 I the Preacher was king over Israel in Jerusalem.

13 And I gave my heart to seek and [a]search out by wisdom concerning all *things* that are done under heaven: [b]this sore travail hath God given to the sons of man to be exercised therewith.

14 I have seen all the works that are done under the sun; and, behold, all *is* vanity and vexation of spirit.

15 [a]*That which is* crooked cannot be made straight: and that which is wanting cannot be numbered.

16 I communed with mine own heart, saying, Lo, I am come to great estate, and have gotten [a]more wisdom than all *they* that have been before me in Jerusalem: yea, my heart had great experience of wisdom and knowledge.

17 [a]And I gave my heart to know wisdom, and to know madness and folly: I perceived that this also is vexation of spirit.

18 For [a]in much wisdom *is* much grief: and he that increaseth knowledge increaseth sorrow.

CHAPTER 1

1 [a]Prov. 1:1
2 [a]Ps. 39:5, 6; 62:9; 144:4; Eccl. 12:8 [b][Rom. 8:20, 21]
3 [a]Eccl. 2:22; 3:9
4 [a]Ps. 104:5; 119:90
5 [a]Ps. 19:4–6
6 [a]Eccl. 11:5; John 3:8
7 [a][Ps. 104:8, 9; Jer. 5:22]
8 [a]Prov. 27:20; Eccl. 4:8
9 [a]Eccl. 3:15
11 [a]Eccl. 2:16
13 [a][Eccl. 7:25; 8:16, 17] [b]Gen. 3:19; Eccl. 3:10
15 [a]Eccl. 7:13
16 [a]1 Kin. 3:12, 13; Eccl. 2:9
17 [a]Eccl. 2:3, 12; 7:23, 25; [1 Thess. 5:21]
18 [a]Eccl. 12:12

NKJV

THE BOOK OF

ECCLESIASTES

The Vanity of Life

1 The words of the Preacher, the son of David, [a]king in Jerusalem.

2 "Vanity[a]* of vanities," says the Preacher;
"Vanity of vanities, [b]all *is* vanity."

3 [a]What profit has a man from all his labor
In which he toils under the sun?
4 *One* generation passes away, and *another*
generation comes;
[a]But the earth abides forever.
5 [a]The sun also rises, and the sun goes down,
And hastens to the place where it arose.
6 [a]The wind goes toward the south,
And turns around to the north;
The wind whirls about continually,
And comes again on its circuit.
7 [a]All the rivers run into the sea,
Yet the sea *is* not full;
To the place from which the rivers come,
There they return again.
8 All things *are* full of labor;
Man cannot express *it.*
[a]The eye is not satisfied with seeing,
Nor the ear filled with hearing.

9 [a]That which has been *is* what will be,
That which *is* done is what will be done,
And *there is* nothing new under the sun.
10 Is there anything of which it may be said,
"See, this *is* new"?
It has already been in ancient times before
us.
11 *There is* [a]no remembrance of former
things,
Nor will there be any remembrance of
things that are to come
By *those* who will come after.

The Grief of Wisdom

12 I, the Preacher, was king over Israel in Jerusalem.

13 And I set my heart to seek and [a]search out by wisdom concerning all that is done under heaven; [b]this burdensome task God has given to the sons of man, by which they may be exercised.

14 I have seen all the works that are done under the sun; and indeed, all *is* vanity and grasping for the wind.

15 [a]*What is* crooked cannot be made straight,
And what is lacking cannot be numbered.

16 I communed with my heart, saying, "Look, I have attained greatness, and have gained [a]more wisdom than all who were before me in Jerusalem. My heart has understood great wisdom and knowledge."

17 [a]And I set my heart to know wisdom and to know madness and folly. I perceived that this also is grasping for the wind.

18 For [a]in much wisdom *is* much grief,
And he who increases knowledge
increases sorrow.

*______

1:2 Or *Absurdity, Frustration, Futility, Nonsense;* and so throughout the book

KJV

The Vanity of Pleasure
(cf. 1 Kin. 4:20–28)

2 I [a]said in mine heart, Go to now, I will prove
thee with [b]mirth, therefore enjoy pleasure:
and, behold, [c]this also *is* vanity.
2 I said of laughter, *It is* mad: and of mirth,
What doeth it?
3 [a]I sought in mine heart to give myself unto
wine, yet acquainting mine heart with wisdom;
and to lay hold on folly, till I might see what *was*
that [b]good for the sons of men, which they should
do under the heaven all the days of their life.
4 I made me great works; I builded me
[a]houses; I planted me vineyards:
5 I made me gardens and orchards, and I
planted trees in them of all *kind of* fruits:
6 I made me pools of water, to water therewith the wood that bringeth forth trees:
7 I got *me* servants and maidens, and had
servants born in my house; also I had great possessions of great and small cattle above all that
were in Jerusalem before me:
8 [a]I gathered me also silver and gold, and
the peculiar treasure of kings and of the provinces: I gat me men singers and women singers,
and the delights of the sons of men, *as* musical
instruments, and that of all sorts.
9 [a]So I was great, and increased [b]more than
all that were before me in Jerusalem: also my wisdom remained with me.
10 And whatsoever mine eyes desired I kept
not from them, I withheld not my heart from any
joy; for my heart rejoiced in all my labour: and
[a]this was my portion of all my labour.
11 Then I looked on all the works that my
hands had wrought, and on the labour that I had
laboured to do: and, behold, all *was* [a]vanity and
vexation of spirit, and *there was* no profit under
the sun.

The End of the Wise and the Fool

12 And I turned myself to behold wisdom,
[a]and madness, and folly: for what *can* the man
do that cometh after the king? *even* that which
hath been already [b]done.
13 Then I saw that wisdom [a]excelleth folly,
as far as light excelleth darkness.
14 [a]The wise man's eyes *are* in his head; but
the fool walketh in darkness: and I myself perceived also that [b]one event happeneth to them
all.
15 Then said I in my heart, As it happeneth
to the fool, so it happeneth even to me; and why
was I then more wise? Then I said in my heart,
that this also *is* vanity.
16 For *there is* [a]no remembrance of the wise
more than of the fool for ever; seeing that which
now *is* in the days to come shall all be forgotten.
And how dieth the wise *man*? as the fool.
17 Therefore I hated life; because the work
that is wrought under the sun *is* grievous unto
me: for all *is* vanity and vexation of spirit.
18 Yea, I hated all my labour which I had
taken under the sun: because [a]I should leave it
unto the man that shall be after me.
19 And who knoweth whether he shall be a
wise *man* or a fool? yet shall he have rule over
all my labour wherein I have laboured, and
wherein I have shewed myself wise under the sun.
This *is* also vanity.

CHAPTER 2

1 [a]Luke 12:19 [b]Prov. 14:13; [Eccl. 7:4; 8:15] [c]Eccl. 1:2
3 [a]Eccl. 1:17 [b][Eccl. 3:12, 13; 5:18; 6:12]
4 [a]1 Kin. 7:1–12
8 [a]1 Kin. 9:28; 10:10, 14, 21
9 [a]Eccl. 1:16 [b]2 Chr. 9:22
10 [a]Eccl. 3:22; 5:18; 9:9
11 [a]Eccl. 1:3, 14
12 [a]Eccl. 1:17; 7:25 [b]Eccl. 1:9
13 [a]Eccl. 7:11, 14, 19; 9:18; 10:10
14 [a]Prov. 17:24; Eccl. 8:1 [b]Ps. 49:10; Eccl. 9:2, 3, 11
16 [a]Eccl. 1:11; 4:16
18 [a]Ps. 49:10

*2:8 Exact meaning unknown

NKJV

The Vanity of Pleasure
(cf. 1 Kin. 4:20–28)

2 I said [a]in my heart, "Come now, I will test
you with [b]mirth; therefore enjoy pleasure";
but surely, [c]this also *was* vanity.
2 I said of laughter—"Madness!"; and of
mirth, "What does it accomplish?"
3 [a]I searched in my heart *how* to gratify my
flesh with wine, while guiding my heart with wisdom, and how to lay hold on folly, till I might
see what *was* [b]good for the sons of men to do
under heaven all the days of their lives.
4 I made my works great, I built myself
[a]houses, and planted myself vineyards.
5 I made myself gardens and orchards, and
I planted all *kinds* of fruit trees in them.
6 I made myself water pools from which to
water the growing trees of the grove.
7 I acquired male and female servants, and
had servants born in my house. Yes, I had greater
possessions of herds and flocks than all who were
in Jerusalem before me.
8 [a]I also gathered for myself silver and gold
and the special treasures of kings and of the provinces. I acquired male and female singers, the delights of the sons of men, *and* *musical instruments of all kinds.
9 [a]So I became great and excelled [b]more
than all who were before me in Jerusalem. Also
my wisdom remained with me.

10 Whatever my eyes desired I did not keep
from them.
I did not withhold my heart from any
pleasure,
For my heart rejoiced in all my labor;
And [a]this was my reward from all my
labor.
11 Then I looked on all the works that my
hands had done
And on the labor in which I had toiled;
And indeed all *was* [a]vanity and grasping
for the wind.
There was no profit under the sun.

The End of the Wise and the Fool

12 Then I turned myself to consider wisdom
[a]and madness and folly;
For what *can* the man *do* who succeeds
the king?—
Only what he has already [b]done.
13 Then I saw that wisdom [a]excels folly
As light excels darkness.
14 [a]The wise man's eyes *are* in his head,
But the fool walks in darkness.
Yet I myself perceived
That [b]the same event happens to them all.

15 So I said in my heart,
"As it happens to the fool,
It also happens to me,
And why was I then more wise?"
Then I said in my heart,
"This also *is* vanity."
16 For *there is* [a]no more remembrance of the
wise than of the fool forever,
Since all that now *is* will be forgotten in
the days to come.
And how does a wise *man* die?
As the fool!

17 Therefore I hated life because the work
that was done under the sun *was* distressing to
me, for all *is* vanity and grasping for the wind.
18 Then I hated all my labor in which I had
toiled under the sun, because [a]I must leave it to
the man who will come after me.
19 And who knows whether he will be wise
or a fool? Yet he will rule over all my labor in
which I toiled and in which I have shown myself
wise under the sun. This also *is* vanity.

KJV

20 Therefore I went about to cause my heart to despair of all the labour which I took under the sun.

21 For there is a man whose labour *is* in wisdom, and in knowledge, and in equity; yet to a man that hath not laboured therein shall he leave it *for* his portion. This also *is* vanity and a great evil.

22 [a]For what hath man of all his labour, and of the vexation of his heart, wherein he hath laboured under the sun?

23 For all his days *are* [a]sorrows, and his travail grief; yea, his heart taketh not rest in the night. This is also vanity.

24 [a]*There is* nothing better for a man, *than* that he should eat and drink, and *that* he should make his soul enjoy good in his labour. This also I saw, that it *was* from the hand of God.

25 For who can eat, or who else can hasten *hereunto*, more than I?

26 For *God* giveth to a man that *is* good in his sight [a]wisdom, and knowledge, and joy: but to the sinner he giveth travail, to gather and to heap up, that [b]he may give to *him that is* good before God. This also *is* vanity and vexation of spirit.

Everything Has Its Time

3 To every *thing there is* a season, and a [a]time to every purpose under the heaven:

2 A time to be born, and [a]a time to die; a time to plant, and a time to pluck up *that which is* planted;

3 A time to kill, and a time to heal; a time to break down, and a time to build up;

4 A time to [a]weep, and a time to laugh; a time to mourn, and a time to dance;

5 A time to cast away stones, and a time to gather stones together; [a]a time to embrace, and a time to refrain from embracing;

6 A time to get, and a time to lose; a time to keep, and a time to cast away;

7 A time to rend, and a time to sew; [a]a time to keep silence, and a time to [b]speak;

8 A time to love, and a time to [a]hate; a time of war, and a time of peace.

The God-Given Task

9 [a]What profit hath he that worketh in that wherein he laboureth?

10 [a]I have seen the travail, which God hath given to the sons of men to be exercised in it.

11 He hath made every *thing* beautiful in his time: also he hath set the world in their heart, so that [a]no man can find out the work that God maketh from the beginning to the end.

12 I know that *there is* no [a]good in them, but for *a man* to rejoice, and to do good in his life.

13 And also [a]that every man should eat and drink, and enjoy the good of all his labour, it *is* the gift of God.

14 I know that, whatsoever God doeth, it shall be for ever: [a]nothing can be put to it, nor any thing taken from it: and God doeth *it*, that *men* should fear before him.

22 [a]Eccl. 1:3; 3:9
23 [a]Job 5:7; 14:1
24 [a]Eccl. 3:12, 13, 22; Is. 56:12; Luke 12:19; 1 Cor. 15:32; [1 Tim. 6:17]
26 [a]Job 32:8; Prov. 2:6; James 1:5 [b]Job 27:16, 17; Prov. 28:8

CHAPTER 3
1 [a]Eccl. 3:17; 8:6
2 [a]Job 14:5; Heb. 9:27
4 [a]Rom. 12:15
5 [a]Joel 2:16; 1 Cor. 7:5
7 [a]Amos 5:13 [b]Prov. 25:11
8 [a]Prov. 13:5; Luke 14:26
9 [a]Eccl. 1:3
10 [a]Eccl. 1:13
11 [a]Job 5:9; Eccl. 7:23; 8:17; Rom. 11:33
12 [a]Eccl. 2:3, 24
13 [a]Eccl. 2:24
14 [a]James 1:17

NKJV

20 Therefore I turned my heart and despaired of all the labor in which I had toiled under the sun.

21 For there is a man whose labor *is* with wisdom, knowledge, and skill; yet he must leave his heritage to a man who has not labored for it. This also *is* vanity and a great evil.

22 [a]For what has man for all his labor, and for the striving of his heart with which he has toiled under the sun?

23 For all his days *are* [a]sorrowful, and his work burdensome; even in the night his heart takes no rest. This also is vanity.

24 [a]Nothing *is* better for a man *than* that he should eat and drink, and *that* his soul should enjoy good in his labor. This also, I saw, was from the hand of God.

25 For who can eat, or who can have enjoyment, *more than I?

26 For *God* gives [a]wisdom and knowledge and joy to a man who *is* good in His sight; but to the sinner He gives the work of gathering and collecting, that [b]he may give to *him who is* good before God. This also *is* vanity and grasping for the wind.

Everything Has Its Time

3 To everything *there is* a season,
A [a]time for every purpose under heaven:

2 A time to be born,
And [a]a time to die;
A time to plant,
And a time to pluck *what is* planted;
3 A time to kill,
And a time to heal;
A time to break down,
And a time to build up;
4 A time to [a]weep,
And a time to laugh;
A time to mourn,
And a time to dance;
5 A time to cast away stones,
And a time to gather stones;
[a]A time to embrace,
And a time to refrain from embracing;
6 A time to gain,
And a time to lose;
A time to keep,
And a time to throw away;
7 A time to tear,
And a time to sew;
[a]A time to keep silence,
And a time to [b]speak;
8 A time to love,
And a time to [a]hate;
A time of war,
And a time of peace.

The God-Given Task

9 [a]What profit has the worker from that in which he labors?

10 [a]I have seen the God-given task with which the sons of men are to be occupied.

11 He has made everything beautiful in its time. Also He has put eternity in their hearts, except that [a]no one can find out the work that God does from beginning to end.

12 I know that nothing *is* [a]better for them than to rejoice, and to do good in their lives,

13 and also that [a]every man should eat and drink and enjoy the good of all his labor—it *is* the gift of God.

14 I know that whatever God does,
It shall be forever.
[a]Nothing can be added to it,
And nothing taken from it.
God does *it*, that men should fear before Him.

*

2:25 So with MT, Tg., Vg.; some Heb. mss., LXX, Syr. *without Him*

KJV

15 [a]That which hath been is now; and that
which is to be hath already been; and God requir-
eth that which is past.

Injustice Seems to Prevail

16 And moreover [a]I saw under the sun the
place of judgment, *that* wickedness *was* there;
and the place of righteousness, *that* iniquity *was*
there.
17 I said in mine heart, [a]God shall judge the
righteous and the wicked: for *there is* a time there
for every purpose and for every work.
18 I said in mine heart concerning the estate
of the sons of men, that God might manifest them,
and that they might see that they themselves are
beasts.
19 [a]For that which befalleth the sons of men
befalleth beasts; even one thing befalleth them:
as the one dieth, so dieth the other; yea, they have
all one breath; so that a man hath no preeminence
above a beast: for all *is* vanity.
20 All go unto one place; [a]all are of the dust,
and all turn to dust again.
21 [a]Who knoweth the spirit of man that
goeth upward, and the spirit of the beast that
goeth downward to the earth?
22 [a]Wherefore I perceive that *there is* nothing better, than that a man should rejoice in his
own works; for [b]that *is* his portion: [c]for who shall
bring him to see what shall be after him?

4 So I returned, and considered all the [a]oppres-
sions that are done under the sun: and behold
the tears of *such as were* oppressed, and they had
no comforter; and on the side of their oppressors
there was power; but they had no comforter.
2 [a]Wherefore I praised the dead which are
already dead more than the living which are yet
alive.
3 [a]Yea, better *is he* than both they, which
hath not yet been, who hath not seen the evil work
that is done under the sun.

The Vanity of Selfish Toil

4 Again, I considered all travail, and every
right work, that for this a man is envied of his
neighbour. This *is* also vanity and vexation of
spirit.
5 [a]The fool foldeth his hands together, and
eateth his own flesh.
6 [a]Better *is* an handful *with* quietness, than
both the hands full *with* travail and vexation of
spirit.
7 Then I returned, and I saw vanity under
the sun.
8 There is one *alone*, and *there is* not a second; yea, he hath neither child nor brother: yet
is there no end of all his labour; neither is his
[a]eye satisfied with riches; [b]neither *saith he*, For
whom do I labour, and bereave my soul [c]of good?
This *is* also vanity, yea, it *is* a sore travail.

The Value of a Friend

9 Two *are* better than one; because they
have a good reward for their labour.

15 [a]Eccl. 1:9
16 [a]Eccl. 5:8
17 [a]Gen. 18:25; Ps. 96:13; Eccl. 11:9; [Matt. 16:27; Rom. 2:6–10; 2 Cor. 5:10; 2 Thess. 1:6–9]
19 [a]Ps. 49:12, 20; 73:22; [Eccl. 2:16]
20 [a]Gen. 3:19; Ps. 103:14
21 [a]Eccl. 12:7
22 [a]Eccl. 2:24; 5:18 [b]Eccl. 2:10 [c]Eccl. 6:12; 8:7

CHAPTER 4

1 [a]Job 35:9; Ps. 12:5; Eccl. 3:16; 5:8; Is. 5:7
2 [a]Job 3:17, 18
3 [a]Job 3:11–22; Eccl. 6:3; Luke 23:29
5 [a]Prov. 6:10; 24:33
6 [a]Prov. 15:16, 17; 16:8
8 [a]Prov. 27:20; Eccl. 5:10; [1 John 2:16] [b]Ps. 39:6 [c]Eccl. 2:18–21

*

3:21 LXX, Syr., Tg., Vg. *Who knows whether the spirit . . . goes upward, and whether . . . goes downward to the earth?*

NKJV

15 [a]That which is has already been,
And what is to be has already been;
And God requires an account of what is past.

Injustice Seems to Prevail

16 Moreover [a]I saw under the sun:

In the place of judgment,
Wickedness *was* there;
And *in* the place of righteousness,
Iniquity *was* there.

17 I said in my heart,

[a]"God shall judge the righteous and the wicked,
For *there is* a time there for every purpose and for every work."

18 I said in my heart, "Concerning the condition of the sons of men, God tests them, that they
may see that they themselves are *like* animals."
19 [a]For what happens to the sons of men also
happens to animals; one thing befalls them: as
one dies, so dies the other. Surely, they all have
one breath; man has no advantage over animals,
for all *is* vanity.
20 All go to one place: [a]all are from the dust,
and all return to dust.
21 [a]Who* knows the spirit of the sons of men,
which goes upward, and the spirit of the animal,
which goes down to the earth?
22 [a]So I perceived that nothing *is* better than
that a man should rejoice in his own works, for
[b]that *is* his heritage. [c]For who can bring him to
see what will happen after him?

4 Then I returned and considered all the [a]oppression that is done under the sun:

And look! The tears of the oppressed,
But they have no comforter—
On the side of their oppressors *there is* power,
But they have no comforter.
2 [a]Therefore I praised the dead who were already dead,
More than the living who are still alive.
3 [a]Yet, better than both *is he* who has never existed,
Who has not seen the evil work that is done under the sun.

The Vanity of Selfish Toil

4 Again, I saw that for all toil and every
skillful work a man is envied by his neighbor.
This also *is* vanity and grasping for the wind.

5 [a]The fool folds his hands
And consumes his own flesh.
6 [a]Better a handful *with* quietness
Than both hands full, *together with* toil and grasping for the wind.

7 Then I returned, and I saw vanity under
the sun:

8 There is one alone, without companion:
He has neither son nor brother.
Yet *there is* no end to all his labors,
Nor is his [a]eye satisfied with riches.
But [b]*he never asks,*
"For whom do I toil and deprive myself of [c]good?"
This also *is* vanity and a grave misfortune.

The Value of a Friend

9 Two *are* better than one,
Because they have a good reward for their labor.

KJV

10 For if they fall, the one will lift up his fellow: but woe to him *that is* alone when he falleth; for *he hath* not another to help him up.

11 Again, if two lie together, then they have heat: but how can one be warm *alone?*

12 And if one prevail against him, two shall withstand him; and a threefold cord is not quickly broken.

Popularity Passes Away

13 Better *is* a poor and a wise child than an old and foolish king, who will no more be admonished.

14 For out of prison he cometh to reign; whereas also *he that is* born in his kingdom becometh poor.

15 I considered all the living which walk under the sun, with the second child that shall stand up in his stead.

16 *There is* no end of all the people, *even* of all that have been before them: they also that come after shall not rejoice in him. Surely this also *is* vanity and vexation of spirit.

Fear God, Keep Your Vows

5 Keep [a]thy foot when thou goest to the house of God, and be more ready to hear, [b]than to give the sacrifice of fools: for they consider not that they do evil.

2 Be not [a]rash with thy mouth, and let not thine heart be hasty to utter *any* thing before God: for God *is* in heaven, and thou upon earth: therefore let thy words [b]be few.

3 For a dream cometh through the multitude of business; and [a]a fool's voice *is known* by multitude of words.

4 [a]When thou vowest a vow unto God, defer not to [b]pay it; for *he hath* no pleasure in fools: pay that which thou hast vowed.

5 [a]Better *is it* that thou shouldest not vow, than that thou shouldest vow and not pay.

6 Suffer not thy [a]mouth to cause thy flesh to sin; [b]neither say thou before the angel, that it *was* an error: wherefore should God be angry at thy voice, and destroy the work of thine hands?

7 For in the multitude of dreams and many words *there are* also *divers* vanities: but [a]fear thou God.

The Vanity of Gain and Honor

8 If thou [a]seest the oppression of the poor, and violent perverting of judgment and justice in a province, marvel not at the matter: for [b]*he that is* higher than the highest regardeth; and *there be* higher than they.

9 Moreover the profit of the earth is for all: the king *himself* is served by the field.

10 He that loveth silver shall not be satisfied with silver; nor he that loveth abundance with increase: this *is* also vanity.

11 When goods increase, they are increased that eat them: and what good *is there* to the owners thereof, saving the beholding *of them* with their eyes?

12 The sleep of a labouring man *is* sweet, whether he eat little or much: but the abundance of the rich will not suffer him to sleep.

CHAPTER 5

1 [a]Ex. 3:5; Is. 1:12 [b][1 Sam. 15:22]; Ps. 50:8; Prov. 15:8; 21:27; [Hos. 6:6]
2 [a]Prov. 20:25 [b]Prov. 10:19; Matt. 6:7
3 [a]Prov. 10:19
4 [a]Num. 30:2; Deut. 23:21–23; Ps. 50:14; 76:11 [b]Ps. 66:13, 14
5 [a]Prov. 20:25; Acts 5:4
6 [a]Prov. 6:2 [b]1 Cor. 11:10
7 [a][Eccl. 12:13]
8 [a]Eccl. 3:16 [b][Ps. 12:5; 58:11; 82:1]

*5:6 Lit. *voice*

NKJV

10 For if they fall, one will lift up his
companion.
But woe to him *who is* alone when he falls,
For *he has* no one to help him up.
11 Again, if two lie down together, they will
keep warm;
But how can one be warm *alone?*
12 Though one may be overpowered by
another, two can withstand him.
And a threefold cord is not quickly
broken.

Popularity Passes Away

13 Better a poor and wise youth
Than an old and foolish king who will be
admonished no more.
14 For he comes out of prison to be king,
Although he was born poor in his
kingdom.
15 I saw all the living who walk under the
sun;
They were with the second youth who
stands in his place.
16 *There was* no end of all the people over
whom he was made king;
Yet those who come afterward will not
rejoice in him.
Surely this also *is* vanity and grasping for
the wind.

Fear God, Keep Your Vows

5 Walk [a]prudently when you go to the house of God; and draw near to hear rather [b]than to give the sacrifice of fools, for they do not know that they do evil.

2 Do not be [a]rash with your mouth,
And let not your heart utter anything
hastily before God.
For God *is* in heaven, and you on earth;
Therefore let your words [b]be few.
3 For a dream comes through much activity,
And [a]a fool's voice *is known* by *his* many
words.

4 [a]When you make a vow to God, do not
delay to [b]pay it;
For *He has* no pleasure in fools.
Pay what you have vowed—
5 [a]Better not to vow than to vow and not pay.

6 Do not let your [a]mouth cause your flesh to sin, [b]nor say before the messenger *of God* that it *was* an error. Why should God be angry at your *excuse and destroy the work of your hands? 7 For in the multitude of dreams and many words *there is* also vanity. But [a]fear God.

The Vanity of Gain and Honor

8 If you [a]see the oppression of the poor, and the violent perversion of justice and righteousness in a province, do not marvel at the matter; for [b]high official watches over high official, and higher officials are over them. 9 Moreover the profit of the land is for all; *even* the king is served from the field.

10 He who loves silver will not be satisfied
with silver;
Nor he who loves abundance, with
increase.
This also *is* vanity.

11 When goods increase,
They increase who eat them;
So what profit have the owners
Except to see *them* with their eyes?

12 The sleep of a laboring man *is* sweet,
Whether he eats little or much;
But the abundance of the rich will not
permit him to sleep.

KJV

13 [a]There is a sore evil *which* I have seen under the sun, *namely,* riches kept for the owners thereof to their hurt.

14 But those riches perish by evil travail: and he begetteth a son, and *there is* nothing in his hand.

15 [a]As he came forth of his mother's womb, naked shall he return to go as he came, and shall take nothing of his labour, which he may carry away in his hand.

16 And this also *is* a sore evil, *that* in all points as he came, so shall he go: and [a]what profit hath he [b]that hath laboured for the wind?

17 All his days also [a]he eateth in darkness, and *he hath* much sorrow and wrath with his sickness.

18 Behold *that* which I have seen: [a]*it is* good and comely *for one* to eat and to drink, and to enjoy the good of all his labour that he taketh under the sun all the days of his life, which God giveth him: [b]for it *is* his portion.

19 [a]Every man also to whom God hath given riches and wealth, and hath given him power to eat thereof, and to take his portion, and to rejoice in his labour; this *is* the [b]gift of God.

20 For he shall not much remember the days of his life; because God answereth *him* in the joy of his heart.

6 There[a] is an evil which I have seen under the sun, and it *is* common among men:

2 A man to whom God hath given riches, wealth, and honour, [a]so that he wanteth nothing for his soul of all that he desireth, [b]yet God giveth him not power to eat thereof, but a stranger eateth it: this *is* vanity, and it *is* an evil disease.

3 If a man beget an hundred *children,* and live many years, so that the days of his years be many, and his soul be not filled with good, and [a]also *that* he have no burial; I say, *that* [b]an untimely birth *is* better than he.

4 For he cometh in with vanity, and departeth in darkness, and his name shall be covered with darkness.

5 Moreover he hath not seen the sun, nor known *any thing:* this hath more rest than the other.

6 Yea, though he live a thousand years twice *told,* yet hath he seen no good: do not all go to one [a]place?

7 [a]All the labour of man *is* for his mouth, and yet the appetite is not filled.

8 For what hath the wise more than the fool? what hath the poor, that knoweth to walk before the living?

9 Better *is* the [a]sight of the eyes than the wandering of the desire: this *is* also vanity and vexation of spirit.

10 That which hath been is named [a]already, and it is known that it *is* man: [b]neither may he contend with him that is mightier than he.

11 Seeing there be many things that increase vanity, what *is* man the better?

12 For who knoweth what *is* good for man in *this* life, all the days of his vain life which he spendeth as [a]a shadow? for [b]who can tell a man what shall be after him under the sun?

13 [a]Eccl. 6:1, 2
15 [a]Job 1:21; Ps. 49:17; 1 Tim. 6:7
16 [a]Eccl. 1:3 [b]Prov. 11:29
17 [a]Ps. 127:2
18 [a]Eccl. 2:24; 3:12, 13; [1 Tim. 6:17] [b]Eccl. 2:10; 3:22
19 [a][Eccl. 6:2] [b]Eccl. 2:24; 3:13

CHAPTER 6

1 [a]Eccl. 5:13
2 [a]Job 21:10; Ps. 17:14; 73:7 [b]Luke 12:20
3 [a]2 Kin. 9:35; Is. 14:19, 20; Jer. 22:19 [b]Job 3:16; Ps. 58:8; Eccl. 4:3
6 [a]Eccl. 2:14, 15
7 [a]Prov. 16:26
9 [a]Eccl. 11:9
10 [a]Eccl. 1:9; 3:15 [b]Job 9:32; Is. 45:9; Jer. 49:19
12 [a]Ps. 102:11; James 4:14 [b]Ps. 39:6; Eccl. 3:22

NKJV

13 [a]There is a severe evil *which* I have seen
under the sun:
Riches kept for their owner to his hurt.
14 But those riches perish through
misfortune;
When he begets a son, *there is* nothing
in his hand.
15 [a]As he came from his mother's womb,
naked shall he return,
To go as he came;
And he shall take nothing from his
labor
Which he may carry away in his hand.

16 And this also *is* a severe evil—
Just exactly as he came, so shall he go.
And [a]what profit has he [b]who has labored
for the wind?
17 All his days [a]he also eats in darkness,
And *he has* much sorrow and sickness and
anger.

18 Here is what I have seen: [a]*It is* good and fitting *for one* to eat and drink, and to enjoy the good of all his labor in which he toils under the sun all the days of his life which God gives him; [b]for it *is* his heritage.

19 As for [a]every man to whom God has given riches and wealth, and given him power to eat of it, to receive his heritage and rejoice in his labor—this *is* the [b]gift of God.

20 For he will not dwell unduly on the days of his life, because God keeps *him* busy with the joy of his heart.

6 There[a] is an evil which I have seen under the sun, and it *is* common among men:

2 A man to whom God has given riches and wealth and honor, [a]so that he lacks nothing for himself of all he desires; [b]yet God does not give him power to eat of it, but a foreigner consumes it. This *is* vanity, and it *is* an evil affliction.

3 If a man begets a hundred *children* and lives many years, so that the days of his years are many, but his soul is not satisfied with goodness, or [a]indeed he has no burial, I say *that* [b]a stillborn child *is* better than he—

4 for it comes in vanity and departs in darkness, and its name is covered with darkness.

5 Though it has not seen the sun or known *anything,* this has more rest than that man,

6 even if he lives a thousand years twice—but has not seen goodness. Do not all go to one [a]place?

7 [a]All the labor of man *is* for his mouth,
And yet the soul is not satisfied.
8 For what more has the wise *man* than the
fool?
What does the poor man have,
Who knows *how* to walk before the
living?
9 Better *is* the [a]sight of the eyes than the
wandering of desire.
This also *is* vanity and grasping for the
wind.

10 Whatever one is, he has been named
[a]already,
For it is known that he *is* man;
[b]And he cannot contend with Him who is
mightier than he.
11 Since there are many things that increase
vanity,
How *is* man the better?

12 For who knows what *is* good for man in life, all the days of his vain life which he passes like [a]a shadow? [b]Who can tell a man what will happen after him under the sun?

KJV

The Value of Practical Wisdom

7 A [a]good name *is* better than precious ointment; and the day of death than the day of
one's [b]birth.
2 *It is* better to go to the house of mourning,
than to go to the house of feasting: for that *is*
the end of all men; and the living will lay *it* to
his [a]heart.
3 Sorrow *is* better than laughter: [a]for by the
sadness of the countenance the heart is made
better.
4 The heart of the wise *is* in the house of
mourning; but the heart of fools *is* in the house
of mirth.
5 [a]*It is* better to hear the rebuke of the wise,
than for a man to hear the song of fools.
6 [a]For as the crackling of thorns under a
pot, so *is* the laughter of the fool: this also *is*
vanity.
7 Surely oppression maketh a wise man
mad; [a]and a gift destroyeth the heart.
8 Better *is* the end of a thing than the beginning thereof: *and* [a]the patient in spirit *is* better
than the proud in spirit.
9 [a]Be not hasty in thy spirit to be angry:
for anger resteth in the bosom of fools.
10 Say not thou, What is *the cause* that the
former days were better than these? for thou dost
not enquire wisely concerning this.
11 Wisdom *is* good with an inheritance: and
by it there is profit [a]to them that see the sun.
12 For wisdom *is* a [a]defence, *and* money *is*
a defence: but the excellency of knowledge *is,*
that wisdom giveth [b]life to them that have it.
13 Consider the work of God: for [a]who can
make *that* straight, which he hath made crooked?
14 [a]In the day of prosperity be joyful, but in
the day of adversity consider: God also hath set
the one over against the other, to the end that
man should find nothing after him.
15 All *things* have I seen in the days of my
vanity: [a]there is a just *man* that perisheth in his
righteousness, and there is a wicked *man* that prolongeth *his life* in his wickedness.
16 [a]Be not righteous over much; [b]neither
make thyself over wise: why shouldest thou destroy thyself?
17 Be not over much wicked, neither be thou
foolish: [a]why shouldest thou die before thy time?
18 *It is* good that thou shouldest take hold
of this; yea, also from this withdraw not thine
hand: for he that [a]feareth God shall come forth
of them all.
19 [a]Wisdom strengtheneth the wise more
than ten mighty *men* which are in the city.
20 [a]For *there is* not a just man upon earth,
that doeth good, and sinneth not.

CHAPTER 7

1 [a]Prov. 22:1 [b]Eccl. 4:2
2 [a][Ps. 90:12]
3 [a][2 Cor. 7:10]
5 [a]Ps. 141:5; [Prov. 13:18; 15:31, 32]
6 [a]Eccl. 2:2
7 [a]Ex. 23:8; Deut. 16:19; [Prov. 17:8, 23]
8 [a]Prov. 14:29; Gal. 5:22; Eph. 4:2
9 [a]Prov. 14:17; James 1:19
11 [a]Eccl. 11:7
12 [a]Eccl. 9:18 [b]Prov. 3:18
13 [a]Job 12:14
14 [a]Deut. 28:47
15 [a]Eccl. 8:12–14
16 [a]Prov. 25:16; Phil. 3:6 [b]Rom. 12:3
17 [a]Job 15:32; Ps. 55:23
18 [a]Eccl. 3:14; 5:7; 8:12, 13
19 [a]Prov. 21:22; Eccl. 9:13–18
20 [a]1 Kin. 8:46; 2 Chr. 6:36; Prov. 20:9; Rom. 3:23; 1 John 1:8

NKJV

The Value of Practical Wisdom

7 A [a]good name *is* better than precious ointment,
And the day of death than the day of one's [b]birth;
2 Better to go to the house of mourning
Than to go to the house of feasting,
For that *is* the end of all men;
And the living will take *it* to [a]heart.
3 Sorrow *is* better than laughter,
[a]For by a sad countenance the heart is made better.
4 The heart of the wise *is* in the house of mourning,
But the heart of fools *is* in the house of mirth.

5 [a]*It is* better to hear the rebuke of the wise
Than for a man to hear the song of fools.
6 [a]For like the crackling of thorns under a pot,
So *is* the laughter of the fool.
This also is vanity.
7 Surely oppression destroys a wise *man's* reason,
[a]And a bribe debases the heart.

8 The end of a thing *is* better than its beginning;
[a]The patient in spirit *is* better than the proud in spirit.
9 [a]Do not hasten in your spirit to be angry,
For anger rests in the bosom of fools.
10 Do not say,
"Why were the former days better than these?"
For you do not inquire wisely concerning this.

11 Wisdom *is* good with an inheritance,
And profitable [a]to those who see the sun.
12 For wisdom *is* a [a]defense *as* money *is* a defense,
But the excellence of knowledge *is that* wisdom gives [b]life to those who have it.

13 Consider the work of God;
For [a]who can make straight what He has made crooked?
14 [a]In the day of prosperity be joyful,
But in the day of adversity consider:
Surely God has appointed the one as well as the other,
So that man can find out nothing *that will come* after him.

15 I have seen everything in my days of vanity:

[a]There is a just *man* who perishes in his righteousness,
And there is a wicked *man* who prolongs *life* in his wickedness.

16 [a]Do not be overly righteous,
[b]Nor be overly wise:
Why should you destroy yourself?
17 Do not be overly wicked,
Nor be foolish:
[a]Why should you die before your time?
18 *It is* good that you grasp this,
And also not remove your hand from the other;
For he who [a]fears God will escape them all.

19 [a]Wisdom strengthens the wise
More than ten rulers of the city.

20 [a]For *there is* not a just man on earth who does good
And does not sin.

KJV

21 Also take no heed unto all words that are spoken; lest thou hear thy servant curse thee:
22 For oftentimes also thine own heart knoweth that thou thyself likewise hast cursed others.
23 All this have I proved by wisdom: [a]I said, I will be wise; but it *was* far from me.
24 [a]That which is far off, and [b]exceeding deep, who can find it out?
25 [a]I applied mine heart to know, and to search, and to seek out wisdom, and the reason *of things*, and to know the wickedness of folly, even of foolishness *and* madness:
26 [a]And I find more bitter than death the woman, whose heart *is* snares and nets, *and* her hands *as* bands: whoso pleaseth God shall escape from her; but the sinner shall be taken by her.
27 Behold, this have I found, saith [a]the preacher, *counting* one by one, to find out the account:
28 Which yet my soul seeketh, but I find not: [a]one man among a thousand have I found; but a woman among all those have I not found.
29 Lo, this only have I found, [a]that God hath made man upright; but [b]they have sought out many inventions.

23 [a]Rom. 1:22
24 [a]Job 28:12; 1 Tim. 6:16 [b]Rom. 11:33
25 [a]Eccl. 1:17
26 [a]Prov. 5:3, 4
27 [a]Eccl. 1:1, 2
28 [a]Job 33:23
29 [a]Gen. 1:27 [b]Gen. 3:6, 7

NKJV

21 Also do not take to heart everything people say,
Lest you hear your servant cursing you.
22 For many times, also, your own heart has known
That even you have cursed others.

23 All this I have proved by wisdom.
[a]I said, "I will be wise";
But it *was* far from me.
24 [a]As for that which is far off and [b]exceedingly deep,
Who can find it out?
25 [a]I applied my heart to know,
To search and seek out wisdom and the reason *of things*,
To know the wickedness of folly,
Even of foolishness *and* madness.
26 [a]And I find more bitter than death
The woman whose heart *is* snares and nets,
Whose hands *are* fetters.
He who pleases God shall escape from her,
But the sinner shall be trapped by her.

27 "Here is what I have found," says [a]the Preacher,
"*Adding* one thing to the other to find out the reason,
28 Which my soul still seeks but I cannot find:
[a]One man among a thousand I have found,
But a woman among all these I have not found.
29 Truly, this only I have found:
[a]That God made man upright,
But [b]they have sought out many schemes."

KJV

8 Who *is* as the wise *man?* and who knoweth the interpretation of a thing? [a]a man's wisdom maketh his face to shine, and [b]the boldness of his face shall be changed.

Obey Authorities for God's Sake

2 I *counsel thee* to keep the king's commandment, [a]and *that* in regard of the oath of God.
3 [a]Be not hasty to go out of his sight: stand not in an evil thing; for he doeth whatsoever pleaseth him.
4 Where the word of a king *is, there is* power: and [a]who may say unto him, What doest thou?
5 Whoso keepeth the commandment shall feel no evil thing: and a wise man's heart discerneth both time and judgment.
6 Because [a]to every purpose there is time and judgment, therefore the misery of man *is* great upon him.
7 [a]For he knoweth not that which shall be: for who can tell him when it shall be?
8 [a]*There is* no man that hath power over the spirit to retain the spirit; neither *hath he* power in the day of death: and *there is* [b]no discharge in *that* war; neither shall wickedness deliver those that are given to it.
9 All this have I seen, and applied my heart unto every work that is done under the sun: *there is* a time wherein one man ruleth over another to his own hurt.

Death Comes to All

10 And so I saw the wicked buried, who had come and gone from the place of the holy, and

CHAPTER 8
1 [a]Prov. 4:8, 9; Acts 6:15 [b]Deut. 28:50
2 [a]Ex. 22:11; 2 Sam. 21:7; 1 Chr. 29:24; Ezek. 17:18; [Rom. 13:5]
3 [a]Eccl. 10:4
4 [a]1 Sam. 13:11, 13; Job 34:18
6 [a]Eccl. 3:1, 17
7 [a]Prov. 24:22; Eccl. 6:12
8 [a]Ps. 49:6, 7; Job 14:5 [b]Deut. 20:5–8

NKJV

8 Who *is* like a wise *man?*
And who knows the interpretation of a thing?
[a]A man's wisdom makes his face shine,
And [b]the sternness of his face is changed.

Obey Authorities for God's Sake

2 I *say*, "Keep the king's commandment [a]for the sake of your oath to God.
3 [a]"Do not be hasty to go from his presence. Do not take your stand for an evil thing, for he does whatever pleases him."

4 Where the word of a king *is, there is* power;
And [a]who may say to him, "What are you doing?"
5 He who keeps his command will experience nothing harmful;
And a wise man's heart discerns both time and judgment,
6 Because [a]for every matter there is a time and judgment,
Though the misery of man increases greatly.
7 [a]For he does not know what will happen;
So who can tell him when it will occur?
8 [a]No one has power over the spirit to retain the spirit,
And no one has power in the day of death.
There is [b]no release from that war,
And wickedness will not deliver those who are given to it.

9 All this I have seen, and applied my heart to every work that is done under the sun: *There is* a time in which one man rules over another to his own hurt.

Death Comes to All

10 Then I saw the wicked buried, who had come and gone from the place of holiness, and

KJV

they were [a]forgotten in the city where they had so done: this *is* also vanity.

11 [a]Because sentence against an evil work is not executed speedily, therefore the heart of the sons of men is fully set in them to do evil.

12 [a]Though a sinner do evil an hundred times, and his *days* be prolonged, yet surely I know that [b]it shall be well with them that fear God, which fear before him:

13 But it shall not be well with the wicked, neither shall he prolong *his* days, *which are* as a shadow; because he feareth not before God.

14 There is a vanity which is done upon the earth; that there be just *men,* unto whom it [a]happeneth according to the work of the wicked; again, there be wicked *men,* to whom it happeneth according to the work of the [b]righteous: I said that this also *is* vanity.

15 [a]Then I commended mirth, because a man hath no better thing under the sun, than to eat, and to drink, and to be merry: for that shall abide with him of his labour the days of his life, which God giveth him under the sun.

16 When I applied mine heart to know wisdom, and to see the business that is done upon the earth: (for also *there is that* neither day nor night seeth sleep with his eyes:)

17 Then I beheld all the work of God, that [a]a man cannot find out the work that is done under the sun: because though a man labour to seek *it* out, yet he shall not find *it;* yea further; though a wise *man* think to know *it,* yet shall he not be able to find *it.*

9 For all this I considered in my heart even to declare all this, [a]that the righteous, and the wise, and their works, *are* in the hand of God: no man knoweth either love or hatred *by* all *that is* before them.

2 [a]All *things come* alike to all: *there is* one event to the righteous, and to the wicked; to the good and to the clean, and to the unclean; to him that sacrificeth, and to him that sacrificeth not: as *is* the good, so *is* the sinner; *and* he that sweareth, as *he* that feareth an oath.

3 This *is* an evil among all *things* that are done under the sun, that *there is* one event unto all: yea, also the heart of the sons of men is full of evil, and madness *is* in their heart while they live, and after that *they go* to the dead.

4 For to him that is joined to all the living there is hope: for a living dog is better than a dead lion.

5 For the living know that they shall die: but [a]the dead know not any thing, neither have they any more a reward; for [b]the memory of them is forgotten.

6 Also their love, and their hatred, and their envy, is now perished; neither have they any more a portion for ever in any *thing* that is done under the sun.

7 Go thy way, [a]eat thy bread with joy, and drink thy wine with a merry heart; for God now accepteth thy works.

8 Let thy garments be always white; and let thy head lack no ointment.

9 Live joyfully with the wife whom thou lovest all the days of the life of thy vanity, which he hath given thee under the sun, all the days of thy vanity: [a]for that *is* thy portion in *this* life, and in thy labour which thou takest under the sun.

10 [a]Whatsoever thy hand findeth to do, do *it* with thy [b]might; for *there is* no work, nor de-

10 [a]Eccl. 2:16; 9:5
11 [a]Ps. 10:6; 50:21; Is. 26:10
12 [a]Is. 65:20; [Rom. 2:5–7] [b][Deut. 4:40; Ps. 37:11, 18, 19; Prov. 1:32, 33; Is. 3:10; Matt. 25:34, 41]
14 [a]Ps. 73:14 [b]Eccl. 2:14; 7:15; 9:1–3
15 [a]Eccl. 2:24
17 [a]Job 5:9; Ps. 73:16; Eccl. 3:11; Rom. 11:33

CHAPTER 9

1 [a]Deut. 33:3; Job 12:10; Eccl. 8:14
2 [a]Gen. 3:17–19; Job 21:7; Ps. 73:3, 12, 13; Mal. 3:15
5 [a]Job 14:21; Is. 63:16 [b]Job 7:8–10; Eccl. 1:11; 2:16; 8:10; Is. 26:14
7 [a]Eccl. 8:15
9 [a]Eccl. 2:10
10 [a][Col. 3:17] [b]Rom. 12:11; Col. 3:23

*

8:10 Some Heb. mss., LXX, Vg. *praised*
9:2 LXX, Syr., Vg. *good and bad,*

NKJV

they were [a]forgotten* in the city where they had so done. This also *is* vanity.

11 [a]Because the sentence against an evil work is not executed speedily, therefore the heart of the sons of men is fully set in them to do evil.

12 [a]Though a sinner does evil a hundred *times,* and his *days* are prolonged, yet I surely know that [b]it will be well with those who fear God, who fear before Him.

13 But it will not be well with the wicked; nor will he prolong *his* days, *which are* as a shadow, because he does not fear before God.

14 There is a vanity which occurs on earth, that there are just *men* to whom it [a]happens according to the work of the wicked; again, there are wicked *men* to whom it happens according to the work of the [b]righteous. I said that this also *is* vanity.

15 [a]So I commended enjoyment, because a man has nothing better under the sun than to eat, drink, and be merry; for this will remain with him in his labor *all* the days of his life which God gives him under the sun.

16 When I applied my heart to know wisdom and to see the business that is done on earth, even though one sees no sleep day or night,

17 then I saw all the work of God, that [a]a man cannot find out the work that is done under the sun. For though a man labors to discover *it,* yet he will not find *it;* moreover, though a wise *man* attempts to know *it,* he will not be able to find *it.*

9 For I considered all this in my heart, so that I could declare it all: [a]that the righteous and the wise and their works *are* in the hand of God. People know neither love nor hatred *by* anything *they see* before them.

2 [a]All things *come* alike to all:

One event *happens* to the righteous and the wicked;
To the *good, the clean, and the unclean;
To him who sacrifices and him who does not sacrifice.
As is the good, so *is* the sinner;
He who takes an oath as *he* who fears an oath.

3 This *is* an evil in all that is done under the sun: that one thing *happens* to all. Truly the hearts of the sons of men are full of evil; madness *is* in their hearts while they live, and after that *they go* to the dead.

4 But for him who is joined to all the living there is hope, for a living dog is better than a dead lion.

5 For the living know that they will die;
But [a]the dead know nothing,
And they have no more reward,
For [b]the memory of them is forgotten.
6 Also their love, their hatred, and their envy have now perished;
Nevermore will they have a share
In anything done under the sun.

7 Go, [a]eat your bread with joy,
And drink your wine with a merry heart;
For God has already accepted your works.
8 Let your garments always be white,
And let your head lack no oil.

9 Live joyfully with the wife whom you love all the days of your vain life which He has given you under the sun, all your days of vanity; [a]for that *is* your portion in life, and in the labor which you perform under the sun.

10 [a]Whatever your hand finds to do, do *it* with your [b]might; for *there is* no work or device

KJV

vice, nor knowledge, nor wisdom, in the grave,
whither thou goest.
11 I returned, [a]and saw under the sun, that
the race *is* not to the swift, nor the battle to the
strong, neither yet bread to the wise, nor yet
riches to men of understanding, nor yet favour
to men of skill; but time and [b]chance happeneth
to them all.
12 For [a]man also knoweth not his time: as
the fishes that are taken in an evil net, and as
the birds that are caught in the snare; so *are* the
sons of men [b]snared in an evil time, when it falleth
suddenly upon them.

Wisdom Superior to Folly

13 This wisdom have I seen also under the
sun, and it *seemed* great unto me:
14 [a]*There was* a little city, and few men
within it; and there came a great king against it,
and besieged it, and built great bulwarks against
it:
15 Now there was found in it a poor wise
man, and he by his wisdom delivered the city;
yet no man remembered that same poor man.
16 Then said I, Wisdom *is* better than
[a]strength: nevertheless [b]the poor man's wisdom
is despised, and his words are not heard.
17 The words of wise *men are* heard in quiet
more than the cry of him that ruleth among fools.
18 Wisdom *is* better than weapons of war:
but [a]one sinner destroyeth much good.

10 Dead flies cause the ointment of the apothecary to send forth a stinking savour: *so
doth* a little folly him that is in reputation for wisdom *and* honour.
2 A wise man's heart *is* at his right hand;
but a fool's heart at his left.
3 Yea also, when he that is a fool walketh
by the way, his wisdom faileth *him*, [a]and he saith
to every one *that* he *is* a fool.
4 If the spirit of the ruler rise up against
thee, [a]leave not thy place; for [b]yielding pacifieth
great offences.
5 There is an evil *which* I have seen under
the sun, as an error *which* proceedeth from the
ruler:
6 [a]Folly is set in great dignity, and the rich
sit in low place.
7 I have seen servants [a]upon horses, and
princes walking as servants upon the earth.
8 [a]He that diggeth a pit shall fall into it; and
whoso breaketh an hedge, a serpent shall bite
him.
9 Whoso removeth stones shall be hurt
therewith; *and* he that cleaveth wood shall be endangered thereby.
10 If the iron be blunt, and he do not whet
the edge, then must he put to more strength: but
wisdom *is* profitable to direct.
11 Surely the serpent will bite [a]without enchantment; and a babbler is no better.
12 [a]The words of a wise man's mouth *are*
gracious; but [b]the lips of a fool will swallow up
himself.
13 The beginning of the words of his mouth
is foolishness: and the end of his talk *is* mischievous madness.

11 [a]Jer. 9:23; Amos 2:14, 15 [b]1 Sam. 6:9 **12** [a]Eccl. 8:7 [b]Prov. 29:6; Luke 12:20, 39; 17:26; 1 Thess. 5:3 **14** [a]2 Sam. 20:16–22 **16** [a]Eccl. 7:12, 19 [b]Mark 6:2, 3 **18** [a]Josh. 7:1–26; 2 Kin. 21:2–17

CHAPTER 10

3 [a]Prov. 13:16; 18:2 **4** [a]Eccl. 8:3 [b]1 Sam. 25:24–33; Prov. 25:15 **6** [a]Esth. 3:1 **7** [a]Prov. 19:10; 30:22 **8** [a]Ps. 7:15; Prov. 26:27 **11** [a]Ps. 58:4, 5; Jer. 8:17 **12** [a]Prov. 10:32; Luke 4:22 [b]Prov. 10:14; Eccl. 4:5

*
9:14 LXX, Syr., Vg. *bulwarks*
10:1 Tg., Vg. omit *putrefy*

NKJV

or knowledge or wisdom in the grave where you
are going.
11 I returned [a]and saw under the sun that—

The race *is* not to the swift,
Nor the battle to the strong,
Nor bread to the wise,
Nor riches to men of understanding,
Nor favor to men of skill;
But time and [b]chance happen to them all.
12 For [a]man also does not know his time:
Like fish taken in a cruel net,
Like birds caught in a snare,
So the sons of men *are* [b]snared in an evil
time,
When it falls suddenly upon them.

Wisdom Superior to Folly

13 This wisdom I have also seen under the
sun, and it *seemed* great to me:
14 [a]*There was* a little city with few men in
it; and a great king came against it, besieged it,
and built great *snares around it.
15 Now there was found in it a poor wise
man, and he by his wisdom delivered the city.
Yet no one remembered that same poor man.
16 Then I said:

"Wisdom *is* better than [a]strength.
Nevertheless [b]the poor man's wisdom *is*
despised,
And his words are not heard.
17 Words of the wise, *spoken* quietly, *should
be* heard
Rather than the shout of a ruler of fools.
18 Wisdom *is* better than weapons of war;
But [a]one sinner destroys much good."

10 Dead flies *putrefy the perfumer's
ointment,
And cause it to give off a foul odor;
So does a little folly to one respected for
wisdom *and* honor.
2 A wise man's heart *is* at his right hand,
But a fool's heart at his left.
3 Even when a fool walks along the way,
He lacks wisdom,
[a]And he shows everyone *that* he *is* a fool.
4 If the spirit of the ruler rises against you,
[a]Do not leave your post;
For [b]conciliation pacifies great offenses.

5 There is an evil I have seen under the sun,
As an error proceeding from the ruler:
6 [a]Folly is set in great dignity,
While the rich sit in a lowly place.
7 I have seen servants [a]on horses,
While princes walk on the ground like
servants.

8 [a]He who digs a pit will fall into it,
And whoever breaks through a wall will
be bitten by a serpent.
9 He who quarries stones may be hurt by
them,
And he who splits wood may be
endangered by it.
10 If the ax is dull,
And one does not sharpen the edge,
Then he must use more strength;
But wisdom brings success.

11 A serpent may bite [a]when *it is* not
charmed;
The babbler is no different.
12 [a]The words of a wise man's mouth *are*
gracious,
But [b]the lips of a fool shall swallow him
up;
13 The words of his mouth begin with
foolishness,
And the end of his talk *is* raving madness.

KJV

14 [a]A fool also is full of words: a man cannot
tell what shall be; and [b]what shall be after him,
who can tell him?
15 The labour of the foolish wearieth every
one of them, because he knoweth not how to go
to the city.
16 [a]Woe to thee, O land, when thy king *is* a
child, and thy princes eat in the morning!
17 Blessed *art* thou, O land, when thy king
is the son of nobles, and thy [a]princes eat in due
season, for strength, and not for drunkenness!
18 By much slothfulness the building decayeth; and [a]through idleness of the hands the house
droppeth through.
19 A feast is made for laughter, and [a]wine
maketh merry: but money answereth all *things*.
20 [a]Curse not the king, no not in thy thought;
and curse not the rich in thy bedchamber: for a
bird of the air shall carry the voice, and that which
hath wings shall tell the matter.

The Value of Diligence

11 Cast thy bread [a]upon the waters: [b]for thou
shalt find it after many days.
2 [a]Give a portion [b]to seven, and also to
eight; [c]for thou knowest not what evil shall be
upon the earth.
3 If the clouds be full of rain, they empty
themselves upon the earth: and if the tree fall
toward the south, or toward the north, in the
place where the tree falleth, there it shall be.
4 He that observeth the wind shall not sow;
and he that regardeth the clouds shall not reap.
5 As [a]thou knowest not what *is* the way of
the spirit, [b]*nor* how the bones *do grow* in the
womb of her that is with child: even so thou knowest not the works of God who maketh all.
6 In the morning sow thy seed, and in the
evening withhold not thine hand: for thou knowest not whether shall prosper, either this or that,
or whether they both *shall be* alike good.
7 Truly the light *is* sweet, and a pleasant
thing it is for the eyes [a]to behold the sun:
8 But if a man live many years, *and* [a]rejoice
in them all; yet let him [b]remember the days of
darkness; for they shall be many. All that cometh
is vanity.

Seek God in Early Life

9 Rejoice, O young man, in thy youth; and
let thy heart cheer thee in the days of thy youth,
[a]and walk in the ways of thine heart, and in the
sight of thine eyes: but know thou, that for all
these *things* [b]God will bring thee into judgment.
10 Therefore remove sorrow from thy heart,
and [a]put away evil from thy flesh: [b]for childhood
and youth *are* vanity.

14 [a][Prov. 15:2]; Eccl. 5:3 [b]Eccl. 3:22; 8:7
16 [a]Is. 3:4, 5; 5:11
17 [a]Prov. 31:4; Is. 5:11
18 [a]Prov. 24:30–34
19 [a]Judg. 9:13; Ps. 104:15; Eccl. 2:3
20 [a]Ex. 22:28; Acts 23:5

CHAPTER 11

1 [a]Is. 32:20 [b][Deut. 15:10; Prov. 19:17; Matt. 10:42; 2 Cor. 9:8; Gal. 6:9, 10; Heb. 6:10]
2 [a]Ps. 112:9; Matt. 5:42; Luke 6:30; [1 Tim. 6:18, 19] [b]Mic. 5:5 [c]Eph. 5:16
5 [a]John 3:8 [b]Ps. 139:14
7 [a]Eccl. 7:11
8 [a]Eccl. 9:7 [b]Eccl. 12:1
9 [a]Num. 15:39; Job 31:7; Eccl. 2:10 [b]Eccl. 3:17; 12:14; [Rom. 14:10]
10 [a]2 Cor. 7:1; 2 Tim. 2:22 [b]Ps. 39:5

NKJV

14 [a]A fool also multiplies words.
No man knows what is to be;
Who can tell him [b]what will be after him?
15 The labor of fools wearies them,
For they do not even know how to go to the city!

16 [a]Woe to you, O land, when your king *is* a child,
And your princes feast in the morning!
17 Blessed *are* you, O land, when your king *is* the son of nobles,
And your [a]princes feast at the proper time—
For strength and not for drunkenness!
18 Because of laziness the building decays,
And [a]through idleness of hands the house leaks.
19 A feast is made for laughter,
And [a]wine makes merry;
But money answers everything.

20 [a]Do not curse the king, even in your thought;
Do not curse the rich, even in your bedroom;
For a bird of the air may carry your voice,
And a bird in flight may tell the matter.

The Value of Diligence

11 Cast your bread [a]upon the waters,
[b]For you will find it after many days.
2 [a]Give a serving [b]to seven, and also to eight,
[c]For you do not know what evil will be on the earth.

3 If the clouds are full of rain,
They empty *themselves* upon the earth;
And if a tree falls to the south or the north,
In the place where the tree falls, there it shall lie.
4 He who observes the wind will not sow,
And he who regards the clouds will not reap.

5 As [a]you do not know what *is* the way of the *wind,
[b]*Or* how the bones *grow* in the womb of her who is with child,
So you do not know the works of God who makes everything.
6 In the morning sow your seed,
And in the evening do not withhold your hand;
For you do not know which will prosper,
Either this or that,
Or whether both alike *will be* good.

7 Truly the light is sweet,
And *it is* pleasant for the eyes [a]to behold the sun;
8 But if a man lives many years
And [a]rejoices in them all,
Yet let him [b]remember the days of darkness,
For they will be many.
All that is coming *is* vanity.

Seek God in Early Life

9 Rejoice, O young man, in your youth,
And let your heart cheer you in the days of your youth;
[a]Walk in the ways of your heart,
And in the sight of your eyes;
But know that for all these
[b]God will bring you into judgment.
10 Therefore remove sorrow from your heart,
And [a]put away evil from your flesh,
[b]For childhood and youth *are* vanity.

*11:5 Or *spirit*

KJV

12 Remember[a] now thy Creator in the days of thy youth, while the evil days come not, nor the years draw nigh, [b]when thou shalt say, I have no pleasure in them;

2 While the sun, or the light, or the moon, or the stars, be not darkened, nor the clouds return after the rain:

3 In the day when the keepers of the house shall tremble, and the strong men shall bow themselves, and the grinders cease because they are few, and those that look out of the windows be darkened,

4 And the doors shall be shut in the streets, when the sound of the grinding is low, and he shall rise up at the voice of the bird, and all [a]the daughters of musick shall be brought low;

5 Also *when* they shall be afraid of *that which is* high, and fears *shall be* in the way, and the almond tree shall flourish, and the grasshopper shall be a burden, and desire shall fail: because man goeth to [a]his long home, and [b]the mourners go about the streets:

6 Or ever the silver cord be loosed, or the golden bowl be broken, or the pitcher be broken at the fountain, or the wheel broken at the cistern.

7 [a]Then shall the dust return to the earth as it was: [b]and the spirit shall return unto God [c]who gave it.

8 [a]Vanity of vanities, saith the preacher; all *is* vanity.

The Whole Duty of Man

9 And moreover, because the preacher was wise, he still taught the people knowledge; yea, he gave good heed, and sought out, *and* [a]set in order many proverbs.

10 The preacher sought to find out acceptable words: and *that which was* written *was* upright, *even* words of truth.

11 The words of the wise *are* as goads, and as nails fastened *by* the masters of assemblies, *which* are given from one shepherd.

12 And further, by these, my son, be admonished: of making many books *there is* no end; and [a]much study *is* a weariness of the flesh.

13 Let us hear the conclusion of the whole matter: [a]Fear God, and keep his commandments: for this *is* the whole *duty* of man.

14 For [a]God shall bring every work into judgment, with every secret thing, whether *it be* good, or whether *it be* evil.

CHAPTER 12

1 [a]2 Chr. 34:3; Prov. 22:6; Lam. 3:27 [b]2 Sam. 19:35
4 [a]2 Sam. 19:35
5 [a]Job 17:13 [b]Gen. 50:10; Jer. 9:17
7 [a]Gen. 3:19; Job 34:15; Ps. 90:3 [b]Eccl. 3:21 [c]Num. 16:22; 27:16; Job 34:14; Is. 57:16; Zech. 12:1
8 [a]Ps. 62:9
9 [a]1 Kin. 4:32
12 [a]Eccl. 1:18
13 [a][Deut. 6:2; 10:12]; Mic. 6:8
14 [a]Eccl. 11:9; Matt. 12:36; [Acts 17:30, 31; Rom. 2:16; 1 Cor. 4:5; 2 Cor. 5:10]

*

12:6 So with Qr., Tg.; Kt. *removed;* LXX, Vg. *broken*
12:11 Lit. *masters of assemblies*

NKJV

12 Remember[a] now your Creator in the days
of your youth,
Before the difficult days come,
And the years draw near [b]when you say,
"I have no pleasure in them":
2 While the sun and the light,
The moon and the stars,
Are not darkened,
And the clouds do not return after the rain;
3 In the day when the keepers of the house tremble,
And the strong men bow down;
When the grinders cease because they are few,
And those that look through the windows grow dim;
4 When the doors are shut in the streets,
And the sound of grinding is low;
When one rises up at the sound of a bird,
And all [a]the daughters of music are brought low.
5 Also they are afraid of height,
And of terrors in the way;
When the almond tree blossoms,
The grasshopper is a burden,
And desire fails.
For man goes to [a]his eternal home,
And [b]the mourners go about the streets.

6 *Remember your Creator* before the silver cord is *loosed,
Or the golden bowl is broken,
Or the pitcher shattered at the fountain,
Or the wheel broken at the well.
7 [a]Then the dust will return to the earth as it was,
[b]And the spirit will return to God [c]who gave it.

8 "Vanity[a] of vanities," says the Preacher,
"All *is* vanity."

The Whole Duty of Man

9 And moreover, because the Preacher was wise, he still taught the people knowledge; yes, he pondered and sought out *and* [a]set in order many proverbs.

10 The Preacher sought to find acceptable words; and *what was* written *was* upright—words of truth.

11 The words of the wise are like goads, and the words of *scholars are like well-driven nails, given by one Shepherd.

12 And further, my son, be admonished by these. Of making many books *there is* no end, and [a]much study *is* wearisome to the flesh.

13 Let us hear the conclusion of the whole matter:

[a]Fear God and keep His commandments,
For this is man's all.
14 For [a]God will bring every work into judgment,
Including every secret thing,
Whether good or evil.

KJV

THE

SONG OF SOLOMON

1 The [a]song of songs, which *is* Solomon's.

The Banquet

2 Let him kiss me with the kisses of his
mouth: [a]for thy love *is* better than wine.
3 Because of the savour of thy good ointments thy name *is as* ointment poured forth,
therefore do the virgins love thee.
4 [a]Draw me, [b]we will run after thee: the
king [c]hath brought me into his chambers: we will
be glad and rejoice in thee, we will remember thy
love more than wine: the upright love thee.
5 I *am* black, but comely, O ye daughters
of Jerusalem, as the tents of Kedar, as the curtains
of Solomon.
6 Look not upon me, because I *am* black, because the sun hath looked upon me: my mother's
children were angry with me; they made me the
keeper of the vineyards; *but* mine own [a]vineyard
have I not kept.
7 Tell me, O thou whom my soul loveth,
where thou feedest, where thou makest *thy flock*
to rest at noon: for why should I be as one that
turneth aside by the flocks of thy companions?
8 If thou know not, [a]O thou fairest among
women, go thy way forth by the footsteps of the
flock, and feed thy kids beside the shepherds'
tents.
9 I have compared thee, [a]O my love, [b]to a
company of horses in Pharaoh's chariots.
10 [a]Thy cheeks are comely with rows *of jewels*, thy neck with chains *of gold*.
11 We will make thee borders of gold with
studs of silver.

CHAPTER 1
1 [a]1 Kin. 4:32
2 [a]Song 4:10
4 [a]Hos. 11:4; John 6:44; 12:32 [b]Phil. 3:12–14 [c]Ps. 45:14, 15; John 14:2; Eph. 2:6
6 [a]Song 8:11, 12
8 [a]Song 5:9
9 [a]Song 2:2, 10, 13; 4:1, 7; John 15:14 [b]2 Chr. 1:16
10 [a]Ezek. 16:11

*

1:2 A Palestinian young woman, Song 6:13. The speaker and audience are identified according to the number, gender, and person of the Hebrew words. Occasionally the identity is not certain. • Masc. sing.: the Beloved **1:4** Masc. sing.: the Beloved • Fem. sing.: the Shulamite • Masc. sing.: the Beloved • Masc. sing.: the Beloved **1:7** LXX, Syr., Vg. *wanders* **1:11** Fem. sing.: the Shulamite

NKJV

THE

SONG OF SOLOMON

1 The [a]song of songs, which *is* Solomon's.

The Banquet

THE *SHULAMITE

2 Let him kiss me with the kisses of his mouth—
[a]For *your love *is* better than wine.
3 Because of the fragrance of your good ointments,
Your name *is* ointment poured forth;
Therefore the virgins love you.
4 [a]Draw me away!

THE DAUGHTERS OF JERUSALEM

[b]We will run after *you.

THE SHULAMITE

The king [c]has brought me into his chambers.

THE DAUGHTERS OF JERUSALEM

We will be glad and rejoice in *you.
We will remember *your love more than wine.

THE SHULAMITE

Rightly do they love *you.

5 I *am* dark, but lovely,
O daughters of Jerusalem,
Like the tents of Kedar,
Like the curtains of Solomon.
6 Do not look upon me, because I *am* dark,
Because the sun has tanned me.
My mother's sons were angry with me;
They made me the keeper of the vineyards,
But my own [a]vineyard I have not kept.

(TO HER BELOVED)

7 Tell me, O you whom I love,
Where you feed *your flock*,
Where you make *it* rest at noon.
For why should I be as one who *veils herself
By the flocks of your companions?

THE BELOVED

8 If you do not know, [a]O fairest among women,
Follow in the footsteps of the flock,
And feed your little goats
Beside the shepherds' tents.
9 I have compared you, [a]my love,
[b]To my filly among Pharaoh's chariots.
10 [a]Your cheeks are lovely with ornaments,
Your neck with chains *of gold*.

THE DAUGHTERS OF JERUSALEM

11 We will make *you ornaments of gold
With studs of silver.

KJV

12 While the king *sitteth* at his table, my
spikenard sendeth forth the smell thereof.
13 A bundle of myrrh *is* my wellbeloved unto
me; he shall lie all night betwixt my breasts.
14 My beloved *is* unto me *as* a cluster of camphire in the vineyards of En–gedi.
15 [a]Behold, thou *art* fair, my love; behold,
thou *art* fair; thou *hast* doves' eyes.
16 Behold, thou *art* [a]fair, my beloved, yea,
pleasant: also our bed *is* green.
17 The beams of our house *are* cedar, *and*
our rafters of fir.

2 I *am* the rose of Sharon, *and* the lily of the
valleys.
2 As the lily among thorns, so *is* my love
among the daughters.
3 As the apple tree among the trees of the
wood, so *is* my beloved among the sons. I sat
down under his shadow with great delight, and
[a]his fruit *was* sweet to my taste.
4 He brought me to the banqueting house,
and his banner over me *was* love.
5 Stay me with flagons, comfort me with apples: for I *am* sick of love.
6 [a]His left hand *is* under my head, and his
right hand doth embrace me.
7 [a]I charge you, O ye daughters of Jerusalem, by the roes, and by the hinds of the field,
that ye stir not up, nor awake *my* love, till he
please.

The Beloved's Request

8 The voice of my beloved! behold, he cometh leaping upon the mountains, skipping upon
the hills.
9 [a]My beloved is like a roe or a young hart:
behold, he standeth behind our wall, he looketh
forth at the windows, shewing himself through
the lattice.
10 My beloved spake, and said unto me, Rise
up, my love, my fair one, and come away.
11 For, lo, the winter is past, the rain is over
and gone;
12 The flowers appear on the earth; the time
of the singing *of birds* is come, and the voice of
the turtle is heard in our land;
13 The fig tree putteth forth her green figs,
and the vines *with* the tender grape give a *good*
smell. Arise, my love, my fair one, and come
away.
14 O my [a]dove, *that art* in the clefts of the
rock, in the secret *places* of the stairs, let me see
thy countenance, [b]let me hear thy voice; for sweet
is thy voice, and thy countenance *is* comely.

15 [a]Song 4:1; 5:12
16 [a]Song 5:10–16

CHAPTER 2
3 [a]Song 4:16; Rev. 22:1, 2
6 [a]Song 8:3
7 [a]Song 3:5; 8:4
9 [a]Prov. 6:5; Song 2:17
14 [a]Song 5:2 [b]Song 8:13

NKJV

THE SHULAMITE

12 While the king *is* at his table,
My spikenard sends forth its fragrance.
13 A bundle of myrrh *is* my beloved to me,
That lies all night between my breasts.
14 My beloved *is* to me a cluster of henna *blooms*
In the vineyards of En Gedi.

THE BELOVED

15 [a]Behold, you *are* fair, my love!
Behold, you *are* fair!
You *have* dove's eyes.

THE SHULAMITE

16 Behold, you *are* [a]handsome, my beloved!
Yes, pleasant!
Also our bed *is* green.
17 The beams of our houses *are* cedar,
And our rafters of fir.

2 I *am* the rose of Sharon,
And the lily of the valleys.

THE BELOVED

2 Like a lily among thorns,
So is my love among the daughters.

THE SHULAMITE

3 Like an apple tree among the trees of the woods,
So *is* my beloved among the sons.
I sat down in his shade with great delight,
And [a]his fruit *was* sweet to my taste.

THE SHULAMITE TO THE DAUGHTERS OF JERUSALEM

4 He brought me to the banqueting house,
And his banner over me *was* love.
5 Sustain me with cakes of raisins,
Refresh me with apples,
For I *am* lovesick.

6 [a]His left hand *is* under my head,
And his right hand embraces me.
7 [a]I charge you, O daughters of Jerusalem,
By the gazelles or by the does of the field,
Do not stir up nor awaken love
Until it pleases.

The Beloved's Request

THE SHULAMITE

8 The voice of my beloved!
Behold, he comes
Leaping upon the mountains,
Skipping upon the hills.
9 [a]My beloved is like a gazelle or a young stag.
Behold, he stands behind our wall;
He is looking through the windows,
Gazing through the lattice.

10 My beloved spoke, and said to me:
"Rise up, my love, my fair one,
And come away.
11 For lo, the winter is past,
The rain is over *and* gone.
12 The flowers appear on the earth;
The time of singing has come,
And the voice of the turtledove
Is heard in our land.
13 The fig tree puts forth her green figs,
And the vines *with* the tender grapes
Give a good smell.
Rise up, my love, my fair one,
And come away!

14 "O my [a]dove, in the clefts of the rock,
In the secret *places* of the cliff,
Let me see your face,
[b]Let me hear your voice;
For your voice *is* sweet,
And your face *is* lovely."

KJV

15 Take us [a]the foxes, the little foxes, that
spoil the vines: for our vines *have* tender grapes.
16 [a]My beloved *is* mine, and I *am* his: he
feedeth among the lilies.
17 [a]Until the day break, and the shadows flee
away, turn, my beloved, and be thou [b]like a roe
or a young hart upon the mountains of Bether.

A Troubled Night

3 By [a]night on my bed I sought him whom my
soul loveth: I sought him, but I found him not.
2 I will rise now, and go about the city in
the streets, and in the broad ways I will seek him
whom my soul loveth: I sought him, but I found
him not.
3 [a]The watchmen that go about the city
found me: *to whom I said,* Saw ye him whom my
soul loveth?
4 *It was* but a little that I passed from them,
but I found him whom my soul loveth: I held him,
and would not let him go, until I had brought him
into my [a]mother's house, and into the chamber
of her that conceived me.
5 [a]I charge you, O ye daughters of Jerusalem, by the roes, and by the hinds of the field,
that ye stir not up, nor awake *my* love, till he
please.

The Coming of Solomon

6 [a]Who *is* this that cometh out of the wilderness like pillars of smoke, perfumed with myrrh
and frankincense, with all powders of the merchant?
7 Behold his bed, which *is* Solomon's;
threescore valiant men *are* about it, of the valiant
of Israel.
8 They all hold swords, *being* expert in war:
every man *hath* his sword upon his thigh because
of fear in the night.
9 King Solomon made himself a chariot of
the wood of Lebanon.
10 He made the pillars thereof *of* silver, the
bottom thereof *of* gold, the covering of it *of* purple,
the midst thereof being paved *with* love, for the
daughters of Jerusalem.
11 Go forth, O ye daughters of Zion, and behold king Solomon with the crown wherewith his
mother crowned him in the day of his espousals,
and in the day of the gladness of his heart.

4 Behold, [a]thou *art* fair, my love; behold, thou
art fair; thou *hast* doves' eyes within thy
locks: thy hair *is* as a [b]flock of goats, that appear
from mount Gilead.
2 [a]Thy teeth *are* like a flock *of sheep* that

---

15 [a]Ps. 80:13; Ezek. 13:4; Luke 13:32
16 [a]Song 6:3
17 [a]Song 4:6 [b]Song 8:14

CHAPTER 3

1 [a]Is. 26:9
3 [a]Song 5:7; Is. 21:6–8, 11, 12
4 [a]Song 8:2
5 [a]Song 2:7; 8:4
6 [a]Song 8:5

CHAPTER 4

1 [a]Song 1:15; 5:12 [b]Song 6:5
2 [a]Song 6:6

*———
2:17 Lit. *Separation*
3:9 A portable enclosed chair

NKJV

HER BROTHERS

15 Catch us [a]the foxes,
The little foxes that spoil the vines,
For our vines *have* tender grapes.

THE SHULAMITE

16 [a]My beloved *is* mine, and I *am* his.
He feeds *his flock* among the lilies.

(TO HER BELOVED)

17 [a]Until the day breaks
And the shadows flee away,
Turn, my beloved,
And be [b]like a gazelle
Or a young stag
Upon the mountains of *Bether.

A Troubled Night

THE SHULAMITE

3 By [a]night on my bed I sought the one I
love;
I sought him, but I did not find him.
2 "I will rise now," *I said,*
"And go about the city;
In the streets and in the squares
I will seek the one I love."
I sought him, but I did not find him.
3 [a]The watchmen who go about the city
found me;
I said,
"Have you seen the one I love?"

4 Scarcely had I passed by them,
When I found the one I love.
I held him and would not let him go,
Until I had brought him to the [a]house of
my mother,
And into the chamber of her who
conceived me.

5 [a]I charge you, O daughters of Jerusalem,
By the gazelles or by the does of the field,
Do not stir up nor awaken love
Until it pleases.

The Coming of Solomon

THE SHULAMITE

6 [a]Who *is* this coming out of the wilderness
Like pillars of smoke,
Perfumed with myrrh and frankincense,
With all the merchant's fragrant powders?
7 Behold, it *is* Solomon's couch,
With sixty valiant men around it,
Of the valiant of Israel.
8 They all hold swords,
Being expert in war.
Every man *has* his sword on his thigh
Because of fear in the night.

9 Of the wood of Lebanon
Solomon the King
Made himself a *palanquin:
10 He made its pillars *of* silver,
Its support *of* gold,
Its seat *of* purple,
Its interior paved *with* love
By the daughters of Jerusalem.
11 Go forth, O daughters of Zion,
And see King Solomon with the crown
With which his mother crowned him
On the day of his wedding,
The day of the gladness of his heart.

THE BELOVED

4 Behold, [a]you *are* fair, my love!
Behold, you *are* fair!
You *have* dove's eyes behind your veil.
Your hair *is* like a [b]flock of goats,
Going down from Mount Gilead.
2 [a]Your teeth *are* like a flock of shorn *sheep*

KJV

are even shorn, which came up from the washing;
whereof every one bear twins, and none *is* barren
among them.
3 Thy lips *are* like a thread of scarlet, and
thy speech *is* comely: [a]thy temples *are* like a piece
of a pomegranate within thy locks.
4 [a]Thy neck *is* like the tower of David
builded [b]for an armoury, whereon there hang a
thousand bucklers, all shields of mighty men.
5 [a]Thy two breasts *are* like two young roes
that are twins, which feed among the lilies.
6 [a]Until the day break, and the shadows flee
away, I will get me to the mountain of myrrh,
and to the hill of frankincense.
7 [a]Thou *art* all fair, my love; *there is* no spot
in thee.
8 Come with me from Lebanon, *my* spouse,
with me from Lebanon: look from the top of
Amana, from the top of Shenir [a]and Hermon,
from the lions' dens, from the mountains of the
leopards.
9 Thou hast ravished my heart, my sister,
my spouse; thou hast ravished my heart with one
of thine eyes, with one chain of thy neck.
10 How fair is thy love, my sister, *my* spouse!
[a]how much better is thy love than wine! and the
smell of thine ointments than all spices!
11 Thy lips, O *my* spouse, drop *as* the honeycomb: [a]honey and milk *are* under thy tongue; and
the smell of thy garments *is* [b]like the smell of
Lebanon.
12 A garden inclosed *is* my sister, *my* spouse;
a spring shut up, a fountain sealed.
13 Thy plants *are* an orchard of pomegranates, with pleasant fruits; camphire, with spikenard,
14 Spikenard and saffron; calamus and cinnamon, with all trees of frankincense; myrrh and
aloes, with all the chief spices:
15 A fountain of gardens, a well of [a]living
waters, and streams from Lebanon.
16 Awake, O north wind; and come, thou
south; blow upon my garden, *that* the spices
thereof may flow out. [a]Let my beloved come into
his garden, and eat his pleasant [b]fruits.

5 I [a]am come into my garden, my [b]sister, *my*
spouse: I have gathered my myrrh with my
spice; [c]I have eaten my honeycomb with my
honey; I have drunk my wine with my milk: eat,
O [d]friends; drink, yea, drink abundantly, O
beloved.

3 [a]Song 6:7
4 [a]Song 7:4
[b]Neh. 3:19
5 [a]Prov. 5:19; Song 7:3
6 [a]Song 2:17
7 [a]Song 1:15; Eph. 5:27
8 [a]Deut. 3:9; 1 Chr. 5:23; Ezek. 27:5
10 [a]Song 1:2, 4
11 [a]Prov. 24:13, 14; Song 5:1
[b]Gen. 27:27; Hos. 14:6, 7
15 [a]Zech. 14:8; John 4:10; 7:38
16 [a]Song 5:1
[b]Song 7:13

CHAPTER 5
1 [a]Song 4:16
[b]Song 4:9
[c]Song 4:11
[d]Luke 15:7, 10; John 3:29

NKJV

Which have come up from the washing,
Every one of which bears twins,
And none *is* barren among them.
3 Your lips *are* like a strand of scarlet,
And your mouth is lovely.
[a]Your temples behind your veil
Are like a piece of pomegranate.
4 [a]Your neck *is* like the tower of David,
Built [b]for an armory,
On which hang a thousand bucklers,
All shields of mighty men.
5 [a]Your two breasts *are* like two fawns,
Twins of a gazelle,
Which feed among the lilies.

6 [a]Until the day breaks
And the shadows flee away,
I will go my way to the mountain of myrrh
And to the hill of frankincense.

7 [a]You *are* all fair, my love,
And *there is* no spot in you.
8 Come with me from Lebanon, *my* spouse,
With me from Lebanon.
Look from the top of Amana,
From the top of Senir [a]and Hermon,
From the lions' dens,
From the mountains of the leopards.

9 You have ravished my heart,
My sister, *my* spouse;
You have ravished my heart
With one *look* of your eyes,
With one link of your necklace.
10 How fair is your love,
My sister, *my* spouse!
[a]How much better than wine is your love,
And the scent of your perfumes
Than all spices!
11 Your lips, O *my* spouse,
Drip as the honeycomb;
[a]Honey and milk *are* under your tongue;
And the fragrance of your garments
Is [b]like the fragrance of Lebanon.

12 A garden enclosed
Is my sister, *my* spouse,
A spring shut up,
A fountain sealed.
13 Your plants *are* an orchard of
pomegranates
With pleasant fruits,
Fragrant henna with spikenard,
14 Spikenard and saffron,
Calamus and cinnamon,
With all trees of frankincense,
Myrrh and aloes,
With all the chief spices—
15 A fountain of gardens,
A well of [a]living waters,
And streams from Lebanon.

THE SHULAMITE

16 Awake, O north *wind*,
And come, O south!
Blow upon my garden,
That its spices may flow out.
[a]Let my beloved come to his garden
And eat its pleasant [b]fruits.

THE BELOVED

5 I [a]have come to my garden, my [b]sister,
my spouse;
I have gathered my myrrh with my spice;
[c]I have eaten my honeycomb with my
honey;
I have drunk my wine with my milk.

(TO HIS FRIENDS)

Eat, O [d]friends!
Drink, yes, drink deeply,
O beloved ones!

KJV

The Shulamite's Troubled Evening

2 I sleep, but my heart waketh: *it is* the voice
of my beloved [a]that knocketh, *saying,* Open to
me, my sister, my love, my dove, my undefiled:
for my head is filled with dew, *and* my locks with
the drops of the night.
3 I have put off my coat; how shall I put it
on? I have washed my feet; how shall I defile
them?
4 My beloved put in his hand by the hole
of the door, and my bowels were moved for him.
5 I rose up to open to my beloved; and my
hands dropped *with* myrrh, and my fingers *with*
sweet smelling myrrh, upon the handles of the
lock.
6 I opened to my beloved; but my beloved
had withdrawn himself, *and* was gone: my soul
failed when he spake: [a]I sought him, but I could
not find him; I called him, but he gave me no
answer.
7 [a]The watchmen that went about the city
found me, they smote me, they wounded me; the
keepers of the walls took away my veil from me.
8 I charge you, O daughters of Jerusalem,
if ye find my beloved, that ye tell him, that I *am*
sick of love.
9 What *is* thy beloved more than *another*
beloved, [a]O thou fairest among women? what *is*
thy beloved more than *another* beloved, that thou
dost so charge us?
10 My beloved *is* white and ruddy, the chiefest among ten thousand.
11 His head *is as* the most fine gold, his locks
are bushy, *and* black as a raven.
12 [a]His eyes *are* as *the eyes* of doves by the
rivers of waters, washed with milk, *and* fitly set.
13 His cheeks *are* as a bed of spices, *as* sweet
flowers: his lips *like* lilies, dropping sweet smelling myrrh.
14 His hands *are as* gold rings set with the
beryl: his belly *is as* bright ivory overlaid *with*
sapphires.
15 His legs *are as* pillars of marble, set upon
sockets of fine gold: his countenance *is* as Lebanon, excellent as the cedars.
16 His mouth *is* most sweet: yea, he *is* altogether lovely. This *is* my beloved, and this *is*
my friend, O daughters of Jerusalem.

6 Whither is thy beloved gone, [a]O thou fairest
among women? whither is thy beloved turned
aside? that we may seek him with thee.

2 [a]Rev. 3:20
6 [a]Song 3:1
7 [a]Song 3:3
9 [a]Song 1:8; 6:1
12 [a]Song 1:15; 4:1

CHAPTER 6
1 [a]Song 1:8; 5:9

NKJV

The Shulamite's Troubled Evening

THE SHULAMITE

2 I sleep, but my heart is awake;
It is the voice of my beloved!
[a]He knocks, *saying,*
"Open for me, my sister, my love,
My dove, my perfect one;
For my head is covered with dew,
My locks with the drops of the night."

3 I have taken off my robe;
How can I put it on *again?*
I have washed my feet;
How can I defile them?
4 My beloved put his hand
By the latch *of the door,*
And my heart yearned for him.
5 I arose to open for my beloved,
And my hands dripped *with* myrrh,
My fingers with liquid myrrh,
On the handles of the lock.

6 I opened for my beloved,
But my beloved had turned away *and* was
gone.
My heart leaped up when he spoke.
[a]I sought him, but I could not find him;
I called him, but he gave me no answer.
7 [a]The watchmen who went about the city
found me.
They struck me, they wounded me;
The keepers of the walls
Took my veil away from me.
8 I charge you, O daughters of Jerusalem,
If you find my beloved,
That you tell him I *am* lovesick!

THE DAUGHTERS OF JERUSALEM

9 What *is* your beloved
More than *another* beloved,
[a]O fairest among women?
What *is* your beloved
More than *another* beloved,
That you so charge us?

THE SHULAMITE

10 My beloved *is* white and ruddy,
Chief among ten thousand.
11 His head *is like* the finest gold;
His locks *are* wavy,
And black as a raven.
12 [a]His eyes *are* like doves
By the rivers of waters,
Washed with milk,
And fitly set.
13 His cheeks *are* like a bed of
spices,
Banks of scented herbs.
His lips *are* lilies,
Dripping liquid myrrh.

14 His hands *are* rods of gold
Set with beryl.
His body *is* carved ivory
Inlaid *with* sapphires.
15 His legs *are* pillars of marble
Set on bases of fine gold.
His countenance *is* like Lebanon,
Excellent as the cedars.
16 His mouth *is* most sweet,
Yes, he *is* altogether lovely.
This *is* my beloved,
And this *is* my friend,
O daughters of Jerusalem!

THE DAUGHTERS OF JERUSALEM

6 Where has your beloved gone,
[a]O fairest among women?
Where has your beloved turned
aside,
That we may seek him with you?

KJV

2 My beloved is gone down into his [a]garden,
to the beds of spices, to feed in the gardens, and
to gather lilies.
3 [a]I *am* my beloved's, and my beloved *is*
mine: he feedeth among the lilies.

Praise of the Shulamite's Beauty

4 Thou *art* beautiful, O my love, as Tirzah,
comely as Jerusalem, terrible as *an army* with
banners.
5 Turn away thine eyes from me, for they
have overcome me: thy hair *is* [a]as a flock of goats
that appear from Gilead.
6 [a]Thy teeth *are* as a flock of sheep which
go up from the washing, whereof every one beareth twins, and *there is* not one barren among
them.
7 [a]As a piece of a pomegranate *are* thy temples within thy locks.
8 There are threescore queens, and fourscore concubines, and [a]virgins without number.
9 My dove, my [a]undefiled is *but* one; she
is the *only* one of her mother, she *is* the choice
one of her that bare her. The daughters saw her,
and blessed her; *yea*, the queens and the concubines, and they praised her.
10 Who *is* she *that* looketh forth as the morning, fair as the moon, clear as the sun, [a]*and* terrible as *an army* with banners?
11 I went down into the garden of nuts to
see the fruits of the valley, *and* [a]to see whether
the vine flourished, *and* the pomegranates
budded.
12 Or ever I was aware, my soul made me
like the chariots of Ammi–nadib.
13 Return, return, O Shulamite; return, return, that we may look upon thee. What will ye
see in the Shulamite? As it were the company of
two armies.

Expressions of Praise

7 How beautiful are thy feet with shoes, [a]O
prince's daughter! the joints of thy thighs *are*
like jewels, the work of the hands of a cunning
workman.
2 Thy navel *is like* a round goblet, *which*
wanteth not liquor: thy belly *is like* an heap of
wheat set about with lilies.
3 [a]Thy two breasts *are* like two young roes
that are twins.
4 [a]Thy neck *is* as a tower of ivory; thine
eyes *like* the fishpools in Heshbon, by the gate
of Bath–rabbim: thy nose *is* as the tower of Lebanon which looketh toward Damascus.

2 [a]Song 4:16; 5:1
3 [a]Song 2:16; 7:10
5 [a]Song 4:1
6 [a]Song 4:2
7 [a]Song 4:3
8 [a]Song 1:3
9 [a]Song 2:14; 5:2
10 [a]Song 6:4
11 [a]Song 7:12

CHAPTER 7
1 [a]Ps. 45:13
3 [a]Song 4:5
4 [a]Song 4:4

*
6:12 Heb. *Ammi Nadib*
6:13 Heb. *Mahanaim*

NKJV

THE SHULAMITE

2 My beloved has gone to his [a]garden,
To the beds of spices,
To feed *his flock* in the gardens,
And to gather lilies.
3 [a]I *am* my beloved's,
And my beloved *is* mine.
He feeds *his flock* among the lilies.

Praise of the Shulamite's Beauty

THE BELOVED

4 O my love, you *are as* beautiful as
Tirzah,
Lovely as Jerusalem,
Awesome as *an army* with banners!
5 Turn your eyes away from me,
For they have overcome me.
Your hair *is* [a]like a flock of goats
Going down from Gilead.
6 [a]Your teeth *are* like a flock of sheep
Which have come up from the washing;
Every one bears twins,
And none *is* barren among them.
7 [a]Like a piece of pomegranate
Are your temples behind your veil.

8 There are sixty queens
And eighty concubines,
And [a]virgins without number.
9 My dove, my [a]perfect one,
Is the only one,
The only one of her mother,
The favorite of the one who bore her.
The daughters saw her
And called her blessed,
The queens and the concubines,
And they praised her.

10 Who is she who looks forth as the
morning,
Fair as the moon,
Clear as the sun,
[a]Awesome as *an army* with banners?

THE SHULAMITE

11 I went down to the garden of nuts
To see the verdure of the valley,
[a]To see whether the vine had budded
And the pomegranates had bloomed.
12 Before I was even aware,
My soul had made me
As the chariots of *my noble people.

THE BELOVED AND HIS FRIENDS

13 Return, return, O Shulamite;
Return, return, that we may look upon
you!

THE SHULAMITE

What would you see in the Shulamite—
As it were, the dance of *the two camps?

Expressions of Praise

THE BELOVED

7 How beautiful are your feet in sandals,
[a]O prince's daughter!
The curves of your thighs *are* like jewels,
The work of the hands of a skillful
workman.
2 Your navel *is* a rounded goblet;
It lacks no blended beverage.
Your waist *is* a heap of wheat
Set about with lilies.
3 [a]Your two breasts *are* like two fawns,
Twins of a gazelle.
4 [a]Your neck *is* like an ivory tower,
Your eyes *like* the pools in Heshbon
By the gate of Bath Rabbim.
Your nose *is* like the tower of Lebanon
Which looks toward Damascus.

KJV

5 Thine head upon thee *is* like Carmel, and
the hair of thine head like purple; the king *is* held
in the galleries.
6 How fair and how pleasant art thou, O
love, for delights!
7 This thy stature is like to a palm tree, and
thy breasts to clusters *of grapes.*
8 I said, I will go up to the palm tree, I will
take hold of the boughs thereof: now also thy
breasts shall be as clusters of the vine, and the
smell of thy nose like apples;
9 And the roof of thy mouth like the best
wine for my beloved, that goeth *down* sweetly,
causing the lips of those that are asleep to speak.
10 [a]I *am* my beloved's, and [b]his desire *is* toward me.
11 Come, my beloved, let us go forth into the
field; let us lodge in the villages.
12 Let us get up early to the vineyards; let
us [a]see if the vine flourish, *whether* the tender
grape appear, *and* the pomegranates bud forth:
there will I give thee my loves.
13 The [a]mandrakes give a smell, and at our
gates [b]*are* all manner of pleasant *fruits,* new and
old, *which* I have laid up for thee, O my beloved.

10 [a]Song 2:16; 6:3 [b]Ps. 45:11
12 [a]Song 6:11
13 [a]Gen. 30:14 [b]Song 2:3; 4:13, 16; Matt. 13:52

NKJV

5 Your head *crowns* you like *Mount*
Carmel,
And the hair of your head *is* like purple;
A king *is* held captive by *your* tresses.

6 How fair and how pleasant you are,
O love, with your delights!
7 This stature of yours is like a palm
tree,
And your breasts *like* its clusters.
8 I said, "I will go up to the palm tree,
I will take hold of its branches."
Let now your breasts be like clusters of
the vine,
The fragrance of your breath like apples,
9 And the roof of your mouth like the best
wine.

THE SHULAMITE

The wine goes *down* smoothly for my
beloved,
Moving gently the *lips of sleepers.
10 [a]I *am* my beloved's,
And [b]his desire *is* toward me.

11 Come, my beloved,
Let us go forth to the field;
Let us lodge in the villages.
12 Let us get up early to the vineyards;
Let us [a]see if the vine has budded,
Whether the grape blossoms are open,
And the pomegranates are in bloom.
There I will give you my love.
13 The [a]mandrakes give off a fragrance,
And at our gates [b]*are* pleasant *fruits,*
All manner, new and old,
Which I have laid up for you, my beloved.

KJV

8 O that thou *wert* as my brother, that sucked
the breasts of my mother! *when* I should find
thee without, I would kiss thee; yea, I should not
be despised.
2 I would lead thee, *and* bring thee into my
mother's [a]house, *who* would instruct me: I would
cause thee to drink of [b]spiced wine of the juice
of my pomegranate.
3 [a]His left hand *should be* under my head,
and his right hand should embrace me.
4 [a]I charge you, O daughters of Jerusalem,
that ye stir not up, nor awake *my* love, until he
please.

Love Renewed in Lebanon

5 [a]Who *is* this that cometh up from the wilderness, leaning upon her beloved? I raised thee
up under the apple tree: there thy mother brought
thee forth: there she brought thee forth *that* bare
thee.
6 [a]Set me as a seal upon thine heart, as a
seal upon thine arm: for love *is* strong as death;
[b]jealousy *is* cruel as the grave: the coals thereof
are coals of fire, *which hath* a most vehement
flame.
7 Many waters cannot quench love, neither
can the floods drown it: [a]if a man would give all
the substance of his house for love, it would utterly be contemned.

CHAPTER 8
2 [a]Song 3:4 [b]Prov. 9:2
3 [a]Song 2:6
4 [a]Song 2:7; 3:5
5 [a]Song 3:6
6 [a]Is. 49:16; Jer. 22:24; Hag. 2:23 [b]Prov. 6:34, 35
7 [a]Prov. 6:35

NKJV

8 Oh, that you were like my brother,
Who nursed at my mother's breasts!
If I should find you outside,
I would kiss you;
I would not be despised.
2 I would lead you *and* bring you
Into the [a]house of my mother,
She *who* used to instruct me.
I would cause you to drink of [b]spiced
wine,
Of the juice of my pomegranate.

(TO THE DAUGHTERS OF JERUSALEM)

3 [a]His left hand *is* under my head,
And his right hand embraces me.
4 [a]I charge you, O daughters of Jerusalem,
Do not stir up nor awaken love
Until it pleases.

Love Renewed in Lebanon

A RELATIVE

5 [a]Who *is* this coming up from the
wilderness,
Leaning upon her beloved?

I awakened you under the apple tree.
There your mother brought you forth;
There she *who* bore you brought *you*
forth.

THE SHULAMITE TO HER BELOVED

6 [a]Set me as a seal upon your heart,
As a seal upon your arm;
For love *is as* strong as death,
[b]Jealousy *as* cruel as *the grave;
Its flames *are* flames of fire,
*A most vehement flame.
7 Many waters cannot quench love,
Nor can the floods drown it.
[a]If a man would give for love
All the wealth of his house,
It would be utterly despised.

7:9 LXX, Syr., Vg. *lips and teeth.*
8:6 Or *Sheol* • Lit. *A flame of* YAH, *a poetic form of* YHWH, *the* LORD

KJV

8 [a]We have a little sister, and she hath no
breasts: what shall we do for our sister in the day
when she shall be spoken for?
9 If she *be* a wall, we will build upon her a
palace of silver: and if she *be* a door, we will in-
close her with boards of cedar.
10 I *am* a wall, and my breasts like towers:
then was I in his eyes as one that found favour.
11 Solomon had a vineyard at Baal–hamon;
[a]he let out the vineyard unto keepers; every one
for the fruit thereof was to bring a thousand *pieces*
of silver.
12 My vineyard, which *is* mine, *is* before me:
thou, O Solomon, *must have* a thousand, and
those that keep the fruit thereof two hundred.
13 Thou that dwellest in the gardens, the
companions hearken to thy voice: [a]cause me to
hear *it*.
14 [a]Make haste, my beloved, and [b]be thou
like to a roe or to a young hart upon the mountains
of spices.

8 [a]Ezek. 23:33
11 [a]Matt. 21:33
13 [a]Song 2:14
14 [a]Rev. 22:17, 20 [b]Song 2:7, 9, 17

NKJV

THE SHULAMITE'S BROTHERS

8 [a]We have a little sister,
And she has no breasts.
What shall we do for our sister
In the day when she is spoken for?
9 If she *is* a wall,
We will build upon her
A battlement of silver;
And if she *is* a door,
We will enclose her
With boards of cedar.

THE SHULAMITE

10 I *am* a wall,
And my breasts like towers;
Then I became in his eyes
As one who found peace.
11 Solomon had a vineyard at Baal Hamon;
[a]He leased the vineyard to keepers;
Everyone was to bring for its fruit
A thousand silver coins.

(TO SOLOMON)

12 My own vineyard *is* before me.
You, O Solomon, *may have* a thousand,
And those who tend its fruit two hundred.

THE BELOVED

13 You who dwell in the gardens,
The companions listen for your voice—
[a]Let me hear it!

THE SHULAMITE

14 [a]Make haste, my beloved,
And [b]be like a gazelle
Or a young stag
On the mountains of spices.

KJV

THE BOOK OF

ISAIAH

1 The [a]vision of Isaiah the son of Amoz, which he saw concerning Judah and Jerusalem in the [b]days of Uzziah, Jotham, Ahaz, *and* Hezekiah, kings of Judah.

The Wickedness of Judah

2 [a]Hear, O heavens, and give ear, O earth: for the LORD hath spoken, I have nourished and brought up children, and they have rebelled against me.

3 [a]The ox knoweth his owner, and the ass his master's crib: *but* Israel [b]doth not know, my people doth not consider.

4 Ah sinful nation, a people laden with iniquity, [a]a seed of evildoers, children that are corrupters: they have forsaken the LORD, they have provoked the Holy One of Israel unto anger, they are gone away backward.

5 [a]Why should ye be stricken any more? ye will revolt more and more: the whole head is sick, and the whole heart faint.

6 From the sole of the foot even unto the head *there is* no soundness in it; *but* wounds, and bruises, and putrifying sores: they have not been closed, neither bound up, neither mollified with ointment.

7 [a]Your country *is* desolate, your cities *are* burned with fire: your land, strangers devour it in your presence, and *it is* desolate, as overthrown by strangers.

8 And the daughter of Zion is left [a]as a cottage in a vineyard, as a lodge in a garden of cucumbers, [b]as a besieged city.

9 [a]Except the LORD of hosts had left unto us a very small remnant, we should have been as [b]Sodom, *and* we should have been like unto Gomorrah.

10 Hear the word of the LORD, ye rulers [a]of Sodom; give ear unto the law of our God, ye people of Gomorrah.

11 To what purpose *is* the multitude of your [a]sacrifices unto me? saith the LORD: I am full of the burnt offerings of rams, and the fat of fed beasts; and I delight not in the blood of bullocks, or of lambs, or of he goats.

CHAPTER 1

1 [a]Num. 12:6 [b]2 Chr. 26—32
2 [a]Jer. 2:12
3 [a]Jer. 8:7 [b]Jer. 9:3, 6
4 [a]Is. 57:3, 4; Matt. 3:7
5 [a]Jer. 5:3
7 [a]Deut. 28:51, 52; 2 Chr. 36:19
8 [a]Job 27:18 [b]Jer. 4:17
9 [a]2 Kin. 25:11, 22; Lam. 3:22 [b]Gen. 19:24; Rom. 9:29
10 [a]Deut. 32:32
11 [a][1 Sam. 15:22]

NKJV

THE BOOK OF

ISAIAH

1 The [a]vision of Isaiah the son of Amoz, which he saw concerning Judah and Jerusalem in the [b]days of Uzziah, Jotham, Ahaz, *and* Hezekiah, kings of Judah.

The Wickedness of Judah

2 [a]Hear, O heavens, and give ear, O earth!
For the LORD has spoken:
"I have nourished and brought up children,
And they have rebelled against Me;
3 [a]The ox knows its owner
And the donkey its master's crib;
But Israel [b]does not know,
My people do not consider."

4 Alas, sinful nation,
A people laden with iniquity,
[a]A brood of evildoers,
Children who are corrupters!
They have forsaken the LORD,
They have provoked to anger
The Holy One of Israel,
They have turned away backward.

5 [a]Why should you be stricken again?
You will revolt more and more.
The whole head is sick,
And the whole heart faints.
6 From the sole of the foot even to the head,
There is no soundness in it,
But wounds and bruises and putrefying sores;
They have not been closed or bound up,
Or soothed with ointment.

7 [a]Your country *is* desolate,
Your cities *are* burned with fire;
Strangers devour your land in your presence;
And *it is* desolate, as overthrown by strangers.
8 So the daughter of Zion is left [a]as a booth in a vineyard,
As a hut in a garden of cucumbers,
[b]As a besieged city.
9 [a]Unless the LORD of hosts
Had left to us a very small remnant,
We would have become like [b]Sodom,
We would have been made like Gomorrah.

10 Hear the word of the LORD,
You rulers [a]of Sodom;
Give ear to the law of our God,
You people of Gomorrah:
11 "To what purpose *is* the multitude of your [a]sacrifices to Me?"
Says the LORD.
"I have had enough of burnt offerings of rams
And the fat of fed cattle.
I do not delight in the blood of bulls,
Or of lambs or goats.

KJV

12 When ye come [a]to appear before me, who
hath required this at your hand, to tread my
courts?
13 Bring no more [a]vain oblations; incense is
an abomination unto me; the new moons and sabbaths, [b]the calling of assemblies, I cannot away
with; *it is* iniquity, even the solemn meeting.
14 Your [a]new moons and your [b]appointed
feasts my soul hateth: they are a trouble unto me;
I am weary to bear *them*.
15 And [a]when ye spread forth your hands, I
will hide mine eyes from you: [b]yea, when ye make
many prayers, I will not hear: your hands are full
of blood.
16 [a]Wash you, make you clean; put away the
evil of your doings from before mine eyes; [b]cease
to do evil;
17 Learn to do well; seek judgment, relieve
the oppressed, judge the fatherless, plead for the
widow.
18 Come now, and let us [a]reason together,
saith the LORD: though your sins be as scarlet,
[b]they shall be as white as snow; though they be
red like crimson, they shall be as wool.
19 If ye be willing and obedient, ye shall eat
the good of the land:
20 But if ye refuse and rebel, ye shall be devoured with the sword: [a]for the mouth of the LORD
hath spoken *it*.

The Degenerate City

21 [a]How is the faithful city become an harlot!
it was full of judgment; righteousness lodged in
it; but now [b]murderers.
22 [a]Thy silver is become dross, thy wine
mixed with water:
23 [a]Thy princes *are* rebellious, and [b]compan-
ions of thieves: [c]every one loveth gifts, and followeth after rewards: they [d]judge not the fatherless, neither doth the cause of the widow come
unto them.
24 Therefore saith the Lord, the LORD of
hosts, the mighty One of Israel, Ah, [a]I will ease
me of mine adversaries, and avenge me of mine
enemies:
25 And I will turn my hand upon thee, and
[a]purely purge away thy dross, and take away all
thy tin:
26 And I will restore thy judges [a]as at the
first, and thy counsellors as at the beginning: afterward [b]thou shalt be called, The city of righteousness, the faithful city.
27 Zion shall be redeemed with judgment,
and her converts with righteousness.
28 And the [a]destruction of the transgressors
and of the sinners *shall be* together, and they that
forsake the LORD shall be consumed.
29 For they shall be ashamed of the oaks
which ye have desired, and ye shall be confounded for the gardens that ye have chosen.

12 [a]Ex. 23:17
13 [a]Matt. 15:9 [b]Joel 1:14
14 [a]Num. 28:11 [b]Lam. 2:6
15 [a]Prov. 1:28 [b]Ps. 66:18; Is. 59:1–3; Mic. 3:4
16 [a]Jer. 4:14 [b]Rom. 12:9
18 [a]Is. 43:26; Mic. 6:2 [b]Ps. 51:7; [Is. 43:25]; Rev. 7:14
20 [a]Is. 40:5; 58:14; Mic. 4:4; [Titus 1:2]
21 [a]Is. 57:3–9; Jer. 2:20 [b]Mic. 3:1–3
22 [a]Jer. 6:28
23 [a]Hos. 9:15 [b]Prov. 29:24 [c]Jer. 22:17 [d]Is. 10:2; Jer. 5:28; Ezek. 22:7; Zech. 7:10
24 [a]Deut. 28:63
25 [a]Is. 48:10; Ezek. 22:19–22; Mal. 3:3
26 [a]Jer. 33:7–11 [b]Is. 33:5; Zech. 8:3
28 [a]Job 31:3; Ps. 9:5; [Is. 66:24; 2 Thess. 1:8, 9]

NKJV

12 "When you come [a]to appear before Me,
Who has required this from your hand,
To trample My courts?
13 Bring no more [a]futile sacrifices;
Incense is an abomination to Me.
The New Moons, the Sabbaths, and [b]the calling of assemblies—
I cannot endure iniquity and the sacred meeting.
14 Your [a]New Moons and your [b]appointed feasts
My soul hates;
They are a trouble to Me,
I am weary of bearing *them*.
15 [a]When you spread out your hands,
I will hide My eyes from you;
[b]Even though you make many prayers,
I will not hear.
Your hands are full of blood.

16 "Wash[a] yourselves, make yourselves clean;
Put away the evil of your doings from before My eyes.
[b]Cease to do evil,
17 Learn to do good;
Seek justice,
Rebuke *the oppressor;
Defend the fatherless,
Plead for the widow.

18 "Come now, and let us [a]reason together,"
Says the LORD,
"Though your sins are like scarlet,
[b]They shall be as white as snow;
Though they are red like crimson,
They shall be as wool.
19 If you are willing and obedient,
You shall eat the good of the land;
20 But if you refuse and rebel,
You shall be devoured by the sword";
[a]For the mouth of the LORD has spoken.

The Degenerate City

21 [a]How the faithful city has become a harlot!
It was full of justice;
Righteousness lodged in it,
But now [b]murderers.
22 [a]Your silver has become dross,
Your wine mixed with water.
23 [a]Your princes *are* rebellious,
And [b]companions of thieves;
[c]Everyone loves bribes,
And follows after rewards.
They [d]do not defend the fatherless,
Nor does the cause of the widow come before them.

24 Therefore the Lord says,
The LORD of hosts, the Mighty One of Israel,
"Ah, [a]I will rid Myself of My adversaries,
And take vengeance on My enemies.
25 I will turn My hand against you,
And [a]thoroughly purge away your dross,
And take away all your alloy.
26 I will restore your judges [a]as at the first,
And your counselors as at the beginning.
Afterward [b]you shall be called the city of righteousness, the faithful city."

27 Zion shall be redeemed with justice,
And her penitents with righteousness.
28 The [a]destruction of transgressors and of sinners *shall be* together,
And those who forsake the LORD shall be consumed.
29 For *they shall be ashamed of the terebinth trees
Which you have desired;
And you shall be embarrassed because of the gardens
Which you have chosen.

*

1:17 Some ancient vss. *the oppressed*
1:29 So with MT, LXX, Vg.; some Heb. mss., Tg. *you*

KJV

30 For ye shall be as an oak whose leaf
fadeth, and as a garden that hath no water.
31 [a]And the strong shall be as tow, and the
maker of it as a spark, and they shall both burn
together, and none shall [b]quench *them.*

The Future House of God
(Mic. 4:1–5)

2 The word that Isaiah the son of Amoz saw
concerning Judah and Jerusalem.
2 And [a]it shall come to pass [b]in the last
days, [c]*that* the mountain of the LORD's house shall
be established in the top of the mountains, and
shall be exalted above the hills; and all nations
shall flow unto it.
3 And many people shall go and say, [a]Come
ye, and let us go up to the mountain of the LORD,
to the house of the God of Jacob; and he will teach
us of his ways, and we will walk in his paths:
[b]for out of Zion shall go forth the law, and the
word of the LORD from Jerusalem.
4 And he shall judge among the nations, and
shall rebuke many people: and they shall beat
their swords into plowshares, and their spears
into pruninghooks: nation shall not lift up sword
against nation, neither shall they learn war any
more.

The Day of the LORD

5 O house of Jacob, come ye, and let us
[a]walk in the light of the LORD.
6 Therefore thou hast forsaken thy people
the house of Jacob, because they be replenished
[a]from the east, and [b]*are* soothsayers like the Philistines, [c]and they please themselves in the children of strangers.
7 [a]Their land also is full of silver and gold,
neither *is there any* end of their treasures; their
land is also full of horses, neither *is there any*
end of their chariots:
8 [a]Their land also is full of idols; they worship the work of their own hands, that which their
own fingers have made:
9 And the mean man boweth down, and the
great man humbleth himself: therefore forgive
them not.
10 [a]Enter into the rock, and hide thee in the
dust, for fear of the LORD, and for the glory of
his majesty.
11 The lofty looks of man shall be [a]humbled,
and the haughtiness of men shall be bowed down,
and the LORD alone shall be exalted [b]in that day.
12 For the day of the LORD of hosts *shall be*
upon every *one that is* proud and lofty, and upon
every *one that is* lifted up; and he shall be brought
low:
13 And upon all [a]the cedars of Lebanon, *that*
are high and lifted up, and upon all the oaks of
Bashan,
14 And [a]upon all the high mountains, and
upon all the hills *that are* lifted up,

31 [a]Ezek. 32:21 [b]Is. 66:24; Matt. 3:12; Mark 9:43

CHAPTER 2

2 [a]Mic. 4:1 [b]Gen. 49:1 [c]Ps. 68:15
3 [a]Jer. 50:5; [Zech. 8:21–23; 14:16–21] [b]Luke 24:47
5 [a]Eph. 5:8
6 [a]Num. 23:7 [b]Deut. 18:14 [c]Ps. 106:35
7 [a]Deut. 17:16; Is. 30:16; 31:1; Mic. 5:10
8 [a]Is. 40:19, 20; Jer. 2:28
10 [a]Is. 2:19, 21; Rev. 6:15, 16
11 [a]Prov. 16:5; Is. 5:15 [b]Hos. 2:16
13 [a]Is. 14:8; Zech. 11:1, 2
14 [a]Is. 30:25

NKJV

30 For you shall be as a terebinth whose leaf
fades,
And as a garden that has no water.
31 [a]The strong shall be as tinder,
And the work of it as a spark;
Both will burn together,
And no one shall [b]quench *them.*

The Future House of God
(Mic. 4:1–5)

2 The word that Isaiah the son of Amoz saw
concerning Judah and Jerusalem.

2 Now [a]it shall come to pass [b]in the latter
days
[c]*That* the mountain of the LORD's house
Shall be established on the top of the
mountains,
And shall be exalted above the hills;
And all nations shall flow to it.
3 Many people shall come and say,
[a]"Come, and let us go up to the mountain
of the LORD,
To the house of the God of Jacob;
He will teach us His ways,
And we shall walk in His paths."
[b]For out of Zion shall go forth the law,
And the word of the LORD from
Jerusalem.
4 He shall judge between the nations,
And rebuke many people;
They shall beat their swords into
plowshares,
And their spears into pruning hooks;
Nation shall not lift up sword against
nation,
Neither shall they learn war anymore.

The Day of the LORD

5 O house of Jacob, come and let us [a]walk
In the light of the LORD.

6 For You have forsaken Your people, the
house of Jacob,
Because they are filled [a]with eastern
ways;
They *are* [b]soothsayers like the Philistines,
[c]And they are pleased with the children of
foreigners.
7 [a]Their land is also full of silver and gold,
And there is no end to their treasures;
Their land is also full of horses,
And there is no end to their chariots.
8 [a]Their land is also full of idols;
They worship the work of their own
hands,
That which their own fingers have
made.
9 People bow down,
And each man humbles himself;
Therefore do not forgive them.

10 [a]Enter into the rock, and hide in the
dust,
From the terror of the LORD
And the glory of His majesty.
11 The lofty looks of man shall be [a]humbled,
The haughtiness of men shall be bowed
down,
And the LORD alone shall be exalted [b]in
that day.

12 For the day of the LORD of hosts
Shall come upon everything proud and
lofty,
Upon everything lifted up—
And it shall be brought low—
13 Upon all [a]the cedars of Lebanon *that are*
high and lifted up,
And upon all the oaks of Bashan;
14 [a]Upon all the high mountains,
And upon all the hills *that are* lifted up;

KJV

15 And upon every high tower, and upon
every fenced wall,
16 [a]And upon all the ships of Tarshish, and
upon all pleasant pictures.
17 And the loftiness of man shall be bowed
down, and the haughtiness of men shall be made
low: and the LORD alone shall be exalted in that
day.
18 And the idols he shall utterly abolish.
19 And they shall go into the [a]holes of the
rocks, and into the caves of the earth, [b]for fear
of the LORD, and for the glory of his majesty, when
he ariseth [c]to shake terribly the earth.
20 In that day a man shall cast his idols of
silver, and his idols of gold, which they made *each*
one for himself to worship, to the moles and to
the bats;
21 To go into the clefts of the rocks, and into
the tops of the ragged rocks, for fear of the LORD,
and for the glory of his majesty, when he ariseth
to shake terribly the earth.
22 [a]Cease ye from man, whose [b]breath *is* in
his nostrils: for wherein is he to be accounted of?

Judgment on Judah and Jerusalem

3 For, behold, the Lord, the LORD of hosts, [a]doth
take away from Jerusalem and from Judah
[b]the stay and the staff, the whole stay of bread,
and the whole stay of water,
2 [a]The mighty man, and the man of war,
the judge, and the prophet, and the prudent, and
the ancient,
3 The captain of fifty, and the honourable
man, and the counsellor, and the cunning artificer,
and the eloquent orator.
4 And I will give [a]children *to be* their
princes, and babes shall rule over them.
5 And the people shall be oppressed, every
one by another, and every one by his neighbour:
the child shall behave himself proudly against the
ancient, and the base against the honourable.
6 When a man shall take hold of his brother
of the house of his father, *saying*, Thou hast clothing, be thou our ruler, and *let* this ruin *be* under
thy hand:
7 In that day shall he swear, saying, I will
not be an healer; for in my house *is* neither bread
nor clothing: make me not a ruler of the people.
8 For [a]Jerusalem is ruined, and Judah is
fallen: because their tongue and their doings *are*
against the LORD, to provoke the eyes of his glory.
9 The shew of their countenance doth witness against them; and they declare their sin as
[a]Sodom, they hide *it* not. Woe unto their soul!
for they have rewarded evil unto themselves.

16 [a]1 Kin. 10:22; Is. 23:1, 14; 60:9
19 [a]Hos. 10:8; [Rev. 9:6] [b][2 Thess. 1:9] [c]Ps. 18:7; Is. 2:21; 13:13; 24:1, 19, 20; Hag. 2:6, 7; Heb. 12:26
22 [a]Ps. 146:3; Jer. 17:5 [b]Job 27:3

CHAPTER 3

1 [a]2 Kin. 25:3; Is. 5:13; Jer. 37:21 [b]Lev. 26:26
2 [a]2 Kin. 24:14; Is. 9:14, 15; Ezek. 17:12, 13
4 [a]Eccl. 10:16
8 [a]2 Chr. 36:16, 17; Mic. 3:12
9 [a]Gen. 13:13; Is. 1:10–15

*
3:6 Lit. *hand*

NKJV

15 Upon every high tower,
And upon every fortified wall;
16 [a]Upon all the ships of Tarshish,
And upon all the beautiful sloops.
17 The loftiness of man shall be bowed down,
And the haughtiness of men shall be
brought low;
The LORD alone will be exalted in that day,
18 But the idols He shall utterly abolish.

19 They shall go into the [a]holes of the rocks,
And into the caves of the earth,
[b]From the terror of the LORD
And the glory of His majesty,
When He arises [c]to shake the earth
mightily.

20 In that day a man will cast away his idols
of silver
And his idols of gold,
Which they made, *each* for himself to
worship,
To the moles and bats,
21 To go into the clefts of the rocks,
And into the crags of the rugged rocks,
From the terror of the LORD
And the glory of His majesty,
When He arises to shake the earth
mightily.

22 [a]Sever yourselves from such a man,
Whose [b]breath *is* in his nostrils;
For of what account is he?

Judgment on Judah and Jerusalem

3 For behold, the Lord, the LORD of hosts,
[a]Takes away from Jerusalem and from
Judah
[b]The stock and the store,
The whole supply of bread and the whole
supply of water;
2 [a]The mighty man and the man of war,
The judge and the prophet,
And the diviner and the elder;
3 The captain of fifty and the honorable
man,
The counselor and the skillful artisan,
And the expert enchanter.

4 "I will give [a]children *to be* their princes,
And babes shall rule over them.
5 The people will be oppressed,
Every one by another and every one by
his neighbor;
The child will be insolent toward the
elder,
And the base toward the honorable."

6 When a man takes hold of his brother
In the house of his father, *saying*,
"You have clothing;
You be our ruler,
And *let* these ruins *be* under your
*power,"
7 In that day he will protest, saying,
"I cannot cure *your* ills,
For in my house *is* neither food nor
clothing;
Do not make me a ruler of the people."

8 For [a]Jerusalem stumbled,
And Judah is fallen,
Because their tongue and their doings
Are against the LORD,
To provoke the eyes of His glory.
9 The look on their countenance witnesses
against them,
And they declare their sin as [a]Sodom;
They do not hide *it*.
Woe to their soul!
For they have brought evil upon
themselves.

KJV

10 Say ye to the righteous, [a]that *it shall be* well *with him:* [b]for they shall eat the fruit of their doings.

11 Woe unto the wicked! [a]*it shall be* ill *with him:* for the reward of his hands shall be given him.

12 *As for* my people, children *are* their oppressors, and women rule over them. O my people, [a]they which lead thee cause *thee* to err, and destroy the way of thy paths.

Oppression and Luxury Condemned

13 The LORD standeth up [a]to plead, and standeth to judge the people.

14 The LORD will enter into judgment with the ancients of his people, and the princes thereof: for ye have eaten up [a]the vineyard; the spoil of the poor *is* in your houses.

15 What mean ye *that* ye [a]beat my people to pieces, and grind the faces of the poor? saith the Lord GOD of hosts.

16 Moreover the LORD saith, Because the daughters of Zion are haughty, and walk with stretched forth necks and wanton eyes, walking and mincing *as* they go, and making a tinkling with their feet:

17 Therefore the LORD will smite with [a]a scab the crown of the head of the daughters of Zion, and the LORD will [b]discover their secret parts.

18 In that day the Lord will take away the bravery of *their* tinkling ornaments *about their feet,* and *their* cauls, and *their* [a]round tires like the moon,

19 The chains, and the bracelets, and the mufflers,

20 The bonnets, and the ornaments of the legs, and the headbands, and the tablets, and the earrings,

21 The rings, and nose jewels,

22 The changeable suits of apparel, and the mantles, and the wimples, and the crisping pins,

23 The glasses, and the fine linen, and the hoods, and the vails.

24 And it shall come to pass, *that* instead of sweet smell there shall be stink; and instead of a girdle a rent; and instead of well set hair [a]baldness; and instead of a stomacher a girding of sackcloth; *and* burning instead of beauty.

25 Thy men shall fall by the sword, and thy mighty in the war.

26 [a]And her gates shall lament and mourn; and she *being* desolate [b]shall sit upon the ground.

4 And [a]in that day seven women shall take hold of one man, saying, We will [b]eat our own bread, and wear our own apparel: only let us be called by thy name, to take away [c]our reproach.

The Renewal of Zion

2 In that day shall [a]the branch of the LORD be beautiful and glorious, and the fruit of the earth

---

10 [a][Deut. 28:1–14; Eccl. 8:12; Is. 54:17] [b]Ps. 128:2
11 [a][Ps. 11:6; Eccl. 8:12, 13]
12 [a]Is. 9:16
13 [a]Is. 66:16; Hos. 4:1; Mic. 6:2
14 [a]Matt. 21:33
15 [a]Mic. 3:2, 3
17 [a]Deut. 28:27 [b]Jer. 13:22
18 [a]Judg. 8:21, 26
24 [a]Is. 22:12; Ezek. 27:31; Amos 8:10
26 [a]Jer. 14:2; Lam. 1:4 [b]Lam. 2:10

CHAPTER 4
1 [a]Is. 2:11, 17 [b]2 Thess. 3:12 [c]Luke 1:25
2 [a]Is. 12:1–6; [Jer. 23:5]; Zech. 3:8

NKJV

10 "Say to the righteous [a]that *it shall be* well
with them,
[b]For they shall eat the fruit of their doings.
11 Woe to the wicked! [a]*It shall be* ill *with him,*
For the reward of his hands shall be given
him.
12 *As for* My people, children *are* their
oppressors,
And women rule over them.
O My people! [a]Those who lead you cause
you to err,
And destroy the way of your paths."

Oppression and Luxury Condemned

13 The LORD stands up [a]to plead,
And stands to judge the people.
14 The LORD will enter into judgment
With the elders of His people
And His princes:
"For you have eaten up [a]the vineyard;
The plunder of the poor *is* in your houses.
15 What do you mean by [a]crushing My
people
And grinding the faces of the poor?"
Says the Lord GOD of hosts.

16 Moreover the LORD says:

"Because the daughters of Zion are
haughty,
And walk with outstretched necks
And wanton eyes,
Walking and mincing *as* they go,
Making a jingling with their feet,
17 Therefore the Lord will strike with [a]a scab
The crown of the head of the daughters
of Zion,
And the LORD will [b]uncover their secret
parts."

18 In that day the Lord will take away the
finery:
The jingling anklets, the scarves, and the
[a]crescents;
19 The pendants, the bracelets, and the veils;
20 The headdresses, the leg ornaments, and
the headbands;
The perfume boxes, the charms,
21 and the rings;
The nose jewels,
22 the festal apparel, and the mantles;
The outer garments, the purses,
23 and the mirrors;
The fine linen, the turbans, and the robes.

24 And so it shall be:

Instead of a sweet smell there will be a
stench;
Instead of a sash, a rope;
Instead of well-set hair, [a]baldness;
Instead of a rich robe, a girding of
sackcloth;
And branding instead of beauty.
25 Your men shall fall by the sword,
And your mighty in the war.

26 [a]Her gates shall lament and mourn,
And she *being* desolate [b]shall sit on the
ground.

4 And [a]in that day seven women shall take
hold of one man, saying,
"We will [b]eat our own food and wear our
own apparel;
Only let us be called by your name,
To take away [c]our reproach."

The Renewal of Zion

2 In that day [a]the Branch of the LORD shall
be beautiful and glorious;

KJV

shall be excellent and comely for them that are
escaped of Israel.
3 And it shall come to pass, *that he that is*
left in Zion, and *he that* remaineth in Jerusalem,
[a]shall be called holy, *even* every one that is [b]writ-
ten among the living in Jerusalem:
4 When [a]the Lord shall have washed away
the filth of the daughters of Zion, and shall have
purged the blood of Jerusalem from the midst
thereof by the spirit of judgment, and by the spirit
of burning.
5 And the LORD will create upon every
dwelling place of mount Zion, and upon her assemblies, [a]a cloud and smoke by day, and [b]the
shining of a flaming fire by night: for upon all
the glory *shall be* a defence.
6 And there shall be a tabernacle for a
shadow in the daytime from the heat, and [a]for a
place of refuge, and for a covert from storm and
from rain.

God's Disappointing Vineyard

5 Now will I sing to my wellbeloved a song of
my beloved [a]touching his vineyard. My wellbeloved hath a vineyard in a very fruitful hill:
2 And he fenced it, and gathered out the
stones thereof, and planted it with the choicest
vine, and built a tower in the midst of it, and also
made a winepress therein: [a]and he looked that it
should bring forth grapes, and it brought forth
wild grapes.
3 And now, O inhabitants of Jerusalem, and
men of Judah, [a]judge, I pray you, betwixt me and
my vineyard.
4 What could have been done more to my
vineyard, that I have not done in [a]it? wherefore,
when I looked that it should bring forth grapes,
brought it forth wild grapes?
5 And now go to; I will tell you what I will
do to my vineyard: [a]I will take away the hedge
thereof, and it shall be eaten up; *and* break down
the wall thereof, and it shall be trodden down:
6 And I will lay it [a]waste: it shall not be
pruned, nor digged; but there shall come up briers
and [b]thorns: I will also command the clouds that
they rain no rain upon it.
7 For the vineyard of the LORD of hosts *is*
the house of Israel, and the men of Judah his
pleasant plant: and he looked for judgment, but
behold oppression; for righteousness, but behold
a cry.

Impending Judgment on Excesses

8 Woe unto them that join [a]house to house,
that lay field to field, till *there be* no place, that
they may be placed alone in the midst of the earth!
9 [a]In mine ears *said* the LORD of hosts, Of
a truth many houses shall be desolate, *even* great
and fair, without inhabitant.
10 Yea, ten acres of vineyard shall yield one
[a]bath, and the seed of an homer shall yield an
ephah.

3 [a]Is. 60:21 [b]Phil. 4:3
4 [a]Mal. 3:2, 3
5 [a]Ex. 13:21, 22; Num. 9:15–23 [b]Zech. 2:5
6 [a]Ps. 27:5; Is. 25:4

CHAPTER 5
1 [a]Ps. 80:8; Jer. 2:21; Matt. 21:33; Mark 12:1; Luke 20:9
2 [a]Deut. 32:6
3 [a][Rom. 3:4]
4 [a]2 Chr. 36:15, 16; Jer. 2:5; 7:25, 26; Mic. 6:3; Matt. 23:37
5 [a]2 Chr. 36:19; Ps. 80:12; 89:40, 41
6 [a]2 Chr. 36:19–21 [b]Is. 7:19–25; Jer. 25:11
8 [a]Jer. 22:13–17; Mic. 2:2; Hab. 2:9–12
9 [a]Is. 22:14
10 [a]Ezek. 45:11

NKJV

And the fruit of the earth *shall be* excellent
and appealing
For those of Israel who have escaped.

3 And it shall come to pass that *he who is*
left in Zion and remains in Jerusalem [a]will be
called holy—everyone who is [b]recorded among
the living in Jerusalem.
4 When [a]the Lord has washed away the filth
of the daughters of Zion, and purged the blood
of Jerusalem from her midst, by the spirit of judgment and by the spirit of burning,
5 then the LORD will create above every
dwelling place of Mount Zion, and above her assemblies, [a]a cloud and smoke by day and [b]the
shining of a flaming fire by night. For over all
the glory there *will be* a covering.
6 And there will be a tabernacle for shade
in the daytime from the heat, [a]for a place of refuge, and for a shelter from storm and rain.

God's Disappointing Vineyard

5 Now let me sing to my Well-beloved
A song of my Beloved [a]regarding His
vineyard:

My Well-beloved has a vineyard
On a very fruitful hill.
2 He dug it up and cleared out its stones,
And planted it with the choicest vine.
He built a tower in its midst,
And also made a winepress in it;
[a]So He expected *it* to bring forth *good*
grapes,
But it brought forth wild grapes.

3 "And now, O inhabitants of Jerusalem and
men of Judah,
[a]Judge, please, between Me and My
vineyard.
4 What more could have been done to My
vineyard
That I have not done in [a]it?
Why then, when I expected *it* to bring
forth *good* grapes,
Did it bring forth wild grapes?
5 And now, please let Me tell you what I
will do to My vineyard:
[a]I will take away its hedge, and it shall be
burned;
And break down its wall, and it shall be
trampled down.
6 I will lay it [a]waste;
It shall not be pruned or dug,
But there shall come up briers and
[b]thorns.
I will also command the clouds
That they rain no rain on it."

7 For the vineyard of the LORD of hosts *is*
the house of Israel,
And the men of Judah are His pleasant
plant.
He looked for justice, but behold,
oppression;
For righteousness, but behold, a cry *for
help.*

Impending Judgment on Excesses

8 Woe to those who join [a]house to house;
They add field to field,
Till *there is* no place
Where they may dwell alone in the midst
of the land!
9 [a]In my hearing the LORD of hosts *said,*
"Truly, many houses shall be desolate,
Great and beautiful ones, without
inhabitant.
10 For ten acres of vineyard shall yield one
[a]bath,
And a homer of seed shall yield one
ephah."

KJV

11 [a]Woe unto them that rise up early in the morning, *that* they may follow strong drink; that continue until night, *till* wine inflame them!

12 And [a]the harp, and the viol, the tabret, and pipe, and wine, are in their feasts: but [b]they regard not the work of the LORD, neither consider the operation of his hands.

13 [a]Therefore my people are gone into captivity, because *they have* no [b]knowledge: and their honourable men *are* famished, and their multitude dried up with thirst.

14 Therefore hell hath enlarged herself, and opened her mouth without measure: and their glory, and their multitude, and their pomp, and he that rejoiceth, shall descend into it.

15 And [a]the mean man shall be brought down, and the mighty man shall be humbled, and the eyes of the lofty shall be humbled:

16 But the LORD of hosts shall be [a]exalted in judgment, and God that is holy shall be sanctified in righteousness.

17 Then shall the lambs feed after their manner, and the waste places of [a]the fat ones shall strangers eat.

18 Woe unto them that draw iniquity with cords of vanity, and sin as it were with a cart rope:

19 [a]That say, Let him make speed, *and* hasten his work, that we may see *it:* and let the counsel of the Holy One of Israel draw nigh and come, that we may know *it!*

20 Woe unto them that call evil good, and good evil; that put darkness for light, and light for darkness; that put bitter for sweet, and sweet for bitter!

21 Woe unto *them that are* [a]wise in their own eyes, and prudent in their own sight!

22 Woe unto *them that are* mighty to drink wine, and men of strength to mingle strong drink:

23 Which [a]justify the wicked for reward, and take away the righteousness of the righteous from him!

24 Therefore [a]as the fire devoureth the stubble, and the flame consumeth the chaff, *so* [b]their root shall be as rottenness, and their blossom shall go up as dust: because they have cast away the law of the LORD of hosts, and despised the word of the Holy One of Israel.

25 [a]Therefore is the anger of the LORD kindled against his people, and he hath stretched forth his hand against them, and hath smitten them: and [b]the hills did tremble, and their carcases *were* torn in the midst of the streets. [c]For all this his anger is not turned away, but his hand *is* stretched out still.

11 [a]Prov. 23:29, 30; Eccl. 10:16, 17; Is. 5:22
12 [a]Amos 6:5 [b]Job 34:27; Ps. 28:5
13 [a]2 Kin. 24:14–16 [b]Is. 1:3; 27:11; Hos. 4:6
15 [a]Is. 2:9, 11
16 [a]Is. 2:11
17 [a]Is. 10:16
19 [a]Jer. 17:15; Amos 5:18
21 [a]Prov. 3:7; Rom. 1:22; 12:16; [1 Cor. 3:18–20]
23 [a]Ex. 23:8; Prov. 17:15; Is. 1:23; Mic. 3:11; 7:3
24 [a]Ex. 15:7 [b]Job 18:16
25 [a]2 Kin. 22:13, 17; Is. 66:15 [b]Ps. 18:7; Is. 64:3; Jer. 4:24; Nah. 1:5 [c]Is. 9:12, 17; Jer. 4:8; Dan. 9:16

NKJV

11 [a]Woe to those who rise early in the morning,
That they may follow intoxicating drink;
Who continue until night, *till* wine inflames them!
12 [a]The harp and the strings,
The tambourine and flute,
And wine are in their feasts;
But [b]they do not regard the work of the LORD,
Nor consider the operation of His hands.

13 [a]Therefore my people have gone into captivity,
Because *they have* no [b]knowledge;
Their honorable men *are* famished,
And their multitude dried up with thirst.
14 Therefore Sheol has enlarged itself
And opened its mouth beyond measure;
Their glory and their multitude and their pomp,
And he who is jubilant, shall descend into it.
15 People shall be brought down,
[a]Each man shall be humbled,
And the eyes of the lofty shall be humbled.
16 But the LORD of hosts shall be [a]exalted in judgment,
And God who is holy shall be hallowed in righteousness.
17 Then the lambs shall feed in their pasture,
And in the waste places of [a]the fat ones strangers shall eat.

18 Woe to those who draw iniquity with cords of vanity,
And sin as if with a cart rope;
19 [a]That say, "Let Him make speed *and* hasten His work,
That we may see *it;*
And let the counsel of the Holy One of Israel draw near and come,
That we may know *it.*"

20 Woe to those who call evil good, and good evil;
Who put darkness for light, and light for darkness;
Who put bitter for sweet, and sweet for bitter!

21 Woe to *those who are* [a]wise in their own eyes,
And prudent in their own sight!

22 Woe to men mighty at drinking wine,
Woe to men valiant for mixing intoxicating drink,
23 Who [a]justify the wicked for a bribe,
And take away justice from the righteous man!

24 Therefore, [a]as the fire devours the stubble,
And the flame consumes the chaff,
So [b]their root will be as rottenness,
And their blossom will ascend like dust;
Because they have rejected the law of the LORD of hosts,
And despised the word of the Holy One of Israel.
25 [a]Therefore the anger of the LORD is aroused against His people;
He has stretched out His hand against them
And stricken them,
And [b]the hills trembled.
Their carcasses *were* as refuse in the midst of the streets.

[c]For all this His anger is not turned away,
But His hand *is* stretched out still.

KJV

26 [a]And he will lift up an ensign to the nations from far, and will [b]hiss unto them from [c]the end of the earth: and, behold, [d]they shall come with speed swiftly:

27 None shall be weary nor stumble among them; none shall slumber nor sleep; neither [a]shall the girdle of their loins be loosed, nor the latchet of their shoes be broken:

28 [a]Whose arrows *are* sharp, and all their bows bent, their horses' hoofs shall be counted like flint, and their wheels like a whirlwind:

29 Their roaring *shall be* like a lion, they shall roar like young lions: yea, they shall roar, and lay hold of the prey, and shall carry *it* away safe, and none shall deliver *it*.

30 And in that day they shall roar against them like the roaring of the sea: and if *one* [a]look unto the land, behold darkness *and* sorrow, and the light is darkened in the heavens thereof.

Isaiah Called to Be a Prophet
(*cf. Ezek. 1:4–28*)

6 In the year that [a]king Uzziah died I [b]saw also the Lord sitting upon a throne, high and lifted up, and his train filled the temple.

2 Above it stood the seraphims: each one had six wings; with twain he covered his face, and [a]with twain he covered his feet, and with twain he did fly.

3 And one cried unto another, and said, [a]Holy, holy, holy, *is* the LORD of hosts: [b]the whole earth *is* full of his glory.

4 And the posts of the door moved at the voice of him that cried, and the house was filled with smoke.

5 Then said I, Woe *is* me! for I am undone; because I *am* a man of [a]unclean lips, and I dwell in the midst of a people of unclean lips: for mine eyes have seen the King, the LORD of hosts.

6 Then flew one of the seraphims unto me, having a live coal in his hand, *which* he had taken with the tongs from off [a]the altar:

7 And he [a]laid *it* upon my mouth, and said, Lo, this hath touched thy lips; and thine iniquity is taken away, and thy sin purged.

8 Also I heard the voice of the Lord, saying, Whom shall I send, and who will go for [a]us? Then said I, Here *am* I; send me.

9 And he said, Go, and [a]tell this people, Hear ye indeed, but understand not; and see ye indeed, but perceive not.

10 Make [a]the heart of this people fat, and make their ears heavy, and shut their eyes; [b]lest they see with their eyes, and hear with their ears, and understand with their heart, and convert, and be healed.

26 [a]Is. 11:10, 12 [b]Is. 7:18; Zech. 10:8 [c]Mal. 1:11 [d]Joel 2:7
27 [a]Dan. 5:6
28 [a]Jer. 5:16
30 [a]Is. 8:22; Jer. 4:23–28; Joel 2:10; Luke 21:25, 26

CHAPTER 6

1 [a]2 Kin. 15:7; 2 Chr. 26:23; Is. 1:1 [b]John 12:41; Rev. 4:2, 3; 20:11
2 [a]Ezek. 1:11
3 [a]Rev. 4:8 [b]Num. 14:21; Ps. 72:19
5 [a]Ex. 6:12, 30
6 [a]Rev. 8:3
7 [a]Jer. 1:9; Dan. 10:16
8 [a]Gen. 1:26
9 [a]Is. 43:8; Matt. 13:14; Mark 4:12; Luke 8:10; John 12:40; Acts 28:26; Rom. 11:8
10 [a]Ps. 119:70; Mark 6:1–6; Acts 7:51; Rom. 10:1–4 [b]Jer. 5:21

NKJV

26 [a]He will lift up a banner to the nations from afar,
And will [b]whistle to them from [c]the end of the earth;
Surely [d]they shall come with speed, swiftly.
27 No one will be weary or stumble among them,
No one will slumber or sleep;
Nor [a]will the belt on their loins be loosed,
Nor the strap of their sandals be broken;
28 [a]Whose arrows *are* sharp,
And all their bows bent;
Their horses' hooves will seem like flint,
And their wheels like a whirlwind.
29 Their roaring *will be* like a lion,
They will roar like young lions;
Yes, they will roar
And lay hold of the prey;
They will carry *it* away safely,
And no one will deliver.
30 In that day they will roar against them
Like the roaring of the sea.
And if *one* [a]looks to the land,
Behold, darkness *and* sorrow;
And the light is darkened by the clouds.

Isaiah Called to Be a Prophet
(*cf. Ezek. 1:4–28*)

6 In the year that [a]King Uzziah died, I [b]saw the Lord sitting on a throne, high and lifted up, and the train of His *robe* filled the temple.

2 Above it stood seraphim; each one had six wings: with two he covered his face, [a]with two he covered his feet, and with two he flew.

3 And one cried to another and said:

[a]"Holy, holy, holy *is* the LORD of hosts;
[b]The whole earth *is* full of His glory!"

4 And the posts of the door were shaken by the voice of him who cried out, and the house was filled with smoke.

5 So I said:

"Woe *is* me, for I am undone!
Because I *am* a man of [a]unclean lips,
And I dwell in the midst of a people of unclean lips;
For my eyes have seen the King,
The LORD of hosts."

6 Then one of the seraphim flew to me, having in his hand a live coal *which* he had taken with the tongs from [a]the altar.

7 And he [a]touched my mouth *with it,* and said:

"Behold, this has touched your lips;
Your iniquity is taken away,
And your sin purged."

8 Also I heard the voice of the Lord, saying:

"Whom shall I send,
And who will go for [a]Us?"

Then I said, "Here *am* I! Send me."

9 And He said, "Go, and [a]tell this people:

'Keep on hearing, but do not understand;
Keep on seeing, but do not perceive.'

10 "Make [a]the heart of this people dull,
And their ears heavy,
And shut their eyes;
[b]Lest they see with their eyes,
And hear with their ears,
And understand with their heart,
And return and be healed."

KJV

11 Then said I, Lord, how long? And he answered, [a]Until the cities be wasted without inhabitant, and the houses without man, and the land be utterly desolate,

12 [a]And the LORD have removed men far away, and *there be* a great forsaking in the midst of the land.

13 But yet in it *shall be* a tenth, and *it* shall return, and shall be eaten: as a teil tree, and as an oak, whose substance *is* in them, when they cast *their leaves: so* [a]the holy seed *shall be* the substance thereof.

Isaiah Sent to King Ahaz
(2 Kin. 16:5; 2 Chr. 28:5–15)

7 And it came to pass in the days of [a]Ahaz the son of Jotham, the son of Uzziah, king of Judah, *that* Rezin the king of Syria, and Pekah the son of Remaliah, king of Israel, went up toward Jerusalem to war against [b]it, but could not prevail against it.

2 And it was told the house of David, saying, Syria is confederate with Ephraim. And his heart was moved, and the heart of his people, as the trees of the wood are moved with the wind.

3 Then said the LORD unto Isaiah, Go forth now to meet Ahaz, thou, and Shear–jashub thy son, at the end of the conduit of the upper pool in the highway of the fuller's field;

4 And say unto him, Take heed, and be [a]quiet; fear not, neither be fainthearted for the two tails of these smoking firebrands, for the fierce anger of Rezin with Syria, and of the son of Remaliah.

5 Because Syria, Ephraim, and the son of Remaliah, have taken evil counsel against thee, saying,

6 Let us go up against Judah, and vex it, and let us make a breach therein for us, and set a king in the midst of it, *even* the son of Tabeal:

7 Thus saith the Lord GOD, [a]It shall not stand, neither shall it come to pass.

8 [a]For the head of Syria *is* Damascus, and the head of Damascus *is* Rezin; and within threescore and five years shall Ephraim be broken, that it be not a people.

9 And the head of Ephraim *is* Samaria, and the head of Samaria *is* Remaliah's son. [a]If ye will not believe, surely ye shall not be established.

The Immanuel Prophecy

10 Moreover the LORD spake again unto Ahaz, saying,

11 [a]Ask thee a sign of the LORD thy God; ask it either in the depth, or in the height above.

12 But Ahaz said, I will not ask, neither will I tempt the LORD.

13 And he said, Hear ye now, O house of David; *Is it* a small thing for you to weary men, but will ye weary my God also?

14 Therefore the Lord himself shall give you a sign; [a]Behold, a virgin shall conceive, and bear [b]a son, and shall call his name [c]Immanuel.

15 Butter and honey shall he eat, that he may know to refuse the evil, and choose the good.

16 [a]For before the child shall know to refuse the evil, and choose the good, the land that thou abhorrest shall be forsaken of [b]both her kings.

17 [a]The LORD shall bring upon thee, and upon thy people, and upon thy father's house, days that have not come, from the day that [b]Ephraim departed from Judah; *even* the king of Assyria.

---

11 [a]Mic. 3:12
12 [a]2 Kin. 25:21; Is. 5:9
13 [a]Deut. 7:6; Ezra 9:2

CHAPTER 7

1 [a]2 Chr. 28 [b]2 Kin. 16:5, 9
4 [a]Ex. 14:13; Is. 30:15; Lam. 3:26
7 [a]2 Kin. 16:5; Is. 8:10; Acts 4:25, 26
8 [a]2 Sam. 8:6; 2 Kin. 17:6
9 [a]2 Chr. 20:20; Is. 5:24
11 [a]Matt. 12:38
14 [a]Matt. 1:23; Luke 1:31; John 1:45; Rev. 12:5 [b][Is. 9:6] [c]Is. 8:8, 10
16 [a]Is. 8:4 [b]2 Kin. 15:30
17 [a]2 Chr. 28:19, 20; Is. 8:7, 8; 10:5, 6 [b]1 Kin. 12:16

*

7:3 Lit. *A Remnant Shall Return*
7:14 Lit. *God-With-Us*

NKJV

11 Then I said, "Lord, how long?" And He answered:

[a]"Until the cities are laid waste and without inhabitant,
The houses are without a man,
The land is utterly desolate,
12 [a]The LORD has removed men far away,
And the forsaken places *are* many in the midst of the land.
13 But yet a tenth *will be* in it,
And will return and be for consuming,
As a terebinth tree or as an oak,
Whose stump *remains* when it is cut down.
So [a]the holy seed *shall be* its stump."

Isaiah Sent to King Ahaz
(2 Kin. 16:5; 2 Chr. 28:5–15)

7 Now it came to pass in the days of [a]Ahaz the son of Jotham, the son of Uzziah, king of Judah, *that* Rezin king of Syria and Pekah the son of Remaliah, king of Israel, went up to Jerusalem to *make* war against [b]it, but could not prevail against it.

2 And it was told to the house of David, saying, "Syria's forces are deployed in Ephraim." So his heart and the heart of his people were moved as the trees of the woods are moved with the wind.

3 Then the LORD said to Isaiah, "Go out now to meet Ahaz, you and *Shear-Jashub your son, at the end of the aqueduct from the upper pool, on the highway to the Fuller's Field,

4 "and say to him: 'Take heed, and be [a]quiet; do not fear or be fainthearted for these two stubs of smoking firebrands, for the fierce anger of Rezin and Syria, and the son of Remaliah.

5 'Because Syria, Ephraim, and the son of Remaliah have plotted evil against you, saying,

6 "Let us go up against Judah and trouble it, and let us make a gap in its wall for ourselves, and set a king over them, the son of Tabel"—

7 'thus says the Lord GOD:

[a]"It shall not stand,
Nor shall it come to pass.
8 [a]For the head of Syria *is* Damascus,
And the head of Damascus *is* Rezin.
Within sixty-five years Ephraim will be broken,
So that it will not *be* a people.
9 The head of Ephraim *is* Samaria,
And the head of Samaria *is* Remaliah's son.
[a]If you will not believe,
Surely you shall not be established." ' "

The Immanuel Prophecy

10 Moreover the LORD spoke again to Ahaz, saying,

11 [a]"Ask a sign for yourself from the LORD your God; ask it either in the depth or in the height above."

12 But Ahaz said, "I will not ask, nor will I test the LORD!"

13 Then he said, "Hear now, O house of David! *Is it* a small thing for you to weary men, but will you weary my God also?

14 "Therefore the Lord Himself will give you a sign: [a]Behold, the virgin shall conceive and bear [b]a Son, and shall call His name [c]Immanuel.*

15 "Curds and honey He shall eat, that He may know to refuse the evil and choose the good.

16 [a]"For before the Child shall know to refuse the evil and choose the good, the land that you dread will be forsaken by [b]both her kings.

17 [a]"The LORD will bring the king of Assyria upon you and your people and your father's house—days that have not come since the day that [b]Ephraim departed from Judah."

KJV

18 And it shall come to pass in that day, *that* the LORD [a]shall hiss for the fly that *is* in the uttermost part of the rivers of Egypt, and for the bee that *is* in the land of Assyria.

19 And they shall come, and shall rest all of them in the desolate valleys, and in [a]the holes of the rocks, and upon all thorns, and upon all bushes.

20 In the same day shall the Lord shave with a [b]razor that is [a]hired, *namely*, by them beyond the river, by the king of Assyria, the head, and the hair of the feet: and it shall also consume the beard.

21 And it shall come to pass in that day, *that* a man shall nourish a young cow, and two sheep;

22 And it shall come to pass, for the abundance of milk *that* they shall give he shall eat butter: for butter and honey shall every one eat that is left in the land.

23 And it shall come to pass in that day, *that* every place shall be, where there were a thousand vines at a thousand silverlings, [a]it shall *even* be for briers and thorns.

24 With arrows and with bows shall *men* come thither; because all the land shall become briers and thorns.

25 And *on* all hills that shall be digged with the mattock, there shall not come thither the fear of briers and thorns: but it shall be for the sending forth of oxen, and for the treading of lesser cattle.

Assyria Will Invade the Land

8 Moreover the LORD said unto me, Take thee a great roll, and [a]write in it with a man's pen concerning Maher–shalal–hashbaz.

2 And I took unto me faithful witnesses to record, [a]Uriah the priest, and Zechariah the son of Jeberechiah.

3 And I went unto the prophetess; and she conceived, and bare a son. Then said the LORD to me, Call his name Maher–shalal–hashbaz.

4 [a]For before the child shall have knowledge to cry, My father, and my mother, [b]the riches of Damascus and the spoil of Samaria shall be taken away before the king of Assyria.

5 The LORD spake also unto me again, saying,

6 Forasmuch as this people refuseth the waters of [a]Shiloah that go softly, and rejoice [b]in Rezin and Remaliah's son;

7 Now therefore, behold, the Lord bringeth up upon them the waters of the river, strong and many, *even* the king of Assyria, and all his glory: and he shall come up over all his channels, and go over all his banks:

8 And he shall pass through Judah; he shall overflow and go over, [a]he shall reach *even* to the neck; and the stretching out of his wings shall fill the breadth of thy land, O [b]Immanuel.

9 [a]Associate yourselves, O ye people, and ye shall be broken in pieces; and give ear, all ye of far countries: gird yourselves, and ye shall be

18 [a]Is. 5:26 **19** [a]Is. 2:19; Jer. 16:16 **20** [a]Is. 10:5, 15 [b]2 Kin. 16:7; 2 Chr. 28:20 **23** [a]Is. 5:6

CHAPTER 8

1 [a]Is. 30:8; Hab. 2:2 **2** [a]2 Kin. 16:10 **4** [a]2 Kin. 17:6; Is. 7:16 [b]2 Kin. 15:29 **6** [a]John 9:7 [b]Is. 7:1, 2 **8** [a]Is. 30:28 [b]Is. 7:14; Matt. 1:23 **9** [a]Joel 3:9

*

7:20 The Euphrates
8:1 Lit. *Speed the Spoil, Hasten the Booty*
8:7 The Euphrates
8:8 Lit. *God-With-Us*

NKJV

18 And it shall come to pass in that day
That the LORD [a]will whistle for the fly
That *is* in the farthest part of the rivers
of Egypt,
And for the bee that *is* in the land of
Assyria.
19 They will come, and all of them will rest
In the desolate valleys and in [a]the clefts
of the rocks,
And on all thorns and in all pastures.

20 In the same day the Lord will shave with
a [a]hired [b]razor,
With those from beyond *the River, with
the king of Assyria,
The head and the hair of the legs,
And will also remove the beard.
21 It shall be in that day
That a man will keep alive a young cow
and two sheep;
22 So it shall be, from the abundance of milk
they give,
That he will eat curds;
For curds and honey everyone will eat
who is left in the land.

23 It shall happen in that day,
That wherever there could be a thousand
vines
Worth a thousand *shekels* of silver,
[a]It will be for briers and thorns.
24 With arrows and bows men will come
there,
Because all the land will become briers
and thorns.
25 And to any hill which could be dug with
the hoe,
You will not go there for fear of briers
and thorns;
But it will become a range for oxen
And a place for sheep to roam.

Assyria Will Invade the Land

8 Moreover the LORD said to me, "Take a large scroll, and [a]write on it with a man's pen concerning *Maher-Shalal-Hash-Baz.

2 "And I will take for Myself faithful witnesses to record, [a]Uriah the priest and Zechariah the son of Jeberechiah."

3 Then I went to the prophetess, and she conceived and bore a son. Then the LORD said to me, "Call his name Maher-Shalal-Hash-Baz;

4 [a]"for before the child shall have knowledge to cry 'My father' and 'My mother,' [b]the riches of Damascus and the spoil of Samaria will be taken away before the king of Assyria."

5 The LORD also spoke to me again, saying:

6 "Inasmuch as these people refused
The waters of [a]Shiloah that flow softly,
And rejoice [b]in Rezin and in Remaliah's
son;
7 Now therefore, behold, the Lord brings up
over them
The waters of *the River, strong and
mighty—
The king of Assyria and all his glory;
He will go up over all his channels
And go over all his banks.
8 He will pass through Judah,
He will overflow and pass over,
[a]He will reach up to the neck;
And the stretching out of his wings
Will fill the breadth of Your land, O
[b]Immanuel.*

9 "Be[a] shattered, O you peoples, and be
broken in pieces!
Give ear, all you from far countries.

KJV

broken in pieces; gird yourselves, and ye shall
be broken in pieces.
10 [a]Take counsel together, and it shall come
to nought; speak the word, [b]and it shall not stand:
[c]for God *is* with us.

Fear God, Heed His Word

11 For the LORD spake thus to me with a
strong hand, and instructed me that I should not
walk in the way of this people, saying,
12 Say ye not, A confederacy, to all *them to*
whom this people shall say, A confederacy; neither fear ye their fear, nor be afraid.
13 Sanctify the LORD of hosts himself; and
let him *be* your fear, and *let* him *be* your dread.
14 And [a]he shall be for a sanctuary; but for
[b]a stone of stumbling and for a rock of offence
to both the houses of Israel, for a gin and for a
snare to the inhabitants of Jerusalem.
15 And many among them shall [a]stumble,
and fall, and be broken, and be snared, and be
taken.
16 Bind up the testimony, seal the law among
my disciples.
17 And I will wait upon the LORD, that [a]hideth
his face from the house of Jacob, and I [b]will look
for him.
18 [a]Behold, I and the children whom the
LORD hath given me [b]*are* for signs and for wonders in Israel from the LORD of hosts, which
dwelleth in mount Zion.
19 And when they shall say unto you, [a]Seek
unto them that have familiar spirits, and unto wizards [b]that peep, and that mutter: should not a people seek unto their God? for the living [c]to the
dead?
20 [a]To the law and to the testimony: if they
speak not according to this word, *it is* because
[b]*there is* no light in them.
21 And they shall pass through it, hardly be-
stead and hungry: and it shall come to pass, that
when they shall be hungry, they shall fret themselves, and [a]curse their king and their God, and
look upward.
22 And they shall look unto the earth; and
behold trouble and darkness, dimness of anguish;
and *they shall be* driven to darkness.

The Government of the Promised Son
(Is. 11:1–9)

9 Nevertheless [a]the dimness *shall* not *be* such
as *was* in her vexation, when at the [b]first he
lightly afflicted the land of Zebulun and the land
of Naphtali, and [c]afterward did more grievously
afflict *her by* the way of the sea, beyond Jordan,
in Galilee of the nations.
2 [a]The people that walked in darkness have
seen a great light: they that dwell in the land of
the shadow of death, upon them hath the light
shined.
3 Thou hast multiplied the nation, *and* not
increased the joy: they joy before thee according
to the joy in harvest, *and* as *men* rejoice [a]when
they divide the spoil.

10 [a]Is. 7:7; Acts 5:38 [b]Is. 7:14 [c]Rom. 8:31
14 [a]Is. 4:6; 25:4; Ezek. 11:16 [b]Luke 2:34; 20:17; Rom. 9:33; 1 Pet. 2:8
15 [a]Matt. 21:44
17 [a]Deut. 31:17; Is. 54:8 [b]Hab. 2:3
18 [a]Heb. 2:13 [b]Ps. 71:7
19 [a]1 Sam. 28:8 [b]Is. 29:4 [c]Ps. 106:28
20 [a]Is. 1:10; 8:16; Luke 16:29 [b]Is. 8:22; Mic. 3:6
21 [a]Rev. 16:11

CHAPTER 9

1 [a]Is. 8:22 [b]2 Kin. 15:29; 2 Chr. 16:4 [c]Matt. 4:13–16
2 [a]Matt. 4:16; Luke 1:79; 2 Cor. 4:6; Eph. 5:8
3 [a]Judg. 5:30

*

8:10 Heb. *Immanuel*
9:3 So with Qr., Tg.; Kt., Vg. *not increased joy;* LXX *Most of the people You brought down in Your joy*

NKJV

Gird yourselves, but be broken in pieces;
Gird yourselves, but be broken in pieces.
10 [a]Take counsel together, but it will come to nothing;
Speak the word, [b]but it will not stand,
[c]For *God *is* with us."

Fear God, Heed His Word

11 For the LORD spoke thus to me with a
strong hand, and instructed me that I should not
walk in the way of this people, saying:

12 "Do not say, 'A conspiracy,'
Concerning all that this people call a conspiracy,
Nor be afraid of their threats, nor be troubled.
13 The LORD of hosts, Him you shall hallow;
Let Him *be* your fear,
And *let* Him *be* your dread.
14 [a]He will be as a sanctuary,
But [b]a stone of stumbling and a rock of offense
To both the houses of Israel,
As a trap and a snare to the inhabitants of Jerusalem.
15 And many among them shall [a]stumble;
They shall fall and be broken,
Be snared and taken."

16 Bind up the testimony,
Seal the law among my disciples.
17 And I will wait on the LORD,
Who [a]hides His face from the house of Jacob;
And I [b]will hope in Him.
18 [a]Here am I and the children whom the LORD has given me!
We [b]*are* for signs and wonders in Israel
From the LORD of hosts,
Who dwells in Mount Zion.

19 And when they say to you, [a]"Seek those
who are mediums and wizards, [b]who whisper and
mutter," should not a people seek their God?
Should they [c]*seek* the dead on behalf of the living?
20 [a]To the law and to the testimony! If they
do not speak according to this word, *it is* because
[b]*there is* no light in them.
21 They will pass through it hard-pressed and
hungry; and it shall happen, when they are hungry, that they will be enraged and [a]curse their
king and their God, and look upward.
22 Then they will look to the earth, and see
trouble and darkness, gloom of anguish; and *they
will be* driven into darkness.

The Government of the Promised Son
(Is. 11:1–9)

9 Nevertheless [a]the gloom *will* not *be* upon her who *is* distressed,
As when at [b]first He lightly esteemed
The land of Zebulun and the land of Naphtali,
And [c]afterward more heavily oppressed *her,*
By the way of the sea, beyond the Jordan,
In Galilee of the Gentiles.
2 [a]The people who walked in darkness
Have seen a great light;
Those who dwelt in the land of the shadow of death,
Upon them a light has shined.

3 You have multiplied the nation
And *increased its joy;
They rejoice before You
According to the joy of harvest,
As *men* rejoice [a]when they divide the spoil.

KJV

4 For thou hast broken the yoke of his burden, and the staff of his shoulder, the rod of his oppressor, as in the day of [a]Midian.

5 For every battle of the warrior *is* with confused noise, and garments rolled in blood; [a]but *this* shall be with burning *and* fuel of fire.

6 [a]For unto us a child is born, unto us a [b]son is given: and [c]the government shall be upon his shoulder: and his name shall be called [d]Wonderful, Counsellor, [e]The mighty God, The everlasting Father, [f]The Prince of Peace.

7 Of the increase of *his* government and peace [a]*there shall be* no end, upon the throne of David, and upon his kingdom, to order it, and to establish it with judgment and with justice from henceforth even for ever. The [b]zeal of the LORD of hosts will perform this.

The Punishment of Samaria

8 The Lord sent a word into [a]Jacob, and it hath lighted upon Israel.

9 And all the people shall know, *even* Ephraim and the inhabitant of Samaria, that say in the pride and stoutness of heart,

10 The bricks are fallen down, but we will build with hewn stones: the sycomores are cut down, but we will change *them into* cedars.

11 Therefore the LORD shall set up the adversaries of Rezin against him, and join his enemies together;

12 The Syrians before, and the Philistines behind; and they shall devour Israel with open mouth. For all this his anger is not turned away, but his hand *is* stretched out still.

13 For the people turneth not unto him that smiteth them, neither do they seek the LORD of hosts.

14 Therefore the LORD will cut off from Israel head and tail, branch and rush, [a]in one day.

15 The ancient and honourable, he *is* the head; and the prophet that teacheth lies, he *is* the tail.

16 For [a]the leaders of this people cause *them* to err; and *they that are* led of them *are* destroyed.

17 Therefore the Lord [a]shall have no joy in their young men, neither shall have mercy on their fatherless and widows: for every one *is* an hypocrite and an evildoer, and every mouth speaketh folly. [b]For all this his anger is not turned away, but his hand *is* stretched out still.

18 For wickedness [a]burneth as the fire: it shall devour the briers and thorns, and shall kindle in the thickets of the forest, and they shall mount up *like* the lifting up of smoke.

19 Through the wrath of the LORD of hosts is [a]the land darkened, and the people shall be as the fuel of the fire: [b]no man shall spare his brother.

4 [a]Judg. 7:22
5 [a]Is. 66:15
6 [a][Is. 7:14; Luke 2:11]; John 1:45 [b]Luke 2:7; [John 3:16; 1 John 4:9] [c][Matt. 28:18; 1 Cor. 15:25]; Rev. 12:5 [d]Judg. 13:18 [e]Titus 2:13 [f]Eph. 2:14
7 [a]Dan. 2:44; Matt. 1:1, 6; Luke 1:32, 33; John 7:42 [b]Is. 37:32
8 [a]Gen. 32:28
14 [a]Rev. 18:8
16 [a]Is. 3:12; Mic. 3:1, 5, 9; Matt. 15:14
17 [a]Ps. 147:10 [b]Is. 5:25
18 [a]Ps. 83:14; [Is. 1:7; 10:17]; Nah. 1:10; Mal. 4:1
19 [a]Is. 8:22 [b]Mic. 7:2, 6

NKJV

4 For You have broken the yoke of his burden
And the staff of his shoulder,
The rod of his oppressor,
As in the day of [a]Midian.
5 For every warrior's sandal from the noisy battle,
And garments rolled in blood,
[a]Will be used for burning *and* fuel of fire.

6 [a]For unto us a Child is born,
Unto us a [b]Son is given;
And [c]the government will be upon His shoulder.
And His name will be called
[d]Wonderful, Counselor, [e]Mighty God,
Everlasting Father, [f]Prince of Peace.
7 Of the increase of *His* government and peace
[a]*There will be* no end,
Upon the throne of David and over His kingdom,
To order it and establish it with judgment and justice
From that time forward, even forever.
The [b]zeal of the LORD of hosts will perform this.

The Punishment of Samaria

8 The Lord sent a word against [a]Jacob,
And it has fallen on Israel.
9 All the people will know—
Ephraim and the inhabitant of Samaria—
Who say in pride and arrogance of heart:
10 "The bricks have fallen down,
But we will rebuild with hewn stones;
The sycamores are cut down,
But we will replace *them* with cedars."
11 Therefore the LORD shall set up
The adversaries of Rezin against him,
And spur his enemies on,
12 The Syrians before and the Philistines behind;
And they shall devour Israel with an open mouth.

For all this His anger is not turned away,
But His hand *is* stretched out still.

13 For the people do not turn to Him who strikes them,
Nor do they seek the LORD of hosts.
14 Therefore the LORD will cut off head and tail from Israel,
Palm branch and bulrush [a]in one day.
15 The elder and honorable, he *is* the head;
The prophet who teaches lies, he *is* the tail.
16 For [a]the leaders of this people cause *them* to err,
And *those who are* led by them are destroyed.
17 Therefore the Lord [a]will have no joy in their young men,
Nor have mercy on their fatherless and widows;
For everyone *is* a hypocrite and an evildoer,
And every mouth speaks folly.
[b]For all this His anger is not turned away,
But His hand *is* stretched out still.

18 For wickedness [a]burns as the fire;
It shall devour the briers and thorns,
And kindle in the thickets of the forest;
They shall mount up *like* rising smoke.
19 Through the wrath of the LORD of hosts
[a]The land is burned up,
And the people shall be as fuel for the fire;
[b]No man shall spare his brother.

KJV

20 And he shall snatch on the right hand, and
be hungry; and he shall eat on the left hand, [a]and
they shall not be satisfied: [b]they shall eat every
man the flesh of his own arm:
21 Manasseh, Ephraim; and Ephraim, Ma-
nasseh: *and* they together *shall be* [a]against Judah.
[b]For all this his anger is not turned away, but
his hand *is* stretched out still.

10 Woe unto them that [a]decree unrighteous
decrees, and that write grievousness *which*
they have prescribed;
2 To turn aside the needy from judgment,
and to take away the right from the poor of my
people, that widows may be their prey, and *that*
they may rob the fatherless!
3 And [a]what will ye do in [b]the day of visitation, and in the desolation *which* shall come from
[c]far? to whom will ye flee for help? and where
will ye leave your glory?
4 Without me they shall bow down under
the [a]prisoners, and they shall fall under the slain.
[b]For all this his anger is not turned away, but
his hand *is* stretched out still.

Arrogant Assyria Also Judged

5 O Assyrian, [a]the rod of mine anger, and
the staff in their hand is mine indignation.
6 I will send him against [a]an hypocritical
nation, and against the people of my wrath will I
[b]give him a charge, to take the spoil, and to take
the prey, and to tread them down like the mire
of the streets.
7 [a]Howbeit he meaneth not so, neither doth
his heart think so; but *it is* in his heart to destroy
and cut off nations not a few.
8 [a]For he saith, *Are* not my princes altogether kings?
9 *Is* not [a]Calno [b]as Carchemish? *is* not Hamath as Arpad? *is* not Samaria [c]as Damascus?
10 As my hand hath found the kingdoms of
the idols, and whose graven images did excel
them of Jerusalem and of Samaria;
11 Shall I not, as I have done unto Samaria
and her idols, so do to Jerusalem and her idols?
12 Wherefore it shall come to pass, *that*
when the Lord hath performed his whole work
[a]upon mount Zion and on Jerusalem, [b]I will punish the fruit of the stout heart of the king of Assyria, and the glory of his high looks.
13 [a]For he saith, By the strength of my hand
I have done *it*, and by my wisdom; for I am prudent: and I have removed the bounds of the people, and have robbed their treasures, and I have
put down the inhabitants like a valiant *man*:
14 And [a]my hand hath found as a nest the
riches of the people: and as one gathereth eggs
that are left, have I gathered all the earth; and

20 [a]Lev. 26:26 [b]Jer. 19:9
21 [a]2 Chr. 28:6, 8; Is. 11:13 [b]Is. 9:12, 17

CHAPTER 10

1 [a]Ps. 58:2
3 [a]Job 31:14 [b]Is. 13:6; Jer. 9:9; Hos. 9:7; Luke 19:44 [c]Is. 5:26
4 [a]Is. 24:22 [b]Is. 5:25
5 [a]Jer. 51:20
6 [a]Is. 9:17 [b]2 Kin. 17:6; Jer. 34:22
7 [a]Gen. 50:20; Mic. 4:11, 12; Acts 2:23, 24
8 [a]2 Kin. 19:10
9 [a]Gen. 10:10; Amos 6:2 [b]2 Chr. 35:20 [c]2 Kin. 16:9
12 [a]2 Kin. 19:31; Is. 28:21 [b]2 Kin. 19:35; 2 Chr. 32:21; Jer. 50:18
13 [a][2 Kin. 19:22–24]; Is. 37:24–27; Ezek. 28:4; Dan. 4:30
14 [a]Job 31:25

NKJV

20 And he shall snatch on the right hand
And be hungry;
He shall devour on the left hand
[a]And not be satisfied;
[b]Every man shall eat the flesh of his own
arm.
21 Manasseh *shall devour* Ephraim, and
Ephraim Manasseh;
Together they *shall be* [a]against Judah.

[b]For all this His anger is not turned away,
But His hand *is* stretched out still.

10 "Woe to those who [a]decree unrighteous
decrees,
Who write misfortune,
Which they have prescribed
2 To rob the needy of justice,
And to take what is right from the poor
of My people,
That widows may be their prey,
And *that* they may rob the fatherless.
3 [a]What will you do in [b]the day of
punishment,
And in the desolation *which* will come
from [c]afar?
To whom will you flee for help?
And where will you leave your glory?
4 Without Me they shall bow down among
the [a]prisoners,
And they shall fall among the slain."

[b]For all this His anger is not turned away,
But His hand *is* stretched out still.

Arrogant Assyria Also Judged

5 "Woe to Assyria, [a]the rod of My anger
And the staff in whose hand is My
indignation.
6 I will send him against [a]an ungodly
nation,
And against the people of My wrath
I will [b]give him charge,
To seize the spoil, to take the prey,
And to tread them down like the mire of
the streets.
7 [a]Yet he does not mean so,
Nor does his heart think so;
But *it is* in his heart to destroy,
And cut off not a few nations.
8 [a]For he says,
'*Are* not my princes altogether kings?
9 *Is* not [a]Calno [b]like Carchemish?
Is not Hamath like Arpad?
Is not Samaria [c]like Damascus?
10 As my hand has found the kingdoms of
the idols,
Whose carved images excelled those of
Jerusalem and Samaria,
11 As I have done to Samaria and her
idols,
Shall I not do also to Jerusalem and her
idols?' "

12 Therefore it shall come to pass, when the
Lord has performed all His work [a]on Mount Zion
and on Jerusalem, *that He will say,* [b]"I will punish
the fruit of the arrogant heart of the king of Assyria, and the glory of his haughty looks."
13 [a]For he says:

"By the strength of my hand I have done
it,
And by my wisdom, for I am prudent;
Also I have removed the boundaries of the
people,
And have robbed their treasuries;
So I have put down the inhabitants like a
valiant *man*.
14 [a]My hand has found like a nest the riches
of the people,
And as one gathers eggs *that are* left,

KJV

there was none that moved the wing, or opened
the mouth, or peeped.
15 Shall [a]the ax boast itself against him that
heweth therewith? *or* shall the saw magnify itself
against him that shaketh it? as if the rod should
shake *itself* against them that lift it up, *or* as if
the staff should lift up *itself, as if it were* no wood.
16 Therefore shall the Lord, the Lord of
hosts, send among his fat ones leanness; and under his glory he shall kindle a burning like the
burning of a fire.
17 And the light of Israel shall be for a fire,
and his Holy One for a flame: [a]and it shall burn
and devour his thorns and his briers in one day;
18 And shall consume the glory of his forest,
and of [a]his fruitful field, both soul and body: and
they shall be as when a standard-bearer fainteth.
19 And the rest of the trees of his forest shall
be few, that a child may write them.

The Returning Remnant of Israel

20 And it shall come to pass in that day, *that*
the remnant of Israel, and such as are escaped
of the house of Jacob, [a]shall no more again stay
upon him that smote them; but shall stay upon
the LORD, the Holy One of Israel, in truth.
21 The remnant shall return, *even* the remnant of Jacob, unto the [a]mighty God.
22 [a]For though thy people Israel be as the
sand of the sea, [b]*yet* a remnant of them shall return: the consumption decreed shall overflow with
righteousness.
23 [a]For the Lord GOD of hosts shall make a
consumption, even determined, in the midst of all
the land.
24 Therefore thus saith the Lord GOD of
hosts, O my people that dwellest in Zion, [a]be not
afraid of the Assyrian: he shall smite thee with a
rod, and shall lift up his staff against thee, after
the manner of [b]Egypt.
25 For yet a very little while, [a]and the indignation shall cease, and mine anger in their
destruction.
26 And the LORD of hosts shall stir up [a]a
scourge for him according to the slaughter of
[b]Midian at the rock of Oreb: and [c]*as* his rod *was*
upon the sea, so shall he lift it up after the manner
of Egypt.
27 And it shall come to pass in that day, *that*
his burden shall be taken away from off thy shoulder, and his yoke from off thy neck, and the yoke
shall be destroyed because of [a]the anointing.
28 He is come to Aiath, he is passed to Migron; at Michmash he hath laid up his carriages:
29 They are gone over [a]the passage: they
have taken up their lodging at Geba; Ramah is
afraid; [b]Gibeah of Saul is fled.

15 [a]Jer. 51:20
17 [a]Is. 9:18
18 [a]2 Kin. 19:23
20 [a]2 Kin. 16:7
21 [a][Is. 9:6]
22 [a]Rom. 9:27, 28 [b]Is. 6:13
23 [a]Is. 28:22; Dan. 9:27; Rom. 9:28
24 [a]Is. 7:4; 12:2 [b]Ex. 14
25 [a]Is. 10:5; 26:20; Dan. 11:36
26 [a]2 Kin. 19:35 [b]Judg. 7:25; Is. 9:4 [c]Ex. 14:26, 27
27 [a]Ps. 105:15; [1 John 2:20]
29 [a]1 Sam. 13:23 [b]1 Sam. 11:4

*_____

10:16 So with Bg.; MT, DSS *YHWH (the* LORD)

NKJV

I have gathered all the earth;
And there was no one who moved *his*
wing,
Nor opened *his* mouth with even a peep."

15 Shall [a]the ax boast itself against him who
chops with it?
Or shall the saw exalt itself against him
who saws with it?
As if a rod could wield *itself* against those
who lift it up,
Or as if a staff could lift up, *as if it were*
not wood!
16 Therefore the Lord, the *Lord of hosts,
Will send leanness among his fat ones;
And under his glory
He will kindle a burning
Like the burning of a fire.
17 So the Light of Israel will be for a fire,
And his Holy One for a flame;
[a]It will burn and devour
His thorns and his briers in one day.
18 And it will consume the glory of his forest
and of [a]his fruitful field,
Both soul and body;
And they will be as when a sick man
wastes away.
19 Then the rest of the trees of his forest
Will be so few in number
That a child may write them.

The Returning Remnant of Israel

20 And it shall come to pass in that day
That the remnant of Israel,
And such as have escaped of the house
of Jacob,
[a]Will never again depend on him who
defeated them,
But will depend on the LORD, the Holy One
of Israel, in truth.
21 The remnant will return, the remnant of
Jacob,
To the [a]Mighty God.
22 [a]For though your people, O Israel, be as
the sand of the sea,
[b]A remnant of them will return;
The destruction decreed shall overflow
with righteousness.
23 [a]For the Lord GOD of hosts
Will make a determined end
In the midst of all the land.

24 Therefore thus says the Lord GOD of hosts:
"O My people, who dwell in Zion, [a]do not be
afraid of the Assyrian. He shall strike you with a
rod and lift up his staff against you, in the manner
of [b]Egypt.
25 "For yet a very little while [a]and the indignation will cease, as will My anger in their
destruction."
26 And the LORD of hosts will stir up [a]a
scourge for him like the slaughter of [b]Midian at
the rock of Oreb; [c]as His rod was on the sea, so
will He lift it up in the manner of Egypt.

27 It shall come to pass in that day
That his burden will be taken away from
your shoulder,
And his yoke from your neck,
And the yoke will be destroyed because
of [a]the anointing oil.

28 He has come to Aiath,
He has passed Migron;
At Michmash he has attended to his
equipment.
29 They have gone along [a]the ridge,
They have taken up lodging at Geba.
Ramah is afraid,
[b]Gibeah of Saul has fled.

KJV

30 Lift up thy voice, O daughter [a]of Gallim:
cause it to be heard unto [b]Laish, O poor Anathoth.
31 [a]Madmenah is removed; the inhabitants
of Gebim gather themselves to flee.
32 As yet shall he remain [a]at Nob that day:
he shall [b]shake his hand *against* the mount of
[c]the daughter of Zion, the hill of Jerusalem.
33 Behold, the Lord, the LORD of hosts, shall
lop the bough with terror: and [a]the high ones of
stature *shall be* hewn down, and the haughty shall
be humbled.
34 And he shall cut down the thickets of the
forest with iron, and Lebanon shall fall by a
mighty one.

The Reign of Jesse's Offspring
(Is. 9:1–7)

11 And [a]there shall come forth a rod out of
the stem of [b]Jesse, and [c]a Branch shall
grow out of his roots:
2 [a]And the spirit of the LORD shall rest upon
him, the spirit of wisdom and understanding, the
spirit of counsel and might, the spirit of knowledge and of the fear of the LORD;
3 And shall make him of quick understanding in the fear of the LORD: and he shall not judge
after the sight of his eyes, neither reprove after
the hearing of his ears:
4 But [a]with righteousness shall he judge the
poor, and reprove with equity for the meek of the
earth: and he shall [b]smite the earth with the rod
of his mouth, and with the breath of his lips shall
he slay the wicked.
5 And righteousness shall be the girdle of
his loins, and faithfulness the girdle of his reins.
6 [a]The wolf also shall dwell with the lamb,
and the leopard shall lie down with the kid; and
the calf and the young lion and the fatling together; and a little child shall lead them.
7 And the cow and the bear shall feed; their
young ones shall lie down together: and the lion
shall eat straw like the ox.
8 And the sucking child shall play on the
hole of the asp, and the weaned child shall put
his hand on the cockatrice' den.
9 [a]They shall not hurt nor destroy in all my
holy mountain: for [b]the earth shall be full of the
knowledge of the LORD, as the waters cover the
sea.
10 [a]And in that day [b]there shall be a root of
Jesse, which shall stand for an [c]ensign of the people; to it shall the [d]Gentiles seek: and his rest shall
be glorious.
11 And it shall come to pass in that day, *that*
the Lord shall set his hand again the second time
to recover the remnant of his people, which shall
be left, [a]from Assyria, and from Egypt, and from
Pathros, and from Cush, and from Elam, and from
Shinar, and from Hamath, and from the islands
of the sea.

30 [a]1 Sam. 25:44 [b]Judg. 18:7
31 [a]Josh. 15:31
32 [a]1 Sam. 21:1; Neh. 11:32 [b]Is. 13:2 [c]Is. 37:22
33 [a]Is. 37:24, 36–38; Ezek. 31:3; Amos 2:9

CHAPTER 11

1 [a][Zech. 6:12]; Rev. 5:5 [b][Is. 9:7; 11:10]; Matt. 1:5; [Acts 13:23] [c]Is. 4:2
2 [a][Is. 42:1; 48:16; 61:1; Matt. 3:16]; Mark 1:10; Luke 3:22; [John 1:32]
4 [a]Rev. 19:11 [b]Job 4:9; Is. 30:28, 33; Mal. 4:6; 2 Thess. 2:8
6 [a]Hos. 2:18
9 [a]Job 5:23; Is. 65:25; Ezek. 34:25; Hos. 2:18 [b]Ps. 98:2, 3; Is. 45:6; Hab. 2:14
10 [a]Is. 2:11 [b]Is. 11:1; Rom. 15:12 [c]Is. 27:12, 13 [d]Rom. 15:10
11 [a]Is. 19:23–25; Hos. 11:11; Zech. 10:10

*———

10:30 So with MT, Tg., Vg.; LXX, Syr. *Listen to her, O Anathoth*

NKJV

30 Lift up your voice,
O daughter [a]of Gallim!
Cause it to be heard as far as [b]Laish—
*O poor Anathoth!
31 [a]Madmenah has fled,
The inhabitants of Gebim seek refuge.
32 As yet he will remain [a]at Nob that day;
He will [b]shake his fist at the mount of [c]the daughter of Zion,
The hill of Jerusalem.

33 Behold, the Lord,
The LORD of hosts,
Will lop off the bough with terror;
[a]Those of high stature *will be* hewn down,
And the haughty will be humbled.
34 He will cut down the thickets of the forest with iron,
And Lebanon will fall by the Mighty One.

The Reign of Jesse's Offspring
(Is. 9:1–7)

11 There [a]shall come forth a Rod from the stem of [b]Jesse,
And [c]a Branch shall grow out of his roots.
2 [a]The Spirit of the LORD shall rest upon Him,
The Spirit of wisdom and understanding,
The Spirit of counsel and might,
The Spirit of knowledge and of the fear of the LORD.

3 His delight *is* in the fear of the LORD,
And He shall not judge by the sight of His eyes,
Nor decide by the hearing of His ears;
4 But [a]with righteousness He shall judge the poor,
And decide with equity for the meek of the earth;
He shall [b]strike the earth with the rod of His mouth,
And with the breath of His lips He shall slay the wicked.
5 Righteousness shall be the belt of His loins,
And faithfulness the belt of His waist.

6 "The[a] wolf also shall dwell with the lamb,
The leopard shall lie down with the young goat,
The calf and the young lion and the fatling together;
And a little child shall lead them.
7 The cow and the bear shall graze;
Their young ones shall lie down together;
And the lion shall eat straw like the ox.
8 The nursing child shall play by the cobra's hole,
And the weaned child shall put his hand in the viper's den.
9 [a]They shall not hurt nor destroy in all My holy mountain,
For [b]the earth shall be full of the knowledge of the LORD
As the waters cover the sea.

10 "And[a] in that day [b]there shall be a Root of Jesse,
Who shall stand as a [c]banner to the people;
For the [d]Gentiles shall seek Him,
And His resting place shall be glorious."

11 It shall come to pass in that day
That the Lord shall set His hand again the second time
To recover the remnant of His people who are left,
[a]From Assyria and Egypt,
From Pathros and Cush,
From Elam and Shinar,
From Hamath and the islands of the sea.

KJV

12 And he shall set up an ensign for the nations, and shall assemble the outcasts of Israel, and gather together [a]the dispersed of Judah from the four corners of the earth.

13 [a]The envy also of Ephraim shall depart, and the adversaries of Judah shall be cut off: Ephraim shall not envy Judah, and Judah shall not vex Ephraim.

14 But they shall fly upon the shoulders of the Philistines toward the west; they shall spoil them of the east together: [a]they shall lay their hand upon Edom and Moab; and the children of Ammon shall obey them.

15 And the LORD [a]shall utterly destroy the tongue of the Egyptian sea; and with his mighty wind shall he shake his hand over the river, and shall smite it in the seven streams, and make *men* go over dryshod.

16 And [a]there shall be an highway for the remnant of his people, which shall be left, from Assyria; [b]like as it was to Israel in the day that he came up out of the land of Egypt.

A Hymn of Praise

12 And [a]in that day thou shalt say, O LORD, I will praise thee: though thou wast angry with me, thine anger is turned away, and thou comfortedst me.

2 Behold, God *is* my salvation; I will trust, and not be afraid: [a]for the [b]LORD JEHOVAH *is* my strength and *my* song; he also is become my salvation.

3 Therefore with joy shall ye draw [a]water out of the wells of salvation.

4 And in that day shall ye say, [a]Praise the LORD, call upon his name, [b]declare his doings among the people, make mention that his [c]name is exalted.

5 [a]Sing unto the LORD; for he hath done excellent things: this *is* known in all the earth.

6 [a]Cry out and shout, thou inhabitant of Zion: for great *is* [b]the Holy One of Israel in the midst of thee.

Proclamation Against Babylon

13 The [a]burden of Babylon, which Isaiah the son of Amoz did see.

2 [a]Lift ye up a banner [b]upon the high mountain, exalt the voice unto them, [c]shake the hand, that they may go into the gates of the nobles.

3 I have commanded my sanctified ones, I have also called [a]my mighty ones for mine anger, *even* them that [b]rejoice in my highness.

4 The [a]noise of a multitude in the mountains, like as of a great people; a tumultuous noise of the kingdoms of nations gathered together: the LORD of hosts mustereth the host of the battle.

---

12 [a]John 7:35
13 [a]Is. 9:21; Jer. 3:18; Ezek. 37:16, 17, 22; Hos. 1:11
14 [a]Is. 63:1; Dan. 11:41; Joel 3:19; Amos 9:12
15 [a]Is. 50:2; 51:10, 11; Zech. 10:10, 11
16 [a]Is. 19:23 [b]Ex. 14:29

CHAPTER 12

1 [a]Is. 2:11
2 [a]Ps. 83:18 [b]Ex. 15:2; Ps. 118:14
3 [a][John 4:10, 14; 7:37, 38]
4 [a]1 Chr. 16:8; Ps. 105:1 [b]Ps. 145:4–6 [c]Ps. 34:3
5 [a]Ex. 15:1; Ps. 98:1; Is. 24:14; 42:10, 11; 44:23
6 [a]Is. 52:9; 54:1; Zeph. 3:14, 15 [b]Ps. 89:18

CHAPTER 13

1 [a]Jer. 50; 51; Matt. 1:11; Rev. 14:8
2 [a]Is. 18:3 [b]Jer. 51:25 [c]Is. 10:32
3 [a]Joel 3:11 [b]Ps. 149:2
4 [a]Is. 17:12; Joel 3:14

*

11:15 So with MT, Vg.; LXX, Syr., Tg. *dry up* • The Euphrates

---

NKJV

12 He will set up a banner for the nations,
And will assemble the outcasts of Israel,
And gather together [a]the dispersed of Judah
From the four corners of the earth.
13 Also [a]the envy of Ephraim shall depart,
And the adversaries of Judah shall be cut off;
Ephraim shall not envy Judah,
And Judah shall not harass Ephraim.
14 But they shall fly down upon the shoulder of the Philistines toward the west;
Together they shall plunder the people of the East;
[a]They shall lay their hand on Edom and Moab;
And the people of Ammon shall obey them.
15 The LORD [a]will utterly *destroy the tongue of the Sea of Egypt;
With His mighty wind He will shake His fist over *the River,
And strike it in the seven streams,
And make *men* cross over dry-shod.
16 [a]There will be a highway for the remnant of His people
Who will be left from Assyria,
[b]As it was for Israel
In the day that he came up from the land of Egypt.

A Hymn of Praise

12 And [a]in that day you will say:

"O LORD, I will praise You;
Though You were angry with me,
Your anger is turned away, and You comfort me.
2 Behold, God *is* my salvation,
I will trust and not be afraid;
[a]'For [b]YAH, the LORD, *is* my strength and song;
He also has become my salvation.' "

3 Therefore with joy you will draw [a]water
From the wells of salvation.

4 And in that day you will say:

[a]"Praise the LORD, call upon His name;
[b]Declare His deeds among the peoples,
Make mention that His [c]name is exalted.
5 [a]Sing to the LORD,
For He has done excellent things;
This *is* known in all the earth.
6 [a]Cry out and shout, O inhabitant of Zion,
For great *is* [b]the Holy One of Israel in your midst!"

Proclamation Against Babylon

13 The [a]burden against Babylon which Isaiah the son of Amoz saw.

2 "Lift[a] up a banner [b]on the high mountain,
Raise your voice to them;
[c]Wave your hand, that they may enter the gates of the nobles.
3 I have commanded My sanctified ones;
I have also called [a]My mighty ones for My anger—
Those who [b]rejoice in My exaltation."

4 The [a]noise of a multitude in the mountains,
Like that of many people!
A tumultuous noise of the kingdoms of nations gathered together!
The LORD of hosts musters
The army for battle.

KJV

5 They come from a far country, from the end of heaven, *even* the [a]LORD, and the weapons of his indignation, to destroy the whole [b]land.

6 Howl ye; [a]for the day of the LORD *is* at hand; [b]it shall come as a destruction from the Almighty.

7 Therefore shall all hands be faint, and every man's heart shall melt:

8 And they shall be afraid: [a]pangs and sorrows shall take hold of them; they shall be in pain as a woman that travaileth: they shall be amazed one at another; their faces *shall be as* flames.

9 Behold, [a]the day of the LORD cometh, cruel both with wrath and fierce anger, to lay the land desolate: and he shall destroy [b]the sinners thereof out of it.

10 For the stars of heaven and the constellations thereof shall not give their light: the sun shall be [a]darkened in his going forth, and the moon shall not cause her light to shine.

11 And I will [a]punish the world for *their* evil, and the wicked for their iniquity; [b]and I will cause the arrogancy of the proud to cease, and will lay low the haughtiness of the terrible.

12 I will make a man more precious than fine gold; even a man than the golden wedge of Ophir.

13 [a]Therefore I will shake the heavens, and the earth shall remove out of her place, in the wrath of the LORD of hosts, and in [b]the day of his fierce anger.

14 And it shall be as the chased roe, and as a sheep that no man taketh up: [a]they shall every man turn to his own people, and flee every one into his own land.

15 Every one that is found shall be thrust through; and every one that is joined *unto them* shall fall by the sword.

16 Their children also shall be [a]dashed to pieces before their eyes; their houses shall be spoiled, and their wives [b]ravished.

17 [a]Behold, I will stir up the Medes against them, which shall not regard silver; and *as for* gold, they shall not delight in it.

18 *Their* bows also shall dash the young men to pieces; and they shall have no pity on the fruit of the womb; their eye shall not spare children.

19 [a]And Babylon, the glory of kingdoms, the beauty of the Chaldees' excellency, shall be as when God overthrew [b]Sodom and Gomorrah.

20 [a]It shall never be inhabited, neither shall it be dwelt in from generation to generation: neither shall the Arabian pitch tent there; neither shall the shepherds make their fold there.

21 [a]But wild beasts of the desert shall lie there; and their houses shall be full of doleful creatures; and owls shall dwell there, and satyrs shall dance there.

22 And the wild beasts of the islands shall cry in their desolate houses, and dragons in *their*

NKJV

5 They come from a far country,
From the end of heaven—
The [a]LORD and His weapons of
indignation,
To destroy the whole [b]land.

6 Wail, [a]for the day of the LORD *is* at hand!
[b]It will come as destruction from the
Almighty.
7 Therefore all hands will be limp,
Every man's heart will melt,
8 And they will be afraid.
[a]Pangs and sorrows will take hold of *them;*
They will be in pain as a woman in
childbirth;
They will be amazed at one another;
Their faces *will be like* flames.

9 Behold, [a]the day of the LORD comes,
Cruel, with both wrath and fierce anger,
To lay the land desolate;
And He will destroy [b]its sinners from it.
10 For the stars of heaven and their
constellations
Will not give their light;
The sun will be [a]darkened in its going
forth,
And the moon will not cause its light to
shine.

11 "I will [a]punish the world for *its* evil,
And the wicked for their iniquity;
[b]I will halt the arrogance of the proud,
And will lay low the haughtiness of the
terrible.
12 I will make a mortal more rare than fine
gold,
A man more than the golden wedge of
Ophir.
13 [a]Therefore I will shake the heavens,
And the earth will move out of her place,
In the wrath of the LORD of hosts
And in [b]the day of His fierce anger.
14 It shall be as the hunted gazelle,
And as a sheep that no man takes up;
[a]Every man will turn to his own people,
And everyone will flee to his own land.
15 Everyone who is found will be thrust
through,
And everyone who is captured will fall by
the sword.
16 Their children also will be [a]dashed to
pieces before their eyes;
Their houses will be plundered
And their wives [b]ravished.

17 "Behold,[a] I will stir up the Medes against
them,
Who will not regard silver;
And *as for* gold, they will not delight in
it.
18 Also *their* bows will dash the young men
to pieces,
And they will have no pity on the fruit of
the womb;
Their eye will not spare children.
19 [a]And Babylon, the glory of kingdoms,
The beauty of the Chaldeans' pride,
Will be as when God overthrew [b]Sodom
and Gomorrah.
20 [a]It will never be inhabited,
Nor will it be settled from generation to
generation;
Nor will the Arabian pitch tents there,
Nor will the shepherds make their
sheepfolds there.
21 [a]But wild beasts of the desert will lie there,
And their houses will be full of owls;
Ostriches will dwell there,
And wild goats will caper there.
22 The hyenas will howl in their citadels,
And jackals in their pleasant palaces.

---

5 [a]Is. 42:13 [b]Is. 24:1; 34:2 **6** [a]Is. 2:12; Ezek. 30:3; Amos 5:18; Zeph. 1:7; Rev. 6:17 [b]Is. 10:25; Job 31:23; Joel 1:15 **8** [a]Ps. 48:6 **9** [a]Mal. 4:1 [b]Ps. 104:35; Prov. 2:22 **10** [a]Is. 24:21–23; Ezek. 32:7; Joel 2:31; Matt. 24:29; Mark 13:24; Luke 21:25 **11** [a]Is. 26:21 [b][Is. 2:17] **13** [a]Is. 34:4; 51:6; Hag. 2:6 [b]Ps. 110:5; Lam. 1:12 **14** [a]Jer. 50:16; 51:9 **16** [a]Ps. 137:8, 9; Is. 13:18; 14:21; Hos. 10:14; Nah. 3:10 [b]Zech. 14:2 **17** [a]Is. 21:2; Jer. 51:11, 28; Dan. 5:28, 31 **19** [a]Is. 14:4; Dan. 4:30; Rev. 18:11–16, 19, 21 [b]Gen. 19:24; Deut. 29:23; Jer. 50:40; Amos 4:11 **20** [a]Jer. 50:3 **21** [a]Is. 34:11–15; Zeph. 2:14; Rev. 18:2

KJV

pleasant palaces: [a]and her time *is* near to come,
and her days shall not be prolonged.

Mercy on Jacob

14 For the LORD [a]will have mercy on Jacob,
and [b]will yet choose Israel, and set them
in their own land: [c]and the strangers shall be
joined with them, and they shall cleave to the
house of Jacob.
2 And the people shall take them, [a]and
bring them to their place: and the house of Israel
shall possess them in the land of the LORD for
servants and handmaids: and they shall take them
captives, whose captives they were; [b]and they
shall rule over their oppressors.

Fall of the King of Babylon

3 And it shall come to pass in the day that
the LORD shall give thee rest from thy sorrow, and
from thy fear, and from the hard bondage wherein
thou wast made to serve,
4 That thou [a]shalt take up this proverb
against the king of Babylon, and say, How hath
the oppressor ceased! the [b]golden city ceased!
5 The LORD hath broken [a]the staff of the
wicked, *and* the sceptre of the rulers.
6 He who smote the people in wrath with a
continual stroke, he that ruled the nations in anger, is persecuted, *and* none hindereth.
7 The whole earth is at rest, *and* is quiet:
they break forth into singing.
8 [a]Yea, the fir trees rejoice at thee, *and* the
cedars of Lebanon, *saying,* Since thou art laid
down, no feller is come up against us.
9 [a]Hell from beneath is moved for thee to
meet *thee* at thy coming: it stirreth up the dead
for thee, *even* all the chief ones of the earth; it
hath raised up from their thrones all the kings of
the nations.
10 All they shall [a]speak and say unto thee,
Art thou also become weak as we? art thou become like unto us?
11 Thy pomp is brought down to the grave,
and the noise of thy viols: the worm is spread
under thee, and the worms cover thee.

The Fall of Lucifer

12 [a]How art thou fallen from heaven, O Lucifer, son of the morning! *how* art thou cut down
to the ground, which didst weaken the nations!
13 For thou hast said in thine heart, [a]I will
ascend into heaven, [b]I will exalt my throne above
the stars of God: I will sit also upon the [c]mount
of the congregation, [d]in the sides of the north:
14 I will ascend above the heights of the
clouds; [a]I will be like the most High.
15 Yet thou [a]shalt be brought down to hell,
to the sides of the pit.
16 They that see thee shall narrowly look
upon thee, *and* consider thee, *saying, Is* this the
man that made the earth to tremble, that did shake
kingdoms;
17 *That* made the world as a wilderness, and
destroyed the cities thereof; *that* opened not the
house of his prisoners?

NKJV

[a]Her time *is* near to come,
And her days will not be prolonged."

Mercy on Jacob

14 For the LORD [a]will have mercy on Jacob,
and [b]will still choose Israel, and settle them
in their own land. [c]The strangers will be joined
with them, and they will cling to the house of
Jacob.
2 Then people will take them [a]and bring
them to their place, and the house of Israel will
possess them for servants and maids in the land
of the LORD; they will take them captive whose
captives they were, [b]and rule over their oppressors.

Fall of the King of Babylon

3 It shall come to pass in the day the LORD
gives you rest from your sorrow, and from your
fear and the hard bondage in which you were
made to serve,
4 that you [a]will take up this proverb against
the king of Babylon, and say:

"How the oppressor has ceased,
The [b]golden* city ceased!
5 The LORD has broken [a]the staff of the
wicked,
The scepter of the rulers;
6 He who struck the people in wrath with
a continual stroke,
He who ruled the nations in anger,
Is persecuted *and* no one hinders.
7 The whole earth is at rest *and* quiet;
They break forth into singing.
8 [a]Indeed the cypress trees rejoice over you,
And the cedars of Lebanon,
Saying, 'Since you were cut down,
No woodsman has come up against us.'

9 "Hell[a] from beneath is excited about you,
To meet *you* at your coming;
It stirs up the dead for you,
All the chief ones of the earth;
It has raised up from their thrones
All the kings of the nations.
10 They all shall [a]speak and say to you:
'Have you also become as weak as we?
Have you become like us?
11 Your pomp is brought down to Sheol,
And the sound of your stringed
instruments;
The maggot is spread under you,
And worms cover you.'

The Fall of Lucifer

12 "How[a] you are fallen from heaven,
O *Lucifer, son of the morning!
How you are cut down to the ground,
You who weakened the nations!
13 For you have said in your heart:
[a]'I will ascend into heaven,
[b]I will exalt my throne above the stars of
God;
I will also sit on the [c]mount of the
congregation
[d]On the farthest sides of the north;
14 I will ascend above the heights of the
clouds,
[a]I will be like the Most High.'
15 Yet you [a]shall be brought down to Sheol,
To the lowest depths of the Pit.

16 "Those who see you will gaze at you,
And consider you, *saying:*
'*Is* this the man who made the earth
tremble,
Who shook kingdoms,
17 Who made the world as a wilderness
And destroyed its cities,
Who did not open the house of his
prisoners?'

---

22 [a]Jer. 51:33

CHAPTER 14

1 [a]Ps. 102:13; Is. 49:13, 15; 54:7, 8 [b]Is. 41:8, 9; Zech. 1:17; 2:12 [c]Is. 60:4, 5, 10
2 [a]Is. 49:22; 60:9; 66:20 [b]Is. 60:14
4 [a]Is. 13:19; Hab. 2:6 [b]Rev. 18:16
5 [a]Ps. 125:3
8 [a]Is. 55:12; Ezek. 31:16
9 [a]Ezek. 32:21
10 [a]Ezek. 32:21
12 [a]Is. 34:4; Luke 10:18; [Rev. 12:7–9]
13 [a]Ezek. 28:2; Matt. 11:23 [b]Dan. 8:10; 2 Thess. 2:4 [c]Ezek. 28:14 [d]Ps. 48:2
14 [a]Is. 47:8; 2 Thess. 2:4
15 [a]Ezek. 28:8; Matt. 11:23; Luke 10:15

14:4 Or *insolent*
14:12 Lit. *Day Star*

KJV

18 All the kings of the nations, *even* all of them, lie in glory, every one in his own house.

19 But thou art cast out of thy grave like an abominable branch, *and as* the raiment of those that are slain, thrust through with a sword, that go down to the stones of the pit; as a carcase trodden under feet.

20 Thou shalt not be joined with them in burial, because thou hast destroyed thy land, *and* slain thy people: [a]the seed of evildoers shall never be renowned.

21 Prepare slaughter for his children [a]for the iniquity of their fathers; that they do not rise, nor possess the land, nor fill the face of the world with cities.

Babylon Destroyed

22 For I will rise up against them, saith the LORD of hosts, and cut off from Babylon [a]the name, and [b]remnant, [c]and son, and nephew, saith the LORD.

23 I will also make it a possession for the [a]bittern, and pools of water: and I will sweep it with the besom of destruction, saith the LORD of hosts.

Assyria Destroyed

24 The LORD of hosts hath sworn, saying, Surely as I have thought, so shall it come to pass; and as I have purposed, *so* shall it [a]stand:

25 That I will break the [a]Assyrian in my land, and upon my mountains tread him under foot: then shall [b]his yoke depart from off them, and his burden depart from off their shoulders.

26 This *is* the [a]purpose that is purposed upon the whole earth: and this *is* the hand that is stretched out upon all the nations.

27 For the LORD of hosts hath [a]purposed, and who shall disannul *it?* and his hand *is* stretched out, and who shall turn it back?

Philistia Destroyed

28 In the year that [a]king Ahaz died was this burden.

29 Rejoice not thou, whole Palestina, [a]because the rod of him that smote thee is broken: for out of the serpent's root shall come forth a cockatrice, [b]and his fruit *shall be* a fiery flying serpent.

30 And the firstborn of the poor shall feed, and the needy shall lie down in safety: and I will kill thy root with famine, and he shall slay thy remnant.

31 Howl, O gate; cry, O city; thou, whole Palestina, *art* dissolved: for there shall come from the north a smoke, and none *shall be* alone in his appointed times.

32 What shall *one* then answer the messengers of the nation? That [a]the LORD hath founded Zion, and [b]the poor of his people shall trust in it.

20 [a]Job 18:19; Ps. 21:10; 109:13; Is. 1:4; 31:2
21 [a]Ex. 20:5; Lev. 26:39; Is. 13:16; Matt. 23:35
22 [a]Prov. 10:7; Is. 26:14; Jer. 51:62 [b]1 Kin. 14:10 [c]Job 18:19; Is. 47:9
23 [a]Is. 34:11; Zeph. 2:14
24 [a]Is. 43:13
25 [a]Mic. 5:5, 6; Zeph. 2:13 [b]Is. 10:27; Nah. 1:13
26 [a]Is. 23:9; Zeph. 3:6, 8
27 [a]2 Chr. 20:6; Job 9:12; 23:13; Ps. 33:11; Prov. 19:21; 21:30; Is. 43:13; Dan. 4:31, 35
28 [a]2 Kin. 16:20; 2 Chr. 28:27
29 [a]2 Chr. 26:6 [b]2 Kin. 18:8
32 [a]Ps. 87:1, 5 [b]Zech. 11:11

NKJV

18 "All the kings of the nations,
All of them, sleep in glory,
Everyone in his own house;
19 But you are cast out of your grave
Like an abominable branch,
Like the garment of those who are slain,
Thrust through with a sword,
Who go down to the stones of the pit,
Like a corpse trodden underfoot.
20 You will not be joined with them in burial,
Because you have destroyed your land
And slain your people.
[a]The brood of evildoers shall never be named.
21 Prepare slaughter for his children
[a]Because of the iniquity of their fathers,
Lest they rise up and possess the land,
And fill the face of the world with cities."

Babylon Destroyed

22 "For I will rise up against them," says the LORD of hosts,
"And cut off from Babylon [a]the name and [b]remnant,
[c]And offspring and posterity," says the LORD.
23 "I will also make it a possession for the [a]porcupine,
And marshes of muddy water;
I will sweep it with the broom of destruction," says the LORD of hosts.

Assyria Destroyed

24 The LORD of hosts has sworn, saying,
"Surely, as I have thought, so it shall come to pass,
And as I have purposed, *so* it shall [a]stand:
25 That I will break the [a]Assyrian in My land,
And on My mountains tread him underfoot.
Then [b]his yoke shall be removed from them,
And his burden removed from their shoulders.
26 This *is* the [a]purpose that is purposed against the whole earth,
And this *is* the hand that is stretched out over all the nations.
27 For the LORD of hosts has [a]purposed,
And who will annul *it?*
His hand *is* stretched out,
And who will turn it back?"

Philistia Destroyed

28 This is the burden which came in the year that [a]King Ahaz died.

29 "Do not rejoice, all you of Philistia,
[a]Because the rod that struck you is broken;
For out of the serpent's roots will come forth a viper,
[b]And its offspring *will be* a fiery flying serpent.
30 The firstborn of the poor will feed,
And the needy will lie down in safety;
I will kill your roots with famine,
And it will slay your remnant.
31 Wail, O gate! Cry, O city!
All you of Philistia *are* dissolved;
For smoke will come from the north,
And no one *will be* alone in his appointed times."

32 What will they answer the messengers of the nation?
That [a]the LORD has founded Zion,
And [b]the poor of His people shall take refuge in it.

KJV

Proclamation Against Moab

15 The [a]burden of Moab. Because in the night
[b]Ar of [c]Moab is laid waste, *and* brought
to silence; because in the night Kir of Moab is
laid waste, *and* brought to silence;
2 He is gone up to Bajith, and to Dibon, the
high places, to weep: Moab shall howl over Nebo,
and over Medeba: [a]on all their heads *shall be*
baldness, *and* every beard cut off.
3 In their streets they shall gird themselves
with sackcloth: on the tops of their houses, and
in their streets, every one shall howl, [a]weeping
abundantly.
4 And Heshbon shall cry, and Elealeh: their
voice shall be heard *even* unto [a]Jahaz: therefore
the armed soldiers of Moab shall cry out; his life
shall be grievous unto him.
5 [a]My heart shall cry out for Moab; his fugitives *shall flee* unto Zoar, an heifer of three years
old: for [b]by the mounting up of Luhith with weeping shall they go it up; for in the way of Horonaim
they shall raise up a cry of destruction.
6 For the waters [a]of Nimrim shall be desolate: for the hay is withered away, the grass faileth, there is no green thing.
7 Therefore the abundance they have gotten, and that which they have laid up, shall they
carry away to the brook of the willows.
8 For the cry is gone round about the borders of Moab; the howling thereof unto Eglaim,
and the howling thereof unto Beer–elim.
9 For the waters of Dimon shall be full of
blood: for I will bring more upon Dimon, [a]lions
upon him that escapeth of Moab, and upon the
remnant of the land.

Moab Destroyed

16 Send [a]ye the lamb to the ruler of the land
[b]from Sela to the wilderness, unto the
mount of the daughter of Zion.
2 For it shall be, *that,* as a [a]wandering bird
cast out of the nest, *so* the daughters of Moab
shall be at the fords of [b]Arnon.
3 Take counsel, execute judgment; make
thy shadow as the night in the midst of the noonday; hide the outcasts; bewray not him that
wandereth.
4 Let mine outcasts dwell with thee, Moab;
be thou a covert to them from the face of the
spoiler: for the extortioner is at an end, the spoiler
ceaseth, the oppressors are consumed out of the
land.
5 And in mercy [a]shall the throne be established: and he shall sit upon it in truth in the tabernacle of David, [b]judging, and seeking judgment,
and hasting [c]righteousness.
6 We have heard of the [a]pride of Moab; *he*
is very proud: *even* of his haughtiness, and his

CHAPTER 15

1 [a]2 Kin. 3:4 [b]Deut. 2:9; Num. 21:28 [c]Is. 15:1—16:14; Jer. 25:21; 48:1–47; Amos 2:1–3; Zeph. 2:8–11
2 [a]Lev. 21:5; Jer. 48:37
3 [a]Jer. 48:38
4 [a]Num. 21:28; 32:3; Jer. 48:34
5 [a]Is. 16:11; Jer. 48:31 [b]Jer. 48:5
6 [a]Num. 32:36
9 [a]2 Kin. 17:25; Jer. 50:17

CHAPTER 16

1 [a]2 Kin. 3:4; Ezra 7:17 [b]2 Kin. 14:7; Is. 42:11
2 [a]Prov. 27:8 [b]Num. 21:13
5 [a][Is. 9:6, 7; 32:1; 55:4; Dan. 7:14; Mic. 4:7; Luke 1:33; Rev. 11:15] [b]Ps. 72:2 [c]Is. 9:7
6 [a]Jer. 48:29; Amos 2:1; Obad. 3, 4; Zeph. 2:8, 10

*

15:2 Heb. *bayith (house)*
15:4 So with MT, Tg., Vg.; LXX, Syr. *loins*
15:5 Or *The Third Eglath,* an unknown city, Jer. 48:34
15:9 So with MT, Tg.; DSS, Vg. *Dibon;* LXX *Rimon*
• See preceding note

NKJV

Proclamation Against Moab

15 The [a]burden against Moab.

Because in the night [b]Ar of [c]Moab is laid waste
And destroyed,
Because in the night Kir of Moab is laid waste
And destroyed,
2 He has gone up to the *temple and Dibon,
To the high places to weep.
Moab will wail over Nebo and over Medeba;
[a]On all their heads *will be* baldness,
And every beard cut off.
3 In their streets they will clothe themselves with sackcloth;
On the tops of their houses
And in their streets
Everyone will wail, [a]weeping bitterly.
4 Heshbon and Elealeh will cry out,
Their voice shall be heard as far as [a]Jahaz;
Therefore the *armed soldiers of Moab will cry out;
His life will be burdensome to him.

5 "My[a] heart will cry out for Moab;
His fugitives *shall flee* to Zoar,
Like *a three-year-old heifer.
For [b]by the Ascent of Luhith
They will go up with weeping;
For in the way of Horonaim
They will raise up a cry of destruction,
6 For the waters [a]of Nimrim will be desolate,
For the green grass has withered away;
The grass fails, there is nothing green.
7 Therefore the abundance they have gained,
And what they have laid up,
They will carry away to the Brook of the Willows.
8 For the cry has gone all around the borders of Moab,
Its wailing to Eglaim
And its wailing to Beer Elim.
9 For the waters of *Dimon will be full of blood;
Because I will bring more upon *Dimon,
[a]Lions upon him who escapes from Moab,
And on the remnant of the land."

Moab Destroyed

16 Send [a]the lamb to the ruler of the land,
[b]From Sela to the wilderness,
To the mount of the daughter of Zion.
2 For it shall be as a [a]wandering bird thrown out of the nest;
So shall be the daughters of Moab at the fords of the [b]Arnon.

3 "Take counsel, execute judgment;
Make your shadow like the night in the middle of the day;
Hide the outcasts,
Do not betray him who escapes.
4 Let My outcasts dwell with you, O Moab;
Be a shelter to them from the face of the spoiler.
For the extortioner is at an end,
Devastation ceases,
The oppressors are consumed out of the land.
5 In mercy [a]the throne will be established;
And One will sit on it in truth, in the tabernacle of David,
[b]Judging and seeking justice and hastening [c]righteousness."

6 We have heard of the [a]pride of Moab—
He is very proud—

KJV

pride, and his wrath: [b]*but* his lies *shall* not *be*
so.
7 Therefore shall Moab [a]howl for Moab,
every one shall howl: for the foundations [b]of Kir-
hareseth shall ye mourn; surely *they are* stricken.
8 For [a]the fields of Heshbon languish, *and*
[b]the vine of Sibmah: the lords of the heathen have
broken down the principal plants thereof, they are
come *even* unto Jazer, they wandered *through* the
wilderness: her branches are stretched out, they
are gone over the [c]sea.
9 Therefore I will bewail with the weeping
of Jazer the vine of Sibmah: I will water thee with
my tears, [a]O Heshbon, and Elealeh: for the shouting for thy summer fruits and for thy harvest is
fallen.
10 And [a]gladness is taken away, and joy out
of the plentiful field; and in the vineyards there
shall be no singing, neither shall there be shouting: the treaders shall tread out no wine in *their*
presses; I have made *their vintage* shouting to
cease.
11 Wherefore [a]my bowels shall sound like
an harp for Moab, and mine inward parts for Kir-
haresh.
12 And it shall come to pass, when it is seen
that Moab is weary on [a]the high place, that he
shall come to his sanctuary to pray; but he shall
not prevail.
13 This *is* the word that the LORD hath spoken
concerning Moab since that time.
14 But now the LORD hath spoken, saying,
Within three years, [a]as the years of an hireling,
and the glory of Moab shall be contemned, with
all that great multitude; and the remnant *shall be*
very small *and* feeble.

Proclamation Against Syria and Israel

17 The [a]burden of Damascus. Behold, Damascus is taken away from *being* a city, and it
shall be a ruinous heap.
2 The cities of [a]Aroer *are* forsaken: they
shall be for flocks, which shall lie down, and
[b]none shall make *them* afraid.
3 [a]The fortress also shall cease from
Ephraim, and the kingdom from Damascus, and
the remnant of Syria: they shall be as the glory
of the children of Israel, saith the LORD of hosts.
4 And in that day it shall come to pass, *that*
the glory of Jacob shall be made thin, and [a]the
fatness of his flesh shall wax lean.
5 [a]And it shall be as when the harvestman
gathereth the corn, and reapeth the ears with his
arm; and it shall be as he that gathereth ears in
the valley of Rephaim.
6 [a]Yet gleaning grapes shall be left in it, as
the shaking of an olive tree, two *or* three berries
in the top of the uppermost bough, four *or* five
in the outmost fruitful branches thereof, saith the
LORD God of Israel.

6 [b]Is. 28:15
7 [a]Jer. 48:20 [b]2 Kin. 3:25; Jer. 48:31
8 [a]Is. 24:7 [b]Is. 16:9 [c]Jer. 48:32
9 [a]Is. 15:4
10 [a]Is. 24:8; Jer. 48:33
11 [a]Is. 15:5; 63:15; Jer. 48:36; Hos. 11:8; Phil. 2:1
12 [a]Is. 15:2
14 [a]Job 7:1; 14:6; Is. 21:16

CHAPTER 17

1 [a]Gen. 14:15; 15:2; 2 Kin. 16:9; Jer. 49:23; Amos 1:3–5; Zech. 9:1; Acts 9:2
2 [a]Num. 32:34 [b]Jer. 7:33
3 [a]Is. 7:16; 8:4
4 [a]Is. 10:16
5 [a]Is. 17:11; Jer. 51:33; Joel 3:13; Matt. 13:30
6 [a]Deut. 4:27; Is. 24:13; Obad. 5

*

17:2 So with MT, Vg.; LXX *It shall be forsaken forever;* Tg. *Its cities shall be forsaken and desolate*

NKJV

Of his haughtiness and his pride and his
wrath;
[b]*But* his lies *shall* not *be* so.
7 Therefore Moab shall [a]wail for Moab;
Everyone shall wail.
For the foundations [b]of Kir Hareseth you
shall mourn;
Surely *they are* stricken.

8 For [a]the fields of Heshbon languish,
And [b]the vine of Sibmah;
The lords of the nations have broken
down its choice plants,
Which have reached to Jazer
And wandered through the wilderness.
Her branches are stretched out,
They are gone over the [c]sea.
9 Therefore I will bewail the vine of Sibmah,
With the weeping of Jazer;
I will drench you with my tears,
[a]O Heshbon and Elealeh;
For battle cries have fallen
Over your summer fruits and your
harvest.

10 [a]Gladness is taken away,
And joy from the plentiful field;
In the vineyards there will be no singing,
Nor will there be shouting;
No treaders will tread out wine in the
presses;
I have made their shouting cease.
11 Therefore [a]my heart shall resound like a
harp for Moab,
And my inner being for Kir Heres.

12 And it shall come to pass,
When it is seen that Moab is weary on
[a]the high place,
That he will come to his sanctuary to pray;
But he will not prevail.

13 This *is* the word which the LORD has spoken concerning Moab since that time.
14 But now the LORD has spoken, saying,
"Within three years, [a]as the years of a hired man,
the glory of Moab will be despised with all that
great multitude, and the remnant *will be* very
small *and* feeble."

Proclamation Against Syria and Israel

17 The [a]burden against Damascus.

"Behold, Damascus will cease from *being*
a city,
And it will be a ruinous heap.
2 *The cities of [a]Aroer *are* forsaken;
They will be for flocks
Which lie down, and [b]no one will make
them afraid.
3 [a]The fortress also will cease from Ephraim,
The kingdom from Damascus,
And the remnant of Syria;
They will be as the glory of the children
of Israel,"
Says the LORD of hosts.

4 "In that day it shall come to pass
That the glory of Jacob will wane,
And [a]the fatness of his flesh grow lean.
5 [a]It shall be as when the harvester gathers
the grain,
And reaps the heads with his arm;
It shall be as he who gathers heads of
grain
In the Valley of Rephaim.
6 [a]Yet gleaning grapes will be left in it,
Like the shaking of an olive tree,
Two *or* three olives at the top of the
uppermost bough,
Four *or* five in its most fruitful branches,"
Says the LORD God of Israel.

KJV

7 At that day shall a man [a]look to his
Maker, and his eyes shall have respect to the Holy
One of Israel.
8 And he shall not look to the altars, the
work of his hands, neither shall respect *that*
which his [a]fingers have made, either the groves,
or the images.
9 In that day shall his strong cities be as a
forsaken bough, and an uppermost branch, which
they left because of the children of Israel: and
there shall be desolation.
10 Because thou hast forgotten [a]the God of
thy salvation, and hast not been mindful of the
rock of thy strength, therefore shalt thou plant
pleasant plants, and shalt set it with strange slips:
11 In the day shalt thou make thy plant to
grow, and in the morning shalt thou make thy
seed to flourish: *but* the harvest *shall be* a heap
in the day of grief and of desperate sorrow.
12 Woe to the multitude of many people,
which make a noise [a]like the noise of the seas;
and to the rushing of nations, *that* make a rushing
like the rushing of mighty waters!
13 The nations shall rush like the rushing of
many waters: but *God* shall [a]rebuke them, and
they shall flee far off, and [b]shall be chased as the
chaff of the mountains before the wind, and like
a rolling thing before the whirlwind.
14 And behold at eveningtide trouble; *and*
before the morning he *is* not. This *is* the portion
of them that spoil us, and the lot of them that
rob us.

Proclamation Against Ethiopia

18 Woe [a]to the land shadowing with wings,
which *is* beyond the rivers of Ethiopia:
2 That sendeth ambassadors by the sea,
even in vessels of bulrushes upon the waters, *say-*
ing, Go, ye swift messengers, to a nation scattered
and peeled, to a people terrible from their beginning hitherto; a nation meted out and trodden
down, whose land the rivers have spoiled!
3 All ye inhabitants of the world, and dwellers on the earth, see ye, [a]when he lifteth up an
ensign on the mountains; and when he bloweth
a trumpet, hear ye.
4 For so the LORD said unto me, I will take
my rest, and I will consider in my dwelling place
like a clear heat upon herbs, *and* like a cloud of
dew in the heat of harvest.
5 For afore the harvest, when the bud is perfect, and the sour grape is ripening in the flower,
he shall both cut off the sprigs with pruninghooks,
and take away *and* cut down the branches.

7 [a]Is. 10:20; Hos. 3:5; Mic. 7:7
8 [a]Is. 2:8; 31:7
10 [a]Ps. 68:19; Is. 51:13
12 [a]Is. 5:30; Jer. 6:23; Ezek. 43:2; Luke 21:25
13 [a]Ps. 9:5; Is. 41:11 [b]Ps. 83:13; Hos. 13:3

CHAPTER 18
1 [a]2 Kin. 19:9; Is. 20:4, 5; Ezek. 30:4, 5, 9; Zeph. 2:12; 3:10
3 [a]Is. 5:26

*
17:8 Heb. *Asherim*, Canaanite deities
17:9 LXX *Hivites;* Tg. *laid waste;* Vg. *as the plows* • LXX *Amorites;* Tg. *in ruins;* Vg. *corn*

NKJV

7 In that day a man will [a]look to his Maker,
And his eyes will have respect for the Holy
One of Israel.
8 He will not look to the altars,
The work of his hands;
He will not respect what his [a]fingers have
made,
Nor the *wooden images nor the incense
altars.

9 In that day his strong cities will be as a
forsaken *bough
And *an uppermost branch,
Which they left because of the children
of Israel;
And there will be desolation.

10 Because you have forgotten [a]the God of
your salvation,
And have not been mindful of the Rock
of your stronghold,
Therefore you will plant pleasant plants
And set out foreign seedlings;
11 In the day you will make your plant to
grow,
And in the morning you will make your
seed to flourish;
But the harvest *will be* a heap of ruins
In the day of grief and desperate sorrow.

12 Woe to the multitude of many people
Who make a noise [a]like the roar of the
seas,
And to the rushing of nations
That make a rushing like the rushing of
mighty waters!
13 The nations will rush like the rushing of
many waters;
But *God* will [a]rebuke them and they will
flee far away,
And [b]be chased like the chaff of the
mountains before the wind,
Like a rolling thing before the whirlwind.
14 Then behold, at eventide, trouble!
And before the morning, he *is* no more.
This *is* the portion of those who plunder
us,
And the lot of those who rob us.

Proclamation Against Ethiopia

18 Woe [a]to the land shadowed with buzzing
wings,
Which *is* beyond the rivers of Ethiopia,
2 Which sends ambassadors by sea,
Even in vessels of reed on the waters,
saying,
"Go, swift messengers, to a nation tall and
smooth *of skin,*
To a people terrible from their beginning
onward,
A nation powerful and treading down,
Whose land the rivers divide."

3 All inhabitants of the world and dwellers
on the earth:
[a]When he lifts up a banner on the
mountains, you see *it;*
And when he blows a trumpet, you hear
it.
4 For so the LORD said to me,
"I will take My rest,
And I will look from My dwelling place
Like clear heat in sunshine,
Like a cloud of dew in the heat of
harvest."
5 For before the harvest, when the bud is
perfect
And the sour grape is ripening in the
flower,
He will both cut off the sprigs with
pruning hooks
And take away *and* cut down the
branches.

KJV

6 They shall be left together unto the fowls
of the mountains, and to the beasts of the earth:
and the fowls shall summer upon them, and all
the beasts of the earth shall winter upon them.
7 In that time [a]shall the present be brought
unto the LORD of hosts of a people scattered and
peeled, and from a people terrible from their beginning hitherto; a nation meted out and trodden
under foot, whose land the rivers have spoiled,
to the place of the name of the LORD of hosts,
the mount Zion.

Proclamation Against Egypt

19 The [a]burden of Egypt. Behold, the LORD
[b]rideth upon a swift cloud, and shall come
into Egypt: and [c]the idols of Egypt shall be moved
at his presence, and the heart of Egypt shall melt
in the midst of it.
2 And I will [a]set the Egyptians against the
Egyptians: and they shall fight every one against
his brother, and every one against his neighbour;
city against city, *and* kingdom against kingdom.
3 And the spirit of Egypt shall fail in the
midst thereof; and I will destroy the counsel
thereof: and they shall [a]seek to the idols, and to
the charmers, and to them that have familiar spirits, and to the wizards.
4 And the Egyptians will I give over [a]into
the hand of a cruel lord; and a fierce king shall
rule over them, saith the Lord, the LORD of hosts.
5 [a]And the waters shall fail from the sea,
and the river shall be wasted and dried up.
6 And they shall turn the rivers far away;
and the brooks [a]of defence shall be emptied and
dried up: the reeds and flags shall wither.
7 The paper reeds by the brooks, by the
mouth of the brooks, and every thing sown by
the brooks, shall wither, be driven away, and be
no *more.*
8 The fishers also shall mourn, and all they
that cast angle into the brooks shall lament, and
they that spread nets upon the waters shall
languish.
9 Moreover they that work in [a]fine flax, and
they that weave networks, shall be confounded.
10 And they shall be broken in the purposes
thereof, all that make sluices *and* ponds for fish.
11 Surely the princes of [a]Zoan *are* fools, the
counsel of the wise counsellors of Pharaoh is become brutish: [b]how say ye unto Pharaoh, I *am*
the son of the wise, the son of ancient kings?
12 [a]Where *are* they? where *are* thy wise
men? and let them tell thee now, and let them
know what the LORD of hosts hath [b]purposed
upon Egypt.
13 The princes of Zoan are become fools,

7 [a]Ps. 68:31; 72:10; Is. 16:1; Zeph. 3:10; Mal. 1:11; Acts 8:27–38

CHAPTER 19

1 [a]Jer. 9:25, 26; Ezek. 29:1—30:19; Joel 3:19 [b]Ps. 18:10; 104:3; Matt. 26:64; Rev. 1:7 [c]Ex. 12:12; Jer. 43:12
2 [a]Judg. 7:22; 1 Sam. 14:16, 20; 2 Chr. 20:23; Matt. 10:21, 36
3 [a]1 Chr. 10:13; Is. 8:19; 47:12; Dan. 2:2
4 [a]Is. 20:4; Jer. 46:26; Ezek. 29:19
5 [a]Is. 50:2; Jer. 51:36; Ezek. 30:12
6 [a]2 Kin. 19:24
9 [a]1 Kin. 10:28; Prov. 7:16; Ezek. 27:7
11 [a]Num. 13:22; Ps. 78:12, 43; Is. 30:4 [b]Gen. 41:38, 39; 1 Kin. 4:29, 30; Acts 7:22
12 [a]1 Cor. 1:20 [b]Ps. 33:11

*______

18:7 So with DSS, LXX, Vg.; MT omits *From;* Tg. *To*
19:7 The Nile

NKJV

6 They will be left together for the mountain
birds of prey
And for the beasts of the earth;
The birds of prey will summer on them,
And all the beasts of the earth will winter
on them.

7 In that time [a]a present will be brought to
the LORD of hosts
*From a people tall and smooth *of skin,*
And from a people terrible from their
beginning onward,
A nation powerful and treading down,
Whose land the rivers divide—
To the place of the name of the LORD of
hosts,
To Mount Zion.

Proclamation Against Egypt

19 The [a]burden against Egypt.

Behold, the LORD [b]rides on a swift
cloud,
And will come into Egypt;
[c]The idols of Egypt will totter at His
presence,
And the heart of Egypt will melt in its
midst.

2 "I will [a]set Egyptians against Egyptians;
Everyone will fight against his brother,
And everyone against his neighbor,
City against city, kingdom against
kingdom.
3 The spirit of Egypt will fail in its
midst;
I will destroy their counsel,
And they will [a]consult the idols and the
charmers,
The mediums and the sorcerers.
4 And the Egyptians I will give
[a]Into the hand of a cruel master,
And a fierce king will rule over them,"
Says the Lord, the LORD of hosts.

5 [a]The waters will fail from the sea,
And the river will be wasted and dried
up.
6 The rivers will turn foul;
The brooks [a]of defense will be emptied
and dried up;
The reeds and rushes will wither.
7 The papyrus reeds by *the River, by the
mouth of the River,
And everything sown by the River,
Will wither, be driven away, and be no
more.
8 The fishermen also will mourn;
All those will lament who cast hooks into
the River,
And they will languish who spread nets
on the waters.
9 Moreover those who work in [a]fine flax
And those who weave fine fabric will be
ashamed;
10 And its foundations will be broken.
All who make wages *will be* troubled of
soul.

11 Surely the princes of [a]Zoan *are* fools;
Pharaoh's wise counselors give foolish
counsel.
[b]How do you say to Pharaoh, "I *am* the
son of the wise,
The son of ancient kings?"
12 [a]Where *are* they?
Where are your wise men?
Let them tell you now,
And let them know what the LORD of hosts
has [b]purposed against Egypt.
13 The princes of Zoan have become fools;

KJV

[a]the princes of Noph are deceived; they have also
seduced Egypt, *even they that are* the stay of the
tribes thereof.
14 The LORD hath mingled [a]a perverse spirit
in the midst thereof: and they have caused Egypt
to err in every work thereof, as a drunken *man*
staggereth in his vomit.
15 Neither shall there be *any* work for Egypt,
which [a]the head or tail, branch or rush, may do.
16 In that day shall Egypt [a]be like unto
women: and it shall be afraid and fear because
of the shaking of the hand of the LORD of hosts,
[b]which he shaketh over it.
17 And the land of Judah shall be a terror
unto Egypt, every one that maketh mention
thereof shall be afraid in himself, because of the
counsel of the LORD of hosts, which he hath [a]de-
termined against it.

Egypt, Assyria, and Israel Blessed

18 In that day shall five cities in the land of
Egypt [a]speak the language of Canaan, and [b]swear
to the LORD of hosts; one shall be called, The city
of destruction.
19 In that day [a]shall there be an altar to the
LORD in the midst of the land of Egypt, and a pillar
at the border thereof to the [b]LORD.
20 And [a]it shall be for a sign and for a witness unto the LORD of hosts in the land of Egypt:
for they shall cry unto the LORD because of the
oppressors, and he shall send them a [b]saviour,
and a great one, and he shall deliver them.
21 And the LORD shall be known to Egypt,
and the Egyptians shall [a]know the LORD in that
day, and [b]shall do sacrifice and oblation; yea, they
shall vow a vow unto the LORD, and perform *it.*
22 And the LORD shall smite Egypt: he shall
smite and [a]heal *it:* and they shall return *even* to
the LORD, and he shall be intreated of them, and
shall heal them.
23 In that day [a]shall there be a highway out
of Egypt to Assyria, and the Assyrian shall come
into Egypt, and the Egyptian into Assyria, and
the Egyptians shall [b]serve with the Assyrians.
24 In that day shall Israel be the third with
Egypt and with Assyria, *even* a blessing in the
midst of the land:
25 Whom the LORD of hosts shall bless, saying, Blessed *be* Egypt my people, and Assyria [a]the
work of my hands, and Israel mine inheritance.

The Sign Against Egypt and Ethiopia

20 In the year that [a]Tartan came unto Ashdod,
(when Sargon the king of Assyria sent
him,) and fought against Ashdod, and took it;
2 At the same time spake the LORD by Isaiah
the son of Amoz, saying, Go and loose [a]the sackcloth from off thy loins, and put off thy shoe from
thy foot. And he did so, [b]walking naked and
barefoot.
3 And the LORD said, Like as my servant
Isaiah hath walked naked and barefoot three
years [a]*for* a sign and wonder upon Egypt and
upon Ethiopia;
4 So shall the [a]king of Assyria lead away
the Egyptians prisoners, and the Ethiopians captives, young and old, naked and barefoot, [b]even
with *their* buttocks uncovered, to the shame of
Egypt.
5 [a]And they shall be afraid and ashamed
of Ethiopia their expectation, and of Egypt their
glory.
6 And the inhabitant of this isle shall say
in that day, Behold, such *is* our expectation,
whither we flee for [a]help to be delivered from the
king of Assyria: and how shall we escape?

13 [a]Jer. 2:16; Ezek. 30:13
14 [a]1 Kin. 22:22; Is. 29:10
15 [a]Is. 9:14–16
16 [a]Jer. 51:30; Nah. 3:13 [b]Is. 11:15
17 [a]Is. 14:24; Dan. 4:35
18 [a]Zeph. 3:9 [b]Is. 45:23
19 [a]Gen. 28:18; Ex. 24:4; Josh. 22:10, 26, 27; Is. 56:7; 60:7 [b]Ps. 68:31
20 [a]Josh. 4:20; 22:27 [b]Is. 43:11
21 [a][Is. 2:3, 4; 11:9] [b]Is. 56:7; 60:7; Zech. 14:16–18; Mal. 1:11
22 [a]Deut. 32:39; Is. 30:26; 57:18; [Heb. 12:11]
23 [a]Is. 11:16; 35:8; 49:11; 62:10 [b]Is. 27:13
25 [a]Deut. 14:2; Ps. 100:3; Is. 29:23; Hos. 2:23; [Eph. 2:10]

CHAPTER 20

1 [a]2 Kin. 18:17
2 [a]Zech. 13:4; Matt. 3:4 [b]1 Sam. 19:24; Mic. 1:8
3 [a]Is. 8:18
4 [a]Is. 19:4 [b]2 Sam. 10:4; Is. 3:17; Jer. 13:22; Mic. 1:11
5 [a]2 Kin. 18:21; Is. 30:3–5; 31:1; Ezek. 29:6, 7
6 [a]Is. 30:5, 7

*

19:13 Ancient Memphis
19:18 Some Heb. mss., Arab., DSS, Tg., Vg. *Sun;* LXX *Asedek,* lit. *Righteousness*
20:1 Or *the Commander in Chief*

NKJV

[a]The princes of *Noph are deceived;
They have also deluded Egypt,
Those who are the mainstay of its tribes.
14 The LORD has mingled [a]a perverse spirit
in her midst;
And they have caused Egypt to err in all
her work,
As a drunken man staggers in his vomit.
15 Neither will there be *any* work for Egypt,
Which [a]the head or tail,
Palm branch or bulrush, may do.

16 In that day Egypt will [a]be like women, and
will be afraid and fear because of the waving of
the hand of the LORD of hosts, [b]which He waves
over it.
17 And the land of Judah will be a terror to
Egypt; everyone who makes mention of it will be
afraid in himself, because of the counsel of the
LORD of hosts which He has [a]determined against
it.

Egypt, Assyria, and Israel Blessed

18 In that day five cities in the land of Egypt
will [a]speak the language of Canaan and [b]swear
by the LORD of hosts; one will be called the City
of *Destruction.
19 In that day [a]there will be an altar to the
LORD in the midst of the land of Egypt, and a pillar
to the [b]LORD at its border.
20 And [a]it will be for a sign and for a witness
to the LORD of hosts in the land of Egypt; for they
will cry to the LORD because of the oppressors,
and He will send them a [b]Savior and a Mighty
One, and He will deliver them.
21 Then the LORD will be known to Egypt,
and the Egyptians will [a]know the LORD in that
day, and [b]will make sacrifice and offering; yes,
they will make a vow to the LORD and perform
it.
22 And the LORD will strike Egypt, He will
strike and [a]heal *it;* they will return to the LORD,
and He will be entreated by them and heal
them.
23 In that day [a]there will be a highway from
Egypt to Assyria, and the Assyrian will come into
Egypt and the Egyptian into Assyria, and the
Egyptians will [b]serve with the Assyrians.
24 In that day Israel will be one of three with
Egypt and Assyria—a blessing in the midst of the
land,
25 whom the LORD of hosts shall bless, saying, "Blessed *is* Egypt My people, and Assyria
[a]the work of My hands, and Israel My inheritance."

The Sign Against Egypt and Ethiopia

20 In the year that [a]Tartan* came to Ashdod,
when Sargon the king of Assyria sent him,
and he fought against Ashdod and took it,
2 at the same time the LORD spoke by Isaiah
the son of Amoz, saying, "Go, and remove [a]the
sackcloth from your body, and take your sandals
off your feet." And he did so, [b]walking naked and
barefoot.
3 Then the LORD said, "Just as My servant
Isaiah has walked naked and barefoot three years
[a]*for* a sign and a wonder against Egypt and
Ethiopia,
4 "so shall the [a]king of Assyria lead away
the Egyptians as prisoners and the Ethiopians as
captives, young and old, naked and barefoot,
[b]with their buttocks uncovered, to the shame of
Egypt.
5 [a]"Then they shall be afraid and ashamed
of Ethiopia their expectation and Egypt their
glory.
6 "And the inhabitant of this territory will
say in that day, 'Surely such *is* our expectation,
wherever we flee for [a]help to be delivered
from the king of Assyria; and how shall we
escape?' "

KJV

The Fall of Babylon Proclaimed

21 The burden of the desert of the sea. As [a]whirlwinds in the south pass through; so it cometh from the desert, from a terrible land.

2 A grievous vision is declared unto me; [a]the treacherous dealer dealeth treacherously, and the spoiler spoileth. [b]Go up, O Elam: besiege, O Media; all the sighing thereof have I made to cease.

3 Therefore [a]are my loins filled with pain: [b]pangs have taken hold upon me, as the pangs of a woman that travaileth: I was bowed down at the hearing *of it;* I was dismayed at the seeing *of it.*

4 My heart panted, fearfulness affrighted me: [a]the night of my pleasure hath he turned into fear unto me.

5 [a]Prepare the table, watch in the watchtower, eat, drink: arise, ye princes, *and* anoint the shield.

6 For thus hath the Lord said unto me, Go, set a watchman, let him declare what he seeth.

7 And he saw a chariot *with* a couple of horsemen, a chariot of asses, *and* a chariot of camels; and he hearkened diligently with much heed:

8 And he cried, A lion: My lord, I stand continually upon the [a]watchtower in the daytime, and I am set in my ward whole nights:

9 And, behold, here cometh a chariot of men, *with* a couple of horsemen. And he answered and said, [a]Babylon is fallen, is fallen; and [b]all the graven images of her gods he hath broken unto the ground.

10 [a]O my threshing, and the corn of my floor: that which I have heard of the LORD of hosts, the God of Israel, have I declared unto you.

Proclamation Against Edom

11 [a]The burden of Dumah. He calleth to me out of [b]Seir, Watchman, what of the night? Watchman, what of the night?

12 The watchman said, The morning cometh, and also the night: if ye will enquire, enquire ye: return, come.

Proclamation Against Arabia

13 [a]The burden upon Arabia. In the forest in Arabia shall ye lodge, O ye travelling companies [b]of Dedanim.

14 The inhabitants of the land of Tema brought water to him that was thirsty, they prevented with their bread him that fled.

15 For they fled from the swords, from the drawn sword, and from the bent bow, and from the grievousness of war.

CHAPTER 21

1 [a]Zech. 9:14 **2** [a]Is. 33:1 [b]Is. 13:17; 22:6; Jer. 49:34 **3** [a]Is. 15:5; 16:11 [b]Is. 13:8 **4** [a]Deut. 28:67 **5** [a]Jer. 51:39; Dan. 5:5 **8** [a]Hab. 2:1 **9** [a]Is. 13:19; 47:5, 9; 48:14; Jer. 51:8; Dan. 5:28, 31; Rev. 14:8; 18:2 [b]Is. 46:1; Jer. 50:2; 51:44 **10** [a]Jer. 51:33; Mic. 4:13 **11** [a]Gen. 25:14; 1 Chr. 1:30; Josh. 15:52 [b]Gen. 32:3; Jer. 49:7; Ezek. 35:2; Obad. 1 **13** [a]Jer. 25:24; 49:28 [b]Gen. 10:7; 1 Chr. 1:9, 32; Jer. 25:23; Ezek. 27:15

NKJV

The Fall of Babylon Proclaimed

21 The burden against the Wilderness of the Sea.

As [a]whirlwinds in the South pass through,
So it comes from the desert, from a terrible land.
2 A distressing vision is declared to me;
[a]The treacherous dealer deals treacherously,
And the plunderer plunders.
[b]Go up, O Elam!
Besiege, O Media!
All its sighing I have made to cease.

3 Therefore [a]my loins are filled with pain;
[b]Pangs have taken hold of me, like the pangs of a woman in labor.
I was distressed when *I* heard *it;*
I was dismayed when *I* saw *it.*
4 My heart wavered, fearfulness frightened me;
[a]The night for which I longed He turned into fear for me.
5 [a]Prepare the table,
Set a watchman in the tower,
Eat and drink.
Arise, you princes,
Anoint the shield!

6 For thus has the Lord said to me:
"Go, set a watchman,
Let him declare what he sees."
7 And he saw a chariot *with* a pair of horsemen,
A chariot of donkeys, *and* a chariot of camels,
And he listened earnestly with great care.
8 *Then he cried, "A lion, my Lord!
I stand continually on the [a]watchtower in the daytime;
I have sat at my post every night.
9 And look, here comes a chariot of men *with* a pair of horsemen!"
Then he answered and said,
[a]"Babylon is fallen, is fallen!
And [b]all the carved images of her gods
He has broken to the ground."

10 [a]Oh, my threshing and the grain of my floor!
That which I have heard from the LORD of hosts,
The God of Israel,
I have declared to you.

Proclamation Against Edom

11 [a]The burden against Dumah.

He calls to me out of [b]Seir,
"Watchman, what of the night?
Watchman, what of the night?"
12 The watchman said,
"The morning comes, and also the night.
If you will inquire, inquire;
Return! Come back!"

Proclamation Against Arabia

13 [a]The burden against Arabia.

In the forest in Arabia you will lodge,
O you traveling companies [b]of Dedanites.
14 O inhabitants of the land of Tema,
Bring water to him who is thirsty;
With their bread they met him who fled.
15 For they fled from the swords, from the drawn sword,
From the bent bow, and from the distress of war.

*

21:8 DSS *Then the observer cried, "My Lord!*

KJV

16 For thus hath the Lord said unto me, Within a year, [a]according to the years of an hireling, and all the glory of [b]Kedar shall fail:

17 And the residue of the number of archers, the mighty men of the children of Kedar, shall be diminished: for the LORD God of Israel hath spoken *it*.

Proclamation Against Jerusalem

22 The burden of the valley of vision. What aileth thee now, that thou art wholly gone up to the housetops?

2 Thou that art full of stirs, a tumultuous city, [a]a joyous city: thy slain *men are* not slain with the sword, nor dead in battle.

3 All thy rulers are fled together, they are bound by the archers: all that are found in thee are bound together, *which* have fled from far.

4 Therefore said I, Look away from me; [a]I will weep bitterly, labour not to comfort me, because of the spoiling of the daughter of my people.

5 [a]For *it is* a day of trouble, and of treading down, and of perplexity [b]by the Lord GOD of hosts in the valley of vision, breaking down the walls, and of crying to the mountains.

6 [a]And Elam bare the quiver with chariots of men *and* horsemen, and [b]Kir uncovered the shield.

7 And it shall come to pass, *that* thy choicest valleys shall be full of chariots, and the horsemen shall set themselves in array at the gate.

8 [a]And he discovered the covering of Judah, and thou didst look in that day to the armour [b]of the house of the forest.

9 [a]Ye have seen also the breaches of the city of David, that they are many: and ye gathered together the waters of the lower pool.

10 And ye have numbered the houses of Jerusalem, and the houses have ye broken down to fortify the wall.

11 [a]Ye made also a ditch between the two walls for the water of the old [b]pool: but ye have not looked unto the maker thereof, neither had respect unto him that fashioned it long ago.

12 And in that day did the Lord GOD of hosts [a]call to weeping, and to mourning, and [b]to baldness, and to girding with sackcloth:

13 And behold joy and gladness, slaying oxen, and killing sheep, eating flesh, and [a]drinking wine: [b]let us eat and drink; for to morrow we shall die.

14 [a]And it was revealed in mine ears by the LORD of hosts, Surely this iniquity [b]shall not be purged from you till ye die, saith the Lord GOD of hosts.

16 [a]Is. 16:14 [b]Ps. 120:5; Song 1:5; Is. 42:11; 60:7; Ezek. 27:21

CHAPTER 22

2 [a]Is. 32:13
4 [a]Jer. 4:19
5 [a]Is. 37:3 [b]Lam. 1:5; 2:2
6 [a]Jer. 49:35 [b]Is. 15:1
8 [a]2 Kin. 18:15, 16 [b]1 Kin. 7:2; 10:17
9 [a]2 Kin. 20:20; 2 Chr. 32:4; Neh. 3:16
11 [a]Neh. 3:16 [b]2 Kin. 20:20; 2 Chr. 32:3, 4
12 [a]Is. 32:11; Joel 1:13; 2:17 [b]Ezra 9:3; Is. 15:2; Mic. 1:16
13 [a]Is. 5:11, 22; 28:7, 8; Luke 17:26–29 [b]Is. 56:12; 1 Cor. 15:32
14 [a]Is. 5:9 [b]1 Sam. 3:14; Ezek. 24:13

NKJV

16 For thus the LORD has said to me: "Within a year, [a]according to the year of a hired man, all the glory of [b]Kedar will fail;

17 "and the remainder of the number of archers, the mighty men of the people of Kedar, will be diminished; for the LORD God of Israel has spoken *it*."

Proclamation Against Jerusalem

22 The burden against the Valley of Vision.

What ails you now, that you have all gone
up to the housetops,
2 You who are full of noise,
A tumultuous city, [a]a joyous city?
Your slain *men are* not slain with the
sword,
Nor dead in battle.
3 All your rulers have fled together;
They are captured by the archers.
All who are found in you are bound
together;
They have fled from afar.
4 Therefore I said, "Look away from
me,
[a]I will weep bitterly;
Do not labor to comfort me
Because of the plundering of the daughter
of my people."

5 [a]For *it is* a day of trouble and treading
down and perplexity
[b]By the Lord GOD of hosts
In the Valley of Vision—
Breaking down the walls
And of crying to the mountain.
6 [a]Elam bore the quiver
With chariots of men *and* horsemen,
And [b]Kir uncovered the shield.
7 It shall come to pass *that* your choicest
valleys
Shall be full of chariots,
And the horsemen shall set themselves in
array at the gate.

8 [a]He removed the protection of Judah.
You looked in that day to the armor [b]of
the House of the Forest;
9 [a]You also saw the damage to the city of
David,
That it was great;
And you gathered together the waters of
the lower pool.
10 You numbered the houses of
Jerusalem,
And the houses you broke down
To fortify the wall.
11 [a]You also made a reservoir between the
two walls
For the water of the old [b]pool.
But you did not look to its Maker,
Nor did you have respect for Him who
fashioned it long ago.

12 And in that day the Lord GOD of hosts
[a]Called for weeping and for mourning,
[b]For baldness and for girding with
sackcloth.
13 But instead, joy and gladness,
Slaying oxen and killing sheep,
Eating meat and [a]drinking wine:
[b]"Let us eat and drink, for tomorrow we
die!"

14 [a]Then it was revealed in my hearing by the
LORD of hosts,
"Surely for this iniquity there [b]will be no
atonement for you,
Even to your death," says the Lord GOD
of hosts.

KJV

The Judgment on Shebna

15 Thus saith the Lord GOD of hosts, Go, get
thee unto this treasurer, *even* unto [a]Shebna,
which *is* over the house, *and say,*
16 What hast thou here? and whom hast thou
here, that thou hast hewed thee out a sepulchre
here, *as* he [a]that heweth him out a sepulchre on
high, *and* that graveth an habitation for himself
in a rock?
17 Behold, the LORD will carry thee away
with a mighty captivity, [a]and will surely cover
thee.
18 He will surely violently turn and toss thee
like a ball into a large country: there shalt thou
die, and there the [a]chariots of thy glory *shall be*
the shame of thy lord's house.
19 And I will drive thee from thy station, and
from thy state shall he pull thee down.
20 And it shall come to pass in that day, that
I will call my servant [a]Eliakim the son of Hilkiah:
21 And I will clothe him with thy robe, and
strengthen him with thy girdle, and I will commit
thy government into his hand: and he shall be a
father to the inhabitants of Jerusalem, and to the
house of Judah.
22 And the key of the house of David will I
lay upon his [a]shoulder; so he shall [b]open, and
none shall shut; and he shall shut, and none shall
open.
23 And I will fasten him *as* [a]a nail in a sure
place; and he shall be for a glorious throne to
his father's house.
24 And they shall hang upon him all the glory
of his father's house, the offspring and the issue,
all vessels of small quantity, from the vessels of
cups, even to all the vessels of flagons.
25 In that day, saith the LORD of hosts, shall
the nail that is fastened in the sure place be removed, and be cut down, and fall; and the burden
that *was* upon it shall be cut off: for the LORD
hath spoken *it.*

Proclamation Against Tyre

23 The [a]burden of Tyre. Howl, ye ships of
Tarshish; for it is laid waste, so that there
is no house, no entering in: from the land of Chittim it is revealed to them.
2 Be still, ye inhabitants of the isle; thou
whom the merchants of Zidon, that pass over the
sea, have replenished.
3 And by great waters the seed of Sihor, the
harvest of the river, *is* her revenue; and [a]she is a
mart of nations.
4 Be thou ashamed, O Zidon: for the sea
hath spoken, *even* the strength of the sea, saying,
I travail not, nor bring forth children, neither do
I nourish up young men, *nor* bring up virgins.
5 [a]As at the report concerning Egypt, *so*
shall they be sorely pained at the report of Tyre.

15 [a]2 Kin. 18:37; Is. 36:3 **16** [a]2 Sam. 18:18; 2 Chr. 16:14; Matt. 27:60 **17** [a]Esth. 7:8 **18** [a]Is. 2:7 **20** [a]2 Kin. 18:18; Is. 36:3, 22; 37:2 **22** [a]Is. 9:6 [b]Job 12:14; Rev. 3:7 **23** [a]Ezra 9:8; Zech. 10:4

CHAPTER 23

1 [a]Jer. 25:22; 47:4; Ezek. 26—28; Amos 1:9; Zech. 9:2, 4 **3** [a]Ezek. 27:3–23 **5** [a]Is. 19:16

*

22:19 LXX omits *he will pull you down;* Syr., Tg., Vg. *I will pull you down*
23:1 Heb. *Kittim,* western lands, especially Cyprus
23:2 So with MT, Vg.; LXX, Tg. *passing over the water;* DSS *your messengers passing over the sea*
23:3 The Nile

NKJV

The Judgment on Shebna

15 Thus says the Lord GOD of hosts:

"Go, proceed to this steward,
To [a]Shebna, who *is* over the house, *and say:*
16 'What have you here, and whom have you here,
That you have hewn a sepulcher here,
As he [a]who hews himself a sepulcher on high,
Who carves a tomb for himself in a rock?
17 Indeed, the LORD will throw you away violently,
O mighty man,
[a]And will surely seize you.
18 He will surely turn violently and toss you like a ball
Into a large country;
There you shall die, and there [a]your glorious chariots
Shall be the shame of your master's house.
19 So I will drive you out of your office,
And from your position *he will pull you down.

20 'Then it shall be in that day,
That I will call My servant [a]Eliakim the son of Hilkiah;
21 I will clothe him with your robe
And strengthen him with your belt;
I will commit your responsibility into his hand.
He shall be a father to the inhabitants of Jerusalem
And to the house of Judah.
22 The key of the house of David
I will lay on his [a]shoulder;
So he shall [b]open, and no one shall shut;
And he shall shut, and no one shall open.
23 I will fasten him *as* [a]a peg in a secure place,
And he will become a glorious throne to his father's house.

24 'They will hang on him all the glory of his father's house, the offspring and the posterity, all vessels of small quantity, from the cups to all the pitchers.
25 'In that day,' says the LORD of hosts, 'the peg that is fastened in the secure place will be removed and be cut down and fall, and the burden that *was* on it will be cut off; for the LORD has spoken.'"

Proclamation Against Tyre

23 The [a]burden against Tyre.

Wail, you ships of Tarshish!
For it is laid waste,
So that there is no house, no harbor;
From the land of *Cyprus it is revealed to them.

2 Be still, you inhabitants of the coastland,
You merchants of Sidon,
*Whom those who cross the sea have filled.
3 And on great waters the grain of Shihor,
The harvest of *the River, *is* her revenue;
And [a]she is a marketplace for the nations.

4 Be ashamed, O Sidon;
For the sea has spoken,
The strength of the sea, saying,
"I do not labor, nor bring forth children;
Neither do I rear young men,
Nor bring up virgins."
5 [a]When the report *reaches* Egypt,
They also will be in agony at the report of Tyre.

KJV

6 Pass ye over to Tarshish; howl, ye inhabitants of the isle.
7 *Is* this your [a]joyous *city*, whose antiquity
is of ancient days? her own feet shall carry her
afar off to sojourn.
8 Who hath taken this counsel against Tyre,
[a]the crowning *city*, whose merchants *are* princes,
whose traffickers *are* the honourable of the earth?
9 The LORD of hosts hath [a]purposed it, to
stain the [b]pride of all glory, *and* to bring into contempt all the honourable of the earth.
10 Pass through thy land as a river, O daughter of Tarshish: *there is* no more strength.
11 He stretched out his hand over the sea,
he shook the kingdoms: the LORD hath given a
commandment [a]against the merchant *city*, to destroy the strong holds thereof.
12 And he said, Thou shalt no more rejoice,
O thou oppressed virgin, daughter of Zidon: arise,
[a]pass over to Chittim; there also shalt thou have
no rest.
13 Behold the land of the [a]Chaldeans; this
people was not, *till* the Assyrian founded it for
[b]them that dwell in the wilderness: they set up
the towers thereof, they raised up the palaces
thereof; *and* he brought it to ruin.
14 [a]Howl, ye ships of Tarshish: for your
strength is laid waste.
15 And it shall come to pass in that day, that
Tyre shall be forgotten seventy years, according
to the days of one king: after the end of seventy
years shall Tyre sing as an harlot.
16 Take an harp, go about the city, thou harlot that hast been forgotten; make sweet melody,
sing many songs, that thou mayest be remembered.
17 And it shall come to pass after the end of
seventy years, that the LORD will visit Tyre, and
she shall turn to her hire, and [a]shall commit fornication with all the kingdoms of the world upon
the face of the earth.
18 And her merchandise and her hire [a]shall
be holiness to the LORD: it shall not be treasured
nor laid up; for her merchandise shall be for them
that dwell before the LORD, to eat sufficiently, and
for durable clothing.

Impending Judgment on the Earth

24 Behold, the LORD maketh the earth empty,
and maketh it waste, and turneth it upside
down, and scattereth abroad the inhabitants
thereof.
2 And it shall be, as with the people, so with
the [a]priest; as with the servant, so with his master;
as with the maid, so with her mistress; [b]as with
the buyer, so with the seller; as with the lender,
so with the borrower; as with the taker of usury,
so with the giver of usury to him.
3 The land shall be utterly emptied, and utterly spoiled: for the LORD hath spoken this word.
4 The earth mourneth *and* fadeth away, the
world languisheth *and* fadeth away, the [a]haughty
people of the earth do languish.

7 [a]Is. 22:2; 32:13
8 [a]Ezek. 28:2, 12
9 [a]Is. 14:26 [b]Job 40:11, 12; Is. 13:11; 24:4; Dan. 4:37
11 [a]Zech. 9:2–4
12 [a]Ezek. 26:13, 14; Rev. 18:22
13 [a]Is. 47:1 [b]Ps. 72:9
14 [a]Ezek. 27:25–30
17 [a]Rev. 17:2
18 [a]Ex. 28:36; Zech. 14:20, 21

CHAPTER 24
2 [a]Hos. 4:9 [b]Ezek. 7:12, 13
4 [a]Is. 25:11

***23:10** The Nile

NKJV

6 Cross over to Tarshish;
Wail, you inhabitants of the coastland!
7 *Is* this your [a]joyous *city*,
Whose antiquity *is* from ancient days,
Whose feet carried her far off to dwell?
8 Who has taken this counsel against Tyre,
[a]the crowning *city*,
Whose merchants *are* princes,
Whose traders *are* the honorable of the earth?
9 The LORD of hosts has [a]purposed it,
To bring to dishonor the [b]pride of all glory,
To bring into contempt all the honorable of the earth.

10 Overflow through your land like *the River,
O daughter of Tarshish;
There is no more strength.
11 He stretched out His hand over the sea,
He shook the kingdoms;
The LORD has given a commandment [a]against Canaan
To destroy its strongholds.
12 And He said, "You will rejoice no more,
O you oppressed virgin daughter of Sidon.
Arise, [a]cross over to Cyprus;
There also you will have no rest."

13 Behold, the land of the [a]Chaldeans,
This people *which* was not;
Assyria founded it for [b]wild beasts of the desert.
They set up its towers,
They raised up its palaces,
And brought it to ruin.

14 [a]Wail, you ships of Tarshish!
For your strength is laid waste.

15 Now it shall come to pass in that day that
Tyre will be forgotten seventy years, according
to the days of one king. At the end of seventy
years it will happen to Tyre as *in* the song of the
harlot:

16 "Take a harp, go about the city,
You forgotten harlot;
Make sweet melody, sing many songs,
That you may be remembered."

17 And it shall be, at the end of seventy years,
that the LORD will deal with Tyre. She will return
to her hire, and [a]commit fornication with all the
kingdoms of the world on the face of the earth.
18 Her gain and her pay [a]will be set apart
for the LORD; it will not be treasured nor laid
up, for her gain will be for those who dwell
before the LORD, to eat sufficiently, and for fine
clothing.

Impending Judgment on the Earth

24 Behold, the LORD makes the earth empty and makes it waste,
Distorts its surface
And scatters abroad its inhabitants.
2 And it shall be:
As with the people, so with the [a]priest;
As with the servant, so with his master;
As with the maid, so with her mistress;
[b]As with the buyer, so with the seller;
As with the lender, so with the borrower;
As with the creditor, so with the debtor.
3 The land shall be entirely emptied and utterly plundered,
For the LORD has spoken this word.

4 The earth mourns *and* fades away,
The world languishes *and* fades away;
The [a]haughty people of the earth languish.

KJV

5 [a]The earth also is defiled under the inhabitants thereof; because they have [b]transgressed the laws, changed the ordinance, broken the [c]everlasting covenant.

6 Therefore hath [a]the curse devoured the earth, and they that dwell therein are desolate: therefore the inhabitants of the earth are [b]burned, and few men left.

7 [a]The new wine mourneth, the vine languisheth, all the merryhearted do sigh.

8 The mirth [a]of tabrets ceaseth, the noise of them that rejoice endeth, the joy of the harp ceaseth.

9 They shall not drink wine with a song; strong drink shall be bitter to them that drink it.

10 The city of confusion is broken down: every house is shut up, that no man may come in.

11 *There is* a crying for wine in the streets; all joy is darkened, the mirth of the land is gone.

12 In the city is left desolation, and the gate is smitten with destruction.

13 When thus it shall be in the midst of the land among the people, [a]*there shall be* as the shaking of an olive tree, *and* as the gleaning grapes when the vintage is done.

14 They shall lift up their voice, they shall sing for the majesty of the LORD, they shall cry aloud from the sea.

15 Wherefore [a]glorify ye the LORD in the fires, *even* [b]the name of the LORD God of Israel in the isles of the sea.

16 From the uttermost part of the earth have we heard songs, *even* glory to the righteous. But I said, My leanness, my leanness, woe unto me! [a]the treacherous dealers have dealt treacherously; yea, the treacherous dealers have dealt very treacherously.

17 [a]Fear, and the pit, and the snare, *are* upon thee, O inhabitant of the earth.

18 And it shall come to pass, *that* he who fleeth from the noise of the fear shall fall into the pit; and he that cometh up out of the midst of the pit shall be taken in the snare: for [a]the windows from on high are open, and [b]the foundations of the earth do shake.

19 [a]The earth is utterly broken down, the earth is clean dissolved, the earth is moved exceedingly.

20 The earth shall [a]reel to and fro like a drunkard, and shall be removed like a cottage; and the transgression thereof shall be heavy upon it; and it shall fall, and not rise again.

21 And it shall come to pass in that day, *that* the LORD shall punish the host of the high ones *that are* on high, [a]and the kings of the earth upon the earth.

22 And they shall be gathered together, *as* prisoners are gathered in the pit, and shall be shut

5 [a]Gen. 3:17; Num. 35:33; Is. 9:17; 10:6 [b]Is. 59:12 [c]1 Chr. 16:14–19; Ps. 105:7–12
6 [a]Mal. 4:6 [b]Is. 9:19
7 [a]Is. 16:8–10; Joel 1:10, 12
8 [a]Is. 5:12, 14; Jer. 7:34; 16:9; 25:10; Ezek. 26:13; Hos. 2:11; Rev. 18:22
13 [a][Is. 17:5, 6; 27:12]
15 [a]Is. 25:3 [b]Mal. 1:11
16 [a]Is. 21:2; 33:1; Jer. 3:20; 5:11
17 [a]Jer. 48:43; Amos 5:19
18 [a]Gen. 7:11 [b]Ps. 18:7; 46:2; Is. 2:19, 21; 13:13
19 [a]Jer. 4:23
20 [a]Is. 19:14; 24:1; 28:7
21 [a]Ps. 76:12

NKJV

5 [a]The earth is also defiled under its
inhabitants,
Because they have [b]transgressed the laws,
Changed the ordinance,
Broken the [c]everlasting covenant.
6 Therefore [a]the curse has devoured the
earth,
And those who dwell in it are desolate.
Therefore the inhabitants of the earth are
[b]burned,
And few men *are* left.

7 [a]The new wine fails, the vine languishes,
All the merry-hearted sigh.
8 The mirth [a]of the tambourine ceases,
The noise of the jubilant ends,
The joy of the harp ceases.
9 They shall not drink wine with a song;
Strong drink is bitter to those who drink
it.
10 The city of confusion is broken down;
Every house is shut up, so that none may
go in.
11 *There is* a cry for wine in the streets,
All joy is darkened,
The mirth of the land is gone.
12 In the city desolation is left,
And the gate is stricken with destruction.
13 When it shall be thus in the midst of the
land among the people,
[a]*It shall be* like the shaking of an olive
tree,
Like the gleaning of grapes when the
vintage is done.

14 They shall lift up their voice, they shall
sing;
For the majesty of the LORD
They shall cry aloud from the sea.
15 Therefore [a]glorify the LORD in the
dawning light,
[b]The name of the LORD God of Israel in the
coastlands of the sea.
16 From the ends of the earth we have heard
songs:
"Glory to the righteous!"
But I said, "I am ruined, ruined!
Woe to me!
[a]The treacherous dealers have dealt
treacherously,
Indeed, the treacherous dealers have dealt
very treacherously."

17 [a]Fear and the pit and the snare
Are upon you, O inhabitant of the earth.
18 And it shall be
That he who flees from the noise of the
fear
Shall fall into the pit,
And he who comes up from the midst of
the pit
Shall be caught in the snare;
For [a]the windows from on high are
open,
And [b]the foundations of the earth are
shaken.

19 [a]The earth is violently broken,
The earth is split open,
The earth is shaken exceedingly.
20 The earth shall [a]reel to and fro like a
drunkard,
And shall totter like a hut;
Its transgression shall be heavy upon it,
And it will fall, and not rise again.

21 It shall come to pass in that day
That the LORD will punish on high the host
of exalted ones,
And on the earth [a]the kings of the earth.
22 They will be gathered together,
As prisoners are gathered in the pit,

KJV

up in the prison, and after many days shall they
be visited.
23 Then the [a]moon shall be confounded, and
the sun ashamed, when the LORD of hosts shall
[b]reign in [c]mount Zion, and in Jerusalem, and before his ancients gloriously.

Praise to God

25 O LORD, thou *art* my God; [a]I will exalt thee,
I will praise thy name; [b]for thou hast done
wonderful *things;* [c]*thy* counsels of old *are* faithfulness *and* truth.
2 For thou hast made [a]of a city an heap; *of*
a defenced city a ruin: a palace of strangers to
be no city; it shall never be built.
3 Therefore shall the strong people [a]glorify
thee, the city of the terrible nations shall fear thee.
4 For thou hast been a strength to the poor,
a strength to the needy in his distress, [a]a refuge
from the storm, a shadow from the heat, when
the blast of the terrible ones *is* as a storm *against*
the wall.
5 Thou shalt bring down the noise of strangers, as the heat in a dry place; *even* the heat with
the shadow of a cloud: the branch of the terrible
ones shall be brought low.
6 And in [a]this mountain shall [b]the LORD of
hosts make unto [c]all people a feast of fat things,
a feast of wines on the lees, of fat things full of
marrow, of wines on the lees well refined.
7 And he will destroy in this mountain the
face of the covering cast over all people, and [a]the
vail that is spread over all nations.
8 He will [a]swallow up death in victory; and
the Lord GOD will [b]wipe away tears from off all
faces; and the rebuke of his people shall he take
away from off all the earth: for the LORD hath
spoken *it.*
9 And it shall be said in that day, Lo, this
is our God; [a]we have waited for him, and he will
save us: this *is* the LORD; we have waited for him,
[b]we will be glad and rejoice in his salvation.
10 For in this mountain shall the hand of the
LORD rest, and [a]Moab shall be trodden down under him, even as straw is trodden down for the
dunghill.
11 And he shall spread forth his hands in the
midst of them, as he that swimmeth spreadeth
forth *his hands* to swim: and he shall bring down
their [a]pride together with the spoils of their
hands.
12 And the [a]fortress of the high fort of thy
walls shall he bring down, lay low, *and* bring to
the ground, *even* to the dust.

23 [a]Is. 13:10; 60:19; Ezek. 32:7; Joel 2:31; 3:15 [b]Rev. 19:4, 6 [c][Heb. 12:22]

CHAPTER 25

1 [a]Ex. 15:2 [b]Ps. 98:1 [c]Num. 23:19
2 [a]Is. 21:9; 23:13; Jer. 51:37
3 [a]Is. 24:15; Rev. 11:13
4 [a]Is. 4:6
6 [a][Is. 2:2–4; 56:7] [b]Prov. 9:2; Matt. 22:4 [c][Dan. 7:14; Matt. 8:11]
7 [a]2 Cor. 3:15; [Eph. 4:18]
8 [a][Hos. 13:14; 1 Cor. 15:54; Rev. 20:14] [b]Is. 30:19; Rev. 7:17; 21:4
9 [a]Gen. 49:18; Is. 8:17; 26:8; [Titus 2:13] [b]Ps. 20:5
10 [a]Is. 16:14; Jer. 48:1–47; Ezek. 25:8–11; Amos 2:1–3; Zeph. 2:9
11 [a]Is. 24:4; 26:5
12 [a]Is. 26:5

NKJV

And will be shut up in the prison;
After many days they will be punished.
23 Then the [a]moon will be disgraced
And the sun ashamed;
For the LORD of hosts will [b]reign
On [c]Mount Zion and in Jerusalem
And before His elders, gloriously.

Praise to God

25 O LORD, You *are* my God.
[a]I will exalt You,
I will praise Your name,
[b]For You have done wonderful *things;*
[c]*Your* counsels of old *are* faithfulness *and*
truth.
2 For You have made [a]a city a ruin,
A fortified city a ruin,
A palace of foreigners to be a city no
more;
It will never be rebuilt.
3 Therefore the strong people will [a]glorify
You;
The city of the terrible nations will fear
You.
4 For You have been a strength to the
poor,
A strength to the needy in his distress,
[a]A refuge from the storm,
A shade from the heat;
For the blast of the terrible ones *is* as a
storm *against* the wall.
5 You will reduce the noise of aliens,
As heat in a dry place;
As heat in the shadow of a cloud,
The song of the terrible ones will be
diminished.
6 And in [a]this mountain
[b]The LORD of hosts will make for [c]all
people
A feast of choice pieces,
A feast of wines on the lees,
Of fat things full of marrow,
Of well-refined wines on the lees.
7 And He will destroy on this mountain
The surface of the covering cast over all
people,
And [a]the veil that is spread over all
nations.
8 He will [a]swallow up death forever,
And the Lord GOD will [b]wipe away tears
from all faces;
The rebuke of His people
He will take away from all the earth;
For the LORD has spoken.

9 And it will be said in that day:
"Behold, this *is* our God;
[a]We have waited for Him, and He will save
us.
This *is* the LORD;
We have waited for Him;
[b]We will be glad and rejoice in His
salvation."

10 For on this mountain the hand of the LORD
will rest,
And [a]Moab shall be trampled down under
Him,
As straw is trampled down for the refuse
heap.
11 And He will spread out His hands in their
midst
As a swimmer reaches out to swim,
And He will bring down their [a]pride
Together with the trickery of their
hands.
12 The [a]fortress of the high fort of your
walls
He will bring down, lay low,
And bring to the ground, down to the
dust.

KJV

A Song of Salvation

26 In [a]that day shall this song be sung in the land of Judah; We have a strong city; [b]salvation will *God* appoint *for* walls and bulwarks.

2 [a]Open ye the gates, that the righteous nation which keepeth the truth may enter in.

3 Thou wilt keep *him* in perfect [a]peace, *whose* mind *is* stayed *on thee:* because he trusteth in thee.

4 Trust ye in the LORD for ever: [a]for in the LORD JEHOVAH *is* everlasting strength:

5 For he bringeth down them that dwell on high; [a]the lofty city, he layeth it low; he layeth it low, *even* to the ground; he bringeth it *even* to the dust.

6 The foot shall tread it down, *even* the feet of the poor, *and* the steps of the needy.

7 The way of the just *is* uprightness: [a]thou, most upright, dost weigh the path of the just.

8 Yea, [a]in the way of thy judgments, O LORD, have we [b]waited for thee; the desire of *our* soul *is* to thy name, and to the remembrance of thee.

9 [a]With my soul have I desired thee in the night; yea, with my spirit within me will I seek thee early: for when thy judgments *are* in the earth, the inhabitants of the world will learn righteousness.

10 [a]Let favour be shewed to the wicked, *yet* will he not learn righteousness: in [b]the land of uprightness will he deal unjustly, and will not behold the majesty of the LORD.

11 LORD, *when* thy hand is lifted up, [a]they will not see: *but* they shall see, and be ashamed for *their* envy at the people; yea, the fire of thine enemies shall devour them.

12 LORD, thou wilt ordain peace for us: for thou also hast wrought all our works in us.

13 O LORD our God, [a]*other* lords beside thee have had dominion over us: *but* by thee only will we make mention of thy name.

14 *They are* dead, they shall not live; *they are* deceased, they shall not rise: therefore hast thou visited and destroyed them, and made all their memory to [a]perish.

15 Thou hast [a]increased the nation, O LORD, thou hast increased the nation: thou art glorified: thou hadst removed *it* far *unto* all the ends of the earth.

16 LORD, [a]in trouble have they visited thee, they poured out a prayer *when* thy chastening *was* upon them.

17 Like as [a]a woman with child, *that* draweth near the time of her delivery, is in pain, *and* crieth out in her pangs; so have we been in thy sight, O LORD.

CHAPTER 26

1 [a]Is. 2:11; 12:1 [b]Is. 60:18
2 [a]Ps. 118:19, 20
3 [a]Is. 57:19; [Phil. 4:6, 7]
4 [a]Is. 12:2; 45:17
5 [a]Is. 25:11, 12
7 [a]Ps. 37:23
8 [a]Is. 64:5 [b]Is. 25:9; 33:2
9 [a]Ps. 63:6; Song 3:1; Is. 50:10; Luke 6:12
10 [a]Eccl. 8:12; [Rom. 2:4] [b]Ps. 143:10
11 [a]Job 34:27; Ps. 28:5; Is. 5:12
13 [a]2 Chr. 12:8
14 [a]Eccl. 9:5; Is. 14:22
15 [a]Is. 9:3
16 [a]Is. 37:3; Hos. 5:15
17 [a]Is. 13:8; [John 16:21]

NKJV

A Song of Salvation

26 In [a]that day this song will be sung in the land of Judah:

"We have a strong city;
[b]*God* will appoint salvation *for* walls and bulwarks.
2 [a]Open the gates,
That the righteous nation which keeps the truth may enter in.
3 You will keep *him* in perfect [a]peace,
Whose mind *is* stayed *on You,*
Because he trusts in You.
4 Trust in the LORD forever,
[a]For in YAH, the LORD, *is* *everlasting strength.
5 For He brings down those who dwell on high,
[a]The lofty city;
He lays it low,
He lays it low to the ground,
He brings it down to the dust.
6 The foot shall tread it down—
The feet of the poor
And the steps of the needy."

7 The way of the just *is* uprightness;
[a]O Most Upright,
You weigh the path of the just.
8 Yes, [a]in the way of Your judgments,
O LORD, we have [b]waited for You;
The desire of *our* soul *is* for Your name
And for the remembrance of You.
9 [a]With my soul I have desired You in the night,
Yes, by my spirit within me I will seek You early;
For when Your judgments *are* in the earth,
The inhabitants of the world will learn righteousness.

10 [a]Let grace be shown to the wicked,
Yet he will not learn righteousness;
In [b]the land of uprightness he will deal unjustly,
And will not behold the majesty of the LORD.
11 LORD, *when* Your hand is lifted up, [a]they will not see.
But they will see and be ashamed
For *their* envy of people;
Yes, the fire of Your enemies shall devour them.

12 LORD, You will establish peace for us,
For You have also done all our works in us.
13 O LORD our God, [a]masters besides You
Have had dominion over us;
But by You only we make mention of Your name.
14 *They are* dead, they will not live;
They are deceased, they will not rise.
Therefore You have punished and destroyed them,
And made all their memory to [a]perish.
15 You have increased the nation, O LORD,
You have [a]increased the nation;
You are glorified;
You have expanded all the borders of the land.

16 LORD, [a]in trouble they have visited You,
They poured out a prayer *when* Your chastening *was* upon them.
17 As [a]a woman with child
Is in pain and cries out in her pangs,
When she draws near the time of her delivery,
So have we been in Your sight, O LORD.

---

*26:4 Or *Rock of Ages*

KJV

18 We have been with child, we have been in pain, we have as it were brought forth wind; we have not wrought any deliverance in the earth; neither have [a]the inhabitants of the world fallen.

19 [a]Thy dead *men* shall live, *together with* my dead body shall they arise. [b]Awake and sing, ye that dwell in dust: for thy dew *is as* the dew of herbs, and the earth shall cast out the dead.

Take Refuge from the Coming Judgment

20 Come, my people, [a]enter thou into thy chambers, and shut thy doors about thee: hide thyself as it were [b]for a little moment, until the indignation be overpast.

21 For, behold, the LORD [a]cometh out of his place to punish the inhabitants of the earth for their iniquity: the earth also shall disclose her blood, and shall no more cover her slain.

27 In that day the LORD with his sore and great and strong sword shall punish leviathan the piercing serpent, [a]even leviathan that crooked serpent; and he shall slay [b]the dragon that *is* in the sea.

The Restoration of Israel

2 In that day [a]sing ye unto her, [b]A vineyard of red wine.

3 [a]I the LORD do keep it; I will water it every moment: lest *any* hurt it, I will keep it night and day.

4 Fury *is* not in me: who would set [a]the briers *and* thorns against me in battle? I would go through them, I would burn them together.

5 Or let him take hold [a]of my strength, *that* he may [b]make peace with me; *and* he shall make peace with me.

6 He shall cause them that come of Jacob [a]to take root: Israel shall blossom and bud, and fill the face of the world with fruit.

7 [a]Hath he smitten him, as he smote those that smote him? *or* is he slain according to the slaughter of them that are slain by him?

8 [a]In measure, when it shooteth forth, thou wilt debate with it: [b]he stayeth his rough wind in the day of the east wind.

9 By this therefore shall the iniquity of Jacob be purged; and this *is* all the fruit to take away his sin; when he maketh all the stones of the altar as chalkstones that are beaten in sunder, the groves and images shall not stand up.

10 Yet the defenced city *shall be* [a]desolate, *and* the habitation forsaken, and left like a wilderness: there shall the calf feed, and there shall he lie down, and consume the branches thereof.

11 When the boughs thereof are withered, they shall be broken off: the women come, *and*

18 [a]Ps. 17:14
19 [a]Is. 25:8; [Ezek. 37:1–14] [b][Dan. 12:2]; Hos. 13:14
20 [a]Ex. 12:22, 23; [Ps. 91:1, 4] [b][Ps. 30:5; Is. 54:7, 8; 2 Cor. 4:17]
21 [a]Mic. 1:3; [Jude 14]

CHAPTER 27
1 [a]Gen. 3:1; Ps. 74:13, 14; Rev. 12:9, 15 [b]Is. 51:9; Ezek. 29:3; 32:2
2 [a]Is. 5:1 [b]Ps. 80:8; Is. 5:7; Jer. 2:21
3 [a]1 Sam. 2:9; Ps. 121:4, 5; Is. 31:5; [John 10:28]
4 [a]2 Sam. 23:6; Is. 9:18
5 [a]Is. 25:4 [b]Job 22:21; Is. 26:3, 12; [Rom. 5:1; 2 Cor. 5:20]
6 [a]Is. 37:31; Hos. 14:5, 6
7 [a]Is. 10:12, 17; 30:30–33
8 [a]Job 23:6; Ps. 6:1; Jer. 10:24; 30:11; 46:28; [1 Cor. 10:13] [b][Ps. 78:38]
10 [a]Is. 5:6, 17; 32:14; Jer. 26:18

*

26:19 So with MT, Vg.; Syr., Tg. *their dead bodies;* LXX *those in the tombs*
27:2 So with MT (Kittel's *Biblia Hebraica*), Bg., Vg.; MT (*Biblia Hebraica Stuttgartensia*), some Heb. mss., LXX *delight;* Tg. *choice vineyard*
27:9 Heb. *Asherim,* Canaanite deities

NKJV

18 We have been with child, we have been in pain;
We have, as it were, brought forth wind;
We have not accomplished any deliverance in the earth,
Nor have [a]the inhabitants of the world fallen.

19 [a]Your dead shall live;
Together with *my dead body they shall arise.
[b]Awake and sing, you who dwell in dust;
For your dew *is like* the dew of herbs,
And the earth shall cast out the dead.

Take Refuge from the Coming Judgment

20 Come, my people, [a]enter your chambers,
And shut your doors behind you;
Hide yourself, as it were, [b]for a little moment,
Until the indignation is past.

21 For behold, the LORD [a]comes out of His place
To punish the inhabitants of the earth for their iniquity;
The earth will also disclose her blood,
And will no more cover her slain.

27 In that day the LORD with His severe sword, great and strong,
Will punish Leviathan the fleeing serpent,
[a]Leviathan that twisted serpent;
And He will slay [b]the reptile that *is* in the sea.

The Restoration of Israel

2 In that day [a]sing to her,
[b]"A vineyard of *red wine!

3 [a]I, the LORD, keep it,
I water it every moment;
Lest any hurt it,
I keep it night and day.

4 Fury *is* not in Me.
Who would set [a]briers *and* thorns
Against Me in battle?
I would go through them,
I would burn them together.

5 Or let him take hold [a]of My strength,
That he may [b]make peace with Me;
And he shall make peace with Me."

6 Those who come He shall cause [a]to take root in Jacob;
Israel shall blossom and bud,
And fill the face of the world with fruit.

7 [a]Has He struck Israel as He struck those who struck him?
Or has He been slain according to the slaughter of those who were slain by Him?

8 [a]In measure, by sending it away,
You contended with it.
[b]He removes *it* by His rough wind
In the day of the east wind.

9 Therefore by this the iniquity of Jacob will be covered;
And this *is* all the fruit of taking away his sin:
When he makes all the stones of the altar
Like chalkstones that are beaten to dust,
*Wooden images and incense altars shall not stand.

10 Yet the fortified city *will be* [a]desolate,
The habitation forsaken and left like a wilderness;
There the calf will feed, and there it will lie down
And consume its branches.

11 When its boughs are withered, they will be broken off;

KJV

set them on fire: for [a]it *is* a people of no understanding: therefore he that made them will [b]not have mercy on them, and [c]he that formed them will shew them no favour.

12 And it shall come to pass in that day, *that* the LORD shall beat off from the channel of the river unto the stream of Egypt, and ye shall be [a]gathered one by one, O ye children of Israel.

13 [a]And it shall come to pass in that day, [b]*that* the great trumpet shall be blown, and they shall come which were ready to perish in the land of Assyria, and the outcasts in the land of [c]Egypt, and shall [d]worship the LORD in the holy mount at Jerusalem.

Woe to Ephraim and Jerusalem

28 Woe to the crown of pride, to the drunkards of Ephraim, whose glorious beauty *is* a fading flower, which *are* on the head of the fat valleys of them that are overcome with wine!

2 Behold, the Lord hath a mighty and strong one, [a]*which* as a tempest of hail *and* a destroying storm, as a flood of mighty waters overflowing, shall cast down to the earth with the hand.

3 The crown of pride, the drunkards of Ephraim, shall be trodden under feet:

4 And the glorious beauty, which *is* on the head of the fat valley, shall be a fading flower, *and* as the hasty fruit before the summer; which *when* he that looketh upon it seeth, while it is yet in his hand he eateth it up.

5 In that day shall the LORD of hosts be for a crown of glory, and for a diadem of beauty, unto the residue of his people,

6 And for a spirit of judgment to him that sitteth in judgment, and for strength to them that turn the battle to the gate.

7 But they also [a]have erred through wine, and through strong drink are out of the way; [b]the priest and the prophet have erred through strong drink, they are swallowed up of wine, they are out of the way through strong drink; they err in vision, they stumble *in* judgment.

8 For all tables are full of vomit *and* filthiness, *so that there is* no place *clean*.

9 [a]Whom shall he teach knowledge? and whom shall he make to understand doctrine? *them that are* weaned from the milk, *and* drawn from the breasts.

10 [a]For precept *must be* upon precept, precept upon precept; line upon line, line upon line; here a little, *and* there a little:

11 For with [a]stammering lips and another tongue will he speak to this people.

11 [a]Deut. 32:28; Is. 1:3 [b]Is. 9:17 [c]Deut. 32:18; Is. 43:1, 7; 44:2, 21, 24 **12** [a][Is. 11:11; 56:8] **13** [a]Is. 2:11 [b]Lev. 25:9; 1 Chr. 15:24; Matt. 24:31; Rev. 11:15 [c]Is. 19:21, 22 [d][Is. 2:3]; Zech. 14:16; [Heb. 12:22]

CHAPTER 28

2 [a]Is. 30:30; Ezek. 13:11 **7** [a]Prov. 20:1; Is. 5:11, 22; Hos. 4:11 [b]Is. 56:10, 12 **9** [a]Jer. 6:10 **10** [a][2 Chr. 36:15; Neh. 9:30; Jer. 25:3, 4; 35:15; 44:4] **11** [a]Is. 33:19; 1 Cor. 14:21

*27:12 The Euphrates

NKJV

The women come *and* set them on fire.
For [a]it *is* a people of no understanding;
Therefore He who made them will [b]not
have mercy on them,
And [c]He who formed them will show them
no favor.

12 And it shall come to pass in that day
That the LORD will thresh,
From the channel of *the River to the
Brook of Egypt;
And you will be [a]gathered one by one,
O you children of Israel.

13 [a]So it shall be in that day:
[b]The great trumpet will be blown;
They will come, who are about to perish
in the land of Assyria,
And they who are outcasts in the land of
[c]Egypt,
And shall [d]worship the LORD in the holy
mount at Jerusalem.

Woe to Ephraim and Jerusalem

28 Woe to the crown of pride, to the
drunkards of Ephraim,
Whose glorious beauty *is* a fading flower
Which *is* at the head of the verdant
valleys,
To those who are overcome with wine!
2 Behold, the Lord has a mighty and strong
one,
[a]Like a tempest of hail and a destroying
storm,
Like a flood of mighty waters overflowing,
Who will bring *them* down to the earth
with *His* hand.
3 The crown of pride, the drunkards of
Ephraim,
Will be trampled underfoot;
4 And the glorious beauty is a fading
flower
Which *is* at the head of the verdant valley,
Like the first fruit before the summer,
Which an observer sees;
He eats it up while it is still in his hand.

5 In that day the LORD of hosts will be
For a crown of glory and a diadem of
beauty
To the remnant of His people,
6 For a spirit of justice to him who sits in
judgment,
And for strength to those who turn back
the battle at the gate.

7 But they also [a]have erred through wine,
And through intoxicating drink are out of
the way;
[b]The priest and the prophet have erred
through intoxicating drink,
They are swallowed up by wine,
They are out of the way through
intoxicating drink;
They err in vision, they stumble *in*
judgment.
8 For all tables are full of vomit *and* filth;
No place *is clean*.

9 "Whom[a] will he teach knowledge?
And whom will he make to understand the
message?
Those *just* weaned from milk?
Those *just* drawn from the breasts?
10 [a]For precept *must be* upon precept, precept
upon precept,
Line upon line, line upon line,
Here a little, there a little."

11 For with [a]stammering lips and another
tongue
He will speak to this people,

KJV

12 To whom he said, This *is* the [a]rest *where-*
with ye may cause the weary to rest; and this *is*
the refreshing: yet they would not hear.
13 But the word of the LORD was unto them
precept upon precept, precept upon precept; line
upon line, line upon line; here a little, *and* there
a little; that they might go, and fall backward,
and be broken, and snared, and taken.
14 Wherefore hear the word of the LORD, ye
scornful men, that rule this people which *is* in
Jerusalem.
15 Because ye have said, We have made a
covenant with death, and with hell are we at
agreement; when the overflowing scourge shall
pass through, it shall not come unto us: [a]for we
have made lies our refuge, and under falsehood
have we hid ourselves:

A Cornerstone in Zion

16 Therefore thus saith the Lord GOD, Behold, I lay in Zion for a foundation [a]a stone, a
tried stone, a precious corner *stone*, a sure foundation: he that believeth shall not make haste.
17 Judgment also will I lay to the line, and
righteousness to the plummet: and the hail shall
sweep away the refuge of lies, and the waters shall
overflow the hiding place.
18 And your covenant with death shall be
disannulled, and your agreement with hell shall
not stand; when the overflowing scourge shall
pass through, then ye shall be trodden down by
it.
19 From the time that it goeth forth it shall
take you: for morning by morning shall it pass
over, by day and by night: and it shall be a vexation only *to* understand the report.
20 For the bed is shorter than that *a man* can
stretch himself *on it:* and the covering narrower
than that he can wrap himself *in it.*
21 For the LORD shall rise up as *in* mount
[a]Perazim, he shall be wroth as *in* the valley of [b]Gib-
eon, that he may do his work, [c]his strange work;
and bring to pass his act, his strange act.
22 Now therefore be ye not mockers, lest
your bands be made strong: for I have heard from
the Lord GOD of hosts [a]a consumption, even determined upon the whole earth.

Listen to the Teaching of God

23 Give ye ear, and hear my voice; hearken,
and hear my speech.
24 Doth the plowman plow all day to sow?
doth he open and break the clods of his ground?

12 [a]Is. 30:15; Jer. 6:16; [Matt. 11:28, 29]
15 [a]Is. 9:15; Ezek. 13:22; Amos 2:4
16 [a]Gen. 49:24; Ps. 118:22; Is. 8:14, 15; Matt. 21:42; Mark 12:10; Luke 20:17; Acts 4:11; Rom. 9:33; 10:11; Eph. 2:20; 1 Pet. 2:6–8
21 [a]2 Sam. 5:20; 1 Chr. 14:11 [b]Josh. 10:10, 12; 2 Sam. 5:25; 1 Chr. 14:16 [c][Lam. 3:33; Luke 19:41–44]
22 [a]Is. 10:22; Dan. 9:27

NKJV

12 To whom He said, "This *is* the [a]rest *with which*
You may cause the weary to rest,"
And, "This *is* the refreshing";
Yet they would not hear.
13 But the word of the LORD was to them,
"Precept upon precept, precept upon precept,
Line upon line, line upon line,
Here a little, there a little,"
That they might go and fall backward, and be broken
And snared and caught.
14 Therefore hear the word of the LORD, you scornful men,
Who rule this people who *are* in Jerusalem,
15 Because you have said, "We have made a covenant with death,
And with Sheol we are in agreement.
When the overflowing scourge passes through,
It will not come to us,
[a]For we have made lies our refuge,
And under falsehood we have hidden ourselves."

A Cornerstone in Zion

16 Therefore thus says the Lord GOD:

"Behold, I lay in Zion [a]a stone for a foundation,
A tried stone, a precious cornerstone, a sure foundation;
Whoever believes will not act hastily.
17 Also I will make justice the measuring line,
And righteousness the plummet;
The hail will sweep away the refuge of lies,
And the waters will overflow the hiding place.
18 Your covenant with death will be annulled,
And your agreement with Sheol will not stand;
When the overflowing scourge passes through,
Then you will be trampled down by it.
19 As often as it goes out it will take you;
For morning by morning it will pass over,
And by day and by night;
It will be a terror just to understand the report."
20 For the bed is too short to stretch out *on,*
And the covering so narrow that one cannot wrap himself *in it.*
21 For the LORD will rise up as *at* Mount [a]Perazim,
He will be angry as in the Valley of [b]Gibeon—
That He may do His work, [c]His awesome work,
And bring to pass His act, His unusual act.
22 Now therefore, do not be mockers,
Lest your bonds be made strong;
For I have heard from the Lord GOD of hosts,
[a]A destruction determined even upon the whole earth.

Listen to the Teaching of God

23 Give ear and hear my voice,
Listen and hear my speech.
24 Does the plowman keep plowing all day to sow?
Does he keep turning his soil and breaking the clods?

KJV

25 When he hath made plain the face thereof,
doth he not cast abroad the fitches, and scatter
the cummin, and cast in the principal wheat and
the appointed barley and the rie in their place?
26 For his God doth instruct him to discretion, *and* doth teach him.
27 For the fitches are not threshed with a
threshing instrument, neither is a cart wheel
turned about upon the cummin; but the fitches
are beaten out with a staff, and the cummin with
a rod.
28 Bread *corn* is bruised; because he will not
ever be threshing it, nor break *it with* the wheel
of his cart, nor bruise it *with* his horsemen.
29 This also cometh forth from the LORD of
hosts, [a]*which* is wonderful in counsel, *and* excellent in working.

Woe to Jerusalem

29 Woe [a]to Ariel, to Ariel, the city [b]*where* David dwelt! add ye year to year; let them kill
sacrifices.
2 Yet I will distress Ariel, and there shall
be heaviness and sorrow: and it shall be unto me
as Ariel.
3 And I will camp against thee round about,
and will lay siege against thee with a mount, and
I will raise forts against thee.
4 And thou shalt be brought down, *and* shalt
speak out of the ground, and thy speech shall be
low out of the dust, and thy voice shall be, as of
one that hath a familiar spirit, [a]out of the ground,
and thy speech shall whisper out of the dust.
5 Moreover the multitude of thy [a]strangers
shall be like small dust, and the multitude of the
terrible ones *shall be* [b]as chaff that passeth away:
yea, it shall be [c]at an instant suddenly.
6 [a]Thou shalt be visited of the LORD of hosts
with thunder, and with [b]earthquake, and great
noise, with storm and tempest, and the flame of
devouring fire.
7 [a]And the multitude of all the nations that
fight against Ariel, even all that fight against her
and her munition, and that distress her, shall be
[b]as a dream of a night vision.
8 [a]It shall even be as when an hungry *man*
dreameth, and, behold, he eateth; but he awaketh,
and his soul is empty: or as when a thirsty man
dreameth, and, behold, he drinketh; but he awaketh, and, behold, *he is* faint, and his soul hath
appetite: so shall the multitude of all the nations
be, that fight against mount Zion.

The Blindness of Disobedience

9 Stay yourselves, and wonder; cry ye out,
and cry: [a]they are drunken, [b]but not with wine;
they stagger, but not with strong drink.
10 For [a]the LORD hath poured out upon you
the spirit of deep sleep, and hath [b]closed your
eyes: the prophets and your rulers, [c]the seers hath
he covered.

29 [a]Ps. 92:5; Is. 9:6; Jer. 32:19

CHAPTER 29

1 [a]Ezek. 24:6, 9 [b]2 Sam. 5:9
4 [a]Is. 8:19
5 [a]Is. 25:5 [b]Job 21:18; Is. 17:13 [c]Is. 30:13; 47:11; 1 Thess. 5:3
6 [a]Is. 28:2; 30:30 [b]1 Sam. 2:10; Zech. 14:4; Matt. 24:7; Mark 13:8; Luke 21:11; Rev. 16:18, 19
7 [a]Is. 37:36; Mic. 4:11, 12; Zech. 12:9 [b]Job 20:8
8 [a]Ps. 73:20
9 [a]Is. 28:7, 8 [b]Is. 51:21
10 [a]Ps. 69:23; Is. 6:9, 10; Mic. 3:6; Rom. 11:8 [b]Ps. 69:23; Is. 6:10 [c]1 Sam. 9:9; Is. 44:18; Mic. 3:6; [2 Thess. 2:9–12]

*———

29:1 Jerusalem, lit. *Lion of God*

NKJV

25 When he has leveled its surface,
Does he not sow the black cummin
And scatter the cummin,
Plant the wheat in rows,
The barley in the appointed place,
And the spelt in its place?
26 For He instructs him in right judgment,
His God teaches him.

27 For the black cummin is not threshed with
a threshing sledge,
Nor is a cartwheel rolled over the cummin;
But the black cummin is beaten out with
a stick,
And the cummin with a rod.
28 Bread *flour* must be ground;
Therefore he does not thresh it forever,
Break *it with* his cartwheel,
Or crush it *with* his horsemen.
29 This also comes from the LORD of hosts,
[a]*Who* is wonderful in counsel *and* excellent
in guidance.

Woe to Jerusalem

29 "Woe [a]to *Ariel, to Ariel, the city [b]*where*
David dwelt!
Add year to year;
Let feasts come around.
2 Yet I will distress Ariel;
There shall be heaviness and sorrow,
And it shall be to Me as Ariel.
3 I will encamp against you all around,
I will lay siege against you with a mound,
And I will raise siegeworks against you.
4 You shall be brought down,
You shall speak out of the ground;
Your speech shall be low, out of the dust;
Your voice shall be like a medium's, [a]out
of the ground;
And your speech shall whisper out of the
dust.

5 "Moreover the multitude of your [a]foes
Shall be like fine dust,
And the multitude of the terrible ones
Like [b]chaff that passes away;
Yes, it shall be [c]in an instant, suddenly.
6 [a]You will be punished by the LORD of hosts
With thunder and [b]earthquake and great
noise,
With storm and tempest
And the flame of devouring fire.
7 [a]The multitude of all the nations who fight
against Ariel,
Even all who fight against her and her
fortress,
And distress her,
Shall be [b]as a dream of a night vision.
8 [a]It shall even be as when a hungry man
dreams,
And look—he eats;
But he awakes, and his soul is still empty;
Or as when a thirsty man dreams,
And look—he drinks;
But he awakes, and indeed *he is* faint,
And his soul still craves:
So the multitude of all the nations shall
be,
Who fight against Mount Zion."

The Blindness of Disobedience

9 Pause and wonder!
Blind yourselves and be blind!
[a]They are drunk, [b]but not with wine;
They stagger, but not with intoxicating
drink.
10 For [a]the LORD has poured out on you
The spirit of deep sleep,
And has [b]closed your eyes, namely, the
prophets;
And He has covered your heads, *namely,*
[c]the seers.

KJV

11 And the vision of all is become unto you as the words of a book [a]that is sealed, which *men* deliver to one that is learned, saying, Read this, I pray thee: [b]and he saith, I cannot; for it *is* sealed:

12 And the book is delivered to him that is not learned, saying, Read this, I pray thee: and he saith, I am not learned.

13 Wherefore the Lord said, [a]Forasmuch as this people draw near *me* with their mouth, and [b]with their lips do honour me, but have removed their heart far from me, and their fear toward me is taught by the precept of men:

14 [a]Therefore, behold, I will proceed to do a marvellous work among this people, *even* a marvellous work and a wonder: [b]for the wisdom of their wise *men* shall perish, and the understanding of their prudent *men* shall be hid.

15 [a]Woe unto them that seek deep to hide their counsel from the LORD, and their works are in the dark, and [b]they say, Who seeth us? and who knoweth us?

16 Surely your turning of things upside down shall be esteemed as the potter's clay: for shall the [a]work say of him that made it, He made me not? or shall the thing framed say of him that framed it, He had no understanding?

Future Recovery of Wisdom

17 *Is* it not yet a very little while, and [a]Lebanon shall be turned into a fruitful field, and the fruitful field shall be esteemed as a forest?

18 And [a]in that day shall the deaf hear the words of the book, and the eyes of the blind shall see out of obscurity, and out of darkness.

19 [a]The meek also shall increase *their* joy in the LORD, and [b]the poor among men shall rejoice in the Holy One of Israel.

20 For the terrible one is brought to nought, and [a]the scorner is consumed, and all that [b]watch for iniquity are cut off:

21 That make a man an offender for a word, and [a]lay a snare for him that reproveth in the gate, and turn aside the just [b]for a thing of nought.

22 Therefore thus saith the LORD, [a]who redeemed Abraham, concerning the house of Jacob, Jacob shall not now be [b]ashamed, neither shall his face now wax pale.

23 But when he seeth his children, [a]the work of mine hands, in the midst of him, they shall sanctify my name, and sanctify the Holy One of Jacob, and shall fear the God of Israel.

24 They also [a]that erred in spirit shall come to understanding, and they that murmured shall learn doctrine.

11 [a]Is. 8:16 [b]Dan. 12:4, 9; [Matt. 13:11–16]; Rev. 5:1–5, 9
13 [a]Ps. 78:36; Ezek. 33:31; Matt. 15:8, 9; Mark 7:6, 7 [b]Col. 2:22
14 [a]Is. 6:9, 10; 28:21; Hab. 1:5 [b]Is. 44:25; Jer. 49:7; Obad. 8; 1 Cor. 1:19
15 [a]Is. 30:1 [b]Ps. 10:11; 94:7; Is. 47:10; Ezek. 8:12; Mal. 2:17
16 [a]Is. 45:9; Jer. 18:1–6; [Rom. 9:19–21]
17 [a]Is. 32:15
18 [a]Is. 35:5; Matt. 11:5; Mark 7:37
19 [a][Ps. 25:9; 37:11; Is. 11:4; 61:1; Matt. 5:5; 11:29] [b]Is. 14:30; [Matt. 5:3; 11:5; James 2:5]
20 [a]Is. 28:14 [b]Is. 59:4; Mic. 2:1
21 [a]Amos 5:10, 12 [b]Prov. 28:21
22 [a]Josh. 24:3 [b]Is. 45:17
23 [a][Is. 45:11; 49:20–26; Eph. 2:10]
24 [a]Is. 28:7

NKJV

11 The whole vision has become to you like the words of a book [a]that is sealed, which *men* deliver to one who is literate, saying, "Read this, please." [b]And he says, "I cannot, for it *is* sealed."

12 Then the book is delivered to one who is illiterate, saying, "Read this, please." And he says, "I am not literate."

13 Therefore the Lord said:

[a]"Inasmuch as these people draw near with their mouths
And honor Me [b]with their lips,
But have removed their hearts far from Me,
And their fear toward Me is taught by the commandment of men,
14 [a]Therefore, behold, I will again do a marvelous work
Among this people,
A marvelous work and a wonder;
[b]For the wisdom of their wise *men* shall perish,
And the understanding of their prudent *men* shall be hidden."

15 [a]Woe to those who seek deep to hide their counsel far from the LORD,
And their works are in the dark;
[b]They say, "Who sees us?" and, "Who knows us?"
16 Surely you have things turned around!
Shall the potter be esteemed as the clay;
For shall the [a]thing made say of him who made it,
"He did not make me"?
Or shall the thing formed say of him who formed it,
"He has no understanding"?

Future Recovery of Wisdom

17 *Is* it not yet a very little while
Till [a]Lebanon shall be turned into a fruitful field,
And the fruitful field be esteemed as a forest?
18 [a]In that day the deaf shall hear the words of the book,
And the eyes of the blind shall see out of obscurity and out of darkness.
19 [a]The humble also shall increase *their* joy in the LORD,
And [b]the poor among men shall rejoice
In the Holy One of Israel.
20 For the terrible one is brought to nothing,
[a]The scornful one is consumed,
And all who [b]watch for iniquity are cut off—
21 Who make a man an offender by a word,
And [a]lay a snare for him who reproves in the gate,
And turn aside the just [b]by empty words.

22 Therefore thus says the LORD, [a]who redeemed Abraham, concerning the house of Jacob:

"Jacob shall not now be [b]ashamed,
Nor shall his face now grow pale;
23 But when he sees his children,
[a]The work of My hands, in his midst,
They will hallow My name,
And hallow the Holy One of Jacob,
And fear the God of Israel.
24 These also [a]who erred in spirit will come to understanding,
And those who complained will learn doctrine."

KJV

Futile Confidence in Egypt

30 Woe to the rebellious children, saith the
LORD, [a]that take counsel, but not of me; and
that cover with a covering, but not of my spirit,
[b]that they may add sin to sin:
2 [a]That walk to go down into Egypt, and
[b]have not asked at my mouth; to strengthen themselves in the strength of Pharaoh, and to trust in
the shadow of Egypt!
3 [a]Therefore shall the strength of Pharaoh
be your shame, and the trust in the shadow of
Egypt *your* confusion.
4 For his princes were at [a]Zoan, and his ambassadors came to Hanes.
5 [a]They were all ashamed of a people *that*
could not profit them, nor be an help nor profit,
but a shame, and also a reproach.
6 [a]The burden of the beasts of the south:
into the land of trouble and anguish, from whence
come the young and old lion, [b]the viper and fiery
flying serpent, they will carry their riches upon
the shoulders of young asses, and their treasures
upon the bunches of camels, to a people *that* shall
not profit *them*.
7 [a]For the Egyptians shall help in vain, and
to no purpose: therefore have I cried concerning
this, Their strength *is* to sit still.

A Rebellious People

8 Now go, [a]write it before them in a table,
and note it in a book, that it may be for the time
to come for ever and ever:
9 That [a]this *is* a rebellious people, lying children, children *that* will not hear the law of the
LORD:
10 [a]Which say to the seers, See not; and to
the prophets, Prophesy not unto us right things,
[b]speak unto us smooth things, prophesy deceits:
11 Get you out of the way, turn aside out of
the path, cause the Holy One of Israel to cease
from before us.
12 Wherefore thus saith the Holy One of Israel, Because ye [a]despise this word, and trust in
oppression and perverseness, and stay thereon:
13 Therefore this iniquity shall be to you [a]as
a breach ready to fall, swelling out in a high wall,
whose breaking [b]cometh suddenly at an instant.
14 And [a]he shall break it as the breaking of
the potters' vessel that is broken in pieces; he shall
not spare: so that there shall not be found in the
bursting of it a sherd to take fire from the hearth,
or to take water *withal* out of the pit.

CHAPTER 30

1 [a]Is. 29:15 [b]Deut. 29:19
2 [a]Is. 31:1; Jer. 43:7 [b]Num. 27:21; Josh. 9:14; 1 Kin. 22:7; Jer. 21:2; 42:2, 20
3 [a]Is. 20:5; Jer. 37:5, 7
4 [a]Is. 19:11
5 [a]Jer. 2:36
6 [a]Is. 57:9; Hos. 8:9; 12:1 [b]Deut. 8:15; Is. 14:29
7 [a]Jer. 37:7
8 [a]Hab. 2:2
9 [a]Deut. 32:20; Is. 1:2, 4; 65:2
10 [a]Is. 5:20; Jer. 11:21; Amos 2:12; Mic. 2:6 [b]1 Kin. 22:8, 13; Jer. 6:14; 23:17, 26; Ezek. 13:7; Mic. 2:11; Rom. 16:18; 2 Tim. 4:3, 4
12 [a]Lev. 26:43; Num. 15:31; Prov. 1:30; 13:13; Is. 5:24; Ezek. 20:13, 16, 24; Amos 2:4
13 [a]1 Kin. 20:30; Ps. 62:3, 4; Is. 58:12 [b]Is. 29:5
14 [a]Ps. 2:9; Jer. 19:11

*______

30:7 Lit. *Rahab Sits Idle*

NKJV

Futile Confidence in Egypt

30 "Woe to the rebellious children," says the
LORD,
[a]"Who take counsel, but not of Me,
And who devise plans, but not of My
Spirit,
[b]That they may add sin to sin;
2 [a]Who walk to go down to Egypt,
And [b]have not asked My advice,
To strengthen themselves in the strength
of Pharaoh,
And to trust in the shadow of Egypt!
3 [a]Therefore the strength of Pharaoh
Shall be your shame,
And trust in the shadow of Egypt
Shall be *your* humiliation.
4 For his princes were at [a]Zoan,
And his ambassadors came to Hanes.
5 [a]They were all ashamed of a people *who*
could not benefit them,
Or be help or benefit,
But a shame and also a reproach."

6 [a]The burden against the beasts of the
South.

Through a land of trouble and
anguish,
From which *came* the lioness and lion,
[b]The viper and fiery flying serpent,
They will carry their riches on the backs
of young donkeys,
And their treasures on the humps of
camels,
To a people *who* shall not profit;
7 [a]For the Egyptians shall help in vain and
to no purpose.
Therefore I have called her
*Rahab-Hem-Shebeth.

A Rebellious People

8 Now go, [a]write it before them on a
tablet,
And note it on a scroll,
That it may be for time to come,
Forever and ever:
9 That [a]this *is* a rebellious people,
Lying children,
Children *who* will not hear the law of the
LORD;
10 [a]Who say to the seers, "Do not see,"
And to the prophets, "Do not prophesy to
us right things;
[b]Speak to us smooth things, prophesy
deceits.
11 Get out of the way,
Turn aside from the path,
Cause the Holy One of Israel
To cease from before us."

12 Therefore thus says the Holy One of
Israel:

"Because you [a]despise this word,
And trust in oppression and
perversity,
And rely on them,
13 Therefore this iniquity shall be to you
[a]Like a breach ready to fall,
A bulge in a high wall,
Whose breaking [b]comes suddenly, in an
instant.
14 And [a]He shall break it like the breaking
of the potter's vessel,
Which is broken in pieces;
He shall not spare.
So there shall not be found among its
fragments
A shard to take fire from the hearth,
Or to take water from the cistern."

KJV

15 For thus saith the Lord GOD, the Holy One
of Israel; [a]In returning and rest shall ye be saved;
in quietness and in confidence shall be your
strength: [b]and ye would not.
16 But ye said, No; for we will flee upon
horses; therefore shall ye flee: and, We will ride
upon the swift; therefore shall they that pursue
you be swift.
17 [a]One thousand *shall flee* at the rebuke of
one; at the rebuke of five shall ye flee: till ye be
left as a beacon upon the top of a mountain, and
as an ensign on an hill.

God Will Be Gracious

18 And therefore will the LORD wait, that he
may be [a]gracious unto you, and therefore will he
be exalted, that he may have mercy upon you:
for the LORD *is* a God of judgment: [b]blessed *are*
all they that [c]wait for him.
19 For the people [a]shall dwell in Zion at Jerusalem: thou shalt [b]weep no more: he will be very
gracious unto thee at the voice of thy cry; when
he shall hear it, he will [c]answer thee.
20 And *though* the Lord give you [a]the bread
of adversity, and the water of affliction, yet shall
not [b]thy teachers be removed into a corner any
more, but thine eyes shall see thy teachers:
21 And thine ears shall hear a word behind
thee, saying, This *is* the way, walk ye in it, when
ye [a]turn to the right hand, and when ye turn to
the left.
22 [a]Ye shall defile also the covering of thy
graven images of silver, and the ornament of thy
molten images of gold: thou shalt cast them away
as a menstruous cloth; [b]thou shalt say unto it,
Get thee hence.
23 [a]Then shall he give the rain of thy seed,
that thou shalt sow the ground withal; and bread
of the increase of the earth, and it shall be fat
and plenteous: in that day shall thy cattle feed in
large pastures.
24 The oxen likewise and the young asses
that ear the ground shall eat clean provender,
which hath been winnowed with the shovel and
with the fan.
25 And there shall be [a]upon every high
mountain, and upon every high hill, rivers *and*
streams of waters in the day of the [b]great slaughter, when the towers fall.
26 Moreover [a]the light of the moon shall be
as the light of the sun, and the light of the sun
shall be sevenfold, as the light of seven days, in
the day that the LORD bindeth up the breach of
his people, and healeth the stroke of their wound.

Judgment on Assyria

27 Behold, the name of the LORD cometh from
far, burning *with* his anger, and the burden

15 [a]Ps. 116:7; Is. 7:4; 28:12 [b]Matt. 23:37
17 [a]Lev. 26:36; Deut. 28:25; 32:30; Josh. 23:10; [Prov. 28:1]
18 [a]Is. 33:2 [b]Ps. 2:12; 34:8; Prov. 16:20; Jer. 17:7 [c]Is. 26:8
19 [a]Is. 65:9; [Ezek. 37:25, 28] [b]Is. 25:8 [c]Ps. 50:15; Is. 65:24; [Matt. 7:7–11]
20 [a]1 Kin. 22:27; Ps. 127:2 [b]Ps. 74:9; Amos 8:11
21 [a]Josh. 1:7
22 [a]2 Chr. 31:1; Is. 2:20; 31:7 [b]Hos. 14:8
23 [a][Matt. 6:33]; 1 Tim. 6:8
25 [a]Is. 2:14, 15 [b]Is. 2:10–21; 34:2
26 [a][Is. 60:19, 20; Rev. 21:23; 22:5]

NKJV

15 For thus says the Lord GOD, the Holy One of Israel:

[a]"In returning and rest you shall be saved;
In quietness and confidence shall be your strength."
[b]But you would not,

16 And you said, "No, for we will flee on horses"—
Therefore you shall flee!
And, "We will ride on swift *horses*"—
Therefore those who pursue you shall be swift!

17 [a]One thousand *shall flee* at the threat of one,
At the threat of five you shall flee,
Till you are left as a pole on top of a mountain
And as a banner on a hill.

God Will Be Gracious

18 Therefore the LORD will wait, that He may be [a]gracious to you;
And therefore He will be exalted, that He may have mercy on you.
For the LORD *is* a God of justice;
[b]Blessed *are* all those who [c]wait for Him.

19 For the people [a]shall dwell in Zion at Jerusalem;
You shall [b]weep no more.
He will be very gracious to you at the sound of your cry;
When He hears it, He will [c]answer you.

20 And *though* the Lord gives you
[a]The bread of adversity and the water of affliction,
Yet [b]your teachers will not be moved into a corner anymore,
But your eyes shall see your teachers.

21 Your ears shall hear a word behind you, saying,
"This *is* the way, walk in it,"
Whenever you [a]turn to the right hand
Or whenever you turn to the left.

22 [a]You will also defile the covering of your images of silver,
And the ornament of your molded images of gold.
You will throw them away as an unclean thing;
[b]You will say to them, "Get away!"

23 [a]Then He will give the rain for your seed
With which you sow the ground,
And bread of the increase of the earth;
It will be fat and plentiful.
In that day your cattle will feed
In large pastures.

24 Likewise the oxen and the young donkeys that work the ground
Will eat cured fodder,
Which has been winnowed with the shovel and fan.

25 There will be [a]on every high mountain
And on every high hill
Rivers *and* streams of waters,
In the day of the [b]great slaughter,
When the towers fall.

26 Moreover [a]the light of the moon will be as the light of the sun,
And the light of the sun will be sevenfold,
As the light of seven days,
In the day that the LORD binds up the bruise of His people
And heals the stroke of their wound.

Judgment on Assyria

27 Behold, the name of the LORD comes from afar,

KJV

thereof is heavy: his lips are full of indignation, and his tongue as a devouring fire:

28 And [a]his breath, as an overflowing stream, [b]shall reach to the midst of the neck, to sift the nations with the sieve of vanity: and *there shall be* [c]a bridle in the jaws of the people, causing *them* to err.

29 Ye shall have a song, as in the night *when* a holy solemnity is kept; and gladness of heart, as when one goeth with a pipe to come into [a]the mountain of the LORD, to the mighty One of Israel.

30 [a]And the LORD shall cause his glorious voice to be heard, and shall shew the lighting down of his arm, with the indignation of *his* anger, and *with* the flame of a devouring fire, *with* scattering, and tempest, [b]and hailstones.

31 For [a]through the voice of the LORD shall the Assyrian be beaten down, [b]*which* smote with a rod.

32 And *in* every place where the grounded staff shall pass, which the LORD shall lay upon him, *it* shall be with tabrets and harps: and in battles of [a]shaking will he fight with it.

33 [a]For Tophet *is* ordained of old; yea, for the king it is prepared; he hath made *it* deep *and* large: the pile thereof *is* fire and much wood; the breath of the LORD, like a stream of brimstone, doth kindle it.

28 [a]Is. 11:4; 2 Thess. 2:8 [b]Is. 8:8 [c]2 Kin. 19:28; Is. 37:29
29 [a][Is. 2:3]
30 [a]Is. 29:6 [b]Is. 28:2
31 [a]Is. 14:25; 37:36 [b]Is. 10:5, 24
32 [a]Is. 11:15
33 [a]2 Kin. 23:10; Jer. 7:31

NKJV

Burning *with* His anger,
And *His* burden *is* heavy;
His lips are full of indignation,
And His tongue like a devouring fire.
28 [a]His breath is like an overflowing stream,
[b]Which reaches up to the neck,
To sift the nations with the sieve of futility;
And *there shall be* [c]a bridle in the jaws
of the people,
Causing *them* to err.

29 You shall have a song
As in the night *when* a holy festival is
kept,
And gladness of heart as when one goes
with a flute,
To come into [a]the mountain of the LORD,
To the Mighty One of Israel.
30 [a]The LORD will cause His glorious voice to
be heard,
And show the descent of His arm,
With the indignation of *His* anger
And the flame of a devouring fire,
With scattering, tempest, [b]and hailstones.
31 For [a]through the voice of the LORD
Assyria will be beaten down,
As He strikes with the [b]rod.
32 And *in* every place where the staff of
punishment passes,
Which the LORD lays on him,
It will be with tambourines and harps;
And in battles of [a]brandishing He will
fight with it.
33 [a]For Tophet *was* established of old,
Yes, for the king it is prepared.
He has made *it* deep and large;
Its pyre *is* fire with much wood;
The breath of the LORD, like a stream of
brimstone,
Kindles it.

KJV

The Folly of Not Trusting God

31 Woe to them [a]that go down to Egypt for help; and [b]stay on horses, and trust in chariots, because *they are* many; and in horsemen, because they are very strong; but they look not unto the Holy One of Israel, [c]neither seek the LORD!

2 Yet he also *is* wise, and will bring evil, and [a]will not call back his words: but will arise against the house of the evildoers, and against the help of them that work iniquity.

3 Now the Egyptians *are* men, and not God; and their horses flesh, and not spirit. When the LORD shall stretch out his hand, both he that helpeth shall fall, and he that is holpen shall fall down, and they all shall fail [a]together.

God Will Deliver Jerusalem

4 For thus hath the LORD spoken unto me, [a]Like as the lion and the young lion roaring on his prey, when a multitude of shepherds is called forth against him, *he* will not be afraid of their voice, nor abase himself for the noise of them: so shall the LORD of hosts come down to fight for mount Zion, and for the hill thereof.

5 [a]As birds flying, so will the LORD of hosts defend Jerusalem; defending also he will deliver *it; and* passing over he will preserve *it*.

CHAPTER 31

1 [a]Is. 30:1, 2 [b]Deut. 17:16; Ps. 20:7; Is. 2:7; 30:16 [c]Is. 9:13; Dan. 9:13; Amos 5:4–8
2 [a]Num. 23:19; Jer. 44:29
3 [a]Is. 20:6
4 [a]Num. 24:9; Hos. 11:10; Amos 3:8
5 [a]Deut. 32:11; Ps. 91:4

NKJV

The Folly of Not Trusting God

31 Woe to those [a]who go down to Egypt for
help,
And [b]rely on horses,
Who trust in chariots because *they are*
many,
And in horsemen because they are very
strong,
But who do not look to the Holy One of
Israel,
[c]Nor seek the LORD!
2 Yet He also *is* wise and will bring
disaster,
And [a]will not call back His words,
But will arise against the house of
evildoers,
And against the help of those who work
iniquity.
3 Now the Egyptians *are* men, and not God;
And their horses are flesh, and not spirit.
When the LORD stretches out His hand,
Both he who helps will fall,
And he who is helped will fall down;
They all will perish [a]together.

God Will Deliver Jerusalem

4 For thus the LORD has spoken to me:

[a]"As a lion roars,
And a young lion over his prey
(When a multitude of shepherds is
summoned against him,
He will not be afraid of their voice
Nor be disturbed by their noise),
So the LORD of hosts will come down
To fight for Mount Zion and for its hill.
5 [a]Like birds flying about,
So will the LORD of hosts defend
Jerusalem.
Defending, He will also deliver *it;*
Passing over, He will preserve *it*."

KJV

6 Turn ye unto *him from* whom the children
of Israel have [a]deeply revolted.
7 For in that day every man shall [a]cast away
his idols of silver, and his idols of gold, which
your own hands have made unto you *for* [b]a sin.
8 Then shall the Assyrian [a]fall with the
sword, not of a mighty man; and the sword, not
of a mean man, shall [b]devour him: but he shall
flee from the sword, and his young men shall be
discomfited.
9 And[a] he shall pass over to his strong hold
for fear, and his princes shall be afraid of the ensign, saith the LORD, whose fire *is* in Zion, and
his furnace in Jerusalem.

6 [a]Hos. 9:9
7 [a]Is. 2:20; 30:22 [b]1 Kin. 12:30
8 [a]2 Kin. 19:35, 36 [b]Is. 37:36
9 [a]Is. 37:37

NKJV

6 Return *to Him* against whom the children
of Israel have [a]deeply revolted.
7 For in that day every man shall [a]throw
away his idols of silver and his idols of gold—
[b]sin, which your own hands have made for yourselves.

8 "Then Assyria shall [a]fall by a sword not of man,
And a sword not of mankind shall [b]devour him.
But he shall flee from the sword,
And his young men shall become forced labor.
9 [a]He shall cross over to his stronghold for fear,
And his princes shall be afraid of the banner,"
Says the LORD,
Whose fire *is* in Zion
And whose furnace *is* in Jerusalem.

A Reign of Righteousness

32 Behold, [a]a king shall reign in righteousness, and princes shall rule in judgment.
2 And a man shall be as an hiding place
from the wind, and [a]a covert from the tempest;
as rivers of water in a dry place, as the shadow
of a great rock in a weary land.
3 And [a]the eyes of them that see shall not
be dim, and the ears of them that hear shall
hearken.
4 The heart also of the rash shall [a]under-
stand knowledge, and the tongue of the stammerers shall be ready to speak plainly.
5 The vile person shall be no more called
liberal, nor the churl said *to be* bountiful.
6 For the vile person will speak villany, and
his heart will work [a]iniquity, to practise hypocrisy, and to utter error against the LORD, to make
empty the soul of the hungry, and he will cause
the drink of the thirsty to fail.
7 The instruments also of the churl *are* evil:
he deviseth wicked devices to destroy the poor
with [a]lying words, even when the needy speaketh
right.
8 But the liberal deviseth liberal things; and
by liberal things shall he stand.

Consequences of Complacency

9 Rise up, ye women [a]that are at ease; hear
my voice, ye careless daughters; give ear unto my
speech.
10 Many days and years shall ye be troubled,
ye careless women: for the vintage shall fail, the
gathering shall not come.
11 Tremble, ye women that are at ease; be
troubled, ye careless ones: strip you, and make
you bare, and gird *sackcloth* upon *your* loins.
12 They shall lament for the teats, for the
pleasant fields, for the fruitful vine.
13 [a]Upon the land of my people shall come
up thorns *and* briers; yea, upon all the houses of
joy *in* [b]the joyous city:
14 [a]Because the palaces shall be forsaken;
the multitude of the city shall be left; the forts

CHAPTER 32
1 [a]Ps. 45:1
2 [a]Is. 4:6
3 [a]Is. 29:18; 35:5
4 [a]Is. 29:24
6 [a]Prov. 24:7–9
7 [a]Jer. 5:26–28; Mic. 7:3
9 [a]Is. 47:8; Amos 6:1; Zeph. 2:15
13 [a]Is. 7:23–25; Hos. 9:6 [b]Is. 22:2
14 [a]Is. 27:10

A Reign of Righteousness

32 Behold, [a]a king will reign in righteousness,
And princes will rule with justice.
2 A man will be as a hiding place from the wind,
And [a]a cover from the tempest,
As rivers of water in a dry place,
As the shadow of a great rock in a weary land.
3 [a]The eyes of those who see will not be dim,
And the ears of those who hear will listen.
4 Also the heart of the rash will [a]understand knowledge,
And the tongue of the stammerers will be ready to speak plainly.

5 The foolish person will no longer be called generous,
Nor the miser said *to be* bountiful;
6 For the foolish person will speak foolishness,
And his heart will work [a]iniquity:
To practice ungodliness,
To utter error against the LORD,
To keep the hungry unsatisfied,
And he will cause the drink of the thirsty to fail.
7 Also the schemes of the schemer *are* evil;
He devises wicked plans
To destroy the poor with [a]lying words,
Even when the needy speaks justice.
8 But a generous man devises generous things,
And by generosity he shall stand.

Consequences of Complacency

9 Rise up, you women [a]who are at ease,
Hear my voice;
You complacent daughters,
Give ear to my speech.
10 In a year and *some* days
You will be troubled, you complacent women;
For the vintage will fail,
The gathering will not come.
11 Tremble, you *women* who are at ease;
Be troubled, you complacent ones;
Strip yourselves, make yourselves bare,
And gird *sackcloth* on *your* waists.

12 People shall mourn upon their breasts
For the pleasant fields, for the fruitful vine.
13 [a]On the land of my people will come up thorns *and* briers,
Yes, on all the happy homes *in* [b]the joyous city;
14 [a]Because the palaces will be forsaken,
The bustling city will be deserted.

KJV

and towers shall be for dens for ever, a joy of
wild asses, a pasture of flocks;
15 Until [a]the spirit be poured upon us from
on high, and [b]the wilderness be a fruitful field,
and the fruitful field be counted for a forest.

The Peace of God's Reign

16 Then judgment shall dwell in the wilderness, and righteousness remain in the fruitful
field.
17 [a]And the work of righteousness shall be
peace; and the effect of righteousness quietness
and assurance for ever.
18 And my people shall dwell in a peaceable
habitation, and in sure dwellings, and in quiet
[a]resting places;
19 [a]When it shall hail, coming down [b]on the
forest; and the city shall be low in a low place.
20 Blessed *are* ye that sow beside all waters,
that send forth *thither* the feet of [a]the ox and the
ass.

A Prayer in Deep Distress

33 Woe to thee [a]that spoilest, and thou *wast*
not spoiled; and dealest treacherously, and
they dealt not treacherously with thee! [b]when
thou shalt cease to spoil, thou shalt be [c]spoiled;
and when thou shalt make an end to deal treacherously, they shall deal treacherously with thee.
2 O LORD, be gracious unto us; [a]we have
waited for thee: be thou their arm every morning,
our salvation also in the time of trouble.
3 At the noise of the tumult the people [a]fled;
at the lifting up of thyself the nations were
scattered.
4 And your spoil shall be gathered *like* the
gathering of the caterpiller: as the running to and
fro of locusts shall he run upon them.
5 [a]The LORD is exalted; for he dwelleth on
high: he hath filled Zion with judgment and
righteousness.
6 And wisdom and knowledge shall be the
stability of thy times, *and* strength of salvation:
the fear of the LORD *is* his treasure.
7 Behold, their valiant ones shall cry without: [a]the ambassadors of peace shall weep
bitterly.
8 [a]The highways lie waste, the wayfaring
man ceaseth: [b]he hath broken the covenant, he
hath despised the cities, he regardeth no man.
9 [a]The earth mourneth *and* languisheth:
Lebanon is ashamed *and* hewn down: Sharon is
like a wilderness; and Bashan and Carmel shake
off *their fruits.*

Impending Judgment on Zion

10 [a]Now will I rise, saith the LORD; now will
I be exalted; now will I lift up myself.
11 [a]Ye shall conceive chaff, ye shall bring

15 [a][Is. 11:2]; Ezek. 39:29; [Joel 2:28] [b]Ps. 107:35; Is. 29:17
17 [a]Ps. 119:165; Is. 2:4; Rom. 14:17; James 3:18
18 [a]Is. 11:10; 14:3; 30:15; [Hos. 2:18–23; Zech. 2:5; 3:10]
19 [a]Is. 30:30 [b]Zech. 11:2
20 [a][Eccl. 11:1]; Is. 30:23, 24

CHAPTER 33

1 [a]Is. 21:2; Hab. 2:8 [b]Rev. 13:10 [c]Is. 10:12; 14:25; 31:8
2 [a]Is. 25:9; 26:8
3 [a]Is. 17:13
5 [a]Ps. 97:9
7 [a]2 Kin. 18:18, 37
8 [a]Judg. 5:6 [b]2 Kin. 18:13–17
9 [a]Is. 24:4
10 [a]Ps. 12:5; Is. 2:19, 21
11 [a][Ps. 7:14; Is. 26:18; 59:4; James 1:15]

NKJV

The forts and towers will become lairs
forever,
A joy of wild donkeys, a pasture of
flocks—
15 Until [a]the Spirit is poured upon us from
on high,
And [b]the wilderness becomes a fruitful
field,
And the fruitful field is counted as a
forest.

The Peace of God's Reign

16 Then justice will dwell in the wilderness,
And righteousness remain in the fruitful
field.
17 [a]The work of righteousness will be peace,
And the effect of righteousness, quietness
and assurance forever.
18 My people will dwell in a peaceful
habitation,
In secure dwellings, and in quiet [a]resting
places,
19 [a]Though hail comes down [b]on the forest,
And the city is brought low in humiliation.

20 Blessed *are* you who sow beside all
waters,
Who send out freely the feet of [a]the ox
and the donkey.

A Prayer in Deep Distress

33 Woe to you [a]who plunder, though you
have not *been* plundered;
And you who deal treacherously, though
they have not dealt treacherously with
you!
[b]When you cease plundering,
You will be [c]plundered;
When you make an end of dealing
treacherously,
They will deal treacherously with you.
2 O LORD, be gracious to us;
[a]We have waited for You.
Be *their arm every morning,
Our salvation also in the time of trouble.
3 At the noise of the tumult the people [a]shall
flee;
When You lift Yourself up, the nations
shall be scattered;
4 And Your plunder shall be gathered
Like the gathering of the caterpillar;
As the running to and fro of locusts,
He shall run upon them.

5 [a]The LORD is exalted, for He dwells on
high;
He has filled Zion with justice and
righteousness.
6 Wisdom and knowledge will be the
stability of your times,
And the strength of salvation;
The fear of the LORD *is* His treasure.

7 Surely their valiant ones shall cry outside,
[a]The ambassadors of peace shall weep
bitterly.
8 [a]The highways lie waste,
The traveling man ceases.
[b]He has broken the covenant,
*He has despised the *cities,
He regards no man.
9 [a]The earth mourns *and* languishes,
Lebanon is shamed *and* shriveled;
Sharon is like a wilderness,
And Bashan and Carmel shake off *their
fruits.*

Impending Judgment on Zion

10 "Now[a] I will rise," says the LORD;
"Now I will be exalted,
Now I will lift Myself up.
11 [a]You shall conceive chaff,

33:2 LXX omits *their;* Syr., Tg., Vg. *our*
33:8 Tg. *They have been removed from their cities* • So with MT, Vg.; DSS *witnesses;* LXX omits *cities*

KJV

forth stubble: your breath, *as* fire, shall devour you.

12 And the people shall be *as* the burnings of lime: [a]*as* thorns cut up shall they be burned in the fire.

13 Hear, [a]ye *that are* far off, what I have done; and, ye *that are* near, acknowledge my might.

14 The sinners in Zion are afraid; fearfulness hath surprised the hypocrites. Who among us shall dwell with the devouring [a]fire? who among us shall dwell with everlasting burnings?

15 He that [a]walketh righteously, and speaketh uprightly; he that despiseth the gain of oppressions, that shaketh his hands from holding of bribes, that stoppeth his ears from hearing of blood, and [b]shutteth his eyes from seeing evil;

16 He shall dwell on high: his place of defence *shall be* the munitions of rocks: bread shall be given him; his waters *shall be* sure.

The Land of the Majestic King

17 Thine eyes shall see the king in his [a]beauty: they shall behold the land that is very far off.

18 Thine heart shall meditate terror. [a]Where *is* the scribe? where *is* the receiver? where *is* he that counted the towers?

19 [a]Thou shalt not see a fierce people, [b]a people of a deeper speech than thou canst perceive; of a stammering tongue, *that thou canst* not understand.

20 [a]Look upon Zion, the city of our solemnities: thine eyes shall see [b]Jerusalem a quiet habitation, a tabernacle *that* shall not be taken down; [c]not one of [d]the stakes thereof shall ever be removed, neither shall any of the cords thereof be broken.

21 But there the glorious LORD *will be* unto us a place of broad rivers *and* streams; wherein shall go no galley with oars, neither shall gallant ship pass thereby.

22 For the LORD *is* our [a]judge, the LORD *is* our [b]lawgiver, [c]the LORD *is* our king; he will save us.

23 Thy tacklings are loosed; they could not well strengthen their mast, they could not spread the sail: then is the prey of a great spoil divided; the lame take the prey.

24 And the inhabitant shall not say, I am sick: [a]the people that dwell therein *shall be* forgiven *their* iniquity.

Judgment on the Nations

34 Come [a]near, ye nations, to hear; and hearken, ye people: [b]let the earth hear, and all that is therein; the world, and all things that come forth of it.

2 For the indignation of the LORD *is* upon all nations, and *his* fury upon all their armies: he hath utterly destroyed them, he hath delivered them to the [a]slaughter.

---

12 [a]Is. 9:18
13 [a]Ps. 48:10; Is. 49:1
14 [a]Is. 30:27, 30; Heb. 12:29
15 [a]Ps. 15:2; 24:3, 4; Is. 58:6–11 [b]Ps. 119:37
17 [a]Ps. 27:4
18 [a]1 Cor. 1:20
19 [a]2 Kin. 19:32 [b]Deut. 28:49, 50; Is. 28:11; Jer. 5:15
20 [a]Ps. 48:12 [b]Ps. 46:5; 125:1; Is. 32:18 [c]Is. 37:33 [d]Is. 54:2
22 [a][Acts 10:42] [b]Is. 1:10; 51:4, 7; James 4:12 [c]Ps. 89:18; Is. 25:9; 35:4; Zech. 9:9
24 [a]Is. 40:2; Jer. 50:20; Mic. 7:18, 19; 1 John 1:7–9

CHAPTER 34
1 [a]Ps. 49:1; Is. 41:1; 43:9 [b]Deut. 32:1; Is. 1:2
2 [a]Is. 13:5

NKJV

You shall bring forth stubble;
Your breath, *as* fire, shall devour you.
12 And the people shall be *like* the burnings of lime;
[a]*Like* thorns cut up they shall be burned in the fire.
13 Hear, [a]you *who are* afar off, what I have done;
And you *who are* near, acknowledge My might."

14 The sinners in Zion are afraid;
Fearfulness has seized the hypocrites:
"Who among us shall dwell with the devouring [a]fire?
Who among us shall dwell with everlasting burnings?"
15 He who [a]walks righteously and speaks uprightly,
He who despises the gain of oppressions,
Who gestures with his hands, refusing bribes,
Who stops his ears from hearing of bloodshed,
And [b]shuts his eyes from seeing evil:
16 He will dwell on high;
His place of defense *will be* the fortress of rocks;
Bread will be given him,
His water *will be* sure.

The Land of the Majestic King

17 Your eyes will see the King in His [a]beauty;
They will see the land that is very far off.
18 Your heart will meditate on terror:
[a]"Where *is* the scribe?
Where *is* he who weighs?
Where *is* he who counts the towers?"
19 [a]You will not see a fierce people,
[b]A people of obscure speech, beyond perception,
Of a stammering tongue *that you* cannot understand.

20 [a]Look upon Zion, the city of our appointed feasts;
Your eyes will see [b]Jerusalem, a quiet home,
A tabernacle *that* will not be taken down;
[c]Not one of [d]its stakes will ever be removed,
Nor will any of its cords be broken.
21 But there the majestic LORD *will be* for us
A place of broad rivers *and* streams,
In which no galley with oars will sail,
Nor majestic ships pass by
22 (For the LORD *is* our [a]Judge,
The LORD *is* our [b]Lawgiver,
[c]The LORD *is* our King;
He will save us);
23 Your tackle is loosed,
They could not strengthen their mast,
They could not spread the sail.

Then the prey of great plunder is divided;
The lame take the prey.
24 And the inhabitant will not say, "I am sick";
[a]The people who dwell in it *will be* forgiven *their* iniquity.

Judgment on the Nations

34 Come [a]near, you nations, to hear;
And heed, you people!
[b]Let the earth hear, and all that is in it,
The world and all things that come forth from it.
2 For the indignation of the LORD *is* against all nations,
And *His* fury against all their armies;
He has utterly destroyed them,
He has given them over to the [a]slaughter.

KJV

3 Their slain also shall be cast out, and
[a]their stink shall come up out of their carcases,
and the mountains shall be melted with their
blood.
4 And [a]all the host of heaven shall be dissolved, and the heavens shall be rolled together
as a scroll: [b]and all their host shall fall down, as
the leaf falleth off from the vine, and as a [c]falling
fig from the fig tree.
5 For [a]my sword shall be bathed in heaven:
behold, it [b]shall come down upon Idumea, and
upon the people of my curse, to judgment.
6 The [a]sword of the LORD is filled with
blood, it is made fat with fatness, *and* with the
blood of lambs and goats, with the fat of the kidneys of rams: for [b]the LORD hath a sacrifice in
Bozrah, and a great slaughter in the land of
Idumea.
7 And the unicorns shall come down with
them, and the bullocks with the bulls; and their
land shall be soaked with blood, and their dust
made fat with fatness.
8 For *it is* the day of the LORD's [a]vengeance,
and the year of recompences for the controversy
of Zion.
9 [a]And the streams thereof shall be turned
into pitch, and the dust thereof into brimstone,
and the land thereof shall become burning pitch.
10 It shall not be quenched night nor day;
[a]the smoke thereof shall go up for ever: [b]from
generation to generation it shall lie waste; none
shall pass through it for ever and ever.
11 [a]But the cormorant and the bittern shall
possess it; the owl also and the raven shall dwell
in it: and [b]he shall stretch out upon it the line of
confusion, and the stones of emptiness.
12 They shall call the nobles thereof to the
kingdom, but none *shall be* there, and all her
princes shall be nothing.
13 And [a]thorns shall come up in her palaces,
nettles and brambles in the fortresses thereof: and
[b]it shall be an habitation of dragons, *and* a court
for owls.
14 The wild beasts of the desert shall also
meet with the wild beasts of the island, and the
satyr shall cry to his fellow; the screech owl also
shall rest there, and find for herself a place of
rest.
15 There shall the great owl make her nest,
and lay, and hatch, and gather under her shadow:
there shall the vultures also be gathered, every
one with her mate.
16 Seek ye out of [a]the book of the LORD, and
read: no one of these shall fail, none shall want
her mate: for my mouth it hath commanded, and
his spirit it hath gathered them.
17 And he hath cast the lot for them, and his
hand hath divided it unto them by line: they shall
possess it for ever, from generation to generation
shall they dwell therein.

3 [a]Joel 2:20; Amos 4:10 **4** [a]Ps. 102:26; Is. 13:13; Ezek. 32:7, 8; Joel 2:31; Matt. 24:29; 2 Pet. 3:10 [b]Is. 14:12 [c]Rev. 6:12–14 **5** [a]Deut. 32:41, 42; Jer. 46:10; Ezek. 21:3–5 [b]Is. 63:1; Jer. 49:7, 8, 20; Ezek. 25:12–14; 35:1–15; Amos 1:11, 12; Obad. 1–14; Mal. 1:4 **6** [a]Is. 66:16 [b]Zeph. 1:7 **8** [a]Is. 63:4 **9** [a]Deut. 29:23; Ps. 11:6; Is. 30:33 **10** [a]Rev. 14:11; 18:18; 19:3 [b]Is. 13:20–22; 24:1; 34:10–15; Mal. 1:3, 4 **11** [a]Is. 14:23; Zeph. 2:14; Rev. 18:2 [b]2 Kin. 21:13; Lam. 2:8 **13** [a]Is. 32:13; Hos. 9:6 [b]Is. 13:21 **16** [a][Mal. 3:16]

NKJV

3 Also their slain shall be thrown out;
[a]Their stench shall rise from their corpses,
And the mountains shall be melted with
their blood.
4 [a]All the host of heaven shall be dissolved,
And the heavens shall be rolled up like a
scroll;
[b]All their host shall fall down
As the leaf falls from the vine,
And as [c]*fruit* falling from a fig tree.

5 "For [a]My sword shall be bathed in heaven;
Indeed it [b]shall come down on Edom,
And on the people of My curse, for
judgment.
6 The [a]sword of the LORD is filled with
blood,
It is made overflowing with fatness,
With the blood of lambs and goats,
With the fat of the kidneys of rams.
For [b]the LORD has a sacrifice in Bozrah,
And a great slaughter in the land of
Edom.
7 The wild oxen shall come down with
them,
And the young bulls with the mighty
bulls;
Their land shall be soaked with blood,
And their dust saturated with fatness."

8 For *it is* the day of the LORD's [a]vengeance,
The year of recompense for the cause of
Zion.
9 [a]Its streams shall be turned into pitch,
And its dust into brimstone;
Its land shall become burning pitch.
10 It shall not be quenched night or day;
[a]Its smoke shall ascend forever.
[b]From generation to generation it shall lie
waste;
No one shall pass through it forever and
ever.
11 [a]But the pelican and the porcupine shall
possess it,
Also the owl and the raven shall dwell in
it.
And [b]He shall stretch out over it
The line of confusion and the stones of
emptiness.
12 They shall call its nobles to the kingdom,
But none *shall be* there, and all its princes
shall be nothing.

13 And [a]thorns shall come up in its palaces,
Nettles and brambles in its fortresses;
[b]It shall be a habitation of jackals,
A courtyard for ostriches.
14 The wild beasts of the desert shall also
meet with the jackals,
And the wild goat shall bleat to its
companion;
Also the night creature shall rest there,
And find for herself a place of rest.
15 There the arrow snake shall make her nest
and lay *eggs*
And hatch, and gather *them* under her
shadow;
There also shall the hawks be gathered,
Every one with her mate.

16 "Search from [a]the book of the LORD, and
read:
Not one of these shall fail;
Not one shall lack her mate.
For My mouth has commanded it, and His
Spirit has gathered them.
17 He has cast the lot for them,
And His hand has divided it among them
with a measuring line.
They shall possess it forever;
From generation to generation they shall
dwell in it."

KJV

The Future Glory of Zion

35 The [a]wilderness and the solitary place shall
be glad for them; and the [b]desert shall rejoice, and blossom as the rose.
2 [a]It shall blossom abundantly, and rejoice
even with joy and singing: the glory of Lebanon
shall be given unto it, the excellency of Carmel
and Sharon, they shall see the [b]glory of the LORD,
and the excellency of our God.
3 [a]Strengthen ye the weak hands, and confirm the feeble knees.
4 Say to them *that are* of a fearful heart,
Be strong, fear not: behold, your God will come
with [a]vengeance, *even* God *with* a recompence;
he will come and [b]save you.
5 Then the [a]eyes of the blind shall be
opened, and [b]the ears of the deaf shall be
unstopped.
6 Then shall the [a]lame *man* leap as an hart,
and the [b]tongue of the dumb sing: for in the wilderness shall [c]waters break out, and streams in
the desert.
7 And the parched ground shall become a
pool, and the thirsty land springs of water: in [a]the
habitation of dragons, where each lay, *shall be*
grass with reeds and rushes.
8 And an [a]highway shall be there, and a
way, and it shall be called The way of holiness;
[b]the unclean shall not pass over it; but it *shall
be* for those: the wayfaring men, though fools,
shall not err *therein.*
9 [a]No lion shall be there, nor *any* ravenous
beast shall go up thereon, it shall not be found
there; but the redeemed shall walk *there:*
10 And the [a]ransomed of the LORD shall return, and come to Zion with songs and everlasting
joy upon their heads: they shall obtain joy and
gladness, and [b]sorrow and sighing shall flee
away.

CHAPTER 35
1 [a]Is. 32:15; 55:12 [b]Is. 41:19; 51:3
2 [a]Is. 32:15 [b]Is. 40:5
3 [a]Job 4:3, 4; Heb. 12:12
4 [a]Is. 34:8 [b]Ps. 145:19; Is. 33:22
5 [a]Is. 29:18; Matt. 9:27; John 9:6, 7 [b][Matt. 11:5]
6 [a]Matt. 11:5; 15:30; John 5:8, 9; Acts 8:7 [b]Is. 32:4; Matt. 9:32; 12:22 [c]Is. 41:18; [John 7:38]
7 [a]Is. 34:13
8 [a]Is. 19:23 [b]Is. 52:1; Joel 3:17; [Matt. 7:13, 14]; 1 Pet. 1:15, 16; Rev. 21:27
9 [a]Lev. 26:6; [Is. 11:7, 9]; Ezek. 34:25
10 [a]Is. 51:11 [b]Is. 25:8; 30:19; 65:19; [Rev. 7:17; 21:4]

NKJV

The Future Glory of Zion

35 The [a]wilderness and the wasteland shall
be glad for them,
And the [b]desert shall rejoice and blossom
as the rose;
2 [a]It shall blossom abundantly and rejoice,
Even with joy and singing.
The glory of Lebanon shall be given to it,
The excellence of Carmel and Sharon.
They shall see the [b]glory of the LORD,
The excellency of our God.

3 [a]Strengthen the weak hands,
And make firm the feeble knees.
4 Say to those *who are* fearful-hearted,
"Be strong, do not fear!
Behold, your God will come *with*
[a]vengeance,
With the recompense of God;
He will come and [b]save you."

5 Then the [a]eyes of the blind shall be
opened,
And [b]the ears of the deaf shall be
unstopped.
6 Then the [a]lame shall leap like a deer,
And the [b]tongue of the dumb sing.
For [c]waters shall burst forth in the
wilderness,
And streams in the desert.
7 The parched ground shall become a pool,
And the thirsty land springs of water;
In [a]the habitation of jackals, where each
lay,
There shall be grass with reeds and
rushes.

8 A [a]highway shall be there, and a road,
And it shall be called the Highway of
Holiness.
[b]The unclean shall not pass over it,
But it *shall be* for others.
Whoever walks the road, although a fool,
Shall not go astray.
9 [a]No lion shall be there,
Nor shall *any* ravenous beast go up on it;
It shall not be found there.
But the redeemed shall walk *there,*
10 And the [a]ransomed of the LORD shall
return,
And come to Zion with singing,
With everlasting joy on their heads.
They shall obtain joy and gladness,
And [b]sorrow and sighing shall flee away.

Sennacherib Boasts Against the LORD
(2 Kin. 18:13–37; 2 Chr. 32:1–19)

36 Now [a]it came to pass in the fourteenth year
of king Hezekiah, *that* Sennacherib king
of Assyria came up against all the defenced cities
of Judah, and took them.
2 And the king of Assyria sent Rabshakeh
from Lachish to Jerusalem unto king Hezekiah
with a great army. And he stood by the conduit of
the upper pool in the highway of the fuller's field.
3 Then came forth unto him [a]Eliakim, Hilkiah's son, which was over the house, and [b]Shebna
the scribe, and Joah, Asaph's son, the recorder.
4 [a]And Rabshakeh said unto them, Say ye
now to Hezekiah, Thus saith the great king, the
king of Assyria, What confidence *is* this wherein
thou trustest?
5 I say, *sayest thou,* (but *they are but* vain
words) *I have* counsel and strength for war: now
on whom dost thou trust, that thou rebellest
against me?
6 Lo, thou trustest in the [a]staff of this broken reed, on Egypt; whereon if a man lean, it will
go into his hand, and pierce it: so *is* Pharaoh king
of Egypt to all that [b]trust in him.
7 But if thou say to me, We trust in the LORD

CHAPTER 36
1 [a]2 Kin. 18:13, 17; 2 Chr. 32:1
3 [a]Is. 22:20 [b]Is. 22:15
4 [a]2 Kin. 18:19
6 [a]Ezek. 29:6 [b]Ps. 146:3; Is. 30:3, 5, 7

*

36:2 A title, probably *Chief of Staff* or *Governor*

Sennacherib Boasts Against the LORD
(2 Kin. 18:13–37; 2 Chr. 32:1–19)

36 Now [a]it came to pass in the fourteenth year
of King Hezekiah *that* Sennacherib king
of Assyria came up against all the fortified cities
of Judah and took them.
2 Then the king of Assyria sent *the* *Rabshakeh with a great army from Lachish to King
Hezekiah at Jerusalem. And he stood by the aqueduct from the upper pool, on the highway to the
Fuller's Field.
3 And [a]Eliakim the son of Hilkiah, who was
over the household, [b]Shebna the scribe, and Joah
the son of Asaph, the recorder, came out to him.
4 [a]Then *the* Rabshakeh said to them, "Say
now to Hezekiah, 'Thus says the great king, the
king of Assyria: "What confidence is this in which
you trust?
5 "I say you speak of having plans and
power for war; but *they are* mere words. Now in
whom do you trust, that you rebel against me?
6 "Look! You are trusting in the [a]staff of
this broken reed, Egypt, on which if a man leans,
it will go into his hand and pierce it. So *is* Pharaoh
king of Egypt to all who [b]trust in him.
7 "But if you say to me, 'We trust in the

KJV

our God: *is it* not he, whose high places and whose altars Hezekiah hath taken away, and said to Judah and to Jerusalem, Ye shall worship before this altar?

8 Now therefore give pledges, I pray thee, to my master the king of Assyria, and I will give thee two thousand horses, if thou be able on thy part to set riders upon them.

9 How then wilt thou turn away the face of one captain of the least of my master's servants, and put thy trust on Egypt for chariots and for horsemen?

10 And am I now come up without the LORD against this land to destroy it? the LORD said unto me, Go up against this land, and destroy it.

11 Then said Eliakim and Shebna and Joah unto Rabshakeh, Speak, I pray thee, unto thy servants in the Syrian language; for we understand *it:* and speak not to us in the Jews' language, in the ears of the people that *are* on the wall.

12 But Rabshakeh said, Hath my master sent me to thy master and to thee to speak these words? *hath he* not *sent me* to the men that sit upon the wall, that they may eat their own dung, and drink their own piss with you?

13 Then Rabshakeh stood, and cried with a loud voice in the Jews' language, and said, Hear ye the words of the great king, the king of Assyria.

14 Thus saith the king, Let not Hezekiah deceive you: for he shall not be able to deliver you.

15 Neither let Hezekiah make you trust in the LORD, saying, The LORD will surely deliver us: this city shall not be delivered into the hand of the king of Assyria.

16 Hearken not to Hezekiah: for thus saith the king of Assyria, Make *an agreement* with me *by* a present, and come out to me: [a]and eat ye every one of his vine, and every one of his fig tree, and drink ye every one the waters of his own cistern;

17 Until I come and take you away to a land like your own land, a land of corn and wine, a land of bread and vineyards.

18 *Beware* lest Hezekiah persuade you, saying, The LORD will deliver us. Hath any of the [a]gods of the nations delivered his land out of the hand of the king of Assyria?

19 Where *are* the gods of Hamath and Arphad? where *are* the gods of Sepharvaim? and have they delivered [a]Samaria out of my hand?

20 Who *are they* among all the gods of these lands, that have delivered their land out of my hand, that the LORD should deliver Jerusalem out of my hand?

21 But they held their peace, and answered him not a word: for the king's commandment was, saying, Answer him not.

22 Then came Eliakim, the son of Hilkiah, that *was* over the household, and Shebna the scribe, and Joah, the son of Asaph, the recorder, to Hezekiah with *their* clothes rent, and told him the words of Rabshakeh.

Isaiah Assures Deliverance
(*2 Kin. 19:1–7*)

37 And [a]it came to pass, when king Hezekiah heard *it*, that he rent his clothes, and covered himself with sackcloth, and went into the house of the LORD.

2 And he sent Eliakim, who *was* over the household, and Shebna the scribe, and the elders of the priests covered with sackcloth, unto Isaiah the prophet the son of Amoz.

3 And they said unto him, Thus saith Hezekiah, This day *is* a day of [a]trouble, and of rebuke, and of blasphemy: for the children are come to the birth, and *there is* not strength to bring forth.

4 It may be the LORD thy God will hear the words of Rabshakeh, whom the king of Assyria his master hath sent to [a]reproach the living God, and will reprove the words which the LORD thy

16 [a]1 Kin. 4:25; Mic. 4:4; Zech. 3:10
18 [a]2 Kin. 19:12; Is. 37:12
19 [a]2 Kin. 17:6

CHAPTER 37

1 [a]2 Kin. 19:1–37; Is. 37:1–38
3 [a]Is. 22:5; 26:16; 33:2
4 [a]Is. 36:15, 18, 20

NKJV

LORD our God,' *is it* not He whose high places and whose altars Hezekiah has taken away, and said to Judah and Jerusalem, 'You shall worship before this altar'?" '

8 "Now therefore, I urge you, give a pledge to my master the king of Assyria, and I will give you two thousand horses—if you are able on your part to put riders on them!

9 "How then will you repel one captain of the least of my master's servants, and put your trust in Egypt for chariots and horsemen?

10 "Have I now come up without the LORD against this land to destroy it? The LORD said to me, 'Go up against this land, and destroy it.' "

11 Then Eliakim, Shebna, and Joah said to *the* Rabshakeh, "Please speak to your servants in Aramaic, for we understand *it;* and do not speak to us in *Hebrew in the hearing of the people who *are* on the wall."

12 But *the* Rabshakeh said, "Has my master sent me to your master and to you to speak these words, and not to the men who sit on the wall, who will eat and drink their own waste with you?"

13 Then *the* Rabshakeh stood and called out with a loud voice in Hebrew, and said, "Hear the words of the great king, the king of Assyria!

14 "Thus says the king: 'Do not let Hezekiah deceive you, for he will not be able to deliver you;

15 'nor let Hezekiah make you trust in the LORD, saying, "The LORD will surely deliver us; this city will not be given into the hand of the king of Assyria." '

16 "Do not listen to Hezekiah; for thus says the king of Assyria: 'Make *peace* with me *by a* present and come out to me; [a]and every one of you eat from his own vine and every one from his own fig tree, and every one of you drink the waters of his own cistern;

17 'until I come and take you away to a land like your own land, a land of grain and new wine, a land of bread and vineyards.

18 '*Beware* lest Hezekiah persuade you, saying, "The LORD will deliver us." Has any one of the [a]gods of the nations delivered its land from the hand of the king of Assyria?

19 'Where *are* the gods of Hamath and Arpad? Where *are* the gods of Sepharvaim? Indeed, have they delivered [a]Samaria from my hand?

20 'Who among all the gods of these lands have delivered their countries from my hand, that the LORD should deliver Jerusalem from my hand?' "

21 But they held their peace and answered him not a word; for the king's commandment was, "Do not answer him."

22 Then Eliakim the son of Hilkiah, who *was* over the household, Shebna the scribe, and Joah the son of Asaph, the recorder, came to Hezekiah with *their* clothes torn, and told him the words of *the* Rabshakeh.

Isaiah Assures Deliverance
(*2 Kin. 19:1–7*)

37 And [a]so it was, when King Hezekiah heard *it*, that he tore his clothes, covered himself with sackcloth, and went into the house of the LORD.

2 Then he sent Eliakim, who *was* over the household, Shebna the scribe, and the elders of the priests, covered with sackcloth, to Isaiah the prophet, the son of Amoz.

3 And they said to him, "Thus says Hezekiah: 'This day *is* a day of [a]trouble and rebuke and blasphemy; for the children have come to birth, but *there is* no strength to bring them forth.

4 'It may be that the LORD your God will hear the words of *the* Rabshakeh, whom his master the king of Assyria has sent to [a]reproach the living God, and will rebuke the words which the

*

36:11 Lit. *Judean*

KJV

God hath heard: wherefore lift up *thy* prayer for the remnant that is left.

5 So the servants of king Hezekiah came to Isaiah.

6 And Isaiah said unto them, Thus shall ye say unto your master, Thus saith the LORD, Be not afraid of the words that thou hast heard, wherewith the servants of the king of Assyria have blasphemed me.

7 Behold, I will send a blast upon him, and he shall hear a rumour, and return to his own land; and I will cause him to fall by the sword in his own land.

Sennacherib's Threat and Hezekiah's Prayer
(2 Kin. 19:8–19)

8 So Rabshakeh returned, and found the king of Assyria warring against Libnah: for he had heard that he was departed from Lachish.

9 And he heard say concerning Tirhakah king of Ethiopia, He is come forth to make war with thee. And when he heard *it,* he sent messengers to Hezekiah, saying,

10 Thus shall ye speak to Hezekiah king of Judah, saying, Let not thy God, in whom thou trustest, deceive thee, saying, Jerusalem shall not be given into the hand of the king of Assyria.

11 Behold, thou hast heard what the kings of Assyria have done to all lands by destroying them utterly; and shalt thou be delivered?

12 Have the [a]gods of the nations delivered them which my fathers have destroyed, *as* Gozan, and Haran, and Rezeph, and the children of Eden which *were* in Telassar?

13 Where *is* the king of [a]Hamath, and the king of Arphad, and the king of the city of Sepharvaim, Hena, and Ivah?

14 And Hezekiah received the letter from the hand of the messengers, and read it: and Hezekiah went up unto the house of the LORD, and spread it before the LORD.

15 And Hezekiah prayed unto the LORD, saying,

16 O LORD of hosts, God of Israel, that dwellest *between* the cherubims, thou *art* the God, *even* thou [a]alone, of all the kingdoms of the earth: thou hast made heaven and earth.

17 [a]Incline thine ear, O LORD, and hear; open thine eyes, O LORD, and see: and [b]hear all the words of Sennacherib, which hath sent to reproach the living God.

18 Of a truth, LORD, the kings of Assyria have laid waste all the nations, and their [a]countries,

19 And have cast their gods into the fire: for they *were* [a]no gods, but the work of men's hands, wood and stone: therefore they have destroyed them.

20 Now therefore, O LORD our God, [a]save us from his hand, that all the kingdoms of the earth may [b]know that thou *art* the LORD, *even* thou only.

The Word of the LORD Concerning Sennacherib
(2 Kin. 19:20–34)

21 Then Isaiah the son of Amoz sent unto Hezekiah, saying, Thus saith the LORD God of Israel, Whereas thou hast prayed to me against Sennacherib king of Assyria:

22 This *is* the word which the LORD hath spoken concerning him; The virgin, the daughter of Zion, hath despised thee, *and* laughed thee to scorn; the daughter of Jerusalem hath shaken her head at thee.

23 Whom hast thou reproached and blasphemed? and against whom hast thou exalted *thy* voice, and lifted up thine eyes on high? *even* against the Holy One of Israel.

12 [a]Is. 36:18, 19
13 [a]Is. 49:23
16 [a]Is. 43:10, 11
17 [a]2 Chr. 6:40; Ps. 17:6; Dan. 9:18 [b]Ps. 74:22
18 [a]2 Kin. 15:29; 16:9; 17:6, 24; 1 Chr. 5:26
19 [a]Is. 40:19, 20
20 [a]Is. 33:22 [b]Ps. 83:18

NKJV

LORD your God has heard. Therefore lift up *your* prayer for the remnant that is left.' "

5 So the servants of King Hezekiah came to Isaiah.

6 And Isaiah said to them, "Thus you shall say to your master, 'Thus says the LORD: "Do not be afraid of the words which you have heard, with which the servants of the king of Assyria have blasphemed Me.

7 "Surely I will send a spirit upon him, and he shall hear a rumor and return to his own land; and I will cause him to fall by the sword in his own land." ' "

Sennacherib's Threat and Hezekiah's Prayer
(2 Kin. 19:8–19)

8 Then *the* Rabshakeh returned, and found the king of Assyria warring against Libnah, for he heard that he had departed from Lachish.

9 And the king heard concerning Tirhakah king of Ethiopia, "He has come out to make war with you." So when he heard *it,* he sent messengers to Hezekiah, saying,

10 "Thus you shall speak to Hezekiah king of Judah, saying: 'Do not let your God in whom you trust deceive you, saying, "Jerusalem shall not be given into the hand of the king of Assyria."

11 'Look! You have heard what the kings of Assyria have done to all lands by utterly destroying them; and shall you be delivered?

12 'Have the [a]gods of the nations delivered those whom my fathers have destroyed, Gozan and Haran and Rezeph, and the people of Eden who *were* in Telassar?

13 'Where *is* the king of [a]Hamath, the king of Arpad, and the king of the city of Sepharvaim, Hena, and Ivah?' "

14 And Hezekiah received the letter from the hand of the messengers, and read it; and Hezekiah went up to the house of the LORD, and spread it before the LORD.

15 Then Hezekiah prayed to the LORD, saying:

16 "O LORD of hosts, God of Israel, *the One* who dwells *between* the cherubim, You *are* God, You [a]alone, of all the kingdoms of the earth. You have made heaven and earth.

17 [a]"Incline Your ear, O LORD, and hear; open Your eyes, O LORD, and see; and [b]hear all the words of Sennacherib, which he has sent to reproach the living God.

18 "Truly, LORD, the kings of Assyria have laid waste all the nations and their [a]lands,

19 "and have cast their gods into the fire; for they *were* [a]not gods, but the work of men's hands—wood and stone. Therefore they destroyed them.

20 "Now therefore, O LORD our God, [a]save us from his hand, that all the kingdoms of the earth may [b]know that You *are* the LORD, You alone."

The Word of the LORD Concerning Sennacherib
(2 Kin. 19:20–34)

21 Then Isaiah the son of Amoz sent to Hezekiah, saying, "Thus says the LORD God of Israel, 'Because you have prayed to Me against Sennacherib king of Assyria,

22 'this *is* the word which the LORD has spoken concerning him:

"The virgin, the daughter of Zion,
Has despised you, laughed you to scorn;
The daughter of Jerusalem
Has shaken *her* head behind your back!

23 "Whom have you reproached and
blasphemed?
Against whom have you raised *your* voice,
And lifted up your eyes on high?
Against the Holy One of Israel.

KJV

24 By thy servants hast thou reproached the
Lord, and hast said, By the multitude of my chariots am I come up to the height of the mountains,
to the sides of Lebanon; and I will cut down the
tall cedars thereof, *and* the choice fir trees thereof:
and I will enter into the height of his border, *and*
the forest of his Carmel.
25 I have digged, and drunk water; and with
the sole of my feet have I dried up all the rivers
of the besieged places.
26 Hast thou not heard [a]long ago, *how* I have
done it; *and* of ancient times, that I have formed
it? now have I brought it to pass, that thou shouldest be to lay waste defenced cities *into* ruinous
heaps.
27 Therefore their inhabitants *were* of small
power, they were dismayed and confounded: they
were *as* the grass of the field, and *as* the green
herb, *as* the grass on the housetops, and *as corn*
blasted before it be grown up.
28 But I know thy abode, and thy going out,
and thy coming in, and thy rage against me.
29 Because thy rage against me, and thy tumult, is come up into mine ears, therefore [a]will I
put my hook in thy nose, and my bridle in thy
lips, and I will [b]turn thee back by the way by
which thou camest.
30 And this *shall be* a sign unto thee, Ye shall
eat *this* year such as groweth of itself; and the
second year that which springeth of the same: and
in the third year sow ye, and reap, and plant vineyards, and eat the fruit thereof.
31 And the remnant that is escaped of the
house of Judah shall again take root downward,
and bear fruit upward:
32 For out of Jerusalem shall go forth a remnant, and they that escape out of mount Zion: the
[a]zeal of the LORD of hosts shall do this.
33 Therefore thus saith the LORD concerning
the king of Assyria, He shall not come into this
city, nor shoot an arrow there, nor come before
it with shields, nor cast a bank against it.
34 By the way that he came, by the same
shall he return, and shall not come into this city,
saith the LORD.
35 For I will [a]defend this city to save it for
mine own sake, and for my servant [b]David's sake.

Sennacherib's Defeat and Death
(*2 Kin. 19:35–37*)

36 Then the [a]angel of the LORD went forth,
and smote in the camp of the Assyrians a hundred
and fourscore and five thousand: and when they
arose early in the morning, behold, they *were* all
dead corpses.
37 So Sennacherib king of Assyria departed,
and went and returned, and dwelt at Nineveh.

26 [a]Is. 25:1; 40:21; 45:21
29 [a]2 Kin. 19:35–37; 2 Chr. 32:21; Is. 30:28; Ezek. 38:4 [b]Ezek. 38:4; 39:2
32 [a]2 Kin. 19:31; Is. 9:7; 59:17; Joel 2:18; Zech. 1:14
35 [a]2 Kin. 20:6; Is. 31:5; 38:6 [b]1 Kin. 11:13
36 [a]2 Kin. 19:35; Is. 10:12, 33, 34

NKJV

24 By your servants you have reproached the
Lord,
And said, 'By the multitude of my chariots
I have come up to the height of the
mountains,
To the limits of Lebanon;
I will cut down its tall cedars
And its choice cypress trees;
I will enter its farthest height,
To its fruitful forest.
25 I have dug and drunk water,
And with the soles of my feet I have
dried up
All the brooks of defense.'

26 "Did you not hear [a]long ago
How I made it,
From ancient times that I formed it?
Now I have brought it to pass,
That you should be
For crushing fortified cities *into* heaps of
ruins.
27 Therefore their inhabitants *had* little
power;
They were dismayed and confounded;
They were *as* the grass of the field
And the green herb,
As the grass on the housetops
And *grain* blighted before it is grown.

28 "But I know your dwelling place,
Your going out and your coming in,
And your rage against Me.
29 Because your rage against Me and your
tumult
Have come up to My ears,
Therefore [a]I will put My hook in your nose
And My bridle in your lips,
And I will [b]turn you back
By the way which you came." '

30 "This *shall be* a sign to you:

You shall eat this year such as grows of
itself,
And the second year what springs from
the same;
Also in the third year sow and reap,
Plant vineyards and eat the fruit of them.
31 And the remnant who have escaped of the
house of Judah
Shall again take root downward,
And bear fruit upward.
32 For out of Jerusalem shall go a remnant,
And those who escape from Mount Zion.
The [a]zeal of the LORD of hosts will do this.

33 "Therefore thus says the LORD concerning
the king of Assyria:

'He shall not come into this city,
Nor shoot an arrow there,
Nor come before it with shield,
Nor build a siege mound against it.
34 By the way that he came,
By the same shall he return;
And he shall not come into this city,'
Says the LORD.
35 'For I will [a]defend this city, to save it
For My own sake and for My servant
[b]David's sake.' "

Sennacherib's Defeat and Death
(*2 Kin. 19:35–37*)

36 Then the [a]angel* of the LORD went out,
and killed in the camp of the Assyrians one hundred and eighty-five thousand; and when *people*
arose early in the morning, there were the
corpses—all dead.
37 So Sennacherib king of Assyria departed
and went away, returned *home*, and remained at
Nineveh.

*
37:36 Or *Angel*

KJV

38 And it came to pass, as he was worshipping in the house of Nisroch his god, that Adrammelech and Sharezer his sons smote him with the
sword; and they escaped into the land of Armenia:
and [a]Esar–haddon his son reigned in his stead.

Hezekiah's Life Extended
(2 Kin. 20:1–11; 2 Chr. 32:24–26)

38 In [a]those days was Hezekiah sick unto
death. And Isaiah the prophet the son of
Amoz came unto him, and said unto him, Thus
saith the LORD, [b]Set thine house in order: for thou
shalt die, and not live.
2 Then Hezekiah turned his face toward the
wall, and prayed unto the LORD,
3 And said, [a]Remember now, O LORD, I beseech thee, how I have walked before thee in truth
and with a perfect heart, and have done *that
which is* good in thy [b]sight. And Hezekiah wept
sore.
4 Then came the word of the LORD to Isaiah,
saying,
5 Go, and say to Hezekiah, Thus saith the
LORD, the God of David thy father, I have heard
thy prayer, I have seen thy tears: behold, I will
add unto thy days fifteen years.
6 And I will deliver thee and this city out
of the hand of the king of Assyria: and [a]I will
defend this city.
7 And this *shall be* [a]a sign unto thee from
the LORD, that the LORD will do this thing that he
hath spoken;
8 Behold, I will bring again the shadow of
the degrees, which is gone down in the sun dial
of Ahaz, ten degrees backward. So the sun returned ten degrees, by which degrees it was gone
down.
9 The writing of Hezekiah king of Judah,
when he had been sick, and was recovered of his
sickness:
10 I said in the cutting off of my days, I shall
go to the gates of the grave: I am deprived of the
residue of my years.
11 I said, I shall not see the LORD, *even* the
LORD, [a]in the land of the living: I shall behold
man no more with the inhabitants of the world.
12 [a]Mine age is departed, and is removed
from me as a shepherd's tent: I have cut off like
a weaver my life: he will cut me off with pining
sickness: from day *even* to night wilt thou make
an end of me.
13 I reckoned till morning, *that,* as a lion,
so will he break all my bones: from day *even* to
night wilt thou make an end of me.
14 Like a crane *or* a swallow, so did I chatter:
[a]I did mourn as a dove: mine eyes fail *with looking* upward: O LORD, I am oppressed; undertake
for me.
15 What shall I say? He hath both spoken
unto me, and himself hath done *it:* I shall go softly
all my years [a]in the bitterness of my soul.
16 O LORD, by these *things men* live, and in
all these *things is* the life of my spirit: so wilt
thou recover me, and make me to live.
17 Behold, for peace I had great bitterness:
but thou hast in love to my soul *delivered it* from
the pit of corruption: for thou hast cast all my
sins behind thy back.

---

38 [a]Ezra 4:2

CHAPTER 38

1 [a]2 Kin. 20:1–6, 9–11; 2 Chr. 32:24; Is. 38:1–8
[b]2 Sam. 17:23
3 [a]Neh. 13:14
[b]2 Kin. 18:5, 6; Ps. 26:3
6 [a]2 Kin. 19:35–37; 2 Chr. 32:21; Is. 31:5; 37:35
7 [a]Judg. 6:17, 21, 36–40; 2 Kin. 20:8; Is. 7:11
11 [a]Ps. 27:13; 116:9
12 [a]Job 7:6
14 [a]Is. 59:11; Ezek. 7:16; Nah. 2:7
15 [a]Job 7:11; 10:1; Is. 38:17

---

*

38:11 Heb. YAH, YAH • LXX omits *among the inhabitants of the world* • So with some Heb. mss.; MT, Vg. *rest;* Tg. *land*
38:14 So with Bg.; MT, DSS *Lord*
38:15 So with MT, Vg.; DSS, Tg. *And shall I say to Him;* LXX omits first half of this verse

---

NKJV

38 Now it came to pass, as he was worshiping
in the house of Nisroch his god, that his sons
Adrammelech and Sharezer struck him down
with the sword; and they escaped into the land
of Ararat. Then [a]Esarhaddon his son reigned in
his place.

Hezekiah's Life Extended
(2 Kin. 20:1–11; 2 Chr. 32:24–26)

38 In [a]those days Hezekiah was sick and near
death. And Isaiah the prophet, the son of
Amoz, went to him and said to him, "Thus says
the LORD: [b]'Set your house in order, for you shall
die and not live.' "
2 Then Hezekiah turned his face toward the
wall, and prayed to the LORD,
3 and said, [a]"Remember now, O LORD, I
pray, how I have walked before You in truth and
with a loyal heart, and have done *what is* good
in Your [b]sight." And Hezekiah wept bitterly.
4 And the word of the LORD came to Isaiah,
saying,
5 "Go and tell Hezekiah, 'Thus says the
LORD, the God of David your father: "I have heard
your prayer, I have seen your tears; surely I will
add to your days fifteen years.
6 "I will deliver you and this city from the
hand of the king of Assyria, and [a]I will defend
this city." '
7 "And this *is* [a]the sign to you from the
LORD, that the LORD will do this thing which He
has spoken:
8 "Behold, I will bring the shadow on the
sundial, which has gone down with the sun on
the sundial of Ahaz, ten degrees backward." So
the sun returned ten degrees on the dial by which
it had gone down.
9 This is the writing of Hezekiah king of Judah, when he had been sick and had recovered
from his sickness:

10 I said,
"In the prime of my life
I shall go to the gates of Sheol;
I am deprived of the remainder of my
years."
11 I said,
"I shall not see *YAH,
The LORD [a]in the land of the living;
I shall observe man no more *among the
inhabitants of *the world.
12 [a]My life span is gone,
Taken from me like a shepherd's tent;
I have cut off my life like a weaver.
He cuts me off from the loom;
From day until night You make an end
of me.
13 I have considered until morning—
Like a lion,
So He breaks all my bones;
From day until night You make an end
of me.
14 Like a crane *or* a swallow, so I chattered;
[a]I mourned like a dove;
My eyes fail *from looking* upward.
O *LORD, I am oppressed;
Undertake for me!

15 "What shall I say?
*He has both spoken to me,
And He Himself has done *it.*
I shall walk carefully all my years
[a]In the bitterness of my soul.
16 O Lord, by these *things men* live;
And in all these *things is* the life of my
spirit;
So You will restore me and make me live.
17 Indeed *it was* for *my own* peace
That I had great bitterness;
But You have lovingly *delivered* my soul
from the pit of corruption,
For You have cast all my sins behind Your
back.

KJV

18 For [a]the grave cannot praise thee, death can *not* celebrate thee: they that go down into the pit cannot hope for thy truth.

19 The living, the living, he shall praise thee, as I *do* this day: [a]the father to the children shall make known thy truth.

20 The LORD *was ready* to save me: therefore we will sing my songs to the stringed instruments all the days of our life in the house of the LORD.

21 For [a]Isaiah had said, Let them take a lump of figs, and lay *it* for a plaister upon the boil, and he shall recover.

22 [a]Hezekiah also had said, What *is* the sign that I shall go up to the house of the LORD?

The Babylonian Envoys
(2 Kin. 20:12–19)

39 At [a]that time Merodach–baladan, the son of Baladan, king of Babylon, sent letters and a present to Hezekiah: for he had heard that he had been sick, and was recovered.

2 [a]And Hezekiah was glad of them, and shewed them the house of his precious things, the silver, and the gold, and the spices, and the precious ointment, and all the house of his armour, and all that was found in his treasures: there was nothing in his house, nor in all his dominion, that Hezekiah shewed them not.

3 Then came Isaiah the prophet unto king Hezekiah, and said unto him, What said these men? and from whence came they unto thee? And Hezekiah said, They are come from a [a]far country unto me, *even* from Babylon.

4 Then said he, What have they seen in thine house? And Hezekiah answered, All that *is* in mine house have they seen: there is nothing among my treasures that I have not shewed them.

5 Then said Isaiah to Hezekiah, Hear the word of the LORD of hosts:

6 Behold, the days come, [a]that all that *is* in thine house, and *that* which thy fathers have laid up in store until this day, shall be carried to Babylon: nothing shall be left, saith the LORD.

7 And of thy [a]sons that shall issue from thee, which thou shalt beget, shall they take away; and they shall be eunuchs in the palace of the king of Babylon.

8 Then said Hezekiah to Isaiah, [a]Good *is* the word of the LORD which thou hast spoken. He said moreover, For there shall be peace and truth in my days.

God's People Are Comforted
(cf. Luke 3:4–6)

40 Comfort ye, comfort ye my people, saith your God.

2 Speak ye comfortably to Jerusalem, and cry unto her, that her warfare is accomplished, that her iniquity is pardoned: [a]for she hath received of the LORD's hand double for all her sins.

3 [a]The voice of him that crieth in the wilderness, [b]Prepare ye the way of the LORD, [c]make straight in the desert a highway for our God.

4 Every valley shall be exalted, and every mountain and hill shall be made low: [a]and the crooked shall be made straight, and the rough places plain:

---

18 [a]Ps. 6:5; 30:9; 88:11; 115:17; [Eccl. 9:10]
19 [a]Deut. 4:9; 6:7; Ps. 78:3, 4
21 [a]2 Kin. 20:7
22 [a]2 Kin. 20:8

CHAPTER 39

1 [a]2 Kin. 20:12–19; 2 Chr. 32:31; Is. 39:1–8
2 [a]2 Chr. 32:25, 31; Job 31:25
3 [a]Deut. 28:49; Jer. 5:15
6 [a]2 Kin. 24:13; 25:13–15; Jer. 20:5
7 [a]Dan. 1:1–7
8 [a]1 Sam. 3:18

CHAPTER 40

2 [a]Is. 61:7
3 [a]Matt. 3:3; Mark 1:3; Luke 3:4–6; John 1:23 [b][Mal. 3:1; 4:5, 6] [c]Ps. 68:4
4 [a]Is. 45:2

*______

39:1 *Berodach-Baladan,* 2 Kin. 20:12
40:3 So with MT, Tg., Vg.; LXX omits *in the desert*

NKJV

18 For [a]Sheol cannot thank You,
Death cannot praise You;
Those who go down to the pit cannot hope for Your truth.
19 The living, the living man, he shall praise You,
As I *do* this day;
[a]The father shall make known Your truth to the children.

20 "The LORD *was ready* to save me;
Therefore we will sing my songs with stringed instruments
All the days of our life, in the house of the LORD."

21 Now [a]Isaiah had said, "Let them take a lump of figs, and apply *it* as a poultice on the boil, and he shall recover."

22 And [a]Hezekiah had said, "What *is* the sign that I shall go up to the house of the LORD?"

The Babylonian Envoys
(2 Kin. 20:12–19)

39 At [a]that time *Merodach-Baladan the son of Baladan, king of Babylon, sent letters and a present to Hezekiah, for he heard that he had been sick and had recovered.

2 [a]And Hezekiah was pleased with them, and showed them the house of his treasures—the silver and gold, the spices and precious ointment, and all his armory—all that was found among his treasures. There was nothing in his house or in all his dominion that Hezekiah did not show them.

3 Then Isaiah the prophet went to King Hezekiah, and said to him, "What did these men say, and from where did they come to you?" So Hezekiah said, "They came to me from a [a]far country, from Babylon."

4 And he said, "What have they seen in your house?" So Hezekiah answered, "They have seen all that *is* in my house; there is nothing among my treasures that I have not shown them."

5 Then Isaiah said to Hezekiah, "Hear the word of the LORD of hosts:

6 'Behold, the days are coming [a]when all that *is* in your house, and what your fathers have accumulated until this day, shall be carried to Babylon; nothing shall be left,' says the LORD.

7 'And they shall take away *some* of your [a]sons who will descend from you, whom you will beget; and they shall be eunuchs in the palace of the king of Babylon.' "

8 So Hezekiah said to Isaiah, [a]"The word of the LORD which you have spoken *is* good!" For he said, "At least there will be peace and truth in my days."

God's People Are Comforted
(cf. Luke 3:4–6)

40 "Comfort, yes, comfort My people!"
Says your God.
2 "Speak comfort to Jerusalem, and cry out to her,
That her warfare is ended,
That her iniquity is pardoned;
[a]For she has received from the LORD's hand
Double for all her sins."

3 [a]The voice of one crying in the wilderness:
[b]"Prepare the way of the LORD;
[c]Make straight *in the desert
A highway for our God.
4 Every valley shall be exalted
And every mountain and hill brought low;
[a]The crooked places shall be made straight
And the rough places smooth;

KJV

5 And the [a]glory of the LORD shall be revealed, and all flesh shall see *it* together: for the
mouth of the LORD hath spoken *it*.
6 The voice said, Cry. And he said, What
shall I cry? [a]All flesh *is* grass, and all the goodli-
ness thereof *is* as the flower of the field:
7 The grass withereth, the flower fadeth: because the spirit of the LORD bloweth upon it: surely
the people *is* grass.
8 The grass withereth, the flower fadeth: but
[a]the word of our God shall stand for ever.
9 O Zion, that bringest good tidings, get thee
up into the high mountain; O Jerusalem, that
bringest good tidings, lift up thy voice with
strength; lift *it* up, be not afraid; say unto the cities
of Judah, Behold your God!
10 Behold, the Lord GOD will come with
strong *hand,* and [a]his arm shall rule for him: behold, [b]his reward *is* with him, and his work before
him.
11 He shall [a]feed his flock like a shepherd:
he shall gather the lambs with his arm, and carry
them in his bosom, *and* shall gently lead those
that are with young.
12 [a]Who hath measured the waters in the
hollow of his hand, and meted out heaven with
the span, and comprehended the dust of the earth
in a measure, and weighed the mountains in
scales, and the hills in a balance?
13 [a]Who hath directed the Spirit of the LORD,
or *being* his counsellor hath taught him?
14 With whom took he counsel, and *who* instructed him, and [a]taught him in the path of judgment, and taught him knowledge, and shewed to
him the way of understanding?
15 Behold, the nations *are* as a drop of a
bucket, and are counted as the small dust of the
balance: behold, he taketh up the isles as a very
little thing.
16 And Lebanon *is* not sufficient to burn, nor
the beasts thereof sufficient for a burnt offering.
17 All nations before him *are* as [a]nothing;
and [b]they are counted to him less than nothing,
and vanity.
18 To whom then will ye [a]liken God? or what
likeness will ye compare unto him?
19 [a]The workman melteth a graven image,
and the goldsmith spreadeth it over with gold, and
casteth silver chains.
20 He that *is* so impoverished that he hath
no oblation chooseth a tree *that* will not rot; he
seeketh unto him a cunning workman [a]to prepare
a graven image, *that* shall not be moved.
21 [a]Have ye not known? have ye not heard?
hath it not been told you from the beginning? have

5 [a]Is. 35:2
6 [a]Job 14:2; James 1:10; 1 Pet. 1:24, 25
8 [a][John 12:34]
10 [a]Is. 59:16, 18 [b]Is. 62:11; Rev. 22:12
11 [a]Jer. 31:10; [Ezek. 34:23, 31]; Mic. 5:4; [John 10:11, 14–16; Heb. 13:20; 1 Pet. 2:25]
12 [a]Prov. 30:4
13 [a]Job 21:22; Rom. 11:34; [1 Cor. 2:16]
14 [a]Job 36:22, 23
17 [a]Dan. 4:35 [b]Ps. 62:9
18 [a]Ex. 8:10; 15:11; 1 Sam. 2:2; Is. 46:5; [Mic. 7:18]; Acts 17:29
19 [a]Ps. 115:4–8; Is. 41:7; 44:10; Hab. 2:18, 19
20 [a]1 Sam. 5:3, 4; Is. 41:7; 46:7; Jer. 10:3
21 [a]Ps. 19:1; Is. 37:26; Acts 14:17; Rom. 1:19

NKJV

5 The [a]glory of the LORD shall be revealed,
And all flesh shall see *it* together;
For the mouth of the LORD has spoken."

6 The voice said, "Cry out!"
And *he said, "What shall I cry?"

[a]"All flesh *is* grass,
And all its loveliness *is* like the flower of the field.
7 The grass withers, the flower fades,
Because the breath of the LORD blows upon it;
Surely the people *are* grass.
8 The grass withers, the flower fades,
But [a]the word of our God stands forever."

9 O Zion,
You who bring good tidings,
Get up into the high mountain;
O Jerusalem,
You who bring good tidings,
Lift up your voice with strength,
Lift *it* up, be not afraid;
Say to the cities of Judah, "Behold your God!"

10 Behold, the Lord GOD shall come with a strong *hand,*
And [a]His arm shall rule for Him;
Behold, [b]His reward *is* with Him,
And His work before Him.
11 He will [a]feed His flock like a shepherd;
He will gather the lambs with His arm,
And carry *them* in His bosom,
And gently lead those who are with young.

12 [a]Who has measured the *waters in the hollow of His hand,
Measured heaven with a span
And calculated the dust of the earth in a measure?
Weighed the mountains in scales
And the hills in a balance?
13 [a]Who has directed the Spirit of the LORD,
Or *as* His counselor has taught Him?
14 With whom did He take counsel, and *who* instructed Him,
And [a]taught Him in the path of justice?
Who taught Him knowledge,
And showed Him the way of understanding?

15 Behold, the nations *are* as a drop in a bucket,
And are counted as the small dust on the scales;
Look, He lifts up the isles as a very little thing.
16 And Lebanon *is* not sufficient to burn,
Nor its beasts sufficient for a burnt offering.
17 All nations before Him *are* as [a]nothing,
And [b]they are counted by Him less than nothing and worthless.

18 To whom then will you [a]liken God?
Or what likeness will you compare to Him?
19 [a]The workman molds an image,
The goldsmith overspreads it with gold,
And the silversmith casts silver chains.
20 Whoever *is* too impoverished for *such* a contribution
Chooses a tree *that* will not rot;
He seeks for himself a skillful workman
[a]To prepare a carved image *that* will not totter.

21 [a]Have you not known?
Have you not heard?

*

40:6 So with MT, Tg.; DSS, LXX, Vg. *I*
40:12 So with MT, LXX, Vg.; DSS adds *of the sea;* Tg. adds *of the world*

KJV

ye not understood from the foundations of the earth?

22 *It is* he that sitteth upon the circle of the earth, and the inhabitants thereof *are* as grasshoppers; that [a]stretcheth out the heavens as a curtain, and spreadeth them out as a [b]tent to dwell in:

23 That bringeth the [a]princes to nothing: he maketh the judges of the earth as vanity.

24 Yea, they shall not be planted; yea, they shall not be sown: yea, their stock shall not take root in the earth: and he shall also blow upon them, and they shall wither, and the whirlwind shall take them away as stubble.

25 [a]To whom then will ye liken me, or shall I be equal? saith the Holy One.

26 Lift up your eyes on high, and behold who hath created these *things*, that bringeth out their host by number: [a]he calleth them all by names by the greatness of his might, for that *he is* strong in power; not one faileth.

27 [a]Why sayest thou, O Jacob, and speakest, O Israel, My way is hid from the LORD, and my judgment is passed over from my God?

28 Hast thou not known? hast thou not heard, *that* the everlasting God, the LORD, the Creator of the ends of the earth, fainteth not, neither is weary? [a]*there is* no searching of his understanding.

29 He giveth power to the faint; and to *them that have* no might he increaseth strength.

30 Even the youths shall faint and be weary, and the young men shall utterly fall:

31 But they that [a]wait upon the LORD [b]shall renew *their* strength; they shall mount up with wings as eagles; they shall run, and not be weary; *and* they shall walk, and not faint.

Israel Assured of God's Help

41 Keep[a] silence before me, O islands; and let the people renew *their* strength: let them come near; then let them speak: let us [b]come near together to judgment.

2 Who raised up the righteous *man* [a]from the east, called him to his foot, [b]gave the nations before him, and made *him* rule over kings? he gave *them* as the dust to his sword, *and* as driven stubble to his bow.

3 He pursued them, *and* passed safely; *even* by the way *that* he had not gone with his feet.

4 [a]Who hath wrought and done *it*, calling the generations from the beginning? I the LORD, the [b]first, and with the last; I *am* [c]he.

5 The isles saw *it*, and feared; the ends of the earth were afraid, drew near, and came.

22 [a]Job 9:8; Ps. 104:2; Is. 42:5; 44:24; Jer. 10:12 [b]Job 36:29; Ps. 19:4
23 [a]Job 12:21; Ps. 107:40; Is. 34:12; [1 Cor. 1:26–29]
25 [a][Deut. 4:15]; Is. 40:18; [John 14:9; Col. 1:15]
26 [a]Ps. 147:4
27 [a]Is. 54:7, 8
28 [a]Ps. 147:5; Eccl. 11:5; Rom. 11:33
31 [a]Is. 30:15; 49:23 [b][Job 17:9]; Ps. 103:5; [2 Cor. 4:8–10, 16]

CHAPTER 41
1 [a]Hab. 2:20; Zech. 2:13 [b]Is. 1:18
2 [a]Is. 46:11 [b]Gen. 14:14; Is. 45:1, 13
4 [a]Is. 41:26 [b]Rev. 1:8, 17; 22:13 [c]Is. 43:10; 44:6

NKJV

Has it not been told you from the
beginning?
Have you not understood from the
foundations of the earth?
22 *It is* He who sits above the circle of the
earth,
And its inhabitants *are* like grasshoppers,
Who [a]stretches out the heavens like a
curtain,
And spreads them out like a [b]tent to dwell
in.
23 He brings the [a]princes to nothing;
He makes the judges of the earth useless.

24 Scarcely shall they be planted,
Scarcely shall they be sown,
Scarcely shall their stock take root in the
earth,
When He will also blow on them,
And they will wither,
And the whirlwind will take them away
like stubble.

25 "To[a] whom then will you liken Me,
Or *to whom* shall I be equal?" says the
Holy One.
26 Lift up your eyes on high,
And see who has created these *things*,
Who brings out their host by number;
[a]He calls them all by name,
By the greatness of His might
And the strength of *His* power;
Not one is missing.

27 [a]Why do you say, O Jacob,
And speak, O Israel:
"My way is hidden from the LORD,
And my just claim is passed over by my
God"?
28 Have you not known?
Have you not heard?
The everlasting God, the LORD,
The Creator of the ends of the earth,
Neither faints nor is weary.
[a]His understanding is unsearchable.
29 He gives power to the weak,
And to *those who have* no might He
increases strength.
30 Even the youths shall faint and be weary,
And the young men shall utterly fall,
31 But those who [a]wait on the LORD
[b]Shall renew *their* strength;
They shall mount up with wings like
eagles,
They shall run and not be weary,
They shall walk and not faint.

Israel Assured of God's Help

41 "Keep [a]silence before Me, O coastlands,
And let the people renew *their* strength!
Let them come near, then let them speak;
Let us [b]come near together for judgment.

2 "Who raised up one [a]from the east?
Who in righteousness called him to His
feet?
Who [b]gave the nations before him,
And made *him* rule over kings?
Who gave *them* as the dust *to* his sword,
As driven stubble to his bow?
3 Who pursued them, *and* passed safely
By the way *that* he had not gone with his
feet?
4 [a]Who has performed and done *it*,
Calling the generations from the
beginning?
'I, the LORD, am [b]the first;
And with the last I *am* [c]He.' "

5 The coastlands saw *it* and feared,
The ends of the earth were afraid;
They drew near and came.

KJV

6 [a]They helped every one his neighbour;
and *every one* said to his brother, Be of good
courage.
7 [a]So the carpenter encouraged the [b]gold-
smith, *and* he that smootheth *with* the hammer
him that smote the anvil, saying, It *is* ready for
the sodering: and he fastened it with nails, [c]*that*
it should not be moved.
8 But thou, Israel, *art* my servant, Jacob
whom I have [a]chosen, the seed of Abraham my
[b]friend.
9 *Thou* whom I have taken from the ends
of the earth, and called thee from the chief men
thereof, and said unto thee, Thou *art* my servant;
I have chosen thee, and not cast thee away.
10 [a]Fear thou not; [b]for I *am* with thee: be
not dismayed; for I *am* thy God: I will strengthen
thee; yea, I will help thee; yea, I will uphold thee
with the right hand of my righteousness.
11 Behold, all they that were incensed
against thee shall be [a]ashamed and confounded:
they shall be as nothing; and they that strive with
thee shall perish.
12 Thou shalt seek them, and shalt not find
them, *even* them that contended with thee: they
that war against thee shall be as nothing, and as
a thing of nought.
13 For I the LORD thy God will hold thy right
hand, saying unto thee, Fear not; I will help thee.
14 Fear not, thou [a]worm Jacob, *and* ye men
of Israel; I will help thee, saith the LORD, and thy
redeemer, the Holy One of Israel.
15 Behold, [a]I will make thee a new sharp
threshing instrument having teeth: thou shalt
thresh the mountains, and beat *them* small, and
shalt make the hills as chaff.
16 Thou shalt [a]fan them, and the wind shall
carry them away, and the whirlwind shall scatter
them: and thou shalt rejoice in the LORD, *and*
[b]shalt glory in the Holy One of Israel.
17 *When* the poor and needy seek water, and
there is none, *and* their tongue faileth for thirst,
I the LORD will hear them, *I* the God of Israel will
not [a]forsake them.
18 I will open [a]rivers in high places, and
fountains in the midst of the valleys: I will make
the [b]wilderness a pool of water, and the dry land
springs of water.
19 I will plant in the wilderness the cedar,
the shittah tree, and the myrtle, and the oil tree;
I will set in the [a]desert the fir tree, *and* the pine,
and the box tree together:
20 [a]That they may see, and know, and consider, and understand together, that the hand of
the LORD hath done this, and the Holy One of Israel hath created it.

6 [a]Is. 40:19
7 [a]Is. 44:13 [b]Is. 40:19 [c]Is. 40:20
8 [a]Deut. 7:6; 10:15; Ps. 135:4; [Is. 43:1] [b]2 Chr. 20:7; James 2:23
10 [a]Is. 41:13, 14; 43:5 [b][Deut. 31:6]
11 [a]Ex. 23:22; Is. 45:24; 60:12; Zech. 12:3
14 [a]Job 25:6; Ps. 22:6
15 [a]Mic. 4:13; Hab. 3:12; [2 Cor. 10:4]
16 [a]Jer. 51:2 [b]Is. 45:25
17 [a]Ps. 94:14; Rom. 11:2
18 [a]Is. 35:6, 7; 43:19; 44:3 [b]Ps. 107:35
19 [a]Is. 35:1
20 [a]Job 12:9; Is. 66:14

NKJV

6 [a]Everyone helped his neighbor,
And said to his brother,
"Be of good courage!"
7 [a]So the craftsman encouraged the
[b]goldsmith;
He who smooths *with* the hammer
inspired him who strikes the anvil,
Saying, "It *is* ready for the soldering";
Then he fastened it with pegs,
[c]*That* it might not totter.

8 "But you, Israel, *are* My servant,
Jacob whom I have [a]chosen,
The descendants of Abraham My
[b]friend.
9 *You* whom I have taken from the ends of
the earth,
And called from its farthest regions,
And said to you,
'You *are* My servant,
I have chosen you and have not cast you
away:
10 [a]Fear not, [b]for I *am* with you;
Be not dismayed, for I *am* your God.
I will strengthen you,
Yes, I will help you,
I will uphold you with My righteous right
hand.'

11 "Behold, all those who were incensed
against you
Shall be [a]ashamed and disgraced;
They shall be as nothing,
And those who strive with you shall
perish.
12 You shall seek them and not find them—
Those who contended with you.
Those who war against you
Shall be as nothing,
As a nonexistent thing.
13 For I, the LORD your God, will hold your
right hand,
Saying to you, 'Fear not, I will help you.'

14 "Fear not, you [a]worm Jacob,
You men of Israel!
I will help you," says the LORD
And your Redeemer, the Holy One of
Israel.
15 "Behold, [a]I will make you into a new
threshing sledge with sharp teeth;
You shall thresh the mountains and beat
them small,
And make the hills like chaff.
16 You shall [a]winnow them, the wind shall
carry them away,
And the whirlwind shall scatter them;
You shall rejoice in the LORD,
And [b]glory in the Holy One of Israel.

17 "The poor and needy seek water, but *there
is* none,
Their tongues fail for thirst.
I, the LORD, will hear them;
I, the God of Israel, will not [a]forsake them.
18 I will open [a]rivers in desolate heights,
And fountains in the midst of the valleys;
I will make the [b]wilderness a pool of
water,
And the dry land springs of water.
19 I will plant in the wilderness the cedar and
the acacia tree,
The myrtle and the oil tree;
I will set in the [a]desert the cypress tree
and the pine
And the box tree together,
20 [a]That they may see and know,
And consider and understand together,
That the hand of the LORD has done
this,
And the Holy One of Israel has created
it.

KJV

The Futility of Idols

21 Produce your cause, saith the LORD; bring forth your strong *reasons*, saith the [a]King of Jacob.

22 [a]Let them bring *them* forth, and shew us what shall happen: let them shew the [b]former things, what they *be*, that we may consider them, and know the latter end of them; or declare us things for to come.

23 [a]Shew the things that are to come hereafter, that we may know that ye *are* gods: yea, [b]do good, or do evil, that we may be dismayed, and behold *it* together.

24 Behold, [a]ye *are* of nothing, and your work of nought: an abomination *is he that* chooseth you.

25 I have raised up *one* from the north, and he shall come: from the rising of the sun [a]shall he call upon my name: [b]and he shall come upon princes as *upon* morter, and as the potter treadeth clay.

26 [a]Who hath declared from the beginning, that we may know? and beforetime, that we may say, *He is* righteous? yea, *there is* none that sheweth, yea, *there is* none that declareth, yea, *there is* none that heareth your words.

27 [a]The first [b]*shall say* to Zion, Behold, behold them: and I will give to Jerusalem one that bringeth good tidings.

28 [a]For I beheld, and *there was* no man; even among them, and *there was* no counsellor, that, when I asked of them, could answer a word.

29 [a]Behold, they *are* all vanity; their works *are* nothing: their molten images *are* wind and confusion.

The Servant of the LORD

42 Behold [a]my servant, whom I uphold; mine elect, *in whom* my soul [b]delighteth; [c]I have put my spirit upon him: he shall bring forth judgment to the Gentiles.

2 He shall not cry, nor lift up, nor cause his voice to be heard in the street.

3 A bruised reed shall he not break, and the smoking flax shall he not quench: he shall bring forth judgment unto truth.

4 He shall not fail nor be discouraged, till he have set judgment in the earth: [a]and the isles shall wait for his law.

5 Thus saith God the LORD, [a]he that created the heavens, and stretched them out; he that spread forth the earth, and that which cometh out of it; [b]he that giveth breath unto the people upon it, and spirit to them that walk therein:

6 [a]I the LORD have called thee in righteousness, and will hold thine hand, and will keep thee, [b]and give thee for a covenant of the people, for [c]a light of the Gentiles;

7 [a]To open the blind eyes, to [b]bring out the prisoners from the prison, *and* them that sit in [c]darkness out of the prison house.

---

21 [a]Is. 43:15
22 [a]Is. 45:21 [b]Is. 43:9
23 [a]Is. 42:9; 44:7, 8; 45:3; [John 13:19] [b]Jer. 10:5
24 [a]Ps. 115:8; Is. 44:9; [Rom. 3:10–20; 1 Cor. 8:4]
25 [a]Ezra 1:2 [b]Is. 41:2; Jer. 50:3
26 [a]Is. 43:9
27 [a]Is. 41:4 [b]Is. 40:9; Nah. 1:15
28 [a]Is. 63:5
29 [a]Is. 41:24

CHAPTER 42

1 [a]Is. 43:10; 49:3, 6; Matt. 12:18; [Phil. 2:7] [b]Matt. 3:17; 17:5; Mark 1:11; Luke 3:22; Eph. 1:6 [c][Is. 11:2]; Matt. 3:16; [Luke 4:18, 19, 21]; John 3:34
4 [a][Gen. 49:10]
5 [a]Is. 44:24; Zech. 12:1 [b]Job 12:10; 33:4; Is. 57:16; Dan. 5:23; Acts 17:25
6 [a]Is. 43:1 [b]Is. 49:8 [c]Is. 49:6; Luke 2:32; [Acts 10:45; 13:47; Gal. 3:14]
7 [a]Is. 35:5 [b]Is. 61:1; Luke 4:18; [2 Tim. 2:26; Heb. 2:14] [c]Is. 9:2

*———

41:29 So with MT, Vg.; DSS, Syr., Tg. *nothing;* LXX omits first line

---

NKJV

The Futility of Idols

21 "Present your case," says the LORD.
"Bring forth your strong *reasons*," says the
[a]King of Jacob.
22 "Let[a] them bring forth and show us what
will happen;
Let them show the [b]former things, what
they *were*,
That we may consider them,
And know the latter end of them;
Or declare to us things to come.
23 [a]Show the things that are to come
hereafter,
That we may know that you *are* gods;
Yes, [b]do good or do evil,
That we may be dismayed and see *it*
together.
24 Indeed [a]you *are* nothing,
And your work *is* nothing;
He who chooses you *is* an abomination.

25 "I have raised up one from the north,
And he shall come;
From the rising of the sun [a]he shall call
on My name;
[b]And he shall come against princes as
though mortar,
As the potter treads clay.
26 [a]Who has declared from the beginning,
that we may know?
And former times, that we may say, '*He
is* righteous'?
Surely *there is* no one who shows,
Surely *there is* no one who declares,
Surely *there is* no one who hears your
words.
27 [a]The first time [b]*I said* to Zion,
'Look, there they are!'
And I will give to Jerusalem one who
brings good tidings.
28 [a]For I looked, and *there was* no man;
I looked among them, but *there was* no
counselor,
Who, when I asked of them, could answer
a word.
29 [a]Indeed they *are* all *worthless;
Their works *are* nothing;
Their molded images *are* wind and
confusion.

The Servant of the LORD

42 "Behold! [a]My Servant whom I uphold,
My Elect One *in whom* My soul [b]delights!
[c]I have put My Spirit upon Him;
He will bring forth justice to the Gentiles.
2 He will not cry out, nor raise *His voice,*
Nor cause His voice to be heard in the
street.
3 A bruised reed He will not break,
And smoking flax He will not quench;
He will bring forth justice for truth.
4 He will not fail nor be discouraged,
Till He has established justice in the earth;
[a]And the coastlands shall wait for His law."

5 Thus says God the LORD,
[a]Who created the heavens and stretched
them out,
Who spread forth the earth and that which
comes from it,
[b]Who gives breath to the people on it,
And spirit to those who walk on it:
6 "I,[a] the LORD, have called You in
righteousness,
And will hold Your hand;
I will keep You [b]and give You as a
covenant to the people,
As [c]a light to the Gentiles,
7 [a]To open blind eyes,
To [b]bring out prisoners from the prison,
Those who sit in [c]darkness from the
prison house.

KJV

8 I *am* the LORD: that *is* my name: and my [a]glory will I not give to another, neither my praise to graven images.

9 Behold, the former things are come to pass, and new things do I declare: before they spring forth I tell you of them.

Praise to the LORD

10 [a]Sing unto the LORD a new song, *and* his praise from the end of the earth, [b]ye that go down to the sea, and all that is therein; the isles, and the inhabitants thereof.

11 Let the wilderness and the cities thereof lift up *their voice,* the villages *that* Kedar doth inhabit: let the inhabitants of the rock sing, let them shout from the top of the mountains.

12 Let them give glory unto the LORD, and declare his praise in the islands.

13 The LORD shall go forth as a mighty man, he shall stir up jealousy like a man of war: he shall cry, [a]yea, roar; he shall prevail against his enemies.

Promise of the LORD's Help

14 I have long time holden my peace; I have been still, *and* refrained myself: *now* will I cry like a travailing woman; I will destroy and devour at once.

15 I will make waste mountains and hills, and dry up all their herbs; and I will make the rivers islands, and I will dry up the pools.

16 And I will bring the blind by a way *that* they knew not; I will lead them in paths *that* they have not known: I will make darkness light before them, and crooked things straight. These things will I do unto them, and not forsake them.

17 They shall be [a]turned back, they shall be greatly ashamed, that trust in graven images, that say to the molten images, Ye *are* our gods.

18 Hear, ye deaf; and look, ye blind, that ye may see.

19 [a]Who *is* blind, but my servant? or deaf, as my messenger *that* I sent? who *is* blind as *he that is* perfect, and blind as the LORD's servant?

20 Seeing many things, [a]but thou observest not; opening the ears, but he heareth not.

Israel's Obstinate Disobedience

21 The LORD is well pleased for his righteousness' sake; he will magnify the law, and make *it* honourable.

22 But this *is* a people robbed and spoiled; *they are* all of them snared in holes, and they are hid in prison houses: they are for a prey, and none delivereth; for a spoil, and none saith, Restore.

23 Who among you will give ear to this? *who* will hearken and hear for the time to come?

24 Who gave Jacob for a spoil, and Israel to the robbers? did not the LORD, he against whom we have sinned? [a]for they would not walk in his ways, neither were they obedient unto his law.

8 [a]Ex. 20:3–5; Is. 48:11
10 [a]Ps. 33:3; 40:3; 98:1 [b]Ps. 107:23
13 [a]Is. 31:4
17 [a]Ps. 97:7; Is. 1:29; 44:11; 45:16
19 [a]Is. 43:8; Ezek. 12:2; [John 9:39, 41]
20 [a]Rom. 2:21
24 [a]Is. 65:2

NKJV

8 I *am* the LORD, that *is* My name;
And My [a]glory I will not give to another,
Nor My praise to carved images.
9 Behold, the former things have come to pass,
And new things I declare;
Before they spring forth I tell you of them."

Praise to the LORD

10 [a]Sing to the LORD a new song,
And His praise from the ends of the earth,
[b]You who go down to the sea, and all that is in it,
You coastlands and you inhabitants of them!
11 Let the wilderness and its cities lift up *their voice,*
The villages *that* Kedar inhabits.
Let the inhabitants of Sela sing,
Let them shout from the top of the mountains.
12 Let them give glory to the LORD,
And declare His praise in the coastlands.
13 The LORD shall go forth like a mighty man;
He shall stir up *His* zeal like a man of war.
He shall cry out, [a]yes, shout aloud;
He shall prevail against His enemies.

Promise of the LORD's Help

14 "I have held My peace a long time,
I have been still and restrained Myself.
Now I will cry like a woman in labor,
I will pant and gasp at once.
15 I will lay waste the mountains and hills,
And dry up all their vegetation;
I will make the rivers coastlands,
And I will dry up the pools.
16 I will bring the blind by a way they did not know;
I will lead them in paths they have not known.
I will make darkness light before them,
And crooked places straight.
These things I will do for them,
And not forsake them.
17 They shall be [a]turned back,
They shall be greatly ashamed,
Who trust in carved images,
Who say to the molded images,
'You *are* our gods.'

18 "Hear, you deaf;
And look, you blind, that you may see.
19 [a]Who *is* blind but My servant,
Or deaf as My messenger *whom* I send?
Who *is* blind as *he who is* perfect,
And blind as the LORD's servant?
20 Seeing many things, [a]but you do not observe;
Opening the ears, but he does not hear."

Israel's Obstinate Disobedience

21 The LORD is well pleased for His righteousness' sake;
He will exalt the law and make *it* honorable.
22 But this *is* a people robbed and plundered;
All of them are snared in holes,
And they are hidden in prison houses;
They are for prey, and no one delivers;
For plunder, and no one says, "Restore!"

23 Who among you will give ear to this?
Who will listen and hear for the time to come?
24 Who gave Jacob for plunder, and Israel to the robbers?
Was it not the LORD,
He against whom we have sinned?
[a]For they would not walk in His ways,
Nor were they obedient to His law.

KJV

25 Therefore he hath poured upon him the fury of his anger, and the strength of battle: [a]and it hath set him on fire round about, [b]yet he knew not; and it burned him, yet he laid *it* not to [c]heart.

The Redeemer of Israel

43 But now thus saith the LORD that created thee, O Jacob, and he that formed thee, O Israel, Fear not: [a]for I have redeemed thee, [b]I have called *thee* by thy name; thou *art* mine.

2 [a]When thou passest through the waters, [b]I *will be* with thee; and through the rivers, they shall not overflow thee: when thou [c]walkest through the fire, thou shalt not be burned; neither shall the flame kindle upon thee.

3 For I *am* the LORD thy God, the Holy One of Israel, thy Saviour: [a]I gave Egypt *for* thy ransom, Ethiopia and Seba for thee.

4 Since thou wast precious in my sight, thou hast been honourable, and I have [a]loved thee: therefore will I give men for thee, and people for thy life.

5 [a]Fear not: for I *am* with thee: I will bring thy seed from the east, and [b]gather thee from the west;

6 I will say to the [a]north, Give up; and to the south, Keep not back: bring my sons from far, and my daughters from the ends of the earth;

7 *Even* every one that is [a]called by my name: for [b]I have created him for my glory, I have formed him; yea, I have made him.

8 [a]Bring forth the blind people that have eyes, and the [b]deaf that have ears.

9 Let all the nations be gathered together, and let the people be assembled: [a]who among them can declare this, and shew us former things? let them bring forth their witnesses, that they may be justified: or let them hear, and say, *It is* truth.

10 [a]Ye *are* my witnesses, saith the LORD, [b]and my servant whom I have chosen: that ye may know and [c]believe me, and understand that I *am* he: before me there was no God formed, neither shall there be after me.

11 I, *even* I, [a]*am* the LORD; and beside me *there is* no saviour.

12 I have declared, and have saved, and I have shewed, when *there was* no [a]strange *god* among you: [b]therefore ye *are* my witnesses, saith the LORD, that I *am* God.

13 [a]Yea, before the day *was* I *am* he; and *there is* none that can deliver out of my hand: I will work, and who shall [b]let it?

14 Thus saith the LORD, your redeemer, the Holy One of Israel; For your sake I have sent to Babylon, and have brought down all their nobles, and the Chaldeans, whose cry *is* in the ships.

15 I *am* the LORD, your Holy One, the creator of Israel, your [a]King.

25 [a]2 Kin. 25:9 [b]Is. 1:3; 5:13; Hos. 7:9 [c]Is. 29:13

CHAPTER 43

1 [a]Is. 43:5; 44:6 [b]Is. 42:6; 45:4
2 [a][Ps. 66:12; 91:3] [b][Deut. 31:6]; Jer. 30:11 [c]Dan. 3:25
3 [a][Prov. 11:8; 21:18]
4 [a]Is. 63:9
5 [a]Is. 41:10; 44:2; Jer. 30:10; 46:27, 28 [b]Is. 54:7
6 [a]Is. 49:12
7 [a]Is. 63:19; James 2:7 [b]Ps. 100:3; Is. 29:23; [John 3:2, 3; 2 Cor. 5:17; Eph. 2:10]
8 [a]Is. 6:9; 42:19; Ezek. 12:2 [b]Is. 29:18
9 [a]Is. 41:21, 22, 26
10 [a]Is. 44:8 [b]Is. 55:4 [c]Is. 41:4; 44:6
11 [a]Is. 45:21; Hos. 13:4
12 [a]Deut. 32:16; Ps. 81:9 [b]Is. 44:8
13 [a]Ps. 90:2; Is. 48:16 [b]Job 9:12; Is. 14:27
15 [a]Is. 41:20, 21

NKJV

25 Therefore He has poured on him the fury
of His anger
And the strength of battle;
[a]It has set him on fire all around,
[b]Yet he did not know;
And it burned him,
Yet he did not take *it* to [c]heart.

The Redeemer of Israel

43 But now, thus says the LORD, who created
you, O Jacob,
And He who formed you, O Israel:
"Fear not, [a]for I have redeemed you;
[b]I have called *you* by your name;
You *are* Mine.
2 [a]When you pass through the waters, [b]I *will be* with you;
And through the rivers, they shall not
overflow you.
When you [c]walk through the fire, you
shall not be burned,
Nor shall the flame scorch you.
3 For I *am* the LORD your God,
The Holy One of Israel, your Savior;
[a]I gave Egypt for your ransom,
Ethiopia and Seba in your place.
4 Since you were precious in My sight,
You have been honored,
And I have [a]loved you;
Therefore I will give men for you,
And people for your life.
5 [a]Fear not, for I *am* with you;
I will bring your descendants from the
east,
And [b]gather you from the west;
6 I will say to the [a]north, 'Give them up!'
And to the south, 'Do not keep them
back!'
Bring My sons from afar,
And My daughters from the ends of the
earth—
7 Everyone who is [a]called by My name,
Whom [b]I have created for My glory;
I have formed him, yes, I have made him."

8 [a]Bring out the blind people who have
eyes,
And the [b]deaf who have ears.
9 Let all the nations be gathered together,
And let the people be assembled.
[a]Who among them can declare this,
And show us former things?
Let them bring out their witnesses, that
they may be justified;
Or let them hear and say, "*It is* truth."
10 "You[a] *are* My witnesses," says the LORD,
[b]"And My servant whom I have chosen,
That you may know and [c]believe Me,
And understand that I *am* He.
Before Me there was no God formed,
Nor shall there be after Me.
11 I, *even* I, [a]*am* the LORD,
And besides Me *there is* no savior.
12 I have declared and saved,
I have proclaimed,
And *there was* no [a]foreign *god* among
you;
[b]Therefore you *are* My witnesses,"
Says the LORD, "that I *am* God.
13 [a]Indeed before the day *was*, I *am* He;
And *there is* no one who can deliver out
of My hand;
I work, and who will [b]reverse it?"

14 Thus says the LORD, your Redeemer,
The Holy One of Israel:
"For your sake I will send to Babylon,
And bring them all down as fugitives—
The Chaldeans, who rejoice in their
ships.
15 I *am* the LORD, your Holy One,
The Creator of Israel, your [a]King."

KJV

16 Thus saith the LORD, which [a]maketh a way
in the sea, and a [b]path in the mighty waters;
17 Which [a]bringeth forth the chariot and
horse, the army and the power; they shall lie down
together, they shall not rise: they are extinct, they
are quenched as tow.
18 [a]Remember ye not the former things, neither consider the things of old.
19 Behold, I will do a [a]new thing; now it shall
spring forth; shall ye not know it? [b]I will even
make a way in the wilderness, *and* rivers in the
desert.
20 The beast of the field shall honour me, the
dragons and the owls: because [a]I give waters in
the wilderness, *and* rivers in the desert, to give
drink to my people, my chosen.
21 [a]This people have I formed for myself;
they shall shew forth my [b]praise.

Pleading with Unfaithful Israel

22 But thou hast not called upon me, O Jacob;
but thou [a]hast been weary of me, O Israel.
23 [a]Thou hast not brought me the small cattle
of thy burnt offerings; neither hast thou honoured
me with thy sacrifices. I have not caused thee to
serve with an offering, nor wearied thee with
incense.
24 Thou hast bought me no sweet cane with
money, neither hast thou filled me with the fat
of thy sacrifices: but thou hast made me to serve
with thy sins, thou hast [a]wearied me with thine
iniquities.
25 I, *even* I, *am* he that [a]blotteth out thy
transgressions [b]for mine own sake, [c]and will not
remember thy sins.
26 Put me in remembrance: let us plead together: declare thou, that thou mayest be justified.
27 Thy first father hath sinned, and thy
teachers have transgressed against me.
28 Therefore I have profaned the princes of
the sanctuary, [a]and have given Jacob to the curse,
and Israel to reproaches.

God's Blessing on Israel

44 Yet now hear, O Jacob my servant; and Israel, whom I have chosen:
2 Thus saith the LORD that made thee, and
formed thee from the womb, *which* will help thee;
Fear not, O Jacob, my servant; and thou, Jesurun,
whom I have chosen.
3 For I will pour water upon him that is
thirsty, and floods upon the dry ground: I will
pour my spirit upon thy seed, and my blessing
upon thine offspring:
4 And they shall spring up *as* among the
grass, as willows by the water courses.
5 One shall say, I *am* the LORD's; and another shall call *himself* by the name of Jacob; and
another shall subscribe *with* his hand unto the
LORD, and surname *himself* by the name of Israel.

16 [a]Ex. 14:16, 21, 22; Ps. 77:19; Is. 51:10 [b]Josh. 3:13
17 [a]Ex. 14:4–9, 25
18 [a]Jer. 16:14
19 [a]Is. 42:9; 48:6; [2 Cor. 5:17; Rev. 21:5] [b]Ex. 17:6; Num. 20:11; Deut. 8:15; Ps. 78:16; Is. 35:1, 6
20 [a]Is. 48:21
21 [a]Ps. 102:18; Is. 42:12; [Luke 1:74, 75; Eph. 1:5, 6; 1 Pet. 2:9] [b]Jer. 13:11
22 [a]Mic. 6:3; Mal. 1:13; 3:14
23 [a]Amos 5:25
24 [a]Ps. 95:10; Is. 1:14; 7:13; Ezek. 6:9; Mal. 2:17
25 [a]Is. 44:22; Jer. 50:20; [Acts 3:19] [b]Ezek. 36:22 [c]Is. 1:18; Jer. 31:34
28 [a]Ps. 79:4; Jer. 24:9; Dan. 9:11; Zech. 8:13

NKJV

16 Thus says the LORD, who [a]makes a way
in the sea
And a [b]path through the mighty waters,
17 Who [a]brings forth the chariot and
horse,
The army and the power
(They shall lie down together, they shall
not rise;
They are extinguished, they are quenched
like a wick):
18 "Do[a] not remember the former things,
Nor consider the things of old.
19 Behold, I will do a [a]new thing,
Now it shall spring forth;
Shall you not know it?
[b]I will even make a road in the
wilderness
And rivers in the desert.
20 The beast of the field will honor Me,
The jackals and the ostriches,
Because [a]I give waters in the wilderness
And rivers in the desert,
To give drink to My people, My chosen.
21 [a]This people I have formed for Myself;
They shall declare My [b]praise.

Pleading with Unfaithful Israel

22 "But you have not called upon Me, O Jacob;
And you [a]have been weary of Me, O
Israel.
23 [a]You have not brought Me the sheep for
your burnt offerings,
Nor have you honored Me with your
sacrifices.
I have not caused you to serve with grain
offerings,
Nor wearied you with incense.
24 You have bought Me no sweet cane with
money,
Nor have you satisfied Me with the fat of
your sacrifices;
But you have burdened Me with your
sins,
You have [a]wearied Me with your
iniquities.

25 "I, *even* I, *am* He who [a]blots out your
transgressions [b]for My own sake;
[c]And I will not remember your sins.
26 Put Me in remembrance;
Let us contend together;
State your *case*, that you may be
acquitted.
27 Your first father sinned,
And your mediators have transgressed
against Me.
28 Therefore I will profane the princes of the
sanctuary;
[a]I will give Jacob to the curse,
And Israel to reproaches.

God's Blessing on Israel

44 "Yet hear now, O Jacob My servant,
And Israel whom I have
chosen.
2 Thus says the LORD who made you
And formed you from the womb, *who* will
help you:
'Fear not, O Jacob My servant;
And you, Jeshurun, whom I have chosen.
3 For I will pour water on him who is thirsty,
And floods on the dry ground;
I will pour My Spirit on your descendants,
And My blessing on your offspring;
4 They will spring up among the grass
Like willows by the watercourses.'
5 One will say, 'I *am* the LORD's';
Another will call *himself* by the name of
Jacob;
Another will write *with* his hand, 'The
LORD's,'
And name *himself* by the name of Israel.

KJV

There Is No Other God

6 Thus saith the LORD the King of Israel, and his redeemer the LORD of hosts; [a]I *am* the first, and I *am* the last; and beside me *there is* no God.

7 And [a]who, as I, shall call, and shall declare it, and set it in order for me, since I appointed the ancient people? and the things that are coming, and shall come, let them shew unto them.

8 Fear ye not, neither be afraid: [a]have not I told thee from that time, and have declared *it?* [b]ye *are* even my witnesses. Is there a God beside me? yea, [c]*there is* no God; I know not *any*.

Idolatry Is Foolishness

9 [a]They that make a graven image *are* all of them vanity; and their delectable things shall not profit; and they *are* their own witnesses; [b]they see not, nor know; that they may be ashamed.

10 Who hath formed a god, or molten a graven image [a]*that* is profitable for nothing?

11 Behold, all his fellows shall be [a]ashamed: and the workmen, they *are* of men: let them all be gathered together, let them stand up; *yet* they shall fear, *and* they shall be ashamed together.

12 [a]The smith with the tongs both worketh in the coals, and fashioneth it with hammers, and worketh it with the strength of his arms: yea, he is hungry, and his strength faileth: he drinketh no water, and is faint.

13 The carpenter stretcheth out *his* rule; he marketh it out with a line; he fitteth it with planes, and he marketh it out with the compass, and maketh it after the figure of a man, according to the beauty of a man; that it may remain in the house.

14 He heweth him down cedars, and taketh the cypress and the oak, which he strengtheneth for himself among the trees of the forest: he planteth an ash, and the rain doth nourish *it*.

15 Then shall it be for a man to burn: for he will take thereof, and warm himself; yea, he kindleth *it*, and baketh bread; yea, he maketh a god, and worshippeth *it;* he maketh it a graven image, and falleth down thereto.

16 He burneth part thereof in the fire; with part thereof he eateth flesh; he roasteth roast, and is satisfied: yea, he warmeth *himself*, and saith, Aha, I am warm, I have seen the fire:

17 And the residue thereof he maketh a god, *even* his graven image: he falleth down unto it, and worshippeth *it*, and prayeth unto it, and saith, Deliver me; for thou *art* my god.

CHAPTER 44

6 [a]Is. 41:4; [Rev. 1:8, 17; 22:13]
7 [a]Is. 41:4, 22, 26
8 [a]Is. 41:22 [b]Is. 43:10, 12 [c]Deut. 4:35; 32:39; 1 Sam. 2:2; 2 Sam. 22:32; Is. 45:5; Joel 2:27
9 [a]Is. 41:24 [b]Ps. 115:4
10 [a]Is. 41:29; Jer. 10:5; Hab. 2:18; Acts 19:26
11 [a]Ps. 97:7; Is. 1:29; 42:17
12 [a]Is. 40:19; Jer. 10:3–5

NKJV

There Is No Other God

6 "Thus says the LORD, the King of Israel,
And his Redeemer, the LORD of hosts:
[a]'I *am* the First and I *am* the Last;
Besides Me *there is* no God.
7 And [a]who can proclaim as I do?
Then let him declare it and set it in order for Me,
Since I appointed the ancient people.
And the things that are coming and shall come,
Let them show these to them.
8 Do not fear, nor be afraid;
[a]Have I not told you from that time, and declared *it?*
[b]You *are* My witnesses.
Is there a God besides Me?
Indeed [c]*there is* no other Rock;
I know not *one*.' "

Idolatry Is Foolishness

9 [a]Those who make an image, all of them *are* useless,
And their precious things shall not profit;
They *are* their own witnesses;
[b]They neither see nor know, that they may be ashamed.
10 Who would form a god or mold an image
[a]*That* profits him nothing?
11 Surely all his companions would be [a]ashamed;
And the workmen, they *are* mere men.
Let them all be gathered together,
Let them stand up;
Yet they shall fear,
They shall be ashamed together.

12 [a]The blacksmith with the tongs works one in the coals,
Fashions it with hammers,
And works it with the strength of his arms.
Even so, he is hungry, and his strength fails;
He drinks no water and is faint.

13 The craftsman stretches out *his* rule,
He marks one out with chalk;
He fashions it with a plane,
He marks it out with the compass,
And makes it like the figure of a man,
According to the beauty of a man, that it may remain in the house.
14 He cuts down cedars for himself,
And takes the cypress and the oak;
He secures *it* for himself among the trees of the forest.
He plants a pine, and the rain nourishes *it*.

15 Then it shall be for a man to burn,
For he will take some of it and warm himself;
Yes, he kindles *it* and bakes bread;
Indeed he makes a god and worships *it;*
He makes it a carved image, and falls down to it.
16 He burns half of it in the fire;
With this half he eats meat;
He roasts a roast, and is satisfied.
He even warms *himself* and says,
"Ah! I am warm,
I have seen the fire."
17 And the rest of it he makes into a god,
His carved image.
He falls down before it and worships *it*,
Prays to it and says,
"Deliver me, for you *are* my god!"

KJV

18 [a]They have not known nor understood: for [b]he hath shut their eyes, that they cannot see; *and* their hearts, that they cannot [c]understand.

19 And none [a]considereth in his heart, neither *is there* knowledge nor understanding to say, I have burned part of it in the fire; yea, also I have baked bread upon the coals thereof; I have roasted flesh, and eaten *it:* and shall I make the residue thereof an abomination? shall I fall down to the stock of a tree?

20 He feedeth on ashes: [a]a deceived heart hath turned him aside, that he cannot deliver his soul, nor say, *Is there* not a [b]lie in my right hand?

Israel Is Not Forgotten

21 Remember these, O Jacob and Israel; for thou *art* my servant: I have formed thee; thou *art* my servant: O Israel, thou shalt not be [a]forgotten of me.

22 [a]I have blotted out, as a thick cloud, thy transgressions, and, as a cloud, thy sins: return unto me; for [b]I have redeemed thee.

23 [a]Sing, O ye heavens; for the LORD hath done *it:* shout, ye lower parts of the earth: break forth into singing, ye mountains, O forest, and every tree therein: for the LORD hath redeemed Jacob, and [b]glorified himself in Israel.

Judah Will Be Restored

24 Thus saith the LORD, [a]thy redeemer, and [b]he that formed thee from the womb, I *am* the LORD that maketh all *things;* [c]that stretcheth forth the heavens alone; that spreadeth abroad the earth by myself;

25 That [a]frustrateth the tokens [b]of the liars, and maketh diviners mad; that turneth wise *men* backward, [c]and maketh their knowledge foolish;

26 [a]That confirmeth the word of his servant, and performeth the counsel of his messengers; that saith to Jerusalem, Thou shalt be inhabited; and to the cities of Judah, Ye shall be built, and I will raise up the decayed places thereof:

27 [a]That saith to the deep, Be dry, and I will dry up thy rivers:

28 That saith of [a]Cyrus, *He is* my shepherd, and shall perform all my pleasure: even saying to Jerusalem, [b]Thou shalt be built; and to the temple, Thy foundation shall be laid.

Cyrus, God's Instrument

45 Thus saith the LORD to his anointed, to [a]Cyrus, whose [b]right hand I have holden, [c]to subdue nations before him; and I will [d]loose the loins of kings, to open before him the two leaved gates; and the gates shall not be shut;

2 I will go before thee, [a]and make the crooked places straight: [b]I will break in pieces the gates of brass, and cut in sunder the bars of iron:

3 And I will give thee the treasures of darkness, and hidden riches of secret places, [a]that thou mayest know that I, the LORD, which [b]call *thee* by thy name, *am* the God of Israel.

---

18 [a]Is. 45:20 [b][Ps. 81:12]; Is. 6:9, 10; 29:10; 2 Thess. 2:11 [c]Jer. 10:14
19 [a]Is. 46:8
20 [a]Job 15:31; Hos. 4:12; Rom. 1:21, 22; 2 Thess. 2:11; 2 Tim. 3:13 [b]Is. 57:11; 59:3, 4, 13; Rom. 1:25
21 [a]Is. 49:15
22 [a]Is. 43:25 [b]Is. 43:1; 1 Cor. 6:20; [1 Pet. 1:18, 19]
23 [a]Ps. 69:34; Is. 42:10; 49:13; Jer. 51:48; Rev. 18:20 [b]Is. 49:3; 60:21
24 [a]Is. 43:14 [b]Is. 43:1 [c]Job 9:8
25 [a]Is. 47:13 [b]Jer. 50:36 [c]2 Sam. 15:31; Job 5:12–14; Ps. 33:10; Is. 29:14; Jer. 51:57; 1 Cor. 1:20, 27
26 [a]Zech. 1:6; Matt. 5:18
27 [a]Jer. 50:38; 51:36
28 [a]2 Chr. 36:22; Ezra 1:1; Is. 45:13 [b]Ezra 6:7

CHAPTER 45

1 [a]Is. 44:28 [b]Ps. 73:23; Is. 41:13 [c]Dan. 5:30 [d]Job 12:21; Is. 45:5
2 [a]Is. 40:4 [b]Ps. 107:16
3 [a]Is. 41:23 [b]Ex. 33:12

---

*

45:2 Tg. *I will trample down the walls;* Vg. *I will humble the great ones of the earth* • DSS, LXX *mountains*

NKJV

18 [a]They do not know nor understand;
For [b]He has shut their eyes, so that they cannot see,
And their hearts, so that they cannot [c]understand.
19 And no one [a]considers in his heart,
Nor *is there* knowledge nor understanding to say,
"I have burned half of it in the fire,
Yes, I have also baked bread on its coals;
I have roasted meat and eaten *it;*
And shall I make the rest of it an abomination?
Shall I fall down before a block of wood?"
20 He feeds on ashes;
[a]A deceived heart has turned him aside;
And he cannot deliver his soul,
Nor say, "*Is there* not a [b]lie in my right hand?"

Israel Is Not Forgotten

21 "Remember these, O Jacob,
And Israel, for you *are* My servant;
I have formed you, you *are* My servant;
O Israel, you will not be [a]forgotten by Me!
22 [a]I have blotted out, like a thick cloud, your transgressions,
And like a cloud, your sins.
Return to Me, for [b]I have redeemed you."
23 [a]Sing, O heavens, for the LORD has done *it!*
Shout, you lower parts of the earth;
Break forth into singing, you mountains,
O forest, and every tree in it!
For the LORD has redeemed Jacob,
And [b]glorified Himself in Israel.

Judah Will Be Restored

24 Thus says the LORD, [a]your Redeemer,
And [b]He who formed you from the womb:
"I *am* the LORD, who makes all *things,*
[c]Who stretches out the heavens all alone,
Who spreads abroad the earth by Myself;
25 Who [a]frustrates the signs [b]of the babblers,
And drives diviners mad;
Who turns wise men backward,
[c]And makes their knowledge foolishness;
26 [a]Who confirms the word of His servant,
And performs the counsel of His messengers;
Who says to Jerusalem, 'You shall be inhabited,'
To the cities of Judah, 'You shall be built,'
And I will raise up her waste places;
27 [a]Who says to the deep, 'Be dry!
And I will dry up your rivers';
28 Who says of [a]Cyrus, '*He is* My shepherd,
And he shall perform all My pleasure,
Saying to Jerusalem, [b]"You shall be built,"
And to the temple, "Your foundation shall be laid." '

Cyrus, God's Instrument

45 "Thus says the LORD to His anointed,
To [a]Cyrus, whose [b]right hand I have held—
[c]To subdue nations before him
And [d]loose the armor of kings,
To open before him the double doors,
So that the gates will not be shut:
2 'I will go before you
[a]And* make the *crooked places straight;
[b]I will break in pieces the gates of bronze
And cut the bars of iron.
3 I will give you the treasures of darkness
And hidden riches of secret places,
[a]That you may know that I, the LORD,
Who [b]call *you* by your name,
Am the God of Israel.

KJV

4 For [a]Jacob my servant's sake, and Israel mine elect, I have even called thee by thy name: I have surnamed thee, though thou hast not known me.

5 I [a]*am* the LORD, and [b]*there is* none else, *there is* no God beside me: [c]I girded thee, though thou hast not known me:

6 [a]That they may [b]know from the rising of the sun, and from the west, that *there is* none beside me. I *am* the LORD, and *there is* none else.

7 I form the light, and create darkness: I make peace, and [a]create evil: I the LORD do all these *things.*

8 [a]Drop down, ye heavens, from above, and let the skies pour down righteousness: let the earth open, and let them bring forth salvation, and let righteousness spring up together; I the LORD have created it.

9 Woe unto him that striveth with [a]his Maker! *Let* the potsherd *strive* with the potsherds of the earth. [b]Shall the clay say to him that fashioneth it, What makest thou? or thy work, He hath no hands?

10 Woe unto him that saith unto *his* father, What begettest thou? or to the woman, What hast thou brought forth?

11 Thus saith the LORD, the Holy One of Israel, and his Maker, [a]Ask me of things to come concerning [b]my sons, and concerning [c]the work of my hands command ye me.

12 [a]I have made the earth, and [b]created man upon it: I, *even* my hands, have stretched out the heavens, and [c]all their host have I commanded.

13 [a]I have raised him up in righteousness, and I will direct all his ways: he shall [b]build my city, and he shall let go my captives, [c]not for price nor reward, saith the LORD of hosts.

The LORD, the Only Savior

14 Thus saith the LORD, [a]The labour of Egypt, and merchandise of Ethiopia and of the Sabeans, men of stature, shall come over unto thee, and they shall be thine: they shall come after thee; [b]in chains they shall come over, and they shall fall down unto thee, they shall make supplication unto thee, *saying,* [c]Surely God *is* in thee; and *there is* none else, [d]*there is* no God.

15 Verily thou *art* a God [a]that hidest thyself, O God of Israel, the Saviour.

16 They shall be [a]ashamed, and also confounded, all of them: they shall go to confusion together *that are* makers of idols.

17 [a]*But* Israel shall be saved in the LORD with an [b]everlasting salvation: ye shall not be ashamed nor [c]confounded world without end.

4 [a]Is. 44:1
5 [a]Deut. 4:35; 32:39; Is. 44:8 [b]Is. 45:14, 18 [c]Ps. 18:32
6 [a]Ps. 102:15; Is. 37:20; Mal. 1:11 [b][Is. 11:9; 52:10]
7 [a]Is. 31:2; 47:11; Amos 3:6
8 [a]Ps. 85:11
9 [a]Is. 64:8 [b]Jer. 18:6; Rom. 9:20, 21
11 [a]Is. 8:19 [b]Jer. 31:9 [c]Is. 29:23; 60:21; 64:8
12 [a]Is. 42:5; Jer. 27:5 [b]Gen. 1:26 [c]Gen. 2:1; Neh. 9:6
13 [a]Is. 41:2 [b]2 Chr. 36:22; Is. 44:28 [c][Rom. 3:24]
14 [a]Ps. 68:31; 72:10, 11; Is. 14:1; 49:23; 60:9, 10, 14, 16; Zech. 8:22, 23 [b]Ps. 149:8 [c]Jer. 16:19; Zech. 8:20–23; 1 Cor. 14:25 [d]Is. 45:5
15 [a]Ps. 44:24; Is. 57:17
16 [a]Is. 44:11
17 [a]Is. 26:4; [Rom. 11:26] [b]Is. 51:6 [c]Is. 29:22

NKJV

4 For [a]Jacob My servant's sake,
And Israel My elect,
I have even called you by your name;
I have named you, though you have not known Me.
5 I [a]*am* the LORD, and [b]*there is* no other;
There is no God besides Me.
[c]I will gird you, though you have not known Me,
6 [a]That they may [b]know from the rising of the sun to its setting
That *there is* none besides Me.
I *am* the LORD, and *there is* no other;
7 I form the light and create darkness,
I make peace and [a]create calamity;
I, the LORD, do all these *things.'*

8 "Rain[a] down, you heavens, from above,
And let the skies pour down righteousness;
Let the earth open, let them bring forth salvation,
And let righteousness spring up together.
I, the LORD, have created it.

9 "Woe to him who strives with [a]his Maker!
Let the potsherd *strive* with the potsherds of the earth!
[b]Shall the clay say to him who forms it, 'What are you making?'
Or shall your handiwork *say,* 'He has no hands'?
10 Woe to him who says to *his* father, 'What are you begetting?'
Or to the woman, 'What have you brought forth?' "

11 Thus says the LORD,
The Holy One of Israel, and his Maker:
[a]"Ask Me of things to come concerning [b]My sons;
And concerning [c]the work of My hands, you command Me.
12 [a]I have made the earth,
And [b]created man on it.
I—My hands—stretched out the heavens,
And [c]all their host I have commanded.
13 [a]I have raised him up in righteousness,
And I will direct all his ways;
He shall [b]build My city
And let My exiles go free,
[c]Not for price nor reward,"
Says the LORD of hosts.

The LORD, the Only Savior

14 Thus says the LORD:

[a]"The labor of Egypt and merchandise of Cush
And of the Sabeans, men of stature,
Shall come over to you, and they shall be yours;
They shall walk behind you,
They shall come over [b]in chains;
And they shall bow down to you.
They will make supplication to you,
saying, [c]'Surely God *is* in you,
And *there is* no other;
[d]*There is* no other God.' "

15 Truly You *are* God, [a]who hide Yourself,
O God of Israel, the Savior!
16 They shall be [a]ashamed
And also disgraced, all of them;
They shall go in confusion together,
Who are makers of idols.
17 [a]*But* Israel shall be saved by the LORD
With an [b]everlasting salvation;
You shall not be ashamed or [c]disgraced
Forever and ever.

KJV

18 For thus saith the LORD [a]that created the
heavens; God himself that formed the earth and
made it; he hath established it, he created it not
in vain, he formed it to be [b]inhabited: [c]I *am* the
LORD; and *there is* none else.
19 I have not spoken in [a]secret, in a dark
place of the earth: I said not unto the seed of Jacob, Seek ye me in vain: [b]I the LORD speak righteousness, I declare things that are right.
20 Assemble yourselves and come; draw
near together, ye *that are* escaped of the nations:
[a]they have no knowledge that set up the wood
of their graven image, and pray unto a god *that*
cannot save.
21 Tell ye, and bring *them* near; yea, let them
take counsel together: [a]who hath declared this
from ancient time? *who* hath told it from that
time? *have* not I the LORD? [b]and *there is* no God
else beside me; a just God and a Saviour; *there
is* none beside me.
22 Look unto me, and be ye saved, [a]all the
ends of the earth: for I *am* God, and *there is* none
else.
23 [a]I have sworn by myself, the word is gone
out of my mouth *in* righteousness, and shall not
return, That unto me every [b]knee shall bow,
[c]every tongue shall swear.
24 Surely, shall *one* say, in the LORD have I
[a]righteousness and strength: *even* to him shall
men come; and [b]all that are incensed against him
shall be ashamed.
25 [a]In the LORD shall all the seed of Israel
be justified, and [b]shall glory.

18 [a]Is. 42:5 [b]Gen. 1:26; Ps. 115:16; Acts 17:26 [c]Is. 45:5
19 [a]Deut. 30:11 [b]Ps. 19:8; Is. 45:23; 63:1
20 [a]Is. 44:9; 46:7; Jer. 10:5
21 [a]Is. 41:22; 43:9 [b]Is. 44:8
22 [a]Ps. 22:27; 65:5
23 [a]Gen. 22:16; Is. 62:8; [Heb. 6:13] [b]Rom. 14:11; [Phil. 2:10] [c]Deut. 6:13; Ps. 63:11; Is. 19:18; 65:16
24 [a]Is. 54:17; [Jer. 23:5; 1 Cor. 1:30] [b]Is. 41:11
25 [a]Is. 45:17 [b]1 Cor. 1:31

NKJV

18 For thus says the LORD,
[a]Who created the heavens,
Who is God,
Who formed the earth and made it,
Who has established it,
Who did not create it in vain,
Who formed it to be [b]inhabited:
[c]"I *am* the LORD, and *there is* no other.
19 I have not spoken in [a]secret,
In a dark place of the earth;
I did not say to the seed of Jacob,
'Seek Me in vain';
[b]I, the LORD, speak righteousness,
I declare things that are right.

20 "Assemble yourselves and come;
Draw near together,
You *who have* escaped from the nations.
[a]They have no knowledge,
Who carry the wood of their carved
image,
And pray to a god *that* cannot save.
21 Tell and bring forth *your case;*
Yes, let them take counsel together.
[a]Who has declared this from ancient
time?
Who has told it from that time?
Have not I, the LORD?
[b]And *there is* no other God besides Me,
A just God and a Savior;
There is none besides Me.

22 "Look to Me, and be saved,
[a]All you ends of the earth!
For I *am* God, and *there is* no other.
23 [a]I have sworn by Myself;
The word has gone out of My mouth *in*
righteousness,
And shall not return,
That to Me every [b]knee shall bow,
[c]Every tongue shall take an oath.
24 He shall say,
'Surely in the LORD I have [a]righteousness
and strength.
To Him *men* shall come,
And [b]all shall be ashamed
Who are incensed against Him.
25 [a]In the LORD all the descendants of Israel
Shall be justified, and [b]shall glory.' "

Dead Idols and the Living God

46 Bel [a]boweth down, Nebo stoopeth, their
idols were upon the beasts, and upon the
cattle: your carriages *were* heavy loaden; [b]*they
are* a burden to the weary *beast.*
2 They stoop, they bow down together; they
could not deliver the burden, [a]but themselves are
gone into captivity.
3 Hearken unto me, O house of Jacob, and
all the remnant of the house of Israel, [a]which are
borne *by me* from the belly, which are carried
from the womb:
4 And *even* to *your* old age [a]I *am* he; and
even to hoar hairs [b]will I carry *you:* I have made,
and I will bear; even I will carry, and will deliver
you.
5 [a]To whom will ye liken me, and make *me*
equal, and compare me, that we may be like?
6 [a]They lavish gold out of the bag, and
weigh silver in the balance, *and* hire a [b]goldsmith;
and he maketh it a god: they fall down, yea, they
worship.
7 [a]They bear him upon the shoulder, they
carry him, and set him in his place, and he stand-

CHAPTER 46

1 [a]Is. 21:9; Jer. 50:2 [b]Jer. 10:5
2 [a]Judg. 18:17, 18, 24; 2 Sam. 5:21; Jer. 48:7; Hos. 10:5, 6
3 [a]Deut. 32:11; Ps. 71:6; Is. 63:9
4 [a]Mal. 3:6 [b]Ps. 48:14
5 [a]Is. 40:18, 25
6 [a]Is. 40:19; 41:6; Jer. 10:4 [b]Is. 44:12
7 [a]Is. 45:20; 46:1; Jer. 10:5

Dead Idols and the Living God

46 Bel [a]bows down, Nebo stoops;
Their idols were on the beasts and on the
cattle.
Your carriages *were* heavily loaded,
[b]A burden to the weary *beast.*
2 They stoop, they bow down together;
They could not deliver the burden,
[a]But have themselves gone into captivity.

3 "Listen to Me, O house of Jacob,
And all the remnant of the house of Israel,
[a]Who have been upheld *by Me* from
birth,
Who have been carried from the womb:
4 Even to *your* old age, [a]I *am* He,
And *even* to gray hairs [b]I will carry *you!*
I have made, and I will bear;
Even I will carry, and will deliver *you.*

5 "To[a] whom will you liken Me, and make
Me equal
And compare Me, that we should be
alike?
6 [a]They lavish gold out of the bag,
And weigh silver on the scales;
They hire a [b]goldsmith, and he makes it
a god;
They prostrate themselves, yes, they
worship.
7 [a]They bear it on the shoulder, they carry
it

KJV

eth; from his place shall he not remove: yea, [b]one shall cry unto him, yet can he not answer, nor save him out of his trouble.

8 Remember this, and shew yourselves men: [a]bring *it* again to mind, O ye transgressors.

9 [a]Remember the former things of old: for I *am* God, and [b]*there is* none else; *I am* God, and *there is* none like me,

10 [a]Declaring the end from the beginning, and from ancient times *the things* that are not *yet* done, saying, [b]My counsel shall stand, and I will do all my pleasure:

11 Calling a ravenous bird [a]from the east, the man [b]that executeth my counsel from a far country: yea, [c]I have spoken *it*, I will also bring it to pass; I have purposed *it*, I will also do it.

12 Hearken unto me, ye [a]stouthearted, [b]that *are* far from righteousness:

13 [a]I bring near my righteousness; it shall not be far off, and my salvation [b]shall not tarry: and I will place [c]salvation in Zion for Israel my glory.

The Humiliation of Babylon

47 Come [a]down, and [b]sit in the dust, O virgin daughter of [c]Babylon, sit on the ground: *there is* no throne, O daughter of the Chaldeans: for thou shalt no more be called tender and delicate.

2 [a]Take the millstones, and grind meal: uncover thy locks, make bare the leg, uncover the thigh, pass over the rivers.

3 [a]Thy nakedness shall be uncovered, yea, thy shame shall be seen: [b]I will take vengeance, and I will not meet *thee as* a man.

4 *As for* [a]our redeemer, the LORD of hosts *is* his name, the Holy One of Israel.

5 Sit thou [a]silent, and get thee into darkness, O daughter of the Chaldeans: [b]for thou shalt no more be called, The lady of kingdoms.

6 [a]I was wroth with my people, [b]I have polluted mine inheritance, and given them into thine hand: thou didst shew them no mercy; [c]upon the ancient hast thou very heavily laid thy yoke.

7 And thou saidst, I shall be [a]a lady for ever: *so* that thou didst not [b]lay these *things* to thy heart, [c]neither didst remember the latter end of it.

8 Therefore hear now this, *thou that art* given to pleasures, that dwellest carelessly, that sayest in thine heart, I *am*, and none else beside me; I shall not sit *as* a widow, neither shall I know the loss of children:

9 But these two *things* shall come to thee [a]in a moment in one day, the loss of children, and widowhood: they shall come upon thee in their perfection for the multitude of thy sorceries,

---

7 [b]Is. 45:20
8 [a]Is. 44:19
9 [a]Deut. 32:7; Is. 42:9; 65:17 [b]Is. 45:5, 21
10 [a]Is. 45:21; 48:3 [b]Ps. 33:11; Prov. 19:21; 21:30; Is. 14:24; 25:1; Acts 5:39; Heb. 6:17
11 [a]Is. 41:2, 25 [b]Is. 44:28 [c]Num. 23:19
12 [a]Ps. 76:5; Is. 48:4; Zech. 7:11, 12; Mal. 3:13 [b][Rom. 10:3]
13 [a][Rom. 1:17] [b]Hab. 2:3 [c]Is. 62:11; Joel 3:17; [1 Pet. 2:6]

CHAPTER 47

1 [a]Jer. 48:18 [b]Is. 3:26 [c]Is. 14:18–23; Jer. 25:12; 50:1—51:64
2 [a]Ex. 11:5; Jer. 25:10
3 [a]Is. 3:17; 20:4 [b][Rom. 12:19]
4 [a]Jer. 50:34
5 [a]1 Sam. 2:9 [b]Is. 13:19; [Dan. 2:37]; Rev. 17:18
6 [a]2 Sam. 24:14 [b]Is. 43:28 [c]Deut. 28:49, 50
7 [a]Rev. 18:7 [b]Is. 42:25; 46:8 [c]Deut. 32:29; Jer. 5:31; Ezek. 7:2, 3
9 [a]Ps. 73:19; 1 Thess. 5:3; Rev. 18:8

NKJV

And set it in its place, and it stands;
From its place it shall not move.
Though [b]*one* cries out to it, yet it cannot
answer
Nor save him out of his trouble.

8 "Remember this, and show yourselves
men;
[a]Recall to mind, O you transgressors.
9 [a]Remember the former things of old,
For I *am* God, and [b]*there is* no other;
I am God, and *there is* none like Me,
10 [a]Declaring the end from the beginning,
And from ancient times *things* that are not
yet done,
Saying, [b]'My counsel shall stand,
And I will do all My pleasure,'
11 Calling a bird of prey [a]from the east,
The man [b]who executes My counsel, from
a far country.
Indeed [c]I have spoken *it;*
I will also bring it to pass.
I have purposed *it;*
I will also do it.

12 "Listen to Me, you [a]stubborn-hearted,
[b]Who *are* far from righteousness:
13 [a]I bring My righteousness near, it shall not
be far off;
My salvation [b]shall not linger.
And I will place [c]salvation in Zion,
For Israel My glory.

The Humiliation of Babylon

47 "Come [a]down and [b]sit in the dust,
O virgin daughter of [c]Babylon;
Sit on the ground without a throne,
O daughter of the Chaldeans!
For you shall no more be called
Tender and delicate.
2 [a]Take the millstones and grind meal.
Remove your veil,
Take off the skirt,
Uncover the thigh,
Pass through the rivers.
3 [a]Your nakedness shall be uncovered,
Yes, your shame will be seen;
[b]I will take vengeance,
And I will not arbitrate with a man."

4 *As for* [a]our Redeemer, the LORD of hosts
is His name,
The Holy One of Israel.

5 "Sit in [a]silence, and go into darkness,
O daughter of the Chaldeans;
[b]For you shall no longer be called
The Lady of Kingdoms.
6 [a]I was angry with My people;
[b]I have profaned My inheritance,
And given them into your hand.
You showed them no mercy;
[c]On the elderly you laid your yoke very
heavily.
7 And you said, 'I shall be [a]a lady forever,'
So that you did not [b]take these *things* to
heart,
[c]Nor remember the latter end of them.

8 "Therefore hear this now, *you who are*
given to pleasures,
Who dwell securely,
Who say in your heart,
'I *am*, and *there is* no one else besides
me;
I shall not sit *as* a widow,
Nor shall I know the loss of children';
9 But these two *things* shall come to you
[a]In a moment, in one day:
The loss of children, and widowhood.
They shall come upon you in their
fullness

KJV

and for the great abundance of thine enchantments.
10 For thou hast trusted in thy wickedness:
thou hast said, None [a]seeth me. Thy wisdom and
thy knowledge, it hath perverted thee; and thou
hast said in thine heart, I *am*, and none else beside
me.
11 Therefore shall evil come upon thee; thou
shalt not know from whence it riseth: and mischief shall fall upon thee; thou shalt not be able
to put it off: and [a]desolation shall come upon thee
[b]suddenly, *which* thou shalt not know.
12 Stand now with thine enchantments, and
with the multitude of thy sorceries, wherein thou
hast laboured from thy youth; if so be thou shalt
be able to profit, if so be thou mayest prevail.
13 [a]Thou art wearied in the multitude of thy
counsels. Let now [b]the astrologers, the stargazers,
the monthly prognosticators, stand up, and save
thee from *these things* that shall come upon thee.
14 Behold, they shall be [a]as stubble; the fire
shall [b]burn them; they shall not deliver themselves from the power of the flame: *there shall*
not *be* a coal to warm at, *nor* fire to sit before it.
15 Thus shall they be unto thee with whom
thou hast laboured, *even* [a]thy merchants, from thy
youth: they shall wander every one to his quarter;
none shall save thee.

Israel Refined for God's Glory

48 Hear ye this, O house of Jacob, which are
called by the name of Israel, and are come
forth out of the waters of Judah, which swear by
the name of the LORD, and make mention of the
God of Israel, *but* [a]not in truth, nor in righteousness.
2 For they call themselves [a]of the holy city,
and [b]stay themselves upon the God of Israel; The
LORD of hosts *is* his name.
3 I have [a]declared the former things from
the beginning; and they went forth out of my
mouth, and I shewed them; I did *them* suddenly,
[b]and they came to pass.
4 Because I knew that thou *art* obstinate,
and [a]thy neck *is* an iron sinew, and thy brow
brass;
5 I have even from the beginning declared
it to thee; before it came to pass I shewed *it* thee:
lest thou shouldest say, Mine idol hath done them,
and my graven image, and my molten image, hath
commanded them.
6 Thou hast heard, see all this; and will not
ye declare *it*? I have shewed thee new things from
this time, even hidden things, and thou didst not
know them.

10 [a]Is. 29:15; Ezek. 8:12; 9:9 **11** [a]Is. 13:6; Jer. 51:8, 43; Luke 17:27; 1 Thess. 5:3 [b]Is. 29:5 **13** [a]Is. 57:10 [b]Is. 8:19; 44:25; 47:9; Dan. 2:2, 10 **14** [a]Is. 5:24; Nah. 1:10; Mal. 4:1 [b][Is. 10:17]; Jer. 51:58 **15** [a]Rev. 18:11

CHAPTER 48

1 [a]Is. 58:2; Jer. 4:2; 5:2 **2** [a]Is. 52:1; 64:10 [b]Is. 10:20; Jer. 7:4; 21:2; Mic. 3:11; Rom. 2:17 **3** [a]Is. 44:7, 8; 46:10 [b]Josh. 21:45; Is. 42:9 **4** [a]Ex. 32:9; Deut. 31:27; Ezek. 2:4; 3:7

NKJV

Because of the multitude of your sorceries,
For the great abundance of your
enchantments.

10 "For you have trusted in your wickedness;
You have said, 'No one [a]sees me';
Your wisdom and your knowledge have
warped you;
And you have said in your heart,
'I *am*, and *there is* no one else besides
me.'
11 Therefore evil shall come upon you;
You shall not know from where it arises.
And trouble shall fall upon you;
You will not be able to put it off.
And [a]desolation shall come upon you
[b]suddenly,
Which you shall not know.

12 "Stand now with your enchantments
And the multitude of your sorceries,
In which you have labored from your
youth—
Perhaps you will be able to profit,
Perhaps you will prevail.
13 [a]You are wearied in the multitude of your
counsels;
Let now [b]the astrologers, the stargazers,
And the monthly prognosticators
Stand up and save you
From what shall come upon you.
14 Behold, they shall be [a]as stubble,
The fire shall [b]burn them;
They shall not deliver themselves
From the power of the flame;
It shall not *be* a coal to be warmed by,
Nor a fire to sit before!
15 Thus shall they be to you
With whom you have labored,
[a]Your merchants from your youth;
They shall wander each one to his quarter.
No one shall save you.

Israel Refined for God's Glory

48 "Hear this, O house of Jacob,
Who are called by the name of Israel,
And have come forth from the wellsprings
of Judah;
Who swear by the name of the LORD,
And make mention of the God of Israel,
But [a]not in truth or in righteousness;
2 For they call themselves [a]after the holy
city,
And [b]lean on the God of Israel;
The LORD of hosts *is* His name:

3 "I have [a]declared the former things from
the beginning;
They went forth from My mouth, and I
caused them to hear it.
Suddenly I did *them*, [b]and they came to
pass.
4 Because I knew that you *were* obstinate,
And [a]your neck *was* an iron sinew,
And your brow bronze,
5 Even from the beginning I have declared
it to you;
Before it came to pass I proclaimed *it* to
you,
Lest you should say, 'My idol has done
them,
And my carved image and my molded
image
Have commanded them.'

6 "You have heard;
See all this.
And will you not declare *it*?
I have made you hear new things from
this time,
Even hidden things, and you did not know
them.

KJV

7 They are created now, and not from the
beginning; even before the day when thou heardest them not; lest thou shouldest say, Behold, I
knew them.
8 Yea, thou heardest not; yea, thou knewest
not; yea, from that time *that* thine ear was not
opened: for I knew that thou wouldest deal very
treacherously, and wast called [a]a transgressor
from the womb.
9 [a]For my name's sake [b]will I defer mine
anger, and for my praise will I refrain for thee,
that I cut thee not off.
10 Behold, [a]I have refined thee, but not with
silver; I have chosen thee in the [b]furnace of
affliction.
11 For mine own sake, *even* for mine own
sake, will I do *it:* for [a]how should *my name* be
polluted? and [b]I will not give my glory unto another.

God's Ancient Plan to Redeem Israel

12 Hearken unto me, O Jacob and Israel, my
called; I *am* he; [a]I *am* the [b]first, I also *am* the
last.
13 [a]Mine hand also hath laid the foundation
of the earth, and my right hand hath spanned the
heavens: *when* [b]I call unto them, they stand up
together.
14 All ye, assemble yourselves, and hear;
which among them hath declared these *things?*
[a]The LORD hath loved him: [b]he will do his pleasure on Babylon, and his arm *shall be on* the
Chaldeans.
15 I, *even* I, have spoken; yea, [a]I have called
him: I have brought him, and he shall make his
way prosperous.
16 Come ye near unto me, hear ye this; [a]I
have not spoken in secret from the beginning;
from the time that it was, there *am* I: and now
[b]the Lord GOD, and his Spirit, hath sent me.
17 Thus saith [a]the LORD, thy Redeemer, the
Holy One of Israel; I *am* the LORD thy God which
teacheth thee to profit, [b]which leadeth thee by
the way *that* thou shouldest go.
18 [a]O that thou hadst hearkened to my commandments! [b]then had thy peace been as a river,
and thy righteousness as the waves of the sea:
19 [a]Thy seed also had been as the sand, and
the offspring of thy bowels like the gravel thereof;
his name should not have been cut off nor destroyed from before me.
20 [a]Go ye forth of Babylon, flee ye from the
Chaldeans, with a voice of singing declare ye, tell

8 [a]Deut. 9:7, 24; Ps. 58:3; Is. 46:3, 8
9 [a]Ps. 79:9; 106:8; Is. 43:25; Ezek. 20:9, 14, 22, 44 [b][Neh. 9:30, 31]; Ps. 78:38; Is. 30:18; 65:8
10 [a]Ps. 66:10; Jer. 9:7 [b]Deut. 4:20; 1 Kin. 8:51; Jer. 11:4
11 [a]Lev. 22:2, 32; Deut. 32:26, 27; Ezek. 20:9 [b]Is. 42:8
12 [a]Deut. 32:39 [b]Is. 44:6; [Rev. 22:13]
13 [a]Ex. 20:11; Ps. 102:25; Is. 42:5; 45:12, 18; Heb. 1:10–12 [b]Is. 40:26
14 [a]Is. 45:1 [b]Is. 44:28; 47:1–15
15 [a]Is. 45:1, 2
16 [a]Is. 45:19 [b]Is. 61:1; Zech. 2:8, 9, 11
17 [a]Is. 43:14 [b]Ps. 32:8; Is. 49:9, 10
18 [a]Deut. 5:29; Ps. 81:13 [b]Deut. 28:1–14; Ps. 119:165; Is. 32:16–18; 66:12
19 [a]Gen. 22:17; Is. 10:22; 44:3, 4; 54:3; Jer. 33:22; Hos. 1:10
20 [a]Jer. 50:8; 51:6, 45; Zech. 2:6, 7; Rev. 18:4

* **48:16** Heb. verb is sing.; or *Has sent Me and His Spirit*

NKJV

7 They are created now and not from the
beginning;
And before this day you have not heard
them,
Lest you should say, 'Of course I knew
them.'
8 Surely you did not hear,
Surely you did not know;
Surely from long ago your ear was not
opened.
For I knew that you would deal very
treacherously,
And were called [a]a transgressor from the
womb.

9 "For[a] My name's sake [b]I will defer My
anger,
And *for* My praise I will restrain it from
you,
So that I do not cut you off.
10 Behold, [a]I have refined you, but not as
silver;
I have tested you in the [b]furnace of
affliction.
11 For My own sake, for My own sake, I will
do *it;*
For [a]how should *My name* be profaned?
And [b]I will not give My glory to another.

God's Ancient Plan to Redeem Israel

12 "Listen to Me, O Jacob,
And Israel, My called:
I *am* He, [a]I *am* the [b]First,
I *am* also the Last.
13 Indeed [a]My hand has laid the foundation
of the earth,
And My right hand has stretched out the
heavens;
When [b]I call to them,
They stand up together.

14 "All of you, assemble yourselves, and
hear!
Who among them has declared these
things?
[a]The LORD loves him;
[b]He shall do His pleasure on Babylon,
And His arm *shall be against* the
Chaldeans.
15 I, *even* I, have spoken;
Yes, [a]I have called him,
I have brought him, and his way will
prosper.

16 "Come near to Me, hear this:
[a]I have not spoken in secret from the
beginning;
From the time that it was, I *was* there.
And now [b]the Lord GOD and His Spirit
*Have sent Me."

17 Thus says [a]the LORD, your Redeemer,
The Holy One of Israel:
"I *am* the LORD your God,
Who teaches you to profit,
[b]Who leads you by the way you should
go.
18 [a]Oh, that you had heeded My
commandments!
[b]Then your peace would have been like a
river,
And your righteousness like the waves of
the sea.
19 [a]Your descendants also would have been
like the sand,
And the offspring of your body like the
grains of sand;
His name would not have been cut off
Nor destroyed from before Me."

20 [a]Go forth from Babylon!
Flee from the Chaldeans!

KJV

this, utter it *even* to the end of the earth; say ye,
The LORD hath [b]redeemed his servant Jacob.
21 And they [a]thirsted not *when* he led them
through the deserts: he [b]caused the waters to flow
out of the rock for them: he clave the rock also,
and the waters gushed out.
22 [a]*There is* no peace, saith the LORD, unto
the wicked.

The Servant, the Light to the Gentiles

49 Listen, [a]O isles, unto me; and hearken, ye
people, from far; [b]The LORD hath called me
from the womb; from the bowels of my mother
hath he made mention of my name.
2 And he hath made [a]my mouth like a sharp
sword; [b]in the shadow of his hand hath he hid
me, and made me [c]a polished shaft; in his quiver
hath he hid me;
3 And said unto me, [a]Thou *art* my servant,
O Israel, [b]in whom I will be glorified.
4 [a]Then I said, I have laboured in vain, I
have spent my strength for nought, and in vain:
yet surely my judgment *is* with the LORD, and my
work with my God.
5 And now, saith the LORD that formed me
from the womb *to be* his servant, to bring Jacob
again to him, Though Israel [a]be not gathered, yet
shall I be glorious in the eyes of the LORD, and
my God shall be my strength.
6 And he said, It is a light thing that thou
shouldest be my servant to raise up the tribes of
Jacob, and to restore the preserved of Israel: I
will also give thee for a [a]light to the Gentiles, that
thou mayest be my salvation unto the end of the
earth.
7 Thus saith the LORD, the Redeemer of Israel, *and* his Holy One, [a]to him whom man despiseth, to him whom the nation abhorreth, to a servant of rulers, [b]Kings shall see and arise, princes
also shall worship, because of the LORD that is
faithful, *and* the Holy One of Israel, and he shall
choose thee.
8 Thus saith the LORD, In an [a]acceptable
time have I heard thee, and in a day of salvation
have I helped thee: and I will preserve thee, [b]and
give thee for a covenant of the people, to establish
the earth, to cause to inherit the desolate
heritages;
9 That thou mayest say [a]to the prisoners,
Go forth; to them that *are* in darkness, Shew yourselves. They shall feed in the ways, and their pastures *shall be* in all high places.

20 [b][Ex. 19:4–6]
21 [a][Is. 41:17, 18] [b]Ex. 17:6; Ps. 105:41
22 [a][Is. 57:21]

CHAPTER 49

1 [a]Is. 41:1 [b]Jer. 1:5; Matt. 1:20; Luke 1:35; John 1:14; 10:36
2 [a]Is. 11:4; Hos. 6:5; [Heb. 4:12]; Rev. 1:16; 2:12 [b]Is. 51:16 [c]Ps. 45:5
3 [a][Is. 41:8; 42:1; Zech. 3:8] [b]Is. 44:23; Matt. 12:18; [John 13:31, 32; 14:13; 15:8; 17:4; Eph. 1:6]
4 [a][Ezek. 3:19]
5 [a]Matt. 23:37; [Rom. 11:25–29]
6 [a]Is. 42:6; 51:4; [Luke 2:32]; Acts 13:47; [Gal. 3:14]
7 [a][Ps. 22:6; Is. 53:3; Matt. 26:67; 27:41]; Mark 15:29; Luke 23:35 [b][Is. 52:15]
8 [a]Ps. 69:13; 2 Cor. 6:2 [b]Is. 42:6
9 [a]Is. 61:1; Zech. 9:12; Luke 4:18

*49:5 Qr., DSS, LXX *gathered to Him;* Kt. *not gathered*

NKJV

With a voice of singing,
Declare, proclaim this,
Utter it to the end of the earth;
Say, "The LORD has [b]redeemed
His servant Jacob!"
21 And they [a]did not thirst
When He led them through the deserts;
He [b]caused the waters to flow from the rock for them;
He also split the rock, and the waters gushed out.

22 "*There*[a] *is* no peace," says the LORD, "for the wicked."

The Servant, the Light to the Gentiles

49 "Listen, [a]O coastlands, to Me,
And take heed, you peoples from afar!
[b]The LORD has called Me from the womb;
From the matrix of My mother He has made mention of My name.
2 And He has made [a]My mouth like a sharp sword;
[b]In the shadow of His hand He has hidden Me,
And made Me [c]a polished shaft;
In His quiver He has hidden Me."

3 "And He said to me,
[a]'You *are* My servant, O Israel,
[b]In whom I will be glorified.'
4 [a]Then I said, 'I have labored in vain,
I have spent my strength for nothing and in vain;
Yet surely my just reward *is* with the LORD,
And my work with my God.'"

5 "And now the LORD says,
Who formed Me from the womb *to be* His Servant,
To bring Jacob back to Him,
So that Israel [a]is *gathered to Him
(For I shall be glorious in the eyes of the LORD,
And My God shall be My strength),
6 Indeed He says,
'It is too small a thing that You should be My Servant
To raise up the tribes of Jacob,
And to restore the preserved ones of Israel;
I will also give You as a [a]light to the Gentiles,
That You should be My salvation to the ends of the earth.'"

7 Thus says the LORD,
The Redeemer of Israel, their Holy One,
[a]To Him whom man despises,
To Him whom the nation abhors,
To the Servant of rulers:
[b]"Kings shall see and arise,
Princes also shall worship,
Because of the LORD who is faithful,
The Holy One of Israel;
And He has chosen You."

8 Thus says the LORD:

"In an [a]acceptable time I have heard You,
And in the day of salvation I have helped You;
I will preserve You [b]and give You
As a covenant to the people,
To restore the earth,
To cause them to inherit the desolate heritages;
9 That You may say [a]to the prisoners, 'Go forth,'
To those who *are* in darkness, 'Show yourselves.'

KJV

10 They shall not [a]hunger nor thirst; [b]neither
shall the heat nor sun smite them: for he that hath
mercy on them [c]shall lead them, even by the
springs of water shall he guide them.
11 [a]And I will make all my mountains a way,
and my highways shall be exalted.
12 Behold, [a]these shall come from far: and,
lo, these from the north and from the west; and
these from the land of Sinim.
13 [a]Sing, O heavens; and be joyful, O earth;
and break forth into singing, O mountains: for
the LORD hath comforted his people, and will have
mercy upon his afflicted.

God Will Remember Zion

14 [a]But Zion said, The LORD hath forsaken
me, and my Lord hath forgotten me.
15 [a]Can a woman forget her sucking child,
that she should not have compassion on the son
of her womb? yea, they may forget, [b]yet will I
not forget thee.
16 Behold, [a]I have graven thee upon the
palms of *my* hands; thy walls *are* continually before me.
17 Thy children shall make haste; thy destroyers and they that made thee waste shall go
forth of thee.
18 [a]Lift up thine eyes round about, and behold: all these gather themselves together, *and*
come to thee. *As* I live, saith the LORD, thou shalt
surely clothe thee with them all, [b]as with an ornament, and bind them *on thee*, as a bride *doeth*.
19 For thy waste and thy desolate places, and
the land of thy destruction, [a]shall even now be
too narrow by reason of the inhabitants, and they
that swallowed thee up shall be far away.
20 [a]The children which thou shalt have,
[b]after thou hast lost the other, shall say again in
thine ears, The place *is* too strait for me: give place
to me that I may dwell.
21 Then shalt thou say in thine heart, Who
hath begotten me these, seeing I have lost my children, and am desolate, a captive, and removing
to and fro? and who hath brought up these? Behold, I was left alone; these, where *had* they *been?*
22 [a]Thus saith the Lord GOD, Behold, I will
lift up mine hand to the Gentiles, and set up my
standard to the people: and they shall bring thy
sons in *their* arms, and thy daughters shall be
carried upon *their* shoulders.
23 [a]And kings shall be thy nursing fathers,
and their queens thy nursing mothers: they shall
bow down to thee with *their* face toward the earth,
and [b]lick up the dust of thy feet; and thou shalt
know that I *am* the LORD: [c]for they shall not be
ashamed that wait for me.

10 [a]Is. 33:16; 48:21; Rev. 7:16 [b]Ps. 121:6 [c]Ps. 23:2; Is. 40:11; 48:17
11 [a]Is. 40:4
12 [a]Is. 43:5, 6
13 [a]Is. 44:23
14 [a]Is. 40:27
15 [a]Ps. 103:13; Mal. 3:17 [b]Rom. 11:29
16 [a]Ex. 13:9; Song 8:6; Hag. 2:23
18 [a]Is. 60:4; John 4:35 [b]Prov. 17:6
19 [a]Is. 54:1, 2; Zech. 10:10
20 [a]Is. 60:4 [b][Matt. 3:9; Rom. 11:11]
22 [a]Is. 60:4
23 [a]Ps. 72:11; Is. 52:15 [b]Ps. 72:9; Mic. 7:17 [c]Ps. 34:22; [Rom. 5:5]

*

49:17 DSS, LXX, Tg., Vg. *builders*

NKJV

"They shall feed along the roads,
And their pastures *shall be* on all desolate
heights.
10 They shall neither [a]hunger nor thirst,
[b]Neither heat nor sun shall strike them;
For He who has mercy on them [c]will lead
them,
Even by the springs of water He will guide
them.
11 [a]I will make each of My mountains a road,
And My highways shall be elevated.
12 Surely [a]these shall come from afar;
Look! Those from the north and the west,
And these from the land of Sinim."

13 [a]Sing, O heavens!
Be joyful, O earth!
And break out in singing, O mountains!
For the LORD has comforted His people,
And will have mercy on His afflicted.

God Will Remember Zion

14 [a]But Zion said, "The LORD has forsaken
me,
And my Lord has forgotten me."

15 "Can[a] a woman forget her nursing child,
And not have compassion on the son of
her womb?
Surely they may forget,
[b]Yet I will not forget you.
16 See, [a]I have inscribed you on the palms
of My hands;
Your walls *are* continually before Me.
17 Your *sons shall make haste;
Your destroyers and those who laid you
waste
Shall go away from you.
18 [a]Lift up your eyes, look around and see;
All these gather together *and* come to you.
As I live," says the LORD,
"You shall surely clothe yourselves with
them all [b]as an ornament,
And bind them *on you* as a bride *does.*

19 "For your waste and desolate places,
And the land of your destruction,
[a]Will even now be too small for the
inhabitants;
And those who swallowed you up will be
far away.
20 [a]The children you will have,
[b]After you have lost the others,
Will say again in your ears,
'The place *is* too small for me;
Give me a place where I may dwell.'
21 Then you will say in your heart,
'Who has begotten these for me,
Since I have lost my children and am
desolate,
A captive, and wandering to and fro?
And who has brought these up?
There I was, left alone;
But these, where *were* they?' "

22 [a]Thus says the Lord GOD:

"Behold, I will lift My hand in an oath to
the nations,
And set up My standard for the peoples;
They shall bring your sons in *their*
arms,
And your daughters shall be carried on
their shoulders;
23 [a]Kings shall be your foster fathers,
And their queens your nursing mothers;
They shall bow down to you with *their*
faces to the earth,
And [b]lick up the dust of your feet.
Then you will know that I *am* the LORD,
[c]For they shall not be ashamed who wait
for Me."

KJV

24 [a]Shall the prey be taken from the mighty,
or the lawful captive delivered?
25 But thus saith the LORD, Even the captives
of the mighty shall be taken away, and the prey
of the terrible shall be delivered: for I will contend
with him that contendeth with thee, and I will save
thy children.
26 And I will [a]feed them that oppress thee
with their own flesh; and they shall be drunken
with their own [b]blood, as with sweet wine: and
all flesh [c]shall know that I the LORD *am* thy
Saviour and thy Redeemer, the mighty One of
Jacob.

The Servant, Israel's Hope

50 Thus saith the LORD, Where *is* [a]the bill of
your mother's divorcement, whom I have
put away? or which of my [b]creditors *is it* to whom
I have sold you? Behold, for your iniquities [c]have
ye sold yourselves, and for your transgressions
is your mother put away.
2 Wherefore, when I came, *was there* no
man? when I called, *was there* none to answer?
Is my hand shortened at all, that it cannot redeem?
or have I no power to deliver? behold, at my [a]re-
buke I dry up the sea, I make the rivers a wilderness: their fish stinketh, because *there is* no water,
and dieth for thirst.
3 [a]I clothe the heavens with blackness, [b]and
I make sackcloth their covering.
4 [a]The Lord GOD hath given me the tongue
of the learned, that I should know how to speak
a word in season to *him that is* [b]weary: he wakeneth morning by morning, he wakeneth mine ear
to hear as the learned.
5 The Lord GOD [a]hath opened mine ear, and
I was not [b]rebellious, neither turned away back.
6 [a]I gave my back to the smiters, and [b]my
cheeks to them that plucked off the hair: I hid
not my face from shame and [c]spitting.
7 For the Lord GOD will help me; therefore
shall I not be confounded: therefore have [a]I set
my face like a flint, and I know that I shall not
be ashamed.
8 [a]*He is* near that justifieth me; who will
contend with me? let us stand together: who *is*
mine adversary? let him come near to me.
9 Behold, the Lord GOD will help me; who
is he *that* shall condemn me? [a]lo, they all shall
wax old as a garment; [b]the moth shall eat them
up.
10 Who *is* among you that feareth the LORD,
that obeyeth the voice of his servant, that [a]walk-
eth *in* darkness, and hath no light? [b]let him trust
in the name of the LORD, and stay upon his God.

24 [a]Matt. 12:29; Luke 11:21, 22
26 [a]Is. 9:20 [b]Rev. 14:20 [c]Ps. 9:16; Is. 60:16

CHAPTER 50
1 [a]Deut. 24:1; Jer. 3:8 [b]Deut. 32:30; 2 Kin. 4:1; Neh. 5:5 [c]Is. 52:3
2 [a]Ps. 106:9; Nah. 1:4
3 [a]Ex. 10:21 [b]Is. 13:10; Rev. 6:12
4 [a]Ex. 4:11 [b]Matt. 11:28
5 [a]Ps. 40:6; Is. 35:5 [b]Matt. 26:39; Mark 14:36; Luke 22:42; John 8:29; 14:31; 15:10; Acts 26:19; [Phil. 2:8; Heb. 5:8; 10:7]
6 [a]Matt. 27:26; John 18:22 [b]Matt. 26:67; 27:30; Mark 14:65; 15:19 [c]Lam. 3:30
7 [a]Ezek. 3:8, 9; Luke 9:51
8 [a]Acts 2:24; [Rom. 8:32–34]
9 [a]Job 13:28; Ps. 102:26; Heb. 1:11 [b]Is. 51:6, 8
10 [a]Ps. 23:4 [b]2 Chr. 20:20

NKJV

24 [a]Shall the prey be taken from the mighty,
Or the captives *of the righteous be
delivered?

25 But thus says the LORD:

"Even the captives of the mighty shall be
taken away,
And the prey of the terrible be delivered;
For I will contend with him who contends
with you,
And I will save your children.
26 I will [a]feed those who oppress you with
their own flesh,
And they shall be drunk with their own
[b]blood as with sweet wine.
All flesh [c]shall know
That I, the LORD, *am* your Savior,
And your Redeemer, the Mighty One of
Jacob."

The Servant, Israel's Hope

50 Thus says the LORD:

"Where *is* [a]the certificate of your mother's
divorce,
Whom I have put away?
Or which of My [b]creditors *is it* to whom
I have sold you?
For your iniquities [c]you have sold
yourselves,
And for your transgressions your mother
has been put away.
2 Why, when I came, *was there* no man?
Why, when I called, *was there* none to
answer?
Is My hand shortened at all that it cannot
redeem?
Or have I no power to deliver?
Indeed with My [a]rebuke I dry up the sea,
I make the rivers a wilderness;
Their fish stink because *there is* no water,
And die of thirst.
3 [a]I clothe the heavens with blackness,
[b]And I make sackcloth their covering."

4 "The[a] Lord GOD has given Me
The tongue of the learned,
That I should know how to speak
A word in season to *him who is* [b]weary.
He awakens Me morning by morning,
He awakens My ear
To hear as the learned.
5 The Lord GOD [a]has opened My ear;
And I was not [b]rebellious,
Nor did I turn away.
6 [a]I gave My back to those who struck *Me*,
And [b]My cheeks to those who plucked out
the beard;
I did not hide My face from shame and
[c]spitting.

7 "For the Lord GOD will help Me;
Therefore I will not be disgraced;
Therefore [a]I have set My face like a flint,
And I know that I will not be ashamed.
8 [a]*He is* near who justifies Me;
Who will contend with Me?
Let us stand together.
Who *is* My adversary?
Let him come near Me.
9 Surely the Lord GOD will help Me;
Who *is* he *who* will condemn Me?
[a]Indeed they will all grow old like a
garment;
[b]The moth will eat them up.

10 "Who among you fears the LORD?
Who obeys the voice of His Servant?
Who [a]walks in darkness
And has no light?
[b]Let him trust in the name of the LORD
And rely upon his God.

*
49:24 So with MT, Tg.; DSS, Syr., Vg. *of the mighty*; LXX *unjustly*

KJV

11 Behold, all ye that kindle a fire, that compass *yourselves* about with sparks: walk in the light of your fire, and in the sparks *that* ye have kindled. [a]This shall ye have of mine hand; ye shall lie down [b]in sorrow.

The LORD *Comforts Zion* (*cf. Gen. 12:1–3*)

51 Hearken to me, [a]ye that follow after righteousness, ye that seek the LORD: look unto the rock *whence* ye are hewn, and to the hole of the pit *whence* ye are digged.

2 [a]Look unto Abraham your father, and unto Sarah *that* bare you: [b]for I called him alone, and [c]blessed him, and increased him.

3 For the LORD shall [a]comfort Zion: he will comfort all her waste places; and he will make her wilderness like Eden, and her desert [b]like the garden of the LORD; joy and gladness shall be found therein, thanksgiving, and the voice of melody.

4 Hearken unto me, my people; and give ear unto me, O my nation: [a]for a law shall proceed from me, and I will make my judgment to rest [b]for a light of the people.

5 [a]My righteousness *is* near; my salvation is gone forth, [b]and mine arms shall judge the people; [c]the isles shall wait upon me, and [d]on mine arm shall they trust.

6 [a]Lift up your eyes to the heavens, and look upon the earth beneath: for [b]the heavens shall vanish away like smoke, [c]and the earth shall wax old like a garment, and they that dwell therein shall die in like manner: but my salvation shall be [d]for ever, and my righteousness shall not be abolished.

7 Hearken unto me, ye that know righteousness, the people [a]in whose heart *is* my law; [b]fear ye not the reproach of men, neither be ye afraid of their revilings.

8 For [a]the moth shall eat them up like a garment, and the worm shall eat them like wool: but my righteousness shall be for ever, and my salvation from generation to generation.

9 [a]Awake, awake, [b]put on strength, O arm of the LORD; awake, [c]as in the ancient days, in the generations of old. [d]*Art* thou not it that hath cut [e]Rahab, *and* wounded the [f]dragon?

10 *Art* thou not it which hath [a]dried the sea, the waters of the great deep; that hath made the depths of the sea a way for the ransomed to pass over?

11 Therefore [a]the redeemed of the LORD shall return, and come with singing unto Zion; and everlasting joy *shall be* upon their head: they shall obtain gladness and joy; *and* sorrow and mourning shall flee away.

11 [a][John 9:39] [b]Ps. 16:4

CHAPTER 51

1 [a][Rom. 9:30–32]
2 [a]Rom. 4:1–3; Heb. 11:11 [b]Gen. 12:1 [c]Gen. 24:35; Deut. 1:10; Ezek. 33:24
3 [a]Is. 40:1; 52:9; Ps. 102:13 [b]Gen. 13:10; Joel 2:3
4 [a]Is. 2:3 [b]Is. 42:6
5 [a]Is. 46:13 [b]Ps. 67:4 [c]Is. 60:9 [d][Rom. 1:16]
6 [a]Is. 40:26 [b]Ps. 102:25, 26; Is. 13:13; 34:4; Matt. 24:35; Heb. 1:10–12; 2 Pet. 3:10 [c]Is. 24:19, 20; 50:9; Heb. 1:10–12 [d]Is. 45:17
7 [a]Ps. 37:31; Jer. 31:33; [Heb. 10:16] [b]Is. 25:8; 54:4; [Matt. 5:11, 12; 10:28; Acts 5:41]
8 [a]Is. 50:9
9 [a]Ps. 44:23 [b]Ps. 93:1 [c]Ps. 44:1 [d]Job 26:12; Ps. 89:10; Is. 30:7 [e]Ps. 87:4 [f]Ps. 74:13; Is. 27:1
10 [a]Ex. 14:21; Is. 63:11–13
11 [a]Is. 35:10; Jer. 31:11, 12

NKJV

11 Look, all you who kindle a fire,
Who encircle *yourselves* with sparks:
Walk in the light of your fire and in the sparks you have kindled—
[a]This you shall have from My hand:
You shall lie down [b]in torment.

The LORD *Comforts Zion* (*cf. Gen. 12:1–3*)

51 "Listen to Me, [a]you who follow after righteousness,
You who seek the LORD:
Look to the rock *from which* you were hewn,
And to the hole of the pit *from which* you were dug.
2 [a]Look to Abraham your father,
And to Sarah *who* bore you;
[b]For I called him alone,
And [c]blessed him and increased him."

3 For the LORD will [a]comfort Zion,
He will comfort all her waste places;
He will make her wilderness like Eden,
And her desert [b]like the garden of the LORD;
Joy and gladness will be found in it,
Thanksgiving and the voice of melody.

4 "Listen to Me, My people;
And give ear to Me, O My nation:
[a]For law will proceed from Me,
And I will make My justice rest
[b]As a light of the peoples.
5 [a]My righteousness *is* near,
My salvation has gone forth,
[b]And My arms will judge the peoples;
[c]The coastlands will wait upon Me,
And [d]on My arm they will trust.
6 [a]Lift up your eyes to the heavens,
And look on the earth beneath.
For [b]the heavens will vanish away like smoke,
[c]The earth will grow old like a garment,
And those who dwell in it will die in like manner;
But My salvation will be [d]forever,
And My righteousness will not be abolished.

7 "Listen to Me, you who know righteousness,
You people [a]in whose heart *is* My law:
[b]Do not fear the reproach of men,
Nor be afraid of their insults.
8 For [a]the moth will eat them up like a garment,
And the worm will eat them like wool;
But My righteousness will be forever,
And My salvation from generation to generation."

9 [a]Awake, awake, [b]put on strength,
O arm of the LORD!
Awake [c]as in the ancient days,
In the generations of old.
[d]*Are* You not *the arm* that cut [e]Rahab apart,
And wounded the [f]serpent?

10 *Are* You not *the One* who [a]dried up the sea,
The waters of the great deep;
That made the depths of the sea a road
For the redeemed to cross over?
11 So [a]the ransomed of the LORD shall return,
And come to Zion with singing,
With everlasting joy on their heads.
They shall obtain joy and gladness;
Sorrow and sighing shall flee away.

KJV

12 I, *even* I, *am* he [a]that comforteth you: who *art* thou, that thou shouldest be afraid [b]of a man *that* shall die, and of the son of man *which* shall be made [c]*as* grass;

13 And [a]forgettest the LORD thy maker, [b]that hath stretched forth the heavens, and laid the foundations of the earth; and hast feared continually every day because of the fury of the oppressor, as if he were ready to destroy? [c]and where *is* the fury of the oppressor?

14 The captive exile hasteneth that he may be loosed, [a]and that he should not die in the pit, nor that his bread should fail.

15 But I *am* the LORD thy God, that [a]divided the sea, whose waves roared: The LORD of hosts *is* his name.

16 And [a]I have put my words in thy mouth, and [b]I have covered thee in the shadow of mine hand, [c]that I may plant the heavens, and lay the foundations of the earth, and say unto Zion, Thou *art* my people.

God's Fury Removed

17 [a]Awake, awake, stand up, O Jerusalem, which [b]hast drunk at the hand of the LORD the cup of his fury; thou hast drunken the dregs of the cup of trembling, *and* wrung *them* out.

18 *There is* none to guide her among all the sons *whom* she hath brought forth; neither *is there any* that taketh her by the hand of all the sons *that* she hath brought up.

19 [a]These two *things* are come unto thee; who shall be sorry for thee? desolation, and destruction, and the famine, and the sword: [b]by whom shall I comfort thee?

20 [a]Thy sons have fainted, they lie at the head of all the streets, as a wild bull in a net: they are full of the fury of the LORD, the rebuke of thy God.

21 Therefore hear now this, thou afflicted, and drunken, [a]but not with wine:

22 Thus saith thy Lord the LORD, and thy God *that* [a]pleadeth the cause of his people, Behold, I have taken out of thine hand the cup of trembling, *even* the dregs of the cup of my fury; thou shalt no more drink it again:

23 [a]But I will put it into the hand of them that afflict thee; which have said to thy soul, Bow down, that we may go over: and thou hast laid thy body as the ground, and as the street, to them that went over.

God Redeems Jerusalem

52 Awake, awake; put on thy strength, O Zion; put on thy beautiful garments, O Jerusalem, the holy city: for henceforth there shall no more come into thee the uncircumcised [a]and the unclean.

2 [a]Shake thyself from the dust; arise, *and* sit down, O Jerusalem: [b]loose thyself from the bands of thy neck, O captive daughter of Zion.

---

12 [a]2 Cor. 1:3 [b]Ps. 118:6; Is. 2:22 [c]Is. 40:6, 7; James 1:10; 1 Pet. 1:24
13 [a]Deut. 6:12; 8:11; Is. 17:10; Jer. 2:32 [b]Ps. 104:2 [c]Job 20:7
14 [a]Zech. 9:11
15 [a]Job 26:12
16 [a]Deut. 18:18; Is. 59:21; John 3:34 [b]Ex. 33:22; Is. 49:2 [c]Is. 65:17
17 [a]Is. 52:1 [b]Job 21:20; Is. 29:9; Jer. 25:15; Rev. 14:10; 16:19
19 [a]Is. 47:9 [b]Amos 7:2
20 [a]Lam. 2:11
21 [a]Lam. 3:15
22 [a]Is. 3:12, 13; 49:25; Jer. 50:34
23 [a]Is. 14:2; Jer. 25:17, 26–28; Zech. 12:2

CHAPTER 52

1 [a]Neh. 11:1; Is. 48:2; 64:10; Zech. 14:20, 21; Matt. 4:5; [Rev. 21:2–27]
2 [a]Is. 3:26 [b]Is. 9:4; 10:27; 14:25; Zech. 2:7

*________

51:23 Lit. *your soul*

NKJV

12 "I, *even* I, *am* He [a]who comforts you.
Who *are* you that you should be afraid
[b]Of a man *who* will die,
And of the son of a man *who* will be made
[c]like grass?
13 And [a]you forget the LORD your Maker,
[b]Who stretched out the heavens
And laid the foundations of the earth;
You have feared continually every day
Because of the fury of the oppressor,
When *he has* prepared to destroy.
[c]And where *is* the fury of the oppressor?
14 The captive exile hastens, that he may be loosed,
[a]That he should not die in the pit,
And that his bread should not fail.
15 But I *am* the LORD your God,
Who [a]divided the sea whose waves roared—
The LORD of hosts *is* His name.
16 And [a]I have put My words in your mouth;
[b]I have covered you with the shadow of My hand,
[c]That I may plant the heavens,
Lay the foundations of the earth,
And say to Zion, 'You *are* My people.' "

God's Fury Removed

17 [a]Awake, awake!
Stand up, O Jerusalem,
You who [b]have drunk at the hand of the LORD
The cup of His fury;
You have drunk the dregs of the cup of trembling,
And drained *it* out.
18 *There is* no one to guide her
Among all the sons she has brought forth;
Nor *is there any* who takes her by the hand
Among all the sons she has brought up.
19 [a]These two *things* have come to you;
Who will be sorry for you?—
Desolation and destruction, famine and sword—
[b]By whom will I comfort you?
20 [a]Your sons have fainted,
They lie at the head of all the streets,
Like an antelope in a net;
They are full of the fury of the LORD,
The rebuke of your God.

21 Therefore please hear this, you afflicted,
And drunk [a]but not with wine.
22 Thus says your Lord,
The LORD and your God,
Who [a]pleads the cause of His people:
"See, I have taken out of your hand
The cup of trembling,
The dregs of the cup of My fury;
You shall no longer drink it.
23 [a]But I will put it into the hand of those who afflict you,
Who have said to *you,
'Lie down, that we may walk over you.'
And you have laid your body like the ground,
And as the street, for those who walk over."

God Redeems Jerusalem

52 Awake, awake!
Put on your strength, O Zion;
Put on your beautiful garments,
O Jerusalem, the holy city!
For the uncircumcised [a]and the unclean
Shall no longer come to you.
2 [a]Shake yourself from the dust, arise;
Sit down, O Jerusalem!
[b]Loose yourself from the bonds of your neck,
O captive daughter of Zion!

KJV

3 For thus saith the LORD, [a]Ye have sold yourselves for nought; and ye shall be redeemed [b]without money.

4 For thus saith the Lord GOD, My people went down aforetime into [a]Egypt to sojourn there; and the Assyrian oppressed them without cause.

5 Now therefore, what have I here, saith the LORD, that my people is taken away for nought? they that rule over them make them to howl, saith the LORD; and my name continually every day *is* [a]blasphemed.

6 Therefore my people shall know my name: therefore *they shall know* in that day that I *am* he that doth speak: behold, *it is* I.

7 [a]How beautiful upon the mountains are the feet of him that bringeth good tidings, that publisheth peace; that bringeth good tidings of good, that publisheth salvation; that saith unto Zion, [b]Thy God reigneth!

8 Thy watchmen shall lift up the voice; with the voice together shall they sing: for they shall see eye to eye, when the LORD shall bring again Zion.

9 Break forth into joy, sing together, ye waste places of Jerusalem: for the LORD hath comforted his people, he hath redeemed Jerusalem.

10 [a]The LORD hath made bare his holy arm in the eyes of [b]all the nations; and all the ends of the earth shall see the salvation of our God.

11 [a]Depart ye, depart ye, go ye out from thence, touch no unclean *thing;* go ye out of the midst of her; [b]be ye clean, that bear the vessels of the LORD.

12 For [a]ye shall not go out with haste, nor go by flight: [b]for the LORD will go before you; [c]and the God of Israel *will be* your rereward.

The Sin-Bearing Servant

13 Behold, [a]my servant shall deal prudently, [b]he shall be exalted and extolled, and be very high.

14 As many were astonied at thee; his [a]visage was so marred more than any man, and his form more than the sons of men:

15 [a]So shall he sprinkle many nations; the kings shall shut their mouths at him: for *that* [b]which had not been told them shall they see; and *that* which they had not heard shall they consider.

53 Who [a]hath believed our report? and to whom is the arm of the LORD revealed?

2 For he shall grow up before him as a tender plant, and as a root out of a dry ground: he hath no form nor comeliness; and when we shall see him, *there is* no beauty that we should desire him.

---

3 [a]Ps. 44:12; Jer. 15:13 [b]Is. 45:13
4 [a]Gen. 46:6
5 [a]Ezek. 36:20, 23; Rom. 2:24
7 [a]Is. 40:9; 61:1; Nah. 1:15; Rom. 10:15; Eph. 6:15 [b]Ps. 93:1; Is. 24:23
10 [a]Ps. 98:1–3 [b]Luke 3:6
11 [a]Is. 48:20; Jer. 50:8; Zech. 2:6, 7; 2 Cor. 6:17 [b]Lev. 22:2; [Is. 1:16]
12 [a]Ex. 12:11, 33; Deut. 16:3 [b]Mic. 2:13 [c]Ex. 14:19, 20; Is. 58:8
13 [a]Is. 42:1 [b]Is. 57:15; Phil. 2:9
14 [a]Ps. 22:6, 7; Matt. 26:67; 27:30; John 19:3
15 [a]Num. 19:18–21; Ezek. 36:25 [b]Rom. 15:21; [Eph. 3:5, 9]; 1 Pet. 1:2

CHAPTER 53

1 [a]John 12:38; Rom. 10:16

*

52:5 DSS *Mock;* LXX *Marvel and wail;* Tg. *Boast themselves;* Vg. *Treat them unjustly*
52:15 Or *startle*

NKJV

3 For thus says the LORD:

[a]"You have sold yourselves for nothing,
And you shall be redeemed [b]without money."

4 For thus says the Lord GOD:

"My people went down at first
Into [a]Egypt to dwell there;
Then the Assyrian oppressed them
without cause.

5 Now therefore, what have I here," says
the LORD,
"That My people are taken away for
nothing?
Those who rule over them
*Make them wail," says the LORD,
"And My name *is* [a]blasphemed continually
every day.

6 Therefore My people shall know My
name;
Therefore *they shall know* in that day
That I *am* He who speaks:
'Behold, *it is* I.' "

7 [a]How beautiful upon the mountains
Are the feet of him who brings good news,
Who proclaims peace,
Who brings glad tidings of good *things,*
Who proclaims salvation,
Who says to Zion,
[b]"Your God reigns!"

8 Your watchmen shall lift up *their* voices,
With their voices they shall sing together;
For they shall see eye to eye
When the LORD brings back Zion.

9 Break forth into joy, sing together,
You waste places of Jerusalem!
For the LORD has comforted His people,
He has redeemed Jerusalem.

10 [a]The LORD has made bare His holy arm
In the eyes of [b]all the nations;
And all the ends of the earth shall see
The salvation of our God.

11 [a]Depart! Depart! Go out from there,
Touch no unclean *thing;*
Go out from the midst of her,
[b]Be clean,
You who bear the vessels of the LORD.

12 For [a]you shall not go out with haste,
Nor go by flight;
[b]For the LORD will go before you,
[c]And the God of Israel *will be* your rear
guard.

The Sin-Bearing Servant

13 Behold, [a]My Servant shall deal prudently;
[b]He shall be exalted and extolled and be
very high.

14 Just as many were astonished at you,
So His [a]visage was marred more than any
man,
And His form more than the sons of men;

15 [a]So shall He *sprinkle many nations.
Kings shall shut their mouths at Him;
For [b]what had not been told them they
shall see,
And what they had not heard they shall
consider.

53 Who [a]has believed our report?
And to whom has the arm of the LORD
been revealed?

2 For He shall grow up before Him as a
tender plant,
And as a root out of dry ground.
He has no form or comeliness;
And when we see Him,
There is no beauty that we should desire
Him.

KJV

3 [a]He is despised and rejected of men; a
man of sorrows, and [b]acquainted with grief: and
we hid as it were *our* faces from him; he was despised, and [c]we esteemed him not.
4 Surely [a]he hath borne our griefs, and carried our sorrows: yet we did esteem him stricken,
smitten of God, and afflicted.
5 But he *was* [a]wounded for our transgressions, *he was* bruised for our iniquities: the chastisement of our peace *was* upon him; and with
his [b]stripes we are healed.
6 All we like sheep have gone astray; we
have turned every one to his own way; and the
LORD hath laid on him the iniquity of us all.
7 He was oppressed, and he was afflicted,
yet [a]he opened not his mouth: [b]he is brought as
a lamb to the slaughter, and as a sheep before
her shearers is dumb, so he openeth not his
mouth.
8 He was [a]taken from prison and from judgment: and who shall declare his generation? for
[b]he was cut off out of the land of the living: for
the transgression of my people was he stricken.
9 [a]And he made his grave with the wicked,
and with the rich in his death; because he had
done no violence, neither *was any* [b]deceit in his
mouth.
10 Yet it pleased the LORD to bruise him; he
hath put *him* to grief: when thou shalt make his
soul [a]an offering for sin, he shall see *his* seed, he
shall prolong *his* days, and the pleasure of the
LORD shall prosper in his hand.
11 He shall see of the travail of his soul, *and*
shall be satisfied: by his knowledge shall [a]my
righteous [b]servant [c]justify many; for he shall bear
their iniquities.
12 [a]Therefore will I divide him *a portion* with
the great, [b]and he shall divide the spoil with the
strong; because he hath [c]poured out his soul unto
death: and he was [d]numbered with the transgressors; and he bare the sin of many, and [e]made intercession for the transgressors.

A Perpetual Covenant of Peace

54 Sing, O [a]barren, thou *that* didst not bear;
break forth into singing, and cry aloud,
thou *that* didst not travail with child: for more
are the children of the desolate than the children
of the married wife, saith the LORD.
2 [a]Enlarge the place of thy tent, and let
them stretch forth the curtains of thine habitations: spare not, lengthen thy cords, and
strengthen thy stakes;

3 [a]Ps. 22:6; [Is. 49:7; Matt. 27:30, 31; Luke 18:31–33; 23:18] [b][Heb. 4:15] [c][John 1:10, 11]
4 [a][Matt. 8:17; Heb. 9:28; 1 Pet. 2:24]
5 [a][Is. 53:10; Rom. 4:25; 1 Cor. 15:3, 4] [b][1 Pet. 2:24, 25]
7 [a]Matt. 26:63; 27:12–14; Mark 14:61; 15:5; Luke 23:9; John 19:9 [b]Acts 8:32, 33; Rev. 5:6
8 [a]Matt. 27:11–26; Luke 23:1–25 [b][Dan. 9:26]
9 [a]Matt. 27:57–60; Luke 23:33 [b]1 Pet. 2:22; 1 John 3:5
10 [a]John 1:29; Acts 2:24; [2 Cor. 5:21]
11 [a][1 John 2:1] [b]Is. 42:1 [c][Acts 13:38, 39; Rom. 5:15–18]
12 [a]Ps. 2:8 [b]Col. 2:15 [c]Is. 50:6; [Rom. 3:25] [d]Matt. 27:38; Mark 15:28; Luke 22:37; 2 Cor. 5:21 [e]Luke 23:34

CHAPTER 54
1 [a]Gal. 4:27
2 [a]Is. 49:19, 20

*

53:9 Lit. *he* or *He*
53:11 So with MT, Tg., Vg.; DSS, LXX *From the labor of His soul He shall see light*

NKJV

3 [a]He is despised and rejected by men,
A Man of sorrows and [b]acquainted with grief.
And we hid, as it were, *our* faces from Him;
He was despised, and [c]we did not esteem Him.

4 Surely [a]He has borne our griefs
And carried our sorrows;
Yet we esteemed Him stricken,
Smitten by God, and afflicted.
5 But He *was* [a]wounded for our transgressions,
He was bruised for our iniquities;
The chastisement for our peace *was* upon Him,
And by His [b]stripes we are healed.
6 All we like sheep have gone astray;
We have turned, every one, to his own way;
And the LORD has laid on Him the iniquity of us all.

7 He was oppressed and He was afflicted,
Yet [a]He opened not His mouth;
[b]He was led as a lamb to the slaughter,
And as a sheep before its shearers is silent,
So He opened not His mouth.
8 He was [a]taken from prison and from judgment,
And who will declare His generation?
For [b]He was cut off from the land of the living;
For the transgressions of My people He was stricken.
9 [a]And *they made His grave with the wicked—
But with the rich at His death,
Because He had done no violence,
Nor *was any* [b]deceit in His mouth.

10 Yet it pleased the LORD to bruise Him;
He has put *Him* to grief.
When You make His soul [a]an offering for sin,
He shall see *His* seed, He shall prolong *His* days,
And the pleasure of the LORD shall prosper in His hand.
11 *He shall see the labor of His soul, *and* be satisfied.
By His knowledge [a]My righteous [b]Servant shall [c]justify many,
For He shall bear their iniquities.
12 [a]Therefore I will divide Him a portion with the great,
[b]And He shall divide the spoil with the strong,
Because He [c]poured out His soul unto death,
And He was [d]numbered with the transgressors,
And He bore the sin of many,
And [e]made intercession for the transgressors.

A Perpetual Covenant of Peace

54 "Sing, O [a]barren,
You *who* have not borne!
Break forth into singing, and cry aloud,
You *who* have not labored with child!
For more *are* the children of the desolate
Than the children of the married woman,"
says the LORD.
2 "Enlarge[a] the place of your tent,
And let them stretch out the curtains of your dwellings;
Do not spare;
Lengthen your cords,
And strengthen your stakes.

KJV

3 For thou shalt break forth on the right
hand and on the left; and thy seed shall [a]inherit
the Gentiles, and make the desolate cities to be
inhabited.
4 [a]Fear not; for thou shalt not be ashamed:
neither be thou confounded; for thou shalt not be
put to shame: for thou shalt forget the shame of
thy youth, and shalt not remember the reproach
of thy widowhood any more.
5 [a]For thy Maker *is* thine husband; the LORD
of hosts *is* his name; and thy Redeemer the Holy
One of Israel; [b]The God of the whole earth shall
he be called.
6 For the LORD [a]hath called thee as a woman
forsaken and grieved in spirit, and a wife of youth,
when thou wast refused, saith thy God.
7 [a]For a small moment have I forsaken thee;
but with great mercies will [b]I gather thee.
8 In a little wrath I hid my face from thee
for a moment; [a]but with everlasting kindness will
I have mercy on thee, saith the LORD thy
Redeemer.
9 For this *is as* the waters of [a]Noah unto
me: for *as* I have sworn that the waters of Noah
should no more go over the earth; so have I sworn
that I would not be wroth with [b]thee, nor rebuke
thee.
10 For [a]the mountains shall depart, and the
hills be removed; [b]but my kindness shall not depart from thee, neither shall the covenant of my
peace be removed, saith the LORD that hath mercy
on thee.
11 O thou afflicted, tossed with tempest, *and*
not comforted, behold, I will lay thy stones with
[a]fair colours, and lay thy foundations with
sapphires.
12 And I will make thy windows of agates,
and thy gates of carbuncles, and all thy borders
of pleasant stones.
13 And all thy children *shall be* [a]taught of
the LORD; and [b]great *shall be* the peace of thy
children.
14 In righteousness shalt thou be established:
thou shalt be far from oppression; for thou shalt
not fear: and from terror; for it shall not come
near thee.
15 Behold, they shall surely gather together,
but not by me: whosoever shall gather together
against thee shall [a]fall for thy sake.
16 Behold, I have created the smith that
bloweth the coals in the fire, and that bringeth
forth an instrument for his work; and I have created the waster to destroy.
17 No weapon that is formed against thee
shall [a]prosper; and every tongue *that* shall rise
against thee in judgment thou shalt condemn.

3 [a]Is. 14:2; 49:22, 23; 60:9
4 [a]Is. 41:10
5 [a]Jer. 3:14; Hos. 2:19 [b]Zech. 14:9; Rom. 3:29
6 [a]Is. 62:4
7 [a]Ps. 30:5; Is. 26:20; 60:10; 2 Cor. 4:17 [b][Is. 43:5; 56:8]
8 [a]Is. 55:3; Jer. 31:3
9 [a]Gen. 8:21; 9:11; [2 Pet. 3:6, 7] [b]Is. 12:1; Ezek. 39:29
10 [a]Ps. 46:2; Is. 51:6; Matt. 5:18 [b]2 Sam. 23:5; Ps. 89:33, 34; Is. 55:3; 59:21; 61:8
11 [a]1 Chr. 29:2; Job 28:16; Rev. 21:18, 19
13 [a]Jer. 31:34; [John 6:45; 1 Cor. 2:10]; 1 Thess. 4:9; [1 John 2:20] [b]Ps. 119:165
15 [a]Is. 41:11–16
17 [a]Is. 17:12–14; 29:8

NKJV

3 For you shall expand to the right and to
the left,
And your descendants will [a]inherit the
nations,
And make the desolate cities inhabited.

4 "Do[a] not fear, for you will not be ashamed;
Neither be disgraced, for you will not be
put to shame;
For you will forget the shame of your
youth,
And will not remember the reproach of
your widowhood anymore.
5 [a]For your Maker *is* your husband,
The LORD of hosts *is* His name;
And your Redeemer *is* the Holy One of
Israel;
He is called [b]the God of the whole
earth.
6 For the LORD [a]has called you
Like a woman forsaken and grieved in
spirit,
Like a youthful wife when you were
refused,"
Says your God.
7 "For[a] a mere moment I have forsaken
you,
But with great mercies [b]I will gather you.
8 With a little wrath I hid My face from you
for a moment;
[a]But with everlasting kindness I will have
mercy on you,"
Says the LORD, your Redeemer.

9 "For this *is* like the waters of [a]Noah to Me;
For as I have sworn
That the waters of Noah would no longer
cover the earth,
So have I sworn
That I would not be angry with [b]you, nor
rebuke you.
10 For [a]the mountains shall depart
And the hills be removed,
[b]But My kindness shall not depart from
you,
Nor shall My covenant of peace be
removed,"
Says the LORD, who has mercy on you.

11 "O you afflicted one,
Tossed with tempest, *and* not comforted,
Behold, I will lay your stones with
[a]colorful gems,
And lay your foundations with
sapphires.
12 I will make your pinnacles of rubies,
Your gates of crystal,
And all your walls of precious stones.
13 All your children *shall be* [a]taught by the
LORD,
And [b]great *shall be* the peace of your
children.
14 In righteousness you shall be established;
You shall be far from oppression, for you
shall not fear;
And from terror, for it shall not come near
you.
15 Indeed they shall surely assemble, *but* not
because of Me.
Whoever assembles against you shall [a]fall
for your sake.

16 "Behold, I have created the blacksmith
Who blows the coals in the fire,
Who brings forth an instrument for his
work;
And I have created the spoiler to
destroy.
17 No weapon formed against you shall
[a]prosper,
And every tongue *which* rises against you
in judgment

KJV

This *is* the heritage of the servants of the
LORD, [b]and their righteousness *is* of me, saith the
LORD.

An Invitation to Abundant Life

55 Ho, [a]every one that thirsteth, come ye to
the waters, and he that hath no money;
[b]come ye, buy, and eat; yea, come, buy wine and
milk without money and without price.
2 Wherefore do ye spend money for *that
which is* not bread? and your labour for *that
which* satisfieth not? hearken diligently unto me,
and eat ye *that which is* good, and let your soul
delight itself in fatness.
3 Incline your ear, and [a]come unto me: hear,
and your soul shall live; [b]and I will make an everlasting covenant with you, *even* the [c]sure mercies
of David.
4 Behold, I have given him *for* [a]a witness
to the people, [b]a leader and commander to the
people.
5 [a]Behold, thou shalt call a nation *that* thou
knowest not, [b]and nations *that* knew not thee
shall run unto thee because of the LORD thy God,
and for the Holy One of Israel; [c]for he hath glorified thee.
6 [a]Seek ye the LORD while he may be
[b]found, call ye upon him while he is near:
7 [a]Let the wicked forsake his way, and the
unrighteous man [b]his thoughts: and let him return
unto the LORD, [c]and he will have mercy upon him;
and to our God, for he will abundantly pardon.
8 [a]For my thoughts *are* not your thoughts,
neither *are* your ways my ways, saith the LORD.
9 [a]For *as* the heavens are higher than the
earth, so are my ways higher than your ways, and
my thoughts than your thoughts.
10 For [a]as the rain cometh down, and the
snow from heaven, and returneth not thither, but
watereth the earth, and maketh it bring forth and
bud, that it may give seed to the sower, and bread
to the eater:
11 [a]So shall my word be that goeth forth out
of my mouth: it shall not return unto me void,
but it shall accomplish that which I please, and
it shall [b]prosper *in the thing* whereto I sent it.
12 [a]For ye shall go out with joy, and be led
forth with peace: the mountains and the hills shall
[b]break forth before you into singing, and [c]all the
trees of the field shall clap *their* hands.
13 [a]Instead of [b]the thorn shall come up the
fir tree, and instead of the brier shall come up
the myrtle tree: and it shall be to the LORD [c]for a
name, for an everlasting sign *that* shall not be
cut off.

17 [b]Is. 45:24, 25; 54:14

CHAPTER 55

1 [a][Matt. 5:6; John 4:14; 7:37; Rev. 21:6; 22:17] [b][Matt. 13:44; Rev. 3:18]
3 [a]Matt. 11:28 [b]Is. 54:8; 61:8; Jer. 32:40 [c]2 Sam. 7:8; Ps. 89:28; [Acts 13:34]
4 [a][John 18:37; Rev. 1:5] [b][Jer. 30:9; Ezek. 34:23; Dan. 9:25]
5 [a]Is. 52:15; Eph. 2:11, 12 [b]Is. 60:5 [c]Is. 60:9
6 [a]Matt. 5:25; 25:11; John 7:34; 8:21; 2 Cor. 6:2; [Heb. 3:13] [b]Ps. 32:6; Is. 49:8
7 [a]Is. 1:16 [b]Is. 59:7; Zech. 8:17 [c]Ps. 130:7; Jer. 3:12
8 [a]2 Sam. 7:19
9 [a]Ps. 103:11
10 [a]Deut. 32:2
11 [a]Is. 45:23; Matt. 24:35 [b]Is. 46:9–11
12 [a]Is. 35:10 [b]Ps. 98:8 [c]1 Chr. 16:33
13 [a]Is. 41:19 [b]Mic. 7:4 [c]Jer. 13:11

NKJV

You shall condemn.
This *is* the heritage of the servants of the
LORD,
[b]And their righteousness *is* from Me,"
Says the LORD.

An Invitation to Abundant Life

55 "Ho! [a]Everyone who thirsts,
Come to the waters;
And you who have no money,
[b]Come, buy and eat.
Yes, come, buy wine and milk
Without money and without price.
2 Why do you spend money for *what is* not
bread,
And your wages for *what* does not satisfy?
Listen carefully to Me, and eat *what is*
good,
And let your soul delight itself in
abundance.
3 Incline your ear, and [a]come to Me.
Hear, and your soul shall live;
[b]And I will make an everlasting covenant
with you—
The [c]sure mercies of David.
4 Indeed I have given him *as* [a]a witness to
the people,
[b]A leader and commander for the people.
5 [a]Surely you shall call a nation you do not
know,
[b]And nations *who* do not know you shall
run to you,
Because of the LORD your God,
And the Holy One of Israel;
[c]For He has glorified you."

6 [a]Seek the LORD while He may be [b]found,
Call upon Him while He is near.
7 [a]Let the wicked forsake his way,
And the unrighteous man [b]his thoughts;
Let him return to the LORD,
[c]And He will have mercy on him;
And to our God,
For He will abundantly pardon.

8 "For[a] My thoughts *are* not your thoughts,
Nor *are* your ways My ways," says the
LORD.
9 "For[a] *as* the heavens are higher than the
earth,
So are My ways higher than your
ways,
And My thoughts than your thoughts.

10 "For [a]as the rain comes down, and the
snow from heaven,
And do not return there,
But water the earth,
And make it bring forth and bud,
That it may give seed to the sower
And bread to the eater,
11 [a]So shall My word be that goes forth from
My mouth;
It shall not return to Me void,
But it shall accomplish what I please,
And it shall [b]prosper *in the thing* for
which I sent it.

12 "For[a] you shall go out with joy,
And be led out with peace;
The mountains and the hills
Shall [b]break forth into singing before
you,
And [c]all the trees of the field shall clap
their hands.
13 [a]Instead of [b]the thorn shall come up the
cypress tree,
And instead of the brier shall come up the
myrtle tree;
And it shall be to the LORD [c]for a name,
For an everlasting sign *that* shall not be
cut off."

KJV

Salvation for the Gentiles

56 Thus saith the LORD, Keep ye judgment, and do justice: [a]for my salvation *is* near to come, and my righteousness to be revealed.

2 Blessed *is* the man *that* doeth this, and the son of man *that* layeth hold on it; [a]that keepeth the sabbath from polluting it, and keepeth his hand from doing any evil.

3 Neither let [a]the son of the stranger, that hath joined himself to the LORD, speak, saying, The LORD hath utterly separated me from his people: neither let the [b]eunuch say, Behold, I *am* a dry tree.

4 For thus saith the LORD unto the eunuchs that keep my sabbaths, and choose *the things* that please me, and take hold of my covenant;

5 Even unto them will I give in [a]mine house and within my walls a place [b]and a name better than of sons and of daughters: I will give them an everlasting name, that shall not be cut off.

6 Also the sons of the stranger, that join themselves to the LORD, to serve him, and to love the name of the LORD, to be his servants, every one that keepeth the sabbath from polluting it, and taketh hold of my covenant;

7 Even them will I [a]bring to my holy mountain, and make them joyful in my [b]house of prayer: [c]their burnt offerings and their sacrifices *shall be* [d]accepted upon mine altar; for [e]mine house shall be called an house of prayer [f]for all people.

8 The Lord GOD [a]which gathereth the outcasts of Israel saith, [b]Yet will I gather *others* to him, beside those that are gathered unto him.

Israel's Irresponsible Leaders

9 [a]All ye beasts of the field, come to devour, *yea,* all ye beasts in the forest.

10 His watchmen *are* [a]blind: they are all ignorant, [b]they *are* all dumb dogs, they cannot bark; sleeping, lying down, loving to slumber.

11 Yea, *they are* [a]greedy dogs *which* [b]can never have enough, and they *are* shepherds *that* cannot understand: they all look to their own way, every one for his gain, from his quarter.

12 Come ye, *say they,* I will fetch wine, and we will fill ourselves with strong [a]drink; [b]and to morrow shall be [c]as this day, *and* much more abundant.

Israel's Futile Idolatry

57 The righteous perisheth, and no man layeth *it* to heart: and [a]merciful men *are* taken away, [b]none considering that the righteous is taken away from the evil *to come.*

2 He shall enter into peace: they shall rest in [a]their beds, *each one* walking *in* his uprightness.

CHAPTER 56

1 [a]Is. 46:13; Matt. 3:2; 4:17; Rom. 13:11, 12
2 [a]Ex. 20:8–11; 31:13–17; Is. 58:13; Jer. 17:21, 22; Ezek. 20:12, 20
3 [a]Is. 14:1; [Eph. 2:12–19] [b]Deut. 23:1; Jer. 38:7; Acts 8:27
5 [a]1 Tim. 3:15 [b][1 John 3:1, 2]
7 [a][Is. 2:2, 3; 60:11; Mic. 4:1, 2] [b]Matt. 21:13; Mark 11:17; Luke 19:46 [c][Rom. 12:1; Heb. 13:15; 1 Pet. 2:5] [d]Is. 60:7 [e]Matt. 21:13 [f][Mal. 1:11]
8 [a]Ps. 147:2; Is. 11:12; 27:12; 54:7 [b]Is. 60:3–11; 66:18–21; [John 10:16]
9 [a]Jer. 12:9
10 [a]Matt. 15:14 [b]Phil. 3:2
11 [a]Is. 28:7; Ezek. 13:19; [Mic. 3:5, 11] [b]Ezek. 34:2–10
12 [a]Is. 28:7 [b]Ps. 10:6; Prov. 23:35; Is. 22:13; Luke 12:19; 1 Cor. 15:32 [c]2 Pet. 3:4

CHAPTER 57

1 [a]Ps. 12:1 [b]1 Kin. 14:13
2 [a]2 Chr. 16:14

*56:5 Lit. *him*

NKJV

Salvation for the Gentiles

56 Thus says the LORD:

"Keep justice, and do righteousness,
[a]For My salvation *is* about to come,
And My righteousness to be revealed.
2 Blessed *is* the man *who* does this,
And the son of man *who* lays hold on it;
[a]Who keeps from defiling the Sabbath,
And keeps his hand from doing any evil."

3 Do not let [a]the son of the foreigner
Who has joined himself to the LORD
Speak, saying,
"The LORD has utterly separated me from His people";
Nor let the [b]eunuch say,
"Here I am, a dry tree."
4 For thus says the LORD:
"To the eunuchs who keep My Sabbaths,
And choose what pleases Me,
And hold fast My covenant,
5 Even to them I will give in [a]My house
And within My walls a place [b]and a name
Better than that of sons and daughters;
I will give *them an everlasting name
That shall not be cut off.

6 "Also the sons of the foreigner
Who join themselves to the LORD, to serve Him,
And to love the name of the LORD, to be His servants—
Everyone who keeps from defiling the Sabbath,
And holds fast My covenant—
7 Even them I will [a]bring to My holy mountain,
And make them joyful in My [b]house of prayer.
[c]Their burnt offerings and their sacrifices
Will be [d]accepted on My altar;
For [e]My house shall be called a house of prayer [f]for all nations."
8 The Lord GOD, [a]who gathers the outcasts of Israel, says,
[b]"Yet I will gather to him
Others besides those who are gathered to him."

Israel's Irresponsible Leaders

9 [a]All you beasts of the field, come to devour,
All you beasts in the forest.
10 His watchmen *are* [a]blind,
They are all ignorant;
[b]They *are* all dumb dogs,
They cannot bark;
Sleeping, lying down, loving to slumber.
11 Yes, *they are* [a]greedy dogs
Which [b]never have enough.
And they *are* shepherds
Who cannot understand;
They all look to their own way,
Every one for his own gain,
From his *own* territory.
12 "Come," *one says,* "I will bring wine,
And we will fill ourselves with intoxicating [a]drink;
[b]Tomorrow will be [c]as today,
And much more abundant."

Israel's Futile Idolatry

57 The righteous perishes,
And no man takes *it* to heart;
[a]Merciful men *are* taken away,
[b]While no one considers
That the righteous is taken away from evil.
2 He shall enter into peace;
They shall rest in [a]their beds,
Each one walking *in* his uprightness.

KJV

3 But draw near hither, [a]ye sons of the sorceress, the seed of the adulterer and the whore.

4 Against whom do ye sport yourselves? against whom make ye a wide mouth, *and* draw out the tongue? *are* ye not children of transgression, a seed of falsehood,

5 Enflaming yourselves with idols [a]under every green tree, [b]slaying the children in the valleys under the clifts of the rocks?

6 Among the smooth [a]*stones* of the stream *is* thy portion; they, they *are* thy lot: even to them hast thou poured a drink offering, thou hast offered a meat offering. Should I receive comfort in [b]these?

7 [a]Upon a lofty and high mountain hast thou set [b]thy bed: even thither wentest thou up to offer sacrifice.

8 Behind the doors also and the posts hast thou set up thy remembrance: for thou hast discovered *thyself to another* than me, and art gone up; thou hast enlarged thy bed, and made thee *a covenant* with them; [a]thou lovedst their bed where thou sawest *it*.

9 And [a]thou wentest to the king with ointment, and didst increase thy perfumes, and didst send thy [b]messengers far off, and didst debase *thyself even* unto hell.

10 Thou art wearied in the greatness of thy way; [a]*yet* saidst thou not, There is no hope: thou hast found the life of thine hand; therefore thou wast not grieved.

11 And [a]of whom hast thou been afraid or feared, that thou hast lied, and hast not remembered me, nor laid *it* to thy heart? [b]have not I held my peace even of old, and thou fearest me not?

12 I will declare thy righteousness, and thy works; for they shall not profit thee.

13 When thou criest, let thy companies deliver thee; but the wind shall carry them all away; vanity shall take *them:* but he that putteth his trust in me shall possess the land, and shall inherit my holy mountain;

Healing for the Backslider

14 And shall say, [a]Cast ye up, cast ye up, prepare the way, take up the stumblingblock out of the way of my people.

15 For thus saith the high and lofty One that inhabiteth eternity, [a]whose name *is* Holy; [b]I dwell in the high and holy *place,* [c]with him also *that is* of a contrite and humble spirit, [d]to revive the spirit of the humble, and to revive the heart of the contrite ones.

16 [a]For I will not contend for ever, neither will I be always wroth: for the spirit should fail before me, and the souls [b]*which* I have made.

3 [a]Is. 1:4; Matt. 16:4
5 [a]2 Kin. 16:4 [b]2 Kin. 23:10; Ps. 106:37, 38; Jer. 7:31; Ezek. 16:20
6 [a]Jer. 3:9; Hab. 2:19 [b]Jer. 5:9, 29; 9:9
7 [a]Jer. 3:6; Ezek. 16:16 [b]Ezek. 23:41
8 [a]Ezek. 16:26
9 [a]Hos. 7:11 [b]Ezek. 23:16, 40
10 [a]Jer. 2:25; 18:12
11 [a]Prov. 29:25; Is. 51:12, 13 [b]Ps. 50:21; Eccl. 8:11; Is. 42:14
14 [a]Is. 40:3; 62:10; Jer. 18:15
15 [a]Job 6:10; Luke 1:49 [b]Ps. 68:35; Zech. 2:13 [c]Ps. 34:18; 51:17; Is. 66:2 [d]Ps. 147:3; Is. 61:1–3
16 [a]Ps. 85:5; 103:9; [Mic. 7:18] [b]Num. 16:22; Job 34:14; Heb. 12:9

*________

57:8 Lit. *hand,* a euphemism

NKJV

3 "But come here,
[a]You sons of the sorceress,
You offspring of the adulterer and the harlot!
4 Whom do you ridicule?
Against whom do you make a wide mouth
And stick out the tongue?
Are you not children of transgression,
Offspring of falsehood,
5 Inflaming yourselves with gods [a]under every green tree,
[b]Slaying the children in the valleys,
Under the clefts of the rocks?
6 Among the smooth [a]*stones* of the stream
Is your portion;
They, they, *are* your lot!
Even to them you have poured a drink offering,
You have offered a grain offering.
Should I receive comfort in [b]these?

7 "On[a] a lofty and high mountain
You have set [b]your bed;
Even there you went up
To offer sacrifice.
8 Also behind the doors and their posts
You have set up your remembrance;
For you have uncovered yourself *to those other* than Me,
And have gone up to them;
You have enlarged your bed
And made *a covenant* with them;
[a]You have loved their bed,
Where you saw *their* *nudity.
9 [a]You went to the king with ointment,
And increased your perfumes;
You sent your [b]messengers far off,
And *even* descended to Sheol.
10 You are wearied in the length of your way;
[a]*Yet* you did not say, 'There is no hope.'
You have found the life of your hand;
Therefore you were not grieved.

11 "And [a]of whom have you been afraid, or feared,
That you have lied
And not remembered Me,
Nor taken *it* to your heart?
Is it not because [b]I have held My peace from of old
That you do not fear Me?
12 I will declare your righteousness
And your works,
For they will not profit you.
13 When you cry out,
Let your collection *of idols* deliver you.
But the wind will carry them all away,
A breath will take *them.*
But he who puts his trust in Me shall possess the land,
And shall inherit My holy mountain."

Healing for the Backslider

14 And one shall say,
[a]"Heap it up! Heap it up!
Prepare the way,
Take the stumbling block out of the way of My people."

15 For thus says the High and Lofty One
Who inhabits eternity, [a]whose name *is* Holy:
[b]"I dwell in the high and holy *place,*
[c]With him *who* has a contrite and humble spirit,
[d]To revive the spirit of the humble,
And to revive the heart of the contrite ones.
16 [a]For I will not contend forever,
Nor will I always be angry;
For the spirit would fail before Me,
And the souls [b]*which* I have made.

KJV

17 For the iniquity of [a]his covetousness was
I wroth, and smote him: [b]I hid me, and was wroth,
[c]and he went on frowardly in the way of his heart.
18 I have seen his ways, and [a]will heal him:
I will lead him also, and restore comforts unto
him and to [b]his mourners.
19 I create [a]the fruit of the lips; Peace, peace
[b]to *him that is* far off, and to *him that is* near,
saith the LORD; and I will heal him.
20 [a]But the wicked *are* like the troubled sea,
when it cannot rest, whose waters cast up mire
and dirt.
21 [a]*There is* no peace, saith my God, to the
wicked.

17 [a]Is. 2:7; 56:11; Jer. 6:13 [b]Is. 8:17; 45:15; 59:2 [c]Is. 9:13
18 [a]Jer. 3:22 [b]Is. 61:2
19 [a]Is. 6:7; 51:16; 59:21; Heb. 13:15 [b]Acts 2:39; Eph. 2:17
20 [a]Job 15:20; Prov. 4:16; Jude 13
21 [a]Is. 48:22

NKJV

17 For the iniquity of [a]his covetousness
I was angry and struck him;
[b]I hid and was angry,
[c]And he went on backsliding in the way
of his heart.
18 I have seen his ways, and [a]will heal him;
I will also lead him,
And restore comforts to him
And to [b]his mourners.

19 "I create [a]the fruit of the lips:
Peace, peace [b]to *him who is* far off and
to *him who is* near,"
Says the LORD,
"And I will heal him."
20 [a]But the wicked *are* like the troubled sea,
When it cannot rest,
Whose waters cast up mire and dirt.

21 "*There*[a] *is* no peace,"
Says my God, "for the wicked."

Fasting that Pleases God

58 Cry aloud, spare not, lift up thy voice like
a trumpet, and [a]shew my people their
transgression, and the house of Jacob their sins.
2 Yet they seek me daily, and delight to
know my ways, as a nation that did righteousness,
and forsook not the ordinance of their God: they
ask of me the ordinances of justice; they take delight in approaching to God.
3 [a]Wherefore have we fasted, *say they,* and
thou seest not? *wherefore* have we [b]afflicted our
soul, and thou takest no knowledge? Behold, in
the day of your fast ye find pleasure, and exact
all your labours.
4 [a]Behold, ye fast for strife and debate, and
to smite with the fist of wickedness: ye shall not
fast as *ye do this* day, to make your voice to be
heard on high.
5 Is it [a]such a fast that I have chosen? [b]a
day for a man to afflict his soul? *is it* to bow down
his head as a bulrush, and [c]to spread sackcloth
and ashes *under him?* wilt thou call this a fast,
and an acceptable day to the LORD?
6 *Is* not this the fast that I have chosen? to
[a]loose the bands of wickedness, [b]to undo the
heavy burdens, and [c]to let the oppressed go free,
and that ye break every yoke?
7 *Is it* not [a]to deal thy bread to the hungry,
and that thou bring the poor that are cast out to
thy house? [b]when thou seest the naked, that thou
cover him; and that thou hide not thyself from
[c]thine own flesh?
8 [a]Then shall thy light break forth as the
morning, and thine health shall spring forth
speedily: and thy righteousness shall go before
thee; [b]the glory of the LORD shall be thy rereward.
9 Then shalt thou call, and the LORD shall
answer; thou shalt cry, and he shall say, Here I
am. If thou take away from the midst of thee the
yoke, the putting forth of the finger, and [a]speak-
ing vanity;

CHAPTER 58

1 [a]Mic. 3:8
3 [a]Mal. 3:13–18; Luke 18:12 [b]Lev. 16:29; 23:27
4 [a]1 Kin. 21:9
5 [a]Zech. 7:5 [b]Lev. 16:29 [c]Esth. 4:3; Job 2:8; Dan. 9:3
6 [a]Luke 4:18, 19 [b]Neh. 5:10–12 [c]Jer. 34:9
7 [a]Ezek. 18:7; Matt. 25:35 [b]Job 31:19–22; James 2:14–17 [c]Gen. 29:14; Neh. 5:5
8 [a]Job 11:17 [b]Ex. 14:19; Is. 52:12
9 [a]Ps. 12:2; Is. 59:13

Fasting that Pleases God

58 "Cry aloud, spare not;
Lift up your voice like a trumpet;
[a]Tell My people their transgression,
And the house of Jacob their sins.
2 Yet they seek Me daily,
And delight to know My ways,
As a nation that did righteousness,
And did not forsake the ordinance of their
God.
They ask of Me the ordinances of justice;
They take delight in approaching God.
3 'Why[a] have we fasted,' *they say,* 'and You
have not seen?
Why have we [b]afflicted our souls, and You
take no notice?'

"In fact, in the day of your fast you find
pleasure,
And exploit all your laborers.
4 [a]Indeed you fast for strife and debate,
And to strike with the fist of wickedness.
You will not fast as *you do* this day,
To make your voice heard on high.
5 Is [a]it a fast that I have chosen,
[b]A day for a man to afflict his soul?
Is it to bow down his head like a
bulrush,
And [c]to spread out sackcloth and ashes?
Would you call this a fast,
And an acceptable day to the LORD?

6 "*Is* this not the fast that I have chosen:
To [a]loose the bonds of wickedness,
[b]To undo the heavy burdens,
[c]To let the oppressed go free,
And that you break every yoke?
7 *Is it* not [a]to share your bread with the
hungry,
And that you bring to your house the poor
who are cast out;
[b]When you see the naked, that you cover
him,
And not hide yourself from [c]your own
flesh?
8 [a]Then your light shall break forth like the
morning,
Your healing shall spring forth speedily,
And your righteousness shall go before
you;
[b]The glory of the LORD shall be your rear
guard.
9 Then you shall call, and the LORD will
answer;
You shall cry, and He will say, 'Here I *am.*'

"If you take away the yoke from your
midst,
The pointing of the finger, and [a]speaking
wickedness,

KJV

10 And *if* thou draw out thy soul to the hungry, and satisfy the afflicted soul; then shall thy light rise in obscurity, and thy darkness *be* as the noon day:

11 And the LORD shall guide thee continually, and satisfy thy soul in drought, and make fat thy bones: and thou shalt be like a watered garden, and like a spring of water, whose waters fail not.

12 And *they that shall be* of thee [a]shall build the old waste places: thou shalt raise up the foundations of many generations; and thou shalt be called, The repairer of the breach, The restorer of paths to dwell in.

13 If [a]thou turn away thy foot from the sabbath, *from* doing thy pleasure on my holy day; and call the sabbath a delight, the holy of the LORD, honourable; and shalt honour him, not doing thine own ways, nor finding thine own pleasure, nor speaking *thine own* words:

14 [a]Then shalt thou delight thyself in the LORD; and I will cause thee to [b]ride upon the high places of the earth, and feed thee with the heritage of Jacob thy father: [c]for the mouth of the LORD hath spoken *it*.

Separated from God

59 Behold, the LORD's hand is not [a]shortened, that it cannot save; neither his ear heavy, that it cannot hear:

2 But your iniquities have separated between you and your God, and your sins have hid *his* face from you, that he will [a]not hear.

3 For [a]your hands are defiled with blood, and your fingers with iniquity; your lips have spoken lies, your tongue hath muttered perverseness.

4 None calleth for justice, nor *any* pleadeth for truth: they trust in [a]vanity, and speak lies; [b]they conceive mischief, and bring forth iniquity.

5 They hatch cockatrice' eggs, and weave the spider's web: he that eateth of their eggs dieth, and that which is crushed breaketh out into a viper.

6 [a]Their webs shall not become garments, neither shall they cover themselves with their works: their works *are* works of iniquity, and the act of violence *is* in their hands.

7 [a]Their feet run to evil, and they make haste to shed [b]innocent blood: [c]their thoughts *are* thoughts of iniquity; wasting and [d]destruction *are* in their paths.

8 The way of [a]peace they know not; and *there is* no judgment in their goings: [b]they have made them crooked paths: whosoever goeth therein shall not know peace.

12 [a]Is. 61:4
13 [a]Ex. 31:16, 17; 35:2, 3; Is. 56:2, 4, 6; Jer. 17:21–27
14 [a]Job 22:26; Is. 61:10 [b]Deut. 32:13; 33:29; Is. 33:16; Hab. 3:19 [c]Is. 1:20; 40:5; Mic. 4:4

CHAPTER 59

1 [a]Num. 11:23; Is. 50:2; Jer. 32:17
2 [a]Is. 1:15
3 [a]Is. 1:15, 21; Jer. 2:30, 34; Ezek. 7:23; Hos. 4:2
4 [a]Is. 30:12; Jer. 7:4 [b]Job 15:35; Ps. 7:14; Is. 33:11
6 [a]Job 8:14
7 [a]Prov. 1:16; Rom. 3:15 [b]Prov. 6:17 [c]Is. 55:7 [d]Rom. 3:16, 17
8 [a]Is. 57:20, 21 [b]Ps. 125:5; Prov. 2:15

NKJV

10 *If* you extend your soul to the hungry
And satisfy the afflicted soul,
Then your light shall dawn in the darkness,
And your darkness shall *be* as the noonday.
11 The LORD will guide you continually,
And satisfy your soul in drought,
And strengthen your bones;
You shall be like a watered garden,
And like a spring of water, whose waters do not fail.
12 Those from among you
[a]Shall build the old waste places;
You shall raise up the foundations of many generations;
And you shall be called the Repairer of the Breach,
The Restorer of Streets to Dwell In.

13 "If [a]you turn away your foot from the Sabbath,
From doing your pleasure on My holy day,
And call the Sabbath a delight,
The holy *day* of the LORD honorable,
And shall honor Him, not doing your own ways,
Nor finding your own pleasure,
Nor speaking *your own* words,
14 [a]Then you shall delight yourself in the LORD;
And I will cause you to [b]ride on the high hills of the earth,
And feed you with the heritage of Jacob your father.
[c]The mouth of the LORD has spoken."

Separated from God

59 Behold, the LORD's hand is not [a]shortened,
That it cannot save;
Nor His ear heavy,
That it cannot hear.
2 But your iniquities have separated you from your God;
And your sins have hidden *His* face from you,
So that He will [a]not hear.
3 For [a]your hands are defiled with blood,
And your fingers with iniquity;
Your lips have spoken lies,
Your tongue has muttered perversity.

4 No one calls for justice,
Nor does *any* plead for truth.
They trust in [a]empty words and speak lies;
[b]They conceive evil and bring forth iniquity.
5 They hatch vipers' eggs and weave the spider's web;
He who eats of their eggs dies,
And *from* that which is crushed a viper breaks out.

6 [a]Their webs will not become garments,
Nor will they cover themselves with their works;
Their works *are* works of iniquity,
And the act of violence *is* in their hands.
7 [a]Their feet run to evil,
And they make haste to shed [b]innocent blood;
[c]Their thoughts *are* thoughts of iniquity;
Wasting and [d]destruction *are* in their paths.
8 The way of [a]peace they have not known,
And *there is* no justice in their ways;
[b]They have made themselves crooked paths;
Whoever takes that way shall not know peace.

KJV

Sin Confessed

9 Therefore is judgment far from us, neither doth justice overtake us: [a]we wait for light, but behold obscurity; for brightness, *but* we walk in darkness.

10 [a]We grope for the wall like the blind, and we grope as if *we had* no eyes: we stumble at noon day as in the night; *we are* in desolate places as dead *men*.

11 We roar all like bears, and [a]mourn sore like doves: we look for judgment, but *there is* none; for salvation, *but* it is far off from us.

12 For our [a]transgressions are multiplied before thee, and our sins testify against us: for our trangressions *are* with us; and *as for* our iniquities, we know them;

13 In transgressing and lying against the LORD, and departing away from our God, speaking oppression and revolt, conceiving and uttering [a]from the heart words of falsehood.

14 And judgment is turned away backward, and justice standeth afar off: for truth is fallen in the street, and equity cannot enter.

15 Yea, truth faileth; and he *that* departeth from evil maketh himself a [a]prey: and the LORD saw *it*, and it displeased him that *there was* no judgment.

The Redeemer of Zion

16 [a]And he saw that *there was* no man, and [b]wondered that *there was* no intercessor: [c]therefore his arm brought salvation unto him; and his righteousness, it sustained him.

17 [a]For he put on righteousness as a breastplate, and an helmet of salvation upon his head; and he put on the garments of vengeance *for* clothing, and was clad with zeal as a cloke.

18 [a]According to *their* deeds, accordingly he will repay, fury to his adversaries, recompence to his enemies; to the islands he will repay recompence.

19 [a]So shall they fear the name of the LORD from the west, and his glory from the rising of the sun. When the enemy shall come in [b]like a flood, the Spirit of the LORD shall lift up a standard against him.

20 And [a]the Redeemer shall come to Zion, and unto them that turn from transgression in Jacob, saith the LORD.

21 [a]As for me, this *is* my covenant with them, saith the LORD; My spirit that *is* upon thee, and my words which I have put in thy mouth, shall not depart out of thy mouth, nor out of the mouth of thy seed, nor out of the mouth of thy seed's seed, saith the LORD, from henceforth and for ever.

The Gentiles Bless Zion

60 Arise, [a]shine; for thy light is come, and [b]the glory of the LORD is risen upon thee.

2 For, behold, the darkness shall cover the earth, and gross darkness the people: but the LORD

---

9 [a]Jer. 8:15
10 [a]Deut. 28:29; Job 5:14; Amos 8:9
11 [a]Is. 38:14; Ezek. 7:16
12 [a]Is. 24:5; 58:1
13 [a]Matt. 12:34
15 [a]Is. 5:23; 10:2; 29:21; 32:7
16 [a]Is. 41:28; 63:5; 64:7; Ezek. 22:30 [b]Mark 6:6 [c]Ps. 98:1; Is. 63:5
17 [a]Eph. 6:14, 17; 1 Thess. 5:8
18 [a]Is. 63:6; Rom. 2:6
19 [a]Ps. 113:3; Mal. 1:11 [b]Rev. 12:15
20 [a]Rom. 11:26
21 [a][Heb. 8:10; 10:16]

CHAPTER 60

1 [a]Eph. 5:14 [b]Mal. 4:2

NKJV

Sin Confessed

9 Therefore justice is far from us,
Nor does righteousness overtake us;
[a]We look for light, but there is darkness!
For brightness, *but* we walk in blackness!
10 [a]We grope for the wall like the blind,
And we grope as if *we had* no eyes;
We stumble at noonday as at twilight;
We are as dead *men* in desolate places.
11 We all growl like bears,
And [a]moan sadly like doves;
We look for justice, but *there is* none;
For salvation, *but* it is far from us.
12 For our [a]transgressions are multiplied
before You,
And our sins testify against us;
For our transgressions *are* with us,
And *as for* our iniquities, we know them:
13 In transgressing and lying against the
LORD,
And departing from our God,
Speaking oppression and revolt,
Conceiving and uttering [a]from the heart
words of falsehood.
14 Justice is turned back,
And righteousness stands afar off;
For truth is fallen in the street,
And equity cannot enter.
15 So truth fails,
And he *who* departs from evil makes
himself a [a]prey.

The Redeemer of Zion

Then the LORD saw *it*, and it displeased
Him
That *there was* no justice.
16 [a]He saw that *there was* no man,
And [b]wondered that *there was* no
intercessor;
[c]Therefore His own arm brought salvation
for Him;
And His own righteousness, it sustained
Him.
17 [a]For He put on righteousness as a
breastplate,
And a helmet of salvation on His head;
He put on the garments of vengeance for
clothing,
And was clad with zeal as a cloak.
18 [a]According to *their* deeds, accordingly He
will repay,
Fury to His adversaries,
Recompense to His enemies;
The coastlands He will fully repay.
19 [a]So shall they fear
The name of the LORD from the west,
And His glory from the rising of the sun;
When the enemy comes in [b]like a flood,
The Spirit of the LORD will lift up a
standard against him.

20 "The[a] Redeemer will come to Zion,
And to those who turn from transgression
in Jacob,"
Says the LORD.

21 "As[a] for Me," says the LORD, "this *is* My covenant with them: My Spirit who *is* upon you, and My words which I have put in your mouth, shall not depart from your mouth, nor from the mouth of your descendants, nor from the mouth of your descendants' descendants," says the LORD, "from this time and forevermore."

The Gentiles Bless Zion

60 Arise, [a]shine;
For your light has come!
And [b]the glory of the LORD is risen upon
you.
2 For behold, the darkness shall cover the
earth,

KJV

shall arise upon thee, and his glory shall be seen upon thee.

3 And the [a]Gentiles shall come to thy light, and kings to the brightness of thy rising.

4 [a]Lift up thine eyes round about, and see: all they gather themselves together, [b]they come to thee: thy sons shall come from far, and thy daughters shall be nursed at *thy* side.

5 Then thou shalt see, and flow together, and thine heart shall fear, and be enlarged; because [a]the abundance of the sea shall be converted unto thee, the forces of the Gentiles shall come unto thee.

6 The multitude of camels shall cover thee, the dromedaries of Midian and [a]Ephah; all they from [b]Sheba shall come: they shall bring [c]gold and incense; and they shall shew forth the praises of the LORD.

7 All the flocks of [a]Kedar shall be gathered together unto thee, the rams of Nebaioth shall minister unto thee: they shall come up with [b]acceptance on mine altar, and [c]I will glorify the house of my glory.

8 Who *are* these *that* fly as a cloud, and as the doves to their windows?

9 [a]Surely the isles shall wait for me, and the ships of Tarshish first, [b]to bring thy sons from far, [c]their silver and their gold with them, unto the name of the LORD thy God, and to the Holy One of Israel, [d]because he hath glorified thee.

10 And [a]the sons of strangers shall build up thy walls, [b]and their kings shall minister unto thee: for [c]in my wrath I smote thee, [d]but in my favour have I had mercy on thee.

11 Therefore thy gates [a]shall be open continually; they shall not be shut day nor night; that *men* may bring unto thee the forces of the Gentiles, and *that* their kings *may be* brought.

12 [a]For the nation and kingdom that will not serve thee shall perish; yea, *those* nations shall be utterly wasted.

13 [a]The glory of Lebanon shall come unto thee, the fir tree, the pine tree, and the box together, to beautify the place of my sanctuary; and I will make [b]the place of my feet glorious.

14 The sons also of them that afflicted thee shall come [a]bending unto thee; and all they that despised thee shall [b]bow themselves down at the soles of thy feet; and they shall call thee, The city of the LORD, [c]The Zion of the Holy One of Israel.

15 Whereas thou hast been forsaken and hated, so that no man went through *thee,* I will make thee an eternal excellency, a joy of many generations.

16 Thou shalt also suck the milk of the Gentiles, [a]and shalt suck the breast of kings: and thou

---

3 [a]Is. 49:6, 23; Rev. 21:24
4 [a]Is. 49:18 [b]Is. 49:20–22
5 [a][Rom. 11:25–27]
6 [a]Gen. 25:4 [b]Gen. 25:3; Ps. 72:10 [c]Is. 61:6; Matt. 2:11
7 [a]Gen. 25:13 [b]Is. 56:7 [c]Is. 60:13; Hag. 2:7, 9
9 [a]Ps. 72:10 [b][Gal. 4:26] [c]Jer. 3:17 [d]Is. 55:5
10 [a]Is. 14:1, 2; 61:5; Zech. 6:15 [b]Is. 49:23; Rev. 21:24 [c]Is. 57:17 [d]Is. 54:7, 8
11 [a]Is. 26:2; 60:18; 62:10; Rev. 21:25, 26
12 [a]Is. 14:2; Zech. 14:17; Matt. 21:44
13 [a]Is. 35:2 [b]1 Chr. 28:2; Ps. 132:7
14 [a]Is. 45:14 [b]Is. 49:23; Rev. 3:9 [c][Heb. 12:22; Rev. 14:1]
16 [a]Is. 49:23

NKJV

And deep darkness the people;
But the LORD will arise over you,
And His glory will be seen upon you.
3 The [a]Gentiles shall come to your light,
And kings to the brightness of your rising.

4 "Lift[a] up your eyes all around, and see:
They all gather together, [b]they come to you;
Your sons shall come from afar,
And your daughters shall be nursed at *your* side.
5 Then you shall see and become radiant,
And your heart shall swell with joy;
Because [a]the abundance of the sea shall be turned to you,
The wealth of the Gentiles shall come to you.
6 The multitude of camels shall cover your *land,*
The dromedaries of Midian and [a]Ephah;
All those from [b]Sheba shall come;
They shall bring [c]gold and incense,
And they shall proclaim the praises of the LORD.
7 All the flocks of [a]Kedar shall be gathered together to you,
The rams of Nebaioth shall minister to you;
They shall ascend with [b]acceptance on My altar,
And [c]I will glorify the house of My glory.

8 "Who *are* these *who* fly like a cloud,
And like doves to their roosts?
9 [a]Surely the coastlands shall wait for Me;
And the ships of Tarshish *will come* first,
[b]To bring your sons from afar,
[c]Their silver and their gold with them,
To the name of the LORD your God,
And to the Holy One of Israel,
[d]Because He has glorified you.

10 "The[a] sons of foreigners shall build up your walls,
[b]And their kings shall minister to you;
For [c]in My wrath I struck you,
[d]But in My favor I have had mercy on you.
11 Therefore your gates [a]shall be open continually;
They shall not be shut day or night,
That *men* may bring to you the wealth of the Gentiles,
And their kings in procession.
12 [a]For the nation and kingdom which will not serve you shall perish,
And *those* nations shall be utterly ruined.

13 "The[a] glory of Lebanon shall come to you,
The cypress, the pine, and the box tree together,
To beautify the place of My sanctuary;
And I will make [b]the place of My feet glorious.
14 Also the sons of those who afflicted you
Shall come [a]bowing to you,
And all those who despised you shall [b]fall prostrate at the soles of your feet;
And they shall call you The City of the LORD,
[c]Zion of the Holy One of Israel.

15 "Whereas you have been forsaken and hated,
So that no one went through *you,*
I will make you an eternal excellence,
A joy of many generations.
16 You shall drink the milk of the Gentiles,
[a]And milk the breast of kings;

KJV

shalt know that [b]I the LORD *am* thy Saviour and
thy Redeemer, the mighty One of Jacob.
17 For brass I will bring gold, and for iron I
will bring silver, and for wood brass, and for
stones iron: I will also make thy officers peace,
and thine exactors righteousness.
18 Violence shall no more be heard in thy
land, wasting nor destruction within thy borders;
but thou shalt call [a]thy walls Salvation, and thy
gates Praise.

God the Glory of His People

19 The [a]sun shall be no more thy light by
day; neither for brightness shall the moon give
light unto thee: but the LORD shall be unto thee
an everlasting light, and [b]thy God thy glory.
20 [a]Thy sun shall no more go down; neither
shall thy moon withdraw itself: for the LORD shall
be thine everlasting light, and the days of thy
mourning shall be ended.
21 [a]Thy people also *shall be* all righteous:
[b]they shall inherit the land for ever, [c]the branch
of my planting, [d]the work of my hands, that I may
be glorified.
22 [a]A little one shall become a thousand, and
a small one a strong nation: I the LORD will hasten
it in his time.

16 [b]Is. 43:3
18 [a]Is. 26:1
19 [a]Rev. 21:23; 22:5 [b]Is. 41:16; 45:25; Zech. 2:5
20 [a]Amos 8:9
21 [a]Is. 52:1; Rev. 21:27 [b]Ps. 37:11; Matt. 5:5 [c]Is. 61:3; [Matt. 15:13; John 15:2] [d]Is. 29:23; [Eph. 2:10]
22 [a]Matt. 13:31, 32

NKJV

You shall know that [b]I, the LORD, *am* your
Savior
And your Redeemer, the Mighty One of
Jacob.

17 "Instead of bronze I will bring gold,
Instead of iron I will bring silver,
Instead of wood, bronze,
And instead of stones, iron.
I will also make your officers peace,
And your magistrates righteousness.
18 Violence shall no longer be heard in your
land,
Neither wasting nor destruction within
your borders;
But you shall call [a]your walls Salvation,
And your gates Praise.

God the Glory of His People

19 "The [a]sun shall no longer be your light by
day,
Nor for brightness shall the moon give
light to you;
But the LORD will be to you an everlasting
light,
And [b]your God your glory.
20 [a]Your sun shall no longer go down,
Nor shall your moon withdraw itself;
For the LORD will be your everlasting light,
And the days of your mourning shall be
ended.
21 [a]Also your people *shall* all *be* righteous;
[b]They shall inherit the land forever,
[c]The branch of My planting,
[d]The work of My hands,
That I may be glorified.
22 [a]A little one shall become a thousand,
And a small one a strong nation.
I, the LORD, will hasten it in its time."

KJV

The Good News of Salvation

61 The [a]Spirit of the Lord GOD *is* upon me;
because the LORD [b]hath anointed me to
preach good tidings unto the meek; he hath sent
me [c]to bind up the brokenhearted, to proclaim
[d]liberty to the captives, and the opening of the
prison to *them that are* bound;
2 [a]To proclaim the acceptable year of the
LORD, and [b]the day of vengeance of our God; [c]to
comfort all that mourn;
3 To appoint unto them that mourn in Zion,
[a]to give unto them beauty for ashes, the oil of
joy for mourning, the garment of praise for the
spirit of heaviness; that they might be called trees
of righteousness, [b]the planting of the LORD, [c]that
he might be glorified.
4 And they shall [a]build the old wastes, they
shall raise up the former desolations, and they
shall repair the waste cities, the desolations of
many generations.
5 And [a]strangers shall stand and feed your
flocks, and the sons of the alien *shall be* your
plowmen and your vinedressers.
6 [a]But ye shall be named the Priests of the
LORD: *men* shall call you the Ministers of our God:
[b]ye shall eat the riches of the Gentiles, and in
their glory shall ye boast yourselves.
7 [a]For your shame *ye shall have* double; and
for confusion they shall rejoice in their portion:

CHAPTER 61

1 [a]Is. 11:2; Matt. 3:17; Luke 4:18, 19; John 1:32; 3:34 [b]Ps. 45:7; Matt. 11:5; Luke 7:22 [c]Ps. 147:3 [d]Is. 42:7; [Acts 10:43]
2 [a]Lev. 25:9 [b]Is. 34:8; Mal. 4:1, 3; [2 Thess. 1:7] [c]Is. 57:18; Jer. 31:13; Matt. 5:4
3 [a]Ps. 30:11 [b]Is. 60:21; [Jer. 17:7, 8] [c][John 15:8]
4 [a]Is. 49:8; 58:12; Ezek. 36:33; Amos 9:14
5 [a][Eph. 2:12]
6 [a]Ex. 19:6 [b]Is. 60:5, 11
7 [a]Is. 40:2; Zech. 9:12

NKJV

The Good News of Salvation

61 "The [a]Spirit of the Lord GOD *is* upon Me,
Because the LORD [b]has anointed Me
To preach good tidings to the poor;
He has sent Me [c]to heal the
brokenhearted,
To proclaim [d]liberty to the captives,
And the opening of the prison to *those
who are* bound;
2 [a]To proclaim the acceptable year of the
LORD,
And [b]the day of vengeance of our God;
[c]To comfort all who mourn,
3 To console those who mourn in Zion,
[a]To give them beauty for ashes,
The oil of joy for mourning,
The garment of praise for the spirit of
heaviness;
That they may be called trees of
righteousness,
[b]The planting of the LORD, [c]that He may
be glorified."

4 And they shall [a]rebuild the old ruins,
They shall raise up the former desolations,
And they shall repair the ruined cities,
The desolations of many generations.
5 [a]Strangers shall stand and feed your
flocks,
And the sons of the foreigner
Shall be your plowmen and your
vinedressers.
6 [a]But you shall be named the priests of the
LORD,
They shall call you the servants of our
God.
[b]You shall eat the riches of the Gentiles,
And in their glory you shall boast.
7 [a]Instead of your shame *you shall have*
double *honor*,
And *instead of* confusion they shall
rejoice in their portion.

KJV

therefore in their land they shall possess the double: everlasting joy shall be unto them.

8 For [a]I the LORD love judgment, [b]I hate robbery for burnt offering; and I will direct their work in truth, [c]and I will make an everlasting covenant with them.

9 And their seed shall be known among the Gentiles, and their offspring among the people: all that see them shall acknowledge them, [a]that they *are* the seed *which* the LORD hath blessed.

10 [a]I will greatly rejoice in the LORD, my soul shall be joyful in my God; for [b]he hath clothed me with the garments of salvation, he hath covered me with the robe of righteousness, [c]as a bridegroom decketh *himself* with ornaments, and as a bride adorneth *herself* with her jewels.

11 For as the earth bringeth forth her bud, and as the garden causeth the things that are sown in it to spring forth; so the Lord GOD will cause [a]righteousness and [b]praise to spring forth before all the nations.

Assurance of Zion's Salvation

62 For Zion's sake will I not hold my peace, and for Jerusalem's sake I will not rest, until the righteousness thereof go forth as brightness, and the salvation thereof as a lamp *that* burneth.

2 [a]And the Gentiles shall see thy righteousness, and all [b]kings thy glory: [c]and thou shalt be called by a new name, which the mouth of the LORD shall name.

3 Thou shalt also be [a]a crown of glory in the hand of the LORD, and a royal diadem in the hand of thy God.

4 [a]Thou shalt no more be termed [b]Forsaken; neither shall thy land any more be termed [c]Desolate: but thou shalt be called Hephzi–bah, and thy land Beulah: for the LORD delighteth in thee, and thy land shall be married.

5 For *as* a young man marrieth a virgin, *so* shall thy sons marry thee: and *as* the bridegroom rejoiceth over the bride, [a]*so* shall thy God rejoice over thee.

6 [a]I have set watchmen upon thy walls, O Jerusalem, *which* shall never hold their peace day nor night: ye that make mention of the LORD, keep not silence,

7 And give him no rest, till he establish, and till he make Jerusalem [a]a praise in the earth.

8 The LORD hath sworn by his right hand, and by the arm of his strength, Surely I will no more [a]give thy corn *to be* meat for thine enemies; and the sons of the stranger shall not drink thy wine, for the which thou hast laboured:

9 But they that have gathered it shall eat it, and praise the LORD; and they that have brought it together shall drink it [a]in the courts of my holiness.

---

8 [a]Ps. 11:7 [b]Is. 1:11, 13 [c]Gen. 17:7; Ps. 105:10; Is. 55:3; Jer. 32:40
9 [a]Is. 65:23
10 [a]Hab. 3:18 [b]Ps. 132:9, 16 [c]Is. 49:18; Rev. 21:2
11 [a]Ps. 72:3; 85:11 [b]Is. 60:18; 62:7

CHAPTER 62
2 [a]Is. 60:3 [b]Ps. 102:15, 16; 138:4, 5; 148:11, 13 [c]Is. 62:4, 12; 65:15
3 [a]Is. 28:5; Zech. 9:16; 1 Thess. 2:19
4 [a]Hos. 1:10; 1 Pet. 2:10 [b]Is. 49:14; 54:6, 7 [c]Is. 54:1
5 [a]Is. 65:19
6 [a]Is. 52:8; Jer. 6:17; Ezek. 3:17; 33:7
7 [a]Is. 60:18; 61:11; Jer. 33:9; Zeph. 3:19, 20
8 [a]Lev. 26:16; Deut. 28:31, 33; Judg. 6:3–6; Is. 1:7; Jer. 5:17
9 [a]Deut. 12:12; 14:23, 26

*

62:4 Lit. *My Delight Is in Her* • Lit. *Married*

NKJV

Therefore in their land they shall possess
double;
Everlasting joy shall be theirs.

8 "For [a]I, the LORD, love justice;
[b]I hate robbery for burnt offering;
I will direct their work in truth,
[c]And will make with them an everlasting
covenant.
9 Their descendants shall be known among
the Gentiles,
And their offspring among the people.
All who see them shall acknowledge them,
[a]That they *are* the posterity *whom* the LORD
has blessed."

10 [a]I will greatly rejoice in the LORD,
My soul shall be joyful in my God;
For [b]He has clothed me with the garments
of salvation,
He has covered me with the robe of
righteousness,
[c]As a bridegroom decks *himself* with
ornaments,
And as a bride adorns *herself* with her
jewels.
11 For as the earth brings forth its bud,
As the garden causes the things that are
sown in it to spring forth,
So the Lord GOD will cause [a]righteousness
and [b]praise to spring forth before all the
nations.

Assurance of Zion's Salvation

62 For Zion's sake I will not hold My peace,
And for Jerusalem's sake I will not rest,
Until her righteousness goes forth as
brightness,
And her salvation as a lamp *that* burns.
2 [a]The Gentiles shall see your righteousness,
And all [b]kings your glory.
[c]You shall be called by a new name,
Which the mouth of the LORD will name.
3 You shall also be [a]a crown of glory
In the hand of the LORD,
And a royal diadem
In the hand of your God.
4 [a]You shall no longer be termed [b]Forsaken,
Nor shall your land any more be termed
[c]Desolate;
But you shall be called *Hephzibah, and
your land *Beulah;
For the LORD delights in you,
And your land shall be married.
5 For *as* a young man marries a virgin,
So shall your sons marry you;
And *as* the bridegroom rejoices over the
bride,
[a]*So* shall your God rejoice over you.

6 [a]I have set watchmen on your walls, O
Jerusalem;
They shall never hold their peace day or
night.
You who make mention of the LORD, do
not keep silent,
7 And give Him no rest till He establishes
And till He makes Jerusalem [a]a praise in
the earth.

8 The LORD has sworn by His right hand
And by the arm of His strength:
"Surely I will no longer [a]give your grain
As food for your enemies;
And the sons of the foreigner shall not
drink your new wine,
For which you have labored.
9 But those who have gathered it shall eat
it,
And praise the LORD;
Those who have brought it together shall
drink it [a]in My holy courts."

KJV

10 Go through, go through the gates; [a]prepare ye the way of the people; cast up, cast up the highway; gather out the stones; [b]lift up a standard for the people.

11 Behold, the LORD hath proclaimed unto the end of the world, [a]Say ye to the daughter of Zion, Behold, thy salvation cometh; behold, his [b]reward *is* with him, and his work before him.

12 And they shall call them, The holy people, The redeemed of the LORD: and thou shalt be called, Sought out, A city not forsaken.

The LORD in Judgment and Salvation

63 Who *is* this that cometh from Edom, with dyed garments from Bozrah? this *that is* glorious in his apparel, travelling in the greatness of his strength? I that speak in righteousness, mighty to save.

2 Wherefore [a]*art thou* red in thine apparel, and thy garments like him that treadeth in the winefat?

3 I have [a]trodden the winepress alone; and of the people *there was* none with me: for I will tread them in mine anger, and trample them in my fury; and their blood shall be sprinkled upon my garments, and I will stain all my raiment.

4 For the [a]day of vengeance *is* in mine heart, and the year of my redeemed is come.

5 [a]And I looked, and [b]*there was* none to help; and I wondered that *there was* none to uphold: therefore mine own [c]arm brought salvation unto me; and my fury, it upheld me.

6 And I will tread down the people in mine anger, and make them drunk in my fury, and I will bring down their strength to the earth.

God's Mercy Remembered

7 I will mention the lovingkindnesses of the LORD, *and* the praises of the LORD, according to all that the LORD hath bestowed on us, and the great goodness toward the house of Israel, which he hath bestowed on them according to his mercies, and according to the multitude of his lovingkindnesses.

8 For he said, Surely they *are* my people, children *that* will not lie: so he was their Saviour.

9 [a]In all their affliction he was afflicted, [b]and the angel of his presence saved them: [c]in his love and in his pity he redeemed them; and [d]he bare them, and carried them all the days of old.

10 But they [a]rebelled, and [b]vexed his holy Spirit: [c]therefore he was turned to be their enemy, *and* he fought against them.

10 [a]Is. 40:3; 57:14 [b]Is. 11:12
11 [a]Zech. 9:9; Matt. 21:5; John 12:15 [b]Is. 40:10; [Rev. 22:12]

CHAPTER 63
2 [a][Rev. 19:13, 15]
3 [a]Lam. 1:15; Rev. 14:19, 20; 19:15
4 [a]Is. 34:8; 35:4; 61:2; Jer. 51:6
5 [a]Is. 41:28; 59:16 [b][John 16:32] [c]Ps. 98:1; Is. 59:16
9 [a]Judg. 10:16 [b]Ex. 14:19 [c]Deut. 7:7 [d]Ex. 19:4
10 [a]Ex. 15:24 [b]Num. 14:11; Ps. 78:40; Acts 7:51; 1 Cor. 10:1–11 [c]Ex. 23:21; Ps. 106:40

NKJV

10 Go through,
Go through the gates!
[a]Prepare the way for the people;
Build up,
Build up the highway!
Take out the stones,
[b]Lift up a banner for the peoples!

11 Indeed the LORD has proclaimed
To the end of the world:
[a]"Say to the daughter of Zion,
'Surely your salvation is coming;
Behold, His [b]reward *is* with Him,
And His work before Him.' "

12 And they shall call them The Holy People,
The Redeemed of the LORD;
And you shall be called Sought Out,
A City Not Forsaken.

The LORD in Judgment and Salvation

63 Who *is* this who comes from Edom,
With dyed garments from Bozrah,
This *One who is* glorious in His apparel,
Traveling in the greatness of His strength?—

"I who speak in righteousness, mighty to save."

2 Why [a]*is* Your apparel red,
And Your garments like one who treads in the winepress?

3 "I have [a]trodden the winepress alone,
And from the peoples no one *was* with Me.
For I have trodden them in My anger,
And trampled them in My fury;
Their blood is sprinkled upon My garments,
And I have stained all My robes.

4 For the [a]day of vengeance *is* in My heart,
And the year of My redeemed has come.

5 [a]I looked, but [b]*there was* no one to help,
And I wondered
That *there was* no one to uphold;
Therefore My own [c]arm brought salvation for Me;
And My own fury, it sustained Me.

6 I have trodden down the peoples in My anger,
Made them drunk in My fury,
And brought down their strength to the earth."

God's Mercy Remembered

7 I will mention the lovingkindnesses of the LORD
And the praises of the LORD,
According to all that the LORD has bestowed on us,
And the great goodness toward the house of Israel,
Which He has bestowed on them according to His mercies,
According to the multitude of His lovingkindnesses.

8 For He said, "Surely they *are* My people,
Children *who* will not lie."
So He became their Savior.

9 [a]In all their affliction He was afflicted,
[b]And the Angel of His Presence saved them;
[c]In His love and in His pity He redeemed them;
And [d]He bore them and carried them
All the days of old.

10 But they [a]rebelled and [b]grieved His Holy Spirit;
[c]So He turned Himself against them as an enemy,
And He fought against them.

KJV

11 Then he [a]remembered the days of old, Moses, *and* his people, *saying,* Where *is* he that [b]brought them up out of the sea with the shepherd of his flock? [c]where *is* he that put his holy Spirit within him?

12 That led *them* by the right hand of Moses [a]with his glorious arm, [b]dividing the water before them, to make himself an everlasting name?

13 [a]That led them through the deep, as an horse in the wilderness, *that* they should not stumble?

14 As a beast goeth down into the valley, the Spirit of the LORD caused him to rest: so didst thou lead thy people, [a]to make thyself a glorious name.

A Prayer of Penitence

15 [a]Look down from heaven, and behold [b]from the habitation of thy holiness and of thy glory: where *is* thy zeal and thy strength, the sounding [c]of thy bowels and of thy mercies toward me? are they restrained?

16 [a]Doubtless thou *art* our father, though Abraham [b]be ignorant of us, and Israel acknowledge us not: thou, O LORD, *art* our father, our redeemer; thy name *is* from everlasting.

17 O LORD, why hast thou [a]made us to err from thy ways, *and* hardened our heart from thy fear? Return for thy servants' sake, the tribes of thine inheritance.

18 [a]The people of thy holiness have possessed *it* but a little while: [b]our adversaries have trodden down thy sanctuary.

19 We are *thine:* thou never barest rule over them; they were not called by thy name.

64 Oh that thou wouldest rend the heavens, that thou wouldest come down, that the mountains might flow down at thy [a]presence,

2 As *when* the melting fire burneth, the fire causeth the waters to boil, to make thy name known to thine adversaries, *that* the nations may tremble at thy presence!

3 When [a]thou didst terrible things *which* we looked not for, thou camest down, the mountains flowed down at thy presence.

4 For since the beginning of the world [a]*men* have not heard, nor perceived by the ear, neither hath the eye seen, O God, beside thee, *what* he hath prepared for him that waiteth for him.

5 Thou meetest him that rejoiceth and worketh righteousness, *those that* remember thee in thy ways: behold, thou art wroth; for we have sinned: [a]in those is continuance, and we shall be saved.

6 But we are all as an unclean *thing,* and all [a]our righteousnesses *are* as filthy rags; and

---

11 [a]Ps. 106:44, 45 [b]Ex. 14:30 [c]Num. 11:17, 25, 29; Hag. 2:5
12 [a]Ex. 15:6 [b]Ex. 14:21, 22; Josh. 3:16; Is. 11:15; 51:10
13 [a]Ps. 106:9
14 [a]2 Sam. 7:23
15 [a]Deut. 26:15; Ps. 80:14 [b]Ps. 33:14 [c]Jer. 31:20; Hos. 11:8
16 [a]Deut. 32:6 [b]Job 14:21
17 [a]Is. 6:9, 10; John 12:40
18 [a]Deut. 7:6 [b]Ps. 74:3–7; Is. 64:11

CHAPTER 64
1 [a]Ex. 19:18; Ps. 18:9; 144:5; Mic. 1:3, 4; [Hab. 3:13]
3 [a]Ex. 34:10
4 [a]Ps. 31:19
5 [a]Mal. 3:6
6 [a][Phil. 3:9]

NKJV

11 Then he [a]remembered the days of old,
Moses *and* his people, *saying:*
"Where *is* He who [b]brought them up out
of the sea
With the shepherd of His flock?
[c]Where *is* He who put His Holy Spirit
within them,
12 Who led *them* by the right hand of Moses,
[a]With His glorious arm,
[b]Dividing the water before them
To make for Himself an everlasting
name,
13 [a]Who led them through the deep,
As a horse in the wilderness,
That they might not stumble?"
14 As a beast goes down into the valley,
And the Spirit of the LORD causes him to
rest,
So You lead Your people,
[a]To make Yourself a glorious name.

A Prayer of Penitence

15 [a]Look down from heaven,
And see [b]from Your habitation, holy and
glorious.
Where *are* Your zeal and Your strength,
The yearning [c]of Your heart and Your
mercies toward me?
Are they restrained?
16 [a]Doubtless You *are* our Father,
Though Abraham [b]was ignorant of us,
And Israel does not acknowledge us.
You, O LORD, *are* our Father;
Our Redeemer from Everlasting *is* Your
name.
17 O LORD, why have You [a]made us stray
from Your ways,
And hardened our heart from Your fear?
Return for Your servants' sake,
The tribes of Your inheritance.
18 [a]Your holy people have possessed *it* but a
little while;
[b]Our adversaries have trodden down Your
sanctuary.
19 We have become *like* those of old, over
whom You never ruled,
Those who were never called by Your
name.

64 Oh, that You would rend the heavens!
That You would come down!
That the mountains might shake at Your
[a]presence—
2 As fire burns brushwood,
As fire causes water to boil—
To make Your name known to Your
adversaries,
That the nations may tremble at Your
presence!
3 When [a]You did awesome things *for which*
we did not look,
You came down,
The mountains shook at Your presence.
4 For since the beginning of the world
[a]*Men* have not heard nor perceived by the
ear,
Nor has the eye seen any God besides
You,
Who acts for the one who waits for
Him.
5 You meet him who rejoices and does
righteousness,
Who remembers You in Your ways.
You are indeed angry, for we have
sinned—
[a]In these ways we continue;
And we need to be saved.

6 But we are all like an unclean *thing,*
And all [a]our righteousnesses *are* like
filthy rags;

KJV

we all do [b]fade as a leaf; and our iniquities, like
the wind, have taken us away.
7 And *there is* none that calleth upon thy
name, that stirreth up himself to take hold of thee:
for thou hast hid thy face from us, and hast consumed us, because of our iniquities.
8 But now, O LORD, thou *art* our father; we
are the clay, and thou our [a]potter; and we all *are*
the work of thy hand.
9 Be not wroth very sore, O LORD, neither
remember iniquity for ever: behold, see, we beseech thee, we *are* all thy people.
10 Thy holy cities are a wilderness, Zion is
a wilderness, Jerusalem a desolation.
11 Our holy and our beautiful house, where
our fathers praised thee, is burned up with fire:
and all [a]our pleasant things are laid waste.
12 [a]Wilt thou refrain thyself for these *things,*
O LORD? [b]wilt thou hold thy peace, and afflict us
very sore?

The Righteousness of God's Judgment

65 I [a]am sought of *them that* asked not *for*
me; I am found of *them that* sought me
not: I said, Behold me, behold me, unto a nation
that [b]was not called by my name.
2 [a]I have spread out my hands all the day
unto a [b]rebellious people, which [c]walketh in a
way *that was* not good, after their own thoughts;
3 A people [a]that provoketh me to anger continually to my face; [b]that sacrificeth in gardens,
and burneth incense upon altars of brick;
4 [a]Which remain among the graves, and
lodge in the monuments, [b]which eat swine's flesh,
and broth of abominable *things is in* their vessels;
5 [a]Which say, Stand by thyself, come not
near to me; for I am holier than thou. These *are*
a smoke in my nose, a fire that burneth all the
day.
6 Behold, [a]*it is* written before me: [b]I will
not keep silence, [c]but will recompense, even recompense into their bosom,
7 Your iniquities, and [a]the iniquities of your
fathers together, saith the LORD, [b]which have
burned incense upon the mountains, [c]and blasphemed me upon the hills: therefore will I measure their former work into their bosom.
8 Thus saith the LORD, As the new wine is
found in the cluster, and *one* saith, Destroy it not;
for [a]a blessing *is* in it: so will I do for my servants'
sakes, that I may not destroy them [b]all.
9 And I will bring forth a seed out of Jacob,
and out of Judah an inheritor of my mountains:
and mine [a]elect shall inherit it, and my servants
shall dwell there.
10 And [a]Sharon shall be a fold of flocks, and

6 [b]Ps. 90:5, 6; Is. 1:30
8 [a]Is. 29:16; 45:9; Jer. 18:6; [Rom. 9:20, 21]
11 [a]Ezek. 24:21
12 [a]Is. 42:14 [b]Ps. 83:1

CHAPTER 65
1 [a]Rom. 9:24; 10:20 [b]Is. 63:19
2 [a]Rom. 10:21 [b]Is. 1:2, 23 [c]Is. 42:24
3 [a]Deut. 32:21 [b]Is. 1:29
4 [a]Deut. 18:11 [b]Lev. 11:7; Is. 66:17
5 [a]Matt. 9:11; Luke 7:39; 18:9–12
6 [a]Deut. 32:34 [b]Ps. 50:3 [c]Ps. 79:12
7 [a]Ex. 20:5 [b]Ezek. 18:6 [c]Is. 57:7; Ezek. 20:27, 28
8 [a]Joel 2:14 [b]Is. 1:9; Amos 9:8, 9
9 [a]Matt. 24:22
10 [a]Is. 33:9

NKJV

We all [b]fade as a leaf,
And our iniquities, like the wind,
Have taken us away.
7 And *there is* no one who calls on Your name,
Who stirs himself up to take hold of You;
For You have hidden Your face from us,
And have consumed us because of our iniquities.

8 But now, O LORD,
You *are* our Father;
We *are* the clay, and You our [a]potter;
And all we *are* the work of Your hand.
9 Do not be furious, O LORD,
Nor remember iniquity forever;
Indeed, please look—we all *are* Your people!
10 Your holy cities are a wilderness,
Zion is a wilderness,
Jerusalem a desolation.
11 Our holy and beautiful temple,
Where our fathers praised You,
Is burned up with fire;
And all [a]our pleasant things are laid waste.
12 [a]Will You restrain Yourself because of these *things,* O LORD?
[b]Will You hold Your peace, and afflict us very severely?

The Righteousness of God's Judgment

65 "I was [a]sought by *those who* did not ask *for Me;*
I was found by *those who* did not seek Me.
I said, 'Here I am, here I am,'
To a nation *that* [b]was not called by My name.
2 [a]I have stretched out My hands all day long to a [b]rebellious people,
Who [c]walk in a way *that is* not good,
According to their own thoughts;
3 A people [a]who provoke Me to anger continually to My face;
[b]Who sacrifice in gardens,
And burn incense on altars of brick;
4 [a]Who sit among the graves,
And spend the night in the tombs;
[b]Who eat swine's flesh,
And the broth of abominable things is *in* their vessels;
5 [a]Who say, 'Keep to yourself,
Do not come near me,
For I am holier than you!'
These *are* smoke in My nostrils,
A fire that burns all the day.

6 "Behold, [a]*it is* written before Me:
[b]I will not keep silence, [c]but will repay—
Even repay into their bosom—
7 Your iniquities and [a]the iniquities of your fathers together,"
Says the LORD,
[b]"Who have burned incense on the mountains
[c]And blasphemed Me on the hills;
Therefore I will measure their former work into their bosom."

8 Thus says the LORD:

"As the new wine is found in the cluster,
And *one* says, 'Do not destroy it,
For [a]a blessing *is* in it,'
So will I do for My servants' sake,
That I may not destroy them [b]all.
9 I will bring forth descendants from Jacob,
And from Judah an heir of My mountains;
My [a]elect shall inherit it,
And My servants shall dwell there.
10 [a]Sharon shall be a fold of flocks,

KJV

[b]the valley of Achor a place for the herds to lie down in, for my people that have [c]sought me.

11 But ye *are* they that forsake the LORD, that forget [a]my holy mountain, that prepare [b]a table for that troop, and that furnish the drink offering unto that number.

12 Therefore will I number you to the sword, and ye shall all bow down to the slaughter: [a]because when I called, ye did not answer; when I spake, ye did not hear; but did evil before mine eyes, and did choose *that* wherein I delighted not.

13 Therefore thus saith the Lord GOD, Behold, my servants shall eat, but ye shall be hungry: behold, my servants shall drink, but ye shall be thirsty: behold, my servants shall rejoice, but ye shall be ashamed:

14 Behold, my servants shall sing for joy of heart, but ye shall cry for sorrow of heart, and [a]shall howl for vexation of spirit.

15 And ye shall leave your name [a]for a curse unto [b]my chosen: for the Lord GOD shall slay thee, and [c]call his servants by another name:

16 [a]That he who blesseth himself in the earth shall bless himself in the God of truth; and [b]he that sweareth in the earth shall swear by the God of truth; because the former troubles are forgotten, and because they are hid from mine eyes.

The Glorious New Creation

17 For, behold, I create [a]new heavens and a new earth: and the former shall not be remembered, nor come into mind.

18 But be ye glad and rejoice for ever *in that* which I create: for, behold, I create Jerusalem a rejoicing, and her people a joy.

19 And [a]I will rejoice in Jerusalem, and joy in my people: and the [b]voice of weeping shall be no more heard in her, nor the voice of crying.

20 There shall be no more thence an infant of days, nor an old man that hath not filled his days: for the child shall die an hundred years old; [a]but the sinner *being* an hundred years old shall be accursed.

21 [a]And they shall build houses, and inhabit *them;* and they shall plant vineyards, and eat the fruit of them.

22 They shall not build, and another inhabit; they shall not plant, and [a]another eat: for [b]as the days of a tree *are* the days of my people, and [c]mine elect shall long enjoy the work of their hands.

23 They shall not labour in vain,[a]nor bring forth for trouble; for [b]they *are* the seed of the blessed of the LORD, and their offspring with them.

10 [b]Josh. 7:24; Hos. 2:15 [c]Is. 55:6
11 [a]Is. 56:7 [b]Ezek. 23:41; [1 Cor. 10:21]
12 [a]2 Chr. 36:15, 16; Prov. 1:24; Is. 41:28; 50:2; 66:4; Jer. 7:13
14 [a]Matt. 8:12; Luke 13:28
15 [a]Jer. 29:22; Zech. 8:13 [b]Is. 65:9, 22 [c][Acts 11:26]
16 [a]Ps. 72:17; Jer. 4:2 [b]Deut. 6:13; Zeph. 1:5
17 [a]Is. 51:16; 66:22; [2 Pet. 3:13]; Rev. 21:1
19 [a]Is. 62:4, 5 [b]Is. 35:10; 51:11; Rev. 7:17; 21:4
20 [a]Eccl. 8:12, 13; Is. 3:11; 22:14
21 [a]Ezek. 28:26; 45:4; Hos. 11:11; Amos 9:14
22 [a]Is. 62:8, 9 [b]Ps. 92:12 [c]Is. 65:9, 15
23 [a]Hos. 9:12 [b]Is. 61:9; [Jer. 32:38, 39; Acts 2:39]

*———

65:11 Lit. *Troop* or *Fortune;* a pagan deity • Lit. *Number* or *Destiny;* a pagan deity

NKJV

And [b]the Valley of Achor a place for herds
to lie down,
For My people who have [c]sought Me.

11 "But you *are* those who forsake the LORD,
Who forget [a]My holy mountain,
Who prepare [b]a table for *Gad,
And who furnish a drink offering for
*Meni.
12 Therefore I will number you for the sword,
And you shall all bow down to the
slaughter;
[a]Because, when I called, you did not
answer;
When I spoke, you did not hear,
But did evil before My eyes,
And chose *that* in which I do not delight."

13 Therefore thus says the Lord GOD:

"Behold, My servants shall eat,
But you shall be hungry;
Behold, My servants shall drink,
But you shall be thirsty;
Behold, My servants shall rejoice,
But you shall be ashamed;
14 Behold, My servants shall sing for joy of
heart,
But you shall cry for sorrow of heart,
And [a]wail for grief of spirit.
15 You shall leave your name [a]as a curse to
[b]My chosen;
For the Lord GOD will slay you,
And [c]call His servants by another name;
16 [a]So that he who blesses himself in the
earth
Shall bless himself in the God of truth;
And [b]he who swears in the earth
Shall swear by the God of truth;
Because the former troubles are forgotten,
And because they are hidden from My
eyes.

The Glorious New Creation

17 "For behold, I create [a]new heavens and a
new earth;
And the former shall not be remembered
or come to mind.
18 But be glad and rejoice forever in what I
create;
For behold, I create Jerusalem *as* a
rejoicing,
And her people a joy.
19 [a]I will rejoice in Jerusalem,
And joy in My people;
The [b]voice of weeping shall no longer be
heard in her,
Nor the voice of crying.

20 "No more shall an infant from there *live
but a few* days,
Nor an old man who has not fulfilled his
days;
For the child shall die one hundred years
old,
[a]But the sinner *being* one hundred years
old shall be accursed.
21 [a]They shall build houses and inhabit
them;
They shall plant vineyards and eat their
fruit.
22 They shall not build and another inhabit;
They shall not plant and [a]another eat;
For [b]as the days of a tree, *so shall be* the
days of My people,
And [c]My elect shall long enjoy the work
of their hands.
23 They shall not labor in vain,
[a]Nor bring forth children for trouble;
For [b]they *shall be* the descendants of the
blessed of the LORD,
And their offspring with them.

KJV

24 And it shall come to pass, that [a]before
they call, I will answer; and while they are yet
speaking, I will [b]hear.
25 The [a]wolf and the lamb shall feed together, and the lion shall eat straw like the bullock: [b]and dust *shall be* the serpent's meat. They
shall not hurt nor destroy in all my holy mountain,
saith the LORD.

True Worship and False

66 Thus saith the LORD, [a]The heaven *is* my
throne, and the earth *is* my footstool: where
is the house that ye build unto me? and where *is*
the place of my rest?
2 For all those *things* hath mine hand made,
and all those *things* have been, saith the LORD:
[a]but to this *man* will I look, [b]*even* to *him that is*
poor and of a contrite spirit, and trembleth at my
word.
3 [a]He that killeth an ox *is as if* he slew a
man; he that sacrificeth a lamb, *as if* he [b]cut off
a dog's neck; he that offereth an oblation, *as if*
he offered swine's blood; he that burneth incense,
as if he blessed an idol. Yea, they have chosen
their own ways, and their soul delighteth in their
abominations.
4 I also will choose their delusions, and will
bring their fears upon them; [a]because when I
called, none did answer; when I spake, they did
not hear: but they did evil before mine eyes, and
chose *that* in which I delighted not.

The LORD Vindicates Zion

5 Hear the word of the LORD, ye that tremble
at his word; Your brethren that [a]hated you, that
cast you out for my name's sake, said, [b]Let the
LORD be glorified: but [c]he shall appear to your
joy, and they shall be ashamed.
6 A voice of noise from the city, a voice from
the temple, a voice of the LORD that rendereth recompence to his enemies.
7 Before she travailed, she brought forth;
before her pain came, she was delivered of a man
child.
8 Who hath heard such a thing? who hath
seen such things? Shall the earth be made to bring
forth in one day? *or* shall a nation be born at once?
for as soon as Zion travailed, she brought forth
her children.
9 Shall I bring to the birth, and not cause
to bring forth? saith the LORD: shall I cause to
bring forth, and shut *the womb?* saith thy God.
10 Rejoice ye with Jerusalem, and be glad
with her, all ye that mourn for her: rejoice for joy with
her, all ye that mourn for her:
11 That ye may suck, and be satisfied with
the breasts of her consolations; that ye may milk
out, and be delighted with the abundance of her
glory.

---

24 [a]Ps. 91:15; Is. 58:9 [b]Is. 30:19; Dan. 9:20–23
25 [a]Is. 11:6–9 [b]Gen. 3:14; Mic. 7:17

CHAPTER 66

1 [a]1 Kin. 8:27; 2 Chr. 6:18; Ps. 11:4; Matt. 5:34; Acts 17:24
2 [a]Ps. 34:18; [Is. 57:15; 61:1; Matt. 5:3, 4; Luke 18:13, 14] [b]Ps. 34:18; 51:17
3 [a][Is. 1:10–17; 58:1–7; Mic. 6:7, 8] [b]Deut. 23:18
4 [a]Prov. 1:24; Is. 65:12; Jer. 7:13
5 [a]Ps. 38:20; Is. 60:15; [Luke 6:22, 23] [b]Is. 5:19 [c][2 Thess. 1:10; Titus 2:13]

NKJV

24 "It shall come to pass
That [a]before they call, I will answer;
And while they are still speaking, I will
[b]hear.
25 The [a]wolf and the lamb shall feed
together,
The lion shall eat straw like the ox,
[b]And dust *shall be* the serpent's food.
They shall not hurt nor destroy in all My
holy mountain,"
Says the LORD.

True Worship and False

66 Thus says the LORD:
[a]"Heaven *is* My throne,
And earth *is* My footstool.
Where *is* the house that you will build Me?
And where *is* the place of My rest?
2 For all those *things* My hand has made,
And all those *things* exist,"
Says the LORD.
[a]"But on this *one* will I look:
[b]On *him who is* poor and of a contrite spirit,
And who trembles at My word.
3 "He[a] who kills a bull *is as if* he slays a man;
He who sacrifices a lamb, *as if* he [b]breaks
a dog's neck;
He who offers a grain offering, *as if he
offers* swine's blood;
He who burns incense, *as if* he blesses an
idol.
Just as they have chosen their own ways,
And their soul delights in their
abominations,
4 So will I choose their delusions,
And bring their fears on them;
[a]Because, when I called, no one answered,
When I spoke they did not hear;
But they did evil before My eyes,
And chose *that* in which I do not delight."

The LORD Vindicates Zion

5 Hear the word of the LORD,
You who tremble at His word:
"Your brethren who [a]hated you,
Who cast you out for My name's sake,
said,
[b]'Let the LORD be glorified,
That [c]we may see your joy.'
But they shall be ashamed."
6 The sound of noise from the city!
A voice from the temple!
The voice of the LORD,
Who fully repays His enemies!

7 "Before she was in labor, she gave birth;
Before her pain came,
She delivered a male child.
8 Who has heard such a thing?
Who has seen such things?
Shall the earth be made to give birth in
one day?
Or shall a nation be born at once?
For as soon as Zion was in labor,
She gave birth to her children.
9 Shall I bring to the time of birth, and not
cause delivery?" says the LORD.
"Shall I who cause delivery shut up *the
womb?*" says your God.
10 "Rejoice with Jerusalem,
And be glad with her, all you who love
her;
Rejoice for joy with her, all you who
mourn for her;
11 That you may feed and be satisfied
With the consolation of her bosom,
That you may drink deeply and be
delighted
With the abundance of her glory."

KJV

12 For thus saith the LORD, Behold, [a]I will extend peace to her like a river, and the glory of the Gentiles like a flowing stream: then shall ye [b]suck, ye shall be [c]borne upon *her* sides, and be dandled upon *her* knees.

13 As one whom his mother comforteth, so will I [a]comfort you; and ye shall be comforted in Jerusalem.

The Reign and Indignation of God

14 And when ye see *this*, your heart shall rejoice, and [a]your bones shall flourish like an herb: and the hand of the LORD shall be known toward his servants, and *his* indignation toward his enemies.

15 [a]For, behold, the LORD will come with fire, and with his chariots like a whirlwind, to render his anger with fury, and his rebuke with flames of fire.

16 For by fire and by [a]his sword will the LORD plead with all flesh: and the slain of the LORD shall be [b]many.

17 [a]They that sanctify themselves, and purify themselves in the gardens behind one *tree* in the midst, eating swine's flesh, and the abomination, and the mouse, shall be consumed together, saith the LORD.

18 For I *know* their works and their [a]thoughts: it shall come, that I will [b]gather all nations and tongues; and they shall come, and see my glory.

19 [a]And I will set a sign among them, and I will send those that escape of them unto the nations, *to* Tarshish, Pul, and Lud, that draw the bow, *to* Tubal, and Javan, *to* the isles afar off, that have not heard my fame, neither have seen my glory; [b]and they shall declare my glory among the Gentiles.

20 And they shall [a]bring all your brethren [b]*for* an offering unto the LORD out of all nations upon horses, and in chariots, and in litters, and upon mules, and upon swift beasts, to my holy mountain Jerusalem, saith the LORD, as the children of Israel bring an offering in a clean vessel into the house of the LORD.

21 And I will also take of them for [a]priests *and* for Levites, saith the LORD.

22 For as [a]the new heavens and the new earth, which I will make, shall remain before me, saith the LORD, so shall your seed and your name remain.

23 And [a]it shall come to pass, *that* from one new moon to another, and from one sabbath to another, [b]shall all flesh come to worship before me, saith the LORD.

24 And they shall go forth, and look upon the carcases of the men that have transgressed against me: for their [a]worm shall not die, neither shall their fire be quenched; and they shall be an abhorring unto all flesh.

12 [a]Is. 48:18; 60:5 [b]Is. 60:16 [c]Is. 49:22; 60:4
13 [a]Is. 51:3; [2 Cor. 1:3, 4]
14 [a]Ezek. 37:1
15 [a]Is. 9:5; [2 Thess. 1:8]
16 [a]Is. 27:1 [b]Is. 34:6
17 [a]Is. 65:3–8
18 [a]Is. 59:7 [b]Is. 45:22–25; Jer. 3:17
19 [a]Luke 2:34 [b]Mal. 1:11
20 [a]Is. 49:22 [b]Is. 18:7; [Rom. 15:16]
21 [a]Ex. 19:6; Is. 61:6; 1 Pet. 2:9; Rev. 1:6
22 [a]Is. 65:17; Heb. 12:26, 27; 2 Pet. 3:13; Rev. 21:1
23 [a]Zech. 14:16 [b]Zech. 14:17–21
24 [a]Is. 14:11; Mark 9:44, 46, 48

NKJV

12 For thus says the LORD:

"Behold, [a]I will extend peace to her like a river,
And the glory of the Gentiles like a flowing stream.
Then you shall [b]feed;
On *her* sides shall you be [c]carried,
And be dandled on *her* knees.
13 As one whom his mother comforts,
So I will [a]comfort you;
And you shall be comforted in Jerusalem."

The Reign and Indignation of God

14 When you see *this*, your heart shall rejoice,
And [a]your bones shall flourish like grass;
The hand of the LORD shall be known to His servants,
And *His* indignation to His enemies.
15 [a]For behold, the LORD will come with fire
And with His chariots, like a whirlwind,
To render His anger with fury,
And His rebuke with flames of fire.
16 For by fire and by [a]His sword
The LORD will judge all flesh;
And the slain of the LORD shall be [b]many.

17 "Those[a] who sanctify themselves and purify themselves,
To go to the gardens
After an *idol* in the midst,
Eating swine's flesh and the abomination and the mouse,
Shall be consumed together," says the LORD.

18 "For I *know* their works and their [a]thoughts. It shall be that I will [b]gather all nations and tongues; and they shall come and see My glory.

19 [a]"I will set a sign among them; and those among them who escape I will send to the nations: *to* Tarshish and *Pul and Lud, who draw the bow, and Tubal and Javan, *to* the coastlands afar off who have not heard My fame nor seen My glory. [b]And they shall declare My glory among the Gentiles.

20 "Then they shall [a]bring all your brethren [b]for an offering to the LORD out of all nations, on horses and in chariots and in litters, on mules and on camels, to My holy mountain Jerusalem," says the LORD, "as the children of Israel bring an offering in a clean vessel into the house of the LORD.

21 "And I will also take some of them for [a]priests *and* Levites," says the LORD.

22 "For as [a]the new heavens and the new earth
Which I will make shall remain before Me," says the LORD,
"So shall your descendants and your name remain.
23 And [a]it shall come to pass
That from one New Moon to another,
And from one Sabbath to another,
[b]All flesh shall come to worship before Me," says the LORD.

24 "And they shall go forth and look
Upon the corpses of the men
Who have transgressed against Me.
For their [a]worm does not die,
And their fire is not quenched.
They shall be an abhorrence to all flesh."

*———

66:19 So with MT, Tg.; LXX *Put* (cf. Jer. 46:9)

KJV

THE BOOK OF

JEREMIAH

1 The words of Jeremiah the son of Hilkiah, of
the priests that *were* [a]in Anathoth in the land
of Benjamin:
2 To whom the word of the LORD came in
the days of [a]Josiah the son of Amon king of Judah, [b]in the thirteenth year of his reign.
3 It came also in the days of [a]Jehoiakim the
son of Josiah king of Judah, [b]unto the end of the
eleventh year of Zedekiah the son of Josiah king
of Judah, [c]unto the carrying away of Jerusalem
captive [d]in the fifth month.

The Prophet Is Called

4 Then the word of the LORD came unto me,
saying,
5 Before I [a]formed thee in the belly [b]I knew
thee; and before thou camest forth out of the
womb I [c]sanctified thee, *and* I ordained thee a
prophet unto the nations.
6 Then said I, [a]Ah, Lord GOD! behold, I cannot speak: for I *am* a child.
7 But the LORD said unto me, Say not, I *am*
a child: for thou shalt go to all that I shall send
thee, and [a]whatsoever I command thee thou shalt
speak.
8 [a]Be not afraid of their faces: for [b]I *am* with
thee to deliver thee, saith the LORD.
9 Then the LORD put forth his hand, and
[a]touched my mouth. And the LORD said unto me,
Behold, I have [b]put my words in thy mouth.
10 [a]See, I have this day set thee over the nations and over the kingdoms, to [b]root out, and to
pull down, and to destroy, and to throw down,
to build, and to plant.
11 Moreover the word of the LORD came unto
me, saying, Jeremiah, what seest thou? And I said,
I see a rod of an almond tree.
12 Then said the LORD unto me, Thou hast
well seen: for I will hasten my word to perform
it.
13 And the word of the LORD came unto me
the second time, saying, What seest thou? And I
said, I see [a]a seething pot; and the face thereof
is toward the north.
14 Then the LORD said unto me, Out of the
[a]north an evil shall break forth upon all the inhabitants of the land.
15 For, lo, I will [a]call all the families of the
kingdoms of the north, saith the LORD; and they
shall come, and they shall [b]set every one his
throne at the entering of the gates of Jerusalem,

CHAPTER 1

1 [a]Josh. 21:18; 1 Kin. 2:26; 1 Chr. 6:60; Is. 10:30; Jer. 29:27
2 [a]1 Kin. 13:2; 2 Kin. 21:24; 2 Chr. 34:1; Jer. 3:6; 36:2 [b]Jer. 25:3
3 [a]2 Kin. 23:34; 1 Chr. 3:15; 2 Chr. 36:5–8; Jer. 25:1 [b]2 Kin. 24:17; 1 Chr. 3:15; 2 Chr. 36:11–13; Jer. 39:2 [c]Jer. 52:12 [d]2 Kin. 25:8
5 [a]Is. 49:1, 5 [b]Ex. 33:12 [c][Luke 1:15]; Gal. 1:15
6 [a]Ex. 4:10; 6:12, 30
7 [a]Num. 22:20, 38; Jer. 1:17; Matt. 28:20
8 [a]Ezek. 2:6; 3:9 [b]Ex. 3:12; Deut. 31:6; Josh. 1:5; Jer. 15:20; Heb. 13:6
9 [a]Is. 6:7; Mark 7:33–35 [b]Ex. 4:11–16; Deut. 18:18; Is. 51:16
10 [a]1 Kin. 19:17 [b]Jer. 18:7–10; Ezek. 22:18; [2 Cor. 10:4, 5]
13 [a]Ezek. 11:3; 24:3
14 [a]Jer. 6:1
15 [a]Jer. 6:22; 25:9 [b]Is. 22:7; Jer. 39:3

NKJV

THE BOOK OF

JEREMIAH

1 The words of Jeremiah the son of Hilkiah, of
the priests who *were* [a]in Anathoth in the land
of Benjamin,
2 to whom the word of the LORD came in
the days of [a]Josiah the son of Amon, king of Judah, [b]in the thirteenth year of his reign.
3 It came also in the days of [a]Jehoiakim the
son of Josiah, king of Judah, [b]until the end of
the eleventh year of Zedekiah the son of Josiah,
king of Judah, [c]until the carrying away of Jerusalem captive [d]in the fifth month.

The Prophet Is Called

4 Then the word of the LORD came to me,
saying:

5 "Before I [a]formed you in the womb [b]I knew
you;
Before you were born I [c]sanctified you;
I ordained you a prophet to the nations."

6 Then said I:

[a]"Ah, Lord GOD!
Behold, I cannot speak, for I *am* a youth."

7 But the LORD said to me:

"Do not say, 'I *am* a youth,'
For you shall go to all to whom I send
you,
And [a]whatever I command you, you shall
speak.
8 [a]Do not be afraid of their faces,
For [b]I *am* with you to deliver you," says
the LORD.

9 Then the LORD put forth His hand and
[a]touched my mouth, and the LORD said to me:

"Behold, I have [b]put My words in your
mouth.
10 [a]See, I have this day set you over the
nations and over the kingdoms,
To [b]root out and to pull down,
To destroy and to throw down,
To build and to plant."

11 Moreover the word of the LORD came to
me, saying, "Jeremiah, what do you see?" And I
said, "I see a branch of an almond tree."
12 Then the LORD said to me, "You have seen
well, for I am ready to perform My word."
13 And the word of the LORD came to me the
second time, saying, "What do you see?" And I
said, "I see [a]a boiling pot, and it is facing away
from the north."
14 Then the LORD said to me:

"Out of the [a]north calamity shall break
forth
On all the inhabitants of the land.
15 For behold, I am [a]calling
All the families of the kingdoms of the
north," says the LORD;
"They shall come and [b]each one set his
throne
At the entrance of the gates of Jerusalem,

KJV

and against all the walls thereof round about, and
against all the cities of Judah.
16 And I will utter my judgments against
them touching all their wickedness, [a]who have
forsaken me, and have burned [b]incense unto
other gods, and worshipped the works of their
own [c]hands.
17 Thou therefore [a]gird up thy loins, and
arise, and speak unto them all that I command
thee: [b]be not dismayed at their faces, lest I confound thee before them.
18 For, behold, I have made thee this day [a]a
defenced city, and an iron pillar, and brasen walls
against the whole land, against the kings of Judah, against the princes thereof, against the
priests thereof, and against the people of the land.
19 And they shall fight against thee; but they
shall not prevail against thee; for I *am* with thee,
saith the LORD, to deliver thee.

God's Case Against Israel

2 Moreover the word of the LORD came to me,
saying,
2 Go and cry in the ears of Jerusalem, saying, Thus saith the LORD; I remember thee, the
kindness of thy [a]youth, the love of thine espousals, [b]when thou wentest after me in the wilderness, in a land *that was* not sown.
3 [a]Israel *was* holiness unto the LORD, *and*
[b]the firstfruits of his increase: [c]all that devour him
shall offend; evil shall [d]come upon them, saith
the LORD.
4 Hear ye the word of the LORD, O house
of Jacob, and all the families of the house of Israel:
5 Thus saith the LORD, [a]What iniquity have
your fathers found in me, that they are gone far
from me, [b]and have walked after vanity, and are
become vain?
6 Neither said they, Where *is* the LORD that
[a]brought us up out of the land of Egypt, that led
us through [b]the wilderness, through a land of deserts and of pits, through a land of drought, and
of the shadow of death, through a land that no
man passed through, and where no man dwelt?
7 And I brought you into [a]a plentiful country, to eat the fruit thereof and the goodness
thereof; but when ye entered, ye [b]defiled my land,
and made mine heritage an abomination.
8 The priests said not, Where *is* the LORD?
and they that handle the [a]law knew me not: the
pastors also transgressed against me, [b]and the
prophets prophesied by Baal, and walked after
things that do not profit.
9 Wherefore [a]I will yet plead with you, saith
the LORD, and with your children's children will
I plead.

16 [a]Deut. 28:20; Jer. 17:13 [b]Is. 65:3, 4; Jer. 7:9 [c]Is. 37:19; Jer. 2:28
17 [a]1 Kin. 18:46; 2 Kin. 4:29; Job 38:3; Luke 12:35; [1 Pet. 1:13] [b]Ezek. 2:6
18 [a]Is. 50:7; Jer. 6:27; 15:20

CHAPTER 2

2 [a]Ezek. 16:8; Hos. 2:15 [b]Deut. 2:7; Jer. 2:6
3 [a][Ex. 19:5, 6; Deut. 7:6; 14:2] [b]James 1:18; Rev. 14:4 [c]Jer. 12:14 [d]Gen. 12:3; Is. 41:11; Jer. 30:15, 16; 50:7
5 [a]Is. 5:4; Mic. 6:3 [b]2 Kin. 17:15; Jer. 8:19; [Jon. 2:8]; Rom. 1:21
6 [a]Ex. 20:2; Is. 63:11 [b]Deut. 8:15; 32:10
7 [a]Num. 13:27 [b]Num. 35:33; Is. 24:5; Hos. 4:3
8 [a]Rom. 2:20 [b]Jer. 23:13
9 [a]Jer. 2:35; Ezek. 20:35, 36; Mic. 6:2

NKJV

Against all its walls all around,
And against all the cities of Judah.
16 I will utter My judgments
Against them concerning all their
wickedness,
Because [a]they have forsaken Me,
Burned [b]incense to other gods,
And worshiped the works of their own
[c]hands.

17 "Therefore [a]prepare yourself and arise,
And speak to them all that I command
you.
[b]Do not be dismayed before their faces,
Lest I dismay you before them.
18 For behold, I have made you this day
[a]A fortified city and an iron pillar,
And bronze walls against the whole
land—
Against the kings of Judah,
Against its princes,
Against its priests,
And against the people of the land.
19 They will fight against you,
But they shall not prevail against you.
For I *am* with you," says the LORD, "to
deliver you."

God's Case Against Israel

2 Moreover the word of the LORD came to me, saying,
2 "Go and cry in the hearing of Jerusalem, saying, 'Thus says the LORD:

"I remember you,
The kindness of your [a]youth,
The love of your betrothal,
[b]When you went after Me in the
wilderness,
In a land not sown.
3 [a]Israel *was* holiness to the LORD,
[b]The firstfruits of His increase.
[c]All that devour him will offend;
Disaster will [d]come upon them," says the
LORD.' "

4 Hear the word of the LORD, O house of Jacob and all the families of the house of Israel.
5 Thus says the LORD:

[a]"What injustice have your fathers found in
Me,
That they have gone far from Me,
[b]Have followed idols,
And have become idolaters?
6 Neither did they say, 'Where *is* the LORD,
Who [a]brought us up out of the land of
Egypt,
Who led us through [b]the wilderness,
Through a land of deserts and pits,
Through a land of drought and the
shadow of death,
Through a land that no one crossed
And where no one dwelt?'
7 I brought you into [a]a bountiful country,
To eat its fruit and its goodness.
But when you entered, you [b]defiled My
land
And made My heritage an abomination.
8 The priests did not say, 'Where *is* the
LORD?'
And those who handle the [a]law did not
know Me;
The rulers also transgressed against Me;
[b]The prophets prophesied by Baal,
And walked after *things that* do not
profit.

9 "Therefore [a]I will yet bring charges against
you," says the LORD,
"And against your children's children I will
bring charges.

KJV

10 For pass over the isles of Chittim, and see; and send unto Kedar, and consider diligently, and see if there be such a [a]thing.

11 [a]Hath a nation changed *their* gods, which *are* [b]yet no gods? [c]but my people have changed their glory for *that which* doth not profit.

12 Be astonished, O ye heavens, at this, and be horribly afraid, be ye very desolate, saith the LORD.

13 For my people have committed two evils; they have forsaken me the [a]fountain of living waters, *and* hewed them out cisterns, broken cisterns, that can hold no water.

14 *Is* Israel [a]a servant? *is* he a homeborn *slave?* why is he spoiled?

15 [a]The young lions roared upon him, *and* yelled, and they made his land waste: his cities are burned without inhabitant.

16 Also the children of Noph and [a]Tahapanes have broken the crown of thy head.

17 [a]Hast thou not procured this unto thyself, in that thou hast forsaken the LORD thy God, when [b]he led thee by the way?

18 And now what hast thou to do [a]in the way of Egypt, to drink the waters of [b]Sihor? or what hast thou to do in the way of [c]Assyria, to drink the waters of the river?

19 Thine own wickedness shall [a]correct thee, and thy backslidings shall reprove thee: know therefore and see that *it is* an evil *thing* and bitter, that thou hast forsaken the LORD thy God, and that my fear *is* not in thee, saith the Lord GOD of hosts.

20 For of old time I have [a]broken thy yoke, *and* burst thy bands; and [b]thou saidst, I will not transgress; when [c]upon every high hill and under every green tree thou wanderest, [d]playing the harlot.

21 Yet I had [a]planted thee a noble vine, wholly a right seed: how then art thou turned into [b]the degenerate plant of a strange vine unto me?

22 For though thou wash thee with nitre, and take thee much sope, *yet* thine iniquity is [a]marked before me, saith the Lord GOD.

23 [a]How canst thou say, I am not polluted, I have not gone after Baalim? see thy way in the valley, know what thou hast done: *thou art* a swift dromedary traversing her ways;

24 A wild ass used to the wilderness, *that* snuffeth up the wind at her pleasure; in her occasion who can turn her away? all they that seek her will not weary themselves; in her month they shall find her.

25 Withhold thy foot from being unshod, and thy throat from thirst: but thou saidst, [a]There is no hope: no; for I have loved [b]strangers, and after them will I go.

26 As the thief is ashamed when he is found,

10 [a]Jer. 18:13
11 [a]Mic. 4:5 [b]Ps. 115:4; Is. 37:19 [c]Ps. 106:20; Rom. 1:23
13 [a]Ps. 36:9; Jer. 17:13; [John 4:14]
14 [a][Ex. 4:22]
15 [a]Is. 1:7; Jer. 50:17
16 [a]2 Kin. 23:29–37; Jer. 43:7–9
17 [a]Jer. 4:18 [b]Deut. 32:10
18 [a]Is. 30:1–3 [b]Josh. 13:3 [c]Hos. 5:13
19 [a]Is. 3:9; Jer. 4:18; Hos. 5:5
20 [a]Lev. 26:13 [b]Ex. 19:8; Josh. 24:18; Judg. 10:16; 1 Sam. 12:10 [c]Deut. 12:2; Is. 57:5, 7; Jer. 3:6 [d]Ex. 34:15
21 [a]Ex. 15:17; Ps. 44:2; 80:8; Is. 5:2 [b]Deut. 32:32; Is. 5:4
22 [a]Job 14:16, 17; Jer. 17:1, 2; Hos. 13:12
23 [a]Prov. 30:12
25 [a]Is. 57:10; Jer. 18:12 [b]Jer. 3:13

NKJV

10 For pass beyond the coasts of *Cyprus and see,
Send to *Kedar and consider diligently,
And see if there has been such *a* [a]*thing.*
11 [a]Has a nation changed *its* gods,
Which *are* [b]not gods?
[c]But My people have changed their Glory
For *what* does not profit.
12 Be astonished, O heavens, at this,
And be horribly afraid;
Be very desolate," says the LORD.
13 "For My people have committed two evils:
They have forsaken Me, the [a]fountain of living waters,
And hewn themselves cisterns—broken cisterns that can hold no water.

14 "*Is* Israel [a]a servant?
Is he a homeborn *slave?*
Why is he plundered?
15 [a]The young lions roared at him, *and* growled;
They made his land waste;
His cities are burned, without inhabitant.
16 Also the people of *Noph and [a]Tahpanhes
Have broken the crown of your head.
17 [a]Have you not brought this on yourself,
In that you have forsaken the LORD your God
When [b]He led you in the way?
18 And now why take [a]the road to Egypt,
To drink the waters of [b]Sihor?
Or why take the road to [c]Assyria,
To drink the waters of *the River?
19 Your own wickedness will [a]correct you,
And your backslidings will rebuke you.
Know therefore and see that *it is* an evil and bitter *thing*
That you have forsaken the LORD your God,
And the fear of Me *is* not in you,"
Says the Lord GOD of hosts.

20 "For of old I have [a]broken your yoke *and* burst your bonds;
And [b]you said, 'I will not transgress,'
When [c]on every high hill and under every green tree
You lay down, [d]playing the harlot.
21 Yet I had [a]planted you a noble vine, a seed of highest quality.
How then have you turned before Me
Into [b]the degenerate plant of an alien vine?
22 For though you wash yourself with lye, and use much soap,
Yet your iniquity is [a]marked before Me,"
says the Lord GOD.

23 "How[a] can you say, 'I am not polluted,
I have not gone after the Baals'?
See your way in the valley;
Know what you have done:
You are a swift dromedary breaking loose in her ways,
24 A wild donkey used to the wilderness,
That sniffs at the wind in her desire;
In her time of mating, who can turn her away?
All those who seek her will not weary themselves;
In her month they will find her.
25 Withhold your foot from being unshod, and your throat from thirst.
But you said, [a]'There is no hope.
No! For I have loved [b]aliens, and after them I will go.'

26 "As the thief is ashamed when he is found out,

*
2:10 Heb. *Kittim,* representative of western cultures • In northern Arabian desert, representative of eastern cultures
2:16 Memphis in ancient Egypt
2:18 The Euphrates

KJV

so is the house of Israel ashamed; they, their kings, their princes, and their priests, and their [a]prophets,

27 Saying to a stock, Thou *art* my father; and to a [a]stone, Thou hast brought me forth: for they have turned *their* back unto me, and not *their* face: but in the time of their [b]trouble they will say, Arise, and save us.

28 But [a]where *are* thy gods that thou hast made thee? let them arise, if they [b]can save thee in the time of thy trouble: for [c]*according to* the number of thy cities are thy gods, O Judah.

29 Wherefore will ye plead with me? ye all have transgressed against me, saith the LORD.

30 In vain have I [a]smitten your children; they [b]received no correction: your own sword hath [c]devoured your prophets, like a destroying lion.

31 O generation, see ye the word of the LORD. Have I been a wilderness unto Israel? a land of darkness? wherefore say my people, We are lords; [a]we will come no more unto thee?

32 Can a maid forget her ornaments, *or* a bride her attire? yet my people [a]have forgotten me days without number.

33 Why trimmest thou thy way to seek love? therefore hast thou also taught the wicked ones thy ways.

34 Also in thy skirts is found [a]the blood of the souls of the poor innocents: I have not found it by secret search, but upon all these.

35 [a]Yet thou sayest, Because I am innocent, surely his anger shall turn from me. Behold, [b]I will plead with thee, [c]because thou sayest, I have not sinned.

36 [a]Why gaddest thou about so much to change thy way? [b]thou also shalt be ashamed of Egypt, [c]as thou wast ashamed of Assyria.

37 Yea, thou shalt go forth from him, and thine hands upon [a]thine head: for the LORD hath rejected thy confidences, and thou shalt [b]not prosper in them.

Israel Is Shameless

3 They say, If a man put away his wife, and she go from him, and become another man's, [a]shall he return unto her again? shall not that [b]land be greatly polluted? but thou hast [c]played the harlot with many lovers; [d]yet return again to me, saith the LORD.

2 Lift up thine eyes unto [a]the high places, and see where thou hast not been lien with. [b]In the ways hast thou sat for them, as the Arabian in the wilderness; [c]and thou hast polluted the land with thy whoredoms and with thy wickedness.

3 Therefore the [a]showers have been withholden, and there hath been no latter rain; and thou hadst a [b]whore's forehead, thou refusedst to be ashamed.

---

26 [a]Is. 28:7; Jer. 5:31
27 [a]Jer. 3:9 [b]Judg. 10:10; Is. 26:16; Hos. 5:15
28 [a]Deut. 32:37; Judg. 10:14 [b]Is. 45:20 [c]2 Kin. 17:30, 31; Jer. 11:13
30 [a]Is. 9:13 [b]Is. 1:5; Jer. 5:3; 7:28 [c]Neh. 9:26; Jer. 26:20–24; Acts 7:52; 1 Thess. 2:15
31 [a]Deut. 32:15; Jer. 2:20, 25
32 [a]Ps. 106:21; Is. 17:10; Jer. 3:21; 13:25; Hos. 8:14
34 [a]2 Kin. 21:16; 24:4; Ps. 106:38; Jer. 7:6; 19:4
35 [a]Jer. 2:23, 29; Mal. 2:17; 3:8 [b]Jer. 2:9 [c][Prov. 28:13; 1 John 1:8, 10]
36 [a]Jer. 31:22; Hos. 5:13; 12:1 [b]Is. 30:3 [c]2 Chr. 28:16
37 [a]2 Sam. 13:19; Jer. 14:3, 4 [b]Jer. 37:7–10

CHAPTER 3

1 [a]Deut. 24:1–4 [b]Jer. 2:7 [c]Jer. 2:20; Ezek. 16:26 [d]Jer. 4:1; [Zech. 1:3]
2 [a]Deut. 12:2; Jer. 2:20; 3:21; 7:29 [b]Prov. 23:28 [c]Jer. 2:7
3 [a]Lev. 26:19; Jer. 14:3–6 [b]Zeph. 3:5

NKJV

So is the house of Israel ashamed;
They and their kings and their princes,
and their priests and their [a]prophets,
27 Saying to a tree, 'You *are* my father,'
And to a [a]stone, 'You gave birth to me.'
For they have turned *their* back to Me,
and not *their* face.
But in the time of their [b]trouble
They will say, 'Arise and save us.'
28 But [a]where *are* your gods that you have
made for yourselves?
Let them arise,
If they [b]can save you in the time of your
trouble;
For [c]*according to* the number of your
cities
Are your gods, O Judah.

29 "Why will you plead with Me?
You all have transgressed against Me,"
says the LORD.
30 "In vain I have [a]chastened your children;
They [b]received no correction.
Your sword has [c]devoured your prophets
Like a destroying lion.

31 "O generation, see the word of the LORD!
Have I been a wilderness to Israel,
Or a land of darkness?
Why do My people say, 'We are lords;
[a]We will come no more to You'?
32 Can a virgin forget her ornaments,
Or a bride her attire?
Yet My people [a]have forgotten Me days
without number.

33 "Why do you beautify your way to seek
love?
Therefore you have also taught
The wicked women your ways.
34 Also on your skirts is found
[a]The blood of the lives of the poor
innocents.
I have not found it by secret search,
But plainly on all these things.
35 [a]Yet you say, 'Because I am innocent,
Surely His anger shall turn from me.'
Behold, [b]I will plead My case against you,
[c]Because you say, 'I have not sinned.'
36 [a]Why do you gad about so much to change
your way?
Also [b]you shall be ashamed of Egypt [c]as
you were ashamed of Assyria.
37 Indeed you will go forth from him
With your hands on [a]your head;
For the LORD has rejected your trusted
allies,
And you will [b]not prosper by them.

Israel Is Shameless

3 "They say, 'If a man divorces his wife,
And she goes from him
And becomes another man's,
[a]May he return to her again?'
Would not that [b]land be greatly polluted?
But you have [c]played the harlot with
many lovers;
[d]Yet return to Me," says the LORD.

2 "Lift up your eyes to [a]the desolate heights
and see:
Where have you not lain *with men?*
[b]By the road you have sat for them
Like an Arabian in the wilderness;
[c]And you have polluted the land
With your harlotries and your
wickedness.
3 Therefore the [a]showers have been
withheld,
And there has been no latter rain.
You have had a [b]harlot's forehead;
You refuse to be ashamed.

KJV

4 Wilt thou not from this time cry unto me, My father, thou *art* [a]the guide of [b]my youth?

5 [a]Will he reserve *his anger* for ever? will he keep *it* to the end? Behold, thou hast spoken and done evil things as thou couldest.

A Call to Repentance

6 The LORD said also unto me in the days of Josiah the king, Hast thou seen *that* which [a]backsliding Israel hath done? she is [b]gone up upon every high mountain and under every green tree, and there hath played the harlot.

7 [a]And I said after she had done all these *things*, Turn thou unto me. But she returned not. And her treacherous [b]sister Judah saw *it*.

8 And I saw, when [a]for all the causes whereby backsliding Israel committed adultery I had [b]put her away, and given her a bill of divorce; [c]yet her treacherous sister Judah feared not, but went and played the harlot also.

9 And it came to pass through the lightness of her whoredom, that she [a]defiled the land, and committed adultery with [b]stones and with stocks.

10 And yet for all this her treacherous sister Judah hath not turned unto me [a]with her whole heart, but feignedly, saith the LORD.

11 And the LORD said unto me, [a]The backsliding Israel hath justified herself more than treacherous Judah.

12 Go and proclaim these words toward [a]the north, and say, Return, thou backsliding Israel, saith the LORD; *and* I will not cause mine anger to fall upon you: for I *am* [b]merciful, saith the LORD, *and* I will not keep *anger* for ever.

13 [a]Only acknowledge thine iniquity, that thou hast transgressed against the LORD thy God, and hast [b]scattered thy ways to the [c]strangers [d]under every green tree, and ye have not obeyed my voice, saith the LORD.

14 Turn, O backsliding children, saith the LORD; [a]for I am married unto you: and I will take you [b]one of a city, and two of a family, and I will bring you to [c]Zion:

15 And I will give you [a]pastors according to mine heart, which shall [b]feed you with knowledge and understanding.

16 And it shall come to pass, when ye be multiplied and [a]increased in the land, in those days, saith the LORD, they shall say no more, The ark of the covenant of the LORD: [b]neither shall it come to mind: neither shall they remember it; neither shall they visit *it;* neither shall *that* be done any more.

17 At that time they shall call Jerusalem the throne of the LORD; and all the nations shall be gathered unto it, [a]to the name of the LORD, to Jerusalem: neither shall they [b]walk any more after the imagination of their evil heart.

18 In those days [a]the house of Judah shall walk with the house of Israel, and they shall come together out of the land of [b]the north to [c]the land that I have given for an inheritance unto your fathers.

19 But I said, How shall I put thee among the children, and give thee [a]a pleasant land, a goodly heritage of the hosts of nations? and I said, Thou shalt call me, [b]My father; and shalt not turn away from me.

4 [a]Ps. 71:17; Prov. 2:17 [b]Jer. 2:2; Hos. 2:15 **5** [a]Ps. 103:9; [Is. 57:16]; Jer. 3:12 **6** [a]Jer. 7:24 [b]Jer. 2:20 **7** [a]2 Kin. 17:13 [b]Jer. 3:11; Ezek. 16:47, 48 **8** [a]Ezek. 23:9 [b]2 Kin. 17:6; Is. 50:1 [c]Ezek. 23:11 **9** [a]Jer. 2:7 [b]Is. 57:6; Jer. 2:27 **10** [a]Jer. 12:2; Hos. 7:14 **11** [a]Ezek. 16:51, 52 **12** [a]2 Kin. 17:6 [b]Ps. 86:15; Jer. 12:15; 31:20; 33:26 **13** [a]Lev. 26:40; Deut. 30:1, 2; [Prov. 28:13; 1 John 1:9] [b]Ezek. 16:15 [c]Jer. 2:25 [d]Deut. 12:2 **14** [a]Jer. 31:32; Hos. 2:19, 20 [b]Jer. 31:6 [c][Rom. 11:5] **15** [a]Jer. 23:4; 31:10; [Ezek. 34:23]; Eph. 4:11 [b]Acts 20:28 **16** [a]Is. 49:19; Jer. 23:3 [b]Is. 65:17 **17** [a]Is. 60:9 [b]Deut. 29:19; Jer. 7:24 **18** [a]Is. 11:13; Jer. 50:4; Ezek. 37:16–22; Hos. 1:11 [b]Jer. 31:8 [c]Amos 9:15 **19** [a]Ps. 106:24 [b]Is. 63:16; Jer. 3:4

NKJV

4 Will you not from this time cry to Me,
'My Father, You *are* [a]the guide of [b]my youth?
5 [a]Will He remain angry forever?
Will He keep it to the end?'
Behold, you have spoken and done evil things,
As you were able."

A Call to Repentance

6 The LORD said also to me in the days of Josiah the king: "Have you seen what [a]backsliding Israel has done? She has [b]gone up on every high mountain and under every green tree, and there played the harlot.

7 [a]"And I said, after she had done all these *things*, 'Return to Me.' But she did not return. And her treacherous [b]sister Judah saw it.

8 "Then I saw that [a]for all the causes for which backsliding Israel had committed adultery, I had [b]put her away and given her a certificate of divorce; [c]yet her treacherous sister Judah did not fear, but went and played the harlot also.

9 "So it came to pass, through her casual harlotry, that she [a]defiled the land and committed adultery with [b]stones and trees.

10 "And yet for all this her treacherous sister Judah has not turned to Me [a]with her whole heart, but in pretense," says the LORD.

11 Then the LORD said to me, [a]"Backsliding Israel has shown herself more righteous than treacherous Judah.

12 "Go and proclaim these words toward [a]the north, and say:

'Return, backsliding Israel,' says the LORD;
'I will not cause My anger to fall on you.
For I *am* [b]merciful,' says the LORD;
'I will not remain angry forever.
13 [a]Only acknowledge your iniquity,
That you have transgressed against the LORD your God,
And have [b]scattered your charms
To [c]alien deities [d]under every green tree,
And you have not obeyed My voice,' says the LORD.

14 "Return, O backsliding children," says the LORD; [a]"for I am married to you. I will take you, [b]one from a city and two from a family, and I will bring you to [c]Zion.

15 "And I will give you [a]shepherds according to My heart, who will [b]feed you with knowledge and understanding.

16 "Then it shall come to pass, when you are multiplied and [a]increased in the land in those days," says the LORD, "that they will say no more, 'The ark of the covenant of the LORD.' [b]It shall not come to mind, nor shall they remember it, nor shall they visit *it*, nor shall it be made anymore.

17 "At that time Jerusalem shall be called The Throne of the LORD, and all the nations shall be gathered to it, [a]to the name of the LORD, to Jerusalem. No more shall they [b]follow the dictates of their evil hearts.

18 "In those days [a]the house of Judah shall walk with the house of Israel, and they shall come together out of the land of [b]the north to [c]the land that I have given as an inheritance to your fathers.

19 "But I said:

'How can I put you among the children
And give you [a]a pleasant land,
A beautiful heritage of the hosts of nations?'

"And I said:

'You shall call Me, [b]"My Father,"
And not turn away from Me.'

KJV

20 Surely *as* a wife treacherously departeth
from her husband, so [a]have ye dealt treacherously
with me, O house of Israel, saith the LORD.
21 A voice was heard upon [a]the high places,
weeping *and* supplications of the children of Israel: for they have perverted their way, *and* they
have forgotten the LORD their God.
22 Return, ye backsliding children, *and* I will
[a]heal your backslidings. Behold, we come unto
thee; for thou *art* the LORD our God.
23 [a]Truly in vain *is salvation hoped for* from
the hills, *and from* the multitude of mountains:
[b]truly in the LORD our God *is* the salvation of
Israel.
24 [a]For shame hath devoured the labour of
our fathers from our youth; their flocks and their
herds, their sons and their daughters.
25 We lie down in our shame, and our confusion covereth us: [a]for we have sinned against the
LORD our God, we and our fathers, from our youth
even unto this day, and [b]have not obeyed the
voice of the LORD our God.

4 If thou wilt return, O Israel, saith the LORD,
[a]return unto me: and if thou wilt put away
thine abominations out of my sight, then shalt
thou not remove.
2 [a]And thou shalt swear, The LORD liveth,
[b]in truth, in judgment, and in righteousness; [c]and
the nations shall bless themselves in him, and in
him shall they [d]glory.
3 For thus saith the LORD to the men of Judah and Jerusalem, [a]Break up your fallow
ground, and [b]sow not among thorns.
4 [a]Circumcise yourselves to the LORD, and
take away the foreskins of your heart, ye men of
Judah and inhabitants of Jerusalem: lest my fury
come forth like fire, and burn that none can
quench *it*, because of the evil of your doings.

An Imminent Invasion

5 Declare ye in Judah, and publish in Jerusalem; and say, [a]Blow ye the trumpet in the land:
cry, gather together, and say, [b]Assemble yourselves, and let us go into the defenced cities.
6 Set up the standard toward Zion: retire,
stay not: for I will bring evil from the [a]north, and
a great destruction.
7 [a]The lion is come up from his thicket, and
[b]the destroyer of the Gentiles is on his way; he
is gone forth from his place [c]to make thy land
desolate; *and* thy cities shall be laid waste, without an inhabitant.
8 For this [a]gird you with sackcloth, lament

20 [a]Is. 48:8
21 [a]Is. 15:2
22 [a]Jer. 30:17; 33:6; Hos. 6:1; 14:4
23 [a]Ps. 121:1, 2 [b]Ps. 3:8; Prov. 21:31; Jer. 17:14; 31:7; Jon. 2:9
24 [a]Jer. 11:13; 14:20; Hos. 9:10
25 [a]Ezra 9:6, 7 [b]Jer. 22:21

CHAPTER 4

1 [a]Jer. 3:1, 22; 15:19; Joel 2:12
2 [a]Deut. 10:20; Is. 45:23; 65:16; Jer. 12:16 [b]Is. 48:1; Zech. 8:8 [c][Gen. 22:18]; Ps. 72:18; Is. 65:16; Jer. 3:17; [Gal. 3:8] [d]Is. 45:25; Jer. 9:24; 1 Cor. 1:31; 2 Cor. 10:17
3 [a]Hos. 10:12 [b]Matt. 13:7
4 [a]Deut. 10:16; 30:6; Jer. 9:25, 26; [Rom. 2:28, 29; Col. 2:11]
5 [a]Jer. 6:1; Hos. 8:1 [b]Josh. 10:20; Jer. 8:14
6 [a]Jer. 1:13–15; 6:1, 22; 50:17
7 [a]2 Kin. 24:1; Dan. 7:4 [b]Jer. 25:9; Ezek. 26:7–10 [c]Is. 1:7; 6:11; Jer. 2:15
8 [a]Is. 22:12; Jer. 6:26

NKJV

20 Surely, *as* a wife treacherously departs
from her husband,
So [a]have you dealt treacherously with Me,
O house of Israel," says the LORD.

21 A voice was heard on [a]the desolate
heights,
Weeping *and* supplications of the children
of Israel.
For they have perverted their way;
They have forgotten the LORD their God.

22 "Return, you backsliding children,
And I will [a]heal your backslidings."

"Indeed we do come to You,
For You are the LORD our God.
23 [a]Truly, in vain *is salvation hoped for* from
the hills,
And from the multitude of mountains;
[b]Truly, in the LORD our God
Is the salvation of Israel.
24 [a]For shame has devoured
The labor of our fathers from our youth—
Their flocks and their herds,
Their sons and their daughters.
25 We lie down in our shame,
And our reproach covers us.
[a]For we have sinned against the LORD our
God,
We and our fathers,
From our youth even to this day,
And [b]have not obeyed the voice of the
LORD our God."

4 "If you will return, O Israel," says the LORD,
[a]"Return to Me;
And if you will put away your
abominations out of My sight,
Then you shall not be moved.
2 [a]And you shall swear, 'The LORD lives,'
[b]In truth, in judgment, and in
righteousness;
[c]The nations shall bless themselves in
Him,
And in Him they shall [d]glory."

3 For thus says the LORD to the men of Judah and Jerusalem:

[a]"Break up your fallow ground,
And [b]do not sow among thorns.
4 [a]Circumcise yourselves to the LORD,
And take away the foreskins of your
hearts,
You men of Judah and inhabitants of
Jerusalem,
Lest My fury come forth like fire,
And burn so that no one can quench *it*,
Because of the evil of your doings."

An Imminent Invasion

5 Declare in Judah and proclaim in Jerusalem, and say:

[a]"Blow the trumpet in the land;
Cry, 'Gather together,'
And say, [b]'Assemble yourselves,
And let us go into the fortified cities.'
6 Set up the standard toward Zion.
Take refuge! Do not delay!
For I will bring disaster from the [a]north,
And great destruction."

7 [a]The lion has come up from his thicket,
And [b]the destroyer of nations is on his
way.
He has gone forth from his place
[c]To make your land desolate.
Your cities will be laid waste,
Without inhabitant.
8 For this, [a]clothe yourself with sackcloth,

KJV

and howl: for the fierce anger of the LORD is not
turned back from us.
9 And it shall come to pass at that day, saith
the LORD, *that* the heart of the king shall perish,
and the heart of the princes; and the priests shall
be astonished, and the prophets shall wonder.
10 Then said I, Ah, Lord GOD! [a]surely thou
hast greatly deceived this people and Jerusalem,
[b]saying, Ye shall have peace; whereas the sword
reacheth unto the soul.
11 At that time shall it be said to this people
and to Jerusalem, [a]A dry wind of the high places
in the wilderness toward the daughter of my people, not to fan, nor to cleanse,
12 *Even* a full wind from those *places* shall
come unto me: now also [a]will I give sentence
against them.
13 Behold, he shall come up as clouds, and
[a]his chariots *shall be* as a whirlwind: [b]his horses
are swifter than eagles. Woe unto us! for we are
spoiled.
14 O Jerusalem, [a]wash thine heart from
wickedness, that thou mayest be saved. How long
shall thy vain thoughts lodge within thee?
15 For a voice declareth [a]from Dan, and publisheth affliction from mount Ephraim.
16 Make ye mention to the nations; behold,
publish against Jerusalem, *that* watchers come
from a [a]far country, and give out their voice
against the cities of Judah.
17 [a]As keepers of a field, are they against
her round about; because she hath been rebellious
against me, saith the LORD.
18 [a]Thy way and thy doings have procured
these *things* unto thee; this *is* thy wickedness, because it is bitter, because it reacheth unto thine
heart.

Sorrow for the Doomed Nation

19 My [a]bowels, my bowels! I am pained at
my very heart; my heart maketh a noise in me; I
cannot hold my peace, because thou hast heard,
O my soul, the sound of the trumpet, the alarm
of war.
20 [a]Destruction upon destruction is cried; for
the whole land is spoiled: suddenly are [b]my tents
spoiled, *and* my curtains in a moment.
21 How long shall I see the standard, *and*
hear the sound of the trumpet?
22 For my people *is* foolish, they have not
known me; they *are* sottish children, and they
have none understanding: [a]they *are* wise to do
evil, but to do good they have no knowledge.
23 [a]I beheld the earth, and, lo, *it was* [b]with-
out form, and void; and the heavens, and they *had*
no light.

10 [a]2 Kin. 25:10–12; Ezek. 14:9; 2 Thess. 2:11 [b]Jer. 5:12; 14:13
11 [a]Jer. 51:1; Ezek. 17:10; Hos. 13:15
12 [a]Jer. 1:16
13 [a]Is. 5:28 [b]Deut. 28:49; Lam. 4:19; Hos. 8:1; Hab. 1:8
14 [a]Prov. 1:22; Is. 1:16; Jer. 13:27; James 4:8
15 [a]Jer. 8:16; 50:17
16 [a]Is. 39:3; Jer. 5:15
17 [a]2 Kin. 25:1, 4
18 [a]Ps. 107:17; Is. 50:1; Jer. 2:17, 19
19 [a]2 Kin. 25:11; 2 Chr. 36:20; Is. 15:5; 16:11; 21:3; 22:4; Jer. 9:1, 10; 20:9
20 [a]Ps. 42:7; Ezek. 7:26 [b]Jer. 10:20
22 [a]Jer. 9:3; 13:23; Rom. 16:19; 1 Cor. 14:20
23 [a]Is. 24:19 [b]Gen. 1:2

NKJV

Lament and wail.
For the fierce anger of the LORD
Has not turned back from us.

9 "And it shall come to pass in that day,"
says the LORD,
"*That* the heart of the king shall perish,
And the heart of the princes;
The priests shall be astonished,
And the prophets shall wonder."

10 Then I said, "Ah, Lord GOD!
[a]Surely You have greatly deceived this
people and Jerusalem,
[b]Saying, 'You shall have peace,'
Whereas the sword reaches to the
heart."

11 At that time it will be said
To this people and to Jerusalem,
[a]"A dry wind of the desolate heights *blows*
in the wilderness
Toward the daughter of My people—
Not to fan or to cleanse—
12 A wind too strong for these will come for
Me;
Now [a]I will also speak judgment against
them."

13 "Behold, he shall come up like clouds,
And [a]his chariots like a whirlwind.
[b]His horses are swifter than eagles.
Woe to us, for we are plundered!"

14 O Jerusalem, [a]wash your heart from
wickedness,
That you may be saved.
How long shall your evil thoughts lodge
within you?
15 For a voice declares [a]from Dan
And proclaims affliction from Mount
Ephraim:
16 "Make mention to the nations,
Yes, proclaim against Jerusalem,
That watchers come from a [a]far country
And raise their voice against the cities of
Judah.
17 [a]Like keepers of a field they are against
her all around,
Because she has been rebellious against
Me," says the LORD.
18 "Your[a] ways and your doings
Have procured these *things* for you.
This *is* your wickedness,
Because it is bitter,
Because it reaches to your heart."

Sorrow for the Doomed Nation

19 O my [a]soul, my soul!
I am pained in my very heart!
My heart makes a noise in me;
I cannot hold my peace,
Because you have heard, O my soul,
The sound of the trumpet,
The alarm of war.
20 [a]Destruction upon destruction is cried,
For the whole land is plundered.
Suddenly [b]my tents are plundered,
And my curtains in a moment.
21 How long will I see the standard,
And hear the sound of the trumpet?

22 "For My people *are* foolish,
They have not known Me.
They *are* silly children,
And they have no understanding.
[a]They *are* wise to do evil,
But to do good they have no knowledge."

23 [a]I beheld the earth, and indeed *it was*
[b]without form, and void;
And the heavens, they *had* no light.

KJV

24 [a]I beheld the mountains, and, lo, they
trembled, and all the hills moved lightly.
25 I beheld, and, lo, *there was* no man, and
[a]all the birds of the heavens were fled.
26 I beheld, and, lo, the fruitful place *was* a
[a]wilderness, and all the cities thereof were broken
down at the presence of the LORD, *and* by his fierce
anger.
27 For thus hath the LORD said, The whole
land shall be desolate; [a]yet will I not make a full
end.
28 For this [a]shall the earth mourn, and [b]the
heavens above be black: because I have spoken
it, I have [c]purposed *it*, and [d]will not repent, neither will I turn back from it.
29 The whole city shall flee for the noise of
the horsemen and bowmen; they shall go into
thickets, and climb up upon the rocks: every city
shall be forsaken, and not a man dwell therein.
30 And *when* thou *art* spoiled, what wilt thou
do? Though thou clothest thyself with crimson,
though thou deckest thee with ornaments of gold,
[a]though thou rentest thy face with painting, in
vain shalt thou make thyself fair; [b]*thy* lovers will
despise thee, they will seek thy life.
31 For I have heard a voice as of a woman
in travail, *and* the anguish as of her that bringeth
forth her first child, the voice of the daughter of
Zion, *that* bewaileth herself, *that* [a]spreadeth her
hands, *saying*, Woe *is* me now! for my soul is wearied because of murderers.

24 [a]Is. 5:25; Jer. 10:10; Ezek. 38:20 **25** [a]Jer. 9:10; 12:4; Zeph. 1:3 **26** [a]Jer. 9:10 **27** [a]Jer. 5:10, 18; 30:11; 46:28 **28** [a]Jer. 12:4, 11; 14:2; Hos. 4:3 [b]Is. 5:30; 50:3; Joel 2:30, 31 [c]Is. 46:10, 11; [Dan. 4:35] [d][Num. 23:19]; Jer. 7:16; 23:30; 30:24 **30** [a]2 Kin. 9:30; Ezek. 23:40 [b]Jer. 22:20, 22; Lam. 1:2, 19; Ezek. 23:9, 10, 22 **31** [a]Is. 1:15; Lam. 1:17

NKJV

24 [a]I beheld the mountains, and indeed they trembled,
And all the hills moved back and forth.
25 I beheld, and indeed *there was* no man,
And [a]all the birds of the heavens had fled.
26 I beheld, and indeed the fruitful land *was* a [a]wilderness,
And all its cities were broken down
At the presence of the LORD,
By His fierce anger.

27 For thus says the LORD:

"The whole land shall be desolate;
[a]Yet I will not make a full end.
28 For this [a]shall the earth mourn,
And [b]the heavens above be black,
Because I have spoken.
I have [c]purposed and [d]will not relent,
Nor will I turn back from it.
29 The whole city shall flee from the noise of the horsemen and bowmen.
They shall go into thickets and climb up on the rocks.
Every city *shall be* forsaken,
And not a man shall dwell in it.

30 "And *when* you *are* plundered,
What will you do?
Though you clothe yourself with crimson,
Though you adorn *yourself* with ornaments of gold,
[a]Though you enlarge your eyes with paint,
In vain you will make yourself fair;
[b]*Your* lovers will despise you;
They will seek your life.

31 "For I have heard a voice as of a woman in labor,
The anguish as of her who brings forth her first child,
The voice of the daughter of Zion bewailing herself;
She [a]spreads her hands, *saying*,
'Woe *is* me now, for my soul is weary
Because of murderers!'

The Justice of God's Judgment

KJV

5 Run ye to and fro through the streets of Jerusalem, and see now, and know, and seek in
the broad places thereof, [a]if ye can find a man,
[b]if there be *any* that executeth judgment, that
seeketh the truth; [c]and I will pardon it.
2 And [a]though they say, [b]The LORD liveth;
surely they [c]swear falsely.
3 O LORD, *are* not [a]thine eyes upon the
truth? thou hast [b]stricken them, but they have not
grieved; thou hast consumed them, *but* [c]they have
refused to receive correction: they have made
their faces harder than a rock; they have refused
to return.
4 Therefore I said, Surely these *are* poor;
they are foolish: for [a]they know not the way of
the LORD, *nor* the judgment of their God.
5 I will get me unto the great men, and will
speak unto them; for [a]they have known the way
of the LORD, *and* the judgment of their God: but
these have altogether [b]broken the yoke, *and* burst
the bonds.

CHAPTER 5

1 [a]Ezek. 22:30 [b]Gen. 18:23–32 [c]Gen. 18:26 **2** [a]Is. 48:1; Titus 1:16 [b]Jer. 4:2 [c]Jer. 7:9 **3** [a]2 Kin. 25:1; [2 Chr. 16:9; Jer. 16:17] [b]Is. 1:5; 9:13; Jer. 2:30 [c]Is. 9:13; Jer. 7:28; Zeph. 3:2 **4** [a]Is. 27:11; Jer. 8:7; Hos. 4:6 **5** [a]Mic. 3:1 [b]Ex. 32:25; Ps. 2:3; Jer. 2:20

NKJV

The Justice of God's Judgment

5 "Run to and fro through the streets of Jerusalem;
See now and know;
And seek in her open places
[a]If you can find a man,
[b]If there is *anyone* who executes judgment,
Who seeks the truth,
[c]And I will pardon her.
2 [a]Though they say, '*As* [b]the LORD lives,'
Surely they [c]swear falsely."

3 O LORD, *are* not [a]Your eyes on the truth?
You have [b]stricken them,
But they have not grieved;
You have consumed them,
But [c]they have refused to receive correction.
They have made their faces harder than rock;
They have refused to return.

4 Therefore I said, "Surely these *are* poor.
They are foolish;
For [a]they do not know the way of the LORD,
The judgment of their God.
5 I will go to the great men and speak to them,
For [a]they have known the way of the LORD,
The judgment of their God."

But these have altogether [b]broken the yoke
And burst the bonds.

KJV

6 Wherefore [a]a lion out of the forest shall
slay them, [b]*and* a wolf of the evenings shall spoil
them, [c]a leopard shall watch over their cities:
every one that goeth out thence shall be torn in
pieces: because their transgressions are many,
and their backslidings are increased.
7 How shall I pardon thee for this? thy children have forsaken me, and [a]sworn by *them* [b]*that
are* no gods: [c]when I had fed them to the full,
they then committed adultery, and assembled
themselves by troops in the harlots' houses.
8 [a]They were *as* fed horses in the morning:
every one neighed after his neighbour's wife.
9 Shall I not visit for these *things?* saith the
LORD: and shall not my soul be [a]avenged on such
a nation as this?
10 Go ye up upon her walls, and destroy; but
make not a [a]full end: take away her battlements;
for they *are* not the LORD'S.
11 For [a]the house of Israel and the house of
Judah have dealt very treacherously against me,
saith the LORD.
12 [a]They have belied the LORD, and said, [b]*It
is* not he; [c]neither shall evil come upon us; neither
shall we see sword nor famine:
13 And the prophets shall become wind, and
the word *is* not in them: thus shall it be done unto
them.
14 Wherefore thus saith the LORD God of
hosts, Because ye speak this word, [a]behold, I will
make my words in thy mouth fire, and this people
wood, and it shall devour them.
15 Lo, I will bring a [a]nation upon you [b]from
far, O house of Israel, saith the LORD: it *is* a mighty
nation, it *is* an ancient nation, a nation whose language thou knowest not, neither understandest
what they say.
16 Their quiver *is* as an open sepulchre, they
are all mighty men.
17 And they shall eat up thine [a]harvest, and
thy bread, *which* thy sons and thy daughters
should eat: they shall eat up thy flocks and thine
herds: they shall eat up thy vines and thy fig trees:
they shall impoverish thy fenced cities, wherein
thou trustedst, with the sword.
18 Nevertheless in those days, saith the LORD,
I [a]will not make a full end with you.
19 And it shall come to pass, when ye shall
say, [a]Wherefore doeth the LORD our God all these
things unto us? then shalt thou answer them, Like
as ye have [b]forsaken me, and served strange gods
in your land, so [c]shall ye serve strangers in a land
that is not your's.
20 Declare this in the house of Jacob, and
publish it in Judah, saying,

6 [a]Jer. 4:7 [b]Ps. 104:20; Ezek. 22:27; Hab. 1:8; Zeph. 3:3 [c]Hos. 13:7 **7** [a]Josh. 23:7; Jer. 12:16; Zeph. 1:5 [b]Deut. 32:21; Jer. 2:11; Gal. 4:8 [c]Deut. 32:15 **8** [a]Jer. 13:27; 29:23; Ezek. 22:11 **9** [a]Jer. 9:9 **10** [a]Jer. 4:27 **11** [a]Jer. 3:6, 7, 20 **12** [a]2 Chr. 36:16; Jer. 4:10 [b]Is. 28:15; 47:8; Jer. 23:17 [c]Jer. 14:13 **14** [a]Is. 24:6; Jer. 1:9; 23:29; Hos. 6:5; Zech. 1:6 **15** [a]Deut. 28:49; Is. 5:26; Jer. 1:15; 6:22 [b]Is. 39:3; Jer. 4:16 **17** [a]Lev. 26:16; Deut. 28:31, 33; Jer. 8:16; 50:7, 17 **18** [a]Jer. 30:11; Amos 9:8 **19** [a]Deut. 29:24–29; 1 Kin. 9:8, 9; Jer. 13:22; 16:10–13 [b]Jer. 1:16; 2:13 [c]Deut. 28:48; Jer. 16:13

NKJV

6 Therefore [a]a lion from the forest shall slay
them,
[b]A wolf of the deserts shall destroy
them;
[c]A leopard will watch over their cities.
Everyone who goes out from there shall
be torn in pieces,
Because their transgressions are many;
Their backslidings have increased.

7 "How shall I pardon you for this?
Your children have forsaken Me
And [a]sworn by *those* [b]*that are* not gods.
[c]When I had fed them to the full,
Then they committed adultery
And assembled themselves by troops in
the harlots' houses.
8 [a]They were *like* well-fed lusty stallions;
Every one neighed after his neighbor's
wife.
9 Shall I not punish *them* for these *things?*"
says the LORD.
"And shall I not [a]avenge Myself on such a
nation as this?

10 "Go up on her walls and destroy,
But do not make a [a]complete end.
Take away her branches,
For they *are* not the LORD'S.
11 For [a]the house of Israel and the house of
Judah
Have dealt very treacherously with Me,"
says the LORD.

12 [a]They have lied about the LORD,
And said, [b]"*It is* not He.
[c]Neither will evil come upon us,
Nor shall we see sword or famine.
13 And the prophets become wind,
For the word *is* not in them.
Thus shall it be done to them."

14 Therefore thus says the LORD God of
hosts:

"Because you speak this word,
[a]Behold, I will make My words in your
mouth fire,
And this people wood,
And it shall devour them.
15 Behold, I will bring a [a]nation against you
[b]from afar,
O house of Israel," says the LORD.
"It *is* a mighty nation,
It *is* an ancient nation,
A nation whose language you do not
know,
Nor can you understand what they say.
16 Their quiver *is* like an open tomb;
They *are* all mighty men.
17 And they shall eat up your [a]harvest and
your bread,
Which your sons and daughters should
eat.
They shall eat up your flocks and your
herds;
They shall eat up your vines and your fig
trees;
They shall destroy your fortified cities,
In which you trust, with the sword.

18 "Nevertheless in those days," says the
LORD, "I [a]will not make a complete end of you.
19 "And it will be when you say, [a]'Why does
the LORD our God do all these *things* to us?' then
you shall answer them, 'Just as you have [b]for-
saken Me and served foreign gods in your land,
so [c]you shall serve aliens in a land *that is* not
yours.'

20 "Declare this in the house of Jacob
And proclaim it in Judah, saying,

KJV

21 Hear now this, O [a]foolish people, and
without understanding; which have eyes, and see
not; which have ears, and hear not:
22 [a]Fear ye not me? saith the LORD: will ye
not tremble at my presence, which have placed
the sand *for* the [b]bound of the sea by a perpetual
decree, that it cannot pass it: and though the
waves thereof toss themselves, yet can they not
prevail; though they roar, yet can they not pass
over it?
23 But this people hath a revolting and a rebellious heart; they are revolted and gone.
24 Neither say they in their heart, Let us now
fear the LORD our God, [a]that giveth rain, both the
[b]former and the latter, in his season: [c]he reserveth
unto us the appointed weeks of the harvest.
25 [a]Your iniquities have turned away these
things, and your sins have withholden good
things from you.
26 For among my people are found wicked
men: they [a]lay wait, as he that setteth snares; they
set a trap, they catch men.
27 As a cage is full of birds, so *are* their
houses full of deceit: therefore they are become
great, and waxen rich.
28 They are waxen [a]fat, they shine: yea, they
overpass the deeds of the wicked: they judge not
[b]the cause, the cause of the fatherless, [c]yet they
prosper; and the right of the needy do they not
judge.
29 [a]Shall I not visit for these *things*? saith
the LORD: shall not my soul be avenged on such
a nation as this?
30 A wonderful and [a]horrible thing is committed in the land;
31 The prophets prophesy [a]falsely, and the
priests bear rule by their means; and my people
[b]love *to have it* so: and what will ye do in the
end thereof?

Impending Destruction from the North

6 O ye children of Benjamin, gather yourselves
to flee out of the midst of Jerusalem, and blow
the trumpet in Tekoa, and set up a sign of fire in
[a]Beth–haccerem: [b]for evil appeareth out of the
north, and great destruction.
2 I have likened the daughter of Zion to a
comely and delicate *woman*.
3 The [a]shepherds with their flocks shall
come unto her; they shall pitch *their* tents against
her round about; they shall feed every one in his
place.
4 [a]Prepare ye war against her; arise, and
let us go up [b]at noon. Woe unto us! for the day
goeth away, for the shadows of the evening are
stretched out.
5 Arise, and let us go by night, and let us
destroy her palaces.
6 For thus hath the LORD of hosts said, Hew

21 [a]Is. 6:9; Jer. 6:10; Ezek. 12:2; Matt. 13:14; John 12:40; Acts 28:26; Rom. 11:8
22 [a]Deut. 28:58; Ps. 119:120; Jer. 2:19; 10:7; [Rev. 15:4] [b]Job 26:10
24 [a]Ps. 147:8; Jer. 14:22; [Matt. 5:45]; Acts 14:17 [b]Deut. 11:14; Joel 2:23; James 5:7 [c][Gen. 8:22]
25 [a]Jer. 3:3
26 [a]Ps. 10:9; Prov. 1:11; Jer. 18:22; Hab. 1:15
28 [a]Deut. 32:15 [b]Is. 1:23; Jer. 7:6; 22:3; Zech. 7:10 [c]Job 12:6; Ps. 73:12
29 [a]Jer. 5:9; Mal. 3:5
30 [a]Jer. 23:14; Hos. 6:10; 2 Tim. 4:3
31 [a]Jer. 14:14; Ezek. 13:6 [b]Mic. 2:11

CHAPTER 6
1 [a]Neh. 3:14 [b]Jer. 4:6
3 [a]2 Kin. 25:1–4; Jer. 4:17; 12:10
4 [a]Jer. 51:27; Joel 3:9 [b]Jer. 15:8; Zeph. 2:4

NKJV

21 'Hear this now, O [a]foolish people,
Without understanding,
Who have eyes and see not,
And who have ears and hear not:
22 [a]Do you not fear Me?' says the LORD.
'Will you not tremble at My presence,
Who have placed the sand as the [b]bound
of the sea,
By a perpetual decree, that it cannot pass
beyond it?
And though its waves toss to and fro,
Yet they cannot prevail;
Though they roar, yet they cannot pass
over it.
23 But this people has a defiant and
rebellious heart;
They have revolted and departed.
24 They do not say in their heart,
"Let us now fear the LORD our God,
[a]Who gives rain, both the [b]former and the
latter, in its season.
[c]He reserves for us the appointed weeks
of the harvest."
25 [a]Your iniquities have turned these *things*
away,
And your sins have withheld good from
you.

26 'For among My people are found wicked
men;
They [a]lie in wait as one who sets snares;
They set a trap;
They catch men.
27 As a cage is full of birds,
So their houses *are* full of deceit.
Therefore they have become great and
grown rich.
28 They have grown [a]fat, they are sleek;
Yes, they surpass the deeds of the wicked;
They do not plead [b]the cause,
The cause of the fatherless;
[c]Yet they prosper,
And the right of the needy they do not
defend.
29 [a]Shall I not punish *them* for these *things*?'
says the LORD.
'Shall I not avenge Myself on such a nation
as this?'

30 "An astonishing and [a]horrible thing
Has been committed in the land:
31 The prophets prophesy [a]falsely,
And the priests rule by their *own* power;
And My people [b]love *to have it* so.
But what will you do in the end?

Impending Destruction from the North

6 "O you children of Benjamin,
Gather yourselves to flee from the midst
of Jerusalem!
Blow the trumpet in Tekoa,
And set up a signal-fire in [a]Beth
Haccerem;
[b]For disaster appears out of the north,
And great destruction.
2 I have likened the daughter of Zion
To a lovely and delicate woman.
3 The [a]shepherds with their flocks shall
come to her.
They shall pitch *their* tents against her all
around.
Each one shall pasture in his own place."

4 "Prepare[a] war against her;
Arise, and let us go up [b]at noon.
Woe to us, for the day goes away,
For the shadows of the evening are
lengthening.
5 Arise, and let us go by night,
And let us destroy her palaces."

6 For thus has the LORD of hosts said:

KJV

ye down trees, and cast a mount against Jerusalem: this *is* the city to be visited; she *is* wholly
oppression in the midst of her.
7 [a]As a fountain casteth out her waters, so
she casteth out her wickedness: [b]violence and
spoil is heard in her; before me continually *is* grief
and wounds.
8 Be thou instructed, O Jerusalem, lest [a]my
soul depart from thee; lest I make thee desolate,
a land not inhabited.
9 Thus saith the LORD of hosts, They shall
throughly glean the remnant of Israel as a vine:
turn back thine hand as a grapegatherer into the
baskets.
10 To whom shall I speak, and give warning,
that they may hear? behold, their [a]ear *is* uncircumcised, and they cannot hearken: behold, [b]the
word of the LORD is unto them a reproach; they
have no delight in it.
11 Therefore I am full of the fury of the LORD;
[a]I am weary with holding in: I will pour it out
[b]upon the children abroad, and upon the assembly of young men together: for even the husband
with the wife shall be taken, the aged with *him
that is* full of days.
12 And [a]their houses shall be turned unto
others, *with their* fields and wives together: for I
will stretch out my hand upon the inhabitants of
the land, saith the LORD.
13 For from the least of them even unto the
greatest of them every one *is* given to [a]covetous-
ness; and from the prophet even unto the [b]priest
every one dealeth falsely.
14 They have [a]healed also the hurt *of the
daughter* of my people slightly, [b]saying, Peace,
peace; when *there is* no peace.
15 Were they [a]ashamed when they had committed abomination? nay, they were not at all
ashamed, neither could they blush: therefore they
shall fall among them that fall: at the time *that* I
visit them they shall be cast down, saith the LORD.
16 Thus saith the LORD, Stand ye in the ways,
and see, and ask for the [a]old paths, where *is* the
good way, and walk therein, and ye shall find
[b]rest for your souls. But they said, We will not
walk *therein*.
17 Also I set [a]watchmen over you, *saying*,
[b]Hearken to the sound of the trumpet. But they
said, We will not hearken.
18 Therefore hear, ye nations, and know, O
congregation, what *is* among them.
19 [a]Hear, O earth: behold, I will bring [b]evil
upon this people, *even* [c]the fruit of their thoughts,
because they have not hearkened unto my words,
nor to my law, but rejected it.

7 [a]Is. 57:20 [b]Ps. 55:9
8 [a]Ezek. 23:18; Hos. 9:12
10 [a]Ex. 6:12; Jer. 5:21; 7:26; [Acts 7:51] [b]Jer. 8:9; 20:8
11 [a]Jer. 20:9 [b]Jer. 9:21
12 [a]Deut. 28:30; Jer. 8:10; 38:22
13 [a]Is. 56:11; Jer. 8:10; 22:17 [b]Jer. 5:31; 23:11; Mic. 3:5, 11
14 [a]Jer. 8:11–15; Ezek. 13:10 [b]Jer. 4:10; 23:17
15 [a]Jer. 3:3; 8:12
16 [a]Is. 8:20; Jer. 18:15; Mal. 4:4; Luke 16:29 [b]Matt. 11:29
17 [a]Is. 21:11; 58:1; Jer. 25:4; Ezek. 3:17; Hab. 2:1 [b]Deut. 4:1
19 [a]Is. 1:2 [b]Jer. 19:3, 15 [c]Prov. 1:31

NKJV

"Cut down trees,
And build a mound against Jerusalem.
This *is* the city to be punished.
She *is* full of oppression in her midst.
7 [a]As a fountain wells up with water,
So she wells up with her wickedness.
[b]Violence and plundering are heard in her.
Before Me continually *are* grief and wounds.
8 Be instructed, O Jerusalem,
Lest [a]My soul depart from you;
Lest I make you desolate,
A land not inhabited."

9 Thus says the LORD of hosts:

"They shall thoroughly glean as a vine the remnant of Israel;
As a grape-gatherer, put your hand back into the branches."

10 To whom shall I speak and give warning,
That they may hear?
Indeed their [a]ear *is* uncircumcised,
And they cannot give heed.
Behold, [b]the word of the LORD is a reproach to them;
They have no delight in it.
11 Therefore I am full of the fury of the LORD.
[a]I am weary of holding *it* in.
"I will pour it out [b]on the children outside,
And on the assembly of young men together;
For even the husband shall be taken with the wife,
The aged with *him who is* full of days.
12 And [a]their houses shall be turned over to others,
Fields and wives together;
For I will stretch out My hand
Against the inhabitants of the land," says the LORD.
13 "Because from the least of them even to the greatest of them,
Everyone *is* given to [a]covetousness;
And from the prophet even to the [b]priest,
Everyone deals falsely.
14 They have also [a]healed the hurt of My people slightly,
[b]Saying, 'Peace, peace!'
When *there is* no peace.
15 Were they [a]ashamed when they had committed abomination?
No! They were not at all ashamed;
Nor did they know how to blush.
Therefore they shall fall among those who fall;
At the time I punish them,
They shall be cast down," says the LORD.

16 Thus says the LORD:

"Stand in the ways and see,
And ask for the [a]old paths, where the good way *is*,
And walk in it;
Then you will find [b]rest for your souls.
But they said, 'We will not walk *in it*.'
17 Also, I set [a]watchmen over you, *saying*,
[b]'Listen to the sound of the trumpet!'
But they said, 'We will not listen.'
18 Therefore hear, you nations,
And know, O congregation, what *is* among them.
19 [a]Hear, O earth!
Behold, I will certainly bring [b]calamity on this people—
[c]The fruit of their thoughts,
Because they have not heeded My words
Nor My law, but rejected it.

KJV

20 [a]To what purpose cometh there to me incense [b]from Sheba, and the [c]sweet cane from a
far country? [d]your burnt offerings *are* not acceptable, nor your sacrifices sweet unto me.
21 Therefore thus saith the LORD, Behold, I
will lay stumblingblocks before this people, and
the fathers and the sons together shall fall upon
them; the neighbour and his friend shall perish.
22 Thus saith the LORD, Behold, a people
cometh from the [a]north country, and a great nation shall be raised from the sides of the earth.
23 They shall lay hold on bow and spear;
they *are* cruel, and have no mercy; their voice
[a]roareth like the sea; and they ride upon horses,
set in array as men for war against thee, O daughter of Zion.
24 We have heard the fame thereof: our
hands wax feeble: [a]anguish hath taken hold of
us, *and* pain, as of a woman in travail.
25 Go not forth into the field, nor walk by
the way; for the sword of the enemy *and* fear *is*
on every side.
26 O daughter of my people, [a]gird *thee* with
sackcloth, [b]and wallow thyself in ashes: [c]make
thee mourning, *as for* an only son, most bitter
lamentation: for the spoiler shall suddenly come
upon us.
27 I have set thee *for* a tower *and* [a]a fortress
among my people, that thou mayest know and
try their way.
28 [a]They *are* all grievous revolters, [b]walking
with slanders: *they are* [c]brass and iron; they *are*
all corrupters.
29 The bellows are burned, the lead is consumed of the fire; the founder melteth in vain:
for the wicked are not plucked away.
30 [a]Reprobate silver shall *men* call them, because the LORD hath rejected them.

Trusting in Lying Words
(cf. Jer. 26:4–6)

7 The word that came to Jeremiah from the
LORD, saying,
2 [a]Stand in the gate of the LORD's house,
and proclaim there this word, and say, Hear the
word of the LORD, all *ye of* Judah, that enter in
at these gates to worship the LORD.
3 Thus saith the LORD of hosts, the God of
Israel, [a]Amend your ways and your doings, and
I will cause you to dwell in this place.
4 [a]Trust ye not in lying words, saying, The
temple of the LORD, The temple of the LORD, The
temple of the LORD, *are* these.
5 For if ye throughly amend your ways and
your doings; if ye throughly [a]execute judgment
between a man and his neighbour;
6 *If* ye oppress not the stranger, the fatherless, and the widow, and shed not innocent blood
in this place, [a]neither walk after other gods to
your hurt:
7 [a]Then will I cause you to dwell in this
place, in [b]the land that I gave to your fathers,
for ever and ever.

20 [a]Ps. 40:6; 50:7–9; Is. 1:11; 66:3; Amos 5:21; Mic. 6:6, 7 [b]Is. 60:6 [c]Is. 43:24 [d]Jer. 7:21–23
22 [a]Jer. 1:15; 10:22; 50:41–43
23 [a]Is. 5:30
24 [a]Jer. 4:31; 13:21; 49:24
26 [a]Jer. 4:8 [b]Jer. 25:34; Mic. 1:10 [c]Amos 8:10; [Zech. 12:10]
27 [a]Jer. 1:18
28 [a]Jer. 5:23 [b]Jer. 9:4 [c]Ezek. 22:18
30 [a]Is. 1:22; Jer. 7:29

CHAPTER 7
2 [a]Jer. 17:19; 26:2
3 [a]Jer. 4:1; 18:11; 26:13
4 [a]Jer. 7:8; Mic. 3:11
5 [a]1 Kin. 6:12; Jer. 21:12; 22:3
6 [a]Deut. 6:14, 15; Jer. 13:10
7 [a]Deut. 4:40 [b]Jer. 3:18

NKJV

20 [a]For what purpose to Me
Comes frankincense [b]from Sheba,
And [c]sweet cane from a far country?
[d]Your burnt offerings *are* not acceptable,
Nor your sacrifices sweet to Me."

21 Therefore thus says the LORD:

"Behold, I will lay stumbling blocks before
this people,
And the fathers and the sons together
shall fall on them.
The neighbor and his friend shall
perish."

22 Thus says the LORD:

"Behold, a people comes from the [a]north
country,
And a great nation will be raised from the
farthest parts of the earth.
23 They will lay hold on bow and spear;
They *are* cruel and have no mercy;
Their voice [a]roars like the sea;
And they ride on horses,
As men of war set in array against you,
O daughter of Zion."

24 We have heard the report of it;
Our hands grow feeble.
[a]Anguish has taken hold of us,
Pain as of a woman in labor.
25 Do not go out into the field,
Nor walk by the way.
Because of the sword of the enemy,
Fear *is* on every side.
26 O daughter of my people,
[a]Dress in sackcloth
[b]And roll about in ashes!
[c]Make mourning *as for* an only son, most
bitter lamentation;
For the plunderer will suddenly come
upon us.

27 "I have set you *as* an assayer *and* [a]a
fortress among My people,
That you may know and test their way.
28 [a]They *are* all stubborn rebels, [b]walking as
slanderers.
They are [c]bronze and iron,
They *are* all corrupters;
29 The bellows blow fiercely,
The lead is consumed by the fire;
The smelter refines in vain,
For the wicked are not drawn off.
30 *People* will call them [a]rejected silver,
Because the LORD has rejected them."

Trusting in Lying Words
(cf. Jer. 26:4–6)

7 The word that came to Jeremiah from the
LORD, saying,
2 [a]"Stand in the gate of the LORD's house,
and proclaim there this word, and say, 'Hear the
word of the LORD, all *you of* Judah who enter in
at these gates to worship the LORD!' "
3 Thus says the LORD of hosts, the God of
Israel: [a]"Amend your ways and your doings, and
I will cause you to dwell in this place.
4 [a]"Do not trust in these lying words, saying, 'The temple of the LORD, the temple of the
LORD, the temple of the LORD *are* these.'
5 "For if you thoroughly amend your ways
and your doings, if you thoroughly [a]execute judgment between a man and his neighbor,
6 "*if* you do not oppress the stranger, the
fatherless, and the widow, and do not shed innocent blood in this place, [a]or walk after other gods
to your hurt,
7 [a]"then I will cause you to dwell in this
place, in [b]the land that I gave to your fathers forever and ever.

KJV

8 Behold, ye trust in [a]lying words, that cannot profit.
9 [a]Will ye steal, murder, and commit adultery, and swear falsely, and burn incense unto Baal, and [b]walk after other gods whom ye know not;
10 [a]And come and stand before me in this house, [b]which is called by my name, and say, We are delivered to do all these abominations?
11 Is [a]this house, which is called by my name, become a [b]den of robbers in your eyes? Behold, even I have seen *it,* saith the LORD.
12 But go ye now unto [a]my place which *was* in Shiloh, [b]where I set my name at the first, and see [c]what I did to it for the wickedness of my people Israel.
13 And now, because ye have done all these works, saith the LORD, and I spake unto you, [a]rising up early and speaking, but ye heard not; and I [b]called you, but ye answered not;
14 Therefore will I do unto *this* house, which is called by my name, wherein ye trust, and unto the place which I gave to you and to your fathers, as I have done to [a]Shiloh.
15 And I will cast you out of my sight, [a]as I have cast out all your brethren, [b]*even* the whole seed of Ephraim.
16 Therefore [a]pray not thou for this people, neither lift up cry nor prayer for them, neither make intercession to me: [b]for I will not hear thee.
17 Seest thou not what they do in the cities of Judah and in the streets of Jerusalem?
18 [a]The children gather wood, and the fathers kindle the fire, and the women knead *their* dough, to make cakes to the queen of heaven, and to [b]pour out drink offerings unto other gods, that they may provoke me to anger.
19 [a]Do they provoke me to anger? saith the LORD: *do they* not *provoke* themselves to the confusion of their own faces?
20 Therefore thus saith the Lord GOD; Behold, mine anger and my fury shall be poured out upon this place, upon man, and upon beast, and upon the trees of the field, and upon the fruit of the ground; and it shall burn, and shall not be quenched.
21 Thus saith the LORD of hosts, the God of Israel; [a]Put your burnt offerings unto your sacrifices, and eat flesh.
22 [a]For I spake not unto your fathers, nor commanded them in the day that I brought them out of the land of Egypt, concerning burnt offerings or sacrifices:
23 But this thing commanded I them, saying, [a]Obey my voice, and [b]I will be your God, and ye shall be my people: and walk ye in all the ways that I have commanded you, that it may be well unto you.
24 [a]But they hearkened not, nor inclined their ear, but [b]walked in the counsels *and* in the imagination of their evil heart, and [c]went backward, and not forward.
25 Since the day that your fathers came forth out of the land of Egypt unto this day I have even [a]sent unto you all my servants the prophets, daily rising up early and sending *them:*
26 [a]Yet they hearkened not unto me, nor inclined their ear, but [b]hardened their neck: [c]they did worse than their fathers.
27 Therefore [a]thou shalt speak all these words unto them; but they will not hearken to thee: thou shalt also call unto them; but they will not answer thee.

Judgment on Obscene Religion

28 But thou shalt say unto them, This *is* a nation that obeyeth not the voice of the LORD their God, [a]nor receiveth correction: [b]truth is perished, and is cut off from their mouth.
29 [a]Cut off thine hair, *O Jerusalem,* and cast *it* away, and take up a lamentation on high places;

8 [a]Jer. 5:31; 14:13, 14 **9** [a]1 Kin. 18:21; Hos. 4:1, 2; Zeph. 1:5 [b]Ex. 20:3; Jer. 7:6; 19:4 **10** [a]Ezek. 23:39 [b]Jer. 7:11, 14; 32:34; 34:15 **11** [a]Is. 56:7 [b]Matt. 21:13; Mark 11:17; Luke 19:46 **12** [a]Josh. 18:1; Judg. 18:31 [b]Deut. 12:11 [c]1 Sam. 4:10; Ps. 78:60; Jer. 26:6 **13** [a]2 Chr. 36:15; Jer. 11:7 [b]Prov. 1:24; Is. 65:12; 66:4 **14** [a]1 Sam. 4:10, 11; Ps. 78:60; Jer. 26:6, 9 **15** [a]2 Kin. 17:23 [b]Ps. 78:67; Hos. 7:13; 9:13; 12:1 **16** [a]Ex. 32:10; Deut. 9:14; Jer. 11:14 [b]Jer. 15:1 **18** [a]Jer. 44:17 [b]Jer. 19:13 **19** [a]Deut. 32:16, 21 **21** [a]Is. 1:11; Jer. 6:20; Hos. 8:13; Amos 5:21, 22 **22** [a]1 Sam. 15:22; Ps. 51:16; [Hos. 6:6] **23** [a]Ex. 15:26; 16:32; Deut. 6:3 [b][Ex. 19:5, 6]; Lev. 26:12; [Jer. 11:4; 13:11] **24** [a]Ps. 81:11; Jer. 11:8 [b]Deut. 29:19; Jer. 9:14 [c]Jer. 32:33 **25** [a]2 Chr. 36:15; Jer. 25:4; 29:19; Mark 12:1–10; Luke 11:47–49 **26** [a]Jer. 11:8 [b]Neh. 9:17 [c]Jer. 16:12; Matt. 23:32 **27** [a]Jer. 1:7; 26:2; 37:14, 15; 43:1–4; Ezek. 2:7 **28** [a]Jer. 5:3 [b]Jer. 9:3 **29** [a]Job 1:20; Is. 15:2; Jer. 48:37; Mic. 1:16

NKJV

8 "Behold, you trust in [a]lying words that cannot profit.
9 [a]"Will you steal, murder, commit adultery, swear falsely, burn incense to Baal, and [b]walk after other gods whom you do not know,
10 [a]"and *then* come and stand before Me in this house [b]which is called by My name, and say, 'We are delivered to do all these abominations'?
11 "Has [a]this house, which is called by My name, become a [b]den of thieves in your eyes? Behold, I, even I, have seen *it,*" says the LORD.
12 "But go now to [a]My place which *was* in Shiloh, [b]where I set My name at the first, and see [c]what I did to it because of the wickedness of My people Israel.
13 "And now, because you have done all these works," says the LORD, "and I spoke to you, [a]rising up early and speaking, but you did not hear, and I [b]called you, but you did not answer,
14 "therefore I will do to the house which is called by My name, in which you trust, and to this place which I gave to you and your fathers, as I have done to [a]Shiloh.
15 "And I will cast you out of My sight, [a]as I have cast out all your brethren—[b]the whole posterity of Ephraim.
16 "Therefore [a]do not pray for this people, nor lift up a cry or prayer for them, nor make intercession to Me; [b]for I will not hear you.
17 "Do you not see what they do in the cities of Judah and in the streets of Jerusalem?
18 [a]"The children gather wood, the fathers kindle the fire, and the women knead dough, to make cakes for the queen of heaven; and *they* [b]pour out drink offerings to other gods, that they may provoke Me to anger.
19 [a]"Do they provoke Me to anger?" says the LORD. "*Do they* not *provoke* themselves, to the shame of their own faces?"
20 Therefore thus says the Lord GOD: "Behold, My anger and My fury will be poured out on this place—on man and on beast, on the trees of the field and on the fruit of the ground. And it will burn and not be quenched."
21 Thus says the LORD of hosts, the God of Israel: [a]"Add your burnt offerings to your sacrifices and eat meat.
22 [a]"For I did not speak to your fathers, or command them in the day that I brought them out of the land of Egypt, concerning burnt offerings or sacrifices.
23 "But this is what I commanded them, saying, [a]'Obey My voice, and [b]I will be your God, and you shall be My people. And walk in all the ways that I have commanded you, that it may be well with you.'
24 [a]"Yet they did not obey or incline their ear, but [b]followed the counsels *and* the dictates of their evil hearts, and [c]went backward and not forward.
25 "Since the day that your fathers came out of the land of Egypt until this day, I have even [a]sent to you all My servants the prophets, daily rising up early and sending *them.*
26 [a]"Yet they did not obey Me or incline their ear, but [b]stiffened their neck. [c]They did worse than their fathers.
27 "Therefore [a]you shall speak all these words to them, but they will not obey you. You shall also call to them, but they will not answer you.

Judgment on Obscene Religion

28 "So you shall say to them, 'This *is* a nation that does not obey the voice of the LORD their God [a]nor receive correction. [b]Truth has perished and has been cut off from their mouth.
29 [a]'Cut off your hair and cast *it* away, and take up a lamentation on the desolate heights; for

KJV

for the LORD hath rejected and forsaken the generation of his wrath.

30 For the children of Judah have done evil in my sight, saith the LORD: [a]they have set their abominations in the house which is called by my name, to pollute it.

31 And they have built the [a]high places of Tophet, which *is* in the valley of the son of Hinnom, to [b]burn their sons and their daughters in the fire; [c]which I commanded *them* not, neither came it into my heart.

32 Therefore, behold, [a]the days come, saith the LORD, that it shall no more be called Tophet, nor the valley of the son of Hinnom, but the valley of slaughter: [b]for they shall bury in Tophet, till there be no place.

33 And the [a]carcases of this people shall be meat for the fowls of the heaven, and for the beasts of the earth; and none shall fray *them* away.

34 Then will I cause to [a]cease from the cities of Judah, and from the streets of Jerusalem, the voice of mirth, and the voice of gladness, the voice of the bridegroom, and the voice of the bride: for [b]the land shall be desolate.

8 At that time, saith the LORD, they shall bring out the bones of the kings of Judah, and the bones of his princes, and the bones of the priests, and the bones of the prophets, and the bones of the inhabitants of Jerusalem, out of their graves:

2 And they shall spread them before the sun, and the moon, and all the host of heaven, whom they have loved, and whom they have served, and after whom they have walked, and whom they have sought, and [a]whom they have worshipped: they shall not be gathered, [b]nor be buried; they shall be for dung upon the face of the earth.

3 And [a]death shall be chosen rather than life by all the residue of them that remain of this evil family, which remain in all the places whither I have driven them, saith the LORD of hosts.

The Peril of False Teaching

4 Moreover thou shalt say unto them, Thus saith the LORD; Shall they fall, and not arise? shall he turn away, and not return?

5 Why *then* is this people of Jerusalem [a]slidden back by a perpetual backsliding? [b]they hold fast deceit, [c]they refuse to return.

6 [a]I hearkened and heard, *but* they spake not aright: [b]no man repented him of his wickedness, saying, What have I done? every one turned to his course, as the horse rusheth into the battle.

7 Yea, [a]the stork in the heaven knoweth her appointed times; and the turtle and the crane and the swallow observe the time of their coming; but [b]my people know not the judgment of the LORD.

8 How do ye say, We *are* wise, [a]and the law of the LORD *is* with us? Lo, certainly in vain made he *it;* the pen of the scribes *is* in vain.

9 [a]The wise *men* are ashamed, they are dismayed and taken: lo, they have rejected the word of the LORD; and [b]what wisdom *is* in them?

10 Therefore [a]will I give their wives unto others, *and* their fields to them that shall inherit

30 [a]2 Kin. 21:4; 2 Chr. 33:3–5, 7; Jer. 32:34, 35; Ezek. 7:20; Dan. 9:27; 11:31
31 [a]2 Kin. 23:10; Jer. 19:5; 32:35 [b]Lev. 18:21; 2 Kin. 17:17; Ps. 106:38 [c]Deut. 17:3
32 [a]Jer. 19:6 [b]2 Kin. 23:10; Jer. 19:11
33 [a]Jer. 9:22; 19:11; Ezek. 6:5
34 [a]Is. 24:7, 8; Jer. 16:9; 25:10; Ezek. 26:13; Hos. 2:11; Rev. 18:23 [b]Lev. 26:33; Is. 1:7; Jer. 4:27

CHAPTER 8

2 [a]2 Kin. 23:5; Jer. 19:13; Ezek. 8:16; Zeph. 1:5; Acts 7:42 [b]Jer. 22:19
3 [a]Job 3:21, 22; 7:15, 16; Jon. 4:3; Rev. 9:6
5 [a]Jer. 7:24 [b]Jer. 9:6 [c]Jer. 5:3
6 [a]Ps. 14:2; [Is. 30:18; Mal. 3:16; 2 Pet. 3:9] [b]Ezek. 22:30; Mic. 7:2; Rev. 9:20
7 [a]Prov. 6:6–8; Song 2:12; Is. 1:3; Matt. 16:2, 3 [b]Jer. 5:4; 9:3
8 [a]Rom. 2:17
9 [a]Is. 19:11; Jer. 6:15; [1 Cor. 1:27] [b]Is. 44:25; Jer. 4:22
10 [a]Deut. 28:30; Amos 5:11; Zeph. 1:13

NKJV

the LORD has rejected and forsaken the generation of His wrath.'

30 "For the children of Judah have done evil in My sight," says the LORD. [a]"They have set their abominations in the house which is called by My name, to pollute it.

31 "And they have built the [a]high places of Tophet, which *is* in the Valley of the Son of Hinnom, to [b]burn their sons and their daughters in the fire, [c]which I did not command, nor did it come into My heart.

32 "Therefore behold, [a]the days are coming," says the LORD, "when it will no more be called Tophet, or the Valley of the Son of Hinnom, but the Valley of Slaughter; [b]for they will bury in Tophet until there is no room.

33 "The [a]corpses of this people will be food for the birds of the heaven and for the beasts of the earth. And no one will frighten *them away.*

34 "Then I will cause to [a]cease from the cities of Judah and from the streets of Jerusalem the voice of mirth and the voice of gladness, the voice of the bridegroom and the voice of the bride. For [b]the land shall be desolate.

8 "At that time," says the LORD, "they shall bring out the bones of the kings of Judah, and the bones of its princes, and the bones of the priests, and the bones of the prophets, and the bones of the inhabitants of Jerusalem, out of their graves.

2 "They shall spread them before the sun and the moon and all the host of heaven, which they have loved and which they have served and after which they have walked, which they have sought and [a]which they have worshiped. They shall not be gathered [b]nor buried; they shall be like refuse on the face of the earth.

3 "Then [a]death shall be chosen rather than life by all the residue of those who remain of this evil family, who remain in all the places where I have driven them," says the LORD of hosts.

The Peril of False Teaching

4 "Moreover you shall say to them, 'Thus says the LORD:

"Will they fall and not rise?
Will one turn away and not return?
5 Why has this people [a]slidden back,
Jerusalem, in a perpetual backsliding?
[b]They hold fast to deceit,
[c]They refuse to return.
6 [a]I listened and heard,
But they do not speak aright.
[b]No man repented of his wickedness,
Saying, 'What have I done?'
Everyone turned to his own course,
As the horse rushes into the battle.

7 "Even [a]the stork in the heavens
Knows her appointed times;
And the turtledove, the swift, and the swallow
Observe the time of their coming.
But [b]My people do not know the judgment of the LORD.

8 "How can you say, 'We *are* wise,
[a]And the law of the LORD *is* with us'?
Look, the false pen of the scribe certainly works falsehood.
9 [a]The wise men are ashamed,
They are dismayed and taken.
Behold, they have rejected the word of the LORD;
So [b]what wisdom do they have?
10 Therefore [a]I will give their wives to others,

KJV

them: for every one from the least even unto the
greatest is given to [b]covetousness, from the
prophet even unto the priest every one dealeth
falsely.
11 For they have [a]healed the hurt of the
daughter of my people slightly, saying, [b]Peace,
peace; when *there is* no peace.
12 Were they [a]ashamed when they had committed abomination? nay, they were not at all
ashamed, neither could they blush: therefore shall
they fall among them that fall: in the time of their
visitation they shall be cast down, saith the LORD.
13 I will surely consume them, saith the
LORD: *there shall be* no grapes [a]on the vine, nor
figs on the [b]fig tree, and the leaf shall fade; and
the things that I have given them shall [c]pass
away from them.
14 Why do we sit still? [a]assemble yourselves,
and let us enter into the defenced cities, and let
us be silent there: for the LORD our God hath put
us to silence, and given us [b]water of gall to drink,
because we have sinned against the LORD.
15 We [a]looked for peace, but no good *came;*
and for a time of health, and behold trouble!
16 The snorting of his horses was heard from
[a]Dan: the whole land trembled at the sound of
the neighing of his [b]strong ones; for they are
come, and have devoured the land, and all that
is in it; the city, and those that dwell therein.
17 For, behold, I will send serpents, cocka-
trices, among you, which *will* not *be* [a]charmed,
and they shall bite you, saith the LORD.

The Prophet Mourns for the People

18 *When* I would comfort myself against sorrow, my heart *is* faint in me.
19 Behold the voice of the cry of the daughter
of my people because of them that dwell in [a]a
far country: *Is* not the LORD in Zion? *is* not her
king in her? Why have they provoked me to anger
with their graven images, *and* with strange
vanities?
20 The harvest is past, the summer is ended,
and we are not saved.
21 [a]For the hurt of the daughter of my people
am I hurt; I am [b]black; astonishment hath taken
hold on me.
22 *Is there* no [a]balm in Gilead; *is there* no
physician there? why then is not the health of the
daughter of my people recovered?

9 Oh [a]that my head were waters, and mine eyes
a fountain of tears, that I might weep day and
night for the slain of the daughter of my people!

---

10 [b]Is. 56:11; 57:17; Jer. 6:13
11 [a]Jer. 6:14 [b]Ezek. 13:10
12 [a]Ps. 52:1, 7; Is. 3:9; Jer. 3:3; 6:15; Zeph. 3:5
13 [a]Jer. 5:17; 7:20; Joel 1:17 [b]Matt. 21:19; Luke 13:6 [c]Deut. 28:39, 40
14 [a]Jer. 4:5 [b]Deut. 29:18; Ps. 69:21; Jer. 9:15; Lam. 3:19; Matt. 27:34
15 [a]Jer. 14:19
16 [a]Judg. 18:29; Jer. 4:15 [b]Jer. 47:3
17 [a]Ps. 58:4, 5
19 [a]Is. 39:3; Jer. 5:15
21 [a]Jer. 9:1 [b]Jer. 14:2; Joel 2:6; Nah. 2:10
22 [a]Gen. 37:25; Jer. 46:11

CHAPTER 9
1 [a]Is. 22:4; Jer. 10:19; Lam. 2:18

NKJV

And their fields to those who will inherit *them;*
Because from the least even to the greatest
Everyone is given to [b]covetousness;
From the prophet even to the priest
Everyone deals falsely.
11 For they have [a]healed the hurt of the daughter of My people slightly,
Saying, [b]'Peace, peace!'
When *there is* no peace.
12 Were they [a]ashamed when they had committed abomination?
No! They were not at all ashamed,
Nor did they know how to blush.
Therefore they shall fall among those who fall;
In the time of their punishment
They shall be cast down," says the LORD.

13 "I will surely consume them," says the LORD.
"No grapes *shall be* [a]on the vine,
Nor figs on the [b]fig tree,
And the leaf shall fade;
And *the things* I have given them shall [c]pass away from them."' "

14 "Why do we sit still?
[a]Assemble yourselves,
And let us enter the fortified cities,
And let us be silent there.
For the LORD our God has put us to silence
And given us [b]water of gall to drink,
Because we have sinned against the LORD.

15 "*We* [a]looked for peace, but no good *came;*
And for a time of health, and there was trouble!
16 The snorting of His horses was heard from [a]Dan.
The whole land trembled at the sound of the neighing of His [b]strong ones;
For they have come and devoured the land and all that is in it,
The city and those who dwell in it."

17 "For behold, I will send serpents among you,
Vipers which cannot be [a]charmed,
And they shall bite you," says the LORD.

The Prophet Mourns for the People

18 I would comfort myself in sorrow;
My heart *is* faint in me.
19 Listen! The voice,
The cry of the daughter of my people
From [a]a far country:
"*Is* not the LORD in Zion?
Is not her King in her?"

"Why have they provoked Me to anger
With their carved images—
With foreign idols?"

20 "The harvest is past,
The summer is ended,
And we are not saved!"

21 [a]For the hurt of the daughter of my people I am hurt.
I am [b]mourning;
Astonishment has taken hold of me.
22 *Is there* no [a]balm in Gilead,
Is there no physician there?
Why then is there no recovery
For the health of the daughter of my people?

9 Oh, [a]that my head were waters,
And my eyes a fountain of tears,
That I might weep day and night
For the slain of the daughter of my people!

KJV

2 Oh that I had in the wilderness a lodging
place of wayfaring men; that I might leave my
people, and go from them! for [a]they *be* all adulterers, an assembly of treacherous men.
3 And [a]they bend their tongues *like* their
bow *for* lies: but they are not valiant for the truth
upon the earth; for they proceed from [b]evil to evil,
and they [c]know not me, saith the LORD.
4 [a]Take ye heed every one of his neighbour,
and trust ye not in any brother: for every brother
will utterly supplant, and every neighbour [b]will
walk with slanders.
5 And they will [a]deceive every one his
neighbour, and will not speak the truth: they have
taught their tongue to speak lies, *and* weary themselves to commit iniquity.
6 Thine habitation *is* in the midst of deceit;
through deceit they refuse to know me, saith the
LORD.
7 Therefore thus saith the LORD of hosts, Behold, [a]I will melt them, and try them; [b]for how
shall I do for the daughter of my people?
8 Their tongue *is as* an arrow shot out; it
speaketh [a]deceit: *one* speaketh [b]peaceably to his
neighbour with his mouth, but in heart he layeth
his wait.
9 [a]Shall I not visit them for these *things?*
saith the LORD: shall not my soul be avenged on
such a nation as this?
10 For the mountains will I take up a weeping
and wailing, and [a]for the habitations of the wilderness a lamentation, because they are burned
up, so that none can pass through *them;* neither
can *men* hear the voice of the cattle; [b]both the
fowl of the heavens and the beast are fled; they
are gone.
11 And I will make Jerusalem [a]heaps, *and*
[b]a den of dragons; and I will make the cities of
Judah desolate, without an inhabitant.
12 [a]Who *is* the wise man, that may understand this? and *who is he* to whom the mouth of
the LORD hath spoken, that he may declare it, for
what the land perisheth *and* is burned up like a
wilderness, that none passeth through?
13 And the LORD saith, Because they have
forsaken my law which I set before them, and
have [a]not obeyed my voice, neither walked
therein;
14 But have [a]walked after the imagination
of their own heart, and after Baalim, [b]which their
fathers taught them:
15 Therefore thus saith the LORD of hosts, the
God of Israel; Behold, I will [a]feed them, *even* this
people, [b]with wormwood, and give them water
of gall to drink.
16 I will [a]scatter them also among the
heathen, whom neither they nor their fathers have
known: [b]and I will send a sword after them, till I
have consumed them.

2 [a]Jer. 5:7, 8; 23:10; Hos. 4:2 **3** [a]Ps. 64:3; Is. 59:4; Jer. 9:8; Hos. 4:1, 2 [b]Jer. 4:22; 13:23 [c]Judg. 2:10; 1 Sam. 2:12; Jer. 4:22; Hos. 4:1; 1 Cor. 15:34 **4** [a]Ps. 12:2; Prov. 26:24, 25; Jer. 9:8; Mic. 7:5, 6 [b]Ps. 15:3; Prov. 10:18; Jer. 6:28 **5** [a]Ps. 36:3, 4; Is. 59:4 **7** [a]Is. 1:25; Jer. 6:27; Mal. 3:3 [b]Hos. 11:8 **8** [a]Ps. 12:2 [b]Ps. 55:21 **9** [a]Is. 1:24; Jer. 5:9, 29 **10** [a]Jer. 4:26; Hos. 4:3 [b]Jer. 4:25; Hos. 4:3 **11** [a]Is. 25:2; Jer. 19:3, 8; 26:9 [b]Is. 13:22; 34:13 **12** [a]Ps. 107:43; Is. 42:23; Hos. 14:9 **13** [a]Jer. 3:25; 7:24 **14** [a]Jer. 7:24; 11:8; Rom. 1:21–24 [b]Gal. 1:14; 1 Pet. 1:18 **15** [a]Ps. 80:5 [b]Deut. 29:18; Jer. 8:14; 23:15; Lam. 3:15 **16** [a]Lev. 26:33; Deut. 28:64; Jer. 15:2–4 [b]Lev. 26:33; Jer. 44:27; Ezek. 5:2

NKJV

2 Oh, that I had in the wilderness
A lodging place for travelers;
That I might leave my people,
And go from them!
For [a]they *are* all adulterers,
An assembly of treacherous men.

3 "And *like* their bow [a]they have bent their
tongues *for* lies.
They are not valiant for the truth on the
earth.
For they proceed from [b]evil to evil,
And they [c]do not know Me," says the
LORD.
4 "Everyone[a] take heed to his neighbor,
And do not trust any brother;
For every brother will utterly supplant,
And every neighbor will [b]walk with
slanders.
5 Everyone will [a]deceive his neighbor,
And will not speak the truth;
They have taught their tongue to speak
lies;
They weary themselves to commit
iniquity.
6 Your dwelling place *is* in the midst of
deceit;
Through deceit they refuse to know Me,"
says the LORD.

7 Therefore thus says the LORD of hosts:

"Behold, [a]I will refine them and try them;
[b]For how shall I deal with the daughter of
My people?
8 Their tongue *is* an arrow shot out;
It speaks [a]deceit;
One speaks [b]peaceably to his neighbor
with his mouth,
But in his heart he lies in wait.
9 [a]Shall I not punish them for these *things*?"
says the LORD.
"Shall I not avenge Myself on such a nation
as this?"

10 I will take up a weeping and wailing for
the mountains,
And [a]for the dwelling places of the
wilderness a lamentation,
Because they are burned up,
So that no one can pass through;
Nor can *men* hear the voice of the
cattle.
[b]Both the birds of the heavens and the
beasts have fled;
They are gone.

11 "I will make Jerusalem [a]a heap of ruins,
[b]a den of jackals.
I will make the cities of Judah desolate,
without an inhabitant."

12 [a]Who *is* the wise man who may understand this? And *who is he* to whom the mouth of
the LORD has spoken, that he may declare it? Why
does the land perish *and* burn up like a wilderness, so that no one can pass through?
13 And the LORD said, "Because they have
forsaken My law which I set before them, and
have [a]not obeyed My voice, nor walked according
to it,
14 "but they have [a]walked according to the
dictates of their own hearts and after the Baals,
[b]which their fathers taught them,"
15 therefore thus says the LORD of hosts, the
God of Israel: "Behold, I will [a]feed them, this people, [b]with wormwood, and give them water of gall
to drink.
16 "I will [a]scatter them also among the Gentiles, whom neither they nor their fathers have
known. [b]And I will send a sword after them until
I have consumed them."

KJV

The People Mourn in Judgment

17 Thus saith the LORD of hosts, Consider ye, and call for [a]the mourning women, that they may come; and send for cunning *women,* that they may come:

18 And let them make haste, and take up a wailing for us, that [a]our eyes may run down with tears, and our eyelids gush out with waters.

19 For a voice of wailing is heard out of Zion, How are we spoiled! we are greatly confounded, because we have forsaken the land, because [a]our dwellings have cast *us* out.

20 Yet hear the word of the LORD, O ye women, and let your ear receive the word of his mouth, and teach your daughters wailing, and every one her neighbour lamentation.

21 For death is come up into our windows, *and* is entered into our palaces, to cut off [a]the children from without, *and* the young men from the streets.

22 Speak, Thus saith the LORD, Even the carcases of men shall fall [a]as dung upon the open field, and as the handful after the harvestman, and none shall gather *them.*

23 Thus saith the LORD, [a]Let not the wise *man* glory in his wisdom, neither let the mighty *man* glory in his [b]might, let not the rich *man* glory in his riches:

24 But [a]let him that glorieth glory in this, that he understandeth and knoweth me, that I *am* the LORD which exercise lovingkindness, judgment, and righteousness, in the earth: [b]for in these *things* I delight, saith the LORD.

25 Behold, the days come, saith the LORD, that [a]I will punish all *them which are* circumcised with the uncircumcised;

26 Egypt, and Judah, and Edom, and the children of Ammon, and Moab, and all *that are* in the [a]utmost corners, that dwell in the wilderness: for all *these* nations *are* uncircumcised, and all the house of Israel *are* [b]uncircumcised in the heart.

Idols and the True God

10 Hear ye the word which the LORD speaketh unto you, O house of Israel:

2 Thus saith the LORD, [a]Learn not the way of the heathen, and be not dismayed at the signs of heaven; for the heathen are dismayed at them.

3 For the customs of the people *are* vain: for [a]*one* cutteth a tree out of the forest, the work of the hands of the workman, with the ax.

4 They deck it with silver and with gold; they [a]fasten it with nails and with hammers, that it move not.

5 They *are* upright as the palm tree, [a]but speak not: they must needs be [b]borne, because they cannot go. Be not afraid of them; for [c]they cannot do evil, neither also *is it* in them to do good.

17 [a]2 Chr. 35:25; Job 3:8; Eccl. 12:5; Amos 5:16; Matt. 9:23
18 [a]Is. 22:4; Jer. 9:1; 14:17
19 [a]Lev. 18:28
21 [a]2 Chr. 36:17; Jer. 6:11; 18:21; Ezek. 9:5, 6
22 [a]Ps. 83:10; Is. 5:25; Jer. 8:1, 2
23 [a][Eccl. 9:11; Is. 47:10]; Ezek. 28:3–7 [b]Ps. 33:16–18
24 [a]Ps. 20:7; 44:8; Is. 41:16; Jer. 4:2; 1 Cor. 1:31; 2 Cor. 10:17; [Gal. 6:14] [b]Is. 61:8; Mic. 7:18
25 [a][Jer. 4:4; Rom. 2:28, 29]
26 [a]Jer. 25:23 [b]Lev. 26:41; Jer. 4:4; 6:10; Ezek. 44:7; [Rom. 2:28]

CHAPTER 10
2 [a][Lev. 18:3; 20:23; Deut. 12:30]
3 [a]Is. 40:19; 45:20
4 [a]Is. 41:7
5 [a]Ps. 115:5; Is. 46:7; Jer. 10:5; 1 Cor. 12:2 [b]Ps. 115:7; Is. 46:1, 7 [c]Is. 41:23, 24

NKJV

The People Mourn in Judgment

17 Thus says the LORD of hosts:

"Consider and call for [a]the mourning
 women,
That they may come;
And send for skillful wailing women,
That they may come.
18 Let them make haste
And take up a wailing for us,
That [a]our eyes may run with tears,
And our eyelids gush with water.
19 For a voice of wailing is heard from Zion:
'How we are plundered!
We are greatly ashamed,
Because we have forsaken the land,
Because we have been cast out of [a]our
 dwellings.' "

20 Yet hear the word of the LORD, O women,
And let your ear receive the word of His
 mouth;
Teach your daughters wailing,
And everyone her neighbor a lamentation.
21 For death has come through our windows,
Has entered our palaces,
To kill off [a]the children—*no longer to be*
 outside!
And the young men—*no longer* on the
 streets!

22 Speak, "Thus says the LORD:

'Even the carcasses of men shall fall [a]as
 refuse on the open field,
Like cuttings after the harvester,
And no one shall gather *them.'* "

23 Thus says the LORD:

[a]"Let not the wise *man* glory in his wisdom,
Let not the mighty *man* glory in his
 [b]might,
Nor let the rich *man* glory in his riches;
24 But [a]let him who glories glory in this,
That he understands and knows Me,
That I *am* the LORD, exercising
 lovingkindness, judgment, and
 righteousness in the earth.
[b]For in these I delight," says the LORD.

25 "Behold, the days are coming," says the LORD, "that [a]I will punish all *who are* circumcised with the uncircumcised—

26 "Egypt, Judah, Edom, the people of Ammon, Moab, and all *who are* in the [a]farthest corners, who dwell in the wilderness. For all *these* nations *are* uncircumcised, and all the house of Israel *are* [b]uncircumcised in the heart."

Idols and the True God

10 Hear the word which the LORD speaks to you, O house of Israel.

2 Thus says the LORD:

[a]"Do not learn the way of the Gentiles;
Do not be dismayed at the signs of heaven,
For the Gentiles are dismayed at them.
3 For the customs of the peoples *are* futile;
For [a]*one* cuts a tree from the forest,
The work of the hands of the workman,
 with the ax.
4 They decorate it with silver and gold;
They [a]fasten it with nails and hammers
So that it will not topple.
5 They *are* upright, like a palm tree,
And [a]they cannot speak;
They must be [b]carried,
Because they cannot go *by themselves.*
Do not be afraid of them,
For [c]they cannot do evil,
Nor can they do any good."

KJV

6 Forasmuch as *there is* none [a]like unto thee, O LORD; thou *art* great, and thy name *is* great in might.

7 [a]Who would not fear thee, O King of nations? for to thee doth it appertain: forasmuch as [b]among all the wise *men* of the nations, and in all their kingdoms, *there is* none like unto thee.

8 But they are altogether [a]brutish and foolish: the stock *is* a doctrine of vanities.

9 Silver spread into plates is brought from Tarshish, and [a]gold from Uphaz, the work of the workman, and of the hands of the founder: blue and purple *is* their clothing: they *are* all [b]the work of cunning *men*.

10 But the LORD *is* the true God, he *is* [a]the living God, and an [b]everlasting king: at his wrath the earth shall tremble, and the nations shall not be able to abide his indignation.

11 Thus shall ye say unto them, [a]The gods that have not made the heavens and the earth, *even* [b]they shall perish from the earth, and from under these heavens.

12 He [a]hath made the earth by his power, he hath [b]established the world by his wisdom, and [c]hath stretched out the heavens by his discretion.

13 [a]When he uttereth his voice, *there is* a multitude of waters in the heavens, and [b]he causeth the vapours to ascend from the ends of the earth; he maketh lightnings with rain, and bringeth forth the wind out of his treasures.

14 [a]Every man is [b]brutish in *his* knowledge: [c]every founder is confounded by the graven image: [d]for his molten image *is* falsehood, and *there is* no breath in them.

15 They *are* vanity, *and* the work of errors: in the time of their visitation they shall perish.

16 [a]The portion of Jacob *is* not like them: for he *is* the former of all *things;* and [b]Israel *is* the rod of his inheritance: [c]The LORD of hosts *is* his name.

The Coming Captivity of Judah

17 [a]Gather up thy wares out of the land, O inhabitant of the fortress.

18 For thus saith the LORD, Behold, I will [a]sling out the inhabitants of the land at this once, and will distress them, [b]that they may find *it so.*

19 [a]Woe is me for my hurt! my wound is grievous: but I said, [b]Truly this *is* a grief, and [c]I must bear it.

20 [a]My tabernacle is spoiled, and all my cords are broken: my children are gone forth of me, and they *are* [b]not: *there is* none to stretch forth my tent any more, and to set up my curtains.

6 [a]Ex. 15:11; Deut. 33:26; Ps. 86:8, 10; Is. 46:5–9; Jer. 10:16
7 [a]Jer. 5:22; Rev. 15:4 [b]Ps. 89:6
8 [a]Ps. 115:8; Hab. 2:18
9 [a]Dan. 10:5 [b]Ps. 115:4
10 [a]1 Tim. 6:17 [b]Ps. 10:16
11 [a]Ps. 96:5 [b]Is. 2:18; Zeph. 2:11
12 [a]Gen. 1:1, 6, 7; Jer. 51:15 [b]Ps. 93:1 [c]Job 9:8; Ps. 104:2; Is. 40:22
13 [a]Job 38:34 [b]Ps. 135:7
14 [a]Jer. 51:17 [b]Prov. 30:2 [c]Is. 42:17; 44:11 [d]Hab. 2:18
16 [a]Ps. 16:5; Jer. 51:19; Lam. 3:24 [b]Deut. 32:9; Ps. 74:2 [c]Is. 47:4
17 [a]Jer. 6:1
18 [a]1 Sam. 25:29; 2 Chr. 36:20 [b]Ezek. 6:10
19 [a]Jer. 8:21 [b]Ps. 77:10 [c]Mic. 7:9
20 [a]Jer. 4:20; Lam. 2:4 [b]Jer. 31:15; Lam. 1:5

NKJV

6 Inasmuch as *there is* none [a]like You, O LORD
(You *are* great, and Your name *is* great in might),
7 [a]Who would not fear You, O King of the nations?
For this is Your rightful due.
For [b]among all the wise *men* of the nations,
And in all their kingdoms,
There is none like You.
8 But they are altogether [a]dull-hearted and foolish;
A wooden idol *is* a worthless doctrine.
9 Silver is beaten into plates;
It is brought from Tarshish,
And [a]gold from Uphaz,
The work of the craftsman
And of the hands of the metalsmith;
Blue and purple *are* their clothing;
They *are* all [b]the work of skillful *men*.
10 But the LORD *is* the true God;
He *is* [a]the living God and the [b]everlasting King.
At His wrath the earth will tremble,
And the nations will not be able to endure His indignation.

11 Thus you shall say to them: [a]"The gods that have not made the heavens and the earth [b]shall perish from the earth and from under these heavens."

12 He [a]has made the earth by His power,
He has [b]established the world by His wisdom,
And [c]has stretched out the heavens at His discretion.
13 [a]When He utters His voice,
There is a multitude of waters in the heavens:
[b]"And He causes the vapors to ascend from the ends of the earth.
He makes lightning for the rain,
He brings the wind out of His treasuries."

14 [a]Everyone is [b]dull-hearted, without knowledge;
[c]Every metalsmith is put to shame by an image;
[d]For his molded image *is* falsehood,
And *there is* no breath in them.
15 They *are* futile, a work of errors;
In the time of their punishment they shall perish.
16 [a]The Portion of Jacob *is* not like them,
For He *is* the Maker of all *things*,
And [b]Israel *is* the tribe of His inheritance;
[c]The LORD of hosts *is* His name.

The Coming Captivity of Judah

17 [a]Gather up your wares from the land,
O inhabitant of the fortress!

18 For thus says the LORD:

"Behold, I will [a]throw out at this time
The inhabitants of the land,
And will distress them,
[b]That they may find *it so.*"

19 [a]Woe is me for my hurt!
My wound is severe.
But I say, [b]"Truly this *is* an infirmity,
And [c]I must bear it."
20 [a]My tent is plundered,
And all my cords are broken;
My children have gone from me,
And they *are* [b]no more.
There is no one to pitch my tent anymore,
Or set up my curtains.

KJV

21 For the pastors are become brutish, and have not sought the LORD: therefore they shall not prosper, and all their flocks shall be [a]scattered.

22 Behold, the noise of the bruit is come, and a great commotion out of the [a]north country, to make the cities of Judah desolate, *and* a [b]den of dragons.

23 O LORD, I know that the [a]way of man *is* not in himself: *it is* not in man that walketh to direct his steps.

24 O LORD, [a]correct me, but with judgment; not in thine anger, lest thou bring me to nothing.

25 [a]Pour out thy fury upon the heathen [b]that know thee not, and upon the families that call not on thy name: for they have eaten up Jacob, and [c]devoured him, and consumed him, and have made his habitation desolate.

The Broken Covenant

11 The word that came to Jeremiah from the LORD, saying,

2 Hear ye the words of this covenant, and speak unto the men of Judah, and to the inhabitants of Jerusalem;

3 And say thou unto them, Thus saith the LORD God of Israel; [a]Cursed *be* the man that obeyeth not the words of this covenant,

4 Which I commanded your fathers in the day *that* I brought them forth out of the land of Egypt, [a]from the iron furnace, saying, [b]Obey my voice, and do them, according to all which I command you: so shall ye be my people, and I will be your God:

5 That I may perform the [a]oath which I have sworn unto your fathers, to give them [b]a land flowing with milk and honey, as *it is* this day. Then answered I, and said, So be it, O LORD.

6 Then the LORD said unto me, Proclaim all these words in the cities of Judah, and in the streets of Jerusalem, saying, Hear ye the words of this covenant, [a]and do them.

7 For I earnestly protested unto your fathers in the day *that* I brought them up out of the land of Egypt, *even* unto this day, [a]rising early and protesting, saying, Obey my voice.

8 [a]Yet they obeyed not, nor inclined their ear, but [b]walked every one in the imagination of their evil heart: therefore I will bring upon them all the words of this covenant, which I commanded *them* to do; but they did *them* not.

9 And the LORD said unto me, [a]A conspiracy is found among the men of Judah, and among the inhabitants of Jerusalem.

10 They are turned back to [a]the iniquities of their forefathers, which refused to hear my words; and they went after other gods to serve them: the house of Israel and the house of Judah have broken my covenant which I made with their fathers.

11 Therefore thus saith the LORD, Behold, I will bring evil upon them, which they shall not be able to escape; and [a]though they shall cry unto me, I will not hearken unto them.

12 Then shall the cities of Judah and inhabitants of Jerusalem go, and [a]cry unto the gods unto whom they offer incense: but they shall not save them at all in the time of their trouble.

13 For *according to* the number of thy [a]cities were thy gods, O Judah; and *according to* the number of the streets of Jerusalem have ye set up altars to *that* shameful thing, *even* altars to burn incense unto Baal.

14 Therefore [a]pray not thou for this people, neither lift up a cry or prayer for them: for I will

---

21 [a]Jer. 23:2
22 [a]Jer. 5:15 [b]Jer. 9:11
23 [a]Prov. 16:1; 20:24
24 [a]Ps. 6:1; 38:1; Jer. 30:11
25 [a]Ps. 79:6, 7; Zeph. 3:8 [b]Job 18:21; 1 Thess. 4:5; [2 Thess. 1:8] [c]Jer. 8:16

CHAPTER 11

3 [a]Deut. 27:26; [Jer. 17:5]; Gal. 3:10
4 [a]Deut. 4:20; 1 Kin. 8:51 [b]Lev. 26:3; Deut. 11:27; Jer. 7:23
5 [a]Ex. 13:5; Deut. 7:12; Ps. 105:9; Jer. 32:22 [b]Ex. 3:8
6 [a]Deut. 17:19; [Rom. 2:13]; James 1:22
7 [a]Jer. 35:15
8 [a]Jer. 7:26 [b]Jer. 13:10
9 [a]Ezek. 22:25; Hos. 6:9
10 [a]1 Sam. 15:11; Jer. 3:10, 11; Ezek. 20:18
11 [a]Ps. 18:41; Prov. 1:28; Is. 1:15; Jer. 14:12; Ezek. 8:18; Mic. 3:4; Zech. 7:13
12 [a]Deut. 32:37; Jer. 44:17
13 [a]2 Kin. 23:13; Jer. 2:28
14 [a]Ex. 32:10; Jer. 7:16; 14:11; [1 John 5:16]

NKJV

21 For the shepherds have become dull-hearted,
And have not sought the LORD;
Therefore they shall not prosper,
And all their flocks shall be [a]scattered.
22 Behold, the noise of the report has come,
And a great commotion out of the [a]north country,
To make the cities of Judah desolate, a [b]den of jackals.

23 O LORD, I know the [a]way of man *is* not in himself;
It is not in man who walks to direct his own steps.
24 O LORD, [a]correct me, but with justice;
Not in Your anger, lest You bring me to nothing.
25 [a]Pour out Your fury on the Gentiles, [b]who do not know You,
And on the families who do not call on Your name;
For they have eaten up Jacob,
[c]Devoured him and consumed him,
And made his dwelling place desolate.

The Broken Covenant

11 The word that came to Jeremiah from the LORD, saying,

2 "Hear the words of this covenant, and speak to the men of Judah and to the inhabitants of Jerusalem;

3 "and say to them, 'Thus says the LORD God of Israel: [a]"Cursed *is* the man who does not obey the words of this covenant

4 "which I commanded your fathers in the day I brought them out of the land of Egypt, [a]from the iron furnace, saying, [b]'Obey My voice, and do according to all that I command you; so shall you be My people, and I will be your God,'

5 "that I may establish the [a]oath which I have sworn to your fathers, to give them [b]'a land flowing with milk and honey,' as *it is* this day." ' " And I answered and said, "So be it, LORD."

6 Then the LORD said to me, "Proclaim all these words in the cities of Judah and in the streets of Jerusalem, saying: 'Hear the words of this covenant [a]and do them.

7 'For I earnestly exhorted your fathers in the day I brought them up out of the land of Egypt, until this day, [a]rising early and exhorting, saying, "Obey My voice."

8 [a]'Yet they did not obey or incline their ear, but [b]everyone followed the dictates of his evil heart; therefore I will bring upon them all the words of this covenant, which I commanded *them* to do, but *which* they have not done.' "

9 And the LORD said to me, [a]"A conspiracy has been found among the men of Judah and among the inhabitants of Jerusalem.

10 "They have turned back to [a]the iniquities of their forefathers who refused to hear My words, and they have gone after other gods to serve them; the house of Israel and the house of Judah have broken My covenant which I made with their fathers."

11 Therefore thus says the LORD: "Behold, I will surely bring calamity on them which they will not be able to escape; and [a]though they cry out to Me, I will not listen to them.

12 "Then the cities of Judah and the inhabitants of Jerusalem will go and [a]cry out to the gods to whom they offer incense, but they will not save them at all in the time of their trouble.

13 "For *according to* the number of your [a]cities were your gods, O Judah; and *according to* the number of the streets of Jerusalem you have set up altars to *that* shameful thing, altars to burn incense to Baal.

14 "So [a]do not pray for this people, or lift up a cry or prayer for them; for I will not hear

KJV

not hear *them* in the time that they cry unto me
for their trouble.
15 [a]What hath my beloved to do in mine
house, *seeing* she hath [b]wrought lewdness with
many, and [c]the holy flesh is passed from thee?
when thou doest evil, then thou [d]rejoicest.
16 The LORD called thy name, [a]A green olive
tree, fair, *and* of goodly fruit: with the noise of a
great tumult he hath kindled fire upon it, and the
branches of it are broken.
17 For the LORD of hosts, [a]that planted thee,
hath pronounced evil against thee, for the evil of
the house of Israel and of the house of Judah,
which they have done against themselves to provoke me to anger in offering incense unto Baal.

Jeremiah's Life Threatened

18 And the LORD hath given me knowledge
of it, and I know *it:* then thou shewedst me their
doings.
19 But I *was* like a lamb *or* an ox *that* is
brought to the slaughter; and I knew not that they
had devised devices against me, *saying,* Let us
destroy the tree with the fruit thereof, [a]and let
us cut him off from [b]the land of the living, that
his name may be no more remembered.
20 But, O LORD of hosts, that judgest righteously, that [a]triest the reins and the heart, let
me see thy [b]vengeance on them: for unto thee
have I revealed my cause.
21 Therefore thus saith the LORD of the men
of [a]Anathoth, that seek thy life, saying, [b]Prophesy
not in the name of the LORD, that thou die not by
our hand:
22 Therefore thus saith the LORD of hosts, Behold, I will punish them: the young men shall die
by the sword; their sons and their daughters shall
[a]die by famine:
23 And there shall be no remnant of them:
for I will bring evil upon the men of Anathoth,
even [a]the year of their visitation.

Jeremiah's Question

12 Righteous [a]*art* thou, O LORD, when I plead
with thee: yet let me talk with thee of *thy*
judgments: [b]Wherefore doth the way of the
wicked prosper? *wherefore* are all they happy that
deal very treacherously?
2 Thou hast planted them, yea, they have
taken root: they grow, yea, they bring forth fruit:
[a]thou *art* near in their mouth, and far from their
reins.
3 But thou, O LORD, [a]knowest me: thou hast
seen me, and [b]tried mine heart toward thee: pull
them out like sheep for the slaughter, and prepare
them for [c]the day of slaughter.
4 How long shall [a]the land mourn, and the
herbs of every field wither, [c]for the wickedness
of them that dwell therein? [b]the beasts are consumed, and the birds; because they said, He shall
not see our last end.

The LORD Answers Jeremiah

5 If thou hast run with the footmen, and
they have wearied thee, then how canst thou
contend with horses? and *if* in the land of peace,

15 [a]Ps. 50:16 [b]Ezek. 16:25 [c][Titus 1:15] [d]Prov. 2:14
16 [a]Ps. 52:8; [Rom. 11:17]
17 [a]Is. 5:2; Jer. 2:21; 12:2
19 [a]Ps. 83:4; Jer. 18:18 [b]Ps. 27:13
20 [a]1 Sam. 16:7; 1 Chr. 28:9; Ps. 7:9 [b]Jer. 15:15
21 [a]Jer. 1:1; 12:5, 6 [b]Is. 30:10; Amos 2:12; Mic. 2:6
22 [a]Jer. 9:21
23 [a]Jer. 23:12; Hos. 9:7; Mic. 7:4

CHAPTER 12

1 [a]Ezra 9:15; Ps. 51:14; Jer. 11:20 [b]Job 12:6; Jer. 5:27, 28; Hab. 1:4; Mal. 3:15
2 [a]Is. 29:13; Ezek. 33:31; Matt. 15:8; Mark 7:6
3 [a]Ps. 17:3 [b]Ps. 7:9; 11:5; Jer. 11:20 [c]Jer. 17:18; 50:27; James 5:5
4 [a]Jer. 23:10; Hos. 4:3 [b]Jer. 9:10; Hos. 4:3; Hab. 3:17 [c]Ps. 107:34

NKJV

them in the time that they cry out to Me because
of their trouble.

15 "What[a] has My beloved to do in My house,
Having [b]done lewd deeds with many?
And [c]the holy flesh has passed from you.
When you do evil, then you [d]rejoice.
16 The LORD called your name,
[a]Green Olive Tree, Lovely *and* of Good
Fruit.
With the noise of a great tumult
He has kindled fire on it,
And its branches are broken.

17 "For the LORD of hosts, [a]who planted you,
has pronounced doom against you for the evil of
the house of Israel and of the house of Judah,
which they have done against themselves to provoke Me to anger in offering incense to Baal."

Jeremiah's Life Threatened

18 Now the LORD gave me knowledge *of*
it, and I know *it;* for You showed me their
doings.
19 But I *was* like a docile lamb brought to
the slaughter; and I did not know that they had
devised schemes against me, *saying,* "Let us destroy the tree with its fruit, [a]and let us cut him
off from [b]the land of the living, that his name may
be remembered no more."

20 But, O LORD of hosts,
You who judge righteously,
[a]Testing the mind and the heart,
Let me see Your [b]vengeance on them,
For to You I have revealed my cause.

21 "Therefore thus says the LORD concerning
the men of [a]Anathoth who seek your life, saying,
[b]'Do not prophesy in the name of the LORD, lest
you die by our hand'—
22 "therefore thus says the LORD of hosts:
'Behold, I will punish them. The young men shall
die by the sword, their sons and their daughters
shall [a]die by famine;
23 'and there shall be no remnant of them,
for I will bring catastrophe on the men of Anathoth, *even* [a]the year of their punishment.' "

Jeremiah's Question

12 Righteous [a]*are* You, O LORD, when I plead
with You;
Yet let me talk with You about *Your*
judgments.
[b]Why does the way of the wicked prosper?
Why are those happy who deal so
treacherously?
2 You have planted them, yes, they have
taken root;
They grow, yes, they bear fruit.
[a]You *are* near in their mouth
But far from their mind.

3 But You, O LORD, [a]know me;
You have seen me,
And You have [b]tested my heart toward
You.
Pull them out like sheep for the slaughter,
And prepare them for [c]the day of
slaughter.
4 How long will [a]the land mourn,
And the herbs of every field wither?
[b]The beasts and birds are consumed,
[c]For the wickedness of those who dwell
there,
Because they said, "He will not see our
final end."

The LORD Answers Jeremiah

5 "If you have run with the footmen, and they
have wearied you,
Then how can you contend with horses?

KJV

wherein thou trustedst, *they wearied thee,* then how wilt thou do in [a]the swelling of Jordan?

6 For even [a]thy brethren, and the house of thy father, even they have dealt treacherously with thee; yea, they have called a multitude after thee: [b]believe them not, though they speak fair words unto thee.

7 I have forsaken mine house, I have left mine heritage; I have given the dearly beloved of my soul into the hand of her enemies.

8 Mine heritage is unto me as a lion in the forest; it crieth out against me: therefore have I [a]hated it.

9 Mine heritage *is* unto me *as* a speckled bird, the birds round about *are* against her; come ye, assemble all the beasts of the field, [a]come to devour.

10 Many [a]pastors have destroyed [b]my vineyard, they have [c]trodden my portion under foot, they have made my pleasant portion a desolate wilderness.

11 They have made it [a]desolate, *and being* desolate it mourneth unto me; the whole land is made desolate, because [b]no man layeth *it* to heart.

12 The spoilers are come upon all high places through the wilderness: for the sword of the LORD shall devour from the *one* end of the land even to the *other* end of the land: no flesh shall have peace.

13 [a]They have sown wheat, but shall reap thorns: they have put themselves to pain, *but* shall not profit: and they shall be ashamed of your revenues because of the fierce anger of the LORD.

14 Thus saith the LORD against all mine evil neighbours, that [a]touch the inheritance which I have caused my people Israel to inherit; Behold, I will [b]pluck them out of their land, and pluck out the house of Judah from among them.

15 [a]And it shall come to pass, after that I have plucked them out I will return, and have compassion on them, [b]and will bring them again, every man to his heritage, and every man to his land.

16 And it shall come to pass, if they will diligently learn the ways of my people, [a]to swear by my name, The LORD liveth; as they taught my people to swear by Baal; then shall they be [b]built in the midst of my people.

17 But if they will not [a]obey, I will utterly pluck up and destroy that nation, saith the LORD.

Symbol of the Linen Sash

13 Thus saith the LORD unto me, Go and get thee a linen girdle, and put it upon thy loins, and put it not in water.

2 So I got a girdle according to the word of the LORD, and put *it* on my loins.

3 And the word of the LORD came unto me the second time, saying,

4 Take the girdle that thou hast got, which *is* upon thy loins, and arise, go to Euphrates, and hide it there in a hole of the rock.

5 So I went, and hid it by Euphrates, as the LORD commanded me.

6 And it came to pass after many days, that the LORD said unto me, Arise, go to Euphrates,

5 [a]Josh. 3:15; 1 Chr. 12:15
6 [a]Gen. 37:4–11; Job 6:15; Ps. 69:8; Jer. 9:4, 5 [b]Ps. 12:2; Prov. 26:25
8 [a]Hos. 9:15; Amos 6:8
9 [a]Lev. 26:22
10 [a]Jer. 6:3; 23:1 [b]Ps. 80:8–16; Is. 5:1–7 [c]Is. 63:18
11 [a]Jer. 10:22; 22:6 [b]Is. 42:25
13 [a]Lev. 26:16; Deut. 28:38; Mic. 6:15; Hag. 1:6
14 [a]Jer. 2:3; 50:11, 12; Zech. 2:8 [b]Deut. 30:3; Ps. 106:47; Is. 11:11–16; Jer. 32:37
15 [a]Jer. 31:20; Lam. 3:32; Ezek. 28:25 [b]Amos 9:14
16 [a][Jer. 4:2]; Zeph. 1:5 [b][Eph. 2:20, 21; 1 Pet. 2:5]
17 [a]Ps. 2:8–12; Is. 60:12

NKJV

And *if* in the land of peace,
In which you trusted, *they wearied you,*
Then how will you do in [a]the *floodplain of the Jordan?
6 For even [a]your brothers, the house of your father,
Even they have dealt treacherously with you;
Yes, they have called a multitude after you.
[b]Do not believe them,
Even though they speak smooth words to you.

7 "I have forsaken My house, I have left My heritage;
I have given the dearly beloved of My soul into the hand of her enemies.
8 My heritage is to Me like a lion in the forest;
It cries out against Me;
Therefore I have [a]hated it.
9 My heritage *is* to Me *like* a speckled vulture;
The vultures all around *are* against her.
Come, assemble all the beasts of the field,
[a]Bring them to devour!

10 "Many [a]rulers* have destroyed [b]My vineyard,
They have [c]trodden My portion underfoot;
They have made My pleasant portion a desolate wilderness.
11 They have made it [a]desolate;
Desolate, it mourns to Me;
The whole land is made desolate,
Because [b]no one takes *it* to heart.
12 The plunderers have come
On all the desolate heights in the wilderness,
For the sword of the LORD shall devour
From *one* end of the land to the *other* end of the land;
No flesh shall have peace.
13 [a]They have sown wheat but reaped thorns;
They have put themselves to pain *but* do not profit.
But be ashamed of your harvest
Because of the fierce anger of the LORD."

14 Thus says the LORD: "Against all My evil neighbors who [a]touch the inheritance which I have caused My people Israel to inherit—behold, I will [b]pluck them out of their land and pluck out the house of Judah from among them.

15 [a]"Then it shall be, after I have plucked them out, that I will return and have compassion on them [b]and bring them back, everyone to his heritage and everyone to his land.

16 "And it shall be, if they will learn carefully the ways of My people, [a]to swear by My name, 'As the LORD lives,' as they taught My people to swear by Baal, then they shall be [b]established in the midst of My people.

17 "But if they do not [a]obey, I will utterly pluck up and destroy that nation," says the LORD.

Symbol of the Linen Sash

13 Thus the LORD said to me: "Go and get yourself a linen sash, and put it around your waist, but do not put it in water."

2 So I got a sash according to the word of the LORD, and put *it* around my waist.

3 And the word of the LORD came to me the second time, saying,

4 "Take the sash that you acquired, which *is* around your waist, and arise, go to the *Euphrates, and hide it there in a hole in the rock."

5 So I went and hid it by the Euphrates, as the LORD commanded me.

6 Now it came to pass after many days that the LORD said to me, "Arise, go to the Euphrates,

*———
12:5 Or *thicket*
12:10 Lit. *shepherds* or *pastors*
13:4 Heb. *Perath*

KJV

and take the girdle from thence, which I commanded thee to hide there.
7 Then I went to Euphrates, and digged, and
took the girdle from the place where I had hid it:
and, behold, the girdle was marred, it was profitable for nothing.
8 Then the word of the LORD came unto me,
saying,
9 Thus saith the LORD, After this manner
[a]will I mar the pride of Judah, and the great [b]pride
of Jerusalem.
10 This evil people, which [a]refuse to hear my
words, which [b]walk in the imagination of their
heart, and walk after other gods, to serve them,
and to worship them, shall even be as this girdle,
which is good for nothing.
11 For as the girdle cleaveth to the loins of
a man, so have I caused to cleave unto me the
whole house of Israel and the whole house of Judah, saith the LORD; that [a]they might be unto me
for a people, and [b]for a name, and for a praise,
and for a [c]glory: but they would [d]not hear.

Symbol of the Wine Bottles

12 Therefore thou shalt speak unto them this
word; Thus saith the LORD God of Israel, Every
bottle shall be filled with wine: and they shall say
unto thee, Do we not certainly know that every
bottle shall be filled with wine?
13 Then shalt thou say unto them, Thus saith
the LORD, Behold, I will fill all the inhabitants of
this land, even the kings that sit upon David's
throne, and the priests, and the prophets, and all
the inhabitants of Jerusalem, [a]with drunkenness.
14 And [a]I will dash them one against another, even the fathers and the sons together, saith
the LORD: I will not pity, nor spare, nor have
mercy, but destroy them.

Pride Precedes Captivity

15 Hear ye, and give ear; be not proud: for
the LORD hath spoken.
16 [a]Give glory to the LORD your God, before
he cause [b]darkness, and before your feet stumble
upon the dark mountains, and, while ye [c]look for
light, he turn it into [d]the shadow of death, *and*
make *it* gross darkness.
17 But if ye will not hear it, my soul shall
[a]weep in secret places for *your* pride; and mine
eye shall weep sore, and run down with tears,
because the LORD's flock is carried away captive.
18 Say unto [a]the king and to the queen, Humble yourselves, sit down: for your principalities
shall come down, *even* the crown of your glory.
19 The cities of the south shall be shut up,
and none shall open *them:* Judah shall be carried
away captive all of it, it shall be wholly carried
away captive.
20 Lift up your eyes, and behold them that
come from the [a]north: where *is* the flock *that* was
given thee, thy beautiful flock?
21 What wilt thou say when he shall punish
thee? for thou hast taught them *to be* captains,
and as chief over thee: shall not [a]sorrows take
thee, as a woman in travail?
22 And if thou say in thine heart, [a]Wherefore
come these things upon me? For the greatness of

CHAPTER 13
9 [a]Lev. 26:19 [b][Is. 2:10–17; 23:9]; Zeph. 3:11
10 [a]Jer. 16:12 [b]Jer. 7:24; 16:12
11 [a][Ex. 19:5, 6; Deut. 32:10, 11] [b]Jer. 33:9 [c]Is. 43:21 [d]Ps. 81:11; Jer. 7:13, 24, 26
13 [a]Ps. 60:3; 75:8; Is. 51:17; 63:6; Jer. 25:27; 51:7, 57
14 [a]2 Chr. 36:17; Ps. 2:9; Is. 9:20, 21; Jer. 19:9–11
16 [a]Josh. 7:19; Ps. 96:8; Mal. 2:2 [b]Is. 5:30; 8:22; Amos 8:9 [c]Is. 59:9 [d]Ps. 44:19; Jer. 2:6
17 [a]Ps. 119:136; Jer. 9:1; 14:17; Luke 19:41, 42
18 [a]2 Kin. 24:12; Jer. 22:26
20 [a]Jer. 10:22; 46:20
21 [a]Jer. 6:24
22 [a]Jer. 16:10

NKJV

and take from there the sash which I commanded
you to hide there."
7 Then I went to the Euphrates and dug, and
I took the sash from the place where I had hidden
it; and there was the sash, ruined. It was profitable
for nothing.
8 Then the word of the LORD came to me,
saying,
9 "Thus says the LORD: 'In this manner [a]I
will ruin the pride of Judah and the great [b]pride
of Jerusalem.
10 'This evil people, who [a]refuse to hear My
words, who [b]follow the dictates of their hearts,
and walk after other gods to serve them and worship them, shall be just like this sash which is
profitable for nothing.
11 'For as the sash clings to the waist of a
man, so I have caused the whole house of Israel
and the whole house of Judah to cling to Me,'
says the LORD, 'that [a]they may become My people,
[b]for renown, for praise, and for [c]glory; but they
would [d]not hear.'

Symbol of the Wine Bottles

12 "Therefore you shall speak to them this
word: 'Thus says the LORD God of Israel: "Every
bottle shall be filled with wine." ' And they will
say to you, 'Do we not certainly know that every
bottle will be filled with wine?'
13 "Then you shall say to them, 'Thus says
the LORD: "Behold, I will fill all the inhabitants
of this land—even the kings who sit on David's
throne, the priests, the prophets, and all the inhabitants of Jerusalem—[a]with drunkenness!
14 "And [a]I will dash them one against another, even the fathers and the sons together,"
says the LORD. "I will not pity nor spare nor have
mercy, but will destroy them." ' "

Pride Precedes Captivity

15 Hear and give ear:
Do not be proud,
For the LORD has spoken.
16 [a]Give glory to the LORD your God
Before He causes [b]darkness,
And before your feet stumble
On the dark mountains,
And while you are [c]looking for light,
He turns it into [d]the shadow of death
And makes *it* dense darkness.
17 But if you will not hear it,
My soul will [a]weep in secret for *your*
pride;
My eyes will weep bitterly
And run down with tears,
Because the LORD's flock has been taken
captive.

18 Say to [a]the king and to the queen mother,
"Humble yourselves;
Sit down,
For your rule shall collapse, the crown of
your glory."
19 The cities of the South shall be shut up,
And no one shall open *them;*
Judah shall be carried away captive, all
of it;
It shall be wholly carried away captive.

20 Lift up your eyes and see
Those who come from the [a]north.
Where *is* the flock *that* was given to
you,
Your beautiful sheep?
21 What will you say when He punishes
you?
For you have taught them
To be chieftains, to be head over you.
Will not [a]pangs seize you,
Like a woman in labor?
22 And if you say in your heart,
[a]"Why have these things come upon me?"

KJV

thine iniquity are [b]thy skirts discovered, *and* thy
heels made bare.
23 Can the Ethiopian change his skin, or the
leopard his spots? *then* may ye also do good, that
are accustomed to do evil.
24 Therefore will I [a]scatter them [b]as the stubble that passeth away by the wind of the
wilderness.
25 [a]This *is* thy lot, the portion of thy measures from me, saith the LORD; because thou hast
forgotten me, and trusted in [b]falsehood.
26 Therefore [a]will I discover thy skirts upon
thy face, that thy shame may appear.
27 I have seen thine adulteries, and thy
[a]neighings, the lewdness of thy whoredom, *and*
thine abominations [b]on the hills in the fields. Woe
unto thee, O Jerusalem! wilt thou not be made
clean? when *shall it* once *be*?

Sword, Famine, and Pestilence

14 The word of the LORD that came to Jeremiah concerning the dearth.
2 Judah mourneth, and [a]the gates thereof
languish; they are [b]black unto the ground; and
[c]the cry of Jerusalem is gone up.
3 And their nobles have sent their little ones
to the waters: they came to the pits, *and* found
no water; they returned with their vessels empty;
they were [a]ashamed and confounded, [b]and covered their heads.
4 Because the ground is chapt, for there was
[a]no rain in the earth, the plowmen were ashamed,
they covered their heads.
5 Yea, the hind also calved in the field, and
forsook *it*, because there was no grass.
6 And [a]the wild asses did stand in the high
places, they snuffed up the wind like dragons;
their eyes did fail, because *there was* no grass.
7 O LORD, though our iniquities testify
against us, do thou *it* [a]for thy name's sake: for
our backslidings are many; we have sinned
against thee.
8 [a]O the hope of Israel, the saviour thereof
in time of trouble, why shouldest thou be as a
stranger in the land, and as a wayfaring man *that*
turneth aside to tarry for a night?
9 Why shouldest thou be as a man astonied,
as a mighty man [a]*that* cannot save? yet thou, O
LORD, [b]*art* in the midst of us, and we are called
by thy name; leave us not.
10 Thus saith the LORD unto this people,
[a]Thus have they loved to wander, they have not
refrained their feet, therefore the LORD doth not
accept them; [b]he will now remember their iniquity, and visit their sins.
11 Then said the LORD unto me, [a]Pray not
for this people for *their* good.

22 [b]Is. 47:2; Ezek. 16:37; Nah. 3:5
24 [a]Lev. 26:33; Jer. 9:16; Ezek. 5:2, 12 [b]Ps. 1:4; Hos. 13:3
25 [a]Job 20:29; Ps. 11:6; Matt. 24:51 [b]Jer. 10:14
26 [a]Lam. 1:8; Ezek. 16:37; Hos. 2:10
27 [a]Jer. 5:7, 8 [b]Is. 65:7; Jer. 2:20; Ezek. 6:13

CHAPTER 14
2 [a]2 Kin. 25:3; Is. 3:26 [b]Jer. 8:21 [c]1 Sam. 5:12; Jer. 11:11; 46:12; Zech. 7:13
3 [a]Job 6:20; Ps. 40:14 [b]2 Sam. 15:30
4 [a]Jer. 3:3; Ezek. 22:24
6 [a]Job 39:5, 6; Jer. 2:24
7 [a]Ps. 25:11; Jer. 14:21
8 [a]Jer. 17:13
9 [a]Is. 59:1 [b]Ex. 29:45; Lev. 26:11; Ps. 46:5; Jer. 8:19
10 [a]Jer. 2:23–25 [b][Jer. 44:21–23]; Hos. 8:13
11 [a]Ex. 32:10; Jer. 7:16; 11:14

NKJV

For the greatness of your iniquity
[b]Your skirts have been uncovered,
Your heels made bare.
23 Can the Ethiopian change his skin or the
leopard its spots?
Then may you also do good who are
accustomed to do evil.

24 "Therefore I will [a]scatter them [b]like
stubble
That passes away by the wind of the
wilderness.
25 [a]This is your lot,
The portion of your measures from Me,"
says the LORD,
"Because you have forgotten Me
And trusted in [b]falsehood.
26 Therefore [a]I will uncover your skirts over
your face,
That your shame may appear.
27 I have seen your adulteries
And your *lustful* [a]neighings,
The lewdness of your harlotry,
Your abominations [b]on the hills in the
fields.
Woe to you, O Jerusalem!
Will you still not be made clean?"

Sword, Famine, and Pestilence

14 The word of the LORD that came to Jeremiah concerning the droughts.

2 "Judah mourns,
And [a]her gates languish;
They [b]mourn for the land,
And [c]the cry of Jerusalem has gone up.
3 Their nobles have sent their lads for
water;
They went to the cisterns *and* found no
water.
They returned with their vessels empty;
They were [a]ashamed and confounded
[b]And covered their heads.
4 Because the ground is parched,
For there was [a]no rain in the land,
The plowmen were ashamed;
They covered their heads.
5 Yes, the deer also gave birth in the field,
But left because there was no grass.
6 And [a]the wild donkeys stood in the
desolate heights;
They sniffed at the wind like jackals;
Their eyes failed because *there was* no
grass."

7 O LORD, though our iniquities testify
against us,
Do it [a]for Your name's sake;
For our backslidings are many,
We have sinned against You.
8 [a]O the Hope of Israel, his Savior in time
of trouble,
Why should You be like a stranger in the
land,
And like a traveler *who* turns aside to
tarry for a night?
9 Why should You be like a man astonished,
Like a mighty one [a]*who* cannot save?
Yet You, O LORD, [b]*are* in our midst,
And we are called by Your name;
Do not leave us!

10 Thus says the LORD to this people:

[a]"Thus they have loved to wander;
They have not restrained their feet.
Therefore the LORD does not accept them;
[b]He will remember their iniquity now,
And punish their sins."

11 Then the LORD said to me, [a]"Do not pray
for this people, for *their* good.

KJV

12 [a]When they fast, I will not hear their cry;
and [b]when they offer burnt offering and an oblation, I will not accept them: but [c]I will consume
them by the sword, and by the famine, and by
the pestilence.
13 [a]Then said I, Ah, Lord GOD! behold, the
prophets say unto them, Ye shall not see the
sword, neither shall ye have famine; but I will
give you assured [b]peace in this place.
14 Then the LORD said unto me, [a]The prophets prophesy lies in my name: [b]I sent them not,
neither have I commanded them, neither spake
unto them: they prophesy unto you a false vision
and divination, and a thing of nought, and the
[c]deceit of their heart.
15 Therefore thus saith the LORD concerning
the prophets that prophesy in my name, and I sent
them not, [a]yet they say, Sword and famine shall
not be in this land; By sword and famine shall
those prophets be consumed.
16 And the people to whom they prophesy
shall be cast out in the streets of Jerusalem because of the famine and the sword; [a]and they shall
have none to bury them, them, their wives, nor
their sons, nor their daughters: for I will pour their
wickedness upon them.
17 Therefore thou shalt say this word unto
them; [a]Let mine eyes run down with tears night
and day, and let them not cease: [b]for the virgin
daughter of my people is broken with a great
breach, with a very grievous blow.
18 If I go forth into [a]the field, then behold
the slain with the sword! and if I enter into the
city, then behold them that are sick with famine!
yea, both the prophet and the [b]priest go about
into a land that they know not.

The People Plead for Mercy

19 [a]Hast thou utterly rejected Judah? hath
thy soul lothed Zion? why hast thou smitten us,
and [b]*there is* no healing for us? [c]we looked for
peace, and *there is* no good; and for the time of
healing, and behold trouble!
20 We acknowledge, O LORD, our wicked-
ness, *and* the iniquity of our [a]fathers: for [b]we have
sinned against thee.
21 Do not abhor *us*, for thy name's sake, do
not disgrace the throne of thy glory: [a]remember,
break not thy covenant with us.
22 [a]Are there *any* among [b]the vanities of the
Gentiles that can cause [c]rain? or can the heavens
give showers? [d]*art* not thou he, O LORD our God?
therefore we will wait upon thee: for thou hast
made all these *things*.

The LORD Will Not Relent

15 Then said the LORD unto me, [a]Though
[b]Moses and [c]Samuel stood before me, *yet*
my mind *could* not *be* toward this people: cast
them out of my sight, and let them go forth.
2 And it shall come to pass, if they say unto
thee, Whither shall we go forth? then thou shalt
tell them, Thus saith the LORD; [a]Such as *are* for
death, to death; and such as *are* for the sword,
to the sword; and such as *are* for the famine, to
the famine; and such as *are* for the [b]captivity, to
the captivity.
3 And I will [a]appoint over them four kinds,
saith the LORD: the sword to slay, and the dogs

12 [a]Prov. 1:28; [Is. 1:15; 58:3–6]; Ezek. 8:18; Mic. 3:4; Zech. 7:13 [b]Jer. 6:20 [c]Jer. 9:16
13 [a]Jer. 4:10 [b]Jer. 8:11; 23:17
14 [a]Jer. 27:10 [b]Jer. 29:8, 9 [c]Jer. 23:16; Ezek. 12:24
15 [a]Jer. 5:12; Ezek. 14:10
16 [a]Ps. 79:2, 3; Jer. 7:32; 15:2, 3
17 [a]Jer. 9:1; 13:17; Lam. 1:16 [b]Is. 37:22; Jer. 8:21; Lam. 1:15; 2:13
18 [a]Jer. 6:25; Lam. 1:20; Ezek. 7:15 [b]Jer. 23:11
19 [a]Jer. 6:30; 7:29; 12:7; Lam. 5:22 [b]Jer. 15:18 [c]Job 30:26; Jer. 8:15; 1 Thess. 5:3
20 [a]Neh. 9:2; Ps. 32:5; Jer. 3:25 [b]Ps. 106:6; Jer. 8:14; 14:7; Dan. 9:8
21 [a]Ps. 106:45
22 [a]Zech. 10:1 [b]Deut. 32:21 [c]1 Kin. 17:1; Jer. 5:24 [d]Ps. 135:7

CHAPTER 15

1 [a]Ps. 99:6; Ezek. 14:14 [b]Ex. 32:11–14; Num. 14:13–20; Ps. 99:6 [c]1 Sam. 7:9
2 [a]Jer. 43:11; Ezek. 5:2, 12; Zech. 11:9; [Rev. 13:10] [b]Jer. 9:16; 16:13
3 [a]Lev. 26:16, 21, 25; Jer. 12:3; Ezek. 14:21

NKJV

12 [a]"When they fast, I will not hear their cry;
and [b]when they offer burnt offering and grain offering, I will not accept them. But [c]I will consume
them by the sword, by the famine, and by the
pestilence."
13 [a]Then I said, "Ah, Lord GOD! Behold, the
prophets say to them, 'You shall not see the
sword, nor shall you have famine, but I will give
you assured [b]peace in this place.' "
14 And the LORD said to me, [a]"The prophets
prophesy lies in My name. [b]I have not sent them,
commanded them, nor spoken to them; they
prophesy to you a false vision, divination, a
worthless thing, and the [c]deceit of their heart.
15 "Therefore thus says the LORD concerning
the prophets who prophesy in My name, whom I
did not send, [a]and who say, 'Sword and famine
shall not be in this land'—'By sword and famine
those prophets shall be consumed!
16 'And the people to whom they prophesy
shall be cast out in the streets of Jerusalem because of the famine and the sword; [a]they will have
no one to bury them—them nor their wives, their
sons nor their daughters—for I will pour their
wickedness on them.'
17 "Therefore you shall say this word to
them:

[a]'Let my eyes flow with tears night and day,
And let them not cease;
[b]For the virgin daughter of my people
Has been broken with a mighty stroke,
with a very severe blow.
18 If I go out to [a]the field,
Then behold, those slain with the sword!
And if I enter the city,
Then behold, those sick from famine!
Yes, both prophet and [b]priest go about in
a land they do not know.' "

The People Plead for Mercy

19 [a]Have You utterly rejected Judah?
Has Your soul loathed Zion?
Why have You stricken us so that [b]*there*
is no healing for us?
[c]We looked for peace, but *there was* no
good;
And for the time of healing, and there was
trouble.
20 We acknowledge, O LORD, our wickedness
And the iniquity of our [a]fathers,
For [b]we have sinned against You.
21 Do not abhor *us*, for Your name's sake;
Do not disgrace the throne of Your glory.
[a]Remember, do not break Your covenant
with us.
22 [a]Are there any among [b]the idols of the
nations that can cause [c]rain?
Or can the heavens give showers?
[d]*Are* You not He, O LORD our God?
Therefore we will wait for You,
Since You have made all these.

The LORD Will Not Relent

15 Then the LORD said to me, [a]"*Even* if [b]Moses
and [c]Samuel stood before Me, My mind
would not *be* favorable toward this people. Cast
them out of My sight, and let them go forth.
2 "And it shall be, if they say to you, 'Where
should we go?' then you shall tell them, 'Thus says
the LORD:

[a]"Such as *are* for death, to death;
And such as *are* for the sword, to the
sword;
And such as *are* for the famine, to the
famine;
And such as *are* for the [b]captivity, to the
captivity." '

3 "And I will [a]appoint over them four forms
of destruction," says the LORD: "the sword to slay,

KJV

to tear, and [b]the fowls of the heaven, and the beasts of the earth, to devour and destroy.

4 And I will cause them to be [a]removed into all kingdoms of the earth, because of [b]Manasseh the son of Hezekiah king of Judah, for *that* which he did in Jerusalem.

5 For who shall have pity upon thee, O Jerusalem? or who shall bemoan thee? or who shall go aside to ask how thou doest?

6 [a]Thou hast forsaken me, saith the LORD, thou art [b]gone backward: therefore will I stretch out my hand against thee, and destroy thee; [c]I am weary with repenting.

7 And I will fan them with a fan in the gates of the land; I will [a]bereave *them* of children, I will destroy my people, *since* they [b]return not from their ways.

8 Their widows are increased to me above the sand of the seas: I have brought upon them against the mother of the young men a spoiler at noonday: I have caused *him* to fall upon it [a]suddenly, and terrors upon the city.

9 [a]She that hath borne seven languisheth: she hath given up the ghost; [b]her sun is gone down while *it was* yet day: she hath been ashamed and confounded: and the residue of them will I deliver to the sword before their enemies, saith the LORD.

Jeremiah's Dejection

10 [a]Woe is me, my mother, that thou hast borne me a man of strife and a man of contention to the whole earth! I have neither lent on usury, nor men have lent to me on usury; *yet* every one of them doth curse me.

11 The LORD said, Verily it shall be well with thy remnant; verily I will cause [a]the enemy to entreat thee *well* in the time of evil and in the time of affliction.

12 Shall iron break the northern iron and the steel?

13 Thy substance and thy treasures will I give to the [a]spoil without price, and *that* for all thy sins, even in all thy borders.

14 And I will make *thee* to pass with thine enemies [a]into a land *which* thou knowest not: for a [b]fire is kindled in mine anger, *which* shall burn upon you.

15 O LORD, [a]thou knowest: remember me, and visit me, and [b]revenge me of my persecutors; take me not away in thy longsuffering: know that [c]for thy sake I have suffered rebuke.

16 Thy words were found, and I did [a]eat them; and [b]thy word was unto me the joy and rejoicing of mine heart: for I am called by thy name, O LORD God of hosts.

3 [b]Jer. 7:33
4 [a]Deut. 28:25 [b]2 Kin. 24:3, 4
6 [a]Jer. 2:13 [b]Is. 1:4; Jer. 7:24 [c]Jer. 20:16; Zech. 8:14
7 [a]Jer. 18:21; Hos. 9:12–16 [b]Is. 9:13; Jer. 5:3; Amos 4:10, 11
8 [a]Is. 29:5
9 [a]1 Sam. 2:5; Is. 47:9 [b]Jer. 6:4; Amos 8:9
10 [a]Job 3:1; Jer. 20:14
11 [a]Jer. 40:4, 5
13 [a]Ps. 44:12; Is. 52:3
14 [a]Deut. 28:36, 64; Jer. 16:13 [b]Deut. 32:22; Ps. 21:9; Jer. 17:4
15 [a]Jer. 12:3 [b]Jer. 20:12 [c]Ps. 69:7–9; Jer. 20:8
16 [a]Ezek. 3:1, 3; Rev. 10:9 [b][Job 23:12; Ps. 119:72]

NKJV

the dogs to drag, [b]the birds of the heavens and the beasts of the earth to devour and destroy.

4 "I will hand them over to [a]trouble, to all kingdoms of the earth, because of [b]Manasseh the son of Hezekiah, king of Judah, for what he did in Jerusalem.

5 "For who will have pity on you, O
Jerusalem?
Or who will bemoan you?
Or who will turn aside to ask how you
are doing?
6 [a]You have forsaken Me," says the LORD,
"You have [b]gone backward.
Therefore I will stretch out My hand
against you and destroy you;
[c]I am weary of relenting!
7 And I will winnow them with a winnowing
fan in the gates of the land;
I will [a]bereave *them* of children;
I will destroy My people,
Since they [b]do not return from their
ways.
8 Their widows will be increased to Me
more than the sand of the seas;
I will bring against them,
Against the mother of the young men,
A plunderer at noonday;
I will cause anguish and terror to fall on
them [a]suddenly.

9 "She[a] languishes who has borne seven;
She has breathed her last;
[b]Her sun has gone down
While *it was* yet day;
She has been ashamed and confounded.
And the remnant of them I will deliver to
the sword
Before their enemies," says the LORD.

Jeremiah's Dejection

10 [a]Woe is me, my mother,
That you have borne me,
A man of strife and a man of contention
to the whole earth!
I have neither lent for interest,
Nor have men lent to me for interest.
Every one of them curses me.

11 The LORD said:

"Surely it will be well with your remnant;
Surely I will cause [a]the enemy to intercede
with you
In the time of adversity and in the time
of affliction.
12 Can anyone break iron,
The northern iron and the bronze?
13 Your wealth and your treasures
I will give as [a]plunder without price,
Because of all your sins,
Throughout your territories.
14 And I will *make *you* cross over with your
enemies
[a]Into a land *which* you do not know;
For a [b]fire is kindled in My anger,
Which shall burn upon you."

15 O LORD, [a]You know;
Remember me and visit me,
And [b]take vengeance for me on my
persecutors.
In Your enduring patience, do not take me
away.
Know that [c]for Your sake I have suffered
rebuke.
16 Your words were found, and I [a]ate them,
And [b]Your word was to me the joy and
rejoicing of my heart;
For I am called by Your name,
O LORD God of hosts.

*

15:14 So with MT, Vg.; LXX, Syr., Tg. *cause you to serve* (cf. 17:4)

KJV

17 [a]I sat not in the assembly of the mockers,
nor rejoiced; I sat alone because of thy hand: for
thou hast filled me with indignation.
18 Why is my [a]pain perpetual, and my
wound incurable, *which* refuseth to be healed?
wilt thou be altogether unto me [b]as a liar, *and*
as waters *that* fail?

The LORD Reassures Jeremiah

19 Therefore thus saith the LORD, [a]If thou return, then will I bring thee again, *and* thou shalt
[b]stand before me: and if thou [c]take forth the precious from the vile, thou shalt be as my mouth:
let them return unto thee; but return not thou unto
them.
20 And I will make thee unto this people a
fenced brasen [a]wall: and they shall fight against
thee, but [b]they shall not prevail against thee: for
I *am* with thee to save thee and to deliver thee,
saith the LORD.
21 And I will deliver thee out of the hand of
the wicked, and I will redeem thee out of the hand
of the terrible.

Jeremiah's Life-Style and Message

16 The word of the LORD came also unto me,
saying,
2 Thou shalt not take thee a wife, neither
shalt thou have sons or daughters in this place.
3 For thus saith the LORD concerning the
sons and concerning the daughters that are born
in this place, and concerning their mothers that
bare them, and concerning their fathers that begat
them in this land;
4 They shall die of [a]grievous deaths; they
shall not be [b]lamented; neither shall they be [c]bur-
ied; *but* they shall be [d]as dung upon the face of
the earth: and they shall be consumed by the
sword, and by famine; and their [e]carcases shall
be meat for the fowls of heaven, and for the beasts
of the earth.
5 For thus saith the LORD, [a]Enter not into
the house of mourning, neither go to lament nor
bemoan them: for I have taken away my peace
from this people, saith the LORD, *even* lovingkindness and mercies.
6 Both the great and the small shall die in
this land: they shall not be buried, [a]neither shall
men lament for them, nor [b]cut themselves, nor
[c]make themselves bald for them:
7 Neither shall *men* tear *themselves* for
them in mourning, to comfort them for the dead;
neither shall *men* give them the cup of consolation
to [a]drink for their father or for their mother.
8 Thou shalt not also go into the house of
feasting, to sit with them to eat and to drink.
9 For thus saith the LORD of hosts, the God
of Israel; Behold, [a]I will cause to cease out of this
place in your eyes, and in your days, the voice
of mirth, and the voice of gladness, the voice of
the bridegroom, and the voice of the bride.
10 And it shall come to pass, when thou shalt
shew this people all these words, and they shall
say unto thee, [a]Wherefore hath the LORD pronounced all this great evil against us? or what *is*
our iniquity? or what *is* our sin that we have committed against the LORD our God?
11 Then shalt thou say unto them, [a]Because
your fathers have forsaken me, saith the LORD,
and have walked after other gods, and have
served them, and have worshipped them, and
have forsaken me, and have not kept my law;
12 And ye have done [a]worse than your fa-

17 [a]Ps. 26:4, 5
18 [a]Job 34:6; Jer. 10:19; 30:15; Mic. 1:9 [b]Job 6:15
19 [a]Jer. 4:1; Zech. 3:7 [b]1 Kin. 17:1; Jer. 15:1 [c]Jer. 6:29; Ezek. 22:26; 44:23
20 [a]Jer. 1:18; 6:27; Ezek. 3:9 [b]Ps. 46:7; Is. 41:10; Jer. 1:8, 19; 20:11; 37:21; 38:13; 39:11, 12

CHAPTER 16

4 [a]Jer. 15:2 [b]Jer. 22:18; 25:33 [c]Jer. 14:16; 19:11 [d]Ps. 83:10; Jer. 8:2; 9:22 [e]Ps. 79:2; Is. 18:6; Jer. 7:33; 34:20
5 [a]Ezek. 24:17, 22, 23
6 [a]Jer. 22:18 [b]Lev. 19:28; Deut. 14:1; Jer. 41:5; 47:5 [c]Is. 22:12; Jer. 7:29
7 [a]Prov. 31:6
9 [a]Is. 24:7, 8; Jer. 7:34; 25:10; Ezek. 26:13; Hos. 2:11; Rev. 18:23
10 [a]Deut. 29:24; 1 Kin. 9:8; Jer. 5:19
11 [a]Deut. 29:25; 1 Kin. 9:9; 2 Chr. 7:22; Neh. 9:26–29; Jer. 22:9
12 [a]Jer. 7:26

NKJV

17 [a]I did not sit in the assembly of the
mockers,
Nor did I rejoice;
I sat alone because of Your hand,
For You have filled me with indignation.
18 Why is my [a]pain perpetual
And my wound incurable,
Which refuses to be healed?
Will You surely be to me [b]like an
unreliable stream,
As waters *that* fail?

The LORD Reassures Jeremiah

19 Therefore thus says the LORD:

[a]"If you return,
Then I will bring you back;
You shall [b]stand before Me;
If you [c]take out the precious from the vile,
You shall be as My mouth.
Let them return to you,
But you must not return to them.
20 And I will make you to this people a
fortified bronze [a]wall;
And they will fight against you,
But [b]they shall not prevail against you;
For I *am* with you to save you
And deliver you," says the LORD.
21 "I will deliver you from the hand of the
wicked,
And I will redeem you from the grip of
the terrible."

Jeremiah's Life-Style and Message

16 The word of the LORD also came to me,
saying,
2 "You shall not take a wife, nor shall you
have sons or daughters in this place."
3 For thus says the LORD concerning the
sons and daughters who are born in this place,
and concerning their mothers who bore them and
their fathers who begot them in this land:
4 "They shall die [a]gruesome deaths; they
shall not be [b]lamented nor shall they be [c]buried,
but they shall be [d]like refuse on the face of the
earth. They shall be consumed by the sword and
by famine, and their [e]corpses shall be meat for
the birds of heaven and for the beasts of the
earth."
5 For thus says the LORD: [a]"Do not enter
the house of mourning, nor go to lament or bemoan them; for I have taken away My peace from
this people," says the LORD, "lovingkindness and
mercies.
6 "Both the great and the small shall die in
this land. They shall not be buried; [a]neither shall
men lament for them, [b]cut themselves, nor [c]make
themselves bald for them.
7 "Nor shall *men* break *bread* in mourning
for them, to comfort them for the dead; nor shall
men give them the cup of consolation to [a]drink
for their father or their mother.
8 "Also you shall not go into the house of
feasting to sit with them, to eat and drink."
9 For thus says the LORD of hosts, the God
of Israel: "Behold, [a]I will cause to cease from this
place, before your eyes and in your days, the voice
of mirth and the voice of gladness, the voice of
the bridegroom and the voice of the bride.
10 "And it shall be, when you show this people all these words, and they say to you, [a]'Why
has the LORD pronounced all this great disaster
against us? Or what *is* our iniquity? Or what *is*
our sin that we have committed against the LORD
our God?'
11 "then you shall say to them, [a]'Because
your fathers have forsaken Me,' says the LORD;
'they have walked after other gods and have
served them and worshiped them, and have forsaken Me and not kept My law.
12 'And you have done [a]worse than your fa-

KJV

thers; for, behold, [b]ye walk every one after the
imagination of his evil heart, that they may not
hearken unto me:
13 [a]Therefore will I cast you out of this land
[b]into a land that ye know not, *neither* ye nor your
fathers; and there shall ye serve other gods day
and night; where I will not shew you favour.

God Will Restore Israel
(cf. Jer. 23:7, 8)

14 Therefore, behold, the [a]days come, saith
the LORD, that it shall no more be said, The LORD
liveth, that brought up the children of Israel out
of the land of Egypt;
15 But, The LORD liveth, that brought up the
children of Israel from the land of the [a]north, and
from all the lands whither he had driven them:
and [b]I will bring them again into their land that
I gave unto their fathers.
16 Behold, I will send for many [a]fishers, saith
the LORD, and they shall fish them; and after will
I send for many hunters, and they shall hunt them
from every mountain, and from every hill, and
out of the holes of the rocks.
17 For mine [a]eyes *are* upon all their ways:
they are not hid from my face, neither is their
iniquity hid from mine eyes.
18 And first I will recompense their iniquity
and their sin [a]double; because [b]they have defiled
my land, they have filled mine inheritance with
the carcases of their detestable and abominable
things.
19 O LORD, [a]my strength, and my fortress,
and [b]my refuge in the day of affliction, the Gentiles shall come unto thee from the ends of the
earth, and shall say, Surely our fathers have inherited lies, vanity, and *things* [c]wherein *there is*
no profit.
20 Shall a man make gods unto himself, and
[a]they *are* no gods?
21 Therefore, behold, I will this once cause
them to know, I will cause them to know mine
hand and my might; and they shall know that [a]my
name *is* The LORD.

Judah's Sin and Punishment

17 The sin of Judah *is* [a]written with a [b]pen
of iron, *and* with the point of a diamond:
it is [c]graven upon the table of their heart, and
upon the horns of your altars;
2 Whilst their children remember their altars and their [a]groves by the green trees upon
the high hills.
3 O my mountain in the field, I will give thy
substance *and* all thy treasures to the spoil, *and*
thy high places for sin, throughout all thy borders.
4 And thou, even thyself, shalt discontinue
from thine heritage that I gave thee; and I will
cause thee to serve thine enemies in [a]the land
which thou knowest not: for [b]ye have kindled a
fire in mine anger, *which* shall burn for ever.
5 Thus saith the LORD; [a]Cursed *be* the man
that trusteth in man, and maketh [b]flesh his arm,
and whose heart departeth from the LORD.
6 For he shall be [a]like the heath in the desert, and [b]shall not see when good cometh; but

12 [b]Jer. 3:17; 18:12
13 [a]Deut. 4:26; 28:36, 63 [b]Jer. 15:14
14 [a]Is. 43:18; Jer. 23:7, 8; [Ezek. 37:21–25]
15 [a]Jer. 3:18 [b]Jer. 24:6; 30:3; 32:37
16 [a]Amos 4:2; Hab. 1:15
17 [a]2 Chr. 16:9; Job 34:21; Ps. 90:8; Prov. 5:21; Jer. 23:24; 32:19; Zech. 4:10; [Luke 12:2; 1 Cor. 4:5]; Heb. 4:13
18 [a]Is. 40:2; Jer. 17:18; Rev. 18:6 [b][Ezek. 43:7]
19 [a]Ps. 18:1, 2; Is. 25:4 [b]Jer. 17:17 [c]Is. 44:10
20 [a]Ps. 115:4–8; Is. 37:19; Jer. 2:11; 5:7; Hos. 8:4–6; Gal. 4:8
21 [a]Ex. 15:3; Ps. 83:18; Is. 43:3; Jer. 33:2; Amos 5:8

CHAPTER 17

1 [a]Jer. 2:22 [b]Job 19:24 [c]Prov. 3:3; 7:3; Is. 49:16; 2 Cor. 3:3
2 [a]Judg. 3:7
4 [a]Jer. 16:13 [b]Is. 5:25; Jer. 15:14
5 [a]Ps. 146:3; Is. 30:1, 2; 31:1 [b]Is. 31:3
6 [a]Jer. 48:6 [b]Job 20:17

*17:2 Heb. *Asherim*, Canaanite deities

NKJV

thers, for behold, [b]each one follows the dictates
of his own evil heart, so that no one listens to
Me.
13 [a]'Therefore I will cast you out of this land
[b]into a land that you do not know, neither you
nor your fathers; and there you shall serve other
gods day and night, where I will not show you
favor.'

God Will Restore Israel
(cf. Jer. 23:7, 8)

14 "Therefore behold, the [a]days are coming,"
says the LORD, "that it shall no more be said, 'The
LORD lives who brought up the children of Israel
from the land of Egypt,'
15 "but, 'The LORD lives who brought up the
children of Israel from the land of the [a]north and
from all the lands where He had driven them.'
For [b]I will bring them back into their land which
I gave to their fathers.
16 "Behold, I will send for many [a]fisher-
men," says the LORD, "and they shall fish them;
and afterward I will send for many hunters, and
they shall hunt them from every mountain
and every hill, and out of the holes of the
rocks.
17 "For My [a]eyes *are* on all their ways; they
are not hidden from My face, nor is their iniquity
hidden from My eyes.
18 "And first I will repay [a]double for their
iniquity and their sin, because [b]they have defiled
My land; they have filled My inheritance with the
carcasses of their detestable and abominable
idols."

19 O LORD, [a]my strength and my fortress,
[b]My refuge in the day of affliction,
The Gentiles shall come to You
From the ends of the earth and say,
"Surely our fathers have inherited lies,
Worthlessness and [c]unprofitable
things."
20 Will a man make gods for himself,
[a]Which *are* not gods?

21 "Therefore behold, I will this once cause
them to know,
I will cause them to know
My hand and My might;
And they shall know that [a]My name *is* the
LORD.

Judah's Sin and Punishment

17 "The sin of Judah *is* [a]written with a [b]pen
of iron;
With the point of a diamond *it is*
[c]engraved
On the tablet of their heart,
And on the horns of your altars,
2 While their children remember
Their altars and their [a]wooden* images
By the green trees on the high hills.
3 O My mountain in the field,
I will give as plunder your wealth, all your
treasures,
And your high places of sin within all your
borders.
4 And you, even yourself,
Shall let go of your heritage which I gave
you;
And I will cause you to serve your enemies
In [a]the land which you do not know;
For [b]you have kindled a fire in My anger
which shall burn forever."

5 Thus says the LORD:

[a]"Cursed *is* the man who trusts in man
And makes [b]flesh his strength,
Whose heart departs from the LORD.
6 For he shall be [a]like a shrub in the desert,
And [b]shall not see when good comes,

KJV

shall inhabit the parched places in the wilderness,
[c]*in* a salt land and not inhabited.
7 [a]Blessed *is* the man that trusteth in the
LORD, and whose hope the LORD is.
8 For he shall be [a]as a tree planted by the
waters, and *that* spreadeth out her roots by the
river, and shall not see when heat cometh, but
her leaf shall be green; and shall not be careful
in the year of drought, neither shall cease from
yielding fruit.
9 The [a]heart *is* deceitful above all *things*,
and desperately wicked: who can know it?
10 I the LORD [a]search the heart, *I* try the
reins, [b]even to give every man according to his
ways, *and* according to the fruit of his doings.
11 *As* the partridge sitteth *on eggs*, and
hatcheth *them* not; *so* he that getteth riches, and
not by right, [a]shall leave them in the midst of his
days, and at his end shall be [b]a fool.
12 A glorious high throne from the beginning
is the place of our sanctuary.
13 O LORD, [a]the hope of Israel, [b]all that forsake thee shall be ashamed, *and* they that depart
from me shall be [c]written in the earth, because
they have forsaken the LORD, the [d]fountain of living waters.

Jeremiah Prays for Deliverance

14 Heal me, O LORD, and I shall be healed;
save me, and I shall be saved: for [a]thou *art* my
praise.
15 Behold, they say unto me, [a]Where *is* the
word of the LORD? let it come now.
16 As for me, [a]I have not hastened from *being* a pastor to follow thee: neither have I desired
the woeful day; thou knowest: that which came
out of my lips was *right* before thee.
17 Be not a terror unto me: [a]thou *art* my hope
in the day of evil.
18 [a]Let them be confounded that persecute
me, but [b]let not me be confounded: let them be
dismayed, but let not me be dismayed: bring upon
them the day of evil, and [c]destroy them with double destruction.

Hallow the Sabbath Day

19 Thus said the LORD unto me; Go and stand
in the gate of the children of the people, whereby
the kings of Judah come in, and by the which
they go out, and in all the gates of Jerusalem;
20 And say unto them, [a]Hear ye the word of
the LORD, ye kings of Judah, and all Judah, and
all the inhabitants of Jerusalem, that enter in by
these gates:
21 Thus saith the LORD; [a]Take heed to yourselves, and bear no burden on the sabbath day,
nor bring *it* in by the gates of Jerusalem;
22 Neither carry forth a burden out of your
houses on the sabbath day, neither do ye any
work, but hallow ye the sabbath day, as I [a]com-
manded your fathers.
23 [a]But they obeyed not, neither inclined
their ear, but made their neck stiff, that they might
not hear, nor receive instruction.
24 And it shall come to pass, [a]if ye diligently

6 [c]Deut. 29:23; Job 39:6
7 [a]Ps. 2:12; 34:8; 125:1; 146:5; Prov. 16:20; [Is. 30:18]; Jer. 39:18
8 [a]Job 8:16; [Ps. 1:3; Ezek. 31:3–9]
9 [a][Eccl. 9:3]; Matt. 15:19; [Mark 7:21, 22]
10 [a]1 Sam. 16:7; 1 Chr. 28:9; Ps. 7:9; 139:23, 24; Prov. 17:3; Jer. 11:20; 20:12; Rom. 8:27; Rev. 2:23 [b]Ps. 62:12; Jer. 32:19; Rom. 2:6
11 [a]Ps. 55:23 [b]Luke 12:20
13 [a]Jer. 14:8 [b][Ps. 73:27; Is. 1:28] [c]Luke 10:20 [d]Jer. 2:13
14 [a]Deut. 10:21; Ps. 109:1
15 [a]Is. 5:19; Ezek. 12:22; 2 Pet. 3:4
16 [a]Jer. 1:4–12
17 [a]Jer. 16:19; Nah. 1:7
18 [a]Ps. 35:4; 70:2; Jer. 15:10; 18:18 [b]Ps. 25:2 [c]Jer. 11:20
20 [a]Ps. 49:1, 2; Jer. 19:3, 4
21 [a]Num. 15:32; Neh. 13:19; [John 5:9–12, 17; 7:22–24]
22 [a]Ex. 20:8; 31:13; Ezek. 20:12
23 [a]Jer. 7:24, 26
24 [a]Jer. 11:4; 26:3

NKJV

But shall inhabit the parched places in the
wilderness,
[c]*In* a salt land *which is* not inhabited.

7 "Blessed[a] *is* the man who trusts in the
LORD,
And whose hope is the LORD.
8 For he shall be [a]like a tree planted by the
waters,
Which spreads out its roots by the river,
And will not *fear when heat comes;
But its leaf will be green,
And will not be anxious in the year of
drought,
Nor will cease from yielding fruit.

9 "The [a]heart *is* deceitful above all *things*,
And desperately wicked;
Who can know it?
10 I, the LORD, [a]search the heart,
I test the mind,
[b]Even to give every man according to his
ways,
According to the fruit of his doings.

11 "*As* a partridge that broods but does not
hatch,
So is he who gets riches, but not by right;
It [a]will leave him in the midst of his days,
And at his end he will be [b]a fool."

12 A glorious high throne from the beginning
Is the place of our sanctuary.
13 O LORD, [a]the hope of Israel,
[b]All who forsake You shall be ashamed.

"Those who depart from Me
Shall be [c]written in the earth,
Because they have forsaken the LORD,
The [d]fountain of living waters."

Jeremiah Prays for Deliverance

14 Heal me, O LORD, and I shall be healed;
Save me, and I shall be saved,
For [a]You *are* my praise.
15 Indeed they say to me,
[a]"Where *is* the word of the LORD?
Let it come now!"
16 As for me, [a]I have not hurried away from
being a shepherd *who* follows You,
Nor have I desired the woeful day;
You know what came out of my lips;
It was right there before You.
17 Do not be a terror to me;
[a]You *are* my hope in the day of doom.
18 [a]Let them be ashamed who persecute me,
But [b]do not let me be put to shame;
Let them be dismayed,
But do not let me be dismayed.
Bring on them the day of doom,
And [c]destroy them with double
destruction!

Hallow the Sabbath Day

19 Thus the LORD said to me: "Go and stand
in the gate of the children of the people, by which
the kings of Judah come in and by which they
go out, and in all the gates of Jerusalem;
20 "and say to them, [a]'Hear the word of the
LORD, you kings of Judah, and all Judah, and all
the inhabitants of Jerusalem, who enter by these
gates.
21 'Thus says the LORD: [a]"Take heed to yourselves, and bear no burden on the Sabbath day,
nor bring *it* in by the gates of Jerusalem;
22 "nor carry a burden out of your houses
on the Sabbath day, nor do any work, but hallow
the Sabbath day, as I [a]commanded your fathers.
23 [a]"But they did not obey nor incline their
ear, but made their neck stiff, that they might not
hear nor receive instruction.
24 "And it shall be, [a]if you heed Me care-

*
17:8 Qr., Tg. *see*

KJV

hearken unto me, saith the LORD, to bring in no
burden through the gates of this city on the [b]sab-
bath day, but hallow the sabbath day, to do no
work therein;
25 [a]Then shall there enter into the gates of
this city kings and princes sitting upon the throne
of David, riding in chariots and on horses, they,
and their princes, the men of Judah, and the inhabitants of Jerusalem: and this city shall remain
for ever.
26 And they shall come from the cities of Judah, and from [a]the places about Jerusalem, and
from the land of Benjamin, and from [b]the plain,
and from the mountains, and from [c]the south,
bringing burnt offerings, and sacrifices, and meat
offerings, and incense, and bringing [d]sacrifices of
praise, unto the house of the LORD.
27 But if ye will not hearken unto me to hallow the sabbath day, and not to bear a burden,
even entering in at the gates of Jerusalem on the
sabbath day; then [a]will I kindle a fire in the gates
thereof, [b]and it shall devour the palaces of Jerusalem, and it shall not be [c]quenched.

The Potter and the Clay

18 The word which came to Jeremiah from the
LORD, saying,
2 Arise, and go down to the potter's house,
and there I will cause thee to hear my words.
3 Then I went down to the potter's house,
and, behold, he wrought a work on the wheels.
4 And the vessel that he made of clay was
marred in the hand of the potter: so he made it
again another vessel, as seemed good to the potter
to make *it.*
5 Then the word of the LORD came to me,
saying,
6 O house of Israel, [a]cannot I do with you
as this potter? saith the LORD. Behold, [b]as the clay
is in the potter's hand, so *are* ye in mine hand, O
house of Israel.
7 *At what* instant I shall speak concerning
a nation, and concerning a kingdom, to [a]pluck
up, and to pull down, and to destroy *it;*
8 [a]If that nation, against whom I have pronounced, turn from their evil, [b]I will repent of the
evil that I thought to do unto them.
9 And *at what* instant I shall speak concerning a nation, and concerning a kingdom, to build
and to plant *it;*
10 If it do evil in my sight, that it obey not
my voice, then I will repent of the good, wherewith I said I would benefit them.
11 Now therefore go to, speak to the men of
Judah, and to the inhabitants of Jerusalem, saying, Thus saith the LORD; Behold, I frame evil
against you, and devise a device against you: [a]re-
turn ye now every one from his evil way, and
make your ways and your doings [b]good.

God's Warning Rejected

12 And they said, [a]There is no hope: but we
will walk after our own devices, and we will every
one do the [b]imagination of his evil heart.
13 Therefore thus saith the LORD; [a]Ask ye
now among the heathen, who hath heard such
things: the virgin of Israel hath done [b]a very horrible thing.
14 Will *a man* leave the snow of Lebanon
which cometh from the rock of the field? *or* shall
the cold flowing waters that come from another
place be forsaken?
15 Because my people hath forgotten [a]me,
they have burned incense to vanity, and they have
caused them to stumble in their ways *from* the

24 [b]Ex. 16:23–30; 20:8–10; Num. 15:32–36; Deut. 5:12–14; Neh. 13:15; [Is. 58:13]
25 [a]Jer. 22:4
26 [a]Jer. 33:13 [b]Zech. 7:7 [c]Judg. 1:9 [d]Ps. 107:22; 116:17; Jer. 33:11
27 [a]Jer. 21:14; Lam. 4:11; Amos 1:4, 7, 10, 12 [b]2 Kin. 25:9; 2 Chr. 36:19; Jer. 39:8; 52:13; Amos 2:5 [c]Jer. 7:20; Ezek. 20:47

CHAPTER 18

6 [a]Is. 45:9; Rom. 9:20, 21 [b]Is. 64:8
7 [a]Jer. 1:10
8 [a]Jer. 7:3–7; 12:16; [Ezek. 18:21; 33:11] [b][Ps. 106:45]; Jer. 26:3; [Hos. 11:8; Joel 2:13]; Jon. 3:10
11 [a]2 Kin. 17:13; Is. 1:16–19; Jer. 4:1; Acts 26:20 [b]Jer. 7:3–7
12 [a]Is. 57:10; Jer. 2:25 [b]Jer. 3:17; 23:17
13 [a]Is. 66:8; Jer. 2:10, 11; 1 Cor. 5:1 [b]Jer. 5:30; Hos. 6:10
15 [a]Jer. 2:13, 32 [b]Jer. 6:16

NKJV

fully," says the LORD, "to bring no burden through
the gates of this city on the [b]Sabbath day, but
hallow the Sabbath day, to do no work in it,
25 [a]"then shall enter the gates of this city
kings and princes sitting on the throne of David,
riding in chariots and on horses, they and their
princes, accompanied by the men of Judah and
the inhabitants of Jerusalem; and this city shall
remain forever.
26 "And they shall come from the cities of
Judah and from [a]the places around Jerusalem,
from the land of Benjamin and from [b]the lowland,
from the mountains and from [c]the South, bringing
burnt offerings and sacrifices, grain offerings and
incense, bringing [d]sacrifices of praise to the house
of the LORD.
27 "But if you will not heed Me to hallow
the Sabbath day, such as not carrying a burden
when entering the gates of Jerusalem on the Sabbath day, then [a]I will kindle a fire in its gates,
[b]and it shall devour the palaces of Jerusalem, and
it shall not be [c]quenched." ' "

The Potter and the Clay

18 The word which came to Jeremiah from the
LORD, saying:
2 "Arise and go down to the potter's house,
and there I will cause you to hear My words."
3 Then I went down to the potter's house,
and there he was, making something at the wheel.
4 And the vessel that he made of clay was
marred in the hand of the potter; so he made it
again into another vessel, as it seemed good to
the potter to make.
5 Then the word of the LORD came to me,
saying:
6 "O house of Israel, [a]can I not do with you
as this potter?" says the LORD. "Look, [b]as the clay
is in the potter's hand, so *are* you in My hand, O
house of Israel!
7 "The instant I speak concerning a nation
and concerning a kingdom, to [a]pluck up, to pull
down, and to destroy *it,*
8 [a]"if that nation against whom I have spoken turns from its evil, [b]I will relent of the disaster
that I thought to bring upon it.
9 "And the instant I speak concerning a nation and concerning a kingdom, to build and to
plant *it,*
10 "if it does evil in My sight so that it does
not obey My voice, then I will relent concerning
the good with which I said I would benefit it.
11 "Now therefore, speak to the men of Judah and to the inhabitants of Jerusalem, saying,
'Thus says the LORD: "Behold, I am fashioning a
disaster and devising a plan against you. [a]Return
now every one from his evil way, and make your
ways and your doings [b]good." ' "

God's Warning Rejected

12 And they said, [a]"That is hopeless! So we
will walk according to our own plans, and we will
every one obey the [b]dictates of his evil heart."
13 Therefore thus says the LORD:

[a]"Ask now among the Gentiles,
Who has heard such things?
The virgin of Israel has done [b]a very
horrible thing.
14 Will *a man* leave the snow water of
Lebanon,
Which comes from the rock of the field?
Will the cold flowing waters be forsaken
for strange waters?

15 "Because My people have forgotten [a]Me,
They have burned incense to worthless
idols.
And they have caused themselves to
stumble in their ways,
From the [b]ancient paths,

KJV

[b]ancient paths, to walk in paths, *in* a way not cast
up;
16 To make their land [a]desolate, *and* a perpetual [b]hissing; every one that passeth thereby
shall be astonished, and wag his head.
17 [a]I will scatter them [b]as with an east wind
before the enemy; [c]I will shew them the back,
and not the face, in the day of their calamity.

Jeremiah Persecuted

18 Then said they, [a]Come, and let us devise
devices against Jeremiah; [b]for the law shall not
perish from the priest, nor counsel from the wise,
nor the word from the prophet. Come, and let us
smite him with the tongue, and let us not give
heed to any of his words.
19 Give heed to me, O LORD, and hearken to
the voice of them that contend with me.
20 [a]Shall evil be recompensed for good? for
they have [b]digged a pit for my soul. Remember
that I [c]stood before thee to speak good for them,
and to turn away thy wrath from them.
21 Therefore [a]deliver up their children to the
famine, and pour out their *blood* by the force of
the sword; and let their wives be [b]bereaved of
their children, and *be* widows; and let their men
be put to death; *let* their young men *be* slain by
the sword in battle.
22 Let a cry be heard from their houses,
when thou shalt bring a troop suddenly upon
them: for they have digged a pit to take me, and
hid snares for my feet.
23 Yet, LORD, thou knowest all their counsel
against me to slay *me:* [a]forgive not their iniquity,
neither blot out their sin from thy sight, but let
them be overthrown before thee; deal *thus* with
them in the time of thine [b]anger.

The Sign of the Broken Flask

19 Thus saith the LORD, Go and get a potter's
earthen bottle, and *take* of the ancients of
the people, and of the ancients of the priests;
2 And go forth unto [a]the valley of the son
of Hinnom, which *is* by the entry of the east gate,
and proclaim there the words that I shall tell thee,
3 [a]And say, Hear ye the word of the LORD,
O kings of Judah, and inhabitants of Jerusalem;
Thus saith the LORD of hosts, the God of Israel;
Behold, I will bring evil upon this place, the which
whosoever heareth, his ears shall [b]tingle.
4 Because they [a]have forsaken me, and
have estranged this place, and have burned incense in it unto other gods, whom neither they
nor their fathers have known, nor the kings of
Judah, and have filled this place with [b]the blood
of innocents;
5 [a]They have built also the high places of
Baal, to burn their sons with fire *for* burnt offerings unto Baal, [b]which I commanded not, nor
spake *it,* neither came *it* into my mind:
6 Therefore, behold, the days come, saith
the LORD, that this place shall no more be called
Tophet, nor [a]The valley of the son of Hinnom,
but The valley of slaughter.
7 And I will make void the counsel of Judah
and Jerusalem in this place; [a]and I will cause them
to fall by the sword before their enemies, and by
the hands of them that seek their lives: and their

15 [b]Jer. 6:16
16 [a]Jer. 19:8
[b]1 Kin. 9:8;
Lam. 2:15;
Mic. 6:16
17 [a]Jer. 13:24
[b]Ps. 48:7 [c]Jer.
2:27
18 [a]Jer. 11:19
[b]Lev. 10:11;
Mal. 2:7;
[John 7:48]
20 [a]Ps. 109:4
[b]Ps. 35:7;
57:6; Jer. 5:26
[c]Jer. 14:7—
15:1
21 [a]Ps. 109:9–
20; Jer. 11:22;
14:16 [b]Jer.
15:7, 8; Ezek.
22:25
23 [a]Neh. 4:5;
Ps. 35:14;
109:14; Is. 2:9;
Jer. 11:20
[b]Jer. 7:20

CHAPTER 19
2 [a]Josh. 15:8;
2 Kin. 23:10;
Jer. 7:31;
32:35
3 [a]Jer. 17:20
[b]1 Sam. 3:11;
2 Kin. 21:12
4 [a]Deut.
28:20; Is.
65:11; Jer.
2:13, 17, 19;
15:6; 17:13
[b]2 Kin. 21:12;
Jer. 2:34; 7:6
5 [a]Num.
22:41; Jer.
7:31; 32:35
[b]Lev. 18:21;
2 Kin. 17:17;
Ps. 106:37, 38
6 [a]Josh. 15:8;
Jer. 7:32
7 [a]Lev. 26:17;
Deut. 28:25;
Jer. 15:2, 9

*

18:17 So with
LXX, Syr.,
Tg., Vg.; MT
look them in

NKJV

To walk in pathways and not on a
highway,
16 To make their land [a]desolate *and* a
perpetual [b]hissing;
Everyone who passes by it will be
astonished
And shake his head.
17 [a]I will scatter them [b]as with an east wind
before the enemy;
[c]I will *show them the back and not the
face
In the day of their calamity."

Jeremiah Persecuted

18 Then they said, [a]"Come and let us devise
plans against Jeremiah; [b]for the law shall not perish from the priest, nor counsel from the wise,
nor the word from the prophet. Come and let us
attack him with the tongue, and let us not give
heed to any of his words."

19 Give heed to me, O LORD,
And listen to the voice of those who
contend with me!
20 [a]Shall evil be repaid for good?
For they have [b]dug a pit for my life.
Remember that I [c]stood before You
To speak good for them,
To turn away Your wrath from them.
21 Therefore [a]deliver up their children to the
famine,
And pour out their *blood*
By the force of the sword;
Let their wives *become* widows
And [b]bereaved of their children.
Let their men be put to death,
Their young men *be* slain
By the sword in battle.
22 Let a cry be heard from their houses,
When You bring a troop suddenly upon
them;
For they have dug a pit to take me,
And hidden snares for my feet.
23 Yet, LORD, You know all their counsel
Which is against me, to slay *me.*
[a]Provide no atonement for their iniquity,
Nor blot out their sin from Your sight;
But let them be overthrown before You.
Deal *thus* with them
In the time of Your [b]anger.

The Sign of the Broken Flask

19 Thus says the LORD: "Go and get a potter's
earthen flask, and *take* some of the elders
of the people and some of the elders of the priests.
2 "And go out to [a]the Valley of the Son of
Hinnom, which *is* by the entry of the Potsherd Gate; and proclaim there the words that I
will tell you,
3 [a]"and say, 'Hear the word of the LORD, O
kings of Judah and inhabitants of Jerusalem. Thus
says the LORD of hosts, the God of Israel: "Behold,
I will bring such a catastrophe on this place, that
whoever hears of it, his ears will [b]tingle.
4 "Because they [a]have forsaken Me and
made this an alien place, because they have
burned incense in it to other gods whom neither
they, their fathers, nor the kings of Judah have
known, and have filled this place with [b]the blood
of the innocents
5 [a]"(they have also built the high places of
Baal, to burn their sons with fire *for* burnt offerings to Baal, [b]which I did not command or speak,
nor did it come into My mind),
6 "therefore behold, the days are coming,"
says the LORD, "that this place shall no more be
called Tophet or [a]the Valley of the Son of Hinnom,
but the Valley of Slaughter.
7 "And I will make void the counsel of Judah and Jerusalem in this place, [a]and I will cause
them to fall by the sword before their enemies
and by the hands of those who seek their lives;

KJV

[b]carcases will I give to be meat for the fowls of
the heaven, and for the beasts of the earth.
8 And I will make this city [a]desolate, and
an hissing; every one that passeth thereby shall
be astonished and hiss because of all the plagues
thereof.
9 And I will cause them to eat the [a]flesh of
their sons and the flesh of their daughters, and
they shall eat every one the flesh of his friend in
the siege and straitness, wherewith their enemies,
and they that seek their lives, shall straiten them.
10 [a]Then shalt thou break the bottle in the
sight of the men that go with thee,
11 And shalt say unto them, Thus saith the
LORD of hosts; [a]Even so will I break this people
and this city, as *one* breaketh a potter's vessel,
that cannot be made whole again: and they shall
[b]bury *them* in Tophet, till *there be* no place to
bury.
12 Thus will I do unto this place, saith the
LORD, and to the inhabitants thereof, and *even*
make this city as Tophet:
13 And the houses of Jerusalem, and the
houses of the kings of Judah, shall be defiled [a]as
the place of Tophet, because of all the houses
upon whose [b]roofs they have burned incense unto
all the host of heaven, and [c]have poured out drink
offerings unto other gods.
14 Then came Jeremiah from Tophet,
whither the LORD had sent him to prophesy; and
he stood in [a]the court of the LORD's house; and
said to all the people,
15 Thus saith the LORD of hosts, the God of
Israel; Behold, I will bring upon this city and upon
all her towns all the evil that I have pronounced
against it, because [a]they have hardened their
necks, that they might not hear my words.

The Word of God to Pashhur

20 Now [a]Pashur the son of [b]Immer the priest,
who *was* also chief governor in the house
of the LORD, heard that Jeremiah prophesied these
things.
2 Then Pashur smote Jeremiah the prophet,
and put him in the stocks that *were* in the high
[a]gate of Benjamin, which *was* by the house of
the LORD.
3 And it came to pass on the morrow, that
Pashur brought forth Jeremiah out of the stocks.
Then said Jeremiah unto him, The LORD hath not
called thy name Pashur, but Magor–missabib.
4 For thus saith the LORD, Behold, I will
make thee a terror to thyself, and to all thy
friends: and they shall fall by the sword of their
enemies, and thine eyes shall behold *it*: and I will
[a]give all Judah into the hand of the king of Babylon, and he shall carry them captive into Babylon,
and shall slay them with the sword.
5 Moreover I [a]will deliver all the strength
of this city, and all the labours thereof, and all
the precious things thereof, and all the treasures
of the kings of Judah will I give into the hand of
their enemies, which shall spoil them, and take
them, and [b]carry them to Babylon.
6 And thou, Pashur, and all that dwell in
thine house shall go into captivity: and thou shalt
come to Babylon, and there thou shalt die, and
shalt be buried there, thou, and all thy friends,
to whom thou hast [a]prophesied lies.

Jeremiah's Unpopular Ministry

7 O LORD, thou hast deceived me, and I was
deceived: [a]thou art stronger than I, and hast prevailed: [b]I am in derision daily, every one mocketh
me.
8 For since I spake, I cried out, [a]I cried violence and spoil; because the word of the LORD was
made a reproach unto me, and a derision, daily.

7 [b]Ps. 79:2; Jer. 7:33; 16:4; 34:20
8 [a]Jer. 18:16; 49:13; 50:13
9 [a]Lev. 26:29; Deut. 28:53, 55; Is. 9:20; Lam. 4:10; Ezek. 5:10
10 [a]Jer. 51:63, 64
11 [a]Ps. 2:9; Is. 30:14; Jer. 13:14; Lam. 4:2; Rev. 2:27 [b]Jer. 7:32
13 [a]2 Kin. 23:10; Ps. 74:7; 79:1; Jer. 52:13; Ezek. 7:21, 22 [b]2 Kin. 23:12; Jer. 32:29; Zeph. 1:5 [c]Jer. 7:18; Ezek. 20:28
14 [a]2 Chr. 20:5; Jer. 26:2–8
15 [a]Neh. 9:17, 29; Jer. 7:26; 17:23

CHAPTER 20

1 [a]Ezra 2:37, 38 [b]1 Chr. 24:14
2 [a]Jer. 37:13; Zech. 14:10
4 [a]Jer. 21:4–10
5 [a]2 Kin. 20:17; 2 Chr. 36:10; Jer. 3:24; 27:21, 22 [b]Is. 39:6
6 [a]Jer. 14:13–15; Lam. 2:14
7 [a]Jer. 1:6, 7 [b]Job 12:4; Lam. 3:14
8 [a]Jer. 6:7

*20:3 Lit. *Fear on Every Side*

NKJV

their [b]corpses I will give as meat for the birds of
the heaven and for the beasts of the earth.
8 "I will make this city [a]desolate and a hissing; everyone who passes by it will be astonished
and hiss because of all its plagues.
9 "And I will cause them to eat the [a]flesh
of their sons and the flesh of their daughters, and
everyone shall eat the flesh of his friend in the
siege and in the desperation with which their enemies and those who seek their lives shall drive
them to despair." '
10 [a]"Then you shall break the flask in the
sight of the men who go with you,
11 "and say to them, 'Thus says the LORD of
hosts: [a]"Even so I will break this people and this
city, as *one* breaks a potter's vessel, which cannot
be made whole again; and they shall [b]bury *them*
in Tophet till *there is* no place to bury.
12 "Thus I will do to this place," says the
LORD, "and to its inhabitants, and make this city
like Tophet.
13 "And the houses of Jerusalem and the
houses of the kings of Judah shall be defiled [a]like
the place of Tophet, because of all the houses on
whose [b]roofs they have burned incense to all the
host of heaven, and [c]poured out drink offerings
to other gods." ' "
14 Then Jeremiah came from Tophet, where
the LORD had sent him to prophesy; and he stood
in [a]the court of the Lord's house and said to all
the people,
15 "Thus says the LORD of hosts, the God of
Israel: 'Behold, I will bring on this city and on
all her towns all the doom that I have pronounced
against it, because [a]they have stiffened their
necks that they might not hear My words.' "

The Word of God to Pashhur

20 Now [a]Pashhur the son of [b]Immer, the priest
who *was* also chief governor in the house
of the LORD, heard that Jeremiah prophesied these
things.
2 Then Pashhur struck Jeremiah the
prophet, and put him in the stocks that *were* in
the high [a]gate of Benjamin, which *was* by the
house of the LORD.
3 And it happened on the next day that
Pashhur brought Jeremiah out of the stocks. Then
Jeremiah said to him, "The LORD has not called
your name Pashhur, but *Magor-Missabib.
4 "For thus says the LORD: 'Behold, I will
make you a terror to yourself and to all your
friends; and they shall fall by the sword of their
enemies, and your eyes shall see *it*. I will [a]give
all Judah into the hand of the king of Babylon,
and he shall carry them captive to Babylon and
slay them with the sword.
5 'Moreover I [a]will deliver all the wealth of
this city, all its produce, and all its precious things;
all the treasures of the kings of Judah I will
give into the hand of their enemies, who will
plunder them, seize them, and [b]carry them to
Babylon.
6 'And you, Pashhur, and all who dwell in
your house, shall go into captivity. You shall go
to Babylon, and there you shall die, and be buried
there, you and all your friends, to whom you have
[a]prophesied lies.' "

Jeremiah's Unpopular Ministry

7 O LORD, You induced me, and I was
persuaded;
[a]You are stronger than I, and have
prevailed.
[b]I am in derision daily;
Everyone mocks me.
8 For when I spoke, I cried out;
[a]I shouted, "Violence and plunder!"
Because the word of the LORD was made
to me
A reproach and a derision daily.

KJV

9 Then I said, I will not make mention of him, nor speak any more in his name. But *his word* was in mine heart as a [a]burning fire shut up in my bones, and I was weary with forbearing, and [b]I could not *stay*.

10 [a]For I heard the defaming of many, fear on every side. Report, *say they*, and we will report it. [b]All my familiars watched for my halting, *saying*, Peradventure he will be enticed, and we shall prevail against him, and we shall take our revenge on him.

11 But the LORD *is* [a]with me as a mighty terrible one: therefore my persecutors shall stumble, and they shall not [b]prevail: they shall be greatly ashamed; for they shall not prosper: *their* [c]everlasting confusion shall never be forgotten.

12 But, O LORD of hosts, that [a]triest the righteous, *and* seest the reins and the heart, [b]let me see thy vengeance on them: for unto thee have I opened my cause.

13 Sing unto the LORD, praise ye the LORD: for [a]he hath delivered the soul of the poor from the hand of evildoers.

14 [a]Cursed *be* the day wherein I was born: let not the day wherein my mother bare me be blessed.

15 Cursed *be* the man who brought tidings to my father, saying, A man child is born unto thee; making him very glad.

16 And let that man be as the cities which the LORD [a]overthrew, and repented not: and let him [b]hear the cry in the morning, and the shouting at noontide;

17 [a]Because he slew me not from the womb; or that my mother might have been my grave, and her womb *to be* always great *with me*.

18 [a]Wherefore came I forth out of the womb to [b]see labour and sorrow, that my days should be consumed with shame?

Jerusalem's Door Is Sealed

21 The word which came unto Jeremiah from the LORD, when [a]king Zedekiah sent unto him [b]Pashur the son of Melchiah, and [c]Zephaniah the son of Maaseiah the priest, saying,

2 [a]Enquire, I pray thee, of the LORD for us; for Nebuchadrezzar king of Babylon maketh war against us; if so be that the LORD will deal with us according to all his wondrous works, that he may go up from us.

3 Then said Jeremiah unto them, Thus shall ye say to Zedekiah:

4 Thus saith the LORD God of Israel; Behold, I will turn back the weapons of war that *are* in your hands, wherewith ye fight against the king of Babylon, and *against* the Chaldeans, which besiege you without the walls, and [a]I will assemble them into the midst of this city.

5 And I [a]myself will fight against you with an [b]outstretched hand and with a strong arm, even in anger, and in fury, and in great wrath.

6 And I will smite the inhabitants of this city, both man and beast: they shall die of a great pestilence.

7 And afterward, saith the LORD, [a]I will deliver Zedekiah king of Judah, and his servants,

---

9 [a]Job 32:18–20; Ps. 39:3; Jer. 4:19; 23:9; [Ezek. 3:14]; Acts 4:20 [b]Job 32:18; Jer. 6:11; Acts 18:5
10 [a]Ps. 31:13 [b]Job 19:19; Ps. 41:9; 55:13, 14; Luke 11:53, 54
11 [a]Jer. 1:18, 19 [b]Jer. 15:20; 17:18 [c]Jer. 23:40
12 [a]Ps. 7:9; 11:5; 17:3; 139:23; [Jer. 11:20; 17:10] [b]Ps. 54:7; 59:10; Jer. 15:15
13 [a]Ps. 35:9, 10; 109:30, 31
14 [a]Job 3:3; Jer. 15:10
16 [a]Gen. 19:25 [b]Jer. 18:22
17 [a]Job 3:10, 11
18 [a]Job 3:20; Jer. 15:10 [b]Lam. 3:1

CHAPTER 21

1 [a]2 Kin. 24:17, 18; Jer. 32:1–3; 37:1; 52:1–3 [b]1 Chr. 9:12; Jer. 38:1 [c]2 Kin. 25:18; Jer. 29:25; 37:3
2 [a]Ex. 9:28; 1 Sam. 9:9; Jer. 37:3, 7; Ezek. 14:7; 20:1–3
4 [a]Is. 13:4; Jer. 39:3; Lam. 2:5, 7; Zech. 14:2
5 [a]Jer. 32:24; 33:5; Is. 63:10 [b]Ex. 6:6; Deut. 4:34; Jer. 6:12
7 [a]2 Kin. 25:5–7, 18–21; Jer. 37:17; 39:5; 52:9

*

21:2 Heb. *Nebuchadrezzar*, and so elsewhere in the book **21:4** Or *Babylonians*, and so elsewhere in the book

---

NKJV

9 Then I said, "I will not make mention of Him,
Nor speak anymore in His name."
But *His word* was in my heart like a [a]burning fire
Shut up in my bones;
I was weary of holding *it* back,
And [b]I could not.

10 [a]For I heard many mocking:
"Fear on every side!"
"Report," *they say*, "and we will report it!"
[b]All my acquaintances watched for my stumbling, *saying*,
"Perhaps he can be induced;
Then we will prevail against him,
And we will take our revenge on him."

11 But the LORD *is* [a]with me as a mighty, awesome One.
Therefore my persecutors will stumble, and will not [b]prevail.
They will be greatly ashamed, for they will not prosper.
Their [c]everlasting confusion will never be forgotten.

12 But, O LORD of hosts,
You who [a]test the righteous,
And see the mind and heart,
[b]Let me see Your vengeance on them;
For I have pleaded my cause before You.

13 Sing to the LORD! Praise the LORD!
For [a]He has delivered the life of the poor
From the hand of evildoers.

14 [a]Cursed *be* the day in which I was born!
Let the day not be blessed in which my mother bore me!

15 Let the man *be* cursed
Who brought news to my father, saying,
"A male child has been born to you!"
Making him very glad.

16 And let that man be like the cities
Which the LORD [a]overthrew, and did not relent;
Let him [b]hear the cry in the morning
And the shouting at noon,

17 [a]Because he did not kill me from the womb,
That my mother might have been my grave,
And her womb always enlarged *with me*.

18 [a]Why did I come forth from the womb to [b]see labor and sorrow,
That my days should be consumed with shame?

Jerusalem's Doom Is Sealed

21 The word which came to Jeremiah from the LORD when [a]King Zedekiah sent to him [b]Pashhur the son of Melchiah, and [c]Zephaniah the son of Maaseiah, the priest, saying,

2 [a]"Please inquire of the LORD for us, for *Nebuchadnezzar king of Babylon makes war against us. Perhaps the LORD will deal with us according to all His wonderful works, that *the king* may go away from us."

3 Then Jeremiah said to them, "Thus you shall say to Zedekiah,

4 'Thus says the LORD God of Israel: "Behold, I will turn back the weapons of war that *are* in your hands, with which you fight against the king of Babylon and the *Chaldeans who besiege you outside the walls; and [a]I will assemble them in the midst of this city.

5 "I [a]Myself will fight against you with an [b]outstretched hand and with a strong arm, even in anger and fury and great wrath.

6 "I will strike the inhabitants of this city, both man and beast; they shall die of a great pestilence.

7 "And afterward," says the LORD, [a]"I will deliver Zedekiah king of Judah, his servants and

KJV

and the people, and such as are left in this city
from the pestilence, from the sword, and from the
famine, into the hand of Nebuchadrezzar king of
Babylon, and into the hand of their enemies, and
into the hand of those that seek their life: and he
shall smite them with the edge of the sword; [b]he
shall not spare them, neither have pity, nor have
mercy.
8 And unto this people thou shalt say, Thus
saith the LORD; Behold, [a]I set before you the way
of life, and the way of death.
9 He that [a]abideth in this city shall die by
the sword, and by the famine, and by the pestilence: but he that goeth out, and falleth to the
Chaldeans that besiege you, he shall [b]live, and
his life shall be unto him for a prey.
10 For I have [a]set my face against this city
for evil, and not for good, saith the LORD: [b]it shall
be given into the hand of the king of Babylon,
and he shall [c]burn it with fire.

Message to the House of David

11 And touching the house of the king of Judah, *say*, Hear ye the word of the LORD;
12 O house of David, thus saith the LORD;
[a]Execute judgment [b]in the morning, and deliver
him that is spoiled out of the hand of the oppressor, lest my fury go out like fire, and burn that
none can quench *it*, because of the evil of your
doings.
13 Behold, [a]I *am* against thee, O inhabitant
of the valley, *and* rock of the plain, saith the LORD;
which say, [b]Who shall come down against us?
or who shall enter into our habitations?
14 But I will punish you according to the
[a]fruit of your doings, saith the LORD: and I will kindle a fire in the forest thereof, and [b]it shall devour
all things round about it.

7 [b]Deut. 28:50; 2 Chr. 36:17; Jer. 13:14; Ezek. 7:9; Hab. 1:6–10
8 [a]Deut. 30:15, 19; Is. 1:19, 20
9 [a]Jer. 38:2 [b]Jer. 39:18
10 [a]Lev. 17:10; Jer. 44:11, 27; Amos 9:4 [b]Jer. 38:3 [c]2 Kin. 25:9; 2 Chr. 36:19; Jer. 34:2, 22; 37:10
12 [a]Ps. 72:1; Is. 1:17; Jer. 22:3; Zech. 7:9 [b]Ps. 101:8; Zeph. 3:5
13 [a][Jer. 23:30–32; Ezek. 13:8] [b]2 Sam. 5:6, 7; Jer. 49:4; Lam. 4:12; Obad. 3, 4
14 [a]Prov. 1:31; Is. 3:10, 11; Jer. 17:10; 32:19 [b]2 Chr. 36:19; Is. 10:16, 18; Jer. 11:16; 17:27; 52:13; Ezek. 20:47, 48

NKJV

the people, and such as are left in this city from
the pestilence and the sword and the famine, into
the hand of Nebuchadnezzar king of Babylon, into
the hand of their enemies, and into the hand of
those who seek their life; and he shall strike them
with the edge of the sword. [b]He shall not spare
them, or have pity or mercy." '
8 "Now you shall say to this people, 'Thus
says the LORD: "Behold, [a]I set before you the way
of life and the way of death.
9 "He who [a]remains in this city shall die
by the sword, by famine, and by pestilence; but
he who goes out and defects to the Chaldeans who
besiege you, he shall [b]live, and his life shall be
as a prize to him.
10 "For I have [a]set My face against this city
for adversity and not for good," says the LORD.
[b]"It shall be given into the hand of the king of
Babylon, and he shall [c]burn it with fire." '

Message to the House of David

11 "And concerning the house of the king of
Judah, *say*, 'Hear the word of the LORD,
12 'O house of David! Thus says the LORD:

[a]"Execute judgment [b]in the morning;
And deliver *him who is* plundered
Out of the hand of the oppressor,
Lest My fury go forth like fire
And burn so that no one can quench *it*,
Because of the evil of your doings.

13 "Behold, [a]I *am* against you, O inhabitant
of the valley,
And rock of the plain," says the LORD,
"Who say, [b]'Who shall come down against
us?
Or who shall enter our dwellings?'
14 But I will punish you according to the
[a]fruit of your doings," says the LORD;
"I will kindle a fire in its forest,
And [b]it shall devour all things around
it." ' "

KJV

22 Thus saith the LORD; Go down to the house
of the king of Judah, and speak there this
word,
2 And say, [a]Hear the word of the LORD, O
king of Judah, that sittest upon the throne of David, thou, and thy servants, and thy people that
enter in by these gates:
3 Thus saith the LORD; [a]Execute ye judgment and righteousness, and deliver the spoiled
out of the hand of the oppressor: and do no wrong,
do no violence to the stranger, the [b]fatherless, nor
the widow, neither shed innocent blood in this
place.
4 For if ye do this thing indeed, [a]then shall
there enter in by the gates of this house kings
sitting upon the throne of David, riding in chariots
and on horses, he, and his servants, and his
people.
5 But if ye will not hear these words, [a]I
swear by myself, saith the LORD, that this house
shall become a desolation.
6 For thus saith the LORD unto the king's
house of Judah; Thou *art* [a]Gilead unto me, *and*
the head of Lebanon: *yet* surely I will make thee
a wilderness, *and* cities *which* are not inhabited.
7 And I will prepare destroyers against thee,
every one with his weapons: and they shall cut
down [a]thy choice cedars, [b]and cast *them* into the
fire.
8 And many nations shall pass by this city,
and they shall say every man to his neighbour,
[a]Wherefore hath the LORD done thus unto this
great city?
9 Then they shall answer, [a]Because they
have forsaken the covenant of the LORD their God,
and worshipped other gods, and served them.

CHAPTER 22

2 [a]Jer. 17:20
3 [a]Is. 58:6; Jer. 21:12; [Mic. 6:8]; Zech. 7:9; 8:16; Matt. 23:23 [b]Jer. 7:6; Zech. 7:10
4 [a]Jer. 17:25
5 [a]Matt. 23:38; Heb. 6:13, 17
6 [a]Gen. 37:25; Num. 32:1; Song 4:1
7 [a]Is. 37:24 [b]Jer. 21:14
8 [a]Deut. 29:24–26; 1 Kin. 9:8, 9; 2 Chr. 7:20–22; Jer. 16:10
9 [a]2 Kin. 22:17; 2 Chr. 34:25; Jer. 11:3

NKJV

22 Thus says the LORD: "Go down to the house
of the king of Judah, and there speak this
word,
2 "and say, [a]'Hear the word of the LORD, O
king of Judah, you who sit on the throne of David,
you and your servants and your people who enter
these gates!
3 'Thus says the LORD: [a]"Execute judgment
and righteousness, and deliver the plundered out
of the hand of the oppressor. Do no wrong and
do no violence to the stranger, the [b]fatherless, or
the widow, nor shed innocent blood in this place.
4 "For if you indeed do this thing, [a]then
shall enter the gates of this house, riding on
horses and in chariots, accompanied by servants
and people, kings who sit on the throne of
David.
5 "But if you will not hear these words, [a]I
swear by Myself," says the LORD, "that this house
shall become a desolation." ' "
6 For thus says the LORD to the house of the
king of Judah:

"You *are* [a]Gilead to Me,
The head of Lebanon;
Yet I surely will make you a wilderness,
Cities *which* are not inhabited.
7 I will prepare destroyers against you,
Everyone with his weapons;
They shall cut down [a]your choice cedars
[b]And cast *them* into the fire.

8 "And many nations will pass by this city;
and everyone will say to his neighbor, [a]'Why has
the LORD done so to this great city?'
9 "Then they will answer, [a]'Because they
have forsaken the covenant of the LORD their God,
and worshiped other gods and served them.' "

KJV

10 Weep ye not for [a]the dead, neither bemoan him: *but* weep sore for him [b]that goeth away: for he shall return no more, nor see his native country.

Message to the Sons of Josiah

11 For thus saith the LORD touching [a]Shallum the son of Josiah king of Judah, which reigned instead of Josiah his father, [b]which went forth out of this place; He shall not return thither any more:

12 But he shall die in the place whither they have led him captive, and shall see this land no more.

13 [a]Woe unto him that buildeth his house by unrighteousness, and his chambers by wrong; [b]*that* useth his neighbour's service without wages, and giveth him not for his work;

14 That saith, I will build me a wide house and large chambers, and cutteth him out windows; and *it is* cieled with cedar, and painted with vermilion.

15 Shalt thou reign, because thou closest *thyself* in cedar? did not thy father eat and drink, and do judgment and justice, *and* then [a]*it was* well with him?

16 He judged the cause of the poor and needy; then *it was* well *with him: was* not this to know me? saith the LORD.

17 [a]But thine eyes and thine heart *are* not but for thy covetousness, and for to shed innocent blood, and for oppression, and for violence, to do *it*.

18 Therefore thus saith the LORD concerning Jehoiakim the son of Josiah king of Judah; [a]They shall not lament for him, *saying*, [b]Ah my brother! or, Ah sister! they shall not lament for him, *saying*, Ah lord! or, Ah his glory!

19 [a]He shall be buried with the burial of an ass, drawn and cast forth beyond the gates of Jerusalem.

20 Go up to Lebanon, and cry; and lift up thy voice in Bashan, and cry from the passages: for all thy lovers are destroyed.

21 I spake unto thee in thy prosperity; *but* thou saidst, I will not hear. [a]This *hath been* thy manner from thy youth, that thou obeyedst not my voice.

22 The wind shall eat up all [a]thy pastors, and thy lovers shall go into captivity: surely then shalt thou be ashamed and confounded for all thy wickedness.

23 O inhabitant of Lebanon, that makest thy nest in the cedars, how gracious shalt thou be when pangs come upon thee, [a]the pain as of a woman in travail!

Message to Coniah

24 *As* I live, saith the LORD, [a]though Coniah the son of Jehoiakim king of Judah [b]were the signet upon my right hand, yet would I pluck thee thence;

25 [a]And I will give thee into the hand of them that seek thy life, and into the hand *of them* whose face thou fearest, even into the hand of Nebuchad-

10 [a]2 Kin. 22:20 [b]Jer. 14:17; 22:11; Lam. 3:48
11 [a]1 Chr. 3:15 [b]2 Kin. 23:34; 2 Chr. 36:4; Ezek. 19:4
13 [a]2 Kin. 23:35; Jer. 17:11; Ezek. 22:13 [b]Lev. 19:13; Deut. 24:14, 15; Mic. 3:10; Hab. 2:9; James 5:4
15 [a]2 Kin. 23:25; Ps. 128:2; Is. 3:10; Jer. 7:23; 42:6
17 [a]Jer. 6:13; 8:10; Ezek. 19:6; [Luke 12:15–20]
18 [a]Jer. 16:4, 6 [b]1 Kin. 13:30
19 [a]1 Kin. 21:23, 24; 2 Chr. 36:6; Jer. 36:30; Dan. 1:2
21 [a]Jer. 3:24, 25; 32:30
22 [a]Jer. 23:1
23 [a]Jer. 6:24
24 [a]2 Kin. 24:6, 8; 1 Chr. 3:16; 2 Chr. 36:9; Jer. 37:1 [b]Song 8:6; Is. 49:16; Hag. 2:23
25 [a]2 Kin. 24:15, 16; Jer. 34:20

NKJV

10 Weep not for [a]the dead, nor bemoan him;
Weep bitterly for him [b]who goes away,
For he shall return no more,
Nor see his native country.

Message to the Sons of Josiah

11 For thus says the LORD concerning [a]Shallum* the son of Josiah, king of Judah, who reigned instead of Josiah his father, [b]who went from this place: "He shall not return here anymore,
12 "but he shall die in the place where they have led him captive, and shall see this land no more.

13 "Woe[a] to him who builds his house by unrighteousness
And his chambers by injustice,
[b]*Who* uses his neighbor's service without wages
And gives him nothing for his work,
14 Who says, 'I will build myself a wide house with spacious chambers,
And cut out windows for it,
Paneling *it* with cedar
And painting *it* with vermilion.'

15 "Shall you reign because you enclose *yourself* in cedar?
Did not your father eat and drink,
And do justice and righteousness?
Then [a]*it was* well with him.
16 He judged the cause of the poor and needy;
Then *it was* well.
Was not this knowing Me?" says the LORD.
17 "Yet[a] your eyes and your heart *are* for nothing but your covetousness,
For shedding innocent blood,
And practicing oppression and violence."

18 Therefore thus says the LORD concerning Jehoiakim the son of Josiah, king of Judah:

[a]"They shall not lament for him,
Saying, [b]'Alas, my brother!' or 'Alas, my sister!'
They shall not lament for him,
Saying, 'Alas, master!' or 'Alas, his glory!'
19 [a]He shall be buried with the burial of a donkey,
Dragged and cast out beyond the gates of Jerusalem.

20 "Go up to Lebanon, and cry out,
And lift up your voice in Bashan;
Cry from Abarim,
For all your lovers are destroyed.
21 I spoke to you in your prosperity,
But you said, 'I will not hear.'
[a]This *has been* your manner from your youth,
That you did not obey My voice.
22 The wind shall eat up all [a]your rulers,
And your lovers shall go into captivity;
Surely then you will be ashamed and humiliated
For all your wickedness.
23 O inhabitant of Lebanon,
Making your nest in the cedars,
How gracious will you be when pangs come upon you,
Like [a]the pain of a woman in labor?

Message to Coniah

24 "*As* I live," says the LORD, [a]"though *Coniah the son of Jehoiakim, king of Judah, [b]were the signet on My right hand, yet I would pluck you off;
25 [a]"and I will give you into the hand of those who seek your life, and into the hand *of those* whose face you fear—the hand of Nebuchadnez-

*

22:11 Or *Jehoahaz*
22:24 Or *Jeconiah* or *Jehoiachin*

KJV

rezzar king of Babylon, and into the hand of the
Chaldeans.
26 [a]And I will cast thee out, and thy mother
that bare thee, into another country, where ye
were not born; and there shall ye die.
27 But to the land whereunto they desire to
return, thither shall they not return.
28 *Is* this man Coniah a despised broken
idol? *is he* [a]a vessel wherein *is* no pleasure?
wherefore are they cast out, he and his seed, and
are cast into a land which they know not?
29 [a]O earth, earth, earth, hear the word of
the LORD.
30 Thus saith the LORD, Write ye this man
[a]childless, a man *that* shall not prosper in his
days: for [b]no man of his seed shall prosper, sitting
upon the throne of David, and ruling any more
in Judah.

The Branch of Righteousness

23 Woe [a]be unto the pastors that destroy and
scatter the sheep of my pasture! saith the
LORD.
2 Therefore thus saith the LORD God of Israel against the pastors that feed my people; Ye
have scattered my flock, and driven them away,
and have not visited them: [a]behold, I will visit
upon you the evil of your doings, saith the LORD.
3 And [a]I will gather the remnant of my flock
out of all countries whither I have driven them,
and will bring them again to their folds; and they
shall be fruitful and increase.
4 And I will set up [a]shepherds over them
which shall feed them: and they shall fear no
more, nor be dismayed, neither shall they be lacking, saith the LORD.
5 Behold, [a]the days come, saith the LORD,
that I will raise unto David a righteous Branch,
and a King shall reign and prosper, [b]and shall
execute judgment and justice in the earth.
6 [a]In his days Judah shall be saved, and Israel [b]shall dwell safely: and [c]this *is* his name
whereby he shall be called, THE LORD OUR
RIGHTEOUSNESS.
7 Therefore, behold, [a]the days come, saith
the LORD, that they shall no more say, The LORD
liveth, which brought up the children of Israel out
of the land of Egypt;
8 But, The LORD liveth, which brought up
and which led the seed of the house of Israel out
of the north country, [a]and from all countries
whither I had driven them; and they shall dwell
in their own [b]land.

False Prophets and Empty Oracles

9 Mine heart within me is broken because
of the prophets; [a]all my bones shake; I am like a
drunken man, and like a man whom wine hath
overcome, because of the LORD, and because of
the words of his holiness.
10 For [a]the land is full of adulterers; for [b]be-
cause of swearing the land mourneth; [c]the pleasant places of the wilderness are dried up, and their
course is evil, and their force *is* not right.

26 [a]2 Kin. 24:15; Jer. 10:18; 16:13 **28** [a]Ps. 31:12; Jer. 48:38; Hos. 8:8 **29** [a]Deut. 32:1; Is. 1:2; 34:1; Mic. 1:2 **30** [a]1 Chr. 3:16, 17; Matt. 1:12 [b]Ps. 94:20; Jer. 36:30

CHAPTER 23

1 [a]Is. 56:9–12; Jer. 10:21 **2** [a]Ex. 32:34 **3** [a]Is. 11:11, 12, 16; Jer. 32:37 **4** [a]Jer. 3:15; [Ezek. 34:23] **5** [a]Is. 4:2; 11:1; 40:10, 11; Jer. 33:14; [Dan. 9:24; Zech. 6:12]; Matt. 1:1, 6; Luke 3:31; [John 1:45; 7:42] [b]Ps. 72:2; Is. 9:7; 32:1, 18; [Dan. 9:24] **6** [a]Deut. 33:28; Jer. 30:10; Zech. 14:11 [b]Jer. 32:37 [c]Is. 45:24; Jer. 33:16; [Dan. 9:24; Rom. 3:22; 1 Cor. 1:30] **7** [a]Is. 43:18, 19; Jer. 16:14 **8** [a]Is. 43:5, 6; Ezek. 34:13; Amos 9:14, 15 [b]Gen. 12:7; Jer. 16:14, 15; 31:8 **9** [a]Jer. 8:18; Hab. 3:16 **10** [a]Jer. 9:2 [b]Hos. 4:2; Mal. 3:5 [c]Ps. 107:34; Jer. 9:10

*23:6 Heb. *YHWH Tsidkenu*

NKJV

zar king of Babylon and the hand of the Chaldeans.
26 [a]"So I will cast you out, and your mother
who bore you, into another country where you
were not born; and there you shall die.
27 "But to the land to which they desire to
return, there they shall not return.

28 "Is this man Coniah a despised, broken
idol—
[a]A vessel in which *is* no pleasure?
Why are they cast out, he and his
descendants,
And cast into a land which they do not
know?
29 [a]O earth, earth, earth,
Hear the word of the LORD!
30 Thus says the LORD:
'Write this man down as [a]childless,
A man *who* shall not prosper in his
days;
For [b]none of his descendants shall
prosper,
Sitting on the throne of David,
And ruling anymore in Judah.' "

The Branch of Righteousness

23 "Woe [a]to the shepherds who destroy and
scatter the sheep of My pasture!" says the
LORD.
2 Therefore thus says the LORD God of Israel
against the shepherds who feed My people: "You
have scattered My flock, driven them away, and
not attended to them. [a]Behold, I will attend to you
for the evil of your doings," says the LORD.
3 "But [a]I will gather the remnant of My
flock out of all countries where I have driven
them, and bring them back to their folds; and they
shall be fruitful and increase.
4 "I will set up [a]shepherds over them who
will feed them; and they shall fear no more, nor
be dismayed, nor shall they be lacking," says the
LORD.

5 "Behold, [a]*the* days are coming," says the
LORD,
"That I will raise to David a Branch of
righteousness;
A King shall reign and prosper,
[b]And execute judgment and righteousness
in the earth.
6 [a]In His days Judah will be saved,
And Israel [b]will dwell safely;
Now [c]this *is* His name by which He will
be called:

*THE LORD OUR RIGHTEOUSNESS.

7 "Therefore, behold, [a]*the* days are coming," says the LORD, "that they shall no longer
say, 'As the LORD lives who brought up the children of Israel from the land of Egypt,'
8 "but, 'As the LORD lives who brought up
and led the descendants of the house of Israel
from the north country [a]and from all the countries
where I had driven them.' And they shall dwell
in their own [b]land."

False Prophets and Empty Oracles

9 My heart within me is broken
Because of the prophets;
[a]All my bones shake.
I am like a drunken man,
And like a man whom wine has
overcome,
Because of the LORD,
And because of His holy words.
10 For [a]the land is full of adulterers;
For [b]because of a curse the land mourns.
[c]The pleasant places of the wilderness are
dried up.
Their course of life is evil,
And their might *is* not right.

KJV

11 For [a]both prophet and priest are profane; yea, [b]in my house have I found their wickedness, saith the LORD.

12 [a]Wherefore their way shall be unto them as slippery *ways* in the darkness: they shall be driven on, and fall therein: for I [b]will bring evil upon them, *even* the year of their visitation, saith the LORD.

13 And I have seen folly in the prophets of Samaria; [a]they prophesied in Baal, and [b]caused my people Israel to err.

14 I have seen also in the prophets of Jerusalem an horrible thing: [a]they commit adultery, and walk in lies: they [b]strengthen also the hands of evildoers, that none doth return from his wickedness: they are all of them unto me as [c]Sodom, and the inhabitants thereof as Gomorrah.

15 Therefore thus saith the LORD of hosts concerning the prophets; Behold, I will feed them with [a]wormwood, and make them drink the water of gall: for from the prophets of Jerusalem is profaneness gone forth into all the land.

16 Thus saith the LORD of hosts, Hearken not unto the words of the prophets that prophesy unto you: they make you vain: [a]they speak a vision of their own heart, *and* not out of the mouth of the LORD.

17 They say still unto them that despise me, The LORD hath said, [a]Ye shall have peace; and they say unto every one that [b]walketh after the imagination of his own heart, [c]No evil shall come upon you.

18 For [a]who hath stood in the counsel of the LORD, and hath perceived and heard his word? who hath marked his word, and heard *it?*

19 Behold, a [a]whirlwind of the LORD is gone forth in fury, even a grievous whirlwind: it shall fall grievously upon the head of the wicked.

20 The [a]anger of the LORD shall not return, until he have executed, and till he have performed the thoughts of his heart: [b]in the latter days ye shall consider it perfectly.

21 [a]I have not sent these prophets, yet they ran: I have not spoken to them, yet they prophesied.

22 But if they had stood in my counsel, and had caused my people to hear my words, then they should have [a]turned them from their evil way, and from the evil of their doings.

23 *Am* I a God at hand, saith the LORD, and not a God afar off?

24 Can any [a]hide himself in secret places that I shall not see him? saith the LORD. [b]Do not I fill heaven and earth? saith the LORD.

11 [a]Jer. 6:13; Zeph. 3:4 [b]Jer. 7:30; 32:34; Ezek. 8:11; 23:39
12 [a]Ps. 35:6; [Prov. 4:19]; Jer. 13:16 [b]Jer. 11:23
13 [a]1 Kin. 18:18–21; Jer. 2:8 [b]Is. 9:16
14 [a]Jer. 29:23 [b]Jer. 23:22; Ezek. 13:22, 23 [c]Gen. 18:20; Deut. 32:32; Is. 1:9, 10
15 [a]Deut. 29:18; Jer. 9:15
16 [a]Jer. 14:14; Ezek. 13:3, 6
17 [a]Jer. 8:11; Ezek. 13:10; Zech. 10:2 [b]Deut. 29:19; Jer. 3:17 [c]Jer. 5:12; Amos 9:10; Mic. 3:11
18 [a]Job 15:8, 9; [Jer. 23:22; 1 Cor. 2:16]
19 [a]Jer. 25:32; 30:23; Amos 1:14
20 [a]2 Kin. 23:26, 27; Jer. 30:24 [b]Gen. 49:1
21 [a]Jer. 14:14; 23:32; 27:15
22 [a]Jer. 25:5
24 [a][Ps. 139:7]; Amos 9:2, 3 [b][1 Kin. 8:27]; Ps. 139:7

NKJV

11 "For [a]both prophet and priest are profane;
Yes, [b]in My house I have found their wickedness," says the LORD.
12 "Therefore[a] their way shall be to them
Like slippery *ways;*
In the darkness they shall be driven on
And fall in them;
For I [b]will bring disaster on them,
The year of their punishment," says the LORD.
13 "And I have seen folly in the prophets of Samaria:
[a]They prophesied by Baal
And [b]caused My people Israel to err.
14 Also I have seen a horrible thing in the prophets of Jerusalem:
[a]They commit adultery and walk in lies;
They also [b]strengthen the hands of evildoers,
So that no one turns back from his wickedness.
All of them are like [c]Sodom to Me,
And her inhabitants like Gomorrah.

15 "Therefore thus says the LORD of hosts concerning the prophets:

'Behold, I will feed them with [a]wormwood,
And make them drink the water of gall;
For from the prophets of Jerusalem
Profaneness has gone out into all the land.' "

16 Thus says the LORD of hosts:

"Do not listen to the words of the prophets who prophesy to you.
They make you worthless;
[a]They speak a vision of their own heart,
Not from the mouth of the LORD.
17 They continually say to those who despise Me,
'The LORD has said, [a]"You shall have peace" ';
And *to* everyone who [b]walks according to the dictates of his own heart, they say,
[c]'No evil shall come upon you.' "

18 For [a]who has stood in the counsel of the LORD,
And has perceived and heard His word?
Who has marked His word and heard *it?*
19 Behold, a [a]whirlwind of the LORD has gone forth in fury—
A violent whirlwind!
It will fall violently on the head of the wicked.
20 The [a]anger of the LORD will not turn back
Until He has executed and performed the thoughts of His heart.
[b]In the latter days you will understand it perfectly.

21 "I[a] have not sent these prophets, yet they ran.
I have not spoken to them, yet they prophesied.
22 But if they had stood in My counsel,
And had caused My people to hear My words,
Then they would have [a]turned them from their evil way
And from the evil of their doings.

23 "*Am* I a God near at hand," says the LORD,
"And not a God afar off?
24 Can anyone [a]hide himself in secret places,
So I shall not see him?" says the LORD;
[b]"Do I not fill heaven and earth?" says the LORD.

KJV

25 I have heard what the prophets said, that
prophesy lies in my name, saying, I have dreamed,
I have dreamed.
26 How long shall *this* be in the heart of the
prophets that prophesy lies? yea, *they are* prophets of the deceit of their own heart;
27 Which think to cause my people to forget
my name by their dreams which they tell every
man to his neighbour, [a]as their fathers have forgotten my name for Baal.
28 The prophet that hath a dream, let him
tell a dream; and he that hath my word, let him
speak my word faithfully. What *is* the chaff to
the wheat? saith the LORD.
29 *Is* not my word like as a [a]fire? saith the
LORD; and like a hammer *that* breaketh the rock
in pieces?
30 Therefore, behold, [a]I *am* against the
prophets, saith the LORD, that steal my words
every one from his neighbour.
31 Behold, I *am* [a]against the prophets, saith
the LORD, that use their tongues, and say, He saith.
32 Behold, I *am* against them that prophesy
false dreams, saith the LORD, and do tell them,
and cause my people to err by their [a]lies, and by
[b]their lightness; yet I sent them not, nor commanded them: therefore they shall not [c]profit this
people at all, saith the LORD.
33 And when this people, or the prophet, or
a priest, shall ask thee, saying, What *is* [a]the burden of the LORD? thou shalt then say unto them,
What burden? I will even forsake you, saith the
LORD.
34 And *as for* the prophet, and the priest, and
the people, that shall say, The burden of the LORD,
I will even punish that man and his house.
35 Thus shall ye say every one to his neighbour, and every one to his brother, What hath
the LORD answered? and, What hath the LORD
spoken?
36 And the burden of the LORD shall ye mention no more: for every man's word shall be his
burden; for ye have [a]perverted the words of the
living God, of the LORD of hosts our God.
37 Thus shalt thou say to the prophet, What
hath the LORD answered thee? and, What hath the
LORD spoken?
38 But since ye say, The burden of the LORD;
therefore thus saith the LORD; Because ye say this
word, The burden of the LORD, and I have sent
unto you, saying, Ye shall not say, The burden
of the LORD;
39 Therefore, behold, I, even I, [a]will utterly
forget you, and I will forsake you, and the city
that I gave you and your fathers, *and cast you*
out of my presence:
40 And I will bring [a]an everlasting reproach
upon you, and a perpetual [b]shame, which shall
not be forgotten.

NKJV

25 "I have heard what the prophets have said
who prophesy lies in My name, saying, 'I have
dreamed, I have dreamed!'
26 "How long will *this* be in the heart of the
prophets who prophesy lies? Indeed *they are*
prophets of the deceit of their own heart,
27 "who try to make My people forget My
name by their dreams which everyone tells his
neighbor, [a]as their fathers forgot My name for
Baal.

28 "The prophet who has a dream, let him tell
a dream;
And he who has My word, let him speak
My word faithfully.
What *is* the chaff to the wheat?" says the
LORD.
29 "*Is* not My word like a [a]fire?" says the
LORD,
"And like a hammer *that* breaks the rock
in pieces?

30 "Therefore behold, [a]I *am* against the
prophets," says the LORD, "who steal My words
every one from his neighbor.
31 "Behold, I *am* [a]against the prophets," says
the LORD, "who use their tongues and say, 'He
says.'
32 "Behold, I *am* against those who prophesy
false dreams," says the LORD, "and tell them, and
cause My people to err by their [a]lies and by [b]their
recklessness. Yet I did not send them or command
them; therefore they shall not [c]profit this people
at all," says the LORD.
33 "So when these people or the prophet or
the priest ask you, saying, 'What is [a]the oracle
of the LORD?' you shall then say to them, *'What
oracle?' I will even forsake you," says the
LORD.
34 "And *as for* the prophet and the priest and
the people who say, 'The oracle of the LORD!' I
will even punish that man and his house.
35 "Thus every one of you shall say to his
neighbor, and every one to his brother, 'What has
the LORD answered?' and, 'What has the LORD
spoken?'
36 "And the oracle of the LORD you shall
mention no more. For every man's word will be
his oracle, for you have [a]perverted the words of
the living God, the LORD of hosts, our God.
37 "Thus you shall say to the prophet, 'What
has the LORD answered you?' and, 'What has the
LORD spoken?'
38 "But since you say, 'The oracle of the
LORD!' therefore thus says the LORD: 'Because you
say this word, "The oracle of the LORD!" and I
have sent to you, saying, "Do not say, 'The oracle
of the LORD!' "
39 'therefore behold, I, even I, [a]will utterly
forget you and forsake you, and the city that I
gave you and your fathers, and *will cast you* out
of My presence.
40 'And I will bring [a]an everlasting reproach
upon you, and a perpetual [b]shame, which shall
not be forgotten.' "

27 [a]Judg. 3:7 **29** [a]Jer. 5:14 **30** [a]Deut. 18:20; Ps. 34:16; Jer. 14:14, 15; Ezek. 13:8, 9 **31** [a]Ezek. 13:9 **32** [a]Jer. 20:6; 27:10; Lam. 2:14; 3:37 [b]Zeph. 3:4 [c]Jer. 7:8; Lam. 2:14 **33** [a]Is. 13:1; Nah. 1:1; Hab. 1:1; Zech. 9:1; Mal. 1:1 **36** [a]Deut. 4:2 **39** [a]Hos. 4:6 **40** [a]Jer. 20:11; Ezek. 5:14, 15 [b]Mic. 3:5–7

KJV

The Sign of Two Baskets of Figs

24 The [a]LORD shewed me, and, behold, two
baskets of figs *were* set before the temple
of the LORD, after that Nebuchadrezzar [b]king of
Babylon had carried away captive [c]Jeconiah the
son of Jehoiakim king of Judah, and the princes
of Judah, with the carpenters and smiths, from
Jerusalem, and had brought them to Babylon.
2 One basket *had* very good figs, *even* like
the figs *that are* first ripe: and the other basket
had very naughty figs, which could not be eaten,
they were so [a]bad.
3 Then said the LORD unto me, What seest
thou, Jeremiah? And I said, Figs; the good figs,
very good; and the evil, very evil, that cannot be
eaten, they are so evil.

NKJV

The Sign of Two Baskets of Figs

24 The [a]LORD showed me, and there were two
baskets of figs set before the temple of the
LORD, after Nebuchadnezzar [b]king of Babylon
had carried away captive [c]Jeconiah the son of Jehoiakim, king of Judah, and the princes of Judah
with the craftsmen and smiths, from Jerusalem,
and had brought them to Babylon.
2 One basket *had* very good figs, like the
figs *that are* first ripe; and the other basket *had*
very bad figs which could not be eaten, they were
so [a]bad.
3 Then the LORD said to me, "What do you
see, Jeremiah?" And I said, "Figs, the good figs,
very good; and the bad, very bad, which cannot
be eaten, they are so bad."

CHAPTER 24

1 [a]Amos 7:1, 4; 8:1 [b]2 Kin. 24:12–16; 2 Chr. 36:10 [c]Jer. 22:24–28; 29:2 **2** [a]Is. 5:4, 7; Jer. 29:17

*———

23:33 LXX, Tg., Vg. *'You are the burden.'*

KJV

4 Again the word of the LORD came unto me, saying,

5 Thus saith the LORD, the God of Israel; Like these good figs, so will I acknowledge them that are carried away captive of Judah, whom I have sent out of this place into the land of the Chaldeans for *their* good.

6 For I will set mine eyes upon them for good, and [a]I will bring them again to this land: and [b]I will build them, and not pull *them* down; and I will plant them, and not pluck *them* up.

7 And I will give them [a]an heart to know me, that I *am* the LORD: and they shall be [b]my people, and I will be their God: for they shall return unto me [c]with their whole heart.

8 And as the evil [a]figs, which cannot be eaten, they are so evil; surely thus saith the LORD, So will I give Zedekiah the king of Judah, and his princes, and the [b]residue of Jerusalem, that remain in this land, and [c]them that dwell in the land of Egypt:

9 And I will deliver them to [a]be removed into all the kingdoms of the earth for *their* hurt, [b]*to be* a reproach and a proverb, a taunt and a curse, in all places whither I shall drive them.

10 And I will send the sword, the famine, and the pestilence, among them, till they be consumed from off the land that I gave unto them and to their fathers.

Seventy Years of Desolation

25 The word that came to Jeremiah concerning all the people of Judah [a]in the fourth year of [b]Jehoiakim the son of Josiah king of Judah, that *was* the first year of Nebuchadrezzar king of Babylon;

2 The which Jeremiah the prophet spake unto all the people of Judah, and to all the inhabitants of Jerusalem, saying,

3 [a]From the thirteenth year of Josiah the son of Amon king of Judah, even unto this day, that *is* the three and twentieth year, the word of the LORD hath come unto me, and I have spoken unto you, rising early and speaking; [b]but ye have not hearkened.

4 And the LORD hath sent unto you all his servants the prophets, [a]rising early and sending *them;* but ye have not hearkened, nor inclined your ear to hear.

5 They said, [a]Turn ye again now every one from his evil way, and from the evil of your doings, and dwell in the land that the LORD hath given unto you and to your fathers for ever and ever:

6 And go not after other gods to serve them, and to worship them, and provoke me not to anger with the works of your hands; and I will do you no hurt.

7 Yet ye have not hearkened unto me, saith the LORD; that ye might [a]provoke me to anger with the works of your hands to your own hurt.

8 Therefore thus saith the LORD of hosts; Because ye have not heard my words,

9 Behold, I will send and take [a]all the families of the north, saith the LORD, and Nebuchadrezzar the king of Babylon, [b]my servant, and will bring them against this land, and against the inhabitants thereof, and against all these nations round about, and will utterly destroy them, and [c]make them an astonishment, and an hissing, and perpetual desolations.

10 Moreover I will take from them the [a]voice of mirth, and the voice of gladness, the voice of the bridegroom, and the voice of the bride, [b]the sound of the millstones, and the light of the candle.

11 And this whole land shall be a desolation, *and* an astonishment; and these nations shall serve the king of Babylon seventy [a]years.

12 And it shall come to pass, [a]when seventy years are accomplished, *that* I will punish the king of Babylon, and that nation, saith the LORD,

6 [a]Jer. 12:15; 29:10; Ezek. 11:17 [b]Jer. 32:41; 33:7; 42:10
7 [a][Deut. 30:6; Jer. 32:39; Ezek. 11:19; 36:26, 27] [b]Is. 51:16; Jer. 30:22; 31:33; 32:38; Ezek. 14:11; Zech. 8:8; [Heb. 8:10] [c]1 Sam. 7:3; Ps. 119:2; Jer. 29:13
8 [a]Jer. 29:17 [b]Jer. 39:9 [c]Jer. 44:1, 26–30
9 [a]Deut. 28:25, 37; 1 Kin. 9:7; 2 Chr. 7:20; Jer. 15:4; 29:18; 34:17 [b]Ps. 44:13, 14

CHAPTER 25

1 [a]Jer. 36:1 [b]2 Kin. 24:1, 2; 2 Chr. 36:4–6; Dan. 1:1, 2
3 [a]Jer. 1:2 [b]Jer. 7:13; 11:7, 8, 10
4 [a]Jer. 7:13, 25
5 [a]2 Kin. 17:13; [Is. 55:6, 7]; Jer. 18:11; Ezek. 18:30; [Jon. 3:8–10]
7 [a]Deut. 32:21; Jer. 7:19; 32:30
9 [a]Jer. 1:15 [b]Is. 45:1; Jer. 27:6 [c]Jer. 18:16
10 [a]Is. 24:7–11; Jer. 7:34; 16:9; Ezek. 26:13; Hos. 2:11; Rev. 18:23 [b]Eccl. 12:4; Is. 47:2
11 [a]2 Chr. 36:21; Jer. 29:10; Dan. 9:2; Zech. 7:5
12 [a]2 Chr. 36:21, 22; Ezra 1:1; Jer. 29:10; Dan. 9:2

NKJV

4 Again the word of the LORD came to me, saying,

5 "Thus says the LORD, the God of Israel: 'Like these good figs, so will I acknowledge those who are carried away captive from Judah, whom I have sent out of this place for *their own* good, into the land of the Chaldeans.

6 'For I will set My eyes on them for good, and [a]I will bring them back to this land; [b]I will build them and not pull *them* down, and I will plant them and not pluck *them* up.

7 'Then I will give them [a]a heart to know Me, that I *am* the LORD; and they shall be [b]My people, and I will be their God, for they shall return to Me [c]with their whole heart.

8 'And as the bad [a]figs which cannot be eaten, they are so bad'—surely thus says the LORD—'so will I give up Zedekiah the king of Judah, his princes, the [b]residue of Jerusalem who remain in this land, and [c]those who dwell in the land of Egypt.

9 'I will deliver them to [a]trouble into all the kingdoms of the earth, for *their* harm, [b]*to be* a reproach and a byword, a taunt and a curse, in all places where I shall drive them.

10 'And I will send the sword, the famine, and the pestilence among them, till they are consumed from the land that I gave to them and their fathers.' "

Seventy Years of Desolation

25 The word that came to Jeremiah concerning all the people of Judah, [a]in the fourth year of [b]Jehoiakim the son of Josiah, king of Judah (which *was* the first year of Nebuchadnezzar king of Babylon),

2 which Jeremiah the prophet spoke to all the people of Judah and to all the inhabitants of Jerusalem, saying:

3 [a]"From the thirteenth year of Josiah the son of Amon, king of Judah, even to this day, this *is* the twenty-third year in which the word of the LORD has come to me; and I have spoken to you, rising early and speaking, [b]but you have not listened.

4 "And the LORD has sent to you all His servants the prophets, [a]rising early and sending *them,* but you have not listened nor inclined your ear to hear.

5 "They said, [a]'Repent now everyone of his evil way and his evil doings, and dwell in the land that the LORD has given to you and your fathers forever and ever.

6 'Do not go after other gods to serve them and worship them, and do not provoke Me to anger with the works of your hands; and I will not harm you.'

7 "Yet you have not listened to Me," says the LORD, "that you might [a]provoke Me to anger with the works of your hands to your own hurt.

8 "Therefore thus says the LORD of hosts: 'Because you have not heard My words,

9 'behold, I will send and take [a]all the families of the north,' says the LORD, 'and Nebuchadnezzar the king of Babylon, [b]My servant, and will bring them against this land, against its inhabitants, and against these nations all around, and will utterly destroy them, and [c]make them an astonishment, a hissing, and perpetual desolations.

10 'Moreover I will take from them the [a]voice of mirth and the voice of gladness, the voice of the bridegroom and the voice of the bride, [b]the sound of the millstones and the light of the lamp.

11 'And this whole land shall be a desolation *and* an astonishment, and these nations shall serve the king of Babylon seventy [a]years.

12 'Then it will come to pass, [a]when seventy years are completed, *that* I will punish the king of Babylon and that nation, the land of the

KJV

for their iniquity, and the land of the Chaldeans,
[b]and will make it perpetual desolations.
13 And I will bring upon that land all my
words which I have pronounced against it, *even*
all that is written in this book, which Jeremiah
hath prophesied against all the nations.
14 [a]For many nations [b]and great kings shall
[c]serve themselves of them also: [d]and I will recompense them according to their deeds, and according to the works of their own hands.

Judgment on the Nations

15 For thus saith the LORD God of Israel unto
me; Take the [a]wine cup of this fury at my hand,
and cause all the nations, to whom I send thee,
to drink it.
16 And [a]they shall drink, and be moved, and
be mad, because of the sword that I will send
among them.
17 Then took I the cup at the LORD's hand,
and made all the nations to drink, unto whom the
LORD had sent me:
18 *To wit,* Jerusalem, and the cities of Judah,
and the kings thereof, and the princes thereof, to
make them [a]a desolation, an astonishment, an
hissing, and [b]a curse; as *it is* this day;
19 Pharaoh king of Egypt, and his servants,
and his princes, and all his people;
20 And all the mingled people, and all the
kings of [a]the land of Uz, and all the kings of the
land of the [b]Philistines, and Ashkelon, and Azzah,
and Ekron, and [c]the remnant of Ashdod,
21 [a]Edom, and Moab, and the children of
Ammon,
22 And all the kings of [a]Tyrus, and all the
kings of Zidon, and the kings of the isles which
are beyond the [b]sea,
23 [a]Dedan, and Tema, and Buz, and all *that*
are in the utmost corners,
24 And all the kings of Arabia, and all the
kings of the [a]mingled people that dwell in the
desert,
25 And all the kings of Zimri, and all the
kings of [a]Elam, and all the kings of the [b]Medes,
26 [a]And all the kings of the north, far and
near, one with another, and all the kingdoms of
the world, which *are* upon the face of the earth:
and the king of Sheshach shall drink after them.
27 Therefore thou shalt say unto them, Thus
saith the LORD of hosts, the God of Israel; [a]Drink
ye, and [b]be drunken, and spue, and fall, and rise
no more, because of the sword which I will send
among you.
28 And it shall be, if they refuse to take the
cup at thine hand to drink, then shalt thou say
unto them, Thus saith the LORD of hosts; Ye shall
certainly drink.
29 For, lo, [a]I begin to bring evil on the city
[b]which is called by my name, and should ye be
utterly unpunished? Ye shall not be unpunished:
for [c]I will call for a sword upon all the inhabitants
of the earth, saith the LORD of hosts.
30 Therefore prophesy thou against them all
these words, and say unto them, The LORD shall
[a]roar from on high, and utter his voice from [b]his
holy habitation; he shall mightily roar upon [c]his
habitation; he shall give [d]a shout, as they that
tread *the grapes,* against all the inhabitants of the
earth.
31 A noise shall come *even* to the ends of
the earth; for the LORD hath [a]a controversy with
the nations, [b]he will plead with all flesh; he will
give them *that are* wicked to the sword, saith the
LORD.
32 Thus saith the LORD of hosts, Behold, evil

12 [b]Is. 13:20; Jer. 50:3 **14** [a]Jer. 50:9; 51:27, 28 [b]Jer. 51:27 [c]Jer. 27:7 [d]Jer. 50:29; 51:6, 24 **15** [a]Job 21:20; Ps. 75:8; Is. 51:17; Rev. 14:10 **16** [a]Jer. 51:7; Ezek. 23:34; Nah. 3:11 **18** [a]Jer. 25:9, 11 [b]Jer. 24:9 **20** [a]Job 1:1; Lam. 4:21 [b]Jer. 47:1–7; Ezek. 25:16, 17 [c]Is. 20:1 **21** [a]Jer. 49:7 **22** [a]Jer. 47:4; Zech. 9:2–4 [b]Jer. 49:23 **23** [a]Is. 21:13; Jer. 49:7, 8 **24** [a]Jer. 25:20; 50:37; Ezek. 30:5 **25** [a]Gen. 10:22; Is. 11:11; Jer. 49:34 [b]Is. 13:17; Jer. 51:11, 28 **26** [a]Jer. 50:9 **27** [a]Jer. 25:16; Hab. 2:16 [b]Is. 63:6 **29** [a][Prov. 11:31]; Is. 10:12; Jer. 13:13; Ezek. 9:6; [Luke 23:31; 1 Pet. 4:17] [b]Dan. 9:18 [c]Ezek. 38:21 **30** [a]Is. 42:13; Joel 3:16; Amos 1:2 [b]Ps. 11:4 [c]1 Kin. 9:3; Ps. 132:14 [d]Is. 16:9; Jer. 48:33 **31** [a]Hos. 4:1; Mic. 6:2 [b]Is. 66:16; Joel 3:2

*———

25:26 A code word for *Babylon,* Jer. 51:41

NKJV

Chaldeans, for their iniquity,' says the LORD;
[b]'and I will make it a perpetual desolation.
13 'So I will bring on that land all My words
which I have pronounced against it, all that is
written in this book, which Jeremiah has prophesied concerning all the nations.
14 [a]'(For many nations [b]and great kings shall
[c]be served by them also; [d]and I will repay them
according to their deeds and according to the
works of their own hands.)' "

Judgment on the Nations

15 For thus says the LORD God of Israel to
me: "Take this [a]wine cup of fury from My hand,
and cause all the nations, to whom I send you,
to drink it.
16 "And [a]they will drink and stagger and go
mad because of the sword that I will send among
them."
17 Then I took the cup from the LORD's hand,
and made all the nations drink, to whom the LORD
had sent me:
18 Jerusalem and the cities of Judah, its
kings and its princes, to make them [a]a desolation,
an astonishment, a hissing, and [b]a curse, as *it is*
this day;
19 Pharaoh king of Egypt, his servants, his
princes, and all his people;
20 all the mixed multitude, all the kings of
[a]the land of Uz, all the kings of the land of the
[b]Philistines (namely, Ashkelon, Gaza, Ekron, and
[c]the remnant of Ashdod);
21 [a]Edom, Moab, and the people of Ammon;
22 all the kings of [a]Tyre, all the kings of Sidon, and the kings of the coastlands which *are*
across the [b]sea;
23 [a]Dedan, Tema, Buz, and all *who are* in
the farthest corners;
24 all the kings of Arabia and all the kings
of the [a]mixed multitude who dwell in the desert;
25 all the kings of Zimri, all the kings of
[a]Elam, and all the kings of the [b]Medes;
26 [a]all the kings of the north, far and near,
one with another; and all the kingdoms of the
world which *are* on the face of the earth. Also
the king of *Sheshach shall drink after them.
27 "Therefore you shall say to them, 'Thus
says the LORD of hosts, the God of Israel: [a]"Drink,
[b]be drunk, and vomit! Fall and rise no more, because of the sword which I will send among
you." '
28 "And it shall be, if they refuse to take the
cup from your hand to drink, then you shall say
to them, 'Thus says the LORD of hosts: "You shall
certainly drink!
29 "For behold, [a]I begin to bring calamity on
the city [b]which is called by My name, and should
you be utterly unpunished? You shall not be
unpunished, for [c]I will call for a sword on all
the inhabitants of the earth," says the LORD of
hosts.'
30 "Therefore prophesy against them all
these words, and say to them:

'The LORD will [a]roar from on high,
And utter His voice from [b]His holy
habitation;
He will roar mightily against [c]His fold.
He will give [d]a shout, as those who tread
the grapes,
Against all the inhabitants of the earth.
31 A noise will come to the ends of the
earth—
For the LORD has [a]a controversy with the
nations;
[b]He will plead His case with all flesh.
He will give those *who are* wicked to the
sword,' says the LORD."

32 Thus says the LORD of hosts:

KJV

shall go forth from nation to nation, and [a]a great whirlwind shall be raised up from the coasts of the earth.

33 [a]And the slain of the LORD shall be at that day from *one* end of the earth even unto the *other* end of the earth: they shall not be [b]lamented, [c]neither gathered, nor buried; they shall be dung upon the ground.

34 [a]Howl, ye shepherds, and cry; and wallow yourselves *in the ashes,* ye principal of the flock: for the days of your slaughter and of your dispersions are accomplished; and ye shall fall like a pleasant vessel.

35 And the shepherds shall have no way to flee, nor the principal of the flock to escape.

36 A voice of the cry of the shepherds, and an howling of the principal of the flock, *shall be heard:* for the LORD hath spoiled their pasture.

37 And the peaceable habitations are cut down because of the fierce anger of the LORD.

38 He hath forsaken his covert, as the lion: for their land is desolate because of the fierceness of the oppressor, and because of his fierce anger.

Jeremiah Saved from Death
(*cf. Jer. 7:1–15*)

26 In the beginning of the reign of Jehoiakim the son of Josiah king of Judah came this word from the LORD, saying,

2 Thus saith the LORD; Stand in [a]the court of the LORD's house, and speak unto all the cities of Judah, which come to worship in the LORD's house, [b]all the words that I command thee to speak unto them; [c]diminish not a word:

3 [a]If so be they will hearken, and turn every man from his evil way, that I may [b]repent me of the evil, which I purpose to do unto them because of the evil of their doings.

4 And thou shalt say unto them, Thus saith the LORD; [a]If ye will not hearken to me, to walk in my law, which I have set before you,

5 To hearken to the words of my servants the prophets, [a]whom I sent unto you, both rising up early, and sending *them,* but ye have not hearkened;

6 Then will I make this house like [a]Shiloh, and will make this city [b]a curse to all the nations of the earth.

7 So the priests and the prophets and all the people heard Jeremiah speaking these words in the house of the LORD.

8 Now it came to pass, when Jeremiah had made an end of speaking all that the LORD had commanded *him* to speak unto all the people, that the priests and the prophets and all the people took him, saying, Thou shalt surely die.

9 Why hast thou prophesied in the name of the LORD, saying, This house shall be like Shiloh, and this city shall be [a]desolate without an inhabitant? And all the people were gathered against Jeremiah in the house of the LORD.

10 When the princes of Judah heard these things, then they came up from the king's house unto the house of the LORD, and sat down in the entry of the new gate of the LORD's *house.*

11 Then spake the priests and the prophets unto the princes and to all the people, saying, This man *is* worthy to [a]die; for he hath prophesied against this city, as ye have heard with your ears.

12 Then spake Jeremiah unto all the princes and to all the people, saying, The LORD sent me to prophesy against this house and against this city all the words that ye have heard.

13 Therefore now [a]amend your ways and

32 [a]Jer. 23:19; 30:23
33 [a]Is. 34:2, 3; 66:16 [b]Jer. 16:4, 6; Ezek. 39:4, 17 [c]Ps. 79:3; Jer. 8:2; Rev. 11:9
34 [a]Jer. 4:8; 6:26; Ezek. 27:30

CHAPTER 26
2 [a]2 Chr. 24:20, 21; Jer. 19:14 [b]Deut. 4:2; Jer. 43:1; Ezek. 3:10; Matt. 28:20; [Rev. 22:19] [c]Acts 20:27
3 [a]Is. 1:16–19; Jer. 36:3–7 [b]Jer. 18:8; Jon. 3:9
4 [a]Lev. 26:14, 15; Deut. 28:15; 1 Kin. 9:6; Is. 1:20; Jer. 17:27; 22:5
5 [a]Jer. 25:4; 29:19
6 [a]1 Sam. 4:10, 11; Ps. 78:60; Jer. 7:12, 14 [b]2 Kin. 22:19; Is. 65:15; Jer. 24:9
9 [a]Jer. 9:11
11 [a]Jer. 38:4
13 [a]Jer. 7:3; [Joel 2:13]; Jon. 3:8

NKJV

"Behold, disaster shall go forth
From nation to nation,
And [a]a great whirlwind shall be raised up
From the farthest parts of the earth.

33 [a]"And at that day the slain of the LORD shall be from *one* end of the earth even to the *other* end of the earth. They shall not be [b]lamented, [c]or gathered, or buried; they shall become refuse on the ground.

34 "Wail,[a] shepherds, and cry!
Roll about *in the ashes,*
You leaders of the flock!
For the days of your slaughter and your
dispersions are fulfilled;
You shall fall like a precious vessel.
35 And the shepherds will have no way to
flee,
Nor the leaders of the flock to escape.
36 A voice of the cry of the shepherds,
And a wailing of the leaders to the flock
will be heard.
For the LORD has plundered their pasture,
37 And the peaceful dwellings are cut down
Because of the fierce anger of the LORD.
38 He has left His lair like the lion;
For their land is desolate
Because of the fierceness of the
Oppressor,
And because of His fierce anger."

Jeremiah Saved from Death
(*cf. Jer. 7:1–15*)

26 In the beginning of the reign of Jehoiakim the son of Josiah, king of Judah, this word came from the LORD, saying,

2 "Thus says the LORD: 'Stand in [a]the court of the LORD's house, and speak to all the cities of Judah, which come to worship *in* the LORD's house, [b]all the words that I command you to speak to them. [c]Do not diminish a word.

3 [a]'Perhaps everyone will listen and turn from his evil way, that I may [b]relent concerning the calamity which I purpose to bring on them because of the evil of their doings.'

4 "And you shall say to them, 'Thus says the LORD: [a]"If you will not listen to Me, to walk in My law which I have set before you,

5 "to heed the words of My servants the prophets [a]whom I sent to you, both rising up early and sending *them* (but you have not heeded),

6 "then I will make this house like [a]Shiloh, and will make this city [b]a curse to all the nations of the earth." ' "

7 So the priests and the prophets and all the people heard Jeremiah speaking these words in the house of the LORD.

8 Now it happened, when Jeremiah had made an end of speaking all that the LORD had commanded *him* to speak to all the people, that the priests and the prophets and all the people seized him, saying, "You will surely die!

9 "Why have you prophesied in the name of the LORD, saying, 'This house shall be like Shiloh, and this city shall be [a]desolate, without an inhabitant'?" And all the people were gathered against Jeremiah in the house of the LORD.

10 When the princes of Judah heard these things, they came up from the king's house to the house of the LORD and sat down in the entry of the New Gate of the LORD's *house.*

11 And the priests and the prophets spoke to the princes and all the people, saying, "This man deserves to [a]die! For he has prophesied against this city, as you have heard with your ears."

12 Then Jeremiah spoke to all the princes and all the people, saying: "The LORD sent me to prophesy against this house and against this city with all the words that you have heard.

13 "Now therefore, [a]amend your ways and

KJV

your doings, and obey the voice of the LORD your
God; and the LORD will repent him of the evil that
he hath pronounced against you.
14 As for me, behold, [a]I *am* in your hand:
do with me as seemeth good and meet unto you.
15 But know ye for certain, that if ye put me
to death, ye shall surely bring innocent blood
upon yourselves, and upon this city, and upon the
inhabitants thereof: for of a truth the LORD hath
sent me unto you to speak all these words in your
ears.
16 Then said the princes and all the people
unto the priests and to the prophets; This man *is*
not worthy to die: for he hath spoken to us in
the name of the LORD our God.
17 [a]Then rose up certain of the elders of the
land, and spake to all the assembly of the people,
saying,
18 [a]Micah the Morasthite prophesied in the
days of Hezekiah king of Judah, and spake to all
the people of Judah, saying, Thus saith the LORD
of hosts; [b]Zion shall be plowed *like* a field, and
Jerusalem shall become [c]heaps, and the mountain
of the house as the high places of a forest.
19 Did Hezekiah king of Judah and all Judah
put him at all to death? [a]did he not fear the LORD,
and [b]besought the LORD, and the LORD [c]repented
him of the evil which he had pronounced against
them? [d]Thus might we procure great evil against
our souls.
20 And there was also a man that prophesied
in the name of the LORD, Urijah the son of Shemaiah of Kirjath-jearim, who prophesied against
this city and against this land according to all the
words of Jeremiah:
21 And when Jehoiakim the king, with all his
mighty men, and all the princes, heard his words,
the king sought to put him to death: but when
Urijah heard it, he was afraid, and fled, and went
into Egypt;
22 And Jehoiakim the king sent men into
Egypt, *namely,* Elnathan the son of Achbor, and
certain men with him into Egypt.
23 And they fetched forth Urijah out of
Egypt, and brought him unto Jehoiakim the king;
who slew him with the sword, and cast his dead
body into the graves of the common people.
24 Nevertheless [a]the hand of Ahikam the son
of Shaphan was with Jeremiah, that they should
not give him into the hand of the people to put
him to death.

Symbol of the Bonds and Yokes

27 In the beginning of the reign of Jehoiakim
the son of Josiah [a]king of Judah came this
word unto Jeremiah from the LORD, saying,
2 Thus saith the LORD to me; Make thee
bonds and yokes, [a]and put them upon thy neck,
3 And send them to the king of Edom, and
to the king of Moab, and to the king of the Ammonites, and to the king of Tyrus, and to the king
of Zidon, by the hand of the messengers which
come to Jerusalem unto Zedekiah king of Judah;
4 And command them to say unto their masters, Thus saith the LORD of hosts, the God of Israel; Thus shall ye say unto your masters;
5 [a]I have made the earth, the man and the
beast that *are* upon the ground, by my great power
and by my outstretched arm, and [b]have given it
unto whom it seemed meet unto me.
6 [a]And now have I given all these lands into
the hand of Nebuchadnezzar the king of Babylon,
[b]my servant; and [c]the beasts of the field have I
given him also to serve him.
7 [a]And all nations shall serve him, and his
son, and his son's son, [b]until the very time of his
land come: [c]and then many nations and great
kings shall serve themselves of him.

14 [a]Jer. 38:5
17 [a]Acts 5:34
18 [a]Mic. 1:1
[b]Mic. 3:12
[c]Neh. 4:2; Ps. 79:1; Jer. 9:11
19 [a]2 Chr. 32:26; Is. 37:1, 4, 15–20
[b]2 Kin. 20:1–19 [c]Ex. 32:14; 2 Sam. 24:16; Jer. 18:8
[d][Acts 5:39]
24 [a]2 Kin. 22:12–14; Jer. 39:14; 40:5–7

CHAPTER 27

1 [a]Jer. 27:3, 12, 20; 28:1
2 [a]Jer. 28:10, 12; Ezek. 4:1; 12:3; 24:3
5 [a]Ps. 115:15; 146:6; Is. 45:12
[b]Deut. 9:29; Ps. 115:16; Jer. 32:17; Dan. 4:17, 25, 32
6 [a]Jer. 28:14
[b]Jer. 25:9; 43:10; Ezek. 29:18, 20 [c]Jer. 28:14; Dan. 2:38
7 [a]2 Chr. 36:20 [b]Jer. 25:12; 50:27; [Dan. 5:26]; Zech. 2:8, 9
[c]Jer. 25:14

*

26:18 Lit. *house*
27:1 LXX omits v. 1 • So with MT, Tg., Vg.; some Heb. mss., Arab., Syr. *Zedekiah* (cf. 27:3, 12; 28:1)

NKJV

your doings, and obey the voice of the LORD your
God; then the LORD will relent concerning the
doom that He has pronounced against you.
14 "As for me, here [a]I am, in your hand; do
with me as seems good and proper to you.
15 "But know for certain that if you put me
to death, you will surely bring innocent blood on
yourselves, on this city, and on its inhabitants;
for truly the LORD has sent me to you to speak
all these words in your hearing."
16 So the princes and all the people said to
the priests and the prophets, "This man does not
deserve to die. For he has spoken to us in the
name of the LORD our God."
17 [a]Then certain of the elders of the land rose
up and spoke to all the assembly of the people,
saying:
18 [a]"Micah of Moresheth prophesied in the
days of Hezekiah king of Judah, and spoke to all
the people of Judah, saying, 'Thus says the LORD
of hosts:

[b]"Zion shall be plowed *like* a field,
Jerusalem shall become [c]heaps of ruins,
And the mountain of the *temple
Like the bare hills of the forest." '

19 "Did Hezekiah king of Judah and all Judah ever put him to death? [a]Did he not fear the
LORD and [b]seek the LORD's favor? And the LORD
[c]relented concerning the doom which He had pronounced against them. [d]But we are doing great
evil against ourselves."
20 Now there was also a man who prophesied in the name of the LORD, Urijah the son of
Shemaiah of Kirjath Jearim, who prophesied
against this city and against this land according
to all the words of Jeremiah.
21 And when Jehoiakim the king, with all his
mighty men and all the princes, heard his words,
the king sought to put him to death; but when
Urijah heard *it,* he was afraid and fled, and went
to Egypt.
22 Then Jehoiakim the king sent men to
Egypt: Elnathan the son of Achbor, and *other* men
who went with him to Egypt.
23 And they brought Urijah from Egypt and
brought him to Jehoiakim the king, who killed
him with the sword and cast his dead body into
the graves of the common people.
24 Nevertheless [a]the hand of Ahikam the son
of Shaphan was with Jeremiah, so that they
should not give him into the hand of the people
to put him to death.

Symbol of the Bonds and Yokes

27 In* the beginning of the reign of *Jehoiakim
the son of Josiah, [a]king of Judah, this word
came to Jeremiah from the LORD, saying,
2 "Thus says the LORD to me: 'Make for
yourselves bonds and yokes, [a]and put them on
your neck,
3 'and send them to the king of Edom, the
king of Moab, the king of the Ammonites, the king
of Tyre, and the king of Sidon, by the hand of
the messengers who come to Jerusalem to Zedekiah king of Judah.
4 'And command them to say to their masters, "Thus says the LORD of hosts, the God of
Israel—thus you shall say to your masters:
5 [a]'I have made the earth, the man and the
beast that *are* on the ground, by My great power
and by My outstretched arm, and [b]have given it
to whom it seemed proper to Me.
6 [a]'And now I have given all these lands into
the hand of Nebuchadnezzar the king of Babylon,
[b]My servant; and [c]the beasts of the field I have
also given him to serve him.
7 [a]'So all nations shall serve him and his
son and his son's son, [b]until the time of his land
comes; [c]and then many nations and great kings
shall make him serve them.

KJV

8 And it shall come to pass, *that* the nation
and kingdom which will not serve the same Nebuchadnezzar the king of Babylon, and that will not
put their neck under the yoke of the king of Babylon, that nation will I punish, saith the LORD, with
the sword, and with the famine, and with the
pestilence, until I have consumed them by his
hand.
9 Therefore hearken not ye to your prophets, nor to your diviners, nor to your dreamers,
nor to your enchanters, nor to your sorcerers,
which speak unto you, saying, Ye shall not serve
the king of Babylon:
10 For they prophesy a [a]lie unto you, to remove you far from your land; and that I should
drive you out, and ye should perish.
11 But the nations that bring their neck under
the yoke of the king of Babylon, and serve him,
those will I let remain still in their own land, saith
the LORD; and they shall till it, and dwell therein.
12 I spake also to [a]Zedekiah king of Judah
according to all these words, saying, Bring your
necks under the yoke of the king of Babylon, and
serve him and his people, and live.
13 [a]Why will ye die, thou and thy people, by
the sword, by the famine, and by the pestilence,
as the LORD hath spoken against the nation that
will not serve the king of Babylon?
14 Therefore [a]hearken not unto the words of
the prophets that speak unto you, saying, Ye shall
not serve the king of Babylon: for they prophesy
[b]a lie unto you.
15 For I have [a]not sent them, saith the LORD,
yet they prophesy a lie in my name; that I might
drive you out, and that ye might perish, ye, and
the prophets that prophesy unto you.
16 Also I spake to the priests and to all this
people, saying, Thus saith the LORD; Hearken not
to the words of your prophets that prophesy unto
you, saying, Behold, [a]the vessels of the LORD's
house shall now shortly be brought again from
Babylon: for they prophesy a lie unto you.
17 Hearken not unto them; serve the king of
Babylon, and live: wherefore should this city be
laid waste?
18 But if they *be* prophets, and if the word
of the LORD be with them, let them now make
intercession to the LORD of hosts, that the vessels
which are left in the house of the LORD, and *in*
the house of the king of Judah, and at Jerusalem,
go not to Babylon.
19 For thus saith the LORD of hosts [a]concern-
ing the pillars, and concerning the sea, and concerning the bases, and concerning the residue of
the vessels that remain in this city,
20 Which Nebuchadnezzar king of Babylon
took not, when he carried away [a]captive Jeconiah
the son of Jehoiakim king of Judah from Jerusalem to Babylon, and all the nobles of Judah and
Jerusalem;
21 Yea, thus saith the LORD of hosts, the God
of Israel, concerning the [a]vessels that remain *in*
the house of the LORD, and *in* the house of the
king of Judah and of Jerusalem;
22 They shall be [a]carried to Babylon, and
there shall they be until the day that I [b]visit them,
saith the LORD; then [c]will I bring them up, and
restore them to this place.

Hananiah's Falsehood and Doom

28 And [a]it came to pass the same year, in the
beginning of the reign of Zedekiah king of
Judah, in the [b]fourth year, *and* in the fifth month,
that Hananiah the son of [c]Azur the prophet,
which *was* of Gibeon, spake unto me in the house
of the LORD, in the presence of the priests and of
all the people, saying,
2 Thus speaketh the LORD of hosts, the God
of Israel, saying, I have broken [a]the yoke of the
king of Babylon.
3 [a]Within two full years will I bring again
into this place all the vessels of the LORD's house,

10 [a]Jer. 23:16, 32; 28:15
12 [a]Jer. 28:1; 38:17
13 [a][Prov. 8:36]; Jer. 27:8; 38:23; [Ezek. 18:31]
14 [a]Jer. 23:16 [b]Jer. 14:14; 23:21; 29:8, 9; Ezek. 13:22
15 [a]Jer. 23:21; 29:9
16 [a]2 Kin. 24:13; 2 Chr. 36:7, 10; Jer. 28:3; Dan. 1:2
19 [a]1 Kin. 7:15; 2 Kin. 25:13–17; Jer. 52:17, 20, 21
20 [a]2 Kin. 24:14, 15; 2 Chr. 36:10, 18; Jer. 24:1
21 [a]Jer. 20:5
22 [a]2 Kin. 25:13; 2 Chr. 36:18 [b]2 Chr. 36:21; Jer. 29:10; 32:5 [c]Ezra 1:7; 7:19

CHAPTER 28
1 [a]Jer. 27:1 [b]Jer. 51:59 [c]Ezek. 11:1
2 [a]Jer. 27:12
3 [a]Jer. 27:16

NKJV

8 'And it shall be, *that* the nation and kingdom which will not serve Nebuchadnezzar the
king of Babylon, and which will not put its neck
under the yoke of the king of Babylon, that nation
I will punish,' says the LORD, 'with the sword, the
famine, and the pestilence, until I have consumed
them by his hand.
9 'Therefore do not listen to your prophets,
your diviners, your dreamers, your soothsayers,
or your sorcerers, who speak to you, saying, "You
shall not serve the king of Babylon."
10 'For they prophesy a [a]lie to you, to remove
you far from your land; and I will drive you out,
and you will perish.
11 'But the nations that bring their necks under the yoke of the king of Babylon and serve
him, I will let them remain in their own land,'
says the LORD, 'and they shall till it and dwell in
it.' " ' "
12 I also spoke to [a]Zedekiah king of Judah
according to all these words, saying, "Bring your
necks under the yoke of the king of Babylon, and
serve him and his people, and live!
13 [a]"Why will you die, you and your people,
by the sword, by the famine, and by the pestilence,
as the LORD has spoken against the nation that
will not serve the king of Babylon?
14 "Therefore [a]do not listen to the words of
the prophets who speak to you, saying, 'You shall
not serve the king of Babylon,' for they prophesy
[b]a lie to you;
15 "for I have [a]not sent them," says the LORD,
"yet they prophesy a lie in My name, that I may
drive you out, and that you may perish, you and
the prophets who prophesy to you."
16 Also I spoke to the priests and to all this
people, saying, "Thus says the LORD: 'Do not listen to the words of your prophets who prophesy
to you, saying, "Behold, [a]the vessels of the LORD's
house will now shortly be brought back from Babylon"; for they prophesy a lie to you.
17 'Do not listen to them; serve the king of
Babylon, and live! Why should this city be laid
waste?
18 'But if they *are* prophets, and if the word
of the LORD is with them, let them now make intercession to the LORD of hosts, that the vessels
which are left in the house of the LORD, *in* the
house of the king of Judah, and at Jerusalem, do
not go to Babylon.'
19 "For thus says the LORD of hosts [a]concern-
ing the pillars, concerning the Sea, concerning
the carts, and concerning the remainder of the
vessels that remain in this city,
20 "which Nebuchadnezzar king of Babylon
did not take, when he carried away [a]captive Jeconiah the son of Jehoiakim, king of Judah, from
Jerusalem to Babylon, and all the nobles of Judah
and Jerusalem—
21 "yes, thus says the LORD of hosts, the God
of Israel, concerning the [a]vessels that remain in
the house of the LORD, and in the house of the
king of Judah and of Jerusalem:
22 'They shall be [a]carried to Babylon, and
there they shall be until the day that I [b]visit them,'
says the LORD. 'Then [c]I will bring them up and
restore them to this place.' "

Hananiah's Falsehood and Doom

28 And [a]it happened in the same year, at the
beginning of the reign of Zedekiah king of
Judah, in the [b]fourth year *and* in the fifth month,
that Hananiah the son of [c]Azur the prophet, who
was from Gibeon, spoke to me in the house of
the LORD in the presence of the priests and of all
the people, saying,
2 "Thus speaks the LORD of hosts, the God
of Israel, saying: 'I have broken [a]the yoke of the
king of Babylon.
3 [a]'Within two full years I will bring back
to this place all the vessels of the LORD's house,

KJV

that Nebuchadnezzar king of Babylon [b]took away from this place, and carried them to Babylon:

4 And I will bring again to this place Jeconiah the son of Jehoiakim king of Judah, with all the captives of Judah, that went into Babylon, saith the LORD: for I will break the yoke of the king of Babylon.

5 Then the prophet Jeremiah said unto the prophet Hananiah in the presence of the priests, and in the presence of all the people that stood in the house of the LORD,

6 Even the prophet Jeremiah said, [a]Amen: the LORD do so: the LORD perform thy words which thou hast prophesied, to bring again the vessels of the LORD's house, and all that is carried away captive, from Babylon into this place.

7 Nevertheless hear thou now this word that I speak in thine ears, and in the ears of all the people;

8 The prophets that have been before me and before thee of old prophesied both against many countries, and against great kingdoms, of war, and of evil, and of pestilence.

9 [a]The prophet which prophesieth of [b]peace, when the word of the prophet shall come to pass, *then* shall the prophet be known, that the LORD hath truly sent him.

10 Then Hananiah the prophet took the [a]yoke from off the prophet Jeremiah's neck, and brake it.

11 And Hananiah spake in the presence of all the people, saying, Thus saith the LORD; Even so will I break the yoke of Nebuchadnezzar king of Babylon [a]from the neck of all nations within the space of two full years. And the prophet Jeremiah went his way.

12 Then the word of the LORD came unto Jeremiah *the prophet,* after that Hananiah the prophet had broken the yoke from off the neck of the prophet Jeremiah, saying,

13 Go and tell Hananiah, saying, Thus saith the LORD; Thou hast broken the yokes of wood; but thou shalt make for them yokes of iron.

14 For thus saith the LORD of hosts, the God of Israel; [a]I have put a yoke of iron upon the neck of all these nations, that they may serve Nebuchadnezzar king of Babylon; and they shall serve him: and [b]I have given him the beasts of the field also.

15 Then said the prophet Jeremiah unto Hananiah the prophet, Hear now, Hananiah; The LORD hath not sent thee; but [a]thou makest this people to trust in a [b]lie.

16 Therefore thus saith the LORD; Behold, I will cast thee from off the face of the earth: this year thou shalt [a]die, because thou hast taught [b]rebellion against the LORD.

17 So Hananiah the prophet died the same year in the seventh month.

Jeremiah's Letter to the Captives

29 Now these *are* the words of the letter that Jeremiah the prophet sent from Jerusalem unto the residue of the elders which were [a]carried away captives, and to the priests, and to the prophets, and to all the people whom Nebuchadnezzar had carried away captive from Jerusalem to Babylon;

2 (After that [a]Jeconiah the king, and the [b]queen, and the eunuchs, the princes of Judah and Jerusalem, and the carpenters, and the smiths, were departed from Jerusalem;)

3 By the hand of Elasah the son of [a]Shaphan, and Gemariah the son of Hilkiah, (whom Zedekiah king of Judah sent unto Babylon to Nebuchadnezzar king of Babylon) saying,

4 Thus saith the LORD of hosts, the God of Israel, unto all that are carried away captives, whom I have caused to be carried away from Jerusalem unto Babylon;

3 [b]2 Kin. 24:13; Dan. 1:2
6 [a]1 Kin. 1:36; Ps. 41:13; Jer. 11:5
9 [a]Deut. 18:22 [b]Jer. 23:17; Ezek. 13:10, 16
10 [a]Jer. 27:2
11 [a]Jer. 27:7
14 [a]Deut. 28:48; Jer. 27:7, 8 [b]Jer. 27:6
15 [a]Jer. 20:6; 29:31; Lam. 2:14; Ezek. 13:22; Zech. 13:3 [b]Jer. 27:10; 29:9
16 [a]Jer. 20:6 [b]Deut. 13:5; Jer. 29:32

CHAPTER 29
1 [a]Jer. 27:20
2 [a]2 Kin. 24:12–16; 2 Chr. 36:9, 10; Jer. 22:24–28 [b]2 Kin. 24:12, 15; Jer. 13:18
3 [a]2 Chr. 34:8

NKJV

that Nebuchadnezzar king of Babylon [b]took away from this place and carried to Babylon.

4 'And I will bring back to this place Jeconiah the son of Jehoiakim, king of Judah, with all the captives of Judah who went to Babylon,' says the LORD, 'for I will break the yoke of the king of Babylon.' "

5 Then the prophet Jeremiah spoke to the prophet Hananiah in the presence of the priests and in the presence of all the people who stood in the house of the LORD,

6 and the prophet Jeremiah said, [a]"Amen! The LORD do so; the LORD perform your words which you have prophesied, to bring back the vessels of the LORD's house and all who were carried away captive, from Babylon to this place.

7 "Nevertheless hear now this word that I speak in your hearing and in the hearing of all the people:

8 "The prophets who have been before me and before you of old prophesied against many countries and great kingdoms—of war and disaster and pestilence.

9 "As for [a]the prophet who prophesies of [b]peace, when the word of the prophet comes to pass, the prophet will be known *as* one whom the LORD has truly sent."

10 Then Hananiah the prophet took the [a]yoke off the prophet Jeremiah's neck and broke it.

11 And Hananiah spoke in the presence of all the people, saying, "Thus says the LORD: 'Even so I will break the yoke of Nebuchadnezzar king of Babylon [a]from the neck of all nations within the space of two full years.' " And the prophet Jeremiah went his way.

12 Now the word of the LORD came to Jeremiah, after Hananiah the prophet had broken the yoke from the neck of the prophet Jeremiah, saying,

13 "Go and tell Hananiah, saying, 'Thus says the LORD: "You have broken the yokes of wood, but you have made in their place yokes of iron."

14 'For thus says the LORD of hosts, the God of Israel: [a]"I have put a yoke of iron on the neck of all these nations, that they may serve Nebuchadnezzar king of Babylon; and they shall serve him. [b]I have given him the beasts of the field also." ' "

15 Then the prophet Jeremiah said to Hananiah the prophet, "Hear now, Hananiah, the LORD has not sent you, but [a]you make this people trust in a [b]lie.

16 "Therefore thus says the LORD: 'Behold, I will cast you from the face of the earth. This year you shall [a]die, because you have taught [b]rebellion against the LORD.' "

17 So Hananiah the prophet died the same year in the seventh month.

Jeremiah's Letter to the Captives

29 Now these *are* the words of the letter that Jeremiah the prophet sent from Jerusalem to the remainder of the elders who were [a]carried away captive—to the priests, the prophets, and all the people whom Nebuchadnezzar had carried away captive from Jerusalem to Babylon.

2 (This happened after [a]Jeconiah the king, the [b]queen mother, the eunuchs, the princes of Judah and Jerusalem, the craftsmen, and the smiths had departed from Jerusalem.)

3 *The letter was sent* by the hand of Elasah the son of [a]Shaphan, and Gemariah the son of Hilkiah, whom Zedekiah king of Judah sent to Babylon, to Nebuchadnezzar king of Babylon, saying,

4 Thus says the LORD of hosts, the God of
Israel, to all who were carried away
captive, whom I have caused to be carried
away from Jerusalem to Babylon:

KJV

5 Build ye houses, and dwell *in them;* and
plant gardens, and eat the fruit of them;
6 Take ye wives, and beget sons and daughters; and take wives for your sons, and give your
daughters to husbands, that they may bear sons
and daughters; that ye may be increased there,
and not diminished.
7 And seek the peace of the city whither I
have caused you to be carried away captives, [a]and
pray unto the LORD for it: for in the peace thereof
shall ye have peace.
8 For thus saith the LORD of hosts, the God
of Israel; Let not your prophets and your diviners,
that *be* in the midst of you, [a]deceive you, neither
hearken to your dreams which ye cause to be
dreamed.
9 For they prophesy [a]falsely unto you in my
name: I have not sent them, saith the LORD.
10 For thus saith the LORD, That after [a]sev-
enty years be accomplished at Babylon I will visit
you, and perform my good word toward you, in
causing you to [b]return to this place.
11 For I know the thoughts that I think toward you, saith the LORD, thoughts of peace, and
not of evil, to give you an expected end.
12 Then shall ye [a]call upon me, and ye shall
go and pray unto me, and I will [b]hearken unto
you.
13 And [a]ye shall seek me, and find *me,* when
ye shall search for me [b]with all your heart.
14 And [a]I will be found of you, saith the
LORD: and I will turn away your captivity, and [b]I
will gather you from all the nations, and from all
the places whither I have driven you, saith the
LORD; and I will bring you again into the place
whence I caused you to be carried away captive.
15 Because ye have said, The LORD hath
raised us up prophets in Babylon;
16 [a]*Know* that thus saith the LORD of the king
that sitteth upon the throne of David, and of all
the people that dwelleth in this city, *and* of your
brethren that are not gone forth with you into
captivity;
17 Thus saith the LORD of hosts; Behold, I will
send upon them the sword, the famine, and the
pestilence, and will make them like [a]vile figs, that
cannot be eaten, they are so evil.
18 And I will persecute them with the sword,
with the famine, and with the pestilence, and [a]will
deliver them to be removed to all the kingdoms
of the earth, to be [b]a curse, and an astonishment,
and an hissing, and a reproach, among all the nations whither I have driven them:
19 Because they have not hearkened to my
words, saith the LORD, which [a]I sent unto them
by my servants the prophets, rising up early and
sending *them;* but ye would not hear, saith the
LORD.
20 Hear ye therefore the word of the LORD,
all ye of the captivity, whom I have sent from Jerusalem to Babylon:
21 Thus saith the LORD of hosts, the God of
Israel, of Ahab the son of Kolaiah, and of Zedekiah the son of Maaseiah, which prophesy a [a]lie
unto you in my name; Behold, I will deliver them
into the hand of Nebuchadrezzar king of Babylon;
and he shall slay them before your eyes;
22 [a]And of them shall be taken up a curse
by all the captivity of Judah which *are* in Babylon,
saying, The LORD make thee like Zedekiah and
like Ahab, [b]whom the king of Babylon roasted
in the fire;
23 Because [a]they have committed villany in
Israel, and have committed adultery with their
neighbours' wives, and have spoken lying words

7 [a]Ezra 6:10; Neh. 1:4–11; Dan. 9:16; 1 Tim. 2:2
8 [a]Jer. 14:14; 23:21; 27:14, 15; Eph. 5:6
9 [a]Jer. 28:15; 37:19
10 [a]2 Chr. 36:21–23; Ezra 1:1–4; Jer. 25:12; 27:22; Dan. 9:2; Zech. 7:5 [b][Jer. 24:6, 7]; Zeph. 2:7
12 [a]Ps. 50:15; Jer. 33:3; Dan. 9:3 [b]Ps. 145:19
13 [a]Lev. 26:39–42; Deut. 30:1–3 [b]1 Chr. 22:19; 2 Chr. 22:9; Jer. 24:7
14 [a][Deut. 4:7]; Ps. 32:6; 46:1; [Is. 55:6, 7]; Jer. 24:7 [b]Is. 43:5, 6; Jer. 23:8; 32:37
16 [a]Jer. 38:2, 3, 17–23
17 [a]Jer. 24:3, 8–10
18 [a]Deut. 28:25; 2 Chr. 29:8; Jer. 15:4; 24:9; 34:17; Ezek. 12:15 [b]Jer. 26:6; 42:18
19 [a]Jer. 25:4; 26:5; 35:15
21 [a]Jer. 14:14, 15; Lam. 2:14; 2 Pet. 2:1
22 [a]Gen. 48:20; Is. 65:15 [b]Dan. 3:6, 21
23 [a]Jer. 23:14

NKJV

5 Build houses and dwell *in them;* plant
gardens and eat their fruit.
6 Take wives and beget sons and daughters;
and take wives for your sons and give
your daughters to husbands, so that they
may bear sons and daughters—that you
may be increased there, and not
diminished.
7 And seek the peace of the city where I
have caused you to be carried away
captive, [a]and pray to the LORD for it; for
in its peace you will have peace.
8 For thus says the LORD of hosts, the God
of Israel: Do not let your prophets and
your diviners who are in your midst
[a]deceive you, nor listen to your dreams
which you cause to be dreamed.
9 For they prophesy [a]falsely to you in My
name; I have not sent them, says the LORD.
10 For thus says the LORD: After [a]seventy
years are completed at Babylon, I will visit
you and perform My good word toward
you, and cause you to [b]return to this place.
11 For I know the thoughts that I think
toward you, says the LORD, thoughts of
peace and not of evil, to give you a future
and a hope.
12 Then you will [a]call upon Me and go and
pray to Me, and I will [b]listen to you.
13 And [a]you will seek Me and find *Me,* when
you search for Me [b]with all your heart.
14 [a]I will be found by you, says the LORD,
and I will bring you back from your
captivity; [b]I will gather you from all the
nations and from all the places where I
have driven you, says the LORD, and I will
bring you to the place from which I cause
you to be carried away captive.
15 Because you have said, "The LORD has
raised up prophets for us in Babylon"—
16 [a]therefore thus says the LORD concerning
the king who sits on the throne of David,
concerning all the people who dwell in
this city, and concerning your brethren
who have not gone out with you into
captivity—
17 thus says the LORD of hosts: Behold, I will
send on them the sword, the famine, and
the pestilence, and will make them like
[a]rotten figs that cannot be eaten, they are
so bad.
18 And I will pursue them with the sword,
with famine, and with pestilence; and I
[a]will deliver them to trouble among all the
kingdoms of the earth—to be [b]a curse, an
astonishment, a hissing, and a reproach
among all the nations where I have driven
them,
19 because they have not heeded My words,
says the LORD, which [a]I sent to them by
My servants the prophets, rising up early
and sending *them;* neither would you
heed, says the LORD.
20 Therefore hear the word of the LORD, all
you of the captivity, whom I have sent
from Jerusalem to Babylon.
21 Thus says the LORD of hosts, the God of
Israel, concerning Ahab the son of
Kolaiah, and Zedekiah the son of
Maaseiah, who prophesy a [a]lie to you in
My name: Behold, I will deliver them into
the hand of Nebuchadnezzar king of
Babylon, and he shall slay them before
your eyes.
22 [a]And because of them a curse shall be
taken up by all the captivity of Judah who
are in Babylon, saying, "The LORD make
you like Zedekiah and Ahab, [b]whom the
king of Babylon roasted in the fire";
23 because [a]they have done disgraceful
things in Israel, have committed adultery
with their neighbors' wives, and have

KJV

in my name, which I have not commanded them;
even I [b]know, and *am* a witness, saith the LORD.
24 *Thus* shalt thou also speak to Shemaiah
the Nehelamite, saying,
25 Thus speaketh the LORD of hosts, the God
of Israel, saying, Because thou hast sent letters
in thy name unto all the people that *are* at Jerusalem, [a]and to Zephaniah the son of Maaseiah the
priest, and to all the priests, saying,
26 The LORD hath made thee priest in the
stead of Jehoiada the priest, that ye should be
[a]officers in the house of the LORD, for every man
that is [b]mad, and maketh himself a prophet, that
thou shouldest [c]put him in prison, and in the
stocks.
27 Now therefore why hast thou not reproved
Jeremiah of Anathoth, which maketh himself a
prophet to you?
28 For therefore he sent unto us *in* Babylon,
saying, This *captivity is* long: build ye houses,
and dwell *in them;* and plant gardens, and eat
the fruit of them.
29 And Zephaniah the priest read this letter
in the ears of Jeremiah the prophet.
30 Then came the word of the LORD unto
Jeremiah, saying,
31 Send to all them of the captivity, saying,
Thus saith the LORD concerning Shemaiah the Nehelamite; Because that Shemaiah hath prophesied
unto you, [a]and I sent him not, and he caused you
to trust in a [b]lie:
32 Therefore thus saith the LORD; Behold, I
will punish Shemaiah the Nehelamite, and his
seed: he shall not have a man to dwell among
this people; neither shall he behold the good that
I will do for my people, saith the LORD; [a]because
he hath taught rebellion against the LORD.

23 [b][Prov. 5:21; Jer. 16:17]; Mal. 3:5; [Heb. 4:13]
25 [a]2 Kin. 25:18; Jer. 21:1
26 [a]Jer. 20:1 [b]2 Kin. 9:11; Hos. 9:7; Mark 3:21; John 10:20; Acts 26:24; [2 Cor. 5:13] [c]Jer. 20:1, 2; Acts 16:24
31 [a]Jer. 28:15 [b]Ezek. 13:8–16, 22, 23
32 [a]Jer. 28:16

NKJV

spoken lying words in My name, which I
have not commanded them. Indeed I
[b]know, and *am* a witness, says the LORD.

24 You shall also speak to Shemaiah the
Nehelamite, saying,
25 Thus speaks the LORD of hosts, the God
of Israel, saying: You have sent letters in
your name to all the people who *are* at
Jerusalem, [a]to Zephaniah the son of
Maaseiah the priest, and to all the priests,
saying,
26 "The LORD has made you priest instead
of Jehoiada the priest, so that there should
be [a]officers *in* the house of the LORD over
every man *who* is [b]demented and
considers himself a prophet, that you
should [c]put him in prison and in the
stocks.
27 Now therefore, why have you not rebuked
Jeremiah of Anathoth who makes himself
a prophet to you?
28 For he has sent to us *in* Babylon, saying,
'This *captivity is* long; build houses and
dwell *in them,* and plant gardens and eat
their fruit.' "
29 Now Zephaniah the priest read this letter
in the hearing of Jeremiah the prophet.
30 Then the word of the LORD came to
Jeremiah, saying:
31 Send to all those in captivity, saying, Thus
says the LORD concerning Shemaiah the
Nehelamite: Because Shemaiah has
prophesied to you, [a]and I have not sent
him, and he has caused you to trust in a
[b]lie—
32 therefore thus says the LORD: Behold, I
will punish Shemaiah the Nehelamite and
his family: he shall not have anyone to
dwell among this people, nor shall he see
the good that I will do for My people, says
the LORD, [a]because he has taught rebellion
against the LORD.

Restoration of Israel and Judah

30 The word that came to Jeremiah from the
LORD, saying,
2 Thus speaketh the LORD God of Israel, saying, Write thee all the words that I have spoken
unto thee in a book.
3 For, lo, the days come, saith the LORD, that
[a]I will bring again the captivity of my people Israel and Judah, saith the LORD: [b]and I will cause
them to return to the land that I gave to their fathers, and they shall possess it.
4 And these *are* the words that the LORD
spake concerning Israel and concerning Judah.
5 For thus saith the LORD; We have heard
a voice of trembling, of fear, and not of peace.
6 Ask ye now, and see whether a man doth
travail with child? wherefore do I see every man
with his hands on his loins, [a]as a woman in travail, and all faces are turned into paleness?
7 [a]Alas! for that day *is* great, [b]so that none
is like it: it *is* even the time of Jacob's trouble;
but he shall be saved out of it.
8 For it shall come to pass in that day, saith
the LORD of hosts, *that* I will break his yoke from
off thy neck, and will burst thy bonds, and strangers shall no more serve themselves of him:
9 But they shall serve the LORD their God,
and [a]David their king, whom I will [b]raise up unto
them.

CHAPTER 30
3 [a]Ps. 53:6; Jer. 29:14; 30:18; 32:44; Ezek. 39:25; Amos 9:14; Zeph. 3:20 [b]Jer. 16:15; Ezek. 20:42; 36:24
6 [a]Jer. 4:31; 6:24
7 [a][Is. 2:12]; Hos. 1:11; Joel 2:11; Amos 5:18; Zeph. 1:14 [b]Lam. 1:12; Dan. 9:12; 12:1
9 [a]Is. 55:3; Ezek. 34:23; 37:24; Hos. 3:5 [b][Luke 1:69; Acts 2:30; 13:23]

Restoration of Israel and Judah

30 The word that came to Jeremiah from the
LORD, saying,
2 "Thus speaks the LORD God of Israel, saying: 'Write in a book for yourself all the words
that I have spoken to you.
3 'For behold, the days are coming,' says the
LORD, 'that [a]I will bring back from captivity My
people Israel and Judah,' says the LORD. [b]'And I
will cause them to return to the land that I gave
to their fathers, and they shall possess it.' "
4 Now these *are* the words that the LORD
spoke concerning Israel and Judah.
5 "For thus says the LORD:

'We have heard a voice of trembling,
Of fear, and not of peace.
6 Ask now, and see,
Whether a man is ever in labor with
child?
So why do I see every man *with* his hands
on his loins
[a]Like a woman in labor,
And all faces turned pale?
7 [a]Alas! For that day *is* great,
[b]So that none *is* like it;
And it *is* the time of Jacob's trouble,
But he shall be saved out of it.

8 'For it shall come to pass in that day,'
Says the LORD of hosts,
'*That* I will break his yoke from your
neck,
And will burst your bonds;
Foreigners shall no more enslave them.
9 But they shall serve the LORD their God,
And [a]David their king,
Whom I will [b]raise up for them.

KJV

10 Therefore [a]fear thou not, O my servant
Jacob, saith the LORD; neither be dismayed, O Israel: for, lo, I will save thee from afar, and thy
seed [b]from the land of their captivity; and Jacob
shall return, and shall be in rest, and be quiet,
and none shall make *him* afraid.
11 For I *am* with [a]thee, saith the LORD, to save
thee: [b]though I make a full end of all nations
whither I have scattered thee, [c]yet will I not make
a full end of thee: but I will correct thee [d]in measure, and will not leave thee altogether unpunished.
12 For thus saith the LORD, [a]Thy bruise *is* incurable, *and* thy wound *is* grievous.
13 *There is* none to plead thy cause, that thou
mayest be bound up: [a]thou hast no healing
medicines.
14 [a]All thy lovers have forgotten thee; they
seek thee not; for I have wounded thee with the
wound [b]of an enemy, with the chastisement [c]of
a cruel one, for the multitude of thine iniquity;
[d]*because* thy sins were increased.
15 Why [a]criest thou for thine affliction? thy
sorrow *is* incurable for the multitude of thine iniquity: *because* thy sins were increased, I have
done these things unto thee.
16 Therefore all they that devour thee [a]shall
be devoured; and all thine adversaries, every one
of them, shall go into [b]captivity; and they that
spoil thee shall be a [c]spoil, and all that prey upon
thee will I give for a [d]prey.
17 [a]For I will restore health unto thee, and I
will heal thee of thy wounds, saith the LORD; because they called thee an Outcast, *saying*, This *is*
Zion, whom no man seeketh after.
18 Thus saith the LORD; Behold, I will bring
again the captivity of Jacob's tents, and [a]have
mercy on his dwellingplaces; and the city shall
be builded upon her own heap, and the palace
shall remain after the manner thereof.
19 And [a]out of them shall proceed thanksgiving and the voice of them that make merry:
[b]and I will multiply them, and they shall not be
few; I will also glorify them, and they shall not
be small.
20 Their children also shall be [a]as aforetime,
and their congregation shall be established before
me, and I will punish all that oppress them.
21 And their nobles shall be of themselves,
[a]and their governor shall proceed from the midst
of them; and I will [b]cause him to draw near, and
he shall approach unto me: for who *is* this that
engaged his heart to approach unto me? saith the
LORD.
22 And ye shall be [a]my people, and I will be
your God.

10 [a]Is. 41:13; 43:5; 44:2; Jer. 46:27, 28 [b]Jer. 3:18
11 [a][Is. 43:2–5] [b]Amos 9:8 [c]Jer. 4:27; 46:27, 28 [d]Ps. 6:1; Is. 27:8; Jer. 10:24; 46:28
12 [a]2 Chr. 36:16; Jer. 15:18
13 [a]Jer. 8:22
14 [a]Jer. 22:20, 22; Lam. 1:2 [b]Job 13:24; 16:9; 19:11 [c]Job 30:21 [d]Jer. 5:6
15 [a]Jer. 15:18
16 [a]Ex. 23:22; Is. 41:11; Jer. 10:25 [b]Is. 14:2; Joel 3:8 [c]Is. 33:1; Ezek. 39:10 [d]Jer. 2:3
17 [a]Ex. 15:26; Ps. 107:20; Is. 30:26; Jer. 33:6
18 [a]Ps. 102:13
19 [a]Ps. 126:1, 2; Is. 51:11; Jer. 31:4; Zeph. 3:14 [b]Is. 49:19–21; Jer. 23:3; 33:22; Zech. 10:8
20 [a]Is. 1:26
21 [a]Gen. 49:10 [b]Num. 16:5; Ps. 65:4
22 [a]Ex. 6:7; Jer. 32:38; Ezek. 36:28; Hos. 2:23; Zech. 13:9

NKJV

10 'Therefore [a]do not fear, O My servant
Jacob,' says the LORD,
'Nor be dismayed, O Israel;
For behold, I will save you from afar,
And your seed [b]from the land of their captivity.
Jacob shall return, have rest and be quiet,
And no one shall make *him* afraid.
11 For I *am* with [a]you,' says the LORD, 'to save you;
[b]Though I make a full end of all nations
where I have scattered you,
[c]Yet I will not make a complete end of you.
But I will correct you [d]in justice,
And will not let you go altogether unpunished.'

12 "For thus says the LORD:

[a]'Your affliction *is* incurable,
Your wound *is* severe.
13 *There is* no one to plead your cause,
That you may be bound up;
[a]You have no healing medicines.
14 [a]All your lovers have forgotten you;
They do not seek you;
For I have wounded you with the wound [b]of an enemy,
With the chastisement [c]of a cruel one,
For the multitude of your iniquities,
[d]*Because* your sins have increased.
15 Why [a]do you cry about your affliction?
Your sorrow *is* incurable.
Because of the multitude of your iniquities,
Because your sins have increased,
I have done these things to you.

16 'Therefore all those who devour you [a]shall be devoured;
And all your adversaries, every one of them, shall go into [b]captivity;
Those who plunder you shall become [c]plunder,
And all who prey upon you I will make a [d]prey.
17 [a]For I will restore health to you
And heal you of your wounds,' says the LORD,
'Because they called you an outcast *saying:*
"This *is* Zion;
No one seeks her." '

18 "Thus says the LORD:

'Behold, I will bring back the captivity of Jacob's tents,
And [a]have mercy on his dwelling places;
The city shall be built upon its own mound,
And the palace shall remain according to its own plan.
19 Then [a]out of them shall proceed thanksgiving
And the voice of those who make merry;
[b]I will multiply them, and they shall not diminish;
I will also glorify them, and they shall not be small.
20 Their children also shall be [a]as before,
And their congregation shall be established before Me;
And I will punish all who oppress them.
21 Their nobles shall be from among them,
[a]And their governor shall come from their midst;
Then I will [b]cause him to draw near,
And he shall approach Me;
For who *is* this who pledged his heart to approach Me?' says the LORD.
22 'You shall be [a]My people,
And I will be your God.' "

KJV

23 Behold, the [a]whirlwind of the LORD goeth forth with fury, a continuing whirlwind: it shall fall with pain upon the head of the wicked.

24 The fierce anger of the LORD shall not return, until he have done *it*, and until he have performed the intents of his heart: [a]in the latter days ye shall consider it.

The Remnant of Israel Saved

31 At [a]the same time, saith the LORD, [b]will I be the God of all the families of Israel, and they shall be my people.

2 Thus saith the LORD, The people *which were* left of the sword found grace in the wilderness; *even* Israel, when [a]I went to cause him to rest.

3 The LORD hath appeared of old unto me, *saying*, Yea, [a]I have loved thee with [b]an everlasting love: therefore with lovingkindness have I [c]drawn thee.

4 Again [a]I will build thee, and thou shalt be built, O virgin of Israel: thou shalt again be adorned with thy [b]tabrets, and shalt go forth in the dances of them that make merry.

5 [a]Thou shalt yet plant vines upon the mountains of Samaria: the planters shall plant, and shall eat *them* as common things.

6 For there shall be a day, *that* the watchmen upon the mount Ephraim shall cry, [a]Arise ye, and let us go up to Zion unto the LORD our God.

7 For thus saith the LORD: [a]Sing with gladness for Jacob, and shout among the chief of the nations: publish ye, praise ye, and say, O LORD, save thy people, the remnant of Israel.

8 Behold, I will bring them [a]from the north country, and [b]gather them from the coasts of the earth, *and* with them the blind and the lame, the woman with child and her that travaileth with child together: a great company shall return thither.

9 [a]They shall come with weeping, and with supplications will I lead them: I will cause them to walk [b]by the rivers of waters in a straight way, wherein they shall not stumble: for I am a father to Israel, and Ephraim *is* my [c]firstborn.

10 Hear the word of the LORD, O ye nations, and declare *it* in the isles afar off, and say, He that scattered Israel [a]will gather him, and keep him, as a shepherd *doth* his flock.

11 For [a]the LORD hath redeemed Jacob, and ransomed him [b]from the hand of *him that was* stronger than he.

12 Therefore they shall come and sing in [a]the height of Zion, and shall flow together to [b]the goodness of the LORD, for wheat, and for wine,

23 [a]Jer. 23:19, 20; 25:32
24 [a]Gen. 49:1

CHAPTER 31

1 [a]Jer. 30:24 [b]Jer. 30:22
2 [a]Ex. 33:14; Num. 10:33; Deut. 1:33; Josh. 1:13; Ps. 95:11; Is. 63:14
3 [a]Deut. 4:37; 7:8; Mal. 1:2 [b]Is. 43:4; Rom. 11:28 [c]Hos. 11:4
4 [a]Jer. 33:7 [b]Ex. 15:20; Judg. 11:34; Ps. 149:3
5 [a]Ps. 107:37; Is. 65:21; Ezek. 28:26; Amos 9:14
6 [a][Is. 2:3; Jer. 31:12; 50:4, 5; Mic. 4:2]
7 [a]Is. 12:5, 6
8 [a]Jer. 3:12, 18; 23:8 [b]Deut. 30:4; Is. 43:6; Ezek. 20:34, 41; 34:13
9 [a][Ps. 126:5; Jer. 50:4] [b]Is. 35:8; 43:19; 49:10, 11 [c]Ex. 4:22
10 [a]Is. 40:11; Ezek. 34:12–14
11 [a]Is. 44:23; 48:20; Jer. 15:21; 50:19 [b]Is. 49:24
12 [a]Ezek. 17:23 [b]Hos. 3:5

NKJV

23 Behold, the [a]whirlwind of the LORD
Goes forth with fury,
A continuing whirlwind;
It will fall violently on the head of the wicked.
24 The fierce anger of the LORD will not return until He has done it,
And until He has performed the intents of His heart.
[a]In the latter days you will consider it.

The Remnant of Israel Saved

31 "At [a]the same time," says the LORD, [b]"I will be the God of all the families of Israel, and they shall be My people."

2 Thus says the LORD:

"The people who survived the sword
Found grace in the wilderness—
Israel, when [a]I went to give him rest."

3 The LORD has appeared of old to me, *saying:*
"Yes, [a]I have loved you with [b]an everlasting love;
Therefore with lovingkindness I have [c]drawn you.
4 Again [a]I will build you, and you shall be rebuilt,
O virgin of Israel!
You shall again be adorned with your [b]tambourines,
And shall go forth in the dances of those who rejoice.
5 [a]You shall yet plant vines on the mountains of Samaria;
The planters shall plant and eat *them* as ordinary food.
6 For there shall be a day
When the watchmen will cry on Mount Ephraim,
[a]'Arise, and let us go up *to* Zion,
To the LORD our God.' "

7 For thus says the LORD:

[a]"Sing with gladness for Jacob,
And shout among the chief of the nations;
Proclaim, give praise, and say,
O LORD, save Your people,
The remnant of Israel!'
8 Behold, I will bring them [a]from the north country,
And [b]gather them from the ends of the earth,
Among them the blind and the lame,
The woman with child
And the one who labors with child, together;
A great throng shall return there.
9 [a]They shall come with weeping,
And with supplications I will lead them.
I will cause them to walk [b]by the rivers of waters,
In a straight way in which they shall not stumble;
For I am a Father to Israel,
And Ephraim *is* My [c]firstborn.

10 "Hear the word of the LORD, O nations,
And declare *it* in the isles afar off, and say,
He who scattered Israel [a]will gather him,
And keep him as a shepherd *does* his flock.'
11 For [a]the LORD has redeemed Jacob,
And ransomed him [b]from the hand of one stronger than he.
12 Therefore they shall come and sing in [a]the height of Zion,
Streaming to [b]the goodness of the LORD—

KJV

and for oil, and for the young of the flock and of
the herd: and their soul shall be as a [c]watered
garden; [d]and they shall not sorrow any more at
all.
13 Then shall the virgin rejoice in the dance,
both young men and old together: for I will turn
their mourning into joy, and will comfort them,
and make them rejoice from their sorrow.
14 And I will satiate the soul of the priests
with fatness, and my people shall be satisfied with
my goodness, saith the LORD.

Mercy on Ephraim

15 Thus saith the LORD; [a]A voice was heard
in [b]Ramah, lamentation, *and* bitter [c]weeping; Ra-
hel weeping for her children refused to be comforted for her children, because [d]they *were* not.
16 Thus saith the LORD; Refrain thy voice
from [a]weeping, and thine eyes from tears: for thy
work shall be rewarded, saith the LORD; and they
shall come again from the land of the enemy.
17 And there is [a]hope in thine end, saith the
LORD, that thy children shall come again to their
own border.
18 I have surely heard Ephraim bemoaning
himself *thus;* Thou hast [a]chastised me, and I was
chastised, as a bullock unaccustomed *to the yoke:*
[b]turn thou me, and I shall be turned; for thou *art*
the LORD my God.
19 Surely [a]after that I was turned, I repented;
and after that I was instructed, I smote upon *my*
thigh: I was [b]ashamed, yea, even confounded, because I did bear the reproach of my youth.
20 *Is* Ephraim my dear son? *is he* a pleasant
child? for since I spake against him, I do earnestly
remember him still: [a]therefore my bowels are
troubled for him; [b]I will surely have mercy upon
him, saith the LORD.
21 Set thee up waymarks, make thee high
heaps: [a]set thine heart toward the highway, *even*
the way *which* thou wentest: turn again, O virgin
of Israel, turn again to these thy cities.
22 How long wilt thou [a]go about, O thou
[b]backsliding daughter? for the LORD hath created
a new thing in the earth, A woman shall compass
a man.

Future Prosperity of Judah

23 Thus saith the LORD of hosts, the God of
Israel; As yet they shall use this speech in the
land of Judah and in the cities thereof, when I
shall bring again their captivity; [a]The LORD bless
thee, O habitation of justice, *and* [b]mountain of
holiness.
24 And there shall dwell in Judah itself, and
[a]in all the cities thereof together, husbandmen,
and they *that* go forth with flocks.
25 For I have satiated the weary soul, and I
have replenished every sorrowful soul.

12 [c]Is. 58:11 [d]Is. 35:10; 65:19; [John 16:22; Rev. 21:4]
15 [a]Matt. 2:17, 18 [b]Josh. 18:25; Judg. 4:5; Is. 10:29; Jer. 40:1 [c]Gen. 37:35 [d]Jer. 10:20
16 [a][Is. 25:8; 30:19]
17 [a]Jer. 29:11
18 [a]Job 5:17; Ps. 94:12 [b]Ps. 80:3, 7, 19; Jer. 17:4; Lam. 5:21; [Acts 3:26]
19 [a]Deut. 30:2 [b]Ezek. 36:31; [Zech. 12:10]
20 [a]Gen. 43:30; Deut. 32:36; Judg. 10:16; Is. 63:15; Hos. 11:8 [b]Is. 57:18; Jer. 3:12; 12:15; [Hos. 14:4]; Mic. 7:18
21 [a]Jer. 50:5
22 [a]Jer. 2:18, 23, 36 [b]Jer. 3:6, 8, 11, 12, 14, 22
23 [a]Ps. 122:5–8; Is. 1:26 [b][Zech. 8:3]
24 [a]Jer. 33:12

NKJV

For wheat and new wine and oil,
For the young of the flock and the herd;
Their souls shall be like a [c]well-watered
garden,
[d]And they shall sorrow no more at all.

13 "Then shall the virgin rejoice in the dance,
And the young men and the old, together;
For I will turn their mourning to joy,
Will comfort them,
And make them rejoice rather than
sorrow.
14 I will satiate the soul of the priests with
abundance,
And My people shall be satisfied with My
goodness, says the LORD."

Mercy on Ephraim

15 Thus says the LORD:

[a]"A voice was heard in [b]Ramah,
Lamentation *and* bitter [c]weeping,
Rachel weeping for her children,
Refusing to be comforted for her children,
Because [d]they *are* no more."

16 Thus says the LORD:

"Refrain your voice from [a]weeping,
And your eyes from tears;
For your work shall be rewarded, says the
LORD,
And they shall come back from the land
of the enemy.
17 There is [a]hope in your future, says the
LORD,
That *your* children shall come back to
their own border.

18 "I have surely heard Ephraim bemoaning
himself:
'You have [a]chastised me, and I was
chastised,
Like an untrained bull;
[b]Restore me, and I will return,
For You *are* the LORD my God.
19 Surely, [a]after my turning, I repented;
And after I was instructed, I struck myself
on the thigh;
I was [b]ashamed, yes, even humiliated,
Because I bore the reproach of my
youth.'
20 *Is* Ephraim My dear son?
Is he a pleasant child?
For though I spoke against him,
I earnestly remember him still;
[a]Therefore My heart yearns for him;
[b]I will surely have mercy on him, says the
LORD.

21 "Set up signposts,
Make landmarks;
[a]Set your heart toward the highway,
The way in *which* you went.
Turn back, O virgin of Israel,
Turn back to these your cities.
22 How long will you [a]gad about,
O you [b]backsliding daughter?
For the LORD has created a new thing in
the earth—
A woman shall encompass a man."

Future Prosperity of Judah

23 Thus says the LORD of hosts, the God of
Israel: "They shall again use this speech in the
land of Judah and in its cities, when I bring back
their captivity: [a]'The LORD bless you, O home of
justice, *and* [b]mountain of holiness!'
24 "And there shall dwell in Judah itself, and
[a]in all its cities together, farmers and those going
out with flocks.
25 "For I have satiated the weary soul, and
I have replenished every sorrowful soul."

KJV

26 Upon this I awaked, and beheld; and my
sleep was [a]sweet unto me.
27 Behold, the days come, saith the LORD,
that [a]I will sow the house of Israel and the house
of Judah with the seed of man, and with the seed
of beast.
28 And it shall come to pass, *that* like as I
have [a]watched over them, [b]to pluck up, and to
break down, and to throw down, and to destroy,
and to afflict; so will I watch over them, [c]to build,
and to plant, saith the LORD.
29 [a]In those days they shall say no more, The
fathers have eaten a sour grape, and the children's
teeth are set on edge.
30 [a]But every one shall die for his own iniquity: every man that eateth the sour grape, his
teeth shall be set on edge.

A New Covenant

31 Behold, the [a]days come, saith the LORD,
that I will make a new covenant with the house
of Israel, and with the house of Judah:
32 Not according to the covenant that I made
with their fathers in the day *that* [a]I took them
by the hand to bring them out of the land of Egypt;
which my covenant they brake, although I was
an husband unto them, saith the LORD:
33 [a]But this *shall be* the covenant that I will
make with the house of Israel; After those days,
saith the LORD, [b]I will put my law in their inward
parts, and write it in their hearts; [c]and will be
their God, and they shall be my people.
34 And they shall teach no more every man
his neighbour, and every man his brother, saying,
Know the LORD: for [a]they shall all know me, from
the least of them unto the greatest of them, saith
the LORD: for [b]I will forgive their iniquity, and I
will remember their sin no more.
35 Thus saith the LORD, [a]which giveth the sun
for a light by day, *and* the ordinances of the moon
and of the stars for a light by night, which divideth
[b]the sea when the waves thereof roar; [c]The LORD
of hosts *is* his name:
36 [a]If those ordinances depart from before
me, saith the LORD, *then* the seed of Israel also
shall cease from being a nation before me for ever.
37 Thus saith the LORD; [a]If heaven above can
be measured, and the foundations of the earth
searched out beneath, I will also [b]cast off all the
seed of Israel for all that they have done, saith
the LORD.
38 Behold, the days come, saith the LORD,
that the city shall be built to the LORD [a]from the
tower of Hananeel unto the gate of the corner.
39 And [a]the measuring line shall yet go forth
over against it upon the hill Gareb, and shall compass about to Goath.
40 And the whole valley of the dead bodies,
and of the ashes, and all the fields unto the brook
of Kidron, [a]unto the corner of the horse gate toward the east, [b]*shall be* holy unto the LORD; it
shall not be plucked up, nor thrown down any
more for ever.

Jeremiah Buys a Field

32 The word that came to Jeremiah from the
LORD [a]in the tenth year of Zedekiah king
of Judah, which *was* the eighteenth year of
Nebuchadrezzar.
2 For then the king of Babylon's army besieged Jerusalem: and Jeremiah the prophet was

26 [a]Prov. 3:24
27 [a]Ezek. 36:9–11; Hos. 2:23
28 [a]Jer. 44:27; Dan. 9:14 [b]Jer. 1:10; 18:7 [c]Jer. 24:6
29 [a]Lam. 5:7; Ezek. 18:2, 3
30 [a]Deut. 24:16; 2 Chr. 25:4; Is. 3:11; [Ezek. 18:4, 20; Gal. 6:5, 7]
31 [a]Jer. 32:40; 33:14; Ezek. 37:26; Heb. 8:8–12; 10:16, 17
32 [a]Deut. 1:31; Is. 63:12
33 [a]Jer. 32:40; Heb. 10:16 [b]Ps. 40:8; [Ezek. 11:19; 36:26, 27; 2 Cor. 3:3] [c]Jer. 24:7; 30:22; 32:38
34 [a]Is. 11:9; 54:13; Jer. 24:7; Hab. 2:14; [John 6:45; 1 Cor. 2:10; 1 John 2:20] [b]Jer. 33:8; 50:20; Mic. 7:18; [Acts 10:43; 13:39; Rom. 11:27]
35 [a]Gen. 1:14–18; Deut. 4:19; Ps. 72:5, 17; 89:2, 36; 119:91 [b]Is. 51:15 [c]Jer. 10:16
36 [a]Ps. 148:6; Is. 54:9, 10; Jer. 33:20
37 [a]Is. 40:12; Jer. 33:22 [b]Jer. 33:24–26; [Rom. 11:2–5, 26, 27]
38 [a]Neh. 3:1; 12:39; Zech. 14:10
39 [a]Ezek. 40:8; Zech. 2:1, 2
40 [a]2 Kin. 11:16; 2 Chr. 23:15; Neh. 3:28 [b][Joel 3:17]; Zech. 14:20

CHAPTER 32

1 [a]2 Kin. 25:1, 2; Jer. 39:1, 2

*———

31:32 So with MT, Tg., Vg.; LXX, Syr. *and I turned away from them*

NKJV

26 After this I awoke and looked around, and
my sleep was [a]sweet to me.
27 "Behold, the days are coming, says the
LORD, that [a]I will sow the house of Israel and the
house of Judah with the seed of man and the seed
of beast.
28 "And it shall come to pass, *that* as I have
[a]watched over them [b]to pluck up, to break down,
to throw down, to destroy, and to afflict, so I will
watch over them [c]to build and to plant, says the
LORD.
29 [a]"In those days they shall say no more:

'The fathers have eaten sour grapes,
And the children's teeth are set on edge.'

30 [a]"But every one shall die for his own iniquity; every man who eats the sour grapes, his
teeth shall be set on edge.

A New Covenant

31 "Behold, the [a]days are coming, says the
LORD, when I will make a new covenant with the
house of Israel and with the house of Judah—
32 "not according to the covenant that I made
with their fathers in the day *that* [a]I took them
by the hand to lead them out of the land of Egypt,
My covenant which they broke, *though I was a
husband to them, says the LORD.
33 [a]"But this *is* the covenant that I will make
with the house of Israel after those days, says the
LORD: [b]I will put My law in their minds, and write
it on their hearts; [c]and I will be their God, and
they shall be My people.
34 "No more shall every man teach his neighbor, and every man his brother, saying, 'Know
the LORD,' for [a]they all shall know Me, from the
least of them to the greatest of them, says the
LORD. For [b]I will forgive their iniquity, and their
sin I will remember no more."

35 Thus says the LORD,
[a]Who gives the sun for a light by day,
The ordinances of the moon and the stars
for a light by night,
Who disturbs [b]the sea,
And its waves roar
[c](The LORD of hosts *is* His name):

36 "If [a]those ordinances depart
From before Me, says the LORD,
Then the seed of Israel shall also cease
From being a nation before Me forever."

37 Thus says the LORD:

[a]"If heaven above can be measured,
And the foundations of the earth searched
out beneath,
I will also [b]cast off all the seed of Israel
For all that they have done, says the LORD.

38 "Behold, the days are coming, says the
LORD, that the city shall be built for the LORD
[a]from the Tower of Hananel to the Corner Gate.
39 [a]"The surveyor's line shall again extend
straight forward over the hill Gareb; then it shall
turn toward Goath.
40 "And the whole valley of the dead bodies
and of the ashes, and all the fields as far as the
Brook Kidron, [a]to the corner of the Horse Gate
toward the east, [b]*shall be* holy to the LORD. It shall
not be plucked up or thrown down anymore forever."

Jeremiah Buys a Field

32 The word that came to Jeremiah from the
LORD [a]in the tenth year of Zedekiah king
of Judah, which was the eighteenth year of
Nebuchadnezzar.
2 For then the king of Babylon's army besieged Jerusalem, and Jeremiah the prophet was

KJV

shut up [a]in the court of the prison, which *was* in the king of Judah's house.

3 For Zedekiah king of Judah had shut him up, saying, Wherefore dost thou [a]prophesy, and say, Thus saith the LORD, [b]Behold, I will give this city into the hand of the king of Babylon, and he shall take it;

4 And Zedekiah king of Judah [a]shall not escape out of the hand of the Chaldeans, but shall surely be delivered into the hand of the king of Babylon, and shall speak with him mouth to mouth, and his eyes shall behold his [b]eyes;

5 And he shall [a]lead Zedekiah to Babylon, and there shall he be [b]until I visit him, saith the LORD: [c]though ye fight with the Chaldeans, ye shall not prosper.

6 And Jeremiah said, The word of the LORD came unto me, saying,

7 Behold, Hanameel the son of Shallum thine uncle shall come unto thee, saying, Buy thee my field that *is* in Anathoth: for the [a]right of redemption *is* thine to buy *it*.

8 So Hanameel mine uncle's son came to me in the court of the prison according to the word of the LORD, and said unto me, Buy my field, I pray thee, that *is* in Anathoth, which *is* in the country of Benjamin: for the right of inheritance *is* thine, and the redemption *is* thine; buy *it* for thyself. Then I knew that this *was* the word of the LORD.

9 And I bought the field of Hanameel my uncle's son, that *was* in Anathoth, and [a]weighed him the money, *even* seventeen shekels of silver.

10 And I subscribed the evidence, and sealed *it*, and took witnesses, and weighed *him* the money in the balances.

11 So I took the evidence of the purchase, *both* that which was sealed *according* to the law and custom, and that which was open:

12 And I gave the evidence of the purchase unto [a]Baruch the son of Neriah, the son of Maaseiah, in the sight of Hanameel mine uncle's *son*, and in the presence of the [b]witnesses that subscribed the book of the purchase, before all the Jews that sat in the court of the prison.

13 And I charged [a]Baruch before them, saying,

14 Thus saith the LORD of hosts, the God of Israel; Take these evidences, this evidence of the purchase, both which is sealed, and this evidence which is open; and put them in an earthen vessel, that they may continue many days.

15 For thus saith the LORD of hosts, the God of Israel; Houses and fields and vineyards shall be [a]possessed again in this land.

Jeremiah Prays for Understanding

16 Now when I had delivered the evidence of the purchase unto Baruch the son of Neriah, I prayed unto the LORD, saying,

17 Ah Lord GOD! behold, [a]thou hast made the heaven and the earth by thy great power and stretched out arm, *and* [b]there is nothing too hard for thee:

18 Thou shewest [a]lovingkindness unto thousands, and recompensest the iniquity of the fathers into the bosom of their children after them: the Great, [b]the Mighty God, [c]the LORD of hosts, *is* his name,

19 [a]Great in counsel, and mighty in work: for thine [b]eyes *are* open upon all the ways of the sons of men: [c]to give every one according to his ways, and according to the fruit of his doings:

20 Which hast set signs and wonders in the land of Egypt, *even* unto this day, and in Israel, and among *other* men; and hast made thee [a]a name, as at this day;

21 And [a]hast brought forth thy people Israel out of the land of Egypt with signs, and with wonders, and with a strong hand, and with a stretched out arm, and with great terror;

22 And hast given them this land, which thou

2 [a]Neh. 3:25; Jer. 33:1; 37:21; 39:14
3 [a]Jer. 26:8, 9 [b]Jer. 21:3–7; 34:2
4 [a]2 Kin. 25:4–7; Jer. 34:3; 38:18, 23; 39:5; 52:9 [b]Jer. 39:5
5 [a]Jer. 27:22; 39:7; Ezek. 12:12, 13 [b]Jer. 27:22 [c]Jer. 21:4; 33:5
7 [a]Lev. 25:24, 25, 32; Ruth 4:4
9 [a]Gen. 23:16; Zech. 11:12
12 [a]Jer. 36:4 [b]Is. 8:2
13 [a]Jer. 36:4
15 [a]Ezra 2:1; [Jer. 31:5, 12, 14]; Amos 9:14, 15; Zech. 3:10
17 [a]2 Kin. 19:15; Ps. 102:25; Is. 40:26–29; Jer. 27:5 [b]Gen. 18:14; Jer. 32:27; Zech. 8:6; Matt. 19:26; Mark 10:27; Luke 18:27
18 [a]Ex. 20:6; 34:7; Deut. 5:9, 10 [b]Ps. 50:1; [Is. 9:6]; Jer. 20:11 [c]Jer. 10:16
19 [a]Is. 28:29 [b]Job 34:21; Ps. 33:13; Prov. 5:21; Jer. 16:17 [c]Ps. 62:12; Jer. 17:10; [Matt. 16:27; John 5:29]
20 [a]Ex. 9:16; 1 Chr. 17:21; Is. 63:12; Jer. 13:11; Dan. 9:15
21 [a]Ex. 6:6; 2 Sam. 7:23; 1 Chr. 17:21; Ps. 136:11, 12

NKJV

shut up [a]in the court of the prison, which *was in* the king of Judah's house.

3 For Zedekiah king of Judah had shut him up, saying, "Why do you [a]prophesy and say, 'Thus says the LORD: [b]"Behold, I will give this city into the hand of the king of Babylon, and he shall take it;

4 "and Zedekiah king of Judah [a]shall not escape from the hand of the Chaldeans, but shall surely be delivered into the hand of the king of Babylon, and shall speak with him *face to face, and see him [b]eye to eye;

5 "then he shall [a]lead Zedekiah to Babylon, and there he shall be [b]until I visit him," says the LORD; [c]"though you fight with the Chaldeans, you shall not succeed" '?"

6 And Jeremiah said, "The word of the LORD came to me, saying,

7 'Behold, Hanamel the son of Shallum your uncle will come to you, saying, "Buy my field which *is* in Anathoth, for the [a]right of redemption *is* yours to buy *it*." '

8 "Then Hanamel my uncle's son came to me in the court of the prison according to the word of the LORD, and said to me, 'Please buy my field that *is* in Anathoth, which *is* in the country of Benjamin; for the right of inheritance *is* yours, and the redemption yours; buy *it* for yourself.' Then I knew that this was the word of the LORD.

9 "So I bought the field from Hanamel, the son of my uncle who *was* in Anathoth, and [a]weighed *out to* him the money—seventeen shekels of silver.

10 "And I signed the deed and sealed *it*, took witnesses, and weighed the money on the scales.

11 "So I took the purchase deed, *both* that which was sealed *according* to the law and custom, and that which was open;

12 "and I gave the purchase deed to [a]Baruch the son of Neriah, son of Mahseiah, in the presence of Hanamel my uncle's *son*, and in the presence of the [b]witnesses who signed the purchase deed, before all the Jews who sat in the court of the prison.

13 "Then I charged [a]Baruch before them, saying,

14 'Thus says the LORD of hosts, the God of Israel: "Take these deeds, both this purchase deed which is sealed and this deed which is open, and put them in an earthen vessel, that they may last many days."

15 'For thus says the LORD of hosts, the God of Israel: "Houses and fields and vineyards shall be [a]possessed again in this land." '

Jeremiah Prays for Understanding

16 "Now when I had delivered the purchase deed to Baruch the son of Neriah, I prayed to the LORD, saying:

17 'Ah, Lord GOD! Behold, [a]You have made the heavens and the earth by Your great power and outstretched arm. [b]There is nothing too hard for You.

18 '*You* show [a]lovingkindness to thousands, and repay the iniquity of the fathers into the bosom of their children after them—the Great, [b]the Mighty God, whose name *is* [c]the LORD of hosts.

19 '*You are* [a]great in counsel and mighty in work, for your [b]eyes *are* open to all the ways of the sons of men, [c]to give everyone according to his ways and according to the fruit of his doings.

20 'You have set signs and wonders in the land of Egypt, to this day, and in Israel and among *other* men; and You have made Yourself [a]a name, as it is this day.

21 'You [a]have brought Your people Israel out of the land of Egypt with signs and wonders, with a strong hand and an outstretched arm, and with great terror;

22 'You have given them this land, of which

*32:4 Lit. *mouth to mouth*

KJV

didst swear to their fathers to give them, [a]a land flowing with milk and honey;

23 And they came in, and possessed it; but [a]they obeyed not thy voice, neither walked in thy law; they have done nothing of all that thou commandedst them to do: therefore thou hast caused all this evil to come upon them:

24 Behold the mounts, they are come unto the city to take it; and the city is given into the hand of the Chaldeans, that fight against it, because of [a]the sword, and of the famine, and of the pestilence: and what thou hast spoken is come to pass; and, behold, thou seest *it*.

25 And thou hast said unto me, O Lord GOD, Buy thee the field for money, and take witnesses; for the city is given into the hand of the Chaldeans.

God's Assurance of the People's Return

26 Then came the word of the LORD unto Jeremiah, saying,

27 Behold, I *am* the LORD, the [a]God of all flesh: is there any thing too hard for me?

28 Therefore thus saith the LORD; Behold, I will give this city into the hand of the Chaldeans, and into the hand of Nebuchadrezzar king of Babylon, and he shall take it:

29 And the Chaldeans, that fight against this city, shall come and [a]set fire on this city, and burn it with the houses, [b]upon whose roofs they have offered incense unto Baal, and poured out drink offerings unto other gods, to provoke me to anger.

30 For the children of Israel and the children of Judah [a]have only done evil before me from their youth: for the children of Israel have only provoked me to anger with the work of their hands, saith the LORD.

31 For this city hath been to me *as* a provocation of mine anger and of my fury from the day that they built it even unto this day; [a]that I should remove it from before my face,

32 Because of all the evil of the children of Israel and of the children of Judah, which they have done to provoke me to anger, [a]they, their kings, their princes, their priests, and [b]their prophets, and the men of Judah, and the inhabitants of Jerusalem.

33 And they have turned unto me the [a]back, and not the face: though I taught them, [b]rising up early and teaching *them*, yet they have not hearkened to receive instruction.

34 But they [a]set their abominations in the house, which is called by my name, to defile it.

35 And they built the high places of Baal, which *are* in the valley of the son of Hinnom, to [a]cause their sons and their daughters to pass through *the fire* unto [b]Molech; [c]which I commanded them not, neither came it into my mind, that they should do this abomination, to cause Judah to sin.

36 And now therefore thus saith the LORD, the God of Israel, concerning this city, whereof ye say, It shall be delivered into the hand of the king of Babylon by the sword, and by the famine, and by the pestilence;

37 Behold, I will [a]gather them out of all countries, whither I have driven them in mine anger, and in my fury, and in great wrath; and I will bring them again unto this place, and I will cause them [b]to dwell safely:

38 And they shall be [a]my people, and I will be their God:

39 And I will [a]give them one heart, and one way, that they may fear me for ever, for the good of them, and of their children after them:

40 And [a]I will make an everlasting covenant with them, that I will not turn away from them, to do them good; but [b]I will put my fear in their hearts, that they shall not depart from me.

41 Yea, [a]I will rejoice over them to do them good, and [b]I will plant them in this land assuredly with my whole heart and with my whole soul.

22 [a]Ex. 3:8, 17; Deut. 1:8; Ps. 105:9–11; Jer. 11:5
23 [a][Neh. 9:26]; Jer. 11:8; [Dan. 9:10–14]
24 [a]Jer. 14:12; Ezek. 14:21
27 [a][Num. 16:22]
29 [a]2 Chr. 36:19; Jer. 21:10; 37:8, 10; 52:13 [b]Jer. 19:13
30 [a]Deut. 9:7–12; Is. 63:10; Jer. 2:7; 3:25; 7:22–26; Ezek. 20:28
31 [a]2 Kin. 23:27; 24:3; Jer. 27:10
32 [a]Ezra 9:7; Is. 1:4, 6; Dan. 9:8 [b]Jer. 23:14
33 [a]Jer. 2:27; 7:24 [b]Jer. 7:13
34 [a]2 Kin. 21:1–7; Jer. 7:10–12, 30; 23:11; Ezek. 8:5, 6
35 [a]2 Chr. 28:2, 3; 33:6; Jer. 7:31; 19:5 [b]Lev. 18:21; 1 Kin. 11:33; 2 Kin. 23:10; Acts 7:43 [c]Jer. 7:31
37 [a]Deut. 30:3; Jer. 23:3; 29:14; 31:10; 50:19; Ezek. 37:21 [b]Jer. 33:16
38 [a][Jer. 24:7; 30:22; 31:33]
39 [a][Jer. 24:7; Ezek. 11:19]
40 [a]Is. 55:3; Jer. 31:31; Ezek. 37:26 [b]Deut. 31:6, 8; [Ezek. 39:29; Jer. 31:33]
41 [a]Deut. 30:9; Is. 62:5; 65:19; Zeph. 3:17 [b]Jer. 24:6; 31:28; Amos 9:15

NKJV

You swore to their fathers to give them—[a]"a land flowing with milk and honey."

23 'And they came in and took possession of it, but [a]they have not obeyed Your voice or walked in Your law. They have done nothing of all that You commanded them to do; therefore You have caused all this calamity to come upon them.

24 'Look, the siege mounds! They have come to the city to take it; and the city has been given into the hand of the Chaldeans who fight against it, because of [a]the sword and famine and pestilence. What You have spoken has happened; there You see *it!*

25 'And You have said to me, O Lord GOD, "Buy the field for money, and take witnesses"!—yet the city has been given into the hand of the Chaldeans.' "

God's Assurance of the People's Return

26 Then the word of the LORD came to Jeremiah, saying,

27 "Behold, I *am* the LORD, the [a]God of all flesh. Is there anything too hard for Me?

28 "Therefore thus says the LORD: 'Behold, I will give this city into the hand of the Chaldeans, into the hand of Nebuchadnezzar king of Babylon, and he shall take it.

29 'And the Chaldeans who fight against this city shall come and [a]set fire to this city and burn it, with the houses [b]on whose roofs they have offered incense to Baal and poured out drink offerings to other gods, to provoke Me to anger;

30 'because the children of Israel and the children of Judah [a]have done only evil before Me from their youth. For the children of Israel have provoked Me only to anger with the work of their hands,' says the LORD.

31 'For this city has been to Me *a provocation of* My anger and My fury from the day that they built it, even to this day; [a]so I will remove it from before My face

32 'because of all the evil of the children of Israel and the children of Judah, which they have done to provoke Me to anger—[a]they, their kings, their princes, their priests, [b]their prophets, the men of Judah, and the inhabitants of Jerusalem.

33 'And they have turned to Me the [a]back, and not the face; though I taught them, [b]rising up early and teaching *them*, yet they have not listened to receive instruction.

34 'But they [a]set their abominations in the house which is called by My name, to defile it.

35 'And they built the high places of Baal which *are* in the Valley of the Son of Hinnom, to [a]cause their sons and their daughters to pass through *the fire* to [b]Molech, [c]which I did not command them, nor did it come into My mind that they should do this abomination, to cause Judah to sin.'

36 "Now therefore, thus says the LORD, the God of Israel, concerning this city of which you say, 'It shall be delivered into the hand of the king of Babylon by the sword, by the famine, and by the pestilence':

37 'Behold, I will [a]gather them out of all countries where I have driven them in My anger, in My fury, and in great wrath; I will bring them back to this place, and I will cause them [b]to dwell safely.

38 'They shall be [a]My people, and I will be their God;

39 'then I will [a]give them one heart and one way, that they may fear Me forever, for the good of them and their children after them.

40 'And [a]I will make an everlasting covenant with them, that I will not turn away from doing them good; but [b]I will put My fear in their hearts so that they will not depart from Me.

41 'Yes, [a]I will rejoice over them to do them good, and [b]I will assuredly plant them in this land, with all My heart and with all My soul.'

KJV

42 For thus saith the LORD; [a]Like as I have brought all this great evil upon this people, so will I bring upon them all the good that I have promised them.

43 And fields shall be bought in this land, [a]whereof ye say, *It is* desolate without man or beast; it is given into the hand of the Chaldeans.

44 Men shall buy fields for money, and subscribe evidences, and seal *them,* and take witnesses in [a]the land of Benjamin, and in the places about Jerusalem, and in the cities of Judah, and in the cities of the mountains, and in the cities of the valley, and in the cities of the south: for [b]I will cause their captivity to return, saith the LORD.

Excellence of the Restored Nation

33 Moreover the word of the LORD came unto Jeremiah the second time, while he was yet [a]shut up in the court of the prison, saying,

2 Thus saith the LORD the [a]maker thereof, the LORD that formed it, to establish it; [b]the LORD *is* his name;

3 [a]Call unto me, and I will answer thee, and shew thee great and mighty things, which thou knowest not.

4 For thus saith the LORD, the God of Israel, concerning the houses of this city, and concerning the houses of the kings of Judah, which are thrown down by [a]the mounts, and by the sword;

5 They come to fight with the Chaldeans, but *it is* to [a]fill them with the dead bodies of men, whom I have slain in mine anger and in my fury, and for all whose wickedness I have hid my face from this city.

6 Behold, [a]I will bring it health and cure, and I will cure them, and will reveal unto them the abundance of peace and truth.

7 And [a]I will cause the captivity of Judah and the captivity of Israel to return, and will build them, [b]as at the first.

8 And I will [a]cleanse them from all their iniquity, whereby they have sinned against me; and I will pardon all their iniquities, whereby they have sinned, and whereby they have transgressed against me.

9 [a]And it shall be to me a name of joy, a praise and an honour before all the nations of the earth, which shall hear all the good that I do unto them: and they shall [b]fear and tremble for all the goodness and for all the prosperity that I procure unto it.

10 Thus saith the LORD; Again there shall be heard in this place, [a]which ye say *shall be* desolate without man and without beast, *even* in the cities of Judah, and in the streets of Jerusalem, that are desolate, without man, and without inhabitant, and without beast,

11 The [a]voice of joy, and the voice of gladness, the voice of the bridegroom, and the voice of the bride, the voice of them that shall say, [b]Praise the LORD of hosts: for the LORD *is* good; for his mercy *endureth* for ever: *and* of them that shall bring [c]the sacrifice of praise into the house of the LORD. For I will cause to return the captivity of the land, as at the first, saith the LORD.

12 Thus saith the LORD of hosts; [a]Again in this place, which is desolate without man and without beast, and in all the cities thereof, shall be an habitation of shepherds causing *their* flocks to lie down.

13 [a]In the cities of the mountains, in the cities of the vale, and in the cities of the south, and in the land of Benjamin, and in the places about Jerusalem, and in the cities of Judah, shall the flocks [b]pass again under the hands of him that telleth *them,* saith the LORD.

---

42 [a]Jer. 31:28; Zech. 8:14, 15
43 [a]Jer. 33:10
44 [a]Jer. 17:26 [b]Jer. 33:7, 11

CHAPTER 33

1 [a]Jer. 32:2, 3
2 [a]Is. 37:26 [b]Ex. 15:3; [Jer. 10:16]; Amos 5:8; 9:6
3 [a]Ps. 91:15; [Is. 55:6, 7]; Jer. 29:12
4 [a]Is. 22:10; Jer. 32:24; Ezek. 4:2; 21:22; Hab. 1:10
5 [a]2 Kin. 23:14; Jer. 21:4–7; 32:5
6 [a]Jer. 30:17; Hos. 6:1
7 [a]Ps. 85:1; Jer. 30:3; 32:44; Amos 9:14 [b]Is. 1:26; Jer. 24:6; 30:20; 31:4, 28; 42:10; Amos 9:14, 15
8 [a]Ps. 51:2; Is. 44:22; Jer. 50:20; Ezek. 36:25, 33; Mic. 7:18, 19; Zech. 13:1; [Heb. 9:11–14]
9 [a]Is. 62:7; Jer. 13:11 [b]Is. 60:5
10 [a]Jer. 32:43
11 [a]Jer. 7:34; 16:9; 25:10; Rev. 18:23 [b]1 Chr. 16:8; 2 Chr. 5:13; Ezra 3:11; Ps. 136:1; Is. 12:4 [c]Lev. 7:12; Ps. 107:22; 116:17; Heb. 13:15
12 [a]Is. 65:10; [Jer. 31:24; 50:19; Ezek. 34:12–15; Zeph. 2:6, 7]
13 [a]Jer. 17:26; 32:44 [b]Lev. 27:33; [Luke 15:4]

NKJV

42 "For thus says the LORD: [a]'Just as I have brought all this great calamity on this people, so I will bring on them all the good that I have promised them.

43 'And fields will be bought in this land [a]of which you say, "*It is* desolate, without man or beast; it has been given into the hand of the Chaldeans."

44 'Men will buy fields for money, sign deeds and seal *them,* and take witnesses, in [a]the land of Benjamin, in the places around Jerusalem, in the cities of Judah, in the cities of the mountains, in the cities of the lowland, and in the cities of the South; for [b]I will cause their captives to return,' says the LORD."

Excellence of the Restored Nation

33 Moreover the word of the LORD came to Jeremiah a second time, while he was still [a]shut up in the court of the prison, saying,

2 "Thus says the LORD [a]who made it, the LORD who formed it to establish it [b](the LORD *is* His name):

3 [a]'Call to Me, and I will answer you, and show you great and mighty things, which you do not know.'

4 "For thus says the LORD, the God of Israel, concerning the houses of this city and the houses of the kings of Judah, which have been pulled down *to fortify* against [a]the siege mounds and the sword:

5 'They come to fight with the Chaldeans, but *only* to [a]fill their places with the dead bodies of men whom I will slay in My anger and My fury, all for whose wickedness I have hidden My face from this city.

6 'Behold, [a]I will bring it health and healing; I will heal them and reveal to them the abundance of peace and truth.

7 'And [a]I will cause the captives of Judah and the captives of Israel to return, and will rebuild those places [b]as at the first.

8 'I will [a]cleanse them from all their iniquity by which they have sinned against Me, and I will pardon all their iniquities by which they have sinned and by which they have transgressed against Me.

9 [a]'Then it shall be to Me a name of joy, a praise, and an honor before all nations of the earth, who shall hear all the good that I do to them; they shall [b]fear and tremble for all the goodness and all the prosperity that I provide for it.'

10 "Thus says the LORD: 'Again there shall be heard in this place—[a]of which you say, "It *is* desolate, without man and without beast"—in the cities of Judah, in the streets of Jerusalem that are desolate, without man and without inhabitant and without beast,

11 'the [a]voice of joy and the voice of gladness, the voice of the bridegroom and the voice of the bride, the voice of those who will say:

[b]"Praise the LORD of hosts,
For the LORD *is* good,
For His mercy *endures* forever"—

and of those *who will* bring [c]the sacrifice of praise into the house of the LORD. For I will cause the captives of the land to return as at the first,' says the LORD.

12 "Thus says the LORD of hosts: [a]'In this place which is desolate, without man and without beast, and in all its cities, there shall again be a dwelling place of shepherds causing *their* flocks to lie down.

13 [a]'In the cities of the mountains, in the cities of the lowland, in the cities of the South, in the land of Benjamin, in the places around Jerusalem, and in the cities of Judah, the flocks shall again [b]pass under the hands of him who counts *them,*' says the LORD.

KJV

14 [a]Behold, the days come, saith the LORD, that [b]I will perform that good thing which I have promised unto the house of Israel and to the house of Judah.

15 In those days, and at that time, will I cause the [a]Branch of righteousness to grow up unto David; and he shall execute judgment and righteousness in the land.

16 In those days shall Judah be saved, and Jerusalem shall dwell safely: and this *is the name* wherewith she shall be called, The LORD our righteousness.

17 For thus saith the LORD; David shall never [a]want a man to sit upon the throne of the house of Israel;

18 Neither shall the [a]priests the Levites want a man before me to [b]offer burnt offerings, and to kindle meat offerings, and to do sacrifice continually.

The Permanence of God's Covenant

19 And the word of the LORD came unto Jeremiah, saying,

20 Thus saith the LORD; If ye can break my covenant of the day, and my covenant of the night, and that there should not be day and night in their season;

21 *Then* may also [a]my covenant be broken with David my servant, that he should not have a son to reign upon his throne; and with the Levites the priests, my ministers.

22 As [a]the host of heaven cannot be numbered, neither the sand of the sea measured: so will I [b]multiply the seed of David my servant, and the [c]Levites that minister unto me.

23 Moreover the word of the LORD came to Jeremiah, saying,

24 Considerest thou not what this people have spoken, saying, The two families which the LORD hath chosen, he hath even cast them off? thus they have [a]despised my people, that they should be no more a nation before them.

25 Thus saith the LORD; If [a]my covenant *be* not with day and night, *and if* I have not [b]appointed the ordinances of heaven and earth;

26 [a]Then will I [b]cast away the seed of Jacob, and David my servant, *so* that I will not take *any* of his seed *to be* rulers over the seed of Abraham, Isaac, and Jacob: for I will cause their captivity to return, and have mercy on them.

Zedekiah Warned by God

34 The word which came unto Jeremiah from the LORD, [a]when Nebuchadnezzar king of Babylon, and all his army, and [b]all the kingdoms of the earth of his dominion, and all the people, fought against Jerusalem, and against all the cities thereof, saying,

2 Thus saith the LORD, the God of Israel; Go and [a]speak to Zedekiah king of Judah, and tell him, Thus saith the LORD; Behold, [b]I will give this city into the hand of the king of Babylon, and he shall burn it with fire:

3 And [a]thou shalt not escape out of his hand, but shalt surely be taken, and delivered into his hand; and thine eyes shall behold the eyes of the king of Babylon, and he shall speak with thee [b]mouth to mouth, and thou shalt go to Babylon.

4 Yet hear the word of the LORD, O Zedekiah king of Judah; Thus saith the LORD of thee, Thou shalt not die by the sword:

5 *But* thou shalt die in peace: and with [a]the burnings of thy fathers, the former kings which were before thee, [b]so shall they burn *odours* for thee; and [c]they will lament thee, *saying*, Ah lord! for I have pronounced the word, saith the LORD.

---

14 [a]Jer. 23:5; 31:27, 31 [b]Is. 32:1; Jer. 29:10; 32:42; Ezek. 34:23–25; Hag. 2:6–9
15 [a]Is. 4:2; 11:1; Jer. 23:5; Zech. 3:8; 6:12, 13
17 [a]2 Sam. 7:16; 1 Kin. 2:4; Ps. 89:29; [Luke 1:32]
18 [a]Num. 3:5–10; Deut. 18:1; 24:8; Josh. 3:3; Ezek. 44:15 [b][Rom. 12:1; 15:16; 1 Pet. 2:5, 9; Rev. 1:6]
21 [a]2 Sam. 23:5; 2 Chr. 7:18; 21:7; Ps. 89:34
22 [a]Gen. 15:5; 22:17; Jer. 31:37 [b]Jer. 30:19; Ezek. 36:10, 11 [c]Is. 66:21; Jer. 33:18
24 [a]Neh. 4:2–4; Esth. 3:6–8; Ps. 44:13, 14; 83:4; Ezek. 36:2
25 [a]Gen. 8:22; Jer. 33:20 [b]Ps. 74:16; 104:19
26 [a]Jer. 31:37 [b]Rom. 11:1, 2

CHAPTER 34

1 [a]2 Kin. 25:1; Jer. 32:1, 2; 39:1; 52:4 [b]Jer. 1:15; 25:9; Dan. 2:37, 38
2 [a]2 Chr. 36:11, 12; Jer. 22:1, 2; 37:1, 2 [b]2 Kin. 25:9; Jer. 21:10; 32:3, 28
3 [a]2 Kin. 25:4, 5; Jer. 21:7; 52:7–11 [b]2 Kin. 25:6, 7; Jer. 32:4; 39:5, 6
5 [a]2 Chr. 16:14; 21:19 [b]Dan. 2:46 [c]Jer. 22:18

*

33:16 Heb. *YHWH Tsidkenu;* cf. Jer. 23:5, 6
34:3 Lit. *mouth to mouth*

NKJV

14 [a]'Behold, the days are coming,' says the LORD, 'that [b]I will perform that good thing which I have promised to the house of Israel and to the house of Judah:

15 'In those days and at that time
I will cause to grow up to David
A [a]Branch of righteousness;
He shall execute judgment and
righteousness in the earth.
16 In those days Judah will be saved,
And Jerusalem will dwell safely.
And this *is the name* by which she will
be called:

*THE LORD OUR RIGHTEOUSNESS.'

17 "For thus says the LORD: 'David shall never [a]lack a man to sit on the throne of the house of Israel;

18 'nor shall the [a]priests, the Levites, lack a man to [b]offer burnt offerings before Me, to kindle grain offerings, and to sacrifice continually.' "

The Permanence of God's Covenant

19 And the word of the LORD came to Jeremiah, saying,

20 "Thus says the LORD: 'If you can break My covenant with the day and My covenant with the night, so that there will not be day and night in their season,

21 'then [a]My covenant may also be broken with David My servant, so that he shall not have a son to reign on his throne, and with the Levites, the priests, My ministers.

22 'As [a]the host of heaven cannot be numbered, nor the sand of the sea measured, so will I [b]multiply the descendants of David My servant and the [c]Levites who minister to Me.' "

23 Moreover the word of the LORD came to Jeremiah, saying,

24 "Have you not considered what these people have spoken, saying, 'The two families which the LORD has chosen, He has also cast them off'? Thus they have [a]despised My people, as if they should no more be a nation before them.

25 "Thus says the LORD: 'If [a]My covenant *is* not with day and night, *and if* I have not [b]appointed the ordinances of heaven and earth,

26 [a]'then I will [b]cast away the descendants of Jacob and David My servant, *so* that I will not take *any* of his descendants *to be* rulers over the descendants of Abraham, Isaac, and Jacob. For I will cause their captives to return, and will have mercy on them.' "

Zedekiah Warned by God

34 The word which came to Jeremiah from the LORD, [a]when Nebuchadnezzar king of Babylon and all his army, [b]all the kingdoms of the earth under his dominion, and all the people, fought against Jerusalem and all its cities, saying,

2 "Thus says the LORD, the God of Israel: 'Go and [a]speak to Zedekiah king of Judah and tell him, "Thus says the LORD: 'Behold, [b]I will give this city into the hand of the king of Babylon, and he shall burn it with fire.

3 'And [a]you shall not escape from his hand, but shall surely be taken and delivered into his hand; your eyes shall see the eyes of the king of Babylon, he shall speak with you [b]face* to face, and you shall go to Babylon.' " '

4 "Yet hear the word of the LORD, O Zedekiah king of Judah! Thus says the LORD concerning you: 'You shall not die by the sword.

5 'You shall die in peace; as in [a]the ceremonies of your fathers, the former kings who were before you, [b]so they shall burn incense for you and [c]lament for you, *saying*, "Alas, lord!" For I have pronounced the word, says the LORD.' "

KJV

6 Then Jeremiah the prophet spake all these words unto Zedekiah king of Judah in Jerusalem,

7 When the king of Babylon's army fought against Jerusalem, and against all the cities of Judah that were left, against Lachish, and against Azekah: for [a]these defenced cities remained of the cities of Judah.

Treacherous Treatment of Slaves

8 *This is* the word that came unto Jeremiah from the LORD, after that the king Zedekiah had made a covenant with all the people which *were* at Jerusalem, to proclaim [a]liberty unto them;

9 [a]That every man should let his manservant, and every man his maidservant, *being* an Hebrew or an Hebrewess, go free; [b]that none should serve himself of them, *to wit,* of a Jew his brother.

10 Now when all the princes, and all the people, which had entered into the covenant, heard that every one should let his manservant, and every one his maidservant, go free, that none should serve themselves of them any more, then they obeyed, and let *them* go.

11 But afterward they turned, and caused the servants and the handmaids, whom they had let go free, to return, and brought them into subjection for servants and for handmaids.

12 Therefore the word of the LORD came to Jeremiah from the LORD, saying,

13 Thus saith the LORD, the God of Israel; I made a [a]covenant with your fathers in the day that I brought them forth out of the land of Egypt, out of the house of bondmen, saying,

14 At the end of [a]seven years let ye go every man his brother an Hebrew, which hath been sold unto thee; and when he hath served thee six years, thou shalt let him go free from thee: but your fathers hearkened not unto me, neither inclined their ear.

15 And ye were now turned, and had done right in my sight, in proclaiming liberty every man to his neighbour; and ye had [a]made a covenant before me [b]in the house which is called by my name:

16 But ye turned and [a]polluted my name, and caused every man his servant, and every man his handmaid, whom he had set at liberty at their pleasure, to return, and brought them into subjection, to be unto you for servants and for handmaids.

17 Therefore thus saith the LORD; Ye have not hearkened unto me, in proclaiming liberty, every one to his brother, and every man to his neighbour: [a]behold, I proclaim a liberty for you, saith the LORD, [b]to the sword, to the pestilence, and to the famine; and I will make you to be [c]removed into all the kingdoms of the earth.

18 And I will give the men that have transgressed my covenant, which have not performed the words of the covenant which they had made before me, when [a]they cut the calf in twain, and passed between the parts thereof,

19 The princes of Judah, and the princes of Jerusalem, the eunuchs, and the priests, and all the people of the land, which passed between the parts of the calf;

20 I will even [a]give them into the hand of their enemies, and into the hand of them that seek their life: and their [b]dead bodies shall be for meat unto the fowls of the heaven, and to the beasts of the earth.

21 And Zedekiah king of Judah and his princes will I give into the hand of their enemies, and into the hand of them that seek their life, and into the hand of the king of Babylon's army, [a]which are gone up from you.

22 [a]Behold, I will command, saith the LORD, and cause them to return to this city; and they shall fight against it, [b]and take it, and burn it with fire: and [c]I will make the cities of Judah a desolation without an inhabitant.

7 [a]2 Kin. 18:13; 19:8; 2 Chr. 11:5, 9
8 [a]Ex. 21:2; Lev. 25:10; Neh. 5:1–13; Is. 58:6; Jer. 34:14, 17
9 [a]Neh. 5:11 [b]Lev. 25:39–46
13 [a]Ex. 24:3, 7, 8; Deut. 5:2, 3, 27; Jer. 31:32
14 [a]Ex. 21:2; 23:10; Deut. 15:12; 1 Kin. 9:22
15 [a]2 Kin. 23:3; Neh. 10:29 [b]Jer. 7:10
16 [a]Ex. 20:7; Lev. 19:12
17 [a]Lev. 26:34, 35; Esth. 7:10; Dan. 6:24; [Matt. 7:2; Gal. 6:7]; James 2:13 [b]Jer. 32:24, 36 [c]Deut. 28:25, 64; Jer. 29:18
18 [a]Gen. 15:10, 17
20 [a]2 Kin. 25:19–21; Jer. 22:25 [b]Deut. 28:26; 1 Sam. 17:44, 46; 1 Kin. 14:11; 16:4; Ps. 79:2; Jer. 7:33; 16:4; 19:7
21 [a]Jer. 37:5–11; 39:4–7
22 [a]Jer. 37:8, 10 [b]Jer. 38:3; 39:1, 2, 8; 52:7, 13 [c]Jer. 9:11; 44:2, 6

NKJV

6 Then Jeremiah the prophet spoke all these words to Zedekiah king of Judah in Jerusalem,

7 when the king of Babylon's army fought against Jerusalem and all the cities of Judah that were left, against Lachish and Azekah; for *only* [a]these fortified cities remained of the cities of Judah.

Treacherous Treatment of Slaves

8 *This is* the word that came to Jeremiah from the LORD, after King Zedekiah had made a covenant with all the people who *were* at Jerusalem to proclaim [a]liberty to them:

9 [a]that every man should set free his male and female slave—a Hebrew man or woman—[b]that no one should keep a Jewish brother in bondage.

10 Now when all the princes and all the people, who had entered into the covenant, heard that everyone should set free his male and female slaves, that no one should keep them in bondage anymore, they obeyed and let *them* go.

11 But afterward they changed their minds and made the male and female slaves return, whom they had set free, and brought them into subjection as male and female slaves.

12 Therefore the word of the LORD came to Jeremiah from the LORD, saying,

13 "Thus says the LORD, the God of Israel: 'I made a [a]covenant with your fathers in the day that I brought them out of the land of Egypt, out of the house of bondage, saying,

14 "At the end of [a]seven years let every man set free his Hebrew brother, who has been sold to him; and when he has served you six years, you shall let him go free from you." But your fathers did not obey Me nor incline their ear.

15 'Then you recently turned and did what was right in My sight—every man proclaiming liberty to his neighbor; and you [a]made a covenant before Me [b]in the house which is called by My name.

16 'Then you turned around and [a]profaned My name, and every one of you brought back his male and female slaves, whom he had set at liberty, at their pleasure, and brought them back into subjection, to be your male and female slaves.'

17 "Therefore thus says the LORD: 'You have not obeyed Me in proclaiming liberty, every one to his brother and every one to his neighbor. [a]Behold, I proclaim liberty to you,' says the LORD—[b]'to the sword, to pestilence, and to famine! And I will deliver you to [c]trouble among all the kingdoms of the earth.

18 'And I will give the men who have transgressed My covenant, who have not performed the words of the covenant which they made before Me, when [a]they cut the calf in two and passed between the parts of it—

19 'the princes of Judah, the princes of Jerusalem, the eunuchs, the priests, and all the people of the land who passed between the parts of the calf—

20 'I will [a]give them into the hand of their enemies and into the hand of those who seek their life. Their [b]dead bodies shall be for meat for the birds of the heaven and the beasts of the earth.

21 'And I will give Zedekiah king of Judah and his princes into the hand of their enemies, into the hand of those who seek their life, and into the hand of the king of Babylon's army [a]which has gone back from you.

22 [a]'Behold, I will command,' says the LORD, 'and cause them to return to this city. They will fight against it [b]and take it and burn it with fire; and [c]I will make the cities of Judah a desolation without inhabitant.' "

KJV

The Obedient Rechabites

35 The word which came unto Jeremiah from the LORD in the days of Jehoiakim the son of Josiah king of Judah, saying,

2 Go unto the house of the [a]Rechabites, and speak unto them, and bring them into the house of the LORD, into one of [b]the chambers, and give them wine to drink.

3 Then I took Jaazaniah the son of Jeremiah, the son of Habaziniah, and his brethren, and all his sons, and the whole house of the Rechabites;

4 And I brought them into the house of the LORD, into the chamber of the sons of Hanan, the son of Igdaliah, a man of God, which *was* by the chamber of the princes, which *was* above the chamber of Maaseiah the son of Shallum, [a]the keeper of the door:

5 And I set before the sons of the house of the Rechabites pots full of wine, and cups, and I said unto them, Drink ye wine.

6 But they said, We will drink no wine: for [a]Jonadab the son of Rechab our father commanded us, saying, Ye shall drink [b]no wine, *neither* ye, nor your sons for ever:

7 Neither shall ye build house, nor sow seed, nor plant vineyard, nor have *any:* but all your days ye shall dwell in tents; [a]that ye may live many days in the land where ye *be* strangers.

8 Thus have we [a]obeyed the voice of Jonadab the son of Rechab our father in all that he hath charged us, to drink no wine all our days, we, our wives, our sons, nor our daughters;

9 Nor to build houses for us to dwell in: neither have we vineyard, nor field, nor seed:

10 But we have dwelt in tents, and have obeyed, and done according to all that Jonadab our father commanded us.

11 But it came to pass, when Nebuchadrezzar king of Babylon came up into the land, that we said, Come, and let us [a]go to Jerusalem for fear of the army of the Chaldeans, and for fear of the army of the Syrians: so we dwell at Jerusalem.

12 Then came the word of the LORD unto Jeremiah, saying,

13 Thus saith the LORD of hosts, the God of Israel; Go and tell the men of Judah and the inhabitants of Jerusalem, Will ye not [a]receive instruction to hearken to my words? saith the LORD.

14 The words of Jonadab the son of Rechab, that he commanded his sons not to drink wine, are performed; for unto this day they drink none, but obey their father's commandment: [a]notwithstanding I have spoken unto you, [b]rising early and speaking; but ye hearkened not unto me.

15 I have sent also unto you all my [a]servants the prophets, rising up early and sending *them,* saying, [b]Return ye now every man from his evil way, and amend your doings, and go not after other gods to serve them, and ye shall [c]dwell in the land which I have given to you and to your fathers: but ye have not inclined your ear, nor hearkened unto me.

16 Because the sons of Jonadab the son of Rechab have performed the commandment of their [a]father, which he commanded them; but this people hath not hearkened unto me:

17 Therefore thus saith the LORD God of hosts, the God of Israel; Behold, I will bring upon Judah and upon all the inhabitants of Jerusalem all the evil that I have pronounced against them: [a]because I have spoken unto them, but they have not heard; and I have called unto them, but they have not answered.

18 And Jeremiah said unto the house of the Rechabites, Thus saith the LORD of hosts, the God of Israel; Because ye have obeyed the commandment of Jonadab your father, and kept all his precepts, and done according unto all that he hath commanded you:

19 Therefore thus saith the LORD of hosts, the

CHAPTER 35

2 [a]2 Sam. 4:2; 2 Kin. 10:15; 1 Chr. 2:55 [b]1 Kin. 6:5, 8; 1 Chr. 9:26, 33
4 [a]2 Kin. 12:9; 25:18; 1 Chr. 9:18, 19
6 [a]2 Kin. 10:15, 23 [b]Lev. 10:9; Num. 6:2–4; Judg. 13:7, 14; Prov. 31:4; Ezek. 44:21; Luke 1:15
7 [a]Ex. 20:12; Eph. 6:2, 3
8 [a][Prov. 1:8, 9; 4:1, 2, 10; 6:20; Eph. 6:1; Col. 3:20]
11 [a]Jer. 4:5–7; 8:14
13 [a][Is. 28:9–12]; Jer. 6:10; 17:23; 32:33
14 [a]2 Chr. 36:15 [b]Jer. 7:13; 25:3
15 [a]Jer. 26:4, 5; 29:19 [b][Is. 1:16, 17]; Jer. 18:11; 25:5, 6; [Ezek. 18:30–32]; Acts 26:20 [c]Jer. 7:7; 25:5, 6
16 [a][Heb. 12:9]
17 [a]Prov. 1:24; Is. 65:12; 66:4; Jer. 7:13

NKJV

The Obedient Rechabites

35 The word which came to Jeremiah from the LORD in the days of Jehoiakim the son of Josiah, king of Judah, saying,

2 "Go to the house of the [a]Rechabites, speak to them, and bring them into the house of the LORD, into one of [b]the chambers, and give them wine to drink."

3 Then I took Jaazaniah the son of Jeremiah, the son of Habazziniah, his brothers and all his sons, and the whole house of the Rechabites,

4 and I brought them into the house of the LORD, into the chamber of the sons of Hanan the son of Igdaliah, a man of God, which *was* by the chamber of the princes, above the chamber of Maaseiah the son of Shallum, [a]the keeper of the door.

5 Then I set before the sons of the house of the Rechabites bowls full of wine, and cups; and I said to them, "Drink wine."

6 But they said, "We will drink no wine, for [a]Jonadab the son of Rechab, our father, commanded us, saying, 'You shall drink [b]no wine, you nor your sons, forever.

7 'You shall not build a house, sow seed, plant a vineyard, nor have *any of these;* but all your days you shall dwell in tents, [a]that you may live many days in the land where you are sojourners.'

8 "Thus we have [a]obeyed the voice of Jonadab the son of Rechab, our father, in all that he charged us, to drink no wine all our days, we, our wives, our sons, or our daughters,

9 "nor to build ourselves houses to dwell in; nor do we have vineyard, field, or seed.

10 "But we have dwelt in tents, and have obeyed and done according to all that Jonadab our father commanded us.

11 "But it came to pass, when Nebuchadnezzar king of Babylon came up into the land, that we said, 'Come, let us [a]go to Jerusalem for fear of the army of the Chaldeans and for fear of the army of the Syrians.' So we dwell at Jerusalem."

12 Then came the word of the LORD to Jeremiah, saying,

13 "Thus says the LORD of hosts, the God of Israel: 'Go and tell the men of Judah and the inhabitants of Jerusalem, "Will you not [a]receive instruction to obey My words?" says the LORD.

14 "The words of Jonadab the son of Rechab, which he commanded his sons, not to drink wine, are performed; for to this day they drink none, and obey their father's commandment. [a]But although I have spoken to you, [b]rising early and speaking, you did not obey Me.

15 "I have also sent to you all My [a]servants the prophets, rising up early and sending *them,* saying, [b]'Turn now everyone from his evil way, amend your doings, and do not go after other gods to serve them; then you will [c]dwell in the land which I have given you and your fathers.' But you have not inclined your ear, nor obeyed Me.

16 "Surely the sons of Jonadab the son of Rechab have performed the commandment of their [a]father, which he commanded them, but this people has not obeyed Me." '

17 "Therefore thus says the LORD God of hosts, the God of Israel: 'Behold, I will bring on Judah and on all the inhabitants of Jerusalem all the doom that I have pronounced against them; [a]because I have spoken to them but they have not heard, and I have called to them but they have not answered.' "

18 And Jeremiah said to the house of the Rechabites, "Thus says the LORD of hosts, the God of Israel: 'Because you have obeyed the commandment of Jonadab your father, and kept all his precepts and done according to all that he commanded you,

19 'therefore thus says the LORD of hosts, the

KJV

God of Israel; Jonadab the son of Rechab shall not want a man to [a]stand before me for ever.

The Scroll Read in the Temple

36 And it came to pass in the [a]fourth year of Jehoiakim the son of Josiah king of Judah, *that* this word came unto Jeremiah from the LORD, saying,

2 Take thee a [a]roll of a book, and [b]write therein all the words that I have spoken unto thee against Israel, and against Judah, and against [c]all the nations, from the day I spake unto thee, from the days of [d]Josiah, even into this day.

3 It [a]may be that the house of Judah will hear all the evil which I purpose to do unto them; that they may [b]return every man from his evil way; that I may forgive their iniquity and their sin.

4 Then Jeremiah [a]called Baruch the son of Neriah: and [b]Baruch wrote from the mouth of Jeremiah all the words of the LORD, which he had spoken unto him, upon a roll of a book.

5 And Jeremiah commanded Baruch, saying, I *am* shut up; I cannot go into the house of the LORD:

6 Therefore go thou, and read in the roll, which thou hast written from my mouth, the words of the LORD in the ears of the people in the LORD's house upon [a]the fasting day: and also thou shalt read them in the ears of all Judah that come out of their cities.

7 It may be they will present their supplication before the LORD, and will return every one from his evil way: for great *is* the anger and the fury that the LORD hath pronounced against this people.

8 And Baruch the son of Neriah did according to all that Jeremiah the prophet commanded him, reading in the book the words of the LORD in the LORD's house.

9 And it came to pass in the fifth year of Jehoiakim the son of Josiah king of Judah, in the ninth month, *that* they proclaimed a fast before the LORD to all the people in Jerusalem, and to all the people that came from the cities of Judah unto Jerusalem.

10 Then read Baruch in the book the words of Jeremiah in the house of the LORD, in the chamber of Gemariah the son of Shaphan the scribe, in the higher court, at the [a]entry of the new gate of the LORD's house, in the ears of all the people.

The Scroll Read in the Palace

11 When Michaiah the son of Gemariah, the son of Shaphan, had heard out of the book all the words of the LORD,

12 Then he went down into the king's house, into the scribe's chamber: and, lo, all the princes sat there, *even* [a]Elishama the scribe, and Delaiah the son of Shemaiah, and [b]Elnathan the son of Achbor, and Gemariah the son of Shaphan, and Zedekiah the son of Hananiah, and all the princes.

13 Then Michaiah declared unto them all the words that he had heard, when Baruch read the book in the ears of the people.

14 Therefore all the princes sent Jehudi the son of Nethaniah, the son of Shelemiah, the son of Cushi, unto Baruch, saying, Take in thine hand the roll wherein thou hast read in the ears of the people, and come. So Baruch the son of Neriah took the roll in his hand, and came unto them.

15 And they said unto him, Sit down now, and read it in our ears. So Baruch read *it* in their ears.

16 Now it came to pass, when they had heard all the words, they were afraid both one and other, and said unto Baruch, We will surely tell the king of all these words.

17 And they asked Baruch, saying, Tell us

19 [a][Ex. 20:12]; Jer. 15:19; [Luke 21:36; Eph. 6:2, 3]

CHAPTER 36

1 [a]2 Kin. 24:1; 2 Chr. 36:5–7; Jer. 25:1, 3; 45:1; Dan. 1:1
2 [a]Is. 8:1; Ezek. 2:9; Zech. 5:1 [b]Jer. 30:2; Hab. 2:2 [c]Jer. 25:15 [d]Jer. 25:3
3 [a]Jer. 26:3; Ezek. 12:3 [b][Deut. 30:2, 8; 1 Sam. 7:3]; Is. 55:7; Jer. 18:8; Jon. 3:8
4 [a]Jer. 32:12 [b]Jer. 45:1
6 [a]Lev. 16:29; 23:27–32; Acts 27:9
10 [a]Jer. 26:10
12 [a]Jer. 41:1 [b]Jer. 26:22

NKJV

God of Israel: "Jonadab the son of Rechab shall not lack a man to [a]stand before Me forever." ' "

The Scroll Read in the Temple

36 Now it came to pass in the [a]fourth year of Jehoiakim the son of Josiah, king of Judah, *that* this word came to Jeremiah from the LORD, saying:

2 "Take a [a]scroll of a book and [b]write on it all the words that I have spoken to you against Israel, against Judah, and against [c]all the nations, from the day I spoke to you, from the days of [d]Josiah even to this day.

3 "It [a]may be that the house of Judah will hear all the adversities which I purpose to bring upon them, that everyone may [b]turn from his evil way, that I may forgive their iniquity and their sin."

4 Then Jeremiah [a]called Baruch the son of Neriah; and [b]Baruch wrote on a scroll of a book, *at the instruction of Jeremiah, all the words of the LORD which He had spoken to him.

5 And Jeremiah commanded Baruch, saying, "I *am* confined, I cannot go into the house of the LORD.

6 "You go, therefore, and read from the scroll which you have written *at my instruction, the words of the LORD, in the hearing of the people in the LORD's house on [a]the day of fasting. And you shall also read them in the hearing of all Judah who come from their cities.

7 "It may be that they will present their supplication before the LORD, and everyone will turn from his evil way. For great *is* the anger and the fury that the LORD has pronounced against this people."

8 And Baruch the son of Neriah did according to all that Jeremiah the prophet commanded him, reading from the book the words of the LORD in the LORD's house.

9 Now it came to pass in the fifth year of Jehoiakim the son of Josiah, king of Judah, in the ninth month, *that* they proclaimed a fast before the LORD to all the people in Jerusalem, and to all the people who came from the cities of Judah to Jerusalem.

10 Then Baruch read from the book the words of Jeremiah in the house of the LORD, in the chamber of Gemariah the son of Shaphan the scribe, in the upper court at the [a]entry of the New Gate of the LORD's house, in the hearing of all the people.

The Scroll Read in the Palace

11 When Michaiah the son of Gemariah, the son of Shaphan, heard all the words of the LORD from the book,

12 he then went down to the king's house, into the scribe's chamber; and there all the princes were sitting—[a]Elishama the scribe, Delaiah the son of Shemaiah, [b]Elnathan the son of Achbor, Gemariah the son of Shaphan, Zedekiah the son of Hananiah, and all the princes.

13 Then Michaiah declared to them all the words that he had heard when Baruch read the book in the hearing of the people.

14 Therefore all the princes sent Jehudi the son of Nethaniah, the son of Shelemiah, the son of Cushi, to Baruch, saying, "Take in your hand the scroll from which you have read in the hearing of the people, and come." So Baruch the son of Neriah took the scroll in his hand and came to them.

15 And they said to him, "Sit down now, and read it in our hearing." So Baruch read *it* in their hearing.

16 Now it happened, when they had heard all the words, that they looked in fear from one to another, and said to Baruch, "We will surely tell the king of all these words."

17 And they asked Baruch, saying, "Tell us

*36:4 Lit. *from Jeremiah's mouth*
36:6 Lit. *from my mouth*

KJV

now, How didst thou write all these words at his
mouth?
18 Then Baruch answered them, He pronounced all these words unto me with his mouth,
and I wrote *them* with ink in the book.
19 Then said the princes unto Baruch, Go,
hide thee, thou and Jeremiah; and let no man
know where ye be.

The King Destroys Jeremiah's Scroll

20 And they went in to the king into the
court, but they laid up the roll in the chamber of
Elishama the scribe, and told all the words in the
ears of the king.
21 So the king sent Jehudi to fetch the roll:
and he took it out of Elishama the scribe's chamber. And Jehudi read it in the ears of the king,
and in the ears of all the princes which stood beside the king.
22 Now the king sat in [a]the winterhouse in
the ninth month: and *there was a fire* on the
hearth burning before him.
23 And it came to pass, *that* when Jehudi had
read three or four leaves, he cut it with the pen-
knife, and cast *it* into the fire that *was* on the
hearth, until all the roll was consumed in the fire
that *was* on the hearth.
24 Yet they were [a]not afraid, nor [b]rent their
garments, *neither* the king, nor any of his servants
that heard all these words.
25 Nevertheless Elnathan and Delaiah and
Gemariah had made intercession to the king that
he would not burn the roll: but he would not hear
them.
26 But the king commanded Jerahmeel the
son of Hammelech, and Seraiah the son of Azriel,
and Shelemiah the son of Abdeel, to take Baruch
the scribe and Jeremiah the prophet: but the LORD
hid them.

Jeremiah Rewrites the Scroll

27 Then the word of the LORD came to Jeremiah, after that the king had burned the roll, and
the words which Baruch wrote at the mouth of
Jeremiah, saying,
28 Take thee again another roll, and write
in it all the former words that were in the first
roll, which Jehoiakim the king of Judah hath
burned.
29 And thou shalt say to Jehoiakim king of
Judah, Thus saith the LORD; Thou hast burned this
roll, saying, [a]Why hast thou written therein, saying, The king of Babylon shall certainly come and
destroy this land, and shall cause to [b]cease from
thence man and beast?
30 Therefore thus saith the LORD of Jehoiakim king of Judah; [a]He shall have none to
sit upon the throne of David: and his dead body
shall be [b]cast out in the day to the heat, and in
the night to the frost.
31 And I will punish him and his seed and
his servants for their iniquity; and I will bring
upon them, and upon the inhabitants of Jerusalem, and upon the men of Judah, all the evil that
I have pronounced against them; but they hearkened not.
32 Then took Jeremiah another roll, and gave
it to Baruch the scribe, the son of Neriah; who
wrote therein from the mouth of Jeremiah all the
words of the book which Jehoiakim king of Judah
had burned in the fire: and there were added besides unto them many like words.

Zedekiah's Vain Hope
(2 Kin. 24:17; 2 Chr. 36:10)

37 And king [a]Zedekiah the son of Josiah
reigned instead of Coniah the son of Jehoiakim, whom Nebuchadrezzar king of Babylon
made king in the land of Judah.
2 [a]But neither he, nor his servants, nor the
people of the land, did hearken unto the words

22 [a]Judg. 3:20; Amos 3:15
24 [a][Ps. 36:1]; Jer. 36:16 [b]Gen. 37:29, 34; 2 Sam. 1:11; 1 Kin. 21:27; 2 Kin. 19:1, 2; 22:11; Is. 36:22; 37:1; Jon. 3:6
29 [a]Jer. 32:3 [b]Jer. 25:9–11; 26:9
30 [a]Jer. 22:30 [b]Jer. 22:19

CHAPTER 37

1 [a]2 Kin. 24:17; 1 Chr. 3:15; 2 Chr. 36:10; Jer. 22:24
2 [a]2 Kin. 24:19, 20; 2 Chr. 36:12–16; [Prov. 29:12]

*

36:17 Lit. *with his mouth*
36:26 Or *son of Hammelech*
36:27 Lit. *from Jeremiah's mouth*
36:32 Lit. *from Jeremiah's mouth*

NKJV

now, how did you write all these words—*at his
instruction?"
18 So Baruch answered them, "He proclaimed with his mouth all these words to me,
and I wrote *them* with ink in the book."
19 Then the princes said to Baruch, "Go and
hide, you and Jeremiah; and let no one know
where you are."

The King Destroys Jeremiah's Scroll

20 And they went to the king, into the court;
but they stored the scroll in the chamber of
Elishama the scribe, and told all the words in the
hearing of the king.
21 So the king sent Jehudi to bring the scroll,
and he took it from Elishama the scribe's chamber. And Jehudi read it in the hearing of the king
and in the hearing of all the princes who stood
beside the king.
22 Now the king was sitting in [a]the winter
house in the ninth month, with *a fire* burning on
the hearth before him.
23 And it happened, when Jehudi had read
three or four columns, *that the king* cut it with
the scribe's knife and cast *it* into the fire that *was*
on the hearth, until all the scroll was consumed
in the fire that *was* on the hearth.
24 Yet they were [a]not afraid, nor did they
[b]tear their garments, the king nor any of his servants who heard all these words.
25 Nevertheless Elnathan, Delaiah, and Gemariah implored the king not to burn the scroll;
but he would not listen to them.
26 And the king commanded Jerahmeel *the
king's son, Seraiah the son of Azriel, and Shelemiah the son of Abdeel, to seize Baruch the scribe
and Jeremiah the prophet, but the LORD hid them.

Jeremiah Rewrites the Scroll

27 Now after the king had burned the scroll
with the words which Baruch had written *at the
instruction of Jeremiah, the word of the LORD
came to Jeremiah, saying:
28 "Take yet another scroll, and write on it
all the former words that were in the first scroll
which Jehoiakim the king of Judah has burned.
29 "And you shall say to Jehoiakim king of
Judah, 'Thus says the LORD: "You have burned
this scroll, saying, [a]'Why have you written in it
that the king of Babylon will certainly come and
destroy this land, and cause man and beast to
[b]cease from here?' "
30 'Therefore thus says the LORD concerning
Jehoiakim king of Judah: [a]"He shall have no one
to sit on the throne of David, and his dead body
shall be [b]cast out to the heat of the day and the
frost of the night.
31 "I will punish him, his family, and his servants for their iniquity; and I will bring on them,
on the inhabitants of Jerusalem, and on the men
of Judah all the doom that I have pronounced
against them; but they did not heed." ' "
32 Then Jeremiah took another scroll and
gave it to Baruch the scribe, the son of Neriah,
who wrote on it *at the instruction of Jeremiah
all the words of the book which Jehoiakim king
of Judah had burned in the fire. And besides, there
were added to them many similar words.

Zedekiah's Vain Hope
(2 Kin. 24:17; 2 Chr. 36:10)

37 Now King [a]Zedekiah the son of Josiah
reigned instead of Coniah the son of Jehoiakim, whom Nebuchadnezzar king of Babylon
made king in the land of Judah.
2 [a]But neither he nor his servants nor the
people of the land gave heed to the words of the

KJV

of the LORD, which he spake by the prophet Jeremiah.

3 And Zedekiah the king sent Jehucal the son of Shelemiah and [a]Zephaniah the son of Maaseiah the priest to the prophet Jeremiah, saying, [b]Pray now unto the LORD our God for us.

4 Now Jeremiah came in and went out among the people: for they had not put him into prison.

5 Then [a]Pharaoh's army was come forth out of Egypt: and when the Chaldeans that besieged Jerusalem heard tidings of them, they departed from Jerusalem.

6 Then came the word of the LORD unto the prophet Jeremiah, saying,

7 Thus saith the LORD, the God of Israel; Thus shall ye say to the king of Judah, [a]that sent you unto me to enquire of me; Behold, Pharaoh's army, which is come forth to help you, shall return to Egypt into their own land.

8 [a]And the Chaldeans shall come again, and fight against this city, and take it, and burn it with fire.

9 Thus saith the LORD; Deceive not yourselves, saying, The Chaldeans shall surely depart from us: for they shall not depart.

10 [a]For though ye had smitten the whole army of the Chaldeans that fight against you, and there remained *but* wounded men among them, *yet* should they rise up every man in his tent, and burn this city with fire.

Jeremiah Imprisoned

11 And it came to pass, that when the army of the Chaldeans was broken up from Jerusalem for fear of Pharaoh's army,

12 Then Jeremiah went forth out of Jerusalem to go into the land of Benjamin, to separate himself thence in the midst of the people.

13 And when he was in the gate of Benjamin, a captain of the ward *was* there, whose name *was* Irijah, the son of Shelemiah, the son of Hananiah; and he took Jeremiah the prophet, saying, Thou fallest away to the Chaldeans.

14 Then said Jeremiah, *It is* false; I fall not away to the Chaldeans. But he hearkened not to him: so Irijah took Jeremiah, and brought him to the princes.

15 Wherefore the princes were wroth with Jeremiah, and smote him, [a]and put him in prison in the [b]house of Jonathan the scribe: for they had made that the prison.

16 When Jeremiah was entered into [a]the dungeon, and into the cabins, and Jeremiah had remained there many days;

17 Then Zedekiah the king sent, and took him out: and the king asked him secretly in his house, and said, Is there *any* word from the LORD? And Jeremiah said, There is: for, said he, thou shalt be [a]delivered into the hand of the king of Babylon.

18 Moreover Jeremiah said unto king Zedekiah, What have I offended against thee, or against thy servants, or against this people, that ye have put me in prison?

19 Where *are* now your prophets which prophesied unto you, saying, The king of Babylon shall not come against you, nor against this land?

20 Therefore hear now, I pray thee, O my lord the king: let my supplication, I pray thee, be accepted before thee; that thou cause me not to return to the house of Jonathan the scribe, lest I die there.

21 Then Zedekiah the king commanded that they should commit Jeremiah [a]into the court of the prison, and that they should give him daily a piece of bread out of the bakers' street, [b]until all the bread in the city were spent. Thus Jeremiah remained in the court of the prison.

3 [a]Jer. 21:1, 2; 29:25; 52:24 [b]1 Kin. 13:6; Jer. 42:2; Acts 8:24
5 [a]2 Kin. 24:7; Jer. 37:7; Ezek. 17:15
7 [a]Is. 36:6; Jer. 21:2; Ezek. 17:17
8 [a]2 Chr. 36:19; Jer. 34:22
10 [a]Lev. 26:36–38; Is. 30:17; Jer. 21:4, 5
15 [a]Jer. 20:2; [Matt. 21:35] [b]Gen. 39:20; 2 Chr. 16:10; 18:26; Jer. 38:26; Acts 5:18
16 [a]Jer. 38:6
17 [a]2 Kin. 25:4–7; Jer. 21:7; Ezek. 12:12, 13; 17:19–21
21 [a]Jer. 32:2; 38:13, 28 [b]2 Kin. 25:3; Jer. 38:9; 52:6

NKJV

LORD which He spoke by the prophet Jeremiah.

3 And Zedekiah the king sent Jehucal the son of Shelemiah, and [a]Zephaniah the son of Maaseiah, the priest, to the prophet Jeremiah, saying, [b]"Pray now to the LORD our God for us."

4 Now Jeremiah was coming and going among the people, for they had not *yet* put him in prison.

5 Then [a]Pharaoh's army came up from Egypt; and when the Chaldeans who were besieging Jerusalem heard news of them, they departed from Jerusalem.

6 Then the word of the LORD came to the prophet Jeremiah, saying,

7 "Thus says the LORD, the God of Israel, 'Thus you shall say to the king of Judah, [a]who sent you to Me to inquire of Me: "Behold, Pharaoh's army which has come up to help you will return to Egypt, to their own land.

8 [a]"And the Chaldeans shall come back and fight against this city, and take it and burn it with fire." '

9 "Thus says the LORD: 'Do not deceive yourselves, saying, "The Chaldeans will surely depart from us," for they will not depart.

10 [a]'For though you had defeated the whole army of the Chaldeans who fight against you, and there remained *only* wounded men among them, they would rise up, every man in his tent, and burn the city with fire.' "

Jeremiah Imprisoned

11 And it happened, when the army of the Chaldeans left *the siege* of Jerusalem for fear of Pharaoh's army,

12 that Jeremiah went out of Jerusalem to go into the land of Benjamin to claim his property there among the people.

13 And when he was in the Gate of Benjamin, a captain of the guard *was* there whose name *was* Irijah the son of Shelemiah, the son of Hananiah; and he seized Jeremiah the prophet, saying, "You are defecting to the Chaldeans!"

14 Then Jeremiah said, "False! I am not defecting to the Chaldeans." But he did not listen to him. So Irijah seized Jeremiah and brought him to the princes.

15 Therefore the princes were angry with Jeremiah, and they struck him [a]and put him in prison in the [b]house of Jonathan the scribe. For they had made that the prison.

16 When Jeremiah entered [a]the dungeon and the cells, and Jeremiah had remained there many days,

17 then Zedekiah the king sent and took him *out*. The king asked him secretly in his house, and said, "Is there *any* word from the LORD?" And Jeremiah said, "There is." Then he said, "You shall be [a]delivered into the hand of the king of Babylon!"

18 Moreover Jeremiah said to King Zedekiah, "What offense have I committed against you, against your servants, or against this people, that you have put me in prison?

19 "Where now *are* your prophets who prophesied to you, saying, 'The king of Babylon will not come against you or against this land'?

20 "Therefore please hear now, O my lord the king. Please, let my petition be accepted before you, and do not make me return to the house of Jonathan the scribe, lest I die there."

21 Then Zedekiah the king commanded that they should commit Jeremiah [a]to the court of the prison, and that they should give him daily a piece of bread from the bakers' street, [b]until all the bread in the city was gone. Thus Jeremiah remained in the court of the prison.

KJV

Jeremiah in the Dungeon

38 Then Shephatiah the son of Mattan, and Gedaliah the son of Pashur, and [a]Jucal the son of Shelemiah, and [b]Pashur the son of Malchiah, [c]heard the words that Jeremiah had spoken unto all the people, saying,

2 Thus saith the LORD, [a]He that remaineth in this city shall die by the sword, by the famine, and by the pestilence: but he that goeth forth to the Chaldeans shall live; for he shall have his life for a prey, and shall live.

3 Thus saith the LORD, [a]This city shall surely be [b]given into the hand of the king of Babylon's army, which shall take it.

4 Therefore the princes said unto the king, We beseech thee, [a]let this man be put to death: for thus he weakeneth the hands of the men of war that remain in this city, and the hands of all the people, in speaking such words unto them: for this man seeketh not the welfare of this people, but the hurt.

5 Then Zedekiah the king said, Behold, he *is* in your hand: for the king *is* not *he that* can do *any* thing against you.

6 [a]Then took they Jeremiah, and cast him into the dungeon of Malchiah the son of Hammelech, that *was* in the court of the prison: and they let down Jeremiah with cords. And in the dungeon *there was* no water, but mire: so Jeremiah sunk in the mire.

7 [a]Now when Ebed–melech the Ethiopian, one of the eunuchs which was in the king's house, heard that they had put Jeremiah in the dungeon; the king then sitting in the gate of Benjamin;

8 Ebed–melech went forth out of the king's house, and spake to the king, saying,

9 My lord the king, these men have done evil in all that they have done to Jeremiah the prophet, whom they have cast into the dungeon; and he is like to die for hunger in the place where he is: for *there is* [a]no more bread in the city.

10 Then the king commanded Ebed–melech the Ethiopian, saying, Take from hence thirty men with thee, and take up Jeremiah the prophet out of the dungeon, before he die.

11 So Ebed–melech took the men with him, and went into the house of the king under the treasury, and took thence old cast clouts and old rotten rags, and let them down by cords into the dungeon to Jeremiah.

12 And Ebed–melech the Ethiopian said unto Jeremiah, Put now *these* old cast clouts and rotten rags under thine armholes under the cords. And Jeremiah did so.

13 So they drew up Jeremiah with cords, and took him up out of the dungeon: and Jeremiah remained [a]in the court of the prison.

Zedekiah's Fears and Jeremiah's Advice

14 Then Zedekiah the king sent, and took Jeremiah the prophet unto him into the third entry that *is* in the house of the LORD: and the king said unto Jeremiah, I will [a]ask thee a thing; hide nothing from me.

15 Then Jeremiah said unto Zedekiah, If I declare *it* unto thee, wilt thou not surely put me to death? and if I give thee counsel, wilt thou not hearken unto me?

16 So Zedekiah the king sware secretly unto Jeremiah, saying, *As* the LORD liveth, [a]that made us this soul, I will not put thee to death, neither will I give thee into the hand of these men that seek thy life.

17 Then said Jeremiah unto Zedekiah, Thus saith the LORD, the God of hosts, the God of Israel; If thou wilt assuredly [a]go forth [b]unto the king of Babylon's princes, then thy soul shall live, and this city shall not be burned with fire; and thou shalt live, and thine house:

18 But if thou wilt not go forth to the king

CHAPTER 38

1 [a]Jer. 37:3 [b]Jer. 21:1 [c]Jer. 21:8
2 [a]Jer. 21:9
3 [a]Jer. 21:10; 32:3 [b]Jer. 34:2
4 [a]Jer. 26:11
6 [a]Jer. 37:21; Lam. 3:55
7 [a]Jer. 39:16
9 [a]Jer. 37:21
13 [a]Neh. 3:25; Jer. 37:21; Acts 23:35; 24:27; 28:16, 30
14 [a]Jer. 21:1, 2; 37:17
16 [a]Num. 16:22; Is. 57:16; Zech. 12:1; [Acts 17:25, 28]
17 [a]2 Kin. 24:12 [b]Jer. 39:3

*

38:1 *Jehucal,* Jer. 37:3
38:6 Or *son of Hammelech*

NKJV

Jeremiah in the Dungeon

38 Now Shephatiah the son of Mattan, Gedaliah the son of Pashhur, [a]Jucal* the son of Shelemiah, and [b]Pashhur the son of Malchiah [c]heard the words that Jeremiah had spoken to all the people, saying,

2 "Thus says the LORD: [a]'He who remains in this city shall die by the sword, by famine, and by pestilence; but he who goes over to the Chaldeans shall live; his life shall be as a prize to him, and he shall live.'

3 "Thus says the LORD: [a]'This city shall surely be [b]given into the hand of the king of Babylon's army, which shall take it.' "

4 Therefore the princes said to the king, "Please, [a]let this man be put to death, for thus he weakens the hands of the men of war who remain in this city, and the hands of all the people, by speaking such words to them. For this man does not seek the welfare of this people, but their harm."

5 Then Zedekiah the king said, "Look, he *is* in your hand. For the king can *do* nothing against you."

6 [a]So they took Jeremiah and cast him into the dungeon of Malchiah *the king's son, which *was* in the court of the prison, and they let Jeremiah down with ropes. And in the dungeon *there was* no water, but mire. So Jeremiah sank in the mire.

7 [a]Now Ebed-Melech the Ethiopian, one of the eunuchs, who was in the king's house, heard that they had put Jeremiah in the dungeon. When the king was sitting at the Gate of Benjamin,

8 Ebed-Melech went out of the king's house and spoke to the king, saying:

9 "My lord the king, these men have done evil in all that they have done to Jeremiah the prophet, whom they have cast into the dungeon, and he is likely to die from hunger in the place where he is. For *there is* [a]no more bread in the city."

10 Then the king commanded Ebed-Melech the Ethiopian, saying, "Take from here thirty men with you, and lift Jeremiah the prophet out of the dungeon before he dies."

11 So Ebed-Melech took the men with him and went into the house of the king under the treasury, and took from there old clothes and old rags, and let them down by ropes into the dungeon to Jeremiah.

12 Then Ebed-Melech the Ethiopian said to Jeremiah, "Please put these old clothes and rags under your armpits, under the ropes." And Jeremiah did so.

13 So they pulled Jeremiah up with ropes and lifted him out of the dungeon. And Jeremiah remained [a]in the court of the prison.

Zedekiah's Fears and Jeremiah's Advice

14 Then Zedekiah the king sent and had Jeremiah the prophet brought to him at the third entrance of the house of the LORD. And the king said to Jeremiah, "I will [a]ask you something. Hide nothing from me."

15 Jeremiah said to Zedekiah, "If I declare *it* to you, will you not surely put me to death? And if I give you advice, you will not listen to me."

16 So Zedekiah the king swore secretly to Jeremiah, saying, "*As* the LORD lives, [a]who made our very souls, I will not put you to death, nor will I give you into the hand of these men who seek your life."

17 Then Jeremiah said to Zedekiah, "Thus says the LORD, the God of hosts, the God of Israel: 'If you surely [a]surrender [b]to the king of Babylon's princes, then your soul shall live; this city shall not be burned with fire, and you and your house shall live.

18 'But if you do not surrender to the king

KJV

of Babylon's princes, then shall this city be given
into the hand of the Chaldeans, and they shall
burn it with fire, and [a]thou shalt not escape out
of their hand.
19 And Zedekiah the king said unto Jere-
miah, I am afraid of the Jews that are [a]fallen to the
Chaldeans, lest they deliver me into their hand,
and they [b]mock me.
20 But Jeremiah said, They shall not deliver
thee. Obey, I beseech thee, the voice of the LORD,
which I speak unto thee: so it shall be [a]well unto
thee, and thy soul shall live.
21 But if thou refuse to go forth, this *is* the
word that the LORD hath shewed me:
22 And, behold, all the [a]women that are left
in the king of Judah's house *shall be* brought forth
to the king of Babylon's princes, and those *women*
shall say, Thy friends have set thee on, and have
prevailed against thee: thy feet are sunk in the
mire, *and* they are turned away back.
23 So they shall bring out all thy wives and
[a]thy children to the Chaldeans: and [b]thou shalt
not escape out of their hand, but shalt be taken
by the hand of the king of Babylon: and thou shalt
cause this city to be burned with fire.
24 Then said Zedekiah unto Jeremiah, Let no
man know of these words, and thou shalt not die.
25 But if the princes hear that I have talked
with thee, and they come unto thee, and say unto
thee, Declare unto us now what thou hast said
unto the king, hide it not from us, and we will
not put thee to death; also what the king said unto
thee:
26 Then thou shalt say unto them, [a]I presented my supplication before the king, that he
would not cause me to return [b]to Jonathan's
house, to die there.
27 Then came all the princes unto Jeremiah,
and asked him: and he told them according to
all these words that the king had commanded.
So they left off speaking with him; for the matter
was not perceived.
28 So [a]Jeremiah abode in the court of the
prison until the day that Jerusalem was taken:
and he was *there* when Jerusalem was taken.

The Fall of Jerusalem
(2 Kin. 25:1–12; Jer. 52:4–16)

39 In the [a]ninth year of Zedekiah king of Judah, in the tenth month, came Nebuchadrezzar king of Babylon and all his army against
Jerusalem, and they besieged it.
2 *And* in the [a]eleventh year of Zedekiah, in
the fourth month, the ninth *day* of the month, the
city was broken up.
3 [a]And all the princes of the king of Babylon
came in, and sat in the middle gate, *even* Nergal–
sharezer, Samgar–nebo, Sarsechim, Rab–saris,
Nergal–sharezer, Rab–mag, with all the residue
of the princes of the king of Babylon.
4 [a]And it came to pass, *that* when Zedekiah
the king of Judah saw them, and all the men of
war, then they fled, and went forth out of the city
by night, by the way of the king's garden, by the
gate betwixt the two walls: and he went out the
way of the plain.
5 But the Chaldeans' army pursued after
them, and [a]overtook Zedekiah in the plains of Jericho: and when they had taken him, they brought
him up to Nebuchadnezzar king of Babylon to
[b]Riblah in the land of Hamath, where he gave
judgment upon him.
6 Then the king of Babylon slew the sons
of Zedekiah in Riblah before his [a]eyes: also the
king of Babylon slew all the [b]nobles of Judah.
7 Moreover [a]he put out Zedekiah's eyes,
and bound him with chains, to carry him to
Babylon.
8 [a]And the Chaldeans burned the king's

NKJV

of Babylon's princes, then this city shall be given
into the hand of the Chaldeans; they shall burn
it with fire, and [a]you shall not escape from their
hand.' "
19 And Zedekiah the king said to Jeremiah,
"I am afraid of the Jews who have [a]defected to
the Chaldeans, lest they deliver me into their
hand, and they [b]abuse me."
20 But Jeremiah said, "They shall not deliver
you. Please, obey the voice of the LORD which I
speak to you. So it shall be [a]well with you, and
your soul shall live.
21 "But if you refuse to surrender, this *is* the
word that the LORD has shown me:
22 'Now behold, all the [a]women who are left
in the king of Judah's house *shall be* surrendered
to the king of Babylon's princes, and those *women*
shall say:

"Your close friends have set upon you
And prevailed against you;
Your feet have sunk in the mire,
And they have turned away again."

23 'So they shall surrender all your wives and
[a]children to the Chaldeans. [b]You shall not escape
from their hand, but shall be taken by the hand
of the king of Babylon. And you shall cause this
city to be burned with fire.' "
24 Then Zedekiah said to Jeremiah, "Let no
one know of these words, and you shall not die.
25 "But if the princes hear that I have talked
with you, and they come to you and say to you,
'Declare to us now what you have said to the king,
and also what the king said to you; do not hide
it from us, and we will not put you to death,'
26 "then you shall say to them, [a]'I presented
my request before the king, that he would not
make me return [b]to Jonathan's house to die
there.' "
27 Then all the princes came to Jeremiah and
asked him. And he told them according to all these
words that the king had commanded. So they
stopped speaking with him, for the conversation
had not been heard.
28 Now [a]Jeremiah remained in the court of
the prison until the day that Jerusalem was taken.
And he was *there* when Jerusalem was taken.

The Fall of Jerusalem
(2 Kin. 25:1–12; Jer. 52:4–16)

39 In the [a]ninth year of Zedekiah king of Judah, in the tenth month, Nebuchadnezzar
king of Babylon and all his army came against
Jerusalem, and besieged it.
2 In the [a]eleventh year of Zedekiah, in the
fourth month, on the ninth *day* of the month, the
city was penetrated.
3 [a]Then all the princes of the king of Babylon came in and sat in the Middle Gate: Nergal-
Sharezer, Samgar-Nebo, Sarsechim, *Rabsaris,
Nergal-Sarezer, *Rabmag, with the rest of the
princes of the king of Babylon.
4 [a]So it was, when Zedekiah the king of Judah and all the men of war saw them, that they
fled and went out of the city by night, by way of
the king's garden, by the gate between the two
walls. And he went out by way of the *plain.
5 But the Chaldean army pursued them and
[a]overtook Zedekiah in the plains of Jericho. And
when they had captured him, they brought him
up to Nebuchadnezzar king of Babylon, to [b]Rib-
lah in the land of Hamath, where he pronounced
judgment on him.
6 Then the king of Babylon killed the sons
of Zedekiah before his [a]eyes in Riblah; the king
of Babylon also killed all the [b]nobles of Judah.
7 Moreover [a]he put out Zedekiah's eyes,
and bound him with bronze fetters to carry him
off to Babylon.
8 [a]And the Chaldeans burned the king's

18 [a]Jer. 32:4; 34:3
19 [a]Jer. 39:9 [b]1 Sam. 31:4
20 [a]Jer. 40:9
22 [a]Jer. 8:10
23 [a]Jer. 39:6; 41:10 [b]Jer. 39:5
26 [a]Jer. 37:20 [b]Jer. 37:15
28 [a][Ps. 23:4]; Jer. 37:21; 39:14

CHAPTER 39

1 [a]2 Kin. 25:1–12; Jer. 52:4; Ezek. 24:1, 2
2 [a]Jer. 1:3
3 [a]Jer. 1:15; 38:17
4 [a]2 Kin. 25:4; Is. 30:16; Jer. 52:7; Amos 2:14
5 [a]Jer. 21:7; 32:4; 38:18, 23 [b]2 Kin. 23:33; Jer. 52:9, 26, 27
6 [a]Deut. 28:34 [b]Jer. 34:19–21
7 [a]2 Kin. 25:7; Jer. 52:11; Ezek. 12:13
8 [a]2 Kin. 25:9; Jer. 38:18; 52:13

*

39:3 A title, probably *Chief Officer;* also v. 13 • A title, probably *Troop Commander;* also v. 13
39:4 Or *Arabah;* the Jordan valley

KJV

house, and the houses of the people, with [b]fire, and brake down the [c]walls of Jerusalem.

9 [a]Then Nebuzar–adan the captain of the guard carried away captive into Babylon the remnant of the people that remained in the city, and those that fell away, that [b]fell to him, with the rest of the people that remained.

10 But Nebuzar–adan the captain of the guard left of the [a]poor of the people, which had nothing, in the land of Judah, and gave them vineyards and fields at the same time.

Jeremiah Goes Free

11 Now Nebuchadrezzar king of Babylon gave charge concerning Jeremiah to Nebuzar–adan the captain of the guard, saying,

12 Take him, and look well to him, and do him no [a]harm; but do unto him even as he shall say unto thee.

13 So Nebuzar–adan the captain of the guard sent, and Nebushasban, Rab–saris, and Nergal–sharezer, Rab–mag, and all the king of Babylon's princes;

14 Even they sent, [a]and took Jeremiah out of the court of the prison, and committed him [b]unto Gedaliah the son of [c]Ahikam the son of Shaphan, that he should carry him home: so he dwelt among the people.

15 Now the word of the LORD came unto Jeremiah, while he was shut up in the court of the prison, saying,

16 Go and speak to [a]Ebed–melech the Ethiopian, saying, Thus saith the LORD of hosts, the God of Israel; Behold, [b]I will bring my words upon this city for evil, and not for good; and they shall be *accomplished* in that day before thee.

17 But I will deliver thee in that day, saith the LORD: and thou shalt not be given into the hand of the men of whom thou *art* afraid.

18 For I will surely deliver thee, and thou shalt not fall by the sword, but [a]thy life shall be for a prey unto thee: [b]because thou hast put thy trust in me, saith the LORD.

Jeremiah with Gedaliah the Governor
(2 Kin. 25:22–26)

40 The word that came to Jeremiah from the LORD, [a]after that Nebuzar–adan the captain of the guard had let him go from Ramah, when he had taken him being bound in chains among all that were carried away captive of Jerusalem and Judah, which were carried away captive unto Babylon.

2 And the captain of the guard took Jeremiah, and [a]said unto him, The LORD thy God hath pronounced this evil upon this place.

3 Now the LORD hath brought *it*, and done according as he hath said: [a]because ye have sinned against the LORD, and have not obeyed his voice, therefore this thing is come upon you.

4 And now, behold, I loose thee this day from the chains which *were* upon thine hand. [a]If it seem good unto thee to come with me into Babylon, come; and I will look well unto thee: but if it seem ill unto thee to come with me into Babylon, forbear: behold, [b]all the land *is* before thee: whither it seemeth good and convenient for thee to go, thither go.

5 Now while he was not yet gone back, *he said,* Go back also to [a]Gedaliah the son of Ahikam the son of Shaphan, [b]whom the king of Babylon hath made governor over the cities of Judah, and dwell with him among the people: or go wheresoever it seemeth convenient unto thee to go. So the captain of the guard gave him victuals and a reward, and let him go.

6 [a]Then went Jeremiah unto Gedaliah the son of Ahikam to [b]Mizpah; and dwelt with him among the people that were left in the land.

7 [a]Now when all the captains of the forces which *were* in the fields, *even* they and their men, heard that the king of Babylon had made Gedaliah

8 [b]Jer. 21:10 [c]2 Kin. 25:10; Neh. 1:3; Jer. 52:14
9 [a]2 Kin. 25:8, 11, 12, 20 [b]Jer. 38:19
10 [a]Jer. 40:7
12 [a]Jer. 1:18, 19; 15:20, 21
14 [a]Jer. 38:28 [b]Jer. 40:5 [c]2 Kin. 22:12, 14; 2 Chr. 34:20; Jer. 26:24
16 [a]Jer. 38:7, 12 [b]Jer. 21:10; [Dan. 9:12; Zech. 1:6]
18 [a]Jer. 21:9; 45:5 [b]1 Chr. 5:20; Ps. 37:40; [Jer. 17:7, 8]

CHAPTER 40

1 [a]Jer. 39:9, 11
2 [a]Jer. 50:7
3 [a]Deut. 29:24, 25; Jer. 50:7; Dan. 9:11; [Rom. 2:5]
4 [a]Jer. 39:12 [b]Gen. 20:15
5 [a]Jer. 39:14 [b]2 Kin. 25:22; Jer. 41:10
6 [a]Jer. 39:14 [b]Judg. 20:1; 1 Sam. 7:5; 2 Chr. 16:6
7 [a]2 Kin. 25:23, 24

NKJV

house and the houses of the people with [b]fire, and broke down the [c]walls of Jerusalem.

9 [a]Then Nebuzaradan the captain of the guard carried away captive to Babylon the remnant of the people who remained in the city and those who [b]defected to him, with the rest of the people who remained.

10 But Nebuzaradan the captain of the guard left in the land of Judah the [a]poor people, who had nothing, and gave them vineyards and fields at the same time.

Jeremiah Goes Free

11 Now Nebuchadnezzar king of Babylon gave charge concerning Jeremiah to Nebuzaradan the captain of the guard, saying,

12 "Take him and look after him, and do him no [a]harm; but do to him just as he says to you."

13 So Nebuzaradan the captain of the guard sent Nebushasban, Rabsaris, Nergal-Sharezer, Rabmag, and all the king of Babylon's chief officers;

14 then they sent *someone* [a]to take Jeremiah from the court of the prison, and committed him [b]to Gedaliah the son of [c]Ahikam, the son of Shaphan, that he should take him home. So he dwelt among the people.

15 Meanwhile the word of the LORD had come to Jeremiah while he was shut up in the court of the prison, saying,

16 "Go and speak to [a]Ebed-Melech the Ethiopian, saying, 'Thus says the LORD of hosts, the God of Israel: "Behold, [b]I will bring My words upon this city for adversity and not for good, and they shall be *performed* in that day before you.

17 "But I will deliver you in that day," says the LORD, "and you shall not be given into the hand of the men of whom you *are* afraid.

18 "For I will surely deliver you, and you shall not fall by the sword; but [a]your life shall be as a prize to you, [b]because you have put your trust in Me," says the LORD.' "

Jeremiah with Gedaliah the Governor
(2 Kin. 25:22-26)

40 The word that came to Jeremiah from the LORD [a]after Nebuzaradan the captain of the guard had let him go from Ramah, when he had taken him bound in chains among all who were carried away captive from Jerusalem and Judah, who were carried away captive to Babylon.

2 And the captain of the guard took Jeremiah and [a]said to him: "The LORD your God has pronounced this doom on this place.

3 "Now the LORD has brought *it*, and has done just as He said. [a]Because you *people* have sinned against the LORD, and not obeyed His voice, therefore this thing has come upon you.

4 "And now look, I free you this day from the chains that *were* on your hand. [a]If it seems good to you to come with me to Babylon, come, and I will look after you. But if it seems wrong for you to come with me to Babylon, remain here. See, [b]all the land *is* before you; wherever it seems good and convenient for you to go, go there."

5 Now while Jeremiah had not yet gone back, *Nebuzaradan said,* "Go back to [a]Gedaliah the son of Ahikam, the son of Shaphan, [b]whom the king of Babylon has made governor over the cities of Judah, and dwell with him among the people. Or go wherever it seems convenient for you to go." So the captain of the guard gave him rations and a gift and let him go.

6 [a]Then Jeremiah went to Gedaliah the son of Ahikam, to [b]Mizpah, and dwelt with him among the people who were left in the land.

7 [a]And when all the captains of the armies who *were* in the fields, they and their men, heard that the king of Babylon had made Gedaliah the

KJV

the son of Ahikam governor in the land, and had committed unto him men, and women, and children, and of [b]the poor of the land, of them that were not carried away captive to Babylon;

8 Then they came to Gedaliah to Mizpah, [a]even Ishmael the son of Nethaniah, and [b]Johanan and Jonathan the sons of Kareah, and Seraiah the son of Tanhumeth, and the sons of Ephai the Netophathite, and [c]Jezaniah the son of a [d]Maachathite, they and their men.

9 And Gedaliah the son of Ahikam the son of Shaphan sware unto them and to their men, saying, Fear not to serve the Chaldeans: dwell in the land, and serve the king of Babylon, and it shall be [a]well with you.

10 As for me, behold, I will dwell at Mizpah, to serve the Chaldeans, which will come unto us: but ye, gather ye wine, and summer fruits, and oil, and put *them* in your vessels, and dwell in your cities that ye have taken.

11 Likewise when all the Jews that *were* in Moab, and among the Ammonites, and in Edom, and that *were* in all the countries, heard that the king of Babylon had left a remnant of Judah, and that he had set over them Gedaliah the son of Ahikam the son of Shaphan;

12 Even all the Jews [a]returned out of all places whither they were driven, and came to the land of Judah, to Gedaliah, unto Mizpah, and gathered wine and summer fruits very much.

13 Moreover Johanan the son of Kareah, and all the captains of the forces that *were* in the fields, came to Gedaliah to Mizpah,

14 And said unto him, Dost thou certainly know that [a]Baalis the king of the Ammonites hath sent Ishmael the son of Nethaniah to slay thee? But Gedaliah the son of Ahikam believed them not.

15 Then Johanan the son of Kareah spake to Gedaliah in Mizpah secretly, saying, Let me go, I pray thee, and I will slay Ishmael the son of Nethaniah, and no man shall know *it:* wherefore should he slay thee, that all the Jews which are gathered unto thee should be scattered, and the [a]remnant in Judah perish?

16 But Gedaliah the son of Ahikam said unto Johanan the son of Kareah, Thou shalt not do this thing: for thou speakest falsely of Ishmael.

Insurrection Against Gedaliah

41 Now it came to pass in the seventh month, [a]*that* Ishmael the son of Nethaniah the son of Elishama, of the seed royal, and the princes of the king, even ten men with him, came unto Gedaliah the son of Ahikam to [b]Mizpah; and there they did eat bread together in Mizpah.

2 Then arose Ishmael the son of Nethaniah, and the ten men that were with him, and [a]smote Gedaliah the son of [b]Ahikam the son of Shaphan with the sword, and slew him, whom the king of Babylon had made [c]governor over the land.

3 Ishmael also slew all the Jews that were with him, *even* with Gedaliah, at Mizpah, and the Chaldeans that were found there, *and* the men of war.

4 And it came to pass the second day after he had slain Gedaliah, and no man knew *it,*

5 That there came certain from Shechem, from Shiloh, and from Samaria, *even* fourscore men, [a]having their beards shaven, and their clothes rent, and having cut themselves, with offerings and incense in their hand, to bring *them* to [b]the house of the LORD.

6 And Ishmael the son of Nethaniah went forth from Mizpah to meet them, weeping all along as he went: and it came to pass, as he met them, he said unto them, Come to Gedaliah the son of Ahikam.

7 And it was *so,* when they came into the midst of the city, that Ishmael the son of Nethaniah [a]slew them, *and cast them* into the midst of the pit, he, and the men that *were* with him.

7 [b]Jer. 39:10
8 [a]Jer. 41:1–10 [b]Jer. 41:11; 43:2 [c]Jer. 42:1 [d]Deut. 3:14; Josh. 12:5; 2 Sam. 10:6
9 [a]Jer. 27:11; 38:17–20
12 [a]Jer. 43:5
14 [a]Jer. 41:10
15 [a]Jer. 42:2

CHAPTER 41

1 [a]2 Kin. 25:25 [b]Jer. 40:6, 10
2 [a]2 Sam. 3:27; 20:9, 10; 2 Kin. 25:25; Ps. 41:9; 109:5; John 13:18 [b]Jer. 26:24 [c]Jer. 40:5
5 [a]Lev. 19:27, 28; Deut. 14:1; Is. 15:2 [b]1 Sam. 1:7; 2 Kin. 25:9; Neh. 10:34, 35
7 [a]Ps. 55:23; Is. 59:7; Ezek. 22:27; 33:24, 26

*

40:8 *Jaazaniah,* 2 Kin. 25:23

NKJV

son of Ahikam governor in the land, and had committed to him men, women, children, and [b]the poorest of the land who had not been carried away captive to Babylon,

8 then they came to Gedaliah at Mizpah—[a]Ishmael the son of Nethaniah, [b]Johanan and Jonathan the sons of Kareah, Seraiah the son of Tanhumeth, the sons of Ephai the Netophathite, and [c]Jezaniah* the son of a [d]Maachathite, they and their men.

9 And Gedaliah the son of Ahikam, the son of Shaphan, took an oath before them and their men, saying, "Do not be afraid to serve the Chaldeans. Dwell in the land and serve the king of Babylon, and it shall be [a]well with you.

10 "As for me, I will indeed dwell at Mizpah and serve the Chaldeans who come to us. But you, gather wine and summer fruit and oil, put *them* in your vessels, and dwell in your cities that you have taken."

11 Likewise, when all the Jews who *were* in Moab, among the Ammonites, in Edom, and who *were* in all the countries, heard that the king of Babylon had left a remnant of Judah, and that he had set over them Gedaliah the son of Ahikam, the son of Shaphan,

12 then all the Jews [a]returned out of all places where they had been driven, and came to the land of Judah, to Gedaliah at Mizpah, and gathered wine and summer fruit in abundance.

13 Moreover Johanan the son of Kareah and all the captains of the forces that *were* in the fields came to Gedaliah at Mizpah,

14 and said to him, "Do you certainly know that [a]Baalis the king of the Ammonites has sent Ishmael the son of Nethaniah to murder you?" But Gedaliah the son of Ahikam did not believe them.

15 Then Johanan the son of Kareah spoke secretly to Gedaliah in Mizpah, saying, "Let me go, please, and I will kill Ishmael the son of Nethaniah, and no one will know *it.* Why should he murder you, so that all the Jews who are gathered to you would be scattered, and the [a]remnant in Judah perish?"

16 But Gedaliah the son of Ahikam said to Johanan the son of Kareah, "You shall not do this thing, for you speak falsely concerning Ishmael."

Insurrection Against Gedaliah

41 Now it came to pass in the seventh month [a]*that* Ishmael the son of Nethaniah, the son of Elishama, of the royal family and of the officers of the king, came with ten men to Gedaliah the son of Ahikam, at [b]Mizpah. And there they ate bread together in Mizpah.

2 Then Ishmael the son of Nethaniah, and the ten men who were with him, arose and [a]struck Gedaliah the son of [b]Ahikam, the son of Shaphan, with the sword, and killed him whom the king of Babylon had made [c]governor over the land.

3 Ishmael also struck down all the Jews who were with him, *that is,* with Gedaliah at Mizpah, and the Chaldeans who were found there, the men of war.

4 And it happened, on the second day after he had killed Gedaliah, when as yet no one knew *it,*

5 that certain men came from Shechem, from Shiloh, and from Samaria, eighty men [a]with their beards shaved and their clothes torn, having cut themselves, with offerings and incense in their hand, to bring *them* to [b]the house of the LORD.

6 Now Ishmael the son of Nethaniah went out from Mizpah to meet them, weeping as he went along; and it happened as he met them that he said to them, "Come to Gedaliah the son of Ahikam!"

7 So it was, when they came into the midst of the city, that Ishmael the son of Nethaniah [a]killed them *and cast them* into the midst of a pit, he and the men who were with him.

KJV

8 But ten men were found among them that said unto Ishmael, Slay us not: for we have treasures in the field, of wheat, and of barley, and of oil, and of honey. So he forbare, and slew them not among their brethren.
9 Now the pit wherein Ishmael had cast all the dead bodies of the men, whom he had slain because of Gedaliah, *was* it [a]which Asa the king had made for fear of Baasha king of Israel: *and* Ishmael the son of Nethaniah filled it with *them that were* slain.
10 Then Ishmael carried away captive all the [a]residue of the people that *were* in Mizpah, [b]*even* the king's daughters, and all the people that remained in Mizpah, [c]whom Nebuzar–adan the captain of the guard had committed to Gedaliah the son of Ahikam: and Ishmael the son of Nethaniah carried them away captive, and departed to go over to [d]the Ammonites.
11 But when [a]Johanan the son of Kareah, and all the captains of the forces that *were* with him, heard of all the evil that Ishmael the son of Nethaniah had done,
12 Then they took all the men, and went to fight with Ishmael the son of Nethaniah, and found him by [a]the great waters that *are* in Gibeon.
13 Now it came to pass, *that* when all the people which *were* with Ishmael saw Johanan the son of Kareah, and all the captains of the forces that *were* with him, then they were glad.
14 So all the people that Ishmael had carried away captive from Mizpah cast about and returned, and went unto Johanan the son of Kareah.
15 But Ishmael the son of Nethaniah escaped from Johanan with eight men, and went to the Ammonites.
16 Then took Johanan the son of Kareah, and all the captains of the forces that *were* with him, all the [a]remnant of the people whom he had recovered from Ishmael the son of Nethaniah, from Mizpah, after *that* he had slain Gedaliah the son of Ahikam, *even* mighty men of war, and the women, and the children, and the eunuchs, whom he had brought again from Gibeon:
17 And they departed, and dwelt in the habitation of [a]Chimham, which is by Beth–lehem, to go to enter into [b]Egypt,
18 Because of the Chaldeans: for they were afraid of them, because Ishmael the son of Nethaniah had slain Gedaliah the son of Ahikam, [a]whom the king of Babylon made governor in the land.

The Flight to Egypt Forbidden

42 Then all the captains of the forces, [a]and Johanan the son of Kareah, and Jezaniah the son of Hoshaiah, and all the people from the least even unto the greatest, came near,
2 And said unto Jeremiah the prophet, Let, we [a]beseech thee, our supplication be accepted before thee, and [b]pray for us unto the LORD thy God, *even* for all this remnant; (for we are left *but* [c]a few of many, as thine eyes do behold us:)
3 That the LORD thy God may shew us [a]the way wherein we may walk, and the thing that we may do.
4 Then Jeremiah the prophet said unto them, I have heard *you;* behold, I will pray unto the LORD your God according to your words; and it shall come to pass, *that* [a]whatsoever thing the LORD shall answer you, I will declare *it* unto you; I will [b]keep nothing back from you.
5 Then they said to Jeremiah, [a]The LORD be a true and faithful witness between us, if we do not even according to all things for the which the LORD thy God shall send thee to us.
6 Whether *it be* good, or whether *it be* evil, we will [a]obey the voice of the LORD our God, to whom we send thee; [b]that it may be well with us, when we obey the voice of the LORD our God.

9 [a]1 Kin. 15:22; 2 Chr. 16:6
10 [a]Jer. 40:11, 12 [b]Jer. 43:6 [c]Jer. 40:7 [d]Jer. 40:14
11 [a]Jer. 40:7, 8, 13–16
12 [a]2 Sam. 2:13
16 [a]Jer. 40:11, 12; 43:4–7
17 [a]2 Sam. 19:37, 38 [b]Jer. 43:7
18 [a]Jer. 40:5

CHAPTER 42

1 [a]Jer. 40:8, 13; 41:11
2 [a]Jer. 15:11 [b]Ex. 8:28; 1 Sam. 7:8; 12:19; 1 Kin. 13:6; Is. 37:4; Jer. 37:3; Acts 8:24; [James 5:16] [c]Lev. 26:22; Deut. 28:62; Is. 1:9; Lam. 1:1
3 [a]Ezra 8:21
4 [a]1 Kin. 22:14; Jer. 23:28 [b]1 Sam. 3:17, 18; Ps. 40:10; Acts 20:20
5 [a]Gen. 31:50; Judg. 11:10; Jer. 43:2; Mic. 1:2; Mal. 2:14; 3:5
6 [a]Ex. 24:7; Deut. 5:27; Josh. 24:24 [b]Deut. 5:29, 33; 6:3; Jer. 7:23

NKJV

8 But ten men were found among them who said to Ishmael, "Do not kill us, for we have treasures of wheat, barley, oil, and honey in the field." So he desisted and did not kill them among their brethren.
9 Now the pit into which Ishmael had cast all the dead bodies of the men whom he had slain, because of Gedaliah, *was* [a]the same one Asa the king had made for fear of Baasha king of Israel. Ishmael the son of Nethaniah filled it with *the* slain.
10 Then Ishmael carried away captive all the [a]rest of the people who *were* in Mizpah, [b]the king's daughters and all the people who remained in Mizpah, [c]whom Nebuzaradan the captain of the guard had committed to Gedaliah the son of Ahikam. And Ishmael the son of Nethaniah carried them away captive and departed to go over to [d]the Ammonites.
11 But when [a]Johanan the son of Kareah and all the captains of the forces that *were* with him heard of all the evil that Ishmael the son of Nethaniah had done,
12 they took all the men and went to fight with Ishmael the son of Nethaniah; and they found him by [a]the great pool that *is* in Gibeon.
13 So it was, when all the people who *were* with Ishmael saw Johanan the son of Kareah, and all the captains of the forces who *were* with him, that they were glad.
14 Then all the people whom Ishmael had carried away captive from Mizpah turned around and came back, and went to Johanan the son of Kareah.
15 But Ishmael the son of Nethaniah escaped from Johanan with eight men and went to the Ammonites.
16 Then Johanan the son of Kareah, and all the captains of the forces that were with him, took from Mizpah all the [a]rest of the people whom he had recovered from Ishmael the son of Nethaniah after he had murdered Gedaliah the son of Ahikam—the mighty men of war and the women and the children and the eunuchs, whom he had brought back from Gibeon.
17 And they departed and dwelt in the habitation of [a]Chimham, which is near Bethlehem, as they went on their way to [b]Egypt,
18 because of the Chaldeans; for they were afraid of them, because Ishmael the son of Nethaniah had murdered Gedaliah the son of Ahikam, [a]whom the king of Babylon had made governor in the land.

The Flight to Egypt Forbidden

42 Now all the captains of the forces, [a]Johanan the son of Kareah, Jezaniah the son of Hoshaiah, and all the people, from the least to the greatest, came near
2 and said to Jeremiah the prophet, [a]"Please, let our petition be acceptable to you, and [b]pray for us to the LORD your God, for all this remnant (since we are left *but* [c]a few of many, as you can see),
3 "that the LORD your God may show us [a]the way in which we should walk and the thing we should do."
4 Then Jeremiah the prophet said to them, "I have heard. Indeed, I will pray to the LORD your God according to your words, and it shall be, *that* [a]whatever the LORD answers you, I will declare *it* to you. I will [b]keep nothing back from you."
5 So they said to Jeremiah, [a]"Let the LORD be a true and faithful witness between us, if we do not do according to everything which the LORD your God sends us by you.
6 "Whether *it is* pleasing or displeasing, we will [a]obey the voice of the LORD our God to whom we send you, [b]that it may be well with us when we obey the voice of the LORD our God."

KJV

7 And it came to pass after ten days, that the word of the LORD came unto Jeremiah.

8 Then called he Johanan the son of Kareah, and all the captains of the forces which *were* with him, and all the people from the least even to the greatest,

9 And said unto them, Thus saith the LORD, the God of Israel, unto whom ye sent me to present your supplication before him;

10 If ye will still abide in this land, then [a]will I build you, and not pull *you* down, and I will plant you, and not pluck *you* up: for I [b]repent me of the evil that I have done unto you.

11 Be not afraid of the king of Babylon, of whom ye are afraid; be not afraid of him, saith the LORD: [a]for I *am* with you to save you, and to deliver you from his hand.

12 And [a]I will shew mercies unto you, that he may have mercy upon you, and cause you to return to your own land.

13 But if [a]ye say, We will not dwell in this land, neither obey the voice of the LORD your God,

14 Saying, No; but we will go into the land of [a]Egypt, where we shall see no war, nor hear the sound of the trumpet, nor have hunger of bread; and there will we dwell:

15 And now therefore hear the word of the LORD, ye remnant of Judah; Thus saith the LORD of hosts, the God of Israel; If ye [a]wholly set [b]your faces to enter into Egypt, and go to sojourn there;

16 Then it shall come to pass, *that* the [a]sword, which ye feared, shall overtake you there in the land of Egypt, and the famine, whereof ye were afraid, shall follow close after you there in Egypt; and there ye shall die.

17 So shall it be with all the men that set their faces to go into Egypt to sojourn there; they shall die by the sword, by the famine, and by the pestilence: and [a]none of them shall remain or escape from the evil that I will bring upon them.

18 For thus saith the LORD of hosts, the God of Israel; As mine anger and my fury hath been [a]poured forth upon the inhabitants of Jerusalem; so shall my fury be poured forth upon you, when ye shall enter into Egypt: and [b]ye shall be an execration, and an astonishment, and a curse, and a reproach; and ye shall see this place no more.

19 The LORD hath said concerning you, O ye remnant of Judah; [a]Go ye not into Egypt: know certainly that I have admonished you this day.

20 For ye dissembled in your hearts, when ye sent me unto the LORD your God, saying, Pray for us unto the LORD our God; and according unto all that the LORD our God shall say, so declare unto us, and we will do *it*.

21 And *now* I have this day declared *it* to you; but ye have [a]not obeyed the voice of the LORD your God, nor any *thing* for the which he hath sent me unto you.

22 Now therefore know certainly that [a]ye shall die by the sword, by the famine, and by the pestilence, in the place whither ye desire to go *and* to sojourn.

Jeremiah Taken to Egypt

43 And it came to pass, *that* when Jeremiah had made an end of speaking unto all the people all the [a]words of the LORD their God, for which the LORD their God had sent him to them, *even* all these words,

2 [a]Then spake Azariah the son of Hoshaiah, and Johanan the son of Kareah, and all the proud men, saying unto Jeremiah, Thou speakest falsely: the LORD our God hath not sent thee to say, Go not into Egypt to sojourn there:

3 But [a]Baruch the son of Neriah setteth thee on against us, for to deliver us into the hand of the Chaldeans, that they might put us to death, and carry us away captives into Babylon.

4 So Johanan the son of Kareah, and all the

10 [a]Jer. 24:6; 31:28; 33:7; Ezek. 36:36 [b]Deut. 32:36; [Jer. 18:8]
11 [a]Num. 14:9; 2 Chr. 32:7, 8; Is. 8:9, 10; 43:2, 5; Jer. 1:19; 15:20; Rom. 8:31
12 [a]Neh. 1:11; Ps. 106:46; Prov. 16:7
13 [a]Jer. 44:16
14 [a]Is. 31:1; Jer. 41:17; 43:7
15 [a]Deut. 17:16; Jer. 44:12–14 [b]Luke 9:51
16 [a]Jer. 44:13, 27; Ezek. 11:8; Amos 9:1–4
17 [a]Jer. 44:14, 28
18 [a]2 Chr. 36:16–19; Jer. 7:20 [b]Deut. 29:21; Is. 65:15; Jer. 18:16; 24:9; 26:6; 29:18, 22; 44:12
19 [a]Deut. 17:16; Is. 30:1–7
21 [a]Is. 30:1–7
22 [a]Jer. 42:17; Ezek. 6:11

CHAPTER 43
1 [a]Jer. 42:9–18
2 [a]Jer. 42:1
3 [a]Jer. 36:4; 45:1

NKJV

7 And it happened after ten days that the word of the LORD came to Jeremiah.

8 Then he called Johanan the son of Kareah, all the captains of the forces which *were* with him, and all the people from the least even to the greatest,

9 and said to them, "Thus says the LORD, the God of Israel, to whom you sent me to present your petition before Him:

10 'If you will still remain in this land, then [a]I will build you and not pull *you* down, and I will plant you and not pluck *you* up. For I [b]relent concerning the disaster that I have brought upon you.

11 'Do not be afraid of the king of Babylon, of whom you are afraid; do not be afraid of him,' says the LORD, [a]'for I *am* with you, to save you and deliver you from his hand.

12 'And [a]I will show you mercy, that he may have mercy on you and cause you to return to your own land.'

13 "But if [a]you say, 'We will not dwell in this land,' disobeying the voice of the LORD your God,

14 "saying, 'No, but we will go to the land of [a]Egypt where we shall see no war, nor hear the sound of the trumpet, nor be hungry for bread, and there we will dwell'—

15 "Then hear now the word of the LORD, O remnant of Judah! Thus says the LORD of hosts, the God of Israel: 'If you [a]wholly set [b]your faces to enter Egypt, and go to dwell there,

16 'then it shall be *that* the [a]sword which you feared shall overtake you there in the land of Egypt; the famine of which you were afraid shall follow close after you there *in* Egypt; and there you shall die.

17 'So shall it be with all the men who set their faces to go to Egypt to dwell there. They shall die by the sword, by famine, and by pestilence. And [a]none of them shall remain or escape from the disaster that I will bring upon them.'

18 "For thus says the LORD of hosts, the God of Israel: 'As My anger and My fury have been [a]poured out on the inhabitants of Jerusalem, so will My fury be poured out on you when you enter Egypt. And [b]you shall be an oath, an astonishment, a curse, and a reproach; and you shall see this place no more.'

19 "The LORD has said concerning you, O remnant of Judah, [a]'Do not go to Egypt!' Know certainly that I have admonished you this day.

20 "For you were hypocrites in your hearts when you sent me to the LORD your God, saying, 'Pray for us to the LORD our God, and according to all that the LORD your God says, so declare to us and we will do *it*.'

21 "And I have this day declared *it* to you, but you have [a]not obeyed the voice of the LORD your God, or anything which He has sent you by me.

22 "Now therefore, know certainly that you [a]shall die by the sword, by famine, and by pestilence in the place where you desire to go to dwell."

Jeremiah Taken to Egypt

43 Now it happened, when Jeremiah had stopped speaking to all the people all the [a]words of the LORD their God, for which the LORD their God had sent him to them, all these words,

2 [a]that Azariah the son of Hoshaiah, Johanan the son of Kareah, and all the proud men spoke, saying to Jeremiah, "You speak falsely! The LORD our God has not sent you to say, 'Do not go to Egypt to dwell there.'

3 "But [a]Baruch the son of Neriah has set you against us, to deliver us into the hand of the Chaldeans, that they may put us to death or carry us away captive to Babylon."

4 So Johanan the son of Kareah, all the

KJV

captains of the forces, and all the people, obeyed
[a]not the voice of the LORD, to dwell in the land
of Judah.
5 But Johanan the son of Kareah, and all
the captains of the forces, took [a]all the remnant
of Judah, that were returned from all nations,
whither they had been driven, to dwell in the land
of Judah;
6 *Even* men, and women, and children, [a]and
the king's daughters, [b]and every person that
Nebuzar–adan the captain of the guard had left
with Gedaliah the son of Ahikam the son of Shaphan, and Jeremiah the prophet, and Baruch the
son of Neriah.
7 [a]So they came into the land of Egypt: for
they obeyed not the voice of the LORD: thus came
they *even* to [b]Tahpanhes.
8 Then came the [a]word of the LORD unto
Jeremiah in Tahpanhes, saying,
9 Take great stones in thine hand, and hide
them in the clay in the brickkiln, which *is* at the
entry of Pharaoh's house in Tahpanhes, in the
sight of the men of Judah;
10 And say unto them, Thus saith the LORD
of hosts, the God of Israel; Behold, I will send
and take Nebuchadrezzar the king of Babylon,
[a]my servant, and will set his throne upon these
stones that I have hid; and he shall spread his
royal pavilion over them.
11 [a]And when he cometh, he shall smite the
land of Egypt, *and deliver* [b]such *as are* for death
to death; and such *as are* for captivity to captivity;
and such *as are* for the sword to the sword.
12 And I will kindle a fire in the houses of
[a]the gods of Egypt; and he shall burn them, and
carry them away captives: and he shall array himself with the land of Egypt, as a shepherd putteth
on his garment; and he shall go forth from thence
in peace.
13 He shall break also the images of Beth–
shemesh, that *is* in the land of Egypt; and the
houses of the gods of the Egyptians shall he burn
with fire.

Israelites Will Be Punished in Egypt

44 The word that came to Jeremiah concerning all the Jews which dwell in the land of
Egypt, which dwell at [a]Migdol, and at [b]Tahpan-
hes, and at [c]Noph, and in the country of [d]Path-
ros, saying,
2 Thus saith the LORD of hosts, the God of
Israel; Ye have seen all the evil that I have brought
upon Jerusalem, and upon all the cities of Judah;
and, behold, this day they *are* [a]a desolation, and
no man dwelleth therein,
3 Because of their wickedness which they
have committed to provoke me to anger, in that
they went [a]to burn incense, *and* to [b]serve other
gods, whom they knew not, *neither* they, ye, nor
your fathers.
4 Howbeit [a]I sent unto you all my servants
the prophets, rising early and sending *them*, saying, Oh, do not this abominable thing that I hate.
5 But they hearkened not, nor inclined their
ear to turn from their wickedness, to burn no incense unto other gods.
6 Wherefore my fury and mine anger was
poured forth, and was kindled in the cities of Judah and in the streets of Jerusalem; and they are
wasted *and* desolate, as at this day.
7 Therefore now thus saith the LORD, the
God of hosts, the God of Israel; Wherefore commit
ye *this* great evil [a]against your souls, to cut off
from you man and woman, child and suckling,
out of Judah, to leave you none to remain;
8 In that ye [a]provoke me unto wrath with
the works of your hands, burning incense unto
other gods in the land of Egypt, whither ye be
gone to dwell, that ye might cut yourselves off,
and that ye might be [b]a curse and a reproach
among all the nations of the earth?
9 Have ye forgotten the wickedness of your

4 [a]2 Kin. 25:26 **5** [a]Jer. 40:11, 12 **6** [a]Jer. 41:10 [b]Jer. 39:10; 40:7 **7** [a]Jer. 42:19 [b]Jer. 2:16; 44:1 **8** [a]Jer. 44:1–30 **10** [a]Jer. 25:9; 27:6; Ezek. 29:18, 20 **11** [a]Is. 19:1–25; Jer. 25:15–19; 44:13; 46:1, 2, 13–26; Ezek. 29:19, 20 [b]Jer. 15:2; Zech. 11:9 **12** [a]Ex. 12:12; Is. 19:1; Jer. 46:25; Ezek. 30:13

CHAPTER 44

1 [a]Ex. 14:2; Jer. 46:14 [b]Jer. 43:7; Ezek. 30:18 [c]Is. 19:13; Jer. 2:16; 46:14; Ezek. 30:13, 16; Hos. 9:6 [d]Is. 11:11; Ezek. 29:14; 30:14 **2** [a]Is. 6:11; Jer. 4:7; 9:11; 34:22; Mic. 3:12 **3** [a]Jer. 19:4 [b]Deut. 13:6; 32:17 **4** [a]2 Chr. 36:15; Jer. 7:25; 25:4; 26:5; 29:19; Zech. 7:7 **7** [a]Num. 16:38; Jer. 7:19; [Ezek. 33:11]; Hab. 2:10 **8** [a]2 Kin. 17:15–17; Jer. 25:6, 7; 44:3; 1 Cor. 10:21, 22 [b]1 Kin. 9:7, 8; 2 Chr. 7:20; Jer. 42:18

*

43:12 So with MT, Tg.; LXX, Syr., Vg. *He*
43:13 Lit. *House of the Sun*, ancient On, later called Heliopolis
44:1 Ancient Memphis

NKJV

captains of the forces, and all the people would
[a]not obey the voice of the LORD, to remain in the
land of Judah.
5 But Johanan the son of Kareah and all the
captains of the forces took [a]all the remnant of
Judah who had returned to dwell in the land of
Judah, from all nations where they had been
driven—
6 men, women, children, [a]the king's daughters, [b]and every person whom Nebuzaradan the
captain of the guard had left with Gedaliah the
son of Ahikam, the son of Shaphan, and Jeremiah
the prophet and Baruch the son of Neriah.
7 [a]So they went to the land of Egypt, for
they did not obey the voice of the LORD. And they
went as far as [b]Tahpanhes.
8 Then the [a]word of the LORD came to Jeremiah in Tahpanhes, saying,
9 "Take large stones in your hand, and hide
them in the sight of the men of Judah, in the clay
in the brick courtyard which *is* at the entrance
to Pharaoh's house in Tahpanhes;
10 "and say to them, 'Thus says the LORD of
hosts, the God of Israel: "Behold, I will send and
bring Nebuchadnezzar the king of Babylon, [a]My
servant, and will set his throne above these stones
that I have hidden. And he will spread his royal
pavilion over them.
11 [a]"When he comes, he shall strike the land
of Egypt *and deliver* to death [b]*those appointed*
for death, and to captivity *those appointed* for
captivity, and to the sword *those appointed* for
the sword.
12 *"I will kindle a fire in the houses of [a]the
gods of Egypt, and he shall burn them and carry
them away captive. And he shall array himself
with the land of Egypt, as a shepherd puts on his
garment, and he shall go out from there in peace.
13 "He shall also break the sacred pillars of
*Beth Shemesh that *are* in the land of Egypt; and
the houses of the gods of the Egyptians he shall
burn with fire." ' "

Israelites Will Be Punished in Egypt

44 The word that came to Jeremiah concerning all the Jews who dwell in the land of
Egypt, who dwell at [a]Migdol, at [b]Tahpanhes, at
[c]Noph*, and in the country of [d]Pathros, saying,
2 "Thus says the LORD of hosts, the God of
Israel: 'You have seen all the calamity that I have
brought on Jerusalem and on all the cities of Judah; and behold, this day they *are* [a]a desolation,
and no one dwells in them,
3 'because of their wickedness which they
have committed to provoke Me to anger, in that
they went [a]to burn incense *and* to [b]serve other
gods whom they did not know, they nor you nor
your fathers.
4 'However [a]I have sent to you all My servants the prophets, rising early and sending *them*,
saying, "Oh, do not do this abominable thing that
I hate!"
5 'But they did not listen or incline their ear
to turn from their wickedness, to burn no incense
to other gods.
6 'So My fury and My anger were poured
out and kindled in the cities of Judah and in the
streets of Jerusalem; and they are wasted *and* desolate, as it is this day.'
7 "Now therefore, thus says the LORD, the
God of hosts, the God of Israel: 'Why do you commit *this* great evil [a]against yourselves, to cut off
from you man and woman, child and infant, out
of Judah, leaving none to remain,
8 'in that you [a]provoke Me to wrath with
the works of your hands, burning incense to other
gods in the land of Egypt where you have gone
to dwell, that you may cut yourselves off and be
[b]a curse and a reproach among all the nations of
the earth?
9 'Have you forgotten the wickedness of

KJV

fathers, and the wickedness of the kings of Judah, and the wickedness of their wives, and your own wickedness, and the wickedness of your wives, which they have committed in the land of Judah, and in the streets of Jerusalem?

10 They are not [a]humbled *even* unto this day, neither have they [b]feared, nor walked in my law, nor in my statutes, that I set before you and before your fathers.

11 Therefore thus saith the LORD of hosts, the God of Israel; Behold, [a]I will set my face against you for evil, and to cut off all Judah.

12 And I will take the remnant of Judah, that have set their faces to go into the land of Egypt to sojourn there, and [a]they shall all be consumed, *and* fall in the land of Egypt; they shall *even* be consumed by the sword *and* by the famine: they shall die, from the least even unto the greatest, by the sword and by the famine: and [b]they shall be an execration, *and* an astonishment, and a curse, and a reproach.

13 [a]For I will punish them that dwell in the land of Egypt, as I have punished Jerusalem, by the sword, by the famine, and by the pestilence:

14 So that none of the remnant of Judah, which are gone into the land of Egypt to sojourn there, shall escape or remain, that they should return into the land of Judah, to the which they have a [a]desire to return to dwell there: for [b]none shall return but such as shall escape.

15 Then all the men which knew that their wives had burned incense unto other gods, and all the women that stood by, a great multitude, even all the people that dwelt in the land of Egypt, in Pathros, answered Jeremiah, saying,

16 *As for* the word that thou hast spoken unto us in the name of the LORD, [a]we will not hearken unto thee.

17 But we will certainly do [a]whatsoever thing goeth forth out of our own mouth, to burn incense unto the [b]queen of heaven, and to pour out drink offerings unto her, as we have done, we, and our fathers, our kings, and our princes, in the cities of Judah, and in the streets of Jerusalem: for *then* had we plenty of victuals, and were well, and saw no evil.

18 But since we left off to burn incense to the queen of heaven, and to pour out drink offerings unto her, we have wanted all *things*, and have been consumed by the sword and by the famine.

19 [a]And when we burned incense to the queen of heaven, and poured out drink offerings unto her, did we make her cakes to worship her, and pour out drink offerings unto her, without our men?

20 Then Jeremiah said unto all the people, to the men, and to the women, and to all the people which had given him *that* answer, saying,

21 The incense that ye burned in the cities of Judah, and in the streets of Jerusalem, ye, and your fathers, your kings, and your princes, and the people of the land, did not the LORD remember them, and came it *not* into his mind?

22 So that the LORD could no longer bear, because of the evil of your doings, *and* because of the abominations which ye have committed; therefore is your land a desolation, and an astonishment, and a curse, without an inhabitant, [a]as at this day.

23 Because ye have burned incense, and because ye have sinned against the LORD, and have not obeyed the voice of the LORD, nor walked in his law, nor in his statutes, nor in his testimonies; [a]therefore this evil is happened unto you, as at this day.

24 Moreover Jeremiah said unto all the people, and to all the women, Hear the word of the LORD, all Judah that *are* in the land of Egypt:

25 Thus saith the LORD of hosts, the God of Israel, saying; Ye and your wives have both spoken with your mouths, and fulfilled with your hand, saying, We will surely perform our vows

10 [a]2 Chr. 36:12; Jer. 6:15; 8:12; Dan. 5:22 [b][Prov. 28:14] **11** [a]Lev. 17:10; 20:5, 6; Jer. 21:10; Amos 9:4 **12** [a]Jer. 42:15–17, 22 [b]Is. 65:15; Jer. 42:18 **13** [a]Jer. 43:11 **14** [a]Jer. 22:26, 27 [b][Is. 4:2; 10:20]; Jer. 44:28; [Rom. 9:27] **16** [a]Jer. 6:16 **17** [a]Num. 30:12; Deut. 23:23; Judg. 11:36 [b]2 Kin. 17:16; Jer. 7:18 **19** [a]Jer. 7:18 **22** [a]Jer. 25:11, 18, 38 **23** [a]1 Kin. 9:9; Neh. 13:18; Jer. 44:2; Dan. 9:11, 12

NKJV

your fathers, the wickedness of the kings of Judah, the wickedness of their wives, your own wickedness, and the wickedness of your wives, which they committed in the land of Judah and in the streets of Jerusalem?

10 'They have not been [a]humbled, to this day, nor have they [b]feared; they have not walked in My law or in My statutes that I set before you and your fathers.'

11 "Therefore thus says the LORD of hosts, the God of Israel: 'Behold, [a]I will set My face against you for catastrophe and for cutting off all Judah.

12 'And I will take the remnant of Judah who have set their faces to go into the land of Egypt to dwell there, and [a]they shall all be consumed *and* fall in the land of Egypt. They shall be consumed by the sword *and* by famine. They shall die, from the least to the greatest, by the sword and by famine; and [b]they shall be an oath, an astonishment, a curse and a reproach!

13 [a]'For I will punish those who dwell in the land of Egypt, as I have punished Jerusalem, by the sword, by famine, and by pestilence,

14 'so that none of the remnant of Judah who have gone into the land of Egypt to dwell there shall escape or survive, lest they return to the land of Judah, to which they [a]desire to return and dwell. For [b]none shall return except those who escape.' "

15 Then all the men who knew that their wives had burned incense to other gods, with all the women who stood by, a great multitude, and all the people who dwelt in the land of Egypt, in Pathros, answered Jeremiah, saying:

16 "*As for* the word that you have spoken to us in the name of the LORD, [a]we will not listen to you!

17 "But we will certainly do [a]whatever has gone out of our own mouth, to burn incense to the [b]queen of heaven and pour out drink offerings to her, as we have done, we and our fathers, our kings and our princes, in the cities of Judah and in the streets of Jerusalem. For *then* we had plenty of food, were well-off, and saw no trouble.

18 "But since we stopped burning incense to the queen of heaven and pouring out drink offerings to her, we have lacked everything and have been consumed by the sword and by famine."

19 *The women also said,* [a]"And when we burned incense to the queen of heaven and poured out drink offerings to her, did we make cakes for her, to worship her, and pour out drink offerings to her without our husbands' *permission?*"

20 Then Jeremiah spoke to all the people—the men, the women, and all the people who had given him *that* answer—saying:

21 "The incense that you burned in the cities of Judah and in the streets of Jerusalem, you and your fathers, your kings and your princes, and the people of the land, did not the LORD remember them, and did it *not* come into His mind?

22 "So the LORD could no longer bear *it,* because of the evil of your doings *and* because of the abominations which you committed. Therefore your land is a desolation, an astonishment, a curse, and without an inhabitant, [a]as *it is* this day.

23 "Because you have burned incense and because you have sinned against the LORD, and have not obeyed the voice of the LORD or walked in His law, in His statutes or in His testimonies, [a]therefore this calamity has happened to you, as *at* this day."

24 Moreover Jeremiah said to all the people and to all the women, "Hear the word of the LORD, all Judah who *are* in the land of Egypt!

25 "Thus says the LORD of hosts, the God of Israel, saying: 'You and your wives have spoken with your mouths and fulfilled with your hands, saying, "We will surely keep our vows that we

KJV

that we have vowed, to burn incense to the queen
of heaven, and to pour out drink offerings unto
her: ye will surely accomplish your vows, and
surely perform your vows.
26 Therefore hear ye the word of the LORD,
all Judah that dwell in the land of Egypt; Behold,
[a]I have sworn by my [b]great name, saith the LORD,
that [c]my name shall no more be named in the
mouth of any man of Judah in all the land of
Egypt, saying, The Lord GOD liveth.
27 Behold, I will watch over them for evil,
and not for good: and all the men of Judah that
are in the land of Egypt [a]shall be consumed by
the sword and by the famine, until there be an
end of them.
28 Yet [a]a small number that escape the
sword shall return out of the land of Egypt into
the land of Judah, and all the remnant of Judah,
that are gone into the land of Egypt to sojourn
there, shall know whose words shall stand, mine,
or their's.
29 And this *shall be* a sign unto you, saith
the LORD, that I will punish you in this place, that
ye may know that my words shall surely [a]stand
against you for evil:
30 Thus saith the LORD; Behold, [a]I will give
Pharaoh–hophra king of Egypt into the hand of
his enemies, and into the hand of them that seek
his life; as I gave [b]Zedekiah king of Judah into
the hand of Nebuchadrezzar king of Babylon, his
enemy, and that sought his life.

Assurance to Baruch

45 The [a]word that Jeremiah the prophet spake
unto [b]Baruch the son of Neriah, when he
had written these words in a book at the mouth
of Jeremiah, in the [c]fourth year of Jehoiakim the
son of Josiah king of Judah, saying,
2 Thus saith the LORD, the God of Israel,
unto thee, O Baruch;
3 Thou didst say, Woe is me now! for the
LORD hath added grief to my sorrow; I [a]fainted
in my sighing, and I find no rest.
4 Thus shalt thou say unto him, The LORD
saith thus; Behold, [a]*that* which I have built will
I break down, and that which I have planted I
will pluck up, even this whole land.
5 And seekest thou great things for thyself?
seek *them* not: for, behold, [a]I will bring evil upon
all flesh, saith the LORD: but thy [b]life will I give
unto thee for a prey in all places whither thou
goest.

Judgment on Egypt

46 The word of the LORD which came to Jeremiah the prophet against [a]the Gentiles;
2 Against [a]Egypt, [b]against the army of
Pharaoh–necho king of Egypt, which was by the
river Euphrates in Carchemish, which Nebuchadrezzar king of Babylon [c]smote in the [d]fourth
year of Jehoiakim the son of Josiah king of Judah.
3 Order ye the buckler and shield, and draw
near to battle.
4 Harness the horses; and get up, ye horsemen, and stand forth with *your* helmets; furbish
the spears, *and* [a]put on the brigandines.
5 Wherefore have I seen them dismayed *and*
turned away back? and their mighty ones are
beaten down, and are fled apace, and look not
back: *for* [a]fear *was* round about, saith the LORD.
6 Let not the swift flee away, nor the mighty
man escape; they shall [a]stumble, and fall toward
the north by the river Euphrates.

26 [a]Gen. 22:16; Deut. 32:40, 41; Jer. 22:5; Amos 6:8; Heb. 6:13 [b]Jer. 10:6 [c]Neh. 9:5; Ps. 50:16; Ezek. 20:39
27 [a]Jer. 1:10; 31:28; Ezek. 7:6
28 [a]Is. 10:19; 27:12, 13
29 [a][Ps. 33:11]
30 [a]Jer. 46:25, 26; Ezek. 29:3; 30:21 [b]2 Kin. 25:4–7; Jer. 39:5

CHAPTER 45

1 [a]Jer. 36:1, 4, 32 [b]Jer. 32:12, 16; 43:3 [c]Jer. 25:1; 36:1; 46:2
3 [a]Ps. 6:6; 69:3; [2 Cor. 4:1, 16; Gal. 6:9]
4 [a]Is. 5:5; Jer. 1:10; 11:17; 18:7–10; 31:28
5 [a]Jer. 25:26 [b]Jer. 21:9; 38:2; 39:18

CHAPTER 46

1 [a]Jer. 25:15
2 [a]Jer. 25:17–19; Ezek. 29:2—32:32 [b]2 Kin. 23:33–35 [c]2 Kin. 23:29; 24:7; 2 Chr. 35:20 [d]Jer. 45:1
4 [a]Is. 21:5; Jer. 51:11, 12; Joel 3:9; Nah. 2:1; 3:14
5 [a]Jer. 49:29
6 [a]Jer. 46:12, 16; Dan. 11:19

NKJV

have made, to burn incense to the queen of heaven
and pour out drink offerings to her." You will
surely keep your vows and perform your vows!'
26 "Therefore hear the word of the LORD, all
Judah who dwell in the land of Egypt: 'Behold,
[a]I have sworn by My [b]great name,' says the LORD,
'that [c]My name shall no more be named in the
mouth of any man of Judah in all the land of
Egypt, saying, "The Lord GOD lives."
27 'Behold, I will watch over them for adversity and not for good. And all the men of Judah
who *are* in the land of Egypt [a]shall be consumed
by the sword and by famine, until there is an end
to them.
28 'Yet [a]a small number who escape the
sword shall return from the land of Egypt to the
land of Judah; and all the remnant of Judah, who
have gone to the land of Egypt to dwell there,
shall know whose words will stand, Mine or
theirs.
29 'And this *shall be* a sign to you,' says the
LORD, 'that I will punish you in this place, that
you may know that My words will surely [a]stand
against you for adversity.'
30 "Thus says the LORD: 'Behold, [a]I will give
Pharaoh Hophra king of Egypt into the hand of
his enemies and into the hand of those who seek
his life, as I gave [b]Zedekiah king of Judah into
the hand of Nebuchadnezzar king of Babylon, his
enemy who sought his life.' "

Assurance to Baruch

45 The [a]word that Jeremiah the prophet spoke
to [b]Baruch the son of Neriah, when he had
written these words in a book *at the instruction
of Jeremiah, in the [c]fourth year of Jehoiakim the
son of Josiah, king of Judah, saying,
2 "Thus says the LORD, the God of Israel,
to you, O Baruch:
3 'You said, "Woe is me now! For the LORD
has added grief to my sorrow. I [a]fainted in my
sighing, and I find no rest." '
4 "Thus you shall say to him, 'Thus says
the LORD: "Behold, [a]what I have built I will break
down, and what I have planted I will pluck up,
that is, this whole land.
5 "And do you seek great things for yourself? Do not seek *them;* for behold, [a]I will bring
adversity on all flesh," says the LORD. "But I will
give your [b]life to you as a prize in all places, wherever you go." ' "

Judgment on Egypt

46 The word of the LORD which came to Jeremiah the prophet against [a]the nations.
2 Against [a]Egypt.
[b]Concerning the army of Pharaoh Necho,
king of Egypt, which was by the River Euphrates in Carchemish, and which Nebuchadnezzar king of Babylon [c]defeated in the [d]fourth
year of Jehoiakim the son of Josiah, king of
Judah:

3 "Order the buckler and shield,
And draw near to battle!
4 Harness the horses,
And mount up, you horsemen!
Stand forth with *your* helmets,
Polish the spears,
[a]Put on the armor!
5 Why have I seen them dismayed *and*
turned back?
Their mighty ones are beaten down;
They have speedily fled,
And did not look back,
For [a]fear *was* all around," says the
LORD.
6 "Do not let the swift flee away,
Nor the mighty man escape;
They will [a]stumble and fall
Toward the north, by the River Euphrates.

---

*45:1 Lit. *from Jeremiah's mouth*

KJV

7 Who *is* this *that* cometh up [a]as a flood, whose waters are moved as the rivers?

8 Egypt riseth up like a flood, and *his* waters are moved like the rivers; and he saith, I will go up, *and* will cover the earth; I will destroy the city and the inhabitants thereof.

9 Come up, ye horses; and rage, ye chariots; and let the mighty men come forth; the Ethiopians and the Libyans, that handle the shield; and the Lydians, [a]that handle *and* bend the bow.

10 For this *is* [a]the day of the Lord GOD of hosts, a day of vengeance, that he may avenge him of his adversaries: and [b]the sword shall devour, and it shall be satiate and made drunk with their blood: for the Lord GOD of hosts [c]hath a sacrifice in the north country by the river Euphrates.

11 [a]Go up into Gilead, and take balm, [b]O virgin, the daughter of Egypt: in vain shalt thou use many medicines; *for* [c]thou shalt not be cured.

12 The nations have heard of thy [a]shame, and thy cry hath filled the land: for the mighty man hath stumbled against the mighty, *and* they are fallen both together.

Babylonia Will Strike Egypt

13 The word that the LORD spake to Jeremiah the prophet, how Nebuchadrezzar king of Babylon should come *and* [a]smite the land of Egypt.

14 Declare ye in Egypt, and publish in [a]Migdol, and publish in Noph and in [b]Tahpanhes: say ye, Stand fast, and prepare thee; for the sword shall devour round about thee.

15 Why are thy valiant *men* swept away? they stood not, because the LORD did drive them.

16 He made many to fall, yea, [a]one fell upon another: and they said, Arise, and [b]let us go again to our own people, and to the land of our nativity, from the oppressing sword.

17 They did cry there, Pharaoh king of Egypt *is but* a noise; he hath passed the time appointed.

18 *As* I live, saith the King, [a]whose name *is* the LORD of hosts, Surely as Tabor *is* among the mountains, and as Carmel by the sea, *so* shall he come.

19 O [a]thou daughter dwelling in Egypt, furnish thyself [b]to go into captivity: for Noph shall be waste and desolate without an inhabitant.

20 Egypt *is like* a very fair [a]heifer, *but* destruction cometh; it cometh [b]out of the north.

21 Also her hired men *are* in the midst of her like fatted bullocks; for they also are turned back, *and* are fled away together: they did not stand, because [a]the day of their calamity was come upon them, *and* the time of their visitation.

22 [a]The voice thereof shall go like a serpent;

7 [a]Is. 8:7, 8; Jer. 47:2; Dan. 11:22
9 [a]Is. 66:19
10 [a]Is. 13:6; Joel 1:15 [b]Deut. 32:42; Is. 31:8; Jer. 12:12 [c]Is. 34:6; Zeph. 1:7; Ezek. 39:17
11 [a]Jer. 8:22 [b]Is. 47:1; Jer. 31:4, 21 [c]Ezek. 30:21
12 [a]Jer. 2:36; Nah. 3:8–10
13 [a]Is. 19:1; Jer. 43:10, 11; Ezek. 29:1–21
14 [a]Jer. 44:1 [b]Ezek. 30:18
16 [a]Lev. 26:36, 37; Jer. 46:6 [b]Jer. 51:9
18 [a]Is. 47:4; Jer. 48:15; Mal. 1:14
19 [a]Jer. 48:18 [b]Is. 20:4
20 [a]Hos. 10:11 [b]Jer. 1:14
21 [a][Ps. 37:13]; Jer. 50:27
22 [a][Is. 29:4]

NKJV

7 "Who *is* this coming up [a]like a flood,
Whose waters move like the rivers?
8 Egypt rises up like a flood,
And *its* waters move like the rivers;
And he says, 'I will go up *and* cover the earth,
I will destroy the city and its inhabitants.'
9 Come up, O horses, and rage, O chariots!
And let the mighty men come forth:
The Ethiopians and the Libyans who handle the shield,
And the Lydians [a]who handle *and* bend the bow.
10 For this *is* [a]the day of the Lord GOD of hosts,
A day of vengeance,
That He may avenge Himself on His adversaries.
[b]The sword shall devour;
It shall be satiated and made drunk with their blood;
For the Lord GOD of hosts [c]has a sacrifice
In the north country by the River Euphrates.

11 "Go[a] up to Gilead and take balm,
[b]O virgin, the daughter of Egypt;
In vain you will use many medicines;
[c]You shall not be cured.
12 The nations have heard of your [a]shame,
And your cry has filled the land;
For the mighty man has stumbled against the mighty;
They both have fallen together."

Babylonia Will Strike Egypt

13 The word that the LORD spoke to Jeremiah the prophet, how Nebuchadnezzar king of Babylon would come *and* [a]strike the land of Egypt.

14 "Declare in Egypt, and proclaim in [a]Migdol;
Proclaim in *Noph and in [b]Tahpanhes;
Say, 'Stand fast and prepare yourselves,
For the sword devours all around you.'
15 Why are your valiant *men* swept away?
They did not stand
Because the LORD drove them away.
16 He made many fall;
Yes, [a]one fell upon another.
And they said, 'Arise!
[b]Let us go back to our own people
And to the land of our nativity
From the oppressing sword.'
17 They cried there,
'Pharaoh, king of Egypt, *is but* a noise.
He has passed by the appointed time!'

18 "*As* I live," says the King,
[a]Whose name *is* the LORD of hosts,
"Surely as Tabor *is* among the mountains
And as Carmel by the sea, *so* he shall come.
19 O [a]you daughter dwelling in Egypt,
Prepare yourself [b]to go into captivity!
For *Noph shall be waste and desolate, without inhabitant.

20 "Egypt *is* a very pretty [a]heifer,
But destruction comes, it comes [b]from the north.
21 Also her mercenaries are in her midst like fat bulls,
For they also are turned back,
They have fled away together.
They did not stand,
For [a]the day of their calamity had come upon them,
The time of their punishment.
22 [a]Her noise shall go like a serpent,

*46:14 Ancient Memphis
46:19 Ancient Memphis

KJV

for they shall march with an army, and come
against her with axes, as hewers of wood.
23 They shall [a]cut down her forest, saith the
LORD, though it cannot be searched; because they
are more than [b]the grasshoppers, and *are*
innumerable.
24 The daughter of Egypt shall be confounded; she shall be delivered into the hand of
[a]the people of the north.
25 The LORD of hosts, the God of Israel, saith;
Behold, I will punish the multitude of [a]No, and
Pharaoh, and Egypt, [b]with their gods, and their
kings; even Pharaoh, and *all* them that [c]trust in
him:
26 [a]And I will deliver them into the hand of
those that seek their lives, and into the hand of
Nebuchadrezzar king of Babylon, and into the
hand of his servants: and [b]afterward it shall be
inhabited, as in the days of old, saith the LORD.

God Will Preserve Israel
(cf. Jer. 30:10, 11)

27 [a]But fear not thou, O my servant Jacob,
and be not dismayed, O Israel: for, behold, I will
[b]save thee from afar off, and thy seed from the
land of their captivity; and Jacob shall return, and
be in rest and at ease, and none shall make *him*
afraid.
28 Fear thou not, O Jacob my servant, saith
the LORD: for I *am* with thee; for I will make a
full end of all the nations whither I have driven
thee: but I will not make [a]a full end of thee, but
[b]correct thee in measure; yet will I not leave thee
wholly unpunished.

Judgment on Philistia

47 The word of the LORD that came to Jeremiah the prophet [a]against the Philistines,
[b]before that Pharaoh smote Gaza.
2 Thus saith the LORD; Behold, [a]waters rise
up [b]out of the north, and shall be an overflowing
flood, and shall overflow the land, and all that is
therein; the city, and them that dwell therein: then
the men shall cry, and all the inhabitants of the
land shall howl.
3 At the [a]noise of the stamping of the hoofs
of his strong *horses*, at the rushing of his chariots,
and at the rumbling of his wheels, the fathers
shall not look back to *their* children for feebleness
of hands;
4 Because of the day that cometh to spoil
all the [a]Philistines, *and* to cut off from [b]Tyrus and
Zidon every helper that remaineth: for the LORD
will spoil the Philistines, [c]the remnant of the country of [d]Caphtor.
5 [a]Baldness is come upon Gaza; [b]Ashkelon
is cut off *with* the remnant of their valley: how
long wilt thou cut thyself?
6 O thou [a]sword of the LORD, how long *will*
it be ere thou be quiet? put up thyself into thy
scabbard, rest, and be still.

23 [a]Is. 10:34 [b]Judg. 6:5; 7:12; Joel 2:25
24 [a]Jer. 1:15
25 [a]Ezek. 30:14–16; Nah. 3:8 [b]Ex. 12:12; Jer. 43:12, 13; Ezek. 30:13; Zeph. 2:11 [c]Is. 30:1–5; 31:1–3
26 [a]Jer. 44:30; Ezek. 32:11 [b]Ezek. 29:8–14
27 [a]Is. 41:13, 14; 43:5; 44:2; Jer. 30:10, 11 [b]Is. 11:11; Jer. 23:3, 4; Mic. 7:12
28 [a]Jer. 10:24; Amos 9:8, 9 [b]Jer. 30:11

CHAPTER 47

1 [a]Is. 14:29–31; Ezek. 25:15–17; Zeph. 2:4, 5; Zech. 9:6 [b]Amos 1:6
2 [a]Is. 8:7, 8; Jer. 46:7, 8 [b]Jer. 1:14
3 [a]Judg. 5:22; Jer. 8:16; Nah. 3:2
4 [a]Is. 14:29–31 [b]Is. 23:1–18; Jer. 25:22; Ezek. 26:1–21; 28:20–24; Amos 1:9, 10; Zech. 9:2–4 [c]Ezek. 25:16; Amos 1:8 [d]Gen. 10:14; Deut. 2:23; Amos 9:7
5 [a]Jer. 48:37; Mic. 1:16; Zeph. 2:4 [b]Judg. 1:18; Jer. 25:20; Amos 1:7, 8; Zech. 9:5
6 [a]Deut. 32:41; Judg. 7:20; Jer. 12:12; Ezek. 21:3–5

*———
46:25 A sun god • Ancient Thebes

NKJV

For they shall march with an army
And come against her with axes,
Like those who chop wood.

23 "They shall [a]cut down her forest," says the
LORD,
"Though it cannot be searched,
Because they *are* innumerable,
And more numerous than [b]grasshoppers.
24 The daughter of Egypt shall be ashamed;
She shall be delivered into the hand
Of [a]the people of the north."

25 The LORD of hosts, the God of Israel, says:
"Behold, I will bring punishment on *Amon of
[a]No,* and Pharaoh and Egypt, [b]with their gods
and their kings—Pharaoh and those who [c]trust
in him.
26 [a]"And I will deliver them into the hand
of those who seek their lives, into the hand of
Nebuchadnezzar king of Babylon and the hand
of his servants. [b]Afterward it shall be inhabited
as in the days of old," says the LORD.

God Will Preserve Israel
(cf. Jer. 30:10, 11)

27 "But[a] do not fear, O My servant Jacob,
And do not be dismayed, O Israel!
For behold, I will [b]save you from afar,
And your offspring from the land of their
captivity;
Jacob shall return, have rest and be at
ease;
No one shall make *him* afraid.
28 Do not fear, O Jacob My servant," says
the LORD,
"For I *am* with you;
For I will make a complete end of all the
nations
To which I have driven you,
But I will not make [a]a complete end of
you.
I will rightly [b]correct you,
For I will not leave you wholly
unpunished."

Judgment on Philistia

47 The word of the LORD that came to Jeremiah the prophet [a]against the Philistines,
[b]before Pharaoh attacked Gaza.
2 Thus says the LORD:

"Behold, [a]waters rise [b]out of the north,
And shall be an overflowing flood;
They shall overflow the land and all that
is in it,
The city and those who dwell within;
Then the men shall cry,
And all the inhabitants of the land shall
wail.
3 At the [a]noise of the stamping hooves of
his strong horses,
At the rushing of his chariots,
At the rumbling of his wheels,
The fathers will not look back for *their*
children,
Lacking courage,
4 Because of the day that comes to plunder
all the [a]Philistines,
To cut off from [b]Tyre and Sidon every
helper who remains;
For the LORD shall plunder the Philistines,
[c]The remnant of the country of [d]Caphtor.
5 [a]Baldness has come upon Gaza,
[b]Ashkelon is cut off
With the remnant of their valley.
How long will you cut yourself?

6 "O you [a]sword of the LORD,
How long until you are quiet?
Put yourself up into your scabbard,
Rest and be still!

KJV

7 How can it be quiet, seeing the LORD hath
[a]given it a charge against Ashkelon, and against
the sea shore? there hath he [b]appointed it.

Judgment on Moab

48 Against [a]Moab thus saith the LORD of hosts,
the God of Israel; Woe unto [b]Nebo! for it
is spoiled: [c]Kiriathaim is confounded *and* taken:
Misgab is confounded and dismayed.
2 [a]*There shall be* no more praise of Moab:
in [b]Heshbon they have devised evil against it;
come, and let us cut it off from *being* a nation.
Also thou shalt be cut down, O [c]Madmen; the
sword shall pursue thee.
3 A voice of crying *shall be* from [a]Horo-
naim, spoiling and great destruction.
4 Moab is destroyed; her little ones have
caused a cry to be heard.
5 [a]For in the going up of Luhith continual
weeping shall go up; for in the going down of
Horonaim the enemies have heard a cry of
destruction.
6 Flee, save your lives, and be like the
[a]heath in the wilderness.
7 For because thou hast trusted in thy works
and in thy [a]treasures, thou shalt also be taken:
and [b]Chemosh shall go forth into captivity *with*
his [c]priests and his princes together.
8 And [a]the spoiler shall come upon every
city, and no city shall escape: the valley also shall
perish, and the plain shall be destroyed, as the
LORD hath spoken.
9 [a]Give wings unto Moab, that it may flee
and get away: for the cities thereof shall be desolate, without any to dwell therein.
10 [a]Cursed *be* he that doeth the work of the
LORD deceitfully, and cursed *be* he that keepeth
back his sword from blood.
11 Moab hath been at ease from his youth,
and he [a]hath settled on his lees, and hath not been
emptied from vessel to vessel, neither hath he
gone into captivity: therefore his taste remained
in him, and his scent is not changed.
12 Therefore, behold, the days come, saith
the LORD, that I will send unto him wanderers,
that shall cause him to wander, and shall empty
his vessels, and break their bottles.
13 And Moab shall be ashamed of [a]Chemosh,
as the house of Israel [b]was ashamed of [c]Beth–el
their confidence.
14 How say ye, [a]We *are* mighty and strong
men for the war?

7 [a]Is. 10:6; Ezek. 14:17 [b]Mic. 6:9

CHAPTER 48

1 [a]Is. 15:1—16:14; 25:10; Ezek. 25:8–11; Amos 2:1–3; Zeph. 2:8–11 [b]Is. 15:2 [c]Num. 32:37; Jer. 48:23; Ezek. 25:9
2 [a]Is. 16:14 [b]Is. 15:4; Jer. 49:3 [c]Is. 10:31
3 [a]Is. 15:5; Jer. 48:5, 34
5 [a]Is. 15:5
6 [a]Jer. 17:6
7 [a]Ps. 52:7; Is. 59:4; Jer. 9:23; [1 Tim. 6:17] [b]Num. 21:29; Judg. 11:24; Jer. 48:7 [c]Jer. 49:3
8 [a]Jer. 6:26
9 [a]Ps. 55:6
10 [a]Judg. 5:23; 1 Sam. 15:3; 1 Kin. 20:42
11 [a]Zeph. 1:12
13 [a]1 Kin. 11:7 [b]Hos. 10:6 [c]1 Kin. 12:29; 13:32–34; Hos. 8:5, 6
14 [a]Is. 16:6

NKJV

7 How can it be quiet,
Seeing the LORD has [a]given it a charge
Against Ashkelon and against the
seashore?
There He has [b]appointed it."

Judgment on Moab

48 Against [a]Moab.
Thus says the LORD of hosts, the God of
Israel:

"Woe to [b]Nebo!
For it is plundered,
[c]Kirjathaim is shamed *and* taken;
*The high stronghold is shamed and
dismayed—
2 [a]No more praise of Moab.
In [b]Heshbon they have devised evil
against her:
'Come, and let us cut her off as a nation.'
You also shall be cut down, O
[c]Madmen!*
The sword shall pursue you;
3 A voice of crying *shall be* from
[a]Horonaim:
'Plundering and great destruction!'

4 "Moab is destroyed;
*Her little ones have caused a cry to be
heard;
5 [a]For in the Ascent of Luhith they ascend
with continual weeping;
For in the descent of Horonaim the
enemies have heard a cry of destruction.

6 "Flee, save your lives!
And be like *the [a]juniper in the
wilderness.
7 For because you have trusted in your
works and your [a]treasures,
You also shall be taken.
And [b]Chemosh shall go forth into
captivity,
His [c]priests and his princes together.
8 And [a]the plunderer shall come against
every city;
No one shall escape.
The valley also shall perish,
And the plain shall be destroyed,
As the LORD has spoken.

9 "Give[a] wings to Moab,
That she may flee and get away;
For her cities shall be desolate,
Without any to dwell in them.
10 [a]Cursed *is* he who does the work of the
LORD deceitfully,
And cursed *is* he who keeps back his
sword from blood.

11 "Moab has been at ease from *his youth;
He [a]has settled on his dregs,
And has not been emptied from vessel to
vessel,
Nor has he gone into captivity.
Therefore his taste remained in him,
And his scent has not changed.

12 "Therefore behold, the days are coming,"
says the LORD,
"That I shall send him wine workers
Who will tip him over
And empty his vessels
And break the bottles.
13 Moab shall be ashamed of [a]Chemosh,
As the house of Israel [b]was ashamed of
[c]Bethel, their confidence.

14 "How can you say, [a]'We *are* mighty
And strong men for the war'?

*———

48:1 Heb. *Misgab*
48:2 A city of Moab
48:4 So with MT, Tg., Vg.; LXX *Proclaim it in Zoar*
48:6 Or *Aroer,* a city of Moab
48:11 Heb. uses masc. and fem. pronouns interchangeably in this chapter.

KJV

15 Moab is spoiled, and gone up *out of* her
cities, and his chosen young men are [a]gone down
to the slaughter, saith [b]the King, whose name *is*
the LORD of hosts.
16 The calamity of Moab *is* near to come, and
his affliction hasteth fast.
17 All ye that are about him, bemoan him;
and all ye that know his name, say, [a]How is the
strong staff broken, *and* the beautiful rod!
18 [a]Thou daughter that dost inhabit [b]Dibon,
come down from *thy* glory, and sit in thirst; for
the spoiler of Moab shall come upon thee, *and*
he shall destroy thy strong holds.
19 O inhabitant of [a]Aroer, [b]stand by the way,
and espy; ask him that fleeth, and her that escapeth, *and* say, What is done?
20 Moab is confounded; for it is broken
down: [a]howl and cry; tell ye it in [b]Arnon, that
Moab is spoiled,
21 And judgment is come upon the plain
country; upon Holon, and upon Jahazah, and
upon Mephaath,
22 And upon Dibon, and upon Nebo, and
upon Beth–diblathaim,
23 And upon Kiriathaim, and upon Beth–
gamul, and upon Beth–meon,
24 And upon [a]Kerioth, and upon Bozrah, and
upon all the cities of the land of Moab, far or near.
25 [a]The horn of Moab is cut off, and his [b]arm
is broken, saith the LORD.
26 [a]Make ye him drunken: for he magnified
himself against the LORD: Moab also shall wallow
in his vomit, and he also shall be in derision.
27 For [a]was not Israel a derision unto thee?
[b]was he found among thieves? for since thou
spakest of him, thou skippedst for [c]joy.
28 O ye that dwell in Moab, leave the cities,
and [a]dwell in the rock, and be like [b]the dove *that*
maketh her nest in the sides of the hole's mouth.
29 We have heard the [a]pride of Moab, (he is
exceeding proud) his loftiness, and his arrogancy,
and his [b]pride, and the haughtiness of his heart.
30 I know his wrath, saith the LORD; but *it
shall* not *be* so; [a]his lies shall not so effect *it*.
31 Therefore [a]will I howl for Moab, and I will
cry out for all Moab; *mine heart* shall mourn for
the men of Kir–heres.
32 [a]O vine of Sibmah, I will weep for thee
with the weeping of [b]Jazer: thy plants are gone
over the sea, they reach *even* to the sea of Jazer:
the spoiler is fallen upon thy summer fruits and
upon thy vintage.
33 And [a]joy and gladness is taken from the
plentiful field, and from the land of Moab; and I
have caused wine to fail from the winepresses:
none shall tread with shouting; *their* shouting
shall be no shouting.
34 [a]From the cry of Heshbon *even* unto [b]Elea-
leh, *and even* unto Jahaz, have they uttered their

15 [a][Is. 40:30, 31]; Jer. 50:27 [b]Jer. 46:18; 51:57; Mal. 1:14
17 [a]Is. 9:4; 14:4, 5
18 [a]Is. 47:1 [b]Num. 21:30; Josh. 13:9, 17; Is. 15:2; Jer. 48:22
19 [a]Deut. 2:36; Josh. 12:2; Is. 17:2 [b]1 Sam. 4:13, 14, 16
20 [a]Is. 16:7 [b]Num. 21:13
24 [a]Jer. 48:41; Amos 2:2
25 [a]Ps. 75:10; Zech. 1:19–21 [b]Ezek. 30:21
26 [a]Jer. 25:15
27 [a]Zeph. 2:8 [b]Jer. 2:26 [c]Lam. 2:15; [Mic. 7:8–10]
28 [a]Ps. 55:6, 7 [b]Song 2:14
29 [a]Is. 16:6; Zeph. 2:8, 10 [b]Jer. 49:16
30 [a]Is. 16:6; Jer. 50:36
31 [a]Is. 15:5; 16:7, 11
32 [a]Is. 16:8, 9 [b]Num. 21:32; Is. 16:10
33 [a]Is. 16:10; Jer. 25:10; Joel 1:12
34 [a]Is. 15:4–6 [b]Num. 32:3, 37

* **48:31** So with DSS, LXX, Vg.; MT *He*

NKJV

15 Moab is plundered and gone up *from* her
cities;
Her chosen young men have [a]gone down
to the slaughter," says [b]the King,
Whose name *is* the LORD of hosts.

16 "The calamity of Moab *is* near at hand,
And his affliction comes quickly.
17 Bemoan him, all you who are around him;
And all you who know his name,
Say, [a]'How the strong staff is broken,
The beautiful rod!'

18 "O [a]daughter inhabiting [b]Dibon,
Come down from *your* glory,
And sit in thirst;
For the plunderer of Moab has come
against you,
He has destroyed your strongholds.
19 O inhabitant of [a]Aroer,
[b]Stand by the way and watch;
Ask him who flees
And her who escapes;
Say, 'What has happened?'
20 Moab is shamed, for he is broken down.
[a]Wail and cry!
Tell it in [b]Arnon, that Moab is plundered.

21 "And judgment has come on the plain
country:
On Holon and Jahzah and Mephaath,
22 On Dibon and Nebo and Beth Diblathaim,
23 On Kirjathaim and Beth Gamul and Beth
Meon,
24 On [a]Kerioth and Bozrah,
On all the cities of the land of Moab,
Far or near.
25 [a]The horn of Moab is cut off,
And his [b]arm is broken," says the LORD.

26 "Make[a] him drunk,
Because he exalted *himself* against the
LORD.
Moab shall wallow in his vomit,
And he shall also be in derision.
27 For [a]was not Israel a derision to you?
[b]Was he found among thieves?
For whenever you speak of him,
You shake *your head in* [c]*scorn.*
28 You who dwell in Moab,
Leave the cities and [a]dwell in the rock,
And be like [b]the dove *which* makes her
nest
In the sides of the cave's mouth.

29 "We have heard the [a]pride of Moab
(He *is* exceedingly proud),
Of his loftiness and arrogance and [b]pride,
And of the haughtiness of his heart."

30 "I know his wrath," says the LORD,
"But it *is* not right;
[a]His lies have made nothing right.
31 Therefore [a]I will wail for Moab,
And I will cry out for all Moab;
*I will mourn for the men of Kir Heres.
32 [a]O vine of Sibmah! I will weep for you with
the weeping of [b]Jazer.
Your plants have gone over the sea,
They reach to the sea of Jazer.
The plunderer has fallen on your summer
fruit and your vintage.
33 [a]Joy and gladness are taken
From the plentiful field
And from the land of Moab;
I have caused wine to fail from the
winepresses;
No one will tread with joyous shouting—
Not joyous shouting!

34 "From[a] the cry of Heshbon to [b]Elealeh and
to Jahaz

KJV

voice, [c]from Zoar *even* unto Horonaim, *as* an
heifer of three years old: for the waters also of
Nimrim shall be desolate.
35 Moreover I will cause to cease in Moab,
saith the LORD, [a]him that offereth in the high
places, and him that burneth incense to his gods.
36 Therefore [a]mine heart shall sound for
Moab like pipes, and mine heart shall sound like
pipes for the men of Kir–heres: because [b]the
riches *that* he hath gotten are perished.
37 For [a]every head *shall be* bald, and every
beard clipped: upon all the hands *shall be* cuttings, and [b]upon the loins sackcloth.
38 *There shall be* lamentation generally upon
all the [a]housetops of Moab, and in the streets
thereof: for I have [b]broken Moab like a vessel
wherein *is* no pleasure, saith the LORD.
39 They shall howl, *saying,* How is it broken
down! how hath Moab turned the back with
shame! so shall Moab be a derision and a dismay-
ing to all them about him.
40 For thus saith the LORD; Behold, [a]he shall
fly as an eagle, and shall [b]spread his wings over
Moab.
41 Kerioth is taken, and the strong holds are
surprised, and [a]the mighty men's hearts in Moab
at that day shall be as the heart of a woman in
her pangs.
42 And Moab shall be destroyed [a]from *being*
a people, because he hath magnified *himself*
against the LORD.
43 [a]Fear, and the pit, and the snare, *shall be*
upon thee, O inhabitant of Moab, saith the LORD.
44 He that fleeth from the fear shall fall into
the pit; and he that getteth up out of the pit shall
be taken in the [a]snare: for [b]I will bring upon it,
even upon Moab, the year of their visitation, saith
the LORD.
45 They that fled stood under the shadow of
Heshbon because of the force: but [a]a fire shall
come forth out of Heshbon, and a flame from the
midst of [b]Sihon, and [c]shall devour the corner of
Moab, and the crown of the head of the tumultuous ones.
46 [a]Woe be unto thee, O Moab! the people
of Chemosh perisheth: for thy sons are taken captives, and thy daughters captives.
47 Yet will I bring again the captivity of
Moab [a]in the latter days, saith the LORD. Thus
far *is* the judgment of Moab.

Judgment on Ammon

49 Concerning [a]the Ammonites, thus saith the
LORD; Hath Israel no sons? hath he no heir?

34 [c]Is. 15:5, 6
35 [a]Is. 15:2; 16:12
36 [a]Is. 15:5; 16:11 [b]Is. 15:7
37 [a]Is. 15:2, 3; Jer. 16:6; 41:5; 47:5 [b]Gen. 37:34; Is. 15:3; 20:2
38 [a]Is. 15:3 [b]Jer. 22:28
40 [a]Deut. 28:49; Jer. 49:22; Hos. 8:1; Hab. 1:8 [b]Is. 8:8
41 [a]Is. 13:8; 21:3; Jer. 30:6; Mic. 4:9, 10
42 [a]Ps. 83:4; Jer. 48:2
43 [a]Is. 24:17, 18; Lam. 3:47
44 [a]1 Kin. 19:17; Is. 24:18; Amos 5:19 [b]Jer. 11:23
45 [a]Num. 21:28, 29 [b]Num. 21:21, 26; Ps. 135:11 [c]Num. 24:17
46 [a]Num. 21:29
47 [a]Jer. 49:6, 39

CHAPTER 49

1 [a]Deut. 23:3, 4; 2 Chr. 20:1; Jer. 25:21; Ezek. 21:28–32; 25:1–7

*______

48:34 Or *The Third Eglath,* an unknown city, Is. 15:5

NKJV

They have uttered their voice,
[c]From Zoar to Horonaim,
Like *a three-year-old heifer;
For the waters of Nimrim also shall be
desolate.

35 "Moreover," says the LORD,
"I will cause to cease in Moab
[a]The one who offers *sacrifices* in the high
places
And burns incense to his gods.
36 Therefore [a]My heart shall wail like flutes
for Moab,
And like flutes My heart shall wail
For the men of Kir Heres.
Therefore [b]the riches they have acquired
have perished.

37 "For [a]every head *shall be* bald, and every
beard clipped;
On all the hands *shall be* cuts, and [b]on
the loins sackcloth—
38 A general lamentation
On all the [a]housetops of Moab,
And in its streets;
For I have [b]broken Moab like a vessel in
which *is* no pleasure," says the LORD.
39 "They shall wail:
'How she is broken down!
How Moab has turned her back with
shame!'
So Moab shall be a derision
And a dismay to all those about her."

40 For thus says the LORD:

"Behold, [a]one shall fly like an eagle,
And [b]spread his wings over Moab.
41 Kerioth is taken,
And the strongholds are surprised;
[a]The mighty men's hearts in Moab on that
day shall be
Like the heart of a woman in birth
pangs.
42 And Moab shall be destroyed [a]as a
people,
Because he exalted *himself* against the
LORD.
43 [a]Fear and the pit and the snare *shall be*
upon you,
O inhabitant of Moab," says the LORD.
44 "He who flees from the fear shall fall into
the pit,
And he who gets out of the pit shall be
caught in the [a]snare.
For upon Moab, upon it [b]I will bring
The year of their punishment," says the
LORD.

45 "Those who fled stood under the shadow
of Heshbon
Because of exhaustion.
But [a]a fire shall come out of Heshbon,
A flame from the midst of [b]Sihon,
And [c]shall devour the brow of Moab,
The crown of the head of the sons of
tumult.
46 [a]Woe to you, O Moab!
The people of Chemosh perish;
For your sons have been taken captive,
And your daughters captive.

47 "Yet I will bring back the captives of
Moab
[a]In the latter days," says the LORD.

Thus far *is* the judgment of Moab.

Judgment on Ammon

49 Against the [a]Ammonites.
Thus says the LORD:

KJV

why *then* doth their king inherit [b]Gad, and his
people dwell in his cities?
2 [a]Therefore, behold, the days come, saith
the LORD, that I will cause an alarm of war to be
heard in [b]Rabbah of the Ammonites; and it shall
be a desolate heap, and her daughters shall be
burned with fire: then shall Israel be heir unto
them that were his heirs, saith the LORD.
3 Howl, O [a]Heshbon, for Ai is spoiled: cry,
ye daughters of Rabbah, [b]gird you with sackcloth;
lament, and run to and fro by the hedges; for their
king shall go into captivity, *and* his [c]priests and
his princes together.
4 Wherefore [a]gloriest thou in the valleys,
thy flowing valley, O [b]backsliding daughter? that
trusted in her [c]treasures, [d]*saying,* Who shall come
unto me?
5 Behold, I will bring a fear upon thee, saith
the Lord GOD of hosts, from all those that be about
thee; and ye shall be driven out every man right
forth; and none shall gather up him that
wandereth.
6 And [a]afterward I will bring again the captivity of the children of Ammon, saith the LORD.

Judgment on Edom

7 [a]Concerning Edom, thus saith the LORD
of hosts; [b]*Is* wisdom no more in Teman? [c]is counsel perished from the prudent? is their wisdom
[d]vanished?
8 Flee ye, turn back, dwell deep, O inhabitants of [a]Dedan; for I will bring the calamity of
Esau upon him, the time *that* I will visit him.
9 If [a]grapegatherers come to thee, would
they not leave *some* gleaning grapes? if thieves
by night, they will destroy till they have enough.
10 [a]But I have made Esau bare, I have uncovered his secret places, and he shall not be able
to hide himself: his seed is spoiled, and his brethren, and his neighbours, and [b]he *is* not.
11 Leave thy fatherless children, I will preserve *them* alive; and let thy widows trust in me.
12 For thus saith the LORD; Behold, [a]they
whose judgment *was* not to drink of the cup have
assuredly drunken; and *art* thou he *that* shall altogether go unpunished? thou shalt not go unpunished, but thou shalt surely drink *of it.*
13 For [a]I have sworn by myself, saith the
LORD, that [b]Bozrah shall become a desolation, a
reproach, a waste, and a curse; and all the cities
thereof shall be perpetual wastes.
14 I have heard a [a]rumour from the LORD,
and an ambassador is sent unto the heathen, *saying,* Gather ye together, and come against her,
and rise up to the battle.

1 [b]Amos 1:13–15; Zeph. 2:8–11
2 [a]Amos 1:13–15 [b]Ezek. 25:5
3 [a]Jer. 48:2 [b]Is. 32:11; Jer. 48:37 [c]Jer. 48:7
4 [a]Jer. 9:23 [b]Jer. 3:14 [c]Jer. 48:7 [d]Jer. 21:13
6 [a]Jer. 48:47
7 [a]Gen. 25:30; 32:3; Is. 34:5, 6; Jer. 25:21; Ezek. 25:12–14; 35:1–15; Joel 3:19; Amos 1:11, 12; Obad. 1–9, 15, 16 [b]Gen. 36:11; Job 2:11 [c]Is. 19:11 [d]Jer. 8:9
8 [a]Is. 21:13; Jer. 25:23
9 [a]Obad. 5, 6
10 [a]Obad. 5, 6; Mal. 1:3 [b]Is. 17:14
12 [a]Jer. 25:29; Obad. 16
13 [a]Gen. 22:16; Is. 45:23; Jer. 44:26; Amos 6:8 [b]Gen. 36:33; 1 Chr. 1:44; Is. 34:6; 63:1; Amos 1:12
14 [a]Obad. 1–4

NKJV

"Has Israel no sons?
Has he no heir?
Why *then* does *Milcom inherit [b]Gad,
And his people dwell in its cities?
2 [a]Therefore behold, the days are coming,"
says the LORD,
"That I will cause to be heard an alarm of war
In [b]Rabbah of the Ammonites;
It shall be a desolate mound,
And her villages shall be burned with fire.
Then Israel shall take possession of his inheritance," says the LORD.

3 "Wail, O [a]Heshbon, for Ai is plundered!
Cry, you daughters of Rabbah,
[b]Gird yourselves with sackcloth!
Lament and run to and fro by the walls;
For Milcom shall go into captivity
With his [c]priests and his princes together.
4 Why [a]do you boast in the valleys,
Your flowing valley, O [b]backsliding daughter?
Who trusted in her [c]treasures, [d]*saying,*
'Who will come against me?'
5 Behold, I will bring fear upon you,"
Says the Lord GOD of hosts,
"From all those who are around you;
You shall be driven out, everyone headlong,
And no one will gather those who wander off.
6 But [a]afterward I will bring back
The captives of the people of Ammon,"
says the LORD.

Judgment on Edom

7 [a]Against Edom.
Thus says the LORD of hosts:
[b]"*Is* wisdom no more in Teman?
[c]Has counsel perished from the prudent?
Has their wisdom [d]vanished?
8 Flee, turn back, dwell in the depths, O inhabitants of [a]Dedan!
For I will bring the calamity of Esau upon him,
The time *that* I will punish him.
9 [a]If grape gatherers came to you,
Would they not leave *some* gleaning grapes?
If thieves by night,
Would they not destroy until they have enough?
10 [a]But I have made Esau bare;
I have uncovered his secret places,
And he shall not be able to hide himself.
His descendants are plundered,
His brethren and his neighbors,
And [b]he *is* no more.
11 Leave your fatherless children,
I will preserve *them* alive;
And let your widows trust in Me."

12 For thus says the LORD: "Behold, [a]those whose judgment *was* not to drink of the cup have assuredly drunk. And *are* you the one who will altogether go unpunished? You shall not go unpunished, but you shall surely drink *of it.*

13 "For [a]I have sworn by Myself," says the LORD, "that [b]Bozrah shall become a desolation, a reproach, a waste, and a curse. And all its cities shall be perpetual wastes."

14 [a]I have heard a message from the LORD,
And an ambassador has been sent to the nations:
"Gather together, come against her,
And rise up to battle!

*________

49:1 Heb. *Malcam,* lit. *their king;* an Ammonite god, 1 Kin. 11:5; *Molech,* Lev. 18:21

KJV

15 For, lo, I will make thee small among the heathen, *and* despised among men.

16 Thy terribleness hath deceived thee, *and* the [a]pride of thine heart, O thou that dwellest in the clefts of the rock, that holdest the height of the hill: [b]though thou shouldest make thy [c]nest as high as the eagle, [d]I will bring thee down from thence, saith the LORD.

17 Also Edom shall be a desolation: [a]every one that goeth by it shall be astonished, and shall hiss at all the plagues thereof.

18 [a]As in the overthrow of Sodom and Gomorrah and the neighbour *cities* thereof, saith the LORD, no man shall abide there, neither shall a son of man dwell in it.

19 [a]Behold, he shall come up like a lion from [b]the swelling of Jordan against the habitation of the strong: but I will suddenly make him run away from her: and who *is* a chosen *man, that* I may appoint over her? for [c]who *is* like me? and who will appoint me the time? and [d]who *is* that shepherd that will stand before me?

20 [a]Therefore hear the counsel of the LORD, that he hath taken against Edom; and his purposes, that he hath purposed against the inhabitants of Teman: Surely the least of the flock shall draw them out: surely he shall make their habitations desolate with them.

21 [a]The earth is moved at the noise of their fall, at the cry the noise thereof was heard in the Red sea.

22 Behold, [a]he shall come up and fly as the eagle, and spread his wings over Bozrah: and at that day shall the heart of the mighty men of Edom be as the heart of a woman in her pangs.

Judgment on Damascus

23 [a]Concerning Damascus. [b]Hamath is confounded, and Arpad: for they have heard evil tidings: they are fainthearted; [c]*there is* sorrow on the sea; it cannot be quiet.

24 Damascus is waxed feeble, *and* turneth herself to flee, and fear hath seized on *her:* [a]anguish and sorrows have taken her, as a woman in travail.

25 How is [a]the city of praise not left, the city of my joy!

26 [a]Therefore her young men shall fall in her streets, and all the men of war shall be cut off in that day, saith the LORD of hosts.

27 And I will kindle a [a]fire in the wall of Damascus, and it shall consume the palaces of Benhadad.

Judgment on Kedar and Hazor

28 [a]Concerning Kedar, and concerning the kingdoms of Hazor, which Nebuchadrezzar king of Babylon shall smite, thus saith the LORD; Arise

16 [a]Jer. 48:29 [b]Obad. 3, 4 [c]Job 39:27; Is. 14:13–15 [d]Amos 9:2
17 [a]Jer. 18:16; 49:13; 50:13; Ezek. 35:7
18 [a]Gen. 19:24, 25; Deut. 29:23; Jer. 50:40; Amos 4:11; Zeph. 2:9
19 [a]Jer. 50:44 [b]Josh. 3:15; Jer. 12:5 [c]Ex. 15:11; Is. 46:9 [d]Job 41:10
20 [a]Is. 14:24, 27; Jer. 50:45
21 [a]Jer. 50:46; Ezek. 26:15, 18
22 [a]Jer. 48:40, 41
23 [a]Is. 17:1–3; Amos 1:3, 5; Zech. 9:1, 2 [b]Jer. 39:5; Zech. 9:2 [c][Is. 57:20]
24 [a]Is. 13:8; Jer. 4:31; 6:24; 48:21
25 [a]Jer. 33:9
26 [a]Jer. 50:30; Amos 4:10
27 [a]Amos 1:4
28 [a]Gen. 25:13; Ps. 120:5; Is. 21:16, 17; Jer. 2:10; Ezek. 27:21

NKJV

15 "For indeed, I will make you small among
nations,
Despised among men.
16 Your fierceness has deceived you,
The [a]pride of your heart,
O you who dwell in the clefts of the
rock,
Who hold the height of the hill!
[b]Though you make your [c]nest as high as
the eagle,
[d]I will bring you down from there," says
the LORD.
17 "Edom also shall be an astonishment;
[a]Everyone who goes by it will be
astonished
And will hiss at all its plagues.
18 [a]As in the overthrow of Sodom and
Gomorrah
And their neighbors," says the LORD,
"No one shall remain there,
Nor shall a son of man dwell in it.

19 "Behold,[a] he shall come up like a lion from
[b]the *floodplain of the Jordan
Against the dwelling place of the strong;
But I will suddenly make him run away
from her.
And who *is* a chosen *man that* I may
appoint over her?
For [c]who *is* like Me?
Who will arraign Me?
And [d]who *is* that shepherd
Who will withstand Me?"

20 [a]Therefore hear the counsel of the LORD
that He has taken against Edom,
And His purposes that He has proposed
against the inhabitants of Teman:
Surely the least of the flock shall draw
them out;
Surely He shall make their dwelling
places desolate with them.
21 [a]The earth shakes at the noise of their fall;
At the cry its noise is heard at the Red
Sea.
22 Behold, [a]He shall come up and fly like the
eagle,
And spread His wings over Bozrah;
The heart of the mighty men of Edom in
that day shall be
Like the heart of a woman in birth
pangs.

Judgment on Damascus

23 [a]Against Damascus.

[b]"Hamath and Arpad are shamed,
For they have heard bad news.
They are fainthearted;
[c]*There is* trouble on the sea;
It cannot be quiet.
24 Damascus has grown feeble;
She turns to flee,
And fear has seized *her.*
[a]Anguish and sorrows have taken her like
a woman in labor.
25 Why is [a]the city of praise not deserted,
the city of My joy?
26 [a]Therefore her young men shall fall in her
streets,
And all the men of war shall be cut off in
that day," says the LORD of hosts.
27 "I[a] will kindle a fire in the wall of
Damascus,
And it shall consume the palaces of
Ben-Hadad."

Judgment on Kedar and Hazor

28 [a]Against Kedar and against the kingdoms of Hazor, which Nebuchadnezzar king of Babylon shall strike.

* **49:19** Or *thicket*

KJV

ye, go up to Kedar, and spoil [b]the men of the east.

29 Their [a]tents and their flocks shall they take away: they shall take to themselves their curtains, and all their vessels, and their camels; and they shall cry unto them, [b]Fear *is* on every side.

30 Flee, get you far off, dwell deep, O ye inhabitants of Hazor, saith the LORD; for Nebuchadrezzar king of Babylon hath taken counsel against you, and hath conceived a purpose against you.

31 Arise, get you up unto [a]the wealthy nation, that dwelleth without care, saith the LORD, which have neither gates nor bars, *which* [b]dwell alone.

32 And their camels shall be a booty, and the multitude of their cattle a spoil: and I will [a]scatter into all winds them *that are* in the utmost corners; and I will bring their calamity from all sides thereof, saith the LORD.

33 And Hazor [a]shall be a dwelling for dragons, *and* a desolation for ever: there shall no man abide there, nor *any* son of man dwell in it.

Judgment on Elam

34 The word of the LORD that came to Jeremiah the prophet against [a]Elam in the [b]beginning of the reign of Zedekiah king of Judah, saying,

35 Thus saith the LORD of hosts; Behold, I will break [a]the bow of Elam, the chief of their might.

36 And upon Elam will I bring the four winds from the four quarters of heaven, and will scatter them toward all those winds; and there shall be no nation whither the outcasts of Elam shall not come.

37 For I will cause Elam to be dismayed before their enemies, and before them that seek their life: and I will bring evil upon them, *even* my fierce anger, saith the LORD; [a]and I will send the sword after them, till I have consumed them:

38 And I will [a]set my throne in Elam, and will destroy from thence the king and the princes, saith the LORD.

39 But it shall come to pass [a]in the latter days, *that* I will bring again the captivity of Elam, saith the LORD.

Judgment on Babylon and Babylonia

50 The word that the LORD spake [a]against Babylon *and* against the land of the Chaldeans by Jeremiah the prophet.

2 Declare ye among the nations, and publish, and set up a standard; publish, *and* conceal not: say, Babylon is [a]taken, [b]Bel is confounded, Merodach is broken in pieces; [c]her idols are confounded, her images are broken in pieces.

3 [a]For out of the north there cometh up [b]a nation against her, which shall make her land desolate, and none shall dwell therein: they shall remove, they shall depart, both man and beast.

28 [b]Judg. 6:3; Job 1:3
29 [a]Ps. 120:5 [b]Jer. 46:5
31 [a]Ezek. 38:11 [b]Num. 23:9; Deut. 33:28; Mic. 7:16
32 [a]Ezek. 5:10
33 [a]Jer. 9:11; 10:22; Zeph. 2:9, 12–15; Mal. 1:3
34 [a]Gen. 10:22; Jer. 25:25; Ezek. 32:24; Dan. 8:2 [b]2 Kin. 24:17, 18; Jer. 28:1
35 [a]Ps. 46:9; Is. 22:6
37 [a]Jer. 9:16
38 [a]Jer. 43:10
39 [a]Jer. 48:47

CHAPTER 50

1 [a]Gen. 10:10; 11:9; 2 Kin. 17:24; Is. 13:1; 47:1; Dan. 1:1; Rev. 14:8
2 [a]Is. 21:9 [b]Is. 46:1; Jer. 51:44 [c]Jer. 43:12, 13
3 [a]Jer. 51:48; Dan. 5:30, 31 [b]Is. 13:17, 18, 20

*———

50:2 Or *Marduk;* a Babylonian god

NKJV

Thus says the LORD:
"Arise, go up to Kedar,
And devastate [b]the men of the East!
29 Their [a]tents and their flocks they shall take away.
They shall take for themselves their curtains,
All their vessels and their camels;
And they shall cry out to them,
[b]'Fear *is* on every side!'

30 "Flee, get far away! Dwell in the depths,
O inhabitants of Hazor!" says the LORD.
"For Nebuchadnezzar king of Babylon has taken counsel against you,
And has conceived a plan against you.

31 "Arise, go up to [a]the wealthy nation that dwells securely," says the LORD,
"Which has neither gates nor bars,
[b]Dwelling alone.
32 Their camels shall be for booty,
And the multitude of their cattle for plunder.
I will [a]scatter to all winds those in the farthest corners,
And I will bring their calamity from all its sides," says the LORD.
33 "Hazor [a]shall be a dwelling for jackals, a desolation forever;
No one shall reside there,
Nor son of man dwell in it."

Judgment on Elam

34 The word of the LORD that came to Jeremiah the prophet against [a]Elam, in the [b]beginning of the reign of Zedekiah king of Judah, saying,
35 "Thus says the LORD of hosts:

'Behold, I will break [a]the bow of Elam,
The foremost of their might.
36 Against Elam I will bring the four winds
From the four quarters of heaven,
And scatter them toward all those winds;
There shall be no nations where the outcasts of Elam will not go.
37 For I will cause Elam to be dismayed before their enemies
And before those who seek their life.
[a]I will bring disaster upon them,
My fierce anger,' says the LORD;
'And I will send the sword after them
Until I have consumed them.
38 I will [a]set My throne in Elam,
And will destroy from there the king and the princes,' says the LORD.

39 'But it shall come to pass [a]in the latter days:
I will bring back the captives of Elam,' says the LORD."

Judgment on Babylon and Babylonia

50 The word that the LORD spoke [a]against Babylon *and* against the land of the Chaldeans by Jeremiah the prophet.

2 "Declare among the nations,
Proclaim, and set up a standard;
Proclaim—do not conceal *it*—
Say, 'Babylon is [a]taken, [b]Bel is shamed.
*Merodach is broken in pieces;
[c]Her idols are humiliated,
Her images are broken in pieces.'
3 [a]For out of the north [b]a nation comes up against her,
Which shall make her land desolate,
And no one shall dwell therein.
They shall move, they shall depart,
Both man and beast.

KJV

4 In those days, and in that time, saith the LORD, the children of Israel shall come, [a]they and the children of Judah together, [b]going and weeping: they shall go, [c]and seek the LORD their God.

5 They shall ask the way to Zion with their faces thitherward, *saying*, Come, and let us join ourselves to the LORD in [a]a perpetual covenant *that* shall not be forgotten.

6 My people hath been [a]lost sheep: their shepherds have caused them to go [b]astray, they have turned them away *on* [c]the mountains: they have gone from mountain to hill, they have forgotten their restingplace.

7 All that found them have [a]devoured them: and [b]their adversaries said, [c]We offend not, because they have sinned against the LORD, [d]the habitation of justice, even the LORD, [e]the hope of their fathers.

8 [a]Remove out of the midst of Babylon, and go forth out of the land of the Chaldeans, and be as the he goats before the flocks.

9 [a]For, lo, I will raise and cause to come up against Babylon an assembly of great nations from the north country: and they shall set themselves in array against her; from thence she shall be taken: their arrows *shall be* as of a mighty expert man; [b]none shall return in vain.

10 And Chaldea shall be a spoil: [a]all that spoil her shall be satisfied, saith the LORD.

11 [a]Because ye were glad, because ye rejoiced, O ye destroyers of mine heritage, because ye are grown fat [b]as the heifer at grass, and bellow as bulls;

12 Your mother shall be sore confounded; she that bare you shall be ashamed: behold, the hindermost of the nations *shall be* a [a]wilderness, a dry land, and a desert.

13 Because of the wrath of the LORD it shall not be inhabited, [a]but it shall be wholly desolate: [b]every one that goeth by Babylon shall be astonished, and hiss at all her plagues.

14 [a]Put yourselves in array against Babylon round about: all ye that bend the bow, shoot at her, spare no arrows: for she hath sinned against the LORD.

15 Shout against her round about: she hath [a]given her hand: her foundations are fallen, [b]her walls are thrown down: for [c]it *is* the vengeance of the LORD: take vengeance upon her; as she hath done, do unto her.

16 Cut off the sower from Babylon, and him that handleth the sickle in the time of harvest: for fear of the oppressing sword [a]they shall turn every one to his people, and they shall flee every one to his own land.

17 Israel *is* a [a]scattered sheep; [b]the lions have driven *him* away: first [c]the king of Assyria

4 [a]Ezra 2:1; Is. 11:12, 13; Jer. 3:18; 31:31; 33:7; Hos. 1:11 [b]Ezra 3:12, 13; [Ps. 126:5]; Jer. 31:9; [Zech. 12:10] [c]Hos. 3:5
5 [a]Jer. 31:31
6 [a]Is. 53:6; [Ezek. 34:15, 16]; Matt. 9:36; 10:6; 1 Pet. 2:25 [b]Jer. 23:1; Ezek. 34:2 [c][Jer. 2:20; 3:6, 23]
7 [a]Ps. 79:7 [b]Jer. 40:2, 3; Zech. 11:5 [c]Jer. 2:3; Dan. 9:16 [d][Ps. 90:1; 91:1] [e]Ps. 22:4; Jer. 14:8; 17:13
8 [a]Is. 48:20; Jer. 51:6, 45; Zech. 2:6, 7; [Rev. 18:4]
9 [a]Jer. 15:14; 51:27 [b]2 Sam. 1:22
10 [a][Rev. 17:16]
11 [a]Is. 47:6 [b]Hos. 10:11
12 [a]Jer. 51:43
13 [a]Jer. 25:12 [b]Jer. 49:17
14 [a]Jer. 51:2
15 [a]1 Chr. 29:24; 2 Chr. 30:8; Lam. 5:6; Ezek. 17:18 [b]Jer. 51:58 [c]Jer. 51:6, 11
16 [a]Is. 13:14; Jer. 51:9
17 [a]2 Kin. 24:10, 14 [b]Jer. 2:15 [c]2 Kin. 15:29; 17:6; 18:9–13

NKJV

4 "In those days and in that time," says the LORD,
"The children of Israel shall come,
[a]They and the children of Judah together;
[b]With continual weeping they shall come,
[c]And seek the LORD their God.
5 They shall ask the way to Zion,
With their faces toward it, *saying*,
Come and let us join ourselves to the LORD
In [a]a perpetual covenant
That will not be forgotten.'

6 "My people have been [a]lost sheep.
Their shepherds have led them [b]astray;
They have turned them away *on* [c]the mountains.
They have gone from mountain to hill;
They have forgotten their resting place.
7 All who found them have [a]devoured them;
And [b]their adversaries said, [c]'We have not offended,
Because they have sinned against the LORD, [d]the habitation of justice,
The LORD, [e]the hope of their fathers.'

8 "Move[a] from the midst of Babylon,
Go out of the land of the Chaldeans;
And be like the rams before the flocks.
9 [a]For behold, I will raise and cause to come up against Babylon
An assembly of great nations from the north country,
And they shall array themselves against her;
From there she shall be captured.
Their arrows *shall be* like *those* of *an expert warrior;
[b]None shall return in vain.
10 And Chaldea shall become plunder;
[a]All who plunder her shall be satisfied," says the LORD.

11 "Because[a] you were glad, because you rejoiced,
You destroyers of My heritage,
Because you have grown fat [b]like a heifer threshing grain,
And you bellow like bulls,
12 Your mother shall be deeply ashamed;
She who bore you shall be ashamed.
Behold, the least of the nations *shall be* a [a]wilderness,
A dry land and a desert.
13 Because of the wrath of the LORD
She shall not be inhabited,
[a]But she shall be wholly desolate.
[b]Everyone who goes by Babylon shall be horrified
And hiss at all her plagues.

14 "Put[a] yourselves in array against Babylon all around,
All you who bend the bow;
Shoot at her, spare no arrows,
For she has sinned against the LORD.
15 Shout against her all around;
She has [a]given her hand,
Her foundations have fallen,
[b]Her walls are thrown down;
For [c]it *is* the vengeance of the LORD.
Take vengeance on her.
As she has done, so do to her.
16 Cut off the sower from Babylon,
And him who handles the sickle at harvest time.
For fear of the oppressing sword
[a]Everyone shall turn to his own people,
And everyone shall flee to his own land.

17 "Israel *is* like [a]scattered sheep;
[b]The lions have driven *him* away.
First [c]the king of Assyria devoured him;

*
50:9 So with some Heb. mss., LXX, Syr.; MT, Tg., Vg. *a warrior who makes childless*

KJV

hath devoured him; and last this [d]Nebuchad-
rezzar king of Babylon hath broken his bones.
18 Therefore thus saith the LORD of hosts, the
God of Israel; Behold, I will punish the king of
Babylon and his land, as I have punished the king
of [a]Assyria.
19 [a]And I will bring Israel again to his habitation, and he shall feed on Carmel and Bashan,
and his soul shall be satisfied upon mount
Ephraim and Gilead.
20 In those days, and in that time, saith the
LORD, [a]the iniquity of Israel shall be sought for,
and *there shall be* none; and the sins of Judah,
and they shall not be found: for I will pardon them
[b]whom I reserve.
21 Go up against the land of Merathaim, *even*
against it, and against the inhabitants of [a]Pekod:
waste and utterly destroy after them, saith the
LORD, and do [b]according to all that I have commanded thee.
22 [a]A sound of battle *is* in the land, and of
great destruction.
23 How is [a]the hammer of the whole earth
cut asunder and broken! how is Babylon become
a desolation among the nations!
24 I have laid a snare for thee, and thou art
also [a]taken, O Babylon, and thou wast not aware:
thou art found, and also caught, because thou hast
[b]striven against the LORD.
25 The LORD hath opened his armoury, and
hath brought forth [a]the weapons of his indignation: for this *is* the work of the Lord GOD of hosts
in the land of the Chaldeans.
26 Come against her from the utmost border,
open her storehouses: cast her up as heaps, and
destroy her utterly: let nothing of her be left.
27 Slay all her [a]bullocks; let them go down
to the slaughter: woe unto them! for their day is
come, the time of [b]their visitation.
28 The voice of them that flee and escape out
of the land of Babylon, [a]to declare in Zion the
vengeance of the LORD our God, the vengeance
of his temple.
29 Call together the archers against Babylon:
all ye that bend the bow, camp against it round
about; let none thereof escape: [a]recompense her
according to her work; according to all that she
hath done, do unto her: [b]for she hath been proud
against the LORD, against the Holy One of Israel.
30 [a]Therefore shall her young men fall in the
streets, and all her men of war shall be cut off in
that day, saith the LORD.
31 Behold, I *am* against thee, *O thou* most
proud, saith the Lord GOD of hosts: for thy day
is come, the time *that* I will visit thee.
32 And the most [a]proud shall stumble and

17 [d]2 Kin. 24:10–14; 25:1–7
18 [a]Is. 10:12; Ezek. 31:3, 11, 12; Nah. 3:7, 18, 19
19 [a]Is. 65:10; Jer. 33:12; Ezek. 34:13
20 [a]Num. 23:21; Is. 43:25; [Jer. 31:34; Mic. 7:19] [b]Is. 1:9
21 [a]Ezek. 23:23 [b]2 Sam. 16:11; 2 Kin. 18:25; 2 Chr. 36:23; Is. 10:6; 44:28; 48:14
22 [a]Jer. 51:54
23 [a]Is. 14:6; Jer. 51:20–24
24 [a]Jer. 51:8, 31; Dan. 5:30 [b][Is. 45:9]
25 [a]Is. 13:5
27 [a]Ps. 22:12; Is. 34:7; Jer. 46:21 [b]Ps. 37:13; Jer. 48:44; Ezek. 7:7
28 [a]Ps. 149:6–9; Jer. 51:10
29 [a]Ps. 137:8; Jer. 51:56; [2 Thess. 1:6]; Rev. 18:6 [b][Is. 47:10]
30 [a]Is. 13:18; Jer. 49:26; 51:4
32 [a]Is. 26:5; Mal. 4:1

*
50:29 Qr., some Heb. mss., LXX, Tg. add *to her*
50:31 So with MT, Tg.; LXX, Vg. *The time of your punishment*

NKJV

Now at last this [d]Nebuchadnezzar king of
Babylon has broken his bones."

18 Therefore thus says the LORD of hosts, the
God of Israel:

"Behold, I will punish the king of Babylon
and his land,
As I have punished the king of [a]Assyria.
19 [a]But I will bring back Israel to his home,
And he shall feed on Carmel and Bashan;
His soul shall be satisfied on Mount
Ephraim and Gilead.
20 In those days and in that time," says the
LORD,
[a]"The iniquity of Israel shall be sought, but
there shall be none;
And the sins of Judah, but they shall not
be found;
For I will pardon those [b]whom I preserve.

21 "Go up against the land of Merathaim,
against it,
And against the inhabitants of [a]Pekod.
Waste and utterly destroy them," says the
LORD,
"And do [b]according to all that I have
commanded you.
22 [a]A sound of battle *is* in the land,
And of great destruction.
23 How [a]the hammer of the whole earth has
been cut apart and broken!
How Babylon has become a desolation
among the nations!
I have laid a snare for you;
24 You have indeed been [a]trapped, O
Babylon,
And you were not aware;
You have been found and also caught,
Because you have [b]contended against the
LORD.
25 The LORD has opened His armory,
And has brought out [a]the weapons of His
indignation;
For this *is* the work of the Lord GOD of
hosts
In the land of the Chaldeans.
26 Come against her from the farthest
border;
Open her storehouses;
Cast her up as heaps of ruins,
And destroy her utterly;
Let nothing of her be left.
27 Slay all her [a]bulls,
Let them go down to the slaughter.
Woe to them!
For their day has come, the time of [b]their
punishment.
28 The voice of those who flee and escape
from the land of Babylon
[a]Declares in Zion the vengeance of the
LORD our God,
The vengeance of His temple.

29 "Call together the archers against Babylon.
All you who bend the bow, encamp
against it all around;
Let none of them *escape.
[a]Repay her according to her work;
According to all she has done, do to her;
[b]For she has been proud against the LORD,
Against the Holy One of Israel.
30 [a]Therefore her young men shall fall in the
streets,
And all her men of war shall be cut off
in that day," says the LORD.
31 "Behold, I *am* against you,
O most haughty one!" says the Lord GOD
of hosts;
"For your day has come,
*The time *that* I will punish you.
32 The most [a]proud shall stumble and fall,

KJV

fall, and none shall raise him up: and [b]I will kindle a fire in his cities, and it shall devour all round about him.

33 Thus saith the LORD of hosts; The children of Israel and the children of Judah *were* oppressed together: and all that took them captives held them fast; they refused to let them go.

34 [a]Their Redeemer *is* strong; [b]the LORD of hosts *is* his name: he shall throughly plead their [c]cause, that he may give rest to the land, and disquiet the inhabitants of Babylon.

35 A sword *is* upon the Chaldeans, saith the LORD, and upon the inhabitants of Babylon, and [a]upon her princes, and upon [b]her wise *men.*

36 A sword *is* [a]upon the liars; and they shall dote: a sword *is* upon her mighty men; and they shall be dismayed.

37 A sword *is* upon their horses, and upon their chariots, and upon all [a]the mingled people that *are* in the midst of her; and [b]they shall become as women: a sword *is* upon her treasures; and they shall be robbed.

38 [a]A drought *is* upon her waters; and they shall be dried up: for it *is* the land of graven images, and they are mad upon *their* idols.

39 [a]Therefore the wild beasts of the desert with the wild beasts of the islands shall dwell *there,* and the owls shall dwell therein: [b]and it shall be no more inhabited for ever; neither shall it be dwelt in from generation to generation.

40 [a]As God overthrew Sodom and Gomorrah and the neighbour *cities* thereof, saith the LORD; *so* shall no man abide there, neither shall any son of man [b]dwell therein.

41 [a]Behold, a people shall come from the north, and a great nation, and many kings shall be raised up from the coasts of the earth.

42 [a]They shall hold the bow and the lance: [b]they *are* cruel, and will not shew mercy: [c]their voice shall roar like the sea, and they shall ride upon horses, *every one* put in array, like a man to the battle, against thee, O daughter of Babylon.

43 The king of Babylon hath [a]heard the report of them, and his hands waxed feeble: anguish took hold of him, *and* pangs as of a woman in [b]travail.

44 [a]Behold, he shall come up like a lion from the swelling of Jordan unto the habitation of the strong: but I will make them suddenly run away from her: and who *is* a chosen *man, that* I may appoint over her? for who *is* like me? and who will appoint me the time? and [b]who *is* that shepherd that will stand before me?

45 Therefore hear ye [a]the counsel of the LORD, that he hath taken against Babylon; and

NKJV

And no one will raise him up;
[b]I will kindle a fire in his cities,
And it will devour all around him."

33 Thus says the LORD of hosts:

"The children of Israel *were* oppressed,
Along with the children of Judah;
All who took them captive have held them fast;
They have refused to let them go.
34 [a]Their Redeemer *is* strong;
[b]The LORD of hosts *is* His name.
He will thoroughly plead their [c]case,
That He may give rest to the land,
And disquiet the inhabitants of Babylon.

35 "A sword *is* against the Chaldeans," says the LORD,
"Against the inhabitants of Babylon,
And [a]against her princes and [b]her wise men.
36 A sword *is* [a]against the soothsayers, and they will be fools.
A sword *is* against her mighty men, and they will be dismayed.
37 A sword *is* against their horses,
Against their chariots,
And against all [a]the mixed peoples who *are* in her midst;
And [b]they will become like women.
A sword *is* against her treasures, and they will be robbed.
38 [a]A *drought *is* against her waters, and they will be dried up.
For it *is* the land of carved images,
And they are insane with *their* idols.

39 "Therefore[a] the wild desert beasts shall dwell *there* with the jackals,
And the ostriches shall dwell in it.
[b]It shall be inhabited no more forever,
Nor shall it be dwelt in from generation to generation.
40 [a]As God overthrew Sodom and Gomorrah
And their neighbors," says the LORD,
"*So* no one shall reside there,
Nor son of man [b]dwell in it.

41 "Behold,[a] a people shall come from the north,
And a great nation and many kings
Shall be raised up from the ends of the earth.
42 [a]They shall hold the bow and the lance;
[b]They *are* cruel and shall not show mercy.
[c]Their voice shall roar like the sea;
They shall ride on horses,
Set in array, like a man for the battle,
Against you, O daughter of Babylon.

43 "The king of Babylon has [a]heard the report about them,
And his hands grow feeble;
Anguish has taken hold of him,
Pangs as of a woman in [b]childbirth.

44 "Behold,[a] he shall come up like a lion from the *floodplain of the Jordan
Against the dwelling place of the strong;
But I will make them suddenly run away from her.
And who *is* a chosen *man that* I may appoint over her?
For who *is* like Me?
Who will arraign Me?
And [b]who *is* that shepherd
Who will withstand Me?"

45 Therefore hear [a]the counsel of the LORD
that He has taken against Babylon,

---

32 [b]Jer. 21:14 **34** [a]Prov. 23:11; Is. 43:14; Jer. 15:21; 31:11; Rev. 18:8 [b]Is. 47:4 [c]Jer. 32:18; 51:19–22 **35** [a]Dan. 5:30 [b]Is. 47:13; Jer. 51:57 **36** [a]Is. 44:25; Jer. 48:30 **37** [a]Jer. 25:20; Ezek. 30:5 [b]Jer. 51:30; Nah. 3:13 **38** [a]Is. 44:27; Jer. 51:36; Rev. 16:12 **39** [a]Is. 13:21, 22; 34:14; Jer. 51:37; Rev. 18:2 [b]Is. 13:20; Jer. 25:12 **40** [a]Gen. 19:24, 25; Is. 13:19; Jer. 49:18; [Luke 17:28–30]; 2 Pet. 2:6; Jude 7 [b]Is. 13:20 **41** [a]Is. 13:2–5; Jer. 6:22; 25:14; 51:27 **42** [a]Jer. 6:23 [b]Is. 13:18 [c]Is. 5:30 **43** [a]Jer. 51:31 [b]Jer. 6:24 **44** [a]Jer. 49:19–21 [b]Job 41:10; Jer. 49:19 **45** [a][Ps. 33:11; Is. 14:24]; Jer. 51:10, 11

***50:38** So with MT, Tg., Vg.; Syr. *sword;* LXX omits *A drought is* **50:44** Or *thicket*

KJV

his [b]purposes, that he hath purposed against the land of the Chaldeans: [c]Surely the least of the flock shall draw them out: surely he shall make *their* habitation desolate with them.

46 [a]At the noise of the taking of Babylon the earth is moved, and the cry is heard among the nations.

The Utter Destruction of Babylon

51 Thus saith the LORD; Behold, I will raise up against [a]Babylon, and against them that dwell in the midst of them that rise up against me, [b]a destroying wind;

2 And will send unto Babylon [a]fanners, that shall fan her, and shall empty her land: [b]for in the day of trouble they shall be against her round about.

3 Against *him that* bendeth [a]let the archer bend his bow, and against *him that* lifteth himself up in his brigandine: and spare ye not her young men; [b]destroy ye utterly all her host.

4 Thus the slain shall fall in the land of the Chaldeans, [a]and *they that are* thrust through in her streets.

5 For Israel *hath* [a]not *been* forsaken, nor Judah of his God, of the LORD of hosts; though their land was filled with sin against the Holy One of Israel.

6 [a]Flee out of the midst of Babylon, and deliver every man his soul: be not cut off in her iniquity; for [b]this *is* the time of the LORD's vengeance; [c]he will render unto her a recompence.

7 [a]Babylon *hath been* a golden cup in the LORD's hand, that made all the earth drunken: [b]the nations have drunken of her wine; therefore the nations [c]are mad.

8 Babylon is suddenly [a]fallen and destroyed: [b]howl for her; [c]take balm for her pain, if so be she may be healed.

9 We would have healed Babylon, but she is not healed: forsake her, and [a]let us go every one into his own country: [b]for her judgment reacheth unto heaven, and is lifted up *even* to the skies.

10 The LORD hath [a]brought forth our righteousness: come, and let us [b]declare in Zion the work of the LORD our God.

11 [a]Make bright the arrows; gather the shields: [b]the LORD hath raised up the spirit of the kings of the Medes: [c]for his device *is* against Babylon, to destroy it; because it *is* [d]the vengeance of the LORD, the vengeance of his temple.

12 [a]Set up the standard upon the walls of Babylon, make the watch strong, set up the watchmen, prepare the ambushes: for the LORD hath both devised and done that which he spake against the inhabitants of Babylon.

13 [a]O thou that dwellest upon many waters, abundant in treasures, thine end is come, *and* the measure of thy covetousness.

45 [b]Jer. 51:29 [c]Jer. 49:19, 20
46 [a]Rev. 18:9

CHAPTER 51

1 [a]Is. 47:1; Jer. 50:1 [b]2 Kin. 19:7; Jer. 4:11; Hos. 13:15
2 [a]Is. 41:16; Jer. 15:7; Matt. 3:12 [b]Jer. 50:14
3 [a]Jer. 50:14, 29 [b]Jer. 50:21
4 [a]Jer. 49:26; 50:30, 37
5 [a][Is. 54:7, 8; Jer. 33:24–26; 46:28]
6 [a]Jer. 50:8; Rev. 18:4 [b]Jer. 50:15 [c]Jer. 25:14
7 [a]Jer. 25:15; Hab. 2:16; Rev. 17:4 [b]Rev. 14:8 [c]Jer. 25:16
8 [a]Is. 21:9; Jer. 50:2; Rev. 14:8; 18:2 [b][Is. 48:20]; Rev. 18:9, 11, 19 [c]Jer. 46:11
9 [a]Is. 13:14; Jer. 46:16; 50:16 [b]Ezra 9:6; Rev. 18:5
10 [a]Ps. 37:6; Mic. 7:9 [b][Is. 40:2]; Jer. 50:28
11 [a]Jer. 46:4, 9; Joel 3:9, 10 [b]Is. 13:17 [c]Jer. 50:45 [d]Jer. 50:28
12 [a]Nah. 2:1; 3:14
13 [a]Rev. 17:1, 15

***51:1** Lit. *The Midst of Those Who Rise Up Against Me;* a code word for Chaldea, Babylonia

NKJV

And His [b]purposes that He has proposed
against the land of the Chaldeans:
[c]Surely the least of the flock shall draw
them out;
Surely He will make their dwelling place
desolate with them.

46 [a]At the noise of the taking of Babylon
The earth trembles,
And the cry is heard among the nations.

The Utter Destruction of Babylon

51 Thus says the LORD:
"Behold, I will raise up against [a]Babylon,
Against those who dwell in *Leb Kamai,
[b]A destroying wind.

2 And I will send [a]winnowers to Babylon,
Who shall winnow her and empty her
land.
[b]For in the day of doom
They shall be against her all around.

3 Against *her* [a]let the archer bend his bow,
And lift himself up against *her* in his
armor.
Do not spare her young men;
[b]Utterly destroy all her army.

4 Thus the slain shall fall in the land of the
Chaldeans,
[a]And *those* thrust through in her streets.

5 For Israel is [a]not forsaken, nor Judah,
By his God, the LORD of hosts,
Though their land was filled with sin
against the Holy One of Israel."

6 [a]Flee from the midst of Babylon,
And every one save his life!
Do not be cut off in her iniquity,
For [b]this *is* the time of the LORD's
vengeance;
[c]He shall recompense her.

7 [a]Babylon *was* a golden cup in the LORD's
hand,
That made all the earth drunk.
[b]The nations drank her wine;
Therefore the nations [c]are deranged.

8 Babylon has suddenly [a]fallen and been
destroyed.
[b]Wail for her!
[c]Take balm for her pain;
Perhaps she may be healed.

9 We would have healed Babylon,
But she is not healed.
Forsake her, and [a]let us go everyone to
his own country;
[b]For her judgment reaches to heaven and
is lifted up to the skies.

10 The LORD has [a]revealed our
righteousness.
Come and let us [b]declare in Zion the work
of the LORD our God.

11 [a]Make the arrows bright!
Gather the shields!
[b]The LORD has raised up the spirit of the
kings of the Medes.
[c]For His plan *is* against Babylon to destroy
it,
Because it *is* [d]the vengeance of the LORD,
The vengeance for His temple.

12 [a]Set up the standard on the walls of
Babylon;
Make the guard strong,
Set up the watchmen,
Prepare the ambushes.
For the LORD has both devised and done
What He spoke against the inhabitants of
Babylon.

13 [a]O you who dwell by many waters,
Abundant in treasures,
Your end has come,
The measure of your covetousness.

KJV

14 [a]The LORD of hosts hath sworn by himself, *saying,* Surely I will fill thee with men, [b]as with caterpillers; and they shall lift [c]up a shout against thee.

15 [a]He hath made the earth by his power, he hath established the world by his wisdom, and [b]hath stretched out the heaven by his understanding.

16 When he uttereth *his* voice, *there is* a multitude of waters in the heavens; and [a]he causeth the vapors to ascend from the ends of the earth: he maketh lightnings with rain, and bringeth forth the wind out of his treasures.

17 [a]Every man is brutish by *his* knowledge; every founder is confounded by the graven image: [b]for his molten image *is* falsehood, and *there is* no breath in them.

18 They *are* vanity, the work of errors: in the time of their visitation they shall perish.

19 The portion of Jacob *is* not like them; for he *is* the former of all things: and *Israel is* the rod of his inheritance: the LORD of hosts *is* his name.

20 [a]Thou *art* my battle ax *and* weapons of war: for with thee will I break in pieces the nations, and with thee will I destroy kingdoms;

21 And with thee will I break in pieces the horse and his rider; and with thee will I break in pieces the chariot and his rider;

22 With thee also will I break in pieces man and woman; and with thee will I break in pieces [a]old and young; and with thee will I break in pieces the young man and the maid;

23 I will also break in pieces with thee the shepherd and his flock; and with thee will I break in pieces the husbandman and his yoke of oxen; and with thee will I break in pieces captains and rulers.

24 [a]And I will render unto Babylon and to all the inhabitants of Chaldea all their evil that they have done in Zion in your sight, saith the LORD.

25 Behold, I *am* against thee, [a]O destroying mountain, saith the LORD, which destroyest all the earth: and I will stretch out mine hand upon thee, and roll thee down from the rocks, [b]and will make thee a burnt mountain.

26 And they shall not take of thee a stone for a corner, nor a stone for foundations; [a]but thou shalt be desolate for ever, saith the LORD.

27 [a]Set ye up a standard in the land, blow the trumpet among the nations, [b]prepare the nations against her, call together against her [c]the kingdoms of Ararat, Minni, and Ashchenaz; appoint a captain against her; cause the horses to come up as the rough caterpillers.

14 [a]Jer. 49:13; Amos 6:8 [b]Jer. 51:27; Nah. 3:15 [c]Jer. 50:15
15 [a]Gen. 1:1, 6; Jer. 10:12–16 [b]Job 9:8; Ps. 104:2; Is. 40:22
16 [a]Ps. 135:7; Jer. 10:13
17 [a][Is. 44:18–20]; Jer. 10:14 [b]Jer. 50:2
20 [a]Is. 10:5, 15; Jer. 50:23
22 [a]2 Chr. 36:17; Is. 13:15, 16
24 [a]Jer. 50:15, 29
25 [a]Is. 13:2; Zech. 4:7 [b]Rev. 8:8
26 [a]Jer. 50:26, 40
27 [a]Is. 13:2; Jer. 50:2; 51:12 [b]Jer. 25:14 [c]Jer. 50:41, 42

NKJV

14 [a]The LORD of hosts has sworn by Himself:
"Surely I will fill you with men, [b]as with locusts,
And they shall lift [c]up a shout against you."

15 [a]He has made the earth by His power;
He has established the world by His wisdom,
And [b]stretched out the heaven by His understanding.
16 When He utters *His* voice—
There is a multitude of waters in the heavens:
[a]"He causes the vapors to ascend from the ends of the earth;
He makes lightnings for the rain;
He brings the wind out of His treasures."

17 [a]Everyone is dull-hearted, without knowledge;
Every metalsmith is put to shame by the carved image;
[b]For his molded image *is* falsehood,
And *there is* no breath in them.
18 They *are* futile, a work of errors;
In the time of their punishment they shall perish.
19 The Portion of Jacob *is* not like them,
For He *is* the Maker of all things;
And *Israel is* the tribe of His inheritance.
The LORD of hosts *is* His name.

20 "You[a] *are* My battle-ax *and* weapons of war:
For with you I will break the nation in pieces;
With you I will destroy kingdoms;
21 With you I will break in pieces the horse and its rider;
With you I will break in pieces the chariot and its rider;
22 With you also I will break in pieces man and woman;
With you I will break in pieces [a]old and young;
With you I will break in pieces the young man and the maiden;
23 With you also I will break in pieces the shepherd and his flock;
With you I will break in pieces the farmer and his yoke of oxen;
And with you I will break in pieces governors and rulers.

24 "And[a] I will repay Babylon
And all the inhabitants of Chaldea
For all the evil they have done
In Zion in your sight," says the LORD.

25 "Behold, I *am* against you, [a]O destroying mountain,
Who destroys all the earth," says the LORD.
"And I will stretch out My hand against you,
Roll you down from the rocks,
[b]And make you a burnt mountain.
26 They shall not take from you a stone for a corner
Nor a stone for a foundation,
[a]But you shall be desolate forever," says the LORD.

27 [a]Set up a banner in the land,
Blow the trumpet among the nations!
[b]Prepare the nations against her,
Call [c]the kingdoms together against her:
Ararat, Minni, and Ashkenaz.
Appoint a general against her;
Cause the horses to come up like the bristling locusts.

KJV

28 Prepare against her the nations with the kings of the Medes, the captains thereof, and all the rulers thereof, and all the land of his dominion.

29 And the land shall tremble and sorrow: for every [a]purpose of the LORD shall be performed against Babylon, [b]to make the land of Babylon a desolation without an inhabitant.

30 The mighty men of Babylon have forborn to fight, they have remained in *their* holds: their might hath failed; [a]they became as women: they have burned her dwelling-places; [b]her bars are broken.

31 [a]One post shall run to meet another, and one messenger to meet another, to shew the king of Babylon that his city is taken at *one* end,

32 And that [a]the passages are stopped, and the reeds they have burned with fire, and the men of war are affrighted.

33 For thus saith the LORD of hosts, the God of Israel; The daughter of Babylon *is* [a]like a threshingfloor, [b]*it is* time to thresh her: yet a little while, [c]and the time of her harvest shall come.

34 Nebuchadrezzar the king of Babylon hath [a]devoured me, he hath crushed me, he hath made me an [b]empty vessel, he hath swallowed me up like a dragon, he hath filled his belly with my delicates, he hath cast me out.

35 The violence done to me and to my flesh *be* upon Babylon, shall the inhabitant of Zion say; and my blood upon the inhabitants of Chaldea, shall Jerusalem say.

36 Therefore thus saith the LORD; Behold, [a]I will plead thy cause, and take vengeance for thee; [b]and I will dry up her sea, and make her springs dry.

37 [a]And Babylon shall become heaps, a dwellingplace for dragons, [b]an astonishment, and an hissing, without an inhabitant.

38 They shall roar together like lions: they shall yell as lions' whelps.

39 In their heat I will make their feasts, and [a]I will make them drunken, that they may rejoice, and sleep a perpetual sleep, and not wake, saith the LORD.

40 I will bring them down like lambs to the slaughter, like rams with he goats.

41 How is [a]Sheshach taken! and how is [b]the praise of the whole earth surprised! how is Babylon become an astonishment among the nations!

42 [a]The sea is come up upon Babylon: she is covered with the multitude of the waves thereof.

43 [a]Her cities are a desolation, a dry land, and a wilderness, a land wherein [b]no man dwelleth, neither doth *any* son of man pass thereby.

29 [a]Jer. 50:45 [b]Is. 13:19, 20; 47:11; Jer. 50:13; 51:26, 43
30 [a]Is. 19:16; Jer. 48:41 [b]Is. 45:1, 2; Lam. 2:9; Amos 1:5; Nah. 3:13
31 [a]Jer. 50:24
32 [a]Jer. 50:38
33 [a]Is. 21:10; Dan. 2:35; Amos 1:3; Mic. 4:13 [b]Is. 41:15; Hab. 3:12 [c]Is. 17:15; Hos. 6:11; Joel 3:13; Rev. 14:15
34 [a]Jer. 50:17 [b]Is. 24:1–3
36 [a][Ps. 140:12]; Jer. 50:34 [b]Jer. 50:38
37 [a]Is. 13:22; Jer. 50:39; [Rev. 18:2] [b]Jer. 25:9, 11
39 [a]Jer. 51:57
41 [a]Jer. 25:26 [b]Is. 13:19; Jer. 49:25; [Dan. 4:30]
42 [a]Is. 8:7, 8; Jer. 51:55; Dan. 9:26
43 [a]Jer. 50:39, 40 [b]Is. 13:20

NKJV

28 Prepare against her the nations,
With the kings of the Medes,
Its governors and all its rulers,
All the land of his dominion.
29 And the land will tremble and sorrow;
For every [a]purpose of the LORD shall be performed against Babylon,
[b]To make the land of Babylon a desolation without inhabitant.
30 The mighty men of Babylon have ceased fighting,
They have remained in their strongholds;
Their might has failed,
[a]They became *like* women;
They have burned her dwelling places,
[b]The bars of her *gate* are broken.
31 [a]One runner will run to meet another,
And one messenger to meet another,
To show the king of Babylon that his city is taken on *all* sides;
32 [a]The passages are blocked,
The reeds they have burned with fire,
And the men of war are terrified.

33 For thus says the LORD of hosts, the God of Israel:

"The daughter of Babylon *is* [a]like a threshing floor
When [b]*it is* time to thresh her;
Yet a little while
[c]And the time of her harvest will come."

34 "Nebuchadnezzar the king of Babylon
Has [a]devoured me, he has crushed me;
He has made me an [b]empty vessel,
He has swallowed me up like a monster;
He has filled his stomach with my delicacies,
He has spit me out.
35 Let the violence *done* to me and my flesh *be* upon Babylon,"
The inhabitant of Zion will say;
"And my blood be upon the inhabitants of Chaldea!"
Jerusalem will say.

36 Therefore thus says the LORD:

"Behold, [a]I will plead your case and take vengeance for you.
[b]I will dry up her sea and make her springs dry.
37 [a]Babylon shall become a heap,
A dwelling place for jackals,
[b]An astonishment and a hissing,
Without an inhabitant.
38 They shall roar together like lions,
They shall growl like lions' whelps.
39 In their excitement I will prepare their feasts;
[a]I will make them drunk,
That they may rejoice,
And sleep a perpetual sleep
And not awake," says the LORD.
40 "I will bring them down
Like lambs to the slaughter,
Like rams with male goats.

41 "Oh, how [a]Sheshach* is taken!
Oh, how [b]the praise of the whole earth is seized!
How Babylon has become desolate among the nations!
42 [a]The sea has come up over Babylon;
She is covered with the multitude of its waves.
43 [a]Her cities are a desolation,
A dry land and a wilderness,
A land where [b]no one dwells,
Through which no son of man passes.

*

51:41 A code word for *Babylon,* Jer. 25:26

KJV

44 And I will punish [a]Bel in Babylon, and I will bring forth out of his mouth that which he hath swallowed up: and the nations shall not flow together any more unto him: yea, [b]the wall of Babylon shall fall.

45 [a]My people, go ye out of the midst of her, and deliver ye every man his soul from the fierce anger of the LORD.

46 And lest your heart faint, and ye fear [a]for the rumour that shall be heard in the land; a rumour shall both come *one* year, and after that in *another* year *shall come* a rumour, and violence in the land, ruler against ruler.

47 Therefore, behold, the days come, that I will do judgment upon the graven images of Babylon: and her whole land shall be confounded, and all her slain shall fall in the midst of her.

48 Then [a]the heaven and the earth, and all that *is* therein, shall sing for Babylon: [b]for the spoilers shall come unto her from the north, saith the LORD.

49 As Babylon *hath caused* the slain of Israel to fall, so at Babylon shall fall the slain of all the earth.

50 [a]Ye that have escaped the sword, go away, stand not still: [b]remember the LORD afar off, and let Jerusalem come into your mind.

51 [a]We are confounded, because we have heard reproach: shame hath covered our faces: for strangers [b]are come into the sanctuaries of the LORD's house.

52 Wherefore, behold, the days come, saith the LORD, that I will do judgment upon her graven images: and through all her land the wounded shall groan.

53 [a]Though Babylon should mount up to heaven, and though she should fortify the height of her strength, *yet* from me shall spoilers come unto her, saith the LORD.

54 [a]A sound of a cry *cometh* from Babylon, and great destruction from the land of the Chaldeans:

55 Because the LORD hath spoiled Babylon, and destroyed out of her the great voice; when her waves do roar like great waters, a noise of their voice is uttered:

56 Because the spoiler is come upon her, *even* upon Babylon, and her mighty men are taken, every one of their bows is broken: [a]for the LORD God of recompences shall surely requite.

57 And I will make drunk her princes, and her [a]wise *men*, her captains, and her rulers, and her mighty men: and they shall sleep a perpetual sleep, and not wake, saith [b]the King, whose name *is* the LORD of hosts.

58 Thus saith the LORD of hosts; The broad

44 [a]Jer. 50:2; Is. 46:1 [b]Jer. 50:15
45 [a]Is. 48:20; [Jer. 50:8, 28; 51:6; Rev. 18:4]
46 [a]2 Kin. 19:7; Is. 13:3–5
48 [a]Is. 44:23; 48:20; 49:13; Rev. 18:20 [b]Jer. 50:3, 41
50 [a]Jer. 44:28 [b][Deut. 4:29–31]; Ezek. 6:9
51 [a]Ps. 44:15; 79:4 [b]Ps. 74:3–8; Jer. 52:13; Lam. 1:10
53 [a]Gen. 11:4; Job 20:6; [Ps. 139:8–10; Is. 14:12–14]; Jer. 49:16; Amos 9:2; Obad. 4
54 [a]Jer. 50:22
56 [a]Ps. 94:1; Jer. 50:29
57 [a]Jer. 50:35 [b]Jer. 46:18; 48:15

NKJV

44 I will punish [a]Bel in Babylon,
And I will bring out of his mouth what
he has swallowed;
And the nations shall not stream to him
anymore.
Yes, [b]the wall of Babylon shall fall.

45 "My[a] people, go out of the midst of her!
And let everyone deliver himself from the
fierce anger of the LORD.
46 And lest your heart faint,
And you fear [a]for the rumor that *will be*
heard in the land
(A rumor will come *one* year,
And after that, in *another* year
A rumor *will come,*
And violence in the land,
Ruler against ruler),
47 Therefore behold, the days are coming
That I will bring judgment on the carved
images of Babylon;
Her whole land shall be ashamed,
And all her slain shall fall in her midst.
48 Then [a]the heavens and the earth and all
that *is* in them
Shall sing joyously over Babylon;
[b]For the plunderers shall come to her from
the north," says the LORD.

49 As Babylon *has caused* the slain of Israel
to fall,
So at Babylon the slain of all the earth
shall fall.
50 [a]You who have escaped the sword,
Get away! Do not stand still!
[b]Remember the LORD afar off,
And let Jerusalem come to your mind.

51 [a]We are ashamed because we have heard
reproach.
Shame has covered our faces,
For strangers [b]have come into the
sanctuaries of the LORD's house.

52 "Therefore behold, the days are coming,"
says the LORD,
"That I will bring judgment on her carved
images,
And throughout all her land the wounded
shall groan.
53 [a]Though Babylon were to mount up to
heaven,
And though she were to fortify the height
of her strength,
Yet from Me plunderers would come to
her," says the LORD.

54 [a]The sound of a cry *comes* from Babylon,
And great destruction from the land of the
Chaldeans,
55 Because the LORD is plundering
Babylon
And silencing her loud voice,
Though her waves roar like great
waters,
And the noise of their voice is uttered,
56 Because the plunderer comes against her,
against Babylon,
And her mighty men are taken.
Every one of their bows is broken;
[a]For the LORD *is* the God of recompense,
He will surely repay.

57 "And I will make drunk
Her princes and [a]wise men,
Her governors, her deputies, and her
mighty men.
And they shall sleep a perpetual sleep
And not awake," says [b]the King,
Whose name *is* the LORD of hosts.

58 Thus says the LORD of hosts:

KJV

walls of Babylon shall be utterly [a]broken, and her high gates shall be burned with fire; and [b]the people shall labour in vain, and the folk in the fire, and they shall be weary.

Jeremiah's Command to Seraiah

59 The word which Jeremiah the prophet commanded Seraiah the son of [a]Neriah, the son of Maaseiah, when he went with Zedekiah the king of Judah into Babylon in the fourth year of his reign. And *this* Seraiah *was* a quiet prince.

60 So Jeremiah [a]wrote in a book all the evil that should come upon Babylon, *even* all these words that are written against Babylon.

61 And Jeremiah said to Seraiah, When thou comest to Babylon, and shalt see, and shalt read all these words;

62 Then shalt thou say, O LORD, thou hast spoken against this place, to cut it off, that [a]none shall remain in it, neither man nor beast, but that it shall be desolate for ever.

63 And it shall be, when thou hast made an end of reading this book, [a]*that* thou shalt bind a stone to it, and cast it into the midst of Euphrates:

64 And thou shalt say, Thus shall Babylon sink, and shall not rise from the evil that I will bring upon her: and they shall be weary. Thus far *are* the words of Jeremiah.

The Fall of Jerusalem Reviewed
(2 Kin. 24:18—25:26; 2 Chr. 36:11–20; Jer. 39:1–10)

52 Zedekiah *was* [a]one and twenty years old when he began to reign, and he reigned eleven years in Jerusalem. And his mother's name *was* Hamutal the daughter of Jeremiah of [b]Libnah.

2 And he did *that which was* evil in the eyes of the LORD, according to all that Jehoiakim had done.

3 For through the anger of the LORD it came to pass in Jerusalem and Judah, till he had cast them out from his presence, that Zedekiah [a]rebelled against the king of Babylon.

4 And it came to pass in the [a]ninth year of his reign, in the tenth month, in the tenth *day* of the month, *that* Nebuchadrezzar king of Babylon came, he and all his army, against Jerusalem, and pitched against it, and built forts against it round about.

5 So the city was besieged unto the eleventh year of king Zedekiah.

6 And in the fourth month, in the ninth *day* of the month, the famine was sore in the city, so that there was no bread for the people of the land.

7 Then the city was broken up, and all the men of war fled, and went forth out of the city by night by the way of the gate between the two walls, which *was* by the king's garden; (now the Chaldeans *were* by the city round about:) and they went by the way of the plain.

8 But the army of the Chaldeans pursued after the king, and overtook Zedekiah in the plains of Jericho; and all his army was scattered from him.

9 [a]Then they took the king, and carried him up unto the king of Babylon to Riblah in the land of Hamath; where he gave judgment upon him.

10 [a]And the king of Babylon slew the sons of Zedekiah before his eyes: he slew also all the princes of Judah in Riblah.

11 Then he [a]put out the eyes of Zedekiah; and the king of Babylon bound him in chains, and carried him to Babylon, and put him in prison till the day of his death.

The Temple and City Plundered and Burned

12 [a]Now in the fifth month, in the tenth *day* of the month, [b]which *was* the nineteenth year of

---

58 [a]Jer. 50:15 [b]Hab. 2:13
59 [a]Jer. 32:12
60 [a]Is. 30:8; Jer. 36:2
62 [a]Is. 13:20; 14:22, 23; Jer. 50:3, 39
63 [a]Jer. 19:10, 11; Rev. 18:21

CHAPTER 52

1 [a]2 Kin. 24:18; 2 Chr. 36:11 [b]Josh. 10:29; 2 Kin. 8:22; Is. 37:8
3 [a]2 Chr. 36:13
4 [a]2 Kin. 25:1; Jer. 39:1; Ezek. 24:1, 2; Zech. 8:19
9 [a]2 Kin. 25:6; Jer. 32:4; 39:5
10 [a]Ezek. 12:13
11 [a]Ezek. 12:13
12 [a]2 Kin. 25:8–21 [b]Jer. 52:29

*52:7 Or *Arabah;* the Jordan valley

NKJV

"The broad walls of Babylon shall be
utterly [a]broken,
And her high gates shall be burned with
fire;
[b]The people will labor in vain,
And the nations, because of the fire;
And they shall be weary."

Jeremiah's Command to Seraiah

59 The word which Jeremiah the prophet commanded Seraiah the son of [a]Neriah, the son of Mahseiah, when he went with Zedekiah the king of Judah to Babylon in the fourth year of his reign. And Seraiah *was* the quartermaster.

60 So Jeremiah [a]wrote in a book all the evil that would come upon Babylon, all these words that are written against Babylon.

61 And Jeremiah said to Seraiah, "When you arrive in Babylon and see it, and read all these words,

62 "then you shall say, 'O LORD, You have spoken against this place to cut it off, so that [a]none shall remain in it, neither man nor beast, but it shall be desolate forever.'

63 "Now it shall be, when you have finished reading this book, [a]*that* you shall tie a stone to it and throw it out into the Euphrates.

64 "Then you shall say, 'Thus Babylon shall sink and not rise from the catastrophe that I will bring upon her. And they shall be weary.' " Thus far *are* the words of Jeremiah.

The Fall of Jerusalem Reviewed
(2 Kin. 24:18—25:26; 2 Chr. 36:11–20; Jer. 39:1–10)

52 Zedekiah *was* [a]twenty-one years old when he became king, and he reigned eleven years in Jerusalem. His mother's name *was* Hamutal the daughter of Jeremiah of [b]Libnah.

2 He also did evil in the sight of the LORD, according to all that Jehoiakim had done.

3 For because of the anger of the LORD *this* happened in Jerusalem and Judah, till He finally cast them out from His presence. Then Zedekiah [a]rebelled against the king of Babylon.

4 Now it came to pass in the [a]ninth year of his reign, in the tenth month, on the tenth *day* of the month, *that* Nebuchadnezzar king of Babylon and all his army came against Jerusalem and encamped against it; and *they* built a siege wall against it all around.

5 So the city was besieged until the eleventh year of King Zedekiah.

6 By the fourth month, on the ninth day of the month, the famine had become so severe in the city that there was no food for the people of the land.

7 Then the city wall was broken through, and all the men of war fled and went out of the city at night by way of the gate between the two walls, which *was* by the king's garden, even though the Chaldeans *were* near the city all around. And they went by way of the *plain.

8 But the army of the Chaldeans pursued the king, and they overtook Zedekiah in the plains of Jericho. All his army was scattered from him.

9 [a]So they took the king and brought him up to the king of Babylon at Riblah in the land of Hamath, and he pronounced judgment on him.

10 [a]Then the king of Babylon killed the sons of Zedekiah before his eyes. And he killed all the princes of Judah in Riblah.

11 He also [a]put out the eyes of Zedekiah; and the king of Babylon bound him in bronze fetters, took him to Babylon, and put him in prison till the day of his death.

The Temple and City Plundered and Burned

12 [a]Now in the fifth month, on the tenth *day* of the month ([b]which *was* the nineteenth year of

KJV

Nebuchadrezzar king of Babylon, [c]came Nebuzar–adan, captain of the guard, *which* served the king of Babylon, into Jerusalem,

13 And burned the house of the LORD, and the king's house; and all the houses of Jerusalem, and all the houses of the great *men,* burned he with fire:

14 And all the army of the Chaldeans, that *were* with the captain of the guard, brake down all the walls of Jerusalem round about.

15 [a]Then Nebuzar–adan the captain of the guard carried away captive *certain* of the poor of the people, and the residue of the people that remained in the city, and those that fell away, that fell to the king of Babylon, and the rest of the multitude.

16 But Nebuzar–adan the captain of the guard left *certain* of the poor of the land for vinedressers and for husbandmen.

17 [a]Also the [b]pillars of brass that *were* in the house of the LORD, and the bases, and the brasen sea that *was* in the house of the LORD, the Chaldeans brake, and carried all the brass of them to Babylon.

18 [a]The caldrons also, and the shovels, and the snuffers, and the bowls, and the spoons, and all the vessels of brass wherewith they ministered, took they away.

19 And the basons, and the firepans, and the bowls, and the caldrons, and the candlesticks, and the spoons, and the cups; *that* which *was* of gold *in* gold, and *that* which *was* of silver *in* silver, took the captain of the guard away.

20 The two pillars, one sea, and twelve brasen bulls that *were* under the bases, which king Solomon had made in the house of the LORD: [a]the brass of all these vessels was without weight.

21 And *concerning* the [a]pillars, the height of one pillar *was* eighteen cubits; and a fillet of twelve cubits did compass it; and the thickness thereof *was* four fingers: *it was* hollow.

22 And a chapiter of brass *was* upon it; and the height of one chapiter *was* five cubits, with network and pomegranates upon the chapiters round about, all *of* brass. The second pillar also and the pomegranates *were* like unto these.

23 And there were ninety and six pomegranates on a side; *and* [a]all the pomegranates upon the network *were* an hundred round about.

The People Taken Captive to Babylonia

24 And [a]the captain of the guard took Seraiah the chief priest, [b]and Zephaniah the second priest, and the three keepers of the door:

25 He took also out of the city an eunuch, which had the charge of the men of war; and seven men of them that were near the king's person, which were found in the city; and the principal scribe of the host, who mustered the people of the land; and threescore men of the people of the land, that were found in the midst of the city.

26 So Nebuzar–adan the captain of the guard took them, and brought them to the king of Babylon to Riblah.

27 And the king of Babylon smote them, and put them to death in Riblah in the land of Hamath. Thus Judah was carried away captive out of his own land.

28 [a]This *is* the people whom Nebuchadrezzar carried away captive: [b]in the seventh year [c]three thousand Jews and three and twenty:

29 [a]In the eighteenth year of Nebuchadrezzar he carried away captive from Jerusalem eight hundred thirty and two persons:

30 In the three and twentieth year of Nebuchadrezzar Nebuzar–adan the captain of the guard carried away captive of the Jews seven hundred forty and five persons: all the persons *were* four thousand and six hundred.

12 [c]Jer. 39:9
15 [a]Jer. 39:9
17 [a]Jer. 27:19 [b]1 Kin. 7:15, 23, 27, 50
18 [a]Ex. 27:3; 1 Kin. 7:40, 45; 2 Kin. 25:14
20 [a]1 Kin. 7:47; 2 Kin. 25:16
21 [a]1 Kin. 7:15; 2 Kin. 25:17; 2 Chr. 3:15
23 [a]1 Kin. 7:20
24 [a]2 Kin. 25:18; 1 Chr. 6:14; Ezra 7:1 [b]Jer. 21:1; 29:25
28 [a]2 Kin. 24:2 [b]2 Kin. 24:12 [c]2 Kin. 24:14
29 [a]2 Kin. 25:11; Jer. 39:9

NKJV

King Nebuchadnezzar king of Babylon), [c]Nebuzaradan, the captain of the guard, *who* served the king of Babylon, came to Jerusalem.

13 He burned the house of the LORD and the king's house; all the houses of Jerusalem, that is, all the houses of the great, he burned with fire.

14 And all the army of the Chaldeans who *were* with the captain of the guard broke down all the walls of Jerusalem all around.

15 [a]Then Nebuzaradan the captain of the guard carried away captive *some* of the poor people, the rest of the people who remained in the city, the defectors who had deserted to the king of Babylon, and the rest of the craftsmen.

16 But Nebuzaradan the captain of the guard left *some* of the poor of the land as vinedressers and farmers.

17 [a]The [b]bronze pillars that *were* in the house of the LORD, and the carts and the bronze Sea that *were* in the house of the LORD, the Chaldeans broke in pieces, and carried all their bronze to Babylon.

18 They also took away [a]the pots, the shovels, the trimmers, the bowls, the spoons, and all the bronze utensils with which the priests ministered.

19 The basins, the firepans, the bowls, the pots, the lampstands, the spoons, and the cups, whatever *was* solid gold and whatever *was* solid silver, the captain of the guard took away.

20 The two pillars, one Sea, the twelve bronze bulls which *were* under *it, and* the carts, which King Solomon had made for the house of the LORD—[a]the bronze of all these articles was beyond measure.

21 Now *concerning* the [a]pillars: the height of one pillar *was* eighteen cubits, a measuring line of twelve cubits could measure its circumference, and its thickness *was* four fingers; *it was* hollow.

22 A capital of bronze *was* on it; and the height of one capital *was* five cubits, with a network and pomegranates all around the capital, all of bronze. The second pillar, with pomegranates was the same.

23 There were ninety-six pomegranates on the sides; [a]all the pomegranates, all around on the network, *were* one hundred.

The People Taken Captive to Babylonia

24 [a]The captain of the guard took Seraiah the chief priest, [b]Zephaniah the second priest, and the three doorkeepers.

25 He also took out of the city an officer who had charge of the men of war, seven men of the king's close associates who were found in the city, the principal scribe of the army who mustered the people of the land, and sixty men of the people of the land who were found in the midst of the city.

26 And Nebuzaradan the captain of the guard took these and brought them to the king of Babylon at Riblah.

27 Then the king of Babylon struck them and put them to death at Riblah in the land of Hamath. Thus Judah was carried away captive from its own land.

28 [a]These *are* the people whom Nebuchadnezzar carried away captive: [b]in the seventh year, [c]three thousand and twenty-three Jews;

29 [a]in the eighteenth year of Nebuchadnezzar he carried away captive from Jerusalem eight hundred and thirty-two persons;

30 in the twenty-third year of Nebuchadnezzar, Nebuzaradan the captain of the guard carried away captive of the Jews seven hundred and forty-five persons. All the persons *were* four thousand six hundred.

KJV

Jehoiachin Released from Prison
(*2 Kin. 25:27–30*)

31 [a]And it came to pass in the seven and thirtieth year of the captivity of Jehoiachin king of
Judah, in the twelfth month, in the five and twentieth *day* of the month, *that* Evil–merodach king
of Babylon in the *first* year of his reign [b]lifted
up the head of Jehoiachin king of Judah, and
brought him forth out of prison,
32 And spake kindly unto him, and set his
throne above the throne of the kings that *were*
with him in Babylon,
33 And changed his prison garments: [a]and
he did continually eat bread before him all the
days of his life.
34 And *for* his diet, there was a continual diet
given him of the king of Babylon, every day a
portion until the day of his death, all the days of
his life.

31 [a]2 Kin. 25:27–30 [b]Gen. 40:13, 20; Ps. 3:3; 27:6
33 [a]2 Sam. 9:7, 13; 1 Kin. 2:7

*
52:31 Or *Awil-Marduk;* lit. *The Man of Marduk*

NKJV

Jehoiachin Released from Prison
(*2 Kin. 25:27–30*)

31 [a]Now it came to pass in the thirty-seventh
year of the captivity of Jehoiachin king of Judah,
in the twelfth month, on the twenty-fifth *day* of
the month, *that* *Evil-Merodach king of Babylon,
in the first *year* of his reign, [b]lifted up the head
of Jehoiachin king of Judah and brought him out
of prison.
32 And he spoke kindly to him and gave him
a more prominent seat than those of the kings
who *were* with him in Babylon.
33 So Jehoiachin changed from his prison
garments, [a]and he ate bread regularly before the
king all the days of his life.
34 And as for his provisions, there was a regular ration given him by the king of Babylon, a
portion for each day until the day of his death,
all the days of his life.

KJV

THE BOOK OF

LAMENTATIONS

Jerusalem in Affliction

1 How doth the city sit solitary, *that was* full of people! [a]*how* is she become as a widow! she *that was* great among the nations, *and* [b]princess among the provinces, *how* is she become tributary!

2 She [a]weepeth sore in the [b]night, and her tears *are* on her cheeks: among all her lovers she hath none to comfort *her:* all her friends have dealt treacherously with her, they are become her enemies.

3 [a]Judah is gone into captivity because of affliction, and because of great servitude: [b]she dwelleth among the heathen, she findeth no [c]rest: all her persecutors overtook her between the straits.

4 The ways of Zion do mourn, because none come to the solemn feasts: all her gates are [a]desolate: her priests sigh, her virgins are afflicted, and she *is* in bitterness.

5 Her adversaries [a]are the chief, her enemies prosper; for the LORD hath afflicted her [b]for the multitude of her transgressions: her [c]children are gone into captivity before the enemy.

6 And from the daughter of Zion all her beauty is departed: her princes are become like harts *that* find no pasture, and they are gone without strength before the pursuer.

7 Jerusalem [a]remembered in the days of her affliction and of her miseries all her pleasant things that she had in the days of old, when her people fell into the hand of the enemy, and none did help her: the adversaries saw her, *and* did mock at her sabbaths.

8 [a]Jerusalem hath grievously sinned; therefore she is removed: all that honoured her despise her, because [b]they have seen her nakedness: yea, she sigheth, and turneth backward.

9 Her filthiness *is* in her skirts; she [a]remembereth not her last end; therefore she came down wonderfully: she had no comforter. O LORD, behold my affliction: for the enemy hath magnified *himself*.

NKJV

THE BOOK OF

LAMENTATIONS

Jerusalem in Affliction

1 How lonely sits the city
That was full of people!
[a]*How* like a widow is she,
Who *was* great among the nations!
The [b]princess among the provinces
Has become a slave!

2 She [a]weeps bitterly in the [b]night,
Her tears *are* on her cheeks;
Among all her lovers
She has none to comfort *her*.
All her friends have dealt treacherously with her;
They have become her enemies.

3 [a]Judah has gone into captivity,
Under affliction and hard servitude;
[b]She dwells among the nations,
She finds no [c]rest;
All her persecutors overtake her in dire straits.

4 The roads to Zion mourn
Because no one comes to the set feasts.
All her gates are [a]desolate;
Her priests sigh,
Her virgins are afflicted,
And she *is* in bitterness.

5 Her adversaries [a]have become the master,
Her enemies prosper;
For the LORD has afflicted her
[b]Because of the multitude of her transgressions.
Her [c]children have gone into captivity before the enemy.

6 And from the daughter of Zion
All her splendor has departed.
Her princes have become like deer
That find no pasture,
That flee without strength
Before the pursuer.

7 In the days of her affliction and roaming,
Jerusalem [a]remembers all her pleasant things
That she had in the days of old.
When her people fell into the hand of the enemy,
With no one to help her,
The adversaries saw her
And mocked at her *downfall.

8 [a]Jerusalem has sinned gravely,
Therefore she has become *vile.
All who honored her despise her
Because [b]they have seen her nakedness;
Yes, she sighs and turns away.

9 Her uncleanness *is* in her skirts;
She [a]did not consider her destiny;
Therefore her collapse was awesome;
She had no comforter.
"O LORD, behold my affliction,
For *the* enemy is exalted!"

CHAPTER 1

1 [a]Is. 47:7–9 [b]1 Kin. 4:21; Ezra 4:20; Jer. 31:7
2 [a]Jer. 13:17 [b]Job 7:3
3 [a]Jer. 52:27 [b]Lam. 2:9 [c]Deut. 28:65
4 [a]Is. 27:10
5 [a]Deut. 28:43 [b]Jer. 30:14, 15; Dan. 9:7, 16 [c]Jer. 52:28
7 [a]Ps. 137:1
8 [a][1 Kin. 8:46] [b]Jer. 13:22; Ezek. 16:37; Hos. 2:10
9 [a]Deut. 32:29; Is. 47:7; Jer. 5:31

*

1:7 Vg. *Sabbaths*
1:8 LXX, Vg. *moved* or *removed*

KJV

10 The adversary hath spread out his hand
upon all her pleasant things: for she hath seen
that [a]the heathen entered into her sanctuary,
whom thou didst command *that* [b]they should not
enter into thy congregation.
11 All her people sigh, [a]they seek bread; they
have given their pleasant things for meat to relieve the soul: see, O LORD, and consider; for I
am become vile.
12 *Is it* nothing to you, all ye that pass by?
behold, and see [a]if there be any sorrow like unto
my sorrow, which is done unto me, where with
the LORD hath afflicted *me* in the day of his fierce
anger.
13 From above hath he sent fire into my
bones, and it prevaileth against them: he hath
[a]spread a net for my feet, he hath turned me back:
he hath made me desolate *and* faint all the day.
14 [a]The yoke of my transgressions is bound
by his hand: they are wreathed, *and* come up upon
my neck: he hath made my strength to fall, the
LORD hath delivered me into *their* hands, *from*
whom I am not able to rise up.
15 The LORD hath trodden under foot all my
mighty *men* in the midst of me: he hath called
an assembly against me to crush my young men:
[a]the LORD hath trodden the virgin, the daughter
of Judah, *as* in a winepress.
16 For these *things* I weep; mine eye, [a]mine
eye runneth down with water, because the comforter that should relieve my soul is far from me:
my children are desolate, because the enemy
prevailed.
17 [a]Zion spreadeth forth her hands, *and*
there is none to comfort her: the LORD hath commanded concerning Jacob, *that* his adversaries
should be [b]round about him: Jerusalem is as a
menstruous woman among them.
18 The LORD is [a]righteous; for I have [b]re-
belled against his commandment: hear, I pray you,
all people, and behold my sorrow: my virgins and
my young men are gone into captivity.
19 I called for my lovers, *but* they deceived
me: my priests and mine elders gave up the ghost
in the city, while they sought their meat to relieve
their souls.
20 Behold, O LORD; for I *am* in distress: my
[a]bowels are troubled; mine heart is turned within
me; for I have grievously rebelled: [b]abroad the
sword bereaveth, at home *there is* as death.

10 [a]Ps. 74:4–8; Is. 64:10, 11; Jer. 51:51 [b]Deut. 23:3; Neh. 13:1
11 [a]Jer. 38:9; 52:6
12 [a]Dan. 9:12
13 [a]Ezek. 12:13; 17:20
14 [a]Deut. 28:48
15 [a]Is. 63:3; [Rev. 14:19]
16 [a]Ps. 69:20; Eccl. 4:1; Jer. 13:17; Lam. 2:18
17 [a][Is. 1:15]; Jer. 4:31 [b]2 Kin. 24:2–4; Jer. 12:9
18 [a]Neh. 9:33; Ps. 119:75; Dan. 9:7, 14 [b]1 Sam. 12:14, 15; Jer. 4:17
20 [a]Job 30:27; Is. 16:11; Jer. 4:19; Lam. 2:11; Hos. 11:8 [b]Deut. 32:25; Ezek. 7:15

NKJV

10 The adversary has spread his hand
Over all her pleasant things;
For she has seen [a]the nations enter her sanctuary,
Those whom You commanded
[b]Not to enter Your assembly.

11 All her people sigh,
[a]They seek bread;
They have given their valuables for food to restore life.
"See, O LORD, and consider,
For I am scorned."

12 "*Is it* nothing to you, all you who pass by?
Behold and see
[a]If there is any sorrow like my sorrow,
Which has been brought on me,
Which the LORD has inflicted
In the day of His fierce anger.

13 "From above He has sent fire into my bones,
And it overpowered them;
He has [a]spread a net for my feet
And turned me back;
He has made me desolate
And faint all the day.

14 "The[a] yoke of my transgressions was *bound;
They were woven together by His hands,
And thrust upon my neck.
He made my strength fail;
The Lord delivered me into the hands of
those whom I am not able to withstand.

15 "The Lord has trampled underfoot all my mighty *men* in my midst;
He has called an assembly against me
To crush my young men;
[a]The Lord trampled *as* in a winepress
The virgin daughter of Judah.

16 "For these *things* I weep;
My eye, [a]my eye overflows with water;
Because the comforter, who should restore my life,
Is far from me.
My children are desolate
Because the enemy prevailed."

17 [a]Zion spreads out her hands,
But no one comforts her;
The LORD has commanded concerning Jacob
That those [b]around him *become* his adversaries;
Jerusalem has become an unclean thing among them.

18 "The LORD is [a]righteous,
For I [b]rebelled against His commandment.
Hear now, all peoples,
And behold my sorrow;
My virgins and my young men
Have gone into captivity.

19 "I called for my lovers,
But they deceived me;
My priests and my elders
Breathed their last in the city,
While they sought food
To restore their life.

20 "See, O LORD, that I *am* in distress;
My [a]soul is troubled;
My heart is overturned within me,
For I have been very rebellious.
[b]Outside the sword bereaves,
At home *it is* like death.

*———

1:14 So with MT, Tg.; LXX, Syr., Vg. *watched over*

KJV

21 They have heard that I sigh: *there is* none
to comfort me: all mine enemies have heard of
my trouble; they are [a]glad that thou hast done
it: thou wilt bring [b]the day *that* thou hast called,
and they shall be like unto me.
22 [a]Let all their wickedness come before
thee; and do unto them, as thou hast done unto
me for all my transgressions: for my sighs *are*
many, and my heart *is* faint.

God's Anger with Jerusalem

2 How hath the LORD covered the daughter of
Zion with a [a]cloud in his anger, [b]*and* cast
down from heaven unto the earth [c]the beauty of
Israel, and remembered not [d]his footstool in the
day of his anger!
2 The LORD hath swallowed up all the habitations of Jacob, and hath [a]not pitied: he hath
thrown down in his wrath the strong holds of the
daughter of Judah; he hath brought *them* down
to the ground: [b]he hath polluted the kingdom and
the princes thereof.
3 He hath cut off in *his* fierce anger all the
horn of Israel: [a]he hath drawn back his right hand
from before the enemy, [b]and he burned against
Jacob like a flaming fire, *which* devoureth round
about.
4 [a]He hath bent his bow like an enemy: he
stood with his right hand as an adversary, and
slew [b]all *that were* pleasant to the eye in the tabernacle of the daughter of Zion: he poured out
his fury like fire.
5 [a]The LORD was as an enemy: he hath swallowed up Israel, he hath swallowed up all her palaces: [b]he hath destroyed his strong holds, and
hath increased in the daughter of Judah mourning
and lamentation.
6 And he hath violently [a]taken away his
tabernacle, [b]as *if it were of* a garden: he hath destroyed his places of the assembly: the LORD hath
caused the solemn feasts and sabbaths to be forgotten in Zion, and hath [c]despised in the indignation of his anger the king and the priest.
7 The LORD hath cast off his altar, he hath
[a]abhorred his sanctuary, he hath given up into
the hand of the enemy the walls of her palaces;
[b]they have made a noise in the house of the LORD,
as in the day of a solemn feast.
8 The LORD hath purposed to destroy the
[a]wall of the daughter of Zion: [b]he hath stretched
out a line, he hath not withdrawn his hand from
destroying: therefore he made the rampart and
the wall to lament; they languished together.

21 [a]Ps. 35:15; Jer. 48:27; 50:11; Lam. 2:15; Obad. 12 [b]Is. 13; [Jer. 46]
22 [a]Neh. 4:4, 5; Ps. 109:15; 137:7, 8; Jer. 30:16

CHAPTER 2

1 [a][Lam. 3:44] [b]Matt. 11:23 [c]2 Sam. 1:19 [d]1 Chr. 28:2; Ps. 99:5; Ezek. 43:7
2 [a]Ps. 21:9; Lam. 3:43 [b]Ps. 89:39, 40; Is. 43:28
3 [a]Ps. 74:11; Jer. 21:4, 5 [b]Ps. 89:46
4 [a]Is. 63:10 [b]Ezek. 24:25
5 [a]Jer. 30:14 [b]2 Kin. 25:9; Jer. 52:13; Lam. 2:2
6 [a]Ps. 80:12; 89:40; Is. 5:5; Jer. 7:14 [b]Is. 1:8; Jer. 52:13 [c]Is. 43:28
7 [a]Ezek. 24:21 [b]Ps. 74:3–8
8 [a]Jer. 52:14 [b][2 Kin. 21:13; Is. 34:11; Amos 7:7–9]

NKJV

21 "They have heard that I sigh,
But no one comforts me.
All my enemies have heard of my trouble;
They are [a]glad that You have done *it.*
Bring on [b]the day You have announced,
That they may become like me.

22 "Let[a] all their wickedness come before
You,
And do to them as You have done to me
For all my transgressions;
For my sighs *are* many,
And my heart *is* faint."

God's Anger with Jerusalem

2 How the Lord has covered the daughter
of Zion
With a [a]cloud in His anger!
[b]He cast down from heaven to the earth
[c]The beauty of Israel,
And did not remember [d]His footstool
In the day of His anger.

2 The Lord has swallowed up and has [a]not
pitied
All the dwelling places of Jacob.
He has thrown down in His wrath
The strongholds of the daughter of
Judah;
He has brought *them* down to the ground;
[b]He has profaned the kingdom and its
princes.

3 He has cut off in fierce anger
Every horn of Israel;
[a]He has drawn back His right hand
From before the enemy.
[b]He has blazed against Jacob like a flaming
fire
Devouring all around.

4 [a]Standing like an enemy, He has bent His
bow;
With His right hand, like an adversary,
He has slain [b]all *who were* pleasing to His
eye;
On the tent of the daughter of Zion,
He has poured out His fury like fire.

5 [a]The Lord was like an enemy.
He has swallowed up Israel,
He has swallowed up all her palaces;
[b]He has destroyed her strongholds,
And has increased mourning and
lamentation
In the daughter of Judah.

6 He has done violence [a]to His tabernacle,
[b]*As if it were* a garden;
He has destroyed His place of assembly;
The LORD has caused
The appointed feasts and Sabbaths to be
forgotten in Zion.
In His burning indignation He has
[c]spurned the king and the priest.

7 The Lord has spurned His altar,
He has [a]abandoned His sanctuary;
He has given up the walls of her palaces
Into the hand of the enemy.
[b]They have made a noise in the house of
the LORD
As on the day of a set feast.

8 The LORD has purposed to destroy
The [a]wall of the daughter of Zion.
[b]He has stretched out a line;
He has not withdrawn His hand from
destroying;
Therefore He has caused the rampart and
wall to lament;
They languished together.

KJV

9 Her gates are sunk into the ground; he hath destroyed and [a]broken her bars: [b]her king and her princes *are* among the Gentiles: [c]the law *is* no *more;* her [d]prophets also find no vision from the LORD.

10 The elders of the daughter of Zion [a]sit upon the ground, *and* keep silence: they have [b]cast up dust upon their heads; they have [c]girded themselves with sackcloth: the virgins of Jerusalem hang down their heads to the ground.

11 [a]Mine eyes do fail with tears, my bowels are troubled, [b]my liver is poured upon the earth, for the destruction of the daughter of my people; because [c]the children and the sucklings swoon in the streets of the city.

12 They say to their mothers, Where *is* corn and wine? when they swooned as the wounded in the streets of the city, when their soul was poured out into their mothers' bosom.

13 What thing shall I take to [a]witness for thee? what thing shall I liken to thee, O daughter of Jerusalem? what shall I equal to thee, that I may comfort thee, O virgin daughter of Zion? for thy breach *is* great like the sea: who can heal thee?

14 Thy [a]prophets have seen vain and foolish things for thee: and they have not [b]discovered thine iniquity, to turn away thy captivity; but have seen for thee false [c]burdens and causes of banishment.

15 All that pass by [a]clap *their* hands at thee; they hiss [b]and wag their head at the daughter of Jerusalem, *saying, Is* this the city that *men* call [c]The perfection of beauty, The joy of the whole earth?

16 [a]All thine enemies have opened their mouth against thee: they hiss and gnash the teeth: they say, [b]We have swallowed *her* up: certainly this *is* the [c]day that we looked for; we have found, [d]we have seen *it.*

17 The LORD hath done *that* which he had [a]devised; he hath fulfilled his word that he had commanded in the days of old: he hath thrown down, and hath not pitied: and he hath caused *thine* enemy to [b]rejoice over thee, he hath set up the horn of thine adversaries.

18 Their heart cried unto the LORD, O wall of the daughter of Zion, [a]let tears run down like a river day and night: give thyself no rest; let not the apple of thine eye cease.

19 Arise, [a]cry out in the night: in the beginning of the watches [b]pour out thine heart like water before the face of the LORD: lift up thy hands toward him for the life of thy young children, that faint for hunger [c]in the top of every street.

9 [a]Jer. 51:30 [b]Deut. 28:36; 2 Kin. 24:15; 25:7; Lam. 1:3; 4:20 [c]2 Chr. 15:3 [d]Ps. 74:9; Mic. 3:6
10 [a]Job 2:13; Is. 3:26 [b]Job 2:12; Ezek. 27:30 [c]Is. 15:3; Jon. 3:6–8
11 [a]Ps. 6:7; Lam. 3:48 [b]Job 16:13; Ps. 22:14 [c]Lam. 4:4
13 [a]Lam. 1:12; Dan. 9:12
14 [a]Jer. 2:8; 23:25–29; 29:8, 9; 37:19; Ezek. 13:2 [b]Is. 58:1; Ezek. 23:36; Mic. 3:8 [c]Jer. 23:33–36; Ezek. 22:25, 28
15 [a]1 Kin. 9:8; Job 27:23; Jer. 18:16; Ezek. 25:6; Nah. 3:19 [b]2 Kin. 19:21; Ps. 44:14 [c][Ps. 48:2; 50:2]; Ezek. 16:14
16 [a]Job 16:9, 10; Ps. 22:13; Lam. 3:46 [b]Ps. 56:2; 124:3; Jer. 51:34 [c]Lam. 1:21; [Obad. 12–15] [d]Ps. 35:21
17 [a]Lev. 26:16 [b]Ps. 38:16
18 [a]Jer. 14:17; Lam. 1:16
19 [a]Ps. 119:147 [b]1 Sam. 1:15; Ps. 42:4; 62:8 [c]Is. 51:20

NKJV

9 Her gates have sunk into the ground;
He has destroyed and [a]broken her bars.
[b]Her king and her princes *are* among the nations;
[c]The Law *is* no *more,*
And her [d]prophets find no vision from the LORD.

10 The elders of the daughter of Zion
[a]Sit on the ground *and* keep silence;
They [b]throw dust on their heads
And [c]gird themselves with sackcloth.
The virgins of Jerusalem
Bow their heads to the ground.

11 [a]My eyes fail with tears,
My heart is troubled;
[b]My bile is poured on the ground
Because of the destruction of the daughter of my people,
Because [c]the children and the infants
Faint in the streets of the city.

12 They say to their mothers,
"Where *is* grain and wine?"
As they swoon like the wounded
In the streets of the city,
As their life is poured out
In their mothers' bosom.

13 How shall I [a]console you?
To what shall I liken you,
O daughter of Jerusalem?
What shall I compare with you, that I may comfort you,
O virgin daughter of Zion?
For your ruin *is* spread wide as the sea;
Who can heal you?

14 Your [a]prophets have seen for you
False and deceptive visions;
They have not [b]uncovered your iniquity,
To bring back your captives,
But have envisioned for you false [c]prophecies and delusions.

15 All who pass by [a]clap *their* hands at you;
They hiss [b]and shake their heads
At the daughter of Jerusalem:
"*Is* this the city that is called
[c]'The perfection of beauty,
The joy of the whole earth'?"

16 [a]All your enemies have opened their mouth against you;
They hiss and gnash *their* teeth.
They say, [b]"We have swallowed *her* up!
Surely this *is* the [c]day we have waited for;
We have found *it,* [d]we have seen *it!*"

17 The LORD has done what He [a]purposed;
He has fulfilled His word
Which He commanded in days of old.
He has thrown down and has not pitied,
And He has caused an enemy to [b]rejoice over you;
He has exalted the horn of your adversaries.

18 Their heart cried out to the Lord,
"O wall of the daughter of Zion,
[a]Let tears run down like a river day and night;
Give yourself no relief;
Give your eyes no rest.

19 "Arise, [a]cry out in the night,
At the beginning of the watches;
[b]Pour out your heart like water before the face of the Lord.
Lift your hands toward Him
For the life of your young children,
Who faint from hunger [c]at the head of every street."

KJV

20 Behold, O LORD, and consider to whom
thou hast done this. [a]Shall the women eat their
fruit, *and* children of a span long? shall the priest
and the prophet be slain in the sanctuary of the
LORD?
21 [a]The young and the old lie on the ground
in the streets: my virgins and my young men are
fallen by the [b]sword; thou hast slain *them* in the
day of thine anger; thou hast killed, *and* not pitied.
22 Thou hast called as in a solemn day [a]my
terrors round about, so that in the day of the
LORD's anger none escaped nor remained: [b]those
that I have swaddled and brought up hath mine
enemy [c]consumed.

The Prophet's Anguish and Hope

3 I *am* the man *that* hath seen affliction by the
rod of his wrath.
2 He hath led me, and brought *me into* darkness, but not *into* light.
3 Surely against me is he turned; he turneth
his hand *against me* all the day.
4 [a]My flesh and my skin hath he made old;
he hath [b]broken my bones.
5 He hath builded against me, and compassed *me* with gall and travel.
6 [a]He hath set me in dark places, as *they*
that be dead of old.
7 [a]He hath hedged me about, that I cannot
get out: he hath made my chain heavy.
8 Also [a]when I cry and shout, he shutteth
out my prayer.
9 He hath inclosed my ways with hewn
stone, he hath made my paths crooked.
10 [a]He *was* unto me *as* a bear lying in wait,
and as a lion in secret places.
11 He hath turned aside my ways, and
[a]pulled me in pieces: he hath made me desolate.
12 He hath bent his bow, and [a]set me as a
mark for the arrow.
13 He hath caused [a]the arrows of his quiver
to enter into my reins.
14 I was a [a]derision to all my people; *and*
[b]their song all the day.
15 [a]He hath filled me with bitterness, he hath
made me drunken with wormwood.
16 He hath also broken my teeth [a]with gravel
stones, he hath covered me with ashes.
17 And thou hast removed my soul far off
from peace: I forgat prosperity.
18 [a]And I said, My strength and my hope is
perished from the LORD:
19 Remembering mine affliction and my misery, [a]the wormwood and the gall.
20 My soul hath *them* still in remembrance,
and is humbled in me.
21 This I recall to my mind, therefore have I
[a]hope.
22 [a]*It is of* the LORD's mercies that we are
not consumed, because his compassions fail [b]not.
23 *They are* new [a]every morning: great *is* thy
faithfulness.

20 [a]Lev. 26:29; Deut. 28:53; Jer. 19:9; Lam. 4:10; Ezek. 5:10
21 [a]2 Chr. 36:17; Jer. 6:11 [b]Jer. 18:21
22 [a]Ps. 31:13; Is. 24:17; Jer. 6:25 [b]Hos. 9:12 [c]Jer. 16:2–4; 44:7

CHAPTER 3
4 [a]Job 16:8 [b]Ps. 51:8; Is. 38:13
6 [a][Ps. 88:5, 6; 143:3]
7 [a]Job 3:23; 19:8; Hos. 2:6
8 [a]Job 30:20; Ps. 22:2
10 [a]Is. 38:13
11 [a]Job 16:12, 13; Jer. 15:3; Hos. 6:1
12 [a]Job 7:20; 16:12; Ps. 38:2
13 [a]Job 6:4
14 [a]Ps. 22:6, 7; 123:4; Jer. 20:7 [b]Job 30:9; Ps. 69:12; Lam. 3:63
15 [a]Jer. 9:15
16 [a][Prov. 20:17]
18 [a]Ps. 31:22
19 [a]Jer. 9:15; Lam. 3:5, 15
21 [a]Ps. 130:7
22 [a][Mal. 3:6] [b]Ps. 78:38; [Jer. 3:12; 30:11]
23 [a]Is. 33:2; Zeph. 3:5

NKJV

20 "See, O LORD, and consider!
To whom have You done this?
[a]Should the women eat their offspring,
The children *they have cuddled?
Should the priest and prophet be slain
In the sanctuary of the Lord?

21 "Young[a] and old lie
On the ground in the streets;
My virgins and my young men
Have fallen by the [b]sword;
You have slain *them* in the day of Your
anger,
You have slaughtered *and* not pitied.

22 "You have invited as to a feast day
[a]The terrors that surround me.
In the day of the LORD's anger
There was no refugee or survivor.
[b]Those whom I have borne and brought up
My enemies have [c]destroyed."

The Prophet's Anguish and Hope

3 I *am* the man *who* has seen affliction by
the rod of His wrath.

2 He has led me and made *me* walk
In darkness and not *in* light.
3 Surely He has turned His hand against me
Time and time again throughout the day.

4 He has aged [a]my flesh and my skin,
And [b]broken my bones.
5 He has besieged me
And surrounded *me* with bitterness and
woe.
6 [a]He has set me in dark places
Like the dead of long ago.

7 [a]He has hedged me in so that I cannot get
out;
He has made my chain heavy.
8 Even [a]when I cry and shout,
He shuts out my prayer.
9 He has blocked my ways with hewn stone;
He has made my paths crooked.

10 [a]He *has been* to me a bear lying in wait,
Like a lion in ambush.
11 He has turned aside my ways and [a]torn
me in pieces;
He has made me desolate.
12 He has bent His bow
And [a]set me up as a target for the arrow.

13 He has caused [a]the arrows of His quiver
To pierce my *loins.
14 I have become the [a]ridicule of all my
people—
[b]Their taunting song all the day.
15 [a]He has filled me with bitterness,
He has made me drink wormwood.

16 He has also broken my teeth [a]with gravel,
And covered me with ashes.
17 You have moved my soul far from peace;
I have forgotten prosperity.
18 [a]And I said, "My strength and my hope
Have perished from the LORD."

19 Remember my affliction and roaming,
[a]The wormwood and the gall.
20 My soul still remembers
And sinks within me.
21 This I recall to my mind,
Therefore I have [a]hope.

22 [a]*Through* the LORD's mercies we are not
consumed,
Because His compassions [b]fail not.
23 *They are* new [a]every morning;
Great *is* Your faithfulness.

*———
2:20 Vg. *a span long*
3:13 Lit. *kidneys*

KJV

24 The LORD *is* my [a]portion, saith my soul;
therefore will I [b]hope in him.
25 The LORD *is* good unto them that [a]wait for
him, to the soul *that* seeketh him.
26 *It is* good that *a man* should both [a]hope
[b]and quietly wait for the salvation of the LORD.
27 [a]*It is* good for a man that he bear the yoke
in his youth.
28 [a]He sitteth alone and keepeth silence, because he hath borne *it* upon him.
29 [a]He putteth his mouth in the dust; if so
be there may be hope.
30 [a]He giveth *his* cheek to him that smiteth
him: he is filled full with reproach.
31 [a]For the LORD will not cast off for ever:
32 But though he cause grief, yet will he have
compassion according to the multitude of his
mercies.
33 For [a]he doth not afflict willingly nor
grieve the children of men.
34 To crush under his feet all the prisoners
of the earth,
35 To turn aside the right of a man before
the face of the most High,
36 To subvert a man in his cause, [a]the LORD
approveth not.
37 Who *is* he [a]*that* saith, and it cometh to
pass, *when* the LORD commandeth *it* not?
38 Out of the mouth of the most High proceedeth not [a]evil and good?
39 [a]Wherefore doth a living man complain,
[b]a man for the punishment of his sins?
40 Let us search and try our ways, and turn
again to the LORD.
41 [a]Let us lift up our heart with *our* hands
unto God in the heavens.
42 [a]We have transgressed and have rebelled:
thou hast not pardoned.
43 Thou hast covered with anger, and persecuted us: thou hast slain, thou hast not pitied.
44 Thou hast covered thyself with a cloud,
that *our* prayer should not pass through.
45 Thou hast made us *as* the [a]offscouring and
refuse in the midst of the people.
46 [a]All our enemies have opened their
mouths against us.
47 [a]Fear and a snare is come upon us, [b]deso-
lation and destruction.
48 [a]Mine eye runneth down with rivers of
water for the destruction of the daughter of my
people.
49 [a]Mine eye trickleth down, and ceaseth
not, without any intermission,
50 Till the LORD [a]look down, and behold from
heaven.
51 Mine eye affecteth mine heart because of
all the daughters of my city.
52 Mine enemies chased me sore, like a bird,
[a]without cause.
53 They have cut off my life [a]in the dungeon,
and [b]cast a stone upon me.
54 [a]Waters flowed over mine head; *then* [b]I
said, I am cut off.
55 [a]I called upon thy name, O LORD, out of
the low [b]dungeon.

24 [a]Ps. 16:5; 73:26; 119:57; Jer. 10:16 [b]Jer. 17:17; Mic. 7:7
25 [a]Ps. 130:6; Is. 30:18
26 [a][Rom. 4:16–18] [b]Ex. 14:13; Ps. 37:7; Is. 7:4
27 [a]Ps. 94:12
28 [a]Jer. 15:17
29 [a]Job 42:6
30 [a]Job 16:10; Is. 50:6; [Matt. 5:39; 26:67]; Mark 14:65; Luke 22:63
31 [a]Ps. 77:7; 94:14; [Is. 54:7–10]
33 [a][Ps. 119:67, 71, 75; Is. 28:21; Ezek. 33:11; Heb. 12:10]
36 [a][Jer. 22:3; Hab. 1:13]
37 [a][Ps. 33:9–11]
38 [a]Job 2:10; [Is. 45:7]; Jer. 32:42; Amos 3:6; [James 3:10, 11]
39 [a]Prov. 19:3 [b]Jer. 30:15; Mic. 7:9; [Heb. 12:5, 6]
41 [a]Ps. 86:4
42 [a]Neh. 9:26; Jer. 14:20; Dan. 9:5
45 [a]1 Cor. 4:13
46 [a]Job 30:9, 10; Ps. 22:6–8; Lam. 2:16
47 [a]Is. 24:17, 18; Jer. 48:43, 44 [b]Is. 51:19
48 [a]Jer. 4:19; 14:17; Lam. 2:11
49 [a]Ps. 77:2; Jer. 14:17
50 [a]Ps. 80:14; Is. 63:15; Lam. 5:1
52 [a]Ps. 35:7, 19
53 [a]Jer. 37:16 [b]Dan. 6:17
54 [a]Ps. 69:2; Jon. 2:3–5 [b]Is. 38:10
55 [a]Ps. 130:1; Jon. 2:2 [b]Jer. 38:6–13

NKJV

24 "The LORD *is* my [a]portion," says my soul,
"Therefore I [b]hope in Him!"
25 The LORD *is* good to those who [a]wait for Him,
To the soul *who* seeks Him.
26 *It is* good that *one* should [a]hope [b]and wait quietly
For the salvation of the LORD.
27 [a]*It is* good for a man to bear
The yoke in his youth.

28 [a]Let him sit alone and keep silent,
Because *God* has laid *it* on him;
29 [a]Let him put his mouth in the dust—
There may yet be hope.
30 [a]Let him give *his* cheek to the one who strikes him,
And be full of reproach.

31 [a]For the Lord will not cast off forever.
32 Though He causes grief,
Yet He will show compassion
According to the multitude of His mercies.
33 For [a]He does not afflict willingly,
Nor grieve the children of men.

34 To crush under one's feet
All the prisoners of the earth,
35 To turn aside the justice *due* a man
Before the face of the Most High,
36 Or subvert a man in his cause—
[a]The Lord does not approve.

37 Who *is* he [a]*who* speaks and it comes to pass,
When the Lord has not commanded *it*?
38 *Is it* not from the mouth of the Most High
That [a]woe and well-being proceed?
39 [a]Why should a living man complain,
[b]A man for the punishment of his sins?

40 Let us search out and examine our ways,
And turn back to the LORD;
41 [a]Let us lift our hearts and hands
To God in heaven.
42 [a]We have transgressed and rebelled;
You have not pardoned.

43 You have covered *Yourself* with anger
And pursued us;
You have slain *and* not pitied.
44 You have covered Yourself with a cloud,
That prayer should not pass through.
45 You have made us an [a]offscouring and refuse
In the midst of the peoples.

46 [a]All our enemies
Have opened their mouths against us.
47 [a]Fear and a snare have come upon us,
[b]Desolation and destruction.
48 [a]My eyes overflow with rivers of water
For the destruction of the daughter of my people.

49 [a]My eyes flow and do not cease,
Without interruption,
50 Till the LORD from heaven
[a]Looks down and sees.
51 My eyes bring suffering to my soul
Because of all the daughters of my city.

52 My enemies [a]without cause
Hunted me down like a bird.
53 They *silenced my life [a]in the pit
And [b]threw stones at me.
54 [a]The waters flowed over my head;
[b]I said, "I am cut off!"

55 [a]I called on Your name, O LORD,
From the lowest [b]pit.

*3:53 LXX *put to death*

KJV

56 [a]Thou hast heard my voice: hide not thine
ear at my breathing, at my cry.
57 Thou [a]drewest near in the day *that* I
called upon thee: thou saidst, [b]Fear not.
58 O LORD, thou hast [a]pleaded the causes of
my soul; [b]thou hast redeemed my life.
59 O LORD, thou hast seen my wrong: [a]judge
thou my cause.
60 Thou hast seen all their vengeance *and*
all their [a]imaginations against me.
61 Thou hast heard their reproach, O LORD,
and all their imaginations against me;
62 The lips of those that rose up against me,
and their device against me all the day.
63 Behold their [a]sitting down, and their rising up; I *am* their musick.
64 [a]Render unto them a recompence, O LORD,
according to the work of their hands.
65 Give them sorrow of heart, thy curse unto
them.
66 Persecute and destroy them in anger
[a]from under the [b]heavens of the LORD.

The Degradation of Zion

4 How is the gold become dim! *how* is the most
fine gold changed! the stones of the sanctuary
are poured out in the top of every street.
2 The precious sons of Zion, comparable to
fine gold, how are they esteemed [a]as earthen
pitchers, the work of the hands of the potter!
3 Even the sea monsters draw out the
breast, they give suck to their young ones: the
daughter of my people *is become* cruel, [a]like the
ostriches in the wilderness.
4 The tongue of the sucking child cleaveth
to the roof of his mouth for thirst: [a]the young children ask bread, *and* no man breaketh *it* unto
them.
5 They that did feed delicately are desolate
in the streets: they that were brought up in scarlet
[a]embrace dunghills.
6 For the punishment of the iniquity of the
daughter of my people is greater than the punishment of the [a]sin of Sodom, that was [b]overthrown
as in a moment, and no hands stayed on her.
7 Her Nazarites were purer than snow, they
were whiter than milk, they were more ruddy in
body than rubies, their polishing *was* of sapphire:
8 Their visage is blacker than a coal; they
are not known in the streets: [a]their skin cleaveth
to their bones; it is withered, it is become like a
stick.
9 *They that be* slain with the sword are better than *they that be* slain with hunger: for these
[a]pine away, stricken through for *want of* the fruits
of the [b]field.

56 [a]Ps. 3:4
57 [a]James 4:8 [b]Is. 41:10, 14; Dan. 10:12
58 [a]Ps. 35:1; Jer. 51:36 [b]Ps. 71:23
59 [a]Ps. 9:4
60 [a]Jer. 11:19
63 [a]Ps. 139:2
64 [a]Ps. 28:4; Jer. 11:20; 2 Tim. 4:14
66 [a]Deut. 25:19; Jer. 10:11 [b]Ps. 8:3

CHAPTER 4

2 [a]Is. 30:14; Jer. 19:11; [2 Cor. 4:7]
3 [a]Job 39:14–17
4 [a]Ps. 22:15
5 [a]Job 24:8
6 [a]Ezek. 16:48 [b]Gen. 19:25; Jer. 20:16
8 [a]Job 19:20; Ps. 102:5
9 [a]Lev. 26:39; Ezek. 24:23 [b]Jer. 16:4

*

3:65 A Jewish tradition *sorrow of*
4:7 Or *nobles*

NKJV

56 [a]You have heard my voice:
"Do not hide Your ear
From my sighing, from my cry for help."
57 You [a]drew near on the day I called on
You,
And said, [b]"Do not fear!"

58 O Lord, You have [a]pleaded the case for
my soul;
[b]You have redeemed my life.
59 O LORD, You have seen *how* I am
wronged;
[a]Judge my case.
60 You have seen all their vengeance,
All their [a]schemes against me.

61 You have heard their reproach, O LORD,
All their schemes against me,
62 The lips of my enemies
And their whispering against me all the
day.
63 Look at their [a]sitting down and their
rising up;
I *am* their taunting song.

64 [a]Repay them, O LORD,
According to the work of their hands.
65 Give them *a veiled heart;
Your curse *be* upon them!
66 In Your anger,
Pursue and destroy them
[a]From under the heavens of the [b]LORD.

The Degradation of Zion

4 How the gold has become dim!
How changed the fine gold!
The stones of the sanctuary are scattered
At the head of every street.

2 The precious sons of Zion,
Valuable as fine gold,
How they are regarded [a]as clay pots,
The work of the hands of the potter!

3 Even the jackals present their breasts
To nurse their young;
But the daughter of my people *is* cruel,
[a]Like ostriches in the wilderness.

4 The tongue of the infant clings
To the roof of its mouth for thirst;
[a]The young children ask for bread,
But no one breaks *it* for them.

5 Those who ate delicacies
Are desolate in the streets;
Those who were brought up in scarlet
[a]Embrace ash heaps.

6 The punishment of the iniquity of the
daughter of my people
Is greater than the punishment of the [a]sin
of Sodom,
Which was [b]overthrown in a moment,
With no hand to help her!

7 Her *Nazirites were brighter than snow
And whiter than milk;
They were more ruddy in body than
rubies,
Like sapphire in their appearance.

8 *Now* their appearance is blacker than
soot;
They go unrecognized in the streets;
[a]Their skin clings to their bones,
It has become as dry as wood.

9 *Those* slain by the sword are better off
Than *those* who die of hunger;
For these [a]pine away,
Stricken *for lack* of the fruits of the [b]field.

KJV

10 The hands of the [a]pitiful women have sodden their [b]own children: they were their [c]meat
in the destruction of the daughter of my people.
11 The LORD hath accomplished his fury; [a]he
hath poured out his fierce anger, and [b]hath kindled a fire in Zion, and it hath devoured the foundations thereof.
12 The kings of the earth, and all the inhabitants of the world, would not have believed that
the adversary and the enemy should have [a]en-
tered into the gates of Jerusalem.
13 [a]For the sins of her prophets, *and* the iniquities of her priests, [b]that have shed the blood
of the just in the midst of her,
14 They have wandered *as* blind *men* in the
streets, [a]they have polluted themselves with
blood, [b]so that men could not touch their
garments.
15 They cried unto them, Depart ye; *it is* [a]un-
clean; depart, depart, touch not: when they fled
away and wandered, they said among the
heathen, They shall no more sojourn *there*.
16 The anger of the LORD hath divided them;
he will no more regard them: [a]they respected not
the persons of the priests, they favoured not the
elders.
17 As for us, [a]our eyes as yet failed for our
vain help: in our watching we have watched for
a nation *that* could not save *us*.
18 [a]They hunt our steps, that we cannot go
in our streets: [b]our end is near, our days are fulfilled; for our end is come.
19 Our persecutors are [a]swifter than the eagles of the heaven: they pursued us upon the
mountains, they laid wait for us in the wilderness.
20 The [a]breath of our nostrils, the anointed
of the LORD, [b]was taken in their pits, of whom
we said, Under his shadow we shall live among
the heathen.
21 Rejoice and be glad, O daughter of [a]Edom,
that dwellest in the land of Uz; [b]the cup also shall
pass through unto thee: thou shalt be drunken,
and shalt make thyself naked.
22 [a]The punishment of thine iniquity is accomplished, O daughter of Zion; he will no more
carry thee away into captivity: [b]he will visit thine
iniquity, O daughter of Edom; he will discover
thy sins.

A Prayer for Restoration

5 Remember, [a]O LORD, what is come upon us:
consider, and behold [b]our reproach.
2 [a]Our inheritance is turned to strangers,
our houses to aliens.

10 [a]Lev. 26:29; Deut. 28:57; 2 Kin. 6:29; Jer. 19:9; Lam. 2:20; Ezek. 5:10 [b]Is. 49:15 [c]Deut. 28:57
11 [a]Jer. 7:20; Lam. 2:17; Ezek. 22:31 [b]Deut. 32:22; Jer. 21:14
12 [a]Jer. 21:13
13 [a]Jer. 5:31; Ezek. 22:26, 28; Zeph. 3:4 [b]Jer. 2:30; 26:8, 9; Matt. 23:31
14 [a]Jer. 2:34 [b]Num. 19:16
15 [a]Lev. 13:45, 46
16 [a]Lam. 5:12
17 [a]2 Kin. 24:7
18 [a]2 Kin. 25:4 [b]Ezek. 7:2, 3, 6; Amos 8:2
19 [a]Deut. 28:49
20 [a]Gen. 2:7 [b]Jer. 52:9; Ezek. 12:13
21 [a]Ps. 83:3–6 [b]Jer. 25:15; Obad. 10
22 [a][Is. 40:2; Jer. 33:7, 8] [b]Ps. 137:7

CHAPTER 5

1 [a]Ps. 89:50 [b]Ps. 79:4; Lam. 2:15
2 [a]Ps. 79:1

*
4:16 Tg. *anger*

NKJV

10 The hands of the [a]compassionate women
Have cooked their [b]own children;
They became [c]food for them
In the destruction of the daughter of my people.

11 The LORD has fulfilled His fury,
[a]He has poured out His fierce anger.
[b]He kindled a fire in Zion,
And it has devoured its foundations.

12 The kings of the earth,
And all inhabitants of the world,
Would not have believed
That the adversary and the enemy
Could [a]enter the gates of Jerusalem—

13 [a]Because of the sins of her prophets
And the iniquities of her priests,
[b]Who shed in her midst
The blood of the just.

14 They wandered blind in the streets;
[a]They have defiled themselves with blood,
[b]So that no one would touch their garments.

15 They cried out to them,
"Go away, [a]unclean!
Go away, go away,
Do not touch us!"
When they fled and wandered,
Those among the nations said,
"They shall no longer dwell *here*."

16 The *face of the LORD scattered them;
He no longer regards them.
[a]*The people* do not respect the priests
Nor show favor to the elders.

17 Still [a]our eyes failed us,
Watching vainly for our help;
In our watching we watched
For a nation *that* could not save *us*.

18 [a]They tracked our steps
So that we could not walk in our streets.
[b]Our end was near;
Our days were over,
For our end had come.

19 Our pursuers were [a]swifter
Than the eagles of the heavens.
They pursued us on the mountains
And lay in wait for us in the wilderness.

20 The [a]breath of our nostrils, the anointed of the LORD,
[b]Was caught in their pits,
Of whom we said, "Under his shadow
We shall live among the nations."

21 Rejoice and be glad, O daughter of [a]Edom,
You who dwell in the land of Uz!
[b]The cup shall also pass over to you
And you shall become drunk and make yourself naked.

22 [a]*The punishment of* your iniquity is accomplished,
O daughter of Zion;
He will no longer send you into captivity.
[b]He will punish your iniquity,
O daughter of Edom;
He will uncover your sins!

A Prayer for Restoration

5 Remember, [a]O LORD, what has come upon us;
Look, and behold [b]our reproach!
2 [a]Our inheritance has been turned over to aliens,
And our houses to foreigners.

KJV

3 We are orphans and fatherless, our
mothers *are* as [a]widows.
4 We have drunken our water for money;
our wood is sold unto us.
5 [a]Our necks *are* under persecution: we labour, *and* have no rest.
6 [a]We have given the hand [b]*to* the Egyptians, *and to* the [c]Assyrians, to be satisfied with
bread.
7 [a]Our fathers have sinned, *and are* not; and
we have borne their iniquities.
8 Servants have ruled over us: *there is* none
that doth deliver *us* out of their hand.
9 We gat our bread with *the peril of* our lives
because of the sword of the wilderness.
10 Our skin was black like an oven because
of the terrible famine.
11 They [a]ravished the women in Zion, *and*
the maids in the cities of Judah.
12 Princes are hanged up by their hand: the
faces of elders were not honoured.
13 They took the young men to [a]grind, and
the children fell under the wood.
14 The elders have ceased from the gate, the
young men from their [a]musick.
15 The joy of our heart is ceased; our dance
is turned into [a]mourning.
16 [a]The crown is fallen *from* our head: woe
unto us, that we have sinned!
17 For this our heart is faint; [a]for these *things*
our eyes are dim.
18 Because of the mountain of Zion, which
is [a]desolate, the foxes walk upon it.
19 Thou, O LORD, [a]remainest for ever; [b]thy
throne from generation to generation.
20 [a]Wherefore dost thou forget us for ever,
and forsake us so long time?
21 [a]Turn thou us unto thee, O LORD, and we
shall be turned; renew our days as of old.
22 But thou hast utterly rejected us; thou art
very wroth against us.

3 [a]Ex. 22:24; Jer. 15:8; 18:21
5 [a]Deut. 28:48; Jer. 28:14
6 [a]Gen. 24:2 [b]Hos. 9:3; 12:1 [c]Jer. 2:18; Hos. 5:13
7 [a]Jer. 31:29
11 [a]Is. 13:16; Zech. 14:2
13 [a]Judg. 16:21
14 [a]Is. 24:8; Jer. 7:34
15 [a]Jer. 25:10; Amos 8:10
16 [a]Job 19:9; Ps. 89:39; Jer. 13:18
17 [a]Ps. 6:7
18 [a]Is. 27:10
19 [a]Ps. 9:7; Hab. 1:12 [b]Ps. 45:6
20 [a]Ps. 13:1; 44:24
21 [a]Ps. 80:3, 7, 19; Jer. 31:18

NKJV

3 We have become orphans and waifs,
Our mothers *are* like [a]widows.

4 We pay for the water we drink,
And our wood comes at a price.
5 [a]*They* pursue at our *heels;
We labor *and* have no rest.
6 [a]We have given our hand [b]to the Egyptians
And the [c]Assyrians, to be satisfied with
bread.

7 [a]Our fathers sinned *and are* no more,
But we bear their iniquities.
8 Servants rule over us;
There is none to deliver *us* from their
hand.
9 We get our bread *at the risk* of our lives,
Because of the sword in the wilderness.

10 Our skin is hot as an oven,
Because of the fever of famine.
11 They [a]ravished the women in Zion,
The maidens in the cities of Judah.
12 Princes were hung up by their hands,
And elders were not respected.
13 Young men [a]ground at the millstones;
Boys staggered under *loads of* wood.
14 The elders have ceased *gathering at* the
gate,
And the young men from their [a]music.

15 The joy of our heart has ceased;
Our dance has turned into [a]mourning.
16 [a]The crown has fallen *from* our head.
Woe to us, for we have sinned!
17 Because of this our heart is faint;
[a]Because of these *things* our eyes grow
dim;
18 Because of Mount Zion which is [a]desolate,
With foxes walking about on it.

19 You, O LORD, [a]remain forever;
[b]Your throne from generation to
generation.
20 [a]Why do You forget us forever,
And forsake us for so long a time?
21 [a]Turn us back to You, O LORD, and we will
be restored;
Renew our days as of old,
22 Unless You have utterly rejected us,
And are very angry with us!

*

5:5 Lit. *necks*

KJV

THE BOOK OF

EZEKIEL

Ezekiel's Vision of God

1 Now it came to pass in the thirtieth year, in
the fourth *month*, in the fifth *day* of the month,
as I *was* among the captives [a]by the river of Chebar, *that* [b]the heavens were opened, and I saw
[c]visions of God.
2 In the fifth *day* of the month, which *was*
the fifth year of king Jehoiachin's captivity,
3 The word of the LORD came expressly unto
Ezekiel the priest, the son of Buzi, in the land of
the Chaldeans by the river Chebar; and [a]the hand
of the LORD was there upon him.
4 And I looked, and, behold, [a]a whirlwind
came [b]out of the north, a great cloud, and a fire
infolding itself, and a brightness *was* about it, and
out of the midst thereof as the colour of amber,
out of the midst of the fire.
5 [a]Also out of the midst thereof *came* the
likeness of four living creatures. And [b]this *was*
their appearance; they had [c]the likeness of a man.
6 And every one had four faces, and every
one had four wings.
7 And their feet *were* straight feet; and the
sole of their feet *was* like the sole of a calf's foot:
and they sparkled [a]like the colour of burnished
brass.
8 [a]And *they had* the hands of a man under
their wings on their four sides; and they four had
their faces and their wings.
9 Their wings *were* joined one to another;
they turned not when they went; they went every
one straight [a]forward.
10 As for [a]the likeness of their faces, they
four [b]had the face of a man, [c]and the face of a
lion, on the right side: [d]and they four had the face
of an ox on the left side; [e]they four also had the
face of an eagle.
11 Thus *were* their faces: and their wings
were stretched upward; two *wings* of every one
were joined one to another, and [a]two covered
their bodies.
12 And [a]they went every one straight forward: whither the spirit was to go, they went; *and*
they turned not when they went.
13 As for the likeness of the living creatures,
their appearance *was* like burning coals of fire,
[a]*and* like the appearance of lamps: it went up and
down among the living creatures; and the fire was
bright, and out of the fire went forth lightning.
14 And the living creatures ran and returned
[a]as the appearance of a flash of lightning.
15 Now as I beheld the living creatures, behold [a]one wheel upon the earth by the living creatures, with his four faces.
16 [a]The appearance of the wheels and their
work *was* [b]like unto the colour of a beryl: and
they four had one likeness: and their appearance
and their work *was* as it were a wheel in the middle of a wheel.
17 When they went, they went upon their
four sides: *and* they turned not when they went.
18 As for their rings, they were so high that
they were dreadful; and their rings *were* [a]full of
eyes round about them four.
19 And [a]when the living creatures went, the
wheels went by them: and when the living crea-

NKJV

THE BOOK OF

EZEKIEL

Ezekiel's Vision of God

1 Now it came to pass in the thirtieth year, in
the fourth *month*, on the fifth *day* of the
month, as I *was* among the captives by [a]the River
Chebar, *that* [b]the heavens were opened and I saw
[c]visions* of God.
2 On the fifth *day* of the month, which *was*
in the fifth year of King Jehoiachin's captivity,
3 the word of the LORD came expressly to
Ezekiel the priest, the son of Buzi, in the land of
the *Chaldeans by the River Chebar; and [a]the
hand of the LORD was upon him there.
4 Then I looked, and behold, [a]a whirlwind
was coming [b]out of the north, a great cloud with
raging fire engulfing itself; and brightness *was*
all around it and radiating out of its midst like
the color of amber, out of the midst of the fire.
5 [a]Also from within it *came* the likeness of
four living creatures. And [b]this *was* their appearance: they had [c]the likeness of a man.
6 Each one had four faces, and each one had
four wings.
7 Their legs *were* straight, and the soles of
their feet *were* like the soles of calves' feet. They
sparkled [a]like the color of burnished bronze.
8 [a]The hands of a man *were* under their
wings on their four sides; and each of the four
had faces and wings.
9 Their wings touched one another. *The
creatures* did not turn when they went, but each
one went straight [a]forward.
10 As for [a]the likeness of their faces, *each*
[b]had the face of a man; each of the four had [c]the
face of a lion on the right side, [d]each of the four
had the face of an ox on the left side, [e]and each
of the four had the face of an eagle.
11 Thus *were* their faces. Their wings
stretched upward; two *wings* of each one touched
one another, and [a]two covered their bodies.
12 And [a]each one went straight forward;
they went wherever the spirit wanted to go, and
they did not turn when they went.
13 As for the likeness of the living creatures,
their appearance *was* like burning coals of fire,
[a]like the appearance of torches going back and
forth among the living creatures. The fire was
bright, and out of the fire went lightning.
14 And the living creatures ran back and
forth, [a]in appearance like a flash of lightning.
15 Now as I looked at the living creatures,
behold, [a]a wheel *was* on the earth beside each
living creature with its four faces.
16 [a]The appearance of the wheels and their
workings *was* [b]like the color of beryl, and all four
had the same likeness. The appearance of their
workings *was*, as it were, a wheel in the middle
of a wheel.
17 When they moved, they went toward any
one of four directions; they did not turn aside
when they went.
18 As for their rims, they were so high they
were awesome; and their rims *were* [a]full of eyes,
all around the four of them.
19 [a]When the living creatures went, the
wheels went beside them; and when the living

CHAPTER 1

1 [a]Ezek. 3:15, 23; 10:15 [b]Matt. 3:16; Mark 1:10; Luke 3:21; Acts 7:56; 10:11; Rev. 4:1; 19:11 [c]Ex. 24:10; Num. 12:6; Is. 1:1; 6:1; Ezek. 8:3; Dan. 8:1, 2
3 [a]1 Kin. 18:46; 2 Kin. 3:15; Ezek. 3:14, 22
4 [a]Is. 21:1; Jer. 23:19; 25:32; Ezek. 13:11, 13 [b]Jer. 1:14
5 [a]Ezek. 10:15, 17, 20; Rev. 4:6–8 [b]Ezek. 10:8 [c]Ezek. 10:14
7 [a]Dan. 10:6; Rev. 1:15
8 [a]Ezek. 10:8, 21
9 [a]Ezek. 1:12; 10:20–22
10 [a]Ezek. 10:14; Rev. 4:7 [b]Num. 2:10 [c]Num. 2:3 [d]Num. 2:18 [e]Num. 2:25
11 [a]Is. 6:2; Ezek. 1:23
12 [a]Ezek. 10:11, 22
13 [a]Ps. 104:4; Rev. 4:5
14 [a]Zech. 4:10; [Matt. 24:27; Luke 17:24]
15 [a]Ezek. 10:9
16 [a]Ezek. 10:9, 10 [b]Dan. 10:6
18 [a]Ezek. 10:12; [Zech. 4:10]; Rev. 4:6, 8
19 [a]Ezek. 10:16, 17

*

1:1 So with MT, LXX, Vg.; Syr., Tg. *a vision*
1:3 Or *Babylonians,* and so elsewhere in the book

KJV

tures were lifted up from the earth, the wheels were lifted up.

20 Whithersoever the spirit was to go, they went, thither *was their* spirit to go; and the wheels were lifted up over against them: [a]for the spirit of the living creature *was* in the wheels.

21 When those went, *these* went; and when those stood, *these* stood; and when those were lifted up from the earth, the wheels were lifted up over against them: for the spirit of the living creature *was* in the wheels.

22 [a]And the likeness of the firmament upon the heads of the living creature *was* as the colour of the terrible [b]crystal, stretched forth over their heads [c]above.

23 And under the firmament *were* their wings straight, the one toward the other: every one had two, which covered on this side, and every one had two, which covered on that side, their bodies.

24 [a]And when they went, I heard the noise of their wings, [b]like the noise of great waters, as [c]the voice of the Almighty, the voice of speech, as the noise of an host: when they stood, they let down their wings.

25 And there was a voice from the firmament that *was* over their heads, when they stood, *and* had let down their wings.

26 [a]And above the firmament that *was* over their heads *was* the likeness of a throne, [b]as the appearance of a sapphire stone: and upon the likeness of the throne *was* the likeness as the appearance of a man above upon [c]it.

27 [a]And I saw as the colour of amber, as the appearance of fire round about within it, from the appearance of his loins even upward, and from the appearance of his loins even downward, I saw as it were the appearance of fire, and it had brightness round about.

28 [a]As the appearance of the bow that is in the cloud in the day of rain, so *was* the appearance of the brightness round about. [b]This *was* the appearance of the likeness of the glory of the LORD. And when I saw *it*, [c]I fell upon my face, and I heard a voice of one that spake.

Ezekiel Sent to Rebellious Israel

2 And he said unto me, Son of man, [a]stand upon thy feet, and I will speak unto thee.

2 And [a]the spirit entered into me when he spake unto me, and set me upon my feet, that I heard him that spake unto me.

3 And he said unto me, Son of man, I send thee to the children of Israel, to a rebellious nation that hath [a]rebelled against me: [b]they and their fathers have transgressed against me, *even* unto this very day.

4 [a]For *they are* impudent children and stiffhearted. I do send thee unto them; and thou shalt say unto them, Thus saith the Lord GOD.

5 [a]And they, whether they will hear, or whether they will forbear, (for they *are* a [b]rebellious house,) yet [c]shall know that there hath been a prophet among them.

6 And thou, son of man, [a]be not afraid of them, neither be afraid of their words, though [b]briers and thorns *be* with thee, and thou dost dwell among scorpions: [c]be not afraid of their words, nor be dismayed at their looks, [d]though they *be* a rebellious house.

7 [a]And thou shalt speak my words unto them, whether they will hear, or whether they will forbear: for they *are* most rebellious.

8 But thou, son of man, hear what I say unto thee; Be not thou rebellious like that rebellious house: open thy mouth, and [a]eat that I give thee.

9 And when I looked, behold, [a]an hand *was* sent unto me; and, lo, [b]a roll of a book *was* therein;

10 And he spread it before me; and it *was*

20 [a]Ezek. 10:17
22 [a]Ezek. 10:1 [b]Rev. 4:6 [c]Ezek. 10:1
24 [a]Ezek. 3:13; 10:5 [b]Rev. 1:15 [c]Job 37:4, 5
26 [a]Ezek. 10:1 [b]Ex. 24:10, 16 [c]Ezek. 8:2
27 [a]Ezek. 8:2
28 [a]Rev. 4:3; 10:1 [b]Ezek. 3:23; 8:4 [c]Dan. 8:17

CHAPTER 2

1 [a]Dan. 10:11
2 [a]Ezek. 3:24
3 [a]Ezek. 5:6; 20:8, 13, 18 [b]Jer. 3:25
4 [a]Ezek. 3:7
5 [a]Ezek. 3:11, 26, 27 [b]Ezek. 3:26 [c]Ezek. 33:33
6 [a]Jer. 1:8, 17 [b]Mic. 7:4 [c][1 Pet. 3:14] [d]Ezek. 3:9, 26, 27
7 [a]Jer. 1:7, 17
8 [a]Rev. 10:9
9 [a][Ezek. 8:3] [b]Ezek. 3:1

*

1:20 Lit. *living creature;* LXX, Vg. *spirit of life;* Tg. *creatures*
1:21 Lit. *living creature;* LXX, Vg. *spirit of life;* Tg. *creatures*
1:22 So with LXX, Tg., Vg.; MT *living creature*

NKJV

creatures were lifted up from the earth, the wheels were lifted up.

20 Wherever the spirit wanted to go, they went, *because* there the spirit went; and the wheels were lifted together with them, [a]for the spirit of the *living creatures *was* in the wheels.

21 When those went, *these* went; when those stood, *these* stood; and when those were lifted up from the earth, the wheels were lifted up together with them, for the spirit of the *living creatures *was* in the wheels.

22 [a]The likeness of the firmament above the heads of the *living creatures *was* like the color of an awesome [b]crystal, stretched out [c]over their heads.

23 And under the firmament their wings *spread out* straight, one toward another. Each one had two which covered one side, and each one had two which covered the other side of the body.

24 [a]When they went, I heard the noise of their wings, [b]like the noise of many waters, like [c]the voice of the Almighty, a tumult like the noise of an army; and when they stood still, they let down their wings.

25 A voice came from above the firmament that *was* over their heads; whenever they stood, they let down their wings.

26 [a]And above the firmament over their heads *was* the likeness of a throne, [b]in appearance like a sapphire stone; on the likeness of the throne *was* a likeness with the appearance of a man high above [c]it.

27 Also from the appearance of His waist and upward [a]I saw, as it were, the color of amber with the appearance of fire all around within it; and from the appearance of His waist and downward I saw, as it were, the appearance of fire with brightness all around.

28 [a]Like the appearance of a rainbow in a cloud on a rainy day, so *was* the appearance of the brightness all around it. [b]This *was* the appearance of the likeness of the glory of the LORD.

Ezekiel Sent to Rebellious Israel

So when I saw *it*, [c]I fell on my face, and I heard a voice of One speaking.

2 And He said to me, "Son of man, [a]stand on your feet, and I will speak to you."

2 Then [a]the Spirit entered me when He spoke to me, and set me on my feet; and I heard Him who spoke to me.

3 And He said to me: "Son of man, I am sending you to the children of Israel, to a rebellious nation that has [a]rebelled against Me; [b]they and their fathers have transgressed against Me to this very day.

4 [a]"For *they are* impudent and stubborn children. I am sending you to them, and you shall say to them, 'Thus says the Lord GOD.'

5 [a]"As for them, whether they hear or whether they refuse—for they *are* a [b]rebellious house—yet they [c]will know that a prophet has been among them.

6 "And you, son of man, [a]do not be afraid of them nor be afraid of their words, though [b]briers and thorns *are* with you and you dwell among scorpions; [c]do not be afraid of their words or dismayed by their looks, [d]though they *are* a rebellious house.

7 [a]"You shall speak My words to them, whether they hear or whether they refuse, for they *are* rebellious.

8 "But you, son of man, hear what I say to you. Do not be rebellious like that rebellious house; open your mouth and [a]eat what I give you."

9 Now when I looked, there was [a]a hand stretched out to me; and behold, [b]a scroll of a book *was* in it.

10 Then He spread it before me; and *there*

KJV

written within and without: and *there was* written therein lamentations, and mourning, and woe.

3 Moreover he said unto me, Son of man, eat that thou findest; [a]eat this roll, and go speak unto the house of Israel.

2 So I opened my mouth, and he caused me to eat that roll.

3 And he said unto me, Son of man, cause thy belly to eat, and fill thy bowels with this roll that I give thee. Then did I [a]eat *it;* and it was in my mouth [b]as honey for sweetness.

4 And he said unto me, Son of man, go, get thee unto the house of Israel, and speak with my words unto them.

5 For thou *art* not sent to a people of a strange speech and of an hard language, *but* to the house of Israel;

6 Not to many people of a strange speech and of an hard language, whose words thou canst not understand. Surely, [a]had I sent thee to them, they would have hearkened unto thee.

7 But the house of Israel will not hearken unto thee; [a]for they will not hearken unto me: [b]for all the house of Israel *are* impudent and hardhearted.

8 Behold, I have made thy face strong against their faces, and thy forehead strong against their foreheads.

9 [a]As an adamant harder than flint have I made thy forehead: [b]fear them not, neither be dismayed at their looks, though they *be* a rebellious house.

10 Moreover he said unto me, Son of man, all my words that I shall speak unto thee receive in thine heart, and hear with thine ears.

11 And go, get thee to them of the captivity, unto the children of thy people, and speak unto them, and tell them, [a]Thus saith the Lord GOD; whether they will hear, or whether they will forbear.

12 Then [a]the spirit took me up, and I heard behind me a voice of a great rushing, *saying,* Blessed *be* the [b]glory of the LORD from his place.

13 *I heard* also the [a]noise of the wings of the living creatures that touched one another, and the noise of the wheels over against them, and a noise of a great rushing.

14 So the spirit lifted me up, and took me away, and I went in bitterness, in the heat of my spirit; but [a]the hand of the LORD was strong upon me.

15 Then I came to them of the captivity at Tel–abib, that dwelt by the river of Chebar, and [a]I sat where they sat, and remained there astonished among them seven days.

Ezekiel Is a Watchman

16 And it [a]came to pass at the end of seven days, that the word of the LORD came unto me, saying,

17 [a]Son of man, I have made thee [b]a watchman unto the house of Israel: therefore hear the word at my mouth, and give them [c]warning from me.

18 When I say unto the wicked, Thou shalt surely die; and thou givest him not warning, nor speakest to warn the wicked from his wicked way, to save his life; the same wicked *man* [a]shall die in his iniquity; but his blood will I require at thine hand.

19 Yet if thou warn the wicked, and he turn not from his wickedness, nor from his wicked way, he shall die in his iniquity; [a]but thou hast delivered thy soul.

20 Again, When a [a]righteous *man* doth turn from his righteousness, and commit iniquity, and I lay a stumblingblock before him, he shall die: because thou hast not given him warning, he shall

CHAPTER 3

1 [a]Ezek. 2:8, 9
3 [a]Jer. 15:16; Rev. 10:9 [b]Ps. 19:10; 119:103
6 [a]Jon. 3:5–10; Matt. 11:21
7 [a]John 15:20, 21 [b]Ezek. 2:4
9 [a]Is. 50:7; Jer. 1:18; Mic. 3:8 [b]Jer. 1:8, 17; Ezek. 2:6
11 [a]Ezek. 2:5, 7
12 [a] 1 Kin. 18:12; Ezek. 8:3; Acts 8:39 [b]Ezek. 1:28; 8:4
13 [a]Ezek. 1:24; 10:5
14 [a]2 Kin. 3:15; Ezek. 1:3; 8:1
15 [a]Job 2:13; Ps. 137:1
16 [a]Jer. 42:7
17 [a]Ezek. 33:7–9 [b]Is. 52:8; 56:10; Jer. 6:17 [c][Lev. 19:17; Prov. 14:25]; Is. 58:1
18 [a]Ezek. 33:6; [John 8:21, 24]
19 [a]Is. 49:4, 5; Ezek. 14:14, 20; Acts 18:6; 20:26; 1 Tim. 4:16
20 [a]Ps. 125:5; Ezek. 18:24; 33:18; Zeph. 1:6

NKJV

was writing on the inside and on the outside, and written on it *were* lamentations and mourning and woe.

3 Moreover He said to me, "Son of man, eat what you find; [a]eat this scroll, and go, speak to the house of Israel."

2 So I opened my mouth, and He caused me to eat that scroll.

3 And He said to me, "Son of man, feed your belly, and fill your stomach with this scroll that I give you." So I [a]ate, and it was in my mouth [b]like honey in sweetness.

4 Then He said to me: "Son of man, go to the house of Israel and speak with My words to them.

5 "For you *are* not sent to a people of unfamiliar speech and of hard language, *but* to the house of Israel,

6 "not to many people of unfamiliar speech and of hard language, whose words you cannot understand. Surely, [a]had I sent you to them, they would have listened to you.

7 "But the house of Israel will not listen to you, [a]because they will not listen to Me; [b]for all the house of Israel *are* impudent and hard-hearted.

8 "Behold, I have made your face strong against their faces, and your forehead strong against their foreheads.

9 [a]"Like adamant stone, harder than flint, I have made your forehead; [b]do not be afraid of them, nor be dismayed at their looks, though they *are* a rebellious house."

10 Moreover He said to me: "Son of man, receive into your heart all My words that I speak to you, and hear with your ears.

11 "And go, get to the captives, to the children of your people, and speak to them and tell them, [a]'Thus says the Lord GOD,' whether they hear, or whether they refuse."

12 Then [a]the Spirit lifted me up, and I heard behind me a great thunderous voice: "Blessed *is* the [b]glory of the LORD from His place!"

13 *I also heard* the [a]noise of the wings of the living creatures that touched one another, and the noise of the wheels beside them, and a great thunderous noise.

14 So the Spirit lifted me up and took me away, and I went in bitterness, in the heat of my spirit; but [a]the hand of the LORD was strong upon me.

15 Then I came to the captives at Tel Abib, who dwelt by the River Chebar; and [a]I sat where they sat, and remained there astonished among them seven days.

Ezekiel Is a Watchman

16 Now it [a]came to pass at the end of seven days that the word of the LORD came to me, saying,

17 [a]"Son of man, I have made you [b]a watchman for the house of Israel; therefore hear a word from My mouth, and give them [c]warning from Me:

18 "When I say to the wicked, 'You shall surely die,' and you give him no warning, nor speak to warn the wicked from his wicked way, to save his life, that same wicked *man* [a]shall die in his iniquity; but his blood I will require at your hand.

19 "Yet, if you warn the wicked, and he does not turn from his wickedness, nor from his wicked way, he shall die in his iniquity; [a]but you have delivered your soul.

20 "Again, when a [a]righteous *man* turns from his righteousness and commits iniquity, and I lay a stumbling block before him, he shall die; because you did not give him warning, he shall

KJV

die in his sin, and his righteousness which he hath done shall not be remembered; but his blood will I require at thine hand.

21 Nevertheless if thou warn the righteous *man,* that the righteous sin not, and he doth not sin, he shall surely live, because he is warned; also thou hast delivered thy soul.

22 [a]And the hand of the LORD was there upon me; and he said unto me, Arise, go forth [b]into the plain, and I will there talk with thee.

23 Then I arose, and went forth into the plain: and, behold, [a]the glory of the LORD stood there, as the glory which I [b]saw by the river of Chebar: [c]and I fell on my face.

24 Then [a]the spirit entered into me, and set me upon my feet, and spake with me, and said unto me, Go, shut thyself within thine house.

25 But thou, O son of man, behold, [a]they shall put bands upon thee, and shall bind thee with them, and thou shalt not go out among them:

26 And [a]I will make thy tongue cleave to the roof of thy mouth, that thou shalt be dumb, and shalt [b]not be to them a reprover: [c]for they *are* a rebellious house.

27 [a]But when I speak with thee, I will open thy mouth, and thou shalt say unto them, [b]Thus saith the Lord GOD; He that heareth, let him hear; and he that forbeareth, let him forbear: for they *are* a rebellious house.

The Siege of Jerusalem Portrayed

4 Thou also, son of man, take thee a tile, and lay it before thee, and pourtray upon it the city, *even* Jerusalem:

2 And [a]lay siege against it, and build a [b]fort against it, and cast a mount against it; set the camp also against it, and set *battering* rams against it round about.

3 Moreover take thou unto thee an iron pan, and set it *for* a wall of iron between thee and the city: and set thy face against it, and it shall be [a]besieged, and thou shalt lay siege against it. [b]This *shall be* a sign to the house of Israel.

4 Lie thou also upon thy left side, and lay the iniquity of the house of Israel upon it: *according* to the number of the days that thou shalt lie upon it thou shalt bear their iniquity.

5 For I have laid upon thee the years of their iniquity, according to the number of the days, three hundred and ninety days: [a]so shalt thou bear the iniquity of the house of Israel.

6 And when thou hast accomplished them, lie again on thy right side, and thou shalt bear the iniquity of the house of Judah forty days: I have appointed thee each day for a year.

7 Therefore thou shalt set thy face toward the siege of Jerusalem, and thine arm *shall be* uncovered, and thou shalt prophesy against it.

8 [a]And, behold, I will lay bands upon thee, and thou shalt not turn thee from one side to another, till thou hast ended the days of thy siege.

9 Take thou also unto thee wheat, and barley, and beans, and lentiles, and millet, and fitches, and put them in one vessel, and make thee bread thereof, *according* to the number of the days that thou shalt lie upon thy side, three hundred and ninety days shalt thou eat thereof.

10 And thy meat which thou shalt eat *shall be* by weight, twenty shekels a day: from time to time shalt thou eat it.

11 Thou shalt drink also water by measure, the sixth part of an hin: from time to time shalt thou drink.

12 And thou shalt eat it *as* barley cakes, and thou shalt bake it with dung that cometh out of man, in their sight.

13 And the LORD said, Even thus [a]shall the children of Israel eat their defiled bread among the Gentiles, whither I will drive them.

14 Then said I, [a]Ah Lord GOD! behold, my soul hath not been polluted: for from my youth up even till now have I not eaten of [b]that which

22 [a]Ezek. 1:3 [b]Ezek. 8:4 **23** [a]Ezek. 1:28 [b]Ezek. 1:1 [c]Ezek. 1:28 **24** [a]Ezek. 2:2 **25** [a]Ezek. 4:8 **26** [a]Luke 1:20, 22 [b]Hos. 4:17 [c]Ezek. 2:5–7 **27** [a]Ezek. 24:27; 33:22 [b]Ezek. 3:11

CHAPTER 4

2 [a]Jer. 6:6 [b]2 Kin. 25:1 **3** [a]Jer. 39:1, 2 [b]Ezek. 12:6, 11; 24:24, 27 **5** [a]Num. 14:34 **8** [a]Ezek. 3:25 **13** [a]Hos. 9:3 **14** [a]Acts 10:14 [b]Lev. 17:15; 22:8

NKJV

die in his sin, and his righteousness which he has done shall not be remembered; but his blood I will require at your hand.

21 "Nevertheless if you warn the righteous *man* that the righteous should not sin, and he does not sin, he shall surely live because he took warning; also you will have delivered your soul."

22 [a]Then the hand of the LORD was upon me there, and He said to me, "Arise, go out [b]into the plain, and there I shall talk with you."

23 So I arose and went out into the plain, and behold, [a]the glory of the LORD stood there, like the glory which I [b]saw by the River Chebar; [c]and I fell on my face.

24 Then [a]the Spirit entered me and set me on my feet, and spoke with me and said to me: "Go, shut yourself inside your house.

25 "And you, O son of man, surely [a]they will put ropes on you and bind you with them, so that you cannot go out among them.

26 [a]"I will make your tongue cling to the roof of your mouth, so that you shall be mute and [b]not be one to rebuke them, [c]for they *are* a rebellious house.

27 [a]"But when I speak with you, I will open your mouth, and you shall say to them, [b]'Thus says the Lord GOD.' He who hears, let him hear; and he who refuses, let him refuse; for they *are* a rebellious house.

The Siege of Jerusalem Portrayed

4 "You also, son of man, take a clay tablet and lay it before you, and portray on it a city, Jerusalem.

2 [a]"Lay siege against it, build a [b]siege wall against it, and heap up a mound against it; set camps against it also, and place battering rams against it all around.

3 "Moreover take for yourself an iron plate, and set it *as* an iron wall between you and the city. Set your face against it, and it shall be [a]besieged, and you shall lay siege against it. [b]This *will be* a sign to the house of Israel.

4 "Lie also on your left side, and lay the iniquity of the house of Israel upon it. *According* to the number of the days that you lie on it, you shall bear their iniquity.

5 "For I have laid on you the years of their iniquity, according to the number of the days, three hundred and ninety days; [a]so you shall bear the iniquity of the house of Israel.

6 "And when you have completed them, lie again on your right side; then you shall bear the iniquity of the house of Judah forty days. I have laid on you a day for each year.

7 "Therefore you shall set your face toward the siege of Jerusalem; your arm *shall be* uncovered, and you shall prophesy against it.

8 [a]"And surely I will restrain you so that you cannot turn from one side to another till you have ended the days of your siege.

9 "Also take for yourself wheat, barley, beans, lentils, millet, and spelt; put them into one vessel, and make bread of them for yourself. *During* the number of days that you lie on your side, three hundred and ninety days, you shall eat it.

10 "And your food which you eat *shall be* by weight, twenty shekels a day; from time to time you shall eat it.

11 "You shall also drink water by measure, one-sixth of a hin; from time to time you shall drink.

12 "And you shall eat it *as* barley cakes; and bake it using fuel of human waste in their sight."

13 Then the LORD said, "So [a]shall the children of Israel eat their defiled bread among the Gentiles, where I will drive them."

14 So I said, [a]"Ah, Lord GOD! Indeed I have never defiled myself from my youth till now; I have never eaten [b]what died of itself or was torn

KJV

dieth of itself, or is torn in pieces; neither came
there [c]abominable flesh into my mouth.
15 Then he said unto me, Lo, I have given
thee cow's dung for man's dung, and thou shalt
prepare thy bread therewith.
16 Moreover he said unto me, Son of man,
behold, I will break the [a]staff of bread in Jerusalem: and they shall [b]eat bread by weight, and with
care; and they shall [c]drink water by measure, and
with astonishment:
17 That they may want bread and water, and
be astonied one with another, and [a]consume away
for their iniquity.

A Sword Against Jerusalem

5 And thou, son of man, take thee a sharp knife,
take thee a barber's razor, [a]and cause *it* to
pass upon thine head and upon thy beard: then
take thee balances to weigh, and divide the *hair.*
2 [a]Thou shalt burn with fire a third part in
the midst of [b]the city, when [c]the days of the siege
are fulfilled: and thou shalt take a third part, *and*
smite about it with a knife: and a third part thou
shalt scatter in the wind; and I will draw out a
sword after [d]them.
3 [a]Thou shalt also take thereof a few in
number, and bind them in thy skirts.
4 Then take of them again, and [a]cast them
into the midst of the fire, and burn them in the
fire; *for* thereof shall a fire come forth into all
the house of Israel.
5 Thus saith the Lord GOD; This *is* Jerusalem: I have set it in the midst of the nations and
countries *that are* round about her.
6 And she hath changed my judgments into
wickedness more than the nations, and my statutes more than the countries that *are* round about
her: for they have refused my judgments and my
statutes, they have not walked in them.
7 Therefore thus saith the Lord GOD; Because ye multiplied more than the nations that
are round about you, *and* have not walked in my
statutes, [a]neither have kept my judgments, neither have done according to the judgments of the
nations that *are* round about you;
8 Therefore thus saith the Lord GOD; Behold, I, even I, *am* against thee, and will execute
judgments in the midst of thee in the sight of the
nations.
9 [a]And I will do in thee that which I have
not done, and whereunto I will not do any more
the like, because of all thine abominations.
10 Therefore the fathers [a]shall eat the sons
in the midst of thee, and the sons shall eat their
fathers; and I will execute judgments in thee, and
the whole remnant of thee will I [b]scatter into all
the winds.
11 Wherefore, *as* I live, saith the Lord GOD;
Surely, because thou hast [a]defiled my sanctuary
with all thy [b]detestable things, and with all thine
abominations, therefore will I also diminish *thee;*
[c]neither shall mine eye spare, neither will I have
any pity.
12 [a]A third part of thee shall die with the pestilence, and with famine shall they be consumed
in the midst of thee: and a third part shall fall by
the sword round about thee; and [b]I will scatter a
third part into all the winds, and I will draw out
a sword after [c]them.
13 Thus shall mine anger [a]be accomplished,
and I will [b]cause my fury to rest upon them, [c]and
I will be comforted: [d]and they shall know that I
the LORD have spoken *it* in my zeal, when I have
accomplished my fury in them.
14 Moreover [a]I will make thee waste, and a
reproach among the nations that *are* round about
thee, in the sight of all that pass by.
15 So it shall be a [a]reproach and a taunt, an
[b]instruction and an astonishment unto the nations
that *are* round about thee, when I shall execute
judgments in thee in anger and in fury and in [c]fu-
rious rebukes. I the LORD have spoken *it.*

14 [c]Deut. 14:3
16 [a]Is. 3:1
[b]Ezek. 4:10, 11; 12:19
[c]Ezek. 4:11
17 [a]Lev. 26:39

CHAPTER 5

1 [a]Is. 7:20
2 [a]Ezek. 5:12
[b]Ezek. 4:1
[c]Ezek. 4:8, 9
[d]Lev. 26:25
3 [a]Jer. 40:6; 52:16
4 [a]Jer. 41:1, 2; 44:14
7 [a]Jer. 2:10, 11
9 [a][Amos 3:2]
10 [a]Jer. 19:9
[b]Zech. 2:6; 7:14
11 [a][Jer. 7:9–11] [b]Ezek. 11:21 [c]Ezek. 7:4, 9; 8:18; 9:10
12 [a]Ezek. 6:12 [b]Jer. 9:16
[c]Jer. 43:10, 11; 44:27
13 [a]Lam. 4:11
[b]Ezek. 21:17
[c]Is. 1:24
[d]Ezek. 36:6; 38:19
14 [a]Lev. 26:31
15 [a]Jer. 24:9
[b][Is. 26:9]
[c]Ezek. 5:8; 25:17

*———

5:7 So with MT, LXX, Tg., Vg.; many Heb. mss., Syr. *but have done* (cf. 11:12)
5:15 LXX, Syr., Tg., Vg. *you*

NKJV

by beasts, nor has [c]abominable flesh ever come
into my mouth."
15 Then He said to me, "See, I am giving you
cow dung instead of human waste, and you shall
prepare your bread over it."
16 Moreover He said to me, "Son of man,
surely I will cut off the [a]supply of bread in Jerusalem; they shall [b]eat bread by weight and with anxiety, and shall [c]drink water by measure and with
dread,
17 "that they may lack bread and water, and
be dismayed with one another, and [a]waste away
because of their iniquity.

A Sword Against Jerusalem

5 "And you, son of man, take a sharp sword,
take it as a barber's razor, [a]and pass *it* over
your head and your beard; then take scales to
weigh and divide the hair.
2 [a]"You shall burn with fire one-third in the
midst of [b]the city, when [c]the days of the siege
are finished; then you shall take one-third and
strike around *it* with the sword, and one-third you
shall scatter in the wind: I will draw out a sword
after [d]them.
3 [a]"You shall also take a small number of
them and bind them in the edge of your *garment.*
4 "Then take some of them again and
[a]throw them into the midst of the fire, and burn
them in the fire. From there a fire will go out into
all the house of Israel.
5 "Thus says the Lord GOD: 'This *is* Jerusalem; I have set her in the midst of the nations
and the countries all around her.
6 'She has rebelled against My judgments
by doing wickedness more than the nations, and
against My statutes more than the countries that
are all around her; for they have refused My judgments, and they have not walked in My statutes.'
7 "Therefore thus says the Lord GOD: 'Because you have multiplied *disobedience* more than
the nations that *are* all around you, have not
walked in My statutes [a]nor kept My judgments,
*nor even done according to the judgments of the
nations that *are* all around you'—
8 "therefore thus says the Lord GOD: 'Indeed I, even I, *am* against you and will execute
judgments in your midst in the sight of the
nations.
9 [a]'And I will do among you what I have
never done, and the like of which I will never do
again, because of all your abominations.
10 'Therefore fathers [a]shall eat *their* sons in
your midst, and sons shall eat their fathers; and
I will execute judgments among you, and all of
you who remain I will [b]scatter to all the winds.
11 'Therefore, *as* I live,' says the Lord GOD,
'surely, because you have [a]defiled My sanctuary
with all your [b]detestable things and with all your
abominations, therefore I will also diminish *you;*
[c]My eye will not spare, nor will I have any pity.
12 [a]'One-third of you shall die of the pestilence, and be consumed with famine in your
midst; and one-third shall fall by the sword all
around you; and [b]I will scatter another third to
all the winds, and I will draw out a sword after
[c]them.
13 'Thus shall My anger [a]be spent, and I will
[b]cause My fury to rest upon them, [c]and I will be
avenged; [d]and they shall know that I, the LORD,
have spoken *it* in My zeal, when I have spent My
fury upon them.
14 'Moreover [a]I will make you a waste and
a reproach among the nations that *are* all around
you, in the sight of all who pass by.
15 'So *it shall be a [a]reproach, a taunt, a [b]les-
son, and an astonishment to the nations that *are*
all around you, when I execute judgments among
you in anger and in fury and in [c]furious rebukes.
I, the LORD, have spoken.

KJV

16 When I shall [a]send upon them the evil arrows of famine, which shall be for *their* destruction, *and* which I will send to destroy you: and I will increase the famine upon you, and will break your [b]staff of bread:

17 So will I send upon you famine and [a]evil beasts, and they shall bereave thee; and [b]pestilence and blood shall pass through thee; and I will bring the sword upon thee. I the LORD have spoken *it*.

Judgment on Idolatrous Israel

6 And the word of the LORD came unto me, saying,

2 Son of man, [a]set thy face toward the [b]mountains of Israel, and prophesy against them,

3 And say, Ye mountains of Israel, hear the word of the Lord GOD; Thus saith the Lord GOD to the mountains, and to the hills, to the rivers, and to the valleys; Behold, I, *even* I, will bring a sword upon you, and [a]I will destroy your high places.

4 And your altars shall be desolate, and your images shall be broken: and [a]I will cast down your slain *men* before your idols.

5 And I will lay the dead carcases of the children of Israel before their idols; and I will scatter your bones round about your altars.

6 In all your dwellingplaces the cities shall be laid waste, and the high places shall be desolate; that your altars may be laid waste and made desolate, and your idols may be broken and cease, and your images may be cut down, and your works may be abolished.

7 And the slain shall fall in the midst of you, and [a]ye shall know that I *am* the LORD.

8 [a]Yet will I leave a remnant, that ye may have *some* that shall escape the sword among the nations, when ye shall be [b]scattered through the countries.

9 And they that escape of you shall [a]remember me among the nations whither they shall be carried captives, because [b]I am broken with their whorish heart, which hath departed from me, and [c]with their eyes, which go a whoring after their idols: and [d]they shall lothe themselves for the evils which they have committed in all their abominations.

10 And they shall know that I *am* the LORD, *and that* I have not said in vain that I would do this evil unto them.

11 Thus saith the Lord GOD; Smite [a]with thine hand, and stamp with thy foot, and say, Alas for all the evil abominations of the house of Israel! [b]for they shall fall by the sword, by the famine, and by the pestilence.

12 He that is far off shall die of the pestilence; and he that is near shall fall by the sword; and he that remaineth and is besieged shall die by the famine: [a]thus will I accomplish my fury upon them.

13 Then shall ye know that I *am* the LORD, when their slain *men* shall be among their idols round about their altars, [a]upon every high hill, [b]in all the tops of the mountains, and [c]under every green tree, and under every thick oak, the place where they did offer sweet savour to all their idols.

14 So will I [a]stretch out my hand upon them, and make the land desolate, yea, more desolate than the wilderness toward [b]Diblath, in all their habitations: and they shall know that I *am* the LORD.

Judgment on Israel Is Near

7 Moreover the word of the LORD came unto me, saying,

2 Also, thou son of man, thus saith the Lord GOD unto the land of Israel; [a]An end, the end is come upon the four corners of the land.

3 Now *is* the end *come* upon thee, and I will

---

16 [a]Deut. 32:23 [b]Lev. 26:26; Ezek. 4:16; 14:13
17 [a]Lev. 26:22; Deut. 32:24; Ezek. 14:21; 33:27; 34:25; Rev. 6:8 [b]Ezek. 38:22

CHAPTER 6

2 [a]Ezek. 20:46; 21:2; 25:2 [b]Ezek. 36:1
3 [a]Lev. 26:30
4 [a]Lev. 26:30
7 [a]Ezek. 7:4, 9
8 [a]Jer. 44:28; Ezek. 5:2, 12; 12:16; 14:22 [b]Ezek. 5:12
9 [a][Deut. 4:29]; Ps. 137; Jer. 51:50 [b]Ps. 78:40; Is. 7:13; 43:24; Hos. 11:8 [c]Num. 15:39; Ezek. 20:7, 24 [d]Lev. 26:39; Job 42:6; Ezek. 20:43; 36:31
11 [a]Ezek. 21:14 [b]Ezek. 5:12
12 [a]Lam. 4:11, 22; Ezek. 5:13
13 [a]Jer. 2:20; 3:6 [b]1 Kin. 14:23; 2 Kin. 16:4; Ezek. 20:28; Hos. 4:13 [c]Is. 57:5
14 [a]Is. 5:25; Ezek. 14:13; 20:33, 34 [b]Num. 33:46

CHAPTER 7

2 [a]Ezek. 7:3, 5, 6; 11:13; Amos 8:2, 10; [Matt. 24:6, 13, 14]

NKJV

16 'When I [a]send against them the terrible arrows of famine which shall be for destruction, which I will send to destroy you, I will increase the famine upon you and cut off your [b]supply of bread.

17 'So I will send against you famine and [a]wild beasts, and they will bereave you. [b]Pestilence and blood shall pass through you, and I will bring the sword against you. I, the LORD, have spoken.' "

Judgment on Idolatrous Israel

6 Now the word of the LORD came to me, saying:

2 "Son of man, [a]set your face toward the [b]mountains of Israel, and prophesy against them,

3 "and say, 'O mountains of Israel, hear the word of the Lord GOD! Thus says the Lord GOD to the mountains, to the hills, to the ravines, and to the valleys: "Indeed I, *even* I, will bring a sword against you, and [a]I will destroy your high places.

4 "Then your altars shall be desolate, your incense altars shall be broken, and [a]I will cast down your slain *men* before your idols.

5 "And I will lay the corpses of the children of Israel before their idols, and I will scatter your bones all around your altars.

6 "In all your dwelling places the cities shall be laid waste, and the high places shall be desolate, so that your altars may be laid waste and made desolate, your idols may be broken and made to cease, your incense altars may be cut down, and your works may be abolished.

7 "The slain shall fall in your midst, and [a]you shall know that I *am* the LORD.

8 [a]"Yet I will leave a remnant, so that you may have *some* who escape the sword among the nations, when you are [b]scattered through the countries.

9 "Then those of you who escape will [a]remember Me among the nations where they are carried captive, because [b]I was crushed by their adulterous heart which has departed from Me, and [c]by their eyes which play the harlot after their idols; [d]they will loathe themselves for the evils which they committed in all their abominations.

10 "And they shall know that I *am* the LORD; I have not said in vain that I would bring this calamity upon them."

11 'Thus says the Lord GOD: [a]"Pound your fists and stamp your feet, and say, 'Alas, for all the evil abominations of the house of Israel! [b]For they shall fall by the sword, by famine, and by pestilence.

12 'He who is far off shall die by the pestilence, he who is near shall fall by the sword, and he who remains and is besieged shall die by the famine. [a]Thus will I spend My fury upon them.

13 'Then you shall know that I *am* the LORD, when their slain are among their idols all around their altars, [a]on every high hill, [b]on all the mountaintops, [c]under every green tree, and under every thick oak, wherever they offered sweet incense to all their idols.

14 'So I will [a]stretch out My hand against them and make the land desolate, yes, more desolate than the wilderness toward [b]Diblah, in all their dwelling places. Then they shall know that I *am* the LORD.' " ' "

Judgment on Israel Is Near

7 Moreover the word of the LORD came to me, saying,

2 "And you, son of man, thus says the Lord GOD to the land of Israel:

[a]'An end! The end has come upon the four
corners of the land.
3 Now the end *has come* upon you,

KJV

send mine anger upon thee, and will judge thee
[a]according to thy ways, and will recompense
upon thee all thine abominations.
4 And [a]mine eye shall not spare thee, neither will I have pity: but I will recompense thy
ways upon thee, and thine abominations shall be
in the midst of thee: [b]and ye shall know that I
am the LORD.
5 Thus saith the Lord GOD; An evil, an only
[a]evil, behold, is come.
6 An end is come, the end is come: it watcheth for thee; behold, it is come.
7 [a]The morning is come unto thee, O thou
that dwellest in the land: [b]the time is come, the
day of trouble *is* near, and not the sounding again
of the mountains.
8 Now will I shortly [a]pour out my fury upon
thee, and accomplish mine anger upon thee: and
I will judge thee according to thy ways, and will
recompense thee for all thine abominations.
9 And mine eye shall not spare, neither will
I have pity: I will recompense thee according to
thy ways and thine abominations *that* are in the
midst of thee; and ye shall know that I *am* the
LORD that smiteth.
10 Behold the day, behold, it is come: [a]the
morning is gone forth; the rod hath blossomed,
pride hath budded.
11 [a]Violence is risen up into a rod of wickedness: none of them *shall remain,* nor of their multitude, nor of any of their's: [b]neither *shall there
be* wailing for them.
12 The time is come, the day draweth near:
let not the buyer [a]rejoice, nor the seller [b]mourn:
for wrath *is* upon all the multitude thereof.
13 For the seller shall not return to that which
is sold, although they were yet alive: for the vision
is touching the whole multitude thereof, *which*
shall not return; neither shall any strengthen himself in the iniquity of his life.
14 They have blown the trumpet, even to
make all ready; but none goeth to the battle: for
my wrath *is* upon all the multitude thereof.
15 [a]The sword *is* without, and the pestilence
and the famine within: he that *is* in the field shall
die with the sword; and he that *is* in the city, famine and pestilence shall devour him.
16 But they that [a]escape of them shall escape,
and shall be on the mountains like doves of the
valleys, all of them mourning, every one for his
iniquity.

3 [a][Rom. 2:6]
4 [a]Ezek. 5:11 [b]Ezek. 12:20
5 [a]2 Kin. 21:12, 13; Nah. 1:9
7 [a]Ezek. 7:10 [b]Zeph. 1:14, 15
8 [a]Ezek. 20:8, 21
10 [a]Ezek. 7:7
11 [a]Jer. 6:7 [b]Jer. 16:5, 6; Ezek. 24:16, 22
12 [a]Prov. 20:14; 1 Cor. 7:30 [b]Is. 24:2
15 [a]Deut. 32:25; Jer. 14:18; Lam. 1:20; Ezek. 5:12
16 [a]Ezra 9:15; Is. 37:31; Ezek. 6:8; 14:22

NKJV

And I will send My anger against you;
I will judge you [a]according to your ways,
And I will repay you for all your
abominations.
4 [a]My eye will not spare you,
Nor will I have pity;
But I will repay your ways,
And your abominations will be in your
midst;
[b]Then you shall know that I *am* the LORD!'

5 "Thus says the Lord GOD:

'A disaster, a singular [a]disaster;
Behold, it has come!
6 An end has come,
The end has come;
It has dawned for you;
Behold, it has come!
7 [a]Doom has come to you, you who dwell
in the land;
[b]The time has come,
A day of trouble *is* near,
And not of rejoicing in the mountains.
8 Now upon you I will soon [a]pour out My
fury,
And spend My anger upon you;
I will judge you according to your ways,
And I will repay you for all your
abominations.

9 'My eye will not spare,
Nor will I have pity;
I will repay you according to your
ways,
And your abominations will be in your
midst.
Then you shall know that I *am* the LORD
who strikes.

10 'Behold, the day!
Behold, it has come!
[a]Doom has gone out;
The rod has blossomed,
Pride has budded.
11 [a]Violence has risen up into a rod of
wickedness;
None of them *shall remain,*
None of their multitude,
None of them;
[b]Nor *shall there be* wailing for them.
12 The time has come,
The day draws near.

'Let not the buyer [a]rejoice,
Nor the seller [b]mourn,
For wrath *is* on their whole multitude.
13 For the seller shall not return to what has
been sold,
Though he may still be alive;
For the vision concerns the whole
multitude,
And it shall not turn back;
No one will strengthen himself
Who lives in iniquity.

14 'They have blown the trumpet and made
everyone ready,
But no one goes to battle;
For My wrath *is* on all their multitude.
15 [a]The sword *is* outside,
And the pestilence and famine within.
Whoever *is* in the field
Will die by the sword;
And whoever *is* in the city,
Famine and pestilence will devour him.

16 'Those who [a]survive will escape and be on
the mountains
Like doves of the valleys,
All of them mourning,
Each for his iniquity.

KJV

17 All [a]hands shall be feeble, and all knees
shall be weak *as* water.
18 They shall also [a]gird *themselves* with
sackcloth, and horror shall cover them; and
shame *shall be* upon all faces, and baldness upon
all their heads.
19 They shall cast their silver in the streets,
and their gold shall be removed: their [a]silver and
their gold shall not be able to deliver them in the
day of the wrath of the LORD: they shall not satisfy
their souls, neither fill their bowels: because it is
the stumblingblock of their iniquity.
20 As for the beauty of his ornament, he set
it in majesty: [a]but they made the images of their
abominations *and* of their detestable things
therein: therefore have I set it far from them.
21 And I will give it into the hands of the
strangers for a [a]prey, and to the wicked of the
earth for a spoil; and they shall pollute it.
22 My face will I turn also from them, and
they shall pollute my secret *place:* for the robbers
shall enter into it, and defile it.
23 Make a chain: for [a]the land is full of
bloody crimes, and the city is full of violence.
24 Wherefore I will bring the [a]worst of the
heathen, and they shall possess their houses: I
will also make the pomp of the strong to cease;
and their holy places shall be [b]defiled.
25 Destruction cometh; and they shall seek
peace, and *there shall be* none.
26 [a]Mischief shall come upon mischief, and
rumour shall be upon rumour; [b]then shall they
seek a vision of the prophet; but the law shall
perish from the priest, and counsel from the
ancients.
27 The king shall mourn, and the prince shall
be clothed with desolation, and the hands of the
people of the land shall be troubled: I will do unto
them after their way, and according to their deserts will I judge them; and they shall know that
I *am* the LORD.

Abominations in the Temple

8 And it came to pass in the sixth year, in the
sixth *month,* in the fifth *day* of the month, *as*
I sat in mine house, and [a]the elders of Judah sat
before me, that [b]the hand of the Lord GOD fell
there upon me.
2 [a]Then I beheld, and lo a likeness as the
appearance of fire: from the appearance of his
loins even downward, fire; and from his loins even
upward, as the appearance of brightness, [b]as the
colour of amber.
3 And he [a]put forth the form of an hand,
and took me by a lock of mine head; and [b]the spirit
lifted me up between the earth and the heaven,
and [c]brought me in the visions of God to Jerusalem, to the door of the inner gate, that looketh
toward the north; [d]where *was* the seat of the image of jealousy, which [e]provoketh to jealousy.

17 [a]Is. 13:7; Jer. 6:24; Ezek. 21:7; Heb. 12:12
18 [a]Is. 3:24; 15:2, 3; Jer. 48:37; Ezek. 27:31; Amos 8:10
19 [a]Prov. 11:4; Jer. 15:13; Zeph. 1:18
20 [a]Jer. 7:30
21 [a]2 Kin. 24:13; Jer. 20:5
23 [a]2 Kin. 21:16
24 [a]Ezek. 21:31; 28:7 [b]2 Chr. 7:20; Ezek. 24:21
26 [a]Deut. 32:23; Is. 47:11; Jer. 4:20 [b]Ps. 74:9; Lam. 2:9; Ezek. 20:1, 3; Mic. 3:6

CHAPTER 8

1 [a]Ezek. 14:1; 20:1; 33:31 [b]Ezek. 1:3; 3:22
2 [a]Ezek. 1:26, 27 [b]Ezek. 1:4, 27
3 [a]Dan. 5:5 [b]Ezek. 3:14; Acts 8:39 [c]Ezek. 11:1, 24; 40:2 [d]Jer. 7:30; 32:34; Ezek. 5:11 [e]Ex. 20:4; Deut. 32:16, 21

NKJV

17 Every [a]hand will be feeble,
And every knee will be *as* weak *as* water.
18 They will also [a]be girded with sackcloth;
Horror will cover them;
Shame *will be* on every face,
Baldness on all their heads.

19 'They will throw their silver into the
streets,
And their gold will be like refuse;
Their [a]silver and their gold will not be
able to deliver them
In the day of the wrath of the LORD;
They will not satisfy their souls,
Nor fill their stomachs,
Because it became their stumbling block
of iniquity.

20 'As for the beauty of his ornaments,
He set it in majesty;
[a]But they made from it
The images of their abominations—
Their detestable things;
Therefore I have made it
Like refuse to them.
21 I will give it as [a]plunder
Into the hands of strangers,
And to the wicked of the earth as spoil;
And they shall defile it.
22 I will turn My face from them,
And they will defile My secret place;
For robbers shall enter it and defile it.

23 'Make a chain,
For [a]the land is filled with crimes of
blood,
And the city is full of violence.
24 Therefore I will bring the [a]worst of the
Gentiles,
And they will possess their houses;
I will cause the pomp of the strong to
cease,
And their holy places shall be [b]defiled.
25 Destruction comes;
They will seek peace, but *there shall be*
none.
26 [a]Disaster will come upon disaster,
And rumor will be upon rumor.
[b]Then they will seek a vision from a
prophet;
But the law will perish from the priest,
And counsel from the elders.

27 'The king will mourn,
The prince will be clothed with
desolation,
And the hands of the common people will
tremble.
I will do to them according to their way,
And according to what they deserve I will
judge them;
Then they shall know that I *am* the
LORD!' "

Abominations in the Temple

8 And it came to pass in the sixth year, in the
sixth *month,* on the fifth *day* of the month,
as I sat in my house with [a]the elders of Judah
sitting before me, that [b]the hand of the Lord GOD
fell upon me there.
2 [a]Then I looked, and there was a likeness,
like the appearance of fire—from the appearance
of His waist and downward, fire; and from His
waist and upward, like the appearance of brightness, [b]like the color of amber.
3 He [a]stretched out the form of a hand, and
took me by a lock of my hair; and [b]the Spirit lifted
me up between earth and heaven, and [c]brought
me in visions of God to Jerusalem, to the door of
the north gate of the inner *court,* [d]where the seat
of the image of jealousy *was,* which [e]provokes
to jealousy.

KJV

4 And, behold, the [a]glory of the God of Israel *was* there, according to the vision that I [b]saw in the plain.

5 Then said he unto me, Son of man, lift up thine eyes now the way toward the north. So I lifted up mine eyes the way toward the north, and behold northward at the gate of the altar this image of jealousy in the entry.

6 He said furthermore unto me, Son of man, seest thou what they do? *even* the great [a]abominations that the house of Israel committeth here, that I should go far off from my sanctuary? but turn thee yet again, *and* thou shalt see greater abominations.

7 And he brought me to the door of the court; and when I looked, behold a hole in the wall.

8 Then said he unto me, Son of man, dig now in the wall: and when I had digged in the wall, behold a door.

9 And he said unto me, Go in, and behold the wicked abominations that they do here.

10 So I went in and saw; and behold every [a]form of [b]creeping things, and abominable beasts, and all the idols of the house of Israel, pourtrayed upon the wall round about.

11 And there stood before them [a]seventy men of the ancients of the house of Israel, and in the midst of them stood Jaazaniah the son of Shaphan, with every man his censer in his hand; and a thick cloud of incense went up.

12 Then said he unto me, Son of man, hast thou seen what the ancients of the house of Israel do in the dark, every man in the chambers of his imagery? for they say, [a]The LORD seeth us not; the LORD hath forsaken the earth.

13 He said also unto me, Turn thee yet again, *and* thou shalt see greater abominations that they do.

14 Then he brought me to the door of the gate of the LORD's house which *was* toward the north; and, behold, there sat women weeping for Tammuz.

15 Then said he unto me, Hast thou seen *this*, O son of man? turn thee yet again, *and* thou shalt see greater abominations than these.

16 And he brought me into the inner court of the LORD's house, and, behold, at the door of the temple of the LORD, [a]between the porch and the altar, [b]*were* about five and twenty men, [c]with their backs toward the temple of the LORD, and their faces toward the east; and they worshipped [d]the sun toward the east.

17 Then he said unto me, Hast thou seen *this*, O son of man? Is it a light thing to the house of Judah that they commit the abominations which they commit here? for they have [a]filled the land with violence, and have returned to provoke me to anger: and, lo, they put the branch to their nose.

18 [a]Therefore will I also deal in fury: mine [b]eye shall not spare, neither will I have pity: and though they [c]cry in mine ears with a loud voice, *yet* will I not hear them.

The Wicked Are Slain

9 He cried also in mine ears with a loud voice, saying, Cause them that have charge over the city to draw near, even every man *with* his destroying weapon in his hand.

2 And, behold, six men came from the way of the higher gate, which lieth toward the north, and every man a slaughter weapon in his hand; [a]and one man among them *was* clothed with linen, with a writer's inkhorn by his side: and they went in, and stood beside the brasen altar.

3 And [a]the glory of the God of Israel was gone up from the cherub, whereupon he was, to the threshold of the house. And he called to the man clothed with linen, which *had* the writer's inkhorn by his side;

4 And the LORD said unto him, Go through the midst of the city, through the midst of Jerusa-

4 [a]Ezek. 3:12; 9:3 [b]Ezek. 1:28; 3:22, 23
6 [a]2 Kin. 23:4, 5; Ezek. 5:11; 8:9, 17
10 [a]Ex. 20:4; Deut. 4:16–18 [b]Rom. 1:23
11 [a]Num. 11:16, 25; Luke 10:1
12 [a]Ps. 14:1; Is. 29:15; Ezek. 9:9
16 [a]Joel 2:17 [b]Ezek. 11:1 [c]2 Chr. 29:6; Jer. 2:27; 32:33; Ezek. 23:39 [d]Deut. 4:19; 2 Kin. 23:5, 11; Job 31:26; Jer. 44:17
17 [a]Ezek. 9:9; Amos 3:10; Mic. 2:2
18 [a]Ezek. 5:13; 16:42; 24:13 [b]Ezek. 5:11; 7:4, 9; 9:5, 10 [c]Prov. 1:28; Is. 1:15; Jer. 11:11; 14:12; Mic. 3:4; Zech. 7:13

CHAPTER 9

2 [a]Lev. 16:4; Ezek. 10:2; Rev. 15:6
3 [a]Ezek. 3:23; 8:4; 10:4, 18; 11:22, 23

*———
9:3 Lit. *house*

NKJV

4 And behold, the [a]glory of the God of Israel *was* there, like the vision that I [b]saw in the plain.

5 Then He said to me, "Son of man, lift your eyes now toward the north." So I lifted my eyes toward the north, and there, north of the altar gate, was this image of jealousy in the entrance.

6 Furthermore He said to me, "Son of man, do you see what they are doing, the great [a]abominations that the house of Israel commits here, to make Me go far away from My sanctuary? Now turn again, you will see greater abominations."

7 So He brought me to the door of the court; and when I looked, there was a hole in the wall.

8 Then He said to me, "Son of man, dig into the wall"; and when I dug into the wall, there was a door.

9 And He said to me, "Go in, and see the wicked abominations which they are doing there."

10 So I went in and saw, and there—every [a]sort of [b]creeping thing, abominable beasts, and all the idols of the house of Israel, portrayed all around on the walls.

11 And there stood before them [a]seventy men of the elders of the house of Israel, and in their midst stood Jaazaniah the son of Shaphan. Each man had a censer in his hand, and a thick cloud of incense went up.

12 Then He said to me, "Son of man, have you seen what the elders of the house of Israel do in the dark, every man in the room of his idols? For they say, [a]'The LORD does not see us, the LORD has forsaken the land.' "

13 And He said to me, "Turn again, *and* you will see greater abominations that they are doing."

14 So He brought me to the door of the north gate of the LORD's house; and to my dismay, women were sitting there weeping for Tammuz.

15 Then He said to me, "Have you seen *this*, O son of man? Turn again, you will see greater abominations than these."

16 So He brought me into the inner court of the LORD's house; and there, at the door of the temple of the LORD, [a]between the porch and the altar, [b]*were* about twenty-five men [c]with their backs toward the temple of the LORD and their faces toward the east, and they were worshiping [d]the sun toward the east.

17 And He said to me, "Have you seen *this*, O son of man? Is it a trivial thing to the house of Judah to commit the abominations which they commit here? For they have [a]filled the land with violence; then they have returned to provoke Me to anger. Indeed they put the branch to their nose.

18 [a]"Therefore I also will act in fury. My [b]eye will not spare nor will I have pity; and though they [c]cry in My ears with a loud voice, I will not hear them."

The Wicked Are Slain

9 Then He called out in my hearing with a loud voice, saying, "Let those who have charge over the city draw near, each *with* a deadly weapon in his hand."

2 And suddenly six men came from the direction of the upper gate, which faces north, each with his battle-ax in his hand. [a]One man among them *was* clothed with linen and had a writer's inkhorn at his side. They went in and stood beside the bronze altar.

3 Now [a]the glory of the God of Israel had gone up from the cherub, where it had been, to the threshold of the *temple. And He called to the man clothed with linen, who *had* the writer's inkhorn at his side;

4 and the LORD said to him, "Go through the midst of the city, through the midst of Jerusa-

KJV

lem, and set [a]a mark upon the foreheads of the men [b]that sigh and that cry for all the abominations that be done in the midst thereof.

5 And to the others he said in mine hearing, Go ye after him through the city, and [a]smite: [b]let not your eye spare, neither have ye pity:

6 [a]Slay utterly old *and* young, both maids, and little children, and women: but [b]come not near any man upon whom *is* the mark; and [c]begin at my sanctuary. [d]Then they began at the ancient men which *were* before the house.

7 And he said unto them, Defile the house, and fill the courts with the slain: go ye forth. And they went forth, and slew in the city.

8 And it came to pass, while they were slaying them, and I was left, that I [a]fell upon my face, and cried, and said, [b]Ah Lord GOD! wilt thou destroy all the residue of Israel in thy pouring out of thy fury upon Jerusalem?

9 Then said he unto me, The iniquity of the house of Israel and Judah *is* exceeding great, and [a]the land is full of blood, and the city full of perverseness: for they say, [b]The LORD hath forsaken the earth, and [c]the LORD seeth not.

10 And as for me also, mine [a]eye shall not spare, neither will I have pity, *but* [b]I will recompense their way upon their head.

11 And, behold, the man clothed with linen, which *had* the inkhorn by his side, reported the matter, saying, I have done as thou hast commanded me.

The Glory Departs from the Temple

10 Then I looked, and, behold, in the [a]firmament that was above the head of the cherubims there appeared over them as it were a sapphire stone, as the appearance of the likeness of a throne.

2 [a]And he spake unto the man clothed with linen, and said, Go in between the wheels, *even* under the cherub, and fill thine hand with [b]coals of fire from between the cherubims, and [c]scatter *them* over the city. And he went in in my sight.

3 Now the cherubims stood on the right side of the house, when the man went in; and the [a]cloud filled the inner court.

4 [a]Then the glory of the LORD went up from the cherub, *and stood* over the threshold of the house; and [b]the house was filled with the cloud, and the court was full of the brightness of the LORD's [c]glory.

5 And the [a]sound of the cherubims' wings was heard *even* to the outer court, as [b]the voice of the Almighty God when he speaketh.

6 And it came to pass, *that* when he had commanded the man clothed with linen, saying, Take fire from between the wheels, from between the cherubims; then he went in, and stood beside the wheels.

7 And *one* cherub stretched forth his hand from between the cherubims unto the fire that *was* between the cherubims, and took *thereof,* and put *it* into the hands of *him that was* clothed with linen: who took *it,* and went out.

8 [a]And there appeared in the cherubims the form of a man's hand under their wings.

9 [a]And when I looked, behold the four wheels by the cherubims, one wheel by one cherub, and another wheel by another cherub: and the appearance of the wheels *was* as the colour of a [b]beryl stone.

10 And *as for* their appearances, they four had one likeness, as if a wheel had been in the midst of a wheel.

11 [a]When they went, they went upon their four sides; they turned not as they went, but to the place whither the head looked they followed it; they turned not as they went.

12 And their whole body, and their backs, and their hands, and their wings, and the wheels, *were* [a]full of eyes round about, *even* the wheels that they four had.

---

4 [a]Ex. 12:7, 13; Ezek. 9:6; [2 Cor. 1:22; 2 Tim. 2:19]; Rev. 7:2, 3; 9:4; 14:1 [b]Ps. 119:53, 136; Jer. 13:17; Ezek. 6:11; 21:6; 2 Cor. 12:21; 2 Pet. 2:8
5 [a]Ezek. 7:9 [b]Ezek. 5:11
6 [a]2 Chr. 36:17 [b]Ex. 12:23; Rev. 9:4 [c]Jer. 25:29; Amos 3:2; [Luke 12:42; 1 Pet. 4:17] [d]Ezek. 8:11, 12, 16
8 [a]Num. 14:5; 16:4, 22, 45; Josh. 7:6 [b]Ezek. 11:13; Amos 7:2–6
9 [a]2 Kin. 21:16; Jer. 2:34; Ezek. 8:17 [b]Job 22:13; Ezek. 8:12 [c]Ps. 10:11; Is. 29:15
10 [a]Is. 65:6; Ezek. 5:11; 7:4; 8:18 [b]Ezek. 11:21; Hos. 9:7

CHAPTER 10

1 [a]Ezek. 1:22, 26
2 [a]Ezek. 9:2, 3; Dan. 10:5 [b]Ps. 18:10–13; Is. 6:6; Ezek. 1:13 [c]Rev. 8:5
3 [a]1 Kin. 8:10, 11
4 [a]Ezek. 1:28 [b]1 Kin. 8:10; Ezek. 43:5 [c]Ezek. 11:22, 23
5 [a][Job 40:9]; Ezek. 1:24; [Rev. 10:3] [b][Ps. 29:3]
8 [a]Ezek. 1:8; 10:21
9 [a]Ezek. 1:15 [b]Ezek. 1:16
11 [a]Ezek. 1:17
12 [a]Rev. 4:6, 8

*10:3 Lit. *house*

NKJV

lem, and put [a]a mark on the foreheads of the men [b]who sigh and cry over all the abominations that are done within it."

5 To the others He said in my hearing, "Go after him through the city and [a]kill; [b]do not let your eye spare, nor have any pity.

6 [a]"Utterly slay old *and* young men, maidens and little children and women; but [b]do not come near anyone on whom *is* the mark; and [c]begin at My sanctuary." [d]So they began with the elders who *were* before the temple.

7 Then He said to them, "Defile the temple, and fill the courts with the slain. Go out!" And they went out and killed in the city.

8 So it was, that while they were killing them, I was left *alone;* and I [a]fell on my face and cried out, and said, [b]"Ah, Lord GOD! Will You destroy all the remnant of Israel in pouring out Your fury on Jerusalem?"

9 Then He said to me, "The iniquity of the house of Israel and Judah *is* exceedingly great, and [a]the land is full of bloodshed, and the city full of perversity; for they say, [b]'The LORD has forsaken the land, and [c]the LORD does not see!'

10 "And as for Me also, My [a]eye will neither spare, nor will I have pity, *but* [b]I will recompense their deeds on their own head."

11 Just then, the man clothed with linen, who *had* the inkhorn at his side, reported back and said, "I have done as You commanded me."

The Glory Departs from the Temple

10 And I looked, and there in the [a]firmament that was above the head of the cherubim, there appeared something like a sapphire stone, having the appearance of the likeness of a throne.

2 [a]Then He spoke to the man clothed with linen, and said, "Go in among the wheels, under the cherub, fill your hands with [b]coals of fire from among the cherubim, and [c]scatter *them* over the city." And he went in as I watched.

3 Now the cherubim were standing on the south side of the *temple when the man went in, and the [a]cloud filled the inner court.

4 [a]Then the glory of the LORD went up from the cherub, *and paused* over the threshold of the temple; and [b]the house was filled with the cloud, and the court was full of the brightness of the LORD's [c]glory.

5 And the [a]sound of the wings of the cherubim was heard *even* in the outer court, like [b]the voice of Almighty God when He speaks.

6 Then it happened, when He commanded the man clothed in linen, saying, "Take fire from among the wheels, from among the cherubim," that he went in and stood beside the wheels.

7 And the cherub stretched out his hand from among the cherubim to the fire that *was* among the cherubim, and took *some of it* and put *it* into the hands of the *man* clothed with linen, who took *it* and went out.

8 [a]The cherubim appeared to have the form of a man's hand under their wings.

9 [a]And when I looked, there were four wheels by the cherubim, one wheel by one cherub and another wheel by each other cherub; the wheels appeared *to have* the color of a [b]beryl stone.

10 *As for* their appearance, all four looked alike—as it were, a wheel in the middle of a wheel.

11 [a]When they went, they went toward *any of* their four directions; they did not turn aside when they went, but followed in the direction the head was facing. They did not turn aside when they went.

12 And their whole body, with their back, their hands, their wings, and the wheels that the four had, *were* [a]full of eyes all around.

KJV

13 As for the wheels, it was cried unto them in my hearing, O wheel.

14 [a]And every one had four faces: the first face *was* the face of a cherub, and the second face *was* the face of a man, and the third the face of a lion, and the fourth the face of an eagle.

15 And the cherubims were lifted up. This *is* [a]the living creature that I saw by the river of Chebar.

16 [a]And when the cherubims went, the wheels went by them: and when the cherubims lifted up their wings to mount up from the earth, the same wheels also turned not from beside them.

17 [a]When they stood, *these* stood; and when they were lifted up, *these* lifted up themselves *also:* for the spirit of the living creature *was* in them.

18 Then [a]the glory of the LORD [b]departed from off the threshold of the house, and stood over the cherubims.

19 And [a]the cherubims lifted up their wings, and mounted up from the earth in my sight: when they went out, the wheels also *were* beside them, and *every one* stood at the door of the [b]east gate of the LORD's house; and the glory of the God of Israel *was* over them above.

20 [a]This *is* the living creature that I saw under the God of Israel [b]by the river of Chebar; and I knew that they *were* the cherubims.

21 [a]Every one had four faces apiece, and every one four wings; and the likeness of the hands of a man *was* under their wings.

22 And [a]the likeness of their faces *was* the same faces which I saw by the river of Chebar, their appearances and themselves: [b]they went every one straight forward.

Judgment on Wicked Counselors

11 Moreover [a]the spirit lifted me up, and brought me unto [b]the east gate of the LORD's house, which looketh eastward: and behold [c]at the door of the gate five and twenty men; among whom I saw Jaazaniah the son of Azur, and Pelatiah the son of Benaiah, princes of the people.

2 Then said he unto me, Son of man, these *are* the men that devise mischief, and give wicked counsel in this city:

3 Which say, *It is* not [a]near; let us build houses: [b]this *city is* the caldron, and we *be* the flesh.

4 Therefore prophesy against them, prophesy, O son of man.

5 And [a]the Spirit of the LORD fell upon me, and said unto me, Speak; Thus saith the LORD; Thus have ye said, O house of Israel: for [b]I know the things that come into your mind, *every one of* them.

6 [a]Ye have multiplied your slain in this city, and ye have filled the streets thereof with the slain.

7 Therefore thus saith the Lord GOD; [a]Your slain whom ye have laid in the midst of it, they *are* the flesh, and this *city is* the caldron: [b]but I will bring you forth out of the midst of it.

8 Ye have [a]feared the sword; and I will bring a sword upon you, saith the Lord GOD.

9 And I will bring you out of the midst thereof, and deliver you into the hands of strangers, and [a]will execute judgments among you.

10 [a]Ye shall fall by the sword; I will judge you in [b]the border of Israel; [c]and ye shall know that I *am* the LORD.

11 [a]This *city* shall not be your caldron, neither shall ye be the flesh in the midst thereof; *but* I will judge you in the border of Israel:

12 And ye shall know that I *am* the LORD: for ye have not walked in my statutes, neither executed my judgments, but [a]have done after the manners of the heathen that *are* round about you.

13 And it came to pass, when I prophesied,

14 [a]1 Kin. 7:29, 36; Ezek. 1:6, 10, 11; Rev. 4:7
15 [a]Ezek. 1:3, 5
16 [a]Ezek. 1:19
17 [a]Ezek. 1:12, 20, 21
18 [a]Ezek. 10:4 [b]Hos. 9:12
19 [a]Ezek. 11:22 [b]Ezek. 11:1
20 [a]Ezek. 1:22 [b]Ezek. 1:1
21 [a]Ezek. 1:6, 8; 10:14; 41:18, 19
22 [a]Ezek. 1:10 [b]Ezek. 1:9, 12

CHAPTER 11

1 [a]Ezek. 3:12, 14 [b]Ezek. 10:19 [c]Ezek. 8:16
3 [a]Ezek. 12:22, 27; 2 Pet. 3:4 [b]Jer. 1:13; Ezek. 11:7, 11; 24:3, 6
5 [a]Ezek. 2:2; 3:24 [b][Jer. 16:17; 17:10]
6 [a]Is. 1:15; Ezek. 7:23; 22:2–6, 9, 12, 27
7 [a]Ezek. 24:3, 6; Mic. 3:2, 3 [b]2 Kin. 25:18–22; Jer. 52:24–27; Ezek. 11:9
8 [a]Jer. 42:16
9 [a]Ezek. 5:8
10 [a]2 Kin. 25:19–21; Jer. 39:6; 52:10 [b]1 Kin. 8:65; 2 Kin. 14:25 [c]Ps. 9:16; Ezek. 6:7; 13:9, 14, 21, 23
11 [a]Ezek. 11:3, 7
12 [a]Lev. 18:3, 24; Deut. 12:30, 31; Ezek. 8:10, 14, 16

*

10:17 Lit. *they* • Lit. *they were* • Lit. *they lifted them*

NKJV

13 As for the wheels, they were called in my hearing, "Wheel."

14 [a]Each one had four faces: the first face *was* the face of a cherub, the second face the face of a man, the third the face of a lion, and the fourth the face of an eagle.

15 And the cherubim were lifted up. This *was* [a]the living creature I saw by the River Chebar.

16 [a]When the cherubim went, the wheels went beside them; and when the cherubim lifted their wings to mount up from the earth, the same wheels also did not turn from beside them.

17 [a]When **the cherubim* stood still, *the wheels* stood still, and when **one* was lifted up, **the other* lifted itself up, for the spirit of the living creature *was* in them.

18 Then [a]the glory of the LORD [b]departed from the threshold of the temple and stood over the cherubim.

19 And [a]the cherubim lifted their wings and mounted up from the earth in my sight. When they went out, the wheels *were* beside them; and they stood at the door of the [b]east gate of the LORD's house, and the glory of the God of Israel *was* above them.

20 [a]This *is* the living creature I saw under the God of Israel [b]by the River Chebar, and I knew they *were* cherubim.

21 [a]Each one had four faces and each one four wings, and the likeness of the hands of a man *was* under their wings.

22 And [a]the likeness of their faces *was* the same *as* the faces which I had seen by the River Chebar, their appearance and their persons. [b]They each went straight forward.

Judgment on Wicked Counselors

11 Then [a]the Spirit lifted me up and brought me to [b]the East Gate of the LORD's house, which faces eastward; and there [c]at the door of the gate were twenty-five men, among whom I saw Jaazaniah the son of Azzur, and Pelatiah the son of Benaiah, princes of the people.

2 And He said to me: "Son of man, these *are* the men who devise iniquity and give wicked counsel in this city,

3 "who say, '*The time is* not [a]near to build houses; [b]this *city is* the caldron, and we *are* the meat.'

4 "Therefore prophesy against them, prophesy, O son of man!"

5 Then [a]the Spirit of the LORD fell upon me, and said to me, "Speak! 'Thus says the LORD: "Thus you have said, O house of Israel; for [b]I know the things that come into your mind.

6 [a]"You have multiplied your slain in this city, and you have filled its streets with the slain."

7 'Therefore thus says the Lord GOD: [a]"Your slain whom you have laid in its midst, they *are* the meat, and this *city is* the caldron; [b]but I shall bring you out of the midst of it.

8 "You have [a]feared the sword; and I will bring a sword upon you," says the Lord GOD.

9 "And I will bring you out of its midst, and deliver you into the hands of strangers, and [a]execute judgments on you.

10 [a]"You shall fall by the sword. I will judge you at [b]the border of Israel. [c]Then you shall know that I *am* the LORD.

11 [a]"This *city* shall not be your caldron, nor shall you be the meat in its midst. I will judge you at the border of Israel.

12 "And you shall know that I *am* the LORD; for you have not walked in My statutes nor executed My judgments, but [a]have done according to the customs of the Gentiles which *are* all around you."'"

13 Now it happened, while I was prophesy-

KJV

that [a]Pelatiah the son of Benaiah died. Then [b]fell I down upon my face, and cried with a loud voice, and said, Ah Lord GOD! wilt thou make a full end of the remnant of Israel?

God Will Restore Israel

14 Again the word of the LORD came unto me, saying,

15 Son of man, thy brethren, *even* thy brethren, the men of thy kindred, and all the house of Israel wholly, *are* they unto whom the inhabitants of Jerusalem have said, Get you far from the LORD: unto us is this land given in possession.

16 Therefore say, Thus saith the Lord GOD; Although I have cast them far off among the heathen, and although I have scattered them among the countries, [a]yet will I be to them as a little sanctuary in the countries where they shall come.

17 Therefore say, Thus saith the Lord GOD; [a]I will even gather you from the people, and assemble you out of the countries where ye have been scattered, and I will give you the land of Israel.

18 And they shall come thither, and they shall take away all the [a]detestable things thereof and all the abominations thereof from thence.

19 And [a]I will give them one heart, and I will put [b]a new spirit within you; and I will take [c]the stony heart out of their flesh, and will give them an heart of flesh:

20 [a]That they may walk in my statutes, and keep mine ordinances, and do them: [b]and they shall be my people, and I will be their God.

21 But *as for them* whose heart walketh after the heart of their detestable things and their abominations, [a]I will recompense their way upon their own heads, saith the Lord GOD.

22 Then did the cherubims [a]lift up their wings, and the wheels beside them; and the glory of the God of Israel *was* over them above.

23 And [a]the glory of the LORD went up from the midst of the city, and stood [b]upon the mountain [c]which *is* on the east side of the city.

24 Afterwards [a]the spirit took me up, and brought me in a vision by the Spirit of God into Chaldea, to them of the captivity. So the vision that I had seen went up from me.

25 Then I spake unto them of the captivity all the things that the LORD had shewed me.

Judah's Captivity Portrayed

12 The word of the LORD also came unto me, saying,

2 Son of man, thou dwellest in the midst of [a]a rebellious house, which [b]have eyes to see, and see not; they have ears to hear, and hear not: [c]for they *are* a rebellious house.

3 Therefore, thou son of man, prepare thee stuff for removing, and remove by day in their sight; and thou shalt remove from thy place to another place in their sight: it may be they will consider, though they *be* a rebellious house.

4 Then shalt thou bring forth thy stuff by day in their sight, as stuff for removing: and thou shalt go forth at even in their sight, as they that go forth into captivity.

5 Dig thou through the wall in their sight, and carry out thereby.

6 In their sight shalt thou bear *it* upon *thy* shoulders, *and* carry *it* forth in the twilight: thou shalt cover thy face, that thou see not the ground: [a]for I have set thee *for* a sign unto the house of Israel.

7 And I did so as I was commanded: I brought forth my stuff by day, as stuff for captivity, and in the even I digged through the wall with mine hand; I brought *it* forth in the twilight, *and* I bare *it* upon *my* shoulder in their sight.

8 And in the morning came the word of the LORD unto me, saying,

13 [a]Acts 5:5 [b]Ezek. 9:8
16 [a]Ps. 90:1; 91:9; Is. 8:14; Jer. 29:7, 11
17 [a]Is. 11:11–16; Jer. 3:12, 18; 24:5; Ezek. 20:41, 42; 28:5
18 [a]Ezek. 37:23
19 [a]Jer. 32:39; Ezek. 36:26; Zeph. 3:9 [b]Ps. 51:10; [Jer. 31:33]; Ezek. 18:31 [c]Zech. 7:12; [Rom. 2:4, 5]
20 [a]Ps. 105:45 [b]Jer. 24:7; Ezek. 14:11; 36:28; 37:27
21 [a]Ezek. 9:10
22 [a]Ezek. 1:19
23 [a]Ezek. 8:4; 9:3 [b]Zech. 14:4 [c]Ezek. 43:2
24 [a]Ezek. 8:3; 2 Cor. 12:2–4

CHAPTER 12

2 [a]Is. 1:23; Ezek. 2:3, 6–8 [b]Is. 6:9; 42:20; Jer. 5:21; Matt. 13:13, 14; Mark 4:12; 8:18; [Luke 8:10; John 9:39–41; 12:40]; Acts 28:26; Rom. 11:8 [c]Ezek. 2:5
6 [a]Is. 8:18; Ezek. 4:3; 24:24

*

11:19 Lit. *you* (pl.)
11:24 Or *Babylon,* and so elsewhere in the book

NKJV

ing, that [a]Pelatiah the son of Benaiah died. Then [b]I fell on my face and cried with a loud voice, and said, "Ah, Lord GOD! Will You make a complete end of the remnant of Israel?"

God Will Restore Israel

14 Again the word of the LORD came to me, saying,

15 "Son of man, your brethren, your relatives, your countrymen, and all the house of Israel in its entirety, *are* those about whom the inhabitants of Jerusalem have said, 'Get far away from the LORD; this land has been given to us as a possession.'

16 "Therefore say, 'Thus says the Lord GOD: "Although I have cast them far off among the Gentiles, and although I have scattered them among the countries, [a]yet I shall be a little sanctuary for them in the countries where they have gone." '

17 "Therefore say, 'Thus says the Lord GOD: [a]"I will gather you from the peoples, assemble you from the countries where you have been scattered, and I will give you the land of Israel." '

18 "And they will go there, and they will take away all its [a]detestable things and all its abominations from there.

19 "Then [a]I will give them one heart, and I will put [b]a new spirit within *them, and take [c]the stony heart out of their flesh, and give them a heart of flesh,

20 [a]"that they may walk in My statutes and keep My judgments and do them; [b]and they shall be My people, and I will be their God.

21 "But *as for those* whose hearts follow the desire for their detestable things and their abominations, [a]I will recompense their deeds on their own heads," says the Lord GOD.

22 So the cherubim [a]lifted up their wings, with the wheels beside them, and the glory of the God of Israel *was* high above them.

23 And [a]the glory of the LORD went up from the midst of the city and stood [b]on the mountain, [c]which *is* on the east side of the city.

24 Then [a]the Spirit took me up and brought me in a vision by the Spirit of God into *Chaldea, to those in captivity. And the vision that I had seen went up from me.

25 So I spoke to those in captivity of all the things the LORD had shown me.

Judah's Captivity Portrayed

12 Now the word of the LORD came to me, saying:

2 "Son of man, you dwell in the midst of [a]a rebellious house, which [b]has eyes to see but does not see, and ears to hear but does not hear; [c]for they *are* a rebellious house.

3 "Therefore, son of man, prepare your belongings for captivity, and go into captivity by day in their sight. You shall go from your place into captivity to another place in their sight. It may be that they will consider, though they *are* a rebellious house.

4 "By day you shall bring out your belongings in their sight, as though going into captivity; and at evening you shall go in their sight, like those who go into captivity.

5 "Dig through the wall in their sight, and carry your belongings out through it.

6 "In their sight you shall bear *them* on *your* shoulders *and* carry *them* out at twilight; you shall cover your face, so that you cannot see the ground, [a]for I have made you a sign to the house of Israel."

7 So I did as I was commanded. I brought out my belongings by day, as though going into captivity, and at evening I dug through the wall with my hand. I brought *them* out at twilight, *and* I bore *them* on *my* shoulder in their sight.

8 And in the morning the word of the LORD came to me, saying,

KJV

9 Son of man, hath not the house of Israel, [a]the rebellious house, said unto thee, [b]What doest thou?

10 Say thou unto them, Thus saith the Lord GOD; This [a]burden *concerneth* the prince in Jerusalem, and all the house of Israel that *are* among them.

11 Say, [a]I *am* your sign: like as I have done, so shall it be done unto them: [b]they shall remove *and* go into captivity.

12 And [a]the prince that *is* among them shall bear upon *his* shoulder in the twilight, and shall go forth: they shall dig through the wall to carry out thereby: he shall cover his face, that he see not the ground with *his* eyes.

13 My [a]net also will I spread upon him, and he shall be taken in my snare: and [b]I will bring him to Babylon *to* the land of the Chaldeans; yet shall he not see it, though he shall die there.

14 And [a]I will scatter toward every wind all that *are* about him to help him, and all his bands; and [b]I will draw out the sword after them.

15 [a]And they shall know that I *am* the LORD, when I shall scatter them among the nations, and disperse them in the countries.

16 [a]But I will leave a few men of them from the sword, from the famine, and from the pestilence; that they may declare all their abominations among the heathen whither they come; and they shall know that I *am* the LORD.

Judgment Not Postponed

17 Moreover the word of the LORD came to me, saying,

18 Son of man, [a]eat thy bread with quaking, and drink thy water with trembling and with carefulness;

19 And say unto the people of the land, Thus saith the Lord GOD of the inhabitants of Jerusalem, *and* of the land of Israel; They shall eat their bread with carefulness, and drink their water with astonishment, that her land may [a]be desolate from all that is therein, [b]because of the violence of all them that dwell therein.

20 And the cities that are inhabited shall be laid waste, and the land shall be desolate; and ye shall know that I *am* the LORD.

21 And the word of the LORD came unto me, saying,

22 Son of man, what *is* that proverb *that* ye have in the land of Israel, saying, [a]The days are prolonged, and every vision faileth?

23 Tell them therefore, Thus saith the Lord GOD; I will make this proverb to cease, and they shall no more use it as a proverb in Israel; but say unto them, [a]The days are at hand, and the effect of every vision.

24 For [a]there shall be no more any [b]vain vision nor flattering divination within the house of Israel.

25 For I *am* the LORD: I will speak, and [a]the word that I shall speak shall come to pass; it shall be no more prolonged: for in your days, O rebellious house, will I say the word, and will [b]perform it, saith the Lord GOD.

26 Again the word of the LORD came to me, saying,

27 [a]Son of man, behold, *they of* the house of Israel say, The vision that he seeth *is* [b]for many days *to come,* and he prophesieth of the times *that are* far off.

28 [a]Therefore say unto them, Thus saith the Lord GOD; There shall none of my words be prolonged any more, but the word which I have spoken [b]shall be done, saith the Lord GOD.

Woe to Foolish Prophets

13 And the word of the LORD came unto me, saying,

2 Son of man, prophesy [a]against the prophets of Israel that prophesy, and say thou unto

---

9 [a]Ezek. 2:5 [b]Ezek. 17:12; 24:19
10 [a]Mal. 1:1
11 [a]Ezek. 12:6 [b]2 Kin. 25:4, 5, 7
12 [a]2 Kin. 25:4; Jer. 39:4; 52:7; Ezek. 12:6
13 [a]Job 19:6; Jer. 52:9; Lam. 1:13; Ezek. 17:20 [b]2 Kin. 25:7; Jer. 52:11; Ezek. 17:16
14 [a]2 Kin. 25:4; Ezek. 5:10 [b]Ezek. 5:2, 12
15 [a][Ps. 9:16]; Ezek. 6:7, 14; 12:16, 20
16 [a]2 Kin. 25:11, 22; Ezek. 6:8–10
18 [a]Lam. 5:9; Ezek. 4:16
19 [a]Jer. 10:22; Ezek. 6:6, 7, 14; Mic. 7:13; Zech. 7:14 [b]Ps. 107:34
22 [a]Jer. 5:12; Ezek. 11:3; 12:27; Amos 6:3; 2 Pet. 3:4
23 [a]Ps. 37:13; Joel 2:1; Zeph. 1:14
24 [a]Jer. 14:13–16; Ezek. 13:6; Zech. 13:2–4 [b]Lam. 2:14
25 [a][Is. 55:11]; Dan. 9:12; [Luke 21:33] [b]Num. 23:19; [Is. 14:24]
27 [a]Ezek. 12:22 [b]Dan. 10:14
28 [a]Ezek. 12:23, 25 [b]Jer. 4:7

CHAPTER 13

2 [a]Is. 28:7; Jer. 23:1–40; Lam. 2:14; Ezek. 22:25–28

NKJV

9 "Son of man, has not the house of Israel, [a]the rebellious house, said to you, [b]'What are you doing?'

10 "Say to them, 'Thus says the Lord GOD: "This [a]burden *concerns* the prince in Jerusalem and all the house of Israel who are among them." '

11 "Say, [a]'I *am* a sign to you. As I have done, so shall it be done to them; [b]they shall be carried away into captivity.'

12 "And [a]the prince who *is* among them shall bear *his belongings* on *his* shoulder at twilight and go out. They shall dig through the wall to carry *them* out through it. He shall cover his face, so that he cannot see the ground with *his* eyes.

13 "I will also spread My [a]net over him, and he shall be caught in My snare. [b]I will bring him to Babylon, *to* the land of the Chaldeans; yet he shall not see it, though he shall die there.

14 [a]"I will scatter to every wind all who *are* around him to help him, and all his troops; and [b]I will draw out the sword after them.

15 [a]"Then they shall know that I *am* the LORD, when I scatter them among the nations and disperse them throughout the countries.

16 [a]"But I will spare a few of their men from the sword, from famine, and from pestilence, that they may declare all their abominations among the Gentiles wherever they go. Then they shall know that I *am* the LORD."

Judgment Not Postponed

17 Moreover the word of the LORD came to me, saying,

18 "Son of man, [a]eat your bread with quaking, and drink your water with trembling and anxiety.

19 "And say to the people of the land, 'Thus says the Lord GOD to the inhabitants of Jerusalem *and* to the land of Israel: "They shall eat their bread with anxiety, and drink their water with dread, so that her land may [a]be emptied of all who are in it, [b]because of the violence of all those who dwell in it.

20 "Then the cities that are inhabited shall be laid waste, and the land shall become desolate; and you shall know that I *am* the LORD." ' "

21 And the word of the LORD came to me, saying,

22 "Son of man, what *is* this proverb *that* you *people* have about the land of Israel, which says, [a]'The days are prolonged, and every vision fails'?

23 "Tell them therefore, 'Thus says the Lord GOD: "I will lay this proverb to rest, and they shall no more use it as a proverb in Israel." But say to them, [a]"The days are at hand, and the fulfillment of every vision.

24 "For [a]no more shall there be any [b]false vision or flattering divination within the house of Israel.

25 "For I *am* the LORD. I speak, and [a]the word which I speak will come to pass; it will no more be postponed; for in your days, O rebellious house, I will say the word and [b]perform it," says the Lord GOD.' "

26 Again the word of the LORD came to me, saying,

27 [a]"Son of man, look, the house of Israel is saying, 'The vision that he sees *is* [b]for many days *from now,* and he prophesies of times far off.'

28 [a]"Therefore say to them, 'Thus says the Lord GOD: "None of My words will be postponed any more, but the word which I speak [b]will be done," says the Lord GOD.' "

Woe to Foolish Prophets

13 And the word of the LORD came to me, saying,

2 "Son of man, prophesy [a]against the prophets of Israel who prophesy, and say to

KJV

[b]them that prophesy out of their own [c]hearts, Hear ye the word of the LORD;

3 Thus saith the Lord GOD; Woe unto the foolish prophets, that follow their own spirit, and have seen nothing!

4 O Israel, thy prophets are [a]like the foxes in the deserts.

5 Ye [a]have not gone up into the gaps, neither made up the hedge for the house of Israel to stand in the battle in the day of the LORD.

6 [a]They have seen vanity and lying divination, saying, The LORD saith: and the LORD hath [b]not sent them: and they have made *others* to hope that they would confirm the word.

7 Have ye not seen a vain vision, and have ye not spoken a lying divination, whereas ye say, The LORD saith *it;* albeit I have not spoken?

8 Therefore thus saith the Lord GOD; Because ye have spoken vanity, and seen lies, therefore, behold, I *am* against you, saith the Lord GOD.

9 And mine hand shall be [a]upon the prophets that see vanity, and that [b]divine lies: they shall not be in the assembly of my people, [c]neither shall they be written in the writing of the house of Israel, [d]neither shall they enter into the land of Israel; [e]and ye shall know that I *am* the Lord GOD.

10 Because, even because they have seduced my people, saying, [a]Peace; and *there was* no peace; and one built up a wall, and, lo, others [b]daubed it with untempered *morter:*

11 Say unto them which daub *it* with untempered *morter,* that it shall fall: [a]there shall be an overflowing shower; and ye, O great hailstones, shall fall; and a stormy wind shall rend *it.*

12 Lo, when the wall is fallen, shall it not be said unto you, Where *is* the daubing wherewith ye have daubed *it?*

13 Therefore thus saith the Lord GOD; I will even rend *it* with a stormy wind in my fury; and there shall be an overflowing shower in mine anger, and great hailstones in *my* fury to consume *it.*

14 So will I break down the wall that ye have daubed with untempered *morter,* and bring it down to the ground, so that the foundation thereof shall be discovered, and it shall fall, and ye shall be consumed in the midst thereof: [a]and ye shall know that I *am* the LORD.

15 Thus will I accomplish my wrath upon the wall, and upon them that have daubed it with untempered *morter,* and will say unto you, The wall *is* no *more,* neither they that daubed it;

16 *To wit,* the prophets of Israel which prophesy concerning Jerusalem, and which [a]see visions of peace for her, and *there is* no peace, saith the Lord GOD.

17 Likewise, thou son of man, [a]set thy face against the daughters of thy people, [b]which prophesy out of their own heart; and prophesy thou against them,

18 And say, Thus saith the Lord GOD; Woe to the *women* that sew pillows to all armholes, and make kerchiefs upon the head of every stature to hunt souls! Will ye [a]hunt the souls of my people, and will ye save the souls alive *that come* unto you?

19 And will ye pollute me among my people [a]for handfuls of barley and for pieces of bread, to slay the souls that should not die, and to save the souls alive that should not live, by your lying to my people that hear *your* lies?

20 Wherefore thus saith the Lord GOD; Behold, I *am* against your pillows, wherewith ye there hunt the souls to make *them* fly, and I will tear them from your arms, and will let the souls go, *even* the souls that ye hunt to make *them* fly.

21 Your kerchiefs also will I tear, and deliver my people out of your hand, and they shall be no more in your hand to be hunted; [a]and ye shall know that I *am* the LORD.

22 Because with [a]lies ye have made the heart of the righteous sad, whom I have not made sad;

2 [b]Ezek. 13:17 [c]Jer. 14:14; 23:16, 26
4 [a]Song 2:15
5 [a]Ps. 106:23; [Jer. 23:22]; Ezek. 22:30
6 [a]Jer. 29:8; Ezek. 22:28 [b]Jer. 27:8–15
9 [a]Jer. 23:30 [b]Jer. 20:3–6 [c]Ezra 2:59, 62; Neh. 7:5; [Ps. 69:28] [d]Jer. 20:3–6 [e]Ezek. 11:10, 12
10 [a]Jer. 6:14; 8:11 [b]Ezek. 22:28
11 [a]Ezek. 38:22
14 [a]Ezek. 13:9, 21, 23; 14:8
16 [a]Jer. 6:14; 8:11; 28:9; Ezek. 13:10
17 [a]Ezek. 20:46; 21:2 [b]Ezek. 13:2; Rev. 2:20
18 [a][2 Pet. 2:14]
19 [a]1 Sam. 2:15–17; Prov. 28:21; Mic. 3:5; Rom. 16:18; 1 Pet. 5:2
21 [a]Ezek. 13:9
22 [a]Jer. 28:15

* **13:18** Lit. *over all the joints of My hands;* Vg. *under every elbow;* LXX, Tg. *on all elbows of the hands*

NKJV

[b]those who prophesy out of their own [c]heart, 'Hear the word of the LORD!' "

3 Thus says the Lord GOD: "Woe to the foolish prophets, who follow their own spirit and have seen nothing!

4 "O Israel, your prophets are [a]like foxes in the deserts.

5 "You [a]have not gone up into the gaps to build a wall for the house of Israel to stand in battle on the day of the LORD.

6 [a]"They have envisioned futility and false divination, saying, 'Thus says the LORD!' But the LORD has [b]not sent them; yet they hope that the word may be confirmed.

7 "Have you not seen a futile vision, and have you not spoken false divination? You say, 'The LORD says,' but I have not spoken."

8 Therefore thus says the Lord GOD: "Because you have spoken nonsense and envisioned lies, therefore I *am* indeed against you," says the Lord GOD.

9 "My hand will be [a]against the prophets who envision futility and who [b]divine lies; they shall not be in the assembly of My people, [c]nor be written in the record of the house of Israel, [d]nor shall they enter into the land of Israel. [e]Then you shall know that I *am* the Lord GOD.

10 "Because, indeed, because they have seduced My people, saying, [a]'Peace!' when *there is* no peace—and one builds a wall, and they [b]plaster it with untempered *mortar*—

11 "say to those who plaster *it* with untempered *mortar,* that it will fall. [a]There will be flooding rain, and you, O great hailstones, shall fall; and a stormy wind shall tear *it* down.

12 "Surely, when the wall has fallen, will it not be said to you, 'Where *is* the mortar with which you plastered *it?*' "

13 Therefore thus says the Lord GOD: "I will cause a stormy wind to break forth in My fury; and there shall be a flooding rain in My anger, and great hailstones in fury to consume *it.*

14 "So I will break down the wall you have plastered with untempered *mortar,* and bring it down to the ground, so that its foundation will be uncovered; it will fall, and you shall be consumed in the midst of it. [a]Then you shall know that I *am* the LORD.

15 "Thus will I accomplish My wrath on the wall and on those who have plastered it with untempered *mortar;* and I will say to you, 'The wall *is* no *more,* nor those who plastered it,

16 '*that is,* the prophets of Israel who prophesy concerning Jerusalem, and who [a]see visions of peace for her when *there is* no peace,' " says the Lord GOD.

17 "Likewise, son of man, [a]set your face against the daughters of your people, [b]who prophesy out of their own heart; prophesy against them,

18 "and say, 'Thus says the Lord GOD: "Woe to the *women* who sew *magic* charms *on their sleeves and make veils for the heads of people of every height to hunt souls! Will you [a]hunt the souls of My people, and keep yourselves alive?

19 "And will you profane Me among My people [a]for handfuls of barley and for pieces of bread, killing people who should not die, and keeping people alive who should not live, by your lying to My people who listen to lies?"

20 'Therefore thus says the Lord GOD: "Behold, I *am* against your *magic* charms by which you hunt souls there like birds. I will tear them from your arms, and let the souls go, the souls you hunt like birds.

21 "I will also tear off your veils and deliver My people out of your hand, and they shall no longer be as prey in your hand. [a]Then you shall know that I *am* the LORD.

22 "Because with [a]lies you have made the heart of the righteous sad, whom I have not made

KJV

and [b]strengthened the hands of the wicked, that he should not return from his wicked way, by promising him life:

23 Therefore [a]ye shall see no more vanity, nor divine divinations: for I will deliver my people out of your hand: and ye shall know that I *am* the LORD.

Idolatry Will Be Punished

14 Then [a]came certain of the elders of Israel unto me, and sat before me.

2 And the word of the LORD came unto me, saying,

3 Son of man, these men have set up their idols in their heart, and put [a]the stumblingblock of their iniquity before their face: [b]should I be enquired of at all by them?

4 Therefore speak unto them, and say unto them, Thus saith the Lord GOD; Every man of the house of Israel that setteth up his idols in his heart, and putteth the stumblingblock of his iniquity before his face, and cometh to the prophet; I the LORD will answer him that cometh according to the multitude of his idols;

5 That I may take the house of Israel in their own heart, because they are all estranged from me through their idols.

6 Therefore say unto the house of Israel, Thus saith the Lord GOD; Repent, and turn *yourselves* from your idols; and [a]turn away your faces from all your abominations.

7 For every one of the house of Israel, or of the stranger that sojourneth in Israel, which separateth himself from me, and setteth up his idols in his heart, and putteth the stumblingblock of his iniquity before his face, and cometh to a prophet to enquire of him concerning me; I the LORD will answer him by myself:

8 And [a]I will set my face against that man, and will make him a [b]sign and a proverb, and I will cut him off from the midst of my people; [c]and ye shall know that I *am* the LORD.

9 And if the prophet be deceived when he hath spoken a thing, I the LORD [a]have deceived that prophet, and I will stretch out my hand upon him, and will destroy him from the midst of my people Israel.

10 And they shall bear the punishment of their iniquity: the punishment of the prophet shall be even as the punishment of him that seeketh *unto him;*

11 That the house of Israel may [a]go no more astray from me, neither be polluted any more with all their transgressions; [b]but that they may be my people, and I may be their God, saith the Lord GOD.

Judgment on Persistent Unfaithfulness

12 The word of the LORD came again to me, saying,

13 Son of man, when the land sinneth against me by trespassing grievously, then will I stretch out mine hand upon it, and will break the [a]staff of the bread thereof, and will send famine upon it, and will cut off man and beast from it:

14 [a]Though these three men, Noah, Daniel, and Job, were in it, they should deliver *but* their own souls [b]by their righteousness, saith the Lord GOD.

15 If I cause [a]noisome beasts to pass through the land, and they spoil it, so that it be desolate, that no man may pass through because of the beasts:

16 [a]*Though* these three men *were* in it, *as* I live, saith the Lord GOD, they shall deliver neither sons nor daughters; they only shall be delivered, but the land shall be [b]desolate.

17 Or *if* [a]I bring a sword upon that land, and say, Sword, go through the land; so that I [b]cut off man and beast from it:

18 [a]Though these three men *were* in it, *as* I live, saith the Lord GOD, they shall deliver neither

---

22 [b]Jer. 23:14
23 [a]Ezek. 12:24; 13:6; Mic. 3:5, 6; Zech. 13:3

CHAPTER 14

1 [a]2 Kin. 6:32; Ezek. 8:1; 20:1; 33:31
3 [a]Ezek. 7:19; Zeph. 1:3 [b]2 Kin. 3:13; Is. 1:15; Jer. 11:11; Ezek. 20:3, 31
6 [a]1 Sam. 7:3; Neh. 1:9; Is. 2:20; 30:22; 55:6, 7; Ezek. 18:30
8 [a]Lev. 17:10; 20:3, 5, 6; Jer. 44:11; Ezek. 15:7 [b]Num. 26:10; Deut. 28:37; Ezek. 5:15 [c]Ezek. 6:7; 13:14
9 [a]1 Kin. 22:23; Job 12:16; Is. 66:4; Jer. 4:10; 2 Thess. 2:11
11 [a]Ps. 119:67, 71; Jer. 31:18, 19; [Heb. 12:11]; 2 Pet. 2:15 [b]Ezek. 11:20; 37:27
13 [a]Lev. 26:26; 2 Kin. 25:3; Is. 3:1; Jer. 52:6; Ezek. 4:16; 5:16
14 [a]Jer. 15:1 [b][Prov. 11:4]
15 [a]Lev. 26:22; Num. 21:6; Ezek. 5:17; 14:21
16 [a]Ezek. 14:14, 18, 20 [b]Ezek. 15:8; 33:28, 29
17 [a]Lev. 26:25; Ezek. 5:12; 21:3, 4; 29:8; 38:21 [b]Ezek. 25:13; Zeph. 1:3
18 [a]Ezek. 14:14

NKJV

sad; and you have [b]strengthened the hands of the wicked, so that he does not turn from his wicked way to save his life.

23 "Therefore [a]you shall no longer envision futility nor practice divination; for I will deliver My people out of your hand, and you shall know that I *am* the LORD." ' "

Idolatry Will Be Punished

14 Now [a]some of the elders of Israel came to me and sat before me.

2 And the word of the LORD came to me, saying,

3 "Son of man, these men have set up their idols in their hearts, and put before them [a]that which causes them to stumble into iniquity. [b]Should I let Myself be inquired of at all by them?

4 "Therefore speak to them, and say to them, 'Thus says the Lord GOD: "Everyone of the house of Israel who sets up his idols in his heart, and puts before him what causes him to stumble into iniquity, and then comes to the prophet, I the LORD will answer him who comes, according to the multitude of his idols,

5 "that I may seize the house of Israel by their heart, because they are all estranged from Me by their idols." '

6 "Therefore say to the house of Israel, 'Thus says the Lord GOD: "Repent, turn away from your idols, and [a]turn your faces away from all your abominations.

7 "For anyone of the house of Israel, or of the strangers who dwell in Israel, who separates himself from Me and sets up his idols in his heart and puts before him what causes him to stumble into iniquity, then comes to a prophet to inquire of him concerning Me, I the LORD will answer him by Myself.

8 [a]"I will set My face against that man and make him a [b]sign and a proverb, and I will cut him off from the midst of My people. [c]Then you shall know that I *am* the LORD.

9 "And if the prophet is induced to speak anything, I the LORD [a]have induced that prophet, and I will stretch out My hand against him and destroy him from among My people Israel.

10 "And they shall bear their iniquity; the punishment of the prophet shall be the same as the punishment of the one who inquired,

11 "that the house of Israel may [a]no longer stray from Me, nor be profaned anymore with all their transgressions, [b]but that they may be My people and I may be their God," says the Lord GOD.' "

Judgment on Persistent Unfaithfulness

12 The word of the LORD came again to me, saying:

13 "Son of man, when a land sins against Me by persistent unfaithfulness, I will stretch out My hand against it; I will cut off its [a]supply of bread, send famine on it, and cut off man and beast from it.

14 [a]"Even *if* these three men, Noah, Daniel, and Job, were in it, they would deliver *only* themselves [b]by their righteousness," says the Lord GOD.

15 "If I cause [a]wild beasts to pass through the land, and they empty it, and make it so desolate that no man may pass through because of the beasts,

16 "*even* [a]*though* these three men *were* in it, *as* I live," says the Lord GOD, "they would deliver neither sons nor daughters; only they would be delivered, and the land would be [b]desolate.

17 "Or *if* [a]I bring a sword on that land, and say, 'Sword, go through the land,' and I [b]cut off man and beast from it,

18 "even [a]*though* these three men *were* in it, *as* I live," says the Lord GOD, "they would de-

KJV

sons nor daughters, but they only shall be delivered themselves.

19 Or *if* I send [a]a pestilence into that land, and [b]pour out my fury upon it in blood, to cut off from it man and beast:

20 [a]Though Noah, Daniel, and Job, *were* in it, *as* I live, saith the Lord GOD, they shall deliver neither son nor daughter; they shall *but* deliver their own souls by their righteousness.

21 For thus saith the Lord GOD; How much more when [a]I send my four sore judgments upon Jerusalem, the sword, and the famine, and the noisome beast, and the pestilence, to cut off from it man and beast?

22 [a]Yet, behold, therein shall be left a remnant that shall be [b]brought forth, *both* sons and daughters: behold, they shall come forth unto you, and [c]ye shall see their way and their doings: and ye shall be comforted concerning the evil that I have brought upon Jerusalem, *even* concerning all that I have brought upon it.

23 And they shall comfort you, when ye see their ways and their doings: and ye shall know that I have not done [a]without cause all that I have done in it, saith the Lord GOD.

The Outcast Vine

15 And the word of the LORD came unto me, saying,

2 Son of man, What is the vine tree more than any tree, *or than* a branch which is among the trees of the forest?

3 Shall wood be taken thereof to do any work? or will *men* take a pin of it to hang any vessel thereon?

4 Behold, [a]it is cast into the fire for fuel; the fire devoureth both the ends of it, and the midst of it is burned. Is it meet for *any* work?

5 Behold, when it was whole, it was meet for no work: how much less shall it be meet yet for *any* work, when the fire hath devoured it, and it is burned?

6 Therefore thus saith the Lord GOD; As the vine tree among the trees of the forest, which I have given to the fire for fuel, so will I give the inhabitants of Jerusalem.

7 And [a]I will set my face against them; [b]they shall go out from *one* fire, and *another* fire shall devour them; [c]and ye shall know that I *am* the LORD, when I set my face against them.

8 And I will make the land desolate, because they have committed a trespass, saith the Lord GOD.

God's Love for Jerusalem

16 Again the word of the LORD came unto me, saying,

2 Son of man, [a]cause Jerusalem to know her abominations,

3 And say, Thus saith the Lord GOD unto Jerusalem; Thy birth [a]and thy nativity *is* of the land of Canaan; [b]thy father *was* an Amorite, and thy mother an Hittite.

4 And *as for* thy nativity, [a]in the day thou wast born thy navel was not cut, neither wast thou washed in water to supple *thee;* thou wast not salted at all, nor swaddled at all.

5 None eye pitied thee, to do any of these unto thee, to have compassion upon thee; but thou wast cast out in the open field, to the lothing of thy person, in the day that thou wast born.

6 And when I passed by thee, and saw thee polluted in thine own blood, I said unto thee *when thou wast* in thy blood, Live; yea, I said unto thee *when thou wast* in thy blood, Live.

7 [a]I have caused thee to multiply as the bud of the field, and thou hast increased and waxen great, and thou art come to excellent ornaments: *thy* breasts are fashioned, and thine hair is grown, whereas thou *wast* naked and bare.

19 [a]2 Sam. 24:15; Ezek. 38:22 [b]Ezek. 7:8
20 [a]Ezek. 14:14
21 [a]Ezek. 5:17; 33:27; Amos 4:6–10; Rev. 6:8
22 [a]2 Kin. 25:11, 12; Ezra 2:1; Ezek. 12:16; 36:20 [b]Ezek. 6:8 [c]Ezek. 20:43
23 [a]Jer. 22:8, 9

CHAPTER 15

4 [a][John 15:6]
7 [a]Lev. 26:17; [Ps. 34:16]; Jer. 21:10; Ezek. 14:8 [b]Is. 24:18 [c]Ezek. 7:4

CHAPTER 16

2 [a]Is. 58:1; Ezek. 20:4; 22:2
3 [a]Ezek. 21:30 [b]Gen. 15:16; Deut. 7:1; Josh. 24:15; Ezek. 16:45
4 [a]Hos. 2:3
7 [a]Ex. 1:7; Deut. 1:10

NKJV

liver neither sons nor daughters, but only they themselves would be delivered.

19 "Or *if* I send [a]a pestilence into that land and [b]pour out My fury on it in blood, and cut off from it man and beast,

20 "even [a]*though* Noah, Daniel, and Job *were* in it, *as* I live," says the Lord GOD, "they would deliver neither son nor daughter; they would deliver *only* themselves by their righteousness."

21 For thus says the Lord GOD: "How much more it shall be when [a]I send My four severe judgments on Jerusalem—the sword and famine and wild beasts and pestilence—to cut off man and beast from it?

22 [a]"Yet behold, there shall be left in it a remnant who will be [b]brought out, *both* sons and daughters; surely they will come out to you, and [c]you will see their ways and their doings. Then you will be comforted concerning the disaster that I have brought upon Jerusalem, all that I have brought upon it.

23 "And they will comfort you, when you see their ways and their doings; and you shall know that I have done nothing [a]without cause that I have done in it," says the Lord GOD.

The Outcast Vine

15 Then the word of the LORD came to me, saying:

2 "Son of man, how is the wood of the vine *better* than any other wood, the vine branch which is among the trees of the forest?

3 "Is wood taken from it to make any object? Or can *men* make a peg from it to hang any vessel on?

4 "Instead, [a]it is thrown into the fire for fuel; the fire devours both ends of it, and its middle is burned. Is it useful for *any* work?

5 "Indeed, when it was whole, no object could be made from it. How much less will it be useful for *any* work when the fire has devoured it, and it is burned?

6 "Therefore thus says the Lord GOD: 'Like the wood of the vine among the trees of the forest, which I have given to the fire for fuel, so I will give up the inhabitants of Jerusalem;

7 'and [a]I will set My face against them. [b]They will go out from *one* fire, but *another* fire shall devour them. [c]Then you shall know that I *am* the LORD, when I set My face against them.

8 'Thus I will make the land desolate, because they have persisted in unfaithfulness,' says the Lord GOD."

God's Love for Jerusalem

16 Again the word of the LORD came to me, saying,

2 "Son of man, [a]cause Jerusalem to know her abominations,

3 "and say, 'Thus says the Lord GOD to Jerusalem: "Your birth [a]and your nativity *are* from the land of Canaan; [b]your father *was* an Amorite and your mother a Hittite.

4 "*As for* your nativity, [a]on the day you were born your navel cord was not cut, nor were you washed in water to cleanse *you;* you were not rubbed with salt nor wrapped in swaddling cloths.

5 "No eye pitied you, to do any of these things for you, to have compassion on you; but you were thrown out into the open field, when you yourself were loathed on the day you were born.

6 "And when I passed by you and saw you struggling in your own blood, I said to you in your blood, 'Live!' Yes, I said to you in your blood, 'Live!'

7 [a]"I made you thrive like a plant in the field; and you grew, matured, and became very beautiful. *Your* breasts were formed, your hair grew, but you *were* naked and bare.

KJV

8 Now when I passed by thee, and looked upon thee, behold, thy time *was* the time of love; [a]and I spread my skirt over thee, and covered thy nakedness: yea, I [b]sware unto thee, and entered into a [c]covenant with thee, saith the Lord GOD, and [d]thou becamest mine.

9 Then washed I thee with water; yea, I throughly washed away thy blood from thee, and I anointed thee with oil.

10 I clothed thee also with broidered work, and shod thee with badgers' skin, and I girded thee about with fine linen, and I covered thee with silk.

11 I decked thee also with ornaments, and I [a]put bracelets upon thy hands, [b]and a chain on thy neck.

12 And I put a jewel on thy forehead, and earrings in thine ears, and a beautiful crown upon thine head.

13 Thus wast thou decked with gold and silver; and thy raiment *was of* fine linen, and silk, and broidered work; [a]thou didst eat fine flour, and honey, and oil: and thou wast exceeding [b]beautiful, and thou didst prosper into a kingdom.

14 And [a]thy renown went forth among the heathen for thy beauty: for it *was* perfect through my comeliness, which I had put upon thee, saith the Lord GOD.

Jerusalem's Harlotry

15 [a]But thou didst trust in thine own beauty, [b]and playedst the harlot because of thy renown, and pouredst out thy fornications on every one that passed by; his it was.

16 [a]And of thy garments thou didst take, and deckedst thy high places with divers colours, and playedst the harlot thereupon: *the like things* shall not come, neither shall it be *so*.

17 Thou hast also taken thy fair jewels of my gold and of my silver, which I had given thee, and madest to thyself images of men, and didst commit whoredom with them,

18 And tookest thy broidered garments, and coveredst them: and thou hast set mine oil and mine incense before them.

19 [a]My meat also which I gave thee, fine flour, and oil, and honey, *wherewith* I fed thee, thou hast even set it before them for a sweet savour: and *thus* it was, saith the Lord GOD.

20 [a]Moreover thou hast taken thy sons and thy daughters, whom thou hast borne unto me, and these hast thou sacrificed unto them to be devoured. *Is this* of thy whoredoms a small matter,

21 That thou hast slain my children, and delivered them to cause them to pass through *the* [a]*fire* for them?

22 And in all thine abominations and thy whoredoms thou hast not remembered the days of thy [a]youth, [b]when thou wast naked and bare, *and* wast polluted in thy blood.

23 And it came to pass after all thy wickedness, (woe, woe unto thee! saith the Lord GOD;)

24 *That* [a]thou hast also built unto thee an eminent place, and [b]hast made thee an high place in every street.

25 Thou hast built thy high place [a]at every head of the way, and hast made thy beauty to be abhorred, and hast opened thy feet to every one that passed by, and multiplied thy whoredoms.

26 Thou hast also committed fornication with [a]the Egyptians thy neighbours, great of flesh; and hast increased thy whoredoms, to [b]provoke me to anger.

27 Behold, therefore I have stretched out my hand over thee, and have diminished thine ordinary *food*, and delivered thee unto the will of them that hate thee, [a]the daughters of the Philistines, which are ashamed of thy lewd way.

28 Thou hast played the whore also with the [a]Assyrians, because thou wast unsatiable; yea,

---

8 [a]Ruth 3:9; Jer. 2:2 [b]Gen. 22:16–18 [c]Ex. 24:6–8 [d][Ex. 19:5]; Jer. 2:2; Ezek. 20:5; [Hos. 2:19, 20]
11 [a]Gen. 24:22, 47; Is. 3:19; Ezek. 23:42 [b]Gen. 41:42; Prov. 1:9
13 [a]Deut. 32:13, 14 [b]Ps. 48:2
14 [a]Ps. 50:2; Lam. 2:15
15 [a]Deut. 32:15; Jer. 7:4; Mic. 3:11 [b]Is. 1:21; 57:8; Jer. 2:20; 3:2, 6, 20; Ezek. 23:11–20; Hos. 1:2
16 [a]2 Kin. 23:7; Ezek. 7:20; Hos. 2:8
19 [a]Hos. 2:8
20 [a]2 Kin. 16:3; Ps. 106:37; Is. 57:5; Jer. 7:31; Ezek. 20:26
21 [a]2 Kin. 17:17; Jer. 19:5; Ezek. 20:31; 23:37
22 [a]Jer. 2:2; Hos. 11:1 [b]Ezek. 16:4–6
24 [a]Jer. 11:13; Ezek. 16:31, 39; 20:28, 29 [b]Ps. 78:58; Is. 57:7; Jer. 2:20; 3:2
25 [a]Prov. 9:14
26 [a]Ezek. 16:26; 20:7, 8 [b]Deut. 31:20
27 [a]2 Chr. 28:18; Is. 9:12; Ezek. 16:57
28 [a]2 Kin. 16:7, 10–18; 2 Chr. 28:16, 20–23; Jer. 2:18, 36; Ezek. 23:12; Hos. 10:6

NKJV

8 "When I passed by you again and looked upon you, indeed your time *was* the time of love; [a]so I spread My wing over you and covered your nakedness. Yes, I [b]swore an oath to you and entered into a [c]covenant with you, and [d]you became Mine," says the Lord GOD.

9 "Then I washed you in water; yes, I thoroughly washed off your blood, and I anointed you with oil.

10 "I clothed you in embroidered cloth and gave you sandals of badger skin; I clothed you with fine linen and covered you with silk.

11 "I adorned you with ornaments, [a]put bracelets on your wrists, [b]and a chain on your neck.

12 "And I put a jewel in your nose, earrings in your ears, and a beautiful crown on your head.

13 "Thus you were adorned with gold and silver, and your clothing *was of* fine linen, silk, and embroidered cloth. [a]You ate *pastry of* fine flour, honey, and oil. You were exceedingly [b]beautiful, and succeeded to royalty.

14 [a]"Your fame went out among the nations because of your beauty, for it *was* perfect through My splendor which I had bestowed on you," says the Lord GOD.

Jerusalem's Harlotry

15 [a]"But you trusted in your own beauty, [b]played the harlot because of your fame, and poured out your harlotry on everyone passing by who *would have* it.

16 [a]"You took some of your garments and adorned multicolored high places for yourself, and played the harlot on them. *Such* things should not happen, nor be.

17 "You have also taken your beautiful jewelry from My gold and My silver, which I had given you, and made for yourself male images and played the harlot with them.

18 "You took your embroidered garments and covered them, and you set My oil and My incense before them.

19 "Also [a]My food which I gave you—the pastry of fine flour, oil, and honey *which* I fed you—you set it before them as sweet incense; and *so* it was," says the Lord GOD.

20 [a]"Moreover you took your sons and your daughters, whom you bore to Me, and these you sacrificed to them to be devoured. *Were* your *acts* of harlotry a small matter,

21 "that you have slain My children and offered them up to them by causing them to pass through *the* [a]*fire?*

22 "And in all your abominations and acts of harlotry you did not remember the days of your [a]youth, [b]when you were naked and bare, struggling in your blood.

23 "Then it was so, after all your wickedness—'Woe, woe to you!' says the Lord GOD—

24 *"that* [a]you also built for yourself a shrine, and [b]made a high place for yourself in every street.

25 "You built your high places [a]at the head of every road, and made your beauty to be abhorred. You offered yourself to everyone who passed by, and multiplied your acts of harlotry.

26 "You also committed harlotry with [a]the Egyptians, your very fleshly neighbors, and increased your acts of harlotry to [b]provoke Me to anger.

27 "Behold, therefore, I stretched out My hand against you, diminished your allotment, and gave you up to the will of those who hate you, [a]the daughters of the Philistines, who were ashamed of your lewd behavior.

28 "You also played the harlot with the [a]Assyrians, because you were insatiable; indeed you

KJV

thou hast played the harlot with them, and yet couldest not be satisfied.

29 Thou hast moreover multiplied thy fornication in the land of Canaan [a]unto Chaldea; and yet thou wast not satisfied herewith.

30 How weak is thine heart, saith the Lord God, seeing thou doest all these *things,* the work of an imperious whorish woman;

Jerusalem's Adultery

31 In that [a]thou buildest thine eminent place in the head of every way, and makest thine high place in every street; and hast not been as an harlot, in that thou scornest [b]hire;

32 *But as* a wife that committeth adultery, *which* taketh strangers instead of her husband!

33 They give gifts to all whores: but [a]thou givest thy gifts to all thy lovers, and hirest them, that they may come unto thee on every side for thy whoredom.

34 And the contrary is in thee from *other* women in thy whoredoms, whereas none followeth thee to commit whoredoms: and in that thou givest a reward, and no reward is given unto thee, therefore thou art contrary.

Jerusalem's Lovers Will Abuse Her

35 Wherefore, O harlot, hear the word of the Lord:

36 Thus saith the Lord God; Because thy filthiness was poured out, and thy nakedness discovered through thy whoredoms with thy lovers, and with all the idols of thy abominations, and by [a]the blood of thy children, which thou didst give unto them;

37 Behold, therefore [a]I will gather all thy lovers, with whom thou hast taken pleasure, and all *them* that thou hast loved, with all *them* that thou hast hated; I will even gather them round about against thee, and will discover thy nakedness unto them, that they may see all thy nakedness.

38 And I will judge thee, as [a]women that break wedlock and [b]shed blood are judged; and I will give thee blood in fury and jealousy.

39 And I will also give thee into their hand, and they shall throw down [a]thine eminent place, and shall break down thy high places: [b]they shall strip thee also of thy clothes, and shall take thy fair jewels, and leave thee naked and bare.

40 [a]They shall also bring up a company against thee, [b]and they shall stone thee with stones, and thrust thee through with their swords.

41 And they shall [a]burn thine houses with fire, and [b]execute judgments upon thee in the sight of many women: and I will cause thee to [c]cease from playing the harlot, and thou also shalt give no hire any more.

42 So [a]will I make my fury toward thee to rest, and my jealousy shall depart from thee, and I will be quiet, and will be no more angry.

43 Because [a]thou hast not remembered the days of thy youth, but hast fretted me in all these *things;* behold, therefore [b]I also will recompense thy way upon *thine* head, saith the Lord God: and thou shalt not commit this lewdness above all thine abominations.

More Wicked than Samaria and Sodom

44 Behold, every one that useth proverbs shall use *this* proverb against thee, saying, As *is* the mother, *so is* her daughter.

45 Thou *art* thy mother's daughter, that lotheth her husband and her children; and thou *art* the [a]sister of thy sisters, which lothed their husbands and their children: [b]your mother *was* an Hittite, and your father an Amorite.

46 And thine elder sister *is* Samaria, she and her daughters that dwell at thy left hand: and [a]thy younger sister, that dwelleth at thy right hand, *is* Sodom and her daughters.

47 Yet hast thou not walked after their ways, nor done after their abominations: but, as *if that*

29 [a]Ezek. 23:14–17
31 [a]Ezek. 16:24, 39 [b]Is. 52:3
33 [a]Is. 30:6; 57:9; Ezek. 16:41; Hos. 8:9, 10
36 [a]Jer. 2:34; Ezek. 16:20
37 [a]Jer. 13:22, 26; Lam. 1:8; Ezek. 23:9, 10, 22, 29; Hos. 2:10; 8:10; Nah. 3:5
38 [a]Lev. 20:10; Deut. 22:22; Ezek. 23:45 [b]Gen. 9:6; Ex. 21:12; Ezek. 16:20, 36
39 [a]Ezek. 16:24, 31 [b]Ezek. 23:26; Hos. 2:3
40 [a]Ezek. 23:45–47; Hab. 1:6–10 [b]John 8:5, 7
41 [a]Deut. 13:16; 2 Kin. 25:9; Jer. 39:8; 52:13 [b]Ezek. 5:8; 23:10, 48 [c]Ezek. 23:27
42 [a]2 Sam. 24:25; Ezek. 5:13; 21:17; Zech. 6:8
43 [a]Ps. 78:42; Ezek. 16:22 [b]Ezek. 9:10; 11:21; 22:31
45 [a]Ezek. 23:2–4 [b]Ezek. 16:3
46 [a]Deut. 32:32; Is. 1:10

NKJV

played the harlot with them and still were not satisfied.

29 "Moreover you multiplied your acts of harlotry as far as the land of the trader, [a]Chaldea; and even then you were not satisfied.

30 "How degenerate is your heart!" says the Lord God, "seeing you do all these *things,* the deeds of a brazen harlot.

Jerusalem's Adultery

31 [a]"You erected your shrine at the head of every road, and built your high place in every street. Yet you were not like a harlot, because you scorned [b]payment.

32 "*You are* an adulterous wife, *who* takes strangers instead of her husband.

33 "Men make payment to all harlots, but [a]you made your payments to all your lovers, and hired them to come to you from all around for your harlotry.

34 "You are the opposite of *other* women in your harlotry, because no one solicited you to be a harlot. In that you gave payment but no payment was given you, therefore you are the opposite."

Jerusalem's Lovers Will Abuse Her

35 'Now then, O harlot, hear the word of the Lord!

36 'Thus says the Lord God: "Because your filthiness was poured out and your nakedness uncovered in your harlotry with your lovers, and with all your abominable idols, and because of [a]the blood of your children which you gave to them,

37 "surely, therefore, [a]I will gather all your lovers with whom you took pleasure, all those you loved, *and* all those you hated; I will gather them from all around against you and will uncover your nakedness to them, that they may see all your nakedness.

38 "And I will judge you as [a]women who break wedlock or [b]shed blood are judged; I will bring blood upon you in fury and jealousy.

39 "I will also give you into their hand, and they shall throw down your shrines and break down [a]your high places. [b]They shall also strip you of your clothes, take your beautiful jewelry, and leave you naked and bare.

40 [a]"They shall also bring up an assembly against you, [b]and they shall stone you with stones and thrust you through with their swords.

41 "They shall [a]burn your houses with fire, and [b]execute judgments on you in the sight of many women; and I will make you [c]cease playing the harlot, and you shall no longer hire lovers.

42 "So [a]I will lay to rest My fury toward you, and My jealousy shall depart from you. I will be quiet, and be angry no more.

43 "Because [a]you did not remember the days of your youth, but *agitated Me with all these *things,* surely [b]I will also recompense your deeds on *your own* head," says the Lord God. "And you shall not commit lewdness in addition to all your abominations.

More Wicked than Samaria and Sodom

44 "Indeed everyone who quotes proverbs will use *this* proverb against you: 'Like mother, like daughter!'

45 "You *are* your mother's daughter, loathing husband and children; and you *are* the [a]sister of your sisters, who loathed their husbands and children; [b]your mother *was* a Hittite and your father an Amorite.

46 "Your elder sister *is* Samaria, who dwells with her daughters to the north of you; and [a]your younger sister, who dwells to the south of you, *is* Sodom and her daughters.

47 "You did not walk in their ways nor act according to their abominations; but, as *if that*

***16:43** So with LXX, Syr., Tg., Vg.; MT *were agitated with Me*

KJV

were a very little *thing*, [a]thou wast corrupted more than they in all thy ways.

48 *As* I live, saith the Lord GOD, [a]Sodom thy sister hath not done, she nor her daughters, as thou hast done, thou and thy daughters.

49 Behold, this was the iniquity of thy sister Sodom, pride, [a]fulness of bread, and abundance of idleness was in her and in her daughters, neither did she strengthen the hand of the poor and needy.

50 And they were haughty, and [a]committed abomination before me: therefore [b]I took them away as I saw *good*.

51 Neither hath Samaria committed [a]half of thy sins; but thou hast multiplied thine abominations more than they, and [b]hast justified thy sisters in all thine abominations which thou hast done.

52 Thou also, which hast judged thy sisters, bear thine own shame for thy sins that thou hast committed more abominable than they: they are more righteous than thou: yea, be thou confounded also, and bear thy shame, in that thou hast justified thy sisters.

53 [a]When I shall bring again their captivity, the captivity of Sodom and her daughters, and the captivity of Samaria and her daughters, then *will I bring again* [b]the captivity of thy captives in the midst of them:

54 That thou mayest bear thine own shame, and mayest be confounded in all that thou hast done, in that thou art [a]a comfort unto them.

55 When thy sisters, Sodom and her daughters, shall return to their former estate, and Samaria and her daughters shall return to their former estate, then thou and thy daughters shall return to your former estate.

56 For thy sister Sodom was not mentioned by thy mouth in the day of thy pride,

57 Before thy wickedness was discovered, as at the time of *thy* [a]reproach of the daughters of Syria, and all *that are* round about her, [b]the daughters of the Philistines, which despise thee round about.

58 [a]Thou hast borne thy lewdness and thine abominations, saith the LORD.

59 For thus saith the Lord GOD; I will even deal with thee as thou hast done, which hast [a]despised [b]the oath in breaking the covenant.

An Everlasting Covenant

60 Nevertheless I will [a]remember my covenant with thee in the days of thy youth, and I will establish unto thee [b]an everlasting covenant.

61 Then [a]thou shalt remember thy ways, and be ashamed, when thou shalt receive thy sisters, thine elder and thy younger: and I will give them unto thee for [b]daughters, [c]but not by thy covenant.

62 [a]And I will establish my covenant with thee; and thou shalt know that I *am* the LORD:

63 That thou mayest [a]remember, and be confounded, [b]and never open thy mouth any more because of thy shame, when I am pacified toward thee for all that thou hast done, saith the Lord GOD.

The Eagles and the Vine

17 And the word of the LORD came unto me, saying,

2 Son of man, put forth a riddle, and speak a [a]parable unto the house of Israel;

3 And say, Thus saith the Lord GOD; [a]A great eagle with great wings, longwinged, full of feathers, which had divers colours, came unto Lebanon, and [b]took the highest branch of the cedar:

4 He cropped off the top of his young twigs,

---

47 [a]2 Kin. 21:9; Ezek. 5:6, 7
48 [a]Is. 3:9; Lam. 4:6; Matt. 10:15; 11:24; Rev. 11:8
49 [a]Gen. 13:10; Is. 22:13; Amos 6:4–6
50 [a]Gen. 13:13; 18:20; 19:5 [b]Gen. 19:24
51 [a]Ezek. 23:11 [b]Jer. 3:8–11; Matt. 12:41
53 [a]Is. 1:9; [Ezek. 16:60] [b]Jer. 20:16
54 [a]Ezek. 14:22
57 [a]2 Kin. 16:5; 2 Chr. 28:18; Is. 7:1; Ezek. 5:14, 15; 22:4 [b]Ezek. 16:27
58 [a]Ezek. 23:49
59 [a]Ezek. 17:13 [b]Deut. 29:12
60 [a]Lev. 26:42–45; Ps. 106:45 [b]Is. 55:3; Jer. 32:40; 50:5; Ezek. 37:26
61 [a]Jer. 50:4, 5; Ezek. 20:43; 36:31 [b]Is. 54:1; 60:4; [Gal. 4:26] [c]Jer. 31:31
62 [a]Hos. 2:19, 20
63 [a]Ezek. 36:31, 32; Dan. 9:7, 8 [b]Ps. 39:9; [Rom. 3:19]

CHAPTER 17

2 [a]Ezek. 20:49; 24:3
3 [a]Jer. 48:40; Ezek. 17:12; Hos. 8:1 [b]2 Kin. 24:12

*

16:50 Vg. *you saw;* LXX *he saw;* Tg. *as was revealed to Me*
16:57 Heb. *Aram;* so with MT, LXX, Tg., Vg.; many Heb. mss., Syr. *Edom*

NKJV

were too little, [a]you became more corrupt than they in all your ways.

48 "*As* I live," says the Lord GOD, "neither [a]your sister Sodom nor her daughters have done as you and your daughters have done.

49 "Look, this was the iniquity of your sister Sodom: She and her daughter had pride, [a]fullness of food, and abundance of idleness; neither did she strengthen the hand of the poor and needy.

50 "And they were haughty and [a]committed abomination before Me; therefore [b]I took them away as *I saw *fit*.

51 "Samaria did not commit [a]half of your sins; but you have multiplied your abominations more than they, and [b]have justified your sisters by all the abominations which you have done.

52 "You who judged your sisters, bear your own shame also, because the sins which you committed were more abominable than theirs; they are more righteous than you. Yes, be disgraced also, and bear your own shame, because you justified your sisters.

53 [a]"When I bring back their captives, the captives of Sodom and her daughters, and the captives of Samaria and her daughters, then *I will also bring back* [b]the captives of your captivity among them,

54 "that you may bear your own shame and be disgraced by all that you did when [a]you comforted them.

55 "When your sisters, Sodom and her daughters, return to their former state, and Samaria and her daughters return to their former state, then you and your daughters will return to your former state.

56 "For your sister Sodom was not a byword in your mouth in the days of your pride,

57 "before your wickedness was uncovered. It was like the time of the [a]reproach of the daughters of *Syria and all *those* around her, and of [b]the daughters of the Philistines, who despise you everywhere.

58 [a]"You have paid for your lewdness and your abominations," says the LORD.

59 'For thus says the Lord GOD: "I will deal with you as you have done, who [a]despised [b]the oath by breaking the covenant.

An Everlasting Covenant

60 "Nevertheless I will [a]remember My covenant with you in the days of your youth, and I will establish [b]an everlasting covenant with you.

61 "Then [a]you will remember your ways and be ashamed, when you receive your older and your younger sisters; for I will give them to you for [b]daughters, [c]but not because of My covenant with you.

62 [a]"And I will establish My covenant with you. Then you shall know that I *am* the LORD,

63 "that you may [a]remember and be ashamed, [b]and never open your mouth anymore because of your shame, when I provide you an atonement for all you have done," says the Lord GOD.' "

The Eagles and the Vine

17 And the word of the LORD came to me, saying,

2 "Son of man, pose a riddle, and speak a [a]parable to the house of Israel,

3 "and say, 'Thus says the Lord GOD:

[a]"A great eagle with large wings and long
pinions,
Full of feathers of various colors,
Came to Lebanon
And [b]took from the cedar the highest
branch.

4 He cropped off its topmost young twig

KJV

and carried it into a land of traffick; he set it in a city of merchants.

5 He took also of the seed of the land, and planted it in [a]a fruitful field; he placed *it* by great waters, *and* set it [b]*as* a willow tree.

6 And it grew, and became a spreading vine [a]of low stature, whose branches turned toward him, and the roots thereof were under him: so it became a vine, and brought forth branches, and shot forth sprigs.

7 There was also another great eagle with great wings and many feathers: and, behold, [a]this vine did bend her roots toward him, and shot forth her branches toward him, that he might water it by the furrows of her plantation.

8 It was planted in a good soil by great waters, that it might bring forth branches, and that it might bear fruit, that it might be a goodly vine.

9 Say thou, Thus saith the Lord GOD; Shall it prosper? [a]shall he not pull up the roots thereof, and cut off the fruit thereof, that it wither? it shall wither in all the leaves of her spring, even without great power or many people to pluck it up by the roots thereof.

10 Yea, behold, *being* planted, shall it prosper? [a]shall it not utterly wither, when the east wind toucheth it? it shall wither in the furrows where it grew.

11 Moreover the word of the LORD came unto me, saying,

12 Say now to [a]the rebellious house, Know ye not what these *things mean?* tell *them,* Behold, [b]the king of Babylon is come to Jerusalem, and hath taken the king thereof, and the princes thereof, and led them with him to Babylon;

13 [a]And hath taken of the king's seed, and made a covenant with him, [b]and hath taken an oath of him: he hath also taken the mighty of the land:

14 That the kingdom might be [a]base, that it might not lift itself up, *but* that by keeping of his covenant it might stand.

15 But [a]he rebelled against him in sending his ambassadors into Egypt, [b]that they might give him horses and much people. [c]Shall he prosper? shall he escape that doeth such *things?* or shall he break the covenant, and be delivered?

16 *As* I live, saith the Lord GOD, surely [a]in the place *where* the king *dwelleth* that made him king, whose oath he despised, and whose covenant he brake, *even* with him in the midst of Babylon he shall die.

17 [a]Neither shall Pharaoh with *his* mighty army and great company make for him in the war, [b]by casting up mounts, and building forts, to cut off many persons:

18 Seeing he despised the oath by breaking the covenant, when, lo, he had [a]given his hand, and hath done all these *things,* he shall not escape.

19 Therefore thus saith the Lord GOD; *As* I live, surely mine oath that he hath despised, and my covenant that he hath broken, even it will I recompense upon his own head.

20 And I will [a]spread my net upon him, and he shall be taken in my snare, and I will bring him to Babylon, and [b]will plead with him there for his trespass that he hath trespassed against me.

5 [a]Deut. 8:7–9 [b]Is. 44:4
6 [a]Ezek. 17:14
7 [a]Ezek. 17:15
9 [a]2 Kin. 25:7
10 [a]Ezek. 19:12; Hos. 13:15
12 [a]Ezek. 2:3–5; 12:9 [b]2 Kin. 24:11–16; Ezek. 1:2; 17:3
13 [a]2 Kin. 24:17; Jer. 37:1; Ezek. 17:5 [b]2 Chr. 36:13
14 [a]Ezek. 29:14
15 [a]2 Kin. 24:20; 2 Chr. 36:13; Jer. 52:3; Ezek. 17:7 [b]Deut. 17:16; Is. 31:1, 3; 36:6, 9 [c]Ezek. 17:9
16 [a]Jer. 52:11; Ezek. 12:13
17 [a]Jer. 37:7; Ezek. 29:6 [b]Jer. 52:4; Ezek. 4:2
18 [a]1 Chr. 29:24; Lam. 5:6
20 [a]Ezek. 12:13 [b]Jer. 2:35; Ezek. 20:36

NKJV

And carried it to a land of trade;
He set it in a city of merchants.
5 Then he took some of the seed of the land
And planted it in [a]a fertile field;
He placed *it* by abundant waters
And set it [b]like a willow tree.
6 And it grew and became a spreading vine
[a]of low stature;
Its branches turned toward him,
But its roots were under it.
So it became a vine,
Brought forth branches,
And put forth shoots.

7 "But there was *another great eagle with
large wings and many feathers;
And behold, [a]this vine bent its roots
toward him,
And stretched its branches toward him,
From the garden terrace where it had been
planted,
That he might water it.
8 It was planted in good soil by many
waters,
To bring forth branches, bear fruit,
And become a majestic vine." '

9 "Say, 'Thus says the Lord GOD:

"Will it thrive?
[a]Will he not pull up its roots,
Cut off its fruit,
And leave it to wither?
All of its spring leaves will wither,
And no great power or many people
Will be needed to pluck it up by its
roots.
10 Behold, *it is* planted,
Will it thrive?
[a]Will it not utterly wither when the east
wind touches it?
It will wither in the garden terrace where
it grew." ' "

11 Moreover the word of the LORD came to me, saying,

12 "Say now to [a]the rebellious house: 'Do you not know what these *things mean?*' Tell *them,* 'Indeed [b]the king of Babylon went to Jerusalem and took its king and princes, and led them with him to Babylon.

13 [a]'And he took the king's offspring, made a covenant with him, [b]and put him under oath. He also took away the mighty of the land,

14 'that the kingdom might be [a]brought low and not lift itself up, *but* that by keeping his covenant it might stand.

15 'But [a]he rebelled against him by sending his ambassadors to Egypt, [b]that they might give him horses and many people. [c]Will he prosper? Will he who does such *things* escape? Can he break a covenant and still be delivered?

16 '*As* I live,' says the Lord GOD, 'surely [a]in the place *where* the king *dwells* who made him king, whose oath he despised and whose covenant he broke—with him in the midst of Babylon he shall die.

17 [a]'Nor will Pharaoh with *his* mighty army and great company do anything in the war, [b]when they heap up a siege mound and build a wall to cut off many persons.

18 'Since he despised the oath by breaking the covenant, and in fact [a]gave his hand and still did all these *things,* he shall not escape.' "

19 Therefore thus says the Lord GOD: "*As* I live, surely My oath which he despised, and My covenant which he broke, I will recompense on his own head.

20 "I will [a]spread My net over him, and he shall be taken in My snare. I will bring him to Babylon and [b]try him there for the treason which he committed against Me.

*17:7 So with LXX, Syr., Vg.; MT, Tg. *one*

KJV

21 And [a]all his fugitives with all his bands
shall fall by the sword, and they that remain shall
be [b]scattered toward all winds: and ye shall know
that I the LORD have spoken *it*.

Israel Exalted at Last
(cf. Ezek. 31:1–9)

22 Thus saith the Lord GOD; I will also take
of the highest [a]branch of the high cedar, and will
set *it;* I will crop off from the top of his young
twigs [b]a tender one, and will [c]plant *it* upon an
high mountain and eminent:
23 [a]In the mountain of the height of Israel
will I plant it: and it shall bring forth boughs, and
bear fruit, and be a goodly cedar: and [b]under it
shall dwell all fowl of every wing; in the shadow
of the branches thereof shall they dwell.
24 And all the trees of the field shall know
that I the LORD [a]have brought down the high tree,
have exalted the low tree, have dried up the green
tree, and have made the dry tree to flourish: [b]I
the LORD have spoken and have done *it*.

A False Proverb Refuted

18 The word of the LORD came unto me again,
saying,
2 What mean ye, that ye use this proverb
concerning the land of Israel, saying, The [a]fathers
have eaten sour grapes, and the children's teeth
are set on edge?
3 *As* I live, saith the Lord GOD, ye shall not
have *occasion* any more to use this proverb in
Israel.
4 Behold, all souls are [a]mine; as the soul
of the father, so also the soul of the son is mine:
[b]the soul that sinneth, it shall die.
5 But if a man be just, and do that which is
lawful and right,
6 [a]*And* hath not eaten upon the mountains,
neither hath lifted up his eyes to the idols of the
house of Israel, neither hath [b]defiled his neighbour's wife, neither hath come near to [c]a menstruous woman,
7 And hath not [a]oppressed any, *but* hath
restored to the debtor his [b]pledge, hath spoiled
none by violence, hath [c]given his bread to the
hungry, and hath covered the naked with a
[d]garment;
8 He *that* hath not given forth upon [a]usury,
neither hath taken any increase, *that* hath withdrawn his hand from iniquity, [b]hath executed true
judgment between man and man,
9 Hath walked in my statutes, and hath kept
my judgments, to deal truly; he *is* just, he shall
surely [a]live, saith the Lord GOD.
10 If he beget a son *that is* a robber, [a]a shedder of blood, and *that* doeth the like to *any* one
of these *things*,
11 And that doeth not any of those *duties*,
but even hath eaten upon the mountains, and defiled his neighbour's wife,
12 Hath oppressed the poor and needy, hath
spoiled by violence, hath not restored the pledge,
and hath lifted up his eyes to the idols, hath
[a]committed abomination,
13 Hath given forth upon usury, and hath
taken increase: shall he then live? he shall not
live: he hath done all these abominations; he shall
surely die; [a]his blood shall be upon him.

21 [a]Ezek. 12:14 [b]Ezek. 12:15; 22:15
22 [a][Is. 11:1; Jer. 23:5; Zech. 3:8] [b]Is. 53:2 [c][Ps. 2:6]
23 [a][Is. 2:2, 3]; Ezek. 20:40; [Mic. 4:1] [b]Ezek. 31:6; Dan. 4:12
24 [a]Ezek. 37:3; Amos 9:11; Luke 1:52; [Rom. 11:23, 24] [b]Ezek. 22:14

CHAPTER 18

2 [a]Jer. 31:29; Lam. 5:7
4 [a]Num. 16:22; 27:16; Is. 42:5; 57:16 [b]Ezek. 18:20; [Rom. 6:23]
6 [a]Ezek. 22:9 [b]Lev. 18:20; 20:10 [c]Lev. 18:19; 20:18
7 [a]Ex. 22:21; Lev. 19:15; 25:14 [b]Ex. 22:26; Deut. 24:12 [c]Deut. 15:7, 11; Ezek. 18:16; [Matt. 25:35–40]; Luke 3:11 [d]Is. 58:7
8 [a]Ex. 22:25; Lev. 25:36; Deut. 23:19; Neh. 5:7; Ps. 15:5 [b]Deut. 1:16; Zech. 8:16
9 [a]Ezek. 20:11; Amos 5:4; [Hab. 2:4; Rom. 1:17]
10 [a]Gen. 9:6; Ex. 21:12; Num. 35:31
12 [a]2 Kin. 21:11; Ezek. 8:6, 17
13 [a]Lev. 20:9, 11–13, 16, 27; Ezek. 3:18; Acts 18:6

*———
17:21 So with MT, Vg.; many Heb. mss., Syr. *choice men;* Tg. *mighty men;* LXX omits *All his fugitives*

NKJV

21 [a]"All his *fugitives with all his troops shall fall by the sword, and those who remain shall be [b]scattered to every wind; and you shall know that I, the LORD, have spoken."

Israel Exalted at Last
(cf. Ezek. 31:1–9)

22 Thus says the Lord GOD: "I will take also *one* of the highest [a]branches of the high cedar and set *it* out. I will crop off from the topmost of its young twigs [b]a tender one, and will [c]plant *it* on a high and prominent mountain.
23 [a]"On the mountain height of Israel I will plant it; and it will bring forth boughs, and bear fruit, and be a majestic cedar. [b]Under it will dwell birds of every sort; in the shadow of its branches they will dwell.
24 "And all the trees of the field shall know that I, the LORD, [a]have brought down the high tree and exalted the low tree, dried up the green tree and made the dry tree flourish; [b]I, the LORD, have spoken and have done *it*."

A False Proverb Refuted

18 The word of the LORD came to me again, saying,
2 "What do you mean when you use this proverb concerning the land of Israel, saying:

'The [a]fathers have eaten sour grapes,
And the children's teeth are set on edge'?

3 "*As* I live," says the Lord GOD, "you shall no longer use this proverb in Israel.

4 "Behold, all souls are [a]Mine;
The soul of the father
As well as the soul of the son is Mine;
[b]The soul who sins shall die.
5 But if a man is just
And does what is lawful and right;
6 [a]If he has not eaten on the mountains,
Nor lifted up his eyes to the idols of the house of Israel,
Nor [b]defiled his neighbor's wife,
Nor approached [c]a woman during her impurity;
7 If he has not [a]oppressed anyone,
But has restored to the debtor his [b]pledge;
Has robbed no one by violence,
But has [c]given his bread to the hungry
And covered the naked with [d]clothing;
8 If he has not exacted [a]usury
Nor taken any increase,
But has withdrawn his hand from iniquity
And [b]executed true judgment between man and man;
9 *If* he has walked in My statutes
And kept My judgments faithfully—
He *is* just;
He shall surely [a]live!"
Says the Lord GOD.

10 "If he begets a son *who is* a robber
Or [a]a shedder of blood,
Who does any of these *things*
11 And does none of those *duties*,
But has eaten on the mountains
Or defiled his neighbor's wife;
12 If he has oppressed the poor and needy,
Robbed by violence,
Not restored the pledge,
Lifted his eyes to the idols,
Or [a]committed abomination;
13 If he has exacted usury
Or taken increase—
Shall he then live?
He shall not live!
If he has done any of these abominations,
He shall surely die;
[a]His blood shall be upon him.

KJV

14 Now, lo, *if* he beget a son, that seeth all his father's sins which he hath done, and considereth, and doeth not such like,

15 [a]*That* hath not eaten upon the mountains, neither hath lifted up his eyes to the idols of the house of Israel, hath not defiled his neighbour's wife,

16 Neither hath oppressed any, hath not withholden the pledge, neither hath spoiled by violence, *but* hath given his bread to the hungry, and hath covered the naked with a garment,

17 *That* hath taken off his hand from the poor, *that* hath not received usury nor increase, hath executed my judgments, hath walked in my statutes; he shall not die for the iniquity of his father, he shall surely live.

18 *As for* his father, because he cruelly oppressed, spoiled his brother by violence, and did *that* which *is* not good among his people, lo, even [a]he shall die in his iniquity.

Turn and Live

19 Yet say ye, Why? [a]doth not the son bear the iniquity of the father? When the son hath done that which is lawful and right, *and* hath kept all my statutes, and hath done them, he shall surely live.

20 [a]The soul that sinneth, it shall die. [b]The son shall not bear the iniquity of the father, neither shall the father bear the iniquity of the son: [c]the righteousness of the righteous shall be upon him, [d]and the wickedness of the wicked shall be upon him.

21 But [a]if the wicked will turn from all his sins that he hath committed, and keep all my statutes, and do that which is lawful and right, he shall surely live, he shall not die.

22 [a]All his transgressions that he hath committed, they shall not be mentioned unto him: in his righteousness that he hath done he shall [b]live.

23 [a]Have I any pleasure at all that the wicked should die? saith the Lord GOD: *and* not that he should return from his ways, and live?

24 But [a]when the righteous turneth away from his righteousness, and committeth iniquity, *and* doeth according to all the abominations that the wicked *man* doeth, shall he live? [b]All his righteousness that he hath done shall not be mentioned: in his trespass that he hath trespassed, and in his sin that he hath sinned, in them shall he die.

25 Yet ye say, [a]The way of the LORD is not equal. Hear now, O house of Israel; Is not my way equal? are not your ways unequal?

26 [a]When a righteous *man* turneth away from his righteousness, and committeth iniquity, and dieth in them; for his iniquity that he hath done shall he die.

27 Again, [a]when the wicked *man* turneth away from his wickedness that he hath committed, and doeth that which is lawful and right, he shall save his soul alive.

28 Because he [a]considereth, and turneth away from all his transgressions that he hath committed, he shall surely live, he shall not die.

29 [a]Yet saith the house of Israel, The way of the LORD is not equal. O house of Israel, are not my ways equal? are not your ways unequal?

30 [a]Therefore I will judge you, O house of Israel, every one according to his ways, saith the Lord GOD. [b]Repent, and turn *yourselves* from all your transgressions; so iniquity shall not be your ruin.

15 [a]Ezek. 18:6
18 [a]Ezek. 3:18
19 [a]Ex. 20:5; Deut. 5:9; 2 Kin. 23:26; 24:3, 4
20 [a]2 Kin. 14:6; 22:18–20; Ezek. 18:4 [b]Deut. 24:16; 2 Kin. 14:6; 2 Chr. 25:4; Jer. 31:29, 30 [c]1 Kin. 8:32; Is. 3:10, 11; [Matt. 16:27] [d]Rom. 2:6–9
21 [a]Ezek. 18:27; 33:12, 19
22 [a]Is. 43:25; Jer. 50:20; Ezek. 18:24; 33:16; Mic. 7:19 [b][Ps. 18:20–24]
23 [a]Lam. 3:33; [Ezek. 18:32; 33:11; 1 Tim. 2:4; 2 Pet. 3:9]
24 [a]1 Sam. 15:11; 2 Chr. 24:2, 17–22; Ezek. 3:20; 18:26; 33:18 [b][2 Pet. 2:20]
25 [a]Ezek. 18:29; 33:17, 20; Mal. 2:17; 3:13–15
26 [a]Ezek. 18:24
27 [a]Ezek. 18:21
28 [a]Ezek. 18:14
29 [a]Ezek. 18:25
30 [a]Ezek. 7:3; 33:20 [b]Matt. 3:2; Rev. 2:5

NKJV

14 "*If,* however, he begets a son
Who sees all the sins which his father has done,
And considers but does not do likewise;
15 [a]*Who* has not eaten on the mountains,
Nor lifted his eyes to the idols of the house of Israel,
Nor defiled his neighbor's wife;
16 Has not oppressed anyone,
Nor withheld a pledge,
Nor robbed by violence,
But has given his bread to the hungry
And covered the naked with clothing;
17 *Who* has withdrawn his hand from *the poor
And not received usury or increase,
But has executed My judgments
And walked in My statutes—
He shall not die for the iniquity of his father;
He shall surely live!

18 "*As for* his father,
Because he cruelly oppressed,
Robbed his brother by violence,
And did what *is* not good among his people,
Behold, [a]he shall die for his iniquity.

Turn and Live

19 "Yet you say, 'Why [a]should the son not bear the guilt of the father?' Because the son has done what is lawful and right, and has kept all My statutes and observed them, he shall surely live.

20 [a]"The soul who sins shall die. [b]The son shall not bear the guilt of the father, nor the father bear the guilt of the son. [c]The righteousness of the righteous shall be upon himself, [d]and the wickedness of the wicked shall be upon himself.

21 "But [a]if a wicked man turns from all his sins which he has committed, keeps all My statutes, and does what is lawful and right, he shall surely live; he shall not die.

22 [a]"None of the transgressions which he has committed shall be remembered against him; because of the righteousness which he has done, he shall [b]live.

23 [a]"Do I have any pleasure at all that the wicked should die?" says the Lord GOD, "*and* not that he should turn from his ways and live?

24 "But [a]when a righteous man turns away from his righteousness and commits iniquity, and does according to all the abominations that the wicked *man* does, shall he live? [b]All the righteousness which he has done shall not be remembered; because of the unfaithfulness of which he is guilty and the sin which he has committed, because of them he shall die.

25 "Yet you say, [a]'The way of the Lord is not fair.' Hear now, O house of Israel, is it not My way which is fair, and your ways which are not fair?

26 [a]"When a righteous *man* turns away from his righteousness, commits iniquity, and dies in it, it is because of the iniquity which he has done that he dies.

27 "Again, [a]when a wicked *man* turns away from the wickedness which he committed, and does what is lawful and right, he preserves himself alive.

28 "Because he [a]considers and turns away from all the transgressions which he committed, he shall surely live; he shall not die.

29 [a]"Yet the house of Israel says, 'The way of the Lord is not fair.' O house of Israel, is it not My ways which are fair, and your ways which are not fair?

30 [a]"Therefore I will judge you, O house of Israel, every one according to his ways," says the Lord GOD. [b]"Repent, and turn from all your transgressions, so that iniquity will not be your ruin.

*18:17 So with MT, Tg., Vg.; LXX *iniquity* (cf. v. 8)

KJV

31 [a]Cast away from you all your transgressions, whereby ye have transgressed; and make
you a [b]new heart and a new spirit: for why will
ye die, O house of Israel?
32 For [a]I have no pleasure in the death of
him that dieth, saith the Lord GOD: wherefore turn
yourselves, and [b]live ye.

Israel Degraded

19 Moreover [a]take thou up a lamentation for
the princes of Israel,
2 And say, What *is* thy mother? A lioness:
she lay down among lions, she nourished her
whelps among young lions.
3 And she brought up one of her whelps:
[a]it became a young lion, and it learned to catch
the prey; it devoured men.
4 The nations also heard of him; he was
taken in their pit, and they brought him with
chains unto the land of [a]Egypt.
5 Now when she saw that she had waited,
and her hope was lost, then she took [a]another of
her whelps, *and* made him a young lion.
6 [a]And he went up and down among the
lions, [b]he became a young lion, and learned to
catch the prey, *and* devoured men.
7 And he knew their desolate palaces, and
he laid waste their cities; and the land was desolate, and the fulness thereof, by the noise of his
roaring.
8 [a]Then the nations set against him on
every side from the provinces, and spread their
net over him: [b]he was taken in their pit.
9 [a]And they put him in ward in chains, and
brought him to the king of Babylon: they brought
him into holds, that his voice should no more be
heard upon [b]the mountains of Israel.
10 Thy mother *is* [a]like a vine in thy blood,
planted by the waters: she was [b]fruitful and full
of branches by reason of many waters.
11 And she had strong rods for the sceptres
of them that bare rule, and her [a]stature was exalted among the thick branches, and she appeared
in her height with the multitude of her branches.
12 But she was [a]plucked up in fury, she was
cast down to the ground, and the [b]east wind dried
up her fruit: her strong rods were broken and
withered; the fire consumed them.
13 And now she *is* planted in the wilderness,
in a dry and thirsty ground.
14 [a]And fire is gone out of a rod of her
branches, *which* hath devoured her fruit, so that
she hath no strong rod *to be* a sceptre to rule.
[b]This *is* a lamentation, and shall be for a
lamentation.

The Rebellions of Israel

20 And it came to pass in the seventh year,
in the fifth *month,* the tenth *day* of the
month, *that* [a]certain of the elders of Israel came
to enquire of the LORD, and sat before me.

---

31 [a]Is. 1:16; 55:7; Ezek. 4:22, 23 [b]Ps. 51:10; Jer. 32:39; Ezek. 11:19; 36:26
32 [a]Lam. 3:33; Ezek. 33:11; [2 Pet. 3:9] [b][Prov. 4:2, 5, 6]

CHAPTER 19

1 [a]Ezek. 26:17; 27:2
3 [a]Ezek. 19:2; 2 Kin. 23:31, 32
4 [a]2 Kin. 23:33, 34; 2 Chr. 36:4
5 [a]2 Kin. 23:34
6 [a]Jer. 22:13–17 [b]Ezek. 19:3
8 [a]2 Kin. 24:2, 11 [b]Ezek. 19:4
9 [a]2 Chr. 36:6; Jer. 22:18 [b]Ezek. 6:2
10 [a]Ezek. 17:6 [b]Deut. 8:7–9
11 [a]Ezek. 31:3; Dan. 4:11
12 [a]Jer. 31:27, 28 [b]Ezek. 17:10; Hos. 13:5
14 [a]Judg. 9:15; 2 Kin. 24:20; Ezek. 17:18 [b]Lam. 2:5

CHAPTER 20

1 [a]Ezek. 8:1, 11, 12; 14:1

*

19:7 LXX *He stood in insolence;* Tg. *He destroyed its palaces;* Vg. *He learned to make widows*
19:10 Lit. *blood;* so with MT, Syr., Vg.; LXX *like a flower on a pomegranate tree;* Tg. *in your likeness*

NKJV

31 [a]"Cast away from you all the transgressions which you have committed, and get yourselves a [b]new heart and a new spirit. For why
should you die, O house of Israel?
32 "For [a]I have no pleasure in the death of
one who dies," says the Lord GOD. "Therefore
turn and [b]live!"

Israel Degraded

19 "Moreover [a]take up a lamentation for the
princes of Israel,
2 "and say:

'What *is* your mother? A lioness:
She lay down among the lions;
Among the young lions she nourished her cubs.
3 She brought up one of her cubs,
And [a]he became a young lion;
He learned to catch prey,
And he devoured men.
4 The nations also heard of him;
He was trapped in their pit,
And they brought him with chains to the land of [a]Egypt.

5 'When she saw that she waited, *that* her hope was lost,
She took [a]another of her cubs *and* made him a young lion.
6 [a]He roved among the lions,
And [b]became a young lion;
He learned to catch prey;
He devoured men.
7 *He knew their desolate places,
And laid waste their cities;
The land with its fullness was desolated
By the noise of his roaring.
8 [a]Then the nations set against him from the provinces on every side,
And spread their net over him;
[b]He was trapped in their pit.
9 [a]They put him in a cage with chains,
And brought him to the king of Babylon;
They brought him in nets,
That his voice should no longer be heard on [b]the mountains of Israel.

10 'Your mother *was* [a]like a vine in your *bloodline,
Planted by the waters,
[b]Fruitful and full of branches
Because of many waters.
11 She had strong branches for scepters of rulers.
[a]She towered in stature above the thick branches,
And was seen in her height amid the dense foliage.
12 But she was [a]plucked up in fury,
She was cast down to the ground,
And the [b]east wind dried her fruit.
Her strong branches were broken and withered;
The fire consumed them.
13 And now she *is* planted in the wilderness,
In a dry and thirsty land.
14 [a]Fire has come out from a rod of her branches
And devoured her fruit,
So that she has no strong branch—
a scepter for ruling.' "

[b]This *is* a lamentation, and has become a lamentation.

The Rebellions of Israel

20 It came to pass in the seventh year, in the fifth *month,* on the tenth *day* of the month, *that* [a]certain of the elders of Israel came to inquire of the LORD, and sat before me.

KJV

2 Then came the word of the LORD unto me,
saying,
3 Son of man, speak unto the elders of Israel, and say unto them, Thus saith the Lord GOD;
Are ye come to enquire of me? *As* I live, saith
the Lord GOD, [a]I will not be enquired of by you.
4 Wilt thou judge them, son of man, wilt
thou judge *them?* [a]cause them to know the abominations of their fathers:
5 And say unto them, Thus saith the Lord
GOD; In the day when [a]I chose Israel, and lifted
up mine hand unto the seed of the house of Jacob,
and made myself [b]known unto them in the land
of Egypt, when I lifted up mine hand unto them,
saying, [c]I *am* the LORD your God;
6 In the day *that* I lifted up mine hand unto
them, [a]to bring them forth of the land of Egypt
into a land that I had espied for them, [b]flowing
with milk and honey, which *is* [c]the glory of all
lands:
7 Then said I unto them, [a]Cast ye away
every man [b]the abominations of his eyes, and defile not yourselves with [c]the idols of Egypt: I *am*
the LORD your God.
8 But they rebelled against me, and would
not hearken unto me: they did not every man cast
away the abominations of their eyes, neither did
they forsake the idols of Egypt: then I said, I will
[a]pour out my fury upon them, to accomplish my
anger against them in the midst of the land of
Egypt.
9 [a]But I wrought for my name's sake, that
it should not be polluted before the heathen,
among whom they *were*, in whose sight I made
myself [b]known unto them, in bringing them forth
out of the land of Egypt.
10 Wherefore I [a]caused them to go forth out
of the land of Egypt, and brought them into the
wilderness.
11 [a]And I gave them my statutes, and shewed
them my judgments, [b]which *if* a man do, he shall
even live in them.
12 Moreover also I gave them my [a]sabbaths,
to be a sign between me and them, that they might
know that I *am* the LORD that sanctify them.
13 But the house of Israel [a]rebelled against
me in the wilderness: they walked not in my statutes, and they [b]despised my judgments, [c]which
if a man do, he shall even live in them; and my
sabbaths they greatly [d]polluted: then I said, I
would pour out my fury upon them in the [e]wilder-
ness, to consume them.
14 [a]But I wrought for my name's sake, that
it should not be polluted before the heathen, in
whose sight I brought them out.
15 Yet also [a]I lifted up my hand unto them
in the wilderness, that I would not bring them into
the land which I had given *them*, [b]flowing with
milk and honey, which *is* [c]the glory of all lands;
16 [a]Because they despised my judgments,
and walked not in my statutes, but polluted my
sabbaths: for [b]their heart went after their idols.
17 [a]Nevertheless mine eye spared them from
destroying them, neither did I make an end of
them in the wilderness.
18 But I said unto their children in the wilderness, Walk ye not in the statutes of your fathers,
neither observe their judgments, nor defile yourselves with their idols:
19 I *am* the LORD your God; [a]walk in my statutes, and keep my judgments, and do them;
20 [a]And hallow my sabbaths; and they shall
be a sign between me and you, that ye may know
that I *am* the LORD your God.
21 Notwithstanding [a]the children rebelled
against me: they walked not in my statutes, neither kept my judgments to do them, [b]which *if* a
man do, he shall even live in them; they polluted
my sabbaths: then I said, I would pour out my
fury upon them, to accomplish my anger against
them in the wilderness.
22 Nevertheless I withdrew mine hand, and

3 [a]Ezek. 7:26; 14:3
4 [a]Ezek. 16:2; 22:2; Matt. 23:32
5 [a]Ex. 6:6–8; Deut. 7:6 [b]Ex. 3:8; 4:31; Deut. 4:34 [c]Ex. 20:2
6 [a]Ex. 3:8, 17; Deut. 8:7–9; Jer. 32:22 [b]Ex. 3:8 [c]Ex. 3:8, 17; 13:5; 33:3; Ps. 48:2; Jer. 11:5; 32:22; Ezek. 20:15; Dan. 8:9; Zech. 7:14
7 [a]Ezek. 18:31 [b]2 Chr. 15:8 [c]Lev. 18:3; Deut. 29:16; Josh. 24:14
8 [a]Ezek. 7:8
9 [a]Num. 14:13 [b]Josh. 2:10; 9:9, 10
10 [a]Ex. 13:18
11 [a]Deut. 4:8; Neh. 9:13; Ps. 147:19 [b]Lev. 18:5; Ezek. 20:13; Rom. 10:5; [Gal. 3:12]
12 [a]Ex. 20:8; Deut. 5:12; Neh. 9:14
13 [a]Num. 14:22; Ps. 78:40; Ezek. 20:8 [b]Prov. 1:25 [c]Lev. 18:5 [d]Ex. 16:27 [e]Num. 14:29; Ps. 106:23
14 [a]Ezek. 20:9, 20
15 [a]Num. 14:28; Ps. 95:11; 106:26 [b]Ex. 3:8 [c]Ezek. 20:6
16 [a]Ezek. 20:13, 24 [b]Num. 15:39; Ps. 78:37; Amos 5:25; Acts 7:42
17 [a][Ps. 78:38]
19 [a]Deut. 5:32
20 [a]Is. 58:13, 14; Jer. 17:22
21 [a]Num. 25:1; Deut. 9:23 [b]Lev. 18:5

NKJV

2 Then the word of the LORD came to me,
saying,
3 "Son of man, speak to the elders of Israel,
and say to them, 'Thus says the Lord GOD: "Have
you come to inquire of Me? *As* I live," says the
Lord GOD, [a]"I will not be inquired of by you." '
4 "Will you judge them, son of man, will
you judge *them?* Then [a]make known to them the
abominations of their fathers.
5 "Say to them, 'Thus says the Lord GOD:
"On the day when [a]I chose Israel and raised My
hand in an oath to the descendants of the house
of Jacob, and made Myself [b]known to them in
the land of Egypt, I raised My hand in an oath
to them, saying, [c]'I *am* the LORD your God.'
6 "On that day I raised My hand in an oath
to them, [a]to bring them out of the land of Egypt
into a land that I had searched out for them, [b]'flowing with milk and honey,' [c]the glory of all lands.
7 "Then I said to them, 'Each of you, [a]throw
away [b]the abominations which are before his
eyes, and do not defile yourselves with [c]the idols
of Egypt. I *am* the LORD your God.'
8 "But they rebelled against Me and would
not obey Me. They did not all cast away the abominations which were before their eyes, nor did
they forsake the idols of Egypt. Then I said, 'I
will [a]pour out My fury on them and fulfill My
anger against them in the midst of the land of
Egypt.'
9 [a]"But I acted for My name's sake, that it
should not be profaned before the Gentiles among
whom they *were*, in whose sight I had made Myself [b]known to them, to bring them out of the land
of Egypt.
10 "Therefore I [a]made them go out of the
land of Egypt and brought them into the wilderness.
11 [a]"And I gave them My statutes and
showed them My judgments, [b]'which, *if* a man
does, he shall live by them.'
12 "Moreover I also gave them My [a]Sab-
baths, to be a sign between them and Me, that
they might know that I *am* the LORD who sanctifies them.
13 "Yet the house of Israel [a]rebelled against
Me in the wilderness; they did not walk in My
statutes; they [b]despised My judgments, [c]'which,
if a man does, he shall live by them'; and they
greatly [d]defiled My Sabbaths. Then I said I would
pour out My fury on them in the [e]wilderness, to
consume them.
14 [a]"But I acted for My name's sake, that it
should not be profaned before the Gentiles, in
whose sight I had brought them out.
15 "So [a]I also raised My hand in an oath to
them in the wilderness, that I would not bring
them into the land which I had given *them*, [b]'flowing with milk and honey,' [c]the glory of all lands,
16 [a]"because they despised My judgments
and did not walk in My statutes, but profaned My
Sabbaths; for [b]their heart went after their idols.
17 [a]"Nevertheless My eye spared them from
destruction. I did not make an end of them in the
wilderness.
18 "But I said to their children in the wilderness, 'Do not walk in the statutes of your fathers,
nor observe their judgments, nor defile yourselves
with their idols.
19 'I *am* the LORD your God: [a]Walk in My
statutes, keep My judgments, and do them;
20 [a]'hallow My Sabbaths, and they will be a
sign between Me and you, that you may know
that I *am* the LORD your God.'
21 "Notwithstanding, [a]the children rebelled
against Me; they did not walk in My statutes, and
were not careful to observe My judgments,
[b]'which, *if* a man does, he shall live by them'; but
they profaned My Sabbaths. Then I said I would
pour out My fury on them and fulfill My anger
against them in the wilderness.
22 "Nevertheless I withdrew My hand and

KJV

wrought for my name's sake, that it should not
be polluted in the sight of the heathen, in whose
sight I brought them forth.
23 I lifted up mine hand unto them also in
the wilderness, that [a]I would scatter them among
the heathen, and disperse them through the
countries;
24 [a]Because they had not executed my judgments, but had despised my statutes, and had polluted my sabbaths, and [b]their eyes were after their
fathers' idols.
25 Wherefore [a]I gave them also statutes *that*
were not good, and judgments whereby they
should not live;
26 And I polluted them in their own gifts, in
that they caused to pass [a]through *the fire* all that
openeth the womb, that I might make them desolate, to the end that they [b]might know that I *am*
the LORD.
27 Therefore, son of man, speak unto the
house of Israel, and say unto them, Thus saith
the Lord GOD; Yet in this your fathers have [a]blas-
phemed me, in that they have committed a trespass against me.
28 *For* when I had brought them into the
land, *for* the which I lifted up mine hand to give
it to them, then [a]they saw every high hill, and
all the thick trees, and they offered there their
sacrifices, and there they presented the provocation of their offering: there also they made their
[b]sweet savour, and poured out there their drink
offerings.
29 Then I said unto them, What *is* the high
place whereunto ye go? And the name thereof is
called Bamah unto this day.
30 Wherefore say unto the house of Israel,
Thus saith the Lord GOD; Are ye polluted after
the manner of your [a]fathers? and commit ye
whoredom after their [b]abominations?
31 For when ye offer [a]your gifts, when ye
make your sons to pass through the fire, ye pollute
yourselves with all your idols, even unto this day:
and shall I be enquired of by you, O house of Israel? *As* I live, saith the Lord GOD, I will [b]not be
enquired of by you.
32 And that [a]which cometh into your mind
shall not be at all, that ye say, We will be as the
heathen, as the families of the countries, to serve
wood and stone.

God Will Restore Israel

33 *As* I live, saith the Lord GOD, surely with
a mighty hand, and [a]with a stretched out arm,
and with fury poured out, will I rule over you:
34 And I will bring you out from the people,
and will gather you out of the countries wherein
ye are scattered, with a mighty hand, and with a
stretched out arm, and with fury poured out.
35 And I will bring you into the wilderness
of the people, and there [a]will I plead with you
face to face.
36 [a]Like as I pleaded with your fathers in the
wilderness of the land of Egypt, so will I plead
with you, saith the Lord GOD.
37 And I will cause you to [a]pass under the
rod, and I will bring you into the bond of the
[b]covenant:
38 And [a]I will purge out from among you the
rebels, and them that transgress against me: I will
bring them forth out of the country where they
sojourn, and [b]they shall not enter into the land
of Israel: and ye shall know that I *am* the LORD.
39 As for you, O house of Israel, thus saith
the Lord GOD; [a]Go ye, serve ye every one his
idols, and hereafter *also*, if ye will not hearken
unto me: [b]but pollute ye my holy name no more
with your gifts, and with your idols.
40 For [a]in mine holy mountain, in the mountain of the height of Israel, saith the Lord GOD,
there shall [b]all the house of Israel, all of them in
the land, serve me: there [c]will I accept them, and
there will I require your offerings, and the first-

NKJV

acted for My name's sake, that it should not be
profaned in the sight of the Gentiles, in whose
sight I had brought them out.
23 "Also I raised My hand in an oath to those
in the wilderness, that [a]I would scatter them
among the Gentiles and disperse them throughout
the countries,
24 [a]"because they had not executed My judgments, but had despised My statutes, profaned My
Sabbaths, and [b]their eyes were fixed on their fathers' idols.
25 "Therefore [a]I also gave them up to statutes *that were* not good, and judgments by which
they could not live;
26 "and I pronounced them unclean because
of their ritual gifts, in that they caused all their
firstborn to pass [a]through *the fire*, that I might
make them desolate and that they [b]might know
that I am the LORD." '
27 "Therefore, son of man, speak to the
house of Israel, and say to them, 'Thus says the
Lord GOD: "In this too your fathers have [a]blas-
phemed Me, by being unfaithful to Me.
28 "When I brought them into the land *concerning* which I had raised My hand in an oath
to give them, and [a]they saw all the high hills and
all the thick trees, there they offered their sacrifices and provoked Me with their offerings. There
they also sent up their [b]sweet aroma and poured
out their drink offerings.
29 "Then I said to them, 'What *is* this high
place to which you go?' So its name is called
*Bamah to this day." '
30 "Therefore say to the house of Israel,
'Thus says the Lord GOD: "Are you defiling yourselves in the manner of your [a]fathers, and committing harlotry according to their [b]abomi-
nations?
31 "For when you offer [a]your gifts and make
your sons pass through the fire, you defile yourselves with all your idols, even to this day. So
shall I be inquired of by you, O house of Israel?
As I live," says the Lord GOD, "I will [b]not be inquired of by you.
32 [a]"What you have in your mind shall never
be, when you say, 'We will be like the Gentiles,
like the families in other countries, serving wood
and stone.'

God Will Restore Israel

33 "*As* I live," says the Lord GOD, "surely
with a mighty hand, [a]with an outstretched arm,
and with fury poured out, I will rule over you.
34 "I will bring you out from the peoples and
gather you out of the countries where you are
scattered, with a mighty hand, with an outstretched arm, and with fury poured out.
35 "And I will bring you into the wilderness
of the peoples, and there [a]I will plead My case
with you face to face.
36 [a]"Just as I pleaded My case with your fathers in the wilderness of the land of Egypt, so I
will plead My case with you," says the Lord GOD.
37 "I will make you [a]pass under the rod, and
I will bring you into the bond of the [b]covenant;
38 [a]"I will purge the rebels from among you,
and those who transgress against Me; I will bring
them out of the country where they dwell, but
[b]they shall not enter the land of Israel. Then you
will know that I *am* the LORD.
39 "As for you, O house of Israel," thus says
the Lord GOD: [a]"Go, serve every one of you his
idols—and hereafter—if you will not obey Me;
[b]but profane My holy name no more with your
gifts and your idols.
40 "For [a]on My holy mountain, on the mountain height of Israel," says the Lord GOD, "there
[b]all the house of Israel, all of them in the land,
shall serve Me; there [c]I will accept them, and there
I will require your offerings and the firstfruits of

23 [a]Lev. 26:33; Deut. 28:64; Ps. 106:27; Jer. 15:4
24 [a]Ezek. 20:13, 16 [b]Ezek. 6:9
25 [a]Ps. 81:12; Rom. 1:24; 2 Thess. 2:11
26 [a]2 Kin. 17:17; 2 Chr. 28:3; Jer. 32:35; Ezek. 16:20 [b]Ezek. 6:7; 20:12, 20
27 [a]Num. 15:30; Is. 65:7; Rom. 2:24
28 [a]1 Kin. 14:23; Ps. 78:58; Is. 57:5–7; Jer. 3:6; Ezek. 6:13 [b]Ezek. 16:19
30 [a]Judg. 2:19 [b]Jer. 7:26; 16:12
31 [a]Ps. 106:37–39; Jer. 7:31; Ezek. 16:20; 20:26 [b]Ezek. 20:3
32 [a]Ezek. 11:5
33 [a]Jer. 21:5
35 [a]Jer. 2:9, 35; Ezek. 17:20
36 [a]Num. 14:21–23, 28
37 [a]Lev. 27:32; Jer. 33:13 [b]Ps. 89:30–34; Ezek. 16:60, 62
38 [a]Ezek. 34:17; Amos 9:9, 10; Zech. 13:8, 9; [Mal. 3:3; 4:1–3; Matt. 25:32] [b]Jer. 44:14
39 [a]Judg. 10:14; Ps. 81:12; Amos 4:4 [b]Is. 1:13–15; Ezek. 23:38
40 [a]Is. 2:2, 3; Ezek. 17:23; Mic. 4:1 [b]Ezek. 37:22 [c]Is. 56:7; 60:7; Ezek. 43:27; Zech. 8:20–22; Mal. 3:4; [Rom. 12:1]

*

20:29 Lit. *High Place*

KJV

fruits of your oblations, with all your holy things.
41 I will accept you with your [a]sweet savour,
when I bring you out from the people, and gather
you out of the countries wherein ye have been
scattered; and I will be sanctified in you before
the heathen.
42 [a]And ye shall know that I *am* the LORD,
[b]when I shall bring you into the land of Israel,
into the country *for* the which I lifted up mine
hand to give it to your fathers.
43 And [a]there shall ye remember your ways,
and all your doings, wherein ye have been defiled;
and [b]ye shall lothe yourselves in your own sight
for all your evils that ye have committed.
44 [a]And ye shall know that I *am* the LORD,
when I have wrought with you [b]for my name's
sake, not according to your wicked ways, nor according to your corrupt doings, O ye house of Israel, saith the Lord GOD.

Fire in the Forest

45 Moreover the word of the LORD came unto
me, saying,
46 [a]Son of man, set thy face toward the
south, and drop *thy word* toward the south, and
prophesy against the forest of the south field;
47 And say to the forest of the south, Hear
the word of the LORD; Thus saith the Lord GOD;
Behold, [a]I will kindle a fire in thee, and it shall
devour [b]every green tree in thee, and every dry
tree: the flaming flame shall not be quenched, and
all faces [c]from the south to the north shall be
burned therein.
48 And all flesh shall see that I the LORD have
kindled it: it shall not be quenched.
49 Then said I, Ah Lord GOD! they say of me,
Doth he not speak [a]parables?

Babylon, the Sword of God

21 And the word of the LORD came unto me,
saying,
2 [a]Son of man, set thy face toward Jerusalem, and [b]drop *thy word* toward the holy places,
and prophesy against the land of Israel,
3 And say to the land of Israel, Thus saith
the LORD; Behold, I *am* [a]against thee, and will
draw forth my sword out of his sheath, and will
cut off from thee [b]the righteous and the wicked.
4 Seeing then that I will cut off from thee
the righteous and the wicked, therefore shall my
sword go forth out of his sheath against all flesh
[a]from the south to the north:
5 That all flesh may know that I the LORD
have drawn forth my sword out of his sheath: it
[a]shall not return any more.
6 [a]Sigh therefore, thou son of man, with the
breaking of *thy* loins; and with bitterness sigh before their eyes.
7 And it shall be, when they say unto thee,
Wherefore sighest thou? that thou shalt answer,
For the tidings; because it cometh: and every heart
shall melt, and [a]all hands shall be feeble, and
every spirit shall faint, and all knees shall be weak
as water: behold, it cometh, and shall be brought
to pass, saith the Lord GOD.
8 Again the word of the LORD came unto
me, saying,
9 Son of man, prophesy, and say, Thus saith
the LORD; Say, [a]A sword, a sword is sharpened,
and also furbished:
10 It is sharpened to make a sore slaughter;
it is furbished that it may glitter: should we then
make mirth? it contemneth the rod of my son, *as*
every tree.
11 And he hath given it to be furbished, that
it may be handled: this sword is sharpened, and
it is furbished, to give it into the hand of [a]the
slayer.

41 [a]Eph. 5:2; Phil. 4:18
42 [a]Ezek. 36:23; 38:23 [b]Ezek. 11:17; 34:13; 36:24
43 [a]Ezek. 16:61 [b]Lev. 26:39; Ezek. 6:9; Hos. 5:15
44 [a]Ezek. 24:24 [b]Ezek. 36:22
46 [a]Ezek. 21:2; Amos 7:16
47 [a]Is. 9:18, 19; Jer. 21:14 [b]Luke 23:31 [c]Ezek. 21:4
49 [a]Ezek. 12:9; 17:2; Matt. 13:13; John 16:25

CHAPTER 21
2 [a]Ezek. 20:46 [b]Amos 7:16
3 [a]Jer. 21:13; Ezek. 5:8; Nah. 2:13; 3:5 [b]Job 9:22
4 [a]Jer. 12:12; Ezek. 20:47
5 [a][Is. 45:23; 55:11]
6 [a]Is. 22:4; Jer. 4:19; Luke 19:41
7 [a]Ezek. 7:17
9 [a]Deut. 32:41; Ezek. 5:1; 21:15, 28
11 [a]Ezek. 21:19

*20:46 Heb. *Negev*

NKJV

your sacrifices, together with all your holy things.
41 "I will accept you as a [a]sweet aroma when
I bring you out from the peoples and gather you
out of the countries where you have been scattered; and I will be hallowed in you before the
Gentiles.
42 [a]"Then you shall know that I *am* the LORD,
[b]when I bring you into the land of Israel, into the
country *for* which I raised My hand in an oath to
give to your fathers.
43 "And [a]there you shall remember your
ways and all your doings with which you were
defiled; and [b]you shall loathe yourselves in your
own sight because of all the evils that you have
committed.
44 [a]"Then you shall know that I *am* the LORD,
when I have dealt with you [b]for My name's sake,
not according to your wicked ways nor according
to your corrupt doings, O house of Israel," says
the Lord GOD.' "

Fire in the Forest

45 Furthermore the word of the LORD came
to me, saying,
46 [a]"Son of man, set your face toward the
south; preach against the south and prophesy
against the forest land, the *South,
47 "and say to the forest of the South, 'Hear
the word of the LORD! Thus says the Lord GOD:
"Behold, [a]I will kindle a fire in you, and it shall
devour [b]every green tree and every dry tree in
you; the blazing flame shall not be quenched, and
all faces [c]from the south to the north shall be
scorched by it.
48 "All flesh shall see that I, the LORD, have
kindled it; it shall not be quenched." ' "
49 Then I said, "Ah, Lord GOD! They say of
me, 'Does he not speak [a]parables?' "

Babylon, the Sword of God

21 And the word of the LORD came to me,
saying,
2 [a]"Son of man, set your face toward Jerusalem, [b]preach against the holy places, and prophesy against the land of Israel;
3 "and say to the land of Israel, 'Thus says
the LORD: "Behold, I *am* [a]against you, and I will
draw My sword out of its sheath and cut off both
[b]righteous and wicked from you.
4 "Because I will cut off both righteous and
wicked from you, therefore My sword shall go
out of its sheath against all flesh [a]from south *to*
north,
5 "that all flesh may know that I, the LORD,
have drawn My sword out of its sheath; it [a]shall
not return anymore." '
6 [a]"Sigh therefore, son of man, with a
breaking heart, and sigh with bitterness before
their eyes.
7 "And it shall be when they say to you,
'Why are you sighing?' that you shall answer, 'Because of the news; when it comes, every heart
will melt, [a]all hands will be feeble, every spirit
will faint, and all knees will be weak *as* water.
Behold, it is coming and shall be brought to pass,'
says the Lord GOD."
8 Again the word of the LORD came to me,
saying,
9 "Son of man, prophesy and say, 'Thus
says the LORD!' Say:

[a]'A sword, a sword is sharpened
And also polished!
10 Sharpened to make a dreadful slaughter,
Polished to flash like lightning!
Should we then make mirth?
It despises the scepter of My son,
As it does all wood.
11 And He has given it to be polished,
That it may be handled;
This sword is sharpened, and it is polished
To be given into the hand of [a]the slayer.'

KJV

12 Cry and howl, son of man: for it shall be upon my people, it *shall be* upon all the princes of Israel: terrors by reason of the sword shall be upon my people: [a]smite therefore upon *thy* thigh.

13 Because *it is* [a]a trial, and what if *the sword* contemn even the rod? [b]it shall be no *more*, saith the Lord GOD.

14 Thou therefore, son of man, prophesy, and [a]smite *thine* hands together, and let the sword be doubled the third time, the sword of the slain: it *is* the sword of the great *men that are* slain, which entereth into their [b]privy chambers.

15 I have set the point of the sword against all their gates, that *their* heart may faint, and *their* ruins be multiplied: ah! [a]*it is* made bright, *it is* wrapped up for the slaughter.

16 [a]Go thee one way or other, *either* on the right hand, *or* on the left, whithersoever thy face *is* set.

17 I will also [a]smite mine hands together, and [b]I will cause my fury to rest: I the LORD have said *it*.

18 The word of the LORD came unto me again, saying,

19 Also, thou son of man, appoint thee two ways, that the sword of the king of Babylon may come: both twain shall come forth out of one land: and choose thou a place, choose *it* at the head of the way to the city.

20 Appoint a way, that the sword may come to [a]Rabbath of the Ammonites, and to Judah in Jerusalem the defenced.

21 For the king of Babylon stood at the parting of the way, at the head of the two ways, to use divination: he made *his* arrows bright, he consulted with images, he looked in the liver.

22 At his right hand was the divination for Jerusalem, to appoint captains, to open the mouth in the slaughter, to [a]lift up the voice with shouting, [b]to appoint *battering* rams against the gates, to cast a mount, *and* to build a fort.

23 And it shall be unto them as a false divination in their sight, to them that [a]have sworn oaths: but he will call to remembrance the iniquity, that they may be taken.

24 Therefore thus saith the Lord GOD; Because ye have made your iniquity to be remembered, in that your transgressions are discovered, so that in all your doings your sins do appear; because, *I say*, that ye are come to remembrance, ye shall be taken with the hand.

25 And thou, [a]profane wicked prince of Israel, [b]whose day is come, when iniquity *shall have* an end,

26 Thus saith the Lord GOD; Remove the diadem, and take off the crown: this *shall* not *be* the same: [a]exalt *him that is* low, and abase *him that is* high.

27 I will overturn, overturn, overturn, it: [a]and it shall be no *more*, until he come whose right it is; and I will give it [b]*him*.

12 [a]Jer. 31:19 **13** [a]Job 9:23; 2 Cor. 8:2 [b]Ezek. 21:27 **14** [a]Num. 24:10; Ezek. 6:11 [b]1 Kin. 20:30 **15** [a]Ezek. 21:10, 28 **16** [a]Ezek. 14:17 **17** [a]Ezek. 22:13 [b]Ezek. 5:13; 16:42; 24:13 **20** [a]Deut. 3:11; Jer. 49:2; Ezek. 25:5; Amos 1:14 **22** [a]Jer. 51:14 [b]Ezek. 4:2 **23** [a]Ezek. 17:16, 18 **25** [a]2 Chr. 36:13; Jer. 52:2; Ezek. 12:10; 17:19 [b]Ezek. 21:29 **26** [a]Luke 1:52 **27** [a]Gen. 49:10; [Luke 1:32, 33; John 1:49] [b]Ps. 2:6; 72:7, 10; [Jer. 23:5, 6; Ezek. 34:24; 37:24]

NKJV

12 "Cry and wail, son of man;
For it will be against My people,
Against all the princes of Israel.
Terrors including the sword will be
against My people;
Therefore [a]strike *your* thigh.

13 "Because *it is* [a]a testing,
And what if *the sword* despises even the
scepter?
[b]*The scepter* shall be no *more*,"

says the Lord GOD.

14 "You therefore, son of man, prophesy,
And [a]strike *your* hands together.
The third time let the sword do double
damage.
It *is* the sword *that* slays,
The sword that slays the great *men*,
That enters their [b]private chambers.
15 I have set the point of the sword against
all their gates,
That the heart may melt and many may
stumble.
Ah! [a]*It is* made bright;
It is grasped for slaughter:

16 "Swords[a] at the ready!
Thrust right!
Set your blade!
Thrust left—
Wherever your edge is ordered!

17 "I also will [a]beat My fists together,
And [b]I will cause My fury to rest;
I, the LORD, have spoken."

18 The word of the LORD came to me again, saying:

19 "And son of man, appoint for yourself two ways for the sword of the king of Babylon to go; both of them shall go from the same land. Make a sign; put *it* at the head of the road to the city.

20 "Appoint a road for the sword to go to [a]Rabbah of the Ammonites, and to Judah, into fortified Jerusalem.

21 "For the king of Babylon stands at the parting of the road, at the fork of the two roads, to use divination: he shakes the arrows, he consults the images, he looks at the liver.

22 "In his right hand is the divination for Jerusalem: to set up battering rams, to call for a slaughter, to [a]lift the voice with shouting, [b]to set battering rams against the gates, to heap up a *siege* mound, and to build a wall.

23 "And it will be to them like a false divination in the eyes of those who [a]have sworn oaths with them; but he will bring their iniquity to remembrance, that they may be taken.

24 "Therefore thus says the Lord GOD: 'Because you have made your iniquity to be remembered, in that your transgressions are uncovered, so that in all your doings your sins appear—because you have come to remembrance, you shall be taken in hand.

25 'Now to you, O [a]profane, wicked prince of Israel, [b]whose day has come, whose iniquity *shall* end,

26 'thus says the Lord GOD:

"Remove the turban, and take off the
crown;
Nothing *shall remain* the same.
[a]Exalt the humble, and humble the exalted.
27 Overthrown, overthrown,
I will make it overthrown!
[a]It shall be no *longer*,
Until He comes whose right it is,
And I will give it *to* [b]*Him*." '

KJV

A Sword Against the Ammonites

28 And thou, son of man, prophesy and say, Thus saith the Lord GOD [a]concerning the Ammonites, and concerning their reproach; even say thou, The sword, the sword *is* drawn: for the slaughter *it is* furbished, to consume because of the glittering:

29 Whiles they [a]see vanity unto thee, whiles they divine a lie unto thee, to bring thee upon the necks of *them that are* slain, of the wicked, [b]whose day is come, when their iniquity *shall have* an end.

30 [a]Shall I cause *it* to return into his sheath? [b]I will judge thee in the place where thou wast created, [c]in the land of thy nativity.

31 And I will [a]pour out mine indignation upon thee, I will [b]blow against thee in the fire of my wrath, and deliver thee into the hand of brutish men, *and* skilful to [c]destroy.

32 Thou shalt be for fuel to the fire; thy blood shall be in the midst of the land; [a]thou shalt be no *more* remembered: for I the LORD have spoken *it*.

Sins of Jerusalem

22 Moreover the word of the LORD came unto me, saying,

2 Now, thou son of man, [a]wilt thou judge, wilt thou judge [b]the bloody city? yea, thou shalt shew her all her abominations.

3 Then say thou, Thus saith the Lord GOD, The city sheddeth [a]blood in the midst of it, that her time may come, and maketh idols against herself to defile herself.

4 Thou art become guilty in thy blood that thou hast [a]shed; and hast defiled thyself in thine idols which thou hast made; and thou hast caused thy days to draw near, and art come *even* unto thy years: [b]therefore have I made thee a reproach unto the heathen, and a mocking to all countries.

5 *Those that be* near, and *those that be* far from thee, shall mock thee, *which art* infamous *and* much vexed.

6 Behold, [a]the princes of Israel, every one were in thee to their power to shed blood.

7 In thee have they [a]set light by father and mother: in the midst of thee have they [b]dealt by oppression with the stranger: in thee have they vexed the fatherless and the widow.

8 Thou hast despised mine holy things, and hast [a]profaned my sabbaths.

9 In thee are [a]men that carry tales to shed blood: [b]and in thee they eat upon the mountains: in the midst of thee they commit lewdness.

10 In thee have they [a]discovered their fathers' nakedness: in thee have they humbled her that was [b]set apart for pollution.

11 And one hath committed abomination [a]with his neighbour's wife; and another [b]hath lewdly defiled his daughter in law; and another in thee hath humbled his sister, his father's [c]daughter.

12 In thee [a]have they taken gifts to shed blood; [b]thou hast taken usury and increase, and thou hast greedily gained of thy neighbours by extortion, and [c]hast forgotten me, saith the Lord GOD.

13 Behold, therefore I have [a]smitten mine hand at thy dishonest gain which thou hast made, and at thy blood which hath been in the midst of thee.

14 [a]Can thine heart endure, or can thine hands be strong, in the days that I shall deal with thee? [b]I the LORD have spoken *it*, and will do *it*.

15 And [a]I will scatter thee among the

---

28 [a]Jer. 25:21; 49:1–6; Ezek. 25:1–7; Amos 1:13; Zeph. 2:8–11
29 [a]Jer. 27:9; Ezek. 12:24; 13:6–9; 22:28 [b]Job 18:20; Ps. 37:17; Is. 10:3; Ezek. 7:2, 3, 7
30 [a]Jer. 47:6, 7 [b]Gen. 15:14 [c]Ezek. 16:3
31 [a]Ezek. 7:8 [b]Ps. 18:15; Is. 30:33; Ezek. 22:20, 21; Hag. 1:9 [c]Jer. 6:22, 23; 51:20, 21; Hab. 1:6–10
32 [a]Ezek. 25:10

CHAPTER 22

2 [a]Ezek. 20:4 [b]Nah. 3:1
3 [a]Ezek. 24:6, 7
4 [a]2 Kin. 21:16; Ezek. 24:7, 8 [b]Deut. 28:37; 1 Kin. 9:7; Ezek. 5:14; Dan. 9:16
6 [a]Is. 1:23; Ezek. 22:27; Mic. 3:1–3; Zeph. 3:3
7 [a]Ex. 20:12; Lev. 20:9; Deut. 5:16; 27:16 [b]Ex. 22:22; Jer. 5:28; Ezek. 22:25; Mal. 3:5
8 [a]Lev. 19:30
9 [a]Lev. 19:16; Jer. 9:4 [b]Ezek. 18:6, 11
10 [a]Lev. 18:7, 8 [b]Lev. 18:19; 20:18; Ezek. 18:6
11 [a]Lev. 18:20; Jer. 5:8; Ezek. 18:11 [b]Lev. 18:15 [c]Lev. 18:9
12 [a]Ex. 23:8; Deut. 16:19; 27:25; Mic. 7:2, 3 [b]Ex. 22:25 [c]Deut. 32:18; Ps. 106:21; Jer. 3:21; Ezek. 23:35
13 [a]Ezek. 21:17
14 [a]Ezek. 21:7 [b]Ezek. 17:24
15 [a]Deut. 4:27; Neh. 1:8; Ezek. 20:23; Zech. 7:14

NKJV

A Sword Against the Ammonites

28 "And you, son of man, prophesy and say, 'Thus says the Lord GOD [a]concerning the Ammonites and concerning their reproach,' and say:

'A sword, a sword *is* drawn,
Polished for slaughter,
For consuming, for flashing—
29 While they [a]see false visions for you,
While they divine a lie to you,
To bring you on the necks of the wicked,
the slain
[b]Whose day has come,
Whose iniquity *shall* end.

30 'Return[a] *it* to its sheath.
[b]I will judge you
In the place where you were created,
[c]In the land of your nativity.
31 I will [a]pour out My indignation on you;
I will [b]blow against you with the fire of
My wrath,
And deliver you into the hands of brutal
men *who are* skillful to [c]destroy.
32 You shall be fuel for the fire;
Your blood shall be in the midst of the
land.
[a]You shall not be remembered,
For I the LORD have spoken.' "

Sins of Jerusalem

22 Moreover the word of the LORD came to me, saying,

2 "Now, son of man, [a]will you judge, will you judge [b]the bloody city? Yes, show her all her abominations!

3 "Then say, 'Thus says the Lord GOD: "The city sheds [a]blood in her own midst, that her time may come; and she makes idols within herself to defile herself.

4 "You have become guilty by the blood which you have [a]shed, and have defiled yourself with the idols which you have made. You have caused your days to draw near, and have come to *the end of* your years; [b]therefore I have made you a reproach to the nations, and a mockery to all countries.

5 "*Those* near and *those* far from you will mock you as infamous *and* full of tumult.

6 "Look, [a]the princes of Israel: each one has used his power to shed blood in you.

7 "In you they have [a]made light of father and mother; in your midst they have [b]oppressed the stranger; in you they have mistreated the fatherless and the widow.

8 "You have despised My holy things and [a]profaned My Sabbaths.

9 "In you are [a]men who slander to cause bloodshed; [b]in you are those who eat on the mountains; in your midst they commit lewdness.

10 "In you men [a]uncover their fathers' nakedness; in you they violate women who are [b]set apart during their impurity.

11 "One commits abomination [a]with his neighbor's wife; [b]another lewdly defiles his daughter-in-law; and another in you violates his sister, his father's [c]daughter.

12 "In you [a]they take bribes to shed blood; [b]you take usury and increase; you have made profit from your neighbors by extortion, and [c]have forgotten Me," says the Lord GOD.

13 "Behold, therefore, I [a]beat My fists at the dishonest profit which you have made, and at the bloodshed which has been in your midst.

14 [a]"Can your heart endure, or can your hands remain strong, in the days when I shall deal with you? [b]I, the LORD, have spoken, and will do *it*.

15 [a]"I will scatter you among the nations,

KJV

heathen, and disperse thee in the countries, and [b]will consume thy filthiness out of thee.
16 And thou shalt take thine inheritance in thyself in the sight of the heathen, and [a]thou shalt know that I *am* the LORD.

Israel in the Furnace

17 And the word of the LORD came unto me, saying,
18 Son of man, [a]the house of Israel is to me become dross: all they *are* brass, and tin, and iron, and lead, in the midst of the [b]furnace; they are *even* the dross of silver.
19 Therefore thus saith the Lord GOD; Because ye are all become dross, behold, therefore I will gather you into the midst of Jerusalem.
20 *As* they gather silver, and brass, and iron, and lead, and tin, into the midst of the furnace, to blow the fire upon it, to [a]melt *it;* so will I gather *you* in mine anger and in my fury, and I will leave *you there,* and melt you.
21 Yea, I will gather you, and blow upon you in the fire of my wrath, and ye shall be melted in the midst thereof.
22 As silver is melted in the midst of the furnace, so shall ye be melted in the midst thereof; and ye shall know that I the LORD have [a]poured out my fury upon you.

Israel's Wicked Leaders

23 And the word of the LORD came unto me, saying,
24 Son of man, say unto her, Thou *art* the land that is [a]not cleansed, nor rained upon in the day of indignation.
25 [a]*There is* a conspiracy of her prophets in the midst thereof, like a roaring lion ravening the prey; they [b]have devoured souls; [c]they have taken the treasure and precious things; they have made her many widows in the midst thereof.
26 [a]Her priests have violated my law, and have [b]profaned mine holy things: they have put no [c]difference between the holy and profane, neither have they shewed *difference* between the unclean and the clean, and have hid their eyes from my sabbaths, and I am profaned among them.
27 Her [a]princes in the midst thereof *are* like wolves ravening the prey, to shed blood, *and* to destroy souls, to get dishonest gain.
28 And [a]her prophets have daubed them with untempered *morter,* [b]seeing vanity, and divining [c]lies unto them, saying, Thus saith the Lord GOD, when the LORD hath not spoken.
29 The people of the land have used oppression, and exercised robbery, and have vexed the poor and needy: yea, they have [a]oppressed the stranger wrongfully.
30 [a]And I sought for a man among them, that should [b]make up the hedge, and [c]stand in the gap before me for the land, that I should not destroy it: but I found none.
31 Therefore have I [a]poured out mine indignation upon them; I have consumed them with the fire of my wrath: [b]their own way have I recompensed upon their heads, saith the Lord GOD.

Two Harlot Sisters

23 The word of the LORD came again unto me, saying,
2 Son of man, there were [a]two women, the daughters of one mother:
3 And [a]they committed whoredoms in Egypt; they committed whoredoms in [b]their youth: there were their breasts pressed, and there they bruised the teats of their virginity.
4 And the names of them *were* Aholah the elder, and Aholibah [a]her sister: and [b]they were mine, and they bare sons and daughters. Thus

---

15 [b]Ezek. 23:27, 48
16 [a]Ps. 9:16
18 [a]Ps. 119:119; Is. 1:22; Jer. 6:28; Lam. 4:1 [b]Prov. 17:3; Is. 48:10
20 [a]Is. 1:25; Jer. 9:7
22 [a]Ezek. 20:8, 33; Hos. 5:10
24 [a]Is. 9:13; Jer. 2:30; Ezek. 24:13; Zeph. 3:2
25 [a]Jer. 11:9; Hos. 6:9 [b]Matt. 23:14 [c]Mic. 3:11; Zeph. 3:3, 4
26 [a]Jer. 32:32; Lam. 4:3; Mal. 2:8 [b]1 Sam. 2:29 [c]Lev. 10:10
27 [a]Is. 1:23; Ezek. 22:6; Mic. 3:1–3, 9–11; Zeph. 3:3
28 [a]Ezek. 13:10 [b]Ezek. 13:6, 7 [c]Jer. 23:25–32; Ezek. 21:29
29 [a]Ex. 23:9; Lev. 19:33
30 [a]Is. 59:16; 63:5; Jer. 5:1 [b]Ezek. 13:5 [c]Ps. 106:23; Jer. 15:1
31 [a]Ezek. 22:22 [b]Ezek. 9:10; [Rom. 2:8, 9]

CHAPTER 23

2 [a]Jer. 3:7, 8; Ezek. 16:44–46
3 [a]Lev. 17:7; Josh. 24:14; Jer. 3:9 [b]Ezek. 16:22
4 [a]Jer. 3:6, 7 [b]Ezek. 16:8, 20

*

22:24 So with MT, Syr., Vg.; LXX *showered upon*
22:25 So with MT, Vg.; LXX *princes;* Tg. *scribes*
23:4 Lit. *Her Own Tabernacle* • Lit. *My Tabernacle Is in Her*

NKJV

disperse you throughout the countries, and [b]remove your filthiness completely from you.
16 "You shall defile yourself in the sight of the nations; then [a]you shall know that I *am* the LORD." ' "

Israel in the Furnace

17 The word of the LORD came to me, saying,
18 "Son of man, [a]the house of Israel has become dross to Me; they *are* all bronze, tin, iron, and lead, in the midst of a [b]furnace; they have become dross from silver.
19 "Therefore thus says the Lord GOD: 'Because you have all become dross, therefore behold, I will gather you into the midst of Jerusalem.
20 '*As men* gather silver, bronze, iron, lead, and tin into the midst of a furnace, to blow fire on it, to [a]melt *it;* so I will gather *you* in My anger and in My fury, and I will leave *you there* and melt you.
21 'Yes, I will gather you and blow on you with the fire of My wrath, and you shall be melted in its midst.
22 'As silver is melted in the midst of a furnace, so shall you be melted in its midst; then you shall know that I, the LORD, have [a]poured out My fury on you.' "

Israel's Wicked Leaders

23 And the word of the LORD came to me, saying,
24 "Son of man, say to her: 'You *are* a land that is [a]not *cleansed or rained on in the day of indignation.'
25 [a]"The conspiracy of her *prophets in her midst is like a roaring lion tearing the prey; they [b]have devoured people; [c]they have taken treasure and precious things; they have made many widows in her midst.
26 [a]"Her priests have violated My law and [b]profaned My holy things; they have not [c]distinguished between the holy and unholy, nor have they made known *the difference* between the unclean and the clean; and they have hidden their eyes from My Sabbaths, so that I am profaned among them.
27 "Her [a]princes in her midst *are* like wolves tearing the prey, to shed blood, to destroy people, and to get dishonest gain.
28 [a]"Her prophets plastered them with untempered *mortar,* [b]seeing false visions, and divining [c]lies for them, saying, 'Thus says the Lord GOD,' when the LORD had not spoken.
29 "The people of the land have used oppressions, committed robbery, and mistreated the poor and needy; and they wrongfully [a]oppress the stranger.
30 [a]"So I sought for a man among them who would [b]make a wall, and [c]stand in the gap before Me on behalf of the land, that I should not destroy it; but I found no one.
31 "Therefore I have [a]poured out My indignation on them; I have consumed them with the fire of My wrath; and I have recompensed [b]their deeds on their own heads," says the Lord GOD.

Two Harlot Sisters

23 The word of the LORD came again to me, saying:

2 "Son of man, there were [a]two women,
The daughters of one mother.
3 [a]They committed harlotry in Egypt,
They committed harlotry in [b]their youth;
Their breasts were there embraced,
Their virgin bosom was there pressed.
4 Their names: *Oholah the elder and
*Oholibah [a]her sister;
[b]They were Mine,
And they bore sons and daughters.
As for their names,

KJV

were their names; Samaria *is* Aholah, and Jerusalem Aholibah.

The Older Sister, Samaria

5 And Aholah played the harlot when she was mine; and she doted on her lovers, on [a]the Assyrians *her* neighbours,

6 *Which were* clothed with blue, captains and rulers, all of them desirable young men, horsemen riding upon horses.

7 Thus she committed her whoredoms with them, with all them *that were* the chosen men of Assyria, and with all on whom she doted: with all their idols she defiled herself.

8 Neither left she her whoredoms *brought* [a]from Egypt: for in her youth they lay with her, and they bruised the breasts of her virginity, and poured their whoredom upon her.

9 Wherefore I have delivered her into the hand of her lovers, into the hand of the [a]Assyrians, upon whom she doted.

10 These discovered her nakedness: they took her sons and her daughters, and slew her with the sword: and she became famous among women; for they had executed judgment upon her.

The Younger Sister, Jerusalem

11 And [a]when her sister Aholibah saw *this,* [b]she was more corrupt in her inordinate love than she, and in her whoredoms more than her sister in *her* whoredoms.

12 She doted upon the [a]Assyrians *her* neighbours, [b]captains and rulers clothed most gorgeously, horsemen riding upon horses, all of them desirable young men.

13 Then I saw that she was defiled, *that* they *took* both one way,

14 And *that* she increased her whoredoms: for when she saw men pourtrayed upon the wall, the images of the [a]Chaldeans pourtrayed with vermilion,

15 Girded with girdles upon their loins, exceeding in dyed attire upon their heads, all of them princes to look to, after the manner of the Babylonians of Chaldea, the land of their nativity:

16 [a]And as soon as she saw them with her eyes, she doted upon them, and sent [b]messengers unto them into Chaldea.

17 And the Babylonians came to her into the bed of love, and they defiled her with their whoredom, and she was polluted with them, and [a]her mind was alienated from them.

18 So she discovered her whoredoms, and discovered her nakedness: then [a]my mind was [b]alienated from her, like as my mind was alienated from her sister.

19 Yet she multiplied her whoredoms, in calling to remembrance the days of her youth, [a]wherein she had played the harlot in the land of Egypt.

20 For she doted upon their paramours, whose flesh *is as* the flesh of asses, and whose issue *is like* the issue of horses.

5 [a]2 Kin. 15:19; 16:7; 17:3; Ezek. 16:28; Hos. 5:13; 8:9, 10
8 [a]Ex. 32:4; 1 Kin. 12:28; 2 Kin. 10:29; 17:16; Ezek. 23:3, 19
9 [a]2 Kin. 17:3
11 [a]Jer. 3:8 [b]Jer. 3:8–11; Ezek. 16:51, 52
12 [a]2 Kin. 16:27, 28; Ezek. 16:28 [b]Ezek. 23:6, 23
14 [a]Jer. 50:2; Ezek. 8:10; 16:29
16 [a]2 Kin. 24:1 [b]Is. 57:9
17 [a]Ezek. 23:22, 28
18 [a]Jer. 6:8 [b]Ps. 78:59; 106:40; Jer. 12:8
19 [a]Lev. 18:3; Ezek. 23:2

NKJV

Samaria *is* Oholah, and Jerusalem *is*
Oholibah.

The Older Sister, Samaria

5 "Oholah played the harlot even though she
was Mine;
And she lusted for her lovers, the
neighboring [a]Assyrians,
6 *Who were* clothed in purple,
Captains and rulers,
All of them desirable young men,
Horsemen riding on horses.
7 Thus she committed her harlotry with
them,
All of them choice men of Assyria;
And with all for whom she lusted,
With all their idols, she defiled herself.
8 She has never given up her harlotry
brought [a]from Egypt,
For in her youth they had lain with her,
Pressed her virgin bosom,
And poured out their immorality upon
her.

9 "Therefore I have delivered her
Into the hand of her lovers,
Into the hand of the [a]Assyrians,
For whom she lusted.
10 They uncovered her nakedness,
Took away her sons and daughters,
And slew her with the sword;
She became a byword among women,
For they had executed judgment on
her.

The Younger Sister, Jerusalem

11 "Now [a]although her sister Oholibah saw *this,* [b]she became more corrupt in her lust than she, and in her harlotry more corrupt than her sister's harlotry.

12 "She lusted for the neighboring [a]Assyrians,
[b]Captains and rulers,
Clothed most gorgeously,
Horsemen riding on horses,
All of them desirable young men.
13 Then I saw that she was defiled;
Both *took* the same way.
14 But she increased her harlotry;
She looked at men portrayed on the wall,
Images of [a]Chaldeans portrayed in
vermilion,
15 Girded with belts around their waists,
Flowing turbans on their heads,
All of them looking like captains,
In the manner of the Babylonians of
Chaldea,
The land of their nativity.
16 [a]As soon as her eyes saw them,
She lusted for them
And sent [b]messengers to them in Chaldea.

17 "Then the Babylonians came to her, into
the bed of love,
And they defiled her with their
immorality;
So she was defiled by them, [a]and
alienated herself from them.
18 She revealed her harlotry and uncovered
her nakedness.
Then [a]I [b]alienated Myself from her,
As I had alienated Myself from her
sister.

19 "Yet she multiplied her harlotry
In calling to remembrance the days of her
youth,
[a]When she had played the harlot in the
land of Egypt.
20 For she lusted for her paramours,
Whose flesh *is like* the flesh of donkeys,
And whose issue *is like* the issue of horses.

KJV

21 Thus thou calledst to remembrance the
lewdness of thy youth, in bruising thy teats by
the [a]Egyptians for the paps of thy youth.

Judgment on Jerusalem

22 Therefore, O Aholibah, thus saith the
Lord GOD; [a]Behold, I will raise up thy lovers
against thee, from whom thy mind is alienated,
and I will bring them against thee on every side;
23 The Babylonians, and all the Chaldeans,
[a]Pekod, and Shoa, and Koa, *and* [b]all the Assyrians with them: all of them desirable young men,
captains and rulers, great lords and renowned,
all of them riding upon horses.
24 And they shall come against thee with
chariots, wagons, and wheels, and with an assembly of people, *which* shall set against thee buckler
and shield and helmet round about: and I will set
judgment before them, and they shall judge thee
according to their judgments.
25 And I will set my [a]jealousy against thee,
and they shall deal furiously with thee: they shall
take away thy nose and thine ears; and thy remnant shall fall by the sword: they shall take thy
sons and thy daughters; and thy residue shall be
devoured by the fire.
26 [a]They shall also strip thee out of thy
clothes, and take away thy fair jewels.
27 Thus [a]will I make thy lewdness to cease
from thee, and thy [b]whoredom *brought* from the
land of Egypt: so that thou shalt not lift up thine
eyes unto them, nor remember Egypt any more.
28 For thus saith the Lord GOD; Behold, I will
deliver thee into the hand *of them* [a]whom thou
hatest, into the hand *of them* [b]from whom thy
mind is alienated:
29 [a]And they shall deal with thee hatefully,
and shall take away all thy labour, and [b]shall
leave thee naked and bare: and the nakedness of
thy whoredoms shall be discovered, both thy
lewdness and thy whoredoms.
30 I will do these *things* unto thee, because
thou hast [a]gone a whoring after the heathen, *and*
because thou art polluted with their idols.
31 Thou hast walked in the way of thy sister;
therefore will I give her [a]cup into thine hand.
32 Thus saith the Lord GOD; Thou shalt drink
of thy sister's cup deep and large: [a]thou shalt be
laughed to scorn and had in derision; it containeth
much.
33 Thou shalt be filled with drunkenness and
sorrow, with the cup of astonishment and desolation, with the cup of thy sister Samaria.
34 Thou shalt [a]even drink it and suck *it* out,
and thou shalt break the sherds thereof, and pluck
off thine own breasts: for I have spoken *it*, saith
the Lord GOD.
35 Therefore thus saith the Lord GOD;

21 [a]Ezek. 16:26
22 [a]Ezek. 16:37–41; 23:28
23 [a]Jer. 50:21 [b]Ezek. 23:12
25 [a]Ex. 34:14; Ezek. 5:13; 8:17, 18; Zeph. 1:18
26 [a]Is. 3:18–23; Ezek. 16:39
27 [a]Ezek. 16:41; 22:15 [b]Ezek. 23:3, 19
28 [a]Jer. 21:7–10; Ezek.16:37–41 [b]Ezek. 23:17
29 [a]Deut. 28:48; Ezek. 23:25, 26, 45–47 [b]Ezek. 16:39
30 [a]Ezek. 6:9
31 [a]2 Kin. 21:13; Jer. 7:14, 15; 25:15; Ezek. 23:33
32 [a]Ezek. 22:4, 5
34 [a]Ps. 75:8; Is. 51:17

NKJV

21 Thus you called to remembrance the
lewdness of your youth,
When the [a]Egyptians pressed your bosom
Because of your youthful breasts.

Judgment on Jerusalem

22 "Therefore, Oholibah, thus says the Lord GOD:

[a]'Behold, I will stir up your lovers against
you,
From whom you have alienated yourself,
And I will bring them against you from
every side:
23 The Babylonians,
All the Chaldeans,
[a]Pekod, Shoa, Koa,
[b]All the Assyrians with them,
All of them desirable young men,
Governors and rulers,
Captains and men of renown,
All of them riding on horses.
24 And they shall come against you
With chariots, wagons, and war-horses,
With a horde of people.
They shall array against you
Buckler, shield, and helmet all around.

'I will delegate judgment to them,
And they shall judge you according to
their judgments.
25 I will set My [a]jealousy against you,
And they shall deal furiously with you;
They shall remove your nose and your
ears,
And your remnant shall fall by the sword;
They shall take your sons and your
daughters,
And your remnant shall be devoured by
fire.
26 [a]They shall also strip you of your clothes
And take away your beautiful jewelry.

27 'Thus [a]I will make you cease your
lewdness and your [b]harlotry
Brought from the land of Egypt,
So that you will not lift your eyes to
them,
Nor remember Egypt anymore.'

28 "For thus says the Lord GOD: 'Surely I will
deliver you into the hand of [a]those you hate, into
the hand *of those* [b]from whom you alienated
yourself.
29 [a]'They will deal hatefully with you, take
away all you have worked for, and [b]leave you
naked and bare. The nakedness of your harlotry
shall be uncovered, both your lewdness and your
harlotry.
30 'I will do these *things* to you because you
have [a]gone as a harlot after the Gentiles, because
you have become defiled by their idols.
31 'You have walked in the way of your sister; therefore I will put her [a]cup in your hand.'
32 "Thus says the Lord GOD:

'You shall drink of your sister's cup,
The deep and wide one;
[a]You shall be laughed to scorn
And held in derision;
It contains much.
33 You will be filled with drunkenness and
sorrow,
The cup of horror and desolation,
The cup of your sister Samaria.
34 You shall [a]drink and drain it,
You shall break its shards,
And tear at your own breasts;
For I have spoken,'
Says the Lord GOD.

35 "Therefore thus says the Lord GOD:

KJV

Because thou [a]hast forgotten me, and [b]cast me behind thy back, therefore bear thou also thy lewdness and thy whoredoms.

Both Sisters Judged

36 The LORD said moreover unto me; Son of man, wilt thou [a]judge Aholah and Aholibah? yea, [b]declare unto them their abominations;

37 That they have committed adultery, and [a]blood *is* in their hands, and with their idols have they committed adultery, and have also caused their sons, [b]whom they bare unto me, to pass for them through *the fire,* to devour *them.*

38 Moreover this they have done unto me: they have [a]defiled my sanctuary in the same day, and [b]have profaned my sabbaths.

39 For when they had slain their children to their idols, then they came the same day into my sanctuary to profane it; and, lo, [a]thus have they done in the midst of mine house.

40 And furthermore, that ye have sent for men to come from far, [a]unto whom a messenger *was* sent; and, lo, they came: for whom thou didst [b]wash thyself, [c]paintedst thy eyes, and deckedst thyself with ornaments,

41 And satest upon a stately [a]bed, and a table prepared before it, [b]whereupon thou hast set mine incense and mine oil.

42 And a voice of a multitude being at ease *was* with her: and with the men of the common sort *were* brought Sabeans from the wilderness, which put bracelets upon their hands, and beautiful crowns upon their heads.

43 Then said I unto *her that was* old in adulteries, Will they now commit whoredoms with her, and she *with them?*

44 Yet they went in unto her, as they go in unto a woman that playeth the harlot: so went they in unto Aholah and unto Aholibah, the lewd women.

45 And the righteous men, they shall [a]judge them after the manner of adulteresses, and after the manner of women that shed blood; because they *are* adulteresses, and [b]blood *is* in their hands.

46 For thus saith the Lord GOD; [a]I will bring up a company upon them, and will give them to be removed and spoiled.

47 [a]And the company shall stone them with stones, and dispatch them with their swords; [b]they shall slay their sons and their daughters, and burn up their houses with fire.

48 Thus [a]will I cause lewdness to cease out of the land, [b]that all women may be taught not to do after your lewdness.

49 And they shall recompense your lewdness upon you, and ye shall [a]bear the sins of your idols: [b]and ye shall know that I *am* the Lord GOD.

Symbol of the Cooking Pot
(cf. Jer. 1:13–19)

24 Again in the ninth year, in the tenth month, in the tenth *day* of the month, the word of the LORD came unto me, saying,

2 Son of man, write thee the name of the day, *even* of this same day: the king of Babylon set himself against Jerusalem [a]this same day.

3 [a]And utter a parable unto the rebellious house, and say unto them, Thus saith the Lord GOD; [b]Set on a pot, set *it* on, and also pour water into it:

4 Gather the pieces thereof into it, *even* every good piece, the thigh, and the shoulder; fill *it* with the choice bones.

5 Take the choice of the flock, and burn also the bones under it, *and* make it boil well, and let them seethe the bones of it therein.

6 Wherefore thus saith the Lord GOD; Woe

---

35 [a]Is. 17:10; Jer. 3:21; Ezek. 22:12; Hos. 8:14; 13:6 [b]1 Kin. 14:9; Jer. 2:27; 32:33; Neh. 9:26
36 [a]Jer. 1:10; Ezek. 20:4; 22:2 [b]Is. 58:1; Ezek. 16:2; Mic. 3:8
37 [a]Ezek. 16:38 [b]Ezek. 16:20, 21, 36, 45; 20:26, 31
38 [a]2 Kin. 21:4, 7; Ezek. 5:11; 7:20 [b]Ezek. 22:8
39 [a]2 Kin. 21:2–8
40 [a]Is. 57:9 [b]Ruth 3:3 [c]2 Kin. 9:30; Jer. 4:30
41 [a]Esth. 1:6; Is. 57:7; Amos 2:8; 6:4 [b]Prov. 7:17; Ezek. 16:18, 19; Hos. 2:8
45 [a]Ezek. 16:38 [b]Ezek. 23:37
46 [a]Ezek. 16:40
47 [a]Lev. 20:10; Ezek. 16:40 [b]2 Chr. 36:17, 19; Ezek. 24:21
48 [a]Ezek. 22:15 [b]Deut. 13:11; Ezek. 22:15; 2 Pet. 2:6
49 [a]Is. 59:18; Ezek. 23:35 [b]Ezek. 20:38, 42, 44; 25:5

CHAPTER 24

2 [a]2 Kin. 25:1; Jer. 39:1; 52:4
3 [a]Ezek. 17:12 [b]Jer. 1:13; Ezek. 11:3

NKJV

'Because you [a]have forgotten Me and [b]cast
Me behind your back,
Therefore you shall bear the *penalty*
Of your lewdness and your harlotry.' "

Both Sisters Judged

36 The LORD also said to me: "Son of man, will you [a]judge Oholah and Oholibah? Then [b]declare to them their abominations.

37 "For they have committed adultery, and [a]blood *is* on their hands. They have committed adultery with their idols, and even sacrificed their sons [b]whom they bore to Me, passing them through *the fire,* to devour *them.*

38 "Moreover they have done this to Me: They have [a]defiled My sanctuary on the same day and [b]profaned My Sabbaths.

39 "For after they had slain their children for their idols, on the same day they came into My sanctuary to profane it; and indeed [a]thus they have done in the midst of My house.

40 "Furthermore you sent for men to come from afar, [a]to whom a messenger *was* sent; and there they came. And you [b]washed yourself for them, [c]painted your eyes, and adorned yourself with ornaments.

41 "You sat on a stately [a]couch, with a table prepared before it, [b]on which you had set My incense and My oil.

42 "The sound of a carefree multitude *was* with her, and Sabeans *were* brought from the wilderness with men of the common sort, who put bracelets on their wrists and beautiful crowns on their heads.

43 "Then I said concerning *her who had grown* old in adulteries, 'Will they commit harlotry with her now, and she *with them?*'

44 "Yet they went in to her, as men go in to a woman who plays the harlot; thus they went in to Oholah and Oholibah, the lewd women.

45 "But righteous men will [a]judge them after the manner of adulteresses, and after the manner of women who shed blood, because they *are* adulteresses, and [b]blood *is* on their hands.

46 "For thus says the Lord GOD: [a]'Bring up an assembly against them, give them up to trouble and plunder.

47 [a]'The assembly shall stone them with stones and execute them with their swords; [b]they shall slay their sons and their daughters, and burn their houses with fire.

48 'Thus [a]I will cause lewdness to cease from the land, [b]that all women may be taught not to practice your lewdness.

49 'They shall repay you for your lewdness, and you shall [a]pay for your idolatrous sins. [b]Then you shall know that I *am* the Lord GOD.' "

Symbol of the Cooking Pot
(cf. Jer. 1:13–19)

24 Again, in the ninth year, in the tenth month, on the tenth *day* of the month, the word of the LORD came to me, saying,

2 "Son of man, write down the name of the day, this very day—the king of Babylon started his siege against Jerusalem [a]this very day.

3 [a]"And utter a parable to the rebellious house, and say to them, 'Thus says the Lord GOD:

[b]"Put on a pot, set *it* on,
And also pour water into it.
4 Gather pieces *of meat* in it,
Every good piece,
The thigh and the shoulder.
Fill *it* with choice cuts;
5 Take the choice of the flock.
Also pile *fuel* bones under it,
Make it boil well,
And let the cuts simmer in it."

6 'Therefore thus says the Lord GOD:

KJV

to [a]the bloody city, to the pot whose scum *is* therein, and whose scum is not gone out of it! bring it out piece by piece; let no [b]lot fall upon it.

7 For her blood is in the midst of her; she set it upon the top of a rock; [a]she poured it not upon the ground, to cover it with dust;

8 That it might cause fury to come up to take vengeance; [a]I have set her blood upon the top of a rock, that it should not be covered.

9 Therefore thus saith the Lord GOD; [a]Woe to the bloody city! I will even make the pile for fire great.

10 Heap on wood, kindle the fire, consume the flesh, and spice it well, and let the bones be burned.

11 Then set it empty upon the coals thereof, that the brass of it may be hot, and may burn, and *that* [a]the filthiness of it may be molten in it, *that* the scum of it may be consumed.

12 She hath wearied *herself* with lies, and her great scum went not forth out of her: her scum *shall be* in the fire.

13 In thy [a]filthiness *is* lewdness: because I have purged thee, and thou wast not purged, thou shalt [b]not be purged from thy filthiness any more, [c]till I have caused my fury to rest upon thee.

14 [a]I the LORD have spoken *it:* [b]it shall come to pass, and I will do *it;* I will not go back, [c]neither will I spare, neither will I repent; according to thy ways, and according to thy doings, shall they judge thee, saith the Lord GOD.

The Prophet's Wife Dies

15 Also the word of the LORD came unto me, saying,

16 Son of man, behold, I take away from thee the desire of thine eyes with a stroke: yet [a]neither shalt thou mourn nor weep, neither shall thy tears run down.

17 Forbear to cry, [a]make no mourning for the dead, [b]bind the tire of thine head upon thee, and [c]put on thy shoes upon thy feet, and [d]cover not *thy* lips, and eat not the bread of men.

18 So I spake unto the people in the morning: and at even my wife died; and I did in the morning as I was commanded.

19 And the people said unto me, [a]Wilt thou not tell us what these *things are* to us, that thou doest *so?*

20 Then I answered them, The word of the LORD came unto me, saying,

21 Speak unto the house of Israel, Thus saith the Lord GOD; Behold, [a]I will profane my sanctuary, the excellency of your strength, the desire of your eyes, and that which your soul pitieth; [b]and your sons and your daughters whom ye have left shall fall by the sword.

22 And ye shall do as I have done: [a]ye shall not cover *your* lips, nor eat the bread of men.

23 And your tires *shall be* upon your heads, and your shoes upon your feet: [a]ye shall not mourn nor weep; but [b]ye shall pine away for your iniquities, and mourn one toward another.

6 [a]2 Kin. 24:3, 4; Ezek. 22:2, 3, 27; Mic. 7:2; Nah. 3:1 [b]2 Sam. 8:2; Joel 3:3; Obad. 11; Nah. 3:10
7 [a]Lev. 17:13; Deut. 12:16
8 [a][Matt. 7:2]
9 [a]Ezek. 24:6; Nah. 3:1; Hab. 2:12
11 [a]Ezek. 22:15
13 [a]Ezek. 23:36–48 [b]Jer. 6:28–30; Ezek. 22:24 [c]Ezek. 5:13; 8:18; 16:42
14 [a][1 Sam. 15:29] [b]Num. 23:19; Ps. 33:9; Is. 55:11 [c]Ezek. 5:11
16 [a]Jer. 16:5
17 [a]Jer. 16:5 [b]Lev. 10:6; 21:10 [c]2 Sam. 15:30 [d]Mic. 3:7
19 [a]Ezek. 12:9; 37:18
21 [a]Jer. 7:14; Lam. 2:7; Ezek. 7:20, 24 [b]Jer. 6:11; 16:3, 4; Ezek. 23:25, 47
22 [a]Jer. 16:6, 7
23 [a]Job 27:15; Ps. 78:64 [b]Lev. 26:39; Ezek. 33:10

*
24:14 LXX, Syr., Tg., Vg. *I*

NKJV

"Woe to [a]the bloody city,
To the pot whose scum *is* in it,
And whose scum is not gone from it!
Bring it out piece by piece,
On which no [b]lot has fallen.
7 For her blood is in her midst;
She set it on top of a rock;
[a]She did not pour it on the ground,
To cover it with dust.
8 That it may raise up fury and take vengeance,
[a]I have set her blood on top of a rock,
That it may not be covered."

9 'Therefore thus says the Lord GOD:

[a]"Woe to the bloody city!
I too will make the pyre great.
10 Heap on the wood,
Kindle the fire;
Cook the meat well,
Mix in the spices,
And let the cuts be burned up.

11 "Then set the pot empty on the coals,
That it may become hot and its bronze may burn,
That [a]its filthiness may be melted in it,
That its scum may be consumed.
12 She has grown weary with lies,
And her great scum has not gone from her.
Let her scum *be* in the fire!
13 In your [a]filthiness *is* lewdness.
Because I have cleansed you, and you were not cleansed,
You will [b]not be cleansed of your filthiness anymore,
[c]Till I have caused My fury to rest upon you.
14 [a]I, the LORD, have spoken *it;*
[b]It shall come to pass, and I will do *it;*
I will not hold back,
[c]Nor will I spare,
Nor will I relent;
According to your ways
And according to your deeds
*They will judge you,"
Says the Lord GOD.'"

The Prophet's Wife Dies

15 Also the word of the LORD came to me, saying,

16 "Son of man, behold, I take away from you the desire of your eyes with one stroke; yet you shall [a]neither mourn nor weep, nor shall your tears run down.

17 "Sigh in silence, [a]make no mourning for the dead; [b]bind your turban on your head, and [c]put your sandals on your feet; [d]do not cover *your* lips, and do not eat man's bread *of sorrow.*"

18 So I spoke to the people in the morning, and at evening my wife died; and the next morning I did as I was commanded.

19 And the people said to me, [a]"Will you not tell us what these *things signify* to us, that you behave so?"

20 Then I answered them, "The word of the LORD came to me, saying,

21 'Speak to the house of Israel, "Thus says the Lord GOD: 'Behold, [a]I will profane My sanctuary, your arrogant boast, the desire of your eyes, the delight of your soul; [b]and your sons and daughters whom you left behind shall fall by the sword.

22 'And you shall do as I have done; [a]you shall not cover *your* lips nor eat man's bread *of sorrow.*

23 'Your turbans shall be on your heads and your sandals on your feet; [a]you shall neither mourn nor weep, but [b]you shall pine away in your iniquities and mourn with one another.

KJV

24 Thus [a]Ezekiel is unto you a sign: according to all that he hath done shall ye do: [b]and when this cometh, [c]ye shall know that I *am* the Lord GOD.

25 Also, thou son of man, *shall it* not *be* in the day when I take from them [a]their strength, the joy of their glory, the desire of their eyes, and that whereupon they set their minds, their sons and their daughters,

26 *That* [a]he that escapeth in that day shall come unto thee, to cause *thee* to hear *it* with *thine* ears?

27 [a]In that day shall thy mouth be opened to him which is escaped, and thou shalt speak, and be no more dumb: and thou shalt be a sign unto them; and they shall know that I *am* the LORD.

Proclamation Against Ammon

25 The word of the LORD came again unto me, saying,

2 Son of man, [a]set thy face [b]against the Ammonites, and prophesy against them;

3 And say unto the Ammonites, Hear the word of the Lord GOD; Thus saith the Lord GOD; [a]Because thou saidst, Aha, against my sanctuary, when it was profaned; and against the land of Israel, when it was desolate; and against the house of Judah, when they went into captivity;

4 Behold, therefore I will deliver thee to the men of the east for a possession, and they shall set their palaces in thee, and make their dwellings in thee: they shall eat thy fruit, and they shall drink thy milk.

5 And I will make [a]Rabbah [b]a stable for camels, and the Ammonites a couchingplace for flocks: [c]and ye shall know that I *am* the LORD.

6 For thus saith the Lord GOD; Because thou [a]hast clapped *thine* hands, and stamped with the feet, and [b]rejoiced in heart with all thy despite against the land of Israel;

7 Behold, therefore I will [a]stretch out mine hand upon thee, and will deliver thee for a spoil to the heathen; and I will cut thee off from the people, and I will cause thee to perish out of the countries: I will destroy thee; and thou shalt know that I *am* the LORD.

Proclamation Against Moab

8 Thus saith the Lord GOD; Because that [a]Moab and [b]Seir do say, Behold, the house of Judah *is* like unto all the heathen;

9 Therefore, behold, I will open the side of Moab from the cities, from his cities *which are* on his frontiers, the glory of the country, Beth–jeshimoth, Baal–meon, and [a]Kiriathaim,

10 [a]Unto the men of the east with the Ammonites, and will give them in possession, that the Ammonites [b]may not be remembered among the nations.

11 And I will execute judgments upon Moab; and they shall know that I *am* the LORD.

Proclamation Against Edom

12 Thus saith the Lord GOD; [a]Because that Edom hath dealt against the house of Judah by taking vengeance, and hath greatly offended, and revenged himself upon them;

13 Therefore thus saith the Lord GOD; I will also stretch out mine hand upon Edom, and will cut off man and beast from it; and I will make it desolate from Teman; and they of Dedan shall fall by the sword.

14 And [a]I will lay my vengeance upon Edom by the hand of my people Israel: and they shall do in Edom according to mine anger and according to my fury; and they shall know my vengeance, saith the Lord GOD.

Proclamation Against Philistia

15 Thus saith the Lord GOD; [a]Because [b]the Philistines have dealt by revenge, and have taken

---

24 [a]Is. 20:3; Ezek. 4:3; 12:6, 11; Luke 11:29, 30 [b]Jer. 17:15; John 13:19; 14:29 [c]Ezek. 6:7; 25:5
25 [a]Ps. 48:2; 50:2; Ezek. 24:21
26 [a]Ezek. 33:21
27 [a]Ezek. 3:26; 33:22

CHAPTER 25

2 [a]Ezek. 35:2 [b]Jer. 49:1; Ezek. 21:28; Amos 1:13–15; Zeph. 2:9
3 [a]Ps. 70:2, 3; [Prov. 17:5]; Ezek. 26:2
5 [a]Deut. 3:11; 2 Sam. 12:26; Jer. 49:2; Ezek. 21:20 [b]Is. 17:2 [c]Ezek. 24:24
6 [a]Job 27:23; Lam. 2:15; Nah. 3:19; Zeph. 2:15 [b]Ezek. 36:5
7 [a]Ezek. 35:3
8 [a]Is. 15:6; Jer. 48:1; Amos 2:1, 2 [b]Ezek. 35:2, 5
9 [a]Num. 32:3, 38; Josh. 13:17; 1 Chr. 5:8; Jer. 48:23
10 [a]Ezek. 25:4 [b]Ezek. 21:32
12 [a]2 Chr. 28:17; Ps. 137:7; Jer. 49:7, 8; Amos 1:11; Obad. 10–14
14 [a]Is. 11:14
15 [a]Jer. 25:20; Amos 1–6 [b]2 Chr. 28:18

NKJV

24 'Thus [a]Ezekiel is a sign to you; according to all that he has done you shall do; [b]and when this comes, [c]you shall know that I *am* the Lord GOD.' "

25 'And you, son of man—*will it* not *be* in the day when I take from them [a]their stronghold, their joy and their glory, the desire of their eyes, and that on which they set their minds, their sons and their daughters:

26 'on that day [a]one who escapes will come to you to let *you* hear *it* with *your* ears;

27 [a]'on that day your mouth will be opened to him who has escaped; you shall speak and no longer be mute. Thus you will be a sign to them, and they shall know that I *am* the LORD.' "

Proclamation Against Ammon

25 The word of the LORD came to me, saying,

2 "Son of man, [a]set your face [b]against the Ammonites, and prophesy against them.

3 "Say to the Ammonites, 'Hear the word of the Lord GOD! Thus says the Lord GOD: [a]"Because you said, 'Aha!' against My sanctuary when it was profaned, and against the land of Israel when it was desolate, and against the house of Judah when they went into captivity,

4 "indeed, therefore, I will deliver you as a possession to the men of the East, and they shall set their encampments among you and make their dwellings among you; they shall eat your fruit, and they shall drink your milk.

5 "And I will make [a]Rabbah [b]a stable for camels and Ammon a resting place for flocks. [c]Then you shall know that I *am* the LORD."

6 'For thus says the Lord GOD: "Because you [a]clapped *your* hands, stamped your feet, and [b]rejoiced in heart with all your disdain for the land of Israel,

7 "indeed, therefore, I will [a]stretch out My hand against you, and give you as plunder to the nations; I will cut you off from the peoples, and I will cause you to perish from the countries; I will destroy you, and you shall know that I *am* the LORD."

Proclamation Against Moab

8 'Thus says the Lord GOD: "Because [a]Moab and [b]Seir say, 'Look! The house of Judah *is* like all the nations,'

9 "therefore, behold, I will clear the territory of Moab of cities, of the cities on its frontier, the glory of the country, Beth Jeshimoth, Baal Meon, and [a]Kirjathaim.

10 [a]"To the men of the East I will give it as a possession, together with the Ammonites, that the Ammonites [b]may not be remembered among the nations.

11 "And I will execute judgments upon Moab, and they shall know that I *am* the LORD."

Proclamation Against Edom

12 'Thus says the Lord GOD: [a]"Because of what Edom did against the house of Judah by taking vengeance, and has greatly offended by avenging itself on them,"

13 'therefore thus says the Lord GOD: "I will also stretch out My hand against Edom, cut off man and beast from it, and make it desolate from Teman; Dedan shall fall by the sword.

14 [a]"I will lay My vengeance on Edom by the hand of My people Israel, that they may do in Edom according to My anger and according to My fury; and they shall know My vengeance," says the Lord GOD.

Proclamation Against Philistia

15 'Thus says the Lord GOD: [a]"Because [b]the Philistines dealt vengefully and took vengeance

KJV

vengeance with a despiteful heart, to destroy *it* for the old hatred;

16 Therefore thus saith the Lord GOD; Behold, [a]I will stretch out mine hand upon the Philistines, and I will cut off the [b]Cherethims, [c]and destroy the remnant of the sea coast.

17 And I will [a]execute great vengeance upon them with furious rebukes; [b]and they shall know that I *am* the LORD, when I shall lay my vengeance upon them.

Proclamation Against Tyre

26 And it came to pass in the eleventh year, in the first *day* of the month, *that* the word of the LORD came unto me, saying,

2 Son of man, [a]because that Tyrus hath said against Jerusalem, [b]Aha, she is broken *that was* the gates of the people: she is turned unto me: I shall be replenished, *now* she is laid waste:

3 Therefore thus saith the Lord GOD; Behold, I *am* against thee, O Tyrus, and will cause many nations to come up against thee, as the sea causeth his waves to come up.

4 And they shall destroy the walls of Tyrus, and break down her towers: I will also scrape her dust from her, and [a]make her like the top of a rock.

5 It shall be *a place for* the spreading of nets [a]in the midst of the sea: for I have spoken *it*, saith the Lord GOD: and it shall become a spoil to the nations.

6 And her daughters which *are* in the field shall be slain by the sword; [a]and they shall know that I *am* the LORD.

7 For thus saith the Lord GOD; Behold, I will bring upon Tyrus [a]Nebuchadrezzar king of Babylon, [b]a king of kings, from the north, with horses, and with chariots, and with horsemen, and companies, and much people.

8 He shall slay with the sword thy daughters in the field: and he shall [a]make a fort against thee, and cast a mount against thee, and lift up the buckler against thee.

9 And he shall set engines of war against thy walls, and with his axes he shall break down thy towers.

10 By reason of the abundance of his horses their dust shall cover thee: thy walls shall shake at the noise of the horsemen, and of the wheels, and of the chariots, when he shall enter into thy gates, as men enter into a city wherein is made a breach.

11 With the hoofs of his [a]horses shall he tread down all thy streets: he shall slay thy people by the sword, and thy strong garrisons shall go down to the ground.

12 And they shall make a spoil of thy riches, and make a prey of thy merchandise: and they shall break down thy walls, and destroy thy pleasant houses: and they shall lay thy stones and thy timber and thy dust in the [a]midst of the water.

13 [a]And I will cause the noise of [b]thy songs to cease; and the sound of thy harps shall be no more heard.

14 And [a]I will make thee like the top of a rock: thou shalt be *a place* to spread nets upon; thou shalt be built no more: for I the LORD have spoken *it*, saith the Lord GOD.

15 Thus saith the Lord GOD to Tyrus; Shall not the isles [a]shake at the sound of thy fall, when the wounded cry, when the slaughter is made in the midst of thee?

16 Then all the [a]princes of the sea shall [b]come down from their thrones, and lay away their robes, and put off their broidered garments: they shall clothe themselves with trembling; [c]they shall sit upon the ground, and [d]shall tremble at *every* moment, and [e]be astonished at thee.

17 And they shall take up a [a]lamentation for thee, and say to thee, How art thou destroyed,

---

16 [a]Zeph. 2:4 [b]1 Sam. 30:14 [c]Jer. 47:4 **17** [a]Ezek. 5:15 [b]Ps. 9:16

CHAPTER 26

2 [a]2 Sam. 5:11; Is. 23:1; Jer. 25:22; Amos 1:9; Zech. 9:2 [b]Ezek. 25:3 **4** [a]Ezek. 26:14 **5** [a]Ezek. 27:32 **6** [a]Ezek. 25:5 **7** [a]Jer. 27:3–6; Ezek. 29:18 [b]Ezra 7:12; Is. 10:8; Jer. 52:32; Dan. 2:37, 47 **8** [a]Jer. 52:4; Ezek. 21:22 **11** [a]Hab. 1:8 **12** [a]Ezek. 27:27, 32 **13** [a]Is. 14:11; 24:8; Jer. 7:34; 25:10; Amos 6:5 [b]Is. 23:16; Ezek. 28:13; Rev. 18:22 **14** [a]Ezek. 26:4, 5 **15** [a]Jer. 49:21; Ezek. 27:28 **16** [a]Is. 23:8 [b]Jon. 3:6 [c]Job 2:13 [d]Ezek. 32:10; Hos. 11:10 [e]Ezek. 27:35 **17** [a]Ezek. 27:2–36; Rev. 18:9

*

26:7 Heb. *Nebuchadrezzar*, and so elsewhere in the book

NKJV

with a spiteful heart, to destroy because of the old hatred,"

16 'therefore thus says the Lord GOD: [a]"I will stretch out My hand against the Philistines, and I will cut off the [b]Cherethites [c]and destroy the remnant of the seacoast.

17 "I will [a]execute great vengeance on them with furious rebukes; [b]and they shall know that I *am* the LORD, when I lay My vengeance upon them." ' "

Proclamation Against Tyre

26 And it came to pass in the eleventh year, on the first *day* of the month, *that* the word of the LORD came to me, saying,

2 "Son of man, [a]because Tyre has said against Jerusalem, [b]'Aha! She is broken who *was* the gateway of the peoples; now she is turned over to me; I shall be filled; she is laid waste.'

3 "Therefore thus says the Lord GOD: 'Behold, I *am* against you, O Tyre, and will cause many nations to come up against you, as the sea causes its waves to come up.

4 'And they shall destroy the walls of Tyre and break down her towers; I will also scrape her dust from her, and [a]make her like the top of a rock.

5 'It shall be *a place for* spreading nets [a]in the midst of the sea, for I have spoken,' says the Lord GOD; 'it shall become plunder for the nations.

6 'Also her daughter *villages* which *are* in the fields shall be slain by the sword. [a]Then they shall know that I am the LORD.'

7 "For thus says the Lord GOD: 'Behold, I will bring against Tyre from the north [a]Nebuchadnezzar* king of Babylon, [b]king of kings, with horses, with chariots, and with horsemen, and an army with many people.

8 'He will slay with the sword your daughter *villages* in the fields; he will [a]heap up a siege mound against you, build a wall against you, and raise a defense against you.

9 'He will direct his battering rams against your walls, and with his axes he will break down your towers.

10 'Because of the abundance of his horses, their dust will cover you; your walls will shake at the noise of the horsemen, the wagons, and the chariots, when he enters your gates, as men enter a city that has been breached.

11 'With the hooves of his [a]horses he will trample all your streets; he will slay your people by the sword, and your strong pillars will fall to the ground.

12 'They will plunder your riches and pillage your merchandise; they will break down your walls and destroy your pleasant houses; they will lay your stones, your timber, and your soil in the [a]midst of the water.

13 [a]'I will put an end to the sound of [b]your songs, and the sound of your harps shall be heard no more.

14 [a]'I will make you like the top of a rock; you shall be *a place for* spreading nets, and you shall never be rebuilt, for I the LORD have spoken,' says the Lord GOD.

15 "Thus says the Lord GOD to Tyre: 'Will the coastlands not [a]shake at the sound of your fall, when the wounded cry, when slaughter is made in the midst of you?

16 'Then all the [a]princes of the sea will [b]come down from their thrones, lay aside their robes, and take off their embroidered garments; they will clothe themselves with trembling; [c]they will sit on the ground, [d]tremble *every* moment, and [e]be astonished at you.

17 'And they will take up a [a]lamentation for you, and say to you:

KJV

that wast inhabited of seafaring men, the renowned city, which wast [b]strong in the sea, she
and her inhabitants, which cause their terror *to*
be on all that haunt it!
18 Now shall [a]the isles tremble in the day
of thy fall; yea, the isles that *are* in the sea shall
be troubled at thy departure.
19 For thus saith the Lord GOD; When I shall
make thee a desolate city, like the cities that are
not inhabited; when I shall bring up the deep upon
thee, and great waters shall cover thee;
20 When I shall bring thee down [a]with them
that descend into the pit, with the people of old
time, and shall set thee in the low parts of the
earth, in places desolate of old, with them that
go down to the pit, that thou be not inhabited;
and I shall set glory [b]in the land of the living;
21 [a]I will make thee a terror, and thou *shalt*
be no *more:* [b]though thou be sought for, yet shalt
thou never be found again, saith the Lord GOD.

Lamentation for Tyre

27 The word of the LORD came again unto me,
saying,
2 Now, thou son of man, [a]take up a lamentation for Tyrus;
3 And say unto Tyrus, [a]O thou that art situate at the entry of the sea, *which art* [b]a merchant
of the people for many isles, Thus saith the Lord
GOD; O Tyrus, thou hast said, [c]I *am* of perfect
beauty.
4 Thy borders *are* in the midst of the seas,
thy builders have perfected thy beauty.
5 They have made all thy *ship* boards of fir
trees of [a]Senir: they have taken cedars from Lebanon to make masts for thee.
6 *Of* the [a]oaks of Bashan have they made
thine oars; the company of the Ashurites have
made thy benches *of* ivory, *brought* out of [b]the
isles of Chittim.
7 Fine linen with broidered work from
Egypt was that which thou spreadest forth to be
thy sail; blue and purple from the isles of Elishah
was that which covered thee.
8 The inhabitants of Zidon and Arvad were
thy mariners: thy wise *men,* O Tyrus, *that* were
in thee, were thy pilots.
9 The ancients of [a]Gebal and the wise *men*
thereof were in thee thy calkers: all the ships of
the sea with their mariners were in thee to occupy
thy merchandise.
10 They of Persia and of Lud and of Phut
were in thine army, thy men of war: they hanged
the shield and helmet in thee; they set forth thy
comeliness.
11 The men of Arvad with thine army *were*
upon thy walls round about, and the Gammadims
were in thy towers: they hanged their shields
upon thy walls round about; they have made [a]thy
beauty perfect.
12 [a]Tarshish *was* thy merchant by reason of
the multitude of all *kind of* riches; with silver, iron,
tin, and lead, they traded in thy fairs.
13 [a]Javan, Tubal, and Meshech, they *were*
thy merchants: they traded [b]the persons of men
and vessels of brass in thy market.

17 [b]Josh. 19:29; Is. 23:4 **18** [a]Ezek. 26:15 **20** [a]Ezek. 32:18 [b]Ezek. 32:23 **21** [a]Ezek. 27:36; 28:19 [b]Ps. 37:10, 36; Ezek. 28:19

CHAPTER 27

2 [a]Ezek. 26:17 **3** [a]Ezek. 26:17; 28:2 [b]Is. 23:3 [c]Ezek. 28:12 **5** [a]Deut. 3:9; 1 Chr. 5:23; Song 4:8 **6** [a]Is. 2:12, 13; Zech. 11:2 [b]Gen. 10:4; Is. 23:1, 12; Jer. 2:10 **9** [a]Josh. 13:5; 1 Kin. 5:18; Ps. 83:7 **11** [a]Ezek. 27:3 **12** [a]Gen. 10:4; 2 Chr. 20:36; Ezek. 38:13 **13** [a]Gen. 10:2; Is. 66:19; Ezek. 27:19 [b]Joel 3:3–6; Rev. 18:13

NKJV

"How you have perished,
O one inhabited by seafaring men,
O renowned city,
Who was [b]strong at sea,
She and her inhabitants,
Who caused their terror *to be* on all her
inhabitants!
18 Now [a]the coastlands tremble on the day
of your fall;
Yes, the coastlands by the sea are troubled
at your departure." '

19 "For thus says the Lord GOD: 'When I
make you a desolate city, like cities that are not
inhabited, when I bring the deep upon you, and
great waters cover you,
20 'then I will bring you down [a]with those
who descend into the Pit, to the people of old,
and I will make you dwell in the lowest part of
the earth, in places desolate from antiquity, with
those who go down to the Pit, so that you may
never be inhabited; and I shall establish glory [b]in
the land of the living.
21 [a]'I will make you a terror, and you *shall*
be no *more;* [b]though you are sought for, you will
never be found again,' says the Lord GOD."

Lamentation for Tyre

27 The word of the LORD came again to me,
saying,
2 "Now, son of man, [a]take up a lamentation
for Tyre,
3 "and say to Tyre, [a]'You who are situated
at the entrance of the sea, [b]merchant of the peoples on many coastlands, thus says the Lord GOD:

"O Tyre, you have said,
[c]'I *am* perfect in beauty.'
4 Your borders *are* in the midst of the seas.
Your builders have perfected your beauty.
5 They made all *your* planks of fir trees from
[a]Senir;
They took a cedar from Lebanon to make
you a mast.
6 *Of* [a]oaks from Bashan they made your
oars;
The company of Ashurites have inlaid
your planks
With ivory from [b]the coasts of *Cyprus.
7 Fine embroidered linen from Egypt was
what you spread for your sail;
Blue and purple from the coasts of Elishah
was what covered you.

8 "Inhabitants of Sidon and Arvad were your
oarsmen;
Your wise men, O Tyre, were in you;
They became your pilots.
9 Elders of [a]Gebal and its wise men
Were in you to caulk your seams;
All the ships of the sea
And their oarsmen were in you
To market your merchandise.

10 "Those from Persia, *Lydia, and *Libya
Were in your army as men of war;
They hung shield and helmet in you;
They gave splendor to you.
11 Men of Arvad with your army *were* on
your walls *all* around,
And the men of Gammad were in your
towers;
They hung their shields on your walls *all*
around;
They made [a]your beauty perfect.

12 [a]"Tarshish *was* your merchant because of
your many luxury goods. They gave you silver,
iron, tin, and lead for your goods.
13 [a]"Javan, Tubal, and Meshech *were* your
traders. They bartered [b]human lives and vessels
of bronze for your merchandise.

*

27:6 Heb. *Kittim,* western lands, especially Cyprus **27:10** Heb. *Lud* • Heb. *Put*

KJV

14 They of the house of [a]Togarmah traded
in thy fairs with horses and horsemen and mules.
15 The men of [a]Dedan *were* thy merchants;
many isles *were* the merchandise of thine hand:
they brought thee *for* a present horns of ivory and
ebony.
16 Syria *was* thy merchant by reason of the
multitude of the wares of thy making: they occupied in thy fairs with emeralds, purple, and broidered work, and fine linen, and coral, and agate.
17 Judah, and the land of Israel, they *were*
thy merchants: they traded in thy market wheat
of [a]Minnith, and Pannag, and honey, and oil, and
[b]balm.
18 Damascus *was* thy merchant in the multitude of the wares of thy making, for the multitude
of all riches; in the wine of Helbon, and white
wool.
19 Dan also and Javan going to and fro occupied in thy fairs: bright iron, cassia, and calamus,
were in thy market.
20 [a]Dedan *was* thy merchant in precious
clothes for chariots.
21 Arabia, and all the princes of [a]Kedar, they
occupied with thee in lambs, and rams, and goats:
in these *were they* thy merchants.
22 The merchants of [a]Sheba and Raamah,
they *were* thy merchants: they occupied in thy
fairs with chief of all spices, and with all precious
stones, and gold.
23 [a]Haran, and Canneh, and Eden, the merchants of [b]Sheba, Asshur, *and* Chilmad, *were* thy
merchants.
24 These *were* thy merchants in all sorts of
things, in blue clothes, and broidered work, and
in chests of rich apparel, bound with cords, and
made of cedar, among thy merchandise.
25 [a]The ships of Tarshish did sing of thee in
thy market: and thou wast replenished, and made
very glorious [b]in the midst of the seas.
26 Thy rowers have brought thee into great
waters: [a]the east wind hath broken thee in the
midst of the seas.
27 Thy [a]riches, and thy fairs, thy merchandise, thy mariners, and thy pilots, thy calkers, and
the occupiers of thy merchandise, and all thy men
of war, that *are* in thee, and in all thy company
which *is* in the midst of thee, shall fall into the
midst of the seas in the day of thy ruin.
28 The [a]suburbs shall shake at the sound of
the cry of thy pilots.
29 And [a]all that handle the oar, the mariners,
and all the pilots of the sea, shall come down from
their ships, they shall stand upon the land;
30 And shall cause their voice to be heard
against thee, and shall cry bitterly, and shall [a]cast
up dust upon their heads, they [b]shall wallow
themselves in the ashes:
31 And they shall [a]make themselves utterly
bald for thee, and gird them with sackcloth, and
they shall weep for thee with bitterness of heart
and bitter wailing.
32 And in their wailing they shall [a]take up
a lamentation for thee, and lament over thee, *saying*, [b]What *city is* like Tyrus, like the destroyed
in the midst of the sea?
33 [a]When thy wares went forth out of the
seas, thou filledst many people; thou didst enrich

14 [a]Gen. 10:3; Ezek. 38:6
15 [a]Gen. 10:7; Is. 21:13
17 [a]Judg. 11:33; 1 Kin. 5:9, 11; Ezra 3:7; Acts 12:20 [b]Jer. 8:22
20 [a]Gen. 25:3
21 [a]Gen. 25:13; Is. 60:7; Jer. 49:28
22 [a]Gen. 10:7; 1 Kin. 10:1, 2; Ps. 72:10; Is. 60:6; Ezek. 38:13
23 [a]Gen. 11:31; 2 Kin. 19:12; Is. 37:12 [b]Gen. 25:3
25 [a]Ps. 48:7; Is. 2:16 [b]Ezek. 27:4
26 [a]Ps. 48:7; Jer. 18:17; Acts 27:14
27 [a][Prov. 11:4]
28 [a]Ezek. 26:15
29 [a]Rev. 18:17
30 [a]1 Sam. 4:12; 2 Sam. 1:2; Job 2:12; Lam. 2:10; Rev. 18:19 [b]Esth. 4:1, 3; Jer. 6:26; Jon. 3:6
31 [a]Is. 15:2; Jer. 16:6; Ezek. 29:18
32 [a]Ezek. 26:17 [b]Ezek. 26:4, 5; Rev. 18:18
33 [a]Rev. 18:19

NKJV

14 "Those from the house of [a]Togarmah
traded for your wares with horses, steeds, and
mules.
15 "The men of [a]Dedan *were* your traders;
many isles *were* the market of your hand. They
brought you ivory tusks and ebony as payment.
16 "Syria *was* your merchant because of the
abundance of goods you made. They gave you
for your wares emeralds, purple, embroidery, fine
linen, corals, and rubies.
17 "Judah and the land of Israel *were* your
traders. They traded for your merchandise wheat
of [a]Minnith, millet, honey, oil, and [b]balm.
18 "Damascus *was* your merchant because
of the abundance of goods you made, because of
your many luxury items, with the wine of Helbon
and with white wool.
19 "Dan and Javan paid for your wares, traversing back and forth. Wrought iron, cassia, and
cane were among your merchandise.
20 [a]"Dedan *was* your merchant in saddle-
cloths for riding.
21 "Arabia and all the princes of [a]Kedar
were your regular merchants. They traded with
you in lambs, rams, and goats.
22 "The merchants of [a]Sheba and Raamah
were your merchants. They traded for your wares
the choicest spices, all kinds of precious stones,
and gold.
23 [a]"Haran, Canneh, Eden, the merchants of
[b]Sheba, Assyria, *and* Chilmad *were* your merchants.
24 "These *were* your merchants in choice
items—in purple clothes, in embroidered
garments, in chests of multicolored apparel, in
sturdy woven cords, which were in your marketplace.

25 "The [a]ships of Tarshish were carriers of
your merchandise.
You were filled and very glorious [b]in the
midst of the seas.
26 Your oarsmen brought you into many
waters,
But [a]the east wind broke you in the midst
of the seas.

27 "Your [a]riches, wares, and merchandise,
Your mariners and pilots,
Your caulkers and merchandisers,
All your men of war who *are* in you,
And the entire company which *is* in your
midst,
Will fall into the midst of the seas on the
day of your ruin.
28 The [a]common-land will shake at the
sound of the cry of your pilots.

29 "All [a]who handle the oar,
The mariners,
All the pilots of the sea
Will come down from their ships *and*
stand on the shore.
30 They will make their voice heard because
of you;
They will cry bitterly and [a]cast dust on
their heads;
They [b]will roll about in ashes;
31 They will [a]shave themselves completely
bald because of you,
Gird themselves with sackcloth,
And weep for you
With bitterness of heart *and* bitter wailing.
32 In their wailing for you
They will [a]take up a lamentation,
And lament for you:
[b]'What *city is* like Tyre,
Destroyed in the midst of the sea?

33 'When[a] your wares went out by sea,
You satisfied many people;

KJV

the kings of the earth with the multitude of thy
riches and of thy merchandise.
34 In the time *when* [a]thou shalt be broken
by the seas in the depths of the waters [b]thy merchandise and all thy company in the midst of thee
shall fall.
35 [a]All the inhabitants of the isles shall be
astonished at thee, and their kings shall be sore
afraid, they shall be troubled in *their* countenance.
36 The merchants among the people [a]shall
hiss at thee; [b]thou shalt be a terror, and never
shalt be any [c]more.

Proclamation Against the King of Tyre

28 The word of the LORD came again unto me,
saying,
2 Son of man, say unto the prince of Tyrus,
Thus saith the Lord GOD; Because thine heart *is*
[a]lifted up, and [b]thou hast said, I *am* a God, I sit
in the seat of God, [c]in the midst of the seas; [d]yet
thou *art* a man, and not God, though thou set thine
heart as the heart of God:
3 Behold, [a]thou *art* wiser than Daniel; there
is no secret that they can hide from thee:
4 With thy wisdom and with thine understanding thou hast gotten thee [a]riches, and hast
gotten gold and silver into thy treasures:
5 [a]By thy great wisdom *and* by thy traffick
hast thou increased thy riches, and thine heart is
lifted up because of thy riches:
6 Therefore thus saith the Lord GOD; Because thou hast set thine heart as the heart of
God;
7 Behold, therefore I will bring [a]strangers
upon thee, [b]the terrible of the nations: and they
shall draw their swords against the beauty of thy
wisdom, and they shall defile thy brightness.
8 They shall bring thee down to the [a]pit, and
thou shalt die the deaths of *them that are* slain
in the midst of the seas.
9 Wilt thou yet [a]say before him that slayeth
thee, I *am* God? but thou *shalt be* a man, and no
God, in the hand of him that slayeth thee.
10 Thou shalt die the deaths of [a]the uncircumcised by the hand of strangers: for I have spoken *it*, saith the Lord GOD.

Lamentation for the King of Tyre

11 Moreover the word of the LORD came unto
me, saying,
12 Son of man, [a]take up a lamentation upon
the king of Tyrus, and say unto him, Thus saith
the Lord GOD; [b]Thou sealest up the sum, full of
wisdom, and perfect in beauty.
13 Thou hast been in [a]Eden the garden of
God; every precious stone *was* thy covering, the
sardius, topaz, and the diamond, the beryl, the
onyx, and the jasper, the sapphire, the emerald,
and the carbuncle, and gold: the workmanship of

---

34 [a]Ezek. 26:19 [b]Ezek. 27:27
35 [a]Is. 23:6; Ezek. 26:15, 16
36 [a]Jer. 18:16; Zeph. 2:15 [b]Ezek. 26:2 [c]Ps. 37:10, 36; Ezek. 28:19

CHAPTER 28
2 [a]Jer. 49:16; Ezek. 31:10 [b]Is. 14:14; 47:8; Ezek. 28:9; 2 Thess. 2:4 [c]Ezek. 27:3, 4 [d]Is. 31:3; Ezek. 28:9
3 [a]Ezek. 14:14; Dan. 1:20; 2:20–23, 28; 5:11, 12; Zech. 9:3
4 [a]Ezek. 27:33; Zech. 9:1–3
5 [a]Ps. 62:10; Zech. 9:3
7 [a]Ezek. 26:7 [b]Ezek. 7:24; 21:31; 30:11; Hab. 1:6–8
8 [a]Is. 14:15
9 [a]Ezek. 28:2
10 [a]1 Sam. 17:26, 36; Ezek. 31:18; 32:19, 21, 25, 27
12 [a]Ezek. 27:2 [b]Ezek. 27:3; 28:3
13 [a]Gen. 2:8; Is. 51:3; Ezek. 31:8, 9; 36:35 [b]Ezek. 26:13

NKJV

You enriched the kings of the earth
With your many luxury goods and your
merchandise.
34 But [a]you are broken by the seas in the
depths of the waters;
[b]Your merchandise and the entire
company will fall in your midst.
35 [a]All the inhabitants of the isles will be
astonished at you;
Their kings will be greatly afraid,
And *their* countenance will be troubled.
36 The merchants among the peoples [a]will
hiss at you;
[b]You will become a horror, and *be* no
[c]more forever.' " ' "

Proclamation Against the King of Tyre

28 The word of the LORD came to me again,
saying,
2 "Son of man, say to the prince of Tyre,
'Thus says the Lord GOD:

"Because your heart *is* [a]lifted up,
And [b]you say, 'I *am* a god,
I sit *in* the seat of gods,
[c]In the midst of the seas,'
[d]Yet you *are* a man, and not a god,
Though you set your heart as the heart
of a god
3 (Behold, [a]you *are* wiser than Daniel!
There is no secret that can be hidden from
you!
4 With your wisdom and your
understanding
You have gained [a]riches for yourself,
And gathered gold and silver into your
treasures;
5 [a]By your great wisdom in trade you have
increased your riches,
And your heart is lifted up because of your
riches),"

6 'Therefore thus says the Lord GOD:

"Because you have set your heart as the
heart of a god,
7 Behold, therefore, I will bring [a]strangers
against you,
[b]The most terrible of the nations;
And they shall draw their swords against
the beauty of your wisdom,
And defile your splendor.
8 They shall throw you down into the [a]Pit,
And you shall die the death of the slain
In the midst of the seas.

9 "Will you still [a]say before him who slays
you,
'I *am* a god'?
But you *shall be* a man, and not a god,
In the hand of him who slays you.
10 You shall die the death of [a]the
uncircumcised
By the hand of aliens;
For I have spoken," says the Lord GOD.' "

Lamentation for the King of Tyre

11 Moreover the word of the LORD came to
me, saying,
12 "Son of man, [a]take up a lamentation for
the king of Tyre, and say to him, 'Thus says the
Lord GOD:

[b]"You *were* the seal of perfection,
Full of wisdom and perfect in beauty.
13 You were in [a]Eden, the garden of God;
Every precious stone *was* your covering:
The sardius, topaz, and diamond,
Beryl, onyx, and jasper,
Sapphire, turquoise, and emerald with
gold.
The workmanship of [b]your timbrels and
pipes

KJV

[b]thy tabrets and of thy pipes was prepared in thee
in the day that thou wast created.
14 Thou *art* the anointed [a]cherub that covereth; and I have set thee *so:* thou wast upon [b]the
holy mountain of God; thou hast walked up and
down in the midst of the stones of fire.
15 Thou *wast* perfect in thy ways from the
day that thou wast created, till [a]iniquity was
found in thee.
16 By the multitude of thy merchandise they
have filled the midst of thee with violence, and
thou hast sinned: therefore I will cast thee as profane out of the mountain of God: and I will destroy
thee, [a]O covering cherub, from the midst of the
stones of fire.
17 [a]Thine heart was lifted up because of thy
beauty, thou hast corrupted thy wisdom by reason
of thy brightness: I will cast thee to the ground,
I will lay thee before kings, that they may behold
thee.
18 Thou hast defiled thy sanctuaries by the
multitude of thine iniquities, by the iniquity of thy
traffick; therefore will I bring forth a fire from
the midst of thee, it shall devour thee, and I will
bring thee to ashes upon the earth in the sight of
all them that behold thee.
19 All they that know thee among the people
shall be astonished at thee: [a]thou shalt be a terror,
and never *shalt* thou *be* any [b]more.

Proclamation Against Sidon

20 Again the word of the LORD came unto
me, saying,
21 Son of man, [a]set thy face [b]against Zidon,
and prophesy against it,
22 And say, Thus saith the Lord GOD; [a]Be-
hold, I *am* against thee, O Zidon; and I will be
glorified in the midst of thee: and [b]they shall
know that I *am* the LORD, when I shall have executed judgments in her, and shall be [c]sanctified
in her.
23 [a]For I will send into her pestilence, and
blood into her street; and the wounded shall be
judged in the midst of her by the sword upon her
on every side; and they shall know that I *am* the
LORD.
24 And there shall be no more a pricking
brier unto the house of Israel, nor [a]*any* grieving
thorn of all *that are* round about them, that [b]de-
spised them; and they shall know that I *am* the
Lord GOD.

Israel's Future Blessing

25 Thus saith the Lord GOD; When I shall
have [a]gathered the house of Israel from the people
among whom they are scattered, and shall be
[b]sanctified in them in the sight of the heathen,
then shall they dwell in their land that I have
given to my servant Jacob.
26 And they shall [a]dwell safely therein, and
shall [b]build houses, and [c]plant vineyards; yea,
they shall dwell with confidence, when I have executed judgments upon all those that despise them
round about them; and they shall know that I *am*
the LORD their God.

Proclamation Against Egypt

29 In the tenth year, in the tenth *month,* in
the twelfth *day* of the month, the word of
the LORD came unto me, saying,

13 [b]Ezek. 26:13
14 [a]Ex. 25:20; Ezek. 28:16 [b]Is. 14:13; Ezek. 20:40
15 [a][Is. 14:12]
16 [a]Ezek. 28:14
17 [a]Ezek. 28:2, 5
19 [a]Ezek. 26:21 [b]Ezek. 27:36
21 [a]Ezek. 6:2; 25:2; 29:2 [b]Gen. 10:15, 19; Is. 23:2, 4, 12; Ezek. 27:8; 32:30
22 [a]Ex. 14:4, 17; Ezek. 39:13 [b]Ps. 9:16 [c]Ezek. 28:25
23 [a]Ezek. 38:22
24 [a]Num. 33:55; Josh. 23:13; Is. 55:13; Ezek. 2:6 [b]Ezek. 16:57; 25:6, 7
25 [a]Ps. 106:47; Is. 11:12, 13; Jer. 32:37; Ezek. 11:17; 20:41; 34:13; 37:21 [b]Ezek. 28:22
26 [a]Jer. 23:6; Ezek. 36:28 [b]Is. 65:21; Jer. 32:15, 43, 44; Amos 9:13, 14 [c]Jer. 31:5; Amos 9:14

NKJV

Was prepared for you on the day you were
created.

14 "You *were* the anointed [a]cherub who
covers;
I established you;
You were on [b]the holy mountain of God;
You walked back and forth in the midst
of fiery stones.
15 You *were* perfect in your ways from the
day you were created,
Till [a]iniquity was found in you.

16 "By the abundance of your trading
You became filled with violence within,
And you sinned;
Therefore I cast you as a profane thing
Out of the mountain of God;
And I destroyed you, [a]O covering cherub,
From the midst of the fiery stones.

17 "Your [a]heart was lifted up because of your
beauty;
You corrupted your wisdom for the sake
of your splendor;
I cast you to the ground,
I laid you before kings,
That they might gaze at you.

18 "You defiled your sanctuaries
By the multitude of your iniquities,
By the iniquity of your trading;
Therefore I brought fire from your midst;
It devoured you,
And I turned you to ashes upon the earth
In the sight of all who saw you.
19 All who knew you among the peoples are
astonished at you;
[a]You have become a horror,
And *shall be* no [b]more forever." ' "

Proclamation Against Sidon

20 Then the word of the LORD came to me,
saying,
21 "Son of man, [a]set your face [b]toward Sidon, and prophesy against her,
22 "and say, 'Thus says the Lord GOD:

[a]"Behold, I *am* against you, O Sidon;
I will be glorified in your midst;
And [b]they shall know that I *am* the LORD,
When I execute judgments in her and am
[c]hallowed in her.
23 [a]For I will send pestilence upon her,
And blood in her streets;
The wounded shall be judged in her midst
By the sword against her on every side;
Then they shall know that I *am* the LORD.

24 "And there shall no longer be a pricking
brier or [a]a painful thorn for the house of Israel
from among all *who are* around them, who [b]de-
spise them. Then they shall know that I *am* the
Lord GOD."

Israel's Future Blessing

25 'Thus says the Lord GOD: "When I have
[a]gathered the house of Israel from the peoples
among whom they are scattered, and am [b]hal-
lowed in them in the sight of the Gentiles, then
they will dwell in their own land which I gave to
My servant Jacob.
26 "And they will [a]dwell safely there, [b]build
houses, and [c]plant vineyards; yes, they will dwell
securely, when I execute judgments on all those
around them who despise them. Then they shall
know that I *am* the LORD their God." ' "

Proclamation Against Egypt

29 In the tenth year, in the tenth *month,* on
the twelfth *day* of the month, the word of
the LORD came to me, saying,

KJV

2 Son of man, [a]set thy face against Pharaoh king of Egypt, and prophesy against him, and [b]against all Egypt:

3 Speak, and say, Thus saith the Lord GOD; [a]Behold, I *am* against thee, Pharaoh king of Egypt, the great [b]dragon that lieth in the midst of his rivers, [c]which hath said, My river *is* mine own, and I have made *it* for myself.

4 But [a]I will put hooks in thy jaws, and I will cause the fish of thy rivers to stick unto thy scales, and I will bring thee up out of the midst of thy rivers, and all the fish of thy rivers shall stick unto thy scales.

5 And I will leave thee *thrown* into the wilderness, thee and all the fish of thy rivers: thou shalt fall upon the open [a]fields; [b]thou shalt not be brought together, nor gathered: [c]I have given thee for meat to the beasts of the field and to the fowls of the heaven.

6 And all the inhabitants of Egypt shall know that I *am* the LORD, because they have been a [a]staff of reed to the house of Israel.

7 [a]When they took hold of thee by thy hand, thou didst break, and rend all their shoulder: and when they leaned upon thee, thou brakest, and madest all their loins to be at a stand.

8 Therefore thus saith the Lord GOD; Behold, I will bring [a]a sword upon thee, and cut off man and beast out of thee.

9 And the land of Egypt shall be [a]desolate and waste; and they shall know that I *am* the LORD: because he hath said, The river *is* mine, and I have made *it*.

10 Behold, therefore I *am* against thee, and against thy rivers, [a]and I will make the land of Egypt utterly waste *and* desolate, [b]from the tower of Syene even unto the border of Ethiopia.

11 [a]No foot of man shall pass through it, nor foot of beast shall pass through it, neither shall it be inhabited forty years.

12 [a]And I will make the land of Egypt desolate in the midst of the countries *that are* desolate, and her cities among the cities *that are* laid waste shall be desolate forty years: and I will [b]scatter the Egyptians among the nations, and will disperse them through the countries.

13 Yet thus saith the Lord GOD; At the [a]end of forty years will I gather the Egyptians from the people whither they were scattered:

14 And I will bring again the captivity of Egypt, and will cause them to return *into* the land of Pathros, into the land of their habitation; and they shall be there a [a]base kingdom.

15 It shall be the basest of the kingdoms; neither shall it exalt itself any more above the nations: for I will diminish them, that they shall no more rule over the nations.

16 And it shall be no more [a]the confidence of the house of Israel, which bringeth *their* iniquity to remembrance, when they shall look after them: but they shall know that I *am* the Lord GOD.

Babylonia Will Plunder Egypt

17 And it came to pass in the seven and twentieth year, in the first *month,* in the first *day* of the month, the word of the LORD came unto me, saying,

18 Son of man, [a]Nebuchadrezzar king of Babylon caused his army to serve a great service against Tyrus: every head *was* made [b]bald, and every shoulder *was* peeled: yet had he no wages,

CHAPTER 29

2 [a]Ezek. 28:21 [b]Is. 19:1; Jer. 25:19; 46:2, 25; Ezek. 30:1—32:32; Joel 3:19
3 [a]Jer. 44:30; Ezek. 28:22; 29:10 [b]Ps. 74:13, 14; Is. 37:1; 51:9; Ezek. 32:2 [c]Ezek. 28:2
4 [a]2 Kin. 19:28; Is. 37:29; Ezek. 38:4
5 [a]Ezek. 32:4–6 [b]Jer. 8:2; 16:4; 25:33 [c]Jer. 7:33; 34:20; Ezek. 39:4
6 [a]2 Kin. 18:21; Is. 36:6; Ezek. 17:15
7 [a]Jer. 37:5, 7, 11; Ezek. 17:17
8 [a]Jer. 46:13; Ezek. 14:17; 32:11–13
9 [a]Ezek. 30:7, 8
10 [a]Ezek. 30:12 [b]Ezek. 30:6
11 [a]Jer. 43:11, 12; 46:19; Ezek. 32:13
12 [a]Jer. 25:15–19; 27:6–11; Ezek. 30:7, 26 [b]Jer. 46:19; Ezek. 30:23, 26
13 [a]Is. 19:23; Jer. 46:26
14 [a]Ezek. 17:6, 14
16 [a]Is. 30:2, 3; 36:4, 6; Lam. 4:17; Ezek. 17:15; 29:6
18 [a]Jer. 25:9; 27:6; Ezek. 26:7–12 [b]Jer. 48:37; Ezek. 27:31

NKJV

2 "Son of man, [a]set your face against Pharaoh king of Egypt, and prophesy against him, and [b]against all Egypt.

3 "Speak, and say, 'Thus says the Lord GOD:

[a]"Behold, I *am* against you,
O Pharaoh king of Egypt,
O great [b]monster who lies in the midst of his rivers,
[c]Who has said, 'My *River *is* my own;
I have made *it* for myself.'

4 But [a]I will put hooks in your jaws,
And cause the fish of your rivers to stick to your scales;
I will bring you up out of the midst of your rivers,
And all the fish in your rivers will stick to your scales.

5 I will leave you in the wilderness,
You and all the fish of your rivers;
You shall fall on the open [a]field;
[b]You shall not be picked up or *gathered.
[c]I have given you as food
To the beasts of the field
And to the birds of the heavens.

6 "Then all the inhabitants of Egypt
Shall know that I *am* the LORD,
Because they have been a [a]staff of reed to the house of Israel.

7 [a]When they took hold of you with the hand,
You broke and tore all their *shoulders;
When they leaned on you,
You broke and made all their backs quiver."

8 'Therefore thus says the Lord GOD: "Surely I will bring [a]a sword upon you and cut off from you man and beast.

9 "And the land of Egypt shall become [a]desolate and waste; then they will know that I *am* the LORD, because he said, 'The River *is* mine, and I have made *it*.'

10 "Indeed, therefore, I *am* against you and against your rivers, [a]and I will make the land of Egypt utterly waste and desolate, [b]from *Migdol *to* Syene, as far as the border of Ethiopia.

11 [a]"Neither foot of man shall pass through it nor foot of beast pass through it, and it shall be uninhabited forty years.

12 [a]"I will make the land of Egypt desolate in the midst of the countries *that are* desolate; and among the cities *that are* laid waste, her cities shall be desolate forty years; and I will [b]scatter the Egyptians among the nations and disperse them throughout the countries."

13 'Yet, thus says the Lord GOD: "At the [a]end of forty years I will gather the Egyptians from the peoples among whom they were scattered.

14 "I will bring back the captives of Egypt and cause them to return to the land of Pathros, to the land of their origin, and there they shall be a [a]lowly kingdom.

15 "It shall be the lowliest of kingdoms; it shall never again exalt itself above the nations, for I will diminish them so that they will not rule over the nations anymore.

16 "No longer shall it be [a]the confidence of the house of Israel, but will remind them of *their* iniquity when they turned to follow them. Then they shall know that I *am* the Lord GOD." ' "

Babylonia Will Plunder Egypt

17 And it came to pass in the twenty-seventh year, in the first *month,* on the first *day* of the month, *that* the word of the LORD came to me, saying,

18 "Son of man, [a]Nebuchadnezzar king of Babylon caused his army to labor strenuously against Tyre; every head *was* made [b]bald, and every shoulder rubbed raw; yet neither he nor his

*

29:3 The Nile
29:5 So with MT, LXX, Vg.; some Heb. mss., Tg. *buried*
29:7 So with MT, Vg.; LXX, Syr. *hand*
29:10 Or *the tower*

KJV

nor his army, for Tyrus, for the service that he
had served against it:
19 Therefore thus saith the Lord GOD; Behold, I will give the land of Egypt unto [a]Nebu-
chadrezzar king of Babylon; and he shall take her
multitude, and take her spoil, and take her prey;
and it shall be the wages for his army.
20 I have given him the land of Egypt *for* his
labour wherewith he [a]served against it, because
they wrought for me, saith the Lord GOD.
21 In that day [a]will I cause the horn of the
house of Israel to bud forth, and I will give thee
[b]the opening of the mouth in the midst of them;
and they shall know that I *am* the LORD.

Egypt and Her Allies Will Fall

30 The word of the LORD came again unto me,
saying,
2 Son of man, prophesy and say, Thus saith
the Lord GOD; [a]Howl ye, Woe worth the day!
3 For [a]the day *is* near, even the day of the
LORD *is* near, a cloudy day; it shall be the time
of the heathen.
4 And the sword shall come upon Egypt,
and great pain shall be in Ethiopia, when the slain
shall fall in Egypt, and they [a]shall take away her
multitude, and [b]her foundations shall be broken
down.
5 Ethiopia, and Libya, and Lydia, and [a]all
the mingled people, and Chub, and the men of
the land that is in league, shall fall with them by
the sword.
6 Thus saith the LORD; They also that uphold Egypt shall fall; and the pride of her power
shall come down: [a]from the tower of Syene shall
they fall in it by the sword, saith the Lord GOD.
7 [a]And they shall be desolate in the midst
of the countries *that are* desolate, and her cities
shall be in the midst of the cities *that are* wasted.
8 And they shall know that I *am* the LORD,
when I have set a fire in Egypt, and *when* all her
helpers shall be destroyed.
9 In that day [a]shall messengers go forth
from me in ships to make the careless Ethiopians
afraid, and great pain shall come upon them, as
in the day of Egypt: for, lo, it cometh.
10 Thus saith the Lord GOD; [a]I will also make
the multitude of Egypt to cease by the hand of
Nebuchadrezzar king of Babylon.
11 He and his people with him, [a]the terrible
of the nations, shall be brought to destroy the
land: and they shall draw their swords against
Egypt, and fill the land with the slain.
12 And [a]I will make the rivers dry, and [b]sell
the land into the hand of the wicked: and I will
make the land waste, and all that is therein, by
the hand of strangers: I the LORD have spoken *it*.

19 [a]Jer. 43:10–13; Ezek. 30:10
20 [a]Is. 10:6, 7; 45:1–3; Jer. 25:9
21 [a]1 Sam. 2:10; Ps. 92:10; 132:17 [b]Ezek. 24:27; Amos 3:7, 8; [Luke 21:15]

CHAPTER 30

2 [a]Is. 13:6; 15:2; Ezek. 21:12; Joel 1:5, 11, 13
3 [a]Ezek. 7:7, 12; Joel 2:1; Obad. 15; Zeph. 1:7
4 [a]Ezek. 29:19 [b]Jer. 50:15
5 [a]Jer. 25:20, 24
6 [a]Ezek. 29:10
7 [a]Jer. 25:18–26; Ezek. 29:12
9 [a]Is. 18:1, 2
10 [a]Ezek. 29:19
11 [a]Ezek. 28:7; 31:12
12 [a]Is. 19:5, 6 [b]Is. 19:4

NKJV

army received wages from Tyre, for the labor
which they expended on it.
19 "Therefore thus says the Lord GOD:
'Surely I will give the land of Egypt to [a]Nebu-
chadnezzar king of Babylon; he shall take away
her wealth, carry off her spoil, and remove her
pillage; and that will be the wages for his
army.
20 'I have given him the land of Egypt *for*
his labor, because they [a]worked for Me,' says the
Lord GOD.
21 'In that day [a]I will cause the horn of the
house of Israel to spring forth, and I will [b]open
your mouth to speak in their midst. Then they
shall know that I *am* the LORD.' "

Egypt and Her Allies Will Fall

30 The word of the LORD came to me again,
saying,
2 "Son of man, prophesy and say, 'Thus
says the Lord GOD:

[a]"Wail, 'Woe to the day!'
3 For [a]the day *is* near,
Even the day of the LORD *is* near;
It will be a day of clouds, the time of the
Gentiles.
4 The sword shall come upon Egypt,
And great anguish shall be in Ethiopia,
When the slain fall in Egypt,
And they [a]take away her wealth,
And [b]her foundations are broken down.

5 "Ethiopia, *Libya, *Lydia, [a]all the mingled
people, Chub, and the men of the lands who are
allied, shall fall with them by the sword."
6 'Thus says the LORD:

"Those who uphold Egypt shall fall,
And the pride of her power shall come
down.
[a]From Migdol *to* Syene
Those within her shall fall by the
sword,"
Says the Lord GOD.

7 "They[a] shall be desolate in the midst of the
desolate countries,
And her cities shall be in the midst of the
cities *that are* laid waste.
8 Then they will know that I *am* the LORD,
When I have set a fire in Egypt
And all her helpers are destroyed.
9 On that day [a]messengers shall go forth
from Me in ships
To make the careless Ethiopians afraid,
And great anguish shall come upon
them,
As on the day of Egypt;
For indeed it is coming!"

10 'Thus says the Lord GOD:

[a]"I will also make a multitude of Egypt to
cease
By the hand of Nebuchadnezzar king of
Babylon.
11 He and his people with him, [a]the most
terrible of the nations,
Shall be brought to destroy the land;
They shall draw their swords against
Egypt,
And fill the land with the slain.
12 [a]I will make the rivers dry,
And [b]sell the land into the hand of the
wicked;
I will make the land waste, and all that is
in it,
By the hand of aliens.
I, the LORD, have spoken."

*———

30:5 Heb. *Put* • Heb. *Lud*

KJV

13 Thus saith the Lord GOD; I will also [a]destroy the idols, and I will cause *their* images to cease out of Noph; [b]and there shall be no more a prince of the land of Egypt: [c]and I will put a fear in the land of Egypt.
14 And I will make [a]Pathros desolate, and will set fire in [b]Zoan, [c]and will execute judgments in No.
15 And I will pour my fury upon Sin, the strength of Egypt; and [a]I will cut off the multitude of No.
16 And I will [a]set fire in Egypt: Sin shall have great pain, and No shall be rent asunder, and Noph *shall have* distresses daily.
17 The young men of Aven and of Pi–beseth shall fall by the sword: and these *cities* shall go into captivity.
18 [a]At Tehaphnehes also the day shall be darkened, when I shall break there the yokes of Egypt: and the pomp of her strength shall cease in her: as for her, a cloud shall cover her, and her daughters shall go into captivity.
19 Thus will I [a]execute judgments in Egypt: and they shall know that I *am* the LORD.

Proclamation Against Pharaoh

20 And it came to pass in the eleventh year, in the first *month,* in the seventh *day* of the month, *that* the word of the LORD came unto me, saying,
21 Son of man, I have [a]broken the arm of Pharaoh king of Egypt; and, lo, [b]it shall not be bound up to be healed, to put a roller to bind it, to make it strong to hold the sword.
22 Therefore thus saith the Lord GOD; Behold, I *am* [a]against Pharaoh king of Egypt, and will [b]break his arms, the strong, and that which was broken; and I will cause the sword to fall out of his hand.
23 [a]And I will scatter the Egyptians among the nations, and will disperse them through the countries.
24 And I will strengthen the arms of the king of Babylon, and put my sword in his hand: but I will break Pharaoh's arms, and he shall groan before him with the groanings of a deadly wounded *man.*
25 But I will strengthen the arms of the king of Babylon, and the arms of Pharaoh shall fall down; and [a]they shall know that I *am* the LORD, when I shall put my sword into the hand of the king of Babylon, and he shall stretch it out upon the land of Egypt.
26 [a]And I will scatter the Egyptians among the nations, and disperse them among the countries; and they shall know that I *am* the LORD.

Egypt Cut Down Like a Great Tree
(cf. Ezek. 17:22–24)

31 And it came to pass in the [a]eleventh year, in the third *month,* in the first *day* of the month, *that* the word of the LORD came unto me, saying,
2 Son of man, speak unto Pharaoh king of Egypt, and to his multitude; [a]Whom art thou like in thy greatness?
3 [a]Behold, the Assyrian *was* a cedar in Lebanon with fair branches, and with a shadowing shroud, and of an high stature; and his top was among the thick boughs.
4 [a]The waters made him great, the deep set him up on high with her rivers running round

13 [a]Is. 19:1; Jer. 43:12; 46:25; Zech. 13:2 [b]Zech. 10:11 [c]Is. 19:16
14 [a]Is. 11:11; Jer. 44:1, 15; Ezek. 29:14 [b]Ps. 78:12, 43; Is. 19:11, 13 [c]Jer. 46:25; Ezek. 30:15, 16; Nah. 3:8–10
15 [a]Jer. 46:25
16 [a]Ezek. 30:8
18 [a]Jer. 2:16
19 [a][Ps. 9:16]; Ezek. 5:8; 25:11
21 [a]Jer. 48:25 [b]Jer. 46:11
22 [a]Jer. 46:25; Ezek. 29:3 [b]Ps. 37:17
23 [a]Ezek. 29:12; 30:17, 18, 26
25 [a]Ps. 9:16
26 [a]Ezek. 29:12

CHAPTER 31

1 [a]Jer. 52:5, 6; Ezek. 30:20; 32:1
2 [a]Ezek. 31:18
3 [a]Is. 10:33, 34; Ezek. 17:3, 4, 22; 31:16; Dan. 4:10, 20–23
4 [a]Jer. 51:36; Ezek. 29:3–9

*

30:13 Ancient Memphis
30:14 Ancient Thebes
30:15 Ancient Pelusium
30:17 Ancient On, Heliopolis
30:18 *Tahpanhes*, Jer. 43:7 • So with many Heb. mss., Bg., LXX, Syr., Tg., Vg.; MT *refrained*

NKJV

13 'Thus says the Lord GOD:

"I will also [a]destroy the idols,
And cause the images to cease from
*Noph;
[b]There shall no longer be princes from the
land of Egypt;
[c]I will put fear in the land of Egypt.
14 I will make [a]Pathros desolate,
Set fire to [b]Zoan,
[c]And execute judgments in *No.
15 I will pour My fury on *Sin, the strength
of Egypt;
[a]I will cut off the multitude of No,
16 And [a]set a fire in Egypt;
Sin shall have great pain,
No shall be split open,
And Noph *shall be in* distress daily.
17 The young men of *Aven and Pi Beseth
shall fall by the sword,
And these *cities* shall go into captivity.
18 [a]At *Tehaphnehes the day shall also be
*darkened,
When I break the yokes of Egypt there.
And her arrogant strength shall cease in
her;
As for her, a cloud shall cover her,
And her daughters shall go into captivity.
19 Thus I will [a]execute judgments on Egypt,
Then they shall know that I *am* the
LORD." ' "

Proclamation Against Pharaoh

20 And it came to pass in the eleventh year, in the first *month,* on the seventh *day* of the month, *that* the word of the LORD came to me, saying,
21 "Son of man, I have [a]broken the arm of Pharaoh king of Egypt; and see, [b]it has not been bandaged for healing, nor a splint put on to bind it, to make it strong enough to hold a sword.
22 "Therefore thus says the Lord GOD: 'Surely I *am* [a]against Pharaoh king of Egypt, and will [b]break his arms, both the strong one and the one that was broken; and I will make the sword fall out of his hand.
23 [a]'I will scatter the Egyptians among the nations, and disperse them throughout the countries.
24 'I will strengthen the arms of the king of Babylon and put My sword in his hand; but I will break Pharaoh's arms, and he will groan before him with the groanings of a mortally wounded *man.*
25 'Thus I will strengthen the arms of the king of Babylon, but the arms of Pharaoh shall fall down; [a]they shall know that I *am* the LORD, when I put My sword into the hand of the king of Babylon and he stretches it out against the land of Egypt.
26 [a]'I will scatter the Egyptians among the nations and disperse them throughout the countries. Then they shall know that I *am* the LORD.' "

Egypt Cut Down Like a Great Tree
(cf. Ezek. 17:22–24)

31 Now it came to pass in the [a]eleventh year, in the third *month,* on the first *day* of the month, *that* the word of the LORD came to me, saying,
2 "Son of man, say to Pharaoh king of Egypt and to his multitude:

[a]'Whom are you like in your greatness?
3 [a]Indeed Assyria *was* a cedar in Lebanon,
With fine branches that shaded the forest,
And of high stature;
And its top was among the thick boughs.
4 [a]The waters made it grow;
Underground waters gave it height,
With their rivers running around the place
where it was planted,

KJV

about his plants, and sent out her little rivers unto
all the trees of the field.
5 Therefore [a]his height was exalted above
all the trees of the field, and his boughs were multiplied, and his branches became long because of
the multitude of waters, when he shot forth.
6 All the [a]fowls of heaven made their nests
in his boughs, and under his branches did all the
beasts of the field bring forth their young, and
under his shadow dwelt all great nations.
7 Thus was he fair in his greatness, in the
length of his branches: for his root was by great
waters.
8 The cedars in the [a]garden of God could
not hide him: the fir trees were not like his
boughs, and the chesnut trees were not like his
branches; nor any tree in the garden of God was
like unto him in his beauty.
9 I have made him fair by the multitude of
his branches: so that all the trees of Eden, that
were in the garden of God, envied him.
10 Therefore thus saith the Lord GOD; Because thou hast lifted up thyself in height, and
he hath shot up his top among the thick boughs,
and [a]his heart is lifted up in his height;
11 I have therefore delivered him into the
hand of the [a]mighty one of the heathen; he shall
surely deal with him: I have driven him out for
his wickedness.
12 And strangers, [a]the terrible of the nations,
have cut him off, and have left him: [b]upon the
mountains and in all the valleys his branches are
fallen, and his boughs are [c]broken by all the rivers
of the land; and all the people of the earth are
gone down from his shadow, and have left him.
13 [a]Upon his ruin shall all the fowls of the
heaven remain, and all the beasts of the field shall
be upon his branches:
14 To the end that none of all the trees by
the waters exalt themselves for their height, neither shoot up their top among the thick boughs,
neither their trees stand up in their height, all that
drink water: for [a]they are all delivered unto death,
[b]to the nether parts of the earth, in the midst of
the children of men, with them that go down to
the pit.
15 Thus saith the Lord GOD; In the day when
he [a]went down to the grave I caused a mourning:
I covered the deep for him, and I restrained the
floods thereof, and the great waters were stayed:
and I caused Lebanon to mourn for him, and all
the trees of the field fainted for him.
16 I made the nations to [a]shake at the sound
of his fall, when I [b]cast him down to hell with
them that descend into the pit: and [c]all the trees
of Eden, the choice and best of Lebanon, all that
drink water, [d]shall be comforted in the nether
parts of the earth.
17 They also went down into hell with him
unto *them that be* slain with the sword; and *they
that were* his arm, *that* [a]dwelt under his shadow
in the midst of the heathen.
18 [a]To whom art thou thus like in glory and
in greatness among the trees of Eden? yet shalt
thou be brought down with the trees of Eden unto

5 [a]Dan. 4:11
6 [a]Ezek. 17:23; 31:13; Dan. 4:12, 21; Matt. 13:32
8 [a]Gen. 2:8, 9; 13:10; Is. 51:3; Ezek. 28:13; 31:16, 18
10 [a]2 Chr. 32:25; Is. 10:12; 14:13, 14; Ezek. 28:17; Dan. 5:20
11 [a]Ezek. 30:10; Dan. 5:18, 19
12 [a]Ezek. 28:7; 30:11; 32:12 [b]Ezek. 32:5; 35:8 [c]Ezek. 30:24, 25
13 [a]Is. 18:6; Ezek. 32:4
14 [a]Ps. 82:7 [b]Ezek. 32:18
15 [a]Ezek. 32:22, 23
16 [a]Ezek. 26:15; Hag. 2:7 [b]Is. 14:15; Ezek. 32:18 [c]Is. 14:8; Hab. 2:17 [d]Ezek. 32:31
17 [a]Lam. 4:20
18 [a]Ezek. 32:19

NKJV

And sent out rivulets to all the trees of
the field.

5 'Therefore [a]its height was exalted above
all the trees of the field;
Its boughs were multiplied,
And its branches became long because of
the abundance of water,
As it sent them out.
6 All the [a]birds of the heavens made their
nests in its boughs;
Under its branches all the beasts of the
field brought forth their young;
And in its shadow all great nations made
their home.

7 'Thus it was beautiful in greatness and in
the length of its branches,
Because its roots reached to abundant
waters.
8 The cedars in the [a]garden of God could
not hide it;
The fir trees were not like its boughs,
And the *chestnut trees were not like its
branches;
No tree in the garden of God was like it
in beauty.
9 I made it beautiful with a multitude of
branches,
So that all the trees of Eden envied it,
That *were* in the garden of God.'

10 "Therefore thus says the Lord GOD: 'Because you have increased in height, and it set its
top among the thick boughs, and [a]its heart was
lifted up in its height,
11 'therefore I will deliver it into the hand
of the [a]mighty one of the nations, and he shall
surely deal with it; I have driven it out for its
wickedness.
12 'And aliens, [a]the most terrible of the nations, have cut it down and left it; its branches
have fallen [b]on the mountains and in all the valleys; its boughs lie [c]broken by all the rivers of
the land; and all the peoples of the earth have
gone from under its shadow and left it.

13 'On [a]its ruin will remain all the birds of
the heavens,
And all the beasts of the field will come
to its branches—

14 'So that no trees by the waters may ever
again exalt themselves for their height, nor set
their tops among the thick boughs, that no tree
which drinks water may ever be high enough to
reach up to them.

'For [a]they have all been delivered to death,
[b]To the depths of the earth,
Among the children of men who go down
to the Pit.'

15 "Thus says the Lord GOD: 'In the day
when it [a]went down to hell, I caused mourning. I
covered the deep because of it. I restrained its
rivers, and the great waters were held back. I
caused Lebanon to mourn for it, and all the trees
of the field wilted because of it.
16 'I made the nations [a]shake at the sound
of its fall, when I [b]cast it down to hell together
with those who descend into the Pit; and [c]all the
trees of Eden, the choice and best of Lebanon,
all that drink water, [d]were comforted in the
depths of the earth.
17 'They also went down to hell with it, with
those *slain* by the sword; and *those who were* its
strong arm [a]dwelt in its shadows among the
nations.
18 [a]'To which of the trees in Eden will you
then be likened in glory and greatness? Yet you
shall be brought down with the trees of Eden to

*

31:8 Or *plane*, Heb. *armon*

KJV

the nether parts of the earth: [b]thou shalt lie in
the midst of the uncircumcised with *them that*
be slain by the sword. This *is* Pharaoh and all
his multitude, saith the Lord GOD.

Lamentation for Pharaoh and Egypt

32 And it came to pass in the twelfth year, in
the [a]twelfth month, in the first *day* of the
month, *that* the word of the LORD came unto me,
saying,
2 Son of man, [a]take up a lamentation for
Pharaoh king of Egypt, and say unto him, [b]Thou
art like a young lion of the nations, [c]and thou
art as a whale in the seas: and thou [d]camest forth
with thy rivers, and troubledst the waters with
thy feet, and [e]fouledst their rivers.
3 Thus saith the Lord GOD; I will therefore
[a]spread out my net over thee with a company of
many people; and they shall bring thee up in my
net.
4 Then [a]will I leave thee upon the land, I
will cast thee forth upon the open field, and [b]will
cause all the fowls of the heaven to remain upon
thee, and I will fill the beasts of the whole earth
with thee.
5 And I will lay thy flesh [a]upon the mountains, and fill the valleys with thy height.
6 I will also water with thy blood the land
wherein thou swimmest, *even* to the mountains;
and the rivers shall be full of thee.
7 And when I shall put thee out, [a]I will cover
the heaven, and make the stars thereof dark; I
will cover the sun with a cloud, and the moon
shall not give her light.
8 All the bright lights of heaven will I make
dark over thee, and set darkness upon thy land,
saith the Lord GOD.
9 I will also vex the hearts of many people,
when I shall bring thy destruction among the nations, into the countries which thou hast not
known.
10 Yea, I will make many people amazed at
thee, and their kings shall be horribly afraid for
thee, when I shall brandish my sword before
them; and [a]they shall tremble at *every* moment,
every man for his own life, in the day of thy fall.
11 [a]For thus saith the Lord GOD; The sword
of the king of Babylon shall come upon thee.
12 By the swords of the mighty will I cause
thy multitude to fall, [a]the terrible of the nations,
all of them: and [b]they shall spoil the pomp of
Egypt, and all the multitude thereof shall be
destroyed.
13 I will destroy also all the beasts thereof
from beside the great waters; [a]neither shall the
foot of man trouble them any more, nor the hoofs
of beasts trouble them.
14 Then will I make their waters deep, and
cause their rivers to run like oil, saith the Lord
GOD.
15 When I shall make the land of Egypt desolate, and the country shall be destitute of that
whereof it was full, when I shall smite all them
that dwell therein, [a]then shall they know that I
am the LORD.
16 This *is* the [a]lamentation wherewith they
shall lament her: the daughters of the nations

18 [b]Jer. 9:25, 26; Ezek. 28:10; 32:19, 21

CHAPTER 32

1 [a]Ezek. 31:1; 33:21
2 [a]Ezek. 27:2 [b]Jer. 4:7; Ezek. 19:2–6; Nah. 2:11–13 [c]Is. 27:1; Ezek. 29:3 [d]Jer. 46:7, 8 [e]Ezek. 34:18
3 [a]Ezek. 12:13; 17:20
4 [a]Ezek. 29:5 [b]Is. 18:6; Ezek. 31:13
5 [a]Ezek. 31:12
7 [a]Is. 13:10; Joel 2:31; 3:15; Amos 8:9; Matt. 24:29; Mark 13:24; Luke 21:25; Rev. 6:12, 13; 8:12
10 [a]Ezek. 26:16
11 [a]Jer. 46:26; Ezek. 30:4
12 [a]Ezek. 28:7; 30:11; 31:12 [b]Ezek. 29:19
13 [a]Ezek. 29:11
15 [a]Ex. 7:5; 14:4, 18; Ps. 9:16; Ezek. 6:7
16 [a]2 Sam. 1:17; 2 Chr. 35:25; Jer. 9:17; Ezek. 26:17

NKJV

the depths of the earth; [b]you shall lie in the midst of the uncircumcised, with *those* slain by the sword. This *is* Pharaoh and all his multitude,' says the Lord GOD."

Lamentation for Pharaoh and Egypt

32 And it came to pass in the twelfth year, in
the [a]twelfth *month,* on the first *day* of the
month, *that* the word of the LORD came to me,
saying,
2 "Son of man, [a]take up a lamentation for
Pharaoh king of Egypt, and say to him:

[b]'You are like a young lion among the nations,
And [c]you *are* like a monster in the seas,
[d]Bursting forth in your rivers,
Troubling the waters with your feet,
And [e]fouling their rivers.'

3 "Thus says the Lord GOD:

'I will therefore [a]spread My net over you with a company of many people,
And they will draw you up in My net.
4 Then [a]I will leave you on the land;
I will cast you out on the open fields,
[b]And cause to settle on you all the birds of the heavens.
And with you I will fill the beasts of the whole earth.
5 I will lay your flesh [a]on the mountains,
And fill the valleys with your carcass.

6 'I will also water the land with the flow of your blood,
Even to the mountains;
And the riverbeds will be full of you.
7 When *I* put out your light,
[a]I will cover the heavens, and make its stars dark;
I will cover the sun with a cloud,
And the moon shall not give her light.
8 All the bright lights of the heavens I will make dark over you,
And bring darkness upon your land,'
Says the Lord GOD.

9 'I will also trouble the hearts of many peoples, when I bring your destruction among the
nations, into the countries which you have not
known.
10 'Yes, I will make many peoples astonished
at you, and their kings shall be horribly afraid
of you when I brandish My sword before them;
and [a]they shall tremble *every* moment, every man
for his own life, in the day of your fall.'
11 [a]"For thus says the Lord GOD: 'The sword
of the king of Babylon shall come upon you.
12 'By the swords of the mighty warriors, all
of them [a]the most terrible of the nations, I will
cause your multitude to fall.

[b]'They shall plunder the pomp of Egypt,
And all its multitude shall be destroyed.
13 Also I will destroy all its animals
From beside its great waters;
[a]The foot of man shall muddy them no more,
Nor shall the hooves of animals muddy them.
14 Then I will make their waters clear,
And make their rivers run like oil,'
Says the Lord GOD.

15 'When I make the land of Egypt desolate,
And the country is destitute of all that once filled it,
When I strike all who dwell in it,
[a]Then they shall know that I *am* the LORD.

16 'This *is* the [a]lamentation
With which they shall lament her;

KJV

shall lament her: they shall lament for her, *even* for Egypt, and for all her multitude, saith the Lord GOD.

Egypt and Others Consigned to the Pit

17 It came to pass also in the twelfth year, in the fifteenth *day* of the month, [a]*that* the word of the LORD came unto me, saying,

18 Son of man, wail for the multitude of Egypt, and [a]cast them down, *even* her, and the daughters of the famous nations, unto the nether parts of the earth, with them that go down into the pit.

19 [a]Whom dost thou pass in beauty? [b]go down, and be thou laid with the uncircumcised.

20 They shall fall in the midst of *them that are* slain by the sword: she is delivered to the sword: [a]draw her and all her multitudes.

21 [a]The strong among the mighty shall speak to him out of the midst of hell with them that help him: they are [b]gone down, they lie uncircumcised, slain by the sword.

22 [a]Asshur *is* there and all her company: his graves *are* about him: all of them slain, fallen by the sword:

23 [a]Whose graves are set in the sides of the pit, and her company is round about her grave: all of them slain, fallen by the sword, which [b]caused terror in the land of the living.

24 There *is* [a]Elam and all her multitude round about her grave, all of them slain, fallen by the sword, which are [b]gone down uncircumcised into the nether parts of the earth, [c]which caused their terror in the land of the living; yet have they borne their shame with them that go down to the pit.

25 They have set her a [a]bed in the midst of the slain with all her multitude: her graves *are* round about him: all of them uncircumcised, slain by the sword: though their terror was caused in the land of the living, yet have they borne their shame with them that go down to the pit: he is put in the midst of *them that be* slain.

26 There *is* [a]Meshech, Tubal, and all her multitude: her graves *are* round about him: all of them [b]uncircumcised, slain by the sword, though they caused their terror in the land of the living.

27 [a]And they shall not lie with the mighty *that are* fallen of the uncircumcised, which are gone down to hell with their weapons of war: and they have laid their swords under their heads, but their iniquities shall be upon their bones, though *they were* the terror of the mighty in the land of the living.

28 Yea, thou shalt be broken in the midst of the uncircumcised, and shalt lie with *them that are* slain with the sword.

17 [a]Ezek. 32:1; 33:21
18 [a]Ezek. 26:20; 31:14
19 [a]Jer. 9:25, 26; Ezek. 31:2, 18 [b]Ezek. 28:10
20 [a]Ps. 28:3
21 [a]Is. 1:31; 14:9, 10; Ezek. 32:27 [b]Ezek. 32:19, 25
22 [a]Ezek. 31:3, 16
23 [a]Is. 14:15 [b]Ezek. 32:24–27, 32
24 [a]Gen. 10:22; 14:1; Is. 11:11; Jer. 25:25; 49:34–39 [b]Ezek. 32:21 [c]Ezek. 32:23
25 [a]Ps. 139:8
26 [a]Gen. 10:2; Ezek. 27:13; 38:2, 3; 39:1 [b]Ezek. 32:19
27 [a]Is. 14:18, 19

NKJV

The daughters of the nations shall lament her;
They shall lament for her, for Egypt,
And for all her multitude,'
Says the Lord GOD."

Egypt and Others Consigned to the Pit

17 It came to pass also in the twelfth year, on the fifteenth *day* of the month, [a]*that* the word of the LORD came to me, saying:

18 "Son of man, wail over the multitude of Egypt,
And [a]cast them down to the depths of the earth,
Her and the daughters of the famous nations,
With those who go down to the Pit:
19 'Whom [a]do you surpass in beauty?
[b]Go down, be placed with the uncircumcised.'

20 "They shall fall in the midst of *those* slain by the sword;
She is delivered to the sword,
[a]Drawing her and all her multitudes.
21 [a]The strong among the mighty
Shall speak to him out of the midst of hell
With those who help him:
'They have [b]gone down,
They lie with the uncircumcised, slain by the sword.'

22 "Assyria[a] *is* there, and all her company,
With their graves all around her,
All of them slain, fallen by the sword.
23 [a]Her graves are set in the recesses of the Pit,
And her company is all around her grave,
All of them slain, fallen by the sword,
Who [b]caused terror in the land of the living.

24 "There *is* [a]Elam and all her multitude,
All around her grave,
All of them slain, fallen by the sword,
Who have [b]gone down uncircumcised to the lower parts of the earth,
[c]Who caused their terror in the land of the living;
Now they bear their shame with those who go down to the Pit.
25 They have set her [a]bed in the midst of the slain,
With all her multitude,
With her graves all around it,
All of them uncircumcised, slain by the sword;
Though their terror was caused
In the land of the living,
Yet they bear their shame
With those who go down to the Pit;
It was put in the midst of the slain.

26 "There *are* [a]Meshech and Tubal and all their multitudes,
With all their graves around it,
All of them [b]uncircumcised, slain by the sword,
Though they caused their terror in the land of the living.
27 [a]They do not lie with the mighty
Who are fallen of the uncircumcised,
Who have gone down to hell with their weapons of war;
They have laid their swords under their heads,
But their iniquities will be on their bones,
Because of the terror of the mighty in the land of the living.
28 Yes, you shall be broken in the midst of the uncircumcised,
And lie with *those* slain by the sword.

KJV

29 There *is* [a]Edom, her kings, and all her
princes, which with their might are laid by *them*
that were slain by the sword: they shall lie with
the uncircumcised, and with them that go down
to the pit.
30 [a]There *be* the princes of the north, all of
them, and all the [b]Zidonians, which are gone
down with the slain; with their terror they are
ashamed of their might; and they lie uncircumcised with *them that be* slain by the sword, and
bear their shame with them that go down to the
pit.
31 Pharaoh shall see them, and shall be
[a]comforted over all his multitude, *even* Pharaoh
and all his army slain by the sword, saith the Lord
GOD.
32 For I have caused my terror in the land
of the living: and he shall be laid in the midst of
the uncircumcised with *them that are* slain with
the sword, *even* Pharaoh and all his multitude,
saith the LORD GOD.

The Watchman and His Message

33 Again the word of the LORD came unto me,
saying,
2 Son of man, speak to [a]the children of thy
people, and say unto them, [b]When I bring the
sword upon a land, if the people of the land take
a man of their coasts, and set him for their
[c]watchman:
3 If when he seeth the sword come upon the
land, he blow the trumpet, and warn the people;
4 Then whosoever heareth the sound of the
trumpet, and taketh [a]not warning; if the sword
come, and take him away, [b]his blood shall be
upon his own head.
5 He heard the sound of the trumpet, and
took not warning; his blood shall be upon him.
But he that taketh warning shall deliver his soul.
6 But if the watchman see the sword come,
and blow not the trumpet, and the people be not
warned; if the sword come, and take *any* person
from among them, [a]he is taken away in his iniquity; but his blood will I require at the watchman's hand.
7 [a]So thou, O son of man, I have set thee a
watchman unto the house of Israel; therefore thou
shalt hear the word at my mouth, and warn them
from me.
8 When I say unto the wicked, O wicked
man, thou shalt surely die; if thou dost not speak
to warn the wicked from his way, that wicked
man shall die in his iniquity; but his blood will I
require at thine hand.
9 Nevertheless, if thou warn the wicked of
his way to turn from it; if he do not turn from
his way, he shall die in his iniquity; but thou hast
delivered thy soul.
10 Therefore, O thou son of man, speak unto
the house of Israel; Thus ye speak, saying, If our
transgressions and our sins *be* upon us, and we
[a]pine away in them, [b]how should we then live?
11 Say unto them, *As* I live, saith the Lord
GOD, [a]I have no pleasure in the death of the
wicked; but that the wicked [b]turn from his way
and live: turn ye, turn ye from your evil ways;
for [c]why will ye die, O house of Israel?

The Fairness of God's Judgment

12 Therefore, thou son of man, say unto the
children of thy people, The [a]righteousness of the
righteous shall not deliver him in the day of his
transgression: as for the wickedness of the

29 [a]Is. 9:25, 26; 34:5, 6; Jer. 49:7–22; Ezek. 25:12–14
30 [a]Jer. 1:15; 25:26; Ezek. 38:6, 15; 39:2 [b]Jer. 25:22; Ezek. 28:21–23
31 [a]Ezek. 14:22; 31:16

CHAPTER 33
2 [a]Ezek. 3:11 [b]Ezek. 14:17 [c]2 Sam. 18:24, 25; 2 Kin. 9:17; Hos. 9:8
4 [a]2 Chr. 25:16; Jer. 6:17; Zech. 1:4 [b]Ezek. 18:13; 35:9; [Acts 18:6]
6 [a]Ezek. 33:8
7 [a]Is. 62:6; Ezek. 3:17–21
10 [a]Lev. 26:39; Ezek. 24:23 [b]Is. 49:14; Ezek. 37:11
11 [a][2 Sam. 14:14; Lam. 3:33]; Ezek. 18:23, 32; Hos. 11:8; [2 Pet. 3:9] [b]Ezek. 18:21, 30; [Hos. 14:1, 4; Acts 3:19] [c][Is. 55:6, 7]; Jer. 3:22; Ezek. 18:30, 31; Hos. 14:1; [Acts 3:19]
12 [a]Ezek. 3:20; 18:24, 26

NKJV

29 "There *is* [a]Edom,
Her kings and all her princes,
Who despite their might
Are laid beside *those* slain by the sword;
They shall lie with the uncircumcised,
And with those who go down to the Pit.
30 [a]There *are* the princes of the north,
All of them, and all the [b]Sidonians,
Who have gone down with the slain
In shame at the terror which they caused
by their might;
They lie uncircumcised with *those* slain
by the sword,
And bear their shame with those who go
down to the Pit.

31 "Pharaoh will see them
And be [a]comforted over all his multitude,
Pharaoh and all his army,
Slain by the sword,"
Says the Lord GOD.

32 "For I have caused My terror in the land
of the living;
And he shall be placed in the midst of the
uncircumcised
With *those* slain by the sword,
Pharaoh and all his multitude,"
Says the Lord GOD.

The Watchman and His Message

33 Again the word of the LORD came to me,
saying,
2 "Son of man, speak to [a]the children of
your people, and say to them: [b]'When I bring the
sword upon a land, and the people of the land
take a man from their territory and make him
their [c]watchman,
3 'when he sees the sword coming upon the
land, if he blows the trumpet and warns the
people,
4 'then whoever hears the sound of the
trumpet and does [a]not take warning, if the sword
comes and takes him away, [b]his blood shall be
on his *own* head.
5 'He heard the sound of the trumpet, but
did not take warning; his blood shall be upon himself. But he who takes warning will save his life.
6 'But if the watchman sees the sword coming and does not blow the trumpet, and the people
are not warned, and the sword comes and takes
any person from among them, [a]he is taken away
in his iniquity; but his blood I will require at the
watchman's hand.'
7 [a]"So you, son of man: I have made you a
watchman for the house of Israel; therefore you
shall hear a word from My mouth and warn them
for Me.
8 "When I say to the wicked, 'O wicked
man, you shall surely die!' and you do not speak
to warn the wicked from his way, that wicked
man shall die in his iniquity; but his blood I will
require at your hand.
9 "Nevertheless if you warn the wicked to
turn from his way, and he does not turn from his
way, he shall die in his iniquity; but you have
delivered your soul.
10 "Therefore you, O son of man, say to the
house of Israel: 'Thus you say, "If our transgressions and our sins *lie* upon us, and we [a]pine away
in them, [b]how can we then live?"'
11 "Say to them: '*As* I live,' says the Lord
GOD, [a]'I have no pleasure in the death of the
wicked, but that the wicked [b]turn from his way
and live. Turn, turn from your evil ways! For [c]why
should you die, O house of Israel?'

The Fairness of God's Judgment

12 "Therefore you, O son of man, say to the
children of your people: 'The [a]righteousness of
the righteous man shall not deliver him in the day
of his transgression; as for the wickedness of the

KJV

wicked, [b]he shall not fall thereby in the day that
he turneth from his wickedness; neither shall the
righteous be able to live for his *righteousness* in
the day that he sinneth.
13 When I shall say to the righteous, *that* he
shall surely live; [a]if he trust to his own righteousness, and commit iniquity, all his righteousnesses
shall not be remembered; but for his iniquity that
he hath committed, he shall die for it.
14 Again, [a]when I say unto the wicked, Thou
shalt surely die; if he turn from his sin, and do
that which is lawful and right;
15 *If* the wicked [a]restore the pledge, [b]give
again that he had robbed, walk in [c]the statutes
of life, without committing iniquity; he shall
surely live, he shall not die.
16 [a]None of his sins that he hath committed
shall be mentioned unto him: he hath done that
which is lawful and right; he shall surely live.
17 [a]Yet the children of thy people say, The
way of the Lord is not equal: but as for them,
their way is not equal.
18 [a]When the righteous turneth from his
righteousness, and committeth iniquity, he shall
even die thereby.
19 But if the wicked turn from his wickedness, and do that which is lawful and right, he
shall live thereby.
20 Yet ye say, [a]The way of the Lord is not
equal. O ye house of Israel, I will judge you every
one after his ways.

The Fall of Jerusalem

21 And it came to pass in the twelfth year
[a]of our captivity, in the tenth *month,* in the fifth
day of the month, [b]*that* one that had escaped out
of Jerusalem came unto me, saying, [c]The city is
smitten.
22 Now [a]the hand of the LORD was upon me
in the evening, afore he that was escaped came;
and had [b]opened my mouth, until he came to me
in the morning; and my mouth was opened, and
I was no more dumb.

The Cause of Judah's Ruin

23 Then the word of the LORD came unto me,
saying,
24 Son of man, [a]they that inhabit those
[b]wastes of the land of Israel speak, saying, [c]Abra-
ham was one, and he inherited the land: [d]but we
are many; the land is given us for [e]inheritance.
25 Wherefore say unto them, Thus saith the
Lord GOD; [a]Ye eat with the blood, and [b]lift up
your eyes toward your idols, and [c]shed blood: and
shall ye possess the [d]land?
26 Ye stand upon your sword, ye work
abomination, and ye [a]defile every one his neighbour's wife: and shall ye possess the land?
27 Say thou thus unto them, Thus saith the
Lord GOD; *As* I live, surely [a]they that *are* in the
wastes shall fall by the sword, and him that *is* in
the open field [b]will I give to the beasts to be devoured, and they that *be* in the forts and [c]in the
caves shall die of the pestilence.
28 [a]For I will lay the land most desolate, and
the [b]pomp of her strength shall cease; and [c]the
mountains of Israel shall be desolate, that none
shall pass through.
29 Then shall they know that I *am* the LORD,
when I have laid the land most desolate because
of all their abominations which they have committed.

Hearing and Not Doing

30 Also, thou son of man, the children of thy
people still are talking against thee by the walls
and in the doors of the houses, and [a]speak one
to another, every one to his brother, saying,
Come, I pray you, and hear what is the word that
cometh forth from the LORD.
31 And [a]they come unto thee as the people

12 [b][2 Chr. 7:14]; Ezek. 8:21; 33:19
13 [a]Ezek. 3:20; 18:24
14 [a][Is. 55:7]; Jer. 18:7, 8; Ezek. 3:18, 19; 18:27; Hos. 14:1, 4
15 [a]Ezek. 18:7 [b]Ex. 22:1–4; Lev. 6:2, 4, 5; Num. 5:6, 7; Luke 19:8 [c]Lev. 18:5; Ps. 119:59; 143:8; Ezek. 20:11, 13, 21
16 [a][Is. 1:18; 43:25]; Ezek. 18:22
17 [a]Ezek. 18:25, 29
18 [a]Ezek. 18:26
20 [a]Ezek. 18:25, 29
21 [a]Ezek. 1:2 [b]Ezek. 24:26 [c]2 Kin. 25:4
22 [a]Ezek. 1:3; 8:1; 37:1 [b]Ezek. 24:27
24 [a]Ezek. 34:2 [b]Ezek. 36:4 [c]Is. 51:2; [Acts 7:5; Rom. 4:12] [d]Mic. 3:11; [Matt. 3:9; John 8:39] [e]Ezek. 11:15
25 [a]Gen. 9:4; Lev. 3:17; 7:26; 17:10–14; 19:26; Deut. 12:16, 23; 15:23 [b]Ezek. 18:6 [c]Ezek. 22:6, 9 [d]Deut. 29:28
26 [a]Ezek. 18:6; 22:11
27 [a]Ezek. 33:24 [b]Ezek. 39:4 [c]Judg. 6:2; 1 Sam. 13:6; Is. 2:19
28 [a]Jer. 44:2, 6, 22; Ezek. 36:34, 35 [b]Ezek. 7:24; 24:21 [c]Ezek. 6:2, 3, 6
30 [a]Is. 29:13; Ezek. 14:3; 20:3, 31
31 [a]Ezek. 14:1

NKJV

wicked, [b]he shall not fall because of it in the day
that he turns from his wickedness; nor shall the
righteous be able to live because of *his righteousness* in the day that he sins.'
13 "When I say to the righteous *that* he shall
surely live, [a]but he trusts in his own righteousness
and commits iniquity, none of his righteous works
shall be remembered; but because of the iniquity
that he has committed, he shall die.
14 "Again, [a]when I say to the wicked, 'You
shall surely die,' if he turns from his sin and does
what is lawful and right,
15 "*if* the wicked [a]restores the pledge, [b]gives
back what he has stolen, and walks in [c]the statutes of life without committing iniquity, he shall
surely live; he shall not die.
16 [a]"None of his sins which he has committed shall be remembered against him; he has done
what is lawful and right; he shall surely live.
17 [a]"Yet the children of your people say, 'The
way of the LORD is not fair.' But it is their way
which is not fair!
18 [a]"When the righteous turns from his righteousness and commits iniquity, he shall die because of it.
19 "But when the wicked turns from his
wickedness and does what is lawful and right, he
shall live because of it.
20 "Yet you say, [a]'The way of the LORD is
not fair.' O house of Israel, I will judge every one
of you according to his own ways."

The Fall of Jerusalem

21 And it came to pass in the twelfth year
[a]of our captivity, in the tenth *month,* on the fifth
day of the month, [b]*that* one who had escaped
from Jerusalem came to me and said, [c]"The city
has been captured!"
22 Now [a]the hand of the LORD had been upon
me the evening before the man came who had
escaped. And He had [b]opened my mouth; so when
he came to me in the morning, my mouth was
opened, and I was no longer mute.

The Cause of Judah's Ruin

23 Then the word of the LORD came to me,
saying:
24 "Son of man, [a]they who inhabit those
[b]ruins in the land of Israel are saying, [c]'Abraham
was only one, and he inherited the land. [d]But we
are many; the land has been given to us as a
[e]possession.'
25 "Therefore say to them, 'Thus says the
Lord GOD: [a]"You eat *meat* with blood, you [b]lift
up your eyes toward your idols, and [c]shed blood.
Should you then possess the [d]land?
26 "You rely on your sword, you commit
abominations, and you [a]defile one another's
wives. Should you then possess the land?"'
27 "Say thus to them, 'Thus says the Lord
GOD: "*As* I live, surely [a]those who *are* in the ruins
shall fall by the sword, and the one who *is* in the
open field [b]I will give to the beasts to be devoured,
and those who *are* in the strongholds and [c]caves
shall die of the pestilence.
28 [a]"For I will make the land most desolate,
her [b]arrogant strength shall cease, and [c]the
mountains of Israel shall be so desolate that no
one will pass through.
29 "Then they shall know that I *am* the LORD,
when I have made the land most desolate because
of all their abominations which they have committed."'

Hearing and Not Doing

30 "As for you, son of man, the children of
your people are talking about you beside the walls
and in the doors of the houses; and they [a]speak
to one another, everyone saying to his brother,
'Please come and hear what the word is that
comes from the LORD.'
31 "So [a]they come to you as people do, they

KJV

cometh, and they [b]sit before thee *as* my people,
and they [c]hear thy words, but they will not do
them: [d]for with their mouth they shew much love,
but [e]their heart goeth after their covetousness.
32 And, lo, thou *art* unto them as a very
lovely song of one that hath a pleasant voice, and
can play well on an instrument: for they hear thy
words, but they do them [a]not.
33 [a]And when this cometh to pass, (lo, it will
come,) then [b]shall they know that a prophet hath
been among them.

Irresponsible Shepherds

34 And the word of the LORD came unto me,
saying,
2 Son of man, prophesy against the shepherds of Israel, prophesy, and say unto them, Thus
saith the Lord GOD unto the shepherds; [a]Woe *be*
to the shepherds of Israel that do feed themselves!
should not the shepherds feed the flocks?
3 [a]Ye eat the fat, and ye clothe you with
the wool, ye [b]kill them that are fed: *but* ye feed
not the flock.
4 [a]The diseased have ye not strengthened,
neither have ye healed that which was sick, neither have ye bound up *that which was* broken,
neither have ye brought again that which was
driven away, neither have ye [b]sought that which
was lost; but with [c]force and with cruelty have
ye ruled them.
5 [a]And they were [b]scattered, because *there
is* no shepherd: [c]and they became meat to all the
beasts of the field, when they were scattered.
6 My sheep [a]wandered through all the
mountains, and upon every high hill: yea, my
flock was scattered upon all the face of the earth,
and none did search or seek *after them.*
7 Therefore, ye shepherds, hear the word
of the LORD;
8 *As* I live saith the Lord GOD, surely because my flock became a prey, and my flock [a]be-
came meat to every beast of the field, because
there was no shepherd, neither did my shepherds
search for my flock, [b]but the shepherds fed themselves, and fed not my flock;
9 Therefore, O ye shepherds, hear the word
of the LORD;
10 Thus saith the Lord GOD; Behold, I *am*
[a]against the shepherds; and [b]I will require my
flock at their hand, and cause them to cease from
feeding the flock; neither shall the shepherds
[c]feed themselves any more; for I will [d]deliver my
flock from their mouth, that they may not be meat
for them.

God, the True Shepherd

11 For thus saith the Lord GOD; Behold, I,
even I, will both search my sheep, and seek them
out.
12 As a [a]shepherd seeketh out his flock in
the day that he is among his sheep *that are* scattered; so will I seek out my sheep, and will deliver
them out of all places where they have been scattered in [b]the cloudy and dark day.
13 And [a]I will bring them out from the people, and gather them from the countries, and will
bring them to their own land, and feed them upon
the mountains of Israel by the rivers, and in all
the inhabited places of the country.
14 [a]I will feed them in a good pasture, and
upon the high mountains of Israel shall their fold
be: [b]there shall they lie in a good fold, and *in* a
fat pasture shall they feed upon the mountains
of Israel.
15 I will feed my flock, and I will cause them
to lie down, saith the Lord GOD.
16 [a]I will seek that which was lost, and bring
again that which was driven away, and will bind
up *that which was* broken, and will strengthen
that which was sick: but I will destroy [b]the fat
and the strong; I will feed them [c]with judgment.
17 And *as for* you, O my flock, thus saith the

31 [b]Ezek. 8:1
[c]Is. 58:2 [d]Ps.
78:36, 37; Is.
29:13; Jer.
12:2; 1 John
3:18 [e][Matt.
13:22]
32 [a][Matt.
7:21–28;
James 1:22–
25]
33 [a]1 Sam.
3:20 [b]Ezek.
2:5

CHAPTER 34
2 [a]Jer. 23:1;
Ezek. 22:25;
Mic. 3:1–3, 11;
Zech. 11:17
3 [a]Is. 56:11;
Zech. 11:16
[b]Ezek. 33:25,
26; Mic. 3:1–3;
Zech. 11:5
4 [a]Zech.
11:16 [b]Matt.
9:36; 10:16;
18:12, 13;
Luke 15:4
[c][1 Pet. 5:3]
5 [a]Ezek.
33:21 [b]Num.
27:17; 1 Kin.
22:17; Jer.
10:21; Matt.
9:36; Mark
6:34 [c]Is. 56:9;
Jer. 12:9
6 [a]Jer. 40:11,
12; 50:6; Ezek.
7:16; 1 Pet.
2:25
8 [a]Ezek. 34:5,
6 [b]Ezek. 34:2,
10
10 [a]Jer. 21:13;
52:24–27;
Ezek. 5:8;
13:8; Zech.
10:3 [b]Ezek.
3:18; Heb.
13:17 [c]Ezek.
34:2, 8 [d]Ps.
72:12–14;
Ezek. 13:23
12 [a]Jer. 31:10
[b]Jer. 13:16;
Ezek. 30:3;
Joel 2:2
13 [a]Is. 65:9,
10; Jer. 23:3;
Ezek. 11:17;
20:41; 28:25;
36:24; 37:21,
22
14 [a]Ps. 23:2;
Jer. 3:15;
[John 10:9]
[b]Jer. 33:12
16 [a]Is. 40:11;
Mic. 4:6;
[Matt. 18:11;
Mark 2:17;
Luke 5:32] [b]Is.
10:16; Amos
4:1 [c]Jer. 10:24

NKJV

[b]sit before you *as* My people, and they [c]hear your
words, but they do not do them; [d]for with their
mouth they show much love, *but* [e]their hearts pursue their *own* gain.
32 "Indeed you *are* to them as a very lovely
song of one who has a pleasant voice and can
play well on an instrument; for they hear your
words, but they do [a]not do them.
33 [a]"And when this comes to pass—surely
it will come—then [b]they will know that a prophet
has been among them."

Irresponsible Shepherds

34 And the word of the LORD came to me,
saying,
2 "Son of man, prophesy against the shepherds of Israel, prophesy and say to them, 'Thus
says the Lord GOD to the shepherds: [a]"Woe to
the shepherds of Israel who feed themselves!
Should not the shepherds feed the flocks?
3 [a]"You eat the fat and clothe yourselves
with the wool; you [b]slaughter the fatlings, *but* you
do not feed the flock.
4 [a]"The weak you have not strengthened,
nor have you healed those who were sick, nor
bound up the broken, nor brought back what was
driven away, nor [b]sought what was lost; but with
[c]force and cruelty you have ruled them.
5 [a]"So they were [b]scattered because *there
was* no shepherd; [c]and they became food for all
the beasts of the field when they were scattered.
6 "My sheep [a]wandered through all the
mountains, and on every high hill; yes, My flock
was scattered over the whole face of the earth,
and no one was seeking or searching *for them.*"
7 'Therefore, you shepherds, hear the word
of the LORD:
8 "As I live," says the Lord GOD, "surely
because My flock became a prey, and My flock
[a]became food for every beast of the field, because
there was no shepherd, nor did My shepherds
search for My flock, [b]but the shepherds fed themselves and did not feed My flock"—
9 'therefore, O shepherds, hear the word of
the LORD!
10 'Thus says the Lord GOD: "Behold, I *am*
[a]against the shepherds, and [b]I will require My
flock at their hand; I will cause them to cease feeding the sheep, and the shepherds shall [c]feed themselves no more; for I will [d]deliver My flock from
their mouths, that they may no longer be food
for them."

God, the True Shepherd

11 'For thus says the Lord GOD: "Indeed I Myself will search for My sheep and seek them out.
12 "As a [a]shepherd seeks out his flock on
the day he is among his scattered sheep, so will
I seek out My sheep and deliver them from all
the places where they were scattered on [b]a cloudy
and dark day.
13 "And [a]I will bring them out from the peoples and gather them from the countries, and will
bring them to their own land; I will feed them
on the mountains of Israel, in the valleys and in
all the inhabited places of the country.
14 [a]"I will feed them in good pasture, and
their fold shall be on the high mountains of Israel.
[b]There they shall lie down in a good fold and feed
in rich pasture on the mountains of Israel.
15 "I will feed My flock, and I will make them
lie down," says the Lord GOD.
16 [a]"I will seek what was lost and bring back
what was driven away, bind up the broken and
strengthen what was sick; but I will destroy [b]the
fat and the strong, and feed them [c]in judgment."
17 'And *as for* you, O My flock, thus says the

KJV

Lord GOD; [a]Behold, I judge between cattle and
cattle, between the rams and the he goats.
18 *Seemeth it* a small thing unto you to have
eaten up the good pasture, but ye must tread down
with your feet the residue of your pastures? and
to have drunk of the deep waters, but ye must
foul the residue with your feet?
19 And *as for* my flock, they eat that which
ye have trodden with your feet; and they drink
that which ye have fouled with your feet.
20 Therefore thus saith the Lord GOD unto
them; [a]Behold, I, *even* I, will judge between the
fat cattle and between the lean cattle.
21 Because ye have thrust with side and with
shoulder, and pushed all the diseased with your
horns, till ye have scattered them abroad;
22 Therefore will I save my flock, and they
shall no more be a prey; and I will judge between
cattle and cattle.
23 And I will set up one [a]shepherd over them,
and he shall feed them, [b]*even* my servant David;
he shall feed them, and he shall be their shepherd.
24 And [a]I the LORD will be their God, and
my servant David [b]a prince among them; I the
LORD have spoken *it*.
25 And [a]I will make with them a covenant
of peace, and [b]will cause the evil beasts to cease
out of the land: and they [c]shall dwell safely in
the wilderness, and sleep in the woods.
26 And I will make them and the places
round about [a]my hill [b]a blessing; and I will [c]cause
the shower to come down in his season; there
shall be [d]showers of blessing.
27 And [a]the tree of the field shall yield her
fruit, and the earth shall yield her increase, and
they shall be safe in their land, and shall know
that I *am* the LORD, when I have [b]broken the bands
of their yoke, and delivered them out of the hand
of those that [c]served themselves of them.
28 And they shall no more be a prey to the
heathen, neither shall the beast of the land devour
them; but [a]they shall dwell safely, and none shall
make *them* afraid.
29 And I will raise up for them a [a]plant of
renown, and they shall [b]be no more consumed
with hunger in the land, [c]neither bear the shame
of the heathen any more.
30 Thus shall they know that [a]I the LORD
their God *am* with them, and *that* they, *even* the
house of Israel, *are* [b]my people, saith the Lord
GOD.
31 And ye my [a]flock, the flock of my pasture,
are men, *and* I *am* your God, saith the Lord GOD.

Judgment on Mount Seir

35 Moreover the word of the LORD came unto
me, saying,
2 Son of man, set thy face against [a]mount
Seir, and [b]prophesy against it,
3 And say unto it, Thus saith the Lord GOD;
Behold, O mount Seir, I *am* against thee, and [a]I
will stretch out mine hand against thee, and I will
make thee most desolate.
4 I will lay thy cities waste, and thou shalt
be desolate, and thou shalt know that I *am* the
LORD.
5 [a]Because thou hast had a perpetual hatred, and hast shed *the blood of* the children of
Israel by the force of the sword in the time of
their calamity, [b]in the time *that their* iniquity *had*
an end:
6 Therefore, *as* I live, saith the Lord GOD, I
will prepare thee unto [a]blood, and blood shall pursue thee: [b]sith thou hast not hated blood, even
blood shall pursue thee.
7 Thus will I make mount Seir most desolate, and cut off from it [a]him that passeth out and
him that returneth.
8 And I will fill his mountains with his slain
men: in thy hills, and in thy valleys, and in all

17 [a]Ezek. 20:37; Mal. 4:1; [Matt. 25:32]
20 [a]Ezek. 34:17
23 [a][Is. 40:11; Jer. 23:4, 5]; Hos. 1:11; [John 10:11; Heb. 13:20; 1 Pet. 2:25; 5:4] [b]Jer. 30:9; Ezek. 37:24; Hos. 3:5
24 [a]Ex. 29:45; Ezek. 37:25 [b]Is. 55:3; Jer. 30:9; Ezek. 37:24, 25; Hos. 3:5
25 [a]Ezek. 37:26 [b]Lev. 26:6; Job 5:22, 23; Is. 11:6–9; Hos. 2:18 [c]Jer. 23:6
26 [a]Is. 56:7 [b]Gen. 12:2; Is. 19:24; Zech. 8:13 [c]Lev. 26:4 [d]Ps. 68:9
27 [a]Lev. 26:4; Ps. 85:12; Is. 4:2 [b]Lev. 26:13; Is. 52:2, 3; Jer. 2:20 [c]Jer. 25:14
28 [a]Jer. 30:10; Ezek. 39:26
29 [a][Is. 11:1] [b]Ezek. 36:29 [c]Ezek. 36:3, 6, 15
30 [a]Ezek. 34:24 [b]Ps. 46:7, 11; Ezek. 14:11; 36:28
31 [a]Ps. 100:3; Jer. 23:1; [John 10:11]

CHAPTER 35

2 [a]Gen. 36:8; Deut. 2:5; Jer. 25:21; 49:7–22; Ezek. 25:12–14; Joel 3:19; Amos 1:11, 12; Obad. 1–9, 15, 16 [b]Amos 1:11
3 [a]Ezek. 6:14
5 [a]Ezek. 25:12 [b]Ps. 137:7; Dan. 9:24; Amos 1:11; Obad. 10
6 [a]Is. 63:1–6; Ezek. 16:38; 32:6 [b]Ps. 109:17
7 [a]Judg. 5:6

NKJV

Lord GOD: [a]"Behold, I shall judge between sheep
and sheep, between rams and goats.
18 "*Is it* too little for you to have eaten up
the good pasture, that you must tread down with
your feet the residue of your pasture—and to have
drunk of the clear waters, that you must foul the
residue with your feet?
19 "And *as for* My flock, they eat what you
have trampled with your feet, and they drink what
you have fouled with your feet."
20 'Therefore thus says the Lord GOD to
them: [a]"Behold, I Myself will judge between the
fat and the lean sheep.
21 "Because you have pushed with side and
shoulder, butted all the weak ones with your
horns, and scattered them abroad,
22 "therefore I will save My flock, and they
shall no longer be a prey; and I will judge between
sheep and sheep.
23 "I will establish one [a]shepherd over them,
and he shall feed them—[b]My servant David. He
shall feed them and be their shepherd.
24 "And [a]I, the LORD, will be their God, and
My servant David [b]a prince among them; I, the
LORD, have spoken.
25 [a]"I will make a covenant of peace with
them, and [b]cause wild beasts to cease from the
land; and they [c]will dwell safely in the wilderness
and sleep in the woods.
26 "I will make them and the places all
around [a]My hill [b]a blessing; and I will [c]cause
showers to come down in their season; there shall
be [d]showers of blessing.
27 "Then [a]the trees of the field shall yield
their fruit, and the earth shall yield her increase.
They shall be safe in their land; and they shall
know that I *am* the LORD, when I have [b]broken
the bands of their yoke and delivered them from
the hand of those who [c]enslaved them.
28 "And they shall no longer be a prey for
the nations, nor shall beasts of the land devour
them; but [a]they shall dwell safely, and no one
shall make *them* afraid.
29 "I will raise up for them a [a]garden of renown, and they shall [b]no longer be consumed
with hunger in the land, [c]nor bear the shame of
the Gentiles anymore.
30 "Thus they shall know that [a]I, the LORD
their God, *am* with them, and they, the house of
Israel, *are* [b]My people," says the Lord GOD.'"
31 "You are My [a]flock, the flock of My pasture; you *are* men, *and* I *am* your God," says the
Lord GOD.

Judgment on Mount Seir

35 Moreover the word of the LORD came to me,
saying,
2 "Son of man, set your face against [a]Mount
Seir and [b]prophesy against it,
3 "and say to it, 'Thus says the Lord GOD:

"Behold, O Mount Seir, I *am* against you;
[a]I will stretch out My hand against you,
And make you most desolate;
4 I shall lay your cities waste,
And you shall be desolate.
Then you shall know that I *am* the LORD.

5 [a]"Because you have had an ancient hatred, and have shed *the blood of* the children of
Israel by the power of the sword at the time of
their calamity, [b]*when* their iniquity *came to an*
end,
6 "therefore, *as* I live," says the Lord GOD,
"I will prepare you for [a]blood, and blood shall
pursue you; [b]since you have not hated blood,
therefore blood shall pursue you.
7 "Thus I will make Mount Seir most desolate, and cut off from it the [a]one who leaves and
the one who returns.
8 "And I will fill its mountains with the
slain; on your hills and in your valleys and in all

KJV

thy rivers, shall they fall that are slain with the
sword.
9 [a]I will make thee perpetual desolations,
and thy cities shall not return: [b]and ye shall know
that I *am* the LORD.
10 Because thou hast said, These two nations
and these two countries shall be mine, and we
will [a]possess it; whereas [b]the LORD was there:
11 Therefore, *as* I live, saith the Lord GOD, I
will even do [a]according to thine anger, and according to thine envy which thou hast used out
of thy hatred against them; and I will make myself
known among them, when I have judged thee.
12 [a]And thou shalt know that I *am* the LORD,
and that I have [b]heard all thy [c]blasphemies which
thou hast spoken against the mountains of Israel,
saying, They are laid desolate, they are given us
to consume.
13 Thus [a]with your mouth ye have boasted
against me, and have multiplied your [b]words
against me: I have heard *them.*
14 Thus saith the Lord GOD; [a]When the
whole earth rejoiceth, I will make thee desolate.
15 [a]As thou didst rejoice at the inheritance
of the house of Israel, because it was desolate,
[b]so will I do unto thee: thou shalt be desolate, O
mount Seir, and all Idumea, *even* all of it: and
they shall know that I *am* the LORD.

Blessing on Israel

36 Also, thou son of man, prophesy unto the
[a]mountains of Israel, and say, Ye mountains of Israel, hear the word of the LORD:
2 Thus saith the Lord GOD; Because [a]the enemy hath said against you, Aha, [b]even the ancient
high places [c]are our's in possession:
3 Therefore prophesy and say, Thus saith
the Lord GOD; Because they have made *you* desolate, and swallowed you up on every side, that
ye might be a possession unto the residue of the
heathen, [a]and ye are taken up in the lips of [b]talk-
ers, and *are* an infamy of the people:
4 Therefore, ye mountains of Israel, hear
the word of the Lord GOD; Thus saith the Lord
GOD to the mountains, and to the hills, to the rivers, and to the valleys, to the desolate wastes, and
to the cities that are forsaken, which [a]became a
prey and [b]derision to the residue of the heathen
that *are* round about;
5 Therefore thus saith the Lord GOD;
[a]Surely in the fire of my jealousy have I spoken
against the residue of the heathen, and against
all Idumea, [b]which have appointed my land
into their possession with the joy of all *their*
heart, with despiteful minds, to cast it out for a
prey.
6 Prophesy therefore concerning the land of
Israel, and say unto the mountains, and to the
hills, to the rivers, and to the valleys, Thus saith
the Lord GOD; Behold, I have spoken in my jealousy and in my fury, because ye have [a]borne the
shame of the heathen:
7 Therefore thus saith the Lord GOD; I have
[a]lifted up mine hand, Surely the heathen that *are*
about you, they shall [b]bear their shame.
8 But ye, O mountains of Israel, ye shall
shoot forth your branches, and yield your fruit
to my people of Israel; for they are at hand to
come.
9 For, behold, I *am* for you, and I will turn
unto you, and ye shall be tilled and sown:
10 And I will multiply men upon you, all the
house of Israel, *even* all of it: and the cities shall
be inhabited, and [a]the wastes shall be builded:
11 And [a]I will multiply upon you man and
beast; and they shall increase and bring fruit: and
I will settle you after your old estates, and will
do [b]better *unto you* than at your beginnings: [c]and
ye shall know that I *am* the LORD.
12 Yea, I will cause men to walk upon you,
even my people Israel; [a]and they shall possess

---

9 [a]Jer. 49:13; Ezek. 25:13 [b]Ezek. 36:11
10 [a]Ps. 83:4–12; Ezek. 36:2, 5 [b][Ps. 48:1–3; 132:13, 14]; Is. 12:6; Ezek. 48:35; Zeph. 3:15
11 [a][Matt. 7:2; James 2:13]
12 [a]Ps. 9:16 [b]Zeph. 2:8 [c]Is. 52:5
13 [a][1 Sam. 2:3] [b]Ezek. 36:3
14 [a]Is. 65:13, 14
15 [a]Obad. 12, 15 [b]Jer. 50:11; Lam. 4:21

CHAPTER 36

1 [a]Ezek. 6:2, 3
2 [a]Jer. 33:24; Ezek. 25:3; 26:2 [b]Deut. 32:13; Ps. 78:69; Is. 58:14; Hab. 3:19 [c]Ezek. 35:10
3 [a]Deut. 28:37; 1 Kin. 9:7; Lam. 2:15; Dan. 9:16 [b]Ps. 44:13, 14; Jer. 18:16; Ezek. 35:13
4 [a]Ezek. 34:8, 28 [b]Ps. 79:4; Jer. 48:27
5 [a]Deut. 4:24; Ezek. 38:19 [b]Ezek. 35:10, 12
6 [a]Ps. 74:10; 123:3, 4; Ezek. 34:29
7 [a]Ezek. 20:5 [b]Jer. 25:9, 15, 29
10 [a]Is. 58:12; 61:4; Amos 9:14
11 [a]Jer. 31:27; 33:12 [b]Job 42:12; Is. 51:3 [c]Ezek. 35:9; 37:6, 13
12 [a]Obad. 17

NKJV

your ravines those who are slain by the sword
shall fall.
9 [a]"I will make you perpetually desolate,
and your cities shall be uninhabited; [b]then you
shall know that I *am* the LORD.
10 "Because you have said, 'These two nations and these two countries shall be mine, and
we will [a]possess them,' although [b]the LORD was
there,
11 "therefore, *as* I live," says the Lord GOD,
"I will do [a]according to your anger and according
to the envy which you showed in your hatred
against them; and I will make Myself known
among them when I judge you.
12 [a]"Then you shall know that I *am* the LORD.
I have [b]heard all your [c]blasphemies which you
have spoken against the mountains of Israel, saying, 'They are desolate; they are given to us to
consume.'
13 "Thus [a]with your mouth you have boasted
against Me and multiplied your [b]words against
Me; I have heard *them.*"
14 'Thus says the Lord GOD: [a]"The whole
earth will rejoice when I make you desolate.
15 [a]"As you rejoiced because the inheritance
of the house of Israel was desolate, [b]so I will do
to you; you shall be desolate, O Mount Seir, as
well as all of Edom—all of it! Then they shall
know that I *am* the LORD." '

Blessing on Israel

36 "And you, son of man, prophesy to the
[a]mountains of Israel, and say, 'O mountains
of Israel, hear the word of the LORD!
2 'Thus says the Lord GOD: "Because [a]the
enemy has said of you, 'Aha! [b]The ancient heights
[c]have become our possession,' " '
3 "therefore prophesy, and say, 'Thus says
the Lord GOD: "Because they made *you* desolate
and swallowed you up on every side, so that you
became the possession of the rest of the nations,
[a]and you are taken up by the lips of [b]talkers and
slandered by the people"—
4 'therefore, O mountains of Israel, hear the
word of the Lord GOD! Thus says the Lord GOD
to the mountains, the hills, the rivers, the valleys,
the desolate wastes, and the cities that have been
forsaken, which [a]became plunder and [b]mockery
to the rest of the nations all around—
5 'therefore thus says the Lord GOD:
[a]"Surely I have spoken in My burning jealousy
against the rest of the nations and against all
Edom, [b]who gave My land to themselves as a possession, with wholehearted joy *and* spiteful
minds, in order to plunder its open country." '
6 "Therefore prophesy concerning the land
of Israel, and say to the mountains, the hills, the
rivers, and the valleys, 'Thus says the Lord GOD:
"Behold, I have spoken in My jealousy and My
fury, because you have [a]borne the shame of the
nations."
7 'Therefore thus says the Lord GOD: "I have
[a]raised My hand in an oath that surely the nations
that *are* around you shall [b]bear their own shame.
8 "But you, O mountains of Israel, you shall
shoot forth your branches and yield your fruit to
My people Israel, for they are about to come.
9 "For indeed I *am* for you, and I will turn
to you, and you shall be tilled and sown.
10 "I will multiply men upon you, all the
house of Israel, all of it; and the cities shall be
inhabited and [a]the ruins rebuilt.
11 [a]"I will multiply upon you man and beast;
and they shall increase and bear young; I will
make you inhabited as in former times, and do
[b]better *for you* than at your beginnings. [c]Then
you shall know that I *am* the LORD.
12 "Yes, I will cause men to walk on you,
My people Israel; [a]they shall take possession of

KJV

thee, and thou shalt be their inheritance, and thou
shalt no more henceforth [b]bereave them *of men.*
13 Thus saith the Lord GOD; Because they
say unto you, [a]Thou *land* devourest up men, and
hast bereaved thy nations;
14 Therefore thou shalt devour men no more,
neither bereave thy nations any more, saith the
Lord GOD.
15 [a]Neither will I cause *men* to hear in thee
the shame of the heathen any more, neither shalt
thou bear the reproach of the people any more,
neither shalt thou cause thy nations to fall any
more, saith the Lord GOD.

The Renewal of Israel

16 Moreover the word of the LORD came unto
me, saying,
17 Son of man, when the house of Israel
dwelt in their own land, [a]they defiled it by their
own way and by their doings: their way was before me as [b]the uncleanness of a removed woman.
18 Wherefore I poured my fury upon them
[a]for the blood that they had shed upon the land,
and for their idols *wherewith* they had polluted
it:
19 And I [a]scattered them among the heathen,
and they were dispersed through the countries:
[b]according to their way and according to their
doings I judged them.
20 And when they entered unto the heathen,
whither they went, they [a]profaned my holy name,
when they said to them, These *are* the people of
the LORD, and are gone forth out of his land.
21 But I had pity [a]for mine holy name, which
the house of Israel had profaned among the
heathen, whither they went.
22 Therefore say unto the house of Israel,
Thus saith the Lord GOD; I do not *this* for your
sakes, O house of Israel, [a]but for mine holy
name's sake, which ye have profaned among the
heathen, whither ye went.
23 And I will sanctify my great name, which
was profaned among the heathen, which ye have
profaned in the midst of them; and the heathen
shall know that I *am* the LORD, saith the Lord
GOD, when I shall be [a]sanctified in you before
their eyes.
24 For [a]I will take you from among the
heathen, and gather you out of all countries, and
will bring you into your own land.
25 [a]Then will I sprinkle clean water upon
you, and ye shall be clean: [b]from all your filthiness, and from all your idols, will I cleanse you.
26 A [a]new heart also will I give you, and a
new spirit will I put within you: and I will take
away the stony heart out of your flesh, and I will
give you an heart of flesh.
27 And I will put my [a]spirit within you, and
cause you to walk in my statutes, and ye shall
keep my judgments, and do *them.*
28 [a]And ye shall dwell in the land that I gave
to your fathers; [b]and ye shall be my people, and
I will be your God.
29 I will also [a]save you from all your un-
cleannesses: and [b]I will call for the corn, and will
increase it, and [c]lay no famine upon you.
30 [a]And I will multiply the fruit of the
tree, and the increase of the field, that ye shall
receive no more reproach of famine among the
heathen.
31 Then [a]shall ye remember your own evil
ways, and your doings that *were* not good, and
[b]shall lothe yourselves in your own sight for your
iniquities and for your abominations.
32 [a]Not for your sakes do I *this,* saith the
Lord GOD, be it known unto you: be ashamed and
confounded for your own ways, O house of Israel.
33 Thus saith the Lord GOD; In the day that
I shall have cleansed you from all your iniquities
I will also cause *you* to dwell in the cities, [a]and
the wastes shall be builded.
34 And the desolate land shall be tilled,

12 [b]Jer. 15:7; Ezek. 22:12, 27
13 [a]Num. 13:32
15 [a]Is. 60:14; Ezek. 34:29
17 [a]Lev. 18:25, 27, 28; Jer. 2:7 [b]Lev. 15:19
18 [a]Ezek. 16:36, 38; 23:37
19 [a]Deut. 28:64; Ezek. 5:12; 22:15; Amos 9:9 [b]Ezek. 7:3; 18:30; 39:24; [Rom. 2:6]
20 [a]Is. 52:5; Ezek. 12:16; Rom. 2:24
21 [a]Ezek. 20:9, 14
22 [a]Ps. 106:8; Ezek. 20:44
23 [a]Is. 5:16; Ezek. 20:41; 28:22
24 [a]Is. 43:5, 6; Ezek. 34:13; 37:21
25 [a]Num. 19:17–19; Ps. 51:7; Is. 52:15; Heb. 9:13, 19; 10:22 [b]Jer. 33:8
26 [a]Ps. 51:10; Jer. 32:39; Ezek. 11:19; [John 3:3]
27 [a]Is. 44:3; 59:21; Ezek. 11:19; 37:14; [Joel 2:28, 29]
28 [a]Ezek. 28:25; 37:25 [b]Jer. 30:22; Ezek. 11:20; 37:27
29 [a]Zech. 13:1; [Matt. 1:21; Rom. 11:26] [b]Ps. 105:16 [c]Ezek. 34:27, 29; Hos. 2:21–23
30 [a]Lev. 26:4; Ezek. 34:27
31 [a]Ezek. 16:61, 63 [b]Lev. 26:39; Ezek. 6:9; 20:43
32 [a]Deut. 9:5
33 [a]Ezek. 36:10

NKJV

you, and you shall be their inheritance; no more
shall you [b]bereave them *of children.*"
13 'Thus says the Lord GOD: "Because they
say to you, [a]'You devour men and bereave your
nation *of children,*'
14 "therefore you shall devour men no more,
nor bereave your nation anymore," says the Lord
GOD.
15 [a]"Nor will I let you hear the taunts of the
nations anymore, nor bear the reproach of the
peoples anymore, nor shall you cause your nation
to stumble anymore," says the Lord GOD.' "

The Renewal of Israel

16 Moreover the word of the LORD came to
me, saying:
17 "Son of man, when the house of Israel
dwelt in their own land, [a]they defiled it by their
own ways and deeds; to Me their way was like
[b]the uncleanness of a woman in her customary
impurity.
18 "Therefore I poured out My fury on them
[a]for the blood they had shed on the land, and for
their idols *with which* they had defiled it.
19 "So I [a]scattered them among the nations,
and they were dispersed throughout the countries;
I judged them [b]according to their ways and their
deeds.
20 "When they came to the nations, wherever they went, they [a]profaned My holy name—
when they said of them, 'These *are* the people of
the LORD, *and* yet they have gone out of His land.'
21 "But I had concern [a]for My holy name,
which the house of Israel had profaned among
the nations wherever they went.
22 "Therefore say to the house of Israel,
'Thus says the Lord GOD: "I do not do *this* for
your sake, O house of Israel, [a]but for My holy
name's sake, which you have profaned among the
nations wherever you went.
23 "And I will sanctify My great name, which
has been profaned among the nations, which you
have profaned in their midst; and the nations shall
know that I *am* the LORD," says the Lord GOD,
"when I am [a]hallowed in you before their eyes.
24 "For [a]I will take you from among the nations, gather you out of all countries, and bring
you into your own land.
25 [a]"Then I will sprinkle clean water on you,
and you shall be clean; I will cleanse you [b]from
all your filthiness and from all your idols.
26 "I will give you a [a]new heart and put a
new spirit within you; I will take the heart of stone
out of your flesh and give you a heart of flesh.
27 "I will put My [a]Spirit within you and cause
you to walk in My statutes, and you will keep
My judgments and do *them.*
28 [a]"Then you shall dwell in the land that I
gave to your fathers; [b]you shall be My people,
and I will be your God.
29 "I will [a]deliver you from all your unclean-
nesses. [b]I will call for the grain and multiply it,
and [c]bring no famine upon you.
30 [a]"And I will multiply the fruit of your trees
and the increase of your fields, so that you need
never again bear the reproach of famine among
the nations.
31 "Then [a]you will remember your evil ways
and your deeds that *were* not good; and you [b]will
loathe yourselves in your own sight, for your iniquities and your abominations.
32 [a]"Not for your sake do I do *this,*" says
the Lord GOD, "let it be known to you. Be ashamed
and confounded for your own ways, O house of
Israel!"
33 'Thus says the Lord GOD: "On the day that
I cleanse you from all your iniquities, I will also
enable *you* to dwell in the cities, [a]and the ruins
shall be rebuilt.
34 "The desolate land shall be tilled instead

KJV

whereas it lay desolate in the sight of all that passed by.

35 And they shall say, This land that was desolate is become like the garden of [a]Eden; and the waste and desolate and ruined cities *are become* fenced, *and* are inhabited.

36 Then the heathen that are left round about you shall know that I the LORD build the ruined *places, and* plant that that was desolate: [a]I the LORD have spoken *it,* and I will do *it.*

37 Thus saith the Lord GOD; [a]I will yet *for* this be enquired of by the house of Israel, to do *it* for them; I will [b]increase them with men like a flock.

38 As the holy flock, as the flock of Jerusalem in her solemn feasts; so shall the waste cities be filled with flocks of men: and they shall know that I *am* the LORD.

The Dry Bones Live

37 The [a]hand of the LORD was upon me, and carried me out [b]in the spirit of the LORD, and set me down in the midst of the valley which *was* full of bones,

2 And caused me to pass by them round about: and, behold, *there were* very many in the open valley; and, lo, *they were* very dry.

3 And he said unto me, Son of man, can these bones live? And I answered, O Lord GOD, [a]thou knowest.

4 Again he said unto me, Prophesy upon these bones, and say unto them, O ye dry bones, hear the word of the LORD.

5 Thus saith the Lord GOD unto these bones; Behold, I will [a]cause breath to enter into you, and ye shall live:

6 And I will lay sinews upon you, and will bring up flesh upon you, and cover you with skin, and put breath in you, and ye shall live; [a]and ye shall know that I *am* the LORD.

7 So I prophesied as I was commanded: and as I prophesied, there was a noise, and behold a shaking, and the bones came together, bone to his bone.

8 And when I beheld, lo, the sinews and the flesh came up upon them, and the skin covered them above: but *there was* no breath in them.

9 Then said he unto me, Prophesy unto the wind, prophesy, son of man, and say to the wind, Thus saith the Lord GOD; [a]Come from the four winds, O breath, and breathe upon these slain, that they may live.

10 So I prophesied as he commanded me, [a]and the breath came into them, and they lived, and stood up upon their feet, an exceeding great army.

11 Then he said unto me, Son of man, these bones are the [a]whole house of Israel: behold, they say, [b]Our bones are dried, and our hope is lost: we are cut off for our parts.

12 Therefore prophesy and say unto them, Thus saith the Lord GOD; Behold, [a]O my people, I will open your graves, and cause you to come up out of your graves, and [b]bring you into the land of Israel.

13 And ye shall know that I *am* the LORD, when I have opened your graves, O my people, and brought you up out of your graves,

14 And [a]shall put my spirit in you, and ye shall live, and I shall place you in your own land: then shall ye know that I the LORD have spoken *it,* and performed *it,* saith the LORD.

One Kingdom, One King

15 The word of the LORD came again unto me, saying,

16 Moreover, thou son of man, [a]take thee one stick, and write upon it, For Judah, and for [b]the children of Israel his companions: then take another stick, and write upon it, For Joseph, the stick of Ephraim, and *for* all the house of Israel his companions:

35 [a]Is. 51:3; Ezek. 28:13; Joel 2:3
36 [a]Ezek. 17:24; 22:14; 37:14; Hos. 14:4–9
37 [a]Ezek. 14:3; 20:3, 31 [b]Ezek. 36:10

CHAPTER 37

1 [a]Ezek. 1:3 [b]Ezek. 3:14; 8:3; 11:24; Acts 8:39
3 [a][Deut. 32:39; 1 Sam. 2:6; John 5:21; Rom. 4:17; 2 Cor. 1:9]
5 [a]Gen. 2:7; Ps. 104:29, 30; Ezek. 37:9, 10, 14
6 [a]Is. 49:23; Ezek. 6:7; 35:12; Joel 2:27; 3:17
9 [a][Ps. 104:30]
10 [a]Rev. 11:11
11 [a]Jer. 33:24; Ezek. 36:10 [b]Ps. 141:7; Is. 49:14
12 [a]Deut. 32:39; 1 Sam. 2:6; Is. 26:19; 66:14; [Dan. 12:2]; Hos. 13:14 [b]Ezek. 36:24
14 [a]Is. 32:15; Ezek. 36:27; [Joel 2:28, 29]; Zech. 12:10
16 [a]Num. 17:2, 3 [b]2 Chr. 11:12, 13, 16; 15:9; 30:11, 18

NKJV

of lying desolate in the sight of all who pass by.

35 "So they will say, 'This land that was desolate has become like the garden of [a]Eden; and the wasted, desolate, and ruined cities *are now* fortified *and* inhabited.'

36 "Then the nations which are left all around you shall know that I, the LORD, have rebuilt the ruined places *and* planted what was desolate. [a]I, the LORD, have spoken *it,* and I will do *it.*"

37 'Thus says the Lord GOD: [a]"I will also let the house of Israel inquire of Me to do this for them: I will [b]increase their men like a flock.

38 "Like a flock *offered as* holy *sacrifices,* like the flock at Jerusalem on its feast days, so shall the ruined cities be filled with flocks of men. Then they shall know that I *am* the LORD." ' "

The Dry Bones Live

37 The [a]hand of the LORD came upon me and brought me out [b]in the Spirit of the LORD, and set me down in the midst of the valley; and it *was* full of bones.

2 Then He caused me to pass by them all around, and behold, *there were* very many in the open valley; and indeed *they were* very dry.

3 And He said to me, "Son of man, can these bones live?" So I answered, "O Lord GOD, [a]You know."

4 Again He said to me, "Prophesy to these bones, and say to them, 'O dry bones, hear the word of the LORD!

5 'Thus says the Lord GOD to these bones: "Surely I will [a]cause breath to enter into you, and you shall live.

6 "I will put sinews on you and bring flesh upon you, cover you with skin and put breath in you; and you shall live. [a]Then you shall know that I *am* the LORD." ' "

7 So I prophesied as I was commanded; and as I prophesied, there was a noise, and suddenly a rattling; and the bones came together, bone to bone.

8 Indeed, as I looked, the sinews and the flesh came upon them, and the skin covered them over; but *there was* no breath in them.

9 Also He said to me, "Prophesy to the breath, prophesy, son of man, and say to the breath, 'Thus says the Lord GOD: [a]"Come from the four winds, O breath, and breathe on these slain, that they may live." ' "

10 So I prophesied as He commanded me, [a]and breath came into them, and they lived, and stood upon their feet, an exceedingly great army.

11 Then He said to me, "Son of man, these bones are the [a]whole house of Israel. They indeed say, [b]'Our bones are dry, our hope is lost, and we ourselves are cut off!'

12 "Therefore prophesy and say to them, 'Thus says the Lord GOD: "Behold, [a]O My people, I will open your graves and cause you to come up from your graves, and [b]bring you into the land of Israel.

13 "Then you shall know that I *am* the LORD, when I have opened your graves, O My people, and brought you up from your graves.

14 "I [a]will put My Spirit in you, and you shall live, and I will place you in your own land. Then you shall know that I, the LORD, have spoken *it* and performed *it,*" says the LORD.' "

One Kingdom, One King

15 Again the word of the LORD came to me, saying,

16 "As for you, son of man, [a]take a stick for yourself and write on it: 'For Judah and for [b]the children of Israel, his companions.' Then take another stick and write on it, 'For Joseph, the stick of Ephraim, and *for* all the house of Israel, his companions.'

KJV

17 And [a]join them one to another into one
stick; and they shall become one in thine hand.
18 And when the children of thy people shall
speak unto thee, saying, [a]Wilt thou not shew us
what thou *meanest* by these?
19 [a]Say unto them, Thus saith the Lord GOD;
Behold, I will take [b]the stick of Joseph, which *is*
in the hand of Ephraim, and the tribes of Israel
his fellows, and will put them with him, *even* with
the stick of Judah, and make them one stick, and
they shall be one in mine hand.
20 And the sticks whereon thou writest shall
be in thine hand [a]before their eyes.
21 And say unto them, Thus saith the Lord
GOD; Behold, [a]I will take the children of Israel
from among the heathen, whither they be gone,
and will gather them on every side, and bring
them into their own land:
22 And [a]I will make them one nation in the
land upon the mountains of Israel; and [b]one king
shall be king to them all: and they shall be no
more two nations, neither shall they be divided
into two kingdoms any more at all:
23 [a]Neither shall they defile themselves any
more with their idols, nor with their detestable
things, nor with any of their transgressions: but
[b]I will save them out of all their dwellingplaces,
wherein they have sinned, and will cleanse them:
so shall they be my people, and I will be their
God.
24 And [a]David my servant *shall be* king over
them; and [b]they all shall have one shepherd: [c]they
shall also walk in my judgments, and observe my
statutes, and do them.
25 [a]And they shall dwell in the land that I
have given unto Jacob my servant, wherein your
fathers have dwelt; and they shall dwell therein,
even they, and their children, and their children's
children [b]for ever: and [c]my servant David *shall
be* their prince for ever.
26 Moreover I will make [a]a covenant of
peace with them; it shall be an everlasting covenant with them: and I will place them, and [b]multi-
ply them, and will set my [c]sanctuary in the midst
of them for evermore.
27 [a]My tabernacle also shall be with them:
yea, I will be [b]their God, and they shall be my
people.
28 [a]And the heathen shall know that I the
LORD do [b]sanctify Israel, when my sanctuary shall
be in the midst of them for evermore.

Gog and Allies Attack Israel

38 And the word of the LORD came unto me,
saying,
2 [a]Son of man, [b]set thy face against [c]Gog,
the land of [d]Magog, the chief prince of [e]Meshech
and Tubal, and prophesy against him,
3 And say, Thus saith the Lord GOD; Behold, I *am* against thee, O Gog, the chief prince
of Meshech and Tubal:
4 And [a]I will turn thee back, and put hooks
into thy jaws, and I will [b]bring thee forth, and
all thine army, horses and horsemen, [c]all of them
clothed with all sorts *of armour, even* a great company *with* bucklers and shields, all of them handling swords:
5 Persia, Ethiopia, and Libya with them; all
of them with shield and helmet:
6 [a]Gomer, and all his bands; the house of
[b]Togarmah of the north quarters, and all his
bands: *and* many people with thee.
7 [a]Be thou prepared, and prepare for
thyself, thou, and all thy company that are assembled unto thee, and be thou a guard unto
them.
8 [a]After many days [b]thou shalt be visited:
in the latter years thou shalt come into the land
that is brought back from the sword, [c]*and is* gathered out of many people, against [d]the mountains
of Israel, which have been always waste: but it

17 [a]Is. 11:13; Jer. 50:4; Ezek. 37:22–24; Hos. 1:11; Zeph. 3:9
18 [a]Ezek. 12:9; 24:19
19 [a]Zech. 10:6 [b]Ezek. 37:16, 17
20 [a]Ezek. 12:3
21 [a]Is. 43:5, 6; Jer. 32:37; Ezek. 36:24; Amos 9:14, 15
22 [a]Is. 11:13; Jer. 3:18; Hos. 1:11 [b]Ezek. 34:23; John 10:16
23 [a]Ezek. 36:25 [b]Ezek. 36:28, 29
24 [a]Is. 40:11; [Jer. 23:5; 30:9]; Ezek. 34:23, 24; Hos. 3:5; [Luke 1:32] [b][John 10:16] [c]Ezek. 36:27
25 [a]Ezek. 36:28 [b]Is. 60:21; Joel 3:20; Amos 9:15 [c]Ps. 89:3, 4; John 12:34
26 [a]Ps. 89:3; Is. 55:3; [Jer. 32:40] [b]Jer. 30:19; Ezek. 36:10 [c][2 Cor. 6:16]
27 [a]Lev. 26:11; [John 1:14]; Rev. 21:3 [b]Ezek. 11:20
28 [a]Ezek. 36:23 [b]Ex. 31:13; Ezek. 20:12

CHAPTER 38

2 [a]Ezek. 39:1 [b]Ezek. 35:2, 3 [c]Ezek. 38:1—39:24; Rev. 20:8 [d]Gen. 10:2; Ezek. 39:6; Rev. 20:8 [e]Ezek. 32:26
4 [a]2 Kin. 19:28; Ezek. 29:4 [b]Is. 43:17 [c]Ezek. 23:12
6 [a]Gen. 10:2 [b]Gen. 10:3; Ezek. 27:14
7 [a]Is. 8:9, 10; Jer. 46:3, 4
8 [a]Deut. 4:30; Is. 24:22 [b]Is. 29:6 [c]Ezek. 34:13 [d]Ezek. 36:1, 4

*

38:2 Tg., Vg., Aquila *the chief prince of Meshech,* also v. 3
38:5 Heb. *Cush* • Heb. *Put*

NKJV

17 "Then [a]join them one to another for yourself into one stick, and they will become one in
your hand.
18 "And when the children of your people
speak to you, saying, [a]'Will you not show us what
you *mean* by these?'—
19 [a]"say to them, 'Thus says the Lord GOD:
"Surely I will take [b]the stick of Joseph, which *is*
in the hand of Ephraim, and the tribes of Israel,
his companions; and I will join them with it, with
the stick of Judah, and make them one stick, and
they will be one in My hand." '
20 "And the sticks on which you write will
be in your hand [a]before their eyes.
21 "Then say to them, 'Thus says the Lord
GOD: "Surely [a]I will take the children of Israel
from among the nations, wherever they have
gone, and will gather them from every side and
bring them into their own land;
22 "and [a]I will make them one nation in the
land, on the mountains of Israel; and [b]one king
shall be king over them all; they shall no longer
be two nations, nor shall they ever be divided into
two kingdoms again.
23 [a]"They shall not defile themselves anymore with their idols, nor with their detestable
things, nor with any of their transgressions; but
[b]I will deliver them from all their dwelling places
in which they have sinned, and will cleanse them.
Then they shall be My people, and I will be their
God.
24 [a]"David My servant *shall be* king over
them, and [b]they shall all have one shepherd; [c]they
shall also walk in My judgments and observe My
statutes, and do them.
25 [a]"Then they shall dwell in the land that I
have given to Jacob My servant, where your fathers dwelt; and they shall dwell there, they, their
children, and their children's children, [b]forever;
and [c]My servant David *shall be* their prince
forever.
26 "Moreover I will make [a]a covenant of
peace with them, and it shall be an everlasting
covenant with them; I will establish them and
[b]multiply them, and I will set My [c]sanctuary in
their midst forevermore.
27 [a]"My tabernacle also shall be with them;
indeed I will be [b]their God, and they shall be My
people.
28 [a]"The nations also will know that I, the
LORD, [b]sanctify Israel, when My sanctuary is in
their midst forevermore." ' "

Gog and Allies Attack Israel

38 Now the word of the LORD came to me,
saying,
2 [a]"Son of man, [b]set your face against [c]Gog,
of the land of [d]Magog, *the prince of Rosh, [e]Me-
shech, and Tubal, and prophesy against him,
3 "and say, 'Thus says the Lord GOD: "Behold, I *am* against you, O Gog, the prince of Rosh,
Meshech, and Tubal.
4 [a]"I will turn you around, put hooks into
your jaws, and [b]lead you out, with all your army,
horses, and horsemen, [c]all splendidly clothed, a
great company *with* bucklers and shields, all of
them handling swords.
5 "Persia, *Ethiopia, and *Libya are with
them, all of them *with* shield and helmet;
6 [a]"Gomer and all its troops; the house of
[b]Togarmah *from* the far north and all its troops—
many people *are* with you.
7 [a]"Prepare yourself and be ready, you and
all your companies that are gathered about you;
and be a guard for them.
8 [a]"After many days [b]you will be visited.
In the latter years you will come into the land of
those brought back from the sword [c]*and* gathered
from many people on [d]the mountains of Israel,
which had long been desolate; they were brought

KJV

is brought forth out of the nations, and they shall [e]dwell safely all of them.

9 Thou shalt ascend and come [a]like a storm, thou shalt be [b]like a cloud to cover the land, thou, and all thy bands, and many people with thee.

10 Thus saith the Lord GOD; It shall also come to pass, *that* at the same time shall things come into thy mind, and thou shalt think an evil thought:

11 And thou shalt say, I will go up to the land of [a]unwalled villages; I will [b]go to them that are at rest, [c]that dwell safely, all of them dwelling without walls, and having neither bars nor gates,

12 To take a spoil, and to take a prey; to turn thine hand upon the desolate places *that are now* inhabited, [a]and upon the people *that are* gathered out of the nations, which have gotten cattle and goods, that dwell in the midst of the land.

13 [a]Sheba, and [b]Dedan, and the merchants [c]of Tarshish, with all [d]the young lions thereof, shall say unto thee, Art thou come to take a spoil? hast thou gathered thy company to take a prey? to carry away silver and gold, to take away cattle and goods, to take a great spoil?

14 Therefore, son of man, prophesy and say unto Gog, Thus saith the Lord GOD; [a]In that day when my people of Israel [b]dwelleth safely, shalt thou not know *it?*

15 [a]And thou shalt come from thy place out of the north parts, thou, and many people with thee, all of them riding upon horses, a great company, and a mighty army:

16 And thou shalt come up against my people of Israel, as a cloud to cover the land; it shall be in the latter days, and I will bring thee against my land, that the heathen may [a]know me, when I shall be [b]sanctified in thee, O Gog, before their eyes.

17 Thus saith the Lord GOD; *Art* thou he of whom I have spoken in old time by my servants the prophets of Israel, which prophesied in those days *many* years that I would bring thee against them?

Judgment on Gog

18 And it shall come to pass at the same time when Gog shall come against the land of Israel, saith the Lord GOD, *that* my fury shall come up in my face.

19 For [a]in my jealousy [b]*and* in the fire of my wrath have I spoken, [c]Surely in that day there shall be a great shaking in the land of Israel;

20 So that [a]the fishes of the sea, and the fowls of the heaven, and the beasts of the field, and all creeping things that creep upon the earth, and all the men that *are* upon the face of the earth, shall shake at my presence, [b]and the mountains shall be thrown down, and the steep places shall fall, and every wall shall fall to the ground.

21 And I will [a]call for [b]a sword against him throughout all my mountains, saith the Lord GOD: [c]every man's sword shall be against his brother.

22 And I will [a]plead against him with [b]pestilence and with blood; and [c]I will rain upon him, and upon his bands, and upon the many people that *are* with him, and overflowing rain, and [d]great hailstones, fire, and brimstone.

23 Thus will I magnify myself, and [a]sanctify myself; [b]and I will be known in the eyes of many nations, and they shall know that I *am* the LORD.

Gog's Armies Destroyed

39 Therefore, [a]thou son of man, prophesy against Gog, and say, Thus saith the Lord GOD; Behold, I *am* against thee, O Gog, the chief prince of Meshech and Tubal:

2 And I will [a]turn thee back, and leave but the sixth part of thee, [b]and will cause thee to come up from the north parts, and will bring thee upon the mountains of Israel:

3 And I will smite thy bow out of thy left

---

8 [e]Jer. 23:6; Ezek. 34:25; 39:26
9 [a]Is. 28:2 [b]Jer. 4:13
11 [a]Zech. 2:4 [b]Jer. 49:31 [c]Ezek. 38:8
12 [a]Ezek. 38:8
13 [a]Ezek. 27:22 [b]Ezek. 27:15, 20 [c]Ezek. 27:12 [d]Ezek. 19:3, 5
14 [a]Is. 4:1 [b]Jer. 23:6; Ezek. 38:8, 11; [Zech. 2:5, 8]
15 [a]Ezek. 39:2
16 [a]Ezek. 35:11 [b]Is. 5:16; 8:13; 29:23; Ezek. 28:22
19 [a]Deut. 32:21, 22; Ps. 18:7, 8; Ezek. 36:5, 6; [Nah. 1:2]; Heb. 12:29 [b]Ps. 89:46 [c]Joel 3:16; Hag. 2:6, 7; Rev. 16:8
20 [a]Hos. 4:3 [b]Jer. 4:24; Nah. 1:5, 6
21 [a]Ps. 105:16 [b]Ezek. 14:17 [c]Judg. 7:22; 1 Sam. 14:20; 2 Chr. 20:23; Hag. 2:22
22 [a]Is. 66:16; Jer. 25:31 [b]Ezek. 5:17 [c]Ps. 11:6; Is. 30:30; Ezek. 13:11 [d]Rev. 16:21
23 [a]Ezek. 36:23 [b]Ps. 9:16; Ezek. 37:28; 38:16

CHAPTER 39

1 [a]Ezek. 38:2, 3
2 [a]Ezek. 38:8 [b]Ezek. 38:15

NKJV

out of the nations, and now all of them [e]dwell safely.

9 "You will ascend, coming [a]like a storm, covering the [b]land like a cloud, you and all your troops and many peoples with you."

10 'Thus says the Lord GOD: "On that day it shall come to pass *that* thoughts will arise in your mind, and you will make an evil plan:

11 "You will say, 'I will go up against a land of [a]unwalled villages; I will [b]go to a peaceful people, [c]who dwell safely, all of them dwelling without walls, and having neither bars nor gates'—

12 "to take plunder and to take booty, to stretch out your hand against the waste places *that are again* inhabited, [a]and against a people gathered from the nations, who have acquired livestock and goods, who dwell in the midst of the land.

13 [a]"Sheba, [b]Dedan, the merchants [c]of Tarshish, and all [d]their young lions will say to you, 'Have you come to take plunder? Have you gathered your army to take booty, to carry away silver and gold, to take away livestock and goods, to take great plunder?' " '

14 "Therefore, son of man, prophesy and say to Gog, 'Thus says the Lord GOD: [a]"On that day when My people Israel [b]dwell safely, will you not know *it?*

15 [a]"Then you will come from your place out of the far north, you and many peoples with you, all of them riding on horses, a great company and a mighty army.

16 "You will come up against My people Israel like a cloud, to cover the land. It will be in the latter days that I will bring you against My land, so that the nations may [a]know Me, when I am [b]hallowed in you, O Gog, before their eyes."

17 'Thus says the Lord GOD: "Are *you* he of whom I have spoken in former days by My servants the prophets of Israel, who prophesied for years in those days that I would bring you against them?

Judgment on Gog

18 "And it will come to pass at the same time, when Gog comes against the land of Israel," says the Lord GOD, "*that* My fury will show in My face.

19 "For [a]in My jealousy [b]*and* in the fire of My wrath I have spoken: [c]'Surely in that day there shall be a great earthquake in the land of Israel,

20 'so that [a]the fish of the sea, the birds of the heavens, the beasts of the field, all creeping things that creep on the earth, and all men who *are* on the face of the earth shall shake at My presence. [b]The mountains shall be thrown down, the steep places shall fall, and every wall shall fall to the ground.'

21 "I will [a]call for [b]a sword against Gog throughout all My mountains," says the Lord GOD. [c]"Every man's sword will be against his brother.

22 "And I will [a]bring him to judgment with [b]pestilence and bloodshed; [c]I will rain down on him, on his troops, and on the many peoples who *are* with him, flooding rain, [d]great hailstones, fire, and brimstone.

23 "Thus I will magnify Myself and [a]sanctify Myself, [b]and I will be known in the eyes of many nations. Then they shall know that I *am* the LORD." '

Gog's Armies Destroyed

39 "And [a]you, son of man, prophesy against Gog, and say, 'Thus says the Lord GOD: "Behold, I *am* against you, O Gog, *the prince of Rosh, Meshech, and Tubal;

2 "and I will [a]turn you around and lead you on, [b]bringing you up from the far north, and bring you against the mountains of Israel.

3 "Then I will knock the bow out of your

---

*39:1 Tg., Vg., Aquila *the chief prince of Meshech*

KJV

hand, and will cause thine arrows to fall out of thy right hand.

4 [a]Thou shalt fall upon the mountains of Israel, thou, and all thy bands, and the people that *is* with thee: [b]I will give thee unto the ravenous birds of every sort, and *to* the beasts of the field to be devoured.

5 Thou shalt fall upon the open field: for I have spoken *it*, saith the Lord GOD.

6 [a]And I will send a fire on Magog, and among them that dwell carelessly in [b]the isles: and they shall know that I *am* the LORD.

7 [a]So will I make my holy name known in the midst of my people Israel; and I will not *let them* [b]pollute my holy name any more: [c]and the heathen shall know that I *am* the LORD, the Holy One in Israel.

8 [a]Behold, it is come, and it is done, saith the Lord GOD; this *is* the day [b]whereof I have spoken.

9 And they that dwell in the cities of Israel shall go forth, and shall set on fire and burn the weapons, both the shields and the bucklers, the bows and the arrows, and the handstaves, and the spears, and they shall burn them with fire seven years:

10 So that they shall take no wood out of the field, neither cut down *any* out of the forests; for they shall burn the weapons with fire: [a]and they shall spoil those that spoiled them, and rob those that robbed them, saith the Lord GOD.

The Burial of Gog

11 And it shall come to pass in that day, *that* I will give unto Gog a place there of graves in Israel, the valley of the passengers on the east of the sea: and it shall stop the *noses* of the passengers: and there shall they bury Gog and all his multitude: and they shall call *it* The valley of Hamon–gog.

12 And seven months shall the house of Israel be burying of them, [a]that they may cleanse the land.

13 Yea, all the people of the land shall bury *them;* and it shall be to them a [a]renown the day that [b]I shall be glorified, saith the Lord GOD.

14 And they shall sever out men of continual employment, passing through the land to bury with the passengers those that remain upon the face of the earth, [a]to cleanse it: after the end of seven months shall they search.

15 And the passengers *that* pass through the land, when *any* seeth a man's bone, then shall he set up a sign by it, till the buriers have buried it in the valley of Hamon–gog.

16 And also the name of the city *shall be* Hamonah. Thus shall they [a]cleanse the land.

A Triumphant Festival

17 And, thou son of man, thus saith the Lord GOD; [a]Speak unto every feathered fowl, and to every beast of the field, [b]Assemble yourselves, and come; gather yourselves on every side to my [c]sacrifice that I do sacrifice for you, *even* a great sacrifice [d]upon the mountains of Israel, that ye may eat flesh, and drink blood.

18 [a]Ye shall eat the flesh of the mighty, and drink the blood of the princes of the earth, of rams, of lambs, and of goats, of bullocks, all of them [b]fatlings of Bashan.

19 And ye shall eat fat till ye be full, and drink blood till ye be drunken, of my sacrifice which I have sacrificed for you.

20 [a]Thus ye shall be filled at my table with horses and chariots, [b]with mighty men, and with all men of war, saith the Lord GOD.

4 [a]Ezek. 38:4, 21 [b]Ezek. 33:27
6 [a]Ezek. 38:22; Amos 1:4, 7, 10; Nah. 1:6 [b]Ps. 72:10; Is. 66:19; Jer. 25:22
7 [a]Ezek. 39:25 [b]Lev. 18:21; Ezek. 36:23 [c]Ezek. 38:16
8 [a]Rev. 16:17; 21:6 [b]Ezek. 38:17
10 [a]Is. 14:2; 33:1; Mic. 5:8; Hab. 2:8
12 [a]Deut. 21:23; Ezek. 39:14, 16
13 [a]Jer. 33:9; Zeph. 3:19, 20 [b]Ezek. 28:22
14 [a]Ezek. 39:12
16 [a]Ezek. 39:12
17 [a]Is. 56:9; [Jer. 12:9]; Ezek. 39:4; Rev. 19:17, 18 [b]Is. 18:6 [c]Is. 34:6, 7; Jer. 46:10; Zeph. 1:7 [d]Ezek. 39:4
18 [a]Ezek. 29:5; Rev. 19:18 [b]Deut. 32:14; Ps. 22:12
20 [a]Ps. 76:5, 6; Ezek. 38:4; Hag. 2:22 [b]Rev. 19:18

NKJV

left hand, and cause the arrows to fall out of your right hand.

4 [a]"You shall fall upon the mountains of Israel, you and all your troops and the peoples who *are* with you; [b]I will give you to birds of prey of every sort and *to* the beasts of the field to be devoured.

5 "You shall fall on the open field; for I have spoken," says the Lord GOD.

6 [a]"And I will send fire on Magog and on those who live in security in [b]the coastlands. Then they shall know that I *am* the LORD.

7 [a]"So I will make My holy name known in the midst of My people Israel, and I will not *let them* [b]profane My holy name anymore. [c]Then the nations shall know that *I am* the LORD, the Holy One in Israel.

8 [a]"Surely it is coming, and it shall be done," says the Lord GOD. "This *is* the day [b]of which I have spoken.

9 "Then those who dwell in the cities of Israel will go out and set on fire and burn the weapons, both the shields and bucklers, the bows and arrows, the javelins and spears; and they will make fires with them for seven years.

10 "They will not take wood from the field nor cut down *any* from the forests, because they will make fires with the weapons; [a]and they will plunder those who plundered them, and pillage those who pillaged them," says the Lord GOD.

The Burial of Gog

11 "It will come to pass in that day *that* I will give Gog a burial place there in Israel, the valley of those who pass by east of the sea; and it will obstruct travelers, because there they will bury Gog and all his multitude. Therefore they will call *it* the Valley of *Hamon Gog.

12 "For seven months the house of Israel will be burying them, [a]in order to cleanse the land.

13 "Indeed all the people of the land will be burying, and they will gain [a]renown for it on the day that [b]I am glorified," says the Lord GOD.

14 "They will set apart men regularly employed, with the help of *a search party, to pass through the land and bury those bodies remaining on the ground, in order [a]to cleanse it. At the end of seven months they will make a search.

15 "The search party will pass through the land; and *when anyone* sees a man's bone, he shall set up a marker by it, till the buriers have buried it in the Valley of Hamon Gog.

16 "*The* name of *the* city *will* also *be* Hamonah. Thus they shall [a]cleanse the land." '

A Triumphant Festival

17 "And as for you, son of man, thus says the Lord GOD, [a]'Speak to every sort of bird and to every beast of the field:

[b]"Assemble yourselves and come;
Gather together from all sides to My
[c]sacrificial meal
Which I am sacrificing for you,
A great sacrificial meal [d]on the mountains
of Israel,
That you may eat flesh and drink blood.
18 [a]You shall eat the flesh of the mighty,
Drink the blood of the princes of the earth,
Of rams and lambs,
Of goats and bulls,
All of them [b]fatlings of Bashan.
19 You shall eat fat till you are full,
And drink blood till you are drunk,
At My sacrificial meal
Which I am sacrificing for you.
20 [a]You shall be filled at My table
With horses and riders,
[b]With mighty men
And with all the men of war," says the
Lord GOD.

39:11 Lit. *The Multitude of Gog*
39:14 Lit. *those who pass through*

KJV

Israel Restored to the Land

21 [a]And I will set my glory among the heathen, and all the heathen shall see my judgment that I have executed, and [b]my hand that I have laid upon them.

22 [a]So the house of Israel shall know that I *am* the LORD their God from that day and forward.

23 [a]And the heathen shall know that the house of Israel went into captivity for their iniquity: because they trespassed against me, therefore [b]hid I my face from them, and [c]gave them into the hand of their enemies: so fell they all by the sword.

24 [a]According to their uncleanness and according to their transgressions have I done unto them, and hid my face from them.

25 Therefore thus saith the Lord GOD; [a]Now will I bring again the captivity of Jacob, and have mercy upon the [b]whole house of Israel, and will be jealous for my holy name;

26 [a]After that they have borne their shame, and all their trespasses whereby they have trespassed against me, when they [b]dwelt safely in their land, and none made *them* afraid.

27 [a]When I have brought them again from the people, and gathered them out of their enemies' lands, and [b]am sanctified in them in the sight of many nations;

28 [a]Then shall they know that I *am* the LORD their God, which caused them to be led into captivity among the heathen: but I have gathered them unto their own land, and have left none of them any more there.

29 [a]Neither will I hide my face any more from them: for I have [b]poured out my spirit upon the house of Israel, saith the Lord GOD.

A New City, a New Temple

40 In the five and twentieth year of our captivity, in the beginning of the year, in the tenth *day* of the month, in the fourteenth year after that [a]the city was smitten, in the selfsame day [b]the hand of the LORD was upon me, and brought me thither.

2 [a]In the visions of God brought he me into the land of Israel, and [b]set me upon a very high mountain, by which *was* as the frame of a city on the south.

3 And he brought me thither, and, behold, *there was* a man, whose appearance *was* [a]like the appearance of brass, [b]with a line of flax in his hand, [c]and a measuring reed; and he stood in the gate.

4 And the man said unto me, [a]Son of man, behold with thine eyes, and hear with thine ears, and set thine heart upon all that I shall shew thee; for to the intent that I might shew *them* unto thee *art* thou brought hither: [b]declare all that thou seest to the house of Israel.

5 And behold [a]a wall on the outside of the house round about, and in the man's hand a measuring reed of six cubits *long* by the cubit and an hand breadth: so he measured the breadth of the building, one reed; and the height, one reed.

The Eastern Gateway of the Temple

6 Then came he unto the gate which looketh toward the [a]east, and went up the stairs thereof, and measured the threshold of the gate, *which was* one reed broad; and the other threshold *of the gate, which was* one reed broad.

7 And *every* little chamber *was* one reed long, and one reed broad; and between the little chambers *were* five cubits; and the threshold of the gate by the porch of the gate within *was* one reed.

8 He measured also the porch of the gate within, one reed.

9 Then measured he the porch of the gate, eight cubits; and the posts thereof, two cubits; and the porch of the gate *was* inward.

NKJV

Israel Restored to the Land

21 [a]"I will set My glory among the nations; all the nations shall see My judgment which I have executed, and [b]My hand which I have laid on them.

22 [a]"So the house of Israel shall know that I *am* the LORD their God from that day forward.

23 [a]"The Gentiles shall know that the house of Israel went into captivity for their iniquity; because they were unfaithful to Me, therefore [b]I hid My face from them. I [c]gave them into the hand of their enemies, and they all fell by the sword.

24 [a]"According to their uncleanness and according to their transgressions I have dealt with them, and hidden My face from them." '

25 "Therefore thus says the Lord GOD: [a]'Now I will bring back the captives of Jacob, and have mercy on the [b]whole house of Israel; and I will be jealous for My holy name—

26 [a]'after they have borne their shame, and all their unfaithfulness in which they were unfaithful to Me, when they [b]dwelt safely in their *own* land and no one made *them* afraid.

27 [a]'When I have brought them back from the peoples and gathered them out of their enemies' lands, and I [b]am hallowed in them in the sight of many nations,

28 [a]'then they shall know that I *am* the LORD their God, who sent them into captivity among the nations, but also brought them back to their land, and left none of them captive any longer.

29 [a]'And I will not hide My face from them anymore; for I shall have [b]poured out My Spirit on the house of Israel,' says the Lord GOD."

A New City, a New Temple

40 In the twenty-fifth year of our captivity, at the beginning of the year, on the tenth *day* of the month, in the fourteenth year after [a]the city was captured, on the very same day [b]the hand of the LORD was upon me; and He took me there.

2 [a]In the visions of God He took me into the land of Israel and [b]set me on a very high mountain; on it toward the south *was* something like the structure of a city.

3 He took me there, and behold, *there was* a man whose appearance *was* [a]like the appearance of bronze. [b]He had a line of flax [c]and a measuring rod in his hand, and he stood in the gateway.

4 And the man said to me, [a]"Son of man, look with your eyes and hear with your ears, and fix your mind on everything I show you; for you *were* brought here so that I might show *them* to you. [b]Declare to the house of Israel everything you see."

5 Now there was [a]a wall all around the outside of the *temple. In the man's hand was a measuring rod six cubits *long, each being a* cubit and a handbreadth; and he measured the width of the wall structure, one rod; and the height, one rod.

The Eastern Gateway of the Temple

6 Then he went to the gateway which faced [a]east; and he went up its stairs and measured the threshold of the gateway, *which was* one rod wide, and the other threshold *was* one rod wide.

7 Each gate chamber *was* one rod long and one rod wide; between the gate chambers *was a space of* five cubits; and the threshold of the gateway by the vestibule of the inside gate *was* one rod.

8 He also measured the vestibule of the inside gate, one rod.

9 Then he measured the vestibule of the gateway, eight cubits; and the gateposts, two cubits. The vestibule of the gate *was* on the inside.

21 [a]Ex. 9:16; Is. 37:20; Ezek. 36:23; 38:23 [b]Ex. 7:4
22 [a]Ex. 39:7, 28
23 [a]Jer. 22:8, 9; 44:22; Ezek. 36:18–20, 23 [b]Deut. 31:17; Is. 1:15; 59:2; Ezek. 39:29 [c]Lev. 26:25
24 [a]2 Kin. 17:7; Jer. 2:17, 19; 4:18; Ezek. 36:19
25 [a]Is. 27:12, 13; Jer. 30:3, 18; Ezek. 34:13; 36:24 [b]Jer. 31:1; Ezek. 20:40; Hos. 1:11
26 [a]Dan. 9:16 [b]Lev. 26:5, 6
27 [a]Ezek. 28:25, 26 [b]Ezek. 36:23, 24; 38:16
28 [a]Ezek. 34:30
29 [a]Is. 54:8, 9 [b]Is. 32:15; Ezek. 36:27; 37:14; [Joel 2:28; Zech. 12:10]; Acts 2:17

CHAPTER 40

1 [a]2 Kin. 25:1–4; Jer. 39:2, 3; 52:4–7; Ezek. 33:21 [b]Ezek. 1:3; 3:14, 22; 37:1
2 [a]Ezek. 1:1; 3:14; 8:3; 37:1; Dan. 7:1, 7 [b][Is. 2:2, 3]; Ezek. 17:23; 20:40; 37:22; [Mic. 4:1]; Rev. 21:10
3 [a]Ezek. 1:7; Dan. 10:6; Rev. 1:15 [b]Ezek. 47:3; Zech. 2:1, 2 [c]Rev. 11:1; 21:15
4 [a]Ezek. 44:5 [b]Ezek. 43:10
5 [a][Is. 26:1]; Ezek. 42:20
6 [a]Ezek. 43:1

*
40:5 Lit. *house*

KJV

10 And the little chambers of the gate eastward *were* three on this side, and three on that side; they three *were* of one measure: and the posts had one measure on this side and on that side.

11 And he measured the breadth of the entry of the gate, ten cubits; *and* the length of the gate, thirteen cubits.

12 The space also before the little chambers *was* one cubit *on this side,* and the space *was* one cubit on that side: and the little chambers *were* six cubits on this side, and six cubits on that side.

13 He measured then the gate from the roof of *one* little chamber to the roof of another: the breadth *was* five and twenty cubits, door against door.

14 He made also posts of threescore cubits, even unto the post of the court round about the gate.

15 And from the face of the gate of the entrance unto the face of the porch of the inner gate *were* fifty cubits.

16 And *there were* [a]narrow windows to the little chambers, and to their posts within the gate round about, and likewise to the arches: and windows *were* round about inward: and upon *each* post *were* [b]palm trees.

The Outer Court

17 Then brought he me into [a]the outward court, and, lo, *there were* [b]chambers, and a pavement made for the court round about: [c]thirty chambers *were* upon the pavement.

18 And the pavement by the side of the gates over against the length of the gates *was* the lower pavement.

19 Then he measured the breadth from the forefront of the lower gate unto the forefront of the inner court without, an hundred cubits eastward and northward.

The Northern Gateway

20 And the gate of the outward court that looked toward the north, he measured the length thereof, and the breadth thereof.

21 And the little chambers thereof *were* three on this side and three on that side; and the posts thereof and the arches thereof were after the measure of the first gate: the length thereof *was* fifty cubits, and the breadth five and twenty cubits.

22 And their windows, and their arches, and their palm trees, *were* after the measure of the gate that looketh toward the east; and they went up unto it by seven steps; and the arches thereof *were* before them.

23 And the gate of the inner court *was* over against the gate toward the north, and toward the east; and he measured from gate to gate an hundred cubits.

The Southern Gateway

24 After that he brought me toward the south, and behold a gate toward the south: and he measured the posts thereof and the arches thereof according to these measures.

25 And *there were* windows in it and in the arches thereof round about, like those windows: the length *was* fifty cubits, and the breadth five and twenty cubits.

26 And *there were* seven steps to go up to it, and the arches thereof *were* before them: and it had palm trees, one on this side, and another on that side, upon the posts thereof.

27 And *there was* a gate in the inner court toward the south: and he measured from gate to gate toward the south an hundred cubits.

Gateways of the Inner Court

28 And he brought me to the inner court by the south gate: and he measured the south gate according to these measures;

16 [a]1 Kin. 6:4; Ezek. 41:16, 26 [b]1 Kin. 6:29, 32, 35; 2 Chr. 3:5; Ezek. 40:22, 26, 31, 34, 37; 41:18–20, 25, 26
17 [a]Ezek. 10:5; 42:1; 46:21; Rev. 11:2 [b]1 Kin. 6:5; 2 Chr. 31:11; Ezek. 40:38 [c]Ezek. 45:5

NKJV

10 In the eastern gateway *were* three gate chambers on one side and three on the other; the three *were* all the same size; also the gateposts were of the same size on this side and that side.

11 He measured the width of the entrance to the gateway, ten cubits; *and* the length of the gate, thirteen cubits.

12 *There was* a space in front of the gate chambers, one cubit *on this side* and one cubit on that side; the gate chambers *were* six cubits on this side and six cubits on that side.

13 Then he measured the gateway from the roof of *one* gate chamber to the roof of the other; the width *was* twenty-five cubits, as door faces door.

14 He measured the gateposts, sixty cubits high, and the court all around the gateway *extended* to the gatepost.

15 *From* the front of the entrance gate to the front of the vestibule of the inner gate *was* fifty cubits.

16 *There were* [a]beveled window *frames* in the gate chambers and in their intervening archways on the inside of the gateway all around, and likewise in the vestibules. *There were* windows all around on the inside. And on each gatepost *were* [b]palm trees.

The Outer Court

17 Then he brought me into [a]the outer court; and *there were* [b]chambers and a pavement made all around the court; [c]thirty chambers faced the pavement.

18 The pavement was by the side of the gateways, corresponding to the length of the gateways; *this was* the lower pavement.

19 Then he measured the width from the front of the lower gateway to the front of the inner court exterior, one hundred cubits toward the east and the north.

The Northern Gateway

20 On the outer court was also a gateway facing north, and he measured its length and its width.

21 Its gate chambers, three on this side and three on that side, its gateposts and its archways, had the same measurements as the first gate; its length *was* fifty cubits and its width twenty-five cubits.

22 Its windows and those of its archways, and also its palm trees, *had* the same measurements as the gateway facing east; it was ascended by seven steps, and its archway *was* in front of it.

23 A gate of the inner court was opposite the northern gateway, just as the eastern *gateway;* and he measured from gateway to gateway, one hundred cubits.

The Southern Gateway

24 After that he brought me toward the south, and there a gateway was facing south; and he measured its gateposts and archways according to these same measurements.

25 *There were* windows in it and in its archways all around like those windows; its length *was* fifty cubits and its width twenty-five cubits.

26 Seven steps led up to it, and its archway *was* in front of them; and it had palm trees on its gateposts, one on this side and one on that side.

27 *There was* also a gateway on the inner court, facing south; and he measured from gateway to gateway toward the south, one hundred cubits.

Gateways of the Inner Court

28 Then he brought me to the inner court through the southern gateway; he measured the southern gateway according to these same measurements.

KJV

29 And the little chambers thereof, and the posts thereof, and the arches thereof, according to these measures: and *there were* windows in it and in the arches thereof round about: *it was* fifty cubits long, and five and twenty cubits broad.

30 And the arches round about *were* [a]five and twenty cubits long, and five cubits broad.

31 And the arches thereof *were* toward the utter court; and palm trees *were* upon the posts thereof: and the going up to it *had* eight steps.

32 And he brought me into the inner court toward the east: and he measured the gate according to these measures.

33 And the little chambers thereof, and the posts thereof, and the arches thereof, *were* according to these measures: and *there were* windows therein and in the arches thereof round about: *it was* fifty cubits long, and five and twenty cubits broad.

34 And the arches thereof *were* toward the outward court; and palm trees *were* upon the posts thereof, on this side, and on that side: and the going up to it *had* eight steps.

35 And he brought me to the north gate, and measured *it* according to these measures;

36 The little chambers thereof, the posts thereof, and the arches thereof, and the windows to it round about: the length *was* fifty cubits, and the breadth five and twenty cubits.

37 And the posts thereof *were* toward the utter court; and palm trees *were* upon the posts thereof, on this side, and on that side: and the going up to it *had* eight steps.

Where Sacrifices Were Prepared

38 And the chambers and the entries thereof *were* by the posts of the gates, where they [a]washed the burnt offering.

39 And in the porch of the gate *were* two tables on this side, and two tables on that side, to slay thereon the burnt offering and [a]the sin offering and [b]the trespass offering.

40 And at the side without, as one goeth up to the entry of the north gate, *were* two tables; and on the other side, which *was* at the porch of the gate, *were* two tables.

41 Four tables *were* on this side, and four tables on that side, by the side of the gate; eight tables, whereupon they slew *their sacrifices.*

42 And the four tables *were* of hewn stone for the burnt offering, of a cubit and an half long, and a cubit and an half broad, and one cubit high: whereupon also they laid the instruments wherewith they slew the burnt offering and the sacrifice.

43 And within *were* hooks, an hand broad, fastened round about: and upon the tables *was* the flesh of the offering.

Chambers for Singers and Priests

44 And without the inner gate *were* the chambers of [a]the singers in the inner court, which *was* at the side of the north gate; and their prospect *was* toward the south: one at the side of the east gate *having* the prospect toward the north.

45 And he said unto me, This chamber, whose prospect *is* toward the south, *is* for the priests, [a]the keepers of the charge of the house.

46 And the chamber whose prospect *is* toward the north *is* for the priests, [a]the keepers of the charge of the altar: these *are* the sons of [b]Zadok among the sons of Levi, which come near to the LORD to minister unto him.

Dimensions of the Inner Court and Vestibule
(cf. 1 Kin. 7:14–22)

47 So he measured the court, an hundred cubits long, and an hundred cubits broad, foursquare; and the altar *that was* before the house.

48 And he brought me to the [a]porch of the house, and measured *each* post of the porch, five cubits on this side, and five cubits on that side:

30 [a]Ezek. 40:21, 25, 33, 36
38 [a]2 Chr. 4:6
39 [a]Lev. 4:2, 3 [b]Lev. 5:6; 6:6; 7:1
44 [a]1 Chr. 6:31, 32; 16:41–43; 25:1–7
45 [a]Lev. 8:35; Num. 3:27, 28, 32, 38; 18:5; 1 Chr. 9:23; 2 Chr. 13:11; Ps. 134:1
46 [a]Lev. 6:12, 13; Num. 18:5; Ezek. 44:15 [b]1 Kin. 2:35; Ezek. 43:19; 44:15, 16
48 [a]1 Kin. 6:3; 2 Chr. 3:4

NKJV

29 Also its gate chambers, its gateposts, and its archways *were* according to these same measurements; *there were* windows in it and in its archways all around; *it was* fifty cubits long and twenty-five cubits wide.

30 *There were* archways all around, [a]twenty-five cubits long and five cubits wide.

31 Its archways faced the outer court, palm trees *were* on its gateposts, and going up to it *were* eight steps.

32 And he brought me into the inner court facing east; he measured the gateway according to these same measurements.

33 Also its gate chambers, its gateposts, and its archways *were* according to these same measurements; and *there were* windows in it and in its archways all around; *it was* fifty cubits long and twenty-five cubits wide.

34 Its archways faced the outer court, and palm trees *were* on its gateposts on this side and on that side; and going up to it *were* eight steps.

35 Then he brought me to the north gateway and measured *it* according to these same measurements—

36 also its gate chambers, its gateposts, and its archways. It had windows all around; its length *was* fifty cubits and its width twenty-five cubits.

37 Its gateposts faced the outer court, palm trees *were* on its gateposts on this side and on that side, and going up to it *were* eight steps.

Where Sacrifices Were Prepared

38 *There was* a chamber and its entrance by the gateposts of the gateway, where they [a]washed the burnt offering.

39 In the vestibule of the gateway *were* two tables on this side and two tables on that side, on which to slay the burnt offering, [a]the sin offering, and [b]the trespass offering.

40 At the outer side of the vestibule, as one goes up to the entrance of the northern gateway, *were* two tables; and on the other side of the vestibule of the gateway *were* two tables.

41 Four tables *were* on this side and four tables on that side, by the side of the gateway, eight tables on which they slaughtered *the sacrifices.*

42 *There were* also four tables of hewn stone for the burnt offering, one cubit and a half long, one cubit and a half wide, and one cubit high; on these they laid the instruments with which they slaughtered the burnt offering and the sacrifice.

43 Inside *were* hooks, a handbreadth wide, fastened all around; and the flesh of the sacrifices *was* on the tables.

Chambers for Singers and Priests

44 Outside the inner gate *were* the chambers for [a]the singers in the inner court, one facing south at the side of the northern gateway, and the other facing north at the side of the southern gateway.

45 Then he said to me, "This chamber which faces south *is* for [a]the priests who have charge of the temple.

46 "The chamber which faces north *is* for the priests [a]who have charge of the altar; these *are* the sons of [b]Zadok, from the sons of Levi, who come near the LORD to minister to Him."

Dimensions of the Inner Court and Vestibule
(cf. 1 Kin. 7:14–22)

47 And he measured the court, one hundred cubits long and one hundred cubits wide, foursquare. The altar *was* in front of the temple.

48 Then he brought me to the [a]vestibule of the temple and measured the doorposts of the vestibule, five cubits on this side and five cubits on

KJV

and the breadth of the gate *was* three cubits on this side, and three cubits on that side.

49 [a]The length of the porch *was* twenty cubits, and the breadth eleven cubits; and *he brought me* by the steps whereby they went up to it: and *there were* [b]pillars by the posts, one on this side, and another on that side.

Dimensions of the Sanctuary

41 Afterward he [a]brought me to the temple, and measured the posts, six cubits broad on the one side, and six cubits broad on the other side, *which was* the breadth of the tabernacle.

2 And the breadth of the door *was* ten cubits; and the sides of the door *were* five cubits on the one side, and five cubits on the other side: and he measured the length thereof, forty cubits: and the breadth, twenty cubits.

3 Then went he inward, and measured the post of the door, two cubits; and the door, six cubits; and the breadth of the door, seven cubits.

4 So [a]he measured the length thereof, twenty cubits; and the breadth, twenty cubits, before the temple: and he said unto me, This *is* the most holy *place*.

The Side Chambers on the Wall

5 After he measured the wall of the house, six cubits; and the breadth of *every* side chamber, four cubits, round about the house on every side.

6 [a]And the side chambers *were* three, one over another, and thirty in order; and they entered into the wall which *was* of the house for the side chambers round about, that they might have hold, but they had [b]not hold in the wall of the house.

7 And [a]*there was* an enlarging, and a winding about still upward to the side chambers: for the winding about of the house went still upward round about the house: therefore the breadth of the house *was still* upward, and so increased *from* the lowest *chamber* to the highest by the midst.

8 I saw also the height of the house round about: the foundations of the side chambers *were* [a]a full reed of six great cubits.

9 The thickness of the wall, which *was* for the side chamber without, *was* five cubits: and *that* which *was* left *was* the place of the side chambers that *were* within.

10 And between the chambers *was* the wideness of twenty cubits round about the house on every side.

11 And the doors of the side chambers *were* toward *the place that was* left, one door toward the north, and another door toward the south: and the breadth of the place that was left *was* five cubits round about.

The Building at the Western End

12 Now the building that *was* before the separate place at the end toward the west *was* seventy cubits broad; and the wall of the building *was* five cubits thick round about, and the length thereof ninety cubits.

Dimensions and Design of the Temple Area

13 So he measured the house, an [a]hundred cubits long; and the separate place, and the building, with the walls thereof, an hundred cubits long;

14 Also the breadth of the face of the house, and of the separate place toward the east, an hundred cubits.

15 And he measured the length of the building over against the separate place which *was* behind it, and the [a]galleries thereof on the one side and on the other side, an hundred cubits, with the inner temple, and the porches of the court;

16 The door posts, and [a]the narrow windows, and the galleries round about on their three stories, over against the door, cieled with [b]wood round about, and from the ground up to the windows, and the windows *were* covered;

49 [a]1 Kin. 6:3 [b]1 Kin. 7:15–22; 2 Chr. 3:17; Jer. 52:17–23; [Rev. 3:12]

CHAPTER 41

1 [a]Ezek. 40:2, 3, 17
4 [a]1 Kin. 6:20; 2 Chr. 3:8
6 [a]1 Kin. 6:5–10 [b]1 Kin. 6:6, 10
7 [a]1 Kin. 6:8
8 [a]Ezek. 40:5
13 [a]Ezek. 40:47
15 [a]Ezek. 42:3, 5
16 [a]1 Kin. 6:4; Ezek. 40:16, 25 [b]1 Kin. 6:15

**41:1* Heb. *heykal;* the main room in the temple, the holy place, Ex. 26:33

NKJV

that side; and the width of the gateway was three cubits on this side and three cubits on that side.

49 [a]The length of the vestibule *was* twenty cubits, and the width eleven cubits; and by the steps which led up to it *there were* [b]pillars by the doorposts, one on this side and another on that side.

Dimensions of the Sanctuary

41 Then he [a]brought me into the *sanctuary and measured the doorposts, six cubits wide on one side and six cubits wide on the other side—the width of the tabernacle.

2 The width of the entryway *was* ten cubits, and the side walls of the entrance *were* five cubits on this side and five cubits on the other side; and he measured its length, forty cubits, and its width, twenty cubits.

3 Also he went inside and measured the doorposts, two cubits; and the entrance, six cubits *high;* and the width of the entrance, seven cubits.

4 [a]He measured the length, twenty cubits; and the width, twenty cubits, beyond the sanctuary; and he said to me, "This *is* the Most Holy *Place*."

The Side Chambers on the Wall

5 Next, he measured the wall of the temple, six cubits. The width of each side chamber all around the temple *was* four cubits on every side.

6 [a]The side chambers *were* in three stories, one above the other, thirty chambers in each story; they rested on ledges which *were* for the side chambers all around, that they might be supported, but [b]not fastened to the wall of the temple.

7 As one went up from story to story, the side chambers [a]became wider all around, because their supporting ledges in the wall of the temple ascended like steps; therefore the width of the structure increased as one went up *from* the lowest *story* to the highest by way of the middle one.

8 I also saw an elevation all around the temple; it was the foundation of the side chambers, [a]a full rod, *that is,* six cubits *high.*

9 The thickness of the outer wall of the side chambers *was* five cubits, and so also the remaining terrace by the place of the side chambers of the temple.

10 And between *it and* the *wall* chambers was a width of twenty cubits all around the temple on every side.

11 The doors of the side chambers opened on the terrace, one door toward the north and another toward the south; and the width of the terrace *was* five cubits all around.

The Building at the Western End

12 The building that faced the separating courtyard at its western end *was* seventy cubits wide; the wall of the building *was* five cubits thick all around, and its length ninety cubits.

Dimensions and Design of the Temple Area

13 So he measured the temple, one [a]hundred cubits long; and the separating courtyard with the building and its walls *was* one hundred cubits long;

14 also the width of the eastern face of the temple, including the separating courtyard, *was* one hundred cubits.

15 He measured the length of the building behind it, facing the separating courtyard, with its [a]galleries on the one side and on the other side, one hundred cubits, as well as the inner temple and the porches of the court,

16 their doorposts and [a]the beveled window frames. And the galleries all around their three stories opposite the threshold were paneled with [b]wood from the ground to the windows—the windows were covered—

KJV

17 To that above the door, even unto the inner house, and without, and by all the wall round about within and without, by measure.

18 And *it was* made [a]with cherubims and [b]palm trees, so that a palm tree *was* between a cherub and a cherub; and *every* cherub had two faces;

19 [a]So that the face of a man *was* toward the palm tree on the one side, and the face of a young lion toward the palm tree on the other side: *it was* made through all the house round about.

20 From the ground unto above the door *were* cherubims and palm trees made, and *on* the wall of the temple.

21 The [a]posts of the temple *were* squared, *and* the face of the sanctuary; the appearance *of the one* as the appearance *of the other.*

22 [a]The altar of wood *was* three cubits high, and the length thereof two cubits; and the corners thereof, and the length thereof, and the walls thereof, *were* of wood: and he said unto me, This *is* [b]the table that *is* [c]before the LORD.

23 [a]And the temple and the sanctuary had two doors.

24 And the doors had two [a]leaves *apiece,* two turning leaves; two *leaves* for the one door, and two leaves for the other *door.*

25 And *there were* made on them, on the doors of the temple, cherubims and palm trees, like as *were* made upon the walls; and *there were* thick planks upon the face of the porch without.

26 And *there were* [a]narrow windows and palm trees on the one side and on the other side, on the sides of the porch, and *upon* the side chambers of the house, and thick planks.

The Chambers for the Priests

42 Then he [a]brought me forth into the utter court, the way toward the [b]north: and he brought me into [c]the chamber that *was* over against the separate place, and which *was* before the building toward the north.

2 Before the length of an hundred cubits *was* the north door, and the breadth *was* fifty cubits.

3 Over against the twenty *cubits* which *were* for the inner court, and over against the [a]pavement which *was* for the utter court, *was* [b]gallery against gallery in three *stories.*

4 And before the chambers *was* a walk of ten cubits breadth inward, a way of one cubit; and their doors toward the north.

5 Now the upper chambers *were* shorter: for the galleries were higher than these, than the lower, and than the middlemost of the building.

6 For they *were* in three *stories,* but had not pillars as the pillars of the courts: therefore *the building* was straitened more than the lowest and the middlemost from the ground.

7 And the wall that *was* without over against the chambers, toward the utter court on the forepart of the chambers, the length thereof *was* fifty cubits.

8 For the length of the chambers that *were* in the utter court *was* fifty cubits: and, lo, before the temple *were* an [a]hundred cubits.

9 And from under these chambers *was* the entry on the east side, as one goeth into them from the utter court.

10 The chambers *were* in the thickness of the wall of the court toward the east, over against the separate place, and over against the building.

11 And [a]the way before them *was* like the appearance of the chambers which *were* toward the north, as long as they, *and* as broad as they: and all their goings out *were* both according to their fashions, and according to their doors.

12 And according to the doors of the chambers that *were* toward the south *was* a door in the head of the way, *even* the way directly before the wall toward the east, as one entereth into them.

---

18 [a]1 Kin. 6:29; 2 Chr. 3:7 [b]2 Chr. 3:5; Ezek. 40:16
19 [a]Ezek. 1:10; 10:14
21 [a]1 Kin. 6:33; Ezek. 40:9, 14, 16; 41:1
22 [a]Ex. 30:1–3; 1 Kin. 6:20; Rev. 8:3 [b]Ex. 25:23, 30; Lev. 24:6; Ezek. 23:41; 44:16; Mal. 1:7, 12 [c]Ex. 30:8
23 [a]1 Kin. 6:31–35
24 [a]1 Kin. 6:34
26 [a]Ezek. 40:16

CHAPTER 42

1 [a]Ezek. 41:1 [b]Ezek. 40:20 [c]Ezek. 41:12, 15
3 [a]Ezek. 40:17 [b]Ezek. 41:15, 16; 42:5
8 [a]Ezek. 41:13, 14
11 [a]Ezek. 42:4

NKJV

17 from the space above the door, even to the inner *room, as well as outside, and on every wall all around, inside and outside, by measure.

18 And *it was* made [a]with cherubim and [b]palm trees, a palm tree between cherub and cherub. *Each* cherub had two faces,

19 [a]so that the face of a man *was* toward a palm tree on one side, and the face of a young lion toward a palm tree on the other side; thus *it was* made throughout the temple all around.

20 From the floor to the space above the door, and on the wall of the sanctuary, cherubim and palm trees *were* carved.

21 The [a]doorposts of the temple *were* square, *as was* the front of the sanctuary; their appearance was similar.

22 [a]The altar *was* of wood, three cubits high, and its length two cubits. Its corners, its length, and its sides *were* of wood; and he said to me, "This *is* [b]the table that *is* [c]before the LORD."

23 [a]The temple and the sanctuary had two doors.

24 The doors had two [a]panels *apiece,* two folding panels: two *panels* for one door and two panels for the other *door.*

25 Cherubim and palm trees *were* carved on the doors of the temple just as they *were* carved on the walls. A wooden canopy *was* on the front of the vestibule outside.

26 *There were* [a]beveled window *frames* and palm trees on one side and on the other, on the sides of the vestibule—also on the side chambers of the temple and on the canopies.

The Chambers for the Priests

42 Then he [a]brought me out into the outer court, by the way toward the [b]north; and he brought me into [c]the chamber which *was* opposite the separating courtyard, and which *was* opposite the building toward the north.

2 Facing the length, *which was* one hundred cubits (the width was fifty cubits), was the north door.

3 Opposite the inner court of twenty *cubits,* and opposite the [a]pavement of the outer court, *was* [b]gallery against gallery in three *stories.*

4 In front of the chambers, toward the inside, *was* a walk ten cubits wide, at a distance of one cubit; and their doors faced north.

5 Now the upper chambers *were* shorter, because the galleries took away *space* from them more than from the lower and middle stories of the building.

6 For they *were* in three *stories* and did not have pillars like the pillars of the courts; therefore *the upper level* was shortened more than the lower and middle levels from the ground up.

7 And a wall which *was* outside ran parallel to the chambers, at the front of the chambers, toward the outer court; its length *was* fifty cubits.

8 The length of the chambers toward the outer court *was* fifty cubits, whereas that facing the temple *was* one [a]hundred cubits.

9 At the lower chambers *was* the entrance on the east side, as one goes into them from the outer court.

10 Also *there were* chambers in the thickness of the wall of the court toward the east, opposite the separating courtyard and opposite the building.

11 [a]*There was* a walk in front of them also, and their appearance *was* like the chambers which *were* toward the north; they *were* as long and as wide as the others, and all their exits and entrances *were* according to plan.

12 And corresponding to the doors of the chambers that *were* facing south, as one enters them, *there was* a door in front of the walk, the way directly in front of the wall toward the east.

---

*__41:17__ Lit. *house;* the Most Holy Place

KJV

13 Then said he unto me, The north chambers *and* the south chambers, which *are* before the separate place, they *be* holy chambers, where the priests that approach unto the LORD [a]shall eat the most holy things: there shall they lay the most holy things, and [b]the meat offering, and the sin offering, and the trespass offering; for the place *is* holy.

14 [a]When the priests enter therein, then shall they not go out of the holy *place* into the utter court, but there they shall lay their garments wherein they minister; for they *are* holy; and shall put on other garments, and shall approach to *those things* which *are* for the people.

Outer Dimensions of the Temple

15 Now when he had made an end of measuring the inner house, he brought me forth toward the gate whose prospect *is* toward the [a]east, and measured it round about.

16 He measured the east side with the measuring reed, five hundred reeds, with the measuring reed round about.

17 He measured the north side, five hundred reeds, with the measuring reed round about.

18 He measured the south side, five hundred reeds, with the measuring reed.

19 He turned about to the west side, *and* measured five hundred reeds with the measuring reed.

20 He measured it by the four sides: [a]it had a wall round about, [b]five hundred *reeds* long, and five hundred broad, to make a separation between the sanctuary and the profane place.

The Temple, The LORD's Dwelling Place

43 Afterward he brought me to the gate, *even* the gate [a]that looketh toward the east:

2 [a]And, behold, the glory of the God of Israel came from the way of the east: and [b]his voice *was* like a noise of many waters: [c]and the earth shined with his glory.

3 And *it was* [a]according to the appearance of the vision which I saw, *even* according to the vision that I saw when I came [b]to destroy the city: and the visions *were* like the vision that I saw [c]by the river Chebar; and I fell upon my face.

4 [a]And the glory of the LORD came into the house by the way of the gate whose prospect *is* toward the east.

5 [a]So the spirit took me up, and brought me into the inner court; and, behold, [b]the glory of the LORD filled the house.

6 And I heard *him* speaking unto me out of the house; and [a]the man stood by me.

7 And he said unto me, Son of man, [a]the place of my throne, and [b]the place of the soles of my feet, [c]where I will dwell in the midst of the children of Israel for ever, and my holy name, shall the house of Israel [d]no more defile, *neither* they, nor their kings, by their whoredom, nor by [e]the carcases of their kings in their high places.

8 [a]In their setting of their threshold by my thresholds, and their post by my posts, and the wall between me and them, they have even defiled my holy name by their abominations that they have committed: wherefore I have consumed them in mine anger.

9 Now let them put away their whoredom, and the carcases of their kings, far from me, and I will dwell in the midst of them for ever.

10 Thou son of man, [a]shew the house to the house of Israel, that they may be ashamed of their iniquities: and let them measure the pattern.

11 And if they be ashamed of all that they have done, shew them the form of the house, and the fashion thereof, and the goings out thereof, and the comings in thereof, and all the forms thereof, and all the [a]ordinances thereof, and all the forms thereof, and all the laws thereof: and write *it* in their sight, that they may keep the whole form thereof, and all the ordinances thereof, and [b]do them.

---

13 [a]Lev. 6:16, 26; 24:9; Ezek. 43:19 [b]Lev. 2:3, 10; 6:14, 17, 25
14 [a]Ezek. 44:19
15 [a]Ezek. 40:6; 43:1
20 [a][Is. 60:18]; Ezek. 40:5; Zech. 2:5 [b]Ezek. 45:2; Rev. 21:16

CHAPTER 43

1 [a]Ezek. 10:19; 46:1
2 [a]Ezek. 11:23 [b]Ezek. 1:24; Rev. 1:15; 14:2 [c]Ezek. 10:4; Rev. 18:1
3 [a]Ezek. 1:4–28 [b]Jer. 1:10; Ezek. 9:1, 5; 32:18 [c]Ezek. 1:28; 3:23
4 [a]Ezek. 10:19; 11:23
5 [a]Ezek. 3:12, 14; 8:3; 2 Cor. 12:2–4 [b]Ezek. 40:34; 1 Kin. 8:10, 11
6 [a]Ezek. 1:26; 40:3
7 [a]Ps. 99:1; Is. 60:13 [b]1 Chr. 28:2; Ps. 99:5 [c]Ex. 29:45; Ps. 68:16; 132:14; Ezek. 37:26–28; Joel 3:17; [John 1:14; 2 Cor. 6:16] [d]Ezek. 39:7 [e]Lev. 26:30; Jer. 16:18; Ezek. 6:5, 13
8 [a]2 Kin. 16:14; 21:4, 5, 7; Ezek. 8:3; 23:39; 44:7
10 [a]Ezek. 40:4
11 [a]Ezek. 44:5 [b]Ezek. 11:20

*

42:16 About 10.5 feet, Ezek. 40:5
43:3 Some Heb. mss., Vg. *He*

NKJV

13 Then he said to me, "The north chambers *and* the south chambers, which *are* opposite the separating courtyard, *are* the holy chambers where the priests who approach the LORD [a]shall eat the most holy offerings. There they shall lay the most holy offerings—[b]the grain offering, the sin offering, and the trespass offering—for the place *is* holy.

14 [a]"When the priests enter them, they shall not go out of the holy *chamber* into the outer court; but there they shall leave their garments in which they minister, for they *are* holy. They shall put on other garments; then they may approach *that* which *is* for the people."

Outer Dimensions of the Temple

15 Now when he had finished measuring the inner temple, he brought me out through the gateway that faces toward the [a]east, and measured it all around.

16 He measured the east side with the *measuring rod, five hundred rods by the measuring rod all around.

17 He measured the north side, five hundred rods by the measuring rod all around.

18 He measured the south side, five hundred rods by the measuring rod.

19 He came around to the west side *and* measured five hundred rods by the measuring rod.

20 He measured it on the four sides; [a]it had a wall all around, [b]five hundred *cubits* long and five hundred wide, to separate the holy areas from the common.

The Temple, the LORD's Dwelling Place

43 Afterward he brought me to the gate, the gate [a]that faces toward the east.

2 [a]And behold, the glory of the God of Israel came from the way of the east. [b]His voice *was* like the sound of many waters; [c]and the earth shone with His glory.

3 *It was* [a]like the appearance of the vision which I saw—like the vision which I saw when *I came [b]to destroy the city. The visions *were* like the vision which I saw [c]by the River Chebar; and I fell on my face.

4 [a]And the glory of the LORD came into the temple by way of the gate which faces toward the east.

5 [a]The Spirit lifted me up and brought me into the inner court; and behold, [b]the glory of the LORD filled the temple.

6 Then I heard *Him* speaking to me from the temple, while [a]a man stood beside me.

7 And He said to me, "Son of man, *this is* [a]the place of My throne and [b]the place of the soles of My feet, [c]where I will dwell in the midst of the children of Israel forever. [d]No more shall the house of Israel defile My holy name, they nor their kings, by their harlotry or with [e]the carcasses of their kings on their high places.

8 [a]"When they set their threshold by My threshold, and their doorpost by My doorpost, with a wall between them and Me, they defiled My holy name by the abominations which they committed; therefore I have consumed them in My anger.

9 "Now let them put their harlotry and the carcasses of their kings far away from Me, and I will dwell in their midst forever.

10 "Son of man, [a]describe the temple to the house of Israel, that they may be ashamed of their iniquities; and let them measure the pattern.

11 "And if they are ashamed of all that they have done, make known to them the design of the temple and its arrangement, its exits and its entrances, its entire design and all its [a]ordinances, all its forms and all its laws. Write *it* down in their sight, so that they may keep its whole design and all its ordinances, and [b]perform them.

KJV

12 This *is* the law of the house; Upon [a]the top of the mountain the whole limit thereof round about *shall be* most holy. Behold, this *is* the law of the house.

Dimensions of the Altar

13 And these *are* the measures of the [a]altar after the cubits: [b]The cubit *is* a cubit and an hand breadth; even the bottom *shall be* a cubit, and the breadth a cubit, and the border thereof by the edge thereof round about *shall be* a span: and this *shall be* the higher place of the altar.

14 And from the bottom *upon* the ground *even* to the lower settle *shall be* two cubits, and the breadth one cubit; and from the lesser settle *even* to the greater settle *shall be* four cubits, and the breadth *one* cubit.

15 So the altar *shall be* four cubits; and from the altar and upward *shall be* four [a]horns.

16 And the altar *shall be* twelve *cubits* long, twelve broad, [a]square in the four squares thereof.

17 And the settle *shall be* fourteen *cubits* long and fourteen broad in the four squares thereof; and the border about it *shall be* half a cubit; and the bottom thereof *shall be* a cubit about; and [a]his stairs shall look toward the east.

Consecrating the Altar

18 And he said unto me, Son of man, thus saith the Lord GOD; These *are* the ordinances of the altar in the day when they shall make it, to offer [a]burnt offerings thereon, and to [b]sprinkle blood thereon.

19 And thou shalt give to [b]the priests the Levites that be of the seed of [c]Zadok, which approach unto me, to minister unto me, saith the Lord GOD, [a]a young bullock for a sin offering.

20 And thou shalt take of the blood thereof, and put *it* on the four horns of it, and on the four corners of the settle, and upon the border round about: thus shalt thou cleanse and purge it.

21 Thou shalt take the bullock also of the sin offering, and he [a]shall burn it in the appointed place of the house, [b]without the sanctuary.

22 And on the second day thou shalt offer a kid of the goats without blemish for a sin offering; and they shall cleanse the altar, as they did cleanse *it* with the bullock.

23 When thou hast made an end of cleansing *it*, thou shalt offer a young bullock without blemish, and a ram out of the flock without blemish.

24 And thou shalt offer them before the LORD, [a]and the priests shall cast salt upon them, and they shall offer them up *for* a burnt offering unto the LORD.

25 [a]Seven days shalt thou prepare every day a goat *for* a sin offering: they shall also prepare a young bullock, and a ram out of the flock, without blemish.

26 Seven days shall they purge the altar and purify it; and they shall consecrate themselves.

27 [a]And when these days are expired, it shall be, *that* upon the eighth day, and *so* forward, the priests shall make your burnt offerings upon the altar, and your peace offerings; and I will [b]accept you, saith the Lord GOD.

The East Gate and the Prince

44 Then he brought me back the way of the gate of the outward sanctuary [a]which looketh toward the east; and it *was* shut.

2 Then said the LORD unto me; This gate shall be shut, it shall not be opened, and no man shall enter in by it; [a]because the LORD, the God of Israel, hath entered in by it, therefore it shall be shut.

3 *It is* for the [a]prince; the prince, he shall sit in it to [b]eat bread before the LORD; he shall enter by the way of the porch of *that* gate, and shall go out by the way of the same.

12 [a]Ezek. 40:2
13 [a]Ex. 27:1–8; 2 Chr. 4:1 [b]Ezek. 41:8
15 [a]Ex. 27:2; Lev. 9:9; 1 Kin. 1:50
16 [a]Ex. 27:1
17 [a]Ex. 20:26
18 [a]Ex. 40:29 [b]Lev. 1:5, 11; [Heb. 9:21, 22]
19 [a]Ex. 29:10; Lev. 8:14; Ezek. 45:18, 19 [b]Ezek. 44:15, 16 [c]1 Kin. 2:35; Ezek. 40:46
21 [a]Ex. 29:14; Lev. 4:12 [b]Heb. 13:11
24 [a]Lev. 2:13; Num. 18:19; [Mark 9:49, 50; Col. 4:6]
25 [a]Ex. 29:35; Lev. 8:33
27 [a]Lev. 9:1–4 [b]Ezek. 20:40, 41; [Rom. 12:1; 1 Pet. 2:5]

CHAPTER 44

1 [a]Ezek. 43:1
2 [a]Ezek. 43:2–4
3 [a]Gen. 31:54; Ex. 24:9–11; [1 Cor. 10:18] [b]Ezek. 46:2, 8

NKJV

12 "This *is* the law of the temple: The whole area surrounding [a]the mountaintop *is* most holy. Behold, this *is* the law of the temple.

Dimensions of the Altar

13 "These are the measurements of the [a]altar in cubits [b](the *cubit is* one cubit and a handbreadth): the base one cubit high and one cubit wide, with a rim all around its edge of one span. This *is* the height of the altar:

14 "from the base on the ground to the lower ledge, two cubits; the width of the ledge, one cubit; from the smaller ledge to the larger ledge, four cubits; and the width of the ledge, *one* cubit.

15 "The altar hearth *is* four cubits high, with four [a]horns extending upward from the hearth.

16 "The altar hearth *is* twelve cubits long, twelve wide, [a]square at its four corners;

17 "the ledge, fourteen *cubits* long and fourteen wide on its four sides, with a rim of half a cubit around it; its base, one cubit all around; and [a]its steps face toward the east."

Consecrating the Altar

18 And He said to me, "Son of man, thus says the Lord GOD: 'These *are* the ordinances for the altar on the day when it is made, for sacrificing [a]burnt offerings on it, and for [b]sprinkling blood on it.

19 'You shall give [a]a young bull for a sin offering to [b]the priests, the Levites, who are of the seed of [c]Zadok, who approach Me to minister to Me,' says the Lord GOD.

20 'You shall take some of its blood and put *it* on the four horns of the altar, on the four corners of the ledge, and on the rim around it; thus you shall cleanse it and make atonement for it.

21 'Then you shall also take the bull of the sin offering, and [a]burn it in the appointed place of the temple, [b]outside the sanctuary.

22 'On the second day you shall offer a kid of the goats without blemish for a sin offering; and they shall cleanse the altar, as they cleansed *it* with the bull.

23 'When you have finished cleansing *it*, you shall offer a young bull without blemish, and a ram from the flock without blemish.

24 'When you offer them before the LORD, [a]the priests shall throw salt on them, and they will offer them up *as* a burnt offering to the LORD.

25 'Every day for [a]seven days you shall prepare a goat *for* a sin offering; they shall also prepare a young bull and a ram from the flock, both without blemish.

26 'Seven days they shall make atonement for the altar and purify it, and so consecrate *it*.

27 [a]'When these days are over it shall be, on the eighth day and thereafter, that the priests shall offer your burnt offerings and your peace offerings on the altar; and I will [b]accept you,' says the Lord GOD."

The East Gate and the Prince

44 Then He brought me back to the outer gate of the sanctuary [a]which faces toward the east, but it *was* shut.

2 And the LORD said to me, "This gate shall be shut; it shall not be opened, and no man shall enter by it, [a]because the LORD God of Israel has entered by it; therefore it shall be shut.

3 "*As for* the [a]prince, *because* he *is* the prince, he may sit in it to [b]eat bread before the LORD; he shall enter by way of the vestibule of the gateway, and go out the same way."

KJV

Those Admitted to the Temple

4 Then brought he me the way of the north gate before the house: and I looked, and, [a]behold, the glory of the LORD filled the house of the LORD: [b]and I fell upon my face.

5 And the LORD said unto me, [a]Son of man, mark well, and behold with thine eyes, and hear with thine ears all that I say unto thee concerning all the [b]ordinances of the house of the LORD, and all the laws thereof; and mark well the entering in of the house, with every going forth of the sanctuary.

6 And thou shalt say to the [a]rebellious, *even* to the house of Israel, Thus saith the Lord GOD; O ye house of Israel, [b]let it suffice you of all your abominations,

7 [a]In that ye have brought *into my sanctuary* [b]strangers, [c]uncircumcised in heart, and uncircumcised in flesh, to be in my sanctuary, to pollute it, *even* my house, when ye offer [d]my bread, [e]the fat and the blood, and they have broken my covenant because of all your abominations.

8 And ye have not [a]kept the charge of mine holy things: but ye have set keepers of my charge in my sanctuary for yourselves.

9 Thus saith the Lord GOD; [a]No stranger, uncircumcised in heart, nor uncircumcised in flesh, shall enter into my sanctuary, of any stranger that *is* among the children of Israel.

Laws Governing Priests

10 [a]And the Levites that are gone away far from me, when Israel went astray, which went astray away from me after their idols; they shall even bear their iniquity.

11 Yet they shall be ministers in my sanctuary, [a]*having* charge at the gates of the house, and ministering to the house: [b]they shall slay the burnt offering and the sacrifice for the people, and [c]they shall stand before them to minister unto them.

12 Because they ministered unto them before their idols, and [a]caused the house of Israel to fall into iniquity; therefore have I [b]lifted up mine hand against them, saith the Lord GOD, and they shall bear their iniquity.

13 [a]And they shall not come near unto me, to do the office of a priest unto me, nor to come near to any of my holy things, in the most holy *place:* but they shall [b]bear their shame, and their abominations which they have committed.

14 But I will make them [a]keepers of the charge of the house, for all the service thereof, and for all that shall be done therein.

15 [a]But the priests the Levites, [b]the sons of Zadok, that kept the charge of my sanctuary [c]when the children of Israel went astray from me, they shall come near to me to minister unto me, and they [d]shall stand before me to offer unto me [e]the fat and the blood, saith the Lord GOD:

16 They shall [a]enter into my sanctuary, and they shall come near to [b]my table, to minister unto me, and they shall keep my charge.

17 And it shall come to pass, *that* when they enter in at the gates of the inner court, [a]they shall be clothed with linen garments; and no wool shall come upon them, whiles they minister in the gates of the inner court, and within.

18 [a]They shall have linen bonnets upon their heads, and shall have linen breeches upon their loins; they shall not gird *themselves* with any thing that causeth sweat.

19 And when they go forth into the utter court, *even* into the utter court to the people, [a]they shall put off their garments wherein they ministered, and lay them in the holy chambers, and they shall put on other garments; and they shall [b]not sanctify the people with their garments.

20 [a]Neither shall they shave their heads, nor

4 [a]Is. 6:3; Ezek. 3:23; 43:5 [b]Ezek. 1:28; 43:3
5 [a]Deut. 32:46; Ezek. 40:4 [b]Deut. 12:32; Ezek. 43:10, 11
6 [a]Ezek. 2:5 [b]Ezek. 45:9; 1 Pet. 4:3
7 [a]Ezek. 43:8; Acts 21:28 [b]Lev. 22:25 [c]Lev. 26:41; Deut. 10:16; Jer. 4:4; 9:26; [Acts 7:51] [d]Lev. 21:17 [e]Lev. 3:16
8 [a]Lev. 22:2; Num. 18:7
9 [a]Ezek. 44:7; Joel 3:17; Zech. 14:21
10 [a]2 Kin. 23:8; Ezek. 48:11
11 [a]1 Chr. 26:1–19 [b]2 Chr. 29:34; 30:17 [c]Num. 16:9
12 [a]Is. 9:16; Mal. 2:8 [b]Ps. 106:26
13 [a]Num. 18:3; 2 Kin. 23:9 [b]Ezek. 32:30
14 [a]Num. 18:4; 1 Chr. 23:28–32; Ezek. 44:11
15 [a]Ezek. 40:46 [b][1 Sam. 2:35]; 2 Sam. 15:27; Ezek. 43:19; 48:11 [c]Ezek. 44:10 [d]Deut. 10:8 [e]Lev. 3:16, 17; 17:5, 6; Ezek. 44:7
16 [a]Num. 18:5, 7, 8 [b]Ezek. 41:22; Mal. 1:7, 12
17 [a]Ex. 28:39–43; 39:27–29; Rev. 19:8
18 [a]Ex. 28:40; 39:28; Is. 3:20; Ezek. 24:17, 23
19 [a]Lev. 6:10; 16:4, 23, 24; Ezek. 42:14 [b]Ex. 30:29; Lev. 6:27; Ezek. 46:20; [Matt. 23:17]
20 [a]Lev. 21:5

NKJV

Those Admitted to the Temple

4 Also He brought me by way of the north gate to the front of the temple; so I looked, and [a]behold, the glory of the LORD filled the house of the LORD; [b]and I fell on my face.

5 And the LORD said to me, [a]"Son of man, mark well, see with your eyes and hear with your ears, all that I say to you concerning all the [b]ordinances of the house of the LORD and all its laws. Mark well who may enter the house and all who go out from the sanctuary.

6 "Now say to the [a]rebellious, to the house of Israel, 'Thus says the Lord GOD: "O house of Israel, [b]let Us have no more of all your abominations.

7 [a]"When you brought in [b]foreigners, [c]uncircumcised in heart and uncircumcised in flesh, to be in My sanctuary to defile it—My house—and when you offered [d]My food, [e]the fat and the blood, then they broke My covenant because of all your abominations.

8 "And you have not [a]kept charge of My holy things, but you have set *others* to keep charge of My sanctuary for you." '

9 'Thus says the Lord GOD: [a]"No foreigner, uncircumcised in heart or uncircumcised in flesh, shall enter My sanctuary, including any foreigner who *is* among the children of Israel.

Laws Governing Priests

10 [a]"And the Levites who went far from Me, when Israel went astray, who strayed away from Me after their idols, they shall bear their iniquity.

11 "Yet they shall be ministers in My sanctuary, [a]*as* gatekeepers of the house and ministers of the house; [b]they shall slay the burnt offering and the sacrifice for the people, and [c]they shall stand before them to minister to them.

12 "Because they ministered to them before their idols and [a]caused the house of Israel to fall into iniquity, therefore I have [b]raised My hand in an oath against them," says the Lord GOD, "that they shall bear their iniquity.

13 [a]"And they shall not come near Me to minister to Me as priest, nor come near any of My holy things, nor into the Most Holy *Place;* but they shall [b]bear their shame and their abominations which they have committed.

14 "Nevertheless I will make them [a]keep charge of the temple, for all its work, and for all that has to be done in it.

15 [a]"But the priests, the Levites, [b]the sons of Zadok, who kept charge of My sanctuary [c]when the children of Israel went astray from Me, they shall come near Me to minister to Me; and they [d]shall stand before Me to offer to Me the [e]fat and the blood," says the Lord GOD.

16 "They shall [a]enter My sanctuary, and they shall come near [b]My table to minister to Me, and they shall keep My charge.

17 "And it shall be, whenever they enter the gates of the inner court, that [a]they shall put on linen garments; no wool shall come upon them while they minister within the gates of the inner court or within the house.

18 [a]"They shall have linen turbans on their heads and linen trousers on their bodies; they shall not clothe themselves with *anything that causes* sweat.

19 "When they go out to the outer court, to the *outer* court to the people, [a]they shall take off their garments in which they have ministered, leave them in the holy chambers, and put on other garments; and in their holy garments they shall [b]not sanctify the people.

20 [a]"They shall neither shave their heads nor

KJV

suffer their locks to grow [b]long; they shall only poll their heads.

21 [a]Neither shall any priest drink wine, when they enter into the inner court.

22 Neither shall they take for their wives a [a]widow, nor her that is put away: but they shall take maidens of the seed of the house of Israel, or a widow that had a priest before.

23 And [a]they shall teach my people *the difference* between the holy and profane, and cause them to [b]discern between the unclean and the clean.

24 And [a]in controversy they shall stand in judgment; *and* they shall judge it according to my judgments: and they shall keep my laws and my statutes in all mine assemblies; [b]and they shall hallow my sabbaths.

25 And they shall come at no dead person to defile themselves: but for father, or for mother, or for son, or for daughter, for brother, or for sister that hath had no husband, they may defile themselves.

26 And [a]after he is cleansed, they shall reckon unto him seven days.

27 And in the day that he goeth into the sanctuary, [b]unto the inner court, to minister in the sanctuary, [a]he shall offer his sin offering, saith the Lord GOD.

28 And it shall be unto them for an inheritance: I [a]*am* their inheritance: and ye shall give them no [b]possession in Israel: I *am* their possession.

29 [a]They shall eat the meat offering, and the sin offering, and the trespass offering; and [b]every dedicated thing in Israel shall be their's.

30 And the [a]first of all the firstfruits of all *things*, and every oblation of all, of every *sort* of your oblations, shall be the priest's: ye [b]shall also give unto the priest the first of your dough, [c]that he may cause the blessing to rest in thine house.

31 The priests shall not eat of any thing that is [a]dead of itself, or torn, whether it be fowl or beast.

The Holy District

45 Moreover, when ye shall [a]divide by lot the land for inheritance, ye shall [b]offer an oblation unto the LORD, an holy portion of the land: the length *shall be* the length of five and twenty thousand *reeds*, and the breadth *shall be* ten thousand. This *shall be* holy in all the borders thereof round about.

2 Of this there shall be for the sanctuary [a]five hundred *in length*, with five hundred *in breadth*, square round about; and fifty cubits round about for the suburbs thereof.

3 And of this measure shalt thou measure the length of five and twenty thousand, and the breadth of ten thousand: [a]and in it shall be the sanctuary *and* the most holy *place*.

4 [a]The holy *portion* of the land shall be for the priests the ministers of the sanctuary, which shall come near to minister unto the LORD: and it shall be a place for their houses, and an holy place for the sanctuary.

5 [a]And the five and twenty thousand of length, and the ten thousand of breadth, shall also the Levites, the ministers of the house, have for themselves, for a possession for [b]twenty chambers.

Properties of the City and the Prince

6 [a]And ye shall appoint the possession of the city five thousand broad, and five and twenty thousand long, over against the oblation of the holy *portion*: it shall be for the whole house of Israel.

7 [a]And *a portion shall be* for the prince on the one side and on the other side of the oblation of the holy *portion*, and of the possession of the city, before the oblation of the holy *portion*, and before the possession of the city, from the west

20 [b]Num. 6:5
21 [a]Lev. 10:9
22 [a]Lev. 21:7, 13, 14
23 [a]Lev. 10:10, 11; Ezek. 22:26; Hos. 4:6; Mic. 3:9–11; Zeph. 3:4; Hag. 2:11–13; Mal. 2:6–8 [b]Lev. 20:25
24 [a]Deut. 17:8, 9; 1 Chr. 23:4; 2 Chr. 19:8–10 [b]Ezek. 22:26
26 [a]Num. 6:10; 19:11, 13–19
27 [a]Lev. 5:3, 6; Num. 6:9–11 [b]Ezek. 44:17
28 [a]Num. 18:20; Deut. 10:9; 18:1, 2; Josh. 13:14, 33 [b]Ezek. 45:4
29 [a]Lev. 7:6 [b]Lev. 27:21, 28; Num. 18:14
30 [a]Ex. 13:2; 22:29; 23:19; Num. 3:13; 18:12 [b]Num. 15:20; Neh. 10:37 [c]Prov. 3:9; [Mal. 3:10]
31 [a]Ex. 22:31; Lev. 22:8; Deut. 14:21; Ezek. 4:14

CHAPTER 45

1 [a]Num. 26:52–56; Ezek. 47:22 [b]Ezek. 48:8, 9
2 [a]Ezek. 42:20
3 [a]Ezek. 48:10
4 [a]Ezek. 48:10, 11
5 [a]Ezek. 48:13 [b]Ezek. 40:17
6 [a]Ezek. 48:15
7 [a]Ezek. 48:21

*

45:5 So with MT, Tg., Vg.; LXX *a possession, cities of dwelling*

NKJV

let their hair grow [b]long, but they shall keep their hair well trimmed.

21 [a]"No priest shall drink wine when he enters the inner court.

22 "They shall not take as wife a [a]widow or a divorced woman, but take virgins of the descendants of the house of Israel, or widows of priests.

23 "And [a]they shall teach My people *the difference* between the holy and the unholy, and cause them to [b]discern between the unclean and the clean.

24 [a]"In controversy they shall stand as judges, *and* judge it according to My judgments. They shall keep My laws and My statutes in all My appointed meetings, [b]and they shall hallow My Sabbaths.

25 "They shall not defile *themselves* by coming near a dead person. Only for father or mother, for son or daughter, for brother or unmarried sister may they defile themselves.

26 [a]"After he is cleansed, they shall count seven days for him.

27 "And on the day that he goes to the sanctuary to minister in the sanctuary, [a]he must offer his sin offering [b]in the inner court," says the Lord GOD.

28 "It shall be, in regard to their inheritance, *that* I [a]*am* their inheritance. You shall give them no [b]possession in Israel, for I *am* their possession.

29 [a]"They shall eat the grain offering, the sin offering, and the trespass offering; [b]every dedicated thing in Israel shall be theirs.

30 "The [a]best of all firstfruits of any kind, and every sacrifice of any kind from all your sacrifices, shall be the priest's; also you [b]shall give to the priest the first of your ground meal, [c]to cause a blessing to rest on your house.

31 "The priests shall not eat anything, bird or beast, that [a]died naturally or was torn *by wild beasts*.

The Holy District

45 "Moreover, when you [a]divide the land by lot into inheritance, you shall [b]set apart a district for the LORD, a holy section of the land; its length *shall be* twenty-five thousand *cubits*, and the width ten thousand. It *shall be* holy throughout its territory all around.

2 "Of this there shall be a square plot for the sanctuary, [a]five hundred by five hundred *rods*, with fifty cubits around it for an open space.

3 "So this is the district you shall measure: twenty-five thousand *cubits* long and ten thousand wide; [a]in it shall be the sanctuary, the Most Holy *Place*.

4 "It shall be [a]a holy *section* of the land, belonging to the priests, the ministers of the sanctuary, who come near to minister to the LORD; it shall be a place for their houses and a holy place for the sanctuary.

5 [a]"*An area* twenty-five thousand *cubits* long and ten thousand wide shall belong to the Levites, the ministers of the temple; they shall have [b]twenty* chambers as a possession.

Properties of the City and the Prince

6 [a]"You shall appoint as the property of the city *an area* five thousand *cubits* wide and twenty-five thousand long, adjacent to the district of the holy *section;* it shall belong to the whole house of Israel.

7 [a]"The prince shall have *a section* on one side and the other of the holy district and the city's property; and bordering on the holy district and the city's property, extending westward on the west side and eastward on the east side, the length

KJV

side westward, and from the east side eastward: and the length *shall be* over against one of the portions, from the west border unto the east border.

8 In the land shall be his possession in Israel: and [a]my princes shall no more oppress my people; and *the rest of* the land shall they give to the house of Israel according to their tribes.

Laws Governing the Prince

9 Thus saith the LORD GOD; [a]Let it suffice you, O princes of Israel: [b]remove violence and spoil, and execute judgment and justice, take away your exactions from my people, saith the Lord GOD.

10 Ye shall have just [a]balances, and a just ephah, and a just bath.

11 The ephah and the bath shall be of one measure, that the bath may contain the tenth part of an homer, and the ephah the tenth part of an homer: the measure thereof shall be after the homer.

12 And the [a]shekel *shall be* twenty gerahs: twenty shekels, five and twenty shekels, fifteen shekels, shall be your maneh.

13 This *is* the oblation that ye shall offer; the sixth part of an ephah of an homer of wheat, and ye shall give the sixth part of an ephah of an homer of barley:

14 Concerning the ordinance of oil, the bath of oil, *ye shall offer* the tenth part of a bath out of the cor, *which is* an homer of ten baths; for ten baths *are* an homer:

15 And one lamb out of the flock, out of two hundred, out of the fat pastures of Israel; for a meat offering, and for a burnt offering, and for peace offerings, [a]to make reconciliation for them, saith the Lord GOD.

16 All the people of the land shall give this oblation for the prince in Israel.

17 And it shall be the [a]prince's part *to give* burnt offerings, and meat offerings, and drink offerings, in the feasts, and in the new moons, and in the sabbaths, in all solemnities of the house of Israel: he shall prepare the sin offering, and the meat offering, and the burnt offering, and the peace offerings, to make reconciliation for the house of Israel.

Keeping the Feasts
(Ex. 12:1–20; Lev. 23:33–43)

18 Thus saith the Lord GOD; In the first *month,* in the first *day* of the month, thou shalt take a young bullock without blemish, and [a]cleanse the sanctuary:

19 [a]And the priest shall take of the blood of the sin offering, and put *it* upon the posts of the house, and upon the four corners of the settle of the altar, and upon the posts of the gate of the inner court.

20 And so thou shalt do the seventh *day* of the month [a]for every one that erreth, and for *him that is* simple: so shall ye reconcile the house.

21 [a]In the first *month,* in the fourteenth day of the month, ye shall have the passover, a feast of seven days; unleavened bread shall be eaten.

22 And upon that day shall the prince prepare for himself and for all the people of the land [a]a bullock *for* a sin offering.

23 And [a]seven days of the feast he shall prepare a burnt offering to the LORD, seven bullocks and seven rams without blemish daily the seven days; [b]and a kid of the goats daily *for* a sin offering.

24 [a]And he shall prepare a meat offering of an ephah for a bullock, and an ephah for a ram, and an hin of oil for an ephah.

25 In the seventh *month,* in the fifteenth day of the month, shall he do the like in the [a]feast of the seven days, according to the sin offering, according to the burnt offering, and according to the meat offering, and according to the oil.

8 [a][Is. 11:3–5]; Jer. 22:17; Ezek. 22:27
9 [a]Ezek. 44:6 [b]Jer. 22:3; Zech. 8:16
10 [a]Lev. 19:36; Deut. 25:15; Prov. 16:11; Amos 8:4–6; Mic. 6:10, 11
12 [a]Ex. 30:13; Lev. 27:25; Num. 3:47
15 [a]Lev. 1:4; 6:30
17 [a]Ezek. 46:4–12
18 [a]Lev. 16:16, 33; Ezek. 43:22, 26
19 [a]Lev. 16:18–20; Ezek. 43:20
20 [a]Lev. 4:27; Ps. 19:12
21 [a]Ex. 12:18; Lev. 23:5, 6; Num. 9:2, 3; 28:16, 17; Deut. 16:1
22 [a]Lev. 4:14
23 [a]Lev. 23:8 [b]Num. 28:15, 22, 30; 29:5, 11, 16, 19
24 [a]Num. 28:12–15; Ezek. 46:5, 7
25 [a]Lev. 23:34; Num. 29:12; Deut. 16:13; 2 Chr. 5:3; 7:8, 10

NKJV

shall be side by side with one of the *tribal* portions, from the west border to the east border.

8 "The land shall be his possession in Israel; and [a]My princes shall no more oppress My people, but they shall give *the rest of* the land to the house of Israel, according to their tribes."

Laws Governing the Prince

9 'Thus says the Lord GOD: [a]"Enough, O princes of Israel! [b]Remove violence and plundering, execute justice and righteousness, and stop dispossessing My people," says the Lord GOD.

10 "You shall have [a]honest scales, an honest ephah, and an honest bath.

11 "The ephah and the bath shall be of the same measure, so that the bath contains one-tenth of a homer, and the ephah one-tenth of a homer; their measure shall be according to the homer.

12 "The [a]shekel *shall be* twenty gerahs; twenty shekels, twenty-five shekels, *and* fifteen shekels shall be your mina.

13 "This *is* the offering which you shall offer: you shall give one-sixth of an ephah from a homer of wheat, and one-sixth of an ephah from a homer of barley.

14 "The ordinance concerning oil, the bath of oil, *is* one-tenth of a bath from a kor. A kor *is* a homer or ten baths, for ten baths *are* a homer.

15 "And one lamb shall be given from a flock of two hundred, from the rich pastures of Israel. These shall be for grain offerings, burnt offerings, and peace offerings, [a]to make atonement for them," says the Lord GOD.

16 "All the people of the land shall give this offering for the prince in Israel.

17 "Then it shall be the [a]prince's part *to give* burnt offerings, grain offerings, and drink offerings, at the feasts, the New Moons, the Sabbaths, and at all the appointed seasons of the house of Israel. He shall prepare the sin offering, the grain offering, the burnt offering, and the peace offerings to make atonement for the house of Israel."

Keeping the Feasts
(Ex. 12:1–20; Lev. 23:33–43)

18 'Thus says the Lord GOD: "In the first *month,* on the first *day* of the month, you shall take a young bull without blemish and [a]cleanse the sanctuary.

19 [a]"The priest shall take some of the blood of the sin offering and put *it* on the doorposts of the temple, on the four corners of the ledge of the altar, and on the gateposts of the gate of the inner court.

20 "And so you shall do on the seventh *day* of the month [a]for everyone who has sinned unintentionally or in ignorance. Thus you shall make atonement for the temple.

21 [a]"In the first *month,* on the fourteenth day of the month, you shall observe the Passover, a feast of seven days; unleavened bread shall be eaten.

22 "And on that day the prince shall prepare for himself and for all the people of the land [a]a bull *for* a sin offering.

23 "On the [a]seven days of the feast he shall prepare a burnt offering to the LORD, seven bulls and seven rams without blemish, daily for seven days, [b]and a kid of the goats daily *for* a sin offering.

24 [a]"And he shall prepare a grain offering of one ephah for each bull and one ephah for each ram, together with a hin of oil for each ephah.

25 "In the seventh *month,* on the fifteenth day of the month, at the [a]feast, he shall do likewise for seven days, according to the sin offering, the burnt offering, the grain offering, and the oil."

KJV

The Manner of Worship

46 Thus saith the Lord GOD; The gate of the inner court that looketh toward the east shall be shut the six [a]working days; but on the sabbath it shall be opened, and in the day of the new moon it shall be opened.

2 [a]And the prince shall enter by the way of the porch of *that* gate without, and shall stand by the post of the gate, and the priests shall prepare his burnt offering and his peace offerings, and he shall worship at the threshold of the gate: then he shall go forth; but the gate shall not be shut until the evening.

3 Likewise the people of the land shall worship at the door of this gate before the LORD in the sabbaths and in the new moons.

4 And the burnt offering that [a]the prince shall offer unto the LORD in the [b]sabbath day *shall be* six lambs without blemish, and a ram without blemish.

5 [a]And the meat offering *shall be* an ephah for a ram, and the meat offering for the lambs as he shall be able to give, and an hin of oil to an ephah.

6 And in the day of the new moon *it shall be* a young bullock without blemish, and six lambs, and a ram: they shall be without blemish.

7 And he shall prepare a meat offering, an ephah for a bullock, and an ephah for a ram, and for the lambs according as his hand shall attain unto, and an hin of oil to an ephah.

8 [a]And when the prince shall enter, he shall go in by the way of the porch of *that* gate, and he shall go forth by the way thereof.

9 But when the people of the land [a]shall come before the LORD in the solemn feasts, he that entereth in by the way of the north [b]gate to worship shall go out by the way of the south gate; and he that entereth by the way of the south gate shall go forth by the way of the north gate: he shall not return by the way of the gate whereby he came in, but shall go forth over against it.

10 And the prince in the midst of them, when they go in, shall go in; and when they go forth, shall go forth.

11 And in the feasts and in the solemnities [a]the meat offering shall be an ephah to a bullock, and an ephah to a ram, and to the lambs as he is able to give, and an hin of oil to an ephah.

12 Now when the prince shall prepare a voluntary burnt offering or peace offerings voluntarily unto the LORD, [a]*one* shall then open him the gate that looketh toward the east, and he shall prepare his burnt offering and his peace offerings, as he did on the sabbath day: then he shall go forth; and after his going forth *one* shall shut the gate.

13 [a]Thou shalt daily prepare a burnt offering unto the LORD *of* a lamb of the first year without blemish: thou shalt prepare it every morning.

14 And thou shalt prepare a meat offering for it every morning, the sixth part of an ephah, and the third part of an hin of oil, to temper with the fine flour; a meat offering continually by a perpetual ordinance unto the LORD.

15 Thus shall they prepare the lamb, and the meat offering, and the oil, every morning *for* a [a]continual burnt offering.

The Prince and Inheritance Laws

16 Thus saith the Lord GOD; If the prince give a gift unto any of his sons, the inheritance thereof shall be his sons'; it *shall be* their possession by inheritance.

17 But if he give a gift of his inheritance to one of his servants, then it shall be his to [a]the year of liberty; after it shall return to the prince: but his inheritance shall be his sons' for them.

18 Moreover [a]the prince shall not take of the people's inheritance by oppression, to thrust them out of their possession; *but* he shall give his sons

CHAPTER 46

1 [a]Ex. 20:9
2 [a]Ezek. 44:3
4 [a]Ezek. 45:17 [b]Num. 28:9, 10
5 [a]Num. 28:12; Ezek. 45:24; 46:7, 11
8 [a]Ezek. 44:3; 46:2
9 [a]Ex. 23:14–17; 34:23; Deut. 16:16, 17; Ps. 84:7; Mic. 6:6 [b]Ezek. 48:31, 33
11 [a]Ezek. 46:5, 7
12 [a]Ezek. 44:3; 46:1, 2, 8
13 [a]Ex. 29:38; Num. 28:3–5
15 [a]Ex. 29:42; Num. 28:6
17 [a]Lev. 25:10
18 [a]Ezek. 45:8

NKJV

The Manner of Worship

46 'Thus says the Lord GOD: "The gateway of the inner court that faces toward the east shall be shut the six [a]working days; but on the Sabbath it shall be opened, and on the day of the New Moon it shall be opened.

2 [a]"The prince shall enter by way of the vestibule of the gateway from the outside, and stand by the gatepost. The priests shall prepare his burnt offering and his peace offerings. He shall worship at the threshold of the gate. Then he shall go out, but the gate shall not be shut until evening.

3 "Likewise the people of the land shall worship at the entrance to this gateway before the LORD on the Sabbaths and the New Moons.

4 "The burnt offering that [a]the prince offers to the LORD on the [b]Sabbath day *shall be* six lambs without blemish, and a ram without blemish;

5 [a]"and the grain offering *shall be one* ephah for a ram, and the grain offering for the lambs, as much as he wants to give, as well as a hin of oil with every ephah.

6 "On the day of the New Moon *it shall be* a young bull without blemish, six lambs, and a ram; they shall be without blemish.

7 "He shall prepare a grain offering of an ephah for a bull, an ephah for a ram, as much as he wants to give for the lambs, and a hin of oil with every ephah.

8 [a]"When the prince enters, he shall go in by way of the vestibule of the gateway, and go out the same way.

9 "But when the people of the land [a]come before the LORD on the appointed feast days, whoever enters by way of the north [b]gate to worship shall go out by way of the south gate; and whoever enters by way of the south gate shall go out by way of the north gate. He shall not return by way of the gate through which he came, but shall go out through the opposite gate.

10 "The prince shall then be in their midst. When they go in, he shall go in; and when they go out, he shall go out.

11 "At the festivals and the appointed feast days [a]the grain offering shall be an ephah for a bull, an ephah for a ram, as much as he wants to give for the lambs, and a hin of oil with every ephah.

12 "Now when the prince makes a voluntary burnt offering or voluntary peace offering to the LORD, the gate that faces toward the east [a]shall then be opened for him; and he shall prepare his burnt offering and his peace offerings as he did on the Sabbath day. Then he shall go out, and after he goes out the gate shall be shut.

13 [a]"You shall daily make a burnt offering to the LORD *of* a lamb of the first year without blemish; you shall prepare it every morning.

14 "And you shall prepare a grain offering with it every morning, a sixth of an ephah, and a third of a hin of oil to moisten the fine flour. This grain offering is a perpetual ordinance, to be made regularly to the LORD.

15 "Thus they shall prepare the lamb, the grain offering, and the oil, *as* a [a]regular burnt offering every morning."

The Prince and Inheritance Laws

16 'Thus says the Lord GOD: "If the prince gives a gift *of some* of his inheritance to any of his sons, it shall belong to his sons; it is their possession by inheritance.

17 "But if he gives a gift of some of his inheritance to one of his servants, it shall be his until [a]the year of liberty, after which it shall return to the prince. But his inheritance shall belong to his sons; it shall become theirs.

18 "Moreover [a]the prince shall not take any of the people's inheritance by evicting them from their property; he shall provide an inheritance for

KJV

inheritance out of his own possession: that my people be not scattered every man from his possession.

How the Offerings Were Prepared

19 After he brought me through the entry, which *was* at the side of the gate, into the holy [a]chambers of the priests, which looked toward the north: and, behold, there *was* a place on the two sides westward.

20 Then said he unto me, This *is* the place where the priests shall [a]boil the trespass offering and the sin offering, where they shall [b]bake the meat offering; that they bear *them* not out into the utter court, [c]to sanctify the people.

21 Then he brought me forth into the utter court, and caused me to pass by the four corners of the court; and, behold, in every corner of the court *there was* a court.

22 In the four corners of the court *there were* courts joined of forty *cubits* long and thirty broad: these four corners *were* of one measure.

23 And *there was* a row *of building* round about in them, round about them four, and *it was* made with boiling places under the rows round about.

24 Then said he unto me, These *are* the places of them that boil, where the ministers of the house shall [a]boil the sacrifice of the people.

The Healing Waters and Trees

47 Afterward he brought me again unto the door of the house; and, behold, [a]waters issued out from under the threshold of the house eastward: for the forefront of the house *stood toward* the east, and the waters came down from under from the right side of the house, at the south *side* of the altar.

2 Then brought he me out of the way of the gate northward, and led me about the way without unto the utter gate by the way that looketh [a]eastward; and, behold, there ran out waters on the right side.

3 And when [a]the man that had the line in his hand went forth eastward, he measured a thousand cubits, and he brought me through the waters; the waters *were* to the ancles.

4 Again he measured a thousand, and brought me through the waters; the waters *were* to the knees. Again he measured a thousand, and brought me through; the waters *were* to the loins.

5 Afterward he measured a thousand; *and it was* a river that I could not pass over: for the waters were risen, waters to swim in, a river that could not be passed over.

6 And he said unto me, Son of man, hast thou seen *this?* Then he brought me, and caused me to return to the brink of the river.

7 Now when I had returned, behold, at the bank of the river *were* very many [a]trees on the one side and on the other.

8 Then said he unto me, These waters issue out toward the east country, and go down into the desert, and go into the sea: *which being* brought forth into the sea, the waters shall be healed.

9 And it shall come to pass, *that* every thing that liveth, which moveth, whithersoever the rivers shall come, shall live: and there shall be a very great multitude of fish, because these waters shall come thither: for they shall be healed; and every thing shall live whither the river cometh.

10 And it shall come to pass, *that* the fishers shall stand upon it from En–gedi even unto En–eglaim; they shall be a *place* to spread forth nets; their fish shall be according to their kinds, as the fish [a]of the great sea, exceeding many.

11 But the miry places thereof and the marishes thereof shall not be healed; they shall be given to salt.

12 And [a]by the river upon the bank thereof, on this side and on that side, shall grow all trees

19 [a]Ezek. 42:13
20 [a]2 Chr. 35:13 [b]Lev. 2:4, 5, 7 [c]Ezek. 44:19
24 [a]Ezek. 46:20

CHAPTER 47

1 [a]Ps. 46:4; Is. 30:25; 55:1; [Jer. 2:13]; Joel 3:18; Zech. 13:1; 14:8; [Rev. 22:1, 17]
2 [a]Ezek. 44:1, 2
3 [a]Ezek. 40:3
7 [a][Is. 60:13, 21; 61:3; Ezek. 47:12; Rev. 22:2]
10 [a]Num. 34:3; Josh. 23:4; Ezek. 48:28
12 [a]Ezek. 47:7; [Rev. 22:2]

NKJV

his sons from his own property, so that none of My people may be scattered from his property." ' "

How the Offerings Were Prepared

19 Now he brought me through the entrance, which *was* at the side of the gate, into the holy [a]chambers of the priests which face toward the north; and there a place *was* situated at their extreme western end.

20 And he said to me, "This *is* the place where the priests shall [a]boil the trespass offering and the sin offering, *and* where they shall [b]bake the grain offering, so that they do not bring *them* out into the outer court [c]to sanctify the people."

21 Then he brought me out into the outer court and caused me to pass by the four corners of the court; and in fact, in every corner of the court *there was another* court.

22 In the four corners of the court *were* enclosed courts, forty *cubits* long and thirty wide; all four corners *were* the same size.

23 *There was* a row *of building stones* all around in them, all around the four of them; and cooking hearths were made under the rows of stones all around.

24 And he said to me, "These *are* the kitchens where the ministers of the temple shall [a]boil the sacrifices of the people."

The Healing Waters and Trees

47 Then he brought me back to the door of the temple; and there was [a]water, flowing from under the threshold of the temple toward the east, for the front of the temple faced east; the water was flowing from under the right side of the temple, south of the altar.

2 He brought me out by way of the north gate, and led me around on the outside to the outer gateway that faces [a]east; and there was water, running out on the right side.

3 And when [a]the man went out to the east with the line in his hand, he measured one thousand cubits, and he brought me through the waters; the water *came up to my* ankles.

4 Again he measured one thousand and brought me through the waters; the water *came up to my* knees. Again he measured one thousand and brought me through; the water *came up to my* waist.

5 Again he measured one thousand, *and it was* a river that I could not cross; for the water was too deep, water in which one must swim, a river that could not be crossed.

6 He said to me, "Son of man, have you seen *this?*" Then he brought me and returned me to the bank of the river.

7 When I returned, there, along the bank of the river, *were* very many [a]trees on one side and the other.

8 Then he said to me: "This water flows toward the eastern region, goes down into the valley, and enters the sea. *When it* reaches the sea, *its* waters are healed.

9 "And it shall be *that* every living thing that moves, wherever the rivers go, will live. There will be a very great multitude of fish, because these waters go there; for they will be healed, and everything will live wherever the river goes.

10 "It shall be *that* fishermen will stand by it from En Gedi to En Eglaim; they will be *places* for spreading their nets. Their fish will be of the same kinds as the fish [a]of the Great Sea, exceedingly many.

11 "But its swamps and marshes will not be healed; they will be given over to salt.

12 [a]"Along the bank of the river, on this side and that, will grow all *kinds of* trees used for food;

KJV

for meat, [b]whose leaf shall not fade, neither shall the fruit thereof be consumed: it shall bring forth new fruit according to his months, because their waters they issued out of the sanctuary: and the fruit thereof shall be for meat, and the leaf thereof for [c]medicine.

Borders of the Land
(cf. Num. 34:1–12)

13 Thus saith the Lord GOD; This *shall be* the [a]border, whereby ye shall inherit the land according to the twelve tribes of Israel: [b]Joseph *shall have two* portions.

14 And ye shall inherit it, one as well as another: *concerning* the which I [a]lifted up mine hand to give it unto your fathers: and this land shall [b]fall unto you for inheritance.

15 And this *shall be* the border of the land toward the north side, from the great sea, [a]the way of Hethlon, as men go to [b]Zedad;

16 [a]Hamath, [b]Berothah, Sibraim, which *is* between the border of Damascus and the border of Hamath; Hazar–hatticon, which *is* by the coast of Hauran.

17 And the border from the sea shall be [a]Hazar–enan, the border of Damascus, and the north northward, and the border of Hamath. And *this is* the north side.

18 And the east side ye shall measure from Hauran, and from Damascus, and from Gilead, and from the land of Israel *by* Jordan, from the border unto the east sea. And *this is* the east side.

19 And the south side southward, from Tamar *even* to [a]the waters of strife *in* Kadesh, the river to the great sea. And *this is* the south side southward.

20 The west side also *shall be* the great sea from the border, till a man come over against Hamath. This *is* the west side.

21 So shall ye [a]divide this land unto you according to the tribes of Israel.

22 And it shall come to pass, *that* ye shall divide it by [a]lot for an inheritance unto you, [b]and to the strangers that sojourn among you, which shall beget children among you: [c]and they shall be unto you as born in the country among the children of Israel; they shall have inheritance with you among the tribes of Israel.

23 And it shall come to pass, *that* in what tribe the stranger sojourneth, there shall ye give *him* his inheritance, saith the Lord GOD.

Division of the Land

48 Now these *are* the names of the tribes. [a]From the north end to the coast of the way of Hethlon, as one goeth to Hamath, Hazar–enan, the border of Damascus northward, to the coast of Hamath; for these are his sides east *and* west; a *portion for* [b]Dan.

2 And by the border of Dan, from the east side unto the west side, a *portion for* [a]Asher.

3 And by the border of Asher, from the east side even unto the west side, a *portion for* [a]Naphtali.

4 And by the border of Naphtali, from the east side unto the west side, a *portion for* [a]Manasseh.

5 And by the border of Manasseh, from the east side unto the west side, a *portion for* [a]Ephraim.

6 And by the border of Ephraim, from the east side even unto the west side, a *portion for* [a]Reuben.

7 And by the border of Reuben, from the east side unto the west side, a *portion for* [a]Judah.

8 And by the border of Judah, from the east side unto the west side, shall be [a]the offering which ye shall offer of five and twenty thousand *reeds in* breadth, and *in* length as one of the *other* parts, from the east side unto the west side: and the [b]sanctuary shall be in the midst of it.

9 The oblation that ye shall offer unto the

12 [b]Job 18:16; [Ps. 1:3; Jer. 17:8] [c][Rev. 22:2]
13 [a]Num. 34:1–29 [b]Gen. 48:5; 1 Chr. 5:1; Ezek. 48:4, 5
14 [a]Gen. 12:7; 13:15; 15:7; 17:8; 26:3; 28:13; Deut. 1:8; Ezek. 20:5, 6, 28, 42 [b]Ezek. 48:29
15 [a]Ezek. 48:1 [b]Num. 34:7, 8
16 [a]Num. 34:8 [b]2 Sam. 8:8
17 [a]Num. 34:9; Ezek. 48:1
19 [a]Num. 20:13; Deut. 32:51; Ps. 81:7; Ezek. 48:28
21 [a]Ezek. 45:1
22 [a]Num. 26:55, 56 [b][Eph. 3:6; Rev. 7:9, 10] [c][Acts 11:18; 15:9; Gal. 3:28; Eph. 2:12–14; Col. 3:11]

CHAPTER 48

1 [a]Ezek. 47:15 [b]Josh. 19:40–48
2 [a]Josh. 19:24–31
3 [a]Josh. 19:32–39
4 [a]Josh. 13:29–31; 17:1–11, 17, 18
5 [a]Josh. 16:5–10; 17:8–10, 14–18
6 [a]Josh. 13:15–23
7 [a]Josh. 15:1–63; 19:9
8 [a]Ezek. 45:1–6 [b][Is. 12:6; 33:20–22]; Ezek. 45:3, 4

NKJV

[b]their leaves will not wither, and their fruit will not fail. They will bear fruit every month, because their water flows from the sanctuary. Their fruit will be for food, and their leaves for [c]medicine."

Borders of the Land
(cf. Num. 34:1–12)

13 Thus says the Lord GOD: "These *are* the [a]borders by which you shall divide the land as an inheritance among the twelve tribes of Israel. [b]Joseph *shall have two* portions.

14 "You shall inherit it equally with one another; for I [a]raised My hand in an oath to give it to your fathers, and this land shall [b]fall to you as your inheritance.

15 "This *shall be* the border of the land on the north: from the Great Sea, *by* [a]the road to Hethlon, as one goes to [b]Zedad,

16 [a]"Hamath, [b]Berothah, Sibraim (which *is* between the border of Damascus and the border of Hamath), to Hazar Hatticon (which *is* on the border of Hauran).

17 "Thus the boundary shall be from the Sea to [a]Hazar Enan, the border of Damascus; and as for the north, northward, it is the border of Hamath. *This is* the north side.

18 "On the east side you shall mark out the border from between Hauran and Damascus, and between Gilead and the land of Israel, along the Jordan, and along the eastern side of the sea. *This is* the east side.

19 "The south side, toward the *South, *shall be* from Tamar to [a]the waters of Meribah by Kadesh, along the brook to the Great Sea. *This is* the south side, toward the South.

20 "The west side *shall be* the Great Sea, from the *southern* boundary until one comes to a point opposite Hamath. This *is* the west side.

21 "Thus you shall [a]divide this land among yourselves according to the tribes of Israel.

22 "It shall be that you will divide it by [a]lot as an inheritance for yourselves, [b]and for the strangers who dwell among you and who bear children among you. [c]They shall be to you as native-born among the children of Israel; they shall have an inheritance with you among the tribes of Israel.

23 "And it shall be *that* in whatever tribe the stranger dwells, there you shall give *him* his inheritance," says the Lord GOD.

Division of the Land

48 "Now these *are* the names of the tribes: [a]From the northern border along the road to Hethlon at the entrance of Hamath, to Hazar Enan, the border of Damascus northward, in the direction of Hamath, *there shall be* one *section for* [b]Dan from its east to its west side;

2 "by the border of Dan, from the east side to the west, one *section for* [a]Asher;

3 "by the border of Asher, from the east side to the west, one *section for* [a]Naphtali;

4 "by the border of Naphtali, from the east side to the west, one *section for* [a]Manasseh;

5 "by the border of Manasseh, from the east side to the west, one *section for* [a]Ephraim;

6 "by the border of Ephraim, from the east side to the west, one *section for* [a]Reuben;

7 "by the border of Reuben, from the east side to the west, one *section for* [a]Judah;

8 "by the border of Judah, from the east side to the west, shall be [a]the district which you shall set apart, twenty-five thousand *cubits* in width, and *in* length the same as one of the *other* portions, from the east side to the west, with the [b]sanctuary in the center.

9 "The district that you shall set apart for

*
47:19 Heb. *Negev*

KJV

LORD *shall be* of five and twenty thousand in length, and of ten thousand in breadth.

10 And for them, *even* for the priests, shall be *this* holy oblation; toward the north five and twenty thousand *in length,* and toward the west ten thousand in breadth, and toward the east ten thousand in breadth, and toward the south five and twenty thousand in length: and the sanctuary of the LORD shall be in the midst thereof.

11 [a]*It shall be* for the priests that are sanctified of the sons of Zadok; which have kept my charge, which went not astray when the children of Israel went astray, [b]as the Levites went astray.

12 And *this* oblation of the land that is offered shall be unto them a thing most [a]holy by the border of the Levites.

13 And over against the border of the priests the [a]Levites *shall have* five and twenty thousand in length, and ten thousand in breadth: all the length *shall be* five and twenty thousand, and the breadth ten thousand.

14 [a]And they shall not sell of it, neither exchange, nor alienate the firstfruits of the land: for *it is* holy unto the LORD.

15 [a]And the five thousand, that are left in the breadth over against the five and twenty thousand, shall be [b]a profane *place* for the city, for dwelling, and for suburbs: and the city shall be in the midst thereof.

16 And these *shall be* the measures thereof; the north side four thousand and five hundred, and the south side four thousand and five hundred, and on the east side four thousand and five hundred, and the west side four thousand and five hundred.

17 And the suburbs of the city shall be toward the north two hundred and fifty, and toward the south two hundred and fifty, and toward the east two hundred and fifty, and toward the west two hundred and fifty.

18 And the residue in length over against the oblation of the holy *portion shall be* ten thousand eastward, and ten thousand westward: and it shall be over against the oblation of the holy *portion;* and the increase thereof shall be for food unto them that serve the city.

19 [a]And they that serve the city shall serve it out of all the tribes of Israel.

20 All the oblation *shall be* five and twenty thousand by five and twenty thousand: ye shall offer the holy oblation foursquare, with the possession of the city.

21 [a]And the residue *shall be* for the prince, on the one side and on the other of the holy oblation, and of the possession of the city, over against the five and twenty thousand of the oblation toward the east border, and westward over against the five and twenty thousand toward the west border, over against the portions for the prince: and it shall be the holy oblation; [b]and the sanctuary of the house *shall be* in the midst thereof.

22 Moreover from the possession of the Levites, and from the possession of the city, *being* in the midst *of that* which is the prince's, between the border of Judah and the border of [a]Benjamin, shall be for the prince.

23 As for the rest of the tribes, from the east side unto the west side, Benjamin *shall have* a *portion.*

24 And by the border of Benjamin, from the east side unto the west side, [a]Simeon *shall have* a *portion.*

25 And by the border of Simeon, from the east side unto the west side, [a]Issachar a *portion.*

26 And by the border of Issachar, from the east side unto the west side, [a]Zebulun a *portion.*

27 And by the border of Zebulun, from the east side unto the west side, [a]Gad a *portion.*

28 And by the border of Gad, at the south side southward, the border shall be even from Tamar *unto* [a]the waters of strife *in* Kadesh, *and* to the river toward the [b]great sea.

NKJV

the LORD *shall be* twenty-five thousand *cubits* in length and ten thousand in width.

10 "To these—to the priests—the holy district shall belong: on the north twenty-five thousand *cubits in length,* on the west ten thousand in width, on the east ten thousand in width, and on the south twenty-five thousand in length. The sanctuary of the LORD shall be in the center.

11 [a]"*It shall be* for the priests of the sons of Zadok, who are sanctified, who have kept My charge, who did not go astray when the children of Israel went astray, [b]as the Levites went astray.

12 "And *this* district of land that is set apart shall be to them a thing most [a]holy by the border of the Levites.

13 "Opposite the border of the priests, the [a]Levites *shall have an area* twenty-five thousand *cubits* in length and ten thousand in width; its entire length *shall be* twenty-five thousand and its width ten thousand.

14 [a]"And they shall not sell or exchange any of it; they may not alienate this best *part* of the land, for *it is* holy to the LORD.

15 [a]"The five thousand *cubits* in width that remain, along the edge of the twenty-five thousand, shall be [b]for general use by the city, for dwellings and common-land; and the city shall be in the center.

16 "These *shall be* its measurements: the north side four thousand five hundred *cubits,* the south side four thousand five hundred, the east side four thousand five hundred, and the west side four thousand five hundred.

17 "The common-land of the city shall be: to the north two hundred and fifty *cubits,* to the south two hundred and fifty, to the east two hundred and fifty, and to the west two hundred and fifty.

18 "The rest of the length, alongside the district of the holy *section, shall be* ten thousand *cubits* to the east and ten thousand to the west. It shall be adjacent to the district of the holy *section,* and its produce shall be food for the workers of the city.

19 [a]"The workers of the city, from all the tribes of Israel, shall cultivate it.

20 "The entire district *shall be* twenty-five thousand *cubits* by twenty-five thousand *cubits,* foursquare. You shall set apart the holy district with the property of the city.

21 [a]"The rest *shall belong* to the prince, on one side and on the other of the holy district and of the city's property, next to the twenty-five thousand *cubits* of the *holy* district as far as the eastern border, and westward next to the twenty-five thousand as far as the western border, adjacent to the *tribal* portions; *it shall belong* to the prince. It shall be the holy district, [b]and the sanctuary of the temple *shall be* in the center.

22 "Moreover, apart from the possession of the Levites and the possession of the city *which are* in the midst of what *belongs* to the prince, *the area* between the border of Judah and the border of [a]Benjamin shall belong to the prince.

23 "As for the rest of the tribes, from the east side to the west, Benjamin *shall have* one *section;*

24 "by the border of Benjamin, from the east side to the west, [a]Simeon *shall have* one *section;*

25 "by the border of Simeon, from the east side to the west, [a]Issachar *shall have* one *section;*

26 "by the border of Issachar, from the east side to the west, [a]Zebulun *shall have* one *section;*

27 "by the border of Zebulun, from the east side to the west, [a]Gad *shall have* one *section;*

28 "by the border of Gad, on the south side, toward the *South, the border shall be from Tamar *to* [a]the waters of Meribah *by* Kadesh, along the brook to the [b]Great Sea.

11 [a]Ezek. 40:46; 44:15 [b]Ezek. 44:10, 12
12 [a]Ezek. 45:4
13 [a]Ezek. 45:5
14 [a]Ex. 22:29; Lev. 27:10, 28, 33; Ezek. 44:30
15 [a]Ezek. 45:6 [b]Ezek. 42:20
19 [a]Ezek. 45:6
21 [a]Ezek. 34:24; 45:7; 48:22 [b]Ezek. 48:8, 10
22 [a]Josh. 18:21–28
24 [a]Josh. 19:1–9
25 [a]Josh. 19:17–23
26 [a]Josh. 19:10–16
27 [a]Josh. 13:24–28
28 [a]Gen. 14:7; 2 Chr. 20:2; Ezek. 47:19 [b]Ezek. 47:10, 15, 19, 20

*

48:28 Heb. *Negev*

KJV

29 [a]This *is* the land which ye shall divide by lot unto the tribes of Israel for inheritance, and these *are* their portions, saith the Lord GOD.

The Gates of the City and Its Name

30 And these *are* the goings out of the city on the north side, four thousand and five hundred measures.
31 [a]And the gates of the city *shall be* after the names of the tribes of Israel: three gates northward; one gate of Reuben, one gate of Judah, one gate of Levi.
32 And at the east side four thousand and five hundred: and three gates; and one gate of Joseph, one gate of Benjamin, one gate of Dan.
33 And at the south side four thousand and five hundred measures: and three gates; one gate of Simeon, one gate of Issachar, one gate of Zebulun.
34 At the west side four thousand and five hundred, *with* their three gates; one gate of Gad, one gate of Asher, one gate of Naphtali.
35 *It was* round about eighteen thousand *measures:* [a]and the name of the city from *that* day *shall be,* [b]The LORD *is* there.

29 [a]Ezek. 47:14, 21, 22
31 [a][Rev. 21:10–14]
35 [a]Jer. 23:6; 33:16 [b]Is. 12:6; 14:32; 24:23; Jer. 3:17; 8:19; 14:9; Ezek. 35:10; Joel 3:21; Zech. 2:10; Rev. 21:3; 22:3

*

48:35 Heb. *YHWH Shammah*

NKJV

29 [a]"This *is* the land which you shall divide by lot as an inheritance among the tribes of Israel, and these *are* their portions," says the Lord GOD.

The Gates of the City and Its Name

30 "These *are* the exits of the city. On the north side, measuring four thousand five hundred *cubits*
31 [a]"(the gates of the city *shall be* named after the tribes of Israel), the three gates northward: one gate for Reuben, one gate for Judah, and one gate for Levi;
32 "on the east side, four thousand five hundred *cubits,* three gates: one gate for Joseph, one gate for Benjamin, and one gate for Dan;
33 "on the south side, measuring four thousand five hundred *cubits,* three gates: one gate for Simeon, one gate for Issachar, and one gate for Zebulun;
34 "on the west side, four thousand five hundred *cubits* with their three gates: one gate for Gad, one gate for Asher, and one gate for Naphtali.
35 "All the way around *shall be* eighteen thousand *cubits;* [a]and the name of the city from *that* day *shall be:* [b]THE* LORD *IS* THERE."

KJV

THE BOOK OF

DANIEL

Daniel and His Friends Obey God
(*cf.* 2 *Kin.* 24:10–17)

1 In the third year of the reign of [a]Jehoiakim king of Judah came Nebuchadnezzar king of Babylon unto Jerusalem, and besieged it.

2 And the LORD gave Jehoiakim king of Judah into his hand, with [a]part of the vessels of the house of God: which he carried [b]into the land of Shinar to the house of his god; [c]and he brought the vessels into the treasure house of his god.

3 And the king spake unto Ashpenaz the master of his eunuchs, that he should bring [a]*certain* of the children of Israel, and of the king's seed, and of the princes;

4 Children [a]in whom *was* no blemish, but well favoured, and skilful in all wisdom, and cunning in knowledge, and understanding science, and such as *had* ability in them to stand in the king's palace, and [b]whom they might teach the learning and the tongue of the Chaldeans.

5 And the king appointed them a daily provision of the king's meat, and of the wine which he drank: so nourishing them three years, that at the end thereof they might [a]stand before the king.

6 Now among these were of the children of Judah, Daniel, Hananiah, Mishael, and Azariah:

7 [a]Unto whom the prince of the eunuchs gave names: [b]for he gave unto Daniel *the name* of Belteshazzar; and to Hananiah, of Shadrach; and to Mishael, of Meshach; and to Azariah, of Abed–nego.

8 But Daniel purposed in his heart that he would not defile himself [a]with the portion of the king's meat, nor with the wine which he drank: therefore he requested of the prince of the eunuchs that he might not defile himself.

9 Now [a]God had brought Daniel into favour and tender love with the prince of the eunuchs.

10 And the prince of the eunuchs said unto Daniel, I fear my lord the king, who hath appointed your meat and your drink: for why should he see your faces worse liking than the children which *are* of your sort? then shall ye make *me* endanger my head to the king.

11 Then said Daniel to Melzar, whom the prince of the eunuchs had set over Daniel, Hananiah, Mishael, and Azariah,

12 Prove thy servants, I beseech thee, ten days; and let them give us pulse to eat, and water to drink.

13 Then let our countenances be looked upon before thee, and the countenance of the children that eat of the portion of the king's meat: and as thou seest, deal with thy servants.

14 So he consented to them in this matter, and proved them ten days.

15 And at the end of ten days their countenances appeared fairer and fatter in flesh than all the children which did eat the portion of the king's meat.

16 Thus Melzar took away the portion of their meat, and the wine that they should drink; and gave them pulse.

17 As for these four children, [a]God gave them [b]knowledge and skill in all learning and

CHAPTER 1

1 [a]2 Kin. 24:1, 2; 2 Chr. 36:5–7; Jer. 25:1; 52:12–30
2 [a]2 Chr. 36:7; Jer. 27:19, 20; Dan. 5:2 [b]Gen. 10:10; 11:2; Is. 11:11; Zech. 5:11 [c]2 Chr. 36:7
3 [a]2 Kin. 20:17, 18; Is. 39:7
4 [a]Lev. 24:19, 20 [b]Acts 7:22
5 [a]Gen. 41:46; 1 Sam. 16:22; 1 Kin. 10:8; Dan. 1:19
7 [a]Gen. 41:45; 2 Kin. 24:17 [b]Dan. 2:26; 4:8; 5:12
8 [a]Lev. 11:47; Deut. 32:38; Ezek. 4:13; Hos. 9:3
9 [a]Gen. 39:21; 1 Kin. 8:50; [Job 5:15, 16]; Ps. 106:46; [Prov. 16:7]; Acts 7:10; 27:3
17 [a]1 Kin. 3:12, 28; 2 Chr. 1:10–12; [Luke 21:15; James 1:5–7] [b]Acts 7:22

*______

1:11 Or *Melzar*

NKJV

THE BOOK OF

DANIEL

Daniel and His Friends Obey God
(*cf.* 2 *Kin.* 24:10–17)

1 In the third year of the reign of [a]Jehoiakim king of Judah, Nebuchadnezzar king of Babylon came to Jerusalem and besieged it.

2 And the Lord gave Jehoiakim king of Judah into his hand, with [a]some of the articles of the house of God, which he carried [b]into the land of Shinar to the house of his god; [c]and he brought the articles into the treasure house of his god.

3 Then the king instructed Ashpenaz, the master of his eunuchs, to bring [a]some of the children of Israel and some of the king's descendants and some of the nobles,

4 young men [a]in whom *there was* no blemish, but good-looking, gifted in all wisdom, possessing knowledge and quick to understand, who *had* ability to serve in the king's palace, and [b]whom they might teach the language and literature of the Chaldeans.

5 And the king appointed for them a daily provision of the king's delicacies and of the wine which he drank, and three years of training for them, so that at the end of *that time* they might [a]serve before the king.

6 Now from among those of the sons of Judah were Daniel, Hananiah, Mishael, and Azariah.

7 [a]To them the chief of the eunuchs gave names: [b]he gave Daniel *the name* Belteshazzar; to Hananiah, Shadrach; to Mishael, Meshach; and to Azariah, Abed-Nego.

8 But Daniel purposed in his heart that he would not defile himself [a]with the portion of the king's delicacies, nor with the wine which he drank; therefore he requested of the chief of the eunuchs that he might not defile himself.

9 Now [a]God had brought Daniel into the favor and goodwill of the chief of the eunuchs.

10 And the chief of the eunuchs said to Daniel, "I fear my lord the king, who has appointed your food and drink. For why should he see your faces looking worse than the young men who *are* your age? Then you would endanger my head before the king."

11 So Daniel said to *the steward whom the chief of the eunuchs had set over Daniel, Hananiah, Mishael, and Azariah,

12 "Please test your servants for ten days, and let them give us vegetables to eat and water to drink.

13 "Then let our appearance be examined before you, and the appearance of the young men who eat the portion of the king's delicacies; and as you see fit, *so* deal with your servants."

14 So he consented with them in this matter, and tested them ten days.

15 And at the end of ten days their features appeared better and fatter in flesh than all the young men who ate the portion of the king's delicacies.

16 Thus the steward took away their portion of delicacies and the wine that they were to drink, and gave them vegetables.

17 As for these four young men, [a]God gave them [b]knowledge and skill in all literature and

KJV

wisdom: and Daniel had [c]understanding in all visions and dreams.
18 Now at the end of the days that the king
had said he should bring them in, then the prince
of the eunuchs brought them in before Nebuchadnezzar.
19 And the king communed with them; and
among them all was found none like Daniel,
Hananiah, Mishael, and Azariah: therefore [a]stood
they before the king.
20 [a]And in all matters of wisdom *and* understanding, that the king enquired of them, he found
them ten times better than all the magicians *and*
astrologers that *were* in all his realm.
21 [a]And Daniel continued *even* unto the first
year of king Cyrus.

Nebuchadnezzar's Dream

2 And in the second year of the reign of
Nebuchadnezzar Nebuchadnezzar dreamed
dreams, [a]wherewith his spirit was troubled, and
[b]his sleep brake from him.
2 [a]Then the king commanded to call the magicians, and the astrologers, and the sorcerers,
and the Chaldeans, for to shew the king his
dreams. So they came and stood before the
king.
3 And the king said unto them, I have
dreamed a dream, and my spirit was troubled to
know the dream.
4 Then spake the Chaldeans to the king in
Syriack, [a]O king, live for ever: tell thy servants
the dream, and we will shew the interpretation.
5 The king answered and said to the Chaldeans, The thing is gone from me: if ye will not make
known unto me the dream, with the interpretation
thereof, ye shall be [a]cut in pieces, and your houses
shall be made a dunghill.
6 [a]But if ye shew the dream, and the interpretation thereof, ye shall receive of me gifts and
rewards and great honour: therefore shew me the
dream, and the interpretation thereof.
7 They answered again and said, Let the
king tell his servants the dream, and we will shew
the interpretation of it.
8 The king answered and said, I know of
certainty that ye would gain the time, because ye
see the thing is gone from me.
9 But if ye will not make known unto me
the dream, *there is but* one decree for you: for
ye have prepared lying and corrupt words to
speak before me, till the time be changed: therefore tell me the dream, and I shall know that ye
can shew me the interpretation thereof.
10 The Chaldeans answered before the king,
and said, There is not a man upon the earth that
can shew the king's matter: therefore *there is* no
king, lord, nor ruler, *that* asked such things at
any magician, or astrologer, or Chaldean.
11 And *it is* a rare thing that the king requir-
eth, and there is none other that can shew it before
the king, [a]except the gods, whose dwelling is not
with flesh.
12 For this cause the king was angry and
very furious, and commanded to destroy all the
wise *men* of Babylon.
13 And the decree went forth that the wise
men should be slain; and they sought [a]Daniel and
his fellows to be slain.

God Reveals Nebuchadnezzar's Dream

14 Then Daniel answered with counsel and
wisdom to Arioch the captain of the king's guard,
which was gone forth to slay the wise *men* of
Babylon:
15 He answered and said to Arioch the king's
captain, Why *is* the decree *so* hasty from the king?
Then Arioch made the thing known to Daniel.
16 Then Daniel went in, and desired of the
king that he would give him time, and that he
would shew the king the interpretation.
17 Then Daniel went to his house, and made

17 [c]Num. 12:6; 2 Chr. 26:5; Dan. 5:11, 12, 14; 10:1
19 [a]Gen. 41:46; [Prov. 22:29]; Dan. 1:5
20 [a]1 Kin. 10:1
21 [a]Dan. 6:28; 10:1

CHAPTER 2

1 [a]Gen. 40:5–8; 41:1, 8; Job 33:15–17; Dan. 2:3; 4:5 [b]Esth. 6:1; Dan. 6:18
2 [a]Gen. 41:8; Ex. 7:11; Is. 47:12, 13; Dan. 1:20; 2:10, 27; 4:6; 5:7
4 [a]1 Kin. 1:31; Dan. 3:9; 5:10; 6:6, 21
5 [a]2 Kin. 10:27; Ezra 6:11; Dan. 3:29
6 [a]Dan. 5:16
11 [a]Gen. 41:39; Dan. 5:11
13 [a]Dan. 1:19, 20

*

1:19 Lit. *talked with them*
2:4 The original language of Dan. 2:4b through 7:28 is Aramaic.

NKJV

wisdom; and Daniel had [c]understanding in all visions and dreams.
18 Now at the end of the days, when the king
had said that they should be brought in, the chief
of the eunuchs brought them in before Nebuchadnezzar.
19 Then the king *interviewed them, and
among them all none was found like Daniel,
Hananiah, Mishael, and Azariah; therefore [a]they
served before the king.
20 [a]And in all matters of wisdom *and* understanding about which the king examined them,
he found them ten times better than all the magicians *and* astrologers who *were* in all his realm.
21 [a]Thus Daniel continued until the first year
of King Cyrus.

Nebuchadnezzar's Dream

2 Now in the second year of Nebuchadnezzar's
reign, Nebuchadnezzar had dreams; [a]and his
spirit was so troubled that [b]his sleep left him.
2 [a]Then the king gave the command to call
the magicians, the astrologers, the sorcerers, and
the Chaldeans to tell the king his dreams. So they
came and stood before the king.
3 And the king said to them, "I have had a
dream, and my spirit is anxious to know the
dream."
4 Then the Chaldeans spoke to the king in
Aramaic, [a]"O* king, live forever! Tell your servants the dream, and we will give the interpretation."
5 The king answered and said to the Chaldeans, "My decision is firm: if you do not make
known the dream to me, and its interpretation,
you shall be [a]cut in pieces, and your houses shall
be made an ash heap.
6 [a]"However, if you tell the dream and its
interpretation, you shall receive from me gifts, rewards, and great honor. Therefore tell me the
dream and its interpretation."
7 They answered again and said, "Let the
king tell his servants the dream, and we will give
its interpretation."
8 The king answered and said, "I know for
certain that you would gain time, because you see
that my decision is firm:
9 "if you do not make known the dream to
me, *there is only* one decree for you! For you have
agreed to speak lying and corrupt words before
me till the time has changed. Therefore tell me
the dream, and I shall know that you can give
me its interpretation."
10 The Chaldeans answered the king, and
said, "There is not a man on earth who can tell
the king's matter; therefore no king, lord, or ruler
has *ever* asked such things of any magician, astrologer, or Chaldean.
11 "*It is* a difficult thing that the king requests, and there is no other who can tell it to
the king [a]except the gods, whose dwelling is not
with flesh."
12 For this reason the king was angry and
very furious, and gave the command to destroy
all the wise *men* of Babylon.
13 So the decree went out, and they began
killing the wise *men;* and they sought [a]Daniel and
his companions, to kill *them.*

God Reveals Nebuchadnezzar's Dream

14 Then with counsel and wisdom Daniel answered Arioch, the captain of the king's guard,
who had gone out to kill the wise *men* of Babylon;
15 he answered and said to Arioch the king's
captain, "Why is the decree from the king so urgent?" Then Arioch made the decision known to
Daniel.
16 So Daniel went in and asked the king to
give him time, that he might tell the king the
interpretation.
17 Then Daniel went to his house, and made

KJV

the thing known to Hananiah, Mishael, and Azariah, his companions:
18 [a]That they would desire mercies of the
God of heaven concerning this secret; that Daniel
and his fellows should not perish with the rest of
the wise *men* of Babylon.
19 Then was the secret revealed unto Daniel
[a]in a night vision. Then Daniel blessed the God
of heaven.
20 Daniel answered and said, [a]Blessed be the
name of God for ever and ever: [b]for wisdom and
might are his:
21 And he changeth [a]the times and the seasons: [b]he removeth kings, and setteth up kings:
[c]he giveth wisdom unto the wise, and knowledge
to them that know understanding:
22 [a]He revealeth the deep and secret things:
[b]he knoweth what *is* in the darkness, and [c]the
light dwelleth with him.
23 I thank thee, and praise thee, O thou God
of my fathers, who hast given me wisdom and
might, and hast made known unto me now what
we [a]desired of thee: for thou hast *now* made
known unto us the king's matter.

Daniel Explains the Dream

24 Therefore Daniel went in unto Arioch,
whom the king had ordained to destroy the wise
men of Babylon: he went and said thus unto him;
Destroy not the wise *men* of Babylon: bring me
in before the king, and I will shew unto the king
the interpretation.
25 Then Arioch brought in Daniel before the
king in haste, and said thus unto him, I have found
a man of the captives of Judah, that will make
known unto the king the interpretation.
26 The king answered and said to Daniel,
whose name *was* Belteshazzar, Art thou able to
make known unto me the dream which I have
seen, and the interpretation thereof?
27 Daniel answered in the presence of the
king, and said, The secret which the king hath
demanded cannot the wise *men*, the astrologers,
the magicians, the soothsayers, shew unto the
king;
28 [a]But there is a God in heaven that revealeth secrets, and maketh known to the king Nebuchadnezzar [b]what shall be in the latter days. Thy
dream, and the visions of thy head upon thy bed,
are these;
29 As for thee, O king, thy thoughts came
into thy mind upon thy bed, what should come
to pass hereafter: [a]and he that revealeth secrets
maketh known to thee what shall come to pass.
30 [a]But as for me, this secret is not revealed
to me for *any* wisdom that I have more than any
living, but for *their* sakes that shall make known
the interpretation to the king, [b]and that thou
mightest know the thoughts of thy heart.
31 Thou, O king, sawest, and behold a great
image. This great image, whose brightness *was*
excellent, stood before thee; and the form thereof
was terrible.
32 [a]This image's head *was* of fine gold, his
breast and his arms of silver, his belly and his
thighs of brass,
33 His legs of iron, his feet part of iron and
part of clay.
34 Thou sawest till that a stone was cut out
[a]without hands, which smote the image upon his
feet *that were* of iron and clay, and brake them
to pieces.
35 [a]Then was the iron, the clay, the brass,
the silver, and the gold, broken to pieces together,
and became [b]like the chaff of the summer

18 [a][Dan. 9:9; Matt. 18:19]
19 [a]Num. 12:6; Job 33:15; [Prov. 3:32]; Amos 3:7
20 [a]Ps. 113:2 [b][1 Chr. 29:11, 12; Job 12:13; Ps. 147:5; Jer. 32:19; Matt. 6:13; Rom. 11:33]
21 [a]Ps. 31:15; Esth. 1:13; Dan. 2:9; 7:25 [b]Job 12:18; [Ps. 75:6, 7; Jer. 27:5; Dan. 4:35] [c]1 Kin. 3:9, 10; 4:29; [James 1:5]
22 [a]Job 12:22; Ps. 25:14; [Prov. 3:22] [b]Job 26:6; Ps. 139:12; [Is. 45:7; Jer. 23:24; Heb. 4:13] [c][Ps. 36:9]; Dan. 5:11, 14; [1 Tim. 6:16; James 1:17; 1 John 1:5]
23 [a]Ps. 21:2, 4; Dan. 2:18, 29, 30
28 [a]Gen. 40:8; Amos 4:13 [b]Gen. 49:1; Is. 2:2; Dan. 10:14; Mic. 4:1
29 [a][Dan. 2:22, 28]
30 [a]Acts 3:12 [b]Dan. 2:47
32 [a]Dan. 2:38, 45
34 [a]Dan. 8:25; [Zech. 4:6]; 2 Cor. 5:1; Heb. 9:24
35 [a]Dan. 7:23–27; [Rev. 16:14] [b]Ps. 1:4; Is. 17:13; 41:15, 16; Hos. 13:3

NKJV

the decision known to Hananiah, Mishael, and
Azariah, his companions,
18 [a]that they might seek mercies from the
God of heaven concerning this secret, so that Daniel and his companions might not perish with the
rest of the wise *men* of Babylon.
19 Then the secret was revealed to Daniel [a]in
a night vision. So Daniel blessed the God of
heaven.
20 Daniel answered and said:

[a]"Blessed be the name of God forever and
ever,
[b]For wisdom and might are His.
21 And He changes [a]the times and the
seasons;
[b]He removes kings and raises up kings;
[c]He gives wisdom to the wise
And knowledge to those who have
understanding.
22 [a]He reveals deep and secret things;
[b]He knows what *is* in the darkness,
And [c]light dwells with Him.

23 "I thank You and praise You,
O God of my fathers;
You have given me wisdom and might,
And have now made known to me what
we [a]asked of You,
For You have made known to us the king's
demand."

Daniel Explains the Dream

24 Therefore Daniel went to Arioch, whom
the king had appointed to destroy the wise *men*
of Babylon. He went and said thus to him: "Do
not destroy the wise *men* of Babylon; take me
before the king, and I will tell the king the
interpretation."
25 Then Arioch quickly brought Daniel before the king, and said thus to him, "I have found
a man of the *captives of Judah, who will make
known to the king the interpretation."
26 The king answered and said to Daniel,
whose name *was* Belteshazzar, "Are you able to
make known to me the dream which I have seen,
and its interpretation?"
27 Daniel answered in the presence of the
king, and said, "The secret which the king has
demanded, the wise *men*, the astrologers, the magicians, and the soothsayers cannot declare to the
king.
28 [a]"But there is a God in heaven who reveals secrets, and He has made known to King
Nebuchadnezzar [b]what will be in the latter days.
Your dream, and the visions of your head upon
your bed, were these:
29 "As for you, O king, thoughts came *to*
your *mind while* on your bed, *about* what would
come to pass after this; [a]and He who reveals secrets has made known to you what will be.
30 [a]"But as for me, this secret has not been
revealed to me because I have more wisdom than
anyone living, but for *our* sakes who make known
the interpretation to the king, [b]and that you may
know the thoughts of your heart.
31 "You, O king, were watching; and behold,
a great image! This great image, whose splendor
was excellent, stood before you; and its form *was*
awesome.
32 [a]"This image's head *was* of fine gold, its
chest and arms of silver, its belly and *thighs of
bronze,
33 "its legs of iron, its feet partly of iron and
partly of *clay.
34 "You watched while a stone was cut out
[a]without hands, which struck the image on its feet
of iron and clay, and broke them in pieces.
35 [a]"Then the iron, the clay, the bronze, the
silver, and the gold were crushed together, and
became [b]like chaff from the summer threshing

*
2:25 Lit. *sons of the captivity*
2:32 Or *sides*
2:33 Or *baked clay,* also vv. 34, 35, 42

KJV

threshingfloors; and the wind carried them away,
that [c]no place was found for them: and the stone
that smote the image [d]became a great mountain,
[e]and filled the whole earth.
36 This *is* the dream; and we will tell the interpretation thereof before the king.
37 [a]Thou, O king, *art* a king of kings: [b]for
the God of heaven hath given thee a kingdom,
power, and strength, and glory.
38 [a]And wheresoever the children of men
dwell, the beasts of the field and the fowls of the
heaven hath he given into thine hand, and hath
made thee ruler over them all. [b]Thou *art* this head
of gold.
39 And after thee shall arise [a]another kingdom [b]inferior to thee, and another third kingdom
of brass, which shall bear rule over all the earth.
40 And [a]the fourth kingdom shall be strong
as iron: forasmuch as iron breaketh in pieces and
subdueth all *things:* and as iron that breaketh all
these, shall it break in pieces and bruise.
41 And whereas thou sawest the feet and
toes, part of potters' clay, and part of iron, the
kingdom shall be divided; but there shall be in it
of the strength of the iron, forasmuch as thou sawest the iron mixed with miry clay.
42 And *as* the toes of the feet *were* part of
iron, and part of clay, [a]*so* the kingdom shall be
partly strong, and partly broken.
43 And whereas thou sawest iron mixed with
miry clay, they shall mingle themselves with the
seed of men: but they shall not cleave one to another, even as iron is not mixed with clay.
44 And in the days of these kings [a]shall the
God of heaven set up a kingdom, [b]which shall
never be destroyed: and the kingdom shall not
be left to other people, [c]*but* it shall break in pieces
and consume all these kingdoms, and it shall
stand for ever.
45 [a]Forasmuch as thou sawest that the stone
was cut out of the mountain without hands, and
that it brake in pieces the iron, the brass, the clay,
the silver, and the gold; the great God hath made
known to the king what shall come to pass hereafter: and the dream *is* certain, and the interpretation thereof sure.

Daniel and His Friends Promoted

46 [a]Then the king Nebuchadnezzar fell upon
his face, and worshipped Daniel, and commanded
that they should offer an oblation [b]and sweet
odours unto him.
47 The king answered unto Daniel, and said,
Of a truth *it is,* that [a]your God *is* a God of [b]gods,
and a LORD of kings, and a revealer of secrets,
seeing thou couldst reveal this secret.
48 [a]Then the king made Daniel a great man,
[b]and gave him many great gifts, and made him
ruler over the whole province of Babylon, and
[c]chief of the governors over all the wise *men* of
Babylon.
49 Then Daniel requested of the king, [a]and
he set Shadrach, Meshach, and Abed–nego, over
the affairs of the province of Babylon: but Daniel
[b]*sat* in the gate of the king.

The Image of Gold

3 Nebuchadnezzar the king made an image of
gold, whose height *was* threescore cubits, *and*
the breadth thereof six cubits: he set it up in the
plain of Dura, in the province of Babylon.
2 Then Nebuchadnezzar the king sent to
gather together the princes, the governors, and
the captains, the judges, the treasurers, the counsellors, the sheriffs, and all the rulers of the provinces, to come to the dedication of the image
which Nebuchadnezzar the king had set up.
3 Then the princes, the governors, and captains, the judges, the treasurers, the counsellors,
the sheriffs, and all the rulers of the provinces,
were gathered together unto the dedication of the
image that Nebuchadnezzar the king had set up;

35 [c]Ps. 37:10,
36 [d][Is. 2:2, 3];
Mic. 4:1 [e]Ps.
80:9
37 [a]Ezra 7:12;
Is. 47:5; Jer.
27:6, 7; Ezek.
26:7; Hos. 8:10
[b]Ezra 1:2
38 [a]Ps. 50:10,
11; Jer. 27:6;
Dan. 4:21, 22
[b]Dan. 2:32
39 [a]Dan. 5:28,
31 [b]Dan. 2:32
40 [a]Dan. 7:7,
23
42 [a]Dan. 7:24
44 [a]Dan. 2:28,
37 [b]Is. 9:6, 7;
Ezek. 37:25;
Dan. 4:3, 34;
6:26; 7:14, 27;
Mic. 4:7;
[Luke 1:32, 33]
[c]Ps. 2:9; Is.
60:12; Dan.
2:34, 35;
[1 Cor. 15:24]
45 [a]Dan. 2:35;
Is. 28:16
46 [a]Dan. 3:5,
7; Acts 10:25;
14:13; Rev.
19:10; 22:8
[b]Lev. 26:31;
Ezra 6:10
47 [a]Dan. 3:28,
29; 4:34–37
[b][Deut. 10:17]
48 [a][Prov.
14:35; 21:1]
[b]Dan. 2:6
[c]Dan. 4:9;
5:11
49 [a]Dan. 1:7;
3:12 [b]Esth.
2:19, 21; 3:2;
Amos 5:15

*———

2:49 The
king's court

NKJV

floors; the wind carried them away so that [c]no
trace of them was found. And the stone that struck
the image [d]became a great mountain [e]and filled
the whole earth.
36 "This *is* the dream. Now we will tell the
interpretation of it before the king.
37 [a]"You, O king, *are* a king of kings. [b]For
the God of heaven has given you a kingdom,
power, strength, and glory;
38 [a]"and wherever the children of men dwell,
or the beasts of the field and the birds of the
heaven, He has given *them* into your hand, and
has made you ruler over them all—[b]you *are* this
head of gold.
39 "But after you shall arise [a]another kingdom [b]inferior to yours; then another, a third kingdom of bronze, which shall rule over all the earth.
40 "And [a]the fourth kingdom shall be as
strong as iron, inasmuch as iron breaks in pieces
and shatters everything; and like iron that
crushes, *that kingdom* will break in pieces and
crush all the others.
41 "Whereas you saw the feet and toes,
partly of potter's clay and partly of iron, the kingdom shall be divided; yet the strength of the iron
shall be in it, just as you saw the iron mixed with
ceramic clay.
42 "And *as* the toes of the feet *were* partly
of iron and partly of clay, [a]*so* the kingdom shall
be partly strong and partly fragile.
43 "As you saw iron mixed with ceramic
clay, they will mingle with the seed of men; but
they will not adhere to one another, just as iron
does not mix with clay.
44 "And in the days of these kings [a]the God
of heaven will set up a kingdom [b]which shall
never be destroyed; and the kingdom shall not
be left to other people; [c]it shall break in pieces
and consume all these kingdoms, and it shall
stand forever.
45 [a]"Inasmuch as you saw that the stone was
cut out of the mountain without hands, and that
it broke in pieces the iron, the bronze, the clay,
the silver, and the gold—the great God has made
known to the king what will come to pass after
this. The dream is certain, and its interpretation
is sure."

Daniel and His Friends Promoted

46 [a]Then King Nebuchadnezzar fell on his
face, prostrate before Daniel, and commanded
that they should present an offering [b]and incense
to him.
47 The king answered Daniel, and said,
"Truly [a]your God *is* the God of [b]gods, the Lord
of kings, and a revealer of secrets, since you could
reveal this secret."
48 [a]Then the king promoted Daniel [b]and
gave him many great gifts; and he made him ruler
over the whole province of Babylon, and [c]chief
administrator over all the wise *men* of Babylon.
49 Also Daniel petitioned the king, [a]and he
set Shadrach, Meshach, and Abed-Nego over the
affairs of the province of Babylon; but Daniel [b]*sat*
in *the gate of the king.

The Image of Gold

3 Nebuchadnezzar the king made an image of
gold, whose height *was* sixty cubits *and* its
width six cubits. He set it up in the plain of Dura,
in the province of Babylon.
2 And King Nebuchadnezzar sent *word* to
gather together the satraps, the administrators,
the governors, the counselors, the treasurers, the
judges, the magistrates, and all the officials of the
provinces, to come to the dedication of the image
which King Nebuchadnezzar had set up.
3 So the satraps, the administrators, the
governors, the counselors, the treasurers, the
judges, the magistrates, and all the officials of the
provinces gathered together for the dedication of
the image that King Nebuchadnezzar had set up;

KJV

and they stood before the image that Nebuchadnezzar had set up.

4 Then an herald cried aloud, To you it is commanded, [a]O people, nations, and languages,

5 *That* at what time ye hear the sound of the cornet, flute, harp, sackbut, psaltery, dulcimer, and all kinds of musick, ye fall down and worship the golden image that Nebuchadnezzar the king hath set up:

6 And whoso falleth not down and worshippeth shall the same hour [a]be cast into the midst of a burning fiery furnace.

7 Therefore at that time, when all the people heard the sound of the cornet, flute, harp, sackbut, psaltery, and all kinds of musick, all the people, the nations, and the languages, fell down *and* worshipped the golden image that Nebuchadnezzar the king had set up.

Daniel's Friends Disobey the King

8 Wherefore at that time certain Chaldeans [a]came near, and accused the Jews.

9 They spake and said to the king Nebuchadnezzar, [a]O king, live for ever.

10 Thou, O king, hast made a decree, that every man that shall hear the sound of the cornet, flute, harp, sackbut, psaltery, and dulcimer, and all kinds of musick, shall fall down and worship the golden image:

11 And whoso falleth not down and worshippeth, *that* he should be cast into the midst of a burning fiery furnace.

12 [a]There are certain Jews whom thou hast set over the affairs of the province of Babylon, Shadrach, Meshach, and Abed–nego; these men, O king, have [b]not regarded thee: they serve not thy gods, nor worship the golden image which thou hast set up.

13 Then Nebuchadnezzar in *his* [a]rage and fury commanded to bring Shadrach, Meshach, and Abed–nego. Then they brought these men before the king.

14 Nebuchadnezzar spake and said unto them, *Is it* true, O Shadrach, Meshach, and Abed–nego, do not ye serve my gods, nor worship the golden image which I have set up?

15 Now if ye be ready that at what time ye hear the sound of the cornet, flute, harp, sackbut, psaltery, and dulcimer, and all kinds of musick, ye fall down and worship the image which I have made; [a]*well:* but if ye worship not, ye shall be cast the same hour into the midst of a burning fiery furnace; [b]and who *is* that God that shall deliver you out of my hands?

16 Shadrach, Meshach, and Abed–nego, answered and said to the king, O Nebuchadnezzar, [a]we *are* not careful to answer thee in this matter.

17 If it be *so*, our [a]God whom we serve is able to [b]deliver us from the burning fiery furnace, and he will deliver *us* out of thine hand, O king.

18 But if not, be it known unto thee, O king, that we will not serve thy gods, nor [a]worship the golden image which thou hast set up.

Saved in Fiery Trial

19 Then was Nebuchadnezzar full of fury, and the form of his visage was changed against Shadrach, Meshach, and Abed–nego: *therefore* he spake, and commanded that they should heat the furnace one seven times more than it was wont to be heated.

20 And he commanded the most mighty men that *were* in his army to bind Shadrach, Meshach, and Abed–nego, *and* to cast *them* into the burning fiery furnace.

21 Then these men were bound in their coats, their hosen, and their hats, and their *other* garments, and were cast into the midst of the burning fiery furnace.

22 Therefore because the king's commandment was urgent, and the furnace exceeding hot,

NKJV

and they stood before the image that Nebuchadnezzar had set up.

4 Then a herald cried aloud: "To you it is commanded, [a]O peoples, nations, and languages,

5 "*that* at the time you hear the sound of the horn, flute, harp, lyre, *and* psaltery, in symphony with all kinds of music, you shall fall down and worship the gold image that King Nebuchadnezzar has set up;

6 "and whoever does not fall down and worship shall [a]be cast immediately into the midst of a burning fiery furnace."

7 So at that time, when all the people heard the sound of the horn, flute, harp, *and* lyre, in symphony with all kinds of music, all the people, nations, and languages fell down *and* worshiped the gold image which King Nebuchadnezzar had set up.

Daniel's Friends Disobey the King

8 Therefore at that time certain Chaldeans [a]came forward and accused the Jews.

9 They spoke and said to King Nebuchadnezzar, [a]"O king, live forever!

10 "You, O king, have made a decree that everyone who hears the sound of the horn, flute, harp, lyre, *and* psaltery, in symphony with all kinds of music, shall fall down and worship the gold image;

11 "and whoever does not fall down and worship shall be cast into the midst of a burning fiery furnace.

12 [a]"There are certain Jews whom you have set over the affairs of the province of Babylon: Shadrach, Meshach, and Abed-Nego; these men, O king, have [b]not paid due regard to you. They do not serve your gods or worship the gold image which you have set up."

13 Then Nebuchadnezzar, in [a]rage and fury, gave the command to bring Shadrach, Meshach, and Abed-Nego. So they brought these men before the king.

14 Nebuchadnezzar spoke, saying to them, "*Is it* true, Shadrach, Meshach, and Abed-Nego, *that* you do not serve my gods or worship the gold image which I have set up?

15 "Now if you are ready at the time you hear the sound of the horn, flute, harp, lyre, *and* psaltery, in symphony with all kinds of music, and you fall down and worship the image which I have made, [a]*good!* But if you do not worship, you shall be cast immediately into the midst of a burning fiery furnace. [b]And who *is* the god who will deliver you from my hands?"

16 Shadrach, Meshach, and Abed-Nego answered and said to the king, "O Nebuchadnezzar, [a]we have no need to answer you in this matter.

17 "If that *is the case*, our [a]God whom we serve is able to [b]deliver us from the burning fiery furnace, and He will deliver *us* from your hand, O king.

18 "But if not, let it be known to you, O king, that we do not serve your gods, nor will we [a]worship the gold image which you have set up."

Saved in Fiery Trial

19 Then Nebuchadnezzar was full of fury, and the expression on his face changed toward Shadrach, Meshach, and Abed-Nego. He spoke and commanded that they heat the furnace seven times more than it was usually heated.

20 And he commanded certain mighty men of valor who *were* in his army to bind Shadrach, Meshach, and Abed-Nego, *and* cast *them* into the burning fiery furnace.

21 Then these men were bound in their coats, their trousers, their turbans, and their *other* garments, and were cast into the midst of the burning fiery furnace.

22 Therefore, because the king's command was urgent, and the furnace exceedingly hot, the

---

CHAPTER 3

4 [a]Dan. 4:1; 6:25
6 [a]Jer. 29:22; Ezek. 22:18–22; Matt. 13:42, 50; Rev. 9:2; 13:15; 14:11
8 [a]Ezra 4:12–16; Esth. 3:8, 9; Dan. 6:12, 13
9 [a]Dan. 2:4; 5:10; 6:6, 21
12 [a]Dan. 2:49 [b]Dan. 1:8; 6:12, 13
13 [a]Dan. 2:12; 3:19
15 [a]Ex. 32:32; Luke 13:9 [b]Ex. 5:2; 2 Kin. 18:35; Is. 36:18–20; Dan. 2:47
16 [a][Matt. 10:19]
17 [a]Job 5:19; [Ps. 27:1, 2; Is. 26:3, 4]; Jer. 1:8; 15:20, 21; Dan. 6:19–22 [b]1 Sam. 17:37; Jer. 1:8; 15:20, 21; 42:11; Dan. 6:16, 19–22; Mic. 7:7; 2 Cor. 1:10
18 [a]Job 13:15

KJV

the flame of the fire slew those men that took up
Shadrach, Meshach, and Abed–nego.
23 And these three men, Shadrach, Meshach,
and Abed–nego, fell down bound into the midst
of the burning fiery furnace.
24 Then Nebuchadnezzar the king was astonied, and rose up in haste, *and* spake, and said
unto his counsellors, Did not we cast three men
bound into the midst of the fire? They answered
and said unto the king, True, O king.
25 He answered and said, Lo, I see four men
loose, [a]walking in the midst of the fire, and they
have no hurt; and the form of the fourth is like
[b]the Son of God.

Nebuchadnezzar Praises God

26 Then Nebuchadnezzar came near to the
mouth of the burning fiery furnace, *and* spake,
and said, Shadrach, Meshach, and Abed–nego, ye
servants of the [a]most high God, come forth, and
come *hither*. Then Shadrach, Meshach, and
Abed–nego, came forth of the midst of the fire.
27 And the princes, governors, and captains,
and the king's counsellors, being gathered together, saw these men, [a]upon whose bodies the
fire had no power, nor was an hair of their head
singed, neither were their coats changed, nor the
smell of fire had passed on them.
28 *Then* Nebuchadnezzar spake, and said,
Blessed *be* the God of Shadrach, Meshach, and
Abed–nego, who hath sent his [a]angel, and delivered his servants that trusted in him, and have
changed the king's word, and yielded their bodies,
that they might not serve nor worship any god,
except their own God.
29 [a]Therefore I make a decree, That every
people, nation, and language, which speak any
thing amiss against the [b]God of Shadrach, Meshach, and Abed–nego, shall be [c]cut in pieces, and
their houses shall be made a dunghill: [d]because
there is no other God that can deliver after this
sort.
30 Then the king promoted Shadrach, Meshach, and Abed–nego, in the province of Babylon.

Nebuchadnezzar's Second Dream

4 Nebuchadnezzar the king, [a]unto all people,
nations, and languages, that dwell in all the
earth; Peace be multiplied unto you.
2 I thought it good to shew the signs and
wonders [a]that the high God hath wrought toward
me.
3 [a]How great *are* his signs! and how mighty
are his wonders! his kingdom *is* [b]an everlasting
kingdom, and his dominion *is* from generation to
generation.
4 I Nebuchadnezzar was at rest in mine
house, and flourishing in my palace:
5 I saw a dream which made me afraid, [a]and
the thoughts upon my bed and the visions of my
head [b]troubled me.
6 Therefore made I a decree to bring in all
the wise *men* of Babylon before me, that they
might make known unto me the interpretation of
the dream.
7 [a]Then came in the magicians, the astrologers, the Chaldeans, and the soothsayers: and I
told the dream before them; but they did not make
known unto me the interpretation thereof.
8 But at the last Daniel came in before me,
[a]whose name *was* Belteshazzar, according to the
name of my god, [b]and in whom *is* the spirit of
the holy gods: and before him I told the dream,
saying,

25 [a][Ps. 91:3–9]; Is. 43:2 [b]Job 1:6; 38:7; [Ps. 34:7]; Dan. 3:28
26 [a][Dan. 4:2, 3, 17, 34, 35]
27 [a][Is. 43:2]; Heb. 11:34
28 [a][Ps. 34:7, 8]; Is. 37:36; [Jer. 17:7]; Dan. 6:22, 23; Acts 5:19; 12:7
29 [a]Dan. 6:26 [b]Dan. 2:46, 47; 4:34–37 [c]Ezra 6:11; Dan. 2:5 [d]Dan. 6:27

CHAPTER 4

1 [a]Ezra 4:17; Dan. 3:4; 6:25
2 [a]Dan. 3:26
3 [a]2 Sam. 7:16; Ps. 89:35–37; Dan. 6:27; 7:13, 14; [Luke 1:31–33] [b][Dan. 2:44; 4:34; 6:26]
5 [a]Dan. 2:28, 29 [b]Dan. 2:1
7 [a]Dan. 2:2
8 [a]Dan. 1:7 [b]Is. 63:11; Dan. 2:11; 4:18; 5:11, 14

*———
3:25 Or *a son of the gods*
3:28 Or *angel*

NKJV

flame of the fire killed those men who took up
Shadrach, Meshach, and Abed-Nego.
23 And these three men, Shadrach, Meshach,
and Abed-Nego, fell down bound into the midst
of the burning fiery furnace.
24 Then King Nebuchadnezzar was astonished; and he rose in haste *and* spoke, saying to
his counselors, "Did we not cast three men bound
into the midst of the fire?" They answered and
said to the king, "True, O king."
25 "Look!" he answered, "I see four men
loose, [a]walking in the midst of the fire; and they
are not hurt, and the form of the fourth is like
[b]the* Son of God."

Nebuchadnezzar Praises God

26 Then Nebuchadnezzar went near the
mouth of the burning fiery furnace *and* spoke,
saying, "Shadrach, Meshach, and Abed-Nego,
servants of the [a]Most High God, come out, and
come *here*." Then Shadrach, Meshach, and Abed-
Nego came from the midst of the fire.
27 And the satraps, administrators, governors, and the king's counselors gathered together,
and they saw these men [a]on whose bodies the
fire had no power; the hair of their head was not
singed nor were their garments affected, and the
smell of fire was not on them.
28 Nebuchadnezzar spoke, saying, "Blessed
be the God of Shadrach, Meshach, and Abed-
Nego, who sent His [a]Angel* and delivered His servants who trusted in Him, and they have frustrated the king's word, and yielded their bodies,
that they should not serve nor worship any god
except their own God!
29 [a]"Therefore I make a decree that any people, nation, or language which speaks anything
amiss against the [b]God of Shadrach, Meshach,
and Abed-Nego shall be [c]cut in pieces, and their
houses shall be made an ash heap; [d]because there
is no other God who can deliver like this."
30 Then the king promoted Shadrach, Meshach, and Abed-Nego in the province of Babylon.

Nebuchadnezzar's Second Dream

4 Nebuchadnezzar the king,

[a]To all peoples, nations, and languages
that dwell in all the earth:

Peace be multiplied to you.

2 I thought it good to declare the signs and
wonders [a]that the Most High God has
worked for me.

3 [a]How great *are* His signs,
And how mighty His wonders!
His kingdom *is* [b]an everlasting kingdom,
And His dominion *is* from generation to
generation.

4 I, Nebuchadnezzar, was at rest in my
house, and flourishing in my palace.
5 I saw a dream which made me afraid, [a]and
the thoughts on my bed and the visions
of my head [b]troubled me.
6 Therefore I issued a decree to bring in all
the wise *men* of Babylon before me, that
they might make known to me the
interpretation of the dream.
7 [a]Then the magicians, the astrologers, the
Chaldeans, and the soothsayers came in,
and I told them the dream; but they did
not make known to me its interpretation.
8 But at last Daniel came before me [a](his
name *is* Belteshazzar, according to the
name of my god; [b]in him *is* the Spirit of
the Holy God), and I told the dream before
him, *saying:*

KJV

9 O Belteshazzar, [a]master of the magicians, because I know that the spirit of the holy gods *is* in thee, and no secret troubleth thee, tell me the visions of my dream that I have seen, and the interpretation thereof.

10 Thus *were* the visions of mine head in my bed; I saw, and behold [a]a tree in the midst of the earth, and the height thereof *was* great.

11 The tree grew, and was strong, and the height thereof reached unto heaven, and the sight thereof to the end of all the earth:

12 The leaves thereof *were* fair, and the fruit thereof much, and in it *was* meat for all: [a]the beasts of the field had shadow under it, and the fowls of the heaven dwelt in the boughs thereof, and all flesh was fed of it.

13 I saw in the visions of my head upon my bed, and, behold, [a]a watcher and [b]an holy one came down from heaven;

14 He cried aloud, and said thus, [a]Hew down the tree, and cut off his branches, shake off his leaves, and scatter his fruit: [b]let the beasts get away from under it, and the fowls from his branches:

15 Nevertheless leave the stump of his roots in the earth, even with a band of iron and brass, in the tender grass of the field; and let it be wet with the dew of heaven, and *let* his portion *be* with the beasts in the grass of the earth:

16 Let his heart be changed from man's, and let a beast's heart be given unto him; and let seven [a]times pass over him.

17 This matter *is* by the decree of the watchers, and the demand by the word of the holy ones: to the intent [a]that the living may know [b]that the most High ruleth in the kingdom of men, and [c]giveth it to whomsoever he will, and setteth up over it the [d]basest of men.

18 This dream I king Nebuchadnezzar have seen. Now thou, O Belteshazzar, declare the interpretation thereof, [a]forasmuch as all the wise *men* of my kingdom are not able to make known unto me the interpretation: but thou *art* able; [b]for the spirit of the holy gods *is* in thee.

Daniel Explains the Second Dream

19 Then Daniel, [a]whose name *was* Belteshazzar, was astonied for one hour, and his thoughts [b]troubled him. The king spake, and said, Belteshazzar, let not the dream, or the interpretation thereof, trouble thee. Belteshazzar answered and said, My lord, [c]the dream *be* to them that hate thee, and the interpretation thereof to thine enemies.

20 [a]The tree that thou sawest, which grew, and was strong, whose height reached unto the heaven, and the sight thereof to all the earth;

21 Whose leaves *were* fair, and the fruit

---

9 [a]Dan. 2:48; 5:11
10 [a]Ezek. 31:3; Dan. 4:20
12 [a]Jer. 27:6; Ezek. 17:23; 31:6; Lam. 4:20
13 [a][Dan. 4:17, 23] [b]Deut. 33:2; Ps. 89:7; Dan. 8:13; Zech. 14:5; Jude 14
14 [a]Ezek. 31:10–14; Dan. 4:23; [Matt. 3:10; 7:19; Luke 13:7–9] [b]Ezek. 31:12, 13; Dan. 4:12
16 [a]Dan. 11:13; 12:7
17 [a]Ps. 9:16; 83:18 [b]Dan. 2:21; 4:25, 32; 5:21 [c]Jer. 27:5–7; Ezek. 29:18–20; Dan. 2:37; 5:18 [d]1 Sam. 2:8; Dan. 11:21
18 [a]Gen. 41:8, 15; Dan. 5:8, 15 [b]Dan. 4:8, 9; 5:11, 14
19 [a]Dan. 4:8 [b]Jer. 4:19; Dan. 7:15, 28; 8:27 [c]2 Sam. 18:32; Jer. 29:7; Dan. 4:24; 10:16
20 [a]Dan. 4:10–12

*4:16 Possibly *years*

NKJV

9 "Belteshazzar, [a]chief of the magicians, because I know that the Spirit of the Holy God *is* in you, and no secret troubles you, explain to me the visions of my dream that I have seen, and its interpretation.

10 "These *were* the visions of my head *while* on my bed:

"I was looking, and behold,
[a]A tree in the midst of the earth,
And its height was great.
11 The tree grew and became strong;
Its height reached to the heavens,
And it could be seen to the ends of all the earth.
12 Its leaves *were* lovely,
Its fruit abundant,
And in it *was* food for all.
[a]The beasts of the field found shade under it,
The birds of the heavens dwelt in its branches,
And all flesh was fed from it.

13 "I saw in the visions of my head *while* on my bed, and there was [a]a watcher, [b]a holy one, coming down from heaven.

14 He cried aloud and said thus:

[a]'Chop down the tree and cut off its branches,
Strip off its leaves and scatter its fruit.
[b]Let the beasts get out from under it,
And the birds from its branches.
15 Nevertheless leave the stump and roots in the earth,
Bound with a band of iron and bronze,
In the tender grass of the field.
Let it be wet with the dew of heaven,
And *let* him graze with the beasts
On the grass of the earth.
16 Let his heart be changed from *that of* a man,
Let him be given the heart of a beast,
And let seven [a]times* pass over him.

17 'This decision *is* by the decree of the watchers,
And the sentence by the word of the holy ones,
In order [a]that the living may know
[b]That the Most High rules in the kingdom of men,
[c]Gives it to whomever He will,
And sets over it the [d]lowest of men.'

18 "This dream I, King Nebuchadnezzar, have seen. Now you, Belteshazzar, declare its interpretation, [a]since all the wise *men* of my kingdom are not able to make known to me the interpretation; but you *are* able, [b]for the Spirit of the Holy God *is* in you."

Daniel Explains the Second Dream

19 Then Daniel, [a]whose name was Belteshazzar, was astonished for a time, and his thoughts [b]troubled him. *So* the king spoke, and said, "Belteshazzar, do not let the dream or its interpretation trouble you." Belteshazzar answered and said, "My lord, *may* [c]the dream concern those who hate you, and its interpretation concern your enemies!

20 [a]The tree that you saw, which grew and became strong, whose height reached to the heavens and which *could be seen* by all the earth,

21 whose leaves *were* lovely and its fruit

KJV

thereof much, and in it *was* meat for all; under which the beasts of the field dwelt, and upon whose branches the fowls of the heaven had their habitation:

22 [a]It *is* thou, O king, that art grown and become strong: for thy greatness is grown, and reacheth unto heaven, [b]and thy dominion to the end of the earth.

23 [a]And whereas the king saw a watcher and an holy one coming down from heaven, and saying, Hew the tree down, and destroy it; yet leave the stump of the roots thereof in the earth, even with a band of iron and brass, in the tender grass of the field; and let it be wet with the dew of heaven, [b]and *let* his portion *be* with the beasts of the field, till seven times pass over him;

24 This *is* the interpretation, O king, and this *is* the decree of the most High, which is come upon my lord the king:

25 That they shall [a]drive thee from men, and thy dwelling shall be with the beasts of the field, and they shall make thee [b]to eat grass as oxen, and they shall wet thee with the dew of heaven, and seven times shall pass over thee, [c]till thou know that the most High ruleth in the kingdom of men, and [d]giveth it to whomsoever he will.

26 And whereas they commanded to leave the stump of the tree roots; thy kingdom shall be sure unto thee, after that thou shalt have known that the [a]heavens do rule.

27 Wherefore, O king, let my counsel be acceptable unto thee, and [a]break off thy sins by righteousness, and thine iniquities by shewing mercy to the poor; [b]if it may be [c]a lengthening of thy tranquillity.

Nebuchadnezzar's Humiliation

28 All this came upon the king Nebuchadnezzar.

29 At the end of twelve months he walked in the palace of the kingdom of Babylon.

30 The king [a]spake, and said, Is not this great Babylon, that I have built for the house of the kingdom by the might of my power, and for the honour of my majesty?

31 [a]While the word *was* in the king's mouth, there fell [b]a voice from heaven, *saying,* O king Nebuchadnezzar, to thee it is spoken; The kingdom is departed from thee.

32 And [a]they shall drive thee from men, and thy dwelling *shall be* with the beasts of the field: they shall make thee to eat grass as oxen, and seven times shall pass over thee, until thou know that the most High ruleth in the kingdom of men, and giveth it to whomsoever he will.

33 The same hour was the thing fulfilled upon Nebuchadnezzar: and he was driven from men, and did eat grass as oxen, and his body was wet with the dew of heaven, till his hairs were grown like eagles' *feathers,* and his nails like birds' *claws.*

Nebuchadnezzar Praises God

34 And [a]at the end of the days I Nebuchadnezzar lifted up mine eyes unto heaven, and mine understanding returned unto me, and I blessed the most High, and I praised and honoured him [b]that liveth for ever, whose dominion *is* [c]an everlasting dominion, and his kingdom *is* from generation to generation:

22 [a]Dan. 2:37, 38 [b]Jer. 27:6–8 **23** [a]Dan. 4:13–15 [b]Dan. 5:21 **25** [a]Dan. 4:32; 5:21 [b]Ps. 106:20 [c]Ps. 83:18; Dan. 4:2; 17:32 [d]Jer. 27:5 **26** [a]Matt. 21:25; Luke 15:18 **27** [a][Prov. 28:13]; Is. 55:7; Ezek. 18:21, 22; [Rom. 2:9–11; 1 Pet. 4:8] [b][Ps. 41:1–3]; Is. 58:6, 7, 10 [c]1 Kin. 21:29 **30** [a]Prov. 16:18; Is. 13:19; Dan. 5:20 **31** [a]Dan. 5:5; Luke 12:20 [b]Dan. 4:24 **32** [a][Dan. 4:25] **34** [a]Dan. 4:26 [b]Ps. 102:24–27; Dan. 6:26; 12:7; [Rev. 4:10] [c][Ps. 10:16]; Dan. 2:44; 7:14; Mic. 4:7; [Luke 1:33]

NKJV

abundant, in which *was* food for all, under which the beasts of the field dwelt, and in whose branches the birds of the heaven had their home—

22 [a]it *is* you, O king, who have grown and become strong; for your greatness has grown and reaches to the heavens, [b]and your dominion to the end of the earth.

23 [a]And inasmuch as the king saw a watcher, a holy one, coming down from heaven and saying, 'Chop down the tree and destroy it, but leave its stump and roots in the earth, *bound* with a band of iron and bronze in the tender grass of the field; let it be wet with the dew of heaven, [b]and let him graze with the beasts of the field, till seven times pass over him';

24 this is the interpretation, O king, and this is the decree of the Most High, which has come upon my lord the king:

25 They shall [a]drive you from men, your dwelling shall be with the beasts of the field, and they shall make you [b]eat grass like oxen. They shall wet you with the dew of heaven, and seven times shall pass over you, [c]till you know that the Most High rules in the kingdom of men, and [d]gives it to whomever He chooses.

26 And inasmuch as they gave the command to leave the stump *and* roots of the tree, your kingdom shall be assured to you, after you come to know that [a]Heaven rules.

27 Therefore, O king, let my advice be acceptable to you; [a]break off your sins by *being* righteous, and your iniquities by showing mercy to *the* poor. [b]Perhaps there may be [c]a lengthening of your prosperity."

Nebuchadnezzar's Humiliation

28 All *this* came upon King Nebuchadnezzar.

29 At the end of the twelve months he was walking about the royal palace of Babylon.

30 The king [a]spoke, saying, "Is not this great Babylon, that I have built for a royal dwelling by my mighty power and for the honor of my majesty?"

31 [a]While the word *was still* in the king's mouth, [b]a voice fell from heaven: "King Nebuchadnezzar, to you it is spoken: the kingdom has departed from you!

32 And [a]they shall drive you from men, and your dwelling *shall be* with the beasts of the field. They shall make you eat grass like oxen; and seven times shall pass over you, until you know that the Most High rules in the kingdom of men, and gives it to whomever He chooses."

33 That very hour the word was fulfilled concerning Nebuchadnezzar; he was driven from men and ate grass like oxen; his body was wet with the dew of heaven till his hair had grown like eagles' *feathers* and his nails like birds' *claws.*

Nebuchadnezzar Praises God

34 And [a]at the end of the *time I, Nebuchadnezzar, lifted my eyes to heaven, and my understanding returned to me; and I blessed the Most High and praised and honored Him [b]who lives forever:

For His dominion *is* [c]an everlasting
dominion,
And His kingdom *is* from generation to
generation.

*———
4:34 Lit. *days*

KJV

35 And [a]all the inhabitants of the earth *are* reputed as nothing: and [b]he doeth according to his will in the army of heaven, and *among* the inhabitants of the earth: and [c]none can stay his hand, or say unto him, [d]What doest thou?

36 At the same time my reason returned unto me; [a]and for the glory of my kingdom, mine honour andbrightness returned unto me; and my counsellors and my lords sought unto me; and I was [b]established in my kingdom, and excellent majesty was [c]added unto me.

37 Now I Nebuchadnezzar [a]praise and extol and honour the King of heaven, [b]all whose works *are* truth, and his ways judgment: [c]and those that walk in pride he is able to abase.

Belshazzar's Feast

5 Belshazzar the king [a]made a great feast to a thousand of his lords, and drank wine before the thousand.

2 Belshazzar, whiles he tasted the wine, commanded to bring the golden and silver vessels [a]which his father Nebuchadnezzar had taken out of the temple which *was* in Jerusalem; that the king, and his princes, his wives, and his concubines, might drink therein.

3 Then they brought the golden [a]vessels that were taken out of the temple of the house of God which *was* at Jerusalem; and the king, and his princes, his wives, and his concubines, drank in them.

4 They drank wine, [a]and praised the gods of gold, and of silver, of brass, of iron, of wood, and of stone.

5 [a]In the same hour came forth fingers of a man's hand, and wrote over against the candlestick upon the plaister of the wall of the king's palace: and the king saw the part of the hand that wrote.

6 Then the king's countenance was changed, and his thoughts troubled him, so that the joints of his loins were loosed, and his [a]knees smote one against another.

7 [a]The king cried aloud to bring in [b]the astrologers, the Chaldeans, and the soothsayers. *And* the king spake, and said to the wise *men* of Babylon, Whosoever shall read this writing, and shew me the interpretation thereof, shall be clothed with scarlet, and *have* a chain of gold about his neck, [c]and shall be the third ruler in the kingdom.

8 Then came in all the king's wise *men:* [a]but they could not read the writing, nor make known to the king the interpretation thereof.

9 Then was king Belshazzar greatly [a]troubled, and his countenance was changed in him, and his lords were astonied.

10 *Now* the queen by reason of the words of the king and his lords came into the banquet house: *and* the queen spake and said, O king, live for ever: let not thy thoughts trouble thee, nor let thy countenance be changed:

11 [a]There is a man in thy kingdom, in whom *is* the spirit of the holy gods; and in the days of thy father light and understanding and wisdom, like the wisdom of the gods, was found in him; whom the king Nebuchadnezzar thy father, the king, *I say,* thy father, made master of the magicians, astrologers, Chaldeans, *and* soothsayers;

12 Forasmuch as an excellent spirit, and knowledge, and understanding, interpreting of dreams, and shewing of hard sentences, and dissolving of doubts, were found in the same Daniel, [a]whom the king named Belteshazzar: now let Daniel be called, and he will shew the interpretation.

35 [a]Ps. 39:5; Is. 40:15, 17 [b]Ps. 115:3; 135:6; Dan. 6:27 [c]Job 34:29; Is. 43:13 [d]Job 9:12; Is. 45:9; Jer. 18:6; Rom. 9:20; [1 Cor. 2:16]
36 [a]Dan. 4:26 [b]2 Chr. 20:20 [c]Job 42:12; [Prov. 22:4; Matt. 6:33]
37 [a]Dan. 2:46, 47; 3:28, 29 [b]Deut. 32:4; [Ps. 33:4]; Is. 5:16; [Rev. 15:3] [c]Ex. 18:11; Job 40:11, 12; Dan. 5:20

CHAPTER 5

1 [a]Esth. 1:3; Is. 22:12–14
2 [a]2 Kin. 24:13; 25:15; Ezra 1:7–11; Jer. 52:19; Dan. 1:2
3 [a]2 Chr. 36:10
4 [a]Is. 42:8; Dan. 5:23; Rev. 9:20
5 [a]Dan. 4:31
6 [a]Dan. 4:6
7 [a]Dan. 4:6, 7; 5:11, 15 [b]Is. 47:13 [c]Dan. 6:2, 3
8 [a]Gen. 41:8; Dan. 2:27; 4:7; 5:15
9 [a]Job 18:11; Is. 21:2–4; Jer. 6:24; Dan. 2:1; 5:6
11 [a]Dan. 2:48; 4:8, 9, 18
12 [a]Dan. 1:7; 4:8

*5:12 Lit. *untying knots*

NKJV

35 [a]All the inhabitants of the earth *are* reputed as nothing;
[b]He does according to His will in the army of heaven
And *among* the inhabitants of the earth.
[c]No one can restrain His hand
Or say to Him, [d]"What have You done?"

36 At the same time my reason returned to me, [a]and for the glory of my kingdom, my honor and splendor returned to me. My counselors and nobles resorted to me, I was [b]restored to my kingdom, and excellent majesty was [c]added to me.

37 Now I, Nebuchadnezzar, [a]praise and extol and honor the King of heaven, [b]all of whose works *are* truth, and His ways justice. [c]And those who walk in pride He is able to put down.

Belshazzar's Feast

5 Belshazzar the king [a]made a great feast for a thousand of his lords, and drank wine in the presence of the thousand.

2 While he tasted the wine, Belshazzar gave the command to bring the gold and silver vessels [a]which his father Nebuchadnezzar had taken from the temple which *had been* in Jerusalem, that the king and his lords, his wives, and his concubines might drink from them.

3 Then they brought the gold [a]vessels that had been taken from the temple of the house of God which *had been* in Jerusalem; and the king and his lords, his wives, and his concubines drank from them.

4 They drank wine, [a]and praised the gods of gold and silver, bronze and iron, wood and stone.

5 [a]In the same hour the fingers of a man's hand appeared and wrote opposite the lampstand on the plaster of the wall of the king's palace; and the king saw the part of the hand that wrote.

6 Then the king's countenance changed, and his thoughts troubled him, so that the joints of his hips were loosened and his [a]knees knocked against each other.

7 [a]The king cried aloud to bring in [b]the astrologers, the Chaldeans, and the soothsayers. The king spoke, saying to the wise *men* of Babylon, "Whoever reads this writing, and tells me its interpretation, shall be clothed with purple and *have* a chain of gold around his neck; [c]and he shall be the third ruler in the kingdom."

8 Now all the king's wise *men* came, [a]but they could not read the writing, or make known to the king its interpretation.

9 Then King Belshazzar was greatly [a]troubled, his countenance was changed, and his lords were astonished.

10 The queen, because of the words of the king and his lords, came to the banquet hall. The queen spoke, saying, "O king, live forever! Do not let your thoughts trouble you, nor let your countenance change.

11 [a]"There is a man in your kingdom in whom *is* the Spirit of the Holy God. And in the days of your father, light and understanding and wisdom, like the wisdom of the gods, were found in him; and King Nebuchadnezzar your father—your father the king—made him chief of the magicians, astrologers, Chaldeans, *and* soothsayers.

12 "Inasmuch as an excellent spirit, knowledge, understanding, interpreting dreams, solving riddles, and *explaining enigmas were found in this Daniel, [a]whom the king named Belteshazzar, now let Daniel be called, and he will give the interpretation."

KJV

The Writing on the Wall Explained

13 Then was Daniel brought in before the king. *And* the king spake and said unto Daniel, *Art* thou that Daniel, which *art* of the children of the captivity of Judah, whom the king my father brought out of Jewry?

14 I have even heard of thee, that [a]the spirit of the gods *is* in thee, and *that* light and understanding and excellent wisdom is found in thee.

15 And now [a]the wise *men,* the astrologers, have been brought in before me, that they should read this writing, and make known unto me the interpretation thereof: but they could not shew the interpretation of the thing:

16 And I have heard of thee, that thou canst make interpretations, and dissolve doubts: [a]now if thou canst read the writing, and make known to me the interpretation thereof, thou shalt be clothed with scarlet, and *have* a chain of gold about thy neck, and shalt be the third ruler in the kingdom.

17 Then Daniel answered and said before the king, Let thy gifts be to thyself, and give thy rewards to another; yet I will read the writing unto the king, and make known to him the interpretation.

18 O thou king, [a]the most high God gave Nebuchadnezzar thy father a kingdom, and majesty, and glory, and honour:

19 And for the majesty that he gave him, [a]all people, nations, and languages, trembled and feared before him: whom he would he [b]slew; and whom he would he kept alive; and whom he would he set up; and whom he would he put down.

20 [a]But when his heart was lifted up, and his mind hardened in pride, he was deposed from his kingly throne, and they took his glory from him:

21 And he was [a]driven from the sons of men; and his heart was made like the beasts, and his dwelling *was* with the wild asses: they fed him with grass like oxen, and his body was wet with the dew of heaven; [b]till he knew that the most high God ruled in the kingdom of men, and *that* he appointeth over it whomsoever he will.

22 And thou his son, O Belshazzar, [a]hast not humbled thine heart, though thou knewest all this;

23 [a]But hast lifted up thyself against the LORD of heaven; and they have brought the [b]vessels of his house before thee, and thou, and thy lords, thy wives, and thy concubines, have drunk wine in them; and thou hast praised the gods of silver, and gold, of brass, iron, wood, and stone, [c]which see not, nor hear, nor know: and the God in whose hand thy breath *is,* [d]and whose *are* all thy ways, hast thou not glorified:

24 Then was the part of the hand sent from him; and this writing was written.

25 And this *is* the writing that was written, MENE, MENE, TEKEL, UPHARSIN.

26 This *is* the interpretation of the thing: MENE; God hath numbered thy kingdom, and finished it.

27 TEKEL; [a]Thou art weighed in the balances, and art found wanting.

28 PERES; Thy kingdom is divided, and given to the [a]Medes and [b]Persians.

29 Then commanded Belshazzar, and they clothed Daniel with scarlet, and *put* a chain of gold about his neck, and made a proclamation concerning him, [a]that he should be the third ruler in the kingdom.

Belshazzar's Fall

30 [a]In that night was Belshazzar the king of the Chaldeans slain.

31 [a]And Darius the Median took the kingdom, *being* about threescore and two years old.

14 [a]Dan. 4:8, 9, 18; 5:11, 12
15 [a]Dan. 5:7, 8
16 [a]Dan. 5:7, 29
18 [a]Jer. 27:5–7; Dan. 2:37, 38; 4:17, 22, 25
19 [a]Jer. 27:7 [b]Dan. 2:12, 13; 3:6
20 [a]Ex. 9:17; Job 15:25; Is. 14:13–15; Dan. 4:30, 37
21 [a]Job 30:3–7; Dan. 4:32, 33 [b]Ex. 9:14–16; Ps. 83:17, 18; Ezek. 17:24; [Dan. 4:17, 34, 35]
22 [a]Ex. 10:3; 2 Chr. 33:23; 36:12
23 [a]Dan. 5:3, 4 [b]Ex. 40:9; Num. 18:3; Is. 52:11; Heb. 9:21 [c]Ps. 115:5, 6; Is. 37:19; Hab. 2:18, 19; Acts 17:24–26; Rom. 1:21 [d]Ps. 139:3; Prov. 20:24; [Jer. 10:23]
27 [a]Job 31:6; Ps. 62:9; Jer. 6:30
28 [a]Is. 21:2; Dan. 5:31; 9:1 [b]Dan. 6:28; Acts 2:9
29 [a]Dan. 5:7, 16
30 [a]Jer. 51:31, 39, 57
31 [a]Dan. 2:39; 9:1

NKJV

The Writing on the Wall Explained

13 Then Daniel was brought in before the king. The king spoke, and said to Daniel, "*Are* you that Daniel *who is one of the captives from Judah, whom my father the king brought from Judah?

14 "I have heard of you, that [a]the Spirit of God *is* in you, and *that* light and understanding and excellent wisdom are found in you.

15 "Now [a]the wise *men,* the astrologers, have been brought in before me, that they should read this writing and make known to me its interpretation, but they could not give the interpretation of the thing.

16 "And I have heard of you, that you can give interpretations and explain enigmas. [a]Now if you can read the writing and make known to me its interpretation, you shall be clothed with purple and *have* a chain of gold around your neck, and shall be the third ruler in the kingdom."

17 Then Daniel answered, and said before the king, "Let your gifts be for yourself, and give your rewards to another; yet I will read the writing to the king, and make known to him the interpretation.

18 "O king, [a]the Most High God gave Nebuchadnezzar your father a kingdom and majesty, glory and honor.

19 "And because of the majesty that He gave him, [a]all peoples, nations, and languages trembled and feared before him. Whomever he wished, he [b]executed; whomever he wished, he kept alive; whomever he wished, he set up; and whomever he wished, he put down.

20 [a]"But when his heart was lifted up, and his spirit was hardened in pride, he was deposed from his kingly throne, and they took his glory from him.

21 "Then he was [a]driven from the sons of men, his heart was made like the beasts, and his dwelling *was* with the wild donkeys. They fed him with grass like oxen, and his body was wet with the dew of heaven, [b]till he knew that the Most High God rules in the kingdom of men, and appoints over it whomever He chooses.

22 "But you his son, Belshazzar, [a]have not humbled your heart, although you knew all this.

23 [a]"And you have lifted yourself up against the Lord of heaven. They have brought the [b]vessels of His house before you, and you and your lords, your wives and your concubines, have drunk wine from them. And you have praised the gods of silver and gold, bronze and iron, wood and stone, [c]which do not see or hear or know; and the God who *holds* your breath in His hand [d]and owns all your ways, you have not glorified.

24 "Then the *fingers of the hand were sent from Him, and this writing was written.

25 "And this is the inscription that was written:

*MENE, MENE, *TEKEL, *UPHARSIN.

26 "This *is* the interpretation of *each* word. MENE: God has numbered your kingdom, and finished it;

27 "TEKEL: [a]You have been weighed in the balances, and found wanting;

28 "PERES: Your kingdom has been divided, and given to the [a]Medes and [b]Persians."*

29 Then Belshazzar gave the command, and they clothed Daniel with purple and *put* a chain of gold around his neck, and made a proclamation concerning him [a]that he should be the third ruler in the kingdom.

Belshazzar's Fall

30 [a]That very night Belshazzar, king of the Chaldeans, was slain.

31 [a]And Darius the Mede received the kingdom, *being* about sixty-two years old.

5:13 Lit. *who is of the sons of the captivity*
5:24 Lit. *palm*
5:25 Lit. *a mina* (50 shekels) from the verb "to number" • Lit. *a shekel* from the verb "to weigh" • Lit. *and half-shekels* from the verb "to divide"; pl. of *Peres,* v. 28
5:28 Aram. *Paras,* consonant with *Peres*

KJV

The Plot Against Daniel

6 It pleased Darius to set over the kingdom an hundred and twenty princes, which should be over the whole kingdom;

2 And over these three presidents; of whom Daniel *was* first: that the princes might give accounts unto them, and the king should have no damage.

3 Then this Daniel was preferred above the presidents and princes, [a]because an excellent spirit *was* in him; and the king thought to set him over the whole realm.

4 [a]Then the presidents and princes sought to find occasion against Daniel concerning the kingdom; but they could find none occasion nor fault; forasmuch as he *was* faithful, neither was there any error or fault found in him.

5 Then said these men, We shall not find any occasion against this Daniel, except we find *it* against him concerning the law of his God.

6 Then these presidents and princes assembled together to the king, and said thus unto him, [a]King Darius, live for ever.

7 All the presidents of the kingdom, the governors, and the princes, the counsellors, and the captains, have [a]consulted together to establish a royal statute, and to make a firm decree, that whosoever shall ask a petition of any God or man for thirty days, save of thee, O king, he shall be cast into the den of lions.

8 Now, O king, establish the decree, and sign the writing, that it be not changed, according to the [a]law of the Medes and Persians, which altereth not.

9 Wherefore king Darius signed the writing and the decree.

Daniel in the Lions' Den

10 Now when Daniel knew that the writing was signed, he went into his house; and his windows being open in his chamber [a]toward Jerusalem, he kneeled upon his knees [b]three times a day, and prayed, and gave thanks before his God, as he did aforetime.

11 Then these men assembled, and found Daniel praying and making supplication before his God.

12 [a]Then they came near, and spake before the king concerning the king's decree; Hast thou not signed a decree, that every man that shall ask *a petition* of any God or man within thirty days, save of thee, O king, shall be cast into the den of lions? The king answered and said, The thing *is* true, [b]according to the law of the Medes and Persians, which altereth not.

13 Then answered they and said before the king, That Daniel, [a]which *is* of the children of the captivity of Judah, [b]regardeth not thee, O king, nor the decree that thou hast signed, but maketh his petition three times a day.

14 Then the king, when he heard *these* words, [a]was sore displeased with himself, and set *his* heart on Daniel to deliver him: and he laboured till the going down of the sun to deliver him.

15 Then these men assembled unto the king, and said unto the king, Know, O king, that [a]the law of the Medes and Persians *is*, That no decree nor statute which the king establisheth may be changed.

16 Then the king commanded, and they brought Daniel, and cast *him* into the den of lions. *Now* the king spake and said unto Daniel, Thy God whom thou servest continually, he will deliver thee.

17 [a]And a stone was brought, and laid upon the mouth of the den; [b]and the king sealed it with his own signet, and with the signet of his lords; that the purpose might not be changed concerning Daniel.

CHAPTER 6

3 [a]Dan. 5:12
4 [a]Eccl. 4:4
6 [a]Neh. 2:3; Dan. 2:4; 6:21
7 [a]Ps. 59:3; 62:4; 64:2–6
8 [a]Esth. 1:19; 8:8; Dan. 6:12, 15
10 [a]1 Kin. 8:29, 30, 46–48; Ps. 5:7; Jon. 2:4 [b]Ps. 55:17; Acts 2:1, 2, 15; [Phil. 4:6]; 1 Thess. 5:17, 18
12 [a]Dan. 3:8–12; Acts 16:19–21 [b]Esth. 1:19; Dan. 6:8, 15
13 [a]Dan. 1:6; 5:13 [b]Esth. 3:8; Dan. 3:12; Acts 5:29
14 [a]Mark 6:26
15 [a]Esth. 8:8; Ps. 94:20, 21; Dan. 6:8, 12
17 [a]Lam. 3:53 [b]Matt. 27:66

NKJV

The Plot Against Daniel

6 It pleased Darius to set over the kingdom one hundred and twenty satraps, to be over the whole kingdom;

2 and over these, three governors, of whom Daniel *was* one, that the satraps might give account to them, so that the king would suffer no loss.

3 Then this Daniel distinguished himself above the governors and satraps, [a]because an excellent spirit *was* in him; and the king gave thought to setting him over the whole realm.

4 [a]So the governors and satraps sought to find *some* charge against Daniel concerning the kingdom; but they could find no charge or fault, because he *was* faithful; nor was there any error or fault found in him.

5 Then these men said, "We shall not find any charge against this Daniel unless we find *it* against him concerning the law of his God."

6 So these governors and satraps thronged before the king, and said thus to him: [a]"King Darius, live forever!

7 "All the governors of the kingdom, the administrators and satraps, the counselors and advisors, have [a]consulted together to establish a royal statute and to make a firm decree, that whoever petitions any god or man for thirty days, except you, O king, shall be cast into the den of lions.

8 "Now, O king, establish the decree and sign the writing, so that it cannot be changed, according to the [a]law of the Medes and Persians, which does not alter."

9 Therefore King Darius signed the written decree.

Daniel in the Lions' Den

10 Now when Daniel knew that the writing was signed, he went home. And in his upper room, with his windows open [a]toward Jerusalem, he knelt down on his knees [b]three times that day, and prayed and gave thanks before his God, as was his custom since early days.

11 Then these men assembled and found Daniel praying and making supplication before his God.

12 [a]And they went before the king, and spoke concerning the king's decree: "Have you not signed a decree that every man who petitions any god or man within thirty days, except you, O king, shall be cast into the den of lions?" The king answered and said, "The thing *is* true, [b]according to the law of the Medes and Persians, which does not alter."

13 So they answered and said before the king, "That Daniel, [a]who is *one of the captives from Judah, [b]does not show due regard for you, O king, or for the decree that you have signed, but makes his petition three times a day."

14 And the king, when he heard *these* words, [a]was greatly displeased with himself, and set *his* heart on Daniel to deliver him; and he labored till the going down of the sun to deliver him.

15 Then these men approached the king, and said to the king, "Know, O king, that *it is* [a]the law of the Medes and Persians that no decree or statute which the king establishes may be changed."

16 So the king gave the command, and they brought Daniel and cast *him* into the den of lions. *But* the king spoke, saying to Daniel, "Your God, whom you serve continually, He will deliver you."

17 [a]Then a stone was brought and laid on the mouth of the den, [b]and the king sealed it with his own signet ring and with the signets of his lords, that the purpose concerning Daniel might not be changed.

---

*__6:13__ Lit. *of the sons of the captivity*

KJV

Daniel Saved from the Lions

18 Then the king went to his palace, and
passed the night fasting: neither were instruments
of musick brought before him: [a]and his sleep went
from him.
19 Then the [a]king arose very early in the
morning, and went in haste unto the den of lions.
20 And when he came to the den, he cried
with a lamentable voice unto Daniel: *and* the king
spake and said to Daniel, O Daniel, servant of
the living God, [a]is thy God, whom thou servest
continually, able to deliver thee from the lions?
21 Then said Daniel unto the king, [a]O king,
live for ever.
22 [a]My God hath sent his angel, and hath
[b]shut the lions' mouths, that they have not hurt
me: forasmuch as before him innocency was
found in me; and also before thee, O king, have
I done no hurt.
23 Then was the king exceeding glad for him,
and commanded that they should take Daniel up
out of the den. So Daniel was taken up out of
the den, and no manner of hurt was found upon
him, [a]because he believed in his God.

Darius Honors God

24 And the king commanded, [a]and they
brought those men which had accused Daniel, and
they cast *them* into the den of lions, them, [b]their
children, and their wives; and the lions had the
mastery of them, and brake all their bones in
pieces or ever they came at the bottom of the den.
25 [a]Then king Darius wrote unto all people,
nations, and languages, that dwell in all the earth;
Peace be multiplied unto you.
26 [a]I make a decree, That in every dominion
of my kingdom men [b]tremble and fear before the
God of Daniel: [c]for he *is* the living God, and stedfast for ever, and his kingdom *that* which shall
not be [d]destroyed, and his dominion *shall be even*
unto the end.
27 He delivereth and rescueth, [a]and he worketh signs and wonders in heaven and in earth,
who hath delivered Daniel from the power of the
lions.
28 So this Daniel prospered in the reign of
Darius, [a]and in the reign of [b]Cyrus the Persian.

Vision of the Four Beasts

7 In the first year of Belshazzar king of Babylon
[a]Daniel had a dream and [b]visions of his head
upon his bed: then he wrote the dream, *and* told
the sum of the matters.
2 Daniel spake and said, I saw in my vision
by night, and, behold, the four winds of the
heaven strove upon the great sea.
3 And four great beasts [a]came up from the
sea, diverse one from another.
4 The first *was* [a]like a lion, and had eagle's
wings: I beheld till the wings thereof were
plucked, and it was lifted up from the earth, and
made stand upon the feet as a man, and a [b]man's
heart was given to it.
5 [a]And behold another beast, a second, like
to a bear, and it raised up itself on one side, and
it had three ribs in the mouth of it between the
teeth of it: and they said thus unto it, Arise, devour
much flesh.
6 After this I beheld, and lo another, like a
leopard, which had upon the back of it four wings
of a fowl; the beast had also [a]four heads; and dominion was given to it.
7 After this I saw in the night visions, and

---

18 [a]Esth. 6:1; Ps. 77:4; Dan. 2:1
19 [a]Dan. 3:24
20 [a]Gen. 18:14; Num. 11:23; Jer. 32:17; Dan. 3:17; [Luke 1:37]
21 [a]Dan. 2:4; 6:6
22 [a]Num. 20:16; Is. 63:9; Dan. 3:28; Acts 12:11; [Heb. 1:14] [b]Ps. 91:11–13; 2 Tim. 4:17; Heb. 11:33
23 [a]Heb. 11:33
24 [a]Deut. 19:18, 19; Esth. 7:10 [b]Deut. 24:16; 2 Kin. 14:6; Esth. 9:10
25 [a]Ezra 1:1, 2; Esth. 3:12; 8:9; Dan. 4:1
26 [a]Ezra 6:8–12; 7:13; Dan. 3:29 [b]Ps. 99:1 [c]Dan. 4:34; 6:20; Hos. 1:10; Rom. 9:26 [d]Dan. 2:44; 4:3; 7:14, 27; [Luke 1:33]
27 [a]Dan. 4:2, 3
28 [a]Dan. 1:21 [b]Ezra 1:1, 2

CHAPTER 7

1 [a]Num. 12:6; [Amos 3:7] [b][Dan. 2:28]
3 [a]Dan. 7:17; Rev. 13:1; 17:8
4 [a]Deut. 28:49; 2 Sam. 1:23; Jer. 48:40; Ezek. 17:3; Hab. 1:8 [b]Dan. 4:16, 34
5 [a]Dan. 2:39
6 [a]Dan. 8:8, 22

*

6:18 Exact meaning unknown
7:1 Lit. *the head* or *chief of the words*

NKJV

Daniel Saved from the Lions

18 Now the king went to his palace and spent
the night fasting; and no *musicians were brought
before him. [a]Also his sleep went from him.
19 Then the [a]king arose very early in the
morning and went in haste to the den of lions.
20 And when he came to the den, he cried
out with a lamenting voice to Daniel. The king
spoke, saying to Daniel, "Daniel, servant of the
living God, [a]has your God, whom you serve continually, been able to deliver you from the lions?"
21 Then Daniel said to the king, [a]"O king,
live forever!
22 [a]"My God sent His angel and [b]shut the
lions' mouths, so that they have not hurt me, because I was found innocent before Him; and also,
O king, I have done no wrong before you."
23 Now the king was exceedingly glad for
him, and commanded that they should take Daniel
up out of the den. So Daniel was taken up out of
the den, and no injury whatever was found on
him, [a]because he believed in his God.

Darius Honors God

24 And the king gave the command, [a]and
they brought those men who had accused Daniel,
and they cast *them* into the den of lions—them,
[b]their children, and their wives; and the lions
overpowered them, and broke all their bones in
pieces before they ever came to the bottom of the
den.
25 [a]Then King Darius wrote:

To all peoples, nations, and languages that
dwell in all the earth:

Peace be multiplied to you.

26 [a]I make a decree that in every dominion
of my kingdom *men must* [b]tremble and
fear before the God of Daniel.

[c]For He *is* the living God,
And steadfast forever;
His kingdom *is the one* which shall not
be [d]destroyed,
And His dominion *shall endure* to the end.
27 He delivers and rescues,
[a]And He works signs and wonders
In heaven and on earth,
Who has delivered Daniel from the power
of the lions.

28 So this Daniel prospered in the reign of
Darius [a]and in the reign of [b]Cyrus the Persian.

Vision of the Four Beasts

7 In the first year of Belshazzar king of Babylon, [a]Daniel had a dream and [b]visions of his
head *while* on his bed. Then he wrote down the
dream, telling *the main facts.
2 Daniel spoke, saying, "I saw in my vision
by night, and behold, the four winds of heaven
were stirring up the Great Sea.
3 "And four great beasts [a]came up from the
sea, each different from the other.
4 "The first *was* [a]like a lion, and had eagle's
wings. I watched till its wings were plucked off;
and it was lifted up from the earth and made to
stand on two feet like a man, and a [b]man's heart
was given to it.
5 [a]"And suddenly another beast, a second,
like a bear. It was raised up on one side, and *had*
three ribs in its mouth between its teeth. And they
said thus to it: 'Arise, devour much flesh!'
6 "After this I looked, and there was another, like a leopard, which had on its back four
wings of a bird. The beast also had [a]four heads,
and dominion was given to it.
7 "After this I saw in the night visions, and

KJV

behold [a]a fourth beast, dreadful and terrible, and
strong exceedingly; and it had great iron teeth:
it devoured and brake in pieces, and stamped the
residue with the feet of it: and it *was* diverse from
all the beasts that *were* before it; [b]and it had ten
horns.
8 I considered the horns, and, behold, [a]there
came up among them another little horn, before
whom there were three of the first horns plucked
up by the roots: and, behold, in this horn *were*
eyes like the eyes [b]of man, [c]and a mouth speaking
great things.

Vision of the Ancient of Days

9 [a]I beheld till the thrones were cast down,
and [b]the Ancient of days did sit, [c]whose garment
was white as snow, and the hair of his head like
the pure wool: his throne *was like* the fiery flame,
[d]*and* his wheels *as* burning fire.
10 [a]A fiery stream issued and came forth
from before him: [b]thousand thousands ministered
unto him, and ten thousand times ten thousand
stood before him: [c]the judgment was set, and the
books were opened.
11 I beheld then because of the voice of the
great words which the horn spake: [a]I beheld *even*
till the beast was slain, and his body destroyed,
and given to the burning flame.
12 As concerning the rest of the beasts, they
had their dominion taken away: yet their lives
were prolonged for a season and time.
13 I saw in the night visions, and, behold,
[a]*one* like the Son of man came with the clouds
of heaven, and came to the Ancient of days, and
they brought him near before him.
14 [a]And there was given him dominion, and
glory, and a kingdom, that all [b]people, nations,
and languages, should serve him: his dominion
is [c]an everlasting dominion, which shall not pass
away, and his kingdom *that* which shall not be
destroyed.

Daniel's Visions Interpreted

15 I Daniel was grieved in my spirit in the
midst of *my* body, and the visions of my head
troubled me.
16 I came near unto one of them that stood
by, and asked him the truth of all this. So he told
me, and made me know the interpretation of the
things.
17 These great beasts, which are four, *are*
four kings, *which* shall arise out of the earth.
18 But [a]the saints of the most High shall take
the kingdom, and possess the kingdom for ever,
even for ever and ever.
19 Then I would know the truth of the fourth
beast, which was diverse from all the others, exceeding dreadful, whose teeth *were of* iron, and
his nails *of* brass; *which* devoured, brake in
pieces, and stamped the residue with his feet;
20 And of the ten horns that *were* in his head,
and *of* the other which came up, and before whom
three fell; even *of* that horn that had eyes, and a
mouth that spake very great things, whose look
was more stout than his fellows.
21 I beheld, [a]and the same horn made war
with the saints, and prevailed against them;
22 Until the Ancient of days came, [a]and judgment was given to the saints of the most High;
and the time came that the saints possessed the
kingdom.
23 Thus he said, The fourth beast shall be

NKJV

behold, [a]a fourth beast, dreadful and terrible, exceedingly strong. It had huge iron teeth; it was
devouring, breaking in pieces, and trampling the
residue with its feet. It *was* different from all
the beasts that *were* before it, [b]and it had ten
horns.
8 "I was considering the horns, and [a]there
was another horn, a little one, coming up among
them, before whom three of the first horns were
plucked out by the roots. And there, in this horn,
were eyes like the eyes [b]of a man, [c]and a mouth
speaking pompous words.

Vision of the Ancient of Days

9 "I[a] watched till thrones were put in place,
And [b]the Ancient of Days was seated;
[c]His garment *was* white as snow,
And the hair of His head *was* like pure
wool.
His throne *was* a fiery flame,
[d]Its wheels a burning fire;
10 [a]A fiery stream issued
And came forth from before Him.
[b]A thousand thousands ministered to Him;
Ten thousand times ten thousand stood
before Him.
[c]The *court was seated,
And the books were opened.

11 "I watched then because of the sound of
the pompous words which the horn was speaking;
[a]I watched till the beast was slain, and its body
destroyed and given to the burning flame.
12 "As for the rest of the beasts, they had
their dominion taken away, yet their lives were
prolonged for a season and a time.

13 "I was watching in the night visions,
And behold, [a]*One* like the Son of Man,
Coming with the clouds of heaven!
He came to the Ancient of Days,
And they brought Him near before Him.
14 [a]Then to Him was given dominion and
glory and a kingdom,
That all [b]peoples, nations, and languages
should serve Him.
His dominion *is* [c]an everlasting dominion,
Which shall not pass away,
And His kingdom *the one*
Which shall not be destroyed.

Daniel's Visions Interpreted

15 "I, Daniel, was grieved in my spirit within
my body, and the visions of my head troubled me.
16 "I came near to one of those who stood
by, and asked him the truth of all this. So he told
me and made known to me the interpretation of
these things:
17 'Those great beasts, which are four, *are*
four *kings *which* arise out of the earth.
18 'But [a]the saints of the Most High shall receive the kingdom, and possess the kingdom forever, even forever and ever.'
19 "Then I wished to know the truth about
the fourth beast, which was different from all the
others, exceedingly dreadful, *with* its teeth of iron
and its nails of bronze, *which* devoured, broke
in pieces, and trampled the residue with its
feet;
20 "and the ten horns that *were* on its head,
and the other *horn* which came up, before which
three fell, namely, that horn which had eyes and
a mouth which spoke pompous words, whose appearance *was* greater than his fellows.
21 "I was watching; [a]and the same horn was
making war against the saints, and prevailing
against them,
22 "until the Ancient of Days came, [a]and a
judgment was made *in favor* of the saints of the
Most High, and the time came for the saints to
possess the kingdom.
23 "Thus he said:

7 [a]Dan. 2:40 [b]Dan. 2:41; Rev. 12:3; 13:1
8 [a]Dan. 8:9 [b]Rev. 9:7 [c]Ps. 12:3; Rev. 13:5, 6
9 [a][Rev. 20:4] [b]Ps. 90:2 [c]Ps. 104:2; Rev. 1:14 [d]Ezek. 1:15
10 [a]Ps. 50:3; Is. 30:33; 66:15 [b]Deut. 33:2; 1 Kin. 22:19; Ps. 68:17; Rev. 5:11 [c]Dan. 12:1; [Rev. 20:11–15]
11 [a][Rev. 19:20; 20:10]
13 [a]Ezek. 1:26; [Matt. 24:30; 26:64; Mark 13:26; 14:62; Luke 21:27; Rev. 1:7, 13; 14:14]
14 [a]Ps. 2:6–8; Dan. 7:27; [Matt. 28:18; John 3:35, 36; 1 Cor. 15:27; Eph. 1:22; Phil 2:9–11; Rev. 1:6; 11:15] [b]Dan. 3:4 [c]Ps. 145:13; Mic. 4:7; [Luke 1:33]; John 12:34; Heb. 12:28
18 [a]Ps. 149:5–9; Is. 60:12–14; Dan. 7:14; [2 Tim. 2:11; Rev. 2:26, 27; 20:4; 22:5]
21 [a]Rev. 11:7; 13:7; 17:14
22 [a][Rev. 1:6]

*——

7:10 Or *judgment*
7:17 Representing their kingdoms, v. 23

KJV

[a]the fourth kingdom upon earth, which shall be
diverse from all kingdoms, and shall devour the
whole earth, and shall tread it down, and break
it in pieces.
24 [a]And the ten horns out of this kingdom
are ten kings *that* shall arise: and another shall
rise after them; and he shall be diverse from the
first, and he shall subdue three kings.
25 [a]And he shall speak *great* words against
the most High, and shall [b]wear out the saints of
the most High, and [c]think to change times and
laws: and [d]they shall be given into his hand [e]until
a time and times and the dividing of time.
26 [a]But the judgment shall sit, and they shall
[b]take away his dominion, to consume and to destroy *it* unto the end.
27 And the [a]kingdom and dominion, and the
greatness of the kingdom under the whole heaven,
shall be given to the people of the saints of the
most High, [b]whose kingdom *is* an everlasting
kingdom, [c]and all dominions shall serve and obey
him.
28 Hitherto *is* the end of the matter. As for
me Daniel, [a]my cogitations much troubled me,
and my countenance changed in me: but I [b]kept
the matter in my heart.

23 [a]Dan. 2:40
24 [a]Dan. 7:7; Rev. 13:1; 17:12
25 [a]Is. 37:23; Dan. 11:36; Rev. 13:1–6 [b]Rev. 17:6 [c]Dan. 2:21 [d]Rev. 13:7; 18:24 [e]Dan. 12:7; Rev. 12:14
26 [a][Dan. 2:35; 7:10, 22] [b]Rev. 19:20
27 [a]Is. 54:3; Dan. 7:14, 18, 22; Rev. 20:4 [b]2 Sam. 7:16; Ps. 89:35–37; Is. 9:7; Dan. 2:44; 4:34; 7:14; [Luke 1:33, 34]; John 12:34; [Rev. 11:15; 22:5] [c]Ps. 2:6–12; 22:27; 72:11; 86:9; Is. 60:12; Rev. 11:1
28 [a]Dan. 8:27 [b]Luke 2:19, 51

NKJV

'The fourth beast shall be
[a]A fourth kingdom on earth,
Which shall be different from all *other*
kingdoms,
And shall devour the whole earth,
Trample it and break it in pieces.
24 [a]The ten horns *are* ten kings
Who shall arise from this kingdom.
And another shall rise after them;
He shall be different from the first
ones,
And shall subdue three kings.
25 [a]He shall speak *pompous* words against
the Most High,
Shall [b]persecute* the saints of the Most
High,
And shall [c]intend to change times and
law.
Then [d]*the saints* shall be given into his
hand
[e]For a time and times and half a time.

26 'But[a] the court shall be seated,
And they shall [b]take away his
dominion,
To consume and destroy *it* forever.
27 Then the [a]kingdom and dominion,
And the greatness of the kingdoms under
the whole heaven,
Shall be given to the people, the saints of
the Most High.
[b]His kingdom *is* an everlasting kingdom,
[c]And all dominions shall serve and obey
Him.'

28 "This *is* the end of the *account. As for
me, Daniel, [a]my thoughts greatly troubled me,
and my countenance changed; but I [b]kept the matter in my heart."

KJV

Vision of a Ram and a Goat

8 In the third year of the reign of king Belshazzar a vision appeared unto me, *even unto* me
Daniel, after that which appeared unto me [a]at the
first.
2 And I saw in a vision; and it came to pass,
when I saw, that I *was* at [a]Shushan *in* the palace,
which *is* in the province of Elam; and I saw in a
vision, and I was by the river of Ulai.
3 Then I lifted up mine eyes, and saw, and,
behold, there stood before the river a ram which
had *two* horns: and the *two* horns *were* high; but
one *was* [a]higher than the other, and the higher
came up last.
4 I saw the ram pushing westward, and
northward, and southward; so that no beasts
might stand before him, neither *was there any*
that could deliver out of his hand; [a]but he did
according to his will, and became great.
5 And as I was considering, behold, an he
goat came from the weston the face of the whole
earth, and touched not the ground: and the goat
had a notable [a]horn between his eyes.
6 And he came to the ram that had *two*
horns, which I had seen standing before the river,
and ran unto him in the fury of his power.
7 And I saw him come close unto the ram,
and he was moved with choler against him, and
smote the ram, and brake his two horns: and there
was no power in the ram to stand before him,
but he cast him down to the ground, and stamped
upon him: and there was none that could deliver
the ram out of his hand.
8 Therefore the he goat waxed very great:
and when he was strong, the great horn was broken; and for it came up [a]four notable ones toward
the four winds of heaven.
9 [a]And out of one of them came forth a little
horn, which waxed exceeding great, toward the
south, and [b]toward the east, and toward the
[c]pleasant *land.*
10 [a]And it waxed great, *even* to [b]the host of

CHAPTER 8
1 [a]Dan. 7:1
2 [a]Neh. 1:1; Esth. 1:2; 2:8
3 [a]Dan. 7:5
4 [a]Dan. 5:19
5 [a]Dan. 8:8, 21; 11:3
8 [a]Dan. 7:6; 8:22; 11:4
9 [a]Dan. 11:21 [b]Dan. 11:25 [c]Ps. 48:2
10 [a]Dan. 11:28 [b]Is. 14:13; Jer. 48:26

NKJV

Vision of a Ram and a Goat

8 In the third year of the reign of King Belshazzar a vision appeared *to* me—to me, Daniel—
after the one that appeared to me [a]the first time.
2 I saw in the vision, and it so happened
while I was looking, that I *was* in [a]Shushan, the
citadel, which *is* in the province of Elam; and I
saw in the vision that I was by the River Ulai.
3 Then I lifted my eyes and saw, and there,
standing beside the river, was a ram which had
two horns, and the two horns *were* high; but one
was [a]higher than the other, and the higher *one*
came up last.
4 I saw the ram pushing westward, northward, and southward, so that no animal could
withstand him; nor *was there any* that could deliver from his hand, [a]but he did according to his
will and became great.
5 And as I was considering, suddenly a male
goat came from the west, across the surface of
the whole earth, without touching the ground; and
the goat *had* a notable [a]horn between his eyes.
6 Then he came to the ram that had two
horns, which I had seen standing beside the river,
and ran at him with furious power.
7 And I saw him confronting the ram; he
was moved with rage against him, attacked the
ram, and broke his two horns. There was no
power in the ram to withstand him, but he cast
him down to the ground and trampled him; and
there was no one that could deliver the ram from
his hand.
8 Therefore the male goat grew very great;
but when he became strong, the large horn was
broken, and in place of it [a]four notable ones came
up toward the four winds of heaven.
9 [a]And out of one of them came a little horn
which grew exceedingly great toward the south,
[b]toward the east, and toward the [c]Glorious *Land.*
10 [a]And it grew up to [b]the host of heaven;

*

7:25 Lit. *wear out*
7:28 Lit. *word*

KJV

heaven; and [c]it cast down *some* of the host and of the stars to the ground, and stamped upon them.

11 Yea, [a]he magnified *himself* even to [b]the prince of the host, [c]and by him [d]the daily *sacrifice* was taken away, and the place of his sanctuary was cast down.

12 And [a]an host was given *him* against the daily *sacrifice* by reason of transgression, and it cast down [b]the truth to the ground; and it [c]practised, and prospered.

13 Then I heard [a]one saint speaking, and another saint said unto that certain *saint* which spake, How long *shall be* the vision *concerning* the daily *sacrifice,* and the transgression of desolation, to give both the sanctuary and the host to be trodden under foot?

14 And he said unto me, Unto two thousand and three hundred days; then shall the sanctuary be cleansed.

Gabriel Interprets the Vision

15 And it came to pass, when I, *even* I Daniel, had seen the vision, and [a]sought for the meaning, then, behold, there stood before me [b]as the appearance of a man.

16 And I heard a man's voice [a]between *the banks of* Ulai, which called, and said, [b]Gabriel, make this *man* to understand the vision.

17 So he came near where I stood: and when he came, I was afraid, and [a]fell upon my face: but he said unto me, Understand, O son of man: for at the time of the end *shall be* the vision.

18 [a]Now as he was speaking with me, I was in a deep sleep on my face toward the ground: [b]but he touched me, and set me upright.

19 And he said, Behold, I will make thee know what shall be in the last end of the indignation: [a]for at the time appointed the end *shall be.*

20 The ram which thou sawest having *two* horns *are* the kings of Media and Persia.

21 And the rough goat *is* the king of Grecia: and the great horn that *is* between his eyes [a]*is* the first king.

22 [a]Now that being broken, whereas four stood up for it, four kingdoms shall stand up out of the nation, but not in his power.

23 And in the latter time of their kingdom, when the transgressors are come to the full, a king [a]of fierce countenance, and understanding dark sentences, shall stand up.

24 And his power shall be mighty, [a]but not by his own power: and he shall destroy wonderfully, [b]and shall prosper, and practise, [c]and shall destroy the mighty and the holy people.

25 And [a]through his policy also he shall cause craft to prosper in his hand; [b]and he shall magnify *himself* in his heart, and by peace shall destroy many: [c]he shall also stand up against the Prince of princes; but he shall be [d]broken without hand.

26 And the vision of the evening and the morning which was told *is* true: [a]wherefore shut thou up the vision; for it *shall be* for many days.

27 [a]And I Daniel fainted, and was sick *certain* days; afterward I rose up, and did the king's business; and I was astonished at the vision, but none understood *it.*

10 [c]Rev. 12:4 **11** [a]2 Kin. 19:22, 23; 2 Chr. 32:15–17; Is. 37:23; Dan. 8:25; 11:36, 37 [b]Josh. 5:14 [c]Ezek. 46:14; Dan. 11:31; 12:11 [d]Ex. 29:38 **12** [a]Dan. 11:31 [b]Ps. 119:43; Is. 59:14 [c]Dan. 8:4; 11:36 **13** [a]Dan. 4:13, 23; 1 Pet. 1:12 **15** [a]1 Pet. 1:10 [b]Ezek. 1:26 **16** [a]Dan. 12:6, 7 [b]Dan. 9:21; Luke 1:19, 26 **17** [a]Ezek. 1:28; 44:4; Dan. 2:46; Rev. 1:17 **18** [a]Dan. 10:9; Luke 9:32 [b]Ezek. 2:2; Dan. 10:10, 16, 18 **19** [a]Hab. 2:3 **21** [a]Dan. 11:3 **22** [a]Dan. 11:4 **23** [a]Deut. 28:50 **24** [a]Rev. 17:13 [b]Dan. 11:36 [c]Dan. 7:25 **25** [a]Dan. 11:21 [b]Dan. 8:11–13; 11:36; 12:7 [c]Dan. 11:36; Rev. 19:19, 20 [d]Job 34:20; Lam. 4:6 **26** [a]Ezek. 12:27; Dan. 12:4, 9; Rev. 22:10 **27** [a]Dan. 7:28; 8:17; Hab. 3:16

NKJV

and [c]it cast down *some* of the host and *some* of the stars to the ground, and trampled them.

11 [a]He even exalted *himself* as high as [b]the Prince of the host; [c]and by him [d]the daily *sacrifices* were taken away, and the place of His sanctuary was cast down.

12 Because of transgression, [a]an army was given over *to the horn* to oppose the daily *sacrifices;* and he cast [b]truth down to the ground. He [c]did *all this* and prospered.

13 Then I heard [a]a holy one speaking; and *another* holy one said to that certain *one* who was speaking, "How long *will* the vision *be, concerning* the daily *sacrifices* and the transgression of desolation, the giving of both the sanctuary and the host to be trampled underfoot?"

14 And he said to me, "For two thousand three hundred *days; then the sanctuary shall be cleansed."

Gabriel Interprets the Vision

15 Then it happened, when I, Daniel, had seen the vision and [a]was seeking the meaning, that suddenly there stood before me [b]one having the appearance of a man.

16 And I heard a man's voice [a]between *the banks of* the Ulai, who called, and said, [b]"Gabriel, make this *man* understand the vision."

17 So he came near where I stood, and when he came I was afraid and [a]fell on my face; but he said to me, "Understand, son of man, that the vision *refers* to the time of the end."

18 [a]Now, as he was speaking with me, I was in a deep sleep with my face to the ground; [b]but he touched me, and stood me upright.

19 And he said, "Look, I am making known to you what shall happen in the latter time of the indignation; [a]for at the appointed time the end *shall be.*

20 "The ram which you saw, having the two horns—*they are* the kings of Media and Persia.

21 "And the male goat *is* the *kingdom of Greece. The large horn that *is* between its eyes [a]*is* the first king.

22 [a]"As for the broken *horn* and the four that stood up in its place, four kingdoms shall arise out of that nation, but not with its power.

23 "And in the latter time of their kingdom,
When the transgressors have reached
their fullness,
A king shall arise,
[a]Having fierce features,
Who understands sinister schemes.
24 His power shall be mighty; [a]but not by
his own power;
He shall destroy fearfully,
[b]And shall prosper and thrive;
[c]He shall destroy the mighty, and *also* the
holy people.

25 "Through[a] his cunning
He shall cause deceit to prosper under his
*rule;
[b]And he shall exalt *himself* in his heart.
He shall destroy many in *their* prosperity.
[c]He shall even rise against the Prince of
princes;
But he shall be [d]broken without *human*
*means.

26 "And the vision of the evenings and
mornings
Which was told is true;
[a]Therefore seal up the vision,
For *it refers* to many days *in the future.*"

27 [a]And I, Daniel, fainted and was sick for days; afterward I arose and went about the king's business. I was astonished by the vision, but no one understood it.

*
8:14 Lit. *evening-mornings* **8:21** Lit. *king,* representing his kingdom, Dan. 7:17, 23 **8:25** Lit. *hand* • Lit. *hand*

KJV

Daniel's Prayer for the People

9 In the first year [a]of Darius the son of Ahasuerus, of the seed of the Medes, which was made king over the realm of the Chaldeans;

2 In the first year of his reign I Daniel understood by books the number of the years, whereof the word of the LORD came to [a]Jeremiah the prophet, that he would accomplish seventy years in the desolations of Jerusalem.

3 [a]And I set my face unto the LORD God, to seek by prayer and supplications, with fasting, and sackcloth, and ashes:

4 And I prayed unto the LORD my God, and made my confession, and said, O [a]Lord, the great and dreadful God, keeping the covenant and mercy to them that love him, and to them that keep his commandments;

5 [a]We have sinned, and have committed iniquity, and have done wickedly, and have rebelled, even by departing from thy precepts and from thy judgments:

6 [a]Neither have we hearkened unto thy servants the prophets, which spake in thy name to our kings, our princes, and our fathers, and to all the people of the land.

7 O LORD, [a]righteousness *belongeth* unto thee, but unto us confusion of faces, as at this day; to the men of Judah, and to the inhabitants of Jerusalem, and unto all Israel, *that are* near, and *that are* far off, through all the countries whither thou hast driven them, because of their trespass that they have trespassed against thee.

8 O LORD, to us *belongeth* confusion of face, to our kings, to our princes, and to our fathers, because we have sinned against thee.

9 [a]To the Lord our God *belong* mercies and forgivenesses, though we have rebelled against him;

10 Neither have we obeyed the voice of the LORD our God, to walk in his laws, which he set before us by his servants the prophets.

11 Yea, [a]all Israel have transgressed thy law, even by departing, that they might not obey thy voice; therefore the curse is poured upon us, and the oath that *is* written in the [b]law of Moses the servant of God, because we have sinned against him.

12 And he hath [a]confirmed his words, which he spake against us, and against our judges that judged us, by bringing upon us a great evil: [b]for under the whole heaven hath not been done as hath been done upon Jerusalem.

13 [a]As *it is* written in the law of Moses, all this evil is come upon us: [b]yet made we not our prayer before the LORD our God, that we might turn from our iniquities, and understand thy truth.

14 Therefore hath the LORD [a]watched upon the evil, and brought it upon us: for [b]the LORD our God *is* righteous in all his works which he doeth: for we obeyed not his voice.

15 And now, O LORD our God, [a]that hast brought thy people forth out of the land of Egypt with a mighty hand, and hast gotten thee [b]renown, as at this day; we have sinned, we have done wickedly.

16 O LORD, [a]according to all thy righteousness, I beseech thee, let thine anger and thy fury be turned away from thy city Jerusalem, [b]thy holy mountain: because for our sins, [c]and for the iniquities of our fathers, [d]Jerusalem and thy people [e]*are become* a reproach to all *that are* about us.

17 Now therefore, O our God, hear the prayer of thy servant, and his supplications, [a]and cause thy face to shine upon thy sanctuary [c]that is desolate, [b]for the LORD's sake.

18 [a]O my God, incline thine ear, and hear; open thine eyes, [b]and behold our desolations, and the city [c]which is called by thy name: for we do not present our supplications before thee for our righteousnesses, but for thy great mercies.

19 O LORD, hear; O LORD, forgive; O LORD,

CHAPTER 9
1 [a]Dan. 1:21
2 [a]2 Chr. 36:21; Ezra 1:1; Jer. 25:11, 12; 29:10; Zech. 7:5
3 [a]Neh. 1:4; Dan. 6:10; 10:15
4 [a]Ex. 20:6
5 [a]1 Kin. 8:47, 48; Neh. 9:33; Ps. 106:6; Is. 64:5–7; Jer. 14:7
6 [a]2 Chr. 36:15; Jer. 44:4, 5
7 [a]Neh. 9:33
9 [a][Neh. 9:17; Ps. 130:4, 7]
11 [a]Is. 1:3–6; Jer. 8:5–10 [b]Lev. 26:14; Neh. 1:6; Ps. 106:6
12 [a]Is. 44:26; Jer. 44:2–6; Lam. 2:17; Zech. 1:6 [b]Lam. 1:12; 2:13; Ezek. 5:9; [Amos 3:2]
13 [a]Lev. 26:14–45; Deut. 28:15–68; Lam. 2:17 [b]Job 36:13; Is. 9:13; Jer. 2:30; Hos. 7:7
14 [a]Jer. 31:28; 44:27 [b]Neh. 9:33
15 [a]Ex. 32:11; 1 Kin. 8:51; Neh. 1:10 [b]Ex. 14:18; Neh. 9:10; Jer. 32:20
16 [a]1 Sam. 12:7; Ps. 31:1; Mic. 6:4, 5 [b]Ps. 87:1–3; Dan. 9:20; Joel 3:17; Zech. 8:3 [c]Ex. 20:5 [d]Ps. 122:6; Jer. 29:7; Lam. 2:16 [e]Ps. 79:4
17 [a]Num. 6:24–26; Ps. 80:3, 7, 19 [b]Lam. 5:18 [c][John 16:24]
18 [a]Is. 37:17 [b]Ex. 3:7 [c]Jer. 25:29

NKJV

Daniel's Prayer for the People

9 In the first year [a]of Darius the son of Ahasuerus, of the lineage of the Medes, who was made king over the realm of the Chaldeans—

2 in the first year of his reign I, Daniel, understood by the books the number of the years *specified* by the word of the LORD through [a]Jeremiah the prophet, that He would accomplish seventy years in the desolations of Jerusalem.

3 [a]Then I set my face toward the Lord God to make request by prayer and supplications, with fasting, sackcloth, and ashes.

4 And I prayed to the LORD my God, and made confession, and said, "O [a]Lord, great and awesome God, who keeps His covenant and mercy with those who love Him, and with those who keep His commandments,

5 [a]"we have sinned and committed iniquity, we have done wickedly and rebelled, even by departing from Your precepts and Your judgments.

6 [a]"Neither have we heeded Your servants the prophets, who spoke in Your name to our kings and our princes, to our fathers and all the people of the land.

7 "O Lord, [a]righteousness *belongs* to You, but to us shame of face, as *it is* this day—to the men of Judah, to the inhabitants of Jerusalem and all Israel, those near and those far off in all the countries to which You have driven them, because of the unfaithfulness which they have committed against You.

8 "O Lord, to us *belongs* shame of face, to our kings, our princes, and our fathers, because we have sinned against You.

9 [a]"To the Lord our God *belong* mercy and forgiveness, though we have rebelled against Him.

10 "We have not obeyed the voice of the LORD our God, to walk in His laws, which He set before us by His servants the prophets.

11 "Yes, [a]all Israel has transgressed Your law, and has departed so as not to obey Your voice; therefore the curse and the oath written in the [b]Law of Moses the servant of God have been poured out on us, because we have sinned against Him.

12 "And He has [a]confirmed His words, which He spoke against us and against our judges who judged us, by bringing upon us a great disaster; [b]for under the whole heaven such has never been done as what has been done to Jerusalem.

13 [a]"As *it is* written in the Law of Moses, all this disaster has come upon us; [b]yet we have not made our prayer before the LORD our God, that we might turn from our iniquities and understand Your truth.

14 "Therefore the LORD has [a]kept the disaster in mind, and brought it upon us; for [b]the LORD our God *is* righteous in all the works which He does, though we have not obeyed His voice.

15 "And now, O Lord our God, [a]who brought Your people out of the land of Egypt with a mighty hand, and made Yourself [b]a name, as *it is* this day—we have sinned, we have done wickedly!

16 "O Lord, [a]according to all Your righteousness, I pray, let Your anger and Your fury be turned away from Your city Jerusalem, [b]Your holy mountain; because for our sins, [c]and for the iniquities of our fathers, [d]Jerusalem and Your people [e]*are* a reproach to all *those* around us.

17 "Now therefore, our God, hear the prayer of Your servant, and his supplications, [a]and [b]for the Lord's sake cause Your face to shine on Your sanctuary, [c]which is desolate.

18 [a]"O my God, incline Your ear and hear; open Your eyes [b]and see our desolations, and the city [c]which is called by Your name; for we do not present our supplications before You because of our righteous deeds, but because of Your great mercies.

19 "O Lord, hear! O Lord, forgive! O Lord,

KJV

hearken and do; defer not, for thine own sake, O my God: for thy city and thy people are called by thy name.

The Seventy-Weeks Prophecy

20 And whiles I *was* speaking, and praying, and confessing my sin and the sin of my people Israel, and presenting my supplication before the LORD my God for the holy mountain of my God;

21 Yea, whiles I *was* speaking in prayer, even the man [a]Gabriel, whom I had seen in the vision at the beginning, being caused to fly swiftly, touched me about the time of the evening oblation.

22 And he informed *me,* and talked with me, and said, O Daniel, I am now come forth to give thee skill and understanding.

23 At the beginning of thy supplications the commandment came forth, and I am come to shew *thee;* for thou *art* greatly [a]beloved: therefore [b]understand the matter, and consider the vision.

24 Seventy weeks are determined upon thy people and upon thy holy city, to finish the transgression, and to make an end of sins, [a]and to make reconciliation for iniquity, [b]and to bring in everlasting righteousness, and to seal up the vision and prophecy, [c]and to anoint the most Holy.

25 Know therefore and understand, *that* from the going forth of the commandment to restore and to build Jerusalem unto [a]the Messiah [b]the Prince *shall be* seven weeks, and threescore and two weeks: the street shall be built again, and the wall, even in troublous times.

26 And after threescore and two weeks [a]shall Messiah be cut off, [b]but not for himself: and [c]the people of the prince that shall come [d]shall destroy the city and the sanctuary; and the end thereof *shall be* with a flood, and unto the end of the war desolations are determined.

27 And he shall confirm [a]the covenant with [b]many for one week: and in the midst of the week he shall cause the sacrifice and the oblation to cease, and for the overspreading of abominations he shall make *it* desolate, [c]even until the consummation, and that determined shall be poured upon the desolate.

Vision of the Glorious Man

10 In the third year of Cyrus king of Persia a thing was revealed unto Daniel, whose [a]name was called Belteshazzar; and the thing *was* true, but the time appointed *was* long: and he understood the thing, and had understanding of the vision.

2 In those days I Daniel was mourning three full weeks.

3 I ate no pleasant bread, neither came flesh nor wine in my mouth, neither did I anoint myself at all, till three whole weeks were fulfilled.

4 And in the four and twentieth day of the first month, as I was by the side of the great river, which *is* Hiddekel;

5 Then I lifted up mine eyes, and looked, and behold a certain man clothed in [a]linen, whose loins *were* [b]girded with fine gold of Uphaz:

6 His body also *was* like the beryl, and his face as the appearance of lightning, and his eyes as lamps of fire, and his arms and his feet like in

21 [a]Dan. 8:16; Luke 1:19, 26 **23** [a]Dan. 10:11, 19 [b]Matt. 24:15 **24** [a]2 Chr. 29:24; [Is. 53:10]; Acts 10:43; [Rom. 5:10]; Heb. 9:12, 14 [b]Rev. 14:6 [c]Ps. 45:7 **25** [a]Luke 2:1, 2; John 1:41; 4:25 [b]Is. 55:4 **26** [a][Is. 53:8]; Matt. 27:50; Mark 9:12; 15:37; [Luke 23:46; 24:26]; John 19:30; Acts 8:32 [b][1 Pet. 2:21] [c]Matt. 22:7 [d]Matt. 24:2; Mark 13:2; Luke 19:43, 44 **27** [a]Is. 42:6 [b][Matt. 26:28] [c]Dan. 11:36

CHAPTER 10

1 [a]Dan. 1:7 **5** [a]Ezek. 9:2; 10:2 [b]Rev. 1:13; 15:6

*———

9:24 Lit. *sevens,* and so throughout the chapter • So with Qr., LXX, Syr., Vg.; Kt., Theodotion *To seal up*
9:25 Or *open square* • Or *moat*
10:1 Or *and of great conflict;*
10:4 Heb. *Hiddekel*

NKJV

listen and act! Do not delay for Your own sake, my God, for Your city and Your people are called by Your name."

The Seventy-Weeks Prophecy

20 Now while I *was* speaking, praying, and confessing my sin and the sin of my people Israel, and presenting my supplication before the LORD my God for the holy mountain of my God,

21 yes, while I *was* speaking in prayer, the man [a]Gabriel, whom I had seen in the vision at the beginning, being caused to fly swiftly, reached me about the time of the evening offering.

22 And he informed *me,* and talked with me, and said, "O Daniel, I have now come forth to give you skill to understand.

23 "At the beginning of your supplications the command went out, and I have come to tell *you,* for you *are* greatly [a]beloved; therefore [b]consider the matter, and understand the vision:

24 "Seventy *weeks are determined
For your people and for your holy city,
To finish the transgression,
*To make an end of sins,
[a]To make reconciliation for iniquity,
[b]To bring in everlasting righteousness,
To seal up vision and prophecy,
[c]And to anoint the Most Holy.

25 "Know therefore and understand,
That from the going forth of the command
To restore and build Jerusalem
Until [a]Messiah [b]the Prince,
There shall be seven weeks and sixty-two weeks;
The *street shall be built again, and the *wall,
Even in troublesome times.

26 "And after the sixty-two weeks
[a]Messiah shall be cut off, [b]but not for Himself;
And [c]the people of the prince who is to come
[d]Shall destroy the city and the sanctuary.
The end of it *shall be* with a flood,
And till the end of the war desolations are determined.

27 Then he shall confirm [a]a covenant with [b]many for one week;
But in the middle of the week
He shall bring an end to sacrifice and offering.
And on the wing of abominations shall be one who makes desolate,
[c]Even until the consummation, which is determined,
Is poured out on the desolate."

Vision of the Glorious Man

10 In the third year of Cyrus king of Persia a message was revealed to Daniel, whose [a]name was called Belteshazzar. The message *was* true, *but the appointed time *was* long; and he understood the message, and had understanding of the vision.

2 In those days I, Daniel, was mourning three full weeks.

3 I ate no pleasant food, no meat or wine came into my mouth, nor did I anoint myself at all, till three whole weeks were fulfilled.

4 Now on the twenty-fourth day of the first month, as I was by the side of the great river, that *is,* the *Tigris,

5 I lifted my eyes and looked, and behold, a certain man clothed in [a]linen, whose waist *was* [b]girded with gold of Uphaz!

6 His body *was* like beryl, his face like the appearance of lightning, his eyes like torches of fire, his arms and feet like burnished bronze in

KJV

colour to polished brass, [a]and the voice of his words like the voice of a multitude.

7 And I Daniel alone saw the vision: for the men that were with me saw not the vision; but a great quaking fell upon them, so that they fled to hide themselves.

8 Therefore I was left alone, and saw this great vision, and there remained no strength in me: for my comeliness was turned in me into corruption, and I retained no strength.

9 Yet heard I the voice of his words: and when I heard the voice of his words, then was I in a deep sleep on my face, and my face toward the ground.

Prophecies Concerning Persia and Greece

10 [a]And, behold, an hand touched me, which set me upon my knees and *upon* the palms of my hands.

11 And he said unto me, O Daniel, [a]a man greatly beloved, understand the words that I speak unto thee, and stand upright: for unto thee am I now sent. And when he had spoken this word unto me, I stood trembling.

12 Then said he unto me, [a]Fear not, Daniel: for from the first day that thou didst set thine heart to understand, and to chasten thyself before thy God, [b]thy words were heard, and I am come for thy words.

13 [a]But the prince of the kingdom of Persia withstood me one and twenty days: but, lo, [b]Michael, one of the chief princes, came to help me; and I remained there with the kings of Persia.

14 Now I am come to make thee understand what shall befall thy people [a]in the latter days: [b]for yet the vision *is* for *many* days.

15 And when he had spoken such words unto me, [a]I set my face toward the ground, and I became dumb.

16 And, behold, [a]*one* like the similitude of the sons of men [b]touched my lips: then I opened my mouth, and spake, and said unto him that stood before me, O my lord, by the vision [c]my sorrows are turned upon me, and I have retained no strength.

17 For how can the servant of this my lord talk with this my lord? for as for me, straightway there remained no strength in me, neither is there breath left in me.

18 Then there came again and touched me *one* like the appearance of a man, and he strengthened me,

19 [a]And said, O man greatly beloved, [b]fear not: peace *be* unto thee, be strong, yea, be strong. And when he had spoken unto me, I was strengthened, and said, Let my lord speak; for thou hast strengthened me.

20 Then said he, Knowest thou wherefore I come unto thee? and now will I return to fight [a]with the prince of Persia: and when I am gone forth, lo, the prince of Grecia shall come.

21 But I will shew thee that which is noted in the scripture of truth: and *there is* none that holdeth with me in these things, [a]but Michael your prince.

11 Also I [a]in the first year of [b]Darius the Mede, *even* I, stood to confirm and to strengthen him.

2 And now will I shew thee the truth. Behold, there shall stand up yet three kings in Persia; and the fourth shall be far richer than *they* all: and by his strength through his riches he shall stir up all against the realm of Grecia.

3 And [a]a mighty king shall stand up, that shall rule with great dominion, and [b]do according to his will.

4 And when he shall stand up, [a]his kingdom shall be broken, and shall be divided toward the four winds of heaven; and not to his posterity, [b]nor according to his dominion which he ruled:

---

6 [a][Rev. 1:15]
10 [a]Dan. 9:21
11 [a]Dan. 9:23
12 [a]Rev. 1:17 [b]Dan. 9:3, 4, 22, 23; Acts 10:4
13 [a]Dan. 10:20 [b]Dan. 10:21; 12:1; Jude 9; [Rev. 12:7]
14 [a]Gen. 49:1; Deut. 31:29; Dan. 2:28 [b]Dan. 8:26; 10:1
15 [a]Dan. 8:18; 10:9
16 [a]Dan. 8:15 [b]Jer. 1:9; Dan. 10:10 [c]Dan. 10:8, 9
19 [a]Dan. 10:11 [b]Judg. 6:23; Is. 43:1; Dan. 10:12
20 [a]Dan. 10:13
21 [a]Dan. 10:13; Jude 9; [Rev. 12:7]

CHAPTER 11

1 [a]Dan. 9:1 [b]Dan. 5:31
3 [a]Dan. 7:6; 8:5 [b]Dan. 8:4; 10:16, 36
4 [a]Jer. 49:36; Ezek. 37:9; Dan. 7:2; 8:8; Zech. 2:6; Rev. 7:1 [b]Dan. 8:22

*

10:16 Theodotion, Vg. *the son;* LXX *a hand*

NKJV

color, [a]and the sound of his words like the voice of a multitude.

7 And I, Daniel, alone saw the vision, for the men who were with me did not see the vision; but a great terror fell upon them, so that they fled to hide themselves.

8 Therefore I was left alone when I saw this great vision, and no strength remained in me; for my vigor was turned to frailty in me, and I retained no strength.

9 Yet I heard the sound of his words; and while I heard the sound of his words I was in a deep sleep on my face, with my face to the ground.

Prophecies Concerning Persia and Greece

10 [a]Suddenly, a hand touched me, which made me tremble on my knees and *on* the palms of my hands.

11 And he said to me, "O Daniel, [a]man greatly beloved, understand the words that I speak to you, and stand upright, for I have now been sent to you." While he was speaking this word to me, I stood trembling.

12 Then he said to me, [a]"Do not fear, Daniel, for from the first day that you set your heart to understand, and to humble yourself before your God, [b]your words were heard; and I have come because of your words.

13 [a]"But the prince of the kingdom of Persia withstood me twenty-one days; and behold, [b]Michael, one of the chief princes, came to help me, for I had been left alone there with the kings of Persia.

14 "Now I have come to make you understand what will happen to your people [a]in the latter days, [b]for the vision *refers* to *many* days yet *to come.*"

15 When he had spoken such words to me, [a]I turned my face toward the ground and became speechless.

16 And suddenly, [a]*one* having the likeness of the *sons of men [b]touched my lips; then I opened my mouth and spoke, saying to him who stood before me, "My lord, because of the vision [c]my sorrows have overwhelmed me, and I have retained no strength.

17 "For how can this servant of my lord talk with you, my lord? As for me, no strength remains in me now, nor is any breath left in me."

18 Then again, *the one* having the likeness of a man touched me and strengthened me.

19 [a]And he said, "O man greatly beloved, [b]fear not! Peace *be* to you; be strong, yes, be strong!" So when he spoke to me I was strengthened, and said, "Let my lord speak, for you have strengthened me."

20 Then he said, "Do you know why I have come to you? And now I must return to fight [a]with the prince of Persia; and when I have gone forth, indeed the prince of Greece will come.

21 "But I will tell you what is noted in the Scripture of Truth. (No one upholds me against these, [a]except Michael your prince.

11 "Also [a]in the first year of [b]Darius the Mede, I, *even* I, stood up to confirm and strengthen him.)

2 "And now I will tell you the truth: Behold, three more kings will arise in Persia, and the fourth shall be far richer than *them* all; by his strength, through his riches, he shall stir up all against the realm of Greece.

3 "Then [a]a mighty king shall arise, who shall rule with great dominion, and [b]do according to his will.

4 "And when he has arisen, [a]his kingdom shall be broken up and divided toward the four winds of heaven, but not among his posterity [b]nor according to his dominion with which he ruled;

KJV

for his kingdom shall be plucked up, even for others beside those.

Warring Kings of North and South

5 And the king of the south shall be strong, and *one* of his princes; and he shall be strong above him, and have dominion; his dominion *shall be* a great dominion.

6 And in the end of years they shall join themselves together; for the king's daughter of the south shall come to the king of the north to make an agreement: but she shall not retain the power of the arm; neither shall he stand, nor his arm: but she shall be given up, and they that brought her, and he that begat her, and he that strengthened her in *these* times.

7 But out of a branch of her roots shall *one* stand up in his estate, which shall come with an army, and shall enter into the fortress of the king of the north, and shall deal against them, and shall prevail:

8 And shall also carry captives into Egypt their gods, with their princes, *and* with their precious vessels of silver and of gold; and he shall continue *more* years than the king of the north.

9 So the king of the south shall come into *his* kingdom, and shall return into his own land.

10 But his sons shall be stirred up, and shall assemble a multitude of great forces: and *one* shall certainly come, [a]and overflow, and pass through: then shall he return, and be stirred up, [b]*even* to his fortress.

11 And the king of the south shall be [a]moved with choler, and shall come forth and fight with him, *even* with the king of the north: and he shall set forth a great multitude; but the [b]multitude shall be given into his hand.

12 *And* when he hath taken away the multitude, his heart shall be lifted up; and he shall cast down *many* ten thousands: but he shall not be strengthened *by it.*

13 For the king of the north shall return, and shall set forth a multitude greater than the former, and shall certainly come after certain years with a great army and with much riches.

14 And in those times there shall many stand up against the king of the south: also the robbers of thy people shall exalt themselves to establish the vision; but they shall [a]fall.

15 So the king of the north shall come, and [a]cast up a mount, and take the most fenced cities: and the arms of the south shall not withstand, neither his chosen people, neither *shall there be any* strength to withstand.

16 But he that cometh against him [a]shall do according to his own will, and [b]none shall stand before him: and he shall stand in the glorious land, which by his hand shall be consumed.

17 He shall also [a]set his face to enter with the strength of his whole kingdom, and upright ones with him; thus shall he do: and he shall give him the daughter of women, corrupting her: but she shall not stand *on his side,* [b]neither be for him.

18 After this shall he turn his face unto the isles, and shall take many: but a prince for his own behalf shall cause the reproach offered by him to cease; without his own reproach he shall cause *it* to turn upon him.

19 Then he shall turn his face toward the fort of his own land: but he shall [a]stumble and fall, [b]and not be found.

20 Then shall stand up in his estate a raiser of taxes *in* the glory of the kingdom: but within few days he shall be destroyed, neither in anger, nor in battle.

21 And in his estate [a]shall stand up a vile person, to whom they shall not give the honour of the kingdom: but he shall come in peaceably, and obtain the kingdom by flatteries.

22 And with the arms of a [a]flood shall they

10 [a]Is. 8:8; Jer. 46:7, 8; 51:42; Dan. 9:26; 11:26, 40 [b]Dan. 11:7
11 [a]Prov. 16:14 [b][Ps. 33:10, 16]
14 [a]Job 9:13
15 [a]Jer. 6:6; Ezek. 4:2; 17:17
16 [a]Dan. 8:4, 7 [b]Josh. 1:5
17 [a]2 Kin. 12:17; 2 Chr. 20:3; Ezek. 4:3, 7 [b]Dan. 9:26
19 [a]Ps. 27:2; Jer. 46:6 [b]Job 20:8; Ps. 37:36; Ezek. 26:21
21 [a]Dan. 7:8
22 [a]Dan. 9:26

*

11:6 Lit. *arm* • Lit. *arm*
11:8 Or *molded images*
11:14 Or *robbers,* lit. *sons of breakage*
11:15 Lit. *arms*
11:16 Lit. *hand*
11:17 Or *bring equitable terms*
11:22 Lit. *arms*

NKJV

for his kingdom shall be uprooted, even for others besides these.

Warring Kings of North and South

5 "Also the king of the South shall become strong, as well as *one* of his princes; and he shall gain power over him and have dominion. His dominion *shall be* a great dominion.

6 "And at the end of *some* years they shall join forces, for the daughter of the king of the South shall go to the king of the North to make an agreement; but she shall not retain the power of her *authority, and neither he nor his *authority shall stand; but she shall be given up, with those who brought her, and with him who begot her, and with him who strengthened her in *those* times.

7 "But from a branch of her roots *one* shall arise in his place, who shall come with an army, enter the fortress of the king of the North, and deal with them and prevail.

8 "And he shall also carry their gods captive to Egypt, with their *princes *and* their precious articles of silver and gold; and he shall continue *more* years than the king of the North.

9 "Also *the king of the North* shall come to the kingdom of the king of the South, but shall return to his own land.

10 "However his sons shall stir up strife, and assemble a multitude of great forces; and *one* shall certainly come [a]and overwhelm and pass through; then he shall return [b]to his fortress and stir up strife.

11 "And the king of the South shall be [a]moved with rage, and go out and fight with him, with the king of the North, who shall muster a great multitude; but the [b]multitude shall be given into the hand of his *enemy.*

12 "When he has taken away the multitude, his heart will be lifted up; and he will cast down tens of thousands, but he will not prevail.

13 "For the king of the North will return and muster a multitude greater than the former, and shall certainly come at the end of some years with a great army and much equipment.

14 "Now in those times many shall rise up against the king of the South. Also, *violent men of your people shall exalt themselves in fulfillment of the vision, but they shall [a]fall.

15 "So the king of the North shall come and [a]build a siege mound, and take a fortified city; and the *forces of the South shall not withstand *him.* Even his choice troops *shall have* no strength to resist.

16 "But he who comes against him [a]shall do according to his own will, and [b]no one shall stand against him. He shall stand in the Glorious Land with destruction in his *power.

17 "He shall also [a]set his face to enter with the strength of his whole kingdom, and *upright ones with him; thus shall he do. And he shall give him the daughter of women to destroy it; but she shall not stand *with him,* [b]or be for him.

18 "After this he shall turn his face to the coastlands, and shall take many. But a ruler shall bring the reproach against them to an end; and with the reproach removed, he shall turn back on him.

19 "Then he shall turn his face toward the fortress of his own land; but he shall [a]stumble and fall, [b]and not be found.

20 "There shall arise in his place one who imposes taxes *on* the glorious kingdom; but within a few days he shall be destroyed, but not in anger or in battle.

21 "And in his place [a]shall arise a vile person, to whom they will not give the honor of royalty; but he shall come in peaceably, and seize the kingdom by intrigue.

22 "With the *force of a [a]flood they shall be

KJV

be overflown from before him, and shall be broken; [b]yea, also the prince of the covenant.

23 And after the league *made* with him [a]he shall work deceitfully: for he shall come up, and shall become strong with a small people.

24 He shall enter peaceably even upon the fattest places of the province; and he shall do *that* which his fathers have not done, nor his fathers' fathers; he shall scatter among them the prey, and spoil, and riches: *yea,* and he shall forecast his devices against the strong holds, even for a time.

25 And he shall stir up his power and his courage against the king of the south with a great army; and the king of the south shall be stirred up to battle with a very great and mighty army; but he shall not stand: for they shall forecast devices against him.

26 Yea, they that feed of the portion of his meat shall destroy him, and his army shall overflow: and many shall fall down slain.

27 And both these kings' hearts *shall be* to do mischief, and they shall speak lies at one table; but it shall not prosper: for yet the end *shall be* at the [a]time appointed.

28 Then shall he return into his land with great riches; and his heart *shall be* against the holy covenant; and he shall do *exploits,* and return to his own land.

The Northern King's Blasphemies

29 At the time appointed he shall return, and come toward the south; but it shall not be as the former, or as the latter.

30 [a]For the ships of Chittim shall come against him: therefore he shall be grieved, and return, and have indignation against the holy covenant: so shall he do; he shall even return, and have intelligence with them that forsake the holy covenant.

31 And arms shall stand on his part, [a]and they shall pollute the sanctuary of strength, and shall take away the daily *sacrifice,* and they shall place the abomination that maketh desolate.

32 And such as do wickedly against the covenant shall he corrupt by flatteries: but the people that do know their God shall be strong, and do *exploits.*

33 And they that understand among the people shall instruct many: yet they shall fall by the sword, and by flame, by captivity, and by spoil, *many* days.

34 Now when they shall fall, they shall be holpen with a little help: but many shall cleave to them with flatteries.

35 And *some* of them of understanding shall fall, [a]to try them, and to purge, and to make *them* white, *even* to the time of the end: because *it is* yet for a time appointed.

36 And the king shall do according to his will; and he shall [a]exalt himself, and magnify himself above every god, and shall speak marvellous things against the God of gods, and shall prosper till the indignation be accomplished: for that that is determined shall be done.

37 Neither shall he regard the God of his fathers, nor the desire of women, [a]nor regard any god: for he shall magnify himself above all.

38 But in his estate shall he honour the God of forces: and a god whom his fathers knew not shall he honour with gold, and silver, and with precious stones, and pleasant things.

39 Thus shall he do in the most strong holds with a strange god, whom he shall acknowledge *and* increase with glory: and he shall cause them to rule over many, and shall divide the land for gain.

The Northern King's Conquests

40 And at the [a]time of the end shall the king of the south push at him: and the king of the north shall come against him [b]like a whirlwind, with chariots, [c]and with horsemen, and with many

22 [b]Dan. 8:10, 11
23 [a]Dan. 8:25
27 [a]Dan. 8:19; Hab. 2:3
30 [a]Gen. 10:4; Num. 24:24; Is. 23:1, 12; Jer. 2:10
31 [a]Dan. 8:11–13; 12:11
35 [a][Deut. 8:16; Prov. 17:3]; Dan. 12:10; Zech. 13:9; Mal. 3:2, 3
36 [a]Dan. 7:8, 25
37 [a]Is. 14:13; 2 Thess. 2:4
40 [a]Dan. 11:27, 35; 12:4, 9 [b]Is. 21:1 [c]Ezek. 38:4; Rev. 9:16

NKJV

swept away from before him and be broken, [b]and also the prince of the covenant.

23 "And after the league *is made* with him [a]he shall act deceitfully, for he shall come up and become strong with a small *number of* people.

24 "He shall enter peaceably, even into the richest places of the province; and he shall do *what* his fathers have not done, nor his forefathers: he shall disperse among them the plunder, spoil, and riches; and he shall devise his plans against the strongholds, but *only* for a time.

25 "He shall stir up his power and his courage against the king of the South with a great army. And the king of the South shall be stirred up to battle with a very great and mighty army; but he shall not stand, for they shall devise plans against him.

26 "Yes, those who eat of the portion of his delicacies shall destroy him; his army shall be swept away, and many shall fall down slain.

27 "Both these kings' hearts *shall be* bent on evil, and they shall speak lies at the same table; but it shall not prosper, for the end *will* still *be* at the [a]appointed time.

28 "While returning to his land with great riches, his heart shall be *moved* against the holy covenant; so he shall do *damage* and return to his own land.

The Northern King's Blasphemies

29 "At the appointed time he shall return and go toward the south; but it shall not be like the former or the latter.

30 [a]"For ships from *Cyprus shall come against him; therefore he shall be grieved, and return in rage against the holy covenant, and do *damage.* So he shall return and show regard for those who forsake the holy covenant.

31 "And *forces shall be mustered by him, [a]and they shall defile the sanctuary fortress; then they shall take away the daily *sacrifices,* and place *there* the abomination of desolation.

32 "Those who do wickedly against the covenant he shall corrupt with flattery; but the people who know their God shall be strong, and carry out *great exploits.*

33 "And those of the people who understand shall instruct many; yet *for many* days they shall fall by sword and flame, by captivity and plundering.

34 "Now when they fall, they shall be aided with a little help; but many shall join with them by intrigue.

35 "And *some* of those of understanding shall fall, [a]to refine them, purify *them,* and make *them* white, *until* the time of the end; because *it is* still for the appointed time.

36 "Then the king shall do according to his own will: he shall [a]exalt and magnify himself above every god, shall speak blasphemies against the God of gods, and shall prosper till the wrath has been accomplished; for what has been determined shall be done.

37 "He shall regard neither the *God of his fathers nor the desire of women, [a]nor regard any god; for he shall exalt himself above *them* all.

38 "But in their place he shall honor a god of fortresses; and a god which his fathers did not know he shall honor with gold and silver, with precious stones and pleasant things.

39 "Thus he shall act against the strongest fortresses with a foreign god, which he shall acknowledge, *and* advance *its* glory; and he shall cause them to rule over many, and divide the land for gain.

The Northern King's Conquests

40 "At the [a]time of the end the king of the South shall attack him; and the king of the North shall come against him [b]like a whirlwind, with chariots, [c]horsemen, and with many ships; and

*

11:30 Heb. *Kittim,* western lands, especially Cyprus
11:31 Lit. *arms*
11:37 Or *gods*

KJV

ships; and he shall enter into the countries, and
shall overflow and pass over.
41 He shall enter also into the glorious land,
and many *countries* shall be overthrown: but
these shall escape out of his hand, [a]*even* Edom,
and Moab, and the chief of the children of
Ammon.
42 He shall stretch forth his hand also upon
the countries: and the land of [a]Egypt shall not
escape.
43 But he shall have power over the treasures
of gold and of silver, and over all the precious
things of Egypt: and the Libyans and the Ethiopians *shall be* [a]at his steps.
44 But tidings out of the east and out of the
north shall trouble him: therefore he shall go forth
with great fury to destroy, and utterly to make
away many.
45 And he shall plant the tabernacles of his
palace between the seas in [a]the glorious holy
mountain; [b]yet he shall come to his end, and none
shall help him.

Prophecy of the End Time

12 And at that time shall Michael stand up,
the great prince which standeth for the children of thy people: [a]and there shall be a time of
trouble, such as never was since there was a nation *even* to that same time: and at that time thy
people [b]shall be delivered, every one that shall
be found [c]written in the book.
2 And many of them that sleep in the dust
of the earth shall awake, [a]some to everlasting life,
and some to shame [b]*and* everlasting contempt.
3 And they that be wise shall [a]shine as the
brightness of the firmament; [b]and they that turn
many to righteousness [c]as the stars for ever and
ever.
4 But thou, O Daniel, [a]shut up the words,
and seal the book, *even* to the time of the end:
many shall [b]run to and fro, and knowledge shall
be increased.
5 Then I Daniel looked, and, behold, there
stood other two, the one on this side of the bank
of the river, and the other on that side of the bank
[a]of the river.
6 And *one* said to the man clothed in [a]linen,
which *was* upon the waters of the river, [b]How
long *shall it be to* the end of these wonders?
7 And I heard the man clothed in linen,
which *was* upon the waters of the river, when he
[a]held up his right hand and his left hand unto
heaven, and sware by him [b]that liveth for ever
[c]that *it shall be* for a time, times, and an half;
[d]and when he shall have accomplished to scatter
the power of [e]the holy people, all these *things*
shall be finished.
8 And I heard, but I understood not: then
said I, O my LORD, what *shall be* the end of these
things?
9 And he said, Go thy way, Daniel: for the
words *are* closed up and sealed till the time of
the end.
10 [a]Many shall be purified, and made white,
and tried; [b]but the wicked shall do wickedly: and
none of the wicked shall understand; but [c]the wise
shall understand.
11 And from the time *that* the daily *sacrifice*
shall be taken away, and the abomination that
maketh desolate set up, *there shall be* a thousand
two hundred and ninety days.
12 Blessed *is* he that waiteth, and cometh to
the thousand three hundred and five and thirty
days.
13 But go thou thy way till the end *be:* [a]for
thou shalt rest, [b]and stand in thy lot at the end
of the days.

41 [a]Is. 11:14
42 [a]Joel 3:19
43 [a]Ex. 11:8
45 [a]Ps. 48:2
[b]Rev. 19:20

CHAPTER 12

1 [a]Is. 26:20; Jer. 30:7; Ezek. 5:9; Dan. 9:12; Matt. 24:21; Mark 13:19 [b]Rom. 11:26 [c]Ex. 32:32; Ps. 56:8
2 [a][Matt. 25:46; John 5:28, 29; Acts 24:15] [b][Is. 66:24; Rom. 9:21]
3 [a]Prov. 3:35; Dan. 11:33, 35; Matt. 13:43 [b]Prov. 11:30; [James 5:19, 20] [c]1 Cor. 15:41
4 [a]Is. 8:16; Dan. 12:9; Rev. 22:10 [b]Amos 8:12
5 [a]Dan. 10:4
6 [a]Ezek. 9:2; Dan. 10:5 [b]Dan. 8:13; 12:8; Matt. 24:3; Mark 13:4
7 [a]Deut. 32:40 [b]Dan. 4:34 [c]Dan. 7:25; Rev. 12:14 [d]Luke 21:24 [e]Dan. 8:24
10 [a]Zech. 13:9 [b]Is. 32:6, 7; Rev. 22:11 [c]Dan. 12:3; Hos. 14:9; John 7:17; 8:47
13 [a]Is. 57:2; Rev. 14:13 [b]Ps. 1:5

NKJV

he shall enter the countries, overwhelm *them,* and
pass through.
41 "He shall also enter the Glorious Land,
and many *countries* shall be overthrown; but
these shall escape from his hand: [a]Edom, Moab,
and the prominent people of Ammon.
42 "He shall stretch out his hand against the
countries, and the land of [a]Egypt shall not escape.
43 "He shall have power over the treasures
of gold and silver, and over all the precious things
of Egypt; also the Libyans and Ethiopians *shall
follow* [a]at his heels.
44 "But news from the east and the north
shall trouble him; therefore he shall go out with
great fury to destroy and annihilate many.
45 "And he shall plant the tents of his palace
between the seas and [a]the glorious holy mountain; [b]yet he shall come to his end, and no one
will help him.

Prophecy of the End Time

12 "At that time Michael shall stand up,
The great prince who stands *watch* over
the sons of your people;
[a]And there shall be a time of trouble,
Such as never was since there was a nation,
Even to that time.
And at that time your people [b]shall be
delivered,
Every one who is found [c]written in the
book.
2 And many of those who sleep in the dust
of the earth shall awake,
[a]Some to everlasting life,
Some to shame [b]*and* everlasting
contempt.
3 Those who are wise shall [a]shine
Like the brightness of the firmament,
[b]And those who turn many to
righteousness
[c]Like the stars forever and ever.

4 "But you, Daniel, [a]shut up the words, and
seal the book until the time of the end; many shall
[b]run to and fro, and knowledge shall increase."
5 Then I, Daniel, looked; and there stood
two others, one on this riverbank and the other
on that [a]riverbank.
6 And *one* said to the man clothed in [a]linen,
who *was* above the waters of the river, [b]"How
long shall the fulfillment of these wonders *be?*"
7 Then I heard the man clothed in linen,
who *was* above the waters of the river, when he
[a]held up his right hand and his left hand to
heaven, and swore by Him [b]who lives forever,
[c]that *it shall be* for a time, times, and half *a time;*
[d]and when the power of [e]the holy people has been
completely shattered, all these *things* shall be
finished.
8 Although I heard, I did not understand.
Then I said, "My lord, what *shall be* the end of
these *things?*"
9 And he said, "Go *your way,* Daniel, for
the words *are* closed up and sealed till the time
of the end.
10 [a]"Many shall be purified, made white, and
refined, [b]but the wicked shall do wickedly; and
none of the wicked shall understand, but [c]the wise
shall understand.
11 "And from the time *that* the daily *sacrifice*
is taken away, and the abomination of desolation
is set up, *there shall be* one thousand two hundred
and ninety days.
12 "Blessed *is* he who waits, and comes to
the one thousand three hundred and thirty-five
days.
13 "But you, go *your way* till the end; [a]for
you shall rest, [b]and will arise to your inheritance
at the end of the days."

KJV

THE BOOK OF

HOSEA

1 The word of the LORD that came unto Hosea, the son of Beeri, in the days of [a]Uzziah, [b]Jotham, [c]Ahaz, *and* [d]Hezekiah, kings of Judah, and in the days of [e]Jeroboam the son of Joash, king of Israel.

The Family of Hosea

2 The beginning of the word of the LORD by Hosea. And the LORD said to Hosea, [a]Go, take unto thee a wife of whoredoms and children of whoredoms: for [b]the land hath committed great whoredom, *departing* from the LORD.

3 So he went and took Gomer the daughter of Diblaim; which conceived, and bare him a son.

4 And the LORD said unto him, Call his name Jezreel; for yet a little *while,* [a]and I will avenge the blood of Jezreel upon the house of Jehu, [b]and will cause to cease the kingdom of the house of Israel.

5 [a]And it shall come to pass at that day, that I will break the bow of Israel in the valley of Jezreel.

6 And she conceived again, and bare a daughter. And *God* said unto him, Call her name Lo–ruhamah: [a]for I will no more have mercy upon the house of Israel; but I will utterly take them away.

7 [a]But I will have mercy upon the house of Judah, and will save them by the LORD their God, and [b]will not save them by bow, nor by sword, nor by battle, by horses, nor by horsemen.

8 Now when she had weaned Lo–ruhamah, she conceived, and bare a son.

9 Then said *God,* Call his name Lo–ammi: for ye *are* not my people, and I will not be your *God.*

The Restoration of Israel

10 Yet [a]the number of the children of Israel shall be as the sand of the sea, which cannot be measured nor numbered; [b]and it shall come to pass, *that* in the place where it was said unto them, Ye *are* not my [c]people, *there* it shall be said unto them, *Ye are* [d]the sons of the living God.

11 [a]Then shall the children of Judah and the children of Israel be gathered together, and

CHAPTER 1

1 [a]2 Chr. 26; Is. 1:1; Amos 1:1 [b]2 Kin. 15:5, 7, 32–38; 2 Chr. 27; Mic. 1:1 [c]2 Kin. 16:1–20; 2 Chr. 28 [d]2 Kin. 18—20; 2 Chr. 29:1—32:33; Mic. 1:1 [e]2 Kin. 13:13; 14:23–29; Amos 1:1
2 [a]Hos. 3:1 [b]Deut. 31:16; Judg. 2:17; Ps. 73:27; Jer. 2:13; Ezek. 16:1–59; 23:1–49
4 [a]2 Kin. 10:11 [b]2 Kin. 15:8–10; 17:6, 23; 18:11
5 [a]2 Kin. 15:29
6 [a]2 Kin. 17:6
7 [a]2 Kin. 19:29–35; Is. 30:18; 37:36, 37 [b]Ps. 44:3–7; [Zech. 4:6]
10 [a]Gen. 22:17; 32:12; Jer. 33:22 [b]1 Pet. 2:10 [c]Rom. 9:26 [d]Is. 63:16; 64:8; [John 1:12]
11 [a]Is. 11:11–13; Jer. 3:18; 50:4; [Ezek. 34:23; 37:15–28]

*

1:6 Lit. *No-Mercy* • Or *That I may forgive them at all*
1:9 Lit. *Not-My-People*
1:10 Heb. *lo-ammi,* v. 9

NKJV

THE BOOK OF

HOSEA

1 The word of the LORD that came to Hosea the son of Beeri, in the days of [a]Uzziah, [b]Jotham, [c]Ahaz, *and* [d]Hezekiah, kings of Judah, and in the days of [e]Jeroboam the son of Joash, king of Israel.

The Family of Hosea

2 When the LORD began to speak by Hosea, the LORD said to Hosea:

[a]"Go, take yourself a wife of harlotry
And children of harlotry,
For [b]the land has committed great harlotry
By departing from the LORD."

3 So he went and took Gomer the daughter of Diblaim, and she conceived and bore him a son.

4 Then the LORD said to him:

"Call his name Jezreel,
For in a little *while*
[a]I will avenge the bloodshed of Jezreel on the house of Jehu,
[b]And bring an end to the kingdom of the house of Israel.
5 [a]It shall come to pass in that day
That I will break the bow of Israel in the Valley of Jezreel."

6 And she conceived again and bore a daughter. Then *God* said to him:

"Call her name *Lo-Ruhamah,
[a]For I will no longer have mercy on the house of Israel,
*But I will utterly take them away.
7 [a]Yet I will have mercy on the house of Judah,
Will save them by the LORD their God,
And [b]will not save them by bow,
Nor by sword or battle,
By horses or horsemen."

8 Now when she had weaned Lo-Ruhamah, she conceived and bore a son.

9 Then *God* said:

"Call his name *Lo-Ammi,
For you *are* not My people,
And I will not be your *God.*

The Restoration of Israel

10 "Yet [a]the number of the children of Israel
Shall be as the sand of the sea,
Which cannot be measured or numbered.
[b]And it shall come to pass
In the place where it was said to them,
'You *are* *not My [c]people,'
There it shall be said to them,
'*You are* [d]sons of the living God.'
11 [a]Then the children of Judah and the children of Israel
Shall be gathered together,

KJV

appoint themselves one head, and they shall come
up out of the land: for great *shall be* the day of
Jezreel.

2 Say ye unto your brethren, Ammi; and to your
sisters, Ruhamah.

God's Unfaithful People

2 Plead with your mother, plead: for [a]she
is not my wife, neither *am* I her husband: let her
therefore put away her [b]whoredoms out of her
sight, and her adulteries from between her
breasts;
3 Lest [a]I strip her naked, and set her as in
the day that she was [b]born, and make her as a
wilderness, and set her like a dry land, and slay
her with [c]thirst.
4 And I will not have mercy upon her children; for they *be* the [a]children of whoredoms.
5 For their mother hath played the harlot:
she that conceived them hath done shamefully:
for she said, I will go after my lovers, [a]that give
me my bread and my water, my wool and my
flax, mine oil and my drink.
6 Therefore, behold, [a]I will hedge up thy
way with thorns, and make a wall, that she shall
not find her paths.
7 And she shall follow after her lovers, but
she shall not overtake them; and she shall seek
them, but shall not find *them:* then shall she say,
[a]I will go and return to my [b]first husband; for
then *was it* better with me than now.
8 For she did not [a]know that I gave her corn,
and wine, and oil, and multiplied her silver and
gold, *which* they prepared for Baal.
9 Therefore will I return, and take away my
corn in the time thereof, and my wine in the season thereof, and will recover my wool and my
flax *given* to cover her nakedness.
10 And now [a]will I discover her lewdness in
the sight of her lovers, and none shall deliver her
out of mine hand.
11 [a]I will also cause all her mirth to cease,
her feast days, her new moons, and her sabbaths,
and all her solemn feasts.
12 And I will destroy her vines and her fig
trees, whereof she hath said, These *are* my rewards that my lovers have given me: and I will
make them a forest, and the beasts of the field
shall eat them.
13 And I will visit upon her the days of Baalim, wherein she burned incense to them, and she
decked herself with her earrings and her jewels,
and she went after her lovers, and forgat me, saith
the LORD.

God's Mercy on His People

14 Therefore, behold, I will allure her, and
bring her into the wilderness, and speak comfortably unto her.

CHAPTER 2
2 [a]Is. 50:1 [b]Ezek. 16:25
3 [a]Jer. 13:22, 26; Ezek. 16:37–39 [b]Ezek. 16:4–7, 22 [c]Jer. 14:3; Amos 8:11–13
4 [a]John 8:41
5 [a]Ezek. 23:5; Hos. 2:8, 12
6 [a]Job 19:8; Lam. 3:7, 9
7 [a]Luke 15:17, 18 [b]Is. 54:5–8; Jer. 2:2; 3:1; Ezek. 16:8; 23:4
8 [a]Is. 1:3; Ezek. 16:19
10 [a]Ezek. 16:37
11 [a]Jer. 7:34; 16:9; Hos. 3:4; Amos 5:21; 8:10

NKJV

And appoint for themselves one head;
And they shall come up out of the land,
For great *will be* the day of Jezreel!

2 Say to your brethren, *'My people,'
And to your sisters, *'Mercy *is shown.'*

God's Unfaithful People

2 "Bring charges against your mother, bring charges;
For [a]she *is* not My wife, nor *am* I her Husband!
Let her put away her [b]harlotries from her sight,
And her adulteries from between her breasts;
3 Lest [a]I strip her naked
And expose her, as in the day she was [b]born,
And make her like a wilderness,
And set her like a dry land,
And slay her with [c]thirst.

4 "I will not have mercy on her children,
For they *are* the [a]children of harlotry.
5 For their mother has played the harlot;
She who conceived them has behaved shamefully.
For she said, 'I will go after my lovers,
[a]Who give *me* my bread and my water,
My wool and my linen,
My oil and my drink.'

6 "Therefore, behold,
[a]I will hedge up your way with thorns,
And wall her in,
So that she cannot find her paths.
7 She will chase her lovers,
But not overtake them;
Yes, she will seek them, but not find *them.*
Then she will say,
[a]'I will go and return to my [b]first husband,
For then *it was* better for me than now.'
8 For she did not [a]know
That I gave her grain, new wine, and oil,
And multiplied her silver and gold—
Which they prepared for Baal.

9 "Therefore I will return and take away
My grain in its time
And My new wine in its season,
And will take back My wool and My linen,
Given to cover her nakedness.
10 Now [a]I will uncover her lewdness in the sight of her lovers,
And no one shall deliver her from My hand.
11 [a]I will also cause all her mirth to cease,
Her feast days,
Her New Moons,
Her Sabbaths—
All her appointed feasts.

12 "And I will destroy her vines and her fig trees,
Of which she has said,
'These *are* my wages that my lovers have given me.'
So I will make them a forest,
And the beasts of the field shall eat them.
13 I will punish her
For the days of the Baals to which she burned incense.
She decked herself with her earrings and jewelry,
And went after her lovers;
But Me she forgot," says the LORD.

God's Mercy on His People

14 "Therefore, behold, I will allure her,
Will bring her into the wilderness,
And speak comfort to her.

*
2:1 Heb. *Ammi,* Hos. 1:9, 10 • Heb. *Ruhamah,* Hos. 1:6

KJV

15 And I will give her her vineyards from
thence, and [a]the valley of Achor for a door of
hope: and she shall sing there, as in [b]the days of
her youth, and [c]as in the day when she came up
out of the land of Egypt.
16 And it shall be at that day, saith the LORD,
that thou shalt call me Ishi; and shalt call me no
more Baali.
17 For [a]I will take away the names of Baalim
out of her mouth, and they shall no more be remembered by their name.
18 And in that day will I make a [a]covenant
for them with the beasts of the field, and with
the fowls of heaven, and *with* the creeping things
of the ground: and [b]I will break the bow and the
sword and the battle out of the earth, and will
make them to [c]lie down safely.
19 And I will betroth thee unto me for ever;
yea, I will betroth thee unto me in righteousness,
and in judgment, and in lovingkindness, and in
mercies.
20 I will even betroth thee unto me in faithfulness: and [a]thou shalt know the LORD.
21 And it shall come to pass in that day, [a]I
will hear, saith the LORD, I will hear the heavens,
and they shall hear the earth;
22 And the earth shall hear the corn, and the
wine, and the oil; and they shall hear Jezreel.
23 And [a]I will sow her unto me in the earth;
[b]and I will have mercy upon her that had not obtained mercy; and I [c]will say to *them which were*
not my people, Thou *art* my people; and they shall
say, *Thou art* my God.

Israel Will Return to God

3 Then said the LORD unto me, Go yet, love a
woman beloved of *her* [a]friend, yet an adulteress, according to the love of the LORD toward the
children of Israel, who look to other gods, and
love flagons of wine.
2 So I bought her to me for fifteen *pieces*
of silver, and *for* an homer of barley, and an half
homer of barley:
3 And I said unto her, Thou shalt [a]abide for
me many days; thou shalt not play the harlot, and
thou shalt not be for *another* man: so *will* I also
be for thee.
4 For the children of Israel shall abide many
days [a]without a king, and without a prince, and
without a sacrifice, and without an image, and
without an [b]ephod, and *without* [c]teraphim:
5 Afterward shall the children of Israel return, and [a]seek the LORD their God, and [b]David
their king; and shall fear the LORD and his goodness in the [c]latter days.

God's Charge Against Israel

4 Hear the word of the LORD, ye children of Israel: for the LORD hath a [a]controversy with
the inhabitants of the land, because *there is* no
truth, nor mercy, nor [b]knowledge of God in the
land.

---

15 [a]Josh. 7:26 [b]Jer. 2:1–3; Ezek. 16:8–14 [c]Ex. 15:1
17 [a]Ex. 23:13; Josh. 23:7; Ps. 16:4
18 [a]Job 5:23; Is. 11:6–9; Ezek. 34:25 [b]Is. 2:4; Ezek. 39:1–10 [c]Lev. 26:5; Is. 32:18; Jer. 23:6; Ezek. 34:25
20 [a][Jer. 31:33, 34]; Hos. 6:6; 13:4; [John 17:3]
21 [a]Is. 55:10; Zech. 8:12; [Mal. 3:10, 11]
23 [a]Jer. 31:27; Amos 9:15 [b]Hos. 1:6 [c]Hos. 1:10; Zech. 13:9; Rom. 9:25, 26; [Eph. 2:11–22]; 1 Pet. 2:10

CHAPTER 3

1 [a]Jer. 3:20
3 [a]Deut. 21:13
4 [a]Hos. 10:3 [b]Ex. 28:4–12; 1 Sam. 23:9–12 [c]Gen. 31:19, 34; Judg. 17:5; 18:14, 17; [1 Sam. 15:23]
5 [a]Jer. 50:4 [b]Jer. 30:9; Ezek. 34:24 [c][Is. 2:2, 3]; Jer. 31:9

CHAPTER 4

1 [a]Is. 1:18; Hos. 12:2; Mic. 6:2 [b]Jer. 4:22

*

2:16 Heb. *Ishi* • Heb. *Baali*
2:22 Lit. *God Will Sow*
2:23 Heb. *lo-ruhamah* • Heb. *lo-ammi*
3:1 Lit. *friend* or *husband*

NKJV

15 I will give her her vineyards from there,
And [a]the Valley of Achor as a door of hope;
She shall sing there,
As in [b]the days of her youth,
[c]As in the day when she came up from the land of Egypt.

16 "And it shall be, in that day,"
Says the LORD,
"*That* you will call Me *'My Husband,'
And no longer call Me *'My Master,'
17 For [a]I will take from her mouth the names of the Baals,
And they shall be remembered by their name no more.
18 In that day I will make a [a]covenant for them
With the beasts of the field,
With the birds of the air,
And *with* the creeping things of the ground.
Bow and sword of battle [b]I will shatter from the earth,
To make them [c]lie down safely.

19 "I will betroth you to Me forever;
Yes, I will betroth you to Me
In righteousness and justice,
In lovingkindness and mercy;
20 I will betroth you to Me in faithfulness,
And [a]you shall know the LORD.

21 "It shall come to pass in that day
That [a]I will answer," says the LORD;
"I will answer the heavens,
And they shall answer the earth.
22 The earth shall answer
With grain,
With new wine,
And with oil;
They shall answer *Jezreel.
23 Then [a]I will sow her for Myself in the earth,
[b]And I will have mercy on *her who had* *not obtained mercy;
Then [c]I will say to *those who were* *not My people,
'You *are* My people!'
And they shall say, '*You are* my God!' "

Israel Will Return to God

3 Then the LORD said to me, "Go again, love a
woman *who is* loved by a [a]lover* and is committing adultery, just like the love of the LORD for the children of Israel, who look to other gods and love *the* raisin cakes *of the pagans.*"

2 So I bought her for myself for fifteen *shekels* of silver, and one and one-half homers of barley.

3 And I said to her, "You shall [a]stay with me many days; you shall not play the harlot, nor shall you have a man—so, too, *will* I *be* toward you."

4 For the children of Israel shall abide many days [a]without king or prince, without sacrifice or sacred pillar, without [b]ephod or [c]teraphim.

5 Afterward the children of Israel shall return and [a]seek the LORD their God and [b]David their king. They shall fear the LORD and His goodness in the [c]latter days.

God's Charge Against Israel

4 Hear the word of the LORD,
You children of Israel,
For the LORD *brings* a [a]charge against the inhabitants of the land:

"There is no truth or mercy
Or [b]knowledge of God in the land.

KJV

2 By swearing, and lying, and killing, and stealing, and committing adultery, they break out, and blood toucheth blood.

3 Therefore [a]shall the land mourn, and [b]every one that dwelleth therein shall languish, with the beasts of the field, and with the fowls of heaven; yea, the fishes of the sea also shall be taken away.

4 Yet let no man strive, nor reprove another: for thy people *are* as they [a]that strive with the priest.

5 Therefore shalt thou fall [a]in the day, and the prophet also shall fall with thee in the night, and I will destroy thy mother.

6 [a]My people are destroyed for lack of knowledge: because thou hast rejected knowledge, I will also reject thee, that thou shalt be no priest to me: [b]seeing thou hast forgotten the law of thy God, I will also forget thy children.

7 As they were increased, so they sinned against me: [a]*therefore* will I change their glory into shame.

8 They eat up the sin of my people, and they set their heart on their iniquity.

9 And there shall be, [a]like people, like priest: and I will punish them for their ways, and reward them their doings.

10 For [a]they shall eat, and not have enough: they shall commit whoredom, and shall not increase: because they have left off to take heed to the LORD.

The Idolatry of Israel

11 Whoredom and wine and new wine [a]take away the heart.

12 My people ask counsel at their [a]stocks, and their staff declareth unto them: for [b]the spirit of whoredoms hath caused *them* to err, and they have gone a whoring from under their God.

13 [a]They sacrifice upon the tops of the mountains, and burn incense upon the hills, under oaks and poplars and elms, because the shadow thereof *is* good: [b]therefore your daughters shall commit whoredom, and your spouses shall commit adultery.

14 I will not punish your daughters when they commit whoredom, nor your spouses when they commit adultery: for themselves are separated with whores, and they sacrifice with [a]harlots: therefore the people *that* doth not understand shall fall.

15 Though thou, Israel, play the harlot, *yet* let not Judah offend; [a]and come not ye unto Gilgal, neither go ye up to [b]Beth–aven, [c]nor swear, The LORD liveth.

16 For Israel [a]slideth back as a backsliding heifer: now the LORD will feed them as a lamb in a large place.

3 [a]Is. 24:4; 33:9; Jer. 4:28; 12:4; Amos 5:16; 8:8 [b]Zeph. 1:3
4 [a]Deut. 17:12
5 [a]Jer. 15:8; Hos. 2:2, 5
6 [a]Is. 5:13 [b]Ezek. 22:26
7 [a]1 Sam. 2:30; Mal. 2:9
9 [a]Is. 24:2; Jer. 5:30, 31; 2 Tim. 4:3, 4
10 [a]Lev. 26:26; Is. 65:13; Mic. 6:14; Hag. 1:6
11 [a]Prov. 20:1; Is. 5:12; 28:7
12 [a]Jer. 2:27 [b]Is. 44:19, 20
13 [a]Is. 1:29; 57:5, 7; Jer. 2:20; Ezek. 6:13; 20:28 [b]Amos 7:17; [Rom. 1:28–32]
14 [a]Deut. 23:18
15 [a]Hos. 9:15; 12:11 [b]1 Kin. 12:29; Josh. 7:2; Hos. 10:8 [c]Jer. 5:2; 44:26; Amos 8:14
16 [a]Jer. 3:6; 7:24; 8:5; Zech. 7:11

NKJV

2 *By* swearing and lying,
Killing and stealing and committing adultery,
They break all restraint,
With bloodshed upon bloodshed.
3 Therefore [a]the land will mourn;
And [b]everyone who dwells there will waste away
With the beasts of the field
And the birds of the air;
Even the fish of the sea will be taken away.

4 "Now let no man contend, or rebuke another;
For your people *are* like those [a]who contend with the priest.
5 Therefore you shall stumble [a]in the day;
The prophet also shall stumble with you in the night;
And I will destroy your mother.
6 [a]My people are destroyed for lack of knowledge.
Because you have rejected knowledge,
I also will reject you from being priest for Me;
[b]Because you have forgotten the law of your God,
I also will forget your children.

7 "The more they increased,
The more they sinned against Me;
[a]I* will change *their glory into shame.
8 They eat up the sin of My people;
They set their heart on their iniquity.
9 And it shall be: [a]like people, like priest.
So I will punish them for their ways,
And reward them for their deeds.
10 For [a]they shall eat, but not have enough;
They shall commit harlotry, but not increase;
Because they have ceased obeying the LORD.

The Idolatry of Israel

11 "Harlotry, wine, and new wine [a]enslave the heart.
12 My people ask counsel from their [a]wooden *idols,*
And their staff informs them.
For [b]the spirit of harlotry has caused *them* to stray,
And they have played the harlot against their God.
13 [a]They offer sacrifices on the mountaintops,
And burn incense on the hills,
Under oaks, poplars, and terebinths,
Because their shade *is* good.
[b]Therefore your daughters commit harlotry,
And your brides commit adultery.

14 "I will not punish your daughters when they commit harlotry,
Nor your brides when they commit adultery;
For *the men* themselves go apart with harlots,
And offer sacrifices with a [a]ritual harlot.
Therefore people *who* do not understand will be trampled.

15 "Though you, Israel, play the harlot,
Let not Judah offend.
[a]Do not come up to Gilgal,
Nor go up to [b]Beth Aven,
[c]Nor swear an oath, *saying,* 'As the LORD lives'—

16 "For Israel [a]is stubborn
Like a stubborn calf;
Now the LORD will let them forage
Like a lamb in open country.

4:7 So with MT, LXX, Vg.; scribal tradition, Syr., Tg. *They will change* • So with MT, LXX, Syr., Tg., Vg.; scribal tradition *My glory*

KJV

17 Ephraim *is* joined to idols: [a]let him alone.
18 Their drink is sour: they have committed
whoredom continually: [a]her rulers *with* shame do
love, Give ye.
19 [a]The wind hath bound her up in her
wings, and [b]they shall be ashamed because of
their sacrifices.

Impending Judgment on Israel and Judah

5 Hear ye this, O priests; and hearken, ye house
of Israel; and give ye ear, O house of the king;
for judgment *is* toward you, because [a]ye have
been a snare on Mizpah, and a net spread upon
Tabor.
2 And the revolters are [a]profound to make
slaughter, though I *have been* a rebuker of them
all.
3 [a]I know Ephraim, and Israel is not hid
from me: for now, O Ephraim, [b]thou committest
whoredom, *and* Israel is defiled.
4 They will not frame their doings to turn
unto their God: for [a]the spirit of whoredoms *is*
in the midst of them, and they have not known
the LORD.
5 And the [a]pride of Israel doth testify to his
face: therefore shall Israel and Ephraim fall in
their iniquity; Judah also shall fall with them.
6 [a]They shall go with their flocks and with
their herds to seek the LORD; but they shall not
find *him;* he hath withdrawn himself from them.
7 They have [a]dealt treacherously against
the LORD: for they have begotten strange children:
now shall a month devour them with their
portions.
8 [a]Blow ye the cornet in Gibeah, *and* the
trumpet in Ramah: [b]cry aloud *at* [c]Beth–aven, after thee, O Benjamin.
9 Ephraim shall be desolate in the day of
rebuke: among the tribes of Israel have I made
known that which shall surely be.
10 The princes of Judah were like them that
[a]remove the bound: *therefore* I will pour out my
wrath upon them like water.
11 Ephraim *is* [a]oppressed *and* broken in
judgment, because he willingly walked after [b]the
commandment.
12 Therefore *will* I *be* unto Ephraim as a
moth, and to the house of Judah [a]as rottenness.
13 When Ephraim saw his sickness, and Judah *saw* his [a]wound, then went Ephraim [b]to the
Assyrian, and sent to king Jareb: yet could he
not heal you, nor cure you of your wound.
14 For [a]I *will be* unto Ephraim as a lion, and
as a young lion to the house of Judah: [b]I, *even* I,
will tear and go away; I will take away, and none
shall rescue *him.*
15 I will go *and* return to my place, till they
acknowledge their offence, and seek my face:

17 [a]Matt. 15:14
18 [a]Mic. 3:11
19 [a]Jer. 51:1 [b]Is. 1:29

CHAPTER 5

1 [a]Hos. 6:9
2 [a]Is. 29:15; Hos. 4:2; 6:9
3 [a]Amos 3:2; 5:12 [b]Hos. 4:17
4 [a]Hos. 4:12
5 [a]Hos. 7:10
6 [a]Prov. 1:28; Is. 1:15; Jer. 11:11; Ezek. 8:18; Mic. 3:4; John 7:34
7 [a]Is. 48:8; Jer. 3:20; Hos. 6:7
8 [a]Hos. 8:1; Joel 2:1 [b]Is. 10:30 [c]Josh. 7:2
10 [a]Deut. 19:14; 27:17
11 [a]Deut. 28:33 [b]Mic. 6:16
12 [a]Prov. 12:4
13 [a]Jer. 30:12–15 [b]2 Kin. 15:19; Hos. 7:11; 10:6
14 [a]Ps. 7:2; Lam. 3:10; Hos. 13:7, 8 [b]Ps. 50:22

NKJV

17 "Ephraim *is* joined to idols,
[a]Let him alone.
18 Their drink is rebellion,
They commit harlotry continually.
[a]Her rulers *dearly love dishonor.
19 [a]The wind has wrapped her up in its wings,
And [b]they shall be ashamed because of their sacrifices.

Impending Judgment on Israel and Judah

5 "Hear this, O priests!
Take heed, O house of Israel!
Give ear, O house of the king!
For yours *is* the judgment,
Because [a]you have been a snare to Mizpah
And a net spread on Tabor.
2 The revolters are [a]deeply involved in slaughter,
Though I rebuke them all.
3 [a]I know Ephraim,
And Israel is not hidden from Me;
For now, O Ephraim, [b]you commit harlotry;
Israel is defiled.

4 "They do not direct their deeds
Toward turning to their God,
For [a]the spirit of harlotry is in their midst,
And they do not know the LORD.
5 The [a]pride of Israel testifies to his face;
Therefore Israel and Ephraim stumble in their iniquity;
Judah also stumbles with them.

6 "With their flocks and herds
[a]They shall go to seek the LORD,
But they will not find *Him;*
He has withdrawn Himself from them.
7 They have [a]dealt treacherously with the LORD,
For they have begotten pagan children.
Now a New Moon shall devour them and their heritage.

8 "Blow[a] the ram's horn in Gibeah,
The trumpet in Ramah!
[b]Cry aloud *at* [c]Beth Aven,
'*Look* behind you, O Benjamin!'
9 Ephraim shall be desolate in the day of rebuke;
Among the tribes of Israel I make known what is sure.

10 "The princes of Judah are like those who [a]remove a landmark;
I will pour out my wrath on them like water.
11 Ephraim is [a]oppressed *and* broken in judgment,
Because he willingly walked by [b]*human* precept.
12 Therefore I *will be* to Ephraim like a moth,
And to the house of Judah [a]like rottenness.

13 "When Ephraim saw his sickness,
And Judah *saw* his [a]wound,
Then Ephraim went [b]to Assyria
And sent to King Jareb;
Yet he cannot cure you,
Nor heal you of your wound.
14 For [a]I *will be* like a lion to Ephraim,
And like a young lion to the house of Judah.
[b]I, *even* I, will tear *them* and go away;
I will take *them* away, and no one shall rescue.
15 I will return again to My place
Till they acknowledge their offense.
Then they will seek My face;

*4:18 Heb. difficult; a Jewish tradition *shamefully love, 'Give!'*

KJV

in their affliction they will seek me early.

A Call to Repentance

6 Come,[a] and let us return unto the LORD: for [b]he hath torn, and [c]he will heal us; he hath smitten, and he will bind us up.

2 [a]After two days will he revive us: in the third day he will raise us up, and we shall live in his sight.

3 [a]Then shall we know, *if* we follow on to know the LORD: his going forth is prepared [b]as the morning; and [c]he shall come unto us [d]as the rain, as the latter *and* former rain unto the earth.

Impenitence of Israel and Judah

4 O Ephraim, what shall I do unto thee? O Judah, what shall I do unto thee? for your goodness *is* as a morning cloud, and as the early dew it goeth away.

5 Therefore have I hewed *them* by the prophets; I have slain them by [a]the words of my mouth: and thy judgments *are as* the light *that* goeth forth.

6 For I desired [a]mercy, and [b]not sacrifice; and the [c]knowledge of God more than burnt offerings.

7 But they like men have transgressed the covenant: there have they dealt treacherously against me.

8 [a]Gilead *is* a city of them that work iniquity, *and is* polluted with blood.

9 And as troops of robbers wait for a man, *so* the company of [a]priests [b]murder in the way by consent: for they commit [c]lewdness.

10 I have seen an horrible thing in the house of Israel: there *is* the whoredom of Ephraim, Israel is defiled.

11 Also, O Judah, he hath set an harvest for thee, when I returned the captivity of my people.

7 When I would have healed Israel, then the iniquity of Ephraim was discovered, and the wickedness of Samaria: for [a]they commit falsehood; and the thief cometh in, *and* the troop of robbers spoileth without.

2 And they consider not in their hearts *that* I [a]remember all their wickedness: now their own doings have beset them about; they are before my face.

3 They make the [a]king glad with their wickedness, and the princes [b]with their lies.

4 [a]They *are* all adulterers, as an oven heated by the baker, *who* ceaseth from raising after he hath kneaded the dough, until it be leavened.

5 In the day of our king the princes have made *him* sick with bottles of [a]wine; he stretched out his hand with scorners.

6 For they have made ready their heart like an oven, whiles they lie in wait: their baker sleepeth all the night; in the morning it burneth as a flaming fire.

CHAPTER 6

1 [a]Is. 1:18; Acts 10:43 [b]Deut. 32:39; Hos. 5:14 [c]Jer. 30:17; Hos. 14:4
2 [a]Luke 24:46; Acts 10:40; [1 Cor. 15:4]
3 [a]Is. 54:13 [b]2 Sam. 23:4 [c]Ps. 72:6; Joel 2:23 [d]Job 29:23
5 [a][Jer. 23:29]
6 [a]Matt. 9:13; 12:7 [b]Is. 1:12, 13; [Mic. 6:6–8] [c][John 17:3]
8 [a]Hos. 12:11
9 [a]Hos. 5:1 [b]Jer. 7:9, 10; Hos. 4:2 [c]Ezek. 22:9; 23:27; Hos. 2:10

CHAPTER 7

1 [a]Ezek. 23:4–8; Hos. 5:1
2 [a]Ps. 25:7; Jer. 14:10; 17:1; Hos. 8:13; 9:9; Amos 8:7
3 [a]Hos. 1:1 [b]Mic. 7:3; [Rom. 1:32]
4 [a]Jer. 9:2; 23:10
5 [a]Is. 28:1, 7

*

6:7 Or *Adam*
7:6 So with MT, Vg.; Syr., Tg. *Their anger;* LXX *Ephraim*

NKJV

In their affliction they will earnestly seek Me."

A Call to Repentance

6 Come,[a] and let us return to the LORD;
For [b]He has torn, but [c]He will heal us;
He has stricken, but He will bind us up.
2 [a]After two days He will revive us;
On the third day He will raise us up,
That we may live in His sight.
3 [a]Let us know,
Let us pursue the knowledge of the LORD.
His going forth is established [b]as the morning;
[c]He will come to us [d]like the rain,
Like the latter *and* former rain to the earth.

Impenitence of Israel and Judah

4 "O Ephraim, what shall I do to you?
O Judah, what shall I do to you?
For your faithfulness is like a morning cloud,
And like the early dew it goes away.
5 Therefore I have hewn *them* by the prophets,
I have slain them by [a]the words of My mouth;
And your judgments *are like* light *that* goes forth.
6 For I desire [a]mercy and [b]not sacrifice,
And the [c]knowledge of God more than burnt offerings.

7 "But like *men they transgressed the covenant;
There they dealt treacherously with Me.
8 [a]Gilead *is* a city of evildoers
And defiled with blood.
9 As bands of robbers lie in wait for a man,
So the company of [a]priests [b]murder on the way to Shechem;
Surely they commit [c]lewdness.
10 I have seen a horrible thing in the house of Israel:
There *is* the harlotry of Ephraim;
Israel is defiled.
11 Also, O Judah, a harvest is appointed for you,
When I return the captives of My people.

7 "When I would have healed Israel,
Then the iniquity of Ephraim was uncovered,
And the wickedness of Samaria.
For [a]they have committed fraud;
A thief comes in;
A band of robbers takes spoil outside.
2 They do not consider in their hearts
That [a]I remember all their wickedness;
Now their own deeds have surrounded them;
They are before My face.
3 They make a [a]king glad with their wickedness,
And princes [b]with their lies.

4 "They[a] *are* all adulterers.
Like an oven heated by a baker—
He ceases stirring *the fire* after kneading the dough,
Until it is leavened.
5 In the day of our king
Princes have made *him* sick, inflamed with [a]wine;
He stretched out his hand with scoffers.
6 They prepare their heart like an oven,
While they lie in wait;
*Their baker sleeps all night;
In the morning it burns like a flaming fire.

KJV

7 They are all hot as an oven, and have devoured their judges; all their kings are fallen: [a]*there is* none among them that calleth unto me.

8 Ephraim, he [a]hath mixed himself among the people; Ephraim is a cake not turned.

9 [a]Strangers have devoured his strength, and he knoweth *it* not: yea, gray hairs are here and there upon him, yet he knoweth not.

10 And the [a]pride of Israel testifieth to his face: and [b]they do not return to the LORD their God, nor seek him for all this.

Futile Reliance on the Nations

11 [a]Ephraim also is like a silly dove without heart: [b]they call to Egypt, they go to [c]Assyria.

12 When they shall go, I will [a]spread my net upon them; I will bring them down as the fowls of the heaven; I will chastise them, [b]as their congregation hath heard.

13 Woe unto them! for they have fled from me: destruction unto them! because they have transgressed against me: though [a]I have redeemed them, yet they have spoken lies against me.

14 [a]And they have not cried unto me with their heart, when they howled upon their beds: they assemble themselves for corn and [b]wine, *and* they rebel against me.

15 Though I have bound *and* strengthened their arms, yet do they imagine mischief against me.

16 They return, *but* not to the most High: [a]they are like a deceitful bow: their princes shall fall by the sword for the [b]rage of their tongue: this *shall be* their derision [c]in the land of Egypt.

The Apostasy of Israel

8 *Set* the trumpet to thy mouth. *He shall come* [a]as an eagle against the house of the LORD, because they have transgressed my covenant, and trespassed against my law.

2 [a]Israel shall cry unto me, My God, [b]we know thee.

3 Israel hath cast off *the thing that is* good: the enemy shall pursue him.

4 [a]They have set up kings, but not by me: they have made princes, and I knew *it* not: of their silver and their gold have they made them idols, that they may be cut off.

5 Thy calf, O Samaria, hath cast *thee* off; mine anger is kindled against them: [a]how long *will it be* ere they attain to innocency?

6 For from Israel *was* it also: the [a]workman made it; therefore it *is* not God: but the calf of Samaria shall be broken in pieces.

7 For [a]they have sown the wind, and they shall reap the whirlwind: it hath no stalk: the bud

7 [a]Is. 64:7
8 [a]Ps. 106:35
9 [a]Is. 1:7; 42:25; Hos. 8:7
10 [a]Hos. 5:5 [b]Is. 9:13
11 [a]Hos. 11:11 [b]Is. 30:3 [c]Hos. 5:13; 8:9
12 [a]Ezek. 12:13 [b]Lev. 26:14; Deut. 28:15; 2 Kin. 17:13
13 [a]Ex. 18:8; Mic. 6:4
14 [a]Job 35:9, 10; Ps. 78:36; Jer. 3:10; Zech. 7:5 [b]Judg. 9:27; Amos 2:8
16 [a]Ps. 78:57 [b]Ps. 73:9; Dan. 7:25; Mal. 3:13, 14 [c]Deut. 28:68; Ezek. 23:32; Hos. 8:13; 9:3

CHAPTER 8

1 [a]Deut. 28:49; Jer. 4:13
2 [a]Ps. 78:34; Hos. 5:15; 7:14 [b]Titus 1:16
4 [a]1 Kin. 12:20; 2 Kin. 15:23, 25; Hos. 13:10, 11
5 [a]Ps. 19:13; Jer. 13:27
6 [a]Is. 40:19
7 [a]Prov. 22:8

*

7:14 So with MT, Tg.; Vg. *thought upon;* LXX *slashed themselves for* (cf. 1 Kin. 18:28) • So with MT, Syr., Tg.; LXX omits *They rebel against Me;* Vg. *They departed from Me*
7:16 Or *upward*
8:1 ram's horn, Heb. *shophar*

NKJV

7 They are all hot, like an oven,
And have devoured their judges;
All their kings have fallen.
[a]None among them calls upon Me.

8 "Ephraim [a]has mixed himself among the peoples;
Ephraim is a cake unturned.
9 [a]Aliens have devoured his strength,
But he does not know *it;*
Yes, gray hairs are here and there on him,
Yet he does not know *it.*
10 And the [a]pride of Israel testifies to his face,
But [b]they do not return to the LORD their God,
Nor seek Him for all this.

Futile Reliance on the Nations

11 "Ephraim[a] also is like a silly dove, without sense—
[b]They call to Egypt,
They go to [c]Assyria.
12 Wherever they go, I will [a]spread My net on them;
I will bring them down like birds of the air;
I will chastise them
[b]According to what their congregation has heard.

13 "Woe to them, for they have fled from Me!
Destruction to them,
Because they have transgressed against Me!
Though [a]I redeemed them,
Yet they have spoken lies against Me.
14 [a]They did not cry out to Me with their heart
When they wailed upon their beds.

"They *assemble together for grain and new [b]wine,
*They rebel against Me;
15 Though I disciplined *and* strengthened their arms,
Yet they devise evil against Me;
16 They return, *but* not *to the Most High;
[a]They are like a treacherous bow.
Their princes shall fall by the sword
For the [b]cursings of their tongue.
This *shall be* their derision [c]in the land of Egypt.

The Apostasy of Israel

8 "Set the *trumpet to your mouth!
He shall come [a]like an eagle against the house of the LORD,
Because they have transgressed My covenant
And rebelled against My law.
2 [a]Israel will cry to Me,
'My God, [b]we know You!'
3 Israel has rejected the good;
The enemy will pursue him.

4 "They[a] set up kings, but not by Me;
They made princes, but I did not acknowledge *them.*
From their silver and gold
They made idols for themselves—
That they might be cut off.
5 Your calf is rejected, O Samaria!
My anger is aroused against them—
[a]How long until they attain to innocence?
6 For from Israel *is* even this:
A [a]workman made it, and it *is* not God;
But the calf of Samaria shall be broken to pieces.

7 "They[a] sow the wind,
And reap the whirlwind.

KJV

shall yield no meal: if so be it yield, the [b]strangers
shall swallow it up.
8 [a]Israel is swallowed up: now shall they
be among the Gentiles [b]as a vessel wherein *is* no
pleasure.
9 For they are gone up to Assyria, [a]a wild
ass alone by himself: Ephraim [b]hath hired lovers.
10 Yea, though they have hired among the
nations, now [a]will I gather them, and they shall
sorrow a little for the burden of [b]the king of
princes.
11 Because Ephraim hath made many altars
to sin, altars shall be unto him to sin.
12 I have written to him [a]the great things of
my law, *but* they were counted as a strange thing.
13 [a]They sacrifice flesh *for* the sacrifices of
mine offerings, and eat *it;* [b]*but* the LORD accepteth
them not; [c]now will he remember their iniquity,
and visit their sins: they shall return to Egypt.
14 [a]For Israel hath forgotten [b]his Maker, and
buildeth temples; and Judah hath multiplied
[c]fenced cities: but [d]I will send a fire upon his cities, and it shall devour the palaces thereof.

7 [b]Hos. 7:9
8 [a]2 Kin. 17:6; Jer. 51:34 [b]Jer. 22:28; 25:34
9 [a]Hos. 7:11; 12:1; Jer. 2:24 [b]Ezek. 16:33, 34
10 [a]Ezek. 16:37; 22:20 [b]Is. 10:8; Ezek. 26:7; Dan. 2:37
12 [a][Deut. 4:6–8]; Ps. 119:18; 147:19, 20
13 [a]Zech. 7:6 [b]Jer. 14:10; Hos. 6:6; 9:4; 1 Cor. 4:5 [c]Hos. 9:9; Amos 8:7; Luke 12:2
14 [a]Deut. 32:18; [Hos. 2:13; 4:6; 13:6] [b]Is. 29:23 [c]Num. 32:17; 2 Kin. 18:13 [d]Jer. 17:27

NKJV

The stalk has no bud;
It shall never produce meal.
If it should produce,
[b]Aliens would swallow it up.
8 [a]Israel is swallowed up;
Now they are among the Gentiles
[b]Like a vessel in which *is* no pleasure.
9 For they have gone up to Assyria,
Like [a]a wild donkey alone by itself;
Ephraim [b]has hired lovers.
10 Yes, though they have hired among the
nations,
Now [a]I will gather them;
And they shall *sorrow a little,
Because of the *burden of [b]the king of
princes.

11 "Because Ephraim has made many altars
for sin,
They have become for him altars for
sinning.
12 I have written for him [a]the great things
of My law,
But they were considered a strange
thing.
13 *For* the sacrifices of My offerings [a]they
sacrifice flesh and eat *it,*
[b]*But* the LORD does not accept them.
[c]Now He will remember their iniquity and
punish their sins.
They shall return to Egypt.

14 "For[a] Israel has forgotten [b]his Maker,
And has built *temples;
Judah also has multiplied [c]fortified
cities;
But [d]I will send fire upon his cities,
And it shall devour his palaces."

Judgment of Israel's Sin

9 Rejoice [a]not, O Israel, for joy, as *other* people:
for thou hast gone a whoring from thy God,
thou hast loved a [b]reward upon every cornfloor.
2 The floor and the winepress shall not feed
them, and the new wine shall fail in her.
3 They shall not dwell in [a]the LORD's land;
[b]but Ephraim shall return to Egypt, and [c]they
shall eat unclean *things* in Assyria.
4 They shall not offer wine *offerings* to the
LORD, [a]neither shall they be pleasing unto him:
their [b]sacrifices *shall be* unto them as the bread
of mourners; all that eat thereof shall be polluted:
for their bread for their soul shall not come into
the house of the LORD.
5 What will ye do in the solemn day, and
in the day of the feast of the LORD?
6 For, lo, they are gone because of destruction: Egypt shall gather them up, Memphis shall
bury them: the pleasant *places* for their silver,
[a]nettles shall possess them: thorns *shall be* in their
tabernacles.
7 The [a]days of visitation are come, the days
of recompence are come; Israel shall know *it:* the
prophet *is* a [b]fool, [c]the spiritual man *is* mad, for
the multitude of thine iniquity, and the great
hatred.

CHAPTER 9

1 [a]Is. 22:12, 13; Hos. 10:5 [b]Jer. 44:17
3 [a][Lev. 25:23]; Jer. 2:7 [b]Hos. 7:16; 8:13 [c]Ezek. 4:13
4 [a]Jer. 6:20 [b]Hos. 8:13; Amos 5:22
6 [a]Is. 5:6; 7:23; Hos. 10:8
7 [a]Is. 10:3; Jer. 10:15; Mic. 7:4; Luke 21:22 [b]Lam. 2:14; [Ezek. 13:3, 10] [c]Mic. 2:11

Judgment of Israel's Sin

9 Do[a] not rejoice, O Israel, with joy like
other peoples,
For you have played the harlot against
your God.
You have made love *for* [b]hire on every
threshing floor.
2 The threshing floor and the winepress
Shall not feed them,
And the new wine shall fail in her.

3 They shall not dwell in [a]the LORD's land,
[b]But Ephraim shall return to Egypt,
And [c]shall eat unclean *things* in
Assyria.
4 They shall not offer wine *offerings* to the
LORD,
Nor [a]shall their [b]sacrifices be pleasing to
Him.
It shall be like bread of mourners to them;
All who eat it shall be defiled.
For their bread *shall be* for their *own*
life;
It shall not come into the house of the
LORD.

5 What will you do in the appointed day,
And in the day of the feast of the LORD?
6 For indeed they are gone because of
destruction.
Egypt shall gather them up;
Memphis shall bury them.
[a]Nettles shall possess their valuables of
silver;
Thorns *shall be* in their tents.

7 The [a]days of punishment have come;
The days of recompense have come.
Israel knows!
The prophet *is* a [b]fool,
[c]The spiritual man *is* insane,
Because of the greatness of your iniquity
and great enmity.

*

8:10 Or *begin to diminish* • Or *oracle* or *proclamation*
8:14 Or *palaces*

KJV

8 The [a]watchman of Ephraim *was* with my God: *but* the prophet *is* a snare of a fowler in all his ways, *and* hatred in the house of his God.

9 [a]They have deeply corrupted *themselves,* as in the days of [b]Gibeah: *therefore* he will remember their iniquity, he will visit their sins.

10 I found Israel like grapes in the [a]wilderness; I saw your fathers as the [b]firstripe in the fig tree at her first time: *but* they went to [c]Baal–peor, and separated themselves unto *that* shame; [d]and *their* abominations were according as they loved.

11 *As for* Ephraim, their glory shall fly away like a bird, from the birth, and from the womb, and from the conception.

12 Though they bring up their children, yet will I bereave them, *that there shall* not *be* a man *left:* yea, [a]woe also to them when I depart from them!

13 Ephraim, [a]as I saw Tyrus, *is* planted in a pleasant place: but Ephraim shall bring forth his children to the murderer.

14 Give them, O LORD: what wilt thou give? give them [a]a miscarrying womb and dry breasts.

15 All their wickedness *is* in [a]Gilgal: for there I hated them: for the wickedness of their doings I will drive them out of mine house, I will love them no more: [b]all their princes *are* revolters.

16 Ephraim is [a]smitten, their root is dried up, they shall bear no fruit: yea, though they bring forth, yet will I slay *even* the beloved *fruit* of their womb.

17 My God will [a]cast them away, because they did not hearken unto him: and they shall be [b]wanderers among the nations.

Israel's Sin and Captivity

10 Israel *is* [a]an empty vine, he bringeth forth fruit unto himself: according to the multitude of his fruit [b]he hath increased the altars; according to the goodness of his land they have made goodly images.

2 Their heart is [a]divided; now shall they be found faulty: he shall break down their altars, he shall spoil their images.

3 For now they shall say, We have no king, because we feared not the LORD; what then should a king do to us?

4 They have spoken words, swearing falsely in making a covenant: [a]thus judgment springeth up as hemlock in the furrows of the field.

5 The inhabitants of Samaria shall fear because of the [a]calves of Beth–aven: for the people thereof shall mourn over it, and the priests thereof *that* rejoiced on it, for the [b]glory thereof, because it is departed from it.

8 [a]Jer. 6:17; 31:6; Ezek. 3:17; 33:7
9 [a]Hos. 10:9 [b]Judg. 19:22
10 [a]Jer. 2:2 [b]Is. 28:4; Mic. 7:1 [c]Num. 25:3; Ps. 106:28 [d]Ps. 81:12
12 [a]Deut. 31:17; Hos. 7:13
13 [a]Ezek. 26—28
14 [a]Luke 23:29
15 [a]Hos. 4:15; 12:11 [b]Is. 1:23; Hos. 5:2
16 [a]Hos. 5:11
17 [a]2 Kin. 17:20; [Zech. 10:6] [b]Lev. 26:33

CHAPTER 10
1 [a]Nah. 2:2 [b]Jer. 2:28; Hos. 8:11; 12:11
2 [a]1 Kin. 18:21; Zeph. 1:5; [Matt. 6:24]
4 [a]Deut. 31:16, 17; 2 Kin. 17:3, 4; Amos 5:7
5 [a]1 Kin. 12:28, 29; Hos. 8:5, 6; 13:2 [b]Hos. 9:11

*

9:8 One who catches birds in a trap or snare
10:5 Lit. *calves,* images

NKJV

8 The [a]watchman of Ephraim *is* with my God;
But the prophet *is* a *fowler's snare in all his ways—
Enmity in the house of his God.
9 [a]They are deeply corrupted,
As in the days of [b]Gibeah.
He will remember their iniquity;
He will punish their sins.

10 "I found Israel
Like grapes in the [a]wilderness;
I saw your fathers
As the [b]firstfruits on the fig tree in its first season.
But they went to [c]Baal Peor,
And separated themselves *to that* shame;
[d]They became an abomination like the thing they loved.
11 *As for* Ephraim, their glory shall fly away like a bird—
No birth, no pregnancy, and no conception!
12 Though they bring up their children,
Yet I will bereave them to the last man.
Yes, [a]woe to them when I depart from them!
13 Just [a]as I saw Ephraim like Tyre, planted in a pleasant place,
So Ephraim will bring out his children to the murderer."

14 Give them, O LORD—
What will You give?
Give them [a]a miscarrying womb
And dry breasts!

15 "All their wickedness *is* in [a]Gilgal,
For there I hated them.
Because of the evil of their deeds
I will drive them from My house;
I will love them no more.
[b]All their princes *are* rebellious.
16 Ephraim is [a]stricken,
Their root is dried up;
They shall bear no fruit.
Yes, were they to bear children,
I would kill the darlings of their womb."

17 My God will [a]cast them away,
Because they did not obey Him;
And they shall be [b]wanderers among the nations.

Israel's Sin and Captivity

10 Israel [a]empties *his* vine;
He brings forth fruit for himself.
According to the multitude of his fruit
[b]He has increased the altars;
According to the bounty of his land
They have embellished *his* sacred pillars.
2 Their heart is [a]divided;
Now they are held guilty.
He will break down their altars;
He will ruin their sacred pillars.

3 For now they say,
"We have no king,
Because we did not fear the LORD.
And as for a king, what would he do for us?"
4 They have spoken words,
Swearing falsely in making a covenant.
Thus judgment springs up [a]like hemlock in the furrows of the field.

5 The inhabitants of Samaria fear
Because of the [a]calf* of Beth Aven.
For its people mourn for it,
And its priests shriek for it—
Because its [b]glory has departed from it.

KJV

6 It shall be also carried unto Assyria *for* a
present to king [a]Jareb: Ephraim shall receive
shame, and Israel shall be ashamed of his own
counsel.
7 *As for* Samaria, her king is cut off as the
foam upon the water.
8 The [a]high places also of Aven, [b]the sin
of Israel, shall be destroyed: the thorn and the
thistle shall come up on their altars; [c]and they
shall say to the mountains, Cover us; and to the
hills, Fall on us.
9 O Israel, thou hast sinned from the days
of [a]Gibeah: there they stood: the [b]battle in Gibeah
against the children of iniquity did not overtake
them.
10 *It is* in my desire that I should chastise
them; and [a]the people shall be gathered against
them, when they shall bind themselves in their
two furrows.
11 And Ephraim *is as* [a]an heifer *that is*
taught, *and* loveth to tread out *the corn;* but I
passed over upon her fair neck: I will make
Ephraim to ride; Judah shall plow, *and* Jacob shall
break his clods.
12 Sow to yourselves in righteousness, reap
in mercy; [a]break up your fallow ground: for *it is*
time to seek the LORD, till he [b]come and rain righteousness upon you.
13 [a]Ye have plowed wickedness, ye have
reaped iniquity; ye have eaten the fruit of lies: because thou didst trust in thy way, in the multitude
of thy mighty men.
14 Therefore shall a tumult arise among thy
people, and all thy fortresses shall be spoiled, as
Shalman spoiled Beth–arbel in the day of battle:
the mother was dashed in pieces upon *her*
children.
15 So shall Beth–el do unto you because of
your great wickedness: in a morning shall the
king of Israel utterly be cut off.

God's Continuing Love for Israel

11 When Israel *was* a child, then I loved him,
and [a]called my [b]son out of Egypt.
2 *As* they called them, so they [a]went from
them: they sacrificed unto Baalim, and burned incense to graven images.
3 [a]I taught Ephraim also to go, taking them
by their arms; but they knew not that [b]I healed
them.
4 I drew them with cords of a man, with
bands of love: and [a]I was to them as they that
take off the yoke on their jaws, and [b]I laid meat
unto them.
5 He shall not return into the land of Egypt,
but the Assyrian shall be his king, because they
refused to return.
6 And the sword shall abide on his cities,
and shall consume his branches, and devour
them, because of their own counsels.

6 [a]Hos. 5:13
8 [a]Hos. 4:15 [b]Deut. 9:21; 1 Kin. 13:34 [c]Is. 2:19; Luke 23:30; Rev. 6:16
9 [a]Hos. 9:9 [b]Judg. 20
10 [a]Jer. 16:16
11 [a][Jer. 50:11; Hos. 4:16; Mic. 4:13]
12 [a]Jer. 4:3 [b]Hos. 6:3
13 [a][Job 4:8; Prov. 22:8; Gal. 6:7, 8]

CHAPTER 11

1 [a]Matt. 2:15 [b]Ex. 4:22, 23
2 [a]2 Kin. 17:13–15
3 [a]Deut. 1:31; 32:10, 11 [b]Ex. 15:26
4 [a]Lev. 26:13 [b]Ex. 16:32; Ps. 78:25

*

10:9 So with many Heb. mss., LXX, Vg.; MT *unruliness*
10:10 Or *in their two habitations*
11:2 So with MT, Vg.; LXX *Just as I called them;* Tg. interprets as *I sent prophets to a thousand of them.* • So with MT, Tg., Vg.; LXX *from My face*
11:3 Some Heb. mss., LXX, Syr., Vg. *My arms*
11:4 Lit. *cords of a man* • Lit. *jaws*

NKJV

6 *The idol* also shall be carried to Assyria
As a present for King [a]Jareb.
Ephraim shall receive shame,
And Israel shall be ashamed of his own
counsel.

7 *As for* Samaria, her king is cut off
Like a twig on the water.
8 Also the [a]high places of Aven, [b]the sin
of Israel,
Shall be destroyed.
The thorn and thistle shall grow on their
altars;
[c]They shall say to the mountains, "Cover
us!"
And to the hills, "Fall on us!"

9 "O Israel, you have sinned from the days
of [a]Gibeah;
There they stood.
The [b]battle in Gibeah against the children
of *iniquity
Did not overtake them.
10 When *it is* My desire, I will chasten them.
[a]Peoples shall be gathered against them
When I bind them *for their two
transgressions.
11 Ephraim *is* [a]a trained heifer
That loves to thresh *grain;*
But I harnessed her fair neck,
I will make Ephraim pull *a plow.*
Judah shall plow;
Jacob shall break his clods."

12 Sow for yourselves righteousness;
Reap in mercy;
[a]Break up your fallow ground,
For *it is* time to seek the LORD,
Till He [b]comes and rains righteousness on
you.

13 [a]You have plowed wickedness;
You have reaped iniquity.
You have eaten the fruit of lies,
Because you trusted in your own way,
In the multitude of your mighty men.
14 Therefore tumult shall arise among your
people,
And all your fortresses shall be plundered
As Shalman plundered Beth Arbel in the
day of battle—
A mother dashed in pieces upon *her*
children.
15 Thus it shall be done to you, O Bethel,
Because of your great wickedness.
At dawn the king of Israel
Shall be cut off utterly.

God's Continuing Love for Israel

11 "When Israel *was* a child, I loved him,
And out of Egypt [a]I called My [b]son.
2 **As* they called them,
So they [a]went *from them;
They sacrificed to the Baals,
And burned incense to carved images.

3 "I[a] taught Ephraim to walk,
Taking them by *their arms;
But they did not know that [b]I healed them.
4 I drew them with *gentle cords,
With bands of love,
And [a]I was to them as those who take the
yoke from their *neck.
[b]I stooped *and* fed them.

5 "He shall not return to the land of Egypt;
But the Assyrian shall be his king,
Because they refused to repent.
6 And the sword shall slash in his cities,
Devour his districts,
And consume *them,*
Because of their own counsels.

KJV

15 Though he be fruitful among *his* brethren, [a]an east wind shall come, the wind of the LORD shall come up from the wilderness, and his spring shall become dry, and his fountain shall be dried up: he shall spoil the treasure of all pleasant vessels.

16 Samaria shall become desolate; for she hath [a]rebelled against her God: they shall fall by the sword: their infants shall be dashed in pieces, and their women with child shall be [b]ripped up.

Israel Restored at Last

14 O Israel, [a]return unto the LORD thy God; for thou hast fallen by thine iniquity.

2 Take with you words, and turn to the LORD: say unto him, Take away all iniquity, and receive *us* graciously: so will we render the [a]calves of our lips.

3 Asshur shall [a]not save us; [b]we will not ride upon horses: neither will we say any more to the work of our hands, *Ye are* our gods: [c]for in thee the fatherless findeth mercy.

4 I will heal their [a]backsliding, I will [b]love them freely: for mine anger is turned away from him.

5 I will be as the [a]dew unto Israel: he shall grow as the lily, and cast forth his roots as Lebanon.

6 His branches shall spread, and [a]his beauty shall be as the olive tree, and [b]his smell as Lebanon.

7 [a]They that dwell under his shadow shall return; they shall revive *as* the corn, and grow as the vine: the scent thereof *shall be* as the wine of Lebanon.

8 Ephraim *shall say,* What have I to do any more with idols? I have heard *him,* and observed him: I *am* like a green fir tree. [a]From me is thy fruit found.

9 Who *is* wise, and he shall understand these *things?* prudent, and he shall know them? for [a]the ways of the LORD *are* right, and the just shall walk in them: but the transgressors shall fall therein.

15 [a]Gen. 41:6; Jer. 4:11, 12; Ezek. 17:10; 19:12
16 [a]2 Kin. 8:12 [b]2 Kin. 15:16

CHAPTER 14

1 [a]Hos. 12:6; [Joel 2:13]
2 [a][Ps. 51:16, 17; Hos. 6:6; Heb. 13:15]
3 [a]Hos. 7:11; 10:13; 12:1 [b][Ps. 33:17]; Is. 31:1 [c]Ps. 10:14; 68:5
4 [a]Jer. 14:7 [b][Eph. 1:6]
5 [a]Job 29:19; Prov. 19:12; Is. 26:19
6 [a]Ps. 52:8; 128:3 [b]Gen. 27:27
7 [a]Dan. 4:12
8 [a][John 15:4]
9 [a][Ps. 111:7, 8; Prov. 10:29]; Zeph. 3:5

*
13:16 LXX *shall be disfigured*
14:2 Lit. *bull calves;* LXX *fruit*
14:7 Lit. *remembrance*

NKJV

15 Though he is fruitful among *his* brethren,
[a]An east wind shall come;
The wind of the LORD shall come up from the wilderness.
Then his spring shall become dry,
And his fountain shall be dried up.
He shall plunder the treasury of every desirable prize.

16 Samaria *is held guilty,
For she has [a]rebelled against her God.
They shall fall by the sword,
Their infants shall be dashed in pieces,
And their women with child [b]ripped open.

Israel Restored at Last

14 O Israel, [a]return to the LORD your God,
For you have stumbled because of your iniquity;
2 Take words with you,
And return to the LORD.
Say to Him,
"Take away all iniquity;
Receive *us* graciously,
For we will offer the [a]sacrifices* of our lips.
3 Assyria shall [a]not save us,
[b]We will not ride on horses,
Nor will we say anymore to the work of our hands,
'*You are* our gods.'
[c]For in You the fatherless finds mercy."

4 "I will heal their [a]backsliding,
I will [b]love them freely,
For My anger has turned away from him.
5 I will be like the [a]dew to Israel;
He shall grow like the lily,
And lengthen his roots like Lebanon.
6 His branches shall spread;
[a]His beauty shall be like an olive tree,
And [b]his fragrance like Lebanon.
7 [a]Those who dwell under his shadow shall return;
They shall be revived *like* grain,
And grow like a vine.
Their *scent *shall be* like the wine of Lebanon.

8 "Ephraim *shall say,*
'What have I to do anymore with idols?'
I have heard and observed him.
I *am* like a green cypress tree;
[a]Your fruit is found in Me."

9 Who *is* wise?
Let him understand these things.
Who is prudent?
Let him know them.
For [a]the ways of the LORD *are* right;
The righteous walk in them,
But transgressors stumble in them.

KJV

THE BOOK OF

JOEL

1 The word of the LORD that came to [a]Joel the son of Pethuel.

The Land Laid Waste
(*Ex. 10:1–20*)

2 Hear this, ye old men, and give ear, all ye inhabitants of the land. [a]Hath this been in your days, or even in the days of your fathers?

3 [a]Tell ye your children of it, and *let* your children *tell* their children, and their children another generation.

4 [a]That which the palmerworm hath left hath the [b]locust eaten; and that which the locust hath left hath the cankerworm eaten; and that which the cankerworm hath left hath the caterpiller eaten.

5 Awake, ye [a]drunkards, and weep; and howl, all ye drinkers of wine, because of the new wine; [b]for it is cut off from your mouth.

6 For [a]a nation is come up upon my land, strong, and without number, [b]whose teeth *are* the teeth of a lion, and he hath the cheek teeth of a great lion.

7 He hath [a]laid my vine waste, and barked my fig tree: he hath made it clean bare, and cast *it* away; the branches thereof are made white.

8 [a]Lament like a virgin girded with sackcloth for [b]the husband of her youth.

9 [a]The meat offering and the drink offering is cut off from the house of the LORD; the priests, the LORD's ministers, [b]mourn.

10 The field is wasted, [a]the land mourneth; for the corn is wasted: [b]the new wine is dried up, the oil languisheth.

11 [a]Be ye ashamed, O ye husbandmen; howl, O ye vinedressers, for the wheat and for the barley; because the harvest of the field is perished.

12 [a]The vine is dried up, and the fig tree languisheth; the pomegranate tree, the palm tree also, and the apple tree, *even* all the trees of the field, are withered: because [b]joy is withered away from the sons of men.

Mourning for the Land

13 [a]Gird yourselves, and lament, ye priests: howl, ye ministers of the altar: come, lie all night

CHAPTER 1

1 [a]Acts 2:16
2 [a]Jer. 30:7; Joel 2:2
3 [a]Ex. 10:2; Ps. 78:4; Is. 38:19
4 [a]Deut. 28:38; Joel 2:25; Amos 4:9 [b]Is. 33:4
5 [a]Is. 5:11; 28:1; Hos. 7:5 [b]Is. 32:10
6 [a]Prov. 30:25; Joel 2:2, 11, 25 [b]Rev. 9:8
7 [a]Is. 5:6; Amos 4:9
8 [a]Is. 22:12 [b]Prov. 2:17; Jer. 3:4
9 [a]Hos. 9:4; Joel 1:13; 2:14 [b]Joel 2:17
10 [a]Jer. 12:11; Hos. 3:4 [b]Is. 24:7
11 [a]Jer. 14:3, 4; Amos 5:16
12 [a]Joel 1:10; Hab. 3:17 [b]Is. 16:10; 24:11; Jer. 48:33
13 [a]Jer. 4:8; Ezek. 7:18

*———

1:4 Exact identity of these locusts unknown

NKJV

THE BOOK OF

JOEL

1 The word of the LORD that came to [a]Joel the son of Pethuel.

The Land Laid Waste
(*Ex. 10:1–20*)

2 Hear this, you elders,
And give ear, all you inhabitants of the land!
[a]Has *anything like* this happened in your days,
Or even in the days of your fathers?
3 [a]Tell your children about it,
Let your children *tell* their children,
And their children another generation.

4 [a]What the chewing *locust left, the [b]swarming locust has eaten;
What the swarming locust left, the crawling locust has eaten;
And what the crawling locust left, the consuming locust has eaten.

5 Awake, you [a]drunkards, and weep;
And wail, all you drinkers of wine,
Because of the new wine,
[b]For it has been cut off from your mouth.
6 For [a]a nation has come up against My land,
Strong, and without number;
[b]His teeth *are* the teeth of a lion,
And he has the fangs of a fierce lion.
7 He has [a]laid waste My vine,
And ruined My fig tree;
He has stripped it bare and thrown *it* away;
Its branches are made white.

8 [a]Lament like a virgin girded with sackcloth
For [b]the husband of her youth.
9 [a]The grain offering and the drink offering
Have been cut off from the house of the LORD;
The priests [b]mourn, who minister to the LORD.
10 The field is wasted,
[a]The land mourns;
For the grain is ruined,
[b]The new wine is dried up,
The oil fails.

11 [a]Be ashamed, you farmers,
Wail, you vinedressers,
For the wheat and the barley;
Because the harvest of the field has perished.
12 [a]The vine has dried up,
And the fig tree has withered;
The pomegranate tree,
The palm tree also,
And the apple tree—
All the trees of the field are withered;
Surely [b]joy has withered away from the sons of men.

Mourning for the Land

13 [a]Gird yourselves and lament, you priests;
Wail, you who minister before the altar;

KJV

in sackcloth, ye ministers of my God: for the meat
offering and the drink offering is withholden from
the house of your God.
14 [a]Sanctify ye a fast, call [b]a solemn assembly, gather the elders *and* [c]call the inhabitants of
the land *into* the house of the LORD your God,
and cry unto the LORD,
15 [a]Alas for the day! for [b]the day of the LORD
is at hand, and as a destruction from the Almighty
shall it come.
16 Is not the meat [a]cut off before our eyes,
yea, [b]joy and gladness from the house of our God?
17 The seed is rotten under their clods, the
garners are laid desolate, the barns are broken
down; for the corn is withered.
18 How do [a]the beasts groan! the herds of
cattle are perplexed, because they have no pasture; yea, the flocks of sheep are made desolate.
19 O LORD, [a]to thee will I cry: for [b]the fire
hath devoured the pastures of the wilderness, and
the flame hath burned all the trees of the field.
20 The beasts of the field [a]cry also unto thee:
for [b]the rivers of waters are dried up, and the
fire hath devoured the pastures of the wilderness.

The Day of the LORD

2 Blow [a]ye the trumpet in Zion, and [b]sound an
alarm in my holy mountain: let all the inhabitants of the land tremble: for [c]the day of the LORD
cometh, for *it is* nigh at hand;
2 [a]A day of darkness and of gloominess, a
day of clouds and of thick darkness, as the morning spread upon the mountains: [b]a great people
and a strong; [c]there hath not been ever the like,
neither shall be any more after it, *even* to the years
of many generations.
3 A fire devoureth before them; and behind
them a flame burneth: the land *is* as [a]the garden
of Eden before them, [b]and behind them a desolate
wilderness; yea, and nothing shall escape them.
4 [a]The appearance of them *is* as the appearance of horses; and as horsemen, so shall they
run.
5 [a]Like the noise of chariots on the tops of
mountains shall they leap, like the noise of a flame
of fire that devoureth the stubble, as a strong people set in battle array.
6 Before their face the people shall be much
pained: [a]all faces shall gather blackness.
7 They shall run like mighty men; they shall
climb the wall like men of war; and they shall
march every one on his ways, and they shall not
break their [a]ranks:
8 Neither shall one thrust another; they
shall walk every one in his path: and *when* they
fall upon the sword, they shall not be wounded.
9 They shall run to and fro in the city; they
shall run upon the wall, they shall climb up upon

14 [a]2 Chr. 20:3; Joel 2:15, 16 [b]Lev. 23:36 [c]2 Chr. 20:13
15 [a][Is. 13:9; Jer. 30:7]; Amos 5:16 [b]Is. 13:6; Ezek. 7:2–12
16 [a]Is. 3:1; Amos 4:6 [b]Deut. 12:7; Ps. 43:4
18 [a]1 Kin. 8:5; Jer. 12:4; 14:5, 6; Hos. 4:3
19 [a][Ps. 50:15]; Mic. 7:7 [b]Jer. 9:10; Amos 7:4
20 [a]Job 38:41; Ps. 104:21; 147:9; Joel 1:18 [b]1 Kin. 17:7; 18:5

CHAPTER 2

1 [a]Jer. 4:5; Joel 2:15; Zeph. 1:16 [b]Num. 10:5 [c]Joel 1:15; 2:11, 31; 3:14; [Obad. 15]; Zeph. 1:14
2 [a]Joel 2:10, 31; Amos 5:18; Zeph. 1:15 [b]Joel 1:6; 2:11, 25 [c]Ex. 10:14; Lam. 1:12; Dan. 9:12; 12:1; Joel 1:2
3 [a]Gen. 2:8; Is. 51:3; Ezek. 36:35 [b]Ex. 10:5, 15; Ps. 105:34, 35; Zech. 7:14
4 [a]Rev. 9:7
5 [a]Rev. 9:9
6 [a]Is. 13:8; Jer. 8:21; Lam. 4:8; Nah. 2:10
7 [a]Prov. 30:27

*———

1:18 LXX, Vg. *are made desolate*
2:6 LXX, Tg., Vg. *gather blackness*
2:8 Lit. *highway* • Halted by losses

NKJV

Come, lie all night in sackcloth,
You who minister to my God;
For the grain offering and the drink
offering
Are withheld from the house of your God.
14 [a]Consecrate a fast,
Call [b]a sacred assembly;
Gather the elders
And [c]call the inhabitants of the land
Into the house of the LORD your God,
And cry out to the LORD.

15 [a]Alas for the day!
For [b]the day of the LORD *is* at hand;
It shall come as destruction from the
Almighty.
16 Is not the food [a]cut off before our eyes,
[b]Joy and gladness from the house of our
God?
17 The seed shrivels under the clods,
Storehouses are in shambles;
Barns are broken down,
For the grain has withered.
18 How [a]the animals groan!
The herds of cattle are restless,
Because they have no pasture;
Even the flocks of sheep *suffer
punishment.

19 O LORD, [a]to You I cry out;
For [b]fire has devoured the open pastures,
And a flame has burned all the trees of
the field.
20 The beasts of the field also [a]cry out to
You,
For [b]the water brooks are dried up,
And fire has devoured the open pastures.

The Day of the LORD

2 Blow [a]the trumpet in Zion,
And [b]sound an alarm in My holy
mountain!
Let all the inhabitants of the land tremble;
For [c]the day of the LORD is coming,
For it is at hand:
2 [a]A day of darkness and gloominess,
A day of clouds and thick darkness,
Like the morning *clouds* spread over the
mountains.
[b]A people *come,* great and strong,
[c]The like of whom has never been;
Nor will there ever be any *such* after
them,
Even for many successive generations.

3 A fire devours before them,
And behind them a flame burns;
The land *is* like [a]the Garden of Eden
before them,
[b]And behind them a desolate wilderness;
Surely nothing shall escape them.
4 [a]Their appearance is like the appearance
of horses;
And like swift steeds, so they run.
5 [a]With a noise like chariots
Over mountaintops they leap,
Like the noise of a flaming fire that
devours the stubble,
Like a strong people set in battle array.

6 Before them the people writhe in pain;
[a]All faces *are drained of color.
7 They run like mighty men,
They climb the wall like men of war;
Every one marches in formation,
And they do not break [a]ranks.
8 They do not push one another;
Every one marches in his own *column.
Though they lunge between the weapons,
They are not *cut down.
9 They run to and fro in the city,
They run on the wall;

KJV

the houses; they shall [a]enter in at the windows
[b]like a thief.
10 [a]The earth shall quake before them; the
heavens shall tremble: [b]the sun and the moon
shall be dark, and the stars shall withdraw their
shining:
11 [a]And the LORD shall utter his voice before
his army: for his camp *is* very great: [b]for *he is*
strong that executeth his word: for the [c]day of
the LORD *is* great and very terrible; and [d]who can
abide it?

A Call to Repentance

12 Therefore also now, saith the LORD, [a]turn
ye *even* to me with all your heart, and with fasting,
and with weeping, and with mourning:
13 And [a]rend your heart, and not [b]your garments, and turn unto the LORD your God: for he
is [c]gracious and merciful, slow to anger, and of
great kindness, and repenteth him of the evil.
14 [a]Who knoweth *if* he will return and repent, and leave [b]a blessing behind him; *even* [c]a
meat offering and a drink offering unto the LORD
your God?
15 [a]Blow the trumpet in Zion, [b]sanctify a
fast, call a solemn assembly:
16 Gather the people, [a]sanctify the congregation, assemble the elders, gather the children, and
those that suck the breasts: [b]let the bridegroom
go forth of his chamber, and the bride out of her
closet.
17 Let the priests, the ministers of the LORD,
weep [a]between the porch and the altar, and let
them say, [b]Spare thy people, O LORD, and give
not thine heritage to reproach, that the heathen
should rule over them: [c]wherefore should they
say among the people, Where *is* their God?

The Land Refreshed
(Acts 2:17)

18 Then will the LORD [a]be jealous for his
land, and pity his people.
19 Yea, the LORD will answer and say unto
his people, Behold, I will send you [a]corn, and
wine, and oil, and ye shall be satisfied therewith:
and I will no more make you a reproach among
the heathen:
20 But [a]I will remove far off from you [b]the
northern *army*, and will drive him into a land barren and desolate, with his face toward the east
sea, and his hinder part [c]toward the utmost sea,
and his stink shall come up, and his ill savour
shall come up, because he hath done great things.
21 Fear not, O land; be glad and rejoice: for
the LORD will do great things.
22 Be not afraid, ye beasts of the field: for
[a]the pastures of the wilderness do spring, for the
tree beareth her fruit, the fig tree and the vine
do yield their strength.

9 [a]Jer. 9:21 [b]John 10:1
10 [a]Ps. 18:7; Joel 3:16; Nah. 1:5 [b]Is. 13:10; 34:4; Jer. 4:23; Ezek. 32:7, 8; Joel 2:31; 3:15; Matt. 24:29; Rev. 8:12
11 [a]Jer. 25:30; Joel 3:16; Amos 1:2 [b]Jer. 50:34; Rev. 18:8 [c]Jer. 30:7; Amos 5:18; Zeph. 1:15 [d][Mal. 3:2]
12 [a][Deut. 4:29]; Jer. 4:1; Ezek. 33:11; Hos. 12:6; 14:1
13 [a][Ps. 34:18; 51:17; Is. 57:15] [b]Gen. 37:34; 2 Sam. 1:11; Job 1:20; Jer. 41:5 [c][Ex. 34:6]
14 [a]Josh. 14:12; 2 Sam. 12:22; 2 Kin. 19:4; Jer. 26:3; Jon. 3:9 [b]Hag. 2:19 [c]Joel 1:9, 13
15 [a]Num. 10:3; 2 Kin. 10:20 [b]Joel 1:14
16 [a]Ex. 19:10 [b]Ps. 19:5
17 [a]Matt. 23:35 [b]Ex. 32:11, 12; [Is. 37:20]; Amos 7:2, 5 [c]Ps. 42:10
18 [a][Is. 60:10; 63:9, 15]
19 [a]Jer. 31:12; Hos. 2:21, 22; Joel 1:10; [Mal. 3:10]
20 [a]Ex. 10:19 [b]Jer. 1:14, 15 [c]Deut. 11:24
22 [a]Joel 1:19

NKJV

They climb into the houses,
They [a]enter at the windows [b]like a thief.

10 [a]The earth quakes before them,
The heavens tremble;
[b]The sun and moon grow dark,
And the stars diminish their brightness.
11 [a]The LORD gives voice before His army,
For His camp is very great;
[b]For strong *is the One* who executes His word.
For the [c]day of the LORD *is* great and very terrible;
[d]Who can endure it?

A Call to Repentance

12 "Now, therefore," says the LORD,
[a]"Turn to Me with all your heart,
With fasting, with weeping, and with mourning."
13 So [a]rend your heart, and not [b]your garments;
Return to the LORD your God,
For He *is* [c]gracious and merciful,
Slow to anger, and of great kindness;
And He relents from doing harm.
14 [a]Who knows *if* He will turn and relent,
And leave [b]a blessing behind Him—
[c]A grain offering and a drink offering
For the LORD your God?

15 [a]Blow the trumpet in Zion,
[b]Consecrate a fast,
Call a sacred assembly;
16 Gather the people,
[a]Sanctify the congregation,
Assemble the elders,
Gather the children and nursing babes;
[b]Let the bridegroom go out from his chamber,
And the bride from her dressing room.
17 Let the priests, who minister to the LORD,
Weep [a]between the porch and the altar;
Let them say, [b]"Spare Your people, O LORD,
And do not give Your heritage to reproach,
That the nations should rule over them.
[c]Why should they say among the peoples,
'Where *is* their God?' "

The Land Refreshed
(Acts 2:17)

18 Then the LORD will [a]be zealous for His land,
And pity His people.
19 The LORD will answer and say to His people,
"Behold, I will send you [a]grain and new wine and oil,
And you will be satisfied by them;
I will no longer make you a reproach among the nations.

20 "But [a]I will remove far from you [b]the northern *army*,
And will drive him away into a barren and desolate land,
With his face toward the eastern sea
And his back [c]toward the western sea;
His stench will come up,
And his foul odor will rise,
Because he has done monstrous things."

21 Fear not, O land;
Be glad and rejoice,
For the LORD has done marvelous things!
22 Do not be afraid, you beasts of the field;
For [a]the open pastures are springing up,
And the tree bears its fruit;
The fig tree and the vine yield their strength.

KJV

23 Be glad then, ye children of Zion, and [a]rejoice in the LORD your God: for he hath given you the former rain moderately, and he [b]will cause to come down for you the rain, the former rain, and the latter rain in the first *month.*

24 And the floors shall be full of wheat, and the fats shall overflow with wine and oil.

25 And I will restore to you the years [a]that the locust hath eaten, the cankerworm, and the caterpiller, and the palmerworm, my great army which I sent among you.

26 And ye shall [a]eat in plenty, and be satisfied, and praise the name of the LORD your God, that hath dealt wondrously with you: and my people shall never be [b]ashamed.

27 And ye shall know that I *am* [a]in the midst of Israel, and *that* [b]I *am* the LORD your God, and none else: and my people shall never be ashamed.

God's Spirit Poured Out

28 [a]And it shall come to pass afterward, *that* [b]I will pour out my spirit upon all flesh; [c]and your sons and your [d]daughters shall prophesy, your old men shall dream dreams, your young men shall see visions:

29 And also upon [a]the servants and upon the handmaids in those days will I pour out my spirit.

30 And [a]I will shew wonders in the heavens and in the earth, blood, and fire, and pillars of smoke.

31 [a]The sun shall be turned into darkness, and the moon into blood, [b]before the great and the terrible day of the LORD come.

32 And it shall come to pass, *that* [a]whosoever shall call on the name of the LORD shall be delivered: for [b]in mount Zion and in Jerusalem shall be deliverance, as the LORD hath said, and in [c]the remnant whom the LORD shall call.

God Judges the Nations

3 For, behold, [a]in those days, and in that time, when I shall bring again the captivity of Judah and Jerusalem,

2 [a]I will also gather all nations, and will bring them down into the valley of Jehoshaphat, and [b]will plead with them there for my people and *for* my heritage Israel, whom they have scattered among the nations, and parted my land.

3 And they have [a]cast lots for my people; and have given a boy for an harlot, and sold a girl for wine, that they might drink.

4 Yea, and what have ye to do with me, [a]O Tyre, and Zidon, and all the coasts of Palestine?

23 [a]Deut. 11:14; Is. 41:16; Jer. 5:24; Hab. 3:18; Zech. 10:7 [b]Lev. 26:4; Hos. 6:3; Zech. 10:1; James 5:7
25 [a]Joel 1:4–7; 2:2–11
26 [a]Lev. 26:5; Deut. 11:15; Is. 62:9 [b]Is. 45:17
27 [a]Lev. 26:11, 12; [Joel 3:17, 21] [b][Is. 45:5, 6]
28 [a]Ezek. 39:29; Acts 2:17–21 [b]Zech. 12:10 [c]Is. 54:13 [d]Acts 21:9
29 [a][1 Cor. 12:13; Gal. 3:28]
30 [a]Matt. 24:29; Mark 13:24, 25; Luke 21:11, 25, 26; Acts 2:19
31 [a]Is. 13:9, 10; 34:4; Joel 2:10; 3:15; Matt. 24:29; Mark 13:24; Luke 21:25; Acts 2:20; Rev. 6:12, 13 [b]Is. 13:9; Zeph. 1:14–16; [Mal. 4:1, 5, 6]
32 [a]Jer. 33:3; Acts 2:21; Rom. 10:13 [b]Is. 46:13; [Rom. 11:26] [c]Is. 11:11; Jer. 31:7; [Mic. 4:7]; Rom. 9:27

CHAPTER 3

1 [a]Jer. 30:3; Ezek. 38:14
2 [a]Is. 66:18; Mic. 4:12; Zech. 14:2 [b]Is. 66:16; Jer. 25:31; Ezek. 38:22
3 [a]Obad. 11; Nah. 3:10
4 [a]Is. 14:29–31; Jer. 47:1–7; Ezek. 25:15–17; Amos 1:6–8; Zech. 9:5–7

* **2:23** Or *teacher of righteousness*

NKJV

23 Be glad then, you children of Zion,
And [a]rejoice in the LORD your God;
For He has given you the *former rain faithfully,
And He [b]will cause the rain to come down for you—
The former rain,
And the latter rain in the first *month.*
24 The threshing floors shall be full of wheat,
And the vats shall overflow with new wine and oil.

25 "So I will restore to you the years [a]that the swarming locust has eaten,
The crawling locust,
The consuming locust,
And the chewing locust,
My great army which I sent among you.
26 You shall [a]eat in plenty and be satisfied,
And praise the name of the LORD your God,
Who has dealt wondrously with you;
And My people shall never be put to [b]shame.
27 Then you shall know that I *am* [a]in the midst of Israel:
[b]I *am* the LORD your God
And there is no other.
My people shall never be put to shame.

God's Spirit Poured Out

28 "And[a] it shall come to pass afterward
That [b]I will pour out My Spirit on all flesh;
[c]Your sons and your [d]daughters shall prophesy,
Your old men shall dream dreams,
Your young men shall see visions.
29 And also on *My* [a]menservants and on *My* maidservants
I will pour out My Spirit in those days.

30 "And [a]I will show wonders in the heavens and in the earth:
Blood and fire and pillars of smoke.
31 [a]The sun shall be turned into darkness,
And the moon into blood,
[b]Before the coming of the great and awesome day of the LORD.
32 And it shall come to pass
That [a]whoever calls on the name of the LORD
Shall be saved.
For [b]in Mount Zion and in Jerusalem there shall be deliverance,
As the LORD has said,
Among [c]the remnant whom the LORD calls.

God Judges the Nations

3 "For behold, [a]in those days and at that time,
When I bring back the captives of Judah and Jerusalem,
2 [a]I will also gather all nations,
And bring them down to the Valley of Jehoshaphat;
And I [b]will enter into judgment with them there
On account of My people, My heritage Israel,
Whom they have scattered among the nations;
They have also divided up My land.
3 They have [a]cast lots for My people,
Have given a boy *as payment* for a harlot,
And sold a girl for wine, that they may drink.

4 "Indeed, what have you to do with Me,
[a]O Tyre and Sidon, and all the coasts of Philistia?

KJV

will ye render me a recompence? and if ye recompense me, swiftly *and* speedily will I return your recompence upon your own head;

5 Because ye have taken my silver and my gold, and have carried into your temples my goodly pleasant things:

6 The children also of Judah and the children of Jerusalem have ye sold unto the Grecians, that ye might remove them far from their border.

7 Behold, [a]I will raise them out of the place whither ye have sold them, and will return your recompence upon your own head:

8 And I will sell your sons and your daughters into the hand of the children of Judah, and they shall sell them to the [a]Sabeans, to a people [b]far off: for the LORD hath spoken *it*.

9 [a]Proclaim ye this among the Gentiles; Prepare war, wake up the mighty men, let all the men of war draw near; let them come up:

10 [a]Beat your plowshares into swords, and your pruninghooks into spears: [b]let the weak say, I *am* strong.

11 Assemble yourselves, and come, all ye heathen, and gather yourselves together round about: thither cause [a]thy mighty ones to come down, O LORD.

12 Let the heathen be wakened, and come up to the valley of Jehoshaphat: for there will I sit to [a]judge all the heathen round about.

13 [a]Put ye in the sickle, for [b]the harvest is ripe: come, get you down; for the [c]press is full, the fats overflow; for their wickedness *is* great.

14 Multitudes, multitudes in the valley of decision: for [a]the day of the LORD *is* near in the valley of decision.

15 The sun and the moon shall be darkened, and the stars shall withdraw their shining.

16 The LORD also shall roar out of Zion, and utter his voice from Jerusalem; and the heavens and the earth shall shake: [a]but the LORD *will be* the hope of his people, and the strength of the children of Israel.

17 So shall ye know that I *am* the LORD your God dwelling in Zion, my [a]holy mountain: then shall Jerusalem be holy, and there shall no strangers pass through her any more.

God Blesses His People

18 And it shall come to pass in that day, *that* the mountains shall drop down new wine, and the hills shall flow with milk, and all the rivers of Judah shall flow with waters, and a [a]fountain shall come forth of the house of the LORD, and shall water the valley of Shittim.

19 Egypt shall be a desolation, and Edom shall be a desolate wilderness, for the violence

7 [a]Is. 43:5, 6; Jer. 23:8; Zech. 9:13
8 [a]Ezek. 23:42 [b]Jer. 6:20
9 [a]Jer. 6:4; Ezek. 38:7; Mic. 3:5
10 [a][Is. 2:4; Mic. 4:3] [b]Zech. 12:8
11 [a]Ps. 103:20; Is. 13:3
12 [a][Ps. 96:13]; Is. 2:4
13 [a][Matt. 13:39]; Rev. 14:15 [b]Jer. 51:33; Hos. 6:11 [c][Is. 63:3]; Lam. 1:5; Rev. 14:19
14 [a]Joel 2:1
16 [a][Is. 51:5, 6]
17 [a]Obad. 16; Zech. 8:3
18 [a]Ps. 46:4; Ezek. 47:1; Zech. 14:8; [Rev. 22:1]

*________

3:8 Lit. *Shebaites,* Is. 60:6; Ezek. 27:22

NKJV

Will you retaliate against Me?
But if you retaliate against Me,
Swiftly and speedily I will return your retaliation upon your own head;
5 Because you have taken My silver and My gold,
And have carried into your temples My prized possessions.
6 Also the people of Judah and the people of Jerusalem
You have sold to the Greeks,
That you may remove them far from their borders.

7 "Behold, [a]I will raise them
Out of the place to which you have sold them,
And will return your retaliation upon your own head.
8 I will sell your sons and your daughters
Into the hand of the people of Judah,
And they will sell them to the [a]Sabeans,*
To a people [b]far off;
For the LORD has spoken."

9 [a]Proclaim this among the nations:
"Prepare for war!
Wake up the mighty men,
Let all the men of war draw near,
Let them come up.
10 [a]Beat your plowshares into swords
And your pruning hooks into spears;
[b]Let the weak say, 'I *am* strong.'"
11 Assemble and come, all you nations,
And gather together all around.
Cause [a]Your mighty ones to go down there, O LORD.
12 "Let the nations be wakened, and come up to the Valley of Jehoshaphat;
For there I will sit to [a]judge all the surrounding nations.
13 [a]Put in the sickle, for [b]the harvest is ripe.
Come, go down;
For the [c]winepress is full,
The vats overflow—
For their wickedness *is* great."

14 Multitudes, multitudes in the valley of decision!
For [a]the day of the LORD *is* near in the valley of decision.
15 The sun and moon will grow dark,
And the stars will diminish their brightness.
16 The LORD also will roar from Zion,
And utter His voice from Jerusalem;
The heavens and earth will shake;
[a]But the LORD will be a shelter for His people,
And the strength of the children of Israel.

17 "So you shall know that I *am* the LORD your God,
Dwelling in Zion My [a]holy mountain.
Then Jerusalem shall be holy,
And no aliens shall ever pass through her again."

God Blesses His People

18 And it will come to pass in that day
That the mountains shall drip with new wine,
The hills shall flow with milk,
And all the brooks of Judah shall be flooded with water;
A [a]fountain shall flow from the house of the LORD
And water the Valley of Acacias.

19 "Egypt shall be a desolation,
And Edom a desolate wilderness,

KJV

against the children of Judah, because they have
shed innocent blood in their land.
20 But Judah shall dwell for ever, and Jerusalem
from generation to generation.
21 For I will [a]cleanse their blood *that* I have
not cleansed: for the LORD dwelleth in Zion.

21 [a]Is. 4:4

NKJV

Because of violence *against* the people of Judah,
For they have shed innocent blood in their land.
20 But Judah shall abide forever,
And Jerusalem from generation to generation.
21 For I will [a]acquit them of the guilt of bloodshed, whom I had not acquitted;
For the LORD dwells in Zion."

KJV

THE BOOK OF

AMOS

1 The words of Amos, who was among the
[a]herdmen of [b]Tekoa, which he saw concerning
Israel in the days of [c]Uzziah king of Judah, and
in the days of [d]Jeroboam the son of Joash king
of Israel, two years before the [e]earthquake.
2 And he said, The LORD will [a]roar from
Zion, and utter his voice from Jerusalem; and the
habitations of the shepherds shall mourn, and the
top of [b]Carmel shall wither.

Judgment on the Nations

3 Thus saith the LORD; For three transgressions of [a]Damascus, and for four, I will not turn
away *the punishment* thereof; because they have
[b]threshed Gilead with threshing instruments of
iron:
4 [a]But I will send a fire into the house of
Hazael, which shall devour the palaces of [b]Ben-
hadad.
5 I will break also the [a]bar of Damascus,
and cut off the inhabitant from the plain of Aven,
and him that holdeth the sceptre from the house
of Eden: and the people of Syria shall go into captivity unto Kir, saith the LORD.
6 Thus saith the LORD; For three transgressions of [a]Gaza, and for four, I will not turn away
the punishment thereof; because they carried
away captive the whole captivity, to deliver *them*
up to Edom:
7 [a]But I will send a fire on the wall of Gaza,
which shall devour the palaces thereof:
8 And I will cut off the inhabitant [a]from
Ashdod, and him that holdeth the sceptre from
Ashkelon, and I will [b]turn mine hand against Ekron: and [c]the remnant of the Philistines shall perish, saith the Lord GOD.
9 Thus saith the LORD; For three transgressions of [a]Tyrus, and for four, I will not turn away
the punishment thereof; because they delivered
up the whole captivity to Edom, and remembered
not the brotherly covenant:
10 But I will send a fire on the wall of Tyrus,
which shall devour the palaces thereof.
11 Thus saith the LORD; For three transgres-

CHAPTER 1

1 [a]2 Kin. 3:4; Amos 7:14 [b]2 Sam. 14:2; Jer. 6:1 [c]2 Kin. 15:1–7; 2 Chr. 26:1–23; Is. 1:1; Hos. 1:1 [d]2 Kin. 14:23–29; Amos 7:10 [e]Zech. 14:5
2 [a]Is. 42:13; Jer. 25:30; Joel 3:16 [b]1 Sam. 25:2; Is. 33:9
3 [a]Is. 8:4; 17:1–3; Jer. 49:23–27; Zech. 9:1 [b]2 Kin. 10:32, 33
4 [a]Jer. 49:27; 51:30 [b]1 Kin. 20:1; 2 Kin. 6:24
5 [a]2 Kin. 14:28; Is. 8:4; Jer. 51:30; Lam. 2:9
6 [a]1 Sam. 6:17; Jer. 47:1, 5; Zeph. 2:4
7 [a]Jer. 47:1
8 [a]Jer. 47:5; Zeph. 2:4 [b]Ps. 81:14 [c]Is. 14:29–31; Jer. 47:1–7; Ezek. 25:16; Joel 3:4–8; Zeph. 2:4–7; Zech. 9:5–7
9 [a]Is. 23:1–18; Jer. 25:22; Ezek. 26:2–4; Joel 3:4–8

NKJV

THE BOOK OF

AMOS

1 The words of Amos, who was among the
[a]sheepbreeders of [b]Tekoa, which he saw concerning Israel in the days of [c]Uzziah king of Judah, and in the days of [d]Jeroboam the son of
Joash, king of Israel, two years before the
[e]earthquake.
2 And he said:

"The LORD [a]roars from Zion,
And utters His voice from Jerusalem;
The pastures of the shepherds mourn,
And the top of [b]Carmel withers."

Judgment on the Nations

3 Thus says the LORD:

"For three transgressions of [a]Damascus,
and for four,
I will not turn away its *punishment*,
Because they have [b]threshed Gilead with
implements of iron.
4 [a]But I will send a fire into the house of
Hazael,
Which shall devour the palaces of [b]Ben-
Hadad.
5 I will also break the *gate* [a]bar of
Damascus,
And cut off the inhabitant from the Valley
of Aven,
And the one who holds the scepter from
Beth Eden.
The people of Syria shall go captive to
Kir,"
Says the LORD.

6 Thus says the LORD:

"For three transgressions of [a]Gaza, and for
four,
I will not turn away its *punishment*,
Because they took captive the whole
captivity
To deliver *them* up to Edom.
7 [a]But I will send a fire upon the wall of
Gaza,
Which shall devour its palaces.
8 I will cut off the inhabitant [a]from Ashdod,
And the one who holds the scepter from
Ashkelon;
I will [b]turn My hand against Ekron,
And [c]the remnant of the Philistines shall
perish,"
Says the Lord GOD.

9 Thus says the LORD:

"For three transgressions of [a]Tyre, and for
four,
I will not turn away its *punishment*,
Because they delivered up the whole
captivity to Edom,
And did not remember the covenant of
brotherhood.
10 But I will send a fire upon the wall of Tyre,
Which shall devour its palaces."

11 Thus says the LORD:

KJV

sions of [a]Edom, and for four, I will not turn away
the punishment thereof; because he did pursue
his [b]brother with the sword, and did cast off all
pity, and his anger did tear perpetually, and he
kept his wrath for ever:
12 But [a]I will send a fire upon Teman, which
shall devour the palaces of Bozrah.
13 Thus saith the LORD; For three transgressions of [a]the children of Ammon, and for four, I
will not turn away *the punishment* thereof; because they have ripped up the women with child
of Gilead, that they might enlarge their border:
14 But I will kindle a fire in the wall of [a]Rab-
bah, and it shall devour the palaces thereof, [b]with
shouting in the day of battle, with a tempest in
the day of the whirlwind:
15 And [a]their king shall go into captivity, he
and his princes together, saith the LORD.

2 Thus saith the LORD; [a]For three transgressions
of Moab, and for four, I will not turn away
the punishment thereof; because he [b]burned the
bones of the king of Edom into lime:
2 But I will send a fire upon Moab, and it
shall devour the palaces of [a]Kirioth: and Moab
shall die with tumult, with shouting, *and* with the
sound of the trumpet:
3 And I will cut off [a]the judge from the midst
thereof, and will slay all the princes thereof with
him, saith the LORD.

Judgment on Judah

4 Thus saith the LORD; For three transgressions of [a]Judah, and for four, I will not turn away
the punishment thereof; [b]because they have despised the law of the LORD, and have not kept
his commandments, and [c]their lies caused them
to err, [d]after the which their fathers have walked:
5 [a]But I will send a fire upon Judah, and it
shall devour the palaces of Jerusalem.

Judgment on Israel

6 Thus saith the LORD; For three transgressions of [a]Israel, and for four, I will not turn away
the punishment thereof; because [b]they sold the
righteous for silver, and the [c]poor for a pair of
shoes;
7 That pant after the dust of the earth on
the head of the poor, and [a]turn aside the way of
the meek: [b]and a man and his father will go in
unto the *same* maid, [c]to profane my holy name:
8 And they lay *themselves* down upon
clothes [b]laid to pledge [a]by every altar, and they
drink the wine of the condemned *in* the house of
their god.

11 [a]Is. 21:11; Jer. 49:8; Ezek. 25:12–14; Mal. 1:2–5 [b]Num. 20:14–21; 2 Chr. 28:17; Obad. 10–12
12 [a]Jer. 49:7, 20; Obad. 9, 10
13 [a]Jer. 49:1; Ezek. 25:2; Zeph. 2:8, 9
14 [a]Deut. 3:11; 1 Chr. 20:1; Jer. 49:2 [b]Ezek. 21:22; Amos 2:2
15 [a]Jer. 49:3

CHAPTER 2

1 [a]Is. 15:1–16; Jer. 25:21; Ezek. 25:8–11; Zeph. 2:8–11 [b]2 Kin. 3:26, 27
2 [a]Jer. 48:24, 41
3 [a]Num. 24:17; Jer. 48:7
4 [a]2 Kin. 17:19; Hos. 12:2; Amos 3:2 [b]Lev. 26:14 [c]Is. 9:15, 16; 28:15; Jer. 16:19; Hab. 2:18 [d]Jer. 9:14; 16:11, 12; Ezek. 20:13, 16, 18
5 [a]Jer. 17:27; Hos. 8:14
6 [a]Judg. 2:17–20; 2 Kin. 17:7–18; 18:12; Ezek. 22:1–13, 23–29 [b]Is. 29:21 [c]Joel 3:3; Amos 4:1; 5:11; 8:6; Mic. 2:2; 3:3
7 [a]Amos 5:12 [b]Lev. 18:6–8; Ezek. 22:11 [c]Lev. 20:3; Ezek. 36:20–22
8 [a]1 Cor. 8:10 [b]Ex. 22:26

*______

2:7 Or *trample on*

NKJV

"For three transgressions of [a]Edom, and
for four,
I will not turn away its *punishment*,
Because he pursued his [b]brother with the
sword,
And cast off all pity;
His anger tore perpetually,
And he kept his wrath forever.
12 But [a]I will send a fire upon Teman,
Which shall devour the palaces of
Bozrah."

13 Thus says the LORD:

"For three transgressions of [a]the people of
Ammon, and for four,
I will not turn away its *punishment*,
Because they ripped open the women with
child in Gilead,
That they might enlarge their territory.
14 But I will kindle a fire in the wall of
[a]Rabbah,
And it shall devour its palaces,
[b]Amid shouting in the day of battle,
And a tempest in the day of the whirlwind.
15 [a]Their king shall go into captivity,
He and his princes together,"
Says the LORD.

2 Thus says the LORD:

[a]"For three transgressions of Moab, and for
four,
I will not turn away its *punishment*,
Because he [b]burned the bones of the king
of Edom to lime.
2 But I will send a fire upon Moab,
And it shall devour the palaces of
[a]Kerioth;
Moab shall die with tumult,
With shouting *and* trumpet sound.
3 And I will cut off [a]the judge from its
midst,
And slay all its princes with him,"
Says the LORD.

Judgment on Judah

4 Thus says the LORD:

"For three transgressions of [a]Judah, and
for four,
I will not turn away its *punishment*,
[b]Because they have despised the law of the
LORD,
And have not kept His commandments.
[c]Their lies lead them astray,
Lies [d]which their fathers followed.
5 [a]But I will send a fire upon Judah,
And it shall devour the palaces of
Jerusalem."

Judgment on Israel

6 Thus says the LORD:

"For three transgressions of [a]Israel, and for
four,
I will not turn away its *punishment*,
Because [b]they sell the righteous for
silver,
And the [c]poor for a pair of sandals.
7 They *pant after the dust of the earth
which is on the head of the poor,
And [a]pervert the way of the humble.
[b]A man and his father go in to the *same*
girl,
[c]To defile My holy name.
8 They lie down [a]by every altar on clothes
[b]taken in pledge,
And drink the wine of the condemned *in*
the house of their god.

KJV

9 Yet destroyed I the [a]Amorite before them, whose height *was* like the [b]height of the cedars, and he *was* strong as the oaks; yet I [c]destroyed his fruit from above, and his roots from beneath.

10 Also [a]I brought you up from the land of Egypt, and [b]led you forty years through the wilderness, to possess the land of the Amorite.

11 And I raised up of your sons for [a]prophets, and of your young men for [b]Nazarites. *Is it* not even thus, O ye children of Israel? saith the LORD.

12 But ye gave the Nazarites wine to drink; and commanded the prophets, [a]saying, Prophesy not.

13 [a]Behold, I am pressed under you, as a cart is pressed *that is* full of sheaves.

14 [a]Therefore the flight shall perish from the swift, and the strong shall not strengthen his force, [b]neither shall the mighty deliver himself:

15 Neither shall he stand that handleth the bow; and *he that is* swift of foot shall not deliver *himself:* neither shall he that rideth the horse deliver himself.

16 And *he that is* courageous among the mighty shall flee away naked in that day, saith the LORD.

Authority of the Prophet's Message

3 Hear this word that the LORD hath spoken against you, O children of Israel, against the whole family which I brought up from the land of Egypt, saying,

2 [a]You only have I known of all the families of the earth: [b]therefore I will punish you for all your iniquities.

3 Can two walk together, except they be agreed?

4 Will a lion roar in the forest, when he hath no prey? will a young lion cry out of his den, if he have taken nothing?

5 Can a bird fall in a snare upon the earth, where no gin *is* for him? shall *one* take up a snare from the earth, and have taken nothing at all?

6 Shall a trumpet be blown in the city, and the people not be afraid? [a]shall there be evil in a city, and the LORD hath not done *it?*

7 Surely the Lord GOD will do nothing, but [a]he revealeth his secret unto his servants the prophets.

8 The lion hath roared, who will not fear? the Lord GOD hath spoken, [a]who can but prophesy?

Punishment of Israel's Sins

9 Publish in the palaces at Ashdod, and in the palaces in the land of Egypt, and say, Assemble yourselves upon the mountains of Samaria, and behold the great tumults in the midst thereof, and the oppressed in the midst thereof.

10 For they [a]know not to do right, saith the LORD, who store up violence and robbery in their palaces.

---

9 [a]Gen. 15:16; Num. 21:25; Deut. 2:31; Josh. 10:12 [b]Ezek. 31:3 [c]Is. 5:24; Ezek. 17:9; [Mal. 4:1]
10 [a]Ex. 12:51; Amos 3:1; 9:7 [b]Deut. 2:7
11 [a]Num. 12:6 [b]Num. 6:2, 3; Judg. 13:5
12 [a]Is. 30:10; Jer. 11:21; Amos 7:13, 16; Mic. 2:6
13 [a]Is. 1:14
14 [a]Jer. 46:6 [b]Ps. 33:16; Jer. 9:23

CHAPTER 3

2 [a][Gen. 18:19; Ex. 19:5, 6; Deut. 7:6; Ps. 147:19] [b]Jer. 14:10; Ezek. 20:36; Dan. 9:12; Matt. 11:22; [Rom. 2:9]
6 [a]Is. 45:7
7 [a]Gen. 6:13; 18:17; [Jer. 23:22]; Dan. 9:22; [John 15:15]
8 [a]Jer. 20:9; [Mic. 3:8]; Acts 4:20; 1 Cor. 9:16
10 [a]Ps. 14:4; Jer. 4:22; Amos 5:7; 6:12

NKJV

9 "Yet *it was* I *who* destroyed the [a]Amorite before them,
Whose height *was* like the [b]height of the cedars,
And he *was as* strong as the oaks;
Yet I [c]destroyed his fruit above
And his roots beneath.

10 Also *it was* [a]I *who* brought you up from the land of Egypt,
And [b]led you forty years through the wilderness,
To possess the land of the Amorite.

11 I raised up some of your sons as [a]prophets,
And some of your young men as [b]Nazirites.
Is it not so, O you children of Israel?"
Says the LORD.

12 "But you gave the Nazirites wine to drink,
And commanded the prophets [a]saying,
'Do not prophesy!'

13 "Behold,[a] I am weighed down by you,
As a cart full of sheaves is weighed down.

14 [a]Therefore flight shall perish from the swift,
The strong shall not strengthen his power,
[b]Nor shall the mighty deliver himself;

15 He shall not stand who handles the bow,
The swift of foot shall not escape,
Nor shall he who rides a horse deliver himself.

16 The most courageous men of might
Shall flee naked in that day,"
Says the LORD.

Authority of the Prophet's Message

3 Hear this word that the LORD has spoken against you, O children of Israel, against the whole family which I brought up from the land of Egypt, saying:

2 "You[a] only have I known of all the families of the earth;
[b]Therefore I will punish you for all your iniquities."

3 Can two walk together, unless they are agreed?

4 Will a lion roar in the forest, when he has no prey?
Will a young lion cry out of his den, if he has caught nothing?

5 Will a bird fall into a snare on the earth, where there is no trap for it?
Will a snare spring up from the earth, if it has caught nothing at all?

6 If a trumpet is blown in a city, will not the people be afraid?
[a]If there is calamity in a city, will not the LORD have done *it?*

7 Surely the Lord GOD does nothing,
Unless [a]He reveals His secret to His servants the prophets.

8 A lion has roared!
Who will not fear?
The Lord GOD has spoken!
[a]Who can but prophesy?

Punishment of Israel's Sins

9 "Proclaim in the palaces at *Ashdod,
And in the palaces in the land of Egypt, and say:
'Assemble on the mountains of Samaria;
See great tumults in her midst,
And the oppressed within her.

10 For they [a]do not know to do right,'
Says the LORD,
'Who store up violence and robbery in their palaces.' "

---

*3:9 So with MT; LXX *Assyria*

KJV

11 Therefore thus saith the Lord GOD; An adversary *there shall be* even round about the land;
and he shall bring down thy strength from thee,
and thy palaces shall be spoiled.
12 Thus saith the LORD; As the shepherd taketh out of the mouth of the lion two legs, or a
piece of an ear; so shall the children of Israel be
taken out that dwell in Samaria in the corner of
a bed, and in Damascus *in* a couch.
13 Hear ye, and testify in the house of Jacob,
saith the Lord GOD, the God of hosts,
14 That in the day that I shall visit the transgressions of Israel upon him I will also visit the
altars of [a]Beth–el: and the horns of the altar shall
be cut off, and fall to the ground.
15 And I will smite [a]the winter house with
[b]the summer house; and the [c]houses of ivory shall
perish, and the great houses shall have an end,
saith the LORD.

4 Hear this word, ye [a]kine of Bashan, that *are*
in the mountain of Samaria, which oppress
the [b]poor, which crush the needy, which say to
their masters, Bring, and let us [c]drink.
2 [a]The Lord GOD hath sworn by his holiness, that, lo, the days shall come upon you, that
he will take you away [b]with hooks, and your posterity with fishhooks.
3 And [a]ye shall go out at the breaches, every
cow at that which is before her; and ye shall cast
them into the palace, saith the LORD.
4 [a]Come to Beth–el, and transgress; at [b]Gil-
gal multiply transgression; and [c]bring your sacrifices every morning, [d]*and* your tithes after three
years:
5 [a]And offer a sacrifice of thanksgiving with
leaven, and proclaim *and* publish [b]the free offerings: for this liketh you, O ye children of Israel,
saith the Lord GOD.

Israel Did Not Accept Correction

6 And I also have given you cleanness of
teeth in all your cities, and want of bread in all
your places: [a]yet have ye not returned unto me,
saith the LORD.
7 And also I have withholden the rain from
you, when *there were* yet three months to the harvest: and I caused it to rain upon one city, and
caused it not to rain upon another city: one piece
was rained upon, and the piece whereupon it
rained not withered.
8 So two *or* three cities wandered unto one
city, to drink water; but they were not satisfied:
yet have ye not returned unto me, saith the LORD.
9 [a]I have smitten you with blasting and mildew: when your gardens and your vineyards and

14 [a]2 Kin. 23:15; Hos. 10:5–8, 14, 15; Amos 4:4
15 [a]Jer. 36:22 [b]Judg. 3:20 [c]1 Kin. 22:39; Ps. 45:8

CHAPTER 4

1 [a]Ps. 22:12; Ezek. 39:18 [b]Amos 2:6 [c]Prov. 23:20
2 [a]Ps. 89:35 [b]Jer. 16:16; Ezek. 29:4; Hab. 1:15
3 [a]Ezek. 12:5
4 [a]Ezek. 20:39; Amos 3:14 [b]Hos. 4:15 [c]Num. 28:3; Amos 5:21, 22 [d]Deut. 14:28
5 [a]Lev. 7:13 [b]Lev. 22:18; Deut. 12:6
6 [a]2 Chr. 28:22; Is. 26:11; Jer. 5:3; Hag. 2:17
9 [a]Deut. 28:22; Hag. 2:17

NKJV

11 Therefore thus says the Lord GOD:
"An adversary *shall be* all around the land;
He shall sap your strength from you,
And your palaces shall be plundered."

12 Thus says the LORD:

"As a shepherd takes from the mouth of a lion
Two legs or a piece of an ear,
So shall the children of Israel be taken out
Who dwell in Samaria—
In the corner of a bed and *on the edge of a couch!
13 Hear and testify against the house of Jacob,"
Says the Lord GOD, the God of hosts,
14 "That in the day I punish Israel for their transgressions,
I will also visit *destruction* on the altars of [a]Bethel;
And the horns of the altar shall be cut off
And fall to the ground.
15 I will destroy [a]the winter house along with [b]the summer house;
The [c]houses of ivory shall perish,
And the great houses shall have an end,"
Says the LORD.

4 Hear this word, you [a]cows of Bashan, who *are* on the mountain of Samaria,
Who oppress the [b]poor,
Who crush the needy,
Who say to *your husbands, "Bring *wine*, let us [c]drink!"
2 [a]The Lord GOD has sworn by His holiness:
"Behold, the days shall come upon you
When He will take you away [b]with fishhooks,
And your posterity with fishhooks.
3 [a]You will go out *through* broken *walls*,
Each one straight ahead of her,
And you will be cast into Harmon,"
Says the LORD.

4 "Come[a] to Bethel and transgress,
At [b]Gilgal multiply transgression;
[c]Bring your sacrifices every morning,
[d]Your tithes every three *days.
5 [a]Offer a sacrifice of thanksgiving with leaven,
Proclaim *and* announce [b]the freewill offerings;
For this you love,
You children of Israel!"
Says the Lord GOD.

Israel Did Not Accept Correction

6 "Also I gave you cleanness of teeth in all your cities.
And lack of bread in all your places;
[a]Yet you have not returned to Me,"
Says the LORD.

7 "I also withheld rain from you,
When *there were* still three months to the harvest.
I made it rain on one city,
I withheld rain from another city.
One part was rained upon,
And where it did not rain the part withered.
8 So two *or* three cities wandered to another city to drink water,
But they were not satisfied;
Yet you have not returned to Me,"
Says the LORD.

9 "I[a] blasted you with blight and mildew.
When your gardens increased,

*

3:12 Heb. uncertain, possibly *on the cover*
4:1 Lit. *their masters* or *lords*
4:4 Or *years*, Deut. 14:28

KJV

your fig trees and your olive trees increased, [b]the
palmerworm devoured *them:* yet have ye not returned unto me, saith the LORD.
10 I have sent among you the pestilence
[a]after the manner of Egypt: your young men have
I slain with the sword, and have taken away your
horses; and I have made the stink of your camps
to come up unto your nostrils: yet have ye not
returned unto me, saith the LORD.
11 I have overthrown *some* of you, as God
overthrew [a]Sodom and Gomorrah, and ye were
as a firebrand plucked out of the burning: yet have
ye not returned unto me, saith the LORD.
12 Therefore thus will I do unto thee, O Israel: *and* because I will do this unto thee, [a]prepare
to meet thy God, O Israel.
13 For, lo, he that formeth the mountains,
and createth the wind, [a]and declareth unto man
what *is* his thought, that maketh the morning
darkness, [b]and treadeth upon the high places of
the earth, [c]The LORD, The God of hosts, *is* his
name.

A Lament for Israel

5 Hear ye this word which I [a]take up against
you, *even* a lamentation, O house of Israel.
2 The virgin of Israel is fallen; she shall no
more rise: she is forsaken upon her land; *there
is* none to raise her up.
3 For thus saith the Lord GOD; The city that
went out *by* a thousand shall leave an hundred,
and that which went forth *by* an hundred shall
leave ten, to the house of Israel.

A Call to Repentance

4 For thus saith the LORD unto the house of
Israel, [a]Seek ye me, [b]and ye shall live:
5 But seek not [a]Beth–el, nor enter into Gilgal, and pass not to [b]Beer–sheba: for Gilgal shall
surely go into captivity, and [c]Beth–el shall come
to nought.
6 [a]Seek the LORD, and ye shall live; lest he
break out like fire in the house of Joseph, and
devour *it,* and *there be* none to quench *it* in
Beth–el.
7 Ye who [a]turn judgment to wormwood,
and leave off righteousness in the earth,
8 *Seek him* that maketh the [a]seven stars and
Orion, and turneth the shadow of death into the
morning, [b]and maketh the day dark with night:
that [c]calleth for the waters of the sea, and poureth
them out upon the face of the earth: [d]The LORD
is his name:
9 That strengtheneth the spoiled against the
strong, so that the spoiled shall come against the
fortress.

9 [b]Joel 1:4, 7; Amos 7:1, 2
10 [a]Ex. 9:3, 6; Lev. 26:25; Deut. 28:27, 60; Ps. 78:50
11 [a]Gen. 19:24, 25; Deut. 29:23; Is. 13:19; Jer. 49:18; Lam. 4:6
12 [a]Amos 4:12
13 [a]Ps. 139:2; Dan. 2:28 [b]Mic. 1:3 [c]Is. 47:4; Jer. 10:16

CHAPTER 5

1 [a]Jer. 7:29; 9:10, 17; Ezek. 19:1
4 [a][Deut. 4:29; 2 Chr. 15:2; Jer. 29:13] [b][Is. 55:3]
5 [a]1 Kin. 12:28, 29; Amos 4:4 [b]Gen. 21:31–33; Amos 8:14 [c]Hos. 4:15
6 [a][Is. 55:3, 6, 7; Amos 5:14]
7 [a]Amos 6:12
8 [a]Job 9:9; 38:31 [b]Ps. 104:20 [c]Job 38:34 [d][Amos 4:13]

*4:13 Or *His*

NKJV

Your vineyards,
Your fig trees,
And your olive trees,
[b]The locust devoured *them;*
Yet you have not returned to Me,"
Says the LORD.

10 "I sent among you a plague [a]after the
manner of Egypt;
Your young men I killed with a sword,
Along with your captive horses;
I made the stench of your camps come up
into your nostrils;
Yet you have not returned to Me,"
Says the LORD.

11 "I overthrew *some* of you,
As God overthrew [a]Sodom and
Gomorrah,
And you were like a firebrand plucked
from the burning;
Yet you have not returned to Me,"
Says the LORD.

12 "Therefore thus will I do to you, O Israel;
Because I will do this to you,
[a]Prepare to meet your God, O Israel!"

13 For behold,
He who forms mountains,
And creates the wind,
[a]Who declares to man what *his thought
is,
And makes the morning darkness,
[b]Who treads the high places of the earth—
[c]The LORD God of hosts *is* His name.

A Lament for Israel

5 Hear this word which I [a]take up against you,
a lamentation, O house of Israel:

2 The virgin of Israel has fallen;
She will rise no more.
She lies forsaken on her land;
There is no one to raise her up.

3 For thus says the Lord GOD:

"The city that goes out by a thousand
Shall have a hundred left,
And that which goes out by a hundred
Shall have ten left to the house of Israel."

A Call to Repentance

4 For thus says the LORD to the house of
Israel:

[a]"Seek Me [b]and live;
5 But do not seek [a]Bethel,
Nor enter Gilgal,
Nor pass over to [b]Beersheba;
For Gilgal shall surely go into captivity,
And [c]Bethel shall come to nothing.
6 [a]Seek the LORD and live,
Lest He break out like fire *in* the house
of Joseph,
And devour *it,*
With no one to quench *it* in Bethel—
7 You who [a]turn justice to wormwood,
And lay righteousness to rest in the
earth!"

8 He made the [a]Pleiades and Orion;
He turns the shadow of death into
morning
[b]And makes the day dark as night;
He [c]calls for the waters of the sea
And pours them out on the face of the
earth;
[d]The LORD *is* His name.
9 He rains ruin upon the strong,
So that fury comes upon the fortress.

KJV

10 [a]They hate him that rebuketh in the gate,
and they [b]abhor him that speaketh uprightly.
11 [a]Forasmuch therefore as your treading *is*
upon the poor, and ye take from him burdens of
wheat: [b]ye have built houses of hewn stone, but
ye shall not dwell in them; ye have planted pleasant vineyards, but ye shall not drink wine of them.
12 For I [a]know your manifold transgressions
and your mighty sins: [b]they afflict the just, they
take a bribe, and they [c]turn aside the poor in the
gate *from their right.*
13 Therefore [a]the prudent shall keep silence
in that time; for it *is* an evil time.
14 Seek good, and not evil, that ye may live:
and so the LORD, the God of hosts, shall be with
you, [a]as ye have spoken.
15 [a]Hate the evil, and love the good, and establish judgment in the gate: [b]it may be that the
LORD God of hosts will be gracious unto the remnant of Joseph.

The Day of the LORD

16 Therefore the LORD, the God of hosts, the
Lord, saith thus; Wailing *shall be* in all streets;
and they shall say in all the highways, Alas! alas!
and they shall call the husbandman to mourning,
and [a]such as are skilful of lamentation to wailing.
17 And in all vineyards *shall be* wailing: for
[a]I will pass through thee, saith the LORD.
18 [a]Woe unto you that desire the day of the
LORD! to what end *is* it for you? [b]the day of the
LORD *is* darkness, and not light.
19 [a]As if a man did flee from a lion, and a
bear met him; or went into the house, and leaned
his hand on the wall, and a serpent bit him.
20 *Shall* not the day of the LORD *be* darkness,
and not light? even very dark, and no brightness
in it?
21 [a]I hate, I despise your feast days, and [b]I
will not smell in your solemn assemblies.
22 [a]Though ye offer me burnt offerings and
your meat offerings, I will not accept *them:* neither will I regard the peace offerings of your fat
beasts.
23 Take thou away from me the noise of thy
songs; for I will not hear the melody of thy viols.
24 [a]But let judgment run down as waters, and
righteousness as a mighty stream.
25 [a]Have ye offered unto me sacrifices and
offerings in the wilderness forty years, O house
of Israel?
26 But ye have borne the tabernacle [a]of your
Moloch and Chiun your images, the star of your
god, which ye made to yourselves.

10 [a]Is. 29:21; 66:5; Amos 5:15 [b]1 Kin. 22:8; Is. 59:15; Jer. 17:16–18
11 [a]Amos 2:6 [b]Deut. 28:30, 38, 39; Mic. 6:15; Zeph. 1:13; Hag. 1:6
12 [a]Hos. 5:3 [b]Is. 1:23; 5:23; Amos 2:6 [c]Is. 29:21
13 [a]Amos 6:10
14 [a]Mic. 3:11
15 [a]Ps. 97:10; Rom. 12:9 [b]Joel 2:14
16 [a]2 Chr. 35:25; Jer. 9:17
17 [a]Ex. 12:12
18 [a]Is. 5:19; Jer. 17:15; Joel 1:15; 2:1, 11, 31 [b]Is. 5:30; Joel 2:2
19 [a]Job 20:24; Is. 24:17, 18; Jer. 48:44
21 [a]Is. 1:11–16; Amos 4:4, 5; 8:10 [b]Lev. 26:31; Jer. 14:12; Hos. 5:6
22 [a]Is. 66:3; Mic. 6:6, 7
24 [a]Jer. 22:3; Ezek. 45:9; Hos. 6:6; Mic. 6:8
25 [a]Deut. 32:17; Josh. 24:14; Neh. 9:18–21; Acts 7:42, 43
26 [a]1 Kin. 11:33

NKJV

10 [a]They hate the one who rebukes in the gate,
And they [b]abhor the one who speaks uprightly.
11 [a]Therefore, because you tread down the poor
And take grain taxes from him,
Though [b]you have built houses of hewn stone,
Yet you shall not dwell in them;
You have planted pleasant vineyards,
But you shall not drink wine from them.
12 For I [a]know your manifold transgressions
And your mighty sins:
[b]Afflicting the just *and* taking bribes;
[c]Diverting the poor *from justice* at the gate.
13 Therefore [a]the prudent keep silent at that time,
For it *is* an evil time.

14 Seek good and not evil,
That you may live;
So the LORD God of hosts will be with you,
[a]As you have spoken.
15 [a]Hate evil, love good;
Establish justice in the gate.
[b]It may be that the LORD God of hosts
Will be gracious to the remnant of Joseph.

The Day of the LORD

16 Therefore the LORD God of hosts, the Lord,
says this:

"*There shall be* wailing in all streets,
And they shall say in all the highways,
'Alas! Alas!'
They shall call the farmer to mourning,
[a]And skillful lamenters to wailing.
17 In all vineyards *there shall be* wailing,
For [a]I will pass through you,"
Says the LORD.

18 [a]Woe to you who desire the day of the LORD!
For what good *is* [b]the day of the LORD to you?
It *will be* darkness, and not light.
19 It *will be* [a]as though a man fled from a lion,
And a bear met him!
Or *as though* he went into the house,
Leaned his hand on the wall,
And a serpent bit him!
20 *Is* not the day of the LORD darkness, and not light?
Is it not very dark, with no brightness in it?

21 "I[a] hate, I despise your feast days,
And [b]I do not savor your sacred assemblies.
22 [a]Though you offer Me burnt offerings and your grain offerings,
I will not accept *them,*
Nor will I regard your fattened peace offerings.
23 Take away from Me the noise of your songs,
For I will not hear the melody of your stringed instruments.
24 [a]But let justice run down like water,
And righteousness like a mighty stream.

25 "Did[a] you offer Me sacrifices and offerings
In the wilderness forty years, O house of Israel?
26 You also carried *Sikkuth* [a]your king
And *Chiun, your idols,
The star of your gods,
Which you made for yourselves.

5:26 LXX, Vg. *tabernacle of Moloch* • A pagan deity • A pagan deity

KJV

27 Therefore will I cause you to go into captivity [a]beyond Damascus, saith the LORD, [b]whose name *is* The God of hosts.

Warnings to Zion and Samaria

6 Woe [a]to them *that are* at [b]ease in Zion, and
[c]trust in the mountain of Samaria, *which are*
named [d]chief of the nations, to whom the house
of Israel came!
2 [a]Pass ye unto [b]Calneh, and see; and from
thence go ye to [c]Hamath the great: then go down
to Gath of the Philistines: [d]*be they* better than
these kingdoms? or their border greater than your
border?
3 Ye that [a]put far away the [b]evil day, [c]and
cause [d]the seat of violence to come near;
4 That lie upon beds of ivory, and stretch
themselves upon their couches, and eat the lambs
out of the flock, and the calves out of the midst
of the stall;
5 [a]That chant to the sound of the viol, *and*
invent to themselves instruments of [b]musick, [c]like
David;
6 That [a]drink wine in bowls, and anoint
themselves with the chief ointments: [b]but they are
not grieved for the affliction of Joseph.
7 Therefore now shall they go [a]captive with
the first that go captive, and the banquet of them
that stretched themselves shall be removed.
8 [a]The Lord GOD hath sworn by himself,
saith the LORD the God of hosts, I abhor [b]the excellency of Jacob, and hate his palaces: therefore
will I deliver up the city with all that is therein.
9 And it shall come to pass, if there remain
ten men in one house, that they shall die.
10 And a man's uncle shall take him up, and
he that burneth him, to bring out the bones out
of the house, and shall say unto him that *is* by
the sides of the house, *Is there* yet *any* with thee?
and he shall say, No. Then shall he say, [a]Hold
thy tongue: [b]for we may not make mention of the
name of the LORD.
11 For, behold, [a]the LORD commandeth, [b]and
he will smite the great house with breaches, and
the little house with clefts.
12 Shall horses run upon the rock? will *one*
plow *there* with oxen? for [a]ye have turned judgment into gall, and the fruit of righteousness into
hemlock:
13 Ye which rejoice in a thing of nought,
which say, Have we not taken to us horns by our
own strength?
14 But, behold, [a]I will raise up against you
a nation, O house of Israel, saith the LORD the
God of hosts; and they shall afflict you from the
[b]entering in of Hemath unto the river of the
wilderness.

Vision of the Locusts

7 Thus hath the Lord GOD shewed unto me; and,
behold, he formed grasshoppers in the begin-

---

27 [a]2 Kin. 17:6; Amos 7:11, 17; Mic. 4:10 [b]Amos 4:13

CHAPTER 6

1 [a]Luke 6:24 [b]Ps. 123:4; Is. 32:9–11; Zeph. 1:12 [c]Is. 31:1; Jer. 49:4 [d]Ex. 19:5; Amos 3:2
2 [a]Jer. 2:10 [b]Gen. 10:10; Is. 10:9 [c]1 Kin. 8:65; 2 Kin. 18:34 [d]Nah. 3:8
3 [a]Is. 56:12; Ezek. 12:27; Amos 9:10; Matt. 24:37–39 [b]Amos 5:18 [c]Amos 5:12 [d]Ps. 94:20
5 [a]Is. 5:12 [b]Amos 5:23; 3:10 [c]1 Chr. 23:5
6 [a]Amos 2:8; 4:1 [b]Gen. 37:25
7 [a]Amos 5:27
8 [a]Gen. 22:16; Jer. 51:14; Amos 4:2; 8:7; Heb. 6:13–17 [b]Ps. 47:4; Ezek. 24:21; Amos 8:7
10 [a]Amos 5:13 [b]Amos 8:3
11 [a]Is. 55:11 [b]2 Kin. 25:9; Amos 3:15
12 [a]1 Kin. 21:7–13; Is. 59:13, 14; Hos. 10:4; Amos 5:7, 11, 12
14 [a]Jer. 5:15 [b]Num. 34:7, 8; 1 Kin. 8:65; 2 Kin. 14:25

*

6:10 Lit. *bones*
6:13 Lit. *Nothing* • Lit. *Horns*, a symbol of strength

NKJV

27 "Therefore I will send you into captivity
[a]beyond Damascus,"
Says the LORD, [b]whose name *is* the God
of hosts.

Warnings to Zion and Samaria

6 Woe [a]to you *who are* at [b]ease in Zion,
And [c]trust in Mount Samaria,
Notable persons in the [d]chief nation,
To whom the house of Israel comes!
2 [a]Go over to [b]Calneh and see;
And from there go to [c]Hamath the
great;
Then go down to Gath of the Philistines.
[d]*Are you* better than these kingdoms?
Or is their territory greater than your
territory?

3 *Woe to* you who [a]put far off the day of
[b]doom,
[c]Who cause [d]the seat of violence to come
near;
4 Who lie on beds of ivory,
Stretch out on your couches,
Eat lambs from the flock
And calves from the midst of the stall;
5 [a]Who sing idly to the sound of stringed
instruments,
And invent for yourselves [b]musical
instruments [c]like David;
6 Who [a]drink wine from bowls,
And anoint yourselves with the best
ointments,
[b]But are not grieved for the affliction of
Joseph.
7 Therefore they shall now go [a]captive as
the first of the captives,
And those who recline at banquets shall
be removed.

8 [a]The Lord GOD has sworn by Himself,
The LORD God of hosts says:
"I abhor [b]the pride of Jacob,
And hate his palaces;
Therefore I will deliver up *the* city
And all that is in it."

9 Then it shall come to pass, that if ten men
remain in one house, they shall die.
10 And when a relative *of the dead,* with one
who will burn *the bodies,* picks up the *bodies to
take them out of the house, he will say to one
inside the house, "*Are there* any more with you?"
Then someone will say, "None." And he will say,
[a]"Hold your tongue! [b]For we dare not mention
the name of the LORD."

11 For behold, [a]the LORD gives a command:
[b]He will break the great house into bits,
And the little house into pieces.

12 Do horses run on rocks?
Does *one* plow *there* with oxen?
Yet [a]you have turned justice into gall,
And the fruit of righteousness into
wormwood,
13 You who rejoice over *Lo Debar,
Who say, "Have we not taken *Karnaim
for ourselves
By our own strength?"

14 "But, behold, [a]I will raise up a nation
against you,
O house of Israel,"
Says the LORD God of hosts;
"And they will afflict you from the
[b]entrance of Hamath
To the Valley of the Arabah."

Vision of the Locusts

7 Thus the Lord GOD showed me: Behold, He
formed locust swarms at the beginning of the

KJV

ning of the shooting up of the latter growth; and,
lo, *it was* the latter growth after the king's
mowings.
2 And it came to pass, *that* when they had
made an end of eating the grass of the land, then
I said, O Lord GOD, forgive, I beseech thee: [a]by
whom shall Jacob arise? for he *is* small.
3 [a]The LORD repented for this: It shall not
be, saith the LORD.

Vision of the Fire

4 Thus hath the Lord GOD shewed unto me:
and, behold, the Lord GOD called to contend by
fire, and it devoured the great deep, and did eat
up a part.
5 Then said I, O Lord GOD, cease, I beseech
thee: [a]by whom shall Jacob arise? for he *is* small.
6 The LORD repented for this: This also shall
not be, saith the Lord GOD.

Vision of the Plumb Line

7 Thus he shewed me: and, behold, the Lord
stood upon a wall *made* by a plumbline, with a
plumbline in his hand.
8 And the LORD said unto me, Amos, what
seest thou? And I said, A plumbline. Then said
the Lord, Behold, [a]I will set a plumbline in the
midst of my people Israel: [b]I will not again pass
by them any more:
9 [a]And the high places of Isaac shall be desolate, and the sanctuaries of Israel shall be laid
waste; and [b]I will rise against the house of Jeroboam with the sword.

Amaziah's Complaint

10 Then Amaziah the [a]priest of [b]Beth–el sent
to [c]Jeroboam king of Israel, saying, Amos hath
conspired against thee in the midst of the house
of Israel: the land is not able to bear all his words.
11 For thus Amos saith, Jeroboam shall die
by the sword, and Israel shall surely be led away
[a]captive out of their own land.
12 Also Amaziah said unto Amos, O thou
seer, go, flee thee away into the land of Judah,
and there eat bread, and prophesy there:
13 But [a]prophesy not again any more at
Beth–el: [b]for it *is* the king's chapel, and it *is* the
king's court.
14 Then answered Amos, and said to Ama-
ziah, I *was* no prophet, neither *was* I [a]a prophet's
son; [b]but I *was* an herdman, and a gatherer of
sycomore fruit:
15 And the LORD took me as I followed the
flock, and the LORD said unto me, Go, [a]prophesy
unto my people Israel.
16 Now therefore hear thou the word of the
LORD: Thou sayest, Prophesy not against Israel,
and [a]drop not *thy word* against the house of Isaac.

CHAPTER 7

2 [a]Is. 51:19
3 [a]Deut. 32:36; Jer. 26:19; Hos. 11:8; Amos 5:15; Jon. 3:10; [James 5:16]
5 [a]Amos 7:2, 3
8 [a]2 Kin. 21:13; Is. 28:17; 34:11; Lam. 2:8 [b]Mic. 7:18
9 [a]Gen. 46:1; Hos. 10:8; Mic. 1:5 [b]2 Kin. 15:8–10; Amos 7:11
10 [a]1 Kin. 12:31, 32; 13:33 [b]1 Kin. 13:32; Amos 4:4 [c]2 Kin. 14:23
11 [a]Amos 5:27; 6:7
13 [a]Amos 2:12; Acts 4:18 [b]1 Kin. 12:29, 32; Amos 7:9
14 [a]1 Kin. 20:35; 2 Kin. 2:5; 2 Chr. 19:2 [b]2 Kin. 3:4; Amos 1:1; Zech. 13:5
15 [a]Amos 3:8
16 [a]Deut. 32:2; Ezek. 21:2; Mic. 2:6

NKJV

late crop; indeed *it was* the late crop after the
king's mowings.
2 And so it was, when they had finished eating the grass of the land, that I said:

"O Lord GOD, forgive, I pray!
[a]Oh, that Jacob may stand,
For he *is* small!"
3 *So* [a]the LORD relented concerning this.
"It shall not be," said the LORD.

Vision of the Fire

4 Thus the Lord GOD showed me: Behold,
the Lord GOD called for conflict by fire, and it
consumed the great deep and devoured the
territory.
5 Then I said:

"O Lord GOD, cease, I pray!
[a]Oh, that Jacob may stand,
For he *is* small!"
6 *So* the LORD relented concerning this.
"This also shall not be," said the Lord
GOD.

Vision of the Plumb Line

7 Thus He showed me: Behold, the Lord
stood on a wall *made* with a plumb line, with a
plumb line in His hand.
8 And the LORD said to me, "Amos, what
do you see?" And I said, "A plumb line." Then
the Lord said:

"Behold, [a]I am setting a plumb line
In the midst of My people Israel;
[b]I will not pass by them anymore.
9 [a]The high places of Isaac shall be desolate,
And the sanctuaries of Israel shall be laid
waste.
[b]I will rise with the sword against the house
of Jeroboam."

Amaziah's Complaint

10 Then Amaziah the [a]priest of [b]Bethel sent
to [c]Jeroboam king of Israel, saying, "Amos has
conspired against you in the midst of the house
of Israel. The land is not able to bear all his
words.
11 "For thus Amos has said:

'Jeroboam shall die by the sword,
And Israel shall surely be led away
[a]captive
From their own land.'"

12 Then Amaziah said to Amos:

"Go, you seer!
Flee to the land of Judah.
There eat bread,
And there prophesy.
13 But [a]never again prophesy at Bethel,
[b]For it *is* the king's sanctuary,
And it *is* the royal residence."

14 Then Amos answered, and said to Amaziah:

"I *was* no prophet,
Nor *was* I [a]a son of a prophet,
But I *was* a [b]sheepbreeder
And a tender of sycamore fruit.
15 Then the LORD took me as I followed the
flock,
And the LORD said to me,
'Go, [a]prophesy to My people Israel.'
16 Now therefore, hear the word of the
LORD:
You say, 'Do not prophesy against
Israel,
And [a]do not spout against the house of
Isaac.'

KJV

17 [a]Therefore thus saith the LORD; [b]Thy wife
shall be an harlot in the city, and thy sons and
thy daughters shall fall by the sword, and thy land
shall be divided by line; and thou shalt die in a
[c]polluted land: and Israel shall surely go into captivity forth of his land.

Vision of the Summer Fruit

8 Thus hath the Lord GOD shewed unto me: and
behold a basket of summer fruit.
2 And he said, Amos, what seest thou? And
I said, A basket of summer fruit. Then said the
LORD unto me, [a]The end is come upon my people
of Israel; [b]I will not again pass by them any more.
3 And [a]the songs of the temple shall be
howlings in that day, saith the Lord GOD: *there
shall be* many dead bodies in every place; [b]they
shall cast *them* forth with silence.
4 Hear this, O ye that swallow up the needy,
even to make the poor of the land to fail,
5 Saying, When will the new moon be gone,
that we may sell corn? and [a]the sabbath, that we
may set forth wheat, [b]making the ephah small,
and the shekel great, and falsifying the balances
by [c]deceit?
6 That we may buy the poor for [a]silver, and
the needy for a pair of shoes; *yea,* and sell the
refuse of the wheat?
7 The LORD hath sworn by [a]the excellency
of Jacob, Surely [b]I will never forget any of their
works.
8 [a]Shall not the land tremble for this, and
every one mourn that dwelleth therein? and it
shall rise up wholly as a flood; and it shall be
cast out and drowned, [b]as *by* the flood of Egypt.
9 And it shall come to pass in that day, saith
the Lord GOD, [a]that I will cause the sun to go down
at noon, and I will darken the earth in the clear
day:
10 And I will turn your feasts into [a]mourning,
[b]and all your songs into lamentation; [c]and I will
bring up sackcloth upon all loins, and baldness
upon every head; and I will make it as the mourning of an only *son,* and the end thereof as a bitter
day.
11 Behold, the days come, saith the Lord
GOD, that I will send a famine in the land, not a
famine of bread, nor a thirst for water, but [a]of
hearing the words of the LORD:
12 And they shall wander from sea to sea,
and from the north even to the east, they shall
run to and fro to seek the word of the LORD, and
shall [a]not find *it.*
13 In that day shall the fair virgins and young
men faint for thirst.
14 They that [a]swear by [b]the sin of Samaria,
and say, Thy god, O Dan, liveth; and, The manner

17 [a]Jer. 28:12; 29:21, 32 [b]Is. 13:16; Lam. 5:11; Hos. 4:13; Zech. 14:2 [c]2 Kin. 17:6; Ezek. 4:13; Hos. 9:3

CHAPTER 8

2 [a]Ezek. 7:2 [b]Amos 7:8
3 [a]Amos 5:23 [b]Amos 6:9, 10
5 [a]Ex. 31:13–17; Neh. 13:15 [b]Mic. 6:10, 11 [c]Lev. 19:35, 36; Deut. 25:13–15
6 [a]Amos 2:6
7 [a]Deut. 33:26, 29; Ps. 68:34; Amos 6:8 [b]Ps. 10:11; Hos. 7:2; 8:13
8 [a]Hos. 4:3 [b]Jer. 46:7, 8; Amos 9:5
9 [a]Job 5:14; Is. 13:10; 59:9, 10; Jer. 15:9; [Mic. 3:6]; Matt. 27:45; Mark 15:32; Luke 23:44
10 [a]Lam. 5:15; Ezek. 7:18 [b]Is. 15:2, 3; Jer. 48:37; Ezek. 27:31 [c]Jer. 6:26; [Zech. 12:10]
11 [a]1 Sam. 3:1; 2 Chr. 15:3; Ps. 74:9; Ezek. 7:26; Mic. 3:6
12 [a]Hos. 5:6
14 [a]Hos. 4:15 [b]Deut. 9:21

*———

8:4 Or *trample on,* Amos 2:7
8:8 The Nile; some Heb. mss., LXX, Syr., Tg., Vg. *River* (cf. Amos 9:5); MT *the light*
8:14 Or *Ashima,* a Syrian goddess

NKJV

17 "Therefore[a] thus says the LORD:

[b]'Your wife shall be a harlot in the city;
Your sons and daughters shall fall by the
sword;
Your land shall be divided by *survey* line;
You shall die in a [c]defiled land;
And Israel shall surely be led away
captive
From his own land.'"

Vision of the Summer Fruit

8 Thus the Lord GOD showed me: Behold, a basket of summer fruit.
2 And He said, "Amos, what do you see?"
So I said, "A basket of summer fruit." Then the
LORD said to me:

[a]"The end has come upon My people Israel;
[b]I will not pass by them anymore.
3 And [a]the songs of the temple
Shall be wailing in that day,"
Says the Lord GOD—
"Many dead bodies everywhere,
[b]They shall be thrown out in silence."

4 Hear this, you who *swallow up the needy,
And make the poor of the land fail,

5 Saying:

"When will the New Moon be past,
That we may sell grain?
And [a]the Sabbath,
That we may trade wheat?
[b]Making the ephah small and the shekel
large,
Falsifying the scales by [c]deceit,
6 That we may buy the poor for [a]silver,
And the needy for a pair of sandals—
Even sell the bad wheat?"

7 The LORD has sworn by [a]the pride of
Jacob:
"Surely [b]I will never forget any of their
works.
8 [a]Shall the land not tremble for this,
And everyone mourn who dwells in it?
All of it shall swell like *the River,
Heave and subside
[b]Like the River of Egypt.

9 "And it shall come to pass in that day,"
says the Lord GOD,
[a]"That I will make the sun go down at noon,
And I will darken the earth in broad
daylight;
10 I will turn your feasts into [a]mourning,
[b]And all your songs into lamentation;
[c]I will bring sackcloth on every waist,
And baldness on every head;
I will make it like mourning for an only
son,
And its end like a bitter day.

11 "Behold, the days are coming," says the
Lord GOD,
"That I will send a famine on the land,
Not a famine of bread,
Nor a thirst for water,
But [a]of hearing the words of the LORD.
12 They shall wander from sea to sea,
And from north to east;
They shall run to and fro, seeking the
word of the LORD,
But shall [a]not find *it.*

13 "In that day the fair virgins
And strong young men
Shall faint from thirst.
14 Those who [a]swear by [b]the *sin of
Samaria,

KJV

of [c]Beer–sheba liveth; even they shall fall, and
never rise up again.

The Destruction of Israel

9 I saw the Lord standing upon the altar: and
he said, Smite the lintel of the door, that the
posts may shake: and [a]cut them in the head, all
of them; and I will slay the last of them with the
sword: [b]he that fleeth of them shall not flee
away, and he that escapeth of them shall not be
delivered.
2 [a]Though they dig into hell, thence shall
mine hand take them; [b]though they climb up to
heaven, thence will I bring them down:
3 And though they [a]hide themselves in the
top of Carmel, I will search and take them out
thence; and though they be hid from my sight in
the bottom of the sea, thence will I command the
serpent, and he shall bite them:
4 And though they go into captivity before
their enemies, [a]thence will I command the sword,
and it shall slay them: and [b]I will set mine eyes
upon them for evil, and not for good.
5 And the Lord GOD of hosts *is* he that
toucheth the land, and it shall [a]melt, [b]and all that
dwell therein shall mourn: and it shall rise up
wholly like a flood; and shall be drowned, as *by*
the flood of Egypt.
6 *It is* he that buildeth his [a]stories in the
heaven, and hath founded his troop in the earth;
he that [b]calleth for the waters of the sea, and poureth them out upon the face of the earth: [c]The LORD
is his name.
7 *Are* ye not as children of the Ethiopians
unto me, O children of Israel? saith the LORD.
Have not I brought up Israel out of the land of
Egypt? and the [a]Philistines from [b]Caphtor, and
the Syrians from [c]Kir?
8 Behold, [a]the eyes of the Lord GOD *are*
upon the sinful kingdom, and I [b]will destroy it
from off the face of the earth; saving that I will
not utterly destroy the house of Jacob, saith the
LORD.
9 For, lo, I will command, and I will sift the
house of Israel among all nations, like as *corn* is
sifted in a sieve, [a]yet shall not the least grain fall
upon the earth.
10 All the sinners of my people shall die by
the sword, [a]which say, The evil shall not overtake
nor prevent us.

Israel Will Be Restored (*cf. Acts 15:16, 17*)

11 [a]In that day will I raise up the tabernacle
of David that is fallen, and close up the breaches

---

14 [c]Amos 5:5

CHAPTER 9

1 [a]Ps. 68:21; Hab. 3:13 [b]Amos 2:14
2 [a]Ps. 139:8; Jer. 23:24 [b]Job 20:6; Jer. 51:53; Obad. 4; Matt. 11:23
3 [a]Jer. 23:24
4 [a]Lev. 26:33 [b]Lev. 17:10; Jer. 21:10; 39:16; 44:11
5 [a]Ps. 104:32; 144:5; Is. 64:1; Mic. 1:4 [b]Amos 8:8
6 [a]Ps. 104:3, 13 [b]Amos 5:8 [c]Amos 4:13; 5:27
7 [a]Jer. 47:4 [b]Deut. 2:23 [c]Amos 1:5
8 [a]Jer. 44:27; Amos 9:4 [b]Jer. 5:10; 30:11; [Joel 2:32]; Amos 3:12; [Obad. 16, 17]
9 [a][Is. 65:8–16]
10 [a][Is. 28:15]; Jer. 5:12; Amos 6:3
11 [a]Acts 15:16–18

NKJV

Who say,
'As your god lives, O Dan!'
And, 'As the way of [c]Beersheba lives!'
They shall fall and never rise again."

The Destruction of Israel

9 I saw the Lord standing by the altar, and He said:

"Strike the doorposts, that the thresholds may shake,
And [a]break them on the heads of them all.
I will slay the last of them with the sword.
[b]He who flees from them shall not get away,
And he who escapes from them shall not be delivered.

2 "Though[a] they dig into *hell,
From there My hand shall take them;
[b]Though they climb up to heaven,
From there I will bring them down;
3 And though they [a]hide themselves on top of Carmel,
From there I will search and take them;
Though they hide from My sight at the bottom of the sea,
From there I will command the serpent, and it shall bite them;
4 Though they go into captivity before their enemies,
From there [a]I will command the sword,
And it shall slay them.
[b]I will set My eyes on them for harm and not for good."

5 The Lord GOD of hosts,
He who touches the earth and it [a]melts,
[b]And all who dwell there mourn;
All of it shall swell like *the River,
And subside like the River of Egypt.
6 He who builds His [a]layers in the sky,
And has founded His strata in the earth;
Who [b]calls for the waters of the sea,
And pours them out on the face of the earth—
[c]The LORD *is* His name.

7 "*Are* you not like the people of Ethiopia to Me,
O children of Israel?" says the LORD.
"Did I not bring up Israel from the land of Egypt,
The [a]Philistines from [b]Caphtor,
And the Syrians from [c]Kir?

8 "Behold, [a]the eyes of the Lord GOD *are* on the sinful kingdom,
And I [b]will destroy it from the face of the earth;
Yet I will not utterly destroy the house of Jacob,"
Says the LORD.

9 "For surely I will command,
And will sift the house of Israel among all nations,
As *grain* is sifted in a sieve;
[a]Yet not the smallest grain shall fall to the ground.
10 All the sinners of My people shall die by the sword,
[a]Who say, 'The calamity shall not overtake nor confront us.'

Israel Will Be Restored (*cf. Acts 15:16, 17*)

11 "On[a] that day I will raise up
The *tabernacle of David, which has fallen down,
And repair its damages;

---

*
9:2 Or *Sheol*
9:5 The Nile
9:11 Lit. *booth;* a figure of a deposed dynasty

KJV

thereof; and I will raise up his ruins, and I will
build it as in the days of old:
12 [a]That they may possess the remnant of
[b]Edom, and of all the heathen, which are called
by my name, saith the LORD that doeth this.
13 Behold, [a]the days come, saith the LORD,
that the plowman shall overtake the reaper, and
the treader of grapes him that soweth seed; [b]and
the mountains shall drop sweet wine, and all the
hills shall melt.
14 [a]And I will bring again the captivity of
my people of Israel, and [b]they shall build the
waste cities, and inhabit *them;* and they shall
plant vineyards, and drink the wine thereof; they
shall also make gardens, and eat the fruit of them.
15 And I will plant them upon their land, and
[a]they shall no more be pulled up out of their land
which I have given them, saith the LORD thy God.

12 [a]Obad. 19 [b]Num. 24:18; Is. 11:14
13 [a]Lev. 26:5 [b]Joel 3:18
14 [a]Ps. 53:6; Is. 60:4; Jer. 30:3, 18 [b]Is. 61:4
15 [a]Is. 60:21; Ezek. 34:28; 37:25

NKJV

I will raise up its ruins,
And rebuild it as in the days of old;
12 [a]That they may possess the remnant of
[b]Edom,*
And all the Gentiles who are called by My
name,"
Says the LORD who does this thing.

13 "Behold, [a]the days are coming," says the
LORD,
"When the plowman shall overtake the
reaper,
And the treader of grapes him who sows
seed;
[b]The mountains shall drip with sweet wine,
And all the hills shall flow *with it.*
14 [a]I will bring back the captives of My people
Israel;
[b]They shall build the waste cities and
inhabit *them;*
They shall plant vineyards and drink wine
from them;
They shall also make gardens and eat fruit
from them.
15 I will plant them in their land,
[a]And no longer shall they be pulled up
From the land I have given them,"
Says the LORD your God.

*9:12 LXX *mankind*

KJV

THE BOOK OF

OBADIAH

The Coming Judgment on Edom

THE vision of Obadiah. Thus saith the Lord
GOD [a]concerning Edom; [b]We have heard a
rumour from the LORD, and an ambassador is sent
among the heathen, Arise ye, and let us rise up
against her in battle.
2 Behold, I have made thee small among the
heathen: thou art greatly despised.
3 The [a]pride of thine heart hath deceived
thee, thou that dwellest in the clefts of the rock,
whose habitation *is* high; [b]that saith in his heart,
Who shall bring me down to the ground?
4 [a]Though thou exalt *thyself* as the eagle,
and though thou [b]set thy nest among the stars,
thence will I bring thee down, saith the LORD.
5 If [a]thieves came to thee, if robbers by
night, (how art thou cut off!) would they not have
stolen till they had enough? if the grapegatherers
came to thee, [b]would they not leave *some* grapes?
6 How are *the things* of Esau searched out!
how are his hidden things sought up!
7 All the men of thy confederacy have
brought thee *even* to the border: [a]the men that
were at peace with thee have deceived thee, *and*
prevailed against thee; *they that eat* thy bread
have laid a wound under thee: [b]*there is* none
understanding in him.
8 [a]Shall I not in that day, saith the LORD,
even destroy the wise *men* out of Edom, and understanding out of the mount of Esau?
9 And thy [a]mighty *men,* O [b]Teman, shall
be dismayed, to the end that every one of the
mount of Esau may be cut off by slaughter.

Edom Mistreated His Brother

10 For *thy* [a]violence against thy brother Jacob shame shall cover thee, and [b]thou shalt be
cut off for ever.
11 In the day that thou [a]stoodest on the other
side, in the day that the strangers carried away
captive his forces, and foreigners entered into his
gates, and [b]cast lots upon Jerusalem, even thou
wast as one of them.

CHAPTER 1

1 [a]Is. 21:11; Ezek. 25:12; Joel 3:19; Mal. 1:3 [b]Jer. 49:14–16; Obad. 1–4
3 [a]Is. 16:6; Jer. 49:16 [b]Is. 14:13–15; Rev. 18:7
4 [a]Job 20:6 [b]Hab. 2:9; Mal. 1:4
5 [a]Jer. 49:9 [b]Deut. 24:21
7 [a]Jer. 38:22 [b]Is. 19:11; Jer. 49:7
8 [a][Job 5:12–14]; Is. 29:14
9 [a]Ps. 76:5 [b]Gen. 36:11; 1 Chr. 1:45; Job 2:11; Jer. 49:7
10 [a]Gen. 27:41; Ezek. 25:12; Amos 1:11 [b]Ezek. 35:9; Joel 3:19
11 [a]Ps. 83:5–8; Amos 1:6, 9 [b]Joel 3:3; Nah. 3:10

NKJV

THE BOOK OF

OBADIAH

The Coming Judgment on Edom

THE vision of Obadiah.

Thus says the Lord GOD [a]concerning Edom
[b](We have heard a report from the LORD,
And a messenger has been sent among the nations, *saying,*
"Arise, and let us rise up against her for battle"):

2 "Behold, I will make you small among the nations;
You shall be greatly despised.
3 The [a]pride of your heart has deceived you,
You who dwell in the clefts of the rock,
Whose habitation is high;
[b]*You* who say in your heart,
'Who will bring me down to the ground?'
4 [a]Though you ascend *as* high as the eagle,
And though you [b]set your nest among the stars,
From there I will bring you down," says the LORD.

5 "If [a]thieves had come to you,
If robbers by night—
Oh, how you will be cut off!—
Would they not have stolen till they had enough?
If grape gatherers had come to you,
[b]Would they not have left *some* gleanings?
6 "Oh, how Esau shall be searched out!
How his hidden treasures shall be sought after!
7 All the men in your confederacy
Shall force you to the border;
[a]The men at peace with you
Shall deceive you *and* prevail against you.
Those who eat your bread shall lay a *trap for you.
[b]No one is aware of it.

8 "Will[a] I not in that day," says the LORD,
"Even destroy the wise *men* from Edom,
And understanding from the mountains of Esau?
9 Then your [a]mighty men, O [b]Teman, shall be dismayed,
To the end that everyone from the mountains of Esau
May be cut off by slaughter.

Edom Mistreated His Brother

10 "For [a]violence against your brother Jacob,
Shame shall cover you,
And [b]you shall be cut off forever.
11 In the day that you [a]stood on the other side—
In the day that strangers carried captive his forces,
When foreigners entered his gates
And [b]cast lots for Jerusalem—
Even you *were* as one of them.

*———

7 Or *wound* or *plot*

KJV

12 But thou shouldest not have [a]looked on the day of thy brother in the day that he became a stranger; neither shouldest thou have [b]rejoiced over the children of Judah in the day of their destruction; neither shouldest thou have spoken proudly in the day of distress.

13 Thou shouldest not have entered into the gate of my people in the day of their calamity; yea, thou shouldest not have looked on their affliction in the day of their calamity, nor have laid *hands* on their substance in the day of their calamity;

14 Neither shouldest thou have stood in the crossway, to cut off those of his that did escape; neither shouldest thou have delivered up those of his that did remain in the day of distress.

15 [a]For the day of the LORD *is* near upon all the heathen: [b]as thou hast done, it shall be done unto thee: thy reward shall return upon thine own head.

16 [a]For as ye have drunk upon my holy mountain, *so* shall all the heathen drink continually, yea, they shall drink, and they shall swallow down, and they shall be as though they had not been.

Israel's Final Triumph

17 But upon mount Zion [a]shall be deliverance, and there shall be holiness; and the house of Jacob shall possess their possessions.

18 And the house of Jacob [a]shall be a fire, and the house of Joseph a flame, and the house of Esau for stubble, and they shall kindle in them, and devour them; and there shall not be *any* remaining of the house of Esau; for the LORD hath spoken *it*.

19 And *they of* the south [a]shall possess the mount of Esau; [b]and *they of* the plain the Philistines: and they shall possess the fields of Ephraim, and the fields of Samaria: and Benjamin *shall possess* Gilead.

20 And the captivity of this host of the children of Israel *shall possess* that of the Canaanites, *even* [a]unto Zarephath; and the captivity of Jerusalem, which *is* in Sepharad, [b]shall possess the cities of the south.

21 And [a]saviours shall come up on mount Zion to judge the mount of Esau; and the [b]kingdom shall be the LORD's.

12 [a]Mic. 4:11; 7:10 [b][Prov. 17:5]; Ezek. 35:15; 36:5
15 [a]Ezek. 30:3; [Joel 1:15; 2:1, 11, 31; Amos 5:18, 20] [b]Jer. 50:29; 51:56; Hab. 2:8
16 [a]Joel 3:17
17 [a]Is. 14:1, 2; Joel 2:32; Amos 9:8
18 [a]Is. 5:24; 9:18, 19; Zech. 12:6
19 [a]Is. 11:14; Amos 9:12 [b]Zeph. 2:7
20 [a]1 Kin. 17:9; Luke 4:26 [b]Jer. 32:44
21 [a][James 5:20] [b]Ps. 22:28; [Dan. 2:44; 7:14; Zech. 14:9; Rev. 11:15]

NKJV

12 "But you should not have [a]gazed on the
day of your brother
*In the day of his captivity;
Nor should you have [b]rejoiced over the
children of Judah
In the day of their destruction;
Nor should you have spoken proudly
In the day of distress.
13 You should not have entered the gate of
My people
In the day of their calamity.
Indeed, you should not have gazed on
their affliction
In the day of their calamity,
Nor laid *hands* on their substance
In the day of their calamity.
14 You should not have stood at the
crossroads
To cut off those among them who escaped;
Nor should you have delivered up those
among them who remained
In the day of distress.

15 "For[a] the day of the LORD upon all the
nations *is* near;
[b]As you have done, it shall be done to you;
Your reprisal shall return upon your own
head.
16 [a]For as you drank on my holy mountain,
So shall all the nations drink continually;
Yes, they shall drink, and swallow,
And they shall be as though they had
never been.

Israel's Final Triumph

17 "But on Mount Zion there [a]shall be
deliverance,
And there shall be holiness;
The house of Jacob shall possess their
possessions.
18 The house of Jacob shall be a fire,
And the house of Joseph [a]a flame;
But the house of Esau *shall be* stubble;
They shall kindle them and devour them,
And no survivor shall *remain* of the house
of Esau,"
For the LORD has spoken.

19 The *South [a]shall possess the mountains
of Esau,
[b]And the Lowland shall possess Philistia.
They shall possess the fields of Ephraim
And the fields of Samaria.
Benjamin *shall possess* Gilead.
20 And the captives of this host of the
children of Israel
Shall possess the land of the Canaanites
As [a]far as Zarephath.
The captives of Jerusalem who are in
Sepharad
[b]Shall possess the cities of the *South.
21 Then [a]saviors* shall come to Mount Zion
To judge the mountains of Esau,
And the [b]kingdom shall be the LORD's.

*
12 Lit. *On the day he became a foreigner*
19 Heb. *Negev*
20 Heb. *Negev*
21 *deliverers*

KJV

THE BOOK OF

JONAH

Jonah's Disobedience

1 Now the word of the LORD came unto [a]Jonah the son of Amittai, saying,

2 Arise, go to [a]Nineveh, that [b]great city, and cry against it; for [c]their wickedness is come up before me.

3 But Jonah rose up to flee unto Tarshish from the presence of the LORD, and went down to [a]Joppa; and he found a ship going to Tarshish: so he paid the fare thereof, and went down into it, to go with them unto [b]Tarshish [c]from the presence of the LORD.

The Storm at Sea

4 But [a]the LORD sent out a great wind into the sea, and there was a mighty tempest in the sea, so that the ship was like to be broken.

5 Then the mariners were afraid, and cried every man unto his god, and cast forth the wares that *were* in the ship into the sea, to lighten *it* of them. But Jonah was gone down [a]into the sides of the ship; and he lay, and was fast asleep.

6 So the shipmaster came to him, and said unto him, What meanest thou, O sleeper? arise, [a]call upon thy God, [b]if so be that God will think upon us, that we perish not.

7 And they said every one to his fellow, Come, and let us [a]cast lots, that we may know for whose cause this evil *is* upon us. So they cast lots, and the lot fell upon Jonah.

8 Then said they unto him, [a]Tell us, we pray thee, for whose cause this evil *is* upon us; What *is* thine occupation? and whence comest thou? what *is* thy country? and of what people *art* thou?

9 And he said unto them, I *am* an Hebrew; and I fear the LORD, the God of heaven, [a]which hath made the sea and the dry *land*.

Jonah Thrown into the Sea

10 Then were the men exceedingly afraid, and said unto him, Why hast thou done this? For the men knew that he fled from the presence of the LORD, because he had told them.

11 Then said they unto him, What shall we do unto thee, that the sea may be calm unto us? for the sea wrought, and was tempestuous.

12 And he said unto them, [a]Take me up, and cast me forth into the sea; so shall the sea be calm unto you: for I know that for my sake this great tempest *is* upon you.

13 Nevertheless the men rowed hard to bring *it* to the land; [a]but they could not: for the sea wrought, and was tempestuous against them.

14 Wherefore they cried unto the LORD, and said, We beseech thee, O LORD, we beseech thee, let us not perish for this man's life, and [a]lay not upon us innocent blood: for thou, O LORD, [b]hast done as it pleased thee.

15 So they took up Jonah, and cast him forth into the sea: [a]and the sea ceased from her raging.

16 Then the men [a]feared the LORD exceedingly, and offered a sacrifice unto the LORD, and made vows.

CHAPTER 1

1 [a]2 Kin. 14:25; Matt. 12:39–41; 16:4; Luke 11:29, 30, 32
2 [a]Is. 37:37 [b]Gen. 10:11, 12; 2 Kin. 19:36; Jon. 4:11; Nah. 1:1; Zeph. 2:13 [c]Gen. 18:20; Hos. 7:2
3 [a]Josh. 19:46; 2 Chr. 2:16; Ezra 3:7; Acts 9:36, 43 [b]Is. 23:1 [c]Gen. 4:16; Job 1:12; 2:7
4 [a]Ps. 107:25
5 [a]1 Sam. 24:3
6 [a]Ps. 107:28 [b]Joel 2:14
7 [a]Josh. 7:14; 1 Sam. 14:41, 42; Prov. 16:33
8 [a]Josh. 7:19; 1 Sam. 14:43
9 [a][Neh. 9:6]; Ps. 146:6; Acts 17:24
12 [a]John 11:50
13 [a][Prov. 21:30]
14 [a]Deut. 21:8 [b]Ps. 115:3; [Dan. 4:35]
15 [a][Ps. 89:9; 107:29]; Luke 8:24
16 [a]Mark 4:41; Acts 5:11

NKJV

THE BOOK OF

JONAH

Jonah's Disobedience

1 Now the word of the LORD came to [a]Jonah the son of Amittai, saying,

2 "Arise, go to [a]Nineveh, that [b]great city, and cry out against it; for [c]their wickedness has come up before Me."

3 But Jonah arose to flee to Tarshish from the presence of the LORD. He went down to [a]Joppa, and found a ship going to Tarshish; so he paid the fare, and went down into it, to go with them to [b]Tarshish [c]from the presence of the LORD.

The Storm at Sea

4 But [a]the LORD sent out a great wind on the sea, and there was a mighty tempest on the sea, so that the ship was about to be broken up.

5 Then the mariners were afraid; and every man cried out to his god, and threw the cargo that *was* in the ship into the sea, to lighten *the load. But Jonah had gone down [a]into the lowest parts of the ship, had lain down, and was fast asleep.

6 So the captain came to him, and said to him, "What do you mean, sleeper? Arise, [a]call on your God; [b]perhaps your God will consider us, so that we may not perish."

7 And they said to one another, "Come, let us [a]cast lots, that we may know for whose cause this trouble *has come* upon us." So they cast lots, and the lot fell on Jonah.

8 Then they said to him, [a]"Please tell us! For whose cause *is* this trouble upon us? What is your occupation? And where do you come from? What is your country? And of what people are you?"

9 So he said to them, "I *am* a Hebrew; and I fear the LORD, the God of heaven, [a]who made the sea and the dry *land*."

Jonah Thrown into the Sea

10 Then the men were exceedingly afraid, and said to him, "Why have you done this?" For the men knew that he fled from the presence of the LORD, because he had told them.

11 Then they said to him, "What shall we do to you that the sea may be calm for us?"—for the sea was growing more tempestuous.

12 And he said to them, [a]"Pick me up and throw me into the sea; then the sea will become calm for you. For I know that this great tempest *is* because of me."

13 Nevertheless the men rowed hard to return to land, [a]but they could not, for the sea continued to grow more tempestuous against them.

14 Therefore they cried out to the LORD and said, "We pray, O LORD, please do not let us perish for this man's life, and [a]do not charge us with innocent blood; for You, O LORD, [b]have done as it pleased You."

15 So they picked up Jonah and threw him into the sea, [a]and the sea ceased from its raging.

16 Then the men [a]feared the LORD exceedingly, and offered a sacrifice to the LORD and took vows.

*———

1:5 Lit. *from upon them*

KJV

Jonah's Prayer and Deliverance

17 Now the LORD had prepared a great fish to swallow up Jonah. And [a]Jonah was in the belly of the fish three days and three nights.

2 Then Jonah prayed unto the LORD his God out of the fish's belly,

2 And said, I [a]cried by reason of mine affliction unto the LORD, [b]and he heard me; out of the belly of hell cried I, *and* thou heardest my voice.

3 [a]For thou hadst cast me into the deep, in the midst of the seas; and the floods compassed me about: [b]all thy billows and thy waves passed over me.

4 [a]Then I said, I am cast out of thy sight; yet I will look again [b]toward thy holy temple.

5 The [a]waters compassed me about, *even* to the soul: the depth closed me round about, the weeds were wrapped about my head.

6 I went down to the bottoms of the mountains; the earth with her bars *was* about me for ever: yet hast thou brought up my [a]life from corruption, O LORD my God.

7 When my soul fainted within me I remembered the LORD: [a]and my prayer came in unto thee, into thine holy temple.

8 They that observe [a]lying vanities forsake their own mercy.

9 But I will [a]sacrifice unto thee with the voice of thanksgiving; I will pay *that* that I have [b]vowed. [c]Salvation *is* of the [d]LORD.

10 And the LORD spake unto the fish, and it vomited out Jonah upon the dry *land*.

Jonah Preaches at Nineveh

3 And the word of the LORD came unto Jonah the second time, saying,

2 Arise, go unto Nineveh, that great city, and preach unto it the preaching that I bid thee.

3 So Jonah arose, and went unto Nineveh, according to the word of the LORD. Now Nineveh was an exceeding great city of three days' journey.

4 And Jonah began to enter into the city a day's journey, and [a]he cried, and said, Yet forty days, and Nineveh shall be overthrown.

The People of Nineveh Believe

5 So the [a]people of Nineveh believed God, and proclaimed a fast, and put on sackcloth, from the greatest of them even to the least of them.

6 For word came unto the king of Nineveh, and he arose from his throne, and he laid his robe from him, and covered *him* with sackcloth, [a]and sat in ashes.

7 [a]And he caused *it* to be proclaimed and published through Nineveh by the decree of the king and his nobles, saying, Let neither man nor beast, herd nor flock, taste any thing: let them not feed, nor drink water:

8 But let man and beast be covered with

17 [a][Matt. 12:40; Luke 11:30]

CHAPTER 2

2 [a]1 Sam. 30:6; Ps. 120:1; Lam. 3:55 [b]Ps. 65:2
3 [a]Ps. 88:6 [b]Ps. 42:7
4 [a]Ps. 31:22; Jer. 7:15 [b]1 Kin. 8:38; 2 Chr. 6:38; Ps. 5:7
5 [a]Ps. 69:1; Lam. 3:54
6 [a]Job 33:28; [Ps. 16:10; Is. 38:17]
7 [a]2 Chr. 30:27; Ps. 18:6
8 [a]2 Kin. 17:15; Ps. 31:6; Jer. 10:8
9 [a]Ps. 50:14, 23; Jer. 33:11; Hos. 14:2 [b]Job 22:27; [Eccl. 5:4, 5] [c]Ps. 3:8; [Is. 45:17] [d][Jer. 3:23]

CHAPTER 3

4 [a][Deut. 18:22]
5 [a][Matt. 12:41; Luke 11:32]
6 [a]Job 2:8
7 [a]2 Chr. 20:3; Dan. 3:29; Joel 2:15

*3:3 Exact meaning unknown

NKJV

Jonah's Prayer and Deliverance

17 Now the LORD had prepared a great fish to swallow up Jonah. And [a]Jonah was in the belly of the fish three days and three nights.

2 Then Jonah prayed to the LORD his God from the fish's belly.

2 And he said:

"I [a]cried out to the LORD because of my affliction,
[b]And He answered me.

"Out of the belly of Sheol I cried,
And You heard my voice.
3 [a]For You cast me into the deep,
Into the heart of the seas,
And the floods surrounded me;
[b]All Your billows and Your waves passed over me.
4 [a]Then I said, 'I have been cast out of Your sight;
Yet I will look again [b]toward Your holy temple.'
5 The [a]waters surrounded me, *even* to my soul;
The deep closed around me;
Weeds were wrapped around my head.
6 I went down to the moorings of the mountains;
The earth with its bars *closed* behind me forever;
Yet You have brought up my [a]life from the pit,
O LORD, my God.

7 "When my soul fainted within me,
I remembered the LORD;
[a]And my prayer went *up* to You,
Into Your holy temple.

8 "Those who regard [a]worthless idols
Forsake their own Mercy.
9 But I will [a]sacrifice to You
With the voice of thanksgiving;
I will pay what I have [b]vowed.
[c]Salvation *is* of the [d]LORD."

10 So the LORD spoke to the fish, and it vomited Jonah onto dry *land*.

Jonah Preaches at Nineveh

3 Now the word of the LORD came to Jonah the second time, saying,

2 "Arise, go to Nineveh, that great city, and preach to it the message that I tell you."

3 So Jonah arose and went to Nineveh, according to the word of the LORD. Now Nineveh was an exceedingly great city, *a three-day journey *in extent*.

4 And Jonah began to enter the city on the first day's walk. Then [a]he cried out and said, "Yet forty days, and Nineveh shall be overthrown!"

The People of Nineveh Believe

5 So the [a]people of Nineveh believed God, proclaimed a fast, and put on sackcloth, from the greatest to the least of them.

6 Then word came to the king of Nineveh; and he arose from his throne and laid aside his robe, covered *himself* with sackcloth [a]and sat in ashes.

7 [a]And he caused *it* to be proclaimed and published throughout Nineveh by the decree of the king and his nobles, saying,

Let neither man nor beast, herd nor flock, taste anything; do not let them eat, or drink water.

8 But let man and beast be covered with

KJV

sackcloth, and cry mightily unto God: yea, [a]let
them turn every one from his evil way, and from
[b]the violence that *is* in their hands.
9 [a]Who can tell *if* God will turn and repent,
and turn away from his fierce anger, that we perish not?
10 [a]And God saw their works, that they
turned from their evil way; and God repented of
the evil, that he had said that he would do unto
them; and he did *it* not.

Jonah's Anger and God's Kindness

4 But it displeased Jonah exceedingly, and he
was very angry.
2 And he prayed unto the LORD, and said, I
pray thee, O LORD, *was* not this my saying, when
I was yet in my country? Therefore I [a]fled before
unto Tarshish: for I knew that thou *art* a [b]gracious
God, and merciful, slow to anger, and of great
kindness, and repentest thee of the evil.
3 [a]Therefore now, O LORD, take, I beseech
thee, my life from me; for [b]*it is* better for me to
die than to live.
4 Then said the LORD, Doest thou well to
be angry?
5 So Jonah went out of the city, and sat on
the east side of the city, and there made him a
booth, and sat under it in the shadow, till he might
see what would become of the city.
6 And the LORD God prepared a gourd, and
made *it* to come up over Jonah, that it might be
a shadow over his head, to deliver him from his
grief. So Jonah was exceeding glad of the gourd.
7 But God prepared a worm when the morning rose the next day, and it smote the gourd that
it withered.
8 And it came to pass, when the sun did
arise, that God prepared a vehement east wind; and
the sun beat upon the head of Jonah, that he
fainted, and wished in himself to die, and said,
[a]*It is* better for me to die than to live.
9 And God said to Jonah, Doest thou well
to be angry for the gourd? And he said, I do well
to be angry, *even* unto death.
10 Then said the LORD, Thou hast had pity
on the gourd, for the which thou hast not laboured, neither madest it grow; which came up in
a night, and perished in a night:
11 And should not I spare Nineveh, [a]that
great city, wherein are more than sixscore thousand persons [b]that cannot discern between their
right hand and their left hand; and *also* much
cattle?

8 [a]Is. 58:6 [b]Is. 59:6
9 [a]2 Sam. 12:22; Joel 2:14; Amos 5:15
10 [a]Ex. 32:14; Jer. 18:8; Amos 7:3, 6

CHAPTER 4

2 [a]Jon. 1:3 [b]Ex. 34:6; Num. 14:18; Ps. 86:5, 15; Joel 2:13
3 [a]1 Kin. 19:4; Job 6:8, 9 [b]Jon. 4:8
8 [a]Jon. 4:3
11 [a]Jon. 1:2; 3:2, 3 [b]Deut. 1:39; Is. 7:16

*________

4:6 Heb. *kikayon,* exact identity unknown

NKJV

sackcloth, and cry mightily to God; yes,
[a]let every one turn from his evil way and
from [b]the violence that is in his hands.
9 [a]Who can tell *if* God will turn and relent,
and turn away from His fierce anger, so
that we may not perish?

10 [a]Then God saw their works, that they
turned from their evil way; and God relented from
the disaster that He had said He would bring upon
them, and He did not do it.

Jonah's Anger and God's Kindness

4 But it displeased Jonah exceedingly, and he
became angry.
2 So he prayed to the LORD, and said, "Ah,
LORD, was not this what I said when I was still
in my country? Therefore I [a]fled previously to
Tarshish; for I know that You *are* a [b]gracious and
merciful God, slow to anger and abundant in
lovingkindness, One who relents from doing
harm.
3 [a]"Therefore now, O LORD, please take my
life from me, for [b]*it is* better for me to die than
to live!"
4 Then the LORD said, "*Is it* right for you
to be angry?"
5 So Jonah went out of the city and sat on
the east side of the city. There he made himself
a shelter and sat under it in the shade, till he might
see what would become of the city.
6 And the LORD God prepared a *plant and
made it come up over Jonah, that it might be
shade for his head to deliver him from his misery.
So Jonah was very grateful for the plant.
7 But as morning dawned the next day God
prepared a worm, and it *so* damaged the plant
that it withered.
8 And it happened, when the sun arose, that
God prepared a vehement east wind; and the sun
beat on Jonah's head, so that he grew faint. Then
he wished death for himself, and said, [a]"*It is* better for me to die than to live."
9 Then God said to Jonah, "*Is it* right for
you to be angry about the plant?" And he said,
"*It is* right for me to be angry, even to death!"
10 But the LORD said, "You have had pity on
the plant for which you have not labored, nor
made it grow, which came up in a night and perished in a night.
11 "And should I not pity Nineveh, [a]that
great city, in which are more than one hundred
and twenty thousand persons [b]who cannot discern between their right hand and their left—and
much livestock?"

KJV

THE BOOK OF

MICAH

1 The word of the LORD that came to [a]Micah the Morasthite in the days of [b]Jotham, Ahaz, *and* Hezekiah, kings of Judah, which he saw concerning Samaria and Jerusalem.

The Coming Judgment on Israel

2 Hear, all ye people; hearken, O earth, and all that therein is: and let the Lord GOD be witness against you, the LORD from [a]his holy temple.

3 For, behold, the LORD cometh forth out of his place, and will come down, and tread upon the high places of the earth.

4 And [a]the mountains shall be molten under him, and the valleys shall be cleft, as wax before the fire, *and* as the waters *that are* poured down a steep place.

5 For the transgression of Jacob *is* all this, and for the sins of the house of Israel. What *is* the transgression of Jacob? *is it* not Samaria? and what *are* the [a]high places of Judah? *are they* not Jerusalem?

6 Therefore I will make Samaria [a]as an heap of the field, *and* as plantings of a vineyard: and I will pour down the stones thereof into the valley, and I will [b]discover the foundations thereof.

7 And all the graven images thereof shall be beaten to pieces, and all the [a]hires thereof shall be burned with the fire, and all the idols thereof will I lay desolate: for she gathered *it* of the hire of an harlot, and they shall return to the [b]hire of an harlot.

Mourning for Israel and Judah

8 Therefore I will wail and howl, I will go stripped and naked: [a]I will make a wailing like the dragons, and mourning as the owls.

9 For her wound *is* incurable; for [a]it is come unto Judah; he is come unto the gate of my people, *even* to Jerusalem.

10 [a]Declare ye *it* not at Gath, weep ye not at all: in the house of Aphrah roll thyself in the dust.

11 Pass ye away, thou inhabitant of Saphir, having thy shame naked: the inhabitant of Zaanan came not forth in the mourning of Beth-ezel; he shall receive of you his standing.

12 For the inhabitant of Maroth waited carefully for good: but [a]evil came down from the LORD unto the gate of Jerusalem.

CHAPTER 1

1 [a][2 Pet. 1:21]; Jer. 26:18 [b]2 Kin. 15:5, 7, 32–38; 2 Chr. 27:1–9; Is. 1:1; Hos. 1:1
2 [a][Ps. 11:4]
4 [a]Amos 9:5
5 [a]Deut. 32:13; 33:29; Amos 4:13
6 [a]2 Kin. 19:25; Mic. 3:12 [b]Ezek. 13:14
7 [a]Hos. 2:5 [b]Deut. 23:18; Is. 23:17
8 [a]Ps. 102:6
9 [a]2 Kin. 18:13; Is. 8:7, 8
10 [a]2 Sam. 1:20
12 [a]Is. 59:9–11; Jer. 14:19; Amos 3:6

*

1:10 Lit. *House of Dust*
1:11 Lit. *Going Out*
1:12 Lit. *was sick*

NKJV

THE BOOK OF

MICAH

1 The word of the LORD that came to [a]Micah of Moresheth in the days of [b]Jotham, Ahaz, *and* Hezekiah, kings of Judah, which he saw concerning Samaria and Jerusalem.

The Coming Judgment on Israel

2 Hear, all you peoples!
Listen, O earth, and all that is in it!
Let the Lord GOD be a witness against you,
The Lord from [a]His holy temple.

3 For behold, the LORD is coming out of His place;
He will come down
And tread on the high places of the earth.
4 [a]The mountains will melt under Him,
And the valleys will split
Like wax before the fire,
Like waters poured down a steep place.
5 All this is for the transgression of Jacob
And for the sins of the house of Israel.
What *is* the transgression of Jacob?
Is it not Samaria?
And what *are* the [a]high places of Judah?
Are they not Jerusalem?

6 "Therefore I will make Samaria [a]a heap of ruins in the field,
Places for planting a vineyard;
I will pour down her stones into the valley,
And I will [b]uncover her foundations.
7 All her carved images shall be beaten to pieces,
And all her [a]pay as a harlot shall be burned with the fire;
All her idols I will lay desolate,
For she gathered *it* from the pay of a harlot,
And they shall return to the [b]pay of a harlot."

Mourning for Israel and Judah

8 Therefore I will wail and howl,
I will go stripped and naked;
[a]I will make a wailing like the jackals
And a mourning like the ostriches,
9 For her wounds *are* incurable.
For [a]it has come to Judah;
It has come to the gate of My people—
To Jerusalem.

10 [a]Tell *it* not in Gath,
Weep not at all;
In *Beth Aphrah
Roll yourself in the dust.
11 Pass by in naked shame, you inhabitant of Shaphir;
The inhabitant of *Zaanan does not go out.
Beth Ezel mourns;
Its place to stand is taken away from you.

12 For the inhabitant of Maroth *pined for good,
But [a]disaster came down from the LORD
To the gate of Jerusalem.

KJV

13 O thou inhabitant of [a]Lachish, bind the
chariot to the swift beast: she *is* the beginning of
the sin to the daughter of Zion: for the transgressions of Israel were [b]found in thee.
14 Therefore shalt thou [a]give presents to
Moresheth–gath: the houses of [b]Achzib *shall be*
a lie to the kings of Israel.
15 Yet will I bring an heir unto thee, O inhabitant of [a]Mareshah: he shall come unto [b]Adullam
the glory of Israel.
16 Make thee [a]bald, and poll thee for thy
[b]delicate children; enlarge thy baldness as the eagle;
for they are gone into [c]captivity from thee.

Woe to Evildoers

2 Woe to them that devise iniquity, and work
evil upon their beds! when the [a]morning is
light, they practise it, because it is in the power
of their hand.
2 And they [a]covet fields, and take *them* by
violence; and houses, and take *them* away: so
they oppress a man and his house, even a man
and his heritage.
3 Therefore thus saith the LORD; Behold,
against this [a]family do I devise an [b]evil, from
which ye shall not remove your necks; neither
shall ye go haughtily: for this time *is* evil.
4 In that day shall *one* take up a parable
against you, and [a]lament with a doleful lamentation, *and* say, We be utterly spoiled: he hath
changed the portion of my people: how hath he
removed *it* from me! turning away he hath divided
our fields.
5 Therefore thou shalt have none that shall
cast a cord by lot in the congregation of the LORD.

Lying Prophets

6 Prophesy ye not, *say they to them that*
prophesy: they shall not prophesy to them, *that*
they shall not take shame.
7 O *thou that art* named the house of Jacob,
is the spirit of the LORD straitened? *are* these his
doings? do not my words do good to him that
walketh uprightly?
8 Even of late my people is risen up as an
enemy: ye pull off the robe with the garment from
them that pass by securely as men averse from
war.
9 The women of my people have ye cast out
from their pleasant houses; from their children
have ye taken away my glory for ever.
10 Arise ye, and depart; for this *is* not *your*
[a]rest: because it is [b]polluted, it shall destroy *you*,
even with a sore destruction.
11 If a man walking in the spirit and falsehood do lie, *saying*, I will prophesy unto thee of

---

13 [a]Josh. 10:3; 2 Kin. 14:19; 18:14; Is. 36:2 [b]Ezek. 23:11
14 [a]2 Sam. 8:2 [b]Josh. 15:44
15 [a]Josh. 15:44 [b]2 Chr. 11:7
16 [a]Job 1:20 [b]Lam. 4:5 [c]2 Kin. 17:6; Amos 7:11, 17; [Mic. 4:10]

CHAPTER 2
1 [a]Hos. 7:6, 7
2 [a]Is. 5:8
3 [a]Ex. 20:5; Jer. 8:3; Amos 3:1, 2 [b]Amos 5:13
4 [a]2 Sam. 1:17
10 [a]Deut. 12:9 [b]Lev. 18:25

NKJV

13 O inhabitant of [a]Lachish,
Harness the chariot to the swift steeds
(She *was* the beginning of sin to the
daughter of Zion),
For the transgressions of Israel were
[b]found in you.

14 Therefore you shall [a]give presents to
*Moresheth Gath;
The houses of [b]Achzib* *shall be* a lie to
the kings of Israel.
15 I will yet bring an heir to you, O inhabitant
of [a]Mareshah;*
The glory of Israel shall come to
[b]Adullam.
16 Make yourself [a]bald and cut off your
hair,
Because of your [b]precious children;
Enlarge your baldness like an eagle,
For they shall go from you into [c]captivity.

Woe to Evildoers

2 Woe to those who devise iniquity,
And work out evil on their beds!
At [a]morning light they practice it,
Because it is in the power of their hand.
2 They [a]covet fields and take *them* by
violence,
Also houses, and seize *them*.
So they oppress a man and his house,
A man and his inheritance.

3 Therefore thus says the LORD:

"Behold, against this [a]family I am devising
[b]disaster,
From which you cannot remove your
necks;
Nor shall you walk haughtily,
For this *is* an evil time.
4 In that day *one* shall take up a proverb
against you,
And [a]lament with a bitter lamentation,
saying:
'We are utterly destroyed!
He has changed the heritage of my people;
How He has removed *it* from me!
To a turncoat He has divided our fields.' "
5 Therefore you will have no *one to
determine boundaries by lot
In the assembly of the LORD.

Lying Prophets

6 "Do not prattle," *you say to those* who
prophesy.
So they shall not prophesy *to you;
*They shall not return insult for insult.
7 *You who are* named the house of
Jacob:
"Is the Spirit of the LORD restricted?
Are these His doings?
Do not My words do good
To him who walks uprightly?

8 "Lately My people have risen up as an
enemy—
You pull off the robe with the garment
From those who trust *you*, as they pass
by,
Like men returned from war.
9 The women of My people you cast out
From their pleasant houses;
From their children
You have taken away My glory forever.

10 "Arise and depart,
For this *is* not *your* [a]rest;
Because it is [b]defiled, it shall destroy,
Yes, with utter destruction.
11 If a man should walk in a false spirit
And speak a lie, *saying*,

---

*

1:14 Lit. *Possession of Gath* • Lit. *Lie*
1:15 Lit. *Inheritance*
2:5 Lit. *one casting a surveyor's line*
2:6 Lit. *to these* • Vg. *He shall not take shame*

KJV

wine and of strong drink; he shall even be the
[a]prophet of this people.

Israel Restored

12 [a]I will surely assemble, O Jacob, all of
thee; I will surely gather the remnant of Israel; I
will put them together [b]as the sheep of Bozrah,
as the flock in the midst of their fold: [c]they shall
make great noise by reason of *the multitude of*
men.
13 The breaker is come up before them: they
have broken up, and have passed through the
gate, and are gone out by it: and [a]their king shall
pass before them, [b]and the LORD on the head of
them.

Wicked Rulers and Prophets

3 And I said, Hear, I pray you, O heads of Jacob,
and ye [a]princes of the house of Israel; [b]*Is it*
not for you to know judgment?
2 Who hate the good, and love the evil; who
pluck off their skin from off them, and their flesh
from off their bones;
3 Who also [a]eat the flesh of my people, and
flay their skin from off them; and they break their
bones, and chop them in pieces, as for the pot,
and [b]as flesh within the caldron.
4 Then [a]shall they cry unto the LORD, but
he will not hear them: he will even hide his face
from them at that time, as they have behaved
themselves ill in their doings.
5 Thus saith the LORD [a]concerning the
prophets that make my people err, that [b]bite with
their teeth, and cry, Peace; and [c]he that putteth
not into their mouths, they even prepare war
against him.
6 [a]Therefore night *shall be* unto you, that
ye shall not have a vision; and it shall be dark
unto you, that ye shall not divine; and the sun
shall go down over the prophets, and the day shall
be dark over [b]them.
7 Then shall the seers be ashamed, and the
diviners confounded: yea, they shall all cover
their lips; [a]for *there is* no answer of God.
8 But truly I am full of power by the spirit
of the LORD, and of judgment, and of might, [a]to
declare unto Jacob his transgression, and to Israel
his sin.
9 Hear this, I pray you, ye heads of the
house of Jacob, and princes of the house of Israel,
that abhor judgment, and pervert all equity.
10 [a]They build up Zion with [b]blood, and Jerusalem with iniquity.
11 [a]The heads thereof judge for reward, and
[b]the priests thereof teach for hire, and the prophets thereof divine for money: [c]yet will they lean
upon the LORD, and say, *Is* not the LORD among
us? none evil can come upon us.
12 Therefore shall Zion for your sake be

11 [a]Is. 30:10; Jer. 5:30, 31; 2 Tim. 4:3, 4 **12** [a][Mic. 4:6, 7] [b]Jer. 31:10 [c]Ezek. 33:22; 36:37 **13** [a][Hos. 3:5] [b]Is. 52:12

CHAPTER 3

1 [a]Ezek. 22:27 [b]Ps. 82:1–5; Jer. 5:4, 5 **3** [a]Ps. 14:4; 27:2; Zeph. 3:3 [b]Ezek. 11:3, 6, 7 **4** [a]Ps. 18:41; Prov. 1:28; Is. 1:15; Jer. 11:11 **5** [a]Is. 56:10, 11; Jer. 6:13; Ezek. 13:10, 19 [b]Matt. 7:15 [c]Ezek. 13:18 **6** [a]Is. 8:20–22; 29:10–12 [b]Is. 29:10; [Jer. 23:33–40]; Ezek. 13:23 **7** [a]Amos 8:11 **8** [a]Is. 58:1 **10** [a]Jer. 22:13, 17 [b]Ezek. 22:27; Hab. 2:12 **11** [a]Is. 1:23; Mic. 7:3 [b]Jer. 6:13 [c]Is. 48:2; Jer. 7:4

*

2:12 Heb. *Bozrah*
3:2 Lit. *them*

NKJV

'I will prophesy to you of wine and drink,'
Even he would be the [a]prattler of this
people.

Israel Restored

12 "I[a] will surely assemble all of you, O
Jacob,
I will surely gather the remnant of Israel;
I will put them together [b]like sheep of *the
fold,
Like a flock in the midst of their
pasture;
[c]They shall make a loud noise because of
so many people.
13 The one who breaks open will come up
before them;
They will break out,
Pass through the gate,
And go out by it;
[a]Their king will pass before them,
[b]With the LORD at their head."

Wicked Rulers and Prophets

3 And I said:

"Hear now, O heads of Jacob,
And you [a]rulers of the house of Israel:
[b]*Is it* not for you to know justice?
2 You who hate good and love evil;
Who strip the skin from *My people,
And the flesh from their bones;
3 Who also [a]eat the flesh of My people,
Flay their skin from them,
Break their bones,
And chop *them* in pieces
Like *meat* for the pot,
[b]Like flesh in the caldron."

4 Then [a]they will cry to the LORD,
But He will not hear them;
He will even hide His face from them at
that time,
Because they have been evil in their
deeds.

5 Thus says the LORD [a]concerning the
prophets
Who make my people stray;
Who chant "Peace"
While they [b]chew with their teeth,
But who prepare war against him
[c]Who puts nothing into their mouths:
6 "Therefore[a] you shall have night without
vision,
And you shall have darkness without
divination;
The sun shall go down on the prophets,
And the day shall be dark for [b]them.
7 So the seers shall be ashamed,
And the diviners abashed;
Indeed they shall all cover their lips;
[a]For *there is* no answer from God."

8 But truly I am full of power by the Spirit
of the LORD,
And of justice and might,
[a]To declare to Jacob his transgression
And to Israel his sin.
9 Now hear this,
You heads of the house of Jacob
And rulers of the house of Israel,
Who abhor justice
And pervert all equity,
10 [a]Who build up Zion with [b]bloodshed
And Jerusalem with iniquity:
11 [a]Her heads judge for a bribe,
[b]Her priests teach for pay,
And her prophets divine for money.
[c]Yet they lean on the LORD, and say,
"Is not the LORD among us?
No harm can come upon us."
12 Therefore because of you

KJV

[a]plowed *as* a field, [b]and Jerusalem shall become
heaps, and [c]the mountain of the house as the high
places of the forest.

The LORD's Reign in Zion
(cf. Is. 2:2–4)

4 But [a]in the last days it shall come to pass,
that the mountain of the house of the LORD
shall be established in the top of the mountains,
and it shall be exalted above the hills; and people
shall flow unto it.
2 And many nations shall come, and say,
Come, and let us go up to the mountain of the
LORD, and to the house of the God of Jacob; and
he will teach us of his ways, and we will walk in
his paths: for the law shall go forth of Zion, and
the word of the LORD from Jerusalem.
3 And he shall judge among many people,
and rebuke strong nations afar off; and they shall
beat their swords into [a]plowshares, and their
spears into pruninghooks: nation shall not lift up
a sword against nation, [b]neither shall they learn
war any more.
4 [a]But they shall sit every man under his
vine and under his fig tree; and none shall make
them afraid: for the mouth of the LORD of hosts
hath spoken *it*.
5 For all people will walk every one in the
name of his god, and [a]we will walk in the name
of the LORD our God for ever and ever.

Zion's Future Triumph

6 In that day, saith the LORD, [a]will I assemble her that halteth, [b]and I will gather her that is
driven out, and her that I have afflicted;
7 And I will make her that halted [a]a remnant, and her that was cast far off a strong nation:
and the LORD [b]shall reign over them in mount
Zion from henceforth, even for ever.
8 And thou, O tower of the flock, the strong
hold of the daughter of Zion, unto thee shall it
come, even the first dominion; the kingdom shall
come to the daughter of Jerusalem.
9 Now why dost thou cry out aloud? [a]*is*
there no king in thee? is thy counsellor perished?
for [b]pangs have taken thee as a woman in travail.
10 Be in pain, and labour to bring forth, O
daughter of Zion, like a woman in travail: for now
shalt thou go forth out of the city, and thou shalt
dwell in the field, and thou shalt go *even* to [a]Bab-
ylon; there shalt thou be delivered; there the
[b]LORD shall [c]redeem thee from the hand of thine
enemies.
11 [a]Now also many nations are gathered
against thee, that say, Let her be defiled, and let
our eye [b]look upon Zion.

12 [a]Jer. 26:18 [b]Ps. 79:1; Jer. 9:11 [c]Mic. 4:1, 2

CHAPTER 4

1 [a]Is. 2:2–4; Ezek. 17:22; Dan. 2:28; 10:14; Hos. 3:5
3 [a]Is. 2:4; Joel 3:10 [b]Ps. 72:7
4 [a]1 Kin. 4:25; Zech. 3:10
5 [a]Zech. 10:12
6 [a]Ezek. 34:16 [b]Ps. 147:2
7 [a]Mic. 2:12 [b][Is. 9:6; 24:23; Luke 1:33; Rev. 11:15]
9 [a]Jer. 8:19 [b]Is. 13:8; Jer. 30:6
10 [a]2 Chr. 36:20; Amos 5:27 [b][Is. 45:13; Mic. 7:8–12] [c]Ezra 1:1–3; 2:1; Ps. 18:17
11 [a]Lam. 2:16 [b]Obad. 12

NKJV

Zion shall be [a]plowed *like* a field,
[b]Jerusalem shall become heaps of ruins,
And [c]the mountain of the *temple
Like the bare hills of the forest.

The LORD's Reign in Zion
(cf. Is. 2:2–4)

4 Now [a]it shall come to pass in the latter
days
That the mountain of the LORD's house
Shall be established on the top of the
mountains,
And shall be exalted above the hills;
And peoples shall flow to it.
2 Many nations shall come and say,
"Come, and let us go up to the mountain
of the LORD,
To the house of the God of Jacob;
He will teach us His ways,
And we shall walk in His paths."
For out of Zion the law shall go forth,
And the word of the LORD from
Jerusalem.
3 He shall judge between many peoples,
And rebuke strong nations afar off;
They shall beat their swords into
[a]plowshares,
And their spears into pruning hooks;
Nation shall not lift up sword against
nation,
[b]Neither shall they learn war anymore.

4 [a]But everyone shall sit under his vine and
under his fig tree,
And no one shall make *them* afraid;
For the mouth of the LORD of hosts has
spoken.
5 For all people walk each in the name of
his god,
But [a]we will walk in the name of the LORD
our God
Forever and ever.

Zion's Future Triumph

6 "In that day," says the LORD,
[a]"I will assemble the lame,
[b]I will gather the outcast
And those whom I have afflicted;
7 I will make the lame [a]a remnant,
And the outcast a strong nation;
So the LORD [b]will reign over them in
Mount Zion
From now on, even forever.
8 And you, O tower of the flock,
The stronghold of the daughter of Zion,
To you shall it come,
Even the former dominion shall come,
The kingdom of the daughter of
Jerusalem."

9 Now why do you cry aloud?
[a]*Is there* no king in your midst?
Has your counselor perished?
For [b]pangs have seized you like a woman
in labor.
10 Be in pain, and labor to bring forth,
O daughter of Zion,
Like a woman in birth pangs.
For now you shall go forth from the
city,
You shall dwell in the field,
And to [a]Babylon you shall go.
There you shall be delivered;
There the [b]LORD will [c]redeem you
From the hand of your enemies.

11 [a]Now also many nations have gathered
against you,
Who say, "Let her be defiled,
And let our eye [b]look upon Zion."

3:12 Lit. *house*

KJV

12 But they know not [a]the thoughts of the
LORD, neither understand they his counsel: for he
shall gather them [b]as the sheaves into the floor.
13 [a]Arise and [b]thresh, O daughter of Zion:
for I will make thine horn iron, and I will make
thy hoofs brass: and thou shalt [c]beat in pieces
many people: [d]and I will consecrate their gain
unto the LORD, and their substance unto [e]the LORD
of the whole earth.

5 Now gather thyself in troops, O daughter of
troops: he hath laid siege against us: they
shall [a]smite the judge of Israel with a rod upon
the cheek.

The Coming Messiah

2 But thou, [a]Beth–lehem [b]Ephratah, *though*
thou be little [c]among the [d]thousands of Judah,
yet out of thee shall he come forth unto me *that*
is to be [e]ruler in Israel; [f]whose goings forth *have*
been from of old, from everlasting.
3 Therefore will he give them up, until the
time *that* [a]she which travaileth hath brought
forth: then [b]the remnant of his brethren shall return unto the children of Israel.
4 And he shall stand and [a]feed in the
strength of the LORD, in the majesty of the name
of the LORD his God; and they shall abide: for now
[b]shall he be great unto the ends of the earth.

Judgment on Israel's Enemies

5 And this *man* [a]shall be the peace, when
the Assyrian shall come into our land: and when
he shall tread in our palaces, then shall we raise
against him seven shepherds, and eight principal
men.
6 And they shall waste the land of Assyria
with the sword, and the land of [a]Nimrod in the
entrances thereof: thus shall he [b]deliver *us* from
the Assyrian, when he cometh into our land, and
when he treadeth within our borders.
7 And [a]the remnant of Jacob shall be in the
midst of many people [b]as a dew from the LORD,
as the showers upon the grass, that tarrieth not
for man, nor waiteth for the sons of men.
8 And the remnant of Jacob shall be among
the Gentiles in the midst of many people as a [a]lion
among the beasts of the forest, as a young lion
among the flocks of sheep: who, if he go through,
both treadeth down, and teareth in pieces, and
none can deliver.
9 Thine hand shall be lifted up upon thine
adversaries, and all thine enemies shall be cut off.
10 And it shall come to pass in that day, saith
the LORD, that I will [a]cut off thy [b]horses out of
the midst of thee, and I will destroy thy [c]chariots:
11 And I will cut off the cities of thy land,
and throw down all thy strong holds:
12 And I will cut off witchcrafts out of thine
hand; and thou shalt have no *more* [a]soothsayers:

12 [a][Is. 55:8, 9] [b]Is. 21:10
13 [a]Jer. 51:33; [Zech. 12:1–8; 14:14] [b]Is. 41:15 [c]Dan. 2:44 [d]Is. 18:7 [e]Zech. 4:14

CHAPTER 5
1 [a]1 Kin. 22:24; Job 16:10; Lam. 3:30; Matt. 27:30; Mark 15:19
2 [a]Is. 11:1; Matt. 2:6; Luke 2:4, 11; John 7:42 [b]Gen. 35:19; 48:7; Ruth 4:11 [c]1 Sam. 23:23 [d]Ex. 18:25 [e][Gen. 49:10; Is. 9:6] [f]Ps. 90:2; [John 1:1]
3 [a]Hos. 11:8; Mic. 4:10 [b]Mic. 4:7; 7:18
4 [a][Is. 40:11; 49:9; Ezek. 34:13–15, 23, 24]; Mic. 7:14 [b]Ps. 72:8; Is. 52:13; Zech. 9:10; [Luke 1:32]
5 [a][Is. 9:6]; Luke 2:14; [Eph. 2:14; Col. 1:20]
6 [a]Gen. 10:8–11 [b]Is. 14:25; Luke 1:71
7 [a]Mic. 5:3 [b]Gen. 27:28; Deut. 32:2; Ps. 72:6; Hos. 14:5
8 [a]Gen. 49:9; Num. 24:9
10 [a]Zech. 9:10 [b]Deut. 17:16 [c]Is. 2:7; 22:18; Hos. 14:3
12 [a]Deut. 18:10–12; Is. 2:6

NKJV

12 But they do not know [a]the thoughts of the
LORD,
Nor do they understand His counsel;
For He will gather them [b]like sheaves to
the threshing floor.

13 "Arise[a] and [b]thresh, O daughter of Zion;
For I will make your horn iron,
And I will make your hooves bronze;
You shall [c]beat in pieces many peoples;
[d]I will consecrate their gain to the LORD,
And their substance to [e]the Lord of the
whole earth."

5 Now gather yourself in troops,
O daughter of troops;
He has laid siege against us;
They will [a]strike the judge of Israel with
a rod on the cheek.

The Coming Messiah

2 "But you, [a]Bethlehem [b]Ephrathah,
Though you are little [c]among the
[d]thousands of Judah,
Yet out of you shall come forth to Me
The One to be [e]Ruler in Israel,
[f]Whose goings forth *are* from of old,
From everlasting."

3 Therefore He shall give them up,
Until the time *that* [a]she who is in labor
has given birth;
Then [b]the remnant of His brethren
Shall return to the children of Israel.
4 And He shall stand and [a]feed *His flock*
In the strength of the LORD,
In the majesty of the name of the LORD
His God;
And they shall abide,
For now He [b]shall be great
To the ends of the earth;
5 And this *One* [a]shall be peace.

Judgment on Israel's Enemies

When the Assyrian comes into our land,
And when he treads in our palaces,
Then we will raise against him
Seven shepherds and eight princely
men.
6 They shall waste with the sword the land
of Assyria,
And the land of [a]Nimrod at its entrances;
Thus He shall [b]deliver *us* from the
Assyrian,
When he comes into our land
And when he treads within our borders.

7 Then [a]the remnant of Jacob
Shall be in the midst of many peoples,
[b]Like dew from the LORD,
Like showers on the grass,
That tarry for no man
Nor wait for the sons of men.
8 And the remnant of Jacob
Shall be among the Gentiles,
In the midst of many peoples,
Like a [a]lion among the beasts of the forest,
Like a young lion among flocks of sheep,
Who, if he passes through,
Both treads down and tears in pieces,
And none can deliver.
9 Your hand shall be lifted against your
adversaries,
And all your enemies shall be cut off.
10 "And it shall be in that day," says the LORD,
"That I will [a]cut off your [b]horses from your
midst
And destroy your [c]chariots.
11 I will cut off the cities of your land
And throw down all your strongholds.
12 I will cut off sorceries from your hand,
And you shall have no [a]soothsayers.

KJV

13 [a]Thy graven images also will I cut off, and thy standing images out of the midst of thee; and thou shalt [b]no more worship the work of thine hands.
14 And I will pluck up thy groves out of the midst of thee: so will I destroy thy cities.
15 And I will [a]execute vengeance in anger and fury upon the heathen, such as they have not heard.

God Pleads with Israel

6 Hear ye now what the LORD saith; Arise, contend thou before the mountains, and let the hills hear thy voice.
2 [a]Hear ye, O mountains, [b]the LORD's controversy, and ye strong foundations of the earth: for [c]the LORD hath a controversy with his people, and he will plead with Israel.
3 O my people, [a]what have I done unto thee? and wherein have I [b]wearied thee? testify against me.
4 [a]For I brought thee up out of the land of Egypt, and redeemed thee out of the house of servants; and I sent before thee Moses, Aaron, and Miriam.
5 O my people, remember now what [a]Balak king of Moab consulted, and what Balaam the son of Beor answered him from Shittim unto Gilgal; that ye may know [b]the righteousness of the LORD.
6 Wherewith shall I come before the LORD, *and* bow myself before the high God? shall I come before him with burnt offerings, with calves of a year old?
7 [a]Will the LORD be pleased with thousands of rams, *or* with ten thousands of [b]rivers of oil? [c]shall I give my firstborn *for* my transgression, the fruit of my body *for* the sin of my soul?
8 He hath [a]shewed thee, O man, what *is* good; and what doth the LORD require of thee, but [b]to do justly, and to love mercy, and to walk humbly with thy God?

Punishment of Israel's Injustice

9 The LORD's voice crieth unto the city, and *the man of* wisdom shall see thy name: hear ye the rod, and who hath appointed it.
10 Are there yet the treasures of wickedness in the house of the wicked, and the scant measure *that is* abominable?
11 Shall I count *them* pure with [a]the wicked balances, and with the bag of deceitful weights?
12 For the rich men thereof are full of [a]violence, and the inhabitants thereof have spoken lies, and [b]their tongue *is* deceitful in their mouth.
13 Therefore also will I [a]make *thee* sick in smiting thee, in making *thee* desolate because of thy sins.

13 [a]Zech. 13:2 [b]Is. 2:8
15 [a][2 Thess. 1:8]

CHAPTER 6

2 [a]Ps. 50:1, 4 [b][Is. 1:18]; Hos. 12:2 [c][Is. 1:18]
3 [a]Is. 5:4; Jer. 2:5, 31 [b]Is. 43:22, 23; Mal. 1:13
4 [a][Deut. 4:20]
5 [a]Num. 22:5, 6; Josh. 24:9 [b]Judg. 5:11
7 [a]Ps. 50:9; Is. 1:11 [b]Job 29:6 [c]Lev. 18:21; 20:1–5; 2 Kin. 16:3; Jer. 7:31; Ezek. 23:37
8 [a][Deut. 10:12; 1 Sam. 15:22]; Hos. 6:6; 12:6 [b]Gen. 18:19; Is. 1:17
11 [a]Lev. 19:36; Hos. 12:7
12 [a]Is. 1:23; 5:7; Amos 6:3, 4; Mic. 2:1, 2 [b]Jer. 9:2–6, 8; Hos. 7:13; Amos 2:4
13 [a]Lev. 26:16; Ps. 107:17

NKJV

13 [a]Your carved images I will also cut off,
And your sacred pillars from your midst;
You shall [b]no more worship the work of your hands;
14 I will pluck your *wooden images from your midst;
Thus I will destroy your cities.
15 And I will [a]execute vengeance in anger and fury
On the nations that have not *heard."

God Pleads with Israel

6 Hear now what the LORD says:

"Arise, plead your case before the mountains,
And let the hills hear your voice.
2 [a]Hear, O you mountains, [b]the LORD's complaint,
And you strong foundations of the earth;
For [c]the LORD has a complaint against His people,
And He will contend with Israel.

3 "O My people, what [a]have I done to you?
And how have I [b]wearied you?
Testify against Me.
4 [a]For I brought you up from the land of Egypt,
I redeemed you from the house of bondage;
And I sent before you Moses, Aaron, and Miriam.
5 O My people, remember now
What [a]Balak king of Moab counseled,
And what Balaam the son of Beor answered him,
From *Acacia Grove to Gilgal,
That you may know [b]the righteousness of the LORD."

6 With what shall I come before the LORD,
And bow myself before the High God?
Shall I come before Him with burnt offerings,
With calves a year old?
7 [a]Will the LORD be pleased with thousands of rams,
Ten thousand [b]rivers of oil?
[c]Shall I give my firstborn *for* my transgression,
The fruit of my body *for* the sin of my soul?

8 He has [a]shown you, O man, what *is* good;
And what does the LORD require of you
But [b]to do justly,
To love mercy,
And to walk humbly with your God?

Punishment of Israel's Injustice

9 The LORD's voice cries to the city—
Wisdom shall see Your name:

"Hear the rod!
Who has appointed it?
10 Are there yet the treasures of wickedness
In the house of the wicked,
And the short measure *that is* an abomination?
11 Shall I count pure *those* with [a]the wicked scales,
And with the bag of deceitful weights?
12 For her rich men are full of [a]violence,
Her inhabitants have spoken lies,
And [b]their tongue is deceitful in their mouth.

13 "Therefore I will also [a]make *you* sick by striking you,
By making *you* desolate because of your sins.

*______

5:14 Heb. *Asherim,* Canaanite deities
5:15 *obeyed*
6:5 Heb. *Shittim,* Num. 25:1; Josh. 2:1; 3:1

KJV

14 [a]Thou shalt eat, but not be satisfied; and thy casting down *shall be* in the midst of thee; and thou shalt take hold, but shalt not deliver; and *that* which thou deliverest will I give up to the sword.

15 Thou shalt [a]sow, but thou shalt not reap; thou shalt tread the olives, but thou shalt not anoint thee with oil; and sweet wine, but shalt not drink wine.

16 For the statutes of [a]Omri are [b]kept, and all the works of the house of Ahab, and ye walk in their counsels; that I should make thee a desolation, and the inhabitants thereof an hissing: therefore ye shall bear the [c]reproach of my people.

Sorrow for Israel's Sins

7 Woe is me! for I am as when they have gathered the summer fruits, as [a]the grapegleanings of the vintage: *there is* no cluster to eat: [b]my soul desired the firstripe fruit.

2 The [a]good *man* is perished out of the earth: and *there is* none upright among men: they all lie in wait for blood; [b]they hunt every man his brother with a net.

3 That they may do evil with both hands earnestly, the prince asketh, and the judge *asketh* for a [a]reward; and the great *man,* he uttereth his mischievous desire: so they wrap it up.

4 The best of them [a]*is* as a brier: the most upright *is sharper* than a thorn hedge: the day of thy watchmen *and* thy visitation cometh; now shall be their perplexity.

5 Trust ye [a]not in a friend, put ye not confidence in a guide: keep the doors of thy mouth from her that lieth in thy [b]bosom.

6 For [a]the son dishonoureth the father, the daughter riseth up against her mother, the daughter in law against her mother in law; a man's enemies *are* the men of his own house.

7 Therefore I will look unto the LORD; I will [a]wait for the God of my salvation: my God will hear me.

Israel's Confession and Comfort

8 [a]Rejoice not against me, O mine enemy: [b]when I fall, I shall arise; when I sit in darkness, the LORD *shall be* a light unto me.

9 [a]I will bear the indignation of the LORD, because I have sinned against him, until he plead my [b]cause, and execute judgment for me: he will bring me forth to the light, *and* I shall behold his righteousness.

10 Then *she that is* mine enemy shall see *it,* and [a]shame shall cover her which said unto me, [b]Where is the LORD thy God? mine eyes shall behold her: now shall she be trodden down as the mire of the streets.

14 [a]Lev. 26:26
15 [a]Deut. 28:38–40; Amos 5:11; Zeph. 1:13; Hag. 1:6
16 [a]1 Kin. 16:25, 26 [b]1 Kin. 16:30; 21:25, 26; 2 Kin. 21:3; Hos. 5:11 [c]Is. 25:8

CHAPTER 7

1 [a]Is. 17:6 [b]Is. 28:4; Hos. 9:10
2 [a]Ps. 12:1; Is. 57:1 [b]Hab. 1:15
3 [a]Amos 5:12; Mic. 3:11
4 [a]Is. 55:13; Ezek. 2:6
5 [a]Jer. 9:4 [b]Deut. 28:56
6 [a]Matt. 10:36; Mark 3:21; Luke 8:19; John 7:5
7 [a]Ps. 130:5; Is. 25:9; Lam. 3:24, 25
8 [a]Prov. 24:17; Obad. 12; [Acts 10:43] [b]Ps. 37:24; [Prov. 24:16]; 2 Cor. 4:9
9 [a]Lam. 3:39, 40; [2 Cor. 5:21] [b]Jer. 50:34
10 [a]Ps. 35:26 [b]Ps. 42:3

NKJV

14 [a]You shall eat, but not be satisfied;
*Hunger *shall be* in your midst.
*You may carry *some* away, but shall not save *them;*
And what you do rescue I will give over to the sword.

15 "You shall [a]sow, but not reap;
You shall tread the olives, but not anoint yourselves with oil;
And *make* sweet wine, but not drink wine.

16 For the statutes of [a]Omri are [b]kept;
All the works of Ahab's house *are done;*
And you walk in their counsels,
That I may make you a desolation,
And your inhabitants a hissing.
Therefore you shall bear the [c]reproach of *My people."

Sorrow for Israel's Sins

7 Woe is me!
For I am like those who gather summer fruits,
Like those who [a]glean vintage grapes;
There is no cluster to eat
Of the first-ripe fruit *which* [b]my soul desires.

2 The [a]faithful *man* has perished from the earth,
And *there is* no one upright among men.
They all lie in wait for blood;
[b]Every man hunts his brother with a net.

3 That they may successfully do evil with both hands—
The prince asks *for gifts,*
The judge *seeks* a [a]bribe,
And the great *man* utters his evil desire;
So they scheme together.

4 The best of them *is* [a]like a brier;
The most upright *is sharper* than a thorn hedge;
The day of your watchman and your punishment comes;
Now shall be their perplexity.

5 [a]Do not trust in a friend;
Do not put your confidence in a companion;
Guard the doors of your mouth
From her who lies in your [b]bosom.

6 For [a]son dishonors father,
Daughter rises against her mother,
Daughter-in-law against her mother-in-law;
A man's enemies *are* the men of his own household.

7 Therefore I will look to the LORD;
I will [a]wait for the God of my salvation;
My God will hear me.

Israel's Confession and Comfort

8 [a]Do not rejoice over me, my enemy;
[b]When I fall, I will arise;
When I sit in darkness,
The LORD *will be* a light to me.

9 [a]I will bear the indignation of the LORD,
Because I have sinned against Him,
Until He pleads my [b]case
And executes justice for me.
He will bring me forth to the light;
I will see His righteousness.

10 Then *she who is* my enemy will see,
And [a]shame will cover her who said to me,
[b]"Where is the LORD your God?"
My eyes will see her;
Now she will be trampled down
Like mud in the streets.

*———

6:14 Or *Emptiness* or *Humiliation* • Tg., Vg. *You shall take hold*
6:16 So with MT, Tg., Vg.; LXX *nations*

KJV

11 *In* the day that thy [a]walls are to be built,
in that day shall the decree be far removed.
12 *In* that day *also* [a]he shall come even to
thee from Assyria, and *from* the fortified cities,
and from the fortress even to the river, and from
sea to sea, and *from* mountain to mountain.
13 Notwithstanding the land shall be desolate because of them that dwell therein, [a]for the
fruit of their doings.

God Will Forgive Israel

14 Feed thy people with thy rod, the flock of
thine heritage, which dwell solitarily *in* [a]the wood,
in the midst of Carmel: let them feed *in* Bashan
and Gilead, as in the days of old.
15 [a]According to the days of thy coming out
of the land of Egypt will I shew unto him [b]marvel-
lous *things*.
16 The nations [a]shall see and be confounded
at all their might: [b]they shall lay *their* hand upon
their mouth, their ears shall be deaf.
17 They shall lick the [a]dust like a serpent,
[b]they shall move out of their holes like worms of
the earth: [c]they shall be afraid of the LORD our
God, and shall fear because of thee.
18 [a]Who *is* a God like unto thee, that [b]par-
doneth iniquity, and passeth by the transgression of
[c]the remnant of his heritage? [d]he retaineth not
his anger for ever, because he delighteth *in*
[e]mercy.
19 He will turn again, he will have compassion upon us; he will subdue our iniquities; and
thou wilt cast all their sins into the depths of the
sea.
20 [a]Thou wilt perform the truth to Jacob, *and*
the mercy to Abraham, [b]which thou hast sworn
unto our fathers from the days of old.

11 [a]Is. 54:11; [Amos 9:11]
12 [a][Is. 11:16; 19:23–25]
13 [a]Jer. 21:14
14 [a]Is. 37:24
15 [a]Ps. 68:22; 78:12 [b]Ex. 34:10
16 [a]Is. 26:11 [b]Job 21:5
17 [a]Ps. 72:9; [Is. 49:23] [b]Ps. 18:45 [c]Jer. 33:9
18 [a]Ex. 15:11 [b]Ex. 34:6, 7, 9; Is. 43:25; Jer. 50:20 [c]Mic. 4:7 [d]Ps. 103:8, 9, 13; [Is. 57:16] [e][Ezek. 33:11]
20 [a]Luke 1:72, 73 [b]Ps. 105:9

NKJV

11 *In* the day when your [a]walls are to be built,
In that day *the decree shall go far and wide.
12 *In* that day [a]they* shall come to you
From Assyria and the *fortified cities,
From the *fortress to *the River,
From sea to sea,
And mountain *to* mountain.
13 Yet the land shall be desolate
Because of those who dwell in it,
And [a]for the fruit of their deeds.

God Will Forgive Israel

14 Shepherd Your people with Your staff,
The flock of Your heritage,
Who dwell solitarily *in* a [a]woodland,
In the midst of Carmel;
Let them feed *in* Bashan and Gilead,
As in days of old.

15 "As[a] in the days when you came out of the land of Egypt,
I will show *them [b]wonders."

16 The nations [a]shall see and be ashamed of all their might;
[b]They shall put *their* hand over *their* mouth;
Their ears shall be deaf.
17 They shall lick the [a]dust like a serpent;
[b]They shall crawl from their holes like snakes of the earth.
[c]They shall be afraid of the LORD our God,
And shall fear because of You.
18 [a]Who *is* a God like You,
[b]Pardoning iniquity
And passing over the transgression of [c]the remnant of His heritage?
[d]He does not retain His anger forever,
Because He delights *in* [e]mercy.
19 He will again have compassion on us,
And will subdue our iniquities.

You will cast all *our sins
Into the depths of the sea.
20 [a]You will give truth to Jacob
And mercy to Abraham,
[b]Which You have sworn to our fathers
From days of old.

*

7:11 Or *the boundary shall be extended* **7:12** Lit. *he,* collective of the captives • Heb. *arey mazor,* possibly *cities of Egypt* • Heb. *mazor,* possibly *Egypt* • The Euphrates **7:15** Lit. *him,* collective for the captives **7:19** Lit. *their*

KJV

THE BOOK OF

NAHUM

1 The burden [a]of Nineveh. The book of the vision of Nahum the Elkoshite.

God's Wrath on His Enemies

2 God *is* [a]jealous, and the LORD revengeth;
the LORD revengeth, and *is* furious; the LORD will
take vengeance on his adversaries, and he reserveth *wrath* for his enemies.
3 The LORD *is* [a]slow to anger, and [b]great in
power, and will not at all acquit *the wicked:* [c]the
LORD *hath* his way in the whirlwind and in the
storm, and the clouds *are* the dust of his feet.
4 [a]He rebuketh the sea, and maketh it dry,
and drieth up all the rivers: [b]Bashan languisheth, and Carmel, and the flower of Lebanon
languisheth.
5 The mountains quake at him, and the hills
melt, and the earth is burned at his presence, yea,
the world, and all that dwell therein.
6 Who can stand before his indignation?
and [a]who can abide in the fierceness of his anger?
his fury is poured out like fire, and the rocks are
thrown down by him.
7 [a]The LORD *is* good, a strong hold in the
day of trouble; and [b]he knoweth them that trust
in him.
8 But with an overrunning flood he will
make an utter end of the place thereof, and darkness shall pursue his enemies.
9 [a]What do ye imagine against the LORD?
[b]he will make an utter end: affliction shall not
rise up the second time.
10 For while *they be* folden together [a]*as*
thorns, [b]and while they are drunken *as* drunkards, [c]they shall be devoured as stubble fully
dry.
11 There is *one* come out of thee, that imag-
ineth evil against the LORD, a wicked counsellor.
12 Thus saith the LORD; Though *they be*
quiet, and likewise many, yet thus shall they be
[a]cut down, when he shall pass through. Though
I have afflicted thee, I will afflict thee no more.
13 For now will I break his yoke from off
thee, and will burst thy bonds in sunder.
14 And the LORD hath given a commandment
concerning thee, *that* no more of thy name be

CHAPTER 1

1 [a]2 Kin. 19:36; Jon. 1:2; Nah. 2:8; Zeph. 2:13
2 [a]Ex. 20:5; Josh. 24:19
3 [a]Ex. 34:6, 7; Neh. 9:17; Ps. 103:8 [b][Job 9:4] [c]Ps. 18:17
4 [a]Josh. 3:15, 16; Ps. 106:9; Is. 50:2; Matt. 8:26 [b]Is. 33:9
6 [a]Jer. 10:10; [Mal. 3:2]
7 [a]Ps. 25:8; 37:39, 40; 100:5; [Jer. 33:11]; Lam. 3:25 [b]Ps. 1:6; John 10:14; 2 Tim. 2:19
9 [a]Ps. 2:1; Nah. 1:11 [b]1 Sam. 3:12
10 [a]2 Sam. 23:6; Mic. 7:4 [b]Is. 56:12; Nah. 3:11 [c]Is. 5:24; 10:17; Mal. 4:1
12 [a][Is. 10:16–19, 33, 34]

1:1 *oracle, prophecy*
1:5 Tg. *burns*

NKJV

THE BOOK OF

NAHUM

1 The *burden [a]against Nineveh. The book of the vision of Nahum the Elkoshite.

God's Wrath on His Enemies

2 God *is* [a]jealous, and the LORD avenges;
The LORD avenges and *is* furious.
The LORD will take vengeance on His adversaries,
And He reserves *wrath* for His enemies;
3 The LORD *is* [a]slow to anger and [b]great in power,
And will not at all acquit *the wicked.*

[c]The LORD has His way
In the whirlwind and in the storm,
And the clouds *are* the dust of His feet.
4 [a]He rebukes the sea and makes it dry,
And dries up all the rivers.
[b]Bashan and Carmel wither,
And the flower of Lebanon wilts.
5 The mountains quake before Him,
The hills melt,
And the earth *heaves at His presence,
Yes, the world and all who dwell in it.

6 Who can stand before His indignation?
And [a]who can endure the fierceness of His anger?
His fury is poured out like fire,
And the rocks are thrown down by Him.

7 [a]The LORD *is* good,
A stronghold in the day of trouble;
And [b]He knows those who trust in Him.
8 But with an overflowing flood
He will make an utter end of its place,
And darkness will pursue His enemies.

9 [a]What do you conspire against the LORD?
[b]He will make an utter end *of it.*
Affliction will not rise up a second time.
10 For while tangled [a]*like* thorns,
[b]And while drunken *like* drunkards,
[c]They shall be devoured like stubble fully dried.
11 From you comes forth *one*
Who plots evil against the LORD,
A wicked counselor.

12 Thus says the LORD:

"Though *they are* safe, and likewise many,
Yet in this manner they will be [a]cut down
When he passes through.
Though I have afflicted you,
I will afflict you no more;
13 For now I will break off his yoke from you,
And burst your bonds apart."

14 The LORD has given a command concerning you:

KJV

sown: out of the house of thy gods will I cut off
the graven image and the molten image: I will
make thy [a]grave; for thou art [b]vile.
15 Behold upon the mountains the [a]feet of
him that bringeth good tidings, that publisheth
peace! O Judah, keep thy solemn feasts, perform
thy vows: for the wicked shall no more pass
through thee; he is [b]utterly cut off.

The Destruction of Nineveh

2 He that dasheth in pieces is come up before
thy face: keep the munition, watch the way,
make *thy* loins strong, fortify *thy* power mightily.
2 For the LORD hath turned away the excellency of Jacob, as the excellency of Israel: for the
emptiers have emptied them out, and marred their
vine branches.
3 The shield of his mighty men is made red,
the valiant men *are* in scarlet: the chariots *shall*
be with flaming torches in the day of his preparation, and the fir trees shall be terribly shaken.
4 The chariots shall rage in the streets, they
shall justle one against another in the broad ways:
they shall seem like torches, they shall run like
the lightnings.
5 He shall recount his worthies: they shall
stumble in their walk; they shall make haste to
the wall thereof, and the defence shall be
prepared.
6 The gates of the rivers shall be opened,
and the palace shall be dissolved.
7 And Huzzab shall be led away captive, she
shall be brought up, and her maids shall lead *her*
as with the voice of doves, tabering upon their
breasts.
8 But Nineveh *is* of old like a pool of water:
yet they shall flee away. Stand, stand, *shall they*
cry; but none shall look back.
9 Take ye the spoil of silver, take the spoil
of [a]gold: for *there is* none end of the store *and*
glory out of all the pleasant furniture.
10 She is empty, and void, and waste: and
the heart melteth, and the knees smite together,
and much pain *is* in all loins, and the faces of
them all gather blackness.
11 Where *is* the dwelling of the [a]lions, and
the feedingplace of the young lions, where the
lion, *even* the old lion, walked, *and* the lion's
whelp, and none made *them* afraid?
12 The lion did tear in pieces enough for his
whelps, and strangled for his lionesses, and [a]filled
his holes with prey, and his dens with ravin.
13 [a]Behold, I *am* against thee, saith the LORD
of hosts, and I will burn her chariots in the smoke,

14 [a]Ezek. 32:22, 23 [b]Nah. 3:6
15 [a]Is. 40:9; 52:7; Rom. 10:15 [b]Is. 29:7, 8

CHAPTER 2

9 [a]Ezek. 7:19; Zeph. 1:18
11 [a]Job 4:10, 11; Ezek. 19:2–7
12 [a]Is. 10:6; Jer. 51:34
13 [a]Jer. 21:13; Ezek. 5:8; Nah. 3:5

NKJV

"Your name shall be perpetuated no
longer.
Out of the house of your gods
I will cut off the carved image and the
molded image.
I will dig your [a]grave,
For you are [b]vile."

15 Behold, on the mountains
The [a]feet of him who brings good tidings,
Who proclaims peace!
O Judah, keep your appointed feasts,
Perform your vows.
For the wicked one shall no more pass
through you;
He is [b]utterly cut off.

The Destruction of Nineveh

2 He* who scatters has come up before your
face.
Man the fort!
Watch the road!
Strengthen *your* flanks!
Fortify *your* power mightily.

2 For the LORD will restore the excellence
of Jacob
Like the excellence of Israel,
For the emptiers have emptied them out
And ruined their vine branches.

3 The shields of his mighty men *are* made
red,
The valiant men *are* in scarlet.
The chariots *come* with flaming torches
In the day of his preparation,
And *the spears are brandished.
4 The chariots rage in the streets,
They jostle one another in the broad
roads;
They seem like torches,
They run like lightning.

5 He remembers his nobles;
They stumble in their walk;
They make haste to her walls,
And the defense is prepared.
6 The gates of the rivers are opened,
And the palace is dissolved.
7 *It is decreed:
She shall be led away captive,
She shall be brought up;
And her maidservants shall lead *her* as
with the voice of doves,
Beating their breasts.

8 Though Nineveh of old *was* like a pool
of water,
Now they flee away.
"Halt! Halt!" *they cry;*
But no one turns back.
9 Take spoil of silver!
Take spoil of [a]gold!
There is no end of treasure,
Or wealth of every desirable prize.
10 She is empty, desolate, and waste!
The heart melts, and the knees shake;
Much pain *is* in every side,
And all their faces *are drained of color.

11 Where *is* the dwelling of the [a]lions,
And the feeding place of the young lions,
Where the lion walked, the lioness *and*
lion's cub,
And no one made *them* afraid?
12 The lion tore in pieces enough for his cubs,
Killed for his lionesses,
[a]Filled his caves with prey,
And his dens with flesh.

13 "Behold, [a]I *am* against you," says the
LORD of hosts, "I will burn *your chariots in

*

2:1 Vg. *He who destroys* **2:3** Lit. *the cypresses are shaken;* LXX, Syr. *the horses rush about;* Vg. *the drivers are stupefied* **2:7** Heb. *Huzzab* **2:10** LXX, Tg., Vg. *gather blackness;* Joel 2:6 **2:13** Lit. *her*

KJV

and the sword shall devour thy young lions: and
I will cut off thy prey from the earth, and the voice
of thy [b]messengers shall no more be heard.

The Woe of Nineveh

3 Woe to the [a]bloody city! it *is* all full of lies
and robbery; the prey departeth not;
2 The noise of a whip, and the noise of the
rattling of the wheels, and of the pransing horses,
and of the jumping chariots.
3 The horseman lifteth up both the bright
sword and the glittering spear: and *there is* a multitude of slain, and a great number of carcases;
and *there is* none end of *their* corpses; they stumble upon their corpses:
4 Because of the multitude of the whoredoms of the wellfavoured harlot, [a]the mistress of
witchcrafts, that selleth nations through her
whoredoms, and families through her witchcrafts.
5 Behold, I *am* [a]against thee, saith the LORD
of hosts; and [b]I will discover thy skirts upon thy
face, and I will shew the nations thy nakedness,
and the kingdoms thy shame.
6 And I will cast abominable filth upon thee,
and make thee [a]vile, and will set thee as [b]a
gazingstock.
7 And it shall come to pass, *that* all they
that look upon thee [a]shall flee from thee, and say,
[b]Nineveh is laid waste: [c]who will bemoan her?
whence shall I seek comforters for thee?
8 [a]Art thou better than populous [b]No, that
was situate among the rivers, *that had* the waters
round about it, whose rampart *was* the sea, *and*
her wall *was* from the sea?
9 Ethiopia and Egypt *were* her strength, and
it was infinite; [a]Put and Lubim were thy helpers.
10 Yet *was* she carried away, she went into
captivity: [a]her young children also were dashed
in pieces [b]at the top of all the streets: and they
[c]cast lots for her honourable men, and all her
great men were bound in chains.
11 Thou also shalt be [a]drunken: thou shalt
be hid, thou also shalt seek strength because of
the enemy.
12 All thy strong holds *shall be like* [a]fig trees
with the firstripe figs: if they be shaken, they shall
even fall into the mouth of the eater.
13 Behold, [a]thy people in the midst of thee
are women: the gates of thy land shall be set wide
open unto thine enemies: the fire shall devour thy
[b]bars.
14 Draw thee waters for the siege, [a]fortify
thy strong holds: go into clay, and tread the
morter, make strong the brickkiln.
15 There shall the fire devour thee; the sword
shall cut thee off, it shall eat thee up like [a]the
cankerworm: make thyself many as the cankerworm, make thyself many as the locusts.

13 [b]2 Kin. 18:17–25; 19:9–13, 23

CHAPTER 3

1 [a]Ezek. 22:2, 3; 24:6–9; Hab. 2:12
4 [a]Is. 47:9–12; Rev. 18:2, 3
5 [a]Jer. 50:31; Ezek. 26:3; Nah. 2:13 [b]Is. 47:2, 3; Jer. 13:26
6 [a]Nah. 1:14 [b]Heb. 10:33
7 [a]Rev. 18:10 [b]Jon. 3:3; 4:11 [c]Is. 51:19; Jer. 15:5
8 [a]Amos 6:2 [b]Jer. 46:25; Ezek. 30:14–16
9 [a]Gen. 10:6; Jer. 46:9; Ezek. 27:10
10 [a]Ps. 137:9; Is. 13:16; Hos. 13:16 [b]Lam. 2:19 [c]Joel 3:3; Obad. 11
11 [a]Is. 49:26; Jer. 25:27; Nah. 1:10
12 [a]Rev. 6:12, 13
13 [a]Is. 19:16; Jer. 50:37; 51:30 [b]Ps. 147:13; Jer. 51:30
14 [a]Nah. 2:1
15 [a]Joel 1:4

NKJV

smoke, and the sword shall devour your young
lions; I will cut off your prey from the earth, and
the voice of your [b]messengers shall be heard no
more."

The Woe of Nineveh

3 Woe to the [a]bloody city!
It *is* all full of lies *and* robbery.
Its victim never departs.
2 The noise of a whip
And the noise of rattling wheels,
Of galloping horses,
Of clattering chariots!
3 Horsemen charge with bright sword and
glittering spear.
There is a multitude of slain,
A great number of bodies,
Countless corpses—
They stumble over the corpses—
4 Because of the multitude of harlotries of
the seductive harlot,
[a]The mistress of sorceries,
Who sells nations through her harlotries,
And families through her sorceries.

5 "Behold, I *am* [a]against you," says the LORD
of hosts;
[b]"I will lift your skirts over your face,
I will show the nations your nakedness,
And the kingdoms your shame.
6 I will cast abominable filth upon you,
Make you [a]vile,
And make you [b]a spectacle.
7 It shall come to pass *that* all who look
upon you
[a]Will flee from you, and say,
[b]'Nineveh is laid waste!
[c]Who will bemoan her?'
Where shall I seek comforters for you?"

8 [a]Are you better than [b]No* Amon
That was situated by the *River,
That had the waters around her,
Whose rampart *was* the sea,
Whose wall *was* the sea?
9 Ethiopia and Egypt *were* her strength,
And *it was* boundless;
[a]Put and Lubim were *your helpers.
10 Yet she *was* carried away,
She went into captivity;
[a]Her young children also were dashed to
pieces
[b]At the head of every street;
They [c]cast lots for her honorable men,
And all her great men were bound in
chains.
11 You also will be [a]drunk;
You will be hidden;
You also will seek refuge from the enemy.

12 All your strongholds *are* [a]fig trees with
ripened figs:
If they are shaken,
They fall into the mouth of the eater.
13 Surely, [a]your people in your midst *are*
women!
The gates of your land are wide open for
your enemies;
Fire shall devour the [b]bars of your
gates.

14 Draw your water for the siege!
[a]Fortify your strongholds!
Go into the clay and tread the mortar!
Make strong the brick kiln!
15 There the fire will devour you,
The sword will cut you off;
It will eat you up like a [a]locust.

Make yourself many—like the locust!
Make yourself many— like the *swarming*
locusts!

*

3:8 Ancient Thebes; Tg., Vg. *populous Alexandria* • Lit. *rivers*, the Nile and the surrounding canals **3:9** LXX *her*

KJV

16 Thou hast multiplied thy [a]merchants
above the stars of heaven: the cankerworm spoileth, and fleeth away.
17 [a]Thy crowned *are* as the locusts, and thy
captains as the great grasshoppers, which camp
in the hedges in the cold day, *but* when the sun
ariseth they flee away, and their place is not
known where they *are*.
18 [a]Thy shepherds slumber, O [b]king of Assyria: thy nobles shall dwell *in the dust*: thy people
is [c]scattered upon the mountains, and no man
gathereth *them*.
19 *There is* no healing of thy bruise; [a]thy
wound is grievous: [b]all that hear the bruit of thee
shall clap the hands over thee: for upon whom
hath not thy wickedness passed continually?

16 [a]Rev. 18:3, 11–19
17 [a]Rev. 9:7
18 [a]Ex. 15:16; Ps. 76:5, 6; Is. 56:10; Jer. 51:57 [b]Jer. 50:18; Ezek. 31:3 [c]1 Kin. 22:17; Is. 13:14
19 [a]Jer. 46:11; Mic. 1:9 [b]Job 27:23; Lam. 2:15; Zeph. 2:15

NKJV

16 You have multiplied your [a]merchants
more than the stars of heaven.
The locust plunders and flies away.
17 [a]Your commanders *are* like *swarming*
locusts,
And your generals like great
grasshoppers,
Which camp in the hedges on a cold day;
When the sun rises they flee away,
And the place where they *are* is not
known.

18 [a]Your shepherds slumber, O [b]king of
Assyria;
Your nobles rest *in the dust*.
Your people are [c]scattered on the
mountains,
And no one gathers them.
19 Your injury *has* no healing,
[a]Your wound is severe.
[b]All who hear news of you
Will clap *their* hands over you,
For upon whom has not your wickedness
passed continually?

KJV

THE BOOK OF

HABAKKUK

1 The burden which Habakkuk the prophet did see.

The Prophet's Question

2 O LORD, how long shall I cry, [a]and thou wilt not hear! *even* cry out unto thee *of* [b]violence, and thou wilt [c]not save!

3 Why dost thou shew me iniquity, and cause *me* to behold grievance? for spoiling and violence *are* before me: and there are *that* raise up strife and contention.

4 Therefore the law is slacked, and judgment doth never go forth: for the [a]wicked doth compass about the righteous; therefore wrong judgment proceedeth.

The LORD's Reply

5 [a]Behold ye among the heathen, and regard, and wonder marvellously: for *I* will work a work in your days, *which* ye will not believe, though it be told *you*.

6 For, lo, I [a]raise up the Chaldeans, *that* bitter and hasty [b]nation, which shall march through the breadth of the land, to possess the dwellingplaces *that are* not their's.

7 They *are* terrible and dreadful: their judgment and their dignity shall proceed of themselves.

8 Their horses also are [a]swifter than the leopards, and are more fierce than the evening wolves: and their horsemen shall spread themselves, and their horsemen shall come from far; they shall fly as the [b]eagle *that* hasteth to eat.

9 They shall come all for violence: their faces shall sup up *as* the east wind, and they shall gather the captivity as the sand.

10 And they shall scoff at the kings, and the princes shall be a scorn unto them: they shall deride every strong hold; for they shall heap dust, and take it.

11 Then shall *his* mind change, and he shall pass over, and offend, [a]*imputing* this his power unto his god.

The Prophet's Second Question

12 *Art* thou not [a]from everlasting, O LORD my God, mine Holy One? we shall not die. O LORD, thou hast ordained them for judgment; and, O mighty God, [b]thou hast established them for [c]correction.

13 *Thou art* of purer eyes than to behold evil, and canst not look on iniquity: wherefore lookest

CHAPTER 1

2 [a]Lam. 3:8 [b]Mic. 2:1, 2; 3:1–3 [c][Job 21:5–16]
4 [a]Jer. 12:1
5 [a]Is. 29:14; Ezek. 12:22–28
6 [a]Deut. 28:49, 50; 2 Kin. 24:2; 2 Chr. 36:17; Jer. 4:11–13; Mic. 4:10 [b]Ezek. 7:24; 21:31
8 [a]Jer. 4:13 [b]Job 9:26; 39:29, 30; Lam. 4:19; Ezek. 17:3; Hos. 8:1; Matt. 24:28; Luke 17:37
11 [a]Dan. 5:4
12 [a]Deut. 33:27; Ps. 90:2; 93:2; Mal. 3:6 [b]Is. 10:5–7; Mal. 3:5 [c]Jer. 25:9

*———

1:1 *oracle, prophecy*
1:11 Lit. *spirit* or *wind*

NKJV

THE BOOK OF

HABAKKUK

1 The *burden which the prophet Habakkuk saw.

The Prophet's Question

2 O LORD, how long shall I cry,
[a]And You will not hear?
Even cry out to You, [b]"Violence!"
And You will [c]not save.
3 Why do You show me iniquity,
And cause *me* to see trouble?
For plundering and violence *are* before me;
There is strife, and contention arises.
4 Therefore the law is powerless,
And justice never goes forth.
For the [a]wicked surround the righteous;
Therefore perverse judgment proceeds.

The LORD's Reply

5 "Look[a] among the nations and watch—
Be utterly astounded!
For *I will* work a work in your days
Which you would not believe, though it were told *you*.
6 For indeed I am [a]raising up the Chaldeans,
A bitter and hasty [b]nation
Which marches through the breadth of the earth,
To possess dwelling places *that are* not theirs.
7 They are terrible and dreadful;
Their judgment and their dignity proceed from themselves.
8 Their horses also are [a]swifter than leopards,
And more fierce than evening wolves.
Their chargers charge ahead;
Their cavalry comes from afar;
They fly as the [b]eagle *that* hastens to eat.

9 "They all come for violence;
Their faces are set *like* the east wind.
They gather captives like sand.
10 They scoff at kings,
And princes are scorned by them.
They deride every stronghold,
For they heap up earthen *mounds* and seize it.
11 Then *his* *mind changes, and he transgresses;
He commits offense,
[a]*Ascribing* this power to his god."

The Prophet's Second Question

12 Are You not [a]from everlasting,
O LORD my God, my Holy One?
We shall not die.
O LORD, [b]You have appointed them for judgment;
O Rock, You have marked them for [c]correction.
13 *You are* of purer eyes than to behold evil,
And cannot look on wickedness.

KJV

thou upon them that deal treacherously, *and* holdest thy tongue when the wicked devoureth *the man that is* more righteous than he?
14 And makest men as the fishes of the sea, as the creeping things, *that have* no ruler over them?
15 They take up all of them with the angle, they catch them in their net, and gather them in their drag: therefore they rejoice and are glad.
16 Therefore [a]they sacrifice unto their net, and burn incense unto their drag; because by them their portion *is* fat, and their meat plenteous.
17 Shall they therefore empty their net, and not spare continually to slay the nations?

2 I will [a]stand upon my watch, and set me upon the tower, and will watch to see what he will say unto me, and what I shall answer when I am reproved.

The Just Live by Faith

2 And the LORD answered me, and said, [a]Write the vision, and make *it* plain upon tables, that he may run that readeth it.
3 For [a]the vision *is* yet for an appointed time, but at the end it shall speak, and [b]not lie: though it tarry, [c]wait for it; because it will [d]surely come, it will not tarry.
4 Behold, his soul *which* is lifted up is not upright in him: but the [a]just shall live by his faith.

Woe to the Wicked

5 Yea also, because he transgresseth by wine, *he is* a proud man, neither keepeth at home, who [a]enlargeth his desire as hell, and *is* as death, and cannot be satisfied, but gathereth unto him all nations, and heapeth unto him all people:
6 Shall not all these [a]take up a parable against him, and a taunting proverb against him, and say, Woe to him that increaseth *that which is* not his! how long? and to him that ladeth himself with thick clay!
7 Shall they not rise up suddenly that shall bite thee, and awake that shall vex thee, and thou shalt be for booties unto them?
8 [a]Because thou hast spoiled many nations, all the remnant of the people shall spoil thee; because of men's blood, and *for* the violence of the land, of the city, and of all that dwell therein.
9 Woe to him that coveteth an evil covetousness to his house, that he may [a]set his nest on high, that he may be delivered from the power of evil!
10 Thou hast consulted shame to thy house by cutting off many people, and hast sinned *against* thy soul.

16 [a]Deut. 8:17

CHAPTER 2

1 [a]Is. 21:8, 11
2 [a]Is. 8:1
3 [a]Dan. 8:17, 19; 10:14 [b]Ezek. 12:24, 25 [c][Heb. 10:37, 38] [d]Ps. 27:13, 14; [James 5:7, 8; 2 Pet. 3:9]
4 [a][John 3:36]; Rom. 1:17; Heb. 10:38
5 [a]Prov. 27:20; 30:16; Is. 5:11–15
6 [a]Mic. 2:4
8 [a]Is. 33:1; Jer. 27:7; Ezek. 39:10; Zech. 2:8
9 [a]Jer. 49:16; Obad. 4

NKJV

Why do You look on those who deal
treacherously,
And hold Your tongue when the wicked
devours
A *person* more righteous than he?
14 *Why* do You make men like fish of the
sea,
Like creeping things *that have* no ruler
over them?

15 They take up all of them with a hook,
They catch them in their net,
And gather them in their dragnet.
Therefore they rejoice and are glad.
16 Therefore [a]they sacrifice to their net,
And burn incense to their dragnet;
Because by them their share *is* sumptuous
And their food plentiful.
17 Shall they therefore empty their net,
And continue to slay nations without pity?

2 I will [a]stand my watch
And set myself on the rampart,
And watch to see what He will say to me,
And what I will answer when I am
corrected.

The Just Live by Faith

2 Then the LORD answered me and said:

[a]"Write the vision
And make *it* plain on tablets,
That he may run who reads it.
3 For [a]the vision *is* yet for an appointed
time;
But at the end it will speak, and it will
[b]not lie.
Though it tarries, [c]wait for it;
Because it will [d]surely come,
It will not tarry.

4 "Behold the proud,
His soul is not upright in him;
But the [a]just shall live by his faith.

Woe to the Wicked

5 "Indeed, because he transgresses by wine,
He is a proud man,
And he does not stay at home.
Because he [a]enlarges his desire as *hell,
And he *is* like death, and cannot be
satisfied,
He gathers to himself all nations
And heaps up for himself all peoples.

6 "Will not all these [a]take up a proverb
against him,
And a taunting riddle against him, and
say,
'Woe to him who increases
What is not his—how long?
And to him who loads himself with *many
pledges'?
7 Will not *your creditors rise up suddenly?
Will they not awaken who oppress you?
And you will become their booty.
8 [a]Because you have plundered many
nations,
All the remnant of the people shall
plunder you,
Because of men's blood
And the violence of the land *and* the city,
And of all who dwell in it.

9 "Woe to him who covets evil gain for his
house,
That he may [a]set his nest on high,
That he may be delivered from the power
of disaster!
10 You give shameful counsel to your house,
Cutting off many peoples,
And sin *against* your soul.

*______

2:5 Or *Sheol*
2:6 Syr., Vg. *thick clay*
2:7 Lit. *those who bite you*

KJV

11 For the stone shall cry out of the wall, and the beam out of the timber shall answer it.

12 Woe to him that buildeth a town with blood, and stablisheth a city by iniquity!

13 Behold, *is it* not of the LORD of hosts that the people shall labour in the very fire, and the people shall weary themselves for very vanity?

14 For the earth shall be filled with the knowledge of the glory of the LORD, as the waters cover the sea.

15 Woe unto him that giveth his neighbour drink, that puttest thy [a]bottle to *him*, and makest *him* drunken also, that thou mayest look on their nakedness!

16 Thou art filled with shame for glory: drink thou also, and let thy foreskin be uncovered: the cup of the LORD's right hand shall be turned unto thee, and shameful spewing *shall be* on thy glory.

17 For the violence of Lebanon shall cover thee, and the spoil of beasts, *which* made them afraid, because of men's blood, and for the violence of the land, of the city, and of all that dwell therein.

18 What profiteth the graven image that the maker thereof hath graven it; the molten image, and a teacher of lies, that the maker of his work trusteth therein, to make dumb idols?

19 Woe unto him that saith to the wood, Awake; to the dumb stone, Arise, it shall teach! Behold, it *is* laid over with gold and silver, and *there is* no breath at all in the midst of it.

20 [a]But the LORD *is* in his holy temple: let all the earth keep silence before him.

15 [a]Hos. 7:5
20 [a]Zeph. 1:7; Zech. 2:13

NKJV

11 For the stone will cry out from the wall,
And the beam from the timbers will answer it.

12 "Woe to him who builds a town with bloodshed,
Who establishes a city by iniquity!
13 Behold, *is it* not of the LORD of hosts
That the peoples labor *to feed the fire,
And nations weary themselves in vain?
14 For the earth will be filled
With the knowledge of the glory of the LORD,
As the waters cover the sea.

15 "Woe to him who gives drink to his neighbor,
*Pressing *him to* your [a]bottle,
Even to make *him* drunk,
That you may look on his nakedness!
16 You are filled with shame instead of glory.
You also—drink!
And *be exposed as uncircumcised!
The cup of the LORD's right hand *will be* turned against you,
And utter shame will be on your glory.
17 For the violence *done to* Lebanon will cover you,
And the plunder of beasts *which* made them afraid,
Because of men's blood
And the violence of the land *and* the city,
And of all who dwell in it.

18 "What profit is the image, that its maker should carve it,
The molded image, a teacher of lies,
That the maker of its mold should trust in it,
To make mute idols?
19 Woe to him who says to wood, 'Awake!'
To silent stone, 'Arise! It shall teach!'
Behold, it is overlaid with gold and silver,
Yet in it there is no breath at all.

20 "But[a] the LORD is in His holy temple.
Let all the earth keep silence before Him."

The Prophet's Prayer

3 A prayer of Habakkuk the prophet upon Shigionoth.

2 O LORD, I have heard thy speech, *and* was afraid: O LORD, revive thy work in the midst of the years, in the midst of the years make known; in wrath remember mercy.

3 God came from Teman, and the Holy One from mount Paran. Selah. His glory covered the heavens, and the earth was full of his praise.

4 And *his* brightness was as the light; he had horns *coming* out of his hand: and there *was* the hiding of his power.

5 Before him went the pestilence, and burning coals went forth at his feet.

6 He stood, and measured the earth: he beheld, and drove asunder the nations; [a]and the everlasting mountains were scattered, the perpetual hills did bow: his ways *are* everlasting.

7 I saw the tents of Cushan in affliction: *and* the curtains of the land of Midian did tremble.

8 Was the LORD displeased against the rivers? *was* thine anger against the rivers? *was* thy

CHAPTER 3
6 [a]Nah. 1:5

The Prophet's Prayer

3 A prayer of Habakkuk the prophet, on *Shigionoth.

2 O LORD, I have heard Your speech *and* was afraid;
O LORD, revive Your work in the midst of the years!
In the midst of the years make *it* known;
In wrath remember mercy.

3 God came from Teman,
The Holy One from Mount Paran. Selah

His glory covered the heavens,
And the earth was full of His praise.
4 *His* brightness was like the light;
He had rays *flashing* from His hand,
And there His power *was* hidden.
5 Before Him went pestilence,
And fever followed at His feet.

6 He stood and measured the earth;
He looked and startled the nations.
[a]And the everlasting mountains were scattered,
The perpetual hills bowed.
His ways *are* everlasting.
7 I saw the tents of Cushan in affliction;
The curtains of the land of Midian trembled.

8 O LORD, were *You* displeased with the rivers,

2:13 Lit. *for what satisfies fire,* for what is of no lasting value
2:15 Lit. *Attaching* or *Joining*
2:16 DSS, LXX *reel!;* Syr., Vg. *fall fast asleep!*
3:1 Exact meaning unknown

KJV

wrath against the sea, that thou didst ride upon
thine horses *and* thy chariots of salvation?
9 Thy bow was made quite naked, *according*
ing to the oaths of the tribes, *even thy* word. Selah.
Thou didst cleave the earth with rivers.
10 The mountains saw thee, *and* they trembled: the overflowing of the water passed by: the
deep uttered his voice, *and* [a]lifted up his hands
on high.
11 The [a]sun *and* moon stood still in their
habitation: at the light of thine arrows they went,
and at the shining of thy glittering spear.
12 Thou didst march through the land in indignation, thou didst thresh the heathen in anger.
13 Thou wentest forth for the salvation of thy
people, *even* for salvation with thine anointed;
thou woundedst the head out of the house of the
wicked, by discovering the foundation unto the
neck. Selah.
14 Thou didst strike through with his staves
the head of his villages: they came out as a whirlwind to scatter me: their rejoicing *was* as to devour the poor secretly.
15 [a]Thou didst walk through the sea with
thine horses, *through* the heap of great waters.
16 When I heard, [a]my belly trembled; my lips
quivered at the voice: rottenness entered into my
bones, and I trembled in myself, that I might rest
in the day of trouble: when he cometh up unto
the people, he will invade them with his troops.

A Hymn of Faith

17 Although the fig tree shall not blossom,
neither *shall* fruit *be* in the vines; the labour of
the olive shall fail, and the fields shall yield no
meat; the flock shall be cut off from the fold, and
there shall be no herd in the stalls:
18 Yet I will [a]rejoice in the LORD, I will joy
in the God of my salvation.
19 The LORD God *is* my strength, and he will
make my feet like [a]hinds' *feet*, and he will make
me to [b]walk upon mine high places. To the chief
singer on my stringed instruments.

10 [a]Ex. 14:22 **11** [a]Josh. 10:12–14 **15** [a]Ps. 77:19; Hab. 3:8 **16** [a]Ps. 119:120 **18** [a]Is. 41:16; 61:10 **19** [a]2 Sam. 22:34; Ps. 18:33 [b]Deut. 32:13; 33:29

* **3:9** Lit. *tribes* or *rods*, cf. v. 14 **3:19** Heb. *YHWH Adonai*

NKJV

Was Your anger against the rivers,
Was Your wrath against the sea,
That You rode on Your horses,
Your chariots of salvation?
9 Your bow was made quite ready;
Oaths were sworn over *Your* *arrows.
Selah

You divided the earth with rivers.
10 The mountains saw You *and* trembled;
The overflowing of the water passed by.
The deep uttered its voice,
And [a]lifted its hands on high.
11 The [a]sun and moon stood still in their
habitation;
At the light of Your arrows they went,
At the shining of Your glittering spear.

12 You marched through the land in
indignation;
You trampled the nations in anger.
13 You went forth for the salvation of Your
people,
For salvation with Your Anointed.
You struck the head from the house of the
wicked,
By laying bare from foundation to neck.
Selah

14 You thrust through with his own arrows
The head of his villages.
They came out like a whirlwind to scatter
me;
Their rejoicing was like feasting on the
poor in secret.
15 [a]You walked through the sea with Your
horses,
Through the heap of great waters.

16 When I heard, [a]my body trembled;
My lips quivered at *the* voice;
Rottenness entered my bones;
And I trembled in myself,
That I might rest in the day of trouble.
When he comes up to the people,
He will invade them with his troops.

A Hymn of Faith

17 Though the fig tree may not blossom,
Nor fruit be on the vines;
Though the labor of the olive may fail,
And the fields yield no food;
Though the flock may be cut off from the
fold,
And there be no herd in the stalls—
18 Yet I will [a]rejoice in the LORD,
I will joy in the God of my salvation.

19 *The LORD God is my strength;
He will make my feet like [a]deer's *feet*,
And He will make me [b]walk on my high
hills.

To the Chief Musician. With my stringed
instruments.

KJV

THE BOOK OF

ZEPHANIAH

1 The word of the LORD which came unto Zephaniah the son of Cushi, the son of Gedaliah,
the son of Amariah, the son of Hizkiah, in the
days of [a]Josiah the son of Amon, king of Judah.

The Great Day of the LORD *(cf. Amos 5:18–20)*

2 I will utterly consume all *things* from off
the land, saith the LORD.
3 [a]I will consume man and beast; I will consume the fowls of the heaven, and the fishes of
the sea, and the stumblingblocks with the wicked;
and I will cut off man from off the land, saith the
LORD.
4 I will also stretch out mine hand upon Judah, and upon all the inhabitants of Jerusalem;
and I will cut off the remnant of Baal from this
place, *and* the name of [a]the Chemarims with the
priests;
5 And them [a]that worship the host of
heaven upon the housetops; and them that worship *and* that swear by the LORD, and that swear
[b]by Malcham;
6 And [a]them that are turned back from the
LORD; and *those* that [b]have not sought the LORD,
nor enquired for him.
7 [a]Hold thy peace at the presence of the
Lord GOD: [b]for the day of the LORD *is* at hand:
for [c]the LORD hath prepared a sacrifice, he hath
bid his guests.
8 And it shall come to pass in the day of
the LORD's sacrifice, that I will punish [a]the
princes, and the king's children, and all such as
are clothed with strange apparel.
9 In the same day also will I punish all those
that [a]leap on the threshold, which fill their masters' houses with violence and deceit.
10 And it shall come to pass in that day, saith
the LORD, *that there shall be* the noise of a cry
from [a]the fish gate, and an howling from the second, and a great crashing from the hills.
11 [a]Howl, ye inhabitants of Maktesh, for all
the merchant people are cut down; all they that
bear silver are cut off.
12 And it shall come to pass at that time, *that*
I will search Jerusalem with candles, and punish
the men that are [a]settled on their lees: [b]that say

CHAPTER 1

1 [a]2 Kin. 22:1, 2; 2 Chr. 34:1–33; Jer. 1:2; 22:11
3 [a]Hos. 4:3
4 [a]2 Kin. 23:5; Hos. 10:5
5 [a]2 Kin. 23:12; Jer. 19:13 [b]Josh. 23:7
6 [a]Is. 1:4; Jer. 2:13 [b]Hos. 7:7
7 [a]Hab. 2:20; Zech. 2:13 [b]Is. 13:6 [c]Deut. 28:26; Is. 34:6; Jer. 46:10; Ezek. 39:17–19
8 [a]Jer. 39:6
9 [a]1 Sam. 5:5
10 [a]2 Chr. 33:14; Neh. 3:3; 12:39
11 [a]James 5:1
12 [a]Jer. 48:11; Amos 6:1 [b]Ps. 94:7

*

1:3 Idols
1:4 Heb. *chemarim*
1:5 Or *Malcam,* an Ammonite god, 1 Kin. 11:5; Jer. 49:1; *Molech,* Lev. 18:21
1:7 Lit. *set apart, consecrated*
1:11 A market district of Jerusalem, lit. *Mortar*
1:12 Lit. *on their lees;* like the dregs of wine

NKJV

THE BOOK OF

ZEPHANIAH

1 The word of the LORD which came to Zephaniah the son of Cushi, the son of Gedaliah,
the son of Amariah, the son of Hezekiah, in the
days of [a]Josiah the son of Amon, king of Judah.

The Great Day of the LORD *(cf. Amos 5:18–20)*

2 "I will utterly consume everything
From the face of the land,"
Says the LORD;
3 "I[a] will consume man and beast;
I will consume the birds of the heavens,
The fish of the sea,
And the *stumbling blocks along with the wicked.
I will cut off man from the face of the land,"
Says the LORD.

4 "I will stretch out My hand against Judah,
And against all the inhabitants of Jerusalem.
I will cut off every trace of Baal from this place,
The names of the [a]idolatrous* priests with the *pagan* priests—
5 Those [a]who worship the host of heaven on the housetops;
Those who worship and swear *oaths* by the LORD,
But who *also* swear [b]by *Milcom;
6 [a]Those who have turned back from *following* the LORD,
And [b]have not sought the LORD, nor inquired of Him."

7 [a]Be silent in the presence of the Lord GOD;
[b]For the day of the LORD *is* at hand,
For [c]the LORD has prepared a sacrifice;
He has *invited His guests.

8 "And it shall be,
In the day of the LORD's sacrifice,
That I will punish [a]the princes and the king's children,
And all such as are clothed with foreign apparel.
9 In the same day I will punish
All those who [a]leap over the threshold,
Who fill their masters' houses with violence and deceit.

10 "And there shall be on that day," says the LORD,
"The sound of a mournful cry from [a]the Fish Gate,
A wailing from the Second Quarter,
And a loud crashing from the hills.
11 [a]Wail, you inhabitants of *Maktesh!
For all the merchant people are cut down;
All those who handle money are cut off.

12 "And it shall come to pass at that time
That I will search Jerusalem with lamps,
And punish the men
Who are [a]settled* in complacency,
[b]Who say in their heart,

KJV

in their heart, The LORD will not do good, neither
will he do evil.
13 Therefore their goods shall become a
booty, and their houses a desolation: they shall
also build houses, but not inhabit *them;* and they
shall plant vineyards, but [a]not drink the wine
thereof.
14 [a]The great day of the LORD *is* near, *it is*
near, and hasteth greatly, *even* the voice of the
day of the LORD: the mighty man shall cry there
bitterly.
15 [a]That day *is* a day of wrath, a day of trouble and distress, a day of wasteness and desolation, a day of darkness and gloominess, a day of
clouds and thick darkness,
16 A day of [a]the trumpet and alarm against
the fenced cities, and against the high towers.
17 And I will bring distress upon men, that
they shall [a]walk like blind men, because they
have sinned against the LORD: and their blood
shall be poured out as dust, and their flesh as the
dung.
18 [a]Neither their silver nor their gold shall
be able to deliver them in the day of the LORD's
wrath; but the whole land shall be devoured by
the fire of his jealousy: for he shall make even a
speedy riddance of all them that dwell in the land.

13 [a]Deut. 28:39
14 [a]Jer. 30:7; Joel 2:1, 11
15 [a]Is. 22:5
16 [a]Is. 27:13; Jer. 4:19
17 [a]Deut. 28:29
18 [a]Ezek. 7:19

NKJV

'The LORD will not do good,
Nor will He do evil.'
13 Therefore their goods shall become booty,
And their houses a desolation;
They shall build houses, but not inhabit
them;
They shall plant vineyards, but [a]not drink
their wine."

14 [a]The great day of the LORD *is* near;
It is near and hastens quickly.
The noise of the day of the LORD is bitter;
There the mighty men shall cry out.
15 [a]That day *is* a day of wrath,
A day of trouble and distress,
A day of devastation and desolation,
A day of darkness and gloominess,
A day of clouds and thick darkness,
16 A day of [a]trumpet and alarm
Against the fortified cities
And against the high towers.

17 "I will bring distress upon men,
And they shall [a]walk like blind men,
Because they have sinned against the
LORD;
Their blood shall be poured out like dust,
And their flesh like refuse."

18 [a]Neither their silver nor their gold
Shall be able to deliver them
In the day of the LORD's wrath;
But the whole land shall be devoured
By the fire of His jealousy,
For He will make speedy riddance
Of all those who dwell in the land.

A Call to Repentance

2 Gather[a] yourselves together, yea, gather together, O nation not desired;
2 Before the decree bring forth, *before* the
day pass as the chaff, before the fierce anger of
the LORD come upon you, before the day of the
LORD's anger come upon you.
3 [a]Seek ye the LORD, [b]all ye meek of the
earth, which have wrought his judgment; seek
righteousness, seek meekness: [c]it may be ye shall
be hid in the day of the LORD's anger.

Judgment on Nations

4 For [a]Gaza shall be forsaken, and Ashkelon a desolation: they shall drive out Ashdod
[b]at the noon day, and Ekron shall be rooted up.
5 Woe unto the inhabitants of [a]the sea
coast, the nation of the Cherethites! the word of
the LORD *is* against you; O [b]Canaan, the land of
the Philistines, I will even destroy thee, that there
shall be no inhabitant.
6 And the sea coast shall be dwellings *and*
cottages for shepherds, [a]and folds for flocks.
7 And the coast shall be for [a]the remnant
of the house of Judah; they shall feed thereupon:
in the houses of Ashkelon shall they lie down in
the evening: for the LORD their God shall [b]visit
them, and [c]turn away their captivity.
8 [a]I have heard the reproach of Moab, and
[b]the revilings of the children of Ammon, whereby
they have reproached my people, and [c]magnified
themselves against their border.

CHAPTER 2

1 [a]2 Chr. 20:4; Joel 1:14; 2:16
3 [a]Ps. 105:4; Amos 5:6 [b]Ps. 76:9 [c]Joel 2:14; Amos 5:14, 15
4 [a]Jer. 47:1, 5; Amos 1:7, 8; Zech. 9:5 [b]Jer. 6:4
5 [a]Ezek. 25:15–17 [b]Josh. 13:3
6 [a]Is. 17:2
7 [a][Mic. 5:7, 8] [b]Luke 1:68 [c]Jer. 29:14
8 [a]Jer. 48:27; Amos 2:1–3 [b]Ezek. 25:3; Amos 1:13 [c]Jer. 49:1

A Call to Repentance

2 Gather[a] yourselves together, yes, gather
together,
O *undesirable nation,
2 Before the decree is issued,
Or the day passes like chaff,
Before the LORD's fierce anger comes upon
you,
Before the day of the LORD's anger comes
upon you!
3 [a]Seek the LORD, [b]all you meek of the earth,
Who have upheld His justice.
Seek righteousness, seek humility.
[c]It may be that you will be hidden
In the day of the LORD's anger.

Judgment on Nations

4 For [a]Gaza shall be forsaken,
And Ashkelon desolate;
They shall drive out Ashdod [b]at noonday,
And Ekron shall be uprooted.
5 Woe to the inhabitants of [a]the seacoast,
The nation of the Cherethites!
The word of the LORD *is* against you,
O [b]Canaan, land of the Philistines:
"I will destroy you;
So there shall be no inhabitant."

6 The seacoast shall be pastures,
With *shelters for shepherds [a]and folds
for flocks.
7 The coast shall be for [a]the remnant of the
house of Judah;
They shall feed *their* flocks there;
In the houses of Ashkelon they shall lie
down at evening.
For the LORD their God will [b]intervene for
them,
And [c]return their captives.

8 "I[a] have heard the reproach of Moab,
And [b]the insults of the people of Ammon,
With which they have reproached My
people,
And [c]made arrogant threats against their
borders.

*

2:1 Or *shameless*
2:6 Underground huts or cisterns, lit. *excavations*

KJV

9 Therefore *as* I live, saith the LORD of hosts, the God of Israel, Surely [a]Moab shall be as Sodom, and [b]the children of Ammon as Gomorrah, [c]*even* the breeding of nettles, and saltpits, and a perpetual desolation: the residue of my people shall spoil them, and the remnant of my people shall possess them.

10 This shall they have [a]for their pride, because they have reproached and magnified *themselves* against the people of the LORD of hosts.

11 The LORD *will be* terrible unto them: for he will famish all the gods of the earth; [a]and *men* shall worship him, every one from his place, *even* all [b]the isles of the heathen.

12 [a]Ye Ethiopians also, ye *shall be* slain by [b]my sword.

13 And he will stretch out his hand against the north, and [a]destroy Assyria; and will make Nineveh a desolation, *and* dry like a wilderness.

14 And flocks shall lie down in the midst of her, all [a]the beasts of the nations: both the [b]cormorant and the bittern shall lodge in the upper lintels of it; *their* voice shall sing in the windows; desolation *shall be* in the thresholds: for he shall uncover the [c]cedar work.

15 This *is* the rejoicing city [a]that dwelt carelessly, [b]that said in her heart, I *am*, and *there is* none beside me: how is she become a desolation, a place for beasts to lie down in! every one that passeth by her [c]shall hiss, *and* [d]wag his hand.

The Wickedness of Jerusalem

3 Woe to her that is filthy and polluted, to the oppressing city!

2 She obeyed not the voice; she received not correction; she trusted not in the LORD; she drew not near to her God.

3 [a]Her princes within her *are* roaring lions; her judges *are* [b]evening wolves; they gnaw not the bones till the morrow.

4 Her [a]prophets *are* light *and* treacherous persons: her priests have polluted the sanctuary, they have done [b]violence to the law.

5 The just LORD *is* in the midst thereof; he will not do iniquity: every morning doth he bring his judgment to light, he faileth not; but [a]the unjust knoweth no shame.

6 I have cut off the nations: their towers are desolate; I made their streets waste, that none passeth by: their cities are destroyed, so that there is no man, that there is none inhabitant.

7 [a]I said, Surely thou wilt fear me, thou wilt receive instruction; so their dwelling should not be cut off, howsoever I punished them: but they rose early, *and* [b]corrupted all their doings.

---

9 [a]Is. 15:1–9; Jer. 48:1–47 [b]Amos 1:13 [c]Deut. 29:23
10 [a]Is. 16:6
11 [a]Mal. 1:11 [b]Gen. 10:5
12 [a]Is. 18:1–7; Ezek. 30:4, 5 [b]Ps. 17:13
13 [a]Is. 10:5–27; 14:24–27; Mic. 5:5, 6
14 [a]Is. 13:21 [b]Is. 14:23; 34:11 [c]Jer. 22:14
15 [a]Is. 47:8 [b]Rev. 18:7 [c]Lam. 2:15 [d]Nah. 3:19

CHAPTER 3

3 [a]Ezek. 22:27 [b]Jer. 5:6; Hab. 1:8
4 [a]Hos. 9:7 [b]Ezek. 22:26; Mal. 2:7, 8
5 [a]Jer. 3:3
7 [a]Jer. 8:6 [b]Gen. 6:12

NKJV

9 Therefore, as I live,"
Says the LORD of hosts, the God of Israel,
"Surely [a]Moab shall be like Sodom,
And [b]the people of Ammon like Gomorrah—
[c]Overrun with weeds and saltpits,
And a perpetual desolation.
The residue of My people shall plunder them,
And the remnant of My people shall possess them."

10 This they shall have [a]for their pride,
Because they have reproached and made arrogant threats
Against the people of the LORD of hosts.
11 The LORD *will be* awesome to them,
For He will reduce to nothing all the gods of the earth;
[a]*People* shall worship Him,
Each one from his place,
Indeed all [b]the shores of the nations.

12 "You[a] Ethiopians also,
You shall be slain by [b]My sword."

13 And He will stretch out His hand against the north,
[a]Destroy Assyria,
And make Nineveh a desolation,
As dry as the wilderness.
14 The herds shall lie down in her midst,
[a]Every beast of the nation.
Both the [b]pelican and the bittern
Shall lodge on the capitals of her *pillars;*
Their voice shall sing in the windows;
Desolation *shall be* at the threshold;
For He will lay bare the [c]cedar work.
15 This is the rejoicing city
[a]That dwelt securely,
[b]That said in her heart,
"I *am it,* and *there is* none besides me."
How has she become a desolation,
A place for beasts to lie down!
Everyone who passes by her
[c]Shall hiss and [d]shake his fist.

The Wickedness of Jerusalem

3 Woe to her who is rebellious and polluted,
To the oppressing city!
2 She has not obeyed *His* voice,
She has not received correction;
She has not trusted in the LORD,
She has not drawn near to her God.

3 [a]Her princes in her midst *are* roaring lions;
Her judges *are* [b]evening wolves
That leave not a bone till morning.
4 Her [a]prophets are insolent, treacherous people;
Her priests have polluted the sanctuary,
They have done [b]violence to the law.
5 The LORD *is* righteous in her midst,
He will do no unrighteousness.
Every morning He brings His justice to light;
He never fails,
But [a]the unjust knows no shame.

6 "I have cut off nations,
Their fortresses are devastated;
I have made their streets desolate,
With none passing by.
Their cities are destroyed;
There is no one, no inhabitant.
7 [a]I said, 'Surely you will fear Me,
You will receive instruction'—
So that her dwelling would not be cut off,
Despite everything for which I punished her.
But they rose early and [b]corrupted all their deeds.

KJV

A Faithful Remnant
(*cf. Gen. 11:1–9; Acts 2:1–11*)

8 Therefore [a]wait ye upon me, saith the
LORD, until the day that I rise up to the prey: for
my determination *is* to [b]gather the nations, that
I may assemble the kingdoms, to pour upon them
mine indignation, *even* all my fierce anger: for
all the earth [c]shall be devoured with the fire of
my jealousy.
9 For then will I turn to the people [a]a pure
language, that they may all call upon the name
of the LORD, to serve him with one consent.
10 [a]From beyond the rivers of Ethiopia my
suppliants, *even* the daughter of my dispersed,
shall bring mine offering.
11 In that day shalt thou not be ashamed for
all thy doings, wherein thou hast transgressed
against me: for then I will take away out of the
midst of thee them that [a]rejoice in thy pride, and
thou shalt no more be haughty because of my holy
mountain.
12 I will also leave in the midst of thee [a]an
afflicted and poor people, and they shall trust in
the name of the LORD.
13 [a]The remnant of Israel [b]shall not do iniquity, [c]nor speak lies; neither shall a deceitful
tongue be found in their mouth: for [d]they shall
feed and lie down, and none shall make *them*
afraid.

Joy in God's Faithfulness

14 [a]Sing, O daughter of Zion; shout, O Israel;
be glad and rejoice with all the heart, O daughter
of Jerusalem.
15 The LORD hath taken away thy judgments,
he hath cast out thine enemy: [a]the king of Israel,
even the LORD, [b]*is* in the midst of thee: thou shalt
not see evil any more.
16 In that day [a]it shall be said to Jerusalem,
Fear thou not: *and to* Zion, [b]Let not thine hands
be slack.
17 The LORD thy God [a]in the midst of thee
is mighty; he will save, [b]he will rejoice over thee
with joy; he will rest in his love, he will joy over
thee with singing.
18 I will gather *them that* [a]*are* sorrowful for
the solemn assembly, *who* are of thee, *to whom*
the reproach of it *was* a burden.
19 Behold, at that time I will undo all that
afflict thee: and I will save her that [a]halteth, and
gather her that was driven out; and I will get them
praise and fame in every land where they have
been put to shame.
20 At that time [a]will I bring you *again*, even
in the time that I gather you: for I will make you
a name and a praise among all people of the earth,
when I turn back your captivity before your eyes,
saith the LORD.

8 [a]Prov. 20:22; Mic. 7:7; Hab. 2:3 [b]Is. 66:18; Ezek. 38:14–23; Joel 3:2; Mic. 4:12; Matt. 25:32 [c]Zeph. 1:18
9 [a]Is. 19:18; 57:19
10 [a]Ps. 68:31; Is. 18:1; Acts 8:27
11 [a]Is. 2:12; 5:15; Matt. 3:9
12 [a]Is. 14:32; Zech. 13:8, 9
13 [a]Is. 10:20–22; [Mic. 4:7] [b]Is. 60:21 [c]Zech. 8:3, 16; Rev. 14:5 [d]Ezek. 34:13–15, 28
14 [a]Is. 12:6
15 [a][John 1:49] [b]Ezek. 48:35; [Rev. 7:15]
16 [a]Is. 35:3, 4 [b]Job 4:3; Heb. 12:12
17 [a]Zeph. 3:5, 15 [b]Deut. 30:9; Is. 62:5; 65:19; Jer. 32:41
18 [a]Lam. 2:6
19 [a][Ezek. 34:16; Mic. 4:6, 7]
20 [a]Is. 11:12; Ezek. 28:25; Amos 9:14

NKJV

A Faithful Remnant
(*cf. Gen. 11:1–9; Acts 2:1–11*)

8 "Therefore [a]wait for Me," says the LORD,
"Until the day I rise up *for plunder;
My determination *is* to [b]gather the nations
To My assembly of kingdoms,
To pour on them My indignation,
All My fierce anger;
All the earth [c]shall be devoured
With the fire of My jealousy.

9 "For then I will restore to the peoples [a]a pure language,
That they all may call on the name of the LORD,
To serve Him with one accord.
10 [a]From beyond the rivers of Ethiopia
My worshipers,
The daughter of My dispersed ones,
Shall bring My offering.
11 In that day you shall not be shamed for any of your deeds
In which you transgress against Me;
For then I will take away from your midst
Those who [a]rejoice in your pride,
And you shall no longer be haughty
In My holy mountain.
12 I will leave in your midst
[a]A meek and humble people,
And they shall trust in the name of the LORD.
13 [a]The remnant of Israel [b]shall do no unrighteousness
[c]And speak no lies,
Nor shall a deceitful tongue be found in their mouth;
For [d]they shall feed *their* flocks and lie down,
And no one shall make *them* afraid."

Joy in God's Faithfulness

14 [a]Sing, O daughter of Zion!
Shout, O Israel!
Be glad and rejoice with all *your* heart,
O daughter of Jerusalem!
15 The LORD has taken away your judgments,
He has cast out your enemy.
[a]The King of Israel, the LORD, [b]*is* in your midst;
You shall *see disaster no more.

16 In that day [a]it shall be said to Jerusalem:
"Do not fear;
Zion, [b]let not your hands be weak.
17 The LORD your God [a]in your midst,
The Mighty One, will save;
[b]He will rejoice over you with gladness,
He will quiet *you* with His love,
He will rejoice over you with singing."

18 "I will gather those who [a]sorrow over the appointed assembly,
Who are among you,
To whom its reproach *is* a burden.
19 Behold, at that time
I will deal with all who afflict you;
I will save the [a]lame,
And gather those who were driven out;
I will appoint them for praise and fame
In every land where they were put to shame.
20 At that time [a]I will bring you back,
Even at the time I gather you;
For I will give you fame and praise
Among all the peoples of the earth,
When I return your captives before your eyes,"
Says the LORD.

---

*

3:8 LXX, Syr. *for witness;* Tg. *for the day of My revelation for judgment;* Vg. *for the day of My resurrection that is to come*
3:15 So with Heb. mss., LXX, Bg; MT, Vg. *fear*

KJV

THE BOOK OF

HAGGAI

The Command to Build God's House
(Ezra 5:1)

1 In [a]the second year of Darius the king, in the sixth month, in the first day of the month, came the word of the LORD by [b]Haggai the prophet unto [c]Zerubbabel the son of Shealtiel, governor of Judah, and to [d]Joshua the son of [e]Josedech, the high priest, saying,

2 Thus speaketh the LORD of hosts, saying, This people say, The time is not come, the time that the LORD's house should be built.

3 Then came the word of the LORD [a]by Haggai the prophet, saying,

4 [a]*Is it* time for you, O ye, to dwell in your cieled houses, and this house *lie* waste?

5 Now therefore thus saith the LORD of hosts; [a]Consider your ways.

6 Ye have [a]sown much, and bring in little; ye eat, but ye have not enough; ye drink, but ye are not filled with drink; ye clothe you, but there is none warm; and [b]he that earneth wages earneth wages *to put it* into a bag with holes.

7 Thus saith the LORD of hosts; Consider your ways.

8 Go up to the [a]mountain, and bring wood, and build the house; and I will take pleasure in it, and I will be glorified, saith the LORD.

9 [a]Ye looked for much, and, lo, *it came* to little; and when ye brought *it* home, [b]I did blow upon it. Why? saith the LORD of hosts. Because of mine house that *is* waste, and ye run every man unto his own house.

10 Therefore [a]the heaven over you is stayed from dew, and the earth is stayed *from* her fruit.

11 And I [a]called for a drought upon the land, and upon the mountains, and upon the corn, and upon the new wine, and upon the oil, and upon *that* which the ground bringeth forth, and upon men, and upon cattle, and [b]upon all the labour of the hands.

The People's Obedience

12 [a]Then Zerubbabel the son of Shealtiel, and Joshua the son of Josedech, the high priest, with all the remnant of the people, obeyed the voice of the LORD their God, and the words of Haggai the prophet, as the LORD their God had sent him, and the people did fear before the LORD.

13 Then spake Haggai the LORD's messenger in the LORD's message unto the people, saying, [a]I *am* with you, saith the LORD.

14 And [a]the LORD stirred up the spirit of Zerubbabel the son of Shealtiel, [b]governor of Judah, and the spirit of Joshua the son of Josedech, the high priest, and the spirit of all the remnant of the people; [c]and they came and did work in the house of the LORD of hosts, their God,

15 In the four and twentieth day of the sixth month, in the second year of Darius the king.

CHAPTER 1

1 [a]Ezra 4:24; Hag. 2:10; Zech. 1:1, 7 [b]Ezra 5:1; 6:14 [c]1 Chr. 3:19; Ezra 2:2; Neh. 7:7; Zech. 4:6; Matt. 1:12, 13 [d]Ezra 5:2, 3; Zech. 6:11 [e]1 Chr. 6:15
3 [a]Ezra 5:1
4 [a]2 Sam. 7:2
5 [a]Lam. 3:40
6 [a]Deut. 28:38–40; Hos. 8:7; Hag. 1:9, 10; 2:16, 17 [b]Zech. 8:10
8 [a]Ezra 3:7
9 [a]Hag. 2:16 [b]Hag. 2:17
10 [a]Lev. 26:19; Deut. 28:23; 1 Kin. 8:35; Joel 1:18–20
11 [a]1 Kin. 17:1; 2 Kin. 8:1 [b]Hag. 2:17
12 [a]Ezra 5:2
13 [a][Matt. 28:20; Rom. 8:31]
14 [a]2 Chr. 36:22; Ezra 1:1 [b]Hag. 2:21 [c]Ezra 5:2, 8; Neh. 4:6

NKJV

THE BOOK OF

HAGGAI

The Command to Build God's House
(Ezra 5:1)

1 In [a]the second year of King Darius, in the sixth month, on the first day of the month, the word of the LORD came by [b]Haggai the prophet to [c]Zerubbabel the son of Shealtiel, governor of Judah, and to [d]Joshua the son of [e]Jehozadak, the high priest, saying,

2 "Thus speaks the LORD of hosts, saying: 'This people says, "The time has not come, the time that the LORD's house should be built." ' "

3 Then the word of the LORD [a]came by Haggai the prophet, saying,

4 "*Is it* [a]time for you yourselves to dwell in your paneled houses, and this *temple *to lie* in ruins?"

5 Now therefore, thus says the LORD of hosts: [a]"Consider your ways!

6 "You have [a]sown much, and bring in little;
You eat, but do not have enough;
You drink, but you are not filled with drink;
You clothe yourselves, but no one is warm;
And [b]he who earns wages,
Earns wages *to put* into a bag with holes."

7 Thus says the LORD of hosts: "Consider your ways!

8 "Go up to the [a]mountains and bring wood and build the temple, that I may take pleasure in it and be glorified," says the LORD.

9 [a]"*You* looked for much, but indeed *it came to* little; and when you brought it home, [b]I blew it away. Why?" says the LORD of hosts. "Because of My house that *is in* ruins, while every one of you runs to his own house.

10 "Therefore [a]the heavens above you withhold the dew, and the earth withholds its fruit.

11 "For I [a]called for a drought on the land and the mountains, on the grain and the new wine and the oil, on whatever the ground brings forth, on men and livestock, and on [b]all the labor of *your* hands."

The People's Obedience

12 [a]Then Zerubbabel the son of Shealtiel, and Joshua the son of Jehozadak, the high priest, with all the remnant of the people, obeyed the voice of the LORD their God, and the words of Haggai the prophet, as the LORD their God had sent him; and the people feared the presence of the LORD.

13 Then Haggai, the LORD's messenger, spoke the LORD's message to the people, saying, [a]"I *am* with you, says the LORD."

14 So [a]the LORD stirred up the spirit of Zerubbabel the son of Shealtiel, [b]governor of Judah, and the spirit of Joshua the son of Jehozadak, the high priest, and the spirit of all the remnant of the people; [c]and they came and worked on the house of the LORD of hosts, their God,

15 on the twenty-fourth day of the sixth month, in the second year of King Darius.

---

*1:4 Lit. *house*

KJV

The Coming Glory of God's House

2 In the seventh *month,* in the one and twentieth *day* of the month, came the word of the LORD by the prophet Haggai, saying,

2 Speak now to Zerubbabel the son of Shealtiel, governor of Judah, and to Joshua the son of Josedech, the high priest, and to the residue of the people, saying,

3 [a]Who *is* left among you that saw this house in her first glory? and how do ye see it now? [b]*is it* not in your eyes in comparison of it as nothing?

4 Yet now [a]be strong, O Zerubbabel, saith the LORD; and be strong, O Joshua, son of Josedech, the high priest; and be strong, all ye people of the land, saith the LORD, and work: for I *am* with you, saith the LORD of hosts:

5 [a]*According to* the word that I covenanted with you when ye came out of Egypt, so [b]my spirit remaineth among you: fear ye not.

6 For thus saith the LORD of hosts; [a]Yet once, it *is* a little while, and [b]I will shake the heavens, and the earth, and the sea, and the dry *land;*

7 And I will shake all nations, [a]and the desire of all nations shall come: and I will fill this house with [b]glory, saith the LORD of hosts.

8 The silver *is* mine, and the gold *is* mine, saith the LORD of hosts.

9 [a]The glory of this latter house shall be greater than of the former, saith the LORD of hosts: and in this place will I give [b]peace, saith the LORD of hosts.

The People Are Defiled

10 In the four and twentieth *day* of the ninth *month,* in the second year of Darius, came the word of the LORD by Haggai the prophet, saying,

11 Thus saith the LORD of hosts; [a]Ask now the priests *concerning* the law, saying,

12 If one bear holy flesh in the skirt of his garment, and with his skirt do touch bread, or pottage, or wine, or oil, or any meat, shall it be holy? And the priests answered and said, No.

13 Then said Haggai, If *one that is* [a]unclean by a dead body touch any of these, shall it be unclean? And the priests answered and said, It shall be unclean.

14 Then answered Haggai, and said, [a]So *is* this people, and so *is* this nation before me, saith the LORD; and so *is* every work of their hands; and that which they offer there *is* unclean.

Promised Blessing

15 And now, I pray you, [a]consider from this day and upward, from before a stone was laid upon a stone in the temple of the LORD:

16 Since those *days* were, [a]when *one* came to an heap of twenty *measures,* there were *but* ten: when *one* came to the pressfat for to draw out fifty *vessels* out of the press, there were *but* twenty.

17 [a]I smote you with blasting and with mildew and with hail [b]in all the labours of your hands; [c]yet ye *turned* not to me, saith the LORD.

18 Consider now from this day and upward, from the four and twentieth day of the ninth *month, even* from [a]the day that the foundation of the LORD's temple was laid, consider *it.*

19 [a]Is the seed yet in the barn? yea, as yet the vine, and the fig tree, and the pomegranate, and the olive tree, hath not brought forth: from this day will I [b]bless *you.*

Zerubbabel Chosen as a Signet

20 And again the word of the LORD came unto Haggai in the four and twentieth *day* of the month, saying,

21 Speak to Zerubbabel, [a]governor of Judah, saying, [b]I will shake the heavens and the earth;

CHAPTER 2

3 [a]Ezra 3:12, 13 [b]Zech. 4:10
4 [a]Deut. 31:23; 1 Chr. 22:13; 28:20; Zech. 8:9; Eph. 6:10
5 [a]Ex. 29:45, 46 [b][Neh. 9:20]; Is. 63:11, 14
6 [a]Heb. 12:26 [b][Joel 3:16]
7 [a]Gen. 49:10; Mal. 3:1 [b]1 Kin. 8:11; Is. 60:7; Zech. 2:5
9 [a][John 1:14] [b]Ps. 85:8, 9; Luke 2:14; [Eph. 2:14]
11 [a]Lev. 10:10, 11; Deut. 33:10; Mal. 2:7
13 [a]Lev. 22:4–6; Num. 19:11, 22
14 [a][Titus 1:15]
15 [a]Hag. 1:5, 7; 2:18
16 [a]Hag. 1:6, 9; Zech. 8:10
17 [a]Deut. 28:22; 1 Kin. 8:37; Amos 4:9 [b]Hag. 1:11 [c]Jer. 5:3; Amos 4:6–11
18 [a]Ezra 5:1, 2, 16; Zech. 8:9
19 [a]Zech. 8:12 [b]Ps. 128:1–6; Jer. 31:12, 14; [Mal. 3:10]
21 [a]Ezra 5:2; Hag. 1:1, 14; Zech. 4:6–10 [b]Hag. 2:6, 7; [Heb. 12:26, 27]

*

2:3 Lit. *house*
2:7 Or *desire of all nations*

NKJV

The Coming Glory of God's House

2 In the seventh *month,* on the twenty-first of the month, the word of the LORD came by Haggai the prophet, saying:

2 "Speak now to Zerubbabel the son of Shealtiel, governor of Judah, and to Joshua the son of Jehozadak, the high priest, and to the remnant of the people, saying:

3 [a]'Who is left among you who saw this *temple in its former glory? And how do you see it now? In comparison with it, [b]*is this* not in your eyes as nothing?

4 'Yet now [a]be strong, Zerubbabel,' says the LORD; 'and be strong, Joshua, son of Jehozadak, the high priest; and be strong, all you people of the land,' says the LORD, 'and work; for I *am* with you,' says the LORD of hosts.

5 [a]'*According to* the word that I covenanted with you when you came out of Egypt, so [b]My Spirit remains among you; do not fear!'

6 "For thus says the LORD of hosts: [a]'Once more (it *is* a little while) [b]I will shake heaven and earth, the sea and dry land;

7 'and I will shake all nations, and they shall come to [a]the *Desire of All Nations, and I will fill this temple with [b]glory,' says the LORD of hosts.

8 'The silver *is* Mine, and the gold *is* Mine,' says the LORD of hosts.

9 [a]'The glory of this latter temple shall be greater than the former,' says the LORD of hosts. 'And in this place I will give [b]peace,' says the LORD of hosts."

The People Are Defiled

10 On the twenty-fourth *day* of the ninth *month,* in the second year of Darius, the word of the LORD came by Haggai the prophet, saying,

11 "Thus says the LORD of hosts: 'Now, [a]ask the priests *concerning the* law, saying,

12 "If one carries holy meat in the fold of his garment, and with the edge he touches bread or stew, wine or oil, or any food, will it become holy?" ' " Then the priests answered and said, "No."

13 And Haggai said, "If *one who is* [a]unclean *because* of a dead body touches any of these, will it be unclean?" So the priests answered and said, "It shall be unclean."

14 Then Haggai answered and said, [a]" 'So is this people, and so is this nation before Me,' says the LORD, 'and so is every work of their hands; and what they offer there is unclean.

Promised Blessing

15 'And now, carefully [a]consider from this day forward: from before stone was laid upon stone in the temple of the LORD—

16 'since those *days,* [a]when *one* came to a heap of twenty ephahs, there were *but* ten; when *one* came to the wine vat to draw out fifty baths from the press, there were *but* twenty.

17 [a]'I struck you with blight and mildew and hail [b]in all the labors of your hands; [c]yet you did not *turn* to Me,' says the LORD.

18 'Consider now from this day forward, from the twenty-fourth day of the ninth month, from [a]the day that the foundation of the LORD's temple was laid—consider it:

19 [a]'Is the seed still in the barn? As yet the vine, the fig tree, the pomegranate, and the olive tree have not yielded *fruit. But* from this day I will [b]bless *you.*' "

Zerubbabel Chosen as a Signet

20 And again the word of the LORD came to Haggai on the twenty-fourth day of the month, saying,

21 "Speak to Zerubbabel, [a]governor of Judah, saying:

[b]'I will shake heaven and earth.

KJV

22 And [a]I will overthrow the throne of kingdoms, and I will destroy the strength of the kingdoms of the heathen; and [b]I will overthrow the chariots, and those that ride in them; and the horses and their riders shall come down, every one by the sword of his brother.

23 In that day, saith the LORD of hosts, will I take thee, O Zerubbabel, my servant, the son of Shealtiel, saith the LORD, [a]and will make thee as a signet: for [b]I have chosen thee, saith the LORD of hosts.

22 [a][Dan. 2:44; Rev. 19:11–21] [b]Ps. 46:9; Ezek. 39:20; Mic. 5:10; Zech. 9:10
23 [a]Song 8:6; Jer. 22:24 [b]Is. 42:1; 43:10

NKJV

22 [a]I will overthrow the throne of kingdoms;
I will destroy the strength of the Gentile kingdoms.
[b]I will overthrow the chariots
And those who ride in them;
The horses and their riders shall come down,
Every one by the sword of his brother.

23 'In that day,' says the LORD of hosts, 'I will take you, Zerubbabel My servant, the son of Shealtiel,' says the LORD, [a]'and will make you like a signet *ring*; for [b]I have chosen you,' says the LORD of hosts."

KJV

THE BOOK OF

ZECHARIAH

A Call to Repentance

1 In the eighth month, [a]in the second year of Darius, came the word of the LORD [b]unto Zechariah, the son of Berechiah, the son of [c]Iddo the prophet, saying,

2 The LORD hath been sore displeased with your fathers.

3 Therefore say thou unto them, Thus saith the LORD of hosts; Turn [a]ye unto me, saith the LORD of hosts, and I will turn unto you, saith the LORD of hosts.

4 Be ye not as your fathers, [a]unto whom the former prophets have cried, saying, Thus saith the LORD of hosts; [b]Turn ye now from your evil ways, and *from* your evil doings: but they did not hear, nor hearken unto me, saith the LORD.

5 Your fathers, where *are* they? and the prophets, do they live for ever?

6 But [a]my words and my statutes, which I commanded my servants the prophets, did they not take hold of your fathers? and they returned and said, [b]Like as the LORD of hosts thought to do unto us, according to our ways, and according to our doings, so hath he dealt with us.

Vision of the Horses

7 Upon the four and twentieth day of the eleventh month, which *is* the month Sebat, in the second year of Darius, came the word of the LORD unto Zechariah, the son of Berechiah, the son of Iddo the prophet, saying,

8 I saw by night, and behold [a]a man riding upon a red horse, and he stood among the myrtle trees that *were* in the bottom; and behind him *were there* [b]red horses, speckled, and white.

9 Then said I, O [a]my lord, what *are* these? And the angel that talked with me said unto me, I will shew thee what these *be*.

10 And the man that stood among the myrtle trees answered and said, [a]These *are they* whom the LORD hath sent to walk to and fro through the earth.

11 [a]And they answered the angel of the LORD that stood among the myrtle trees, and said, We have walked to and fro through the earth, and, behold, all the earth sitteth still, and is at rest.

The LORD Will Comfort Zion

12 Then the angel of the LORD answered and said, O LORD of hosts, [a]how long wilt thou not have mercy on Jerusalem and on the cities of Judah, against which thou hast had indignation [b]these threescore and ten years?

13 And the LORD answered the angel that talked with me *with* [a]good words *and* comfortable words.

14 So the angel that communed with me said

CHAPTER 1

1 [a]Ezra 4:24; 6:15; Hag. 1:1; Zech. 7:1 [b]Ezra 5:1; 6:14; Zech. 7:1; Matt. 23:35; Luke 11:51 [c]Neh. 12:4, 16
3 [a]Is. 31:6; 44:22; [Mic. 7:19; Mal. 3:7–10; Luke 15:20; James 4:8]
4 [a]2 Chr. 36:15, 16 [b]Is. 31:6; Jer. 3:12; 18:11; Ezek. 18:30; [Hos. 14:1]
6 [a][Is. 55:11] [b]Lam. 1:18; 2:17
8 [a]Is. 55:13; Zech. 6:2; [Rev. 6:4] [b][Zech. 6:2–7; Rev. 6:2]
9 [a]Zech. 4:4, 5, 13; 6:4
10 [a][Heb. 1:14]
11 [a][Ps. 103:20, 21]
12 [a]Ps. 74:10; Jer. 12:4; Hab. 1:2 [b]2 Chr. 36:21; Jer. 25:11, 12; 29:10; Dan. 9:2; Zech. 7:5
13 [a]Jer. 29:10

NKJV

THE BOOK OF

ZECHARIAH

A Call to Repentance

1 In the eighth month [a]of the second year of Darius, the word of the LORD came [b]to Zechariah the son of Berechiah, the son of [c]Iddo the prophet, saying,

2 "The LORD has been very angry with your fathers.

3 "Therefore say to them, 'Thus says the LORD of hosts: "Return [a]to Me," says the LORD of hosts, "and I will return to you," says the LORD of hosts.

4 "Do not be like your fathers, [a]to whom the former prophets preached, saying, 'Thus says the LORD of hosts: [b]"Turn now from your evil ways and your evil deeds." ' But they did not hear nor heed Me," says the LORD.

5 "Your fathers, where *are* they?
And the prophets, do they live
forever?
6 Yet surely [a]My words and My statutes,
Which I commanded My servants the
prophets,
Did they not overtake your fathers?

"So they returned and said:

[b]'Just as the LORD of hosts determined to
do to us,
According to our ways and according to
our deeds,
So He has dealt with us.' " ' "

Vision of the Horses

7 On the twenty-fourth day of the eleventh month, which is the month Shebat, in the second year of Darius, the word of the LORD came to Zechariah the son of Berechiah, the son of Iddo the prophet:

8 I saw by night, and behold, [a]a man riding on a red horse, and it stood among the myrtle trees in the hollow; and behind him *were* [b]horses: red, sorrel, and white.

9 Then I said, [a]"My lord, what *are* these?" So the angel who talked with me said to me, "I will show you what they *are*."

10 And the man who stood among the myrtle trees answered and said, [a]"These *are the ones* whom the LORD has sent to walk to and fro throughout the earth."

11 [a]So they answered the Angel of the LORD, who stood among the myrtle trees, and said, "We have walked to and fro throughout the earth, and behold, all the earth is resting quietly."

The LORD Will Comfort Zion

12 Then the Angel of the LORD answered and said, "O LORD of hosts, [a]how long will You not have mercy on Jerusalem and on the cities of Judah, against which You were angry [b]these seventy years?"

13 And the LORD answered the angel who talked to me, *with* [a]good *and* comforting words.

14 So the angel who spoke with me said to

KJV

unto me, Cry thou, saying, Thus saith the LORD
of hosts; I am [a]jealous for Jerusalem and for Zion
with a great jealousy.
15 And I am very sore displeased with the
heathen *that are* at ease: for [a]I was but a little
displeased, and they helped forward the affliction.
16 Therefore thus saith the LORD; [a]I am returned to Jerusalem with mercies: my [b]house
[c]shall be built in it, saith the LORD of hosts, and
[d]a line shall be stretched forth upon Jerusalem.
17 Cry yet, saying, Thus saith the LORD of
hosts; My cities through prosperity shall yet be
spread abroad; [a]and the LORD shall yet comfort
Zion, and [b]shall yet choose Jerusalem.

Vision of the Horns

18 Then lifted I up mine eyes, and saw, and
behold four [a]horns.
19 And I said unto the angel that talked with
me, What *be* these? And he answered me, [a]These
are the horns which have scattered Judah, Israel,
and Jerusalem.
20 And the LORD shewed me four carpenters.
21 Then said I, What come these to do? And
he spake, saying, These *are* the [a]horns which have
scattered Judah, so that no man did lift up his
head: but these are come to fray them, to cast
out the horns of the Gentiles, which [b]lifted up
their horn over the land of Judah to scatter it.

Vision of the Measuring Line

2 I lifted up mine eyes again, and looked, and
behold [a]a man with a measuring line in his
hand.
2 Then said I, Whither goest thou? And he
said unto me, [a]To measure Jerusalem, to see what
is the breadth thereof, and what *is* the length
thereof.
3 And, behold, the angel that talked with
me went forth, and another angel went out to meet
him,
4 And said unto him, Run, speak to this
young man, saying, [a]Jerusalem shall be inhabited
as towns without walls for the multitude of men
and cattle therein:
5 For I, saith the LORD, will be unto her [a]a
wall of fire round about, [b]and will be the glory
in the midst of her.

Future Joy of Zion and Many Nations

6 Ho, ho, *come forth,* and flee [a]from the
land of the north, saith the LORD: for I have
[b]spread you abroad as the four winds of the
heaven, saith the LORD.
7 [a]Deliver thyself, O Zion, that dwellest
with the daughter of Babylon.
8 For thus saith the LORD of hosts; After the
glory hath he sent me unto the nations which
spoiled you: for he that [a]toucheth you toucheth
the apple of his eye.
9 For, behold, I will [a]shake mine hand upon
them, and they shall be a spoil to their servants:
and [b]ye shall know that the LORD of hosts hath
sent me.
10 [a]Sing and rejoice, O daughter of Zion: for,
lo, I come, and I [b]will dwell in the midst of thee,
saith the LORD.
11 [a]And many nations shall be joined to the
LORD [b]in that day, and shall be [c]my people: and
I will dwell in the midst of thee, and [d]thou shalt

14 [a]Joel 2:18; Zech. 8:2
15 [a]Is. 47:6
16 [a][Is. 12:1; 54:8; Zech. 2:10; 8:3] [b]Ezra 6:14, 15; Hag. 1:4; Zech. 4:9 [c]2 Chr. 36:23; Ezra 1:2, 3; Is. 44:28 [d]Zech. 2:1–3
17 [a][Is. 40:1, 2; 51:3] [b]Is. 14:1; Zech. 2:12
18 [a][Lam. 2:17]
19 [a]Ezra 4:1, 4, 7
21 [a][Ps. 75:10] [b]Ps. 75:4, 5

CHAPTER 2

1 [a]Jer. 31:39; Ezek. 40:3; 47:3; Zech. 1:16
2 [a]Rev. 11:1
4 [a]Jer. 31:27
5 [a][Is. 26:1] [b][Is. 60:19]
6 [a]Is. 48:20 [b]Deut. 28:64
7 [a]Is. 48:20; Jer. 51:6; [Rev. 18:4]
8 [a]Deut. 32:10; Ps. 17:8
9 [a]Is. 19:16 [b]Zech. 4:9
10 [a]Is. 12:6 [b][Lev. 26:12]
11 [a][Is. 2:2, 3] [b]Zech. 3:10 [c]Ex. 12:49 [d]Ezek. 33:33

*

1:21 Lit. *these*

NKJV

me, "Proclaim, saying, 'Thus says the LORD of
hosts:

"I am [a]zealous for Jerusalem
And for Zion with great zeal.
15 I am exceedingly angry with the nations
at ease;
For [a]I was a little angry,
And they helped—*but* with evil *intent.*"

16 'Therefore thus says the LORD:

[a]"I am returning to Jerusalem with mercy;
My [b]house [c]shall be built in it," says the
LORD of hosts,
"And [d]a *surveyor's* line shall be stretched
out over Jerusalem." '

17 "Again proclaim, saying, 'Thus says the
LORD of hosts:

"My cities shall again spread out through
prosperity;
[a]The LORD will again comfort Zion,
And [b]will again choose Jerusalem." ' "

Vision of the Horns

18 Then I raised my eyes and looked, and
there *were* four [a]horns.
19 And I said to the angel who talked with
me, "What *are* these?" So he answered me,
[a]"These *are* the horns that have scattered Judah,
Israel, and Jerusalem."
20 Then the LORD showed me four craftsmen.
21 And I said, "What are these coming to
do?" So he said, "These *are* the [a]horns that scattered Judah, so that no one could lift up his head;
but *the craftsmen are coming to terrify them, to
cast out the horns of the nations that [b]lifted up
their horn against the land of Judah to scatter
it."

Vision of the Measuring Line

2 Then I raised my eyes and looked, and behold,
[a]a man with a measuring line in his hand.
2 So I said, "Where are you going?" And
he said to me, [a]"To measure Jerusalem, to see
what *is* its width and what *is* its length."
3 And there *was* the angel who talked with
me, going out; and another angel was coming out
to meet him,
4 who said to him, "Run, speak to this
young man, saying: [a]'Jerusalem shall be inhabited *as* towns without walls, because of the multitude of men and livestock in it.
5 'For I,' says the LORD, 'will be [a]a wall of
fire all around her, [b]and I will be the glory in
her midst.' "

Future Joy of Zion and Many Nations

6 "Up, up! Flee [a]from the land of the north,"
says the LORD; "for I have [b]spread you abroad
like the four winds of heaven," says the LORD.
7 "Up, Zion! [a]Escape, you who dwell with
the daughter of Babylon."
8 For thus says the LORD of hosts: "He sent
Me after glory, to the nations which plunder you;
for he who [a]touches you touches the apple of His
eye.
9 "For surely I will [a]shake My hand against
them, and they shall become spoil for their servants. Then [b]you will know that the LORD of hosts
has sent Me.
10 [a]"Sing and rejoice, O daughter of Zion!
For behold, I am coming and I [b]will dwell in your
midst," says the LORD.
11 [a]"Many nations shall be joined to the
LORD [b]in that day, and they shall become [c]My
people. And I will dwell in your midst. Then [d]you

KJV

know that the LORD of hosts hath sent me unto thee.

12 And the LORD shall [a]inherit Judah his portion in the holy land, and shall choose Jerusalem again.

13 [a]Be silent, O all flesh, before the LORD: for he is raised up [b]out of his holy habitation.

Vision of the High Priest

3 And he shewed me [a]Joshua the high priest standing before the angel of the LORD, and [b]Satan standing at his right hand to resist him.

2 And the LORD said unto Satan, [a]The LORD rebuke thee, O Satan; even the LORD that [b]hath chosen Jerusalem rebuke thee: [c]*is* not this a brand plucked out of the fire?

3 Now Joshua was clothed with [a]filthy garments, and stood before the angel.

4 And he answered and spake unto those that stood before him, saying, Take away the filthy garments from him. And unto him he said, Behold, I have caused thine iniquity to pass from thee, [a]and I will clothe thee with change of raiment.

5 And I said, Let them set a fair [a]mitre upon his head. So they set a fair mitre upon his head, and clothed him with garments. And the angel of the LORD stood by.

The Coming Branch

6 And the angel of the LORD protested unto Joshua, saying,

7 Thus saith the LORD of hosts; If thou wilt walk in my ways, and if thou wilt [a]keep my charge, then thou shalt also [b]judge my house, and shalt also keep my courts, and I will give thee places to walk among these that [c]stand by.

8 Hear now, O Joshua the high priest, thou, and thy fellows that sit before thee: for they *are* [a]men wondered at: for, behold, I will bring forth [b]my servant the [c]BRANCH.

9 For behold the stone that I have laid before Joshua; [a]upon one stone *shall be* [b]seven eyes: behold, I will engrave the graving thereof, saith the LORD of hosts, and [c]I will remove the iniquity of that land in one day.

10 [a]In that day, saith the LORD of hosts, shall ye call every man his neighbour [b]under the vine and under the fig tree.

Vision of the Lampstand and Olive Trees

4 And [a]the angel that talked with me came again, and waked me, [b]as a man that is wakened out of his sleep,

2 And said unto me, What seest thou? And I said, I have looked, and behold [a]a candlestick all *of* gold, with a bowl upon the top of it, [b]and his seven lamps thereon, and seven pipes to the seven lamps, which *are* upon the top thereof:

3 [a]And two olive trees by it, one upon the right *side* of the bowl, and the other upon the left *side* thereof.

4 So I answered and spake to the angel that talked with me, saying, What *are* these, my lord?

5 Then the angel that talked with me answered and said unto me, Knowest thou not what these be? And I said, No, my lord.

6 Then he answered and spake unto me, saying, This *is* the word of the LORD unto [a]Zerubbabel, saying, [b]Not by might, nor by power, but by my spirit, saith the LORD of hosts.

---

12 [a][Deut. 32:9]; Ps. 33:12; Jer. 10:16
13 [a]Hab. 2:20; Zeph. 1:7 [b]Ps. 68:5

CHAPTER 3

1 [a]Ezra 5:2; Hag. 1:1; Zech. 6:11 [b]1 Chr. 21:1; Job 1:6; Ps. 109:6; [Rev. 12:9, 10]
2 [a]Mark 9:25; [Jude 9] [b][Rom. 8:33] [c]Amos 4:11; Jude 23
3 [a]Ezra 9:15; Is. 64:6
4 [a]Gen. 3:21; Is. 61:10
5 [a]Ex. 29:6
7 [a]Lev. 8:35; Ezek. 44:16 [b]Deut. 17:9, 12 [c]Zech. 4:4
8 [a]Ps. 71:7 [b]Is. 42:1 [c]Is. 11:1; 53:2; Jer. 23:5; 33:15; Zech. 6:12
9 [a][Zech. 4:10; Rev. 5:6] [b]Ps. 118:22 [c]Jer. 31:34; 50:20; Zech. 3:4
10 [a]Zech. 2:11 [b]1 Kin. 4:25; Is. 36:16; Mic. 4:4

CHAPTER 4

1 [a]Zech. 1:9; 2:3 [b]Dan. 8:18
2 [a]Rev. 1:12 [b]Ex. 25:37; [Rev. 4:5]
3 [a]Rev. 11:3, 4
6 [a]Hag. 1:1 [b]Is. 30:1; Hos. 1:7; Hag. 2:4, 5

NKJV

will know that the LORD of hosts has sent Me to you.

12 "And the LORD will [a]take possession of Judah as His inheritance in the Holy Land, and will again choose Jerusalem.

13 [a]"Be silent, all flesh, before the LORD, for He is aroused [b]from His holy habitation!"

Vision of the High Priest

3 Then he showed me [a]Joshua the high priest standing before the Angel of the LORD, and [b]Satan standing at his right hand to oppose him.

2 And the LORD said to Satan, [a]"The LORD rebuke you, Satan! The LORD who [b]has chosen Jerusalem rebuke you! [c]*Is* this not a brand plucked from the fire?"

3 Now Joshua was clothed with [a]filthy garments, and was standing before the Angel.

4 Then He answered and spoke to those who stood before Him, saying, "Take away the filthy garments from him." And to him He said, "See, I have removed your iniquity from you, [a]and I will clothe you with rich robes."

5 And I said, "Let them put a clean [a]turban on his head." So they put a clean turban on his head, and they put the clothes on him. And the Angel of the LORD stood by.

The Coming Branch

6 Then the Angel of the LORD admonished Joshua, saying,

7 "Thus says the LORD of hosts:

'If you will walk in My ways,
And if you will [a]keep My command,
Then you shall also [b]judge My house,
And likewise have charge of My courts;
I will give you places to walk
Among these who [c]stand here.

8 'Hear, O Joshua, the high priest,
You and your companions who sit before you,
For they are [a]a wondrous sign;
For behold, I am bringing forth [b]My Servant the [c]BRANCH.
9 For behold, the stone
That I have laid before Joshua:
[a]Upon the stone *are* [b]seven eyes.
Behold, I will engrave its inscription,'
Says the LORD of hosts,
'And [c]I will remove the iniquity of that land in one day.
10 [a]In that day,' says the LORD of hosts,
'Everyone will invite his neighbor
[b]Under his vine and under his fig tree.' "

Vision of the Lampstand and Olive Trees

4 Now [a]the angel who talked with me came back and wakened me, [b]as a man who is wakened out of his sleep.

2 And he said to me, "What do you see?" So I said, "I am looking, and there *is* [a]a lampstand of solid gold with a bowl on top of it, [b]and on the *stand* seven lamps with seven pipes to the seven lamps.

3 [a]"Two olive trees *are* by it, one at the right of the bowl and the other at its left."

4 So I answered and spoke to the angel who talked with me, saying, "What *are* these, my lord?"

5 Then the angel who talked with me answered and said to me, "Do you not know what these are?" And I said, "No, my lord."

6 So he answered and said to me:

"This *is* the word of the LORD to
[a]Zerubbabel:
[b]'Not by might nor by power, but by My Spirit,'
Says the LORD of hosts.

KJV

7 Who *art* thou, [a]O great mountain? before
Zerubbabel *thou shalt become* a plain: and he
shall bring forth [b]the headstone *thereof* [c]*with*
shoutings, *crying,* Grace, grace unto it.
8 Moreover the word of the LORD came unto
me, saying,
9 The hands of Zerubbabel [a]have laid the
foundation of this house; his hands [b]shall also finish it; and [c]thou shalt know that the [d]LORD of
hosts hath sent me unto you.
10 For who hath despised the day of [a]small
things? for they shall rejoice, and shall see the
plummet in the hand of Zerubbabel *with* those
seven; [b]they *are* the eyes of the LORD, which run
to and fro through the whole earth.
11 Then answered I, and said unto him, What
are these [a]two olive trees upon the right *side* of
the candlestick and upon the left *side* thereof?
12 And I answered again, and said unto him,
What *be these* two olive branches which through
the two golden pipes empty the golden *oil* out of
themselves?
13 And he answered me and said, Knowest
thou not what these *be?* And I said, No, my lord.
14 Then said he, [a]These *are* the two anointed
ones, [b]that stand by the Lord of the whole earth.

Vision of the Flying Scroll

5 Then I turned, and lifted up mine eyes, and
looked, and behold a flying [a]roll.
2 And he said unto me, What seest thou?
And I answered, I see a flying roll; the length
thereof *is* twenty cubits, and the breadth thereof
ten cubits.
3 Then said he unto me, This *is* the [a]curse
that goeth forth over the face of the whole earth:
for every one that stealeth shall be cut off *as* on
this side according to it; and every one that sweareth shall be cut off *as* on that side according to
it.
4 I will bring it forth, saith the LORD of hosts,
and it shall enter into the house of the [a]thief, and
into the house of [b]him that sweareth falsely by
my name: and it shall remain in the midst of his
house, and [c]shall consume it with the timber
thereof and the stones thereof.

Vision of the Woman in a Basket

5 Then the angel that talked with me went
forth, and said unto me, Lift up now thine eyes,
and see what *is* this that goeth forth.
6 And I said, What *is* it? And he said, This
is an ephah that goeth forth. He said moreover,
This *is* their resemblance through all the earth.
7 And, behold, there was lifted up a talent
of lead: and this *is* a woman that sitteth in the
midst of the ephah.
8 And he said, This *is* wickedness. And he
cast it into the midst of the ephah; and he cast
the weight of lead upon the mouth thereof.
9 Then lifted I up mine eyes, and looked,
and, behold, there came out two women, and the
wind *was* in their wings; for they had wings like
the wings of a [a]stork: and they lifted up the ephah
between the earth and the heaven.
10 Then said I to the [a]angel that talked with
me, Whither do these bear the ephah?
11 And he said unto me, To [a]build it an house
in [b]the land of Shinar: and it shall be established,
and set there upon her own base.

7 [a]Ps. 114:4, 6; Is. 40:4; Jer. 51:25; Nah. 1:5; Zech. 14:4, 5; [Matt. 21:21] [b]Ps. 118:22 [c]Ezra 3:10, 11, 13; Ps. 84:11
9 [a]Ezra 3:8–10; 5:16; Hag. 2:18 [b]Ezra 6:14, 15; Zech. 6:12, 13 [c]Zech. 2:9, 11; 6:15 [d][Is. 43:16]; Zech. 2:8
10 [a]Neh. 4:2–4; Amos 7:2, 5; Hag. 2:3 [b]2 Chr. 16:9; Prov. 15:3; Zech. 3:9
11 [a]Zech. 4:3; Rev. 11:4
14 [a]Rev. 11:4 [b]Zech. 3:1–7

CHAPTER 5

1 [a]Jer. 36:2; Ezek. 2:9; Rev. 5:1
3 [a]Mal. 4:6
4 [a]Ex. 20:15; Lev. 19:11 [b]Ex. 20:7; Lev. 19:12; Is. 48:1; Jer. 5:2; Zech. 8:17; Mal. 3:5 [c]Lev. 14:34, 35; Job 18:15
9 [a]Lev. 11:13, 19; Ps. 104:17; Jer. 8:7
10 [a]Zech. 5:5
11 [a]Jer. 29:5, 28 [b]Gen. 10:10; Is. 11:11; Dan. 1:2

*

4:9 Lit. *house*
4:12 Lit. *into the hands of*
5:6 Heb. *ephah,* a measuring container, and so elsewhere
5:8 Lit. *stone*
5:11 Babylon

NKJV

7 'Who *are* you, [a]O great mountain?
Before Zerubbabel *you shall become* a plain!
And he shall bring forth [b]the capstone
[c]With shouts of "Grace, grace to it!" ' "

8 Moreover the word of the LORD came to
me, saying:

9 "The hands of Zerubbabel
[a]Have laid the foundation of this *temple;
His hands [b]shall also finish *it.*
Then [c]you will know
That the [d]LORD of hosts has sent Me to you.
10 For who has despised the day of [a]small things?
For these seven rejoice to see
The plumb line in the hand of Zerubbabel.
[b]They are the eyes of the LORD,
Which scan to and fro throughout the whole earth."

11 Then I answered and said to him, "What
are these [a]two olive trees—at the right of the
lampstand and at its left?"
12 And I further answered and said to him,
"What *are these* two olive branches that *drip* *into
the receptacles of the two gold pipes from which
the golden *oil* drains?"
13 Then he answered me and said, "Do you
not know what these *are?*" And I said, "No, my
lord."
14 So he said, [a]"These *are* the two anointed
ones, [b]who stand beside the Lord of the whole
earth."

Vision of the Flying Scroll

5 Then I turned and raised my eyes, and saw
there a flying [a]scroll.
2 And he said to me, "What do you see?"
So I answered, "I see a flying scroll. Its length *is*
twenty cubits and its width ten cubits."
3 Then he said to me, "This *is* the [a]curse
that goes out over the face of the whole earth:
'Every thief shall be expelled,' according *to* this
side of *the scroll;* and, 'Every perjurer shall be
expelled,' according *to* that side of it."

4 "I will send out *the curse,*" says the LORD of hosts;
"It shall enter the house of the [a]thief
And the house of [b]the one who swears falsely by My name.
It shall remain in the midst of his house
And consume [c]it, with its timber and stones."

Vision of the Woman in a Basket

5 Then the angel who talked with me came
out and said to me, "Lift your eyes now, and see
what this *is* that goes forth."
6 So I asked, "What *is* it?" And he said,
"It *is* a *basket that is going forth." He also
said, "This *is* their resemblance throughout the
earth:
7 "Here *is* a lead disc lifted up, and this *is*
a woman sitting inside the basket";
8 then he said, "This *is* Wickedness!" And
he thrust her down into the basket, and threw
the lead *cover over its mouth.
9 Then I raised my eyes and looked, and
there *were* two women, coming with the wind in
their wings; for they had wings like the wings of
a [a]stork, and they lifted up the basket between
earth and heaven.
10 So I said to the [a]angel who talked with
me, "Where are they carrying the basket?"
11 And he said to me, "To [a]build a house for
it in [b]the land of *Shinar; when it is ready, *the
basket* will be set there on its base."

KJV

Vision of the Four Chariots

6 And I turned, and lifted up mine eyes, and looked, and, behold, there came four chariots out from between two mountains; and the mountains *were* mountains of brass.

2 In the first chariot *were* [a]red horses; and in the second chariot [b]black horses;

3 And in the third chariot white horses; and in the fourth chariot grisled and bay horses.

4 Then I answered [a]and said unto the angel that talked with me, What *are* these, my lord?

5 And the angel answered and said unto me, [a]These *are* the four spirits of the heavens, which go forth from [b]standing before the Lord of all the earth.

6 The black horses which *are* therein go forth into [a]the north country; and the white go forth after them; and the grisled go forth toward the south country.

7 And the bay went forth, and sought to go that they might [a]walk to and fro through the earth: and he said, Get you hence, walk to and fro through the earth. So they walked to and fro through the earth.

8 Then cried he upon me, and spake unto me, saying, Behold, these that go toward the north country have quieted my [a]spirit in the north country.

The Command to Crown Joshua

9 And the word of the LORD came unto me, saying,

10 Take of *them of* the captivity, *even* of Heldai, of Tobijah, and of Jedaiah, which are come from Babylon, and come thou the same day, and go into the house of Josiah the son of Zephaniah;

11 Then take silver and gold, and make [a]crowns, and set *them* upon the head of [b]Joshua the son of Josedech, the high priest;

12 And speak unto him, saying, Thus speaketh the LORD of hosts, saying, Behold [a]the man whose name *is* The [b]BRANCH; and he shall grow up out of his place, [c]and he shall build the temple of the LORD:

13 Even he shall build the temple of the LORD; and he [a]shall bear the glory, and shall sit and rule upon his throne; and [b]he shall be a priest upon his throne: and the counsel of peace shall be between them both.

14 And the crowns shall be to Helem, and to Tobijah, and to Jedaiah, and to Hen the son of Zephaniah, [a]for a memorial in the temple of the LORD.

15 And [a]they *that are* far off shall come and build in the temple of the LORD, and ye shall know that the LORD of hosts hath sent me unto you. And *this* shall come to pass, if ye will diligently obey the voice of the LORD your God.

Obedience Better than Fasting

7 And it came to pass in the fourth year of king Darius, *that* the word of the LORD came unto Zechariah in the fourth *day* of the ninth month, *even* in Chisleu;

2 When they had sent unto the house of God Sherezer and Regem-melech, and their men, to pray before the LORD,

3 *And* to [a]speak unto the priests which *were* in the house of the LORD of hosts, and to the prophets, saying, Should I weep in [b]the fifth month, separating myself, as I have done these so many years?

4 Then came the word of the LORD of hosts unto me, saying,

5 Speak unto all the people of the land, and to the priests, saying, When ye [a]fasted and mourned in the fifth [b]and seventh *month*, [c]even

CHAPTER 6

2 [a]Zech. 1:8; Rev. 6:4 [b]Rev. 6:5
4 [a]Zech. 5:10
5 [a][Ps. 104:4; Heb. 1:7, 14] [b]1 Kin. 22:19; Dan. 7:10; Zech. 4:14; Luke 1:19
6 [a]Jer. 1:14; Ezek. 1:4
7 [a]Gen. 13:17; Gen. 1:10
8 [a]Eccl. 10:4
11 [a]Ex. 29:6 [b]Ezra 3:2; Hag. 1:1; Zech. 3:1
12 [a]John 1:45 [b]Is. 4:2; 11:1; Jer. 23:5; 33:15; Zech. 3:8 [c][Matt. 16:18; Eph. 2:20; Heb. 3:3]
13 [a]Is. 22:24 [b]Ps. 110:4; [Heb. 3:1]
14 [a]Ex. 12:14; Mark 14:9
15 [a]Is. 57:19; [Eph. 2:13]

CHAPTER 7

3 [a]Deut. 17:9; Mal. 2:7 [b]Zech. 8:19
5 [a][Is. 58:1–9] [b]Jer. 41:1 [c]Zech. 1:12

*

6:14 So with MT, Tg., Vg.; Syr. *for Heldai* (cf. v. 10); LXX *for the patient ones*
7:2 Lit. *they*, cf. v. 5 • Or *Sar-Ezer* • Heb. *Bethel*

NKJV

Vision of the Four Chariots

6 Then I turned and raised my eyes and looked, and behold, four chariots *were* coming from between two mountains, and the mountains *were* mountains of bronze.

2 With the first chariot *were* [a]red horses, with the second chariot [b]black horses,

3 with the third chariot white horses, and with the fourth chariot dappled horses—strong *steeds.*

4 Then I answered [a]and said to the angel who talked with me, "What *are* these, my lord?"

5 And the angel answered and said to me, [a]"These *are* four spirits of heaven, who go out from *their* [b]station before the Lord of all the earth.

6 "The one with the black horses is going to [a]the north country, the white are going after them, and the dappled are going toward the south country."

7 Then the strong *steeds* went out, eager to go, that they might [a]walk to and fro throughout the earth. And He said, "Go, walk to and fro throughout the earth." So they walked to and fro throughout the earth.

8 And He called to me, and spoke to me, saying, "See, those who go toward the north country have given rest to My [a]Spirit in the north country."

The Command to Crown Joshua

9 Then the word of the LORD came to me, saying:

10 "Receive *the gift* from the captives—from Heldai, Tobijah, and Jedaiah, who have come from Babylon—and go the same day and enter the house of Josiah the son of Zephaniah.

11 "Take the silver and gold, make [a]an elaborate crown, and set *it* on the head of [b]Joshua the son of Jehozadak, the high priest.

12 "Then speak to him, saying, 'Thus says the LORD of hosts, saying:

"Behold, [a]the Man whose name *is* the
[b]BRANCH!
From His place He shall branch out,
[c]And He shall build the temple of the LORD;
13 Yes, He shall build the temple of the LORD.
He [a]shall bear the glory,
And shall sit and rule on His throne;
So [b]He shall be a priest on His throne,
And the counsel of peace shall be between
them both." '

14 "Now the elaborate crown shall be [a]for a memorial in the temple of the LORD *for Helem, Tobijah, Jedaiah, and Hen the son of Zephaniah.

15 "Even [a]those from afar shall come and build the temple of the LORD. Then you shall know that the LORD of hosts has sent Me to you. And *this* shall come to pass if you diligently obey the voice of the LORD your God."

Obedience Better than Fasting

7 Now in the fourth year of King Darius it came to pass *that* the word of the LORD came to Zechariah, on the fourth day of the ninth month, Chislev,

2 when **the people* sent *Sherezer, with Regem-Melech and his men, *to* *the house of God, to pray before the LORD,

3 *and* to [a]ask the priests who *were* in the house of the LORD of hosts, and the prophets, saying, "Should I weep in [b]the fifth month and fast as I have done for so many years?"

4 Then the word of the LORD of hosts came to me, saying,

5 "Say to all the people of the land, and to the priests: 'When you [a]fasted and mourned in the fifth [b]and seventh *months* [c]during those

KJV

those seventy years, did ye at all fast [d]unto me,
even to me?
6 [a]And when ye did eat, and when ye did
drink, did not ye eat *for yourselves,* and drink *for*
yourselves?
7 *Should* ye not *hear* the words which the
LORD hath cried by the [a]former prophets, when
Jerusalem was inhabited and in prosperity, and
the cities thereof round about her, when *men* inhabited [b]the south and the plain?

Disobedience Resulted in Captivity

8 And the word of the LORD came unto
Zechariah, saying,
9 Thus speaketh the LORD of hosts, saying,
[a]Execute true judgment, and shew mercy and
compassions every man to his brother:
10 And [a]oppress not the widow, nor the
fatherless, the stranger, nor the poor; [b]and let
none of you imagine evil against his brother in
your heart.
11 But they refused to hearken, and [a]pulled
away the shoulder, and [b]stopped their ears, that
they should not hear.
12 Yea, they made their [a]hearts *as* an adamant stone, [b]lest they should hear the law, and
the words which the LORD of hosts hath sent in
his spirit by the former prophets: [c]therefore came
a great wrath from the LORD of hosts.
13 Therefore it is come to pass, *that* as he
cried, and they would not hear; so [a]they cried,
and I would not hear, saith the LORD of hosts:
14 But [a]I scattered them with a whirlwind
among all the nations whom they knew not. Thus
the land was desolate after them, that no man
passed through nor returned: for they laid the
pleasant land desolate.

Jerusalem, Holy City of the Future

8 Again the word of the LORD of hosts came *to*
me, saying,
2 Thus saith the LORD of hosts; [a]I was jealous for Zion with great jealousy, and I was jealous
for her with great fury.
3 Thus saith the LORD; I am [a]returned unto
Zion, and will [b]dwell in the midst of Jerusalem:
and Jerusalem [c]shall be called a city of truth; and
[d]the mountain of the LORD of hosts [e]the holy
mountain.
4 Thus saith the LORD of hosts; [a]There shall
yet old men and old women dwell in the streets
of Jerusalem, and every man with his staff in his
hand for very age.
5 And the streets of the city shall be [a]full
of boys and girls playing in the streets thereof.
6 Thus saith the LORD of hosts; If it be marvellous in the eyes of the remnant of this people
in these days, [a]should it also be marvellous in
mine eyes? saith the LORD of hosts.
7 Thus saith the LORD of hosts; Behold, [a]I
will save my people from the east country, and
from the west country;

5 [d][Rom. 14:6]
6 [a]Deut. 12:7; 14:26; 1 Chr. 29:22
7 [a]Is. 1:16–20; Jer. 7:5, 23; Zech. 1:4 [b]Jer. 17:26
9 [a]Is. 58:6, 7; Jer. 7:28
10 [a]Ex. 22:22; Ps. 72:4; Is. 1:17; Jer. 5:28 [b]Ps. 36:4; Ezek. 38:10; 45:9; Mic. 2:1; Zech. 8:16, 17
11 [a]Neh. 9:29 [b]Jer. 17:23; Acts 7:57
12 [a]Ezek. 11:19 [b]Neh. 9:29, 30 [c]2 Chr. 36:16; Dan. 9:11, 12
13 [a]Prov. 1:24–28; Is. 1:15; Jer. 11:11; Mic. 3:4
14 [a]Lev. 26:33; Deut. 4:27; 28:64; Neh. 1:8

CHAPTER 8
2 [a]Joel 2:18; Nah. 1:2; Zech. 1:14
3 [a]Zech. 1:16 [b]Zech. 2:10, 11 [c]Is. 1:21 [d][Is. 2:2, 3] [e]Jer. 31:23
4 [a]1 Sam. 2:31; Is. 65:20
5 [a]Jer. 30:19, 20
6 [a][Gen. 18:14; Luke 1:37]
7 [a]Ps. 107:3; Is. 11:11; Ezek. 37:21

NKJV

seventy years, did you really fast [d]for Me—for
Me?
6 [a]'When you eat and when you drink, do
you not eat and drink *for yourselves?*
7 *'Should you* not *have obeyed* the words
which the LORD proclaimed through the [a]former
prophets when Jerusalem and the cities around
it were inhabited and prosperous, and [b]the *South
and the Lowland were inhabited?' "

Disobedience Resulted in Captivity

8 Then the word of the LORD came to Zechariah, saying,
9 "Thus says the LORD of hosts:

[a]'Execute true justice,
Show mercy and compassion
Everyone to his brother.
10 [a]Do not oppress the widow or the
fatherless,
The alien or the poor.
[b]Let none of you plan evil in his heart
Against his brother.'

11 "But they refused to heed, [a]shrugged their
shoulders, and [b]stopped their ears so that they
could not hear.
12 "Yes, they made their [a]hearts like flint,
[b]refusing to hear the law and the words which
the LORD of hosts had sent by His Spirit through
the former prophets. [c]Thus great wrath came
from the LORD of hosts.
13 "Therefore it happened, *that* just as He
proclaimed and they would not hear, so [a]they
called out and I would not listen," says the LORD
of hosts.
14 "But [a]I scattered them with a whirlwind
among all the nations which they had not known.
Thus the land became desolate after them, so that
no one passed through or returned; for they made
the pleasant land desolate."

Jerusalem, Holy City of the Future

8 Again the word of the LORD of hosts came,
saying,
2 "Thus says the LORD of hosts:

[a]'I am zealous for Zion with great zeal;
With great fervor I am zealous for her.'

3 "Thus says the LORD:

[a]'I will return to Zion,
And [b]dwell in the midst of Jerusalem.
Jerusalem [c]shall be called the City of
Truth,
[d]The Mountain of the LORD of hosts,
[e]The Holy Mountain.'

4 "Thus says the LORD of hosts:

[a]'Old men and old women shall again sit
In the streets of Jerusalem,
Each one with his staff in his hand
Because of great age.
5 The streets of the city
Shall be [a]full of boys and girls
Playing in its streets.'

6 "Thus says the LORD of hosts:

'If it is marvelous in the eyes of the
remnant of this people in these days,
[a]Will it also be marvelous in My eyes?'
Says the LORD of hosts.

7 "Thus says the LORD of hosts:

'Behold, [a]I will save My people from the
land of the east
And from the land of the west;

---
*7:7 Heb. *Negev*

KJV

8 And I will [a]bring them, and they shall
dwell in the midst of Jerusalem: [b]and they shall
be my people, and I will be their God, [c]in truth
and in righteousness.
9 Thus saith the LORD of hosts; [a]Let your
hands be strong, ye that hear in these days these
words by the mouth of [b]the prophets, which *were*
in [c]the day *that* the foundation of the house of
the LORD of hosts was laid, that the temple might
be built.
10 For before these days there was no [a]hire
for man, nor any hire for beast; neither *was there*
any peace to him that went out or came in because
of the affliction: for I set all men every one against
his neighbour.
11 [a]But now I *will* not *be* unto the residue
of this people as in the former days, saith the LORD
of hosts.
12 [a]For the seed *shall be* prosperous; the vine
shall give her fruit, and [b]the ground shall give
her increase, and [c]the heavens shall give their
dew; and I will cause the remnant of this people
to possess all these *things*.
13 And it shall come to pass, *that* as ye were
[a]a curse among the heathen, O house of Judah,
and house of Israel; so will I save you, and [b]ye
shall be a blessing: fear not, *but* let your hands
be strong.
14 For thus saith the LORD of hosts; [a]As I
thought to punish you, when your fathers provoked me to wrath, saith the LORD of hosts, [b]and
I repented not:
15 So again have I thought in these days to
do well unto Jerusalem and to the house of Judah:
fear ye not.
16 These *are* the things that ye shall [a]do;
[b]Speak ye every man the truth to his neighbour;
execute the judgment of truth and peace in your
gates:
17 [a]And let none of you imagine evil in your
hearts against his neighbour; and love no false
oath: for all these *are things* that I hate, saith the
LORD.
18 And the word of the LORD of hosts came
unto me, saying,
19 Thus saith the LORD of hosts; [a]The fast
of the fourth *month*, [b]and the fast of the fifth,
[c]and the fast of the seventh, [d]and the fast of the
tenth, shall be to the house of Judah [e]joy and gladness, and cheerful feasts; [f]therefore love the truth
and peace.
20 Thus saith the LORD of hosts; *It shall* yet
come to pass, that there shall come people, and
the inhabitants of many cities:

8 [a]Zeph. 3:20; Zech. 10:10 [b][Jer. 30:22; 31:1, 33; Zech. 13:9] [c]Jer. 4:2
9 [a]1 Chr. 22:13; Is. 35:4; Hag. 2:4 [b]Ezra 5:1, 2; 6:14; Zech. 4:9 [c]Hag. 2:18
10 [a]Hag. 1:6, 9
11 [a][Ps. 103:9]; Is. 12:1; Hag. 2:15–19
12 [a]Joel 2:22 [b]Ps. 67:6 [c]Hag. 1:10
13 [a]Jer. 42:18 [b]Gen. 12:2; Ruth 4:11, 12; Is. 19:24, 25; Ezek. 34:26; [Zeph. 3:20]
14 [a]Jer. 31:28 [b][2 Chr. 36:16]
16 [a]Zech. 7:9, 10 [b]Ps. 15:2; [Prov. 12:17–19]; Zech. 8:3; [Eph. 4:25]
17 [a]Prov. 3:29; Jer. 4:14; Zech. 7:10
19 [a]Jer. 52:6 [b]Jer. 52:12 [c]2 Kin. 25:25; Jer. 41:1, 2 [d]Jer. 52:4 [e]Esth. 8:17 [f]Zech. 8:16; Luke 1:74, 75

*8:17 Lit. *his*

NKJV

8 I will [a]bring them *back*,
And they shall dwell in the midst of
Jerusalem.
[b]They shall be My people
And I will be their God,
[c]In truth and righteousness.'

9 "Thus says the LORD of hosts:

[a]'Let your hands be strong,
You who have been hearing in these days
These words by the mouth of [b]the
prophets,
Who *spoke* in [c]the day the foundation was
laid
For the house of the LORD of hosts,
That the temple might be built.
10 For before these days
There were no [a]wages for man nor any
hire for beast;
There was no peace from the enemy for
whoever went out or came in;
For I set all men, everyone, against his
neighbor.

11 [a]'But now I *will* not *treat* the remnant of
this people as in the former days,' says the LORD
of hosts.

12 'For[a] the seed *shall be* prosperous,
The vine shall give its fruit,
[b]The ground shall give her increase,
And [c]the heavens shall give their dew—
I will cause the remnant of this people
To possess all these.
13 And it shall come to pass
That just as you were [a]a curse among the
nations,
O house of Judah and house of Israel,
So I will save you, and [b]you shall be a
blessing.
Do not fear,
Let your hands be strong.'

14 "For thus says the LORD of hosts:

[a]'Just as I determined to punish you
When your fathers provoked Me to
wrath,'
Says the LORD of hosts,
[b]'And I would not relent,
15 So again in these days
I am determined to do good
To Jerusalem and to the house of Judah.
Do not fear.
16 These *are* the things you shall [a]do:
[b]Speak each man the truth to his neighbor;
Give judgment in your gates for truth,
justice, and peace;
17 [a]Let none of you think evil in *your heart
against your neighbor;
And do not love a false oath.
For all these *are things* that I hate,'
Says the LORD."

18 Then the word of the LORD of hosts came
to me, saying,
19 "Thus says the LORD of hosts:

[a]'The fast of the fourth *month*,
[b]The fast of the fifth,
[c]The fast of the seventh,
[d]And the fast of the tenth,
Shall be [e]joy and gladness and cheerful
feasts
For the house of Judah.
[f]Therefore love truth and peace.'

20 "Thus says the LORD of hosts:

'Peoples shall yet come,
Inhabitants of many cities;

KJV

21 And the inhabitants of one *city* shall go
to another, saying, [a]Let us go speedily to pray
before the LORD, and to seek the LORD of hosts: I
will go also.
22 Yea, [a]many people and strong nations
shall come to seek the LORD of hosts in Jerusalem,
and to pray before the LORD.
23 Thus saith the LORD of hosts; In those days
it shall come to pass, that ten men shall [a]take
hold out of all languages of the nations, even shall
[b]take hold of the skirt of him that is a Jew, saying,
We will go with you: for we have heard [c]*that* God
is with you.

Israel Defended Against Enemies

9 The burden of the word of the LORD in the
land of Hadrach, and [a]Damascus *shall be* the
rest thereof: when [b]the eyes of man, as of all the
tribes of Israel, *shall be* toward the LORD.
2 And [a]Hamath also shall border thereby;
[b]Tyrus, and [c]Zidon, though it be very [d]wise.
3 And Tyrus did build herself a strong hold,
and heaped up silver as the dust, and fine gold
as the mire of the streets.
4 Behold, [a]the LORD will cast her out, and
he will smite [b]her power in the sea; and she shall
be devoured with fire.
5 Ashkelon shall see *it,* and fear; Gaza also
shall see it, and be very sorrowful, and [a]Ekron;
for her expectation shall be ashamed; and the
king shall perish from Gaza, and Ashkelon shall
not be inhabited.
6 And a bastard shall dwell [a]in Ashdod, and
I will cut off the pride of the [b]Philistines.
7 And I will take away his blood out of his
mouth, and his abominations from between his
teeth: but he that remaineth, even he, *shall be* for
our God, and he shall be as a governor in Judah,
and Ekron as a Jebusite.
8 And [a]I will encamp about mine house because of the army, because of him that passeth
by, and because of him that returneth: and no oppressor shall pass through them any more: for
now have I seen with mine eyes.

The Coming King
(*Matt. 21:5; John 12:14, 15*)

9 [a]Rejoice greatly, O daughter of Zion;
shout, O daughter of Jerusalem: behold, [b]thy King
cometh unto thee: he *is* just, and having salvation;
lowly, and riding upon an ass, and upon a colt
the foal of an ass.
10 And I [a]will cut off the chariot from
Ephraim, and the horse from Jerusalem, and the
[b]battle bow shall be cut off: and he shall speak
peace unto the heathen: and his [c]dominion *shall
be* from sea *even* to sea, and from the river *even*
to the ends of the earth.

God Will Save His People

11 As for thee also, by the blood of thy covenant I have sent forth thy [a]prisoners out of the
pit wherein *is* no water.

21 [a][Is. 2:2, 3; Mic. 4:1, 2]
22 [a]Is. 60:3; 66:23; [Zech. 14:16–21]
23 [a]Is. 3:6 [b][Is. 45:14] [c]1 Cor. 14:25

CHAPTER 9

1 [a]Is. 17:1; Jer. 23:33 [b]Amos 1:3–5
2 [a]Jer. 49:23 [b]Is. 23; Jer. 25:22; 47:4; Ezek. 26; Amos 1:9, 10 [c]1 Kin. 17:9 [d]Ezek. 28:3
4 [a]Is. 23:1 [b]Ezek. 26:17
5 [a]Zeph. 2:4, 5
6 [a]Amos 1:8; Zeph. 2:4 [b]Ezek. 25:15–17
8 [a][Ps. 34:7]
9 [a]Zeph. 3:14, 15; Zech. 2:10 [b][Ps. 110:1; Is. 9:6, 7; Jer. 23:5, 6]; Matt. 21:5; Mark 11:7, 9; Luke 19:38; John 12:15
10 [a]Hos. 1:7; Mic. 5:10 [b]Ps. 46:9; Is. 2:4; Hos. 2:18; Mic. 4:3 [c]Ps. 72:8
11 [a]Is. 42:7

NKJV

21 The inhabitants of one *city* shall go to
another, saying,
[a]"Let us continue to go and pray before the
LORD,
And seek the LORD of hosts.
I myself will go also."
22 Yes, [a]many peoples and strong nations
Shall come to seek the LORD of hosts in
Jerusalem,
And to pray before the LORD.'

23 "Thus says the LORD of hosts: 'In those
days ten men [a]from every language of the nations
shall [b]grasp the sleeve of a Jewish man, saying,
"Let us go with you, for we have heard [c]*that* God
is with you." ' "

Israel Defended Against Enemies

9 The *burden of the word of the LORD
Against the land of Hadrach,
And [a]Damascus its resting place
(For [b]the eyes of men
And all the tribes of Israel
Are on the LORD);
2 Also *against* [a]Hamath, *which* borders on
it,
And *against* [b]Tyre and [c]Sidon, though
they are very [d]wise.

3 For Tyre built herself a tower,
Heaped up silver like the dust,
And gold like the mire of the streets.
4 Behold, [a]the LORD will cast her out;
He will destroy [b]her power in the sea,
And she will be devoured by fire.
5 Ashkelon shall see *it* and fear;
Gaza also shall be very sorrowful;
And [a]Ekron, for He dried up her
expectation.
The king shall perish from Gaza,
And Ashkelon shall not be inhabited.

6 "A mixed race shall settle [a]in Ashdod,
And I will cut off the pride of the
[b]Philistines.
7 I will take away the blood from his mouth,
And the abominations from between his
teeth.
But he who remains, even he *shall be* for
our God,
And shall be like a leader in Judah,
And Ekron like a Jebusite.
8 [a]I will camp around My house
Because of the army,
Because of him who passes by and him
who returns.
No more shall an oppressor pass through
them,
For now I have seen with My eyes.

The Coming King
(*Matt. 21:5; John 12:14, 15*)

9 "Rejoice [a]greatly, O daughter of Zion!
Shout, O daughter of Jerusalem!
Behold, [b]your King is coming to you;
He *is* just and having salvation,
Lowly and riding on a donkey,
A colt, the foal of a donkey.
10 I [a]will cut off the chariot from Ephraim
And the horse from Jerusalem;
The [b]battle bow shall be cut off.
He shall speak peace to the nations;
His dominion *shall be* [c]'from sea to sea,
And from the River to the ends of the
earth.'

God Will Save His People

11 "As for you also,
Because of the blood of your covenant,
I will set your [a]prisoners free from the
waterless pit.

*
9:1 *oracle, prophecy*

KJV

12 Turn you to the strong hold, [a]ye prisoners
of hope: even to day do I declare *that* I will render
[b]double unto thee;
13 When I have bent Judah for me, filled the
bow with Ephraim, and raised up thy sons, O
Zion, against thy sons, O Greece, and made thee
as the sword of a mighty man.
14 And the LORD shall be seen over them, and
[a]his arrow shall go forth as the lightning: and the
Lord GOD shall blow the trumpet, and shall go
[b]with whirlwinds of the south.
15 The LORD of hosts shall [a]defend them; and
they shall devour, and subdue with sling stones;
and they shall drink, *and* make a noise as through
wine; and they shall be filled like bowls, *and* as
the corners of the altar.
16 And the LORD their God shall [a]save them
in that day as the flock of his people: for [b]*they
shall be as* the stones of a crown, [c]lifted up as
an ensign upon his land.
17 For [a]how great *is* his goodness, and how
great *is* his [b]beauty! [c]corn shall make the young
men cheerful, and new wine the maids.

Restoration of Judah and Israel

10 Ask ye [a]of the LORD [b]rain [c]in the time of
the latter rain; *so* the LORD shall make
bright clouds, and give them showers of rain, to
every one grass in the field.
2 For the [a]idols have spoken vanity, and the
diviners have seen a [b]lie, and have told false
dreams; they [c]comfort in vain: therefore they
went their way as a [d]flock, they were troubled,
[e]because *there was* no shepherd.
3 Mine anger was kindled against the
[a]shepherds, [b]and I punished the goats: for the LORD
of hosts [c]hath visited his flock the house of Judah,
and [d]hath made them as his goodly horse in the
battle.
4 Out of him came forth [a]the corner, out of
him [b]the nail, out of him the battle bow, out of
him every oppressor together.
5 And they shall be as mighty *men,* which
[a]tread down *their enemies* in the mire of the
streets in the battle: and they shall fight, because
the LORD *is* with them, and the riders on horses
shall be confounded.
6 And I will strengthen the house of Judah,
and I will save the house of Joseph, and [a]I will
bring them again to place them; for I [b]have mercy
upon them: and they shall be as though I had not
cast them off: for I *am* the LORD their God, and
[c]will hear them.
7 And *they of* Ephraim shall be like a
mighty *man,* and their [a]heart shall rejoice as
through wine: yea, their children shall see *it,* and
be glad; their heart shall rejoice in the LORD.

12 [a]Is. 49:9; Jer. 17:13; Heb. 6:18–20 [b]Is. 61:7
14 [a]Ps. 18:14; Hab. 3:11 [b]Is. 21:1
15 [a]Is. 37:35; Zech. 12:8
16 [a]Jer. 31:10, 11 [b]Is. 62:3; Mal. 3:17 [c]Is. 11:12
17 [a][Ps. 31:19] [b][Ps. 45:1–16] [c]Joel 3:18

CHAPTER 10

1 [a][Jer. 14:22] [b][Deut. 11:13, 14] [c][Joel 2:23]
2 [a]Jer. 10:8 [b]Jer. 27:9; [Ezek. 13] [c]Job 13:4 [d]Jer. 50:6, 17 [e]Ezek. 34:5–8; Matt. 9:36; Mark 6:34
3 [a]Jer. 25:34–36; Ezek. 34:2; Zech. 11:17 [b]Ezek. 34:17 [c]Luke 1:68 [d]Song 1:9
4 [a]Is. 28:16 [b]Is. 22:23
5 [a]Ps. 18:42
6 [a]Jer. 3:18; Ezek. 37:21 [b]Hos. 1:7; Zech. 1:16 [c]Zech. 13:9
7 [a]Ps. 104:15

NKJV

12 Return to the stronghold,
[a]You prisoners of hope.
Even today I declare
That I will restore [b]double to you.
13 For I have bent Judah, My *bow,*
Fitted the bow with Ephraim,
And raised up your sons, O Zion,
Against your sons, O Greece,
And made you like the sword of a mighty man."

14 Then the LORD will be seen over them,
And [a]His arrow will go forth like lightning.
The Lord GOD will blow the trumpet,
And go [b]with whirlwinds from the south.
15 The LORD of hosts will [a]defend them;
They shall devour and subdue with slingstones.
They shall drink *and* roar as if with wine;
They shall be filled *with blood* like basins,
Like the corners of the altar.
16 The LORD their God will [a]save them in that day,
As the flock of His people.
For [b]they *shall be like* the jewels of a crown,
[c]Lifted like a banner over His land—
17 For [a]how great is *its goodness
And how great *its [b]beauty!
[c]Grain shall make the young men thrive,
And new wine the young women.

Restoration of Judah and Israel

10 Ask [a]the LORD for [b]rain
In [c]the time of the *latter rain.
The LORD will make flashing clouds;
He will give them showers of rain,
Grass in the field for everyone.

2 For the [a]idols* speak delusion;
The diviners envision [b]lies,
And tell false dreams;
They [c]comfort in vain.
Therefore *the people* wend their way like [d]sheep;
They are in trouble [e]because *there is* no shepherd.

3 "My anger is kindled against the [a]shepherds,
[b]And I will punish the goatherds.
For the LORD of hosts [c]will visit His flock,
The house of Judah,
And [d]will make them as His royal horse in the battle.
4 From him comes [a]the cornerstone,
From him [b]the tent peg,
From him the battle bow,
From him every *ruler together.
5 They shall be like mighty men,
Who [a]tread down *their enemies*
In the mire of the streets in the battle.
They shall fight because the LORD is with them,
And the riders on horses shall be put to shame.

6 "I will strengthen the house of Judah,
And I will save the house of Joseph.
[a]I will bring them back,
Because I [b]have mercy on them.
They shall be as though I had not cast them aside;
For I *am* the LORD their God,
And I [c]will hear them.
7 *Those of* Ephraim shall be like a mighty man,
And their [a]heart shall rejoice as if with wine.
Yes, their children shall see *it* and be glad;
Their heart shall rejoice in the LORD.

9:17 Or *His* • Or *His*
10:1 Spring rain
10:2 Heb. *teraphim*
10:4 Or *despot*

KJV

8 I will [a]hiss for them, and gather them; for I have redeemed them: [b]and they shall increase as they have increased.

9 And [a]I will sow them among the people: and they shall [b]remember me in far countries; and they shall live with their children, and turn again.

10 [a]I will bring them again also out of the land of Egypt, and gather them out of Assyria; and I will bring them into the land of Gilead and Lebanon; [b]and *place* shall not be found for them.

11 [a]And he shall pass through the sea with affliction, and shall smite the waves in the sea, and all the deeps of the river shall dry up: and [b]the pride of Assyria shall be brought down, and [c]the sceptre of Egypt shall depart away.

12 And I will strengthen them in the LORD; and [a]they shall walk up and down in his name, saith the LORD.

Desolation of Israel

11 Open [a]thy doors, O Lebanon, that the fire may devour thy cedars.

2 Howl, fir tree; for the [a]cedar is fallen; because the mighty are spoiled: howl, O ye oaks of Bashan; [b]for the forest of the vintage is come down.

3 *There is* a voice of the howling of the [a]shepherds; for their glory is spoiled: a voice of the roaring of young lions; for the pride of Jordan is spoiled.

Prophecy of the Shepherds

4 Thus saith the LORD my God; Feed the flock of the slaughter;

5 Whose possessors slay them, and [a]hold themselves not guilty: and they that sell them [b]say, Blessed *be* the LORD; for I am rich: and their own shepherds pity them [c]not.

6 For I will no more pity the inhabitants of the land, saith the LORD: but, lo, I will deliver the men every one into his neighbour's hand, and into the hand of his king: and they shall smite the land, and out of their hand I will not deliver *them*.

7 And I will feed the flock of slaughter, *even* you, [a]O poor of the flock. And I took unto me two staves; the one I called Beauty, and the other I called Bands; and I fed the flock.

8 Three shepherds also I cut off [a]in one month; and my soul lothed them, and their soul also abhorred me.

9 Then said I, I will not feed you: [a]that that dieth, let it die; and that that is to be cut off, let it be cut off; and let the rest eat every one the flesh of another.

10 And I took my staff, *even* Beauty, and cut it asunder, that I might break my covenant which I had made with all the people.

11 And it was broken in that day: and so [a]the poor of the flock that waited upon me knew that it *was* the word of the LORD.

12 And I said unto them, If ye think good, give *me* my price; and if not, forbear. So they [a]weighed for my price thirty *pieces* of silver.

13 And the LORD said unto me, Cast it unto the [a]potter: a goodly price that I was prised at of them. And I took the thirty *pieces* of silver, and cast them to the potter in the house of the LORD.

14 Then I cut asunder mine other staff, *even* Bands, that I might break the brotherhood between Judah and Israel.

8 [a]Is. 5:26 [b]Is. 49:19; Ezek. 36:37; Zech. 2:4
9 [a]Hos. 2:23 [b]Deut. 30:1
10 [a]Is. 11:11; Hos. 11:11 [b]Is. 49:19, 20
11 [a]Is. 11:15 [b]Is. 14:25; Zeph. 2:13 [c]Ezek. 30:13
12 [a]Mic. 4:5

CHAPTER 11
1 [a]Zech. 10:10
2 [a]Ezek. 31:3 [b]Is. 32:19
3 [a]Jer. 25:34–36
5 [a][Jer. 2:3]; 50:7 [b]Deut. 29:19; Hos. 12:8; 1 Tim. 6:9 [c]Ezek. 34:2, 3
7 [a]Jer. 39:10; Zeph. 3:12; Matt. 11:5
8 [a]Hos. 5:7
9 [a]Jer. 15:2
11 [a]Zeph. 3:12; Matt. 27:50; Mark 15:37; Luke 23:46; Acts 8:32
12 [a]Gen. 37:28; Ex. 21:32; Matt. 26:15; 27:9, 10
13 [a]Matt. 27:3–10; Acts 1:18, 19

*

10:11 The Nile
11:3 Or *flood-plain, thicket*
11:7 So with MT, Tg., Vg.; LXX *for the Canaanites* • Or *Grace* • Or *Unity*
11:11 So with MT, Tg., Vg.; LXX *the Canaanites*

NKJV

8 I will [a]whistle for them and gather them,
For I will redeem them;
[b]And they shall increase as they once increased.

9 "I[a] will sow them among the peoples,
And they shall [b]remember Me in far countries;
They shall live, together with their children,
And they shall return.

10 [a]I will also bring them back from the land of Egypt,
And gather them from Assyria.
I will bring them into the land of Gilead and Lebanon,
[b]Until no *more room* is found for them.

11 [a]He shall pass through the sea with affliction,
And strike the waves of the sea:
All the depths of *the River shall dry up.
Then [b]the pride of Assyria shall be brought down,
And [c]the scepter of Egypt shall depart.

12 "So I will strengthen them in the LORD,
And [a]they shall walk up and down in His name,"
Says the LORD.

Desolation of Israel

11 Open [a]your doors, O Lebanon,
That fire may devour your cedars.
2 Wail, O cypress, for the [a]cedar has fallen,
Because the mighty *trees* are ruined.
Wail, O oaks of Bashan,
[b]For the thick forest has come down.
3 *There is* the sound of wailing [a]shepherds!
For their glory is in ruins.
There is the sound of roaring lions!
For the *pride of the Jordan is in ruins.

Prophecy of the Shepherds

4 Thus says the LORD my God, "Feed the flock for slaughter,

5 "whose owners slaughter them and [a]feel no guilt; those who sell them [b]say, 'Blessed be the LORD, for I am rich'; and their shepherds do [c]not pity them.

6 "For I will no longer pity the inhabitants of the land," says the LORD. "But indeed I will give everyone into his neighbor's hand and into the hand of his king. They shall attack the land, and I will not deliver *them* from their hand."

7 So I fed the flock for slaughter, *in particular [a]the poor of the flock. I took for myself two staffs: the one I called *Beauty, and the other I called *Bonds; and I fed the flock.

8 I dismissed the three shepherds [a]in one month. My soul loathed them, and their soul also abhorred me.

9 Then I said, "I will not feed you. [a]Let what is dying die, and what is perishing perish. Let those that are left eat each other's flesh."

10 And I took my staff, Beauty, and cut it in two, that I might break the covenant which I had made with all the peoples.

11 So it was broken on that day. Thus [a]the* poor of the flock, who were watching me, knew that it *was* the word of the LORD.

12 Then I said to them, "If it is agreeable to you, give *me* my wages; and if not, refrain." So they [a]weighed out for my wages thirty *pieces* of silver.

13 And the LORD said to me, "Throw it to the [a]potter"—that princely price they set on me. So I took the thirty *pieces* of silver and threw them into the house of the LORD for the potter.

14 Then I cut in two my other staff, Bonds, that I might break the brotherhood between Judah and Israel.

KJV

15 And the LORD said unto me, [a]Take unto
thee yet the instruments of a foolish shepherd.
16 For, lo, I will raise up a shepherd in the
land, *which* shall not visit those that be cut off,
neither shall seek the young one, nor heal that
that is broken, nor feed that that standeth still:
but he shall eat the flesh of the fat, and tear their
claws in [a]pieces.
17 [a]Woe to the idol shepherd that leaveth the
flock! the sword *shall be* upon his arm, and upon
his right eye: his arm shall be clean dried up, and
his right eye shall be utterly darkened.

The Coming Deliverance of Judah

12 The burden of the word of the LORD for Israel, saith the LORD, [a]which stretcheth forth
the heavens, and layeth the foundation of the
earth, and [b]formeth the spirit of man within him.
2 Behold, I will make Jerusalem [a]a cup of
trembling unto all the people round about, when
they shall be in the siege both against Judah *and*
against Jerusalem.
3 [a]And in that day will I make Jerusalem
[b]a burdensome stone for all people: all that burden themselves with it shall be cut in pieces,
though all the people of the earth be gathered together against it.
4 In that day, saith the LORD, [a]I will smite
every horse with astonishment, and his rider with
madness: and I will open mine eyes upon the
house of Judah, and will smite every horse of the
people with blindness.
5 And the governors of Judah shall say in
their heart, The inhabitants of Jerusalem *shall be*
my strength in the LORD of hosts their God.
6 In that day will I make the governors of
Judah [a]like an hearth of fire among the wood,
and like a torch of fire in a sheaf; and they shall
devour all the people round about, on the right
hand and on the left: and Jerusalem shall be
inhabited again in her own place, *even* in Jerusalem.
7 The LORD also shall save the tents of Judah first, that the glory of the house of David and
the glory of the inhabitants of Jerusalem do not
magnify *themselves* against Judah.
8 In that day shall the LORD defend the inhabitants of Jerusalem; and he that is feeble
among them at that day shall be as David; and
the house of David *shall be* as God, as the angel
of the LORD before them.
9 And it shall come to pass in that day, *that*
I will seek to [a]destroy all the nations that come
against Jerusalem.

Mourning for the Pierced One

10 [a]And I will pour upon the house of David,
and upon the inhabitants of Jerusalem, the spirit
of grace and of supplications: and they shall [b]look
upon me whom they have pierced, and they shall
mourn for him, [c]as one mourneth for *his* only *son*,
and shall be in bitterness for him, as one that is
in bitterness for *his* firstborn.
11 In that day shall there be a great [a]mourn-
ing in Jerusalem, [b]as the mourning of Hadadrim-
mon in the valley of Megiddon.
12 [a]And the land shall mourn, every family
apart; the family of the house of David apart, and
their wives apart; the family of the house of [b]Na-
than apart, and their wives apart;
13 The family of the house of Levi apart, and
their wives apart; the family of Shimei apart, and
their wives apart;
14 All the families that remain, every family
apart, and their wives apart.

Idolatry Cut Off

13 In that [a]day there shall be [b]a fountain
opened to the house of David and to the

---

15 [a]Is. 56:11; Ezek. 34:2
16 [a]Ezek. 34:1–10; Mic. 3:1–3
17 [a]Jer. 23:1; Ezek. 34:2; Zech. 10:2; 11:15; John 10:12, 13

CHAPTER 12

1 [a]Is. 42:5; 44:24 [b]Num. 16:22; [Eccl. 12:7; Is. 57:16]; Heb. 12:9
2 [a]Is. 51:17
3 [a]Zech. 12:4, 6, 8; 13:1 [b]Matt. 21:44
4 [a]Ps. 76:6; Ezek. 38:4
6 [a]Is. 10:17, 18; Obad. 18; Zech. 11:1
9 [a]Hag. 2:22
10 [a]Jer. 31:9; 50:4; Ezek. 39:29; [Joel 2:28, 29] [b]John 19:34, 37; 20:27; [Rev. 1:7] [c]Jer. 6:26; Amos 8:10
11 [a][Matt. 24:30]; Acts 2:37; [Rev. 1:7] [b]2 Kin. 23:39
12 [a][Matt. 24:30; Rev. 1:7] [b]Luke 3:31

CHAPTER 13

1 [a]Acts 10:43; [Rev. 21:6, 7] [b]Ps. 36:9; [Heb. 9:14; 1 John 1:7]

*

12:1 *oracle, prophecy*
12:11 Heb. *Megiddon*

NKJV

15 And the LORD said to me, [a]"Next, take for
yourself the implements of a foolish shepherd.
16 "For indeed I will raise up a shepherd in
the land *who* will not care for those who are cut
off, nor seek the young, nor heal those that are
broken, nor feed those that still stand. But he will
eat the flesh of the fat and tear their hooves in
[a]pieces.

17 "Woe[a] to the worthless shepherd,
Who leaves the flock!
A sword *shall be* against his arm
And against his right eye;
His arm shall completely wither,
And his right eye shall be totally blinded."

The Coming Deliverance of Judah

12 The *burden of the word of the LORD
against Israel. Thus says the LORD, [a]who
stretches out the heavens, lays the foundation of
the earth, and [b]forms the spirit of man within him:
2 "Behold, I will make Jerusalem [a]a cup of
drunkenness to all the surrounding peoples, when
they lay siege against Judah and Jerusalem.
3 [a]"And it shall happen in that day that I
will make Jerusalem [b]a very heavy stone for all
peoples; all who would heave it away will surely
be cut in pieces, though all nations of the earth
are gathered against it.
4 "In that day," says the LORD, [a]"I will strike
every horse with confusion, and its rider with
madness; I will open My eyes on the house of
Judah, and will strike every horse of the peoples
with blindness.
5 "And the governors of Judah shall say in
their heart, 'The inhabitants of Jerusalem *are* my
strength in the LORD of hosts, their God.'
6 "In that day I will make the governors of
Judah [a]like a firepan in the woodpile, and like a
fiery torch in the sheaves; they shall devour all
the surrounding peoples on the right hand and
on the left, but Jerusalem shall be inhabited again
in her own place—Jerusalem.
7 "The LORD will save the tents of Judah
first, so that the glory of the house of David and
the glory of the inhabitants of Jerusalem shall not
become greater than that of Judah.
8 "In that day the LORD will defend the inhabitants of Jerusalem; the one who is feeble
among them in that day shall be like David, and
the house of David *shall be* like God, like the Angel of the LORD before them.
9 "It shall be in that day *that* I will seek to
[a]destroy all the nations that come against Jerusalem.

Mourning for the Pierced One

10 [a]"And I will pour on the house of David
and on the inhabitants of Jerusalem the Spirit of
grace and supplication; then they will [b]look on
Me whom they pierced. Yes, they will mourn for
Him [c]as one mourns for *his* only *son*, and grieve
for Him as one grieves for a firstborn.
11 "In that day there shall be a great [a]mourn-
ing in Jerusalem, [b]like the mourning at Hadad
Rimmon in the plain of *Megiddo.
12 [a]"And the land shall mourn, every family
by itself: the family of the house of David by itself,
and their wives by themselves; the family of the
house of [b]Nathan by itself, and their wives by
themselves;
13 "the family of the house of Levi by itself,
and their wives by themselves; the family of
Shimei by itself, and their wives by themselves;
14 "all the families that remain, every family
by itself, and their wives by themselves.

Idolatry Cut Off

13 "In that [a]day [b]a fountain shall be opened
for the house of David and for the inhab-

KJV

inhabitants of Jerusalem for sin and for [c]uncleanness.

2 And it shall come to pass in that day, saith the LORD of hosts, *that* I will [a]cut off the names of the idols out of the land, and they shall no more be remembered: and also I will cause [b]the prophets and the unclean spirit to pass out of the land.

3 And it shall come to pass, *that* when any shall yet prophesy, then his father and his mother that begat him shall say unto him, Thou shalt [a]not live; for thou speakest lies in the name of the LORD: and his father and his mother that begat him [b]shall thrust him through when he prophesieth.

4 And it shall come to pass in that day, *that* [a]the prophets shall be ashamed every one of his vision, when he hath prophesied; neither shall they wear [b]a rough garment to deceive:

5 [a]But he shall say, I *am* no prophet, I *am* an husbandman; for man taught me to keep cattle from my youth.

6 And *one* shall say unto him, What *are* these wounds in thine hands? Then he shall answer, *Those* with which I was wounded *in* the house of my friends.

The Shepherd Savior

7 Awake, O sword, against [a]my shepherd, and against the man [b]*that is* my fellow, saith the LORD of hosts: [c]smite the shepherd, and the sheep shall be scattered: and I will turn mine hand upon [d]the little ones.

8 And it shall come to pass, *that* in all the land, saith the LORD, [a]two parts therein shall be cut off *and* die; [b]but the third shall be left therein.

9 And I will bring the third part [a]through the fire, and will [b]refine them as silver is refined, and will try them as gold is tried: [c]they shall call on my name, and I will hear them: [d]I will say, It *is* my people: and they shall say, The LORD *is* my God.

The Day of the LORD
(cf. Ezek. 38; 39; Mark 13; Rev. 20—22)

14 Behold, [a]the day of the LORD cometh, and thy spoil shall be divided in the midst of thee.

2 For [a]I will gather all nations against Jerusalem to battle; and the city shall be taken, and the houses rifled, and the women ravished; and half of the city shall go forth into captivity, and the residue of the people shall not be cut off from the city.

3 Then shall the LORD go forth, and fight against those nations, as when he fought in the day of battle.

4 And his feet shall stand in that day [a]upon the mount of Olives, which *is* before Jerusalem on the east, and the mount of Olives shall cleave in the midst thereof toward the east and toward the west, [b]*and there shall be* a very great valley; and half of the mountain shall remove toward the north, and half of it toward the south.

5 And ye shall flee *to* the valley of the mountains; for the valley of the mountains shall

---

1 [c]Num. 19:17; Is. 4:4; Ezek. 36:25
2 [a]Ex. 23:13; Hos. 2:17 [b]Jer. 23:14, 15; 2 Pet. 2:1
3 [a]Deut. 18:20; [Ezek. 14:9] [b]Deut. 13:6–11; [Matt. 10:37]
4 [a]Jer. 6:15; 8:9; [Mic. 3:6, 7] [b]2 Kin. 1:8; Is. 20:2; Matt. 3:4
5 [a]Amos 7:14
7 [a]Is. 40:11; Ezek. 34:23, 24; 37:24; Mic. 5:2, 4 [b][John 10:30] [c]Matt. 26:31, 56, 67; Mark 14:27; 1 Pet. 5:4; Rev. 7:16, 17 [d]Luke 12:32
8 [a]Is. 6:13; Ezek. 5:2, 4, 12 [b][Rom. 11:5]
9 [a]Is. 48:10; Ezek. 20:38; Mal. 3:3 [b]1 Pet. 1:6 [c]Ps. 50:15; Zeph. 3:9; [Zech. 12:10] [d]Jer. 30:22; Hos. 2:23

CHAPTER 14

1 [a][Is. 13:6, 9; Joel 2:1; Mal. 4:1]
2 [a]Joel 3:2; Zech. 12:2, 3
4 [a]Ezek. 11:23; Acts 1:9–12 [b]Joel 3:12

NKJV

itants of Jerusalem, for sin and for [c]uncleanness.

2 "It shall be in that day," says the LORD of hosts, "*that* I will [a]cut off the names of the idols from the land, and they shall no longer be remembered. I will also cause [b]the prophets and the unclean spirit to depart from the land.

3 "It shall come to pass *that* if anyone still prophesies, then his father and mother who begot him will say to him, 'You shall [a]not live, because you have spoken lies in the name of the LORD.' And his father and mother who begot him [b]shall thrust him through when he prophesies.

4 "And it shall be in that day *that* [a]every prophet will be ashamed of his vision when he prophesies; they will not wear [b]a robe of coarse hair to deceive.

5 [a]"But he will say, 'I *am* no prophet, I *am* a farmer; for a man taught me to keep cattle from my youth.'

6 "And *one* will say to him, 'What are these wounds between your *arms?' Then he will answer, '*Those* with which I was wounded in the house of my friends.'

The Shepherd Savior

7 "Awake, O sword, against [a]My
Shepherd,
Against the Man [b]who is My Companion,"
Says the LORD of hosts.
[c]"Strike the Shepherd,
And the sheep will be scattered;
Then I will turn My hand against [d]the little
ones.
8 And it shall come to pass in all the
land,"
Says the LORD,
"*That* [a]two-thirds in it shall be cut off *and*
die,
[b]But *one*-third shall be left in it:
9 I will bring the *one*-third [a]through the
fire,
Will [b]refine them as silver is refined,
And test them as gold is tested.
[c]They will call on My name,
And I will answer them.
[d]I will say, 'This *is* My people';
And each one will say, 'The LORD *is* my
God.'"

The Day of the LORD
(cf. Ezek. 38; 39; Mark 13; Rev. 20—22)

14 Behold, [a]the day of the LORD is
coming,
And your spoil will be divided in your
midst.
2 For [a]I will gather all the nations to battle
against Jerusalem;
The city shall be taken,
The houses rifled,
And the women ravished.
Half of the city shall go into captivity,
But the remnant of the people shall not
be cut off from the city.

3 Then the LORD will go forth
And fight against those nations,
As He fights in the day of battle.
4 And in that day His feet will stand [a]on
the Mount of Olives,
Which faces Jerusalem on the east.
And the Mount of Olives shall be split in
two,
From east to west,
[b]*Making* a very large valley;
Half of the mountain shall move toward
the north
And half of it toward the south.

5 Then you shall flee *through* My mountain
valley,

***13:6** Or *hands*

KJV

reach unto Azal: yea, ye shall flee, like as ye fled
from before the [a]earthquake in the days of Uzziah
king of Judah: [b]and the LORD my God shall come,
and [c]all the saints with thee.
6 And it shall come to pass in that day, *that*
the light shall not be clear, *nor* dark:
7 But it shall be one day [a]which shall be
known to the LORD, not day, nor night: but it shall
come to pass, *that* at [b]evening time it shall be
light.
8 And it shall be in that day, *that* living [a]wa-
ters shall go out from Jerusalem; half of them
toward the former sea, and half of them toward
the hinder sea: in summer and in winter shall it
be.
9 And the LORD shall be [a]king over all the
earth: in that day shall there be [b]one LORD, and
his name one.
10 All the land shall be turned as a plain from
Geba to Rimmon south of Jerusalem: and it shall
be lifted up, and [a]inhabited in her place, from Benjamin's gate unto the place of the first gate, unto
the corner gate, [b]and *from* the tower of Hananeel
unto the king's winepresses.
11 And *men* shall dwell in it, and there shall
be [a]no more utter destruction; [b]but Jerusalem
shall be safely inhabited.
12 And this shall be the plague wherewith
the LORD will smite all the people that have fought
against Jerusalem; Their flesh shall consume
away while they stand upon their feet, and their
eyes shall consume away in their holes, and their
tongue shall consume away in their mouth.
13 And it shall come to pass in that day, *that*
[a]a great tumult from the LORD shall be among
them; and they shall lay hold every one on the
hand of his neighbour, and [b]his hand shall rise
up against the hand of his neighbour.
14 And Judah also shall fight at Jerusalem;
[a]and the wealth of all the heathen round about
shall be gathered together, gold, and silver, and
apparel, in great abundance.
15 And [a]so shall be the plague of the horse,
of the mule, of the camel, and of the ass, and of
all the beasts that shall be in these tents, as this
plague.

The Nations Worship the King

16 And it shall come to pass, *that* every one
that is left of all the nations which came against
Jerusalem shall even [a]go up from year to year to
[b]worship the King, the LORD of hosts, and to keep
[c]the feast of tabernacles.
17 [a]And it shall be, *that* whoso will not come
up of *all* the families of the earth unto Jerusalem

5 [a]Is. 29:6; Amos 1:1 [b][Ps. 96:13]; Is. 66:15, 16; Matt. 24:30, 31; 25:31; Jude 14 [c]Joel 3:11
7 [a]Matt. 24:36 [b]Is. 30:26
8 [a]Ezek. 47:1–12; Joel 3:18; [John 7:38; Rev. 22:1, 2]
9 [a][Jer. 23:5, 6; Rev. 11:15] [b][Eph. 4:5, 6]; Deut. 6:4
10 [a]Jer. 30:18; Zech. 12:6 [b]Neh. 3:1; Jer. 31:38
11 [a]Jer. 31:40 [b]Jer. 23:6; Ezek. 34:25–28; Hos. 2:18
13 [a]1 Sam. 14:15, 20 [b]Judg. 7:22; 2 Chr. 20:23; Ezek. 38:21
14 [a]Ezek. 39:10, 17
15 [a]Zech. 14:12
16 [a][Is. 2:2, 3; 60:6–9; 66:18–21; Mic. 4:1, 2] [b]Is. 27:13 [c]Lev. 23:34–44; Neh. 8:14; Hos. 12:9; John 7:2
17 [a]Is. 60:12

NKJV

For the mountain valley shall reach to
Azal.
Yes, you shall flee
As you fled from the [a]earthquake
In the days of Uzziah king of Judah.

[b]Thus the LORD my God will come,
And [c]all the saints with *You.

6 It shall come to pass in that day
That there will be no light;
The lights will diminish.
7 It shall be one day
[a]Which is known to the LORD—
Neither day nor night.
But at [b]evening time it shall happen
That it will be light.

8 And in that day it shall be
That living [a]waters shall flow from
Jerusalem,
Half of them toward the eastern sea
And half of them toward the western
sea;
In both summer and winter it shall occur.
9 And the LORD shall be [a]King over all the
earth.
In that day it shall be—
[b]"The LORD *is* one,"
And His name one.

10 All the land shall be turned into a plain
from Geba to Rimmon south of Jerusalem. *Jeru-
salem shall be raised up and [a]inhabited in her
place from Benjamin's Gate to the place of the
First Gate and the Corner Gate, [b]and *from* the
Tower of Hananel to the king's winepresses.

11 *The people* shall dwell in it;
And [a]no longer shall there be utter
destruction,
[b]But Jerusalem shall be safely inhabited.

12 And this shall be the plague with which
the LORD will strike all the people who fought
against Jerusalem:

Their flesh shall dissolve while they stand
on their feet,
Their eyes shall dissolve in their sockets,
And their tongues shall dissolve in their
mouths.

13 It shall come to pass in that day
That [a]a great panic from the LORD will
be among them.
Everyone will seize the hand of his
neighbor,
And raise [b]his hand against his neighbor's
hand;
14 Judah also will fight at Jerusalem.
[a]And the wealth of all the surrounding
nations
Shall be gathered together:
Gold, silver, and apparel in great
abundance.

15 [a]Such also shall be the plague
On the horse *and* the mule,
On the camel and the donkey,
And on all the cattle that will be in those
camps.
So *shall* this plague *be*.

The Nations Worship the King

16 And it shall come to pass *that* everyone
who is left of all the nations which came against
Jerusalem shall [a]go up from year to year to [b]wor-
ship the King, the LORD of hosts, and to keep [c]the
Feast of Tabernacles.
17 [a]And it shall be *that* whichever of the
families of the earth do not come up to Jerusalem

*

14:5 Or *you;* LXX, Tg., Vg. *Him*
14:10 Lit. *She*

KJV

to worship the King, the LORD of hosts, even upon
them shall be no rain.
18 And if the family of [a]Egypt go not up, and
come not, [b]that *have* no *rain;* there shall be the
plague, wherewith the LORD will smite the
heathen that come not up to keep the feast of
tabernacles.
19 This shall be the punishment of Egypt, and
the punishment of all nations that come not up
to keep the feast of tabernacles.
20 In that day shall there be upon the bells
of the horses, [a]HOLINESS UNTO THE LORD;
and the [b]pots in the LORD's house shall be like
the bowls before the altar.
21 Yea, every pot in Jerusalem and in Judah
shall be holiness unto the LORD of hosts: and all
they that sacrifice shall come and take of them,
and seethe therein: and in that day there shall
be no more the [a]Canaanite [b]in the house of the
LORD of hosts.

18 [a]Is. 19:21 [b]Deut. 11:10 **20** [a]Ex. 28:36; 39:30; Is. 23:18; Jer. 2:3 [b]Ezek. 46:20 **21** [a]Is. 35:8; Ezek. 44:9; Joel 3:17; Rev. 21:27; 22:15 [b][Eph. 2:19–22]

*______

14:21 Or *on every pot . . . shall be engraved "HOLINESS TO THE LORD OF HOSTS"*

NKJV

to worship the King, the LORD of hosts, on them
there will be no rain.
18 If the family of [a]Egypt will not come up
and enter in, [b]they *shall have* no *rain;* they shall
receive the plague with which the LORD strikes
the nations who do not come up to keep the Feast
of Tabernacles.
19 This shall be the punishment of Egypt and
the punishment of all the nations that do not come
up to keep the Feast of Tabernacles.
20 In that day [a]"HOLINESS TO THE LORD"
shall be *engraved* on the bells of the horses. The
[b]pots in the LORD's house shall be like the bowls
before the altar.
21 Yes, *every pot in Jerusalem and Judah
shall be holiness to the LORD of hosts. Everyone
who sacrifices shall come and take them and cook
in them. In that day there shall no longer be a
[a]Canaanite [b]in the house of the LORD of hosts.

KJV

THE BOOK OF

MALACHI

1 The burden of the word of the LORD to Israel by Malachi.

Israel Beloved of God

2 [a]I have loved you, saith the LORD. Yet ye say, Wherein hast thou loved us? *Was* not Esau Jacob's brother? saith the LORD: yet [b]I loved Jacob,

3 And I hated Esau, and [a]laid his mountains and his heritage waste for the dragons of the wilderness.

4 Whereas Edom saith, We are impoverished, but we will return and build the desolate places; thus saith the LORD of hosts, They shall build, but I will [a]throw down; and they shall call them, The border of wickedness, and, The people against whom the LORD hath indignation for ever.

5 And your eyes shall see, and ye shall say, [a]The LORD will be magnified from the border of Israel.

Polluted Offerings

6 A son [a]honoureth *his* father, and a servant his master: [b]if then I *be* a father, where *is* mine honour? and if I *be* a master, where *is* my fear? saith the LORD of hosts unto you, O priests, that despise my name. [c]And ye say, Wherein have we despised thy name?

7 Ye offer [a]polluted bread upon mine altar; and ye say, Wherein have we polluted thee? In that ye say, [b]The table of the LORD *is* contemptible.

8 And [a]if ye offer the blind for sacrifice, *is it* not evil? and if ye offer the lame and sick, *is it* not evil? offer it now unto thy governor; will he be pleased with thee, or [b]accept thy person? saith the LORD of hosts.

9 And now, I pray you, beseech God that he will be gracious unto us: [a]this hath been by your means: will he regard your persons? saith the LORD of hosts.

CHAPTER 1

2 [a]Deut. 4:37; 7:8; 23:5; Is. 41:8, 9; [Jer. 31:3]; John 15:12 [b]Rom. 9:13
3 [a]Jer. 49:18; Ezek. 35:9, 15
4 [a]Jer. 49:16–18
5 [a]Ps. 35:27; Mic. 5:4
6 [a][Ex. 20:12]; Prov. 30:11, 17; [Matt. 15:4–8; Eph. 6:2, 3] [b][Is. 63:16; 64:8]; Jer. 31:9; Luke 6:46 [c]Mal. 2:14
7 [a]Deut. 15:21 [b]Ezek. 41:22
8 [a]Lev. 22:22; Deut. 15:19–23 [b][Job 42:8]
9 [a]Hos. 13:9

*———

1:1 *oracle, prophecy*

NKJV

THE BOOK OF

MALACHI

1 The *burden of the word of the LORD to Israel by Malachi.

Israel Beloved of God

2 "I[a] have loved you," says the LORD.
"Yet you say, 'In what way have You loved us?'
Was not Esau Jacob's brother?"
Says the LORD.
"Yet [b]Jacob I have loved;
3 But Esau I have hated,
And [a]laid waste his mountains and his heritage
For the jackals of the wilderness."

4 Even though Edom has said,
"We have been impoverished,
But we will return and build the desolate places,"

Thus says the LORD of hosts:

"They may build, but I will [a]throw down;
They shall be called the Territory of Wickedness,
And the people against whom the LORD will have indignation forever.
5 Your eyes shall see,
And you shall say,
[a]'The LORD is magnified beyond the border of Israel.'

Polluted Offerings

6 "A son [a]honors *his* father,
And a servant *his* master.
[b]If then I am the Father,
Where *is* My honor?
And if I *am* a Master,
Where *is* My reverence?
Says the LORD of hosts
To you priests who despise My name.
[c]Yet you say, 'In what way have we despised Your name?'

7 "You offer [a]defiled food on My altar,
But say,
'In what way have we defiled You?'
By saying,
[b]'The table of the LORD is contemptible.'
8 And [a]when you offer the blind as a sacrifice,
Is it not evil?
And when you offer the lame and sick,
Is it not evil?
Offer it then to your governor!
Would he be pleased with you?
Would he [b]accept you favorably?"
Says the LORD of hosts.

9 "But now entreat God's favor,
That He may be gracious to us.
[a]*While* this is being *done* by your hands,
Will He accept you favorably?"
Says the LORD of hosts.

KJV

10 Who *is there* even among you that would
shut the doors *for nought?* [a]neither do ye kindle
fire on mine altar for nought. I have no pleasure
in you, saith the LORD of hosts, [b]neither will I accept an offering at your hand.
11 For [a]from the rising of the sun even unto
the going down of the same my name *shall be*
great [b]among the Gentiles; [c]and in every place
[d]incense *shall be* offered unto my name, and a
pure offering: [e]for my name *shall be* great among
the heathen, saith the LORD of hosts.
12 But ye have profaned it, in that ye say,
[a]The table of the LORD *is* polluted; and the fruit
thereof, *even* his meat, *is* contemptible.
13 Ye said also, Behold, what a [a]weariness
is it! and ye have snuffed at it, saith the LORD of
hosts; and ye brought *that which was* torn, and
the lame, and the sick; thus ye brought an offering: [b]should I accept this of your hand? saith the
LORD.
14 But cursed *be* [a]the deceiver, which hath
in his flock a male, and voweth, and sacrificeth
unto the Lord a [b]corrupt thing: for [c]I *am* a great
King, saith the LORD of hosts, and my name *is*
dreadful among the heathen.

Corrupt Priests

2 And now, O ye [a]priests, this commandment
is for you.
2 [a]If ye will not hear, and if ye will not lay
it to heart, to give glory unto my name, saith the
LORD of hosts, I will even send a curse upon you,
and I will curse your blessings: yea, I have cursed
them [b]already, because ye do not lay *it* to heart.
3 Behold, I will corrupt your seed, and
spread [a]dung upon your faces, *even* the dung of
your solemn feasts; and *one* shall [b]take you away
with it.
4 And ye shall know that I have sent this
commandment unto you, that my covenant might
be with Levi, saith the LORD of hosts.
5 [a]My covenant was with him of life and
peace; and I gave them to him [b]*for* the fear wherewith he feared me, and was afraid before my
name.
6 [a]The law of truth was in his mouth, and
iniquity was not found in his lips: he walked with
me in peace and equity, and did [b]turn many away
from iniquity.
7 [a]For the priest's lips should keep knowledge, and they should seek the law at his mouth:
[b]for he *is* the messenger of the LORD of hosts.
8 But ye are departed out of the way; ye

10 [a]1 Cor. 9:13 [b]Is. 1:11 **11** [a]Is. 59:19 [b]Is. 60:3, 5 [c]1 Tim. 2:8 [d]Rev. 8:3 [e]Is. 66:18, 19 **12** [a]Mal. 1:7 **13** [a]Is. 43:22 [b]Lev. 22:20 **14** [a]Mal. 1:8 [b]Lev. 22:18–20 [c]Ps. 47:2

CHAPTER 2

1 [a]Mal. 1:6 **2** [a][Lev. 26:14, 15; Deut. 28:15] [b]Mal. 3:9 **3** [a]Ex. 29:14 [b]1 Kin. 14:10 **5** [a]Num. 25:12; Ezek. 34:25 [b]Deut. 33:9 **6** [a]Deut. 33:10 [b]Jer. 23:22; [James 5:20] **7** [a]Num. 27:21; Deut. 17:8–11; Jer. 18:18 [b][Gal. 4:14]

*

1:12 So with Bg.; MT *Lord*
2:6 Or *True instruction*

NKJV

10 "Who *is there* even among you who would
shut the doors,
[a]So that you would not kindle fire *on* My
altar in vain?
I have no pleasure in you,"
Says the LORD of hosts,
[b]"Nor will I accept an offering from your
hands.
11 For [a]from the rising of the sun, even to
its going down,
My name *shall be* great [b]among the
Gentiles;
[c]In every place [d]incense *shall be* offered
to My name,
And a pure offering;
[e]For My name shall be great among the
nations,"
Says the LORD of hosts.

12 "But you profane it,
In that you say,
[a]'The table of the *LORD is defiled;
And its fruit, its food, *is* contemptible.'
13 You also say,
'Oh, what a [a]weariness!'
And you sneer at it,"
Says the LORD of hosts.
"And you bring the stolen, the lame, and
the sick;
Thus you bring an offering!
[b]Should I accept this from your hand?"
Says the LORD.
14 "But cursed *be* [a]the deceiver
Who has in his flock a male,
And takes a vow,
But sacrifices to the Lord [b]what is
blemished—
For [c]I *am* a great King,"
Says the LORD of hosts,
"And My name *is to be* feared among the
nations.

Corrupt Priests

2 "And now, O [a]priests, this commandment
is for you.
2 [a]If you will not hear,
And if you will not take *it* to heart,
To give glory to My name,"
Says the LORD of hosts,
"I will send a curse upon you,
And I will curse your blessings.
Yes, I have cursed them [b]already,
Because you do not take *it* to heart.

3 "Behold, I will rebuke your descendants
And spread [a]refuse on your faces,
The refuse of your solemn feasts;
And *one* will [b]take you away with it.
4 Then you shall know that I have sent this
commandment to you,
That My covenant with Levi may
continue,"
Says the LORD of hosts.
5 "My[a] covenant was with him, *one* of life
and peace,
And I gave them to him [b]*that he might*
fear Me;
So he feared Me
And was reverent before My name.
6 [a]The* law of truth was in his mouth,
And injustice was not found on his lips.
He walked with Me in peace and equity,
And [b]turned many away from iniquity.

7 "For[a] the lips of a priest should keep
knowledge,
And *people* should seek the law from his
mouth;
[b]For he is the messenger of the LORD of
hosts.
8 But you have departed from the way;

KJV

[a]have caused many to stumble at the law; [b]ye
have corrupted the covenant of Levi, saith the
LORD of hosts.
9 Therefore [a]have I also made you contemptible and base before all the people, according as ye have not kept my ways, but have been
[b]partial in the law.

Treachery of Infidelity

10 [a]Have we not all one father? [b]hath not one
God created us? why do we deal treacherously
every man against his brother, by profaning the
covenant of our fathers?
11 Judah hath dealt treacherously, and an
abomination is committed in Israel and in Jerusalem; for Judah hath [a]profaned the holiness of the
LORD which he loved, and hath married the
daughter of a strange god.
12 The LORD will cut off the man that doeth
this, the master and the scholar, out of the tabernacles of Jacob, [a]and him that offereth an offering
unto the LORD of hosts.
13 And this have ye done again, covering the
altar of the LORD with tears, with weeping, and
with crying out, insomuch that he regardeth not
the offering any more, or receiveth *it* with good
will at your hand.
14 Yet ye say, Wherefore? Because the LORD
hath been witness between thee and [a]the wife of
thy youth, against whom thou hast dealt treacherously: [b]yet *is* she thy companion, and the wife of
thy covenant.
15 And [a]did not he make one? Yet had he
the residue of the spirit. And wherefore one? That
he might seek [b]a godly seed. Therefore take heed
to your spirit, and let none deal treacherously
against the wife of his youth.
16 For [a]the LORD, the God of Israel, saith that
he hateth putting away: for *one* covereth violence
with his garment, saith the LORD of hosts: therefore take heed to your spirit, that ye deal not
treacherously.
17 [a]Ye have wearied the LORD with your
words. Yet ye say, Wherein have we wearied *him?*
When ye say, [b]Every one that doeth evil *is* good
in the sight of the LORD, and he delighteth in them;
or, Where *is* the God of judgment?

The Coming Messenger

3 Behold, [a]I will send my messenger, and he
shall [b]prepare the way before me: and the
Lord, whom ye seek, shall suddenly come to his
temple, [c]even the messenger of the covenant,
whom ye delight in: behold, [d]he shall come, saith
the LORD of hosts.

8 [a]Jer. 18:15 [b]Num. 25:12, 13; Neh. 13:29; Ezek. 44:10
9 [a]1 Sam. 2:30 [b]Deut. 1:17; Mic. 3:11; 1 Tim. 5:21
10 [a]Jer. 31:9; 1 Cor. 8:6; [Eph. 4:6] [b]Job 31:15
11 [a]Ezra 9:1, 2; Neh. 13:23
12 [a]Neh. 13:29
14 [a]Prov. 5:18; Jer. 9:2; Mal. 3:5 [b]Prov. 2:17
15 [a]Gen. 2:24; Matt. 19:4, 5 [b]Ezra 9:2; [1 Cor. 7:14]
16 [a]Deut. 24:1; [Matt. 5:31; 19:6–8]
17 [a]Is. 43:22, 24 [b]Is. 5:20; Zeph. 1:12

CHAPTER 3

1 [a]Matt. 11:10; Mark 1:2; Luke 1:76; 7:27; John 1:23; 2:14, 15 [b][Is. 40:3] [c]Is. 63:9 [d]Hab. 2:7

*

2:12 Talmud, Vg. *teacher and student*

NKJV

You [a]have caused many to stumble at the law.
[b]You have corrupted the covenant of Levi,"
Says the LORD of hosts.
9 "Therefore [a]I also have made you contemptible and base
Before all the people,
Because you have not kept My ways
But have shown [b]partiality in the law."

Treachery of Infidelity

10 [a]Have we not all one Father?
[b]Has not one God created us?
Why do we deal treacherously with one another
By profaning the covenant of the fathers?
11 Judah has dealt treacherously,
And an abomination has been committed in Israel and in Jerusalem,
For Judah has [a]profaned
The LORD's holy *institution* which He loves:
He has married the daughter of a foreign god.
12 May the LORD cut off from the tents of Jacob
The man who does this, being *awake and aware,
Yet [a]who brings an offering to the LORD of hosts!

13 And this is the second thing you do:
You cover the altar of the LORD with tears,
With weeping and crying;
So He does not regard the offering anymore,
Nor receive *it* with goodwill from your hands.
14 Yet you say, "For what reason?"
Because the LORD has been witness
Between you and [a]the wife of your youth,
With whom you have dealt treacherously;
[b]Yet she is your companion
And your wife by covenant.
15 But [a]did He not make *them* one,
Having a remnant of the Spirit?
And why one?
He seeks [b]godly offspring.
Therefore take heed to your spirit,
And let none deal treacherously with the wife of his youth.

16 "For [a]the LORD God of Israel says
That He hates divorce,
For it covers one's garment with violence,"
Says the LORD of hosts.
"Therefore take heed to your spirit,
That you do not deal treacherously."

17 [a]You have wearied the LORD with your words;
Yet you say,
"In what way have we wearied *Him?*"
In that you say,
[b]"Everyone who does evil
Is good in the sight of the LORD,
And He delights in them,"
Or, "Where *is* the God of justice?"

The Coming Messenger

3 "Behold, [a]I send My messenger,
And he will [b]prepare the way before Me.
And the Lord, whom you seek,
Will suddenly come to His temple,
[c]Even the Messenger of the covenant,
In whom you delight.
Behold, [d]He is coming,"
Says the LORD of hosts.

KJV

2 But who may abide [a]the day of his coming? and [b]who shall stand when he appeareth? for [c]he *is* like a refiner's fire, and like fullers' sope:

3 And [a]he shall sit *as* a refiner and purifier of silver: and he shall purify the sons of Levi, and purge them as gold and silver, that they may [b]offer unto the LORD an offering in righteousness.

4 Then [a]shall the offering of Judah and Jerusalem be pleasant unto the LORD, as in the days of old, and as in former years.

5 And I will come near to you to judgment; and I will be a swift witness against the sorcerers, and against the adulterers, [a]and against false swearers, and against those that [b]oppress the hireling in *his* wages, the [c]widow, and the fatherless, and that turn aside the stranger *from his right,* and fear not me, saith the LORD of hosts.

6 For I *am* the LORD, [a]I change not; [b]therefore ye sons of Jacob are not consumed.

7 Even from the days of [a]your fathers ye are gone away from mine ordinances, and have not kept *them.* [b]Return unto me, and I will return unto you, saith the LORD of hosts. [c]But ye said, Wherein shall we return?

Do Not Rob God

8 Will a man rob God? Yet ye have robbed me. But ye say, Wherein have we robbed thee? [a]In tithes and offerings.

9 Ye *are* cursed with a curse: for ye have robbed me, *even* this whole nation.

10 [a]Bring ye all the tithes into the [b]storehouse, that there may be meat in mine house, and prove me now herewith, saith the LORD of hosts, if I will not open you the [c]windows of heaven, and [d]pour you out a blessing, that *there shall* not *be room* enough *to receive it.*

11 And I will rebuke [a]the devourer for your sakes, and he shall not destroy the fruits of your ground; neither shall your vine cast her fruit before the time in the field, saith the LORD of hosts.

12 And all nations shall call you blessed: for ye shall be [a]a delightsome land, saith the LORD of hosts.

The People Complain Harshly

13 [a]Your words have been stout against me, saith the LORD. Yet ye say, What have we spoken *so much* against thee?

14 [a]Ye have said, It *is* vain to serve God: and what profit *is it* that we have kept his ordinance, and that we have walked mournfully before the LORD of hosts?

2 [a]Jer. 10:10; Joel 2:11; Nah. 1:6; [Mal. 4:1] [b]Is. 33:14; Ezek. 22:14; Rev. 6:17 [c]Is. 4:4; Zech. 13:9; [Matt. 3:10–12; 1 Cor. 3:13–15]
3 [a]Is. 1:25; Dan. 12:10; Zech. 13:9 [b][1 Pet. 2:5]
4 [a]Mal. 1:11
5 [a]Lev. 19:12; Zech. 5:4; [James 5:12] [b]Lev. 19:13; James 5:4 [c]Ex. 22:22
6 [a][Num. 23:19; Rom. 11:29; James 1:17] [b][Lam. 3:22]
7 [a]Acts 7:51 [b]Zech. 1:3 [c]Mal. 1:6
8 [a]Neh. 13:10–12
10 [a]Prov. 3:9, 10 [b]1 Chr. 26:20 [c]Gen. 7:11 [d]2 Chr. 31:10
11 [a]Amos 4:9
12 [a]Dan. 8:9
13 [a]Mal. 2:17
14 [a]Job 21:14

NKJV

2 "But who can endure [a]the day of His coming?
And [b]who can stand when He appears?
For [c]He *is* like a refiner's fire
And like launderers' soap.
3 [a]He will sit as a refiner and a purifier of silver;
He will purify the sons of Levi,
And purge them as gold and silver,
That they may [b]offer to the LORD
An offering in righteousness.

4 "Then [a]the offering of Judah and Jerusalem
Will be pleasant to the LORD,
As in the days of old,
As in former years.
5 And I will come near you for judgment;
I will be a swift witness
Against sorcerers,
Against adulterers,
[a]Against perjurers,
Against those who [b]exploit wage earners and [c]widows and orphans,
And against those who turn away an alien—
Because they do not fear Me,"
Says the LORD of hosts.

6 "For I *am* the LORD, [a]I do not change;
[b]Therefore you are not consumed, O sons of Jacob.
7 Yet from the days of [a]your fathers
You have gone away from My ordinances
And have not kept *them.*
[b]Return to Me, and I will return to you,"
Says the LORD of hosts.
[c]"But you said,
'In what way shall we return?'

Do Not Rob God

8 "Will a man rob God?
Yet you have robbed Me!
But you say,
'In what way have we robbed You?'
[a]In tithes and offerings.
9 You are cursed with a curse,
For you have robbed Me,
Even this whole nation.
10 [a]Bring all the tithes into the [b]storehouse,
That there may be food in My house,
And try Me now in this,"
Says the LORD of hosts,
"If I will not open for you the [c]windows of heaven
And [d]pour out for you *such* blessing
That *there will* not *be room* enough *to receive it.*

11 "And I will rebuke [a]the devourer for your sakes,
So that he will not destroy the fruit of your ground,
Nor shall the vine fail to bear fruit for you in the field,"
Says the LORD of hosts;
12 "And all nations will call you blessed,
For you will be [a]a delightful land,"
Says the LORD of hosts.

The People Complain Harshly

13 "Your[a] words have been harsh against Me,"
Says the LORD,
"Yet you say,
'What have we spoken against You?'
14 [a]You have said,
'It is useless to serve God;
What profit *is it* that we have kept His ordinance,
And that we have walked as mourners
Before the LORD of hosts?

KJV

15 And now [a]we call the proud happy; yea, they that work wickedness are set up; yea, *they that* [b]tempt God are even delivered.

A Book of Remembrance

16 Then they [a]that feared the LORD [b]spake often one to another: and the LORD hearkened, and heard *it*, and [c]a book of remembrance was written before him for them that feared the LORD, and that thought upon his name.

17 And [a]they shall be mine, saith the LORD of hosts, in that day when I make up my [b]jewels; and [c]I will spare them, as a man spareth his own son that serveth him.

18 [a]Then shall ye return, and discern between the righteous and the wicked, between him that serveth God and him that serveth him not.

The Great Day of God

4 For, behold, [a]the day cometh, that shall burn as an oven; and all [b]the proud, yea, and all that do wickedly, shall be [c]stubble: and the day that cometh shall burn them up, saith the LORD of hosts, that it shall [d]leave them neither root nor branch.

2 But unto you that [a]fear my name shall the [b]Sun of righteousness arise with healing in his wings; and ye shall go forth, and grow up as calves of the stall.

3 [a]And ye shall tread down the wicked; for they shall be ashes under the soles of your feet in the day that I shall do *this*, saith the LORD of hosts.

4 Remember ye the [a]law of Moses my servant, which I commanded unto him in Horeb for all Israel, *with* [b]the statutes and judgments.

5 Behold, I will send you [a]Elijah the prophet [b]before the coming of the great and dreadful day of the LORD:

6 And he shall turn the heart of the fathers to the children, and the heart of the children to their fathers, lest I come and [a]smite the earth with [b]a curse.

---

15 [a]Ps. 73:12 [b]Ps. 95:9
16 [a]Ps. 66:16 [b]Heb. 3:13 [c]Ps. 56:8
17 [a]Ex. 19:5; Deut. 7:6; Is. 43:21; [1 Pet. 2:9] [b]Is. 62:3 [c]Ps. 103:13
18 [a][Ps. 58:11]

CHAPTER 4

1 [a]Ps. 21:9; [Nah. 1:5, 6; Mal. 3:2, 3; 2 Pet. 3:7] [b]Mal. 3:18 [c]Is. 5:24; Obad. 18 [d]Amos 2:9
2 [a]Mal. 3:16 [b]Matt. 4:16; Luke 1:78; Acts 10:43; 2 Cor. 4:6; Eph. 5:14
3 [a]Mic. 7:10
4 [a]Ex. 20:3 [b]Deut. 4:10
5 [a][Matt. 11:14; 17:10–13; Mark 9:11–13; Luke 1:17]; John 1:21 [b]Joel 2:31
6 [a]Zech. 14:12 [b]Zech. 5:3

*
3:17 Lit. *special treasure*

NKJV

15 So now [a]we call the proud blessed,
For those who do wickedness are raised up;
They even [b]tempt God and go free.' "

A Book of Remembrance

16 Then those [a]who feared the LORD [b]spoke to one another,
And the LORD listened and heard *them;*
So [c]a book of remembrance was written before Him
For those who fear the LORD
And who meditate on His name.

17 "They[a] shall be Mine," says the LORD of hosts,
"On the day that I make them My [b]jewels.*
And [c]I will spare them
As a man spares his own son who serves him."
18 [a]Then you shall again discern
Between the righteous and the wicked,
Between one who serves God
And one who does not serve Him.

The Great Day of God

4 "For behold, [a]the day is coming,
Burning like an oven,
And all [b]the proud, yes, all who do wickedly will be [c]stubble.
And the day which is coming shall burn them up,"
Says the LORD of hosts,
"That will [d]leave them neither root nor branch.
2 But to you who [a]fear My name
The [b]Sun of Righteousness shall arise
With healing in His wings;
And you shall go out
And grow fat like stall-fed calves.
3 [a]You shall trample the wicked,
For they shall be ashes under the soles of your feet
On the day that I do *this*,"
Says the LORD of hosts.

4 "Remember the [a]Law of Moses, My servant,
Which I commanded him in Horeb for all Israel,
With [b]*the* statutes and judgments.
5 Behold, I will send you [a]Elijah the prophet
[b]Before the coming of the great and dreadful day of the LORD.
6 And he will turn
The hearts of the fathers to the children,
And the hearts of the children to their fathers,
Lest I come and [a]strike the earth with [b]a curse."

The
New Testament

KJV

THE GOSPEL ACCORDING TO

MATTHEW

The Genealogy of Jesus Christ
(Ruth 4:18–22; 1 Chr. 2:1–15; Luke 3:23–38)

1 The book of the [a]generation of Jesus Christ,
[b]the son of David, [c]the son of Abraham.
2 [a]Abraham begat Isaac; and [b]Isaac begat
Jacob; and Jacob begat [c]Judas and his brethren;
3 And [a]Judas begat Phares and Zara of Tha-
mar; and [b]Phares begat Esrom; and Esrom begat
Aram;
4 And Aram begat Aminadab; and Aminadab begat Naasson; and Naasson begat Salmon;
5 And Salmon begat [a]Booz of Rachab; and
Booz begat Obed of Ruth; and Obed begat Jesse;
6 And [a]Jesse begat David the king; and
[b]David the king begat Solomon of her *that had
been the wife* of Urias;
7 And [a]Solomon begat Roboam; and Roboam begat [b]Abia; and Abia begat Asa;
8 And Asa begat [a]Josaphat; and Josaphat
begat Joram; and Joram begat [b]Ozias;
9 And Ozias begat Joatham; and Joatham
begat [a]Achaz; and Achaz begat Ezekias;
10 And [a]Ezekias begat Manasses; and Manasses begat Amon; and Amon begat [b]Josias;
11 And [a]Josias begat Jechonias and his
brethren, about the time they were [b]carried away
to Babylon:
12 And after they were brought to Babylon,
[a]Jechonias begat Salathiel; and Salathiel begat
[b]Zorobabel;
13 And Zorobabel begat Abiud; and Abiud
begat Eliakim; and Eliakim begat Azor;
14 And Azor begat Sadoc; and Sadoc begat
Achim; and Achim begat Eliud;
15 And Eliud begat Eleazar; and Eleazar begat Matthan; and Matthan begat Jacob;
16 And Jacob begat Joseph the husband of
[a]Mary, of whom was born Jesus, who is called
Christ.
17 So all the generations from Abraham to
David *are* fourteen generations; and from David
until the carrying away into Babylon *are* fourteen
generations; and from the carrying away into
Babylon unto Christ *are* fourteen generations.

Christ Born of Mary
(Luke 2:1–7)

18 Now the [a]birth of Jesus Christ was on this
wise: When as his mother Mary was espoused to
Joseph, before they came together, she was found
with child [b]of the Holy Ghost.
19 Then Joseph her husband, being a just
man, and not willing [a]to make her a publick example, was minded to put her away privily.
20 But while he thought on these things, behold, the angel of the Lord appeared unto him in
a dream, saying, Joseph, thou son of David, fear
not to take unto thee Mary thy wife: [a]for that
which is conceived in her is of the Holy Ghost.
21 [a]And she shall bring forth a son, and thou
shalt call his name JESUS: for [b]he shall save his
people from their sins.
22 Now all this was done, that it might be
fulfilled which was spoken of the Lord by the
prophet, saying,
23 [a]BEHOLD, A VIRGIN SHALL BE WITH CHILD,

CHAPTER 1
1 [a]Luke 3:23 [b]John 7:42 [c]Gen. 12:3; 22:18
2 [a]Gen. 21:2, 12 [b]Gen. 25:26; 28:14 [c]Gen. 29:35
3 [a]Gen. 38:27; 49:10 [b]Ruth 4:18–22
5 [a]Ruth 2:1; 4:1–13
6 [a]1 Sam. 16:1 [b]2 Sam. 7:12; 12:24
7 [a]1 Chr. 3:10 [b]2 Chr. 11:20
8 [a]1 Chr. 3:10 [b]2 Kin. 15:13
9 [a]2 Kin. 15:38
10 [a]2 Kin. 20:21 [b]1 Kin. 13:2
11 [a]1 Chr. 3:15, 16 [b]2 Kin. 24:14–16
12 [a]1 Chr. 3:17 [b]Ezra 3:2
16 [a]Matt. 13:55
18 [a]Luke 1:27 [b]Luke 1:35
19 [a]Deut. 24:1
20 [a]Luke 1:35
21 [a]Luke 1:31; 2:21 [b]John 1:29
23 [a]Is. 7:14

*

1:6 Words in italic type have been added for clarity. They are not found in the original Greek.
1:7 NU *Asaph*
1:10 NU *Amos*
1:23 Words in oblique type in the New Testament are quoted from the Old Testament.

NKJV

THE GOSPEL ACCORDING TO

MATTHEW

The Genealogy of Jesus Christ
(Ruth 4:18–22; 1 Chr. 2:1–15; Luke 3:23–38)

1 The book of the [a]genealogy of Jesus Christ,
[b]the Son of David, [c]the Son of Abraham:
2 [a]Abraham begot Isaac, [b]Isaac begot Jacob, and Jacob begot [c]Judah and his brothers.
3 [a]Judah begot Perez and Zerah by Tamar,
[b]Perez begot Hezron, and Hezron begot Ram.
4 Ram begot Amminadab, Amminadab begot Nahshon, and Nahshon begot Salmon.
5 Salmon begot [a]Boaz by Rahab, Boaz begot Obed by Ruth, Obed begot Jesse,
6 and [a]Jesse begot David the king.
[b]David the king begot Solomon by her
**who had been the wife* of Uriah.
7 [a]Solomon begot Rehoboam, Rehoboam
begot [b]Abijah, and Abijah begot *Asa.
8 Asa begot [a]Jehoshaphat, Jehoshaphat begot Joram, and Joram begot [b]Uzziah.
9 Uzziah begot Jotham, Jotham begot
[a]Ahaz, and Ahaz begot Hezekiah.
10 [a]Hezekiah begot Manasseh, Manasseh begot *Amon, and Amon begot [b]Josiah.
11 [a]Josiah begot Jeconiah and his brothers
about the time they were [b]carried away to
Babylon.
12 And after they were brought to Babylon,
[a]Jeconiah begot Shealtiel, and Shealtiel begot
[b]Zerubbabel.
13 Zerubbabel begot Abiud, Abiud begot
Eliakim, and Eliakim begot Azor.
14 Azor begot Zadok, Zadok begot Achim,
and Achim begot Eliud.
15 Eliud begot Eleazar, Eleazar begot Matthan, and Matthan begot Jacob.
16 And Jacob begot Joseph the husband of
[a]Mary, of whom was born Jesus who is called
Christ.
17 So all the generations from Abraham to
David *are* fourteen generations, from David until
the captivity in Babylon *are* fourteen generations,
and from the captivity in Babylon until the Christ
are fourteen generations.

Christ Born of Mary
(Luke 2:1–7)

18 Now the [a]birth of Jesus Christ was as follows: After His mother Mary was betrothed to Joseph, before they came together, she was found
with child [b]of the Holy Spirit.
19 Then Joseph her husband, being a just
man, and not wanting [a]to make her a public example, was minded to put her away secretly.
20 But while he thought about these things,
behold, an angel of the Lord appeared to him in
a dream, saying, "Joseph, son of David, do not
be afraid to take to you Mary your wife, [a]for that
which is conceived in her is of the Holy Spirit.
21 [a]"And she will bring forth a Son, and you
shall call His name JESUS, [b]for He will save His
people from their sins."
22 So all this was done that it might be fulfilled which was spoken by the Lord through the
prophet, saying:
23 [a]*"Behold,* the virgin shall be with child,*

KJV

AND SHALL BRING FORTH A SON, AND THEY SHALL CALL HIS NAME EMMANUEL, which being interpreted is, God with us.

24 Then Joseph being raised from sleep did as the angel of the Lord had bidden him, and took unto him his wife:

25 And knew her not till she had brought forth [a]her firstborn son: and he called his name JESUS.

Wise Men from the East

2 Now when [a]Jesus was born in Bethlehem of Judaea in the days of Herod the king, behold, there came wise men [b]from the east to Jerusalem,

2 Saying, [a]Where is he that is born King of the Jews? for we have seen [b]his star in the east, and are come to worship him.

3 When Herod the king had heard *these things,* he was troubled, and all Jerusalem with him.

4 And when he had gathered all [a]the chief priests and [b]scribes of the people together, [c]he demanded of them where Christ should be born.

5 And they said unto him, In Bethlehem of Judaea: for thus it is written by the prophet,

6 [a]AND THOU BETHLEHEM, *IN* THE LAND OF JUDA, ART NOT THE LEAST AMONG THE PRINCES OF JUDA: FOR OUT OF THEE SHALL COME A GOVERNOR, [b]THAT SHALL RULE MY PEOPLE ISRAEL.

7 Then Herod, when he had privily called the wise men, enquired of them diligently what time the [a]star appeared.

8 And he sent them to Bethlehem, and said, Go and search diligently for the young child; and when ye have found *him,* bring me word again, that I may come and worship him also.

9 When they had heard the king, they departed; and, lo, the star, which they saw in the east, went before them, till it came and stood over where the young child was.

10 When they saw the star, they rejoiced with exceeding great joy.

11 And when they were come into the house, they saw the young child with Mary his mother, and fell down, and worshipped him: and when they had opened their treasures, [a]they presented unto him gifts; gold, and frankincense, and myrrh.

12 And being warned of God [a]in a dream that they should not return to Herod, they departed into their own country another way.

The Flight into Egypt

13 And when they were departed, behold, the angel of the Lord appeareth to Joseph in a dream, saying, Arise, and take the young child and his mother, and flee into Egypt, and be thou there until I bring thee word: for Herod will seek the young child to destroy him.

14 When he arose, he took the young child and his mother by night, and departed into Egypt:

15 And was there until the death of Herod: that it might be fulfilled which was spoken of the Lord by the prophet, saying, [a]OUT OF EGYPT HAVE I CALLED MY SON.

Massacre of the Innocents

16 Then Herod, when he saw that he was mocked of the wise men, was exceeding wroth, and sent forth, and slew all the children that were in Bethlehem, and in all the coasts thereof, from two years old and under, according to the time which he had diligently enquired of the wise men.

17 Then was fulfilled that which was spoken by Jeremy the prophet, saying,

18 [a]IN RAMA WAS THERE A VOICE HEARD, LAMENTATION, AND WEEPING, AND GREAT MOURNING,

---

25 [a]Ex. 13:2; Luke 2:7, 21

CHAPTER 2

1 [a]Mic. 5:2; Luke 2:4–7 [b]Gen. 25:6; 1 Kin. 4:30
2 [a]Luke 2:11 [b][Num. 24:17; Is. 60:3]
4 [a]2 Chr. 36:14 [b]2 Chr. 34:13 [c]Mal. 2:7
6 [a]Mic. 5:2; John 7:42 [b]Gen. 49:10; [Rev. 2:27]
7 [a]Num. 24:17
11 [a]Ps. 72:10; Is. 60:6
12 [a][Job 33:15, 16]; Matt. 1:20
15 [a]Num. 24:8; Hos. 11:1
18 [a]Jer. 31:15

*______

1:25 NU *a Son*

NKJV

and bear a Son, and they shall call His name Immanuel," which is translated, "God with us."

24 Then Joseph, being aroused from sleep, did as the angel of the Lord commanded him and took to him his wife,

25 and did not know her till she had brought forth [a]her* firstborn Son. And he called His name JESUS.

Wise Men from the East

2 Now after [a]Jesus was born in Bethlehem of Judea in the days of Herod the king, behold, wise men [b]from the East came to Jerusalem,

2 saying, [a]"Where is He who has been born King of the Jews? For we have seen [b]His star in the East and have come to worship Him."

3 When Herod the king heard *this,* he was troubled, and all Jerusalem with him.

4 And when he had gathered all [a]the chief priests and [b]scribes of the people together, [c]he inquired of them where the Christ was to be born.

5 So they said to him, "In Bethlehem of Judea, for thus it is written by the prophet:

6 *'But[a] you, Bethlehem, in the land of Judah,*
Are not the least among the rulers of
Judah;
For out of you shall come a Ruler
[b] Who will shepherd My people Israel.'"

7 Then Herod, when he had secretly called the wise men, determined from them what time the [a]star appeared.

8 And he sent them to Bethlehem and said, "Go and search carefully for the young Child, and when you have found *Him,* bring back word to me, that I may come and worship Him also."

9 When they heard the king, they departed; and behold, the star which they had seen in the East went before them, till it came and stood over where the young Child was.

10 When they saw the star, they rejoiced with exceedingly great joy.

11 And when they had come into the house, they saw the young Child with Mary His mother, and fell down and worshiped Him. And when they had opened their treasures, [a]they presented gifts to Him: gold, frankincense, and myrrh.

12 Then, being divinely warned [a]in a dream that they should not return to Herod, they departed for their own country another way.

The Flight into Egypt

13 Now when they had departed, behold, an angel of the Lord appeared to Joseph in a dream, saying, "Arise, take the young Child and His mother, flee to Egypt, and stay there until I bring you word; for Herod will seek the young Child to destroy Him."

14 When he arose, he took the young Child and His mother by night and departed for Egypt,

15 and was there until the death of Herod, that it might be fulfilled which was spoken by the Lord through the prophet, saying, [a]*"Out of Egypt I called My Son."*

Massacre of the Innocents

16 Then Herod, when he saw that he was deceived by the wise men, was exceedingly angry; and he sent forth and put to death all the male children who were in Bethlehem and in all its districts, from two years old and under, according to the time which he had determined from the wise men.

17 Then was fulfilled what was spoken by Jeremiah the prophet, saying:

18 *"A[a] voice was heard in Ramah,*
Lamentation, weeping, and great
mourning,
Rachel weeping for her children,

KJV

RACHEL WEEPING *FOR* HER CHILDREN, AND WOULD
NOT BE COMFORTED, BECAUSE THEY ARE NOT.

The Home in Nazareth
(*Luke 2:39*)

19 But when Herod was dead, behold, an angel of the Lord appeareth in a dream to Joseph
in Egypt,
20 [a]Saying, Arise, and take the young child
and his mother, and go into the land of Israel:
for they are dead which [b]sought the young child's
life.
21 And he arose, and took the young child
and his mother, and came into the land of Israel.
22 But when he heard that Archelaus did
reign in Judaea in the room of his father Herod,
he was afraid to go thither: notwithstanding, being warned of God in a [a]dream, he turned aside
[b]into the parts of Galilee:
23 And he came and dwelt in a city called
[a]Nazareth: that it might be fulfilled [b]which was
spoken by the prophets, He shall be called a
Nazarene.

John the Baptist Prepares the Way
(*Mark 1:2–8; Luke 3:1–20*)

3 In those days came [a]John the Baptist, preaching [b]in the wilderness of Judaea,
2 And saying, Repent ye: for [a]the kingdom
of heaven is at hand.
3 For this is he that was spoken of by the
prophet Esaias, saying, [a]THE VOICE OF ONE CRYING
IN THE WILDERNESS, [b]PREPARE YE THE WAY OF THE
LORD, MAKE HIS PATHS STRAIGHT.
4 And [a]the same John had his raiment of
camel's hair, and a leathern girdle about his loins;
and his meat was [b]locusts and [c]wild honey.
5 [a]Then went out to him Jerusalem, and all
Judaea, and all the region round about Jordan,
6 [a]And were baptized of him in Jordan, confessing their sins.
7 But when he saw many of the Pharisees
and Sadducees come to his baptism, he said unto
them, [a]O generation of vipers, who hath warned
you to flee from [b]the wrath to come?
8 Bring forth therefore fruits meet for
repentance:
9 And think not to say within yourselves,
[a]We have Abraham to *our* father: for I say unto
you, that God is able of these stones to raise up
children unto Abraham.
10 And now also the ax is laid unto the root
of the trees: [a]therefore every tree which bringeth
not forth good fruit is hewn down, and cast into
the fire.
11 [a]I indeed baptize you with water unto repentance: but he that cometh after me is mightier
than I, whose shoes I am not worthy to bear: [b]he
shall baptize you with the Holy Ghost, and *with*
fire:
12 [a]Whose fan *is* in his hand, and he will
throughly purge his floor, and gather his wheat
into the garner; but he will [b]burn up the chaff
with unquenchable fire.

John Baptizes Jesus
(*Mark 1:9–11; Luke 3:21, 22; John 1:29–34*)

13 [a]Then cometh Jesus [b]from Galilee to Jordan unto John, to be baptized of him.
14 But John forbad him, saying, I have need
to be baptized of thee, and comest thou to me?
15 And Jesus answering said unto him, Suffer *it to be so* now: for thus it becometh us to
fulfil all righteousness. Then he suffered him.
16 [a]And Jesus, when he was baptized, went
up straightway out of the water: and, lo, the heavens were opened unto him, and he saw [b]the Spirit
of God descending like a dove, and lighting upon
him:

20 [a]Luke 2:39 [b]Matt. 2:16 **22** [a]Matt. 2:12, 13, 19 [b]Matt. 3:13; Luke 2:39 **23** [a]Luke 1:26; 2:39; John 1:45, 46 [b]Judg. 13:5

CHAPTER 3

1 [a]Matt. 3:1–12; Mark 1:3–8; Luke 3:2–17; John 1:6–8, 19–28 [b]Josh. 14:10 **2** [a]Dan. 2:44; Mal. 4:6; Matt. 4:17; Mark 1:15; Luke 1:17; 10:9; 11:20; 21:31 **3** [a]Is. 40:3; Luke 3:4; John 1:23 [b]Luke 1:76 **4** [a]2 Kin. 1:8; Zech. 13:4; Matt. 11:8; Mark 1:6 [b]Lev. 11:22 [c]1 Sam. 14:25, 26 **5** [a]Mark 1:5 **6** [a]Acts 19:4, 18 **7** [a]Matt. 12:34; Luke 3:7–9 [b][Rom. 5:9; 1 Thess. 1:10] **9** [a]John 8:33; Acts 13:26; [Rom. 4:1, 11, 16; Gal. 3:29] **10** [a][Ps. 92:12–14]; Matt. 7:19; Luke 13:7, 9; [John 15:6] **11** [a]Mark 1:4, 8; Luke 3:16; John 1:26; Acts 1:5 [b][Is. 4:4; John 20:22; Acts 2:3, 4; 1 Cor. 12:13] **12** [a]Mal. 3:3 [b]Mal. 4:1; Matt. 13:30 **13** [a]Matt. 3:13–17; Mark 1:9–11; Luke 3:21, 22; John 1:31–34 [b]Matt. 2:22 **16** [a]Mark 1:10 [b][Is. 11:2]; Luke 3:22; John 1:32; Acts 7:56

*———

3:11 M omits *and fire*
3:16 Or *he*

NKJV

Refusing to be comforted,
Because they are no more."

The Home in Nazareth
(*Luke 2:39*)

19 Now when Herod was dead, behold, an
angel of the Lord appeared in a dream to Joseph
in Egypt,
20 [a]saying, "Arise, take the young Child and
His mother, and go to the land of Israel, for those
who [b]sought the young Child's life are dead."
21 Then he arose, took the young Child and
His mother, and came into the land of Israel.
22 But when he heard that Archelaus was
reigning over Judea instead of his father Herod,
he was afraid to go there. And being warned by
God in a [a]dream, he turned aside [b]into the region
of Galilee.
23 And he came and dwelt in a city called
[a]Nazareth, that it might be fulfilled [b]which was
spoken by the prophets, "He shall be called a
Nazarene."

John the Baptist Prepares the Way
(*Mark 1:2–8; Luke 3:1–20*)

3 In those days [a]John the Baptist came preaching [b]in the wilderness of Judea,
2 and saying, "Repent, for [a]the kingdom of
heaven is at hand!"
3 For this is he who was spoken of by the
prophet Isaiah, saying:

[a]*"The voice of one crying in the wilderness:*
[b]*'Prepare the way of the LORD;*
Make His paths straight.' "

4 Now [a]John himself was clothed in camel's
hair, with a leather belt around his waist; and his
food was [b]locusts and [c]wild honey.
5 [a]Then Jerusalem, all Judea, and all the region around the Jordan went out to him
6 [a]and were baptized by him in the Jordan,
confessing their sins.
7 But when he saw many of the Pharisees
and Sadducees coming to his baptism, he said to
them, [a]"Brood of vipers! Who warned you to flee
from [b]the wrath to come?
8 "Therefore bear fruits worthy of repentance,
9 "and do not think to say to yourselves,
[a]'We have Abraham as *our* father.' For I say to
you that God is able to raise up children to Abraham from these stones.
10 "And even now the ax is laid to the root
of the trees. [a]Therefore every tree which does not
bear good fruit is cut down and thrown into the
fire.
11 [a]"I indeed baptize you with water unto repentance, but He who is coming after me is mightier than I, whose sandals I am not worthy to carry.
[b]He will baptize you with the Holy Spirit *and fire.
12 [a]"His winnowing fan *is* in His hand, and
He will thoroughly clean out His threshing floor,
and gather His wheat into the barn; but He will
[b]burn up the chaff with unquenchable fire."

John Baptizes Jesus
(*Mark 1:9–11; Luke 3:21, 22; John 1:29–34*)

13 [a]Then Jesus came [b]from Galilee to John
at the Jordan to be baptized by him.
14 And John *tried to* prevent Him, saying,
"I need to be baptized by You, and are You coming to me?"
15 But Jesus answered and said to him, "Permit *it to be so* now, for thus it is fitting for us to
fulfill all righteousness." Then he allowed Him.
16 [a]When He had been baptized, Jesus came
up immediately from the water; and behold, the
heavens were opened to Him, and *He saw [b]the
Spirit of God descending like a dove and alighting
upon Him.

KJV

17 [a]And lo a voice from heaven, saying, [b]This is my beloved Son, in whom I am well pleased.

Satan Tempts Jesus
(*Mark 1:12, 13; Luke 4:1–13*)

4 Then was [a]Jesus led up of [b]the spirit into the wilderness to be tempted of the devil.

2 And when he had fasted forty days and forty nights, he was afterward an hungred.

3 And when the tempter came to him, he said, If thou be the Son of God, command that these stones be made bread.

4 But he answered and said, It is written, [a]MAN SHALL NOT LIVE BY BREAD ALONE, BUT BY EVERY WORD THAT PROCEEDETH OUT OF THE MOUTH OF GOD.

5 Then the devil taketh him up [a]into the holy city, and setteth him on a pinnacle of the temple,

6 And saith unto him, If thou be the Son of God, cast thyself down: for it is written, [a]HE SHALL GIVE HIS ANGELS CHARGE CONCERNING THEE: and [b]IN *THEIR* HANDS THEY SHALL BEAR THEE UP, LEST AT ANY TIME THOU DASH THY FOOT AGAINST A STONE.

7 Jesus said unto him, It is written again, [a]THOU SHALT NOT TEMPT THE LORD THY GOD.

8 Again, the devil taketh him up into an exceeding high mountain, and [a]sheweth him all the kingdoms of the world, and the glory of them;

9 And saith unto him, All these things will I give thee, if thou wilt fall down and worship me.

10 Then saith Jesus unto him, Get thee hence, Satan: for it is written, [a]THOU SHALT WORSHIP THE LORD THY GOD, AND HIM ONLY SHALT THOU SERVE.

11 Then the devil [a]leaveth him, and, behold, [b]angels came and ministered unto him.

Jesus Begins His Galilean Ministry
(*Mark 1:14, 15; Luke 4:14, 15*)

12 [a]Now when Jesus had heard that John was cast into prison, he departed into Galilee;

13 And leaving Nazareth, he came and dwelt in Capernaum, which is upon the sea coast, in the borders of Zabulon and Nephthalim:

14 That it might be fulfilled which was spoken by Esaias the prophet, saying,

15 [a]THE LAND OF ZABULON, AND THE LAND OF NEPHTHALIM, BY THE WAY OF THE SEA, BEYOND JORDAN, GALILEE OF THE GENTILES;

16 [a]THE PEOPLE WHICH SAT IN DARKNESS SAW GREAT LIGHT; AND TO THEM WHICH SAT IN THE REGION AND SHADOW OF DEATH LIGHT IS SPRUNG UP.

17 [a]From that time Jesus began to preach, and to say, [b]Repent: for the kingdom of heaven is at hand.

Four Fishermen Called as Disciples
(*Mark 1:16–20; Luke 5:1–11*)

18 [a]And Jesus, walking by the sea of Galilee, saw two brethren, Simon [b]called Peter, and Andrew his brother, casting a net into the sea: for they were fishers.

19 And he saith unto them, Follow me, and [a]I will make you fishers of men.

20 [a]And they straightway left *their* nets, and followed him.

21 [a]And going on from thence, he saw other two brethren, James *the son* of Zebedee, and John his brother, in a ship with Zebedee their father, mending their nets; and he called them.

22 And they immediately left the ship and their father, and followed him.

17 [a]John 12:28 [b]Ps. 2:7; Is. 42:1; Mark 1:11; Luke 1:35; 9:35; Col. 1:13

CHAPTER 4

1 [a]Matt. 4:1–11; Mark 1:12; Luke 4:1 [b]Ezek. 3:14; Acts 8:39
4 [a]Deut. 8:3
5 [a]Neh. 11:1, 18; Dan. 9:24; Matt. 27:53
6 [a]Ps. 91:11 [b]Ps. 91:12
7 [a]Deut. 6:16
8 [a][Matt. 16:26; 1 John 2:15–17]
10 [a]Deut. 6:13; 10:20; Josh. 24:14
11 [a][James 4:7] [b]Matt. 26:53; Luke 22:43; [Heb. 1:14]
12 [a]Matt. 14:3; Mark 1:14; Luke 3:20; John 4:43
15 [a]Is. 9:1, 2
16 [a]Is. 42:7; Luke 2:32
17 [a]Mark 1:14, 15 [b]Matt. 3:2; 10:7
18 [a]Matt. 4:18–22; Mark 1:16–20; Luke 5:2–11; John 1:40–42 [b]Matt. 10:2; 16:18; John 1:40–42
19 [a]Luke 5:10
20 [a]Matt. 19:27; Mark 10:28
21 [a]Mark 1:19

*
4:10 M *Get behind Me*

NKJV

17 [a]And suddenly a voice *came* from heaven, saying, [b]"This is My beloved Son, in whom I am well pleased."

Satan Tempts Jesus
(*Mark 1:12, 13; Luke 4:1–13*)

4 Then [a]Jesus was led up by [b]the Spirit into the wilderness to be tempted by the devil.

2 And when He had fasted forty days and forty nights, afterward He was hungry.

3 Now when the tempter came to Him, he said, "If You are the Son of God, command that these stones become bread."

4 But He answered and said, "It is written, [a]*'Man shall not live by bread alone, but by every word that proceeds from the mouth of God.'* "

5 Then the devil took Him up [a]into the holy city, set Him on the pinnacle of the temple,

6 and said to Him, "If You are the Son of God, throw Yourself down. For it is written:

[a]*'He shall give His angels charge over you,'*

and,

[b]*'In their hands they shall bear you up,*
Lest you dash your foot against a stone.' "

7 Jesus said to him, "It is written again, [a]*'You shall not tempt the LORD your God.'* "

8 Again, the devil took Him up on an exceedingly high mountain, and [a]showed Him all the kingdoms of the world and their glory.

9 And he said to Him, "All these things I will give You if You will fall down and worship me."

10 Then Jesus said to him, *"Away with you, Satan! For it is written, [a]*'You shall worship the LORD your God, and Him only you shall serve.'* "

11 Then the devil [a]left Him, and behold, [b]angels came and ministered to Him.

Jesus Begins His Galilean Ministry
(*Mark 1:14, 15; Luke 4:14, 15*)

12 [a]Now when Jesus heard that John had been put in prison, He departed to Galilee.

13 And leaving Nazareth, He came and dwelt in Capernaum, which is by the sea, in the regions of Zebulun and Naphtali,

14 that it might be fulfilled which was spoken by Isaiah the prophet, saying:

15 *"The[a] land of Zebulun and the land of*
Naphtali,
By the way of the sea, beyond the Jordan,
Galilee of the Gentiles:
16 [a]*The people who sat in darkness have seen*
a great light,
And upon those who sat in the region and
shadow of death
Light has dawned."

17 [a]From that time Jesus began to preach and to say, [b]"Repent, for the kingdom of heaven is at hand."

Four Fishermen Called as Disciples
(*Mark 1:16–20; Luke 5:1–11*)

18 [a]And Jesus, walking by the Sea of Galilee, saw two brothers, Simon [b]called Peter, and Andrew his brother, casting a net into the sea; for they were fishermen.

19 Then He said to them, "Follow Me, and [a]I will make you fishers of men."

20 [a]They immediately left *their* nets and followed Him.

21 [a]Going on from there, He saw two other brothers, James *the son* of Zebedee, and John his brother, in the boat with Zebedee their father, mending their nets. He called them,

22 and immediately they left the boat and their father, and followed Him.

KJV

Jesus Heals a Great Multitude
(Mark 1:35–39; Luke 4:44; 6:17–19)

23 And Jesus went about all Galilee, [a]teach-
ing in their synagogues, and preaching [b]the gospel of the kingdom, [c]and healing all manner of
sickness and all manner of disease among the
people.
24 And his fame went throughout all Syria:
and they [a]brought unto him all sick people that
were taken with divers diseases and torments, and
those which were possessed with devils, and those
which were lunatick, and those that had the palsy;
and he healed them.
25 [a]And there followed him great multitudes
of people from Galilee, and *from* Decapolis, and
from Jerusalem, and *from* Judaea, and *from* beyond Jordan.

The Beatitudes
(Luke 6:20–26)

5 And seeing the multitudes, [a]he went up into
a mountain: and when he was set, his disciples
came unto him:
2 And he opened his mouth, and [a]taught
them, saying,
3 [a]Blessed *are* the poor in spirit: for their's
is the kingdom of heaven.
4 [a]Blessed *are* they that mourn: for they
shall be comforted.
5 [a]Blessed *are* the meek: for [b]they shall inherit the earth.
6 Blessed *are* they which do [a]hunger and
thirst after righteousness: [b]for they shall be filled.
7 Blessed *are* the merciful: [a]for they shall
obtain mercy.
8 [a]Blessed *are* the pure in heart: for [b]they
shall see God.
9 Blessed *are* the peacemakers: for they
shall be called the children of God.
10 [a]Blessed *are* they which are persecuted
for righteousness' sake: for their's is the kingdom
of heaven.
11 [a]Blessed are ye, when *men* shall revile
you, and persecute *you*, and shall say all manner
of [b]evil against you falsely, for my sake.
12 [a]Rejoice, and be exceeding glad: for great
is your reward in heaven: for [b]so persecuted they
the prophets which were before you.

Believers Are Salt and Light
(Mark 9:50; Luke 14:34, 35)

13 Ye are the salt of the earth: [a]but if the
salt have lost his savour, wherewith shall it be
salted? it is thenceforth good for nothing, but to
be cast out, and to be trodden under foot of men.
14 [a]Ye are the light of the world. A city that
is set on an hill cannot be hid.
15 Neither do men [a]light a candle, and put
it under a bushel, but on a candlestick; and it giveth light unto all that are in the house.
16 Let your light so shine before men, [a]that
they may see your good works, and [b]glorify your
Father which is in heaven.

Christ Fulfills the Law

17 [a]Think not that I am come to destroy the
law, or the prophets: I am not come to destroy,
but to fulfil.
18 For verily I say unto you, [a]Till heaven and
earth pass, one jot or one tittle shall in no wise
pass from the law, till all be fulfilled.
19 [a]Whosoever therefore shall break one of
these least commandments, and shall teach men
so, he shall be called the least in the kingdom of
heaven: but whosoever shall do and teach *them*,
the same shall be called great in the kingdom of
heaven.
20 For I say unto you, That except your righteousness shall exceed [a]*the righteousness* of the

23 [a]Matt. 9:35 [b][Matt. 24:14] [c]Mark 1:34
24 [a]Luke 4:40
25 [a]Mark 3:7, 8

CHAPTER 5
1 [a]Mark 3:13
2 [a][Matt. 7:29]
3 [a]Luke 6:20–23
4 [a]Rev. 21:4
5 [a]Ps. 37:11 [b][Rom. 4:13]
6 [a]Luke 1:53 [b][Is. 55:1; 65:13]
7 [a]Ps. 41:1
8 [a]Ps. 15:2; 24:4 [b]1 Cor. 13:12
10 [a]1 Pet. 3:14
11 [a]Luke 6:22 [b]1 Pet. 4:14
12 [a]1 Pet. 4:13, 14 [b]Acts 7:52
13 [a]Luke 14:34
14 [a][John 8:12]
15 [a]Luke 8:16
16 [a]1 Pet. 2:12 [b][John 15:8]
17 [a]Rom. 10:4
18 [a]Luke 16:17
19 [a][James 2:10]
20 [a][Rom. 10:3]

NKJV

Jesus Heals a Great Multitude
(Mark 1:35–39; Luke 4:44; 6:17–19)

23 And Jesus went about all Galilee, [a]teach-
ing in their synagogues, preaching [b]the gospel
of the kingdom, [c]and healing all kinds of sickness
and all kinds of disease among the people.
24 Then His fame went throughout all Syria;
and they [a]brought to Him all sick people who
were afflicted with various diseases and torments,
and those who were demon-possessed, epileptics,
and paralytics; and He healed them.
25 [a]Great multitudes followed Him—from
Galilee, and *from* Decapolis, Jerusalem, Judea,
and beyond the Jordan.

The Beatitudes
(Luke 6:20–26)

5 And seeing the multitudes, [a]He went up on a
mountain, and when He was seated His disciples came to Him.
2 Then He opened His mouth and [a]taught
them, saying:

3 "Blessed[a] *are* the poor in spirit,
For theirs is the kingdom of heaven.
4 [a]Blessed *are* those who mourn,
For they shall be comforted.
5 [a]Blessed *are* the meek,
For [b]they shall inherit the earth.
6 Blessed *are* those who [a]hunger and thirst
for righteousness,
[b]For they shall be filled.
7 Blessed *are* the merciful,
[a]For they shall obtain mercy.
8 [a]Blessed *are* the pure in heart,
For [b]they shall see God.
9 Blessed *are* the peacemakers,
For they shall be called sons of God.
10 [a]Blessed are those who are persecuted for
righteousness' sake,
For theirs is the kingdom of heaven.

11 [a]"Blessed are you when they revile and
persecute you, and say all kinds of [b]evil against
you falsely for My sake.
12 [a]"Rejoice and be exceedingly glad, for
great *is* your reward in heaven, for [b]so they persecuted the prophets who were before you.

Believers Are Salt and Light
(Mark 9:50; Luke 14:34, 35)

13 "You are the salt of the earth; [a]but if the
salt loses its flavor, how shall it be seasoned? It
is then good for nothing but to be thrown out and
trampled underfoot by men.
14 [a]"You are the light of the world. A city
that is set on a hill cannot be hidden.
15 "Nor do they [a]light a lamp and put it under a basket, but on a lampstand, and it gives
light to all *who are* in the house.
16 "Let your light so shine before men, [a]that
they may see your good works and [b]glorify your
Father in heaven.

Christ Fulfills the Law

17 [a]"Do not think that I came to destroy the
Law or the Prophets. I did not come to destroy
but to fulfill.
18 "For assuredly, I say to you, [a]till heaven
and earth pass away, one jot or one tittle will
by no means pass from the law till all is fulfilled.
19 [a]"Whoever therefore breaks one of the
least of these commandments, and teaches men
so, shall be called least in the kingdom of heaven;
but whoever does and teaches *them*, he shall be
called great in the kingdom of heaven.
20 "For I say to you, that unless your righteousness exceeds [a]*the righteousness* of the

KJV

scribes and Pharisees, ye shall in no case enter into the kingdom of heaven.

Murder Begins in the Heart
(*Luke 12:57–59*)

21 Ye have heard that it was said by them of old time, [a]THOU SHALT NOT KILL; and whosoever shall kill shall be in danger of the judgment:

22 But I say unto you, That [a]whosoever is angry with his brother without a cause shall be in danger of the judgment: and whosoever shall say to his brother, [b]Raca, shall be in danger of the council: but whosoever shall say, Thou fool, shall be in danger of hell fire.

23 Therefore [a]if thou bring thy gift to the altar, and there rememberest that thy brother hath ought against thee;

24 [a]Leave there thy gift before the altar, and go thy way; first be reconciled to thy brother, and then come and offer thy gift.

25 [a]Agree with thine adversary quickly, [b]whiles thou art in the way with him; lest at any time the adversary deliver thee to the judge, and the judge deliver thee to the officer, and thou be cast into prison.

26 Verily I say unto thee, Thou shalt by no means come out thence, till thou hast paid the uttermost farthing.

Adultery in the Heart

27 Ye have heard that it was said by them of old time, [a]THOU SHALT NOT COMMIT ADULTERY:

28 But I say unto you, That whosoever [a]looketh on a woman to lust after her hath committed adultery with her already in his heart.

29 [a]And if thy right eye offend thee, [b]pluck it out, and cast *it* from thee: for it is profitable for thee that one of thy members should perish, and not *that* thy whole body should be cast into hell.

30 And if thy right hand offend thee, cut it off, and cast *it* from thee: for it is profitable for thee that one of thy members should perish, and not *that* thy whole body should be cast into hell.

Marriage Is Sacred and Binding
(*Matt. 19:9; Mark 10:11, 12; Luke 16:18*)

31 It hath been said, [a]WHOSOEVER SHALL PUT AWAY HIS WIFE, LET HIM GIVE HER A WRITING OF DIVORCEMENT:

32 But I say unto you, That [a]whosoever shall put away his wife, saving for the cause of fornication, causeth her to commit adultery: and whosoever shall marry her that is divorced committeth adultery.

Jesus Forbids Oaths

33 Again, ye have heard that [a]it hath been said by them of old time, [b]Thou shalt not forswear thyself, but [c]shalt perform unto the Lord thine oaths:

34 But I say unto you, [a]Swear not at all; neither by heaven; for it is [b]God's throne:

35 Nor by the earth; for it is his footstool: neither by Jerusalem; for it is the city of [a]the great King.

36 Neither shalt thou swear by thy head, because thou canst not make one hair white or black.

37 [a]But let your communication be, Yea, yea; Nay, nay: for whatsoever is more than these cometh of evil.

Go the Second Mile
(*Luke 6:29–31*)

38 Ye have heard that it hath been said, [a]AN EYE FOR AN EYE, AND A TOOTH FOR A TOOTH:

39 But I say unto you, [a]That ye resist not evil: [b]but whosoever shall smite thee on thy right cheek, turn to him the other also.

21 [a]Ex. 20:13; Deut. 5:17
22 [a][1 John 3:15] [b][James 2:20; 3:6]
23 [a]Matt. 8:4
24 [a][Job 42:8; 1 Tim. 2:8; 1 Pet. 3:7]
25 [a][Prov. 25:8]; Luke 12:58, 59 [b][Ps. 32:6; Is. 55:6]
27 [a]Ex. 20:14; Deut. 5:18
28 [a]2 Sam. 11:2–5; Job 31:1; Prov. 6:25; [Matt. 15:19; James 1:14, 15]
29 [a]Mark 9:43 [b][Col. 3:5]
31 [a]Deut. 24:1; [Jer. 3:1]; Mark 10:2
32 [a][Matt. 19:9; Mark 10:11; Luke 16:18; Rom. 7:3]; 1 Cor. 7:11
33 [a]Matt. 23:16 [b][Ex. 20:7]; Lev. 19:12; Num. 30:2 [c]Deut. 23:23
34 [a]Matt. 23:16; James 5:12 [b]Is. 66:1
35 [a]Ps. 48:2; [Matt. 5:2, 19; 6:10]
37 [a][Col. 4:6]; James 5:12
38 [a]Ex. 21:24; Lev. 24:20; Deut. 19:21
39 [a][Prov. 20:22]; Luke 6:29; [Rom. 12:17; 1 Cor. 6:7; 1 Pet. 3:9] [b]Is. 50:6; Lam. 3:30

NKJV

scribes and Pharisees, you will by no means enter the kingdom of heaven.

Murder Begins in the Heart
(*Luke 12:57–59*)

21 "You have heard that it was said to those of old, [a]*'You shall not murder,* and whoever murders will be in danger of the judgment.'

22 "But I say to you that [a]whoever is angry with his brother *without a cause shall be in danger of the judgment. And whoever says to his brother, [b]'Raca!' shall be in danger of the council. But whoever says, 'You fool!' shall be in danger of hell fire.

23 "Therefore [a]if you bring your gift to the altar, and there remember that your brother has something against you,

24 [a]"leave your gift there before the altar, and go your way. First be reconciled to your brother, and then come and offer your gift.

25 [a]"Agree with your adversary quickly, [b]while you are on the way with him, lest your adversary deliver you to the judge, the judge hand you over to the officer, and you be thrown into prison.

26 "Assuredly, I say to you, you will by no means get out of there till you have paid the last penny.

Adultery in the Heart

27 "You have heard that it was said *to those of old, [a]*'You shall not commit adultery.'*

28 "But I say to you that whoever [a]looks at a woman to lust for her has already committed adultery with her in his heart.

29 [a]"If your right eye causes you to sin, [b]pluck it out and cast *it* from you; for it is more profitable for you that one of your members perish, than for your whole body to be cast into hell.

30 "And if your right hand causes you to sin, cut it off and cast *it* from you; for it is more profitable for you that one of your members perish, than for your whole body to be cast into hell.

Marriage Is Sacred and Binding
(*Matt. 19:9; Mark 10:11, 12; Luke 16:18*)

31 "Furthermore it has been said, [a]'Whoever divorces his wife, let him give her a certificate of divorce.'

32 "But I say to you that [a]whoever divorces his wife for any reason except *sexual immorality causes her to commit adultery; and whoever marries a woman who is divorced commits adultery.

Jesus Forbids Oaths

33 "Again you have heard that [a]it was said to those of old, [b]'You shall not swear falsely, but [c]shall perform your oaths to the Lord.'

34 "But I say to you, [a]do not swear at all: neither by heaven, for it is [b]God's throne;

35 "nor by the earth, for it is His footstool; nor by Jerusalem, for it is the city of [a]the great King.

36 "Nor shall you swear by your head, because you cannot make one hair white or black.

37 [a]"But let your 'Yes' be 'Yes,' and your 'No,' 'No.' For whatever is more than these is from the evil one.

Go the Second Mile
(*Luke 6:29–31*)

38 "You have heard that it was said, [a]*'An eye for an eye and a tooth for a tooth.'*

39 [a]"But I tell you not to resist an evil person. [b]But whoever slaps you on your right cheek, turn the other to him also.

5:22 NU omits *without a cause*
5:27 NU, M omit *to those of old*
5:32 Or *fornication*

KJV

40 And if any man will sue thee at the law,
and take away thy coat, let him have *thy* cloke
also.
41 And whosoever [a]shall compel thee to go
a mile, go with him twain.
42 Give to him that asketh thee, and [a]from
him that would borrow of thee turn not thou away.

Love Your Enemies
(*Luke 6:27, 28, 32–36*)

43 Ye have heard that it hath been said,
[a]THOU SHALT LOVE THY NEIGHBOUR, [b]and hate thine
enemy.
44 But I say unto you, [a]Love your enemies,
bless them that curse you, [b]do good to them that
hate you, and pray [c]for them which despitefully
use you, and persecute you;
45 That ye may be the children of your Father
which is in heaven: for [a]he maketh his sun to rise
on the evil and on the good, and sendeth rain on
the just and on the unjust.
46 [a]For if ye love them which love you, what
reward have ye? do not even the publicans the
same?
47 And if ye salute your brethren only, what
do ye more *than others?* do not even the publicans
so?
48 [a]Be ye therefore perfect, even [b]as your Father
which is in heaven is perfect.

Do Good to Please God

6 Take heed that ye do not your alms before
men, to be seen of them: otherwise ye have
no reward of your Father which is in heaven.
2 Therefore [a]when thou doest *thine* alms,
do not sound a trumpet before thee, as the hypocrites
do in the synagogues and in the streets, that
they may have glory of men. Verily I say unto
you, They have their reward.
3 But when thou doest alms, let not thy left
hand know what thy right hand doeth:
4 That thine alms may be in secret: and thy
Father which seeth in secret himself [a]shall reward
thee openly.

The Model Prayer
(*Luke 11:2–4*)

5 And when thou prayest, thou shalt not be
as the hypocrites *are:* for they love to pray standing
in the synagogues and in the corners of the
streets, that they may be seen of men. Verily I
say unto you, They have their reward.
6 But thou, when thou prayest, [a]enter into
thy closet, and when thou hast shut thy door, pray
to thy Father which is in secret; and thy Father
which seeth in secret shall reward thee openly.
7 But when ye pray, [a]use not vain repetitions,
as the heathen *do:* [b]for they think that they
shall be heard for their much speaking.
8 Be not ye therefore like unto them: for
your Father [a]knoweth what things ye have need
of, before ye ask him.
9 After this [a]manner therefore pray ye:
[b]Our Father which art in heaven, Hallowed be thy
[c]name.
10 Thy kingdom come. [a]Thy will be done in
earth, [b]as *it is* in heaven.
11 Give us this day our [a]daily bread.
12 And [a]forgive us our debts, as we forgive
our debtors.
13 [a]And lead us not into temptation, but [b]deliver
us from evil: For thine is the kingdom, and
the power, and the glory, for ever. Amen.
14 [a]For if ye forgive men their trespasses,
your heavenly Father will also forgive you:

41 [a]Matt. 27:32
42 [a]Deut. 15:7–11; Luke 6:30–34; 1 Tim. 6:18
43 [a]Lev. 19:18 [b]Deut. 23:3–6; Ps. 41:10
44 [a]Luke 6:27; Rom. 12:14 [b][Rom. 12:20] [c]Luke 23:34; Acts 7:60; 1 Cor. 4:12; 1 Pet. 2:23
45 [a]Job 25:3; Ps. 65:9–13; Luke 12:16, 17; Acts 14:17
46 [a]Luke 6:32
48 [a]Gen. 17:1; Lev. 11:44; 19:2; Luke 6:36; [Col. 1:28; 4:12]; James 1:4; 1 Pet. 1:15 [b]Eph. 5:1

CHAPTER 6

2 [a]Rom. 12:8
4 [a]Luke 14:12–14
6 [a]2 Kin. 4:33
7 [a]Eccl. 5:2 [b]1 Kin. 18:26
8 [a][Rom. 8:26, 27]
9 [a]Matt. 6:9–13; Luke 11:2–4; [John 16:24; Eph. 6:18; Jude 20] [b][Matt. 5:9, 16] [c]Mal. 1:11
10 [a]Matt. 26:42; Luke 22:42; Acts 21:14 [b]Ps. 103:20
11 [a][Job 23:12]; Prov. 30:8; Is. 33:16; Luke 11:3
12 [a][Matt. 18:21, 22]
13 [a][Matt. 26:41; 1 Cor. 10:31; 2 Pet. 2:9; Rev. 3:10] [b]John 17:15; [2 Thess. 3:3]; 2 Tim. 4:18; [1 John 5:18]
14 [a][Matt. 7:2]; Mark 11:25; [Eph. 4:32; Col. 3:13]

*________

5:44 NU *But I say to you, love your enemies and pray for those who persecute you*
5:47 M *friends* • NU *Gentiles*
6:4 NU omits *openly*
6:6 NU omits *openly*
6:13 NU omits the rest of v. 13.

NKJV

40 "If anyone wants to sue you and take
away your tunic, let him have *your* cloak also.
41 "And whoever [a]compels you to go one
mile, go with him two.
42 "Give to him who asks you, and [a]from him
who wants to borrow from you do not turn away.

Love Your Enemies
(*Luke 6:27, 28, 32–36*)

43 "You have heard that it was said, [a]*'You
shall love your neighbor* [b]and hate your enemy.'
44 *"But I say to you, [a]love your enemies,
bless those who curse you, [b]do good to those who
hate you, and pray [c]for those who spitefully use
you and persecute you,
45 "that you may be sons of your Father in
heaven; for [a]He makes His sun rise on the evil
and on the good, and sends rain on the just and
on the unjust.
46 [a]"For if you love those who love you, what
reward have you? Do not even the tax collectors
do the same?
47 "And if you greet your *brethren only,
what do you do more *than others?* Do not even
the *tax collectors do so?
48 [a]"Therefore you shall be perfect, just [b]as
your Father in heaven is perfect.

Do Good to Please God

6 "Take heed that you do not do your charitable
deeds before men, to be seen by them. Otherwise
you have no reward from your Father in
heaven.
2 "Therefore, [a]when you do a charitable
deed, do not sound a trumpet before you as the
hypocrites do in the synagogues and in the streets,
that they may have glory from men. Assuredly, I
say to you, they have their reward.
3 "But when you do a charitable deed, do
not let your left hand know what your right hand
is doing,
4 "that your charitable deed may be in secret;
and your Father who sees in secret [a]will
Himself reward you *openly.

The Model Prayer
(*Luke 11:2–4*)

5 "And when you pray, you shall not be like
the hypocrites. For they love to pray standing in
the synagogues and on the corners of the streets,
that they may be seen by men. Assuredly, I say
to you, they have their reward.
6 "But you, when you pray, [a]go into your
room, and when you have shut your door, pray
to your Father who *is* in the secret *place;* and
your Father who sees in secret will reward you
*openly.
7 "And when you pray, [a]do not use vain repetitions
as the heathen *do.* [b]For they think that
they will be heard for their many words.
8 "Therefore do not be like them. For your
Father [a]knows the things you have need of before
you ask Him.
9 "In this [a]manner, therefore, pray:

[b]Our Father in heaven,
Hallowed be Your [c]name.
10 Your kingdom come.
[a]Your will be done
On earth [b]as *it is* in heaven.
11 Give us this day our [a]daily bread.
12 And [a]forgive us our debts,
As we forgive our debtors.
13 [a]And do not lead us into temptation,
But [b]deliver us from the evil one.
*For Yours is the kingdom and the power
and the glory forever. Amen.

14 [a]"For if you forgive men their trespasses,
your heavenly Father will also forgive you.

KJV

15 But [a]if ye forgive not men their trespasses, neither will your Father forgive your trespasses.

Fasting to Be Seen Only by God

16 Moreover [a]when ye fast, be not, as the hypocrites, of a sad countenance: for they disfigure their faces, that they may appear unto men to fast. Verily I say unto you, They have their reward.
17 But thou, when thou fastest, [a]anoint thine head, and wash thy face;
18 That thou appear not unto men to fast, but unto thy Father which is in secret: and thy Father, which seeth in secret, shall reward thee openly.

Lay Up Treasures in Heaven
(Luke 12:33, 34)

19 [a]Lay not up for yourselves treasures upon earth, where moth and rust doth corrupt, and where thieves break through and steal:
20 [a]But lay up for yourselves treasures in heaven, where neither moth nor rust doth corrupt, and where thieves do not break through nor steal:
21 For where your treasure is, there will your heart be also.

The Lamp of the Body
(Luke 11:34–36)

22 [a]The light of the body is the eye: if therefore thine eye be single, thy whole body shall be full of light.
23 But if thine eye be evil, thy whole body shall be full of darkness. If therefore the light that is in thee be darkness, how great *is* that darkness!

You Cannot Serve God and Riches

24 [a]No man can serve two masters: for either he will hate the one, and love the other; or else he will hold to the one, and despise the other. [b]Ye cannot serve God and mammon.

Do Not Worry
(Luke 12:22–31)

25 Therefore I say unto you, [a]Take no thought for your life, what ye shall eat, or what ye shall drink; nor yet for your body, what ye shall put on. Is not the life more than meat, and the body than raiment?
26 [a]Behold the fowls of the air: for they sow not, neither do they reap, nor gather into barns; yet your heavenly Father feedeth them. Are ye not much better than they?
27 Which of you by taking thought can add one cubit unto his stature?
28 And why take ye thought for raiment? Consider the lilies of the field, how they grow; they toil not, neither do they spin:
29 And yet I say unto you, That even Solomon in all his glory was not arrayed like one of these.
30 Wherefore, if God so clothe the grass of the field, which to day is, and to morrow is cast into the oven, *shall he* not much more *clothe* you, O ye of little faith?
31 Therefore take no thought, saying, What shall we eat? or, What shall we drink? or, Wherewithal shall we be clothed?
32 (For after all these things do the Gentiles seek:) for your heavenly Father knoweth that ye have need of all these things.
33 But [a]seek ye first the kingdom of God, and his righteousness; and all these things shall be added unto you.
34 Take therefore no thought for the morrow: for the morrow shall take thought for the things of itself. Sufficient unto the day *is* the evil thereof.

Do Not Judge
(Luke 6:37–42)

7 Judge [a]not, that ye be not judged.
2 For with what judgment ye judge, ye shall

NKJV

15 "But [a]if you do not forgive men their trespasses, neither will your Father forgive your trespasses.

Fasting to Be Seen Only by God

16 "Moreover, [a]when you fast, do not be like the hypocrites, with a sad countenance. For they disfigure their faces that they may appear to men to be fasting. Assuredly, I say to you, they have their reward.
17 "But you, when you fast, [a]anoint your head and wash your face,
18 "so that you do not appear to men to be fasting, but to your Father who *is* in the secret *place;* and your Father who sees in secret will reward you *openly.

Lay Up Treasures in Heaven
(Luke 12:33, 34)

19 [a]"Do not lay up for yourselves treasures on earth, where moth and rust destroy and where thieves break in and steal;
20 [a]"but lay up for yourselves treasures in heaven, where neither moth nor rust destroys and where thieves do not break in and steal.
21 "For where your treasure is, there your heart will be also.

The Lamp of the Body
(Luke 11:34–36)

22 [a]"The lamp of the body is the eye. If therefore your eye is good, your whole body will be full of light.
23 "But if your eye is bad, your whole body will be full of darkness. If therefore the light that is in you is darkness, how great *is* that darkness!

You Cannot Serve God and Riches

24 [a]"No one can serve two masters; for either he will hate the one and love the other, or else he will be loyal to the one and despise the other. [b]You cannot serve God and mammon.

Do Not Worry
(Luke 12:22–31)

25 "Therefore I say to you, [a]do not worry about your life, what you will eat or what you will drink; nor about your body, what you will put on. Is not life more than food and the body more than clothing?
26 [a]"Look at the birds of the air, for they neither sow nor reap nor gather into barns; yet your heavenly Father feeds them. Are you not of more value than they?
27 "Which of you by worrying can add one cubit to his stature?
28 "So why do you worry about clothing? Consider the lilies of the field, how they grow: they neither toil nor spin;
29 "and yet I say to you that even Solomon in all his glory was not arrayed like one of these.
30 "Now if God so clothes the grass of the field, which today is, and tomorrow is thrown into the oven, *will He* not much more *clothe* you, O you of little faith?
31 "Therefore do not worry, saying, 'What shall we eat?' or 'What shall we drink?' or 'What shall we wear?'
32 "For after all these things the Gentiles seek. For your heavenly Father knows that you need all these things.
33 "But [a]seek first the kingdom of God and His righteousness, and all these things shall be added to you.
34 "Therefore do not worry about tomorrow, for tomorrow will worry about its own things. Sufficient for the day *is* its own trouble.

Do Not Judge
(Luke 6:37–42)

7 "Judge [a]not, that you be not judged.
2 "For with what judgment you judge, you

---

15 [a]Matt. 18:35; James 2:13
16 [a]Is. 58:3–7; Luke 18:12
17 [a]Ruth 3:3; 2 Sam. 12:20; Dan. 10:3
19 [a]Prov. 23:4; [1 Tim. 6:17; Heb. 13:5]; James 5:1
20 [a]Matt. 19:21; Luke 12:33; 18:22; 1 Tim. 6:19; 1 Pet. 1:4
22 [a]Luke 11:34, 35
24 [a]Luke 16:9, 11, 13 [b][Gal. 1:10; 1 Tim. 6:17; James 4:4; 1 John 2:15]
25 [a][Ps. 55:22]; Luke 12:22; [Phil. 4:6; 1 Pet. 5:7]
26 [a]Job 38:41; Ps. 147:9; Matt. 10:29; Luke 12:24
33 [a]1 Kin. 3:13; Luke 12:31; [1 Tim. 4:8]

CHAPTER 7

1 [a]Matt. 7:1–5; Luke 6:37; Rom. 14:3; [1 Cor. 4:3, 4]

*______

6:18 NU, M omit *openly*

KJV

be judged: [a]and with what measure ye mete, it shall be measured to you again.

3 [a]And why beholdest thou the mote that is in thy brother's eye, but considerest not the beam that is in thine own eye?

4 Or how wilt thou say to thy brother, Let me pull out the mote out of thine eye; and, behold, a beam *is* in thine own eye?

5 Thou hypocrite, first cast out the beam out of thine own eye; and then shalt thou see clearly to cast out the mote out of thy brother's eye.

6 [a]Give not that which is holy unto the dogs, neither cast ye your pearls before swine, lest they trample them under their feet, and turn again and rend you.

Keep Asking, Seeking, Knocking
(Luke 11:9–13)

7 [a]Ask, and it shall be given you; seek, and ye shall find; knock, and it shall be opened unto you:

8 For [a]every one that asketh receiveth; and he that seeketh findeth; and to him that knocketh it shall be opened.

9 [a]Or what man is there of you, whom if his son ask bread, will he give him a stone?

10 Or if he ask a fish, will he give him a serpent?

11 If ye then, [a]being evil, know how to give good gifts unto your children, how much more shall your Father which is in heaven give good things to them that ask him?

12 Therefore all things [a]whatsoever ye would that men should do to you, do ye even so to them: for [b]this is the law and the prophets.

The Narrow Way
(Luke 13:24)

13 [a]Enter ye in at the strait gate: for wide *is* the gate, and broad *is* the way, that leadeth to destruction, and many there be which go in thereat:

14 Because strait *is* the gate, and narrow *is* the way, which leadeth unto life, and few there be that find it.

You Will Know Them by Their Fruits
(Matt. 12:33; Luke 6:43–45)

15 [a]Beware of false prophets, [b]which come to you in sheep's clothing, but inwardly they are ravening wolves.

16 [a]Ye shall know them by their fruits. [b]Do men gather grapes of thorns, or figs of thistles?

17 Even so [a]every good tree bringeth forth good fruit; but a corrupt tree bringeth forth evil fruit.

18 A good tree cannot bring forth evil fruit, neither *can* a corrupt tree bring forth good fruit.

19 [a]Every tree that bringeth not forth good fruit is hewn down, and cast into the fire.

20 Wherefore by their fruits ye shall know them.

I Never Knew You
(Luke 6:46; 13:26, 27)

21 Not every one that saith unto me, [a]Lord, Lord, shall enter into the kingdom of heaven; but he that [b]doeth the will of my Father which is in heaven.

22 Many will say to me in that day, Lord, Lord, have we [a]not prophesied in thy name? and in thy name have cast out devils? and in thy name done many wonderful works?

23 And [a]then will I profess unto them, I never knew you: [b]depart from me, ye that work iniquity.

Build on the Rock
(Luke 6:47–49)

24 Therefore [a]whosoever heareth these sayings of mine, and doeth them, I will liken him unto a wise man, which built his house upon a rock:

---

2 [a]Mark 4:24; Luke 6:38 **3** [a]Luke 6:41 **6** [a]Prov. 9:7, 8; Acts 13:45 **7** [a][Matt. 21:22; Mark 11:24]; Luke 11:9–13; 18:1–8; [John 15:7; James 1:5, 6; 1 John 3:22] **8** [a]Prov. 8:17; Jer. 29:12 **9** [a]Luke 11:11 **11** [a]Gen. 6:5; 8:21; Ps. 84:11; Is. 63:7; [Rom. 8:32; James 1:17]; 1 John 3:1 **12** [a]Luke 6:31 [b]Matt. 22:40; Rom. 13:8; Gal. 5:14; [1 Tim. 1:5] **13** [a]Luke 13:24 **15** [a]Deut. 13:3; Jer. 23:16; Ezek. 22:28; Mark 13:22; [Luke 6:26]; Rom. 16:17; Eph. 5:6; [Col. 2:8; 2 Pet. 2:1; 1 John 4:1–3] [b]Mic. 3:5 **16** [a]Matt. 7:20; 12:33; Luke 6:44; James 3:12 [b]Luke 6:43 **17** [a]Jer. 11:19; Matt. 12:33 **19** [a]Matt. 3:10; Luke 3:9; [John 15:2, 6] **21** [a]Hos. 8:2; Matt. 25:11; Luke 6:46; Acts 19:13 [b]Rom. 2:13; James 1:22 **22** [a]Num. 24:4 **23** [a]Matt. 25:12; Luke 13:25; [2 Tim. 2:19] [b]Ps. 5:5; 6:8; [Matt. 25:41]; Luke 13:27 **24** [a]Matt. 7:24–27; Luke 6:47–49

NKJV

will be judged; [a]and with the measure you use, it will be measured back to you.

3 [a]"And why do you look at the speck in your brother's eye, but do not consider the plank in your own eye?

4 "Or how can you say to your brother, 'Let me remove the speck from your eye'; and look, a plank *is* in your own eye?

5 "Hypocrite! First remove the plank from your own eye, and then you will see clearly to remove the speck from your brother's eye.

6 [a]"Do not give what is holy to the dogs; nor cast your pearls before swine, lest they trample them under their feet, and turn and tear you in pieces.

Keep Asking, Seeking, Knocking
(Luke 11:9–13)

7 [a]"Ask, and it will be given to you; seek, and you will find; knock, and it will be opened to you.

8 "For [a]everyone who asks receives, and he who seeks finds, and to him who knocks it will be opened.

9 [a]"Or what man is there among you who, if his son asks for bread, will give him a stone?

10 "Or if he asks for a fish, will he give him a serpent?

11 "If you then, [a]being evil, know how to give good gifts to your children, how much more will your Father who is in heaven give good things to those who ask Him!

12 "Therefore, [a]whatever you want men to do to you, do also to them, for [b]this is the Law and the Prophets.

The Narrow Way
(Luke 13:24)

13 [a]"Enter by the narrow gate; for wide *is* the gate and broad *is* the way that leads to destruction, and there are many who go in by it.

14 *"Because narrow *is* the gate and difficult *is* the way which leads to life, and there are few who find it.

You Will Know Them by Their Fruits
(Matt. 12:33; Luke 6:43–45)

15 [a]"Beware of false prophets, [b]who come to you in sheep's clothing, but inwardly they are ravenous wolves.

16 [a]"You will know them by their fruits. [b]Do men gather grapes from thornbushes or figs from thistles?

17 "Even so, [a]every good tree bears good fruit, but a bad tree bears bad fruit.

18 "A good tree cannot bear bad fruit, nor *can* a bad tree bear good fruit.

19 [a]"Every tree that does not bear good fruit is cut down and thrown into the fire.

20 "Therefore by their fruits you will know them.

I Never Knew You
(Luke 6:46; 13:26, 27)

21 "Not everyone who says to Me, [a]'Lord, Lord,' shall enter the kingdom of heaven, but he who [b]does the will of My Father in heaven.

22 "Many will say to Me in that day, 'Lord, Lord, have we [a]not prophesied in Your name, cast out demons in Your name, and done many wonders in Your name?'

23 "And [a]then I will declare to them, 'I never knew you; [b]depart from Me, you who practice lawlessness!'

Build on the Rock
(Luke 6:47–49)

24 "Therefore [a]whoever hears these sayings of Mine, and does them, I will liken him to a wise man who built his house on the rock:

---

*7:14 NU, M *How narrow . . . !*

KJV

25 And the rain descended, and the floods came, and the winds blew, and beat upon that house; and it fell not: for it was founded upon a rock.

26 And every one that heareth these sayings of mine, and doeth them not, shall be likened unto a foolish man, which built his house upon the sand:

27 And the rain descended, and the floods came, and the winds blew, and beat upon that house; and it fell: and great was the fall of it.

28 And it came to pass, when Jesus had ended these sayings, [a]the people were astonished at his doctrine:

29 [a]For he taught them as *one* having authority, and not as the scribes.

Jesus Cleanses a Leper
(Mark 1:40–45; Luke 5:12–16)

8 When he was come down from the mountain, great multitudes followed him.

2 [a]And, behold, there came a leper and [b]worshipped him, saying, Lord, if thou wilt, thou canst make me clean.

3 And Jesus put forth *his* hand, and touched him, saying, I will; be thou clean. And immediately his leprosy [a]was cleansed.

4 And Jesus saith unto him, [a]See thou tell no man; but go thy way, shew thyself to the priest, and offer the gift that [b]Moses [c]commanded, for a testimony unto them.

Jesus Heals a Centurion's Servant
(Luke 7:1–10)

5 [a]And when Jesus was entered into Capernaum, there came unto him a [b]centurion, beseeching him,

6 And saying, Lord, my servant lieth at home sick of the palsy, grievously tormented.

7 And Jesus saith unto him, I will come and heal him.

8 The centurion answered and said, Lord, [a]I am not worthy that thou shouldest come under my roof: but [b]speak the word only, and my servant shall be healed.

9 For I am a man under authority, having soldiers under me: and I say to this *man*, Go, and he goeth; and to another, Come, and he cometh; and to my servant, Do this, and he doeth *it*.

10 When Jesus heard *it*, he marvelled, and said to them that followed, Verily I say unto you, I have not found so great faith, no, not in Israel.

11 And I say unto you, That [a]many shall come from the east and west, and shall sit down with Abraham, and Isaac, and Jacob, in the kingdom of heaven.

12 But [a]the children of the kingdom [b]shall be cast out into outer darkness: there shall be weeping and gnashing of teeth.

13 And Jesus said unto the centurion, Go thy way; and as thou hast believed, *so* be it done unto thee. And his servant was healed in the selfsame hour.

Peter's Mother-in-Law Healed
(Mark 1:29–31; Luke 4:38, 39)

14 [a]And when Jesus was come into Peter's house, he saw [b]his wife's mother laid, and sick of a fever.

15 And he touched her hand, and the fever left her: and she arose, and ministered unto them.

Many Healed After Sabbath Sunset
(Mark 1:32–34; Luke 4:40, 41)

16 [a]When the even was come, they brought unto him many that were possessed with devils: and he cast out the spirits with *his* word, and healed all that were sick:

28 [a]Matt. 13:54; Mark 1:22; 6:2; Luke 4:32; John 7:46
29 [a][John 7:46]

CHAPTER 8

2 [a]Matt. 8:2–4; Mark 1:40–45; Luke 5:12–14 [b]Matt. 2:11; 9:18; 15:25; John 9:38; Acts 10:25
3 [a]Matt. 11:5; Luke 4:27
4 [a]Matt. 9:30; Mark 5:43; Luke 4:41; 8:56; 9:21 [b]Lev. 14:3, 4, 10; Mark 1:44; Luke 5:14 [c]Lev. 14:4–32; Deut. 24:8
5 [a]Luke 7:1–3 [b]Matt. 27:54; Acts 10:1
8 [a]Luke 15:19, 21 [b]Ps. 107:20
11 [a][Gen. 12:3; Is. 2:2, 3; 11:10]; Mal. 1:11; Luke 13:29; [Acts 10:45; 11:18; 14:27; Rom. 15:9–13; Eph. 3:6]
12 [a][Matt. 21:43] [b]Matt. 13:42, 50; 22:13; 24:51; 25:30; Luke 13:28; 2 Pet. 2:17; Jude 13
14 [a]Matt. 8:14–16; Mark 1:29–31; Luke 4:38, 39 [b]1 Cor. 9:5
16 [a]Mark 1:32–34; Luke 4:40, 41

NKJV

25 "and the rain descended, the floods came, and the winds blew and beat on that house; and it did not fall, for it was founded on the rock.

26 "But everyone who hears these sayings of Mine, and does not do them, will be like a foolish man who built his house on the sand:

27 "and the rain descended, the floods came, and the winds blew and beat on that house; and it fell. And great was its fall."

28 And so it was, when Jesus had ended these sayings, that [a]the people were astonished at His teaching,

29 [a]for He taught them as one having authority, and not as the scribes.

Jesus Cleanses a Leper
(Mark 1:40–45; Luke 5:12–16)

8 When He had come down from the mountain, great multitudes followed Him.

2 [a]And behold, a leper came and [b]worshiped Him, saying, "Lord, if You are willing, You can make me clean."

3 Then Jesus put out *His* hand and touched him, saying, "I am willing; be cleansed." Immediately his leprosy [a]was cleansed.

4 And Jesus said to him, [a]"See that you tell no one; but go your way, show yourself to the priest, and offer the gift that [b]Moses [c]commanded, as a testimony to them."

Jesus Heals a Centurion's Servant
(Luke 7:1–10)

5 [a]Now when Jesus had entered Capernaum, a [b]centurion came to Him, pleading with Him,

6 saying, "Lord, my servant is lying at home paralyzed, dreadfully tormented."

7 And Jesus said to him, "I will come and heal him."

8 The centurion answered and said, "Lord, [a]I am not worthy that You should come under my roof. But only [b]speak a word, and my servant will be healed.

9 "For I also am a man under authority, having soldiers under me. And I say to this *one*, 'Go,' and he goes; and to another, 'Come,' and he comes; and to my servant, 'Do this,' and he does *it*."

10 When Jesus heard *it*, He marveled, and said to those who followed, "Assuredly, I say to you, I have not found such great faith, not even in Israel!

11 "And I say to you that [a]many will come from east and west, and sit down with Abraham, Isaac, and Jacob in the kingdom of heaven.

12 "But [a]the sons of the kingdom [b]will be cast out into outer darkness. There will be weeping and gnashing of teeth."

13 Then Jesus said to the centurion, "Go your way; and as you have believed, *so* let it be done for you." And his servant was healed that same hour.

Peter's Mother-in-Law Healed
(Mark 1:29–31; Luke 4:38, 39)

14 [a]Now when Jesus had come into Peter's house, He saw [b]his wife's mother lying sick with a fever.

15 So He touched her hand, and the fever left her. And she arose and served *them.

Many Healed After Sabbath Sunset
(Mark 1:32–34; Luke 4:40, 41)

16 [a]When evening had come, they brought to Him many who were demon-possessed. And He cast out the spirits with a word, and healed all who were sick,

*———

8:15 NU, M *Him*

KJV

17 That it might be fulfilled which was spoken by Esaias the prophet, saying, [a]HIMSELF TOOK OUR INFIRMITIES, AND BARE OUR SICKNESSES.

The Cost of Discipleship
(Luke 9:57–62)

18 Now when Jesus saw great multitudes about him, he gave commandment to depart unto the other side.

19 [a]And a certain scribe came, and said unto him, Master, I will follow thee whithersoever thou goest.

20 And Jesus saith unto him, The foxes have holes, and the birds of the air *have* nests; but the Son of man hath not where to lay *his* head.

21 [a]And another of his disciples said unto him, Lord, [b]suffer me first to go and bury my father.

22 But Jesus said unto him, Follow me; and let the dead bury their dead.

Wind and Wave Obey Jesus
(Mark 4:35–41; Luke 8:22–25)

23 And when he was entered into a ship, his disciples followed him.

24 [a]And, behold, there arose a great tempest in the sea, insomuch that the ship was covered with the waves: but he was asleep.

25 And his disciples came to *him*, and awoke him, saying, Lord, save us: we perish.

26 And he saith unto them, Why are ye fearful, O ye of little faith? Then [a]he arose, and rebuked the winds and the sea; and there was a great calm.

27 But the men marvelled, saying, What manner of man is this, that even the winds and the sea obey him!

Two Demon-Possessed Men Healed
(Mark 5:1–20; Luke 8:26–39)

28 [a]And when he was come to the other side into the country of the Gergesenes, there met him two possessed with devils, coming out of the tombs, exceeding fierce, so that no man might pass by that way.

29 And, behold, they cried out, saying, What have we to do with thee, Jesus, thou Son of God? art thou come hither to torment us before the time?

30 And there was a good way off from them an herd of many swine feeding.

31 So the devils besought him, saying, If thou cast us out, suffer us to go away into the herd of swine.

32 And he said unto them, Go. And when they were come out, they went into the herd of swine: and, behold, the whole herd of swine ran violently down a steep place into the sea, and perished in the waters.

33 And they that kept them fled, and went their ways into the city, and told every thing, and what was befallen to the possessed of the devils.

34 And, behold, the whole city came out to meet Jesus: and when they saw him, [a]they besought *him* that he would depart out of their coasts.

Jesus Forgives and Heals a Paralytic
(Mark 2:1–12; Luke 5:17–26)

9 And he entered into a ship, and passed over, [a]and came into his own city.

2 [a]And, behold, they brought to him a man sick of the palsy, lying on a bed: [b]and Jesus seeing their faith said unto the sick of the palsy; Son, be of good cheer; thy sins be forgiven thee.

3 And, behold, certain of the scribes said within themselves, This *man* blasphemeth.

4 And Jesus [a]knowing their thoughts said, Wherefore think ye evil in your hearts?

5 For whether is easier, to say, *Thy* sins be forgiven thee; or to say, Arise, and walk?

17 [a]Is. 53:4; 1 Pet. 2:24
19 [a]Matt. 8:19–22; Luke 9:57, 58
21 [a]Luke 9:59, 60 [b]1 Kin. 19:20
24 [a]Mark 4:37; Luke 8:23–25
26 [a]Ps. 65:7; 89:9; 107:29
28 [a]Mark 5:1–4; Luke 8:26–33
34 [a]Deut. 5:25; 1 Kin. 17:18; Amos 7:12; Luke 5:8; Acts 16:39

CHAPTER 9

1 [a]Matt. 4:13; 11:23; Mark 5:21
2 [a]Mark 2:3–12; Luke 5:18–26 [b]Matt. 8:10
4 [a]Ps. 139:2; Matt. 12:25; Mark 12:15; Luke 5:22; 6:8; 9:47; 11:17

*

8:28 NU *Gadarenes*
8:31 NU *send us into*

NKJV

17 that it might be fulfilled which was spoken by Isaiah the prophet, saying:

[a]*"He Himself took our infirmities*
And bore our sicknesses."

The Cost of Discipleship
(Luke 9:57–62)

18 And when Jesus saw great multitudes about Him, He gave a command to depart to the other side.

19 [a]Then a certain scribe came and said to Him, "Teacher, I will follow You wherever You go."

20 And Jesus said to him, "Foxes have holes and birds of the air *have* nests, but the Son of Man has nowhere to lay *His* head."

21 [a]Then another of His disciples said to Him, "Lord, [b]let me first go and bury my father."

22 But Jesus said to him, "Follow Me, and let the dead bury their own dead."

Wind and Wave Obey Jesus
(Mark 4:35–41; Luke 8:22–25)

23 Now when He got into a boat, His disciples followed Him.

24 [a]And suddenly a great tempest arose on the sea, so that the boat was covered with the waves. But He was asleep.

25 Then His disciples came to *Him* and awoke Him, saying, "Lord, save us! We are perishing!"

26 But He said to them, "Why are you fearful, O you of little faith?" Then [a]He arose and rebuked the winds and the sea, and there was a great calm.

27 So the men marveled, saying, "Who can this be, that even the winds and the sea obey Him?"

Two Demon-Possessed Men Healed
(Mark 5:1–20; Luke 8:26–39)

28 [a]When He had come to the other side, to the country of the *Gergesenes, there met Him two demon-possessed *men,* coming out of the tombs, exceedingly fierce, so that no one could pass that way.

29 And suddenly they cried out, saying, "What have we to do with You, Jesus, You Son of God? Have You come here to torment us before the time?"

30 Now a good way off from them there was a herd of many swine feeding.

31 So the demons begged Him, saying, "If You cast us out, *permit us to go away into the herd of swine."

32 And He said to them, "Go." So when they had come out, they went into the herd of swine. And suddenly the whole herd of swine ran violently down the steep place into the sea, and perished in the water.

33 Then those who kept *them* fled; and they went away into the city and told everything, including what *had happened* to the demon-possessed *men.*

34 And behold, the whole city came out to meet Jesus. And when they saw Him, [a]they begged *Him* to depart from their region.

Jesus Forgives and Heals a Paralytic
(Mark 2:1–12; Luke 5:17–26)

9 So He got into a boat, crossed over, [a]and came to His own city.

2 [a]Then behold, they brought to Him a paralytic lying on a bed. [b]When Jesus saw their faith, He said to the paralytic, "Son, be of good cheer; your sins are forgiven you."

3 And at once some of the scribes said within themselves, "This Man blasphemes!"

4 But Jesus, [a]knowing their thoughts, said, "Why do you think evil in your hearts?

5 "For which is easier, to say, '*Your* sins are forgiven you,' or to say, 'Arise and walk'?

KJV

6 But that ye may know that the Son of man
hath power on earth to forgive sins, (then saith
he to the sick of the palsy,) Arise, take up thy
bed, and go unto thine house.
7 And he arose, and departed to his house.
8 But when the multitudes saw *it*, they
[a]marvelled, and glorified God, which had given
such power unto men.

Matthew the Tax Collector
(Mark 2:13–17; Luke 5:27–32)

9 [a]And as Jesus passed forth from thence,
he saw a man, named Matthew, sitting at the receipt of custom: and he saith unto him, Follow
me. And he arose, and followed him.
10 [a]And it came to pass, as Jesus sat at meat
in the house, behold, many publicans and sinners
came and sat down with him and his disciples.
11 And when the Pharisees saw *it*, they said
unto his disciples, Why eateth your Master with
[a]publicans and [b]sinners?
12 But when Jesus heard *that*, he said unto
them, They that be whole need not a physician,
but they that are sick.
13 But go ye and learn what *that* meaneth,
[a]I WILL HAVE MERCY, AND NOT SACRIFICE: for I am
not come to call the righteous, [b]but sinners to repentance.

Jesus Is Questioned About Fasting
(Mark 2:18–22; Luke 5:33–39)

14 Then came to him the disciples of John,
saying, [a]Why do we and the Pharisees fast oft,
but thy disciples fast not?
15 And Jesus said unto them, Can [a]the children of the bridechamber mourn, as long as the
bridegroom is with them? but the days will come,
when the bridegroom shall be taken from them,
and [b]then shall they fast.
16 No man putteth a piece of new cloth unto
an old garment, for that which is put in to fill it
up taketh from the garment, and the rent is made
worse.
17 Neither do men put new wine into old bottles: else the bottles break, and the wine runneth
out, and the bottles perish: but they put new wine
into new bottles, and both are preserved.

A Girl Restored to Life and a Woman Healed
(Mark 5:21–43; Luke 8:40–56)

18 [a]While he spake these things unto them,
behold, there came a certain ruler, and worshipped him, saying, My daughter is even now
dead: but come and lay thy hand upon her, and
she shall live.
19 And Jesus arose, and followed him, and
so did his [a]disciples.
20 [a]And, behold, a woman, which was diseased with an issue of blood twelve years, came
behind *him*, and [b]touched the hem of his garment:
21 For she said within herself, If I may but
touch his garment, I shall be whole.
22 But Jesus turned him about, and when he
saw her, he said, Daughter, be of good comfort;
[a]thy faith hath made thee whole. And the woman
was made whole from that hour.
23 [a]And when Jesus came into the ruler's
house, and saw [b]the minstrels and the people
making a noise,
24 He said unto them, [a]Give place: for the
maid is not dead, but sleepeth. And they laughed
him to scorn.
25 But when the people were put forth, he
went in, and [a]took her by the hand, and the maid
arose.
26 And the [a]fame hereof went abroad into
all that land.

Two Blind Men Healed

27 And when Jesus departed thence, [a]two
blind men followed him, crying, and saying,
[b]*Thou* son of David, have mercy on us.

8 [a]Matt. 8:27; John 7:15
9 [a]Mark 2:14; Luke 5:27
10 [a]Mark 2:15; Luke 5:29
11 [a]Matt. 11:19; Mark 2:16; Luke 5:30; 15:2 [b][Gal. 2:15]
13 [a]Hos. 6:6; [Mic. 6:6–8]; Matt. 12:7 [b]Mark 2:17; Luke 5:32; 1 Tim. 1:15
14 [a]Mark 2:18; Luke 5:33–35; 18:12
15 [a]John 3:29 [b]Acts 13:2, 3; 14:23
18 [a]Mark 5:22–43; Luke 8:41–56
19 [a]Matt. 10:2–4
20 [a]Mark 5:25; Luke 8:43 [b]Num. 15:38; Deut. 22:12; Matt. 14:36; 23:5; Mark 6:56
22 [a]Matt. 9:29; 15:28; Mark 5:34; 10:52; Luke 7:50; 8:48; 17:19; 18:42
23 [a]Mark 5:38; Luke 8:51 [b]2 Chr. 35:25; Jer. 9:17; 16:6; Ezek. 24:17
24 [a]John 11:3; Acts 20:10
25 [a]Matt. 8:3, 15; Mark 1:31
26 [a]Matt. 4:24; Mark 1:28, 45; Luke 4:14, 37; 5:15; 7:17
27 [a]Matt. 20:29–34 [b]Matt. 15:22; Mark 10:47; Luke 18:38, 39

NKJV

6 "But that you may know that the Son of
Man has power on earth to forgive sins"—then
He said to the paralytic, "Arise, take up your bed,
and go to your house."
7 And he arose and departed to his house.
8 Now when the multitudes saw *it*, they
[a]marveled* and glorified God, who had given such
power to men.

Matthew the Tax Collector
(Mark 2:13–17; Luke 5:27–32)

9 [a]As Jesus passed on from there, He saw
a man named Matthew sitting at the tax office.
And He said to him, "Follow Me." So he arose
and followed Him.
10 [a]Now it happened, as Jesus sat at the table
in the house, *that* behold, many tax collectors and
sinners came and sat down with Him and His
disciples.
11 And when the Pharisees saw *it*, they said
to His disciples, "Why does your Teacher eat with
[a]tax collectors and [b]sinners?"
12 When Jesus heard *that*, He said to them,
"Those who are well have no need of a physician,
but those who are sick.
13 "But go and learn what *this* means: [a]*'I de-*
sire mercy and not sacrifice.' For I did not come
to call the righteous, [b]but sinners, *to repentance."

Jesus Is Questioned About Fasting
(Mark 2:18–22; Luke 5:33–39)

14 Then the disciples of John came to Him,
saying, [a]"Why do we and the Pharisees fast *often, but Your disciples do not fast?"
15 And Jesus said to them, "Can [a]the friends
of the bridegroom mourn as long as the bridegroom is with them? But the days will come when
the bridegroom will be taken away from them,
and [b]then they will fast.
16 "No one puts a piece of unshrunk cloth
on an old garment; for the patch pulls away from
the garment, and the tear is made worse.
17 "Nor do they put new wine into old wineskins, or else the wineskins break, the wine is
spilled, and the wineskins are ruined. But they
put new wine into new wineskins, and both are
preserved."

A Girl Restored to Life and a Woman Healed
(Mark 5:21–43; Luke 8:40–56)

18 [a]While He spoke these things to them, behold, a ruler came and worshiped Him, saying,
"My daughter has just died, but come and lay
Your hand on her and she will live."
19 So Jesus arose and followed him, and so
did His [a]disciples.
20 [a]And suddenly, a woman who had a flow
of blood for twelve years came from behind and
[b]touched the hem of His garment.
21 For she said to herself, "If only I may
touch His garment, I shall be made well."
22 But Jesus turned around, and when He
saw her He said, "Be of good cheer, daughter;
[a]your faith has made you well." And the woman
was made well from that hour.
23 [a]When Jesus came into the ruler's house,
and saw [b]the flute players and the noisy crowd
wailing,
24 He said to them, [a]"Make room, for the girl
is not dead, but sleeping." And they ridiculed Him.
25 But when the crowd was put outside, He
went in and [a]took her by the hand, and the girl
arose.
26 And the [a]report of this went out into all
that land.

Two Blind Men Healed

27 When Jesus departed from there, [a]two
blind men followed Him, crying out and saying,
[b]"Son of David, have mercy on us!"

*———

9:8 NU *were afraid*
9:13 NU omits *to repentance*
9:14 NU brackets *often* as disputed.

KJV

28 And when he was come into the house, the blind men came to him: and Jesus saith unto them, Believe ye that I am able to do this? They said unto him, Yea, Lord.
29 Then touched he their eyes, saying, According to your faith be it unto you.
30 And their eyes were opened; and Jesus straitly charged them, saying, [a]See *that* no man know *it*.
31 [a]But they, when they were departed, spread abroad his fame in all that country.

A Mute Man Speaks

32 [a]As they went out, behold, they brought to him a dumb man possessed with a devil.
33 And when the devil was cast out, the dumb spake: and the multitudes marvelled, saying, It was never so seen in Israel.
34 But the Pharisees said, [a]He casteth out devils through the prince of the devils.

The Compassion of Jesus
(Luke 10:2, 3)

35 And Jesus went about all the cities and villages, [a]teaching in their synagogues, and preaching the gospel of the kingdom, and healing every sickness and every disease among the people.
36 [a]But when he saw the multitudes, he was moved with compassion on them, because they fainted, and were scattered abroad, [b]as sheep having no shepherd.
37 Then saith he unto his disciples, [a]The harvest truly *is* plenteous, but the labourers *are* few;
38 [a]Pray ye therefore the Lord of the harvest, that he will send forth labourers into his harvest.

The Twelve Apostles
(Mark 3:13–19; Luke 6:12–16)

10 And [a]when he had called unto *him* his twelve disciples, he gave them power *against* unclean spirits, to cast them out, and to heal all manner of sickness and all manner of disease.
2 Now the names of the twelve apostles are these; The first, Simon, [a]who is called Peter, and Andrew his brother; James *the son* of Zebedee, and John his brother;
3 Philip, and Bartholomew; Thomas, and Matthew the publican; James *the son* of Alphaeus, and Lebbaeus, whose surname was Thaddaeus;
4 [a]Simon the Canaanite, and Judas [b]Iscariot, who also betrayed him.

Sending Out the Twelve
(Mark 6:7–13; Luke 9:1–6)

5 These twelve Jesus sent forth, and commanded them, saying, [a]Go not into the way of the Gentiles, and into *any* city of [b]the Samaritans enter ye not:
6 [a]But go rather to the [b]lost sheep of the house of Israel.
7 [a]And as ye go, preach, saying, [b]The kingdom of heaven is at hand.
8 Heal the sick, cleanse the lepers, raise the dead, cast out devils: [a]freely ye have received, freely give.
9 [a]Provide neither gold, nor silver, nor [b]brass in your purses,
10 Nor scrip for *your* journey, neither two coats, neither shoes, nor yet staves: [a]for the workman is worthy of his meat.
11 [a]And into whatsoever city or town ye shall enter, enquire who in it is worthy; and there abide till ye go thence.
12 And when ye come into an house, salute it.
13 [a]And if the house be worthy, let your peace come upon it: [b]but if it be not worthy, let your peace return to you.
14 [a]And whosoever shall not receive you, nor

30 [a]Matt. 8:4
31 [a]Mark 7:36
32 [a]Matt. 12:22, 24
34 [a]Luke 11:15
35 [a]Matt. 4:23
36 [a]Mark 6:34 [b]Num. 27:17
37 [a]Luke 10:2
38 [a]2 Thess. 3:1

CHAPTER 10

1 [a]Luke 6:13
2 [a]John 1:42
4 [a]Acts 1:13 [b]John 13:2, 26
5 [a]Matt. 4:15 [b]John 4:9
6 [a]Matt. 15:24 [b]Jer. 50:6
7 [a]Luke 9:2 [b]Matt. 3:2
8 [a][Acts 8:18]
9 [a]1 Sam. 9:7 [b]Mark 6:8
10 [a]1 Tim. 5:18
11 [a]Luke 10:8
13 [a]Luke 10:5 [b]Ps. 35:13
14 [a]Mark 6:11

NKJV

28 And when He had come into the house, the blind men came to Him. And Jesus said to them, "Do you believe that I am able to do this?" They said to Him, "Yes, Lord."
29 Then He touched their eyes, saying, "According to your faith let it be to you."
30 And their eyes were opened. And Jesus sternly warned them, saying, [a]"See *that* no one knows *it*."
31 [a]But when they had departed, they spread the news about Him in all that country.

A Mute Man Speaks

32 [a]As they went out, behold, they brought to Him a man, mute and demon-possessed.
33 And when the demon was cast out, the mute spoke. And the multitudes marveled, saying, "It was never seen like this in Israel!"
34 But the Pharisees said, [a]"He casts out demons by the ruler of the demons."

The Compassion of Jesus
(Luke 10:2, 3)

35 Then Jesus went about all the cities and villages, [a]teaching in their synagogues, preaching the gospel of the kingdom, and healing every sickness and every disease *among the people.
36 [a]But when He saw the multitudes, He was moved with compassion for them, because they were *weary and scattered, [b]like sheep having no shepherd.
37 Then He said to His disciples, [a]"The harvest truly *is* plentiful, but the laborers *are* few.
38 [a]"Therefore pray the Lord of the harvest to send out laborers into His harvest."

The Twelve Apostles
(Mark 3:13–19; Luke 6:12–16)

10 And [a]when He had called His twelve disciples to *Him,* He gave them power *over* unclean spirits, to cast them out, and to heal all kinds of sickness and all kinds of disease.
2 Now the names of the twelve apostles are these: first, Simon, [a]who is called Peter, and Andrew his brother; James the *son* of Zebedee, and John his brother;
3 Philip and Bartholomew; Thomas and Matthew the tax collector; James the *son* of Alphaeus, and *Lebbaeus, whose surname was Thaddaeus;
4 [a]Simon the *Cananite, and Judas [b]Iscariot, who also betrayed Him.

Sending Out the Twelve
(Mark 6:7–13; Luke 9:1–6)

5 These twelve Jesus sent out and commanded them, saying: [a]"Do not go into the way of the Gentiles, and do not enter a city of [b]the Samaritans.
6 [a]"But go rather to the [b]lost sheep of the house of Israel.
7 [a]"And as you go, preach, saying, [b]'The kingdom of heaven is at hand.'
8 "Heal the sick, *cleanse the lepers, *raise the dead, cast out demons. [a]Freely you have received, freely give.
9 [a]"Provide neither gold nor silver nor [b]copper in your money belts,
10 "nor bag for *your* journey, nor two tunics, nor sandals, nor staffs; [a]for a worker is worthy of his food.
11 [a]"Now whatever city or town you enter, inquire who in it is worthy, and stay there till you go out.
12 "And when you go into a household, greet it.
13 [a]"If the household is worthy, let your peace come upon it. [b]But if it is not worthy, let your peace return to you.
14 [a]"And whoever will not receive you nor

9:35 NU omits *among the people*
9:36 NU, M *harassed*
10:3 NU omits *Lebbaeus, whose surname was*
10:4 NU *Cananaean*
10:8 NU *raise the dead, cleanse the lepers* • M omits *raise the dead*

KJV

hear your words, when ye depart out of that house or city, [b]shake off the dust of your feet.

15 Verily I say unto you, [a]It shall be more tolerable for the land of Sodom and Gomorrha in the day of judgment, than for that city.

Persecutions Are Coming
(Mark 13:9–13; Luke 21:12–17)

16 [a]Behold, I send you forth as sheep in the midst of wolves: [b]be ye therefore wise as serpents, and [c]harmless as doves.

17 But beware of men: for [a]they will deliver you up to the councils, and [b]they will scourge you in their synagogues;

18 And [a]ye shall be brought before governors and kings for my sake, for a testimony against them and the Gentiles.

19 [a]But when they deliver you up, take no thought how or what ye shall speak: for [b]it shall be given you in that same hour what ye shall speak.

20 [a]For it is not ye that speak, but the Spirit of your Father which speaketh in you.

21 [a]And the brother shall deliver up the brother to death, and the father the child: and the children shall rise up against *their* parents, and cause them to be put to death.

22 And [a]ye shall be hated of all *men* for my name's sake: [b]but he that endureth to the end shall be saved.

23 But [a]when they persecute you in this city, flee ye into another: for verily I say unto you, Ye shall not have [b]gone over the cities of Israel, [c]till the Son of man be come.

24 [a]The disciple is not above *his* master, nor the servant above his lord.

25 It is enough for the disciple that he be as his master, and the servant as his lord. If [a]they have called the master of the house Beelzebub, how much more *shall they call* them of his household?

26 Fear them not therefore: [a]for there is nothing covered, that shall not be revealed; and hid, that shall not be known.

Jesus Teaches the Fear of God
(Luke 12:3–7)

27 What I tell you in darkness, *that* [a]speak ye in light: and what ye hear in the ear, *that* preach ye upon the housetops.

28 [a]And fear not them which kill the body, but are not able to kill the soul: but rather [b]fear him which is able to destroy both soul and body in hell.

29 Are not two [a]sparrows sold for a farthing? and one of them shall not fall on the ground without your Father.

30 [a]But the very hairs of your head are all numbered.

31 Fear ye not therefore, ye are of more value than many sparrows.

Confess Christ Before Men
(Luke 12:8, 9)

32 [a]Whosoever therefore shall confess me before men, [b]him will I confess also before my Father which is in heaven.

33 [a]But whosoever shall deny me before men, him will I also deny before my Father which is in heaven.

Christ Brings Division
(Luke 12:51–53; 14:26, 27)

34 [a]Think not that I am come to send peace on earth: I came not to send peace, but a sword.

35 For I am come to [a]SET A MAN AT VARIANCE AGAINST HIS FATHER, AND THE DAUGHTER AGAINST HER MOTHER, AND THE DAUGHTER IN LAW AGAINST HER MOTHER IN LAW.

36 And [a]A MAN'S FOES *SHALL BE* THEY OF HIS OWN HOUSEHOLD.

37 [a]He that loveth father or mother more

14 [b]Acts 13:51
15 [a]Matt. 11:22, 24
16 [a]Luke 10:3 [b]Eph. 5:15 [c][Phil. 2:14–16]
17 [a]Mark 13:9 [b]Acts 5:40; 22:19; 26:11
18 [a]2 Tim. 4:16
19 [a]Luke 12:11, 12; 21:14, 15 [b]Ex. 4:12
20 [a]2 Sam. 23:2
21 [a]Mic. 7:6
22 [a]Luke 21:17 [b]Mark 13:13
23 [a]Acts 8:1 [b][Mark 13:10] [c]Matt. 16:28
24 [a]John 15:20
25 [a]John 8:48, 52
26 [a]Mark 4:22
27 [a]Acts 5:20
28 [a]Luke 12:4 [b]Luke 12:5
29 [a]Luke 12:6, 7
30 [a]Luke 21:18
32 [a]Luke 12:8 [b][Rev. 3:5]
33 [a]2 Tim. 2:12
34 [a][Luke 12:49]
35 [a]Mic. 7:6
36 [a]John 13:18
37 [a]Luke 14:26

NKJV

hear your words, when you depart from that house or city, [b]shake off the dust from your feet.

15 "Assuredly, I say to you, [a]it will be more tolerable for the land of Sodom and Gomorrah in the day of judgment than for that city!

Persecutions Are Coming
(Mark 13:9–13; Luke 21:12–17)

16 [a]"Behold, I send you out as sheep in the midst of wolves. [b]Therefore be wise as serpents and [c]harmless as doves.

17 "But beware of men, for [a]they will deliver you up to councils and [b]scourge you in their synagogues.

18 [a]"You will be brought before governors and kings for My sake, as a testimony to them and to the Gentiles.

19 [a]"But when they deliver you up, do not worry about how or what you should speak. For [b]it will be given to you in that hour what you should speak;

20 [a]"for it is not you who speak, but the Spirit of your Father who speaks in you.

21 [a]"Now brother will deliver up brother to death, and a father *his* child; and children will rise up against parents and cause them to be put to death.

22 "And [a]you will be hated by all for My name's sake. [b]But he who endures to the end will be saved.

23 [a]"When they persecute you in this city, flee to another. For assuredly, I say to you, you will not have [b]gone through the cities of Israel [c]before the Son of Man comes.

24 [a]"A disciple is not above *his* teacher, nor a servant above his master.

25 "It is enough for a disciple that he be like his teacher, and a servant like his master. If [a]they have called the master of the house *Beelzebub, how much more *will they call* those of his household!

26 "Therefore do not fear them. [a]For there is nothing covered that will not be revealed, and hidden that will not be known.

Jesus Teaches the Fear of God
(Luke 12:3–7)

27 "Whatever I tell you in the dark, [a]speak in the light; and what you hear in the ear, preach on the housetops.

28 [a]"And do not fear those who kill the body but cannot kill the soul. But rather [b]fear Him who is able to destroy both soul and body in hell.

29 "Are not two [a]sparrows sold for a copper coin? And not one of them falls to the ground apart from your Father's will.

30 [a]"But the very hairs of your head are all numbered.

31 "Do not fear therefore; you are of more value than many sparrows.

Confess Christ Before Men
(Luke 12:8, 9)

32 [a]"Therefore whoever confesses Me before men, [b]him I will also confess before My Father who is in heaven.

33 [a]"But whoever denies Me before men, him I will also deny before My Father who is in heaven.

Christ Brings Division
(Luke 12:51–53; 14:26, 27)

34 [a]"Do not think that I came to bring peace on earth. I did not come to bring peace but a sword.

35 "For I have come to [a]*'set a man against his father, a daughter against her mother, and a daughter-in-law against her mother-in-law'*;

36 "and [a]*'a man's enemies will be those of his own household.'*

37 [a]"He who loves father or mother more

*10:25 NU, M *Beelzebul;* a Philistine deity, 2 Kin. 1:2, 3

KJV

than me is not worthy of me: and he that loveth
son or daughter more than me is not worthy of
me.
38 [a]And he that taketh not his cross, and followeth after me, is not worthy of me.
39 [a]He that findeth his life shall lose it: and
he that loseth his life for my sake shall find it.

A Cup of Cold Water
(*Mark 9:41*)

40 [a]He that receiveth you receiveth me, and
he that receiveth me receiveth him that sent me.
41 [a]He that receiveth a prophet in the name
of a prophet shall receive a prophet's reward; and
he that receiveth a righteous man in the name of
a righteous man shall receive a righteous man's
reward.
42 [a]And whosoever shall give to drink unto
one of these little ones a cup of cold *water* only
in the name of a disciple, verily I say unto you,
he shall in no wise lose his reward.

John the Baptist Sends Messengers to Jesus
(*Luke 7:18–35*)

11 And it came to pass, when Jesus had made
an end of commanding his twelve disciples,
he departed thence to [a]teach and to preach in their
cities.
2 [a]Now when John had heard [b]in the prison
the works of Christ, he sent two of his disciples,
3 And said unto him, Art thou [a]he that
should come, or do we look for another?
4 Jesus answered and said unto them, Go
and shew John again those things which ye do
hear and see:
5 [a]The blind receive their sight, and the
lame walk, the lepers are cleansed, and the deaf
hear, the dead are raised up, and [b]the poor have
the gospel preached to them.
6 And blessed is *he*, whosoever shall not [a]be
offended in me.
7 [a]And as they departed, Jesus began to say
unto the multitudes concerning John, What went
ye out into the wilderness to see? [b]A reed shaken
with the wind?
8 But what went ye out for to see? A man
clothed in soft raiment? behold, they that wear
soft *clothing* are in kings' houses.
9 But what went ye out for to see? A
prophet? yea, I say unto you, [a]and more than a
prophet.
10 For this is *he*, of whom it is written, [a]BE-
HOLD, I SEND MY MESSENGER BEFORE THY FACE,
WHICH SHALL PREPARE THY WAY BEFORE THEE.
11 Verily I say unto you, Among them that
are born of women there hath not risen a greater
than John the Baptist: notwithstanding he that is
least in the kingdom of heaven is greater than
he.
12 [a]And from the days of John the Baptist
until now the kingdom of heaven suffereth violence, and the violent take it by force.
13 [a]For all the prophets and the law prophesied until John.
14 And if ye will receive *it*, this is [a]Elias,
which was for to come.
15 [a]He that hath ears to hear, let him hear.
16 [a]But whereunto shall I liken this generation? It is like unto children sitting in the markets,
and calling unto their fellows,
17 And saying, We have piped unto you, and
ye have not danced; we have mourned unto you,
and ye have not lamented.
18 For John came neither eating nor drinking, and they say, He hath a devil.
19 The Son of man came eating and drinking,

38 [a][Matt. 16:24; Mark 8:34; Luke 9:23; 14:27] **39** [a]Matt. 16:25; Mark 8:35; Luke 9:24; 17:33; John 12:25 **40** [a]Mark 9:37; Luke 9:48; John 12:44; Gal. 4:14 **41** [a]1 Kin. 17:10; 2 Kin. 4:8 **42** [a][Matt. 25:40]; Mark 9:41; Heb. 6:10

CHAPTER 11

1 [a]Matt. 9:35; Luke 23:5 **2** [a]Luke 7:18–35 [b]Matt. 4:12; 14:3; Mark 6:17; Luke 9:7 **3** [a]Gen. 49:10; Num. 24:17; Deut. 18:15, 18; Dan. 9:24; John 6:14 **5** [a]Is. 29:18; 35:4–6; John 2:23 [b]Ps. 22:26; Is. 61:1; Luke 4:18; James 2:5 **6** [a]Is. 8:14, 15; [Rom. 9:32]; 1 Pet. 2:8 **7** [a]Luke 7:24 [b][Eph. 4:14] **9** [a]Matt. 14:5; 21:26; Luke 1:76; 20:6 **10** [a]Mal. 3:1; Mark 1:2; Luke 1:76 **12** [a]Luke 16:16 **13** [a]Mal. 4:4–6 **14** [a]Mal. 4:5; Matt. 17:10–13; Mark 9:11–13; Luke 1:17; John 1:21 **15** [a]Matt. 13:9; Luke 8:8; Rev. 2:7, 11, 17, 29; 3:6, 13 **16** [a]Luke 7:31

*———

11:2 NU *sent by his*

NKJV

than Me is not worthy of Me. And he who loves
son or daughter more than Me is not worthy of
Me.
38 [a]"And he who does not take his cross and
follow after Me is not worthy of Me.
39 [a]"He who finds his life will lose it, and
he who loses his life for My sake will find it.

A Cup of Cold Water
(*Mark 9:41*)

40 [a]"He who receives you receives Me, and
he who receives Me receives Him who sent Me.
41 [a]"He who receives a prophet in the name
of a prophet shall receive a prophet's reward. And
he who receives a righteous man in the name of
a righteous man shall receive a righteous man's
reward.
42 [a]"And whoever gives one of these little
ones only a cup of cold *water* in the name of a
disciple, assuredly, I say to you, he shall by no
means lose his reward."

John the Baptist Sends Messengers to Jesus
(*Luke 7:18–35*)

11 Now it came to pass, when Jesus finished
commanding His twelve disciples, that He
departed from there to [a]teach and to preach in
their cities.
2 [a]And when John had heard [b]in prison
about the works of Christ, he *sent two of his
disciples
3 and said to Him, "Are You [a]the Coming
One, or do we look for another?"
4 Jesus answered and said to them, "Go and
tell John the things which you hear and see:
5 [a]"*The* blind see and *the* lame walk; *the*
lepers are cleansed and *the* deaf hear; *the* dead
are raised up and [b]*the* poor have the gospel
preached to them.
6 "And blessed is he who is not [a]offended
because of Me."
7 [a]As they departed, Jesus began to say to
the multitudes concerning John: "What did you
go out into the wilderness to see? [b]A reed shaken
by the wind?
8 "But what did you go out to see? A man
clothed in soft garments? Indeed, those who wear
soft *clothing* are in kings' houses.
9 "But what did you go out to see? A
prophet? Yes, I say to you, [a]and more than a
prophet.
10 "For this is *he* of whom it is written:

[a]'Behold, I send My messenger before Your
face,
Who will prepare Your way before You.'

11 "Assuredly, I say to you, among those
born of women there has not risen one greater
than John the Baptist; but he who is least in the
kingdom of heaven is greater than he.
12 [a]"And from the days of John the Baptist
until now the kingdom of heaven suffers violence,
and the violent take it by force.
13 [a]"For all the prophets and the law prophesied until John.
14 "And if you are willing to receive *it*, he
is [a]Elijah who is to come.
15 [a]"He who has ears to hear, let him hear!
16 [a]"But to what shall I liken this generation?
It is like children sitting in the marketplaces and
calling to their companions,
17 "and saying:

'We played the flute for you,
And you did not dance;
We mourned to you,
And you did not lament.'

18 "For John came neither eating nor drinking, and they say, 'He has a demon.'
19 "The Son of Man came eating and drink-

KJV

and they say, Behold a man gluttonous, and a winebibber, [a]a friend of publicans and sinners. [b]But wisdom is justified of her children.

Woe to the Impenitent Cities
(Gen. 19:12–14; Luke 10:13–15)

20 [a]Then began he to upbraid the cities wherein most of his mighty works were done, because they repented not:

21 Woe unto thee, Chorazin! woe unto thee, Bethsaida! for if the mighty works, which were done in you, had been done in Tyre and Sidon, they would have repented long ago [a]in sackcloth and ashes.

22 But I say unto you, [a]It shall be more tolerable for Tyre and Sidon at the day of judgment, than for you.

23 And thou, Capernaum, [a]which art exalted unto heaven, shalt be brought down to hell: for if the mighty works, which have been done in thee, had been done in Sodom, it would have remained until this day.

24 But I say unto you, [a]That it shall be more tolerable for the land of Sodom in the day of judgment, than for thee.

Jesus Gives True Rest
(Luke 10:21, 22)

25 [a]At that time Jesus answered and said, I thank thee, O Father, Lord of heaven and earth, because [b]thou hast hid these things from the wise and prudent, [c]and hast revealed them unto babes.

26 Even so, Father: for so it seemed good in thy sight.

27 [a]All things are delivered unto me of my Father: and no man knoweth the Son, but the Father; [b]neither knoweth any man the Father, save the Son, and *he* to whomsoever the Son will reveal *him*.

28 Come unto [a]me, all *ye* that labour and are heavy laden, and I will give you rest.

29 Take my yoke upon you, [a]and learn of me; for I am meek and [b]lowly in heart: [c]and ye shall find rest unto your souls.

30 [a]For my yoke *is* easy, and my burden is light.

Jesus Is Lord of the Sabbath
(Mark 2:23–28; Luke 6:1–5)

12 At that time [a]Jesus went on the sabbath day through the corn; and his disciples were an hungred, and began to [b]pluck the ears of corn, and to eat.

2 But when the Pharisees saw *it*, they said unto him, Behold, thy disciples do that which is not lawful to do upon the sabbath day.

3 But he said unto them, Have ye not read [a]what David did, when he was an hungred, and they that were with him;

4 How he entered into the house of God, and did eat [a]the shewbread, which was not lawful for him to eat, neither for them which were with him, [b]but only for the priests?

5 Or have ye not read in the [a]law, how that on the sabbath days the priests in the temple profane the sabbath, and are blameless?

6 But I say unto you, That in this place is [a]*one* greater than the temple.

7 But if ye had known what *this* meaneth, [a]I WILL HAVE MERCY, AND NOT SACRIFICE, ye would not have condemned the guiltless.

8 For the Son of man is Lord even of the sabbath day.

Healing on the Sabbath
(Mark 3:1–6; Luke 6:6–11)

9 [a]And when he was departed thence, he went into their synagogue:

10 And, behold, there was a man which had *his* hand withered. And they asked him, saying, [a]Is it lawful to heal on the sabbath days? that they might accuse him.

19 [a]Matt. 9:10 [b]Luke 7:35; John 2:1–11 **20** [a]Luke 10:13–15, 18 **21** [a]Jon. 3:6–8 **22** [a]Matt. 10:15; 11:24 **23** [a]Is. 14:13; Lam. 2:1; Ezek. 26:20; 31:14; 32:18, 24 **24** [a]Matt. 10:15 **25** [a]Luke 10:21, 22 [b]Ps. 8:2; 1 Cor. 1:19; [2 Cor. 3:14] [c]Matt. 16:17 **27** [a]Matt. 28:18; Luke 10:22; John 3:35; 13:3; 1 Cor. 15:27 [b]John 1:18; 6:46; 10:15 **28** [a][John 6:35–37] **29** [a][John 13:15]; Eph. 4:2; [Phil. 2:5; 1 Pet. 2:21; 1 John 2:6] [b]Zech. 9:9; [Phil. 2:7, 8] [c]Jer. 6:16 **30** [a][1 John 5:3]

CHAPTER 12

1 [a]Mark 2:23; Luke 6:1–5 [b]Deut. 23:25 **3** [a]Ex. 31:15; 35:2; 1 Sam. 21:6 **4** [a]Ex. 25:30; Lev. 24:5 [b]Ex. 29:32; Lev. 8:31; 24:9 **5** [a]Num. 28:9; [John 7:22] **6** [a][2 Chr. 6:18; Is. 66:1, 2; Mal. 3:1]; Matt. 12:41, 42 **7** [a][1 Sam. 15:22; Hos. 6:6; Mic. 6:6–8]; Matt. 9:13 **9** [a]Mark 3:1–6; Luke 6:6–11 **10** [a]Luke 13:14; 14:3; John 9:16

*

11:19 NU *works*
11:23 NU *will you be exalted to heaven? No, you will be*
12:8 NU, M omit *even*

NKJV

ing, and they say, 'Look, a glutton and a winebibber, [a]a friend of tax collectors and sinners!' [b]But wisdom is justified by her *children."

Woe to the Impenitent Cities
(Gen. 19:12–14; Luke 10:13–15)

20 [a]Then He began to rebuke the cities in which most of His mighty works had been done, because they did not repent:

21 "Woe to you, Chorazin! Woe to you, Bethsaida! For if the mighty works which were done in you had been done in Tyre and Sidon, they would have repented long ago [a]in sackcloth and ashes.

22 "But I say to you, [a]it will be more tolerable for Tyre and Sidon in the day of judgment than for you.

23 "And you, Capernaum, [a]who* are exalted to heaven, will be brought down to Hades; for if the mighty works which were done in you had been done in Sodom, it would have remained until this day.

24 "But I say to you [a]that it shall be more tolerable for the land of Sodom in the day of judgment than for you."

Jesus Gives True Rest
(Luke 10:21, 22)

25 [a]At that time Jesus answered and said, "I thank You, Father, Lord of heaven and earth, that [b]You have hidden these things from *the* wise and prudent [c]and have revealed them to babes.

26 "Even so, Father, for so it seemed good in Your sight.

27 [a]"All things have been delivered to Me by My Father, and no one knows the Son except the Father. [b]Nor does anyone know the Father except the Son, and *the one* to whom the Son wills to reveal *Him*.

28 "Come to [a]Me, all *you* who labor and are heavy laden, and I will give you rest.

29 "Take My yoke upon you [a]and learn from Me, for I am gentle and [b]lowly in heart, [c]and you will find rest for your souls.

30 [a]"For My yoke *is* easy and My burden is light."

Jesus Is Lord of the Sabbath
(Mark 2:23–28; Luke 6:1–5)

12 At that time [a]Jesus went through the grainfields on the Sabbath. And His disciples were hungry, and began to [b]pluck heads of grain and to eat.

2 And when the Pharisees saw *it*, they said to Him, "Look, Your disciples are doing what is not lawful to do on the Sabbath!"

3 But He said to them, "Have you not read [a]what David did when he was hungry, he and those who were with him:

4 "how he entered the house of God and ate [a]the showbread which was not lawful for him to eat, nor for those who were with him, [b]but only for the priests?

5 "Or have you not read in the [a]law that on the Sabbath the priests in the temple profane the Sabbath, and are blameless?

6 "Yet I say to you that in this place there is [a]*One* greater than the temple.

7 "But if you had known what *this* means, [a]*'I desire mercy and not sacrifice,'* you would not have condemned the guiltless.

8 "For the Son of Man is Lord *even of the Sabbath."

Healing on the Sabbath
(Mark 3:1–6; Luke 6:6–11)

9 [a]Now when He had departed from there, He went into their synagogue.

10 And behold, there was a man who had a withered hand. And they asked Him, saying, [a]"Is it lawful to heal on the Sabbath?"—that they might accuse Him.

KJV

11 And he said unto them, What man shall there be among you, that shall have one sheep, and if it fall into a pit on the sabbath day, will he not lay hold on it, and lift *it* out?

12 How much then is a man better than a sheep? Wherefore it is lawful to do well on the sabbath days.

13 Then saith he to the man, Stretch forth thine hand. And he stretched *it* forth; and it was restored whole, like as the other.

14 Then [a]the Pharisees went out, and held a council against him, how they might destroy him.

Behold, My Servant

15 But when Jesus knew *it,* [a]he withdrew himself from thence: [b]and great multitudes followed him, and he healed them all;

16 And [a]charged them that they should not make him known:

17 That it might be fulfilled which was spoken by Esaias the prophet, saying,

18 [a]BEHOLD MY SERVANT, WHOM I HAVE CHOSEN; MY BELOVED, [b]IN WHOM MY SOUL IS WELL PLEASED: I WILL PUT MY SPIRIT UPON HIM, AND HE SHALL SHEW JUDGMENT TO THE GENTILES.

19 HE SHALL NOT STRIVE, NOR CRY; NEITHER SHALL ANY MAN HEAR HIS VOICE IN THE STREETS.

20 A BRUISED REED SHALL HE NOT BREAK, AND SMOKING FLAX SHALL HE NOT QUENCH, TILL HE SEND FORTH JUDGMENT UNTO VICTORY.

21 AND IN HIS NAME SHALL THE GENTILES TRUST.

A House Divided Cannot Stand
(*Mark 3:22–27; Luke 11:14–23*)

22 [a]Then was brought unto him one possessed with a devil, blind, and dumb: and he healed him, insomuch that the blind and dumb both spake and saw.

23 And all the people were amazed, and said, Is not this the [a]son of David?

24 [a]But when the Pharisees heard *it,* they said, This *fellow* doth not cast out devils, but by Beelzebub the prince of the devils.

25 And Jesus [a]knew their thoughts, and said unto them, Every kingdom divided against itself is brought to desolation; and every city or house divided against itself shall not stand:

26 And if Satan cast out Satan, he is divided against himself; how shall then his kingdom stand?

27 And if I by Beelzebub cast out devils, by whom do your children cast *them* out? therefore they shall be your judges.

28 But if I cast out devils by the Spirit of God, then [a]the kingdom of God is come unto you.

29 [a]Or else how can one enter into a strong man's house, and spoil his goods, except he first bind the strong man? and then he will spoil his house.

30 He that is not with me is against me; and he that gathereth not with me scattereth abroad.

The Unpardonable Sin
(*Mark 3:28–30*)

31 Wherefore I say unto you, [a]All manner of sin and blasphemy shall be forgiven unto men: [b]but the blasphemy *against* the *Holy* Ghost shall not be forgiven unto men.

32 And whosoever [a]speaketh a word against the Son of man, [b]it shall be forgiven him: but whosoever speaketh against the Holy Ghost, it shall not be forgiven him, neither in this world, neither in the *world* to come.

A Tree Known by Its Fruit
(*Matt. 7:15–20*)

33 Either make the tree good, and [a]his fruit good; or else make the tree corrupt, and his fruit corrupt: for the tree is known by *his* fruit.

34 O [a]generation of vipers, how can ye, being

14 [a]Ps. 2:2; Matt. 27:1; Mark 3:6; [Luke 6:11]; John 5:18; 10:39; 11:53
15 [a]Matt. 10:23; Mark 3:7 [b]Matt. 19:2
16 [a]Matt. 8:4; 9:30; 17:9
18 [a]Is. 42:1–4; 49:3 [b]Matt. 3:17; 17:5
22 [a]Matt. 9:32; [Mark 3:11]; Luke 11:14, 15
23 [a]Matt. 9:27; 21:9
24 [a]Matt. 9:34; Mark 3:22; Luke 11:15
25 [a]Matt. 9:4; John 2:25; Rev. 2:23
28 [a][Dan. 2:44; 7:14; Luke 1:33]; 11:20; [17:20, 21; 1 John 3:8]
29 [a]Is. 49:24; [Luke 11:21–23]
31 [a]Mark 3:28–30; Luke 12:10; [Heb. 6:4–6; 10:26, 29; 1 John 5:16] [b]Acts 7:51
32 [a]Matt. 11:19; 13:55; John 7:12, 52 [b]1 Tim. 1:13
33 [a]Matt. 7:16–18; Luke 6:43, 44; [John 15:4–7]
34 [a]Matt. 3:7; 23:33; Luke 3:7

NKJV

11 Then He said to them, "What man is there among you who has one sheep, and if it falls into a pit on the Sabbath, will not lay hold of it and lift *it* out?

12 "Of how much more value then is a man than a sheep? Therefore it is lawful to do good on the Sabbath."

13 Then He said to the man, "Stretch out your hand." And he stretched *it* out, and it was restored as whole as the other.

14 Then [a]the Pharisees went out and plotted against Him, how they might destroy Him.

Behold, My Servant

15 But when Jesus knew *it,* [a]He withdrew from there. [b]And great *multitudes followed Him, and He healed them all.

16 Yet He [a]warned them not to make Him known,

17 that it might be fulfilled which was spoken by Isaiah the prophet, saying:

18 *"Behold![a] My Servant whom I have chosen,*
My Beloved [b]in whom My soul is well
pleased!
I will put My Spirit upon Him,
And He will declare justice to the Gentiles.
19 *He will not quarrel nor cry out,*
Nor will anyone hear His voice in the
streets.
20 *A bruised reed He will not break,*
And smoking flax He will not quench,
Till He sends forth justice to victory;
21 *And in His name Gentiles will trust."*

A House Divided Cannot Stand
(*Mark 3:22–27; Luke 11:14–23*)

22 [a]Then one was brought to Him who was demon-possessed, blind and mute; and He healed him, so that the *blind and mute man both spoke and saw.

23 And all the multitudes were amazed and said, "Could this be the [a]Son of David?"

24 [a]Now when the Pharisees heard *it* they said, "This *fellow* does not cast out demons except by *Beelzebub, the ruler of the demons."

25 But Jesus [a]knew their thoughts, and said to them: "Every kingdom divided against itself is brought to desolation, and every city or house divided against itself will not stand.

26 "If Satan casts out Satan, he is divided against himself. How then will his kingdom stand?

27 "And if I cast out demons by Beelzebub, by whom do your sons cast *them* out? Therefore they shall be your judges.

28 "But if I cast out demons by the Spirit of God, [a]surely the kingdom of God has come upon you.

29 [a]"Or how can one enter a strong man's house and plunder his goods, unless he first binds the strong man? And then he will plunder his house.

30 "He who is not with Me is against Me, and he who does not gather with Me scatters abroad.

The Unpardonable Sin
(*Mark 3:28–30*)

31 "Therefore I say to you, [a]every sin and blasphemy will be forgiven men, [b]but the blasphemy *against* the Spirit will not be forgiven men.

32 "Anyone who [a]speaks a word against the Son of Man, [b]it will be forgiven him; but whoever speaks against the Holy Spirit, it will not be forgiven him, either in this age or in the *age* to come.

A Tree Known by Its Fruit
(*Matt. 7:15–20*)

33 "Either make the tree good and [a]its fruit good, or else make the tree bad and its fruit bad; for a tree is known by *its* fruit.

34 [a]"Brood of vipers! How can you, being

*

12:15 NU brackets *multitudes* as disputed.
12:22 NU omits *blind and*
12:24 NU, M *Beelzebul,* a Philistine deity

KJV

evil, speak good things? [b]for out of the abundance of the heart the mouth speaketh.

35 A good man out of the good treasure of the heart bringeth forth good things: and an evil man out of the evil treasure bringeth forth evil things.

36 But I say unto you, That every idle word that men shall speak, they shall give account thereof in the day of judgment.

37 For by thy words thou shalt be justified, and by thy words thou shalt be condemned.

The Scribes and Pharisees Ask for a Sign
(Luke 11:29–32)

38 [a]Then certain of the scribes and of the Pharisees answered, saying, Master, we would see a sign from thee.

39 But he answered and said unto them, An evil and [a]adulterous generation seeketh after a sign; and there shall no sign be given to it, but the sign of the prophet Jonas:

40 [a]For as Jonas was three days and three nights in the whale's belly; so shall the Son of man be three days and three nights in the heart of the earth.

41 [a]The men of Nineveh shall rise in judgment with this generation, and [b]shall condemn it: [c]because they repented at the preaching of Jonas; and, behold, a greater than Jonas *is* here.

42 [a]The queen of the south shall rise up in the judgment with this generation, and shall condemn it: for she came from the uttermost parts of the earth to hear the wisdom of Solomon; and, behold, a greater than Solomon *is* here.

An Unclean Spirit Returns
(Luke 11:24–26)

43 [a]When the unclean spirit is gone out of a man, [b]he walketh through dry places, seeking rest, and findeth none.

44 Then he saith, I will return into my house from whence I came out; and when he is come, he findeth *it* empty, swept, and garnished.

45 Then goeth he, and taketh with himself seven other spirits more wicked than himself, and they enter in and dwell there: [a]and the last *state* of that man is worse than the first. Even so shall it be also unto this wicked generation.

Jesus' Mother and Brothers Send for Him
(Mark 3:31–35; Luke 8:19–21)

46 While he yet talked to the people, [a]behold, *his* mother and [b]his brethren stood without, desiring to speak with him.

47 Then one said unto him, Behold, [a]thy mother and thy brethren stand without, desiring to speak with thee.

48 But he answered and said unto him that told him, Who is my mother? and who are my brethren?

49 And he stretched forth his hand toward his disciples, and said, Behold my mother and my [a]brethren!

50 For [a]whosoever shall do the will of my Father which is in heaven, the same is my brother, and sister, and mother.

The Parable of the Sower
(Mark 4:1–9; Luke 8:4–8)

13 The same day went Jesus out of the house, [a]and sat by the sea side.

2 [a]And great multitudes were gathered together unto him, so that [b]he went into a ship, and sat; and the whole multitude stood on the shore.

3 And he spake many things unto them in parables, saying, [a]Behold, a sower went forth to sow;

4 And when he sowed, some *seeds* fell by the way side, and the fowls came and devoured them up:

5 Some fell upon stony places, where they

34 [b]1 Sam. 24:13; Is. 32:6; [Matt. 15:18]; Luke 6:45; Eph. 4:29; [James 3:2–12]
38 [a]Matt. 16:1; Mark 8:11; Luke 11:16; John 2:18; 1 Cor. 1:22
39 [a]Is. 57:3; Matt. 16:4; Mark 8:38; [Luke 11:29–32]; John 4:48
40 [a]Jon. 1:17; Luke 24:46; Acts 10:40; 1 Cor. 15:4
41 [a]Jon. 3:5; Luke 11:32 [b]Jer. 3:11; Ezek. 16:51; [Rom. 2:27] [c]Jon. 3:5
42 [a]1 Kin. 10:1–13; 2 Chr. 9:1; Luke 11:31
43 [a]Luke 11:24–26 [b][Job 1:7; 1 Pet. 5:8]
45 [a]Mark 5:9; Luke 11:26; [Heb. 6:4–8; 10:26; 2 Pet. 2:20–22]
46 [a]Mark 3:31–35; Luke 8:19–21 [b]Matt. 13:55; Mark 6:3; John 2:12; 7:3, 5; Acts 1:14; 1 Cor. 9:5; Gal. 1:19
47 [a]Matt. 13:55, 56; John 2:12; Acts 1:14
49 [a]John 20:17; [Rom. 8:29]
50 [a]John 15:14; [Gal. 5:6; 6:15; Col. 3:11; Heb. 2:11]

CHAPTER 13

1 [a]Matt. 13:1–15; Mark 4:1–12; Luke 8:4–10
2 [a]Luke 8:4 [b]Luke 5:3
3 [a]Luke 8:5

*12:35 NU, M omit *of his heart*

NKJV

evil, speak good things? [b]For out of the abundance of the heart the mouth speaks.

35 "A good man out of the good treasure *of his heart brings forth good things, and an evil man out of the evil treasure brings forth evil things.

36 "But I say to you that for every idle word men may speak, they will give account of it in the day of judgment.

37 "For by your words you will be justified, and by your words you will be condemned."

The Scribes and Pharisees Ask for a Sign
(Luke 11:29–32)

38 [a]Then some of the scribes and Pharisees answered, saying, "Teacher, we want to see a sign from You."

39 But He answered and said to them, "An evil and [a]adulterous generation seeks after a sign, and no sign will be given to it except the sign of the prophet Jonah.

40 [a]"For as Jonah was three days and three nights in the belly of the great fish, so will the Son of Man be three days and three nights in the heart of the earth.

41 [a]"The men of Nineveh will rise up in the judgment with this generation and [b]condemn it, [c]because they repented at the preaching of Jonah; and indeed a greater than Jonah *is* here.

42 [a]"The queen of the South will rise up in the judgment with this generation and condemn it, for she came from the ends of the earth to hear the wisdom of Solomon; and indeed a greater than Solomon *is* here.

An Unclean Spirit Returns
(Luke 11:24–26)

43 [a]"When an unclean spirit goes out of a man, [b]he goes through dry places, seeking rest, and finds none.

44 "Then he says, 'I will return to my house from which I came.' And when he comes, he finds *it* empty, swept, and put in order.

45 "Then he goes and takes with him seven other spirits more wicked than himself, and they enter and dwell there; [a]and the last *state* of that man is worse than the first. So shall it also be with this wicked generation."

Jesus' Mother and Brothers Send for Him
(Mark 3:31–35; Luke 8:19–21)

46 While He was still talking to the multitudes, [a]behold, His mother and [b]brothers stood outside, seeking to speak with Him.

47 Then one said to Him, "Look, [a]Your mother and Your brothers are standing outside, seeking to speak with You."

48 But He answered and said to the one who told Him, "Who is My mother and who are My brothers?"

49 And He stretched out His hand toward His disciples and said, "Here are My mother and My [a]brothers!

50 "For [a]whoever does the will of My Father in heaven is My brother and sister and mother."

The Parable of the Sower
(Mark 4:1–9; Luke 8:4–8)

13 On the same day Jesus went out of the house [a]and sat by the sea.

2 [a]And great multitudes were gathered together to Him, so that [b]He got into a boat and sat; and the whole multitude stood on the shore.

3 Then He spoke many things to them in parables, saying: [a]"Behold, a sower went out to sow.

4 "And as he sowed, some *seed* fell by the wayside; and the birds came and devoured them.

5 "Some fell on stony places, where they did

KJV

had not much earth: and forthwith they sprung up, because they had no deepness of earth:

6 And when the sun was up, they were scorched; and because they had no root, they withered away.

7 And some fell among thorns; and the thorns sprung up, and choked them:

8 But other fell into good ground, and brought forth fruit, some [a]an hundredfold, some sixtyfold, some thirtyfold.

9 [a]Who hath ears to hear, let him hear.

The Purpose of Parables
(*Mark 4:10–12; Luke 8:9, 10*)

10 And the disciples came, and said unto him, Why speakest thou unto them in parables?

11 He answered and said unto them, Because [a]it is given unto you to know the mysteries of the kingdom of heaven, but to them it is not given.

12 [a]For whosoever hath, to him shall be given, and he shall have more abundance: but whosoever hath not, from him shall be taken away even that he hath.

13 Therefore speak I to them in parables: because they seeing see not; and hearing they hear not, neither do they understand.

14 And in them is fulfilled the prophecy of Esaias, which saith, [a]BY HEARING YE SHALL HEAR, AND SHALL NOT UNDERSTAND; AND SEEING YE SHALL SEE, AND SHALL NOT [b]PERCEIVE:

15 FOR THIS PEOPLE'S HEART IS WAXED GROSS, AND *THEIR* EARS [a]ARE DULL OF HEARING, AND THEIR EYES THEY HAVE [b]CLOSED; LEST AT ANY TIME THEY SHOULD SEE WITH *THEIR* EYES AND HEAR WITH *THEIR* EARS, AND SHOULD UNDERSTAND WITH *THEIR* HEART, AND SHOULD BE CONVERTED, AND I SHOULD [c]HEAL THEM.

16 But [a]blessed *are* your eyes, for they see: and your ears, for they hear.

17 For verily I say unto you, [a]That many prophets and righteous *men* have desired to see *those things* which ye see, and have not seen *them;* and to hear *those things* which ye hear, and have not heard *them.*

The Parable of the Sower Explained
(*Mark 4:13–20; Luke 8:11–15*)

18 [a]Hear ye therefore the parable of the sower.

19 When any one heareth the word [a]of the kingdom, and understandeth *it* not, then cometh the wicked *one,* and catcheth away that which was sown in his heart. This is he which received seed by the way side.

20 But he that received the seed into stony places, the same is he that heareth the word, and anon [a]with joy receiveth it;

21 Yet hath he not root in himself, but dureth for a while: for when [a]tribulation or persecution ariseth because of the word, by and by [b]he is offended.

22 [a]He also that received seed [b]among the thorns is he that heareth the word; and the care of this world, and the deceitfulness of riches, choke the word, and he becometh unfruitful.

23 But he that received seed into the good ground is he that heareth the word, and understandeth *it;* which also beareth [a]fruit, and bringeth forth, some an hundredfold, some sixty, some thirty.

The Parable of the Wheat and the Tares

24 Another parable put he forth unto them, saying, The kingdom of heaven is likened unto a man which sowed good seed in his field:

25 But while men slept, his enemy came and sowed tares among the wheat, and went his way.

26 But when the blade was sprung up, and brought forth fruit, then appeared the tares also.

8 [a]Gen. 26:12; Matt. 13:23
9 [a]Matt. 11:15; Mark 4:9; Rev. 2:7, 11, 17, 29; 3:6, 13, 22
11 [a][Matt. 11:25; 16:17]; Mark 4:10, 11; [John 6:65; 1 Cor. 2:10; Col. 1:27; 1 John 2:20, 27]
12 [a]Matt. 25:29; Mark 4:25; Luke 8:18; 19:26
14 [a]Is. 6:9, 10; Ezek. 12:2; Mark 4:12; Luke 8:10; John 12:40; Acts 28:26, 27; Rom. 11:8; [2 Cor. 3:14, 15] [b][John 3:36]
15 [a]Ps. 119:70; Zech. 7:11; 2 Tim. 4:4; Heb. 5:11 [b]Luke 19:42 [c]Acts 28:26, 27
16 [a][Prov. 20:12; Matt. 16:17]; Luke 10:23, 24; [John 20:29]
17 [a]John 8:56; Heb. 11:13; 1 Pet. 1:10, 11
18 [a]Mark 4:13–20; Luke 8:11–15
19 [a]Matt. 4:23
20 [a]Is. 58:2; Ezek. 33:31, 32; John 5:35
21 [a][Acts 14:22] [b]Matt. 11:6; 2 Tim. 1:15
22 [a]Matt. 19:23; Mark 10:23; Luke 18:24; 1 Tim. 6:9; 2 Tim. 4:10 [b]Jer. 4:3
23 [a][John 15:5]; Phil. 1:11; Col. 1:6

NKJV

not have much earth; and they immediately sprang up because they had no depth of earth.

6 "But when the sun was up they were scorched, and because they had no root they withered away.

7 "And some fell among thorns, and the thorns sprang up and choked them.

8 "But others fell on good ground and yielded a crop: some [a]a hundredfold, some sixty, some thirty.

9 [a]"He who has ears to hear, let him hear!"

The Purpose of Parables
(*Mark 4:10–12; Luke 8:9, 10*)

10 And the disciples came and said to Him, "Why do You speak to them in parables?"

11 He answered and said to them, "Because [a]it has been given to you to know the mysteries of the kingdom of heaven, but to them it has not been given.

12 [a]"For whoever has, to him more will be given, and he will have abundance; but whoever does not have, even what he has will be taken away from him.

13 "Therefore I speak to them in parables, because seeing they do not see, and hearing they do not hear, nor do they understand.

14 "And in them the prophecy of Isaiah is fulfilled, which says:

[a]'Hearing you will hear and shall not understand,
And seeing you will see and not [b]perceive;
15 *For the hearts of this people have grown dull.*
Their ears [a]are hard of hearing,
And their eyes they have [b]closed,
Lest they should see with their eyes and hear with their ears,
Lest they should understand with their hearts and turn,
*So that I *should [c]heal them.'*

16 "But [a]blessed *are* your eyes for they see, and your ears for they hear;

17 "for assuredly, I say to you [a]that many prophets and righteous *men* desired to see what you see, and did not see *it,* and to hear what you hear, and did not hear *it.*

The Parable of the Sower Explained
(*Mark 4:13–20; Luke 8:11–15*)

18 [a]"Therefore hear the parable of the sower:

19 "When anyone hears the word [a]of the kingdom, and does not understand *it,* then the wicked *one* comes and snatches away what was sown in his heart. This is he who received seed by the wayside.

20 "But he who received the seed on stony places, this is he who hears the word and immediately [a]receives it with joy;

21 "yet he has no root in himself, but endures only for a while. For when [a]tribulation or persecution arises because of the word, immediately [b]he stumbles.

22 "Now [a]he who received seed [b]among the thorns is he who hears the word, and the cares of this world and the deceitfulness of riches choke the word, and he becomes unfruitful.

23 "But he who received seed on the good ground is he who hears the word and understands *it,* who indeed bears [a]fruit and produces: some a hundredfold, some sixty, some thirty."

The Parable of the Wheat and the Tares

24 Another parable He put forth to them, saying: "The kingdom of heaven is like a man who sowed good seed in his field;

25 "but while men slept, his enemy came and sowed tares among the wheat and went his way.

26 "But when the grain had sprouted and produced a crop, then the tares also appeared.

*13:15 NU, M *would*

KJV

27 So the servants of the householder came and said unto him, Sir, didst not thou sow good seed in thy field? from whence then hath it tares?

28 He said unto them, An enemy hath done this. The servants said unto him, Wilt thou then that we go and gather them up?

29 But he said, Nay; lest while ye gather up the tares, ye root up also the wheat with them.

30 Let both grow together until the harvest: and in the time of harvest I will say to the reapers, Gather ye together first the tares, and bind them in bundles to burn them: but [a]gather the wheat into my barn.

The Parable of the Mustard Seed
(Mark 4:30–32; Luke 13:18, 19)

31 Another parable put he forth unto them, saying, [a]The kingdom of heaven is like to a grain of mustard seed, which a man took, and sowed in his field:

32 Which indeed is the least of all seeds: but when it is grown, it is the greatest among herbs, and becometh a [a]tree, so that the birds of the air come and lodge in the branches thereof.

The Parable of the Leaven
(Luke 13:20, 21)

33 [a]Another parable spake he unto them; The kingdom of heaven is like unto leaven, which a woman took, and hid in three measures of meal, till the [b]whole was leavened.

Prophecy and the Parables

34 [a]All these things spake Jesus unto the multitude in parables; and without a parable spake he not unto them:

35 That it might be fulfilled which was spoken by the prophet, saying, [a]I WILL OPEN MY MOUTH IN PARABLES; [b]I WILL UTTER THINGS WHICH HAVE BEEN KEPT SECRET FROM THE FOUNDATION OF THE WORLD.

The Parable of the Tares Explained

36 Then Jesus sent the multitude away, and went into the house: and his disciples came unto him, saying, Declare unto us the parable of the tares of the field.

37 He answered and said unto them, He that soweth the good seed is the Son of man;

38 [a]The field is the world; the good seed are the children of the kingdom; but the tares are [b]the children of the wicked *one;*

39 The enemy that sowed them is the devil; [a]the harvest is the end of the world; and the reapers are the angels.

40 As therefore the tares are gathered and burned in the fire; so shall it be in the end of this world.

41 The Son of man shall send forth his angels, [a]and they shall gather out of his kingdom all things that offend, and them which do iniquity;

42 [a]And shall cast them into a furnace of fire: [b]there shall be wailing and gnashing of teeth.

43 [a]Then shall the righteous shine forth as the sun in the kingdom of their Father. [b]Who hath ears to hear, let him hear.

The Parable of the Hidden Treasure

44 Again, the kingdom of heaven is like unto treasure hid in a field; the which when a man hath found, he hideth, and for joy thereof goeth and [a]selleth all that he hath, and [b]buyeth that field.

The Parable of the Pearl of Great Price

45 Again, the kingdom of heaven is like unto a merchant man, seeking goodly pearls:

46 Who, when he had found [a]one pearl of great price, went and sold all that he had, and bought it.

NKJV

27 "So the servants of the owner came and said to him, 'Sir, did you not sow good seed in your field? How then does it have tares?'

28 "He said to them, 'An enemy has done this.' The servants said to him, 'Do you want us then to go and gather them up?'

29 "But he said, 'No, lest while you gather up the tares you also uproot the wheat with them.

30 'Let both grow together until the harvest, and at the time of harvest I will say to the reapers, "First gather together the tares and bind them in bundles to burn them, but [a]gather the wheat into my barn." ' "

The Parable of the Mustard Seed
(Mark 4:30–32; Luke 13:18, 19)

31 Another parable He put forth to them, saying: [a]"The kingdom of heaven is like a mustard seed, which a man took and sowed in his field,

32 "which indeed is the least of all the seeds; but when it is grown it is greater than the herbs and becomes a [a]tree, so that the birds of the air come and nest in its branches."

The Parable of the Leaven
(Luke 13:20, 21)

33 [a]Another parable He spoke to them: "The kingdom of heaven is like leaven, which a woman took and hid in three *measures of meal till [b]it was all leavened."

Prophecy and the Parables

34 [a]All these things Jesus spoke to the multitude in parables; and without a parable He did not speak to them,

35 that it might be fulfilled which was spoken by the prophet, saying:

> [a]*"I will open My mouth in parables;*
> [b]*I will utter things kept secret from the foundation of the world."*

The Parable of the Tares Explained

36 Then Jesus sent the multitude away and went into the house. And His disciples came to Him, saying, "Explain to us the parable of the tares of the field."

37 He answered and said to them: "He who sows the good seed is the Son of Man.

38 [a]"The field is the world, the good seeds are the sons of the kingdom, but the tares are [b]the sons of the wicked *one.*

39 "The enemy who sowed them is the devil, [a]the harvest is the end of the age, and the reapers are the angels.

40 "Therefore as the tares are gathered and burned in the fire, so it will be at the end of this age.

41 "The Son of Man will send out His angels, [a]and they will gather out of His kingdom all things that offend, and those who practice lawlessness,

42 [a]"and will cast them into the furnace of fire. [b]There will be wailing and gnashing of teeth.

43 [a]"Then the righteous will shine forth as the sun in the kingdom of their Father. [b]He who has ears to hear, let him hear!

The Parable of the Hidden Treasure

44 "Again, the kingdom of heaven is like treasure hidden in a field, which a man found and hid; and for joy over it he goes and [a]sells all that he has and [b]buys that field.

The Parable of the Pearl of Great Price

45 "Again, the kingdom of heaven is like a merchant seeking beautiful pearls,

46 "who, when he had found [a]one pearl of great price, went and sold all that he had and bought it.

---

30 [a]Matt. 3:12
31 [a][Is. 2:2, 3; Mic. 4:1]; Mark 4:30; Luke 13:18, 19
32 [a]Ps. 104:12; Ezek. 17:22–24; 31:3–9; Dan. 4:12
33 [a]Luke 13:20, 21 [b][1 Cor. 5:6; Gal. 5:9]
34 [a]Mark 4:33, 34; John 10:6; 16:25
35 [a]Ps. 78:2 [b]Rom. 16:25, 26; 1 Cor. 2:7; Eph. 3:9; Col. 1:26
38 [a]Matt. 24:14; 28:19; Mark 16:15; Luke 24:47; Rom. 10:18; Col. 1:6 [b]Gen. 3:15; John 8:44; Acts 13:10
39 [a]Joel 3:13; Rev. 14:15
41 [a]Matt. 18:7; 2 Pet. 2:1, 2
42 [a]Matt. 3:12; Rev. 19:20; 20:10 [b]Matt. 8:12; 13:50
43 [a][Dan. 12:3; 1 Cor. 15:42, 43, 58] [b]Matt. 13:9
44 [a]Phil. 3:7, 8 [b][Is. 55:1; Rev. 3:18]
46 [a]Prov. 2:4; 3:14, 15; 8:10, 19

*________

13:33 Gr. *sata,* same as a Heb. *seah;* approximately 2 pecks in all

KJV

The Parable of the Dragnet

47 Again, the kingdom of heaven is like unto
a net, that was cast into the sea, and [a]gathered
of every kind:
48 Which, when it was full, they drew to
shore, and sat down, and gathered the good into
vessels, but cast the bad away.
49 So shall it be at the end of the world: the
angels shall come forth, and [a]sever the wicked
from among the just,
50 And shall cast them into the furnace of
fire: there shall be wailing and gnashing of teeth.
51 Jesus saith unto them, Have ye understood all these things? They say unto him, Yea,
Lord.
52 Then said he unto them, Therefore every
scribe *which is* instructed unto the kingdom of
heaven is like unto a man *that is* an householder,
which bringeth forth out of his treasure [a]*things*
new and old.

Jesus Rejected at Nazareth
(Mark 6:1–6; Luke 4:16–30)

53 And it came to pass, *that* when Jesus had
finished these parables, he departed thence.
54 [a]And when he was come into his own
country, he taught them in their synagogue, insomuch that they were astonished, and said,
Whence hath this *man* this wisdom, and *these*
mighty works?
55 [a]Is not this the carpenter's son? is not his
mother called Mary? and [b]his brethren, [c]James,
and Joses, and Simon, and Judas?
56 And his sisters, are they not all with us?
Whence then hath this *man* all these things?
57 And they [a]were offended in him. But
Jesus said unto them, [b]A prophet is not without
honour, save in his own country, and in his own
house.
58 And [a]he did not many mighty works there
because of their unbelief.

John the Baptist Beheaded
(Mark 6:14–29; Luke 9:7–9)

14 At that time [a]Herod the tetrarch heard of
the fame of Jesus,
2 And said unto his servants, This is John
the Baptist; he is risen from the dead; and therefore mighty works do shew forth themselves in
him.
3 [a]For Herod had laid hold on John, and
bound him, and put *him* in prison for Herodias'
sake, his brother Philip's wife.
4 For John said unto him, [a]It is not lawful
for thee to have her.
5 And when he would have put him to
death, he feared the multitude, [a]because they
counted him as a prophet.
6 But when Herod's birthday was kept, the
daughter of Herodias danced before them, and
pleased Herod.
7 Whereupon he promised with an oath to
give her whatsoever she would ask.
8 And she, being before instructed of her
mother, said, Give me here John Baptist's head
in a charger.
9 And the king was sorry: nevertheless for
the oath's sake, and them which sat with him at
meat, he commanded *it* to be given *her*.
10 And he sent, and beheaded John in the
prison.
11 And his head was brought in a charger,
and given to the damsel: and she brought *it* to
her mother.
12 And his disciples came, and took up the
body, and buried it, and went and told Jesus.

Feeding the Five Thousand
(Mark 6:30–44; Luke 9:10–17; John 6:1–14)

13 [a]When Jesus heard *of it*, he departed
thence by ship into a desert place apart: and when

47 [a]Matt. 22:9, 10
49 [a]Matt. 25:32
52 [a]Song 7:13
54 [a]Ps. 22:22; Matt. 2:23; Mark 6:1; Luke 4:16; John 7:15
55 [a]Is. 49:7; Mark 6:3; [Luke 3:23]; John 6:42 [b]Matt. 12:46 [c]Mark 15:40
57 [a]Matt. 11:6; Mark 6:3, 4 [b]Luke 4:24; John 4:44
58 [a]Mark 6:5, 6; John 5:44, 46, 47

CHAPTER 14

1 [a]Mark 6:14–29; Luke 9:7–9
3 [a]Matt. 4:12; Mark 6:17; Luke 3:19, 20
4 [a]Lev. 18:16; 20:21
5 [a]Matt. 21:26; Luke 20:6
13 [a]Matt. 10:23; 12:15; Mark 6:32–44; Luke 9:10–17; John 6:1, 2

*

13:51 NU omits *Jesus said to them* • NU omits *Lord*
13:52 Or *for*
13:55 NU *Joseph*

NKJV

The Parable of the Dragnet

47 "Again, the kingdom of heaven is like a
dragnet that was cast into the sea and [a]gathered
some of every kind,
48 "which, when it was full, they drew to
shore; and they sat down and gathered the good
into vessels, but threw the bad away.
49 "So it will be at the end of the age. The
angels will come forth, [a]separate the wicked from
among the just,
50 "and cast them into the furnace of fire.
There will be wailing and gnashing of teeth."
51 *Jesus said to them, "Have you understood all these things?" They said to Him, "Yes,
*Lord."
52 Then He said to them, "Therefore every
scribe instructed *concerning the kingdom of
heaven is like a householder who brings out of
his treasure [a]*things* new and old."

Jesus Rejected at Nazareth
(Mark 6:1–6; Luke 4:16–30)

53 Now it came to pass, when Jesus had finished these parables, that He departed from there.
54 [a]When He had come to His own country,
He taught them in their synagogue, so that they
were astonished and said, "Where did this *Man*
get this wisdom and *these* mighty works?
55 [a]"Is this not the carpenter's son? Is not
His mother called Mary? And [b]His brothers
[c]James, *Joses, Simon, and Judas?
56 "And His sisters, are they not all with us?
Where then did this *Man* get all these things?"
57 So they [a]were offended at Him. But Jesus
said to them, [b]"A prophet is not without honor
except in his own country and in his own house."
58 Now [a]He did not do many mighty works
there because of their unbelief.

John the Baptist Beheaded
(Mark 6:14–29; Luke 9:7–9)

14 At that time [a]Herod the tetrarch heard the
report about Jesus
2 and said to his servants, "This is John the
Baptist; he is risen from the dead, and therefore
these powers are at work in him."
3 [a]For Herod had laid hold of John and
bound him, and put *him* in prison for the sake of
Herodias, his brother Philip's wife.
4 Because John had said to him, [a]"It is not
lawful for you to have her."
5 And although he wanted to put him to
death, he feared the multitude, [a]because they
counted him as a prophet.
6 But when Herod's birthday was celebrated, the daughter of Herodias danced before
them and pleased Herod.
7 Therefore he promised with an oath to
give her whatever she might ask.
8 So she, having been prompted by her
mother, said, "Give me John the Baptist's head
here on a platter."
9 And the king was sorry; nevertheless, because of the oaths and because of those who sat
with him, he commanded *it* to be given to *her*.
10 So he sent and had John beheaded in
prison.
11 And his head was brought on a platter and
given to the girl, and she brought *it* to her mother.
12 Then his disciples came and took away
the body and buried it, and went and told Jesus.

Feeding the Five Thousand
(Mark 6:30–44; Luke 9:10–17; John 6:1–14)

13 [a]When Jesus heard *it*, He departed from
there by boat to a deserted place by Himself. But

KJV

the people had heard *thereof*, they followed him
on foot out of the cities.
14 And Jesus went forth, and saw a great
multitude, and [a]was moved with compassion toward them, and he healed their sick.
15 [a]And when it was evening, his disciples
came to him, saying, This is a desert place, and
the time is now past; send the multitude away,
that they may go into the villages, and buy themselves victuals.
16 But Jesus said unto them, They need not
depart; give ye them to eat.
17 And they say unto him, We have here but
five loaves, and two fishes.
18 He said, Bring them hither to me.
19 And he commanded the multitude to sit
down on the grass, and took the five loaves, and
the two fishes, and looking up to heaven, [a]he
blessed, and brake, and gave the loaves to *his* disciples, and the disciples to the multitude.
20 And they did all eat, and were filled: and
they took up of the fragments that remained
twelve baskets full.
21 And they that had eaten were about five
thousand men, beside women and children.

Jesus Walks on the Sea
(Mark 6:45–52; John 6:15–21)

22 And straightway Jesus constrained his
disciples to get into a ship, and to go before him
unto the other side, while he sent the multitudes
away.
23 [a]And when he had sent the multitudes
away, he went up into a mountain apart to pray:
[b]and when the evening was come, he was there
alone.
24 But the ship was now in the midst of the
sea, tossed with waves: for the wind was contrary.
25 And in the fourth watch of the night Jesus
went unto them, walking on the sea.
26 And when the disciples saw him [a]walking
on the sea, they were troubled, saying, It is a
spirit; and they cried out for fear.
27 But straightway Jesus spake unto them,
saying, Be of good [a]cheer; it is I; be not afraid.
28 And Peter answered him and said, Lord,
if it be thou, bid me come unto thee on the water.
29 And he said, Come. And when Peter was
come down out of the ship, he walked on the water, to go to Jesus.
30 But when he saw the wind boisterous, he
was afraid; and beginning to sink, he cried, saying, Lord, save me.
31 And immediately Jesus stretched forth *his*
hand, and caught him, and said unto him, O thou
of [a]little faith, wherefore didst thou doubt?
32 And when they were come into the ship,
the wind ceased.
33 Then they that were in the ship came and
worshipped him, saying, Of a truth [a]thou art the
Son of God.

Many Touch Him and Are Made Well
(Mark 6:53–56)

34 [a]And when they were gone over, they
came into the land of Gennesaret.
35 And when the men of that place had
knowledge of him, they sent out into all that country round about, and brought unto him all that
were diseased;
36 And besought him that they might only
[a]touch the hem of his garment: and [b]as many as
touched were made perfectly whole.

Defilement Comes from Within
(Mark 7:1–23)

15 Then [a]came to Jesus scribes and Pharisees,
which were of Jerusalem, saying,
2 [a]Why do thy disciples transgress the tradition of the elders? for they wash not their hands
when they eat bread.
3 But he answered and said unto them, Why

14 [a]Matt. 9:36; Mark 6:34
15 [a]Mark 6:35; Luke 9:12
19 [a]1 Sam. 9:13; Matt. 15:36; 26:26; Mark 6:41; 8:7; 14:22; Luke 24:30; Acts 27:35; [Rom. 14:6]
23 [a]Mark 6:46; Luke 9:28; John 6:15 [b]John 6:16
26 [a]Job 9:8
27 [a]Acts 23:11; 27:22, 25, 36
31 [a]Matt. 6:30; 8:26
33 [a]Ps. 2:7; Matt. 16:16; 26:63; Mark 1:1; Luke 4:41; John 1:49; 6:69; 11:27; Acts 8:37; Rom. 1:4
34 [a]Mark 6:53; Luke 5:1
36 [a][Mark 5:24–34] [b]Matt. 9:20; Mark 3:10; [Luke 6:19]; Acts 19:12

CHAPTER 15

1 [a]Mark 7:1; John 1:19; Acts 25:7
2 [a]Mark 7:5

*———

14:24 NU *many furlongs away from the land*
14:30 NU brackets *that* and *boisterous* as disputed.
14:33 NU omits *came and*
14:34 NU *to land at*

NKJV

when the multitudes heard it, they followed Him
on foot from the cities.
14 And when Jesus went out He saw a great
multitude; and He [a]was moved with compassion
for them, and healed their sick.
15 [a]When it was evening, His disciples came
to Him, saying, "This is a deserted place, and the
hour is already late. Send the multitudes away,
that they may go into the villages and buy themselves food."
16 But Jesus said to them, "They do not need
to go away. You give them something to eat."
17 And they said to Him, "We have here only
five loaves and two fish."
18 He said, "Bring them here to Me."
19 Then He commanded the multitudes to sit
down on the grass. And He took the five loaves
and the two fish, and looking up to heaven, [a]He
blessed and broke and gave the loaves to the disciples; and the disciples gave to the multitudes.
20 So they all ate and were filled, and they
took up twelve baskets full of the fragments that
remained.
21 Now those who had eaten were about five
thousand men, besides women and children.

Jesus Walks on the Sea
(Mark 6:45–52; John 6:15–21)

22 Immediately Jesus made His disciples get
into the boat and go before Him to the other side,
while He sent the multitudes away.
23 [a]And when He had sent the multitudes
away, He went up on the mountain by Himself
to pray. [b]Now when evening came, He was alone
there.
24 But the boat was now *in the middle of
the sea, tossed by the waves, for the wind was
contrary.
25 Now in the fourth watch of the night Jesus
went to them, walking on the sea.
26 And when the disciples saw Him [a]walking
on the sea, they were troubled, saying, "It is a
ghost!" And they cried out for fear.
27 But immediately Jesus spoke to them, saying, "Be of good [a]cheer! It is I; do not be afraid."
28 And Peter answered Him and said, "Lord,
if it is You, command me to come to You on the
water."
29 So He said, "Come." And when Peter had
come down out of the boat, he walked on the water to go to Jesus.
30 But when he saw *that the wind *was* boisterous, he was afraid; and beginning to sink he
cried out, saying, "Lord, save me!"
31 And immediately Jesus stretched out *His*
hand and caught him, and said to him, "O you
of [a]little faith, why did you doubt?"
32 And when they got into the boat, the wind
ceased.
33 Then those who were in the boat *came
and worshiped Him, saying, "Truly [a]You are the
Son of God."

Many Touch Him and Are Made Well
(Mark 6:53–56)

34 [a]When they had crossed over, they came
*to the land of Gennesaret.
35 And when the men of that place recognized Him, they sent out into all that surrounding
region, brought to Him all who were sick,
36 and begged Him that they might only
[a]touch the hem of His garment. And [b]as many
as touched *it* were made perfectly well.

Defilement Comes from Within
(Mark 7:1–23)

15 Then [a]the scribes and Pharisees who were
from Jerusalem came to Jesus, saying,
2 [a]"Why do Your disciples transgress the
tradition of the elders? For they do not wash their
hands when they eat bread."
3 He answered and said to them, "Why do

KJV

do ye also transgress the commandment of God
by your tradition?
4 For God commanded, saying, [a]HONOUR
THY FATHER AND MOTHER: and, [b]HE THAT CURSETH
FATHER OR MOTHER, LET HIM DIE THE DEATH.
5 But ye say, Whosoever shall say to *his* father or *his* mother, [a]*It is* a gift, by whatsoever
thou mightest be profited by me;
6 And honour not his father or his mother,
he shall be free. Thus have ye made the commandment of God of none effect by your tradition.
7 *Ye* [a]hypocrites, well did Esaias prophesy
of you, saying,
8 [a]THIS PEOPLE DRAWETH NIGH UNTO ME WITH
THEIR MOUTH, AND HONOURETH ME WITH *THEIR* LIPS;
BUT THEIR HEART IS FAR FROM ME.
9 BUT IN VAIN THEY DO WORSHIP ME, [a]TEACH-
ING *FOR* DOCTRINES THE COMMANDMENTS OF MEN.
10 [a]And he called the multitude, and said
unto them, Hear, and understand:
11 [a]Not that which goeth into the mouth defileth a man; but that which cometh out of the
mouth, this defileth a man.
12 Then came his disciples, and said unto
him, Knowest thou that the Pharisees were offended, after they heard this saying?
13 But he answered and said, [a]Every plant,
which my heavenly Father hath not planted, shall
be rooted up.
14 Let them alone: [a]they be blind leaders of
the blind. And if the blind lead the blind, both
shall fall into the ditch.
15 [a]Then answered Peter and said unto him,
Declare unto us this parable.
16 And Jesus said, [a]Are ye also yet without
understanding?
17 Do not ye yet understand, that [a]whatso-
ever entereth in at the mouth goeth into the belly,
and is cast out into the draught?
18 But [a]those things which proceed out of the
mouth come forth from the heart; and they defile
the man.
19 [a]For out of the heart proceed evil
thoughts, murders, adulteries, fornications, thefts,
false witness, blasphemies:
20 These are *the things* which defile a man:
but to eat with unwashen hands defileth not a
man.

A Gentile Shows Her Faith
(*Mark 7:24–30*)

21 [a]Then Jesus went thence, and departed
into the coasts of Tyre and Sidon.
22 And, behold, a woman of Canaan came
out of the same coasts, and cried unto him, saying,
Have mercy on me, O Lord, *thou* [a]son of David;
my daughter is grievously vexed with a devil.
23 But he answered her not a word. And his
disciples came and besought him, saying, Send
her away; for she crieth after us.
24 But he answered and said, [a]I am not sent
but unto the lost sheep of the house of Israel.
25 Then came she and worshipped him, saying, Lord, help me.
26 But he answered and said, It is not meet
to take the children's bread, and to cast *it* to
[a]dogs.
27 And she said, Truth, Lord: yet the dogs
eat of the crumbs which fall from their masters'
table.
28 Then Jesus answered and said unto her,
O woman, [a]great *is* thy faith: be it unto thee even
as thou wilt. And her daughter was made whole
from that very hour.

4 [a]Ex. 20:1, 12; Lev. 19:3; [Deut. 5:16]; Prov. 23:22; [Eph. 6:2, 3] [b]Ex. 21:17; Lev. 20:9; Deut. 27:16; Prov. 20:20; 30:17
5 [a]Mark 7:11, 12
7 [a]Mark 7:6
8 [a]Ps. 78:36; Is. 29:13; Ezek. 33:31
9 [a]Is. 29:13; [Col. 2:18–22]; Titus 1:14
10 [a]Mark 7:14
11 [a][Acts 10:15; Rom. 14:14, 17, 20; 1 Tim. 4:4; Titus 1:15]
13 [a][Is. 60:21; 61:3; John 15:2; 1 Cor. 3:12, 13]
14 [a]Is. 9:16; Mal. 2:8; Matt. 23:16, 24; Luke 6:39; Rom. 2:19
15 [a]Mark 7:17
16 [a]Matt. 16:9; Mark 7:18
17 [a][1 Cor. 6:13]
18 [a][Matt. 12:34]; Mark 7:20; [James 3:6]
19 [a]Gen. 6:5; 8:21; Prov. 6:14; Jer. 17:9; Mark 7:21; [Rom. 1:29–32; Gal. 5:19–21]
21 [a]Mark 7:24–30
22 [a]Matt. 1:1; 22:41, 42
24 [a]Matt. 10:5, 6; [Rom. 15:8]
26 [a]Matt. 7:6; Phil. 3:2
28 [a]Luke 7:9

NKJV

you also transgress the commandment of God because of your tradition?
4 "For God commanded, saying, [a]*'Honor*
your father and your mother'; and, [b]*'He who*
curses father or mother, let him be put to
death.'
5 "But you say, 'Whoever says to his father
or mother, [a]"Whatever profit you might have received from me *is* a gift *to God*"—
6 'then he need not honor his father *or
mother.' Thus you have made the *commandment
of God of no effect by your tradition.
7 [a]"Hypocrites! Well did Isaiah prophesy
about you, saying:

8 *'These[a] people *draw near to Me with their*
mouth,
And honor Me with their lips,
But their heart is far from Me.
9 *And in vain they worship Me,*
[a]*Teaching as doctrines the commandments*
of men.' "

10 [a]When He had called the multitude
to *Himself*, He said to them, "Hear and understand:
11 [a]"Not what goes into the mouth defiles a
man; but what comes out of the mouth, this defiles
a man."
12 Then His disciples came and said to Him,
"Do You know that the Pharisees were offended
when they heard this saying?"
13 But He answered and said, [a]"Every plant
which My heavenly Father has not planted will
be uprooted.
14 "Let them alone. [a]They are blind leaders
of the blind. And if the blind leads the blind, both
will fall into a ditch."
15 [a]Then Peter answered and said to Him,
"Explain this parable to us."
16 So Jesus said, [a]"Are you also still without
understanding?
17 "Do you not yet understand that [a]what-
ever enters the mouth goes into the stomach and
is eliminated?
18 "But [a]those things which proceed out of
the mouth come from the heart, and they defile
a man.
19 [a]"For out of the heart proceed evil
thoughts, murders, adulteries, fornications, thefts,
false witness, blasphemies.
20 "These are *the things* which defile a man,
but to eat with unwashed hands does not defile
a man."

A Gentile Shows Her Faith
(*Mark 7:24–30*)

21 [a]Then Jesus went out from there and departed to the region of Tyre and Sidon.
22 And behold, a woman of Canaan came
from that region and cried out to Him, saying,
"Have mercy on me, O Lord, [a]Son of David! My
daughter is severely demon-possessed."
23 But He answered her not a word. And His
disciples came and urged Him, saying, "Send her
away, for she cries out after us."
24 But He answered and said, [a]"I was not
sent except to the lost sheep of the house of
Israel."
25 Then she came and worshiped Him, saying, "Lord, help me!"
26 But He answered and said, "It is not good
to take the children's bread and throw *it* to the
little [a]dogs."
27 And she said, "Yes, Lord, yet even the little dogs eat the crumbs which fall from their masters' table."
28 Then Jesus answered and said to her, "O
woman, [a]great *is* your faith! Let it be to you as
you desire." And her daughter was healed from
that very hour.

15:6 NU omits *or mother* • NU *word*
15:8 NU omits *draw near to Me with their mouth, And*

KJV

Jesus Heals Great Multitudes
(*Mark 7:31–37*)

29 [a]And Jesus departed from thence, and came nigh [b]unto the sea of Galilee; and went up into a mountain, and sat down there.
30 [a]And great multitudes came unto him, having with them *those that were* lame, blind, dumb, maimed, and many others, and cast them down at Jesus' [b]feet; and he healed them:
31 Insomuch that the multitude wondered, when they saw the dumb to speak, the maimed to be whole, the lame to walk, and the blind to see: and they [a]glorified the God of Israel.

Feeding the Four Thousand
(*Mark 8:1–10*)

32 [a]Then Jesus called his disciples *unto him,* and said, I have compassion on the multitude, because they continue with me now three days, and have nothing to eat: and I will not send them away fasting, lest they faint in the way.
33 [a]And his disciples say unto him, Whence should we have so much bread in the wilderness, as to fill so great a multitude?
34 And Jesus saith unto them, How many loaves have ye? And they said, Seven, and a few little fishes.
35 And he commanded the multitude to sit down on the ground.
36 And [a]he took the seven loaves and the fishes, and [b]gave thanks, and brake *them,* and gave to his disciples, and the disciples to the multitude.
37 And they did all eat, and were filled: and they took up of the broken *meat* that was left seven baskets full.
38 And they that did eat were four thousand men, beside women and children.
39 [a]And he sent away the multitude, and took ship, and came into the coasts of Magdala.

The Pharisees and Sadducees Seek a Sign
(*Mark 8:11–13; Luke 12:54–56*)

16 The [a]Pharisees also with the Sadducees came, and tempting desired him that he would shew them a sign from heaven.
2 He answered and said unto them, When it is evening, ye say, *It will be* fair weather: for the sky is red.
3 And in the morning, *It will be* foul weather to day: for the sky is red and lowring. O *ye* hypocrites, ye can discern the face of the sky; but can ye not *discern* the signs of the times?
4 [a]A wicked and adulterous generation seeketh after a sign; and there shall no sign be given unto it, but the sign of the prophet Jonas. And he left them, and departed.

The Leaven of the Pharisees and Sadducees
(*Mark 8:14–21*)

5 And [a]when his disciples were come to the other side, they had forgotten to take bread.
6 Then Jesus said unto them, [a]Take heed and beware of the leaven of the Pharisees and of the Sadducees.
7 And they reasoned among themselves, saying, *It is* because we have taken no bread.
8 *Which* when Jesus perceived, he said unto them, O ye of little faith, why reason ye among yourselves, because ye have brought no bread?
9 [a]Do ye not yet understand, neither remember the five loaves of the five thousand, and how many baskets ye took up?
10 [a]Neither the seven loaves of the four thousand, and how many baskets ye took up?
11 How is it that ye do not understand that I spake *it* not to you concerning bread, that ye should beware of the leaven of the Pharisees and of the Sadducees?

29 [a]Matt. 15:29–31; Mark 7:31–37 [b]Matt. 4:18
30 [a]Is. 35:5, 6; Matt. 11:5; Luke 7:22 [b]Mark 7:25; Luke 7:38; 8:41; 10:39
31 [a]Luke 5:25, 26; 19:37, 38
32 [a]Mark 8:1–10
33 [a]2 Kin. 4:43
36 [a]Matt. 14:19; 26:27; Luke 22:17, 19; John 6:11, 23; Acts 27:35; [Rom. 14:6] [b]1 Sam. 9:13; Luke 22:19
39 [a]Mark 8:10

CHAPTER 16

1 [a]Matt. 12:38; Mark 8:11; Luke 11:16; 12:54–56; 1 Cor. 1:22
4 [a]Prov. 30:12; Matt. 12:39; Luke 11:29; 24:46
5 [a]Mark 8:14
6 [a]Mark 8:15; Luke 12:1
9 [a]Matt. 14:15–21; Mark 6:30–44; Luke 9:10–17; John 6:1–14
10 [a]Matt. 15:32–38; Mark 8:1–9

NKJV

Jesus Heals Great Multitudes
(*Mark 7:31–37*)

29 [a]Jesus departed from there, [b]skirted the Sea of Galilee, and went up on the mountain and sat down there.
30 [a]Then great multitudes came to Him, having with them *the* lame, blind, mute, maimed, and many others; and they laid them down at Jesus' [b]feet, and He healed them.
31 So the multitude marveled when they saw *the* mute speaking, *the* maimed made whole, *the* lame walking, and *the* blind seeing; and they [a]glorified the God of Israel.

Feeding the Four Thousand
(*Mark 8:1–10*)

32 [a]Now Jesus called His disciples to *Himself* and said, "I have compassion on the multitude, because they have now continued with Me three days and have nothing to eat. And I do not want to send them away hungry, lest they faint on the way."
33 [a]Then His disciples said to Him, "Where could we get enough bread in the wilderness to fill such a great multitude?"
34 Jesus said to them, "How many loaves do you have?" And they said, "Seven, and a few little fish."
35 So He commanded the multitude to sit down on the ground.
36 And [a]He took the seven loaves and the fish and [b]gave thanks, broke *them* and gave *them* to His disciples; and the disciples *gave* to the multitude.
37 So they all ate and were filled, and they took up seven large baskets full of the fragments that were left.
38 Now those who ate were four thousand men, besides women and children.
39 [a]And He sent away the multitude, got into the boat, and came to the region of *Magdala.

The Pharisees and Sadducees Seek a Sign
(*Mark 8:11–13; Luke 12:54–56*)

16 Then the [a]Pharisees and Sadducees came, and testing Him asked that He would show them a sign from heaven.
2 He answered and said to them, "When it is evening you say, *'It will be* fair weather, for the sky is red';
3 "and in the morning, *'It will be* foul weather today, for the sky is red and threatening.' *Hypocrites! You know how to discern the face of the sky, but you cannot *discern* the signs of the times.
4 [a]"A wicked and adulterous generation seeks after a sign, and no sign shall be given to it except the sign of *the prophet Jonah." And He left them and departed.

The Leaven of the Pharisees and Sadducees
(*Mark 8:14–21*)

5 Now [a]when His disciples had come to the other side, they had forgotten to take bread.
6 Then Jesus said to them, [a]"Take heed and beware of the leaven of the Pharisees and the Sadducees."
7 And they reasoned among themselves, saying, *"It is* because we have taken no bread."
8 But Jesus, being aware of *it,* said to them, "O you of little faith, why do you reason among yourselves because you *have brought no bread?
9 [a]"Do you not yet understand, or remember the five loaves of the five thousand and how many baskets you took up?
10 [a]"Nor the seven loaves of the four thousand and how many large baskets you took up?
11 "How is it you do not understand that I did not speak to you concerning bread?—*but* to beware of the leaven of the Pharisees and Sadducees."

*

15:39 NU *Magadan*
16:3 NU omits *Hypocrites*
16:4 NU omits *the prophet*
16:8 NU *have no bread*

KJV

12 Then understood they how that he bade *them* not beware of the leaven of bread, but of the doctrine of the Pharisees and of the Sadducees.

Peter Confesses Jesus as the Christ
(Mark 8:27–30; Luke 9:18–20)

13 When Jesus came into the coasts of Caesarea Philippi, he asked his disciples, saying, [a]Whom do men say that I the Son of man am?

14 And they said, [a]Some *say that thou art* John the Baptist: some, Elias; and others, Jeremias, or [b]one of the prophets.

15 He saith unto them, But whom say [a]ye that I am?

16 And Simon Peter answered and said, [a]Thou art the Christ, the Son of the living God.

17 And Jesus answered and said unto him, Blessed art thou, Simon Bar–jona: [a]for flesh and blood hath not revealed *it* unto thee, but [b]my Father which is in heaven.

18 And I say also unto thee, That [a]thou art Peter, and [b]upon this rock I will build my church; and [c]the gates of hell shall not prevail against it.

19 [a]And I will give unto thee the keys of the kingdom of heaven: and whatsoever thou shalt bind on earth shall be bound in heaven: and whatsoever thou shalt loose on earth shall be loosed in heaven.

20 [a]Then charged he his disciples that they should tell no man that he was Jesus the Christ.

Jesus Predicts His Death and Resurrection
(Mark 8:31–33; Luke 9:21, 22)

21 From that time forth began Jesus [a]to shew unto his disciples, how that he must go unto Jerusalem, and suffer many things of the elders and chief priests and scribes, and be killed, and be raised again the third day.

22 Then Peter took him, and began to rebuke him, saying, Be it far from thee, Lord: this shall not be unto thee.

23 But he turned, and said unto Peter, Get thee behind me, [a]Satan: [b]thou art an offence unto me: for thou savourest not the things that be of God, but those that be of men.

Take Up the Cross and Follow Him
(Mark 8:34–38; Luke 9:23–26)

24 [a]Then said Jesus unto his disciples, If any *man* will come after me, let him deny himself, and take up his cross, and [b]follow me.

25 For [a]whosoever will save his life shall lose it: and whosoever will lose his life for my sake shall find it.

26 For what is a man [a]profited, if he shall gain the whole world, and lose his own soul? or [b]what shall a man give in exchange for his soul?

27 For [a]the Son of man shall come in the glory of his Father [b]with his angels; [c]and then he shall reward every man according to his works.

Jesus Transfigured on the Mount
(Mark 9:1–13; Luke 9:27–36; 2 Pet. 1:16–18)

28 Verily I say unto you, [a]There be some standing here, which shall not taste of death, till they see the Son of man coming in his kingdom.

17 And [a]after six days Jesus taketh Peter, James, and John his brother, and bringeth them up into an high mountain apart,

2 And was transfigured before them: and his face did shine as the sun, and his raiment was white as the light.

3 And, behold, there appeared unto them Moses and Elias talking with him.

4 Then answered Peter, and said unto Jesus, Lord, it is good for us to be here: if thou wilt, let us make here three tabernacles; one for thee, and one for Moses, and one for Elias.

5 [a]While he yet spake, behold, a bright cloud overshadowed them: and behold a voice out

13 [a]Mark 8:27; Luke 9:18
14 [a]Matt. 14:2; Luke 9:7–9 [b]Matt. 21:11
15 [a]John 6:67
16 [a]Matt. 14:33; Mark 8:29; Luke 9:20; John 6:69; 11:27; Acts 8:37; 9:20; Heb. 1:2, 5; 1 John 4:15
17 [a][Eph. 2:8] [b][Matt. 11:27; 1 Cor. 2:10]; Gal. 1:16
18 [a]John 1:42 [b]Acts 2:41; [Eph. 2:20; Rev. 21:14] [c]Job 33:17; Ps. 9:13; 107:18; Is. 38:10
19 [a]Matt. 18:18; John 20:23
20 [a]Matt. 17:9; Mark 8:30; Luke 9:21
21 [a]Matt. 20:17; Mark 8:31; 9:31; Luke 9:22; 18:31; 24:46; John 2:19
23 [a]Matt. 4:10 [b][Rom. 8:7]
24 [a]Mark 8:34; Luke 9:23; [Acts 14:22; 2 Cor. 4:10, 11; 1 Thess. 3:3; 2 Tim. 3:12] [b][1 Pet. 2:21]
25 [a]Luke 17:33; John 12:25
26 [a]Luke 12:20, 21 [b]Ps. 49:7, 8
27 [a]Matt. 26:64; Mark 8:38; Luke 9:26 [b][Dan. 7:10]; Zech. 14:5 [c]Job 34:11; Ps. 62:12; Prov. 24:12; Rom. 2:6; 2 Cor. 5:10; 1 Pet. 1:17; Rev. 2:23
28 [a]Mark 9:1; Luke 9:27; Acts 7:55, 56; Rev. 19:11

CHAPTER 17

1 [a]Matt. 17:1–8; Mark 9:2–8; Luke 9:28–36
5 [a]2 Pet. 1:17

*______

16:19 Or *will have been bound . . . will have been loosed*
17:4 NU *I will make*

NKJV

12 Then they understood that He did not tell *them* to beware of the leaven of bread, but of the doctrine of the Pharisees and Sadducees.

Peter Confesses Jesus as the Christ
(Mark 8:27–30; Luke 9:18–20)

13 When Jesus came into the region of Caesarea Philippi, He asked His disciples, saying, [a]"Who do men say that I, the Son of Man, am?"

14 So they said, [a]"Some *say* John the Baptist, some Elijah, and others Jeremiah or [b]one of the prophets."

15 He said to them, "But who do [a]you say that I am?"

16 Simon Peter answered and said, [a]"You are the Christ, the Son of the living God."

17 Jesus answered and said to him, "Blessed are you, Simon Bar-Jonah, [a]for flesh and blood has not revealed *this* to you, but [b]My Father who is in heaven.

18 "And I also say to you that [a]you are Peter, and [b]on this rock I will build My church, and [c]the gates of Hades shall not prevail against it.

19 [a]"And I will give you the keys of the kingdom of heaven, and whatever you bind on earth *will be bound in heaven, and whatever you loose on earth will be loosed in heaven."

20 [a]Then He commanded His disciples that they should tell no one that He was Jesus the Christ.

Jesus Predicts His Death and Resurrection
(Mark 8:31–33; Luke 9:21, 22)

21 From that time Jesus began [a]to show to His disciples that He must go to Jerusalem, and suffer many things from the elders and chief priests and scribes, and be killed, and be raised the third day.

22 Then Peter took Him aside and began to rebuke Him, saying, "Far be it from You, Lord; this shall not happen to You!"

23 But He turned and said to Peter, "Get behind Me, [a]Satan! [b]You are an offense to Me, for you are not mindful of the things of God, but the things of men."

Take Up the Cross and Follow Him
(Mark 8:34–38; Luke 9:23–26)

24 [a]Then Jesus said to His disciples, "If anyone desires to come after Me, let him deny himself, and take up his cross, and [b]follow Me.

25 "For [a]whoever desires to save his life will lose it, but whoever loses his life for My sake will find it.

26 "For what [a]profit is it to a man if he gains the whole world, and loses his own soul? Or [b]what will a man give in exchange for his soul?

27 "For [a]the Son of Man will come in the glory of His Father [b]with His angels, [c]and then He will reward each according to his works.

Jesus Transfigured on the Mount
(Mark 9:1–13; Luke 9:27–36; 2 Pet. 1:16–18)

28 "Assuredly, I say to you, [a]there are some standing here who shall not taste death till they see the Son of Man coming in His kingdom."

17 Now [a]after six days Jesus took Peter, James, and John his brother, led them up on a high mountain by themselves;

2 and He was transfigured before them. His face shone like the sun, and His clothes became as white as the light.

3 And behold, Moses and Elijah appeared to them, talking with Him.

4 Then Peter answered and said to Jesus, "Lord, it is good for us to be here; if You wish, *let us make here three tabernacles: one for You, one for Moses, and one for Elijah."

5 [a]While he was still speaking, behold, a bright cloud overshadowed them; and suddenly

KJV

of the cloud, which said, [b]This is my beloved Son, [c]in whom I am well pleased; [d]hear ye him.

6 [a]And when the disciples heard *it*, they fell on their face, and were sore afraid.

7 And Jesus came and [a]touched them, and said, Arise, and be not afraid.

8 And when they had lifted up their eyes, they saw no man, save Jesus only.

9 And as they came down from the mountain, Jesus charged them, saying, Tell the vision to no man, until the Son of man be risen again from the dead.

10 And his disciples asked him, saying, [a]Why then say the scribes that Elias must first come?

11 And Jesus answered and said unto them, Elias truly shall first come, and [a]restore all things.

12 [a]But I say unto you, That Elias is come already, and they knew him not, but [b]have done unto him whatsoever they listed. Likewise [c]shall also the Son of man suffer of them.

13 [a]Then the disciples understood that he spake unto them of John the Baptist.

A Boy Is Healed
(Mark 9:14–29; Luke 9:37–42)

14 [a]And when they were come to the multitude, there came to him a *certain* man, kneeling down to him, and saying,

15 Lord, have mercy on my son: for he is lunatick, and sore vexed: for ofttimes he falleth into the fire, and oft into the water.

16 And I brought him to thy disciples, and they could not cure him.

17 Then Jesus answered and said, O faithless and [a]perverse generation, how long shall I be with you? how long shall I suffer you? bring him hither to me.

18 And Jesus [a]rebuked the devil; and he departed out of him: and the child was cured from that very hour.

19 Then came the disciples to Jesus apart, and said, Why could not we cast him out?

20 And Jesus said unto them, Because of your unbelief: for verily I say unto you, [a]If ye have faith as a grain of mustard seed, ye shall say unto this mountain, Remove hence to yonder place; and it shall remove; and nothing shall be impossible unto you.

21 Howbeit this kind goeth not out but by prayer and fasting.

Jesus Again Predicts His Death and Resurrection
(Mark 9:30–32; Luke 9:43–45)

22 [a]And while they abode in Galilee, Jesus said unto them, The Son of man shall be betrayed into the hands of men:

23 And they shall kill him, and the third day he shall be raised again. And they were exceeding [a]sorry.

Peter and His Master Pay Their Taxes

24 And [a]when they were come to Capernaum, they that received tribute *money* came to Peter, and said, Doth not your master pay tribute?

25 He saith, Yes. And when he was come into the house, Jesus prevented him, saying, What thinkest thou, Simon? of whom do the kings of the earth take custom or tribute? of their own children, or of [a]strangers?

26 Peter saith unto him, Of strangers. Jesus saith unto him, Then are the children free.

27 Notwithstanding, lest we should offend them, go thou to the sea, and cast an hook, and take up the fish that first cometh up; and when thou hast opened his mouth, thou shalt find a piece of money: that take, and give unto them for me and thee.

5 [b]Ps. 2:7; Matt. 3:17; Mark 1:11; Luke 1:35; 3:22; [John 12:28–30] [c]Is. 42:1; Matt. 3:17; 12:18; 2 Pet. 1:17 [d][Deut. 18:15, 19; Acts 3:22, 23]
6 [a]2 Pet. 1:18
7 [a]Dan. 8:18
10 [a]Mal. 4:5; Matt. 11:14; 16:14; Mark 9:11
11 [a][Mal. 4:6]; Luke 1:17
12 [a]Matt. 11:14; Mark 9:12, 13 [b]Matt. 14:3, 10 [c]Matt. 16:21
13 [a]Matt. 11:14
14 [a]Matt. 17:14–19; Mark 9:14–28; Luke 9:37–42
17 [a]Deut. 32:5; Phil. 2:15
18 [a]Luke 4:41
20 [a]Matt. 21:21; Mark 11:23; Luke 17:6; [1 Cor. 12:9]
22 [a]Matt. 16:21; 26:57; Mark 8:31; Luke 9:22, 44; John 18:12
23 [a]Matt. 26:22; 27:50; Luke 23:46; 24:46; John 16:6; 19:30; Acts 10:40
24 [a]Mark 9:33
25 [a][Is. 60:10–17]

*———

17:11 NU omits *first*
17:15 Lit. *moonstruck*
17:20 NU *little faith*
17:21 NU omits v. 21.
17:22 NU *gathering together*
17:24 NU *Capharnaum,* here and elsewhere
17:27 Gr. *stater,* the exact temple tax for two

NKJV

a voice came out of the cloud, saying, [b]"This is My beloved Son, [c]in whom I am well pleased. [d]Hear Him!"

6 [a]And when the disciples heard *it,* they fell on their faces and were greatly afraid.

7 But Jesus came and [a]touched them and said, "Arise, and do not be afraid."

8 When they had lifted up their eyes, they saw no one but Jesus only.

9 Now as they came down from the mountain, Jesus commanded them, saying, "Tell the vision to no one until the Son of Man is risen from the dead."

10 And His disciples asked Him, saying, [a]"Why then do the scribes say that Elijah must come first?"

11 Jesus answered and said to them, "Indeed, Elijah is coming *first and will [a]restore all things.

12 [a]"But I say to you that Elijah has come already, and they [b]did not know him but did to him whatever they wished. Likewise [c]the Son of Man is also about to suffer at their hands."

13 [a]Then the disciples understood that He spoke to them of John the Baptist.

A Boy Is Healed
(Mark 9:14–29; Luke 9:37–42)

14 [a]And when they had come to the multitude, a man came to Him, kneeling down to Him and saying,

15 "Lord, have mercy on my son, for he is *an epileptic and suffers severely; for he often falls into the fire and often into the water.

16 "So I brought him to Your disciples, but they could not cure him."

17 Then Jesus answered and said, "O faithless and [a]perverse generation, how long shall I be with you? How long shall I bear with you? Bring him here to Me."

18 And Jesus [a]rebuked the demon, and it came out of him; and the child was cured from that very hour.

19 Then the disciples came to Jesus privately and said, "Why could we not cast it out?"

20 So Jesus said to them, "Because of your *unbelief; for assuredly, I say to you, [a]if you have faith as a mustard seed, you will say to this mountain, 'Move from here to there,' and it will move; and nothing will be impossible for you.

21 *"However, this kind does not go out except by prayer and fasting."

Jesus Again Predicts His Death and Resurrection
(Mark 9:30–32; Luke 9:43–45)

22 [a]Now while they were *staying in Galilee, Jesus said to them, "The Son of Man is about to be betrayed into the hands of men,

23 "and they will kill Him, and the third day He will be raised up." And they were exceedingly [a]sorrowful.

Peter and His Master Pay Their Taxes

24 [a]When they had come to *Capernaum, those who received the *temple* tax came to Peter and said, "Does your Teacher not pay the *temple* tax?"

25 He said, "Yes." And when he had come into the house, Jesus anticipated him, saying, "What do you think, Simon? From whom do the kings of the earth take customs or taxes, from their sons or from [a]strangers?"

26 Peter said to Him, "From strangers." Jesus said to him, "Then the sons are free.

27 "Nevertheless, lest we offend them, go to the sea, cast in a hook, and take the fish that comes up first. And when you have opened its mouth, you will find a *piece of money; take that and give it to them for Me and you."

KJV

Who Is the Greatest?
(Mark 9:33–37; Luke 9:46–48)

18 At [a]the same time came the disciples unto Jesus, saying, Who is the greatest in the kingdom of heaven?

2 And Jesus called a little [a]child unto him, and set him in the midst of them,

3 And said, Verily I say unto you, [a]Except ye be converted, and become as little children, ye shall not enter into the kingdom of heaven.

4 [a]Whosoever therefore shall humble himself as this little child, the same is greatest in the kingdom of heaven.

5 And [a]whoso shall receive one such little child in my name receiveth me.

Jesus Warns of Offenses
(Mark 9:42–48; Luke 17:1, 2)

6 [a]But whoso shall offend one of these little ones which believe in me, it were better for him that a millstone were hanged about his neck, and *that* he were drowned in the depth of the sea.

7 Woe unto the world because of offences! for [a]it must needs be that offences come; but [b]woe to that man by whom the offence cometh!

8 [a]Wherefore if thy hand or thy foot offend thee, cut them off, and cast *them* from thee: it is better for thee to enter into life halt or maimed, rather than having two hands or two feet to be cast into everlasting fire.

9 And if thine eye offend thee, pluck it out, and cast *it* from thee: it is better for thee to enter into life with one eye, rather than having two eyes to be cast into hell fire.

The Parable of the Lost Sheep
(Luke 15:1–7)

10 Take heed that ye despise not one of these little ones; for I say unto you, That in heaven [a]their angels do always [b]behold the face of my Father which is in heaven.

11 [a]For the Son of man is come to save that which was lost.

12 [a]How think ye? if a man have an hundred sheep, and one of them be gone astray, doth he not leave the ninety and nine, and goeth into the mountains, and seeketh that which is gone astray?

13 And if so be that he find it, verily I say unto you, he rejoiceth more of that *sheep*, than of the ninety and nine which went not astray.

14 Even so it is not the [a]will of your Father which is in heaven, that one of these little ones should perish.

Dealing with a Sinning Brother

15 Moreover [a]if thy brother shall trespass against thee, go and tell him his fault between thee and him alone: if he shall hear thee, [b]thou hast gained thy brother.

16 But if he will not hear *thee, then* take with thee one or two more, that in [a]THE MOUTH OF TWO OR THREE WITNESSES EVERY WORD MAY BE ESTABLISHED.

17 And if he shall neglect to hear them, tell *it* unto the church: but if he neglect to hear the church, let him be unto thee as an [a]heathen man and a publican.

18 Verily I say unto you, [a]Whatsoever ye shall bind on earth shall be bound in heaven: and whatsoever ye shall loose on earth shall be loosed in heaven.

19 [a]Again I say unto you, That if two of you shall agree on earth as touching any thing that they shall ask, [b]it shall be done for them of my Father which is in heaven.

20 For where two or three are gathered [a]together in my name, there am I in the midst of them.

NKJV

Who Is the Greatest?
(Mark 9:33–37; Luke 9:46–48)

18 At [a]that time the disciples came to Jesus, saying, "Who then is greatest in the kingdom of heaven?"

2 Then Jesus called a little [a]child to Him, set him in the midst of them,

3 and said, "Assuredly, I say to you, [a]unless you are converted and become as little children, you will by no means enter the kingdom of heaven.

4 [a]"Therefore whoever humbles himself as this little child is the greatest in the kingdom of heaven.

5 [a]"Whoever receives one little child like this in My name receives Me.

Jesus Warns of Offenses
(Mark 9:42–48; Luke 17:1, 2)

6 [a]"But whoever causes one of these little ones who believe in Me to sin, it would be better for him if a millstone were hung around his neck, and he were drowned in the depth of the sea.

7 "Woe to the world because of offenses! For [a]offenses must come, but [b]woe to that man by whom the offense comes!

8 [a]"If your hand or foot causes you to sin, cut it off and cast *it* from you. It is better for you to enter into life lame or maimed, rather than having two hands or two feet, to be cast into the everlasting fire.

9 "And if your eye causes you to sin, pluck it out and cast *it* from you. It is better for you to enter into life with one eye, rather than having two eyes, to be cast into hell fire.

The Parable of the Lost Sheep
(Luke 15:1–7)

10 "Take heed that you do not despise one of these little ones, for I say to you that in heaven [a]their angels always [b]see the face of My Father who is in heaven.

11 [a]"For* the Son of Man has come to save that which was lost.

12 [a]"What do you think? If a man has a hundred sheep, and one of them goes astray, does he not leave the ninety-nine and go to the mountains to seek the one that is straying?

13 "And if he should find it, assuredly, I say to you, he rejoices more over that *sheep* than over the ninety-nine that did not go astray.

14 "Even so it is not the [a]will of your Father who is in heaven that one of these little ones should perish.

Dealing with a Sinning Brother

15 "Moreover [a]if your brother sins against you, go and tell him his fault between you and him alone. If he hears you, [b]you have gained your brother.

16 "But if he will not hear, take with you one or two more, that [a]*'by the mouth of two or three witnesses every word may be established.'*

17 "And if he refuses to hear them, tell *it* to the church. But if he refuses even to hear the church, let him be to you like a [a]heathen and a tax collector.

18 "Assuredly, I say to you, [a]whatever you bind on earth will be bound in heaven, and whatever you loose on earth will be loosed in heaven.

19 [a]"Again* I say to you that if two of you agree on earth concerning anything that they ask, [b]it will be done for them by My Father in heaven.

20 "For where two or three are gathered [a]together in My name, I am there in the midst of them."

CHAPTER 18

1 [a]Mark 9:33–37; Luke 9:46–48; 22:24–27
2 [a]Matt. 19:14; Mark 10:14; Luke 18:14–17
3 [a]Ps. 131:2; Matt. 19:14; Mark 10:15; Luke 18:16; [1 Cor. 14:20; 1 Pet. 2:2]
4 [a][Matt. 20:27; 23:11]
5 [a][Matt. 10:42]; Luke 9:48
6 [a]Mark 9:42; Luke 17:2; [1 Cor. 8:12]
7 [a]Luke 17:1; [1 Cor. 11:19]; 1 Tim. 4:1 [b]Matt. 26:24; 27:4, 5
8 [a]Matt. 5:29, 30; Mark 9:43, 45
10 [a][Ps. 34:7]; Zech. 13:7; [Heb. 1:14] [b]Esth. 1:14; Luke 1:19; Acts 12:15; [Rev. 8:2]
11 [a]Luke 9:56; John 3:17
12 [a]Matt. 18:12–14; Luke 15:4–7
14 [a][1 Tim. 2:4]
15 [a]Lev. 19:17; [Luke 17:3, 4; Gal. 6:1]; 2 Thess. 3:15; [James 5:19] [b][James 5:20]; 1 Pet. 3:1
16 [a]Deut. 17:6; 19:15; John 8:17; 2 Cor. 13:1; 1 Tim. 5:19; Heb. 10:28
17 [a]Rom. 16:17; 1 Cor. 5:9; [2 Thess. 3:6, 14; 2 John 10]
18 [a]Matt. 16:19; [John 20:22, 23; 1 Cor. 5:4]
19 [a][1 Cor. 1:10] [b][1 John 3:22; 5:14]
20 [a]Acts 20:7; 1 Cor. 14:26

*

18:11 NU omits v. 11.
18:19 NU, M *Again, assuredly, I say*

KJV

The Parable of the Unforgiving Servant

21 Then came Peter to him, and said, Lord, how oft shall my brother sin against me, and I forgive him? [a]till seven times?

22 Jesus saith unto him, I say not unto thee, [a]Until seven times: but, Until seventy times seven.

23 Therefore is the kingdom of heaven likened unto a certain king, which would take account of his servants.

24 And when he had begun to reckon, one was brought unto him, which owed him ten thousand talents.

25 But forasmuch as he had not to pay, his lord commanded him [a]to be sold, and his wife, and children, and all that he had, and payment to be made.

26 The servant therefore fell down, and worshipped him, saying, Lord, have patience with me, and I will pay thee all.

27 Then the lord of that servant was moved with compassion, and loosed him, and forgave him the debt.

28 But the same servant went out, and found one of his fellowservants, which owed him an hundred pence: and he laid hands on him, and took *him* by the throat, saying, Pay me that thou owest.

29 And his fellowservant fell down at his feet, and besought him, saying, Have patience with me, and I will pay thee all.

30 And he would not: but went and cast him into prison, till he should pay the debt.

31 So when his fellowservants saw what was done, they were very sorry, and came and told unto their lord all that was done.

32 Then his lord, after that he had called him, said unto him, O thou wicked servant, I forgave thee [a]all that debt, because thou desiredst me:

33 Shouldest not thou also have had compassion on thy fellowservant, even as I had pity on thee?

34 And his lord was wroth, and delivered him to the tormentors, till he should pay all that was due unto him.

35 [a]So likewise shall my heavenly Father do also unto you, if ye from your hearts forgive not every one his brother their trespasses.

Marriage and Divorce
(*Mark 10:1–12*)

19 And it came to pass, [a]*that* when Jesus had finished these sayings, he departed from Galilee, and came into the coasts of Judaea beyond Jordan;

2 [a]And great multitudes followed him; and he healed them there.

3 The Pharisees also came unto him, tempting him, and saying unto him, Is it lawful for a man to put away his wife for every cause?

4 And he answered and said unto them, Have ye not read, that he which made *them* at the beginning [a]MADE THEM MALE AND FEMALE,

5 And said, [a]FOR THIS CAUSE SHALL A MAN LEAVE FATHER AND MOTHER, AND SHALL CLEAVE TO HIS WIFE: AND [b]THEY TWAIN SHALL BE ONE FLESH?

6 Wherefore they are no more twain, but one flesh. What therefore God hath joined together, let not man put asunder.

7 They say unto him, [a]Why did Moses then command to give a writing of divorcement, and to put her away?

8 He saith unto them, Moses because of the [a]hardness of your hearts suffered you to put away your [b]wives: but from the beginning it was not so.

9 [a]And I say unto you, Whosoever shall put away his wife, except *it be* for fornication, and shall marry another, committeth adultery: and whoso marrieth her which is put away doth commit adultery.

10 His disciples say unto him, [a]If the case

21 [a]Luke 17:4
22 [a][Matt. 6:14; Mark 11:25]; Col. 3:13
25 [a]Ex. 21:2; Lev. 25:39; 2 Kin. 4:1; Neh. 5:5, 8
32 [a]Luke 7:41–43
35 [a]Prov. 21:13; Matt. 6:12; Mark 11:26; James 2:13

CHAPTER 19

1 [a]Matt. 19:1–9; Mark 10:1–12; John 10:40
2 [a]Matt. 12:15
4 [a]Gen. 1:27; 5:2; [Mal. 2:15]
5 [a]Gen. 2:24; Mark 10:5–9; Eph. 5:31 [b][1 Cor. 6:16; 7:2]
7 [a]Deut. 24:1–4; Matt. 5:31
8 [a]Heb. 3:15 [b]Mal. 2:16
9 [a][Matt. 5:32]; Mark 10:11; Luke 16:18; 1 Cor. 7:10
10 [a][Prov. 21:19]

*________

18:29 NU omits *at his feet* • NU, M omit *all*
18:35 NU omits *his trespasses*
19:4 NU *created*
19:9 Or *fornication*

NKJV

The Parable of the Unforgiving Servant

21 Then Peter came to Him and said, "Lord, how often shall my brother sin against me, and I forgive him? [a]Up to seven times?"

22 Jesus said to him, "I do not say to you, [a]up to seven times, but up to seventy times seven.

23 "Therefore the kingdom of heaven is like a certain king who wanted to settle accounts with his servants.

24 "And when he had begun to settle accounts, one was brought to him who owed him ten thousand talents.

25 "But as he was not able to pay, his master commanded [a]that he be sold, with his wife and children and all that he had, and that payment be made.

26 "The servant therefore fell down before him, saying, 'Master, have patience with me, and I will pay you all.'

27 "Then the master of that servant was moved with compassion, released him, and forgave him the debt.

28 "But that servant went out and found one of his fellow servants who owed him a hundred denarii; and he laid hands on him and took *him* by the throat, saying, 'Pay me what you owe!'

29 "So his fellow servant fell down *at his feet and begged him, saying, 'Have patience with me, and I will pay you *all.'

30 "And he would not, but went and threw him into prison till he should pay the debt.

31 "So when his fellow servants saw what had been done, they were very grieved, and came and told their master all that had been done.

32 "Then his master, after he had called him, said to him, 'You wicked servant! I forgave you [a]all that debt because you begged me.

33 'Should you not also have had compassion on your fellow servant, just as I had pity on you?'

34 "And his master was angry, and delivered him to the torturers until he should pay all that was due to him.

35 [a]"So My heavenly Father also will do to you if each of you, from his heart, does not forgive his brother *his trespasses."

Marriage and Divorce
(*Mark 10:1–12*)

19 Now it came to pass, [a]when Jesus had finished these sayings, *that* He departed from Galilee and came to the region of Judea beyond the Jordan.

2 [a]And great multitudes followed Him, and He healed them there.

3 The Pharisees also came to Him, testing Him, and saying to Him, "Is it lawful for a man to divorce his wife for *just* any reason?"

4 And He answered and said to them, "Have you not read that He who *made *them* at the beginning [a]*'made them male and female,'*

5 "and said, [a]*'For this reason a man shall leave his father and mother and be joined to his wife, and* [b]*the two shall become one flesh'*?

6 "So then, they are no longer two but one flesh. Therefore what God has joined together, let not man separate."

7 They said to Him, [a]"Why then did Moses command to give a certificate of divorce, and to put her away?"

8 He said to them, "Moses, because of the [a]hardness of your hearts, permitted you to divorce your [b]wives, but from the beginning it was not so.

9 [a]"And I say to you, whoever divorces his wife, except for *sexual immorality, and marries another, commits adultery; and whoever marries her who is divorced commits adultery."

10 His disciples said to Him, [a]"If such is the

KJV

of the man be so with *his* wife, it is not good to
marry.

Jesus Teaches on Celibacy

11 But he said unto them, [a]All *men* cannot receive this saying, save *they* to whom it is
given.
12 For there are some eunuchs, which were
so born from *their* mother's womb: and [a]there
are some eunuchs, which were made eunuchs of
men: and there be eunuchs, which have made
themselves eunuchs for the kingdom of heaven's
sake. He that is able to receive *it*, let him receive
it.

Jesus Blesses Little Children
(Mark 10:13–16; Luke 18:15–17)

13 [a]Then were there brought unto him little
children, that he should put *his* hands on them,
and pray: and the disciples rebuked them.
14 But Jesus said, Suffer little children, and
forbid them not, to come unto me: for [a]of such is
the kingdom of heaven.
15 And he laid *his* hands on them, and departed thence.

Jesus Counsels the Rich Young Ruler
(Mark 10:17–22; Luke 18:18–23)

16 [a]And, behold, one came and said unto
him, [b]Good Master, what good thing shall I do,
that I may have eternal life?
17 And he said unto him, Why callest thou
me good? *there is* none [a]good but one, *that is*,
God: but if thou wilt enter into life, [b]keep the
commandments.
18 He saith unto him, Which? Jesus said,
[a]THOU SHALT DO NO MURDER, THOU SHALT NOT COM-
MIT ADULTERY, THOU SHALT NOT STEAL, THOU SHALT
NOT BEAR FALSE WITNESS,
19 [a]HONOUR THY FATHER AND *THY* MOTHER:
and, [b]THOU SHALT LOVE THY NEIGHBOUR AS THYSELF.
20 The young man saith unto him, All these
things have I [a]kept from my youth up: what lack
I yet?
21 Jesus said unto him, If thou wilt be perfect,
[a]go *and* sell that thou hast, and give to the poor,
and thou shalt have treasure in heaven: and come
and follow me.
22 But when the young man heard that saying, he went away sorrowful: for he had great
possessions.

With God All Things Are Possible
(Mark 10:23–31; Luke 18:24–30)

23 Then said Jesus unto his disciples, Verily
I say unto you, That [a]a rich man shall hardly enter
into the kingdom of heaven.
24 And again I say unto you, It is easier for
a camel to go through the eye of a needle, than
for a rich man to enter into the kingdom of
God.
25 When his disciples heard *it*, they were exceedingly amazed, saying, Who then can be
saved?
26 But Jesus beheld *them*, and said unto
them, With men this is impossible; but [a]with God
all things are possible.
27 Then answered Peter and said unto him,
Behold, [a]we have forsaken all, and followed thee;
what shall we have therefore?
28 And Jesus said unto them, Verily I say
unto you, That ye which have followed me, in the
regeneration when the Son of man shall sit in the
throne of his glory, [a]ye also shall sit upon twelve
thrones, judging the twelve tribes of Israel.
29 [a]And every one that hath forsaken
houses, or brethren, or sisters, or father, or
mother, or wife, or children, or lands, for my
name's sake, shall receive an hundredfold, and
shall inherit everlasting life.
30 [a]But many *that are* first shall be last; and
the last *shall be* first.

NKJV

case of the man with *his* wife, it is better not to
marry."

Jesus Teaches on Celibacy

11 But He said to them, [a]"All cannot accept
this saying, but only *those* to whom it has been
given:
12 "For there are eunuchs who were born
thus from *their* mother's womb, and [a]there are
eunuchs who were made eunuchs by men, and
there are eunuchs who have made themselves eunuchs for the kingdom of heaven's sake. He who
is able to accept *it*, let him accept *it*."

Jesus Blesses Little Children
(Mark 10:13–16; Luke 18:15–17)

13 [a]Then little children were brought to Him
that He might put *His* hands on them and pray,
but the disciples rebuked them.
14 But Jesus said, "Let the little children
come to Me, and do not forbid them; for [a]of such
is the kingdom of heaven."
15 And He laid *His* hands on them and departed from there.

Jesus Counsels the Rich Young Ruler
(Mark 10:17–22; Luke 18:18–23)

16 [a]Now behold, one came and said to Him,
[b]"Good* Teacher, what good thing shall I do that
I may have eternal life?"
17 So He said to him, *"Why do you call Me
good? *No one *is* [a]good but One, *that is*, God.
But if you want to enter into life, [b]keep the
commandments."
18 He said to Him, "Which ones?" Jesus said,
[a]"*'You shall not murder,' 'You shall not commit
adultery,' 'You shall not steal,' 'You shall not bear
false witness,'*
19 [a]*'Honor your father and your mother,'*
and, [b]*'You shall love your neighbor as yourself.'* "
20 The young man said to Him, "All these
things I have [a]kept *from my youth. What do I
still lack?"
21 Jesus said to him, "If you want to be perfect, [a]go, sell what you have and give to the poor,
and you will have treasure in heaven; and come,
follow Me."
22 But when the young man heard that saying, he went away sorrowful, for he had great possessions.

With God All Things Are Possible
(Mark 10:23–31; Luke 18:24–30)

23 Then Jesus said to His disciples, "Assuredly, I say to you that [a]it is hard for a rich
man to enter the kingdom of heaven.
24 "And again I say to you, it is easier for a
camel to go through the eye of a needle than for
a rich man to enter the kingdom of God."
25 When His disciples heard *it*, they were
greatly astonished, saying, "Who then can be
saved?"
26 But Jesus looked at *them* and said to them,
"With men this is impossible, but [a]with God all
things are possible."
27 Then Peter answered and said to Him,
"See, [a]we have left all and followed You. Therefore what shall we have?"
28 So Jesus said to them, "Assuredly I say
to you, that in the regeneration, when the Son of
Man sits on the throne of His glory, [a]you who
have followed Me will also sit on twelve thrones,
judging the twelve tribes of Israel.
29 [a]"And everyone who has left houses or
brothers or sisters or father or mother *or wife
or children or lands, for My name's sake, shall
receive a hundredfold, and inherit eternal life.
30 [a]"But many *who are* first will be last, and
the last first.

11 [a][1 Cor. 7:2, 7, 9, 17] **12** [a][1 Cor. 7:32] **13** [a]Luke 18:15 **14** [a]Matt. 18:3, 4 **16** [a]Mark 10:17–30 [b]Luke 10:25 **17** [a]Nah. 1:7 [b]Lev. 18:5 **18** [a]Ex. 20:13–16 **19** [a]Ex. 20:12–16; Deut. 5:16–20 [b]Lev. 19:18 **20** [a][Phil. 3:6, 7] **21** [a]Acts 2:45; 4:34, 35 **23** [a][1 Tim. 6:9] **26** [a]Jer. 32:17 **27** [a]Deut. 33:9 **28** [a]Luke 22:28–30 **29** [a]Mark 10:29, 30 **30** [a]Luke 13:30

*

19:16 NU omits *Good*
19:17 NU *Why do you ask Me about what is good?* • NU *There is One who is good. But*
19:20 NU omits *from my youth*
19:29 NU omits *or wife*

KJV

The Parable of the Workers in the Vineyard

20 For the kingdom of heaven is like unto a man *that is* an householder, which went out early in the morning to hire labourers into his vineyard.

2 And when he had agreed with the labourers for a penny a day, he sent them into his vineyard.

3 And he went out about the third hour, and saw others standing idle in the marketplace,

4 And said unto them; Go ye also into the vineyard, and whatsoever is right I will give you. And they went their way.

5 Again he went out about the sixth and ninth hour, and did likewise.

6 And about the eleventh hour he went out, and found others standing idle, and saith unto them, Why stand ye here all the day idle?

7 They say unto him, Because no man hath hired us. He saith unto them, Go ye also into the vineyard; and whatsoever is right, *that* shall ye receive.

8 So when even was come, the lord of the vineyard saith unto his steward, Call the labourers, and give them *their* hire, beginning from the last unto the first.

9 And when they came that *were hired* about the eleventh hour, they received every man a penny.

10 But when the first came, they supposed that they should have received more; and they likewise received every man a penny.

11 And when they had received *it*, they murmured against the goodman of the house,

12 Saying, These last have wrought *but* one hour, and thou hast made them equal unto us, which have borne the burden and heat of the day.

13 But he answered one of them, and said, Friend, I do thee no wrong: didst not thou agree with me for a penny?

14 Take *that* thine *is*, and go thy way: I will give unto this last, even as unto thee.

15 [a]Is it not lawful for me to do what I will with mine own? [b]Is thine eye evil, because I am good?

16 [a]So the last shall be first, and the first last: [b]for many be called, but few chosen.

Jesus a Third Time Predicts His Death and Resurrection
(Mark 10:32–34; Luke 18:31–34)

17 [a]And Jesus going up to Jerusalem took the twelve disciples apart in the way, and said unto them,

18 [a]Behold, we go up to Jerusalem; and the Son of man shall be betrayed unto the chief priests and unto the scribes, and they shall condemn him to death,

19 [a]And shall deliver him to the Gentiles to [b]mock, and to [c]scourge, and to [d]crucify *him:* and the third day he shall [e]rise again.

Greatness Is Serving
(Mark 10:35–45)

20 [a]Then came to him the mother of [b]Zebedee's children with her sons, worshipping *him*, and desiring a certain thing of him.

21 And he said unto her, What wilt thou? She saith unto him, Grant that these my two sons [a]may sit, the one on thy right hand, and the other on the left, in thy kingdom.

22 But Jesus answered and said, Ye know not what ye ask. Are ye able to drink of [a]the cup that I shall drink of, and to be baptized with [b]the baptism that I am baptized with? They say unto him, We are able.

23 And he saith unto them, [a]Ye shall drink indeed of my cup, and be baptized with the baptism that I am baptized with: but to sit on my

CHAPTER 20

15 [a][Rom. 9:20, 21] [b]Deut. 15:9; Prov. 23:6; [Matt. 6:23]; Mark 7:22
16 [a]Matt. 19:30; Mark 10:31; Luke 13:30 [b]Matt. 22:14
17 [a]Matt. 20:17–19; Mark 10:32–34; Luke 18:31–33; John 12:12
18 [a]Matt. 16:21; 26:47–57; Mark 14:42, 64; John 18:5; 19:7
19 [a]Matt. 27:2; Mark 15:1, 16; Luke 23:1; John 18:28; Acts 3:13 [b]Matt. 26:67, 68; 27:29, 41; Mark 15:20, 31 [c]Matt. 27:26; Mark 15:15; John 19:1 [d]Matt. 27:35; Luke 23:33; Acts 3:13–15 [e]Matt. 28:5, 6; Mark 16:6, 9; Luke 24:5–8, 46; Acts 10:40; 1 Cor. 15:4
20 [a]Mark 10:35–45 [b]Matt. 4:21; 10:2
21 [a][Matt. 19:28]
22 [a]Is. 51:17, 22; Jer. 49:12; Matt. 26:39, 42; Mark 14:36; Luke 22:42; John 18:11 [b]Luke 12:50
23 [a][Acts 12:2; Rom. 8:17; 2 Cor. 1:7; Rev. 1:9]

*________

20:6 NU omits *idle*
20:7 NU omits the rest of v. 7.
20:16 NU omits the rest of v. 16.
20:22 NU omits *and be baptized with the baptism that I am baptized with*
20:23 NU omits *and be baptized with the baptism that I am baptized with*

NKJV

The Parable of the Workers in the Vineyard

20 "For the kingdom of heaven is like a landowner who went out early in the morning to hire laborers for his vineyard.

2 "Now when he had agreed with the laborers for a denarius a day, he sent them into his vineyard.

3 "And he went out about the third hour and saw others standing idle in the marketplace,

4 "and said to them, 'You also go into the vineyard, and whatever is right I will give you.' So they went.

5 "Again he went out about the sixth and the ninth hour, and did likewise.

6 "And about the eleventh hour he went out and found others standing *idle, and said to them, 'Why have you been standing here idle all day?'

7 "They said to him, 'Because no one hired us.' He said to them, 'You also go into the vineyard, *and whatever is right you will receive.'

8 "So when evening had come, the owner of the vineyard said to his steward, 'Call the laborers and give them *their* wages, beginning with the last to the first.'

9 "And when those came who *were hired* about the eleventh hour, they each received a denarius.

10 "But when the first came, they supposed that they would receive more; and they likewise received each a denarius.

11 "And when they had received *it*, they complained against the landowner,

12 "saying, 'These last *men* have worked *only* one hour, and you made them equal to us who have borne the burden and the heat of the day.'

13 "But he answered one of them and said, 'Friend, I am doing you no wrong. Did you not agree with me for a denarius?

14 'Take *what is* yours and go your way. I wish to give to this last man *the same* as to you.

15 [a]'Is it not lawful for me to do what I wish with my own things? Or [b]is your eye evil because I am good?'

16 [a]"So the last will be first, and the first last. [b]For* many are called, but few chosen."

Jesus a Third Time Predicts His Death and Resurrection
(Mark 10:32–34; Luke 18:31–34)

17 [a]Now Jesus, going up to Jerusalem, took the twelve disciples aside on the road and said to them,

18 [a]"Behold, we are going up to Jerusalem, and the Son of Man will be betrayed to the chief priests and to the scribes; and they will condemn Him to death,

19 [a]"and deliver Him to the Gentiles to [b]mock and to [c]scourge and to [d]crucify. And the third day He will [e]rise again."

Greatness Is Serving
(Mark 10:35–45)

20 [a]Then the mother of [b]Zebedee's sons came to Him with her sons, kneeling down and asking something from Him.

21 And He said to her, "What do you wish?" She said to Him, "Grant that these two sons of mine [a]may sit, one on Your right hand and the other on the left, in Your kingdom."

22 But Jesus answered and said, "You do not know what you ask. Are you able to drink [a]the cup that I am about to drink, *and be baptized with [b]the baptism that I am baptized with?" They said to Him, "We are able."

23 So He said to them, [a]"You will indeed drink My cup, *and be baptized with the baptism that I am baptized with; but to sit on My right

KJV

right hand, and on my left, is not mine to give,
but *it shall be given to them* for whom it is prepared of my Father.
24 [a]And when the ten heard *it*, they were
moved with indignation against the two brethren.
25 But Jesus called them *unto him*, and said,
Ye know that the princes of the Gentiles exercise
dominion over them, and they that are great exercise authority upon them.
26 But [a]it shall not be so among you: but
[b]whosoever will be great among you, let him be
your minister;
27 [a]And whosoever will be chief among you,
let him be your servant:
28 [a]Even as the [b]Son of man came not to be
ministered unto, [c]but to minister, and [d]to give his
life a ransom [e]for many.

Two Blind Men Receive Their Sight
(Mark 10:46–52; Luke 18:35–43)

29 [a]And as they departed from Jericho, a
great multitude followed him.
30 And, behold, [a]two blind men sitting by the
way side, when they heard that Jesus passed by,
cried out, saying, Have mercy on us, O Lord, *thou*
[b]son of David.
31 And the multitude [a]rebuked them, because they should hold their peace: but they cried
the more, saying, Have mercy on us, O Lord, *thou*
son of David.
32 And Jesus stood still, and called them, and
said, What will ye that I shall do unto you?
33 They say unto him, Lord, that our eyes
may be opened.
34 So Jesus had [a]compassion *on them*, and
touched their eyes: and immediately their eyes
received sight, and they followed him.

The Triumphal Entry
(Mark 11:1–10; Luke 19:28–40; John 12:12–19)

21 And [a]when they drew nigh unto Jerusalem,
and were come to Bethphage, unto [b]the
mount of Olives, then sent Jesus two disciples,
2 Saying unto them, Go into the village over
against you, and straightway ye shall find an ass
tied, and a colt with her: loose *them*, and bring
them unto me.
3 And if any *man* say ought unto you, ye
shall say, The Lord hath need of them; and
straightway he will send them.
4 All this was done, that it might be fulfilled
which was spoken by the prophet, saying,
5 [a]TELL YE THE DAUGHTER OF SION, BEHOLD,
THY KING COMETH UNTO THEE, MEEK, AND SITTING
UPON AN ASS, AND A COLT THE FOAL OF AN ASS.
6 [a]And the disciples went, and did as Jesus
commanded them,
7 And brought the ass, and the colt, and [a]put
on them their clothes, and they set *him* thereon.
8 And a very great multitude spread their
garments in the way; [a]others cut down branches
from the trees, and strawed *them* in the way.
9 And the multitudes that went before, and
that followed, cried, saying, Hosanna to the son
of David: [a]BLESSED *IS* HE THAT COMETH IN THE
NAME OF THE LORD; Hosanna in the highest.
10 [a]And when he was come into Jerusalem,
all the city was moved, saying, Who is this?
11 And the multitude said, This is Jesus [a]the
prophet of Nazareth of Galilee.

Jesus Cleanses the Temple
(Mark 11:15–19; Luke 19:45–48; John 2:13–22)

12 [a]And Jesus went into the temple of God,
and cast out all them that sold and bought in the

24 [a]Mark 10:41; Luke 22:24, 25
26 [a][1 Pet. 5:3] [b]Matt. 23:11; Mark 9:35; 10:43; Luke 22:26
27 [a][Matt. 18:4]
28 [a]John 13:4 [b][Matt. 26:28; John 13:13; 2 Cor. 8:9; Phil. 2:6, 7; 1 Tim. 2:5, 6; Titus 2:14; Heb. 9:28; Rev. 1:5] [c]Luke 22:27; John 13:14 [d][Is. 53:10, 11; Dan. 9:24, 26; John 11:51, 52; 1 Pet. 1:18, 19] [e][Rom. 5:15, 19; Heb. 9:28]
29 [a]Mark 10:46–52; Luke 18:35–43
30 [a]Matt. 9:27 [b][2 Sam. 7:14–17; Ps. 89:3–5, 19–37; Is. 11:10–12; Ezek. 37:21–25]; Matt. 1:1; Luke 1:31, 32; [Acts 15:14–17]
31 [a]Matt. 19:13
34 [a]Matt. 9:36; 14:14; 15:32; 18:27

CHAPTER 21

1 [a]Mark 11:1–10; Luke 19:29–38 [b][Zech. 14:4]
5 [a]Is. 62:11; Zech. 9:9; John 12:15
6 [a]Mark 11:4
7 [a]2 Kin. 9:13
8 [a]Lev. 23:40; John 12:13
9 [a]Ps. 118:26; Matt. 23:39
10 [a]John 2:13, 15
11 [a][Deut. 18:15, 18]; Matt. 2:23; 16:14; Luke 4:16–29; John 6:14; 7:40; 9:17; [Acts 3:22, 23]
12 [a]Mal. 3:1; Mark 11:15–18; Luke 19:45–47; John 2:13–16

*

21:1 M *Bethsphage*
21:4 NU omits *All*
21:7 NU *and He sat*
21:12 NU omits *of God*

NKJV

hand and on My left is not Mine to give, but *it is
for those* for whom it is prepared by My Father."
24 [a]And when the ten heard *it*, they were
greatly displeased with the two brothers.
25 But Jesus called them to *Himself* and said,
"You know that the rulers of the Gentiles lord it
over them, and those who are great exercise authority over them.
26 "Yet [a]it shall not be so among you; but
[b]whoever desires to become great among you, let
him be your servant.
27 [a]"And whoever desires to be first among
you, let him be your slave—
28 [a]"just as the [b]Son of Man did not come
to be served, [c]but to serve, and [d]to give His life
a ransom [e]for many."

Two Blind Men Receive Their Sight
(Mark 10:46–52; Luke 18:35–43)

29 [a]Now as they went out of Jericho, a great
multitude followed Him.
30 And behold, [a]two blind men sitting by the
road, when they heard that Jesus was passing by,
cried out, saying, "Have mercy on us, O Lord,
[b]Son of David!"
31 Then the multitude [a]warned them that
they should be quiet; but they cried out all the
more, saying, "Have mercy on us, O Lord, Son
of David!"
32 So Jesus stood still and called them, and
said, "What do you want Me to do for you?"
33 They said to Him, "Lord, that our eyes
may be opened."
34 So Jesus had [a]compassion and touched
their eyes. And immediately their eyes received
sight, and they followed Him.

The Triumphal Entry
(Mark 11:1–10; Luke 19:28–40; John 12:12–19)

21 Now [a]when they drew near Jerusalem, and
came to *Bethphage, at [b]the Mount of
Olives, then Jesus sent two disciples,
2 saying to them, "Go into the village opposite you, and immediately you will find a donkey
tied, and a colt with her. Loose *them* and bring
them to Me.
3 "And if anyone says anything to you, you
shall say, 'The Lord has need of them,' and immediately he will send them."
4 *All this was done that it might be fulfilled
which was spoken by the prophet, saying:

5 *"Tell[a] the daughter of Zion,*
'Behold, your King is coming to you,
Lowly, and sitting on a donkey,
A colt, the foal of a donkey.' "

6 [a]So the disciples went and did as Jesus
commanded them.
7 They brought the donkey and the colt,
[a]laid their clothes on them, *and set *Him* on them.
8 And a very great multitude spread their
clothes on the road; [a]others cut down branches
from the trees and spread *them* on the road.
9 Then the multitudes who went before and
those who followed cried out, saying:

"Hosanna to the Son of David!
[a]*'Blessed is He who comes in the name of*
the LORD!'
Hosanna in the highest!"

10 [a]And when He had come into Jerusalem,
all the city was moved, saying, "Who is this?"
11 So the multitudes said, "This is Jesus, [a]the
prophet from Nazareth of Galilee."

Jesus Cleanses the Temple
(Mark 11:15–19; Luke 19:45–48; John 2:13–22)

12 [a]Then Jesus went into the temple *of God
and drove out all those who bought and sold in

KJV

temple, and overthrew the tables of the [b]money-
changers, and the seats of them that sold doves,
13 And said unto them, It is written, [a]MY
HOUSE SHALL BE CALLED THE HOUSE OF PRAYER; but
ye have made it a [b]DEN OF THIEVES.
14 And the blind and the lame came to him
in the temple; and he healed them.
15 And when the chief priests and scribes
saw the wonderful things that he did, and the children crying in the temple, and saying, Hosanna
to the [a]son of David; they were sore displeased,
16 And said unto him, Hearest thou what
these say? And Jesus saith unto them, Yea; have
ye never read, [a]OUT OF THE MOUTH OF BABES AND
SUCKLINGS THOU HAST PERFECTED PRAISE?
17 And he left them, and [a]went out of the
city into Bethany; and he lodged there.

The Fig Tree Withered
(Mark 11:12–14)

18 [a]Now in the morning as he returned into
the city, he hungered.
19 [a]And when he saw a fig tree in the way,
he came to it, and found nothing thereon, but
leaves only, and said unto it, Let no fruit grow
on thee henceforward for ever. And presently the
fig tree withered away.

The Lesson of the Withered Fig Tree
(Mark 11:20–24)

20 [a]And when the disciples saw *it*, they marvelled, saying, How soon is the fig tree withered
away!
21 Jesus answered and said unto them, Verily I say unto you, [a]If ye have faith, and [b]doubt
not, ye shall not only do this *which is done* to
the fig tree, [c]but also if ye shall say unto this
mountain, Be thou removed, and be thou cast into
the sea; it shall be done.
22 And [a]all things, whatsoever ye shall ask
in prayer, believing, ye shall receive.

Jesus' Authority Questioned
(Mark 11:27–33; Luke 20:1–8)

23 [a]And when he was come into the temple,
the chief priests and the elders of the people came
unto him as he was teaching, and [b]said, By what
authority doest thou these things? and who gave
thee this authority?
24 And Jesus answered and said unto them,
I also will ask you one thing, which if ye tell me,
I in like wise will tell you by what authority I do
these things.
25 The [a]baptism of [b]John, whence was it?
from heaven, or of men? And they reasoned with
themselves, saying, If we shall say, From heaven;
he will say unto us, Why did ye not then believe
him?
26 But if we shall say, Of men; we [a]fear the
people; [b]for all hold John as a prophet.
27 And they answered Jesus, and said, We
cannot tell. And he said unto them, Neither tell I
you by what authority I do these things.

The Parable of the Two Sons

28 But what think ye? A *certain* man had two
sons; and he came to the first, and said, Son, go
work to day in my [a]vineyard.
29 He answered and said, I will not: but afterward he repented, and went.
30 And he came to the second, and said likewise. And he answered and said, I go, sir: and
went not.
31 Whether of them twain did the will of *his*
father? They say unto him, The first. Jesus saith
unto them, [a]Verily I say unto you, That the publicans and the harlots go into the kingdom of God
before you.

12 [b]Deut. 14:25
13 [a]Is. 56:7 [b]Jer. 7:11
15 [a]Matt. 1:1; John 7:42
16 [a]Ps. 8:2; Matt. 11:25
17 [a]Matt. 26:6; Mark 11:1, 11, 12; 14:3; Luke 19:29; 24:50; John 11:1, 18; 12:1
18 [a]Mark 11:12–14, 20–24
19 [a]Mark 11:13
20 [a]Mark 11:20
21 [a]Matt. 17:20 [b]James 1:6 [c]1 Cor. 13:2
22 [a]Matt. 7:7–11; Mark 11:24; Luke 11:9; [John 15:7; James 5:16; 1 John 3:22; 5:14]
23 [a]Mark 11:27–33; Luke 20:1–8 [b]Ex. 2:14; Acts 4:7; 7:27
25 [a][John 1:29–34] [b]John 1:15–28
26 [a]Matt. 14:5; 21:46; Luke 20:6 [b]Matt. 14:5; Mark 6:20
28 [a]Matt. 20:1; 21:33
31 [a]Luke 7:29, 37–50

NKJV

the temple, and overturned the tables of the
[b]money changers and the seats of those who sold
doves.
13 And He said to them, "It is written, [a]*'My
house shall be called a house of prayer,'* but you
have made it a [b]*'den of thieves.'* "
14 Then *the* blind and *the* lame came to Him
in the temple, and He healed them.
15 But when the chief priests and scribes saw
the wonderful things that He did, and the children
crying out in the temple and saying, "Hosanna
to the [a]Son of David!" they were indignant
16 and said to Him, "Do You hear what these
are saying?" And Jesus said to them, "Yes. Have
you never read,

[a]*'Out of the mouth of babes and nursing
infants
You have perfected praise'?* "

17 Then He left them and [a]went out of the
city to Bethany, and He lodged there.

The Fig Tree Withered
(Mark 11:12–14)

18 [a]Now in the morning, as He returned to
the city, He was hungry.
19 [a]And seeing a fig tree by the road, He
came to it and found nothing on it but leaves, and
said to it, "Let no fruit grow on you ever again."
Immediately the fig tree withered away.

The Lesson of the Withered Fig Tree
(Mark 11:20–24)

20 [a]And when the disciples saw *it*, they marveled, saying, "How did the fig tree wither away
so soon?"
21 So Jesus answered and said to them, "Assuredly, I say to you, [a]if you have faith and [b]do
not doubt, you will not only do what was done
to the fig tree, [c]but also if you say to this mountain, 'Be removed and be cast into the sea,' it will
be done.
22 "And [a]whatever things you ask in prayer,
believing, you will receive."

Jesus' Authority Questioned
(Mark 11:27–33; Luke 20:1–8)

23 [a]Now when He came into the temple, the
chief priests and the elders of the people confronted Him as He was teaching, and [b]said, "By
what authority are You doing these things? And
who gave You this authority?"
24 But Jesus answered and said to them, "I
also will ask you one thing, which if you tell Me,
I likewise will tell you by what authority I do these
things:
25 "The [a]baptism of [b]John—where was it
from? From heaven or from men?" And they reasoned among themselves, saying, "If we say,
'From heaven,' He will say to us, 'Why then did
you not believe him?'
26 "But if we say, 'From men,' we [a]fear the
multitude, [b]for all count John as a prophet."
27 So they answered Jesus and said, "We do
not know." And He said to them, "Neither will I
tell you by what authority I do these things.

The Parable of the Two Sons

28 "But what do you think? A man had two
sons, and he came to the first and said, 'Son, go,
work today in my [a]vineyard.'
29 "He answered and said, 'I will not,' but
afterward he regretted it and went.
30 "Then he came to the second and said
likewise. And he answered and said, 'I *go*, sir,'
but he did not go.
31 "Which of the two did the will of *his* father?" They said to Him, "The first." Jesus said
to them, [a]"Assuredly, I say to you that tax collectors and harlots enter the kingdom of God before
you.

KJV

32 For [a]John came unto you in the way of righteousness, and ye believed him not: [b]but the publicans and the harlots believed him: and ye, when ye had seen *it*, repented not afterward, that ye might believe him.

The Parable of the Wicked Vinedressers
(*Mark 12:1–12; Luke 20:9–19*)

33 Hear another parable: There was a certain householder, [a]which planted a vineyard, and hedged it round about, and digged a winepress in it, and built a tower, and let it out to husbandmen, and [b]went into a far country:

34 And when the time of the fruit drew near, he sent his servants to the husbandmen, that they might receive the fruits of it.

35 [a]And the husbandmen took his servants, and beat one, and killed another, and stoned another.

36 Again, he sent other servants more than the first: and they did unto them likewise.

37 But last of all he sent unto them his [a]son, saying, They will reverence my son.

38 But when the husbandmen saw the son, they said among themselves, [a]This is the heir; [b]come, let us kill him, and let us seize on his inheritance.

39 [a]And they caught him, and cast *him* out of the vineyard, and slew *him*.

40 When the lord therefore of the vineyard cometh, what will he do unto those husbandmen?

41 [a]They say unto him, [b]He will miserably destroy those wicked men, [c]and will let out *his* vineyard unto other husbandmen, which shall render him the fruits in their seasons.

42 Jesus saith unto them, Did ye never read in the scriptures, [a]THE STONE WHICH THE BUILDERS REJECTED, THE SAME IS BECOME THE HEAD OF THE CORNER: THIS IS THE LORD'S DOING, AND IT IS MARVELLOUS IN OUR EYES?

43 Therefore say I unto you, [a]The kingdom of God shall be taken from you, and given to a nation bringing forth the fruits thereof.

44 And whosoever [a]shall fall on this stone shall be broken: but on whomsoever it shall fall, [b]it will grind him to powder.

45 And when the chief priests and Pharisees had heard his parables, they perceived that he spake of them.

46 But when they sought to lay hands on him, they [a]feared the multitude, because [b]they took him for a prophet.

The Parable of the Wedding Feast
(*Luke 14:15–24*)

22 And Jesus answered [a]and spake unto them again by parables, and said,

2 The kingdom of heaven is like unto a certain king, which made a marriage for his son,

3 And sent forth his servants to call them that were bidden to the wedding: and they would not come.

4 Again, he sent forth other servants, saying, Tell them which are bidden, Behold, I have prepared my dinner: [a]my oxen and *my* fatlings *are* killed, and all things *are* ready: come unto the marriage.

5 But they made light of *it*, and went their ways, one to his farm, another to his merchandise:

6 And the remnant took his servants, and entreated *them* spitefully, and slew *them*.

7 But when the king heard *thereof*, he was wroth: and he sent forth [a]his armies, and destroyed those murderers, and burned up their city.

8 Then saith he to his servants, The wedding is ready, but they which were bidden were not [a]worthy.

9 Go ye therefore into the highways, and as many as ye shall find, bid to the marriage.

10 So those servants went out into the

32 [a]Luke 3:1–12; 7:29 [b]Luke 3:12, 13
33 [a]Ps. 80:9; Mark 12:1–12; Luke 20:9–19 [b]Matt. 25:14
35 [a]2 Chr. 24:21; 36:16; [Matt. 23:34, 37; Acts 7:52; 1 Thess. 2:15]; Heb. 11:36, 37
37 [a][John 3:16]
38 [a][Ps. 2:8; Heb. 1:2] [b][Ps. 2:2]; John 11:53; Acts 4:27
39 [a][Matt. 26:50]; Mark 14:46; Luke 22:54; John 18:12; [Acts 2:23]
41 [a]Luke 20:16 [b][Luke 21:24] [c][Matt. 8:11; Acts 13:46; Rom. 9; 10]
42 [a]Ps. 118:22, 23; Is. 28:16; Mark 12:10; Luke 20:17; Acts 4:11; [Rom. 9:33]; Eph. 2:20; [1 Pet. 2:6, 7]
43 [a][Matt. 8:12]; Acts 13:46
44 [a]Is. 8:14, 15; Zech. 12:3; Luke 20:18; [Rom. 9:33]; 1 Pet. 2:8 [b][Is. 60:12; Dan. 2:44]
46 [a]Matt. 21:26; Mark 11:18, 32 [b]Matt. 21:11; Luke 7:16; John 7:40

CHAPTER 22

1 [a]Luke 14:16; [Rev. 19:7–9]
4 [a]Prov. 9:2
7 [a][Dan. 9:26]
8 [a]Matt. 10:11

NKJV

32 "For [a]John came to you in the way of righteousness, and you did not believe him; [b]but tax collectors and harlots believed him; and when you saw *it*, you did not afterward relent and believe him.

The Parable of the Wicked Vinedressers
(*Mark 12:1–12; Luke 20:9–19*)

33 "Hear another parable: There was a certain landowner [a]who planted a vineyard and set a hedge around it, dug a winepress in it and built a tower. And he leased it to vinedressers and [b]went into a far country.

34 "Now when vintage-time drew near, he sent his servants to the vinedressers, that they might receive its fruit.

35 [a]"And the vinedressers took his servants, beat one, killed one, and stoned another.

36 "Again he sent other servants, more than the first, and they did likewise to them.

37 "Then last of all he sent his [a]son to them, saying, 'They will respect my son.'

38 "But when the vinedressers saw the son, they said among themselves, [a]'This is the heir. [b]Come, let us kill him and seize his inheritance.'

39 [a]"So they took him and cast *him* out of the vineyard and killed *him*.

40 "Therefore, when the owner of the vineyard comes, what will he do to those vinedressers?"

41 [a]They said to Him, [b]"He will destroy those wicked men miserably, [c]and lease *his* vineyard to other vinedressers who will render to him the fruits in their seasons."

42 Jesus said to them, "Have you never read in the Scriptures:

[a]'The stone which the builders rejected
Has become the chief cornerstone.
This was the LORD's doing,
And it is marvelous in our eyes'?

43 "Therefore I say to you, [a]the kingdom of God will be taken from you and given to a nation bearing the fruits of it.

44 "And [a]whoever falls on this stone will be broken; but on whomever it falls, [b]it will grind him to powder."

45 Now when the chief priests and Pharisees heard His parables, they perceived that He was speaking of them.

46 But when they sought to lay hands on Him, they [a]feared the multitudes, because [b]they took Him for a prophet.

The Parable of the Wedding Feast
(*Luke 14:15–24*)

22 And Jesus answered [a]and spoke to them again by parables and said:

2 "The kingdom of heaven is like a certain king who arranged a marriage for his son,

3 "and sent out his servants to call those who were invited to the wedding; and they were not willing to come.

4 "Again, he sent out other servants, saying, 'Tell those who are invited, "See, I have prepared my dinner; [a]my oxen and fatted cattle *are* killed, and all things *are* ready. Come to the wedding." '

5 "But they made light of it and went their ways, one to his own farm, another to his business.

6 "And the rest seized his servants, treated *them* spitefully, and killed *them*.

7 "But when the king heard *about it*, he was furious. And he sent out [a]his armies, destroyed those murderers, and burned up their city.

8 "Then he said to his servants, 'The wedding is ready, but those who were invited were not [a]worthy.

9 'Therefore go into the highways, and as many as you find, invite to the wedding.'

10 "So those servants went out into the

KJV

highways, and [a]gathered together all as many as they found, both bad and good: and the wedding was furnished with guests.

11 And when the king came in to see the guests, he saw there a man [a]which had not on a wedding garment:

12 And he saith unto him, Friend, how camest thou in hither not having a wedding garment? And he was [a]speechless.

13 Then said the king to the servants, Bind him hand and foot, and take him away, and cast *him* [a]into outer darkness; there shall be weeping and gnashing of teeth.

14 [a]For many are called, but few *are* chosen.

The Pharisees: Is It Lawful to Pay Taxes to Caesar?

(*Mark 12:13–17; Luke 20:20–26*)

15 [a]Then went the Pharisees, and took counsel how they might entangle him in *his* talk.

16 And they sent out unto him their disciples with the [a]Herodians, saying, Master, we know that thou art true, and teachest the way of God in truth, neither carest thou for any *man:* for thou regardest not the person of men.

17 Tell us therefore, What thinkest thou? Is it lawful to give tribute unto Caesar, or not?

18 But Jesus perceived their wickedness, and said, Why tempt ye me, *ye* hypocrites?

19 Shew me the tribute money. And they brought unto him a penny.

20 And he saith unto them, Whose *is* this image and superscription?

21 They say unto him, Caesar's. Then saith he unto them, [a]Render therefore unto Caesar the things which are [b]Caesar's; and unto God the things that are [c]God's.

22 When they had heard *these words,* they marvelled, and left him, and went their way.

The Sadducees: What About the Resurrection?

(*Mark 12:18–27; Luke 20:27–40*)

23 [a]The same day came to him the Sadducees, [b]which say that there is no resurrection, and asked him,

24 Saying, Master, [a]Moses said, If a man die, having no children, his brother shall marry his wife, and raise up seed unto his brother.

25 Now there were with us seven brethren: and the first, when he had married a wife, deceased, and, having no issue, left his wife unto his brother:

26 Likewise the second also, and the third, unto the seventh.

27 And last of all the woman died also.

28 Therefore in the resurrection whose wife shall she be of the seven? for they all had her.

29 Jesus answered and said unto them, Ye do err, [a]not knowing the scriptures, nor the power of God.

30 For in the resurrection they neither marry, nor are given in marriage, but [a]are as the angels of God in heaven.

31 But as touching the resurrection of the dead, have ye not read that which was spoken unto you by God, saying,

32 [a]I AM THE GOD OF ABRAHAM, AND THE GOD OF ISAAC, AND THE GOD OF JACOB? God is not the God of the dead, but of the living.

33 And when the multitude heard *this,* [a]they were astonished at his doctrine.

The Scribes: Which Is the First Commandment of All?

(*Mark 12:28–34; Luke 10:25–28*)

34 [a]But when the Pharisees had heard that he had put the Sadducees to silence, they were gathered together.

35 Then one of them, *which was* [a]a lawyer, asked *him a question,* tempting him, and saying,

10 [a]Matt. 13:38, 47, 48; [Acts 28:28]
11 [a][2 Cor. 5:3; Eph. 4:24; Col. 3:10, 12; Rev. 3:4; 16:15; 19:8]
12 [a][Rom. 3:19]
13 [a]Matt. 8:12; 25:30; Luke 13:28
14 [a]Matt. 20:16
15 [a]Mark 12:13–17; Luke 20:20–26
16 [a]Mark 3:6; 8:15; 12:13
21 [a]Matt. 17:25 [b][Rom. 13:1–7; 1 Pet. 2:13–15] [c][1 Cor. 3:23; 6:19, 20; 12:27]
23 [a]Mark 12:18–27; Luke 20:27–40 [b]Acts 23:8
24 [a]Deut. 25:5
29 [a]John 20:9
30 [a][1 John 3:2]
32 [a]Gen. 17:7; 26:24; 28:21; Ex. 3:6, 15; Mark 12:26; Luke 20:37; Acts 7:32; [Heb. 11:16]
33 [a]Matt. 7:28
34 [a]Mark 12:28–31; Luke 10:25–37
35 [a]Luke 7:30; 10:25; 11:45, 46, 52; 14:3; Titus 3:13

*________

22:13 NU omits *take him away, and*
22:30 NU omits *of God*

NKJV

highways and [a]gathered together all whom they found, both bad and good. And the wedding *hall* was filled with guests.

11 "But when the king came in to see the guests, he saw a man there [a]who did not have on a wedding garment.

12 "So he said to him, 'Friend, how did you come in here without a wedding garment?' And he was [a]speechless.

13 "Then the king said to the servants, 'Bind him hand and foot, *take him away, and cast *him* [a]into outer darkness; there will be weeping and gnashing of teeth.'

14 [a]"For many are called, but few *are* chosen."

The Pharisees: Is It Lawful to Pay Taxes to Caesar?

(*Mark 12:13–17; Luke 20:20–26*)

15 [a]Then the Pharisees went and plotted how they might entangle Him in *His* talk.

16 And they sent to Him their disciples with the [a]Herodians, saying, "Teacher, we know that You are true, and teach the way of God in truth; nor do You care about anyone, for You do not regard the person of men.

17 "Tell us, therefore, what do You think? Is it lawful to pay taxes to Caesar, or not?"

18 But Jesus perceived their wickedness, and said, "Why do you test Me, *you* hypocrites?

19 "Show Me the tax money." So they brought Him a denarius.

20 And He said to them, "Whose image and inscription *is* this?"

21 They said to Him, "Caesar's." And He said to them, [a]"Render therefore to Caesar the things that are [b]Caesar's, and to God the things that are [c]God's."

22 When they had heard *these words,* they marveled, and left Him and went their way.

The Sadducees: What About the Resurrection?

(*Mark 12:18–27; Luke 20:27–40*)

23 [a]The same day the Sadducees, [b]who say there is no resurrection, came to Him and asked Him,

24 saying: "Teacher, [a]Moses said that if a man dies, having no children, his brother shall marry his wife and raise up offspring for his brother.

25 "Now there were with us seven brothers. The first died after he had married, and having no offspring, left his wife to his brother.

26 "Likewise the second also, and the third, even to the seventh.

27 "Last of all the woman died also.

28 "Therefore, in the resurrection, whose wife of the seven will she be? For they all had her."

29 Jesus answered and said to them, "You are mistaken, [a]not knowing the Scriptures nor the power of God.

30 "For in the resurrection they neither marry nor are given in marriage, but [a]are like angels *of God in heaven.

31 "But concerning the resurrection of the dead, have you not read what was spoken to you by God, saying,

32 [a]*'I am the God of Abraham, the God of Isaac, and the God of Jacob'*? God is not the God of the dead, but of the living."

33 And when the multitudes heard *this,* [a]they were astonished at His teaching.

The Scribes: Which Is the First Commandment of All?

(*Mark 12:28–34; Luke 10:25–28*)

34 [a]But when the Pharisees heard that He had silenced the Sadducees, they gathered together.

35 Then one of them, [a]a lawyer, asked *Him a question,* testing Him, and saying,

KJV

36 Master, which *is* the great commandment in the law?

37 Jesus said unto him, [a]THOU SHALT LOVE THE LORD THY GOD WITH ALL THY HEART, AND WITH ALL THY SOUL, AND WITH ALL THY MIND.

38 This is the first and great commandment.

39 And the second *is* like unto it, [a]THOU SHALT LOVE THY NEIGHBOUR AS THYSELF.

40 [a]On these two commandments hang all the law and the prophets.

Jesus: How Can David Call His Descendant Lord?
(Mark 12:35–37; Luke 20:41–44)

41 [a]While the Pharisees were gathered together, Jesus asked them,

42 Saying, What think ye of Christ? whose son is he? They say unto him, *The* [a]*son* of David.

43 He saith unto them, How then doth David in spirit call him Lord, saying,

44 [a]THE LORD SAID UNTO MY LORD, SIT THOU ON MY RIGHT HAND, TILL I MAKE THINE ENEMIES THY FOOTSTOOL?

45 If David then call him Lord; how is he his son?

46 [a]And no man was able to answer him a word, [b]neither durst any *man* from that day forth ask him any more *questions*.

Woe to the Scribes and Pharisees
(Mark 12:38–40; Luke 20:45–47)

23 Then spake Jesus to the multitude, and to his disciples,

2 Saying, [a]The scribes and the Pharisees sit in Moses' seat:

3 All therefore whatsoever they bid you observe, *that* observe and do; but do not ye after their works: for [a]they say, and do not.

4 [a]For they bind heavy burdens and grievous to be borne, and lay *them* on men's shoulders; but they *themselves* will not move them with one of their fingers.

5 But all their works they do for to [a]be seen of men: they make broad their phylacteries, and enlarge the borders of their garments,

6 [a]And love the uppermost rooms at feasts, and the chief seats in the synagogues,

7 And greetings in the markets, and to be called of men, Rabbi, Rabbi.

8 [a]But be not ye called Rabbi: for one is your Master, *even* Christ; and all ye are brethren.

9 And call no *man* your father upon the earth: [a]for one is your Father, which is in heaven.

10 Neither be ye called masters: for one is your Master, *even* Christ.

11 But [a]he that is greatest among you shall be your servant.

12 [a]And whosoever shall exalt himself shall be abased; and he that shall humble himself shall be exalted.

13 But [a]woe unto you, scribes and Pharisees, hypocrites! for ye shut up the kingdom of heaven against men: for ye neither go in *yourselves*, neither suffer ye them that are entering to go in.

14 Woe unto you, scribes and Pharisees, hypocrites! [a]for ye devour widows' houses, and for a pretence make long prayer: therefore ye shall receive the greater damnation.

15 Woe unto you, scribes and Pharisees, hypocrites! for ye compass sea and land to make one proselyte, and when he is made, ye make him twofold more the child of hell than yourselves.

16 Woe unto you, [a]*ye* blind guides, which say, [b]Whosoever shall swear by the temple, it is nothing; but whosoever shall swear by the gold of the temple, he is a debtor!

37 [a]Deut. 6:5; 10:12; 30:6
39 [a]Lev. 19:18
40 [a][Matt. 7:12]
41 [a]Luke 20:41–44
42 [a]Matt. 1:1; 21:9
44 [a]Ps. 110:1
46 [a]Luke 14:6 [b]Mark 12:34

CHAPTER 23
2 [a]Neh. 8:4, 8
3 [a][Rom. 2:19]
4 [a]Luke 11:46
5 [a][Matt. 6:1–6, 16–18]
6 [a]Luke 11:43; 20:46
8 [a][James 3:1]
9 [a][Mal. 1:6]
11 [a]Matt. 20:26, 27
12 [a]Luke 14:11; 18:14
13 [a]Luke 11:52
14 [a]Mark 12:40
16 [a]Matt. 15:14; 23:24 [b][Matt. 5:33, 34]

*

23:3 NU omits *to observe*
23:8 NU omits *the Christ*
23:14 NU omits v. 14.

NKJV

36 "Teacher, which *is* the great commandment in the law?"

37 Jesus said to him, [a]"'*You shall love the* LORD *your God with all your heart, with all your soul, and with all your mind.*'

38 "This is *the* first and great commandment.

39 "And *the* second *is* like it: [a]'*You shall love your neighbor as yourself.*'

40 [a]"On these two commandments hang all the Law and the Prophets."

Jesus: How Can David Call His Descendant Lord?
(Mark 12:35–37; Luke 20:41–44)

41 [a]While the Pharisees were gathered together, Jesus asked them,

42 saying, "What do you think about the Christ? Whose Son is He?" They said to Him, "*The* [a]*Son* of David."

43 He said to them, "How then does David in the Spirit call Him *'Lord,'* saying:

44 *'The[a]* LORD *said to my Lord,*
"Sit at My right hand,
Till I make Your enemies Your
footstool" '?

45 "If David then calls Him *'Lord,'* how is He his Son?"

46 [a]And no one was able to answer Him a word, [b]nor from that day on did anyone dare question Him anymore.

Woe to the Scribes and Pharisees
(Mark 12:38–40; Luke 20:45–47)

23 Then Jesus spoke to the multitudes and to His disciples,

2 saying: [a]"The scribes and the Pharisees sit in Moses' seat.

3 "Therefore whatever they tell you *to observe, *that* observe and do, but do not do according to their works; for [a]they say, and do not do.

4 [a]"For they bind heavy burdens, hard to bear, and lay *them* on men's shoulders; but they *themselves* will not move them with one of their fingers.

5 "But all their works they do to [a]be seen by men. They make their phylacteries broad and enlarge the borders of their garments.

6 [a]"They love the best places at feasts, the best seats in the synagogues,

7 "greetings in the marketplaces, and to be called by men, 'Rabbi, Rabbi.'

8 [a]"But you, do not be called 'Rabbi'; for One is your Teacher, *the Christ, and you are all brethren.

9 "Do not call anyone on earth your father; [a]for One is your Father, He who is in heaven.

10 "And do not be called teachers; for One is your Teacher, the Christ.

11 "But [a]he who is greatest among you shall be your servant.

12 [a]"And whoever exalts himself will be humbled, and he who humbles himself will be exalted.

13 "But [a]woe to you, scribes and Pharisees, hypocrites! For you shut up the kingdom of heaven against men; for you neither go in *yourselves*, nor do you allow those who are entering to go in.

14 *"Woe to you, scribes and Pharisees, hypocrites! [a]For you devour widows' houses, and for a pretense make long prayers. Therefore you will receive greater condemnation.

15 "Woe to you, scribes and Pharisees, hypocrites! For you travel land and sea to win one proselyte, and when he is won, you make him twice as much a son of hell as yourselves.

16 "Woe to you, [a]blind guides, who say, [b]'Whoever swears by the temple, it is nothing; but whoever swears by the gold of the temple, he is obliged *to perform it.*'

KJV

17 *Ye* fools and blind: for whether is greater,
the gold, [a]or the temple that sanctifieth the gold?
18 And, Whosoever shall swear by the altar,
it is nothing; but whosoever sweareth by the gift
that is upon it, he is guilty.
19 *Ye* fools and blind: for whether *is* greater,
the gift, or [a]the altar that sanctifieth the gift?
20 Whoso therefore shall swear by the altar,
sweareth by it, and by all things thereon.
21 And whoso shall swear by the temple,
sweareth by it, and by [a]him that dwelleth therein.
22 And he that shall swear by heaven, sweareth by [a]the throne of God, and by him that sitteth
thereon.
23 Woe unto you, scribes and Pharisees, hypocrites! [a]for ye pay tithe of mint and anise and
cummin, and [b]have omitted the weightier *matters*
of the law, judgment, mercy, and faith: these
ought ye to have done, and not to leave the other
undone.
24 *Ye* blind guides, which strain at a gnat,
and swallow a camel.
25 Woe unto you, scribes and Pharisees, hypocrites! [a]for ye make clean the outside of the cup
and of the platter, but within they are full of extortion and excess.
26 *Thou* blind Pharisee, cleanse first that
which is within the cup and platter, that the outside of them may be clean also.
27 Woe unto you, scribes and Pharisees, hypocrites! [a]for ye are like unto whited sepulchres,
which indeed appear beautiful outward, but are
within full of dead *men's* bones, and of all
uncleanness.
28 Even so ye also outwardly appear righteous unto men, but within ye are full of hypocrisy
and iniquity.
29 [a]Woe unto you, scribes and Pharisees,
hypocrites! because ye build the tombs of the
prophets, and garnish the sepulchres of the
righteous,
30 And say, If we had been in the days of
our fathers, we would not have been partakers
with them in the blood of the prophets.
31 Wherefore ye be witnesses unto yourselves, that [a]ye are the children of them which
killed the prophets.
32 [a]Fill ye up then the measure of your
fathers.
33 *Ye* serpents, *ye* [a]generation of vipers, how
can ye escape the damnation of hell?
34 [a]Wherefore, behold, I send unto you
prophets, and wise men, and scribes: and [b]*some*
of them ye shall kill and crucify; and [c]*some* of
them shall ye scourge in your synagogues, and
persecute *them* from city to city:
35 [a]That upon you may come all the righteous blood shed upon the earth, [b]from the blood
of righteous Abel unto [c]the blood of Zacharias
son of Barachias, whom ye slew between the temple and the altar.
36 Verily I say unto you, All these things
shall come upon this generation.

Jesus Laments over Jerusalem
(*Luke 13:34, 35*)

37 [a]O Jerusalem, Jerusalem, *thou* that killest
the prophets, [b]and stonest them which are sent
unto thee, how often would [c]I have gathered thy
children together, even as a hen gathereth her
chickens [d]under *her* wings, and ye would not!
38 Behold, your house is left unto you
desolate.
39 For I say unto you, Ye shall not see me
henceforth, till ye shall say, [a]BLESSED *IS* HE THAT
COMETH IN THE NAME OF THE LORD.

Jesus Predicts the Destruction of the Temple
(*Mark 13:1, 2; Luke 21:5, 6*)

24 And [a]Jesus went out, and departed from
the temple: and his disciples came to *him*
for to shew him the buildings of the temple.

---

17 [a]Ex. 30:29
19 [a]Ex. 29:37
21 [a]1 Kin. 8:13; 2 Chr. 6:2; Ps. 26:8; 132:14
22 [a]Ps. 11:4; Is. 66:1; Matt. 5:34; Acts 7:49
23 [a]Matt. 23:13; Luke 11:42; 18:12 [b][1 Sam. 15:22; Hos. 6:6; Mic. 6:8]; Matt. 9:13; 12:7
25 [a]Mark 7:4; Luke 11:39
27 [a]Luke 11:44; Acts 23:3
29 [a]Luke 11:47, 48
31 [a]Matt. 23:34, 37; [Acts 7:51, 52]; 1 Thess. 2:15
32 [a]Gen. 15:16; [1 Thess. 2:16]
33 [a]Matt. 3:7; 12:34; Luke 3:7
34 [a]Matt. 21:34, 35; Luke 11:49 [b]John 16:2; Acts 7:54–60; 22:19 [c]Matt. 10:17; Acts 5:40; 2 Cor. 11:24, 25
35 [a]Rev. 18:24 [b]Gen. 4:8; Heb. 11:4; 1 John 3:12 [c]2 Chr. 24:20, 21
37 [a]Luke 13:34, 35 [b]2 Chr. 24:20, 21; 36:15, 16; Neh. 9:26; Matt. 21:35, 36 [c]Deut. 32:11, 12; Matt. 11:28–30 [d]Ps. 17:8; 91:4; Is. 49:5
39 [a]Ps. 118:26; Matt. 21:9

CHAPTER 24

1 [a]Mark 13:1; Luke 21:5–36

*

23:17 NU *sanctified*
23:21 M *dwelt*
23:25 M *unrighteousness*

NKJV

17 "Fools and blind! For which is greater, the
gold [a]or the temple that *sanctifies the gold?
18 "And, 'Whoever swears by the altar, it is
nothing; but whoever swears by the gift that is
on it, he is obliged *to perform it.*'
19 "Fools and blind! For which is greater, the
gift [a]or the altar that sanctifies the gift?
20 "Therefore he who swears by the altar,
swears by it and by all things on it.
21 "He who swears by the temple, swears by
it and by [a]Him who *dwells in it.
22 "And he who swears by heaven, swears
by [a]the throne of God and by Him who sits on
it.
23 "Woe to you, scribes and Pharisees, hypocrites! [a]For you pay tithe of mint and anise and
cummin, and [b]have neglected the weightier *matters* of the law: justice and mercy and faith. These
you ought to have done, without leaving the others undone.
24 "Blind guides, who strain out a gnat and
swallow a camel!
25 "Woe to you, scribes and Pharisees, hypocrites! [a]For you cleanse the outside of the cup and
dish, but inside they are full of extortion and *self-
indulgence.
26 "Blind Pharisee, first cleanse the inside of
the cup and dish, that the outside of them may
be clean also.
27 "Woe to you, scribes and Pharisees, hypocrites! [a]For you are like whitewashed tombs
which indeed appear beautiful outwardly, but
inside are full of dead *men's* bones and all
uncleanness.
28 "Even so you also outwardly appear righteous to men, but inside you are full of hypocrisy
and lawlessness.
29 [a]"Woe to you, scribes and Pharisees, hypocrites! Because you build the tombs of the prophets and adorn the monuments of the righteous,
30 "and say, 'If we had lived in the days of
our fathers, we would not have been partakers
with them in the blood of the prophets.'
31 "Therefore you are witnesses against
yourselves that [a]you are sons of those who murdered the prophets.
32 [a]"Fill up, then, the measure of your fathers' *guilt.*
33 "Serpents, [a]brood of vipers! How can you
escape the condemnation of hell?
34 [a]"Therefore, indeed, I send you prophets,
wise men, and scribes: [b]*some* of them you will
kill and crucify, and [c]*some* of them you will
scourge in your synagogues and persecute from
city to city,
35 [a]"that on you may come all the righteous
blood shed on the earth, [b]from the blood of righteous Abel to [c]the blood of Zechariah, son of Berechiah, whom you murdered between the temple
and the altar.
36 "Assuredly, I say to you, all these things
will come upon this generation.

Jesus Laments over Jerusalem
(*Luke 13:34, 35*)

37 [a]"O Jerusalem, Jerusalem, the one who
kills the prophets [b]and stones those who are sent
to her! How often [c]I wanted to gather your children together, as a hen gathers her chicks [d]under
her wings, but you were not willing!
38 "See! Your house is left to you desolate;
39 "for I say to you, you shall see Me no more
till you say, [a]*'Blessed is He who comes in the
name of the LORD!'"*

Jesus Predicts the Destruction of the Temple
(*Mark 13:1, 2; Luke 21:5, 6*)

24 Then [a]Jesus went out and departed from
the temple, and His disciples came up to
show Him the buildings of the temple.

KJV

2 And Jesus said unto them, See ye not all these things? verily I say unto you, [a]There shall not be left here one stone upon another, that shall not be thrown down.

The Signs of the Times and the End of the Age
(Mark 13:3–13; Luke 21:7–19)

3 And as he sat upon the mount of Olives, [a]the disciples came unto him privately, saying, [b]Tell us, when shall these things be? and what *shall be* the sign of thy coming, and of the end of the world?

4 And Jesus answered and said unto them, [a]Take heed that no man deceive you.

5 For [a]many shall come in my name, saying, I am Christ; [b]and shall deceive many.

6 And ye shall hear of [a]wars and rumours of wars: see that ye be not troubled: for all *these things* must come to pass, but the end is not yet.

7 For [a]nation shall rise against nation, and kingdom against kingdom: and there shall be [b]famines, and pestilences, and earthquakes, in divers places.

8 All these *are* the beginning of sorrows.

9 [a]Then shall they deliver you up to be afflicted, and shall kill you: and ye shall be hated of all nations for my name's sake.

10 And then shall many be offended, and shall betray one another, and shall hate one another.

11 And [a]many false prophets shall rise, and [b]shall deceive many.

12 And because iniquity shall abound, the love of many shall wax [a]cold.

13 [a]But he that shall endure unto the end, the same shall be saved.

14 And this [a]gospel of the kingdom [b]shall be preached in all the world for a witness unto all nations; and then shall the end come.

The Great Tribulation
(Mark 13:14–23; Luke 17:23, 24, 37; 21:20–24)

15 [a]When ye therefore shall see the ABOMINATION OF DESOLATION, spoken of by [b]Daniel the prophet, stand in the holy place, ([c]whoso readeth, let him understand:)

16 Then let them which be in Judaea flee into the mountains:

17 Let him which is on the housetop not come down to take any thing out of his house:

18 Neither let him which is in the field return back to take his clothes.

19 And [a]woe unto them that are with child, and to them that give suck in those days!

20 But pray ye that your flight be not in the winter, neither on the sabbath day:

21 For [a]then shall be great tribulation, such as was not since the beginning of the world to this time, no, nor ever shall be.

22 And except those days should be shortened, there should no flesh be saved: [a]but for the elect's sake those days shall be shortened.

23 [a]Then if any man shall say unto you, Lo, here *is* Christ, or there; believe *it* not.

24 For [a]there shall arise false Christs, and false prophets, and shall shew great signs and wonders; insomuch that, [b]if *it were* possible, they shall deceive the very elect.

25 Behold, I have told you before.

26 Wherefore if they shall say unto you, Behold, he is in the desert; go not forth: behold, *he is* in the secret chambers; believe *it* not.

27 [a]For as the lightning cometh out of the east, and shineth even unto the west; so shall also the coming of the Son of man be.

28 [a]For wheresoever the carcase is, there will the eagles be gathered together.

The Coming of the Son of Man
(Mark 13:24–27; Luke 21:25–28)

29 [a]Immediately after the tribulation of those days [b]shall the sun be darkened, and the moon

2 [a]Luke 19:44
3 [a]Mark 13:3 [b][1 Thess. 5:1–3]
4 [a][Col. 2:8, 18]
5 [a]John 5:43 [b]Matt. 24:11
6 [a][Rev. 6:2–4]
7 [a]Hag. 2:22 [b]Rev. 6:5, 6
9 [a]Matt. 10:17
11 [a]2 Pet. 2:1 [b][1 Tim. 4:1]
12 [a][2 Thess. 2:3]
13 [a]Matt. 10:22
14 [a]Matt. 4:23 [b]Rom. 10:18
15 [a]Mark 13:14 [b]Dan. 9:27; 11:31; 12:11 [c]Dan. 9:23
19 [a]Luke 23:29
21 [a]Dan. 9:26
22 [a]Is. 65:8, 9
23 [a]Luke 17:23
24 [a][2 Thess. 2:9] [b][2 Tim. 2:19]
27 [a]Luke 17:24
28 [a]Luke 17:37
29 [a][Dan. 7:11] [b]Ezek. 32:7

NKJV

2 And Jesus said to them, "Do you not see all these things? Assuredly, I say to you, [a]not *one* stone shall be left here upon another, that shall not be thrown down."

The Signs of the Times and the End of the Age
(Mark 13:3–13; Luke 21:7–19)

3 Now as He sat on the Mount of Olives, [a]the disciples came to Him privately, saying, [b]"Tell us, when will these things be? And what *will be* the sign of Your coming, and of the end of the age?"

4 And Jesus answered and said to them: [a]"Take heed that no one deceives you.

5 "For [a]many will come in My name, saying, 'I am the Christ,' [b]and will deceive many.

6 "And you will hear of [a]wars and rumors of wars. See that you are not troubled; for *all *these things* must come to pass, but the end is not yet.

7 "For [a]nation will rise against nation, and kingdom against kingdom. And there will be [b]famines, *pestilences, and earthquakes in various places.

8 "All these *are* the beginning of sorrows.

9 [a]"Then they will deliver you up to tribulation and kill you, and you will be hated by all nations for My name's sake.

10 "And then many will be offended, will betray one another, and will hate one another.

11 "Then [a]many false prophets will rise up and [b]deceive many.

12 "And because lawlessness will abound, the love of many will grow [a]cold.

13 [a]"But he who endures to the end shall be saved.

14 "And this [a]gospel of the kingdom [b]will be preached in all the world as a witness to all the nations, and then the end will come.

The Great Tribulation
(Mark 13:14–23; Luke 17:23, 24, 37; 21:20–24)

15 [a]"Therefore when you see the [b]*'abomination of desolation,'* spoken of by Daniel the prophet, standing in the holy place" [c](whoever reads, let him understand),

16 "then let those who are in Judea flee to the mountains.

17 "Let him who is on the housetop not go down to take anything out of his house.

18 "And let him who is in the field not go back to get his clothes.

19 "But [a]woe to those who are pregnant and to those who are nursing babies in those days!

20 "And pray that your flight may not be in winter or on the Sabbath.

21 "For [a]then there will be great tribulation, such as has not been since the beginning of the world until this time, no, nor ever shall be.

22 "And unless those days were shortened, no flesh would be saved; [a]but for the elect's sake those days will be shortened.

23 [a]"Then if anyone says to you, 'Look, here *is* the Christ!' or 'There!' do not believe *it*.

24 "For [a]false christs and false prophets will rise and show great signs and wonders to deceive, [b]if possible, even the elect.

25 "See, I have told you beforehand.

26 "Therefore if they say to you, 'Look, He is in the desert!' do not go out; *or* 'Look, *He is* in the inner rooms!' do not believe *it*.

27 [a]"For as the lightning comes from the east and flashes to the west, so also will the coming of the Son of Man be.

28 [a]"For wherever the carcass is, there the eagles will be gathered together.

The Coming of the Son of Man
(Mark 13:24–27; Luke 21:25–28)

29 [a]"Immediately after the tribulation of those days [b]the sun will be darkened, and the

---

*

24:6 NU omits *all*
24:7 NU omits *pestilences*

KJV

shall not give her light, and the stars shall fall
from heaven, and the powers of the heavens shall
be shaken:
30 [a]And then shall appear the sign of the Son
of man in heaven: [b]and then shall all the tribes
of the earth mourn, and they shall see the Son
of man coming in the clouds of heaven with power
and great glory.
31 [a]And he shall send his angels with a great
sound of a trumpet, and they shall gather together
his elect from the four winds, from one end of
heaven to the other.

The Parable of the Fig Tree
(Mark 13:28–31; Luke 21:29–33)

32 Now learn [a]a parable of the fig tree; When
his branch is yet tender, and putteth forth leaves,
ye know that summer *is* nigh:
33 So likewise ye, when ye shall see all these
things, know [a]that it is near, *even* at the doors.
34 Verily I say unto you, [a]This generation
shall not pass, till all these things be fulfilled.
35 [a]Heaven and earth shall pass away, but
my words shall not pass away.

No One Knows the Day or Hour
(Mark 13:32–37; Luke 17:26, 27, 34, 35; 21:34–36)

36 [a]But of that day and hour knoweth no
man, no, not the angels of heaven, [b]but my Father
only.
37 But as the days of Noe *were,* so shall also
the coming of the Son of man be.
38 [a]For as in the days that were before the
flood they were eating and drinking, marrying
and giving in marriage, until the day that Noe
entered into the ark,
39 And knew not until the flood came, and
took them all away; so shall also the coming of
the Son of man be.
40 [a]Then shall two be in the field; the one
shall be taken, and the other left.
41 Two *women shall be* grinding at the mill;
the one shall be taken, and the other left.
42 [a]Watch therefore: for ye know not what
hour your Lord doth come.
43 [a]But know this, that if the goodman of the
house had known in what watch the thief would
come, he would have watched, and would not
have suffered his house to be broken up.
44 [a]Therefore be ye also ready: for in such
an hour as ye think not the Son of man cometh.

The Faithful Servant and the Evil Servant
(Luke 12:41–48)

45 [a]Who then is a faithful and wise servant,
whom his lord hath made ruler over his household, to give them meat in due season?
46 [a]Blessed *is* that servant, whom his lord
when he cometh shall find so doing.
47 Verily I say unto you, That [a]he shall make
him ruler over all his goods.
48 But and if that evil servant shall say in
his heart, My lord [a]delayeth his coming;
49 And shall begin to smite *his* fellowservants, and to eat and drink with the drunken;
50 The lord of that servant shall come in a
day when he looketh not for *him,* and in an hour
that he is [a]not aware of,
51 And shall cut him asunder, and appoint
him his portion with the hypocrites: [a]there shall
be weeping and gnashing of teeth.

The Parable of the Wise and Foolish Virgins

25 Then shall the kingdom of heaven be likened unto ten virgins, which took their
lamps, and went forth to meet [a]the bridegroom.
2 [a]And five of them were wise, and five
were foolish.
3 They that *were* foolish took their lamps,
and took no oil with them:

30 [a][Dan. 7:13, 14; Matt. 16:27; 24:3, 37, 39] [b]Zech. 12:12
31 [a]Ex. 19:16; Deut. 30:4; Is. 27:13; Zech. 9:14; [1 Cor. 15:52; 1 Thess. 4:16]; Heb. 12:19; Rev. 8:2; 11:15
32 [a]Luke 21:29
33 [a][James 5:9; Rev. 3:20]
34 [a][Matt. 10:23; 16:28; 23:36]
35 [a]Ps. 102:25, 26; Is. 51:6; Mark 13:31; Luke 21:33; [1 Pet. 1:23–25; 2 Pet. 3:10]
36 [a]Mark 13:32; Acts 1:7; 1 Thess. 5:2; 2 Pet. 3:10 [b]Zech. 14:7
38 [a][Gen. 6:3–5]; Luke 17:26; [1 Pet. 3:20]
40 [a]Luke 17:34
42 [a]Matt. 25:13; Luke 21:36; 1 Thess. 5:6
43 [a]Luke 12:39; 1 Thess. 5:2; Rev. 3:3
44 [a]Luke 12:35–40; [1 Thess. 5:6]
45 [a]Luke 12:42–46; [Acts 20:28]
46 [a]Rev. 16:15
47 [a]Matt. 25:21, 23; Luke 22:29
48 [a][2 Pet. 3:4–9]
50 [a]Mark 13:32
51 [a]Matt. 8:12; 25:30

CHAPTER 25

1 [a][Eph. 5:29, 30; Rev. 19:7; 21:2, 9]
2 [a]Matt. 13:47; 22:10

*

24:33 Or *He*
24:36 NU adds *nor the Son*
24:42 NU *day*
24:48 NU omits *his coming*

NKJV

moon will not give its light; the stars will fall from
heaven, and the powers of the heavens will be
shaken.
30 [a]"Then the sign of the Son of Man will
appear in heaven, [b]and then all the tribes of the
earth will mourn, and they will see the Son of
Man coming on the clouds of heaven with power
and great glory.
31 [a]"And He will send His angels with a
great sound of a trumpet, and they will gather
together His elect from the four winds, from one
end of heaven to the other.

The Parable of the Fig Tree
(Mark 13:28–31; Luke 21:29–33)

32 "Now learn [a]this parable from the fig tree:
When its branch has already become tender and
puts forth leaves, you know that summer *is*
near.
33 "So you also, when you see all these
things, know [a]that *it is near—at the doors!
34 "Assuredly, I say to you, [a]this generation
will by no means pass away till all these things
take place.
35 [a]"Heaven and earth will pass away, but
My words will by no means pass away.

No One Knows the Day or Hour
(Mark 13:32–37; Luke 17:26, 27, 34, 35; 21:34–36)

36 [a]"But of that day and hour no one knows,
not even the angels of *heaven, [b]but My Father
only.
37 "But as the days of Noah *were,* so also
will the coming of the Son of Man be.
38 [a]"For as in the days before the flood, they
were eating and drinking, marrying and giving
in marriage, until the day that Noah entered the
ark,
39 "and did not know until the flood came
and took them all away, so also will the coming
of the Son of Man be.
40 [a]"Then two *men* will be in the field: one
will be taken and the other left.
41 "Two *women will be* grinding at the mill:
one will be taken and the other left.
42 [a]"Watch therefore, for you do not know
what *hour your Lord is coming.
43 [a]"But know this, that if the master of the
house had known what hour the thief would
come, he would have watched and not allowed
his house to be broken into.
44 [a]"Therefore you also be ready, for the Son
of Man is coming at an hour you do not expect.

The Faithful Servant and the Evil Servant
(Luke 12:41–48)

45 [a]"Who then is a faithful and wise servant,
whom his master made ruler over his household,
to give them food in due season?
46 [a]"Blessed *is* that servant whom his master, when he comes, will find so doing.
47 "Assuredly, I say to you that [a]he will
make him ruler over all his goods.
48 "But if that evil servant says in his heart,
'My master [a]is delaying *his coming,'
49 "and begins to beat *his* fellow servants,
and to eat and drink with the drunkards,
50 "the master of that servant will come on
a day when he is not looking for *him* and at an
hour that he is [a]not aware of,
51 "and will cut him in two and appoint *him*
his portion with the hypocrites. [a]There shall be
weeping and gnashing of teeth.

The Parable of the Wise and Foolish Virgins

25 "Then the kingdom of heaven shall be likened to ten virgins who took their lamps
and went out to meet [a]the bridegroom.
2 [a]"Now five of them were wise, and five
were foolish.
3 "Those who *were* foolish took their lamps
and took no oil with them,

KJV

4 But the wise took oil in their vessels with their lamps.

5 While the bridegroom tarried, [a]they all slumbered and slept.

6 And at midnight [a]there was a cry made, Behold, the bridegroom cometh; go ye out to meet him.

7 Then all those virgins arose, and [a]trimmed their lamps.

8 And the foolish said unto the wise, Give us of your oil; for our lamps are gone out.

9 But the wise answered, saying, *Not so;* lest there be not enough for us and you: but go ye rather to them that sell, and buy for yourselves.

10 And while they went to buy, the bridegroom came; and they that were ready went in with him to the marriage: and [a]the door was shut.

11 Afterward came also the other virgins, saying, [a]Lord, Lord, open to us.

12 But he answered and said, Verily I say unto you, [a]I know you not.

13 [a]Watch therefore, for ye [b]know neither the day nor the hour wherein the Son of man cometh.

The Parable of the Talents
(*Luke 19:11–27*)

14 [a]For *the kingdom of heaven is* [b]as a man travelling into a far country, *who* called his own servants, and delivered unto them his goods.

15 And unto one he gave five talents, to another two, and to another one; [a]to every man according to his several ability; and straightway took his journey.

16 Then he that had received the five talents went and traded with the same, and made *them* other five talents.

17 And likewise he that *had received* two, he also gained other two.

18 But he that had received one went and digged in the earth, and hid his lord's money.

19 After a long time the lord of those servants cometh, and reckoneth with them.

20 And so he that had received five talents came and brought other five talents, saying, LORD, thou deliveredst unto me five talents: behold, I have gained beside them five talents more.

21 His lord said unto him, Well done, *thou* good and faithful servant: thou hast been [a]faithful over a few things, [b]I will make thee ruler over many things: enter thou into [c]the joy of thy lord.

22 He also that had received two talents came and said, Lord, thou deliveredst unto me two talents: behold, I have gained two other talents beside them.

23 His lord said unto him, [a]Well done, good and faithful servant; thou hast been faithful over a few things, I will make thee ruler over many things: enter thou into the [b]joy of thy lord.

24 Then he which had received the one talent came and said, Lord, I knew thee that thou art an hard man, reaping where thou hast not sown, and gathering where thou hast not strawed:

25 And I was afraid, and went and hid thy talent in the earth: lo, *there* thou hast *that is* thine.

26 His lord answered and said unto him, *Thou* [a]wicked and slothful servant, thou knewest that I reap where I sowed not, and gather where I have not strawed:

27 Thou oughtest therefore to have put my money to the exchangers, and *then* at my coming I should have received mine own with usury.

28 Take therefore the talent from him, and give *it* unto him which hath ten talents.

29 [a]For unto every one that hath shall be given, and he shall have abundance: but from him that hath not shall be taken away even that which he hath.

30 And cast ye the unprofitable servant [a]into

5 [a]1 Thess. 5:6
6 [a][Matt. 24:31; 1 Thess. 4:16]
7 [a]Luke 12:35
10 [a][Matt. 7:21]; Luke 13:25
11 [a][Matt. 7:21–23; Luke 13:25–30]
12 [a][Ps. 5:5; Hab. 1:13; John 9:31]
13 [a]Mark 13:35; [Luke 21:36]; 1 Thess. 5:6 [b]Matt. 24:36, 42
14 [a]Luke 19:12–27 [b]Matt. 21:33
15 [a][Rom. 12:6; 1 Cor. 12:7, 11, 29; Eph. 4:11]
21 [a][Luke 16:10; 1 Cor. 4:2; 2 Tim. 4:7, 8] [b][Matt. 24:47; 25:34, 46; Luke 12:44; 22:29, 30; Rev. 3:21; 21:7] [c][2 Tim. 2:12; Heb. 12:2; 1 Pet. 1:8]
23 [a]Matt. 24:45, 47; 25:21 [b][Ps. 16:11; John 15:10, 11]
26 [a]Matt. 18:32; Luke 19:22
29 [a]Matt. 13:12; Mark 4:25; Luke 8:18; [John 15:2]
30 [a]Matt. 8:12; 22:13; [Luke 13:28]

*

25:6 NU omits *is coming*
25:13 NU omits the rest of v. 13.

NKJV

4 "but the wise took oil in their vessels with their lamps.

5 "But while the bridegroom was delayed, [a]they all slumbered and slept.

6 "And at midnight [a]a cry was *heard:* 'Behold, the bridegroom *is coming; go out to meet him!'

7 "Then all those virgins arose and [a]trimmed their lamps.

8 "And the foolish said to the wise, 'Give us *some* of your oil, for our lamps are going out.'

9 "But the wise answered, saying, '*No,* lest there should not be enough for us and you; but go rather to those who sell, and buy for yourselves.'

10 "And while they went to buy, the bridegroom came, and those who were ready went in with him to the wedding; and [a]the door was shut.

11 "Afterward the other virgins came also, saying, [a]'Lord, Lord, open to us!'

12 "But he answered and said, 'Assuredly, I say to you, [a]I do not know you.'

13 [a]"Watch therefore, for you [b]know neither the day nor the hour *in which the Son of Man is coming.

The Parable of the Talents
(*Luke 19:11–27*)

14 [a]"For *the kingdom of heaven is* [b]like a man traveling to a far country, *who* called his own servants and delivered his goods to them.

15 "And to one he gave five talents, to another two, and to another one, [a]to each according to his own ability; and immediately he went on a journey.

16 "Then he who had received the five talents went and traded with them, and made another five talents.

17 "And likewise he who *had received* two gained two more also.

18 "But he who had received one went and dug in the ground, and hid his lord's money.

19 "After a long time the lord of those servants came and settled accounts with them.

20 "So he who had received five talents came and brought five other talents, saying, 'Lord, you delivered to me five talents; look, I have gained five more talents besides them.'

21 "His lord said to him, 'Well *done,* good and faithful servant; you were [a]faithful over a few things, [b]I will make you ruler over many things. Enter into [c]the joy of your lord.'

22 "He also who had received two talents came and said, 'Lord, you delivered to me two talents; look, I have gained two more talents besides them.'

23 "His lord said to him, [a]'Well *done,* good and faithful servant; you have been faithful over a few things, I will make you ruler over many things. Enter into [b]the joy of your lord.'

24 "Then he who had received the one talent came and said, 'Lord, I knew you to be a hard man, reaping where you have not sown, and gathering where you have not scattered seed.

25 'And I was afraid, and went and hid your talent in the ground. Look, *there* you have *what is* yours.'

26 "But his lord answered and said to him, 'You [a]wicked and lazy servant, you knew that I reap where I have not sown, and gather where I have not scattered seed.

27 'So you ought to have deposited my money with the bankers, and at my coming I would have received back my own with interest.

28 'Therefore take the talent from him, and give *it* to him who has ten talents.

29 [a]'For to everyone who has, more will be given, and he will have abundance; but from him who does not have, even what he has will be taken away.

30 'And cast the unprofitable servant [a]into

KJV

outer darkness: [b]there shall be weeping and [c]gnashing of teeth.

The Son of Man Will Judge the Nations

31 [a]When the Son of man shall come in his glory, and all the holy angels with him, then shall he sit upon the throne of his glory:

32 And [a]before him shall be gathered all nations: and [b]he shall separate them one from another, as a shepherd divideth *his* sheep from the goats:

33 And he shall set the [a]sheep on his right hand, but the goats on the left.

34 Then shall the King say unto them on his right hand, Come, ye blessed of my Father, [a]inherit the kingdom [b]prepared for you from the foundation of the world:

35 [a]For I was an hungred, and ye gave me meat: I was thirsty, and ye gave me drink: [b]I was a stranger, and ye took me in:

36 [a]Naked, and ye clothed me: I was sick, and ye visited me: [b]I was in prison, and ye came unto me.

37 Then shall the righteous answer him, saying, Lord, when saw we thee an hungred, and fed *thee?* or thirsty, and gave *thee* drink?

38 When saw we thee a stranger, and took *thee* in? or naked, and clothed *thee?*

39 Or when saw we thee sick, or in prison, and came unto thee?

40 And the King shall answer and say unto them, Verily I say unto you, [a]Inasmuch as ye have done *it* unto one of the least of these my brethren, ye have done *it* unto me.

41 Then shall he say also unto them on the left hand, [a]Depart from me, ye cursed, [b]into everlasting fire, prepared for [c]the devil and his angels:

42 For I was an hungred, and ye gave me no meat: I was thirsty, and ye gave me no drink:

43 I was a stranger, and ye took me not in: naked, and ye clothed me not: sick, and in prison, and ye visited me not.

44 Then shall they also answer him, saying, Lord, when saw we thee an hungred, or athirst, or a stranger, or naked, or sick, or in prison, and did not minister unto thee?

45 Then shall he answer them, saying, Verily I say unto you, [a]Inasmuch as ye did *it* not to one of the least of these, ye did *it* not to me.

46 And [a]these shall go away into everlasting punishment: but the righteous into life eternal.

The Plot to Kill Jesus
(Mark 14:1, 2; Luke 22:1, 2; John 11:45–53)

26 And it came to pass, when Jesus had finished all these sayings, he said unto his disciples,

2 [a]Ye know that after two days is *the feast of* the passover, and the Son of man is betrayed to be crucified.

3 [a]Then assembled together the chief priests, and the scribes, and the elders of the people, unto the palace of the high priest, who was called Caiaphas,

4 And [a]consulted that they might take Jesus by subtilty, and kill *him.*

5 But they said, Not on the feast *day,* lest there be an uproar among the [a]people.

The Anointing at Bethany
(Mark 14:3–9; John 12:1–8)

6 Now when Jesus was in [a]Bethany, in the house of Simon the leper,

7 There came unto him a woman having an alabaster box of very precious ointment, and poured it on his head, as he sat *at meat.*

8 [a]But when his disciples saw *it,* they had indignation, saying, To what purpose *is* this waste?

30 [b]Matt. 7:23; 8:12; 24:51 [c]Ps. 112:10
31 [a][Zech. 14:5]; Matt. 16:27; Mark 8:38; Acts 1:11; [1 Thess. 4:16]; 2 Thess. 1:7; [Jude 14]; Rev. 1:7
32 [a][Rom. 14:10; 2 Cor. 5:10; Rev. 20:12] [b]Ezek. 20:38
33 [a]Ps. 79:13; 100:3; [John 10:11, 27, 28]
34 [a][Rom. 8:17; 1 Pet. 1:4, 9; Rev. 21:7] [b]Matt. 20:23; Mark 10:40; 1 Cor. 2:9; Heb. 11:16
35 [a]Is. 58:7; Ezek. 18:7, 16; [James 1:27; 2:15, 16] [b]Job 31:32; [Heb. 13:2]; 3 John 5
36 [a]Is. 58:7; Ezek. 18:7, 16; [James 2:15, 16] [b]2 Tim. 1:16
40 [a]Prov. 14:31; Matt. 10:42; Mark 9:41; Heb. 6:10
41 [a]Ps. 6:8; Matt. 7:23; Luke 13:27 [b]Matt. 13:40, 42 [c][2 Pet. 2:4]; Jude 6
45 [a]Prov. 14:31; Zech. 2:8; Acts 9:5
46 [a][Dan. 12:2; John 5:29; Acts 24:15; Rom. 2:7]

CHAPTER 26

2 [a]Matt. 27:35; Mark 14:1, 2; Luke 22:1, 2; John 13:1; 19:18
3 [a]Ps. 2:2; John 11:47; Acts 4:25
4 [a]John 11:47; Acts 4:25–28
5 [a]Matt. 21:26
6 [a]Matt. 8:2; Mark 14:3–9; Luke 7:37–39; John 11:1, 2; 12:1–8
8 [a]John 12:4

NKJV

the outer darkness. [b]There will be weeping and [c]gnashing of teeth.'

The Son of Man Will Judge the Nations

31 [a]"When the Son of Man comes in His glory, and all the *holy angels with Him, then He will sit on the throne of His glory.

32 [a]"All the nations will be gathered before Him, and [b]He will separate them one from another, as a shepherd divides *his* sheep from the goats.

33 "And He will set the [a]sheep on His right hand, but the goats on the left.

34 "Then the King will say to those on His right hand, 'Come, you blessed of My Father, [a]inherit the kingdom [b]prepared for you from the foundation of the world:

35 [a]'for I was hungry and you gave Me food; I was thirsty and you gave Me drink; [b]I was a stranger and you took Me in;

36 'I *was* [a]naked and you clothed Me; I was sick and you visited Me; [b]I was in prison and you came to Me.'

37 "Then the righteous will answer Him, saying, 'Lord, when did we see You hungry and feed *You,* or thirsty and give *You* drink?

38 'When did we see You a stranger and take *You* in, or naked and clothe *You?*

39 'Or when did we see You sick, or in prison, and come to You?'

40 "And the King will answer and say to them, 'Assuredly, I say to you, [a]inasmuch as you did *it* to one of the least of these My brethren, you did *it* to Me.'

41 "Then He will also say to those on the left hand, [a]'Depart from Me, you cursed, [b]into the everlasting fire prepared for [c]the devil and his angels:

42 'for I was hungry and you gave Me no food; I was thirsty and you gave Me no drink;

43 'I was a stranger and you did not take Me in, naked and you did not clothe Me, sick and in prison and you did not visit Me.'

44 "Then they also will answer *Him, saying, 'Lord, when did we see You hungry or thirsty or a stranger or naked or sick or in prison, and did not minister to You?'

45 "Then He will answer them, saying, 'Assuredly, I say to you, [a]inasmuch as you did not do *it* to one of the least of these, you did not do *it* to Me.'

46 "And [a]these will go away into everlasting punishment, but the righteous into eternal life."

The Plot to Kill Jesus
(Mark 14:1, 2; Luke 22:1, 2; John 11:45–53)

26 Now it came to pass, when Jesus had finished all these sayings, *that* He said to His disciples,

2 [a]"You know that after two days is the Passover, and the Son of Man will be delivered up to be crucified."

3 [a]Then the chief priests, *the scribes, and the elders of the people assembled at the palace of the high priest, who was called Caiaphas,

4 and [a]plotted to take Jesus by trickery and kill *Him.*

5 But they said, "Not during the feast, lest there be an uproar among the [a]people."

The Anointing at Bethany
(Mark 14:3–9; John 12:1–8)

6 And when Jesus was in [a]Bethany at the house of Simon the leper,

7 a woman came to Him having an alabaster flask of very costly fragrant oil, and she poured *it* on His head as He sat *at the table.*

8 [a]But when His disciples saw *it,* they were indignant, saying, "Why this waste?

*

25:31 NU omits *holy*
25:44 NU, M omit *Him*
26:3 NU omits *the scribes*

KJV

9 For this ointment might have been sold
for much, and given to the poor.
10 When Jesus understood *it,* he said unto
them, Why trouble ye the woman? for she hath
wrought a good work upon me.
11 [a]For ye have the poor always with you;
but [b]me ye have not always.
12 For in that she hath poured this ointment
on my body, she did *it* for my [a]burial.
13 Verily I say unto you, Wheresoever this
gospel shall be preached in the whole world, *there*
shall also this, that this woman hath done, be told
for a memorial of her.

Judas Agrees to Betray Jesus
(Mark 14:10, 11; Luke 22:3–6)

14 [a]Then one of the twelve, called [b]Judas Iscariot, went unto the chief priests,
15 And said *unto them,* [a]What will ye give
me, and I will deliver him unto you? And they
covenanted with him for thirty pieces of silver.
16 And from that time he sought opportunity
to betray him.

Jesus Celebrates Passover with His Disciples
(Mark 14:12–21; Luke 22:7–13)

17 [a]Now the first *day* of the *feast of* unleavened bread the disciples came to Jesus, saying
unto him, Where wilt thou that we prepare for
thee to eat the passover?
18 And he said, Go into the city to such a
man, and say unto him, The Master saith, [a]My
time is at hand; I will keep the passover at thy
house with my disciples.
19 And the disciples did as Jesus had appointed them; and they made ready the passover.
20 [a]Now when the even was come, he sat
down with the twelve.
21 And as they did eat, he said, Verily I say
unto you, that one of you shall [a]betray me.
22 And they were exceeding sorrowful, and
began every one of them to say unto him, Lord,
is it I?
23 And he answered and said, [a]He that dippeth *his* hand with me in the dish, the same shall
betray me.
24 The Son of man goeth [a]as it is written of
him: but [b]woe unto that man by whom the Son
of man is betrayed! [c]it had been good for that
man if he had not been born.
25 Then Judas, which betrayed him, answered and said, Master, is it I? He said unto him,
Thou hast said.

Jesus Institutes the Lord's Supper
(Mark 14:22–26; Luke 22:14–23; 1 Cor. 11:23–26)

26 [a]And as they were eating, [b]Jesus took
bread, and blessed *it,* and brake *it,* and gave *it*
to the disciples, and said, Take, eat; [c]this is my
body.
27 And he took the cup, and gave thanks, and
gave *it* to them, saying, [a]Drink ye all of it;
28 For [a]this is my blood [b]of the new testament, which is shed [c]for many for the remission
of sins.
29 But [a]I say unto you, I will not drink henceforth of this fruit of the vine, [b]until that day when
I drink it new with you in my Father's kingdom.
30 [a]And when they had sung an hymn, they
went out into the mount of Olives.

Jesus Predicts Peter's Denial
(Mark 14:27–31; Luke 22:31–34; John 13:36–38)

31 Then saith Jesus unto them, [a]All ye shall
[b]be offended because of me this night: for it is
written, [c]I WILL SMITE THE SHEPHERD, AND THE
SHEEP OF THE FLOCK SHALL BE SCATTERED ABROAD.
32 But after I am risen again, [a]I will go before
you into Galilee.

11 [a][Deut. 15:11] [b][John 13:33; 14:19; 16:5, 28; 17:11]
12 [a]John 19:38–42
14 [a]Mark 14:10, 11; Luke 22:3–6 [b]Matt. 10:4
15 [a]Zech. 11:12
17 [a]Ex. 12:6, 18–20
18 [a]Luke 9:51
20 [a]Mark 14:17–21
21 [a]John 6:70, 71; 13:21
23 [a]Ps. 41:9
24 [a]1 Cor. 15:3 [b]Luke 17:1 [c]John 17:12
26 [a]Mark 14:22–25 [b]1 Cor. 11:23–25 [c][1 Pet. 2:24]
27 [a]Mark 14:23
28 [a][Ex. 24:8] [b]Jer. 31:31 [c]Matt. 20:28
29 [a]Mark 14:25 [b]Acts 10:41
30 [a]Mark 14:26–31
31 [a]John 16:32 [b][Matt. 11:6] [c]Zech. 13:7
32 [a]Matt. 28:7, 10, 16

*

26:26 M *gave thanks for*
26:28 NU omits *new*

NKJV

9 "For this fragrant oil might have been sold
for much and given to *the* poor."
10 But when Jesus was aware of *it,* He said
to them, "Why do you trouble the woman? For
she has done a good work for Me.
11 [a]"For you have the poor with you always,
but [b]Me you do not have always.
12 "For in pouring this fragrant oil on My
body, she did *it* for My [a]burial.
13 "Assuredly, I say to you, wherever this
gospel is preached in the whole world, what this
woman has done will also be told as a memorial
to her."

Judas Agrees to Betray Jesus
(Mark 14:10, 11; Luke 22:3–6)

14 [a]Then one of the twelve, called [b]Judas Iscariot, went to the chief priests
15 and said, [a]"What are you willing to give
me if I deliver Him to you?" And they counted
out to him thirty pieces of silver.
16 So from that time he sought opportunity
to betray Him.

Jesus Celebrates Passover with His Disciples
(Mark 14:12–21; Luke 22:7–13)

17 [a]Now on the first *day of the Feast* of Unleavened Bread the disciples came to Jesus, saying to Him, "Where do You want us to prepare
for You to eat the Passover?"
18 And He said, "Go into the city to a certain
man, and say to him, 'The Teacher says, [a]"My
time is at hand; I will keep the Passover at your
house with My disciples." ' "
19 So the disciples did as Jesus had directed
them; and they prepared the Passover.
20 [a]When evening had come, He sat down
with the twelve.
21 Now as they were eating, He said, "Assuredly, I say to you, one of you will [a]betray Me."
22 And they were exceedingly sorrowful, and
each of them began to say to Him, "Lord, is it
I?"
23 He answered and said, [a]"He who dipped
his hand with Me in the dish will betray Me.
24 "The Son of Man indeed goes just [a]as it
is written of Him, but [b]woe to that man by whom
the Son of Man is betrayed! [c]It would have been
good for that man if he had not been born."
25 Then Judas, who was betraying Him, answered and said, "Rabbi, is it I?" He said to him,
"You have said it."

Jesus Institutes the Lord's Supper
(Mark 14:22–26; Luke 22:14–23; 1 Cor. 11:23–26)

26 [a]And as they were eating, [b]Jesus took
bread, *blessed and broke *it,* and gave *it* to the
disciples and said, "Take, eat; [c]this is My body."
27 Then He took the cup, and gave thanks,
and gave *it* to them, saying, [a]"Drink from it, all
of you.
28 "For [a]this is My blood [b]of the *new covenant, which is shed [c]for many for the remission
of sins.
29 "But [a]I say to you, I will not drink of this
fruit of the vine from now on [b]until that day when
I drink it new with you in My Father's kingdom."
30 [a]And when they had sung a hymn, they
went out to the Mount of Olives.

Jesus Predicts Peter's Denial
(Mark 14:27–31; Luke 22:31–34; John 13:36–38)

31 Then Jesus said to them, [a]"All of you will
[b]be made to stumble because of Me this night,
for it is written:

> [c]*'I will strike the Shepherd,*
> *And the sheep of the flock will be*
> *scattered.'*

32 "But after I have been raised, [a]I will go
before you to Galilee."

KJV

33 Peter answered and said unto him, Though all *men* shall be offended because of thee, *yet* will I never be offended.

34 Jesus said unto him, [a]Verily I say unto thee, That this night, before the cock crow, thou shalt deny me thrice.

35 Peter said unto him, Though I should die with thee, yet will I not deny thee. Likewise also said all the disciples.

The Prayer in the Garden
(Mark 14:32–42; Luke 22:39–46)

36 [a]Then cometh Jesus with them unto a place called Gethsemane, and saith unto the disciples, Sit ye here, while I go and pray yonder.

37 And he took with him Peter and [a]the two sons of Zebedee, and began to be sorrowful and very heavy.

38 Then saith he unto them, [a]My soul is exceeding sorrowful, even unto death: tarry ye here, and watch with me.

39 And he went a little farther, and fell on his face, and [a]prayed, saying, [b]O my Father, if it be possible, [c]let this cup pass from me: nevertheless [d]not as I will, but as thou *wilt*.

40 And he cometh unto the disciples, and findeth them asleep, and saith unto Peter, What, could ye not watch with me one hour?

41 [a]Watch and pray, that ye enter not into temptation: [b]the spirit indeed *is* willing, but the flesh *is* weak.

42 He went away again the second time, and prayed, saying, O my Father, if this cup may not pass away from me, except I drink it, thy will be done.

43 And he came and found them asleep again: for their eyes were heavy.

44 And he left them, and went away again, and prayed the third time, saying the same words.

45 Then cometh he to his disciples, and saith unto them, Sleep on now, and take *your* rest: behold, the hour is at hand, and the Son of man is [a]betrayed into the hands of sinners.

46 Rise, let us be going: behold, he is at hand that doth betray me.

Betrayal and Arrest in Gethsemane
(Mark 14:43–52; Luke 22:47–53; John 18:1–11)

47 And [a]while he yet spake, lo, Judas, one of the twelve, came, and with him a great multitude with swords and staves, from the chief priests and elders of the people.

48 Now he that betrayed him gave them a sign, saying, Whomsoever I shall kiss, that same is he: hold him fast.

49 And forthwith he came to Jesus, and said, Hail, master; [a]and kissed him.

50 And Jesus said unto him, [a]Friend, wherefore art thou come? Then came they, and laid hands on Jesus, and took him.

51 And, behold, [a]one of them which were with Jesus stretched out *his* hand, and drew his sword, and struck a servant of the high priest's, and smote off his ear.

52 Then said Jesus unto him, Put up again thy sword into his place: [a]for all they that take the sword shall perish with the sword.

53 Thinkest thou that I cannot now pray to my Father, and he shall presently give me [a]more than twelve legions of angels?

54 But how then shall the scriptures be fulfilled, [a]that thus it must be?

55 In that same hour said Jesus to the multitudes, Are ye come out as against a thief with swords and staves for to take me? I sat daily with you teaching in the temple, and ye laid no hold on me.

56 But all this was done, that the [a]scriptures of the prophets might be fulfilled. Then [b]all the disciples forsook him, and fled.

34 [a]Matt. 26:74, 75; Mark 14:30; Luke 22:34; John 13:38
36 [a]Mark 14:32–35; Luke 22:39, 40; John 18:1
37 [a]Matt. 4:21; 17:1; Mark 5:37
38 [a]John 12:27
39 [a]Mark 14:36; Luke 22:42; [Heb. 5:7–9] [b]John 12:27 [c]Matt. 20:22 [d]Ps. 40:8; Is. 50:5; John 5:30; 6:38; Phil. 2:8
41 [a]Mark 13:33; 14:38; Luke 22:40, 46; [Eph. 6:18] [b]Ps. 103:14–16; [Rom. 7:15; 8:23; Gal. 5:17]
45 [a]Matt. 17:22, 23; 20:18, 19
47 [a]Mark 14:43–50; Luke 22:47–53; John 18:3–11; Acts 1:16
49 [a]2 Sam. 20:9; [Prov. 27:6]
50 [a]Ps. 41:9; 55:13
51 [a]Mark 14:47; Luke 22:50; John 18:10
52 [a]Gen. 9:6; Rev. 13:10
53 [a]2 Kin. 6:17; Dan. 7:10
54 [a]Is. 50:6; 53:2–11; Luke 24:25–27, 44–46; John 19:28; Acts 13:29; 17:3; 26:23
56 [a]Lam. 4:20 [b]Zech. 13:7; Matt. 26:31; Mark 14:27; John 18:15

NKJV

33 Peter answered and said to Him, "Even if all are made to stumble because of You, I will never be made to stumble."

34 Jesus said to him, [a]"Assuredly, I say to you that this night, before the rooster crows, you will deny Me three times."

35 Peter said to Him, "Even if I have to die with You, I will not deny You!" And so said all the disciples.

The Prayer in the Garden
(Mark 14:32–42; Luke 22:39–46)

36 [a]Then Jesus came with them to a place called Gethsemane, and said to the disciples, "Sit here while I go and pray over there."

37 And He took with Him Peter and [a]the two sons of Zebedee, and He began to be sorrowful and deeply distressed.

38 Then He said to them, [a]"My soul is exceedingly sorrowful, even to death. Stay here and watch with Me."

39 He went a little farther and fell on His face, and [a]prayed, saying, [b]"O My Father, if it is possible, [c]let this cup pass from Me; nevertheless, [d]not as I will, but as You *will*."

40 Then He came to the disciples and found them sleeping, and said to Peter, "What? Could you not watch with Me one hour?

41 [a]"Watch and pray, lest you enter into temptation. [b]The spirit indeed *is* willing, but the flesh *is* weak."

42 Again, a second time, He went away and prayed, saying, "O My Father, *if this cup cannot pass away from Me unless I drink it, Your will be done."

43 And He came and found them asleep again, for their eyes were heavy.

44 So He left them, went away again, and prayed the third time, saying the same words.

45 Then He came to His disciples and said to them, "Are *you* still sleeping and resting? Behold, the hour is at hand, and the Son of Man is being [a]betrayed into the hands of sinners.

46 "Rise, let us be going. See, My betrayer is at hand."

Betrayal and Arrest in Gethsemane
(Mark 14:43–52; Luke 22:47–53; John 18:1–11)

47 And [a]while He was still speaking, behold, Judas, one of the twelve, with a great multitude with swords and clubs, came from the chief priests and elders of the people.

48 Now His betrayer had given them a sign, saying, "Whomever I kiss, He is the One; seize Him."

49 Immediately he went up to Jesus and said, "Greetings, Rabbi!" [a]and kissed Him.

50 But Jesus said to him, [a]"Friend, why have you come?" Then they came and laid hands on Jesus and took Him.

51 And suddenly, [a]one of those *who were* with Jesus stretched out *his* hand and drew his sword, struck the servant of the high priest, and cut off his ear.

52 But Jesus said to him, "Put your sword in its place, [a]for all who take the sword will *perish by the sword.

53 "Or do you think that I cannot now pray to My Father, and He will provide Me with [a]more than twelve legions of angels?

54 "How then could the Scriptures be fulfilled, [a]that it must happen thus?"

55 In that hour Jesus said to the multitudes, "Have you come out, as against a robber, with swords and clubs to take Me? I sat daily with you, teaching in the temple, and you did not seize Me.

56 "But all this was done that the [a]Scriptures of the prophets might be fulfilled." Then [b]all the disciples forsook Him and fled.

*

26:42 NU *if this may not pass away unless*
26:52 M *die*

KJV

Jesus Faces the Sanhedrin
(Mark 14:53–65; Luke 22:66–71; John 18:12–14, 19–24)

57 [a]And they that had laid hold on Jesus led *him* away to Caiaphas the high priest, where the scribes and the elders were assembled.

58 But [a]Peter followed him afar off unto the high priest's palace, and went in, and sat with the servants, to see the end.

59 Now the chief priests, and elders, and all the council, sought [a]false witness against Jesus, to put him to death;

60 But found none: yea, though [a]many false witnesses came, *yet* found they none. At the last came [b]two false witnesses,

61 And said, This *fellow* said, [a]I am able to destroy the temple of God, and to build it in three days.

62 [a]And the high priest arose, and said unto him, Answerest thou nothing? what *is it which* these witness against thee?

63 But [a]Jesus held his peace. And the high priest answered and said unto him, [b]I adjure thee by the living God, that thou tell us whether thou be the Christ, the Son of God.

64 Jesus saith unto him, Thou hast said: nevertheless I say unto you, [a]Hereafter shall ye see the Son of man [b]sitting on the right hand of power, and coming in the clouds of heaven.

65 [a]Then the high priest rent his clothes, saying, He hath spoken blasphemy; what further need have we of witnesses? behold, now ye have heard his [b]blasphemy.

66 What think ye? They answered and said, [a]He is guilty of death.

67 [a]Then did they spit in his face, and buffeted him; and [b]others smote *him* with the palms of their hands,

68 Saying, [a]Prophesy unto us, thou Christ, Who is he that smote thee?

Peter Denies Jesus, and Weeps Bitterly
(Mark 14:66–72; Luke 22:54–62; John 18:15–18, 25–27)

69 [a]Now Peter sat without in the palace: and a damsel came unto him, saying, Thou also wast with Jesus of Galilee.

70 But he denied before *them* all, saying, I know not what thou sayest.

71 And when he was gone out into the porch, another *maid* saw him, and said unto them that were there, This *fellow* was also with Jesus of Nazareth.

72 And again he denied with an oath, I do not know the man.

73 And after a while came unto *him* they that stood by, and said to Peter, Surely thou also art *one* of them; for thy [a]speech bewrayeth thee.

74 Then [a]began he to curse and to swear, *saying,* I know not the man. And immediately the cock crew.

75 And Peter remembered the word of Jesus, which said unto him, [a]Before the cock crow, thou shalt deny me thrice. And he went out, and wept bitterly.

Jesus Handed Over to Pontius Pilate
(Mark 15:1; Luke 23:1; John 18:28)

27 When the morning was come, [a]all the chief priests and elders of the people took counsel against Jesus to put him to death:

2 And when they had bound him, they led *him* away, and [a]delivered him to Pontius Pilate the governor.

Judas Hangs Himself
(Acts 1:18, 19)

3 [a]Then Judas, which had betrayed him, when he saw that he was condemned, repented himself, and brought again the thirty [b]pieces of silver to the chief priests and elders,

---

57 [a]John 18:12, 19–24
58 [a]John 18:15, 16
59 [a]Ps. 35:11
60 [a]Mark 14:55 [b]Deut. 19:15
61 [a]John 2:19
62 [a]Mark 14:60
63 [a]Is. 53:7 [b]Lev. 5:1
64 [a]Dan. 7:13 [b][Acts 7:55]
65 [a]2 Kin. 18:37 [b]John 10:30–36
66 [a]Lev. 24:16
67 [a]Is. 50:6; 53:3 [b]Luke 22:63–65
68 [a]Mark 14:65
69 [a]John 18:16–18, 25–27
73 [a]Luke 22:59
74 [a]Mark 14:71
75 [a]Matt. 26:34

CHAPTER 27

1 [a]John 18:28
2 [a]Acts 3:13
3 [a]Matt. 26:14 [b]Matt. 26:15

*

26:59 NU omits *the elders*
26:60 NU *but found none, even though many false witnesses came forward.* • NU omits *false witnesses*
27:2 NU omits *Pontius*

NKJV

Jesus Faces the Sanhedrin
(Mark 14:53–65; Luke 22:66–71; John 18:12–14, 19–24)

57 [a]And those who had laid hold of Jesus led *Him* away to Caiaphas the high priest, where the scribes and the elders were assembled.

58 But [a]Peter followed Him at a distance to the high priest's courtyard. And he went in and sat with the servants to see the end.

59 Now the chief priests, *the elders, and all the council sought [a]false testimony against Jesus to put Him to death,

60 *but found none. Even though [a]many false witnesses came forward, they found none. But at last [b]two *false witnesses came forward

61 and said, "This *fellow* said, [a]'I am able to destroy the temple of God and to build it in three days.' "

62 [a]And the high priest arose and said to Him, "Do You answer nothing? What *is it* these men testify against You?"

63 But [a]Jesus kept silent. And the high priest answered and said to Him, [b]"I put You under oath by the living God: Tell us if You are the Christ, the Son of God!"

64 Jesus said to him, "*It is as* you said. Nevertheless, I say to you, [a]hereafter you will see the Son of Man [b]sitting at the right hand of the Power, and coming on the clouds of heaven."

65 [a]Then the high priest tore his clothes, saying, "He has spoken blasphemy! What further need do we have of witnesses? Look, now you have heard His [b]blasphemy!

66 "What do you think?" They answered and said, [a]"He is deserving of death."

67 [a]Then they spat in His face and beat Him; and [b]others struck *Him* with the palms of their hands,

68 saying, [a]"Prophesy to us, Christ! Who is the one who struck You?"

Peter Denies Jesus, and Weeps Bitterly
(Mark 14:66–72; Luke 22:54–62; John 18:15–18, 25–27)

69 [a]Now Peter sat outside in the courtyard. And a servant girl came to him, saying, "You also were with Jesus of Galilee."

70 But he denied it before *them* all, saying, "I do not know what you are saying."

71 And when he had gone out to the gateway, another *girl* saw him and said to those *who were* there, "This *fellow* also was with Jesus of Nazareth."

72 But again he denied with an oath, "I do not know the Man!"

73 And a little later those who stood by came up and said to Peter, "Surely you also are *one* of them, for your [a]speech betrays you."

74 Then [a]he began to curse and swear, *saying,* "I do not know the Man!" Immediately a rooster crowed.

75 And Peter remembered the word of Jesus who had said to him, [a]"Before the rooster crows, you will deny Me three times." So he went out and wept bitterly.

Jesus Handed Over to Pontius Pilate
(Mark 15:1; Luke 23:1; John 18:28)

27 When morning came, [a]all the chief priests and elders of the people plotted against Jesus to put Him to death.

2 And when they had bound Him, they led Him away and [a]delivered Him to *Pontius Pilate the governor.

Judas Hangs Himself
(Acts 1:18, 19)

3 [a]Then Judas, His betrayer, seeing that He had been condemned, was remorseful and brought back the thirty [b]pieces of silver to the chief priests and elders,

KJV

4 Saying, I have sinned in that I have betrayed the innocent blood. And they said, What *is that* to us? see thou *to that.*

5 And he cast down the pieces of silver in the temple, [a]and departed, and went and hanged himself.

6 And the chief priests took the silver pieces, and said, It is not lawful for to put them into the treasury, because it is the price of blood.

7 And they took counsel, and bought with them the potter's field, to bury strangers in.

8 Wherefore that field was called, [a]The field of blood, unto this day.

9 Then was fulfilled that which was spoken by Jeremy the prophet, saying, [a]AND THEY TOOK THE THIRTY PIECES OF SILVER, THE PRICE OF HIM THAT WAS VALUED, whom they of the children of Israel did value;

10 AND [a]GAVE THEM FOR THE POTTER'S FIELD, AS THE LORD APPOINTED ME.

Jesus Faces Pilate
(*Mark 15:2–5; Luke 23:2–5; John 18:29–38*)

11 And Jesus stood before the governor: [a]and the governor asked him, saying, Art thou the King of the Jews? And Jesus said unto him, [b]Thou sayest.

12 And when he was accused of the chief priests and elders, [a]he answered nothing.

13 Then said Pilate unto him, [a]Hearest thou not how many things they witness against thee?

14 And he answered him to never a word; insomuch that the governor marvelled greatly.

Taking the Place of Barabbas
(*Mark 15:6–15; Luke 23:13–25; John 18:39, 40*)

15 [a]Now at *that* feast the governor was wont to release unto the people a prisoner, whom they would.

16 And they had then a notable prisoner, called Barabbas.

17 Therefore when they were gathered together, Pilate said unto them, Whom will ye that I release unto you? Barabbas, or Jesus which is called Christ?

18 For he knew that for [a]envy they had delivered him.

19 When he was set down on the judgment seat, his wife sent unto him, saying, Have thou nothing to do with that just man: for I have suffered many things this day in a dream because of him.

20 [a]But the chief priests and elders persuaded the multitude that they should ask Barabbas, and destroy Jesus.

21 The governor answered and said unto them, Whether of the twain will ye that I release unto you? They said, [a]Barabbas.

22 Pilate saith unto them, What shall I do then with Jesus which is called Christ? *They* all say unto him, Let him be crucified.

23 And the governor said, [a]Why, what evil hath he done? But they cried out the more, saying, Let him be crucified.

24 When Pilate saw that he could prevail nothing, but *that* rather a tumult was made, he [a]took water, and washed *his* hands before the multitude, saying, I am innocent of the blood of this just person: see ye *to it.*

25 Then answered all the people, and said, [a]His blood *be* on us, and on our children.

26 Then released he Barabbas unto them: and when [a]he had scourged Jesus, he delivered *him* to be crucified.

The Soldiers Mock Jesus
(*Mark 15:16–20*)

27 [a]Then the soldiers of the governor took Jesus into the common hall, and gathered unto him the whole band *of soldiers.*

28 And they [a]stripped him, and [b]put on him a scarlet robe.

NKJV

4 saying, "I have sinned by betraying innocent blood." And they said, "What *is that* to us? You see *to it!*"

5 Then he threw down the pieces of silver in the temple and [a]departed, and went and hanged himself.

6 But the chief priests took the silver pieces and said, "It is not lawful to put them into the treasury, because they are the price of blood."

7 And they consulted together and bought with them the potter's field, to bury strangers in.

8 Therefore that field has been called [a]the Field of Blood to this day.

9 Then was fulfilled what was spoken by Jeremiah the prophet, saying, [a]*"And they took the thirty pieces of silver, the value of Him who was priced,* whom they of the children of Israel priced,

10 *"and [a]gave them for the potter's field, as the LORD directed me."*

Jesus Faces Pilate
(*Mark 15:2–5; Luke 23:2–5; John 18:29–38*)

11 Now Jesus stood before the governor. [a]And the governor asked Him, saying, "Are You the King of the Jews?" Jesus said to him, [b]"*It is* as you say."

12 And while He was being accused by the chief priests and elders, [a]He answered nothing.

13 Then Pilate said to Him, [a]"Do You not hear how many things they testify against You?"

14 But He answered him not one word, so that the governor marveled greatly.

Taking the Place of Barabbas
(*Mark 15:6–15; Luke 23:13–25; John 18:39, 40*)

15 [a]Now at the feast the governor was accustomed to releasing to the multitude one prisoner whom they wished.

16 And at that time they had a notorious prisoner called *Barabbas.

17 Therefore, when they had gathered together, Pilate said to them, "Whom do you want me to release to you? Barabbas, or Jesus who is called Christ?"

18 For he knew that they had handed Him over because of [a]envy.

19 While he was sitting on the judgment seat, his wife sent to him, saying, "Have nothing to do with that just Man, for I have suffered many things today in a dream because of Him."

20 [a]But the chief priests and elders persuaded the multitudes that they should ask for Barabbas and destroy Jesus.

21 The governor answered and said to them, "Which of the two do you want me to release to you?" They said, [a]"Barabbas!"

22 Pilate said to them, "What then shall I do with Jesus who is called Christ?" *They* all said to him, "Let Him be crucified!"

23 Then the governor said, [a]"Why, what evil has He done?" But they cried out all the more, saying, "Let Him be crucified!"

24 When Pilate saw that he could not prevail at all, but rather *that* a tumult was rising, he [a]took water and washed *his* hands before the multitude, saying, "I am innocent of the blood of this *just Person. You see *to it.*"

25 And all the people answered and said, [a]"His blood *be* on us and on our children."

26 Then he released Barabbas to them; and when [a]he had scourged Jesus, he delivered *Him* to be crucified.

The Soldiers Mock Jesus
(*Mark 15:16–20*)

27 [a]Then the soldiers of the governor took Jesus into the Praetorium and gathered the whole garrison around Him.

28 And they [a]stripped Him and [b]put a scarlet robe on Him.

---

5 [a]2 Sam. 17:23; Matt. 18:7; 26:24; John 17:12; Acts 1:18
8 [a]Acts 1:19
9 [a]Zech. 11:12
10 [a]Jer. 32:6–9; Zech. 11:12, 13
11 [a]Mark 15:2–5; Luke 23:2, 3; John 18:29–38 [b]John 18:37; 1 Tim. 6:13
12 [a]Ps. 38:13, 14; Matt. 26:63; John 19:9
13 [a]Matt. 26:62; John 19:10
15 [a]Mark 15:6–15; Luke 23:17–25; John 18:39—19:16
18 [a]Matt. 21:38; [John 15:22–25]
20 [a]Mark 15:11; Luke 23:18; John 18:40; Acts 3:14
21 [a]Acts 3:14
23 [a]Acts 3:13
24 [a]Deut. 21:6–8
25 [a]Deut. 19:10; Josh. 2:19; 2 Sam. 1:16; 1 Kin. 2:32; Acts 5:28
26 [a][Is. 50:6; 53:5]; Matt. 20:19; Mark 15:15; Luke 23:16, 24, 25; John 19:1, 16
27 [a]Mark 15:16–20; John 19:2
28 [a]Mark 15:17; John 19:2 [b]Luke 23:11

*

27:16 NU *Jesus Barabbas*
27:24 NU omits *just*

KJV

29 [a]And when they had platted a crown of thorns, they put *it* upon his head, and a reed in his right hand: and they bowed the knee before him, and mocked him, saying, Hail, King of the Jews!

30 And [a]they spit upon him, and took the reed, and smote him on the head.

31 And after that they had mocked him, they took the robe off from him, and put his own raiment on him, [a]and led him away to crucify *him*.

The King on a Cross
(*Mark 15:21–32; Luke 23:26–43; John 19:17–27*)

32 [a]And as they came out, [b]they found a man of Cyrene, Simon by name: him they compelled to bear his cross.

33 [a]And when they were come unto a place called Golgotha, that is to say, a place of a skull,

34 [a]They gave him vinegar to drink mingled with gall: and when he had tasted *thereof*, he would not drink.

35 [a]And they crucified him, and parted his garments, casting lots: that it might be fulfilled which was spoken by the prophet, [b]THEY PARTED MY GARMENTS AMONG THEM, AND UPON MY VESTURE DID THEY CAST LOTS.

36 [a]And sitting down they watched him there;

37 And [a]set up over his head his accusation written, THIS IS JESUS THE KING OF THE JEWS.

38 [a]Then were there two thieves crucified with him, one on the right hand, and another on the left.

39 And [a]they that passed by reviled him, wagging their heads,

40 And saying, [a]Thou that destroyest the temple, and buildest *it* in three days, save thyself. [b]If thou be the Son of God, come down from the cross.

41 Likewise also the chief priests mocking *him*, with the scribes and elders, said,

42 He [a]saved others; himself he cannot save. If he be the King of Israel, let him now come down from the cross, and we will believe him.

43 [a]He trusted in God; let him deliver him now, if he will have him: for he said, I am the Son of God.

44 [a]The thieves also, which were crucified with him, cast the same in his teeth.

Jesus Dies on the Cross
(*Mark 15:33–41; Luke 23:44–49; John 19:28–30*)

45 [a]Now from the sixth hour there was darkness over all the land unto the ninth hour.

46 And about the ninth hour [a]Jesus cried with a loud voice, saying, Eli, Eli, lama sabachthani? that is to say, [b]MY GOD, MY GOD, WHY HAST THOU FORSAKEN ME?

47 Some of them that stood there, when they heard *that*, said, This *man* calleth for Elias.

48 And straightway one of them ran, and took a spunge, [a]and filled *it* with vinegar, and put *it* on a reed, and gave him to drink.

49 The rest said, Let be, let us see whether Elias will come to save him.

50 [a]Jesus, when he had cried again with a loud voice, [b]yielded up the ghost.

51 And, behold, [a]the veil of the temple was rent in twain from the top to the bottom; and the earth did quake, and the rocks rent;

52 And the graves were opened; and many bodies of the saints which slept arose,

53 And came out of the graves after his resurrection, and went into the holy city, and appeared unto many.

54 [a]Now when the centurion, and they that were with him, watching Jesus, saw the earthquake, and those things that were done, they

29 [a]Is. 53:3
30 [a]Matt. 26:67
31 [a]Is. 53:7
32 [a]Heb. 13:12 [b]Mark 15:21
33 [a]John 19:17
34 [a]Ps. 69:21
35 [a]Luke 23:34 [b]Ps. 22:18
36 [a]Matt. 27:54
37 [a]John 19:19
38 [a]Is. 53:9, 12
39 [a]Mark 15:29
40 [a]John 2:19 [b]Matt. 26:63
42 [a][John 3:14, 15]
43 [a]Ps. 22:8
44 [a]Luke 23:39–43
45 [a]Mark 15:33–41
46 [a][Heb. 5:7] [b]Ps. 22:1
48 [a]Ps. 69:21
50 [a]Luke 23:46 [b][John 10:18]
51 [a]Ex. 26:31
54 [a]Mark 15:39

NKJV

29 [a]When they had twisted a crown of thorns, they put *it* on His head, and a reed in His right hand. And they bowed the knee before Him and mocked Him, saying, "Hail, King of the Jews!"

30 Then [a]they spat on Him, and took the reed and struck Him on the head.

31 And when they had mocked Him, they took the robe off Him, put His *own* clothes on Him, [a]and led Him away to be crucified.

The King on a Cross
(*Mark 15:21–32; Luke 23:26–43; John 19:17–27*)

32 [a]Now as they came out, [b]they found a man of Cyrene, Simon by name. Him they compelled to bear His cross.

33 [a]And when they had come to a place called Golgotha, that is to say, Place of a Skull,

34 [a]they gave Him *sour wine mingled with gall to drink. But when He had tasted *it*, He would not drink.

35 [a]Then they crucified Him, and divided His garments, casting lots, *that it might be fulfilled which was spoken by the prophet:

[b]*"They divided My garments among them,*
And for My clothing they cast lots."

36 [a]Sitting down, they kept watch over Him there.

37 And they [a]put up over His head the accusation written against Him:

THIS IS JESUS THE KING OF THE JEWS.

38 [a]Then two robbers were crucified with Him, one on the right and another on the left.

39 And [a]those who passed by blasphemed Him, wagging their heads

40 and saying, [a]"You who destroy the temple and build *it* in three days, save Yourself! [b]If You are the Son of God, come down from the cross."

41 Likewise the chief priests also, mocking with the *scribes and elders, said,

42 "He [a]saved others; Himself He cannot save. *If He is the King of Israel, let Him now come down from the cross, and we will believe *Him.

43 [a]"He trusted in God; let Him deliver Him now if He will have Him; for He said, 'I am the Son of God.' "

44 [a]Even the robbers who were crucified with Him reviled Him with the same thing.

Jesus Dies on the Cross
(*Mark 15:33–41; Luke 23:44–49; John 19:28–30*)

45 [a]Now from the sixth hour until the ninth hour there was darkness over all the land.

46 And about the ninth hour [a]Jesus cried out with a loud voice, saying, "Eli, Eli, lama sabachthani?" that is, [b]*"My God, My God, why have You forsaken Me?"*

47 Some of those who stood there, when they heard *that*, said, "This Man is calling for Elijah!"

48 Immediately one of them ran and took a sponge, [a]filled *it* with sour wine and put *it* on a reed, and offered it to Him to drink.

49 The rest said, "Let Him alone; let us see if Elijah will come to save Him."

50 And Jesus [a]cried out again with a loud voice, and [b]yielded up His spirit.

51 Then, behold, [a]the veil of the temple was torn in two from top to bottom; and the earth quaked, and the rocks were split,

52 and the graves were opened; and many bodies of the saints who had fallen asleep were raised;

53 and coming out of the graves after His resurrection, they went into the holy city and appeared to many.

54 [a]So when the centurion and those with him, who were guarding Jesus, saw the earthquake and the things that had happened, they

---

*
27:34 NU omits *sour*
27:35 NU, M omit the rest of v. 35.
27:41 M *scribes, the Pharisees, and the elders*
27:42 NU omits *If* • NU, M *in Him*

KJV

feared greatly, saying, [b]Truly this was the Son
of God.
55 And many women were there beholding
afar off, [a]which followed Jesus from Galilee, ministering unto him:
56 [a]Among which was Mary Magdalene, and
Mary the mother of James and Joses, and the
mother of Zebedee's children.

Jesus Buried in Joseph's Tomb
(Mark 15:42–47; Luke 23:50–56; John 19:38–42)

57 [a]When the even was come, there came a
rich man of Arimathaea, named Joseph, who also
himself was Jesus' disciple:
58 He went to Pilate, and begged the body
of Jesus. Then Pilate commanded the body to be
delivered.
59 And when Joseph had taken the body, he
wrapped it in a clean linen cloth,
60 And [a]laid it in his own new tomb, which
he had hewn out in the rock: and he rolled a great
stone to the door of the sepulchre, and departed.
61 And there was Mary Magdalene, and the
other Mary, sitting over against the sepulchre.

Pilate Sets a Guard

62 Now the next day, that followed the day
of the preparation, the chief priests and Pharisees
came together unto Pilate,
63 Saying, Sir, we remember that that deceiver said, while he was yet alive, [a]After three
days I will rise again.
64 Command therefore that the sepulchre be
made sure until the third day, lest his disciples
come by night, and steal him away, and say unto
the people, He is risen from the dead: so the last
error shall be worse than the first.
65 Pilate said unto them, Ye have a watch:
go your way, make *it* as sure as ye can.
66 So they went, and made the sepulchre
sure, [a]sealing the stone, and setting a watch.

He Is Risen
(Mark 16:1–8; Luke 24:1–12; John 20:1–10)

28 In the [a]end of the sabbath, as it began to
dawn toward the first *day* of the week,
came Mary Magdalene [b]and the other Mary to
see the sepulchre.
2 And, behold, there was a great earthquake: for [a]the angel of the Lord descended from
heaven, and came and rolled back the stone from
the door, and sat upon it.
3 [a]His countenance was like lightning, and
his raiment white as snow:
4 And for fear of him the keepers did shake,
and became as [a]dead *men*.
5 And the angel answered and said unto the
women, Fear not ye: for I know that ye seek Jesus,
which was crucified.
6 He is not here: for he is risen, [a]as he said.
Come, see the place where the Lord lay.
7 And go quickly, and tell his disciples that
he is risen from the dead; and, behold, [a]he goeth
before you into Galilee; there shall ye see him:
lo, I have told you.
8 And they departed quickly from the sepulchre with fear and great joy; and did run to bring
his disciples word.

The Women Worship the Risen Lord

9 And as they went to tell his disciples, behold, [a]Jesus met them, saying, All hail. And they
came and held him by the feet, and worshipped
him.
10 Then said Jesus unto them, Be not afraid:
go tell [a]my brethren that they go into Galilee, and
there shall they see me.

The Soldiers Are Bribed

11 Now when they were going, behold, some
of the watch came into the city, and shewed unto
the chief priests all the things that were done.

---

54 [b]Matt. 14:33
55 [a]Luke 8:2, 3
56 [a]Mark 15:40, 47; 16:9
57 [a]John 19:38–42
60 [a]Is. 53:9
63 [a]Mark 8:31; 10:34
66 [a]Dan. 6:17

CHAPTER 28

1 [a]Luke 24:1–10 [b]Matt. 27:56, 61
2 [a]Mark 16:5
3 [a]Dan. 7:9; 10:6
4 [a]Rev. 1:17
6 [a]Matt. 12:40; 16:21; 17:23; 20:19
7 [a]Mark 16:7
9 [a]John 20:14
10 [a]John 20:17

*
27:56 NU *Joseph*
27:64 NU omits *by night*
28:2 NU omits *from the door*
28:9 NU omits *as they went to tell His disciples*

NKJV

feared greatly, saying, [b]"Truly this was the Son
of God!"
55 And many women [a]who followed Jesus
from Galilee, ministering to Him, were there looking on from afar,
56 [a]among whom were Mary Magdalene,
Mary the mother of James and *Joses, and the
mother of Zebedee's sons.

Jesus Buried in Joseph's Tomb
(Mark 15:42–47; Luke 23:50–56; John 19:38–42)

57 Now [a]when evening had come, there
came a rich man from Arimathea, named Joseph,
who himself had also become a disciple of Jesus.
58 This man went to Pilate and asked for the
body of Jesus. Then Pilate commanded the body
to be given to him.
59 When Joseph had taken the body, he
wrapped it in a clean linen cloth,
60 and [a]laid it in his new tomb which he had
hewn out of the rock; and he rolled a large stone
against the door of the tomb, and departed.
61 And Mary Magdalene was there, and the
other Mary, sitting opposite the tomb.

Pilate Sets a Guard

62 On the next day, which followed the Day
of Preparation, the chief priests and Pharisees
gathered together to Pilate,
63 saying, "Sir, we remember, while He was
still alive, how that deceiver said, [a]'After three
days I will rise.'
64 "Therefore command that the tomb be
made secure until the third day, lest His disciples
come *by night and steal Him *away*, and say to
the people, 'He has risen from the dead.' So the
last deception will be worse than the first."
65 Pilate said to them, "You have a guard;
go your way, make *it* as secure as you know how."
66 So they went and made the tomb secure,
[a]sealing the stone and setting the guard.

He Is Risen
(Mark 16:1–8; Luke 24:1–12; John 20:1–10)

28 Now [a]after the Sabbath, as the first *day* of
the week began to dawn, Mary Magdalene
[b]and the other Mary came to see the tomb.
2 And behold, there was a great earthquake;
for [a]an angel of the Lord descended from heaven,
and came and rolled back the stone *from the
door, and sat on it.
3 [a]His countenance was like lightning, and
his clothing as white as snow.
4 And the guards shook for fear of him, and
became like [a]dead *men*.
5 But the angel answered and said to the
women, "Do not be afraid, for I know that you
seek Jesus who was crucified.
6 "He is not here; for He is risen, [a]as He
said. Come, see the place where the Lord lay.
7 "And go quickly and tell His disciples that
He is risen from the dead, and indeed [a]He is going
before you into Galilee; there you will see Him.
Behold, I have told you."
8 So they went out quickly from the tomb
with fear and great joy, and ran to bring His disciples word.

The Women Worship the Risen Lord

9 And *as they went to tell His disciples, behold, [a]Jesus met them, saying, "Rejoice!" So they
came and held Him by the feet and worshiped
Him.
10 Then Jesus said to them, "Do not be
afraid. Go *and* tell [a]My brethren to go to Galilee,
and there they will see Me."

The Soldiers Are Bribed

11 Now while they were going, behold, some
of the guard came into the city and reported to
the chief priests all the things that had happened.

KJV

12 And when they were assembled with the elders, and had taken counsel, they gave large money unto the soldiers,
13 Saying, Say ye, His disciples came by night, and stole him *away* while we slept.
14 And if this come to the governor's ears, we will persuade him, and secure you.
15 So they took the money, and did as they were taught: and this saying is commonly reported among the Jews until this day.

The Great Commission
(Mark 16:14–18; Luke 24:36–49; John 20:19–23; Acts 1:6–8)

16 Then the eleven disciples went away into Galilee, into a mountain [a]where Jesus had appointed them.
17 And when they saw him, they worshipped him: but some [a]doubted.
18 And Jesus came and spake unto them, saying, [a]All power is given unto me in heaven and in earth.
19 [a]Go ye therefore, and [b]teach all nations, baptizing them in the name of the Father, and of the Son, and of the Holy Ghost:
20 [a]Teaching them to observe all things whatsoever I have commanded you: and, lo, I am [b]with you alway, *even* unto the end of the world. Amen.

16 [a]Matt. 26:32; 28:7, 10
17 [a]John 20:24–29
18 [a][Dan. 7:13, 14]
19 [a]Mark 16:15 [b]Luke 24:47
20 [a][Acts 2:42] [b][Acts 4:31; 18:10; 23:11]

*
28:19 M omits *therefore*
28:20 NU omits *Amen*

NKJV

12 When they had assembled with the elders and consulted together, they gave a large sum of money to the soldiers,
13 saying, "Tell them, 'His disciples came at night and stole Him *away* while we slept.'
14 "And if this comes to the governor's ears, we will appease him and make you secure."
15 So they took the money and did as they were instructed; and this saying is commonly reported among the Jews until this day.

The Great Commission
(Mark 16:14–18; Luke 24:36–49; John 20:19–23; Acts 1:6–8)

16 Then the eleven disciples went away into Galilee, to the mountain [a]which Jesus had appointed for them.
17 When they saw Him, they worshiped Him; but some [a]doubted.
18 And Jesus came and spoke to them, saying, [a]"All authority has been given to Me in heaven and on earth.
19 [a]"Go *therefore and [b]make disciples of all the nations, baptizing them in the name of the Father and of the Son and of the Holy Spirit,
20 [a]"teaching them to observe all things that I have commanded you; and lo, I am [b]with you always, *even* to the end of the age." *Amen.

KJV

THE GOSPEL ACCORDING TO

MARK

John the Baptist Prepares the Way
(Matt. 3:1–12; Luke 3:1–20; John 1:19–28)

1 The [a]beginning of the gospel of Jesus Christ,
[b]the Son of God;
2 As it is written in the prophets,[a]BEHOLD,
I SEND MY MESSENGER BEFORE THY FACE, WHICH
SHALL PREPARE THY WAY BEFORE THEE.
3 [a]THE VOICE OF ONE CRYING IN THE WILDER-
NESS, PREPARE YE THE WAY OF THE LORD, MAKE HIS
PATHS STRAIGHT.
4 [a]John did baptize in the wilderness, and
preach the baptism of repentance for the remission of sins.
5 [a]And there went out unto him all the land
of Judaea, and they of Jerusalem, and were all
baptized of him in the river of Jordan, confessing
their sins.
6 And John was [a]clothed with camel's hair,
and with a girdle of a skin about his loins; and
he did eat locusts and wild honey;
7 And preached, saying, [a]There cometh one
mightier than I after me, the latchet of whose
shoes I am not worthy to stoop down and unloose.
8 [a]I indeed have baptized you with water:
but he shall baptize you [b]with the Holy Ghost.

John Baptizes Jesus
(Matt. 3:13–17; Luke 3:21, 22; John 1:29–34)

9 [a]And it came to pass in those days, that
Jesus came from Nazareth of Galilee, and was
baptized of John in Jordan.
10 [a]And straightway coming up out of the
water, he saw the heavens opened, and the Spirit
like a dove [b]descending upon him:
11 And there came a voice from heaven, *saying*, [a]Thou art my beloved Son, in whom I am
well pleased.

Satan Tempts Jesus
(Matt. 4:1–11; Luke 4:1–13)

12 [a]And immediately the spirit driveth him
into the wilderness.
13 And he was there in the wilderness forty
days, tempted of Satan; and was with the wild
beasts; [a]and the angels ministered unto him.

Jesus Begins His Galilean Ministry
(Matt. 4:12–17; Luke 4:14, 15)

14 [a]Now after that John was put in prison,
Jesus came into Galilee, [b]preaching the gospel of
the kingdom of God,
15 And saying, [a]The time is fulfilled, and [b]the
kingdom of God is at hand: repent ye, and believe
the gospel.

Four Fishermen Called as Disciples
(Matt. 4:18–22; Luke 5:1–11)

16 [a]Now as he walked by the sea of Galilee,
he saw Simon and Andrew his brother casting a
net into the sea: for they were fishers.
17 And Jesus said unto them, Come ye after
me, and I will make you to become [a]fishers of
men.
18 And straightway [a]they forsook their nets,
and followed him.

CHAPTER 1
1 [a]Matt. 1:1; 3:1; Luke 3:22 [b]Ps. 2:7; Matt. 14:33; Luke 1:35
2 [a]Mal. 3:1; Matt. 11:10; Luke 7:27
3 [a]Is. 40:3; Matt. 3:3; Luke 3:4; John 1:23
4 [a]Mal. 4:6; Matt. 3:1; Luke 3:3
5 [a]Matt. 3:5
6 [a]Matt. 3:4
7 [a]Matt. 3:11; John 1:27; Acts 13:25
8 [a]Acts 1:5; 11:16 [b]Is. 44:3; John 20:22; [Acts 2:4; 10:45, 46; 1 Cor. 12:13]
9 [a]Matt. 3:13–17; Luke 3:21, 22
10 [a]Ezek. 1:1; Matt. 3:16; John 1:32 [b]Is. 11:2; 61:1; Acts 10:38
11 [a][Ps. 2:7]; Is. 42:1; Matt. 3:17; 12:18; Mark 9:7; Luke 3:22
12 [a]Matt. 4:1–11; Luke 4:1–13
13 [a]Matt. 4:10, 11
14 [a]Matt. 4:12 [b]Matt. 4:23
15 [a]Dan. 9:25; [Gal. 4:4; Eph. 1:10; 1 Tim. 2:6]; Titus 1:3 [b]Matt. 3:2; 4:17; [Acts 20:21]
16 [a]Matt. 4:18–22; Luke 5:2–11; John 1:40–42
17 [a]Matt. 13:47, 48
18 [a]Matt. 19:27; [Luke 14:26]

*

1:2 NU *Isaiah the prophet*
1:10 NU *out of*
1:14 NU omits *of the kingdom*

NKJV

THE GOSPEL ACCORDING TO

MARK

John the Baptist Prepares the Way
(Matt. 3:1–12; Luke 3:1–20; John 1:19–28)

1 The [a]beginning of the gospel of Jesus Christ,
[b]the Son of God.
2 As it is written in *the Prophets:

[a]*"Behold, I send My messenger before Your*
face,
Who will prepare Your way before You."
3 *"The[a] voice of one crying in the wilderness:*
'Prepare the way of the LORD;
Make His paths straight.'"

4 [a]John came baptizing in the wilderness
and preaching a baptism of repentance for the
remission of sins.
5 [a]Then all the land of Judea, and those
from Jerusalem, went out to him and were all baptized by him in the Jordan River, confessing their
sins.
6 Now John was [a]clothed with camel's hair
and with a leather belt around his waist, and he
ate locusts and wild honey.
7 And he preached, saying, [a]"There comes
One after me who is mightier than I, whose sandal
strap I am not worthy to stoop down and loose.
8 [a]"I indeed baptized you with water, but
He will baptize you [b]with the Holy Spirit."

John Baptizes Jesus
(Matt. 3:13–17; Luke 3:21, 22; John 1:29–34)

9 [a]It came to pass in those days *that* Jesus
came from Nazareth of Galilee, and was baptized
by John in the Jordan.
10 [a]And immediately, coming up *from the
water, He saw the heavens parting and the Spirit
[b]descending upon Him like a dove.
11 Then a voice came from heaven, [a]"You
are My beloved Son, in whom I am well pleased."

Satan Tempts Jesus
(Matt. 4:1–11; Luke 4:1–13)

12 [a]Immediately the Spirit drove Him into
the wilderness.
13 And He was there in the wilderness forty
days, tempted by Satan, and was with the wild
beasts; [a]and the angels ministered to Him.

Jesus Begins His Galilean Ministry
(Matt. 4:12–17; Luke 4:14, 15)

14 [a]Now after John was put in prison, Jesus
came to Galilee, [b]preaching the gospel *of the
kingdom of God,
15 and saying, [a]"The time is fulfilled, and
[b]the kingdom of God is at hand. Repent, and believe in the gospel."

Four Fishermen Called as Disciples
(Matt. 4:18–22; Luke 5:1–11)

16 [a]And as He walked by the Sea of Galilee,
He saw Simon and Andrew his brother casting a
net into the sea; for they were fishermen.
17 Then Jesus said to them, "Follow Me, and
I will make you become [a]fishers of men."
18 [a]They immediately left their nets and followed Him.

KJV

19 And when he had gone a little farther thence, he saw James the *son* of Zebedee, and John his brother, who also were in the ship mending their nets.

20 And straightway he called them: and they left their father Zebedee in the ship with the hired servants, and went after him.

Jesus Casts Out an Unclean Spirit
(Luke 4:31–37)

21 [a]And they went into Capernaum; and straightway on the sabbath day he entered into the [b]synagogue, and taught.

22 [a]And they were astonished at his doctrine: for he taught them as one that had authority, and not as the scribes.

23 And there was in their synagogue a man with an [a]unclean spirit; and he cried out,

24 Saying, Let *us* alone; [a]what have we to do with thee, thou Jesus of Nazareth? art thou come to destroy us? I [b]know thee who thou art, the [c]Holy One of God.

25 And Jesus [a]rebuked him, saying, Hold thy peace, and come out of him.

26 And when the unclean spirit [a]had torn him, and cried with a loud voice, he came out of him.

27 And they were all amazed, insomuch that they questioned among themselves, saying, What thing is this? what new doctrine *is* this? for with authority commandeth he even the unclean spirits, and they do obey him.

28 And immediately his [a]fame spread abroad throughout all the region round about Galilee.

Peter's Mother-in-Law Healed
(Matt. 8:14, 15; Luke 4:38, 39)

29 [a]And forthwith, when they were come out of the synagogue, they entered into the house of Simon and Andrew, with James and John.

30 But Simon's wife's mother lay sick of a fever, and anon they tell him of her.

31 And he came and took her by the hand, and lifted her up; and immediately the fever left her, and she ministered unto them.

Many Healed After Sabbath Sunset
(Matt. 8:16, 17; Luke 4:40, 41)

32 [a]And at even, when the sun did set, they brought unto him all that were diseased, and them that were possessed with devils.

33 And all the city was gathered together at the door.

34 And he healed many that were sick of divers diseases, and [a]cast out many devils; and [b]suffered not the devils to speak, because they knew him.

Preaching in Galilee
(Matt. 4:23–25; Luke 4:42–44)

35 And [a]in the morning, rising up a great while before day, he went out, and departed into a solitary place, and there [b]prayed.

36 And Simon and they that were with him followed after him.

37 And when they had found him, they said unto him, [a]All *men* [b]seek for thee.

38 And he said unto them, [a]Let us go into the next towns, that I may preach there also: for [b]therefore came I forth.

39 [a]And he preached in their synagogues throughout all Galilee, and [b]cast out devils.

Jesus Cleanses a Leper
(Matt. 8:1–4; Luke 5:12–16)

40 [a]And there came a leper to him, beseeching him, and kneeling down to him, and saying unto him, If thou wilt, thou canst make me clean.

41 And Jesus, moved with [a]compassion, put forth *his* hand, and touched him, and saith unto him, I will; be thou clean.

21 [a]Matt. 4:13; Luke 4:31–37 [b]Ps. 22:22; Matt. 4:23; Luke 4:16; 13:10
22 [a]Matt. 7:28, 29; 13:54
23 [a][Matt. 12:43]; Mark 5:2; 7:25; Luke 4:33
24 [a]Matt. 8:28, 29; Mark 5:7, 8; Luke 8:28 [b]Mark 3:11; Luke 4:41; James 2:19 [c]Ps. 16:10
25 [a][Luke 4:39]
26 [a]Mark 9:20
28 [a]Matt. 4:24; 9:31
29 [a]Matt. 8:14, 15; Luke 4:38, 39
32 [a]Matt. 8:16, 17; Luke 4:40, 41
34 [a]Matt. 9:33; Luke 13:32 [b]Mark 3:12; Luke 4:41; Acts 16:17, 18
35 [a]Luke 4:42, 43 [b]Matt. 26:39, 44; Mark 6:46; Luke 5:16; 6:12; 9:28, 29; Heb. 5:7
37 [a]Matt. 4:25; John 3:26; 12:19 [b][Heb. 11:6]
38 [a]Luke 4:43 [b][Is. 61:1, 2; Mark 10:45; John 16:28; 17:4, 8]
39 [a]Ps. 22:22; Matt. 4:23; 9:35; Mark 1:21; 3:1; Luke 4:44 [b]Mark 5:8, 13; 7:29, 30
40 [a]Matt. 8:2–4; Luke 5:12–14
41 [a]Luke 7:13

*———

1:27 NU *What is this? A new doctrine with authority. He*

NKJV

19 When He had gone a little farther from there, He saw James the *son* of Zebedee, and John his brother, who also *were* in the boat mending their nets.

20 And immediately He called them, and they left their father Zebedee in the boat with the hired servants, and went after Him.

Jesus Casts Out an Unclean Spirit
(Luke 4:31–37)

21 [a]Then they went into Capernaum, and immediately on the Sabbath He entered the [b]synagogue and taught.

22 [a]And they were astonished at His teaching, for He taught them as one having authority, and not as the scribes.

23 Now there was a man in their synagogue with an [a]unclean spirit. And he cried out,

24 saying, "Let *us* alone! [a]What have we to do with You, Jesus of Nazareth? Did You come to destroy us? I [b]know who You are—the [c]Holy One of God!"

25 But Jesus [a]rebuked him, saying, "Be quiet, and come out of him!"

26 And when the unclean spirit [a]had convulsed him and cried out with a loud voice, he came out of him.

27 Then they were all amazed, so that they questioned among themselves, saying, *"What is this? What new doctrine *is* this? For with authority He commands even the unclean spirits, and they obey Him."

28 And immediately His [a]fame spread throughout all the region around Galilee.

Peter's Mother-in-Law Healed
(Matt. 8:14, 15; Luke 4:38, 39)

29 [a]Now as soon as they had come out of the synagogue, they entered the house of Simon and Andrew, with James and John.

30 But Simon's wife's mother lay sick with a fever, and they told Him about her at once.

31 So He came and took her by the hand and lifted her up, and immediately the fever left her. And she served them.

Many Healed After Sabbath Sunset
(Matt. 8:16, 17; Luke 4:40, 41)

32 [a]At evening, when the sun had set, they brought to Him all who were sick and those who were demon-possessed.

33 And the whole city was gathered together at the door.

34 Then He healed many who were sick with various diseases, and [a]cast out many demons; and He [b]did not allow the demons to speak, because they knew Him.

Preaching in Galilee
(Matt. 4:23–25; Luke 4:42–44)

35 Now [a]in the morning, having risen a long while before daylight, He went out and departed to a solitary place; and there He [b]prayed.

36 And Simon and those *who were* with Him searched for Him.

37 When they found Him, they said to Him, [a]"Everyone [b]is looking for You."

38 But He said to them, [a]"Let us go into the next towns, that I may preach there also, because [b]for this purpose I have come forth."

39 [a]And He was preaching in their synagogues throughout all Galilee, and [b]casting out demons.

Jesus Cleanses a Leper
(Matt. 8:1–4; Luke 5:12–16)

40 [a]Now a leper came to Him, imploring Him, kneeling down to Him and saying to Him, "If You are willing, You can make me clean."

41 Then Jesus, moved with [a]compassion, stretched out *His* hand and touched him, and said to him, "I am willing; be cleansed."

KJV

42 And as soon as he had spoken, [a]immedi-
ately the leprosy departed from him, and he was
cleansed.
43 And he straitly charged him, and forthwith sent him away;
44 And saith unto him, See thou say nothing
to any man: but go thy way, shew thyself to the
priest, and offer for thy cleansing those things
[a]which Moses commanded, for a testimony unto
them.
45 [a]But he went out, and began to publish *it*
much, and to blaze abroad the matter, insomuch
that Jesus could no more openly enter into the
city, but was without in desert places: [b]and they
came to him from every quarter.

Jesus Forgives and Heals a Paralytic
(Matt. 9:2–8; Luke 5:17–26)

2 And again [a]he entered into Capernaum after
some days; and it was noised that he was in
the house.
2 And straightway many were gathered together, insomuch that there was no room to receive *them,* no, not so much as about the door:
and he preached the word unto them.
3 And they come unto him, bringing one
sick of the [a]palsy, which was borne of four.
4 And when they could not come nigh unto
him for the press, they uncovered the roof where
he was: and when they had broken *it* up, they
let down the bed wherein the sick of the palsy
lay.
5 When Jesus saw their faith, he said unto
the sick of the palsy, Son, thy sins be forgiven
thee.
6 But there were certain of the scribes sitting there, and reasoning in their hearts,
7 Why doth this *man* thus speak blasphemies? [a]who can forgive sins but God only?
8 And immediately when Jesus perceived in
his spirit that they so reasoned within themselves,
he said unto them, Why reason ye these things
in your hearts?
9 [a]Whether is it easier to say to the sick of
the palsy, *Thy* sins be forgiven thee; or to say,
Arise, and take up thy bed, and walk?
10 But that ye may know that the Son of man
hath power on earth to forgive sins, (he saith to
the sick of the palsy,)
11 I say unto thee, Arise, and take up thy bed,
and go thy way into thine house.
12 And immediately he arose, took up the
bed, and went forth before them all; insomuch
that they were all amazed, and [a]glorified God,
saying, We never saw it on this fashion.

Matthew the Tax Collector
(Matt. 9:9–13; Luke 5:27–32)

13 [a]And he went forth again by the sea side;
and all the multitude resorted unto him, and he
taught them.
14 [a]And as he passed by, he saw Levi the
son of Alphaeus sitting at the receipt of custom,
and said unto him, [b]Follow me. And he arose and
[c]followed him.
15 [a]And it came to pass, that, as Jesus sat
at meat in his house, many publicans and sinners
sat also together with Jesus and his disciples: for
there were many, and they followed him.
16 And when the scribes and Pharisees saw
him eat with publicans and sinners, they said unto
his disciples, How is it that he eateth and drinketh
with publicans and sinners?
17 When Jesus heard *it,* he saith unto them,
[a]They that are whole have no need of the physician, but they that are sick: I came not to call
the righteous, but sinners to repentance.

Jesus Is Questioned About Fasting
(Matt. 9:14–17; Luke 5:33–39)

18 [a]And the disciples of John and of the
Pharisees used to fast: and they come and say

42 [a]Matt. 15:28; Mark 5:29
44 [a]Lev. 14:1–32
45 [a]Matt. 28:15; Luke 5:15 [b]Mark 2:2, 13; 3:7; Luke 5:17; John 6:2

CHAPTER 2

1 [a]Matt. 9:1
3 [a]Matt. 4:24; 8:6; Acts 8:7; 9:33
7 [a]Job 14:4; Is. 43:25; Dan. 9:9
9 [a]Matt. 9:5
12 [a]Matt. 15:31; [Phil. 2:11]
13 [a]Matt. 9:9
14 [a]Matt. 9:9–13; Luke 5:27–32 [b]Matt. 4:19; 8:22; 19:21; John 1:43; 12:26; 21:22 [c]Luke 18:28
15 [a]Matt. 9:10
17 [a]Matt. 9:12, 13; 18:11; Luke 5:31, 32; 19:10
18 [a]Matt. 9:14–17; Luke 5:33–38

*

2:2 NU omits *Immediately*
2:16 NU of *the*
2:17 NU omits *to repentance*

NKJV

42 As soon as He had spoken, [a]immediately
the leprosy left him, and he was cleansed.
43 And He strictly warned him and sent him
away at once,
44 and said to him, "See that you say nothing
to anyone; but go your way, show yourself to the
priest, and offer for your cleansing those things
[a]which Moses commanded, as a testimony to
them."
45 [a]However, he went out and began to proclaim *it* freely, and to spread the matter, so that
Jesus could no longer openly enter the city, but
was outside in deserted places; [b]and they came
to Him from every direction.

Jesus Forgives and Heals a Paralytic
(Matt. 9:2–8; Luke 5:17–26)

2 And again [a]He entered Capernaum after *some*
days, and it was heard that He was in the
house.
2 *Immediately many gathered together, so
that there was no longer room to receive *them,*
not even near the door. And He preached the word
to them.
3 Then they came to Him, bringing a [a]para-
lytic who was carried by four *men.*
4 And when they could not come near Him
because of the crowd, they uncovered the roof
where He was. So when they had broken through,
they let down the bed on which the paralytic was
lying.
5 When Jesus saw their faith, He said to the
paralytic, "Son, your sins are forgiven you."
6 And some of the scribes were sitting there
and reasoning in their hearts,
7 "Why does this *Man* speak blasphemies
like this? [a]Who can forgive sins but God alone?"
8 But immediately, when Jesus perceived in
His spirit that they reasoned thus within themselves, He said to them, "Why do you reason
about these things in your hearts?
9 [a]"Which is easier, to say to the paralytic,
'*Your* sins are forgiven you,' or to say, 'Arise, take
up your bed and walk'?
10 "But that you may know that the Son of
Man has power on earth to forgive sins"—He said
to the paralytic,
11 "I say to you, arise, take up your bed, and
go to your house."
12 Immediately he arose, took up the bed,
and went out in the presence of them all, so that
all were amazed and [a]glorified God, saying, "We
never saw *anything* like this!"

Matthew the Tax Collector
(Matt. 9:9–13; Luke 5:27–32)

13 [a]Then He went out again by the sea; and
all the multitude came to Him, and He taught
them.
14 [a]As He passed by, He saw Levi the *son*
of Alphaeus sitting at the tax office. And He said
to him, [b]"Follow Me." So he arose and [c]followed
Him.
15 [a]Now it happened, as He was dining in
Levi's house, that many tax collectors and sinners
also sat together with Jesus and His disciples; for
there were many, and they followed Him.
16 And when the scribes *and Pharisees saw
Him eating with the tax collectors and sinners,
they said to His disciples, "How *is it* that He eats
and drinks with tax collectors and sinners?"
17 When Jesus heard *it,* He said to them,
[a]"Those who are well have no need of a physician,
but those who are sick. I did not come to call *the*
righteous, but sinners, *to repentance."

Jesus Is Questioned About Fasting
(Matt. 9:14–17; Luke 5:33–39)

18 [a]The disciples of John and of the Pharisees were fasting. Then they came and said to

KJV

unto him, Why do the disciples of John and of the Pharisees fast, but thy disciples fast not?

19 And Jesus said unto them, Can the children of the bridechamber fast, while the bridegroom is with them? as long as they have the bridegroom with them, they cannot fast.

20 But the days will come, when the bridegroom shall be [a]taken away from them, and then shall they fast in those days.

21 No man also seweth a piece of new cloth on an old garment: else the new piece that filled it up taketh away from the old, and the rent is made worse.

22 And no man putteth new wine into old bottles: else the new wine doth burst the bottles, and the wine is spilled, and the bottles will be marred: but new wine must be put into new bottles.

Jesus Is Lord of the Sabbath
(Matt. 12:1–8; Luke 6:1–5)

23 [a]And it came to pass, that he went through the corn fields on the sabbath day; and his disciples began, as they went, [b]to pluck the ears of corn.

24 And the Pharisees said unto him, Behold, why do they on the sabbath day that which is [a]not lawful?

25 And he said unto them, Have ye never read [a]what David did, when he had need, and was an hungred, he, and they that were with him?

26 How he went into the house of God in the days of Abiathar the high priest, and did eat the shewbread, [a]which is not lawful to eat but for the priests, and gave also to them which were with him?

27 And he said unto them, The sabbath was made for man, and not man for the [a]sabbath:

28 Therefore [a]the Son of man is Lord also of the sabbath.

Healing on the Sabbath
(Matt. 12:9–14; Luke 6:6–11)

3 And [a]he entered again into the synagogue; and there was a man there which had a withered hand.

2 And they [a]watched him, whether he would [b]heal him on the sabbath day; that they might accuse him.

3 And he saith unto the man which had the withered hand, Stand forth.

4 And he saith unto them, Is it lawful to do good on the sabbath days, or to do evil? to save life, or to kill? But they held their peace.

5 And when he had looked round about on them with anger, being grieved for the [a]hardness of their hearts, he saith unto the man, Stretch forth thine hand. And he stretched *it* out: and his hand was restored whole as the other.

6 [a]And the Pharisees went forth, and straightway took counsel with [b]the Herodians against him, how they might destroy him.

A Great Multitude Follows Jesus
(Matt. 12:15–21)

7 But Jesus withdrew himself with his disciples to the sea: and a great multitude from Galilee followed him, [a]and from Judaea,

8 And from Jerusalem, and from Idumaea, and *from* beyond Jordan; and they about Tyre and Sidon, a great multitude, when they had heard what [a]great things he did, came unto him.

9 And he spake to his disciples, that a small ship should wait on him because of the multitude, lest they should throng him.

10 For he had healed [a]many; insomuch that they pressed upon him for to [b]touch him, as many as had plagues.

11 [a]And unclean spirits, when they saw him, fell down before him, and cried, saying, [b]Thou art the Son of God.

20 [a]Acts 1:9; 13:2, 3; 14:23
23 [a]Matt. 12:1–8; Luke 6:1–5 [b]Deut. 23:25
24 [a]Ex. 20:10; 31:15
25 [a]1 Sam. 21:1–6
26 [a]Ex. 29:32, 33; Lev. 24:5–9
27 [a]Gen. 2:3; Ex. 23:12; Deut. 5:14; Neh. 9:14; Ezek. 20:12
28 [a]Matt. 12:8

CHAPTER 3
1 [a]Matt. 12:9–14; Luke 6:6–11
2 [a][Ps. 37:32]; Luke 14:1; 20:20 [b]Luke 13:14
5 [a]Zech. 7:12
6 [a]Ps. 2:2; Mark 12:13 [b]Matt. 22:16
7 [a]Matt. 4:25; Luke 6:17
8 [a]Mark 5:19
10 [a]Mark 5:29, 34; Luke 7:21 [b]Matt. 9:21; 14:36; Mark 6:56; 8:22
11 [a]Mark 1:23, 24; Luke 4:41 [b]Matt. 8:29; 14:33; Mark 1:1; 5:7; Luke 8:28

*3:5 NU omits *as whole as the other*

NKJV

Him, "Why do the disciples of John and of the Pharisees fast, but Your disciples do not fast?"

19 And Jesus said to them, "Can the friends of the bridegroom fast while the bridegroom is with them? As long as they have the bridegroom with them they cannot fast.

20 "But the days will come when the bridegroom will be [a]taken away from them, and then they will fast in those days.

21 "No one sews a piece of unshrunk cloth on an old garment; or else the new piece pulls away from the old, and the tear is made worse.

22 "And no one puts new wine into old wineskins; or else the new wine bursts the wineskins, the wine is spilled, and the wineskins are ruined. But new wine must be put into new wineskins."

Jesus Is Lord of the Sabbath
(Matt. 12:1–8; Luke 6:1–5)

23 [a]Now it happened that He went through the grainfields on the Sabbath; and as they went His disciples began [b]to pluck the heads of grain.

24 And the Pharisees said to Him, "Look, why do they do what is [a]not lawful on the Sabbath?"

25 But He said to them, "Have you never read [a]what David did when he was in need and hungry, he and those with him:

26 "how he went into the house of God *in the days* of Abiathar the high priest, and ate the showbread, [a]which is not lawful to eat except for the priests, and also gave some to those who were with him?"

27 And He said to them, "The Sabbath was made for man, and not man for the [a]Sabbath.

28 "Therefore [a]the Son of Man is also Lord of the Sabbath."

Healing on the Sabbath
(Matt. 12:9–14; Luke 6:6–11)

3 And [a]He entered the synagogue again, and a man was there who had a withered hand.

2 So they [a]watched Him closely, whether He would [b]heal him on the Sabbath, so that they might accuse Him.

3 And He said to the man who had the withered hand, "Step forward."

4 Then He said to them, "Is it lawful on the Sabbath to do good or to do evil, to save life or to kill?" But they kept silent.

5 And when He had looked around at them with anger, being grieved by the [a]hardness of their hearts, He said to the man, "Stretch out your hand." And he stretched *it* out, and his hand was restored *as whole as the other.

6 [a]Then the Pharisees went out and immediately plotted with [b]the Herodians against Him, how they might destroy Him.

A Great Multitude Follows Jesus
(Matt. 12:15–21)

7 But Jesus withdrew with His disciples to the sea. And a great multitude from Galilee followed Him, [a]and from Judea

8 and Jerusalem and Idumea and beyond the Jordan; and those from Tyre and Sidon, a great multitude, when they heard how [a]many things He was doing, came to Him.

9 So He told His disciples that a small boat should be kept ready for Him because of the multitude, lest they should crush Him.

10 For He healed [a]many, so that as many as had afflictions pressed about Him to [b]touch Him.

11 [a]And the unclean spirits, whenever they saw Him, fell down before Him and cried out, saying, [b]"You are the Son of God."

KJV

12 And [a]he straitly charged them that they
should not make him known.

The Twelve Apostles
(Matt. 10:1–4; Luke 6:12–16)

13 [a]And he goeth up into a mountain, and
calleth *unto him* whom he would: and they came
unto him.
14 And he ordained twelve, that they should
be with him, and that he might send them forth
to preach,
15 And to have power to heal sicknesses, and
to cast out devils:
16 And Simon [a]he surnamed Peter;
17 And James the *son* of Zebedee, and John
the brother of James; and he surnamed them Boa-
nerges, which is, The sons of thunder:
18 And Andrew, and Philip, and Bartholomew, and Matthew, and Thomas, and James the
son of Alphaeus, and Thaddaeus, and Simon the
Canaanite,
19 And Judas Iscariot, which also betrayed
him: and they went into an house.

A House Divided Cannot Stand
(Matt. 12:22–30; Luke 11:14–23)

20 And the multitude cometh together again,
[a]so that they could not so much as eat bread.
21 And when his [a]friends heard *of it,* they
went out to lay hold on him: [b]for they said, He
is beside himself.
22 And the scribes which came down from
Jerusalem said, [a]He hath Beelzebub, and by the
[b]prince of the devils casteth he out devils.
23 [a]And he called them *unto him,* and said
unto them in parables, How can Satan cast out
Satan?
24 And if a kingdom be divided against itself,
that kingdom cannot stand.
25 And if a house be divided against itself,
that house cannot stand.
26 And if Satan rise up against himself,
and be divided, he cannot stand, but hath an
end.
27 [a]No man can enter into a strong man's
house, and spoil his goods, except he will first
bind the strong man; and then he will spoil his
house.

The Unpardonable Sin
(Matt. 12:31, 32; Luke 12:10)

28 [a]Verily I say unto you, All sins shall be
forgiven unto the sons of men, and blasphemies
wherewith soever they shall blaspheme:
29 But he that shall blaspheme against the
Holy Ghost hath never forgiveness, but is in danger of eternal damnation:
30 Because they [a]said, He hath an unclean
spirit.

Jesus' Mother and Brothers Send for Him
(Matt. 12:46–50; Luke 8:19–21)

31 [a]There came then his brethren and his
mother, and, standing without, sent unto him,
calling him.
32 And the multitude sat about him, and they
said unto him, Behold, thy mother and thy brethren without seek for thee.
33 And he answered them, saying, Who is
my mother, or my brethren?
34 And he looked round about on them
which sat about him, and said, Behold my mother
and my brethren!
35 For whosoever shall do the [a]will of God,
the same is my brother, and my sister, and
mother.

The Parable of the Sower
(Matt. 13:1–9; Luke 8:4–8)

4 And [a]he began again to teach by the sea side:
and there was gathered unto him a great multitude, so that he entered into a ship, and sat in

12 [a]Matt. 12:16; Mark 1:25, 34
13 [a]Matt. 10:1; Mark 6:7; Luke 9:1
16 [a]Matt. 16:18; John 1:42
20 [a]Mark 6:31
21 [a]Ps. 69:8; Matt. 13:55; Mark 6:3; John 2:12 [b]John 7:5; 10:20; Acts 26:24; [2 Cor. 5:13]
22 [a]Matt. 9:34; 10:25; Luke 11:15; John 7:20; 8:48, 52; 10:20 [b][John 12:31; 14:30; 16:11; Eph. 2:2]
23 [a]Matt. 12:25–29; Luke 11:17–22
27 [a][Is. 49:24, 25]; Matt. 12:29
28 [a]Matt. 12:31, 32; Luke 12:10; [1 John 5:16]
30 [a]Matt. 9:34; John 7:20; 8:48, 52; 10:20
31 [a]Matt. 12:46–50; Luke 8:19–21
35 [a]Eph. 6:6; Heb. 10:36; 1 Pet. 4:2; [1 John 2:17]

CHAPTER 4

1 [a]Matt. 13:1–15; Luke 8:4–10

*———

3:14 NU adds *whom He also named apostles*
3:15 NU omits *to heal sicknesses and*
3:16 NU *and He appointed the twelve: Simon . . .*
3:32 NU, M add *and Your sisters*

NKJV

12 But [a]He sternly warned them that they
should not make Him known.

The Twelve Apostles
(Matt. 10:1–4; Luke 6:12–16)

13 [a]And He went up on the mountain and
called to *Him* those He Himself wanted. And they
came to Him.
14 Then He appointed twelve, *that they
might be with Him and that He might send them
out to preach,
15 and to have power *to heal sicknesses and
to cast out demons:
16 *Simon, [a]to whom He gave the name
Peter;
17 James the *son* of Zebedee and John the
brother of James, to whom He gave the name Boa-
nerges, that is, "Sons of Thunder";
18 Andrew, Philip, Bartholomew, Matthew,
Thomas, James the *son* of Alphaeus, Thaddaeus,
Simon the Cananite;
19 and Judas Iscariot, who also betrayed
Him. And they went into a house.

A House Divided Cannot Stand
(Matt. 12:22–30; Luke 11:14–23)

20 Then the multitude came together again,
[a]so that they could not so much as eat bread.
21 But when His [a]own people heard *about
this,* they went out to lay hold of Him, [b]for they
said, "He is out of His mind."
22 And the scribes who came down from Jerusalem said, [a]"He has Beelzebub," and, "By the
[b]ruler of the demons He casts out demons."
23 [a]So He called them to *Himself* and said
to them in parables: "How can Satan cast out
Satan?
24 "If a kingdom is divided against itself, that
kingdom cannot stand.
25 "And if a house is divided against itself,
that house cannot stand.
26 "And if Satan has risen up against himself, and is divided, he cannot stand, but has an
end.
27 [a]"No one can enter a strong man's house
and plunder his goods, unless he first binds the
strong man. And then he will plunder his house.

The Unpardonable Sin
(Matt. 12:31, 32; Luke 12:10)

28 [a]"Assuredly, I say to you, all sins will be
forgiven the sons of men, and whatever blasphemies they may utter;
29 "but he who blasphemes against the Holy
Spirit never has forgiveness, but is subject to eternal condemnation"—
30 because they [a]said, "He has an unclean
spirit."

Jesus' Mother and Brothers Send for Him
(Matt. 12:46–50; Luke 8:19–21)

31 [a]Then His brothers and His mother came,
and standing outside they sent to Him, calling
Him.
32 And a multitude was sitting around Him;
and they said to Him, "Look, Your mother and
Your brothers *are outside seeking You."
33 But He answered them, saying, "Who is
My mother, or My brothers?"
34 And He looked around in a circle at those
who sat about Him, and said, "Here are My
mother and My brothers!
35 "For whoever does the [a]will of God is My
brother and My sister and mother."

The Parable of the Sower
(Matt. 13:1–9; Luke 8:4–8)

4 And [a]again He began to teach by the sea. And
a great multitude was gathered to Him, so that
He got into a boat and sat *in it* on the sea; and

KJV

the sea; and the whole multitude was by the sea on the land.

2 And he taught them many things by parables, [a]and said unto them in his doctrine,

3 Hearken; Behold, there went out a sower to sow:

4 And it came to pass, as he sowed, some fell by the way side, and the fowls of the air came and devoured it up.

5 And some fell on stony ground, where it had not much earth; and immediately it sprang up, because it had no depth of earth:

6 But when the sun was up, it was scorched; and because it had no root, it withered away.

7 And some fell among thorns, and the thorns grew up, and choked it, and it yielded no fruit.

8 And other fell on good ground, and did yield fruit that sprang up and increased; and brought forth, some thirty, and some sixty, and some an hundred.

9 And he said unto them, He that hath ears to hear, let him hear.

The Purpose of Parables
(Matt. 13:10–17; Luke 8:9, 10)

10 [a]And when he was alone, they that were about him with the twelve asked of him the parable.

11 And he said unto them, Unto you it is given to [a]know the mystery of the kingdom of God: but unto [b]them that are without, all *these* things are done in parables:

12 [a]That SEEING THEY MAY SEE, AND NOT PERCEIVE; AND HEARING THEY MAY HEAR, AND NOT UNDERSTAND; LEST AT ANY TIME THEY SHOULD BE CONVERTED, AND *THEIR* SINS SHOULD BE FORGIVEN THEM.

The Parable of the Sower Explained
(Matt. 13:18–23; Luke 8:11–15)

13 And he said unto them, Know ye not this parable? and how then will ye know all parables?

14 [a]The sower soweth the word.

15 And these are they by the way side, where the word is sown; but when they have heard, Satan cometh immediately, and taketh away the word that was sown in their hearts.

16 And these are they likewise which are sown on stony ground; who, when they have heard the word, immediately receive it with gladness;

17 And have no root in themselves, and so endure but for a time: afterward, when affliction or persecution ariseth for the word's sake, immediately they are offended.

18 And these are they which are sown among thorns; such as hear the word,

19 And the [a]cares of this world, [b]and the deceitfulness of riches, and the lusts of other things entering in, choke the word, and it becometh unfruitful.

20 And these are they which are sown on good ground; such as hear the word, and receive *it*, and bring forth [a]fruit, some thirtyfold, some sixty, and some an hundred.

Light Under a Basket
(Luke 8:16–18)

21 [a]And he said unto them, Is a candle brought to be put under a bushel, or under a bed? and not to be set on a candlestick?

22 [a]For there is nothing hid, which shall not be manifested; neither was any thing kept secret, but that it should come abroad.

23 [a]If any man have ears to hear, let him hear.

24 And he said unto them, Take heed what ye hear: [a]with what measure ye mete, it shall be measured to you: and unto you that hear shall more be given.

25 [a]For he that hath, to him shall be given:

2 [a]Mark 12:38
10 [a]Matt. 13:10; Luke 8:9
11 [a][Matt. 11:25; 1 Cor. 2:10–16; 2 Cor. 4:6] [b][1 Cor. 5:12, 13; Col. 4:5; 1 Thess. 4:12; 1 Tim. 3:7]
12 [a]Is. 6:9, 10; 43:8; Jer. 5:21; Ezek. 12:2; Matt. 13:14; Luke 8:10; John 12:40; Rom. 11:8
14 [a]Matt. 13:18–23; Luke 8:11–15
19 [a]Luke 21:34 [b]Prov. 23:5; Eccl. 5:13; Luke 18:24; 1 Tim. 6:9, 10, 17
20 [a][John 15:2, 5; Rom. 7:4]
21 [a]Matt. 5:15; Luke 8:16; 11:33
22 [a]Eccl. 12:14; Matt. 10:26, 27; Luke 12:3; [1 Cor. 4:5]
23 [a]Matt. 11:15; 13:9, 43; Mark 4:9; Luke 8:8; 14:35; Rev. 3:6, 13, 22; 13:9
24 [a]Matt. 7:2; Luke 6:38; 2 Cor. 9:6
25 [a]Matt. 13:12; 25:29; Luke 8:18; 19:26

NKJV

the whole multitude was on the land facing the sea.

2 Then He taught them many things by parables, [a]and said to them in His teaching:

3 "Listen! Behold, a sower went out to sow.

4 "And it happened, as he sowed, *that* some *seed* fell by the wayside; and the birds *of the air came and devoured it.

5 "Some fell on stony ground, where it did not have much earth; and immediately it sprang up because it had no depth of earth.

6 "But when the sun was up it was scorched, and because it had no root it withered away.

7 "And some *seed* fell among thorns; and the thorns grew up and choked it, and it yielded no crop.

8 "But other *seed* fell on good ground and yielded a crop that sprang up, increased and produced: some thirtyfold, some sixty, and some a hundred."

9 And He said *to them, "He who has ears to hear, let him hear!"

The Purpose of Parables
(Matt. 13:10–17; Luke 8:9, 10)

10 [a]But when He was alone, those around Him with the twelve asked Him about the parable.

11 And He said to them, "To you it has been given to [a]know the mystery of the kingdom of God; but to [b]those who are outside, all things come in parables,

12 "so that

[a]'Seeing they may see and not perceive,
And hearing they may hear and not understand;
Lest they should turn,
And their sins be forgiven them.'"

The Parable of the Sower Explained
(Matt. 13:18–23; Luke 8:11–15)

13 And He said to them, "Do you not understand this parable? How then will you understand all the parables?

14 [a]"The sower sows the word.

15 "And these are the ones by the wayside where the word is sown. When they hear, Satan comes immediately and takes away the word that was sown in their hearts.

16 "These likewise are the ones sown on stony ground who, when they hear the word, immediately receive it with gladness;

17 "and they have no root in themselves, and so endure only for a time. Afterward, when tribulation or persecution arises for the word's sake, immediately they stumble.

18 "Now these are the ones sown among thorns; *they are* the ones who hear the word,

19 "and the [a]cares of this world, [b]the deceitfulness of riches, and the desires for other things entering in choke the word, and it becomes unfruitful.

20 "But these are the ones sown on good ground, those who hear the word, accept *it*, and bear [a]fruit: some thirtyfold, some sixty, and some a hundred."

Light Under a Basket
(Luke 8:16–18)

21 [a]Also He said to them, "Is a lamp brought to be put under a basket or under a bed? Is it not to be set on a lampstand?

22 [a]"For there is nothing hidden which will not be revealed, nor has anything been kept secret but that it should come to light.

23 [a]"If anyone has ears to hear, let him hear."

24 Then He said to them, "Take heed what you hear. [a]With the same measure you use, it will be measured to you; and to you who hear, more will be given.

25 [a]"For whoever has, to him more will be

*

4:4 NU, M omit *of the air*
4:9 NU, M omit *to them*

KJV

and he that hath not, from him shall be taken even that which he hath.

The Parable of the Growing Seed

26 And he said, [a]So is the kingdom of God, as if a man should cast seed into the ground;

27 And should sleep, and rise night and day, and the seed should spring and [a]grow up, he knoweth not how.

28 For the earth [a]bringeth forth fruit of herself; first the blade, then the ear, after that the full corn in the ear.

29 But when the fruit is brought forth, immediately [a]he putteth in the sickle, because the harvest is come.

The Parable of the Mustard Seed
(Matt. 13:31, 32; Luke 13:18, 19)

30 And he said, [a]Whereunto shall we liken the kingdom of God? or with what comparison shall we compare it?

31 *It is* like a grain of mustard seed, which, when it is sown in the earth, is less than all the seeds that be in the earth:

Jesus' Use of Parables

32 But when it is sown, it groweth up, and becometh greater than all herbs, and shooteth out great branches; so that the fowls of the air may lodge under the shadow of it.

33 [a]And with many such parables spake he the word unto them, as they were able to hear *it.*

34 But without a parable spake he not unto them: and when they were alone, he [a]expounded all things to his disciples.

Wind and Wave Obey Jesus
(Matt. 8:23–27; Luke 8:22–25)

35 [a]And the same day, when the even was come, he saith unto them, Let us pass over unto the other side.

36 And when they had sent away the multitude, they took him even as he was in the ship. And there were also with him other little ships.

37 And there arose a great storm of wind, and the waves beat into the ship, so that it was now full.

38 And he was in the hinder part of the ship, asleep on a pillow: and they awake him, and say unto him, [a]Master, [b]carest thou not that we perish?

39 And he arose, and [a]rebuked the wind, and said unto the sea, [b]Peace, be still. And the wind ceased, and there was a great calm.

40 And he said unto them, Why are ye so fearful? [a]how is it that ye have no faith?

41 And they feared exceedingly, and said one to another, What manner of man is this, that even the wind and the sea obey him?

A Demon-Possessed Man Healed
(Matt. 8:28—9:1; Luke 8:26–39)

5 And [a]they came over unto the other side of the sea, into the country of the Gadarenes.

2 And when he was come out of the ship, immediately there met him out of the tombs a man with an [a]unclean spirit,

3 Who had *his* dwelling among the tombs; and no man could bind him, no, not with chains:

4 Because that he had been often bound with fetters and chains, and the chains had been plucked asunder by him, and the fetters broken in pieces: neither could any *man* tame him.

5 And always, night and day, he was in the mountains, and in the tombs, crying, and cutting himself with stones.

6 But when he saw Jesus afar off, he ran and worshipped him,

7 And cried with a loud voice, and said, What have I to do with thee, Jesus, *thou* Son of the most high God? I [a]adjure thee by God, that thou torment me not.

26 [a][Matt. 13:24–30, 36–43]; Luke 8:1
27 [a][2 Cor. 3:18; 2 Pet. 3:18]
28 [a][John 12:24]
29 [a][Mark 13:30, 39]; Rev. 14:15
30 [a]Matt. 13:31, 32; Luke 13:18, 19; [Acts 2:41; 4:4; 5:14; 19:20]
33 [a]Matt. 13:34, 35; [John 16:12]
34 [a]Luke 24:27, 45
35 [a]Matt. 8:18, 23–27; Luke 8:22, 25
38 [a][Matt. 23:8–10] [b]Ps. 44:23
39 [a]Mark 9:25; Luke 4:39 [b]Ps. 65:7; 89:9; 93:4; 104:6, 7; Matt. 8:26; Luke 8:24
40 [a]Matt. 14:31, 32; Luke 8:25

CHAPTER 5

1 [a]Matt. 8:28–34; Luke 8:26–37
2 [a]Mark 1:23; 7:25; [Rev. 16:13, 14]
7 [a]Matt. 26:63; Mark 1:24; Acts 19:13

NKJV

given; but whoever does not have, even what he has will be taken away from him."

The Parable of the Growing Seed

26 And He said, [a]"The kingdom of God is as if a man should scatter seed on the ground,

27 "and should sleep by night and rise by day, and the seed should sprout and [a]grow, he himself does not know how.

28 "For the earth [a]yields crops by itself: first the blade, then the head, after that the full grain in the head.

29 "But when the grain ripens, immediately [a]he puts in the sickle, because the harvest has come."

The Parable of the Mustard Seed
(Matt. 13:31, 32; Luke 13:18, 19)

30 Then He said, [a]"To what shall we liken the kingdom of God? Or with what parable shall we picture it?

31 "*It is* like a mustard seed which, when it is sown on the ground, is smaller than all the seeds on earth;

32 "but when it is sown, it grows up and becomes greater than all herbs, and shoots out large branches, so that the birds of the air may nest under its shade."

Jesus' Use of Parables

33 [a]And with many such parables He spoke the word to them as they were able to hear *it.*

34 But without a parable He did not speak to them. And when they were alone, [a]He explained all things to His disciples.

Wind and Wave Obey Jesus
(Matt. 8:23–27; Luke 8:22–25)

35 [a]On the same day, when evening had come, He said to them, "Let us cross over to the other side."

36 Now when they had left the multitude, they took Him along in the boat as He was. And other little boats were also with Him.

37 And a great windstorm arose, and the waves beat into the boat, so that it was already filling.

38 But He was in the stern, asleep on a pillow. And they awoke Him and said to Him, [a]"Teacher, [b]do You not care that we are perishing?"

39 Then He arose and [a]rebuked the wind, and said to the sea, [b]"Peace, be still!" And the wind ceased and there was a great calm.

40 But He said to them, "Why are you so fearful? [a]How* *is it* that you have no faith?"

41 And they feared exceedingly, and said to one another, "Who can this be, that even the wind and the sea obey Him!"

A Demon-Possessed Man Healed
(Matt. 8:28—9:1; Luke 8:26–39)

5 Then [a]they came to the other side of the sea, to the country of the *Gadarenes.

2 And when He had come out of the boat, immediately there met Him out of the tombs a man with an [a]unclean spirit,

3 who had *his* dwelling among the tombs; and no one could bind *him, not even with chains,

4 because he had often been bound with shackles and chains. And the chains had been pulled apart by him, and the shackles broken in pieces; neither could anyone tame him.

5 And always, night and day, he was in the mountains and in the tombs, crying out and cutting himself with stones.

6 When he saw Jesus from afar, he ran and worshiped Him.

7 And he cried out with a loud voice and said, "What have I to do with You, Jesus, Son of the Most High God? I [a]implore You by God that You do not torment me."

*______

4:40 NU *Have you still no faith?*
5:1 NU *Gerasenes*
5:3 NU adds *anymore*

KJV

8 For he said unto him, [a]Come out of the man, *thou* unclean spirit.
9 And he asked him, What *is* thy name? And he answered, saying, My name *is* Legion: for we are many.
10 And he besought him much that he would not send them away out of the country.
11 Now there was there nigh unto the mountains a great herd of [a]swine feeding.
12 And all the devils besought him, saying, Send us into the swine, that we may enter into them.
13 And forth with Jesus gave them leave. And the unclean spirits went out, and entered into the swine: and the herd ran violently down a steep place into the sea, (they were about two thousand;) and were choked in the sea.
14 And they that fed the swine fled, and told *it* in the city, and in the country. And they went out to see what it was that was done.
15 And they come to Jesus, and see him that was [a]possessed with the devil, and had the legion, [b]sitting, and [c]clothed, and in his right mind: and they were afraid.
16 And they that saw *it* told them how it befell to him that was possessed with the devil, and *also* concerning the swine.
17 And [a]they began to pray him to depart out of their coasts.
18 And when he was come into the ship, [a]he that had been possessed with the devil prayed him that he might be with him.
19 Howbeit Jesus suffered him not, but saith unto him, Go home to thy friends, and tell them how great things the Lord hath done for thee, and hath had compassion on thee.
20 And he departed, and began to [a]publish in Decapolis how great things Jesus had done for him: and all *men* did [b]marvel.

A Girl Restored to Life and a Woman Healed *(Matt. 9:18–26; Luke 8:40–56)*

21 [a]And when Jesus was passed over again by ship unto the other side, much people gathered unto him: and he was nigh unto the sea.
22 [a]And, behold, there cometh one of the rulers of the synagogue, Jairus by name; and when he saw him, he fell at his feet,
23 And besought him greatly, saying, My little daughter lieth at the point of death: *I pray thee,* come and [a]lay thy hands on her, that she may be healed; and she shall live.
24 And *Jesus* went with him; and much people followed him, and thronged him.
25 And a certain woman, [a]which had an issue of blood twelve years,
26 And had suffered many things of many physicians, and had spent all that she had, and was nothing bettered, but rather grew worse,
27 When she had heard of Jesus, came in the press behind, and [a]touched his garment.
28 For she said, If I may touch but his clothes, I shall be whole.
29 And straightway the fountain of her blood was dried up; and she felt in *her* body that she was healed of that plague.
30 And Jesus, immediately knowing in himself that [a]virtue had gone out of him, turned him about in the press, and said, Who touched my clothes?
31 And his disciples said unto him, Thou seest the multitude thronging thee, and sayest thou, Who touched me?
32 And he looked round about to see her that had done this thing.
33 But the woman [a]fearing and trembling, knowing what was done in her, came and fell down before him, and told him all the truth.
34 And he said unto her, Daughter, [a]thy faith hath made thee whole; [b]go in peace, and be whole of thy plague.

8 [a]Mark 1:25; 9:25; [Acts 16:18] **11** [a]Lev. 11:7, 8; Deut. 14:8; Luke 15:15, 16 **15** [a]Matt. 4:24; 8:16; Mark 1:32 [b]Luke 10:39 [c][Is. 61:10] **17** [a]Matt. 8:34; Acts 16:39 **18** [a]Luke 8:38, 39 **20** [a]Ex. 15:2; Ps. 66:16 [b]Matt. 9:8, 33; John 5:20; 7:21; Acts 3:12; 4:13 **21** [a]Matt. 9:1; Luke 8:40 **22** [a]Matt. 9:18–26; Luke 8:41–56; Acts 13:15 **23** [a]Matt. 8:15; Mark 6:5; 7:32; 8:23, 25; 16:18; Luke 4:40; Acts 9:17; 28:8 **25** [a]Lev. 15:19, 25; Matt. 9:20 **27** [a]Matt. 14:35, 36; Mark 3:10; 6:56 **30** [a]Luke 6:19; 8:46 **33** [a][Ps. 89:7] **34** [a]Matt. 9:22; Mark 10:52; Acts 14:9 [b]1 Sam. 1:17; 20:42; 2 Kin. 5:19; Luke 7:50; 8:48; Acts 16:36; [James 2:16]

NKJV

8 For He said to him, [a]"Come out of the man, unclean spirit!"
9 Then He asked him, "What *is* your name?" And he answered, saying, "My name *is* Legion; for we are many."
10 Also he begged Him earnestly that He would not send them out of the country.
11 Now a large herd of [a]swine was feeding there near the mountains.
12 So all the demons begged Him, saying, "Send us to the swine, that we may enter them."
13 And *at once Jesus gave them permission. Then the unclean spirits went out and entered the swine (there were about two thousand); and the herd ran violently down the steep place into the sea, and drowned in the sea.
14 So those who fed the swine fled, and they told *it* in the city and in the country. And they went out to see what it was that had happened.
15 Then they came to Jesus, and saw the one *who had been* [a]demon-possessed and had the legion, [b]sitting and [c]clothed and in his right mind. And they were afraid.
16 And those who saw it told them how it happened to him *who had been* demon-possessed, and about the swine.
17 Then [a]they began to plead with Him to depart from their region.
18 And when He got into the boat, [a]he who had been demon-possessed begged Him that he might be with Him.
19 However, Jesus did not permit him, but said to him, "Go home to your friends, and tell them what great things the Lord has done for you, and how He has had compassion on you."
20 And he departed and began to [a]proclaim in Decapolis all that Jesus had done for him; and all [b]marveled.

A Girl Restored to Life and a Woman Healed *(Matt. 9:18–26; Luke 8:40–56)*

21 [a]Now when Jesus had crossed over again by boat to the other side, a great multitude gathered to Him; and He was by the sea.
22 [a]And behold, one of the rulers of the synagogue came, Jairus by name. And when he saw Him, he fell at His feet
23 and begged Him earnestly, saying, "My little daughter lies at the point of death. Come and [a]lay Your hands on her, that she may be healed, and she will live."
24 So *Jesus* went with him, and a great multitude followed Him and thronged Him.
25 Now a certain woman [a]had a flow of blood for twelve years,
26 and had suffered many things from many physicians. She had spent all that she had and was no better, but rather grew worse.
27 When she heard about Jesus, she came behind *Him* in the crowd and [a]touched His garment.
28 For she said, "If only I may touch His clothes, I shall be made well."
29 Immediately the fountain of her blood was dried up, and she felt in *her* body that she was healed of the affliction.
30 And Jesus, immediately knowing in Himself that [a]power had gone out of Him, turned around in the crowd and said, "Who touched My clothes?"
31 But His disciples said to Him, "You see the multitude thronging You, and You say, 'Who touched Me?' "
32 And He looked around to see her who had done this thing.
33 But the woman, [a]fearing and trembling, knowing what had happened to her, came and fell down before Him and told Him the whole truth.
34 And He said to her, "Daughter, [a]your faith has made you well. [b]Go in peace, and be healed of your affliction."

*________
5:13 NU *He gave*

KJV

35 [a]While he yet spake, there came from the ruler of the synagogue's *house certain* which said, Thy daughter is dead: why troublest thou the Master any further?

36 As soon as Jesus heard the word that was spoken, he saith unto the ruler of the synagogue, Be not afraid, only [a]believe.

37 And he suffered no man to follow him, save Peter, and James, and John the brother of James.

38 And he cometh to the house of the ruler of the synagogue, and seeth the tumult, and them that [a]wept and wailed greatly.

39 And when he was come in, he saith unto them, Why make ye this ado, and weep? the damsel is not dead, but [a]sleepeth.

40 And they laughed him to scorn. [a]But when he had put them all out, he taketh the father and the mother of the damsel, and them that were with him, and entereth in where the damsel was lying.

41 And he took the damsel by the hand, and said unto her, Talitha cumi; which is, being interpreted, Damsel, I say unto thee, arise.

42 And straightway the damsel arose, and walked; for she was *of the age* of twelve years. And they were [a]astonished with a great astonishment.

43 And [a]he charged them straitly that no man should know it; and commanded that something should be given her to eat.

Jesus Rejected at Nazareth
(Matt. 13:53–58; Luke 4:16–30)

6 And [a]he went out from thence, and came into his own country; and his disciples follow him.

2 And when the sabbath day was come, he began to teach in the synagogue: and many hearing *him* were [a]astonished, saying, [b]From whence hath this *man* these things? and what wisdom *is* this which is given unto him, that even such mighty works are wrought by his hands?

3 Is not this the carpenter, the son of Mary, [a]the brother of James, and Joses, and of Juda, and Simon? and are not his sisters here with us? And they [b]were offended at him.

4 But Jesus said unto them, [a]A prophet is not without honour, but in his own country, and among his own kin, and in his own house.

5 [a]And he could there do no mighty work, save that he laid his hands upon a few sick folk, and healed *them*.

6 And [a]he marvelled because of their unbelief. [b]And he went round about the villages, teaching.

Sending Out the Twelve
(Matt. 10:1, 5–15, Luke 9:1–6)

7 [a]And he called *unto him* the twelve, and began to send them forth by [b]two and two; and gave them power over unclean spirits;

8 And commanded them that they should take nothing for *their* journey, save a staff only; no scrip, no bread, no money in *their* purse:

9 But [a]*be* shod with sandals; and not put on two coats.

10 [a]And he said unto them, In what place soever ye enter into an house, there abide till ye depart from that place.

11 [a]And whosoever shall not receive you, nor hear you, when ye depart thence, [b]shake off the dust under your feet for a testimony against them. Verily I say unto you, It shall be more tolerable for Sodom and Gomorrha in the day of judgment, than for that city.

12 And they went out, and preached that men should repent.

13 And they cast out many devils, [a]and anointed with oil many that were sick, and healed *them*.

NKJV

35 [a]While He was still speaking, *some* came from the ruler of the synagogue's *house* who said, "Your daughter is dead. Why trouble the Teacher any further?"

36 As soon as Jesus heard the word that was spoken, He said to the ruler of the synagogue, "Do not be afraid; only [a]believe."

37 And He permitted no one to follow Him except Peter, James, and John the brother of James.

38 Then He came to the house of the ruler of the synagogue, and saw a tumult and those who [a]wept and wailed loudly.

39 When He came in, He said to them, "Why make this commotion and weep? The child is not dead, but [a]sleeping."

40 And they ridiculed Him. [a]But when He had put them all outside, He took the father and the mother of the child, and those *who were* with Him, and entered where the child was lying.

41 Then He took the child by the hand, and said to her, "Talitha, cumi," which is translated, "Little girl, I say to you, arise."

42 Immediately the girl arose and walked, for she was twelve years *of age*. And they were [a]overcome with great amazement.

43 But [a]He commanded them strictly that no one should know it, and said that *something* should be given her to eat.

Jesus Rejected at Nazareth
(Matt. 13:53–58; Luke 4:16–30)

6 Then [a]He went out from there and came to His own country, and His disciples followed Him.

2 And when the Sabbath had come, He began to teach in the synagogue. And many hearing *Him* were [a]astonished, saying, [b]"Where *did* this Man *get* these things? And what wisdom *is* this which is given to Him, that such mighty works are performed by His hands!

3 "Is this not the carpenter, the Son of Mary, and [a]brother of James, Joses, Judas, and Simon? And are not His sisters here with us?" So they [b]were offended at Him.

4 But Jesus said to them, [a]"A prophet is not without honor except in his own country, among his own relatives, and in his own house."

5 [a]Now He could do no mighty work there, except that He laid His hands on a few sick people and healed *them*.

6 And [a]He marveled because of their unbelief. [b]Then He went about the villages in a circuit, teaching.

Sending Out the Twelve
(Matt. 10:1, 5–15; Luke 9:1–6)

7 [a]And He called the twelve to *Himself*, and began to send them out [b]two *by* two, and gave them power over unclean spirits.

8 He commanded them to take nothing for the journey except a staff—no bag, no bread, no copper in *their* money belts—

9 but [a]to wear sandals, and not to put on two tunics.

10 [a]Also He said to them, "In whatever place you enter a house, stay there till you depart from that place.

11 [a]"And *whoever will not receive you nor hear you, when you depart from there, [b]shake off the dust under your feet as a testimony against them. *Assuredly, I say to you, it will be more tolerable for Sodom and Gomorrah in the day of judgment than for that city!"

12 So they went out and preached that *people* should repent.

13 And they cast out many demons, [a]and anointed with oil many who were sick, and healed *them*.

---

35 [a]Luke 8:49 **36** [a][Mark 9:23; John 11:40] **38** [a]Mark 16:10; Acts 9:39 **39** [a]John 11:4, 11 **40** [a]Acts 9:40 **42** [a]Mark 1:27; 7:37 **43** [a][Matt. 8:4; 12:16–19; 17:9]; Mark 3:12

CHAPTER 6

1 [a]Matt. 13:54; Luke 4:16 **2** [a]Matt. 7:28; Luke 4:32; Acts 4:13 [b]John 6:42 **3** [a]Matt. 12:46; Gal. 1:19 [b][Matt. 11:6] **4** [a]Matt. 13:57; Luke 4:24; John 4:44 **5** [a]Gen. 19:22; 32:25; Matt. 13:58; [Mark 9:23] **6** [a]Is. 59:16; Matt. 17:17, 20; [Heb. 3:18, 19; 4:2] [b]Matt. 9:35; Luke 13:22; Acts 10:38; Eph. 2:17 **7** [a]Matt. 10:1; 28:19, 20; Mark 3:13, 14; Luke 9:1 [b][Eccl. 4:9, 10] **9** [a][Eph. 6:15] **10** [a]Matt. 10:11; Luke 9:4; 10:7, 8 **11** [a]Matt. 10:14; Luke 10:10 [b]Acts 13:51; 18:6 **13** [a][James 5:14]

*________

6:11 NU *whatever place* • NU omits the rest of v. 11.

KJV

John the Baptist Beheaded
(Matt. 14:1–12; Luke 9:7–9)

14 [a]And king Herod heard *of him;* (for his name was spread abroad:) and he said, That John the Baptist was risen from the dead, and therefore [b]mighty works do shew forth themselves in him.

15 [a]Others said, That it is Elias. And others said, That it is a prophet, [b]or as one of the prophets.

16 [a]But when Herod heard *thereof,* he said, It is John, whom I beheaded: he is risen from the dead.

17 For Herod himself had sent forth and laid hold upon John, and bound him in prison for Herodias' sake, his brother Philip's wife: for he had married her.

18 For John had said unto Herod, [a]It is not lawful for thee to have thy brother's wife.

19 Therefore Herodias had a quarrel against him, and would have killed him; but she could not:

20 For Herod [a]feared John, knowing that he was a just man and an holy, and observed him; and when he heard him, he did many things, and heard him gladly.

21 [a]And when a convenient day was come, that Herod [b]on his birthday made a supper to his lords, high captains, and chief *estates* of Galilee;

22 And when the daughter of the said Herodias came in, and danced, and pleased Herod and them that sat with him, the king said unto the damsel, Ask of me whatsoever thou wilt, and I will give *it* thee.

23 And he sware unto her, [a]Whatsoever thou shalt ask of me, I will give *it* thee, unto the half of my kingdom.

24 And she went forth, and said unto her mother, What shall I ask? And she said, The head of John the Baptist.

25 And she came in straightway with haste unto the king, and asked, saying, I will that thou give me by and by in a charger the head of John the Baptist.

26 [a]And the king was exceeding sorry; *yet* for his oath's sake, and for their sakes which sat with him, he would not reject her.

27 And immediately the king sent an executioner, and commanded his head to be brought: and he went and beheaded him in the prison,

28 And brought his head in a charger, and gave it to the damsel: and the damsel gave it to her mother.

29 And when his disciples heard *of it,* they came and [a]took up his corpse, and laid it in a tomb.

Feeding the Five Thousand
(Matt. 14:13–21; Luke 9:10–17; John 6:1–14)

30 [a]And the apostles gathered themselves together unto Jesus, and told him all things, both what they had done, and what they had taught.

31 [a]And he said unto them, Come ye yourselves apart into a desert place, and rest a while: for [b]there were many coming and going, and they had no leisure so much as to eat.

32 [a]And they departed into a desert place by ship privately.

33 And the people saw them departing, and many [a]knew him, and ran afoot thither out of all cities, and outwent them, and came together unto him.

34 [a]And Jesus, when he came out, saw much people, and was moved with compassion toward them, because they were as [b]sheep not having a shepherd: and [c]he began to teach them many things.

35 [a]And when the day was now far spent, his disciples came unto him, and said, This is a desert place, and now the time *is* far passed:

36 Send them away, that they may go into

NKJV

John the Baptist Beheaded
(Matt. 14:1–12; Luke 9:7–9)

14 [a]Now King Herod heard *of Him,* for His name had become well known. And he said, "John the Baptist is risen from the dead, and therefore [b]these powers are at work in him."

15 [a]Others said, "It is Elijah." And others said, "It is the Prophet, [b]or* like one of the prophets."

16 [a]But when Herod heard, he said, "This is John, whom I beheaded; he has been raised from the dead!"

17 For Herod himself had sent and laid hold of John, and bound him in prison for the sake of Herodias, his brother Philip's wife; for he had married her.

18 Because John had said to Herod, [a]"It is not lawful for you to have your brother's wife."

19 Therefore Herodias held it against him and wanted to kill him, but she could not;

20 for Herod [a]feared John, knowing that he *was* a just and holy man, and he protected him. And when he heard him, he *did many things, and heard him gladly.

21 [a]Then an opportune day came when Herod [b]on his birthday gave a feast for his nobles, the high officers, and the chief *men* of Galilee.

22 And when Herodias' daughter herself came in and danced, and pleased Herod and those who sat with him, the king said to the girl, "Ask me whatever you want, and I will give *it* to you."

23 He also swore to her, [a]"Whatever you ask me, I will give you, up to half my kingdom."

24 So she went out and said to her mother, "What shall I ask?" And she said, "The head of John the Baptist!"

25 Immediately she came in with haste to the king and asked, saying, "I want you to give me at once the head of John the Baptist on a platter."

26 [a]And the king was exceedingly sorry; *yet,* because of the oaths and because of those who sat with him, he did not want to refuse her.

27 Immediately the king sent an executioner and commanded his head to be brought. And he went and beheaded him in prison,

28 brought his head on a platter, and gave it to the girl; and the girl gave it to her mother.

29 When his disciples heard *of it,* they came and [a]took away his corpse and laid it in a tomb.

Feeding the Five Thousand
(Matt. 14:13–21; Luke 9:10–17; John 6:1–14)

30 [a]Then the apostles gathered to Jesus and told Him all things, both what they had done and what they had taught.

31 [a]And He said to them, "Come aside by yourselves to a deserted place and rest a while." For [b]there were many coming and going, and they did not even have time to eat.

32 [a]So they departed to a deserted place in the boat by themselves.

33 But *the multitudes saw them departing, and many [a]knew Him and ran there on foot from all the cities. They arrived before them and came together to Him.

34 [a]And Jesus, when He came out, saw a great multitude and was moved with compassion for them, because they were like [b]sheep not having a shepherd. So [c]He began to teach them many things.

35 [a]When the day was now far spent, His disciples came to Him and said, "This is a deserted place, and already the hour *is* late.

36 "Send them away, that they may go into

14 [a]Matt. 14:1–12; Mark 6:14–16; Luke 9:7–9 [b]Luke 19:37
15 [a]Matt. 16:14; Mark 8:28; Luke 9:19 [b]Matt. 21:11
16 [a]Matt. 14:2; Luke 3:19
18 [a]Lev. 18:16; 20:21
20 [a]Matt. 14:5; 21:26
21 [a]Matt. 14:6 [b]Gen. 40:20
23 [a]Esth. 5:3, 6; 7:2
26 [a]Matt. 14:9
29 [a]1 Kin. 13:29, 30; Matt. 27:58–61; Acts 8:2
30 [a]Luke 9:10
31 [a]Matt. 14:13 [b]Mark 3:20
32 [a]Matt. 14:13–21; Luke 9:10–17; John 6:5–13
33 [a][Col. 1:6]
34 [a]Matt. 9:36; 14:14; [Heb. 5:2] [b]Num. 27:17; 1 Kin. 22:17; 2 Chr. 18:16; Zech. 10:2 [c][Is. 48:17; 61:1–3]; Luke 9:11
35 [a]Matt. 14:15; Luke 9:12

---

*

6:15 NU, M *a prophet, like one*
6:20 NU *was very perplexed, yet*
6:33 NU, M *they*

KJV

the country round about, and into the villages, and buy themselves bread: for they have nothing to eat.

37 He answered and said unto them, Give ye them to eat. And they say unto him, [a]Shall we go and buy two hundred pennyworth of bread, and give them to eat?

38 He saith unto them, How many loaves have ye? go and see. And when they knew, they say, [a]Five, and two fishes.

39 And he [a]commanded them to make all sit down by companies upon the green grass.

40 And they sat down in ranks, by hundreds, and by fifties.

41 And when he had taken the five loaves and the two fishes, he [a]looked up to heaven, [b]and blessed, and brake the loaves, and gave *them* to his disciples to set before them; and the two fishes divided he among them all.

42 And they did all eat, and were filled.

43 And they took up twelve baskets full of the fragments, and of the fishes.

44 And they that did eat of the loaves were about five thousand men.

Jesus Walks on the Sea
(*Matt. 14:22–33; John 6:15–21*)

45 [a]And straightway he constrained his disciples to get into the ship, and to go to the other side before unto Bethsaida, while he sent away the people.

46 And when he had sent them away, he [a]departed into a mountain to pray.

47 And when even was come, the ship was in the midst of the sea, and he alone on the land.

48 And he saw them toiling in rowing; for the wind was contrary unto them: and about the fourth watch of the night he cometh unto them, walking upon the sea, and [a]would have passed by them.

49 But when they saw him walking upon the sea, they supposed it had been a [a]spirit, and cried out:

50 For they all saw him, and were troubled. And immediately he talked with them, and saith unto them, [a]Be of good cheer: it is I; be not [b]afraid.

51 And he went up unto them into the ship; and the wind [a]ceased: and they were sore [b]amazed in themselves beyond measure, and wondered.

52 For [a]they considered not *the miracle* of the loaves: for their [b]heart was hardened.

Many Touch Him and Are Made Well
(*Matt. 14:34–36*)

53 [a]And when they had passed over, they came into the land of Gennesaret, and drew to the shore.

54 And when they were come out of the ship, straightway they knew him,

55 And ran through that whole region round about, and began to carry about in beds those that were sick, where they heard he was.

56 And whithersoever he entered, into villages, or cities, or country, they laid the sick in the streets, and besought him that [a]they might touch if it were but the [b]border of his garment: and as many as touched him were made whole.

Defilement Comes from Within
(*Matt. 15:1–20*)

7 Then [a]came together unto him the Pharisees, and certain of the scribes, which came from Jerusalem.

2 And when they saw some of his disciples eat bread with defiled, that is to say, with [a]unwashen, hands, they found fault.

3 For the Pharisees, and all the Jews, except they wash *their* hands oft, eat not, holding the [a]tradition of the elders.

4 And *when they come* from the market, except they wash, they eat not. And many other

---

37 [a]Num. 11:13, 22; 2 Kin. 4:43
38 [a]Matt. 14:17; Luke 9:13; John 6:9
39 [a]Matt. 15:35; Mark 8:6
41 [a]John 11:41, 42 [b]1 Sam. 9:13; Matt. 15:36; 26:26; Mark 8:7; Luke 24:30
45 [a]Matt. 14:22–32; John 6:15–21
46 [a]Mark 1:35; Luke 5:16
48 [a]Luke 24:28
49 [a]Matt. 14:26; Luke 24:37
50 [a]Matt. 9:2; John 16:33 [b]Is. 41:10
51 [a]Ps. 107:29 [b]Mark 1:27; 2:12; 5:42; 7:37
52 [a]Matt. 16:9–11; Mark 8:17, 18 [b]Is. 63:17; Mark 3:5; 16:14
53 [a]Matt. 14:34–36; John 6:24, 25
56 [a]Matt. 9:20; Mark 5:27, 28; [Acts 19:12] [b]Num. 15:38, 39

CHAPTER 7

1 [a]Matt. 15:1–20
2 [a]Matt. 15:20
3 [a]Mark 7:5, 8, 9, 13; Gal. 1:14; 1 Pet. 1:18

*

6:36 NU *something to eat* and omits the rest of v. 36.
6:44 NU, M omit *about*
7:2 NU omits *when* • NU omits *they found fault*

NKJV

the surrounding country and villages and buy themselves *bread; for they have nothing to eat."

37 But He answered and said to them, "You give them something to eat." And they said to Him, [a]"Shall we go and buy two hundred denarii worth of bread and give them *something* to eat?"

38 But He said to them, "How many loaves do you have? Go and see." And when they found out they said, [a]"Five, and two fish."

39 Then He [a]commanded them to make them all sit down in groups on the green grass.

40 So they sat down in ranks, in hundreds and in fifties.

41 And when He had taken the five loaves and the two fish, He [a]looked up to heaven, [b]blessed and broke the loaves, and gave *them* to His disciples to set before them; and the two fish He divided among *them* all.

42 So they all ate and were filled.

43 And they took up twelve baskets full of fragments and of the fish.

44 Now those who had eaten the loaves were *about five thousand men.

Jesus Walks on the Sea
(*Matt. 14:22–33; John 6:15–21*)

45 [a]Immediately He made His disciples get into the boat and go before Him to the other side, to Bethsaida, while He sent the multitude away.

46 And when He had sent them away, He [a]departed to the mountain to pray.

47 Now when evening came, the boat was in the middle of the sea; and He *was* alone on the land.

48 Then He saw them straining at rowing, for the wind was against them. Now about the fourth watch of the night He came to them, walking on the sea, and [a]would have passed them by.

49 And when they saw Him walking on the sea, they supposed it was a [a]ghost, and cried out;

50 for they all saw Him and were troubled. But immediately He talked with them and said to them, [a]"Be of good cheer! It is I; do not be [b]afraid."

51 Then He went up into the boat to them, and the wind [a]ceased. And they were greatly [b]amazed in themselves beyond measure, and marveled.

52 For [a]they had not understood about the loaves, because their [b]heart was hardened.

Many Touch Him and Are Made Well
(*Matt. 14:34–36*)

53 [a]When they had crossed over, they came to the land of Gennesaret and anchored there.

54 And when they came out of the boat, immediately the people recognized Him,

55 ran through that whole surrounding region, and began to carry about on beds those who were sick to wherever they heard He was.

56 Wherever He entered, into villages, cities, or the country, they laid the sick in the marketplaces, and begged Him that [a]they might just touch the [b]hem of His garment. And as many as touched Him were made well.

Defilement Comes from Within
(*Matt. 15:1–20*)

7 Then [a]the Pharisees and some of the scribes came together to Him, having come from Jerusalem.

2 Now *when they saw some of His disciples eat bread with defiled, that is, with [a]unwashed hands, *they found fault.

3 For the Pharisees and all the Jews do not eat unless they wash *their* hands in a special way, holding the [a]tradition of the elders.

4 *When they come* from the marketplace, they do not eat unless they wash. And there are

KJV

things there be, which they have received to hold, *as* the washing of cups, and pots, brasen vessels, and of tables.

5 [a]Then the Pharisees and scribes asked him, Why walk not thy disciples according to the tradition of the elders, but eat bread with unwashen hands?

6 He answered and said unto them, Well hath Esaias prophesied of you [a]hypocrites, as it is written, [b]THIS PEOPLE HONOURETH ME WITH *THEIR* LIPS, BUT THEIR HEART IS FAR FROM ME.

7 HOWBEIT IN VAIN DO THEY WORSHIP ME, TEACHING *FOR* DOCTRINES THE COMMANDMENTS OF MEN.

8 For laying aside the commandment of God, ye hold the tradition of men, *as* the washing of pots and cups: and many other such like things ye do.

9 And he said unto them, Full well ye [a]reject the commandment of God, that ye may keep your own tradition.

10 For Moses said, [a]HONOUR THY FATHER AND THY MOTHER; and, [b]WHOSO CURSETH FATHER OR MOTHER, LET HIM DIE THE DEATH:

11 But ye say, If a man shall say to his father or mother, *It is* [a]Corban, that is to say, a gift, by whatsoever thou mightest be profited by me; *he shall be free.*

12 And ye suffer him no more to do ought for his father or his mother;

13 Making the word of God of none effect through your tradition, which ye have delivered: and many such like things do ye.

14 [a]And when he had called all the people *unto him,* he said unto them, Hearken unto me every one *of you,* and [b]understand:

15 There is nothing from without a man, that entering into him can defile him: but the things which come out of him, those are they that [a]defile the man.

16 [a]If any man have ears to hear, let him hear.

17 [a]And when he was entered into the house from the people, his disciples asked him concerning the parable.

18 And he saith unto them, [a]Are ye so without understanding also? Do ye not perceive, that whatsoever thing from without entereth into the man, *it* cannot defile him;

19 Because it entereth not into his heart, but into the belly, and goeth out into the draught, purging all meats?

20 And he said, [a]That which cometh out of the man, that defileth the man.

21 [a]For from within, out of the heart of men, [b]proceed evil thoughts, [c]adulteries, [d]fornications, murders,

22 Thefts, [a]covetousness, wickedness, [b]deceit, [c]lasciviousness, an evil eye, [d]blasphemy, [e]pride, foolishness:

23 All these evil things come from within, and defile the man.

A Gentile Shows Her Faith
(Matt. 15:21–28)

24 [a]And from thence he arose, and went into the borders of Tyre and Sidon, and entered into an house, and would have no man know *it:* but he could not be [b]hid.

25 For a *certain* woman, whose young daughter had an unclean spirit, heard of him, and came and [a]fell at his feet:

26 The woman was a Greek, a Syrophenician by nation; and she besought him that he would cast forth the devil out of her daughter.

27 But Jesus said unto her, Let the children first be filled: for it is not meet to take the children's bread, and to cast *it* unto the dogs.

28 And she answered and said unto him, Yes,

---

5 [a]Matt. 15:2
6 [a]Matt. 23:13–29 [b]Is. 29:13
9 [a]Prov. 1:25; Jer. 7:23, 24; Is. 24:5
10 [a]Ex. 20:12; Deut. 5:16; Matt. 15:4 [b]Ex. 21:17; Lev. 20:9; Prov. 20:20
11 [a]Matt. 15:5; 23:18
14 [a]Matt. 15:10 [b]Matt. 16:9, 11, 12
15 [a]Is. 59:3; [Heb. 12:15]
16 [a]Matt. 11:15
17 [a]Matt. 15:15
18 [a][Is. 28:9–11; 1 Cor. 3:2; Heb. 5:11–14]
20 [a]Ps. 39:1; [Matt. 12:34–37; James 3:6]
21 [a]Gen. 6:5; 8:21; Prov. 6:18; Jer. 17:9; Matt. 15:19 [b][Gal. 5:19–21] [c]2 Pet. 2:14 [d]1 Thess. 4:3
22 [a]Luke 12:15 [b]Rom. 1:28, 29 [c]1 Pet. 4:3 [d]Rev. 2:9 [e]1 John 2:16
24 [a]Matt. 15:29 [b]Mark 2:1, 2
25 [a]Mark 5:22; John 11:32; Rev. 1:17

NKJV

many other things which they have received and hold, *like* the washing of cups, pitchers, copper vessels, and couches.

5 [a]Then the Pharisees and scribes asked Him, "Why do Your disciples not walk according to the tradition of the elders, but eat bread with unwashed hands?"

6 He answered and said to them, "Well did Isaiah prophesy of you [a]hypocrites, as it is written:

[b]'This people honors Me with their lips,
But their heart is far from Me.
7 *And in vain they worship Me,*
Teaching as doctrines the commandments of men.'

8 "For laying aside the commandment of God, you hold the tradition of men—*the washing of pitchers and cups, and many other such things you do."

9 He said to them, "*All too* well [a]you reject the commandment of God, that you may keep your tradition.

10 "For Moses said, [a]*'Honor your father and your mother'*; and, [b]*'He who curses father or mother, let him be put to death.'*

11 "But you say, 'If a man says to his father or mother, [a]"Whatever profit you might have received from me *is* Corban"—' (that is, a gift *to God*),

12 "then you no longer let him do anything for his father or his mother,

13 "making the word of God of no effect through your tradition which you have handed down. And many such things you do."

14 [a]When He had called all the multitude to *Himself,* He said to them, "Hear Me, everyone, and [b]understand:

15 "There is nothing that enters a man from outside which can defile him; but the things which come out of him, those are the things that [a]defile a man.

16 [a]"If* anyone has ears to hear, let him hear!"

17 [a]When He had entered a house away from the crowd, His disciples asked Him concerning the parable.

18 So He said to them, [a]"Are you thus without understanding also? Do you not perceive that whatever enters a man from outside cannot defile him,

19 "because it does not enter his heart but his stomach, and is eliminated, **thus* purifying all foods?"

20 And He said, [a]"What comes out of a man, that defiles a man.

21 [a]"For from within, out of the heart of men, [b]proceed evil thoughts, [c]adulteries, [d]fornications, murders,

22 "thefts, [a]covetousness, wickedness, [b]deceit, [c]lewdness, an evil eye, [d]blasphemy, [e]pride, foolishness.

23 "All these evil things come from within and defile a man."

A Gentile Shows Her Faith
(Matt. 15:21–28)

24 [a]From there He arose and went to the region of Tyre *and Sidon. And He entered a house and wanted no one to know *it,* but He could not be [b]hidden.

25 For a woman whose young daughter had an unclean spirit heard about Him, and she came and [a]fell at His feet.

26 The woman was a Greek, a Syro-Phoenician by birth, and she kept asking Him to cast the demon out of her daughter.

27 But Jesus said to her, "Let the children be filled first, for it is not good to take the children's bread and throw *it* to the little dogs."

28 And she answered and said to Him, "Yes,

---

*

7:8 NU omits the rest of v. 8. **7:16** NU omits v. 16. **7:19** NU sets off the final phrase as Mark's comment that Jesus has declared all foods clean. **7:24** NU omits *and Sidon*

KJV

Lord: yet the dogs under the table eat of the children's crumbs.
29 And he said unto her, For this saying go
thy way; the devil is gone out of thy daughter.
30 And when she was come to her house, she
found the devil gone out, and her daughter laid
upon the bed.

Jesus Heals a Deaf-Mute
(*Matt. 15:29–31*)

31 [a]And again, departing from the coasts of
Tyre and Sidon, he came unto the sea of Galilee,
through the midst of the coasts of Decapolis.
32 And [a]they bring unto him one that was
deaf, and had an impediment in his speech; and
they beseech him to put his hand upon him.
33 And he took him aside from the multitude,
and put his fingers into his ears, and [a]he spit, and
touched his tongue;
34 And [a]looking up to heaven, [b]he sighed,
and saith unto him, Ephphatha, that is, Be opened.
35 [a]And straightway his ears were opened,
and the string of his tongue was loosed, and he
spake plain.
36 And [a]he charged them that they should
tell no man: but the more he charged them, so
much the more a great deal they published *it;*
37 And were [a]beyond measure astonished,
saying, He hath done all things well: he [b]maketh
both the deaf to hear, and the dumb to speak.

Feeding the Four Thousand
(*Matt. 15:32–39*)

8 In those days [a]the multitude being very great,
and having nothing to eat, Jesus called his
disciples *unto him,* and saith unto them,
2 I have [a]compassion on the multitude, because they have now been with me three days,
and have nothing to eat:
3 And if I send them away fasting to their
own houses, they will faint by the way: for divers
of them came from far.
4 And his disciples answered him, From
whence can a man satisfy these *men* with bread
here in the wilderness?
5 [a]And he asked them, How many loaves
have ye? And they said, Seven.
6 And he commanded the people to sit down
on the ground: and he took the seven loaves, and
gave thanks, and brake, and gave to his disciples
to set before *them;* and they did set *them* before
the people.
7 And they had a few small fishes: and [a]he
blessed, and commanded to set them also before
them.
8 So they did eat, and were filled: and they
took up of the broken *meat* that was left seven
baskets.
9 And they that had eaten were about four
thousand: and he sent them away.
10 And [a]straightway he entered into a ship
with his disciples, and came into the parts of Dalmanutha.

The Pharisees Seek a Sign
(*Matt. 16:1–4*)

11 [a]And the Pharisees came forth, and began
to question with him, seeking of him a sign from
heaven, tempting him.
12 And he [a]sighed deeply in his spirit, and
saith, Why doth this generation seek after a sign?
verily I say unto you, There shall [b]no sign be given
unto this generation.

Beware of the Leaven of the Pharisees and Herod
(*Matt. 16:5–12*)

13 And he left them, and entering into the
ship again departed to the other side.
14 [a]Now *the disciples* had forgotten to take

31 [a]Matt. 15:29; Mark 15:37; Luke 23:46; 24:46; Acts 10:40; 1 Cor. 15:4
32 [a]Matt. 9:32; Luke 11:14
33 [a]Mark 8:23; John 9:6
34 [a]Mark 6:41; John 11:41; 17:1 [b]John 11:33, 38
35 [a]Is. 35:5, 6
36 [a]Mark 5:43
37 [a]Mark 6:51; 10:26 [b]Matt. 12:22

CHAPTER 8

1 [a]Matt. 15:32–39; Mark 6:34–44; Luke 9:12
2 [a]Matt. 9:36; 14:14; Mark 1:41; 6:34
5 [a]Matt. 15:34; Mark 6:38; John 6:9
7 [a]Matt. 14:19; Mark 6:41
10 [a]Matt. 15:39
11 [a]Matt. 12:38; 16:1; Luke 11:16; John 2:18; 6:30; 1 Cor. 1:22
12 [a]Mark 7:34 [b]Matt. 12:39
14 [a]Matt. 16:5

* **8:14** NU, M *they*

NKJV

Lord, yet even the little dogs under the table eat
from the children's crumbs."
29 Then He said to her, "For this saying go
your way; the demon has gone out of your
daughter."
30 And when she had come to her house, she
found the demon gone out, and her daughter lying
on the bed.

Jesus Heals a Deaf-Mute
(*Matt. 15:29–31*)

31 [a]Again, departing from the region of Tyre
and Sidon, He came through the midst of the region of Decapolis to the Sea of Galilee.
32 Then [a]they brought to Him one who was
deaf and had an impediment in his speech, and
they begged Him to put His hand on him.
33 And He took him aside from the multitude, and put His fingers in his ears, and [a]He spat
and touched his tongue.
34 Then, [a]looking up to heaven, [b]He sighed,
and said to him, "Ephphatha," that is, "Be
opened."
35 [a]Immediately his ears were opened, and
the impediment of his tongue was loosed, and he
spoke plainly.
36 Then [a]He commanded them that they
should tell no one; but the more He commanded
them, the more widely they proclaimed *it.*
37 And they were [a]astonished beyond measure, saying, "He has done all things well. He
[b]makes both the deaf to hear and the mute to
speak."

Feeding the Four Thousand
(*Matt. 15:32–39*)

8 In those days, [a]the multitude being very great
and having nothing to eat, Jesus called His
disciples *to Him* and said to them,
2 "I have [a]compassion on the multitude, because they have now continued with Me three
days and have nothing to eat.
3 "And if I send them away hungry to their
own houses, they will faint on the way; for some
of them have come from afar."
4 Then His disciples answered Him, "How
can one satisfy these people with bread here in
the wilderness?"
5 [a]He asked them, "How many loaves do
you have?" And they said, "Seven."
6 So He commanded the multitude to sit
down on the ground. And He took the seven
loaves and gave thanks, broke *them* and gave
them to His disciples to set before *them;* and they
set *them* before the multitude.
7 They also had a few small fish; and [a]hav-
ing blessed them, He said to set them also before
them.
8 So they ate and were filled, and they took
up seven large baskets of leftover fragments.
9 Now those who had eaten were about four
thousand. And He sent them away,
10 [a]immediately got into the boat with His
disciples, and came to the region of Dalmanutha.

The Pharisees Seek a Sign
(*Matt. 16:1–4*)

11 [a]Then the Pharisees came out and began
to dispute with Him, seeking from Him a sign
from heaven, testing Him.
12 But He [a]sighed deeply in His spirit, and
said, "Why does this generation seek a sign? Assuredly, I say to you, [b]no sign shall be given to
this generation."

Beware of the Leaven of the Pharisees and Herod
(*Matt. 16:5–12*)

13 And He left them, and getting into the boat
again, departed to the other side.
14 [a]Now *the disciples had forgotten to take

KJV

bread, neither had they in the ship with them more than one loaf.

15 [a]And he charged them, saying, Take heed, beware of the leaven of the Pharisees, and *of* the leaven of Herod.

16 And they reasoned among themselves, saying, *It is* because we have no bread.

17 And when Jesus knew *it,* he saith unto them, Why reason ye, because ye have no bread? [a]perceive ye not yet, neither understand? have ye your heart yet hardened?

18 Having eyes, see ye not? and having ears, hear ye not? and do ye not remember?

19 [a]When I brake the five loaves among five thousand, how many baskets full of fragments took ye up? They say unto him, Twelve.

20 And [a]when the seven among four thousand, how many baskets full of fragments took ye up? And they said, Seven.

21 And he said unto them, How is it that [a]ye do not understand?

A Blind Man Healed at Bethsaida

22 And he cometh to Bethsaida; and they bring a [a]blind man unto him, and besought him to [b]touch him.

23 And he took the blind man by the hand, and led him out of the town; and when [a]he had spit on his eyes, and put his hands upon him, he asked him if he saw ought.

24 And he looked up, and said, I see men as trees, walking.

25 After that he put *his* hands again upon his eyes, and made him look up: and he was restored, and saw every man clearly.

26 And he sent him away to his house, saying, Neither go into the town, [a]nor tell *it* to any in the town.

Peter Confesses Jesus as the Christ
(Matt. 16:13–20; Luke 9:18–20)

27 [a]And Jesus went out, and his disciples, into the towns of Caesarea Philippi: and by the way he asked his disciples, saying unto them, Whom do men say that I am?

28 And they answered, [a]John the Baptist: but some *say,* [b]Elias; and others, One of the prophets.

29 And he saith unto them, But whom say ye that I am? And Peter answereth and saith unto him, [a]Thou art the Christ.

30 [a]And he charged them that they should tell no man of him.

Jesus Predicts His Death and Resurrection
(Matt. 16:21–23; Luke 9:21, 22)

31 And [a]he began to teach them, that the Son of man must suffer many things, and be [b]rejected of the elders, and *of* the chief priests, and scribes, and be [c]killed, and after three days rise again.

32 And he spake that saying openly. And Peter took him, and began to rebuke him.

33 But when he had turned about and looked on his disciples, he [a]rebuked Peter, saying, Get thee behind me, Satan: for thou savourest not the things that be of God, but the things that be of men.

Take Up the Cross and Follow Him
(Matt. 16:24–27; Luke 9:23–26)

34 And when he had called the people *unto him* with his disciples also, he said unto them, [a]Whosoever will come after me, let him deny himself, and take up his cross, and follow me.

35 For [a]whosoever will save his life shall lose it; but whosoever shall lose his life for my sake and the gospel's, the same shall save it.

36 For what shall it profit a man, if he shall gain the whole world, and lose his own soul?

37 Or what shall a man give in exchange for his soul?

38 [a]Whosoever therefore [b]shall be ashamed

---

15 [a]Matt. 16:6; Luke 12:1
17 [a]Mark 6:52; 16:14
19 [a]Matt. 14:20; Mark 6:43; Luke 9:17; John 6:13
20 [a]Matt. 15:37
21 [a][Mark 6:52]
22 [a]Matt. 9:27; John 9:1 [b]Luke 18:15
23 [a]Mark 7:33
26 [a]Matt. 8:4; Mark 5:43; 7:36
27 [a]Matt. 16:13–16; Luke 9:18–20
28 [a]Matt. 14:2 [b]Mark 6:14, 15; Luke 9:7, 8
29 [a]John 1:41; 4:42; 6:69; 11:27; Acts 2:36; 8:37; 9:20
30 [a]Matt. 8:4; 16:20; Luke 9:21
31 [a][Is. 53:3–11]; Matt. 16:21; 20:19; Luke 18:31–33; 1 Pet. 1:11 [b]Mark 10:33 [c]Mark 9:31; 10:34
33 [a]Mark 16:14; [Rev. 3:19]
34 [a][Matt. 10:38]; Luke 14:27
35 [a]Matt. 10:39; Luke 17:33; John 12:25
38 [a]Matt. 10:33; Luke 9:26; 12:9 [b]Rom. 1:16; 2 Tim. 1:8, 9; 2:12

*

8:17 NU omits *still*
8:26 NU *"Do not even go into the town."*

NKJV

bread, and they did not have more than one loaf with them in the boat.

15 [a]Then He charged them, saying, "Take heed, beware of the leaven of the Pharisees and the leaven of Herod."

16 And they reasoned among themselves, saying, *"It is* because we have no bread."

17 But Jesus, being aware of *it,* said to them, "Why do you reason because you have no bread? [a]Do you not yet perceive nor understand? Is your heart *still hardened?

18 "Having eyes, do you not see? And having ears, do you not hear? And do you not remember?

19 [a]"When I broke the five loaves for the five thousand, how many baskets full of fragments did you take up?" They said to Him, "Twelve."

20 "Also, [a]when I broke the seven for the four thousand, how many large baskets full of fragments did you take up?" And they said, "Seven."

21 So He said to them, "How *is it* [a]you do not understand?"

A Blind Man Healed at Bethsaida

22 Then He came to Bethsaida; and they brought a [a]blind man to Him, and begged Him to [b]touch him.

23 So He took the blind man by the hand and led him out of the town. And when [a]He had spit on his eyes and put His hands on him, He asked him if he saw anything.

24 And he looked up and said, "I see men like trees, walking."

25 Then He put *His* hands on his eyes again and made him look up. And he was restored and saw everyone clearly.

26 Then He sent him away to his house, saying, *"Neither go into the town, [a]nor tell anyone in the town."

Peter Confesses Jesus as the Christ
(Matt. 16:13–20; Luke 9:18–20)

27 [a]Now Jesus and His disciples went out to the towns of Caesarea Philippi; and on the road He asked His disciples, saying to them, "Who do men say that I am?"

28 So they answered, [a]"John the Baptist; but some *say,* [b]Elijah; and others, one of the prophets."

29 He said to them, "But who do you say that I am?" Peter answered and said to Him, [a]"You are the Christ."

30 [a]Then He strictly warned them that they should tell no one about Him.

Jesus Predicts His Death and Resurrection
(Matt. 16:21–23; Luke 9:21, 22)

31 And [a]He began to teach them that the Son of Man must suffer many things, and be [b]rejected by the elders and chief priests and scribes, and be [c]killed, and after three days rise again.

32 He spoke this word openly. Then Peter took Him aside and began to rebuke Him.

33 But when He had turned around and looked at His disciples, He [a]rebuked Peter, saying, "Get behind Me, Satan! For you are not mindful of the things of God, but the things of men."

Take Up the Cross and Follow Him
(Matt. 16:24–27; Luke 9:23–26)

34 When He had called the people to *Himself,* with His disciples also, He said to them, [a]"Whoever desires to come after Me, let him deny himself, and take up his cross, and follow Me.

35 "For [a]whoever desires to save his life will lose it, but whoever loses his life for My sake and the gospel's will save it.

36 "For what will it profit a man if he gains the whole world, and loses his own soul?

37 "Or what will a man give in exchange for his soul?

38 [a]"For whoever [b]is ashamed of Me and My

KJV

of me and of my words in this adulterous and sinful generation; of him also shall the Son of man be ashamed, when he cometh in the glory of his Father with the holy angels.

Jesus Transfigured on the Mount
(Matt. 16:28—17:13; Luke 9:27–36; 2 Pet. 1:16–18)

9 And he said unto them, [a]Verily I say unto you, That there be some of them that stand here, which shall not taste of death, till they have seen [b]the kingdom of God come with power.

2 [a]And after six days Jesus taketh *with him* Peter, and James, and John, and leadeth them up into an high mountain apart by themselves: and he was transfigured before them.

3 And his raiment became shining, exceeding [a]white as snow; so as no fuller on earth can white them.

4 And there appeared unto them Elias with Moses: and they were talking with Jesus.

5 And Peter answered and said to Jesus, Master, it is good for us to be here: and let us make three tabernacles; one for thee, and one for Moses, and one for Elias.

6 For he wist not what to say; for they were sore afraid.

7 And there was a [a]cloud that overshadowed them: and a voice came out of the cloud, saying, This is [b]my beloved Son: [c]hear him.

8 And suddenly, when they had looked round about, they saw no man any more, save Jesus only with themselves.

9 [a]And as they came down from the mountain, he charged them that they should tell no man what things they had seen, till the Son of man were risen from the dead.

10 And they kept that saying with themselves, questioning one with another [a]what the rising from the dead should mean.

11 And they asked him, saying, Why say the scribes [a]that Elias must first come?

12 And he answered and told them, Elias verily cometh first, and restoreth all things; and [a]how it is written of the Son of man, that he must suffer many things, and [b]be set at nought.

13 But I say unto you, That [a]Elias is indeed come, and they have done unto him whatsoever they listed, as it is written of him.

A Boy Is Healed
(Matt. 17:14–21; Luke 9:37–42)

14 [a]And when he came to *his* disciples, he saw a great multitude about them, and the scribes questioning with them.

15 And straightway all the people, when they beheld him, were greatly amazed, and running to *him* saluted him.

16 And he asked the scribes, What question ye with them?

17 And [a]one of the multitude answered and said, Master, I have brought unto thee my son, which hath a dumb spirit;

18 And wheresoever he taketh him, he teareth him: and he foameth, and gnasheth with his teeth, and pineth away: and I spake to thy disciples that they should cast him out; and they could not.

19 He answereth him, and saith, O [a]faithless generation, how long shall I be with you? how long shall I suffer you? bring him unto me.

20 And they brought him unto him: and [a]when he saw him, straightway the spirit tare him; and he fell on the ground, and wallowed foaming.

21 And he asked his father, How long is it ago since this came unto him? And he said, Of a child.

22 And ofttimes it hath cast him into the fire, and into the waters, to destroy him: but if thou canst do any thing, have compassion on us, and help us.

CHAPTER 9
1 [a]Matt. 16:28; Mark 13:26; Luke 9:27; Acts 7:55, 56; Rev. 20:4 [b][Matt. 24:30]
2 [a]Matt. 17:1–8; Luke 9:28–36
3 [a]Dan. 7:9; Matt. 28:3
7 [a]Ex. 40:34; 1 Kin. 8:10; Acts 1:9; Rev. 1:7 [b]Ps. 2:7; [Is. 42:1]; Matt. 3:17; Mark 1:11; Luke 1:35; 3:22; 2 Pet. 1:17 [c]Acts 3:22
9 [a]Matt. 17:9–13; Mark 16:6; Luke 24:6, 7, 46
10 [a]John 2:19–22
11 [a]Mal. 4:5; Matt. 17:10
12 [a]Ps. 22:6; Is. 53:3; Dan. 9:26 [b]Luke 23:11; Phil. 2:7
13 [a]Mal. 4:5; Matt. 11:14; 17:12; Luke 1:17
14 [a]Matt. 17:14–19; Luke 9:37–42
17 [a]Matt. 17:14; Luke 9:38
19 [a]John 4:48
20 [a]Mark 1:26; Luke 9:42

NKJV

words in this adulterous and sinful generation, of him the Son of Man also will be ashamed when He comes in the glory of His Father with the holy angels."

Jesus Transfigured on the Mount
(Matt. 16:28—17:13; Luke 9:27–36; 2 Pet. 1:16–18)

9 And He said to them, [a]"Assuredly, I say to you that there are some standing here who will not taste death till they see [b]the kingdom of God present with power."

2 [a]Now after six days Jesus took Peter, James, and John, and led them up on a high mountain apart by themselves; and He was transfigured before them.

3 His clothes became shining, exceedingly [a]white, like snow, such as no launderer on earth can whiten them.

4 And Elijah appeared to them with Moses, and they were talking with Jesus.

5 Then Peter answered and said to Jesus, "Rabbi, it is good for us to be here; and let us make three tabernacles: one for You, one for Moses, and one for Elijah"—

6 because he did not know what to say, for they were greatly afraid.

7 And a [a]cloud came and overshadowed them; and a voice came out of the cloud, saying, "This is [b]My beloved Son. [c]Hear Him!"

8 Suddenly, when they had looked around, they saw no one anymore, but only Jesus with themselves.

9 [a]Now as they came down from the mountain, He commanded them that they should tell no one the things they had seen, till the Son of Man had risen from the dead.

10 So they kept this word to themselves, questioning [a]what the rising from the dead meant.

11 And they asked Him, saying, "Why do the scribes say [a]that Elijah must come first?"

12 Then He answered and told them, "Indeed, Elijah is coming first and restores all things. And [a]how is it written concerning the Son of Man, that He must suffer many things and [b]be treated with contempt?

13 "But I say to you that [a]Elijah has also come, and they did to him whatever they wished, as it is written of him."

A Boy Is Healed
(Matt. 17:14–21; Luke 9:37–42)

14 [a]And when He came to the disciples, He saw a great multitude around them, and scribes disputing with them.

15 Immediately, when they saw Him, all the people were greatly amazed, and running to *Him,* greeted Him.

16 And He asked the scribes, "What are you discussing with them?"

17 Then [a]one of the crowd answered and said, "Teacher, I brought You my son, who has a mute spirit.

18 "And wherever it seizes him, it throws him down; he foams at the mouth, gnashes his teeth, and becomes rigid. So I spoke to Your disciples, that they should cast it out, but they could not."

19 He answered him and said, "O [a]faithless generation, how long shall I be with you? How long shall I bear with you? Bring him to Me."

20 Then they brought him to Him. And [a]when he saw Him, immediately the spirit convulsed him, and he fell on the ground and wallowed, foaming at the mouth.

21 So He asked his father, "How long has this been happening to him?" And he said, "From childhood.

22 "And often he has thrown him both into the fire and into the water to destroy him. But if You can do anything, have compassion on us and help us."

KJV

23 Jesus said unto him, [a]If thou canst believe, all things *are* possible to him that believeth.

24 And straightway the father of the child cried out, and said with tears, Lord, I believe; [a]help thou mine unbelief.

25 When Jesus saw that the people came running together, he [a]rebuked the foul spirit, saying unto him, *Thou* dumb and deaf spirit, I charge thee, come out of him, and enter no more into him.

26 And *the spirit* cried, and rent him sore, and came out of him: and he was as one dead; insomuch that many said, He is dead.

27 But Jesus took him by the hand, and lifted him up; and he arose.

28 [a]And when he was come into the house, his disciples asked him privately, Why could not we cast him out?

29 And he said unto them, This kind can come forth by nothing, but by [a]prayer and fasting.

Jesus Again Predicts His Death and Resurrection
(Matt. 17:22, 23; Luke 9:43–45)

30 And they departed thence, and passed through Galilee; and he would not that any man should know *it*.

31 [a]For he taught his disciples, and said unto them, The Son of man is delivered into the hands of men, and they shall [b]kill him; and after that he is killed, he shall [c]rise the third day.

32 But they understood [a]not that saying, and were afraid to ask him.

Who Is the Greatest?
(Matt. 18:1–5; Luke 9:46–48)

33 [a]And he came to Capernaum: and being in the house he asked them, What was it that ye disputed among yourselves by the way?

34 But they held their peace: for by the way they had [a]disputed among themselves, who *should be* the [b]greatest.

35 And he sat down, and called the twelve, and saith unto them, [a]If any man desire to be first, *the same* shall be last of all, and servant of all.

36 And [a]he took a child, and set him in the midst of them: and when he had taken him in his arms, he said unto them,

37 Whosoever shall receive one of such children in my name, receiveth me: and [a]whosoever shall receive me, receiveth not me, but him that sent me.

Jesus Forbids Sectarianism
(Matt. 10:40–42; Luke 9:49, 50)

38 [a]And John answered him, saying, Master, we saw one casting out devils in thy name, and he followeth not us: and we forbad him, because he followeth not us.

39 But Jesus said, Forbid him not: [a]for there is no man which shall do a miracle in my name, that can lightly speak evil of me.

40 For [a]he that is not against us is on our part.

41 [a]For whosoever shall give you a cup of water to drink in my name, because ye belong to Christ, verily I say unto you, he shall not lose his reward.

Jesus Warns of Offenses
(Matt. 18:6–9; Luke 17:1, 2)

42 [a]And whosoever shall offend one of *these* little ones that believe in me, it is better for him that a millstone were hanged about his neck, and he were cast into the sea.

43 [a]And if thy hand offend thee, cut it off: it is better for thee to enter into life maimed, than having two hands to go into hell, into the fire that never shall be quenched:

44 Where [a]THEIR WORM DIETH NOT, AND THE FIRE IS NOT QUENCHED.

23 [a]Matt. 17:20; Mark 11:23; Luke 17:6; John 11:40
24 [a]Luke 17:5
25 [a]Mark 1:25
28 [a]Matt. 17:19
29 [a][James 5:16]
31 [a]Matt. 17:22; Luke 9:44 [b]Matt. 16:21; 27:50; Luke 18:33; 23:46; Acts 2:23 [c]Matt. 20:19; Luke 24:46; Acts 10:40; 1 Cor. 15:4
32 [a]Luke 2:50; 18:34; John 12:16
33 [a]Matt. 18:1–5; Mark 14:53, 64; Luke 9:46–48; 22:24; John 18:12; 19:7
34 [a][Prov. 13:10]; Mark 15:20, 31 [b]Matt. 18:4; [Mark 9:50]; 14:65; 15:15, 37; Luke 22:24; 23:46; 24:46
35 [a]Matt. 20:26, 27; 23:11; Mark 10:43, 44; Luke 22:26, 27
36 [a]Mark 10:13–16
37 [a]Matt. 10:40; Luke 10:16; John 13:20
38 [a]Num. 11:27–29; Luke 9:49
39 [a]1 Cor. 12:3
40 [a][Matt. 12:30]; Luke 11:23
41 [a]Matt. 10:42
42 [a]Matt. 18:6; Luke 17:1, 2; [1 Cor. 8:12]
43 [a][Deut. 13:6]; Matt. 5:29, 30; 18:8, 9
44 [a]Is. 66:24

NKJV

23 Jesus said to him, [a]"If* you can believe, all things *are* possible to him who believes."

24 Immediately the father of the child cried out and said with tears, "Lord, I believe; [a]help my unbelief!"

25 When Jesus saw that the people came running together, He [a]rebuked the unclean spirit, saying to it: "Deaf and dumb spirit, I command you, come out of him and enter him no more!"

26 Then *the spirit* cried out, convulsed him greatly, and came out of him. And he became as one dead, so that many said, "He is dead."

27 But Jesus took him by the hand and lifted him up, and he arose.

28 [a]And when He had come into the house, His disciples asked Him privately, "Why could we not cast it out?"

29 So He said to them, "This kind can come out by nothing but [a]prayer *and fasting."

Jesus Again Predicts His Death and Resurrection
(Matt. 17:22, 23; Luke 9:43–45)

30 Then they departed from there and passed through Galilee, and He did not want anyone to know *it*.

31 [a]For He taught His disciples and said to them, "The Son of Man is being betrayed into the hands of men, and they will [b]kill Him. And after He is killed, He will [c]rise the third day."

32 But they [a]did not understand this saying, and were afraid to ask Him.

Who Is the Greatest?
(Matt. 18:1–5; Luke 9:46–48)

33 [a]Then He came to Capernaum. And when He was in the house He asked them, "What was it you disputed among yourselves on the road?"

34 But they kept silent, for on the road they had [a]disputed among themselves who *would be the* [b]greatest.

35 And He sat down, called the twelve, and said to them, [a]"If anyone desires to be first, he shall be last of all and servant of all."

36 Then [a]He took a little child and set him in the midst of them. And when He had taken him in His arms, He said to them,

37 "Whoever receives one of these little children in My name receives Me; and [a]whoever receives Me, receives not Me but Him who sent Me."

Jesus Forbids Sectarianism
(Matt. 10:40–42; Luke 9:49, 50)

38 [a]Now John answered Him, saying, "Teacher, we saw someone who does not follow us casting out demons in Your name, and we forbade him because he does not follow us."

39 But Jesus said, "Do not forbid him, [a]for no one who works a miracle in My name can soon afterward speak evil of Me.

40 "For [a]he who is not against *us is on *our side.

41 [a]"For whoever gives you a cup of water to drink in My name, because you belong to Christ, assuredly, I say to you, he will by no means lose his reward.

Jesus Warns of Offenses
(Matt. 18:6–9; Luke 17:1, 2)

42 [a]"But whoever causes one of these little ones who believe in Me to stumble, it would be better for him if a millstone were hung around his neck, and he were thrown into the sea.

43 [a]"If your hand causes you to sin, cut it off. It is better for you to enter into life maimed, rather than having two hands, to go to hell, into the fire that shall never be quenched—

44 *"where

[a]*'Their worm does not die,*
And the fire is not quenched.'

---

*
9:23 NU *If you can! All things*
9:29 NU omits *and fasting*
9:40 M *you* • M *your*
9:44 NU omits v. 44.

KJV

45 And if thy foot offend thee, cut it off: it is better for thee to enter halt into life, than having two feet to be cast into hell, into the fire that never shall be quenched:

46 Where [a]THEIR WORM DIETH NOT, AND THE FIRE IS NOT QUENCHED.

47 And if thine eye offend thee, pluck it out: it is better for thee to enter into the kingdom of God with one eye, than having two eyes to be cast into hell fire:

48 Where THEIR [a]WORM DIETH NOT, AND THE [b]FIRE IS NOT QUENCHED.

Tasteless Salt Is Worthless

49 For every one shall be [a]salted with fire, [b]and every sacrifice shall be salted with salt.

50 [a]Salt *is* good: but if the salt have lost his saltness, wherewith will ye season it? [b]Have salt in yourselves, and [c]have peace one with another.

Marriage and Divorce
(*Matt. 19:1–9*)

10 And [a]he arose from thence, and cometh into the coasts of Judaea by the farther side of Jordan: and the people resort unto him again; and, as he was wont, he taught them again.

2 [a]And the Pharisees came to him, and asked him, Is it lawful for a man to put away *his* wife? tempting him.

3 And he answered and said unto them, What did Moses command you?

4 And they said, [a]Moses suffered to write a bill of divorcement, and to put *her* away.

5 And Jesus answered and said unto them, For the hardness of your heart he wrote you this precept.

6 But from the beginning of the creation [a]God MADE THEM MALE AND FEMALE.

7 [a]FOR THIS CAUSE SHALL A MAN LEAVE HIS FATHER AND MOTHER, AND CLEAVE TO HIS WIFE;

8 AND THEY TWAIN SHALL BE ONE FLESH: so then they are no more twain, but one flesh.

9 What therefore God hath joined together, let not man put asunder.

10 And in the house his disciples asked him again of the same *matter*.

11 And he saith unto them, [a]Whosoever shall put away his wife, and marry another, committeth adultery against her.

12 And if a woman shall put away her husband, and be married to another, she committeth adultery.

Jesus Blesses Little Children
(*Matt. 19:13–15; Luke 18:15–17*)

13 [a]And they brought young children to him, that he should touch them: and *his* disciples rebuked those that brought *them*.

14 But when Jesus saw *it*, he was much displeased, and said unto them, Suffer the little children to come unto me, and forbid them not: for [a]of such is the kingdom of God.

15 Verily I say unto you, [a]Whosoever shall not receive the kingdom of God as a little child, he shall [b]not enter therein.

16 And he took them up in his arms, put *his* hands upon them, and blessed them.

Jesus Counsels the Rich Young Ruler
(*Matt. 19:16–22; Luke 18:18–23*)

17 [a]And when he was gone forth into the way, there came one running, and kneeled to him, and asked him, Good Master, what shall I [b]do that I may inherit eternal life?

18 And Jesus said unto him, Why callest thou me good? *there is* none good but one, *that is*, [a]God.

---

46 [a]Is. 66:24 **48** [a]Is. 66:24 [b]Jer. 7:20; [Rev. 21:8] **49** [a][Matt. 3:11] [b]Lev. 2:13; Ezek. 43:24 **50** [a]Matt. 5:13; Luke 14:34 [b][Eph. 4:29]; Col. 4:6 [c]Rom. 12:18; 14:19; 2 Cor. 13:11; 1 Thess. 5:13; Heb. 12:14

CHAPTER 10

1 [a]Matt. 19:1–9; John 10:40; 11:7 **2** [a]Matt. 19:3 **4** [a]Deut. 24:1–4; Matt. 5:31; 19:7 **6** [a]Gen. 1:27; 5:2 **7** [a]Gen. 2:24; [1 Cor. 6:16]; Eph. 5:31 **11** [a]Ex. 20:14; [Matt. 5:32; 19:9]; Luke 16:18; [Rom. 7:3]; 1 Cor. 7:10, 11 **13** [a]Matt. 19:13–15; Luke 18:15–17 **14** [a][1 Cor. 14:20; 1 Pet. 2:2] **15** [a]Matt. 18:3, 4; 19:14; Luke 18:17 [b]Luke 13:28 **17** [a]Matt. 19:16–30; Luke 18:18–30 [b]John 6:28; Acts 2:37 **18** [a]1 Sam. 2:2

NKJV

45 "And if your foot causes you to sin, cut it off. It is better for you to enter life lame, rather than having two feet, to be cast into hell, *into the fire that shall never be quenched—

46 "where

[a]'Their worm does not die,
And the fire is not quenched.'

47 "And if your eye causes you to sin, pluck it out. It is better for you to enter the kingdom of God with one eye, rather than having two eyes, to be cast into hell fire—

48 "where

[a]'Their worm does not die,
And the [b]fire is not quenched.'

Tasteless Salt Is Worthless

49 "For everyone will be [a]seasoned with fire, [b]and* every sacrifice will be seasoned with salt.

50 [a]"Salt *is* good, but if the salt loses its flavor, how will you season it? [b]Have salt in yourselves, and [c]have peace with one another."

Marriage and Divorce
(*Matt. 19:1–9*)

10 Then [a]He arose from there and came to the region of Judea by the other side of the Jordan. And multitudes gathered to Him again, and as He was accustomed, He taught them again.

2 [a]The Pharisees came and asked Him, "Is it lawful for a man to divorce *his* wife?" testing Him.

3 And He answered and said to them, "What did Moses command you?"

4 They said, [a]"Moses permitted *a man* to write a certificate of divorce, and to dismiss *her*."

5 And Jesus answered and said to them, "Because of the hardness of your heart he wrote you this precept.

6 "But from the beginning of the creation, God [a]*'made them male and female.'*

7 [a]*'For this reason a man shall leave his father and mother and be joined to his wife,*

8 *'and the two shall become one flesh'*; so then they are no longer two, but one flesh.

9 "Therefore what God has joined together, let not man separate."

10 In the house His disciples also asked Him again about the same *matter*.

11 So He said to them, [a]"Whoever divorces his wife and marries another commits adultery against her.

12 "And if a woman divorces her husband and marries another, she commits adultery."

Jesus Blesses Little Children
(*Matt. 19:13–15; Luke 18:15–17*)

13 [a]Then they brought little children to Him, that He might touch them; but the disciples rebuked those who brought *them*.

14 But when Jesus saw *it*, He was greatly displeased and said to them, "Let the little children come to Me, and do not forbid them; for [a]of such is the kingdom of God.

15 "Assuredly, I say to you, [a]whoever does not receive the kingdom of God as a little child will [b]by no means enter it."

16 And He took them up in His arms, laid *His* hands on them, and blessed them.

Jesus Counsels the Rich Young Ruler
(*Matt. 19:16–22; Luke 18:18–23*)

17 [a]Now as He was going out on the road, one came running, knelt before Him, and asked Him, "Good Teacher, what shall I [b]do that I may inherit eternal life?"

18 So Jesus said to him, "Why do you call Me good? No one *is* good but One, *that is*, [a]God.

---

*

9:45 NU omits the rest of v. 45 and all of v. 46. **9:49** NU omits the rest of v. 49.

KJV

19 Thou knowest the commandments, [a]DO NOT COMMIT ADULTERY, DO NOT KILL, DO NOT STEAL, DO NOT BEAR FALSE WITNESS, Defraud not, HONOUR THY FATHER AND MOTHER.

20 And he answered and said unto him, Master, all these have I [a]observed from my youth.

21 Then Jesus beholding him loved him, and said unto him, One thing thou lackest: go thy way, [a]sell whatsoever thou hast, and give to the poor, and thou shalt have [b]treasure in heaven: and come, [c]take up the cross, and follow me.

22 And he was sad at that saying, and went away grieved: for he had great possessions.

With God All Things Are Possible
(Matt. 19:23–30; Luke 18:24–30)

23 [a]And Jesus looked round about, and saith unto his disciples, How hardly shall they that have riches enter into the kingdom of God!

24 And the disciples were astonished at his words. But Jesus answereth again, and saith unto them, Children, how hard is it for them [a]that trust in riches to enter into the kingdom of God!

25 It is easier for a camel to go through the eye of a needle, than for a [a]rich man to enter into the kingdom of God.

26 And they were astonished out of measure, saying among themselves, Who then can be saved?

27 And Jesus looking upon them saith, With men *it is* impossible, but not [a]with God: for with God all things are possible.

28 [a]Then Peter began to say unto him, Lo, we have left all, and have followed thee.

29 And Jesus answered and said, Verily I say unto you, There is no man that hath left house, or brethren, or sisters, or father, or mother, or wife, or children, or lands, for my sake, and the gospel's,

30 [a]But he shall receive an hundredfold now in this time, houses, and brethren, and sisters, and mothers, and children, and lands, with [b]persecutions; and in the world to come eternal life.

31 [a]But many *that are* first shall be last; and the last first.

Jesus a Third Time Predicts His Death and Resurrection
(Matt. 20:17–19; Luke 18:31–34)

32 [a]And they were in the way going up to Jerusalem; and Jesus went before them: and they were amazed; and as they followed, they were afraid. [b]And he took again the twelve, and began to tell them what things should happen unto him,

33 *Saying,* Behold, we go up to Jerusalem; and the Son of man shall be delivered unto the chief priests, and unto the scribes; and they shall condemn him to death, and shall deliver him to the Gentiles:

34 And they shall mock him, and shall scourge him, and shall spit upon him, and shall kill him: and the third day he shall rise again.

Greatness Is Serving
(Matt. 20:20–28)

35 [a]And James and John, the sons of Zebedee, come unto him, saying, Master, we would that thou shouldest do for us whatsoever we shall desire.

36 And he said unto them, What would ye that I should do for you?

37 They said unto him, Grant unto us that we may sit, one on thy right hand, and the other on thy left hand, in thy glory.

38 But Jesus said unto them, Ye know not what ye ask: can ye drink of the [a]cup that I drink of? and be baptized with the [b]baptism that I am baptized with?

39 And they said unto him, We can. And Jesus said unto them, [a]Ye shall indeed drink of the cup that I drink of; and with the baptism that I am baptized withal shall ye be baptized:

19 [a]Ex. 20:12–16; Deut. 5:16–20; [Rom. 13:9; James 2:10, 11]
20 [a]Phil. 3:6
21 [a][Luke 12:33; 16:9] [b]Matt. 6:19, 20; 19:21 [c][Mark 8:34]
23 [a]Matt. 19:23; [Mark 4:19]; Luke 18:24
24 [a]Job 31:24; Ps. 52:7; 62:10; [Prov. 11:28; 1 Tim. 6:17]
25 [a][Matt. 13:22; 19:24]
27 [a]Job 42:2; Jer. 32:17; Matt. 19:26; Luke 1:37
28 [a]Matt. 19:27; Luke 18:28
30 [a]2 Chr. 25:9; Luke 18:29, 30 [b]1 Thess. 3:3; 2 Tim. 3:12; [1 Pet. 4:12, 13]
31 [a]Matt. 19:30; 20:16; Luke 13:30
32 [a]Matt. 20:17–19; Luke 18:31–33 [b]Mark 8:31; 9:31; Luke 9:22; 18:31
35 [a][James 4:3]
38 [a]Matt. 26:39, 42; Mark 14:36; Luke 22:42; John 18:11 [b]Luke 12:50
39 [a]Matt. 10:17, 18, 21, 22; 24:9; John 16:33; Acts 12:2; Rev. 1:9

*
10:24 NU omits *for those who trust in riches*
10:29 NU omits *or wife*

NKJV

19 "You know the commandments: [a]*'Do not commit adultery,' 'Do not murder,' 'Do not steal,' 'Do not bear false witness,'* 'Do not defraud,' *'Honor your father and your mother.'* "

20 And he answered and said to Him, "Teacher, all these things I have [a]kept from my youth."

21 Then Jesus, looking at him, loved him, and said to him, "One thing you lack: Go your way, [a]sell whatever you have and give to the poor, and you will have [b]treasure in heaven; and come, [c]take up the cross, and follow Me."

22 But he was sad at this word, and went away sorrowful, for he had great possessions.

With God All Things Are Possible
(Matt. 19:23–30; Luke 18:24–30)

23 [a]Then Jesus looked around and said to His disciples, "How hard it is for those who have riches to enter the kingdom of God!"

24 And the disciples were astonished at His words. But Jesus answered again and said to them, "Children, how hard it is *for those [a]who trust in riches to enter the kingdom of God!

25 "It is easier for a camel to go through the eye of a needle than for a [a]rich man to enter the kingdom of God."

26 And they were greatly astonished, saying among themselves, "Who then can be saved?"

27 But Jesus looked at them and said, "With men *it is* impossible, but not [a]with God; for with God all things are possible."

28 [a]Then Peter began to say to Him, "See, we have left all and followed You."

29 So Jesus answered and said, "Assuredly, I say to you, there is no one who has left house or brothers or sisters or father or mother *or wife or children or lands, for My sake and the gospel's,

30 [a]"who shall not receive a hundredfold now in this time—houses and brothers and sisters and mothers and children and lands, with [b]persecutions—and in the age to come, eternal life.

31 [a]"But many *who are* first will be last, and the last first."

Jesus a Third Time Predicts His Death and Resurrection
(Matt. 20:17–19; Luke 18:31–34)

32 [a]Now they were on the road, going up to Jerusalem, and Jesus was going before them; and they were amazed. And as they followed they were afraid. [b]Then He took the twelve aside again and began to tell them the things that would happen to Him:

33 "Behold, we are going up to Jerusalem, and the Son of Man will be betrayed to the chief priests and to the scribes; and they will condemn Him to death and deliver Him to the Gentiles;

34 "and they will mock Him, and scourge Him, and spit on Him, and kill Him. And the third day He will rise again."

Greatness Is Serving
(Matt. 20:20–28)

35 [a]Then James and John, the sons of Zebedee, came to Him, saying, "Teacher, we want You to do for us whatever we ask."

36 And He said to them, "What do you want Me to do for you?"

37 They said to Him, "Grant us that we may sit, one on Your right hand and the other on Your left, in Your glory."

38 But Jesus said to them, "You do not know what you ask. Are you able to drink the [a]cup that I drink, and be baptized with the [b]baptism that I am baptized with?"

39 They said to Him, "We are able." So Jesus said to them, [a]"You will indeed drink the cup that I drink, and with the baptism I am baptized with you will be baptized;

KJV

40 But to sit on my right hand and on my
left hand is not mine to give; but *it shall be given*
to them [a]for whom it is prepared.
41 [a]And when the ten heard *it,* they began
to be much displeased with James and John.
42 But Jesus called them *to him,* and saith
unto them, [a]Ye know that they which are accounted to rule over the Gentiles exercise lordship
over them; and their great ones exercise authority
upon them.
43 [a]But so shall it not be among you: but
whosoever will be great among you, shall be your
minister:
44 And whosoever of you will be the chiefest,
shall be servant of all.
45 For even [a]the Son of man came not to be
ministered unto, but to minister, and [b]to give his
life a ransom for many.

Jesus Heals Blind Bartimaeus
(Matt. 20:29–34; Luke 18:35–43)

46 [a]And they came to Jericho: and as he went
out of Jericho with his disciples and a great number of people, blind Bartimaeus, the son of Timaeus, sat by the highway side begging.
47 And when he heard that it was Jesus of
Nazareth, he began to cry out, and say, Jesus,
thou [a]son of David, [b]have mercy on me.
48 And many charged him that he should
hold his peace: but he cried the more a great deal,
Thou son of David, have mercy on me.
49 And Jesus stood still, and commanded
him to be called. And they call the blind man,
saying unto him, Be of good comfort, rise; he calleth thee.
50 And he, casting away his garment, rose,
and came to Jesus.
51 And Jesus answered and said unto him,
What wilt thou that I should do unto thee? The
blind man said unto him, Lord, that I might receive my sight.
52 And Jesus said unto him, Go thy way; [a]thy
faith hath made thee whole. And immediately he
received his sight, and followed Jesus in the way.

The Triumphal Entry
(Matt. 21:1–11; Luke 19:28–40; John 12:12–19)

11 And [a]when they came nigh to Jerusalem,
unto Bethphage and Bethany, at the mount
of Olives, he sendeth forth two of his disciples,
2 And saith unto them, Go your way into
the village over against you: and as soon as ye
be entered into it, ye shall find a colt tied, whereon
never man sat; loose him, and bring *him.*
3 And if any man say unto you, Why do ye
this? say ye that the Lord hath need of him; and
straightway he will send him hither.
4 And they went their way, and found the
colt tied by the door without in a place where
two ways met; and they loose him.
5 And certain of them that stood there said
unto them, What do ye, loosing the colt?
6 And they said unto them even as Jesus
had commanded: and they let them go.
7 And they brought the colt to Jesus, and
cast their garments on him; and he sat upon him.
8 [a]And many spread their garments in the
way: and others cut down branches off the trees,
and strawed *them* in the way.
9 And they that went before, and they that
followed, cried, saying, [a]HOSANNA; BLESSED *IS* HE
THAT COMETH IN THE NAME OF THE LORD:
10 Blessed *be* the kingdom of our father David, that cometh in the name of the Lord: [a]Ho-
sanna in the highest.
11 [a]And Jesus entered into Jerusalem, and
into the temple: and when he had looked round

40 [a][Matt. 25:34; John 17:2, 6, 24; Rom. 8:30; Heb. 11:16] **41** [a]Matt. 20:24 **42** [a]Luke 22:25 **43** [a]Matt. 20:26, 28; Mark 9:35; Luke 9:48 **45** [a]Luke 22:27; John 13:14; [Phil. 2:7, 8] [b]Matt. 20:28; [2 Cor. 5:21; 1 Tim. 2:5, 6; Titus 2:14] **46** [a]Matt. 20:29–34; Luke 18:35–43 **47** [a]Jer. 23:5; Matt. 22:42; Rom. 1:3, 4; Rev. 22:16 [b]Matt. 15:22; Luke 17:13 **52** [a]Matt. 9:22; Mark 5:34

CHAPTER 11

1 [a]Matt. 21:1–9; Luke 19:29; John 2:13 **8** [a]Matt. 21:8 **9** [a]Ps. 118:25, 26; Matt. 21:9 **10** [a]Ps. 148:1 **11** [a]Matt. 21:12

NKJV

40 "but to sit on My right hand and on My
left is not Mine to give, but *it is for those* [a]for
whom it is prepared."
41 [a]And when the ten heard *it,* they began
to be greatly displeased with James and John.
42 But Jesus called them to *Himself* and said
to them, [a]"You know that those who are considered rulers over the Gentiles lord it over them,
and their great ones exercise authority over
them.
43 [a]"Yet it shall not be so among you; but
whoever desires to become great among you shall
be your servant.
44 "And whoever of you desires to be first
shall be slave of all.
45 "For even [a]the Son of Man did not come
to be served, but to serve, and [b]to give His life a
ransom for many."

Jesus Heals Blind Bartimaeus
(Matt. 20:29–34; Luke 18:35–43)

46 [a]Now they came to Jericho. As He went
out of Jericho with His disciples and a great multitude, blind Bartimaeus, the son of Timaeus, sat
by the road begging.
47 And when he heard that it was Jesus of
Nazareth, he began to cry out and say, "Jesus,
[a]Son of David, [b]have mercy on me!"
48 Then many warned him to be quiet; but
he cried out all the more, "Son of David, have
mercy on me!"
49 So Jesus stood still and commanded him
to be called. Then they called the blind man, saying to him, "Be of good cheer. Rise, He is calling
you."
50 And throwing aside his garment, he rose
and came to Jesus.
51 So Jesus answered and said to him, "What
do you want Me to do for you?" The blind man
said to Him, "Rabboni, that I may receive my
sight."
52 Then Jesus said to him, "Go your way;
[a]your faith has made you well." And immediately
he received his sight and followed Jesus on the
road.

The Triumphal Entry
(Matt. 21:1–11; Luke 19:28–40; John 12:12–19)

11 Now [a]when they drew near Jerusalem, to
*Bethphage and Bethany, at the Mount of
Olives, He sent two of His disciples;
2 and He said to them, "Go into the village
opposite you; and as soon as you have entered it
you will find a colt tied, on which no one has sat.
Loose it and bring *it.*
3 "And if anyone says to you, 'Why are you
doing this?' say, 'The Lord has need of it,' and
immediately he will send it here."
4 So they went their way, and found *the
colt tied by the door outside on the street, and
they loosed it.
5 But some of those who stood there said
to them, "What are you doing, loosing the colt?"
6 And they spoke to them just as Jesus had
commanded. So they let them go.
7 Then they brought the colt to Jesus and
threw their clothes on it, and He sat on it.
8 [a]And many spread their clothes on the
road, and others cut down leafy branches from
the trees and spread *them* on the road.
9 Then those who went before and those
who followed cried out, saying:

"Hosanna!
[a]'*Blessed is He who comes in the name of*
the LORD!'
10 Blessed *is* the kingdom of our father David
That comes *in the name of the Lord!
[a]Hosanna in the highest!"

11 [a]And Jesus went into Jerusalem and into
the temple. So when He had looked around at

---

*11:1 M *Bethsphage*
11:4 NU, M *a*
11:10 NU omits *in the name of the Lord*

KJV

about upon all things, and now the eventide was come, he went out unto Bethany with the twelve.

The Fig Tree Withered
(Matt. 21:18, 19)

12 [a]And on the morrow, when they were come from Bethany, he was hungry:

13 [a]And seeing a fig tree afar off having leaves, he came, if haply he might find any thing thereon: and when he came to it, he found nothing but leaves; for the time of figs was not *yet.*

14 And Jesus answered and said unto it, No man eat fruit of thee hereafter for ever. And his disciples heard *it.*

Jesus Cleanses the Temple
(Matt. 21:12–17; Luke 19:45–48; John 2:13–22)

15 [a]And they come to Jerusalem: and Jesus went into the temple, and began to cast out them that sold and bought in the temple, and overthrew the tables of the moneychangers, and the seats of them that sold [b]doves;

16 And would not suffer that any man should carry *any* vessel through the temple.

17 And he taught, saying unto them, Is it not written, [a]MY HOUSE SHALL BE CALLED OF ALL NATIONS THE HOUSE OF PRAYER? but [b]ye have made it a DEN OF THIEVES.

18 And [a]the scribes and chief priests heard *it,* and sought how they might destroy him: for they feared him, because [b]all the people was astonished at his doctrine.

19 And when even was come, he went out of the city.

The Lesson of the Withered Fig Tree
(Matt. 21:20–22)

20 [a]And in the morning, as they passed by, they saw the fig tree dried up from the roots.

21 And Peter calling to remembrance saith unto him, Master, behold, the fig tree which thou cursedst is withered away.

22 And Jesus answering saith unto them, Have faith in God.

23 For [a]verily I say unto you, That whosoever shall say unto this mountain, Be thou removed, and be thou cast into the sea; and shall not doubt in his heart, but shall believe that those things which he saith shall come to pass; he shall have whatsoever he saith.

24 Therefore I say unto you, [a]What things soever ye desire, when ye pray, believe that ye receive *them,* and ye shall have *them.*

Forgiveness and Prayer
(Matt. 6:14, 15)

25 And when ye stand praying, [a]forgive, if ye have ought against any: that your Father also which is in heaven may forgive you your trespasses.

26 But [a]if ye do not forgive, neither will your Father which is in heaven forgive your trespasses.

Jesus' Authority Questioned
(Matt. 21:23–27; Luke 20:1–8)

27 And they come again to Jerusalem: [a]and as he was walking in the temple, there come to him the chief priests, and the scribes, and the elders,

28 And say unto him, By what [a]authority doest thou these things? and who gave thee this authority to do these things?

29 And Jesus answered and said unto them, I will also ask of you one question, and answer me, and I will tell you by what authority I do these things.

30 The [a]baptism of John, was *it* from heaven, or of men? answer me.

31 And they reasoned with themselves, saying, If we shall say, From heaven; he will say, Why then did ye not believe him?

32 But if we shall say, Of men; they feared

---

12 [a]Matt. 21:18–22
13 [a]Matt. 21:19
15 [a]Mal. 3:1; Matt. 21:12–16; Luke 19:45–47; John 2:13–16 [b]Lev. 14:22
17 [a]Is. 56:7 [b]Jer. 7:11
18 [a]Ps. 2:2; Matt. 21:45, 46; Luke 19:47 [b]Matt. 7:28; Mark 1:22; 6:2; Luke 4:32
20 [a]Matt. 21:19–22
23 [a]Matt. 17:20; 21:21; Luke 17:6
24 [a]Matt. 7:7; Luke 11:9; [John 14:13; 15:7; 16:24; James 1:5, 6]
25 [a]Matt. 6:14; 18:23–35; Eph. 4:32; [Col. 3:13]
26 [a]Matt. 6:15; 18:35
27 [a]Matt. 21:23–27; Luke 20:1–8
28 [a]John 5:27
30 [a][Mark 1:4, 5, 8]; Luke 7:29, 30

NKJV

all things, as the hour was already late, He went out to Bethany with the twelve.

The Fig Tree Withered
(Matt. 21:18, 19)

12 [a]Now the next day, when they had come out from Bethany, He was hungry.

13 [a]And seeing from afar a fig tree having leaves, He went to see if perhaps He would find something on it. When He came to it, He found nothing but leaves, for it was not the season for figs.

14 In response Jesus said to it, "Let no one eat fruit from you ever again." And His disciples heard *it.*

Jesus Cleanses the Temple
(Matt. 21:12–17; Luke 19:45–48; John 2:13–22)

15 [a]So they came to Jerusalem. Then Jesus went into the temple and began to drive out those who bought and sold in the temple, and overturned the tables of the money changers and the seats of those who sold [b]doves.

16 And He would not allow anyone to carry wares through the temple.

17 Then He taught, saying to them, "Is it not written, [a]*'My house shall be called a house of prayer for all nations'*? But you have made it a [b]*'den of thieves.'* "

18 And [a]the scribes and chief priests heard it and sought how they might destroy Him; for they feared Him, because [b]all the people were astonished at His teaching.

19 When evening had come, He went out of the city.

The Lesson of the Withered Fig Tree
(Matt. 21:20–22)

20 [a]Now in the morning, as they passed by, they saw the fig tree dried up from the roots.

21 And Peter, remembering, said to Him, "Rabbi, look! The fig tree which You cursed has withered away."

22 So Jesus answered and said to them, "Have faith in God.

23 "For [a]assuredly, I say to you, whoever says to this mountain, 'Be removed and be cast into the sea,' and does not doubt in his heart, but believes that those things he says will be done, he will have whatever he says.

24 "Therefore I say to you, [a]whatever things you ask when you pray, believe that you receive *them,* and you will have *them.*

Forgiveness and Prayer
(Matt. 6:14, 15)

25 "And whenever you stand praying, [a]if you have anything against anyone, forgive him, that your Father in heaven may also forgive you your trespasses.

26 *"But [a]if you do not forgive, neither will your Father in heaven forgive your trespasses."

Jesus' Authority Questioned
(Matt. 21:23–27; Luke 20:1–8)

27 Then they came again to Jerusalem. [a]And as He was walking in the temple, the chief priests, the scribes, and the elders came to Him.

28 And they said to Him, "By what [a]authority are You doing these things? And who gave You this authority to do these things?"

29 But Jesus answered and said to them, "I also will ask you one question; then answer Me, and I will tell you by what authority I do these things:

30 "The [a]baptism of John—was it from heaven or from men? Answer Me."

31 And they reasoned among themselves, saying, "If we say, 'From heaven,' He will say, 'Why then did you not believe him?'

32 "But if we say, 'From men' "—they feared

***11:26** NU omits v. 26.

KJV

the people: for [a]all *men* counted John, that he was a prophet indeed.

33 And they answered and said unto Jesus, We cannot tell. And Jesus answering saith unto them, Neither do I tell you by what authority I do these things.

The Parable of the Wicked Vinedressers
(Matt. 21:33–46; Luke 20:9–19)

12 And [a]he began to speak unto them by parables. A *certain* man planted a vineyard, and set an hedge about *it*, and digged *a place for* the winefat, and built a tower, and let it out to husbandmen, and went into a far country.

2 And at the season he sent to the husbandmen a servant, that he might receive from the husbandmen of the fruit of the vineyard.

3 And they caught *him*, and beat him, and sent *him* away empty.

4 And again he sent unto them another servant; and at him they cast stones, and wounded *him* in the head, and sent *him* away shamefully handled.

5 And again he sent another; and him they killed, and many others; [a]beating some, and killing some.

6 Having yet therefore one son, his wellbeloved, he sent him also last unto them, saying, They will reverence my son.

7 But those husbandmen said among themselves, This is the heir; come, let us kill him, and the inheritance shall be our's.

8 And they took him, and [a]killed *him*, and cast *him* out of the vineyard.

9 What shall therefore the lord of the vineyard do? he will come and destroy the husbandmen, and will give the vineyard unto others.

10 And have ye not read this scripture; [a]THE STONE WHICH THE BUILDERS REJECTED IS BECOME THE HEAD OF THE CORNER:

11 THIS WAS THE LORD'S DOING, AND IT IS MARVELLOUS IN OUR EYES?

12 [a]And they sought to lay hold on him, but feared the people: for they knew that he had spoken the parable against them: and they left him, and went their way.

The Pharisees: Is It Lawful to Pay Taxes to Caesar?
(Matt. 22:15–22; Luke 20:20–26)

13 [a]And they send unto him certain of the Pharisees and of the Herodians, to catch him in *his* words.

14 And when they were come, they say unto him, Master, we know that thou art true, and carest for no man: for thou regardest not the person of men, but teachest the [a]way of God in truth: Is it lawful to give tribute to Caesar, or not?

15 Shall we give, or shall we not give? But he, knowing their [a]hypocrisy, said unto them, Why tempt ye me? bring me a penny, that I may see *it*.

16 And they brought *it*. And he saith unto them, Whose *is* this image and superscription? And they said unto him, Caesar's.

17 And Jesus answering said unto them, Render to Caesar the things that are Caesar's, and to [a]God the things that are God's. And they marvelled at him.

The Sadducees: What About the Resurrection?
(Matt. 22:23–33; Luke 20:27–40)

18 [a]Then come unto him the Sadducees, [b]which say there is no resurrection; and they asked him, saying,

19 Master, [a]Moses wrote unto us, If a man's brother die, and leave *his* wife *behind him*, and leave no children, that his brother should take his wife, and raise up seed unto his brother.

20 Now there were seven brethren: and the first took a wife, and dying left no seed.

32 [a]Matt. 3:5; 14:5; Mark 6:20

CHAPTER 12

1 [a]Matt. 21:33–46; Luke 20:9–19
5 [a]2 Chr. 36:16
8 [a][Acts 2:23]
10 [a]Ps. 118:22, 23
12 [a]Matt. 21:45, 46; Mark 11:18; John 7:25, 30, 44
13 [a]Matt. 22:15–22; Luke 20:20–26
14 [a]Acts 18:26
15 [a]Matt. 23:28; Luke 12:1
17 [a][Eccl. 5:4, 5]
18 [a]Matt. 22:23–33; Luke 20:27–38 [b]Acts 23:8
19 [a]Deut. 25:5

*———

12:4 NU omits *and at him they threw stones*

NKJV

the people, for [a]all counted John to have been a prophet indeed.

33 So they answered and said to Jesus, "We do not know." And Jesus answered and said to them, "Neither will I tell you by what authority I do these things."

The Parable of the Wicked Vinedressers
(Matt. 21:33–46; Luke 20:9–19)

12 Then [a]He began to speak to them in parables: "A man planted a vineyard and set a hedge around *it*, dug *a place for* the wine vat and built a tower. And he leased it to vinedressers and went into a far country.

2 "Now at vintage-time he sent a servant to the vinedressers, that he might receive some of the fruit of the vineyard from the vinedressers.

3 "And they took *him* and beat him and sent *him* away empty-handed.

4 "Again he sent them another servant, *and at him they threw stones, wounded *him* in the head, and sent *him* away shamefully treated.

5 "And again he sent another, and him they killed; and many others, [a]beating some and killing some.

6 "Therefore still having one son, his beloved, he also sent him to them last, saying, 'They will respect my son.'

7 "But those vinedressers said among themselves, 'This is the heir. Come, let us kill him, and the inheritance will be ours.'

8 "So they took him and [a]killed *him* and cast *him* out of the vineyard.

9 "Therefore what will the owner of the vineyard do? He will come and destroy the vinedressers, and give the vineyard to others.

10 "Have you not even read this Scripture:

[a]'The stone which the builders rejected
Has become the chief cornerstone.
11 *This was the LORD's doing,*
And it is marvelous in our eyes'?"

12 [a]And they sought to lay hands on Him, but feared the multitude, for they knew He had spoken the parable against them. So they left Him and went away.

The Pharisees: Is It Lawful to Pay Taxes to Caesar?
(Matt. 22:15–22; Luke 20:20–26)

13 [a]Then they sent to Him some of the Pharisees and the Herodians, to catch Him in *His* words.

14 When they had come, they said to Him, "Teacher, we know that You are true, and care about no one; for You do not regard the person of men, but teach the [a]way of God in truth. Is it lawful to pay taxes to Caesar, or not?

15 "Shall we pay, or shall we not pay?" But He, knowing their [a]hypocrisy, said to them, "Why do you test Me? Bring Me a denarius that I may see *it*."

16 So they brought *it*. And He said to them, "Whose image and inscription *is* this?" They said to Him, "Caesar's."

17 And Jesus answered and said to them, "Render to Caesar the things that are Caesar's, and to [a]God the things that are God's." And they marveled at Him.

The Sadducees: What About the Resurrection?
(Matt. 22:23–33; Luke 20:27–40)

18 [a]Then *some* Sadducees, [b]who say there is no resurrection, came to Him; and they asked Him, saying:

19 "Teacher, [a]Moses wrote to us that if a man's brother dies, and leaves *his* wife behind, and leaves no children, his brother should take his wife and raise up offspring for his brother.

20 "Now there were seven brothers. The first took a wife; and dying, he left no offspring.

KJV

21 And the second took her, and died, neither left he any seed: and the third likewise.
22 And the seven had her, and left no seed: last of all the woman died also.
23 In the resurrection therefore, when they shall rise, whose wife shall she be of them? for the seven had her to wife.
24 And Jesus answering said unto them, Do ye not therefore err, because ye know not the scriptures, neither the power of God?
25 For when they shall rise from the dead, they neither marry, nor are given in marriage; but [a]are as the angels which are in heaven.
26 And as touching the dead, that they [a]rise: have ye not read in the book of Moses, how in the bush God spake unto him, saying, [b]I AM THE GOD OF ABRAHAM, AND THE GOD OF ISAAC, AND THE GOD OF JACOB?
27 He is not the God of the dead, but the God of the living: ye therefore do greatly err.

The Scribes: Which Is the First Commandment of All?
(*Matt. 22:34–40; Luke 10:25–28*)

28 [a]And one of the scribes came, and having heard them reasoning together, and perceiving that he had answered them well, asked him, Which is the first commandment of all?
29 And Jesus answered him, The first of all the commandments *is*, [a]HEAR, O ISRAEL; THE LORD OUR GOD IS ONE LORD:
30 AND THOU SHALT [a]LOVE THE LORD THY GOD WITH ALL THY HEART, AND WITH ALL THY SOUL, AND WITH ALL THY MIND, AND WITH ALL THY STRENGTH: this *is* the first commandment.
31 And the second *is* like, *namely* this, [a]THOU SHALT LOVE THY NEIGHBOUR AS THYSELF. There is none other commandment greater than [b]these.
32 And the scribe said unto him, Well, Master, thou hast said the truth: for there is one God; [a]and there is none other but he:
33 And to love him with all the heart, and with all the understanding, and with all the soul, and with all the strength, and to love *his* neighbour as himself, [a]is more than all whole burnt offerings and sacrifices.
34 And when Jesus saw that he answered discreetly, he said unto him, Thou art not far from the kingdom of God. [a]And no man after that durst ask him *any question*.

Jesus: How Can David Call His Descendant Lord?
(*Matt. 22:41–46; Luke 20:41–44*)

35 [a]And Jesus answered and said, while he taught in the temple, How say the scribes that Christ is the son of David?
36 For David himself said [a]by the Holy Ghost, [b]THE LORD SAID TO MY LORD, SIT THOU ON MY RIGHT HAND, TILL I MAKE THINE ENEMIES THY FOOTSTOOL.
37 David therefore himself calleth him Lord; and whence is he *then* his [a]son? And the common people heard him gladly.

Beware of the Scribes
(*Matt. 23:1–7; Luke 20:45–47*)

38 And [a]he said unto them in his doctrine, [b]Beware of the scribes, which love to go in long clothing, and [c]*love* salutations in the marketplaces,
39 And the [a]chief seats in the synagogues, and the uppermost rooms at feasts:
40 [a]Which devour widows' houses, and for a pretence make long prayers: these shall receive greater damnation.

NKJV

21 "And the second took her, and he died; nor did he leave any offspring. And the third likewise.
22 "So the seven had her and left no offspring. Last of all the woman died also.
23 "Therefore, in the resurrection, when they rise, whose wife will she be? For all seven had her as wife."
24 Jesus answered and said to them, "Are you not therefore mistaken, because you do not know the Scriptures nor the power of God?
25 "For when they rise from the dead, they neither marry nor are given in marriage, but [a]are like angels in heaven.
26 "But concerning the dead, that they [a]rise, have you not read in the book of Moses, in the *burning* bush *passage*, how God spoke to him, saying, [b]*'I am the God of Abraham, the God of Isaac, and the God of Jacob'*?
27 "He is not the God of the dead, but the God of the living. You are therefore greatly mistaken."

The Scribes: Which Is the First Commandment of All?
(*Matt. 22:34–40; Luke 10:25–28*)

28 [a]Then one of the scribes came, and having heard them reasoning together, *perceiving that He had answered them well, asked Him, "Which is the first commandment of all?"
29 Jesus answered him, "The first of all the commandments *is*: [a]*'Hear, O Israel, the LORD our God, the LORD is one.*
30 *'And you shall [a]love the LORD your God with all your heart, with all your soul, with all your mind, and with all your strength.'* *This *is* the first commandment.
31 "And the second, like *it, is* this: [a]*'You shall love your neighbor as yourself.'* There is no other commandment greater than [b]these."
32 So the scribe said to Him, "Well *said*, Teacher. You have spoken the truth, for there is one God, [a]and there is no other but He.
33 "And to love Him with all the heart, with all the understanding, *with all the soul, and with all the strength, and to love one's neighbor as oneself, [a]is more than all the whole burnt offerings and sacrifices."
34 Now when Jesus saw that he answered wisely, He said to him, "You are not far from the kingdom of God." [a]But after that no one dared question Him.

Jesus: How Can David Call His Descendant Lord?
(*Matt. 22:41–46; Luke 20:41–44*)

35 [a]Then Jesus answered and said, while He taught in the temple, "How *is it* that the scribes say that the Christ is the Son of David?
36 "For David himself said [a]by the Holy Spirit:

[b]*'The LORD said to my Lord,*
"Sit at My right hand,
Till I make Your enemies Your
footstool."'

37 "Therefore David himself calls Him *'Lord'*; how is He *then* his [a]Son?" And the common people heard Him gladly.

Beware of the Scribes
(*Matt. 23:1–7; Luke 20:45–47*)

38 Then [a]He said to them in His teaching, [b]"Beware of the scribes, who desire to go around in long robes, [c]*love* greetings in the marketplaces,
39 "the [a]best seats in the synagogues, and the best places at feasts,
40 [a]"who devour widows' houses, and for a pretense make long prayers. These will receive greater condemnation."

25 [a][1 Cor. 15:42, 49, 52] **26** [a][John 5:25, 28, 29]; Acts 26:8; Rom. 4:17; [Rev. 20:12, 13] [b]Ex. 3:6, 15 **28** [a]Matt. 22:34–40; Luke 10:25–28; 20:39 **29** [a]Deut. 6:4, 5; Is. 44:8; 45:22; 46:9; 1 Cor. 8:6 **30** [a][Deut. 10:12; 30:6]; Luke 10:27 **31** [a]Lev. 19:18; Matt. 22:39; Gal. 5:14; James 2:8 [b][Rom. 13:9] **32** [a]Deut. 4:39; Is. 45:6, 14; 46:9; [John 1:14, 17; 14:6] **33** [a][1 Sam. 15:22; Hos. 6:6; Mic. 6:6–8; Matt. 9:13; 12:7] **34** [a]Matt. 22:46 **35** [a]Matt. 22:41–46; Luke 20:41–44 **36** [a]2 Sam. 23:2 [b]Ps. 110:1 **37** [a][Acts 2:29–31] **38** [a]Mark 4:2 [b]Matt. 23:1–7; Luke 20:45–47 [c]Matt. 23:7; Luke 11:43 **39** [a]Luke 14:7 **40** [a]Matt. 23:14

*

12:28 NU *seeing*
12:30 NU omits the rest of v. 30.
12:33 NU omits *with all the soul*

KJV

The Widow's Two Mites
(Luke 21:1–4)

41 [a]And Jesus sat over against the treasury,
and beheld how the people cast money [b]into the
treasury: and many that were rich cast in much.
42 And there came a certain poor widow, and
she threw in two mites, which make a farthing.
43 And he called *unto him* his disciples, and
saith unto them, Verily I say unto you, That [a]this
poor widow hath cast more in, than all they which
have cast into the treasury:
44 For all *they* did cast in of their abundance;
but she of her want did cast in all that she had,
[a]*even* all her living.

Jesus Predicts the Destruction of the Temple
(Matt. 24:1, 2; Luke 21:5, 6)

13 And [a]as he went out of the temple, one of
his disciples saith unto him, Master, see
what manner of stones and what buildings *are
here!*
2 And Jesus answering said unto him, Seest
thou these great buildings? [a]there shall not be left
one stone upon another, that shall not be thrown
down.

The Signs of the Times and the End of the Age
(Matt. 24:3–14; Luke 21:7–19)

3 And as he sat upon the mount of Olives
over against the temple, [a]Peter and [b]James and
[c]John and [d]Andrew asked him privately,
4 [a]Tell us, when shall these things be? and
what *shall be* the sign when all these things shall
be fulfilled?
5 And Jesus answering them began to say,
[a]Take heed lest any *man* deceive you:
6 For many shall come in my name, saying,
I am *Christ;* and shall deceive many.
7 And when ye shall hear of wars and rumours of wars, be ye not troubled: for *such things*
must needs be; but the end *shall* not *be* yet.
8 For nation shall rise against nation, and
[a]kingdom against kingdom: and there shall be
earthquakes in divers places, and there shall be
famines and troubles: [b]these *are* the beginnings
of sorrows.
9 But [a]take heed to yourselves: for they
shall deliver you up to councils; and in the synagogues ye shall be beaten: and ye shall be brought
before rulers and kings for my sake, for a testimony against them.
10 And [a]the gospel must first be published
among all nations.
11 [a]But when they shall lead *you,* and deliver you up, take no thought beforehand what
ye shall speak, neither do ye premeditate: but
whatsoever shall be given you in that hour, that
speak ye: for it is not ye that speak, [b]but the Holy
Ghost.
12 Now [a]the brother shall betray the brother
to death, and the father the son; and children shall
rise up against *their* parents, and shall cause them
to be put to death.
13 [a]And ye shall be hated of all *men* for my
name's sake: but [b]he that shall endure unto the
end, the same shall be saved.

The Great Tribulation
(Matt. 24:15–28; Luke 21:20–24)

14 [a]But when ye shall see the ABOMINATION
OF DESOLATION, [b]spoken of by Daniel the prophet,
standing where it ought not, (let him that readeth
understand,) then [c]let them that be in Judaea flee
to the mountains:
15 And let him that is on the housetop not
go down into the house, neither enter *therein,* to
take any thing out of his house:
16 And let him that is in the field not turn
back again for to take up his garment.
17 [a]But woe to them that are with child, and
to them that give suck in those days!

NKJV

The Widow's Two Mites
(Luke 21:1–4)

41 [a]Now Jesus sat opposite the treasury and
saw how the people put money [b]into the treasury.
And many *who were* rich put in much.
42 Then one poor widow came and threw in
two *mites, which make a quadrans.
43 So He called His disciples to *Himself* and
said to them, "Assuredly, I say to you that [a]this
poor widow has put in more than all those who
have given to the treasury;
44 "for they all put in out of their abundance,
but she out of her poverty put in all that she had,
[a]her whole livelihood."

Jesus Predicts the Destruction of the Temple
(Matt. 24:1, 2; Luke 21:5, 6)

13 Then [a]as He went out of the temple, one
of His disciples said to Him, "Teacher, see
what manner of stones and what buildings *are
here!*"
2 And Jesus answered and said to him, "Do
you see these great buildings? [a]Not *one* stone
shall be left upon another, that shall not be thrown
down."

The Signs of the Times and the End of the Age
(Matt. 24:3–14; Luke 21:7–19)

3 Now as He sat on the Mount of Olives opposite the temple, [a]Peter, [b]James, [c]John, and
[d]Andrew asked Him privately,
4 [a]"Tell us, when will these things be? And
what *will be* the sign when all these things will
be fulfilled?"
5 And Jesus, answering them, began to say:
[a]"Take heed that no one deceives you.
6 "For many will come in My name, saying,
'I am *He,*' and will deceive many.
7 "But when you hear of wars and rumors
of wars, do not be troubled; for *such things* must
happen, but the end *is* not yet.
8 "For nation will rise against nation, and
[a]kingdom against kingdom. And there will be
earthquakes in various places, and there will be
famines *and troubles. [b]These *are* the beginnings
of sorrows.
9 "But [a]watch out for yourselves, for they
will deliver you up to councils, and you will be
beaten in the synagogues. You will *be brought
before rulers and kings for My sake, for a testimony to them.
10 "And [a]the gospel must first be preached
to all the nations.
11 [a]"But when they arrest *you* and deliver
you up, do not worry beforehand, *or premeditate
what you will speak. But whatever is given you
in that hour, speak that; for it is not you who
speak, [b]but the Holy Spirit.
12 "Now [a]brother will betray brother to
death, and a father *his* child; and children will
rise up against parents and cause them to be put
to death.
13 [a]"And you will be hated by all for My
name's sake. But [b]he who endures to the end shall
be saved.

The Great Tribulation
(Matt. 24:15–28; Luke 21:20–24)

14 [a]"So when you see the [b]*'abomination of
desolation,'* *spoken of by Daniel the prophet,
standing where it ought not" (let the reader understand), "then [c]let those who are in Judea flee to
the mountains.
15 "Let him who is on the housetop not go
down into the house, nor enter to take anything
out of his house.
16 "And let him who is in the field not go
back to get his clothes.
17 [a]"But woe to those who are pregnant and
to those who are nursing babies in those days!

---

41 [a]Luke 21:1–4 [b]2 Kin. 12:9
43 [a][2 Cor. 8:12]
44 [a]Deut. 24:6; [1 John 3:17]

CHAPTER 13

1 [a]Matt. 24:1; Luke 21:5–36
2 [a]Luke 19:44
3 [a]Matt. 16:18; Mark 1:16 [b]Mark 1:19 [c]Mark 1:19 [d]John 1:40
4 [a]Matt. 24:3; Luke 21:7
5 [a]Jer. 29:8; Eph. 5:6; [Col. 2:8]; 1 Thess. 2:3; 2 Thess. 2:3
8 [a]Hag. 2:22 [b]Matt. 24:8
9 [a]Matt. 10:17, 18; 24:9; Acts 12:4; [Rev. 2:10]
10 [a]Matt. 24:14
11 [a]Matt. 10:19–22; Luke 12:11; 21:12–17 [b]Acts 2:4; 4:8, 31
12 [a]Mic. 7:6; Matt. 10:21; 24:10; Luke 21:16
13 [a]Matt. 24:9; Luke 21:17; John 15:21 [b]Dan. 12:12; Matt. 10:22; 24:13; [Rev. 2:10]
14 [a]Matt. 24:15 [b]Dan. 9:27; 11:31; 12:11 [c]Luke 21:21
17 [a]Luke 21:23

*———

12:42 Gr. *lepta,* very small copper coins
13:8 NU omits *and troubles*
13:9 NU, M *stand*
13:11 NU omits *or premeditate*
13:14 NU omits *spoken of by Daniel the prophet*

KJV

18 And pray ye that your flight be not in the
winter.
19 [a]For *in* those days shall be affliction, such
as was not from the beginning of the creation
which God created unto this time, neither shall
be.
20 And except that the Lord had shortened
those days, no flesh should be saved: but for the
elect's sake, whom he hath chosen, he hath shortened the days.
21 [a]And then if any man shall say to you,
Lo, here *is* Christ; or, lo, *he is* there; believe *him*
not:
22 For false Christs and false prophets shall
rise, and shall shew signs and [a]wonders, to seduce, if *it were* possible, even the elect.
23 But [a]take ye heed: behold, I have foretold
you all things.

The Coming of the Son of Man
(Matt. 24:29–31; Luke 21:25–28)

24 [a]But in those days, after that tribulation,
the sun shall be darkened, and the moon shall
not give her light,
25 And the stars of heaven shall fall, and the
powers that are in heaven shall be [a]shaken.
26 [a]And then shall they see the Son of
man coming in the clouds with great power and
glory.
27 And then shall he send his angels, and
shall gather together his elect from the four
winds, from the uttermost part of the earth to
the uttermost part of heaven.

The Parable of the Fig Tree
(Matt. 24:32–35; Luke 21:29–33)

28 [a]Now learn a parable of the fig tree; When
her branch is yet tender, and putteth forth leaves,
ye know that summer is near:
29 So ye in like manner, when ye shall see
these things come to pass, know that it is nigh,
even at the doors.
30 Verily I say unto you, that this generation
shall not pass, till all these things be done.
31 Heaven and earth shall pass away: but
[a]my words shall not pass away.

No One Knows the Day or Hour
(Matt. 24:36–44; Luke 21:34–36)

32 But of that day and *that* hour [a]knoweth
no man, no, not the angels which are in heaven,
neither the Son, but the [b]Father.
33 [a]Take ye heed, watch and pray: for ye
know not when the time is.
34 [a]*For the Son of man is* as a man taking a
far journey, who left his house, and gave [b]author-
ity to his servants, and to every man his work,
and commanded the porter to watch.
35 [a]Watch ye therefore: for ye know not
when the master of the house cometh, at even,
or at midnight, or at the cockcrowing, or in the
morning:
36 Lest coming suddenly he find you
sleeping.
37 And what I say unto you I say unto all,
Watch.

The Plot to Kill Jesus
(Matt. 26:1–5; Luke 22:1, 2; John 11:45–53)

14 After [a]two days was *the feast of* the passover, and of [b]unleavened bread: and
the chief priests and the scribes sought how
they might take him by craft, and put *him* to
death.
2 But they said, Not on the feast *day*, lest
there be an uproar of the people.

The Anointing at Bethany
(Matt. 26:6–13; John 12:1–8)

3 [a]And being in Bethany in the house of Simon the leper, as he sat at meat, there came a
woman having an alabaster box of ointment of

19 [a]Dan. 9:26; 12:1; Joel 2:2; Matt. 24:21; Mark 10:6
21 [a]Matt. 24:23; Luke 17:23; 21:8
22 [a]Deut. 13:1–3; Rev. 13:13, 14
23 [a]John 16:1–4; [2 Pet. 3:17]
24 [a]Zeph. 1:15; Matt. 24:29
25 [a]Is. 13:10; 34:4; Heb. 12:26; Rev. 6:13
26 [a][Dan. 7:13, 14; Matt. 16:27; 24:30]; Mark 14:62; Acts 1:11; [1 Thess. 4:16; 2 Thess. 1:7, 10]; Rev. 1:7
28 [a]Matt. 24:32; Luke 21:29
31 [a]Is. 40:8; [2 Pet. 3:7, 10, 12]
32 [a]Matt. 25:13 [b]Matt. 24:36; Acts 1:7
33 [a]Matt. 24:42; 25:13; Luke 12:40; 21:34; [Rom. 13:11]; 1 Thess. 5:6; 1 Pet. 4:7
34 [a]Matt. 24:45; 25:14 [b][Matt. 16:19]
35 [a]Matt. 24:42, 44

CHAPTER 14

1 [a]Matt. 26:2–5; Luke 22:1, 2; John 11:55; 13:1 [b]Ex. 12:1–27; Mark 14:12
3 [a]Matt. 26:6; Luke 7:37; John 12:1, 3

NKJV

18 "And pray that your flight may not be in
winter.
19 [a]"For *in* those days there will be tribulation, such as has not been since the beginning of
the creation which God created until this time,
nor ever shall be.
20 "And unless the Lord had shortened those
days, no flesh would be saved; but for the elect's
sake, whom He chose, He shortened the days.
21 [a]"Then if anyone says to you, 'Look, here
is the Christ!' or, 'Look, *He is* there!' do not believe
it.
22 "For false christs and false prophets will
rise and show signs and [a]wonders to deceive, if
possible, even the elect.
23 "But [a]take heed; see, I have told you all
things beforehand.

The Coming of the Son of Man
(Matt. 24:29–31; Luke 21:25–28)

24 [a]"But in those days, after that tribulation,
the sun will be darkened, and the moon will not
give its light;
25 "the stars of heaven will fall, and the powers in the heavens will be [a]shaken.
26 [a]"Then they will see the Son of Man coming in the clouds with great power and glory.
27 "And then He will send His angels, and
gather together His elect from the four winds,
from the farthest part of earth to the farthest part
of heaven.

The Parable of the Fig Tree
(Matt. 24:32–35; Luke 21:29–33)

28 [a]"Now learn this parable from the fig tree:
When its branch has already become tender, and
puts forth leaves, you know that summer is near.
29 "So you also, when you see these things
happening, know that *it is near—at the doors!
30 "Assuredly, I say to you, this generation
will by no means pass away till all these things
take place.
31 "Heaven and earth will pass away, but
[a]My words will by no means pass away.

No One Knows the Day or Hour
(Matt. 24:36–44; Luke 21:34–36)

32 "But of that day and hour [a]no one knows,
not even the angels in heaven, nor the Son, but
only the [b]Father.
33 [a]"Take heed, watch and pray; for you do
not know when the time is.
34 [a]"*It is* like a man going to a far country,
who left his house and gave [b]authority to his servants, and to each his work, and commanded the
doorkeeper to watch.
35 [a]"Watch therefore, for you do not know
when the master of the house is coming—in the
evening, at midnight, at the crowing of the
rooster, or in the morning—
36 "lest, coming suddenly, he find you
sleeping.
37 "And what I say to you, I say to all:
Watch!"

The Plot to Kill Jesus
(Matt. 26:1–5; Luke 22:1, 2; John 11:45–53)

14 After [a]two days it was the Passover and
[b]*the Feast* of Unleavened Bread. And the
chief priests and the scribes sought how they
might take Him by trickery and put *Him* to death.
2 But they said, "Not during the feast, lest
there be an uproar of the people."

The Anointing at Bethany
(Matt. 26:6–13; John 12:1–8)

3 [a]And being in Bethany at the house of Simon the leper, as He sat at the table, a woman
came having an alabaster flask of very costly oil

*———
13:29 Or *He*

KJV

spikenard very precious; and she brake the box, and poured *it* on his head.

4 And there were some that had indignation within themselves, and said, Why was this waste of the ointment made?

5 For it might have been sold for more than three hundred [a]pence, and have been given to the poor. And they [b]murmured against her.

6 And Jesus said, Let her alone; why trouble ye her? she hath wrought a good work on me.

7 [a]For ye have the poor with you always, and whensoever ye will ye may do them good: [b]but me ye have not always.

8 She hath done what she could: she is come aforehand to anoint my body to the burying.

9 Verily I say unto you, Wheresoever this gospel shall be [a]preached throughout the whole world, *this* also that she hath done shall be spoken of for a memorial of her.

Judas Agrees to Betray Jesus
(Matt. 26:14–16; Luke 22:3–6)

10 [a]And Judas Iscariot, one of the twelve, went unto the chief priests, to betray him unto them.

11 And when they heard *it*, they were glad, and promised to give him money. And he sought how he might conveniently betray him.

Jesus Celebrates the Passover with His Disciples
(Matt. 26:17–25; Luke 22:7–13; John 13:21–30)

12 [a]And the first day of unleavened bread, when they killed the passover, his disciples said unto him, Where wilt thou that we go and prepare that thou mayest eat the passover?

13 And he sendeth forth two of his disciples, and saith unto them, Go ye into the city, and there shall meet you a man bearing a pitcher of water: follow him.

14 And wheresoever he shall go in, say ye to the goodman of the house, The Master saith, Where is the guestchamber, where I shall eat the passover with my disciples?

15 And he will shew you a large upper room furnished *and* prepared: there make ready for us.

16 And his disciples went forth, and came into the city, and found as he had said unto them: and they made ready the passover.

17 [a]And in the evening he cometh with the twelve.

18 And as they sat and did eat, Jesus said, Verily I say unto you, [a]One of you which eateth with me shall betray me.

19 And they began to be sorrowful, and to say unto him one by one, *Is* it I? and another *said*, *Is* it I?

20 And he answered and said unto them, *It is* one of the twelve, that dippeth with me in the dish.

21 [a]The Son of man indeed goeth, as it is written of him: but woe to that man by whom the Son of man is betrayed! good were it for that man if he had never been born.

Jesus Institutes the Lord's Supper
(Matt. 26:26–29; Luke 22:14–23; 1 Cor. 11:23–26)

22 [a]And as they did eat, Jesus took bread, and blessed, and brake *it*, and gave to them, and said, Take, eat: this is my [b]body.

23 And he took the cup, and when he had given thanks, he gave *it* to them: and they all drank of it.

24 And he said unto them, This is my blood of the new testament, which is shed for many.

25 Verily I say unto you, I will drink no more of the fruit of the vine, until that day that I drink it new in the kingdom of God.

26 [a]And when they had sung an hymn, they went out into the mount of Olives.

5 [a]Matt. 18:28; Mark 12:15 [b]Matt. 20:11; John 6:61
7 [a]Deut. 15:11; Matt. 26:11; John 12:8 [b][John 7:33; 8:21; 14:2, 12; 16:10, 17, 28]
9 [a]Matt. 28:19, 20; Mark 16:15; Luke 24:47
10 [a]Ps. 41:9; 55:12–14; Matt. 10:2–4
12 [a]Ex. 12:8; Matt. 26:17–19; Luke 22:7–13
17 [a]Matt. 26:20–24; Luke 22:14, 21–23
18 [a]Ps. 41:9; Matt. 26:46; Mark 14:42; John 6:70, 71; 13:18
21 [a]Matt. 26:24; Luke 22:22; Acts 1:16–20
22 [a]Matt. 26:26–29; Luke 22:17–20; 1 Cor. 11:23–25 [b][1 Pet. 2:24]
26 [a]Matt. 26:30

*
14:19 NU omits the rest of v. 19.
14:22 NU omits *eat*
14:24 NU omits *new*

NKJV

of spikenard. Then she broke the flask and poured *it* on His head.

4 But there were some who were indignant among themselves, and said, "Why was this fragrant oil wasted?

5 "For it might have been sold for more than three hundred [a]denarii and given to the poor." And they [b]criticized her sharply.

6 But Jesus said, "Let her alone. Why do you trouble her? She has done a good work for Me.

7 [a]"For you have the poor with you always, and whenever you wish you may do them good; [b]but Me you do not have always.

8 "She has done what she could. She has come beforehand to anoint My body for burial.

9 "Assuredly, I say to you, wherever this gospel is [a]preached in the whole world, what this woman has done will also be told as a memorial to her."

Judas Agrees to Betray Jesus
(Matt. 26:14–16; Luke 22:3–6)

10 [a]Then Judas Iscariot, one of the twelve, went to the chief priests to betray Him to them.

11 And when they heard *it*, they were glad, and promised to give him money. So he sought how he might conveniently betray Him.

Jesus Celebrates the Passover with His Disciples
(Matt. 26:17–25; Luke 22:7–13; John 13:21–30)

12 [a]Now on the first day of Unleavened Bread, when they killed the Passover *lamb*, His disciples said to Him, "Where do You want us to go and prepare, that You may eat the Passover?"

13 And He sent out two of His disciples and said to them, "Go into the city, and a man will meet you carrying a pitcher of water; follow him.

14 "Wherever he goes in, say to the master of the house, 'The Teacher says, "Where is the guest room in which I may eat the Passover with My disciples?" '

15 "Then he will show you a large upper room, furnished *and* prepared; there make ready for us."

16 So His disciples went out, and came into the city, and found it just as He had said to them; and they prepared the Passover.

17 [a]In the evening He came with the twelve.

18 Now as they sat and ate, Jesus said, "Assuredly, I say to you, [a]one of you who eats with Me will betray Me."

19 And they began to be sorrowful, and to say to Him one by one, "*Is* it I?" *And another *said*, "*Is* it I?"

20 He answered and said to them, "*It is* one of the twelve, who dips with Me in the dish.

21 [a]"The Son of Man indeed goes just as it is written of Him, but woe to that man by whom the Son of Man is betrayed! It would have been good for that man if he had never been born."

Jesus Institutes the Lord's Supper
(Matt. 26:26–29; Luke 22:14–23; 1 Cor. 11:23–26)

22 [a]And as they were eating, Jesus took bread, blessed and broke *it*, and gave *it* to them and said, "Take, *eat; this is My [b]body."

23 Then He took the cup, and when He had given thanks He gave *it* to them, and they all drank from it.

24 And He said to them, "This is My blood of the *new covenant, which is shed for many.

25 "Assuredly, I say to you, I will no longer drink of the fruit of the vine until that day when I drink it new in the kingdom of God."

26 [a]And when they had sung a hymn, they went out to the Mount of Olives.

KJV

Jesus Predicts Peter's Denial
(Matt. 26:31–35; Luke 22:31–34; John 13:36–38)

27 [a]And Jesus saith unto them, All ye shall
be offended because of me this night: for it is written, [b]I WILL SMITE THE SHEPHERD, AND THE SHEEP
SHALL BE SCATTERED.
28 But [a]after that I am risen, I will go before
you into Galilee.
29 [a]But Peter said unto him, Although all
shall be offended, yet *will* not I.
30 And Jesus saith unto him, Verily I say
unto thee, That this day, *even* in this night, before
the cock crow twice, thou shalt deny me thrice.
31 But he spake the more vehemently, If I
should die with thee, I will not deny thee in any
wise. Likewise also said they all.

The Prayer in the Garden
(Matt. 26:36–46; Luke 22:39–46)

32 [a]And they came to a place which was
named Gethsemane: and he saith to his disciples,
Sit ye here, while I shall pray.
33 And he [a]taketh with him Peter and James
and John, and began to be sore amazed, and to
be very heavy;
34 And saith unto them, [a]My soul is exceeding sorrowful unto death: tarry ye here, and
watch.
35 And he went forward a little, and fell on
the ground, and prayed that, if it were possible,
the hour might pass from him.
36 And he said, [a]Abba, Father, [b]all things *are*
possible unto thee; take away this cup from me:
[c]nevertheless not what I will, but what thou wilt.
37 And he cometh, and findeth them sleeping, and saith unto Peter, Simon, sleepest thou?
couldest not thou watch one hour?
38 [a]Watch ye and pray, lest ye enter into
temptation. [b]The spirit truly *is* ready, but the flesh
is weak.
39 And again he went away, and prayed, and
spake the same words.
40 And when he returned, he found them
asleep again, (for their eyes were heavy,) neither
wist they what to answer him.
41 And he cometh the third time, and saith
unto them, Sleep on now, and take *your* rest: it
is enough, [a]the hour is come; behold, the Son of
man is betrayed into the hands of sinners.
42 [a]Rise up, let us go; lo, he that betrayeth
me is at hand.

Betrayal and Arrest in Gethsemane
(Matt. 26:47–56; Luke 22:47–53; John 18:1–11)

43 [a]And immediately, while he yet spake,
cometh Judas, one of the twelve, and with him a
great multitude with swords and staves, from the
chief priest and the scribes and the elders.
44 And he that betrayed him had given them
a token, saying, Whomsoever I shall [a]kiss, that
same is he; take him, and lead *him* away safely.
45 And as soon as he was come, he goeth
straightway to him, and saith, Master, master; and
kissed him.
46 And they laid their hands on him, and
took him.
47 And one of them that stood by drew a
sword, and smote a servant of the high priest, and
cut off his ear.
48 [a]And Jesus answered and said unto them,
Are ye come out, as against a thief, with swords
and *with* staves to take me?
49 I was daily with you in the temple [a]teach-
ing, and ye took me not: but [b]the scriptures must
be fulfilled.
50 [a]And they all forsook him, and fled.

NKJV

Jesus Predicts Peter's Denial
(Matt. 26:31–35; Luke 22:31–34; John 13:36–38)

27 [a]Then Jesus said to them, "All of you will
be made to stumble *because of Me this night,
for it is written:

[b]'I will strike the Shepherd,
And the sheep will be scattered.'

28 "But [a]after I have been raised, I will go
before you to Galilee."
29 [a]Peter said to Him, "Even if all are made
to stumble, yet I *will* not *be.*"
30 Jesus said to him, "Assuredly, I say to you
that today, *even* this night, before the rooster
crows twice, you will deny Me three times."
31 But he spoke more vehemently, "If I have
to die with You, I will not deny You!" And they
all said likewise.

The Prayer in the Garden
(Matt. 26:36–46; Luke 22:39–46)

32 [a]Then they came to a place which was
named Gethsemane; and He said to His disciples,
"Sit here while I pray."
33 And He [a]took Peter, James, and John with
Him, and He began to be troubled and deeply
distressed.
34 Then He said to them, [a]"My soul is exceedingly sorrowful, *even* to death. Stay here and
watch."
35 He went a little farther, and fell on the
ground, and prayed that if it were possible, the
hour might pass from Him.
36 And He said, [a]"Abba, Father, [b]all things
are possible for You. Take this cup away from
Me; [c]nevertheless, not what I will, but what You
will."
37 Then He came and found them sleeping,
and said to Peter, "Simon, are you sleeping?
Could you not watch one hour?
38 [a]"Watch and pray, lest you enter into
temptation. [b]The spirit indeed *is* willing, but the
flesh *is* weak."
39 Again He went away and prayed, and
spoke the same words.
40 And when He returned, He found them
asleep again, for their eyes were heavy; and they
did not know what to answer Him.
41 Then He came the third time and said to
them, "Are you still sleeping and resting? It is
enough! [a]The hour has come; behold, the Son
of Man is being betrayed into the hands of sinners.
42 [a]"Rise, let us be going. See, My betrayer
is at hand."

Betrayal and Arrest in Gethsemane
(Matt. 26:47–56; Luke 22:47–53; John 18:1–11)

43 [a]And immediately, while He was still
speaking, Judas, one of the twelve, with a
great multitude with swords and clubs, came
from the chief priests and the scribes and the
elders.
44 Now His betrayer had given them a signal,
saying, "Whomever I [a]kiss, He is the One; seize
Him and lead *Him* away safely."
45 As soon as He had come, immediately he
went up to Him and said to Him, "Rabbi, Rabbi!"
and kissed Him.
46 Then they laid their hands on Him and
took Him.
47 And one of those who stood by drew his
sword and struck the servant of the high priest,
and cut off his ear.
48 [a]Then Jesus answered and said to them,
"Have you come out, as against a robber, with
swords and clubs to take Me?
49 "I was daily with you in the temple [a]teach-
ing, and you did not seize Me. But [b]the Scriptures
must be fulfilled."
50 [a]Then they all forsook Him and fled.

27 [a]Matt. 26:31–35; Mark 14:50; John 16:32 [b][Is. 53:5, 10]; Zech. 13:7
28 [a]Matt. 28:16; Mark 16:7; John 21:1
29 [a]Matt. 26:33, 34; Luke 22:33, 34; John 13:37, 38
32 [a]Matt. 26:36–46; Luke 22:40–46; John 18:1
33 [a]Mark 5:37; 9:2; 13:3
34 [a]Is. 53:3, 4; Matt. 26:38; John 12:27
36 [a]Rom. 8:15; Gal. 4:6 [b][Heb. 5:7] [c]Is. 50:5; John 5:30; 6:38
38 [a]Luke 21:36 [b][Rom. 7:18, 21–24; Gal. 5:17]
41 [a]John 13:1; 17:1
42 [a]Matt. 26:46; Mark 14:18; Luke 9:44; John 13:21; 18:1, 2
43 [a]Ps. 3:1; Matt. 26:47–56; Luke 22:47–53; John 18:3–11
44 [a][Prov. 27:6]
48 [a]Matt. 26:55; Luke 22:52
49 [a]Matt. 21:23 [b]Ps. 22:6; Is. 53:7; Luke 22:37; 24:44
50 [a]Ps. 88:8; Zech. 13:7; Matt. 26:31; Mark 14:27

*_________

14:27 NU omits *because of Me this night*

KJV

A Young Man Flees Naked

51 And there followed him a certain young
man, having a linen cloth cast about *his* naked
body; and the young men laid hold on him:
52 And he left the linen cloth, and fled from
them naked.

Jesus Faces the Sanhedrin
(Matt. 26:57–68; Luke 22:66–71;
John 18:12–14, 19–24)

53 [a]And they led Jesus away to the high
priest: and with him were [b]assembled all the
[c]chief priests and the elders and the scribes.
54 And [a]Peter followed him afar off, even
into the palace of the high priest: and he sat with
the servants, and warmed himself at the fire.
55 [a]And the chief priests and all the council
sought for witness against Jesus to put him to
death; and found none.
56 For many bare [a]false witness against him,
but their witness agreed not together.
57 And there arose certain, and bare false
witness against him, saying,
58 We heard him say, [a]I will destroy this temple that is made with hands, and within three days
I will build another made without hands.
59 But neither so did their witness agree
together.
60 [a]And the high priest stood up in the midst,
and asked Jesus, saying, Answerest thou nothing?
what *is it which* these witness against thee?
61 But [a]he held his peace, and answered
nothing. [b]Again the high priest asked him, and
said unto him, Art thou the Christ, the Son of the
Blessed?
62 And Jesus said, I am: [a]and ye shall see
the Son of man sitting on the right hand of power,
and coming in the clouds of heaven.
63 Then the high priest rent his clothes, and
saith, What need we any further witnesses?
64 Ye have heard the [a]blasphemy: what
think ye? And they all condemned him to be guilty
of [b]death.
65 And some began to [a]spit on him, and to
cover his face, and to buffet him, and to say unto
him, Prophesy: and the servants did strike him
with the palms of their hands.

Peter Denies Jesus, and Weeps
(Matt. 26:69–75; Luke 22:54–62;
John 18:15–18, 25–27)

66 [a]And as Peter was beneath in the palace,
there cometh one of the maids of the high priest:
67 And when she saw Peter warming himself, she looked upon him, and said, And thou also
wast with [a]Jesus of Nazareth.
68 But he denied, saying, I know not, neither
understand I what thou sayest. And he went out
into the porch; and the cock crew.
69 [a]And a maid saw him again, and began
to say to them that stood by, This is *one* of them.
70 And he denied it again. [a]And a little after,
they that stood by said again to Peter, Surely thou
art *one* of them: [b]for thou art a Galilaean, and
thy speech agreeth *thereto.*
71 But he began to curse and to swear, *saying,* I know not this man of whom ye speak.
72 [a]And the second time the cock crew. And
Peter called to mind the word that Jesus said unto
him, Before the cock crow twice, thou shalt deny
me thrice. And when he thought thereon, he wept.

Jesus Faces Pilate
(Matt. 27:1, 2, 11–14; Luke 23:1–5; John 18:28–38)

15 And [a]straightway in the morning the chief
priests held a consultation with the elders
and scribes and the whole council, and bound Jesus, and carried *him* away, and [b]delivered *him*
to Pilate.

53 [a]Matt. 26:57–68; Mark 10:33; Luke 22:54; John 18:12, 13, 19–24 [b]Mark 15:1 [c]Matt. 16:21; 27:12; Luke 9:22; 23:23; John 7:32; 18:3; 19:6
54 [a]John 18:15
55 [a]Matt. 26:59
56 [a]Ex. 20:16; Ps. 27:12; 35:11; Prov. 6:16–19; 19:5
58 [a]Matt. 26:61; Mark 15:29; John 2:19; [2 Cor. 5:1]
60 [a]Matt. 26:62; Mark 15:3–5
61 [a]Is. 53:7; John 19:9; Acts 8:32; [1 Pet. 2:23] [b]Matt. 26:63; Luke 22:67–71
62 [a]Matt. 24:30; 26:64; Luke 22:69
64 [a]John 10:33, 36 [b]Matt. 20:18; Mark 10:33; John 19:7
65 [a]Job 16:10; Is. 50:6; 52:14; Lam. 3:30; Mark 10:34; Luke 18:32
66 [a]Matt. 26:58, 69–75; Luke 22:55–62; John 18:16–18, 25–27
67 [a]Mark 10:47; John 1:45; Acts 10:38
69 [a]Matt. 26:71; Luke 22:58; John 18:25
70 [a]Matt. 26:73; Luke 22:59; John 18:26 [b]Acts 2:7
72 [a]Matt. 26:75; Mark 14:30; Luke 22:34; John 13:38

CHAPTER 15

1 [a]Ps. 2:2; Matt. 27:1; Luke 22:66; 23:1; John 18:28; Acts 3:13; 4:26 [b]Luke 18:32; Acts 3:13

*———

14:65 NU *received Him with slaps*
14:70 NU omits the rest of v. 70.

NKJV

A Young Man Flees Naked

51 Now a certain young man followed Him,
having a linen cloth thrown around *his* naked
body. And the young men laid hold of him,
52 and he left the linen cloth and fled from
them naked.

Jesus Faces the Sanhedrin
(Matt. 26:57–68; Luke 22:66–71;
John 18:12–14, 19–24)

53 [a]And they led Jesus away to the high
priest; and with him were [b]assembled all the
[c]chief priests, the elders, and the scribes.
54 But [a]Peter followed Him at a distance,
right into the courtyard of the high priest. And
he sat with the servants and warmed himself at
the fire.
55 [a]Now the chief priests and all the council
sought testimony against Jesus to put Him to
death, but found none.
56 For many bore [a]false witness against Him,
but their testimonies did not agree.
57 Then some rose up and bore false witness
against Him, saying,
58 "We heard Him say, [a]'I will destroy this
temple made with hands, and within three days I
will build another made without hands.'"
59 But not even then did their testimony
agree.
60 [a]And the high priest stood up in the midst
and asked Jesus, saying, "Do You answer nothing? What *is it* these men testify against You?"
61 But [a]He kept silent and answered nothing.
[b]Again the high priest asked Him, saying to Him,
"Are You the Christ, the Son of the Blessed?"
62 Jesus said, "I am. [a]And you will see the
Son of Man sitting at the right hand of the Power,
and coming with the clouds of heaven."
63 Then the high priest tore his clothes and
said, "What further need do we have of witnesses?
64 "You have heard the [a]blasphemy! What
do you think?" And they all condemned Him to
be deserving of [b]death.
65 Then some began to [a]spit on Him, and to
blindfold Him, and to beat Him, and to say to Him,
"Prophesy!" And the officers *struck Him with
the palms of their hands.

Peter Denies Jesus, and Weeps
(Matt. 26:69–75; Luke 22:54–62;
John 18:15–18, 25–27)

66 [a]Now as Peter was below in the courtyard,
one of the servant girls of the high priest came.
67 And when she saw Peter warming himself, she looked at him and said, "You also were
with [a]Jesus of Nazareth."
68 But he denied it, saying, "I neither know
nor understand what you are saying." And he
went out on the porch, and a rooster crowed.
69 [a]And the servant girl saw him again, and
began to say to those who stood by, "This is one
of them."
70 But he denied it again. [a]And a little later
those who stood by said to Peter again, "Surely
you are *one* of them; [b]for you are a Galilean, *and
your speech shows *it.*"
71 Then he began to curse and swear, "I do
not know this Man of whom you speak!"
72 [a]A second time *the* rooster crowed. Then
Peter called to mind the word that Jesus had said
to him, "Before the rooster crows twice, you will
deny Me three times." And when he thought about
it, he wept.

Jesus Faces Pilate
(Matt. 27:1, 2, 11–14; Luke 23:1–5; John 18:28–38)

15 Immediately, [a]in the morning, the chief
priests held a consultation with the elders
and scribes and the whole council; and they
bound Jesus, led *Him* away, and [b]delivered *Him*
to Pilate.

KJV

2 [a]And Pilate asked him, Art thou the King of the Jews? And he answering said unto him, Thou sayest *it*.

3 And the chief priests accused him of many things: but he [a]answered nothing.

4 [a]And Pilate asked him again, saying, Answerest thou nothing? behold how many things they witness against thee.

5 [a]But Jesus yet answered nothing; so that Pilate marvelled.

Taking the Place of Barabbas
(Matt. 27:15–26; Luke 23:17–25; John 18:39—19:16)

6 Now [a]at *that* feast he released unto them one prisoner, whomsoever they desired.

7 And there was *one* named Barabbas, *which lay* bound with them that had made insurrection with him, who had committed murder in the insurrection.

8 And the multitude crying aloud began to desire *him to do* as he had ever done unto them.

9 But Pilate answered them, saying, Will ye that I release unto you the King of the Jews?

10 For he knew that the chief priests had delivered him for envy.

11 But [a]the chief priests moved the people, that he should rather release Barabbas unto them.

12 And Pilate answered and said again unto them, What will ye then that I shall do *unto him* whom ye call the [a]King of the Jews?

13 And they cried out again, Crucify him.

14 Then Pilate said unto them, Why, [a]what evil hath he done? And they cried out the more exceedingly, Crucify him.

15 [a]And *so* Pilate, willing to content the people, released Barabbas unto them, and delivered Jesus, when he had scourged *him*, to be [b]crucified.

The Soldiers Mock Jesus
(Matt. 27:27–31)

16 [a]And the soldiers led him away into the hall, called Praetorium; and they call together the whole band.

17 And they clothed him with purple, and platted a crown of thorns, and put it about his *head*,

18 And began to salute him, Hail, King of the Jews!

19 And they [a]smote him on the head with a reed, and did spit upon him, and bowing *their* knees worshipped him.

20 And when they had [a]mocked him, they took off the purple from him, and put his own clothes on him, and led him out to crucify him.

The King on a Cross
(Matt. 27:32–44; Luke 23:26–43; John 19:17–27)

21 [a]And they compel one Simon a Cyrenian, who passed by, coming out of the country, the father of Alexander and Rufus, to bear his cross.

22 [a]And they bring him unto the place Golgotha, which is, being interpreted, The place of a skull.

23 [a]And they gave him to drink wine mingled with myrrh: but he received *it* not.

24 And when they had crucified him, [a]they parted his garments, casting lots upon them, what every man should take.

25 And [a]it was the third hour, and they crucified him.

26 And [a]the superscription of his accusation was written over, THE KING OF THE JEWS.

27 And [a]with him they crucify two thieves; the one on his right hand, and the other on his left.

28 And the scripture was fulfilled, which saith, [a]AND HE WAS NUMBERED WITH THE TRANSGRESSORS.

29 And [a]they that passed by railed on him,

2 [a]Matt. 27:11–14; Luke 23:2, 3; John 18:29–38
3 [a]Is. 53:7; John 19:9; Acts 8:32
4 [a]Matt. 27:13
5 [a]Ps. 38:13, 14; Is. 53:7; John 19:9
6 [a]Matt. 27:15–26; Luke 23:18–25; John 18:39—19:16
11 [a]Matt. 27:20; Acts 3:14
12 [a]Ps. 2:6; [Is. 9:7]; Jer. 23:5; 33:15; Mic. 5:2
14 [a]Is. 53:9; John 8:46; 1 Pet. 2:21–23
15 [a]Is. 50:6; Matt. 27:26; Mark 10:34; John 19:1, 16 [b][Is. 53:8]
16 [a]Matt. 27:27–31
19 [a][Is. 50:6; 52:14; 53:5]; Mic. 5:1; Mark 14:65
20 [a]Ps. 35:16; 69:19; Is. 53:3; Matt. 20:19; Mark 10:34; Luke 22:63; 23:11
21 [a]Matt. 27:32; Luke 23:26
22 [a]Matt. 27:33–44; Luke 23:33–43; John 19:17–24; Heb. 13:12
23 [a]Ps. 69:21; Matt. 27:34
24 [a]Ps. 22:18; Luke 23:34; John 19:23
25 [a]Matt. 27:45; Luke 23:44; John 19:14
26 [a]Matt. 27:37; John 19:19
27 [a]Is. 53:9, 12; Matt. 27:38; Luke 22:37
28 [a]Is. 53:12; Luke 22:37
29 [a]Ps. 22:6, 7; 69:7

*————

15:4 NU *of which they accuse You*
15:8 NU *going up*
15:28 NU omits v. 28.

NKJV

2 [a]Then Pilate asked Him, "Are You the King of the Jews?" He answered and said to him, "*It is as* you say."

3 And the chief priests accused Him of many things, but He [a]answered nothing.

4 [a]Then Pilate asked Him again, saying, "Do You answer nothing? See how many things *they testify against You!"

5 [a]But Jesus still answered nothing, so that Pilate marveled.

Taking the Place of Barabbas
(Matt. 27:15–26; Luke 23:17–25; John 18:39—19:16)

6 Now [a]at the feast he was accustomed to releasing one prisoner to them, whomever they requested.

7 And there was one named Barabbas, *who was* chained with his fellow rebels; they had committed murder in the rebellion.

8 Then the multitude, *crying aloud, began to ask *him to do* just as he had always done for them.

9 But Pilate answered them, saying, "Do you want me to release to you the King of the Jews?"

10 For he knew that the chief priests had handed Him over because of envy.

11 But [a]the chief priests stirred up the crowd, so that he should rather release Barabbas to them.

12 Pilate answered and said to them again, "What then do you want me to do *with Him* whom you call the [a]King of the Jews?"

13 So they cried out again, "Crucify Him!"

14 Then Pilate said to them, "Why, [a]what evil has He done?" But they cried out all the more, "Crucify Him!"

15 [a]So Pilate, wanting to gratify the crowd, released Barabbas to them; and he delivered Jesus, after he had scourged *Him*, to be [b]crucified.

The Soldiers Mock Jesus
(Matt. 27:27–31)

16 [a]Then the soldiers led Him away into the hall called Praetorium, and they called together the whole garrison.

17 And they clothed Him with purple; and they twisted a crown of thorns, put it on His *head*,

18 and began to salute Him, "Hail, King of the Jews!"

19 Then they [a]struck Him on the head with a reed and spat on Him; and bowing the knee, they worshiped Him.

20 And when they had [a]mocked Him, they took the purple off Him, put His own clothes on Him, and led Him out to crucify Him.

The King on a Cross
(Matt. 27:32–44; Luke 23:26–43; John 19:17–27)

21 [a]Then they compelled a certain man, Simon a Cyrenian, the father of Alexander and Rufus, as he was coming out of the country and passing by, to bear His cross.

22 [a]And they brought Him to the place Golgotha, which is translated, Place of a Skull.

23 [a]Then they gave Him wine mingled with myrrh to drink, but He did not take *it*.

24 And when they crucified Him, [a]they divided His garments, casting lots for them to determine what every man should take.

25 Now [a]it was the third hour, and they crucified Him.

26 And [a]the inscription of His accusation was written above:

THE KING OF THE JEWS.

27 [a]With Him they also crucified two robbers, one on His right and the other on His left.

28 *So the Scripture was fulfilled which says, [a]*"And He was numbered with the transgressors."*

29 And [a]those who passed by blasphemed

KJV

[b]wagging their heads, and saying, Ah, [c]thou that
destroyest the temple, and buildest *it* in three
days,
30 Save thyself, and come down from the
cross.
31 Likewise also the chief priests [a]mocking
said among themselves with the scribes, He saved
[b]others; himself he cannot save.
32 Let Christ the King of Israel descend now
from the cross, that we may see and believe. And
[a]they that were crucified with him reviled him.

Jesus Dies on the Cross
(Matt. 27:45–56; Luke 23:44–49; John 19:28–30)

33 And [a]when the sixth hour was come, there
was darkness over the whole land until the ninth
hour.
34 And at the ninth hour Jesus cried with a
loud voice, saying, Eloi, Eloi, lama sabachthani?
which is, being interpreted, [a]MY GOD, MY GOD,
WHY HAST THOU FORSAKEN ME?
35 And some of them that stood by, when
they heard *it*, said, Behold, he calleth Elias.
36 And [a]one ran and filled a spunge full of
vinegar, and put *it* on a reed, and [b]gave him to
drink, saying, Let alone; let us see whether Elias
will come to take him down.
37 [a]And Jesus cried with a loud voice, and
gave up the ghost.
38 And [a]the veil of the temple was rent in
twain from the top to the bottom.
39 And [a]when the centurion, which stood
over against him, saw that he so cried out, and
gave up the ghost, he said, Truly this man was
the Son of God.
40 [a]There were also women looking on [b]afar
off: among whom was Mary Magdalene, and
Mary the mother of James the less and of Joses,
and Salome;
41 (Who also, when he was in Galilee, [a]fol-
lowed him, and ministered unto him;) and many
other women which came up with him unto Jerusalem.

Jesus Buried in Joseph's Tomb
(Matt. 27:57–61; Luke 23:50–56; John 19:38–42)

42 [a]And now when the even was come, because it was the preparation, that is, the day
before the sabbath,
43 Joseph of Arimathaea, an honourable
counsellor, which also [a]waited for the kingdom
of God, came, and went in boldly unto Pilate, and
craved the body of Jesus.
44 And Pilate marvelled if he were already
dead: and calling *unto him* the centurion, he
asked him whether he had been any while dead.
45 And when he knew *it* of the centurion,
he gave the body to Joseph.
46 [a]And he bought fine linen, and took him
down, and wrapped him in the linen, and laid him
in a sepulchre which was hewn out of a rock, and
rolled a stone unto the door of the sepulchre.
47 And Mary Magdalene and Mary *the
mother* of Joses beheld where he was laid.

He Is Risen
(Matt. 28:1–8; Luke 24:1–12; John 20:1–10)

16 And [a]when the sabbath was past, Mary
Magdalene, and Mary the *mother* of James,
and Salome, [b]had bought sweet spices, that they
might come and anoint him.
2 [a]And very early in the morning the first
day of the week, they came unto the sepulchre
at the rising of the sun.
3 And they said among themselves, Who
shall roll us away the stone from the door of the
sepulchre?
4 And when they looked, they saw that the
stone was rolled away: for it was very great.
5 [a]And entering into the sepulchre, they

29 [b]Ps. 109:25 [c]Mark 14:58; John 2:19–21
31 [a]Luke 18:32 [b]Luke 7:14, 15; John 11:43, 44
32 [a]Amos 8:9; Matt. 27:44; Luke 23:39
33 [a]Matt. 27:45–56; Luke 23:44–49
34 [a]Ps. 22:1; Matt. 27:46
36 [a]Matt. 27:48; John 19:29 [b]Ps. 69:21
37 [a]Dan. 9:26; Zech. 11:10, 11; Matt. 27:50; Mark 8:31; Luke 23:46; John 19:30
38 [a]Ex. 26:31–33; Matt. 27:51; Luke 23:45
39 [a]Matt. 27:54; Luke 23:47
40 [a]Matt. 27:55; Luke 23:49; John 19:25 [b]Ps. 38:11
41 [a]Luke 8:2, 3
42 [a]Matt. 27:57–61; Luke 23:50–56; John 19:38–42
43 [a]Matt. 27:57; Luke 2:25, 38; 23:51; John 19:38
46 [a]Is. 53:9; Matt. 27:59, 60; Luke 23:53; John 19:40

CHAPTER 16

1 [a]Matt. 28:1–8; Luke 24:1–10; John 20:1–8 [b]Luke 23:56; John 19:39
2 [a]Luke 24:1; John 20:1
5 [a]Luke 24:3; John 20:11, 12

*

15:32 M *believe Him*
15:39 NU *He thus breathed His last*

NKJV

Him, [b]wagging their heads and saying, "Aha!
[c]*You* who destroy the temple and build *it* in three
days,
30 "save Yourself, and come down from the
cross!"
31 Likewise the chief priests also, [a]mocking
among themselves with the scribes, said, "He
saved [b]others; Himself He cannot save.
32 "Let the Christ, the King of Israel, descend
now from the cross, that we may see and *believe." Even [a]those who were crucified with Him
reviled Him.

Jesus Dies on the Cross
(Matt. 27:45–56; Luke 23:44–49; John 19:28–30)

33 Now [a]when the sixth hour had come,
there was darkness over the whole land until the
ninth hour.
34 And at the ninth hour Jesus cried out
with a loud voice, saying, "Eloi, Eloi, lama
sabachthani?" which is translated, [a]*"My God, My
God, why have You forsaken Me?"*
35 Some of those who stood by, when they
heard *that*, said, "Look, He is calling for Elijah!"
36 Then [a]someone ran and filled a sponge
full of sour wine, put *it* on a reed, and [b]offered *it*
to Him to drink, saying, "Let Him alone; let us
see if Elijah will come to take Him down."
37 [a]And Jesus cried out with a loud voice,
and breathed His last.
38 Then [a]the veil of the temple was torn in
two from top to bottom.
39 So [a]when the centurion, who stood opposite Him, saw that *He cried out like this and
breathed His last, he said, "Truly this Man was
the Son of God!"
40 [a]There were also women looking on [b]from
afar, among whom were Mary Magdalene, Mary
the mother of James the Less and of Joses, and
Salome,
41 who also [a]followed Him and ministered
to Him when He was in Galilee, and many other
women who came up with Him to Jerusalem.

Jesus Buried in Joseph's Tomb
(Matt. 27:57–61; Luke 23:50–56; John 19:38–42)

42 [a]Now when evening had come, because
it was the Preparation Day, that is, the day before
the Sabbath,
43 Joseph of Arimathea, a prominent council
member, who [a]was himself waiting for the kingdom of God, coming and taking courage, went
in to Pilate and asked for the body of Jesus.
44 Pilate marveled that He was already dead;
and summoning the centurion, he asked him if
He had been dead for some time.
45 So when he found out from the centurion,
he granted the body to Joseph.
46 [a]Then he bought fine linen, took Him
down, and wrapped Him in the linen. And he laid
Him in a tomb which had been hewn out of the
rock, and rolled a stone against the door of the
tomb.
47 And Mary Magdalene and Mary *the
mother* of Joses observed where He was laid.

He Is Risen
(Matt. 28:1–8; Luke 24:1–12; John 20:1–10)

16 Now [a]when the Sabbath was past, Mary
Magdalene, Mary *the mother* of James, and
Salome [b]bought spices, that they might come and
anoint Him.
2 [a]Very early in the morning, on the first
day of the week, they came to the tomb when the
sun had risen.
3 And they said among themselves, "Who
will roll away the stone from the door of the tomb
for us?"
4 But when they looked up, they saw that
the stone had been rolled away—for it was very
large.
5 [a]And entering the tomb, they saw a young

KJV

saw a young man sitting on the right side, clothed in a long white garment; and they were affrighted.

6 [a]And he saith unto them, Be not affrighted: Ye seek Jesus of Nazareth, which was crucified: he is risen; he is not here: behold the place where they laid him.

7 But go your way, tell his disciples and Peter that he goeth before you into Galilee: there shall ye see him, [a]as he said unto you.

8 And they went out quickly, and fled from the sepulchre; for they trembled and were amazed: [a]neither said they any thing to any *man*; for they were afraid.

Mary Magdalene Sees the Risen Lord
(Matt. 28:9, 10; John 20:11–18)

9 Now when *Jesus* was risen early the first *day* of the week, he appeared first to Mary Magdalene, [a]out of whom he had cast seven devils.

10 [a]*And* she went and told them that had been with him, as they mourned and wept.

11 [a]And they, when they had heard that he was alive, and had been seen of her, believed not.

Jesus Appears to Two Disciples
(Luke 24:13–35)

12 After that he appeared in another form [a]unto two of them, as they walked, and went into the country.

13 And they went and told *it* unto the residue: neither believed they them.

The Great Commission
(Matt. 28:16–20; Luke 24:44–49; Acts 1:6–8)

14 [a]Afterward he appeared unto the eleven as they sat at meat, and upbraided them with their unbelief and hardness of heart, because they believed not them which had seen him after he was risen.

15 [a]And he said unto them, Go ye into all the world, [b]and preach the gospel to every creature.

16 [a]He that believeth and is baptized shall be saved; [b]but he that believeth not shall be damned.

17 And these [a]signs shall follow them that believe; [b]In my name shall they cast out devils; [c]they shall speak with new tongues;

18 [a]They shall take up serpents; and if they drink any deadly thing, it shall not hurt them; [b]they shall lay hands on the sick, and they shall recover.

Christ Ascends to God's Right Hand
(Luke 24:50–53)

19 So then [a]after the Lord had spoken unto them, he was [b]received up into heaven, and [c]sat on the right hand of God.

20 And they went forth, and preached every where, the Lord working with *them,* [a]and confirming the word with signs following. Amen.

NKJV

man clothed in a long white robe sitting on the right side; and they were alarmed.

6 [a]But he said to them, "Do not be alarmed. You seek Jesus of Nazareth, who was crucified. He is risen! He is not here. See the place where they laid Him.

7 "But go, tell His disciples—and Peter—that He is going before you into Galilee; there you will see Him, [a]as He said to you."

8 So they went out *quickly and fled from the tomb, for they trembled and were amazed. [a]And they said nothing to anyone, for they were afraid.

Mary Magdalene Sees the Risen Lord
(Matt. 28:9, 10; John 20:11–18)

9 *Now when *He* rose early on the first *day* of the week, He appeared first to Mary Magdalene, [a]out of whom He had cast seven demons.

10 [a]She went and told those who had been with Him, as they mourned and wept.

11 [a]And when they heard that He was alive and had been seen by her, they did not believe.

Jesus Appears to Two Disciples
(Luke 24:13–35)

12 After that, He appeared in another form [a]to two of them as they walked and went into the country.

13 And they went and told *it* to the rest, *but* they did not believe them either.

The Great Commission
(Matt. 28:16–20; Luke 24:44–49; Acts 1:6–8)

14 [a]Later He appeared to the eleven as they sat at the table; and He rebuked their unbelief and hardness of heart, because they did not believe those who had seen Him after He had risen.

15 [a]And He said to them, "Go into all the world [b]and preach the gospel to every creature.

16 [a]"He who believes and is baptized will be saved; [b]but he who does not believe will be condemned.

17 "And these [a]signs will follow those who believe: [b]In My name they will cast out demons; [c]they will speak with new tongues;

18 [a]"they* will take up serpents; and if they drink anything deadly, it will by no means hurt them; [b]they will lay hands on the sick, and they will recover."

Christ Ascends to God's Right Hand
(Luke 24:50–53)

19 So then, [a]after the Lord had spoken to them, He was [b]received up into heaven, and [c]sat down at the right hand of God.

20 And they went out and preached everywhere, the Lord working with *them* [a]and confirming the word through the accompanying signs. Amen.

---

6 [a]Matt. 28:6
7 [a]Matt. 26:32; 28:16, 17
8 [a]Matt. 28:8
9 [a]Luke 8:2
10 [a]Luke 24:10
11 [a]Luke 24:11, 41
12 [a]Luke 24:13–35
14 [a]1 Cor. 15:5
15 [a]Matt. 28:19 [b][Col. 1:23]
16 [a][John 3:18, 36] [b][John 12:48]
17 [a]Acts 5:12 [b]Luke 10:17 [c][Acts 2:4]
18 [a]Acts 28:3–6 [b]James 5:14
19 [a]Acts 1:2, 3 [b]Luke 9:51; 24:51 [c][Ps. 110:1]
20 [a][Heb. 2:4]

*

16:8 NU, M omit *quickly*
16:9 Vv. 9–20 are bracketed in NU as not in the original text. They are lacking in Codex Sinaiticus and Codex Vaticanus, although nearly all other mss. of Mark contain them.
16:18 NU *and in their hands they will*

KJV

THE GOSPEL ACCORDING TO

LUKE

Dedication to Theophilus

1 Forasmuch as many have taken in hand to set forth in order a declaration of those [a]things which are most surely believed among us,

2 Even as they [c]delivered them unto us, which [a]from the beginning were [b]eyewitnesses, and ministers of the word;

3 It seemed good to me also, having had perfect understanding of all things from the very first, to write unto thee in order, [a]most excellent Theophilus,

4 [a]That thou mightest know the certainty of those things, wherein thou hast been instructed.

John's Birth Announced to Zacharias

5 There was [a]in the days of Herod, the king of Judaea, a certain priest named Zacharias, [b]of the course of [c]Abia: and his [d]wife *was* of the daughters of Aaron, and her name *was* Elisabeth.

6 And they were both righteous before God, walking in all the commandments and ordinances of the Lord blameless.

7 And they had no child, because that Elisabeth was barren, and they both were *now* well stricken in years.

8 And it came to pass, that while he executed the priest's office before God in the order of his course,

9 According to the custom of the priest's office, his lot was [a]to burn incense when he went into the temple of the Lord.

10 [a]And the whole multitude of the people were praying without at the time of incense.

11 And there appeared unto him an angel of the Lord standing on the right side of [a]the altar of incense.

12 And when Zacharias saw *him,* [a]he was troubled, and fear fell upon him.

13 But the angel said unto him, Fear not, Zacharias: for thy prayer is heard; and thy wife Elisabeth shall bear thee a son, and [a]thou shalt call his name John.

14 And thou shalt have joy and gladness; and [a]many shall rejoice at his birth.

15 For he shall be [a]great in the sight of the Lord, and [b]shall drink neither wine nor strong drink; and he shall be filled with the Holy Ghost, [c]even from his mother's womb.

16 And many of the children of Israel shall he turn to the Lord their God.

17 [a]And he shall go before him in the spirit and power of Elias, TO TURN THE HEARTS OF THE FATHERS TO THE CHILDREN, and the disobedient to the wisdom of the just; to make ready a people prepared for the Lord.

18 And Zacharias said unto the angel, [a]Whereby shall I know this? for I am an old man, and my wife well stricken in years.

19 And the angel answering said unto him, I am [a]Gabriel, that stand in the presence of God; and am sent to speak unto thee, and to shew thee these glad [b]tidings.

20 And, behold, [a]thou shalt be dumb, and not able to speak, until the day that these things shall be performed, because thou believest not my words, which shall be fulfilled in their season.

CHAPTER 1

1 [a]John 20:31
2 [a]Mark 1:1; John 15:27; Acts 1:21, 22 [b]Acts 1:2 [c]Acts 1:3; 10:39; Heb. 2:3; 1 Pet. 5:1; 2 Pet. 1:16; 1 John 1:1
3 [a]Acts 1:1
4 [a][John 20:31]
5 [a]Matt. 2:1 [b]1 Chr. 24:1, 10 [c]Neh. 12:4 [d]Lev. 21:13, 14
9 [a]Ex. 30:7, 8; 1 Chr. 23:13; 2 Chr. 29:11
10 [a]Lev. 16:17
11 [a]Ex. 30:1
12 [a]Judg. 6:22; Dan. 10:8; Luke 2:9; Acts 10:4; Rev. 1:17
13 [a]Luke 1:57, 60, 63
14 [a]Luke 1:58
15 [a][Luke 7:24–28] [b]Num. 6:3; Judg. 13:4; Matt. 11:18 [c]Jer. 1:5; Gal. 1:15
17 [a]Mal. 4:5, 6; Matt. 3:2; 11:14; Mark 1:4; 9:12
18 [a]Gen. 17:17
19 [a]Dan. 8:16; [Matt. 18:10]; Heb. 1:4 [b]Luke 2:10
20 [a]Ezek. 3:26; 24:27

*

1:1 Or *are most surely believed*

NKJV

THE GOSPEL ACCORDING TO

LUKE

Dedication to Theophilus

1 Inasmuch as many have taken in hand to set in order a narrative of those [a]things which *have been fulfilled among us,

2 just as those who [a]from the beginning were [b]eyewitnesses and ministers of the word [c]delivered them to us,

3 it seemed good to me also, having had perfect understanding of all things from the very first, to write to you an orderly account, [a]most excellent Theophilus,

4 [a]that you may know the certainty of those things in which you were instructed.

John's Birth Announced to Zacharias

5 There was [a]in the days of Herod, the king of Judea, a certain priest named Zacharias, [b]of the division of [c]Abijah. His [d]wife *was* of the daughters of Aaron, and her name *was* Elizabeth.

6 And they were both righteous before God, walking in all the commandments and ordinances of the Lord blameless.

7 But they had no child, because Elizabeth was barren, and they were both well advanced in years.

8 So it was, that while he was serving as priest before God in the order of his division,

9 according to the custom of the priesthood, his lot fell [a]to burn incense when he went into the temple of the Lord.

10 [a]And the whole multitude of the people was praying outside at the hour of incense.

11 Then an angel of the Lord appeared to him, standing on the right side of [a]the altar of incense.

12 And when Zacharias saw *him,* [a]he was troubled, and fear fell upon him.

13 But the angel said to him, "Do not be afraid, Zacharias, for your prayer is heard; and your wife Elizabeth will bear you a son, and [a]you shall call his name John.

14 "And you will have joy and gladness, and [a]many will rejoice at his birth.

15 "For he will be [a]great in the sight of the Lord, and [b]shall drink neither wine nor strong drink. He will also be filled with the Holy Spirit, [c]even from his mother's womb.

16 "And he will turn many of the children of Israel to the Lord their God.

17 [a]"He will also go before Him in the spirit and power of Elijah, *'to turn the hearts of the fathers to the children,'* and the disobedient to the wisdom of the just, to make ready a people prepared for the Lord."

18 And Zacharias said to the angel, [a]"How shall I know this? For I am an old man, and my wife is well advanced in years."

19 And the angel answered and said to him, "I am [a]Gabriel, who stands in the presence of God, and was sent to speak to you and bring you these glad [b]tidings.

20 "But behold, [a]you will be mute and not able to speak until the day these things take place, because you did not believe my words which will be fulfilled in their own time."

KJV

21 And the people waited for Zacharias, and marvelled that he tarried so long in the temple.

22 And when he came out, he could not speak unto them: and they perceived that he had seen a vision in the temple: for he beckoned unto them, and remained speechless.

23 And it came to pass, that, as soon as [a]the days of his ministration were accomplished, he departed to his own house.

24 And after those days his wife Elisabeth conceived, and hid herself five months, saying,

25 Thus hath the Lord dealt with me in the days wherein he looked on *me,* to [a]take away my reproach among men.

Christ's Birth Announced to Mary

26 And in the sixth month the angel Gabriel was sent from God unto a city of Galilee, named Nazareth,

27 To a virgin [a]espoused to a man whose name was Joseph, of the house of David; and the virgin's name *was* Mary.

28 And the angel came in unto her, and said, [a]Hail, *thou that art* highly favoured, [b]the Lord *is* with thee: blessed *art* thou among women.

29 And when she saw *him,* [a]she was troubled at his saying, and cast in her mind what manner of salutation this should be.

30 And the angel said unto her, Fear not, Mary: for thou hast found [a]favour with God.

31 [a]And, behold, thou shalt conceive in thy womb, and bring forth a son, and [b]shalt call his name JESUS.

32 He shall be great, [a]and shall be called the Son of the Highest: and [b]the Lord God shall give unto him the [c]throne of his [d]father David:

33 [a]And he shall reign over the house of Jacob for ever; and of his kingdom there shall be no end.

34 Then said Mary unto the angel, How shall this be, seeing I know not a man?

35 And the angel answered and said unto her, [a]The Holy Ghost shall come upon thee, and the power of the Highest shall overshadow thee: therefore also that holy thing which shall be born of thee shall be called [b]the Son of God.

36 And, behold, thy cousin Elisabeth, she hath also conceived a son in her old age: and this is the sixth month with her, who was called barren.

37 For [a]with God nothing shall be impossible.

38 And Mary said, Behold the handmaid of the Lord; be it unto me according to thy word. And the angel departed from her.

Mary Visits Elisabeth

39 And Mary arose in those days, and went into the hill country with haste, [a]into a city of Juda;

40 And entered into the house of Zacharias, and saluted Elisabeth.

41 And it came to pass, that, when Elisabeth heard the salutation of Mary, the babe leaped in her womb; and Elisabeth was [a]filled with the Holy Ghost:

42 And she spake out with a loud voice, and said, [a]Blessed *art* thou among women, and blessed *is* the fruit of thy womb.

43 And whence *is* this to me, that the mother of my Lord should come to me?

44 For, lo, as soon as the voice of thy salutation sounded in mine ears, the babe leaped in my womb for joy.

45 And [a]blessed *is* she that believed: for there shall be a performance of those things which were told her from the Lord.

The Song of Mary

46 And Mary said, [a]My soul doth magnify the Lord,

23 [a]2 Kin. 11:5; 1 Chr. 9:25
25 [a]Gen. 30:23; Is. 4:1; 54:1, 4
27 [a]Matt. 1:18; Luke 2:4, 5
28 [a]Dan. 9:23 [b]Judg. 6:12
29 [a]Luke 1:12
30 [a]Luke 2:52
31 [a]Is. 7:14; Matt. 1:21, 25; Gal. 4:4 [b]Luke 2:21; [Phil. 2:9–11]
32 [a]Matt. 3:17; 17:5; Mark 5:7; Luke 1:35, 76; 6:35; Acts 7:48 [b]2 Sam. 7:12, 13, 16; Ps. 132:11; [Is. 9:6, 7; 16:5; Jer. 23:5] [c]2 Sam. 7:14–17; Acts 2:33; 7:55 [d]Matt. 1:1
33 [a][Dan. 2:44; Obad. 21; Mic. 4:7]; John 12:34; [Heb. 1:8]; 2 Pet. 1:11
35 [a]Matt. 1:20 [b]Ps. 2:7; Matt. 3:17; 14:33; 17:5; Mark 1:1; John 1:34; 20:31; Acts 8:37; [Rom. 1:1–4; Heb. 1:2, 8]
37 [a]Gen. 18:14; Jer. 32:17; Matt. 19:26; Mark 10:27; Rom. 4:21
39 [a]Josh. 21:9
41 [a]Acts 6:3
42 [a]Judg. 5:24
45 [a]John 20:29
46 [a]1 Sam. 2:1–10; Ps. 34:2, 3; Hab. 3:18

*

1:28 NU omits *blessed are you among women*
1:29 NU omits *when she saw him*

NKJV

21 And the people waited for Zacharias, and marveled that he lingered so long in the temple.

22 But when he came out, he could not speak to them; and they perceived that he had seen a vision in the temple, for he beckoned to them and remained speechless.

23 So it was, as soon as [a]the days of his service were completed, that he departed to his own house.

24 Now after those days his wife Elizabeth conceived; and she hid herself five months, saying,

25 "Thus the Lord has dealt with me, in the days when He looked on *me,* to [a]take away my reproach among people."

Christ's Birth Announced to Mary

26 Now in the sixth month the angel Gabriel was sent by God to a city of Galilee named Nazareth,

27 to a virgin [a]betrothed to a man whose name was Joseph, of the house of David. The virgin's name *was* Mary.

28 And having come in, the angel said to her, [a]"Rejoice, highly favored *one,* [b]the Lord *is* with you; *blessed *are* you among women!"

29 But *when she saw *him,* [a]she was troubled at his saying, and considered what manner of greeting this was.

30 Then the angel said to her, "Do not be afraid, Mary, for you have found [a]favor with God.

31 [a]"And behold, you will conceive in your womb and bring forth a Son, and [b]shall call His name JESUS.

32 "He will be great, [a]and will be called the Son of the Highest; and [b]the Lord God will give Him the [c]throne of His [d]father David.

33 [a]"And He will reign over the house of Jacob forever, and of His kingdom there will be no end."

34 Then Mary said to the angel, "How can this be, since I do not know a man?"

35 And the angel answered and said to her, [a]"*The* Holy Spirit will come upon you, and the power of the Highest will overshadow you; therefore, also, that Holy One who is to be born will be called [b]the Son of God.

36 "Now indeed, Elizabeth your relative has also conceived a son in her old age; and this is now the sixth month for her who was called barren.

37 "For [a]with God nothing will be impossible."

38 Then Mary said, "Behold the maidservant of the Lord! Let it be to me according to your word." And the angel departed from her.

Mary Visits Elizabeth

39 Now Mary arose in those days and went into the hill country with haste, [a]to a city of Judah,

40 and entered the house of Zacharias and greeted Elizabeth.

41 And it happened, when Elizabeth heard the greeting of Mary, that the babe leaped in her womb; and Elizabeth was [a]filled with the Holy Spirit.

42 Then she spoke out with a loud voice and said, [a]"Blessed *are* you among women, and blessed *is* the fruit of your womb!

43 "But why *is* this *granted* to me, that the mother of my Lord should come to me?

44 "For indeed, as soon as the voice of your greeting sounded in my ears, the babe leaped in my womb for joy.

45 [a]"Blessed *is* she who believed, for there will be a fulfillment of those things which were told her from the Lord."

The Song of Mary

46 And Mary said:

[a]"My soul magnifies the Lord,

KJV

47 And my spirit hath [a]rejoiced in [b]God my Saviour.
48 For [a]he hath regarded the low estate of his handmaiden: for, behold, from henceforth [b]all generations shall call me blessed.
49 For he that is mighty [a]hath done to me great things; and [b]holy *is* his name.
50 And [a]his mercy *is* on them that fear him from generation to generation.
51 [a]He hath shewed strength with his arm; [b]he hath scattered the proud in the imagination of their hearts.
52 [a]He hath put down the mighty from *their* seats, and exalted them of low degree.
53 He hath [a]filled the hungry with good things; and the rich he hath sent empty away.
54 He hath holpen his [a]servant Israel, [b]in remembrance of *his* mercy;
55 [a]As he spake to our [b]fathers, to Abraham, and to his [c]seed for ever.
56 And Mary abode with her about three months, and returned to her own house.

Birth of John the Baptist

57 Now Elisabeth's full time came that she should be delivered; and she brought forth a son.
58 And her neighbours and her cousins heard how the Lord had shewed great mercy upon her; and they [a]rejoiced with her.

Circumcision of John the Baptist

59 And it came to pass, that [a]on the eighth day they came to circumcise the child; and they called him Zacharias, after the name of his father.
60 And his mother answered and said, [a]Not *so;* but he shall be called John.
61 And they said unto her, There is none of thy kindred that is called by this name.
62 And they made signs to his father, how he would have him called.
63 And he asked for a writing table, and wrote, saying, His name is John. And they marvelled all.
64 And his mouth was opened immediately, and his tongue *loosed,* and he spake, and praised God.
65 And fear came on all that dwelt round about them: and all these sayings were noised abroad throughout all the hill country of Judaea.
66 And all they that heard *them* [a]laid *them* up in their hearts, saying, What manner of child shall this be! And [b]the hand of the Lord was with him.

Zacharias' Prophecy

67 And his father Zacharias [a]was filled with the Holy Ghost, and prophesied, saying,
68 [a]Blessed *be* the Lord God of Israel; for [b]he hath visited and redeemed his people,
69 [a]And hath raised up an horn of salvation for us in the house of his servant David;
70 [a]As he spake by the mouth of his holy prophets, which have been [b]since the world began:
71 That we should be saved from our enemies, and from the hand of all that hate us;
72 [a]To perform the mercy *promised* to our fathers, and to remember his holy covenant;
73 [a]The oath which he sware to our father Abraham,
74 That he would grant unto us, that we

47 [a]Ps. 35:9; Hab. 3:18 [b]1 Tim. 1:1; 2:3; Titus 1:3; 2:10; 3:4; Jude 25
48 [a]1 Sam. 1:11; Ps. 138:6 [b]Luke 11:27
49 [a]Ps. 71:19; 126:2, 3 [b]Ps. 111:9; Rev. 4:8
50 [a]Gen. 17:7; Ex. 20:6; 34:6, 7; Ps. 103:17
51 [a]Ps. 98:1; 118:15; Is. 40:10 [b]Ps. 33:10; [1 Pet. 5:5]
52 [a]1 Sam. 2:7, 8
53 [a][Matt. 5:6]
54 [a]Is. 41:8 [b]Ps. 98:3; [Jer. 31:3]
55 [a]Gen. 17:19; Ps. 132:11; [Gal. 3:16] [b][Rom. 11:28] [c]Gen. 17:7
58 [a][Rom. 12:15]
59 [a]Gen. 17:12; Lev. 12:3; Luke 2:21; Phil. 3:5
60 [a]Luke 1:13, 63
66 [a]Luke 2:19 [b]Gen. 39:2; Acts 11:21
67 [a]Joel 2:28
68 [a]1 Kin. 1:48; Ps. 106:48 [b]Ex. 3:16
69 [a]2 Sam. 22:3; Ps. 132:17; Ezek. 29:21
70 [a]Jer. 23:5; Rom. 1:2 [b]Acts 3:21
72 [a]Lev. 26:42
73 [a]Gen. 12:3; 22:16–18; [Heb. 6:13]

NKJV

47 And my spirit has [a]rejoiced in [b]God my
Savior.
48 For [a]He has regarded the lowly state of
His maidservant;
For behold, henceforth [b]all generations
will call me blessed.
49 For He who is mighty [a]has done great
things for me,
And [b]holy *is* His name.
50 And [a]His mercy *is* on those who fear Him
From generation to generation.
51 [a]He has shown strength with His arm;
[b]He has scattered *the* proud in the
imagination of their hearts.
52 [a]He has put down the mighty from *their*
thrones,
And exalted *the* lowly.
53 He has [a]filled *the* hungry with good
things,
And *the* rich He has sent away empty.
54 He has helped His [a]servant Israel,
[b]In remembrance of *His* mercy,
55 [a]As He spoke to our [b]fathers,
To Abraham and to his [c]seed forever."

56 And Mary remained with her about three months, and returned to her house.

Birth of John the Baptist

57 Now Elizabeth's full time came for her to be delivered, and she brought forth a son.
58 When her neighbors and relatives heard how the Lord had shown great mercy to her, they [a]rejoiced with her.

Circumcision of John the Baptist

59 So it was, [a]on the eighth day, that they came to circumcise the child; and they would have called him by the name of his father, Zacharias.
60 His mother answered and said, [a]"No; he shall be called John."
61 But they said to her, "There is no one among your relatives who is called by this name."
62 So they made signs to his father—what he would have him called.
63 And he asked for a writing tablet, and wrote, saying, "His name is John." So they all marveled.
64 Immediately his mouth was opened and his tongue *loosed,* and he spoke, praising God.
65 Then fear came on all who dwelt around them; and all these sayings were discussed throughout all the hill country of Judea.
66 And all those who heard *them* [a]kept *them* in their hearts, saying, "What kind of child will this be?" And [b]the hand of the Lord was with him.

Zacharias' Prophecy

67 Now his father Zacharias [a]was filled with the Holy Spirit, and prophesied, saying:

68 "Blessed[a] *is* the Lord God of Israel,
For [b]He has visited and redeemed His
people,
69 [a]And has raised up a horn of salvation
for us
In the house of His servant David,
70 [a]As He spoke by the mouth of His holy
prophets,
Who *have been* [b]since the world began,
71 That we should be saved from our
enemies
And from the hand of all who hate us,
72 [a]To perform the mercy *promised* to our
fathers
And to remember His holy covenant,
73 [a]The oath which He swore to our father
Abraham:
74 To grant us that we,

KJV

being delivered out of the hand of our enemies
might [a]serve him without fear,
75 [a]In holiness and righteousness before
him, all the days of our life.
76 And thou, child, shalt be called the
[a]prophet of the Highest: for [b]thou shalt go before
the face of the Lord to prepare his ways;
77 To give [a]knowledge of salvation unto his
people by the remission of their sins,
78 Through the tender mercy of our God;
whereby the dayspring from on high hath visited
us,
79 [a]To give light to them that sit in darkness
and *in* the shadow of death, to [b]guide our feet
into the way of peace.
80 And [a]the child grew, and waxed strong
in spirit, and [b]was in the deserts till the day of
his shewing unto Israel.

Christ Born of Mary
(Matt. 1:18–25)

2 And it came to pass in those days, that there
went out a decree from Caesar Augustus, that
all the world should be taxed.
2 ([a]*And* this taxing was first made when
Cyrenius was governor of Syria.)
3 And all went to be taxed, every one into
his own city.
4 And Joseph also went up from Galilee, out
of the city of Nazareth, into Judaea, unto [a]the city
of David, which is called Bethlehem; ([b]because
he was of the house and lineage of David:)
5 To be taxed with Mary [a]his espoused wife,
being great with child.
6 And so it was, that, while they were there,
the days were accomplished that she should be
delivered.
7 And [a]she brought forth her firstborn son,
and wrapped him in swaddling clothes, and laid
him in a manger; because there was no room for
them in the inn.

Glory in the Highest

8 And there were in the same country shepherds abiding in the field, keeping watch over
their flock by night.
9 And, lo, the angel of the Lord came upon
them, and the glory of the Lord shone round about
them: [a]and they were sore afraid.
10 And the angel said unto them, [a]Fear not:
for, behold, I bring you good tidings of great joy,
[b]which shall be to all people.
11 [a]For unto you is born this day in the city
of David [b]a Saviour, [c]which is Christ the Lord.
12 And this *shall be* a sign unto you; Ye shall
find the babe wrapped in swaddling clothes, lying
in a manger.
13 [a]And suddenly there was with the angel
a multitude of the heavenly host praising God,
and saying,
14 [a]Glory to God in the highest, and on earth
[b]peace, [c]good will toward men.
15 And it came to pass, as the angels were
gone away from them into heaven, the shepherds
said one to another, Let us now go even unto Bethlehem, and see this thing which is come to pass,
which the Lord hath made known unto us.
16 And they came with haste, and found
Mary, and Joseph, and the babe lying in a manger.
17 And when they had seen *it*, they made
known abroad the saying which was told them
concerning this child.
18 And all they that heard *it* wondered at
those things which were told them by the
shepherds.

74 [a][Rom. 6:18; Heb. 9:14] **75** [a]Jer. 32:39; [Eph. 4:24; 2 Thess. 2:13] **76** [a]Matt. 3:3; 11:9; Mark 3:2, 3; Luke 3:4; John 1:23 [b]Is. 40:3; Mal. 3:1; Matt. 11:10 **77** [a][Jer. 31:34; Mark 1:4]; Luke 3:3 **79** [a]Is. 9:2; Matt. 4:16; [Acts 26:18; 2 Cor. 4:6; Eph. 5:14] [b][John 10:4; 14:27; 16:33] **80** [a]Luke 2:40 [b]Matt. 3:1

CHAPTER 2

2 [a]Dan. 9:25; Acts 5:37 **4** [a]1 Sam. 16:1; Mic. 5:2 [b]Matt. 1:16 **5** [a][Matt. 1:18] **7** [a]Matt. 1:25; Luke 1:31 **9** [a]Luke 1:12 **10** [a]Luke 1:13, 30 [b]Gen. 12:3; Is. 49:6; [Matt. 28:19; Mark 1:15; Col. 1:23] **11** [a]Is. 9:6 [b]Matt. 1:21; John 4:42; [Acts 5:31] [c]Matt. 1:16; 16:16, 20; John 11:27; Acts 2:36; Phil. 2:11 **13** [a]Gen. 28:12; Ps. 103:20; 148:2; Dan. 7:10; [Heb. 1:14]; Rev. 5:11 **14** [a]Matt. 21:9; Luke 19:38; Eph. 1:6 [b]Is. 57:19; [Rom. 5:1]; Eph. 2:17; [Col. 1:20] [c][John 3:16; Eph. 2:4, 7; 2 Thess. 2:16; 1 John 4:9]

*

1:78 NU *shall visit*
2:5 NU omits *wife*
2:9 NU omits *behold*
2:14 NU *toward men of goodwill*
2:17 NU omits *widely*

NKJV

Being delivered from the hand of our enemies,
Might [a]serve Him without fear,
75 [a]In holiness and righteousness before Him all the days of our life.

76 "And you, child, will be called the [a]prophet of the Highest;
For [b]you will go before the face of the Lord to prepare His ways,
77 To give [a]knowledge of salvation to His people
By the remission of their sins,
78 Through the tender mercy of our God,
With which the Dayspring from on high
*has visited us;
79 [a]To give light to those who sit in darkness and the shadow of death,
To [b]guide our feet into the way of peace."

80 So [a]the child grew and became strong in
spirit, and [b]was in the deserts till the day of his
manifestation to Israel.

Christ Born of Mary
(Matt. 1:18–25)

2 And it came to pass in those days *that* a decree went out from Caesar Augustus that all
the world should be registered.
2 [a]This census first took place while Qui-
rinius was governing Syria.
3 So all went to be registered, everyone to
his own city.
4 Joseph also went up from Galilee, out of
the city of Nazareth, into Judea, to [a]the city of
David, which is called Bethlehem, [b]because he
was of the house and lineage of David,
5 to be registered with Mary, [a]his betrothed
*wife, who was with child.
6 So it was, that while they were there, the
days were completed for her to be delivered.
7 And [a]she brought forth her firstborn Son,
and wrapped Him in swaddling cloths, and laid
Him in a manger, because there was no room for
them in the inn.

Glory in the Highest

8 Now there were in the same country shepherds living out in the fields, keeping watch over
their flock by night.
9 And *behold, an angel of the Lord stood
before them, and the glory of the Lord shone
around them, [a]and they were greatly afraid.
10 Then the angel said to them, [a]"Do not be
afraid, for behold, I bring you good tidings of
great joy [b]which will be to all people.
11 [a]"For there is born to you this day in the
city of David [b]a Savior, [c]who is Christ the Lord.
12 "And this *will be* the sign to you: You will
find a Babe wrapped in swaddling cloths, lying
in a manger."
13 [a]And suddenly there was with the angel
a multitude of the heavenly host praising God and
saying:

14 "Glory[a] to God in the highest,
And on earth [b]peace, [c]goodwill* toward men!"

15 So it was, when the angels had gone away
from them into heaven, that the shepherds said
to one another, "Let us now go to Bethlehem and
see this thing that has come to pass, which the
Lord has made known to us."
16 And they came with haste and found Mary
and Joseph, and the Babe lying in a manger.
17 Now when they had seen *Him*, they made
*widely known the saying which was told them
concerning this Child.
18 And all those who heard *it* marveled at
those things which were told them by the
shepherds.

KJV

19 [a]But Mary kept all these things, and pondered *them* in her heart.

20 And the shepherds returned, glorifying and [a]praising God for all the things that they had heard and seen, as it was told unto them.

Circumcision of Jesus

21 [a]And when eight days were accomplished for the circumcising of the child, his name was called [b]JESUS, which was so named of the angel [c]before he was conceived in the womb.

Jesus Presented in the Temple

22 And when [a]the days of her purification according to the law of Moses were accomplished, they brought him to Jerusalem, to present *him* to the Lord;

23 [a](As it is written in the law of the Lord, [b]EVERY MALE THAT OPENETH THE WOMB SHALL BE CALLED HOLY TO THE LORD;)

24 And to offer a sacrifice according to that which is said in the law of the LORD, [a]A PAIR OF TURTLEDOVES, OR TWO YOUNG PIGEONS.

Simeon Sees God's Salvation

25 And, behold, there was a man in Jerusalem, whose name *was* Simeon; and the same man *was* just and devout, [a]waiting for the consolation of Israel: and the Holy Ghost was upon him.

26 And it was revealed unto him by the Holy Ghost, that he should not [a]see death, before he had seen the LORD's Christ.

27 And he came [a]by the Spirit into the temple: and when the parents brought in the child Jesus, to do for him after the custom of the law,

28 Then took he him up in his arms, and blessed God, and said,

29 LORD, [a]now lettest thou thy servant depart in peace, according to thy word:

30 For mine eyes [a]have seen thy salvation,

31 Which thou hast prepared before the face of all people;

32 [a]A light to lighten the Gentiles, and the glory of thy people Israel.

33 And Joseph and his mother marvelled at those things which were spoken of him.

34 And Simeon blessed them, and said unto Mary his mother, Behold, this *child* is set for the [a]fall and rising again of many in Israel; and for [b]a sign which shall be spoken against;

35 (Yea, [a]a sword shall pierce through thy own soul also,) that the thoughts of many hearts may be revealed.

Anna Bears Witness to the Redeemer

36 And there was one Anna, a prophetess, the daughter of Phanuel, of the tribe of [a]Aser: she was of a great age, and had lived with an husband seven years from her virginity;

37 And she *was* a widow of about fourscore and four years, which departed not from the temple, but served *God* with fastings and prayers [a]night and day.

38 And she coming in that instant gave thanks likewise unto the Lord, and spake of him to all them that [a]looked for redemption in Jerusalem.

The Family Returns to Nazareth

39 And when they had performed all things according to the law of the Lord, they returned into Galilee, to their own city Nazareth.

40 [a]And the child grew, and waxed strong in spirit, filled with wisdom: and the grace of God was upon him.

The Boy Jesus Amazes the Scholars

41 Now his parents went to [a]Jerusalem [b]every year at the feast of the passover.

42 And when he was twelve years old, they

NKJV

19 [a]But Mary kept all these things and pondered *them* in her heart.

20 Then the shepherds returned, glorifying and [a]praising God for all the things that they had heard and seen, as it was told them.

Circumcision of Jesus

21 [a]And when eight days were completed *for the circumcision of the Child, His name was called [b]JESUS, the name given by the angel [c]before He was conceived in the womb.

Jesus Presented in the Temple

22 Now when [a]the days of her purification according to the law of Moses were completed, they brought Him to Jerusalem to present *Him* to the Lord

23 [a](as it is written in the law of the Lord, [b]*"Every male who opens the womb shall be called holy to the LORD"*),

24 and to offer a sacrifice according to what is said in the law of the Lord, [a]*"A pair of turtledoves or two young pigeons."*

Simeon Sees God's Salvation

25 And behold, there was a man in Jerusalem whose name was Simeon, and this man was just and devout, [a]waiting for the Consolation of Israel, and the Holy Spirit was upon him.

26 And it had been revealed to him by the Holy Spirit that he would not [a]see death before he had seen the Lord's Christ.

27 So he came [a]by the Spirit into the temple. And when the parents brought in the Child Jesus, to do for Him according to the custom of the law,

28 he took Him up in his arms and blessed God and said:

29 "Lord, [a]now You are letting Your servant
depart in peace,
According to Your word;
30 For my eyes [a]have seen Your salvation
31 Which You have prepared before the face
of all peoples,
32 [a]A light to *bring* revelation to the Gentiles,
And the glory of Your people Israel."

33 *And Joseph and His mother marveled at those things which were spoken of Him.

34 Then Simeon blessed them, and said to Mary His mother, "Behold, this *Child* is destined for the [a]fall and rising of many in Israel, and for [b]a sign which will be spoken against

35 (yes, [a]a sword will pierce through your own soul also), that the thoughts of many hearts may be revealed."

Anna Bears Witness to the Redeemer

36 Now there was one, Anna, a prophetess, the daughter of Phanuel, of the tribe of [a]Asher. She was of a great age, and had lived with a husband seven years from her virginity;

37 and this woman *was* a widow *of about eighty-four years, who did not depart from the temple, but served *God* with fastings and prayers [a]night and day.

38 And coming in that instant she gave thanks to *the Lord, and spoke of Him to all those who [a]looked for redemption in Jerusalem.

The Family Returns to Nazareth

39 So when they had performed all things according to the law of the Lord, they returned to Galilee, to their *own* city, Nazareth.

40 [a]And the Child grew and became strong *in spirit, filled with wisdom; and the grace of God was upon Him.

The Boy Jesus Amazes the Scholars

41 His parents went to [a]Jerusalem [b]every year at the Feast of the Passover.

42 And when He was twelve years old, they

---

19 [a]Gen. 37:11
20 [a]Luke 19:37
21 [a]Lev. 12:3 [b][Matt. 1:21] [c]Luke 1:31
22 [a]Lev. 12:2–8
23 [a]Deut. 18:4 [b]Ex. 13:2, 12, 15
24 [a]Lev. 12:2, 8
25 [a]Mark 15:43
26 [a][Heb. 11:5]
27 [a]Matt. 4:1
29 [a]Gen. 46:30
30 [a][Is. 52:10]
32 [a]Acts 10:45; 13:47; 28:28
34 [a][1 Pet. 2:7, 8] [b]Acts 4:2; 17:32; 28:22
35 [a]Ps. 42:10
36 [a]Josh. 19:24
37 [a]1 Tim. 5:5
38 [a]Mark 15:43
40 [a]Luke 1:80; 2:52
41 [a]John 4:20 [b]Deut. 16:1, 16

*

2:21 NU *for His circumcision*
2:33 NU *And His father and mother*
2:37 NU *until she was eighty-four*
2:38 NU *God*
2:40 NU omits *in spirit*

KJV

went up to Jerusalem after the [a]custom of the feast.

43 And when they had fulfilled the [a]days, as they returned, the child Jesus tarried behind in Jerusalem; and Joseph and his mother knew not *of it.*

44 But they, supposing him to have been in the company, went a day's journey; and they sought him among *their* kinsfolk and acquaintance.

45 And when they found him not, they turned back again to Jerusalem, seeking him.

46 And it came to pass, that after three days they found him in the temple, sitting in the midst of the doctors, both hearing them, and asking them questions.

47 And [a]all that heard him were astonished at his understanding and answers.

48 And when they saw him, they were amazed: and his mother said unto him, Son, why hast thou thus dealt with us? behold, thy father and I have sought thee sorrowing.

49 And he said unto them, How is it that ye sought me? wist ye not that I must be [a]about [b]my Father's business?

50 And [a]they understood not the saying which he spake unto them.

Jesus Advances in Wisdom and Favor

51 And he went down with them, and came to Nazareth, and was subject unto them: but his mother [a]kept all these sayings in her heart.

52 And Jesus [a]increased in wisdom and stature, [b]and in favour with God and man.

John the Baptist Prepares the Way
(Matt. 3:1–6; Mark 1:2–6; John 1:19–23)

3 Now in the fifteenth year of the reign of Tiberius Caesar, [a]Pontius Pilate being governor of Judaea, and Herod being tetrarch of Galilee, and his brother Philip tetrarch of Ituraea and of the region of Trachonitis, and Lysanias the tetrarch of Abilene,

2 [a]Annas and Caiaphas being the high priests, the word of God came unto [b]John the son of Zacharias in the wilderness.

3 [a]And he came into all the country about Jordan, preaching the baptism of repentance [b]for the remission of sins;

4 As it is written in the book of the words of Esaias the prophet, saying, [a]THE VOICE OF ONE CRYING IN THE WILDERNESS, PREPARE YE THE WAY OF THE LORD, MAKE HIS PATHS STRAIGHT.

5 EVERY VALLEY SHALL BE FILLED, AND EVERY MOUNTAIN AND HILL SHALL BE BROUGHT LOW; AND THE CROOKED SHALL BE MADE STRAIGHT, AND THE ROUGH WAYS *SHALL BE* MADE SMOOTH;

6 AND [a]ALL FLESH SHALL SEE THE SALVATION OF GOD.

John Preaches to the People
(Matt. 3:7–12; Mark 1:7, 8; John 1:24–28)

7 Then said he to the multitude that came forth to be baptized of him, [a]O generation of vipers, who hath warned you to flee from the wrath to come?

8 Bring forth therefore fruits [a]worthy of repentance, and begin not to say within yourselves, We have Abraham to *our* father: for I say unto you, That God is able of these stones to raise up children unto Abraham.

9 And now also the axe is laid unto the root of the trees: [a]every tree therefore which bringeth not forth good fruit is hewn down, and cast into the fire.

10 And the people asked him, saying, [a]What shall we do then?

11 He answereth and saith unto them, [a]He that hath two coats, let him impart to him that hath none; and he that hath meat, [b]let him do likewise.

---

42 [a]Ex. 23:14, 15
43 [a]Ex. 12:15
47 [a]Matt. 7:28; 13:54; 22:33; Mark 1:22; 6:2; 11:18; Luke 4:32; John 7:15
49 [a]John 9:4 [b][Mark 1:22; Luke 4:22, 32; John 4:34; 5:17, 36]
50 [a]Mark 9:32; Luke 9:45; 18:34; John 7:15, 46
51 [a]Dan. 7:28
52 [a][Is. 11:2, 3; Col. 2:2, 3] [b]1 Sam. 2:26; [Prov. 3:1–4]

CHAPTER 3
1 [a]Matt. 27:2
2 [a]John 11:49; 18:13; Acts 4:6 [b]Luke 1:13
3 [a]Matt. 3:1; Mark 1:4 [b]Luke 1:77
4 [a]Is. 40:3–5; Matt. 3:3; Mark 1:3
6 [a]Ps. 98:2; Is. 52:10; Luke 2:10; [Rom. 10:8–18]
7 [a]Matt. 3:7; 12:34; 23:33
8 [a][2 Cor.7:9–11]
9 [a]Matt. 7:19; Luke 13:6–9
10 [a]Luke 3:12, 14; [Acts 2:37, 38; 16:30, 31]
11 [a]Luke 11:41; 2 Cor. 8:14; James 2:15, 16; [1 John 3:17; 4:20] [b]Is. 58:7; [1 Tim. 6:17, 18]

*

2:43 NU *His parents*
3:2 NU, M *in the high priesthood of Annas and Caiaphas*

NKJV

went up to Jerusalem according to the [a]custom of the feast.

43 When they had finished the [a]days, as they returned, the Boy Jesus lingered behind in Jerusalem. And *Joseph and His mother did not know *it;*

44 but supposing Him to have been in the company, they went a day's journey, and sought Him among *their* relatives and acquaintances.

45 So when they did not find Him, they returned to Jerusalem, seeking Him.

46 Now so it was *that* after three days they found Him in the temple, sitting in the midst of the teachers, both listening to them and asking them questions.

47 And [a]all who heard Him were astonished at His understanding and answers.

48 So when they saw Him, they were amazed; and His mother said to Him, "Son, why have You done this to us? Look, Your father and I have sought You anxiously."

49 And He said to them, "Why did you seek Me? Did you not know that I must be [a]about [b]My Father's business?"

50 But [a]they did not understand the statement which He spoke to them.

Jesus Advances in Wisdom and Favor

51 Then He went down with them and came to Nazareth, and was subject to them, but His mother [a]kept all these things in her heart.

52 And Jesus [a]increased in wisdom and stature, [b]and in favor with God and men.

John the Baptist Prepares the Way
(Matt. 3:1–6; Mark 1:2–6; John 1:19–23)

3 Now in the fifteenth year of the reign of Tiberius Caesar, [a]Pontius Pilate being governor of Judea, Herod being tetrarch of Galilee, his brother Philip tetrarch of Iturea and the region of Trachonitis, and Lysanias tetrarch of Abilene,

2 *while [a]Annas and Caiaphas were high priests, the word of God came to [b]John the son of Zacharias in the wilderness.

3 [a]And he went into all the region around the Jordan, preaching a baptism of repentance [b]for the remission of sins,

4 as it is written in the book of the words of Isaiah the prophet, saying:

[a]"The voice of one crying in the wilderness:
'Prepare the way of the LORD;
Make His paths straight.
5 *Every valley shall be filled*
And every mountain and hill brought low;
The crooked places shall be made straight
And the rough ways smooth;
6 *And [a]all flesh shall see the salvation of*
God.' "

John Preaches to the People
(Matt. 3:7–12; Mark 1:7, 8; John 1:24–28)

7 Then he said to the multitudes that came out to be baptized by him, [a]"Brood of vipers! Who warned you to flee from the wrath to come?

8 "Therefore bear fruits [a]worthy of repentance, and do not begin to say to yourselves, 'We have Abraham as *our* father.' For I say to you that God is able to raise up children to Abraham from these stones.

9 "And even now the ax is laid to the root of the trees. Therefore [a]every tree which does not bear good fruit is cut down and thrown into the fire."

10 So the people asked him, saying, [a]"What shall we do then?"

11 He answered and said to them, [a]"He who has two tunics, let him give to him who has none; and he who has food, [b]let him do likewise."

KJV

12 Then [a]came also publicans to be baptized, and said unto him, Master, what shall we
do?
13 And he said unto them, [a]Exact no more
than that which is appointed you.
14 And the soldiers likewise demanded of
him, saying, And what shall we do? And he said
unto them, Do violence to no man, [a]neither accuse
any falsely; and be content with your wages.
15 And as the people were in expectation,
and all men mused in their hearts of John,
whether he were the Christ, or not;
16 John answered, saying unto *them* all, [a]I
indeed baptize you with water; but one mightier
than I cometh, the latchet of whose shoes I am
not worthy to unloose: he shall [b]baptize you with
the Holy Ghost and with fire:
17 Whose fan *is* in his hand, and he will
throughly purge his floor, and [a]will gather the
wheat into his garner; but the chaff he will burn
with fire unquenchable.
18 And many other things in his exhortation
preached he unto the people.
19 [a]But Herod the tetrarch, being reproved
by him for Herodias his brother Philip's wife, and
for all the evils which Herod had done,
20 Added yet this above all, that he shut up
John in prison.

John Baptizes Jesus
(Matt. 3:13–17; Mark 1:9–11; John 1:29–34)

21 Now when all the people were baptized,
[a]it came to pass, that Jesus also being baptized,
and praying, the heaven was opened,
22 And the Holy Ghost descended in a bodily
shape like a dove upon him, and a voice came
from heaven, which said, Thou art my beloved
Son; in thee I am [a]well pleased.

The Genealogy of Jesus Christ
(Gen. 5:1–32; 11:10–26; Ruth 4:18–22; 1 Chr. 1:1–4, 24–27, 34; 2:1–15; Matt. 1:2–16)

23 And Jesus himself began to be [a]about
thirty years of age, being (as was supposed) [b]the
son of Joseph, which was *the son* of Heli,
24 Which was *the son* of Matthat, which was
the son of Levi, which was *the son* of Melchi,
which was *the son* of Janna, which was *the son*
of Joseph,
25 Which was *the son* of Mattathias, which
was *the son* of Amos, which was *the son* of Naum,
which was *the son* of Esli, which was *the son* of
Nagge,
26 Which was *the son* of Maath, which was
the son of Mattathias, which was *the son* of
Semei, which was *the son* of Joseph, which was
the son of Juda,
27 Which was *the son* of Joanna, which was
the son of Rhesa, which was *the son* of [a]Zorob-
abel, which was *the son* of Salathiel, which was
the son of Neri,
28 Which was *the son* of Melchi, which was
the son of Addi, which was *the son* of Cosam,
which was *the son* of Elmodam, which was *the
son* of Er,
29 Which was *the son* of Jose, which was *the
son* of Eliezer, which was *the son* of Jorim, which
was *the son* of Matthat, which was *the son* of
Levi,
30 Which was *the son* of Simeon, which was
the son of Juda, which was *the son* of Joseph,
which was *the son* of Jonan, which was *the son*
of Eliakim,
31 Which was *the son* of Melea, which was
the son of Menan, which was *the son* of Mattatha,
which was *the son* of [a]Nathan, [b]which was *the
son* of David,
32 [a]Which was *the son* of Jesse, which was
the son of Obed, which was *the son* of Booz,
which was *the son* of Salmon, which was *the son*
of Naasson,
33 Which was *the son* of Aminadab, which

12 [a]Matt. 21:32; Luke 7:29
13 [a]Luke 19:8
14 [a]Ex. 20:16; 23:1; Lev. 19:11
16 [a]Matt. 3:11, 12; Mark 1:7, 8 [b]John 7:39; 20:22; Acts 2:1–4
17 [a]Mic. 4:12; Matt. 13:24–30
19 [a]Matt. 14:3; Mark 6:17
21 [a]Matt. 3:13–17; John 1:32
22 [a]Ps. 2:7; [Is. 42:1]; Matt. 3:17; 17:5; Mark 1:11; Luke 1:35; 9:35; 2 Pet. 1:17
23 [a][Num. 4:3, 35, 39, 43, 47] [b]Matt. 13:55; John 6:42
27 [a]Ezra 2:2; 3:8
31 [a]Zech. 12:12 [b]2 Sam. 5:14; 7:12; 1 Chr. 3:5; 17:11; Is. 9:7; Jer. 23:5
32 [a]Ruth 4:18–22; 1 Chr. 2:10–12; Is. 11:1, 10

*

3:19 NU *brother's wife*

NKJV

12 Then [a]tax collectors also came to be baptized, and said to him, "Teacher, what shall we
do?"
13 And he said to them, [a]"Collect no more
than what is appointed for you."
14 Likewise the soldiers asked him, saying,
"And what shall we do?" So he said to them, "Do
not intimidate anyone [a]or accuse falsely, and be
content with your wages."
15 Now as the people were in expectation,
and all reasoned in their hearts about John,
whether he was the Christ *or* not,
16 John answered, saying to all, [a]"I indeed
baptize you with water; but One mightier than I
is coming, whose sandal strap I am not worthy
to loose. He will [b]baptize you with the Holy Spirit
and fire.
17 "His winnowing fan *is* in His hand, and
He will thoroughly clean out His threshing floor,
and [a]gather the wheat into His barn; but the chaff
He will burn with unquenchable fire."
18 And with many other exhortations he
preached to the people.
19 [a]But Herod the tetrarch, being rebuked by
him concerning Herodias, his *brother Philip's
wife, and for all the evils which Herod had done,
20 also added this, above all, that he shut
John up in prison.

John Baptizes Jesus
(Matt. 3:13–17; Mark 1:9–11; John 1:29–34)

21 When all the people were baptized, [a]it
came to pass that Jesus also was baptized; and
while He prayed, the heaven was opened.
22 And the Holy Spirit descended in bodily
form like a dove upon Him, and a voice came from
heaven which said, "You are My beloved Son; in
You I am [a]well pleased."

The Genealogy of Jesus Christ
(Gen. 5:1–32; 11:10–26; Ruth 4:18–22; 1 Chr. 1:1–4, 24–27, 34; 2:1–15; Matt. 1:2–16)

23 Now Jesus Himself began *His ministry at*
[a]about thirty years of age, being (as was supposed) [b]*the* son of Joseph, *the son* of Heli,
24 *the son* of Matthat, *the son* of Levi, *the
son* of Melchi, *the son* of Janna, *the son* of Joseph,
25 *the son* of Mattathiah, *the son* of Amos,
the son of Nahum, *the son* of Esli, *the son* of
Naggai,
26 *the son* of Maath, *the son* of Mattathiah,
the son of Semei, *the son* of Joseph, *the son* of
Judah,
27 *the son* of Joannas, *the son* of Rhesa, *the
son* of [a]Zerubbabel, *the son* of Shealtiel, *the son*
of Neri,
28 *the son* of Melchi, *the son* of Addi, *the
son* of Cosam, *the son* of Elmodam, *the son* of
Er,
29 *the son* of Jose, *the son* of Eliezer, *the
son* of Jorim, *the son* of Matthat, *the son* of Levi,
30 *the son* of Simeon, *the son* of Judah, *the
son* of Joseph, *the son* of Jonan, *the son* of
Eliakim,
31 *the son* of Melea, *the son* of Menan, *the
son* of Mattathah, *the son* of [a]Nathan, [b]*the son*
of David,
32 [a]*the son* of Jesse, *the son* of Obed, *the
son* of Boaz, *the son* of Salmon, *the son* of
Nahshon,
33 *the son* of Amminadab, *the son* of Ram,

KJV

was *the son* of Aram, which was *the son* of Esrom,
which was *the son* of Phares, which was *the son*
of Juda,
34 Which was *the son* of Jacob, which was
the son of Isaac, which was *the son* of Abraham,
[a]which was *the son* of Thara, which was *the son*
of Nachor,
35 Which was *the son* of Saruch, which was
the son of Ragau, which was *the son* of Phalec,
which was *the son* of Heber, which was *the son*
of Sala,
36 [a]Which was *the son* of Cainan, which was
the son of [b]Arphaxad, [c]which was *the son* of Sem,
which was *the son* of Noe, which was *the son* of
Lamech,
37 Which was *the son* of Mathusala, which
was *the son* of Enoch, which was *the son* of Jared,
which was *the son* of Maleleel, which was *the
son* of Cainan,
38 Which was *the son* of Enos, which was
the son of Seth, which was *the son* of Adam,
[a]which was *the son* of God.

Satan Tempts Jesus
(*Matt. 4:1–11; Mark 1:12, 13*)

4 And [a]Jesus being full of the Holy Ghost returned from Jordan, and [b]was led by the Spirit
into the wilderness,
2 Being forty days tempted of the devil. And
[a]in those days he did eat nothing: and when they
were ended, he afterward hungered.
3 And the devil said unto him, If thou be
the [a]Son of God, command this stone that it be
made bread.
4 And Jesus answered him, saying, It is written, [a]THAT MAN SHALL NOT LIVE BY BREAD ALONE,
BUT BY EVERY WORD OF GOD.
5 And the devil, taking him up into an high
mountain, shewed unto him all the kingdoms of
the world in a moment of time.
6 And the devil said unto him, All this power
will I give thee, and the glory of them: for [a]that
is delivered unto me; and to whomsoever I will I
give it.
7 If thou therefore wilt worship me, all shall
be thine.
8 And Jesus answered and said unto him,
Get thee behind me, Satan: for it is written, [a]THOU
SHALT WORSHIP THE LORD THY GOD, AND HIM ONLY
SHALT THOU SERVE.
9 [a]And he brought him to Jerusalem, and
set him on a pinnacle of the temple, and said unto
him, If thou be the Son of God, cast thyself down
from hence:
10 For it is written, [a]HE SHALL GIVE HIS ANGELS
CHARGE OVER THEE, TO KEEP THEE:
11 And [a]IN *THEIR* HANDS THEY SHALL BEAR THEE
UP, LEST AT ANY TIME THOU DASH THY FOOT AGAINST
A STONE.
12 And Jesus answering said unto him, It is
said, [a]THOU SHALT NOT TEMPT THE LORD THY
GOD.
13 And when the devil had ended all the
temptation, he departed from him [a]for a season.

Jesus Begins His Galilean Ministry
(*Matt. 4:12–17; Mark 1:14, 15*)

14 [a]And Jesus returned [b]in the power of the
Spirit into [c]Galilee: and there went out a [d]fame
of him through all the region round about.
15 And he [a]taught in their synagogues, [b]be-
ing glorified of all.

Jesus Rejected at Nazareth
(*Matt. 13:54–58; Mark 6:1–6*)

16 And he came to [a]Nazareth, where he had
been brought up: and, as his custom was, [b]he went

---

34 [a]Gen. 11:24, 26–30; 12:3; Num. 24:17; 1 Chr. 1:24–27
36 [a]Gen. 11:12 [b]Gen. 10:22, 24; 11:10–13; 1 Chr. 1:17, 18 [c]Gen. 5:6–32; 9:27; 11:10
38 [a]Gen. 5:1, 2

CHAPTER 4

1 [a][Is. 11:2; 61:1]; Matt. 4:1–11; Mark 1:12, 13 [b]Ezek. 3:12; Luke 2:27
2 [a]Ex. 34:28; 1 Kin. 19:8
3 [a]Mark 3:11; John 20:31
4 [a]Deut. 8:3
6 [a][John 12:31; 14:30; Rev. 13:2, 7]
8 [a]Deut. 6:13; 10:20; Matt. 4:10
9 [a]Matt. 4:5–7
10 [a]Ps. 91:11
11 [a]Ps. 91:12
12 [a]Deut. 6:16
13 [a][John 14:30; Heb. 4:15; James 4:7]
14 [a]Matt. 4:12 [b]John 4:43 [c]Acts 10:37 [d]Matt. 4:24
15 [a]Ps. 22:22; Matt. 4:23 [b]Is. 52:13
16 [a]Matt. 2:23; 13:54; Mark 6:1 [b]Mark 1:21; John 18:20; Acts 13:14–16; 17:2

NKJV

the son of Hezron, *the son* of Perez, *the son* of
Judah,
34 *the son* of Jacob, *the son* of Isaac, *the son*
of Abraham, [a]*the son* of Terah, *the son* of Nahor,
35 *the son* of Serug, *the son* of Reu, *the son*
of Peleg, *the son* of Eber, *the son* of Shelah,
36 [a]*the son* of Cainan, *the son* of [b]Arphaxad,
[c]*the son* of Shem, *the son* of Noah, *the son* of
Lamech,
37 *the son* of Methuselah, *the son* of Enoch,
the son of Jared, *the son* of Mahalalel, *the son*
of Cainan,
38 *the son* of Enosh, *the son* of Seth, *the son*
of Adam, [a]*the son* of God.

Satan Tempts Jesus
(*Matt. 4:1–11; Mark 1:12, 13*)

4 Then [a]Jesus, being filled with the Holy Spirit,
returned from the Jordan and [b]was led by the
Spirit *into the wilderness,
2 being tempted for forty days by the devil.
And [a]in those days He ate nothing, and afterward,
when they had ended, He was hungry.
3 And the devil said to Him, "If You are [a]the
Son of God, command this stone to become
bread."
4 But Jesus answered him, saying, "It is
written, [a]*'Man shall not live by bread alone, *but
by every word of God.'*"
5 *Then the devil, taking Him up on a high
mountain, showed Him all the kingdoms of the
world in a moment of time.
6 And the devil said to Him, "All this authority I will give You, and their glory; for [a]*this*
has been delivered to me, and I give it to whomever I wish.
7 "Therefore, if You will worship before me,
all will be Yours."
8 And Jesus answered and said to him,
*"Get behind Me, Satan! *For it is written, [a]*'You
shall worship the LORD your God, and Him only
you shall serve.'*"
9 [a]Then he brought Him to Jerusalem, set
Him on the pinnacle of the temple, and said to
Him, "If You are the Son of God, throw Yourself
down from here.
10 "For it is written:

> [a]*'He shall give His angels charge over you,*
> *To keep you,'*

11 "and,

> [a]*'In their hands they shall bear you up,*
> *Lest you dash your foot against a stone.'*"

12 And Jesus answered and said to him, "It
has been said, [a]*'You shall not tempt the LORD your
God.'*"
13 Now when the devil had ended every
temptation, he departed from Him [a]until an opportune time.

Jesus Begins His Galilean Ministry
(*Matt. 4:12–17; Mark 1:14, 15*)

14 [a]Then Jesus returned [b]in the power of the
Spirit to [c]Galilee, and [d]news of Him went out
through all the surrounding region.
15 And He [a]taught in their synagogues, [b]be-
ing glorified by all.

Jesus Rejected at Nazareth
(*Matt. 13:54–58; Mark 6:1–6*)

16 So He came to [a]Nazareth, where He had
been brought up. And as His custom was, [b]He

---

*

4:1 NU *in*
4:4 NU omits *but by every word of God*
4:5 NU *And taking Him up, he showed Him*
4:8 NU omits *Get behind Me, Satan* • NU, M omit *For*

KJV

into the synagogue on the sabbath day, and stood up for to read.

17 And there was delivered unto him the book of the prophet Esaias. And when he had opened the book, he found the place where it was written,

18 [a]THE SPIRIT OF THE LORD *IS* UPON ME, BECAUSE HE HATH ANOINTED ME TO PREACH THE GOSPEL TO THE POOR; HE HATH SENT ME TO HEAL THE BROKENHEARTED, TO PREACH DELIVERANCE TO THE CAPTIVES, AND RECOVERING OF SIGHT TO THE BLIND, TO [b]SET AT LIBERTY THEM THAT ARE BRUISED,

19 TO PREACH THE ACCEPTABLE YEAR OF THE LORD.

20 And he closed the book, and he gave *it* again to the minister, and sat down. And the eyes of all them that were in the synagogue were fastened on him.

21 And he began to say unto them, This day is this scripture [a]fulfilled in your ears.

22 And all bare him witness, and [a]wondered at the gracious words which proceeded out of his mouth. And they said, [b]Is not this Joseph's son?

23 And he said unto them, Ye will surely say unto me this proverb, Physician, heal thyself: whatsoever we have heard done in [a]Capernaum, do also here in [b]thy country.

24 And he said, Verily I say unto you, No [a]prophet is accepted in his own country.

25 But I tell you of a truth, [a]many widows were in Israel in the days of Elias, when the heaven was shut up three years and six months, when great famine was throughout all the land;

26 But unto none of them was Elias sent, save unto Sarepta, *a city* of Sidon, unto a woman *that was* a widow.

27 [a]And many lepers were in Israel in the time of Eliseus the prophet; and none of them was cleansed, saving Naaman the Syrian.

28 And all they in the synagogue, when they heard these things, were [a]filled with wrath,

29 [a]And rose up, and thrust him out of the city, and led him unto the brow of the hill whereon their city was built, that they might cast him down headlong.

30 But he [a]passing through the midst of them went his way,

Jesus Casts Out an Unclean Spirit
(*Mark 1:21–28*)

31 And [a]came down to Capernaum, a city of Galilee, and taught them on the sabbath days.

32 And they were [a]astonished at his doctrine: [b]for his word was with power.

33 [a]And in the synagogue there was a man, which had a spirit of an unclean devil, and cried out with a loud voice,

34 Saying, Let *us* alone; what have we to do with thee, *thou* Jesus of Nazareth? art thou come to destroy us? [a]I know thee who thou art; [b]the Holy One of God.

35 And Jesus rebuked him, saying, Hold thy peace, and come out of him. And when the devil had thrown him in the midst, he came out of him, and hurt him not.

36 And they were all amazed, and spake among themselves, saying, What a word *is* this! for with authority and power he commandeth the unclean spirits, and they come out.

37 And the fame of him went out into every place of the country round about.

Peter's Mother-in-Law Healed
(*Matt. 8:14, 15; Mark 1:29–31*)

38 [a]And he arose out of the synagogue, and entered into Simon's house. And Simon's wife's mother was taken with a great fever; and they [b]besought him for her.

39 And he stood over her, and [a]rebuked the

18 [a]Is. 49:8, 9; 61:1, 2; Matt. 11:5; 12:18; John 3:34 [b][Dan. 9:24]
21 [a]Matt. 1:22, 23; Acts 13:29
22 [a][Ps. 45:2]; Matt. 13:54; Mark 6:2; Luke 2:47; [John 1:14, 17] [b]John 6:42
23 [a]Matt. 4:13; 11:23 [b]Matt. 13:54; Mark 6:1
24 [a]Matt. 13:57; Mark 6:4; John 4:44
25 [a]1 Kin. 17:9; James 5:17
27 [a]2 Kin. 5:1–14
28 [a]Luke 6:11
29 [a]Luke 17:25; John 8:37; 10:31
30 [a]John 8:59; 10:39
31 [a]Is. 9:1; Matt. 4:13; Mark 1:21
32 [a]Matt. 7:28, 29 [b]Luke 4:36; [John 6:63; 7:46; 8:26, 28, 38, 47; 12:49, 50]
33 [a]Mark 1:23
34 [a]Luke 4:41 [b]Ps. 16:10; Is. 49:7; Dan. 9:24; Luke 1:35
38 [a]Matt. 8:14, 15; Mark 1:29–31 [b]Mark 5:23
39 [a]Luke 8:24

*

4:18 NU omits *to heal the brokenhearted*
4:23 NU *Capharnaum,* here and elsewhere
4:26 Gr. *Sarepta*

NKJV

went into the synagogue on the Sabbath day, and stood up to read.

17 And He was handed the book of the prophet Isaiah. And when He had opened the book, He found the place where it was written:

18 *"The[a] Spirit of the LORD is upon Me,*
Because He has anointed Me
To preach the gospel to the poor;
*He has sent Me *to heal the*
brokenhearted,
To proclaim liberty to the captives
And recovery of sight to the blind,
To [b]set at liberty those who are oppressed;
19 *To proclaim the acceptable year of the*
LORD."

20 Then He closed the book, and gave *it* back to the attendant and sat down. And the eyes of all who were in the synagogue were fixed on Him.

21 And He began to say to them, "Today this Scripture is [a]fulfilled in your hearing."

22 So all bore witness to Him, and [a]marveled at the gracious words which proceeded out of His mouth. And they said, [b]"Is this not Joseph's son?"

23 He said to them, "You will surely say this proverb to Me, 'Physician, heal yourself! Whatever we have heard done in [a]Capernaum,* do also here in [b]Your country.' "

24 Then He said, "Assuredly, I say to you, no [a]prophet is accepted in his own country.

25 "But I tell you truly, [a]many widows were in Israel in the days of Elijah, when the heaven was shut up three years and six months, and there was a great famine throughout all the land;

26 "but to none of them was Elijah sent except to *Zarephath, *in the region* of Sidon, to a woman *who was* a widow.

27 [a]"And many lepers were in Israel in the time of Elisha the prophet, and none of them was cleansed except Naaman the Syrian."

28 So all those in the synagogue, when they heard these things, were [a]filled with wrath,

29 [a]and rose up and thrust Him out of the city; and they led Him to the brow of the hill on which their city was built, that they might throw Him down over the cliff.

30 Then [a]passing through the midst of them, He went His way.

Jesus Casts Out an Unclean Spirit
(*Mark 1:21–28*)

31 Then [a]He went down to Capernaum, a city of Galilee, and was teaching them on the Sabbaths.

32 And they were [a]astonished at His teaching, [b]for His word was with authority.

33 [a]Now in the synagogue there was a man who had a spirit of an unclean demon. And he cried out with a loud voice,

34 saying, "Let *us* alone! What have we to do with You, Jesus of Nazareth? Did You come to destroy us? [a]I know who You are—[b]the Holy One of God!"

35 But Jesus rebuked him, saying, "Be quiet, and come out of him!" And when the demon had thrown him in *their* midst, it came out of him and did not hurt him.

36 Then they were all amazed and spoke among themselves, saying, "What a word this *is!* For with authority and power He commands the unclean spirits, and they come out."

37 And the report about Him went out into every place in the surrounding region.

Peter's Mother-in-Law Healed
(*Matt. 8:14, 15; Mark 1:29–31*)

38 [a]Now He arose from the synagogue and entered Simon's house. But Simon's wife's mother was sick with a high fever, and they [b]made request of Him concerning her.

39 So He stood over her and [a]rebuked the

KJV

fever; and it left her: and immediately she arose and ministered unto them.

Many Healed After Sabbath Sunset
(Matt. 8:16, 17; Mark 1:32–34)

40 [a]Now when the sun was setting, all they that had any sick with divers diseases brought them unto him; and he laid his hands on every one of them, and healed them.

41 [a]And devils also came out of many, crying out, and saying, [b]Thou art Christ the Son of God. And [c]he rebuking *them* suffered them not to speak: for they knew that he was Christ.

Jesus Preaches in Galilee
(Matt. 4:23–25; Mark 1:35–39)

42 [a]And when it was day, he departed and went into a desert place: and the people sought him, and came unto him, and stayed him, that he should not depart from them.

43 And he said unto them, I must [a]preach the kingdom of God to other cities also: for therefore am I sent.

44 [a]And he preached in the synagogues of Galilee.

Four Fishermen Called as Disciples
(Matt. 4:18–22; Mark 1:16–20)

5 And [a]it came to pass, that, as the people pressed upon him to [b]hear the word of God, he stood by the lake of Gennesaret,

2 And saw two ships standing by the lake: but the fishermen were gone out of them, and were washing *their* nets.

3 And he entered into one of the ships, which was Simon's, and prayed him that he would thrust out a little from the land. And he [a]sat down, and taught the people out of the ship.

4 Now when he had left speaking, he said unto Simon, [a]Launch out into the deep, and let down your nets for a draught.

5 And Simon answering said unto him, Master, we have toiled all the night, and have taken [a]nothing: nevertheless [b]at thy word I will let down the net.

6 And when they had this done, they inclosed a great multitude of fishes: and their net brake.

7 And they beckoned unto *their* partners, which were in the other ship, that they should come and help them. And they came, and filled both the ships, so that they began to sink.

8 When Simon Peter saw *it,* he fell down at Jesus' knees, saying, [a]Depart from me; for I am a sinful man, O Lord.

9 For he was [a]astonished, and all that were with him, at the draught of the fishes which they had taken:

10 And so *was* also James, and John, the sons of Zebedee, which were partners with Simon. And Jesus said unto Simon, Fear not; [a]from henceforth thou shalt catch men.

11 And when they had brought their ships to land, [a]they forsook all, and followed him.

Jesus Cleanses a Leper
(Matt. 8:1–4; Mark 1:40–45)

12 [a]And it came to pass, when he was in a certain city, behold a man full of [b]leprosy: who seeing Jesus fell on *his* face, and besought him, saying, Lord, if thou wilt, thou canst make me clean.

13 And he put forth *his* hand, and touched him, saying, I will: be thou clean. And [a]immediately the leprosy departed from him.

14 [a]And he charged him to tell no man: but go, and shew thyself to the priest, and offer for thy cleansing, [b]according as Moses commanded, for a testimony unto them.

15 But so much the more went there a [a]fame abroad of him: [b]and great multitudes came to-

40 [a]Matt. 8:16, 17; Mark 1:32–34
41 [a]Mark 1:34; 3:11; Acts 8:7 [b]Mark 8:29 [c]Mark 1:25, 34; 3:11; Luke 4:34, 35
42 [a]Mark 1:35–38; Luke 9:10
43 [a]Mark 1:14; [John 9:4]
44 [a]Matt. 4:23; 9:35; Mark 1:39

CHAPTER 5

1 [a]Matt. 4:18–22; Mark 1:16–20; John 1:40–42 [b]Acts 13:44
3 [a]John 8:2
4 [a]John 21:6
5 [a]John 21:3 [b]Ps. 33:9
8 [a]2 Sam. 6:9; 1 Kin. 17:18
9 [a]Mark 5:42; 10:24, 26
10 [a]Matt. 4:19; Mark 1:17
11 [a]Matt. 4:20; 19:27; [Mark 1:18; 8:34, 35; Luke 9:59–62]; John 12:26
12 [a]Matt. 8:2–4; Mark 1:40–44 [b]Lev. 13:14
13 [a]Matt. 20:34; Luke 8:44; John 5:9
14 [a]Matt. 8:4; Luke 17:14 [b]Lev. 13:1–3; 14:2–32
15 [a]Mark 1:45 [b]Matt. 4:25; Mark 3:7; John 6:2

*

4:41 NU omits *the Christ*
4:44 NU *Judea*

NKJV

fever, and it left her. And immediately she arose and served them.

Many Healed After Sabbath Sunset
(Matt. 8:16, 17; Mark 1:32–34)

40 [a]When the sun was setting, all those who had any that were sick with various diseases brought them to Him; and He laid His hands on every one of them and healed them.

41 [a]And demons also came out of many, crying out and saying, [b]"You are *the Christ, the Son of God!" And He, [c]rebuking *them,* did not allow them to speak, for they knew that He was the Christ.

Jesus Preaches in Galilee
(Matt. 4:23–25; Mark 1:35–39)

42 [a]Now when it was day, He departed and went into a deserted place. And the crowd sought Him and came to Him, and tried to keep Him from leaving them;

43 but He said to them, "I must [a]preach the kingdom of God to the other cities also, because for this purpose I have been sent."

44 [a]And He was preaching in the synagogues of *Galilee.

Four Fishermen Called as Disciples
(Matt. 4:18–22; Mark 1:16–20)

5 So [a]it was, as the multitude pressed about Him to [b]hear the word of God, that He stood by the Lake of Gennesaret,

2 and saw two boats standing by the lake; but the fishermen had gone from them and were washing *their* nets.

3 Then He got into one of the boats, which was Simon's, and asked him to put out a little from the land. And He [a]sat down and taught the multitudes from the boat.

4 When He had stopped speaking, He said to Simon, [a]"Launch out into the deep and let down your nets for a catch."

5 But Simon answered and said to Him, "Master, we have toiled all night and caught [a]nothing; nevertheless [b]at Your word I will let down the net."

6 And when they had done this, they caught a great number of fish, and their net was breaking.

7 So they signaled to *their* partners in the other boat to come and help them. And they came and filled both the boats, so that they began to sink.

8 When Simon Peter saw *it,* he fell down at Jesus' knees, saying, [a]"Depart from me, for I am a sinful man, O Lord!"

9 For he and all who were with him were [a]astonished at the catch of fish which they had taken;

10 and so also *were* James and John, the sons of Zebedee, who were partners with Simon. And Jesus said to Simon, "Do not be afraid. [a]From now on you will catch men."

11 So when they had brought their boats to land, [a]they forsook all and followed Him.

Jesus Cleanses a Leper
(Matt. 8:1–4; Mark 1:40–45)

12 [a]And it happened when He was in a certain city, that behold, a man who was full of [b]leprosy saw Jesus; and he fell on *his* face and implored Him, saying, "Lord, if You are willing, You can make me clean."

13 Then He put out *His* hand and touched him, saying, "I am willing; be cleansed." [a]Immediately the leprosy left him.

14 [a]And He charged him to tell no one, "But go and show yourself to the priest, and make an offering for your cleansing, as a testimony to them, [b]just as Moses commanded."

15 However, [a]the report went around concerning Him all the more; and [b]great multitudes

KJV

gether to hear, and to be healed by him of their infirmities.

16 [a]And he withdrew himself into the wilderness, and [b]prayed.

Jesus Forgives and Heals a Paralytic
(Matt. 9:2–8; Mark 2:1–12)

17 And it came to pass on a certain day, as he was teaching, that there were Pharisees and doctors of the law sitting by, which were come out of every town of Galilee, and Judaea, and Jerusalem: and the power of the Lord was *present* to heal them.

18 [a]And, behold, men brought in a bed a man which was taken with a palsy: and they sought *means* to bring him in, and to lay *him* before him.

19 And when they could not find by what *way* they might bring him in because of the multitude, they went upon the housetop, and let him down through the tiling with *his* couch into the midst [a]before Jesus.

20 And when he saw their faith, he said unto him, Man, thy sins are forgiven thee.

21 [a]And the scribes and the Pharisees began to reason, saying, Who is this which speaketh blasphemies? [b]Who can forgive sins, but God alone?

22 But when Jesus [a]perceived their thoughts, he answering said unto them, What reason ye in your hearts?

23 Whether is easier, to say, Thy sins be forgiven thee; or to say, Rise up and walk?

24 But that ye may know that the Son of man hath power upon earth to forgive sins, (he said unto the sick of the palsy,) [a]I say unto thee, Arise, and take up thy couch, and go into thine house.

25 And immediately he rose up before them, and took up that whereon he lay, and departed to his own house, [a]glorifying God.

26 And they were all amazed, and they [a]glorified God, and were filled with fear, saying, We have seen strange things to day.

Matthew the Tax Collector
(Matt. 9:9–13; Mark 2:13–17)

27 [a]And after these things he went forth, and saw a publican, named Levi, sitting at the receipt of custom: and he said unto him, [b]Follow me.

28 And he left all, rose up, and [a]followed him.

29 [a]And Levi made him a great feast in his own house: and [b]there was a great company of publicans and of others that sat down with them.

30 But their scribes and Pharisees murmured against his disciples, saying, [a]Why do ye eat and drink with publicans and sinners?

31 And Jesus answering said unto them, They that are whole need not a physician; but they that are sick.

32 [a]I came not to call the righteous, but sinners to repentance.

Jesus Is Questioned About Fasting
(Matt. 9:14–17; Mark 2:18–22)

33 And they said unto him, [a]Why do the disciples of John fast often, and make prayers, and likewise *the disciples* of the Pharisees; but thine eat and drink?

34 And he said unto them, Can ye make the children of the bridechamber fast, while the [a]bridegroom is with them?

35 But the days will come, when the bridegroom shall be taken away from them, and then shall they fast in those days.

36 [a]And he spake also a parable unto them; No man putteth a piece of a new garment upon an old; if otherwise, then both the new maketh a rent, and the piece that was *taken* out of the new agreeth not with the old.

37 And no man putteth new wine into old bottles; else the new wine will burst the bottles, and be spilled, and the bottles shall perish.

16 [a]Luke 9:10 [b]Matt. 14:23; Mark 1:35; Luke 6:12; 9:18; 11:1
18 [a]Matt. 9:2–8; Mark 2:3–12
19 [a]Matt. 15:30
21 [a]Matt. 9:3; 26:65; Mark 2:6, 7; John 10:33 [b]Ps. 32:5; 130:4; Is. 43:25
22 [a]Luke 9:47; John 2:25
24 [a]Mark 2:11; 5:41; Luke 7:14
25 [a]Luke 17:15, 18; Acts 3:8
26 [a]Luke 1:65; 7:16
27 [a]Matt. 9:9–17; Mark 2:13–22 [b][Mark 8:34]; Luke 9:59; John 12:26; 21:19, 22
28 [a]Matt. 4:22; 19:27; Mark 10:28
29 [a]Matt. 9:9, 10; Mark 2:15 [b]Luke 15:1
30 [a]Matt. 11:19; Luke 15:2; Acts 23:9
32 [a]Matt. 9:13; 1 Tim. 1:15
33 [a]Matt. 9:14; Mark 2:18; Luke 7:33
34 [a]John 3:29
36 [a]Matt. 9:16, 17; Mark 2:21, 22

*

5:17 NU *with Him to heal*
5:30 NU *But the Pharisees and their scribes*
5:33 NU omits *Why do,* making the verse a statement
5:36 NU *tears a piece from a new garment and puts it on an old one*

NKJV

came together to hear, and to be healed by Him of their infirmities.

16 [a]So He Himself *often* withdrew into the wilderness and [b]prayed.

Jesus Forgives and Heals a Paralytic
(Matt. 9:2–8; Mark 2:1–12)

17 Now it happened on a certain day, as He was teaching, that there were Pharisees and teachers of the law sitting by, who had come out of every town of Galilee, Judea, and Jerusalem. And the power of the Lord was *present* *to heal them.

18 [a]Then behold, men brought on a bed a man who was paralyzed, whom they sought to bring in and lay before Him.

19 And when they could not find how they might bring him in, because of the crowd, they went up on the housetop and let him down with *his* bed through the tiling into the midst [a]before Jesus.

20 When He saw their faith, He said to him, "Man, your sins are forgiven you."

21 [a]And the scribes and the Pharisees began to reason, saying, "Who is this who speaks blasphemies? [b]Who can forgive sins but God alone?"

22 But when Jesus [a]perceived their thoughts, He answered and said to them, "Why are you reasoning in your hearts?

23 "Which is easier, to say, 'Your sins are forgiven you,' or to say, 'Rise up and walk'?

24 "But that you may know that the Son of Man has power on earth to forgive sins"—He said to the man who was paralyzed, [a]"I say to you, arise, take up your bed, and go to your house."

25 Immediately he rose up before them, took up what he had been lying on, and departed to his own house, [a]glorifying God.

26 And they were all amazed, and they [a]glorified God and were filled with fear, saying, "We have seen strange things today!"

Matthew the Tax Collector
(Matt. 9:9–13; Mark 2:13–17)

27 [a]After these things He went out and saw a tax collector named Levi, sitting at the tax office. And He said to him, [b]"Follow Me."

28 So he left all, rose up, and [a]followed Him.

29 [a]Then Levi gave Him a great feast in his own house. And [b]there were a great number of tax collectors and others who sat down with them.

30 *And their scribes and the Pharisees complained against His disciples, saying, [a]"Why do You eat and drink with tax collectors and sinners?"

31 Jesus answered and said to them, "Those who are well have no need of a physician, but those who are sick.

32 [a]"I have not come to call *the* righteous, but sinners, to repentance."

Jesus Is Questioned About Fasting
(Matt. 9:14–17; Mark 2:18–22)

33 Then they said to Him, [a]"Why* do the disciples of John fast often and make prayers, and likewise those of the Pharisees, but Yours eat and drink?"

34 And He said to them, "Can you make the friends of the bridegroom fast while the [a]bridegroom is with them?

35 "But the days will come when the bridegroom will be taken away from them; then they will fast in those days."

36 [a]Then He spoke a parable to them: "No one *puts a piece from a new garment on an old one; otherwise the new makes a tear, and also the piece that was *taken* out of the new does not match the old.

37 "And no one puts new wine into old wineskins; or else the new wine will burst the wineskins and be spilled, and the wineskins will be ruined.

KJV

38 But new wine must be put into new bottles; and both are preserved.

39 No man also having drunk old *wine* straightway desireth new: for he saith, The old is better.

Jesus Is Lord of the Sabbath
(*Matt. 12:1–8; Mark 2:23–28*)

6 And [a]it came to pass on the second sabbath after the first, that he went through the corn fields; and his disciples plucked the ears of corn, and did eat, rubbing *them* in *their* hands.

2 And certain of the Pharisees said unto them, Why do ye that [a]which is not lawful to do on the sabbath days?

3 And Jesus answering them said, Have ye not read so much as this, [a]what David did, when himself was an hungred, and they which were with him;

4 How he went into the house of God, and did take and eat the shewbread, and gave also to them that were with him; [a]which it is not lawful to eat but for the priests alone?

5 And he said unto them, That the Son of man is Lord also of the sabbath.

Healing on the Sabbath
(*Matt. 12:9–14; Mark 3:1–6*)

6 [a]And it came to pass also on another sabbath, that he entered into the synagogue and taught: and there was a man whose right hand was withered.

7 And the scribes and Pharisees watched him, whether he would [a]heal on the sabbath day; that they might find an [b]accusation against him.

8 But he [a]knew their thoughts, and said to the man which had the withered hand, Rise up, and stand forth in the midst. And he arose and stood forth.

9 Then said Jesus unto them, I will ask you one thing; [a]Is it lawful on the sabbath days to do good, or to do evil? to save life, or to destroy *it?*

10 And looking round about upon them all, he said unto the man, Stretch forth thy hand. And he did so: and his hand was restored whole as the other.

11 And they were filled with madness; and communed one with another what they might do to Jesus.

The Twelve Apostles
(*Matt. 10:1–4; Mark 3:13–19*)

12 And it came to pass in those days, that he went out into a mountain to pray, and continued all night in [a]prayer to God.

13 And when it was day, he called *unto him* his disciples: [a]and of them he chose [b]twelve, whom also he named apostles;

14 Simon, ([a]whom he also named Peter,) and Andrew his brother, James and John, Philip and Bartholomew,

15 Matthew and Thomas, James the *son* of Alphaeus, and Simon called Zelotes,

16 And Judas [a]*the brother* of James, and [b]Judas Iscariot, which also was the traitor.

Jesus Heals a Great Multitude
(*cf. Matt. 4:24, 25; Mark 3:7–12*)

17 And he came down with them, and stood in the plain, and the company of his disciples, [a]and a great multitude of people out of all Judaea and Jerusalem, and from the sea coast of Tyre and Sidon, which came to hear him, and to be healed of their diseases;

18 And they that were vexed with unclean spirits: and they were healed.

19 And the whole multitude [a]sought to [b]touch him: for [c]there went virtue out of him, and healed *them* all.

CHAPTER 6
1 [a]Matt. 12:1–8; Mark 2:23–28
2 [a]Ex. 20:10
3 [a]1 Sam. 21:6
4 [a]Lev. 24:9
6 [a]Matt. 12:9–14; Mark 3:1–6; Luke 13:14; 14:3; John 9:16
7 [a]Luke 13:14; 14:1–6 [b]Luke 20:20
8 [a]Matt. 9:4; John 2:24, 25
9 [a]John 7:23
12 [a]Matt. 14:23; Mark 1:35; Luke 5:16; 9:18; 11:1
13 [a]John 6:70 [b]Matt. 10:1
14 [a]John 1:42
16 [a]Jude 1 [b]Luke 22:3–6
17 [a]Matt. 4:25; Mark 3:7, 8
19 [a]Matt. 9:21; 14:36; Mark 3:10 [b]Mark 5:27, 28; Luke 8:44–47 [c]Mark 5:30; Luke 8:46

NKJV

38 "But new wine must be put into new wineskins, *and both are preserved.

39 "And no one, having drunk old *wine,* *immediately desires new; for he says, 'The old is *better.' "

Jesus Is Lord of the Sabbath
(*Matt. 12:1–8; Mark 2:23–28*)

6 Now [a]it happened *on the second Sabbath after the first that He went through the grainfields. And His disciples plucked the heads of grain and ate *them,* rubbing *them* in *their* hands.

2 And some of the Pharisees said to them, "Why are you doing [a]what is not lawful to do on the Sabbath?"

3 But Jesus answering them said, "Have you not even read this, [a]what David did when he was hungry, he and those who were with him:

4 "how he went into the house of God, took and ate the showbread, and also gave some to those with him, [a]which is not lawful for any but the priests to eat?"

5 And He said to them, "The Son of Man is also Lord of the Sabbath."

Healing on the Sabbath
(*Matt. 12:9–14; Mark 3:1–6*)

6 [a]Now it happened on another Sabbath, also, that He entered the synagogue and taught. And a man was there whose right hand was withered.

7 So the scribes and Pharisees watched Him closely, whether He would [a]heal on the Sabbath, that they might find an [b]accusation against Him.

8 But He [a]knew their thoughts, and said to the man who had the withered hand, "Arise and stand here." And he arose and stood.

9 Then Jesus said to them, "I will ask you one thing: [a]Is it lawful on the Sabbath to do good or to do evil, to save life or *to destroy?"

10 And when He had looked around at them all, He said to *the man, "Stretch out your hand." And he did so, and his hand was restored *as whole as the other.

11 But they were filled with rage, and discussed with one another what they might do to Jesus.

The Twelve Apostles
(*Matt. 10:1–4; Mark 3:13–19*)

12 Now it came to pass in those days that He went out to the mountain to pray, and continued all night in [a]prayer to God.

13 And when it was day, He called His disciples to *Himself;* [a]and from them He chose [b]twelve whom He also named apostles:

14 Simon, [a]whom He also named Peter, and Andrew his brother; James and John; Philip and Bartholomew;

15 Matthew and Thomas; James the *son* of Alphaeus, and Simon called the Zealot;

16 Judas [a]*the son* of James, and [b]Judas Iscariot who also became a traitor.

Jesus Heals a Great Multitude
(*cf. Matt. 4:24, 25; Mark 3:7–12*)

17 And He came down with them and stood on a level place with a crowd of His disciples [a]and a great multitude of people from all Judea and Jerusalem, and from the seacoast of Tyre and Sidon, who came to hear Him and be healed of their diseases,

18 as well as those who were tormented with unclean spirits. And they were healed.

19 And the whole multitude [a]sought to [b]touch Him, for [c]power went out from Him and healed *them* all.

*

5:38 NU omits *and both are preserved*
5:39 NU omits *immediately* • NU *good*
6:1 NU *on a Sabbath that He went*
6:9 M *to kill*
6:10 NU, M *him* • NU omits *as whole as the other*

KJV

The Beatitudes
(*Matt. 5:1–12*)

20 And he lifted up his eyes on his disciples, and said, [a]Blessed *be ye* poor: for your's is the kingdom of God.

21 [a]Blessed *are ye* that hunger now: for ye shall be [b]filled. [c]Blessed *are ye* that weep now: for ye shall [d]laugh.

22 [a]Blessed are ye, when men shall hate you, and when they [b]shall separate you *from their company,* and shall reproach *you,* and cast out your name as evil, for the Son of man's sake.

23 [a]Rejoice ye in that day, and leap for joy: for, behold, your reward *is* great in heaven: for [b]in the like manner did their fathers unto the prophets.

Jesus Pronounces Woes

24 [a]But woe unto you [b]that are rich! for [c]ye have received your consolation.

25 [a]Woe unto you that are full! for ye shall hunger. [b]Woe unto you that laugh now! for ye shall mourn and [c]weep.

26 [a]Woe unto you, when all men shall speak well of you! for so did their fathers to the false prophets.

Love Your Enemies
(*Matt. 5:38–48*)

27 [a]But I say unto you which hear, Love your enemies, do good to them which hate you,

28 [a]Bless them that curse you, and [b]pray for them which despitefully use you.

29 [a]And unto him that smiteth thee on the *one* cheek offer also the other; [b]and him that taketh away thy cloke forbid not *to take thy* coat also.

30 [a]Give to every man that asketh of thee; and of him that taketh away thy goods ask *them* not again.

31 [a]And as ye would that men should do to you, do ye also to them likewise.

32 [a]For if ye love them which love you, what thank have ye? for sinners also love those that love them.

33 And if ye do good to them which do good to you, what thank have ye? for sinners also do even the same.

34 [a]And if ye lend *to them* of whom ye hope to receive, what thank have ye? for sinners also lend to sinners, to receive as much again.

35 But [a]love ye your enemies, and [b]do good, and [c]lend, hoping for nothing again; and your reward shall be great, and [d]ye shall be the children of the Highest: for he is kind unto the unthankful and *to* the evil.

36 [a]Be ye therefore merciful, as your Father also is merciful.

Do Not Judge
(*Matt. 7:1–5*)

37 [a]Judge not, and ye shall not be judged: condemn not, and ye shall not be condemned: [b]forgive, and ye shall be forgiven:

38 [a]Give, and it shall be given unto you; good measure, pressed down, and shaken together, and running over, shall men give into your [b]bosom. For [c]with the same measure that ye mete withal it shall be measured to you again.

39 And he spake a parable unto them, [a]Can the blind lead the blind? shall they not both fall into the ditch?

20 [a]Matt. 5:3–12; [11:5]; Luke 6:20–23; [James 2:5]
21 [a]Is. 55:1; 65:13; Matt. 5:6 [b][Rev. 7:16] [c][Is. 61:3; Rev. 7:17] [d]Ps. 126:5
22 [a]Matt. 5:11; 1 Pet. 2:19; 3:14; 4:14 [b][John 16:2]
23 [a]Matt. 5:12; Acts 5:41; [Col. 1:24]; James 1:2 [b]Acts 7:51
24 [a]Amos 6:1; Luke 12:21; James 5:1–6 [b]Luke 12:21 [c]Matt. 6:2, 5, 16; Luke 16:25
25 [a][Is. 65:13] [b][Prov. 14:13] [c]James 4:9
26 [a][John 15:19; 1 John 4:5]
27 [a]Ex. 23:4; Prov. 25:21; Matt. 5:44; Rom. 12:20
28 [a]Rom. 12:14 [b]Luke 23:24; Acts 7:60
29 [a]Matt. 5:39–42 [b][1 Cor. 6:7]
30 [a]Deut. 15:7, 8; Prov. 3:27; 21:26; Matt. 5:42
31 [a]Matt. 7:12
32 [a]Matt. 5:45
34 [a]Matt. 5:42
35 [a][Rom. 13:10] [b]Heb. 13:16 [c]Lev. 25:35–37; Ps. 37:26 [d]Matt. 5:46
36 [a]Matt. 5:48; Eph. 4:32
37 [a]Matt. 7:1–5; Rom. 14:4; [1 Cor. 4:5] [b]Matt. 18:21–35
38 [a][Prov. 19:17; 28:27] [b]Ps. 79:12; Is. 65:6, 7; Jer. 32:18 [c]Matt. 7:2; Mark 4:24; James 2:13
39 [a]Matt. 15:14; 23:16; Rom. 2:19

NKJV

The Beatitudes
(*Matt. 5:1–12*)

20 Then He lifted up His eyes toward His disciples, and said:

[a]"Blessed *are you* poor,
For yours is the kingdom of God.
21 [a]Blessed *are you* who hunger now,
For you shall be [b]filled.
[c]Blessed *are you* who weep now,
For you shall [d]laugh.
22 [a]Blessed are you when men hate you,
And when they [b]exclude you,
And revile *you,* and cast out your name as evil,
For the Son of Man's sake.
23 [a]Rejoice in that day and leap for joy!
For indeed your reward *is* great in heaven,
For [b]in like manner their fathers did to the prophets.

Jesus Pronounces Woes

24 "But[a] woe to you [b]who are rich,
For [c]you have received your consolation.
25 [a]Woe to you who are full,
For you shall hunger.
[b]Woe to you who laugh now,
For you shall mourn and [c]weep.
26 [a]Woe *to you when *all men speak well of you,
For so did their fathers to the false prophets.

Love Your Enemies
(*Matt. 5:38–48*)

27 [a]"But I say to you who hear: Love your enemies, do good to those who hate you,

28 [a]"bless those who curse you, and [b]pray for those who spitefully use you.

29 [a]"To him who strikes you on the *one* cheek, offer the other also. [b]And from him who takes away your cloak, do not withhold *your* tunic either.

30 [a]"Give to everyone who asks of you. And from him who takes away your goods do not ask *them* back.

31 [a]"And just as you want men to do to you, you also do to them likewise.

32 [a]"But if you love those who love you, what credit is that to you? For even sinners love those who love them.

33 "And if you do good to those who do good to you, what credit is that to you? For even sinners do the same.

34 [a]"And if you lend *to those* from whom you hope to receive back, what credit is that to you? For even sinners lend to sinners to receive as much back.

35 "But [a]love your enemies, [b]do good, and [c]lend, hoping for nothing in return; and your reward will be great, and [d]you will be sons of the Most High. For He is kind to the unthankful and evil.

36 [a]"Therefore be merciful, just as your Father also is merciful.

Do Not Judge
(*Matt. 7:1–5*)

37 [a]"Judge not, and you shall not be judged. Condemn not, and you shall not be condemned. [b]Forgive, and you will be forgiven.

38 [a]"Give, and it will be given to you: good measure, pressed down, shaken together, and running over will be put into your [b]bosom. For [c]with the same measure that you use, it will be measured back to you."

39 And He spoke a parable to them: [a]"Can the blind lead the blind? Will they not both fall into the ditch?

*
6:26 NU, M omit *to you* • M omits *all*

KJV

40 [a]The disciple is not above his master: but every one that is perfect shall be as his master.

41 [a]And why beholdest thou the mote that is in thy brother's eye, but perceivest not the beam that is in thine own eye?

42 Either how canst thou say to thy brother, Brother, let me pull out the mote that is in thine eye, when thou thyself beholdest not the beam that is in thine own eye? Thou hypocrite, cast out first the beam out of thine own eye, and then shalt thou see clearly to pull out the mote that is in thy brother's eye.

A Tree Is Known by Its Fruit
(*Matt. 7:15–20*)

43 [a]For a good tree bringeth not forth corrupt fruit; neither doth a corrupt tree bring forth good fruit.

44 For [a]every tree is known by his own fruit. For of thorns men do not gather figs, nor of a bramble bush gather they grapes.

45 [a]A good man out of the good treasure of his heart bringeth forth that which is good; and an evil man out of the evil treasure of his heart bringeth forth that which is evil: for [b]of the abundance of the heart his mouth speaketh.

Build on the Rock
(*Matt. 7:21–27*)

46 [a]And why call ye me, Lord, Lord, and do not the things which I say?

47 [a]Whosoever cometh to me, and heareth my sayings, and doeth them, I will shew you to whom he is like:

48 He is like a man which built an house, and digged deep, and laid the foundation on a rock: and when the flood arose, the stream beat vehemently upon that house, and could not shake it: for it was founded upon a rock.

49 But he that heareth, and doeth not, is like a man that without a foundation built an house upon the earth; against which the stream did beat vehemently, and immediately it fell; and the ruin of that house was great.

Jesus Heals a Centurion's Servant
(*Matt. 8:5–13*)

7 Now when he had ended all his sayings in the audience of the people, he [a]entered into Capernaum.

2 And a certain centurion's servant, who was dear unto him, was sick, and ready to die.

3 And when he heard of Jesus, he sent unto him the elders of the Jews, beseeching him that he would come and heal his servant.

4 And when they came to Jesus, they besought him instantly, saying, That he was worthy for whom he should do this:

5 For he loveth our nation, and he hath built us a synagogue.

6 Then Jesus went with them. And when he was now not far from the house, the centurion sent friends to him, saying unto him, Lord, trouble not thyself: for I am not worthy that thou shouldest enter under my roof:

7 Wherefore neither thought I myself worthy to come unto thee: but [a]say in a word, and my servant shall be healed.

8 For I also am a man set under [a]authority, having under me soldiers, and I say unto one, Go, and he goeth; and to another, Come, and he cometh; and to my servant, Do this, and he doeth *it*.

9 When Jesus heard these things, he marvelled at him, and turned him about, and said unto the people that followed him, I say unto you, I have not found so great faith, no, not in Israel.

10 And they that were sent, returning to the house, found the servant whole that had been sick.

40 [a]Matt. 10:24; [John 13:16; 15:20]
41 [a]Matt. 7:3
43 [a]Matt. 7:16–18, 20
44 [a]Matt. 12:33
45 [a]Matt. 12:35 [b]Prov. 15:2, 28; 16:23; 18:21; Matt. 12:34
46 [a]Mal. 1:6; Matt. 7:21; 25:11; Luke 13:25
47 [a]Matt. 7:24–27; [John 14:21]; James 1:22–25

CHAPTER 7
1 [a]Matt. 8:5–13
7 [a]Ps. 33:9; 107:20
8 [a][Mark 13:34]

NKJV

40 [a]"A disciple is not above his teacher, but everyone who is perfectly trained will be like his teacher.

41 [a]"And why do you look at the speck in your brother's eye, but do not perceive the plank in your own eye?

42 "Or how can you say to your brother, 'Brother, let me remove the speck that *is* in your eye,' when you yourself do not see the plank that *is* in your own eye? Hypocrite! First remove the plank from your own eye, and then you will see clearly to remove the speck that is in your brother's eye.

A Tree Is Known by Its Fruit
(*Matt. 7:15–20*)

43 [a]"For a good tree does not bear bad fruit, nor does a bad tree bear good fruit.

44 "For [a]every tree is known by its own fruit. For *men* do not gather figs from thorns, nor do they gather grapes from a bramble bush.

45 [a]"A good man out of the good treasure of his heart brings forth good; and an evil man out of the evil *treasure of his heart brings forth evil. For out [b]of the abundance of the heart his mouth speaks.

Build on the Rock
(*Matt. 7:21–27*)

46 [a]"But why do you call Me 'Lord, Lord,' and not do the things which I say?

47 [a]"Whoever comes to Me, and hears My sayings and does them, I will show you whom he is like:

48 "He is like a man building a house, who dug deep and laid the foundation on the rock. And when the flood arose, the stream beat vehemently against that house, and could not shake it, for it was *founded on the rock.

49 "But he who heard and did nothing is like a man who built a house on the earth without a foundation, against which the stream beat vehemently; and immediately it *fell. And the ruin of that house was great."

Jesus Heals a Centurion's Servant
(*Matt. 8:5–13*)

7 Now when He concluded all His sayings in the hearing of the people, He [a]entered Capernaum.

2 And a certain centurion's servant, who was dear to him, was sick and ready to die.

3 So when he heard about Jesus, he sent elders of the Jews to Him, pleading with Him to come and heal his servant.

4 And when they came to Jesus, they begged Him earnestly, saying that the one for whom He should do this was deserving,

5 "for he loves our nation, and has built us a synagogue."

6 Then Jesus went with them. And when He was already not far from the house, the centurion sent friends to Him, saying to Him, "Lord, do not trouble Yourself, for I am not worthy that You should enter under my roof.

7 "Therefore I did not even think myself worthy to come to You. But [a]say the word, and my servant will be healed.

8 "For I also am a man placed under [a]authority, having soldiers under me. And I say to one, 'Go,' and he goes; and to another, 'Come,' and he comes; and to my servant, 'Do this,' and he does *it*."

9 When Jesus heard these things, He marveled at him, and turned around and said to the crowd that followed Him, "I say to you, I have not found such great faith, not even in Israel!"

10 And those who were sent, returning to the house, found the servant well *who had been sick.

6:45 NU omits *treasure of his heart*
6:48 NU *well built*
6:49 NU *collapsed*
7:10 NU omits *who had been sick*

KJV

Jesus Raises the Son of the Widow of Nain

11 And it came to pass the day after, that he went into a city called Nain; and many of his disciples went with him, and much people.

12 Now when he came nigh to the gate of the city, behold, there was a dead man carried out, the only son of his mother, and she was a widow: and much people of the city was with her.

13 And when the Lord saw her, he had [a]compassion on her, and said unto her, [b]Weep not.

14 And he came and touched the bier: and they that bare *him* stood still. And he said, Young man, I say unto thee, [a]Arise.

15 And he that was dead [a]sat up, and began to speak. And he [b]delivered him to his mother.

16 [a]And there came a fear on all: and they [b]glorified God, saying, [c]That a great prophet is risen up among us; and, [d]That God hath visited his people.

17 And this rumour of him went forth throughout all Judaea, and throughout all the region round about.

John the Baptist Sends Messengers to Jesus
(*Matt. 11:2–19*)

18 [a]And the disciples of John shewed him of all these things.

19 And John calling *unto him* two of his disciples sent *them* to Jesus, saying, Art thou he that should [a]come? or look we for another?

20 When the men were come unto him, they said, John Baptist hath sent us unto thee, saying, Art thou he that should come? or look we for another?

21 And in that same hour he cured many of *their* infirmities and plagues, and of evil spirits; and unto many *that were* blind he gave sight.

22 [a]Then Jesus answering said unto them, Go your way, and tell John what things ye have seen and heard; [b]how that the blind [c]see, the lame [d]walk, the lepers are [e]cleansed, the deaf [f]hear, the dead are raised, [g]to the poor the gospel is preached.

23 And blessed is *he,* whosoever shall not be offended in me.

24 [a]And when the messengers of John were departed, he began to speak unto the people concerning John, What went ye out into the wilderness for to see? A reed shaken with the wind?

25 But what went ye out for to see? A man clothed in soft raiment? Behold, they which are gorgeously apparelled, and live delicately, are in kings' courts.

26 But what went ye out for to see? A prophet? Yea, I say unto you, and much more than a prophet.

27 This is *he,* of whom it is written, [a]BEHOLD, I SEND MY MESSENGER BEFORE THY FACE, WHICH SHALL PREPARE THY WAY BEFORE THEE.

28 For I say unto you, Among those that are born of women there is not a [a]greater prophet than John the Baptist: but he that is least in the kingdom of God is greater than he.

29 And all the people that heard *him,* and the publicans, justified God, [a]being baptized with the baptism of John.

30 But the Pharisees and lawyers rejected [a]the counsel of God against themselves, being not baptized of him.

31 And the Lord said, [a]Whereunto then shall I liken the men of this generation? and to what are they like?

32 They are like unto children sitting in the marketplace, and calling one to another, and saying, We have piped unto you, and ye have not danced; we have mourned to you, and ye have not wept.

NKJV

Jesus Raises the Son of the Widow of Nain

11 Now it happened, the day after, *that* He went into a city called Nain; and many of His disciples went with Him, and a large crowd.

12 And when He came near the gate of the city, behold, a dead man was being carried out, the only son of his mother; and she was a widow. And a large crowd from the city was with her.

13 When the Lord saw her, He had [a]compassion on her and said to her, [b]"Do not weep."

14 Then He came and touched the open coffin, and those who carried *him* stood still. And He said, "Young man, I say to you, [a]arise."

15 So he who was dead [a]sat up and began to speak. And He [b]presented him to his mother.

16 [a]Then fear came upon all, and they [b]glorified God, saying, [c]"A great prophet has risen up among us"; and, [d]"God has visited His people."

17 And this report about Him went throughout all Judea and all the surrounding region.

John the Baptist Sends Messengers to Jesus
(*Matt. 11:2–19*)

18 [a]Then the disciples of John reported to him concerning all these things.

19 And John, calling two of his disciples to *him,* sent *them* to *Jesus, saying, "Are You [a]the Coming One, or do we look for another?"

20 When the men had come to Him, they said, "John the Baptist has sent us to You, saying, 'Are You the Coming One, or do we look for another?' "

21 And that very hour He cured many of infirmities, afflictions, and evil spirits; and to many blind He gave sight.

22 [a]Jesus answered and said to them, "Go and tell John the things you have seen and heard: [b]that *the* blind [c]see, *the* lame [d]walk, *the* lepers are [e]cleansed, *the* deaf [f]hear, *the* dead are raised, [g]*the* poor have the gospel preached to them.

23 "And blessed is *he* who is not offended because of Me."

24 [a]When the messengers of John had departed, He began to speak to the multitudes concerning John: "What did you go out into the wilderness to see? A reed shaken by the wind?

25 "But what did you go out to see? A man clothed in soft garments? Indeed those who are gorgeously appareled and live in luxury are in kings' courts.

26 "But what did you go out to see? A prophet? Yes, I say to you, and more than a prophet.

27 "This is *he* of whom it is written:

[a]*'Behold, I send My messenger before Your face,*
Who will prepare Your way before You.'

28 "For I say to you, among those born of women there is *not a [a]greater prophet than John the Baptist; but he who is least in the kingdom of God is greater than he."

29 And when all the people heard *Him,* even the tax collectors justified God, [a]having been baptized with the baptism of John.

30 But the Pharisees and lawyers rejected [a]the will of God for themselves, not having been baptized by him.

31 *And the Lord said, [a]"To what then shall I liken the men of this generation, and what are they like?

32 "They are like children sitting in the marketplace and calling to one another, saying:

'We played the flute for you,
And you did not dance;
We mourned to you,
And you did not weep.'

13 [a]Lam. 3:32; John 11:35; [Heb. 4:15] [b]Luke 8:52
14 [a]Mark 5:41; Luke 8:54; John 11:43; Acts 9:40; [Rom. 4:17]
15 [a]Matt. 11:5; Luke 8:55; John 11:44 [b]1 Kin. 17:23; 2 Kin. 4:36
16 [a]Luke 1:65 [b]Luke 5:26 [c]Luke 24:19; John 4:19; 6:14; 9:17 [d]Luke 1:68
18 [a]Matt. 11:2–19
19 [a][Mic. 5:2; Zech. 9:9; Mal. 3:1–3]
22 [a]Matt. 11:4 [b]Is. 35:5 [c]John 9:7 [d]Matt. 15:31 [e]Luke 17:12–14 [f]Mark 7:37 [g][Is. 61:1–3; Luke 4:18]
24 [a]Matt. 11:7
27 [a]Is. 40:3; Mal. 3:1; Matt. 11:10; Mark 1:2
28 [a][Luke 1:15]
29 [a]Matt. 3:5; Luke 3:12
30 [a]Acts 20:27
31 [a]Matt. 11:16

*

7:19 NU *the Lord*
7:28 NU *none greater than John;*
7:31 NU, M omit *And the Lord said*

KJV

33 For [a]John the Baptist came [b]neither eating bread nor drinking wine; and ye say, He hath a devil.

34 The Son of man is come [a]eating and drinking; and ye say, Behold a gluttonous man, and a winebibber, a friend of publicans and sinners!

35 [a]But wisdom is justified of all her children.

A Sinful Woman Forgiven

36 [a]And one of the Pharisees desired him that he would eat with him. And he went into the Pharisee's house, and sat down to meat.

37 And, behold, a woman in the city, which was a sinner, when she knew that *Jesus* sat at meat in the Pharisee's house, brought an alabaster box of ointment,

38 And stood at his feet behind *him* weeping, and began to wash his feet with tears, and did wipe *them* with the hairs of her head, and kissed his feet, and anointed *them* with the ointment.

39 Now when the Pharisee which had bidden him saw *it*, he spake within himself, saying, [a]This man, if he were a prophet, would have known who and what manner of woman *this is* that toucheth him: for she is a sinner.

40 And Jesus answering said unto him, Simon, I have somewhat to say unto thee. And he saith, Master, say on.

41 There was a certain creditor which had two debtors: the one owed five hundred [a]pence, and the other fifty.

42 And when they had nothing to pay, he frankly forgave them both. Tell me therefore, which of them will love him most?

43 Simon answered and said, I suppose that *he*, to whom he forgave most. And he said unto him, Thou hast rightly judged.

44 And he turned to the woman, and said unto Simon, Seest thou this woman? I entered into thine house, thou gavest me no [a]water for my feet: but she hath washed my feet with tears, and wiped *them* with the hairs of her head.

45 Thou gavest me no [a]kiss: but this woman since the time I came in hath not ceased to kiss my feet.

46 [a]My head with oil thou didst not anoint: but this woman hath anointed my feet with ointment.

47 [a]Wherefore I say unto thee, Her sins, which are many, are forgiven; for she loved much: but to whom little is forgiven, *the same* loveth little.

48 And he said unto her, [a]Thy sins are forgiven.

49 And they that sat at meat with him began to say within themselves, [a]Who is this that forgiveth sins also?

50 And he said to the woman, [a]Thy faith hath saved thee; go in peace.

Many Women Minister to Jesus

8 And it came to pass afterward, that he went throughout every city and village, preaching and shewing the glad tidings of the kingdom of God: and the twelve *were* with him,

2 And [a]certain women, which had been healed of evil spirits and infirmities, Mary called Magdalene, [b]out of whom went seven devils,

3 And Joanna the wife of Chuza Herod's steward, and Susanna, and many others, which ministered unto him of their substance.

The Parable of the Sower
(Matt. 13:1–9; Mark 4:1–9)

4 [a]And when much people were gathered together, and were come to him out of every city, he spake by a parable:

5 A sower went out to sow his seed: and as he sowed, some fell by the way side; and it was trodden down, and the fowls of the air devoured it.

33 [a]Matt. 3:1 [b][Matt. 3:4]; Luke 1:15
34 [a]Luke 15:2
35 [a]Matt. 11:19
36 [a]Matt. 26:6; Mark 14:3; John 11:2
39 [a]Luke 15:2
41 [a]Matt. 18:28; Mark 6:37
44 [a]Gen. 18:4; 19:2; 43:24; Judg. 19:21; 1 Tim. 5:10
45 [a]Rom. 16:16
46 [a]2 Sam. 12:20; Ps. 23:5; Eccl. 9:8; Dan. 10:3
47 [a][1 Tim. 1:14]
48 [a]Matt. 9:2; Mark 2:5
49 [a]Matt. 9:3; [Mark 2:7]; Luke 5:21
50 [a]Matt. 9:22; Mark 5:34; 10:52; Luke 8:48; 18:42

CHAPTER 8
2 [a]Matt. 27:55; Mark 15:40, 41; Luke 23:49, 55 [b]Matt. 27:56; Mark 16:9
4 [a]Matt. 13:2–9; Mark 4:1–9

*
8:3 NU, M *them*

NKJV

33 "For [a]John the Baptist came [b]neither eating bread nor drinking wine, and you say, 'He has a demon.'

34 "The Son of Man has come [a]eating and drinking, and you say, 'Look, a glutton and a winebibber, a friend of tax collectors and sinners!'

35 [a]"But wisdom is justified by all her children."

A Sinful Woman Forgiven

36 [a]Then one of the Pharisees asked Him to eat with him. And He went to the Pharisee's house, and sat down to eat.

37 And behold, a woman in the city who was a sinner, when she knew that *Jesus* sat at the table in the Pharisee's house, brought an alabaster flask of fragrant oil,

38 and stood at His feet behind *Him* weeping; and she began to wash His feet with her tears, and wiped *them* with the hair of her head; and she kissed His feet and anointed *them* with the fragrant oil.

39 Now when the Pharisee who had invited Him saw *this*, he spoke to himself, saying, [a]"This man, if He were a prophet, would know who and what manner of woman *this is* who is touching Him, for she is a sinner."

40 And Jesus answered and said to him, "Simon, I have something to say to you." So he said, "Teacher, say it."

41 "There was a certain creditor who had two debtors. One owed five hundred [a]denarii, and the other fifty.

42 "And when they had nothing with which to repay, he freely forgave them both. Tell Me, therefore, which of them will love him more?"

43 Simon answered and said, "I suppose the *one* whom he forgave more." And He said to him, "You have rightly judged."

44 Then He turned to the woman and said to Simon, "Do you see this woman? I entered your house; you gave Me no [a]water for My feet, but she has washed My feet with her tears and wiped *them* with the hair of her head.

45 "You gave Me no [a]kiss, but this woman has not ceased to kiss My feet since the time I came in.

46 [a]"You did not anoint My head with oil, but this woman has anointed My feet with fragrant oil.

47 [a]"Therefore I say to you, her sins, *which are* many, are forgiven, for she loved much. But to whom little is forgiven, *the same* loves little."

48 Then He said to her, [a]"Your sins are forgiven."

49 And those who sat at the table with Him began to say to themselves, [a]"Who is this who even forgives sins?"

50 Then He said to the woman, [a]"Your faith has saved you. Go in peace."

Many Women Minister to Jesus

8 Now it came to pass, afterward, that He went through every city and village, preaching and bringing the glad tidings of the kingdom of God. And the twelve *were* with Him,

2 and [a]certain women who had been healed of evil spirits and infirmities—Mary called Magdalene, [b]out of whom had come seven demons,

3 and Joanna the wife of Chuza, Herod's steward, and Susanna, and many others who provided for *Him from their substance.

The Parable of the Sower
(Matt. 13:1–9; Mark 4:1–9)

4 [a]And when a great multitude had gathered, and they had come to Him from every city, He spoke by a parable:

5 "A sower went out to sow his seed. And as he sowed, some fell by the wayside; and it was trampled down, and the birds of the air devoured it.

KJV

6 And some fell upon a rock; and as soon as it was sprung up, it withered away, because it lacked moisture.

7 And some fell among thorns; and the thorns sprang up with it, and choked it.

8 And other fell on good ground, and sprang up, and bare fruit an hundredfold. And when he had said these things, he cried, [a]He that hath ears to hear, let him hear.

The Purpose of Parables
(Matt. 13:10–17; Mark 4:10–12)

9 [a]And his disciples asked him, saying, What might this parable be?

10 And he said, Unto you it is given to know the mysteries of the kingdom of God: but to others in parables; [a]THAT SEEING THEY MIGHT NOT SEE, AND HEARING THEY MIGHT NOT UNDERSTAND.

The Parable of the Sower Explained
(Matt. 13:18–23; Mark 4:13–20)

11 [a]Now the parable is this: The seed is the [b]word of God.

12 Those by the way side are they that hear; then cometh the devil, and taketh away the word out of their hearts, lest they should believe and be saved.

13 They on the rock *are they*, which, when they hear, receive the word with joy; and these have no root, which for a while believe, and in time of temptation fall away.

14 And that which fell among thorns are they, which, when they have heard, go forth, and are choked with cares and [a]riches and pleasures of *this* life, and bring no fruit to perfection.

15 But that on the good ground are they, which in an honest and good heart, having heard the word, keep *it*, and bring forth fruit with [a]patience.

The Parable of the Revealed Light
(Mark 4:21–25)

16 [a]No man, when he hath lighted a candle, covereth it with a vessel, or putteth *it* under a bed; but setteth *it* on a candlestick, that they which enter in may see the [b]light.

17 [a]For nothing is secret, that shall not be [b]made manifest; neither *any thing* hid, that shall not be known and come abroad.

18 Take heed therefore how ye hear: [a]for whosoever hath, to him shall be given; and whosoever hath not, from him shall be taken even that which he seemeth to [b]have.

Jesus' Mother and Brothers Come to Him
(Matt. 12:46–50, Mark 3:31–35)

19 [a]Then came to him *his* mother and his brethren, and could not come at him for the press.

20 And it was told him *by certain* which said, Thy mother and thy brethren stand without, desiring to see thee.

21 And he answered and said unto them, My mother and my brethren are these which hear the word of God, and do it.

Wind and Wave Obey Jesus
(Matt. 8:23–27; Mark 4:35–41)

22 [a]Now it came to pass on a certain day, that he went into a ship with his disciples: and he said unto them, Let us go over unto the other side of the lake. And they launched forth.

23 But as they sailed he fell asleep: and there came down a storm of wind on the lake; and they were filled *with water*, and were in jeopardy.

24 And they came to him, and awoke him, saying, Master, master, we perish. Then he arose, and rebuked the wind and the raging of the water: and they ceased, and there was a calm.

8 [a]Matt. 11:15; Mark 7:16; Luke 14:35; Rev. 2:7, 11, 17, 29; 3:6, 13, 22; 13:9
9 [a]Matt. 13:10–23; Mark 4:10–20
10 [a]Is. 6:9; Matt. 13:14; Acts 28:26
11 [a]Matt. 13:18; Mark 4:14; [1 Pet. 1:23] [b]Luke 5:1; 11:28
14 [a]Matt. 19:23; 1 Tim. 6:9, 10
15 [a][Rom. 2:7; Heb. 10:36–39; James 5:7, 8]
16 [a]Matt. 5:15; Mark 4:21; Luke 11:33 [b]Matt. 5:14
17 [a]Matt. 10:26; Luke 12:2; [1 Cor. 4:5] [b][Eccl. 12:14; 2 Cor. 5:10]
18 [a]Matt. 25:29 [b]Matt. 13:12
19 [a]Ps. 69:8; Matt. 12:46–50; Mark 3:31–35
22 [a]Matt. 8:23–27; Mark 4:36–41

NKJV

6 "Some fell on rock; and as soon as it sprang up, it withered away because it lacked moisture.

7 "And some fell among thorns, and the thorns sprang up with it and choked it.

8 "But others fell on good ground, sprang up, and yielded a crop a hundredfold." When He had said these things He cried, [a]"He who has ears to hear, let him hear!"

The Purpose of Parables
(Matt. 13:10–17; Mark 4:10–12)

9 [a]Then His disciples asked Him, saying, "What does this parable mean?"

10 And He said, "To you it has been given to know the mysteries of the kingdom of God, but to the rest *it is given* in parables, that

[a]*'Seeing they may not see,*
And hearing they may not understand.'

The Parable of the Sower Explained
(Matt. 13:18–23; Mark 4:13–20)

11 [a]"Now the parable is this: The seed is the [b]word of God.

12 "Those by the wayside are the ones who hear; then the devil comes and takes away the word out of their hearts, lest they should believe and be saved.

13 "But the ones on the rock *are those* who, when they hear, receive the word with joy; and these have no root, who believe for a while and in time of temptation fall away.

14 "Now the ones *that* fell among thorns are those who, when they have heard, go out and are choked with cares, [a]riches, and pleasures of life, and bring no fruit to maturity.

15 "But the ones *that* fell on the good ground are those who, having heard the word with a noble and good heart, keep *it* and bear fruit with [a]patience.

The Parable of the Revealed Light
(Mark 4:21–25)

16 [a]"No one, when he has lit a lamp, covers it with a vessel or puts *it* under a bed, but sets *it* on a lampstand, that those who enter may see the [b]light.

17 [a]"For nothing is secret that will not be [b]revealed, nor *anything* hidden that will not be known and come to light.

18 "Therefore take heed how you hear. [a]For whoever has, to him *more* will be given; and whoever does not have, even what he seems to [b]have will be taken from him."

Jesus' Mother and Brothers Come to Him
(Matt. 12:46–50; Mark 3:31–35)

19 [a]Then His mother and brothers came to Him, and could not approach Him because of the crowd.

20 And it was told Him *by some,* who said, "Your mother and Your brothers are standing outside, desiring to see You."

21 But He answered and said to them, "My mother and My brothers are these who hear the word of God and do it."

Wind and Wave Obey Jesus
(Matt. 8:23–27; Mark 4:35–41)

22 [a]Now it happened, on a certain day, that He got into a boat with His disciples. And He said to them, "Let us cross over to the other side of the lake." And they launched out.

23 But as they sailed He fell asleep. And a windstorm came down on the lake, and they were filling *with water,* and were in jeopardy.

24 And they came to Him and awoke Him, saying, "Master, Master, we are perishing!" Then He arose and rebuked the wind and the raging of the water. And they ceased, and there was a calm.

KJV

25 And he said unto them, [a]Where is your faith? And they being afraid wondered, saying one to another, [b]What manner of man is this! for he commandeth even the winds and water, and they obey him.

A Demon-Possessed Man Healed
(Matt. 8:28—9:1; Mark 5:1–20)

26 [a]And they arrived at the country of the Gadarenes, which is over against Galilee.

27 And when he went forth to land, there met him out of the city a certain man, which had devils long time, and ware no clothes, neither abode in *any* house, but in the tombs.

28 When he saw Jesus, he [a]cried out, and fell down before him, and with a loud voice said, [b]What have I to do with thee, Jesus, [c]*thou* Son of God most high? I beseech thee, torment me not.

29 (For he had commanded the unclean spirit to come out of the man. For oftentimes it had caught him: and he was kept bound with chains and in fetters; and he brake the bands, and was driven of the devil into the wilderness.)

30 And Jesus asked him, saying, What is thy name? And he said, Legion: because many devils were entered into him.

31 And they besought him that he would not command them to go out [a]into the deep.

32 And there was there an herd of many [a]swine feeding on the mountain: and they besought him that he would suffer them to enter into them. And he suffered them.

33 Then went the devils out of the man, and entered into the swine: and the herd ran violently down a steep place into the lake, and were choked.

34 When they that fed *them* saw what was done, they fled, and went and told *it* in the city and in the country.

35 Then they went out to see what was done; and came to Jesus, and found the man, out of whom the devils were departed, [a]sitting at the [b]feet of Jesus, clothed, and in his [c]right mind: and they were afraid.

36 They also which saw *it* told them by what means he that was possessed of the devils was healed.

37 [a]Then the whole multitude of the country of the Gadarenes round about [b]besought him to [c]depart from them; for they were taken with great [d]fear: and he went up into the ship, and returned back again.

38 Now [a]the man out of whom the devils were departed besought him that he might be with him: but Jesus sent him away, saying,

39 Return to thine own house, and shew how great things God hath done unto thee. And he went his way, and published throughout the whole city how great things Jesus had done unto him.

A Girl Restored to Life and a Woman Healed
(Matt. 9:18–26; Mark 5:21–43)

40 And it came to pass, that, when Jesus was returned, the people *gladly* received him: for they were all waiting for him.

41 [a]And, behold, there came a man named Jairus, and he was a ruler of the synagogue: and he fell down at Jesus' feet, and besought him that he would come into his house:

42 For he had one only daughter, about twelve years of age, and she lay [a]a dying. But as he went the people thronged him.

43 [a]And a woman having an [b]issue of blood twelve years, which had spent all her living upon physicians, neither could be healed of any,

44 Came behind *him*, and [a]touched the border of his garment: and immediately her issue of blood stanched.

45 And Jesus said, Who touched me? When all denied, Peter and they that were with him said,

25 [a]Luke 9:41 [b]Luke 4:36; 5:26
26 [a]Matt. 8:28–34; Mark 5:1–17
28 [a]Mark 1:26; 9:26 [b]Mark 1:23, 24 [c]Luke 4:41
31 [a]Rom. 10:7; [Rev. 20:1, 3]
32 [a]Lev. 11:7; Deut. 14:8
35 [a][Matt. 11:28] [b]Matt. 28:9; Mark 7:25; Luke 10:39; 17:16; John 11:32 [c][2 Tim. 1:7]
37 [a]Matt. 8:34 [b]Mark 1:24; Luke 4:34 [c]Job 21:14; Acts 16:39 [d]Luke 5:26
38 [a]Mark 5:18–20
41 [a]Matt. 9:18–26; Mark 5:22–43
42 [a]Luke 7:2
43 [a]Matt. 9:20 [b]Luke 15:19–22
44 [a]Mark 6:56; Luke 5:13

NKJV

25 But He said to them, [a]"Where is your faith?" And they were afraid, and marveled, saying to one another, [b]"Who can this be? For He commands even the winds and water, and they obey Him!"

A Demon-Possessed Man Healed
(Matt. 8:28—9:1; Mark 5:1–20)

26 [a]Then they sailed to the country of the *Gadarenes, which is opposite Galilee.

27 And when He stepped out on the land, there met Him a certain man from the city who had demons *for a long time. And he wore no clothes, nor did he live in a house but in the tombs.

28 When he saw Jesus, he [a]cried out, fell down before Him, and with a loud voice said, [b]"What have I to do with [c]You, Jesus, Son of the Most High God? I beg You, do not torment me!"

29 For He had commanded the unclean spirit to come out of the man. For it had often seized him, and he was kept under guard, bound with chains and shackles; and he broke the bonds and was driven by the demon into the wilderness.

30 Jesus asked him, saying, "What is your name?" And he said, "Legion," because many demons had entered him.

31 And they begged Him that He would not command them to go out [a]into the abyss.

32 Now a herd of many [a]swine was feeding there on the mountain. So they begged Him that He would permit them to enter them. And He permitted them.

33 Then the demons went out of the man and entered the swine, and the herd ran violently down the steep place into the lake and drowned.

34 When those who fed *them* saw what had happened, they fled and told *it* in the city and in the country.

35 Then they went out to see what had happened, and came to Jesus, and found the man from whom the demons had departed, [a]sitting at the [b]feet of Jesus, clothed and in his [c]right mind. And they were afraid.

36 They also who had seen *it* told them by what means he who had been demon-possessed was healed.

37 [a]Then the whole multitude of the surrounding region of the *Gadarenes [b]asked Him to [c]depart from them, for they were seized with great [d]fear. And He got into the boat and returned.

38 Now [a]the man from whom the demons had departed begged Him that he might be with Him. But Jesus sent him away, saying,

39 "Return to your own house, and tell what great things God has done for you." And he went his way and proclaimed throughout the whole city what great things Jesus had done for him.

A Girl Restored to Life and a Woman Healed
(Matt. 9:18–26; Mark 5:21–43)

40 So it was, when Jesus returned, that the multitude welcomed Him, for they were all waiting for Him.

41 [a]And behold, there came a man named Jairus, and he was a ruler of the synagogue. And he fell down at Jesus' feet and begged Him to come to his house,

42 for he had an only daughter about twelve years of age, and she [a]was dying. But as He went, the multitudes thronged Him.

43 [a]Now a woman, having a [b]flow of blood for twelve years, who had spent all her livelihood on physicians and could not be healed by any,

44 came from behind and [a]touched the border of His garment. And immediately her flow of blood stopped.

45 And Jesus said, "Who touched Me?" When all denied it, Peter *and those with him said,

---

8:26 NU *Gerasenes*
8:27 NU *and for a long time wore no clothes*
8:37 NU *Gerasenes*
8:45 NU omits *and those with him*

KJV

Master, the multitude throng thee and press *thee*, and sayest thou, Who touched me?

46 And Jesus said, Somebody hath touched me: for I perceive that [a]virtue is gone out of me.

47 And when the woman saw that she was not hid, she came trembling, and falling down before him, she declared unto him before all the people for what cause she had touched him, and how she was healed immediately.

48 And he said unto her, Daughter, be of good comfort: [a]thy faith hath made thee whole; [b]go in peace.

49 [a]While he yet spake, there cometh one from the ruler of the synagogue's *house*, saying to him, Thy daughter is dead; trouble not the Master.

50 But when Jesus heard *it*, he answered him, saying, Fear not: [a]believe only, and she shall be made whole.

51 And when he came into the house, he suffered no man to go in, save Peter, and James, and John, and the father and the mother of the maiden.

52 And all wept, and bewailed her: but he said, [a]Weep not; she is not dead, [b]but sleepeth.

53 And they laughed him to scorn, knowing that she was dead.

54 And he put them all out, and took her by the hand, and called, saying, Maid, [a]arise.

55 And her spirit came again, and she arose straightway: and he commanded to give her meat.

56 And her parents were astonished: but [a]he charged them that they should tell no man what was done.

Sending Out the Twelve
(Matt. 10:5–15)

9 Then [a]he called his twelve disciples together, and [b]gave them power and authority over all devils, and to cure diseases.

2 And [a]he sent them to preach the kingdom of God, and to heal the sick.

3 [a]And he said unto them, Take nothing for *your* journey, neither staves, nor scrip, neither bread, neither money; neither have two coats apiece.

4 [a]And whatsoever house ye enter into, there abide, and thence depart.

5 [a]And whosoever will not receive you, when ye go out of that city, [b]shake off the very dust from your feet for a testimony against them.

6 [a]And they departed, and went through the towns, preaching the gospel, and healing every where.

Herod Seeks to See Jesus
(Matt. 14:1–12; Mark 6:14–29)

7 [a]Now Herod the tetrarch heard of all that was done by him: and he was perplexed, because that it was said of some, that John was risen from the dead;

8 And of some, that Elias had appeared; and of others, that one of the old prophets was risen again.

9 And Herod said, John have I beheaded: but who is this, of whom I hear such things? [a]And he desired to see him.

Feeding the Five Thousand
(Matt. 14:13–21; Mark 6:30–44; John 6:1–15)

10 [a]And the apostles, when they were returned, told him all that they had done. [b]And he took them, and went aside privately into a desert place belonging to the city called Bethsaida.

11 And the people, when they knew *it*, followed him: and he received them, and spake unto them of the kingdom of God, and healed them that had need of healing.

12 [a]And when the day began to wear away, then came the twelve, and said unto him, Send the multitude away, that they may go into the

NKJV

"Master, the multitudes throng and press You, *and You say, 'Who touched Me?' "

46 But Jesus said, "Somebody touched Me, for I perceived [a]power going out from Me."

47 Now when the woman saw that she was not hidden, she came trembling; and falling down before Him, she declared to Him in the presence of all the people the reason she had touched Him and how she was healed immediately.

48 And He said to her, "Daughter, *be of good cheer; [a]your faith has made you well. [b]Go in peace."

49 [a]While He was still speaking, someone came from the ruler of the synagogue's *house*, saying to him, "Your daughter is dead. Do not trouble the *Teacher."

50 But when Jesus heard *it*, He answered him, saying, "Do not be afraid; [a]only believe, and she will be made well."

51 When He came into the house, He permitted no one to go *in except *Peter, James, and John, and the father and mother of the girl.

52 Now all wept and mourned for her; but He said, [a]"Do not weep; she is not dead, [b]but sleeping."

53 And they ridiculed Him, knowing that she was dead.

54 But He *put them all outside, took her by the hand and called, saying, "Little girl, [a]arise."

55 Then her spirit returned, and she arose immediately. And He commanded that she be given *something* to eat.

56 And her parents were astonished, but [a]He charged them to tell no one what had happened.

Sending Out the Twelve
(Matt. 10:5–15)

9 Then [a]He called His twelve disciples together and [b]gave them power and authority over all demons, and to cure diseases.

2 [a]He sent them to preach the kingdom of God and to heal the sick.

3 [a]And He said to them, "Take nothing for the journey, neither staffs nor bag nor bread nor money; and do not have two tunics apiece.

4 [a]"Whatever house you enter, stay there, and from there depart.

5 [a]"And whoever will not receive you, when you go out of that city, [b]shake off the very dust from your feet as a testimony against them."

6 [a]So they departed and went through the towns, preaching the gospel and healing everywhere.

Herod Seeks to See Jesus
(Matt. 14:1–12; Mark 6:14–29)

7 [a]Now Herod the tetrarch heard of all that was done by Him; and he was perplexed, because it was said by some that John had risen from the dead,

8 and by some that Elijah had appeared, and by others that one of the old prophets had risen again.

9 Herod said, "John I have beheaded, but who is this of whom I hear such things?" [a]So he sought to see Him.

Feeding the Five Thousand
(Matt. 14:13–21; Mark 6:30–44; John 6:1–15)

10 [a]And the apostles, when they had returned, told Him all that they had done. [b]Then He took them and went aside privately into a deserted place belonging to the city called Bethsaida.

11 But when the multitudes knew *it*, they followed Him; and He received them and spoke to them about the kingdom of God, and healed those who had need of healing.

12 [a]When the day began to wear away, the twelve came and said to Him, "Send the multitude away, that they may go into the surrounding

---

46 [a]Mark 5:30; Luke 6:19
48 [a]Mark 5:34; Luke 7:50 [b]John 8:11
49 [a]Mark 5:35
50 [a][Mark 11:22–24]
52 [a]Luke 7:13 [b][John 11:11, 13]
54 [a]Luke 7:14; John 11:43
56 [a]Matt. 8:4; 9:30; Mark 5:43

CHAPTER 9

1 [a]Matt. 10:1, 2; Mark 3:13; 6:7 [b]Mark 16:17, 18; [John 14:12]
2 [a]Matt. 10:7, 8; Mark 6:12; Luke 10:1, 9
3 [a]Matt. 10:9–15; Mark 6:8–11; Luke 10:4–12; 22:35
4 [a]Matt. 10:11; Mark 6:10
5 [a]Matt. 10:14 [b]Luke 10:11; Acts 13:51
6 [a]Mark 6:12; Luke 8:1
7 [a]Matt. 14:1, 2; Mark 6:14
9 [a]Luke 23:8
10 [a]Mark 6:30 [b]Matt. 14:13
12 [a]Matt. 14:15; Mark 6:35; John 6:1, 5

---

*

8:45 NU omits the rest of v. 45.
8:48 NU omits *be of good cheer*
8:49 NU adds *anymore*
8:51 NU adds *with Him* • NU, M *Peter, John, and James*
8:54 NU omits *put them all outside*

KJV

towns and country round about, and lodge, and get victuals: for we are here in a desert place.

13 But he said unto them, Give ye them to eat. And they said, We have no more but five loaves and two fishes; except we should go and buy meat for all this people.

14 For they were about five thousand men. And he said to his disciples, Make them sit down by fifties in a company.

15 And they did so, and made them all sit down.

16 Then he took the five loaves and the two fishes, and looking up to heaven, he [a]blessed them, and brake, and gave to the disciples to set before the multitude.

17 And they did eat, and were all filled: and there was taken up of fragments that remained to them twelve baskets.

Peter Confesses Jesus as the Christ
(Matt. 16:13–20; Mark 8:27–30)

18 [a]And it came to pass, as he was alone praying, his disciples were with him: and he asked them, saying, Whom say the people that I am?

19 They answering said, [a]John the Baptist; but some *say*, Elias; and others *say*, that one of the old prophets is risen again.

20 He said unto them, But whom say ye that I am? [a]Peter answering said, The Christ of God.

Jesus Predicts His Death and Resurrection
(Matt. 16:20–23; Mark 8:30–33)

21 [a]And he straitly charged them, and commanded *them* to tell no man that thing;

22 Saying, [a]The Son of man must suffer many things, and be rejected of the elders and chief priests and scribes, and be slain, and be raised the third day.

Take Up the Cross and Follow Him
(Matt. 16:24–27; Mark 8:34–38)

23 [a]And he said to *them* all, If any *man* will come after me, let him deny himself, and take up his cross daily, and follow me.

24 [a]For whosoever will save his life shall lose it: but whosoever will lose his life for my sake, the same shall save it.

25 [a]For what is a man advantaged, if he gain the whole world, and lose himself, or be cast away?

26 [a]For whosoever shall be ashamed of me and of my words, of him shall the Son of man be [b]ashamed, when he shall come in his own glory, and *in his* Father's, and of the holy angels.

Jesus Transfigured on the Mount
(Matt. 16:28—17:9; Mark 9:2–10; 2 Pet. 1:16–18)

27 [a]But I tell you of a truth, there be some standing here, which shall not taste of death, till they see the kingdom of God.

28 [a]And it came to pass about an eight days after these sayings, he took Peter and John and James, and went up into a mountain to pray.

29 And as he prayed, the fashion of his countenance was altered, and his raiment *was* white *and* glistering.

30 And, behold, there talked with him two men, which were [a]Moses and [b]Elias:

31 Who appeared in glory, and spake of his decease which he should accomplish at Jerusalem.

32 But Peter and they that were with him [a]were heavy with sleep: and when they were awake, they saw his glory, and the two men that stood with him.

33 And it came to pass, as they departed from him, Peter said unto Jesus, Master, it is good for us to be here: and let us make three tabernacles; one for thee, and one for Moses, and one for Elias: not knowing what he said.

34 While he thus spake, there came a cloud,

16 [a]Luke 22:19; 24:30
18 [a]Matt. 16:13–16; Mark 8:27–29
19 [a]Matt. 14:2
20 [a]Matt. 16:16; John 6:68, 69
21 [a]Matt. 8:4; 16:20; Mark 8:30
22 [a]Matt. 16:21; 17:22; Luke 18:31–33; 23:46; 24:46
23 [a]Matt. 10:38; 16:24; Mark 8:34; Luke 14:27
24 [a]Matt. 10:39; Luke 17:33; [John 12:25]
25 [a]Matt. 16:26; Mark 8:36; [Luke 16:19–31]; Acts 1:18, 25
26 [a][Rom. 1:16] [b]Matt. 10:33; Mark 8:38; Luke 12:9; 2 Tim. 2:12
27 [a]Matt. 16:28; Mark 9:1; Acts 7:55, 56; Rev. 20:4
28 [a]Matt. 17:1–8; Mark 9:2–8
30 [a]Heb. 11:23–29 [b]2 Kin. 2:1–11
32 [a]Dan. 8:18; 10:9; Matt. 26:40, 43; Mark 14:40

*

9:23 M omits *daily*

NKJV

towns and country, and lodge and get provisions; for we are in a deserted place here."

13 But He said to them, "You give them something to eat." And they said, "We have no more than five loaves and two fish, unless we go and buy food for all these people."

14 For there were about five thousand men. Then He said to His disciples, "Make them sit down in groups of fifty."

15 And they did so, and made them all sit down.

16 Then He took the five loaves and the two fish, and looking up to heaven, He [a]blessed and broke *them*, and gave *them* to the disciples to set before the multitude.

17 So they all ate and were filled, and twelve baskets of the leftover fragments were taken up by them.

Peter Confesses Jesus as the Christ
(Matt. 16:13–20; Mark 8:27–30)

18 [a]And it happened, as He was alone praying, *that* His disciples joined Him, and He asked them, saying, "Who do the crowds say that I am?"

19 So they answered and said, [a]"John the Baptist, but some *say* Elijah; and others *say* that one of the old prophets has risen again."

20 He said to them, "But who do you say that I am?" [a]Peter answered and said, "The Christ of God."

Jesus Predicts His Death and Resurrection
(Matt. 16:20–23; Mark 8:30–33)

21 [a]And He strictly warned and commanded them to tell this to no one,

22 saying, [a]"The Son of Man must suffer many things, and be rejected by the elders and chief priests and scribes, and be killed, and be raised the third day."

Take Up the Cross and Follow Him
(Matt. 16:24–27; Mark 8:34–38)

23 [a]Then He said to *them* all, "If anyone desires to come after Me, let him deny himself, and take up his cross *daily, and follow Me.

24 [a]"For whoever desires to save his life will lose it, but whoever loses his life for My sake will save it.

25 [a]"For what profit is it to a man if he gains the whole world, and is himself destroyed or lost?

26 [a]"For whoever is ashamed of Me and My words, of him the Son of Man will be [b]ashamed when He comes in His *own* glory, and *in His* Father's, and of the holy angels.

Jesus Transfigured on the Mount
(Matt. 16:28—17:9; Mark 9:2–10; 2 Pet. 1:16–18)

27 [a]"But I tell you truly, there are some standing here who shall not taste death till they see the kingdom of God."

28 [a]Now it came to pass, about eight days after these sayings, that He took Peter, John, and James and went up on the mountain to pray.

29 As He prayed, the appearance of His face was altered, and His robe *became* white *and* glistening.

30 And behold, two men talked with Him, who were [a]Moses and [b]Elijah,

31 who appeared in glory and spoke of His decease which He was about to accomplish at Jerusalem.

32 But Peter and those with him [a]were heavy with sleep; and when they were fully awake, they saw His glory and the two men who stood with Him.

33 Then it happened, as they were parting from Him, *that* Peter said to Jesus, "Master, it is good for us to be here; and let us make three tabernacles: one for You, one for Moses, and one for Elijah"—not knowing what he said.

34 While he was saying this, a cloud came

KJV

and overshadowed them: and they feared as they entered into the [a]cloud.

35 And there came a voice out of the cloud, saying, [a]This is my beloved Son: [b]hear him.

36 And when the voice was past, Jesus was found alone. [a]And they kept *it* close, and told no man in those days any of those things which they had seen.

A Boy Is Healed
(*Matt. 17:14–21; Mark 9:14–29*)

37 [a]And it came to pass, that on the next day, when they were come down from the hill, much people met him.

38 And, behold, a man of the company cried out, saying, Master, I beseech thee, look upon my son: for he is mine only child.

39 And, lo, a spirit taketh him, and he suddenly crieth out; and it teareth him that he foameth again, and bruising him hardly departeth from him.

40 And I besought thy disciples to cast him out; and they could not.

41 And Jesus answering said, O faithless and perverse generation, how long shall I be with you, and suffer you? Bring thy son hither.

42 And as he was yet a coming, the devil threw him down, and tare *him*. And Jesus rebuked the unclean spirit, and healed the child, and delivered him again to his father.

Jesus Again Predicts His Death
(*Matt. 17:22, 23; Mark 9:30–32*)

43 And they were all amazed at the mighty power of God. But while they wondered every one at all things which Jesus did, he said unto his disciples,

44 [a]Let these sayings sink down into your ears: for the Son of man shall be delivered into the hands of men.

45 [a]But they understood not this saying, and it was hid from them, that they perceived it not: and they feared to ask him of that saying.

Who Is the Greatest?
(*Matt: 18:1–5; Mark 9:33–37*)

46 [a]Then there arose a reasoning among them, which of them should be greatest.

47 And Jesus, [a]perceiving the thought of their heart, took a [b]child, and set him by him,

48 And said unto them, [a]Whosoever shall receive this child in my name receiveth me: and [b]whosoever shall receive me [c]receiveth him that sent me: [d]for he that is least among you all, the same shall be great.

Jesus Forbids Sectarianism
(*Mark 9:38–41*)

49 [a]And John answered and said, Master, we saw one casting out devils in thy name; and we forbad him, because he followeth not with us.

50 And Jesus said unto him, Forbid *him* not: for [a]he that is not against us is for us.

A Samaritan Village Rejects the Savior

51 And it came to pass, when the time was come that [a]he should be received up, he stedfastly set his face to go to Jerusalem,

52 And sent messengers before his face: and they went, and entered into a village of the Samaritans, to make ready for him.

53 And [a]they did not receive him, because his face was as though he would go to Jerusalem.

54 And when his disciples [a]James and John saw *this*, they said, Lord, wilt thou that we command fire to come down from heaven, and consume them, even as [b]Elias did?

55 But he turned, and rebuked them, and said, Ye know not what manner of [a]spirit ye are of.

56 For [a]the Son of man is not come to destroy

NKJV

and overshadowed them; and they were fearful as they entered the [a]cloud.

35 And a voice came out of the cloud, saying, [a]"This is *My beloved Son. [b]Hear Him!"

36 When the voice had ceased, Jesus was found alone. [a]But they kept quiet, and told no one in those days any of the things they had seen.

A Boy Is Healed
(*Matt. 17:14–21; Mark 9:14–29*)

37 [a]Now it happened on the next day, when they had come down from the mountain, that a great multitude met Him.

38 Suddenly a man from the multitude cried out, saying, "Teacher, I implore You, look on my son, for he is my only child.

39 "And behold, a spirit seizes him, and he suddenly cries out; it convulses him so that he foams *at the mouth;* and it departs from him with great difficulty, bruising him.

40 "So I implored Your disciples to cast it out, but they could not."

41 Then Jesus answered and said, "O faithless and perverse generation, how long shall I be with you and bear with you? Bring your son here."

42 And as he was still coming, the demon threw him down and convulsed *him*. Then Jesus rebuked the unclean spirit, healed the child, and gave him back to his father.

Jesus Again Predicts His Death
(*Matt. 17:22, 23; Mark 9:30–32*)

43 And they were all amazed at the majesty of God. But while everyone marveled at all the things which Jesus did, He said to His disciples,

44 [a]"Let these words sink down into your ears, for the Son of Man is about to be betrayed into the hands of men."

45 [a]But they did not understand this saying, and it was hidden from them so that they did not perceive it; and they were afraid to ask Him about this saying.

Who Is the Greatest?
(*Matt. 18:1–5; Mark 9:33–37*)

46 [a]Then a dispute arose among them as to which of them would be greatest.

47 And Jesus, [a]perceiving the thought of their heart, took a [b]little child and set him by Him,

48 and said to them, [a]"Whoever receives this little child in My name receives Me; and [b]whoever receives Me [c]receives Him who sent Me. [d]For he who is least among you all will be great."

Jesus Forbids Sectarianism
(*Mark 9:38–41*)

49 [a]Now John answered and said, "Master, we saw someone casting out demons in Your name, and we forbade him because he does not follow with us."

50 But Jesus said to him, "Do not forbid *him*, for [a]he who is not against *us is on *our side."

A Samaritan Village Rejects the Savior

51 Now it came to pass, when the time had come for [a]Him to be received up, that He steadfastly set His face to go to Jerusalem,

52 and sent messengers before His face. And as they went, they entered a village of the Samaritans, to prepare for Him.

53 But [a]they did not receive Him, because His face was *set* for the journey to Jerusalem.

54 And when His disciples [a]James and John saw *this*, they said, "Lord, do You want us to command fire to come down from heaven and consume them, *just as [b]Elijah did?"

55 But He turned and rebuked them, *and said, "You do not know what manner of [a]spirit you are of.

56 *"For [a]the Son of Man did not come to

---

34 [a]Ex. 13:21; Acts 1:9
35 [a]Ps. 2:7; [Is. 42:1; Matt. 3:17; 12:18]; Mark 1:11; Luke 3:22 [b]Acts 3:22
36 [a]Matt. 17:9; Mark 9:9
37 [a]Matt. 17:14–18; Mark 9:14–27
44 [a]Matt. 17:22; Mark 10:33; 14:53; Luke 22:54; John 18:12
45 [a]Mark 9:32; Luke 2:50; 18:34
46 [a]Matt. 18:1–5; Mark 9:33–37; Luke 22:24
47 [a]Matt. 9:4; John 2:24, 25 [b]Luke 18:17
48 [a]Matt. 18:5 [b]Matt. 10:40; Mark 9:37; John 12:44 [c]John 13:20 [d][Matt. 23:11, 12]; 1 Cor. 15:9; Eph. 3:8
49 [a]Mark 9:38–40
50 [a]Matt. 12:30; Luke 11:23
51 [a]Is. 50:7; Mark 16:19; Acts 1:2
53 [a]John 4:4, 9
54 [a]Mark 3:17 [b]2 Kin. 1:10, 12
55 [a][Rom. 8:15; 2 Tim. 1:7]
56 [a]Luke 19:10; John 3:17; 12:47

*

9:35 NU *My Son, the Chosen One*
9:50 NU *you* • NU *your*
9:54 NU omits *just as Elijah did*
9:55 NU omits the rest of v. 55.
9:56 NU omits *For the Son of Man did not come to destroy men's lives but to save them.*

KJV

men's lives, but to save *them*. And they went to
another village.

The Cost of Discipleship
(Matt: 8:18–22)

57 [a]And it came to pass, that, as they went
in the way, a certain *man* said unto him, Lord, I
will follow thee whithersoever thou goest.
58 And Jesus said unto him, Foxes have
holes, and birds of the air *have* nests; but the Son
of man [a]hath not where to lay *his* head.
59 [a]And he said unto another, Follow me. But
he said, Lord, suffer me first to go and bury my
father.
60 Jesus said unto him, Let the dead bury
their dead: but go thou and preach the kingdom
of God.
61 And another also said, Lord, [a]I will follow
thee; but let me first go bid them farewell, which
are at home at my house.
62 And Jesus said unto him, No man, having
put his hand to the plough, and looking back, is
[a]fit for the kingdom of God.

The Seventy Send Out

10 After these things the Lord appointed other
seventy also, and [a]sent them two and two
before his face into every city and place, whither
he himself would come.
2 Therefore said he unto them, [a]The harvest
truly *is* great, but the labourers *are* few: [b]pray
ye therefore the Lord of the harvest, that he would
send forth labourers into his harvest.
3 Go your ways: [a]behold, I send you forth
as lambs among wolves.
4 [a]Carry neither purse, nor scrip, nor shoes:
and [b]salute no man by the way.
5 [a]And into whatsoever house ye enter, first
say, Peace *be* to this house.
6 And if the son of peace be there, your
peace shall rest upon it: if not, it shall turn to
you again.
7 [a]And in the same house remain, [b]eating
and drinking such things as they give: for [c]the
labourer is worthy of his hire. Go not from house
to house.
8 And into whatsoever city ye enter, and
they receive you, eat such things as are set before
you:
9 [a]And heal the sick that are therein, and
say unto them, [b]The kingdom of God is come nigh
unto you.
10 But into whatsoever city ye enter, and
they receive you not, go your ways out into the
streets of the same, and say,
11 [a]Even the very dust of your city, which
cleaveth on us, we do wipe off against you: notwithstanding be ye sure of this, that the kingdom
of God is come nigh unto you.
12 But I say unto you, that [a]it shall be more
tolerable in that day for Sodom, than for that
city.

Woe to the Impenitent Cities
(Matt. 11:20–24)

13 [a]Woe unto thee, Chorazin! woe unto thee,
Bethsaida! [b]for if the mighty works had been done
in Tyre and Sidon, which have been done in you,
they had a great while ago repented, sitting in
sackcloth and ashes.
14 But it shall be more tolerable for Tyre and
Sidon at the judgment, than for you.
15 [a]And thou, Capernaum, which art [b]ex-
alted to heaven, [c]shalt be thrust down to hell.
16 [a]He that heareth you heareth me; and [b]he
that despiseth you despiseth me; [c]and he that despiseth me despiseth him that sent me.

The Seventy Return with Joy

17 And [a]the seventy returned again with joy,
saying, Lord, even the devils are subject unto us
through thy name.

57 [a]Matt. 8:19–22
58 [a]Luke 2:7; 8:23
59 [a]Matt. 8:21, 22
61 [a]1 Kin. 19:20
62 [a]2 Tim. 4:10

CHAPTER 10

1 [a]Matt. 10:1; Mark 6:7
2 [a]Matt. 9:37, 38; John 4:35 [b]2 Thess. 3:1; [1 Cor. 3:9]
3 [a]Matt. 10:16
4 [a]Matt. 10:9–14; Mark 6:8–11; Luke 9:3–5 [b]2 Kin. 4:29
5 [a]1 Sam. 25:6; Matt. 10:12
7 [a]Matt. 10:11 [b]1 Cor. 10:27 [c][Matt. 10:10]; 1 Cor. 9:4–8; 1 Tim. 5:18
9 [a]Mark 3:15 [b]Matt. 3:2; 10:7; Luke 10:11
11 [a]Matt. 10:14; Mark 6:11; Luke 9:5; Acts 13:51
12 [a]Gen. 19:24–28; Lam. 4:6; Matt. 10:15; 11:24; Mark 6:11
13 [a]Matt. 11:21–23 [b]Ezek. 3:6
15 [a]Matt. 11:23 [b]Gen. 11:4; Deut. 1:28; Is. 14:13–15; Jer. 51:53 [c]Ezek. 26:20
16 [a]Matt. 10:40; Mark 9:37; John 13:20; Gal. 4:14 [b][John 12:48]; 1 Thess. 4:8 [c]John 5:23
17 [a]Luke 10:1

*———

10:1 NU *seventy-two*
10:11 NU *our feet*
10:12 NU, M omit *But*
10:15 NU *will you be exalted to heaven? You will be thrust down to Hades!*
10:17 NU *seventy-two*

NKJV

destroy men's lives but to save *them*." And they
went to another village.

The Cost of Discipleship
(Matt. 8:18–22)

57 [a]Now it happened as they journeyed on
the road, *that* someone said to Him, "Lord, I will
follow You wherever You go."
58 And Jesus said to him, "Foxes have holes
and birds of the air *have* nests, but the Son of
Man [a]has nowhere to lay *His* head."
59 [a]Then He said to another, "Follow Me."
But he said, "Lord, let me first go and bury my
father."
60 Jesus said to him, "Let the dead bury their
own dead, but you go and preach the kingdom
of God."
61 And another also said, "Lord, [a]I will follow You, but let me first go *and* bid them farewell
who are at my house."
62 But Jesus said to him, "No one, having
put his hand to the plow, and looking back, is
[a]fit for the kingdom of God."

The Seventy Sent Out

10 After these things the Lord appointed *seventy others also, and [a]sent them two by two
before His face into every city and place where
He Himself was about to go.
2 Then He said to them, [a]"The harvest truly
is great, but the laborers *are* few; therefore [b]pray
the Lord of the harvest to send out laborers into
His harvest.
3 "Go your way; [a]behold, I send you out as
lambs among wolves.
4 [a]"Carry neither money bag, knapsack,
nor sandals; and [b]greet no one along the road.
5 [a]"But whatever house you enter, first say,
'Peace to this house.'
6 "And if a son of peace is there, your peace
will rest on it; if not, it will return to you.
7 [a]"And remain in the same house, [b]eating
and drinking such things as they give, for [c]the
laborer is worthy of his wages. Do not go from
house to house.
8 "Whatever city you enter, and they receive you, eat such things as are set before you.
9 [a]"And heal the sick there, and say to
them, [b]'The kingdom of God has come near to
you.'
10 "But whatever city you enter, and they do
not receive you, go out into its streets and say,
11 [a]'The very dust of your city which clings
to *us we wipe off against you. Nevertheless know
this, that the kingdom of God has come near you.'
12 *"But I say to you that [a]it will be more
tolerable in that Day for Sodom than for that city.

Woe to the Impenitent Cities
(Matt. 11:20–24)

13 [a]"Woe to you, Chorazin! Woe to you,
Bethsaida! [b]For if the mighty works which were
done in you had been done in Tyre and Sidon,
they would have repented long ago, sitting in
sackcloth and ashes.
14 "But it will be more tolerable for Tyre and
Sidon at the judgment than for you.
15 [a]"And you, Capernaum, *who are [b]ex-
alted to heaven, [c]will be brought down to Hades.
16 [a]"He who hears you hears Me, [b]he who
rejects you rejects Me, and [c]he who rejects Me
rejects Him who sent Me."

The Seventy Return with Joy

17 Then [a]the *seventy returned with joy, saying, "Lord, even the demons are subject to us in
Your name."

KJV

18 And he said unto them, [a]I beheld Satan as lightning fall from heaven.

19 Behold, [a]I give unto you power to tread on serpents and scorpions, and over all the power of the enemy: and nothing shall by any means hurt you.

20 Notwithstanding in this rejoice not, that the spirits are subject unto you; but rather rejoice, because [a]your names are written in heaven.

Jesus Rejoices in the Spirit
(Matt. 11:25–27)

21 [a]In that hour Jesus rejoiced in spirit, and said, I thank thee, O Father, Lord of heaven and earth, that thou hast hid these things from the wise and prudent, and hast revealed them unto babes: even so, Father; for so it seemed good in thy sight.

22 [a]All things are delivered to me of my Father: and [b]no man knoweth who the Son is, but the Father; and who the Father is, but the Son, and *he* to whom the Son will reveal *him.*

23 And he turned him unto *his* disciples, and said privately, [a]Blessed *are* the eyes which see the things that ye see:

24 For I tell you, [a]that many prophets and kings have desired to see those things which ye see, and have not seen *them;* and to hear those things which ye hear, and have not heard *them.*

The Parable of the Good Samaritan
(Matt. 22:34–40; Mark 12:28–34)

25 And, behold, a certain lawyer stood up, and tempted him, saying, [a]Master, what shall I do to inherit eternal life?

26 He said unto him, What is written in the law? how readest thou?

27 And he answering said, [a]THOU SHALT LOVE THE LORD THY GOD WITH ALL THY HEART, AND WITH ALL THY SOUL, AND WITH ALL THY STRENGTH, AND WITH ALL THY MIND; and [b]THY NEIGHBOUR AS THYSELF.

28 And he said unto him, Thou hast answered right: this do, and [a]thou shalt live.

29 But he, willing to [a]justify himself, said unto Jesus, And who is my neighbour?

30 And Jesus answering said, A certain *man* went down from Jerusalem to Jericho, and fell among thieves, which stripped him of his raiment, and wounded *him,* and departed, leaving *him* half dead.

31 And by chance there came down a certain priest that way: and when he saw him, [a]he passed by on the other side.

32 And likewise a Levite, when he was at the place, came and looked *on him,* and passed by on the other side.

33 But a certain [a]Samaritan, as he journeyed, came where he was: and when he saw him, he had [b]compassion *on him,*

34 And went to *him,* and bound up his wounds, pouring in oil and wine, and set him on his own beast, and brought him to an inn, and took care of him.

35 And on the morrow when he departed, he took out two [a]pence, and gave *them* to the host, and said unto him, Take care of him; and whatsoever thou spendest more, when I come again, I will repay thee.

36 Which now of these three, thinkest thou, was neighbour unto him that fell among the thieves?

37 And he said, He that shewed mercy on him. Then said Jesus unto him, [a]Go, and do thou likewise.

Mary and Martha Worship and Serve

38 Now it came to pass, as they went, that he entered into a certain village: and a certain woman named [a]Martha received him into her house.

39 And she had a sister called Mary, [a]which also [b]sat at Jesus' feet, and heard his word.

18 [a]John 12:31; Rev. 9:1; 12:8, 9 **19** [a]Ps. 91:13; Mark 16:18; Acts 28:5 **20** [a][Ex. 32:32, 33]; Ps. 69:28; Is. 4:3; Dan. 12:1; Phil. 4:3; Heb. 12:23; Rev. 13:8 **21** [a]Matt. 11:25–27 **22** [a]Matt. 28:18; John 3:35; 5:27; 17:2 [b][John 1:18; 6:44, 46] **23** [a]Matt. 13:16, 17 **24** [a]1 Pet. 1:10, 11 **25** [a]Matt. 19:16–19; 22:35 **27** [a]Deut. 6:5 [b]Lev. 19:18; Matt. 19:19 **28** [a]Lev. 18:5; Neh. 9:29; Ezek. 20:11, 13, 21; Matt. 19:17; Rom. 10:5 **29** [a]Luke 16:15 **31** [a]Ps. 38:11 **33** [a]John 4:9 [b]Luke 15:20 **35** [a]Matt. 20:2 **37** [a]Prov. 14:21; [Matt. 9:13; 12:7] **38** [a]John 11:1; 12:2, 3 **39** [a][1 Cor. 7:32–40] [b]Luke 8:35; Acts 22:3

NKJV

18 And He said to them, [a]"I saw Satan fall like lightning from heaven.

19 "Behold, [a]I give you the authority to trample on serpents and scorpions, and over all the power of the enemy, and nothing shall by any means hurt you.

20 "Nevertheless do not rejoice in this, that the spirits are subject to you, but *rather rejoice because [a]your names are written in heaven."

Jesus Rejoices in the Spirit
(Matt. 11:25–27)

21 [a]In that hour Jesus rejoiced in the Spirit and said, "I thank You, Father, Lord of heaven and earth, that You have hidden these things from *the* wise and prudent and revealed them to babes. Even so, Father, for so it seemed good in Your sight.

22 [a]"All* things have been delivered to Me by My Father, and [b]no one knows who the Son is except the Father, and who the Father is except the Son, and *the one* to whom the Son wills to reveal *Him.*"

23 Then He turned to *His* disciples and said privately, [a]"Blessed *are* the eyes which see the things you see;

24 "for I tell you [a]that many prophets and kings have desired to see what you see, and have not seen *it,* and to hear what you hear, and have not heard *it.*"

The Parable of the Good Samaritan
(Matt. 22:34–40; Mark 12:28–34)

25 And behold, a certain lawyer stood up and tested Him, saying, [a]"Teacher, what shall I do to inherit eternal life?"

26 He said to him, "What is written in the law? What is your reading *of it?*"

27 So he answered and said, [a]"*'You shall love the LORD your God with all your heart, with all your soul, with all your strength, and with all your mind,'* and [b]*'your neighbor as yourself.'* "

28 And He said to him, "You have answered rightly; do this and [a]you will live."

29 But he, wanting to [a]justify himself, said to Jesus, "And who is my neighbor?"

30 Then Jesus answered and said: "A certain *man* went down from Jerusalem to Jericho, and fell among thieves, who stripped him of his clothing, wounded *him,* and departed, leaving *him* half dead.

31 "Now by chance a certain priest came down that road. And when he saw him, [a]he passed by on the other side.

32 "Likewise a Levite, when he arrived at the place, came and looked, and passed by on the other side.

33 "But a certain [a]Samaritan, as he journeyed, came where he was. And when he saw him, he had [b]compassion.

34 "So he went to *him* and bandaged his wounds, pouring on oil and wine; and he set him on his own animal, brought him to an inn, and took care of him.

35 "On the next day, *when he departed, he took out two [a]denarii, gave *them* to the innkeeper, and said to him, 'Take care of him; and whatever more you spend, when I come again, I will repay you.'

36 "So which of these three do you think was neighbor to him who fell among the thieves?"

37 And he said, "He who showed mercy on him." Then Jesus said to him, [a]"Go and do likewise."

Mary and Martha Worship and Serve

38 Now it happened as they went that He entered a certain village; and a certain woman named [a]Martha welcomed Him into her house.

39 And she had a sister called Mary, [a]who also [b]sat at *Jesus' feet and heard His word.

*______

10:20 NU, M omit *rather*
10:22 M *And turning to the disciples He said, "All . . .*
10:35 NU omits *when he departed*
10:39 NU *the Lord's*

KJV

40 But Martha was cumbered about much
serving, and came to him, and said, LORD, dost
thou not care that my sister hath left me to serve
alone? bid her therefore that she help me.
41 And Jesus answered and said unto her,
Martha, Martha, thou art careful and troubled
about many things:
42 But [a]one thing is needful: and Mary hath
chosen that good part, which shall not be taken
away from her.

The Model Prayer
(Matt. 6:9–15)

11 And it came to pass, that, as he was praying
in a certain place, when he ceased, one of
his disciples said unto him, Lord, teach us to pray,
as John also taught his disciples.
2 And he said unto them, When ye pray,
say, [a]Our Father which art in heaven, Hallowed
be thy name. Thy kingdom come. Thy will be
done, as in heaven, so in earth.
3 Give us day by day our daily bread.
4 And [a]forgive us our sins; for we also forgive every one that is indebted to us. And lead
us not into temptation; but deliver us from evil.

A Friend Comes at Midnight

5 And he said unto them, Which of you shall
have a friend, and shall go unto him at midnight,
and say unto him, Friend, lend me three loaves;
6 For a friend of mine in his journey is come
to me, and I have nothing to set before him?
7 And he from within shall answer and say,
Trouble me not: the door is now shut, and my
children are with me in bed; I cannot rise and
give thee.
8 I say unto you, [a]Though he will not rise
and give him, because he is his friend, yet because
of his importunity he will rise and give him as
many as he needeth.

Keep Asking, Seeking, Knocking
(Matt. 7:7–11)

9 [a]And I say unto you, Ask, and it shall be
given you; [b]seek, and ye shall find; knock, and it
shall be opened unto you.
10 For every one that asketh receiveth; and
he that seeketh findeth; and to him that knocketh
it shall be opened.
11 [a]If a son shall ask bread of any of you
that is a father, will he give him a stone? or if *he
ask* a fish, will he for a fish give him a serpent?
12 Or if he shall ask an egg, will he offer him
a scorpion?
13 If ye then, being evil, know how to give
[a]good gifts unto your children: how much more
shall *your* heavenly Father give the Holy Spirit
to them that ask him?

A House Divided Cannot Stand
(Matt. 12:22–30; Mark 3:22–27)

14 [a]And he was casting out a devil, and it
was dumb. And it came to pass, when the devil
was gone out, the dumb spake; and the people
wondered.
15 But some of them said, [a]He casteth out
devils through Beelzebub the chief of the devils.
16 And others, tempting *him*, [a]sought of him
a sign from heaven.
17 [a]But [b]he, knowing their thoughts, said
unto them, Every kingdom divided against itself
is brought to desolation; and a house *divided*
against a house falleth.
18 If Satan also be divided against himself,
how shall his kingdom stand? because ye say that
I cast out devils through Beelzebub.

42 [a][Ps. 27:4; John 6:27]

CHAPTER 11

2 [a]Matt. 6:9–13
4 [a][Eph. 4:32]
8 [a][Luke 18:1–5]
9 [a]Ps. 50:14, 15; Jer. 33:3; [Matt. 7:7; 21:22; Mark 11:24; John 15:7; James 1:5, 6; 1 John 3:22; 5:14, 15] [b]Is. 55:6
11 [a]Matt. 7:9
13 [a]James 1:17
14 [a]Matt. 9:32–34; 12:22, 24
15 [a]Matt. 9:34; 12:24
16 [a]Matt. 12:38; 16:1; Mark 8:11
17 [a]Matt. 12:25–29; Mark 3:23–27 [b]Matt. 9:4; John 2:25

*

10:41 NU *the Lord*
11:2 NU omits *Our* • NU omits *in heaven* • NU omits the rest of v. 2.
11:4 NU omits *But deliver us from the evil one*
11:11 NU omits *bread from any father among you, will he give him a stone? Or if he asks for*
11:15 NU, M *Beelzebul*

NKJV

40 But Martha was distracted with much
serving, and she approached Him and said, "Lord,
do You not care that my sister has left me to serve
alone? Therefore tell her to help me."
41 And *Jesus answered and said to her,
"Martha, Martha, you are worried and troubled
about many things.
42 "But [a]one thing is needed, and Mary has
chosen that good part, which will not be taken
away from her."

The Model Prayer
(Matt. 6:9–15)

11 Now it came to pass, as He was praying
in a certain place, when He ceased, *that*
one of His disciples said to Him, "Lord, teach us
to pray, as John also taught his disciples."
2 So He said to them, "When you pray, say:

[a]Our* Father *in heaven,
Hallowed be Your name.
Your kingdom come.
*Your will be done
On earth as *it is* in heaven.
3 Give us day by day our daily bread.
4 And [a]forgive us our sins,
For we also forgive everyone who is
indebted to us.
And do not lead us into temptation,
*But deliver us from the evil one."

A Friend Comes at Midnight

5 And He said to them, "Which of you shall
have a friend, and go to him at midnight and say
to him, 'Friend, lend me three loaves;
6 'for a friend of mine has come to me on
his journey, and I have nothing to set before him';
7 "and he will answer from within and say,
'Do not trouble me; the door is now shut, and my
children are with me in bed; I cannot rise and
give to you'?
8 "I say to you, [a]though he will not rise and
give to him because he is his friend, yet because
of his persistence he will rise and give him as
many as he needs.

Keep Asking, Seeking, Knocking
(Matt. 7:7–11)

9 [a]"So I say to you, ask, and it will be given
to you; [b]seek, and you will find; knock, and it
will be opened to you.
10 "For everyone who asks receives, and he
who seeks finds, and to him who knocks it will
be opened.
11 [a]"If a son asks for *bread from any father
among you, will he give him a stone? Or if *he
asks* for a fish, will he give him a serpent instead
of a fish?
12 "Or if he asks for an egg, will he offer
him a scorpion?
13 "If you then, being evil, know how to give
[a]good gifts to your children, how much more will
your heavenly Father give the Holy Spirit to those
who ask Him!"

A House Divided Cannot Stand
(Matt. 12:22–30; Mark 3:22–27)

14 [a]And He was casting out a demon, and it
was mute. So it was, when the demon had gone
out, that the mute spoke; and the multitudes
marveled.
15 But some of them said, [a]"He casts out demons by *Beelzebub, the ruler of the demons."
16 Others, testing *Him*, [a]sought from Him a
sign from heaven.
17 [a]But [b]He, knowing their thoughts, said to
them: "Every kingdom divided against itself is
brought to desolation, and a house *divided* against
a house falls.
18 "If Satan also is divided against himself,
how will his kingdom stand? Because you say I
cast out demons by Beelzebub.

KJV

19 And if I by Beelzebub cast out devils, by whom do your sons cast *them* out? therefore shall they be your judges.

20 But if I [a]with the finger of God cast out devils, no doubt the kingdom of God is come upon you.

21 [a]When a strong man armed keepeth his palace, his goods are in peace:

22 But [a]when a stronger than he shall come upon him, and overcome him, he taketh from him all his armour wherein he trusted, and divideth his spoils.

23 [a]He that is not with me is against me: and he that gathereth not with me scattereth.

An Unclean Spirit Returns
(*Matt. 12:43–45*)

24 [a]When the unclean spirit is gone out of a man, he walketh through dry places, seeking rest; and finding none, he saith, I will return unto my house whence I came out.

25 And when he cometh, he findeth *it* swept and garnished.

26 Then goeth he, and taketh *to him* seven other spirits more wicked than himself; and they enter in, and dwell there: and [a]the last *state* of that man is worse than the first.

Keeping the Word

27 And it came to pass, as he spake these things, a certain woman of the company lifted up her voice, and said unto him, [a]Blessed *is* the womb that bare thee, and the paps which thou hast sucked.

28 But he said, Yea [a]rather, blessed *are* they that hear the word of God, and keep it.

Seeking a Sign
(*Matt. 12:38–42*)

29 [a]And when the people were gathered thick together, he began to say, This is an evil generation: they seek a [b]sign; and there shall no sign be given it, but the sign of Jonas the prophet.

30 For as [a]Jonas was a sign unto the Ninevites, so shall also the Son of man be to this generation.

31 [a]The queen of the south shall rise up in the judgment with the men of this generation, and condemn them: for she came from the utmost parts of the earth to hear the wisdom of Solomon; and, behold, a [b]greater than Solomon *is* here.

32 The men of Nineve shall rise up in the judgment with this generation, and shall condemn it: for [a]they repented at the preaching of Jonas; and, behold, a greater than Jonas *is* here.

The Lamp of the Body
(*Matt. 6:22, 23*)

33 [a]No man, when he hath lighted a candle, putteth *it* in a secret place, neither under a [b]bushel, but on a candlestick, that they which come in may see the light.

34 [a]The light of the body is the eye: therefore when thine eye is single, thy whole body also is full of light; but when *thine eye* is evil, thy body also *is* full of darkness.

35 Take heed therefore that the light which is in thee be not darkness.

36 If thy whole body therefore *be* full of light, having no part dark, the whole shall be full of light, as when the bright shining of a candle doth give thee light.

Woe to the Pharisees and Lawyers

37 And as he spake, a certain Pharisee besought him to dine with him: and he went in, and sat down to meat.

38 And [a]when the Pharisee saw *it*, he marvelled that he had not first washed before dinner.

39 [a]And the Lord said unto him, Now do ye Pharisees make clean the outside of the cup and

NKJV

19 "And if I cast out demons by Beelzebub, by whom do your sons cast *them* out? Therefore they will be your judges.

20 "But if I cast out demons [a]with the finger of God, surely the kingdom of God has come upon you.

21 [a]"When a strong man, fully armed, guards his own palace, his goods are in peace.

22 "But [a]when a stronger than he comes upon him and overcomes him, he takes from him all his armor in which he trusted, and divides his spoils.

23 [a]"He who is not with Me is against Me, and he who does not gather with Me scatters.

An Unclean Spirit Returns
(*Matt. 12:43–45*)

24 [a]"When an unclean spirit goes out of a man, he goes through dry places, seeking rest; and finding none, he says, 'I will return to my house from which I came.'

25 "And when he comes, he finds *it* swept and put in order.

26 "Then he goes and takes with *him* seven other spirits more wicked than himself, and they enter and dwell there; and [a]the last *state* of that man is worse than the first."

Keeping the Word

27 And it happened, as He spoke these things, that a certain woman from the crowd raised her voice and said to Him, [a]"Blessed *is* the womb that bore You, and *the* breasts which nursed You!"

28 But He said, [a]"More than that, blessed *are* those who hear the word of God and keep it!"

Seeking a Sign
(*Matt. 12:38–42*)

29 [a]And while the crowds were thickly gathered together, He began to say, "This is an evil generation. It seeks a [b]sign, and no sign will be given to it except the sign of Jonah *the prophet.

30 "For as [a]Jonah became a sign to the Ninevites, so also the Son of Man will be to this generation.

31 [a]"The queen of the South will rise up in the judgment with the men of this generation and condemn them, for she came from the ends of the earth to hear the wisdom of Solomon; and indeed a [b]greater than Solomon *is* here.

32 "The men of Nineveh will rise up in the judgment with this generation and condemn it, for [a]they repented at the preaching of Jonah; and indeed a greater than Jonah *is* here.

The Lamp of the Body
(*Matt. 6:22, 23*)

33 [a]"No one, when he has lit a lamp, puts *it* in a secret place or under a [b]basket, but on a lampstand, that those who come in may see the light.

34 [a]"The lamp of the body is the eye. Therefore, when your eye is good, your whole body also is full of light. But when *your eye* is bad, your body also *is* full of darkness.

35 "Therefore take heed that the light which is in you is not darkness.

36 "If then your whole body *is* full of light, having no part dark, *the* whole *body* will be full of light, as when the bright shining of a lamp gives you light."

Woe to the Pharisees and Lawyers

37 And as He spoke, a certain Pharisee asked Him to dine with him. So He went in and sat down to eat.

38 [a]When the Pharisee saw *it*, he marveled that He had not first washed before dinner.

39 [a]Then the Lord said to him, "Now you Pharisees make the outside of the cup and dish

20 [a]Ex. 8:19
21 [a]Matt. 12:29; Mark 3:27
22 [a][Is. 53:12; Col. 2:15]
23 [a]Matt. 12:30; Mark 9:40
24 [a]Matt. 12:43–45; Mark 1:27; 3:11; 5:13; Acts 5:16; 8:7
26 [a]John 5:14; [Heb. 6:4–6; 10:26; 2 Pet. 2:20]
27 [a]Luke 1:28, 48
28 [a]Ps. 1:1, 2; 112:1; 119:1, 2; Is. 48:17, 18; [Matt. 7:21; Luke 8:21]; James 1:25
29 [a]Matt. 12:38–42 [b]1 Cor. 1:22
30 [a]Jon. 1:17; 2:10; 3:3–10; Luke 24:46; Acts 10:40; 1 Cor. 15:4
31 [a]1 Kin. 10:1–9; 2 Chr. 9:1–8 [b][Is. 9:6; Rom. 9:5]
32 [a]Jon. 3:5
33 [a]Matt. 5:15; Mark 4:21; Luke 8:16 [b]Matt. 5:15
34 [a]Matt. 6:22, 23
38 [a]Matt. 15:2; Mark 7:2, 3
39 [a]Matt. 23:25

*_____

11:29 NU omits *the prophet*

KJV

the platter; but [b]your inward part is full of ravening and wickedness.
40 *Ye* fools, did not [a]he that made that which
is without make that which is within also?
41 [a]But rather give alms of such things as
ye have; and, behold, all things are clean unto
you.
42 [a]But woe unto you, Pharisees! for ye tithe
mint and rue and all manner of herbs, and [b]pass
over judgment and the [c]love of God: these ought
ye to have done, and not to leave the other
undone.
43 [a]Woe unto you, Pharisees! for ye love the
uppermost seats in the synagogues, and greetings
in the markets.
44 [a]Woe unto you, scribes and Pharisees,
hypocrites! [b]for ye are as graves which appear
not, and the men that walk over *them* are not
aware *of them*.
45 Then answered one of the lawyers, and
said unto him, Master, thus saying thou re-
proachest us also.
46 And he said, Woe unto you also, *ye* lawyers! [a]for ye lade men with burdens grievous to
be borne, and ye yourselves touch not the burdens
with one of your fingers.
47 [a]Woe unto you! for ye build the sepulchres
of the prophets, and your fathers killed them.
48 Truly ye bear witness that ye allow the
deeds of your fathers: for they indeed killed them,
and ye build their sepulchres.
49 Therefore also said the wisdom of God,
[a]I will send them prophets and apostles, and *some*
of them they shall slay and persecute:
50 That the blood of all the prophets, which
was shed from the foundation of the world, may
be required of this generation;
51 [a]From the blood of Abel unto [b]the blood
of Zacharias, which perished between the altar
and the temple: verily I say unto you, It shall be
required of this generation.
52 [a]Woe unto you, lawyers! for ye have taken
away the key of knowledge: ye entered not in
yourselves, and them that were entering in ye
hindered.
53 And as he said these things unto them,
the scribes and the Pharisees began to urge *him*
vehemently, and to provoke him to speak of many
things:
54 Laying wait for him, and [a]seeking to catch
something out of his mouth, that they might accuse him.

Beware of Hypocrisy
(*Matt. 10:26, 27*)

12 In [a]the mean time, when there were gathered together an innumerable multitude of
people, insomuch that they trode one upon another, he began to say unto his disciples first of
all, [b]Beware ye of the leaven of the Pharisees,
which is hypocrisy.
2 [a]For there is nothing covered, that shall
not be revealed; neither hid, that shall not be
known.
3 Therefore whatsoever ye have spoken in
darkness shall be heard in the light; and that
which ye have spoken in the ear in closets shall
be proclaimed upon the housetops.

Jesus Teaches the Fear of God
(*Matt. 10:8–31*)

4 [a]And I say unto you [b]my friends, Be not
afraid of them that kill the body, and after that
have no more that they can do.
5 But I will forewarn you whom ye shall
fear: Fear him, which after he hath killed hath
power to cast into hell; yea, I say unto you, [a]Fear
him.
6 Are not five sparrows sold for two far-
things, and [a]not one of them is forgotten before
God?
7 But even the very hairs of your head are

39 [b]Gen. 6:5; Titus 1:15
40 [a]Gen. 1:26, 27
41 [a]Is. 58:7; Dan. 4:27; [Luke 12:33; 16:9]
42 [a]Matt. 23:23 [b][Mic. 6:7, 8] [c]John 5:42
43 [a]Matt. 23:6; Mark 12:38, 39; Luke 14:7; 20:46
44 [a]Matt. 23:27 [b]Ps. 5:9
46 [a]Matt. 23:4
47 [a]Matt. 23:29; Acts 7:52
49 [a]Prov. 1:20; Matt. 23:34
51 [a]Gen. 4:8; 2 Chr. 36:16 [b]2 Chr. 24:20, 21
52 [a]Matt. 23:13
54 [a]Mark 12:13

CHAPTER 12

1 [a]Matt. 16:6; Mark 8:15 [b]Matt. 16:12; Luke 11:39
2 [a]Matt. 10:26; Mark 4:22; Luke 8:17; [1 Cor. 4:5]
4 [a]Is. 51:7, 8, 12, 13; Jer. 1:8; Matt. 10:28 [b][John 15:13–15]
5 [a]Ps. 119:120
6 [a]Matt. 6:26

*———

11:44 NU omits *scribes and Pharisees, hypocrites*
11:53 NU *And when He left there*
11:54 NU omits *and seeking* • NU omits *that they might accuse Him*
12:6 Gr. *assarion*, a coin worth about 1/16 of a denarius

NKJV

clean, but [b]your inward part is full of greed and
wickedness.
40 "Foolish ones! Did not [a]He who made the
outside make the inside also?
41 [a]"But rather give alms of such things as
you have; then indeed all things are clean to you.
42 [a]"But woe to you Pharisees! For you tithe
mint and rue and all manner of herbs, and [b]pass
by justice and the [c]love of God. These you ought
to have done, without leaving the others undone.
43 [a]"Woe to you Pharisees! For you love the
best seats in the synagogues and greetings in the
marketplaces.
44 [a]"Woe to you, *scribes and Pharisees,
hypocrites! [b]For you are like graves which are
not seen, and the men who walk over *them* are
not aware *of them*."
45 Then one of the lawyers answered and
said to Him, "Teacher, by saying these things You
reproach us also."
46 And He said, "Woe to you also, lawyers!
[a]For you load men with burdens hard to bear,
and you yourselves do not touch the burdens with
one of your fingers.
47 [a]"Woe to you! For you build the tombs
of the prophets, and your fathers killed them.
48 "In fact, you bear witness that you approve the deeds of your fathers; for they indeed
killed them, and you build their tombs.
49 "Therefore the wisdom of God also said,
[a]'I will send them prophets and apostles, and
some of them they will kill and persecute,'
50 "that the blood of all the prophets which
was shed from the foundation of the world may
be required of this generation,
51 [a]"from the blood of Abel to [b]the blood of
Zechariah who perished between the altar and
the temple. Yes, I say to you, it shall be required
of this generation.
52 [a]"Woe to you lawyers! For you have taken
away the key of knowledge. You did not enter in
yourselves, and those who were entering in you
hindered."
53 *And as He said these things to them, the
scribes and the Pharisees began to assail *Him* vehemently, and to cross-examine Him about many
things,
54 lying in wait for Him, *and [a]seeking to
catch Him in something He might say, *that they
might accuse Him.

Beware of Hypocrisy
(*Matt. 10:26, 27*)

12 In [a]the meantime, when an innumerable
multitude of people had gathered together,
so that they trampled one another, He began to
say to His disciples first *of all*, [b]"Beware of the
leaven of the Pharisees, which is hypocrisy.
2 [a]"For there is nothing covered that will
not be revealed, nor hidden that will not be
known.
3 "Therefore whatever you have spoken in
the dark will be heard in the light, and what you
have spoken in the ear in inner rooms will be proclaimed on the housetops.

Jesus Teaches the Fear of God
(*Matt. 10:8–31*)

4 [a]"And I say to you, [b]My friends, do not
be afraid of those who kill the body, and after
that have no more that they can do.
5 "But I will show you whom you should
fear: Fear Him who, after He has killed, has power
to cast into hell; yes, I say to you, [a]fear Him!
6 "Are not five sparrows sold for two *copper coins? And [a]not one of them is forgotten before God.
7 "But the very hairs of your head are all

KJV

all numbered. Fear not therefore: ye are of more value than many sparrows.

Confess Christ Before Men
(Matt. 10:32, 33)

8 [a]Also I say unto you, Whosoever shall confess me [b]before men, him shall the Son of man also confess before the angels of God:

9 But he that [a]denieth me before men shall be denied before the angels of God.

10 And [a]whosoever shall speak a word against the Son of man, it shall be forgiven him: but unto him that blasphemeth against the Holy Ghost it shall not be forgiven.

11 [a]And when they bring you unto the synagogues, and *unto* magistrates, and powers, take ye no thought how or what thing ye shall answer, or what ye shall say:

12 For the Holy Ghost shall [a]teach you in the same hour what ye ought to say.

The Parable of the Rich Fool

13 And one of the company said unto him, Master, speak to my brother, that he divide the inheritance with me.

14 And he said unto him, [a]Man, who made me a judge or a divider over you?

15 And he said unto them, [a]Take heed, and beware of covetousness: for a man's life consisteth not in the abundance of the things which he possesseth.

16 And he spake a parable unto them, saying, The ground of a certain rich man brought forth plentifully:

17 And he thought within himself, saying, What shall I do, because I have no room where to bestow my fruits?

18 And he said, This will I do: I will pull down my barns, and build greater; and there will I bestow all my fruits and my goods.

19 And I will say to my soul, [a]Soul, thou hast much goods laid up for many years; take thine ease, [b]eat, drink, *and* be merry.

20 But God said unto him, *Thou* fool, this night [a]thy soul shall be required of thee: [b]then whose shall those things be, which thou hast provided?

21 So *is* he that layeth up treasure for himself, [a]and is not rich toward God.

Do Not Worry
(Matt. 6:19–21, 25–34)

22 And he said unto his disciples, Therefore I say unto you, [a]Take no thought for your life, what ye shall eat; neither for the body, what ye shall put on.

23 The life is more than meat, and the body *is more* than raiment.

24 Consider the ravens: for they neither sow nor reap; which neither have storehouse nor barn; and [a]God feedeth them: how much more are ye better than the fowls?

25 And which of you with taking thought can add to his stature one cubit?

26 If ye then be not able to do that thing which is least, why take ye thought for the rest?

27 Consider the lilies how they grow: they toil not, they spin not; and yet I say unto you, that [a]Solomon in all his glory was not arrayed like one of these.

28 If then God so clothe the grass, which is to day in the field, and to morrow is cast into the oven; how much more *will he clothe* you, O ye of [a]little faith?

29 And seek not ye what ye shall eat, or what ye shall drink, neither be ye of doubtful mind.

30 For all these things do the nations of the world seek after: and your Father [a]knoweth that ye have need of these things.

31 [a]But rather seek ye the kingdom of God; and all these things shall be added unto you.

8 [a]1 Sam. 2:30; Matt. 10:32; [Mark 8:38; Rom. 10:9; 2 Tim. 2:12; 1 John 2:23] [b]Ps. 119:46
9 [a]Matt. 10:33; [Mark 8:38; 2 Tim. 2:12]
10 [a][Matt. 12:31, 32; Mark 3:28; 1 John 5:16]
11 [a]Matt. 6:25; 10:19; Mark 13:11
12 [a][John 14:26]
14 [a][John 18:36]
15 [a][1 Tim. 6:6–10]
19 [a]Eccl. 11:9; 1 Cor. 15:32; James 5:5 [b][Eccl. 2:24; 3:13; 5:18; 8:15]
20 [a]Job 27:8; Ps. 52:7; [James 4:14] [b]Ps. 39:6; Jer. 17:11
21 [a][Matt. 6:20; Luke 12:33; 1 Tim. 6:18, 19; James 2:5; 5:1–5]
22 [a]Matt. 6:25–33
24 [a]Job 38:41; Ps. 147:9
27 [a]1 Kin. 10:4–7; 2 Chr. 9:3–6
28 [a]Matt. 6:30; 8:26; 14:31; 16:8
30 [a]Matt. 6:31, 32
31 [a]Matt. 6:33

*
12:15 NU *all covetousness*
12:31 NU *His kingdom, and these things*

NKJV

numbered. Do not fear therefore; you are of more value than many sparrows.

Confess Christ Before Men
(Matt. 10:32, 33)

8 [a]"Also I say to you, whoever confesses Me [b]before men, him the Son of Man also will confess before the angels of God.

9 "But he who [a]denies Me before men will be denied before the angels of God.

10 "And [a]anyone who speaks a word against the Son of Man, it will be forgiven him; but to him who blasphemes against the Holy Spirit, it will not be forgiven.

11 [a]"Now when they bring you to the synagogues and magistrates and authorities, do not worry about how or what you should answer, or what you should say.

12 "For the Holy Spirit will [a]teach you in that very hour what you ought to say."

The Parable of the Rich Fool

13 Then one from the crowd said to Him, "Teacher, tell my brother to divide the inheritance with me."

14 But He said to him, [a]"Man, who made Me a judge or an arbitrator over you?"

15 And He said to them, [a]"Take heed and beware of *covetousness, for one's life does not consist in the abundance of the things he possesses."

16 Then He spoke a parable to them, saying: "The ground of a certain rich man yielded plentifully.

17 "And he thought within himself, saying, 'What shall I do, since I have no room to store my crops?'

18 "So he said, 'I will do this: I will pull down my barns and build greater, and there I will store all my crops and my goods.

19 'And I will say to my soul, [a]"Soul, you have many goods laid up for many years; take your ease; [b]eat, drink, *and* be merry." '

20 "But God said to him, 'Fool! This night [a]your soul will be required of you; [b]then whose will those things be which you have provided?'

21 "So *is* he who lays up treasure for himself, [a]and is not rich toward God."

Do Not Worry
(Matt. 6:19–21, 25–34)

22 Then He said to His disciples, "Therefore I say to you, [a]do not worry about your life, what you will eat; nor about the body, what you will put on.

23 "Life is more than food, and the body *is more* than clothing.

24 "Consider the ravens, for they neither sow nor reap, which have neither storehouse nor barn; and [a]God feeds them. Of how much more value are you than the birds?

25 "And which of you by worrying can add one cubit to his stature?

26 "If you then are not able to do *the* least, why are you anxious for the rest?

27 "Consider the lilies, how they grow: they neither toil nor spin; and yet I say to you, even [a]Solomon in all his glory was not arrayed like one of these.

28 "If then God so clothes the grass, which today is in the field and tomorrow is thrown into the oven, how much more *will He clothe* you, O *you* of [a]little faith?

29 "And do not seek what you should eat or what you should drink, nor have an anxious mind.

30 "For all these things the nations of the world seek after, and your Father [a]knows that you need these things.

31 [a]"But seek *the kingdom of God, and all these things shall be added to you.

KJV

32 Fear not, little flock; for [a]it is your Father's good pleasure to give you the kingdom.

33 [a]Sell that ye have, and give [b]alms; [c]provide yourselves bags which wax not old, a treasure in the heavens that faileth not, where no thief approacheth, neither moth corrupteth.

34 For where your treasure is, there will your heart be also.

The Faithful Servant and the Evil Servant
(Matt. 24:42–51)

35 [a]Let your loins be girded about, and [b]*your* lights burning;

36 And ye yourselves like unto men that wait for their lord, when he will return from the wedding; that when he cometh and knocketh, they may open unto him immediately.

37 [a]Blessed *are* those servants, whom the lord when he cometh shall find watching: verily I say unto you, that he shall gird himself, and make them to sit down to meat, and will come forth and serve them.

38 And if he shall come in the second watch, or come in the third watch, and find *them* so, blessed are those servants.

39 [a]And this know, that if the goodman of the house had known what hour the thief would come, he would have watched, and not have suffered his house to be broken through.

40 [a]Be ye therefore ready also: for the Son of man cometh at an hour when ye think not.

41 Then Peter said unto him, Lord, speakest thou this parable unto us, or even to all?

42 And the Lord said, [a]Who then is that faithful and wise steward, whom *his* lord shall make ruler over his household, to give *them their* portion of meat in due season?

43 Blessed *is* that servant, whom his lord when he cometh shall find so doing.

44 [a]Of a truth I say unto you, that he will make him ruler over all that he hath.

45 [a]But and if that servant say in his heart, My lord delayeth his coming; and shall begin to beat the menservants and maidens, and to eat and drink, and to be drunken;

46 The lord of that servant will come in a [a]day when he looketh not for *him,* and at an hour when he is not aware, and will cut him in sunder, and will appoint him his portion with the unbelievers.

47 And [a]that servant, which [b]knew his lord's will, and prepared not *himself,* neither did according to his will, shall be beaten with many *stripes.*

48 [a]But he that knew not, and did commit things worthy of stripes, shall be beaten with few *stripes.* For unto whomsoever much is given, of him shall be much required: and to whom men have committed much, of him they will ask the more.

Christ Brings Division
(Matt. 10:34–39)

49 [a]I am come to send fire on the earth; and what will I, if it be already kindled?

50 But [a]I have a baptism to be baptized with; and how am I straitened till it be [b]accomplished!

51 [a]Suppose ye that I am come to give peace on earth? I tell you, Nay; [b]but rather division:

52 [a]For from henceforth there shall be five in one house divided, three against two, and two against three.

53 The [a]father shall be divided against the son, and the son against the father; the mother against the daughter, and the daughter against the mother; the mother in law against her daughter in law, and the daughter in law against her mother in law.

32 [a][Dan. 7:18, 27]; Zech. 13:7; [Matt. 11:25, 26; Luke 22:29, 30]
33 [a]Matt. 19:21; Acts 2:45; 4:34 [b]Luke 11:41 [c]Matt. 6:20; Luke 16:9; [1 Tim. 6:19]
35 [a][Eph. 6:14; 1 Pet. 1:13] [b][Matt. 25:1–13]
37 [a]Matt. 24:46
39 [a]Matt. 24:43; 1 Thess. 5:2; [2 Pet. 3:10]; Rev. 3:3; 16:15
40 [a]Matt. 24:44; 25:13; Mark 13:33; [Luke 21:34, 36]; 1 Thess. 5:6; [2 Pet. 3:12]
42 [a]Matt. 24:45, 46; 25:21; [1 Cor. 4:2]
44 [a]Matt. 24:47; 25:21; [Rev. 3:21]
45 [a]Matt. 24:48; 2 Pet. 3:3, 4
46 [a]1 Thess. 5:3
47 [a]Num. 15:30; Deut. 25:2; [John 9:41; 15:22; Acts 17:30] [b][James 4:17]
48 [a][Lev. 5:17]; Num. 15:29; [1 Tim. 1:13]
49 [a]Luke 12:51
50 [a]Matt. 20:18, 22, 23; Mark 10:38 [b]John 12:27; 19:30
51 [a]Matt. 10:34–36 [b]Mic. 7:6; John 7:43; 9:16; 10:19; Acts 14:4
52 [a]Matt. 10:35; Mark 13:12
53 [a]Matt. 10:21, 36

*
12:39 NU *not have allowed*

NKJV

32 "Do not fear, little flock, for [a]it is your Father's good pleasure to give you the kingdom.

33 [a]"Sell what you have and give [b]alms; [c]provide yourselves money bags which do not grow old, a treasure in the heavens that does not fail, where no thief approaches nor moth destroys.

34 "For where your treasure is, there your heart will be also.

The Faithful Servant and the Evil Servant
(Matt. 24:42–51)

35 [a]"Let your waist be girded and [b]*your* lamps burning;

36 "and you yourselves be like men who wait for their master, when he will return from the wedding, that when he comes and knocks they may open to him immediately.

37 [a]"Blessed *are* those servants whom the master, when he comes, will find watching. Assuredly, I say to you that he will gird himself and have them sit down *to eat,* and will come and serve them.

38 "And if he should come in the second watch, or come in the third watch, and find *them* so, blessed are those servants.

39 [a]"But know this, that if the master of the house had known what hour the thief would come, he would *have watched and not allowed his house to be broken into.

40 [a]"Therefore you also be ready, for the Son of Man is coming at an hour you do not expect."

41 Then Peter said to Him, "Lord, do You speak this parable *only* to us, or to all *people?*"

42 And the Lord said, [a]"Who then is that faithful and wise steward, whom *his* master will make ruler over his household, to give *them their* portion of food in due season?

43 "Blessed *is* that servant whom his master will find so doing when he comes.

44 [a]"Truly, I say to you that he will make him ruler over all that he has.

45 [a]"But if that servant says in his heart, 'My master is delaying his coming,' and begins to beat the male and female servants, and to eat and drink and be drunk,

46 "the master of that servant will come on a [a]day when he is not looking for *him,* and at an hour when he is not aware, and will cut him in two and appoint *him* his portion with the unbelievers.

47 "And [a]that servant who [b]knew his master's will, and did not prepare *himself* or do according to his will, shall be beaten with many *stripes.*

48 [a]"But he who did not know, yet committed things deserving of stripes, shall be beaten with few. For everyone to whom much is given, from him much will be required; and to whom much has been committed, of him they will ask the more.

Christ Brings Division
(Matt. 10:34–39)

49 [a]"I came to send fire on the earth, and how I wish it were already kindled!

50 "But [a]I have a baptism to be baptized with, and how distressed I am till it is [b]accomplished!

51 [a]"Do *you* suppose that I came to give peace on earth? I tell you, not at all, [b]but rather division.

52 [a]"For from now on five in one house will be divided: three against two, and two against three.

53 [a]"Father will be divided against son and son against father, mother against daughter and daughter against mother, mother-in-law against her daughter-in-law and daughter-in-law against her mother-in-law."

KJV

Discern the Time
(Matt. 16:1–4)

54 And he said also to the people, [a]When ye
see a cloud rise out of the west, straightway ye
say, There cometh a shower; and so it is.
55 And when *ye see* the [a]south wind blow,
ye say, There will be heat; and it cometh to pass.
56 *Ye* hypocrites, ye can discern the face of
the sky and of the earth; but how is it that ye do
not discern [a]this time?

Make Peace with Your Adversary

57 Yea, and why even of yourselves judge
ye not what is right?
58 [a]When thou goest with thine adversary to
the magistrate, [b]*as thou art* in the way, give diligence that thou mayest be delivered from him;
lest he hale thee to the judge, and the judge deliver
thee to the officer, and the officer cast thee into
prison.
59 I tell thee, thou shalt not depart thence,
till thou hast paid the very last mite.

Repent or Perish

13 There were present at that season some
that told him of the Galilaeans, whose
blood Pilate had mingled with their sacrifices.
2 And Jesus answering said unto them, Suppose ye that these Galilaeans were sinners above
all the Galilaeans, because they suffered such
things?
3 I tell you, Nay: but, except ye repent, ye
shall all likewise perish.
4 Or those eighteen, upon whom the tower
in Siloam fell, and slew them, think ye that they
were sinners above all men that dwelt in
Jerusalem?
5 I tell you, Nay: but, except ye repent, ye
shall all likewise perish.

The Parable of the Barren Fig Tree

6 He spake also this parable; [a]A certain
man had a fig tree planted in his vineyard; and
he came and sought fruit thereon, and found none.
7 Then said he unto the dresser of his vineyard, Behold, these three years I come seeking
fruit on this fig tree, and find none: cut it down;
why cumbereth it the ground?
8 And he answering said unto him, Lord,
let it alone this year also, till I shall dig about it,
and dung *it:*
9 And if it bear fruit, *well:* and if not, *then*
after that thou shalt [a]cut it down.

A Spirit of Infirmity

10 And he was teaching in one of the synagogues on the sabbath.
11 And, behold, there was a woman which
had a spirit of infirmity eighteen years, and was
bowed together, and could in no wise lift up
herself.
12 And when Jesus saw her, he called *her
to him,* and said unto her, Woman, thou art loosed
from thine [a]infirmity.
13 [a]And he laid *his* hands on her: and immediately she was made straight, and glorified God.
14 And the ruler of the synagogue answered
with indignation, because that Jesus had [a]healed
on the sabbath day, and said unto the people,
[b]There are six days in which men ought to work:
in them therefore come and be healed, and [c]not
on the sabbath day.
15 The Lord then answered him, and said,
Thou hypocrite, [a]doth not each one of you on the
sabbath loose his ox or *his* ass from the stall, and
lead *him* away to watering?
16 And ought not this woman, [a]being a
daughter of Abraham, whom Satan hath bound,
lo, these eighteen years, be loosed from this bond
on the sabbath day?
17 And when he had said these things, all

54 [a]Matt. 16:2, 3
55 [a]Job 37:17
56 [a]Luke 19:41–44
58 [a]Prov. 25:8; Matt. 5:25, 26 [b][Ps. 32:6; Is. 55:6]

CHAPTER 13

6 [a]Is. 5:2; Matt. 21:19
9 [a][John 15:2]
12 [a]Luke 7:21; 8:2
13 [a]Mark 16:18; Acts 9:17
14 [a][Luke 6:6–11; 14:1–6]; John 5:16 [b]Ex. 20:9; 23:12 [c]Matt. 12:10; Mark 3:2; Luke 6:7; 14:3
15 [a][Matt. 7:5; 23:13]; Luke 14:5
16 [a]Luke 19:9

*———

13:9 NU *And if it bears fruit after that, well. But if not, you can*
13:15 NU, M *Hypocrites*

NKJV

Discern the Time
(Matt. 16:1–4)

54 Then He also said to the multitudes,
[a]"Whenever you see a cloud rising out of the west,
immediately you say, 'A shower is coming'; and
so it is.
55 "And when you see the [a]south wind blow,
you say, 'There will be hot weather'; and there
is.
56 "Hypocrites! You can discern the face of
the sky and of the earth, but how *is it* you do
not discern [a]this time?

Make Peace with Your Adversary

57 "Yes, and why, even of yourselves, do you
not judge what is right?
58 [a]"When you go with your adversary to the
magistrate, make every effort [b]along the way to
settle with him, lest he drag you to the judge, the
judge deliver you to the officer, and the officer
throw you into prison.
59 "I tell you, you shall not depart from there
till you have paid the very last mite."

Repent or Perish

13 There were present at that season some
who told Him about the Galileans whose
blood Pilate had mingled with their sacrifices.
2 And Jesus answered and said to them,
"Do you suppose that these Galileans were worse
sinners than all *other* Galileans, because they suffered such things?
3 "I tell you, no; but unless you repent you
will all likewise perish.
4 "Or those eighteen on whom the tower in
Siloam fell and killed them, do you think that they
were worse sinners than all *other* men who dwelt
in Jerusalem?
5 "I tell you, no; but unless you repent you
will all likewise perish."

The Parable of the Barren Fig Tree

6 He also spoke this parable: [a]"A certain
man had a fig tree planted in his vineyard, and
he came seeking fruit on it and found none.
7 "Then he said to the keeper of his vineyard, 'Look, for three years I have come seeking
fruit on this fig tree and find none. Cut it down;
why does it use up the ground?'
8 "But he answered and said to him, 'Sir,
let it alone this year also, until I dig around it
and fertilize *it.*
9 *'And if it bears fruit, *well.* But if not, after
that you can [a]cut it down.'"

A Spirit of Infirmity

10 Now He was teaching in one of the synagogues on the Sabbath.
11 And behold, there was a woman who had
a spirit of infirmity eighteen years, and was bent
over and could in no way raise *herself* up.
12 But when Jesus saw her, He called *her* to
Him and said to her, "Woman, you are loosed
from your [a]infirmity."
13 [a]And He laid *His* hands on her, and immediately she was made straight, and glorified God.
14 But the ruler of the synagogue answered
with indignation, because Jesus had [a]healed on
the Sabbath; and he said to the crowd, [b]"There
are six days on which men ought to work; therefore come and be healed on them, and [c]not on
the Sabbath day."
15 The Lord then answered him and said,
*"Hypocrite! [a]Does not each one of you on the
Sabbath loose his ox or donkey from the stall,
and lead *it* away to water it?
16 "So ought not this woman, [a]being a
daughter of Abraham, whom Satan has bound—
think of it—for eighteen years, be loosed from this
bond on the Sabbath?"
17 And when He said these things, all His

KJV

his adversaries were ashamed: and all the people rejoiced for all the glorious things that were [a]done by him.

The Parable of the Mustard Seed
(Matt. 13:31, 32; Mark 4:30–32)

18 [a]Then said he, Unto what is the kingdom of God like? and whereunto shall I resemble it?

19 It is like a grain of mustard seed, which a man took, and cast into his garden; and it grew, and waxed a great tree; and the fowls of the air lodged in the branches of it.

The Parable of the Leaven
(Matt. 13:33)

20 And again he said, Whereunto shall I liken the kingdom of God?

21 It is like leaven, which a woman took and hid in three [a]measures of meal, till the whole was leavened.

The Narrow Way
(Matt. 7:13, 14)

22 [a]And he went through the cities and villages, teaching, and journeying toward Jerusalem.

23 Then said one unto him, Lord, are there [a]few that be saved? And he said unto them,

24 [a]Strive to enter in at the strait gate: for [b]many, I say unto you, will seek to enter in, and shall not be able.

25 [a]When once the master of the house is risen up, and [b]hath shut to the door, and ye begin to stand without, and to knock at the door, saying, [c]Lord, Lord, open unto us; and he shall answer and say unto you, [d]I know you not whence ye are:

26 Then shall ye begin to say, We have eaten and drunk in thy presence, and thou hast taught in our streets.

27 [a]But he shall say, I tell you, I know you not whence ye are; [b]depart from me, all *ye* workers of iniquity.

28 [a]There shall be weeping and gnashing of teeth, [b]when ye shall see Abraham, and Isaac, and Jacob, and all the prophets, in the kingdom of God, and you *yourselves* thrust out.

29 And they shall come from the east, and *from* the west, and from the north, and *from* the south, and shall sit down in the kingdom of God.

30 [a]And, behold, there are last which shall be first, and there are first which shall be last.

31 The same day there came certain of the Pharisees, saying unto him, Get thee out, and depart hence: for Herod will kill thee.

32 And he said unto them, Go ye, and tell that fox, Behold, I cast out devils, and I do cures to day and to morrow, and the third *day* [a]I shall be perfected.

33 Nevertheless I must walk to day, and to morrow, and the *day* following: for it cannot be that a prophet perish out of Jerusalem.

Jesus Laments over Jerusalem
(Matt. 23:37–39)

34 [a]O Jerusalem, Jerusalem, which killest the prophets, and stonest them that are sent unto thee; how often would I have gathered thy children together, as a hen *doth gather* her brood under *her* wings, and ye would not!

35 Behold, [a]your house is left unto you desolate: and verily I say unto you, Ye shall not see me, until *the time* come when ye shall say, [b]BLESSED *IS* HE THAT COMETH IN THE NAME OF THE LORD.

A Man with Dropsy Healed on the Sabbath

14 And it came to pass, as he went into the house of one of the chief Pharisees to eat bread on the sabbath day, that they watched him.

17 [a]Mark 5:19, 20
18 [a]Matt. 13:31, 32; Mark 4:30–32
21 [a]Matt. 13:33
22 [a]Matt. 9:35; Mark 6:6
23 [a][Matt. 7:14; 20:16]
24 [a][Matt. 7:13] [b][John 7:34; 8:21; 13:33; Rom. 9:31]
25 [a][Ps. 32:6]; Is. 55:6 [b]Matt. 25:10; Rev. 22:11 [c]Luke 6:46 [d]Matt. 7:23; 25:12
27 [a][Matt. 7:23; 25:41] [b]Ps. 6:8; [Matt. 25:41]; Titus 1:16
28 [a]Matt. 8:12; 13:42; 24:51 [b]Matt. 8:11
30 [a][Matt. 19:30; 20:16]; Mark 10:31
32 [a]Luke 24:46; Acts 10:40; 1 Cor. 15:4; [Heb. 2:10; 5:9; 7:28]
34 [a]Matt. 23:37–39; 2 Chr. 24:20, 21; 36:15, 16
35 [a]Lev. 26:31, 32; Ps. 69:25; Is. 1:7; Jer. 22:5; Dan. 9:27; Mic. 3:12 [b]Ps. 118:26; Matt. 21:9; Mark 11:10; Luke 19:38; John 12:13

*

13:19 NU omits *large*
13:21 Gr. *sata,* same as Heb. *seah;* approximately 2 pecks in all
13:31 NU *In that very hour*
13:35 NU, M omit *assuredly*

NKJV

adversaries were put to shame; and all the multitude rejoiced for all the glorious things that were [a]done by Him.

The Parable of the Mustard Seed
(Matt. 13:31, 32; Mark 4:30–32)

18 [a]Then He said, "What is the kingdom of God like? And to what shall I compare it?

19 "It is like a mustard seed, which a man took and put in his garden; and it grew and became a *large tree, and the birds of the air nested in its branches."

The Parable of the Leaven
(Matt. 13:33)

20 And again He said, "To what shall I liken the kingdom of God?

21 "It is like leaven, which a woman took and hid in three [a]measures* of meal till it was all leavened."

The Narrow Way
(Matt. 7:13, 14)

22 [a]And He went through the cities and villages, teaching, and journeying toward Jerusalem.

23 Then one said to Him, "Lord, are there [a]few who are saved?" And He said to them,

24 [a]"Strive to enter through the narrow gate, for [b]many, I say to you, will seek to enter and will not be able.

25 [a]"When once the Master of the house has risen up and [b]shut the door, and you begin to stand outside and knock at the door, saying, [c]'Lord, Lord, open for us,' and He will answer and say to you, [d]'I do not know you, where you are from,'

26 "then you will begin to say, 'We ate and drank in Your presence, and You taught in our streets.'

27 [a]"But He will say, 'I tell you I do not know you, where you are from. [b]Depart from Me, all you workers of iniquity.'

28 [a]"There will be weeping and gnashing of teeth, [b]when you see Abraham and Isaac and Jacob and all the prophets in the kingdom of God, and yourselves thrust out.

29 "They will come from the east and the west, from the north and the south, and sit down in the kingdom of God.

30 [a]"And indeed there are last who will be first, and there are first who will be last."

31 *On that very day some Pharisees came, saying to Him, "Get out and depart from here, for Herod wants to kill You."

32 And He said to them, "Go, tell that fox, 'Behold, I cast out demons and perform cures today and tomorrow, and the third *day* [a]I shall be perfected.'

33 "Nevertheless I must journey today, tomorrow, and the *day* following; for it cannot be that a prophet should perish outside of Jerusalem.

Jesus Laments over Jerusalem
(Matt. 23:37–39)

34 [a]"O Jerusalem, Jerusalem, the one who kills the prophets and stones those who are sent to her! How often I wanted to gather your children together, as a hen *gathers* her brood under *her* wings, but you were not willing!

35 "See! [a]Your house is left to you desolate; and *assuredly, I say to you, you shall not see Me until *the time* comes when you say, [b]*'Blessed is He who comes in the name of the LORD!'* "

A Man with Dropsy Healed on the Sabbath

14 Now it happened, as He went into the house of one of the rulers of the Pharisees to eat bread on the Sabbath, that they watched Him closely.

KJV

2 And, behold, there was a certain man before him which had the dropsy.

3 And Jesus answering spake unto the lawyers and Pharisees, saying, [a]Is it lawful to heal on the sabbath day?

4 And they held their peace. And he took *him*, and healed him, and let him go;

5 And answered them, saying, [a]Which of you shall have an ass or an ox fallen into a pit, and will not straightway pull him out on the sabbath day?

6 And they could not answer him again to these things.

Take the Lowly Place

7 And he put forth a parable to those which were bidden, when he marked how they chose out the chief rooms; saying unto them,

8 When thou art bidden of any *man* to a wedding, sit not down in the highest room; lest a more honourable man than thou be bidden of him;

9 And he that bade thee and him come and say to thee, Give this man place; and thou begin with shame to take the lowest room.

10 [a]But when thou art bidden, go and sit down in the lowest room; that when he that bade thee cometh, he may say unto thee, Friend, go up higher: then shalt thou have worship in the presence of them that sit at meat with thee.

11 [a]For whosoever exalteth himself shall be abased; and he that humbleth himself shall be exalted.

12 Then said he also to him that bade him, When thou makest a dinner or a supper, call not thy friends, nor thy brethren, neither thy kinsmen, nor *thy* rich neighbours; lest they also bid thee again, and a recompence be made thee.

13 But when thou makest a feast, call [a]the poor, the maimed, the lame, the blind:

14 And thou shalt be [a]blessed; for they cannot recompense thee: for thou shalt be recompensed at the resurrection of the just.

The Parable of the Great Supper
(*Matt. 22:1–14*)

15 And when one of them that sat at meat with him heard these things, he said unto him, [a]Blessed *is* he that shall eat bread in the kingdom of God.

16 [a]Then said he unto him, A certain man made a great supper, and bade many:

17 And [a]sent his servant at supper time to say to them that were bidden, Come; for all things are now ready.

18 And they all with one *consent* began to make excuse. The first said unto him, I have bought a piece of ground, and I must needs go and see it: I pray thee have me excused.

19 And another said, I have bought five yoke of oxen, and I go to prove them: I pray thee have me excused.

20 And another said, I have married a wife, and therefore I cannot come.

21 So that servant came, and shewed his lord these things. Then the master of the house being angry said to his servant, Go out quickly into the streets and lanes of the city, and bring in hither the poor, and the maimed, and the halt, and the blind.

22 And the servant said, LORD, it is done as thou hast commanded, and yet there is room.

23 And the lord said unto the servant, Go out into the highways and hedges, and compel *them* to come in, that my house may be filled.

24 For I say unto you, [a]That none of those men which were bidden shall taste of my supper.

Leaving All to Follow Christ
(*Matt. 10:34–39*)

25 And there went great multitudes with him: and he turned, and said unto them,

CHAPTER 14
3 [a]Matt. 12:10
5 [a][Ex. 23:5; Deut. 22:4]; Luke 13:15
10 [a]Prov. 25:6, 7
11 [a]Job 22:29; Ps. 18:27; Prov. 29:23; Matt. 23:12; Luke 18:14; James 4:6; [1 Pet. 5:5]
13 [a]Neh. 8:10, 12
14 [a][Matt. 25:34–40]
15 [a]Rev. 19:9
16 [a]Matt. 22:2–14
17 [a]Prov. 9:2, 5
24 [a][Matt. 21:43; 22:8; Acts 13:46]

*

14:3 NU adds *or not*
14:5 NU, M *son*
14:15 M *dinner*

NKJV

2 And behold, there was a certain man before Him who had dropsy.

3 And Jesus, answering, spoke to the lawyers and Pharisees, saying, [a]"Is it lawful to heal on the *Sabbath?"

4 But they kept silent. And He took *him* and healed him, and let him go.

5 Then He answered them, saying, [a]"Which of you, having a *donkey or an ox that has fallen into a pit, will not immediately pull him out on the Sabbath day?"

6 And they could not answer Him regarding these things.

Take the Lowly Place

7 So He told a parable to those who were invited, when He noted how they chose the best places, saying to them:

8 "When you are invited by anyone to a wedding feast, do not sit down in the best place, lest one more honorable than you be invited by him;

9 "and he who invited you and him come and say to you, 'Give place to this man,' and then you begin with shame to take the lowest place.

10 [a]"But when you are invited, go and sit down in the lowest place, so that when he who invited you comes he may say to you, 'Friend, go up higher.' Then you will have glory in the presence of those who sit at the table with you.

11 [a]"For whoever exalts himself will be humbled, and he who humbles himself will be exalted."

12 Then He also said to him who invited Him, "When you give a dinner or a supper, do not ask your friends, your brothers, your relatives, nor rich neighbors, lest they also invite you back, and you be repaid.

13 "But when you give a feast, invite [a]*the* poor, *the* maimed, *the* lame, *the* blind.

14 "And you will be [a]blessed, because they cannot repay you; for you shall be repaid at the resurrection of the just."

The Parable of the Great Supper
(*Matt. 22:1–14*)

15 Now when one of those who sat at the table with Him heard these things, he said to Him, [a]"Blessed *is* he who shall eat *bread in the kingdom of God!"

16 [a]Then He said to him, "A certain man gave a great supper and invited many,

17 "and [a]sent his servant at supper time to say to those who were invited, 'Come, for all things are now ready.'

18 "But they all with one *accord* began to make excuses. The first said to him, 'I have bought a piece of ground, and I must go and see it. I ask you to have me excused.'

19 "And another said, 'I have bought five yoke of oxen, and I am going to test them. I ask you to have me excused.'

20 "Still another said, 'I have married a wife, and therefore I cannot come.'

21 "So that servant came and reported these things to his master. Then the master of the house, being angry, said to his servant, 'Go out quickly into the streets and lanes of the city, and bring in here *the* poor and *the* maimed and *the* lame and *the* blind.'

22 "And the servant said, 'Master, it is done as you commanded, and still there is room.'

23 "Then the master said to the servant, 'Go out into the highways and hedges, and compel *them* to come in, that my house may be filled.

24 'For I say to you [a]that none of those men who were invited shall taste my supper.' "

Leaving All to Follow Christ
(*Matt. 10:34–39*)

25 Now great multitudes went with Him. And He turned and said to them,

KJV

26 [a]If any *man* come to me, [b]and hate not
his father, and mother, and wife, and children,
and brethren, and sisters, [c]yea, and his own life
also, he cannot be my disciple.
27 And [a]whosoever doth not bear his cross,
and come after me, cannot be my disciple.
28 For [a]which of you, intending to build a
tower, sitteth not down first, and counteth the
cost, whether he have *sufficient* to finish *it?*
29 Lest haply, after he hath laid the foundation, and is not able to finish *it,* all that behold *it*
begin to mock him,
30 Saying, This man began to build, and was
not able to finish.
31 Or what king, going to make war against
another king, sitteth not down first, and con-
sulteth whether he be able with ten thousand to
meet him that cometh against him with twenty
thousand?
32 Or else, while the other is yet a great way
off, he sendeth an ambassage, and desireth conditions of peace.
33 So likewise, whosoever he be of you that
[a]forsaketh not all that he hath, he cannot be my
disciple.

Tasteless Salt Is Worthless
(Matt. 5:13; Mark 9:50)

34 [a]Salt *is* good: but if the salt have lost his
savour, wherewith shall it be seasoned?
35 It is neither fit for the land, nor yet for
the dunghill; *but* men cast it out. He that hath
ears to hear, let him hear.

The Parable of the Lost Sheep
(Matt. 18:10–14)

15 Then [a]drew near unto him all the publicans
and sinners for to hear him.
2 And the Pharisees and scribes murmured,
saying, This man receiveth sinners, [a]and eateth
with them.
3 And he spake this parable unto them,
saying,
4 [a]What man of you, having an hundred
sheep, if he lose one of them, doth not leave the
ninety and nine in the wilderness, and go after
that which is lost, until he find it?
5 And when he hath found *it,* he layeth *it*
on his shoulders, rejoicing.
6 And when he cometh home, he calleth together *his* friends and neighbours, saying unto
them, [a]Rejoice with me; for I have found my sheep
[b]which was lost.
7 I say unto you, that likewise joy shall be
in heaven over one sinner that repenteth, [a]more
than over ninety and nine just persons, which
[b]need no repentance.

The Parable of the Lost Coin

8 Either what woman having ten pieces of
silver, if she lose one piece, doth not light a candle,
and sweep the house, and seek diligently till she
find *it?*
9 And when she hath found *it,* she calleth
her friends and *her* neighbours together, saying,
Rejoice with me; for I have found the piece which
I had lost.
10 Likewise, I say unto you, there is joy in
the presence of the angels of God over one sinner
that repenteth.

The Parable of the Lost Son

11 And he said, A certain man had two
sons:
12 And the younger of them said to *his* father,
Father, give me the portion of goods that falleth
to me. And he divided unto them [a]*his* living.
13 And not many days after the younger son
gathered all together, and took his journey into
a far country, and there wasted his substance with
riotous living.
14 And when he had spent all, there arose a

26 [a]Deut. 13:6; 33:9; Matt. 10:37 [b]Rom. 9:13 [c]Rev. 12:11
27 [a]Matt. 16:24; Mark 8:34; Luke 9:23; [2 Tim. 3:12]
28 [a]Prov. 24:27
33 [a]Matt. 19:27
34 [a]Matt. 5:13; [Mark 9:50]

CHAPTER 15
1 [a][Matt. 9:10–15]
2 [a]Acts 11:3; Gal. 2:12
4 [a]Matt. 18:12–14; 1 Pet. 2:25
6 [a][Rom. 12:15] [b][Luke 19:10; 1 Pet. 2:10, 25]
7 [a][Luke 5:32] [b][Mark 2:17]
12 [a]Mark 12:44

*
15:8 Gr. *drachma,* a valuable coin often worn in a ten-piece garland by married women

NKJV

26 [a]"If anyone comes to Me [b]and does not
hate his father and mother, wife and children,
brothers and sisters, [c]yes, and his own life also,
he cannot be My disciple.
27 "And [a]whoever does not bear his cross
and come after Me cannot be My disciple.
28 "For [a]which of you, intending to build a
tower, does not sit down first and count the cost,
whether he has *enough* to finish *it*—
29 "lest, after he has laid the foundation, and
is not able to finish, all who see *it* begin to mock
him,
30 "saying, 'This man began to build and was
not able to finish.'
31 "Or what king, going to make war against
another king, does not sit down first and consider
whether he is able with ten thousand to meet him
who comes against him with twenty thousand?
32 "Or else, while the other is still a great
way off, he sends a delegation and asks conditions
of peace.
33 "So likewise, whoever of you [a]does not
forsake all that he has cannot be My disciple.

Tasteless Salt Is Worthless
(Matt. 5:13; Mark 9:50)

34 [a]"Salt *is* good; but if the salt has lost its
flavor, how shall it be seasoned?
35 "It is neither fit for the land nor for the
dunghill, *but* men throw it out. He who has ears
to hear, let him hear!"

The Parable of the Lost Sheep
(Matt. 18:10–14)

15 Then [a]all the tax collectors and the sinners
drew near to Him to hear Him.
2 And the Pharisees and scribes complained, saying, "This Man receives sinners [a]and
eats with them."
3 So He spoke this parable to them, saying:
4 [a]"What man of you, having a hundred
sheep, if he loses one of them, does not leave the
ninety-nine in the wilderness, and go after the one
which is lost until he finds it?
5 "And when he has found *it,* he lays *it* on
his shoulders, rejoicing.
6 "And when he comes home, he calls together *his* friends and neighbors, saying to them,
[a]'Rejoice with me, for I have found my sheep
[b]which was lost!'
7 "I say to you that likewise there will be
more joy in heaven over one sinner who repents
[a]than over ninety-nine just persons who [b]need no
repentance.

The Parable of the Lost Coin

8 "Or what woman, having ten silver *coins,
if she loses one coin, does not light a lamp, sweep
the house, and search carefully until she finds *it?*
9 "And when she has found *it,* she calls *her*
friends and neighbors together, saying, 'Rejoice
with me, for I have found the piece which I lost!'
10 "Likewise, I say to you, there is joy in the
presence of the angels of God over one sinner
who repents."

The Parable of the Lost Son

11 Then He said: "A certain man had two
sons.
12 "And the younger of them said to *his* father, 'Father, give me the portion of goods that
falls *to me.*' So he divided to them [a]*his* livelihood.
13 "And not many days after, the younger
son gathered all together, journeyed to a far country, and there wasted his possessions with prodi-
gal living.
14 "But when he had spent all, there arose

KJV

mighty famine in that land; and he began to be in want.

15 And he went and joined himself to a citizen of that country; and he sent him into his fields to feed swine.

16 And he would fain have filled his belly with the husks that the swine did eat: and no man gave unto him.

17 And when he came to himself, he said, How many hired servants of my father's have bread enough and to spare, and I perish with hunger!

18 I will arise and go to my father, and will say unto him, Father, [a]I have sinned against heaven, and before thee,

19 And am no more worthy to be called thy son: make me as one of thy hired servants.

20 And he arose, and came to his father. But [a]when he was yet a great way off, his father saw him, and had compassion, and ran, and fell on his neck, and kissed him.

21 And the son said unto him, Father, I have sinned against heaven, [a]and in thy sight, and am no more worthy to be called thy son.

22 But the father said to his servants, Bring forth the best robe, and put *it* on him; and put a ring on his hand, and shoes on *his* feet:

23 And bring hither the fatted calf, and kill *it;* and let us eat, and be merry:

24 [a]For this my son was dead, and is alive again; he was lost, and is found. And they began to be merry.

25 Now his elder son was in the field: and as he came and drew nigh to the house, he heard musick and dancing.

26 And he called one of the servants, and asked what these things meant.

27 And he said unto him, Thy brother is come; and thy father hath killed the fatted calf, because he hath received him safe and sound.

28 And he was angry, and would not go in: therefore came his father out, and intreated him.

29 And he answering said to *his* father, Lo, these many years do I serve thee, neither transgressed I at any time thy commandment: and yet thou never gavest me a kid, that I might make merry with my friends:

30 But as soon as this thy son was come, which hath devoured thy living with harlots, thou hast killed for him the fatted calf.

31 And he said unto him, Son, thou art ever with me, and all that I have is thine.

32 It was meet that we should make merry, and be glad: [a]for this thy brother was dead, and is alive again; and was lost, and is found.

The Parable of the Unjust Steward

16 And he said also unto his disciples, There was a certain rich man, which had a steward; and the same was accused unto him that he had wasted his goods.

2 And he called him, and said unto him, How is it that I hear this of thee? give an [a]account of thy stewardship; for thou mayest be no longer steward.

3 Then the steward said within himself, What shall I do? for my lord taketh away from me the stewardship: I cannot dig; to beg I am ashamed.

4 I am resolved what to do, that, when I am put out of the stewardship, they may receive me into their houses.

5 So he called every one of his lord's debtors *unto him,* and said unto the first, How much owest thou unto my lord?

6 And he said, An hundred measures of oil. And he said unto him, Take thy bill, and sit down quickly, and write fifty.

7 Then said he to another, And how much owest thou? And he said, An hundred measures

18 [a]Ex. 9:27; 10:16; Num. 22:34; Josh. 7:20; 1 Sam. 15:24, 30; 26:21; 2 Sam. 12:13; 24:10, 17; Ps. 51:4; Matt. 27:4
20 [a][Jer. 3:12]; Matt. 9:36; [Acts 2:39; Eph. 2:13, 17]
21 [a]Ps. 51:4
24 [a]Matt. 8:22; Luke 9:60; 15:32; Rom. 11:15; [Eph. 2:1, 5; 5:14; Col. 2:13; 1 Tim. 5:6]
32 [a]Luke 15:24

CHAPTER 16

2 [a][Rom. 14:12; 2 Cor. 5:10; 1 Pet. 4:5, 6]

*———

15:22 NU *Quickly bring*
16:6 Gr. *batos,* same as Heb. *bath;* 8 or 9 gallons each
16:7 Gr. *koros,* same as Heb. *kor;* 10 or 12 bushels each

NKJV

a severe famine in that land, and he began to be in want.

15 "Then he went and joined himself to a citizen of that country, and he sent him into his fields to feed swine.

16 "And he would gladly have filled his stomach with the pods that the swine ate, and no one gave him *anything.*

17 "But when he came to himself, he said, 'How many of my father's hired servants have bread enough and to spare, and I perish with hunger!

18 'I will arise and go to my father, and will say to him, "Father, [a]I have sinned against heaven and before you,

19 "and I am no longer worthy to be called your son. Make me like one of your hired servants." '

20 "And he arose and came to his father. But [a]when he was still a great way off, his father saw him and had compassion, and ran and fell on his neck and kissed him.

21 "And the son said to him, 'Father, I have sinned against heaven [a]and in your sight, and am no longer worthy to be called your son.'

22 "But the father said to his servants, *'Bring out the best robe and put *it* on him, and put a ring on his hand and sandals on *his* feet.

23 'And bring the fatted calf here and kill *it,* and let us eat and be merry;

24 [a]'for this my son was dead and is alive again; he was lost and is found.' And they began to be merry.

25 "Now his older son was in the field. And as he came and drew near to the house, he heard music and dancing.

26 "So he called one of the servants and asked what these things meant.

27 "And he said to him, 'Your brother has come, and because he has received him safe and sound, your father has killed the fatted calf.'

28 "But he was angry and would not go in. Therefore his father came out and pleaded with him.

29 "So he answered and said to *his* father, 'Lo, these many years I have been serving you; I never transgressed your commandment at any time; and yet you never gave me a young goat, that I might make merry with my friends.

30 'But as soon as this son of yours came, who has devoured your livelihood with harlots, you killed the fatted calf for him.'

31 "And he said to him, 'Son, you are always with me, and all that I have is yours.

32 'It was right that we should make merry and be glad, [a]for your brother was dead and is alive again, and was lost and is found.' "

The Parable of the Unjust Steward

16 He also said to His disciples: "There was a certain rich man who had a steward, and an accusation was brought to him that this man was wasting his goods.

2 "So he called him and said to him, 'What is this I hear about you? Give an [a]account of your stewardship, for you can no longer be steward.'

3 "Then the steward said within himself, 'What shall I do? For my master is taking the stewardship away from me. I cannot dig; I am ashamed to beg.

4 'I have resolved what to do, that when I am put out of the stewardship, they may receive me into their houses.'

5 "So he called every one of his master's debtors to *him,* and said to the first, 'How much do you owe my master?'

6 "And he said, 'A hundred *measures of oil.' So he said to him, 'Take your bill, and sit down quickly and write fifty.'

7 "Then he said to another, 'And how much do you owe?' So he said, 'A hundred *measures

KJV

of wheat. And he said unto him, Take thy bill, and write fourscore.

8 And the lord commended the unjust steward, because he had done wisely: for the children of this world are in their generation wiser than [a]the children of light.

9 And I say unto you, [a]Make to yourselves friends of the mammon of unrighteousness; that, when ye fail, they may receive you into everlasting habitations.

10 [a]He that is faithful in that which is least is faithful also in much: and he that is unjust in the least is unjust also in much.

11 If therefore ye have not been faithful in the unrighteous mammon, who will commit to your trust the true *riches?*

12 And if ye have not been faithful in that which is another man's, who shall give you that which is your [a]own?

13 [a]No servant can serve two masters: for either he will hate the one, and love the other; or else he will hold to the one, and despise the other. Ye cannot serve God and mammon.

The Law, the Prophets, and the Kingdom

14 And the Pharisees also, [a]who were covetous, heard all these things: and they derided him.

15 And he said unto them, Ye are they which [a]justify yourselves [b]before men; but [c]God knoweth your hearts: for [d]that which is highly esteemed among men is abomination in the sight of God.

16 [a]The law and the prophets *were* until John: since that time the kingdom of God is preached, and every man presseth into it.

17 [a]And it is easier for heaven and earth to pass, than one tittle of the law to fail.

18 [a]Whosoever putteth away his wife, and marrieth another, committeth adultery: and whosoever marrieth her that is put away from *her* husband committeth adultery.

The Rich Man and Lazarus

19 There was a certain rich man, which was clothed in purple and fine linen, and fared sumptuously every day:

20 And there was a certain beggar named Lazarus, which was laid at his gate, full of sores,

21 And desiring to be fed with the crumbs which fell from the rich man's table: moreover the dogs came and licked his sores.

22 And it came to pass, that the beggar died, and was carried by the angels into [a]Abraham's bosom: the rich man also died, and was buried;

23 And in hell he lift up his eyes, being in torments, and seeth Abraham afar off, and Lazarus in his bosom.

24 And he cried and said, Father Abraham, have mercy on me, and send Lazarus, that he may dip the tip of his finger in water, and [a]cool my tongue; for I [b]am tormented in this flame.

25 But Abraham said, Son, [a]remember that thou in thy lifetime receivedst thy good things, and likewise Lazarus evil things: but now he is comforted, and thou art tormented.

26 And beside all this, between us and you there is a great gulf fixed: so that they which would pass from hence to you cannot; neither can they pass to us, that *would come* from thence.

27 Then he said, I pray thee therefore, father, that thou wouldest send him to my father's house:

28 For I have five brethren; that he may testify unto them, lest they also come into this place of torment.

29 Abraham saith unto him, [a]They have Moses and the prophets; let them hear them.

30 And he said, Nay, father Abraham: but if one went unto them from the dead, they will repent.

31 And he said unto him, [a]If they hear not

---

8 [a][John 12:36; Eph. 5:8]; 1 Thess. 5:5
9 [a]Dan. 4:27; [Matt. 6:19; 19:21]; Luke 11:41; [1 Tim. 6:17–19]
10 [a]Matt. 25:21; Luke 19:17
12 [a][1 Pet. 1:3, 4]
13 [a]Matt. 6:24; Gal. 1:10
14 [a]Matt. 23:14
15 [a]Luke 10:29 [b][Matt. 6:2, 5, 16] [c]1 Chr. 28:9; 2 Chr. 6:30; Ps. 7:9; Prov. 15:11; Jer. 17:10 [d]1 Sam. 16:7; Ps. 10:3; Prov. 6:16–19; 16:5
16 [a]Matt. 3:1–12; 4:17; 11:12, 13; Luke 7:29
17 [a]Ps. 102:26, 27; Is. 40:8; 51:6; Matt. 5:18; 1 Pet. 1:25
18 [a]Matt. 5:32; 19:9; Mark 10:11; 1 Cor. 7:10, 11
22 [a]Matt. 8:11
24 [a]Zech. 14:12 [b][Is. 66:24; Mark 9:42–48]
25 [a]Job 21:13; Luke 6:24; James 5:5
29 [a]Is. 8:20; 34:16; [John 5:39, 45]; Acts 15:21; 17:11; [2 Tim. 3:15]
31 [a][John 5:46]

---

*

16:9 NU *it fails*
16:21 NU *what fell*

NKJV

of wheat.' And he said to him, 'Take your bill, and write eighty.'

8 "So the master commended the unjust steward because he had dealt shrewdly. For the sons of this world are more shrewd in their generation than [a]the sons of light.

9 "And I say to you, [a]make friends for yourselves by unrighteous mammon, that when *you fail, they may receive you into an everlasting home.

10 [a]"He who *is* faithful in *what is* least is faithful also in much; and he who is unjust in *what is* least is unjust also in much.

11 "Therefore if you have not been faithful in the unrighteous mammon, who will commit to your trust the true *riches?*

12 "And if you have not been faithful in what is another man's, who will give you what is your [a]own?

13 [a]"No servant can serve two masters; for either he will hate the one and love the other, or else he will be loyal to the one and despise the other. You cannot serve God and mammon."

The Law, the Prophets, and the Kingdom

14 Now the Pharisees, [a]who were lovers of money, also heard all these things, and they derided Him.

15 And He said to them, "You are those who [a]justify yourselves [b]before men, but [c]God knows your hearts. For [d]what is highly esteemed among men is an abomination in the sight of God.

16 [a]"The law and the prophets *were* until John. Since that time the kingdom of God has been preached, and everyone is pressing into it.

17 [a]"And it is easier for heaven and earth to pass away than for one tittle of the law to fail.

18 [a]"Whoever divorces his wife and marries another commits adultery; and whoever marries her who is divorced from *her* husband commits adultery.

The Rich Man and Lazarus

19 "There was a certain rich man who was clothed in purple and fine linen and fared sumptuously every day.

20 "But there was a certain beggar named Lazarus, full of sores, who was laid at his gate,

21 "desiring to be fed with *the crumbs which fell from the rich man's table. Moreover the dogs came and licked his sores.

22 "So it was that the beggar died, and was carried by the angels to [a]Abraham's bosom. The rich man also died and was buried.

23 "And being in torments in Hades, he lifted up his eyes and saw Abraham afar off, and Lazarus in his bosom.

24 "Then he cried and said, 'Father Abraham, have mercy on me, and send Lazarus that he may dip the tip of his finger in water and [a]cool my tongue; for I [b]am tormented in this flame.'

25 "But Abraham said, 'Son, [a]remember that in your lifetime you received your good things, and likewise Lazarus evil things; but now he is comforted and you are tormented.

26 'And besides all this, between us and you there is a great gulf fixed, so that those who want to pass from here to you cannot, nor can those from there pass to us.'

27 "Then he said, 'I beg you therefore, father, that you would send him to my father's house,

28 'for I have five brothers, that he may testify to them, lest they also come to this place of torment.'

29 "Abraham said to him, [a]'They have Moses and the prophets; let them hear them.'

30 "And he said, 'No, father Abraham; but if one goes to them from the dead, they will repent.'

31 "But he said to him, [a]'If they do not hear

KJV

Moses and the prophets, [b]neither will they be persuaded, though one rose from the dead.

Jesus Warns of Offenses
(*Matt. 18:6, 7; Mark 9:42*)

17 Then said he unto the disciples, [a]It is impossible but that offences will come: but
[b]woe *unto him,* through whom they come!
2 It were better for him that a millstone
were hanged about his neck, and he cast into the
sea, than that he should offend one of these little
ones.
3 Take heed to yourselves: [a]If thy brother
trespass against thee, [b]rebuke him; and if he repent, forgive him.
4 And if he trespass against thee seven
times in a day, and seven times in a day turn again
to thee, saying, I repent; thou shalt forgive him.

Faith and Duty
(*Matt. 17:19–21; Mark 9:28, 29*)

5 And the apostles said unto the Lord, Increase our faith.
6 [a]And the Lord said, If ye had faith as a
grain of mustard seed, ye might say unto this
sycamine tree, Be thou plucked up by the root,
and be thou planted in the sea; and it should obey
you.
7 But which of you, having a servant plowing or feeding cattle, will say unto him by and
by, when he is come from the field, Go and sit
down to meat?
8 And will not rather say unto him, Make
ready wherewith I may sup, and gird thyself, [a]and
serve me, till I have eaten and drunken; and afterward thou shalt eat and drink?
9 Doth he thank that servant because he did
the things that were commanded him? I trow not.
10 So likewise ye, when ye shall have done
all those things which are commanded you, say,
We are [a]unprofitable servants: we have done that
which was our duty to do.

Ten Lepers Cleansed

11 And it came to pass, [a]as he went to Jerusalem, that he passed through the midst of Samaria
and Galilee.
12 And as he entered into a certain village,
there met him ten men that were lepers, [a]which
stood afar off:
13 And they lifted up *their* voices, and said,
Jesus, Master, have mercy on us.
14 And when he saw *them,* he said unto
them, [a]Go shew yourselves unto the priests. And
it came to pass, that, as they went, they were
cleansed.
15 And one of them, when he saw that he
was healed, turned back, and with a loud voice
[a]glorified God,
16 And fell down on *his* face at his feet, giving him thanks: and he was a [a]Samaritan.
17 And Jesus answering said, Were there not
ten cleansed? but where *are* the nine?
18 There are not found that returned to give
glory to God, save this stranger.
19 [a]And he said unto him, Arise, go thy way:
thy faith hath made thee whole.

The Coming of the Kingdom
(*Gen. 6:5—8:22; 19:12–14*)

20 And when he was demanded of the Pharisees, when the kingdom of God should come, he
answered them and said, The kingdom of God
cometh not with observation:
21 [a]Neither shall they say, Lo here! or, lo
there! for, behold, [b]the kingdom of God is within
you.
22 And he said unto the disciples, [a]The days
will come, when ye shall desire to see one of the
days of the Son of man, and ye shall not see *it.*
23 [a]And they shall say to you, See here; or,
see there: go not after *them,* nor follow *them.*

NKJV

Moses and the prophets, [b]neither will they be persuaded though one rise from the dead.' "

Jesus Warns of Offenses
(*Matt. 18:6, 7; Mark 9:42*)

17 Then He said to the disciples, [a]"It is impossible that no offenses should come, but
[b]woe *to him* through whom they do come!
2 "It would be better for him if a millstone
were hung around his neck, and he were thrown
into the sea, than that he should offend one of
these little ones.
3 "Take heed to yourselves. [a]If your brother
sins *against you, [b]rebuke him; and if he repents,
forgive him.
4 "And if he sins against you seven times
in a day, and seven times in a day returns *to
you, saying, 'I repent,' you shall forgive him."

Faith and Duty
(*Matt. 17:19–21; Mark 9:28, 29*)

5 And the apostles said to the Lord, "Increase our faith."
6 [a]So the Lord said, "If you have faith as a
mustard seed, you can say to this mulberry tree,
'Be pulled up by the roots and be planted in the
sea,' and it would obey you.
7 "And which of you, having a servant
plowing or tending sheep, will say to him when
he has come in from the field, 'Come at once and
sit down to eat'?
8 "But will he not rather say to him, 'Prepare something for my supper, and gird yourself
[a]and serve me till I have eaten and drunk, and
afterward you will eat and drink'?
9 "Does he thank that servant because he
did the things that were commanded *him? I think
not.
10 "So likewise you, when you have done all
those things which you are commanded, say, 'We
are [a]unprofitable servants. We have done what
was our duty to do.' "

Ten Lepers Cleansed

11 Now it happened [a]as He went to Jerusalem that He passed through the midst of Samaria
and Galilee.
12 Then as He entered a certain village, there
met Him ten men who were lepers, [a]who stood
afar off.
13 And they lifted up *their* voices and said,
"Jesus, Master, have mercy on us!"
14 So when He saw *them,* He said to them,
[a]"Go, show yourselves to the priests." And so it
was that as they went, they were cleansed.
15 And one of them, when he saw that he
was healed, returned, and with a loud voice [a]glori-
fied God,
16 and fell down on *his* face at His feet, giving Him thanks. And he was a [a]Samaritan.
17 So Jesus answered and said, "Were there
not ten cleansed? But where *are* the nine?
18 "Were there not any found who returned
to give glory to God except this foreigner?"
19 [a]And He said to him, "Arise, go your way.
Your faith has made you well."

The Coming of the Kingdom
(*Gen. 6:5—8:22; 19:12–14*)

20 Now when He was asked by the Pharisees
when the kingdom of God would come, He answered them and said, "The kingdom of God does
not come with observation;
21 [a]"nor will they say, *'See here!' or 'See
there!' For indeed, [b]the kingdom of God is within
you."
22 Then He said to the disciples, [a]"The days
will come when you will desire to see one of the
days of the Son of Man, and you will not see *it.*
23 [a]"And they will say to you, *'Look here!'
or 'Look there!' Do not go after *them* or follow
them.

---

31 [b]John 12:10, 11

CHAPTER 17

1 [a][1 Cor. 11:19] [b]Matt. 18:6, 7; 26:24; Mark 9:42; [2 Thess. 1:6]; Jude 11
3 [a][Matt. 18:15, 21] [b]Lev. 19:17; [Prov. 17:10; Gal. 6:1; James 5:19, 20]
6 [a]Matt. 17:20; 21:21; [Mark 9:23; 11:23]; Luke 13:19
8 [a][Luke 12:37]
10 [a]Job 22:3; 35:7; Ps. 16:2; Matt. 25:30; Rom. 3:12; 11:35; [1 Cor. 9:16, 17]; Philem. 11
11 [a]Luke 9:51, 52; John 4:4
12 [a]Lev. 13:46; Num. 5:2
14 [a]Lev. 13:1–59; 14:1–32; Matt. 8:4; Luke 5:14
15 [a]Luke 5:25; 18:43
16 [a]2 Kin. 17:24; Luke 9:52, 53; John 4:9
19 [a]Matt. 9:22; Mark 5:34; 10:52; Luke 7:50; 8:48; 18:42
21 [a]Luke 17:23 [b][Rom. 14:17]
22 [a]Matt. 9:15; Mark 2:20; Luke 5:35; [John 17:12]
23 [a]Matt. 24:23; Mark 13:21; [Luke 21:8]

*

17:3 NU omits *against you*
17:4 M omits *to you*
17:9 NU omits the rest of v. 9; M omits *him*
17:21 NU reverses *here* and *there*
17:23 NU reverses *here* and *there*

KJV

24 [a]For as the lightning, that lighteneth out of the one *part* under heaven, shineth unto the other *part* under heaven; so shall also the Son of man be in his day.

25 [a]But first must he suffer many things, and be [b]rejected of this generation.

26 [a]And as it [b]was in the [c]days of [d]Noe, so shall it be also in the days of the Son of man.

27 They did eat, they drank, they married wives, they were given in marriage, until the [a]day that Noe entered into the ark, and the flood came, and [b]destroyed them all.

28 [a]Likewise also as it was in the days of Lot; they did eat, they drank, they bought, they sold, they planted, they builded;

29 But [a]the same day that Lot went out of Sodom it rained fire and brimstone from heaven, and destroyed *them* all.

30 Even thus shall it be in the day when the Son of man [a]is revealed.

31 In that day, he [a]which shall be upon the housetop, and his stuff in the house, let him not come down to take it away: and he that is in the field, let him likewise not return back.

32 [a]Remember Lot's wife.

33 [a]Whosoever shall seek to save his life shall lose it; and whosoever shall lose his life shall preserve it.

34 [a]I tell you, in that night there shall be two *men* in one bed; the one shall be taken, and the other shall be left.

35 [a]Two *women* shall be grinding together; the one shall be taken, and the other left.

36 Two *men* shall be in the field; the one shall be taken, and the other left.

37 And they answered and said unto him, [a]Where, Lord? And he said unto them, Wheresoever the body *is,* thither will the eagles be gathered together.

The Parable of the Persistent Widow

18 And he spake a parable unto them *to this end,* that men ought [a]always to pray, and not to faint;

2 Saying, There was in a city a judge, which feared not God, neither regarded man:

3 And there was a widow in that city; and she came unto him, saying, Avenge me of mine adversary.

4 And he would not for a while: but afterward he said within himself, Though I fear not God, nor regard man;

5 [a]Yet because this widow troubleth me, I will avenge her, lest by her continual coming she weary me.

6 And the Lord said, Hear what the unjust judge saith.

7 And [a]shall not God avenge his own elect, which cry day and night unto him, though he bear long with them?

8 I tell you [a]that he will avenge them speedily. Nevertheless when the Son of man cometh, shall he find faith on the earth?

The Parable of the Pharisee and the Tax Collector

9 And he spake this parable unto certain [a]which trusted in themselves that they were righteous, and despised others:

10 Two men went up into the temple to pray; the one a Pharisee, and the other a publican.

11 The Pharisee [a]stood and prayed thus with himself, [b]God, I thank thee, that I am not as other men *are,* extortioners, unjust, adulterers, or even as this publican.

12 I fast twice in the week, I give tithes of all that I possess.

13 And the publican, standing afar off, would not lift up so much as *his* eyes unto heaven, but smote upon his breast, saying, God be merciful to me a sinner.

14 I tell you, this man went down to his house justified *rather* than the other: [a]for every one that

---

24 [a]Matt. 24:27
25 [a]Matt. 26:67; 27:29–31; Mark 8:31; 9:31; 10:33 [b]Luke 9:22
26 [a]Matt. 24:37–39 [b][Gen. 6:5–7] [c][Gen. 6:8–13] [d]1 Pet. 3:20
27 [a]Gen. 7:1–16 [b]Gen. 7:19–23
28 [a]Gen. 19
29 [a]Gen. 19:16, 24, 29; 2 Pet. 2:6, 7
30 [a][Matt. 16:27]; 1 Cor. 1:7; [Col. 3:4; 2 Thess. 1:7]; 1 Pet. 1:7; 4:13; 1 John 2:28
31 [a]Matt. 24:17, 18; Mark 13:15
32 [a]Gen. 19:26
33 [a]Matt. 10:39; 16:25; Mark 8:35; Luke 9:24; John 12:25
34 [a]Matt. 24:40, 41; [1 Thess. 4:17]
35 [a]Matt. 24:40, 41
37 [a]Job 39:30; Matt. 24:28

CHAPTER 18

1 [a]Luke 11:5–10; Rom. 12:12; [Eph. 6:18]; Col. 4:2; 1 Thess. 5:17
5 [a]Luke 11:8
7 [a]Rev. 6:10
8 [a]Heb. 10:37; [2 Pet. 3:8, 9]
9 [a]Prov. 30:12; Luke 10:29; 16:15
11 [a]Ps. 135:2 [b]Is. 1:15; 58:2; Rev. 3:17
14 [a]Job 22:29; Matt. 23:12; Luke 14:11; [James 4:6; 1 Pet. 5:5]

*________

17:36 NU, M omit v. 36.

NKJV

24 [a]"For as the lightning that flashes out of one *part* under heaven shines to the other *part* under heaven, so also the Son of Man will be in His day.

25 [a]"But first He must suffer many things and be [b]rejected by this generation.

26 [a]"And as it [b]was in the [c]days of [d]Noah, so it will be also in the days of the Son of Man:

27 "They ate, they drank, they married wives, they were given in marriage, until the [a]day that Noah entered the ark, and the flood came and [b]destroyed them all.

28 [a]"Likewise as it was also in the days of Lot: They ate, they drank, they bought, they sold, they planted, they built;

29 "but on [a]the day that Lot went out of Sodom it rained fire and brimstone from heaven and destroyed *them* all.

30 "Even so will it be in the day when the Son of Man [a]is revealed.

31 "In that day, he [a]who is on the housetop, and his goods *are* in the house, let him not come down to take them away. And likewise the one who is in the field, let him not turn back.

32 [a]"Remember Lot's wife.

33 [a]"Whoever seeks to save his life will lose it, and whoever loses his life will preserve it.

34 [a]"I tell you, in that night there will be two *men* in one bed: the one will be taken and the other will be left.

35 [a]"Two *women* will be grinding together: the one will be taken and the other left.

36 *"Two *men* will be in the field: the one will be taken and the other left."

37 And they answered and said to Him, [a]"Where, Lord?" So He said to them, "Wherever the body is, there the eagles will be gathered together."

The Parable of the Persistent Widow

18 Then He spoke a parable to them, that men [a]always ought to pray and not lose heart,

2 saying: "There was in a certain city a judge who did not fear God nor regard man.

3 "Now there was a widow in that city; and she came to him, saying, 'Get justice for me from my adversary.'

4 "And he would not for a while; but afterward he said within himself, 'Though I do not fear God nor regard man,

5 [a]'yet because this widow troubles me I will avenge her, lest by her continual coming she weary me.' "

6 Then the Lord said, "Hear what the unjust judge said.

7 "And [a]shall God not avenge His own elect who cry out day and night to Him, though He bears long with them?

8 "I tell you [a]that He will avenge them speedily. Nevertheless, when the Son of Man comes, will He really find faith on the earth?"

The Parable of the Pharisee and the Tax Collector

9 Also He spoke this parable to some [a]who trusted in themselves that they were righteous, and despised others:

10 "Two men went up to the temple to pray, one a Pharisee and the other a tax collector.

11 "The Pharisee [a]stood and prayed thus with himself, [b]'God, I thank You that I am not like other men—extortioners, unjust, adulterers, or even as this tax collector.

12 'I fast twice a week; I give tithes of all that I possess.'

13 "And the tax collector, standing afar off, would not so much as raise *his* eyes to heaven, but beat his breast, saying, 'God, be merciful to me a sinner!'

14 "I tell you, this man went down to his house justified *rather* than the other; [a]for every-

KJV

exalteth himself shall be abased; and he that humbleth himself shall be exalted.

Jesus Blesses Little Children
(Matt. 19:13–15; Mark 10:13–16)

15 [a]And they brought unto him also infants, that he would touch them: but when *his* disciples saw *it,* they rebuked them.

16 But Jesus called them *unto him,* and said, Suffer little children to come unto me, and forbid them not: for [a]of such is the kingdom of God.

17 [a]Verily I say unto you, Whosoever shall not receive the kingdom of God as a little child shall in no wise enter therein.

Jesus Counsels the Rich Young Ruler
(Matt. 19:16–22; Mark 10:17–22)

18 [a]And a certain ruler asked him, saying, Good Master, what shall I do to inherit eternal life?

19 And Jesus said unto him, Why callest thou me good? none *is* good, save [a]one, *that is,* God.

20 Thou knowest the commandments, [a]DO NOT COMMIT ADULTERY, DO NOT KILL, DO NOT STEAL, DO NOT BEAR FALSE WITNESS, [b]HONOUR THY FATHER AND THY MOTHER.

21 And he said, All [a]these have I kept from my youth up.

22 Now when Jesus heard these things, he said unto him, Yet lackest thou one thing: [a]sell all that thou hast, and distribute unto the poor, and thou shalt have treasure in heaven: and come, follow me.

23 And when he heard this, he was very sorrowful: for he was very rich.

With God All Things Are Possible
(Matt. 19:23–30; Mark 10:23–31)

24 And when Jesus saw that he was very sorrowful, he said, [a]How hardly shall they that have riches enter into the kingdom of God!

25 For it is easier for a camel to go through a needle's eye, than for a rich man to enter into the kingdom of God.

26 And they that heard *it* said, Who then can be saved?

27 And he said, [a]The things which are impossible with men are possible with God.

28 [a]Then Peter said, Lo, we have left all, and followed thee.

29 And he said unto them, Verily I say unto you, [a]There is no man that hath left house, or parents, or brethren, or wife, or children, for the kingdom of God's sake,

30 [a]Who shall not receive manifold more in this present time, and in the world to come life everlasting.

Jesus a Third Time Predicts His Death and Resurrection
(Matt. 20:17–19; Mark 10:32–34)

31 [a]Then he took *unto him* the twelve, and said unto them, Behold, we go up to Jerusalem, and all things [b]that are written by the prophets concerning the Son of man shall be accomplished.

32 For [a]he shall be delivered unto the Gentiles, and shall be mocked, and spitefully entreated, and spitted on:

33 And they shall scourge *him,* and put him to death: and the third day he shall rise again.

34 [a]And they understood none of these things: and this saying was hid from them, neither knew they the things which were spoken.

A Blind Man Receives His Sight
(Matt. 20:29–34; Mark 10:46–52)

35 [a]And it came to pass, that as he was come nigh unto Jericho, a certain blind man sat by the way side begging:

36 And hearing the multitude pass by, he asked what it meant.

15 [a]Matt. 19:13–15; Mark 10:13–16
16 [a]Matt. 18:3; 1 Cor. 14:20; 1 Pet. 2:2
17 [a]Matt. 18:3; 19:14; Mark 10:15
18 [a]Matt. 19:16–29; Mark 10:17–30
19 [a]Ps. 86:5; 119:68
20 [a]Ex. 20:12–16; Deut. 5:16–20; Mark 10:19; Rom. 13:9 [b]Eph. 6:2; Col. 3:20
21 [a]Phil. 3:6
22 [a]Matt. 6:19, 20; 19:21; [1 Tim. 6:19]
24 [a]Prov. 11:28; Matt. 19:23; Mark 10:23
27 [a]Job 42:2; Jer. 32:17; Zech. 8:6; Matt. 19:26; Luke 1:37
28 [a]Matt. 19:27
29 [a]Deut. 33:9
30 [a]Job 42:10
31 [a]Matt. 16:21; 17:22; 20:17; Mark 10:32; Luke 9:51 [b]Ps. 22; [Is. 53]
32 [a]Matt. 26:67; 27:2, 29, 41; Mark 14:65; 15:1, 19, 20, 31; Luke 23:1; John 18:28; Acts 3:13
34 [a]Mark 9:32; Luke 2:50; 9:45; [John 10:6; 12:16]
35 [a]Matt. 20:29–34; Mark 10:46–52

NKJV

one who exalts himself will be humbled, and he who humbles himself will be exalted."

Jesus Blesses Little Children
(Matt. 19:13–15; Mark 10:13–16)

15 [a]Then they also brought infants to Him that He might touch them; but when the disciples saw *it,* they rebuked them.

16 But Jesus called them to *Him* and said, "Let the little children come to Me, and do not forbid them; for [a]of such is the kingdom of God.

17 [a]"Assuredly, I say to you, whoever does not receive the kingdom of God as a little child will by no means enter it."

Jesus Counsels the Rich Young Ruler
(Matt. 19:16–22; Mark 10:17–22)

18 [a]Now a certain ruler asked Him, saying, "Good Teacher, what shall I do to inherit eternal life?"

19 So Jesus said to him, "Why do you call Me good? No one *is* good but [a]One, *that is,* God.

20 "You know the commandments: [a]*'Do not commit adultery,' 'Do not murder,' 'Do not steal,' 'Do not bear false witness,'* [b]*'Honor your father and your mother.'* "

21 And he said, "All [a]these things I have kept from my youth."

22 So when Jesus heard these things, He said to him, "You still lack one thing. [a]Sell all that you have and distribute to the poor, and you will have treasure in heaven; and come, follow Me."

23 But when he heard this, he became very sorrowful, for he was very rich.

With God All Things Are Possible
(Matt. 19:23–30; Mark 10:23–31)

24 And when Jesus saw that he became very sorrowful, He said, [a]"How hard it is for those who have riches to enter the kingdom of God!

25 "For it is easier for a camel to go through the eye of a needle than for a rich man to enter the kingdom of God."

26 And those who heard it said, "Who then can be saved?"

27 But He said, [a]"The things which are impossible with men are possible with God."

28 [a]Then Peter said, "See, we have left *all and followed You."

29 So He said to them, "Assuredly, I say to you, [a]there is no one who has left house or parents or brothers or wife or children, for the sake of the kingdom of God,

30 [a]"who shall not receive many times more in this present time, and in the age to come eternal life."

Jesus a Third Time Predicts His Death and Resurrection
(Matt. 20:17–19; Mark 10:32–34)

31 [a]Then He took the twelve aside and said to them, "Behold, we are going up to Jerusalem, and all things [b]that are written by the prophets concerning the Son of Man will be accomplished.

32 "For [a]He will be delivered to the Gentiles and will be mocked and insulted and spit upon.

33 "They will scourge *Him* and kill Him. And the third day He will rise again."

34 [a]But they understood none of these things; this saying was hidden from them, and they did not know the things which were spoken.

A Blind Man Receives His Sight
(Matt. 20:29–34; Mark 10:46–52)

35 [a]Then it happened, as He was coming near Jericho, that a certain blind man sat by the road begging.

36 And hearing a multitude passing by, he asked what it meant.

*______

18:28 NU *our own*

KJV

37 And they told him, that Jesus of Nazareth passeth by.

38 And he cried, saying, Jesus, *thou* [a]son of David, have mercy on me.

39 And they which went before rebuked him, that he should hold his peace: but he cried so much the more, *Thou* son of David, have mercy on me.

40 And Jesus stood, and commanded him to be brought unto him: and when he was come near, he asked him,

41 Saying, What wilt thou that I shall do unto thee? And he said, Lord, that I may receive my sight.

42 And Jesus said unto him, Receive thy sight: [a]thy faith hath saved thee.

43 And immediately he received his sight, and followed him, [a]glorifying God: and all the people, when they saw *it*, gave praise unto God.

Jesus Comes to Zacchaeus' House

19 And *Jesus* entered and passed through [a]Jericho.

2 And, behold, *there was* a man named Zacchaeus, which was the chief among the publicans, and he was rich.

3 And he sought to [a]see Jesus who he was; and could not for the press, because he was little of stature.

4 And he ran before, and climbed up into a sycomore tree to see him: for he was to pass that *way*.

5 And when Jesus came to the place, he looked up, and saw him, and said unto him, Zacchaeus, make haste, and come down; for to day I must abide at thy house.

6 And he made haste, and came down, and received him joyfully.

7 And when they saw *it*, they all murmured, saying, [a]That he was gone to be guest with a man that is a sinner.

8 And Zacchaeus stood, and said unto the Lord; Behold, Lord, the half of my goods I give to the [a]poor; and if I have taken any thing from any man by [b]false accusation, [c]I restore *him* fourfold.

9 And Jesus said unto him, This day is salvation come to this house, forsomuch as [a]he also is [b]a son of Abraham.

10 [a]For the Son of man is come to seek and to save that which was lost.

The Parable of the Minas
(Matt. 25:14–30)

11 And as they heard these things, he added and spake a parable, because he was nigh to Jerusalem, and because [a]they thought that the kingdom of God should immediately appear.

12 [a]He said therefore, A certain nobleman went into a far country to receive for himself a kingdom, and to return.

13 And he called his ten servants, and delivered them ten pounds, and said unto them, Occupy till I come.

14 [a]But his citizens hated him, and sent a message after him, saying, We will not have this *man* to reign over us.

15 And it came to pass, that when he was returned, having received the kingdom, then he commanded these servants to be called unto him, to whom he had given the money, that he might know how much every man had gained by trading.

16 Then came the first, saying, Lord, thy pound hath gained ten pounds.

17 And he said unto him, [a]Well, thou good servant: because thou hast been [b]faithful in a very little, have thou authority over ten cities.

18 And the second came, saying, Lord, thy pound hath gained five pounds.

19 And he said likewise to him, Be thou also over five cities.

NKJV

37 So they told him that Jesus of Nazareth was passing by.

38 And he cried out, saying, "Jesus, [a]Son of David, have mercy on me!"

39 Then those who went before warned him that he should be quiet; but he cried out all the more, "Son of David, have mercy on me!"

40 So Jesus stood still and commanded him to be brought to Him. And when he had come near, He asked him,

41 saying, "What do you want Me to do for you?" He said, "Lord, that I may receive my sight."

42 Then Jesus said to him, "Receive your sight; [a]your faith has made you well."

43 And immediately he received his sight, and followed Him, [a]glorifying God. And all the people, when they saw *it*, gave praise to God.

Jesus Comes to Zacchaeus' House

19 Then *Jesus* entered and passed through [a]Jericho.

2 Now behold, *there was* a man named Zacchaeus who was a chief tax collector, and he was rich.

3 And he sought to [a]see who Jesus was, but could not because of the crowd, for he was of short stature.

4 So he ran ahead and climbed up into a sycamore tree to see Him, for He was going to pass that *way*.

5 And when Jesus came to the place, He looked up *and saw him, and said to him, "Zacchaeus, make haste and come down, for today I must stay at your house."

6 So he made haste and came down, and received Him joyfully.

7 But when they saw *it*, they all complained, saying, [a]"He has gone to be a guest with a man who is a sinner."

8 Then Zacchaeus stood and said to the Lord, "Look, Lord, I give half of my goods to the [a]poor; and if I have taken anything from anyone by [b]false accusation, [c]I restore fourfold."

9 And Jesus said to him, "Today salvation has come to this house, because [a]he also is [b]a son of Abraham;

10 [a]"for the Son of Man has come to seek and to save that which was lost."

The Parable of the Minas
(Matt. 25:14–30)

11 Now as they heard these things, He spoke another parable, because He was near Jerusalem and because [a]they thought the kingdom of God would appear immediately.

12 [a]Therefore He said: "A certain nobleman went into a far country to receive for himself a kingdom and to return.

13 "So he called ten of his servants, delivered to them ten *minas, and said to them, 'Do business till I come.'

14 [a]"But his citizens hated him, and sent a delegation after him, saying, 'We will not have this *man* to reign over us.'

15 "And so it was that when he returned, having received the kingdom, he then commanded these servants, to whom he had given the money, to be called to him, that he might know how much every man had gained by trading.

16 "Then came the first, saying, 'Master, your mina has earned ten minas.'

17 "And he said to him, [a]'Well *done*, good servant; because you were [b]faithful in a very little, have authority over ten cities.'

18 "And the second came, saying, 'Master, your mina has earned five minas.'

19 "Likewise he said to him, 'You also be over five cities.'

---

38 [a]Matt. 9:27
42 [a]Luke 17:19
43 [a]Luke 5:26; Acts 4:21; 11:18

CHAPTER 19

1 [a]Josh. 6:26; 1 Kin. 16:34
3 [a]John 12:21
7 [a]Matt. 9:11; Luke 5:30; 15:2
8 [a][Ps. 41:1] [b]Luke 3:14 [c]Ex. 22:1; Lev. 6:5; Num. 5:7; 1 Sam. 12:3; 2 Sam. 12:6
9 [a]Luke 3:8; 13:16; [Rom. 4:16; Gal. 3:7] [b][Luke 13:16]
10 [a]Matt. 18:11; [Luke 5:32; Rom. 5:8]
11 [a]Acts 1:6
12 [a]Matt. 25:14–30; Mark 13:34
14 [a][John 1:11]
17 [a]Matt. 25:21, 23 [b]Luke 16:10

*

19:5 NU omits *and saw him*
19:13 Gr. *mna*, same as Heb. *minah*, each worth about three months' salary

KJV

20 And another came, saying, Lord, behold, *here is* thy pound, which I have kept laid up in a napkin:

21 [a]For I feared thee, because thou art an austere man: thou takest up that thou layedst not down, and reapest that thou didst not sow.

22 And he saith unto him, [a]Out of thine own mouth will I judge thee, *thou* wicked servant. [b]Thou knewest that I was an austere man, taking up that I laid not down, and reaping that I did not sow:

23 Wherefore then gavest not thou my money into the bank, that at my coming I might have required mine own with usury?

24 And he said unto them that stood by, Take from him the pound, and give *it* to him that hath ten pounds.

25 (And they said unto him, Lord, he hath ten pounds.)

26 For I say unto you, [a]That unto every one which hath shall be given; and from him that hath not, even that he hath shall be taken away from him.

27 But those mine enemies, which would not that I should reign over them, bring hither, and slay *them* before me.

The Triumphal Entry
(*Matt. 21:1–11; Mark 11:1–11; John 12:12–19*)

28 And when he had thus spoken, [a]he went before, ascending up to Jerusalem.

29 [a]And it came to pass, when he was come nigh to Bethphage and [b]Bethany, at the mount called *the* [c]*mount* of Olives, he sent two of his disciples,

30 Saying, Go ye into the village over against *you;* in the which at your entering ye shall find a colt tied, whereon yet never man sat: loose him, and bring *him hither.*

31 And if any man ask you, Why do ye loose *him?* thus shall ye say unto him, Because the Lord hath need of him.

32 And they that were sent went their way, and found even [a]as he had said unto them.

33 And as they were loosing the colt, the owners thereof said unto them, Why loose ye the colt?

34 And they said, The Lord hath need of him.

35 And they brought him to Jesus: [a]and they cast their garments upon the colt, and they set Jesus thereon.

36 And as he went, they spread their clothes in the way.

37 And when he was come nigh, even now at the descent of the mount of Olives, the whole multitude of the disciples began to [a]rejoice and praise God with a loud voice for all the mighty works that they had seen;

38 Saying, [a]BLESSED *BE* THE KING THAT COMETH IN THE NAME OF THE LORD: [b]peace in heaven, and glory in the highest.

39 And some of the Pharisees from among the multitude said unto him, Master, rebuke thy disciples.

40 And he answered and said unto them, I tell you that, if these should hold their peace, [a]the stones would immediately cry out.

Jesus Weeps over Jerusalem

41 And when he was come near, he beheld the city, and [a]wept over it,

42 Saying, If thou hadst known, even thou, at least in this [a]thy day, the things *which* [b]*belong* unto thy [c]peace! but now they are hid from thine eyes.

43 For the days shall come upon thee, that thine enemies shall [a]cast a trench about thee, and compass thee round, and keep thee in on every side,

44 And [a]shall lay thee even with the ground, and thy children within thee; and [b]they shall not

21 [a]Matt. 25:24
22 [a]2 Sam. 1:16; Job 15:6; [Matt. 12:37] [b]Matt. 25:26
26 [a]Matt. 13:12; 25:29; Mark 4:25; Luke 8:18
28 [a]Mark 10:32
29 [a]Matt. 21:1; Mark 11:1 [b]Matt. 26:6; John 12:1 [c]John 8:1; Acts 1:12
32 [a]Luke 22:13
35 [a]2 Kin. 9:13; Matt. 21:7; Mark 11:7
37 [a]Luke 13:17; 18:43
38 [a]Ps. 118:26; Luke 13:35 [b]Luke 2:14; [Eph. 2:14]
40 [a]Hab. 2:11
41 [a]Is. 53:3; John 11:35
42 [a]Ps. 95:7, 8; Heb. 3:13 [b][Luke 1:77–79; Acts 10:36] [c][Rom. 5:1]
43 [a]Is. 29:3, 4; Jer. 6:3, 6; Luke 21:20
44 [a]1 Kin. 9:7, 8; Mic. 3:12 [b]Matt. 24:2; Mark 13:2; Luke 21:6

*———

19:29 M *Bethsphage*

NKJV

20 "Then another came, saying, 'Master, here is your mina, which I have kept put away in a handkerchief.

21 [a]'For I feared you, because you are an austere man. You collect what you did not deposit, and reap what you did not sow.'

22 "And he said to him, [a]'Out of your own mouth I will judge you, *you* wicked servant. [b]You knew that I was an austere man, collecting what I did not deposit and reaping what I did not sow.

23 'Why then did you not put my money in the bank, that at my coming I might have collected it with interest?'

24 "And he said to those who stood by, 'Take the mina from him, and give *it* to him who has ten minas.'

25 ("But they said to him, 'Master, he has ten minas.')

26 'For I say to you, [a]that to everyone who has will be given; and from him who does not have, even what he has will be taken away from him.

27 'But bring here those enemies of mine, who did not want me to reign over them, and slay *them* before me.' "

The Triumphal Entry
(*Matt. 21:1–11; Mark 11:1–11; John 12:12–19*)

28 When He had said this, [a]He went on ahead, going up to Jerusalem.

29 [a]And it came to pass, when He drew near to *Bethphage and [b]Bethany, at the mountain called [c]Olivet, *that* He sent two of His disciples,

30 saying, "Go into the village opposite *you,* where as you enter you will find a colt tied, on which no one has ever sat. Loose it and bring *it here.*

31 "And if anyone asks you, 'Why are you loosing *it?'* thus you shall say to him, 'Because the Lord has need of it.' "

32 So those who were sent went their way and found *it* just [a]as He had said to them.

33 But as they were loosing the colt, the owners of it said to them, "Why are you loosing the colt?"

34 And they said, "The Lord has need of him."

35 Then they brought him to Jesus. [a]And they threw their own clothes on the colt, and they set Jesus on him.

36 And as He went, *many* spread their clothes on the road.

37 Then, as He was now drawing near the descent of the Mount of Olives, the whole multitude of the disciples began to [a]rejoice and praise God with a loud voice for all the mighty works they had seen,

38 saying:

> [a]" *'Blessed is the King who comes in the*
> *name of the LORD!'*
> [b]Peace in heaven and glory in the highest!"

39 And some of the Pharisees called to Him from the crowd, "Teacher, rebuke Your disciples."

40 But He answered and said to them, "I tell you that if these should keep silent, [a]the stones would immediately cry out."

Jesus Weeps over Jerusalem

41 Now as He drew near, He saw the city and [a]wept over it,

42 saying, "If you had known, even you, especially in this [a]your day, the things *that* [b]*make* for your [c]peace! But now they are hidden from your eyes.

43 "For days will come upon you when your enemies will [a]build an embankment around you, surround you and close you in on every side,

44 [a]"and level you, and your children within you, to the ground; and [b]they will not leave in

KJV

leave in thee one stone upon another; [c]because
thou knewest not the time of thy visitation.

Jesus Cleanses the Temple
(Matt. 21:12–17; Mark 11:15–19; John 2:12–25)

45 [a]And he went into the temple, and began
to cast out them that sold therein, and them that
bought;
46 Saying unto them, [a]It is written, MY HOUSE
IS THE HOUSE OF PRAYER: but ye have made it a
[b]DEN OF THIEVES.
47 And he [a]taught daily in the temple. But
[b]the chief priests and the scribes and the chief
of the people sought to destroy him,
48 And could not find what they might do:
for all the people were very attentive to [a]hear him.

Jesus' Authority Questioned
(Matt. 21:23–27; Mark 11:27–33)

20 And [a]it came to pass, *that* on one of those
days, as he taught the people in the temple,
and preached the gospel, the chief priests and the
scribes came upon *him* with the elders,
2 And spake unto him, saying, Tell us, [a]by
what authority doest thou these things? or who
is he that gave thee this authority?
3 And he answered and said unto them, I
will also ask you one thing; and answer me:
4 The [a]baptism of John, was it from heaven,
or of men?
5 And they reasoned with themselves, saying, If we shall say, From heaven; he will say,
Why then believed ye him not?
6 But and if we say, Of men; all the people
will stone us: [a]for they be persuaded that John
was a prophet.
7 And they answered, that they could not
tell whence *it was.*
8 And Jesus said unto them, Neither tell I
you by what authority I do these things.

The Parable of the Wicked Vinedressers
(Matt. 21:33–46; Mark 12:1–12)

9 Then began he to speak to the people this
parable; [a]A certain man planted a vineyard, and
let it forth to husbandmen, and went into a far
country for a long time.
10 And at the season he [a]sent a servant to
the husbandmen, that they should give him of the
fruit of the vineyard: but the husbandmen beat
him, and sent *him* away empty.
11 And again he sent another servant: and
they beat him also, and entreated *him* shamefully,
and sent *him* away empty.
12 And again he sent a third: and they
wounded him also, and cast *him* out.
13 Then said the lord of the vineyard, What
shall I do? I will send my beloved son: it may be
they will reverence *him* when they see him.
14 But when the husbandmen saw him, they
reasoned among themselves, saying, This is the
[a]heir: come, [b]let us kill him, that the inheritance
may be [c]our's.
15 So they cast him out of the vineyard, and
[a]killed *him.* What therefore shall the lord of the
vineyard do unto them?
16 He shall come and destroy these husbandmen, and shall give the vineyard to [a]others. And
when they heard *it,* they said, God forbid.
17 And he beheld them, and said, What is
this then that is written, [a]THE STONE WHICH THE
BUILDERS REJECTED, THE SAME IS BECOME THE HEAD
OF THE CORNER?
18 Whosoever shall fall upon that stone shall
be [a]broken; but [b]on whomsoever it shall fall, it
will grind him to powder.
19 And the chief priests and the scribes the
same hour sought to lay hands on him; and they

44 [c][Dan. 9:24; Luke 1:68, 78; 1 Pet. 2:12]
45 [a]Mal. 3:1; Matt. 21:12, 13; Mark 11:11, 15–17; John 2:13–16
46 [a]Is. 56:7 [b]Jer. 7:11
47 [a]Luke 21:37; 22:53 [b]Mark 11:18; Luke 20:19; John 7:19; 8:37
48 [a]Luke 21:38

CHAPTER 20
1 [a]Matt. 21:23–27; Mark 11:27–33
2 [a]Acts 4:7; 7:27
4 [a]John 1:26, 31
6 [a]Matt. 14:5; 21:26; Mark 6:20; Luke 7:24–30
9 [a]Ps. 80:8; Matt. 21:33–46; Mark 12:1–12
10 [a]2 Kin. 17:13, 14; 2 Chr. 36:15, 16; [Acts 7:52; 1 Thess. 2:15]
14 [a][Heb. 1:1–3] [b]Matt. 27:21–23 [c]John 11:47, 48
15 [a]Luke 23:33; Acts 2:22, 23; 3:15
16 [a][John 1:11–13]; Rom. 11:1, 11; 1 Cor. 6:15; Gal. 2:17; 3:21; 6:14
17 [a]Ps. 118:22; Matt. 21:42; 1 Pet. 2:7, 8
18 [a]Is. 8:14, 15 [b][Dan. 2:34, 35, 44, 45]; Matt. 21:44

NKJV

you one stone upon another, [c]because you did not
know the time of your visitation."

Jesus Cleanses the Temple
(Matt. 21:12–17; Mark 11:15–19; John 2:12–25)

45 [a]Then He went into the temple and began
to drive out those who *bought and sold in it,
46 saying to them, "It is written, [a]*'My house
is a house of prayer,' but you have made it a
[b]*'den of thieves.'*"
47 And He [a]was teaching daily in the temple.
But [b]the chief priests, the scribes, and the leaders
of the people sought to destroy Him,
48 and were unable to do anything; for all
the people were very attentive to [a]hear Him.

Jesus' Authority Questioned
(Matt. 21:23–27; Mark 11:27–33)

20 Now [a]it happened on one of those days,
as He taught the people in the temple and
preached the gospel, *that* the chief priests and
the scribes, together with the elders, confronted
Him
2 and spoke to Him, saying, "Tell us, [a]by
what authority are You doing these things? Or
who is he who gave You this authority?"
3 But He answered and said to them, "I also
will ask you one thing, and answer Me:
4 "The [a]baptism of John—was it from
heaven or from men?"
5 And they reasoned among themselves,
saying, "If we say, 'From heaven,' He will say,
'Why *then did you not believe him?'
6 "But if we say, 'From men,' all the people
will stone us, [a]for they are persuaded that John
was a prophet."
7 So they answered that they did not know
where *it was* from.
8 And Jesus said to them, "Neither will I
tell you by what authority I do these things."

The Parable of the Wicked Vinedressers
(Matt. 21:33–46; Mark 12:1–12)

9 Then He began to tell the people this parable: [a]"A certain man planted a vineyard, leased
it to vinedressers, and went into a far country for
a long time.
10 "Now at vintage-time he [a]sent a servant
to the vinedressers, that they might give him some
of the fruit of the vineyard. But the vinedressers
beat him and sent *him* away empty-handed.
11 "Again he sent another servant; and they
beat him also, treated *him* shamefully, and sent
him away empty-handed.
12 "And again he sent a third; and they
wounded him also and cast *him* out.
13 "Then the owner of the vineyard said,
'What shall I do? I will send my beloved son.
Probably they will respect *him* when they see
him.'
14 "But when the vinedressers saw him, they
reasoned among themselves, saying, 'This is the
[a]heir. Come, [b]let us kill him, that the inheritance
may be [c]ours.'
15 "So they cast him out of the vineyard and
[a]killed *him.* Therefore what will the owner of the
vineyard do to them?
16 "He will come and destroy those vinedressers and give the vineyard to [a]others." And
when they heard *it* they said, "Certainly not!"
17 Then He looked at them and said, "What
then is this that is written:

[a]*'The stone which the builders rejected*
Has become the chief cornerstone'?

18 "Whoever falls on that stone will be [a]bro-
ken; but [b]on whomever it falls, it will grind him
to powder."
19 And the chief priests and the scribes that
very hour sought to lay hands on Him, but they

*
19:45 NU *were selling, saying*
19:46 NU *shall be*
20:5 NU, M omit *then*

KJV

feared the people: for they perceived that he had spoken this parable against them.

The Pharisees: Is It Lawful to Pay Taxes to Caesar?
(Matt. 22:15–22; Mark 12:13–17)

20 [a]And they watched *him*, and sent forth spies, which should feign themselves just men, that they might take hold of his words, that so they might deliver him unto the power and authority of the governor.

21 And they asked him, saying, [a]Master, we know that thou sayest and teachest rightly, neither acceptest thou the person *of any*, but teachest the way of God truly:

22 Is it lawful for us to give tribute unto Caesar, or no?

23 But he perceived their craftiness, and said unto them, Why tempt ye me?

24 Shew me a penny. Whose image and superscription hath it? They answered and said, Caesar's.

25 And he said unto them, [a]Render therefore unto Caesar the things which be Caesar's, and unto God the things which be God's.

26 And they could not take hold of his words before the people: and they marvelled at his answer, and held their peace.

The Sadducees: What About the Resurrection?
(Matt. 22:23–33; Mark 12:18–27)

27 [a]Then came to *him* certain of the Sadducees, [b]which deny that there is any resurrection; and they asked him,

28 Saying, Master, Moses wrote unto us, If any man's brother die, having a wife, and he die without children, that his brother should take his wife, and raise up seed unto his brother.

29 There were therefore seven brethren: and the first took a wife, and died without children.

30 And the second took her to wife, and he died childless.

31 And the third took her; and in like manner the seven also: and they left no children, and died.

32 Last of all the woman died also.

33 Therefore in the resurrection whose wife of them is she? for seven had her to wife.

34 And Jesus answering said unto them, The children of this world marry, and are given in marriage:

35 But they which shall be [a]accounted worthy to obtain that world, and the resurrection from the dead, neither marry, nor are given in marriage:

36 Neither can they die any more: for [a]they are equal unto the angels; and are the children of God, [b]being the children of the resurrection.

37 Now that the dead are raised, even Moses shewed at the bush, when he calleth the Lord [a]THE GOD OF ABRAHAM, AND THE GOD OF ISAAC, AND THE GOD OF JACOB.

38 For he is not a God of the dead, but of the living: for [a]all live unto him.

39 Then certain of the scribes answering said, Master, thou hast well said.

40 And after that they durst not ask him any *question at all*.

Jesus: How Can David Call His Descendant Lord?
(Matt. 22:41–46; Mark 12:35–37)

41 And he said unto them, [a]How say they that Christ is David's son?

42 And David himself saith in the book of Psalms, [a]THE LORD SAID UNTO MY LORD, SIT THOU ON MY RIGHT HAND,

43 TILL I MAKE THINE ENEMIES THY FOOTSTOOL.

44 David therefore calleth him LORD, [a]how is he then his son?

20 [a]Matt. 22:15
21 [a]Matt. 22:16; Mark 12:14
25 [a]Matt. 17:24–27; Rom. 13:7; [1 Pet. 2:13–17]
27 [a]Matt. 22:23–33; Mark 12:18–27 [b]Acts 23:6, 8
35 [a]Phil. 3:11
36 [a][1 Cor. 15:42, 49, 52; 1 John 3:2] [b]Rom. 8:23
37 [a]Ex. 3:1–6, 15; Acts 7:30–32
38 [a][Rom. 6:10, 11; 14:8, 9; Heb. 11:16]
41 [a]Matt. 22:41–46; Mark 12:35–37
42 [a]Ps. 110:1; Acts 2:34, 35
44 [a]Acts 13:22, 23; Rom. 1:3; 9:4, 5

NKJV

*feared the people—for they knew He had spoken this parable against them.

The Pharisees: Is It Lawful to Pay Taxes to Caesar?
(Matt. 22:15–22; Mark 12:13–17)

20 [a]So they watched *Him*, and sent spies who pretended to be righteous, that they might seize on His words, in order to deliver Him to the power and the authority of the governor.

21 Then they asked Him, saying, [a]"Teacher, we know that You say and teach rightly, and You do not show personal favoritism, but teach the way of God in truth:

22 "Is it lawful for us to pay taxes to Caesar or not?"

23 But He perceived their craftiness, and said to them, *"Why do you test Me?

24 "Show Me a denarius. Whose image and inscription does it have?" They answered and said, "Caesar's."

25 And He said to them, [a]"Render therefore to Caesar the things that are Caesar's, and to God the things that are God's."

26 But they could not catch Him in His words in the presence of the people. And they marveled at His answer and kept silent.

The Sadducees: What About the Resurrection?
(Matt. 22:23–33; Mark 12:18–27)

27 [a]Then some of the Sadducees, [b]who deny that there is a resurrection, came to *Him* and asked Him,

28 saying: "Teacher, Moses wrote to us *that* if a man's brother dies, having a wife, and he dies without children, his brother should take his wife and raise up offspring for his brother.

29 "Now there were seven brothers. And the first took a wife, and died without children.

30 "And the second *took her as wife, and he died childless.

31 "Then the third took her, and in like manner the seven *also; and they left no children, and died.

32 "Last of all the woman died also.

33 "Therefore, in the resurrection, whose wife does she become? For all seven had her as wife."

34 Jesus answered and said to them, "The sons of this age marry and are given in marriage.

35 "But those who are [a]counted worthy to attain that age, and the resurrection from the dead, neither marry nor are given in marriage;

36 "nor can they die anymore, for [a]they are equal to the angels and are sons of God, [b]being sons of the resurrection.

37 "But even Moses showed in the *burning* bush *passage* that the dead are raised, when he called the Lord [a]*'the God of Abraham, the God of Isaac, and the God of Jacob.'*

38 "For He is not the God of the dead but of the living, for [a]all live to Him."

39 Then some of the scribes answered and said, "Teacher, You have spoken well."

40 But after that they dared not question Him anymore.

Jesus: How Can David Call His Descendant Lord?
(Matt. 22:41–46; Mark 12:35–37)

41 And He said to them, [a]"How can they say that the Christ is the Son of David?

42 "Now David himself said in the Book of Psalms:

[a]'The LORD said to my Lord,
"Sit at My right hand,
43 *Till I make Your enemies Your*
footstool."'

44 "Therefore David calls Him *'Lord'*; [a]how is He then his Son?"

---

*

20:19 M *were afraid—for*
20:23 NU omits *Why do you test Me?*
20:30 NU omits the rest of v. 30.
20:31 NU, M *also left no children*

KJV

Beware of the Scribes
(Matt. 23:1–7; Mark 12:38–40)

45 [a]Then in the audience of all the people
he said unto his disciples,
46 [a]Beware of the scribes, which desire to
walk in long robes, and [b]love greetings in the
markets, and the highest seats in the synagogues,
and the chief rooms at feasts;
47 [a]Which devour widows' houses, and for
a [b]shew make long prayers: the same shall receive
greater damnation.

The Widow's Two Mites
(Mark 12:41–44)

21 And he looked up, [a]and saw the rich men
casting their gifts into the treasury.
2 And he saw also a certain [a]poor widow
casting in thither two [b]mites.
3 And he said, Of a truth I say unto you,
[a]that this poor widow hath cast in more than they
all:
4 For all these have of their abundance cast
in unto the offerings of God: but she of her penury
hath cast in [a]all the living that she had.

Jesus Predicts the Destruction of the Temple
(Matt. 24:1, 2; Mark 13:1, 2)

5 [a]And as some spake of the temple, how
it was adorned with goodly stones and gifts, he
said,
6 *As for* these things which ye behold, the
days will come, in the which [a]there shall not be
left one stone upon another, that shall not be
thrown down.

The Signs of the Times and the End of the Age
(Matt. 24:3–14; Mark 13:3–13)

7 And they asked him, saying, Master, but
when shall these things be? and what sign *will*
there be when these things shall come to pass?
8 And he said, [a]Take heed that ye be not
deceived: for many shall come in my name, saying,
I am *Christ;* and the time draweth near: go
ye not therefore after them.
9 But when ye shall hear of [a]wars and commotions,
be not terrified: for these things must
first come to pass; but the end *is* not by and by.
10 [a]Then said he unto them, Nation shall rise
against nation, and kingdom against kingdom:
11 And great [a]earthquakes shall be in divers
places, and famines, and pestilences; and fearful
sights and great signs shall there be from heaven.
12 [a]But before all these, they shall lay their
hands on you, and persecute *you,* delivering *you*
up to the synagogues, and [b]into prisons, [c]being
brought before kings and rulers [d]for my name's
sake.
13 And [a]it shall turn to you for a testimony.
14 [a]Settle *it* therefore in your hearts, not to
meditate before what ye shall answer:
15 For I will give you a mouth and wisdom,
[a]which all your adversaries shall not be able to
gainsay nor resist.
16 [a]And ye shall be betrayed both by parents,
and brethren, and kinsfolks, and friends; and
[b]*some* of you shall they cause to be put to death.
17 And [a]ye shall be hated of all *men* for my
name's sake.
18 [a]But there shall not an hair of your head
perish.
19 In your patience possess ye your souls.

The Destruction of Jerusalem
(Matt. 24:15–28; Mark 13:14–23)

20 [a]And when ye shall see Jerusalem compassed
with armies, then know that the desolation
thereof is nigh.
21 Then let them which are in Judaea flee
to the mountains; and let them which are in the
midst of it depart out; and let not them that are
in the countries enter thereinto.

45 [a]Matt. 23:1–7; Mark 12:38–40
46 [a]Matt. 23:5 [b]Luke 11:43; 14:7
47 [a]Matt. 23:14 [b][Matt. 6:5, 6]

CHAPTER 21

1 [a]Mark 12:41–44
2 [a][2 Cor. 6:10] [b]Mark 12:42
3 [a][2 Cor. 8:12]
4 [a][2 Cor. 8:12]
5 [a]Matt. 24:1; Mark 13:1
6 [a]Is. 64:10, 11; Lam. 2:6–9; Mic. 3:12; Luke 19:41–44
8 [a]Matt. 24:4; Mark 13:5; Eph. 5:6; 2 Thess. 2:3; [1 John 4:1]
9 [a]Rev. 6:4
10 [a]Matt. 24:7
11 [a]Rev. 6:12
12 [a]Mark 13:9; John 16:2; [Rev. 2:10] [b]Acts 4:3; 5:18; 12:4; 16:24 [c]Acts 25:23 [d]1 Pet. 2:13
13 [a][Phil. 1:12–14, 28; 2 Thess. 1:5]
14 [a]Matt. 10:19; Mark 13:11; Luke 12:11
15 [a]Acts 6:10
16 [a]Mic. 7:6; Mark 13:12 [b]Acts 7:59; 12:2
17 [a]Matt. 10:22
18 [a]Matt. 10:30; Luke 12:7
20 [a]Matt. 24:15; Mark 13:14

*

21:4 NU omits *for God*
21:8 NU omits *Therefore*

NKJV

Beware of the Scribes
(Matt. 23:1–7; Mark 12:38–40)

45 [a]Then, in the hearing of all the people, He
said to His disciples,
46 [a]"Beware of the scribes, who desire to go
around in long robes, [b]love greetings in the
marketplaces, the best seats in the synagogues,
and the best places at feasts,
47 [a]"who devour widows' houses, and for a
[b]pretense make long prayers. These will receive
greater condemnation."

The Widow's Two Mites
(Mark 12:41–44)

21 And He looked up [a]and saw the rich putting
their gifts into the treasury,
2 and He saw also a certain [a]poor widow
putting in two [b]mites.
3 So He said, "Truly I say to you [a]that this
poor widow has put in more than all;
4 "for all these out of their abundance have
put in offerings *for God, but she out of her poverty
put in [a]all the livelihood that she had."

Jesus Predicts the Destruction of the Temple
(Matt. 24:1, 2; Mark 13:1, 2)

5 [a]Then, as some spoke of the temple, how
it was adorned with beautiful stones and donations,
He said,
6 "These things which you see—the days
will come in which [a]not *one* stone shall be left
upon another that shall not be thrown down."

The Signs of the Times and the End of the Age
(Matt. 24:3–14; Mark 13:3–13)

7 So they asked Him, saying, "Teacher, but
when will these things be? And what sign *will*
there be when these things are about to take
place?"
8 And He said: [a]"Take heed that you not
be deceived. For many will come in My name,
saying, 'I am *He,*' and, 'The time has drawn near.'
*Therefore do not go after them.
9 "But when you hear of [a]wars and commotions,
do not be terrified; for these things must
come to pass first, but the end *will not come*
immediately."
10 [a]Then He said to them, "Nation will rise
against nation, and kingdom against kingdom.
11 "And there will be great [a]earthquakes in
various places, and famines and pestilences; and
there will be fearful sights and great signs from
heaven.
12 [a]"But before all these things, they will lay
their hands on you and persecute *you,* delivering
you up to the synagogues and [b]prisons. [c]You will
be brought before kings and rulers [d]for My
name's sake.
13 "But [a]it will turn out for you as an occasion
for testimony.
14 [a]"Therefore settle *it* in your hearts not to
meditate beforehand on what you will answer;
15 "for I will give you a mouth and wisdom
[a]which all your adversaries will not be able to
contradict or resist.
16 [a]"You will be betrayed even by parents
and brothers, relatives and friends; and they will
put [b]*some* of you to death.
17 "And [a]you will be hated by all for My
name's sake.
18 [a]"But not a hair of your head shall be lost.
19 "By your patience possess your souls.

The Destruction of Jerusalem
(Matt. 24:15–28; Mark 13:14–23)

20 [a]"But when you see Jerusalem surrounded
by armies, then know that its desolation
is near.
21 "Then let those who are in Judea flee to
the mountains, let those who are in the midst of
her depart, and let not those who are in the country
enter her.

KJV

22 For these be the days of vengeance, that
[a]all things which are written may be fulfilled.
23 [a]But woe unto them that are with child,
and to them that give suck, in those days! for there
shall be great distress in the land, and wrath upon
this people.
24 And they shall fall by the edge of the
sword, and shall be led away captive into all nations: and Jerusalem shall be trodden down of
the Gentiles, [a]until the times of the Gentiles be
fulfilled.

The Coming of the Son of Man
(Matt. 24:29–31; Mark 13:24–27)

25 [a]And there shall be signs in the sun, and
in the moon, and in the stars; and upon the earth
distress of nations, with perplexity; the sea and
the waves roaring;
26 Men's hearts failing them for fear, and for
looking after those things which are coming on
the earth: [a]for the powers of heaven shall be
shaken.
27 And then shall they see the Son of
man [a]coming in a cloud with power and great
glory.
28 And when these things begin to come to
pass, then look up, and lift up your heads; for
[a]your redemption draweth nigh.

The Parable of the Fig Tree
(Matt. 24:32–35; Mark 13:28–31)

29 [a]And he spake to them a parable; Behold
the fig tree, and all the trees;
30 When they now shoot forth, ye see and
know of your own selves that summer is now nigh
at hand.
31 So likewise ye, when ye see these things
come to pass, know ye that the kingdom of God
is nigh at hand.
32 Verily I say unto you, This generation
shall not pass away, till all be fulfilled.
33 [a]Heaven and earth shall pass away: but
my [b]words shall not pass away.

The Importance of Watching
(Matt. 24:36–44; Mark 13:32–37)

34 And [a]take heed to yourselves, lest at any
time your hearts be overcharged with surfeiting,
and drunkenness, and [b]cares of this life, and so
that day come upon you unawares.
35 For [a]as a snare shall it come on all them
that dwell on the face of the whole earth.
36 [a]Watch ye therefore, and [b]pray always,
that ye may be accounted [c]worthy to escape all
these things that shall come to pass, and [d]to stand
before the Son of man.
37 [a]And in the day time he was teaching
in the temple; and [b]at night he went out, and
abode in the mount that is called *the mount* of
Olives.
38 And all the people came early in the morning to him in the temple, for to hear him.

The Plot to Kill Jesus
(Matt. 26:1–5, 14–16; Mark 14:1, 2, 10, 11;
John 11:45–53)

22 Now [a]the feast of unleavened bread drew
nigh, which is called the Passover.
2 And [a]the chief priests and scribes sought
how they might kill him; for they feared the
people.
3 [a]Then entered Satan into Judas surnamed
Iscariot, being of the number of the [b]twelve.
4 And he went his way, and communed with
the chief priests and captains, how he might betray him unto them.
5 And they were glad, and [a]covenanted to
give him money.
6 And he promised, and sought opportunity
to [a]betray him unto them in the absence of the
multitude.

22 [a]Is. 63:4; [Dan. 9:24–27]; Hos. 9:7; [Zech. 11:1]
23 [a]Matt. 24:19
24 [a][Dan. 9:27; 12:7]
25 [a]Is. 13:9, 10, 13; Matt. 24:29; Mark 13:24; [2 Pet. 3:10–12]
26 [a]Matt. 24:29
27 [a]Dan. 7:13; [Matt. 16:27; 24:30; 26:64]; Mark 13:26; Rev. 1:7; 14:14
28 [a][Rom. 8:19, 23]
29 [a]Matt. 24:32; Mark 13:28
33 [a]Is. 51:6; Matt. 24:35; Heb. 1:10, 11; [2 Pet. 3:7, 10, 12] [b]Is. 40:8; Luke 16:17; 1 Pet. 1:24, 25
34 [a]Matt. 24:42–44; Mark 4:19; Luke 12:40, 45; Rom. 13:13; 1 Thess. 5:6; 1 Pet. 4:7 [b]Luke 8:14
35 [a]1 Thess. 5:2; [2 Pet. 3:10]; Rev. 3:3; 16:15
36 [a]Matt. 24:42; 25:13; Mark 13:33; Luke 12:40 [b]Luke 18:1; [Eph. 6:18]; Col. 4:2; 1 Thess. 5:17 [c]Luke 20:35 [d]Ps. 1:5; [Eph. 6:13]
37 [a]John 8:1, 2 [b]Luke 22:39

CHAPTER 22

1 [a]Matt. 26:2–5; Mark 14:1, 2
2 [a]Ps. 2:2; John 11:47; Acts 4:27
3 [a]Matt. 26:14–16; Mark 14:10, 11; John 13:2, 27 [b]Matt. 10:2–4
5 [a]Zech. 11:12
6 [a]Ps. 41:9

*———

21:36 NU *have strength to*

NKJV

22 "For these are the days of vengeance, that
[a]all things which are written may be fulfilled.
23 [a]"But woe to those who are pregnant and
to those who are nursing babies in those days!
For there will be great distress in the land and
wrath upon this people.
24 "And they will fall by the edge of the
sword, and be led away captive into all nations.
And Jerusalem will be trampled by Gentiles [a]until
the times of the Gentiles are fulfilled.

The Coming of the Son of Man
(Matt. 24:29–31; Mark 13:24–27)

25 [a]"And there will be signs in the sun, in
the moon, and in the stars; and on the earth distress of nations, with perplexity, the sea and the
waves roaring;
26 "men's hearts failing them from fear and
the expectation of those things which are coming
on the earth, [a]for the powers of the heavens will
be shaken.
27 "Then they will see the Son of Man [a]com-
ing in a cloud with power and great glory.
28 "Now when these things begin to happen,
look up and lift up your heads, because [a]your redemption draws near."

The Parable of the Fig Tree
(Matt. 24:32–35; Mark 13:28–31)

29 [a]Then He spoke to them a parable: "Look
at the fig tree, and all the trees.
30 "When they are already budding, you see
and know for yourselves that summer is now
near.
31 "So you also, when you see these things
happening, know that the kingdom of God is near.
32 "Assuredly, I say to you, this generation
will by no means pass away till all things take
place.
33 [a]"Heaven and earth will pass away, but
My [b]words will by no means pass away.

The Importance of Watching
(Matt. 24:36–44; Mark 13:32–37)

34 "But [a]take heed to yourselves, lest your
hearts be weighed down with carousing, drunkenness, and [b]cares of this life, and that Day come
on you unexpectedly.
35 "For [a]it will come as a snare on all those
who dwell on the face of the whole earth.
36 [a]"Watch therefore, and [b]pray always that
you may *be counted [c]worthy to escape all these
things that will come to pass, and [d]to stand before
the Son of Man."
37 [a]And in the daytime He was teaching in
the temple, but [b]at night He went out and stayed
on the mountain called Olivet.
38 Then early in the morning all the people
came to Him in the temple to hear Him.

The Plot to Kill Jesus
(Matt. 26:1–5, 14–16; Mark 14:1, 2, 10, 11;
John 11:45–53)

22 Now [a]the Feast of Unleavened Bread drew
near, which is called Passover.
2 And [a]the chief priests and the scribes
sought how they might kill Him, for they feared
the people.
3 [a]Then Satan entered Judas, surnamed Iscariot, who was numbered among the [b]twelve.
4 So he went his way and conferred with
the chief priests and captains, how he might betray Him to them.
5 And they were glad, and [a]agreed to give
him money.
6 So he promised and sought opportunity
to [a]betray Him to them in the absence of the
multitude.

KJV

Jesus and His Disciples Prepare the Passover (Matt. 26:17–19; Mark 14:12–16)

7 [a]Then came the day of unleavened bread, when the passover must be killed.

8 And he sent Peter and John, saying, Go and prepare us the passover, that we may eat.

9 And they said unto him, Where wilt thou that we prepare?

10 And he said unto them, Behold, when ye are entered into the city, there shall a man meet you, bearing a pitcher of water; follow him into the house where he entereth in.

11 And ye shall say unto the goodman of the house, The Master saith unto thee, Where is the guestchamber, where I shall eat the passover with my disciples?

12 And he shall shew you a large upper room furnished: there make ready.

13 And they went, and [a]found as he had said unto them: and they made ready the passover.

Jesus Institutes the Lord's Supper (Matt. 26:20–30; Mark 14:17–26; John 13:21–30)

14 [a]And when the hour was come, he sat down, and the twelve apostles with him.

15 And he said unto them, With desire I have desired to eat this passover with you before I suffer:

16 For I say unto you, I will not any more eat thereof, [a]until it be fulfilled in the kingdom of God.

17 And he took the cup, and gave thanks, and said, Take this, and divide *it* among yourselves:

18 For [a]I say unto you, I will not drink of the fruit of the vine, until the kingdom of God shall come.

19 [a]And he took bread, and gave thanks, and brake *it,* and gave unto them, saying, This is my [b]body which is given for you: [c]this do in remembrance of me.

20 Likewise also the cup after supper, saying, [a]This cup *is* the new testament in my blood, which is shed for you.

21 [a]But, behold, the hand of him that betrayeth me *is* with me on the table.

22 [a]And truly the Son of man goeth, [b]as it was determined: but woe unto that man by whom he is betrayed!

23 [a]And they began to enquire among themselves, which of them it was that should do this thing.

The Disciples Argue About Greatness

24 [a]And there was also a strife among them, which of them should be accounted the greatest.

25 [a]And he said unto them, The kings of the Gentiles exercise lordship over them; and they that exercise authority upon them are called benefactors.

26 [a]But ye *shall* not *be* so: [b]but he that is greatest among you, let him be as the younger; and he that is chief, as he that doth serve.

27 [a]For whether *is* greater, he that sitteth at meat, or he that serveth? *is* not he that sitteth at meat? but [b]I am among you as he that serveth.

28 Ye are they which have continued with me in [a]my temptations.

29 And [a]I appoint unto you a kingdom, as my Father hath appointed unto me;

30 That [a]ye may eat and drink at my table in my kingdom, [b]and sit on thrones judging the twelve tribes of Israel.

Jesus Predicts Peter's Denial (Matt. 26:31–35; Mark 14:27–31; John 13:36–38)

31 And the Lord said, Simon, Simon, behold, [a]Satan hath desired *to have* you, that he may [b]sift *you* as wheat:

32 But [a]I have prayed for thee, that thy faith fail not: and when thou art converted, [b]strengthen thy brethren.

NKJV

Jesus and His Disciples Prepare the Passover (Matt. 26:17–19; Mark 14:12–16)

7 [a]Then came the Day of Unleavened Bread, when the Passover must be killed.

8 And He sent Peter and John, saying, "Go and prepare the Passover for us, that we may eat."

9 So they said to Him, "Where do You want us to prepare?"

10 And He said to them, "Behold, when you have entered the city, a man will meet you carrying a pitcher of water; follow him into the house which he enters.

11 "Then you shall say to the master of the house, 'The Teacher says to you, "Where is the guest room where I may eat the Passover with My disciples?" '

12 "Then he will show you a large, furnished upper room; there make ready."

13 So they went and [a]found it just as He had said to them, and they prepared the Passover.

Jesus Institutes the Lord's Supper (Matt. 26:20–30; Mark 14:17–26; John 13:21–30)

14 [a]When the hour had come, He sat down, and the *twelve apostles with Him.

15 Then He said to them, "With *fervent* desire I have desired to eat this Passover with you before I suffer;

16 "for I say to you, I will no longer eat of it [a]until it is fulfilled in the kingdom of God."

17 Then He took the cup, and gave thanks, and said, "Take this and divide *it* among yourselves;

18 "for [a]I say to you, *I will not drink of the fruit of the vine until the kingdom of God comes."

19 [a]And He took bread, gave thanks and broke *it,* and gave *it* to them, saying, "This is My [b]body which is given for you; [c]do this in remembrance of Me."

20 Likewise He also *took* the cup after supper, saying, [a]"This cup *is* the new covenant in My blood, which is shed for you.

21 [a]"But behold, the hand of My betrayer *is* with Me on the table.

22 [a]"And truly the Son of Man goes [b]as it has been determined, but woe to that man by whom He is betrayed!"

23 [a]Then they began to question among themselves, which of them it was who would do this thing.

The Disciples Argue About Greatness

24 [a]Now there was also a dispute among them, as to which of them should be considered the greatest.

25 [a]And He said to them, "The kings of the Gentiles exercise lordship over them, and those who exercise authority over them are called 'benefactors.'

26 [a]"But not so *among* you; on the contrary, [b]he who is greatest among you, let him be as the younger, and he who governs as he who serves.

27 [a]"For who *is* greater, he who sits at the table, or he who serves? *Is* it not he who sits at the table? Yet [b]I am among you as the One who serves.

28 "But you are those who have continued with Me in [a]My trials.

29 "And [a]I bestow upon you a kingdom, just as My Father bestowed *one* upon Me,

30 "that [a]you may eat and drink at My table in My kingdom, [b]and sit on thrones judging the twelve tribes of Israel."

Jesus Predicts Peter's Denial (Matt. 26:31–35; Mark 14:27–31; John 13:36–38)

31 *And the Lord said, "Simon, Simon! Indeed, [a]Satan has asked for you, that he may [b]sift *you* as wheat.

32 "But [a]I have prayed for you, that your faith should not fail; and when you have returned to *Me,* [b]strengthen your brethren."

---

7 [a]Matt. 26:17–19; Mark 14:12–16
13 [a]Luke 19:32
14 [a]Matt. 26:20; Mark 14:17
16 [a]Luke 14:15; [Acts 10:41; Rev. 19:9]
18 [a]Matt. 26:29; Mark 14:25
19 [a]Matt. 26:26; Mark 14:22 [b][1 Pet. 2:24] [c]1 Cor. 11:23–26
20 [a]1 Cor. 10:16
21 [a]Ps. 41:9; Matt. 26:21, 23; Mark 14:18; Luke 22:48; John 13:21, 26, 27
22 [a]Matt. 26:24 [b]John 17:12; Acts 2:23
23 [a]Matt. 26:22; John 13:22, 25
24 [a]Mark 9:34; Luke 9:46–48
25 [a][Matt. 20:25–28]; Mark 10:42–45
26 [a]Matt. 20:26; [1 Pet. 5:3] [b]Luke 9:48
27 [a][Luke 12:37] [b]Matt. 20:28; John 13:13, 14; Phil. 2:7
28 [a][Heb. 2:18; 4:15]
29 [a]Matt. 24:47
30 [a][Matt. 8:11; Rev. 19:9] [b]Ps. 49:14; [Matt. 19:28; 1 Cor. 6:2; Rev. 3:21]
31 [a]1 Pet. 5:8 [b]Amos 9:9
32 [a][John 17:9, 11, 15] [b]John 21:15–17; Acts 1:15; 2:14; 2 Pet. 1:10–15

*

22:14 NU omits *twelve*
22:18 NU adds *from now on*
22:31 NU omits *And the Lord said*

KJV

33 And he said unto him, Lord, I am ready to go with thee, both into prison, and to death.

34 [a]And he said, I tell thee, Peter, the cock shall not crow this day, before that thou shalt thrice deny that thou knowest me.

Supplies for the Road

35 [a]And he said unto them, When I sent you without purse, and scrip, and shoes, lacked ye any thing? And they said, Nothing.

36 Then said he unto them, But now, he that hath a purse, let him take *it,* and likewise *his* scrip: and he that hath no sword, let him sell his garment, and buy one.

37 For I say unto you, that this that is written must yet be accomplished in me, [a]AND HE WAS RECKONED AMONG THE TRANSGRESSORS: for the things concerning me have an end.

38 And they said, Lord, behold, here *are* two swords. And he said unto them, It is enough.

The Prayer in the Garden
(Matt. 26:36–46; Mark 14:32–42; John 18:1)

39 [a]And he came out, and [b]went, as he was wont, to the mount of Olives; and his disciples also followed him.

40 [a]And when he was at the place, he said unto them, Pray that ye enter not into temptation.

41 [a]And he was withdrawn from them about a stone's cast, and kneeled down, and prayed,

42 Saying, Father, if thou be willing, remove this cup from me: nevertheless [a]not my will, but thine, be done.

43 And there appeared [a]an angel unto him from heaven, strengthening him.

44 [a]And being in an agony he prayed more earnestly: and his sweat was as it were great drops of blood falling down to the ground.

45 And when he rose up from prayer, and was come to his disciples, he found them sleeping for sorrow,

46 And said unto them, Why [a]sleep ye? rise and [b]pray, lest ye enter into temptation.

Betrayal and Arrest in Gethsemane
(Matt. 26:47–56; Mark 14:43–52; John 18:1–11)

47 And while he yet spake, [a]behold a multitude, and he that was called [b]Judas, one of the twelve, went before them, and drew near unto Jesus to kiss him.

48 But Jesus said unto him, Judas, betrayest thou the Son of man with a [a]kiss?

49 When they which were about him saw what would follow, they said unto him, Lord, shall we smite with the sword?

50 And [a]one of them smote the servant of the high priest, and cut off his right ear.

51 And Jesus answered and said, Suffer ye thus far. And he touched his ear, and healed him.

52 [a]Then Jesus said unto the chief priests, and captains of the temple, and the elders, which were come to him, Be ye come out, as against a [b]thief, with swords and staves?

53 When I was daily with you in the [a]temple, ye stretched forth no hands against me: but this is your [b]hour, and the power of darkness.

Peter Denies Jesus, and Weeps Bitterly
(Matt. 26:69–75; Mark 14:66–72; John 18:13–18, 25–27)

54 [a]Then took they him, and led *him,* and brought him into the high priest's house. [b]And Peter followed afar off.

55 [a]And when they had kindled a fire in the midst of the hall, and were set down together, Peter sat down among them.

56 But a certain maid beheld him as he sat by the fire, and earnestly looked upon him, and said, This man was also with him.

34 [a]Matt. 26:33–35; Mark 14:29–31; Luke 22:61; John 13:37, 38
35 [a]Matt. 10:9; Mark 6:8; Luke 9:3; 10:4
37 [a]Is. 53:12; Matt. 27:38; Mark 15:28; Luke 22:32
39 [a]Matt. 26:36; John 18:1 [b]Luke 21:37
40 [a]Matt. 26:36–46; Mark 14:32–42
41 [a]Matt. 26:39; Mark 14:35; [Luke 18:11–14]
42 [a]Is. 50:5; John 4:34; 5:30; 6:38; 8:29
43 [a]Matt. 4:11
44 [a]John 12:27; [Heb. 5:7]
46 [a]Luke 9:32 [b]1 Chr. 16:11; Luke 22:40; [Eph. 6:18]; 1 Thess. 5:17
47 [a]Matt. 26:47–56; Mark 14:43–50; John 18:3–11 [b]Ps. 41:9; Matt. 20:18; Luke 9:44; 22:21; Acts 1:16, 17
48 [a][Prov. 27:6]
50 [a]Matt. 26:51
52 [a]Matt. 26:55 [b]Luke 23:32
53 [a]Luke 19:47, 48 [b][John 12:27]
54 [a]Is. 53:7, 8; Matt. 26:57; Mark 14:53; Luke 9:44; Acts 8:32 [b]Matt. 26:58; Mark 14:54; John 18:15
55 [a]Matt. 26:69–75; Mark 14:66–72; John 18:15, 17, 18

NKJV

33 But he said to Him, "Lord, I am ready to go with You, both to prison and to death."

34 [a]Then He said, "I tell you, Peter, the rooster shall not crow this day before you will deny three times that you know Me."

Supplies for the Road

35 [a]And He said to them, "When I sent you without money bag, knapsack, and sandals, did you lack anything?" So they said, "Nothing."

36 Then He said to them, "But now, he who has a money bag, let him take *it,* and likewise a knapsack; and he who has no sword, let him sell his garment and buy one.

37 "For I say to you that this which is written must still be accomplished in Me: [a]*'And He was numbered with the transgressors.'* For the things concerning Me have an end."

38 So they said, "Lord, look, here *are* two swords." And He said to them, "It is enough."

The Prayer in the Garden
(Matt. 26:36–46; Mark 14:32–42; John 18:1)

39 [a]Coming out, [b]He went to the Mount of Olives, as He was accustomed, and His disciples also followed Him.

40 [a]When He came to the place, He said to them, "Pray that you may not enter into temptation."

41 [a]And He was withdrawn from them about a stone's throw, and He knelt down and prayed,

42 saying, "Father, if it is Your will, take this cup away from Me; nevertheless [a]not My will, but Yours, be done."

43 *Then [a]an angel appeared to Him from heaven, strengthening Him.

44 [a]And being in agony, He prayed more earnestly. Then His sweat became like great drops of blood falling down to the ground.

45 When He rose up from prayer, and had come to His disciples, He found them sleeping from sorrow.

46 Then He said to them, "Why [a]do you sleep? Rise and [b]pray, lest you enter into temptation."

Betrayal and Arrest in Gethsemane
(Matt. 26:47–56; Mark 14:43–52; John 18:1–11)

47 And while He was still speaking, [a]behold, a multitude; and he who was called [b]Judas, one of the twelve, went before them and drew near to Jesus to kiss Him.

48 But Jesus said to him, "Judas, are you betraying the Son of Man with a [a]kiss?"

49 When those around Him saw what was going to happen, they said to Him, "Lord, shall we strike with the sword?"

50 And [a]one of them struck the servant of the high priest and cut off his right ear.

51 But Jesus answered and said, "Permit even this." And He touched his ear and healed him.

52 [a]Then Jesus said to the chief priests, captains of the temple, and the elders who had come to Him, "Have you come out, as against a [b]robber, with swords and clubs?

53 "When I was with you daily in the [a]temple, you did not try to seize Me. But this is your [b]hour, and the power of darkness."

Peter Denies Jesus, and Weeps Bitterly
(Matt. 26:69–75; Mark 14:66–72; John 18:13–18, 25–27)

54 [a]Having arrested Him, they led *Him* and brought Him into the high priest's house. [b]But Peter followed at a distance.

55 [a]Now when they had kindled a fire in the midst of the courtyard and sat down together, Peter sat among them.

56 And a certain servant girl, seeing him as he sat by the fire, looked intently at him and said, "This man was also with Him."

---

* **22:43** NU brackets vv. 43 and 44 as not in the original text.

KJV

57 And he denied him, saying, Woman, I know him not.
58 [a]And after a little while another saw him, and said, Thou art also of them. And Peter said, Man, I am not.
59 [a]And about the space of one hour after another confidently affirmed, saying, Of a truth this *fellow* also was with him: for he is a [b]Galilaean.
60 And Peter said, Man, I know not what thou sayest. And immediately, while he yet spake, the cock crew.
61 And the Lord turned, and looked upon Peter. And [a]Peter remembered the word of the Lord, how he had said unto him, [b]Before the cock crow, thou shalt deny me thrice.
62 And Peter went out, and wept bitterly.

Jesus Mocked and Beaten
(Matt. 26:67, 68; Mark 14:65)

63 [a]And the men that held Jesus mocked him, and [b]smote *him.*
64 And when they had blindfolded him, they [a]struck him on the face, and asked him, saying, Prophesy, who is it that smote thee?
65 And many other things blasphemously spake they against him.

Jesus Faces the Sanhedrin
(Matt. 26:57–68; Mark 14:61–64; John 18;12–14, 19–24)

66 [a]And as soon as it was day, [b]the elders of the people and the chief priests and the scribes came together, and led him into their council, saying,
67 [a]Art thou the Christ? tell us. And he said unto them, If I tell you, ye will [b]not believe:
68 And if I also ask *you,* ye will not answer me, nor let *me* go.
69 [a]Hereafter shall the Son of man sit on the right hand of the power of God.
70 Then said they all, Art thou then the Son of God? And he said unto them, [a]Ye say that I am.
71 [a]And they said, What need we any further witness? for we ourselves have heard of his own mouth.

Jesus Handed Over to Pontius Pilate
(Matt. 27:1, 2, 11–14; Mark 15:1–5; John 18:28–38)

23 And [a]the whole multitude of them arose, and led him unto [b]Pilate.
2 And they began to [a]accuse him, saying, We found this *fellow* [b]perverting the nation, and [c]forbidding to give tribute to Caesar, saying [d]that he himself is Christ a King.
3 [a]And Pilate asked him, saying, Art thou the King of the Jews? And he answered him and said, Thou sayest *it.*
4 Then said Pilate to the chief priests and *to* the people, [a]I find no fault in this man.
5 And they were the more fierce, saying, He stirreth up the people, teaching throughout all Jewry, beginning from [a]Galilee to this place.

Jesus Faces Herod

6 When Pilate heard of Galilee, he asked whether the man were a Galilaean.
7 And as soon as he knew that he belonged unto [a]Herod's jurisdiction, he sent him to Herod, who himself also was at Jerusalem at that time.
8 And when Herod saw Jesus, [a]he was exceeding glad: for he was desirous to see him of a long *season,* because [b]he had heard many things of him; and he hoped to have seen some miracle done by him.
9 Then he questioned with him in many words; but he answered him [a]nothing.
10 And the chief priests and scribes stood and vehemently accused him.
11 [a]And Herod with his men of war set him

58 [a]John 18:25
59 [a]Mark 14:70 [b]Acts 1:11; 2:7
61 [a]Matt. 26:75 [b]John 13:38
63 [a]Ps. 69:1, 4, 7–9 [b]Is. 50:6
64 [a]Zech. 13:7
66 [a]Matt. 27:1 [b]Acts 4:26
67 [a]Matt. 26:63–66 [b]Luke 20:5–7
69 [a]Heb. 1:3; 8:1
70 [a]Matt. 26:64; 27:11
71 [a]Mark 14:63

CHAPTER 23

1 [a]John 18:28 [b]Luke 3:1; 13:1
2 [a]Acts 24:2 [b]Acts 17:7 [c]Matt. 17:27 [d]John 19:12
3 [a]1 Tim. 6:13
4 [a][1 Pet. 2:22]
5 [a]John 7:41
7 [a]Luke 3:1; 9:7; 13:31
8 [a]Luke 9:9 [b]Matt. 14:1
9 [a]John 19:9
11 [a]Is. 53:3

*———

22:57 NU *it*
22:60 NU, M *a rooster*
22:61 NU adds *today*
22:64 NU *And having blindfolded Him, they asked Him*
22:68 NU omits *also* • NU omits the rest of v. 68.
23:2 NU *our*
23:6 NU omits *of Galilee*

NKJV

57 But he denied *Him, saying, "Woman, I do not know Him."
58 [a]And after a little while another saw him and said, "You also are of them." But Peter said, "Man, I am not!"
59 [a]Then after about an hour had passed, another confidently affirmed, saying, "Surely this *fellow* also was with Him, for he is a [b]Galilean."
60 But Peter said, "Man, I do not know what you are saying!" Immediately, while he was still speaking, *the rooster crowed.
61 And the Lord turned and looked at Peter. Then [a]Peter remembered the word of the Lord, how He had said to him, [b]"Before the rooster *crows, you will deny Me three times."
62 So Peter went out and wept bitterly.

Jesus Mocked and Beaten
(Matt. 26:67, 68; Mark 14:65)

63 [a]Now the men who held Jesus mocked Him and [b]beat Him.
64 *And having blindfolded Him, they [a]struck Him on the face and asked Him, saying, "Prophesy! Who is the one who struck You?"
65 And many other things they blasphemously spoke against Him.

Jesus Faces the Sanhedrin
(Matt. 26:57–68; Mark 14:61–64; John 18:12–14, 19–24)

66 [a]As soon as it was day, [b]the elders of the people, both chief priests and scribes, came together and led Him into their council, saying,
67 [a]"If You are the Christ, tell us." But He said to them, "If I tell you, you will [b]by no means believe.
68 "And if I *also ask *you,* you will by no means answer *Me or let *Me* go.
69 [a]"Hereafter the Son of Man will sit on the right hand of the power of God."
70 Then they all said, "Are You then the Son of God?" So He said to them, [a]"You *rightly* say that I am."
71 [a]And they said, "What further testimony do we need? For we have heard it ourselves from His own mouth."

Jesus Handed Over to Pontius Pilate
(Matt. 27:1, 2, 11–14; Mark 15:1–5; John 18:28–38)

23 Then [a]the whole multitude of them arose and led Him to [b]Pilate.
2 And they began to [a]accuse Him, saying, "We found this *fellow* [b]perverting *the nation, and [c]forbidding to pay taxes to Caesar, saying [d]that He Himself is Christ, a King."
3 [a]Then Pilate asked Him, saying, "Are You the King of the Jews?" He answered him and said, "*It is as* you say."
4 So Pilate said to the chief priests and the crowd, [a]"I find no fault in this Man."
5 But they were the more fierce, saying, "He stirs up the people, teaching throughout all Judea, beginning from [a]Galilee to this place."

Jesus Faces Herod

6 When Pilate heard *of Galilee, he asked if the Man were a Galilean.
7 And as soon as he knew that He belonged to [a]Herod's jurisdiction, he sent Him to Herod, who was also in Jerusalem at that time.
8 Now when Herod saw Jesus, [a]he was exceedingly glad; for he had desired for a long *time* to see Him, because [b]he had heard many things about Him, and he hoped to see some miracle done by Him.
9 Then he questioned Him with many words, but He answered him [a]nothing.
10 And the chief priests and scribes stood and vehemently accused Him.
11 [a]Then Herod, with his men of war, treated

KJV

at nought, and mocked *him*, and arrayed him in
a gorgeous robe, and sent him again to Pilate.
12 And the same day [a]Pilate and Herod were
made friends together: for before they were at enmity between themselves.

Taking the Place of Barabbas
(*Matt. 27:15–26; Mark 15:6–15; John 18:38—19:16*)

13 [a]And Pilate, when he had called together
the chief priests and the rulers and the people,
14 Said unto them, [a]Ye have brought this
man unto me, as one that perverteth the people:
and, behold, [b]I, having examined *him* before you,
have found no fault in this man touching those
things whereof ye accuse him:
15 No, nor yet Herod: for I sent you to him;
and, lo, nothing worthy of death is done unto him.
16 [a]I will therefore chastise him, and release
him.
17 [a](For of necessity he must release one
unto them at the feast.)
18 And [a]they cried out all at once, saying,
Away with this *man*, and release unto us
Barabbas:
19 (Who for a certain sedition made in the
city, and for murder, was cast into prison.)
20 Pilate therefore, willing to release Jesus,
spake again to them.
21 But they cried, saying, Crucify *him*, crucify him.
22 And he said unto them the third time,
Why, what evil hath he done? I have found no
cause of death in him: I will therefore chastise
him, and let *him* go.
23 And they were instant with loud voices,
requiring that he might be crucified. And the
voices of them and of the chief priests prevailed.
24 And [a]Pilate gave sentence that it should
be as they required.
25 [a]And he released unto them him that for
sedition and murder was cast into prison, whom
they had desired; but he delivered Jesus to their
will.

The King on a Cross
(*Matt. 27:32–44; Mark 15:21–32; John 19:17–24*)

26 [a]And as they led him away, they laid hold
upon one Simon, a Cyrenian, coming out of the
country, and on him they laid the cross, that he
might bear *it* after Jesus.
27 And there followed him a great company
of people, and of women, which also bewailed and
lamented him.
28 But Jesus turning unto them said, Daughters of Jerusalem, weep not for me, but weep for
yourselves, and for your children.
29 [a]For, behold, the days are coming, in the
which they shall say, Blessed *are* the barren, and
the wombs that never bare, and the paps which
never gave suck.
30 Then shall they begin [a]TO SAY TO THE
MOUNTAINS, FALL ON US; AND TO THE HILLS, COVER
US.
31 [a]For if they do these things in a green tree,
what shall be done in the dry?
32 [a]And there were also two others, malefactors, led with him to be put to death.
33 And [a]when they were come to the place,
which is called Calvary, there they crucified him,
and the malefactors, one on the right hand, and
the other on the left.
34 Then said Jesus, Father, [a]forgive them; for
[b]they know not what they do. And [c]they parted
his raiment, and cast lots.
35 And [a]the people stood beholding. And the
[b]rulers also with them derided *him*, saying, He
saved others; let him save himself, if he be Christ,
the chosen of God.

12 [a]Acts 4:26, 27
13 [a]Matt. 27:23; Mark 15:14; John 18:38
14 [a]Luke 23:1, 2 [b]Luke 23:4
16 [a]Matt. 27:26; Mark 15:15; Luke 23:22; John 19:1; Acts 16:37
17 [a]Matt. 27:15; Mark 15:6; John 18:39
18 [a]Is. 53:3; Acts 3:13–15
24 [a]Matt. 27:26; Mark 15:15; John 19:16
25 [a]Is. 53:8
26 [a]Matt. 27:32; Mark 15:21; John 19:17
29 [a]Matt. 24:19; Luke 21:23
30 [a]Is. 2:19; Hos. 10:8; Rev. 6:16, 17; 9:6
31 [a][Prov. 11:31; Jer. 25:29]; Ezek. 20:47; 21:3, 4; 1 Pet. 4:17
32 [a]Is. 53:9, 12; Matt. 27:38; Mark 15:27; John 19:18
33 [a]Ps. 22:16–18; Matt. 27:33–44; Mark 15:22–32; John 19:17–24
34 [a]Ps. 109:4; [Matt. 5:44]; Acts 7:60; 1 Cor. 4:12 [b]Acts 3:17 [c]Ps. 22:18; Matt. 27:35; Mark 15:24; John 19:23
35 [a]Ps. 22:17; [Zech. 12:10] [b]Ps. 22:8; Matt. 27:39; Mark 15:29

*

23:15 NU *he sent Him back to us*
23:17 NU omits v. 17.
23:23 NU omits *and of the chief priests*
23:25 NU, M omit *to them*
23:34 NU brackets the first sentence as a later addition.

NKJV

Him with contempt and mocked *Him*, arrayed
Him in a gorgeous robe, and sent Him back to
Pilate.
12 That very day [a]Pilate and Herod became
friends with each other, for previously they had
been at enmity with each other.

Taking the Place of Barabbas
(*Matt. 27:15–26; Mark 15:6–15; John 18:38—19:16*)

13 [a]Then Pilate, when he had called together
the chief priests, the rulers, and the people,
14 said to them, [a]"You have brought this
Man to me, as one who misleads the people. And
indeed, [b]having examined *Him* in your presence,
I have found no fault in this Man concerning those
things of which you accuse Him;
15 "no, neither did Herod, for *I sent you
back to him; and indeed nothing deserving of
death has been done by Him.
16 [a]"I will therefore chastise Him and release
Him"
17 [a](for* it was necessary for him to release
one to them at the feast).
18 And [a]they all cried out at once, saying,
"Away with this *Man*, and release to us Barabbas"—
19 who had been thrown into prison for a
certain rebellion made in the city, and for murder.
20 Pilate, therefore, wishing to release Jesus,
again called out to them.
21 But they shouted, saying, "Crucify *Him*,
crucify Him!"
22 Then he said to them the third time, "Why,
what evil has He done? I have found no reason
for death in Him. I will therefore chastise Him
and let *Him* go."
23 But they were insistent, demanding with
loud voices that He be crucified. And the voices
of these men *and of the chief priests prevailed.
24 So [a]Pilate gave sentence that it should be
as they requested.
25 [a]And he released *to them the one they
requested, who for rebellion and murder had been
thrown into prison; but he delivered Jesus to their
will.

The King on a Cross
(*Matt. 27:32–44; Mark 15:21–32; John 19:17–24*)

26 [a]Now as they led Him away, they laid hold
of a certain man, Simon a Cyrenian, who was
coming from the country, and on him they laid
the cross that he might bear *it* after Jesus.
27 And a great multitude of the people followed Him, and women who also mourned and
lamented Him.
28 But Jesus, turning to them, said, "Daughters of Jerusalem, do not weep for Me, but weep
for yourselves and for your children.
29 [a]"For indeed the days are coming in
which they will say, 'Blessed *are* the barren,
wombs that never bore, and breasts which never
nursed!'
30 "Then they will begin [a]*'to say to the
mountains, "Fall on us!" and to the hills, "Cover
us!"'*
31 [a]"For if they do these things in the green
wood, what will be done in the dry?"
32 [a]There were also two others, criminals,
led with Him to be put to death.
33 And [a]when they had come to the place
called Calvary, there they crucified Him, and the
criminals, one on the right hand and the other
on the left.
34 *Then Jesus said, "Father, [a]forgive them,
for [b]they do not know what they do." And [c]they
divided His garments and cast lots.
35 And [a]the people stood looking on. But
even the [b]rulers with them sneered, saying, "He
saved others; let Him save Himself if He is the
Christ, the chosen of God."

KJV

36 And the soldiers also mocked him, coming to him, and offering him [a]vinegar,

37 And saying, If thou be the king of the Jews, save thyself.

38 [a]And a superscription also was written over him in letters of Greek, and Latin, and Hebrew, THIS IS THE KING OF THE JEWS.

39 [a]And one of the malefactors which were hanged railed on him, saying, If thou be Christ, save thyself and us.

40 But the other answering rebuked him, saying, Dost not thou fear God, seeing thou art in the same condemnation?

41 And we indeed justly; for we receive the due reward of our deeds: but this man hath done [a]nothing amiss.

42 And he said unto Jesus, Lord, remember me when thou comest into thy kingdom.

43 And Jesus said unto him, Verily I say unto thee, to day shalt thou be with me in [a]paradise.

Jesus Dies on the Cross
(Matt. 27:45–56; Mark 15:33–41; John 19:25–30)

44 [a]And it was about the sixth hour, and there was a darkness over all the earth until the ninth hour.

45 And the sun was darkened, and [a]the veil of the temple was rent in the midst.

46 And when Jesus had cried with a loud voice, he said, Father, [a]INTO THY HANDS I COMMEND MY SPIRIT: [b]and having said thus, he gave up the ghost.

47 [a]Now when the centurion saw what was done, he glorified God, saying, Certainly this was a righteous man.

48 And all the people that came together to that sight, beholding the things which were done, smote their breasts, and returned.

49 [a]And all his acquaintance, and the women that followed him from Galilee, stood afar off, beholding these things.

Jesus Buried in Joseph's Tomb
(Matt. 27:57–61; Mark 15:42–47; John 19:38–42)

50 [a]And, behold, *there was* a man named Joseph, a counsellor; *and he was* a good man, and a just:

51 (The same had not consented to the counsel and deed of them;) *he was* of Arimathaea, a city of the Jews: [a]who also himself waited for the kingdom of God.

52 This *man* went unto Pilate, and begged the body of Jesus.

53 [a]And he took it down, and wrapped it in linen, and laid it in a sepulchre that was hewn in stone, wherein never man before was laid.

54 And that day was [a]the preparation, and the sabbath drew on.

55 And the women also, [a]which came with him from Galilee, followed after, and [b]beheld the sepulchre, and how his body was laid.

56 And they returned, and [a]prepared spices and ointments; and rested the sabbath day [b]according to the commandment.

He Is Risen
(Matt. 28:1–10; Mark 16:1–8; John 20:1–10)

24 Now [a]upon the first *day* of the week, very early in the morning, they came unto the sepulchre, [b]bringing the spices which they had prepared, and certain *others* with them.

2 [a]And they found the stone rolled away from the sepulchre.

3 [a]And they entered in, and found not the body of the Lord Jesus.

4 And it came to pass, as they were much perplexed thereabout, [a]behold, two men stood by them in shining garments:

5 And as they were afraid, and bowed down *their* faces to the earth, they said unto them, Why seek ye the living among the dead?

NKJV

36 The soldiers also mocked Him, coming and offering Him [a]sour wine,

37 and saying, "If You are the King of the Jews, save Yourself."

38 [a]And an inscription also was *written over Him in letters of Greek, Latin, and Hebrew:

THIS IS THE KING OF THE JEWS.

39 [a]Then one of the criminals who were hanged blasphemed Him, saying, *"If You are the Christ, save Yourself and us."

40 But the other, answering, rebuked him, saying, "Do you not even fear God, seeing you are under the same condemnation?

41 "And we indeed justly, for we receive the due reward of our deeds; but this Man has done [a]nothing wrong."

42 Then he said *to Jesus, "Lord, remember me when You come into Your kingdom."

43 And Jesus said to him, "Assuredly, I say to you, today you will be with Me in [a]Paradise."

Jesus Dies on the Cross
(Matt. 27:45–56; Mark 15:33–41; John 19:25–30)

44 [a]Now it *was about the sixth hour, and there was darkness over all the earth until the ninth hour.

45 Then the sun was *darkened, and [a]the veil of the temple was torn in two.

46 And when Jesus had cried out with a loud voice, He said, "Father, [a]*'into Your hands I commit My spirit.'*" [b]Having said this, He breathed His last.

47 [a]So when the centurion saw what had happened, he glorified God, saying, "Certainly this was a righteous Man!"

48 And the whole crowd who came together to that sight, seeing what had been done, beat their breasts and returned.

49 [a]But all His acquaintances, and the women who followed Him from Galilee, stood at a distance, watching these things.

Jesus Buried in Joseph's Tomb
(Matt. 27:57–61; Mark 15:42–47; John 19:38–42)

50 [a]Now behold, *there was* a man named Joseph, a council member, a good and just man.

51 He had not consented to their decision and deed. *He was* from Arimathea, a city of the Jews, [a]who* himself was also waiting for the kingdom of God.

52 This man went to Pilate and asked for the body of Jesus.

53 [a]Then he took it down, wrapped it in linen, and laid it in a tomb *that was* hewn out of the rock, where no one had ever lain before.

54 That day was [a]the Preparation, and the Sabbath drew near.

55 And the women [a]who had come with Him from Galilee followed after, and [b]they observed the tomb and how His body was laid.

56 Then they returned and [a]prepared spices and fragrant oils. And they rested on the Sabbath [b]according to the commandment.

He Is Risen
(Matt. 28:1–10; Mark 16:1–8; John 20:1–10)

24 Now [a]on the first *day* of the week, very early in the morning, they, *and certain *other women* with them, came to the tomb [b]bringing the spices which they had prepared.

2 [a]But they found the stone rolled away from the tomb.

3 [a]Then they went in and did not find the body of the Lord Jesus.

4 And it happened, as they were *greatly perplexed about this, that [a]behold, two men stood by them in shining garments.

5 Then, as they were afraid and bowed *their* faces to the earth, they said to them, "Why do you seek the living among the dead?

---

36 [a]Ps. 69:21
38 [a]John 19:19
39 [a]Mark 15:32
41 [a][Heb. 7:26]
43 [a][Rev. 2:7]
44 [a]Matt. 27:45–56
45 [a]Matt. 27:51
46 [a]Ps. 31:5 [b]John 19:30
47 [a]Mark 15:39
49 [a]Ps. 38:11
50 [a]Matt. 27:57–61
51 [a]Luke 2:25, 38
53 [a]Mark 15:46
54 [a]Matt. 27:62
55 [a]Luke 8:2 [b]Mark 15:47
56 [a]Mark 16:1 [b]Ex. 20:10

CHAPTER 24

1 [a]John 20:1–8 [b]Luke 23:56
2 [a]Mark 16:4
3 [a]Mark 16:5
4 [a]John 20:12

*

23:38 NU omits *written* and *in letters of Greek, Latin, and Hebrew*
23:39 NU *Are You not the Christ? Save*
23:42 NU *"Jesus, remember me*
23:44 NU adds *already*
23:45 NU *obscured*
23:51 NU *who was waiting*
24:1 NU omits *and certain other women with them*
24:4 NU omits *greatly*

KJV

6 He is not here, but is risen: [a]remember how he spake unto you when he was yet in Galilee,

7 Saying, The Son of man must be [a]delivered into the hands of sinful men, and be crucified, and the third day rise again.

8 And [a]they remembered his words,

9 [a]And returned from the sepulchre, and told all these things unto the eleven, and to all the rest.

10 It was Mary Magdalene, and [a]Joanna, and Mary *the mother* of James, and other *women that were* with them, which told these things unto the apostles.

11 [a]And their words seemed to them as idle tales, and they believed them not.

12 [a]Then arose Peter, and ran unto the sepulchre; and stooping down, he beheld the linen clothes laid by themselves, and departed, wondering in himself at that which was come to pass.

The Road to Emmaus
(Mark 16:12, 13)

13 [a]And, behold, two of them went that same day to a village called Emmaus, which was from Jerusalem *about* threescore furlongs.

14 And they talked together of all these things which had happened.

15 And it came to pass, that, while they communed *together* and reasoned, [a]Jesus himself drew near, and went with them.

16 But [a]their eyes were holden that they should not know him.

17 And he said unto them, What manner of communications *are* these that ye have one to another, as ye walk, and are sad?

18 And the one of them, [a]whose name was Cleopas, answering said unto him, Art thou only a stranger in Jerusalem, and hast not known the things which are come to pass there in these days?

19 And he said unto them, What things? And they said unto him, Concerning Jesus of Nazareth, [a]which was a prophet [b]mighty in deed and word before God and all the people:

20 [a]And how the chief priests and our rulers delivered him to be condemned to death, and have crucified him.

21 But we trusted [a]that it had been he which should have redeemed Israel: and beside all this, to day is the third day since these things were done.

22 Yea, and [a]certain women also of our company made us astonished, which were early at the sepulchre;

23 And when they found not his body, they came, saying, that they had also seen a vision of angels, which said that he was alive.

24 And [a]certain of them which were with us went to the sepulchre, and found *it* even so as the women had said: but him they saw not.

25 Then he said unto them, O fools, and slow of heart to believe all that the prophets have spoken:

26 [a]Ought not Christ to have suffered these things, and to enter into his [b]glory?

27 And beginning at [a]Moses and [b]all the prophets, he expounded unto them in all the scriptures the things concerning himself.

The Disciples' Eyes Opened

28 And they drew nigh unto the village, whither they went: and [a]he made as though he would have gone further.

29 But [a]they constrained him, saying, [b]Abide with us: for it is toward evening, and the day is far spent. And he went in to tarry with them.

30 And it came to pass, as [a]he sat at meat with them, he took bread, and blessed *it*, and brake, and gave to them.

31 And their eyes were opened, and they knew him; and he vanished out of their sight.

32 And they said one to another, Did not our

---

6 [a]Matt. 16:21; Mark 8:31; Luke 9:22
7 [a]Hos. 6:1, 2; Luke 9:44; 11:29, 30; 18:31–33
8 [a]Luke 9:22, 44; John 2:19–22
9 [a]Matt. 28:8; Mark 16:10
10 [a]Luke 8:3
11 [a]Luke 24:25
12 [a]John 20:3–6
13 [a]Mark 16:12
15 [a][Matt. 18:20]
16 [a]John 20:14; 21:4
18 [a]John 19:25
19 [a]Matt. 21:11; Luke 7:16; John 3:2; Acts 2:22 [b]Acts 7:22
20 [a]Luke 23:1; Acts 13:27, 28
21 [a]Luke 1:68; 2:38; [Acts 1:6]
22 [a]Matt. 28:8; Mark 16:10; Luke 24:9, 10
24 [a]Luke 24:12
26 [a]Acts 17:2, 3; [Heb. 2:9, 10] [b][1 Pet. 1:10–12]
27 [a][Gen. 3:15; 12:3; Num. 21:9; Deut. 18:15]; John 5:46 [b][Ps. 16:9, 10; 22; 132:11; Is. 7:14; 9:6; Jer. 23:5; 33:14, 15; Ezek. 34:23; 37:25; Dan. 9:24]; Mic. 7:20; [Mal. 3:1; 4:2]; John 1:45; 5:39; [Rom. 1:1–6]
28 [a]Gen. 32:26; 42:7; Mark 6:48
29 [a]Gen. 19:2, 3; Acts 16:15 [b][John 14:23]
30 [a]Matt. 14:19; Mark 8:6; Luke 9:16

NKJV

6 "He is not here, but is risen! [a]Remember how He spoke to you when He was still in Galilee,

7 "saying, 'The Son of Man must be [a]delivered into the hands of sinful men, and be crucified, and the third day rise again.' "

8 And [a]they remembered His words.

9 [a]Then they returned from the tomb and told all these things to the eleven and to all the rest.

10 It was Mary Magdalene, [a]Joanna, Mary *the mother* of James, and the other *women* with them, who told these things to the apostles.

11 [a]And their words seemed to them like idle tales, and they did not believe them.

12 [a]But Peter arose and ran to the tomb; and stooping down, he saw the linen cloths *lying by themselves; and he departed, marveling to himself at what had happened.

The Road to Emmaus
(Mark 16:12, 13)

13 [a]Now behold, two of them were traveling that same day to a village called Emmaus, which was *seven miles from Jerusalem.

14 And they talked together of all these things which had happened.

15 So it was, while they conversed and reasoned, that [a]Jesus Himself drew near and went with them.

16 But [a]their eyes were restrained, so that they did not know Him.

17 And He said to them, "What kind of conversation *is* this that you have with one another as you *walk and are sad?"

18 Then the one [a]whose name was Cleopas answered and said to Him, "Are You the only stranger in Jerusalem, and have You not known the things which happened there in these days?"

19 And He said to them, "What things?" So they said to Him, "The things concerning Jesus of Nazareth, [a]who was a Prophet [b]mighty in deed and word before God and all the people,

20 [a]"and how the chief priests and our rulers delivered Him to be condemned to death, and crucified Him.

21 "But we were hoping [a]that it was He who was going to redeem Israel. Indeed, besides all this, today is the third day since these things happened.

22 "Yes, and [a]certain women of our company, who arrived at the tomb early, astonished us.

23 "When they did not find His body, they came saying that they had also seen a vision of angels who said He was alive.

24 "And [a]certain of those *who were* with us went to the tomb and found *it* just as the women had said; but Him they did not see."

25 Then He said to them, "O foolish ones, and slow of heart to believe in all that the prophets have spoken!

26 [a]"Ought not the Christ to have suffered these things and to enter into His [b]glory?"

27 And beginning at [a]Moses and [b]all the Prophets, He expounded to them in all the Scriptures the things concerning Himself.

The Disciples' Eyes Opened

28 Then they drew near to the village where they were going, and [a]He indicated that He would have gone farther.

29 But [a]they constrained Him, saying, [b]"Abide with us, for it is toward evening, and the day is far spent." And He went in to stay with them.

30 Now it came to pass, as [a]He sat at the table with them, that He took bread, blessed and broke *it*, and gave it to them.

31 Then their eyes were opened and they knew Him; and He vanished from their sight.

32 And they said to one another, "Did not

---

*

24:12 NU omits *lying*
24:13 Lit. *60 stadia*
24:17 NU *walk? And they stood still, looking sad.*

KJV

heart burn within us, while he talked with us by
the way, and while he opened to us the scriptures?
33 And they rose up the same hour, and returned to Jerusalem, and found the eleven gathered together, and them that were with them,
34 Saying, The Lord is risen indeed, and
[a]hath appeared to Simon.
35 And they told what things *were done* in
the way, and how he was known of them in breaking of bread.

Jesus Appears to His Disciples
(*John 20:19–23; Acts 1:3–5; 1 Cor. 15:5*)

36 [a]And as they thus spake, Jesus himself
stood in the midst of them, and saith unto them,
Peace *be* unto you.
37 But they were terrified and affrighted, and
supposed that they had seen [a]a spirit.
38 And he said unto them, Why are ye troubled? and why do thoughts arise in your hearts?
39 Behold my hands and my feet, that it is I
myself: [a]handle me, and see; for a [b]spirit hath
not flesh and bones, as ye see me have.
40 And when he had thus spoken, he shewed
them *his* hands and *his* feet.
41 And while they yet believed not [a]for joy,
and wondered, he said unto them, [b]Have ye here
any meat?
42 And they gave him a piece of a broiled
fish, and of an honeycomb.
43 [a]And he took *it*, and did eat before them.

The Scriptures Opened

44 And he said unto them, [a]These *are* the
words which I spake unto you, while I was yet
with you, that all things must be fulfilled, which
were written in the law of Moses, and *in* the
prophets, and *in* the psalms, concerning me.
45 Then [a]opened he their understanding, that
they might understand the scriptures,
46 And said unto them, [a]Thus it is written,
and thus it behoved Christ to suffer, and to rise
from the dead the third day:
47 And that repentance and [a]remission of
sins should be preached in his name [b]among all
nations, beginning at Jerusalem.
48 And [a]ye are witnesses of these things.
49 [a]And, behold, I send the promise of my
Father upon you: but tarry ye in the city of Jerusalem, until ye be endued with power from on high.

The Ascension
(*Mark 16:19, 20; Acts 1:9*)

50 And he led them out [a]as far as to Bethany,
and he lifted up his hands, and blessed them.
51 [a]And it came to pass, while he blessed
them, he was parted from them, and carried up
into heaven.
52 [a]And they worshipped him, and returned
to Jerusalem with great joy:
53 And were continually [a]in the temple,
praising and blessing God. Amen.

34 [a]1 Cor. 15:5
36 [a]Mark 16:14
37 [a]Mark 6:49
39 [a]John 20:20, 27 [b][1 Cor. 15:50]
41 [a]Gen. 45:26 [b]John 21:5
43 [a]Acts 10:39–41
44 [a]Matt. 16:21; 17:22; 20:18
45 [a]Acts 16:14
46 [a]Acts 17:3
47 [a]Acts 5:31; 10:43; 13:38; 26:18 [b][Jer. 31:34]
48 [a][Acts 1:8]
49 [a]Joel 2:28
50 [a]Acts 1:12
51 [a]Mark 16:19
52 [a]Matt. 28:9
53 [a]Acts 2:46

*

24:40 Some printed New Testaments omit v. 40. It is found in nearly all Gr. mss.
24:42 NU omits *and some honeycomb*
24:46 NU *that the Christ should suffer and rise*
24:49 NU omits *of Jerusalem*
24:53 NU omits *praising and* • NU omits *Amen.*

NKJV

our heart burn within us while He talked with us
on the road, and while He opened the Scriptures
to us?"
33 So they rose up that very hour and returned to Jerusalem, and found the eleven and
those *who were* with them gathered together,
34 saying, "The Lord is risen indeed, and
[a]has appeared to Simon!"
35 And they told about the things *that had
happened* on the road, and how He was known
to them in the breaking of bread.

Jesus Appears to His Disciples
(*John 20:19–23; Acts 1:3–5; 1 Cor. 15:5*)

36 [a]Now as they said these things, Jesus
Himself stood in the midst of them, and said to
them, "Peace to you."
37 But they were terrified and frightened,
and supposed they had seen [a]a spirit.
38 And He said to them, "Why are you troubled? And why do doubts arise in your hearts?
39 "Behold My hands and My feet, that it is
I Myself. [a]Handle Me and see, for a [b]spirit does
not have flesh and bones as you see I have."
40 *When He had said this, He showed them
His hands and His feet.
41 But while they still did not believe [a]for
joy, and marveled, He said to them, [b]"Have you
any food here?"
42 So they gave Him a piece of a broiled fish
*and some honeycomb.
43 [a]And He took *it* and ate in their presence.

The Scriptures Opened

44 Then He said to them, [a]"These *are* the
words which I spoke to you while I was still with
you, that all things must be fulfilled which were
written in the Law of Moses and *the* Prophets and
the Psalms concerning Me."
45 And [a]He opened their understanding, that
they might comprehend the Scriptures.
46 Then He said to them, [a]"Thus it is written,
*and thus it was necessary for the Christ to suffer
and to rise from the dead the third day,
47 "and that repentance and [a]remission of
sins should be preached in His name [b]to all nations, beginning at Jerusalem.
48 "And [a]you are witnesses of these things.
49 [a]"Behold, I send the Promise of My Father
upon you; but tarry in the city *of Jerusalem until
you are endued with power from on high."

The Ascension
(*Mark 16:19, 20; Acts 1:9*)

50 And He led them out [a]as far as Bethany,
and He lifted up His hands and blessed them.
51 [a]Now it came to pass, while He blessed
them, that He was parted from them and carried
up into heaven.
52 [a]And they worshiped Him, and returned
to Jerusalem with great joy,
53 and were continually [a]in the temple
*praising and blessing God. *Amen.

KJV

THE GOSPEL ACCORDING TO

JOHN

The Eternal Word
(Gen. 1:1—2:3)

1 In the beginning [a]was the Word, and the [b]Word was [c]with God, and the Word was [d]God.

2 [a]The same was in the beginning with God.

3 [a]All things were made by him; and without him was not any thing made that was made.

4 [a]In him was life; and [b]the life was the light of men.

5 And [a]the light shineth in darkness; and the darkness comprehended it not.

John's Witness: The True Light

6 There was a [a]man sent from God, whose name *was* John.

7 The same came for a [a]witness, to bear witness of the Light, that all *men* through him might [b]believe.

8 He was not that Light, but *was sent* to bear witness of that [a]Light.

9 [a]*That* was the true Light, which lighteth every man that cometh into the world.

10 He was in the world, and the world was made by him, and [a]the world knew him not.

11 [a]He came unto his own, and his own received him not.

12 But [a]as many as received him, to them gave he power to become the sons of God, *even* to them that believe on his name:

13 [a]Which were born, not of blood, nor of the will of the flesh, nor of the will of man, but of God.

The Word Becomes Flesh

14 [a]And the Word [b]was made [c]flesh, and dwelt among us, (and [d]we beheld his glory, the glory as of the only begotten of the Father,) [e]full of grace and truth.

15 [a]John bare witness of him, and cried, saying, This was he of whom I spake, [b]He that cometh after me is preferred before me: [c]for he was before me.

16 And of his [a]fulness have all we received, and grace for grace.

17 For [a]the law was given by Moses, *but* [b]grace and [c]truth came by Jesus Christ.

18 [a]No man hath seen God at any time; [b]the only begotten Son, which is in the bosom of the Father, he hath declared *him*.

A Voice in the Wilderness
(Matt. 3:1–12; Mark 1:1–8; Luke 3:1–20)

19 And this is [a]the record of John, when the Jews sent priests and Levites from Jerusalem to ask him, Who art thou?

20 And [a]he confessed, and denied not; but confessed, I am not the Christ.

21 And they asked him, What then? Art thou Elias? And he saith, I am not. Art thou [a]that prophet? And he answered, No.

22 Then said they unto him, Who art thou? that we may give an answer to them that sent us. What sayest thou of thyself?

23 He said, [a]I *am* THE VOICE OF ONE CRYING IN

NKJV

THE GOSPEL ACCORDING TO

JOHN

The Eternal Word
(Gen. 1:1—2:3)

1 In the beginning [a]was the Word, and the [b]Word was [c]with God, and the Word was [d]God.

2 [a]He was in the beginning with God.

3 [a]All things were made through Him, and without Him nothing was made that was made.

4 [a]In Him was life, and [b]the life was the light of men.

5 And [a]the light shines in the darkness, and the darkness did not *comprehend it.

John's Witness: The True Light

6 There was a [a]man sent from God, whose name *was* John.

7 This man came for a [a]witness, to bear witness of the Light, that all through him might [b]believe.

8 He was not that Light, but *was sent* to bear witness of that [a]Light.

9 [a]That* was the true Light which gives light to every man coming into the world.

10 He was in the world, and the world was made through Him, and [a]the world did not know Him.

11 [a]He came to His *own, and His *own did not receive Him.

12 But [a]as many as received Him, to them He gave the right to become children of God, to those who believe in His name:

13 [a]who were born, not of blood, nor of the will of the flesh, nor of the will of man, but of God.

The Word Becomes Flesh

14 [a]And the Word [b]became [c]flesh and dwelt among us, and [d]we beheld His glory, the glory as of the only begotten of the Father, [e]full of grace and truth.

15 [a]John bore witness of Him and cried out, saying, "This was He of whom I said, [b]'He who comes after me is preferred before me, [c]for He was before me.' "

16 *And of His [a]fullness we have all received, and grace for grace.

17 For [a]the law was given through Moses, *but* [b]grace and [c]truth came through Jesus Christ.

18 [a]No one has seen God at any time. [b]The only begotten *Son, who is in the bosom of the Father, He has declared *Him*.

A Voice in the Wilderness
(Matt. 3:1–12; Mark 1:1–8; Luke 3:1–20)

19 Now this is [a]the testimony of John, when the Jews sent priests and Levites from Jerusalem to ask him, "Who are you?"

20 [a]He confessed, and did not deny, but confessed, "I am not the Christ."

21 And they asked him, "What then? Are you Elijah?" He said, "I am not." "Are you [a]the Prophet?" And he answered, "No."

22 Then they said to him, "Who are you, that we may give an answer to those who sent us? What do you say about yourself?"

23 He said: [a]"I *am*

CHAPTER 1

1 [a][1 John 1:1 [b]Rev. 19:13 [c][John 17:5] [d][1 John 5:20]
2 [a]Gen. 1:1
3 [a][Col. 1:16, 17]
4 [a][1 John 5:11] [b]John 8:12; 9:5; 12:46
5 [a][John 3:19]
6 [a]Matt. 3:1–17
7 [a]John 3:25–36; 5:33–35 [b][John 3:16]
8 [a]Is. 9:2; 49:6
9 [a]Is. 49:6
10 [a]Heb. 1:2
11 [a][Luke 19:14]
12 [a]Gal. 3:26
13 [a][1 Pet. 1:23]
14 [a]Rev. 19:13 [b]Gal. 4:4 [c]Heb. 2:11 [d]Is. 40:5 [e][John 8:32; 14:6; 18:37]
15 [a]John 3:32 [b][Matt. 3:11] [c][Col. 1:17]
16 [a][Col. 1:19; 2:9]
17 [a][Ex. 20:1] [b][Rom. 5:21; 6:14] [c][John 8:32; 14:6; 18:37]
18 [a]Ex. 33:20 [b]1 John 4:9
19 [a]John 5:33
20 [a]Luke 3:15
21 [a]Deut. 18:15, 18
23 [a]Matt. 3:3

*

1:5 Or *overcome*
1:9 Or *That was the true Light which, coming into the world, gives light to every man.*
1:11 His own things or domain • His own people
1:16 NU *For*
1:18 NU *God*

KJV

THE WILDERNESS, MAKE STRAIGHT THE WAY OF THE LORD, as [b]said the prophet Esaias.

24 And they which were sent were of the Pharisees.

25 And they asked him, and said unto him, Why baptizest thou then, if thou be not that Christ, nor Elias, neither that prophet?

26 John answered them, saying, [a]I baptize with water: [b]but there standeth one among you, whom ye know not;

27 [a]He it is, who coming after me is preferred before me, whose shoe's latchet I am not worthy to unloose.

28 These things were done [a]in Bethabara beyond Jordan, where John was baptizing.

The Lamb of God
(Matt. 3:13–17; Mark 1:9–11; Luke 3:21, 22)

29 The next day John seeth Jesus coming unto him, and saith, Behold [a]the Lamb of God, [b]which taketh away the sin of the world.

30 This is he of whom I said, After me cometh a man which is preferred before me: for he was before me.

31 And I knew him not: but that he should be made manifest to Israel, [a]therefore am I come baptizing with water.

32 [a]And John bare record, saying, I saw the Spirit descending from heaven like a dove, and it abode upon him.

33 And I knew him not: but he that sent me to baptize with water, the same said unto me, Upon whom thou shalt see the Spirit descending, and remaining on him, [a]the same is he which baptizeth with the Holy Ghost.

34 And I saw, and bare record that this is the [a]Son of God.

The First Disciples

35 Again the next day after John stood, and two of his disciples;

36 And looking upon Jesus as he walked, he saith, [a]Behold the Lamb of God!

37 And the two disciples heard him speak, and they [a]followed Jesus.

38 Then Jesus turned, and saw them following, and saith unto them, What seek ye? They said unto him, Rabbi, (which is to say, being interpreted, Master,) where dwellest thou?

39 He saith unto them, Come and see. They came and saw where he dwelt, and abode with him that day: for it was about the tenth hour.

40 One of the two which heard John *speak*, and followed him, was [a]Andrew, Simon Peter's brother.

41 He first findeth his own brother Simon, and saith unto him, We have found the Messias, which is, being interpreted, the Christ.

42 And he brought him to Jesus. And when Jesus beheld him, he said, Thou art Simon the son of Jona: [a]thou shalt be called Cephas, which is by interpretation, A stone.

Philip and Nathanael

43 The day following Jesus would go forth into Galilee, and findeth [a]Philip, and saith unto him, Follow me.

44 Now [a]Philip was of Bethsaida, the city of Andrew and Peter.

45 Philip findeth [a]Nathanael, and saith unto him, We have found him, of whom [b]Moses in the law, and the [c]prophets, did write, Jesus [d]of Nazareth, the [e]son of Joseph.

46 And Nathanael said unto him, [a]Can there any good thing come out of Nazareth? Philip saith unto him, Come and see.

47 Jesus saw Nathanael coming to him, and saith of him, Behold [a]an Israelite indeed, in whom is no guile!

23 [b]Is. 40:3
26 [a]Matt. 3:11 [b]Mal. 3:1
27 [a]Acts 19:4
28 [a]Judg. 7:24
29 [a]Rev. 5:6–14 [b][1 Pet. 2:24]
31 [a]Matt. 3:6
32 [a]Mark 1:10
33 [a]Matt. 3:11
34 [a]John 11:27
36 [a]John 1:29
37 [a]Matt. 4:20, 22
40 [a]Matt. 4:18
42 [a]Matt. 16:18
43 [a]John 6:5; 12:21, 22; 14:8, 9
44 [a]John 12:21
45 [a]John 21:2 [b]Luke 24:27 [c][Zech. 6:12] [d][Matt. 2:23] [e]Luke 3:23
46 [a]John 7:41, 42, 52
47 [a]Ps. 32:2; 73:1

NKJV

[b]*'The voice of one crying in the wilderness: "Make straight the way of the LORD,"'*
as the prophet Isaiah said."

24 Now those who were sent were from the Pharisees.

25 And they asked him, saying, "Why then do you baptize if you are not the Christ, nor Elijah, nor the Prophet?"

26 John answered them, saying, [a]"I baptize with water, [b]but there stands One among you whom you do not know.

27 [a]"It is He who, coming after me, is preferred before me, whose sandal strap I am not worthy to loose."

28 These things were done [a]in *Bethabara beyond the Jordan, where John was baptizing.

The Lamb of God
(Matt. 3:13–17; Mark 1:9–11; Luke 3:21, 22)

29 The next day John saw Jesus coming toward him, and said, "Behold! [a]The Lamb of God [b]who takes away the sin of the world!

30 "This is He of whom I said, 'After me comes a Man who is preferred before me, for He was before me.'

31 "I did not know Him; but that He should be revealed to Israel, [a]therefore I came baptizing with water."

32 [a]And John bore witness, saying, "I saw the Spirit descending from heaven like a dove, and He remained upon Him.

33 "I did not know Him, but He who sent me to baptize with water said to me, 'Upon whom you see the Spirit descending, and remaining on Him, [a]this is He who baptizes with the Holy Spirit.'

34 "And I have seen and testified that this is the [a]Son of God."

The First Disciples

35 Again, the next day, John stood with two of his disciples.

36 And looking at Jesus as He walked, he said, [a]"Behold the Lamb of God!"

37 The two disciples heard him speak, and they [a]followed Jesus.

38 Then Jesus turned, and seeing them following, said to them, "What do you seek?" They said to Him, "Rabbi" (which is to say, when translated, Teacher), "where are You staying?"

39 He said to them, "Come and see." They came and saw where He was staying, and remained with Him that day (now it was about the tenth hour).

40 One of the two who heard John *speak*, and followed Him, was [a]Andrew, Simon Peter's brother.

41 He first found his own brother Simon, and said to him, "We have found the Messiah" (which is translated, the Christ).

42 And he brought him to Jesus. Now when Jesus looked at him, He said, "You are Simon the son of *Jonah. [a]You shall be called Cephas" (which is translated, A Stone).

Philip and Nathanael

43 The following day Jesus wanted to go to Galilee, and He found [a]Philip and said to him, "Follow Me."

44 Now [a]Philip was from Bethsaida, the city of Andrew and Peter.

45 Philip found [a]Nathanael and said to him, "We have found Him of whom [b]Moses in the law, and also the [c]prophets, wrote—Jesus [d]of Nazareth, the [e]son of Joseph."

46 And Nathanael said to him, [a]"Can anything good come out of Nazareth?" Philip said to him, "Come and see."

47 Jesus saw Nathanael coming toward Him, and said of him, "Behold, [a]an Israelite indeed, in whom is no deceit!"

*———
1:28 NU, M *Bethany*
1:42 NU *John*

KJV

48 Nathanael saith unto him, Whence knowest thou me? Jesus answered and said unto him, Before that Philip called thee, when thou wast under the fig tree, I saw thee.

49 Nathanael answered and saith unto him, Rabbi, [a]thou art the Son of God; thou art [b]the King of Israel.

50 Jesus answered and said unto him, Because I said unto thee, I saw thee under the fig tree, believest thou? thou shalt see greater things than these.

51 And he saith unto him, Verily, verily, I say unto you, [a]Hereafter ye shall see heaven open, and the angels of God ascending and descending upon the Son of man.

Water Turned to Wine

2 And the third day there was a [a]marriage in [b]Cana of Galilee; and the [c]mother of Jesus was there:

2 And both Jesus was called, and his disciples, to the marriage.

3 And when they wanted wine, the mother of Jesus saith unto him, They have no wine.

4 Jesus saith unto her, [a]Woman, [b]what have I to do with thee? [c]mine hour is not yet come.

5 His mother saith unto the servants, Whatsoever he saith unto you, do *it*.

6 And there were set there six waterpots of stone, [a]after the manner of the purifying of the Jews, containing two or three firkins apiece.

7 Jesus saith unto them, Fill the waterpots with water. And they filled them up to the brim.

8 And he saith unto them, Draw out now, and bear unto the governor of the feast. And they bare *it*.

9 When the ruler of the feast had tasted [a]the water that was made wine, and knew not whence it was: (but the servants which drew the water knew;) the governor of the feast called the bridegroom,

10 And saith unto him, Every man at the beginning doth set forth good wine; and when men have well drunk, then that which is worse: *but* thou hast kept the good wine until now.

11 This [a]beginning of miracles did Jesus in Cana of Galilee, [b]and manifested forth his glory; and his disciples believed on him.

12 After this he went down to [a]Capernaum, he, and his mother, and [b]his brethren, and his disciples: and they continued there not many days.

Jesus Cleanses the Temple
(Matt. 21:12–17; Mark 11:15–19; Luke 19:45–48)

13 [a]And the Jews' passover was at hand, and Jesus went up to Jerusalem,

14 [a]And found in the temple those that sold oxen and sheep and doves, and the changers of money sitting:

15 And when he had made a scourge of small cords, he drove them all out of the temple, and the sheep, and the oxen; and poured out the changers' money, and overthrew the tables;

16 And said unto them that sold doves, Take these things hence; make not [a]my Father's house an house of merchandise.

17 And his disciples remembered that it was written, [a]THE ZEAL OF THINE HOUSE HATH EATEN ME UP.

18 Then answered the Jews and said unto him, [a]What sign shewest thou unto us, seeing that thou doest these things?

19 Jesus answered and said unto them, [a]Destroy this temple, and in three days I will raise it up.

20 Then said the Jews, Forty and six years was this temple in building, and wilt thou rear it up in three days?

21 But he spake [a]of the temple of his body.

---

49 [a]Ps. 2:7; Matt. 14:33; Luke 1:35 [b]Matt. 21:5
51 [a]Gen. 28:12; [Luke 2:9, 13]; Acts 1:10; 7:55, 56

CHAPTER 2

1 [a][Heb. 13:4] [b]Josh. 19:28 [c]John 19:25
4 [a]John 19:26 [b]2 Sam. 16:10 [c]John 7:6, 8, 30; 8:20
6 [a]Matt. 15:2; [Mark 7:3; Luke 11:39]; John 3:25
9 [a]John 4:46
11 [a]John 4:54 [b][John 1:14]
12 [a]Matt. 4:13; John 4:46 [b]Matt. 12:46; 13:55
13 [a]Ex. 12:14; Deut. 16:1–6; John 5:1; 6:4; 11:55
14 [a]Mal. 3:1; Matt. 21:12; Mark 11:15, 17; Luke 19:45
16 [a]Luke 2:49
17 [a]Ps. 69:9
18 [a]Matt. 12:38; John 6:30
19 [a]Matt. 26:61; 27:40; [Mark 14:58; 15:29]; Luke 24:46; Acts 6:14; 10:40; 1 Cor. 15:4
21 [a][Col. 2:9; Heb. 8:2; 1 Cor. 3:16; 6:19; 2 Cor. 6:16]

*

1:51 NU omits *hereafter*
2:17 NU, M *will eat*

NKJV

48 Nathanael said to Him, "How do You know me?" Jesus answered and said to him, "Before Philip called you, when you were under the fig tree, I saw you."

49 Nathanael answered and said to Him, "Rabbi, [a]You are the Son of God! You are [b]the King of Israel!"

50 Jesus answered and said to him, "Because I said to you, 'I saw you under the fig tree,' do you believe? You will see greater things than these."

51 And He said to him, "Most assuredly, I say to you, [a]hereafter* you shall see heaven open, and the angels of God ascending and descending upon the Son of Man."

Water Turned to Wine

2 On the third day there was a [a]wedding in [b]Cana of Galilee, and the [c]mother of Jesus was there.

2 Now both Jesus and His disciples were invited to the wedding.

3 And when they ran out of wine, the mother of Jesus said to Him, "They have no wine."

4 Jesus said to her, [a]"Woman, [b]what does your concern have to do with Me? [c]My hour has not yet come."

5 His mother said to the servants, "Whatever He says to you, do *it*."

6 Now there were set there six waterpots of stone, [a]according to the manner of purification of the Jews, containing twenty or thirty gallons apiece.

7 Jesus said to them, "Fill the waterpots with water." And they filled them up to the brim.

8 And He said to them, "Draw *some* out now, and take *it* to the master of the feast." And they took *it*.

9 When the master of the feast had tasted [a]the water that was made wine, and did not know where it came from (but the servants who had drawn the water knew), the master of the feast called the bridegroom.

10 And he said to him, "Every man at the beginning sets out the good wine, and when the *guests* have well drunk, then the inferior. You have kept the good wine until now!"

11 This [a]beginning of signs Jesus did in Cana of Galilee, [b]and manifested His glory; and His disciples believed in Him.

12 After this He went down to [a]Capernaum, He, His mother, [b]His brothers, and His disciples; and they did not stay there many days.

Jesus Cleanses the Temple
(Matt. 21:12–17; Mark 11:15–19; Luke 19:45–48)

13 [a]Now the Passover of the Jews was at hand, and Jesus went up to Jerusalem.

14 [a]And He found in the temple those who sold oxen and sheep and doves, and the money changers doing business.

15 When He had made a whip of cords, He drove them all out of the temple, with the sheep and the oxen, and poured out the changers' money and overturned the tables.

16 And He said to those who sold doves, "Take these things away! Do not make [a]My Father's house a house of merchandise!"

17 Then His disciples remembered that it was written, [a]*"Zeal for Your house *has eaten Me up."*

18 So the Jews answered and said to Him, [a]"What sign do You show to us, since You do these things?"

19 Jesus answered and said to them, [a]"Destroy this temple, and in three days I will raise it up."

20 Then the Jews said, "It has taken forty-six years to build this temple, and will You raise it up in three days?"

21 But He was speaking [a]of the temple of His body.

KJV

22 When therefore he was risen from the dead, [a]his disciples remembered that he had said this unto them; and they believed the scripture, and the word which Jesus had said.

The Discerner of Hearts

23 Now when he was in Jerusalem at the passover, in the feast *day,* many believed in his name, when they saw [a]the miracles which he did.

24 But Jesus did not commit himself unto them, because he [a]knew all *men,*

25 And needed not that any should testify of man: for [a]he knew what was in man.

The New Birth

3 There was a man of the Pharisees, named Nicodemus, a ruler of the Jews:

2 [a]The same came to Jesus by night, and said unto him, Rabbi, we know that thou art a teacher come from God: for [b]no man can do these miracles that thou doest, except [c]God be with him.

3 Jesus answered and said unto him, Verily, verily, I say unto thee, [a]Except a man be born again, he cannot see the kingdom of God.

4 Nicodemus saith unto him, How can a man be born when he is old? can he enter the second time into his mother's womb, and be born?

5 Jesus answered, Verily, verily, I say unto thee, [a]Except a man be born of water and *of* the Spirit, he cannot enter into the kingdom of God.

6 That which is born of the flesh is [a]flesh; and that which is born of the Spirit is spirit.

7 Marvel not that I said unto thee, Ye must be born again.

8 [a]The wind bloweth where it listeth, and thou hearest the sound thereof, but canst not tell whence it cometh, and whither it goeth: so is every one that is born of the Spirit.

9 Nicodemus answered and said unto him, [a]How can these things be?

10 Jesus answered and said unto him, Art thou a master of Israel, and knowest not these things?

11 [a]Verily, verily, I say unto thee, We speak that we do know, and testify that we have seen; and [b]ye receive not our witness.

12 If I have told you earthly things, and ye believe not, how shall ye believe, if I tell you *of* heavenly things?

13 And [a]no man hath ascended up to heaven, but he that came down from heaven, *even* the Son of man which is in heaven.

14 [a]And as Moses lifted up the serpent in the wilderness, even so [b]must the Son of man be lifted up:

15 That whosoever [a]believeth in him should not perish, but [b]have eternal life.

16 [a]For God so loved the world, that he gave his only begotten [b]Son, that whosoever believeth in him should not perish, but have everlasting life.

17 [a]For God sent not his Son into the world to condemn the world; but that the world through him might be saved.

18 [a]He that believeth on him is not condemned: but he that believeth not is condemned already, because he hath not believed in the name of the only begotten Son of God.

19 And this is the condemnation, [a]that light is come into the world, and men loved darkness rather than light, because their deeds were evil.

20 For [a]every one that doeth evil hateth the light, neither cometh to the light, lest his deeds should be reproved.

21 But he that doeth truth cometh to the light, that his deeds may be made manifest, that they are [a]wrought in God.

John the Baptist Exalts Christ

22 After these things came Jesus and his disciples into the land of Judaea; and there he tarried with them, [a]and baptized.

22 [a]Luke 24:8
23 [a][Acts 2:22]
24 [a]Rev. 2:23
25 [a]Matt. 9:4

CHAPTER 3

2 [a]John 7:50; 19:39 [b]John 9:16, 33 [c][Acts 10:38]
3 [a][1 Pet. 1:23]
5 [a][Acts 2:38]
6 [a]1 Cor. 15:50
8 [a]Eccl. 11:5
9 [a]John 6:52, 60
11 [a][Matt. 11:27] [b]John 3:32; 8:14
13 [a]Eph. 4:9
14 [a]Num. 21:9 [b]John 8:28; 12:34; 19:18
15 [a]John 6:47 [b]John 3:36
16 [a]Rom. 5:8 [b][Is. 9:6]
17 [a]Luke 9:56
18 [a]John 5:24; 6:40, 47; 20:31
19 [a][John 1:4, 9–11]
20 [a]Eph. 5:11, 13
21 [a]1 Cor. 15:10
22 [a]John 4:1, 2

NKJV

22 Therefore, when He had risen from the dead, [a]His disciples remembered that He had said this *to them; and they believed the Scripture and the word which Jesus had said.

The Discerner of Hearts

23 Now when He was in Jerusalem at the Passover, during the feast, many believed in His name when they saw the [a]signs which He did.

24 But Jesus did not commit Himself to them, because He [a]knew all *men,*

25 and had no need that anyone should testify of man, for [a]He knew what was in man.

The New Birth

3 There was a man of the Pharisees named Nicodemus, a ruler of the Jews.

2 [a]This man came to Jesus by night and said to Him, "Rabbi, we know that You are a teacher come from God; for [b]no one can do these signs that You do unless [c]God is with him."

3 Jesus answered and said to him, "Most assuredly, I say to you, [a]unless one is born again, he cannot see the kingdom of God."

4 Nicodemus said to Him, "How can a man be born when he is old? Can he enter a second time into his mother's womb and be born?"

5 Jesus answered, "Most assuredly, I say to you, [a]unless one is born of water and the Spirit, he cannot enter the kingdom of God.

6 "That which is born of the flesh is [a]flesh, and that which is born of the Spirit is spirit.

7 "Do not marvel that I said to you, 'You must be born again.'

8 [a]"The wind blows where it wishes, and you hear the sound of it, but cannot tell where it comes from and where it goes. So is everyone who is born of the Spirit."

9 Nicodemus answered and said to Him, [a]"How can these things be?"

10 Jesus answered and said to him, "Are you the teacher of Israel, and do not know these things?

11 [a]"Most assuredly, I say to you, We speak what We know and testify what We have seen, and [b]you do not receive Our witness.

12 "If I have told you earthly things and you do not believe, how will you believe if I tell you heavenly things?

13 [a]"No one has ascended to heaven but He who came down from heaven, *that is,* the Son of Man *who is in heaven.

14 [a]"And as Moses lifted up the serpent in the wilderness, even so [b]must the Son of Man be lifted up,

15 "that whoever [a]believes in Him should *not perish but [b]have eternal life.

16 [a]"For God so loved the world that He gave His only begotten [b]Son, that whoever believes in Him should not perish but have everlasting life.

17 [a]"For God did not send His Son into the world to condemn the world, but that the world through Him might be saved.

18 [a]"He who believes in Him is not condemned; but he who does not believe is condemned already, because he has not believed in the name of the only begotten Son of God.

19 "And this is the condemnation, [a]that the light has come into the world, and men loved darkness rather than light, because their deeds were evil.

20 "For [a]everyone practicing evil hates the light and does not come to the light, lest his deeds should be exposed.

21 "But he who does the truth comes to the light, that his deeds may be clearly seen, that they have been [a]done in God."

John the Baptist Exalts Christ

22 After these things Jesus and His disciples came into the land of Judea, and there He remained with them [a]and baptized.

*

2:22 NU, M omit *to them*
3:13 NU omits *who is in heaven*
3:15 NU omits *not perish but*

KJV

23 And John also was baptizing in Aenon near to [a]Salim, because there was much water there: [b]and they came, and were baptized.

24 For [a]John was not yet cast into prison.

25 Then there arose a question between *some* of John's disciples and the Jews about purifying.

26 And they came unto John, and said unto him, Rabbi, he that was with thee beyond Jordan, [a]to whom thou barest witness, behold, the same baptizeth, and all *men* [b]come to him.

27 John answered and said, [a]A man can receive nothing, except it be given him from heaven.

28 Ye yourselves bear me witness, that I said, [a]I am not the Christ, but [b]that I am sent before him.

29 [a]He that hath the bride is the bridegroom: but [b]the friend of the bridegroom, which standeth and heareth him, rejoiceth greatly because of the bridegroom's voice: this my joy therefore is fulfilled.

30 [a]He must increase, but I *must* decrease.

31 [a]He that cometh from above [b]is above all: [c]he that is of the earth is earthly, and speaketh of the earth: [d]he that cometh from heaven is above all.

32 And [a]what he hath seen and heard, that he testifieth; and no man receiveth his testimony.

33 He that hath received his testimony [a]hath set to his seal that God is true.

34 [a]For he whom God hath sent speaketh the words of God: for God giveth not the Spirit [b]by measure *unto him*.

35 [a]The Father loveth the Son, and hath given all things into his hand.

36 [a]He that believeth on the Son hath everlasting life: and he that believeth not the Son shall not see life; but the [b]wrath of God abideth on him.

A Samaritan Woman Meets Her Messiah

4 When therefore the Lord knew how the Pharisees had heard that Jesus made and [a]baptized more disciples than John,

2 (Though Jesus himself baptized not, but his disciples,)

3 He left Judaea, and departed again into Galilee.

4 And he must needs go through Samaria.

5 Then cometh he to a city of Samaria, which is called Sychar, near to the parcel of ground that [a]Jacob [b]gave to his son Joseph.

6 Now Jacob's well was there. Jesus therefore, being wearied with *his* journey, sat thus on the well: *and* it was about the sixth hour.

7 There cometh a woman of Samaria to draw water: Jesus saith unto her, Give me to drink.

8 (For his disciples were gone away unto the city to buy meat.)

9 Then saith the woman of Samaria unto him, How is it that thou, being a Jew, askest drink of me, which am a woman of Samaria? for [a]the Jews have no dealings with the [b]Samaritans.

10 Jesus answered and said unto her, If thou knewest the [a]gift of God, and who it is that saith to thee, Give me to drink; thou wouldest have asked of him, and he would have given thee [b]living water.

11 The woman saith unto him, Sir, thou hast nothing to draw with, and the well is deep: from whence then hast thou that living water?

12 Art thou greater than our father Jacob, which gave us the well, and drank thereof himself, and his children, and his cattle?

13 Jesus answered and said unto her, Whosoever drinketh of this water shall thirst again:

14 But [a]whosoever drinketh of the water that I shall give him shall never thirst; but the water that I shall give him [b]shall be in him a well of water springing up into everlasting life.

23 [a]1 Sam. 9:4 [b]Matt. 3:5, 6
24 [a]Matt. 4:12; 14:3; Mark 6:17; Luke 3:20
26 [a]John 1:7, 15, 27, 34 [b]Mark 2:2; 3:10; 5:24; Luke 8:19
27 [a][Rom. 12:5–8]; 1 Cor. 3:5, 6; 4:7; Heb. 5:4; [James 1:17; 1 Pet. 4:10, 11]
28 [a]John 1:19–27 [b]Mal. 3:1; Mark 1:2; [Luke 1:17]
29 [a]Matt. 22:2; [2 Cor. 11:2; Eph. 5:25, 27]; Rev. 21:9 [b]Song 5:1
30 [a][Is. 9:7]
31 [a]John 3:13; 8:23 [b]Matt. 28:18; John 1:15, 27; 13:13; Rom. 9:5; [Col. 1:17, 18] [c]1 Cor. 15:47 [d]John 6:33; 1 Cor. 15:47; Eph. 1:21; Phil. 2:9
32 [a]Is. 53:1, 3; John 3:11; 15:15
33 [a]Rom. 3:4; 1 John 5:10
34 [a]Deut. 18:18; John 7:16 [b]John 1:16
35 [a]Matt. 11:27; Luke 10:22; John 5:20; [Heb. 2:8]
36 [a]John 3:16, 17; 6:47; Rom. 1:17; 1 John 5:10 [b]Rom. 1:18; Eph. 5:6; 1 Thess. 1:10

CHAPTER 4

1 [a]John 3:22, 26; 1 Cor. 1:17
5 [a]Gen. 33:19; Josh. 24:32 [b]Gen. 48:22; Josh. 4:12
9 [a]Acts 10:28 [b]2 Kin. 17:24; Matt. 10:5, 6; Luke 9:52; 10:33; 17:16; John 8:48
10 [a][Rom. 5:15] [b]Is. 12:3; 44:3; Jer. 2:13; Zech. 13:1; 14:8; John 7:38
14 [a][John 6:35, 58] [b]John 7:37, 38

NKJV

23 Now John also was baptizing in Aenon near [a]Salim, because there was much water there. [b]And they came and were baptized.

24 For [a]John had not yet been thrown into prison.

25 Then there arose a dispute between *some* of John's disciples and the Jews about purification.

26 And they came to John and said to him, "Rabbi, He who was with you beyond the Jordan, [a]to whom you have testified—behold, He is baptizing, and all [b]are coming to Him!"

27 John answered and said, [a]"A man can receive nothing unless it has been given to him from heaven.

28 "You yourselves bear me witness, that I said, [a]'I am not the Christ,' but, [b]'I have been sent before Him.'

29 [a]"He who has the bride is the bridegroom; but [b]the friend of the bridegroom, who stands and hears him, rejoices greatly because of the bridegroom's voice. Therefore this joy of mine is fulfilled.

30 [a]"He must increase, but I *must* decrease.

31 [a]"He who comes from above [b]is above all; [c]he who is of the earth is earthly and speaks of the earth. [d]He who comes from heaven is above all.

32 "And [a]what He has seen and heard, that He testifies; and no one receives His testimony.

33 "He who has received His testimony [a]has certified that God is true.

34 [a]"For He whom God has sent speaks the words of God, for God does not give the Spirit [b]by measure.

35 [a]"The Father loves the Son, and has given all things into His hand.

36 [a]"He who believes in the Son has everlasting life; and he who does not believe the Son shall not see life, but the [b]wrath of God abides on him."

A Samaritan Woman Meets Her Messiah

4 Therefore, when the Lord knew that the Pharisees had heard that Jesus made and [a]baptized more disciples than John

2 (though Jesus Himself did not baptize, but His disciples),

3 He left Judea and departed again to Galilee.

4 But He needed to go through Samaria.

5 So He came to a city of Samaria which is called Sychar, near the plot of ground that [a]Jacob [b]gave to his son Joseph.

6 Now Jacob's well was there. Jesus therefore, being wearied from *His* journey, sat thus by the well. It was about the sixth hour.

7 A woman of Samaria came to draw water. Jesus said to her, "Give Me a drink."

8 For His disciples had gone away into the city to buy food.

9 Then the woman of Samaria said to Him, "How is it that You, being a Jew, ask a drink from me, a Samaritan woman?" For [a]Jews have no dealings with [b]Samaritans.

10 Jesus answered and said to her, "If you knew the [a]gift of God, and who it is who says to you, 'Give Me a drink,' you would have asked Him, and He would have given you [b]living water."

11 The woman said to Him, "Sir, You have nothing to draw with, and the well is deep. Where then do You get that living water?

12 "Are You greater than our father Jacob, who gave us the well, and drank from it himself, as well as his sons and his livestock?"

13 Jesus answered and said to her, "Whoever drinks of this water will thirst again,

14 "but [a]whoever drinks of the water that I shall give him will never thirst. But the water that I shall give him [b]will become in him a fountain of water springing up into everlasting life."

KJV

15 [a]The woman saith unto him, Sir, give me this water, that I thirst not, neither come hither to draw.

16 Jesus saith unto her, Go, call thy husband, and come hither.

17 The woman answered and said, I have no husband. Jesus said unto her, Thou hast well said, I have no husband:

18 For thou hast had five husbands; and he whom thou now hast is not thy husband: in that saidst thou truly.

19 The woman saith unto him, Sir, [a]I perceive that thou art a prophet.

20 Our fathers worshipped in [a]this mountain; and ye say, that in [b]Jerusalem is the place where men ought to worship.

21 Jesus saith unto her, Woman, believe me, the hour cometh, [a]when ye shall neither in this mountain, nor yet at Jerusalem, worship the Father.

22 Ye worship [a]ye know not what: we know what we worship: for [b]salvation is of the Jews.

23 But the hour cometh, and now is, when the true worshippers shall [a]worship the Father in [b]spirit [c]and in truth: for the Father seeketh such to worship him.

24 [a]God *is* a Spirit: and they that worship him must worship *him* in spirit and in truth.

25 The woman saith unto him, I know that Messias [a]cometh, which is called Christ: when he is come, [b]he will tell us all things.

26 Jesus saith unto her, [a]I that speak unto thee am *he*.

The Whitened Harvest

27 And upon this came his disciples, and marvelled that he talked with the woman: yet no man said, What seekest thou? or, Why talkest thou with her?

28 The woman then left her waterpot, and went her way into the city, and saith to the men,

29 Come, see a man, [a]which told me all things that ever I did: is not this the Christ?

30 Then they went out of the city, and came unto him.

31 In the mean while his disciples prayed him, saying, Master, eat.

32 But he said unto them, I have meat to eat that ye know not of.

33 Therefore said the disciples one to another, Hath any man brought him *ought* to eat?

34 Jesus saith unto them, [a]My meat is to do the will of him that sent me, and to [b]finish his work.

35 Say not ye, There are yet four months, and *then* cometh [a]harvest? behold, I say unto you, Lift up your eyes, and look on the fields; [b]for they are white already to harvest.

36 [a]And he that reapeth receiveth wages, and gathereth fruit unto life eternal: that [b]both he that soweth and he that reapeth may rejoice together.

37 And herein is that saying true, [a]One soweth, and another reapeth.

38 I sent you to reap that whereon ye bestowed no labour: [a]other men laboured, and ye are entered into their labours.

The Savior of the World

39 And many of the Samaritans of that city believed on him [a]for the saying of the woman, which testified, He told me all that ever I did.

40 So when the Samaritans were come unto him, they besought him that he would tarry with them: and he abode there two days.

41 And many more believed because of his own [a]word;

42 And said unto the woman, Now we believe, not because of thy saying: for [a]we have heard *him* ourselves, and know that this is indeed the Christ, the Saviour of the world.

15 [a]John 6:34, 35; 17:2, 3; [Rom. 6:23; 1 John 5:20]
19 [a]Matt. 21:11; Luke 7:16, 39; 24:19; John 6:14; 7:40; 9:17
20 [a]Gen. 12:6–8; 33:18, 20; Judg. 9:7 [b]Deut. 12:5, 11; 1 Kin. 9:3; 2 Chr. 7:12; Ps. 122:1–9
21 [a][Mal. 1:11]; 1 Tim. 2:8
22 [a][2 Kin. 17:28–41] [b][Is. 2:3; Luke 24:47; Rom. 3:1; 9:4, 5]
23 [a]Matt. 18:20; [Heb. 13:10–14] [b]Phil. 3:3 [c][John 1:17]
24 [a]2 Cor. 3:17
25 [a]Deut. 18:15 [b]John 4:29, 39
26 [a]Dan. 9:25; Matt. 26:63, 64; Mark 14:61, 62
29 [a]John 4:25
34 [a]Ps. 40:7, 8; Heb. 10:9 [b]Job 23:12; [John 6:38; 17:4; 19:30]
35 [a]Gen. 8:22 [b]Matt. 9:37; Luke 10:2
36 [a]Dan. 12:3; Rom. 6:22 [b]1 Thess. 2:19
37 [a]1 Cor. 3:5–9
38 [a]Jer. 44:4; [1 Pet. 1:12]
39 [a]John 4:29
41 [a]Luke 4:32; [John 6:63]
42 [a]John 17:8; 1 John 4:14

*———

4:42 NU omits *the Christ*

NKJV

15 [a]The woman said to Him, "Sir, give me this water, that I may not thirst, nor come here to draw."

16 Jesus said to her, "Go, call your husband, and come here."

17 The woman answered and said, "I have no husband." Jesus said to her, "You have well said, 'I have no husband,'

18 "for you have had five husbands, and the one whom you now have is not your husband; in that you spoke truly."

19 The woman said to Him, "Sir, [a]I perceive that You are a prophet.

20 "Our fathers worshiped on [a]this mountain, and you *Jews* say that in [b]Jerusalem is the place where one ought to worship."

21 Jesus said to her, "Woman, believe Me, the hour is coming [a]when you will neither on this mountain, nor in Jerusalem, worship the Father.

22 "You worship [a]what you do not know; we know what we worship, for [b]salvation is of the Jews.

23 "But the hour is coming, and now is, when the true worshipers will [a]worship the Father in [b]spirit [c]and truth; for the Father is seeking such to worship Him.

24 [a]"God *is* Spirit, and those who worship Him must worship in spirit and truth."

25 The woman said to Him, "I know that Messiah [a]is coming" (who is called Christ). "When He comes, [b]He will tell us all things."

26 Jesus said to her, [a]"I who speak to you am *He*."

The Whitened Harvest

27 And at this *point* His disciples came, and they marveled that He talked with a woman; yet no one said, "What do You seek?" or, "Why are You talking with her?"

28 The woman then left her waterpot, went her way into the city, and said to the men,

29 "Come, see a Man [a]who told me all things that I ever did. Could this be the Christ?"

30 Then they went out of the city and came to Him.

31 In the meantime His disciples urged Him, saying, "Rabbi, eat."

32 But He said to them, "I have food to eat of which you do not know."

33 Therefore the disciples said to one another, "Has anyone brought Him *anything* to eat?"

34 Jesus said to them, [a]"My food is to do the will of Him who sent Me, and to [b]finish His work.

35 "Do you not say, 'There are still four months and *then* comes [a]the harvest'? Behold, I say to you, lift up your eyes and look at the fields, [b]for they are already white for harvest!

36 [a]"And he who reaps receives wages, and gathers fruit for eternal life, that [b]both he who sows and he who reaps may rejoice together.

37 "For in this the saying is true: [a]'One sows and another reaps.'

38 "I sent you to reap that for which you have not labored; [a]others have labored, and you have entered into their labors."

The Savior of the World

39 And many of the Samaritans of that city believed in Him [a]because of the word of the woman who testified, "He told me all that I *ever* did."

40 So when the Samaritans had come to Him, they urged Him to stay with them; and He stayed there two days.

41 And many more believed because of His own [a]word.

42 Then they said to the woman, "Now we believe, not because of what you said, for [a]we ourselves have heard *Him* and we know that this is indeed *the Christ, the Savior of the world."

KJV

Welcome at Galilee

43 Now after two days he departed thence, and went into Galilee.

44 For [a]Jesus himself testified, that a prophet hath no honour in his own country.

45 Then when he was come into Galilee, the Galilaeans received him, [a]having seen all the things that he did at Jerusalem at the feast: [b]for they also went unto the feast.

A Nobleman's Son Healed

46 So Jesus came again into Cana of Galilee, [a]where he made the water wine. And there was a certain nobleman, whose son was sick at Capernaum.

47 When he heard that Jesus was come out of Judaea into Galilee, he went unto him, and besought him that he would come down, and heal his son: for he was at the point of death.

48 Then said Jesus unto him, [a]Except ye see signs and wonders, ye will not believe.

49 The nobleman saith unto him, Sir, come down ere my child die.

50 Jesus saith unto him, Go thy way; thy son liveth. And the man believed the word that Jesus had spoken unto him, and he went his way.

51 And as he was now going down, his servants met him, and told *him,* saying, Thy son liveth.

52 Then enquired he of them the hour when he began to amend. And they said unto him, Yesterday at the seventh hour the fever left him.

53 So the father knew that *it was* at the same hour, in the which Jesus said unto him, Thy son liveth: and himself believed, and his whole house.

54 This *is* again the second miracle *that* Jesus did, when he was come out of Judaea into Galilee.

A Man Healed at the Pool of Bethesda

5 After [a]this there was a feast of the Jews; and Jesus [b]went up to Jerusalem.

2 Now there is at Jerusalem [a]by the sheep *market* a pool, which is called in the Hebrew tongue Bethesda, having five porches.

3 In these lay a great multitude of impotent folk, of blind, halt, withered, waiting for the moving of the water.

4 For an angel went down at a certain season into the pool, and troubled the water: whosoever then first after the troubling of the water stepped in was made whole of whatsoever disease he had.

5 And a certain man was there, which had an infirmity thirty and eight years.

6 When Jesus saw him lie, and knew that he had been now a long time *in that case,* he saith unto him, Wilt thou be made whole?

7 The impotent man answered him, Sir, I have no man, when the water is troubled, to put me into the pool: but while I am coming, another steppeth down before me.

8 Jesus saith unto him, [a]Rise, take up thy bed, and walk.

9 And immediately the man was made whole, and took up his bed, and walked: and [a]on the same day was the sabbath.

10 The Jews therefore said unto him that was cured, It is the sabbath day: [a]it is not lawful for thee to carry *thy* bed.

11 He answered them, He that made me whole, the same said unto me, Take up thy bed, and walk.

12 Then asked they him, What man is that which said unto thee, Take up thy bed, and walk?

13 And he that was [a]healed wist not who it was: for Jesus had conveyed himself away, a multitude being in *that* place.

14 Afterward Jesus findeth him in the temple, and said unto him, Behold, thou art made whole: [a]sin no more, lest a worse thing come unto thee.

---

44 [a]Matt. 13:57; Mark 6:4; Luke 4:24
45 [a]John 2:13, 23; 3:2 [b]Deut. 16:16
46 [a]John 2:1, 11
48 [a]John 6:30; Rom. 15:19; 1 Cor. 1:22; 2 Cor. 12:12; [2 Thess. 2:9]; Heb. 2:4

CHAPTER 5

1 [a]Lev. 23:2; Deut. 16:16 [b]John 2:13
2 [a]Neh. 3:1, 32; 12:39
8 [a]Matt. 9:6; Mark 2:11; Luke 5:24
9 [a]John 9:14
10 [a]Ex. 20:10; Neh. 13:19; Jer. 17:21, 22; Matt. 12:2; Mark 2:24; Luke 6:2
13 [a]Luke 13:14; 22:51
14 [a]Matt. 12:45; [Mark 2:5]; John 8:11

*

5:2 NU *Bethzatha*
5:3 NU omits the rest of v. 3 and all of v. 4

NKJV

Welcome at Galilee

43 Now after the two days He departed from there and went to Galilee.

44 For [a]Jesus Himself testified that a prophet has no honor in his own country.

45 So when He came to Galilee, the Galileans received Him, [a]having seen all the things He did in Jerusalem at the feast; [b]for they also had gone to the feast.

A Nobleman's Son Healed

46 So Jesus came again to Cana of Galilee [a]where He had made the water wine. And there was a certain nobleman whose son was sick at Capernaum.

47 When he heard that Jesus had come out of Judea into Galilee, he went to Him and implored Him to come down and heal his son, for he was at the point of death.

48 Then Jesus said to him, [a]"Unless you *people* see signs and wonders, you will by no means believe."

49 The nobleman said to Him, "Sir, come down before my child dies!"

50 Jesus said to him, "Go your way; your son lives." So the man believed the word that Jesus spoke to him, and he went his way.

51 And as he was now going down, his servants met him and told *him,* saying, "Your son lives!"

52 Then he inquired of them the hour when he got better. And they said to him, "Yesterday at the seventh hour the fever left him."

53 So the father knew that *it was* at the same hour in which Jesus said to him, "Your son lives." And he himself believed, and his whole household.

54 This again *is* the second sign Jesus did when He had come out of Judea into Galilee.

A Man Healed at the Pool of Bethesda

5 After [a]this there was a feast of the Jews, and Jesus [b]went up to Jerusalem.

2 Now there is in Jerusalem [a]by the Sheep *Gate* a pool, which is called in Hebrew, *Bethesda, having five porches.

3 In these lay a great multitude of sick people, blind, lame, paralyzed, *waiting for the moving of the water.

4 For an angel went down at a certain time into the pool and stirred up the water; then whoever stepped in first, after the stirring of the water, was made well of whatever disease he had.

5 Now a certain man was there who had an infirmity thirty-eight years.

6 When Jesus saw him lying there, and knew that he already had been *in that condition* a long time, He said to him, "Do you want to be made well?"

7 The sick man answered Him, "Sir, I have no man to put me into the pool when the water is stirred up; but while I am coming, another steps down before me."

8 Jesus said to him, [a]"Rise, take up your bed and walk."

9 And immediately the man was made well, took up his bed, and walked. And [a]that day was the Sabbath.

10 The Jews therefore said to him who was cured, "It is the Sabbath; [a]it is not lawful for you to carry your bed."

11 He answered them, "He who made me well said to me, 'Take up your bed and walk.' "

12 Then they asked him, "Who is the Man who said to you, 'Take up your bed and walk'?"

13 But the one who was [a]healed did not know who it was, for Jesus had withdrawn, a multitude being in *that* place.

14 Afterward Jesus found him in the temple, and said to him, "See, you have been made well. [a]Sin no more, lest a worse thing come upon you."

KJV

15 The man departed, and told the Jews that
it was Jesus, which had made him whole.

Honor the Father and the Son

16 And therefore did the Jews [a]persecute
Jesus, and sought to slay him, because he had
done these things on the sabbath day.
17 But Jesus answered them, [a]My Father
worketh hitherto, and I work.
18 Therefore the Jews [a]sought the more to
kill him, because he not only had broken the sabbath, but said also that God was his Father, [b]mak-
ing himself equal with God.
19 Then answered Jesus and said unto them,
Verily, verily, I say unto you, [a]The Son can do
nothing of himself, but what he seeth the Father
do: for what things soever he doeth, these also
doeth the Son likewise.
20 For [a]the Father loveth the Son, and
[b]sheweth him all things that himself doeth: and
he will shew him greater works than these, that
ye may marvel.
21 For as the Father raiseth up the dead, and
quickeneth *them;* [a]even so the Son quickeneth
whom he will.
22 For the Father judgeth no man, but [a]hath
committed all judgment unto the Son:
23 That all *men* should honour the Son, even
as they honour the Father. [a]He that honoureth
not the Son honoureth not the Father which hath
sent him.

Life and Judgment Are Through the Son

24 Verily, verily, I say unto you, [a]He that
heareth my word, and believeth on him that sent
me, hath everlasting life, and shall not come into
condemnation; [b]but is passed from death unto life.
25 Verily, verily, I say unto you, The hour is
coming, and now is, when [a]the dead shall hear
the voice of the Son of God: and they that hear
shall live.
26 For [a]as the Father hath life in himself; so
hath he given to the Son to have [b]life in himself;
27 And [a]hath given him authority to execute
judgment also, [b]because he is the Son of man.
28 Marvel not at this: for the hour is coming,
in the which all that are in the graves shall [a]hear
his voice,
29 [a]And shall come forth; [b]they that have
done good, unto the resurrection of life; and they
that have done evil, unto the resurrection of
damnation.
30 [a]I can of mine own self do nothing: as I
hear, I judge: and my judgment is just; because
[b]I seek not mine own will, but the will of the Father which hath sent me.

The Fourfold Witness

31 [a]If I bear witness of myself, my witness
is not true.
32 [a]There is another that beareth witness of
me; and I know that the witness which he witnesseth of me is true.
33 Ye sent unto John, [a]and he bare witness
unto the truth.
34 But I receive not testimony from man: but
these things I say, that ye might be saved.
35 He was a burning and [a]a shining light:
and [b]ye were willing for a season to rejoice in
his light.
36 But [a]I have greater witness than *that* of
John: for [b]the works which the Father hath given
me to finish, the same [c]works that I do, bear witness of me, that the Father hath sent me.
37 And the Father himself, which hath sent
me, [a]hath borne witness of me. Ye have neither
heard his voice at any time, [b]nor seen his shape.
38 And ye have not his word abiding in you:
for whom he hath sent, him ye believe not.
39 [a]Search the scriptures; for in them ye

16 [a]John 8:37; 10:39
17 [a][John 9:4; 17:4]
18 [a]John 7:1, 19 [b]John 10:30
19 [a]John 5:30; 6:38; 8:28; 12:49; 14:10
20 [a]Matt. 3:17 [b][Matt. 11:27]
21 [a][John 11:25]
22 [a][Acts 17:31]
23 [a]1 John 2:23
24 [a]John 3:16, 18; 6:47 [b][1 John 3:14]
25 [a][Col. 2:13]
26 [a]Ps. 36:9 [b]1 Cor. 15:45
27 [a][Acts 10:42; 17:31] [b]Dan. 7:13
28 [a][1 Thess. 4:15–17]
29 [a]Is. 26:19 [b]Dan. 12:2
30 [a]John 5:19 [b]Matt. 26:39
31 [a]John 8:14
32 [a][Matt. 3:17]
33 [a][John 1:15, 19, 27, 32]
35 [a]2 Pet. 1:19 [b]Mark 6:20
36 [a]1 John 5:9 [b]John 3:2; 10:25; 17:4 [c]John 9:16; 10:38
37 [a]Matt. 3:17 [b]1 John 4:12
39 [a]Is. 8:20; 34:16

*
5:16 NU omits *and sought to kill Him*

NKJV

15 The man departed and told the Jews that
it was Jesus who had made him well.

Honor the Father and the Son

16 For this reason the Jews [a]persecuted
Jesus, *and sought to kill Him, because He had
done these things on the Sabbath.
17 But Jesus answered them, [a]"My Father
has been working until now, and I have been
working."
18 Therefore the Jews [a]sought all the more
to kill Him, because He not only broke the Sabbath, but also said that God was His Father, [b]mak-
ing Himself equal with God.
19 Then Jesus answered and said to them,
"Most assuredly, I say to you, [a]the Son can do
nothing of Himself, but what He sees the Father
do; for whatever He does, the Son also does in
like manner.
20 "For [a]the Father loves the Son, and
[b]shows Him all things that He Himself does; and
He will show Him greater works than these, that
you may marvel.
21 "For as the Father raises the dead and
gives life to *them,* [a]even so the Son gives life to
whom He will.
22 "For the Father judges no one, but [a]has
committed all judgment to the Son,
23 "that all should honor the Son just as they
honor the Father. [a]He who does not honor the
Son does not honor the Father who sent Him.

Life and Judgment Are Through the Son

24 "Most assuredly, I say to you, [a]he who
hears My word and believes in Him who sent Me
has everlasting life, and shall not come into judgment, [b]but has passed from death into life.
25 "Most assuredly, I say to you, the hour is
coming, and now is, when [a]the dead will hear the
voice of the Son of God; and those who hear will
live.
26 "For [a]as the Father has life in Himself,
so He has granted the Son to have [b]life in Himself,
27 "and [a]has given Him authority to execute
judgment also, [b]because He is the Son of Man.
28 "Do not marvel at this; for the hour is
coming in which all who are in the graves will
[a]hear His voice
29 [a]"and come forth—[b]those who have done
good, to the resurrection of life, and those who
have done evil, to the resurrection of condemnation.
30 [a]"I can of Myself do nothing. As I hear, I
judge; and My judgment is righteous, because [b]I
do not seek My own will but the will of the Father
who sent Me.

The Fourfold Witness

31 [a]"If I bear witness of Myself, My witness
is not true.
32 [a]"There is another who bears witness of
Me, and I know that the witness which He witnesses of Me is true.
33 "You have sent to John, [a]and he has borne
witness to the truth.
34 "Yet I do not receive testimony from man,
but I say these things that you may be saved.
35 "He was the burning and [a]shining lamp,
and [b]you were willing for a time to rejoice in his
light.
36 "But [a]I have a greater witness than
John's; for [b]the works which the Father has given
Me to finish—the very [c]works that I do—bear witness of Me, that the Father has sent Me.
37 "And the Father Himself, who sent Me,
[a]has testified of Me. You have neither heard His
voice at any time, [b]nor seen His form.
38 "But you do not have His word abiding
in you, because whom He sent, Him you do not
believe.
39 [a]"You search the Scriptures, for in them

KJV

think ye have eternal life: and [b]they are they
which testify of me.
40 [a]And ye will not come to me, that ye might
have life.
41 [a]I receive not honour from men.
42 But I know you, that ye have not the love
of God in you.
43 I am come in my Father's name, and ye
receive me not: if another shall come in his own
name, him ye will receive.
44 [a]How can ye believe, which receive honour one of another, and seek not [b]the honour that
cometh from God only?
45 Do not think that I will accuse you to the
Father: [a]there is *one* that accuseth you, *even* Moses, in whom ye trust.
46 For had ye believed Moses, ye would have
believed me: [a]for he wrote of me.
47 But if ye believe [a]not his writings, how
shall ye believe my words?

Feeding the Five Thousand
(Matt. 14:13–21; Mark 6:30–44; Luke 9:10–17)

6 After [a]these things Jesus went over the sea
of Galilee, which is *the sea* of [b]Tiberias.
2 And a great multitude followed him, because they saw his miracles which he did on them
that were [a]diseased.
3 And Jesus went up into a mountain, and
there he sat with his disciples.
4 [a]And the passover, a feast of the Jews,
was nigh.
5 [a]When Jesus then lifted up *his* eyes, and
saw a great company come unto him, he saith
unto [b]Philip, Whence shall we buy bread, that
these may eat?
6 And this he said to prove him: for he himself knew what he would do.
7 Philip answered him, [a]Two hundred
pennyworth of bread is not sufficient for them,
that every one of them may take a little.
8 One of his disciples, [a]Andrew, Simon Peter's brother, saith unto him,
9 There is a lad here, which hath five barley
loaves, and two small fishes: [a]but what are they
among so many?
10 And Jesus said, Make the men sit down.
Now there was much grass in the place. So the
men sat down, in number about five thousand.
11 And Jesus took the loaves; and when he
had given thanks, he distributed to the disciples,
and the disciples to them that were set down; and
likewise of the fishes as much as they would.
12 When they were filled, he said unto his
disciples, Gather up the fragments that remain,
that nothing be lost.
13 Therefore they gathered *them* together,
and filled twelve baskets with the fragments of
the five barley loaves, which remained over and
above unto them that had eaten.
14 Then those men, when they had seen the
miracle that Jesus did, said, This is of a truth [a]that
prophet that should come into the world.

Jesus Walks on the Sea
(Matt. 14:22–33; Mark 6:45–52)

15 When Jesus therefore perceived that they
would come and take him by force, to make him
a [a]king, he departed again into a mountain himself alone.
16 [a]And when even was *now* come, his disciples went down unto the sea,
17 And entered into a ship, and went over
the sea toward Capernaum. And it was now dark,
and Jesus was not come to them.
18 And the sea arose by reason of a great
wind that blew.
19 So when they had rowed about five and
twenty or thirty furlongs, they see Jesus walking
on the sea, and drawing nigh unto the ship: and
they were [a]afraid.

NKJV

you think you have eternal life; and [b]these are
they which testify of Me.
40 [a]"But you are not willing to come to Me
that you may have life.
41 [a]"I do not receive honor from men.
42 "But I know you, that you do not have
the love of God in you.
43 "I have come in My Father's name, and
you do not receive Me; if another comes in his
own name, him you will receive.
44 [a]"How can you believe, who receive
honor from one another, and do not seek [b]the
honor that *comes* from the only God?
45 "Do not think that I shall accuse you to
the Father; [a]there is *one* who accuses you—Moses, in whom you trust.
46 "For if you believed Moses, you would believe Me; [a]for he wrote about Me.
47 "But if you [a]do not believe his writings,
how will you believe My words?"

Feeding the Five Thousand
(Matt. 14:13–21; Mark 6:30–44; Luke 9:10–17)

6 After [a]these things Jesus went over the Sea
of Galilee, which is *the Sea* of [b]Tiberias.
2 Then a great multitude followed Him, because they saw His signs which He performed on
those who were [a]diseased.
3 And Jesus went up on the mountain, and
there He sat with His disciples.
4 [a]Now the Passover, a feast of the Jews,
was near.
5 [a]Then Jesus lifted up *His* eyes, and seeing
a great multitude coming toward Him, He said
to [b]Philip, "Where shall we buy bread, that these
may eat?"
6 But this He said to test him, for He Himself
knew what He would do.
7 Philip answered Him, [a]"Two hundred denarii worth of bread is not sufficient for them,
that every one of them may have a little."
8 One of His disciples, [a]Andrew, Simon Peter's brother, said to Him,
9 "There is a lad here who has five barley
loaves and two small fish, [a]but what are they
among so many?"
10 Then Jesus said, "Make the people sit
down." Now there was much grass in the place.
So the men sat down, in number about five
thousand.
11 And Jesus took the loaves, and when
He had given thanks He distributed *them* *to
the disciples, and the disciples to those sitting
down; and likewise of the fish, as much as they
wanted.
12 So when they were filled, He said to His
disciples, "Gather up the fragments that remain,
so that nothing is lost."
13 Therefore they gathered *them* up, and
filled twelve baskets with the fragments of the
five barley loaves which were left over by those
who had eaten.
14 Then those men, when they had seen the
sign that Jesus did, said, "This is truly [a]the
Prophet who is to come into the world."

Jesus Walks on the Sea
(Matt. 14:22–33; Mark 6:45–52)

15 Therefore when Jesus perceived that they
were about to come and take Him by force to
make Him [a]king, He departed again to the mountain by Himself alone.
16 [a]Now when evening came, His disciples
went down to the sea,
17 got into the boat, and went over the sea
toward Capernaum. And it was already dark, and
Jesus had not come to them.
18 Then the sea arose because a great wind
was blowing.
19 So when they had rowed about *three or
four miles, they saw Jesus walking on the sea and
drawing near the boat; and they were [a]afraid.

39 [b]Luke 24:27
40 [a][John 1:11; 3:19]
41 [a]1 Thess. 2:6
44 [a]John 12:43 [b][Rom. 2:29]
45 [a]Rom. 2:12
46 [a]Deut. 18:15, 18
47 [a]Luke 16:29, 31

CHAPTER 6
1 [a]Mark 6:32 [b]John 6:23; 21:1
2 [a]Matt. 4:23; 8:16; 9:35; 14:36; 15:30; 19:2
4 [a]Deut. 16:1
5 [a]Matt. 14:14 [b]John 1:43
7 [a]Num. 11:21, 22
8 [a]John 1:40
9 [a]2 Kin. 4:43
14 [a]Gen. 49:10
15 [a][John 18:36]
16 [a]Matt. 14:23
19 [a]Matt. 17:6

*

6:11 NU omits *to the disciples, and the disciples*
6:19 Lit. *25 or 30 stadia*

KJV

20 But he saith unto them, [a]It is I; be not afraid.

21 Then they willingly received him into the ship: and immediately the ship was at the land whither they went.

The Bread from Heaven

22 The day following, when the people which stood on the other side of the sea saw that there was none other boat there, save that one whereinto his disciples were entered, and that Jesus went not with his disciples into the boat, but *that* his disciples were gone away alone;

23 (Howbeit there came other boats from Tiberias nigh unto the place where they did eat bread, after that the Lord had given thanks:)

24 When the people therefore saw that Jesus was not there, neither his disciples, they also took shipping, and came to Capernaum, [a]seeking for Jesus.

25 And when they had found him on the other side of the sea, they said unto him, Rabbi, when camest thou hither?

26 Jesus answered them and said, Verily, verily, I say unto you, Ye seek me, not because ye saw the miracles, but because ye did eat of the loaves, and were filled.

27 [a]Labour not for the meat which perisheth, but [b]for that meat which endureth unto everlasting life, which the Son of man shall give unto you: [c]for him hath God the Father sealed.

28 Then said they unto him, What shall we do, that we might work the works of God?

29 Jesus answered and said unto them, [a]This is the work of God, that ye believe on him whom he hath sent.

30 They said therefore unto him, [a]What sign shewest thou then, that we may see, and believe thee? what dost thou work?

31 [a]Our fathers did eat manna in the desert; as it is written, [b]HE GAVE THEM BREAD FROM HEAVEN TO EAT.

32 Then Jesus said unto them, Verily, verily, I say unto you, Moses gave you not that bread from heaven; but [a]my Father giveth you the true bread from heaven.

33 For the bread of God is he which cometh down from heaven, and giveth life unto the world.

34 [a]Then said they unto him, Lord, evermore give us this bread.

35 And Jesus said unto them, [a]I am the bread of life: [b]he that cometh to me shall never hunger; and he that believeth on me shall never [c]thirst.

36 [a]But I said unto you, That ye also have seen me, and believe [b]not.

37 [a]All that the Father giveth me shall come to me; and [b]him that cometh to me I will in no wise cast out.

38 For I came down from heaven, [a]not to do mine own will, [b]but the will of him that sent me.

39 And this is the Father's will which hath sent me, [a]that of all which he hath given me I should lose nothing, but should raise it up again at the last day.

40 And this is the will of him that sent me, [a]that every one which seeth the Son, and believeth on him, may have everlasting life: and I will raise him up at the last day.

Rejected by His Own

41 The Jews then murmured at him, because he said, I am the bread which came down from heaven.

42 And they said, [a]Is not this Jesus, the son of Joseph, whose father and mother we know? how is it then that he saith, I came down from heaven?

43 Jesus therefore answered and said unto them, Murmur not among yourselves.

44 [a]No man can come to me, except the Father which hath sent me [b]draw him: and I will raise him up at the last day.

20 [a]Is. 43:1, 2
24 [a]Mark 1:37; Luke 4:42
27 [a]Matt. 6:19 [b]John 4:14; [Eph. 2:8, 9] [c]Ps. 2:7; Is. 42:1; Matt. 3:17; 17:5; Mark 1:11; 9:7; Luke 3:22; 9:35; John 5:37; Acts 2:22; 2 Pet. 1:17
29 [a]1 Thess. 1:3; James 2:22; [1 John 3:23]; Rev. 2:26
30 [a]Matt. 12:38; 16:1; Mark 8:11; 1 Cor. 1:22
31 [a]Ex. 16:15; Num. 11:7; 1 Cor. 10:3 [b]Ex. 16:4, 15; Neh. 9:15; Ps. 78:24
32 [a]John 3:13, 16
34 [a]John 4:15
35 [a]John 6:48, 58 [b]John 4:14; 7:37; Rev. 7:16 [c]Is. 55:1, 2
36 [a]John 6:26, 64; 15:24 [b]John 10:26
37 [a]John 6:45 [b][Matt. 24:24; John 10:28, 29]; 2 Tim. 2:19; 1 John 2:19
38 [a]Matt. 26:39; John 5:30 [b]John 4:34
39 [a]John 10:28; 17:12; 18:9
40 [a]John 3:15, 16; 4:14; 6:27, 47, 54
42 [a]Matt. 13:55; Mark 6:3; Luke 4:22
44 [a]Song 1:4 [b][Eph. 2:8, 9; Phil. 1:29; 2:12, 13]

NKJV

20 But He said to them, [a]"It is I; do not be afraid."

21 Then they willingly received Him into the boat, and immediately the boat was at the land where they were going.

The Bread from Heaven

22 On the following day, when the people who were standing on the other side of the sea saw that there was no other boat there, except *that one *which His disciples had entered, and that Jesus had not entered the boat with His disciples, but His disciples had gone away alone—

23 however, other boats came from Tiberias, near the place where they ate bread after the Lord had given thanks—

24 when the people therefore saw that Jesus was not there, nor His disciples, they also got into boats and came to Capernaum, [a]seeking Jesus.

25 And when they found Him on the other side of the sea, they said to Him, "Rabbi, when did You come here?"

26 Jesus answered them and said, "Most assuredly, I say to you, you seek Me, not because you saw the signs, but because you ate of the loaves and were filled.

27 [a]"Do not labor for the food which perishes, but [b]for the food which endures to everlasting life, which the Son of Man will give you, [c]because God the Father has set His seal on Him."

28 Then they said to Him, "What shall we do, that we may work the works of God?"

29 Jesus answered and said to them, [a]"This is the work of God, that you believe in Him whom He sent."

30 Therefore they said to Him, [a]"What sign will You perform then, that we may see it and believe You? What work will You do?

31 [a]"Our fathers ate the manna in the desert; as it is written, [b]*'He gave them bread from heaven to eat.'* "

32 Then Jesus said to them, "Most assuredly, I say to you, Moses did not give you the bread from heaven, but [a]My Father gives you the true bread from heaven.

33 "For the bread of God is He who comes down from heaven and gives life to the world."

34 [a]Then they said to Him, "Lord, give us this bread always."

35 And Jesus said to them, [a]"I am the bread of life. [b]He who comes to Me shall never hunger, and he who believes in Me shall never [c]thirst.

36 [a]"But I said to you that you have seen Me and yet [b]do not believe.

37 [a]"All that the Father gives Me will come to Me, and [b]the one who comes to Me I will by no means cast out.

38 "For I have come down from heaven, [a]not to do My own will, [b]but the will of Him who sent Me.

39 "This is the will of the Father who sent Me, [a]that of all He has given Me I should lose nothing, but should raise it up at the last day.

40 "And this is the will of Him who sent Me, [a]that everyone who sees the Son and believes in Him may have everlasting life; and I will raise him up at the last day."

Rejected by His Own

41 The Jews then complained about Him, because He said, "I am the bread which came down from heaven."

42 And they said, [a]"Is not this Jesus, the son of Joseph, whose father and mother we know? How is it then that He says, 'I have come down from heaven'?"

43 Jesus therefore answered and said to them, "Do not murmur among yourselves.

44 [a]"No one can come to Me unless the Father who sent Me [b]draws him; and I will raise him up at the last day.

*______

6:22 NU omits *that* • NU omits *which His disciples had entered*

KJV

45 [a]It is written in the prophets, AND THEY SHALL BE ALL TAUGHT OF GOD. [b]Every man therefore that hath heard, and hath learned of the Father, cometh unto me.

46 [a]Not that any man hath seen the Father, [b]save he which is of God, he hath seen the Father.

47 Verily, verily, I say unto you, [a]He that believeth on me hath everlasting life.

48 [a]I am that bread of life.

49 [a]Your fathers did eat manna in the wilderness, and are dead.

50 [a]This is the bread which cometh down from heaven, that a man may eat thereof, and not die.

51 I am the living bread [a]which came down from heaven: if any man eat of this bread, he shall live for ever: and [b]the bread that I will give is my flesh, which I will give for the life of the world.

52 The Jews therefore [a]strove among themselves, saying, How can this man give us *his* flesh to eat?

53 Then Jesus said unto them, Verily, verily, I say unto you, Except [a]ye eat the flesh of the Son of man, and drink his blood, ye have no life in you.

54 [a]Whoso eateth my flesh, and drinketh my blood, hath eternal life; and I will raise him up at the last day.

55 For my flesh is meat indeed, and my blood is drink indeed.

56 He that eateth my flesh, and drinketh my blood, [a]dwelleth in me, and I in him.

57 As the living Father hath sent me, and I live by the Father: so he that eateth me, even he shall live by me.

58 [a]This is that bread which came down from heaven: not [b]as your fathers did eat manna, and are dead: he that eateth of this bread shall live for ever.

59 These things said he in the synagogue, as he taught in Capernaum.

Many Disciples Turn Away

60 [a]Many therefore of his disciples, when they had heard *this,* said, This is an hard saying; who can hear it?

61 When Jesus knew in himself that his disciples murmured at it, he said unto them, Doth this offend you?

62 [a]*What* and if ye shall see the Son of man ascend up where he was before?

63 [a]It is the spirit that quickeneth; the [b]flesh profiteth nothing: the [c]words that I speak unto you, *they* are spirit, and *they* are life.

64 But [a]there are some of you that believe not. For [b]Jesus knew from the beginning who they were that believed not, and who should betray him.

65 And he said, Therefore [a]said I unto you, that no man can come unto me, except it were given unto him of my Father.

66 [a]From that *time* many of his disciples went back, and walked no more with him.

67 Then said Jesus unto the twelve, Will ye also go away?

68 Then Simon Peter answered him, Lord, to whom shall we go? thou hast [a]the words of eternal life.

69 [a]And we believe and are sure that thou art that Christ, the Son of the living God.

70 Jesus answered them, [a]Have not I chosen you twelve, [b]and one of you is a devil?

71 He spake of [a]Judas Iscariot *the son* of Simon: for he it was that should [b]betray him, being one of the twelve.

Jesus' Brothers Disbelieve

7 After these things Jesus walked in Galilee: for he would not walk in Jewry, [a]because the Jews sought to kill him.

---

45 [a]Is. 54:13; Jer. 31:34; Mic. 4:2; [Heb. 8:10] [b]John 6:37
46 [a]John 1:18 [b]Matt. 11:27; [Luke 10:22]; John 7:29
47 [a][John 3:16, 18]
48 [a]John 6:33, 35; [Gal. 2:20; Col. 3:3, 4]
49 [a]John 6:31, 58
50 [a]John 6:51, 58
51 [a]John 3:13 [b]Heb. 10:5
52 [a]John 7:43; 9:16; 10:19
53 [a]Matt. 26:26
54 [a]John 4:14; 6:27, 40
56 [a][1 John 3:24; 4:15, 16]
58 [a]John 6:49–51 [b]Ex. 16:14–35
60 [a]Matt. 11:6; John 6:66
62 [a]Mark 16:19; John 3:13; Acts 1:9; 2:32, 33; Eph. 4:8
63 [a]Gen. 2:7; 2 Cor. 3:6 [b]John 3:6 [c][John 6:68; 14:24]
64 [a]John 6:36 [b]John 2:24, 25; 13:11
65 [a]John 6:37, 44, 45
66 [a]Luke 9:62; John 6:60
68 [a]Acts 5:20
69 [a]Matt. 16:16; Mark 8:29; Luke 9:20; John 1:49; 11:27
70 [a]Luke 6:13 [b][John 13:27]
71 [a]John 12:4; 13:2, 26 [b]Matt. 26:14–16

CHAPTER 7

1 [a]Matt. 21:38; 26:4; John 5:18; 7:19, 25; 8:37, 40

*

6:45 M *hears and has learned*
6:47 NU omits *in Me*
6:55 NU *true food* • NU *true drink*
6:69 NU *Holy One of God.*
7:1 The ruling authorities

NKJV

45 "It is written in the prophets, [a]*'And they shall all be taught by God.'* [b]Therefore everyone who *has heard and learned from the Father comes to Me.

46 [a]"Not that anyone has seen the Father, [b]except He who is from God; He has seen the Father.

47 "Most assuredly, I say to you, [a]he who believes *in Me has everlasting life.

48 [a]"I am the bread of life.

49 [a]"Your fathers ate the manna in the wilderness, and are dead.

50 [a]"This is the bread which comes down from heaven, that one may eat of it and not die.

51 "I am the living bread [a]which came down from heaven. If anyone eats of this bread, he will live forever; and [b]the bread that I shall give is My flesh, which I shall give for the life of the world."

52 The Jews therefore [a]quarreled among themselves, saying, "How can this Man give us *His* flesh to eat?"

53 Then Jesus said to them, "Most assuredly, I say to you, unless [a]you eat the flesh of the Son of Man and drink His blood, you have no life in you.

54 [a]"Whoever eats My flesh and drinks My blood has eternal life, and I will raise him up at the last day.

55 "For My flesh is *food indeed, and My blood is *drink indeed.

56 "He who eats My flesh and drinks My blood [a]abides in Me, and I in him.

57 "As the living Father sent Me, and I live because of the Father, so he who feeds on Me will live because of Me.

58 [a]"This is the bread which came down from heaven—not [b]as your fathers ate the manna, and are dead. He who eats this bread will live forever."

59 These things He said in the synagogue as He taught in Capernaum.

Many Disciples Turn Away

60 [a]Therefore many of His disciples, when they heard *this,* said, "This is a hard saying; who can understand it?"

61 When Jesus knew in Himself that His disciples complained about this, He said to them, "Does this offend you?

62 [a]"*What* then if you should see the Son of Man ascend where He was before?

63 [a]"It is the Spirit who gives life; the [b]flesh profits nothing. The [c]words that I speak to you are spirit, and *they* are life.

64 "But [a]there are some of you who do not believe." For [b]Jesus knew from the beginning who they were who did not believe, and who would betray Him.

65 And He said, "Therefore [a]I have said to you that no one can come to Me unless it has been granted to him by My Father."

66 [a]From that *time* many of His disciples went back and walked with Him no more.

67 Then Jesus said to the twelve, "Do you also want to go away?"

68 But Simon Peter answered Him, "Lord, to whom shall we go? You have [a]the words of eternal life.

69 [a]"Also we have come to believe and know that You are the *Christ, the Son of the living God."

70 Jesus answered them, [a]"Did I not choose you, the twelve, [b]and one of you is a devil?"

71 He spoke of [a]Judas Iscariot, *the son* of Simon, for it was he who would [b]betray Him, being one of the twelve.

Jesus' Brothers Disbelieve

7 After these things Jesus walked in Galilee; for He did not want to walk in Judea, [a]because the *Jews sought to kill Him.

KJV

2 [a]Now the Jews' feast of tabernacles was at hand.

3 [a]His brethren therefore said unto him, Depart hence, and go into Judaea, that thy disciples also may see the works that thou doest.

4 For *there is* no man *that* doeth any thing in secret, and he himself seeketh to be known openly. If thou do these things, shew thyself to the world.

5 For [a]neither did his [b]brethren believe in him.

6 Then Jesus said unto them, [a]My time is not yet come: but your time is alway ready.

7 [a]The world cannot hate you; but me it hateth, [b]because I testify of it, that the works thereof are evil.

8 Go ye up unto this feast: I go not up yet unto this feast; [a]for my time is not yet full come.

9 When he had said these words unto them, he abode *still* in Galilee.

The Heavenly Scholar

10 But when his brethren were gone up, then went he also up unto the feast, not openly, but as it were in secret.

11 Then [a]the Jews sought him at the feast, and said, Where is he?

12 And [a]there was much murmuring among the people concerning him: for [b]some said, He is a good man: others said, Nay; but he deceiveth the people.

13 Howbeit no man spake openly of him [a]for fear of the Jews.

14 Now about the midst of the feast Jesus went up into the temple, and [a]taught.

15 [a]And the Jews marvelled, saying, How knoweth this man letters, having never learned?

16 Jesus answered them, and said, [a]My doctrine is not mine, but his that sent me.

17 [a]If any man will do his will, he shall know of the doctrine, whether it be of God, or *whether* I speak of myself.

18 [a]He that speaketh of himself seeketh his own glory: but he that [b]seeketh his glory that sent him, the same is true, and [c]no unrighteousness is in him.

19 [a]Did not Moses give you the law, and *yet* none of you keepeth the law? [b]Why go ye about to kill me?

20 The people answered and said, [a]Thou hast a devil: who goeth about to kill thee?

21 Jesus answered and said unto them, I have done one work, and ye all marvel.

22 [a]Moses therefore gave unto you circumcision; (not because it is of Moses, [b]but of the fathers;) and ye on the sabbath day circumcise a man.

23 If a man on the sabbath day receive circumcision, that the law of Moses should not be broken; are ye angry at me, because [a]I have made a man every whit whole on the sabbath day?

24 [a]Judge not according to the appearance, but judge righteous judgment.

Could This Be the Christ?

25 Then said some of them of Jerusalem, Is not this he, whom they seek to [a]kill?

26 But, lo, he speaketh boldly, and they say nothing unto him. [a]Do the rulers know indeed that this is the very Christ?

27 [a]Howbeit we know this man whence he is: but when Christ cometh, no man knoweth whence he is.

28 Then cried Jesus in the temple as he taught, saying, [a]Ye both know me, and ye know whence I am: and [b]I am not come of myself, but he that sent me [c]is true, [d]whom ye know not.

29 But [a]I know him: for I am from him, and he hath sent me.

30 Then [a]they sought to take him: but [b]no man laid hands on him, because his hour was not yet come.

2 [a]Lev. 23:34
3 [a]Matt. 12:46
5 [a]Ps. 69:8 [b]Mark 3:21
6 [a]John 2:4; 8:20
7 [a][John 15:19] [b]John 3:19
8 [a]John 8:20
11 [a]John 11:56
12 [a]John 9:16; 10:19 [b]Luke 7:16
13 [a][John 9:22; 12:42; 19:38]
14 [a]Mark 6:34
15 [a]Matt. 13:54
16 [a]John 3:11
17 [a]John 3:21; 8:43
18 [a]John 5:41 [b]John 8:50 [c][2 Cor. 5:21]
19 [a]Deut. 33:4 [b]Matt. 12:14
20 [a]John 8:48, 52
22 [a]Lev. 12:3 [b]Gen. 17:9–14
23 [a]John 5:8, 9, 16
24 [a]Prov. 24:23
25 [a]Matt. 21:38; 26:4
26 [a]John 7:48
27 [a]Luke 4:22
28 [a]John 8:14 [b]John 5:43 [c]Rom. 3:4 [d]John 1:18; 8:55
29 [a]Matt. 11:27
30 [a]Mark 11:18 [b]John 7:32, 44; 8:20; 10:39

*

7:8 NU omits *yet*
7:16 NU, M *So Jesus*
7:26 NU omits *truly*
7:29 NU, M omit *But*

NKJV

2 [a]Now the Jews' Feast of Tabernacles was at hand.

3 [a]His brothers therefore said to Him, "Depart from here and go into Judea, that Your disciples also may see the works that You are doing.

4 "For no one does anything in secret while he himself seeks to be known openly. If You do these things, show Yourself to the world."

5 For [a]even His [b]brothers did not believe in Him.

6 Then Jesus said to them, [a]"My time has not yet come, but your time is always ready.

7 [a]"The world cannot hate you, but it hates Me [b]because I testify of it that its works are evil.

8 "You go up to this feast. I am not *yet going up to this feast, [a]for My time has not yet fully come."

9 When He had said these things to them, He remained in Galilee.

The Heavenly Scholar

10 But when His brothers had gone up, then He also went up to the feast, not openly, but as it were in secret.

11 Then [a]the Jews sought Him at the feast, and said, "Where is He?"

12 And [a]there was much complaining among the people concerning Him. [b]Some said, "He is good"; others said, "No, on the contrary, He deceives the people."

13 However, no one spoke openly of Him [a]for fear of the Jews.

14 Now about the middle of the feast Jesus went up into the temple and [a]taught.

15 [a]And the Jews marveled, saying, "How does this Man know letters, having never studied?"

16 *Jesus answered them and said, [a]"My doctrine is not Mine, but His who sent Me.

17 [a]"If anyone wills to do His will, he shall know concerning the doctrine, whether it is from God or *whether* I speak on My own *authority*.

18 [a]"He who speaks from himself seeks his own glory; but He who [b]seeks the glory of the One who sent Him is true, and [c]no unrighteousness is in Him.

19 [a]"Did not Moses give you the law, yet none of you keeps the law? [b]Why do you seek to kill Me?"

20 The people answered and said, [a]"You have a demon. Who is seeking to kill You?"

21 Jesus answered and said to them, "I did one work, and you all marvel.

22 [a]"Moses therefore gave you circumcision (not that it is from Moses, [b]but from the fathers), and you circumcise a man on the Sabbath.

23 "If a man receives circumcision on the Sabbath, so that the law of Moses should not be broken, are you angry with Me because [a]I made a man completely well on the Sabbath?

24 [a]"Do not judge according to appearance, but judge with righteous judgment."

Could This Be the Christ?

25 Now some of them from Jerusalem said, "Is this not He whom they seek to [a]kill?

26 "But look! He speaks boldly, and they say nothing to Him. [a]Do the rulers know indeed that this is *truly the Christ?

27 [a]"However, we know where this Man is from; but when the Christ comes, no one knows where He is from."

28 Then Jesus cried out, as He taught in the temple, saying, [a]"You both know Me, and you know where I am from; and [b]I have not come of Myself, but He who sent Me [c]is true, [d]whom you do not know.

29 *"But [a]I know Him, for I am from Him, and He sent Me."

30 Therefore [a]they sought to take Him; but [b]no one laid a hand on Him, because His hour had not yet come.

KJV

31 And [a]many of the people believed on him,
and said, When Christ cometh, will he do more
miracles than these which this *man* hath done?

Jesus and the Religious Leaders

32 The Pharisees heard that the people murmured such things concerning him; and the Pharisees and the chief priests sent officers to take him.
33 Then said Jesus unto them, [a]Yet a little
while am I with you, and *then* I [b]go unto him
that sent me.
34 Ye [a]shall seek me, and shall not find *me:*
and where I am, *thither* ye [b]cannot come.
35 Then said the Jews among themselves,
Whither will he go, that we shall not find him?
will he go unto [a]the dispersed among the Gentiles,
and teach the Gentiles?
36 What *manner of* saying is this that he said,
Ye shall seek me, and shall not find *me:* and where
I am, *thither* ye cannot come?

The Promise of the Holy Spirit

37 [a]In the last day, that great *day* of the feast,
Jesus stood and cried, saying, [b]If any man thirst,
let him come unto me, and drink.
38 [a]He that believeth on me, as the scripture
hath said, [b]out of his belly shall flow rivers of
living water.
39 ([a]But this spake he of the Spirit, which
they that believe on him should receive: for the
Holy Ghost was not yet *given;* because that Jesus
was not yet [b]glorified.)

Who Is He?

40 Many of the people therefore, when they
heard this saying, said, Of a truth this is [a]the
Prophet.
41 Others said, This is [a]the Christ. But some
said, Shall Christ come out of Galilee?
42 [a]Hath not the scripture said, That Christ
cometh of the seed of David, and out of the town
of Bethlehem, [b]where David was?
43 So [a]there was a division among the people
because of him.
44 And [a]some of them would have taken him;
but no man laid hands on him.

Rejected by the Authorities

45 Then came the officers to the chief priests
and Pharisees; and they said unto them, Why
have ye not brought him?
46 The officers answered, [a]Never man spake
like this man.
47 Then answered them the Pharisees, Are
ye also deceived?
48 Have any of the rulers or of the Pharisees
believed on him?
49 But this people who knoweth not the law
are cursed.
50 Nicodemus saith unto them, [a](he that
came to Jesus by night, being one of them,)
51 [a]Doth our law judge *any* man, before it
hear him, and know what he doeth?
52 They answered and said unto him, Art
thou also of Galilee? Search, and look: for [a]out
of Galilee ariseth no prophet.

An Adultress Faces the Light of the World

53 And every man went unto his own house.

8 Jesus went unto the mount of Olives.
2 And early in the morning he came again
into the temple, and all the people came unto him;
and he sat down, and [a]taught them.
3 And the scribes and Pharisees brought
unto him a woman taken in adultery; and when
they had set her in the midst,
4 They say unto him, Master, this woman
was taken in [a]adultery, in the very act.
5 [a]Now Moses in the law commanded us,
that such should be stoned: but what sayest thou?

31 [a]Matt. 12:23
33 [a]John 13:33 [b][1 Pet. 3:22]
34 [a]Hos. 5:6 [b][Matt. 5:20]
35 [a]James 1:1
37 [a]Lev. 23:36 [b][Is. 55:1]
38 [a]Deut. 18:15 [b]Is. 12:3; 43:20; 44:3; 55:1
39 [a]Is. 44:3 [b]John 12:16; 13:31; 17:5
40 [a]Deut. 18:15, 18
41 [a]John 4:42; 6:69
42 [a]Mic. 5:2 [b]1 Sam. 16:1, 4
43 [a]John 7:12
44 [a]John 7:30
46 [a]Luke 4:22
50 [a]John 3:1, 2; 19:39
51 [a]Deut. 1:16, 17; 19:15
52 [a][Is. 9:1, 2]

CHAPTER 8

2 [a]John 8:20; 18:20
4 [a]Ex. 20:14
5 [a]Lev. 20:10

*———

7:33 NU, M omit *to them*
7:39 NU *who believed* • NU omits *Holy*
7:40 NU *some*
7:50 NU *before*
7:52 NU *is to rise*
7:53 NU brackets 7:53 through 8:11 as not in the original text. They are present in over 900 mss. of John.
8:2 M *very early*
8:4 M *we found this woman*
8:5 M *in our law Moses commanded* • NU, M *to stone such* • M adds *about her*

NKJV

31 And [a]many of the people believed in Him,
and said, "When the Christ comes, will He do
more signs than these which this *Man* has done?"

Jesus and the Religious Leaders

32 The Pharisees heard the crowd murmuring these things concerning Him, and the Pharisees and the chief priests sent officers to take Him.
33 Then Jesus said *to them, [a]"I shall be with
you a little while longer, and *then* I [b]go to Him
who sent Me.
34 "You [a]will seek Me and not find *Me,* and
where I am you [b]cannot come."
35 Then the Jews said among themselves,
"Where does He intend to go that we shall not
find Him? Does He intend to go to [a]the Dispersion
among the Greeks and teach the Greeks?
36 "What is this thing that He said, 'You will
seek Me and not find Me, and where I am you
cannot come'?"

The Promise of the Holy Spirit

37 [a]On the last day, that great *day* of the
feast, Jesus stood and cried out, saying, [b]"If anyone thirsts, let him come to Me and drink.
38 [a]"He who believes in Me, as the Scripture
has said, [b]out of his heart will flow rivers of living
water."
39 [a]But this He spoke concerning the Spirit,
whom those *believing in Him would receive; for
the *Holy Spirit was not yet *given,* because Jesus
was not yet [b]glorified.

Who Is He?

40 Therefore *many from the crowd, when
they heard this saying, said, "Truly this is [a]the
Prophet."
41 Others said, "This is [a]the Christ." But
some said, "Will the Christ come out of Galilee?
42 [a]"Has not the Scripture said that the
Christ comes from the seed of David and from
the town of Bethlehem, [b]where David was?"
43 So [a]there was a division among the people
because of Him.
44 Now [a]some of them wanted to take Him,
but no one laid hands on Him.

Rejected by the Authorities

45 Then the officers came to the chief priests
and Pharisees, who said to them, "Why have you
not brought Him?"
46 The officers answered, [a]"No man ever
spoke like this Man!"
47 Then the Pharisees answered them, "Are
you also deceived?
48 "Have any of the rulers or the Pharisees
believed in Him?
49 "But this crowd that does not know the
law is accursed."
50 Nicodemus [a](he who came to Jesus *by
night, being one of them) said to them,
51 [a]"Does our law judge a man before it
hears him and knows what he is doing?"
52 They answered and said to him, "Are you
also from Galilee? Search and look, for [a]no
prophet *has arisen out of Galilee."

An Adulteress Faces the Light of the World

53 *And everyone went to his *own* house.

8 But Jesus went to the Mount of Olives.
2 Now *early in the morning He came again
into the temple, and all the people came to Him;
and He sat down and [a]taught them.
3 Then the scribes and Pharisees brought
to Him a woman caught in adultery. And when
they had set her in the midst,
4 they said to Him, "Teacher, *this woman
was caught in [a]adultery, in the very act.
5 [a]"Now *Moses, in the law, commanded us
*that such should be stoned. But what do You
*say?"

KJV

6 This they said, tempting him, that they
[a]might have to accuse him. But Jesus stooped
down, and with *his* finger wrote on the ground,
as though he heard them not.
7 So when they continued asking him, he
lifted up himself, and said unto them, [a]He that is
without sin among you, let him first cast a stone
at her.
8 And again he stooped down, and wrote
on the ground.
9 And they which heard *it*, [a]being convicted
by *their own* conscience, went out one by one,
beginning at the eldest, *even* unto the last: and
Jesus was left alone, and the woman standing in
the midst.
10 When Jesus had lifted up himself, and saw
none but the woman, he said unto her, Woman,
where are those thine accusers? hath no man condemned thee?
11 She said, No man, Lord. And Jesus said
unto her, [a]Neither do I condemn thee: go, and
[b]sin no more.
12 Then spake Jesus again unto them, say-
ing, [a]I am the light of the world: he that [b]followeth
me shall not walk in darkness, but shall have the
light of life.

Jesus Defends His Self-Witness

13 The Pharisees therefore said unto him,
[a]Thou bearest record of thyself; thy record is not
true.
14 Jesus answered and said unto them,
Though I bear record of myself, *yet* my record is
true: for I know whence I came, and whither I
go; but [a]ye cannot tell whence I come, and
whither I go.
15 [a]Ye judge after the flesh; [b]I judge no man.
16 And yet if I judge, my judgment is true:
for [a]I am not alone, but I and the Father that sent
me.
17 [a]It is also written in your law, that the testimony of two men is true.
18 I am one that bear witness of myself, and
[a]the Father that sent me beareth witness of me.
19 Then said they unto him, Where is thy Father? Jesus answered, [a]Ye neither know me, nor
my Father: [b]if ye had known me, ye should have
known my Father also.
20 These words spake Jesus in [a]the treasury,
as he taught in the temple: and [b]no man laid
hands on him; for [c]his hour was not yet come.

Jesus Predicts His Departure

21 Then said Jesus again unto them, I go my
way, and [a]ye shall seek me, and [b]shall die in your
sins: whither I go, ye cannot come.
22 Then said the Jews, Will he kill himself?
because he saith, Whither I go, ye cannot come.
23 And he said unto them, [a]Ye are from beneath; I am from above: [b]ye are of this world; I
am not of this world.
24 [a]I said therefore unto you, that ye shall
die in your sins: [b]for if ye believe not that I am
he, ye shall die in your sins.
25 Then said they unto him, Who art thou?
And Jesus saith unto them, Even *the same* that I
[a]said unto you from the beginning.
26 I have many things to say and to judge
of you: but [a]he that sent me is true; and [b]I speak
to the world those things which I have heard of
him.
27 They understood not that he spake to
them of the Father.
28 Then said Jesus unto them, When ye have
[a]lifted up the Son of man, [b]then shall ye know
that I am *he*, and [c]*that* I do nothing of myself;
but [d]as my Father hath taught me, I speak these
things.
29 And [a]he that sent me is with me: [b]the Father hath not left me alone; [c]for I do always those
things that please him.

6 [a]Matt. 22:15
7 [a]Deut. 17:7; [Rom. 2:1]
9 [a]Rom. 2:22
11 [a][Luke 9:56; 12:14; John 3:17] [b][John 5:14]
12 [a]Is. 9:2; Mal. 4:2; John 1:4; 9:5; 12:35; [2 Tim. 1:10] [b]1 Thess. 5:5
13 [a]John 5:31
14 [a]John 7:28; 9:29
15 [a]1 Sam. 16:7; John 7:24 [b][John 3:17; 12:47; 18:36]
16 [a]John 16:32
17 [a]Deut. 17:6; 19:15; Matt. 18:16; 2 Cor. 13:1; Heb. 10:28
18 [a]John 5:37; 1 John 5:9
19 [a]John 16:3 [b]John 14:7
20 [a]Mark 12:41, 43; Luke 21:1 [b]John 2:4; 7:30 [c]John 7:8
21 [a]John 7:34; 13:33 [b]John 8:24
23 [a]John 3:31 [b]John 15:19; 17:16; 1 John 4:5
24 [a]John 8:21 [b][Mark 16:16]
25 [a]John 4:26
26 [a]John 7:28 [b]John 3:32; 15:15
28 [a]Matt. 27:35; Mark 15:24; Luke 23:33; John 3:14; 12:32; 19:18 [b][Rom. 1:4] [c]John 5:19, 30 [d]Deut. 18:15, 18, 19; John 3:11
29 [a]John 14:10 [b]John 8:16; 16:32 [c]John 4:34; 5:30; 6:38

*

8:6 NU, M omit *as though He did not hear*
8:7 M *looked up*
8:9 NU, M omit *being convicted by their conscience*
8:10 NU omits *and saw no one but the woman;* M *He saw her and said,* • NU, M omit *of yours*
8:11 NU, M add *from now on*

NKJV

6 This they said, testing Him, that they
[a]might have *something* of which to accuse Him.
But Jesus stooped down and wrote on the ground
with *His* finger, *as though He did not hear.
7 So when they continued asking Him, He
*raised Himself up and said to them, [a]"He who
is without sin among you, let him throw a stone
at her first."
8 And again He stooped down and wrote
on the ground.
9 Then those who heard *it*, [a]being* convicted by *their* conscience, went out one by one,
beginning with the oldest *even* to the last. And
Jesus was left alone, and the woman standing in
the midst.
10 When Jesus had raised Himself up *and
saw no one but the woman, He said to her,
"Woman, where are those accusers *of yours?
Has no one condemned you?"
11 She said, "No one, Lord." And Jesus said
to her, [a]"Neither do I condemn you; go *and [b]sin
no more."
12 Then Jesus spoke to them again, saying,
[a]"I am the light of the world. He who [b]follows
Me shall not walk in darkness, but have the light
of life."

Jesus Defends His Self-Witness

13 The Pharisees therefore said to Him,
[a]"You bear witness of Yourself; Your witness is
not true."
14 Jesus answered and said to them, "Even
if I bear witness of Myself, My witness is true,
for I know where I came from and where I am
going; but [a]you do not know where I come from
and where I am going.
15 [a]"You judge according to the flesh; [b]I
judge no one.
16 "And yet if I do judge, My judgment is
true; for [a]I am not alone, but I *am* with the Father
who sent Me.
17 [a]"It is also written in your law that the
testimony of two men is true.
18 "I am One who bears witness of Myself,
and [a]the Father who sent Me bears witness of
Me."
19 Then they said to Him, "Where is Your
Father?" Jesus answered, [a]"You know neither Me
nor My Father. [b]If you had known Me, you would
have known My Father also."
20 These words Jesus spoke in [a]the treasury,
as He taught in the temple; and [b]no one laid hands
on Him, for [c]His hour had not yet come.

Jesus Predicts His Departure

21 Then Jesus said to them again, "I am going away, and [a]you will seek Me, and [b]will die
in your sin. Where I go you cannot come."
22 So the Jews said, "Will He kill Himself,
because He says, 'Where I go you cannot come'?"
23 And He said to them, [a]"You are from beneath; I am from above. [b]You are of this world;
I am not of this world.
24 [a]"Therefore I said to you that you will die
in your sins; [b]for if you do not believe that I am
He, you will die in your sins."
25 Then they said to Him, "Who are You?"
And Jesus said to them, "Just what I [a]have been
saying to you from the beginning.
26 "I have many things to say and to judge
concerning you, but [a]He who sent Me is true; and
[b]I speak to the world those things which I heard
from Him."
27 They did not understand that He spoke
to them of the Father.
28 Then Jesus said to them, "When you [a]lift
up the Son of Man, [b]then you will know that I
am *He*, and [c]*that* I do nothing of Myself; but [d]as
My Father taught Me, I speak these things.
29 "And [a]He who sent Me is with Me. [b]The
Father has not left Me alone, [c]for I always do
those things that please Him."

KJV

30 As he spake these words, [a]many believed
on him.

The Truth Shall Make You Free

31 Then said Jesus to those Jews which believed on him, If ye [a]continue in my word, *then*
are ye my disciples indeed;
32 And ye shall know the [a]truth, and [b]the
truth shall make you free.
33 They answered him, [a]We be Abraham's
seed, and were never in bondage to any man: how
sayest thou, Ye shall be made free?
34 Jesus answered them, Verily, verily, I say
unto you, [a]Whosoever committeth sin is the servant of sin.
35 And [a]the servant abideth not in the house
for ever: *but* the Son abideth ever.
36 [a]If the Son therefore shall make you free,
ye shall be free indeed.

Abraham's Seed and Satan's

37 I know that ye are Abraham's seed; but
[a]ye seek to kill me, because my word hath no
place in you.
38 [a]I speak that which I have seen with my
Father: and ye do that which ye have seen with
your father.
39 They answered and said unto him, [a]Abra-
ham is our father. Jesus saith unto them, [b]If ye
were Abraham's children, ye would do the works
of Abraham.
40 [a]But now ye seek to kill me, a man that
hath told you the truth, [b]which I have heard of
God: this did not Abraham.
41 Ye do the deeds of your father. Then said
they to him, We be not born of fornication; [a]we
have one Father, *even* God.
42 Jesus said unto them, [a]If God were your
Father, ye would love me: [b]for I proceeded forth
and came from God; [c]neither came I of myself,
but he sent me.
43 [a]Why do ye not understand my speech?
even because ye cannot hear my word.
44 [a]Ye are of *your* father the devil, and the
[b]lusts of your father ye will [c]do. He was a murderer from the beginning, and [d]abode not in the
truth, because there is no truth in him. When he
speaketh a lie, he speaketh of his own: for he is
a liar, and the father of it.
45 And because I tell *you* the truth, ye believe
me not.
46 Which of you convinceth me of sin? And
if I say the truth, why do ye not believe me?
47 [a]He that is of God heareth God's words:
ye therefore hear *them* not, because ye are not
of God.

Before Abraham Was, I AM

48 Then answered the Jews, and said unto
him, Say we not well that thou art a Samaritan,
and [a]hast a devil?
49 Jesus answered, I have not a devil; but I
honour my Father, and [a]ye do dishonour me.
50 And [a]I seek not mine own glory: there is
one that seeketh and judgeth.
51 Verily, verily, I say unto you, [a]If a man
keep my saying, he shall never see death.
52 Then said the Jews unto him, Now we
know that thou [a]hast a devil. [b]Abraham is dead,
and the prophets; and thou sayest, If a man keep
my saying, he shall never taste of death.
53 Art thou greater than our father Abraham,
which is dead? and the prophets are dead: [a]whom
makest thou thyself?
54 Jesus answered, [a]If I honour myself, my
honour is nothing: [b]it is my Father that honoureth
me; of whom ye say, that he is your God:
55 Yet [a]ye have not known him; but I know
him: and if I should say, I know him not, I shall

30 [a]John 7:31; 10:42; 11:45
31 [a][John 14:15, 23]
32 [a][John 1:14, 17; 14:6] [b][Rom. 6:14, 18, 22; James 1:25; 2:12]
33 [a]Lev. 25:42; [Matt. 3:9]; Luke 3:8
34 [a]Prov. 5:22; Rom. 6:16; 2 Pet. 2:19
35 [a]Gen. 21:10; Gal. 4:30
36 [a][Rom. 8:2; 2 Cor. 3:17]; Gal. 5:1
37 [a]John 7:19
38 [a][John 3:32; 5:19, 30; 14:10, 24]
39 [a]Matt. 3:9; John 8:37 [b][Rom. 2:28; Gal. 3:7, 29]
40 [a]John 8:37 [b]John 8:26
41 [a]Deut. 32:6; Is. 63:16; Mal. 1:6
42 [a]1 John 5:1 [b]John 16:27; 17:8, 25 [c]John 5:43; Gal. 4:4
43 [a][John 7:17]
44 [a]Matt. 13:38; 1 John 3:8 [b]1 John 2:16, 17 [c][1 John 3:8–10, 15] [d][Jude 6]
47 [a]Luke 8:15; John 10:26; 1 John 4:6
48 [a]John 7:20; 10:20
49 [a]John 5:41
50 [a]John 5:41; 7:18; [Phil. 2:6–8]
51 [a]John 5:24; 11:26
52 [a]John 7:20; 10:20 [b]Zech. 1:5; Heb. 11:13
53 [a]John 10:33; 19:7
54 [a]John 5:31, 32 [b]John 5:41; Acts 3:13
55 [a]John 7:28, 29

*

8:38 NU *heard from*
8:54 NU, M *our*

NKJV

30 As He spoke these words, [a]many believed
in Him.

The Truth Shall Make You Free

31 Then Jesus said to those Jews who believed Him, "If you [a]abide in My word, you are
My disciples indeed.
32 "And you shall know the [a]truth, and [b]the
truth shall make you free."
33 They answered Him, [a]"We are Abraham's
descendants, and have never been in bondage to
anyone. How *can* you say, 'You will be made
free'?"
34 Jesus answered them, "Most assuredly, I
say to you, [a]whoever commits sin is a slave of
sin.
35 "And [a]a slave does not abide in the house
forever, *but* a son abides forever.
36 [a]"Therefore if the Son makes you free,
you shall be free indeed.

Abraham's Seed and Satan's

37 "I know that you are Abraham's descendants, but [a]you seek to kill Me, because My word
has no place in you.
38 [a]"I speak what I have seen with My Father, and you do what you have *seen with your
father."
39 They answered and said to Him, [a]"Abraham is our father." Jesus said to them, [b]"If you
were Abraham's children, you would do the
works of Abraham.
40 [a]"But now you seek to kill Me, a Man who
has told you the truth [b]which I heard from God.
Abraham did not do this.
41 "You do the deeds of your father." Then
they said to Him, "We were not born of fornication; [a]we have one Father—God."
42 Jesus said to them, [a]"If God were your
Father, you would love Me, for [b]I proceeded forth
and came from God; [c]nor have I come of Myself,
but He sent Me.
43 [a]"Why do you not understand My
speech? Because you are not able to listen to My
word.
44 [a]"You are of *your* father the devil, and
the [b]desires of your father you want to [c]do. He
was a murderer from the beginning, and [d]*does
not* stand in the truth, because there is no truth
in him. When he speaks a lie, he speaks from his
own *resources,* for he is a liar and the father of
it.
45 "But because I tell the truth, you do not
believe Me.
46 "Which of you convicts Me of sin? And if
I tell the truth, why do you not believe Me?
47 [a]"He who is of God hears God's words;
therefore you do not hear, because you are not
of God."

Before Abraham Was, I AM

48 Then the Jews answered and said to Him,
"Do we not say rightly that You are a Samaritan
and [a]have a demon?"
49 Jesus answered, "I do not have a demon;
but I honor My Father, and [a]you dishonor Me.
50 "And [a]I do not seek My *own* glory; there
is One who seeks and judges.
51 "Most assuredly, I say to you, [a]if anyone
keeps My word he shall never see death."
52 Then the Jews said to Him, "Now we
know that You [a]have a demon! [b]Abraham is dead,
and the prophets; and You say, 'If anyone keeps
My word he shall never taste death.'
53 "Are You greater than our father Abraham, who is dead? And the prophets are dead.
[a]Who do You make Yourself out to be?"
54 Jesus answered, [a]"If I honor Myself, My
honor is nothing. [b]It is My Father who honors
Me, of whom you say that He is *your God.
55 "Yet [a]you have not known Him, but I
know Him. And if I say, 'I do not know Him,' I

KJV

be a liar like unto you: but I know him, and [b]keep his saying.

56 Your father Abraham [a]rejoiced to see my day: [b]and he saw *it,* and was glad.

57 Then said the Jews unto him, Thou art not yet fifty years old, and hast thou seen Abraham?

58 Jesus said unto them, Verily, verily, I say unto you, [a]Before Abraham was, [b]I am.

59 Then [a]took they up stones to cast at him: but Jesus hid himself, and went out of the temple, [b]going through the midst of them, and so passed by.

A Man Born Blind Receives Sight

9 And as *Jesus* passed by, he saw a man which was blind from *his* birth.

2 And his disciples asked him, saying, Master, [a]who did sin, this man, or his parents, that he was born blind?

3 Jesus answered, Neither hath this man sinned, nor his parents: [a]but that the works of God should be made manifest in him.

4 [a]I must work the works of him that sent me, while it is [b]day: the night cometh, when no man can work.

5 As long as I am in the world, [a]I am the light of the world.

6 When he had thus spoken, [a]he spat on the ground, and made clay of the spittle, and he anointed the eyes of the blind man with the clay,

7 And said unto him, Go, wash [a]in the pool of Siloam, (which is by interpretation, Sent.) [b]He went his way therefore, and washed, and came seeing.

8 The neighbours therefore, and they which before had seen him that he was blind, said, Is not this he that sat and begged?

9 Some said, This is he: others *said,* He is like him: *but* he said, I am *he.*

10 Therefore said they unto him, How were thine eyes opened?

11 He answered and said, [a]A man that is called Jesus made clay, and anointed mine eyes, and said unto me, Go to the pool of Siloam, and wash: and I went and washed, and I received sight.

12 Then said they unto him, Where is he? He said, I know not.

The Pharisees Excommunicate the Healed Man

13 They brought to the Pharisees him that aforetime was blind.

14 And it was the sabbath day when Jesus made the clay, and opened his eyes.

15 Then again the Pharisees also asked him how he had received his sight. He said unto them, He put clay upon mine eyes, and I washed, and do see.

16 Therefore said some of the Pharisees, This man is not of God, because he keepeth not the sabbath day. Others said, [a]How can a man that is a sinner do such miracles? And [b]there was a division among them.

17 They say unto the blind man again, What sayest thou of him, that he hath opened thine eyes? He said, [a]He is a prophet.

18 But the Jews did not believe concerning him, that he had been blind, and received his sight, until they called the parents of him that had received his sight.

19 And they asked them, saying, Is this your son, who ye say was born blind? how then doth he now see?

20 His parents answered them and said, We know that this is our son, and that he was born blind:

21 But by what means he now seeth, we know not; or who hath opened his eyes, we know not: he is of age; ask him: he shall speak for himself.

22 These *words* spake his parents, because [a]they feared the Jews: for the Jews had agreed

55 [b][John 15:10]
56 [a]Luke 10:24 [b]Matt. 13:17; Heb. 11:13
58 [a]Mic. 5:2; John 17:5; Heb. 7:3; Rev. 22:13 [b]Ex. 3:14; Is. 43:13; John 17:5, 24; Col. 1:17; Rev. 1:8
59 [a]John 10:31; 11:8 [b]Luke 4:30; John 10:39

CHAPTER 9

2 [a]Luke 13:2; John 9:34; Acts 28:4
3 [a]John 11:4
4 [a][John 4:34; 5:19, 36; 17:4] [b]John 11:9, 10; 12:35; Gal. 6:10
5 [a][John 1:5, 9; 3:19; 8:12; 12:35, 46]
6 [a]Mark 7:33; 8:23
7 [a]Neh. 3:15; Is. 8:6; Luke 13:4; John 9:11 [b]2 Kin. 5:14
11 [a]John 9:6, 7
16 [a]John 3:2; 9:33 [b]John 7:12, 43; 10:19
17 [a][John 4:19; 6:14]
22 [a]John 7:13; 12:42; 19:38; Acts 5:13

NKJV

shall be a liar like you; but I do know Him and [b]keep His word.

56 "Your father Abraham [a]rejoiced to see My day, [b]and he saw *it* and was glad."

57 Then the Jews said to Him, "You are not yet fifty years old, and have You seen Abraham?"

58 Jesus said to them, "Most assuredly, I say to you, [a]before Abraham was, [b]I AM."

59 Then [a]they took up stones to throw at Him; but Jesus hid Himself and went out of the temple, [b]going* through the midst of them, and so passed by.

A Man Born Blind Receives Sight

9 Now as *Jesus* passed by, He saw a man who was blind from birth.

2 And His disciples asked Him, saying, "Rabbi, [a]who sinned, this man or his parents, that he was born blind?"

3 Jesus answered, "Neither this man nor his parents sinned, [a]but that the works of God should be revealed in him.

4 [a]"I* must work the works of Him who sent Me while it is [b]day; *the* night is coming when no one can work.

5 "As long as I am in the world, [a]I am the light of the world."

6 When He had said these things, [a]He spat on the ground and made clay with the saliva; and He anointed the eyes of the blind man with the clay.

7 And He said to him, "Go, wash [a]in the pool of Siloam" (which is translated, Sent). So [b]he went and washed, and came back seeing.

8 Therefore the neighbors and those who previously had seen that he was *blind said, "Is not this he who sat and begged?"

9 Some said, "This is he." Others *said,* *"He is like him." He said, "I am *he.*"

10 Therefore they said to him, "How were your eyes opened?"

11 He answered and said, [a]"A Man called Jesus made clay and anointed my eyes and said to me, 'Go to *the pool of Siloam and wash.' So I went and washed, and I received sight."

12 Then they said to him, "Where is He?" He said, "I do not know."

The Pharisees Excommunicate the Healed Man

13 They brought him who formerly was blind to the Pharisees.

14 Now it was a Sabbath when Jesus made the clay and opened his eyes.

15 Then the Pharisees also asked him again how he had received his sight. He said to them, "He put clay on my eyes, and I washed, and I see."

16 Therefore some of the Pharisees said, "This Man is not from God, because He does not keep the Sabbath." Others said, [a]"How can a man who is a sinner do such signs?" And [b]there was a division among them.

17 They said to the blind man again, "What do you say about Him because He opened your eyes?" He said, [a]"He is a prophet."

18 But the Jews did not believe concerning him, that he had been blind and received his sight, until they called the parents of him who had received his sight.

19 And they asked them, saying, "Is this your son, who you say was born blind? How then does he now see?"

20 His parents answered them and said, "We know that this is our son, and that he was born blind;

21 "but by what means he now sees we do not know, or who opened his eyes we do not know. He is of age; ask him. He will speak for himself."

22 His parents said these *things* because [a]they feared the Jews, for the Jews had agreed

*

8:59 NU omits the rest of v. 59.
9:4 NU *We*
9:8 NU *a beggar*
9:9 NU *"No, but he is like him."*
9:11 NU omits *the pool of*

KJV

already, that if any man did confess that he was Christ, he [b]should be put out of the synagogue.

23 Therefore said his parents, He is of age; ask him.

24 Then again called they the man that was blind, and said unto him, [a]Give God the praise: [b]we know that this man is a sinner.

25 He answered and said, Whether he be a sinner *or no,* I know not: one thing I know, that, whereas I was blind, now I see.

26 Then said they to him again, What did he to thee? how opened he thine eyes?

27 He answered them, I have told you already, and ye did not hear: wherefore would ye hear *it* again? will ye also be his disciples?

28 Then they reviled him, and said, Thou art his disciple; but we are Moses' disciples.

29 We know that God [a]spake unto [b]Moses: *as for* this *fellow,* [c]we know not from whence he is.

30 The man answered and said unto them, [a]Why herein is a marvellous thing, that ye know not from whence he is, and *yet* he hath opened mine eyes.

31 Now we know that [a]God heareth not sinners: but if any man be a worshipper of God, and doeth his will, him he heareth.

32 Since the world began was it not heard that any man opened the eyes of one that was born blind.

33 [a]If this man were not of God, he could do nothing.

34 They answered and said unto him, [a]Thou wast altogether born in sins, and dost thou teach us? And they cast him out.

True Vision and True Blindness

35 Jesus heard that they had cast him out; and when he had [a]found him, he said unto him, Dost thou [b]believe on [c]the Son of God?

36 He answered and said, Who is he, Lord, that I might believe on him?

37 And Jesus said unto him, Thou hast both seen him, and [a]it is he that talketh with thee.

38 And he said, Lord, I believe. And he [a]worshipped him.

39 And Jesus said, [a]For judgment I am come into this world, [b]that they which see not might see; and that they which see might be made blind.

40 And *some* of the Pharisees which were with him heard these words, [a]and said unto him, Are we blind also?

41 Jesus said unto them, [a]If ye were blind, ye should have no sin: but now ye say, We see; therefore your sin remaineth.

Jesus the True Shepherd

10 Verily, verily, I say unto you, He that entereth not by the door into the sheepfold, but climbeth up some other way, the same is a thief and a robber.

2 But he that entereth in by the door is the shepherd of the sheep.

3 To him the porter openeth; and the sheep hear his voice: and he calleth his own sheep by [a]name, and leadeth them out.

4 And when he putteth forth his own sheep, he goeth before them, and the sheep follow him: for they know his voice.

5 And a [a]stranger will they not follow, but will flee from him: for they know not the voice of strangers.

6 This parable spake Jesus unto them: but they understood not what things they were which he spake unto them.

Jesus the Good Shepherd

7 Then said Jesus unto them again, Verily, verily, I say unto you, I am the door of the sheep.

---

22 [b]John 16:2 **24** [a]Josh. 7:19; 1 Sam. 6:5; Ezra 10:11; Rev. 11:13 [b]John 9:16 **29** [a]Ex. 19:19, 20; 33:11; 34:29; Num. 12:6–8 [b][John 5:45–47] [c]John 7:27, 28; 8:14 **30** [a]John 3:10 **31** [a]Job 27:9; 35:12; Ps. 18:41; Prov. 1:28; 15:29; 28:9; Is. 1:15; Jer. 11:11; 14:12; Ezek. 8:18; Mic. 3:4; Zech. 7:13; [James 5:16] **33** [a]John 3:2; 9:16 **34** [a]Ps. 51:5; John 9:2 **35** [a]John 5:14 [b]John 1:7; 16:31 [c]Matt. 14:33; 16:16; Mark 1:1; John 10:36; 1 John 5:13 **37** [a]John 4:26 **38** [a]Matt. 8:2 **39** [a][John 3:17; 5:22, 27; 12:47] [b]Matt. 13:13; 15:14 **40** [a][Rom. 2:19] **41** [a]John 15:22, 24

CHAPTER 10

3 [a]John 20:16 **5** [a][2 Cor. 11:13–15]

NKJV

already that if anyone confessed *that* He *was* Christ, he [b]would be put out of the synagogue.

23 Therefore his parents said, "He is of age; ask him."

24 So they again called the man who was blind, and said to him, [a]"Give God the glory! [b]We know that this Man is a sinner."

25 He answered and said, "Whether He is a sinner *or not* I do not know. One thing I know: that though I was blind, now I see."

26 Then they said to him again, "What did He do to you? How did He open your eyes?"

27 He answered them, "I told you already, and you did not listen. Why do you want to hear *it* again? Do you also want to become His disciples?"

28 Then they reviled him and said, "You are His disciple, but we are Moses' disciples.

29 "We know that God [a]spoke to [b]Moses; *as for* this *fellow,* [c]we do not know where He is from."

30 The man answered and said to them, [a]"Why, this is a marvelous thing, that you do not know where He is from; yet He has opened my eyes!

31 "Now we know that [a]God does not hear sinners; but if anyone is a worshiper of God and does His will, He hears him.

32 "Since the world began it has been unheard of that anyone opened the eyes of one who was born blind.

33 [a]"If this Man were not from God, He could do nothing."

34 They answered and said to him, [a]"You were completely born in sins, and are you teaching us?" And they cast him out.

True Vision and True Blindness

35 Jesus heard that they had cast him out; and when He had [a]found him, He said to him, "Do you [b]believe in [c]the Son of *God?"

36 He answered and said, "Who is He, Lord, that I may believe in Him?"

37 And Jesus said to him, "You have both seen Him and [a]it is He who is talking with you."

38 Then he said, "Lord, I believe!" And he [a]worshiped Him.

39 And Jesus said, [a]"For judgment I have come into this world, [b]that those who do not see may see, and that those who see may be made blind."

40 Then *some* of the Pharisees who were with Him heard these words, [a]and said to Him, "Are we blind also?"

41 Jesus said to them, [a]"If you were blind, you would have no sin; but now you say, 'We see.' Therefore your sin remains.

Jesus the True Shepherd

10 "Most assuredly, I say to you, he who does not enter the sheepfold by the door, but climbs up some other way, the same is a thief and a robber.

2 "But he who enters by the door is the shepherd of the sheep.

3 "To him the doorkeeper opens, and the sheep hear his voice; and he calls his own sheep by [a]name and leads them out.

4 "And when he brings out his own sheep, he goes before them; and the sheep follow him, for they know his voice.

5 "Yet they will by no means follow a [a]stranger, but will flee from him, for they do not know the voice of strangers."

6 Jesus used this illustration, but they did not understand the things which He spoke to them.

Jesus the Good Shepherd

7 Then Jesus said to them again, "Most assuredly, I say to you, I am the door of the sheep.

---

*9:35 NU *Man*

KJV

8 All that ever came before me are thieves
and robbers: but the sheep did not hear them.
9 [a]I am the door: by me if any man enter
in, he shall be saved, and shall go in and out, and
find pasture.
10 The thief cometh not, but for to steal, and
to kill, and to destroy: I am come that they might
have life, and that they might have *it* more
abundantly.
11 [a]I am the good shepherd: the good shepherd giveth his life for the sheep.
12 But he that is an hireling, and not the
shepherd, whose own the sheep are not, seeth the
wolf coming, and [a]leaveth the sheep, and fleeth:
and the wolf catcheth them, and scattereth the
sheep.
13 The hireling fleeth, because he is an hireling, and careth not for the sheep.
14 I am the good shepherd, and [a]know my
sheep, and [b]am known of mine.
15 [a]As the Father knoweth me, even so know
I the Father: [b]and I lay down my life for the sheep.
16 And [a]other sheep I have, which are not
of this fold: them also I must bring, and they shall
hear my voice; [b]and there shall be one fold, *and*
one shepherd.
17 Therefore doth my Father [a]love me,
[b]because I lay down my life, that I might take it
again.
18 No man taketh it from me, but I lay it
down of myself. I [a]have power to lay it down,
and I have power to take it again. [b]This commandment have I received of my Father.
19 [a]There was a division therefore again
among the Jews for these sayings.
20 And many of them said, [a]He hath a devil,
and is mad; why hear ye him?
21 Others said, These are not the words of
him that hath a devil. [a]Can a devil [b]open the eyes
of the blind?

The Shepherd Knows His Sheep

22 And it was at Jerusalem the feast of the
dedication, and it was winter.
23 And Jesus walked in the temple [a]in Solomon's porch.
24 Then came the Jews round about him, and
said unto him, How long dost thou make us to
doubt? If thou be the Christ, tell us plainly.
25 Jesus answered them, I told you, and ye
believed not: [a]the works that I do in my Father's
name, they [b]bear witness of me.
26 But [a]ye believe not, because ye are not
of my sheep, as I said unto you.
27 [a]My sheep hear my voice, and I know
them, and they follow me:
28 And I give unto them eternal life; and they
shall never perish, neither shall any *man* pluck
them out of my hand.
29 [a]My Father, [b]which gave *them* me, is
greater than all; and no *man* is able to pluck *them*
out of my Father's hand.
30 [a]I and *my* Father are one.

Renewed Efforts to Stone Jesus

31 Then [a]the Jews took up stones again to
stone him.
32 Jesus answered them, Many good works
have I shewed you from my Father; for which of
those works do ye stone me?
33 The Jews answered him, saying, For a
good work we stone thee not; but for [a]blasphemy;
and because that thou, being a man, [b]makest thyself God.
34 Jesus answered them, [a]Is it not written in
your law, I SAID, YE ARE GODS?
35 If he called them gods, [a]unto whom the
word of God came, and the scripture [b]cannot be
broken;
36 Say ye of him, [a]whom the Father hath
sanctified, and [b]sent into the world, Thou blas-
phemest; [c]because I said, I am [d]the Son of God?

9 [a][John 14:6; Eph. 2:18]
11 [a]Gen. 49:24; Is. 40:11; Ezek. 34:23; [Heb. 13:20]; 1 Pet. 2:25; 5:4; Rev. 7:17
12 [a]Zech. 11:16, 17
14 [a]Is. 40:11; Nah. 1:7; Zech. 13:7; John 6:64; 2 Tim. 2:19 [b]2 Tim. 1:12
15 [a]Matt. 11:27 [b]Matt. 27:50; Mark 15:37; Luke 23:46; [John 15:13; 19:30]; 1 John 3:16
16 [a]Is. 42:6; 56:8; Acts 10:45; 11:18; 13:46 [b]Ezek. 37:22; John 11:52; 17:20; Eph. 2:13–18; 1 Pet. 2:25
17 [a]John 5:20 [b][Is. 53:7, 8, 12; Heb. 2:9]
18 [a]Matt. 26:53; [John 2:19; 5:26] [b][John 6:38; 14:31; 17:4; Acts 2:24, 32]
19 [a]John 7:43; 9:16
20 [a]John 7:20
21 [a][Ex. 4:11] [b]John 9:6, 7, 32, 33
23 [a]Acts 3:11; 5:12
25 [a]John 5:36; 10:38 [b]Matt. 11:4; John 2:11; 20:30
26 [a][John 8:47]
27 [a]John 10:4, 14
29 [a]John 14:28 [b][John 17:2, 6, 12, 24]
30 [a]John 17:11, 21–24
31 [a]John 8:59
33 [a]John 5:18 [b]Matt. 9:3
34 [a]Ps. 82:6
35 [a]Matt. 5:17, 18 [b]1 Pet. 1:25
36 [a]John 6:27 [b]John 3:17 [c]John 5:17, 18 [d]Luke 1:35

NKJV

8 "All who *ever* came *before Me are thieves
and robbers, but the sheep did not hear them.
9 [a]"I am the door. If anyone enters by Me,
he will be saved, and will go in and out and find
pasture.
10 "The thief does not come except to steal,
and to kill, and to destroy. I have come that they
may have life, and that they may have *it* more
abundantly.
11 [a]"I am the good shepherd. The good shepherd gives His life for the sheep.
12 "But a hireling, *he who is* not the shepherd, one who does not own the sheep, sees the
wolf coming and [a]leaves the sheep and flees; and
the wolf catches the sheep and scatters them.
13 "The hireling flees because he is a hireling
and does not care about the sheep.
14 "I am the good shepherd; and [a]I know My
sheep, and [b]am known by My own.
15 [a]"As the Father knows Me, even so I know
the Father; [b]and I lay down My life for the sheep.
16 "And [a]other sheep I have which are not
of this fold; them also I must bring, and they will
hear My voice; [b]and there will be one flock *and*
one shepherd.
17 "Therefore My Father [a]loves Me, [b]be-
cause I lay down My life that I may take it again.
18 "No one takes it from Me, but I lay it down
of Myself. I [a]have power to lay it down, and I
have power to take it again. [b]This command I
have received from My Father."
19 Therefore [a]there was a division again
among the Jews because of these sayings.
20 And many of them said, [a]"He has a demon
and is mad. Why do you listen to Him?"
21 Others said, "These are not the words of
one who has a demon. [a]Can a demon [b]open the
eyes of the blind?"

The Shepherd Knows His Sheep

22 Now it was the Feast of Dedication in Jerusalem, and it was winter.
23 And Jesus walked in the temple, [a]in Solomon's porch.
24 Then the Jews surrounded Him and said
to Him, "How long do You keep us in doubt? If
You are the Christ, tell us plainly."
25 Jesus answered them, "I told you, and you
do not believe. [a]The works that I do in My Father's
name, they [b]bear witness of Me.
26 "But [a]you do not believe, because you are
not of My sheep, *as I said to you.
27 [a]"My sheep hear My voice, and I know
them, and they follow Me.
28 "And I give them eternal life, and they
shall never perish; neither shall anyone snatch
them out of My hand.
29 [a]"My Father, [b]who has given *them* to Me,
is greater than all; and no one is able to snatch
them out of My Father's hand.
30 [a]"I and *My* Father are one."

Renewed Efforts to Stone Jesus

31 Then [a]the Jews took up stones again to
stone Him.
32 Jesus answered them, "Many good works
I have shown you from My Father. For which of
those works do you stone Me?"
33 The Jews answered Him, saying, "For a
good work we do not stone You, but for [a]blas-
phemy, and because You, being a Man, [b]make
Yourself God."
34 Jesus answered them, "Is it not written
in your law, [a]*'I said, "You are gods"'*?
35 "If He called them gods, [a]to whom the
word of God came (and the Scripture [b]cannot be
broken),
36 "do you say of Him [a]whom the Father
sanctified and [b]sent into the world, 'You are blaspheming,' [c]because I said, 'I am [d]the Son of God'?

10:8 M omits *before Me*
10:26 NU omits *as I said to you*

KJV

37 [a]If I do not the works of my Father, believe
me not.
38 But if I do, though ye believe not me, [a]be-
lieve the works: that ye may know, and believe,
[b]that the Father *is* in me, and I in him.
39 [a]Therefore they sought again to take him:
but he escaped out of their hand,

The Believers Beyond Jordan

40 And went away again beyond Jordan into
the place [a]where John at first baptized; and there
he abode.
41 And many resorted unto him, and said,
John did no miracle: [a]but all things that John
spake of this man were true.
42 And many believed on him there.

The Death of Lazarus

11 Now a certain *man* was sick, *named* Lazarus, of Bethany, the town of [a]Mary and her
sister Martha.
2 ([a]It was *that* Mary which anointed the
Lord with ointment, and wiped his feet with her
hair, whose brother Lazarus was sick.)
3 Therefore his sisters sent unto him, saying, Lord, behold, he whom thou lovest is sick.
4 When Jesus heard *that,* he said, This sickness is not unto death, but for the glory of God,
that the Son of God might be glorified thereby.
5 Now Jesus loved Martha, and her sister,
and Lazarus.
6 When he had heard therefore that he was
sick, [a]he abode two days still in the same place
where he was.
7 Then after that saith he to *his* disciples,
Let us go into Judaea again.
8 *His* disciples say unto him, Master, the
Jews of late sought to [a]stone thee; and goest thou
thither again?
9 Jesus answered, Are there not twelve
hours in the day? [a]If any man walk in the day,
he stumbleth not, because he seeth the [b]light of
this world.
10 But [a]if a man walk in the night, he stumbleth, because there is no light in him.
11 These things said he: and after that he
saith unto them, Our friend Lazarus [a]sleepeth; but
I go, that I may awake him out of sleep.
12 Then said his disciples, Lord, if he sleep,
he shall do well.
13 Howbeit Jesus spake of his death: but they
thought that he had spoken of taking of rest in
sleep.
14 Then said Jesus unto them plainly, Lazarus is dead.
15 And I am glad for your sakes that I was
not there, to the intent ye may believe; nevertheless let us go unto him.
16 Then said [a]Thomas, which is called Didymus, unto his fellowdisciples, Let us also go, that
we may die with him.

I Am the Resurrection and the Life

17 Then when Jesus came, he found that he
had *lain* in the grave four days already.
18 Now Bethany was nigh unto Jerusalem,
about fifteen furlongs off:
19 And many of the Jews came to Martha
and Mary, to comfort them concerning their
brother.
20 Then Martha, as soon as she heard that
Jesus was coming, went and met him: but Mary
sat *still* in the house.
21 Then said Martha unto Jesus, Lord, if thou
hadst been here, my brother had not died.
22 But I know, that even now, [a]whatsoever
thou wilt ask of God, God will give *it* thee.
23 Jesus saith unto her, Thy brother shall rise
again.
24 Martha saith unto him, [a]I know that he
shall rise again in the resurrection at the last day.
25 Jesus said unto her, I am [a]the resur-

37 [a]John 10:25; 15:24 **38** [a]John 5:36 [b]John 14:10, 11 **39** [a]John 7:30, 44 **40** [a]John 1:28 **41** [a][John 1:29, 36; 3:28–36; 5:33]

CHAPTER 11

1 [a]Luke 10:38, 39; John 11:5, 19 **2** [a]Matt. 26:7 **6** [a]John 10:40 **8** [a]John 8:59; 10:31 **9** [a]Luke 13:33; John 9:4; 12:35 [b]Is. 9:2 **10** [a]John 12:35 **11** [a]Deut. 31:16; [Dan. 12:2]; Matt. 9:24; Acts 7:60; [1 Cor. 15:18, 51] **16** [a]Matt. 10:3; Mark 3:18; Luke 6:15; John 14:5; 20:26–28; Acts 1:13 **22** [a][John 9:31; 11:41] **24** [a][Luke 14:14; John 5:29] **25** [a]John 5:21; 6:39, 40, 44; [Rev. 1:18]

NKJV

37 [a]"If I do not do the works of My Father,
do not believe Me;
38 "but if I do, though you do not believe Me,
[a]believe the works, that you may know and *believe [b]that the Father *is* in Me, and I in Him."
39 [a]Therefore they sought again to seize
Him, but He escaped out of their hand.

The Believers Beyond Jordan

40 And He went away again beyond the Jordan to the place [a]where John was baptizing at
first, and there He stayed.
41 Then many came to Him and said, "John
performed no sign, [a]but all the things that John
spoke about this Man were true."
42 And many believed in Him there.

The Death of Lazarus

11 Now a certain *man* was sick, Lazarus of
Bethany, the town of [a]Mary and her sister
Martha.
2 [a]It was *that* Mary who anointed the Lord
with fragrant oil and wiped His feet with her hair,
whose brother Lazarus was sick.
3 Therefore the sisters sent to Him, saying,
"Lord, behold, he whom You love is sick."
4 When Jesus heard *that,* He said, "This
sickness is not unto death, but for the glory of
God, that the Son of God may be glorified through
it."
5 Now Jesus loved Martha and her sister
and Lazarus.
6 So, when He heard that he was sick, [a]He
stayed two more days in the place where He was.
7 Then after this He said to *the* disciples,
"Let us go to Judea again."
8 *The* disciples said to Him, "Rabbi, lately
the Jews sought to [a]stone You, and are You going
there again?"
9 Jesus answered, "Are there not twelve
hours in the day? [a]If anyone walks in the day,
he does not stumble, because he sees the [b]light
of this world.
10 "But [a]if one walks in the night, he stumbles, because the light is not in him."
11 These things He said, and after that He
said to them, "Our friend Lazarus [a]sleeps, but I
go that I may wake him up."
12 Then His disciples said, "Lord, if he sleeps
he will get well."
13 However, Jesus spoke of his death, but
they thought that He was speaking about taking
rest in sleep.
14 Then Jesus said to them plainly, "Lazarus
is dead.
15 "And I am glad for your sakes that I was
not there, that you may believe. Nevertheless let
us go to him."
16 Then [a]Thomas, who is called the Twin,
said to his fellow disciples, "Let us also go, that
we may die with Him."

I Am the Resurrection and the Life

17 So when Jesus came, He found that he
had already been in the tomb four days.
18 Now Bethany was near Jerusalem, about
*two miles away.
19 And many of the Jews had joined the
women around Martha and Mary, to comfort them
concerning their brother.
20 Then Martha, as soon as she heard that
Jesus was coming, went and met Him, but Mary
was sitting in the house.
21 Now Martha said to Jesus, "Lord, if You
had been here, my brother would not have died.
22 "But even now I know that [a]whatever You
ask of God, God will give You."
23 Jesus said to her, "Your brother will rise
again."
24 Martha said to Him, [a]"I know that he will
rise again in the resurrection at the last day."
25 Jesus said to her, "I am [a]the resurrection

*———

10:38 NU *understand*
11:18 Lit. *15 stadia*

KJV

rection, and the life: [b]he that believeth in me, though he were [c]dead, yet shall he live:
26 And whosoever liveth and believeth in me shall never die. Believest thou this?
27 She saith unto him, Yea, Lord: [a]I believe that thou art the Christ, the Son of God, which should come into the world.

Jesus and Death, the Last Enemy

28 And when she had so said, she went her way, and called Mary her sister secretly, saying, The Master is come, and calleth for thee.
29 As soon as she heard *that*, she arose quickly, and came unto him.
30 Now Jesus was not yet come into the town, but was in that place where Martha met him.
31 [a]The Jews then which were with her in the house, and comforted her, when they saw Mary, that she rose up hastily and went out, followed her, saying, She goeth unto the grave to weep there.
32 Then when Mary was come where Jesus was, and saw him, she [a]fell down at his feet, saying unto him, [b]Lord, if thou hadst been here, my brother had not died.
33 When Jesus therefore saw her weeping, and the Jews also weeping which came with her, he groaned in the spirit, and was troubled,
34 And said, Where have ye laid him? They said unto him, Lord, come and see.
35 [a]Jesus wept.
36 Then said the Jews, Behold how he loved him!
37 And some of them said, Could not this man, [a]which opened the eyes of the blind, have caused that even this man should not have died?

Lazarus Raised from the Dead

38 Jesus therefore again groaning in himself cometh to the grave. It was a cave, and a [a]stone lay upon it.
39 Jesus said, Take ye away the stone. Martha, the sister of him that was dead, saith unto him, Lord, by this time he stinketh: for he hath been *dead* four days.
40 Jesus saith unto her, Said I not unto thee, that, if thou wouldest believe, thou shouldest [a]see the glory of God?
41 Then they took away the stone *from the place* where the dead was laid. And Jesus lifted up *his* eyes, and said, Father, I thank thee that thou hast heard me.
42 And I knew that thou hearest me always: but [a]because of the people which stand by I said *it*, that they may believe that thou hast sent me.
43 And when he thus had spoken, he cried with a loud voice, Lazarus, come forth.
44 And he that was dead came forth, bound hand and foot with [a]graveclothes: and [b]his face was bound about with a napkin. Jesus saith unto them, Loose him, and let him go.

The Plot to Kill Jesus
(Matt. 26:1–5; Mark 14:1, 2; Luke 22:1, 2)

45 Then many of the Jews which came to Mary, [a]and had seen the things which Jesus did, believed on him.
46 But some of them went their ways to the Pharisees, and [a]told them what things Jesus had done.
47 [a]Then gathered the chief priests and the Pharisees a council, and said, [b]What do we? for this man doeth many miracles.
48 If we let him thus alone, all *men* will believe on him: and the Romans shall come and take away both our place and nation.
49 And one of them, *named* [a]Caiaphas, being the high priest that same year, said unto them, Ye know nothing at all,
50 [a]Nor consider that it is expedient for us,

25 [b]John 3:16, 36; 1 John 5:10 [c]1 Cor. 15:22; [Heb. 9:27]
27 [a]Matt. 16:16; Luke 2:11; John 4:42; 6:14, 69
31 [a]John 11:19, 33
32 [a]Mark 5:22; 7:25; Rev. 1:17 [b]John 11:21
35 [a]Luke 19:41
37 [a]John 9:6, 7
38 [a]Matt. 27:60, 66; Mark 15:46; Luke 24:2; John 20:1
40 [a][John 11:4, 23]
42 [a]John 12:30; 17:21
44 [a]John 19:40 [b]John 20:7
45 [a]John 2:23; 10:42; 12:11, 18
46 [a]John 5:15
47 [a]Ps. 2:2; Matt. 26:3; Mark 14:1; Luke 22:2 [b]John 12:19; Acts 4:16
49 [a]Matt. 26:3; Luke 3:2; John 18:14; Acts 4:6
50 [a]John 18:14

NKJV

and the life. [b]He who believes in Me, though he may [c]die, he shall live.
26 "And whoever lives and believes in Me shall never die. Do you believe this?"
27 She said to Him, "Yes, Lord, [a]I believe that You are the Christ, the Son of God, who is to come into the world."

Jesus and Death, the Last Enemy

28 And when she had said these things, she went her way and secretly called Mary her sister, saying, "The Teacher has come and is calling for you."
29 As soon as she heard *that*, she arose quickly and came to Him.
30 Now Jesus had not yet come into the town, but *was in the place where Martha met Him.
31 [a]Then the Jews who were with her in the house, and comforting her, when they saw that Mary rose up quickly and went out, followed her, *saying, "She is going to the tomb to weep there."
32 Then, when Mary came where Jesus was, and saw Him, she [a]fell down at His feet, saying to Him, [b]"Lord, if You had been here, my brother would not have died."
33 Therefore, when Jesus saw her weeping, and the Jews who came with her weeping, He groaned in the spirit and was troubled.
34 And He said, "Where have you laid him?" They said to Him, "Lord, come and see."
35 [a]Jesus wept.
36 Then the Jews said, "See how He loved him!"
37 And some of them said, "Could not this Man, [a]who opened the eyes of the blind, also have kept this man from dying?"

Lazarus Raised from the Dead

38 Then Jesus, again groaning in Himself, came to the tomb. It was a cave, and a [a]stone lay against it.
39 Jesus said, "Take away the stone." Martha, the sister of him who was dead, said to Him, "Lord, by this time there is a stench, for he has been *dead* four days."
40 Jesus said to her, "Did I not say to you that if you would believe you would [a]see the glory of God?"
41 Then they took away the stone **from the place* where the dead man was lying. And Jesus lifted up *His* eyes and said, "Father, I thank You that You have heard Me.
42 "And I know that You always hear Me, but [a]because of the people who are standing by I said *this*, that they may believe that You sent Me."
43 Now when He had said these things, He cried with a loud voice, "Lazarus, come forth!"
44 And he who had died came out bound hand and foot with [a]graveclothes, and [b]his face was wrapped with a cloth. Jesus said to them, "Loose him, and let him go."

The Plot to Kill Jesus
(Matt. 26:1–5; Mark 14:1, 2; Luke 22:1, 2)

45 Then many of the Jews who had come to Mary, [a]and had seen the things Jesus did, believed in Him.
46 But some of them went away to the Pharisees and [a]told them the things Jesus did.
47 [a]Then the chief priests and the Pharisees gathered a council and said, [b]"What shall we do? For this Man works many signs.
48 "If we let Him alone like this, everyone will believe in Him, and the Romans will come and take away both our place and nation."
49 And one of them, [a]Caiaphas, being high priest that year, said to them, "You know nothing at all,
50 [a]"nor do you consider that it is expedient

11:30 NU *was still*
11:31 NU *supposing that she was going*
11:41 NU omits *from the place where the dead man was lying*

KJV

that one man should die for the people, and that the whole nation perish not.

51 And this spake he not of himself: but being high priest that year, he prophesied that Jesus should die for that nation;

52 And not [a]for that nation only, [b]but that also he should gather together in one the children of God that were scattered abroad.

53 Then from that day forth they took counsel together for to [a]put him to death.

54 Jesus [a]therefore walked no more openly among the Jews; but went thence unto a country near to the wilderness, into a city called [b]Ephraim, and there continued with his disciples.

55 [a]And the Jews' passover was nigh at hand: and many went out of the country up to Jerusalem before the passover, to [b]purify themselves.

56 [a]Then sought they for Jesus, and spake among themselves, as they stood in the temple, What think ye, that he will not come to the feast?

57 Now both the chief priests and the Pharisees had given a commandment, that, if any man knew where he were, he should shew *it,* that they might [a]take him.

The Anointing at Bethany
(Matt. 26:6–13; Mark 14:3–9)

12 Then Jesus six days before the passover came to Bethany, [a]where Lazarus was which had been dead, whom he raised from the dead.

2 [a]There they made him a supper; and Martha served: but Lazarus was one of them that sat at the table with him.

3 Then took [a]Mary a pound of ointment of [b]spikenard, very costly, and anointed the feet of Jesus, and wiped his feet with her hair: and the house was filled with the odour of the ointment.

4 Then saith one of his disciples, [a]Judas Iscariot, Simon's *son,* which should betray him,

5 Why was not this ointment sold for three hundred pence, and given to the poor?

6 This he said, not that he cared for the poor; but because he was a thief, and [a]had the bag, and bare what was put therein.

7 Then said Jesus, Let her alone: against the day of my burying hath she kept this.

8 For [a]the poor always ye have with you; but me ye have not always.

The Plot to Kill Lazarus

9 Much people of the Jews therefore knew that he was there: and they came not for Jesus' sake only, but that they might see Lazarus also, [a]whom he had raised from the dead.

10 [a]But the chief priests consulted that they might put Lazarus also to death;

11 [a]Because that by reason of him many of the Jews went away, and believed on Jesus.

The Triumphal Entry
(Matt. 21:1–11; Mark 11:1–11; Luke 19:28–40)

12 [a]On the next day much people that were come to the feast, when they heard that Jesus was coming to Jerusalem,

13 Took branches of palm trees, and went forth to meet him, and cried, Hosanna: [a]BLESSED *IS* THE KING OF ISRAEL THAT COMETH IN THE NAME OF THE LORD.

14 [a]And Jesus, when he had found a young ass, sat thereon; as it is written,

15 [a]FEAR NOT, DAUGHTER OF SION: BEHOLD, THY KING COMETH, SITTING ON AN ASS'S COLT.

---

52 [a]Is. 49:6; Acts 10:45; 11:18; 13:46; [1 John 2:2] [b]Ps. 22:27; John 10:16; [Eph. 2:14–17] **53** [a]Matt. 26:4; Luke 6:11; 19:47; 22:2; John 5:16 **54** [a]John 4:1, 3; 7:1 [b]2 Chr. 13:19 **55** [a]Matt. 26:1; Mark 14:1; Luke 22:1; John 2:13; 5:1; 6:4 [b]Num. 9:10, 13; 31:19, 20; 2 Chr. 30:17; Luke 2:22 **56** [a]John 7:11 **57** [a]Matt. 26:14–16

CHAPTER 12

1 [a]Matt. 21:17; John 11:1, 43 **2** [a]Matt. 26:6; Mark 14:3; Luke 10:38–41 **3** [a]Luke 10:38, 39; John 11:2 [b]Song 1:12 **4** [a]John 13:26 **6** [a]John 13:29 **8** [a]Deut. 15:11; Matt. 26:11; Mark 14:7; John 17:11 **9** [a]John 11:43, 44 **10** [a]Luke 16:31 **11** [a]John 11:45; 12:18 **12** [a]Matt. 21:4–9; Mark 11:7–10; Luke 19:35–38 **13** [a]Ps. 118:25, 26 **14** [a]Matt. 21:7 **15** [a]Is. 40:9; Zech. 9:9

NKJV

for *us that one man should die for the people, and not that the whole nation should perish."

51 Now this he did not say on his own *authority;* but being high priest that year he prophesied that Jesus would die for the nation,

52 and [a]not for that nation only, but [b]also that He would gather together in one the children of God who were scattered abroad.

53 Then, from that day on, they plotted to [a]put Him to death.

54 [a]Therefore Jesus no longer walked openly among the Jews, but went from there into the country near the wilderness, to a city called [b]Ephraim, and there remained with His disciples.

55 [a]And the Passover of the Jews was near, and many went from the country up to Jerusalem before the Passover, to [b]purify themselves.

56 [a]Then they sought Jesus, and spoke among themselves as they stood in the temple, "What do you think—that He will not come to the feast?"

57 Now both the chief priests and the Pharisees had given a command, that if anyone knew where He was, he should report *it,* that they might [a]seize Him.

The Anointing at Bethany
(Matt. 26:6–13; Mark 14:3–9)

12 Then, six days before the Passover, Jesus came to Bethany, [a]where Lazarus was *who had been dead, whom He had raised from the dead.

2 [a]There they made Him a supper; and Martha served, but Lazarus was one of those who sat at the table with Him.

3 Then [a]Mary took a pound of very costly oil of [b]spikenard, anointed the feet of Jesus, and wiped His feet with her hair. And the house was filled with the fragrance of the oil.

4 But one of His disciples, [a]Judas Iscariot, Simon's *son,* who would betray Him, said,

5 "Why was this fragrant oil not sold for *three hundred denarii and given to the poor?"

6 This he said, not that he cared for the poor, but because he was a thief, and [a]had the money box; and he used to take what was put in it.

7 But Jesus said, "Let her alone; *she has kept this for the day of My burial.

8 "For [a]the poor you have with you always, but Me you do not have always."

The Plot to Kill Lazarus

9 Now a great many of the Jews knew that He was there; and they came, not for Jesus' sake only, but that they might also see Lazarus, [a]whom He had raised from the dead.

10 [a]But the chief priests plotted to put Lazarus to death also,

11 [a]because on account of him many of the Jews went away and believed in Jesus.

The Triumphal Entry
(Matt. 21:1–11; Mark 11:1–11; Luke 19:28–40)

12 [a]The next day a great multitude that had come to the feast, when they heard that Jesus was coming to Jerusalem,

13 took branches of palm trees and went out to meet Him, and cried out:

"Hosanna!
[a]*'Blessed is He who comes in the name of the LORD!'*
The King of Israel!"

14 [a]Then Jesus, when He had found a young donkey, sat on it; as it is written:

15 *"Fear[a] not, daughter of Zion;*
Behold, your King is coming,
Sitting on a donkey's colt."

---

*

11:50 NU *you* **12:1** NU omits *who had been dead* **12:5** About one year's wages for a worker **12:7** NU *that she may keep*

KJV

16 These things [a]understood not his disciples at the first: [b]but when Jesus was glorified, [c]then remembered they that these things were written of him, and *that* they had done these things unto him.
17 The people therefore that was with him when he called Lazarus out of his grave, and raised him from the dead, bare record.
18 [a]For this cause the people also met him, for that they heard that he had done this miracle.
19 The Pharisees therefore said among themselves, [a]Perceive ye how ye prevail nothing? behold, the world is gone after him.

The Fruitful Grain of Wheat

20 And there [a]were certain Greeks among them [b]that came up to worship at the feast:
21 The same came therefore to Philip, [a]which was of Bethsaida of Galilee, and desired him, saying, Sir, we would see Jesus.
22 Philip cometh and telleth Andrew: and again Andrew and Philip tell Jesus.
23 And Jesus answered them, saying, [a]The hour is come, that the Son of man should be glorified.
24 Verily, verily, I say unto you, [a]Except a corn of wheat fall into the ground and die, it abideth alone: but if it die, it bringeth forth much fruit.
25 [a]He that loveth his life shall lose it; and he that hateth his life in this world shall keep it unto life eternal.
26 If any man serve me, let him [a]follow me; and [b]where I am, there shall also my servant be: if any man serve me, him will *my* Father honour.

Jesus Predicts His Death on the Cross

27 [a]Now is my soul troubled; and what shall I say? Father, save me from this hour: [b]but for this cause came I unto this hour.
28 Father, glorify thy name. [a]Then came there a voice from heaven, *saying*, I have both glorified *it*, and will glorify *it* again.
29 The people therefore, that stood by, and heard *it*, said that it thundered: others said, An angel spake to him.
30 Jesus answered and said, [a]This voice came not because of me, but for your sakes.
31 Now is the judgment of this world: now shall [a]the prince of this world be cast out.
32 And I, [a]if I be lifted up from the earth, will draw [b]all *men* unto me.
33 [a]This he said, signifying what death he should die.
34 The people answered him, [a]We have heard out of the law that Christ abideth for ever: and how sayest thou, The Son of man must be lifted up? who is this Son of man?
35 Then Jesus said unto them, Yet a little while [a]is the light with you. [b]Walk while ye have the light, lest darkness come upon you: for [c]he that walketh in darkness knoweth not whither he goeth.
36 While ye have light, believe in the light, that ye may be [a]the children of light. These things spake Jesus, and departed, and [b]did hide himself from them.

Who Has Believed Our Report?

37 But though he had done so many [a]miracles before them, yet they believed not on him:
38 That the saying of Esaias the prophet might be fulfilled, which he spake, [a]LORD, WHO HATH BELIEVED OUR REPORT? AND TO WHOM HATH THE ARM OF THE LORD BEEN REVEALED?
39 Therefore they could not believe, because that Esaias said again,

16 [a]Luke 18:34 [b]John 7:39; 12:23 [c][John 14:26]
18 [a]John 12:11
19 [a]John 11:47, 48
20 [a]Mark 7:26; Acts 17:4 [b]1 Kin. 8:41, 42; Acts 8:27
21 [a]John 1:43, 44; 14:8–11
23 [a]Matt. 26:18, 45; John 13:32; Acts 3:13
24 [a][Rom. 14:9]; 1 Cor. 15:36
25 [a]Matt. 10:39; Mark 8:35; Luke 9:24
26 [a][Matt. 16:24] [b]John 14:3; 17:24; [1 Thess. 4:17]
27 [a][Matt. 26:38, 39]; Mark 14:34; Luke 12:50; John 11:33 [b]Luke 22:53; John 18:37
28 [a]Matt. 3:17; 17:5; Mark 1:11; 9:7; Luke 3:22; 9:35
30 [a]John 11:42
31 [a]Matt. 12:29; Luke 10:18; [Acts 26:18; 2 Cor. 4:4]
32 [a]John 3:14; 8:28 [b][Rom. 5:18; Heb. 2:9]
33 [a]John 18:32; 21:19
34 [a]Ps. 89:36, 37; Is. 9:6, 7; Mic. 4:7
35 [a][John 1:9; 7:33; 8:12] [b]Jer. 13:16; [Gal. 6:10]; Eph. 5:8 [c]John 11:10; [1 John 2:9–11]
36 [a]Luke 16:8; John 8:12 [b]John 8:59
37 [a]John 11:47
38 [a]Is. 53:1; Rom. 10:16

NKJV

16 [a]His disciples did not understand these things at first; [b]but when Jesus was glorified, [c]then they remembered that these things were written about Him and *that* they had done these things to Him.
17 Therefore the people, who were with Him when He called Lazarus out of his tomb and raised him from the dead, bore witness.
18 [a]For this reason the people also met Him, because they heard that He had done this sign.
19 The Pharisees therefore said among themselves, [a]"You see that you are accomplishing nothing. Look, the world has gone after Him!"

The Fruitful Grain of Wheat

20 Now there [a]were certain Greeks among those [b]who came up to worship at the feast.
21 Then they came to Philip, [a]who was from Bethsaida of Galilee, and asked him, saying, "Sir, we wish to see Jesus."
22 Philip came and told Andrew, and in turn Andrew and Philip told Jesus.
23 But Jesus answered them, saying, [a]"The hour has come that the Son of Man should be glorified.
24 "Most assuredly, I say to you, [a]unless a grain of wheat falls into the ground and dies, it remains alone; but if it dies, it produces much grain.
25 [a]"He who loves his life will lose it, and he who hates his life in this world will keep it for eternal life.
26 "If anyone serves Me, let him [a]follow Me; and [b]where I am, there My servant will be also. If anyone serves Me, him *My* Father will honor.

Jesus Predicts His Death on the Cross

27 [a]"Now My soul is troubled, and what shall I say? 'Father, save Me from this hour'? [b]But for this purpose I came to this hour.
28 "Father, glorify Your name." [a]Then a voice came from heaven, *saying*, "I have both glorified *it* and will glorify *it* again."
29 Therefore the people who stood by and heard *it* said that it had thundered. Others said, "An angel has spoken to Him."
30 Jesus answered and said, [a]"This voice did not come because of Me, but for your sake.
31 "Now is the judgment of this world; now [a]the ruler of this world will be cast out.
32 "And I, [a]if I am lifted up from the earth, will draw [b]all *peoples* to Myself."
33 [a]This He said, signifying by what death He would die.
34 The people answered Him, [a]"We have heard from the law that the Christ remains forever; and how *can* You say, 'The Son of Man must be lifted up'? Who is this Son of Man?"
35 Then Jesus said to them, "A little while longer [a]the light is with you. [b]Walk while you have the light, lest darkness overtake you; [c]he who walks in darkness does not know where he is going.
36 "While you have the light, believe in the light, that you may become [a]sons of light." These things Jesus spoke, and departed, and [b]was hidden from them.

Who Has Believed Our Report?

37 But although He had done so many [a]signs before them, they did not believe in Him,
38 that the word of Isaiah the prophet might be fulfilled, which he spoke:

> [a]*"Lord, who has believed our report?*
> *And to whom has the arm of the LORD*
> *been revealed?"*

39 Therefore they could not believe, because Isaiah said again:

KJV

40 [a]HE HATH BLINDED THEIR EYES, AND HARDENED THEIR HEART; [b]THAT THEY SHOULD NOT SEE WITH *THEIR* EYES, NOR UNDERSTAND WITH *THEIR* HEART, AND BE CONVERTED, AND I SHOULD HEAL THEM.

41 [a]These things said Esaias, when he saw his glory, and spake of him.

Walk in the Light

42 Nevertheless among the chief rulers also many believed on him; but [a]because of the Pharisees they did not confess *him,* lest they should be put out of the synagogue:

43 [a]For they loved the praise of men more than the praise of God.

44 Jesus cried and said, [a]He that believeth on me, [b]believeth not on me, [c]but on him that sent me.

45 And [a]he that seeth me seeth him that sent me.

46 [a]I am come a light into the world, that whosoever believeth on me should not abide in darkness.

47 And if any man hear my words, and believe not, [a]I judge him not: for [b]I came not to judge the world, but to save the world.

48 [a]He that rejecteth me, and receiveth not my words, hath one that judgeth him: [b]the word that I have spoken, the same shall judge him in the last day.

49 For [a]I have not spoken of myself; but the Father which sent me, he gave me a commandment, [b]what I should say, and what I should speak.

50 And I know that his commandment is life everlasting: whatsoever I speak therefore, even as the Father said unto me, so I [a]speak.

Jesus Washes the Disciples' Feet

13 Now [a]before the feast of the passover, when Jesus knew that [b]his hour was come that he should depart out of this world unto the Father, having loved his own which were in the world, he [c]loved them unto the end.

2 And supper being ended, [a]the devil having now put into the heart of Judas Iscariot, Simon's *son,* to betray him;

3 Jesus knowing [a]that the Father had given all things into his hands, and that he was [b]come from God, and [c]went to God;

4 [a]He riseth from supper, and laid aside his garments; and took a towel, and girded himself.

5 After that he poureth water into a bason, and began to wash the disciples' feet, and to wipe *them* with the towel wherewith he was girded.

6 Then cometh he to Simon Peter: and Peter saith unto him, Lord, [a]dost thou wash my feet?

7 Jesus answered and said unto him, What I do thou [a]knowest not now; [b]but thou shalt know hereafter.

8 Peter saith unto him, Thou shalt never wash my feet. Jesus answered him, [a]If I wash thee not, thou hast no part with me.

9 Simon Peter saith unto him, Lord, not my feet only, but also *my* hands and *my* head.

10 Jesus saith to him, He that is washed needeth not save to wash *his* feet, but is clean every whit: and [a]ye are clean, but not all.

11 For [a]he knew who should betray him; therefore said he, Ye are not all clean.

12 So after he had washed their feet, and had taken his garments, and was set down again, he said unto them, Know ye what I have done to you?

13 [a]Ye call me Master and Lord: and ye say well; for *so* I am.

14 [a]If I then, *your* Lord and Master, have washed your feet; [b]ye also ought to wash one another's feet.

15 For [a]I have given you an example, that ye should do as I have done to you.

16 [a]Verily, verily, I say unto you, The servant

---

40 [a]Is. 6:9, 10 [b]Matt. 13:14
41 [a]Is. 6:1
42 [a]John 7:13; 9:22
43 [a]John 5:41, 44
44 [a]Mark 9:37 [b][John 3:16, 18, 36; 11:25, 26] [c][John 5:24]
45 [a][John 14:9]
46 [a]John 1:4, 5; 8:12; 12:35, 36
47 [a]John 5:45 [b]John 3:17
48 [a][Luke 10:16] [b]Deut. 18:18, 19
49 [a]John 8:38 [b]Deut. 18:18
50 [a]John 5:19; 8:28

CHAPTER 13

1 [a]Matt. 26:2 [b]John 12:23; 17:1 [c]John 15:9
2 [a]Luke 22:3
3 [a]Acts 2:36 [b]John 8:42; 16:28 [c]John 17:11; 20:17
4 [a][Luke 22:27]
6 [a]Matt. 3:14
7 [a]John 12:16; 16:12 [b]John 13:19
8 [a][1 Cor. 6:11]
10 [a][John 15:3]
11 [a]John 6:64; 18:4
13 [a]Matt. 23:8, 10
14 [a]Luke 22:27 [b][Rom. 12:10]
15 [a][1 Pet. 2:21–24]
16 [a]Matt. 10:24

NKJV

40 *"He[a] has blinded their eyes and hardened their hearts,*
[b]Lest they should see with their eyes,
Lest they should understand with their hearts and turn,
So that I should heal them."

41 [a]These things Isaiah said *when he saw His glory and spoke of Him.

Walk in the Light

42 Nevertheless even among the rulers many believed in Him, but [a]because of the Pharisees they did not confess *Him,* lest they should be put out of the synagogue;

43 [a]for they loved the praise of men more than the praise of God.

44 Then Jesus cried out and said, [a]"He who believes in Me, [b]believes not in Me [c]but in Him who sent Me.

45 "And [a]he who sees Me sees Him who sent Me.

46 [a]"I have come *as* a light into the world, that whoever believes in Me should not abide in darkness.

47 "And if anyone hears My words and does not *believe, [a]I do not judge him; for [b]I did not come to judge the world but to save the world.

48 [a]"He who rejects Me, and does not receive My words, has that which judges him—[b]the word that I have spoken will judge him in the last day.

49 "For [a]I have not spoken on My own *authority;* but the Father who sent Me gave Me a command, [b]what I should say and what I should speak.

50 "And I know that His command is everlasting life. Therefore, whatever I speak, just as the Father has told Me, so I [a]speak."

Jesus Washes the Disciples' Feet

13 Now [a]before the Feast of the Passover, when Jesus knew that [b]His hour had come that He should depart from this world to the Father, having loved His own who were in the world, He [c]loved them to the end.

2 And *supper being ended, [a]the devil having already put it into the heart of Judas Iscariot, Simon's *son,* to betray Him,

3 Jesus, knowing [a]that the Father had given all things into His hands, and that He [b]had come from God and [c]was going to God,

4 [a]rose from supper and laid aside His garments, took a towel and girded Himself.

5 After that, He poured water into a basin and began to wash the disciples' feet, and to wipe *them* with the towel with which He was girded.

6 Then He came to Simon Peter. And *Peter* said to Him, [a]"Lord, are You washing my feet?"

7 Jesus answered and said to him, "What I am doing you [a]do not understand now, [b]but you will know after this."

8 Peter said to Him, "You shall never wash my feet!" Jesus answered him, [a]"If I do not wash you, you have no part with Me."

9 Simon Peter said to Him, "Lord, not my feet only, but also *my* hands and *my* head!"

10 Jesus said to him, "He who is bathed needs only to wash *his* feet, but is completely clean; and [a]you are clean, but not all of you."

11 For [a]He knew who would betray Him; therefore He said, "You are not all clean."

12 So when He had washed their feet, taken His garments, and sat down again, He said to them, "Do you know what I have done to you?

13 [a]"You call Me Teacher and Lord, and you say well, for *so* I am.

14 [a]"If I then, *your* Lord and Teacher, have washed your feet, [b]you also ought to wash one another's feet.

15 "For [a]I have given you an example, that you should do as I have done to you.

16 [a]"Most assuredly, I say to you, a servant

---

*

12:41 NU *because*
12:47 NU *keep them*
13:2 NU *during supper*

KJV

is not greater than his lord; neither he that is sent
greater than he that sent him.
17 [a]If ye know these things, happy are ye if
ye do them.

Jesus Identifies His Betrayer
(Matt. 26:21–25; Mark 14:18, 19; Luke 22:21–23)

18 I speak not of you all: I know whom I have
chosen: but that the [a]scripture may be fulfilled,
[b]HE THAT EATETH BREAD WITH ME HATH LIFTED UP
HIS HEEL AGAINST ME.
19 [a]Now I tell you before it come, that, when
it is come to pass, ye may believe that I am *he*.
20 [a]Verily, verily, I say unto you, He that receiveth whomsoever I send receiveth me; and he
that receiveth me receiveth him that sent me.
21 [a]When Jesus had thus said, [b]he was troubled in spirit, and testified, and said, Verily, verily,
I say unto you, that [c]one of you shall betray me.
22 Then the disciples looked one on another,
doubting of whom he spake.
23 Now [a]there was leaning on Jesus' bosom
one of his disciples, whom Jesus loved.
24 Simon Peter therefore beckoned to him,
that he should ask who it should be of whom he
spake.
25 He then lying on Jesus' breast saith unto
him, Lord, who is it?
26 Jesus answered, He it is, to whom I shall
give a sop, when I have dipped *it*. And when he
had dipped the sop, he gave *it* to [a]Judas Iscariot,
the son of Simon.
27 [a]And after the sop Satan entered into him.
Then said Jesus unto him, That thou doest, do
quickly.
28 Now no man at the table knew for what
intent he spake this unto him.
29 For some *of them* thought, because [a]Judas
had the bag, that Jesus had said unto him, Buy
those things that we have need of against the
feast; or, that he should give something to the
poor.
30 He then having received the sop went immediately out: and it was night.

The New Commandment

31 Therefore, when he was gone out, Jesus
said, [a]Now is the Son of man glorified, and [b]God
is glorified in him.
32 If God be glorified in him, God shall also
glorify him in himself, and [a]shall straightway glorify him.
33 Little children, yet a [a]little while I am with
you. Ye shall seek me: [b]and as I said unto the
Jews, Whither I go, ye cannot come; so now I
say to you.
34 [a]A new commandment I give unto you,
That ye love one another; as I have loved you,
that ye also love one another.
35 [a]By this shall all *men* know that ye are
my disciples, if ye have love one to another.

Jesus Predicts Peter's Denial

36 Simon Peter said unto him, Lord, whither
goest thou? Jesus answered him, Whither I [a]go,
thou canst not follow me now; but [b]thou shalt follow me afterwards.
37 Peter said unto him, Lord, why cannot I
follow thee now? I will [a]lay down my life for thy
sake.
38 Jesus answered him, Wilt thou lay down
thy life for my sake? Verily, verily, I say unto thee,
The cock shall not [a]crow, till thou hast denied
me thrice.

The Way, the Truth, and the Life

14 Let [a]not your heart be troubled: ye believe
in God, believe also in me.
2 In my Father's house are many mansions:
if *it were* not *so*, I would have told you. [a]I go to
prepare a place for you.
3 And if I go and prepare a place for you,

17 [a][James 1:25]
18 [a]John 15:25; 17:12 [b]Ps. 41:9
19 [a]John 14:29; 16:4
20 [a]Matt. 10:40
21 [a]Luke 22:21 [b]John 12:27 [c]1 John 2:19
23 [a]John 19:26; 20:2; 21:7, 20
26 [a]John 6:70, 71; 12:4
27 [a]Luke 22:3
29 [a]John 12:6
31 [a]John 12:23 [b][1 Pet. 4:11]
32 [a]John 12:23
33 [a]John 12:35; 14:19; 16:16–19 [b][John 7:34; 8:21]
34 [a]1 Thess. 4:9
35 [a]1 John 2:5
36 [a]John 13:33; 14:2; 16:5 [b]2 Pet. 1:14
37 [a]Mark 14:29–31
38 [a]John 18:25–27

CHAPTER 14
1 [a][John 14:27; 16:22, 24]
2 [a]John 13:33, 36

*13:18 NU *My bread has*
13:25 NU, M add *thus*
14:2 Lit. *dwellings* • NU *would I have told you that I go* or *I would have told you; for I go*

NKJV

is not greater than his master; nor is he who is
sent greater than he who sent him.
17 [a]"If you know these things, blessed are
you if you do them.

Jesus Identifies His Betrayer
(Matt. 26:21–25; Mark 14:18, 19; Luke 22:21–23)

18 "I do not speak concerning all of you. I
know whom I have chosen; but that the [a]Scripture
may be fulfilled, [b]*'He who eats *bread with Me
has lifted up his heel against Me.'*
19 [a]"Now I tell you before it comes, that
when it does come to pass, you may believe that
I am *He*.
20 [a]"Most assuredly, I say to you, he who
receives whomever I send receives Me; and he
who receives Me receives Him who sent Me."
21 [a]When Jesus had said these things, [b]He
was troubled in spirit, and testified and said,
"Most assuredly, I say to you, [c]one of you will
betray Me."
22 Then the disciples looked at one another,
perplexed about whom He spoke.
23 Now [a]there was leaning on Jesus' bosom
one of His disciples, whom Jesus loved.
24 Simon Peter therefore motioned to him to
ask who it was of whom He spoke.
25 Then, leaning *back on Jesus' breast, he
said to Him, "Lord, who is it?"
26 Jesus answered, "It is he to whom I shall
give a piece of bread when I have dipped *it*." And
having dipped the bread, He gave *it* to [a]Judas
Iscariot, *the son* of Simon.
27 [a]Now after the piece of bread, Satan entered him. Then Jesus said to him, "What you do,
do quickly."
28 But no one at the table knew for what reason He said this to him.
29 For some thought, because [a]Judas had the
money box, that Jesus had said to him, "Buy *those
things* we need for the feast," or that he should
give something to the poor.
30 Having received the piece of bread, he
then went out immediately. And it was night.

The New Commandment

31 So, when he had gone out, Jesus said,
[a]"Now the Son of Man is glorified, and [b]God is
glorified in Him.
32 "If God is glorified in Him, God will also
glorify Him in Himself, and [a]glorify Him
immediately.
33 "Little children, I shall be with you a [a]little
while longer. You will seek Me; [b]and as I said to
the Jews, 'Where I am going, you cannot come,'
so now I say to you.
34 [a]"A new commandment I give to you, that
you love one another; as I have loved you, that
you also love one another.
35 [a]"By this all will know that you are My
disciples, if you have love for one another."

Jesus Predicts Peter's Denial

36 Simon Peter said to Him, "Lord, where are
You going?" Jesus answered him, "Where I [a]am
going you cannot follow Me now, but [b]you shall
follow Me afterward."
37 Peter said to Him, "Lord, why can I not
follow You now? I will [a]lay down my life for Your
sake."
38 Jesus answered him, "Will you lay down
your life for My sake? Most assuredly, I say to
you, the rooster shall not [a]crow till you have denied Me three times.

The Way, the Truth, and the Life

14 "Let [a]not your heart be troubled; you believe in God, believe also in Me.
2 "In My Father's house are many *man-
sions; if *it were* not *so*, *I would have told you.
[a]I go to prepare a place for you.
3 "And if I go and prepare a place for you,

KJV

[a]I will come again, and receive you unto myself;
that [b]where I am, *there* ye may be also.
4 And whither I go ye know, and the way
ye know.
5 [a]Thomas saith unto him, Lord, we know
not whither thou goest; and how can we know
the way?
6 Jesus saith unto him, I am [a]the way, [b]the
truth, and [c]the life: [d]no man cometh unto the Father, [e]but by me.

The Father Revealed

7 [a]If ye had known me, ye should have
known my Father also: and from henceforth ye
know him, and have seen him.
8 Philip saith unto him, Lord, shew us the
Father, and it sufficeth us.
9 Jesus saith unto him, Have I been so long
time with you, and yet hast thou not known me,
Philip? [a]he that hath seen me hath seen the Father; and how sayest thou *then,* Shew us the
Father?
10 Believest thou not that [a]I am in the Father,
and the Father in me? the words that I speak unto
you [b]I speak not of myself: but the Father that
dwelleth in me, he doeth the works.
11 Believe me that I *am* in the Father, and
the Father in me: [a]or else believe me for the very
works' sake.

The Answered Prayer

12 [a]Verily, verily, I say unto you, He that believeth on me, the works that I do shall he do
also; and greater *works* than these shall he do;
because I go unto my Father.
13 [a]And whatsoever ye shall ask in my name,
that will I do, that the Father may be [b]glorified
in the Son.
14 If ye shall ask any thing in my name, I
will do *it.*

Jesus Promises Another Helper

15 [a]If ye love me, keep my commandments.
16 And I will pray the Father, and [a]he shall
give you another Comforter, that he may abide
with you for ever;
17 *Even* [a]the Spirit of truth; [b]whom the world
cannot receive, because it seeth him not, neither
knoweth him: but ye know him; for he dwelleth
with you, [c]and shall be in you.
18 [a]I will not leave you comfortless: [b]I will
come to you.

Indwelling of the Father and the Son

19 Yet a little while, and the world seeth me
no more; but [a]ye see me: [b]because I live, ye shall
live also.
20 At that day ye shall know that [a]I *am* in
my Father, and ye in me, and I in you.
21 [a]He that hath my commandments, and
keepeth them, he it is that loveth me: and he that
loveth me shall be loved of my Father, and I will
love him, and will manifest myself to him.
22 [a]Judas saith unto him, not Iscariot, Lord,
how is it that thou wilt manifest thyself unto us,
and not unto the world?
23 Jesus answered and said unto him, If a
man love me, he will keep my words: and my Father will love him, [a]and we will come unto him,
and make our abode with him.
24 He that loveth me not keepeth not my sayings: and [a]the word which ye hear is not mine,
but the Father's which sent me.

The Gift of His Peace

25 These things have I spoken unto you, being *yet* present with you.
26 But [a]the Comforter, *which is* the Holy
Ghost, whom the Father will [b]send in my name,
[c]he shall teach you all things, and bring all things
to your [d]remembrance, whatsoever I have said
unto you.

3 [a][Acts 1:11] [b][John 12:26; 1 Thess. 4:17]
5 [a]Matt. 10:3; John 11:16; 20:24–29; 21:2
6 [a][John 10:9; Rom. 5:2; Eph. 2:18; Heb. 9:8; 10:19, 20] [b][John 1:14, 17; 8:32; 18:37] [c][John 11:25] [d]1 Tim. 2:5 [e][John 10:7–9; Acts 4:12]
7 [a]John 8:19
9 [a]John 12:45; Col. 1:15; Heb. 1:3
10 [a]John 10:38; 14:11, 20 [b]Deut. 18:18; John 5:19; 14:24
11 [a]John 5:36; 10:38
12 [a]Matt. 21:21; Mark 16:17; Luke 10:17
13 [a]Matt. 7:7; [Mark 11:24]; Luke 11:9; John 15:16; 16:23, 24; [James 1:5–7; 1 John 3:22] [b]John 13:31
15 [a]1 John 5:3
16 [a][John 15:26; 20:22]; Acts 2:4, 33; Rom. 8:15
17 [a][John 15:26; 16:13; 1 John 4:6; 5:7] [b][1 Cor. 2:14] [c][1 John 2:27]
18 [a][Matt. 28:20] [b][John 14:3, 28]
19 [a]John 16:16, 22 [b][Rom. 5:10; 1 Cor. 15:20; 2 Cor. 4:10]
20 [a]John 10:38; 14:11
21 [a]1 John 2:5
22 [a]Luke 6:16; Acts 1:13
23 [a]2 Cor. 6:16; Eph. 3:17; [1 John 2:24]; Rev. 3:20; 21:3
24 [a]John 5:19
26 [a]Luke 24:49 [b]John 15:26 [c]1 Cor. 2:13 [d]John 2:22; 12:16; 1 John 2:20

*

14:14 NU *ask Me*
14:15 NU *you will keep*

NKJV

[a]I will come again and receive you to Myself; that
[b]where I am, *there* you may be also.
4 "And where I go you know, and the way
you know."
5 [a]Thomas said to Him, "Lord, we do not
know where You are going, and how can we know
the way?"
6 Jesus said to him, "I am [a]the way, [b]the
truth, and [c]the life. [d]No one comes to the Father
[e]except through Me.

The Father Revealed

7 [a]"If you had known Me, you would have
known My Father also; and from now on you
know Him and have seen Him."
8 Philip said to Him, "Lord, show us the Father, and it is sufficient for us."
9 Jesus said to him, "Have I been with you
so long, and yet you have not known Me, Philip?
[a]He who has seen Me has seen the Father; so how
can you say, 'Show us the Father'?
10 "Do you not believe that [a]I am in the Father, and the Father in Me? The words that I speak
to you [b]I do not speak on My own *authority;* but
the Father who dwells in Me does the works.
11 "Believe Me that I *am* in the Father and
the Father in Me, [a]or else believe Me for the sake
of the works themselves.

The Answered Prayer

12 [a]"Most assuredly, I say to you, he who
believes in Me, the works that I do he will do also;
and greater *works* than these he will do, because
I go to My Father.
13 [a]"And whatever you ask in My name, that
I will do, that the Father may be [b]glorified in the
Son.
14 "If you *ask anything in My name, I will
do *it.*

Jesus Promises Another Helper

15 [a]"If you love Me, *keep My commandments.
16 "And I will pray the Father, and [a]He will
give you another Helper, that He may abide with
you forever—
17 [a]"the Spirit of truth, [b]whom the world
cannot receive, because it neither sees Him nor
knows Him; but you know Him, for He dwells
with you [c]and will be in you.
18 [a]"I will not leave you orphans; [b]I will
come to you.

Indwelling of the Father and the Son

19 "A little while longer and the world will
see Me no more, but [a]you will see Me. [b]Because
I live, you will live also.
20 "At that day you will know that [a]I *am* in
My Father, and you in Me, and I in you.
21 [a]"He who has My commandments and
keeps them, it is he who loves Me. And he who
loves Me will be loved by My Father, and I will
love him and manifest Myself to him."
22 [a]Judas (not Iscariot) said to Him, "Lord,
how is it that You will manifest Yourself to us,
and not to the world?"
23 Jesus answered and said to him, "If anyone loves Me, he will keep My word; and My Father will love him, [a]and We will come to him and
make Our home with him.
24 "He who does not love Me does not keep
My words; and [a]the word which you hear is not
Mine but the Father's who sent Me.

The Gift of His Peace

25 "These things I have spoken to you while
being present with you.
26 "But [a]the Helper, the Holy Spirit, whom
the Father will [b]send in My name, [c]He will teach
you all things, and bring to your [d]remembrance
all things that I said to you.

KJV

27 [a]Peace I leave with you, my peace I give
unto you: not as the world giveth, give I unto you.
Let not your heart be troubled, neither let it be
afraid.
28 Ye have heard how [a]I said unto you, I go
away, and come *again* unto you. If ye loved me,
ye would rejoice, because I said, [b]I go unto the
Father: for [c]my Father is greater than I.
29 And [a]now I have told you before it come
to pass, that, when it is come to pass, ye might
believe.
30 Hereafter I will not talk much with you:
[a]for the prince of this world cometh, and hath
[b]nothing in me.
31 But that the world may know that I love
the Father; and [a]as the Father gave me commandment, even so I do. Arise, let us go hence.

The True Vine

15 I am the true vine, and my Father is the
husbandman.
2 [a]Every branch in me that beareth not fruit
he taketh away: and every *branch* that beareth
fruit, he purgeth it, that it may bring forth [b]more
fruit.
3 [a]Now ye are clean through the word
which I have spoken unto you.
4 [a]Abide in me, and I in you. As the branch
cannot bear fruit of itself, except it abide in the
vine; no more can ye, except ye abide in me.
5 I am the vine, ye *are* the branches: He that
abideth in me, and I in him, the same bringeth
forth much [a]fruit: for without me ye can do
[b]nothing.
6 If a man abide not in me, [a]he is cast forth
as a branch, and is withered; and men gather
them, and cast *them* into the fire, and they are
burned.
7 If ye abide in me, and my words [a]abide
in you, [b]ye shall ask what ye will, and it shall be
done unto you.
8 [a]Herein is my Father glorified, that ye
bear much fruit; [b]so shall ye be my disciples.

Love and Joy Perfected

9 As the Father hath [a]loved me, so have I
loved you: continue ye in my love.
10 [a]If ye keep my commandments, ye shall
abide in my love; even as I have kept my Father's
commandments, and abide in his love.
11 These things have I spoken unto you, that
my joy might remain in you, and [a]*that* your joy
might be full.
12 [a]This is my [b]commandment, That ye love
one another, as I have loved you.
13 [a]Greater love hath no man than this, that
a man lay down his life for his friends.
14 [a]Ye are my friends, if ye do whatsoever I
command you.
15 Henceforth I call you not servants; for the
servant knoweth not what his lord doeth: but I
have called you friends; [a]for all things that I have
heard of my Father I have made known unto
you.
16 [a]Ye have not chosen me, but I have chosen
you, and [b]ordained you, that ye should go and
bring forth fruit, and *that* your fruit should remain: that whatsoever ye shall ask of the Father
[c]in my name, he may give it you.
17 These things I command you, that ye love
one another.

The World's Hatred

18 [a]If the world hate you, ye know that it
hated me before *it hated* you.
19 [a]If ye were of the world, the world would
love his own: but [b]because ye are not of the world,
but I have chosen you out of the world, therefore
the world hateth you.
20 Remember the word that I said unto you,
[a]The servant is not greater than his lord. If they

NKJV

27 [a]"Peace I leave with you, My peace I give
to you; not as the world gives do I give to you.
Let not your heart be troubled, neither let it be
afraid.
28 "You have heard Me [a]say to you, 'I am
going away and coming *back* to you.' If you loved
Me, you would rejoice because *I said, [b]'I am
going to the Father,' for [c]My Father is greater
than I.
29 "And [a]now I have told you before it
comes, that when it does come to pass, you may
believe.
30 "I will no longer talk much with you, [a]for
the ruler of this world is coming, and he has [b]noth-
ing in Me.
31 "But that the world may know that I love
the Father, and [a]as the Father gave Me commandment, so I do. Arise, let us go from here.

The True Vine

15 "I am the true vine, and My Father is the
vinedresser.
2 [a]"Every branch in Me that does not bear
fruit He *takes away; and every *branch* that bears
fruit He prunes, that it may bear [b]more fruit.
3 [a]"You are already clean because of the
word which I have spoken to you.
4 [a]"Abide in Me, and I in you. As the branch
cannot bear fruit of itself, unless it abides in the
vine, neither can you, unless you abide in Me.
5 "I am the vine, you *are* the branches. He
who abides in Me, and I in him, bears much [a]fruit;
for without Me you can do [b]nothing.
6 "If anyone does not abide in Me, [a]he is
cast out as a branch and is withered; and they
gather them and throw *them* into the fire, and
they are burned.
7 "If you abide in Me, and My words [a]abide
in you, [b]you* will ask what you desire, and it shall
be done for you.
8 [a]"By this My Father is glorified, that you
bear much fruit; [b]so you will be My disciples.

Love and Joy Perfected

9 "As the Father [a]loved Me, I also have
loved you; abide in My love.
10 [a]"If you keep My commandments, you
will abide in My love, just as I have kept My Father's commandments and abide in His love.
11 "These things I have spoken to you, that
My joy may remain in you, and [a]*that* your joy
may be full.
12 [a]"This is My [b]commandment, that you
love one another as I have loved you.
13 [a]"Greater love has no one than this, than
to lay down one's life for his friends.
14 [a]"You are My friends if you do whatever
I command you.
15 "No longer do I call you servants, for a
servant does not know what his master is doing;
but I have called you friends, [a]for all things that
I heard from My Father I have made known to
you.
16 [a]"You did not choose Me, but I chose you
and [b]appointed you that you should go and bear
fruit, and *that* your fruit should remain, that
whatever you ask the Father [c]in My name He may
give you.
17 "These things I command you, that you
love one another.

The World's Hatred

18 [a]"If the world hates you, you know that
it hated Me before *it hated* you.
19 [a]"If you were of the world, the world
would love its own. Yet [b]because you are not of
the world, but I chose you out of the world, therefore the world hates you.
20 "Remember the word that I said to you,
[a]'A servant is not greater than his master.' If they

---

27 [a]Luke 1:79; [John 16:33; 20:19; Phil. 4:7]; Col. 3:15
28 [a]John 14:3, 18 [b]John 16:16 [c][John 5:18; Phil. 2:6]
29 [a]John 13:19
30 [a][John 12:31] [b][John 8:46; 2 Cor. 5:21; Heb. 4:15; 1 Pet. 1:19; 2:22]
31 [a]Is. 50:5; John 10:18; Phil. 2:8

CHAPTER 15

2 [a]Matt. 15:13 [b][Matt. 13:12]
3 [a][John 13:10; 17:17]; Eph. 5:26
4 [a]John 17:23; Eph. 3:17; [Col. 1:23]
5 [a]Hos. 14:8; [Gal. 5:22, 23] [b]2 Cor. 3:5
6 [a]Matt. 3:10
7 [a]1 John 2:14 [b]John 14:13; 16:23
8 [a]Ps. 22:23; [Matt. 5:16]; John 13:31; 17:4; [Phil. 1:11]; 1 Pet. 4:11 [b]John 8:31
9 [a]John 5:20; 17:26
10 [a]John 14:15
11 [a][John 16:24]; 1 John 1:4
12 [a]John 13:34; 1 John 3:11 [b]Rom. 12:9
13 [a]Eph. 5:2; 1 John 3:16
14 [a][Matt. 12:50; 28:20]; John 14:15, 21; Acts 10:42; 1 John 3:23, 24
15 [a]Gen. 18:17
16 [a]John 6:70; 13:18; 15:19; 1 John 4:10 [b][Matt. 28:19; Mark 16:15; Col. 1:6] [c]John 14:13; 16:23, 24
18 [a]John 7:7; 1 John 3:13
19 [a]1 John 4:5 [b]John 17:14
20 [a]Matt. 10:24; John 13:16

*

14:28 NU omits *I said*
15:2 Or *lifts up*
15:7 NU omits *you will*

KJV

have persecuted me, they will also persecute you;
[b]if they have kept my saying, they will keep your's
also.
21 But [a]all these things will they do unto you
for my name's sake, because they know not him
that sent me.
22 [a]If I had not come and spoken unto them,
they had not had sin: [b]but now they have no cloke
for their sin.
23 [a]He that hateth me hateth my Father also.
24 If I had not done among them [a]the works
which none other man did, they had not had sin:
but now have they both [b]seen and hated both me
and my Father.
25 But *this cometh to pass,* that the word
might be fulfilled that is written in their law,
[a]THEY HATED ME WITHOUT A CAUSE.

The Coming Rejection

26 [a]But when the Comforter is come, whom
I will send unto you from the Father, *even* the
Spirit of truth, which proceedeth from the Father,
[b]he shall testify of me:
27 And [a]ye also shall bear witness, because
[b]ye have been with me from the beginning.

16 These things have I spoken unto you, that
ye [a]should not be offended.
2 [a]They shall put you out of the synagogues:
yea, the time cometh, [b]that whosoever killeth you
will think that he doeth God service.
3 And [a]these things will they do unto you,
because they have not known the Father, nor me.
4 But these things have I told you, that when
the time shall come, ye may remember that I told
you of them. And these things I said not unto you
at the beginning, because I was with you.

The Work of the Holy Spirit

5 But now I [a]go my way to him that sent
me; and none of you asketh me, Whither goest
thou?
6 But because I have said these things unto
you, [a]sorrow hath filled your heart.
7 Nevertheless I tell you the truth; It is expedient for you that I go away: for if I go not away,
the Comforter will not come unto you; but [a]if I
depart, I will send him unto you.
8 And when he is [a]come, he will reprove
the world of sin, and of righteousness, and of
judgment:
9 [a]Of sin, because they believe not on me;
10 [a]Of righteousness, [b]because I go to my Father, and ye see me no more;
11 [a]Of judgment, because [b]the prince of this
world is judged.
12 I have yet many things to say unto you,
[a]but ye cannot bear them now.
13 Howbeit when he, [a]the Spirit of truth, is
come, [b]he will guide you into all truth: for he shall
not speak of himself; but whatsoever he shall
hear, *that* shall he speak: and he will shew you
things to come.
14 [a]He shall glorify me: for he shall receive
of mine, and shall shew *it* unto you.
15 [a]All things that the Father hath are mine:
therefore said I, that he shall take of mine, and
shall shew *it* unto you.

Sorrow Will Turn to Joy

16 A [a]little while, and ye shall not see me:
and again, a little while, and ye shall see me, [b]be-
cause I go to the Father.
17 Then said *some* of his disciples among
themselves, What is this that he saith unto us, A
little while, and ye shall not see me: and again, a
little while, and ye shall see me: and, Because I
go to the Father?
18 They said therefore, What is this that he
saith, A little while? we cannot tell what he saith.
19 Now Jesus knew that they were desirous

20 [b]Ezek. 3:7
21 [a]Matt. 10:22; 24:9; [1 Pet. 4:14]; Rev. 2:3
22 [a]John 9:41; 15:24 [b][Rom. 1:20; James 4:17]
23 [a]1 John 2:23
24 [a]John 3:2 [b]John 14:9
25 [a]Ps. 35:19; 69:4; 109:3–5
26 [a]Luke 24:49; [John 14:17]; Acts 2:4, 33 [b]1 John 5:6
27 [a]Luke 24:48; 1 Pet. 5:1; 2 Pet. 1:16 [b]Matt. 3:14; Luke 1:2; 1 John 1:1

CHAPTER 16

1 [a]Matt. 11:6
2 [a]John 9:22 [b]Acts 8:1
3 [a]John 8:19; 15:21; Acts 13:27; Rom. 10:2
5 [a]John 7:33; 13:33; 14:28; 17:11
6 [a]Matt. 17:23; [John 16:20, 22]
7 [a]Acts 2:33
8 [a]Acts 1:8; 2:1–4, 37
9 [a]Acts 2:22
10 [a]Acts 2:32 [b]John 5:32
11 [a]Acts 26:18 [b][Luke 10:18]
12 [a]Mark 4:33
13 [a][John 14:17] [b]John 14:26; Acts 11:28; Rev. 1:19
14 [a]John 15:26
15 [a]Matt. 11:27; John 3:35
16 [a]John 7:33; 12:35; 13:33; 14:19; 19:40–42; 20:19 [b]John 13:3

*______

16:3 NU, M omit *to you*
16:4 NU *their*
16:15 NU, M *takes of Mine and will declare*

NKJV

persecuted Me, they will also persecute you. [b]If
they kept My word, they will keep yours also.
21 "But [a]all these things they will do to you
for My name's sake, because they do not know
Him who sent Me.
22 [a]"If I had not come and spoken to them,
they would have no sin, [b]but now they have no
excuse for their sin.
23 [a]"He who hates Me hates My Father also.
24 "If I had not done among them [a]the works
which no one else did, they would have no sin;
but now they have [b]seen and also hated both Me
and My Father.
25 "But *this happened* that the word might
be fulfilled which is written in their law, [a]*'They
hated Me without a cause.'*

The Coming Rejection

26 [a]"But when the Helper comes, whom I
shall send to you from the Father, the Spirit of
truth who proceeds from the Father, [b]He will testify of Me.
27 "And [a]you also will bear witness, because
[b]you have been with Me from the beginning.

16 "These things I have spoken to you, that
you [a]should not be made to stumble.
2 [a]"They will put you out of the synagogues;
yes, the time is coming [b]that whoever kills you
will think that he offers God service.
3 "And [a]these things they will do *to you
because they have not known the Father nor Me.
4 "But these things I have told you, that
when *the time comes, you may remember that I
told you of them. And these things I did not say
to you at the beginning, because I was with you.

The Work of the Holy Spirit

5 "But now I [a]go away to Him who sent Me,
and none of you asks Me, 'Where are You going?'
6 "But because I have said these things to
you, [a]sorrow has filled your heart.
7 "Nevertheless I tell you the truth. It is to
your advantage that I go away; for if I do not go
away, the Helper will not come to you; but [a]if I
depart, I will send Him to you.
8 "And when He has [a]come, He will convict
the world of sin, and of righteousness, and of
judgment:
9 [a]"of sin, because they do not believe in
Me;
10 [a]"of righteousness, [b]because I go to My
Father and you see Me no more;
11 [a]"of judgment, because [b]the ruler of this
world is judged.
12 "I still have many things to say to you,
[a]but you cannot bear *them* now.
13 "However, when He, [a]the Spirit of truth,
has come, [b]He will guide you into all truth; for
He will not speak on His own *authority,* but whatever He hears He will speak; and He will tell you
things to come.
14 [a]"He will glorify Me, for He will take of
what is Mine and declare *it* to you.
15 [a]"All things that the Father has are Mine.
Therefore I said that He *will take of Mine and
declare *it* to you.

Sorrow Will Turn to Joy

16 "A [a]little while, and you will not see Me;
and again a little while, and you will see Me, [b]be-
cause I go to the Father."
17 Then *some* of His disciples said among
themselves, "What is this that He says to us, 'A
little while, and you will not see Me; and again a
little while, and you will see Me'; and, 'because I
go to the Father'?"
18 They said therefore, "What is this that He
says, 'A little while'? We do not know what He
is saying."
19 Now Jesus knew that they desired to ask

KJV

to ask him, and said unto them, Do ye enquire
among yourselves of that I said, A little while,
and ye shall not see me: and again, a little while,
and ye shall see me?
20 Verily, verily, I say unto you, That ye shall
weep and [a]lament, but the world shall rejoice: and
ye shall be sorrowful, but your sorrow shall be
turned into [b]joy.
21 [a]A woman when she is in travail hath sorrow, because her hour is come: but as soon as
she is delivered of the child, she remembereth no
more the anguish, for joy that a man is born into
the world.
22 And ye now therefore have sorrow: but I
will see you again, and [a]your heart shall rejoice,
and your joy no man taketh from you.
23 And in that day ye shall ask me nothing.
[a]Verily, verily, I say unto you, Whatsoever ye
shall ask the Father in my name, he will give *it*
you.
24 Hitherto have ye asked nothing in my
name: ask, and ye shall receive, [a]that your joy
may be [b]full.

Jesus Christ Has Overcome the World

25 These things have I spoken unto you in
proverbs: but the time cometh, when I shall no
more speak unto you in proverbs, but I shall shew
you [a]plainly of the Father.
26 At that day ye shall ask in my name: and
I say not unto you, that I will pray the Father for
you:
27 [a]For the Father himself loveth you, because ye have loved me, and [b]have believed that
I came out from God.
28 [a]I came forth from the Father, and am
come into the world: again, I leave the world, and
go to the Father.
29 His disciples said unto him, Lo, now
speakest thou plainly, and speakest no proverb.
30 Now are we sure that [a]thou knowest all
things, and needest not that any man should ask
thee: by this [b]we believe that thou camest forth
from God.
31 Jesus answered them, Do ye now believe?
32 [a]Behold, the hour cometh, yea, is now
come, that ye shall be scattered, [b]every man to
his own, and shall leave me alone: and [c]yet I am
not alone, because the Father is with me.
33 These things I have spoken unto you, that
[a]in me ye might have peace. [b]In the world ye shall
have tribulation: but be of good cheer; [c]I have
overcome the world.

Jesus Prays for Himself

17 These words spake Jesus, and lifted up his
eyes to heaven, and said, Father, [a]the hour
is come; glorify thy Son, that thy Son also may
glorify thee:
2 [a]As thou hast given him power over all
flesh, that he should give eternal life to as many
[b]as thou hast given him.
3 And [a]this is life eternal, that they might
know thee [b]the only true God, and Jesus Christ,
[c]whom thou hast sent.
4 [a]I have glorified thee on the earth: [b]I have
finished the work [c]which thou gavest me to do.
5 And now, O Father, glorify thou me with
thine own self with the glory [a]which I had with
thee before the world was.

Jesus Prays for His Disciples

6 [a]I have manifested thy name unto the men
[b]which thou gavest me out of the world: [c]thine
they were, and thou gavest them me; and they
have kept thy word.
7 Now they have known that all things
whatsoever thou hast given me are of thee.
8 For I have given unto them the words
[a]which thou gavest me; and they have received

NKJV

Him, and He said to them, "Are you inquiring
among yourselves about what I said, 'A little
while, and you will not see Me; and again a little
while, and you will see Me'?
20 "Most assuredly, I say to you that you will
weep and [a]lament, but the world will rejoice; and
you will be sorrowful, but your sorrow will be
turned into [b]joy.
21 [a]"A woman, when she is in labor, has sorrow because her hour has come; but as soon as
she has given birth to the child, she no longer
remembers the anguish, for joy that a human being has been born into the world.
22 "Therefore you now have sorrow; but I
will see you again and [a]your heart will rejoice,
and your joy no one will take from you.
23 "And in that day you will ask Me nothing.
[a]Most assuredly, I say to you, whatever you ask
the Father in My name He will give you.
24 "Until now you have asked nothing in My
name. Ask, and you will receive, [a]that your joy
may be [b]full.

Jesus Christ Has Overcome the World

25 "These things I have spoken to you in figurative language; but the time is coming when I
will no longer speak to you in figurative language,
but I will tell you [a]plainly about the Father.
26 "In that day you will ask in My name, and
I do not say to you that I shall pray the Father
for you;
27 [a]"for the Father Himself loves you, because you have loved Me, and [b]have believed that
I came forth from God.
28 [a]"I came forth from the Father and have
come into the world. Again, I leave the world and
go to the Father."
29 His disciples said to Him, "See, now You
are speaking plainly, and using no figure of
speech!
30 "Now we are sure that [a]You know all
things, and have no need that anyone should
question You. By this [b]we believe that You came
forth from God."
31 Jesus answered them, "Do you now
believe?
32 [a]"Indeed the hour is coming, yes, has now
come, that you will be scattered, [b]each to his own,
and will leave Me alone. And [c]yet I am not alone,
because the Father is with Me.
33 "These things I have spoken to you, that
[a]in Me you may have peace. [b]In the world you
*will have tribulation; but be of good cheer, [c]I
have overcome the world."

Jesus Prays for Himself

17 Jesus spoke these words, lifted up His eyes
to heaven, and said: "Father, [a]the hour has
come. Glorify Your Son, that Your Son also may
glorify You,
2 [a]"as You have given Him authority over
all flesh, that He *should give eternal life to as
many [b]as You have given Him.
3 "And [a]this is eternal life, that they may
know You, [b]the only true God, and Jesus Christ
[c]whom You have sent.
4 [a]"I have glorified You on the earth. [b]I
have finished the work [c]which You have given
Me to do.
5 "And now, O Father, glorify Me together
with Yourself, with the glory [a]which I had with
You before the world was.

Jesus Prays for His Disciples

6 [a]"I have manifested Your name to the
men [b]whom You have given Me out of the world.
[c]They were Yours, You gave them to Me, and they
have kept Your word.
7 "Now they have known that all things
which You have given Me are from You.
8 "For I have given to them the words
[a]which You have given Me; and they have re-

20 [a]Mark 16:10 [b]Luke 24:32, 41
21 [a]Is. 13:8; 26:17; 42:14
22 [a]1 Pet. 1:8
23 [a]Matt. 7:7
24 [a]John 17:13 [b]John 15:11
25 [a]John 7:13
27 [a][John 14:21, 23] [b]John 3:13
28 [a]John 13:1, 3; 16:5, 10, 17
30 [a]John 21:17 [b]John 17:8
32 [a]Matt. 26:31, 56 [b]John 20:10 [c]John 8:29
33 [a][Eph. 2:14] [b]2 Tim. 3:12 [c]Rom. 8:37

CHAPTER 17

1 [a]John 12:23
2 [a]John 3:35 [b]John 6:37, 39; 17:6, 9, 24
3 [a]Jer. 9:23, 24 [b]1 Cor. 8:4 [c]John 3:34
4 [a]John 13:31 [b]John 4:34; 19:30 [c]John 14:31
5 [a]Phil. 2:6
6 [a]Ps. 22:22 [b]John 6:37 [c]Ezek. 18:4
8 [a]John 8:28

*

16:33 NU, M omit *will*
17:2 M *shall*

KJV

them, [b]and have known surely that I came out from thee, and they have believed that [c]thou didst send me.

9 I pray for them: [a]I pray not for the world, but for them which thou hast given me; for they are thine.

10 And all mine are thine, and [a]thine are mine; and I am glorified in them.

11 [a]And now I am no more in the world, but these are in the world, and I come to thee. Holy Father, [b]keep through thine own name those whom thou hast given me, that they may be one, [c]as we *are.*

12 While I was with them in the world, [a]I kept them in thy name: those that thou gavest me I have kept, and [b]none of them is lost, [c]but the son of perdition; [d]that the scripture might be fulfilled.

13 And now come I to thee; and these things I speak in the world, that they might have my joy fulfilled in themselves.

14 I have given them thy word; [a]and the world hath hated them, because they are not of the world, [b]even as I am not of the world.

15 I pray not that thou shouldest take them out of the world, but [a]that thou shouldest keep them from the evil.

16 They are not of the world, even as I am not of the world.

17 [a]Sanctify them through thy truth: [b]thy word is truth.

18 [a]As thou hast sent me into the world, even so have I also sent them into the world.

19 And [a]for their sakes I sanctify myself, that they also might be sanctified through the truth.

Jesus Prays for All Believers

20 Neither pray I for these alone, but for them also which shall believe on me through their word;

21 [a]That they all may be one; as [b]thou, Father, *art* in me, and I in thee, that they also may be one in us: that the world may believe that thou hast sent me.

22 And the [a]glory which thou gavest me I have given them; [b]that they may be one, even as we are one:

23 I in them, and thou in me, [a]that they may be made perfect in one; and that the world may know that thou hast sent me, and hast loved them, as thou hast loved me.

24 [a]Father, I will that they also, whom thou hast given me, be with me where I am; that they may behold my glory, which thou hast given me: [b]for thou lovedst me before the foundation of the world.

25 O righteous Father, [a]the world hath not known thee: but [b]I have known thee, and [c]these have known that thou hast sent me.

26 [a]And I have declared unto them thy name, and will declare *it:* that the love [b]wherewith thou hast loved me may be in them, and I in them.

Betrayal and Arrest in Gethsemane
(Matt. 26:47–56; Mark 14:43–52; Luke 22:47–53)

18 When Jesus had spoken these words, [a]he went forth with his disciples over [b]the brook Cedron, where was a garden, into the which he entered, and his disciples.

2 And Judas also, which betrayed him, knew the place: [a]for Jesus ofttimes resorted thither with his disciples.

3 [a]Judas then, having received a band *of men* and officers from the chief priests and Pharisees, cometh thither with lanterns and torches and weapons.

4 Jesus therefore, [a]knowing all things that should come upon him, went forth, and said unto them, Whom seek ye?

5 They answered him, [a]Jesus of Nazareth. Jesus saith unto them, I am *he.* And Judas also, which [b]betrayed him, stood with them.

8 [b]John 8:42; 16:27, 30 [c]Deut. 18:15, 18
9 [a][1 John 5:19]
10 [a]John 16:15
11 [a]John 13:1 [b][1 Pet. 1:5] [c]John 10:30
12 [a]Heb. 2:13 [b]1 John 2:19 [c]John 6:70 [d]Ps. 41:9; 109:8
14 [a]John 15:19 [b]John 8:23
15 [a]1 John 5:18
17 [a][Eph. 5:26] [b]Ps. 119:9, 142, 151
18 [a]John 4:38; 20:21
19 [a][Heb. 10:10]
21 [a][Gal. 3:28] [b]John 10:38; 17:11, 23
22 [a]1 John 1:3 [b][2 Cor. 3:18]
23 [a][Col. 3:14]
24 [a][1 Thess. 4:17] [b]John 17:5
25 [a]John 15:21 [b]John 7:29; 8:55; 10:15 [c]John 3:17; 17:3, 8, 18, 21, 23
26 [a]John 17:6 [b]John 15:9

CHAPTER 18
1 [a]Mark 14:26, 32 [b]2 Sam. 15:23
2 [a]Luke 21:37; 22:39
3 [a]Luke 22:47–53
4 [a]John 6:64; 13:1, 3; 19:28
5 [a]Matt. 21:11 [b]Ps. 41:9

*

17:11 NU, M *keep them through Your name which You have given Me*
17:12 NU omits *in the world* • NU *Your name which You gave Me. And I guarded them;* (or *it;*)
17:20 NU, M omit *will*

NKJV

ceived *them,* [b]and have known surely that I came forth from You; and they have believed that [c]You sent Me.

9 "I pray for them. [a]I do not pray for the world but for those whom You have given Me, for they are Yours.

10 "And all Mine are Yours, and [a]Yours are Mine, and I am glorified in them.

11 [a]"Now I am no longer in the world, but these are in the world, and I come to You. Holy Father, [b]keep* through Your name those whom You have given Me, that they may be one [c]as We *are.*

12 "While I was with them *in the world, [a]I kept them in *Your name. Those whom You gave Me I have kept; and [b]none of them is lost [c]except the son of perdition, [d]that the Scripture might be fulfilled.

13 "But now I come to You, and these things I speak in the world, that they may have My joy fulfilled in themselves.

14 "I have given them Your word; [a]and the world has hated them because they are not of the world, [b]just as I am not of the world.

15 "I do not pray that You should take them out of the world, but [a]that You should keep them from the evil one.

16 "They are not of the world, just as I am not of the world.

17 [a]"Sanctify them by Your truth. [b]Your word is truth.

18 [a]"As You sent Me into the world, I also have sent them into the world.

19 "And [a]for their sakes I sanctify Myself, that they also may be sanctified by the truth.

Jesus Prays for All Believers

20 "I do not pray for these alone, but also for those who *will believe in Me through their word;

21 [a]"that they all may be one, as [b]You, Father, *are* in Me, and I in You; that they also may be one in Us, that the world may believe that You sent Me.

22 "And the [a]glory which You gave Me I have given them, [b]that they may be one just as We are one:

23 "I in them, and You in Me; [a]that they may be made perfect in one, and that the world may know that You have sent Me, and have loved them as You have loved Me.

24 [a]"Father, I desire that they also whom You gave Me may be with Me where I am, that they may behold My glory which You have given Me; [b]for You loved Me before the foundation of the world.

25 "O righteous Father! [a]The world has not known You, but [b]I have known You; and [c]these have known that You sent Me.

26 [a]"And I have declared to them Your name, and will declare *it,* that the love [b]with which You loved Me may be in them, and I in them."

Betrayal and Arrest in Gethsemane
(Matt. 26:47–56; Mark 14:43–52; Luke 22:47–53)

18 When Jesus had spoken these words, [a]He went out with His disciples over [b]the Brook Kidron, where there was a garden, which He and His disciples entered.

2 And Judas, who betrayed Him, also knew the place; [a]for Jesus often met there with His disciples.

3 [a]Then Judas, having received a detachment *of troops,* and officers from the chief priests and Pharisees, came there with lanterns, torches, and weapons.

4 Jesus therefore, [a]knowing all things that would come upon Him, went forward and said to them, "Whom are you seeking?"

5 They answered Him, [a]"Jesus of Nazareth." Jesus said to them, "I am *He.*" And Judas, who [b]betrayed Him, also stood with them.

KJV

6 As soon then as he had said unto them, I am *he,* they went backward, and fell to the ground.

7 Then asked he them again, Whom seek ye? And they said, Jesus of Nazareth.

8 Jesus answered, I have told you that I am *he:* if therefore ye seek me, let these go their way:

9 That the saying might be fulfilled, which he spake, [a]Of them which thou gavest me have I lost none.

10 [a]Then Simon Peter having a sword drew it, and smote the high priest's servant, and cut off his right ear. The servant's name was Malchus.

11 Then said Jesus unto Peter, Put up thy sword into the sheath: [a]the cup which my Father hath given me, shall I not drink it?

Before the High Priest

12 Then the band and the captain and officers of the Jews took Jesus, and bound him,

13 And [a]led him away to [b]Annas first; for he was father in law to [c]Caiaphas, which was the high priest that same year.

14 [a]Now Caiaphas was he, which gave counsel to the Jews, that it was expedient that one man should die for the people.

Peter Denies Jesus
(Matt. 26:69–75; Mark 14:66–72; Luke 22:54–62)

15 [a]And Simon Peter followed Jesus, and *so did* [b]another disciple: that disciple was known unto the high priest, and went in with Jesus into the palace of the high priest.

16 [a]But Peter stood at the door without. Then went out that other disciple, which was known unto the high priest, and spake unto her that kept the door, and brought in Peter.

17 Then saith the damsel that kept the door unto Peter, Art not thou also *one* of this man's disciples? He saith, I am [a]not.

18 And the servants and officers stood there, who had made a fire of coals; for it was cold: and they warmed themselves: and Peter stood with them, and warmed himself.

Jesus Questioned by the High Priest

19 The high priest then asked Jesus of his disciples, and of his doctrine.

20 Jesus answered him, [a]I spake openly to the world; I ever taught [b]in the synagogue, and [c]in the temple, whither the Jews always resort; and in secret have I said nothing.

21 Why askest thou me? ask [a]them which heard me, what I have said unto them: behold, they know what I said.

22 And when he had thus spoken, one of the officers which stood by [a]struck Jesus with the palm of his hand, saying, Answerest thou the high priest so?

23 Jesus answered him, If I have spoken evil, bear witness of the evil: but if well, why smitest thou me?

24 [a]Now Annas had sent him bound unto [b]Caiaphas the high priest.

Peter Denies Twice More

25 And Simon Peter stood and warmed himself. [a]They said therefore unto him, Art not thou also *one* of his disciples? He denied *it,* and said, I am not.

26 One of the servants of the high priest, being *his* kinsman whose ear Peter cut off, saith, Did not I see thee in the garden with him?

27 Peter then denied again: and [a]immediately the cock crew.

In Pilate's Court
(Matt. 27:1, 2, 11–14; Mark 15:1–5; Luke 23:1–5)

28 [a]Then led they Jesus from Caiaphas unto the hall of judgment: and it was early; [b]and they themselves went not into the judgment hall, lest

9 [a][John 6:39; 17:12]
10 [a]Matt. 26:51; Mark 14:47; Luke 22:49, 50
11 [a]Matt. 20:22; 26:39; Mark 14:36; Luke 22:42
13 [a]Matt. 26:57 [b]Luke 3:2; John 18:24; Acts 4:6 [c]Matt. 26:3; John 11:49, 51
14 [a]John 11:50
15 [a]Matt. 26:58; Mark 14:54; Luke 22:54 [b]John 20:2–5
16 [a]Matt. 26:69; Mark 14:66–68; Luke 22:55–57
17 [a]Matt. 26:34
20 [a]Matt. 26:55; Luke 4:15; John 8:26 [b]John 6:59 [c]Mark 14:49; John 7:14, 28
21 [a]Mark 12:37
22 [a]Job 16:10; Is. 50:6; Jer. 20:2; Lam. 3:30; Acts 23:2
24 [a]Matt. 26:57; Luke 3:2; Acts 4:6 [b]John 11:49
25 [a]Matt. 26:71–75; Mark 14:69–72; Luke 22:58–62
27 [a]Matt. 26:74; Mark 14:72; Luke 22:60; John 13:38
28 [a]Matt. 27:2; Mark 15:1; Luke 23:1; Acts 3:13 [b]John 11:55; Acts 10:28; 11:3

NKJV

6 Now when He said to them, "I am *He,*" they drew back and fell to the ground.

7 Then He asked them again, "Whom are you seeking?" And they said, "Jesus of Nazareth."

8 Jesus answered, "I have told you that I am *He.* Therefore, if you seek Me, let these go their way,"

9 that the saying might be fulfilled which He spoke, [a]"Of those whom You gave Me I have lost none."

10 [a]Then Simon Peter, having a sword, drew it and struck the high priest's servant, and cut off his right ear. The servant's name was Malchus.

11 So Jesus said to Peter, "Put your sword into the sheath. Shall I not drink [a]the cup which My Father has given Me?"

Before the High Priest

12 Then the detachment *of troops* and the captain and the officers of the Jews arrested Jesus and bound Him.

13 And [a]they led Him away to [b]Annas first, for he was the father-in-law of [c]Caiaphas who was high priest that year.

14 [a]Now it was Caiaphas who advised the Jews that it was expedient that one man should die for the people.

Peter Denies Jesus
(Matt. 26:69–75; Mark 14:66–72; Luke 22:54–62)

15 [a]And Simon Peter followed Jesus, and so *did* [b]another* disciple. Now that disciple was known to the high priest, and went with Jesus into the courtyard of the high priest.

16 [a]But Peter stood at the door outside. Then the other disciple, who was known to the high priest, went out and spoke to her who kept the door, and brought Peter in.

17 Then the servant girl who kept the door said to Peter, "You are not also *one* of this Man's disciples, are you?" He said, "I am [a]not."

18 Now the servants and officers who had made a fire of coals stood there, for it was cold, and they warmed themselves. And Peter stood with them and warmed himself.

Jesus Questioned by the High Priest

19 The high priest then asked Jesus about His disciples and His doctrine.

20 Jesus answered him, [a]"I spoke openly to the world. I always taught [b]in synagogues and [c]in the temple, where *the Jews always meet, and in secret I have said nothing.

21 "Why do you ask Me? Ask [a]those who have heard Me what I said to them. Indeed they know what I said."

22 And when He had said these things, one of the officers who stood by [a]struck Jesus with the palm of His hand, saying, "Do You answer the high priest like that?"

23 Jesus answered him, "If I have spoken evil, bear witness of the evil; but if well, why do you strike Me?"

24 [a]Then Annas sent Him bound to [b]Caiaphas the high priest.

Peter Denies Twice More

25 Now Simon Peter stood and warmed himself. [a]Therefore they said to him, "You are not also *one* of His disciples, are you?" He denied *it* and said, "I am not!"

26 One of the servants of the high priest, a relative *of him* whose ear Peter cut off, said, "Did I not see you in the garden with Him?"

27 Peter then denied again; and [a]immediately a rooster crowed.

In Pilate's Court
(Matt. 27:1, 2, 11–14; Mark 15:1–5; Luke 23:1–5)

28 [a]Then they led Jesus from Caiaphas to the Praetorium, and it was early morning. [b]But they themselves did not go into the Praetorium, lest

*

18:15 M *the other*
18:20 NU *all the Jews meet*

KJV

they should be defiled; but that they might eat the passover.

29 [a]Pilate then went out unto them, and said, What accusation bring ye against this man?

30 They answered and said unto him, If he were not a malefactor, we would not have delivered him up unto thee.

31 Then said Pilate unto them, Take ye him, and judge him according to your law. The Jews therefore said unto him, It is not lawful for us to put any man to death:

32 [a]That the saying of Jesus might be fulfilled, which he spake, [b]signifying what death he should die.

33 [a]Then Pilate entered into the judgment hall again, and called Jesus, and said unto him, Art thou the King of the Jews?

34 Jesus answered him, Sayest thou this thing of thyself, or did others tell it thee of me?

35 Pilate answered, Am I a Jew? Thine own nation and the chief priests have delivered thee unto me: what hast thou done?

36 [a]Jesus answered, [b]My kingdom is not of this world: if my kingdom were of this world, then would my servants fight, that I should not be delivered to the Jews: but now is my kingdom not from hence.

37 Pilate therefore said unto him, Art thou a king then? Jesus answered, Thou sayest that I am a king. To this end was I born, and for this cause came I into the world, [a]that I should bear [b]witness unto the truth. Every one that [c]is of the truth [d]heareth my voice.

38 Pilate saith unto him, What is truth? And when he had said this, he went out again unto the Jews, and saith unto them, [a]I find in him no fault *at all.*

Taking the Place of Barabbas
(Matt. 27:15–23; Mark 15:6–14; Luke 23:13–23)

39 [a]But ye have a custom, that I should release unto you one at the passover: will ye therefore that I release unto you the King of the Jews?

40 [a]Then cried they all again, saying, Not this man, but Barabbas. [b]Now Barabbas was a robber.

The Soldiers Mock Jesus
(Matt. 27:27–31; Mark 15:16–20)

19 Then [a]Pilate therefore took Jesus, and scourged *him.*

2 And the soldiers platted a crown of thorns, and put *it* on his head, and they put on him a purple robe,

3 And said, Hail, King of the Jews! and they [a]smote him with their hands.

4 Pilate therefore went forth again, and saith unto them, Behold, I bring him forth to you, [a]that ye may know that I find no fault in him.

Pilate's Decision

5 Then came Jesus forth, wearing the crown of thorns, and the purple robe. And *Pilate* saith unto them, Behold the man!

6 [a]When the chief priests therefore and officers saw him, they cried out, saying, Crucify *him,* crucify *him.* Pilate saith unto them, Take ye him, and crucify *him:* for I find no fault in him.

7 The Jews answered him, [a]We have a law, and by our law he ought to die, because [b]he made himself the Son of God.

8 When Pilate therefore heard that saying, he was the more afraid;

9 And went again into the judgment hall, and saith unto Jesus, Whence art thou? [a]But Jesus gave him no answer.

10 Then saith Pilate unto him, Speakest thou not unto me? knowest thou not that I have power to crucify thee, and have power to release thee?

29 [a]Matt. 27:11–14; Mark 15:2–5; Luke 23:2, 3 **32** [a]Matt. 20:17–19; 26:2; Mark 10:33; Luke 18:32 [b]John 3:14; 8:28; 12:32, 33 **33** [a]Matt. 27:11 **36** [a]1 Tim. 6:13 [b][Dan. 2:44; 7:14]; Luke 12:14; John 6:15; 8:15 **37** [a][Matt. 5:17; 20:28; Luke 4:43; 12:49; 19:10; John 3:17; 9:39; 10:10; 12:47] [b]Is. 55:4; Rev. 1:5 [c][John 14:6] [d]John 8:47; 10:27; [1 John 3:19; 4:6] **38** [a]Is. 53:9; Matt. 27:24; Luke 23:4; John 19:4, 6; 1 Pet. 2:22–24 **39** [a]Matt. 27:15–26; Mark 15:6–15; Luke 23:17–25 **40** [a]Is. 53:3; Acts 3:14 [b]Luke 23:19

CHAPTER 19

1 [a]Matt. 20:19; 27:26; Mark 15:15; Luke 18:33 **3** [a]Is. 50:6 **4** [a]Is. 53:9; John 18:33, 38; 1 Pet. 2:22–24 **6** [a]Acts 3:13 **7** [a]Lev. 24:16 [b]Matt. 26:63–66; John 5:18; 10:33 **9** [a]Is. 53:7; Matt. 27:12, 14; Luke 23:9

*__________

19:3 NU *And they came up to Him and said*
19:7 NU *the law*

NKJV

they should be defiled, but that they might eat the Passover.

29 [a]Pilate then went out to them and said, "What accusation do you bring against this Man?"

30 They answered and said to him, "If He were not an evildoer, we would not have delivered Him up to you."

31 Then Pilate said to them, "You take Him and judge Him according to your law." Therefore the Jews said to him, "It is not lawful for us to put anyone to death,"

32 [a]that the saying of Jesus might be fulfilled which He spoke, [b]signifying by what death He would die.

33 [a]Then Pilate entered the Praetorium again, called Jesus, and said to Him, "Are You the King of the Jews?"

34 Jesus answered him, "Are you speaking for yourself about this, or did others tell you this concerning Me?"

35 Pilate answered, "Am I a Jew? Your own nation and the chief priests have delivered You to me. What have You done?"

36 [a]Jesus answered, [b]"My kingdom is not of this world. If My kingdom were of this world, My servants would fight, so that I should not be delivered to the Jews; but now My kingdom is not from here."

37 Pilate therefore said to Him, "Are You a king then?" Jesus answered, "You say *rightly* that I am a king. For this cause I was born, and for this cause I have come into the world, [a]that I should bear [b]witness to the truth. Everyone who [c]is of the truth [d]hears My voice."

38 Pilate said to Him, "What is truth?" And when he had said this, he went out again to the Jews, and said to them, [a]"I find no fault in Him at all."

Taking the Place of Barabbas
(Matt. 27:15–23; Mark 15:6–14; Luke 23:13–23)

39 [a]"But you have a custom that I should release someone to you at the Passover. Do you therefore want me to release to you the King of the Jews?"

40 [a]Then they all cried again, saying, "Not this Man, but Barabbas!" [b]Now Barabbas was a robber.

The Soldiers Mock Jesus
(Matt. 27:27–31; Mark 15:16–20)

19 So then [a]Pilate took Jesus and scourged *Him.*

2 And the soldiers twisted a crown of thorns and put *it* on His head, and they put on Him a purple robe.

3 *Then they said, "Hail, King of the Jews!" And they [a]struck Him with their hands.

4 Pilate then went out again, and said to them, "Behold, I am bringing Him out to you, [a]that you may know that I find no fault in Him."

Pilate's Decision

5 Then Jesus came out, wearing the crown of thorns and the purple robe. And *Pilate* said to them, "Behold the Man!"

6 [a]Therefore, when the chief priests and officers saw Him, they cried out, saying, "Crucify *Him,* crucify *Him!*" Pilate said to them, "You take Him and crucify *Him,* for I find no fault in Him."

7 The Jews answered him, [a]"We have a law, and according to *our law He ought to die, because [b]He made Himself the Son of God."

8 Therefore, when Pilate heard that saying, he was the more afraid,

9 and went again into the Praetorium, and said to Jesus, "Where are You from?" [a]But Jesus gave him no answer.

10 Then Pilate said to Him, "Are You not speaking to me? Do You not know that I have power to crucify You, and power to release You?"

KJV

11 Jesus answered, [a]Thou couldest have no power *at all* against me, except it were given thee from above: therefore [b]he that delivered me unto thee hath the greater sin.

12 And from thenceforth Pilate sought to release him: but the Jews cried out, saying, If thou let this man go, thou art not Caesar's friend: [a]whosoever maketh himself a king speaketh against Caesar.

13 [a]When Pilate therefore heard that saying, he brought Jesus forth, and sat down in the judgment seat in a place that is called the Pavement, but in the Hebrew, Gabbatha.

14 And [a]it was the preparation of the passover, and about the sixth hour: and he saith unto the Jews, Behold your King!

15 But they cried out, Away with *him,* away with *him,* crucify him. Pilate saith unto them, Shall I crucify your King? The chief priests answered, [a]We have no king but Caesar.

16 [a]Then delivered he him therefore unto them to be crucified. And they took Jesus, and led *him* away.

The King on a Cross
(Matt. 27:32–56; Mark 15:21–41; Luke 23:26–49)

17 [a]And he bearing his cross [b]went forth into a place called *the place* of a skull, which is called in the Hebrew Golgotha:

18 Where they crucified him, and [a]two other with him, on either side one, and Jesus in the midst.

19 [a]And Pilate wrote a title, and put *it* on the cross. And the writing was, JESUS OF NAZARETH THE KING OF THE JEWS.

20 This title then read many of the Jews: for the place where Jesus was crucified was nigh to the city: and it was written in Hebrew, *and* Greek, *and* Latin.

21 Then said the chief priests of the Jews to Pilate, Write not, The King of the Jews; but that he said, I am King of the Jews.

22 Pilate answered, What I have written I have written.

23 [a]Then the soldiers, when they had crucified Jesus, took his garments, and made four parts, to every soldier a part; and also *his* coat: now the coat was without seam, woven from the top throughout.

24 They said therefore among themselves, Let us not rend it, but cast lots for it, whose it shall be: that the scripture might be fulfilled, which saith, [a]THEY PARTED MY RAIMENT AMONG THEM, AND FOR MY VESTURE THEY DID CAST LOTS. These things therefore the soldiers did.

Behold Your Mother

25 [a]Now there stood by the cross of Jesus his mother, and his mother's sister, Mary the *wife* of [b]Cleophas, and Mary Magdalene.

26 When Jesus therefore saw his mother, and [a]the disciple standing by, whom he loved, he saith unto his mother, [b]Woman, behold thy son!

27 Then saith he to the disciple, Behold thy mother! And from that hour that disciple took her [a]unto his own *home.*

It Is Finished

28 After this, Jesus knowing that all things were now accomplished, [a]that the scripture might be fulfilled, saith, I thirst.

29 Now there was set a vessel full of vinegar: and [a]they filled a spunge with vinegar, and put *it* upon hyssop, and put *it* to his mouth.

30 When Jesus therefore had received the vinegar, he said, [a]It is finished: and he bowed his head, and gave up the ghost.

11 [a][Luke 22:53]; John 7:30 [b]John 3:27; Rom. 13:1
12 [a]Luke 23:2; John 18:33; Acts 17:7
13 [a]Deut. 1:17; 1 Sam. 15:24; Prov. 29:25; Is. 51:12; Acts 4:19
14 [a]Matt. 27:62; John 19:31, 42
15 [a][Gen. 49:10]
16 [a]Matt. 27:26, 31; Mark 15:15; Luke 23:24
17 [a]Matt. 27:31, 33; Mark 15:21, 22; Luke 23:26, 33 [b]Num. 15:36; Heb. 13:12
18 [a]Ps. 22:16–18; Is. 53:12; Matt. 20:19; 26:2
19 [a]Matt. 27:37; Mark 15:26; Luke 23:38
23 [a]Matt. 27:35; Mark 15:24; Luke 23:34
24 [a]Ps. 22:18
25 [a]Matt. 27:55; Mark 15:40; Luke 2:35; 23:49 [b]Luke 24:18
26 [a]John 13:23; 20:2; 21:7, 20, 24 [b]John 2:4
27 [a]Luke 18:28; John 1:11; 16:32; Acts 21:6
28 [a]Ps. 22:15
29 [a]Ps. 69:21; Matt. 27:48, 50; Mark 15:36; Luke 23:36
30 [a]Dan. 9:26; Zech. 11:10, 11; John 17:4

*______

19:16 NU omits *and led Him away*
19:28 M *seeing*

NKJV

11 Jesus answered, [a]"You could have no power at all against Me unless it had been given you from above. Therefore [b]the one who delivered Me to you has the greater sin."

12 From then on Pilate sought to release Him, but the Jews cried out, saying, "If you let this Man go, you are not Caesar's friend. [a]Whoever makes himself a king speaks against Caesar."

13 [a]When Pilate therefore heard that saying, he brought Jesus out and sat down in the judgment seat in a place that is called *The* Pavement, but in Hebrew, Gabbatha.

14 Now [a]it was the Preparation Day of the Passover, and about the sixth hour. And he said to the Jews, "Behold your King!"

15 But they cried out, "Away with *Him,* away with *Him!* Crucify Him!" Pilate said to them, "Shall I crucify your King?" The chief priests answered, [a]"We have no king but Caesar!"

16 [a]Then he delivered Him to them to be crucified. So they took Jesus *and led *Him* away.

The King on a Cross
(Matt. 27:32–56; Mark 15:21–41; Luke 23:26–49)

17 [a]And He, bearing His cross, [b]went out to a place called *the Place* of a Skull, which is called in Hebrew, Golgotha,

18 where they crucified Him, and [a]two others with Him, one on either side, and Jesus in the center.

19 [a]Now Pilate wrote a title and put *it* on the cross. And the writing was:

JESUS OF NAZARETH, THE KING OF THE JEWS.

20 Then many of the Jews read this title, for the place where Jesus was crucified was near the city; and it was written in Hebrew, Greek, *and* Latin.

21 Therefore the chief priests of the Jews said to Pilate, "Do not write, 'The King of the Jews,' but, 'He said, "I am the King of the Jews." ' "

22 Pilate answered, "What I have written, I have written."

23 [a]Then the soldiers, when they had crucified Jesus, took His garments and made four parts, to each soldier a part, and also the tunic. Now the tunic was without seam, woven from the top in one piece.

24 They said therefore among themselves, "Let us not tear it, but cast lots for it, whose it shall be," that the Scripture might be fulfilled which says:

[a]*"They divided My garments among them,*
And for My clothing they cast lots."

Therefore the soldiers did these things.

Behold Your Mother

25 [a]Now there stood by the cross of Jesus His mother, and His mother's sister, Mary the *wife* of [b]Clopas, and Mary Magdalene.

26 When Jesus therefore saw His mother, and [a]the disciple whom He loved standing by, He said to His mother, [b]"Woman, behold your son!"

27 Then He said to the disciple, "Behold your mother!" And from that hour that disciple took her [a]to his own *home.*

It Is Finished

28 After this, Jesus, *knowing that all things were now accomplished, [a]that the Scripture might be fulfilled, said, "I thirst!"

29 Now a vessel full of sour wine was sitting there; and [a]they filled a sponge with sour wine, put *it* on hyssop, and put *it* to His mouth.

30 So when Jesus had received the sour wine, He said, [a]"It is finished!" And bowing His head, He gave up His spirit.

KJV

Jesus' Side Is Pierced

31 The Jews therefore, [a]because it was the
preparation, [b]that the bodies should not remain
upon the cross on the sabbath day, (for that sabbath day was an [c]high day,) besought Pilate that
their legs might be broken, and *that* they might
be taken away.
32 Then came the soldiers, and brake the legs
of the first, and of the other which was crucified
with him.
33 But when they came to Jesus, and saw that
he was dead already, they brake not his legs:
34 But one of the soldiers with a spear
pierced his side, and forthwith [a]came there out
blood and water.
35 And he that saw *it* bare record, and his
record is [a]true: and he knoweth that he saith true,
that ye might [b]believe.
36 For these things were done, [a]that the
scripture should be fulfilled, A BONE OF HIM SHALL
NOT BE BROKEN.
37 And again another scripture saith, [a]THEY
SHALL LOOK ON HIM WHOM THEY PIERCED.

Jesus Buried in Joseph's Tomb
(Matt. 27:57–61; Mark 15:42–47; Luke 23:50–56)

38 [a]And after this Joseph of Arimathaea, being a disciple of Jesus, but secretly [b]for fear of
the Jews, besought Pilate that he might take away
the body of Jesus: and Pilate gave *him* leave. He
came therefore, and took the body of Jesus.
39 And there came also [a]Nicodemus, which
at the first came to Jesus by night, and brought
a mixture of [b]myrrh and aloes, about an hundred
pound *weight.*
40 Then took they the body of Jesus, and
[a]wound it in linen clothes with the spices, as the
manner of the Jews is to bury.
41 Now in the place where he was crucified
there was a garden; and in the garden a new
sepulchre, wherein was never man yet laid.
42 [a]There laid they Jesus therefore [b]because
of the Jews' preparation *day;* for the sepulchre
was nigh at hand.

The Empty Tomb
(Matt. 28:1–10; Mark 16:1–8; Luke 24:1–12)

20 The [a]first *day* of the week cometh Mary
Magdalene early, when it was yet dark,
unto the sepulchre, and seeth the [b]stone taken
away from the sepulchre.
2 Then she runneth, and cometh to Simon
Peter, and to the [a]other disciple, [b]whom Jesus
loved, and saith unto them, They have taken away
the Lord out of the sepulchre, and we know not
where they have laid him.
3 [a]Peter therefore went forth, and that other
disciple, and came to the sepulchre.
4 So they ran both together: and the other
disciple did outrun Peter, and came first to the
sepulchre.
5 And he stooping down, *and looking in,*
saw [a]the linen clothes lying; yet went he not in.
6 Then cometh Simon Peter following him,
and went into the sepulchre, and seeth the linen
clothes lie,
7 And [a]the napkin, that was about his head,
not lying with the linen clothes, but wrapped together in a place by itself.
8 Then went in also that [a]other disciple,
which came first to the sepulchre, and he saw,
and believed.
9 For as yet they knew not the [a]scripture,
that he must rise again from the dead.
10 Then the disciples went away again unto
their own home.

Mary Magdalene Sees the Risen Lord

11 [a]But Mary stood without at the sepulchre
weeping: and as she wept, she stooped down, *and
looked* into the sepulchre,

31 [a]Matt. 27:62; Mark 15:42; Luke 23:54 [b]Deut. 21:23; Josh. 8:29; 10:26 [c]Ex. 12:16; Lev. 23:6, 7
34 [a][1 John 5:6, 8]
35 [a]John 21:24 [b][John 20:31]
36 [a][Ex. 12:46; Num. 9:12]; Ps. 34:20
37 [a]Ps. 22:16, 17; Zech. 12:10; 13:6; Rev. 1:7
38 [a]Matt. 27:57–61; Mark 15:42–47; Luke 23:50–56 [b][John 7:13; 9:22; 12:42]
39 [a]John 3:1, 2; 7:50 [b]Ps. 45:8; Prov. 7:17; Song 4:14; Matt. 2:11
40 [a]Luke 24:12; John 20:5, 7; Acts 5:6
42 [a]Is. 53:9; Matt. 26:12; Mark 14:8 [b]John 19:14, 31

CHAPTER 20
1 [a]Matt. 28:1–8; Mark 16:1–8; Luke 24:1–10; Acts 20:7; 1 Cor. 16:2 [b]Matt. 27:60, 66; 28:2; Mark 15:46; 16:4; Luke 24:2; John 11:38
2 [a]John 21:23, 24 [b]John 13:23; 19:26; 21:7, 20, 24
3 [a]Luke 24:12
5 [a]John 19:40
7 [a]John 11:44
8 [a]John 21:23, 24
9 [a]Ps. 16:10; Acts 2:25, 31; 13:34, 35
11 [a]Mark 16:5

NKJV

Jesus' Side Is Pierced

31 [a]Therefore, because it was the Preparation *Day,* [b]that the bodies should not remain on
the cross on the Sabbath (for that Sabbath was a
[c]high day), the Jews asked Pilate that their legs
might be broken, and *that* they might be taken
away.
32 Then the soldiers came and broke the legs
of the first and of the other who was crucified
with Him.
33 But when they came to Jesus and saw that
He was already dead, they did not break His legs.
34 But one of the soldiers pierced His side
with a spear, and immediately [a]blood and water
came out.
35 And he who has seen has testified, and
his testimony is [a]true; and he knows that he is
telling the truth, so that you may [b]believe.
36 For these things were done that the Scripture should be fulfilled, [a]*"Not one of His bones
shall be broken."*
37 And again another Scripture says, [a]*"They
shall look on Him whom they pierced."*

Jesus Buried in Joseph's Tomb
(Matt. 27:57–61; Mark 15:42–47; Luke 23:50–56)

38 [a]After this, Joseph of Arimathea, being a
disciple of Jesus, but secretly, [b]for fear of the
Jews, asked Pilate that he might take away the
body of Jesus; and Pilate gave *him* permission.
So he came and took the body of Jesus.
39 And [a]Nicodemus, who at first came to
Jesus by night, also came, bringing a mixture of
[b]myrrh and aloes, about a hundred pounds.
40 Then they took the body of Jesus, and
[a]bound it in strips of linen with the spices, as the
custom of the Jews is to bury.
41 Now in the place where He was crucified
there was a garden, and in the garden a new tomb
in which no one had yet been laid.
42 So [a]there they laid Jesus, [b]because of the
Jews' Preparation *Day,* for the tomb was nearby.

The Empty Tomb
(Matt. 28:1–10; Mark 16:1–8; Luke 24:1–12)

20 Now on the [a]first *day* of the week Mary
Magdalene went to the tomb early, while
it was still dark, and saw *that* the [b]stone had been
taken away from the tomb.
2 Then she ran and came to Simon Peter,
and to the [a]other disciple, [b]whom Jesus loved,
and said to them, "They have taken away the Lord
out of the tomb, and we do not know where they
have laid Him."
3 [a]Peter therefore went out, and the other
disciple, and were going to the tomb.
4 So they both ran together, and the other
disciple outran Peter and came to the tomb first.
5 And he, stooping down and looking in,
saw [a]the linen cloths lying *there;* yet he did not
go in.
6 Then Simon Peter came, following him,
and went into the tomb; and he saw the linen
cloths lying *there,*
7 and [a]the handkerchief that had been
around His head, not lying with the linen cloths,
but folded together in a place by itself.
8 Then the [a]other disciple, who came to the
tomb first, went in also; and he saw and believed.
9 For as yet they did not know the [a]Scrip-
ture, that He must rise again from the dead.
10 Then the disciples went away again to
their own homes.

Mary Magdalene Sees the Risen Lord

11 [a]But Mary stood outside by the tomb
weeping, and as she wept she stooped down *and
looked* into the tomb.

KJV

12 And seeth two angels in white sitting, the one at the head, and the other at the feet, where the body of Jesus had lain.

13 And they say unto her, Woman, why weepest thou? She saith unto them, Because they have taken away my Lord, and I know not where they have laid him.

14 [a]And when she had thus said, she turned herself back, and saw Jesus standing, and [b]knew not that it was Jesus.

15 Jesus saith unto her, Woman, why weepest thou? whom seekest thou? She, supposing him to be the gardener, saith unto him, Sir, if thou have borne him hence, tell me where thou hast laid him, and I will take him away.

16 Jesus saith unto her, [a]Mary. She turned herself, and saith unto him, Rabboni; which is to say, Master.

17 Jesus saith unto her, Touch me not; for I am not yet [a]ascended to my Father: but go to [b]my brethren, and say unto them, [c]I ascend unto my Father, and your Father; and *to* [d]my God, and your God.

18 [a]Mary Magdalene came and told the disciples that she had seen the Lord, and *that* he had spoken these things unto her.

The Apostles Commissioned (*Luke 24:36–43; 1 Cor. 15:5*)

19 [a]Then the same day at evening, being the first *day* of the week, when the doors were shut where the disciples were assembled for [b]fear of the Jews, came Jesus and stood in the midst, and saith unto them, [c]Peace *be* unto you.

20 And when he had so said, he [a]shewed unto them *his* hands and his side. [b]Then were the disciples glad, when they saw the Lord.

21 Then said Jesus to them again, Peace *be* unto you: [a]as *my* Father hath sent me, even so send I you.

22 And when he had said this, he breathed on *them,* and saith unto them, Receive ye the Holy Ghost:

23 [a]Whose soever sins ye remit, they are remitted unto them; *and* whose soever *sins* ye retain, they are retained.

Seeing and Believing

24 But Thomas, one of the twelve, [a]called Didymus, was not with them when Jesus came.

25 The other disciples therefore said unto him, We have seen the Lord. But he said unto them, Except I shall see in his hands the print of the nails, and put my finger into the print of the nails, and thrust my hand into his side, I will not believe.

26 And after eight days again his disciples were within, and Thomas with them: *then* came Jesus, the doors being shut, and stood in the midst, and said, Peace *be* unto you.

27 Then saith he to Thomas, Reach hither thy finger, and behold my hands; and [a]reach hither thy hand, and thrust *it* into my side: and be not [b]faithless, but believing.

28 And Thomas answered and said unto him, My Lord and my God.

29 Jesus saith unto him, Thomas, because thou hast seen me, thou hast believed: [a]blessed *are* they that have not seen, and *yet* have believed.

That You May Believe

30 And [a]many other signs truly did Jesus in the presence of his disciples, which are not written in this book:

31 [a]But these are written, that [b]ye might believe that Jesus [c]is the Christ, the Son of God; [d]and that believing ye might have life through his name.

14 [a]Matt. 28:9; Mark 16:9 [b][Luke 24:16, 31]; John 21:4
16 [a]John 10:3
17 [a]Mark 16:19; Luke 24:5; Acts 1:9; 2:34–36; Eph. 4:8–10; Heb. 4:14 [b]Ps. 22:22; Matt. 18:10; Rom. 8:29; Heb. 2:11 [c]John 16:28; 17:11 [d]Eph. 1:17
18 [a]Matt. 28:10; Luke 24:10, 23
19 [a]Mark 16:14; Luke 24:36; John 14:27; 1 Cor. 15:5 [b]John 9:22; 19:38 [c]John 14:27; 16:16; Eph. 2:17
20 [a]Acts 1:3 [b]John 16:20, 22
21 [a][Matt. 28:18–20]; John 17:18, 19; [2 Tim. 2:2]; Heb. 3:1
23 [a]Matt. 16:19; 18:18
24 [a]John 11:16
27 [a]Ps. 22:16; Zech. 12:10; 13:6; 1 John 1:1 [b]Mark 16:14
29 [a]2 Cor. 5:7; 1 Pet. 1:8
30 [a]John 21:25
31 [a]Luke 1:4 [b]John 19:35; 1 John 5:13 [c]Luke 2:11; 1 John 5:1 [d]John 3:15, 16; 5:24; [1 Pet. 1:8, 9]

NKJV

12 And she saw two angels in white sitting, one at the head and the other at the feet, where the body of Jesus had lain.

13 Then they said to her, "Woman, why are you weeping?" She said to them, "Because they have taken away my Lord, and I do not know where they have laid Him."

14 [a]Now when she had said this, she turned around and saw Jesus standing *there,* and [b]did not know that it was Jesus.

15 Jesus said to her, "Woman, why are you weeping? Whom are you seeking?" She, supposing Him to be the gardener, said to Him, "Sir, if You have carried Him away, tell me where You have laid Him, and I will take Him away."

16 Jesus said to her, [a]"Mary!" She turned and said to *Him, "Rabboni!" (which is to say, Teacher).

17 Jesus said to her, "Do not cling to Me, for I have not yet [a]ascended to My Father; but go to [b]My brethren and say to them, [c]'I am ascending to My Father and your Father, and *to* [d]My God and your God.' "

18 [a]Mary Magdalene came and told the *disciples that she had seen the Lord, and *that* He had spoken these things to her.

The Apostles Commissioned (*Luke 24:36–43; 1 Cor. 15:5*)

19 [a]Then, the same day at evening, being the first *day* of the week, when the doors were shut where the disciples were *assembled, for [b]fear of the Jews, Jesus came and stood in the midst, and said to them, [c]"Peace *be* with you."

20 When He had said this, He [a]showed them *His* hands and His side. [b]Then the disciples were glad when they saw the Lord.

21 So Jesus said to them again, "Peace to you! [a]As the Father has sent Me, I also send you."

22 And when He had said this, He breathed on *them,* and said to them, "Receive the Holy Spirit.

23 [a]"If you forgive the sins of any, they are forgiven them; if you retain the *sins* of any, they are retained."

Seeing and Believing

24 Now Thomas, [a]called the Twin, one of the twelve, was not with them when Jesus came.

25 The other disciples therefore said to him, "We have seen the Lord." So he said to them, "Unless I see in His hands the print of the nails, and put my finger into the print of the nails, and put my hand into His side, I will not believe."

26 And after eight days His disciples were again inside, and Thomas with them. Jesus came, the doors being shut, and stood in the midst, and said, "Peace to you!"

27 Then He said to Thomas, "Reach your finger here, and look at My hands; and [a]reach your hand *here,* and put *it* into My side. Do not be [b]unbelieving, but believing."

28 And Thomas answered and said to Him, "My Lord and my God!"

29 Jesus said to him, *"Thomas, because you have seen Me, you have believed. [a]Blessed *are* those who have not seen and *yet* have believed."

That You May Believe

30 And [a]truly Jesus did many other signs in the presence of His disciples, which are not written in this book;

31 [a]but these are written that [b]you may believe that Jesus [c]is the Christ, the Son of God, [d]and that believing you may have life in His name.

20:16 NU adds *in Hebrew*
20:18 NU *disciples, "I have seen the Lord,"*
20:19 NU omits *assembled*
20:29 NU, M omit *Thomas*

KJV

Breakfast by the Sea

21 After these things Jesus shewed himself
again to the disciples at the [a]sea of Tiberias; and on this wise shewed he *himself.*
2 There were together Simon Peter, and
[a]Thomas called Didymus, and [b]Nathanael of
[c]Cana in Galilee, and [d]the *sons* of Zebedee, and
two other of his disciples.
3 Simon Peter saith unto them, I go a fishing. They say unto him, We also go with thee.
They went forth, and entered into a ship immediately; and that night they caught nothing.
4 But when the morning was now come,
Jesus stood on the shore: but the disciples [a]knew
not that it was Jesus.
5 Then [a]Jesus saith unto them, Children,
have ye any meat? They answered him, No.
6 And he said unto them, [a]Cast the net on
the right side of the ship, and ye shall find. They
cast therefore, and now they were not able to
draw it for the multitude of fishes.
7 Therefore [a]that disciple whom Jesus loved
saith unto Peter, It is the Lord. Now when Simon
Peter heard that it was the Lord, he girt *his* fisher's
coat *unto him,* (for he was naked,) and did cast
himself into the sea.
8 And the other disciples came in a little
ship; (for they were not far from land, but as it
were two hundred cubits,) dragging the net with
fishes.
9 As soon then as they were come to land,
they saw a fire of coals there, and fish laid thereon, and bread.
10 Jesus saith unto them, Bring of the fish
which ye have now caught.
11 Simon Peter went up, and drew the net
to land full of great fishes, an hundred and fifty
and three: and for all there were so many, yet
was not the net broken.
12 Jesus saith unto them, [a]Come *and* dine.
And none of the disciples durst ask him, Who art
thou? knowing that it was the Lord.
13 Jesus then cometh, and taketh bread, and
giveth them, and fish likewise.
14 This is now [a]the third time that Jesus
shewed himself to his disciples, after that he was
risen from the dead.

Jesus Restores Peter

15 So when they had dined, Jesus saith to
Simon Peter, Simon, *son* of Jonas, lovest thou me
more than these? He saith unto him, Yea, Lord;
thou knowest that I love thee. He saith unto him,
[a]Feed my lambs.
16 He saith to him again the second time, Simon, *son* of Jonas, lovest thou me? He saith unto
him, Yea, Lord; thou knowest that I love thee.
[a]He saith unto him, Feed my [b]sheep.
17 He saith unto him the third time, Simon,
son of Jonas, lovest thou me? Peter was grieved
because he said unto him the third time, Lovest
thou me? And he said unto him, Lord, [a]thou
knowest all things; thou knowest that I love thee.
Jesus saith unto him, Feed my sheep.
18 [a]Verily, verily, I say unto thee, When thou
wast young, thou girdedst thyself, and walkedst
whither thou wouldest: but when thou shalt be
old, thou shalt stretch forth thy hands, and another shall gird thee, and carry *thee* whither thou
wouldest not.
19 This spake he, signifying [a]by what death
he should glorify God. And when he had spoken
this, he saith unto him, [b]Follow me.

The Beloved Disciple and His Book

20 Then Peter, turning about, seeth the disciple [a]whom Jesus loved following; [b]which also
leaned on his breast at supper, and said, Lord,
which is he that betrayeth thee?
21 Peter seeing him saith to Jesus, Lord, and
what *shall* this man *do?*

CHAPTER 21
1 [a]Matt. 26:32; Mark 14:28; John 6:1
2 [a]John 20:24 [b]John 1:45–51 [c]John 2:1 [d]Matt. 4:21; Mark 1:19; Luke 5:10
4 [a]Luke 24:16; John 20:14
5 [a]Luke 24:41
6 [a]Luke 5:4, 6, 7
7 [a]John 13:23; 20:2
12 [a]Acts 10:41
14 [a]John 20:19, 26
15 [a]Acts 20:28; 1 Tim. 4:6; 1 Pet. 5:2
16 [a]Matt. 2:6; Acts 20:28; Heb. 13:20; 1 Pet. 2:25; 5:2, 4 [b]Ps. 79:13; Matt. 10:16; 15:24; 25:33; 26:31
17 [a]John 2:24, 25; 16:30
18 [a]John 13:36; Acts 12:3, 4
19 [a]2 Pet. 1:13, 14 [b][Matt. 4:19; 16:24]; John 21:22
20 [a]John 13:23; 20:2 [b]John 13:25

*
21:3 NU omits *immediately*
21:15 NU *John*
21:16 NU *John*
21:17 NU *John*

NKJV

Breakfast by the Sea

21 After these things Jesus showed Himself
again to the disciples at the [a]Sea of Tiberias, and in this way He showed *Himself:*
2 Simon Peter, [a]Thomas called the Twin,
[b]Nathanael of [c]Cana in Galilee, [d]the *sons* of Zebedee, and two others of His disciples were together.
3 Simon Peter said to them, "I am going
fishing." They said to him, "We are going with
you also." They went out and *immediately got
into the boat, and that night they caught nothing.
4 But when the morning had now come,
Jesus stood on the shore; yet the disciples [a]did
not know that it was Jesus.
5 Then [a]Jesus said to them, "Children, have
you any food?" They answered Him, "No."
6 And He said to them, [a]"Cast the net on
the right side of the boat, and you will find *some.*"
So they cast, and now they were not able to draw
it in because of the multitude of fish.
7 Therefore [a]that disciple whom Jesus loved
said to Peter, "It is the Lord!" Now when Simon
Peter heard that it was the Lord, he put on *his*
outer garment (for he had removed it), and
plunged into the sea.
8 But the other disciples came in the little
boat (for they were not far from land, but about
two hundred cubits), dragging the net with fish.
9 Then, as soon as they had come to land,
they saw a fire of coals there, and fish laid on it,
and bread.
10 Jesus said to them, "Bring some of the fish
which you have just caught."
11 Simon Peter went up and dragged the net
to land, full of large fish, one hundred and fifty-
three; and although there were so many, the net
was not broken.
12 Jesus said to them, [a]"Come *and* eat breakfast." Yet none of the disciples dared ask Him,
"Who are You?"—knowing that it was the Lord.
13 Jesus then came and took the bread and
gave it to them, and likewise the fish.
14 This *is* now [a]the third time Jesus showed
Himself to His disciples after He was raised from
the dead.

Jesus Restores Peter

15 So when they had eaten breakfast, Jesus
said to Simon Peter, "Simon, *son* of *Jonah, do
you love Me more than these?" He said to Him,
"Yes, Lord; You know that I love You." He said
to him, [a]"Feed My lambs."
16 He said to him again a second time, "Simon, *son* of *Jonah, do you love Me?" He said to
Him, "Yes, Lord; You know that I love You." [a]He
said to him, "Tend My [b]sheep."
17 He said to him the third time, "Simon, *son*
of *Jonah, do you love Me?" Peter was grieved
because He said to him the third time, "Do you
love Me?" And he said to Him, "Lord, [a]You know
all things; You know that I love You." Jesus said
to him, "Feed My sheep.
18 [a]"Most assuredly, I say to you, when you
were younger, you girded yourself and walked
where you wished; but when you are old, you will
stretch out your hands, and another will gird you
and carry *you* where you do not wish."
19 This He spoke, signifying [a]by what death
he would glorify God. And when He had spoken
this, He said to him, [b]"Follow Me."

The Beloved Disciple and His Book

20 Then Peter, turning around, saw the disciple [a]whom Jesus loved following, [b]who also had
leaned on His breast at the supper, and said,
"Lord, who is the one who betrays You?"
21 Peter, seeing him, said to Jesus, "But
Lord, what *about* this man?"

KJV

22 Jesus saith unto him, If I will that he tarry
[a]till I come, what *is that* to thee? follow thou me.
23 Then went this saying abroad among the
brethren, that that disciple should not die: yet
Jesus said not unto him, He shall not die; but, If
I will that he tarry till I come, what *is that* to
thee?
24 This is the disciple which [a]testifieth of
these things, and wrote these things: and we know
that his testimony is true.
25 [a]And there are also many other things
which Jesus did, the which, if they should be written every one, [b]I suppose that even the world itself
could not contain the books that should be written. Amen.

22 [a][Matt. 16:27, 28; 25:31; 1 Cor. 4:5; 11:26; Rev. 2:25; 3:11; 22:7, 20] **24** [a]John 19:35; 3 John 12 **25** [a]John 20:30 [b]Amos 7:10

NKJV

22 Jesus said to him, "If I will that he remain
[a]till I come, what *is that* to you? You follow Me."
23 Then this saying went out among the
brethren that this disciple would not die. Yet Jesus
did not say to him that he would not die, but, "If
I will that he remain till I come, what *is that* to
you?"
24 This is the disciple who [a]testifies of these
things, and wrote these things; and we know that
his testimony is true.
25 [a]And there are also many other things
that Jesus did, which if they were written one by
one, [b]I suppose that even the world itself could
not contain the books that would be written.
Amen.

KJV

THE ACTS

OF THE APOSTLES

Prologue

1 The former treatise have I made, O [a]Theophilus, of all that Jesus began both to do and teach,

2 [a]Until the day in which he was taken up, after that he through the Holy Ghost [b]had given commandments unto the apostles whom he had chosen:

3 [a]To whom also he shewed himself alive after his passion by many infallible proofs, being seen of them forty days, and speaking of the things pertaining to the kingdom of God:

The Holy Spirit Promised

4 [a]And, being assembled together with *them,* commanded them that they should not depart from Jerusalem, but wait for the promise of the Father, which, *saith he,* ye have [b]heard of me.

5 [a]For John truly baptized with water; [b]but ye shall be baptized with the Holy Ghost not many days hence.

6 When they therefore were come together, they asked of him, saying, Lord, wilt thou at this time restore again the kingdom to Israel?

7 And he said unto them, [a]It is not for you to [b]know the times or the seasons, which the Father hath put in his own power.

8 [a]But ye shall receive power, [b]after that the Holy Ghost is come upon you: and [c]ye shall be witnesses unto me both in Jerusalem, and in all Judaea, and in [d]Samaria, and unto the [e]uttermost part of the earth.

Jesus Ascends to Heaven
(Mark 16:19, 20; Luke 24:50–53)

9 [a]And when he had spoken these things, while they beheld, [b]he was taken up; and a cloud received him out of their sight.

10 And while they looked stedfastly toward heaven as he went up, behold, two men stood by them [a]in white apparel;

11 Which also said, Ye men of Galilee, why stand ye gazing up into heaven? this same Jesus, which is taken up from you into heaven, [a]shall so come in like manner as ye have seen him go into heaven.

The Upper Room Prayer Meeting

12 [a]Then returned they unto Jerusalem from the mount called Olivet, which is from Jerusalem a sabbath day's journey.

13 And when they were come in, they went up [a]into an upper room, where abode both [b]Peter, and James, and John, and Andrew, Philip, and Thomas, Bartholomew, and Matthew, James *the son* of Alphaeus, and [c]Simon Zelotes, and [d]Judas *the brother* of James.

14 [a]These all continued with one accord in prayer and supplication, with [b]the women, and Mary the mother of Jesus, and with [c]his brethren.

Matthias Chosen
(cf. Ps. 109:8)

15 And in those days Peter stood up in the midst of the disciples, and said, (the number [a]of

CHAPTER 1

1 [a]Luke 1:3 **2** [a]Mark 16:19 [b]Matt. 28:19 **3** [a]Mark 16:12, 14 **4** [a]Luke 24:49 [b][John 14:16, 17, 26; 15:26] **5** [a]Matt. 3:11 [b][Joel 2:28] **7** [a]1 Thess. 5:1 [b]Matt. 24:36 **8** [a][Acts 2:1, 4] [b]Luke 24:49 [c]Luke 24:48 [d]Acts 8:1, 5, 14 [e]Col. 1:23 **9** [a]Luke 24:50, 51 [b]Acts 1:2 **10** [a]John 20:12 **11** [a]Dan. 7:13 **12** [a]Luke 24:52 **13** [a]Acts 9:37, 39; 20:8 [b]Matt. 10:2–4 [c]Luke 6:15 [d]Jude 1 **14** [a]Acts 2:1, 46 [b]Luke 23:49, 55 [c]Matt. 13:55 **15** [a]Rev. 3:4

NKJV

THE ACTS

OF THE APOSTLES

Prologue

1 The former account I made, O [a]Theophilus, of all that Jesus began both to do and teach,

2 [a]until the day in which He was taken up, after He through the Holy Spirit [b]had given commandments to the apostles whom He had chosen,

3 [a]to whom He also presented Himself alive after His suffering by many infallible proofs, being seen by them during forty days and speaking of the things pertaining to the kingdom of God.

The Holy Spirit Promised

4 [a]And being assembled together with *them,* He commanded them not to depart from Jerusalem, but to wait for the Promise of the Father, "which," *He said,* "you have [b]heard from Me;

5 [a]"for John truly baptized with water, [b]but you shall be baptized with the Holy Spirit not many days from now."

6 Therefore, when they had come together, they asked Him, saying, "Lord, will You at this time restore the kingdom to Israel?"

7 And He said to them, [a]"It is not for you to [b]know times or seasons which the Father has put in His own authority.

8 [a]"But you shall receive power [b]when the Holy Spirit has come upon you; and [c]you shall be *witnesses to Me in Jerusalem, and in all Judea and [d]Samaria, and to the [e]end of the earth."

Jesus Ascends to Heaven
(Mark 16:19, 20; Luke 24:50–53)

9 [a]Now when He had spoken these things, while they watched, [b]He was taken up, and a cloud received Him out of their sight.

10 And while they looked steadfastly toward heaven as He went up, behold, two men stood by them [a]in white apparel,

11 who also said, "Men of Galilee, why do you stand gazing up into heaven? This *same* Jesus, who was taken up from you into heaven, [a]will so come in like manner as you saw Him go into heaven."

The Upper Room Prayer Meeting

12 [a]Then they returned to Jerusalem from the mount called Olivet, which is near Jerusalem, a Sabbath day's journey.

13 And when they had entered, they went up [a]into the upper room where they were staying: [b]Peter, James, John, and Andrew; Philip and Thomas; Bartholomew and Matthew; James *the son* of Alphaeus and [c]Simon the Zealot; and [d]Judas *the son* of James.

14 [a]These all continued with one accord in prayer *and supplication, with [b]the women and Mary the mother of Jesus, and with [c]His brothers.

Matthias Chosen
(cf. Ps. 109:8)

15 And in those days Peter stood up in the midst of the *disciples (altogether the number [a]of

*

1:8 NU *My witnesses* **1:14** NU omits *and supplication* **1:15** NU *brethren*

KJV

names together were about an hundred and twenty,)

16 Men *and* brethren, this scripture must needs have been fulfilled, [a]which the Holy Ghost by the mouth of David spake before concerning Judas, [b]which was guide to them that took Jesus.

17 For [a]he was numbered with us, and had obtained part of [b]this ministry.

18 [a]Now this man purchased a field with [b]the reward of iniquity; and falling headlong, he burst asunder in the midst, and all his bowels gushed out.

19 And it was known unto all the dwellers at Jerusalem; insomuch as that field is called in their proper tongue, Aceldama, that is to say, The field of blood.

20 For it is written in the book of Psalms, [a]LET HIS HABITATION BE DESOLATE, AND LET NO MAN DWELL THEREIN: and [b]HIS BISHOPRICK LET ANOTHER TAKE.

21 Wherefore of these men which have companied with us all the time that the Lord Jesus went in and out among us,

22 Beginning from the baptism of John, unto that same day that [a]he was taken up from us, must one be ordained [b]to be a witness with us of his resurrection.

23 And they appointed two, Joseph called [a]Barsabas, who was surnamed Justus, and Matthias.

24 And they prayed, and said, Thou, Lord, [a]which knowest the hearts of all *men*, shew whether of these two thou hast chosen,

25 [a]That he may take part of this ministry and apostleship, from which Judas by transgression fell, that he might go to his own place.

26 And they gave forth their lots; and the lot fell upon Matthias; and he was numbered with the eleven apostles.

Coming of the Holy Spirit

2 And when [a]the day of Pentecost was fully come, [b]they were all with one accord in one place.

2 And suddenly there came a sound from heaven as of a rushing mighty wind, and [a]it filled all the house where they were sitting.

3 And there appeared unto them cloven tongues like as of fire, and it sat upon each of them.

4 And [a]they were all filled with the Holy Ghost, and began [b]to speak with other tongues, as the Spirit gave them utterance.

The Crowd's Response

5 And there were dwelling at Jerusalem Jews, [a]devout men, out of every nation under heaven.

6 Now when this was noised abroad, the [a]multitude came together, and were confounded, because that every man heard them speak in his own language.

7 And they were all amazed and marvelled, saying one to another, Behold, are not all these which speak [a]Galilaeans?

8 And how hear we every man in our own tongue, wherein we were born?

9 Parthians, and Medes, and Elamites, and the dwellers in Mesopotamia, and in Judaea, and [a]Cappadocia, in Pontus, and Asia,

10 Phrygia, and Pamphylia, in Egypt, and in the parts of Libya about Cyrene, and strangers of Rome, Jews and proselytes,

11 Cretes and Arabians, we do hear them speak in our tongues the wonderful works of God.

12 And they were all amazed, and were in doubt, saying one to another, What meaneth this?

NKJV

names was about a hundred and twenty), and said,

16 "Men *and* brethren, this Scripture had to be fulfilled, [a]which the Holy Spirit spoke before by the mouth of David concerning Judas, [b]who became a guide to those who arrested Jesus;

17 "for [a]he was numbered with us and obtained a part in [b]this ministry."

18 [a](Now this man purchased a field with [b]the wages of iniquity; and falling headlong, he burst open in the middle and all his entrails gushed out.

19 And it became known to all those dwelling in Jerusalem; so that field is called in their own language, Akel Dama, that is, Field of Blood.)

20 "For it is written in the Book of Psalms:

> [a]*'Let his dwelling place be desolate,*
> *And let no one live in it';*

and,

> [b]*'Let another take his *office.'*

21 "Therefore, of these men who have accompanied us all the time that the Lord Jesus went in and out among us,

22 "beginning from the baptism of John to that day when [a]He was taken up from us, one of these must [b]become a witness with us of His resurrection."

23 And they proposed two: Joseph called [a]Barsabas, who was surnamed Justus, and Matthias.

24 And they prayed and said, "You, O Lord, [a]who know the hearts of all, show which of these two You have chosen

25 [a]"to take part in this ministry and apostleship from which Judas by transgression fell, that he might go to his own place."

26 And they cast their lots, and the lot fell on Matthias. And he was numbered with the eleven apostles.

Coming of the Holy Spirit

2 When [a]the Day of Pentecost had fully come, [b]they were all *with one accord in one place.

2 And suddenly there came a sound from heaven, as of a rushing mighty wind, and [a]it filled the whole house where they were sitting.

3 Then there appeared to them divided tongues, as of fire, and *one* sat upon each of them.

4 And [a]they were all filled with the Holy Spirit and began [b]to speak with other tongues, as the Spirit gave them utterance.

The Crowd's Response

5 And there were dwelling in Jerusalem Jews, [a]devout men, from every nation under heaven.

6 And when this sound occurred, the [a]multitude came together, and were confused, because everyone heard them speak in his own language.

7 Then they were all amazed and marveled, saying to one another, "Look, are not all these who speak [a]Galileans?

8 "And how *is it that* we hear, each in our own language in which we were born?

9 "Parthians and Medes and Elamites, those dwelling in Mesopotamia, Judea and [a]Cappadocia, Pontus and Asia,

10 "Phrygia and Pamphylia, Egypt and the parts of Libya adjoining Cyrene, visitors from Rome, both Jews and proselytes,

11 "Cretans and Arabs—we hear them speaking in our own tongues the wonderful works of God."

12 So they were all amazed and perplexed, saying to one another, "Whatever could this mean?"

16 [a]Ps. 41:9 [b]Matt. 26:47; Mark 14:43; Luke 22:47; John 18:3 **17** [a]Matt. 10:4 [b]Acts 1:25 **18** [a]Matt. 27:3–10 [b]Matt. 18:7; 26:24; Mark 14:21; 26:14, 15; Luke 22:22; John 17:12 **20** [a]Ps. 69:25 [b]Ps. 109:8 **22** [a]Acts 1:9 [b]Acts 1:8; 2:32 **23** [a]Acts 15:22 **24** [a]1 Sam. 16:7; Jer. 17:10; Acts 1:2 **25** [a]Acts 1:17

CHAPTER 2

1 [a]Lev. 23:15; Deut. 16:9; Acts 20:16; 1 Cor. 16:8 [b]Acts 1:14 **2** [a]Acts 4:31 **4** [a]Matt. 3:11; 5:6; 10:20; Luke 3:16; John 14:16; 16:7–15; Acts 1:5 [b]Mark 16:17; Acts 10:46; 19:6; [1 Cor. 12:10, 28, 30; 13:1] **5** [a]Luke 2:25; Acts 8:2 **6** [a]Acts 4:32 **7** [a]Matt. 26:73; Acts 1:11 **9** [a]1 Pet. 1:1

*

1:20 Gr. *episkopen, position of overseer*
2:1 NU *together*

KJV

13 Others mocking said, These men are full
of new wine.

Peter's Sermon
(*Joel 2:28–32*)

14 But Peter, standing up with the eleven,
lifted up his voice, and said unto them, Ye men
of Judaea, and all *ye* that dwell at Jerusalem, be
this known unto you, and hearken to my words:
15 For these are not drunken, as ye suppose,
[a]seeing it is *but* the third hour of the day.
16 But this is that which was spoken by the
prophet Joel;
17 [a]AND IT SHALL COME TO PASS IN THE LAST
DAYS, SAITH GOD, [b]I WILL POUR OUT OF MY SPIRIT
UPON ALL FLESH: AND YOUR SONS AND [c]YOUR DAUGH-
TERS SHALL PROPHESY, AND YOUR YOUNG MEN SHALL
SEE VISIONS, AND YOUR OLD MEN SHALL DREAM
DREAMS:
18 AND ON MY SERVANTS AND ON MY HAND-
MAIDENS I WILL POUR OUT IN THOSE DAYS OF MY
SPIRIT; [a]AND THEY SHALL PROPHESY:
19 [a]AND I WILL SHEW WONDERS IN HEAVEN
ABOVE, AND SIGNS IN THE EARTH BENEATH; BLOOD,
AND FIRE, AND VAPOUR OF SMOKE:
20 [a]THE SUN SHALL BE TURNED INTO DARKNESS,
AND THE MOON INTO BLOOD, BEFORE THAT GREAT
AND NOTABLE DAY OF THE LORD COME:
21 AND IT SHALL COME TO PASS, *THAT* [a]WHOSO-
EVER SHALL CALL ON THE NAME OF THE LORD SHALL
BE SAVED.
22 Ye men of Israel, hear these words; Jesus
of Nazareth, a man approved of God among you
[a]by miracles and wonders and signs, which God
did by him in the midst of you, as ye yourselves
also know:
23 Him, [a]being delivered by the determinate
counsel and foreknowledge of God, [b]ye have
taken, and by wicked hands have crucified and
slain:
24 [a]Whom God hath raised up, having loosed
the pains of death: because it was not possible
that he should be holden of it.
25 For David speaketh concerning him, [a]I
FORESAW THE LORD ALWAYS BEFORE MY FACE, FOR
HE IS ON MY RIGHT HAND, THAT I SHOULD NOT BE
MOVED:
26 THEREFORE DID MY HEART REJOICE, AND MY
TONGUE WAS GLAD; MOREOVER ALSO MY FLESH SHALL
REST IN HOPE:
27 BECAUSE THOU WILT NOT LEAVE MY SOUL IN
HELL, NEITHER WILT THOU SUFFER THINE HOLY ONE
TO SEE [a]CORRUPTION.
28 THOU HAST MADE KNOWN TO ME THE WAYS
OF LIFE; THOU SHALT MAKE ME FULL OF JOY WITH THY
COUNTENANCE.
29 Men *and* brethren, let me freely speak
unto you [a]of the patriarch David, that he is both
dead and buried, and his sepulchre is with us unto
this day.
30 Therefore being a prophet, [a]and knowing
that God had sworn with an oath to him, that of
the fruit of his loins, according to the flesh, he
would raise up Christ to sit on his throne;
31 He seeing this before spake of the resurrection of Christ, [a]that his soul was not left in
hell, neither his flesh did see corruption.
32 [a]This Jesus hath God raised up, [b]whereof
we all are witnesses.
33 Therefore being by [b]the right hand of God
[a]exalted, and [c]having received of the Father the

15 [a]1 Thess. 5:7
17 [a]Is. 44:3; Ezek. 11:19; Joel 2:28–32; [Zech. 12:10; John 7:38] [b]Acts 10:45 [c]Acts 21:9
18 [a]Acts 21:4, 9; 1 Cor. 12:10
19 [a]Joel 2:30
20 [a]Is. 13:10; Ezek. 32:7; Matt. 24:29; Mark 13:24, 25; Luke 21:25; Rev. 6:12
21 [a]Rom. 10:13
22 [a]Is. 50:5; John 3:2; 5:6; Acts 10:38
23 [a]Matt. 26:4; Luke 22:22; Acts 3:18; 4:28; [1 Pet. 1:20] [b]Acts 5:30
24 [a][Rom. 8:11; 1 Cor. 6:14; 2 Cor. 4:14; Eph. 1:20; Col. 2:12]; 1 Thess. 1:10; Heb. 13:20
25 [a]Ps. 16:8–11
27 [a]Acts 13:30–37
29 [a]Acts 13:36
30 [a]2 Sam. 7:12; Ps. 132:11; Luke 1:32; Rom. 1:3; 2 Tim. 2:8
31 [a]Ps. 16:10; Is. 50:8; 53:10
32 [a]Acts 2:24 [b]Acts 1:8; 3:15
33 [a]Ps. 68:18; [Acts 5:31]; Phil. 2:9 [b]Ps. 110:1; Mark 16:19; [Heb. 10:12] [c]Luke 24:49; [John 14:26]

NKJV

13 Others mocking said, "They are full of
new wine."

Peter's Sermon
(*Joel 2:28–32*)

14 But Peter, standing up with the eleven,
raised his voice and said to them, "Men of Judea
and all who dwell in Jerusalem, let this be known
to you, and heed my words.
15 "For these are not drunk, as you suppose,
[a]since it is *only* the third hour of the day.
16 "But this is what was spoken by the
prophet Joel:
17 *'And[a] it shall come to pass in the last days,*
says God,
[b]That I will pour out of My Spirit on all
flesh;
Your sons and [c]your daughters shall
prophesy,
Your young men shall see visions,
Your old men shall dream dreams.
18 *And on My menservants and on My*
maidservants
I will pour out My Spirit in those days;
[a]And they shall prophesy.
19 *[a]I will show wonders in heaven above*
And signs in the earth beneath:
Blood and fire and vapor of smoke.
20 *[a]The sun shall be turned into darkness,*
And the moon into blood,
Before the coming of the great and
awesome day of the LORD.
21 *And it shall come to pass*
That [a]whoever calls on the name of the
LORD
Shall be saved.'

22 "Men of Israel, hear these words: Jesus
of Nazareth, a Man attested by God to you [a]by
miracles, wonders, and signs which God did
through Him in your midst, as you yourselves also
know—
23 "Him, [a]being delivered by the determined
purpose and foreknowledge of God, [b]you *have
taken by lawless hands, have crucified, and put
to death;
24 [a]"whom God raised up, having loosed the
pains of death, because it was not possible that
He should be held by it.
25 "For David says concerning Him:
[a]'I foresaw the LORD always before my face,
For He is at my right hand, that I may
not be shaken.
26 *Therefore my heart rejoiced, and my*
tongue was glad;
Moreover my flesh also will rest in hope.
27 *For You will not leave my soul in Hades,*
Nor will You allow Your Holy One to see
[a]corruption.
28 *You have made known to me the ways*
of life;
You will make me full of joy in Your
presence.'

29 "Men *and* brethren, let *me* speak freely
to you [a]of the patriarch David, that he is both
dead and buried, and his tomb is with us to this
day.
30 "Therefore, being a prophet, [a]and knowing that God had sworn with an oath to him
that of the fruit of his body, *according to the
flesh, He would raise up the Christ to sit on his
throne,
31 "he, foreseeing this, spoke concerning the
resurrection of the Christ, [a]that His soul was not
left in Hades, nor did His flesh see corruption.
32 [a]"This Jesus God has raised up, [b]of which
we are all witnesses.
33 "Therefore [a]being exalted to [b]the right
hand of God, and [c]having received from the Fa-

*

2:23 NU omits *have taken*
2:30 NU *He would seat one on his throne,*

KJV

promise of the Holy Ghost, he [d]hath shed forth
this, which ye now see and hear.
34 For David is not ascended into the heavens: but he saith himself, [a]THE LORD SAID UNTO
MY LORD, SIT THOU ON MY RIGHT HAND,
35 UNTIL I MAKE THY FOES THY FOOTSTOOL.
36 Therefore let all the house of Israel know
assuredly, that God hath made that same Jesus,
whom ye have crucified, both Lord and Christ.
37 Now when they heard *this,* [a]they were
pricked in their heart, and said unto Peter and to
the rest of the apostles, Men *and* brethren, what
shall we do?
38 Then Peter said unto them, [a]Repent, and
be baptized every one of you in the name of Jesus
Christ for the remission of sins, and ye shall receive the gift of the Holy Ghost.
39 For the promise is unto you, and [a]to your
children, and [b]to all that are afar off, *even* as many
as the Lord our God shall call.

A Vital Church Grows

40 And with many other words did he testify
and exhort, saying, Save yourselves from this un-
toward generation.
41 Then they that gladly received his word
were baptized: and the same day there were
added *unto them* about three thousand souls.
42 [a]And they continued stedfastly in the
apostles' doctrine and fellowship, and in breaking
of bread, and in prayers.
43 And fear came upon every soul: and
[a]many wonders and signs were done by the
apostles.
44 And all that believed were together, and
[a]had all things common;
45 And sold their possessions and goods, and
[a]parted them to all *men,* as every man had need.
46 [a]And they, continuing daily with one accord [b]in the temple, and [c]breaking bread from
house to house, did eat their meat with gladness
and singleness of heart,
47 Praising God, and having favour with all
the people. And[a] the Lord added to the church
daily such as should be saved.

A Lame Man Healed

3 Now Peter and John went up together [a]into
the temple at the hour of prayer, [b]*being* the
ninth *hour.*
2 And [a]a certain man lame from his
mother's womb was carried, whom they laid daily
at the gate of the temple which is called Beautiful,
[b]to ask alms of them that entered into the temple;
3 Who seeing Peter and John about to go
into the temple asked an alms.
4 And Peter, fastening his eyes upon him
with John, said, Look on us.
5 And he gave heed unto them, expecting
to receive something of them.
6 Then Peter said, Silver and gold have I
none; but such as I have give I thee: [a]In the name
of Jesus Christ of Nazareth rise up and walk.
7 And he took him by the right hand, and
lifted *him* up: and immediately his feet and ancle
bones received strength.
8 And he [a]leaping up stood, and walked,
and entered with them into the temple, walking,
and leaping, and praising God.
9 [a]And all the people saw him walking and
praising God:
10 And they knew that it was he which [a]sat
for alms at the Beautiful gate of the temple: and
they were filled with wonder and amazement at
that which had happened unto him.

Preaching in Solomon's Portico

11 And as the lame man which was healed
held Peter and John, all the people ran together

NKJV

ther the promise of the Holy Spirit, He [d]poured
out this which you now see and hear.
34 "For David did not ascend into the heavens, but he says himself:

[a]'*The LORD said to my Lord,*
"*Sit at My right hand,*
35 *Till I make Your enemies Your*
footstool." '

36 "Therefore let all the house of Israel know
assuredly that God has made this Jesus, whom
you crucified, both Lord and Christ."
37 Now when they heard *this,* [a]they were cut
to the heart, and said to Peter and the rest of the
apostles, "Men *and* brethren, what shall we do?"
38 Then Peter said to them, [a]"Repent, and
let every one of you be baptized in the name of
Jesus Christ for the remission of sins; and you
shall receive the gift of the Holy Spirit.
39 "For the promise is to you and [a]to your
children, and [b]to all who are afar off, as many
as the Lord our God will call."

A Vital Church Grows

40 And with many other words he testified
and exhorted them, saying, "Be saved from this
perverse generation."
41 Then those who *gladly received his word
were baptized; and that day about three thousand
souls were added *to them.*
42 [a]And they continued steadfastly in the
apostles' doctrine and fellowship, in the breaking
of bread, and in prayers.
43 Then fear came upon every soul, and
[a]many wonders and signs were done through the
apostles.
44 Now all who believed were together, and
[a]had all things in common,
45 and sold their possessions and goods, and
[a]divided them among all, as anyone had need.
46 [a]So continuing daily with one accord [b]in
the temple, and [c]breaking bread from house to
house, they ate their food with gladness and simplicity of heart,
47 praising God and having favor with all the
people. And [a]the Lord added *to the church daily
those who were being saved.

A Lame Man Healed

3 Now Peter and John went up together [a]to the
temple at the hour of prayer, [b]the ninth *hour.*
2 And [a]a certain man lame from his
mother's womb was carried, whom they laid daily
at the gate of the temple which is called Beautiful,
[b]to ask alms from those who entered the temple;
3 who, seeing Peter and John about to go
into the temple, asked for alms.
4 And fixing his eyes on him, with John, Peter said, "Look at us."
5 So he gave them his attention, expecting
to receive something from them.
6 Then Peter said, "Silver and gold I do not
have, but what I do have I give you: [a]In the name
of Jesus Christ of Nazareth, rise up and walk."
7 And he took him by the right hand and
lifted *him* up, and immediately his feet and ankle
bones received strength.
8 So he, [a]leaping up, stood and walked and
entered the temple with them—walking, leaping,
and praising God.
9 [a]And all the people saw him walking and
praising God.
10 Then they knew that it was he who [a]sat
begging alms at the Beautiful Gate of the temple;
and they were filled with wonder and amazement
at what had happened to him.

Preaching in Solomon's Portico

11 Now as the lame man who was healed
held on to Peter and John, all the people ran to-

---

33 [d]Matt. 3:11; 5:6; Luke 3:16; 22:69; John 14:16;16:7–15; Acts 2:1–11, 17; 10:45; Eph. 4:8
34 [a]Ps. 68:18; 110:1; Matt. 22:44; Luke 23:43; John 20:17; 1 Cor. 15:25; Eph. 1:20; Heb. 1:13
37 [a][Zech. 12:10]; Luke 3:10, 12, 14; John 16:8
38 [a]Luke 24:47
39 [a]Joel 2:28, 32 [b]Acts 11:15, 18; Eph. 2:13
42 [a]Acts 1:14; Rom. 12:12; Eph. 6:18; Col. 4:2; Heb. 10:25
43 [a]Mark 16:17; Acts 2:22
44 [a]Acts 4:32, 34, 37; 5:2
45 [a]Is. 58:7
46 [a]Acts 1:14 [b]Luke 24:53 [c]Luke 24:30; Acts 2:42; 20:7; [1 Cor. 10:16]
47 [a]Acts 5:14

CHAPTER 3

1 [a]Acts 2:46 [b]Ps. 55:17; Matt. 27:45; Acts 10:30
2 [a]Acts 14:8 [b]John 9:8; Acts 3:10
6 [a]Acts 4:10
8 [a]Is. 35:6
9 [a]Acts 4:16, 21
10 [a]John 9:8; Acts 3:2

*

2:41 NU omits *gladly*
2:47 NU omits *to the church*

KJV

unto them in the porch [a]that is called Solomon's, greatly wondering.

12 And when Peter saw *it,* he answered unto the people, Ye men of Israel, why marvel ye at this? or why look ye so earnestly on us, as though by our own power or holiness we had made this man to walk?

13 [a]The God of Abraham, and of Isaac, and of Jacob, the God of our fathers, [b]hath glorified his Son Jesus; whom ye [c]delivered up, and [d]denied him in the presence of Pilate, when he was determined to let *him* go.

14 But ye denied [a]the Holy One [b]and the Just, and [c]desired a murderer to be granted unto you;

15 And killed the Prince of life, [a]whom God hath raised from the dead; [b]whereof we are witnesses.

16 [a]And his name through faith in his name hath made this man strong, whom ye see and know: yea, the faith which is by him hath given him this perfect soundness in the presence of you all.

17 And now, brethren, I wot that [a]through ignorance ye did *it,* as *did* also your rulers.

18 But [a]those things, which God before had shewed [b]by the mouth of all his prophets, that Christ should suffer, he hath so fulfilled.

19 [a]Repent ye therefore, and be converted, that your sins may be blotted out, when the times of refreshing shall come from the presence of the Lord;

20 And he shall send Jesus Christ, which before was preached unto you:

21 [a]Whom the heaven must receive until the times of [b]restitution of all things, [c]which God hath spoken by the mouth of all his holy prophets since the world began.

22 For Moses truly said unto the fathers, [a]A PROPHET SHALL THE LORD YOUR GOD RAISE UP UNTO YOU OF YOUR BRETHREN, LIKE UNTO ME; HIM SHALL YE HEAR IN ALL THINGS WHATSOEVER HE SHALL SAY UNTO YOU.

23 AND IT SHALL COME TO PASS, *THAT* EVERY SOUL, WHICH WILL NOT HEAR THAT PROPHET, SHALL BE DESTROYED FROM AMONG THE PEOPLE.

24 Yea, and [a]all the prophets from Samuel and those that follow after, as many as have spoken, have likewise foretold of these days.

25 [a]Ye are the children of the prophets, and of the covenant which God made with our fathers, saying unto Abraham, [b]AND IN THY SEED SHALL ALL THE KINDREDS OF THE EARTH BE BLESSED.

26 Unto you [a]first God, having raised up his Son Jesus, sent him to bless you, [b]in turning away every one of you from his iniquities.

Peter and John Arrested

4 And as they spake unto the people, the priests, and the captain of the temple, and the [a]Sadducees, came upon them,

2 Being grieved that they taught the people, and preached through Jesus the resurrection from the dead.

3 And they laid hands on them, and put *them* in hold unto the next day: for it was now eventide.

4 Howbeit many of them which heard the word believed; and the number of the men was about five thousand.

Addressing the Sanhedrin

5 And it came to pass on the morrow, that their rulers, and elders, and scribes,

6 And [a]Annas the high priest, and Caiaphas, and John, and Alexander, and as many as were of the kindred of the high priest, were gathered together at Jerusalem.

7 And when they had set them in the midst, they asked, [a]By what power, or by what name, have ye done this?

8 [a]Then Peter, filled with the Holy Ghost,

11 [a]John 10:23; Acts 5:12
13 [a]John 5:30 [b]Is. 49:3; John 7:39; 12:23; 13:31 [c]Matt. 27:2 [d]Matt. 27:20; Mark 15:11; Luke 23:18; John 18:40; Acts 13:28
14 [a]Ps. 16:10; Mark 1:24; Luke 1:35 [b]Acts 7:52; 2 Cor. 5:21 [c]John 18:40
15 [a]Acts 2:24 [b]Acts 2:32
16 [a]Matt. 9:22; Acts 4:10; 14:9
17 [a]Luke 23:34; John 16:3; [Acts 13:27; 17:30]; 1 Cor. 2:8; 1 Tim. 1:13
18 [a]Luke 24:44; Acts 26:22 [b]Ps. 22; Is. 50:6; 53:5; Dan. 9:26; Hos. 6:1; Zech. 13:6; 1 Pet. 1:10
19 [a][Acts 2:38; 26:20]
21 [a]Acts 1:11 [b]Matt. 17:11; [Rom. 8:21] [c]Luke 1:70
22 [a]Deut. 18:15, 18, 19; Acts 7:37
24 [a]2 Sam. 7:12; Luke 24:25
25 [a]Acts 2:39; [Rom. 9:4, 8; Gal. 3:26] [b]Gen. 12:3; 18:18; 22:18; 26:4; 28:14
26 [a]Matt. 15:24; John 4:22; Acts 13:46; [Rom. 1:16; 2:9] [b]Is. 42:1; Matt. 1:21

CHAPTER 4

1 [a]Matt. 22:23
6 [a]Luke 3:2; John 11:49; 18:13
7 [a]Ex. 2:14; Matt. 21:23; Acts 7:27
8 [a]Luke 12:11, 12

*

3:20 NU, M *Christ Jesus*
• NU, M *ordained for you before*
3:24 NU, M *proclaimed*

NKJV

gether to them in the porch [a]which is called Solomon's, greatly amazed.

12 So when Peter saw *it,* he responded to the people: "Men of Israel, why do you marvel at this? Or why look so intently at us, as though by our own power or godliness we had made this man walk?

13 [a]"The God of Abraham, Isaac, and Jacob, the God of our fathers, [b]glorified His Servant Jesus, whom you [c]delivered up and [d]denied in the presence of Pilate, when he was determined to let *Him* go.

14 "But you denied [a]the Holy One [b]and the Just, and [c]asked for a murderer to be granted to you,

15 "and killed the Prince of life, [a]whom God raised from the dead, [b]of which we are witnesses.

16 [a]"And His name, through faith in His name, has made this man strong, whom you see and know. Yes, the faith which *comes* through Him has given him this perfect soundness in the presence of you all.

17 "Yet now, brethren, I know that [a]you did *it* in ignorance, as *did* also your rulers.

18 "But [a]those things which God foretold [b]by the mouth of all His prophets, that the Christ would suffer, He has thus fulfilled.

19 [a]"Repent therefore and be converted, that your sins may be blotted out, so that times of refreshing may come from the presence of the Lord,

20 "and that He may send *Jesus Christ, who was *preached to you before,

21 [a]"whom heaven must receive until the times of [b]restoration of all things, [c]which God has spoken by the mouth of all His holy prophets since the world began.

22 "For Moses truly said to the fathers, [a]*'The LORD your God will raise up for you a Prophet like me from your brethren. Him you shall hear in all things, whatever He says to you.*

23 *'And it shall be that every soul who will not hear that Prophet shall be utterly destroyed from among the people.'*

24 "Yes, and [a]all the prophets, from Samuel and those who follow, as many as have spoken, have also *foretold these days.

25 [a]"You are sons of the prophets, and of the covenant which God made with our fathers, saying to Abraham, [b]*'And in your seed all the families of the earth shall be blessed.'*

26 "To you [a]first, God, having raised up His Servant Jesus, sent Him to bless you, [b]in turning away every one *of you* from your iniquities."

Peter and John Arrested

4 Now as they spoke to the people, the priests, the captain of the temple, and the [a]Sadducees came upon them,

2 being greatly disturbed that they taught the people and preached in Jesus the resurrection from the dead.

3 And they laid hands on them, and put *them* in custody until the next day, for it was already evening.

4 However, many of those who heard the word believed; and the number of the men came to be about five thousand.

Addressing the Sanhedrin

5 And it came to pass, on the next day, that their rulers, elders, and scribes,

6 as well as [a]Annas the high priest, Caiaphas, John, and Alexander, and as many as were of the family of the high priest, were gathered together at Jerusalem.

7 And when they had set them in the midst, they asked, [a]"By what power or by what name have you done this?"

8 [a]Then Peter, filled with the Holy Spirit,

KJV

said unto them, Ye rulers of the people, and elders of Israel,

9 If we this day be examined of the good deed done to the impotent man, by what means he is made whole;

10 Be it known unto you all, and to all the people of Israel, [a]that by the name of Jesus Christ of Nazareth, whom ye crucified, [b]whom God raised from the dead, *even* by him doth this man stand here before you whole.

11 [a]This is THE STONE WHICH WAS SET AT NOUGHT OF YOU BUILDERS, WHICH IS BECOME THE HEAD OF THE CORNER.

12 [a]Neither is there salvation in any other: for there is none other name under heaven given among men, whereby we must be saved.

The Name of Jesus Forbidden

13 Now when they saw the boldness of Peter and John, [a]and perceived that they were unlearned and ignorant men, they marvelled; and they took knowledge of them, that they had been with Jesus.

14 And beholding the man which was healed [a]standing with them, they could say nothing against it.

15 But when they had commanded them to go aside out of the council, they conferred among themselves,

16 Saying, [a]What shall we do to these men? for that indeed a notable miracle hath been done by them *is* [b]manifest to all them that dwell in Jerusalem; and we cannot deny *it*.

17 But that it spread no further among the people, let us straitly threaten them, that they speak henceforth to no man in this name.

18 [a]And they called them, and commanded them not to speak at all nor teach in the name of Jesus.

19 But Peter and John answered and said unto them, [a]Whether it be right in the sight of God to hearken unto you more than unto God, judge ye.

20 [a]For we cannot but speak the things which [b]we have seen and heard.

21 So when they had further threatened them, they let them go, finding nothing how they might punish them, [a]because of the people: for all *men* [b]glorified God for [c]that which was done.

22 For the man was above forty years old, on whom this miracle of healing was shewed.

Prayer for Boldness
(cf. Ps. 2:1, 2)

23 And being let go, [a]they went to their own company, and reported all that the chief priests and elders had said unto them.

24 And when they heard that, they lifted up their voice to God with one accord, and said, Lord, [a]thou *art* God, which hast made heaven, and earth, and the sea, and all that in them is:

25 Who by the mouth of thy servant David hast said, [a]WHY DID THE HEATHEN RAGE, AND THE PEOPLE IMAGINE VAIN THINGS?

26 THE KINGS OF THE EARTH STOOD UP, AND THE RULERS WERE GATHERED TOGETHER AGAINST THE LORD, AND AGAINST HIS CHRIST.

27 For [a]of a truth against [b]thy holy child Jesus, [c]whom thou hast anointed, both Herod, and Pontius Pilate, with the Gentiles, and the people of Israel, were gathered together,

28 [a]For to do whatsoever thy hand and thy counsel determined before to be done.

29 And now, Lord, behold their threatenings: and grant unto thy servants, [a]that with all boldness they may speak thy word,

30 By stretching forth thine hand to heal; [a]and that signs and wonders may be done [b]by the name of [c]thy holy child Jesus.

31 And when they had prayed, [a]the place was shaken where they were assembled together;

10 [a]Acts 2:22; 3:6, 16 [b]Acts 2:24
11 [a]Ps. 118:22; Is. 28:16; Matt. 21:42
12 [a]Is. 42:1, 6, 7; 53:11; Dan. 9:24; [Matt. 1:21; John 14:6; Acts 10:43; 1 Tim. 2:5, 6]
13 [a]Matt. 11:25; [1 Cor. 1:27]
14 [a]Acts 3:11
16 [a]John 11:47 [b]Acts 3:7–10
18 [a]Acts 5:28, 40
19 [a]Acts 5:29
20 [a]Acts 1:8; 2:32 [b]Acts 22:15; [1 John 1:1, 3]
21 [a]Matt. 21:26; Luke 20:6, 19; 22:2; Acts 5:26 [b]Matt. 15:31 [c]Acts 3:7, 8
23 [a]Acts 2:44–46; 12:12
24 [a]Ex. 20:11; 2 Kin. 19:15; Neh. 9:6; Ps. 146:6
25 [a]Ps. 2:1, 2
27 [a]Matt. 26:3; Luke 22:2; 23:1, 8 [b][Luke 1:35] [c]Luke 4:18; John 10:36
28 [a]Acts 2:23; 3:18
29 [a]Acts 4:13, 31; 9:27; 13:46; 14:3; 19:8; 26:26; Eph. 6:19
30 [a]Acts 2:43; 5:12 [b]Acts 3:6, 16 [c]Acts 4:27
31 [a]Matt. 5:6; Acts 2:2, 4; 16:26

NKJV

said to them, "Rulers of the people and elders of Israel:

9 "If we this day are judged for a good deed *done* to a helpless man, by what means he has been made well,

10 "let it be known to you all, and to all the people of Israel, [a]that by the name of Jesus Christ of Nazareth, whom you crucified, [b]whom God raised from the dead, by Him this man stands here before you whole.

11 "This is the [a]*'stone which was rejected by you builders, which has become the chief cornerstone.'*

12 [a]"Nor is there salvation in any other, for there is no other name under heaven given among men by which we must be saved."

The Name of Jesus Forbidden

13 Now when they saw the boldness of Peter and John, [a]and perceived that they were uneducated and untrained men, they marveled. And they realized that they had been with Jesus.

14 And seeing the man who had been healed [a]standing with them, they could say nothing against it.

15 But when they had commanded them to go aside out of the council, they conferred among themselves,

16 saying, [a]"What shall we do to these men? For, indeed, that a notable miracle has been done through them *is* [b]evident to all who dwell in Jerusalem, and we cannot deny *it*.

17 "But so that it spreads no further among the people, let us severely threaten them, that from now on they speak to no man in this name."

18 [a]So they called them and commanded them not to speak at all nor teach in the name of Jesus.

19 But Peter and John answered and said to them, [a]"Whether it is right in the sight of God to listen to you more than to God, you judge.

20 [a]"For we cannot but speak the things which [b]we have seen and heard."

21 So when they had further threatened them, they let them go, finding no way of punishing them, [a]because of the people, since they all [b]glorified God for [c]what had been done.

22 For the man was over forty years old on whom this miracle of healing had been performed.

Prayer for Boldness
(cf. Ps. 2:1, 2)

23 And being let go, [a]they went to their own *companions* and reported all that the chief priests and elders had said to them.

24 So when they heard that, they raised their voice to God with one accord and said: "Lord, [a]You *are* God, who made heaven and earth and the sea, and all that is in them,

25 "who *by the mouth of Your servant David have said:

[a]*'Why did the nations rage,*
And the people plot vain things?
26 *The kings of the earth took their stand,*
And the rulers were gathered together
Against the LORD and against His Christ.'

27 "For [a]truly against [b]Your holy Servant Jesus, [c]whom You anointed, both Herod and Pontius Pilate, with the Gentiles and the people of Israel, were gathered together

28 [a]"to do whatever Your hand and Your purpose determined before to be done.

29 "Now, Lord, look on their threats, and grant to Your servants [a]that with all boldness they may speak Your word,

30 "by stretching out Your hand to heal, [a]and that signs and wonders may be done [b]through the name of [c]Your holy Servant Jesus."

31 And when they had prayed, [a]the place where they were assembled together was shaken;

*

4:25 NU *through the Holy Spirit, by the mouth of our father, Your servant David,*

KJV

and they were all filled with the Holy Ghost, [b]and they spake the word of God with boldness.

Sharing in All Things

32 And the multitude of them that believed [a]were of one heart and of one soul: [b]neither said any *of them* that ought of the things which he possessed was his own; but they had all things common.

33 And with [a]great power gave the apostles [b]witness of the resurrection of the Lord Jesus: and [c]great grace was upon them all.

34 Neither was there any among them that lacked: [a]for as many as were possessors of lands or houses sold them, and brought the prices of the things that were sold,

35 [a]And laid *them* down at the apostles' feet: [b]and distribution was made unto every man according as he had need.

36 And Joses, who by the apostles was surnamed Barnabas, (which is, being interpreted, The son of consolation,) a Levite, *and* of the country of Cyprus,

37 [a]Having land, sold *it*, and brought the money, and laid *it* at the apostles' feet.

Lying to the Holy Spirit

5 But a certain man named Ananias, with Sapphira his wife, sold a possession,

2 And kept back *part* of the price, his wife also being privy *to it*, and brought a certain part, and laid *it* at the apostles' feet.

3 [a]But Peter said, Ananias, why hath [b]Satan filled thine heart to lie to the Holy Ghost, and to keep back *part* of the price of the land?

4 Whiles it remained, was it not thine own? and after it was sold, was it not in thine own power? why hast thou conceived this thing in thine heart? thou hast not lied unto men, but unto God.

5 And Ananias hearing these words [a]fell down, and gave up the ghost: and great fear came on all them that heard these things.

6 And the young men arose, [a]wound him up, and carried *him* out, and buried *him*.

7 And it was about the space of three hours after, when his wife, not knowing what was done, came in.

8 And Peter answered unto her, Tell me whether ye sold the land for so much? And she said, Yea, for so much.

9 Then Peter said unto her, How is it that ye have agreed together [a]to tempt the Spirit of the Lord? behold, the feet of them which have buried thy husband *are* at the door, and shall carry thee out.

10 [a]Then fell she down straightway at his feet, and yielded up the ghost: and the young men came in, and found her dead, and, carrying *her* forth, buried *her* by her husband.

11 [a]And great fear came upon all the church, and upon as many as heard these things.

Continuing Power in the Church

12 And [a]by the hands of the apostles were many signs and wonders wrought among the people; ([b]and they were all with one accord in Solomon's porch.

13 And [a]of the rest durst no man join himself to them: [b]but the people magnified them.

14 And believers were the more added to the Lord, multitudes both of men and women.)

15 Insomuch that they brought forth the sick into the streets, and laid *them* on beds and couches, [a]that at the least the shadow of Peter passing by might overshadow some of them.

16 There came also a multitude *out* of the cities round about unto Jerusalem, bringing [a]sick folks, and them which were vexed with unclean spirits: and they were healed every one.

31 [b]Acts 4:29
32 [a]Acts 5:12; Rom. 15:5, 6; 2 Cor. 13:11; Phil. 1:27; 2:2; 1 Pet. 3:8 [b]Acts 2:44
33 [a][Acts 1:8] [b]Acts 1:22 [c]Rom. 6:15
34 [a][Matt. 19:21]; Acts 2:45
35 [a]Acts 4:37; 5:2 [b]Acts 2:45; 6:1
37 [a]Acts 4:34, 35; 5:1, 2

CHAPTER 5

3 [a]Num. 30:2; Deut. 23:21; Eccl. 5:4 [b]Matt. 4:10; Luke 22:3; John 13:2, 27
5 [a]Ezek. 11:13; Acts 5:10, 11
6 [a]John 19:40
9 [a]Matt. 4:7; Acts 5:3, 4
10 [a]Ezek. 11:13; Acts 5:5
11 [a]Acts 2:43; 5:5; 19:17
12 [a]Acts 2:43; 4:30; 6:8; 14:3; 15:12; [Rom. 15:19]; 2 Cor. 12:12; Heb. 2:4 [b]Acts 3:11; 4:32
13 [a]John 9:22 [b]Acts 2:47; 4:21
15 [a]Matt. 9:21; 14:36; Acts 19:12
16 [a]Mark 16:17, 18; [John 14:12]

*———
4:36 NU *Joseph*

NKJV

and they were all filled with the Holy Spirit, [b]and they spoke the word of God with boldness.

Sharing in All Things

32 Now the multitude of those who believed [a]were of one heart and one soul; [b]neither did anyone say that any of the things he possessed was his own, but they had all things in common.

33 And with [a]great power the apostles gave [b]witness to the resurrection of the Lord Jesus. And [c]great grace was upon them all.

34 Nor was there anyone among them who lacked; [a]for all who were possessors of lands or houses sold them, and brought the proceeds of the things that were sold,

35 [a]and laid *them* at the apostles' feet; [b]and they distributed to each as anyone had need.

36 And *Joses, who was also named Barnabas by the apostles (which is translated Son of Encouragement), a Levite of the country of Cyprus,

37 [a]having land, sold *it*, and brought the money and laid *it* at the apostles' feet.

Lying to the Holy Spirit

5 But a certain man named Ananias, with Sapphira his wife, sold a possession.

2 And he kept back *part* of the proceeds, his wife also being aware *of it*, and brought a certain part and laid *it* at the apostles' feet.

3 [a]But Peter said, "Ananias, why has [b]Satan filled your heart to lie to the Holy Spirit and keep back *part* of the price of the land for yourself?

4 "While it remained, was it not your own? And after it was sold, was it not in your own control? Why have you conceived this thing in your heart? You have not lied to men but to God."

5 Then Ananias, hearing these words, [a]fell down and breathed his last. So great fear came upon all those who heard these things.

6 And the young men arose and [a]wrapped him up, carried *him* out, and buried *him*.

7 Now it was about three hours later when his wife came in, not knowing what had happened.

8 And Peter answered her, "Tell me whether you sold the land for so much?" She said, "Yes, for so much."

9 Then Peter said to her, "How is it that you have agreed together [a]to test the Spirit of the Lord? Look, the feet of those who have buried your husband *are* at the door, and they will carry you out."

10 [a]Then immediately she fell down at his feet and breathed her last. And the young men came in and found her dead, and carrying *her* out, buried *her* by her husband.

11 [a]So great fear came upon all the church and upon all who heard these things.

Continuing Power in the Church

12 And [a]through the hands of the apostles many signs and wonders were done among the people. [b]And they were all with one accord in Solomon's Porch.

13 Yet [a]none of the rest dared join them, [b]but the people esteemed them highly.

14 And believers were increasingly added to the Lord, multitudes of both men and women,

15 so that they brought the sick out into the streets and laid *them* on beds and couches, [a]that at least the shadow of Peter passing by might fall on some of them.

16 Also a multitude gathered from the surrounding cities to Jerusalem, bringing [a]sick people and those who were tormented by unclean spirits, and they were all healed.

KJV

Imprisoned Apostles Freed

17 [a]Then the high priest rose up, and all they that were with him, (which is the sect of the Sadducees,) and were filled with indignation,

18 [a]And laid their hands on the apostles, and put them in the common prison.

19 But [a]the angel of the Lord by night opened the prison doors, and brought them forth, and said,

20 Go, stand and speak in the temple to the people [a]all the words of this life.

21 And when they heard *that,* they entered into the temple early in the morning, and taught. [a]But the high priest came, and they that were with him, and called the council together, and all the senate of the children of Israel, and sent to the prison to have them brought.

Apostles on Trial Again

22 But when the officers came, and found them not in the prison, they returned, and told,

23 Saying, The prison truly found we shut with all safety, and the keepers standing without before the doors: but when we had opened, we found no man within.

24 Now when the high priest and [a]the captain of the temple and the chief priests heard these things, they doubted of them whereunto this would grow.

25 Then came one and told them, saying, Behold, the men whom ye put in prison are standing in the temple, and teaching the people.

26 Then went the captain with the officers, and brought them without violence: [a]for they feared the people, lest they should have been stoned.

27 And when they had brought them, they set *them* before the council: and the high priest asked them,

28 Saying, [a]Did not we straitly command you that ye should not teach in this name? and, behold, ye have filled Jerusalem with your doctrine, [b]and intend to bring this man's [c]blood upon us.

29 Then Peter and the *other* apostles answered and said, [a]We ought to obey God rather than men.

30 [a]The God of our fathers raised up Jesus, whom ye slew and [b]hanged on a tree.

31 [a]Him hath God exalted with his right hand *to be* [b]a Prince and [c]a Saviour, [d]for to give repentance to Israel, and forgiveness of sins.

32 And [a]we are his witnesses of these things; and *so is* also the Holy Ghost, [b]whom God hath given to them that obey him.

Gamaliel's Advice

33 When they heard *that,* they were [a]cut *to the heart,* and took counsel to slay them.

34 Then stood there up one in the council, a Pharisee, named [a]Gamaliel, a doctor of the law, had in reputation among all the people, and commanded to put the apostles forth a little space;

35 And said unto them, Ye men of Israel, take heed to yourselves what ye intend to do as touching these men.

36 For before these days rose up Theudas, boasting himself to be somebody; to whom a number of men, about four hundred, joined themselves: who was slain; and all, as many as obeyed him, were scattered, and brought to nought.

37 After this man rose up Judas of Galilee in the days of the taxing, and drew away much people after him: he also perished; and all, *even* as many as obeyed him, were dispersed.

38 And now I say unto you, Refrain from these men, and let them alone: for if this counsel or this work be of men, it will come to nought:

39 [a]But if it be of God, ye cannot overthrow it; lest haply ye be found even [b]to fight against God.

40 And to him they agreed: and when they had [a]called the apostles, [b]and beaten *them,* they

17 [a]Matt. 3:7; Acts 4:1, 2, 6
18 [a]Luke 21:12; Acts 4:3; 16:37
19 [a]Matt. 1:20, 24; 2:13, 19; 28:2; Luke 1:11; 2:9; Acts 12:7; 16:26
20 [a][John 6:63, 68; 17:3; 1 John 5:11]
21 [a]Acts 4:5, 6
24 [a]Luke 22:4; Acts 4:1; 5:26
26 [a]Matt. 21:26
28 [a]Acts 4:17, 18 [b]Acts 2:23, 36 [c]Matt. 23:35
29 [a]Acts 4:19
30 [a]Acts 3:13, 15 [b]Acts 10:39; 13:29; [Gal. 3:13; 1 Pet. 2:24]
31 [a]Mark 16:19; [Acts 2:33, 36; Phil. 2:9–11] [b]Acts 3:15; Rev. 1:5 [c]Matt. 1:21 [d]Luke 24:47; [Eph. 1:7; Col. 1:14]
32 [a]John 15:26, 27; Acts 15:28; Rom. 8:16; Heb. 2:4 [b]Acts 2:4; 10:44
33 [a]Acts 2:37; 7:54
34 [a]Acts 22:3
39 [a]Luke 21:15; 1 Cor. 1:25 [b]Acts 7:51; 9:5
40 [a]Acts 4:18 [b]Matt. 10:17; Mark 13:9; Acts 16:22, 23; 21:32; 2 Cor. 11:25

*

5:23 NU, M omit *outside*
5:24 NU omits *the high priest*
5:25 NU, M omit *saying*

NKJV

Imprisoned Apostles Freed

17 [a]Then the high priest rose up, and all those who *were* with him (which is the sect of the Sadducees), and they were filled with indignation,

18 [a]and laid their hands on the apostles and put them in the common prison.

19 But at night [a]an angel of the Lord opened the prison doors and brought them out, and said,

20 "Go, stand in the temple and speak to the people [a]all the words of this life."

21 And when they heard *that,* they entered the temple early in the morning and taught. [a]But the high priest and those with him came and called the council together, with all the elders of the children of Israel, and sent to the prison to have them brought.

Apostles on Trial Again

22 But when the officers came and did not find them in the prison, they returned and reported,

23 saying, "Indeed we found the prison shut securely, and the guards standing *outside before the doors; but when we opened them, we found no one inside!"

24 Now when *the high priest, [a]the captain of the temple, and the chief priests heard these things, they wondered what the outcome would be.

25 So one came and told them, *saying, "Look, the men whom you put in prison are standing in the temple and teaching the people!"

26 Then the captain went with the officers and brought them without violence, [a]for they feared the people, lest they should be stoned.

27 And when they had brought them, they set *them* before the council. And the high priest asked them,

28 saying, [a]"Did we not strictly command you not to teach in this name? And look, you have filled Jerusalem with your doctrine, [b]and intend to bring this Man's [c]blood on us!"

29 But Peter and the *other* apostles answered and said: [a]"We ought to obey God rather than men.

30 [a]"The God of our fathers raised up Jesus whom you murdered by [b]hanging on a tree.

31 [a]"Him God has exalted to His right hand *to be* [b]Prince and [c]Savior, [d]to give repentance to Israel and forgiveness of sins.

32 "And [a]we are His witnesses to these things, and *so* also *is* the Holy Spirit [b]whom God has given to those who obey Him."

Gamaliel's Advice

33 When they heard *this,* they were [a]furious and plotted to kill them.

34 Then one in the council stood up, a Pharisee named [a]Gamaliel, a teacher of the law held in respect by all the people, and commanded them to put the apostles outside for a little while.

35 And he said to them: "Men of Israel, take heed to yourselves what you intend to do regarding these men.

36 "For some time ago Theudas rose up, claiming to be somebody. A number of men, about four hundred, joined him. He was slain, and all who obeyed him were scattered and came to nothing.

37 "After this man, Judas of Galilee rose up in the days of the census, and drew away many people after him. He also perished, and all who obeyed him were dispersed.

38 "And now I say to you, keep away from these men and let them alone; for if this plan or this work is of men, it will come to nothing;

39 [a]"but if it is of God, you cannot overthrow it—lest you even be found [b]to fight against God."

40 And they agreed with him, and when they had [a]called for the apostles [b]and beaten *them,*

KJV

commanded that they should not speak in the name of Jesus, and let them go.

41 And they departed from the presence of the council, [a]rejoicing that they were counted worthy to suffer shame for his name.

42 And daily [a]in the temple, and in every house, [b]they ceased not to teach and preach Jesus Christ.

Seven Chosen to Serve

6 And in those days, [a]when the number of the disciples was multiplied, there arose a murmuring of the [b]Grecians against the Hebrews, because their widows were neglected [c]in the daily ministration.

2 Then the twelve called the multitude of the disciples *unto them,* and said, [a]It is not reason that we should leave the word of God, and serve tables.

3 Wherefore, brethren, [a]look ye out among you seven men of honest report, full of the Holy Ghost and wisdom, whom we may appoint over this [b]business.

4 But we [a]will give ourselves continually to prayer, and to the ministry of the word.

5 And the saying pleased the whole multitude: and they chose Stephen, [a]a man full of faith and of the Holy Ghost, and [b]Philip, and Prochorus, and Nicanor, and Timon, and Parmenas, and [c]Nicolas a proselyte of Antioch:

6 Whom they set before the apostles: and [a]when they had prayed, [b]they laid *their* hands on them.

7 And [a]the word of God increased; and the number of the disciples multiplied in Jerusalem greatly; and a great company [b]of the priests were obedient to the faith.

Stephen Accused of Blasphemy

8 And Stephen, full of faith and power, did great [a]wonders and miracles among the people.

9 Then there arose certain of the synagogue, which is called *the synagogue* of the Libertines, and Cyrenians, and Alexandrians, and of them of Cilicia and of Asia, disputing with Stephen.

10 And [a]they were not able to resist the wisdom and the spirit by which he spake.

11 [a]Then they suborned men, which said, We have heard him speak blasphemous words against Moses, and *against* God.

12 And they stirred up the people, and the elders, and the scribes, and came upon *him,* and caught him, and brought *him* to the council,

13 And set up false witnesses, which said, This man ceaseth not to speak blasphemous words against this holy place, and the law:

14 [a]For we have heard him say, that this Jesus of Nazareth shall destroy this place, and shall change the customs which Moses delivered us.

15 And all that sat in the council, looking stedfastly on him, saw his face as it had been the face of an angel.

Stephen's Address: The Call of Abraham

7 Then said the high priest, Are these things so?

2 And he said, [a]Men, brethren, and fathers, hearken; The [b]God of glory appeared unto our father Abraham, when he was in Mesopotamia, before he dwelt in [c]Charran,

3 And said unto him, [a]GET THEE OUT OF THY COUNTRY, AND FROM THY KINDRED, AND COME INTO THE LAND WHICH I SHALL SHEW THEE.

4 Then [a]came he out of the land of the Chaldaeans, and dwelt in Charran: and from thence, when his father was [b]dead, he removed him into this land, wherein ye now dwell.

5 And he gave him none inheritance in it, no, not *so much as* to set his foot on: [a]yet he promised that he would give it to him for a possession, and to his seed after him, when *as yet* he had no child.

---

41 [a]Matt. 5:10–12; Rom. 5:3; 2 Cor. 12:10; Heb. 10:34; [James 1:2; 1 Pet. 4:13–16]
42 [a]Acts 2:46 [b]Acts 4:20, 29

CHAPTER 6

1 [a]Acts 2:41; 4:4 [b]Acts 9:29; 11:20 [c]Acts 4:35; 11:29
2 [a]Ex. 18:17
3 [a]Deut. 1:13; 1 Tim. 3:7 [b]Phil. 1:1; 1 Tim. 3:8–13
4 [a]Acts 2:42
5 [a]Acts 6:3; 11:24 [b]Acts 8:5, 26; 21:8 [c]Rev. 2:6, 15
6 [a]Acts 1:24 [b]Num. 8:10; 27:18; Deut. 34:9; [Mark 5:23; Acts 8:17; 9:17; 13:3; 19:6; 1 Tim. 4:14; 2 Tim. 1:6]; Heb. 6:2
7 [a]Acts 12:24; Col. 1:6 [b]John 12:42
8 [a]Acts 2:43; 5:12; 8:15; 14:3
10 [a]Ex. 4:12; Is. 54:17; Luke 21:15
11 [a]1 Kin. 21:10, 13; Matt. 26:59, 60
14 [a]Acts 10:38; 25:8

CHAPTER 7

2 [a]Acts 22:1 [b]Ps. 29:3; 1 Cor. 2:8 [c]Gen. 11:31, 32
3 [a]Gen. 12:1
4 [a]Gen. 11:31; 15:17; Heb. 11:8–10 [b]Gen. 11:32
5 [a]Gen. 12:7; 13:15; 15:3, 18; 17:8; 26:3

*

5:41 NU *the name;* M *the name of Jesus*
6:1 Greek-speaking Jews
6:8 NU *grace*
6:13 NU omits *blasphemous*

NKJV

they commanded that they should not speak in the name of Jesus, and let them go.

41 So they departed from the presence of the council, [a]rejoicing that they were counted worthy to suffer shame for *His name.

42 And daily [a]in the temple, and in every house, [b]they did not cease teaching and preaching Jesus *as* the Christ.

Seven Chosen to Serve

6 Now in those days, [a]when *the number of* the disciples was multiplying, there arose a complaint against the Hebrews by the [b]Hellenists,* because their widows were neglected [c]in the daily distribution.

2 Then the twelve summoned the multitude of the disciples and said, [a]"It is not desirable that we should leave the word of God and serve tables.

3 "Therefore, brethren, [a]seek out from among you seven men of *good* reputation, full of the Holy Spirit and wisdom, whom we may appoint over this [b]business;

4 "but we [a]will give ourselves continually to prayer and to the ministry of the word."

5 And the saying pleased the whole multitude. And they chose Stephen, [a]a man full of faith and the Holy Spirit, and [b]Philip, Prochorus, Nicanor, Timon, Parmenas, and [c]Nicolas, a proselyte from Antioch,

6 whom they set before the apostles; and [a]when they had prayed, [b]they laid hands on them.

7 Then [a]the word of God spread, and the number of the disciples multiplied greatly in Jerusalem, and a great many [b]of the priests were obedient to the faith.

Stephen Accused of Blasphemy

8 And Stephen, full of *faith and power, did great [a]wonders and signs among the people.

9 Then there arose some from what is called the Synagogue of the Freedmen (Cyrenians, Alexandrians, and those from Cilicia and Asia), disputing with Stephen.

10 And [a]they were not able to resist the wisdom and the Spirit by which he spoke.

11 [a]Then they secretly induced men to say, "We have heard him speak blasphemous words against Moses and God."

12 And they stirred up the people, the elders, and the scribes; and they came upon *him,* seized him, and brought *him* to the council.

13 They also set up false witnesses who said, "This man does not cease to speak *blasphemous words against this holy place and the law;

14 [a]"for we have heard him say that this Jesus of Nazareth will destroy this place and change the customs which Moses delivered to us."

15 And all who sat in the council, looking steadfastly at him, saw his face as the face of an angel.

Stephen's Address: The Call of Abraham

7 Then the high priest said, "Are these things so?"

2 And he said, [a]"Brethren and fathers, listen: The [b]God of glory appeared to our father Abraham when he was in Mesopotamia, before he dwelt in [c]Haran,

3 "and said to him, [a]*'Get out of your country and from your relatives, and come to a land that I will show you.'*

4 "Then [a]he came out of the land of the Chaldeans and dwelt in Haran. And from there, when his father was [b]dead, He moved him to this land in which you now dwell.

5 "And *God* gave him no inheritance in it, not even *enough* to set his foot on. But even when *Abraham* had no child, [a]He promised to give it to him for a possession, and to his descendants after him.

KJV

6 And God spake on this wise, [a]That his seed should sojourn in a strange land; and that they should bring them into [b]bondage, and entreat *them* evil four hundred years.

7 [a]And the nation to whom they shall be in bondage will I [b]judge, said God: [c]and after that shall they come forth, and serve me in this place.

8 [a]And he gave him the covenant of circumcision: [b]and so *Abraham* begat Isaac, and circumcised him the eighth day; [c]and Isaac *begat* Jacob; and [d]Jacob *begat* the twelve patriarchs.

The Patriarchs in Egypt

9 [a]And the patriarchs, moved with envy, [b]sold Joseph into Egypt: [c]but God was with him,

10 And delivered him out of all his afflictions, [a]and gave him favour and wisdom in the sight of Pharaoh king of Egypt; and he made him governor over Egypt and all his house.

11 [a]Now there came a dearth over all the land of Egypt and Chanaan, and great affliction: and our fathers found no sustenance.

12 [a]But when Jacob heard that there was corn in Egypt, he sent out our fathers first.

13 And at the [a]second *time* Joseph was made known to his brethren; and Joseph's kindred was made known unto Pharaoh.

14 [a]Then sent Joseph, and called his father Jacob to *him,* and [b]all his kindred, threescore and fifteen souls.

15 [a]So Jacob went down into Egypt, [b]and died, he, and our fathers,

16 And [a]were carried over into Sychem, and laid in [b]the sepulchre that Abraham bought for a sum of money of the sons of Emmor *the father* of Sychem.

God Delivers Israel by Moses

17 But when [a]the time of the promise drew nigh, which God had sworn to Abraham, [b]the people grew and multiplied in Egypt,

18 Till another king [a]arose, which knew not Joseph.

19 The same dealt subtilly with our kindred, and evil entreated our fathers, [a]so that they cast out their young children, to the end they might not live.

20 [a]In which time Moses was born, and [b]was exceeding fair, and nourished up in his father's house three months:

21 And [a]when he was cast out, [b]Pharaoh's daughter took him up, and nourished him for her own son.

22 And Moses was learned in all the wisdom of the Egyptians, and was [a]mighty in words and in deeds.

23 [a]And when he was full forty years old, it came into his heart to visit his brethren the children of Israel.

24 And seeing one *of them* suffer wrong, he defended *him,* and avenged him that was oppressed, and smote the Egyptian:

25 For he supposed his brethren would have understood how that God by his hand would deliver them: but they understood not.

26 And the next day he shewed himself unto them as they strove, and would have set them at one again, saying, Sirs, ye are brethren; why do ye wrong one to another?

27 But he that did his neighbour wrong thrust him away, saying, [a]Who made thee a ruler and a judge over us?

28 Wilt thou kill me, as thou didst the Egyptian yesterday?

29 [a]Then fled Moses at this saying, and was a stranger in the land of Madian, where he [b]begat two sons.

30 [a]And when forty years were expired, there appeared to him in the wilderness of mount Sina an angel of the Lord in a flame of fire in a bush.

6 [a]Gen. 15:13, 14, 16; 47:11, 12 [b]Ex. 1:8–14; 12:40, 41; Gal. 3:17
7 [a]Gen. 15:14 [b]Ex. 14:13–31 [c]Ex. 3:12; Josh. 3:1–17
8 [a]Gen. 17:9–14 [b]Gen. 21:1–5 [c]Gen. 25:21–26 [d]Gen. 29:31—30:24; 35:18, 22–26
9 [a]Gen. 37:4, 11, 28; Ps. 105:17 [b]Gen. 37:28 [c]Gen. 39:2, 21, 23
10 [a]Gen. 41:38–44
11 [a]Gen. 41:54; 42:5
12 [a]Gen. 42:1, 2
13 [a]Gen. 45:4, 16
14 [a]Gen. 45:9, 27 [b]Gen. 46:26, 27; Deut. 10:22
15 [a]Gen. 46:1–7 [b]Gen. 49:33; Ex. 1:6
16 [a]Gen. 50:13; Ex. 13:19; Josh. 24:32 [b]Gen. 23:16
17 [a]Gen. 15:13; Ex. 2:23–25; Acts 7:6, 7 [b]Ex. 1:7–9; Ps. 105:24, 25
18 [a]Ex. 1:8
19 [a]Ex. 1:22
20 [a]Ex. 2:1, 2 [b]Heb. 11:23
21 [a]Ex. 2:3, 4 [b]Ex. 2:5–10
22 [a]Luke 24:19
23 [a]Ex. 2:11, 12; Heb. 11:24–26
27 [a]Luke 12:14; Ex. 2:14; Acts 7:35
29 [a]Heb. 11:27 [b]Ex. 2:15, 21, 22; 4:20; 18:3
30 [a]Ex. 3:1–10; Is. 63:9

NKJV

6 "But God spoke in this way: [a]that his descendants would dwell in a foreign land, and that they would bring them into [b]bondage and oppress *them* four hundred years.

7 [a]*'And the nation to whom they will be in bondage I will* [b]*judge,'* said God, [c]*'and after that they shall come out and serve Me in this place.'*

8 [a]"Then He gave him the covenant of circumcision; [b]and so *Abraham* begot Isaac and circumcised him on the eighth day; [c]and Isaac *begot* Jacob, and [d]Jacob *begot* the twelve patriarchs.

The Patriarchs in Egypt

9 [a]"And the patriarchs, becoming envious, [b]sold Joseph into Egypt. [c]But God was with him

10 "and delivered him out of all his troubles, [a]and gave him favor and wisdom in the presence of Pharaoh, king of Egypt; and he made him governor over Egypt and all his house.

11 [a]"Now a famine and great trouble came over all the land of Egypt and Canaan, and our fathers found no sustenance.

12 [a]"But when Jacob heard that there was grain in Egypt, he sent out our fathers first.

13 "And the [a]second *time* Joseph was made known to his brothers, and Joseph's family became known to the Pharaoh.

14 [a]"Then Joseph sent and called his father Jacob and [b]all his relatives to *him,* *seventy-five people.

15 [a]"So Jacob went down to Egypt; [b]and he died, he and our fathers.

16 "And [a]they were carried back to Shechem and laid in [b]the tomb that Abraham bought for a sum of money from the sons of Hamor, *the father* of Shechem.

God Delivers Israel by Moses

17 "But when [a]the time of the promise drew near which God had sworn to Abraham, [b]the people grew and multiplied in Egypt

18 "till another king [a]arose who did not know Joseph.

19 "This man dealt treacherously with our people, and oppressed our forefathers, [a]making them expose their babies, so that they might not live.

20 [a]"At this time Moses was born, and [b]was well pleasing to God; and he was brought up in his father's house for three months.

21 "But [a]when he was set out, [b]Pharaoh's daughter took him away and brought him up as her own son.

22 "And Moses was learned in all the wisdom of the Egyptians, and was [a]mighty in words and deeds.

23 [a]"Now when he was forty years old, it came into his heart to visit his brethren, the children of Israel.

24 "And seeing one of *them* suffer wrong, he defended and avenged him who was oppressed, and struck down the Egyptian.

25 "For he supposed that his brethren would have understood that God would deliver them by his hand, but they did not understand.

26 "And the next day he appeared to two of them as they were fighting, and *tried to* reconcile them, saying, 'Men, you are brethren; why do you wrong one another?'

27 "But he who did his neighbor wrong pushed him away, saying, [a]*'Who made you a ruler and a judge over us?*

28 *'Do you want to kill me as you did the Egyptian yesterday?'*

29 [a]"Then, at this saying, Moses fled and became a dweller in the land of Midian, where he [b]had two sons.

30 [a]"And when forty years had passed, an Angel *of the Lord appeared to him in a flame of fire in a bush, in the wilderness of Mount Sinai.

7:14 Or *seventy,* Ex. 1:5
7:30 NU omits *of the Lord*

KJV

31 When Moses saw *it*, he wondered at the
sight: and as he drew near to behold *it*, the voice
of the Lord came unto him,
32 *Saying*, [a]I *AM* THE GOD OF THY FATHERS,
THE GOD OF ABRAHAM, AND THE GOD OF ISAAC,
AND THE GOD OF JACOB. Then Moses trembled, and
durst not behold.
33 [a]THEN SAID THE LORD TO HIM, PUT OFF THY
SHOES FROM THY FEET: FOR THE PLACE WHERE THOU
STANDEST IS HOLY GROUND.
34 [a]I HAVE SEEN, I HAVE SEEN THE AFFLICTION
OF MY PEOPLE WHICH IS IN EGYPT, AND I HAVE HEARD
THEIR GROANING, AND AM COME DOWN TO DELIVER
THEM. AND NOW COME, I WILL [b]SEND THEE INTO
EGYPT.
35 This Moses whom they refused, saying,
[a]WHO MADE THEE A RULER AND A JUDGE? the same
did God send *to be* a ruler and a deliverer [b]by
the hand of the angel which appeared to him in
the bush.
36 [a]He brought them out, after that he had
[b]shewed wonders and signs in the land of Egypt,
[c]and in the Red sea, [d]and in the wilderness forty
years.

Israel Rebels Against God

37 This is that Moses, which said unto the
children of Israel, [a]A PROPHET SHALL THE LORD
YOUR GOD RAISE UP UNTO YOU OF YOUR BRETHREN,
LIKE UNTO ME; [b]HIM SHALL YE HEAR.
38 [a]This is he, that was in the church in the
wilderness with [b]the angel which spake to him
in the mount Sina, and *with* our fathers: [c]who
received the lively [d]oracles to give unto us:
39 To whom our fathers [a]would not obey, but
thrust *him* from them, and in their hearts turned
back again into Egypt,
40 [a]Saying unto Aaron, MAKE US GODS TO GO
BEFORE US: FOR *AS FOR* THIS MOSES, WHICH BROUGHT
US OUT OF THE LAND OF EGYPT, WE WOT NOT WHAT
IS BECOME OF HIM.
41 [a]And they made a calf in those days, and
offered sacrifice unto the idol, and [b]rejoiced in
the works of their own hands.
42 Then [a]God turned, and gave them up to
worship [b]the host of heaven; as it is written in
the book of the prophets, [c]O YE HOUSE OF ISRAEL,
HAVE YE OFFERED TO ME SLAIN BEASTS AND SACRI-
FICES *BY THE SPACE OF* FORTY YEARS IN THE WILDER-
NESS?
43 YEA, YE TOOK UP THE TABERNACLE OF MO-
LOCH, AND THE STAR OF YOUR GOD REMPHAN, FIG-
URES WHICH YE MADE TO WORSHIP THEM: AND [a]I
WILL CARRY YOU AWAY BEYOND BABYLON.

God's True Tabernacle

44 Our fathers had the tabernacle of witness
in the wilderness, as he had appointed, speaking
unto Moses, [a]that he should make it according
to the fashion that he had seen.
45 [a]Which also our fathers that came after
brought in with Jesus into the possession of the
Gentiles, [b]whom God drave out before the face
of our fathers, unto the [c]days of David;
46 [a]Who found favour before God, and [b]de-
sired to find a tabernacle for the God of Jacob.
47 [a]But Solomon built him an house.
48 Howbeit [a]the most High dwelleth not in
temples made with hands; as saith the prophet,
49 [a]HEAVEN *IS* MY THRONE, AND EARTH *IS* MY
FOOTSTOOL: WHAT HOUSE WILL YE BUILD ME? SAITH
THE LORD: OR WHAT *IS* THE PLACE OF MY REST?
50 HATH NOT MY HAND [a]MADE ALL THESE
THINGS?

32 [a]Ex. 3:6, 15; [Matt. 22:32]; Heb. 11:16
33 [a]Ex. 3:5, 7, 8, 10
34 [a]Ex. 2:24, 25 [b]Ps. 105:26
35 [a]Ex. 2:14; Acts 7:27 [b]Ex. 14:21
36 [a]Ex. 12:41; 33:1; Deut. 6:21, 23; Heb. 8:9 [b]Ex. 7:8, 9; Deut. 6:22; Ps. 105:27; John 4:48 [c]Ex. 14:21 [d]Ex. 16:1, 35; Num. 14:33; Ps. 95:8–10; Acts 7:42; 13:18; Heb. 3:8
37 [a]Deut. 18:15, 18, 19; Acts 3:22 [b]Matt. 17:5
38 [a]Ex. 19:3 [b]Is. 63:9; Gal. 3:19; Heb. 2:2 [c]Ex. 21:1; Deut. 5:27; John 1:17 [d]Rom. 3:2; Heb. 5:12; 1 Pet. 4:11
39 [a]Ps. 95:8–11
40 [a]Ex. 32:1, 23
41 [a]Ex. 32:2–4; Deut. 9:16; Ps. 106:19 [b]Ex. 32:6, 18, 19
42 [a]Ps. 81:12; [2 Thess. 2:11] [b]Deut. 4:19; 2 Kin. 21:3 [c]Amos 5:25–27
43 [a]2 Chr. 36:11–21; Jer. 25:9–12
44 [a]Ex. 25:40; [Heb. 8:5]
45 [a]Deut. 32:49; Josh. 3:14; 18:1; 23:9 [b]Neh. 9:24; Ps. 44:2 [c]2 Sam. 6:2–15
46 [a]2 Sam. 7:1–13; 1 Kin. 8:17 [b]1 Chr. 22:7; Ps. 132:4, 5
47 [a]1 Kin. 6:1–38; 8:20, 21; 2 Chr. 3:1–17
48 [a]1 Kin. 8:27; 2 Chr. 2:6; Acts 17:24
49 [a]Is. 66:1, 2; Matt. 5:34
50 [a]Ps. 102:25

*
7:37 NU, M omit *Him you shall hear*

NKJV

31 "When Moses saw *it*, he marveled at the
sight; and as he drew near to observe, the voice
of the Lord came to him,
32 *"saying,* [a]*'I am the God of your fathers—*
the God of Abraham, the God of Isaac, and the
God of Jacob.' And Moses trembled and dared
not look.
33 [a]*'Then the LORD said to him, "Take your*
sandals off your feet, for the place where you
stand is holy ground.
34 *"I have surely* [a]*seen the oppression of My*
people who are in Egypt; I have heard their groan-
ing and have come down to deliver them. And
now come, I will [b]*send you to Egypt."'*
35 "This Moses whom they rejected, saying,
[a]*'Who made you a ruler and a judge?'* is the one
God sent *to be* a ruler and a deliverer [b]by the
hand of the Angel who appeared to him in the
bush.
36 [a]"He brought them out, after he had
[b]shown wonders and signs in the land of Egypt,
[c]and in the Red Sea, [d]and in the wilderness forty
years.

Israel Rebels Against God

37 "This is that Moses who said to the children of Israel, [a]*'The LORD your God will raise up*
for you a Prophet like me from your brethren.
[b]*Him* you shall hear.'*
38 [a]"This is he who was in the congregation
in the wilderness with [b]the Angel who spoke to
him on Mount Sinai, and *with* our fathers, [c]the
one who received the living [d]oracles to give to
us,
39 "whom our fathers [a]would not obey, but
rejected. And in their hearts they turned back to
Egypt,
40 [a]"saying to Aaron, *'Make us gods to go*
before us; as for this Moses who brought us out
of the land of Egypt, we do not know what has
become of him.'
41 [a]"And they made a calf in those days, offered sacrifices to the idol, and [b]rejoiced in the
works of their own hands.
42 "Then [a]God turned and gave them up to
worship [b]the host of heaven, as it is written in
the book of the Prophets:

[c]*'Did you offer Me slaughtered animals and*
sacrifices during forty years in the
wilderness,
O house of Israel?
43 *You also took up the tabernacle of*
Moloch,
And the star of your god Remphan,
Images which you made to worship;
And [a]*I will carry you away beyond*
Babylon.'

God's True Tabernacle

44 "Our fathers had the tabernacle of witness
in the wilderness, as He appointed, instructing
Moses [a]to make it according to the pattern that
he had seen,
45 [a]"which our fathers, having received it in
turn, also brought with Joshua into the land possessed by the Gentiles, [b]whom God drove out before the face of our fathers until the [c]days of
David,
46 [a]"who found favor before God and [b]asked
to find a dwelling for the God of Jacob.
47 [a]"But Solomon built Him a house.
48 "However, [a]the Most High does not dwell
in temples made with hands, as the prophet
says:

49 *'Heaven*[a] *is My throne,*
And earth is My footstool.
What house will you build for Me? says
the LORD,
Or what is the place of My rest?
50 *Has My hand not* [a]*made all these things?'*

KJV

Israel Resists the Holy Spirit

51 Ye [a]stiffnecked and [b]uncircumcised in
heart and ears, ye do always resist the Holy
Ghost: as your fathers *did*, so *do* ye.
52 [a]Which of the prophets have not your fathers persecuted? and they have slain them which
shewed before of the coming of [b]the Just One;
of whom ye have been now the betrayers and
murderers:
53 [a]Who have received the law by the dispo-
sition of angels, and have not kept *it*.

Stephen the Martyr

54 [a]When they heard these things, they were
cut to the heart, and they gnashed on him with
their teeth.
55 But he, [a]being full of the Holy Ghost,
looked up stedfastly into heaven, and saw the
[b]glory of God, and Jesus standing on the right
hand of God,
56 And said, Behold, [a]I see the heavens
opened, and the [b]Son of man standing on the right
hand of God.
57 Then they cried out with a loud voice, and
stopped their ears, and ran upon him with one
accord,
58 And cast *him* out of the city, and stoned
him: and [a]the witnesses laid down their clothes
at a young man's feet, whose name was Saul.
59 And they stoned Stephen, calling upon
God, and saying, Lord Jesus, [a]receive my
spirit.
60 And he kneeled down, and cried with a
loud voice, [a]Lord, lay not this sin to their charge.
And when he had said this, he fell asleep.

Saul Persecutes the Church

8 And Saul was consenting unto his death. And
at that time there was a great persecution
against the church which was at Jerusalem; and
[a]they were all scattered abroad throughout the
regions of Judaea and Samaria, except the
apostles.
2 And devout men carried Stephen *to his
burial*, and [a]made great lamentation over him.
3 As for Saul, [a]he made havock of the
church, entering into every house, and haling men
and women committed *them* to prison.

Christ Is Preached in Samaria

4 Therefore [a]they that were scattered
abroad went every where preaching the word.
5 Then [a]Philip went down to the city of Samaria, and preached Christ unto them.
6 And the people with one accord gave heed
unto those things which Philip spake, hearing and
seeing the miracles which he did.
7 For [a]unclean spirits, crying with loud
voice, came out of many that were possessed *with
them*: and many taken with palsies, and that were
lame, were healed.
8 And there was great joy in that city.

The Sorcerer's Profession of Faith

9 But there was a certain man, called Simon,
which beforetime in the same city [a]used sorcery,
and bewitched the people of Samaria, [b]giving out
that himself was some great one:
10 To whom they all gave heed, from the
least to the greatest, saying, This man is the great
power of God.
11 And to him they had regard, because that
of long time he had bewitched them with
sorceries.
12 But when they believed Philip preaching
the things [a]concerning the kingdom of God, and
the name of Jesus Christ, they were baptized, both
men and women.
13 Then Simon himself believed also: and
when he was baptized, he continued with Philip,
and wondered, beholding the miracles and signs
which were done.

51 [a]Ex. 32:9; Is. 6:10 [b]Lev. 26:41
52 [a]2 Chr. 36:16; Matt. 21:35; 23:35; 1 Thess. 2:15 [b]Acts 3:14; 22:14; 1 John 2:1
53 [a]Ex. 20:1; Deut. 33:2; Acts 7:38; Gal. 3:19; Heb. 2:2
54 [a]Acts 5:33
55 [a]Matt. 5:8; 16:28; Mark 9:1; Luke 9:27; Acts 6:5 [b][Ex. 24:17]
56 [a]Matt. 3:16 [b]Dan. 7:13
58 [a]Acts 22:20
59 [a]Ps. 31:5
60 [a]Matt. 5:44; Luke 23:34

CHAPTER 8

1 [a]John 16:2; Acts 8:4; 11:19
2 [a]Gen. 23:2
3 [a]Acts 7:58; 1 Cor. 15:9; Gal. 1:13; Phil. 3:6; 1 Tim. 1:13
4 [a]Matt. 10:23
5 [a]Acts 6:5; 8:26, 30
7 [a]Mark 16:17
9 [a]Acts 8:11; 13:6 [b]Acts 5:36
12 [a]Acts 1:3; 8:4

*
8:5 Or *a*

NKJV

Israel Resists the Holy Spirit

51 "*You* [a]stiff-necked and [b]uncircumcised in
heart and ears! You always resist the Holy Spirit;
as your fathers *did*, so *do* you.
52 [a]"Which of the prophets did your fathers
not persecute? And they killed those who foretold
the coming of [b]the Just One, of whom you now
have become the betrayers and murderers,
53 [a]"who have received the law by the direction of angels and have not kept *it*."

Stephen the Martyr

54 [a]When they heard these things they were
cut to the heart, and they gnashed at him with
their teeth.
55 But he, [a]being full of the Holy Spirit,
gazed into heaven and saw the [b]glory of God, and
Jesus standing at the right hand of God,
56 and said, "Look! [a]I see the heavens
opened and the [b]Son of Man standing at the right
hand of God!"
57 Then they cried out with a loud voice,
stopped their ears, and ran at him with one
accord;
58 and they cast *him* out of the city and
stoned *him*. And [a]the witnesses laid down their
clothes at the feet of a young man named Saul.
59 And they stoned Stephen as he was calling
on *God* and saying, "Lord Jesus, [a]receive my
spirit."
60 Then he knelt down and cried out with a
loud voice, [a]"Lord, do not charge them with this
sin." And when he had said this, he fell asleep.

Saul Persecutes the Church

8 Now Saul was consenting to his death. At that
time a great persecution arose against the
church which was at Jerusalem; and [a]they were
all scattered throughout the regions of Judea and
Samaria, except the apostles.
2 And devout men carried Stephen *to his
burial*, and [a]made great lamentation over him.
3 As for Saul, [a]he made havoc of the church,
entering every house, and dragging off men and
women, committing *them* to prison.

Christ Is Preached in Samaria

4 Therefore [a]those who were scattered went
everywhere preaching the word.
5 Then [a]Philip went down to *the city of Samaria and preached Christ to them.
6 And the multitudes with one accord
heeded the things spoken by Philip, hearing and
seeing the miracles which he did.
7 For [a]unclean spirits, crying with a loud
voice, came out of many who were possessed; and
many who were paralyzed and lame were healed.
8 And there was great joy in that city.

The Sorcerer's Profession of Faith

9 But there was a certain man called Simon,
who previously [a]practiced sorcery in the city and
[b]astonished the people of Samaria, claiming that
he was someone great,
10 to whom they all gave heed, from the least
to the greatest, saying, "This man is the great
power of God."
11 And they heeded him because he had astonished them with his sorceries for a long time.
12 But when they believed Philip as he
preached the things [a]concerning the kingdom of
God and the name of Jesus Christ, both men and
women were baptized.
13 Then Simon himself also believed; and
when he was baptized he continued with Philip,
and was amazed, seeing the miracles and signs
which were done.

KJV

The Sorcerer's Sin

14 Now when the [a]apostles which were at
Jerusalem heard that Samaria had received the
word of God, they sent unto them Peter and John:
15 Who, when they were come down, prayed
for them, [a]that they might receive the Holy Ghost:
16 (For [a]as yet he was fallen upon none of
them: only [b]they were baptized in [c]the name of
the Lord Jesus.)
17 Then [a]laid they *their* hands on them, and
they received the Holy Ghost.
18 And when Simon saw that through laying
on of the apostles' hands the Holy Ghost was
given, he offered them money,
19 Saying, Give me also this power, that on
whomsoever I lay hands, he may receive the Holy
Ghost.
20 But Peter said unto him, Thy money perish with thee, because [a]thou hast thought that
[b]the gift of God may be purchased with money.
21 Thou hast neither part nor lot in this matter: for thy [a]heart is not right in the sight of God.
22 Repent therefore of this thy wickedness,
and pray God, [a]if perhaps the thought of thine
heart may be forgiven thee.
23 For I perceive that thou art in [a]the gall of
bitterness, and *in* the bond of iniquity.
24 Then answered Simon, and said, [a]Pray ye
to the Lord for me, that none of these things
which ye have spoken come upon me.
25 And they, when they had testified and
preached the word of the Lord, returned to Jerusalem, and preached the gospel in many villages
of the Samaritans.

Christ Is Preached to an Ethiopian
(*cf. Is. 53:7, 8*)

26 And the angel of the Lord spake unto
[a]Philip, saying, Arise, and go toward the south
unto the way that goeth down from Jerusalem
unto Gaza, which is desert.
27 And he arose and went: and, behold, [a]a
man of Ethiopia, an eunuch of great authority under Candace queen of the Ethiopians, who had
the charge of all her treasure, and [b]had come to
Jerusalem for to worship,
28 Was returning, and sitting in his chariot
read Esaias the prophet.
29 Then the Spirit said unto Philip, Go near,
and join thyself to this chariot.
30 And Philip ran thither to *him*, and heard
him read the prophet Esaias, and said, Understandest thou what thou readest?
31 And he said, How can I, except some man
should guide me? And he desired Philip that he
would come up and sit with him.
32 The place of the scripture which he read
was this, [a]HE WAS LED AS A SHEEP TO THE SLAUGH-
TER; AND LIKE A LAMB DUMB BEFORE HIS SHEARER,
[b]SO OPENED HE NOT HIS MOUTH:
33 IN HIS HUMILIATION HIS [a]JUDGMENT WAS
TAKEN AWAY: AND WHO SHALL DECLARE HIS GEN-
ERATION? FOR HIS LIFE IS [b]TAKEN FROM THE EARTH.
34 And the eunuch answered Philip, and
said, I pray thee, of whom speaketh the prophet
this? of himself, or of some other man?
35 Then Philip opened his mouth, [a]and began
at the same scripture, and preached unto him
Jesus.
36 And as they went on *their* way, they came
unto a certain water: and the eunuch said, See,
here is water; [a]what doth hinder me to be
baptized?
37 And Philip said, [a]If thou believest with all
thine heart, thou mayest. And he answered and
said, [b]I believe that Jesus Christ is the Son of God.
38 And he commanded the chariot to stand

14 [a]Acts 5:12, 29, 40
15 [a]Acts 2:38; 19:2
16 [a]Acts 19:2 [b]Matt. 28:19; Acts 2:38 [c]Acts 10:48; 19:5
17 [a]Acts 6:6; 19:6; Heb. 6:2
20 [a]2 Kin. 5:16; Is. 55:1; Dan. 5:17; [Matt. 10:8] [b][Acts 2:38; 10:45; 11:17]
21 [a]Jer. 17:9
22 [a]Dan. 4:27; 2 Tim. 2:25
23 [a]Heb. 12:15
24 [a]Gen. 20:7, 17; Ex. 8:8; Num. 21:7; 1 Kin. 13:6; Job 42:8; James 5:16
26 [a]Acts 6:5
27 [a]Ps. 68:31; 87:4; Is. 56:3; Zeph. 3:10 [b]1 Kin. 8:41, 42; John 12:20
32 [a]Is. 53:7, 8 [b]Matt. 26:62, 63; 27:12, 14; John 19:9
33 [a]Luke 23:1–25 [b]Luke 23:33–46
35 [a]Luke 24:27; Acts 17:2; 18:28; 28:23
36 [a]Acts 10:47; 16:33
37 [a]Matt. 28:19; [Mark 16:16; Rom. 10:9, 10] [b]Matt. 16:16; John 6:69; 9:35, 38; 11:27

NKJV

The Sorcerer's Sin

14 Now when the [a]apostles who were at Jerusalem heard that Samaria had received the word
of God, they sent Peter and John to them,
15 who, when they had come down, prayed
for them [a]that they might receive the Holy Spirit.
16 For [a]as yet He had fallen upon none of
them. [b]They had only been baptized in [c]the name
of the Lord Jesus.
17 Then [a]they laid hands on them, and they
received the Holy Spirit.
18 And when Simon saw that through the
laying on of the apostles' hands the Holy Spirit
was given, he offered them money,
19 saying, "Give me this power also, that
anyone on whom I lay hands may receive the Holy
Spirit."
20 But Peter said to him, "Your money perish
with you, because [a]you thought that [b]the gift of
God could be purchased with money!
21 "You have neither part nor portion in this
matter, for your [a]heart is not right in the sight of
God.
22 "Repent therefore of this your wickedness, and pray God [a]if perhaps the thought of
your heart may be forgiven you.
23 "For I see that you are [a]poisoned by bitterness and bound by iniquity."
24 Then Simon answered and said, [a]"Pray
to the Lord for me, that none of the things which
you have spoken may come upon me."
25 So when they had testified and preached
the word of the Lord, they returned to Jerusalem,
preaching the gospel in many villages of the Samaritans.

Christ Is Preached to an Ethiopian
(*cf. Is. 53:7, 8*)

26 Now an angel of the Lord spoke to [a]Philip,
saying, "Arise and go toward the south along the
road which goes down from Jerusalem to Gaza."
This is desert.
27 So he arose and went. And behold, [a]a man
of Ethiopia, a eunuch of great authority under
Candace the queen of the Ethiopians, who had
charge of all her treasury, and [b]had come to Jerusalem to worship,
28 was returning. And sitting in his chariot,
he was reading Isaiah the prophet.
29 Then the Spirit said to Philip, "Go near
and overtake this chariot."
30 So Philip ran to him, and heard him reading the prophet Isaiah, and said, "Do you understand what you are reading?"
31 And he said, "How can I, unless someone
guides me?" And he asked Philip to come up and
sit with him.
32 The place in the Scripture which he read
was this:

[a]*"He was led as a sheep to the slaughter;*
And as a lamb before its shearer is silent,
[b]*So He opened not His mouth.*
33 *In His humiliation His [a]justice was taken*
away,
And who will declare His generation?
For His life is [b]taken from the earth."

34 So the eunuch answered Philip and said,
"I ask you, of whom does the prophet say this,
of himself or of some other man?"
35 Then Philip opened his mouth, [a]and beginning at this Scripture, preached Jesus to him.
36 Now as they went down the road, they
came to some water. And the eunuch said, "See,
here is water. [a]What hinders me from being
baptized?"
37 *Then Philip said, [a]"If you believe with
all your heart, you may." And he answered and
said, [b]"I believe that Jesus Christ is the Son of
God."
38 So he commanded the chariot to stand

*8:37 NU, M omit v. 37. It is found in Western texts, including the Latin tradition.

KJV

still: and they went down both into the water, both Philip and the eunuch; and he baptized him.

39 And when they were come up out of the water, [a]the Spirit of the Lord caught away Philip, that the eunuch saw him no more: and he went on his way rejoicing.

40 But Philip was found at Azotus: and passing through he preached in all the cities, till he came to [a]Caesarea.

The Damascus Road: Saul Converted
(Acts 22:6–16; 26:12–18)

9 And [a]Saul, yet breathing out threatenings and slaughter against the disciples of the Lord, went unto the high priest,

2 And desired of him [a]letters to Damascus to the synagogues, that if he found any of this way, whether they were men or women, he might bring them bound unto Jerusalem.

3 And [a]as he journeyed, he came near Damascus: and suddenly there shined round about him a light from heaven:

4 And he fell to the earth, and heard a voice saying unto him, Saul, Saul, [a]why persecutest thou me?

5 And he said, Who art thou, Lord? And the Lord said, I am Jesus whom thou persecutest: *it is* hard for thee to kick against the pricks.

6 And he trembling and astonished said, Lord, what wilt thou have me to do? And the Lord *said* unto him, Arise, and go into the city, and it shall be told thee what thou must do.

7 And [a]the men which journeyed with him stood speechless, hearing a voice, but seeing no man.

8 And Saul arose from the earth; and when his eyes were opened, he saw no man: but they led him by the hand, and brought *him* into Damascus.

9 And he was three days without sight, and neither did eat nor drink.

Ananias Baptizes Saul

10 And there was a certain disciple at Damascus, [a]named Ananias; and to him said the Lord in a vision, Ananias. And he said, Behold, I *am here,* Lord.

11 And the Lord *said* unto him, Arise, and go into the street which is called Straight, and enquire in the house of Judas for *one* called Saul, [a]of Tarsus: for, behold, he prayeth,

12 And hath seen in a vision a man named Ananias coming in, and putting *his* hand on him, that he might receive his sight.

13 Then Ananias answered, Lord, I have heard by many of this man, [a]how much evil he hath done to thy saints at Jerusalem:

14 And here he hath authority from the chief priests to bind all [a]that call on thy name.

15 But the Lord said unto him, Go thy way: for [a]he is a chosen vessel unto me, to bear my name before [b]the Gentiles, and [c]kings, and the [d]children of Israel:

16 For [a]I will shew him how great things he must suffer for my [b]name's sake.

17 [a]And Ananias went his way, and entered into the house; and [b]putting his hands on him said, Brother Saul, the Lord, *even* Jesus, that appeared unto thee in the way as thou camest, hath sent me, that thou mightest receive thy sight, and [c]be filled with the Holy Ghost.

18 And immediately there fell from his eyes as it had been scales: and he received sight forthwith, and arose, and was baptized.

19 And when he had received meat, he was strengthened. [a]Then was Saul certain days with the disciples which were at Damascus.

Saul Preaches Christ

20 And straightway he preached Christ in the synagogues, that he is the Son of God.

21 But all that heard *him* were amazed, and

39 [a]1 Kin. 18:12; 2 Kin. 2:16; Ezek. 3:12, 14; 2 Cor. 12:2
40 [a]Acts 21:8

CHAPTER 9

1 [a]Acts 7:57; 8:1, 3; 26:10, 11; Gal. 1:13; 1 Tim. 1:13
2 [a]Acts 22:5
3 [a]Acts 22:6; 26:12, 13; 1 Cor. 15:8
4 [a][Matt. 25:40]
7 [a]Dan. 10:7; John 12:29; [Acts 22:9; 26:13]
10 [a]Acts 22:12
11 [a]Acts 21:39; 22:3
13 [a]Acts 9:1
14 [a]Acts 7:59; 9:2, 21; 1 Cor. 1:2; 2 Tim. 2:22
15 [a]Acts 13:2; 22:21; Rom. 1:1; 1 Cor. 15:10; Gal. 1:15; Eph. 3:7, 8; 1 Tim. 2:7; 2 Tim. 1:11 [b]Rom. 1:5; 11:13; Gal. 2:7, 8 [c]Acts 25:22, 23; 26:1 [d]Acts 21:40; Rom. 1:16; 9:1–5
16 [a]Acts 20:23; 2 Cor. 11:23–28; 12:7–10; Gal. 6:17; Phil. 1:29, 30 [b]2 Cor. 4:11
17 [a]Acts 22:12, 13 [b]Acts 8:17 [c]Acts 2:4; 4:31; 8:17; 13:52
19 [a]Acts 26:20

NKJV

still. And both Philip and the eunuch went down into the water, and he baptized him.

39 Now when they came up out of the water, [a]the Spirit of the Lord caught Philip away, so that the eunuch saw him no more; and he went on his way rejoicing.

40 But Philip was found at Azotus. And passing through, he preached in all the cities till he came to [a]Caesarea.

The Damascus Road: Saul Converted
(Acts 22:6–16; 26:12–18)

9 Then [a]Saul, still breathing threats and murder against the disciples of the Lord, went to the high priest

2 and asked [a]letters from him to the synagogues of Damascus, so that if he found any who were of the Way, whether men or women, he might bring them bound to Jerusalem.

3 [a]As he journeyed he came near Damascus, and suddenly a light shone around him from heaven.

4 Then he fell to the ground, and heard a voice saying to him, "Saul, Saul, [a]why are you persecuting Me?"

5 And he said, "Who are You, Lord?" Then the Lord said, "I am Jesus, whom you are persecuting. *It *is* hard for you to kick against the goads."

6 So he, trembling and astonished, said, "Lord, what do You want me to do?" Then the Lord *said* to him, "Arise and go into the city, and you will be told what you must do."

7 And [a]the men who journeyed with him stood speechless, hearing a voice but seeing no one.

8 Then Saul arose from the ground, and when his eyes were opened he saw no one. But they led him by the hand and brought *him* into Damascus.

9 And he was three days without sight, and neither ate nor drank.

Ananias Baptizes Saul

10 Now there was a certain disciple at Damascus [a]named Ananias; and to him the Lord said in a vision, "Ananias." And he said, "Here I am, Lord."

11 So the Lord *said* to him, "Arise and go to the street called Straight, and inquire at the house of Judas for *one* called Saul [a]of Tarsus, for behold, he is praying.

12 "And in a vision he has seen a man named Ananias coming in and putting *his* hand on him, so that he might receive his sight."

13 Then Ananias answered, "Lord, I have heard from many about this man, [a]how much harm he has done to Your saints in Jerusalem.

14 "And here he has authority from the chief priests to bind all [a]who call on Your name."

15 But the Lord said to him, "Go, for [a]he is a chosen vessel of Mine to bear My name before [b]Gentiles, [c]kings, and the [d]children of Israel.

16 "For [a]I will show him how many things he must suffer for My [b]name's sake."

17 [a]And Ananias went his way and entered the house; and [b]laying his hands on him he said, "Brother Saul, the Lord *Jesus, who appeared to you on the road as you came, has sent me that you may receive your sight and [c]be filled with the Holy Spirit."

18 Immediately there fell from his eyes *something* like scales, and he received his sight at once; and he arose and was baptized.

19 So when he had received food, he was strengthened. [a]Then Saul spent some days with the disciples at Damascus.

Saul Preaches Christ

20 Immediately he preached *the Christ in the synagogues, that He is the Son of God.

21 Then all who heard were amazed, and

---

*9:5 NU, M omit the rest of v. 5 and begin v. 6 with *But arise and go*
9:17 M omits *Jesus*
9:20 NU *Jesus*

KJV

said; [a]Is not this he that destroyed them which
called on this name in Jerusalem, and came hither
for that intent, that he might bring them bound
unto the chief priests?
22 But Saul increased the more in strength,
[a]and confounded the Jews which dwelt at Damascus, proving that this is very Christ.

Saul Escapes Death

23 And after that many days were fulfilled,
[a]the Jews took counsel to kill him:
24 [a]But their laying await was known of
Saul. And they watched the gates day and night
to kill him.
25 Then the disciples took him by night, and
[a]let *him* down by the wall in a basket.

Saul at Jersualem

26 And [a]when Saul was come to Jerusalem,
he assayed to join himself to the disciples: but
they were all afraid of him, and believed not that
he was a disciple.
27 [a]But Barnabas took him, and brought *him*
to the apostles, and declared unto them how he
had seen the Lord in the way, and that he had
spoken to him, [b]and how he had preached boldly
at Damascus in the name of Jesus.
28 And [a]he was with them coming in and going out at Jerusalem.
29 And he spake boldly in the name of the
Lord Jesus, and disputed against the [a]Grecians:
[b]but they went about to slay him.
30 *Which* when the brethren knew, they
brought him down to Caesarea, and sent him forth
to Tarsus.

The Church Prospers

31 [a]Then had the churches rest throughout
all Judaea and Galilee and Samaria, and were
[b]edified; and walking in the [c]fear of the Lord, and
in the [d]comfort of the Holy Ghost, were [e]multi-
plied.

Aeneas Healed

32 And it came to pass, as Peter passed
[a]throughout all *quarters*, he came down also to the
saints which dwelt at Lydda.
33 And there he found a certain man named
Aeneas, which had kept his bed eight years, and
was sick of the palsy.
34 And Peter said unto him, Aeneas, [a]Jesus
Christ maketh thee whole: arise, and make thy
bed. And he arose immediately.
35 And all that dwelt at Lydda and [a]Saron
saw him, and [b]turned to the Lord.

Dorcas Restored to Life

36 Now there was at Joppa a certain disciple
named Tabitha, which by interpretation is called
Dorcas: this woman was full [a]of good works and
almsdeeds which she did.
37 And it came to pass in those days, that
she was sick, and died: whom when they had
washed, they laid *her* in [a]an upper chamber.
38 And forasmuch as Lydda was nigh to
Joppa, and the disciples had heard that Peter was
there, they sent unto him two men, desiring *him*
that he would not delay to come to them.
39 Then Peter arose and went with them.
When he was come, they brought him into the
upper chamber: and all the widows stood by him
weeping, and shewing the coats and garments
which Dorcas made, while she was with them.
40 But Peter [a]put them all forth, and
[b]kneeled down, and prayed; and turning *him* to
the body [c]said, Tabitha, arise. And she opened
her eyes: and when she saw Peter, she sat up.
41 And he gave her *his* hand, and lifted her
up, and when he had called the saints and widows,
presented her alive.
42 And it was known throughout all Joppa;
[a]and many believed in the Lord.

21 [a]Acts 8:3; 9:13; Gal. 1:13, 23
22 [a]Acts 18:28
23 [a]Acts 23:12; 2 Cor. 11:26
24 [a]2 Cor. 11:32
25 [a]Josh. 2:15; 1 Sam. 19:12
26 [a]Acts 22:17–20; 26:20; Gal. 1:17, 18
27 [a]Acts 4:36; 13:2 [b]Acts 9:20, 22
28 [a]Gal. 1:18
29 [a]Acts 6:1; 11:20 [b]Acts 9:23; 2 Cor. 11:26
31 [a]Acts 5:11; 8:1; 16:5 [b][Eph. 4:16, 29] [c]Ps. 34:9 [d]John 14:16 [e]Acts 16:5
32 [a]Acts 8:14
34 [a][Acts 3:6, 16; 4:10]
35 [a]1 Chr. 5:16; 27:29; Is. 33:9; 35:2; 65:10 [b]Acts 11:21; 15:19
36 [a]1 Tim. 2:10; Titus 3:8
37 [a]Acts 1:13; 9:39
40 [a]Matt. 9:25 [b]Luke 22:41; Acts 7:60 [c]Mark 5:41, 42; John 11:43
42 [a]John 11:45

*

9:31 NU *church . . . was*

NKJV

said, [a]"Is this not he who destroyed those who
called on this name in Jerusalem, and has come
here for that purpose, so that he might bring them
bound to the chief priests?"
22 But Saul increased all the more in
strength, [a]and confounded the Jews who dwelt
in Damascus, proving that this *Jesus* is the Christ.

Saul Escapes Death

23 Now after many days were past, [a]the Jews
plotted to kill him.
24 [a]But their plot became known to Saul.
And they watched the gates day and night, to kill
him.
25 Then the disciples took him by night and
[a]let *him* down through the wall in a large basket.

Saul at Jersualem

26 And [a]when Saul had come to Jerusalem,
he tried to join the disciples; but they were all
afraid of him, and did not believe that he was a
disciple.
27 [a]But Barnabas took him and brought *him*
to the apostles. And he declared to them how he
had seen the Lord on the road, and that He had
spoken to him, [b]and how he had preached boldly
at Damascus in the name of Jesus.
28 So [a]he was with them at Jerusalem, coming in and going out.
29 And he spoke boldly in the name of the
Lord Jesus and disputed against the [a]Hellenists,
[b]but they attempted to kill him.
30 When the brethren found out, they
brought him down to Caesarea and sent him out
to Tarsus.

The Church Prospers

31 [a]Then the *churches throughout all Judea,
Galilee, and Samaria had peace and were [b]edified.
And walking in the [c]fear of the Lord and in the
[d]comfort of the Holy Spirit, they were [e]multiplied.

Aeneas Healed

32 Now it came to pass, as Peter went
[a]through all *parts of the country*, that he also came
down to the saints who dwelt in Lydda.
33 There he found a certain man named Aeneas, who had been bedridden eight years and
was paralyzed.
34 And Peter said to him, "Aeneas, [a]Jesus
the Christ heals you. Arise and make your bed."
Then he arose immediately.
35 So all who dwelt at Lydda and [a]Sharon
saw him and [b]turned to the Lord.

Dorcas Restored to Life

36 At Joppa there was a certain disciple
named Tabitha, which is translated Dorcas. This
woman was full [a]of good works and charitable
deeds which she did.
37 But it happened in those days that she became sick and died. When they had washed her,
they laid *her* in [a]an upper room.
38 And since Lydda was near Joppa, and the
disciples had heard that Peter was there, they sent
two men to him, imploring *him* not to delay in
coming to them.
39 Then Peter arose and went with them.
When he had come, they brought *him* to the upper
room. And all the widows stood by him weeping,
showing the tunics and garments which Dorcas
had made while she was with them.
40 But Peter [a]put them all out, and [b]knelt
down and prayed. And turning to the body he
[c]said, "Tabitha, arise." And she opened her eyes,
and when she saw Peter she sat up.
41 Then he gave her *his* hand and lifted her
up; and when he had called the saints and widows,
he presented her alive.
42 And it became known throughout all
Joppa, [a]and many believed on the Lord.

KJV

43 And it came to pass, that he tarried many days in Joppa with one [a]Simon a tanner.

Cornelius Sends a Delegation

10 There was a certain man in [a]Caesarea called Cornelius, a centurion of the band called the Italian *band,*

2 [a]A devout *man,* and one that [b]feared God with all his house, which gave much alms to the people, and prayed to God alway.

3 [a]He saw in a vision evidently about the ninth hour of the day an angel of God coming in to him, and saying unto him, Cornelius.

4 And when he looked on him, he was afraid, and said, What is it, Lord? And he said unto him, Thy prayers and thine alms are come up for a memorial before God.

5 And now [a]send men to Joppa, and call for *one* Simon, whose surname is Peter:

6 He lodgeth with one [a]Simon a tanner, whose house is by the sea side: [b]he shall tell thee what thou oughtest to do.

7 And when the angel which spake unto Cornelius was departed, he called two of his household servants, and a devout soldier of them that waited on him continually;

8 And when he had declared all *these* things unto them, he sent them to Joppa.

Peter's Vision

9 On the morrow, as they went on their journey, and drew nigh unto the city, [a]Peter went up upon the housetop to pray about the sixth hour:

10 And he became very hungry, and would have eaten: but while they made ready, he fell into a trance,

11 And [a]saw heaven opened, and a certain vessel descending unto him, as it had been a great sheet knit at the four corners, and let down to the earth:

12 Wherein were all manner of fourfooted beasts of the earth, and wild beasts, and creeping things, and fowls of the air.

13 And there came a voice to him, Rise, Peter; kill, and eat.

14 But Peter said, Not so, Lord; [a]for I have never eaten any thing that is common or unclean.

15 And the voice *spake* unto him again the second time, [a]What God hath cleansed, *that* call not thou common.

16 This was done thrice: and the vessel was received up again into heaven.

Summoned to Caesarea

17 Now while Peter doubted in himself what this vision which he had seen should mean, behold, the men which were sent from Cornelius had made enquiry for Simon's house, and stood before the gate,

18 And called, and asked whether Simon, which was surnamed Peter, were lodged there.

19 While Peter thought on the vision, [a]the Spirit said unto him, Behold, three men seek thee.

20 [a]Arise therefore, and get thee down, and go with them, doubting nothing: for I have sent them.

21 Then Peter went down to the men which were sent unto him from Cornelius; and said, Behold, I am he whom ye seek: what *is* the cause wherefore ye are come?

22 And they said, Cornelius the centurion, a just man, and one that feareth God, and [a]of good report among all the nation of the Jews, was warned from God by an holy angel to send for thee into his house, and to hear words of thee.

23 Then called he them in, and lodged *them.* And on the morrow Peter went away with them, [a]and certain brethren from Joppa accompanied him.

43 [a]Acts 10:6

CHAPTER 10

1 [a]Acts 8:40; 23:23
2 [a]Acts 8:2; 9:22; 22:12 [b][Acts 10:22, 35; 13:16, 26]
3 [a]Acts 10:30; 11:13
5 [a]Acts 11:13, 14
6 [a]Acts 9:43 [b]Acts 11:14
9 [a]Acts 10:9–32; 11:5–14
11 [a]Ezek. 1:1; Matt. 3:16; Acts 7:56; Rev. 4:1; 19:11
14 [a]Lev. 11:4; 20:25; Deut. 14:3, 7; Ezek. 4:14
15 [a][Matt. 15:11; Mark 7:19]; Acts 10:28; [Rom. 14:14]; 1 Cor. 10:25; [1 Tim. 4:4; Titus 1:15]
19 [a]Acts 11:12
20 [a]Acts 15:7–9
22 [a]Acts 22:12
23 [a]Acts 10:45; 11:12

*

10:6 NU, M omit the rest of v. 6.
10:21 NU, M omit *who had been sent to him from Cornelius*

NKJV

43 So it was that he stayed many days in Joppa with [a]Simon, a tanner.

Cornelius Sends a Delegation

10 There was a certain man in [a]Caesarea called Cornelius, a centurion of what was called the Italian Regiment,

2 [a]a devout *man* and one who [b]feared God with all his household, who gave alms generously to the people, and prayed to God always.

3 About the ninth hour of the day [a]he saw clearly in a vision an angel of God coming in and saying to him, "Cornelius!"

4 And when he observed him, he was afraid, and said, "What is it, lord?" So he said to him, "Your prayers and your alms have come up for a memorial before God.

5 "Now [a]send men to Joppa, and send for Simon whose surname is Peter.

6 "He is lodging with [a]Simon, a tanner, whose house is by the sea. [b]He* will tell you what you must do."

7 And when the angel who spoke to him had departed, Cornelius called two of his household servants and a devout soldier from among those who waited on him continually.

8 So when he had explained all *these* things to them, he sent them to Joppa.

Peter's Vision

9 The next day, as they went on their journey and drew near the city, [a]Peter went up on the housetop to pray, about the sixth hour.

10 Then he became very hungry and wanted to eat; but while they made ready, he fell into a trance

11 and [a]saw heaven opened and an object like a great sheet bound at the four corners, descending to him and let down to the earth.

12 In it were all kinds of four-footed animals of the earth, wild beasts, creeping things, and birds of the air.

13 And a voice came to him, "Rise, Peter; kill and eat."

14 But Peter said, "Not so, Lord! [a]For I have never eaten anything common or unclean."

15 And a voice *spoke* to him again the second time, [a]"What God has cleansed you must not call common."

16 This was done three times. And the object was taken up into heaven again.

Summoned to Caesarea

17 Now while Peter wondered within himself what this vision which he had seen meant, behold, the men who had been sent from Cornelius had made inquiry for Simon's house, and stood before the gate.

18 And they called and asked whether Simon, whose surname was Peter, was lodging there.

19 While Peter thought about the vision, [a]the Spirit said to him, "Behold, three men are seeking you.

20 [a]"Arise therefore, go down and go with them, doubting nothing; for I have sent them."

21 Then Peter went down to the men *who had been sent to him from Cornelius, and said, "Yes, I am he whom you seek. For what reason have you come?"

22 And they said, "Cornelius *the* centurion, a just man, one who fears God and [a]has a good reputation among all the nation of the Jews, was divinely instructed by a holy angel to summon you to his house, and to hear words from you."

23 Then he invited them in and lodged *them.* On the next day Peter went away with them, [a]and some brethren from Joppa accompanied him.

KJV

Peter Meets Cornelius

24 And the morrow after they entered into
Caesarea. And Cornelius waited for them, and
had called together his kinsmen and near friends.
25 And as Peter was coming in, Cornelius
met him, and fell down at his feet, and worshipped
him.
26 But Peter took him up, saying, [a]Stand up;
I myself also am a man.
27 And as he talked with him, he went in,
and found many that were come together.
28 And he said unto them, Ye know how
[a]that it is an unlawful thing for a man that is a
Jew to keep company, or come unto one of another nation; but [b]God hath shewed me that I
should not call any man common or unclean.
29 Therefore came I *unto you* without gainsaying, as soon as I was sent for: I ask therefore
for what intent ye have sent for me?
30 And Cornelius said, Four days ago I was
fasting until this hour; and at the ninth hour I
prayed in my house, and, behold, [a]a man stood
before me [b]in bright clothing,
31 And said, Cornelius, [a]thy prayer is heard,
[b]and thine alms are had in remembrance in the
sight of God.
32 Send therefore to Joppa, and call hither
Simon, whose surname is Peter; he is lodged in
the house of *one* Simon a tanner by the sea side:
who, when he cometh, shall speak unto thee.
33 Immediately therefore I sent to thee; and
thou hast well done that thou art come. Now
therefore are we all here present before God, to
hear all things that are commanded thee of God.

Preaching to Cornelius' Household

34 Then Peter opened *his* mouth, and said,
[a]Of a truth I perceive that God is no respecter of
persons:
35 But [a]in every nation he that feareth him,
and worketh righteousness, is [b]accepted with
him.
36 The word which *God* sent unto the children of Israel, [a]preaching peace by Jesus Christ:
([b]he is Lord of all:)
37 That word, *I say,* ye know, which was published throughout all Judaea, and [a]began from
Galilee, after the baptism which John preached;
38 How [a]God anointed Jesus of Nazareth
with the Holy Ghost and with power: who [b]went
about doing good, and healing all that were oppressed of the devil; [c]for God was with him.
39 And we are [a]witnesses of all things which
he did both in the land of the Jews, and in Jerusalem; whom they [b]slew and hanged on a tree:
40 Him [a]God raised up the third day, and
shewed him openly;
41 [a]Not to all the people, but unto witnesses
chosen before of God, *even* to us, [b]who did eat
and drink with him after he rose from the dead.
42 And [a]he commanded us to preach unto
the people, and to testify [b]that it is he which was
ordained of God *to be* the Judge [c]of quick and
dead.
43 [a]To him give all the prophets witness, that
through his name [b]whosoever believeth in him
shall receive [c]remission of sins.

The Holy Spirit Falls on the Gentiles

44 While Peter yet spake these words, [a]the
Holy Ghost fell on all them which heard the word.
45 [a]And they of the circumcision which believed were astonished, as many as came with Peter, [b]because that on the Gentiles also was poured
out the gift of the Holy Ghost.
46 For they heard them speak with tongues,
and magnify God. Then answered Peter,
47 Can any man forbid water, that these
should not be baptized, which have received the
Holy Ghost [a]as well as we?
48 [a]And he commanded them to be baptized

26 [a]Acts 14:14, 15
28 [a]John 4:9; 18:28 [b][Acts 10:14, 35; 15:8, 9]
30 [a]Acts 1:10 [b]Matt. 28:3
31 [a]Dan. 10:12 [b]Heb. 6:10
34 [a]Deut. 10:17
35 [a][Eph. 2:13] [b]Ps. 15:1, 2
36 [a]Is. 57:19 [b]Rom. 10:12
37 [a]Luke 4:14
38 [a]Luke 4:18 [b]Matt. 4:23 [c]John 3:2; 8:29
39 [a]Acts 1:8 [b]Acts 2:23
40 [a]Acts 2:24
41 [a][John 14:17, 19, 22; 15:27] [b]Luke 24:30, 41–43
42 [a]Matt. 28:19 [b]John 5:22, 27 [c]1 Pet. 4:5
43 [a]Zech. 13:1 [b]Gal. 3:22 [c]Acts 13:38, 39
44 [a]Acts 4:31
45 [a]Acts 10:23 [b]Acts 11:18
47 [a]Acts 2:4; 10:44; 11:17; 15:8
48 [a]1 Cor. 1:14–17

NKJV

Peter Meets Cornelius

24 And the following day they entered
Caesarea. Now Cornelius was waiting for them,
and had called together his relatives and close
friends.
25 As Peter was coming in, Cornelius met
him and fell down at his feet and worshiped *him.*
26 But Peter lifted him up, saying, [a]"Stand
up; I myself am also a man."
27 And as he talked with him, he went in and
found many who had come together.
28 Then he said to them, "You know how
[a]unlawful it is for a Jewish man to keep company
with or go to one of another nation. But [b]God
has shown me that I should not call any man common or unclean.
29 "Therefore I came without objection as
soon as I was sent for. I ask, then, for what reason
have you sent for me?"
30 So Cornelius said, *"Four days ago I was
fasting until this hour; and at the ninth hour I
prayed in my house, and behold, [a]a man stood
before me [b]in bright clothing,
31 "and said, 'Cornelius, [a]your prayer has
been heard, and [b]your alms are remembered in
the sight of God.
32 'Send therefore to Joppa and call Simon
here, whose surname is Peter. He is lodging in
the house of Simon, a tanner, by the sea. *When
he comes, he will speak to you.'
33 "So I sent to you immediately, and you
have done well to come. Now therefore, we are
all present before God, to hear all the things commanded you by God."

Preaching to Cornelius' Household

34 Then Peter opened *his* mouth and said:
[a]"In truth I perceive that God shows no partiality.
35 "But [a]in every nation whoever fears Him
and works righteousness is [b]accepted by Him.
36 "The word which *God* sent to the children
of Israel, [a]preaching peace through Jesus Christ—
[b]He is Lord of all—
37 "that word you know, which was proclaimed throughout all Judea, and [a]began from
Galilee after the baptism which John preached:
38 "how [a]God anointed Jesus of Nazareth
with the Holy Spirit and with power, who [b]went
about doing good and healing all who were oppressed by the devil, [c]for God was with Him.
39 "And we are [a]witnesses of all things
which He did both in the land of the Jews and in
Jerusalem, whom *they [b]killed by hanging on a
tree.
40 "Him [a]God raised up on the third day, and
showed Him openly,
41 [a]"not to all the people, but to witnesses
chosen before by God, *even* to us [b]who ate and
drank with Him after He arose from the dead.
42 "And [a]He commanded us to preach to the
people, and to testify [b]that it is He who was ordained by God *to be* Judge [c]of the living and the
dead.
43 [a]"To Him all the prophets witness that,
through His name, [b]whoever believes in Him will
receive [c]remission of sins."

The Holy Spirit Falls on the Gentiles

44 While Peter was still speaking these
words, [a]the Holy Spirit fell upon all those who
heard the word.
45 [a]And those of the circumcision who believed were astonished, as many as came with Peter, [b]because the gift of the Holy Spirit had been
poured out on the Gentiles also.
46 For they heard them speak with tongues
and magnify God. Then Peter answered,
47 "Can anyone forbid water, that these
should not be baptized who have received the
Holy Spirit [a]just as we *have?"*
48 [a]And he commanded them to be baptized

*

10:30 NU *Four days ago to this hour, at the ninth hour*
10:32 NU omits the rest of v. 32.
10:39 NU, M *they also*

KJV

[b]in the name of the Lord. Then prayed they him
to tarry certain days.

Peter Defends God's Grace

11 And the apostles and brethren that were
in Judaea heard that the Gentiles had also
received the word of God.
2 And when Peter was come up to Jerusalem, [a]they that were of the circumcision contended with him,
3 Saying, [a]Thou wentest in to men uncircumcised, [b]and didst eat with them.
4 But Peter rehearsed *the matter* from the
beginning, and expounded *it* [a]by order unto them,
saying,
5 [a]I was in the city of Joppa praying: and
in a trance I saw a vision, A certain vessel descend, as it had been a great sheet, let down from
heaven by four corners; and it came even to me:
6 Upon the which when I had fastened mine
eyes, I considered, and saw fourfooted beasts of
the earth, and wild beasts, and creeping things,
and fowls of the air.
7 And I heard a voice saying unto me, Arise,
Peter; slay and eat.
8 But I said, Not so, Lord: for nothing common or unclean hath at any time entered into my
mouth.
9 But the voice answered me again from
heaven, What God hath cleansed, *that* call not
thou common.
10 And this was done three times: and all
were drawn up again into heaven.
11 And, behold, immediately there were
three men already come unto the house where I
was, sent from Caesarea unto me.
12 And [a]the Spirit bade me go with them,
nothing doubting. Moreover [b]these six brethren
accompanied me, and we entered into the man's
house:
13 [a]And he shewed us how he had seen an
angel in his house, which stood and said unto him,
Send men to Joppa, and call for Simon, whose
surname is Peter;
14 Who shall tell thee words, whereby thou
and all thy house shall be saved.
15 And as I began to speak, the Holy Ghost
fell on them, [a]as on us at the beginning.
16 Then remembered I the word of the Lord,
how that he said, [a]John indeed baptized with water; but [b]ye shall be baptized with the Holy Ghost.
17 [a]Forasmuch then as God gave them the
like gift as *he did* unto us, who believed on the
Lord Jesus Christ; [b]what was I, that I could withstand God?
18 When they heard these things, they held
their peace, and glorified God, saying, [a]Then hath
God also to the Gentiles granted repentance unto
life.

Barnabas and Saul at Antioch

19 [a]Now they which were scattered abroad
upon the persecution that arose about Stephen
travelled as far as Phenice, and Cyprus, and Antioch, preaching the word to none but unto the Jews
only.
20 And some of them were men of Cyprus
and Cyrene, which, when they were come to Antioch, spake unto [a]the Grecians, preaching the Lord
Jesus.
21 And [a]the hand of the Lord was with them:
and a great number believed, and [b]turned unto
the Lord.
22 Then tidings of these things came unto the
ears of the church which was in Jerusalem: and
they sent forth [a]Barnabas, that he should go as
far as Antioch.
23 Who, when he came, and had seen the
grace of God, was glad, and [a]exhorted them all,
that with purpose of heart they would cleave unto
the Lord.
24 For he was a good man, and [a]full of the

48 [b]Acts 2:38; 8:16; 19:5

CHAPTER 11

2 [a]Acts 10:45
3 [a]Acts 10:28 [b]Gal. 2:12
4 [a]Luke 1:3
5 [a]Acts 10:9
12 [a][John 16:13] [b]Acts 10:23
13 [a]Acts 10:30
15 [a]Acts 2:1–4; 15:7–9
16 [a]John 1:26, 33 [b]Is. 44:3
17 [a][Acts 15:8, 9] [b]Acts 10:47
18 [a]Rom. 10:12, 13; 15:9, 16
19 [a]Acts 8:1, 4
20 [a]Acts 6:1; 9:29
21 [a]Luke 1:66 [b]Acts 9:35; 14:1
22 [a]Acts 4:36; 9:27
23 [a]Acts 13:43; 14:22
24 [a]Acts 6:5

NKJV

[b]in the name of the Lord. Then they asked him
to stay a few days.

Peter Defends God's Grace

11 Now the apostles and brethren who were
in Judea heard that the Gentiles had also
received the word of God.
2 And when Peter came up to Jerusalem,
[a]those of the circumcision contended with him,
3 saying, [a]"You went in to uncircumcised
men [b]and ate with them!"
4 But Peter explained *it* to them [a]in order
from the beginning, saying:
5 [a]"I was in the city of Joppa praying; and
in a trance I saw a vision, an object descending
like a great sheet, let down from heaven by four
corners; and it came to me.
6 "When I observed it intently and considered, I saw four-footed animals of the earth, wild
beasts, creeping things, and birds of the air.
7 "And I heard a voice saying to me, 'Rise,
Peter; kill and eat.'
8 "But I said, 'Not so, Lord! For nothing
common or unclean has at any time entered my
mouth.'
9 "But the voice answered me again from
heaven, 'What God has cleansed you must not
call common.'
10 "Now this was done three times, and all
were drawn up again into heaven.
11 "At that very moment, three men stood
before the house where I was, having been sent
to me from Caesarea.
12 "Then [a]the Spirit told me to go with them,
doubting nothing. Moreover [b]these six brethren
accompanied me, and we entered the man's
house.
13 [a]"And he told us how he had seen an angel standing in his house, who said to him, 'Send
men to Joppa, and call for Simon whose surname
is Peter,
14 'who will tell you words by which you and
all your household will be saved.'
15 "And as I began to speak, the Holy Spirit
fell upon them, [a]as upon us at the beginning.
16 "Then I remembered the word of the Lord,
how He said, [a]'John indeed baptized with water,
but [b]you shall be baptized with the Holy Spirit.'
17 [a]"If therefore God gave them the same gift
as *He gave* us when we believed on the Lord Jesus
Christ, [b]who was I that I could withstand God?"
18 When they heard these things they became silent; and they glorified God, saying,
[a]"Then God has also granted to the Gentiles repentance to life."

Barnabas and Saul at Antioch

19 [a]Now those who were scattered after the
persecution that arose over Stephen traveled as
far as Phoenicia, Cyprus, and Antioch, preaching
the word to no one but the Jews only.
20 But some of them were men from Cyprus
and Cyrene, who, when they had come to Antioch,
spoke to [a]the Hellenists, preaching the Lord
Jesus.
21 And [a]the hand of the Lord was with them,
and a great number believed and [b]turned to the
Lord.
22 Then news of these things came to the
ears of the church in Jerusalem, and they sent
out [a]Barnabas to go as far as Antioch.
23 When he came and had seen the grace of
God, he was glad, and [a]encouraged them all that
with purpose of heart they should continue with
the Lord.
24 For he was a good man, [a]full of the Holy

KJV

Holy Ghost and of faith: [b]and much people was
added unto the Lord.
25 Then departed Barnabas to [a]Tarsus, for
to seek Saul:
26 And when he had found him, he brought
him unto Antioch. And it came to pass, that a
whole year they assembled themselves with the
church, and taught much people. And the disciples were called Christians first in Antioch.

Relief to Judea

27 And in these days came [a]prophets from
Jerusalem unto Antioch.
28 And there stood up one of them named
[a]Agabus, and signified by the Spirit that there
should be great dearth throughout all the world:
which came to pass in the days of [b]Claudius
Caesar.
29 Then the disciples, every man according
to his ability, determined to send [a]relief unto the
brethren which dwelt in Judaea:
30 [a]Which also they did, and sent it to the
elders by the hands of Barnabas and Saul.

Herod's Violence to the Church

12 Now about that time Herod the king
stretched forth *his* hands to vex certain of
the church.
2 And he killed James [a]the brother of John
with the sword.
3 And because he saw it pleased the Jews,
he proceeded further to take Peter also. (Then
were [a]the days of unleavened bread.)
4 And [a]when he had apprehended him, he
put *him* in prison, and delivered *him* to four
quaternions of soldiers to keep him; intending after Easter to bring him forth to the people.

Peter Freed from Prison

5 Peter therefore was kept in prison: but
prayer was made without ceasing of the church
unto God for him.
6 And when Herod would have brought him
forth, the same night Peter was sleeping between
two soldiers, bound with two chains: and the
keepers before the door kept the prison.
7 And, behold, [a]the angel of the Lord came
upon *him*, and a light shined in the prison: and
he smote Peter on the side, and raised him up,
saying, Arise up quickly. And his chains fell off
from *his* hands.
8 And the angel said unto him, Gird thyself,
and bind on thy sandals. And so he did. And he
saith unto him, Cast thy garment about thee, and
follow me.
9 And he went out, and followed him; and
[a]wist not that it was true which was done by the
angel; but thought [b]he saw a vision.
10 When they were past the first and the second ward, they came unto the iron gate that leadeth unto the city; [a]which opened to them of his
own accord: and they went out, and passed on
through one street; and forthwith the angel departed from him.
11 And when Peter was come to himself, he
said, Now I know of a surety, that [a]the Lord hath
sent his angel, and [b]hath delivered me out of the
hand of Herod, and *from* all the expectation of
the people of the Jews.
12 And when he had considered *the thing*,
[a]he came to the house of Mary the mother of
[b]John, whose surname was Mark; where many
were gathered together [c]praying.
13 And as Peter knocked at the door of the
gate, a damsel came to hearken, named Rhoda.
14 And when she knew Peter's voice, she
opened not the gate for gladness, but ran in, and
told how Peter stood before the gate.
15 And they said unto her, Thou art mad. But
she constantly affirmed that it was even so. Then
said they, [a]It is his angel.
16 But Peter continued knocking: and when

24 [b]Acts 5:14; 11:21
25 [a]Acts 9:11, 30
27 [a]1 Cor. 12:28
28 [a]Acts 21:10 [b]Acts 18:2
29 [a]1 Cor. 16:1
30 [a]Acts 12:25

CHAPTER 12

2 [a]Matt. 4:21; 20:23
3 [a]Ex. 12:15; 23:15
4 [a]John 21:18
7 [a]Acts 5:19
9 [a]Ps. 126:1 [b]Acts 10:3, 17; 11:5
10 [a]Acts 5:19; 16:26
11 [a][Ps. 34:7] [b]Job 5:19
12 [a]Acts 4:23 [b]Acts 13:5, 13; 15:37 [c]Acts 12:5
15 [a][Matt. 18:10]

*______

12:5 NU *constantly* or *earnestly*

NKJV

Spirit and of faith. [b]And a great many people were
added to the Lord.
25 Then Barnabas departed for [a]Tarsus to
seek Saul.
26 And when he had found him, he brought
him to Antioch. So it was that for a whole year
they assembled with the church and taught a great
many people. And the disciples were first called
Christians in Antioch.

Relief to Judea

27 And in these days [a]prophets came from
Jerusalem to Antioch.
28 Then one of them, named [a]Agabus, stood
up and showed by the Spirit that there was going
to be a great famine throughout all the world,
which also happened in the days of [b]Claudius
Caesar.
29 Then the disciples, each according to his
ability, determined to send [a]relief to the brethren
dwelling in Judea.
30 [a]This they also did, and sent it to the elders by the hands of Barnabas and Saul.

Herod's Violence to the Church

12 Now about that time Herod the king
stretched out *his* hand to harass some from
the church.
2 Then he killed James [a]the brother of John
with the sword.
3 And because he saw that it pleased the
Jews, he proceeded further to seize Peter also.
Now it was *during* [a]the Days of Unleavened
Bread.
4 So [a]when he had arrested him, he put *him*
in prison, and delivered *him* to four squads of soldiers to keep him, intending to bring him before
the people after Passover.

Peter Freed from Prison

5 Peter was therefore kept in prison, but
*constant prayer was offered to God for him by
the church.
6 And when Herod was about to bring him
out, that night Peter was sleeping, bound with two
chains between two soldiers; and the guards before the door were keeping the prison.
7 Now behold, [a]an angel of the Lord stood
by *him*, and a light shone in the prison; and he
struck Peter on the side and raised him up, saying,
"Arise quickly!" And his chains fell off *his* hands.
8 Then the angel said to him, "Gird yourself
and tie on your sandals"; and so he did. And he
said to him, "Put on your garment and follow me."
9 So he went out and followed him, and [a]did
not know that what was done by the angel was
real, but thought [b]he was seeing a vision.
10 When they were past the first and the second guard posts, they came to the iron gate that
leads to the city, [a]which opened to them of its
own accord; and they went out and went down
one street, and immediately the angel departed
from him.
11 And when Peter had come to himself, he
said, "Now I know for certain that [a]the Lord has
sent His angel, and [b]has delivered me from the
hand of Herod and *from* all the expectation of
the Jewish people."
12 So, when he had considered *this*, [a]he
came to the house of Mary, the mother of [b]John
whose surname was Mark, where many were
gathered together [c]praying.
13 And as Peter knocked at the door of the
gate, a girl named Rhoda came to answer.
14 When she recognized Peter's voice, because of *her* gladness she did not open the gate,
but ran in and announced that Peter stood before
the gate.
15 But they said to her, "You are beside yourself!" Yet she kept insisting that it was so. So they
said, [a]"It is his angel."
16 Now Peter continued knocking; and when

KJV

they had opened *the door,* and saw him, they were
astonished.
17 But he, [a]beckoning unto them with the
hand to hold their peace, declared unto them how
the Lord had brought him out of the prison. And
he said, Go shew these things unto James, and
to the brethren. And he departed, and went into
another place.
18 Now as soon as it was day, there was no
small stir among the soldiers, what was become
of Peter.
19 And when Herod had sought for him, and
found him not, he examined the keepers, and
commanded that *they* should be put to death. And
he went down from Judaea to Caesarea, and *there*
abode.

Herod's Violent Death

20 And Herod was highly displeased with
them of [a]Tyre and Sidon: but they came with one
accord to him, and, having made Blastus the
king's chamberlain their friend, desired peace; because [b]their country was nourished by the king's
country.
21 And upon a set day Herod, arrayed in
royal apparel, sat upon his throne, and made an
oration unto them.
22 And the people gave a shout, *saying, It is*
the voice of a god, and not of a man.
23 And immediately the angel of the Lord
[a]smote him, because [b]he gave not God the glory:
and he was eaten of worms, and gave up the
ghost.
24 But [a]the word of God grew and multiplied.

Barnabas and Saul Appointed

25 And [a]Barnabas and Saul returned from
Jerusalem, when they had [b]fulfilled *their* ministry, and [c]took with them [d]John, whose surname
was Mark.

13 Now there were [a]in the church that was
at Antioch certain prophets and teachers;
as [b]Barnabas, and Simeon that was called Niger,
and [c]Lucius of Cyrene, and Manaen, which had
been brought up with Herod the tetrarch, and
Saul.
2 As they ministered to the Lord, and
fasted, the Holy Ghost said, [a]Separate me Barnabas and Saul for the work [b]whereunto I have
called them.
3 And [a]when they had fasted and prayed,
and laid *their* hands on them, they sent *them*
away.

Preaching in Cyprus

4 So they, being sent forth by the Holy
Ghost, departed unto Seleucia; and from thence
they sailed to [a]Cyprus.
5 And when they were at Salamis, [a]they
preached the word of God in the synagogues of
the Jews: and they had also [b]John to *their*
minister.
6 And when they had gone through the isle
unto Paphos, they found [a]a certain sorcerer, a
false prophet, a Jew, whose name *was* Bar–jesus:
7 Which was with the deputy of the country,
Sergius Paulus, a prudent man; who called for
Barnabas and Saul, and desired to hear the word
of God.
8 But [a]Elymas the sorcerer (for so is his
name by interpretation) withstood them, seeking
to turn away the deputy from the faith.
9 Then Saul, (who also *is called* Paul,) [a]filled
with the Holy Ghost, set his eyes on him,
10 And said, O full of all subtilty and all mischief, [a]*thou* child of the devil, *thou* enemy of all
righteousness, wilt thou not cease to pervert the
right ways of the Lord?
11 And now, behold, [a]the hand of the Lord
is upon thee, and thou shalt be blind, not seeing
the sun for a season. And immediately there fell

17 [a]Acts 13:16; 19:33; 21:40
20 [a]Matt. 11:21 [b]1 Kin. 5:11; Ezra 3:7; Ezek. 27:17
23 [a]1 Sam. 25:38; 2 Sam. 24:16, 17; 2 Kin. 19:35; Acts 5:19 [b]Ps. 115:1
24 [a]Is. 55:11; Acts 6:7; 19:20
25 [a]Acts 11:30 [b]Acts 11:30 [c]Acts 13:5, 13 [d]Acts 12:12; 15:37

CHAPTER 13

1 [a]Acts 14:26 [b]Acts 11:22 [c]Rom. 16:21
2 [a]Num. 8:14; Acts 9:15; 22:21; Rom. 1:1; Gal. 1:15; 2:9 [b]Matt. 9:38; Acts 14:26; Rom. 10:15; Eph. 3:7, 8; 1 Tim. 2:7; 2 Tim. 1:11; Heb. 5:4
3 [a]Matt. 9:15; Mark 2:20; Luke 5:35; Acts 6:6
4 [a]Acts 4:36
5 [a][Acts 13:46] [b]Acts 12:25; 15:37
6 [a]Acts 8:9
8 [a]Ex. 7:11; 2 Tim. 3:8
9 [a]Acts 2:4; 4:8
10 [a]Matt. 13:38; John 8:44; [1 John 3:8]
11 [a]Ex. 9:3; 1 Sam. 5:6; Job 19:21; Ps. 32:4; Heb. 10:31

*
12:25 NU, M *to*
13:6 NU *the whole island*

NKJV

they opened *the door* and saw him, they were
astonished.
17 But [a]motioning to them with his hand to
keep silent, he declared to them how the Lord
had brought him out of the prison. And he said,
"Go, tell these things to James and to the brethren." And he departed and went to another place.
18 Then, as soon as it was day, there was
no small stir among the soldiers about what had
become of Peter.
19 But when Herod had searched for him and
not found him, he examined the guards and commanded that *they* should be put to death. And
he went down from Judea to Caesarea, and stayed
there.

Herod's Violent Death

20 Now Herod had been very angry with the
people of [a]Tyre and Sidon; but they came to him
with one accord, and having made Blastus the
king's personal aide their friend, they asked for
peace, because [b]their country was supplied with
food by the king's *country.*
21 So on a set day Herod, arrayed in royal
apparel, sat on his throne and gave an oration to
them.
22 And the people kept shouting, "The voice
of a god and not of a man!"
23 Then immediately an angel of the Lord
[a]struck him, because [b]he did not give glory to
God. And he was eaten by worms and died.
24 But [a]the word of God grew and multiplied.

Barnabas and Saul Appointed

25 And [a]Barnabas and Saul returned *from
Jerusalem when they had [b]fulfilled *their* ministry,
and they also [c]took with them [d]John whose surname was Mark.

13 Now [a]in the church that was at Antioch
there were certain prophets and teachers:
[b]Barnabas, Simeon who was called Niger, [c]Lucius
of Cyrene, Manaen who had been brought up with
Herod the tetrarch, and Saul.
2 As they ministered to the Lord and fasted,
the Holy Spirit said, [a]"Now separate to Me Barnabas and Saul for the work [b]to which I have called
them."
3 Then, [a]having fasted and prayed, and laid
hands on them, they sent *them* away.

Preaching in Cyprus

4 So, being sent out by the Holy Spirit, they
went down to Seleucia, and from there they sailed
to [a]Cyprus.
5 And when they arrived in Salamis, [a]they
preached the word of God in the synagogues of
the Jews. They also had [b]John as *their* assistant.
6 Now when they had gone through *the island to Paphos, they found [a]a certain sorcerer, a
false prophet, a Jew whose name *was* Bar-Jesus,
7 who was with the proconsul, Sergius Paulus, an intelligent man. This man called for Barnabas and Saul and sought to hear the word of God.
8 But [a]Elymas the sorcerer (for so his name
is translated) withstood them, seeking to turn the
proconsul away from the faith.
9 Then Saul, who also *is called* Paul, [a]filled
with the Holy Spirit, looked intently at him
10 and said, "O full of all deceit and all fraud,
[a]*you* son of the devil, *you* enemy of all righteousness, will you not cease perverting the straight
ways of the Lord?
11 "And now, indeed, [a]the hand of the Lord
is upon you, and you shall be blind, not seeing
the sun for a time." And immediately a dark mist

KJV

on him a mist and a darkness; and he went about
seeking some to lead him by the hand.
12 Then the deputy, when he saw what was
done, believed, being astonished at the doctrine
of the Lord.

At Antioch in Pisidia

13 Now when Paul and his company loosed
from Paphos, they came to Perga in Pamphylia:
and [a]John departing from them returned to
Jerusalem.
14 But when they departed from Perga, they
came to Antioch in Pisidia, and [a]went into the
synagogue on the sabbath day, and sat down.
15 And [a]after the reading of the law and the
prophets the rulers of the synagogue sent unto
them, saying, *Ye* men *and* brethren, if ye have
[b]any word of exhortation for the people, say on.
16 Then Paul stood up, and beckoning with
his hand said, Men of Israel, and [a]ye that fear
God, give audience.
17 The God of this people of Israel [a]chose
our fathers, and exalted the people [b]when they
dwelt as strangers in the land of Egypt, and with
an high arm [c]brought he them out of it.
18 And [a]about the time of forty years suffered he their manners in the wilderness.
19 And when he had destroyed [a]seven nations in the land of Chanaan, [b]he divided their
land to them by lot.
20 And after that [a]he gave *unto them* judges
about the space of four hundred and fifty years,
[b]until Samuel the prophet.
21 [a]And afterward they desired a king: and
God gave unto them [b]Saul the son of Cis, a man
of the tribe of Benjamin, by the space of forty
years.
22 And [a]when he had removed him, [b]he
raised up unto them David to be their king; to
whom also he gave testimony, and said, [c]I HAVE
FOUND DAVID the *son* of Jesse, [d]A MAN AFTER MINE
OWN HEART, which shall fulfil all my will.
23 [a]Of this man's seed hath God according
[b]to *his* promise raised unto Israel [c]a Saviour,
Jesus:
24 [a]When John had first preached before his
coming the baptism of repentance to all the people
of Israel.
25 And as John fulfilled his course, he said,
[a]Whom think ye that I am? I am not *he*. But, behold, [b]there cometh one after me, whose shoes
of *his* feet I am not worthy to loose.
26 Men *and* brethren, children of the stock
of Abraham, and [a]whosoever among you feareth
God, [b]to you is the word of this salvation sent.
27 For they that dwell at Jerusalem, and their
rulers, [a]because they knew him not, nor yet the
voices of the prophets which are read every sabbath day, they have fulfilled *them* in condemning
him.
28 [a]And though they found no cause of death
in him, yet desired they Pilate that he should be
slain.
29 [a]And when they had fulfilled all that was
written of him, [b]they took *him* down from the tree,
and laid *him* in a sepulchre.
30 [a]But God raised him from the dead:
31 And [a]he was seen many days of them
which came up with him from Galilee to Jerusalem, who are his witnesses unto the people.
32 And we declare unto you glad tidings, how
that [a]the promise which was made unto the
fathers,
33 God hath fulfilled the same unto us their
children, in that he hath raised up Jesus again;
as it is also written in the second psalm, [a]THOU
ART MY SON, THIS DAY HAVE I BEGOTTEN THEE.
34 And as concerning that he raised him up
from the dead, *now* no more to return to corruption, he said on this wise, [a]I WILL GIVE YOU THE
SURE MERCIES OF DAVID.

13 [a]Acts 15:38
14 [a]Acts 16:13
15 [a]Luke 4:16 [b]Heb. 13:22
16 [a]Acts 10:35
17 [a]Ex. 6:1, 6; 13:14, 16; Deut. 7:6–8 [b]Acts 7:17 [c]Ex. 14:8
18 [a]Ex. 16:35; Num. 14:34; Acts 7:36
19 [a]Deut. 7:1 [b]Josh. 14:1, 2; 19:51; Ps. 78:55
20 [a]Judg. 2:16; 1 Sam. 4:18; 7:15 [b]1 Sam. 3:20; Acts 3:24
21 [a]1 Sam. 8:5 [b]1 Sam. 10:20–24
22 [a]1 Sam. 15:23, 26, 28 [b]1 Sam. 16:1, 12, 13 [c]Ps. 89:20 [d]1 Sam. 13:14
23 [a]Is. 11:1 [b]Ps. 132:11 [c][Matt. 1:21]
24 [a]Matt. 3:1; [Luke 3:3]
25 [a]Matt. 3:11; Mark 1:7; Luke 3:16 [b]John 1:20, 27
26 [a]Ps. 66:16 [b]Matt. 10:6
27 [a]Luke 23:34
28 [a]Matt. 27:22, 23; Mark 15:13, 14; Luke 23:21–23; John 19:15; Acts 3:14; [2 Cor. 5:21; Heb. 4:15]; 1 Pet. 2:22
29 [a]Luke 18:31 [b]Matt. 27:57–61; Mark 15:42–47; Luke 23:50–56; John 19:38–42
30 [a]Ps. 16:10, 11; Hos. 6:2; Matt. 12:39, 40; 28:6
31 [a]Matt. 28:16; Acts 1:3, 11; 1 Cor. 15:5–8
32 [a][Gen. 3:15]
33 [a]Ps. 2:7; Heb. 1:5
34 [a]Is. 55:3

*———

13:17 M omits *Israel*
13:23 M *salvation, after*

NKJV

fell on him, and he went around seeking someone
to lead him by the hand.
12 Then the proconsul believed, when he saw
what had been done, being astonished at the
teaching of the Lord.

At Antioch in Pisidia

13 Now when Paul and his party set sail from
Paphos, they came to Perga in Pamphylia; and
[a]John, departing from them, returned to Jerusalem.
14 But when they departed from Perga, they
came to Antioch in Pisidia, and [a]went into the
synagogue on the Sabbath day and sat down.
15 And [a]after the reading of the Law and the
Prophets, the rulers of the synagogue sent to
them, saying, "Men *and* brethren, if you have
[b]any word of exhortation for the people, say on."
16 Then Paul stood up, and motioning with
his hand said, "Men of Israel, and [a]you who fear
God, listen:
17 "The God of this people *Israel [a]chose our
fathers, and exalted the people [b]when they dwelt
as strangers in the land of Egypt, and with an
uplifted arm He [c]brought them out of it.
18 "Now [a]for a time of about forty years He
put up with their ways in the wilderness.
19 "And when He had destroyed [a]seven nations in the land of Canaan, [b]He distributed their
land to them by allotment.
20 "After that [a]He gave *them* judges for
about four hundred and fifty years, [b]until Samuel
the prophet.
21 [a]"And afterward they asked for a king;
so God gave them [b]Saul the son of Kish, a man
of the tribe of Benjamin, for forty years.
22 "And [a]when He had removed him, [b]He
raised up for them David as king, to whom also
He gave testimony and said, [c]'*I have found David*
the son of Jesse, [d]*a man after My own heart*, who
will do all My will.'
23 [a]"From this man's seed, according [b]to *the*
promise, God raised up for Israel [c]a* Savior—
Jesus—
24 [a]"after John had first preached, before His
coming, the baptism of repentance to all the people of Israel.
25 "And as John was finishing his course, he
said, [a]'Who do you think I am? I am not *He*. But
behold, [b]there comes One after me, the sandals
of whose feet I am not worthy to loose.'
26 "Men *and* brethren, sons of the family of
Abraham, and [a]those among you who fear God,
[b]to you the word of this salvation has been sent.
27 "For those who dwell in Jerusalem, and
their rulers, [a]because they did not know Him, nor
even the voices of the Prophets which are read
every Sabbath, have fulfilled *them* in condemning
Him.
28 [a]"And though they found no cause for
death *in Him*, they asked Pilate that He should
be put to death.
29 [a]"Now when they had fulfilled all that was
written concerning Him, [b]they took *Him* down
from the tree and laid *Him* in a tomb.
30 [a]"But God raised Him from the dead.
31 [a]"He was seen for many days by those
who came up with Him from Galilee to Jerusalem,
who are His witnesses to the people.
32 "And we declare to you glad tidings—
[a]that promise which was made to the fathers.
33 "God has fulfilled this for us their children, in that He has raised up Jesus. As it is also
written in the second Psalm:

> [a]'*You are My Son,*
> *Today I have begotten You.*'

34 "And that He raised Him from the dead,
no more to return to corruption, He has spoken
thus:

> [a]'*I will give you the sure mercies of David.*'

KJV

35 Wherefore he saith also in another *psalm*,
[a]THOU SHALT NOT SUFFER THINE HOLY ONE TO SEE
CORRUPTION.
36 For David, after he had served his own
generation by the will of God, [a]fell on sleep, and
was laid unto his fathers, and saw corruption:
37 But he, whom God raised again, saw no
corruption.
38 Be it known unto you therefore, men *and*
brethren, that [a]through this man is preached unto
you the forgiveness of sins:
39 And [a]by him all that believe are justified
from all things, from which ye could not be justified by the law of Moses.
40 Beware therefore, lest that come upon
you, which is spoken of in the prophets;
41 [a]BEHOLD, YE DESPISERS, AND WONDER, AND
PERISH: FOR I WORK A WORK IN YOUR DAYS, A WORK
WHICH YE SHALL IN NO WISE BELIEVE, THOUGH A MAN
DECLARE IT UNTO YOU.

Blessing and Conflict at Antioch

42 And when the Jews were gone out of the
synagogue, the Gentiles besought that these
words might be preached to them the next
sabbath.
43 Now when the congregation was broken
up, many of the Jews and religious proselytes followed Paul and Barnabas: who, speaking to them,
[a]persuaded them to continue in [b]the grace of God.
44 And the next sabbath day came almost the
whole city together to hear the word of God.
45 But when the Jews saw the multitudes,
they were filled with envy, and [a]spake against
those things which were spoken by Paul, contradicting and blaspheming.
46 Then Paul and Barnabas waxed bold, and
said, [a]It was necessary that the word of God
should first have been spoken to you: but [b]seeing
ye put it from you, and judge yourselves unworthy
of everlasting life, lo, [c]we turn to the Gentiles.
47 For so hath the Lord commanded us, [a]*saying*, I HAVE SET THEE TO BE A LIGHT OF THE GEN-
TILES, THAT THOU SHOULDEST BE FOR SALVATION
UNTO THE ENDS OF THE EARTH.
48 And when the Gentiles heard this, they
were glad, and glorified the word of the Lord:
[a]and as many as were ordained to eternal life
believed.
49 And the word of the Lord was published
throughout all the region.
50 But the Jews stirred up the devout and
honourable women, and the chief men of the city,
and [a]raised persecution against Paul and Barnabas, and expelled them out of their coasts.
51 [a]But they shook off the dust of their feet
against them, and came unto Iconium.
52 And the disciples [a]were filled with joy,
and [b]with the Holy Ghost.

At Iconium

14 And it came to pass in Iconium, that they
went both together into the synagogue of
the Jews, and so spake, that a great multitude both
of the Jews and also of the [a]Greeks believed.
2 But the unbelieving Jews stirred up the
Gentiles, and made their minds evil affected
against the brethren.
3 Long time therefore abode they speaking
boldly in the Lord, [a]which gave testimony unto
the word of his grace, and granted signs and
[b]wonders to be done by their hands.
4 But the multitude of the city was [a]divided:
and part held with the Jews, and part with the
[b]apostles.
5 And when there was an assault made both

35 [a]Ps. 16:10; Acts 2:27
36 [a]Acts 2:29
38 [a]Jer. 31:34
39 [a][Is. 53:11; John 3:16]
41 [a]Hab. 1:5
43 [a]Acts 11:23 [b]Titus 2:11; Heb. 12:15; 1 Pet. 5:12
45 [a]Acts 18:6; 1 Pet. 4:4; Jude 10
46 [a]Matt. 10:6; Acts 3:26; Rom. 1:16 [b]Ex. 32:10; Deut. 32:21; Is. 55:5; Matt. 21:43; Rom. 10:19 [c]Acts 18:6
47 [a]Is. 42:6; 49:6; Luke 2:32
48 [a][Acts 2:47]
50 [a]Acts 7:52; 2 Tim. 3:11
51 [a]Matt. 10:14; Mark 6:11; [Luke 9:5]
52 [a]Matt. 5:12; John 16:22 [b]Acts 2:4; 4:8, 31; 13:9

CHAPTER 14

1 [a]John 7:35; Acts 18:4; Rom. 1:14, 16; 1 Cor. 1:22
3 [a]Mark 16:20; Acts 4:29; 20:32; Heb. 2:4 [b]Acts 5:12
4 [a]Luke 12:51 [b]Acts 13:2, 3

*———

13:42 Or *And when they went out of the synagogue of the Jews;* NU *And when they went out of the synagogue, they begged*

NKJV

35 "Therefore He also says in another *Psalm:*

[a]*'You will not allow Your Holy One to see*
corruption.'

36 "For David, after he had served his own
generation by the will of God, [a]fell asleep, was
buried with his fathers, and saw corruption;
37 "but He whom God raised up saw no
corruption.
38 "Therefore let it be known to you, brethren, that [a]through this Man is preached to you
the forgiveness of sins;
39 "and [a]by Him everyone who believes is
justified from all things from which you could not
be justified by the law of Moses.
40 "Beware therefore, lest what has been
spoken in the prophets come upon you:

41 *'Behold,*[a] *you despisers,*
Marvel and perish!
For I work a work in your days,
A work which you will by no means
believe,
Though one were to declare it to you.'"

Blessing and Conflict at Antioch

42 *So when the Jews went out of the synagogue, the Gentiles begged that these words might
be preached to them the next Sabbath.
43 Now when the congregation had broken
up, many of the Jews and devout proselytes followed Paul and Barnabas, who, speaking to them,
[a]persuaded them to continue in [b]the grace of God.
44 On the next Sabbath almost the whole city
came together to hear the word of God.
45 But when the Jews saw the multitudes,
they were filled with envy; and contradicting and
blaspheming, they [a]opposed the things spoken by
Paul.
46 Then Paul and Barnabas grew bold and
said, [a]"It was necessary that the word of God
should be spoken to you first; but [b]since you reject
it, and judge yourselves unworthy of everlasting
life, behold, [c]we turn to the Gentiles.
47 "For so the Lord has commanded us:

[a]*'I have set you as a light to the Gentiles,*
That you should be for salvation to the
ends of the earth.'"

48 Now when the Gentiles heard this, they
were glad and glorified the word of the Lord.
[a]And as many as had been appointed to eternal
life believed.
49 And the word of the Lord was being
spread throughout all the region.
50 But the Jews stirred up the devout and
prominent women and the chief men of the city,
[a]raised up persecution against Paul and Barnabas, and expelled them from their region.
51 [a]But they shook off the dust from their
feet against them, and came to Iconium.
52 And the disciples [a]were filled with joy and
[b]with the Holy Spirit.

At Iconium

14 Now it happened in Iconium that they went
together to the synagogue of the Jews, and
so spoke that a great multitude both of the Jews
and of the [a]Greeks believed.
2 But the unbelieving Jews stirred up the
Gentiles and poisoned their minds against the
brethren.
3 Therefore they stayed there a long time,
speaking boldly in the Lord, [a]who was bearing
witness to the word of His grace, granting signs
and [b]wonders to be done by their hands.
4 But the multitude of the city was [a]divided:
part sided with the Jews, and part with the
[b]apostles.
5 And when a violent attempt was made by

KJV

of the Gentiles, and also of the Jews with their rulers, [a]to use *them* despitefully, and to stone them,

6 They were ware of *it*, and [a]fled unto Lystra and Derbe, cities of Lycaonia, and unto the region that lieth round about:

7 And there they preached the gospel.

Idolatry at Lystra

8 [a]And there sat a certain man at Lystra, impotent in his feet, being a cripple from his mother's womb, who never had walked:

9 The same heard Paul speak: who stedfastly beholding him, and perceiving that he had faith to be healed,

10 Said with a loud voice, [a]Stand upright on thy feet. And he leaped and walked.

11 And when the people saw what Paul had done, they lifted up their voices, saying in the speech of Lycaonia, [a]The gods are come down to us in the likeness of men.

12 And they called Barnabas, Jupiter; and Paul, Mercurius, because he was the chief speaker.

13 Then the priest of Jupiter, which was before their city, brought oxen and garlands unto the gates, [a]and would have done sacrifice with the people.

14 *Which* when the apostles, Barnabas and Paul, heard *of*, [a]they rent their clothes, and ran in among the people, crying out,

15 And saying, Sirs, [a]why do ye these things? [b]We also are men of like passions with you, and preach unto you that ye should turn from [c]these vanities [d]unto the living God, [e]which made heaven, and earth, and the sea, and all things that are therein:

16 [a]Who in times past suffered all nations to walk in their own ways.

17 [a]Nevertheless he left not himself without witness, in that he did good, and [b]gave us rain from heaven, and fruitful seasons, filling our hearts with [c]food and gladness.

18 And with these sayings scarce restrained they the people, that they had not done sacrifice unto them.

Stoning, Escape to Derbe

19 [a]And there came thither *certain* Jews from Antioch and Iconium, who persuaded the people, [b]and, having stoned Paul, drew *him* out of the city, supposing he had been [c]dead.

20 Howbeit, as the disciples stood round about him, he rose up, and came into the city: and the next day he departed with Barnabas to Derbe.

Strengthening the Converts

21 And when they had preached the gospel to that city, [a]and had taught many, they returned again to Lystra, and *to* Iconium, and Antioch,

22 Confirming the souls of the disciples, *and* [a]exhorting them to continue in the faith, and that [b]we must through much tribulation enter into the kingdom of God.

23 And when they had [a]ordained them elders in every church, and had prayed with fasting, they commended them to the Lord, on whom they believed.

24 And after they had passed throughout Pisidia, they came to Pamphylia.

25 And when they had preached the word in Perga, they went down into Attalia:

26 And thence sailed to Antioch, from whence they had been recommended to the grace of God for the work which they fulfilled.

27 And when they were come, and had gathered the church together, [a]they rehearsed all that God had done with them, and how he had [b]opened the door of faith unto the Gentiles.

28 And there they abode long time with the disciples.

5 [a]2 Tim. 3:11
6 [a]Matt. 10:23
8 [a]Acts 3:2
10 [a][Is. 35:6]
11 [a]Acts 8:10; 28:6
13 [a]Dan. 2:46
14 [a]Num. 14:6; Matt. 26:65; Mark 14:63
15 [a]Acts 10:26 [b]James 5:17 [c]1 Sam. 12:21; Jer. 8:19; 14:22; Amos 2:4; 1 Cor. 8:4 [d]1 Thess. 1:9 [e]Gen. 1:1; Ex. 20:11; Ps. 146:6; Acts 4:24; 17:24; Rev. 14:7
16 [a]Ps. 81:12; Mic. 4:5; 1 Pet. 4:3
17 [a]Acts 17:24–27; Rom. 1:19, 20 [b]Lev. 26:4; Deut. 11:14; [Matt. 5:45] [c]Ps. 145:16
19 [a]Acts 13:45, 50; 14:2–5; 1 Thess. 2:14 [b]Acts 14:5; 2 Cor. 11:25; 2 Tim. 3:11 [c][2 Cor. 12:1–4]
21 [a]Matt. 28:19
22 [a]Acts 11:23 [b]Matt. 10:38; Luke 22:28; [Rom. 8:17; 2 Tim. 2:12; 3:12]
23 [a]Matt. 9:15; Mark 2:20; Luke 5:35; 2 Cor. 8:19; Titus 1:5
27 [a]Acts 15:4, 12 [b]1 Cor. 16:9; 2 Cor. 2:12; Col. 4:3; Rev. 3:8

NKJV

both the Gentiles and Jews, with their rulers, [a]to abuse and stone them,

6 they became aware of it and [a]fled to Lystra and Derbe, cities of Lycaonia, and to the surrounding region.

7 And they were preaching the gospel there.

Idolatry at Lystra

8 [a]And in Lystra a certain man without strength in his feet was sitting, a cripple from his mother's womb, who had never walked.

9 *This* man heard Paul speaking. Paul, observing him intently and seeing that he had faith to be healed,

10 said with a loud voice, [a]"Stand up straight on your feet!" And he leaped and walked.

11 Now when the people saw what Paul had done, they raised their voices, saying in the Lycaonian *language*, [a]"The gods have come down to us in the likeness of men!"

12 And Barnabas they called Zeus, and Paul, Hermes, because he was the chief speaker.

13 Then the priest of Zeus, whose temple was in front of their city, brought oxen and garlands to the gates, [a]intending to sacrifice with the multitudes.

14 But when the apostles Barnabas and Paul heard this, [a]they tore their clothes and ran in among the multitude, crying out

15 and saying, "Men, [a]why are you doing these things? [b]We also are men with the same nature as you, and preach to you that you should turn from [c]these useless things [d]to the living God, [e]who made the heaven, the earth, the sea, and all things that are in them,

16 [a]"who in bygone generations allowed all nations to walk in their own ways.

17 [a]"Nevertheless He did not leave Himself without witness, in that He did good, [b]gave us rain from heaven and fruitful seasons, filling our hearts with [c]food and gladness."

18 And with these sayings they could scarcely restrain the multitudes from sacrificing to them.

Stoning, Escape to Derbe

19 [a]Then Jews from Antioch and Iconium came there; and having persuaded the multitudes, [b]they stoned Paul *and* dragged *him* out of the city, supposing him to be [c]dead.

20 However, when the disciples gathered around him, he rose up and went into the city. And the next day he departed with Barnabas to Derbe.

Strengthening the Converts

21 And when they had preached the gospel to that city [a]and made many disciples, they returned to Lystra, Iconium, and Antioch,

22 strengthening the souls of the disciples, [a]exhorting *them* to continue in the faith, and *saying*, [b]"We must through many tribulations enter the kingdom of God."

23 So when they had [a]appointed elders in every church, and prayed with fasting, they commended them to the Lord in whom they had believed.

24 And after they had passed through Pisidia, they came to Pamphylia.

25 Now when they had preached the word in Perga, they went down to Attalia.

26 From there they sailed to Antioch, where they had been commended to the grace of God for the work which they had completed.

27 Now when they had come and gathered the church together, [a]they reported all that God had done with them, and that He had [b]opened the door of faith to the Gentiles.

28 So they stayed there a long time with the disciples.

KJV

Conflict over Circumcision

15 And [a]certain men which came down from Judaea taught the brethren, *and said,* [b]Except ye be circumcised after the manner of Moses, ye cannot be saved.

2 When therefore Paul and Barnabas had no small dissension and disputation with them, they determined that [a]Paul and Barnabas, and certain other of them, should go up to Jerusalem unto the apostles and elders about this question.

3 And [a]being brought on their way by the church, they passed through Phenice and Samaria, [b]declaring the conversion of the Gentiles: and they caused great joy unto all the brethren.

4 And when they were come to Jerusalem, they were received of the church, and *of* the apostles and elders, and they declared all things that God had done with them.

5 But there rose up certain of the sect of the Pharisees which believed, saying, That it was needful to circumcise them, and to command *them* to keep the law of Moses.

The Jerusalem Council

6 And the apostles and elders came together for to consider of this matter.

7 And when there had been much disputing, Peter rose up, and said unto them, [a]Men *and* brethren, ye know how that a good while ago God made choice among us, that the Gentiles by my mouth should hear the word of the gospel, and believe.

8 And God, [a]which knoweth the hearts, bare them witness, [b]giving them the Holy Ghost, even as *he did* unto us;

9 [a]And put no difference between us and them, [b]purifying their hearts by faith.

10 Now therefore why tempt ye God, [a]to put a yoke upon the neck of the disciples, which neither our fathers nor we were able to bear?

11 But [a]we believe that through the grace of the Lord Jesus Christ we shall be saved, even as they.

12 Then all the multitude kept silence, and gave audience to Barnabas and Paul, declaring what miracles and wonders God had [a]wrought among the Gentiles by them.

13 And after they had held their peace, [a]James answered, saying, Men *and* brethren, hearken unto me:

14 [a]Simeon hath declared how God at the first did visit the Gentiles, to take out of them a people for his name.

15 And to this agree the words of the prophets; as it is written,

16 [a]AFTER THIS I WILL RETURN, AND WILL BUILD AGAIN THE TABERNACLE OF DAVID, WHICH IS FALLEN DOWN; AND I WILL BUILD AGAIN THE RUINS THEREOF, AND I WILL SET IT UP:

17 THAT THE RESIDUE OF MEN MIGHT SEEK AFTER THE LORD, AND ALL THE GENTILES, UPON WHOM MY NAME IS CALLED, SAITH THE LORD, WHO DOETH ALL THESE THINGS.

18 Known unto God are all his works from the beginning of the world.

19 Wherefore [a]my sentence is, that we trouble not them, which from among the Gentiles [b]are turned to God:

20 But that we [a]write unto them, that they abstain [b]from pollutions of idols, and [c]*from* fornication, [d]and *from* things strangled, and *from* blood.

21 For Moses of old time hath in every city them that preach him, [a]being read in the synagogues every sabbath day.

The Jerusalem Decree

22 Then pleased it the apostles and elders, with the whole church, to send chosen men of

CHAPTER 15

1 [a]Gal. 2:12 [b]John 7:22; Acts 15:5; Gal. 5:2; Phil. 3:2; [Col. 2:8, 11, 16]
2 [a]Gal. 2:1
3 [a]Acts 20:38; 21:5; Rom. 15:24; 1 Cor. 16:6, 11; 2 Cor. 1:16; Titus 3:13; 3 John 6 [b]Acts 14:27; 15:4, 12
7 [a]Acts 10:20
8 [a]1 Chr. 28:9; Acts 1:24 [b]Acts 2:4; 10:44, 47
9 [a]Rom. 10:12 [b]Acts 10:15, 28
10 [a]Matt. 23:4; Gal. 5:1
11 [a]Rom. 3:4; 5:15; 2 Cor. 13:14; [Eph. 2:5–8; Titus 2:11]
12 [a]Acts 14:27; 15:3, 4
13 [a]Acts 12:17
14 [a]Acts 15:7; 2 Pet. 1:1
16 [a]Amos 9:11, 12
19 [a]Acts 15:28; 21:25 [b]1 Thess. 1:9
20 [a]Acts 21:25 [b]Gen. 35:2; Ex. 20:3, 23; Ezek. 20:30; [1 Cor. 8:1; 10:20, 28]; Rev. 2:14 [c][1 Cor. 6:9]; Gal. 5:19; Eph. 5:3; Col. 3:5; 1 Thess. 4:3; 1 Pet. 4:3 [d]Gen. 9:4; Lev. 3:17; Deut. 12:16; 1 Sam. 14:33
21 [a]Acts 13:15, 27; 2 Cor. 3:14

*

15:11 NU, M omit *Christ*
15:18 NU (continuing v. 17) *known from eternity (of old).'*
15:20 Or *fornication*

NKJV

Conflict over Circumcision

15 And [a]certain *men* came down from Judea and taught the brethren, [b]"Unless you are circumcised according to the custom of Moses, you cannot be saved."

2 Therefore, when Paul and Barnabas had no small dissension and dispute with them, they determined that [a]Paul and Barnabas and certain others of them should go up to Jerusalem, to the apostles and elders, about this question.

3 So, [a]being sent on their way by the church, they passed through Phoenicia and Samaria, [b]describing the conversion of the Gentiles; and they caused great joy to all the brethren.

4 And when they had come to Jerusalem, they were received by the church and the apostles and the elders; and they reported all things that God had done with them.

5 But some of the sect of the Pharisees who believed rose up, saying, "It is necessary to circumcise them, and to command *them* to keep the law of Moses."

The Jerusalem Council

6 Now the apostles and elders came together to consider this matter.

7 And when there had been much dispute, Peter rose up and said to them: [a]"Men and brethren, you know that a good while ago God chose among us, that by my mouth the Gentiles should hear the word of the gospel and believe.

8 "So God, [a]who knows the heart, acknowledged them by [b]giving them the Holy Spirit, just as *He did* to us,

9 [a]"and made no distinction between us and them, [b]purifying their hearts by faith.

10 "Now therefore, why do you test God [a]by putting a yoke on the neck of the disciples which neither our fathers nor we were able to bear?

11 "But [a]we believe that through the grace of the Lord Jesus *Christ we shall be saved in the same manner as they."

12 Then all the multitude kept silent and listened to Barnabas and Paul declaring how many miracles and wonders God had [a]worked through them among the Gentiles.

13 And after they had become silent, [a]James answered, saying, "Men *and* brethren, listen to me:

14 [a]"Simon has declared how God at the first visited the Gentiles to take out of them a people for His name.

15 "And with this the words of the prophets agree, just as it is written:

16 *'After[a] this I will return*
And will rebuild the tabernacle of David,
which has fallen down;
I will rebuild its ruins,
And I will set it up;
17 *So that the rest of mankind may seek the* LORD,
Even all the Gentiles who are called by My name,
Says the LORD *who does all these things.'*

18 *"Known to God from eternity are all His works.

19 "Therefore [a]I judge that we should not trouble those from among the Gentiles who [b]are turning to God,

20 "but that we [a]write to them to abstain [b]from things polluted by idols, [c]*from* *sexual immorality, [d]*from* things strangled, and *from* blood.

21 "For Moses has had throughout many generations those who preach him in every city, [a]being read in the synagogues every Sabbath."

The Jerusalem Decree

22 Then it pleased the apostles and elders, with the whole church, to send chosen men of

KJV

their own company to Antioch with Paul and Barnabas; *namely*, Judas surnamed [a]Barsabas, and
Silas, chief men among the brethren:
23 And they wrote *letters* by them after this
manner; The apostles and elders and brethren
send greeting unto the brethren which are of the
Gentiles in Antioch and Syria and Cilicia:
24 Forasmuch as we have heard, that [a]cer-
tain which went out from us have troubled you
with words, [b]subverting your souls, saying, *Ye*
must be circumcised, and keep the law: to whom
we gave no *such* commandment:
25 It seemed good unto us, being assembled
with one accord, to send chosen men unto you
with our beloved Barnabas and Paul,
26 [a]Men that have hazarded their lives for
the name of our Lord Jesus Christ.
27 We have sent therefore Judas and Silas,
who shall also tell *you* the same things by mouth.
28 For it seemed good to the Holy Ghost, and
to us, to lay upon you no greater burden than
these necessary things;
29 [a]That ye abstain from meats offered to
idols, and [b]from blood, and from things strangled,
and from [c]fornication: from which if ye keep
yourselves, ye shall do well. Fare ye well.

Continuing Ministry in Syria

30 So when they were dismissed, they came
to Antioch: and when they had gathered the multitude together, they delivered the epistle:
31 *Which* when they had read, they rejoiced
for the consolation.
32 And Judas and Silas, being [a]prophets also
themselves, [b]exhorted the brethren with many
words, and confirmed *them*.
33 And after they had tarried *there* a space,
they were let [a]go in peace from the brethren unto
the apostles.
34 Notwithstanding it pleased Silas to abide
there still.
35 [a]Paul also and Barnabas continued in Antioch, teaching and preaching the word of the
Lord, with many others also.

Division over John Mark

36 And some days after Paul said unto Barnabas, Let us go again and visit our brethren in
every city where we have preached the word of
the Lord, *and see* how they do.
37 And Barnabas determined to take with
them [a]John, whose surname was Mark.
38 But Paul thought not good to take him
with them, [a]who departed from them from Pamphylia, and went not with them to the work.
39 And the contention was so sharp between
them, that they departed asunder one from the
other: and so Barnabas took Mark, and sailed
unto [a]Cyprus;
40 And Paul chose Silas, and departed, [a]be-
ing recommended by the brethren unto the grace
of God.
41 And he went through Syria and Cilicia,
[a]confirming the churches.

Timothy Joins Paul and Silas

16 Then came he to [a]Derbe and Lystra: and,
behold, a certain disciple was there,
[b]named Timotheus, [c]the son of a certain woman,
which was a Jewess, and believed; but his father
was a Greek:
2 Which was well reported of by the brethren that were at Lystra and Iconium.
3 Him would Paul have to go forth with him;

22 [a]Acts 1:23
24 [a]Acts 15:1; Gal. 2:4; 5:12; Titus 1:10, 11 [b]Gal. 1:7; 5:10
26 [a]Acts 13:50; 14:19; 1 Cor. 15:30; 2 Cor. 11:23–26
29 [a]Acts 15:20; 21:25; Rev. 2:14, 20 [b]Lev. 17:14 [c]1 Cor. 5:1; 6:18; 7:2; Col. 3:5; 1 Thess. 4:3
32 [a]Acts 11:27; 1 Cor. 12:28; Eph. 4:11; Rev. 18:20 [b]Acts 14:22; 18:23
33 [a]Mark 5:34; Acts 16:36; 1 Cor. 16:11; Heb. 11:31
35 [a]Acts 13:1
37 [a]Acts 12:12, 25; Col. 4:10; 2 Tim. 4:11; Philem. 24
38 [a]Acts 13:13
39 [a]Acts 4:36; 13:4
40 [a]Acts 11:23; 14:26
41 [a]Acts 16:5

CHAPTER 16

1 [a]Acts 14:6 [b]Acts 19:22; Rom. 16:21; 1 Cor. 4:17; 16:10; Phil. 1:1; 2:19; 1 Thess. 3:2; 2 Tim. 1:2 [c]2 Tim. 1:5; 3:15

*———

15:22 NU, M *Barsabbas*
15:24 NU omits *saying, "You must be circumcised and keep the law"*
15:29 Or *fornication*
15:33 NU *those who had sent them*
15:34 NU, M omit v. 34.

NKJV

their own company to Antioch with Paul and
Barnabas, *namely*, Judas who was also named
[a]Barsabas,* and Silas, leading men among the
brethren.

23 They wrote this *letter* by them:

The apostles, the elders, and the brethren,
To the brethren who are of the Gentiles
in Antioch, Syria, and Cilicia:

Greetings.

24 Since we have heard that [a]some who went
out from us have troubled you with words,
[b]unsettling your souls, *saying, "*You*
must be circumcised and keep the law"—
to whom we gave no *such*
commandment—
25 it seemed good to us, being assembled
with one accord, to send chosen men to
you with our beloved Barnabas and Paul,
26 [a]men who have risked their lives for the
name of our Lord Jesus Christ.
27 We have therefore sent Judas and Silas,
who will also report the same things by
word of mouth.
28 For it seemed good to the Holy Spirit, and
to us, to lay upon you no greater burden
than these necessary things:
29 [a]that you abstain from things offered to
idols, [b]from blood, from things strangled,
and from [c]sexual* immorality. If you keep
yourselves from these, you will do well.
Farewell.

Continuing Ministry in Syria

30 So when they were sent off, they came to
Antioch; and when they had gathered the multitude together, they delivered the letter.
31 When they had read it, they rejoiced over
its encouragement.
32 Now Judas and Silas, themselves being
[a]prophets also, [b]exhorted and strengthened the
brethren with many words.
33 And after they had stayed *there* for a time,
they were [a]sent back with greetings from the
brethren to *the apostles.
34 *However, it seemed good to Silas to remain there.
35 [a]Paul and Barnabas also remained in Antioch, teaching and preaching the word of the
Lord, with many others also.

Division over John Mark

36 Then after some days Paul said to Barnabas, "Let us now go back and visit our brethren
in every city where we have preached the word
of the Lord, *and see* how they are doing."
37 Now Barnabas was determined to take
with them [a]John called Mark.
38 But Paul insisted that they should not take
with them [a]the one who had departed from them
in Pamphylia, and had not gone with them to the
work.
39 Then the contention became so sharp that
they parted from one another. And so Barnabas
took Mark and sailed to [a]Cyprus;
40 but Paul chose Silas and departed, [a]being
commended by the brethren to the grace of God.
41 And he went through Syria and Cilicia,
[a]strengthening the churches.

Timothy Joins Paul and Silas

16 Then he came to [a]Derbe and Lystra. And
behold, a certain disciple was there,
[b]named Timothy, [c]*the* son of a certain Jewish
woman who believed, but his father *was* Greek.
2 He was well spoken of by the brethren
who were at Lystra and Iconium.
3 Paul wanted to have him go on with him.

KJV

and [a]took and circumcised him because of the
Jews which were in those quarters: for they knew
all that his father was a Greek.
4 And as they went through the cities, they
delivered them the [a]decrees for to keep, [b]that
were ordained of the apostles and elders which
were at Jerusalem.
5 And [a]so were the churches established in
the faith, and increased in number daily.

The Macedonian Call

6 Now when they had gone throughout
Phrygia and the region of [a]Galatia, and were forbidden of the Holy Ghost to preach the word in
Asia,
7 After they were come to Mysia, they assayed to go into Bithynia: but the Spirit suffered
them not.
8 And they passing by Mysia [a]came down
to Troas.
9 And a vision appeared to Paul in the night;
There stood a [a]man of Macedonia, and prayed
him, saying, Come over into Macedonia, and help
us.
10 And after he had seen the vision, immediately we endeavoured to go [a]into Macedonia, assuredly gathering that the Lord had called us for
to preach the gospel unto them.

Lydia Baptized at Philippi

11 Therefore loosing from Troas, we came
with a straight course to Samothracia, and the
next *day* to Neapolis;
12 And from thence to [a]Philippi, which is the
chief city of that part of Macedonia, *and* a colony:
and we were in that city abiding certain days.
13 And on the sabbath we went out of the
city by a river side, where prayer was wont to
be made; and we sat down, and spake unto the
women which resorted *thither*.
14 And a certain woman named Lydia, a
seller of purple, of the city of [a]Thyatira, which
worshipped God, heard *us*: whose [b]heart the Lord
opened, that she attended unto the things which
were spoken of Paul.
15 And when she was baptized, and her
household, she besought *us*, saying, If ye have
judged me to be faithful to the Lord, come into my
house, and abide *there*. And [a]she constrained us.

Paul and Silas Imprisoned

16 And it came to pass, as we went to prayer,
a certain damsel [a]possessed with a spirit of divination met us, which brought her masters [b]much
gain by soothsaying:
17 The same followed Paul and us, and cried,
saying, These men are the servants of the most
high God, which shew unto us the way of salvation.
18 And this did she many days. But Paul, [a]be-
ing grieved, turned and said to the spirit, I command thee in the name of Jesus Christ to come
out of her. [b]And he came out the same hour.
19 And [a]when her masters saw that the hope
of their gains was gone, they caught Paul and Silas, and [b]drew *them* into the marketplace unto
the rulers,
20 And brought them to the magistrates, saying, These men, being Jews, [a]do exceedingly trouble our city,
21 And teach customs, which are not lawful
for us to receive, neither to observe, being
Romans.
22 And the multitude rose up together
against them: and the magistrates rent off their
clothes, [a]and commanded to beat *them*.
23 And when they had laid many stripes
upon them, they cast *them* into prison, charging
the jailor to keep them safely:
24 Who, having received such a charge,
thrust them into the inner prison, and made their
feet fast in the stocks.

3 [a][1 Cor. 9:20; Gal. 2:3; 5:2]
4 [a]Acts 15:19–21 [b]Acts 15:28, 29
5 [a]Acts 2:47; 15:41
6 [a]Acts 18:23; Gal. 1:1, 2
8 [a]Acts 16:11; 20:5; 2 Cor. 2:12; 2 Tim. 4:13
9 [a]Acts 10:30
10 [a]2 Cor. 2:13
12 [a]Acts 20:6; Phil. 1:1; 1 Thess. 2:2
14 [a]Rev. 1:11; 2:18, 24 [b]Luke 24:45
15 [a]Gen. 19:3; 33:11; Judg. 19:21; Luke 24:29; [Heb. 13:2]
16 [a]Lev. 19:31; 20:6, 27; Deut. 18:11; 1 Sam. 28:3, 7; 2 Kin. 21:6; 1 Chr. 10:13; Is. 8:19 [b]Acts 19:24
18 [a]Mark 1:25, 34 [b]Mark 16:17
19 [a]Acts 16:16; 19:25, 26 [b]Matt. 10:18
20 [a]1 Kin. 18:17; Acts 17:8
22 [a]2 Cor. 6:5; 11:23, 25; 1 Thess. 2:2

*16:7 NU adds *of Jesus*

NKJV

And he [a]took *him* and circumcised him because
of the Jews who were in that region, for they all
knew that his father was Greek.
4 And as they went through the cities, they
delivered to them the [a]decrees to keep, [b]which
were determined by the apostles and elders at
Jerusalem.
5 [a]So the churches were strengthened in the
faith, and increased in number daily.

The Macedonian Call

6 Now when they had gone through Phrygia
and the region of [a]Galatia, they were forbidden
by the Holy Spirit to preach the word in Asia.
7 After they had come to Mysia, they tried
to go into Bithynia, but the *Spirit did not permit
them.
8 So passing by Mysia, they [a]came down
to Troas.
9 And a vision appeared to Paul in the night.
A [a]man of Macedonia stood and pleaded with
him, saying, "Come over to Macedonia and help
us."
10 Now after he had seen the vision, immediately we sought to go [a]to Macedonia, concluding
that the Lord had called us to preach the gospel
to them.

Lydia Baptized at Philippi

11 Therefore, sailing from Troas, we ran a
straight course to Samothrace, and the next *day*
came to Neapolis,
12 and from there to [a]Philippi, which is the
foremost city of that part of Macedonia, a colony.
And we were staying in that city for some days.
13 And on the Sabbath day we went out of
the city to the riverside, where prayer was cus-
tomarily made; and we sat down and spoke to
the women who met *there*.
14 Now a certain woman named Lydia heard
us. She was a seller of purple from the city of
[a]Thyatira, who worshiped God. [b]The Lord opened
her heart to heed the things spoken by Paul.
15 And when she and her household were
baptized, she begged *us*, saying, "If you have
judged me to be faithful to the Lord, come to my
house and stay." So [a]she persuaded us.

Paul and Silas Imprisoned

16 Now it happened, as we went to prayer,
that a certain slave girl [a]possessed with a spirit
of divination met us, who brought her masters
[b]much profit by fortune-telling.
17 This girl followed Paul and us, and cried
out, saying, "These men are the servants of the
Most High God, who proclaim to us the way of
salvation."
18 And this she did for many days. But Paul,
[a]greatly annoyed, turned and said to the spirit,
"I command you in the name of Jesus Christ to
come out of her." [b]And he came out that very
hour.
19 But [a]when her masters saw that their hope
of profit was gone, they seized Paul and Silas and
[b]dragged *them* into the marketplace to the
authorities.
20 And they brought them to the magistrates,
and said, "These men, being Jews, [a]exceedingly
trouble our city;
21 "and they teach customs which are not
lawful for us, being Romans, to receive or
observe."
22 Then the multitude rose up together
against them; and the magistrates tore off their
clothes [a]and commanded *them* to be beaten with
rods.
23 And when they had laid many stripes on
them, they threw *them* into prison, commanding
the jailer to keep them securely.
24 Having received such a charge, he put
them into the inner prison and fastened their feet
in the stocks.

KJV

The Philippian Jailer Saved

25 And at midnight Paul and Silas prayed,
and sang praises unto God: and the prisoners
heard them.
26 [a]And suddenly there was a great earthquake, so that the foundations of the prison were
shaken: and immediately [b]all the doors were
opened, and every one's bands were loosed.
27 And the keeper of the prison awaking out
of his sleep, and seeing the prison doors open,
he drew out his sword, and would have killed himself, supposing that the prisoners had been fled.
28 But Paul cried with a loud voice, saying,
Do thyself no harm: for we are all here.
29 Then he called for a light, and sprang in,
and came trembling, and fell down before Paul
and Silas,
30 And brought them out, and said, [a]Sirs,
what must I do to be saved?
31 And they said, [a]Believe on the Lord Jesus
Christ, and thou shalt be saved, and thy house.
32 And they spake unto him the word of the
Lord, and to all that were in his house.
33 And he took them the same hour of the
night, and washed *their* stripes; and was baptized,
he and all his, straightway.
34 And when he had brought them into his
house, [a]he set meat before them, and rejoiced, believing in God with all his house.

Paul Refuses to Depart Secretly

35 And when it was day, the magistrates sent
the serjeants, saying, Let those men go.
36 And the keeper of the prison told this saying to Paul, The magistrates have sent to let you
go: now therefore depart, and go in peace.
37 But Paul said unto them, They have
beaten us openly uncondemned, [a]being Romans,
and have cast *us* into prison; and now do they
thrust us out privily? nay verily; but let them come
themselves and fetch us out.
38 And the serjeants told these words unto
the magistrates: and they feared, when they heard
that they were Romans.
39 And they came and besought them, and
brought *them* out, and [a]desired *them* to depart
out of the city.
40 And they went out of the prison, [a]and entered into *the house of* Lydia: and when they had
seen the brethren, they comforted them, and
departed.

Preaching Christ at Thessalonica

17 Now when they had passed through Am-
phipolis and Apollonia, they came to [a]Thes-
salonica, where was a synagogue of the Jews:
2 And Paul, as his manner was, [a]went in
unto them, and three sabbath days [b]reasoned with
them out of the scriptures,
3 Opening and alleging, [a]that Christ must
needs have suffered, and risen again from the
dead; and that this Jesus, whom I preach unto
you, is Christ.
4 [a]And some of them believed, and con-
sorted with Paul and [b]Silas; and of the devout
Greeks a great multitude, and of the chief women
not a few.

Assault on Jason's House

5 But the Jews which believed not, moved
with [a]envy, took unto them certain lewd fellows
of the baser sort, and gathered a company, and
set all the city on an uproar, and assaulted the
house of [b]Jason, and sought to bring them out to
the people.
6 And when they found them not, they drew
Jason and certain brethren unto the rulers of the
city, crying, [a]These that have turned the world
upside down are come hither also;
7 Whom Jason hath received: and these all

26 [a]Acts 4:31 [b]Acts 5:19; 12:7, 10
30 [a]Luke 3:10; Acts 2:37; 9:6; 22:10
31 [a][John 3:16, 36; 6:47; Acts 13:38, 39; Rom. 10:9–11; 1 John 5:10]
34 [a]Matt. 5:4; Luke 5:29; 19:6
37 [a]Acts 22:25–29
39 [a]Matt. 8:34
40 [a]Acts 16:14

CHAPTER 17

1 [a]Acts 17:11, 13; 20:4; 27:2; Phil. 4:16; 1 Thess. 1:1; 2 Thess. 1:1; 2 Tim. 4:10
2 [a]Luke 4:16; Acts 9:20; 13:5, 14; 14:1; 16:13; 19:8 [b]1 Thess. 2:1–16
3 [a]Luke 24:26, 46; Acts 18:5, 28; Gal. 3:1
4 [a]Acts 28:24 [b]Acts 15:22, 27, 32, 40
5 [a]Acts 13:45 [b]Acts 17:6, 7, 9; Rom. 16:21
6 [a][Acts 16:20]

*

17:5 NU omits *who were not persuaded* • M omits *becoming envious*

NKJV

The Philippian Jailer Saved

25 But at midnight Paul and Silas were praying and singing hymns to God, and the prisoners
were listening to them.
26 [a]Suddenly there was a great earthquake,
so that the foundations of the prison were shaken;
and immediately [b]all the doors were opened and
everyone's chains were loosed.
27 And the keeper of the prison, awaking
from sleep and seeing the prison doors open, supposing the prisoners had fled, drew his sword and
was about to kill himself.
28 But Paul called with a loud voice, saying,
"Do yourself no harm, for we are all here."
29 Then he called for a light, ran in, and fell
down trembling before Paul and Silas.
30 And he brought them out and said, [a]"Sirs,
what must I do to be saved?"
31 So they said, [a]"Believe on the Lord Jesus
Christ, and you will be saved, you and your
household."
32 Then they spoke the word of the Lord to
him and to all who were in his house.
33 And he took them the same hour of the
night and washed *their* stripes. And immediately
he and all his family were baptized.
34 Now when he had brought them into his
house, [a]he set food before them; and he rejoiced,
having believed in God with all his household.

Paul Refuses to Depart Secretly

35 And when it was day, the magistrates sent
the officers, saying, "Let those men go."
36 So the keeper of the prison reported these
words to Paul, saying, "The magistrates have sent
to let you go. Now therefore depart, and go in
peace."
37 But Paul said to them, "They have beaten
us openly, uncondemned [a]Romans, *and* have
thrown *us* into prison. And now do they put us
out secretly? No indeed! Let them come themselves and get us out."
38 And the officers told these words to the
magistrates, and they were afraid when they
heard that they were Romans.
39 Then they came and pleaded with them
and brought *them* out, and [a]asked *them* to depart
from the city.
40 So they went out of the prison [a]and entered *the house of* Lydia; and when they had seen
the brethren, they encouraged them and departed.

Preaching Christ at Thessalonica

17 Now when they had passed through Am-
phipolis and Apollonia, they came to
[a]Thessalonica, where there was a synagogue of the
Jews.
2 Then Paul, as his custom was, [a]went in
to them, and for three Sabbaths [b]reasoned with
them from the Scriptures,
3 explaining and demonstrating [a]that the
Christ had to suffer and rise again from the dead,
and *saying*, "This Jesus whom I preach to you is
the Christ."
4 [a]And some of them were persuaded; and
a great multitude of the devout Greeks, and not
a few of the leading women, joined Paul and
[b]Silas.

Assault on Jason's House

5 But the Jews *who were not persuaded,
*becoming [a]envious, took some of the evil men
from the marketplace, and gathering a mob, set
all the city in an uproar and attacked the house
of [b]Jason, and sought to bring them out to the
people.
6 But when they did not find them, they
dragged Jason and some brethren to the rulers
of the city, crying out, [a]"These who have turned
the world upside down have come here too.
7 "Jason has harbored them, and these are

KJV

do contrary to the decrees of Caesar, [a]saying that
there is another king, *one* Jesus.
8 And they troubled the people and the rulers of the city, when they heard these things.
9 And when they had taken security of Jason, and of the other, they let them go.

Ministering at Berea

10 And [a]the brethren immediately sent away
Paul and Silas by night unto Berea: who coming
thither went into the synagogue of the Jews.
11 These were more noble than those in
Thessalonica, in that they received the word with
all readiness of mind, and [a]searched the scriptures daily, whether those things were so.
12 Therefore many of them believed; also of
honourable women which were Greeks, and of
men, not a few.
13 But when the Jews of Thessalonica had
knowledge that the word of God was preached
of Paul at Berea, they came thither also, and
stirred up the people.
14 [a]And then immediately the brethren sent
away Paul to go as it were to the sea: but Silas
and Timotheus abode there still.
15 And they that conducted Paul brought him
unto Athens: and [a]receiving a commandment
unto Silas and Timotheus for to come to him with
all speed, they departed.

The Philosophers at Athens

16 Now while Paul waited for them at Athens, [a]his spirit was stirred in him, when he saw
the city wholly given to idolatry.
17 Therefore disputed he in the synagogue
with the Jews, and with the devout persons, and
in the market daily with them that met with him.
18 Then certain philosophers of the Epicureans, and of the Stoicks, encountered him. And
some said, What will this babbler say? other some,
He seemeth to be a setter forth of strange gods:
because he preached unto them [a]Jesus, and the
resurrection.
19 And they took him, and brought him unto
Areopagus, saying, May we know what this new
doctrine, whereof thou speakest, *is?*
20 For thou bringest certain strange things
to our ears: we would know therefore what these
things mean.
21 (For all the Athenians and strangers
which were there spent their time in nothing else,
but either to tell, or to hear some new thing.)

Addressing the Areopagus

22 Then Paul stood in the midst of Mars' hill,
and said, *Ye* men of Athens, I perceive that in
all things ye are too superstitious.
23 For as I passed by, and beheld your devotions, I found an altar with this inscription, TO
THE UNKNOWN GOD. Whom therefore ye ignorantly worship, him declare I unto you.
24 [a]God that made the world and all things
therein, seeing that he is [b]Lord of heaven and
earth, [c]dwelleth not in temples made with hands;
25 Neither is worshipped with men's hands,
as though he needed any thing, seeing he [a]giveth
to all life, and breath, and all things;
26 And hath made of one blood all nations
of men for to dwell on all the face of the earth,
and hath determined the times before appointed,
and [a]the bounds of their habitation;
27 [a]That they should seek the Lord, if haply
they might feel after him, and find him, [b]though
he be not far from every one of us:
28 For [a]in him we live, and move, and have
our being; [b]as certain also of your own poets have
said, For we are also his offspring.
29 Forasmuch then as we are the offspring

7 [a]Luke 23:2; John 19:12; 1 Pet. 2:13
10 [a]Acts 9:25; 17:14
11 [a]Is. 34:16; Luke 16:29; John 5:39
14 [a]Matt. 10:23
15 [a]Acts 18:5
16 [a]2 Pet. 2:8
18 [a]1 Cor. 15:12
24 [a]Is. 42:5; Acts 14:15 [b]Deut. 10:14; Ps. 115:16; Matt. 11:25 [c]1 Kin. 8:27; Acts 7:48–50
25 [a]Gen. 2:7; Is. 42:5; Dan. 5:23
26 [a]Deut. 32:8; Job 12:23; Dan. 4:35
27 [a][Rom. 1:20] [b]Deut. 4:7; Ps. 139:7, 10; Jer. 23:23, 24; [Acts 14:17]
28 [a][Col. 1:17; Heb. 1:3] [b]Titus 1:12

*———
17:18 NU, M add *also*
17:26 NU omits *blood*

NKJV

all acting contrary to the decrees of Caesar, [a]saying there is another king—Jesus."
8 And they troubled the crowd and the rulers of the city when they heard these things.
9 So when they had taken security from Jason and the rest, they let them go.

Ministering at Berea

10 Then [a]the brethren immediately sent Paul
and Silas away by night to Berea. When they arrived, they went into the synagogue of the Jews.
11 These were more fair-minded than those
in Thessalonica, in that they received the word
with all readiness, and [a]searched the Scriptures
daily *to find out* whether these things were so.
12 Therefore many of them believed, and
also not a few of the Greeks, prominent women
as well as men.
13 But when the Jews from Thessalonica
learned that the word of God was preached by
Paul at Berea, they came there also and stirred
up the crowds.
14 [a]Then immediately the brethren sent Paul
away, to go to the sea; but both Silas and Timothy
remained there.
15 So those who conducted Paul brought him
to Athens; and [a]receiving a command for Silas
and Timothy to come to him with all speed, they
departed.

The Philosophers at Athens

16 Now while Paul waited for them at Athens, [a]his spirit was provoked within him when
he saw that the city was given over to idols.
17 Therefore he reasoned in the synagogue
with the Jews and with the *Gentile* worshipers,
and in the marketplace daily with those who happened to be there.
18 *Then certain Epicurean and Stoic philosophers encountered him. And some said, "What
does this babbler want to say?" Others said, "He
seems to be a proclaimer of foreign gods," because he preached to them [a]Jesus and the
resurrection.
19 And they took him and brought him to
the Areopagus, saying, "May we know what this
new doctrine *is* of which you speak?
20 "For you are bringing some strange things
to our ears. Therefore we want to know what
these things mean."
21 For all the Athenians and the foreigners
who were there spent their time in nothing else
but either to tell or to hear some new thing.

Addressing the Areopagus

22 Then Paul stood in the midst of the Areopagus and said, "Men of Athens, I perceive that
in all things you are very religious;
23 "for as I was passing through and considering the objects of your worship, I even found
an altar with this inscription:

TO THE UNKNOWN GOD.

Therefore, the One whom you worship without
knowing, Him I proclaim to you:
24 [a]"God, who made the world and everything in it, since He is [b]Lord of heaven and earth,
[c]does not dwell in temples made with hands.
25 "Nor is He worshiped with men's hands,
as though He needed anything, since He [a]gives
to all life, breath, and all things.
26 "And He has made from one *blood every
nation of men to dwell on all the face of the earth,
and has determined their preappointed times and
[a]the boundaries of their dwellings,
27 [a]"so that they should seek the Lord, in
the hope that they might grope for Him and find
Him, [b]though He is not far from each one of us;
28 "for [a]in Him we live and move and have
our being, [b]as also some of your own poets have
said, 'For we are also His offspring.'
29 "Therefore, since we are the offspring of

KJV

of God, [a]we ought not to think that the Godhead is like unto gold, or silver, or stone, graven by art and man's device.

30 And [a]the times of this ignorance God winked at; but [b]now commandeth all men every where to repent:

31 Because he hath appointed a day, in the which [a]he will judge the world in righteousness by *that* man whom he hath ordained; *whereof* he hath given assurance unto all *men,* in that [b]he hath raised him from the dead.

32 And when they heard of the resurrection of the dead, some mocked: and others said, We will hear thee again of this *matter.*

33 So Paul departed from among them.

34 Howbeit certain men clave unto him, and believed: among the which *was* Dionysius the Areopagite, and a woman named Damaris, and others with them.

Ministering at Corinth

18 After these things Paul departed from Athens, and came to Corinth;

2 And found a certain Jew named [a]Aquila, born in Pontus, lately come from Italy, with his wife Priscilla; (because that Claudius had commanded all Jews to depart from Rome:) and came unto them.

3 And because he was of the same craft, he abode with them, [a]and wrought: for by their occupation they were tentmakers.

4 [a]And he reasoned in the synagogue every sabbath, and persuaded the Jews and the Greeks.

5 And [a]when Silas and Timotheus were come from Macedonia, Paul was [b]pressed in the spirit, and testified to the Jews *that* Jesus *was* Christ.

6 And [a]when they opposed themselves, and blasphemed, [b]he shook *his* raiment, and said unto them, [c]Your blood *be* upon your own heads; [d]I *am* clean: [e]from henceforth I will go unto the Gentiles.

7 And he departed thence, and entered into a certain *man's* house, named Justus, *one* that worshipped God, whose house joined hard to the synagogue.

8 [a]And Crispus, the chief ruler of the synagogue, believed on the Lord with all his house; and many of the Corinthians hearing believed, and were baptized.

9 Then [a]spake the Lord to Paul in the night by a vision, Be not afraid, but speak, and hold not thy peace:

10 [a]For I am with thee, and no man shall set on thee to hurt thee: for I have much people in this city.

11 And he continued *there* a year and six months, teaching the word of God among them.

12 And when Gallio was the deputy of Achaia, the Jews made insurrection with one accord against Paul, and brought him to the judgment seat,

13 Saying, This *fellow* persuadeth men to worship God contrary to the law.

14 And when Paul was now about to open *his* mouth, Gallio said unto the Jews, If it were a matter of wrong or wicked lewdness, O *ye* Jews, reason would that I should bear with you:

15 But if it be a [a]question of words and names, and *of* your law, look ye *to it;* for I will be no judge of such *matters.*

16 And he drave them from the judgment seat.

17 Then all the Greeks took [a]Sosthenes, the chief ruler of the synagogue, and beat *him* before the judgment seat. And Gallio cared for none of those things.

Paul Returns to Antioch

18 And Paul *after this* tarried *there* yet a good while, and then took his leave of the breth-

---

29 [a]Ps. 115:4–7; Is. 40:18, 19; Rom. 1:23
30 [a]Acts 14:16; [Rom. 3:25] [b]Luke 24:47; Acts 26:20; [Titus 2:11, 12]; 1 Pet. 1:14; 4:3
31 [a]Ps. 9:8; 96:13; 98:9; John 5:22, 27; Acts 10:42; Rom. 2:16 [b]Acts 2:24

CHAPTER 18
2 [a]Rom. 16:3; 1 Cor. 16:19; 2 Tim. 4:19
3 [a]Acts 20:34; 1 Cor. 4:12; 9:14; 2 Cor. 11:7; 12:13; 1 Thess. 2:9; 4:11; 2 Thess. 3:8
4 [a]Acts 17:2
5 [a]Acts 17:14, 15 [b]Acts 18:28
6 [a]Acts 13:45 [b]Neh. 5:13; Matt. 10:14; Acts 13:51 [c]Lev. 20:9, 11, 12; 2 Sam. 1:16; 1 Kin. 2:33; Ezek. 18:13; 33:4, 6, 8; Matt. 27:25; Acts 20:26 [d][Ezek. 3:18, 19] [e]Acts 13:46–48; 28:28
8 [a]1 Cor. 1:14
9 [a]Acts 23:11
10 [a]Jer. 1:18, 19
15 [a]Acts 23:29; 25:19
17 [a]1 Cor. 1:1

*

18:7 NU *Titius Justus*
18:17 NU *they all*

NKJV

God, [a]we ought not to think that the Divine Nature is like gold or silver or stone, something shaped by art and man's devising.

30 "Truly, [a]these times of ignorance God overlooked, but [b]now commands all men everywhere to repent,

31 "because He has appointed a day on which [a]He will judge the world in righteousness by the Man whom He has ordained. He has given assurance of this to all by [b]raising Him from the dead."

32 And when they heard of the resurrection of the dead, some mocked, while others said, "We will hear you again on this *matter.*"

33 So Paul departed from among them.

34 However, some men joined him and believed, among them Dionysius the Areopagite, a woman named Damaris, and others with them.

Ministering at Corinth

18 After these things Paul departed from Athens and went to Corinth.

2 And he found a certain Jew named [a]Aquila, born in Pontus, who had recently come from Italy with his wife Priscilla (because Claudius had commanded all the Jews to depart from Rome); and he came to them.

3 So, because he was of the same trade, he stayed with them [a]and worked; for by occupation they were tentmakers.

4 [a]And he reasoned in the synagogue every Sabbath, and persuaded both Jews and Greeks.

5 [a]When Silas and Timothy had come from Macedonia, Paul was [b]compelled by the Spirit, and testified to the Jews *that* Jesus *is* the Christ.

6 But [a]when they opposed him and blasphemed, [b]he shook *his* garments and said to them, [c]"Your blood *be* upon your *own* heads; [d]I *am* clean. [e]From now on I will go to the Gentiles."

7 And he departed from there and entered the house of a certain *man* named *Justus, *one* who worshiped God, whose house was next door to the synagogue.

8 [a]Then Crispus, the ruler of the synagogue, believed on the Lord with all his household. And many of the Corinthians, hearing, believed and were baptized.

9 Now [a]the Lord spoke to Paul in the night by a vision, "Do not be afraid, but speak, and do not keep silent;

10 [a]"for I am with you, and no one will attack you to hurt you; for I have many people in this city."

11 And he continued *there* a year and six months, teaching the word of God among them.

12 When Gallio was proconsul of Achaia, the Jews with one accord rose up against Paul and brought him to the judgment seat,

13 saying, "This *fellow* persuades men to worship God contrary to the law."

14 And when Paul was about to open *his* mouth, Gallio said to the Jews, "If it were a matter of wrongdoing or wicked crimes, O Jews, there would be reason why I should bear with you.

15 "But if it is a [a]question of words and names and your own law, look *to it* yourselves; for I do not want to be a judge of such *matters.*"

16 And he drove them from the judgment seat.

17 Then *all the Greeks took [a]Sosthenes, the ruler of the synagogue, and beat *him* before the judgment seat. But Gallio took no notice of these things.

Paul Returns to Antioch

18 So Paul still remained a good while. Then he took leave of the brethren and sailed for Syria,

KJV

ren, and sailed thence into Syria, and with him
Priscilla and Aquila; having [a]shorn *his* head in
[b]Cenchrea: for he had a vow.
19 And he came to Ephesus, and left them
there: but he himself entered into the synagogue,
and reasoned with the Jews.
20 When they desired *him* to tarry longer
time with them, he consented not;
21 But bade them farewell, saying, [a]I must
by all means keep this feast that cometh in Jerusalem: but I will return again unto you, [b]if God will.
And he sailed from Ephesus.
22 And when he had landed at [a]Caesarea,
and gone up, and saluted the church, he went
down to Antioch.
23 And after he had spent some time *there,*
he departed, and went over *all* the country of [a]Ga-
latia and Phrygia in order, [b]strengthening all the
disciples.

Ministry of Apollos

24 [a]And a certain Jew named Apollos, born
at Alexandria, an eloquent man, *and* mighty in
the scriptures, came to Ephesus.
25 This man was instructed in the way of the
Lord; and being [a]fervent in the spirit, he spake
and taught diligently the things of the Lord,
[b]knowing only the baptism of John.
26 And he began to speak boldly in the synagogue: whom when Aquila and Priscilla had
heard, they took him unto *them,* and expounded
unto him the way of God more perfectly.
27 And when he was disposed to pass into
Achaia, the brethren wrote, exhorting the disciples to receive him: who, when he was come,
[a]helped them much which had believed through
grace:
28 For he mightily convinced the Jews, *and*
that publickly, [a]shewing by the scriptures that
Jesus was Christ.

Paul at Ephesus

19 And it came to pass, that, while [a]Apollos
was at Corinth, Paul having passed through
the [b]upper coasts came to Ephesus: and finding
certain disciples,
2 He said unto them, Have ye received the
Holy Ghost since ye believed? And they said unto
him, [a]We have not so much as heard whether
there be any Holy Ghost.
3 And he said unto them, Unto what then
were ye baptized? And they said, [a]Unto John's
baptism.
4 Then said Paul, [a]John verily baptized with
the baptism of repentance, saying unto the people,
that they should believe on him which should
come after him, that is, on Christ Jesus.
5 When they heard *this,* they were baptized
[a]in the name of the Lord Jesus.
6 And when Paul had [a]laid *his* hands upon
them, the Holy Ghost came on them; and [b]they
spake with tongues, and prophesied.
7 And all the men were about twelve.
8 [a]And he went into the synagogue, and
spake boldly for the space of three months, disputing and persuading the things [b]concerning the
kingdom of God.
9 But [a]when divers were hardened, and believed not, but spake evil [b]of that way before the
multitude, he departed from them, and separated
the disciples, disputing daily in the school of one
Tyrannus.
10 And [a]this continued by the space of
two years; so that all they which dwell in Asia
heard the word of the Lord Jesus, both Jews and
Greeks.

Miracles Glorify Christ

11 And [a]God wrought special miracles by the
hands of Paul:
12 [a]So that from his body were brought unto
the sick handkerchiefs or aprons, and the diseases

18 [a]Num. 6:2, 5, 9, 18; Acts 21:24 [b]Rom. 16:1
21 [a]Acts 19:21; 20:16 [b]1 Cor. 4:19; Heb. 6:3; James 4:15
22 [a]Acts 8:40
23 [a]Gal. 1:2 [b]Acts 14:22; 15:32, 41
24 [a]Acts 19:1; 1 Cor. 1:12; 3:4; 16:12; Titus 3:13
25 [a]Rom. 12:11 [b][Matt. 3:1–11; Mark 1:7, 8; Luke 3:16, 17; 7:29; John 1:26, 33]; Acts 19:3
27 [a]1 Cor. 3:6
28 [a]Acts 9:22; 17:3; 18:5

CHAPTER 19
1 [a]1 Cor. 1:12; 3:5, 6; Titus 3:13 [b]Acts 18:23
2 [a]1 Sam. 3:7; Acts 8:16
3 [a]Luke 7:29; Acts 18:25
4 [a]Matt. 3:11; Mark 1:4, 7, 8; Luke 3:16; [John 1:15, 26, 27]; Acts 13:24
5 [a]Matt. 28:19; Acts 8:12, 16; 10:48
6 [a]Acts 6:6; 8:17 [b]Mark 16:17; Acts 2:4; 10:46
8 [a]Acts 17:2; 18:4 [b]Acts 1:3; 28:23
9 [a]2 Tim. 1:15; 2 Pet. 2:2; Jude 10 [b]Acts 9:2; 19:23; 22:4; 24:14
10 [a]Acts 19:8; 20:31
11 [a]Mark 16:20; Acts 14:3
12 [a]2 Kin. 4:29; Acts 5:15

*
18:21 NU omits *I must by all means keep this coming feast in Jerusalem*

NKJV

and Priscilla and Aquila *were* with him. [a]He had
his hair cut off at [b]Cenchrea, for he had taken a
vow.
19 And he came to Ephesus, and left them
there; but he himself entered the synagogue and
reasoned with the Jews.
20 When they asked *him* to stay a longer time
with them, he did not consent,
21 but took leave of them, saying, [a]"I* must
by all means keep this coming feast in Jerusalem;
but I will return again to you, [b]God willing." And
he sailed from Ephesus.
22 And when he had landed at [a]Caesarea,
and gone up and greeted the church, he went
down to Antioch.
23 After he had spent some time *there,* he
departed and went over the region of [a]Galatia and
Phrygia in order, [b]strengthening all the disciples.

Ministry of Apollos

24 [a]Now a certain Jew named Apollos, born
at Alexandria, an eloquent man *and* mighty in the
Scriptures, came to Ephesus.
25 This man had been instructed in the way
of the Lord; and being [a]fervent in spirit, he spoke
and taught accurately the things of the Lord,
[b]though he knew only the baptism of John.
26 So he began to speak boldly in the synagogue. When Aquila and Priscilla heard him, they
took him aside and explained to him the way of
God more accurately.
27 And when he desired to cross to Achaia,
the brethren wrote, exhorting the disciples to receive him; and when he arrived, [a]he greatly
helped those who had believed through grace;
28 for he vigorously refuted the Jews pub-
licly, [a]showing from the Scriptures that Jesus is
the Christ.

Paul at Ephesus

19 And it happened, while [a]Apollos was at
Corinth, that Paul, having passed through
[b]the upper regions, came to Ephesus. And finding
some disciples
2 he said to them, "Did you receive the Holy
Spirit when you believed?" So they said to him,
[a]"We have not so much as heard whether there
is a Holy Spirit."
3 And he said to them, "Into what then were
you baptized?" So they said, [a]"Into John's
baptism."
4 Then Paul said, [a]"John indeed baptized
with a baptism of repentance, saying to the people
that they should believe on Him who would come
after him, that is, on Christ Jesus."
5 When they heard *this,* they were baptized
[a]in the name of the Lord Jesus.
6 And when Paul had [a]laid hands on them,
the Holy Spirit came upon them, and [b]they spoke
with tongues and prophesied.
7 Now the men were about twelve in all.
8 [a]And he went into the synagogue and
spoke boldly for three months, reasoning and persuading [b]concerning the things of the kingdom
of God.
9 But [a]when some were hardened and did
not believe, but spoke evil [b]of the Way before the
multitude, he departed from them and withdrew
the disciples, reasoning daily in the school of
Tyrannus.
10 And [a]this continued for two years, so that
all who dwelt in Asia heard the word of the Lord
Jesus, both Jews and Greeks.

Miracles Glorify Christ

11 Now [a]God worked unusual miracles by
the hands of Paul,
12 [a]so that even handkerchiefs or aprons
were brought from his body to the sick, and the

KJV

departed from them, and the evil spirits went out
of them.
13 [a]Then certain of the vagabond Jews, exor-
cists, [b]took upon them to call over them which
had evil spirits the name of the Lord Jesus, saying, We adjure you by Jesus whom Paul
[c]preacheth.
14 And there were seven sons of *one* Sceva,
a Jew, *and* chief of the priests, which did so.
15 And the evil spirit answered and said,
Jesus I know, and Paul I know; but who are ye?
16 And the man in whom the evil spirit was
leaped on them, and overcame them, and prevailed against them, so that they fled out of that
house naked and wounded.
17 And this was known to all the Jews and
Greeks also dwelling at Ephesus; and [a]fear fell
on them all, and the name of the Lord Jesus was
magnified.
18 And many that believed came, and [a]con-
fessed, and shewed their deeds.
19 Many of them also which used curious
arts brought their books together, and burned
them before all *men:* and they counted the price
of them, and found *it* fifty thousand *pieces* of
silver.
20 [a]So mightily grew the word of God and
prevailed.

The Riot at Ephesus

21 [a]After these things were ended, Paul
[b]purposed in the spirit, when he had passed
through [c]Macedonia and Achaia, to go to Jerusalem, saying, After I have been there, [d]I must also
see Rome.
22 So he sent into Macedonia two of them
that ministered unto him, [a]Timotheus and [b]Eras-
tus; but he himself stayed in Asia for a season.
23 And [a]the same time there arose no small
stir about [b]that way.
24 For a certain *man* named Demetrius, a
silversmith, which made silver shrines for Diana,
brought [a]no small gain unto the craftsmen;
25 Whom he called together with the workmen of like occupation, and said, Sirs, ye know
that by this craft we have our wealth.
26 Moreover ye see and hear, that not alone
at Ephesus, but almost throughout all Asia, this
Paul hath persuaded and turned away much people, saying that [a]they be no gods, which are made
with hands:
27 So that not only this our craft is in danger
to be set at nought; but also that the temple of
the great goddess Diana should be despised, and
her magnificence should be destroyed, whom all
Asia and the world worshippeth.
28 And when they heard *these sayings,* they
were full of wrath, and cried out, saying, Great
is Diana of the Ephesians.
29 And the whole city was filled with confusion: and having caught [a]Gaius and [b]Aristarchus,
men of Macedonia, Paul's companions in travel,
they rushed with one accord into the theatre.
30 And when Paul would have entered in
unto the people, the disciples suffered him not.
31 And certain of the chief of Asia, which
were his friends, sent unto him, desiring *him* that
he would not adventure himself into the theatre.
32 Some therefore cried one thing, and some
another: for the assembly was confused; and the
more part knew not wherefore they were come
together.
33 And they drew Alexander out of the multitude, the Jews putting him forward. And [a]Alexan-
der [b]beckoned with the hand, and would have
made his defence unto the people.
34 But when they knew that he was a Jew,
all with one voice about the space of two hours
cried out, Great *is* Diana of the Ephesians.
35 And when the townclerk had appeased
the people, he said, *Ye* men of Ephesus, what man
is there that knoweth not how that the city of the

13 [a]Matt. 12:27; Luke 11:19 [b]Mark 9:38; Luke 9:49 [c]1 Cor. 1:23; 2:2
17 [a]Luke 1:65; 7:16; Acts 2:43; 5:5, 11
18 [a]Matt. 3:6
20 [a]Acts 6:7; 12:24
21 [a]Rom. 15:25; Gal. 2:1 [b]Acts 20:22; 2 Cor. 1:16 [c]Acts 20:1; 1 Cor. 16:5 [d]Acts 18:21; 23:11; Rom. 1:13; 15:22–29
22 [a]1 Tim. 1:2 [b]Rom. 16:23; 2 Tim. 4:20
23 [a]2 Cor. 1:8 [b]Acts 9:2
24 [a]Acts 16:16, 19
26 [a]Deut. 4:28; Ps. 115:4; Is. 44:10–20; Jer. 10:3; Acts 17:29; 1 Cor. 8:4; 10:19; Rev. 9:20
29 [a]Acts 20:4; Rom. 16:23; 1 Cor. 1:14; 3 John 1 [b]Acts 20:4; 27:2; Col. 4:10; Philem. 24
33 [a]1 Tim. 1:20; 2 Tim. 4:14 [b]Acts 12:17

*

19:13 NU *I*
19:16 M *and they overpowered them* • NU *both of them*
19:24 Gr. *Artemis*
19:27 NU *she be deposed from her magnificence*

NKJV

diseases left them and the evil spirits went out
of them.
13 [a]Then some of the itinerant Jewish exor-
cists [b]took it upon themselves to call the name
of the Lord Jesus over those who had evil spirits,
saying, *"We exorcise you by the Jesus whom
Paul [c]preaches."
14 Also there were seven sons of Sceva, a
Jewish chief priest, who did so.
15 And the evil spirit answered and said, "Jesus I know, and Paul I know; but who are you?"
16 Then the man in whom the evil spirit was
leaped on them, *overpowered them, and prevailed against *them, so that they fled out of that
house naked and wounded.
17 This became known both to all Jews and
Greeks dwelling in Ephesus; and [a]fear fell on
them all, and the name of the Lord Jesus was
magnified.
18 And many who had believed came [a]con-
fessing and telling their deeds.
19 Also, many of those who had practiced
magic brought their books together and burned
them in the sight of all. And they counted up the
value of them, and *it* totaled fifty thousand *pieces*
of silver.
20 [a]So the word of the Lord grew mightily
and prevailed.

The Riot at Ephesus

21 [a]When these things were accomplished,
Paul [b]purposed in the Spirit, when he had passed
through [c]Macedonia and Achaia, to go to Jerusalem, saying, "After I have been there, [d]I must also
see Rome."
22 So he sent into Macedonia two of those
who ministered to him, [a]Timothy and [b]Erastus,
but he himself stayed in Asia for a time.
23 And [a]about that time there arose a great
commotion about [b]the Way.
24 For a certain man named Demetrius, a silversmith, who made silver shrines of *Diana,
brought [a]no small profit to the craftsmen.
25 He called them together with the workers
of similar occupation, and said: "Men, you know
that we have our prosperity by this trade.
26 "Moreover you see and hear that not only
at Ephesus, but throughout almost all Asia, this
Paul has persuaded and turned away many people, saying that [a]they are not gods which are made
with hands.
27 "So not only is this trade of ours in danger
of falling into disrepute, but also the temple of
the great goddess Diana may be despised and *her
magnificence destroyed, whom all Asia and the
world worship."
28 Now when they heard *this,* they were full
of wrath and cried out, saying, "Great *is* Diana
of the Ephesians!"
29 So the whole city was filled with confusion, and rushed into the theater with one accord,
having seized [a]Gaius and [b]Aristarchus, Macedonians, Paul's travel companions.
30 And when Paul wanted to go in to the people, the disciples would not allow him.
31 Then some of the officials of Asia, who
were his friends, sent to him pleading that he
would not venture into the theater.
32 Some therefore cried one thing and some
another, for the assembly was confused, and most
of them did not know why they had come
together.
33 And they drew Alexander out of the multitude, the Jews putting him forward. And [a]Alexan-
der [b]motioned with his hand, and wanted to make
his defense to the people.
34 But when they found out that he was a
Jew, all with one voice cried out for about two
hours, "Great *is* Diana of the Ephesians!"
35 And when the city clerk had quieted the
crowd, he said: "Men of Ephesus, what man is
there who does not know that the city of the Ephe-

KJV

Ephesians is a worshipper of the great goddess Diana, and of the *image* which fell down from Jupiter?

36 Seeing then that these things cannot be spoken against, ye ought to be quiet, and to do nothing rashly.

37 For ye have brought hither these men, which are neither robbers of churches, nor yet blasphemers of your goddess.

38 Wherefore if Demetrius, and the craftsmen which are with him, have a matter against any man, the law is open, and there are deputies: let them implead one another.

39 But if ye enquire any thing concerning other matters, it shall be determined in a lawful assembly.

40 For we are in danger to be called in question for this day's uproar, there being no cause whereby we may give an account of this concourse.

41 And when he had thus spoken, he dismissed the assembly.

Journeys in Greece

20 And after the uproar was ceased, Paul called unto *him* the disciples, and embraced *them,* and [a]departed for to go into Macedonia.

2 And when he had gone over those parts, and had given them much exhortation, he came into [a]Greece,

3 And *there* abode three months. And [a]when the Jews laid wait for him, as he was about to sail into Syria, he purposed to return through Macedonia.

4 And there accompanied him into Asia Sopater of Berea; and of the Thessalonians, [a]Aristarchus and Secundus; and [b]Gaius of Derbe, and [c]Timotheus; and of Asia, [d]Tychicus and [e]Trophimus.

5 These going before tarried for us at [a]Troas.

6 And we sailed away from Philippi after [a]the days of unleavened bread, and came unto them [b]to Troas in five days; where we abode seven days.

Ministering at Troas

7 And upon [a]the first *day* of the week, when the disciples came together [b]to break bread, Paul preached unto them, ready to depart on the morrow; and continued his speech until midnight.

8 And there were many lights [a]in the upper chamber, where they were gathered together.

9 And there sat in a window a certain young man named Eutychus, being fallen into a deep sleep: and as Paul was long preaching, he sunk down with sleep, and fell down from the third loft, and was taken up dead.

10 And Paul went down, and [a]fell on him, and embracing *him* said, [b]Trouble not yourselves; for his life is in him.

11 When he therefore was come up again, and had broken bread, and eaten, and talked a long while, even till break of day, so he departed.

12 And they brought the young man alive, and were not a little comforted.

From Troas to Miletus

13 And we went before to ship, and sailed unto Assos, there intending to take in Paul: for so had he appointed, minding himself to go afoot.

14 And when he met with us at Assos, we took him in, and came to Mitylene.

15 And we sailed thence, and came the next *day* over against Chios; and the next *day* we arrived at Samos, and tarried at Trogyllium; and the next *day* we came to Miletus.

16 For Paul had determined to sail by Ephesus, because he would not spend the time in Asia: for [a]he hasted, if it were possible for him, [b]to be at Jerusalem [c]the day of Pentecost.

CHAPTER 20
1 [a]1 Cor. 16:5; 1 Tim. 1:3
2 [a]Acts 17:15; 18:1
3 [a]Acts 9:23; 23:12; 25:3; 2 Cor. 11:26
4 [a]Acts 19:29; Col. 4:10 [b]Acts 19:29 [c]Acts 16:1 [d]Eph. 6:21; Col. 4:7; 2 Tim. 4:12; Titus 3:12 [e]Acts 21:29; 2 Tim. 4:20
5 [a]2 Cor. 2:12; 2 Tim. 4:13
6 [a]Ex. 12:14, 15 [b]Acts 16:8; 2 Cor. 2:12; 2 Tim. 4:13
7 [a]1 Cor. 16:2; Rev. 1:10 [b]Acts 2:42, 46; 20:11; 1 Cor. 10:16
8 [a]Acts 1:13
10 [a]1 Kin. 17:21; 2 Kin. 4:34 [b]Matt. 9:23, 24; Mark 5:39
16 [a]Acts 18:21; 19:21; 21:4 [b]Acts 24:17 [c]Acts 2:1; 1 Cor. 16:8

*

19:37 NU *our*
20:8 NU, M *we*

NKJV

sians is temple guardian of the great goddess Diana, and of the *image* which fell down from Zeus?

36 "Therefore, since these things cannot be denied, you ought to be quiet and do nothing rashly.

37 "For you have brought these men here who are neither robbers of temples nor blasphemers of *your goddess.

38 "Therefore, if Demetrius and his fellow craftsmen have a case against anyone, the courts are open and there are proconsuls. Let them bring charges against one another.

39 "But if you have any other inquiry to make, it shall be determined in the lawful assembly.

40 "For we are in danger of being called in question for today's uproar, there being no reason which we may give to account for this disorderly gathering."

41 And when he had said these things, he dismissed the assembly.

Journeys in Greece

20 After the uproar had ceased, Paul called the disciples to *himself,* embraced *them,* and [a]departed to go to Macedonia.

2 Now when he had gone over that region and encouraged them with many words, he came to [a]Greece

3 and stayed three months. And [a]when the Jews plotted against him as he was about to sail to Syria, he decided to return through Macedonia.

4 And Sopater of Berea accompanied him to Asia—also [a]Aristarchus and Secundus of the Thessalonians, and [b]Gaius of Derbe, and [c]Timothy, and [d]Tychicus and [e]Trophimus of Asia.

5 These men, going ahead, waited for us at [a]Troas.

6 But we sailed away from Philippi after [a]the Days of Unleavened Bread, and in five days joined them [b]at Troas, where we stayed seven days.

Ministering at Troas

7 Now on [a]the first *day* of the week, when the disciples came together [b]to break bread, Paul, ready to depart the next day, spoke to them and continued his message until midnight.

8 There were many lamps [a]in the upper room where *they were gathered together.

9 And in a window sat a certain young man named Eutychus, who was sinking into a deep sleep. He was overcome by sleep; and as Paul continued speaking, he fell down from the third story and was taken up dead.

10 But Paul went down, [a]fell on him, and embracing *him* said, [b]"Do not trouble yourselves, for his life is in him."

11 Now when he had come up, had broken bread and eaten, and talked a long while, even till daybreak, he departed.

12 And they brought the young man in alive, and they were not a little comforted.

From Troas to Miletus

13 Then we went ahead to the ship and sailed to Assos, there intending to take Paul on board; for so he had given orders, intending himself to go on foot.

14 And when he met us at Assos, we took him on board and came to Mitylene.

15 We sailed from there, and the next *day* came opposite Chios. The following *day* we arrived at Samos and stayed at Trogyllium. The next *day* we came to Miletus.

16 For Paul had decided to sail past Ephesus, so that he would not have to spend time in Asia; for [a]he was hurrying [b]to be at Jerusalem, if possible, on [c]the Day of Pentecost.

KJV

The Ephesian Elders Exhorted

17 And from Miletus he sent to Ephesus, and
called the elders of the church.
18 And when they were come to him, he said
unto them, Ye know, [a]from the first day that I
came into Asia, after what manner I have been
with you at all seasons,
19 Serving the Lord with all humility of
mind, and with many tears, and temptations,
which befell me [a]by the lying in wait of the Jews:
20 *And* how [a]I kept back nothing that was
profitable *unto you,* but have shewed you, and
have taught you publickly, and from house to
house,
21 [a]Testifying both to the Jews, and also to
the Greeks, [b]repentance toward God, and faith
toward our Lord Jesus Christ.
22 And now, behold, [a]I go bound in the spirit
unto Jerusalem, not knowing the things that shall
befall me there:
23 Save that [a]the Holy Ghost witnesseth in
every city, saying that bonds and afflictions abide
me.
24 But [a]none of these things move me, neither count I my life dear unto myself, [b]so that I
might finish my course with joy, [c]and the ministry, [d]which I have received of the Lord Jesus, to
testify the gospel of the grace of God.
25 And now, behold, I know that ye all,
among whom I have gone preaching the kingdom
of God, shall see my face no more.
26 Wherefore I take you to record this day,
that I *am* [a]pure from the blood of all *men.*
27 For I have not shunned to declare unto
you all [a]the counsel of God.
28 [a]Take heed therefore unto yourselves, and
to all the flock, over the which the Holy Ghost
[b]hath made you overseers, to feed the church of
God, [c]which he hath purchased [d]with his own
blood.
29 For I know this, that after my departing
[a]shall grievous wolves enter in among you, not
sparing the flock.
30 Also [a]of your own selves shall men arise,
speaking perverse things, to draw away disciples
after them.
31 Therefore watch, and remember, that [a]by
the space of three years I ceased not to warn every
one night and day with tears.
32 And now, brethren, I commend you to
God, and [a]to the word of his grace, which is able
[b]to build you up, and to give you [c]an inheritance
among all them which are sanctified.
33 I have coveted no man's silver, or gold,
or apparel.
34 Yea, ye yourselves know, [a]that these
hands have ministered unto my necessities, and
to them that were with me.
35 I have shewed you all things, [a]how that
so labouring ye ought to support the weak, and
to remember the words of the Lord Jesus, how
he said, It is more blessed to give than to receive.
36 And when he had thus spoken, he kneeled
down, and prayed with them all.
37 And they all [a]wept sore, and [b]fell on
Paul's neck, and kissed him,
38 Sorrowing most of all for the words which
he spake, that they should see his face no more.
And they accompanied him unto the ship.

Warnings on the Journey to Jerusalem

21 And it came to pass, that after we were gotten from them, and had launched, we came
with a straight course unto Coos, and the *day* following unto Rhodes, and from thence unto Patara:
2 And finding a ship sailing over unto Phe-
nicia, we went aboard, and set forth.
3 Now when we had discovered Cyprus, we
left it on the left hand, and sailed into Syria, and
landed at Tyre: for there the ship was to unlade
her burden.
4 And finding disciples, we tarried there

18 [a]Acts 18:19; 19:1, 10; 20:4, 16
19 [a]Acts 20:3
20 [a]Acts 20:27
21 [a]Acts 18:5; 19:10 [b]Mark 1:15
22 [a]Acts 19:21
23 [a]Acts 21:4, 11
24 [a]Acts 21:13 [b]Acts 13:25; 2 Tim. 4:7 [c]Acts 1:17 [d]Gal. 1:1
26 [a]Acts 18:6; 2 Cor. 7:2
27 [a]Luke 7:30; John 15:15; Eph. 1:11
28 [a]Luke 12:32; John 21:15–17; Acts 20:29; [1 Tim. 4:16]; 1 Pet. 5:2 [b]1 Cor. 12:28 [c]Eph. 1:7, 14; Col. 1:14; Titus 2:14; Heb. 9:12; [1 Pet. 1:19]; Rev. 5:9 [d]Heb. 9:14
29 [a]Ezek. 22:27; Matt. 7:15
30 [a]1 Tim. 1:20; 2 Tim. 1:15
31 [a]Acts 19:8, 10; 24:17
32 [a]Heb. 13:9 [b]Acts 9:31 [c]Acts 26:18; Eph. 1:14, 18; 5:5; Col. 1:12; 3:24; [Heb. 9:15; 1 Pet. 1:4]
34 [a]Acts 18:3; 1 Cor. 4:12; 1 Thess. 2:9; 2 Thess. 3:8
35 [a]Rom. 15:1; 1 Cor. 9:12; 2 Cor. 11:9, 12; Eph. 4:28; 1 Thess. 4:11; 2 Thess. 3:8
37 [a]Acts 21:13 [b]Gen. 45:14

*

20:24 NU *But I do not count my life of any value or dear to myself*
20:28 M *of the Lord and God*
20:34 NU, M omit *Yes*
21:4 NU *the disciples*

NKJV

The Ephesian Elders Exhorted

17 From Miletus he sent to Ephesus and
called for the elders of the church.
18 And when they had come to him, he said
to them: "You know, [a]from the first day that I
came to Asia, in what manner I always lived
among you,
19 "serving the Lord with all humility, with
many tears and trials which happened to me [a]by
the plotting of the Jews;
20 "how [a]I kept back nothing that was helpful, but proclaimed it to you, and taught you pub-
licly and from house to house,
21 [a]"testifying to Jews, and also to Greeks,
[b]repentance toward God and faith toward our
Lord Jesus Christ.
22 "And see, now [a]I go bound in the spirit
to Jerusalem, not knowing the things that will
happen to me there,
23 "except that [a]the Holy Spirit testifies in
every city, saying that chains and tribulations
await me.
24 *"But [a]none of these things move me; nor
do I count my life dear to myself, [b]so that I may
finish my race with joy, [c]and the ministry [d]which
I received from the Lord Jesus, to testify to the
gospel of the grace of God.
25 "And indeed, now I know that you all,
among whom I have gone preaching the kingdom
of God, will see my face no more.
26 "Therefore I testify to you this day that I
am [a]innocent of the blood of all *men.*
27 "For I have not shunned to declare to you
[a]the whole counsel of God.
28 [a]"Therefore take heed to yourselves and
to all the flock, among which the Holy Spirit [b]has
made you overseers, to shepherd the church *of
God [c]which He purchased [d]with His own blood.
29 "For I know this, that after my departure
[a]savage wolves will come in among you, not sparing the flock.
30 "Also [a]from among yourselves men will
rise up, speaking perverse things, to draw away
the disciples after themselves.
31 "Therefore watch, and remember that [a]for
three years I did not cease to warn everyone night
and day with tears.
32 "So now, brethren, I commend you to God
and [a]to the word of His grace, which is able [b]to
build you up and give you [c]an inheritance among
all those who are sanctified.
33 "I have coveted no one's silver or gold or
apparel.
34 *"Yes, you yourselves know [a]that these
hands have provided for my necessities, and for
those who were with me.
35 "I have shown you in every way, [a]by laboring like this, that you must support the weak.
And remember the words of the Lord Jesus, that
He said, 'It is more blessed to give than to
receive.' "
36 And when he had said these things, he
knelt down and prayed with them all.
37 Then they all [a]wept freely, and [b]fell on
Paul's neck and kissed him,
38 sorrowing most of all for the words which
he spoke, that they would see his face no more.
And they accompanied him to the ship.

Warnings on the Journey to Jerusalem

21 Now it came to pass, that when we had departed from them and set sail, running a
straight course we came to Cos, the following *day*
to Rhodes, and from there to Patara.
2 And finding a ship sailing over to Phoenicia, we went aboard and set sail.
3 When we had sighted Cyprus, we passed
it on the left, sailed to Syria, and landed at Tyre;
for there the ship was to unload her cargo.
4 And finding *disciples, we stayed there

KJV

seven days: [a]who said to Paul through the Spirit, that he should not go up to Jerusalem.

5 And when we had accomplished those days, we departed and went our way; and they all brought us on our way, with wives and children, till *we were* out of the city: and [a]we kneeled down on the shore, and prayed.

6 And when we had taken our leave one of another, we took ship; and they returned [a]home again.

7 And when we had finished *our* course from Tyre, we came to Ptolemais, and saluted the brethren, and abode with them one day.

8 And the next *day* we that were of Paul's company departed, and came unto [a]Caesarea: and we entered into the house of Philip [b]the evangelist, [c]which was *one* of the seven; and abode with him.

9 And the same man had four daughters, virgins, [a]which did prophesy.

10 And as we tarried *there* many days, there came down from Judaea a certain prophet, named [a]Agabus.

11 And when he was come unto us, he took Paul's girdle, and bound his own hands and feet, and said, Thus saith the Holy Ghost, [a]So shall the Jews at Jerusalem bind the man that owneth this girdle, and shall deliver *him* into the hands of the Gentiles.

12 And when we heard these things, both we, and they of that place, besought him not to go up to Jerusalem.

13 Then Paul answered, [a]What mean ye to weep and to break mine heart? for I am ready not to be bound only, but also to die at Jerusalem for the name of the Lord Jesus.

14 And when he would not be persuaded, we ceased, saying, [a]The will of the Lord be done.

Paul Urged to Make Peace

15 And after those days we took up our carriages, and went up to Jerusalem.

16 There went with us also *certain* of the disciples of Caesarea, and brought with them one Mnason of Cyprus, an old disciple, with whom we should lodge.

17 [a]And when we were come to Jerusalem, the brethren received us gladly.

18 And the *day* following Paul went in with us unto [a]James; and all the elders were present.

19 And when he had saluted them, [a]he declared particularly what things God had wrought among the Gentiles [b]by his ministry.

20 And when they heard *it*, they glorified the Lord, and said unto him, Thou seest, brother, how many thousands of Jews there are which believe; and they are all [a]zealous of the law:

21 And they are informed of thee, that thou teachest all the Jews which are among the Gentiles to forsake Moses, saying that they ought not to circumcise *their* children, neither to walk after the customs.

22 What is it therefore? the multitude must needs come together: for they will hear that thou art come.

23 Do therefore this that we say to thee: We have four men which have a vow on them;

24 Them take, and purify thyself with them, and be at charges with them, that they may [a]shave *their* heads: and all may know that those things, whereof they were informed concerning thee, are nothing; but *that* thou thyself also walkest orderly, and keepest the law.

25 As touching the Gentiles which believe, [a]we have written *and* concluded that they observe no such thing, save only that they keep themselves from *things* offered to idols, and from blood, and from strangled, and from fornication.

Arrested in the Temple

26 Then Paul took the men, and the next day purifying himself with them [a]entered into the

NKJV

seven days. [a]They told Paul through the Spirit not to go up to Jerusalem.

5 When we had come to the end of those days, we departed and went on our way; and they all accompanied us, with wives and children, till *we were* out of the city. And [a]we knelt down on the shore and prayed.

6 When we had taken our leave of one another, we boarded the ship, and they returned [a]home.

7 And when we had finished *our* voyage from Tyre, we came to Ptolemais, greeted the brethren, and stayed with them one day.

8 On the next *day* we *who were Paul's companions departed and came to [a]Caesarea, and entered the house of Philip [b]the evangelist, [c]who was *one* of the seven, and stayed with him.

9 Now this man had four virgin daughters [a]who prophesied.

10 And as we stayed many days, a certain prophet named [a]Agabus came down from Judea.

11 When he had come to us, he took Paul's belt, bound his *own* hands and feet, and said, "Thus says the Holy Spirit, [a]'So shall the Jews at Jerusalem bind the man who owns this belt, and deliver *him* into the hands of the Gentiles.' "

12 Now when we heard these things, both we and those from that place pleaded with him not to go up to Jerusalem.

13 Then Paul answered, [a]"What do you mean by weeping and breaking my heart? For I am ready not only to be bound, but also to die at Jerusalem for the name of the Lord Jesus."

14 So when he would not be persuaded, we ceased, saying, [a]"The will of the Lord be done."

Paul Urged to Make Peace

15 And after those days we packed and went up to Jerusalem.

16 Also some of the disciples from Caesarea went with us and brought with them a certain Mnason of Cyprus, an early disciple, with whom we were to lodge.

17 [a]And when we had come to Jerusalem, the brethren received us gladly.

18 On the following *day* Paul went in with us to [a]James, and all the elders were present.

19 When he had greeted them, [a]he told in detail those things which God had done among the Gentiles [b]through his ministry.

20 And when they heard *it*, they glorified the Lord. And they said to him, "You see, brother, how many myriads of Jews there are who have believed, and they are all [a]zealous for the law;

21 "but they have been informed about you that you teach all the Jews who are among the Gentiles to forsake Moses, saying that they ought not to circumcise *their* children nor to walk according to the customs.

22 *"What then? The assembly must certainly meet, for they will hear that you have come.

23 "Therefore do what we tell you: We have four men who have taken a vow.

24 "Take them and be purified with them, and pay their expenses so that they may [a]shave *their* heads, and that all may know that those things of which they were informed concerning you are nothing, but *that* you yourself also walk orderly and keep the law.

25 "But concerning the Gentiles who believe, [a]we have written *and* decided *that they should observe no such thing, except that they should keep themselves from *things* offered to idols, from blood, from things strangled, and from sexual immorality."

Arrested in the Temple

26 Then Paul took the men, and the next day, having been purified with them, [a]entered the

---

CHAPTER 21
4 [a][Acts 20:23; 21:12]
5 [a]Luke 22:41; Acts 9:40; 20:36
6 [a]John 1:11
8 [a]Acts 8:40; 21:16 [b]Acts 8:5, 26, 40; Eph. 4:11; 2 Tim. 4:5 [c]Acts 6:5
9 [a]Joel 2:28; Acts 2:17
10 [a]Acts 11:28
11 [a]Acts 20:23; 21:33; 22:25
13 [a]Acts 20:24, 37
14 [a]Matt. 6:10; 26:42; Luke 11:2; 22:42
17 [a]Acts 15:4
18 [a]Acts 15:13; Gal. 1:19; 2:9
19 [a]Acts 15:4, 12; Rom. 15:18, 19 [b]Acts 1:17; 20:24; 1 Tim. 2:7
20 [a]Acts 15:1; 22:3; [Rom. 10:2]; Gal. 1:14
24 [a]Num. 6:2, 13, 18; Acts 18:18
25 [a]Acts 15:19, 20, 29
26 [a]John 11:55; Acts 21:24; 24:18

---

*
21:8 NU omits *who were Paul's companions*
21:22 NU *What then is to be done? They will certainly hear*
21:25 NU omits *that they should observe no such thing, except*

KJV

temple, [b]to signify the accomplishment of the days of purification, until that an offering should be offered for every one of them.
27 And when the seven days were almost ended, [a]the Jews which were of Asia, when they saw him in the temple, stirred up all the people, and [b]laid hands on him,
28 Crying out, Men of Israel, help: This is the man, [a]that teacheth all *men* every where against the people, and the law, and this place: and further brought Greeks also into the temple, and hath polluted this holy place.
29 (For they had seen before with him in the city [a]Trophimus an Ephesian, whom they supposed that Paul had brought into the temple.)
30 And [a]all the city was moved, and the people ran together: and they took Paul, and drew him out of the temple: and forthwith the doors were shut.
31 And as they went [a]about to kill him, tidings came unto the chief captain of the band, that all Jerusalem was in an uproar.
32 [a]Who immediately took soldiers and centurions, and ran down unto them: and when they saw the chief captain and the soldiers, they left beating of Paul.
33 Then the [a]chief captain came near, and took him, and [b]commanded *him* to be bound with two chains; and demanded who he was, and what he had done.
34 And some cried one thing, some another, among the multitude: and when he could not know the certainty for the tumult, he commanded him to be carried into the castle.
35 And when he came upon the stairs, so it was, that he was borne of the soldiers for the violence of the people.
36 For the multitude of the people followed after, crying, [a]Away with him.

Addressing the Jerusalem Mob
(Acts 9:1–19; 26:12–18)

37 And as Paul was to be led into the castle, he said unto the chief captain, May I speak unto thee? Who said, Canst thou speak Greek?
38 [a]Art not thou that Egyptian, which before these days madest an uproar, and leddest out into the wilderness four thousand men that were murderers?
39 But Paul said, [a]I am a man *which am* a Jew of Tarsus, *a city* in Cilicia, a citizen of no mean city: and, I beseech thee, suffer me to speak unto the people.
40 And when he had given him licence, Paul stood on the stairs, and [a]beckoned with the hand unto the people. And when there was made a great silence, he spake unto *them* in the [b]Hebrew tongue, saying,

22 Men, [a]brethren, and fathers, hear ye my defence *which I make* now unto you.
2 (And when they heard that he spake in the [a]Hebrew tongue to them, they kept the more silence: and he saith,)
3 [a]I am verily a man *which am* a Jew, born in Tarsus, *a city* in Cilicia, yet brought up in this city [b]at the feet of [c]Gamaliel, *and* taught [d]according to the perfect manner of the law of the fathers, and [e]was zealous toward God, [f]as ye all are this day.
4 [a]And I persecuted this way unto the death, binding and delivering into prisons both men and women.
5 As also the high priest doth bear me witness, and [a]all the estate of the elders: [b]from whom also I received letters unto the brethren, and went to Damascus, [c]to bring them which were there bound unto Jerusalem, for to be punished.
6 And [a]it came to pass, that, as I made my journey, and was come nigh unto Damascus about noon, suddenly there shone from heaven a great light round about me.

26 [b]Num. 6:13; Acts 24:18
27 [a]Acts 20:19; 24:18 [b]Acts 26:21
28 [a][Matt. 24:15]; Acts 6:13; 24:6
29 [a]Acts 20:4
30 [a]2 Kin. 11:15; Acts 16:19; 26:21
31 [a]2 Cor. 11:23
32 [a]Acts 23:27; 24:7
33 [a]Acts 24:7 [b]Acts 20:23; 21:11; Eph. 6:20; 2 Tim. 1:16; 2:9
36 [a]Luke 23:18; John 19:15; Acts 22:22
38 [a]Acts 5:36
39 [a]Acts 9:11; 22:3; 2 Cor. 11:22; Phil. 3:4–6
40 [a]Acts 12:17 [b]John 5:2; Acts 22:2

CHAPTER 22

1 [a]Acts 7:2
2 [a]Acts 21:40
3 [a]Acts 21:39; 2 Cor. 11:22 [b]Deut. 33:3 [c]Acts 5:34 [d]Acts 23:6; 26:5; Phil. 3:6 [e]Acts 21:20; Gal. 1:14 [f][Rom. 10:2]
4 [a]Acts 8:3; 26:9–11; Phil. 3:6; 1 Tim. 1:13
5 [a]Acts 23:14; 24:1; 25:15 [b]Luke 22:66; Acts 4:5; 1 Tim. 4:4 [c]Acts 9:2
6 [a]Acts 9:3; 26:12, 13

*

21:29 M omits *previously*

NKJV

temple [b]to announce the expiration of the days of purification, at which time an offering should be made for each one of them.
27 Now when the seven days were almost ended, [a]the Jews from Asia, seeing him in the temple, stirred up the whole crowd and [b]laid hands on him,
28 crying out, "Men of Israel, help! This is the man [a]who teaches all *men* everywhere against the people, the law, and this place; and furthermore he also brought Greeks into the temple and has defiled this holy place."
29 (For they had *previously seen [a]Trophimus the Ephesian with him in the city, whom they supposed that Paul had brought into the temple.)
30 And [a]all the city was disturbed; and the people ran together, seized Paul, and dragged him out of the temple; and immediately the doors were shut.
31 Now as they were [a]seeking to kill him, news came to the commander of the garrison that all Jerusalem was in an uproar.
32 [a]He immediately took soldiers and centurions, and ran down to them. And when they saw the commander and the soldiers, they stopped beating Paul.
33 Then the [a]commander came near and took him, and [b]commanded *him* to be bound with two chains; and he asked who he was and what he had done.
34 And some among the multitude cried one thing and some another. So when he could not ascertain the truth because of the tumult, he commanded him to be taken into the barracks.
35 When he reached the stairs, he had to be carried by the soldiers because of the violence of the mob.
36 For the multitude of the people followed after, crying out, [a]"Away with him!"

Addressing the Jerusalem Mob
(Acts 9:1–19; 26:12–18)

37 Then as Paul was about to be led into the barracks, he said to the commander, "May I speak to you?" He replied, "Can you speak Greek?
38 [a]"Are you not the Egyptian who some time ago stirred up a rebellion and led the four thousand assassins out into the wilderness?"
39 But Paul said, [a]"I am a Jew from Tarsus, in Cilicia, a citizen of no mean city; and I implore you, permit me to speak to the people."
40 So when he had given him permission, Paul stood on the stairs and [a]motioned with his hand to the people. And when there was a great silence, he spoke to *them* in the [b]Hebrew language, saying,

22 "Brethren[a] and fathers, hear my defense before you now."
2 And when they heard that he spoke to them in the [a]Hebrew language, they kept all the more silent. Then he said:
3 [a]"I am indeed a Jew, born in Tarsus of Cilicia, but brought up in this city [b]at the feet of [c]Gamaliel, taught [d]according to the strictness of our fathers' law, and [e]was zealous toward God [f]as you all are today.
4 [a]"I persecuted this Way to the death, binding and delivering into prisons both men and women,
5 "as also the high priest bears me witness, and [a]all the council of the elders, [b]from whom I also received letters to the brethren, and went to Damascus [c]to bring in chains even those who were there to Jerusalem to be punished.
6 "Now [a]it happened, as I journeyed and came near Damascus at about noon, suddenly a great light from heaven shone around me.

KJV

7 And I fell unto the ground, and heard a
voice saying unto me, Saul, Saul, why persecutest
thou me?
8 And I answered, Who art thou, Lord? And
he said unto me, I am Jesus of Nazareth, whom
thou persecutest.
9 And [a]they that were with me saw indeed
the light, and were afraid; but they heard not the
voice of him that spake to me.
10 And I said, What shall I do, Lord? And
the Lord said unto me, Arise, and go into Damascus; and there it shall be told thee of all things
which are appointed for thee to do.
11 And when I could not see for the glory of
that light, being led by the hand of them that were
with me, I came into Damascus.
12 And [a]one Ananias, a devout man according to the law, [b]having a good report of all the
[c]Jews which dwelt *there*,
13 Came unto me, and stood, and said unto
me, Brother Saul, receive thy sight. And the same
hour I looked up upon him.
14 And he said, [a]The God of our fathers
[b]hath chosen thee, that thou shouldest [c]know his
will, and [d]see that Just One, and [e]shouldest hear
the voice of his mouth.
15 [a]For thou shalt be his witness unto all men
of [b]what thou hast seen and heard.
16 And now why tarriest thou? arise, and be
baptized, [a]and wash away thy sins, [b]calling on
the name of the Lord.
17 And [a]it came to pass, that, when I was
come again to Jerusalem, even while I prayed in
the temple, I was in a trance;
18 And [a]saw him saying unto me, [b]Make
haste, and get thee quickly out of Jerusalem: for
they will not receive thy testimony concerning
me.
19 And I said, Lord, [a]they know that I imprisoned and [b]beat in every synagogue them that believed on thee:
20 [a]And when the blood of thy martyr Stephen was shed, I also was standing by, and [b]con-
senting unto his death, and kept the raiment of
them that slew him.
21 And he said unto me, Depart: [a]for I will
send thee far hence unto the Gentiles.

Paul's Roman Citizenship

22 And they gave him audience unto this
word, and *then* lifted up their voices, and said,
[a]Away with such a *fellow* from the earth: for it
is not fit that [b]he should live.
23 And as they cried out, and cast off *their*
clothes, and threw dust into the air,
24 The chief captain commanded him to be
brought into the castle, and bade that he should
be examined by scourging; that he might know
wherefore they cried so against him.
25 And as they bound him with thongs, Paul
said unto the centurion that stood by, [a]Is it lawful
for you to scourge a man that is a Roman, and
uncondemned?
26 When the centurion heard *that*, he went
and told the chief captain, saying, Take heed what
thou doest: for this man is a Roman.
27 Then the chief captain came, and said
unto him, Tell me, art thou a Roman? He said,
Yea.
28 And the chief captain answered, With a
great sum obtained I this freedom. And Paul said,
But I was *free* born.
29 Then straightway they departed from
him which should have examined him: and the
chief captain also was afraid, after he knew that
he was a Roman, and because he had bound
him.

The Sanhedrin Divided

30 On the morrow, because he would have
known the certainty wherefore he was accused
of the Jews, he loosed him from *his* bands, and

9 [a]Dan. 10:7; Acts 9:7
12 [a]Acts 9:17 [b]Acts 10:22 [c]1 Tim. 3:7
14 [a]Acts 3:13; 5:30 [b]Acts 9:15; 26:16; Gal. 1:15 [c]Acts 3:14; 7:52 [d]Acts 9:17; 26:16; 1 Cor. 9:1; 15:8 [e]1 Cor. 11:23; Gal. 1:12
15 [a]Acts 23:11 [b]Acts 4:20; 26:16
16 [a]Acts 2:38; 1 Cor. 6:11; [Eph. 5:26]; Heb. 10:22 [b]Acts 9:14; Rom. 10:13
17 [a]Acts 9:26; 26:20; 2 Cor. 12:2
18 [a]Acts 22:14 [b]Matt. 10:14
19 [a]Acts 8:3; 22:4 [b]Matt. 10:17; Acts 26:11
20 [a]Acts 7:54—8:1 [b]Luke 11:48
21 [a]Acts 9:15; Rom. 1:5; 11:13; Gal. 2:7, 8; Eph. 3:7, 8; 1 Tim. 2:7; 2 Tim. 1:11
22 [a]Acts 21:36; 1 Thess. 2:16 [b]Acts 25:24
25 [a]Acts 16:37

NKJV

7 "And I fell to the ground and heard a voice
saying to me, 'Saul, Saul, why are you persecuting
Me?'
8 "So I answered, 'Who are You, Lord?' And
He said to me, 'I am Jesus of Nazareth, whom
you are persecuting.'
9 "And [a]those who were with me indeed
saw the light *and were afraid, but they did not
hear the voice of Him who spoke to me.
10 "So I said, 'What shall I do, Lord?' And
the Lord said to me, 'Arise and go into Damascus,
and there you will be told all things which are
appointed for you to do.'
11 "And since I could not see for the glory
of that light, being led by the hand of those who
were with me, I came into Damascus.
12 "Then [a]a certain Ananias, a devout man
according to the law, [b]having a good testimony
with all the [c]Jews who dwelt *there*,
13 "came to me; and he stood and said to
me, 'Brother Saul, receive your sight.' And at that
same hour I looked up at him.
14 "Then he said, [a]'The God of our fathers
[b]has chosen you that you should [c]know His will,
and [d]see the Just One, [e]and hear the voice of His
mouth.
15 [a]'For you will be His witness to all men
of [b]what you have seen and heard.
16 'And now why are you waiting? Arise and
be baptized, [a]and wash away your sins, [b]calling
on the name of the Lord.'
17 "Now [a]it happened, when I returned to
Jerusalem and was praying in the temple, that I
was in a trance
18 "and [a]saw Him saying to me, [b]'Make
haste and get out of Jerusalem quickly, for they
will not receive your testimony concerning Me.'
19 "So I said, 'Lord, [a]they know that in every
synagogue I imprisoned and [b]beat those who believe on You.
20 [a]'And when the blood of Your martyr Stephen was shed, I also was standing by [b]consent-
ing *to his death, and guarding the clothes of
those who were killing him.'
21 "Then He said to me, 'Depart, [a]for I will
send you far from here to the Gentiles.' "

Paul's Roman Citizenship

22 And they listened to him until this word,
and *then* they raised their voices and said,
[a]"Away with such a *fellow* from the earth, for [b]he
is not fit to live!"
23 Then, as they cried out and tore off *their*
clothes and threw dust into the air,
24 the commander ordered him to be brought
into the barracks, and said that he should be examined under scourging, so that he might know
why they shouted so against him.
25 And as they bound him with thongs, Paul
said to the centurion who stood by, [a]"Is it lawful
for you to scourge a man who is a Roman, and
uncondemned?"
26 When the centurion heard *that*, he went
and told the commander, saying, "Take care what
you do, for this man is a Roman."
27 Then the commander came and said to
him, "Tell me, are you a Roman?" He said, "Yes."
28 The commander answered, "With a large
sum I obtained this citizenship." And Paul said,
"But I was born *a citizen*."
29 Then immediately those who were about
to examine him withdrew from him; and the commander was also afraid after he found out that
he was a Roman, and because he had bound him.

The Sanhedrin Divided

30 The next day, because he wanted to know
for certain why he was accused by the Jews, he
released him from *his* bonds, and commanded the

*
22:9 NU omits *and were afraid*
22:20 NU omits *to his death*

KJV

commanded the chief priests and all their council to appear, and brought Paul down, and set him before them.

23 And Paul, earnestly beholding the council, said, Men *and* brethren, [a]I have lived in all good conscience before God until this day.

2 And the high priest Ananias commanded them that stood by him [a]to smite him on the mouth.

3 Then said Paul unto him, God shall smite thee, *thou* whited wall: for sittest thou to judge me after the law, and [a]commandest me to be smitten contrary to the law?

4 And they that stood by said, Revilest thou God's high priest?

5 Then said Paul, [a]I wist not, brethren, that he was the high priest: for it is written, [b]THOU SHALT NOT SPEAK EVIL OF THE RULER OF THY PEOPLE.

6 But when Paul perceived that the one part were Sadducees, and the other Pharisees, he cried out in the council, Men *and* brethren, [a]I am a Pharisee, the son of a Pharisee: [b]of the hope and resurrection of the dead I am called in question.

7 And when he had so said, there arose a dissension between the Pharisees and the Sadducees: and the multitude was divided.

8 [a]For the Sadducees say that there is no resurrection, neither angel, nor spirit: but the Pharisees confess both.

9 And there arose a great cry: and the scribes *that were* of the Pharisees' part arose, and strove, saying, [a]We find no evil in this man: but [b]if a spirit or an angel hath spoken to him, [c]let us not fight against God.

10 And when there arose a great dissension, the chief captain, fearing lest Paul should have been pulled in pieces of them, commanded the soldiers to go down, and to take him by force from among them, and to bring *him* into the castle.

The Plot Against Paul

11 And [a]the night following the Lord stood by him, and said, Be of good cheer, Paul: for as thou hast testified of me in [b]Jerusalem, so must thou bear witness also at [c]Rome.

12 And when it was day, [a]certain of the Jews banded together, and bound themselves under a curse, saying that they would neither eat nor drink till they had [b]killed Paul.

13 And they were more than forty which had made this conspiracy.

14 And they came to the chief priests and [a]elders, and said, We have bound ourselves under a great curse, that we will eat nothing until we have slain Paul.

15 Now therefore ye with the council signify to the chief captain that he bring him down unto you to morrow, as though ye would enquire something more perfectly concerning him: and we, or ever he come near, are ready to kill him.

16 And when Paul's sister's son heard of their lying in wait, he went and entered into the castle, and told Paul.

17 Then Paul called one of the centurions unto *him*, and said, Bring this young man unto the chief captain: for he hath a certain thing to tell him.

18 So he took him, and brought *him* to the chief captain, and said, Paul the prisoner called me unto *him*, and prayed me to bring this young man unto thee, who hath something to say unto thee.

19 Then the chief captain took him by the hand, and went *with him* aside privately, and asked *him*, What is that thou hast to tell me?

20 And he said, [a]The Jews have agreed to desire thee that thou wouldest bring down Paul to morrow into the council, as though they would enquire somewhat of him more perfectly.

21 But do not thou yield unto them: for there

CHAPTER 23
1 [a]Acts 24:16; 1 Cor. 4:4; 2 Cor. 1:12; 4:2; 2 Tim. 1:3; Heb. 13:18
2 [a]1 Kin. 22:24; Jer. 20:2; John 18:22
3 [a]Lev. 19:35; Deut. 25:1, 2; John 7:51
5 [a]Lev. 5:17, 18 [b]Ex. 22:28; Eccl. 10:20; 2 Pet. 2:10
6 [a]Acts 26:5; Phil. 3:5 [b]Acts 24:15, 21; 26:6; 28:20
8 [a]Matt. 22:23; Mark 12:18; Luke 20:27
9 [a]Acts 25:25; 26:31 [b]John 12:29; Acts 22:6, 7, 17, 18 [c]Acts 5:39
11 [a]Acts 18:9; 27:23, 24 [b]Acts 21:18, 19; 22:1–21 [c]Acts 28:16, 17, 23
12 [a]Acts 23:21, 30; 25:3 [b]Acts 9:23, 24; 25:3; 26:21; 27:42; 1 Thess. 2:15
14 [a]Acts 4:5, 23; 6:12; 22:5; 24:1; 25:15
20 [a]Acts 23:12

*———

23:9 NU *what if a spirit or an angel has spoken to him?* omitting the last clause
23:15 NU omits *tomorrow*

NKJV

chief priests and all their council to appear, and brought Paul down and set him before them.

23 Then Paul, looking earnestly at the council, said, "Men *and* brethren, [a]I have lived in all good conscience before God until this day."

2 And the high priest Ananias commanded those who stood by him [a]to strike him on the mouth.

3 Then Paul said to him, "God will strike you, *you* whitewashed wall! For you sit to judge me according to the law, and [a]do you command me to be struck contrary to the law?"

4 And those who stood by said, "Do you revile God's high priest?"

5 Then Paul said, [a]"I did not know, brethren, that he was the high priest; for it is written, [b]*'You shall not speak evil of a ruler of your people.'* "

6 But when Paul perceived that one part were Sadducees and the other Pharisees, he cried out in the council, "Men *and* brethren, [a]I am a Pharisee, the son of a Pharisee; [b]concerning the hope and resurrection of the dead I am being judged!"

7 And when he had said this, a dissension arose between the Pharisees and the Sadducees; and the assembly was divided.

8 [a]For Sadducees say that there is no resurrection—and no angel or spirit; but the Pharisees confess both.

9 Then there arose a loud outcry. And the scribes of the Pharisees' party arose and protested, saying, [a]"We find no evil in this man; *but [b]if a spirit or an angel has spoken to him, [c]let us not fight against God."

10 Now when there arose a great dissension, the commander, fearing lest Paul might be pulled to pieces by them, commanded the soldiers to go down and take him by force from among them, and bring *him* into the barracks.

The Plot Against Paul

11 But [a]the following night the Lord stood by him and said, "Be of good cheer, Paul; for as you have testified for Me in [b]Jerusalem, so you must also bear witness at [c]Rome."

12 And when it was day, [a]some of the Jews banded together and bound themselves under an oath, saying that they would neither eat nor drink till they had [b]killed Paul.

13 Now there were more than forty who had formed this conspiracy.

14 They came to the chief priests and [a]elders, and said, "We have bound ourselves under a great oath that we will eat nothing until we have killed Paul.

15 "Now you, therefore, together with the council, suggest to the commander that he be brought down to you *tomorrow, as though you were going to make further inquiries concerning him; but we are ready to kill him before he comes near."

16 So when Paul's sister's son heard of their ambush, he went and entered the barracks and told Paul.

17 Then Paul called one of the centurions to *him* and said, "Take this young man to the commander, for he has something to tell him."

18 So he took him and brought *him* to the commander and said, "Paul the prisoner called me to *him* and asked *me* to bring this young man to you. He has something to say to you."

19 Then the commander took him by the hand, went aside, and asked privately, "What is it that you have to tell me?"

20 And he said, [a]"The Jews have agreed to ask that you bring Paul down to the council tomorrow, as though they were going to inquire more fully about him.

21 "But do not yield to them, for more than

KJV

lie in wait for him of them more than forty men,
which have bound themselves with an oath, that
they will neither eat nor drink till they have killed
him: and now are they ready, looking for a promise from thee.
22 So the chief captain *then* let the young
man depart, and charged *him*, *See thou* tell no
man that thou hast shewed these things to me.

Sent to Felix

23 And he called unto *him* two centurions,
saying, Make ready two hundred soldiers to go
to [a]Caesarea, and horsemen threescore and ten,
and spearmen two hundred, at the third hour of
the night;
24 And provide *them* beasts, that they may
set Paul on, and bring *him* safe unto Felix the
governor.
25 And he wrote a letter after this manner:
26 Claudius Lysias unto the most excellent
governor Felix *sendeth* greeting.
27 [a]This man was taken of the Jews, and
should have been killed of them: then came I with
an army, and rescued him, having understood that
he was a Roman.
28 [a]And when I would have known the cause
wherefore they accused him, I brought him forth
into their council:
29 Whom I perceived to be accused [a]of questions of their law, [b]but to have nothing laid to
his charge worthy of death or of bonds.
30 And [a]when it was told me how that the
Jews laid wait for the man, I sent straightway to
thee, and [b]gave commandment to his accusers
also to say before thee what *they had* against him.
Farewell.
31 Then the soldiers, as it was commanded
them, took Paul, and brought *him* by night to
Antipatris.
32 On the morrow they left the horsemen to
go with him, and returned to the castle:
33 Who, when they came to [a]Caesarea, and
delivered the [b]epistle to the governor, presented
Paul also before him.
34 And when the governor had read *the letter*, he asked of what province he was. And when
he understood that *he was* of [a]Cilicia;
35 [a]I will hear thee, said he, when thine accusers are also come. And he commanded him to
be kept in [b]Herod's judgment hall.

Accused of Sedition

24 And after [a]five days [b]Ananias the high
priest descended with the elders, and *with*
a certain orator *named* Tertullus, who informed
the governor against Paul.
2 And when he was called forth, Tertullus
began to accuse *him*, saying, Seeing that by thee
we enjoy great quietness, and that very worthy
deeds are done unto this nation by thy providence,
3 We accept *it* always, and in all places,
most noble Felix, with all thankfulness.
4 Notwithstanding, that I be not further tedious unto thee, I pray thee that thou wouldest
hear us of thy clemency a few words.
5 [a]For we have found this man *a* pestilent
fellow, and a mover of sedition among all the Jews
throughout the world, and a ringleader of the sect
of the Nazarenes:
6 [a]Who also hath gone about to profane the
temple: whom we took, and would [b]have judged
according to our law.
7 [a]But the chief captain Lysias came *upon
us*, and with great violence took *him* away out of
our hands,
8 [a]Commanding his accusers to come unto

23 [a]Acts 8:40; 23:33
27 [a]Acts 21:30, 33; 24:7
28 [a]Acts 22:30
29 [a]Acts 18:15; 25:19 [b]Acts 25:25; 26:31
30 [a]Acts 23:20 [b]Acts 24:8; 25:6
33 [a]Acts 8:40 [b]Acts 23:26–30
34 [a]Acts 6:9; 21:39
35 [a]Acts 24:1, 10; 25:16 [b]Matt. 27:27

CHAPTER 24

1 [a]Acts 21:27 [b]Acts 23:2, 30, 35; 25:2
5 [a]Luke 23:2; Acts 6:13; 16:20; 17:6; 21:28; 1 Pet. 2:12, 15
6 [a]Acts 21:28 [b]John 18:31
7 [a]Acts 21:33; 23:10
8 [a]Acts 23:30

*———

23:30 NU *there would be a plot against the man*
24:6 NU ends the sentence here and omits the rest of v. 6, all of v. 7, and the first clause of v. 8.

NKJV

forty of them lie in wait for him, men who have
bound themselves by an oath that they will neither eat nor drink till they have killed him; and
now they are ready, waiting for the promise from
you."
22 So the commander let the young man depart, and commanded *him*, "Tell no one that you
have revealed these things to me."

Sent to Felix

23 And he called for two centurions, saying,
"Prepare two hundred soldiers, seventy horsemen, and two hundred spearmen to go to
[a]Caesarea at the third hour of the night;
24 "and provide mounts to set Paul on, and
bring *him* safely to Felix the governor."
25 He wrote a letter in the following manner:

26 Claudius Lysias,

To the most excellent governor Felix:

Greetings.

27 [a]This man was seized by the Jews and was
about to be killed by them. Coming with
the troops I rescued him, having learned
that he was a Roman.
28 [a]And when I wanted to know the reason
they accused him, I brought him before
their council.
29 I found out that he was accused
[a]concerning questions of their law, [b]but
had nothing charged against him
deserving of death or chains.
30 And [a]when it was told me that *the Jews
lay in wait for the man, I sent him
immediately to you, and [b]also
commanded his accusers to state before
you the charges against him.
Farewell.

31 Then the soldiers, as they were commanded, took Paul and brought *him* by night to
Antipatris.
32 The next day they left the horsemen to
go on with him, and returned to the barracks.
33 When they came to [a]Caesarea and had delivered the [b]letter to the governor, they also presented Paul to him.
34 And when the governor had read *it*, he
asked what province he was from. And when he
understood that *he was* from [a]Cilicia,
35 he said, [a]"I will hear you when your accusers also have come." And he commanded him
to be kept in [b]Herod's Praetorium.

Accused of Sedition

24 Now after [a]five days [b]Ananias the high
priest came down with the elders and a certain orator *named* Tertullus. These gave evidence
to the governor against Paul.
2 And when he was called upon, Tertullus
began his accusation, saying: "Seeing that
through you we enjoy great peace, and prosperity
is being brought to this nation by your foresight,
3 "we accept *it* always and in all places,
most noble Felix, with all thankfulness.
4 "Nevertheless, not to be tedious to you
any further, I beg you to hear, by your courtesy,
a few words from us.
5 [a]"For we have found this man a plague,
a creator of dissension among all the Jews
throughout the world, and a ringleader of the sect
of the Nazarenes.
6 [a]"He even tried to profane the temple, and
we seized him, *and wanted [b]to judge him according to our law.
7 [a]"But the commander Lysias came by and
with great violence took *him* out of our hands,
8 [a]"commanding his accusers to come to

KJV

thee: by examining of whom thyself mayest take
knowledge of all these things, whereof we accuse
him.
9 And the Jews also assented, saying that
these things were so.

The Defense Before Felix

10 Then Paul, after that the governor had
beckoned unto him to speak, answered, Forasmuch as I know that thou hast been of many years
a judge unto this nation, I do the more cheerfully
answer for myself:
11 Because that thou mayest understand,
that there are yet but twelve days since I went
up to Jerusalem [a]for to worship.
12 [a]And they neither found me in the temple
disputing with any man, neither raising up the
people, neither in the synagogues, nor in the city:
13 Neither can they prove the things whereof
they now accuse me.
14 But this I confess unto thee, that after [a]the
way which they call heresy, so worship I the [b]God
of my fathers, believing all things which are written in [c]the law and in the prophets:
15 And [a]have hope toward God, which they
themselves also allow, [b]that there shall be a resurrection of the dead, both of the just and unjust.
16 And [a]herein do I exercise myself, to have
always a conscience void of offence toward God,
and *toward* men.
17 Now after many years [a]I came to bring
alms to my nation, and offerings.
18 [a]Whereupon certain Jews from Asia
found me [b]purified in the temple, neither with
multitude, nor with tumult.
19 [a]Who ought to have been here before
thee, and object, if they had ought against me.
20 Or else let these same *here* say, if they
have found any evil doing in me, while I stood
before the council,
21 Except it be for this one voice, that I cried
standing among them, [a]Touching the resurrection
of the dead I am called in question by you this
day.

Felix Procrastinates

22 And when Felix heard these things, having more perfect knowledge of *that* [a]way, he deferred them, and said, When [b]Lysias the chief captain shall come down, I will know the uttermost
of your matter.
23 And he commanded a centurion to keep
Paul, and to let *him* have liberty, and [a]that he
should forbid none of his acquaintance to minister
or come unto him.
24 And after certain days, when Felix came
with his wife Drusilla, which was a Jewess, he
sent for Paul, and heard him concerning the [a]faith
in Christ.
25 And as he reasoned of righteousness, temperance, and judgment to come, Felix trembled,
and answered, Go thy way for this time; when I
have a convenient season, I will call for thee.
26 He hoped also that [a]money should have
been given him of Paul, that he might loose him:
wherefore he sent for him the oftener, and communed with him.
27 But after two years Porcius Festus came
into Felix' room: and Felix, [a]willing to shew the
Jews a pleasure, left Paul bound.

Paul Appeals to Caesar

25 Now when Festus was come into the province, after three days he ascended from
[a]Caesarea to Jerusalem.
2 [a]Then the high priest and the chief of the
Jews informed him against Paul, and besought
him,
3 And desired favour against him, that he
would send for him to Jerusalem, [a]laying wait in
the way to kill him.
4 But Festus answered, that Paul should be

NKJV

you. By examining him yourself you may ascertain all these things of which we accuse him."
9 And the Jews also *assented, maintaining
that these things were so.

The Defense Before Felix

10 Then Paul, after the governor had nodded
to him to speak, answered: "Inasmuch as I know
that you have been for many years a judge of this
nation, I do the more cheerfully answer for
myself,
11 "because you may ascertain that it is no
more than twelve days since I went up to Jerusalem [a]to worship.
12 [a]"And they neither found me in the temple
disputing with anyone nor inciting the crowd, either in the synagogues or in the city.
13 "Nor can they prove the things of which
they now accuse me.
14 "But this I confess to you, that according
to [a]the Way which they call a sect, so I worship
the [b]God of my fathers, believing all things which
are written in [c]the Law and in the Prophets.
15 [a]"I have hope in God, which they themselves also accept, [b]that there will be a resurrection *of *the* dead, both of *the* just and *the*
unjust.
16 [a]"This *being* so, I myself always strive to
have a conscience without offense toward God
and men.
17 "Now after many years [a]I came to bring
alms and offerings to my nation,
18 [a]"in the midst of which some Jews from
Asia found me [b]purified in the temple, neither
with a mob nor with tumult.
19 [a]"They ought to have been here before
you to object if they had anything against me.
20 "Or else let those who are *here* themselves
say *if they found any wrongdoing in me while I
stood before the council,
21 "unless *it is* for this one statement which
I cried out, standing among them, [a]'Concerning
the resurrection of the dead I am being judged
by you this day.'"

Felix Procrastinates

22 But when Felix heard these things, having
more accurate knowledge of *the* [a]Way, he ad-
journed the proceedings and said, "When [b]Lysias
the commander comes down, I will make a decision on your case."
23 So he commanded the centurion to keep
Paul and to let *him* have liberty, and [a]told him
not to forbid any of his friends to provide for or
visit him.
24 And after some days, when Felix came
with his wife Drusilla, who was Jewish, he sent
for Paul and heard him concerning the [a]faith in
Christ.
25 Now as he reasoned about righteousness,
self-control, and the judgment to come, Felix was
afraid and answered, "Go away for now; when I
have a convenient time I will call for you."
26 Meanwhile he also hoped that [a]money
would be given him by Paul, *that he might release him. Therefore he sent for him more often
and conversed with him.
27 But after two years Porcius Festus succeeded Felix; and Felix, [a]wanting to do the Jews
a favor, left Paul bound.

Paul Appeals to Caesar

25 Now when Festus had come to the province, after three days he went up from
[a]Caesarea to Jerusalem.
2 [a]Then the *high priest and the chief men
of the Jews informed him against Paul; and they
petitioned him,
3 asking a favor against him, that he would
summon him to Jerusalem—[a]while *they* lay in
ambush along the road to kill him.
4 But Festus answered that Paul should be

---

11 [a]Acts 21:15, 18, 26, 27; 24:17
12 [a]Acts 25:8; 28:17
14 [a]Amos 8:14; Acts 9:2; 24:22 [b]2 Tim. 1:3 [c]Acts 26:22; 28:23
15 [a]Acts 23:6; 26:6, 7; 28:20 [b][Dan. 12:2; John 5:28, 29; 11:24]
16 [a]Acts 23:1
17 [a]Acts 11:29, 30; Rom. 15:25–28; 1 Cor. 16:1–4; 2 Cor. 8:1–4; 9:1, 2, 12; Gal. 2:10
18 [a]Acts 21:27; 26:21 [b]Acts 21:26
19 [a][Acts 23:30; 25:16]
21 [a][Acts 23:6; 24:15; 28:20]
22 [a]Acts 9:2; 18:26; 19:9, 23; 22:4 [b]Acts 23:26; 24:7
23 [a]Acts 23:16; 27:3; 28:16
24 [a][John 3:15; 5:24; 11:25; 12:46; 20:31; Rom. 10:9]
26 [a]Ex. 23:8
27 [a]Ex. 23:2; Acts 12:3; 23:35; 25:9, 14

CHAPTER 25

1 [a]Acts 8:40; 25:4, 6, 13
2 [a]Acts 24:1; 25:15
3 [a]Acts 23:12, 15

*

24:9 NU, M *joined the attack*
24:15 NU omits *of the dead*
24:20 NU, M *what wrongdoing they found*
24:26 NU omits *that he might release him*
25:2 NU *chief priests*

KJV

kept at Caesarea, and that he himself would depart shortly *thither.*

5 Let them therefore, said he, which among you are able, go down with *me,* and accuse this man, [a]if there be any wickedness in him.

6 And when he had tarried among them more than ten days, he went down unto Caesarea; and the next day sitting on the judgment seat commanded Paul to be brought.

7 And when he was come, the Jews which came down from Jerusalem stood round about, [a]and laid many and grievous complaints against Paul, which they could not prove.

8 While he answered for himself, [a]Neither against the law of the Jews, neither against the temple, nor yet against Caesar, have I offended any thing at all.

9 But Festus, [a]willing to do the Jews a pleasure, answered Paul, and said, [b]Wilt thou go up to Jerusalem, and there be judged of these things before me?

10 Then said Paul, I stand at Caesar's judgment seat, where I ought to be judged: to the Jews have I done no wrong, as thou very well knowest.

11 [a]For if I be an offender, or have committed any thing worthy of death, I refuse not to die: but if there be none of these things whereof these accuse me, no man may deliver me unto them. [b]I appeal unto Caesar.

12 Then Festus, when he had conferred with the council, answered, Hast thou appealed unto Caesar? unto Caesar shalt thou go.

Paul Before Agrippa

13 And after certain days king Agrippa and Bernice came unto Caesarea to salute Festus.

14 And when they had been there many days, Festus declared Paul's cause unto the king, saying, [a]There is a certain man left in bonds by Felix:

15 [a]About whom, when I was at Jerusalem, the chief priests and the elders of the Jews informed *me,* desiring *to have* judgment against him.

16 [a]To whom I answered, It is not the manner of the Romans to deliver any man to die, before that he which is accused have the accusers face to face, and have licence to answer for himself concerning the crime laid against him.

17 Therefore, when they were come hither, [a]without any delay on the morrow I sat on the judgment seat, and commanded the man to be brought forth.

18 Against whom when the accusers stood up, they brought none accusation of such things as I supposed:

19 [a]But had certain questions against him of their own superstition, and of one Jesus, which was dead, whom Paul affirmed to be alive.

20 And because I doubted of such manner of questions, I asked *him* whether he would go to Jerusalem, and there be judged of these matters.

21 But when Paul had [a]appealed to be reserved unto the hearing of Augustus, I commanded him to be kept till I might send him to Caesar.

22 Then [a]Agrippa said unto Festus, I would also hear the man myself. To morrow, said he, thou shalt hear him.

23 And on the morrow, when Agrippa was come, and Bernice, with great pomp, and was entered into the place of hearing, with the chief captains, and principal men of the city, at Festus' commandment [a]Paul was brought forth.

24 And Festus said, King Agrippa, and all men which are here present with us, ye see this man, about whom [a]all the multitude of the Jews have dealt with me, both at Jerusalem, and *also* here, crying that he ought [b]not to live any longer.

25 But when I found that [a]he had committed nothing worthy of death, [b]and that he himself

5 [a]Acts 18:14; 25:18
7 [a]Mark 15:3; Luke 23:2, 10; Acts 24:5, 13
8 [a]Acts 6:13; 24:12; 28:17
9 [a]Acts 12:2; 24:27 [b]Acts 25:20
11 [a]Acts 18:14; 23:29; 25:25; 26:31 [b]Acts 26:32; 28:19
14 [a]Acts 24:27
15 [a]Acts 24:1; 25:2, 3
16 [a]Acts 25:4, 5
17 [a]Matt. 27:19; Acts 25:6, 10
19 [a]Acts 18:14, 15; 23:29
21 [a]Acts 25:11, 12
22 [a]Acts 9:15
23 [a]Acts 9:15
24 [a]Acts 25:2, 3, 7 [b]Acts 21:36; 22:22
25 [a]Acts 23:9, 29; 26:31 [b]Acts 25:11, 12

NKJV

kept at Caesarea, and that he himself was going *there* shortly.

5 "Therefore," he said, "let those who have authority among you go down with *me* and accuse this man, to see [a]if there is any fault in him."

6 And when he had remained among them more than ten days, he went down to Caesarea. And the next day, sitting on the judgment seat, he commanded Paul to be brought.

7 When he had come, the Jews who had come down from Jerusalem stood about [a]and laid many serious complaints against Paul, which they could not prove,

8 while he answered for himself, [a]"Neither against the law of the Jews, nor against the temple, nor against Caesar have I offended in anything at all."

9 But Festus, [a]wanting to do the Jews a favor, answered Paul and said, [b]"Are you willing to go up to Jerusalem and there be judged before me concerning these things?"

10 So Paul said, "I stand at Caesar's judgment seat, where I ought to be judged. To the Jews I have done no wrong, as you very well know.

11 [a]"For if I am an offender, or have committed anything deserving of death, I do not object to dying; but if there is nothing in these things of which these men accuse me, no one can deliver me to them. [b]I appeal to Caesar."

12 Then Festus, when he had conferred with the council, answered, "You have appealed to Caesar? To Caesar you shall go!"

Paul Before Agrippa

13 And after some days King Agrippa and Bernice came to Caesarea to greet Festus.

14 When they had been there many days, Festus laid Paul's case before the king, saying: [a]"There is a certain man left a prisoner by Felix,

15 [a]"about whom the chief priests and the elders of the Jews informed *me,* when I was in Jerusalem, asking for a judgment against him.

16 [a]"To them I answered, 'It is not the custom of the Romans to deliver any man *to destruction before the accused meets the accusers face to face, and has opportunity to answer for himself concerning the charge against him.'

17 "Therefore when they had come together, [a]without any delay, the next day I sat on the judgment seat and commanded the man to be brought in.

18 "When the accusers stood up, they brought no accusation against him of such things as I supposed,

19 [a]"but had some questions against him about their own religion and about a certain Jesus, who had died, whom Paul affirmed to be alive.

20 "And because I was uncertain of such questions, I asked whether he was willing to go to Jerusalem and there be judged concerning these matters.

21 "But when Paul [a]appealed to be reserved for the decision of Augustus, I commanded him to be kept till I could send him to Caesar."

22 Then [a]Agrippa said to Festus, "I also would like to hear the man myself." "Tomorrow," he said, "you shall hear him."

23 So the next day, when Agrippa and Bernice had come with great pomp, and had entered the auditorium with the commanders and the prominent men of the city, at Festus' command [a]Paul was brought in.

24 And Festus said: "King Agrippa and all the men who are here present with us, you see this man about whom [a]the whole assembly of the Jews petitioned me, both at Jerusalem and here, crying out that he was [b]not fit to live any longer.

25 "But when I found that [a]he had committed nothing deserving of death, [b]and that he himself

---

***25:16** NU omits *to destruction,* although it is implied

KJV

hath appealed to Augustus, I have determined to send him.

26 Of whom I have no certain thing to write unto my lord. Wherefore I have brought him forth before you, and specially before thee, O king Agrippa, that, after examination had, I might have somewhat to write.

27 For it seemeth to me unreasonable to send a prisoner, and not withal to signify the crimes *laid* against him.

Paul's Early Life

26 Then Agrippa said unto Paul, Thou art permitted to speak for thyself. Then Paul stretched forth the hand, and answered for himself:

2 I think myself [a]happy, king Agrippa, because I shall answer [b]for myself this day before thee touching all the things whereof I am [c]accused of the Jews:

3 Especially *because I know* thee to be expert in all customs and questions which are among the Jews: wherefore I beseech thee to hear me patiently.

4 My manner of life from my youth, which was at the first among mine own nation at Jerusalem, know all the Jews;

5 Which knew me from the beginning, if they would testify, that after [a]the most straitest sect of our religion I lived a Pharisee.

6 [a]And now I stand and am judged for the hope of [b]the promise made of God unto our fathers:

7 Unto which *promise* [a]our twelve tribes, instantly serving *God* [b]day and night, [c]hope to come. For which hope's sake, king Agrippa, I am accused of the Jews.

8 Why should it be thought a thing incredible with you, that God should raise the dead?

9 [a]I verily thought with myself, that I ought to do many things contrary to the name of [b]Jesus of Nazareth.

10 [a]Which thing I also did in Jerusalem: and many of the saints did I shut up in prison, having received authority [b]from the chief priests; and when they were put to death, I gave my voice against *them*.

11 [a]And I punished them oft in every synagogue, and compelled *them* to blaspheme; and being exceedingly mad against them, I persecuted *them* even unto strange cities.

Paul Recounts His Conversion
(Acts 9:1–19; 22:6–16)

12 [a]Whereupon as I went to Damascus with authority and commission from the chief priests,

13 At midday, O king, I saw in the way a light from heaven, above the brightness of the sun, shining round about me and them which journeyed with me.

14 And when we were all fallen to the earth, I heard a voice speaking unto me, and saying in the Hebrew tongue, Saul, Saul, why persecutest thou me? *it is* hard for thee to kick against the pricks.

15 And I said, Who art thou, Lord? And he said, I am Jesus whom thou persecutest.

16 But rise, and stand upon thy feet: for I have appeared unto thee for this purpose, [a]to make thee a minister and a witness both of these things which thou hast seen, and of those things in the which I will appear unto thee;

17 Delivering thee from the people, and *from* the Gentiles, [a]unto whom now I send thee,

18 [a]To open their eyes, *and* [b]to turn *them* from darkness to light, and *from* the power of Satan unto God, [c]that they may receive forgiveness of sins, and [d]inheritance among them which are [e]sanctified by faith that is in me.

NKJV

had appealed to Augustus, I decided to send him.

26 "I have nothing certain to write to my lord concerning him. Therefore I have brought him out before you, and especially before you, King Agrippa, so that after the examination has taken place I may have something to write.

27 "For it seems to me unreasonable to send a prisoner and not to specify the charges against him."

Paul's Early Life

26 Then Agrippa said to Paul, "You are permitted to speak for yourself." So Paul stretched out his hand and answered for himself:

2 "I think myself [a]happy, King Agrippa, because today I shall answer [b]for myself before you concerning all the things of which I am [c]accused by the Jews,

3 "especially because you are expert in all customs and questions which have to do with the Jews. Therefore I beg you to hear me patiently.

4 "My manner of life from my youth, which was spent from the beginning among my own nation at Jerusalem, all the Jews know.

5 "They knew me from the first, if they were willing to testify, that according to [a]the strictest sect of our religion I lived a Pharisee.

6 [a]"And now I stand and am judged for the hope of [b]the promise made by God to our fathers.

7 "To this *promise* [a]our twelve tribes, earnestly serving *God* [b]night and day, [c]hope to attain. For this hope's sake, King Agrippa, I am accused by the Jews.

8 "Why should it be thought incredible by you that God raises the dead?

9 [a]"Indeed, I myself thought I must do many things contrary to the name of [b]Jesus of Nazareth.

10 [a]"This I also did in Jerusalem, and many of the saints I shut up in prison, having received authority [b]from the chief priests; and when they were put to death, I cast my vote against *them*.

11 [a]"And I punished them often in every synagogue and compelled *them* to blaspheme; and being exceedingly enraged against them, I persecuted *them* even to foreign cities.

Paul Recounts His Conversion
(Acts 9:1–19; 22:6–16)

12 [a]"While thus occupied, as I journeyed to Damascus with authority and commission from the chief priests,

13 "at midday, O king, along the road I saw a light from heaven, brighter than the sun, shining around me and those who journeyed with me.

14 "And when we all had fallen to the ground, I heard a voice speaking to me and saying in the Hebrew language, 'Saul, Saul, why are you persecuting Me? *It is* hard for you to kick against the goads.'

15 "So I said, 'Who are You, Lord?' And He said, 'I am Jesus, whom you are persecuting.

16 'But rise and stand on your feet; for I have appeared to you for this purpose, [a]to make you a minister and a witness both of the things which you have seen and of the things which I will yet reveal to you.

17 'I will deliver you from the *Jewish* people, as well as *from* the Gentiles, [a]to whom I *now send you,

18 [a]'to open their eyes, *in order* [b]to turn *them* from darkness to light, and *from* the power of Satan to God, [c]that they may receive forgiveness of sins and [d]an inheritance among those who are [e]sanctified by faith in Me.'

CHAPTER 26

2 [a][1 Pet. 3:14; 4:14] [b][1 Pet. 3:15, 16] [c]Acts 21:28; 24:5, 6 **5** [a][Acts 22:3; 23:6; 24:15, 21]; Phil. 3:5 **6** [a]Acts 23:6 [b][Gen. 3:15; 22:18; 26:4; 49:10; Deut. 18:15; 2 Sam. 7:12; Ps. 132:11; Is. 4:2; 7:14; 9:6; 40:10; Jer. 23:5; 33:14–16; Ezek. 34:23; 37:24; Dan. 9:24]; Acts 13:32; Rom. 15:8; [Titus 2:13] **7** [a]James 1:1 [b]Luke 2:37; 1 Thess. 3:10; 1 Tim. 5:5 [c]Phil. 3:11 **9** [a]John 16:2; 1 Cor. 15:9; 1 Tim. 1:12, 13 [b]Acts 2:22; 10:38 **10** [a]Acts 8:1–3; 9:13; Gal. 1:13 [b]Acts 9:14 **11** [a]Matt. 10:17; Acts 22:19 **12** [a]Acts 9:3–8; 22:6–11; 26:12–18 **16** [a]Acts 22:15; Eph. 3:6–8 **17** [a]Acts 22:21 **18** [a]Is. 35:5; 42:7, 16; Luke 1:79; [John 8:12; 2 Cor. 4:4]; Eph. 1:18; 1 Thess. 5:5 [b]2 Cor. 6:14; Eph. 4:18; 5:8; [Col. 1:13]; 1 Pet. 2:9 [c]Luke 1:77 [d]Eph. 1:11; Col. 1:12 [e]Acts 20:32

*______

26:17 NU, M omit *now*

KJV

Paul's Post-Conversion Life

19 Whereupon, O king Agrippa, I was not disobedient unto the heavenly vision:

20 But [a]shewed first unto them of Damascus, and at Jerusalem, and throughout all the coasts of Judaea, and *then* to the Gentiles, that they should repent and turn to God, and do [b]works meet for repentance.

21 For these causes the Jews caught me in the temple, and went about to kill *me*.

22 Having therefore obtained help of God, I continue unto this day, witnessing both to small and great, saying none other things than those [a]which the prophets and [b]Moses did say should come:

23 [a]That Christ should suffer, *and* [b]that he should be the first that should rise from the dead, and [c]should shew light unto the people, and to the Gentiles.

Agrippa Parries Paul's Challenge

24 And as he thus spake for himself, Festus said with a loud voice, Paul, [a]thou art beside thyself; much learning doth make thee mad.

25 But he said, I am not mad, most noble Festus; but speak forth the words of truth and soberness.

26 For the king [a]knoweth of these things, before whom also I speak freely: for I am persuaded that none of these things are hidden from him; for this thing was not done in a corner.

27 King Agrippa, believest thou the prophets? I know that thou believest.

28 Then Agrippa said unto Paul, Almost thou persuadest me to be a Christian.

29 And Paul said, [a]I would to God, that not only thou, but also all that hear me this day, were both almost, and altogether such as I am, except these bonds.

30 And when he had thus spoken, the king rose up, and the governor, and Bernice, and they that sat with them:

31 And when they were gone aside, they talked between themselves, saying, [a]This man doeth nothing worthy of death or of bonds.

32 Then said Agrippa unto Festus, This man might have been set at [a]liberty, [b]if he had not appealed unto Caesar.

The Voyage to Rome Begins

27 And when [a]it was determined that we should sail into Italy, they delivered Paul and certain other prisoners unto *one* named Julius, a centurion of Augustus' band.

2 And entering into a ship of Adramyttium, we launched, meaning to sail by the coasts of Asia; *one* [a]Aristarchus, a Macedonian of Thessalonica, being with us.

3 And the next *day* we touched at Sidon. And Julius [a]courteously entreated Paul, and gave *him* liberty to go unto his friends to refresh himself.

4 And when we had launched from thence, we sailed under Cyprus, because the winds were contrary.

5 And when we had sailed over the sea of Cilicia and Pamphylia, we came to Myra, *a city* of Lycia.

6 And there the centurion found a ship of [a]Alexandria sailing into Italy; and he put us therein.

7 And when we had sailed slowly many days, and scarce were come over against Cnidus, the wind not suffering us, we sailed under [a]Crete, over against Salmone;

8 And, hardly passing it, came unto a place which is called The fair havens; nigh whereunto was the city *of* Lasea.

20 [a]Acts 9:19, 20, 22; 11:26 [b]Matt. 3:8; Luke 3:8
22 [a]Luke 24:27; Acts 24:14; 28:23; Rom. 3:21 [b]John 5:46
23 [a]Luke 24:26 [b]1 Cor. 15:20, 23; Col. 1:18; Rev. 1:5 [c]Is. 42:6; 49:6; Luke 2:32; 2 Cor. 4:4
24 [a]2 Kin. 9:11; John 10:20; [1 Cor. 1:23; 2:13, 14; 4:10]
26 [a]Acts 26:3
29 [a]1 Cor. 7:7
31 [a]Acts 23:9, 29; 25:25
32 [a]Acts 28:18 [b]Acts 25:11

CHAPTER 27

1 [a]Acts 25:12, 25
2 [a]Acts 19:29
3 [a]Acts 24:23; 28:16
6 [a]Acts 28:11
7 [a]Acts 2:11; 27:12, 21; Titus 1:5, 12

NKJV

Paul's Post-Conversion Life

19 "Therefore, King Agrippa, I was not disobedient to the heavenly vision,

20 "but [a]declared first to those in Damascus and in Jerusalem, and throughout all the region of Judea, and *then* to the Gentiles, that they should repent, turn to God, and do [b]works befitting repentance.

21 "For these reasons the Jews seized me in the temple and tried to kill *me*.

22 "Therefore, having obtained help from God, to this day I stand, witnessing both to small and great, saying no other things than those [a]which the prophets and [b]Moses said would come—

23 [a]"that the Christ would suffer, [b]that He would be the first to rise from the dead, and [c]would proclaim light to the *Jewish* people and to the Gentiles."

Agrippa Parries Paul's Challenge

24 Now as he thus made his defense, Festus said with a loud voice, "Paul, [a]you are beside yourself! Much learning is driving you mad!"

25 But he said, "I am not mad, most noble Festus, but speak the words of truth and reason.

26 "For the king, before whom I also speak freely, [a]knows these things; for I am convinced that none of these things escapes his attention, since this thing was not done in a corner.

27 "King Agrippa, do you believe the prophets? I know that you do believe."

28 Then Agrippa said to Paul, "You almost persuade me to become a Christian."

29 And Paul said, [a]"I would to God that not only you, but also all who hear me today, might become both almost and altogether such as I am, except for these chains."

30 When he had said these things, the king stood up, as well as the governor and Bernice and those who sat with them;

31 and when they had gone aside, they talked among themselves, saying, [a]"This man is doing nothing deserving of death or chains."

32 Then Agrippa said to Festus, "This man might have been set [a]free [b]if he had not appealed to Caesar."

The Voyage to Rome Begins

27 And when [a]it was decided that we should sail to Italy, they delivered Paul and some other prisoners to *one* named Julius, a centurion of the Augustan Regiment.

2 So, entering a ship of Adramyttium, we put to sea, meaning to sail along the coasts of Asia. [a]Aristarchus, a Macedonian of Thessalonica, was with us.

3 And the next *day* we landed at Sidon. And Julius [a]treated Paul kindly and gave *him* liberty to go to his friends and receive care.

4 When we had put to sea from there, we sailed under *the shelter of* Cyprus, because the winds were contrary.

5 And when we had sailed over the sea which is off Cilicia and Pamphylia, we came to Myra, *a city* of Lycia.

6 There the centurion found [a]an Alexandrian ship sailing to Italy, and he put us on board.

7 When we had sailed slowly many days, and arrived with difficulty off Cnidus, the wind not permitting us to proceed, we sailed under *the shelter of* [a]Crete off Salmone.

8 Passing it with difficulty, we came to a place called Fair Havens, near the city *of* Lasea.

KJV

Paul's Warning Ignored

9 Now when much time was spent, and when sailing was now dangerous, [a]because the fast was now already past, Paul admonished *them,*

10 And said unto them, Sirs, I perceive that this voyage will be with hurt and much damage, not only of the lading and ship, but also of our lives.

11 Nevertheless the centurion believed the master and the owner of the ship, more than those things which were spoken by Paul.

12 And because the haven was not commodious to winter in, the more part advised to depart thence also, if by any means they might attain to Phenice, *and there* to winter; *which is* an haven of Crete, and lieth toward the south west and north west.

In the Tempest

13 And when the south wind blew softly, supposing that they had obtained *their* purpose, loosing *thence,* they sailed close by Crete.

14 But not long after there arose against it a tempestuous wind, called Euroclydon.

15 And when the ship was caught, and could not bear up into the wind, we let *her* drive.

16 And running under a certain island which is called Clauda, we had much work to come by the boat:

17 Which when they had taken up, they used helps, undergirding the ship; and, fearing lest they should fall into the quicksands, strake sail, and so were driven.

18 And we being exceedingly tossed with a tempest, the next *day* they lightened the ship;

19 And the third *day* [a]we cast out with our own hands the tackling of the ship.

20 And when neither sun nor stars in many days appeared, and no small tempest lay on *us,* all hope that we should be saved was then taken away.

21 But after long abstinence Paul stood forth in the midst of them, and said, Sirs, ye should have hearkened unto me, and not have loosed from Crete, and to have gained this harm and loss.

22 And now I exhort you to be of good cheer: for there shall be no loss of *any man's* life among you, but of the ship.

23 [a]For there stood by me this night the angel of God, whose I am, and [b]whom I serve,

24 Saying, Fear not, Paul; thou must be brought before Caesar: and, lo, God hath given thee all them that sail with thee.

25 Wherefore, sirs, be of good cheer: [a]for I believe God, that it shall be even as it was told me.

26 Howbeit [a]we must be cast upon a certain island.

27 But when the fourteenth night was come, as we were driven up and down in Adria, about midnight the shipmen deemed that they drew near to some country;

28 And sounded, and found *it* twenty fathoms: and when they had gone a little further, they sounded again, and found *it* fifteen fathoms.

29 Then fearing lest we should have fallen upon rocks, they cast four anchors out of the stern, and wished for the day.

30 And as the shipmen were about to flee out of the ship, when they had let down the boat into the sea, under colour as though they would have cast anchors out of the foreship,

31 Paul said to the centurion and to the soldiers, Except these abide in the ship, ye cannot be saved.

32 Then the soldiers cut off the ropes of the boat, and let her fall off.

9 [a]Lev. 16:29–31; 23:27–29; Num. 29:7
19 [a]Jon. 1:5
23 [a]Acts 18:9; 23:11; 2 Tim. 4:17 [b]Dan. 6:16; Rom. 1:9; 2 Tim. 1:3
25 [a]Luke 1:45; Rom. 4:20, 21; 2 Tim. 1:12
26 [a]Acts 28:1

*__________

27:14 A southeast wind that stirs up broad waves; NU *Euraquilon,* a northeaster
27:16 NU *Cauda*
27:17 M *Syrtes*

NKJV

Paul's Warning Ignored

9 Now when much time had been spent, and sailing was now dangerous [a]because the Fast was already over, Paul advised them,

10 saying, "Men, I perceive that this voyage will end with disaster and much loss, not only of the cargo and ship, but also our lives."

11 Nevertheless the centurion was more persuaded by the helmsman and the owner of the ship than by the things spoken by Paul.

12 And because the harbor was not suitable to winter in, the majority advised to set sail from there also, if by any means they could reach Phoenix, a harbor of Crete opening toward the southwest and northwest, *and* winter *there.*

In the Tempest

13 When the south wind blew softly, supposing that they had obtained *their* desire, putting out to sea, they sailed close by Crete.

14 But not long after, a tempestuous head wind arose, called *Euroclydon.

15 So when the ship was caught, and could not head into the wind, we let *her* drive.

16 And running under *the shelter of* an island called *Clauda, we secured the skiff with difficulty.

17 When they had taken it on board, they used cables to undergird the ship; and fearing lest they should run aground on the *Syrtis *Sands,* they struck sail and so were driven.

18 And because we were exceedingly tempest-tossed, the next *day* they lightened the ship.

19 On the third *day* [a]we threw the ship's tackle overboard with our own hands.

20 Now when neither sun nor stars appeared for many days, and no small tempest beat on *us,* all hope that we would be saved was finally given up.

21 But after long abstinence from food, then Paul stood in the midst of them and said, "Men, you should have listened to me, and not have sailed from Crete and incurred this disaster and loss.

22 "And now I urge you to take heart, for there will be no loss of life among you, but only of the ship.

23 [a]"For there stood by me this night an angel of the God to whom I belong and [b]whom I serve,

24 "saying, 'Do not be afraid, Paul; you must be brought before Caesar; and indeed God has granted you all those who sail with you.'

25 "Therefore take heart, men, [a]for I believe God that it will be just as it was told me.

26 "However, [a]we must run aground on a certain island."

27 Now when the fourteenth night had come, as we were driven up and down in the Adriatic *Sea,* about midnight the sailors sensed that they were drawing near some land.

28 And they took soundings and found *it* to be twenty fathoms; and when they had gone a little farther, they took soundings again and found *it* to be fifteen fathoms.

29 Then, fearing lest we should run aground on the rocks, they dropped four anchors from the stern, and prayed for day to come.

30 And as the sailors were seeking to escape from the ship, when they had let down the skiff into the sea, under pretense of putting out anchors from the prow,

31 Paul said to the centurion and the soldiers, "Unless these men stay in the ship, you cannot be saved."

32 Then the soldiers cut away the ropes of the skiff and let it fall off.

KJV

33 And while the day was coming on, Paul besought *them* all to take meat, saying, This day is the fourteenth day that ye have tarried and continued fasting, having taken nothing.

34 Wherefore I pray you to take *some* meat: for this is for your health: for [a]there shall not an hair fall from the head of any of you.

35 And when he had thus spoken, he took bread, and [a]gave thanks to God in presence of them all: and when he had broken *it*, he began to eat.

36 Then were they all of good cheer, and they also took *some* meat.

37 And we were in all in the ship two hundred threescore and sixteen [a]souls.

38 And when they had eaten enough, they lightened the ship, and cast out the wheat into the sea.

Shipwrecked on Malta

39 And when it was day, they knew not the land: but they discovered a certain creek with a shore, into the which they were minded, if it were possible, to thrust in the ship.

40 And when they had taken up the anchors, they committed *themselves* unto the sea, and loosed the rudder bands, and hoised up the mainsail to the wind, and made toward shore.

41 And falling into a place where two seas met, [a]they ran the ship aground; and the forepart stuck fast, and remained unmoveable, but the hinder part was broken with the violence of the waves.

42 And the soldiers' counsel was to kill the prisoners, lest any of them should swim out, and escape.

43 But the centurion, willing to save Paul, kept them from *their* purpose; and commanded that they which could swim should cast *themselves* first *into the sea*, and get to land:

44 And the rest, some on boards, and some on *broken pieces* of the ship. And so it came to pass, [a]that they escaped all safe to land.

Paul's Ministry on Malta

28 And when they were escaped, then they knew that [a]the island was called Melita.

2 And the [a]barbarous people shewed us no little kindness: for they kindled a fire, and received us every one, because of the present rain, and because of the cold.

3 And when Paul had gathered a bundle of sticks, and laid *them* on the fire, there came a viper out of the heat, and fastened on his hand.

4 And when the barbarians saw the *venomous* beast hang on his hand, they said among themselves, No doubt this man is a murderer, whom, though he hath escaped the sea, yet vengeance suffereth not to live.

5 And he shook off the beast into the fire, and [a]felt no harm.

6 Howbeit they looked when he should have swollen, or fallen down dead suddenly: but after they had looked a great while, and saw no harm come to him, they changed their minds, and [a]said that he was a god.

7 In the same quarters were possessions of the chief man of the island, whose name was Publius; who received us, and lodged us three days courteously.

8 And it came to pass, that the father of Publius lay sick of a fever and of a bloody flux: to whom Paul entered in, and [a]prayed, and [b]laid his hands on him, and healed him.

9 So when this was done, others also, which had diseases in the island, came, and were healed:

10 Who also honoured us with many [a]honours; and when we departed, they laded *us* with such things as were [b]necessary.

34 [a]1 Kin. 1:52; [Matt. 10:30; Luke 12:7; 21:18]
35 [a]1 Sam. 9:13; Matt. 15:36; Mark 8:6; John 6:11; [1 Tim. 4:3, 4]
37 [a]Acts 2:41; 7:14; Rom. 13:1; 1 Pet. 3:20
41 [a]2 Cor. 11:25
44 [a]Acts 27:22, 31

CHAPTER 28
1 [a]Acts 27:26
2 [a]Acts 28:4; Rom. 1:14; 1 Cor. 14:11; Col. 3:11
5 [a]Mark 16:18; Luke 10:19
6 [a]Acts 12:22; 14:11
8 [a]Acts 9:40; [James 5:14, 15] [b]Matt. 9:18; Mark 5:23; 6:5; 7:32; 16:18; Luke 4:40; Acts 19:11, 12; [1 Cor. 12:9, 28]
10 [a]Matt. 15:6; 1 Tim. 5:17 [b][Phil. 4:19]

NKJV

33 And as day was about to dawn, Paul implored *them* all to take food, saying, "Today is the fourteenth day you have waited and continued without food, and eaten nothing.

34 "Therefore I urge you to take nourishment, for this is for your survival, [a]since not a hair will fall from the head of any of you."

35 And when he had said these things, he took bread and [a]gave thanks to God in the presence of them all; and when he had broken *it* he began to eat.

36 Then they were all encouraged, and also took food themselves.

37 And in all we were two hundred and seventy-six [a]persons on the ship.

38 So when they had eaten enough, they lightened the ship and threw out the wheat into the sea.

Shipwrecked on Malta

39 When it was day, they did not recognize the land; but they observed a bay with a beach, onto which they planned to run the ship if possible.

40 And they let go the anchors and left *them* in the sea, meanwhile loosing the rudder ropes; and they hoisted the mainsail to the wind and made for shore.

41 But striking a place where two seas met, [a]they ran the ship aground; and the prow stuck fast and remained immovable, but the stern was being broken up by the violence of the waves.

42 And the soldiers' plan was to kill the prisoners, lest any of them should swim away and escape.

43 But the centurion, wanting to save Paul, kept them from *their* purpose, and commanded that those who could swim should jump *overboard* first and get to land,

44 and the rest, some on boards and some on *parts* of the ship. And so it was [a]that they all escaped safely to land.

Paul's Ministry on Malta

28 Now when they had escaped, they then found out that [a]the island was called Malta.

2 And the [a]natives showed us unusual kindness; for they kindled a fire and made us all welcome, because of the rain that was falling and because of the cold.

3 But when Paul had gathered a bundle of sticks and laid *them* on the fire, a viper came out because of the heat, and fastened on his hand.

4 So when the natives saw the creature hanging from his hand, they said to one another, "No doubt this man is a murderer, whom, though he has escaped the sea, yet justice does not allow to live."

5 But he shook off the creature into the fire and [a]suffered no harm.

6 However, they were expecting that he would swell up or suddenly fall down dead. But after they had looked for a long time and saw no harm come to him, they changed their minds and [a]said that he was a god.

7 In that region there was an estate of the leading citizen of the island, whose name was Publius, who received us and entertained us courteously for three days.

8 And it happened that the father of Publius lay sick of a fever and dysentery. Paul went in to him and [a]prayed, and [b]he laid his hands on him and healed him.

9 So when this was done, the rest of those on the island who had diseases also came and were healed.

10 They also honored us in many [a]ways; and when we departed, they provided such things as were [b]necessary.

KJV

Arrival at Rome

11 And after three months we departed in a
ship of [a]Alexandria, which had wintered in the
isle, whose sign was Castor and Pollux.
12 And landing at Syracuse, we tarried *there*
three days.
13 And from thence we fetched a compass,
and came to Rhegium: and after one day the south
wind blew, and we came the next day to Puteoli:
14 Where we found [a]brethren, and were desired to tarry with them seven days: and so we
went toward Rome.
15 And from thence, when the brethren
heard of us, they came to meet us as far as Appii
forum, and The three taverns: whom when Paul
saw, he thanked God, and took courage.
16 And when we came to Rome, the centurion delivered the prisoners to the captain of the
guard: but [a]Paul was suffered to dwell by himself
with a soldier that kept him.

Paul's Ministry at Rome

17 And it came to pass, that after three days
Paul called the chief of the Jews together: and
when they were come together, he said unto them,
Men *and* brethren, [a]though I have committed
nothing against the people, or customs of our fathers, yet [b]was I delivered prisoner from Jerusalem into the hands of the Romans.
18 Who, [a]when they had examined me,
would have let *me* go, because there was no cause
of death in me.
19 But when the Jews spake against *it*, [a]I was
constrained to appeal unto Caesar; not that I had
ought to accuse my nation of.
20 For this cause therefore have I called for
you, to see *you*, and to speak with *you*: because
that [a]for the hope of Israel I am bound with [b]this
chain.
21 And they said unto him, We neither received letters out of Judaea concerning thee, neither any of the brethren that came shewed or
spake any harm of thee.
22 But we desire to hear of thee what thou
thinkest: for as concerning this sect, we know that
every where [a]it is spoken against.
23 And when they had appointed him a day,
there came many to him into *his* lodging; [a]to
whom he expounded and testified the kingdom
of God, persuading them concerning Jesus, [b]both
out of the law of Moses, and *out of* the prophets,
from morning till evening.
24 And [a]some believed the things which
were spoken, and some believed not.
25 And when they agreed not among themselves, they departed, after that Paul had spoken
one word, Well spake the Holy Ghost by Esaias
the prophet unto our fathers,
26 Saying, [a]GO UNTO THIS PEOPLE, AND SAY,
HEARING YE SHALL HEAR, AND SHALL NOT UNDER-
STAND; AND SEEING YE SHALL SEE, AND NOT PER-
CEIVE:
27 FOR THE HEART OF THIS PEOPLE IS WAXED
GROSS, AND THEIR EARS ARE DULL OF HEARING, AND
THEIR EYES HAVE THEY CLOSED; LEST THEY SHOULD
SEE WITH *THEIR* EYES, AND HEAR WITH *THEIR* EARS,
AND UNDERSTAND WITH *THEIR* HEART, AND SHOULD
BE CONVERTED, AND I SHOULD HEAL THEM.
28 Be it known therefore unto you, that the
salvation of God is sent [a]unto the Gentiles, and
that they will hear it.
29 And when he had said these words, the
Jews departed, and had great reasoning among
themselves.

11 [a]Acts 27:6
14 [a]Rom. 1:8
16 [a]Acts 23:11; 24:25; 27:3
17 [a]Acts 23:29; 24:12, 13; 26:31 [b]Acts 21:33
18 [a]Acts 22:24; 24:10; 25:8; 26:32
19 [a]Acts 25:11, 21, 25
20 [a]Acts 26:6, 7 [b]Acts 26:29; Eph. 3:1; 4:1; 6:20; 2 Tim. 1:8, 16; Philem. 10, 13
22 [a]Luke 2:34; Acts 24:5, 14; [1 Pet. 2:12; 3:16; 4:14, 16]
23 [a]Luke 24:27; [Acts 17:3; 19:8] [b]Acts 26:6, 22
24 [a]Acts 14:4; 19:9
26 [a]Is. 6:9, 10; Jer. 5:21; Ezek. 12:2; Matt. 13:14, 15; Mark 4:12; Luke 8:10; John 12:40, 41; Rom. 11:8
28 [a]Is. 42:1, 6; 49:6; Matt. 21:41; Luke 2:32; Rom. 11:11

NKJV

Arrival at Rome

11 After three months we sailed in [a]an Alexandrian ship whose figurehead was the Twin
Brothers, which had wintered at the island.
12 And landing at Syracuse, we stayed three
days.
13 From there we circled round and reached
Rhegium. And after one day the south wind blew;
and the next day we came to Puteoli,
14 where we found [a]brethren, and were invited to stay with them seven days. And so we
went toward Rome.
15 And from there, when the brethren heard
about us, they came to meet us as far as Appii
Forum and Three Inns. When Paul saw them, he
thanked God and took courage.
16 Now when we came to Rome, the centurion delivered the prisoners to the captain of the
guard; but [a]Paul was permitted to dwell by himself with the soldier who guarded him.

Paul's Ministry at Rome

17 And it came to pass after three days that
Paul called the leaders of the Jews together. So
when they had come together, he said to them:
"Men *and* brethren, [a]though I have done nothing
against our people or the customs of our fathers,
yet [b]I was delivered as a prisoner from Jerusalem
into the hands of the Romans,
18 "who, [a]when they had examined me,
wanted to let *me* go, because there was no cause
for putting me to death.
19 "But when the *Jews spoke against *it*, [a]I
was compelled to appeal to Caesar, not that I had
anything of which to accuse my nation.
20 "For this reason therefore I have called
for you, to see *you* and speak with *you*, because
[a]for the hope of Israel I am bound with [b]this
chain."
21 Then they said to him, "We neither received letters from Judea concerning you, nor
have any of the brethren who came reported or
spoken any evil of you.
22 "But we desire to hear from you what you
think; for concerning this sect, we know that [a]it
is spoken against everywhere."
23 So when they had appointed him a day,
many came to him at *his* lodging, [a]to whom he
explained and solemnly testified of the kingdom
of God, persuading them concerning Jesus [b]from
both the Law of Moses and the Prophets, from
morning till evening.
24 And [a]some were persuaded by the things
which were spoken, and some disbelieved.
25 So when they did not agree among themselves, they departed after Paul had said one
word: "The Holy Spirit spoke rightly through
Isaiah the prophet to *our fathers,
26 "saying,

[a]'Go to this people and say:
"Hearing you will hear, and shall not
understand;
And seeing you will see, and not perceive;
27 *For the hearts of this people have grown*
dull.
Their ears are hard of hearing,
And their eyes they have closed,
Lest they should see with their eyes and
hear with their ears,
Lest they should understand with their
hearts and turn,
So that I should heal them."'

28 "Therefore let it be known to you that the
salvation of God has been sent [a]to the Gentiles,
and they will hear it!"
29 *And when he had said these words, the
Jews departed and had a great dispute among
themselves.

*———

28:19 The ruling authorities
28:25 NU *your*
28:29 NU omits v. 29.

KJV

30 And Paul dwelt two whole years in his own hired house, and received all that came in unto him,
31 [a]Preaching the kingdom of God, and teaching those things which concern the Lord Jesus Christ, with all confidence, no man forbidding him.

31 [a]Acts 4:31; Eph. 6:19

NKJV

30 Then Paul dwelt two whole years in his own rented house, and received all who came to him,
31 [a]preaching the kingdom of God and teaching the things which concern the Lord Jesus Christ with all confidence, no one forbidding him.

KJV

THE EPISTLE OF PAUL THE APOSTLE TO THE

ROMANS

Greeting

1 Paul, a servant of Jesus Christ, [a]called *to be* an apostle, [b]separated unto the gospel of God,

2 ([a]Which he had promised afore [b]by his prophets in the holy scriptures,)

3 Concerning his Son Jesus Christ our Lord, which was [a]made of the seed of David according to the flesh;

4 And [a]declared *to be* the Son of God with power, according [b]to the spirit of holiness, by the resurrection from the dead:

5 By whom [a]we have received grace and apostleship, for [b]obedience to the faith among all nations, [c]for his name:

6 Among whom are ye also the called of Jesus Christ:

7 To all that be in Rome, beloved of God, [a]called *to be* saints: [b]Grace to you and peace from God our Father, and the Lord Jesus Christ.

Desire to Visit Rome

8 First, [a]I thank my God through Jesus Christ for you all, that [b]your faith is spoken of throughout the whole world.

9 For [a]God is my witness, [b]whom I serve with my spirit in the gospel of his Son, that [c]without ceasing I make mention of you always in my prayers;

10 Making request, if by any means now at length I might have a prosperous journey by the will of God to come unto you.

11 For I long to see you, that [a]I may impart unto you some spiritual gift, to the end ye may be established;

12 That is, that I may be comforted together with you by [a]the mutual faith both of you and me.

13 Now I would not have you ignorant, brethren, that oftentimes I purposed to come unto you, (but [a]was let hitherto,) that I might have some [b]fruit among you also, even as among other Gentiles.

14 I am debtor both to the Greeks, and to the Barbarians; both to the wise, and to the unwise.

15 So, as much as in me is, I am ready to preach the gospel to you that are at Rome also.

The Just Live by Faith

16 For [a]I am not ashamed of the gospel of Christ: for [b]it is the power of God unto salvation to every one that believeth; [c]to the Jew first, and also to the Greek.

17 For [a]therein is the righteousness of God revealed from faith to faith: as it is written, [b]THE JUST SHALL LIVE BY FAITH.

God's Wrath on Unrighteousness

18 [a]For the wrath of God is revealed from heaven against all ungodliness and [b]unrighteousness of men, who hold the truth in unrighteousness;

CHAPTER 1

1 [a]1 Tim. 1:11 [b]Acts 9:15; 13:2
2 [a]Acts 26:6 [b]Gal. 3:8
3 [a]Gal. 4:4
4 [a]Acts 9:20; 13:33 [b][Heb. 9:14]
5 [a]Eph. 3:8 [b]Acts 6:7 [c]Acts 9:15
7 [a]1 Cor. 1:2, 24 [b]1 Cor. 1:3
8 [a]1 Cor. 1:4 [b]Rom. 16:19
9 [a]Rom. 9:1 [b]Acts 27:23 [c]1 Thess. 3:10
11 [a]Rom. 15:29
12 [a]Titus 1:4
13 [a][1 Thess. 2:18] [b]Phil. 4:17
16 [a]Ps. 40:9, 10 [b]1 Cor. 1:18, 24 [c]Acts 3:26
17 [a]Rom. 3:21; 9:30 [b]Hab. 2:4
18 [a][Acts 17:30] [b]2 Thess. 2:10

*_____

1:16 NU omits *of Christ*

NKJV

THE EPISTLE OF PAUL THE APOSTLE TO THE

ROMANS

Greeting

1 Paul, a bondservant of Jesus Christ, [a]called *to be* an apostle, [b]separated to the gospel of God

2 [a]which He promised before [b]through His prophets in the Holy Scriptures,

3 concerning His Son Jesus Christ our Lord, who was [a]born of the seed of David according to the flesh,

4 *and* [a]declared *to be* the Son of God with power according [b]to the Spirit of holiness, by the resurrection from the dead.

5 Through Him [a]we have received grace and apostleship for [b]obedience to the faith among all nations [c]for His name,

6 among whom you also are the called of Jesus Christ;

7 To all who are in Rome, beloved of God, [a]called *to be* saints:

[b]Grace to you and peace from God our Father and the Lord Jesus Christ.

Desire to Visit Rome

8 First, [a]I thank my God through Jesus Christ for you all, that [b]your faith is spoken of throughout the whole world.

9 For [a]God is my witness, [b]whom I serve with my spirit in the gospel of His Son, that [c]without ceasing I make mention of you always in my prayers,

10 making request if, by some means, now at last I may find a way in the will of God to come to you.

11 For I long to see you, that [a]I may impart to you some spiritual gift, so that you may be established—

12 that is, that I may be encouraged together with you by [a]the mutual faith both of you and me.

13 Now I do not want you to be unaware, brethren, that I often planned to come to you (but [a]was hindered until now), that I might have some [b]fruit among you also, just as among the other Gentiles.

14 I am a debtor both to Greeks and to barbarians, both to wise and to unwise.

15 So, as much as is in me, *I am* ready to preach the gospel to you who are in Rome also.

The Just Live by Faith

16 For [a]I am not ashamed of the gospel *of Christ, for [b]it is the power of God to salvation for everyone who believes, [c]for the Jew first and also for the Greek.

17 For [a]in it the righteousness of God is revealed from faith to faith; as it is written, [b]*"The just shall live by faith."*

God's Wrath on Unrighteousness

18 [a]For the wrath of God is revealed from heaven against all ungodliness and [b]unrighteousness of men, who suppress the truth in unrighteousness,

KJV

19 Because [a]that which may be known of God is manifest in them; for [b]God hath shewed *it* unto them.

20 For [a]the invisible things of him from the creation of the world are clearly seen, being understood by the things that are made, *even* his eternal power and Godhead; so that they are without excuse:

21 Because that, when they knew God, they glorified *him* not as God, neither were thankful; but [a]became vain in their imaginations, and their foolish heart was darkened.

22 [a]Professing themselves to be wise, they became fools,

23 And changed the glory of the [a]uncorruptible [b]God into an image made like to corruptible man, and to birds, and fourfooted beasts, and creeping things.

24 [a]Wherefore God also gave them up to uncleanness through the lusts of their own hearts, [b]to dishonour their own bodies [c]between themselves:

25 Who changed [a]the truth of God [b]into a lie, and worshipped and served the creature more than the Creator, who is blessed for ever. Amen.

26 For this cause God gave them up unto [a]vile affections: for even their women did change the natural use into that which is against nature:

27 And likewise also the men, leaving the natural use of the woman, burned in their lust one toward another; men with men working that which is unseemly, and receiving in themselves that recompence of their error which was meet.

28 And even as they did not like to retain God in *their* knowledge, God gave them over to a reprobate mind, to do those things [a]which are not convenient;

29 Being filled with all unrighteousness, fornication, wickedness, covetousness, maliciousness; full of envy, murder, debate, deceit, malignity; whisperers,

30 Backbiters, haters of God, despiteful, proud, boasters, inventors of evil things, disobedient to parents,

31 Without understanding, covenantbreakers, without natural affection, implacable, unmerciful:

32 Who [a]knowing the judgment of God, that they which commit such things [b]are worthy of death, not only do the same, but [c]have pleasure in them that do them.

God's Righteous Judgment

2 Therefore thou art [a]inexcusable, O man, whosoever thou art that judgest: [b]for wherein thou judgest another, thou condemnest thyself; for thou that judgest doest the same things.

2 But we are sure that the judgment of God is according to truth against them which commit such things.

3 And thinkest thou this, O man, that judgest them which do such things, and doest the same, that thou shalt escape the judgment of God?

4 Or despisest thou [a]the riches of his goodness and [b]forbearance and [c]longsuffering; [d]not knowing that the goodness of God leadeth thee to repentance?

5 But after thy hardness and impenitent heart [a]treasurest up unto thyself wrath against the day of wrath and revelation of the righteous judgment of God;

6 [a]WHO WILL RENDER TO EVERY MAN ACCORDING TO HIS DEEDS:

7 To them who by patient continuance in well doing seek for glory and honour and immortality, eternal life:

8 But unto them that are contentious, and [a]do not obey the truth, but obey unrighteousness, indignation and wrath,

9 Tribulation and anguish, upon every soul of man that doeth evil, of the Jew [a]first, and also of the Gentile;

19 [a][Acts 14:17; 17:24] [b][John 1:9]
20 [a]Job 12:7–9; Ps. 19:1–6; Jer. 5:22
21 [a]2 Kin. 17:15; Jer. 2:5; Eph. 4:17
22 [a]Jer. 10:14; [1 Cor. 1:20]
23 [a]1 Tim. 1:17; 6:15, 16 [b]Deut. 4:16–18; Ps. 106:20; Jer. 2:11; Acts 17:29
24 [a]Ps. 81:12; Acts 7:42; Eph. 4:18, 19 [b]1 Cor. 6:18 [c]Lev. 18:22
25 [a]1 Thess. 1:9 [b]Is. 44:20; Jer. 10:14; 13:25; 16:19
26 [a]Lev. 18:22; Eph. 5:12
28 [a]Eph. 5:4
32 [a][Rom. 2:2] [b][Rom. 6:21] [c][Ps. 50:18]; Hos. 7:3

CHAPTER 2

1 [a][Rom. 1:20] [b]2 Sam. 12:5–7; [Matt. 7:1–5; Luke 6:37]; John 8:9; Rom. 14:22
4 [a]Rom. 9:23; 11:33; [2 Cor. 8:2; Eph. 1:7, 18; 2:7; Phil. 4:19; Col. 1:27; 2:2; Titus 3:6] [b][Rom. 3:25] [c]Ex. 34:6; [Rom. 9:22; 1 Tim. 1:16]; 1 Pet. 3:20 [d]Is. 30:18; [2 Pet. 3:9, 15]
5 [a][Deut. 32:34]; Prov. 1:18; James 5:3
6 [a][Job 34:11]; Ps. 62:12; Prov. 24:12; Jer. 17:10; [2 Cor. 5:10; Rev. 20:12, 13]
8 [a]Job 24:13; [2 Thess. 1:8]
9 [a]Amos 3:2; Luke 12:47; Acts 3:26; Rom. 1:16; 1 Pet. 4:17

* **1:29** NU omits *sexual immorality*
1:31 NU omits *unforgiving*

NKJV

19 because [a]what may be known of God is manifest in them, for [b]God has shown *it* to them.

20 For since the creation of the world [a]His invisible *attributes* are clearly seen, being understood by the things that are made, *even* His eternal power and Godhead, so that they are without excuse,

21 because, although they knew God, they did not glorify *Him* as God, nor were thankful, but [a]became futile in their thoughts, and their foolish hearts were darkened.

22 [a]Professing to be wise, they became fools,

23 and changed the glory of the [a]incorruptible [b]God into an image made like corruptible man—and birds and four-footed animals and creeping things.

24 [a]Therefore God also gave them up to uncleanness, in the lusts of their hearts, [b]to dishonor their bodies [c]among themselves,

25 who exchanged [a]the truth of God [b]for the lie, and worshiped and served the creature rather than the Creator, who is blessed forever. Amen.

26 For this reason God gave them up to [a]vile passions. For even their women exchanged the natural use for what is against nature.

27 Likewise also the men, leaving the natural use of the woman, burned in their lust for one another, men with men committing what is shameful, and receiving in themselves the penalty of their error which was due.

28 And even as they did not like to retain God in *their* knowledge, God gave them over to a debased mind, to do those things [a]which are not fitting;

29 being filled with all unrighteousness, *sexual immorality, wickedness, covetousness, maliciousness; full of envy, murder, strife, deceit, evil-mindedness; *they are* whisperers,

30 backbiters, haters of God, violent, proud, boasters, inventors of evil things, disobedient to parents,

31 undiscerning, untrustworthy, unloving, *unforgiving, unmerciful;

32 who, [a]knowing the righteous judgment of God, that those who practice such things [b]are deserving of death, not only do the same but also [c]approve of those who practice them.

God's Righteous Judgment

2 Therefore you are [a]inexcusable, O man, whoever you are who judge, [b]for in whatever you judge another you condemn yourself; for you who judge practice the same things.

2 But we know that the judgment of God is according to truth against those who practice such things.

3 And do you think this, O man, you who judge those practicing such things, and doing the same, that you will escape the judgment of God?

4 Or do you despise [a]the riches of His goodness, [b]forbearance, and [c]longsuffering, [d]not knowing that the goodness of God leads you to repentance?

5 But in accordance with your hardness and your impenitent heart [a]you are treasuring up for yourself wrath in the day of wrath and revelation of the righteous judgment of God,

6 who [a]*"will render to each one according to his deeds"*:

7 eternal life to those who by patient continuance in doing good seek for glory, honor, and immortality;

8 but to those who are self-seeking and [a]do not obey the truth, but obey unrighteousness—indignation and wrath,

9 tribulation and anguish, on every soul of man who does evil, of the Jew [a]first and also of the Greek;

KJV

10 [a]But glory, honour, and peace, to every man that worketh good, to the Jew first, and also to the Gentile:

11 For [a]there is no respect of persons with God.

12 For as many as have sinned without law shall also perish without law: and as many as have sinned in the law shall be judged by the law;

13 (For [a]not the hearers of the law *are* just before God, but the doers of the law shall be justified.

14 For when the Gentiles, which have not the law, do by nature the things contained in the law, these, having not the law, are a law unto themselves:

15 Which shew the [a]work of the law written in their hearts, their [b]conscience also bearing witness, and *their* thoughts the mean while accusing or else excusing one another;)

16 [a]In the day when God shall judge the secrets of men [b]by Jesus Christ [c]according to my gospel.

The Jews Guilty as the Gentiles

17 Behold, [a]thou art called a Jew, and [b]restest in the law, [c]and makest thy boast of God,

18 And [a]knowest *his* will, and [b]approvest the things that are more excellent, being instructed out of the law;

19 And [a]art confident that thou thyself art a guide of the blind, a light of them which are in darkness,

20 An instructor of the foolish, a teacher of babes, [a]which hast the form of knowledge and of the truth in the law.

21 [a]Thou therefore which teachest another, teachest thou not thyself? thou that preachest a man should not steal, dost thou steal?

22 Thou that sayest a man should not commit adultery, dost thou commit adultery? thou that abhorrest idols, [a]dost thou commit sacrilege?

23 Thou that [a]makest thy boast of the law, through breaking the law dishonourest thou God?

24 For [a]THE NAME OF GOD IS [b]BLASPHEMED AMONG THE GENTILES THROUGH YOU, as it is [c]written.

Circumcision of No Avail

25 [a]For circumcision verily profiteth, if thou keep the law: but if thou be a breaker of the law, thy circumcision is made uncircumcision.

26 Therefore [a]if the uncircumcision keep the righteousness of the law, shall not his uncircumcision be counted for circumcision?

27 And shall not uncircumcision which is by nature, if it fulfil the law, [a]judge thee, who by the letter and circumcision dost transgress the law?

28 For [a]he is not a Jew, which is one outwardly; neither *is that* circumcision, which is outward in the flesh:

29 But he *is* a Jew, [a]which is one inwardly; and [b]circumcision *is that* of the heart, [c]in the spirit, *and* not in the letter; [d]whose praise *is* not of men, but of God.

God's Judgment Defended

3 What advantage then hath the Jew? or what profit *is there* of circumcision?

2 Much every way: chiefly, because that [a]unto them were committed the oracles of God.

3 For what if [a]some did not believe? [b]shall their unbelief make the faith of God without effect?

4 [a]God forbid: yea, let [b]God be true, but [c]every man a liar; as it is written, [d]THAT THOU MIGHTEST BE JUSTIFIED IN THY SAYINGS, AND MIGHTEST OVERCOME WHEN THOU ART JUDGED.

---

10 [a]Rom. 2:7; Heb. 2:7; [1 Pet. 1:7] **11** [a]Deut. 10:17; [Job 34:19]; Acts 10:34; [Eph. 6:9] **13** [a]Matt. 7:21, 22; John 13:17; [James 1:22, 25; 1 John 3:7] **15** [a]1 Cor. 5:1 [b]Acts 24:25 **16** [a]Eccl. 12:14; [Matt. 25:31]; Rev. 20:12 [b]John 5:22; Acts 10:42; 17:31; Rom. 3:6; 14:10 [c]1 Tim. 1:11 **17** [a][Matt. 3:9]; John 8:33 [b]Mic. 3:11; John 5:45; Rom. 2:23; 9:4 [c]Is. 48:1, 2 **18** [a]Deut. 4:8 [b]Phil. 1:10 **19** [a]Matt. 15:14; John 9:34 **20** [a][2 Tim. 3:5] **21** [a]Ps. 50:16; Matt. 23:3 **22** [a]Mal. 3:8 **23** [a]Mic. 3:11; John 5:45; Rom. 2:17; 9:4 **24** [a]Ezek. 16:27 [b]2 Sam. 12:14; Is. 52:5; Ezek. 36:22 **25** [a]Gen. 17:10–14; [Gal. 5:3] **26** [a][Acts 10:34] **27** [a]Matt. 12:41 **28** [a][Matt. 3:9]; John 8:39; Rom. 2:17; 9:6; [Gal. 6:15] **29** [a][1 Pet. 3:4] [b]Phil. 3:3; Col. 2:11 [c]Deut. 30:6; Rom. 2:27; 7:6; [2 Cor. 3:6] [d]John 5:44; 12:43; [1 Cor. 4:5; 2 Cor. 10:18]; 1 Thess. 2:4

CHAPTER 3

2 [a]Deut. 4:5–8; Ps. 147:19; Rom. 9:4 **3** [a]Rom. 10:16; Heb. 4:2 [b]Num. 23:19; [2 Tim. 2:13] **4** [a]Job 40:8 [b][John 3:33] [c]Ps. 62:9 [d]Ps. 51:4

*

2:17 NU *But if*

NKJV

10 [a]but glory, honor, and peace to everyone who works what is good, to the Jew first and also to the Greek.

11 For [a]there is no partiality with God.

12 For as many as have sinned without law will also perish without law, and as many as have sinned in the law will be judged by the law

13 (for [a]not the hearers of the law *are* just in the sight of God, but the doers of the law will be justified;

14 for when Gentiles, who do not have the law, by nature do the things in the law, these, although not having the law, are a law to themselves,

15 who show the [a]work of the law written in their hearts, their [b]conscience also bearing witness, and between themselves *their* thoughts accusing or else excusing *them*)

16 [a]in the day when God will judge the secrets of men [b]by Jesus Christ, [c]according to my gospel.

The Jews Guilty as the Gentiles

17 *Indeed [a]you are called a Jew, and [b]rest on the law, [c]and make your boast in God,

18 and [a]know *His* will, and [b]approve the things that are excellent, being instructed out of the law,

19 and [a]are confident that you yourself are a guide to the blind, a light to those who are in darkness,

20 an instructor of the foolish, a teacher of babes, [a]having the form of knowledge and truth in the law.

21 [a]You, therefore, who teach another, do you not teach yourself? You who preach that a man should not steal, do you steal?

22 You who say, "Do not commit adultery," do you commit adultery? You who abhor idols, [a]do you rob temples?

23 You who [a]make your boast in the law, do you dishonor God through breaking the law?

24 For [a]*"the name of God is* [b]*blasphemed among the Gentiles because of you,"* as it is written.

Circumcision of No Avail

25 [a]For circumcision is indeed profitable if you keep the law; but if you are a breaker of the law, your circumcision has become uncircumcision.

26 Therefore, [a]if an uncircumcised man keeps the righteous requirements of the law, will not his uncircumcision be counted as circumcision?

27 And will not the physically uncircumcised, if he fulfills the law, [a]judge you who, *even* with *your* written *code* and circumcision, *are* a transgressor of the law?

28 For [a]he is not a Jew who *is one* outwardly, nor *is* circumcision that which *is* outward in the flesh;

29 but *he is* a Jew [a]who *is one* inwardly; and [b]circumcision *is that* of the heart, [c]in the Spirit, not in the letter; [d]whose praise *is* not from men but from God.

God's Judgment Defended

3 What advantage then has the Jew, or what *is* the profit of circumcision?

2 Much in every way! Chiefly because [a]to them were committed the oracles of God.

3 For what if [a]some did not believe? [b]Will their unbelief make the faithfulness of God without effect?

4 [a]Certainly not! Indeed, let [b]God be true but [c]every man a liar. As it is written:

> [d]*"That You may be justified in Your words,*
> *And may overcome when You are*
> *judged."*

KJV

5 But if our unrighteousness commend the
righteousness of God, what shall we say? *Is* God
unrighteous who taketh vengeance? [a](I speak as
a man)
6 God forbid: for then [a]how shall God judge
the world?
7 For if the truth of God hath more
abounded through my lie unto his glory; why yet
am I also judged as a sinner?
8 And not *rather,* (as we be slanderously reported, and as some affirm that we say,) [a]Let us
do evil, that good may come? whose damnation
is just.

All Have Sinned
(Ps. 14:1–3; 53:1–4)

9 What then? are we better *than they*? No,
in no wise: for we have before proved both Jews
and Gentiles, that [a]they are all under sin;
10 As it is written, [a]THERE IS NONE RIGHTEOUS,
NO, NOT ONE:
11 THERE IS NONE THAT UNDERSTANDETH,
THERE IS NONE THAT SEEKETH AFTER GOD.
12 THEY ARE ALL GONE OUT OF THE WAY, THEY
ARE TOGETHER BECOME UNPROFITABLE; THERE IS
NONE THAT DOETH GOOD, NO, NOT ONE.
13 [a]THEIR THROAT *IS* AN OPEN SEPULCHRE; WITH
THEIR TONGUES THEY HAVE USED DECEIT; [b]THE
POISON OF ASPS *IS* UNDER THEIR LIPS:
14 [a]WHOSE MOUTH *IS* FULL OF CURSING AND
BITTERNESS:
15 [a]THEIR FEET *ARE* SWIFT TO SHED BLOOD:
16 DESTRUCTION AND MISERY *ARE* IN THEIR
WAYS:
17 AND THE WAY OF PEACE HAVE THEY NOT
KNOWN:
18 [a]THERE IS NO FEAR OF GOD BEFORE
THEIR EYES.
19 Now we know that what things soever
[a]the law saith, it saith to them who are under the
law: that [b]every mouth may be stopped, and all
the world may become guilty before God.
20 Therefore [a]by the deeds of the law there
shall no flesh be justified in his sight: for by the
law *is* the knowledge of sin.

God's Righteousness Through Faith

21 But now [a]the righteousness of God without the law is manifested, [b]being witnessed by
the law [c]and the prophets;
22 Even the righteousness of God *which is*
by faith of Jesus Christ unto all and upon all them
that believe: for [a]there is no difference:
23 For [a]all have sinned, and come short of
the glory of God;
24 Being justified freely [a]by his grace
[b]through the redemption that is in Christ Jesus:
25 Whom God hath set forth [a]*to be* a propitiation through faith [b]in his blood, to declare his
righteousness for the remission of [c]sins that are
past, through the forbearance of God;
26 To declare, *I say,* at this time his righteousness: that he might be just, and the justifier
of him which believeth in Jesus.

Boasting Excluded

27 [a]Where *is* boasting then? It is excluded.
By what law? of works? Nay: but by the law of
faith.
28 Therefore we conclude [a]that a man is justified by faith without the deeds of the law.
29 *Is he* the God of the Jews only? *is he* not
also of the Gentiles? Yes, of the Gentiles also:
30 Seeing [a]*it is* one God, which shall justify
the circumcision by faith, and uncircumcision
through faith.

5 [a]Rom. 6:19; 1 Cor. 9:8; 15:32; Gal. 3:15
6 [a][Gen. 18:25]
8 [a]Rom. 5:20
9 [a]Rom. 3:19, 23; 11:32; Gal. 3:22
10 [a]Ps. 14:1–3; 53:1–3; Eccl. 7:20
13 [a]Ps. 5:9 [b]Ps. 140:3
14 [a]Ps. 10:7
15 [a]Prov. 1:16; Is. 59:7, 8
18 [a]Ps. 36:1
19 [a]John 10:34 [b]Job 5:16; Ps. 107:42
20 [a]Ps. 143:2; [Acts 13:39; Gal. 2:16]
21 [a]Acts 15:11 [b]John 5:46 [c]1 Pet. 1:10
22 [a]Rom. 10:12; [Gal. 3:28; Col. 3:11]
23 [a]Gal. 3:22
24 [a]Rom. 4:4, 16; [Eph. 2:8; Titus 3:5, 7] [b][Matt. 20:28; Eph. 1:7; Col. 1:14; 1 Tim. 2:6; Heb. 9:12, 15; 1 Pet. 1:18, 19]
25 [a]Lev. 16:15 [b]Col. 1:20 [c]Acts 14:16; 17:30; [Rom. 2:4]
27 [a]Rom. 2:17, 23; [1 Cor. 1:29]; Eph. 2:9
28 [a]Gal. 2:16
30 [a]Rom. 10:12; [Gal. 3:8, 20]

NKJV

5 But if our unrighteousness demonstrates
the righteousness of God, what shall we say? *Is*
God unjust who inflicts wrath? [a](I speak as a
man.)
6 Certainly not! For then [a]how will God
judge the world?
7 For if the truth of God has increased
through my lie to His glory, why am I also still
judged as a sinner?
8 And *why* not *say,* [a]"Let us do evil that
good may come"?—as we are slanderously reported and as some affirm that we say. Their condemnation is just.

All Have Sinned
(Ps. 14:1–3; 53:1–4)

9 What then? Are we better *than they*? Not
at all. For we have previously charged both Jews
and Greeks that [a]they are all under sin.
10 As it is written:

[a]*"There is none righteous, no, not one;*
11 *There is none who understands;*
There is none who seeks after God.
12 *They have all turned aside;*
They have together become unprofitable;
There is none who does good, no, not
one."
13 *"Their[a] throat is an open tomb;*
With their tongues they have practiced
deceit";
[b]*"The poison of asps is under their lips";*
14 *"Whose[a] mouth is full of cursing and*
bitterness."
15 *"Their[a] feet are swift to shed blood;*
16 *Destruction and misery are in their ways;*
17 *And the way of peace they have not*
known."
18 *"There[a] is no fear of God before their*
eyes."

19 Now we know that whatever [a]the law
says, it says to those who are under the law, that
[b]every mouth may be stopped, and all the world
may become guilty before God.
20 Therefore [a]by the deeds of the law no
flesh will be justified in His sight, for by the law
is the knowledge of sin.

God's Righteousness Through Faith

21 But now [a]the righteousness of God apart
from the law is revealed, [b]being witnessed by the
Law [c]and the Prophets,
22 even the righteousness of God, through
faith in Jesus Christ, to all *and on all who believe.
For [a]there is no difference;
23 for [a]all have sinned and fall short of the
glory of God,
24 being justified freely [a]by His grace
[b]through the redemption that is in Christ
Jesus,
25 whom God set forth [a]*as* a propitiation [b]by
His blood, through faith, to demonstrate His righteousness, because in His forbearance God had
passed over [c]the sins that were previously
committed,
26 to demonstrate at the present time His
righteousness, that He might be just and the justifier of the one who has faith in Jesus.

Boasting Excluded

27 [a]Where *is* boasting then? It is excluded.
By what law? Of works? No, but by the law of
faith.
28 Therefore we conclude [a]that a man is justified by faith apart from the deeds of the law.
29 Or *is He* the God of the Jews only? *Is He*
not also the God of the Gentiles? Yes, of the Gentiles also,
30 since [a]*there is* one God who will justify
the circumcised by faith and the uncircumcised
through faith.

*———
3:22 NU omits *and on all*

KJV

31 Do we then make void the law through faith? God forbid: yea, we establish the law.

Abraham Justified by Faith
(*Gen. 17:10*)

4 What shall we say then that [a]Abraham our [b]father, as pertaining to the flesh, hath found?

2 For if Abraham were [a]justified by works, he hath *whereof* to glory; but not before God.

3 For what saith the scripture? [a]ABRAHAM BELIEVED GOD, AND IT WAS COUNTED UNTO HIM FOR RIGHTEOUSNESS.

4 Now [a]to him that worketh is the reward not reckoned of grace, but of debt.

David Celebrates the Same Truth

5 But to him that worketh [a]not, but believeth on him that justifieth [b]the ungodly, his faith is counted for righteousness.

6 Even as David also [a]describeth the blessedness of the man, unto whom God imputeth righteousness without works,

7 *Saying,* [a]BLESSED *ARE* THEY WHOSE INIQUITIES ARE FORGIVEN, AND WHOSE SINS ARE COVERED.

8 BLESSED *IS* THE MAN TO WHOM THE LORD WILL NOT IMPUTE SIN.

Abraham Justified Before Circumcision

9 *Cometh* this blessedness then upon the circumcision *only,* or upon the uncircumcision also? for we say that faith was reckoned to Abraham for righteousness.

10 How was it then reckoned? when he was in circumcision, or in uncircumcision? Not in circumcision, but in uncircumcision.

11 And [a]he received the sign of circumcision, a seal of the righteousness of the faith which *he had yet* being uncircumcised: that [b]he might be the father of all them that believe, though they be not circumcised; that righteousness might be imputed unto them also:

12 And the father of circumcision to them who are not of the circumcision only, but who also walk in the steps of that faith of our father [a]Abraham, which *he had* being *yet* uncircumcised.

The Promise Granted Through Faith

13 For the promise, that he should be the [a]heir of the world, *was* not to Abraham, or to his seed, through the law, but through the righteousness of faith.

14 For [a]if they which are of the law *be* heirs, faith is made void, and the promise made of none effect:

15 Because [a]the law worketh wrath: for where no law is, *there is* no transgression.

16 Therefore *it is* of faith, that *it might be* [a]by grace; [b]to the end the promise might be sure to all the seed; not to that only which is of the law, but to that also which is of the faith of Abraham; [c]who is the father of us all,

17 (As it is written, [a]I HAVE MADE THEE A FATHER OF MANY NATIONS,) before him whom he believed, *even* God, [b]who quickeneth the dead, and calleth those [c]things which be not as though they were.

18 Who against hope believed in hope, that he might become the father of many nations, according to that which was spoken, [a]SO SHALL THY SEED BE.

19 And being not weak in faith, [a]he considered not his own body now dead, when he was about an hundred years old, [b]neither yet the deadness of Sarah's womb:

20 He staggered not at the promise of God through unbelief; but was strong in faith, giving glory to God;

CHAPTER 4

1 [a]Gen. 11:27—25:9; Is. 51:2; [Matt. 3:9]; John 8:33 [b][Luke 3:8]; John 8:53; James 2:21
2 [a]Rom. 3:20, 27
3 [a]Gen. 15:6; Rom. 4:9, 22; Gal. 3:6; James 2:23
4 [a]Rom. 11:6
5 [a][Gal. 2:16; Eph. 2:8, 9] [b]Josh. 24:2
6 [a]Ps. 32:1, 2
7 [a]Ps. 32:1, 2
11 [a]Gen. 17:10 [b]Luke 19:9; Rom. 4:16
12 [a]Rom. 4:18–22
13 [a]Gen. 17:4–6; 22:17
14 [a]Gal. 3:18
15 [a]Rom. 3:20
16 [a][Rom. 3:24] [b][Gal. 3:22] [c]Is. 51:2
17 [a]Gen. 17:5 [b][Rom. 8:11] [c]Rom. 9:26
18 [a]Gen. 15:5
19 [a]Gen. 17:17 [b]Heb. 11:11

NKJV

31 Do we then make void the law through faith? Certainly not! On the contrary, we establish the law.

Abraham Justified by Faith
(*Gen. 17:10*)

4 What then shall we say that [a]Abraham our [b]father* has found according to the flesh?

2 For if Abraham was [a]justified by works, he has *something* to boast about, but not before God.

3 For what does the Scripture say? [a]*"Abraham believed God, and it was accounted to him for righteousness."*

4 Now [a]to him who works, the wages are not counted as grace but as debt.

David Celebrates the Same Truth

5 But to him who [a]does not work but believes on Him who justifies [b]the ungodly, his faith is accounted for righteousness,

6 just as David also [a]describes the blessedness of the man to whom God imputes righteousness apart from works:

7 *"Blessed[a] are those whose lawless deeds*
are forgiven,
And whose sins are covered;
8 *Blessed is the man to whom the* LORD *shall*
not impute sin."

Abraham Justified Before Circumcision

9 *Does* this blessedness then *come* upon the circumcised *only,* or upon the uncircumcised also? For we say that faith was accounted to Abraham for righteousness.

10 How then was it accounted? While he was circumcised, or uncircumcised? Not while circumcised, but while uncircumcised.

11 And [a]he received the sign of circumcision, a seal of the righteousness of the faith which *he had while still* uncircumcised, that [b]he might be the father of all those who believe, though they are uncircumcised, that righteousness might be imputed to them also,

12 and the father of circumcision to those who not only *are* of the circumcision, but who also walk in the steps of the faith which our father [a]Abraham *had while still* uncircumcised.

The Promise Granted Through Faith

13 For the promise that he would be the [a]heir of the world *was* not to Abraham or to his seed through the law, but through the righteousness of faith.

14 For [a]if those who are of the law *are* heirs, faith is made void and the promise made of no effect,

15 because [a]the law brings about wrath; for where there is no law *there is* no transgression.

16 Therefore *it is* of faith that *it might be* [a]according to grace, [b]so that the promise might be sure to all the seed, not only to those who are of the law, but also to those who are of the faith of Abraham, [c]who is the father of us all

17 (as it is written, [a]*"I have made you a father of many nations"*) in the presence of Him whom he believed—God, [b]who gives life to the dead and calls those [c]things which do not exist as though they did;

18 who, contrary to hope, in hope believed, so that he became the father of many nations, according to what was spoken, [a]*"So shall your descendants be."*

19 And not being weak in faith, [a]he did not consider his own body, already dead (since he was about a hundred years old), [b]and the deadness of Sarah's womb.

20 He did not waver at the promise of God through unbelief, but was strengthened in faith, giving glory to God,

---

*4:1 Or (fore-) *father according to the flesh has found?*

KJV

21 And being fully persuaded that, what he
had promised, [a]he was able also to perform.
22 And therefore [a]IT WAS IMPUTED TO HIM FOR
RIGHTEOUSNESS.
23 Now [a]it was not written for his sake alone,
that it was imputed to him;
24 But for us also, to whom it shall be imputed, if we believe [a]on him that raised up Jesus
our Lord from the dead;
25 [a]Who was delivered for our offences, and
[b]was raised again for our justification.

Faith Triumphs in Trouble

5 Therefore [a]being justified by faith, we have
[b]peace with God through our Lord Jesus
Christ:
2 [a]By whom also we have access by faith
into this grace [b]wherein we stand, and [c]rejoice
in hope of the glory of God.
3 And not only so, but [a]we glory in tribulations also: [b]knowing that tribulation worketh
patience;
4 [a]And patience, experience; and experience, hope:
5 [a]And hope maketh not ashamed; [b]be-
cause the love of God is shed abroad in our hearts
by the Holy Ghost which is given unto us.

Christ in Our Place

6 For when we were yet without strength,
in due time [a]Christ died for the ungodly.
7 For scarcely for a righteous man will one
die: yet peradventure for a good man some would
even dare to die.
8 But [a]God commendeth his love toward us,
in that, while we were yet sinners, Christ died
for us.
9 Much more then, being now justified [a]by
his blood, we shall be saved [b]from wrath through
him.
10 For [a]if, when we were enemies, [b]we were
reconciled to God by the death of his Son, much
more, being reconciled, we shall be saved [c]by his
life.
11 And not only *so,* but we also [a]joy in God
through our Lord Jesus Christ, by whom we have
now received the atonement.

Death in Adam, Life in Christ
(Gen. 3:1–19)

12 Wherefore, as [a]by one man sin entered
into the world, and [b]death by sin; and so death
passed upon all men, for that all have sinned:
13 (For until the law sin was in the world:
but [a]sin is not imputed when there is no law.
14 Nevertheless death reigned from Adam to
Moses, even over them that had not sinned after
the similitude of Adam's transgression, [a]who is
the figure of him that was to come.
15 But not as the offence, so also *is* the free
gift. For if through the offence of one many be
dead, much more the grace of God, and the gift
by grace, *which is* by one man, Jesus Christ, hath
abounded [a]unto many.
16 And not as *it was* by one that sinned, *so*
is the gift: for the judgment *was* by one to condemnation, but the free gift *is* of many offences unto
justification.
17 For if by one man's offence death reigned
by one; much more they which receive abundance
of grace and of the gift of righteousness shall
reign in life by one, Jesus Christ.)
18 Therefore as by the offence of one *judg-*
ment came upon all men to condemnation; even
so by the righteousness of [a]one *the free gift came*
[b]upon all men unto justification of life.
19 For as by one man's disobedience many
were made sinners, so by the [a]obedience of one
shall many be made righteous.

21 [a]Gen. 18:14; [Ps. 115:3; Luke 1:37; Heb. 11:19]
22 [a]Gen. 15:6
23 [a]Rom. 15:4; 1 Cor. 10:6
24 [a]Acts 2:24
25 [a]Is. 53:4, 5; [Rom. 5:6, 8; 8:32; Gal. 2:20; Eph. 5:2; Heb. 9:28] [b][Rom. 5:18; 1 Cor. 15:17; 2 Cor. 5:15]

CHAPTER 5

1 [a]Is. 32:17; John 16:33 [b][Is. 53:5]; Acts 10:36; [Eph. 2:14]
2 [a][John 10:9; Eph. 2:18; 3:12; Heb. 10:19; 1 Pet. 3:18] [b]1 Cor. 15:1 [c]Heb. 3:6
3 [a]Matt. 5:11, 12; [John 16:33; Acts 5:41; 2 Cor. 12:9]; James 1:2 [b]James 1:3
4 [a]Phil. 2:22; [James 1:12]
5 [a]Phil. 1:20 [b]2 Cor. 1:22; Eph. 1:13
6 [a]Is. 53:5; [Rom. 4:25; 5:8; 8:32; Gal. 2:20; Eph. 5:2]
8 [a][John 3:16; 15:13; Rom. 8:39]
9 [a]Eph. 2:13; [1 John 1:7] [b]Rom. 1:18; 1 Thess. 1:10
10 [a][Rom. 8:32] [b]Rom. 11:28; 2 Cor. 5:18; [Eph. 2:5, 6]; Col. 1:21 [c]John 14:19
11 [a][Gal. 4:9]
12 [a]Gen. 2:17; 3:6, 19; [Rom. 5:15–17; 1 Cor. 15:21] [b]Gen. 2:17
13 [a]1 John 3:4
14 [a][1 Cor. 15:21, 22]
15 [a][Is. 53:11]
18 [a][1 Cor. 15:21, 45] [b]Matt. 1:21; [John 12:32]
19 [a]Is. 53:11, 12; [Phil. 2:8]

NKJV

21 and being fully convinced that what He
had promised [a]He was also able to perform.
22 And therefore [a]*"it was accounted to him*
for righteousness."
23 Now [a]it was not written for his sake alone
that it was imputed to him,
24 but also for us. It shall be imputed to us
who believe [a]in Him who raised up Jesus our Lord
from the dead,
25 [a]who was delivered up because of our offenses, and [b]was raised because of our justification.

Faith Triumphs in Trouble

5 Therefore, [a]having been justified by faith, *we
have [b]peace with God through our Lord Jesus
Christ,
2 [a]through whom also we have access by
faith into this grace [b]in which we stand, and [c]re-
joice in hope of the glory of God.
3 And not only *that,* but [a]we also glory in
tribulations, [b]knowing that tribulation produces
perseverance;
4 [a]and perseverance, character; and character, hope.
5 [a]Now hope does not disappoint, [b]because
the love of God has been poured out in our hearts
by the Holy Spirit who was given to us.

Christ in Our Place

6 For when we were still without strength,
in due time [a]Christ died for the ungodly.
7 For scarcely for a righteous man will one
die; yet perhaps for a good man someone would
even dare to die.
8 But [a]God demonstrates His own love toward us, in that while we were still sinners, Christ
died for us.
9 Much more then, having now been justified [a]by His blood, we shall be saved [b]from wrath
through Him.
10 For [a]if when we were enemies [b]we were
reconciled to God through the death of His Son,
much more, having been reconciled, we shall be
saved [c]by His life.
11 And not only *that,* but we also [a]rejoice
in God through our Lord Jesus Christ, through
whom we have now received the reconciliation.

Death in Adam, Life in Christ
(Gen. 3:1–19)

12 Therefore, just as [a]through one man sin
entered the world, and [b]death through sin, and
thus death spread to all men, because all sinned—
13 (For until the law sin was in the world,
but [a]sin is not imputed when there is no law.
14 Nevertheless death reigned from Adam to
Moses, even over those who had not sinned according to the likeness of the transgression of
Adam, [a]who is a type of Him who was to come.
15 But the free gift *is* not like the offense.
For if by the one man's offense many died, much
more the grace of God and the gift by the grace
of the one Man, Jesus Christ, abounded [a]to many.
16 And the gift *is* not like *that which came*
through the one who sinned. For the judgment
which came from one *offense resulted* in condemnation, but the free gift *which came* from many
offenses *resulted* in justification.
17 For if by the one man's offense death
reigned through the one, much more those who
receive abundance of grace and of the gift of righteousness will reign in life through the One, Jesus
Christ.)
18 Therefore, as through one man's offense
judgment came to all men, resulting in condemnation, even so through [a]one Man's righteous act
the free gift came [b]to all men, resulting in justification of life.
19 For as by one man's disobedience many
were made sinners, so also by [a]one Man's obedience many will be made righteous.

*

5:1 Some ancient mss. *let us have*

KJV

20 Moreover [a]the law entered, that the offence might abound. But where sin abounded, grace did much [b]more abound:

21 That as sin hath reigned unto death, even so might grace reign through righteousness unto eternal life by Jesus Christ our Lord.

Dead to Sin, Alive to God

6 What shall we say then? [a]Shall we continue in sin, that grace may abound?

2 God forbid. How shall we, that are [a]dead to sin, live any longer therein?

3 Know ye not, that [a]so many of us as were baptized into Jesus Christ [b]were baptized into his death?

4 Therefore we are [a]buried with him by baptism into death: that [b]like as Christ was raised up from the dead by [c]the glory of the Father, [d]even so we also should walk in newness of life.

5 [a]For if we have been planted together in the likeness of his death, we shall be also *in the likeness* of *his* resurrection:

6 Knowing this, that [a]our old man is crucified with *him,* that [b]the body of sin might be destroyed, that henceforth we should not serve sin.

7 For [a]he that is dead is freed from sin.

8 Now [a]if we be dead with Christ, we believe that we shall also live with him:

9 Knowing that [a]Christ being raised from the dead dieth no more; death hath no more dominion over him.

10 For in that he died, [a]he died unto sin once: but in that he liveth, [b]he liveth unto God.

11 Likewise reckon ye also yourselves to be [a]dead indeed unto sin, but [b]alive unto God through Jesus Christ our Lord.

12 [a]Let not sin therefore reign in your mortal body, that ye should obey it in the lusts thereof.

13 Neither yield ye your [a]members *as* instruments of unrighteousness unto sin: but [b]yield yourselves unto God, as those that are alive from the dead, and your members *as* instruments of righteousness unto God.

14 For [a]sin shall not have dominion over you: for ye are not under the law, but under grace.

From Slaves of Sin to Slaves of God

15 What then? shall we sin, [a]because we are not under the law, but under grace? God forbid.

16 Know ye not, that [a]to whom ye yield yourselves servants to obey, his servants ye are to whom ye obey; whether of sin unto death, or of obedience unto righteousness?

17 But God be thanked, that ye were the servants of sin, but ye have obeyed from the heart [a]that form of doctrine which was delivered you.

18 Being then [a]made free from sin, ye became the servants of righteousness.

19 I speak after the manner of men because of the infirmity of your flesh: for as ye have yielded your members servants to uncleanness and to iniquity unto iniquity; even so now yield your members servants to righteousness unto holiness.

20 For when ye were [a]the servants of sin, ye were free from righteousness.

21 [a]What fruit had ye then in those things whereof ye are now ashamed? for [b]the end of those things *is* death.

22 But now [a]being made free from sin, and become servants to God, ye have your fruit unto holiness, and the end everlasting life.

23 For [a]the wages of sin *is* death; but [b]the gift of God *is* eternal life through Jesus Christ our Lord.

---

20 [a]John 15:22 [b]Luke 7:47; Rom. 6:1; 1 Tim. 1:14

CHAPTER 6

1 [a]Rom. 3:8; 6:15
2 [a][Rom. 6:11; 7:4, 6; Gal. 2:19; Col. 2:20; 3:3]; 1 Pet. 2:24
3 [a]Acts 2:38; 8:16; 19:5; [Gal. 3:27]; Col. 2:12 [b][1 Cor. 15:29]
4 [a]Col. 2:12 [b]1 Cor. 6:14 [c]John 2:11 [d]Rom. 7:6; [2 Cor. 5:17; Gal. 6:15; Eph. 4:23; Col. 3:10]
5 [a]2 Cor. 4:10; Phil. 3:10; Col. 2:12; 3:1
6 [a]Gal. 2:20; 5:24; 6:14 [b]Col. 2:11
7 [a]1 Pet. 4:1
8 [a]Rom. 6:4; 2 Cor. 4:10; 2 Tim. 2:11
9 [a]Rev. 1:18
10 [a]Heb. 9:27 [b]Luke 20:38
11 [a][Rom. 6:2; 7:4, 6] [b][Gal. 2:19; Col. 2:20; 3:3]; 1 Pet. 2:24
12 [a]Ps. 19:13
13 [a]Rom. 6:16, 19; 7:5; Col. 3:5; James 4:1 [b]Rom. 12:1; 2 Cor. 5:14; 1 Pet. 2:24; 4:2
14 [a][Rom. 7:4, 6; 8:2; Gal. 5:18]
15 [a]1 Cor. 9:21
16 [a]Prov. 5:22; [Matt. 6:24]; John 8:34; 2 Pet. 2:19
17 [a]2 Tim. 1:13
18 [a]John 8:32; Rom. 6:22; 8:2; 1 Cor. 7:22; Gal. 5:1; 1 Pet. 2:16
20 [a]John 8:34
21 [a]Jer. 12:13; Ezek. 16:63; Rom. 7:5 [b]Rom. 1:32; Gal. 6:8
22 [a][John 8:32]; Rom. 6:18; 8:2
23 [a]Gen. 2:17 [b]Rom. 2:7; 1 Pet. 1:4

NKJV

20 Moreover [a]the law entered that the offense might abound. But where sin abounded, grace [b]abounded much more,

21 so that as sin reigned in death, even so grace might reign through righteousness to eternal life through Jesus Christ our Lord.

Dead to Sin, Alive to God

6 What shall we say then? [a]Shall we continue in sin that grace may abound?

2 Certainly not! How shall we who [a]died to sin live any longer in it?

3 Or do you not know that [a]as many of us as were baptized into Christ Jesus [b]were baptized into His death?

4 Therefore we were [a]buried with Him through baptism into death, that [b]just as Christ was raised from the dead by [c]the glory of the Father, [d]even so we also should walk in newness of life.

5 [a]For if we have been united together in the likeness of His death, certainly we also shall be *in the likeness* of *His* resurrection,

6 knowing this, that [a]our old man was crucified with *Him,* that [b]the body of sin might be done away with, that we should no longer be slaves of sin.

7 For [a]he who has died has been freed from sin.

8 Now [a]if we died with Christ, we believe that we shall also live with Him,

9 knowing that [a]Christ, having been raised from the dead, dies no more. Death no longer has dominion over Him.

10 For *the death* that He died, [a]He died to sin once for all; but *the life* that He lives, [b]He lives to God.

11 Likewise you also, reckon yourselves to be [a]dead indeed to sin, but [b]alive to God in Christ Jesus our Lord.

12 [a]Therefore do not let sin reign in your mortal body, that you should obey it in its lusts.

13 And do not present your [a]members *as* instruments of unrighteousness to sin, but [b]present yourselves to God as being alive from the dead, and your members *as* instruments of righteousness to God.

14 For [a]sin shall not have dominion over you, for you are not under law but under grace.

From Slaves of Sin to Slaves of God

15 What then? Shall we sin [a]because we are not under law but under grace? Certainly not!

16 Do you not know that [a]to whom you present yourselves slaves to obey, you are that one's slaves whom you obey, whether of sin *leading* to death, or of obedience *leading* to righteousness?

17 But God be thanked that *though* you were slaves of sin, yet you obeyed from the heart [a]that form of doctrine to which you were delivered.

18 And [a]having been set free from sin, you became slaves of righteousness.

19 I speak in human *terms* because of the weakness of your flesh. For just as you presented your members *as* slaves of uncleanness, and of lawlessness *leading* to *more* lawlessness, so now present your members *as* slaves *of* righteousness for holiness.

20 For when you were [a]slaves of sin, you were free in regard to righteousness.

21 [a]What fruit did you have then in the things of which you are now ashamed? For [b]the end of those things *is* death.

22 But now [a]having been set free from sin, and having become slaves of God, you have your fruit to holiness, and the end, everlasting life.

23 For [a]the wages of sin *is* death, but [b]the gift of God *is* eternal life in Christ Jesus our Lord.

KJV

Freed from the Law

7 Know ye not, brethren, (for I speak to them
that know the law,) how that the law hath dominion over a man as long as he liveth?
2 For [a]the woman which hath an husband
is bound by the law to *her* husband so long as
he liveth; but if the husband be dead, she is loosed
from the law of *her* husband.
3 So then [a]if, while *her* husband liveth, she
be married to another man, she shall be called
an adulteress: but if her husband be dead, she is
free from that law; so that she is no adulteress,
though she be married to another man.
4 Wherefore, my brethren, ye also are become [a]dead to the law by the body of Christ; that
ye should be married to another, *even* to him who
is raised from the dead, that we should [b]bring
forth fruit unto God.
5 For when we were in the flesh, the mo-
tions of sins, which were by the law, [a]did work
in our members [b]to bring forth fruit unto death.
6 But now we are delivered from the law,
that being dead wherein we were held; that we
should serve [a]in newness of spirit, and not *in* the
oldness of the letter.

Sin's Advantage in the Law

7 What shall we say then? *Is* the law sin?
God forbid. Nay, [a]I had not known sin, but by
the law: for I had not known lust, except the law
had said, [b]THOU SHALT NOT COVET.
8 But [a]sin, taking occasion by the commandment, wrought in me all manner of concupiscence. For [b]without the law sin *was* dead.
9 For I was alive without the law once: but
when the commandment came, sin revived, and
I died.
10 And the commandment, [a]which *was ordained* to life, I found *to be* unto death.
11 For sin, taking occasion by the commandment, deceived me, and by it slew *me*.
12 Wherefore [a]the law *is* holy, and the commandment holy, and just, and good.

Law Cannot Save from Sin

13 Was then that which is good made death
unto me? God forbid. But sin, that it might appear
sin, working death in me by that which is good;
that sin by the commandment might become exceeding sinful.
14 For we know that the law is spiritual: but
I am carnal, [a]sold under sin.
15 For that which I do I allow not: for [a]what
I would, that do I not; but what I hate, that do I.
16 If then I do that which I would not, I consent unto the law that *it is* good.
17 Now then it is no more I that do it, but
sin that dwelleth in me.
18 For I know that [a]in me (that is, in my
flesh,) dwelleth no good thing: for to will is present with me; but *how* to perform that which is
good I find not.
19 For the good that I would I do not: but
the evil which I would not, that I do.
20 Now if I do that I would not, it is no more
I that do it, but sin that dwelleth in me.
21 I find then a law, that, when I would do
good, evil is present with me.
22 For I [a]delight in the law of God after [b]the
inward man:
23 But [a]I see another law in [b]my members,
warring against the law of my mind, and bringing
me into captivity to the law of sin which is in
my members.
24 O wretched man that I am! who shall deliver me [a]from the body of this death?
25 [a]I thank God through Jesus Christ our
Lord. So then with the mind I myself serve the
law of God; but with the flesh the law of sin.

CHAPTER 7

2 [a]1 Cor. 7:39
3 [a][Matt. 5:32]
4 [a]Rom. 8:2; Gal. 2:19; 5:18; [Col. 2:14] [b]Gal. 5:22
5 [a]Rom. 6:13 [b]Rom. 6:21; Gal. 5:19; James 1:15
6 [a]Rom. 2:29; 2 Cor. 3:6
7 [a]Rom. 3:20 [b]Ex. 20:17; Deut. 5:21; Acts 20:33
8 [a]Rom. 4:15 [b]1 Cor. 15:56
10 [a]Lev. 18:5; Ezek. 20:11, 13, 21; Luke 10:28; Rom. 10:5; 2 Cor. 3:7; Gal. 3:12
12 [a]Ps. 19:8
14 [a]1 Kin. 21:20, 25; 2 Kin. 17:17; Rom. 6:16
15 [a]Rom. 7:19; [Gal. 5:17]
18 [a][Gen. 6:5; 8:21]
22 [a]Ps. 1:2 [b][2 Cor. 4:16; Eph. 3:16; 1 Pet. 3:4]
23 [a]Rom. 6:19; [Gal. 5:17]; James 4:1; 1 Pet. 2:11 [b]Rom. 6:13, 19
24 [a][Rom. 8:11; 1 Cor. 15:51, 52; 1 Thess. 4:14–17]
25 [a]1 Cor. 15:57

NKJV

Freed from the Law

7 Or do you not know, brethren (for I speak to
those who know the law), that the law has
dominion over a man as long as he lives?
2 For [a]the woman who has a husband is
bound by the law to *her* husband as long as he
lives. But if the husband dies, she is released from
the law of *her* husband.
3 So then [a]if, while *her* husband lives, she
marries another man, she will be called an adulteress; but if her husband dies, she is free from
that law, so that she is no adulteress, though she
has married another man.
4 Therefore, my brethren, you also have become [a]dead to the law through the body of Christ,
that you may be married to another—to Him who
was raised from the dead, that we should [b]bear
fruit to God.
5 For when we were in the flesh, the sinful
passions which were aroused by the law [a]were
at work in our members [b]to bear fruit to death.
6 But now we have been delivered from the
law, having died to what we were held by, so that
we should serve [a]in the newness of the Spirit and
not *in* the oldness of the letter.

Sin's Advantage in the Law

7 What shall we say then? *Is* the law sin?
Certainly not! On the contrary, [a]I would not have
known sin except through the law. For I would
not have known covetousness unless the law had
said, [b]"*You shall not covet.*"
8 But [a]sin, taking opportunity by the commandment, produced in me all *manner of evil* desire. For [b]apart from the law sin *was* dead.
9 I was alive once without the law, but when
the commandment came, sin revived and I died.
10 And the commandment, [a]which *was* to
bring life, I found to *bring* death.
11 For sin, taking occasion by the commandment, deceived me, and by it killed *me*.
12 Therefore [a]the law *is* holy, and the commandment holy and just and good.

Law Cannot Save from Sin

13 Has then what is good become death to
me? Certainly not! But sin, that it might appear
sin, was producing death in me through what is
good, so that sin through the commandment
might become exceedingly sinful.
14 For we know that the law is spiritual, but
I am carnal, [a]sold under sin.
15 For what I am doing, I do not understand.
[a]For what I will to do, that I do not practice; but
what I hate, that I do.
16 If, then, I do what I will not to do, I agree
with the law that *it is* good.
17 But now, *it is* no longer I who do it, but
sin that dwells in me.
18 For I know that [a]in me (that is, in my flesh)
nothing good dwells; for to will is present with
me, but *how* to perform what is good I do not
find.
19 For the good that I will *to do,* I do not
do; but the evil I will not *to do,* that I practice.
20 Now if I do what I will not *to do,* it is no
longer I who do it, but sin that dwells in me.
21 I find then a law, that evil is present with
me, the one who wills to do good.
22 For I [a]delight in the law of God according
to [b]the inward man.
23 But [a]I see another law in [b]my members,
warring against the law of my mind, and bringing
me into captivity to the law of sin which is in
my members.
24 O wretched man that I am! Who will deliver me [a]from this body of death?
25 [a]I thank God—through Jesus Christ
our Lord! So then, with the mind I myself serve
the law of God, but with the flesh the law of
sin.

KJV

Free from Indwelling Sin

8 *There is* therefore now no condemnation to them which are in Christ Jesus, who [a]walk not after the flesh, but after the Spirit.

2 For [a]the law of [b]the Spirit of life in Christ Jesus hath made me free from [c]the law of sin and death.

3 For [a]what the law could not do, in that it was weak through the flesh, [b]God sending his own Son in the likeness of sinful flesh, and for sin, condemned sin in the flesh:

4 That the righteousness of the law might be fulfilled in us, who [a]walk not after the flesh, but after the Spirit.

5 For [a]they that are after the flesh do mind the things of the flesh; but they that are after the Spirit [b]the things of the Spirit.

6 For [a]to be carnally minded *is* death; but to be spiritually minded *is* life and peace.

7 Because [a]the carnal mind *is* enmity against God: for it is not subject to the law of God, [b]neither indeed can be.

8 So then they that are in the flesh cannot please God.

9 But ye are not in the flesh, but in the Spirit, if so be that the Spirit of God dwell in you. Now if any man have not the Spirit of Christ, he is none of his.

10 And if Christ *be* in you, the body *is* dead because of sin; but the Spirit *is* life because of righteousness.

11 But if the Spirit of [a]him that raised up Jesus from the dead dwell in you, [b]he that raised up Christ from the dead shall also quicken your mortal bodies by his Spirit that dwelleth in you.

Sonship Through the Spirit

12 [a]Therefore, brethren, we are debtors, not to the flesh, to live after the flesh.

13 For [a]if ye live after the flesh, ye shall die: but if ye through the Spirit do [b]mortify the deeds of the body, ye shall live.

14 For [a]as many as are led by the Spirit of God, they are the sons of God.

15 For [a]ye have not received the spirit of bondage again [b]to fear; but ye have received the [c]Spirit of adoption, whereby we cry, [d]Abba, Father.

16 [a]The Spirit itself beareth witness with our spirit, that we are the children of God:

17 And if children, then [a]heirs; heirs of God, and joint-heirs with Christ; [b]if so be that we suffer with *him*, that we may be also glorified together.

From Suffering to Glory

18 For I reckon that [a]the sufferings of this present time *are* not worthy *to be compared* with the glory which shall be revealed in us.

19 For [a]the earnest expectation of the creature waiteth for the manifestation of the sons of God.

20 For [a]the creature was made subject to vanity, not willingly, but by reason of him who hath subjected *the same* in hope,

21 Because the creature itself also shall be delivered from the bondage of corruption into the glorious [a]liberty of the children of God.

22 For we know that the whole creation [a]groaneth and travaileth in pain together until now.

23 And not only *they*, but ourselves also, which have [a]the firstfruits of the Spirit, [b]even we ourselves groan [c]within ourselves, waiting for the adoption, *to wit*, the [d]redemption of our body.

24 For we are saved by hope: but [a]hope that is seen is not hope: for what a man seeth, why doth he yet hope for?

25 But if we hope for that we see not, *then* do we with patience wait for *it*.

CHAPTER 8

1 [a]Gal. 5:16
2 [a]Rom. 6:18, 22 [b][1 Cor. 15:45] [c]Rom. 7:24, 25
3 [a]Acts 13:39; [Heb. 7:18] [b][2 Cor. 5:21; Gal. 3:13]
4 [a][Rom. 6:4; 2 Cor. 5:7]; Gal. 5:16, 25; Eph. 4:1; 5:2, 15; [1 John 1:7; 2:6]
5 [a]John 3:6 [b][Gal. 5:22–25]
6 [a]Gal. 6:8
7 [a]James 4:4 [b]1 Cor. 2:14
11 [a]Acts 2:24; Rom. 6:4 [b]1 Cor. 6:14
12 [a][Rom. 6:7, 14]
13 [a]Gal. 6:8 [b]Eph. 4:22; [Col. 3:5–10]
14 [a][Gal. 5:18]
15 [a][1 Cor. 2:12]; Heb. 2:15 [b]2 Tim. 1:7 [c][Is. 56:5] [d]Mark 14:36; Gal. 4:6
16 [a]Eph. 1:13
17 [a]Acts 26:18 [b]Phil. 1:29
18 [a]2 Cor. 4:17; [1 Pet. 1:6; 4:13]
19 [a][2 Pet. 3:13]
20 [a]Gen. 3:17–19
21 [a][2 Cor. 3:17]; Gal. 5:1, 13
22 [a]Jer. 12:4, 11
23 [a]2 Cor. 5:5; Eph. 1:14 [b]2 Cor. 5:2, 4 [c][Luke 20:36] [d]Luke 21:28; Eph. 1:14; 4:30; [Phil. 3:20, 21]
24 [a]Rom. 4:18; 2 Cor. 5:7; Heb. 11:1

*

8:1 NU omits the rest of v. 1.

NKJV

Free from Indwelling Sin

8 *There is* therefore now no condemnation to those who are in Christ Jesus, [a]who* do not walk according to the flesh, but according to the Spirit.

2 For [a]the law of [b]the Spirit of life in Christ Jesus has made me free from [c]the law of sin and death.

3 For [a]what the law could not do in that it was weak through the flesh, [b]God *did* by sending His own Son in the likeness of sinful flesh, on account of sin: He condemned sin in the flesh,

4 that the righteous requirement of the law might be fulfilled in us who [a]do not walk according to the flesh but according to the Spirit.

5 For [a]those who live according to the flesh set their minds on the things of the flesh, but those *who live* according to the Spirit, [b]the things of the Spirit.

6 For [a]to be carnally minded *is* death, but to be spiritually minded *is* life and peace.

7 Because [a]the carnal mind *is* enmity against God; for it is not subject to the law of God, [b]nor indeed can be.

8 So then, those who are in the flesh cannot please God.

9 But you are not in the flesh but in the Spirit, if indeed the Spirit of God dwells in you. Now if anyone does not have the Spirit of Christ, he is not His.

10 And if Christ *is* in you, the body *is* dead because of sin, but the Spirit *is* life because of righteousness.

11 But if the Spirit of [a]Him who raised Jesus from the dead dwells in you, [b]He who raised Christ from the dead will also give life to your mortal bodies through His Spirit who dwells in you.

Sonship Through the Spirit

12 [a]Therefore, brethren, we are debtors—not to the flesh, to live according to the flesh.

13 For [a]if you live according to the flesh you will die; but if by the Spirit you [b]put to death the deeds of the body, you will live.

14 For [a]as many as are led by the Spirit of God, these are sons of God.

15 For [a]you did not receive the spirit of bondage again [b]to fear, but you received the [c]Spirit of adoption by whom we cry out, [d]"Abba, Father."

16 [a]The Spirit Himself bears witness with our spirit that we are children of God,

17 and if children, then [a]heirs—heirs of God and joint heirs with Christ, [b]if indeed we suffer with *Him*, that we may also be glorified together.

From Suffering to Glory

18 For I consider that [a]the sufferings of this present time are not worthy *to be compared* with the glory which shall be revealed in us.

19 For [a]the earnest expectation of the creation eagerly waits for the revealing of the sons of God.

20 For [a]the creation was subjected to futility, not willingly, but because of Him who subjected *it* in hope;

21 because the creation itself also will be delivered from the bondage of corruption into the glorious [a]liberty of the children of God.

22 For we know that the whole creation [a]groans and labors with birth pangs together until now.

23 Not only *that*, but we also who have [a]the firstfruits of the Spirit, [b]even we ourselves groan [c]within ourselves, eagerly waiting for the adoption, the [d]redemption of our body.

24 For we were saved in this hope, but [a]hope that is seen is not hope; for why does one still hope for what he sees?

25 But if we hope for what we do not see, we eagerly wait for *it* with perseverance.

KJV

26 Likewise the Spirit also helpeth our infirmities: for [a]we know not what we should pray
for as we ought: but [b]the Spirit itself maketh intercession for us with groanings which cannot be
uttered.
27 And [a]he that searcheth the hearts knoweth what *is* the mind of the Spirit, because he maketh intercession for the saints [b]according to *the*
will of God.
28 And we know that all things work together for good to them that love God, to them
[a]who are the called according to *his* purpose.
29 For whom [a]he did foreknow, [b]he also did
predestinate [c]*to be* conformed to the image of his
Son, [d]that he might be the firstborn among many
brethren.
30 Moreover whom he did predestinate, them
he also [a]called: and whom he called, them he also
[b]justified: and whom he justified, them he also
[c]glorified.

God's Everlasting Love

31 What shall we then say to these things?
[a]If God *be* for us, who *can be* against us?
32 [a]He that spared not his own Son, but [b]de-
livered him up for us all, how shall he not with
him also freely give us all things?
33 Who shall lay any thing to the charge of
God's elect? [a]*It is* God that justifieth.
34 [a]Who *is* he that condemneth? *It is* Christ
that died, yea rather, that is risen again, [b]who is
even at the right hand of God, [c]who also maketh
intercession for us.
35 Who shall separate us from the love of
Christ? *shall* tribulation, or distress, or persecution, or famine, or nakedness, or peril, or sword?
36 As it is written, [a]FOR THY SAKE WE ARE
KILLED ALL THE DAY LONG; WE ARE ACCOUNTED AS
SHEEP FOR THE SLAUGHTER.
37 [a]Nay, in all these things we are more than
conquerors through him that loved us.
38 For I am persuaded, that neither death,
nor life, nor angels, nor [a]principalities, nor powers, nor things present, nor things to come,
39 Nor height, nor depth, nor any other creature, shall be able to separate us from the love
of God, which is in Christ Jesus our Lord.

Israel's Rejection of Christ

9 I [a]say the truth in Christ, I lie not, my conscience also bearing me witness in the Holy
Ghost,
2 [a]That I have great heaviness and continual sorrow in my heart.
3 For [a]I could wish that myself were accursed from Christ for my brethren, my kinsmen
according to the flesh:
4 Who are Israelites; [a]to whom *pertaineth*
the adoption, and [b]the glory, and [c]the covenants,
and [d]the giving of the law, and [e]the service *of*
God, and [f]the promises;
5 [a]Whose *are* the fathers, and of [b]whom as
concerning the flesh Christ *came,* [c]who is over
all, God blessed for ever. Amen.

Israel's Rejection and God's Purpose
(Gen. 25:19–23)

6 [a]Not as though the word of God hath
taken none effect. For [b]they *are* not all Israel,
which are of Israel:
7 [a]Neither, because they are the seed of
Abraham, *are they* all children: but, IN [b]ISAAC
SHALL THY SEED BE CALLED.
8 That is, They which are the children of
the flesh, these *are* not the children of God: but
[a]the children of the promise are counted for the
seed.
9 For this *is* the word of promise, [a]AT THIS
TIME WILL I COME, AND SARAH SHALL HAVE A SON.

26 [a]Matt. 20:22 [b]Eph. 6:18
27 [a]1 Chr. 28:9 [b]1 John 5:14
28 [a]2 Tim. 1:9
29 [a]2 Tim. 2:19 [b]Eph. 1:5, 11 [c][2 Cor. 3:18] [d]Heb. 1:6
30 [a][1 Pet. 2:9; 3:9] [b][Gal. 2:16] [c]John 17:22
31 [a]Num. 14:9
32 [a]Rom. 5:6, 10 [b][Rom. 4:25]
33 [a]Is. 50:8, 9
34 [a]John 3:18 [b]Mark 16:19 [c]Heb. 7:25; 9:24
36 [a]Ps. 44:22
37 [a]1 Cor. 15:57
38 [a][Eph. 1:21]

CHAPTER 9

1 [a]2 Cor. 1:23
2 [a]Rom. 10:1
3 [a]Ex. 32:32
4 [a]Ex. 4:22 [b]1 Sam. 4:21 [c]Acts 3:25 [d]Ps. 147:19 [e]Heb. 9:1, 6 [f][Acts 2:39; 13:32]
5 [a]Deut. 10:15 [b][Luke 1:34, 35; 3:23] [c]Jer. 23:6
6 [a]Num. 23:19 [b][Gal. 6:16]
7 [a][Gal. 4:23] [b]Gen. 21:12
8 [a]Gal. 4:28
9 [a]Gen. 18:10, 14

*

8:26 NU omits *for us*
9:3 Or *relatives*

NKJV

26 Likewise the Spirit also helps in our weaknesses. For [a]we do not know what we should pray
for as we ought, but [b]the Spirit Himself makes
intercession *for us with groanings which cannot
be uttered.
27 Now [a]He who searches the hearts knows
what the mind of the Spirit *is,* because He makes
intercession for the saints [b]according to *the will*
of God.
28 And we know that all things work together for good to those who love God, to those
[a]who are the called according to *His* purpose.
29 For whom [a]He foreknew, [b]He also predestined [c]*to be* conformed to the image of His Son,
[d]that He might be the firstborn among many
brethren.
30 Moreover whom He predestined, these He
also [a]called; whom He called, these He also [b]justi-
fied; and whom He justified, these He also [c]glori-
fied.

God's Everlasting Love

31 What then shall we say to these things?
[a]If God *is* for us, who *can be* against us?
32 [a]He who did not spare His own Son, but
[b]delivered Him up for us all, how shall He not
with Him also freely give us all things?
33 Who shall bring a charge against God's
elect? [a]*It is* God who justifies.
34 [a]Who *is* he who condemns? *It is* Christ
who died, and furthermore is also risen, [b]who is
even at the right hand of God, [c]who also makes
intercession for us.
35 Who shall separate us from the love of
Christ? *Shall* tribulation, or distress, or persecution, or famine, or nakedness, or peril, or sword?
36 As it is written:

> [a]*"For Your sake we are killed all day long;*
> *We are accounted as sheep for the*
> *slaughter."*

37 [a]Yet in all these things we are more than
conquerors through Him who loved us.
38 For I am persuaded that neither death nor
life, nor angels nor [a]principalities nor powers, nor
things present nor things to come,
39 nor height nor depth, nor any other created thing, shall be able to separate us from the
love of God which is in Christ Jesus our Lord.

Israel's Rejection of Christ

9 I [a]tell the truth in Christ, I am not lying, my
conscience also bearing me witness in the
Holy Spirit,
2 [a]that I have great sorrow and continual
grief in my heart.
3 For [a]I could wish that I myself were accursed from Christ for my brethren, my *countrymen according to the flesh,
4 who are Israelites, [a]to whom *pertain* the
adoption, [b]the glory, [c]the covenants, [d]the giving
of the law, [e]the service *of God,* and [f]the promises;
5 [a]of whom *are* the fathers and from
[b]whom, according to the flesh, Christ *came,* [c]who
is over all, *the* eternally blessed God. Amen.

Israel's Rejection and God's Purpose
(Gen. 25:19–23)

6 [a]But it is not that the word of God has
taken no effect. For [b]they *are* not all Israel who
are of Israel,
7 [a]nor *are they* all children because they are
the seed of Abraham; but, [b]*"In Isaac your seed*
shall be called."
8 That is, those who *are* the children of the
flesh, these *are* not the children of God; but [a]the
children of the promise are counted as the seed.
9 For this *is* the word of promise: [a]*"At this*
time I will come and Sarah shall have a son."

KJV

10 And not only *this;* but when [a]Rebecca also had conceived by one, *even* by our father Isaac;

11 (For *the children* being not yet born, neither having done any good or evil, that the purpose of God according to election might stand, not of works, but of [a]him that calleth;)

12 It was said unto her, [a]The elder shall serve the younger.

13 As it is written, [a]Jacob have I loved, but Esau have I hated.

Israel's Rejection and God's Justice

14 What shall we say then? [a]*Is there* unrighteousness with God? God forbid.

15 For he saith to Moses, [a]I will have mercy on whom I will have mercy, and I will have compassion on whom I will have compassion.

16 So then *it is* not of him that willeth, nor of him that runneth, but of God that sheweth mercy.

17 For [a]the scripture saith unto Pharaoh, [b]Even for this same purpose have I raised thee up, that I might shew my power in thee, and that my name might be declared throughout all the earth.

18 Therefore hath he mercy on whom he will *have mercy,* and whom he will he [a]hardeneth.

19 Thou wilt say then unto me, Why doth he yet find fault? For [a]who hath resisted his will?

20 Nay but, O man, who art thou that repliest against God? [a]Shall the thing formed say to him that formed *it,* Why hast thou made me thus?

21 Hath not the [a]potter power over the clay, of the same lump to make [b]one vessel unto honour, and another unto dishonour?

22 *What* if God, willing to shew *his* wrath, and to make his power known, endured with much longsuffering [a]the vessels of wrath [b]fitted to destruction:

23 And that he might make known [a]the riches of his glory on the vessels of mercy, which he had [b]afore prepared unto glory,

24 Even us, whom he hath [a]called, [b]not of the Jews only, but also of the Gentiles?

25 As he saith also in Osee, [a]I will call them my people, which were not my people; and her beloved, which was not beloved.

26 [a]And it shall come to pass, *that* in the place where it was said unto them, Ye *are* not my people; there shall they be called the children of the living God.

27 Esaias also crieth concerning Israel, [a]Though the number of the children of Israel be as the sand of the sea, [b]a remnant shall be saved:

28 For he will finish the work, and cut *it* short in righteousness: [a]because a short work will the Lord make upon the earth.

29 And as Esaias said before, [a]Except the Lord of Sabaoth had left us a seed, [b]we had been as Sodoma, and been made like unto Gomorrha.

Present Condition of Israel

30 What shall we say then? [a]That the Gentiles, which followed not after righteousness, have attained to righteousness, [b]even the righteousness which is of faith.

31 But Israel, [a]which followed after the law of righteousness, [b]hath not attained to the law of righteousness.

10 [a]Gen. 25:21
11 [a][Rom. 4:17; 8:28]
12 [a]Gen. 25:23
13 [a]Mal. 1:2, 3
14 [a]Deut. 32:4
15 [a]Ex. 33:19
17 [a]Gal. 3:8 [b]Ex. 9:16
18 [a]Ex. 4:21; Deut. 2:30; Josh. 11:20; John 12:40; Rom. 11:7, 25
19 [a]2 Chr. 20:6; Job 9:12; Dan. 4:35
20 [a]Is. 29:16; Jer. 18:6; Rom. 9:22; 2 Tim. 2:20
21 [a]Prov. 16:4 [b]2 Tim. 2:20
22 [a][1 Thess. 5:9] [b]Prov. 16:4; [1 Pet. 2:8]
23 [a][Col. 1:27] [b][Rom. 8:28–30]
24 [a][Rom. 8:28] [b]Is. 42:6, 7; 49:6; Luke 2:32; Rom. 3:29
25 [a]Hos. 2:23; 1 Pet. 2:10
26 [a]Hos. 1:10
27 [a]Is. 10:22, 23 [b]Rom. 11:5
28 [a]Is. 10:23; 28:22
29 [a]Is. 1:9 [b]Deut. 29:23; Is. 13:19; Jer. 49:18; 50:40; Amos 4:11
30 [a]Rom. 4:11 [b]Rom. 1:17; 3:21; 10:6; [Gal. 2:16; 3:24; Phil. 3:9]; Heb. 11:7
31 [a][Rom. 10:2–4] [b][Gal. 5:4]

**

9:28 NU *the Lord will finish the work and cut it short upon the earth*
9:29 Lit., in Heb., *Hosts*
9:31 NU omits *of righteousness*

NKJV

10 And not only *this,* but when [a]Rebecca also had conceived by one man, *even* by our father Isaac

11 (for *the children* not yet being born, nor having done any good or evil, that the purpose of God according to election might stand, not of works but of [a]Him who calls),

12 it was said to her, [a]*"The older shall serve the younger."*

13 As it is written, [a]*"Jacob I have loved, but Esau I have hated."*

Israel's Rejection and God's Justice

14 What shall we say then? [a]*Is there* unrighteousness with God? Certainly not!

15 For He says to Moses, [a]*"I will have mercy on whomever I will have mercy, and I will have compassion on whomever I will have compassion."*

16 So then *it is* not of him who wills, nor of him who runs, but of God who shows mercy.

17 For [a]the Scripture says to the Pharaoh, [b]*"For this very purpose I have raised you up, that I may show My power in you, and that My name may be declared in all the earth."*

18 Therefore He has mercy on whom He wills, and whom He wills He [a]hardens.

19 You will say to me then, "Why does He still find fault? For [a]who has resisted His will?"

20 But indeed, O man, who are you to reply against God? [a]Will the thing formed say to him who formed *it,* "Why have you made me like this?"

21 Does not the [a]potter have power over the clay, from the same lump to make [b]one vessel for honor and another for dishonor?

22 *What* if God, wanting to show *His* wrath and to make His power known, endured with much longsuffering [a]the vessels of wrath [b]prepared for destruction,

23 and that He might make known [a]the riches of His glory on the vessels of mercy, which He had [b]prepared beforehand for glory,

24 *even* us whom He [a]called, [b]not of the Jews only, but also of the Gentiles?

25 As He says also in Hosea:

[a]*"I will call them My people, who were not*
My people,
And her beloved, who was not beloved."

26 *"And[a] it shall come to pass in the place*
where it was said to them,
'You are not My people,'
There they shall be called sons of the
living God."

27 Isaiah also cries out concerning Israel:

[a]*"Though the number of the children of*
Israel be as the sand of the sea,
[b]*The remnant will be saved.*

28 *For *He will finish the work and cut it*
short in righteousness,
[a]*Because the* Lord *will make a short work*
upon the earth."

29 And as Isaiah said before:

[a]*"Unless the* Lord *of *Sabaoth had left us*
a seed,
[b]*We would have become like Sodom,*
And we would have been made like
Gomorrah."

Present Condition of Israel

30 What shall we say then? [a]That Gentiles, who did not pursue righteousness, have attained to righteousness, [b]even the righteousness of faith;

31 but Israel, [a]pursuing the law of righteousness, [b]has not attained to the law *of righteousness.

KJV

32 Wherefore? Because *they sought it* not by
faith, but as it were by the works of the law. For
[a]they stumbled at that stumblingstone;
33 As it is written, [a]BEHOLD, I LAY IN SION A
STUMBLINGSTONE AND ROCK OF OFFENCE: AND [b]WHO-
SOEVER BELIEVETH ON HIM SHALL NOT BE ASHAMED.

Israel Needs the Gospel

10 Brethren, my heart's desire and prayer to
God for Israel is, that they might be saved.
2 For I bear them record [a]that they have a
zeal of God, but not according to knowledge.
3 For they being ignorant of [a]God's righteousness, and going about to establish their own
[b]righteousness, have not submitted themselves
unto the righteousness of God.
4 For [a]Christ *is* the end of the law for righteousness to every one that believeth.
5 For Moses describeth the righteousness
which is of the law, [a]THAT THE MAN WHICH DOETH
THOSE THINGS SHALL LIVE BY THEM.
6 But the righteousness which is of faith
speaketh on this wise, [a]SAY NOT IN THINE HEART,
WHO SHALL ASCEND INTO HEAVEN? (that is, to bring
Christ down *from above:*)
7 Or, [a]WHO SHALL DESCEND INTO THE DEEP?
(that is, to bring up Christ again from the dead.)
8 But what saith it? [a]THE WORD IS NIGH THEE,
EVEN IN THY MOUTH, AND IN THY HEART: that is, the
word of faith, which we preach;
9 That [a]if thou shalt confess with thy mouth
the Lord Jesus, and shalt believe in thine heart
that God hath raised him from the dead, thou shalt
be saved.
10 For with the heart man believeth unto
righteousness; and with the mouth confession is
made unto salvation.
11 For the scripture saith, [a]WHOSOEVER BE-
LIEVETH ON HIM SHALL NOT BE ASHAMED.
12 For [a]there is no difference between the
Jew and the Greek: for [b]the same Lord over all
[c]is rich unto all that call upon him.
13 [a]FOR WHOSOEVER SHALL CALL [b]UPON THE
NAME OF THE LORD SHALL BE SAVED.

Israel Rejects the Gospel

14 How then shall they call on him in whom
they have not believed? and how shall they believe in him of whom they have not heard? and
how shall they hear [a]without a preacher?
15 And how shall they preach, except they
be sent? as it is written, [a]HOW BEAUTIFUL ARE THE
FEET OF THEM THAT PREACH THE GOSPEL OF PEACE,
AND BRING GLAD TIDINGS OF GOOD THINGS!
16 But they have not all obeyed the gospel.
For Esaias saith, [a]LORD, WHO HATH BELIEVED OUR
REPORT?
17 So then faith *cometh* by hearing, and
hearing by the word of God.
18 But I say, Have they not heard? Yes verily,
[a]THEIR SOUND WENT INTO ALL THE EARTH, [b]AND
THEIR WORDS UNTO THE ENDS OF THE WORLD.
19 But I say, Did not Israel know? First Moses
saith, [a]I WILL PROVOKE YOU TO JEALOUSY BY *THEM
THAT ARE* NO PEOPLE, *AND* BY A [b]FOOLISH NATION I
WILL ANGER YOU.
20 But Esaias is very bold, and saith, [a]I WAS
FOUND OF THEM THAT SOUGHT ME NOT; I WAS MADE
MANIFEST UNTO THEM THAT ASKED NOT AFTER ME.

32 [a][Luke 2:34; 1 Cor. 1:23]
33 [a][Ps. 118:22]; Is. 8:14; 28:16; [Matt. 21:42; 1 Pet. 2:6–8] [b]Rom. 5:5; 10:11

CHAPTER 10

2 [a]Acts 21:20; Gal. 1:14
3 [a][Rom. 1:17] [b][Phil. 3:9]
4 [a]Matt. 5:17; [Rom. 7:1–4; Gal. 3:24; 4:5]
5 [a]Lev. 18:5; Neh. 9:29; Ezek. 20:11, 13, 21; Rom. 7:10; Gal. 3:12
6 [a]Deut. 30:12–14
7 [a]Deut. 30:13
8 [a]Deut. 30:14
9 [a]Matt. 10:32; Luke 12:8; Acts 8:37; Rom. 14:9; [1 Cor. 12:3]; Phil. 2:11
11 [a]Is. 28:16; Jer. 17:7; Rom. 9:33
12 [a]Acts 15:9; Rom. 3:22, 29; Gal. 3:28 [b]Acts 10:36; 1 Tim. 2:5 [c]Eph. 1:7
13 [a]Joel 2:32; Acts 2:21 [b]Acts 9:14
14 [a]Acts 8:31; Titus 1:3
15 [a]Is. 52:7; Nah. 1:15
16 [a]Is. 53:1; John 12:38
18 [a]Ps. 19:4; Matt. 24:14; Mark 16:15; Rom. 1:8; Col. 1:6, 23; 1 Thess. 1:8 [b]1 Kin. 18:10; Matt. 4:8
19 [a]Deut. 32:21; Rom. 11:11 [b]Titus 3:3
20 [a]Is. 65:1; Rom. 9:30

*
9:32 NU *by works*, omitting *of the law*
10:1 NU *them*
10:15 NU omits *preach the gospel of peace, Who*

NKJV

32 Why? Because *they did* not *seek it* by
faith, but as it were, *by the works of the law.
For [a]they stumbled at that stumbling stone.
33 As it is written:

[a]"Behold, I lay in Zion a stumbling stone
and rock of offense,
And [b]whoever believes on Him will not
be put to shame."

Israel Needs the Gospel

10 Brethren, my heart's desire and prayer to
God for *Israel is that they may be saved.
2 For I bear them witness [a]that they have
a zeal for God, but not according to knowledge.
3 For they being ignorant of [a]God's righteousness, and seeking to establish their own
[b]righteousness, have not submitted to the righteousness of God.
4 For [a]Christ *is* the end of the law for righteousness to everyone who believes.
5 For Moses writes about the righteousness
which is of the law, [a]*"The man who does those
things shall live by them."*
6 But the righteousness of faith speaks in
this way, [a]*"Do not say in your heart, 'Who will
ascend into heaven?' "* (that is, to bring Christ
down *from above*)
7 or, [a]*" 'Who will descend into the abyss?' "*
(that is, to bring Christ up from the dead).
8 But what does it say? [a]*"The word is near
you, in your mouth and in your heart"* (that is,
the word of faith which we preach):
9 that [a]if you confess with your mouth the
Lord Jesus and believe in your heart that God
has raised Him from the dead, you will be saved.
10 For with the heart one believes unto righteousness, and with the mouth confession is made
unto salvation.
11 For the Scripture says, [a]*"Whoever believes on Him will not be put to shame."*
12 For [a]there is no distinction between Jew
and Greek, for [b]the same Lord over all [c]is rich
to all who call upon Him.
13 For [a]*"whoever calls [b]on the name of the
LORD shall be saved."*

Israel Rejects the Gospel

14 How then shall they call on Him in whom
they have not believed? And how shall they believe in Him of whom they have not heard? And
how shall they hear [a]without a preacher?
15 And how shall they preach unless they are
sent? As it is written:

[a]"How beautiful are the feet of those who
**preach the gospel of peace,*
Who bring glad tidings of good things!"

16 But they have not all obeyed the gospel.
For Isaiah says, [a]*"Lord, who has believed our
report?"*
17 So then faith *comes* by hearing, and hearing by the word of God.
18 But I say, have they not heard? Yes indeed:

[a]"Their sound has gone out to all the earth,
[b]And their words to the ends of the world."

19 But I say, did Israel not know? First Moses
says:

[a]"I will provoke you to jealousy by those
who are not a nation,
I will move you to anger by a [b]foolish
nation."

20 But Isaiah is very bold and says:

[a]"I was found by those who did not seek
Me;

KJV

21 But to Israel he saith, [a]ALL DAY LONG I HAVE STRETCHED FORTH MY HANDS UNTO A DISOBEDIENT AND GAINSAYING PEOPLE.

Israel's Rejection Not Total

11 I say then, [a]Hath God cast away his people? [b]God forbid. For [c]I also am an Israelite, of the seed of Abraham, *of* the tribe of Benjamin.

2 God hath not cast away his people which [a]he foreknew. Wot ye not what the scripture saith of Elias? how he maketh intercession to God against Israel, saying,

3 [a]LORD, THEY HAVE KILLED THY PROPHETS, AND DIGGED DOWN THINE ALTARS; AND I AM LEFT ALONE, AND THEY SEEK MY LIFE.

4 But what saith the answer of God unto him? [a]I HAVE RESERVED TO MYSELF SEVEN THOUSAND MEN, WHO HAVE NOT BOWED THE KNEE TO *THE IMAGE OF* BAAL.

5 [a]Even so then at this present time also there is a remnant according to the election of grace.

6 And [a]if by grace, then *is it* no more of works: otherwise grace is no more grace. But if *it be* of works, then is it no more grace: otherwise work is no more work.

7 What then? [a]Israel hath not obtained that which he seeketh for; but the election hath obtained it, and the rest were [b]blinded.

8 (According as it is written, [a]GOD HATH GIVEN THEM THE SPIRIT OF SLUMBER, [b]EYES THAT THEY SHOULD NOT SEE, AND EARS THAT THEY SHOULD NOT HEAR;) UNTO THIS DAY.

9 And David saith, [a]LET THEIR TABLE BE MADE A SNARE, AND A TRAP, AND A STUMBLINGBLOCK, AND A RECOMPENCE UNTO THEM:

10 LET THEIR EYES BE DARKENED, THAT THEY MAY NOT SEE, AND BOW DOWN THEIR BACK ALWAY.

Israel's Rejection Not Final

11 I say then, Have they stumbled that they should fall? God forbid: but *rather* [a]through their fall salvation *is come* unto the Gentiles, for to provoke them to [b]jealousy.

12 Now if the fall of them *be* the riches of the world, and the diminishing of them the riches of the Gentiles; how much more their fulness?

13 For I speak to you Gentiles, inasmuch as [a]I am the apostle of the Gentiles, I magnify mine office:

14 If by any means I may provoke to emulation *them which are* my flesh, and [a]might save some of them.

15 For if the casting away of them *be* the reconciling of the world, what *shall* the receiving *of them be*, [a]but life from the dead?

16 For if [a]the firstfruit *be* holy, the lump *is* also *holy*: and if the root *be* holy, so *are* the branches.

17 And if [a]some of the branches be broken off, [b]and thou, being a wild olive tree, wert graffed in among them, and with them partakest of the root and fatness of the olive tree;

18 [a]Boast not against the branches. But if thou boast, thou bearest not the root, but the root thee.

19 Thou wilt say then, The branches were broken off, that I might be graffed in.

20 Well; because of [a]unbelief they were broken off, and thou standest by faith. Be not highminded, but fear:

21 For if God spared not the natural branches, *take heed* lest he also spare not thee.

22 Behold therefore the goodness and sever-

NKJV

I was made manifest to those who did not
ask for Me."

21 But to Israel he says:

[a]*"All day long I have stretched out My*
hands
To a disobedient and contrary people."

Israel's Rejection Not Total

11 I say then, [a]has God cast away His people? [b]Certainly not! For [c]I also am an Israelite, of the seed of Abraham, *of* the tribe of Benjamin.

2 God has not cast away His people whom [a]He foreknew. Or do you not know what the Scripture says of Elijah, how he pleads with God against Israel, saying,

3 [a]*"LORD, they have killed Your prophets and torn down Your altars, and I alone am left, and they seek my life"*?

4 But what does the divine response say to him? [a]*"I have reserved for Myself seven thousand men who have not bowed the knee to Baal."*

5 [a]Even so then, at this present time there is a remnant according to the election of grace.

6 And [a]if by grace, then *it is* no longer of works; otherwise grace is no longer grace. *But if *it is* of works, it is no longer grace; otherwise work is no longer work.

7 What then? [a]Israel has not obtained what it seeks; but the elect have obtained it, and the rest were [b]blinded.

8 Just as it is written:

[a]*"God has given them a spirit of stupor,*
[b]*Eyes that they should not see*
And ears that they should not hear,
To this very day."

9 And David says:

[a]*"Let their table become a snare and a trap,*
A stumbling block and a recompense to
them.
10 *Let their eyes be darkened, so that they*
do not see,
And bow down their back always."

Israel's Rejection Not Final

11 I say then, have they stumbled that they should fall? Certainly not! But [a]through their fall, to provoke them to [b]jealousy, salvation *has come* to the Gentiles.

12 Now if their fall *is* riches for the world, and their failure riches for the Gentiles, how much more their fullness!

13 For I speak to you Gentiles; inasmuch as [a]I am an apostle to the Gentiles, I magnify my ministry,

14 if by any means I may provoke to jealousy *those who are* my flesh and [a]save some of them.

15 For if their being cast away *is* the reconciling of the world, what *will* their acceptance *be* [a]but life from the dead?

16 For if [a]the firstfruit *is* holy, the lump *is* also *holy;* and if the root *is* holy, so *are* the branches.

17 And if [a]some of the branches were broken off, [b]and you, being a wild olive tree, were grafted in among them, and with them became a partaker of the root and fatness of the olive tree,

18 [a]do not boast against the branches. But if you do boast, *remember that* you do not support the root, but the root supports you.

19 You will say then, "Branches were broken off that I might be grafted in."

20 Well *said.* Because of [a]unbelief they were broken off, and you stand by faith. Do not be haughty, but fear.

21 For if God did not spare the natural branches, He may not spare you either.

22 Therefore consider the goodness and se-

---

21 [a]Is. 65:2

CHAPTER 11

1 [a]Ps. 94:14; Jer. 46:28 [b]1 Sam. 12:22; Jer. 31:37 [c]2 Cor. 11:22; Phil. 3:5
2 [a][Rom. 8:29]
3 [a]1 Kin. 19:10, 14
4 [a]1 Kin. 19:18
5 [a]2 Kin. 19:4; Rom. 9:27
6 [a]Rom. 4:4
7 [a]Rom. 9:31 [b]Mark 6:52; Rom. 9:18; 11:25; 2 Cor. 3:14
8 [a]Is. 29:10, 13 [b]Deut. 29:3, 4; Is. 6:9; Matt. 13:13, 14; John 12:40; Acts 28:26, 27
9 [a]Ps. 69:22, 23
11 [a]Is. 42:6, 7; Acts 28:28 [b]Deut. 32:21; Acts 13:46; Rom. 10:19
13 [a]Acts 9:15; 22:21; Gal. 1:16; 2:7–9; Eph. 3:8
14 [a]1 Cor. 9:22; 1 Tim. 4:16; James 5:20
15 [a][Is. 26:16–19]
16 [a]Lev. 23:10; [James 1:18]
17 [a]Jer. 11:16; [John 15:2] [b]Acts 2:39; [Eph. 2:12]
18 [a][1 Cor. 10:12]
20 [a]Heb. 3:19

*

11:6 NU omits the rest of v. 6.

KJV

ity of God: on them which fell, severity; but toward thee, goodness, [a]if thou continue in *his*
goodness: otherwise [b]thou also shalt be cut off.
23 And they also, [a]if they abide not still in
unbelief, shall be graffed in: for God is able to
graff them in again.
24 For if thou wert cut out of the olive tree
which is wild by nature, and wert graffed contrary
to nature into a good olive tree: how much more
shall these, which be the natural *branches*, be
graffed into their own olive tree?
25 For I would not, brethren, that ye should
be ignorant of this mystery, lest ye should be
[a]wise in your own conceits; that [b]blindness in part
is happened to Israel, [c]until the fulness of the Gentiles be come in.
26 And so all Israel shall be saved: as it is
written, [a]There shall come out of Sion the Deliverer, and shall turn away ungodliness from
Jacob:
27 [a]For this *is* my covenant unto them,
when I shall take away their sins.
28 As concerning the gospel, *they are* enemies for your sakes: but as touching the election,
they are [a]beloved for the fathers' sakes.
29 For the gifts and calling of God *are* [a]with-
out repentance.
30 For as ye [a]in times past have not believed
God, yet have now obtained mercy through their
unbelief:
31 Even so have these also now not believed,
that through your mercy they also may obtain
mercy.
32 For God hath concluded them [a]all in unbelief, that he might have mercy upon all.
33 O the depth of the riches both of the wisdom and knowledge of God! how unsearchable
are his judgments, and his ways past finding out!
34 For who hath known the [a]mind of the
Lord? or [b]who hath been his counsellor?
35 [a]Or who hath first given to him, and it
shall be recompensed unto him again?
36 For [a]of him, and through him, and to him,
are all things: [b]to whom *be* glory for ever. Amen.

Living Sacrifices to God

12 I [a]beseech you therefore, brethren, by the
mercies of God, that ye present your bodies
a [b]living sacrifice, holy, acceptable unto God,
which is your reasonable service.
2 And [a]be not conformed to this world: but
[b]be ye transformed by the renewing of your mind,
that ye may [c]prove what *is* that good, and acceptable, and perfect, will of God.

Serve God with Spiritual Gifts

3 For I say, [a]through the grace given unto
me, to every man that is among you, [b]not to think
of himself more highly than he ought to think;
but to think soberly, according as God hath dealt
[c]to every man the measure of faith.
4 For [a]as we have many members in one
body, and all members have not the same office:
5 So [a]we, *being* many, are one body in
Christ, and every one members one of another.
6 Having then gifts differing according to
the grace that is [a]given to us, whether prophecy,
let us [b]*prophesy* according to the proportion of
faith;
7 Or ministry, *let us wait* on *our* ministering: or [a]he that teacheth, on teaching;
8 Or [a]he that exhorteth, on exhortation: [b]he
that giveth, *let him do it* with simplicity; [c]he that
ruleth, with diligence; he that sheweth mercy,
[d]with cheerfulness.

NKJV

verity of God: on those who fell, severity; but toward you, *goodness, [a]if you continue in *His*
goodness. Otherwise [b]you also will be cut off.
23 And they also, [a]if they do not continue in
unbelief, will be grafted in, for God is able to graft
them in again.
24 For if you were cut out of the olive tree
which is wild by nature, and were grafted contrary to nature into a cultivated olive tree, how
much more will these, who *are* natural *branches*,
be grafted into their own olive tree?
25 For I do not desire, brethren, that you
should be ignorant of this mystery, lest you should
be [a]wise in your own opinion, that [b]blindness in
part has happened to Israel [c]until the fullness of
the Gentiles has come in.
26 And so all Israel will be *saved, as it is
written:

[a]*"The Deliverer will come out of Zion,*
And He will turn away ungodliness from
Jacob;
27 *For* [a]*this is My covenant with them,*
When I take away their sins."

28 Concerning the gospel *they are* enemies
for your sake, but concerning the election *they*
are [a]beloved for the sake of the fathers.
29 For the gifts and the calling of God *are*
[a]irrevocable.
30 For as you [a]were once disobedient to God,
yet have now obtained mercy through their
disobedience,
31 even so these also have now been disobedient, that through the mercy shown you they also
may obtain mercy.
32 For God has committed them [a]all to disobedience, that He might have mercy on all.
33 Oh, the depth of the riches both of the wisdom and knowledge of God! How unsearchable
are His judgments and His ways past finding out!

34 *"For who has known the* [a]*mind of the*
Lord?
Or [b]*who has become His counselor?"*
35 *"Or*[a] *who has first given to Him*
And it shall be repaid to him?"

36 For [a]of Him and through Him and to Him
are all things, [b]to whom *be* glory forever. Amen.

Living Sacrifices to God

12 I [a]beseech you therefore, brethren, by the
mercies of God, that you present your bodies [b]a living sacrifice, holy, acceptable to God,
which is your reasonable service.
2 And [a]do not be conformed to this world,
but [b]be transformed by the renewing of your
mind, that you may [c]prove what *is* that good and
acceptable and perfect will of God.

Serve God with Spiritual Gifts

3 For I say, [a]through the grace given to me,
to everyone who is among you, [b]not to think *of*
himself more highly than he ought to think, but
to think soberly, as God has dealt [c]to each one a
measure of faith.
4 For [a]as we have many members in one
body, but all the members do not have the same
function,
5 so [a]we, *being* many, are one body in
Christ, and individually members of one another.
6 Having then gifts differing according to
the grace that is [a]given to us, *let us use them:* if
prophecy, *let us* [b]*prophesy* in proportion to our
faith;
7 or ministry, *let us use it* in *our* ministering; [a]he who teaches, in teaching;
8 [a]he who exhorts, in exhortation; [b]he who
gives, with liberality; [c]he who leads, with diligence; he who shows mercy, [d]with cheerfulness.

---

22 [a]1 Cor. 15:2; Heb. 3:6, 14 [b][John 15:2]
23 [a][2 Cor. 3:16]
25 [a]Rom. 12:16 [b]2 Cor. 3:14 [c]Luke 21:24; John 10:16; Rom. 11:12
26 [a]Ps. 14:7; Is. 59:20, 21
27 [a]Is. 27:9; Heb. 8:12
28 [a]Deut. 7:8; 10:15; Rom. 9:5
29 [a]Num. 23:19
30 [a][Eph. 2:2]
32 [a]Rom. 3:9; [Gal. 3:22]
34 [a]Is. 40:13; Jer. 23:18; 1 Cor. 2:16 [b]Job 36:22
35 [a]Job 41:11
36 [a][1 Cor. 8:6; 11:12]; Col. 1:16; Heb. 2:10 [b]Heb. 13:21

CHAPTER 12

1 [a]1 Cor. 1:10; 2 Cor. 10:1–4 [b]Phil. 4:18; Heb. 10:18, 20
2 [a]Matt. 13:22; Gal. 1:4; 1 John 2:15 [b]Eph. 4:23; [Titus 3:5] [c][1 Thess. 4:3]
3 [a]Rom. 1:5; 15:15; 1 Cor. 3:10; 15:10; Gal. 2:9; Eph. 3:7 [b]Prov. 25:27 [c][Eph. 4:7]
4 [a]1 Cor. 12:12–14; [Eph. 4:4, 16]
5 [a][1 Cor. 10:17]; Gal. 3:28
6 [a][John 3:27] [b]Acts 11:27
7 [a]Eph. 4:11
8 [a]Acts 15:32 [b][Matt. 6:1–3] [c][Acts 20:28] [d]2 Cor. 9:7

*

11:22 NU adds *of God*
11:26 Or *delivered*

KJV

Behave Like a Christian

9 [a]*Let* love be without dissimulation. [b]Ab-
hor that which is evil; cleave to that which is
good.
10 [a]*Be* kindly affectioned one to another with
brotherly love; [b]in honour preferring one another;
11 Not slothful in business; fervent in spirit;
serving the Lord;
12 [a]Rejoicing in hope; [b]patient in tribulation;
[c]continuing instant in prayer;
13 [a]Distributing to the necessity of saints;
[b]given to hospitality.
14 [a]Bless them which persecute you: bless,
and curse not.
15 [a]Rejoice with them that do rejoice, and
weep with them that weep.
16 [a]*Be* of the same mind one toward another.
[b]Mind not high things, but condescend to men of
low estate. Be not wise in your own conceits.
17 [a]Recompense to no man evil for evil.
[b]Provide things honest in the sight of all men.
18 If it be possible, as much as lieth in you,
[a]live peaceably with all men.
19 Dearly beloved, [a]avenge not yourselves,
but *rather* give place unto wrath: for it is written, [b]VENGEANCE *IS* MINE; I WILL REPAY, saith the
Lord.
20 [a]Therefore IF THINE ENEMY HUNGER, FEED
HIM; IF HE THIRST, GIVE HIM DRINK: FOR IN SO DOING
THOU SHALT HEAP COALS OF FIRE ON HIS HEAD.
21 Be not overcome of evil, but [a]overcome
evil with good.

Submit to Government

13 Let every soul be [a]subject unto the higher
powers. For there is no power but of God:
the powers that be are ordained of God.
2 Whosoever therefore resisteth [a]the power,
resisteth the ordinance of God: and they that resist shall receive to themselves damnation.
3 For rulers are not a terror to good works,
but to the evil. Wilt thou then not be afraid of
the power? [a]do that which is good, and thou shalt
have praise of the same:
4 For he is the minister of God to thee for
good. But if thou do that which is evil, be afraid;
for he beareth not the sword in vain: for he is
the minister of God, a revenger to *execute* wrath
upon him that doeth evil.
5 Wherefore [a]*ye* must needs be subject, not
only for wrath, [b]but also for conscience sake.
6 For for this cause pay ye tribute also: for
they are God's ministers, attending continually
upon this very thing.
7 [a]Render therefore to all their dues: tribute
to whom tribute *is due;* custom to whom custom;
fear to whom fear; honour to whom honour.

Love Your Neighbor
(cf. Mark 12:31; James 2:8)

8 Owe no man any thing, but to love one
another: for [a]he that loveth another hath fulfilled
the law.
9 For this, [a]THOU SHALT NOT COMMIT ADUL-
TERY, THOU SHALT NOT KILL, THOU SHALT NOT STEAL,
THOU SHALT NOT BEAR FALSE WITNESS, THOU SHALT
NOT COVET; and if *there be* any other commandment, it is briefly comprehended in this saying,
namely, [b]THOU SHALT LOVE THY NEIGHBOUR AS
THYSELF.
10 Love worketh no ill to his neighbour:
therefore [a]love *is* the fulfilling of the law.

Put on Christ

11 And that, knowing the time, that now *it*
is high time [a]to awake out of sleep: for now

9 [a]1 Tim. 1:5 [b]Ps. 34:14
10 [a]Heb. 13:1 [b]Phil. 2:3
12 [a]Luke 10:20 [b]Luke 21:19 [c]Luke 18:1
13 [a]1 Cor. 16:1 [b]1 Tim. 3:2
14 [a][Matt. 5:44]
15 [a][1 Cor. 12:26]
16 [a][Phil. 2:2; 4:2] [b]Jer. 45:5
17 [a][Matt. 5:39] [b]2 Cor. 8:21
18 [a]Heb. 12:14
19 [a]Lev. 19:18 [b]Deut. 32:35
20 [a]Prov. 25:21, 22
21 [a][Rom. 12:1, 2]

CHAPTER 13

1 [a]1 Pet. 2:13
2 [a][Titus 3:1]
3 [a]1 Pet. 2:14
5 [a]Eccl. 8:2 [b][1 Pet. 2:13, 19]
7 [a]Matt. 22:21
8 [a][Gal. 5:13, 14]
9 [a]Ex. 20:13–17; Deut. 5:17–21 [b]Lev. 19:18
10 [a][Matt. 7:12; 22:39, 40]
11 [a][1 Cor. 15:34]

NKJV

Behave Like a Christian

9 [a]*Let* love *be* without hypocrisy. [b]Abhor
what is evil. Cling to what is good.
10 [a]*Be* kindly affectionate to one another
with brotherly love, [b]in honor giving preference
to one another;
11 not lagging in diligence, fervent in spirit,
serving the Lord;
12 [a]rejoicing in hope, [b]patient in tribulation,
[c]continuing steadfastly in prayer;
13 [a]distributing to the needs of the saints,
[b]given to hospitality.
14 [a]Bless those who persecute you; bless and
do not curse.
15 [a]Rejoice with those who rejoice, and weep
with those who weep.
16 [a]Be of the same mind toward one another.
[b]Do not set your mind on high things, but associate with the humble. Do not be wise in your own
opinion.
17 [a]Repay no one evil for evil. [b]Have regard
for good things in the sight of all men.
18 If it is possible, as much as depends on
you, [a]live peaceably with all men.
19 Beloved, [a]do not avenge yourselves, but
rather give place to wrath; for it is written, [b]*"Ven-*
geance is Mine, I will repay," says the Lord.
20 Therefore

[a]*"If your enemy is hungry, feed him;*
If he is thirsty, give him a drink;
For in so doing you will heap coals of fire
on his head."

21 Do not be overcome by evil, but [a]over-
come evil with good.

Submit to Government

13 Let every soul be [a]subject to the governing
authorities. For there is no authority except
from God, and the authorities that exist are appointed by God.
2 Therefore whoever resists [a]the authority
resists the ordinance of God, and those who resist
will bring judgment on themselves.
3 For rulers are not a terror to good works,
but to evil. Do you want to be unafraid of the
authority? [a]Do what is good, and you will have
praise from the same.
4 For he is God's minister to you for good.
But if you do evil, be afraid; for he does not bear
the sword in vain; for he is God's minister, an
avenger to *execute* wrath on him who practices
evil.
5 Therefore [a]*you* must be subject, not only
because of wrath [b]but also for conscience' sake.
6 For because of this you also pay taxes,
for they are God's ministers attending continually
to this very thing.
7 [a]Render therefore to all their due: taxes
to whom taxes *are due,* customs to whom customs,
fear to whom fear, honor to whom honor.

Love Your Neighbor
(cf. Mark 12:31; James 2:8)

8 Owe no one anything except to love one
another, for [a]he who loves another has fulfilled
the law.
9 For the commandments, [a]*"You shall not*
commit adultery," "You shall not murder," "You
shall not steal," **"You shall not bear false wit-*
ness," "You shall not covet," and if *there is* any
other commandment, are *all* summed up in this
saying, namely, [b]*"You shall love your neighbor*
as yourself."
10 Love does no harm to a neighbor; therefore [a]love *is* the fulfillment of the law.

Put on Christ

11 And *do* this, knowing the time, that now
it is high time [a]to awake out of sleep; for now

*

13:9 NU omits *"You shall not bear false witness."*

KJV

is our salvation nearer than when we believed.
12 The night is far spent, the day is at hand:
[a]let us therefore cast off the works of darkness,
and [b]let us put on the armour of light.
13 [a]Let us walk honestly, as in the day; [b]not
in rioting and drunkenness, [c]not in chambering
and wantonness, [d]not in strife and envying.
14 But [a]put ye on the Lord Jesus Christ, and
[b]make not provision for the flesh, to *fulfil* the lusts
thereof.

The Law of Liberty

14 Him that [a]is weak in the faith receive ye,
but not to doubtful disputations.
2 For one believeth that he [a]may eat all
things: another, who is weak, eateth herbs.
3 Let not him that eateth despise him that
eateth not; and [a]let not him which eateth not judge
him that eateth: for God hath received him.
4 [a]Who art thou that judgest another man's
servant? to his own master he standeth or falleth.
Yea, he shall be holden up: for God is able to
make him stand.
5 [a]One man esteemeth one day above another: another esteemeth every day *alike.* Let every man be fully persuaded in his own mind.
6 He that [a]regardeth the day, regardeth *it*
unto the Lord; and he that regardeth not the day,
to the Lord he doth not regard *it.* He that eateth,
eateth to the Lord, for [b]he giveth God thanks; and
he that eateth not, to the Lord he eateth not, and
giveth God thanks.
7 For [a]none of us liveth to himself, and no
man dieth to himself.
8 For whether we [a]live, we live unto the
Lord; and whether we die, we die unto the Lord:
whether we live therefore, or die, we are the
Lord's.
9 For [a]to this end Christ both died, and rose,
and revived, that he might be [b]Lord both of the
dead and living.
10 But why dost thou judge thy brother? or
why dost thou set at nought thy brother? for [a]we
shall all stand before the judgment seat of Christ.
11 For it is written, [a]*As* I LIVE, SAITH THE LORD,
EVERY KNEE SHALL BOW TO ME, AND EVERY TONGUE
SHALL CONFESS TO GOD.
12 So then [a]every one of us shall give account of himself to God.
13 Let us not therefore judge one another any
more: but judge this rather, that [a]no man put a
stumblingblock or an occasion to fall in *his*
brother's way.

The Law of Love

14 I know, and am persuaded by the Lord
Jesus, [a]that *there is* nothing unclean of itself: but
to him that esteemeth any thing to be unclean,
to him *it is* unclean.
15 But if thy brother be grieved with *thy*
meat, now walkest thou not charitably. [a]Destroy
not him with thy meat, for whom Christ died.
16 [a]Let not then your good be evil spoken
of:
17 [a]For the kingdom of God is not meat and
drink; but righteousness, and [b]peace, and joy in
the Holy Ghost.
18 For he that in these things serveth Christ
[a]*is* acceptable to God, and approved of men.
19 [a]Let us therefore follow after the things
which make for peace, and things wherewith [b]one
may edify another.
20 [a]For meat destroy not the work of God.
[b]All things indeed *are* pure; [c]but *it is* evil for that
man who eateth with offence.
21 *It is* good neither to eat [a]flesh, nor to drink
wine, nor *any thing* whereby thy brother stumbleth, or is offended, or is made weak.

12 [a]Eph. 5:11 [b][Eph. 6:11, 13]
13 [a]Phil. 4:8 [b]Prov. 23:20 [c][1 Cor. 6:9] [d]James 3:14
14 [a]Gal. 3:27 [b][Gal. 5:16]

CHAPTER 14

1 [a][1 Cor. 8:9; 9:22]
2 [a][Titus 1:15]
3 [a][Col. 2:16]
4 [a]James 4:11, 12
5 [a]Gal. 4:10
6 [a]Gal. 4:10 [b][1 Tim. 4:3]
7 [a][Gal. 2:20]
8 [a]2 Cor. 5:14, 15
9 [a]2 Cor. 5:15 [b]Acts 10:36
10 [a]2 Cor. 5:10
11 [a]Is. 45:23
12 [a]1 Pet. 4:5
13 [a]1 Cor. 8:9
14 [a]1 Cor. 10:25
15 [a]1 Cor. 8:11
16 [a][Rom. 12:17]
17 [a]1 Cor. 8:8 [b][Rom. 8:6]
18 [a]2 Cor. 8:21
19 [a]Rom. 12:18 [b]1 Cor. 14:12
20 [a]Rom. 14:15 [b]Acts 10:15 [c]1 Cor. 8:9–12
21 [a]1 Cor. 8:13

NKJV

our salvation *is* nearer than when we *first*
believed.
12 The night is far spent, the day is at hand.
[a]Therefore let us cast off the works of darkness,
and [b]let us put on the armor of light.
13 [a]Let us walk properly, as in the day, [b]not
in revelry and drunkenness, [c]not in lewdness and
lust, [d]not in strife and envy.
14 But [a]put on the Lord Jesus Christ, and
[b]make no provision for the flesh, to *fulfill its* lusts.

The Law of Liberty

14 Receive[a] one who is weak in the faith, *but*
not to disputes over doubtful things.
2 For one believes he [a]may eat all things,
but he who is weak eats *only* vegetables.
3 Let not him who eats despise him who
does not eat, and [a]let not him who does not eat
judge him who eats; for God has received him.
4 [a]Who are you to judge another's servant?
To his own master he stands or falls. Indeed, he
will be made to stand, for God is able to make
him stand.
5 [a]One person esteems *one* day above another; another esteems every day *alike.* Let each
be fully convinced in his own mind.
6 He who [a]observes the day, observes *it* to
the Lord; *and he who does not observe the day,
to the Lord he does not observe *it.* He who eats,
eats to the Lord, for [b]he gives God thanks; and
he who does not eat, to the Lord he does not eat,
and gives God thanks.
7 For [a]none of us lives to himself, and no
one dies to himself.
8 For if we [a]live, we live to the Lord; and
if we die, we die to the Lord. Therefore, whether
we live or die, we are the Lord's.
9 For [a]to this end Christ died *and rose and
lived again, that He might be [b]Lord of both the
dead and the living.
10 But why do you judge your brother? Or
why do you show contempt for your brother? For
[a]we shall all stand before the judgment seat of
*Christ.
11 For it is written:

[a]*"As I live, says the* LORD,
Every knee shall bow to Me,
And every tongue shall confess to God."

12 So then [a]each of us shall give account of
himself to God.
13 Therefore let us not judge one another
anymore, but rather resolve this, [a]not to put a
stumbling block or a cause to fall in *our* brother's
way.

The Law of Love

14 I know and am convinced by the Lord Jesus [a]that *there is* nothing unclean of itself; but
to him who considers anything to be unclean, to
him *it is* unclean.
15 Yet if your brother is grieved because of
your food, you are no longer walking in love. [a]Do
not destroy with your food the one for whom
Christ died.
16 [a]Therefore do not let your good be spoken
of as evil;
17 [a]for the kingdom of God is not eating and
drinking, but righteousness and [b]peace and joy
in the Holy Spirit.
18 For he who serves Christ in *these things
[a]*is* acceptable to God and approved by men.
19 [a]Therefore let us pursue the things *which
make* for peace and the things by which [b]one may
edify another.
20 [a]Do not destroy the work of God for the
sake of food. [b]All things indeed *are* pure, [c]but *it
is* evil for the man who eats with offense.
21 *It is* good neither to eat [a]meat nor drink
wine nor *do anything* by which your brother
stumbles *or is offended or is made weak.

*———

14:6 NU omits the rest of this sentence.
14:9 NU omits *and rose*
14:10 NU *God*
14:18 NU *this thing*
14:21 NU omits the rest of v. 21.

KJV

22 Hast thou faith? have *it* to thyself before God. [a]Happy *is* he that condemneth not himself in that thing which he alloweth.

23 And he that doubteth is damned if he eat, because *he eateth* not of faith: for [a]whatsoever *is* not of faith is sin.

Bearing Others' Burdens

15 We [a]then that are strong ought to bear the infirmities of the weak, and not to please ourselves.

2 [a]Let every one of us please *his* neighbour for *his* good to edification.

3 [a]For even Christ pleased not himself; but, as it is written, THE [b]REPROACHES OF THEM THAT REPROACHED THEE FELL ON ME.

4 For [a]whatsoever things were written aforetime were written for our learning, that we through patience and comfort of the scriptures might have hope.

5 [a]Now the God of patience and consolation grant you to be likeminded one toward another according to Christ Jesus:

6 That ye may [a]with one mind *and* one mouth glorify God, even the Father of our Lord Jesus Christ.

Glorify God Together

7 Wherefore [a]receive ye one another, [b]as Christ also received us to the glory of God.

8 Now I say that [a]Jesus Christ was a minister of the circumcision for the truth of God, [b]to confirm the promises *made* unto the fathers:

9 And [a]that the Gentiles might glorify God for *his* mercy; as it is written, [b]FOR THIS CAUSE I WILL CONFESS TO THEE AMONG THE GENTILES, AND SING UNTO THY NAME.

10 And again he saith, [a]REJOICE, YE GENTILES, WITH HIS PEOPLE.

11 And again, [a]PRAISE THE LORD, ALL YE GENTILES; AND LAUD HIM, ALL YE PEOPLE.

12 And again, Esaias saith, [a]THERE SHALL BE A ROOT OF JESSE, AND HE THAT SHALL RISE TO REIGN OVER THE GENTILES; IN HIM SHALL THE GENTILES TRUST.

13 Now the God of hope fill you with all [a]joy and peace in believing, that ye may abound in hope, through the power of the Holy Ghost.

From Jerusalem to Illyricum

14 And [a]I myself also am persuaded of you, my brethren, that ye also are full of goodness, [b]filled with all knowledge, able also to admonish one another.

15 Nevertheless, brethren, I have written the more boldly unto you in some sort, as putting you in mind, [a]because of the grace that is given to me of God,

16 That [a]I should be the minister of Jesus Christ to the Gentiles, ministering the gospel of God, that the [b]offering up of the Gentiles might be acceptable, being sanctified by the Holy Ghost.

17 I have therefore whereof I may glory through Jesus Christ [a]in those things which pertain to God.

18 For I will not dare to speak of any of those things [a]which Christ hath not wrought by me, [b]to make the Gentiles obedient, by word and deed,

19 [a]Through mighty signs and wonders, by the power of the Spirit of God; so that from Jerusalem, and round about unto Illyricum, I have fully preached the gospel of Christ.

20 Yea, so have I strived to preach the gospel,

---

22 [a][1 John 3:21]
23 [a]Titus 1:15

CHAPTER 15

1 [a]Rom. 14:1; [Gal. 6:1, 2]; 1 Thess. 5:14
2 [a]1 Cor. 9:22; 10:24, 33; 2 Cor. 13:9
3 [a]Matt. 26:39; [Phil. 2:5–8] [b]Ps. 69:9
4 [a]Rom. 4:23, 24; 1 Cor. 10:11; 2 Tim. 3:16, 17
5 [a]1 Cor. 1:10; Phil. 1:27
6 [a]Acts 4:24
7 [a]Rom. 14:1, 3 [b]Rom. 5:2
8 [a]Matt. 15:24; Acts 3:26 [b][Rom. 4:16]; 2 Cor. 1:20
9 [a]John 10:16 [b]2 Sam. 22:50; Ps. 18:49
10 [a]Deut. 32:43
11 [a]Ps. 117:1
12 [a]Is. 11:1, 10
13 [a]Rom. 12:12; 14:17
14 [a]2 Pet. 1:12 [b]1 Cor. 1:5; 8:1, 7, 10
15 [a]Rom. 1:5; 12:3
16 [a]Acts 9:15; Rom. 11:13 [b][Is. 66:20]
17 [a]Heb. 2:17; 5:1
18 [a]Acts 15:12; 21:19; 2 Cor. 3:5; Gal. 2:8 [b]Rom. 1:5
19 [a]Acts 19:11

*

14:22 NU *The faith which you have—have*
14:23 M puts Rom. 16:25–27 here.
15:7 NU, M *you*
15:14 M *others*

NKJV

22 *Do you have faith? Have *it* to yourself before God. [a]Happy *is* he who does not condemn himself in what he approves.

23 But he who doubts is condemned if he eats, because *he does* not *eat* from faith; for [a]whatever *is* not from faith is *sin.

Bearing Others' Burdens

15 We [a]then who are strong ought to bear with the scruples of the weak, and not to please ourselves.

2 [a]Let each of us please *his* neighbor for *his* good, leading to edification.

3 [a]For even Christ did not please Himself; but as it is written, [b]*"The reproaches of those who reproached You fell on Me."*

4 For [a]whatever things were written before were written for our learning, that we through the patience and comfort of the Scriptures might have hope.

5 [a]Now may the God of patience and comfort grant you to be like-minded toward one another, according to Christ Jesus,

6 that you may [a]with one mind *and* one mouth glorify the God and Father of our Lord Jesus Christ.

Glorify God Together

7 Therefore [a]receive one another, just [b]as Christ also received *us, to the glory of God.

8 Now I say that [a]Jesus Christ has become a servant to the circumcision for the truth of God, [b]to confirm the promises *made* to the fathers,

9 and [a]that the Gentiles might glorify God for *His* mercy, as it is written:

[b]*"For this reason I will confess to You*
among the Gentiles,
And sing to Your name."

10 And again he says:

[a]*"Rejoice, O Gentiles, with His people!"*

11 And again:

[a]*"Praise the LORD, all you Gentiles!*
Laud Him, all you peoples!"

12 And again, Isaiah says:

[a]*"There shall be a root of Jesse;*
And He who shall rise to reign over the
Gentiles,
In Him the Gentiles shall hope."

13 Now may the God of hope fill you with all [a]joy and peace in believing, that you may abound in hope by the power of the Holy Spirit.

From Jerusalem to Illyricum

14 Now [a]I myself am confident concerning you, my brethren, that you also are full of goodness, [b]filled with all knowledge, able also to admonish *one another.

15 Nevertheless, brethren, I have written more boldly to you on *some* points, as reminding you, [a]because of the grace given to me by God,

16 that [a]I might be a minister of Jesus Christ to the Gentiles, ministering the gospel of God, that the [b]offering of the Gentiles might be acceptable, sanctified by the Holy Spirit.

17 Therefore I have reason to glory in Christ Jesus [a]in the things *which pertain* to God.

18 For I will not dare to speak of any of those things [a]which Christ has not accomplished through me, in word and deed, [b]to make the Gentiles obedient—

19 [a]in mighty signs and wonders, by the power of the Spirit of God, so that from Jerusalem and round about to Illyricum I have fully preached the gospel of Christ.

20 And so I have made it my aim to preach

KJV

not where Christ was named, [a]lest I should build upon another man's foundation:

21 But as it is written, [a]TO WHOM HE WAS NOT SPOKEN OF, THEY SHALL SEE: AND THEY THAT HAVE NOT HEARD SHALL UNDERSTAND.

Plan to Visit Rome

22 For which cause also [a]I have been much hindered from coming to you.

23 But now having no more place in these parts, and [a]having a great desire these many years to come unto you;

24 Whensoever I take my journey into Spain, I will come to you: for I trust to see you in my journey, [a]and to be brought on my way thitherward by you, if first I be somewhat [b]filled with your *company*.

25 But now [a]I go unto Jerusalem to minister unto the saints.

26 For [a]it hath pleased them of Macedonia and Achaia to make a certain contribution for the poor saints which are at Jerusalem.

27 It hath pleased them verily; and their debtors they are. For [a]if the Gentiles have been made partakers of their spiritual things, [b]their duty is also to minister unto them in carnal things.

28 When therefore I have performed this, and have sealed to them [a]this fruit, I will come by you into Spain.

29 [a]And I am sure that, when I come unto you, I shall come in the fulness of the blessing of the gospel of Christ.

30 Now I beseech you, brethren, for the Lord Jesus Christ's sake, and [a]for the love of the Spirit, [b]that ye strive together with me in *your* prayers to God for me;

31 [a]That I may be delivered from them that do not believe in Judaea; and that [b]my service which *I have* for Jerusalem may be accepted of the saints;

32 [a]That I may come unto you with joy [b]by the will of God, and may with you [c]be refreshed.

33 Now [a]the God of peace *be* with you all. Amen.

Sister Phoebe Commended

16 I commend unto you Phebe our sister, which is a servant of the church which is at [a]Cenchrea:

2 [a]That ye receive her in the Lord, [b]as becometh saints, and that ye assist her in whatsoever business she hath need of you: for she hath been a succourer of many, and of myself also.

Greeting Roman Saints

3 Greet [a]Priscilla and Aquila my helpers in Christ Jesus:

4 Who have for my life laid down their own necks: unto whom not only I give thanks, but also all the churches of the Gentiles.

5 Likewise *greet* [a]the church that is in their house. Salute my wellbeloved Epaenetus, who is [b]the first fruits of Achaia unto Christ.

6 Greet Mary, who bestowed much labour on us.

7 Salute Andronicus and Junia, my kinsmen, and my fellowprisoners, who are of note among the [a]apostles, who also [b]were in Christ before me.

8 Greet Amplias my beloved in the Lord.

9 Salute Urbane, our helper in Christ, and Stachys my beloved.

10 Salute Apelles approved in Christ. Salute them which are of Aristobulus' *household*.

11 Salute Herodion my kinsman. Greet them that be of the *household* of Narcissus, which are in the Lord.

12 Salute Tryphena and Tryphosa, who labour in the Lord. Salute the beloved Persis, which laboured much in the Lord.

20 [a]1 Cor. 3:10; [2 Cor. 10:13, 15, 16]
21 [a]Is. 52:15
22 [a]Rom. 1:13; 1 Thess. 2:17, 18
23 [a]Acts 19:21; 23:11; Rom. 1:10, 11
24 [a]Acts 15:3 [b]Rom. 1:12
25 [a]Acts 19:21
26 [a]1 Cor. 16:1; 2 Cor. 8:1–15
27 [a]Rom. 11:17 [b]1 Cor. 9:11
28 [a]Phil. 4:17
29 [a][Rom. 1:11]
30 [a]Phil. 2:1 [b]2 Cor. 1:11; Col. 4:12
31 [a]2 Tim. 3:11; 4:17 [b]2 Cor. 8:4
32 [a]Rom. 1:10 [b]Acts 18:21 [c]1 Cor. 16:18
33 [a]Rom. 16:20; 1 Cor. 14:33; 2 Cor. 13:11; Phil. 4:9; [1 Thess. 5:23]; 2 Thess. 3:16; Heb. 13:20

CHAPTER 16
1 [a]Acts 18:18
2 [a]Phil. 2:29 [b]Phil. 1:27
3 [a]Acts 18:2, 18, 26; 1 Cor. 16:19; 2 Tim. 4:19
5 [a]1 Cor. 16:19; Col. 4:15; Philem. 2 [b]1 Cor. 16:15
7 [a]Acts 1:13, 26 [b]Rom. 8:11; 16:3, 9, 10; 2 Cor. 5:17; 12:2; Gal. 1:22

NKJV

the gospel, not where Christ was named, [a]lest I should build on another man's foundation,

21 but as it is written:

> [a]*"To whom He was not announced, they*
> *shall see;*
> *And those who have not heard shall*
> *understand."*

Plan to Visit Rome

22 For this reason [a]I also have been much hindered from coming to you.

23 But now no longer having a place in these parts, and [a]having a great desire these many years to come to you,

24 whenever I journey to Spain, *I shall come to you. For I hope to see you on my journey, [a]and to be helped on my way there by you, if first I may [b]enjoy your *company* for a while.

25 But now [a]I am going to Jerusalem to minister to the saints.

26 For [a]it pleased those from Macedonia and Achaia to make a certain contribution for the poor among the saints who are in Jerusalem.

27 It pleased them indeed, and they are their debtors. For [a]if the Gentiles have been partakers of their spiritual things, [b]their duty is also to minister to them in material things.

28 Therefore, when I have performed this and have sealed to them [a]this fruit, I shall go by way of you to Spain.

29 [a]But I know that when I come to you, I shall come in the fullness of the blessing *of the gospel of Christ.

30 Now I beg you, brethren, through the Lord Jesus Christ, and [a]through the love of the Spirit, [b]that you strive together with me in prayers to God for me,

31 [a]that I may be delivered from those in Judea who do not believe, and that [b]my service for Jerusalem may be acceptable to the saints,

32 [a]that I may come to you with joy [b]by the will of God, and may [c]be refreshed together with you.

33 Now [a]the God of peace *be* with you all. Amen.

Sister Phoebe Commended

16 I commend to you Phoebe our sister, who is a servant of the church in [a]Cenchrea,

2 [a]that you may receive her in the Lord [b]in a manner worthy of the saints, and assist her in whatever business she has need of you; for indeed she has been a helper of many and of myself also.

Greeting Roman Saints

3 Greet [a]Priscilla and Aquila, my fellow workers in Christ Jesus,

4 who risked their own necks for my life, to whom not only I give thanks, but also all the churches of the Gentiles.

5 Likewise *greet* [a]the church that is in their house. Greet my beloved Epaenetus, who is [b]the firstfruits of *Achaia to Christ.

6 Greet Mary, who labored much for us.

7 Greet Andronicus and Junia, my countrymen and my fellow prisoners, who are of note among the [a]apostles, who also [b]were in Christ before me.

8 Greet Amplias, my beloved in the Lord.

9 Greet Urbanus, our fellow worker in Christ, and Stachys, my beloved.

10 Greet Apelles, approved in Christ. Greet those who are of the *household* of Aristobulus.

11 Greet Herodion, my *countryman. Greet those who are of the *household* of Narcissus who are in the Lord.

12 Greet Tryphena and Tryphosa, who have labored in the Lord. Greet the beloved Persis, who labored much in the Lord.

15:24 NU omits *I shall come to you* and joins *Spain* with the next sentence.
15:29 NU omits *of the gospel*
16:5 NU *Asia*
16:11 Or *relative*

KJV

13 Salute Rufus [a]chosen in the Lord, and his
mother and mine.
14 Salute Asyncritus, Phlegon, Hermas,
Patrobas, Hermes, and the brethren which are with
them.
15 Salute Philologus, and Julia, Nereus, and
his sister, and Olympas, and all the saints which
are with them.
16 [a]Salute one another with an holy kiss. The
churches of Christ salute you.

Avoid Divisive Persons

17 Now I beseech you, brethren, mark them
[a]which cause divisions and offences contrary to
the doctrine which ye have learned; and [b]avoid
them.
18 For they that are such serve not our Lord
Jesus Christ, but [a]their own belly; and [b]by good
words and fair speeches deceive the hearts of the
simple.
19 For [a]your obedience is come abroad unto
all *men.* I am glad therefore on your behalf: but
yet I would have you [b]wise unto that which is
good, and simple concerning evil.
20 And [a]the God of peace [b]shall bruise Satan
under your feet shortly. [c]The grace of our Lord
Jesus Christ *be* with you. Amen.

Greetings from Paul's Friends

21 [a]Timotheus my workfellow, and [b]Lucius,
and [c]Jason, and [d]Sosipater, my kinsmen, salute
you.
22 I Tertius, who wrote *this* epistle, salute
you in the Lord.
23 [a]Gaius mine host, and of the whole
church, saluteth you. [b]Erastus the chamberlain of
the city saluteth you, and Quartus a brother.
24 [a]The grace of our Lord Jesus Christ *be*
with you all. Amen.

Benediction

25 Now [a]to him that is of power to stablish
you [b]according to my gospel, and the preaching
of Jesus Christ, [c]according to the revelation of
the mystery, [d]which was kept secret since the
world began,
26 But [a]now is made manifest, and by the
scriptures of the prophets, according to the commandment of the everlasting God, made known
to all nations for [b]the obedience of faith:
27 To [a]God only wise, *be* glory through Jesus
Christ for ever. Amen.

13 [a]2 John 1
16 [a]1 Cor. 16:20
17 [a][Acts 15:1] [b][1 Cor. 5:9]
18 [a]Phil. 3:19 [b]Col. 2:4
19 [a]Rom. 1:8 [b]Matt. 10:16
20 [a]Rom. 15:33 [b]Gen. 3:15 [c]1 Cor. 16:23
21 [a]Acts 16:1 [b]Acts 13:1 [c]Acts 17:5 [d]Acts 20:4
23 [a]1 Cor. 1:14 [b]Acts 19:22
24 [a]1 Thess. 5:28
25 [a][Eph. 3:20] [b]Rom. 2:16 [c]Eph. 1:9 [d]Col. 1:26; 2:2; 4:3
26 [a]Eph. 1:9 [b]Rom. 1:5
27 [a]Jude 25

*

16:16 NU *All the churches*
16:18 NU, M omit *Jesus*
16:24 NU omits v. 24.
16:25 M puts Rom. 16:25–27 after Rom. 14:23.

NKJV

13 Greet Rufus, [a]chosen in the Lord, and his
mother and mine.
14 Greet Asyncritus, Phlegon, Hermas,
Patrobas, Hermes, and the brethren who are with
them.
15 Greet Philologus and Julia, Nereus and his
sister, and Olympas, and all the saints who are
with them.
16 [a]Greet one another with a holy kiss. *The
churches of Christ greet you.

Avoid Divisive Persons

17 Now I urge you, brethren, note those [a]who
cause divisions and offenses, contrary to the doctrine which you learned, and [b]avoid them.
18 For those who are such do not serve our
Lord *Jesus Christ, but [a]their own belly, and [b]by
smooth words and flattering speech deceive the
hearts of the simple.
19 For [a]your obedience has become known
to all. Therefore I am glad on your behalf; but I
want you to be [b]wise in what is good, and simple
concerning evil.
20 And [a]the God of peace [b]will crush Satan
under your feet shortly. [c]The grace of our Lord
Jesus Christ *be* with you. Amen.

Greetings from Paul's Friends

21 [a]Timothy, my fellow worker, and [b]Lucius,
[c]Jason, and [d]Sosipater, my countrymen, greet
you.
22 I, Tertius, who wrote *this* epistle, greet you
in the Lord.
23 [a]Gaius, my host and *the host* of the whole
church, greets you. [b]Erastus, the treasurer of the
city, greets you, and Quartus, a brother.
24 [a]The* grace of our Lord Jesus Christ *be*
with you all. Amen.

Benediction

25 *Now [a]to Him who is able to establish you
[b]according to my gospel and the preaching of Jesus Christ, [c]according to the revelation of the
mystery [d]kept secret since the world began
26 but [a]now made manifest, and by the
prophetic Scriptures made known to all nations,
according to the commandment of the everlasting
God, for [b]obedience to the faith—
27 to [a]God, alone wise, *be* glory through Jesus Christ forever. Amen.

KJV

THE FIRST EPISTLE OF PAUL THE APOSTLE TO THE

CORINTHIANS

Greeting

1 Paul, [a]called *to be* an apostle of Jesus Christ [b]through the will of God, and [c]Sosthenes *our* brother,

2 Unto the church of God which is at Corinth, to them that [a]are sanctified in Christ Jesus, [b]called *to be* saints, with all that in every place call upon the name of Jesus Christ [c]our Lord, [d]both their's and our's:

3 [a]Grace *be* unto you, and peace, from God our Father, and *from* the Lord Jesus Christ.

Spiritual Gifts at Corinth

4 [a]I thank my God always on your behalf, for the grace of God which is given you by Jesus Christ;

5 That in every thing ye are enriched by him, [a]in all utterance, and *in* all knowledge;

6 Even as [a]the testimony of Christ was confirmed in you:

7 So that ye come behind in no gift; [a]waiting for the coming of our Lord Jesus Christ:

8 [a]Who shall also confirm you unto the end, [b]*that ye may be* blameless in the day of our Lord Jesus Christ.

9 [a]God *is* faithful, by whom ye were called unto [b]the fellowship of his Son Jesus Christ our Lord.

Sectarianism Is Sin

10 Now I beseech you, brethren, by the name of our Lord Jesus Christ, [a]that ye all speak the same thing, and *that* there be no divisions among you; but *that* ye be perfectly joined together in the same mind and in the same judgment.

11 For it hath been declared unto me of you, my brethren, by them *which are of the house* of Chloe, that there are contentions among you.

12 Now this I say, [a]that every one of you saith, I am of Paul; and I of [b]Apollos; and I of [c]Cephas; and I of Christ.

13 [a]Is Christ divided? was Paul crucified for you? or were ye baptized in the name of Paul?

14 I thank God that I baptized [a]none of you, but [b]Crispus and [c]Gaius;

15 Lest any should say that I had baptized in mine own name.

16 And I baptized also the household of [a]Stephanas: besides, I know not whether I baptized any other.

17 For Christ sent me not to baptize, but to preach the gospel: [a]not with wisdom of words, lest the cross of Christ should be made of none effect.

Christ the Power and Wisdom of God
(cf. Is. 29:14)

18 For the preaching of the cross is to [b]them that perish [a]foolishness; but unto us [c]which are saved it is the [d]power of God.

CHAPTER 1

1 [a]Rom. 1:1 [b]2 Cor. 1:1 [c]Acts 18:17
2 [a][Acts 15:9] [b]Rom. 1:7; Eph. 4:1; 1 Thess. 2:12 [c][1 Cor. 8:6] [d][Rom. 3:22]
3 [a]Rom. 1:7
4 [a]Rom. 1:8
5 [a][1 Cor. 12:8]
6 [a]2 Thess. 1:10; 1 Tim. 2:6; 2 Tim. 1:8; Rev. 1:2
7 [a]Luke 17:30; Rom. 8:19, 23; Phil. 3:20; Titus 2:13; [2 Pet. 3:12]
8 [a]1 Thess. 3:13; 5:23 [b]Phil. 1:6; Col. 1:22; 2:7
9 [a]Deut. 7:9; Is. 49:7; 1 Cor. 10:13; 2 Cor. 1:18; 1 Thess. 5:24; 2 Thess. 3:3 [b][John 15:4]
10 [a]2 Cor. 13:11; 1 Pet. 3:8
12 [a]Matt. 3:8–10; 1 Cor. 3:4 [b]Acts 18:24; 1 Cor. 3:22 [c]John 1:42; 1 Cor. 3:22; 9:5; 15:5
13 [a]2 Cor. 11:4
14 [a]John 4:2 [b]Acts 18:8 [c]Rom. 16:23
16 [a]1 Cor. 16:15, 17
17 [a][1 Cor. 2:1, 4, 13]
18 [a]2 Cor. 2:15 [b]Acts 17:18 [c][1 Cor. 2:14; 15:2] [d]Rom. 1:16; 1 Cor. 1:24

NKJV

THE FIRST EPISTLE OF PAUL THE APOSTLE TO THE

CORINTHIANS

Greeting

1 Paul, [a]called *to be* an apostle of Jesus Christ [b]through the will of God, and [c]Sosthenes *our* brother,

2 To the church of God which is at Corinth, to those who [a]are sanctified in Christ Jesus, [b]called *to be* saints, with all who in every place call on the name of Jesus Christ [c]our Lord, [d]both theirs and ours:

3 [a]Grace to you and peace from God our Father and the Lord Jesus Christ.

Spiritual Gifts at Corinth

4 [a]I thank my God always concerning you for the grace of God which was given to you by Christ Jesus,

5 that you were enriched in every thing by Him [a]in all utterance and all knowledge,

6 even as [a]the testimony of Christ was confirmed in you,

7 so that you come short in no gift, eagerly [a]waiting for the revelation of our Lord Jesus Christ,

8 [a]who will also confirm you to the end, [b]*that you may be* blameless in the day of our Lord Jesus Christ.

9 [a]God *is* faithful, by whom you were called into [b]the fellowship of His Son, Jesus Christ our Lord.

Sectarianism Is Sin

10 Now I plead with you, brethren, by the name of our Lord Jesus Christ, [a]that you all speak the same thing, and *that* there be no divisions among you, but *that* you be perfectly joined together in the same mind and in the same judgment.

11 For it has been declared to me concerning you, my brethren, by those of Chloe's *household,* that there are contentions among you.

12 Now I say this, that [a]each of you says, "I am of Paul," or "I am of [b]Apollos," or "I am of [c]Cephas," or "I am of Christ."

13 [a]Is Christ divided? Was Paul crucified for you? Or were you baptized in the name of Paul?

14 I thank God that I baptized [a]none of you except [b]Crispus and [c]Gaius,

15 lest anyone should say that I had baptized in my own name.

16 Yes, I also baptized the household of [a]Stephanas. Besides, I do not know whether I baptized any other.

17 For Christ did not send me to baptize, but to preach the gospel, [a]not with wisdom of words, lest the cross of Christ should be made of no effect.

Christ the Power and Wisdom of God
(cf. Is. 29:14)

18 For the message of the cross is [a]foolishness to [b]those who are perishing, but to us [c]who are being saved it is the [d]power of God.

KJV

19 For it is written, [a]I WILL DESTROY THE WIS-
DOM OF THE WISE, AND WILL BRING TO NOTHING THE
UNDERSTANDING OF THE PRUDENT.
20 [a]Where *is* the wise? where *is* the scribe?
where *is* the disputer of this world? [b]hath not God
made foolish the wisdom of this world?
21 For after that in the [a]wisdom of God the
world by wisdom knew not God, it pleased God
by the foolishness of preaching to save them that
believe.
22 For the [a]Jews require a sign, and the
Greeks seek after wisdom:
23 But we preach Christ crucified, [a]unto the
Jews a stumblingblock, and unto the Greeks
[b]foolishness;
24 But unto them which are called, both Jews
and Greeks, Christ [a]the power of God, and [b]the
wisdom of God.
25 Because the foolishness of God is wiser
than men; and the weakness of God is stronger
than men.

Glory Only in the Lord

26 For ye see your calling, brethren, how that
[a]not many wise men after the flesh, not many
mighty, not many noble, *are called:*
27 But [a]God hath chosen the foolish things
of the world to confound the wise; and God hath
chosen the weak things of the world to confound
the things which are mighty;
28 And base things of the world, and things
which are despised, hath God chosen, *yea,* and
things which are not, to bring to nought things
that are:
29 That no flesh should glory in his presence.
30 But of him are ye in Christ Jesus, who of
God is made unto us wisdom, and [a]righteousness,
and sanctification, and redemption:
31 That, according as it is written, [a]HE THAT
GLORIETH, LET HIM GLORY IN THE LORD.

Christ Crucified

2 And I, brethren, when I came to you, came
not with excellency of speech or of wisdom,
declaring unto you the testimony of God.
2 For I determined not to know any thing
among you, [a]save Jesus Christ, and him crucified.
3 And [a]I was with you [b]in weakness, and
in fear, and in much trembling.
4 And my speech and my preaching [a]*was*
not with enticing words of man's wisdom, [b]but
in demonstration of the Spirit and of power:
5 That your faith should not stand in the
wisdom of men, but in the [a]power of God.

Spiritual Wisdom

6 Howbeit we speak wisdom among them
that are perfect: yet not the wisdom of this world,
nor of the princes of this world, that come to
nought:
7 But we speak the wisdom of God in a
mystery, *even* the hidden *wisdom,* which God ordained before the world unto our glory:
8 Which none of the princes of this world
knew: for [a]had they known *it,* they would not
have [b]crucified the Lord of glory.
9 But as it is written, [a]EYE HATH NOT SEEN,
NOR EAR HEARD, NEITHER HAVE ENTERED INTO THE
HEART OF MAN, THE THINGS WHICH GOD HATH PRE-
PARED FOR THEM THAT LOVE HIM.
10 But [a]God hath revealed *them* unto us by
his Spirit: for the Spirit searcheth all things, yea,
the deep things of God.
11 For what man knoweth the things of a
man, save the [a]spirit of man which is in him?

19 [a]Is. 29:14 **20** [a]Is. 19:12; 33:18 [b]Job 12:17; Matt. 13:22; 1 Cor. 2:6, 8; 3:18, 19 **21** [a]Dan. 2:20; [Rom. 11:33] **22** [a]Matt. 12:38; Mark 8:11; John 2:18; 4:48 **23** [a]Is. 8:14; Luke 2:34; John 6:60; Gal. 5:11; [1 Pet. 2:8] [b][1 Cor. 2:14] **24** [a][Rom. 1:4] [b]Col. 2:3 **26** [a]John 7:48 **27** [a]Ps. 8:2; Matt. 11:25 **30** [a]Jer. 23:5; 33:16; [2 Cor. 5:21; Phil. 3:9] **31** [a]Jer. 9:23, 24; 2 Cor. 10:17

CHAPTER 2

2 [a]1 Cor. 1:23; Gal. 6:14 **3** [a]Acts 18:1 [b][2 Cor. 4:7] **4** [a]2 Pet. 1:16 [b]Rom. 15:19; 1 Cor. 4:20 **5** [a]Rom. 1:16; 1 Thess. 1:5 **8** [a]Luke 23:34 [b]Matt. 27:33–50 **9** [a][Is. 64:4; 65:17] **10** [a]Matt. 11:25; 13:11; 16:17; [Gal. 1:12; Eph. 3:3, 5] **11** [a]Job 32:8; Eccl. 12:7; [1 Cor. 6:20; James 2:26]

NKJV

19 For it is written:

[a]"I will destroy the wisdom of the wise,
And bring to nothing the understanding
of the prudent."

20 [a]Where *is* the wise? Where *is* the scribe?
Where *is* the disputer of this age? [b]Has not God
made foolish the wisdom of this world?
21 For since, in the [a]wisdom of God, the
world through wisdom did not know God, it
pleased God through the foolishness of the message preached to save those who believe.
22 For [a]Jews request a sign, and Greeks seek
after wisdom;
23 but we preach Christ crucified, [a]to the
Jews a stumbling block and to the *Greeks
[b]foolishness,
24 but to those who are called, both Jews and
Greeks, Christ [a]the power of God and [b]the wisdom of God.
25 Because the foolishness of God is wiser
than men, and the weakness of God is stronger
than men.

Glory Only in the Lord

26 For you see your calling, brethren, [a]that
not many wise according to the flesh, not many
mighty, not many noble, *are called.*
27 But [a]God has chosen the foolish things of
the world to put to shame the wise, and God has
chosen the weak things of the world to put to
shame the things which are mighty;
28 and the base things of the world and the
things which are despised God has chosen, and
the things which are not, to bring to nothing the
things that are,
29 that no flesh should glory in His presence.
30 But of Him you are in Christ Jesus, who
became for us wisdom from God—and [a]righ-
teousness and sanctification and redemption—
31 that, as it is written, *[a]"He who glories, let*
him glory in the LORD."

Christ Crucified

2 And I, brethren, when I came to you, did not
come with excellence of speech or of wisdom
declaring to you the *testimony of God.
2 For I determined not to know anything
among you [a]except Jesus Christ and Him crucified.
3 [a]I was with you [b]in weakness, in fear, and
in much trembling.
4 And my speech and my preaching [a]*were*
not with persuasive words of *human wisdom,
[b]but in demonstration of the Spirit and of power,
5 that your faith should not be in the wisdom of men but in the [a]power of God.

Spiritual Wisdom

6 However, we speak wisdom among those
who are mature, yet not the wisdom of this age,
nor of the rulers of this age, who are coming to
nothing.
7 But we speak the wisdom of God in a
mystery, the hidden *wisdom* which God ordained
before the ages for our glory,
8 which none of the rulers of this age knew;
for [a]had they known, they would not have [b]cruci-
fied the Lord of glory.
9 But as it is written:

[a]"Eye has not seen, nor ear heard,
Nor have entered into the heart of man
The things which God has prepared for
those who love Him."

10 But [a]God has revealed *them* to us through
His Spirit. For the Spirit searches all things, yes,
the deep things of God.
11 For what man knows the things of a man
except the [a]spirit of the man which is in him?

1:23 NU *Gentiles*
2:1 NU *mystery*
2:4 NU omits *human*

KJV

[b]even so the things of God knoweth no man, but
the Spirit of God.
12 Now we have received, not the spirit of
the world, but [a]the spirit which is of God; that
we might know the things that are freely given
to us of God.
13 Which things also we speak, not in the
words which man's wisdom teacheth, but which
the Holy Ghost teacheth; comparing spiritual
things with spiritual.
14 [a]But the natural man receiveth not the
things of the Spirit of God: for they are foolishness
unto him: neither can he know *them,* because they
are spiritually discerned.
15 But he that is spiritual judgeth all things,
yet he himself is judged of no man.
16 [a]For who hath known the mind of the
Lord, that he may instruct him? [b]But we have
the mind of Christ.

Sectarianism Is Carnal

3 And I, brethren, could not speak unto you as
unto spiritual, but as unto carnal, *even* as unto
[a]babes in Christ.
2 I have fed you with [a]milk, and not with
meat: [b]for hitherto ye were not able *to bear it,*
neither yet now are ye able.
3 For ye are yet carnal: for whereas *there
is* among you envying, and strife, and divisions,
are ye not carnal, and walk as men?
4 For while one saith, I am of Paul; and another, I *am* of Apollos; are ye not carnal?

Watering, Working, Warning

5 Who then is Paul, and who *is* Apollos, but
[a]ministers by whom ye believed, even as the Lord
gave to every man?
6 [a]I have planted, [b]Apollos watered; [c]but
God gave the increase.
7 So then [a]neither is he that planteth any
thing, neither he that watereth; but God that giveth the increase.
8 Now he that planteth and he that watereth
are one: [a]and every man shall receive his own
reward according to his own labour.
9 For [a]we are labourers together with God:
ye are God's husbandry, *ye are* [b]God's building.
10 [a]According to the grace of God which is
given unto me, as a wise masterbuilder, I have
laid [b]the foundation, and another buildeth thereon. But let every man take heed how he buildeth
thereupon.
11 For other foundation can no man lay than
[a]that is laid, [b]which is Jesus Christ.
12 Now if any man build upon this foundation gold, silver, precious stones, wood, hay,
stubble;
13 Every man's work shall be made manifest:
for the day [a]shall declare it, because [b]it shall be
revealed by fire; and the fire shall try every man's
work of what sort it is.
14 If any man's work abide which he hath
built thereupon, he shall receive a reward.
15 If any man's work shall be burned, he
shall suffer loss: but he himself shall be saved;
yet so as by fire.
16 [a]Know ye not that ye are the temple of
God, and *that* the Spirit of God dwelleth in
you?
17 If any man defile the temple of God, him
shall God destroy; for the temple of God is holy,
which *temple* ye are.

Avoid Worldly Wisdom

18 [a]Let no man deceive himself. If any man
among you seemeth to be wise in this world, let
him become a fool, that he may be wise.
19 For the wisdom of this world is foolishness
with God. For it is written, [a]He taketh the wise
in their own craftiness.
20 And again, [a]The Lord knoweth the
thoughts of the wise, that they are vain.

11 [b]Rom. 11:33
12 [a][Rom. 8:15]
14 [a]Matt. 16:23
16 [a]Job 15:8; Is. 40:13; Rom. 11:34 [b][John 15:15]

CHAPTER 3

1 [a]1 Cor. 2:6; Eph. 4:14; Heb. 5:13
2 [a]Heb. 5:12; 1 Pet. 2:2 [b]John 16:12
5 [a]Rom. 15:16; 2 Cor. 3:3, 6; 4:1; 5:18; 6:4; Eph. 3:7; Col. 1:25; 1 Tim. 1:12
6 [a]Acts 18:4; 1 Cor. 4:15; 9:1; 15:1; 2 Cor. 10:14 [b]Acts 18:24–27; 1 Cor. 1:12 [c][2 Cor. 3:5]
7 [a]2 Cor. 12:11; [Gal. 6:3]
8 [a]Ps. 62:12; Rom. 2:6
9 [a]Mark 16:20; Acts 15:4; 2 Cor. 6:1 [b][1 Cor. 3:16; Eph. 2:20–22]; Col. 2:7; Heb. 3:3, 4; [1 Pet. 2:5]
10 [a]Rom. 1:5 [b]1 Cor. 4:15
11 [a]Is. 28:16; Matt. 16:18; 2 Cor. 11:4 [b]Eph. 2:20; 1 Pet. 2:4
13 [a]1 Pet. 1:7 [b]Mal. 3:1–3; Luke 2:35
16 [a]Rom. 8:9; 1 Cor. 6:19; 2 Cor. 6:16; Eph. 2:21
18 [a]Prov. 3:7
19 [a]Job 5:13
20 [a]Ps. 94:11

*2:13 NU omits *Holy*

NKJV

[b]Even so no one knows the things of God except
the Spirit of God.
12 Now we have received, not the spirit of
the world, but [a]the Spirit who is from God, that
we might know the things that have been freely
given to us by God.
13 These things we also speak, not in words
which man's wisdom teaches but which the *Holy
Spirit teaches, comparing spiritual things with
spiritual.
14 [a]But the natural man does not receive the
things of the Spirit of God, for they are foolishness
to him; nor can he know *them,* because they are
spiritually discerned.
15 But he who is spiritual judges all things,
yet he himself is *rightly* judged by no one.
16 For [a]*"who has known the mind of the
Lord that he may instruct Him?"* [b]But we have
the mind of Christ.

Sectarianism Is Carnal

3 And I, brethren, could not speak to you as to
spiritual *people* but as to carnal, as to [a]babes
in Christ.
2 I fed you with [a]milk and not with solid
food; [b]for until now you were not able *to receive
it,* and even now you are still not able;
3 for you are still carnal. For where *there
are* envy, strife, and divisions among you, are you
not carnal and behaving like *mere* men?
4 For when one says, "I am of Paul," and
another, "I *am* of Apollos," are you not carnal?

Watering, Working, Warning

5 Who then is Paul, and who *is* Apollos, but
[a]ministers through whom you believed, as the
Lord gave to each one?
6 [a]I planted, [b]Apollos watered, [c]but God
gave the increase.
7 So then [a]neither he who plants is anything, nor he who waters, but God who gives the
increase.
8 Now he who plants and he who waters
are one, [a]and each one will receive his own reward according to his own labor.
9 For [a]we are God's fellow workers; you are
God's field, *you are* [b]God's building.
10 [a]According to the grace of God which was
given to me, as a wise master builder I have laid
[b]the foundation, and another builds on it. But let
each one take heed how he builds on it.
11 For no other foundation can anyone lay
than [a]that which is laid, [b]which is Jesus Christ.
12 Now if anyone builds on this foundation
with gold, silver, precious stones, wood, hay,
straw,
13 each one's work will become clear; for the
Day [a]will declare it, because [b]it will be revealed
by fire; and the fire will test each one's work, of
what sort it is.
14 If anyone's work which he has built on *it*
endures, he will receive a reward.
15 If anyone's work is burned, he will suffer
loss; but he himself will be saved, yet so as
through fire.
16 [a]Do you not know that you are the temple
of God and *that* the Spirit of God dwells in you?
17 If anyone defiles the temple of God, God
will destroy him. For the temple of God is holy,
which *temple* you are.

Avoid Worldly Wisdom

18 [a]Let no one deceive himself. If anyone
among you seems to be wise in this age, let him
become a fool that he may become wise.
19 For the wisdom of this world is foolishness
with God. For it is written, [a]*"He catches the wise
in their own craftiness"*;
20 and again, [a]*"The Lord knows the
thoughts of the wise, that they are futile."*

KJV

21 Therefore let no man glory in men. For
[a]all things are your's;
22 Whether Paul, or Apollos, or Cephas, or
the world, or life, or death, or things present, or
things to come; all are your's;
23 And [a]ye are Christ's; and Christ *is* God's.

Stewards of the Mysteries of God

4 Let a man so account of us, as of [a]the ministers of Christ, [b]and stewards of the mysteries
of God.
2 Moreover it is required in stewards, that
a man be found faithful.
3 But with me it is a very small thing that I
should be judged of you, or of man's judgment:
yea, I judge not mine own self.
4 For I know nothing by myself; yet am I
not hereby justified: but he that judgeth me is the
Lord.
5 [a]Therefore judge nothing before the time,
until the Lord come, who both will bring to [b]light
the hidden things of darkness, and will make
[c]manifest the counsels of the hearts: and [d]then
shall every man have praise of God.

Fools for Christ's Sake

6 And these things, brethren, I have in a figure transferred to myself and *to* Apollos for your
sakes; that ye might learn in us not to think *of*
men above that which is written, that no one of
you be puffed up for one against another.
7 For who maketh thee to differ *from an-*
other? and [a]what hast thou that thou didst not
receive? now if thou didst receive *it,* why dost
thou glory, as if thou hadst not received *it?*
8 Now ye are full, [a]now ye are rich, ye have
reigned as kings without us: and I would to God
ye did reign, that we also might reign with you.
9 For I think that God hath set forth us the
apostles last, as it were appointed to death: for
we are made a [a]spectacle unto the world, and to
angels, and to men.
10 We *are* [a]fools for Christ's sake, but ye *are*
wise in Christ; [b]we *are* weak, but ye *are* strong;
ye *are* honourable, but we *are* despised.
11 Even unto this present hour we both hunger, and thirst, and are naked, and are buffeted,
and have no certain dwellingplace;
12 [a]And labour, working with our own
hands: [b]being reviled, we bless; being persecuted,
we suffer it:
13 Being defamed, we intreat: [a]we are made
as the filth of the world, *and are* the offscouring
of all things unto this day.

Paul's Paternal Care

14 I write not these things to shame you, but
[a]as my beloved sons I warn *you.*
15 For though ye have ten thousand instruc-
ters in Christ, yet *have ye* not many fathers: for
[a]in Christ Jesus I have begotten you through the
gospel.
16 Wherefore I beseech you, [a]be ye followers
of me.
17 For this cause have I sent unto you [a]Timo-
theus, [b]who is my beloved son, and faithful in
the Lord, who shall bring you [c]into remembrance
of my ways which be in Christ, as I [d]teach every
where [e]in every church.
18 [a]Now some are puffed up, as though I
would not come to you.
19 [a]But I will come to you shortly, [b]if the
Lord will, and will know, not the speech of them
which are puffed up, but the power.
20 For [a]the kingdom of God *is* not in word,
but in [b]power.
21 What will ye? [a]shall I come unto you with
a rod, or in love, and *in* the spirit of meekness?

Immorality Defiles the Church

5 It is reported commonly *that there is* fornication among you, and such fornication as is

---

21 [a][2 Cor. 4:5]
23 [a][Rom. 14:8]; 1 Cor. 15:23; 2 Cor. 10:7; [Gal. 3:29]

CHAPTER 4

1 [a]Matt. 24:45; Rom. 13:6; 2 Cor. 3:6; Col. 1:25 [b]Luke 12:42; 1 Cor. 9:17; Titus 1:7; 1 Pet. 4:10
5 [a]Matt. 7:1; Rom. 2:1; [Rev. 20:12] [b]Matt. 10:26 [c]1 Cor. 3:13 [d]Rom. 2:29; 1 Cor. 3:8; [2 Cor. 5:10]
7 [a]John 3:27; Rom. 12:3, 6; 1 Pet. 4:10
8 [a]Rev. 3:17
9 [a]Heb. 10:33
10 [a]Acts 17:18; 26:24; 1 Cor. 1:18 [b]1 Cor. 2:3; 2 Cor. 13:9
12 [a]Acts 18:3; 20:34 [b]Matt. 5:44
13 [a]Lam. 3:45
14 [a]2 Cor. 6:13; 12:14; 1 Thess. 2:11; 1 John 2:1; 3 John 4
15 [a]Num. 11:12; Acts 18:11; 1 Cor. 3:8; Gal. 4:19; Philem. 10
16 [a][1 Cor. 11:1]; Phil. 3:17; 4:9; [1 Thess. 1:6]; 2 Thess. 3:9
17 [a]Acts 19:22; Phil. 2:19 [b]1 Cor. 4:14; 1 Tim. 1:2, 18; 2 Tim. 1:2 [c]1 Cor. 11:2 [d]1 Cor. 7:17; Titus 1:5 [e]1 Cor. 14:33
18 [a]1 Cor. 5:2
19 [a]Acts 19:21; 20:2; 1 Cor. 11:34; 16:5, 7–9; 2 Cor. 1:15 [b]Acts 18:21; Heb. 6:3; James 4:15
20 [a]1 Thess. 1:5 [b]1 Cor. 2:4
21 [a]2 Cor. 10:2

---

*
4:3 Lit. *day*

NKJV

21 Therefore let no one boast in men. For [a]all
things are yours:
22 whether Paul or Apollos or Cephas, or the
world or life or death, or things present or things
to come—all are yours.
23 And [a]you *are* Christ's, and Christ *is* God's.

Stewards of the Mysteries of God

4 Let a man so consider us, as [a]servants of
Christ [b]and stewards of the mysteries of God.
2 Moreover it is required in stewards that
one be found faithful.
3 But with me it is a very small thing that I
should be judged by you or by a human *court.
In fact, I do not even judge myself.
4 For I know of nothing against myself, yet
I am not justified by this; but He who judges me
is the Lord.
5 [a]Therefore judge nothing before the time,
until the Lord comes, who will both bring to [b]light
the hidden things of darkness and [c]reveal the
counsels of the hearts. [d]Then each one's praise
will come from God.

Fools for Christ's Sake

6 Now these things, brethren, I have figura-
tively transferred to myself and Apollos for your
sakes, that you may learn in us not to think beyond what is written, that none of you may be
puffed up on behalf of one against the other.
7 For who makes you differ *from another?*
And [a]what do you have that you did not receive?
Now if you did indeed receive *it,* why do you boast
as if you had not received *it?*
8 You are already full! [a]You are already
rich! You have reigned as kings without us—and
indeed I could wish you did reign, that we also
might reign with you!
9 For I think that God has displayed us, the
apostles, last, as men condemned to death; for
we have been made a [a]spectacle to the world, both
to angels and to men.
10 We *are* [a]fools for Christ's sake, but you
are wise in Christ! [b]We *are* weak, but you *are*
strong! You *are* distinguished, but we *are*
dishonored!
11 To the present hour we both hunger and
thirst, and we are poorly clothed, and beaten, and
homeless.
12 [a]And we labor, working with our own
hands. [b]Being reviled, we bless; being persecuted,
we endure;
13 being defamed, we entreat. [a]We have
been made as the filth of the world, the offscouring of all things until now.

Paul's Paternal Care

14 I do not write these things to shame you,
but [a]as my beloved children I warn *you.*
15 For though you might have ten thousand
instructors in Christ, yet *you do* not *have* many
fathers; for [a]in Christ Jesus I have begotten you
through the gospel.
16 Therefore I urge you, [a]imitate me.
17 For this reason I have sent [a]Timothy to
you, [b]who is my beloved and faithful son in the
Lord, who will [c]remind you of my ways in Christ,
as I [d]teach everywhere [e]in every church.
18 [a]Now some are puffed up, as though I
were not coming to you.
19 [a]But I will come to you shortly, [b]if the
Lord wills, and I will know, not the word of those
who are puffed up, but the power.
20 For [a]the kingdom of God *is* not in word
but in [b]power.
21 What do you want? [a]Shall I come to you
with a rod, or in love and a spirit of gentleness?

Immorality Defiles the Church

5 It is actually reported *that there is* sexual immorality among you, and such sexual immo-

KJV

not so much as named among the Gentiles, that
one should have his father's [a]wife.
2 [a]And ye are puffed up, and have not rather
[b]mourned, that he that hath done this deed might
be taken away from among you.
3 [a]For I verily, as absent in body, but present in spirit, have judged already, as though I were
present, *concerning* him that hath so done this
deed,
4 In the [a]name of our Lord Jesus Christ,
when ye are gathered together, and my spirit,
[b]with the power of our Lord Jesus Christ,
5 [a]To deliver such an one unto [b]Satan for
the destruction of the flesh, that the spirit may
be saved in the day of the Lord Jesus.
6 [a]Your glorying *is* not good. Know ye not
that [b]a little leaven leaveneth the whole lump?
7 Purge out therefore the old leaven, that
ye may be a new lump, as ye are unleavened. For
even [a]Christ our [b]passover is sacrificed for us:
8 Therefore [a]let us keep the feast, [b]not with
old leaven, neither [c]with the leaven of malice and
wickedness; but with the unleavened *bread* of sincerity and truth.

Immorality Must Be Judged

9 I wrote unto you in an epistle [a]not to company with fornicators:
10 Yet not altogether with the fornicators of
this world, or with the covetous, or extortioners,
or with idolaters; for then must ye needs go [a]out
of the world.
11 But now I have written unto you not to
keep company, [a]if any man that is called a brother
be a fornicator, or covetous, or an idolater, or a
railer, or a drunkard, or an extortioner; with such
an one [b]no not to eat.
12 For what have I to do to judge them also
that are without? do not ye judge them that are
within?
13 But them that are without God judgeth.
Therefore [a]PUT AWAY FROM AMONG YOURSELVES
THAT WICKED PERSON.

Do Not Sue the Brethren

6 Dare any of you, having a matter against another, go to law before the unjust, and not
before the [a]saints?
2 Do ye not know that [a]the saints shall
judge the world? and if the world shall be judged
by you, are ye unworthy to judge the smallest
matters?
3 Know ye not that we shall [a]judge angels?
how much more things that pertain to this
life?
4 If then ye have judgments of things pertaining to this life, set them to judge who are least
esteemed in the church.
5 I speak to your shame. Is it so, that there
is not a wise man among you? no, not one that
shall be able to judge between his brethren?
6 But brother goeth to law with brother, and
that before the unbelievers.
7 Now therefore there is utterly a fault
among you, because ye go to law one with
another. [a]Why do ye not rather take wrong?
why do ye not rather *suffer yourselves to* be
defrauded?
8 Nay, ye do wrong, and defraud, and that
your brethren.
9 Know ye not that the unrighteous shall not
inherit the kingdom of God? Be not deceived:
[a]neither fornicators, nor idolaters, nor adulterers,
nor effeminate, nor abusers of themselves with
mankind,
10 Nor thieves, nor covetous, nor drunkards,
nor revilers, nor extortioners, shall inherit the
kingdom of God.
11 And such were [a]some of you: [b]but ye are
washed, but ye are sanctified, but ye are justified
in the name of the Lord Jesus, and by the Spirit
of our God.

NKJV

rality as is not even *named among the Gentiles—
that a man has his father's [a]wife!
2 [a]And you are puffed up, and have not
rather [b]mourned, that he who has done this deed
might be taken away from among you.
3 [a]For I indeed, as absent in body but present in spirit, have already judged (as though I
were present) him who has so done this deed.
4 In the [a]name of our Lord Jesus Christ,
when you are gathered together, along with my
spirit, [b]with the power of our Lord Jesus Christ,
5 [a]deliver such a one to [b]Satan for the destruction of the flesh, that his spirit may be saved
in the day of the Lord *Jesus.
6 [a]Your glorying *is* not good. Do you not
know that [b]a little leaven leavens the whole lump?
7 Therefore purge out the old leaven, that
you may be a new lump, since you truly are unleavened. For indeed [a]Christ, our [b]Passover, was
sacrificed *for us.
8 Therefore [a]let us keep the feast, [b]not with
old leaven, nor [c]with the leaven of malice and
wickedness, but with the unleavened *bread* of sincerity and truth.

Immorality Must Be Judged

9 I wrote to you in my epistle [a]not to keep
company with sexually immoral people.
10 Yet *I* certainly *did* not *mean* with the sexually immoral people of this world, or with the
covetous, or extortioners, or idolaters, since then
you would need to go [a]out of the world.
11 But now I have written to you not to keep
company [a]with anyone named a brother, who is
sexually immoral, or covetous, or an idolater, or
a reviler, or a drunkard, or an extortioner—[b]not
even to eat with such a person.
12 For what *have* I *to do* with judging those
also who are outside? Do you not judge those who
are inside?
13 But those who are outside God judges.
Therefore [a]*"put away from yourselves the evil
person."*

Do Not Sue the Brethren

6 Dare any of you, having a matter against another, go to law before the unrighteous, and
not before the [a]saints?
2 Do you not know that [a]the saints will
judge the world? And if the world will be judged
by you, are you unworthy to judge the smallest
matters?
3 Do you not know that we shall [a]judge angels? How much more, things that pertain to this
life?
4 If then you have judgments concerning
things pertaining to this life, do you appoint those
who are least esteemed by the church to judge?
5 I say this to your shame. Is it so, that there
is not a wise man among you, not even one, who
will be able to judge between his brethren?
6 But brother goes to law against brother,
and that before unbelievers!
7 Now therefore, it is already an utter failure for you that you go to law against one another.
[a]Why do you not rather accept wrong? Why do
you not rather *let yourselves* be cheated?
8 No, you yourselves do wrong and cheat,
and *you do* these things *to your* brethren!
9 Do you not know that the unrighteous will
not inherit the kingdom of God? Do not be deceived. [a]Neither fornicators, nor idolaters, nor
adulterers, nor *homosexuals, nor sodomites,
10 nor thieves, nor covetous, nor drunkards,
nor revilers, nor extortioners will inherit the kingdom of God.
11 And such were [a]some of you. [b]But you
were washed, but you were sanctified, but you
were justified in the name of the Lord Jesus and
by the Spirit of our God.

CHAPTER 5

1 [a]Lev. 18:6–8; Deut. 22:30; 27:20
2 [a]1 Cor. 4:18 [b]2 Cor. 7:7–10
3 [a]Col. 2:5; 1 Thess. 2:17
4 [a][Matt. 18:20] [b][Matt. 16:19; John 20:23]; 2 Cor. 12:9
5 [a]Ps. 109:6; Prov. 23:14; Luke 22:31; 1 Tim. 1:20 [b][Acts 26:18]
6 [a]1 Cor. 3:21 [b]Hos. 7:4; Matt. 16:6, 12; Gal. 5:9; 2 Tim. 2:17
7 [a]Is. 53:7 [b]John 19:14
8 [a]Ex. 12:15 [b]Deut. 16:3 [c]Matt. 16:6
9 [a]2 Cor. 6:14; Eph. 5:11; 2 Thess. 3:6
10 [a]John 17:15
11 [a]Matt. 18:17 [b]Gal. 2:12
13 [a]Deut. 13:5; 17:7, 12; 19:19; 21:21; 22:21, 24; 24:7; 1 Cor. 5:2

CHAPTER 6

1 [a]Dan. 7:22; Matt. 19:28
2 [a]Ps. 49:14
3 [a]2 Pet. 2:4
7 [a][Prov. 20:22]
9 [a]Acts 20:32; [1 Cor. 15:50]; Gal. 5:21; Eph. 5:5; 1 Tim. 1:9
11 [a][1 Cor. 12:2; Col. 3:5–7; Titus 3:3–7] [b]Heb. 10:22

*

5:1 NU omits *named*
5:5 NU omits *Jesus*
5:7 NU omits *for us*
6:9 *catamites,* those submitting to homosexuals

KJV

Glorify God in Body and Spirit

12 [a]All things are lawful unto me, but all things are not expedient: all things are lawful for me, but I will not be brought under the power of any.

13 [a]Meats for the belly, and the belly for meats: but God shall destroy both it and them. Now the body *is* not for [b]fornication, but [c]for the Lord; [d]and the Lord for the body.

14 And [a]God hath both raised up the Lord, and will also raise up us [b]by his own power.

15 Know ye not that [a]your bodies are the members of Christ? shall I then take the members of Christ, and make *them* the members of an harlot? God forbid.

16 What? know ye not that he which is joined to an harlot is one body? for [a]TWO, saith he, SHALL BE ONE FLESH.

17 [a]But he that is joined unto the Lord is one spirit.

18 [a]Flee fornication. Every sin that a man doeth is without the body; but he that committeth fornication sinneth [b]against his own body.

19 What? [a]know ye not that your body is the temple of the Holy Ghost *which is* in you, which ye have of God, [b]and ye are not your own?

20 For [a]ye are bought with a price: therefore glorify God in your body, and in your spirit, which are God's.

Principles of Marriage

7 Now concerning the things whereof ye wrote unto me: [a]*It is* good for a man not to touch a woman.

2 Nevertheless, *to avoid* fornication, let every man have his own wife, and let every woman have her own husband.

3 [a]Let the husband render unto the wife due benevolence: and likewise also the wife unto the husband.

4 The wife hath not power of her own body, but the husband: and likewise also the husband hath not power of his own body, but the wife.

5 [a]Defraud ye not one the other, except *it be* with consent for a time, that ye may give yourselves to fasting and prayer; and come together again, that [b]Satan tempt you not for your incontinency.

6 But I speak this by permission, [a]*and* not of commandment.

7 For [a]I would that all men were even as I myself. But every man hath his proper gift of God, one after this manner, and another after that.

8 I say therefore to the unmarried and widows, [a]It is good for them if they abide even as I.

9 But [a]if they cannot contain, let them marry: for it is better to marry than to burn.

Keep Your Marriage Vows

10 And unto the married I command, *yet* not I, but the [a]Lord, [b]Let not the wife depart from *her* husband:

11 But and if she depart, let her remain unmarried, or be reconciled to *her* husband: and let not the husband put away *his* wife.

12 But to the rest speak I, not the Lord: If any brother hath a wife that believeth not, and she be pleased to dwell with him, let him not put her away.

13 And the woman which hath an husband that believeth not, and if he be pleased to dwell with her, let her not leave him.

14 For the unbelieving husband is sanctified by the wife, and the unbelieving wife is sanctified by the husband: else [a]were your children unclean; but now are they holy.

15 But if the unbelieving depart, let him de-

12 [a]1 Cor. 10:23
13 [a]Matt. 15:17; [Rom. 14:17]; Col. 2:22 [b]1 Cor. 5:1; Gal. 5:19; Eph. 5:3; Col. 3:5; 1 Thess. 4:3 [c]1 Thess. 4:3 [d][Eph. 5:23]
14 [a]Rom. 6:5, 8; 2 Cor. 4:14 [b]Eph. 1:19
15 [a]Rom. 12:5; 1 Cor. 6:13; 12:27; Eph. 5:30
16 [a]Gen. 2:24; Matt. 19:5; Mark 10:8; Eph. 5:31
17 [a][John 17:21–23; Rom. 8:9–11]; 1 Cor. 6:15; [Gal. 2:20]; Eph. 4:4
18 [a]Rom. 6:12; 1 Cor. 6:9; 2 Cor. 12:21; Eph. 5:3; Col. 3:5; Heb. 13:4 [b]Rom. 1:24; 1 Thess. 4:4
19 [a]John 2:21; 1 Cor. 3:16; 2 Cor. 6:16 [b]Rom. 14:7
20 [a]Acts 20:28; 1 Cor. 7:23; Gal. 3:13; 1 Pet. 1:18; 2 Pet. 2:1; Rev. 5:9

CHAPTER 7

1 [a]1 Cor. 7:8, 26
3 [a]Ex. 21:10
5 [a]Joel 2:16 [b]1 Thess. 3:5
6 [a]2 Cor. 8:8
7 [a]Acts 26:29
8 [a]1 Cor. 7:1, 26
9 [a]1 Tim. 5:14
10 [a]Mark 10:6–10 [b]Mal. 2:14; [Matt. 5:32]
14 [a]Ezra 9:2; Mal. 2:15

*————

6:20 NU omits the rest of v. 20.

NKJV

Glorify God in Body and Spirit

12 [a]All things are lawful for me, but all things are not helpful. All things are lawful for me, but I will not be brought under the power of any.

13 [a]Foods for the stomach and the stomach for foods, but God will destroy both it and them. Now the body *is* not for [b]sexual immorality but [c]for the Lord, [d]and the Lord for the body.

14 And [a]God both raised up the Lord and will also raise us up [b]by His power.

15 Do you not know that [a]your bodies are members of Christ? Shall I then take the members of Christ and make *them* members of a harlot? Certainly not!

16 Or do you not know that he who is joined to a harlot is one body *with her*? For [a]*"the two,"* He says, *"shall become one flesh."*

17 [a]But he who is joined to the Lord is one spirit *with Him.*

18 [a]Flee sexual immorality. Every sin that a man does is outside the body, but he who commits sexual immorality sins [b]against his own body.

19 Or [a]do you not know that your body is the temple of the Holy Spirit *who is* in you, whom you have from God, [b]and you are not your own?

20 For [a]you were bought at a price; therefore glorify God in your body *and in your spirit, which are God's.

Principles of Marriage

7 Now concerning the things of which you wrote to me: [a]*It is* good for a man not to touch a woman.

2 Nevertheless, because of sexual immorality, let each man have his own wife, and let each woman have her own husband.

3 [a]Let the husband render to his wife the affection due her, and likewise also the wife to her husband.

4 The wife does not have authority over her own body, but the husband *does.* And likewise the husband does not have authority over his own body, but the wife *does.*

5 [a]Do not deprive one another except with consent for a time, that you may give yourselves to fasting and prayer; and come together again so that [b]Satan does not tempt you because of your lack of self-control.

6 But I say this as a concession, [a]not as a commandment.

7 For [a]I wish that all men were even as I myself. But each one has his own gift from God, one in this manner and another in that.

8 But I say to the unmarried and to the widows: [a]It is good for them if they remain even as I am;

9 but [a]if they cannot exercise self-control, let them marry. For it is better to marry than to burn *with passion.*

Keep Your Marriage Vows

10 Now to the married I command, *yet* not I but the [a]Lord: [b]A wife is not to depart from *her* husband.

11 But even if she does depart, let her remain unmarried or be reconciled to *her* husband. And a husband is not to divorce *his* wife.

12 But to the rest I, not the Lord, say: If any brother has a wife who does not believe, and she is willing to live with him, let him not divorce her.

13 And a woman who has a husband who does not believe, if he is willing to live with her, let her not divorce him.

14 For the unbelieving husband is sanctified by the wife, and the unbelieving wife is sanctified by the husband; otherwise [a]your children would be unclean, but now they are holy.

15 But if the unbeliever departs, let him de-

KJV

part. A brother or a sister is not under bondage
in such *cases:* but God hath called us [a]to peace.
16 For what knowest thou, O wife, whether
thou shalt [a]save *thy* husband? or how knowest
thou, O man, whether thou shalt save *thy* wife?

Live as You Are Called

17 But as God hath distributed to every man,
as the Lord hath called every one, so let him walk.
And [a]so ordain I in all churches.
18 Is any man called being circumcised? let
him not become uncircumcised. Is any called in
uncircumcision? [a]let him not be circumcised.
19 [a]Circumcision is nothing, and uncircumcision is nothing, but [b]the keeping of the commandments of God.
20 Let every man abide in the same calling
wherein he was called.
21 Art thou called *being* a servant? care not
for it: but if thou mayest be made free, use *it*
rather.
22 For he that is called in the Lord, *being* a
servant, is [a]the Lord's freeman: likewise also he
that is called, *being* free, is [b]Christ's servant.
23 [a]Ye are bought with a price; be not ye the
servants of men.
24 Brethren, let every man, wherein he is
called, therein abide with [a]God.

To the Unmarried and Widows

25 Now concerning virgins [a]I have no commandment of the Lord: yet I give my judgment,
as one [b]that hath obtained mercy of the Lord [c]to
be faithful.
26 I suppose therefore that this is good for
the present distress, *I say,* [a]that *it is* good for a
man so to be.
27 Art thou bound unto a wife? seek not to
be loosed. Art thou loosed from a wife? seek not
a wife.
28 But and if thou marry, thou hast not
sinned; and if a virgin marry, she hath not sinned.
Nevertheless such shall have trouble in the flesh:
but I spare you.
29 But [a]this I say, brethren, the time *is* short:
it remaineth, that both they that have wives be
as though they had none;
30 And they that weep, as though they wept
not; and they that rejoice, as though they rejoiced
not; and they that buy, as though they possessed
not;
31 And they that use this world, as not [a]abus-
ing *it:* for [b]the fashion of this world passeth away.
32 But I would have you without carefulness.
[a]He that is unmarried careth for the things that
belong to the Lord, how he may please the Lord:
33 But he that is married careth for the things
that are of the world, how he may please *his* wife.
34 There is difference *also* between a wife
and a virgin. The unmarried woman [a]careth for
the things of the Lord, that she may be holy both
in body and in spirit: but she that is married careth
for the things of the world, how she may please
her husband.
35 And this I speak for your own profit; not
that I may cast a snare upon you, but for that
which is comely, and that ye may attend upon
the Lord without distraction.
36 But if any man think that he behaveth
himself uncomely toward his virgin, if she pass
the flower of *her* age, and need so require, let him
do what he will, he sinneth not: let them marry.
37 Nevertheless he that standeth stedfast in
his heart, having no necessity, but hath power
over his own will, and hath so decreed in his heart
that he will keep his virgin, doeth well.
38 [a]So then he that giveth *her* in marriage
doeth well; but he that giveth *her* not in marriage
doeth better.

15 [a]Rom. 12:18
16 [a]Rom. 11:14; 1 Pet. 3:1
17 [a]1 Cor. 4:17
18 [a]Acts 15:1
19 [a][Rom. 2:27, 29; Gal. 3:28; 5:6; 6:15; Col. 3:11] [b][John 15:14]
22 [a][John 8:36]; Rom. 6:18; Philem. 16 [b][1 Cor. 9:21; Gal. 5:13]; Eph. 6:6; Col. 3:24; 1 Pet. 2:16
23 [a]Lev. 25:42; 1 Cor. 6:20; 1 Pet. 1:18, 19; Rev. 5:9
24 [a][Eph. 6:5–8; Col. 3:22–24]
25 [a]2 Cor. 8:8 [b]2 Cor. 4:1; 1 Tim. 1:13, 16 [c]1 Tim. 1:12
26 [a]1 Cor. 7:1, 8
29 [a][Rom. 13:11]; 1 Cor. 7:31; 1 Pet. 4:7; [2 Pet. 3:8, 9]
31 [a]1 Cor. 9:18 [b]Ps. 39:6; 1 Cor. 7:29; James 1:10; 4:14; 1 Pet. 1:24; 4:7; [1 John 2:17]
32 [a]1 Tim. 5:5
34 [a]Luke 10:40
38 [a]Heb. 13:4

*______

7:34 M adds *also*
7:37 Or *virgin daughter*
7:38 NU *his own virgin*

NKJV

part; a brother or a sister is not under bondage
in such *cases.* But God has called us [a]to peace.
16 For how do you know, O wife, whether
you will [a]save *your* husband? Or how do you
know, O husband, whether you will save *your*
wife?

Live as You Are Called

17 But as God has distributed to each one,
as the Lord has called each one, so let him walk.
And [a]so I ordain in all the churches.
18 Was anyone called while circumcised? Let
him not become uncircumcised. Was anyone
called while uncircumcised? [a]Let him not be
circumcised.
19 [a]Circumcision is nothing and uncircumcision is nothing, but [b]keeping the commandments
of God *is what matters.*
20 Let each one remain in the same calling
in which he was called.
21 Were you called *while* a slave? Do not be
concerned about it; but if you can be made free,
rather use *it.*
22 For he who is called in the Lord *while* a
slave is [a]the Lord's freedman. Likewise he who
is called *while* free is [b]Christ's slave.
23 [a]You were bought at a price; do not become slaves of men.
24 Brethren, let each one remain with [a]God
in that *state* in which he was called.

To the Unmarried and Widows

25 Now concerning virgins: [a]I have no commandment from the Lord; yet I give judgment as
one [b]whom the Lord in His mercy *has made*
[c]trustworthy.
26 I suppose therefore that this is good because of the present distress—[a]that *it is* good for
a man to remain as he is:
27 Are you bound to a wife? Do not seek to
be loosed. Are you loosed from a wife? Do not
seek a wife.
28 But even if you do marry, you have not
sinned; and if a virgin marries, she has not sinned.
Nevertheless such will have trouble in the flesh,
but I would spare you.
29 But [a]this I say, brethren, the time *is* short,
so that from now on even those who have wives
should be as though they had none,
30 those who weep as though they did not
weep, those who rejoice as though they did not
rejoice, those who buy as though they did not
possess,
31 and those who use this world as not
[a]misusing *it.* For [b]the form of this world is passing
away.
32 But I want you to be without care. [a]He
who is unmarried cares for the things of the
Lord—how he may please the Lord.
33 But he who is married cares about the
things of the world—how he may please *his* wife.
34 There *is a difference between a wife and
a virgin. The unmarried woman [a]cares about the
things of the Lord, that she may be holy both in
body and in spirit. But she who is married cares
about the things of the world—how she may
please *her* husband.
35 And this I say for your own profit, not that
I may put a leash on you, but for what is proper,
and that you may serve the Lord without
distraction.
36 But if any man thinks he is behaving im-
properly toward his virgin, if she is past the flower
of youth, and thus it must be, let him do what he
wishes. He does not sin; let them marry.
37 Nevertheless he who stands steadfast in
his heart, having no necessity, but has power over
his own will, and has so determined in his heart
that he will keep his *virgin, does well.
38 [a]So then he who gives **her* in marriage
does well, but he who does not give *her* in marriage does better.

KJV

39 [a]The wife is bound by the law as long as her husband liveth; but if her husband be dead, she is at liberty to be married to whom she will; [b]only in the Lord.

40 But she is happier if she so abide, [a]after my judgment: and [b]I think also that I have the Spirit of God.

Be Sensitive to Conscience

8 Now [a]as touching things offered unto idols, we know that we all have [b]knowledge. [c]Knowledge puffeth up, but charity edifieth.

2 And [a]if any man think that he knoweth any thing, he knoweth nothing yet as he ought to know.

3 But if any man love God, the same is known of him.

4 As concerning therefore the eating of those things that are offered in sacrifice unto idols, we know that [a]an idol *is* nothing in the world, [b]and that *there is* none other God but one.

5 For though there be that are [a]called gods, whether in heaven or in earth, (as there be gods many, and lords many,)

6 But [a]to us *there is but* one God, the Father, [b]of whom *are* all things, and we in him; and [c]one Lord Jesus Christ, [d]by whom *are* all things, and [e]we by him.

7 Howbeit *there is* not in every man that knowledge: for some [a]with conscience of the idol unto this hour eat *it* as a thing offered unto an idol; and their conscience being weak is [b]defiled.

8 But [a]meat commendeth us not to God: for neither, if we eat, are we the better; neither, if we eat not, are we the worse.

9 But [a]take heed lest by any means this liberty of your's become [b]a stumblingblock to them that are weak.

10 For if any man see thee which hast knowledge sit at meat in the idol's temple, shall not [a]the conscience of him which is weak be emboldened to eat those things which are offered to idols;

11 And [a]through thy knowledge shall the weak brother perish, for whom Christ died?

12 But [a]when ye sin so against the brethren, and wound their weak conscience, ye sin against Christ.

13 Wherefore, [a]if meat make my brother to offend, I will eat no flesh while the world standeth, lest I make my brother to offend.

A Pattern of Self-Denial

9 Am [a]I not an apostle? am I not free? [b]have I not seen Jesus Christ our Lord? [c]are not ye my work in the Lord?

2 If I be not an apostle unto others, yet doubtless I am to you: for [a]the seal of mine apostleship are ye in the Lord.

3 Mine answer to them that do examine me is this,

4 [a]Have we not power to eat and to drink?

5 Have we not power to lead about a sister, a wife, as well as other apostles, and *as* [a]the brethren of the Lord, and [b]Cephas?

6 Or I only and Barnabas, [a]have not we power to forbear working?

7 Who [a]goeth a warfare any time at his own charges? who [b]planteth a vineyard, and eateth not of the fruit thereof? or who [c]feedeth a flock, and eateth not of the milk of the flock?

8 Say I these things as a man? or saith not the law the same also?

9 For it is written in the law of Moses, [a]THOU SHALT NOT MUZZLE THE MOUTH OF THE OX THAT TREADETH OUT THE CORN. Doth God take care for oxen?

10 Or saith he *it* altogether for our sakes? For our sakes, no doubt, *this* is written: that [a]he that ploweth should plow in hope; and that he that thresheth in hope should be partaker of his hope.

11 [a]If we have sown unto you spiritual

---

39 [a]Rom. 7:2 [b]2 Cor. 6:14
40 [a]1 Cor. 7:6, 25 [b]1 Thess. 4:8

CHAPTER 8

1 [a]Acts 15:20 [b]Rom. 14:14 [c]Rom. 14:3
2 [a][1 Cor. 13:8–12]
4 [a]Is. 41:24 [b]Deut. 4:35, 39; 6:4
5 [a][John 10:34]
6 [a]Mal. 2:10 [b]Acts 17:28 [c]John 13:13 [d]John 1:3 [e]Rom. 5:11
7 [a][1 Cor. 10:28] [b]Rom. 14:14, 22
8 [a][Rom. 14:17]
9 [a]Gal. 5:13 [b]Rom. 12:13, 21
10 [a]1 Cor. 10:28
11 [a]Rom. 14:15, 20
12 [a]Matt. 25:40
13 [a]Rom. 14:21

CHAPTER 9

1 [a]Acts 9:15 [b]1 Cor. 15:8 [c]1 Cor. 3:6; 4:15
2 [a]2 Cor. 12:12
4 [a][1 Thess. 2:6, 9]
5 [a]Matt. 13:55 [b]Matt. 8:14
6 [a]Acts 4:36
7 [a]2 Cor. 10:4 [b]Deut. 20:6 [c]John 21:15
9 [a]Deut. 25:4
10 [a]2 Tim. 2:6
11 [a]Rom. 15:27

NKJV

39 [a]A wife is bound by law as long as her husband lives; but if her husband dies, she is at liberty to be married to whom she wishes, [b]only in the Lord.

40 But she is happier if she remains as she is, [a]according to my judgment—and [b]I think I also have the Spirit of God.

Be Sensitive to Conscience

8 Now [a]concerning things offered to idols: We know that we all have [b]knowledge. [c]Knowledge puffs up, but love edifies.

2 And [a]if anyone thinks that he knows anything, he knows nothing yet as he ought to know.

3 But if anyone loves God, this one is known by Him.

4 Therefore concerning the eating of things offered to idols, we know that [a]an idol *is* nothing in the world, [b]and that *there is* no other God but one.

5 For even if there are [a]so-called gods, whether in heaven or on earth (as there are many gods and many lords),

6 yet [a]for us *there is* one God, the Father, [b]of whom *are* all things, and we for Him; and [c]one Lord Jesus Christ, [d]through whom *are* all things, and [e]through whom we *live.*

7 However, *there is* not in everyone that knowledge; for some, [a]with consciousness of the idol, until now eat *it* as a thing offered to an idol; and their conscience, being weak, is [b]defiled.

8 But [a]food does not commend us to God; for neither if we eat are we the better, nor if we do not eat are we the worse.

9 But [a]beware lest somehow this liberty of yours become [b]a stumbling block to those who are weak.

10 For if anyone sees you who have knowledge eating in an idol's temple, will not [a]the conscience of him who is weak be emboldened to eat those things offered to idols?

11 And [a]because of your knowledge shall the weak brother perish, for whom Christ died?

12 But [a]when you thus sin against the brethren, and wound their weak conscience, you sin against Christ.

13 Therefore, [a]if food makes my brother stumble, I will never again eat meat, lest I make my brother stumble.

A Pattern of Self-Denial

9 Am [a]I not an apostle? Am I not free? [b]Have I not seen Jesus Christ our Lord? [c]Are you not my work in the Lord?

2 If I am not an apostle to others, yet doubtless I am to you. For you are [a]the seal of my apostleship in the Lord.

3 My defense to those who examine me is this:

4 [a]Do we have no right to eat and drink?

5 Do we have no right to take along a believing wife, as *do* also the other apostles, [a]the brothers of the Lord, and [b]Cephas?

6 Or *is it* only Barnabas and I [a]*who* have no right to refrain from working?

7 Who ever [a]goes to war at his own expense? Who [b]plants a vineyard and does not eat of its fruit? Or who [c]tends a flock and does not drink of the milk of the flock?

8 Do I say these things as a *mere* man? Or does not the law say the same also?

9 For it is written in the law of Moses, [a]*"You shall not muzzle an ox while it treads out the grain."* Is it oxen God is concerned about?

10 Or does He say *it* altogether for our sakes? For our sakes, no doubt, *this* is written, that [a]he who plows should plow in hope, and he who threshes in hope should be partaker of his hope.

11 [a]If we have sown spiritual things for you,

KJV

things, *is it* a great thing if we shall reap your carnal things?

12 If others be partakers of *this* power over you, *are* not we rather? [a]Nevertheless we have not used this power; but suffer all things, [b]lest we should hinder the gospel of Christ.

13 [a]Do ye not know that they which minister about holy things live *of the things* of the [b]temple? and they which wait at the altar are partakers with the altar?

14 Even so [a]hath the Lord ordained [b]that they which preach the gospel should live of the gospel.

15 But [a]I have used none of these things: neither have I written these things, that it should be so done unto me: for [b]*it were* better for me to die, than that any man should make my glorying void.

16 For though I preach the gospel, I have nothing to glory of: for [a]necessity is laid upon me; yea, woe is unto me, if I preach not the gospel!

17 For if I do this thing willingly, [a]I have a reward: but if against my will, [b]a dispensation *of the gospel* is committed unto me.

18 What is my reward then? *Verily* that, [a]when I preach the gospel, I may make the gospel of Christ without charge, that I [b]abuse not my power in the gospel.

Serving All Men

19 For though I be [a]free from all *men,* yet have [b]I made myself servant unto all, [c]that I might gain the more.

20 And [a]unto the Jews I became as a Jew, that I might gain the Jews; to them that are under the law, as under the law, that I might gain them that are under the law;

21 [a]To [b]them that are without law, as without law, [c](being not without law to God, but under the law to Christ,) that I might gain them that are without law.

22 [a]To the weak became I as weak, that I might gain the weak: [b]I am made all things to all *men,* [c]that I might by all means save some.

23 And this I do for the gospel's sake, that I might be partaker thereof with *you.*

Striving for a Crown

24 Know ye not that they which run in a race run all, but one receiveth the prize? [a]So run, that ye may obtain.

25 And every man that striveth for the mastery is temperate in all things. Now they *do it* to obtain a corruptible crown; but we [a]an incorruptible.

26 I therefore so run, [a]not as uncertainly; so fight I, not as one that beateth the air:

27 [a]But I keep under my body, and [b]bring *it* into subjection: lest that by any means, when I have preached to others, I myself should be [c]a castaway.

Old Testament Examples

10 Moreover, brethren, I would not that ye should be ignorant, how that all our fathers were under [a]the cloud, and all passed through [b]the sea;

2 And were all baptized unto Moses in the cloud and in the sea;

3 And did all eat the same [a]spiritual meat;

4 And did all drink the same [a]spiritual drink: for they drank of that spiritual Rock that followed them: and that Rock was Christ.

5 But with many of them God was not well pleased: for they [a]were overthrown in the wilderness.

6 Now these things were our examples, to the intent we should not lust after evil things, as [a]they also lusted.

7 [a]Neither be ye idolaters, as *were* some of them; as it is written, [b]THE PEOPLE SAT DOWN TO EAT AND DRINK, AND ROSE UP TO PLAY.

NKJV

is it a great thing if we reap your material things?

12 If others are partakers of *this* right over you, *are* we not even more? [a]Nevertheless we have not used this right, but endure all things [b]lest we hinder the gospel of Christ.

13 [a]Do you not know that those who minister the holy things eat *of the things* of the [b]temple, and those who serve at the altar partake of *the offerings of* the altar?

14 Even so [a]the Lord has commanded [b]that those who preach the gospel should live from the gospel.

15 But [a]I have used none of these things, nor have I written these things that it should be done so to me; for [b]it *would be* better for me to die than that anyone should make my boasting void.

16 For if I preach the gospel, I have nothing to boast of, for [a]necessity is laid upon me; yes, woe is me if I do not preach the gospel!

17 For if I do this willingly, [a]I have a reward; but if against my will, [b]I have been entrusted with a stewardship.

18 What is my reward then? That [a]when I preach the gospel, I may present the gospel *of Christ without charge, that I [b]may not abuse my authority in the gospel.

Serving All Men

19 For though I am [a]free from all *men,* [b]I have made myself a servant to all, [c]that I might win the more;

20 and [a]to the Jews I became as a Jew, that I might win Jews; to those *who are* under the law, as under the *law, that I might win those *who are* under the law;

21 [a]to [b]those *who are* without law, as without law [c](not being without *law toward God, but under *law toward Christ), that I might win those *who are* without law;

22 [a]to the weak I became *as weak, that I might win the weak. [b]I have become all things to all *men,* [c]that I might by all means save some.

23 Now this I do for the gospel's sake, that I may be partaker of it with *you.*

Striving for a Crown

24 Do you not know that those who run in a race all run, but one receives the prize? [a]Run in such a way that you may obtain *it.*

25 And everyone who competes *for the prize* is temperate in all things. Now they *do it* to obtain a perishable crown, but we *for* [a]an imperishable *crown.*

26 Therefore I run thus: [a]not with uncertainty. Thus I fight: not as *one who* beats the air.

27 [a]But I discipline my body and [b]bring *it* into subjection, lest, when I have preached to others, I myself should become [c]disqualified.

Old Testament Examples

10 Moreover, brethren, I do not want you to be unaware that all our fathers were under [a]the cloud, all passed through [b]the sea,

2 all were baptized into Moses in the cloud and in the sea,

3 all ate the same [a]spiritual food,

4 and all drank the same [a]spiritual drink. For they drank of that spiritual Rock that followed them, and that Rock was Christ.

5 But with most of them God was not well pleased, for *their bodies* [a]were scattered in the wilderness.

6 Now these things became our examples, to the intent that we should not lust after evil things as [a]they also lusted.

7 [a]And do not become idolaters as *were* some of them. As it is written, [b]*"The people sat down to eat and drink, and rose up to play."*

---

12 [a][Acts 18:3; 20:33] [b]2 Cor. 11:12
13 [a]Lev. 6:16, 26; 7:6, 31 [b]Num. 18:8–31
14 [a]Matt. 10:10 [b]Rom. 10:15
15 [a]Acts 18:3; 20:33 [b]2 Cor. 11:10
16 [a][Rom. 1:14]
17 [a]1 Cor. 3:8, 14; 9:18 [b]Gal. 2:7
18 [a]1 Cor. 10:33 [b]1 Cor. 7:31; 9:12
19 [a]1 Cor. 9:1 [b]Gal. 5:13 [c]Matt. 18:15
20 [a]Acts 16:3; 21:23–26
21 [a][Gal. 2:3; 3:2] [b][Rom. 2:12, 14] [c][1 Cor. 7:22]
22 [a]Rom. 14:1; 15:1 [b]1 Cor. 10:33 [c]Rom. 11:14
24 [a]Gal. 2:2
25 [a]James 1:12
26 [a]2 Tim. 2:5
27 [a][Rom. 8:13] [b][Rom. 6:18] [c]Jer. 6:30

CHAPTER 10

1 [a]Ex. 13:21, 22 [b]Ex. 14:21, 22, 29
3 [a]Ex. 16:4, 15, 35
4 [a]Ex. 17:5–7
5 [a]Num. 14:29, 37; 26:65
6 [a]Num. 11:4, 34
7 [a]1 Cor. 5:11; 10:14 [b]Ex. 32:6

---

*
9:18 NU omits *of Christ*
9:20 NU adds *though not being myself under the law*
9:21 NU *God's law* • NU *Christ's law*
9:22 NU omits *as*

KJV

8 [a]Neither let us commit fornication, as [b]some of them committed, and [c]fell in one day three and twenty thousand.
9 Neither let us tempt Christ, as [a]some of them also tempted, and [b]were destroyed of serpents.
10 Neither murmur ye, as [a]some of them also murmured, and [b]were destroyed of [c]the destroyer.
11 Now all these things happened unto them for ensamples: and [a]they are written for our admonition, [b]upon whom the ends of the world are come.
12 Wherefore [a]let him that thinketh he standeth take heed lest he fall.
13 There hath no temptation taken you but such as is common to man: but [a]God *is* faithful, [b]who will not suffer you to be tempted above that ye are able; but will with the temptation also make a way to escape, that ye may be able to bear *it*.

Flee from Idolatry

14 Wherefore, my dearly beloved, [a]flee from idolatry.
15 I speak as to [a]wise men; judge ye what I say.
16 [a]The cup of blessing which we bless, is it not the communion of the blood of Christ? [b]The bread which we break, is it not the communion of the body of Christ?
17 For [a]we *being* many are one bread, *and* one body: for we are all partakers of that one bread.
18 Behold [a]Israel [b]after the flesh: [c]are not they which eat of the sacrifices partakers of the altar?
19 What say I then? [a]that the idol is any thing, or that which is offered in sacrifice to idols is any thing?
20 But *I say*, that the things which the Gentiles [a]sacrifice, [b]they sacrifice to devils, and not to God: and I would not that ye should have fellowship with devils.
21 [a]Ye cannot drink the cup of the Lord, and [b]the cup of devils: ye cannot be partakers of the [c]Lord's table, and of the table of devils.
22 Do we [a]provoke the Lord to jealousy? [b]are we stronger than he?

All to the Glory of God
(cf. Ps. 24:1)

23 All things are lawful for me, but all things are not [a]expedient: all things are lawful for me, but all things edify not.
24 Let no man seek his own, but every man [a]another's *wealth*.
25 [a]Whatsoever is sold in the shambles, *that* eat, asking no question for conscience sake:
26 For [a]THE EARTH *IS* THE LORD'S, AND THE FULNESS THEREOF.
27 If any of them that believe not bid you *to a feast*, and ye be disposed to go; [a]whatsoever is set before you, eat, asking no question for conscience sake.
28 But if any man say unto you, This is offered in sacrifice unto idols, eat not [a]for his sake that shewed it, and for conscience sake: for [b]THE EARTH *IS* THE LORD'S, AND THE FULNESS THEREOF:
29 Conscience, I say, not thine own, but of the other: for [a]why is my liberty judged of another *man's* conscience?
30 For if I by grace be a partaker, why am I evil spoken of for that [a]for which I give thanks?
31 [a]Whether therefore ye eat, or drink, or whatsoever ye do, do all to the glory of God.
32 [a]Give none offence, neither to the Jews, nor to the Gentiles, nor to the church of God:
33 Even [a]as I please all *men* in all *things*, not seeking mine own profit, but the *profit* of many, that they may be saved.

8 [a]Rev. 2:14 [b]Num. 25:1–9 [c]Ps. 106:29
9 [a]Ex. 17:2, 7 [b]Num. 21:6–9
10 [a]Ex. 16:2 [b]Num. 14:37 [c]Ex. 12:23
11 [a]Rom. 15:4 [b]Phil. 4:5
12 [a]Rom. 11:20
13 [a]1 Cor. 1:9 [b]Ps. 125:3
14 [a]2 Cor. 6:17
15 [a]1 Cor. 8:1
16 [a]Matt. 26:26–28 [b]Acts 2:42
17 [a]1 Cor. 12:12, 27
18 [a]Rom. 4:12 [b]Rom. 4:1 [c]Lev. 3:3; 7:6, 14
19 [a]1 Cor. 8:4
20 [a]Lev. 17:7 [b]Deut. 32:17
21 [a]2 Cor. 6:15, 16 [b]Deut. 32:38 [c][1 Cor. 11:23–29]
22 [a]Deut. 32:21 [b]Ezek. 22:14
23 [a]1 Cor. 6:12
24 [a]Phil. 2:4
25 [a][1 Tim. 4:4]
26 [a]Ps. 24:1
27 [a]Luke 10:7, 8
28 [a][1 Cor. 8:7, 10, 12] [b]Ps. 24:1
29 [a]Rom. 14:16
30 [a]Rom. 14:6
31 [a]Col. 3:17
32 [a]Rom. 14:13
33 [a]Rom. 15:2

*

10:11 NU omits *all*
10:23 NU omits *for me*
• See preceding note
10:28 NU omits the rest of v. 28.

NKJV

8 [a]Nor let us commit sexual immorality, as [b]some of them did, and [c]in one day twenty-three thousand fell;
9 nor let us tempt Christ, as [a]some of them also tempted, and [b]were destroyed by serpents;
10 nor complain, as [a]some of them also complained, and [b]were destroyed by [c]the destroyer.
11 Now *all these things happened to them as examples, and [a]they were written for our admonition, [b]upon whom the ends of the ages have come.
12 Therefore [a]let him who thinks he stands take heed lest he fall.
13 No temptation has overtaken you except such as is common to man; but [a]God *is* faithful, [b]who will not allow you to be tempted beyond what you are able, but with the temptation will also make the way of escape, that you may be able to bear *it*.

Flee from Idolatry

14 Therefore, my beloved, [a]flee from idolatry.
15 I speak as to [a]wise men; judge for yourselves what I say.
16 [a]The cup of blessing which we bless, is it not the communion of the blood of Christ? [b]The bread which we break, is it not the communion of the body of Christ?
17 For [a]we, *though* many, are one bread *and* one body; for we all partake of that one bread.
18 Observe [a]Israel [b]after the flesh: [c]Are not those who eat of the sacrifices partakers of the altar?
19 What am I saying then? [a]That an idol is anything, or what is offered to idols is anything?
20 Rather, that the things which the Gentiles [a]sacrifice [b]they sacrifice to demons and not to God, and I do not want you to have fellowship with demons.
21 [a]You cannot drink the cup of the Lord and [b]the cup of demons; you cannot partake of the [c]Lord's table and of the table of demons.
22 Or do we [a]provoke the Lord to jealousy? [b]Are we stronger than He?

All to the Glory of God
(cf. Ps. 24:1)

23 All things are lawful *for me, but not all things are [a]helpful; all things are lawful *for me, but not all things edify.
24 Let no one seek his own, but each one [a]the other's *well-being*.
25 [a]Eat whatever is sold in the meat market, asking no questions for conscience' sake;
26 for [a]*"the earth is the LORD's, and all its fullness."*
27 If any of those who do not believe invites you *to dinner*, and you desire to go, [a]eat whatever is set before you, asking no question for conscience' sake.
28 But if anyone says to you, "This was offered to idols," do not eat it [a]for the sake of the one who told you, and for conscience' sake; *for [b]*"the earth is the LORD's, and all its fullness."*
29 "Conscience," I say, not your own, but that of the other. For [a]why is my liberty judged by another *man's* conscience?
30 But if I partake with thanks, why am I evil spoken of for *the food* [a]over which I give thanks?
31 [a]Therefore, whether you eat or drink, or whatever you do, do all to the glory of God.
32 [a]Give no offense, either to the Jews or to the Greeks or to the church of God,
33 just [a]as I also please all *men* in all *things*, not seeking my own profit, but the *profit* of many, that they may be saved.

KJV

11 Be [a]ye followers of me, even as I also *am* of Christ.

Head Coverings

2 Now I praise you, brethren, that ye remember me in all things, and keep the ordinances, as I delivered *them* to you.

3 But I would have you know, that [a]the head of every man is Christ; and [b]the head of the woman *is* the man; and [c]the head of Christ *is* God.

4 Every man praying or [a]prophesying, having *his* head covered, dishonoureth his head.

5 But every woman that prayeth or prophesieth with *her* head uncovered dishonoureth her head: for that is even all one as if she were [a]shaven.

6 For if the woman be not covered, let her also be shorn: but if it be [a]a shame for a woman to be shorn or shaven, let her be covered.

7 For a man indeed ought not to cover *his* head, forasmuch as [a]he is the image and glory of God: but the woman is the glory of the man.

8 For the man is not of the woman; but the woman [a]of the man.

9 Neither was the man created for the woman; but the woman [a]for the man.

10 For this cause ought the woman to have power on *her* head because of the angels.

11 Nevertheless [a]neither is the man without the woman, neither the woman without the man, in the Lord.

12 For as the woman *is* of the man, even so *is* the man also by the woman; but all things of God.

13 Judge in yourselves: is it comely that a woman pray unto God uncovered?

14 Doth not even nature itself teach you, that, if a man have long hair, it is a shame unto him?

15 But if a woman have long hair, it is a glory to her: for *her* hair is given her for a covering.

16 But [a]if any man seem to be contentious, we have no such custom, [b]neither the churches of God.

Conduct at the Lord's Supper

17 Now in this that I declare *unto you* I praise *you* not, that ye come together not for the better, but for the worse.

18 For first of all, when ye come together in the church, [a]I hear that there be divisions among you: and I partly believe it.

19 For [a]there must be also heresies among you, [b]that they which are approved may be made manifest among you.

20 When ye come together therefore into one place, *this* is not to eat the Lord's supper.

21 For in eating every one taketh before *other* his own supper: and one is hungry, and [a]another is drunken.

22 What? have ye not houses to eat and to drink in? or despise ye [a]the church of God, and [b]shame them that have not? What shall I say to you? shall I praise you in this? I praise *you* not.

Institution of the Lord's Supper
(Matt. 26:26–29; Mark 14:22–25; Luke 22:14–23)

23 For [a]I have received of the Lord that which also I delivered unto you, [b]That the Lord Jesus the *same* night in which he was betrayed took bread:

24 And when he had given thanks, he brake *it,* and said, Take, eat: this is my body, which is broken for you: this do in remembrance of me.

25 After the same manner also *he took* the cup, when he had supped, saying, This cup is the new testament in my blood: this do ye, as oft as ye drink *it,* in remembrance of me.

26 For as often as ye eat this bread, and drink this cup, ye do shew the Lord's death [a]till he come.

NKJV

11 Imitate[a] me, just as I also *imitate* Christ.

Head Coverings

2 Now I praise you, brethren, that you remember me in all things and keep the traditions just as I delivered *them* to you.

3 But I want you to know that [a]the head of every man is Christ, [b]the head of woman *is* man, and [c]the head of Christ *is* God.

4 Every man praying or [a]prophesying, having *his* head covered, dishonors his head.

5 But every woman who prays or prophesies with *her* head uncovered dishonors her head, for that is one and the same as if her head were [a]shaved.

6 For if a woman is not covered, let her also be shorn. But if it is [a]shameful for a woman to be shorn or shaved, let her be covered.

7 For a man indeed ought not to cover *his* head, since [a]he is the image and glory of God; but woman is the glory of man.

8 For man is not from woman, but woman [a]from man.

9 Nor was man created for the woman, but woman [a]for the man.

10 For this reason the woman ought to have *a symbol of* authority on *her* head, because of the angels.

11 Nevertheless, [a]neither *is* man independent of woman, nor woman independent of man, in the Lord.

12 For as woman *came* from man, even so man also *comes* through woman; but all things are from God.

13 Judge among yourselves. Is it proper for a woman to pray to God with her head uncovered?

14 Does not even nature itself teach you that if a man has long hair, it is a dishonor to him?

15 But if a woman has long hair, it is a glory to her; for *her* hair is given *to her for a covering.

16 But [a]if anyone seems to be contentious, we have no such custom, [b]nor *do* the churches of God.

Conduct at the Lord's Supper

17 Now in giving these instructions I do not praise *you,* since you come together not for the better but for the worse.

18 For first of all, when you come together as a church, [a]I hear that there are divisions among you, and in part I believe it.

19 For [a]there must also be factions among you, [b]that those who are approved may be recognized among you.

20 Therefore when you come together in one place, it is not to eat the Lord's Supper.

21 For in eating, each one takes his own supper ahead of *others;* and one is hungry and [a]another is drunk.

22 What! Do you not have houses to eat and drink in? Or do you despise [a]the church of God and [b]shame those who have nothing? What shall I say to you? Shall I praise you in this? I do not praise *you.*

Institution of the Lord's Supper
(Matt. 26:26–29; Mark 14:22–25; Luke 22:14–23)

23 For [a]I received from the Lord that which I also delivered to you: [b]that the Lord Jesus on the *same* night in which He was betrayed took bread;

24 and when He had given thanks, He broke *it* and said, *"Take, eat; this is My body which is *broken for you; do this in remembrance of Me."

25 In the same manner *He* also *took* the cup after supper, saying, "This cup is the new covenant in My blood. This do, as often as you drink *it,* in remembrance of Me."

26 For as often as you eat this bread and drink this cup, you proclaim the Lord's death [a]till He comes.

CHAPTER 11

1 [a]Eph. 5:1
3 [a]Eph. 1:22; 4:15; 5:23; Col. 1:18; 2:19 [b]Gen. 3:16; [Eph. 5:23] [c]John 14:28
4 [a]1 Cor. 12:10
5 [a]Deut. 21:12
6 [a]Num. 5:18
7 [a]Gen. 1:26, 27; 5:1; 9:6; James 3:9
8 [a]Gen. 2:21–23; 1 Tim. 2:13
9 [a]Gen. 2:18
11 [a][Gal. 3:28]
16 [a]1 Tim. 6:4 [b]1 Cor. 7:17
18 [a]1 Cor. 1:10–12; 3:3
19 [a]Matt. 18:7; Luke 17:1; 1 Tim. 4:1; 2 Pet. 2:1 [b][Deut. 13:3]; Luke 2:35; 1 John 2:19
21 [a]2 Pet. 2:13; Jude 12
22 [a]1 Cor. 10:32 [b]James 2:6
23 [a]1 Cor. 15:3; Gal. 1:12; Col. 3:24 [b]Matt. 26:26–28; Mark 14:22–24; Luke 22:17–20; 1 Cor. 10:16
26 [a]John 14:3; [Acts 1:11]

*

11:15 M omits *to her*
11:24 NU omits *Take, eat* • NU omits *broken*

KJV

Examine Yourself

27 Wherefore whosoever shall eat [a]this
bread, and drink *this* cup of the Lord, unworthily,
shall be guilty of the body and blood of the Lord.
28 But [a]let a man examine himself, and so
let him eat of *that* bread, and drink of *that* cup.
29 For he that eateth and drinketh unworthily, eateth and drinketh damnation to himself,
not discerning the Lord's body.
30 For this cause many *are* weak and sickly
among you, and many sleep.
31 For [a]if we would judge ourselves, we
should not be judged.
32 But when we are judged, [a]we are chastened of the Lord, that we should not be condemned with the world.
33 Wherefore, my brethren, when ye [a]come
together to eat, tarry one for another.
34 And if any man hunger, let him eat at
home; that ye come not together unto condemnation. And the rest will I set in order when I come.

Spiritual Gifts: Unity in Diversity

12 Now [a]concerning spiritual *gifts*, brethren,
I would not have you ignorant.
2 Ye know [a]that ye were Gentiles, carried
away unto these [b]dumb idols, even as ye were
led.
3 Wherefore I give you to understand, that
no man speaking by the Spirit of God calleth Jesus
accursed: and [a]*that* no man can say that Jesus
is the Lord, but by the Holy Ghost.
4 Now [a]there are diversities of gifts, but
[b]the same Spirit.
5 [a]And there are differences of administra-
tions, but the same Lord.
6 And there are diversities of operations,
but it is the same God [a]which worketh all in all.
7 But the manifestation of the Spirit is given
to every man to profit withal.
8 For to one is given by the Spirit [a]the word
of wisdom; to another [b]the word of knowledge
by the same Spirit;
9 [a]To another faith by the same Spirit; to
another [b]the gifts of healing by the same Spirit;
10 [a]To another the working of miracles; to
another [b]prophecy; to another [c]discerning of spirits; to another [d]*divers* kinds of tongues; to another
the interpretation of tongues:
11 But all these worketh that one and the
selfsame Spirit, [a]dividing to every man severally
[b]as he will.

Unity and Diversity in One Body
(cf. Eph. 4:1–16)

12 For [a]as the body is one, and hath many
members, and all the members of that one body,
being many, are one body: [b]so also *is* Christ.
13 For [a]by one Spirit are we all baptized into
one body, [b]whether *we be* Jews or Gentiles,
whether *we be* bond or free; and [c]have been all
made to drink into one Spirit.
14 For the body is not one member, but
many.
15 If the foot shall say, Because I am not the
hand, I am not of the body; is it therefore not of
the body?
16 And if the ear shall say, Because I am not
the eye, I am not of the body; is it therefore not
of the body?
17 If the whole body *were* an eye, where *were*
the hearing? If the whole *were* hearing, where
were the smelling?
18 But now hath [a]God set the members every
one of them in the body, [b]as it hath pleased him.
19 And if they were all one member, where
were the body?
20 But now *are they* many members, yet but
one body.
21 And the eye cannot say unto the hand, I

27 [a][John 6:51]
28 [a]Matt. 26:22; 2 Cor. 13:5; Gal. 6:4
31 [a][Ps. 32:5; 1 John 1:9]
32 [a]2 Sam. 7:14; Ps. 94:12; [Heb. 12:5–10; Rev. 3:19]
33 [a]1 Cor. 14:26

CHAPTER 12

1 [a]1 Cor. 12:4; 14:1, 37
2 [a]1 Cor. 6:11; Eph. 2:11; 1 Pet. 4:3 [b]Ps. 115:5; Is. 46:7; Jer. 10:5; Hab. 2:18
3 [a]Matt. 16:17
4 [a]Rom. 12:3–8; 1 Cor. 12:11; Eph. 4:4, 11; Heb. 2:4 [b]Eph. 4:4
5 [a]Rom. 12:6
6 [a]1 Cor. 15:28; Eph. 1:23; 4:6
8 [a]1 Cor. 2:6, 7; 2 Cor. 1:12 [b]Rom. 15:14; [1 Cor. 2:11, 16]; 2 Cor. 8:7
9 [a]Matt. 17:19; [1 Cor. 13:2]; 2 Cor. 4:13 [b]Matt. 10:1; Mark 3:15; 16:18; James 5:14
10 [a]Mark 16:17 [b]Rom. 12:6 [c]1 John 4:1 [d]Acts 2:4–11
11 [a]Rom. 12:6; 2 Cor. 10:13 [b][John 3:8]
12 [a]Rom. 12:4, 5; 1 Cor. 10:17; Eph. 4:4 [b][Gal. 3:16]
13 [a][Rom. 6:5] [b]Rom. 3:22; Gal. 3:28; [Eph. 2:13–18]; Col. 3:11 [c][John 7:37–39]
18 [a]1 Cor. 12:28 [b]Rom. 12:3

*

11:27 NU, M *the blood*
11:29 NU omits *in an unworthy manner* • NU omits *Lord's*
12:2 NU, M *that when*
12:9 NU *one*
12:13 NU omits *into*

NKJV

Examine Yourself

27 Therefore whoever eats [a]this bread or
drinks *this* cup of the Lord in an unworthy manner will be guilty of the body and *blood of the
Lord.
28 But [a]let a man examine himself, and so
let him eat of the bread and drink of the cup.
29 For he who eats and drinks *in an unworthy manner eats and drinks judgment to himself,
not discerning the *Lord's body.
30 For this reason many *are* weak and sick
among you, and many sleep.
31 For [a]if we would judge ourselves, we
would not be judged.
32 But when we are judged, [a]we are chastened by the Lord, that we may not be condemned
with the world.
33 Therefore, my brethren, when you [a]come
together to eat, wait for one another.
34 But if anyone is hungry, let him eat at
home, lest you come together for judgment. And
the rest I will set in order when I come.

Spiritual Gifts: Unity in Diversity

12 Now [a]concerning spiritual *gifts*, brethren,
I do not want you to be ignorant:
2 You know [a]that* you were Gentiles, carried away to these [b]dumb idols, however you were
led.
3 Therefore I make known to you that no
one speaking by the Spirit of God calls Jesus accursed, and [a]no one can say that Jesus is Lord
except by the Holy Spirit.
4 [a]There are diversities of gifts, but [b]the
same Spirit.
5 [a]There are differences of ministries, but
the same Lord.
6 And there are diversities of activities, but
it is the same God [a]who works all in all.
7 But the manifestation of the Spirit is given
to each one for the profit *of all:*
8 for to one is given [a]the word of wisdom
through the Spirit, to another [b]the word of knowledge through the same Spirit,
9 [a]to another faith by the same Spirit, to another [b]gifts of healings by *the same Spirit,
10 [a]to another the working of miracles, to another [b]prophecy, to another [c]discerning of spirits,
to another [d]*different* kinds of tongues, to another
the interpretation of tongues.
11 But one and the same Spirit works all
these things, [a]distributing to each one individually [b]as He wills.

Unity and Diversity in One Body
(cf. Eph. 4:1–16)

12 For [a]as the body is one and has many
members, but all the members of that one body,
being many, are one body, [b]so also *is* Christ.
13 For [a]by one Spirit we were all baptized
into one body—[b]whether Jews or Greeks,
whether slaves or free—and [c]have all been made
to drink *into one Spirit.
14 For in fact the body is not one member
but many.
15 If the foot should say, "Because I am not
a hand, I am not of the body," is it therefore not
of the body?
16 And if the ear should say, "Because I am
not an eye, I am not of the body," is it therefore
not of the body?
17 If the whole body *were* an eye, where
would be the hearing? If the whole *were* hearing,
where *would be* the smelling?
18 But now [a]God has set the members, each
one of them, in the body [b]just as He pleased.
19 And if they *were* all one member, where
would the body *be?*
20 But now indeed *there are* many members,
yet one body.
21 And the eye cannot say to the hand, "I

have no need of thee: nor again the head to the feet, I have no need of you.

22 Nay, much more those members of the body, which seem to be more feeble, are necessary:

23 And those *members* of the body, which we think to be less honourable, upon these we bestow more abundant honour; and our uncomely *parts* have more abundant comeliness.

24 For our comely *parts* have no need: but God hath tempered the body together, having given more abundant honour to that *part* which lacked:

25 That there should be no schism in the body; but *that* the members should have the same care one for another.

26 And whether one member suffer, all the members suffer with it; or one member be honoured, all the members rejoice with it.

27 Now [a]ye are the body of Christ, and [b]members in particular.

28 And [a]God hath set some in the church, first [b]apostles, secondarily [c]prophets, thirdly teachers, after that [d]miracles, then [e]gifts of healings, [f]helps, [g]governments, diversities of tongues.

29 *Are* all apostles? *are* all prophets? *are* all teachers? *are* all workers of miracles?

30 Have all the gifts of healing? do all speak with tongues? do all interpret?

31 But [a]covet earnestly the best gifts: and yet shew I unto you a more excellent way.

The Greatest Gift

13 Though I speak with the tongues of men and of angels, and have not charity, I am become *as* sounding brass, or a tinkling cymbal.

2 And though I have *the gift of* [a]prophecy, and understand all mysteries, and all knowledge; and though I have all faith, [b]so that I could remove mountains, and have not charity, I am nothing.

3 And [a]though I bestow all my goods to feed *the poor,* and though I give my body to be burned, and have not charity, it profiteth me nothing.

4 [a]Charity suffereth long, *and* is [b]kind; charity [c]envieth not; charity vaunteth not itself, is not puffed up,

5 Doth not behave itself unseemly, [a]seeketh not her own, is not easily provoked, thinketh no evil;

6 [a]Rejoiceth not in iniquity, but [b]rejoiceth in the truth;

7 [a]Beareth all things, believeth all things, hopeth all things, endureth all things.

8 Charity never faileth: but whether *there be* prophecies, they shall fail; whether *there be* tongues, they shall cease; whether *there be* knowledge, it shall vanish away.

9 [a]For we know in part, and we prophesy in part.

10 But when that which is perfect is come, then that which is in part shall be done away.

11 When I was a child, I spake as a child, I understood as a child, I thought as a child: but when I became a man, I put away childish things.

12 For [a]now we see through a glass, darkly; but then [b]face to face: now I know in part; but then shall I know even as also I am known.

13 And now abideth faith, hope, charity, these three; but the greatest of these *is* charity.

Prophecy and Tongues

14 Follow after charity, and [a]desire spiritual *gifts,* [b]but rather that ye may prophesy.

2 For he that [a]speaketh in an *unknown* tongue speaketh not unto men, but unto God: for no man understandeth *him;* howbeit in the spirit he speaketh mysteries.

3 But he that prophesieth speaketh unto men *to* [a]edification, and [b]exhortation, and comfort.

27 [a]Rom. 12:5; Eph. 1:23; 4:12; 5:23, 30; Col. 1:24 [b]Eph. 5:30
28 [a]Eph. 4:11 [b][Eph. 2:20; 3:5] [c]Acts 13:1; Rom. 12:6 [d]1 Cor. 12:10, 29; Gal. 3:5 [e]Mark 16:18; 1 Cor. 12:9, 30 [f]Num. 11:17 [g]Rom. 12:8; 1 Tim. 5:17; Heb. 13:17, 24
31 [a]1 Cor. 14:1, 39

CHAPTER 13

2 [a]Matt. 7:22; 1 Cor. 12:8–10, 28; 14:1 [b]Matt. 17:20; 21:21; Mark 11:23; Luke 17:6
3 [a]Matt. 6:1, 2
4 [a]Prov. 10:12; 17:9; 1 Thess. 5:14; [1 Pet. 4:8] [b]Eph. 4:32 [c]Gal. 5:26
5 [a]1 Cor. 10:24; Phil. 2:4
6 [a]Ps. 10:3; Rom. 1:32 [b]2 John 4; 3 John 3
7 [a]Rom. 15:1; Gal. 6:2; 2 Tim. 2:24
9 [a]1 Cor. 8:2; 13:12
12 [a][2 Cor. 3:18; 5:7]; Phil. 3:12; James 1:23 [b]Gen. 32:30; Num. 12:8; Matt. 18:10; [1 John 3:2]

CHAPTER 14

1 [a]1 Cor. 12:31; 14:39 [b]Num. 11:25, 29
2 [a]Acts 2:4; 10:46
3 [a]Rom. 14:19; 15:2; 2 Cor. 10:8; 12:19; Eph. 4:12, 29 [b]1 Tim. 4:13; 2 Tim. 4:2; Titus 1:9; 2:15; Heb. 3:13; 10:25

*

12:31 NU *greater*
13:3 NU *so I may boast*

have no need of you"; nor again the head to the feet, "I have no need of you."

22 No, much rather, those members of the body which seem to be weaker are necessary.

23 And those *members* of the body which we think to be less honorable, on these we bestow greater honor; and our unpresentable *parts* have greater modesty,

24 but our presentable *parts* have no need. But God composed the body, having given greater honor to that *part* which lacks it,

25 that there should be no schism in the body, but *that* the members should have the same care for one another.

26 And if one member suffers, all the members suffer with *it;* or if one member is honored, all the members rejoice with *it.*

27 Now [a]you are the body of Christ, and [b]members individually.

28 And [a]God has appointed these in the church: first [b]apostles, second [c]prophets, third teachers, after that [d]miracles, then [e]gifts of healings, [f]helps, [g]administrations, varieties of tongues.

29 *Are* all apostles? *Are* all prophets? *Are* all teachers? *Are* all workers of miracles?

30 Do all have gifts of healings? Do all speak with tongues? Do all interpret?

31 But [a]earnestly desire the *best gifts. And yet I show you a more excellent way.

The Greatest Gift

13 Though I speak with the tongues of men and of angels, but have not love, I have become sounding brass or a clanging cymbal.

2 And though I have *the gift of* [a]prophecy, and understand all mysteries and all knowledge, and though I have all faith, [b]so that I could remove mountains, but have not love, I am nothing.

3 And [a]though I bestow all my goods to feed *the poor,* and though I give my body *to be burned, but have not love, it profits me nothing.

4 [a]Love suffers long *and* is [b]kind; love [c]does not envy; love does not parade itself, is not puffed up;

5 does not behave rudely, [a]does not seek its own, is not provoked, thinks no evil;

6 [a]does not rejoice in iniquity, but [b]rejoices in the truth;

7 [a]bears all things, believes all things, hopes all things, endures all things.

8 Love never fails. But whether *there are* prophecies, they will fail; whether *there are* tongues, they will cease; whether *there is* knowledge, it will vanish away.

9 [a]For we know in part and we prophesy in part.

10 But when that which is perfect has come, then that which is in part will be done away.

11 When I was a child, I spoke as a child, I understood as a child, I thought as a child; but when I became a man, I put away childish things.

12 For [a]now we see in a mirror, dimly, but then [b]face to face. Now I know in part, but then I shall know just as I also am known.

13 And now abide faith, hope, love, these three; but the greatest of these *is* love.

Prophecy and Tongues

14 Pursue love, and [a]desire spiritual *gifts,* [b]but especially that you may prophesy.

2 For he who [a]speaks in a tongue does not speak to men but to God, for no one understands *him;* however, in the spirit he speaks mysteries.

3 But he who prophesies speaks [a]edification and [b]exhortation and comfort to men.

KJV

4 He that speaketh in an *unknown* tongue edifieth himself; but he that prophesieth edifieth the church.

5 I would that ye all spake with tongues, but rather that ye prophesied: for greater *is* he that prophesieth than he that speaketh with tongues, except he interpret, that the church may receive edifying.

Tongues Must Be Interpreted

6 Now, brethren, if I come unto you speaking with tongues, what shall I profit you, except I shall speak to you either by [a]revelation, or by knowledge, or by prophesying, or by doctrine?

7 And even things without life giving sound, whether pipe or harp, except they give a distinction in the sounds, how shall it be known what is piped or harped?

8 For if the trumpet give an uncertain sound, who shall prepare himself to the battle?

9 So likewise ye, except ye utter by the tongue words easy to be understood, how shall it be known what is spoken? for ye shall speak into the air.

10 There are, it may be, so many kinds of voices in the world, and none of them *is* without signification.

11 Therefore if I know not the meaning of the voice, I shall be unto him that speaketh a barbarian, and he that speaketh *shall be* a barbarian unto me.

12 Even so ye, forasmuch as ye are zealous of spiritual *gifts,* seek that ye may excel to the edifying of the church.

13 Wherefore let him that speaketh in an *unknown* tongue pray that he may [a]interpret.

14 For if I pray in an *unknown* tongue, my spirit prayeth, but my understanding is unfruitful.

15 What is it then? I will pray with the spirit, and I will pray with the understanding also: [a]I will sing with the spirit, and I will sing [b]with the understanding also.

16 Else when thou shalt bless with the spirit, how shall he that occupieth the room of the unlearned say Amen [a]at thy giving of thanks, seeing he understandeth not what thou sayest?

17 For thou verily givest thanks well, but the other is not edified.

18 I thank my God, I speak with tongues more than ye all:

19 Yet in the church I had rather speak five words with my understanding, that *by my voice* I might teach others also, than ten thousand words in an *unknown* tongue.

Tongues a Sign to Unbelievers

20 Brethren, [a]be not children in understanding: howbeit in malice [b]be ye children, but in understanding be men.

21 [a]In the law it is [b]written, WITH *MEN OF* OTHER TONGUES AND OTHER LIPS WILL I SPEAK UNTO THIS PEOPLE; AND YET FOR ALL THAT WILL THEY NOT HEAR ME, saith the Lord.

22 Wherefore tongues are for a [a]sign, not to them that believe, but to them that believe not: but prophesying *serveth* not for them that believe not, but for them which believe.

23 If therefore the whole church be come together into one place, and all speak with tongues, and there come in *those that are* unlearned, or unbelievers, [a]will they not say that ye are mad?

24 But if all prophesy, and there come in one that believeth not, or *one* unlearned, he is convinced of all, he is judged of all:

25 And thus are the secrets of his heart made manifest; and so falling down on *his* face he will worship God, and report [a]that God is in you of a truth.

NKJV

4 He who speaks in a tongue edifies himself, but he who prophesies edifies the church.

5 I wish you all spoke with tongues, but even more that you prophesied; *for he who prophesies *is* greater than he who speaks with tongues, unless indeed he interprets, that the church may receive edification.

Tongues Must Be Interpreted

6 But now, brethren, if I come to you speaking with tongues, what shall I profit you unless I speak to you either by [a]revelation, by knowledge, by prophesying, or by teaching?

7 Even things without life, whether flute or harp, when they make a sound, unless they make a distinction in the sounds, how will it be known what is piped or played?

8 For if the trumpet makes an uncertain sound, who will prepare for battle?

9 So likewise you, unless you utter by the tongue words easy to understand, how will it be known what is spoken? For you will be speaking into the air.

10 There are, it may be, so many kinds of languages in the world, and none of them *is* without significance.

11 Therefore, if I do not know the meaning of the language, I shall be a foreigner to him who speaks, and he who speaks *will be* a foreigner to me.

12 Even so you, since you are zealous for spiritual *gifts, let it be* for the edification of the church *that* you seek to excel.

13 Therefore let him who speaks in a tongue pray that he may [a]interpret.

14 For if I pray in a tongue, my spirit prays, but my understanding is unfruitful.

15 What is *the conclusion* then? I will pray with the spirit, and I will also pray with the understanding. [a]I will sing with the spirit, and I will also sing [b]with the understanding.

16 Otherwise, if you bless with the spirit, how will he who occupies the place of the uninformed say "Amen" [a]at your giving of thanks, since he does not understand what you say?

17 For you indeed give thanks well, but the other is not edified.

18 I thank my God I speak with tongues more than you all;

19 yet in the church I would rather speak five words with my understanding, that I may teach others also, than ten thousand words in a tongue.

Tongues a Sign to Unbelievers

20 Brethren, [a]do not be children in understanding; however, in malice [b]be babes, but in understanding be mature.

21 [a]In the law it is written:

> [b]"*With men of other tongues and other lips*
> *I will speak to this people;*
> *And yet, for all that, they will not hear*
> *Me,"*

says the Lord.

22 Therefore tongues are for a [a]sign, not to those who believe but to unbelievers; but prophesying is not for unbelievers but for those who believe.

23 Therefore if the whole church comes together in one place, and all speak with tongues, and there come in *those who are* uninformed or unbelievers, [a]will they not say that you are out of your mind?

24 But if all prophesy, and an unbeliever or an uninformed person comes in, he is convinced by all, he is convicted by all.

25 *And thus the secrets of his heart are revealed; and so, falling down on *his* face, he will worship God and report [a]that God is truly among you.

---

6 [a]1 Cor. 14:26; Eph. 1:17
13 [a]1 Cor. 12:10
15 [a]Eph. 5:19; Col. 3:16 [b]Ps. 47:7
16 [a]Deut. 27:15–26; 1 Chr. 16:36; Neh. 5:13; 8:6; Ps. 106:48; Jer. 11:5; 28:6; 1 Cor. 11:24; Rev. 5:14; 7:12
20 [a]Ps. 131:2; [Matt. 11:25; 18:3; 19:14]; Rom. 16:19; 1 Cor. 3:1; Eph. 4:14; Heb. 5:12, 13 [b][Matt. 18:3; 1 Pet. 2:2]
21 [a]John 10:34; 1 Cor. 14:34 [b]Is. 28:11, 12
22 [a]Mark 16:17
23 [a]Acts 2:13
25 [a]Is. 45:14; Dan. 2:47; Zech. 8:23; Acts 4:13

---

*

14:5 NU *and*
14:25 NU omits *And thus*

KJV

Order in Church Meetings

26 How is it then, brethren? when ye come
together, every one of you hath a psalm, [a]hath a
doctrine, hath a tongue, hath a revelation, hath
an interpretation. [b]Let all things be done unto
edifying.
27 If any man speak in an *unknown* tongue,
let it be by two, or at the most *by* three, and *that*
by course; and let one interpret.
28 But if there be no interpreter, let him keep
silence in the church; and let him speak to himself,
and to God.
29 Let the prophets speak two or three, and
[a]let the other judge.
30 If *any thing* be revealed to another that
sitteth by, [a]let the first hold his peace.
31 For ye may all prophesy one by one, that
all may learn, and all may be comforted.
32 And [a]the spirits of the prophets are subject to the prophets.
33 For God is not *the author* of confusion,
but of peace, [a]as in all churches of the saints.
34 [a]Let your women keep silence in the
churches: for it is not permitted unto them to
speak; but *they are commanded* to be under obedience, as also saith the [b]law.
35 And if they will learn any thing, let them
ask their husbands at home: for it is a shame for
women to speak in the church.
36 What? came the word of God out from
you? or came it unto you only?
37 [a]If any man think himself to be a prophet,
or spiritual, let him acknowledge that the things
that I write unto you are the commandments of
the Lord.
38 But if any man be ignorant, let him be
ignorant.
39 Wherefore, brethren, [a]covet to prophesy,
and forbid not to speak with tongues.
40 [a]Let all things be done decently and in
order.

The Risen Christ, Faith's Reality
(cf. Mark 16:9–20)

15 Moreover, brethren, I declare unto you the
gospel [a]which I preached unto you, which
also ye have received, and [b]wherein ye stand;
2 [a]By which also ye are saved, if ye keep
in memory what I preached unto you, unless [b]ye
have believed in vain.
3 For [a]I delivered unto you first of all that
[b]which I also received, how that Christ died for
our sins [c]according to the scriptures;
4 And that he was buried, and that he rose
again the third day [a]according to the scriptures:
5 [a]And that he was seen of Cephas, then
[b]of the twelve:
6 After that, he was seen of above five hundred brethren at once; of whom the greater part
remain unto this present, but some are fallen
asleep.
7 After that, he was seen of James; then [a]of
all the apostles.
8 [a]And last of all he was seen of me also,
as of one born out of due time.
9 For I am [a]the least of the apostles, that
am not meet to be called an apostle, because [b]I
persecuted the church of God.
10 But [a]by the grace of God I am what I am:
and his grace which *was bestowed* upon me was
not in vain; but I laboured more abundantly than
they all: [b]yet not I, but the grace of God which
was with me.
11 Therefore whether *it were* I or they, so
we preach, and so ye believed.

The Risen Christ, Our Hope
(cf. 1 Thess. 4:13–18)

12 Now if Christ be preached that he rose
from the dead, how say some among you that
there is no resurrection of the dead?

NKJV

Order in Church Meetings

26 How is it then, brethren? Whenever you
come together, each of you has a psalm, [a]has a
teaching, has a tongue, has a revelation, has an
interpretation. [b]Let all things be done for
edification.
27 If anyone speaks in a tongue, *let there be*
two or at the most three, *each* in turn, and let
one interpret.
28 But if there is no interpreter, let him keep
silent in church, and let him speak to himself and
to God.
29 Let two or three prophets speak, and [a]let
the others judge.
30 But if *anything* is revealed to another who
sits by, [a]let the first keep silent.
31 For you can all prophesy one by one, that
all may learn and all may be encouraged.
32 And [a]the spirits of the prophets are subject to the prophets.
33 For God is not *the author* of confusion but
of peace, [a]as in all the churches of the saints.
34 [a]Let *your women keep silent in the
churches, for they are not permitted to speak; but
they are to be submissive, as the [b]law also says.
35 And if they want to learn something, let
them ask their own husbands at home; for it is
shameful for women to speak in church.
36 Or did the word of God come *originally*
from you? Or *was it* you only that it reached?
37 [a]If anyone thinks himself to be a prophet
or spiritual, let him acknowledge that the things
which I write to you are the commandments of
the Lord.
38 But *if anyone is ignorant, let him be
ignorant.
39 Therefore, brethren, [a]desire earnestly to
prophesy, and do not forbid to speak with
tongues.
40 [a]Let all things be done decently and in
order.

The Risen Christ, Faith's Reality
(cf. Mark 16:9–20)

15 Moreover, brethren, I declare to you the
gospel [a]which I preached to you, which
also you received and [b]in which you stand,
2 [a]by which also you are saved, if you hold
fast that word which I preached to you—unless
[b]you believed in vain.
3 For [a]I delivered to you first of all that
[b]which I also received: that Christ died for our
sins [c]according to the Scriptures,
4 and that He was buried, and that He rose
again the third day [a]according to the Scriptures,
5 [a]and that He was seen by Cephas, then
[b]by the twelve.
6 After that He was seen by over five hundred brethren at once, of whom the greater part
remain to the present, but some have fallen
asleep.
7 After that He was seen by James, then [a]by
all the apostles.
8 [a]Then last of all He was seen by me also,
as by one born out of due time.
9 For I am [a]the least of the apostles, who
am not worthy to be called an apostle, because
[b]I persecuted the church of God.
10 But [a]by the grace of God I am what I am,
and His grace toward me was not in vain; but I
labored more abundantly than they all, [b]yet not
I, but the grace of God *which was* with me.
11 Therefore, whether *it was* I or they, so we
preach and so you believed.

The Risen Christ, Our Hope
(cf. 1 Thess. 4:13–18)

12 Now if Christ is preached that He has been
raised from the dead, how do some among you
say that there is no resurrection of the dead?

---

26 [a]1 Cor. 12:8–10; 14:6 [b]1 Cor. 12:7; [2 Cor. 12:19]
29 [a]1 Cor. 12:10
30 [a][1 Thess. 5:19, 20]
32 [a]1 John 4:1
33 [a]1 Cor. 11:16
34 [a]1 Tim. 2:11; 1 Pet. 3:1 [b]Gen. 3:16
37 [a]2 Cor. 10:7; [1 John 4:6]
39 [a]1 Cor. 12:31; 1 Thess. 5:20
40 [a]1 Cor. 14:33

CHAPTER 15

1 [a]Rom. 2:16; [Gal. 1:11] [b][Rom. 5:2; 11:20; 2 Cor. 1:24]
2 [a]Rom. 1:16; 1 Cor. 1:21 [b]Gal. 3:4
3 [a]1 Cor. 11:2, 23 [b][Gal. 1:12] [c]Ps. 22:15; Is. 53:5–12; Acts 3:18; 1 Pet. 1:11
4 [a]Gen. 1:9–13; 2 Kin. 20:8; Ps. 16:9–11; 68:18; 110:1; Is. 53:10; Hos. 6:2; Jon. 1:17; 2:10; Matt. 12:39, 40; Mark 8:31; Luke 11:29, 30; 24:26; John 2:19–21; Acts 2:25
5 [a]Luke 24:34 [b]Matt. 28:17
7 [a]Luke 24:50; Acts 1:3, 4
8 [a][Acts 9:3–8; 22:6–11; 26:12–18]; 1 Cor. 9:1
9 [a]2 Cor. 12:11; Eph. 3:8; 1 Tim. 1:15 [b]Acts 8:3
10 [a]Eph. 3:7, 8 [b]Matt. 10:20; Rom. 15:18; Gal. 2:8; Phil. 2:13

*

14:34 NU omits *your*
14:38 NU *if anyone does not recognize this, he is not recognized.*

KJV

13 But if there be no resurrection of the dead,
[a]then is Christ not risen:
14 And if Christ be not risen, then *is* our
preaching vain, and your faith *is* also vain.
15 Yea, and we are found false witnesses of
God; because [a]we have testified of God that he
raised up Christ: whom he raised not up, if so be
that the dead rise not.
16 For if the dead rise not, then is not Christ
raised:
17 And if Christ be not raised, your faith *is*
vain; [a]ye are yet in your sins.
18 Then they also which are fallen [a]asleep
in Christ are perished.
19 [a]If in this life only we have hope in Christ,
we are of all men most miserable.

The Last Enemy Destroyed

20 But now [a]is Christ risen from the dead,
and become [b]the firstfruits of them that slept.
21 For [a]since by man *came* death, [b]by man
came also the resurrection of the dead.
22 For as in Adam all die, even so in Christ
shall all [a]be made alive.
23 But [a]every man in his own order: Christ
the firstfruits; afterward they that are Christ's at
his coming.
24 Then *cometh* the end, when he shall have
delivered up [a]the kingdom to God, even the Father; when he shall have put down all rule and
all authority and power.
25 For he must reign, [a]till he hath put all enemies under his feet.
26 [a]The last enemy *that* shall be destroyed
is death.
27 For HE [a]HATH PUT ALL THINGS UNDER HIS
FEET. But when he saith all things are put under
him, it is manifest that he is excepted, which did
put all things under him.
28 [a]And when all things shall be subdued
unto him, then [b]shall the Son also himself be subject unto him that put all things under him, that
God may be all in all.

Effects of Denying the Resurrection

29 Else what shall they do which are baptized
for the dead, if the dead rise not at all? why are
they then baptized for the dead?
30 And [a]why stand we in jeopardy every
hour?
31 I protest by [a]your rejoicing which I have
in Christ Jesus our Lord, [b]I die daily.
32 If after the manner of men [a]I have fought
with beasts at Ephesus, what advantageth it me,
if the dead rise not? [b]LET US EAT AND DRINK; FOR
TO MORROW WE DIE.
33 Be not deceived: [a]evil communications
corrupt good manners.
34 [a]Awake to righteousness, and sin not; [b]for
some have not the knowledge of God: [c]I speak
this to your shame.

A Glorious Body

35 But some *man* will say, [a]How are the dead
raised up? and with what body do they come?
36 *Thou* fool, [a]that which thou sowest is not
quickened, except it die:
37 And that which thou sowest, thou sowest
not that body that shall be, but bare grain, it may
chance of wheat, or of some other *grain:*
38 But God giveth it a body as it hath pleased
him, and to every seed his own body.
39 All flesh *is* not the same flesh: but *there*
is one *kind of* flesh of men, another flesh of beasts,
another of fishes, *and* another of birds.
40 *There are* also celestial bodies, and bodies
terrestrial: but the glory of the celestial *is* one,
and the *glory* of the terrestrial *is* another.
41 *There is* one glory of the sun, and another
glory of the moon, and another glory of the stars:
for *one* star differeth from *another* star in glory.
42 [a]So also *is* the resurrection of the dead.

13 [a][1 Thess. 4:14]
15 [a]Acts 2:24
17 [a][Rom. 4:25]
18 [a]Job 14:12; Ps. 13:3
19 [a]1 Cor. 4:9; 2 Tim. 3:12
20 [a]Acts 2:24; 1 Pet. 1:3 [b]Acts 26:23; 1 Cor. 15:23; Rev. 1:5
21 [a]Gen. 3:19; Ezek. 18:4; Rom. 5:12; 6:23; Heb. 9:27 [b]John 11:25
22 [a][John 5:28, 29]
23 [a][1 Thess. 4:15–17]
24 [a][Dan. 2:44; 7:14, 27; 2 Pet. 1:11]
25 [a]Ps. 110:1; Matt. 22:44
26 [a][2 Tim. 1:10; Rev. 20:14; 21:4]
27 [a]Ps. 8:6
28 [a][Phil. 3:21] [b]1 Cor. 3:23; 11:3; 12:6
30 [a]2 Cor. 11:26
31 [a]1 Thess. 2:19 [b]Rom. 8:36
32 [a]2 Cor. 1:8 [b]Eccl. 2:24; Is. 22:13; 56:12; Luke 12:19
33 [a][1 Cor. 5:6]
34 [a]Rom. 13:11; Eph. 5:14 [b][1 Thess. 4:5] [c]1 Cor. 6:5
35 [a]Ezek. 37:3
36 [a]John 12:24
42 [a][Dan. 12:3; Matt. 13:43]

*

15:39 NU, M omit *of flesh*

NKJV

13 But if there is no resurrection of the dead,
[a]then Christ is not risen.
14 And if Christ is not risen, then our preaching *is* empty and your faith *is* also empty.
15 Yes, and we are found false witnesses of
God, because [a]we have testified of God that He
raised up Christ, whom He did not raise up—if
in fact the dead do not rise.
16 For if *the* dead do not rise, then Christ is
not risen.
17 And if Christ is not risen, your faith *is* futile; [a]you are still in your sins!
18 Then also those who have fallen [a]asleep
in Christ have perished.
19 [a]If in this life only we have hope in Christ,
we are of all men the most pitiable.

The Last Enemy Destroyed

20 But now [a]Christ is risen from the dead,
and has become [b]the firstfruits of those who have
fallen asleep.
21 For [a]since by man *came* death, [b]by Man
also *came* the resurrection of the dead.
22 For as in Adam all die, even so in Christ
all shall [a]be made alive.
23 But [a]each one in his own order: Christ the
firstfruits, afterward those *who are* Christ's at His
coming.
24 Then *comes* the end, when He delivers
[a]the kingdom to God the Father, when He puts
an end to all rule and all authority and power.
25 For He must reign [a]till He has put all enemies under His feet.
26 [a]The last enemy *that* will be destroyed *is*
death.
27 For [a]*"He has put all things under His
feet."* But when He says "all things are put under
Him," it is evident that He who put all things under Him is excepted.
28 [a]Now when all things are made subject
to Him, then [b]the Son Himself will also be subject
to Him who put all things under Him, that God
may be all in all.

Effects of Denying the Resurrection

29 Otherwise, what will they do who are baptized for the dead, if the dead do not rise at all?
Why then are they baptized for the dead?
30 And [a]why do we stand in jeopardy every
hour?
31 I affirm, by [a]the boasting in you which I
have in Christ Jesus our Lord, [b]I die daily.
32 If, in the manner of men, [a]I have fought
with beasts at Ephesus, what advantage *is it* to
me? If *the* dead do not rise, [b]*"Let us eat and drink,
for tomorrow we die!"*
33 Do not be deceived: [a]"Evil company cor-
rupts good habits."
34 [a]Awake to righteousness, and do not sin;
[b]for some do not have the knowledge of God. [c]I
speak *this* to your shame.

A Glorious Body

35 But someone will say, [a]"How are the dead
raised up? And with what body do they come?"
36 Foolish one, [a]what you sow is not made
alive unless it dies.
37 And what you sow, you do not sow that
body that shall be, but mere grain—perhaps
wheat or some other *grain.*
38 But God gives it a body as He pleases, and
to each seed its own body.
39 All flesh *is* not the same flesh, but *there
is* one *kind* **of* flesh of men, another flesh of animals, another of fish, *and* another of birds.
40 *There are* also celestial bodies and terrestrial bodies; but the glory of the celestial *is* one,
and the *glory* of the terrestrial *is* another.
41 *There is* one glory of the sun, another
glory of the moon, and another glory of the stars;
for *one* star differs from *another* star in glory.
42 [a]So also *is* the resurrection of the dead.

KJV

It is sown in corruption; it is raised in incorruption:
43 [a]It is sown in dishonour; it is raised
in glory: it is sown in weakness; it is raised in
power:
44 It is sown a natural body; it is raised a
spiritual body. There is a natural body, and there
is a spiritual body.
45 And so it is written, [a]The first MAN Adam
WAS MADE A LIVING SOUL; [b]the last Adam *was made*
[c]a quickening spirit.
46 Howbeit that *was* not first which is spiritual, but that which is natural; and afterward that
which is spiritual.
47 [a]The first man *is* of the earth, [b]earthy: the
second man *is* the Lord [c]from heaven.
48 As *is* the earthy, such *are* they also that
are earthy: [a]and as *is* the heavenly, such *are* they
also that are heavenly.
49 And [a]as we have borne the image of the
earthy, [b]we shall also bear the image of the heavenly.

Our Final Victory

50 Now this I say, brethren, that [a]flesh and
blood cannot inherit the kingdom of God; neither
doth corruption inherit incorruption.
51 Behold, I shew you a mystery; [a]We shall
not all sleep, [b]but we shall all be changed,
52 In a moment, in the twinkling of an eye,
at the last trump: [a]for the trumpet shall sound,
and the dead shall be raised incorruptible, and
we shall be changed.
53 For this corruptible must put on incorruption, and [a]this mortal *must* put on immortality.
54 So when this corruptible shall have put
on incorruption, and this mortal shall have put
on immortality, then shall be brought to pass the
saying that is written, [a]DEATH IS SWALLOWED UP
IN VICTORY.
55 [a]O DEATH, WHERE *IS* THY STING? O GRAVE,
WHERE *IS* THY VICTORY?
56 The sting of death *is* sin; and [a]the strength
of sin *is* the law.
57 [a]But thanks *be* to God, which giveth us
[b]the victory through our Lord Jesus Christ.
58 [a]Therefore, my beloved brethren, be ye
stedfast, unmoveable, always abounding in the
work of the Lord, forasmuch as ye know [b]that
your labour is not in vain in the Lord.

Collection for the Saints

16 Now concerning [a]the collection for the
saints, as I have given order to the churches
of Galatia, even so do ye.
2 [a]Upon the first *day* of the week let every
one of you lay by him in store, as *God* hath prospered him, that there be no gatherings when I
come.
3 And when I come, [a]whomsoever ye shall
approve by *your* letters, them will I send to bring
your liberality unto Jerusalem.
4 [a]And if it be meet that I go also, they shall
go with me.

Personal Plans
(cf. Acts 19:21)

5 Now I will come unto you, [a]when I shall
pass through Macedonia: for I do pass through
Macedonia.
6 And it may be that I will abide, yea, and
winter with you, that ye may [a]bring me on my
journey whithersoever I go.
7 For I will not see you now by the way;
but I trust to tarry a while with you, [a]if the Lord
permit.
8 But I will tarry at Ephesus until [a]Pente-
cost.
9 For [a]a great door and effectual is opened
unto me, and [b]*there are* many adversaries.
10 Now [a]if Timotheus come, see that he may

43 [a][Phil. 3:21]
45 [a]Gen. 2:7 [b][Rom. 5:14] [c]John 5:21; 6:57
47 [a]John 3:31 [b]Gen. 2:7; 3:19 [c]John 3:13
48 [a]Phil. 3:20
49 [a]Gen. 5:3 [b]Rom. 8:29
50 [a][John 3:3, 5]
51 [a][1 Thess. 4:15] [b][Phil. 3:21]
52 [a]Matt. 24:31
53 [a]2 Cor. 5:4
54 [a]Is. 25:8
55 [a]Hos. 13:14
56 [a][Rom. 3:20; 4:15; 7:8]
57 [a][Rom. 7:25] [b][1 John 5:4]
58 [a]2 Pet. 3:14 [b][1 Cor. 3:8]

CHAPTER 16
1 [a]Gal. 2:10
2 [a]Acts 20:7
3 [a]2 Cor. 3:1; 8:18
4 [a]2 Cor. 8:4, 19
5 [a]2 Cor. 1:15, 16
6 [a]Acts 15:3
7 [a]James 4:15
8 [a]Lev. 23:15–22
9 [a]Acts 14:27 [b]Acts 19:9
10 [a]Acts 19:22

*
15:47 NU omits *the Lord*
15:49 M *let us also bear*
15:55 NU *O Death, where is your victory? O Death, where is your sting?*

NKJV

The body is sown in corruption, it is raised in
incorruption.
43 [a]It is sown in dishonor, it is raised in glory.
It is sown in weakness, it is raised in power.
44 It is sown a natural body, it is raised a
spiritual body. There is a natural body, and there
is a spiritual body.
45 And so it is written, [a]*"The first man Adam
became a living being."* [b]The last Adam *became*
[c]a life-giving spirit.
46 However, the spiritual is not first, but the
natural, and afterward the spiritual.
47 [a]The first man *was* of the earth, [b]*made*
of dust; the second Man *is* *the Lord [c]from
heaven.
48 As *was* the *man* of dust, so also *are* those
who are made of dust; [a]and as *is* the heavenly
Man, so also *are* those *who are* heavenly.
49 And [a]as we have borne the image of the
man of dust, [b]we* shall also bear the image of
the heavenly *Man.*

Our Final Victory

50 Now this I say, brethren, that [a]flesh and
blood cannot inherit the kingdom of God; nor
does corruption inherit incorruption.
51 Behold, I tell you a mystery: [a]We shall
not all sleep, [b]but we shall all be changed—
52 in a moment, in the twinkling of an eye,
at the last trumpet. [a]For the trumpet will sound,
and the dead will be raised incorruptible, and we
shall be changed.
53 For this corruptible must put on incorruption, and [a]this mortal *must* put on immortality.
54 So when this corruptible has put on incorruption, and this mortal has put on immortality,
then shall be brought to pass the saying that is
written: [a]*"Death is swallowed up in victory."*

55 *"O[a]* Death, where is your sting?*
O Hades, where is your victory?"

56 The sting of death *is* sin, and [a]the strength
of sin *is* the law.
57 [a]But thanks *be* to God, who gives us [b]the
victory through our Lord Jesus Christ.
58 [a]Therefore, my beloved brethren, be steadfast, immovable, always abounding in the work
of the Lord, knowing [b]that your labor is not in
vain in the Lord.

Collection for the Saints

16 Now concerning [a]the collection for the
saints, as I have given orders to the
churches of Galatia, so you must do also:
2 [a]On the first *day* of the week let each one
of you lay something aside, storing up as he may
prosper, that there be no collections when I come.
3 And when I come, [a]whomever you ap-
prove by *your* letters I will send to bear your gift
to Jerusalem.
4 [a]But if it is fitting that I go also, they will
go with me.

Personal Plans
(cf. Acts 19:21)

5 Now I will come to you [a]when I pass
through Macedonia (for I am passing through
Macedonia).
6 And it may be that I will remain, or even
spend the winter with you, that you may [a]send
me on my journey, wherever I go.
7 For I do not wish to see you now on the
way; but I hope to stay a while with you, [a]if the
Lord permits.
8 But I will tarry in Ephesus until [a]Pente-
cost.
9 For [a]a great and effective door has opened
to me, and [b]*there are* many adversaries.
10 And [a]if Timothy comes, see that he may

KJV

be with you without fear: for [b]he worketh the work of the Lord, as I also *do.*
11 [a]Let no man therefore despise him: but conduct him forth [b]in peace, that he may come unto me: for I look for him with the brethren.
12 As touching *our* brother [a]Apollos, I greatly desired him to come unto you with the brethren: but his will was not at all to come at this time; but he will come when he shall have convenient time.

Final Exhortations

13 [a]Watch ye, [b]stand fast in the faith, quit you like men, [c]be strong.
14 [a]Let all your things be done with charity.
15 I beseech you, brethren, (ye know [a]the house of Stephanas, that it is [b]the firstfruits of Achaia, and *that* they have addicted themselves to [c]the ministry of the saints,)
16 [a]That ye submit yourselves unto such, and to every one that helpeth with *us,* and [b]laboureth.
17 I am glad of the coming of Stephanas and Fortunatus and Achaicus: [a]for that which was lacking on your part they have supplied.
18 [a]For they have refreshed my spirit and your's: therefore [b]acknowledge ye them that are such.

Greetings and a Solemn Farewell

19 The churches of Asia salute you. Aquila and Priscilla salute you much in the Lord, [a]with the church that is in their house.
20 All the brethren greet you. [a]Greet ye one another with an holy kiss.
21 [a]The salutation of *me* Paul with mine own hand.
22 If any man [a]love not the Lord Jesus Christ, [b]let him be Anathema [c]Maranatha.
23 [a]The grace of our Lord Jesus Christ *be* with you.
24 My love *be* with you all in Christ Jesus. Amen.

10 [b]Phil. 2:20 **11** [a]1 Tim. 4:12 [b]Acts 15:33 **12** [a]1 Cor. 1:12; 3:5 **13** [a]Matt. 24:42 [b]Phil. 1:27; 4:1 [c][Eph. 3:16; 6:10] **14** [a][1 Pet. 4:8] **15** [a]1 Cor. 1:16 [b]Rom. 16:5 [c]2 Cor. 8:4 **16** [a]Heb. 13:17 [b][Heb. 6:10] **17** [a]2 Cor. 11:9 **18** [a]Col. 4:8 [b]Phil. 2:29 **19** [a]Rom. 16:5 **20** [a]Rom. 16:16 **21** [a]Col. 4:18 **22** [a]Eph. 6:24 [b]Gal. 1:8, 9 [c]Jude 14, 15 **23** [a]Rom. 16:20

*

16:22 Gr. *anathema* • Aram. *Marana tha* or *Maranatha;* possibly *Maran atha, Our Lord has come*

NKJV

be with you without fear; for [b]he does the work of the Lord, as I also *do.*
11 [a]Therefore let no one despise him. But send him on his journey [b]in peace, that he may come to me; for I am waiting for him with the brethren.
12 Now concerning *our* brother [a]Apollos, I strongly urged him to come to you with the brethren, but he was quite unwilling to come at this time; however, he will come when he has a convenient time.

Final Exhortations

13 [a]Watch, [b]stand fast in the faith, be brave, [c]be strong.
14 [a]Let all *that* you *do* be done with love.
15 I urge you, brethren—you know [a]the household of Stephanas, that it is [b]the firstfruits of Achaia, and *that* they have devoted themselves to [c]the ministry of the saints—
16 [a]that you also submit to such, and to everyone who works and [b]labors with *us.*
17 I am glad about the coming of Stephanas, Fortunatus, and Achaicus, [a]for what was lacking on your part they supplied.
18 [a]For they refreshed my spirit and yours. Therefore [b]acknowledge such men.

Greetings and a Solemn Farewell

19 The churches of Asia greet you. Aquila and Priscilla greet you heartily in the Lord, [a]with the church that is in their house.
20 All the brethren greet you. [a]Greet one another with a holy kiss.
21 [a]The salutation with my own hand—Paul's.
22 If anyone [a]does not love the Lord Jesus Christ, [b]let him be *accursed. [c]O* Lord, come!
23 [a]The grace of our Lord Jesus Christ *be* with you.
24 My love *be* with you all in Christ Jesus. Amen.

KJV

THE SECOND EPISTLE OF PAUL THE APOSTLE TO THE

CORINTHIANS

Greeting

1 Paul, [a]an apostle of Jesus Christ by the will
of God, and [b]Timothy *our* brother, unto the
church of God which is at Corinth, [c]with all the
saints which are in all Achaia:
2 [a]Grace *be* to you and peace from God our
Father, and *from* the Lord Jesus Christ.

Comfort in Suffering

3 [a]Blessed *be* God, even the Father of our
Lord Jesus Christ, the Father of mercies, and the
God of all comfort;
4 Who [a]comforteth us in all our tribulation,
that we may be able to comfort them which are
in any trouble, by the comfort wherewith we ourselves are comforted of God.
5 For as [a]the sufferings of Christ abound in
us, so our consolation also aboundeth by Christ.
6 And whether we be afflicted, [a]*it is* for your
consolation and salvation, which is effectual in
the enduring of the same sufferings which we also
suffer: or whether we be comforted, *it is* for your
consolation and salvation.
7 And our hope of you *is* stedfast, knowing,
that [a]as ye are partakers of the sufferings, so *shall
ye be* also of the consolation.

Delivered from Suffering

8 For we would not, brethren, have you ignorant of [a]our trouble which came to us in Asia,
that we were pressed out of measure, above
strength, insomuch that we despaired even of life:
9 But we had the sentence of death in ourselves, that we should [a]not trust in ourselves, but
in God which raiseth the dead:
10 [a]Who delivered us from so great a death,
and doth deliver: in whom we trust that he will
yet deliver *us;*
11 Ye also [a]helping together by prayer for
us, that [b]for the gift *bestowed* upon us by the
means of many persons thanks may be given by
many on our behalf.

Paul's Sincerity

12 For our rejoicing is this, the testimony of
our conscience, that in simplicity and [a]godly sincerity, [b]not with fleshly wisdom, but by the grace
of God, we have had our conversation in the
world, and more abundantly to you-ward.
13 For we write none other things unto you,
than what ye read or acknowledge; and I trust
ye shall acknowledge even to the end;
14 As also ye have acknowledged us in part,
[a]that we are your rejoicing, even as [b]ye also *are*
our's in the day of the Lord Jesus.

Sparing the Church

15 And in this confidence [a]I was minded to
come unto you before, that ye might have [b]a second benefit;
16 And to pass by you into Macedonia, and
[a]to come again out of Macedonia unto you, and
of you to be brought on my way toward Judaea.

CHAPTER 1
1 [a]1 Cor. 1:1; Eph. 1:1; Col. 1:1; 1 Tim. 1:1; 2 Tim. 1:1 [b]Acts 16:1; 1 Cor. 16:10 [c]Phil. 1:1; Col. 1:2
2 [a]Rom. 1:7
3 [a]Eph. 1:3; 1 Pet. 1:3
4 [a]Is. 51:12; 66:13; 2 Cor. 7:6, 7, 13
5 [a][Acts 9:4]; 2 Cor. 4:10; Phil. 3:10; Col. 1:24
6 [a]2 Cor. 4:15; 12:15; Eph. 3:1, 13; 2 Tim. 2:10
7 [a][Rom. 8:17; 2 Tim. 2:12]
8 [a]Acts 19:23; 1 Cor. 15:32; 16:9
9 [a]Jer. 17:5, 7
10 [a][2 Pet. 2:9]
11 [a]Rom. 15:30; Phil. 1:19; Philem. 22 [b]2 Cor. 4:15; 9:11
12 [a]2 Cor. 2:17 [b][1 Cor. 2:4]
14 [a]2 Cor. 5:12 [b]Phil. 2:16; 1 Thess. 2:19
15 [a]1 Cor. 4:19 [b]Rom. 1:11; 15:29
16 [a]Acts 19:21; 1 Cor. 16:3–6

*
1:10 NU *shall*
1:11 M *your behalf*

NKJV

THE SECOND EPISTLE OF PAUL THE APOSTLE TO THE

CORINTHIANS

Greeting

1 Paul, [a]an apostle of Jesus Christ by the will
of God, and [b]Timothy *our* brother,

To the church of God which is at Corinth,
[c]with all the saints who are in all Achaia:

2 [a]Grace to you and peace from God our
Father and the Lord Jesus Christ.

Comfort in Suffering

3 [a]Blessed *be* the God and Father of our
Lord Jesus Christ, the Father of mercies and God
of all comfort,
4 who [a]comforts us in all our tribulation,
that we may be able to comfort those who are in
any trouble, with the comfort with which we ourselves are comforted by God.
5 For as [a]the sufferings of Christ abound in
us, so our consolation also abounds through
Christ.
6 Now if we are afflicted, [a]*it is* for your consolation and salvation, which is effective for enduring the same sufferings which we also suffer.
Or if we are comforted, *it is* for your consolation
and salvation.
7 And our hope for you *is* steadfast, because
we know that [a]as you are partakers of the sufferings, so also *you will partake* of the consolation.

Delivered from Suffering

8 For we do not want you to be ignorant,
brethren, of [a]our trouble which came to us in
Asia: that we were burdened beyond measure,
above strength, so that we despaired even of life.
9 Yes, we had the sentence of death in ourselves, that we should [a]not trust in ourselves but
in God who raises the dead,
10 [a]who delivered us from so great a death,
and *does deliver us; in whom we trust that He
will still deliver *us,*
11 you also [a]helping together in prayer for
us, that thanks may be given by many persons
on *our behalf [b]for the gift *granted* to us through
many.

Paul's Sincerity

12 For our boasting is this: the testimony of
our conscience that we conducted ourselves in the
world in simplicity and [a]godly sincerity, [b]not with
fleshly wisdom but by the grace of God, and more
abundantly toward you.
13 For we are not writing any other things
to you than what you read or understand. Now I
trust you will understand, even to the end
14 (as also you have understood us in part),
[a]that we are your boast as [b]you also *are* ours, in
the day of the Lord Jesus.

Sparing the Church

15 And in this confidence [a]I intended to come
to you before, that you might have [b]a second benefit—
16 to pass by way of you to Macedonia, [a]to
come again from Macedonia to you, and be helped
by you on my way to Judea.

KJV

17 When I therefore was thus minded, did I use lightness? or the things that I purpose, do I purpose [a]according to the flesh, that with me there should be yea yea, and nay nay?

18 But *as* God *is* [a]true, our word toward you was not yea and nay.

19 For [a]the Son of God, Jesus Christ, who was preached among you by us, *even* by me and [b]Silvanus and [c]Timotheus, was not yea and nay, [d]but in him was yea.

20 [a]For all the promises of God in him *are* yea, and in him Amen, unto the glory of God by us.

21 Now he which stablisheth us with you in Christ, and [a]hath anointed us, *is* God;

22 Who [a]hath also sealed us, and [b]given the earnest of the Spirit in our hearts.

23 Moreover [a]I call God for a record upon my soul, [b]that to spare you I came not as yet unto Corinth.

24 Not for [a]that we have dominion over your faith, but are helpers of your joy: for [b]by faith ye stand.

2 But I determined this with myself, [a]that I would not come again to you in heaviness.

2 For if I make you [a]sorry, who is he then that maketh me glad, but the same which is made sorry by me?

Forgive the Offender

3 And I wrote this same unto you, lest, when I came, [a]I should have sorrow from them of whom I ought to rejoice; [b]having confidence in you all, that my joy is *the joy* of you all.

4 For out of much affliction and anguish of heart I wrote unto you with many tears; [a]not that ye should be grieved, but that ye might know the love which I have more abundantly unto you.

5 But [a]if any have caused grief, he hath not [b]grieved me, but in part: that I may not overcharge you all.

6 Sufficient to such a man *is* this punishment, which *was inflicted* [a]of many.

7 [a]So that contrariwise ye *ought* rather to forgive *him,* and comfort *him,* lest perhaps such a one should be swallowed up with overmuch sorrow.

8 Wherefore I beseech you that ye would confirm *your* love toward him.

9 For to this end also did I write, that I might know the proof of you, whether ye be [a]obedient in all things.

10 To whom ye forgive any thing, I *forgive* also: for if I forgave any thing, to whom I forgave *it,* for your sakes *forgave I it* in the person of Christ;

11 Lest Satan should get an advantage of us: for we are not ignorant of his devices.

Triumph in Christ

12 Furthermore, [a]when I came to Troas to *preach* Christ's gospel, and [b]a door was opened unto me of the Lord,

13 [a]I had no rest in my spirit, because I found not Titus my brother: but taking my leave of them, I went from thence into Macedonia.

14 Now thanks *be* unto God, which always causeth us to triumph in Christ, and maketh manifest the savour of his knowledge by us in every place.

15 For we are unto God a sweet savour of Christ, [a]in them that are saved, and [b]in them that perish:

16 [a]To the one *we are* the savour of death unto death; and to the other the savour of life unto life. And [b]who *is* sufficient for these things?

17 For we are not as many, which [a]corrupt the word of God: but as [b]of sincerity, but as of God, in the sight of God speak we in Christ.

17 [a]2 Cor. 10:2; 11:18
18 [a]1 John 5:20
19 [a]Mark 1:1; Luke 1:35; John 1:34; 20:31; 1 John 5:5, 20 [b]1 Thess. 1:1; 2 Thess. 1:1; 1 Pet. 5:12 [c]Acts 18:5; 2 Cor. 1:1 [d][Heb. 13:8]
20 [a][Rom. 15:8, 9]
21 [a][1 John 2:20, 27]
22 [a][Eph. 4:30] [b]Rom. 8:16; 2 Cor. 5:5; [Eph. 1:14]
23 [a]Rom. 1:9; Gal. 1:20; Phil. 1:8 [b]1 Cor. 4:21; 2 Cor. 2:3; 12:20
24 [a]1 Cor. 3:5; 2 Cor. 4:5; 11:20; [1 Pet. 5:3] [b]Rom. 11:20; 1 Cor. 15:1

CHAPTER 2

1 [a]2 Cor. 1:23
2 [a]2 Cor. 7:8
3 [a]1 Cor. 4:21; 2 Cor. 12:21 [b]2 Cor. 8:22; Gal. 5:10; 2 Thess. 3:4; Philem. 21
4 [a][2 Cor. 2:9; 7:8, 12]
5 [a][1 Cor. 5:1] [b]Gal. 4:12
6 [a]1 Cor. 5:4, 5; 2 Cor. 7:11; 1 Tim. 5:20
7 [a]Gal. 6:1; Eph. 4:32
9 [a]2 Cor. 7:15; 10:6
12 [a]Acts 16:8 [b]1 Cor. 16:9
13 [a]2 Cor. 7:6, 13; 8:6; Gal. 2:1, 3; 2 Tim. 4:10; Titus 1:4
15 [a][1 Cor. 1:18] [b][2 Cor. 4:3]
16 [a]Luke 2:34; [John 9:39; 1 Pet. 2:7] [b][1 Cor. 15:10]
17 [a]2 Pet. 2:3 [b]1 Cor. 5:8; 2 Cor. 1:12; 1 Thess. 2:4; 1 Pet. 4:11

*

2:10 NU *indeed, what I have forgiven, if I have forgiven anything, I did it for your sakes*
2:17 M *the rest*

NKJV

17 Therefore, when I was planning this, did I do it lightly? Or the things I plan, do I plan [a]according to the flesh, that with me there should be Yes, Yes, and No, No?

18 But *as* God *is* [a]faithful, our word to you was not Yes and No.

19 For [a]the Son of God, Jesus Christ, who was preached among you by us—by me, [b]Silvanus, and [c]Timothy—was not Yes and No, [d]but in Him was Yes.

20 [a]For all the promises of God in Him *are* Yes, and in Him Amen, to the glory of God through us.

21 Now He who establishes us with you in Christ and [a]has anointed us *is* God,

22 who [a]also has sealed us and [b]given us the Spirit in our hearts as a guarantee.

23 Moreover [a]I call God as witness against my soul, [b]that to spare you I came no more to Corinth.

24 Not [a]that we have dominion over your faith, but are fellow workers for your joy; for [b]by faith you stand.

2 But I determined this within myself, [a]that I would not come again to you in sorrow.

2 For if I make you [a]sorrowful, then who is he who makes me glad but the one who is made sorrowful by me?

Forgive the Offender

3 And I wrote this very thing to you, lest, when I came, [a]I should have sorrow over those from whom I ought to have joy, [b]having confidence in you all that my joy is *the joy* of you all.

4 For out of much affliction and anguish of heart I wrote to you, with many tears, [a]not that you should be grieved, but that you might know the love which I have so abundantly for you.

5 But [a]if anyone has caused grief, he has not [b]grieved me, but all of you to some extent—not to be too severe.

6 This punishment which *was inflicted* [a]by the majority *is* sufficient for such a man,

7 [a]so that, on the contrary, you *ought* rather to forgive and comfort *him,* lest perhaps such a one be swallowed up with too much sorrow.

8 Therefore I urge you to reaffirm *your* love to him.

9 For to this end I also wrote, that I might put you to the test, whether you are [a]obedient in all things.

10 Now whom you forgive anything, I also *forgive.* For *if indeed I have forgiven anything, I have forgiven that one for your sakes in the presence of Christ,

11 lest Satan should take advantage of us; for we are not ignorant of his devices.

Triumph in Christ

12 Furthermore, [a]when I came to Troas to *preach* Christ's gospel, and [b]a door was opened to me by the Lord,

13 [a]I had no rest in my spirit, because I did not find Titus my brother; but taking my leave of them, I departed for Macedonia.

14 Now thanks *be* to God who always leads us in triumph in Christ, and through us diffuses the fragrance of His knowledge in every place.

15 For we are to God the fragrance of Christ [a]among those who are being saved and [b]among those who are perishing.

16 [a]To the one *we are* the aroma of death *leading* to death, and to the other the aroma of life *leading* to life. And [b]who *is* sufficient for these things?

17 For we are not, as *so many, [a]peddling the word of God; but as [b]of sincerity, but as from God, we speak in the sight of God in Christ.

KJV

Christ's Epistle
(cf. Jer. 31:31–34)

3 Do [a]we begin again to commend ourselves? or need we, as some *others*, [b]epistles of commendation to you, or *letters* of commendation from you?

2 [a]Ye are our epistle written in our hearts, known and read of all men:

3 *Forasmuch as ye are* manifestly declared to be the epistle of Christ [a]ministered by us, written not with ink, but with the Spirit of the living God; not [b]in tables of stone, but [c]in fleshy tables of the heart.

The Spirit, Not the Letter

4 And such trust have we through Christ to God-ward:

5 [a]Not that we are sufficient of ourselves to think any thing as of ourselves; but [b]our sufficiency *is* of God;

6 Who also hath made us able [a]ministers of [b]the new testament; not [c]of the letter, but of the spirit: for [d]the letter killeth, [e]but the spirit giveth life.

Glory of the New Covenant

7 But if [a]the ministration of death, [b]written *and* engraven in stones, was glorious, [c]so that the children of Israel could not stedfastly behold the face of Moses for the glory of his countenance; which *glory* was to be done away:

8 How shall not [a]the ministration of the spirit be rather glorious?

9 For if the ministration of condemnation *be* glory, much more doth the ministration [a]of righteousness exceed in glory.

10 For even that which was made glorious had no glory in this respect, by reason of the glory that excelleth.

11 For if that which is done away *was* glorious, much more that which remaineth *is* glorious.

12 Seeing then that we have such hope, [a]we use great plainness of speech:

13 And not as Moses, [a]*which* put a vail over his face, that the children of Israel could not stedfastly look to [b]the end of that which is abolished:

14 But [a]their minds were blinded: for until this day remaineth the same vail untaken away in the reading of the old testament; which *vail* is done away in Christ.

15 But even unto this day, when Moses is read, the vail is upon their heart.

16 Nevertheless [a]when it shall turn to the Lord, [b]the vail shall be taken away.

17 Now [a]the Lord is that Spirit: and where the Spirit of the Lord *is*, there *is* [b]liberty.

18 But we all, with open face beholding [a]as in a glass [b]the glory of the Lord, [c]are changed into the same image from glory to glory, *even* as by the Spirit of the Lord.

The Light of Christ's Gospel

4 Therefore seeing we have this ministry, [a]as we have received mercy, we faint [b]not;

2 But have renounced the hidden things of dishonesty, not walking in craftiness, nor handling the word of God deceitfully; but by manifestation of the truth [a]commending ourselves to every man's conscience in the sight of God.

3 But if our gospel be hid, [a]it is hid to them that are lost:

4 In whom [a]the god of this world [b]hath blinded the minds of them which believe not, lest [c]the light of the glorious gospel of Christ, [d]who is the image of God, should shine unto them.

5 [a]For we preach not ourselves, but Christ Jesus the Lord; and [b]ourselves your servants for Jesus' sake.

6 For God, [a]who commanded the light to shine out of darkness, hath [b]shined in our hearts,

CHAPTER 3

1 [a]2 Cor. 5:12; 10:12, 18; 12:11 [b]Acts 18:27
2 [a]1 Cor. 9:2
3 [a]1 Cor. 3:5 [b]Ex. 24:12; 31:18; 32:15; 2 Cor. 3:7 [c]Ps. 40:8
5 [a][John 15:5] [b]1 Cor. 15:10
6 [a]1 Cor. 3:5; Eph. 3:7 [b]Jer. 31:31; Matt. 26:28; Luke 22:20 [c]Rom. 2:27 [d][Rom. 3:20]; Gal. 3:10 [e]John 6:63; Rom. 8:2
7 [a]Rom. 7:10 [b]Ex. 34:1; Deut. 10:1 [c]Ex. 34:29
8 [a][Gal. 3:5]
9 [a][Rom. 1:17; 3:21]
12 [a]Acts 4:13, 29; 2 Cor. 7:4; Eph. 6:19
13 [a]Ex. 34:33–35; 2 Cor. 3:7 [b]Rom. 10:4; [Gal. 3:23]
14 [a]Is. 6:10; 29:10; Acts 28:26; Rom. 11:7, 8; 2 Cor. 4:4
16 [a]Ex. 34:34; Rom. 11:23 [b]Is. 25:7
17 [a][1 Cor. 15:45] [b]John 8:32; Gal. 5:1, 13
18 [a]1 Cor. 13:12 [b][2 Cor. 4:4, 6] [c][Rom. 8:29, 30]

CHAPTER 4

1 [a]1 Cor. 7:25 [b]Luke 18:1; 2 Cor. 4:16; Gal. 6:9; Eph. 3:13; 2 Thess. 3:13
2 [a]2 Cor. 5:11
3 [a][1 Cor. 1:18]; 2 Cor. 2:15
4 [a]John 12:31; [Eph. 6:12] [b]John 12:40 [c][2 Cor. 3:8, 9] [d][John 1:18]; Phil. 2:6; Col. 1:15; Heb. 1:3
5 [a]1 Cor. 1:13 [b]1 Cor. 9:19
6 [a]Gen. 1:3 [b]Is. 9:2; Mal. 4:2; Luke 1:78; 2 Pet. 1:19

*———
3:6 Or *spirit*

NKJV

Christ's Epistle
(cf. Jer. 31:31–34)

3 Do [a]we begin again to commend ourselves? Or do we need, as some *others*, [b]epistles of commendation to you or *letters* of commendation from you?

2 [a]You are our epistle written in our hearts, known and read by all men;

3 clearly *you are* an epistle of Christ, [a]ministered by us, written not with ink but by the Spirit of the living God, not [b]on tablets of stone but [c]on tablets of flesh, *that is*, of the heart.

The Spirit, Not the Letter

4 And we have such trust through Christ toward God.

5 [a]Not that we are sufficient of ourselves to think of anything as *being* from ourselves, but [b]our sufficiency *is* from God,

6 who also made us sufficient as [a]ministers of [b]the new covenant, not [c]of the letter but of the *Spirit; for [d]the letter kills, [e]but the Spirit gives life.

Glory of the New Covenant

7 But if [a]the ministry of death, [b]written *and* engraved on stones, was glorious, [c]so that the children of Israel could not look steadily at the face of Moses because of the glory of his countenance, which *glory* was passing away,

8 how will [a]the ministry of the Spirit not be more glorious?

9 For if the ministry of condemnation *had* glory, the ministry [a]of righteousness exceeds much more in glory.

10 For even what was made glorious had no glory in this respect, because of the glory that excels.

11 For if what is passing away *was* glorious, what remains *is* much more glorious.

12 Therefore, since we have such hope, [a]we use great boldness of speech—

13 unlike Moses, [a]*who* put a veil over his face so that the children of Israel could not look steadily at [b]the end of what was passing away.

14 But [a]their minds were blinded. For until this day the same veil remains unlifted in the reading of the Old Testament, because the *veil* is taken away in Christ.

15 But even to this day, when Moses is read, a veil lies on their heart.

16 Nevertheless [a]when one turns to the Lord, [b]the veil is taken away.

17 Now [a]the Lord is the Spirit; and where the Spirit of the Lord *is*, there *is* [b]liberty.

18 But we all, with unveiled face, beholding [a]as in a mirror [b]the glory of the Lord, [c]are being transformed into the same image from glory to glory, just as by the Spirit of the Lord.

The Light of Christ's Gospel

4 Therefore, since we have this ministry, [a]as we have received mercy, we [b]do not lose heart.

2 But we have renounced the hidden things of shame, not walking in craftiness nor handling the word of God deceitfully, but by manifestation of the truth [a]commending ourselves to every man's conscience in the sight of God.

3 But even if our gospel is veiled, [a]it is veiled to those who are perishing,

4 whose minds [a]the god of this age [b]has blinded, who do not believe, lest [c]the light of the gospel of the glory of Christ, [d]who is the image of God, should shine on them.

5 [a]For we do not preach ourselves, but Christ Jesus the Lord, and [b]ourselves your bondservants for Jesus' sake.

6 For it is the God [a]who commanded light to shine out of darkness, who has [b]shone in our

to *give* the light of the knowledge of the glory of
God in the face of Jesus Christ.

Cast Down but Unconquered

7 But we have this treasure in earthen vessels, [a]that the excellency of the power may be of
God, and not of us.
8 *We are* [a]troubled on every side, yet not
distressed; *we are* perplexed, but not in despair;
9 Persecuted, but not [a]forsaken; [b]cast
down, but not destroyed;
10 [a]Always bearing about in the body the
dying of the Lord Jesus, [b]that the life also of Jesus
might be made manifest in our body.
11 For we which live [a]are alway delivered
unto death for Jesus' sake, that the life also of
Jesus might be made manifest in our mortal flesh.
12 So then death worketh in us, but life in
you.
13 We having [a]the same spirit of faith, according as it is written, [b]I BELIEVED, AND THEREFORE
HAVE I SPOKEN; we also believe, and therefore
speak;
14 Knowing that [a]he which raised up the
Lord Jesus shall raise up us also by Jesus, and
shall present *us* with you.
15 For [a]all things *are* for your sakes, that [b]the
abundant grace might through the thanksgiving
of many redound to the glory of God.

Seeing the Invisible

16 For which cause we faint [a]not; but though
our outward man perish, yet the inward *man* is
[b]renewed day by day.
17 For [a]our light affliction, which is but for
a moment, worketh for us a far more exceeding
and eternal weight of glory;
18 [a]While we look not at the things which
are seen, but at the things which are not seen:
for the things which are seen *are* temporal; but
the things which are not seen *are* eternal.

Assurance of the Resurrection

5 For we know that if [a]our earthly house of *this*
tabernacle were dissolved, we have a building
of God, an house [b]not made with hands, eternal
in the heavens.
2 For in this [a]we groan, earnestly desiring
to be clothed upon with our house which is from
heaven:
3 If so be that [a]being clothed we shall not
be found naked.
4 For we that are in *this* tabernacle do
groan, being burdened: not for that we would be
unclothed, but [a]clothed upon, that mortality might
be swallowed up of life.
5 Now he that hath wrought us for the selfsame thing *is* God, who also [a]hath given unto us
the earnest of the Spirit.
6 Therefore *we are* always confident, knowing that, whilst we are at home in the body, we
are absent from the Lord:
7 (For [a]we walk by faith, not by sight:)
8 We are confident, *I say*, and [a]willing
rather to be absent from the body, and to be present with the Lord.

The Judgment Seat of Christ

9 Wherefore we labour, that, whether present or absent, we may be accepted of him.
10 [a]For we must all appear before the judgment seat of Christ; [b]that every one may receive
the things *done* in *his* body, according to that he
hath done, whether *it be* good or bad.
11 Knowing therefore [a]the terror of the Lord,
we persuade men; but we are made manifest unto
God; and I trust also are made manifest in your
consciences.

Be Reconciled to God

12 For [a]we commend not ourselves again
unto you, but give you occasion [b]to glory on our

7 [a]Judg. 7:2; 1 Cor. 2:5
8 [a]2 Cor. 1:8; 7:5
9 [a]Ps. 37:24 [b]Ps. 129:2; [Heb. 13:5]
10 [a]Phil. 3:10 [b]Rom. 8:17
11 [a]Rom. 8:36
13 [a]2 Pet. 1:1 [b]Ps. 116:10
14 [a][Rom. 8:11]
15 [a]Col. 1:24 [b]1 Cor. 9:19; 2 Cor. 1:11
16 [a]2 Cor. 4:1; Gal. 6:9 [b][Is. 40:29, 31; Col. 3:10]
17 [a]Matt. 5:12; Rom. 8:18; 1 Pet. 1:6
18 [a]Rom. 8:24; [2 Cor. 5:7; Heb. 11:1, 13]

CHAPTER 5

1 [a]Job 4:19; 1 Cor. 15:47; 2 Cor. 4:7 [b]Mark 14:58; Acts 7:48; Heb. 9:11, 24
2 [a]Rom. 8:23; 2 Cor. 5:4
3 [a]Rev. 3:18
4 [a]1 Cor. 15:53
5 [a]Rom. 8:23; [2 Cor. 1:22]; Eph. 1:14
7 [a]Rom. 8:24; Heb. 11:1
8 [a]Phil. 1:23
10 [a]Matt. 16:27; Acts 10:42; Rom. 2:16; 14:10, 12 [b]Gal. 6:7; Eph. 6:8
11 [a][Heb. 10:31; 12:29; Jude 23]
12 [a]2 Cor. 3:1 [b]2 Cor. 1:14; Phil. 1:26

hearts to *give* the light of the knowledge of the
glory of God in the face of Jesus Christ.

Cast Down but Unconquered

7 But we have this treasure in earthen vessels, [a]that the excellence of the power may be of
God and not of us.
8 *We are* [a]hard-pressed on every side, yet
not crushed; *we are* perplexed, but not in despair;
9 persecuted, but not [a]forsaken; [b]struck
down, but not destroyed—
10 [a]always carrying about in the body the
dying of the Lord Jesus, [b]that the life of Jesus
also may be manifested in our body.
11 For we who live [a]are always delivered to
death for Jesus' sake, that the life of Jesus also
may be manifested in our mortal flesh.
12 So then death is working in us, but life
in you.
13 And since we have [a]the same spirit of
faith, according to what is written, [b]*"I believed
and therefore I spoke,"* we also believe and therefore speak,
14 knowing that [a]He who raised up the Lord
Jesus will also raise us up with Jesus, and will
present *us* with you.
15 For [a]all things *are* for your sakes, that
[b]grace, having spread through the many, may
cause thanksgiving to abound to the glory of God.

Seeing the Invisible

16 Therefore we [a]do not lose heart. Even
though our outward man is perishing, yet the inward *man* is [b]being renewed day by day.
17 For [a]our light affliction, which is but for
a moment, is working for us a far more exceeding
and eternal weight of glory,
18 [a]while we do not look at the things which
are seen, but at the things which are not seen.
For the things which are seen *are* temporary, but
the things which are not seen *are* eternal.

Assurance of the Resurrection

5 For we know that if [a]our earthly house, *this*
tent, is destroyed, we have a building from
God, a house [b]not made with hands, eternal in
the heavens.
2 For in this [a]we groan, earnestly desiring
to be clothed with our habitation which is from
heaven,
3 if indeed, [a]having been clothed, we shall
not be found naked.
4 For we who are in *this* tent groan, being
burdened, not because we want to be unclothed,
[a]but further clothed, that mortality may be swallowed up by life.
5 Now He who has prepared us for this very
thing *is* God, who also [a]has given us the Spirit
as a guarantee.
6 So *we are* always confident, knowing that
while we are at home in the body we are absent
from the Lord.
7 For [a]we walk by faith, not by sight.
8 We are confident, yes, [a]well pleased
rather to be absent from the body and to be present with the Lord.

The Judgment Seat of Christ

9 Therefore we make it our aim, whether
present or absent, to be well pleasing to Him.
10 [a]For we must all appear before the judgment seat of Christ, [b]that each one may receive
the things *done* in the body, according to what
he has done, whether good or bad.
11 Knowing, therefore, [a]the terror of the
Lord, we persuade men; but we are well known
to God, and I also trust are well known in your
consciences.

Be Reconciled to God

12 For [a]we do not commend ourselves again
to you, but give you opportunity [b]to boast on our

KJV

behalf, that ye may have somewhat to *answer* them which glory in appearance, and not in heart.

13 For [a]whether we be beside ourselves, *it is* to God: or whether we be sober, *it is* for your cause.

14 For the love of Christ constraineth us; because we thus judge, that [a]if one died for all, then were all dead:

15 And *that* he died for all, [a]that they which live should not henceforth live unto themselves, but unto him which died for them, and rose again.

16 [a]Wherefore henceforth know we no man after the flesh: yea, though we have known Christ after the flesh, [b]yet now henceforth know we *him* no more.

17 Therefore if any man [a]*be* in Christ, *he is* [b]a new creature: [c]old things are passed away; behold, all things are become [d]new.

18 And all things *are* of God, [a]who hath reconciled us to himself by Jesus Christ, and hath given to us the ministry of reconciliation;

19 To wit, that [a]God was in Christ, reconciling the world unto himself, not imputing their trespasses unto them; and hath committed unto us the word of reconciliation.

20 Now then we are [a]ambassadors for Christ, as though God did beseech *you* by us: we pray *you* in Christ's stead, be ye reconciled to God.

21 For [a]he hath made him *to be* sin for us, who knew no sin; that we might be made [b]the righteousness of God in him.

Marks of the Ministry

6 We then, *as* [a]workers together *with him*, [b]beseech *you* also that ye receive not the grace of God in vain.

2 (For he saith, [a]I HAVE HEARD THEE IN A TIME ACCEPTED, AND IN THE DAY OF SALVATION HAVE I SUCCOURED THEE: behold, now *is* the accepted time; behold, now *is* the day of salvation.)

3 [a]Giving no offence in any thing, that the ministry be not blamed:

4 But in all *things* approving ourselves [a]as the ministers of God, in much patience, in afflictions, in necessities, in distresses,

5 [a]In stripes, in imprisonments, in tumults, in labours, in watchings, in fastings;

6 By pureness, by knowledge, by longsuffering, by kindness, by the Holy Ghost, by love unfeigned,

7 [a]By the word of truth, by [b]the power of God, by [c]the armour of righteousness on the right hand and on the left,

8 By honour and dishonour, by evil report and good report: as deceivers, and *yet* true;

9 As unknown, and [a]*yet* well known; [b]as dying, and, behold, we live; [c]as chastened, and not killed;

10 As sorrowful, yet alway rejoicing; as poor, yet making many [a]rich; as having nothing, and *yet* possessing all things.

Be Holy

11 O *ye* Corinthians, our mouth is open unto you, [a]our heart is enlarged.

12 Ye are not straitened in us, but [a]ye are straitened in your own bowels.

13 Now for a recompence in the same, [a](I speak as unto *my* children,) be ye also enlarged.

14 [a]Be ye not unequally yoked together with unbelievers: for [b]what fellowship hath righteousness with unrighteousness? and what communion hath light with darkness?

15 And what concord hath Christ with Belial? or what part hath he that believeth with an infidel?

16 And what agreement hath the temple of

13 [a]Mark 3:21; 2 Cor. 11:1, 16; 12:11
14 [a][Rom. 5:15; 6:6; Gal. 2:20; Col. 3:3]
15 [a][Rom. 6:11]
16 [a]2 Cor. 10:3 [b][Matt. 12:50]
17 [a][John 6:63] [b][Rom. 8:9] [c]Is. 43:18; 65:17; [Eph. 4:24]; Rev. 21:4 [d][Rom. 6:3–10; Col. 3:3]
18 [a]Rom. 5:10; [Eph. 2:16; Col. 1:20]
19 [a][Rom. 3:24]
20 [a]Mal. 2:7; Eph. 6:20
21 [a]Is. 53:6, 9 [b][Rom. 1:17; 3:21]; 1 Cor. 1:30

CHAPTER 6

1 [a]1 Cor. 3:9 [b]2 Cor. 5:20
2 [a]Is. 49:8
3 [a]Rom. 14:13
4 [a]1 Cor. 4:1
5 [a]2 Cor. 11:23
7 [a]2 Cor. 7:14 [b]1 Cor. 2:4 [c]Rom. 13:12; 2 Cor. 10:4
9 [a]2 Cor. 4:2; 5:11 [b]1 Cor. 4:9, 11 [c]Ps. 118:18
10 [a]1 Cor. 1:5; [2 Cor. 8:9]
11 [a]Is. 60:5; 2 Cor. 7:3
12 [a]2 Cor. 12:15
13 [a]1 Cor. 4:14
14 [a]Deut. 7:2, 3; 22:10; 1 Cor. 5:9 [b]1 Sam. 5:2, 3; 1 Kin. 18:21; Eph. 5:6, 7, 11; 1 John 1:6

NKJV

behalf, that you may have *an answer* for those who boast in appearance and not in heart.

13 For [a]if we are beside ourselves, *it is* for God; or if we are of sound mind, *it is* for you.

14 For the love of Christ compels us, because we judge thus: that [a]if One died for all, then all died;

15 and He died for all, [a]that those who live should live no longer for themselves, but for Him who died for them and rose again.

16 [a]Therefore, from now on, we regard no one according to the flesh. Even though we have known Christ according to the flesh, [b]yet now we know *Him thus* no longer.

17 Therefore, if anyone [a]*is* in Christ, *he is* [b]a new creation; [c]old things have passed away; behold, all things have become [d]new.

18 Now all things *are* of God, [a]who has reconciled us to Himself through Jesus Christ, and has given us the ministry of reconciliation,

19 that is, that [a]God was in Christ reconciling the world to Himself, not imputing their trespasses to them, and has committed to us the word of reconciliation.

20 Now then, we are [a]ambassadors for Christ, as though God were pleading through us: we implore *you* on Christ's behalf, be reconciled to God.

21 For [a]He made Him who knew no sin *to be* sin for us, that we might become [b]the righteousness of God in Him.

Marks of the Ministry

6 We then, *as* [a]workers together *with Him* also [b]plead with *you* not to receive the grace of God in vain.

2 For He says:

> [a]*"In an acceptable time I have heard you,*
> *And in the day of salvation I have helped you."*

Behold, now *is* the accepted time; behold, now *is* the day of salvation.

3 [a]We give no offense in anything, that our ministry may not be blamed.

4 But in all *things* we commend ourselves [a]as ministers of God: in much patience, in tribulations, in needs, in distresses,

5 [a]in stripes, in imprisonments, in tumults, in labors, in sleeplessness, in fastings;

6 by purity, by knowledge, by longsuffering, by kindness, by the Holy Spirit, by sincere love,

7 [a]by the word of truth, by [b]the power of God, by [c]the armor of righteousness on the right hand and on the left,

8 by honor and dishonor, by evil report and good report; as deceivers, and *yet* true;

9 as unknown, and [a]*yet* well known; [b]as dying, and behold we live; [c]as chastened, and *yet* not killed;

10 as sorrowful, yet always rejoicing; as poor, yet making many [a]rich; as having nothing, and *yet* possessing all things.

Be Holy

11 O Corinthians! We have spoken openly to you, [a]our heart is wide open.

12 You are not restricted by us, but [a]you are restricted by your *own* affections.

13 Now in return for the same [a](I speak as to children), you also be open.

14 [a]Do not be unequally yoked together with unbelievers. For [b]what fellowship has righteousness with lawlessness? And what communion has light with darkness?

15 And what accord has Christ with Belial? Or what part has a believer with an unbeliever?

16 And what agreement has the temple of

KJV

God with idols? for [a]ye are the temple of the living
God; as God hath said, [b]I WILL DWELL IN THEM, AND
WALK IN *THEM;* AND I WILL BE THEIR GOD, AND THEY
SHALL BE MY PEOPLE.
17 [a]Wherefore COME OUT FROM AMONG THEM,
AND BE YE SEPARATE, saith the Lord, AND TOUCH NOT
THE UNCLEAN *THING;* AND I WILL RECEIVE YOU,
18 [a]AND WILL BE A FATHER UNTO YOU, AND YE
SHALL BE MY [b]SONS AND DAUGHTERS, saith the Lord
Almighty.

7 Having [a]therefore these promises, dearly beloved, let us cleanse ourselves from all filthiness of the flesh and spirit, perfecting holiness
in the fear of God.

The Corinthians' Repentance

2 Receive us; we have wronged no man, we
have corrupted no man, [a]we have defrauded no
man.
3 I speak not *this* to condemn *you:* for [a]I
have said before, that ye are in our hearts to die
and live with *you.*
4 [a]Great *is* my boldness of speech toward
you, [b]great *is* my glorying of you: [c]I am filled with
comfort, I am exceeding joyful in all our
tribulation.
5 For, [a]when we were come into Macedonia,
our flesh had no rest, but [b]we were troubled on
every side; [c]without *were* fightings, within *were*
fears.
6 Nevertheless [a]God, that comforteth those
that are cast down, comforted us by [b]the coming
of Titus;
7 And not by his coming only, but by the
consolation wherewith he was comforted in you,
when he told us your earnest desire, your mourning, your fervent mind toward me; so that I rejoiced the more.
8 For though I made you [a]sorry with a letter,
I do not repent, [b]though I did repent: for I perceive
that the same epistle hath made you sorry, though
it were but for a season.
9 Now I rejoice, not that ye were made
sorry, but that ye sorrowed to repentance: for ye
were made sorry after a godly manner, that ye
might receive damage by us in nothing.
10 For [a]godly sorrow worketh repentance to
salvation not to be repented of: [b]but the sorrow
of the world worketh death.
11 For behold this selfsame thing, that ye sorrowed after a godly sort, what carefulness it
wrought in you, yea, *what* [a]clearing of yourselves,
yea, *what* indignation, yea, *what* fear, yea, *what*
vehement desire, yea, *what* zeal, yea, *what* revenge! In all *things* ye have approved yourselves
to be [b]clear in this matter.
12 Wherefore, though I wrote unto you, *I did*
it not for his cause that had done the wrong, nor
for his cause that suffered wrong, [a]but that our
care for you in the sight of God might appear unto
you.

The Joy of Titus

13 Therefore we were comforted in your
comfort: yea, and exceedingly the more joyed we
for the joy of Titus, because his spirit [a]was refreshed by you all.
14 For if I have boasted any thing to him of
you, I am not ashamed; but as we spake all things
to you in truth, even so our boasting, which *I made*
before Titus, is found a truth.
15 And his inward affection is more abun-

16 [a][1 Cor. 3:16, 17; 6:19]; Eph. 2:21; [Heb. 3:6] [b]Ex. 29:45; Lev. 26:12; Jer. 31:33; 32:38; Ezek. 37:26, 27; Zech. 8:8
17 [a]Num. 33:51–56; Is. 52:11; Rev. 18:4
18 [a]2 Sam. 7:14; Jer. 31:1, 9; [Rev. 21:7] [b][John 1:12; Rom. 8:14; Gal. 4:5–7]; Phil. 2:15; 1 John 3:1

CHAPTER 7

1 [a][1 John 3:3]
2 [a]Acts 20:33
3 [a]2 Cor. 6:11, 12
4 [a]2 Cor. 3:12 [b]1 Cor. 1:4 [c]Phil. 2:17; Col. 1:24
5 [a]Rom. 15:26; 2 Cor. 2:13 [b]2 Cor. 4:8 [c]Deut. 32:25
6 [a]Is. 49:13; 2 Cor. 1:3, 4 [b]2 Cor. 2:13; 7:13
8 [a]2 Cor. 2:2 [b]2 Cor. 2:4
10 [a]2 Sam. 12:13; Ps. 32:10; Matt. 26:75 [b]Prov. 17:22
11 [a]Eph. 5:11 [b]2 Cor. 2:5–11
12 [a]2 Cor. 2:4
13 [a]Rom. 15:32

*__________
6:16 NU *we*

NKJV

God with idols? For [a]you* are the temple of the
living God. As God has said:

[b]*"I will dwell in them*
And walk among them.
I will be their God,
And they shall be My people."

17 Therefore

[a]*"Come out from among them*
And be separate, says the Lord.
Do not touch what is unclean,
And I will receive you."
18 *"I [a]will be a Father to you,*
And you shall be My [b]sons and daughters,
Says the LORD *Almighty."*

7 Therefore,[a] having these promises, beloved,
let us cleanse ourselves from all filthiness of
the flesh and spirit, perfecting holiness in the fear
of God.

The Corinthians' Repentance

2 Open *your hearts* to us. We have wronged
no one, we have corrupted no one, [a]we have
cheated no one.
3 I do not say *this* to condemn; for [a]I have
said before that you are in our hearts, to die together and to live together.
4 [a]Great *is* my boldness of speech toward
you, [b]great *is* my boasting on your behalf. [c]I am
filled with comfort. I am exceedingly joyful in all
our tribulation.
5 For indeed, [a]when we came to Macedonia,
our bodies had no rest, but [b]we were troubled
on every side. [c]Outside *were* conflicts, inside *were*
fears.
6 Nevertheless [a]God, who comforts the
downcast, comforted us by [b]the coming of Titus,
7 and not only by his coming, but also by
the consolation with which he was comforted in
you, when he told us of your earnest desire, your
mourning, your zeal for me, so that I rejoiced even
more.
8 For even if I made you [a]sorry with my
letter, I do not regret it; [b]though I did regret it.
For I perceive that the same epistle made you
sorry, though only for a while.
9 Now I rejoice, not that you were made
sorry, but that your sorrow led to repentance. For
you were made sorry in a godly manner, that you
might suffer loss from us in nothing.
10 For [a]godly sorrow produces repentance
leading to salvation, not to be regretted; [b]but the
sorrow of the world produces death.
11 For observe this very thing, that you sorrowed in a godly manner: What diligence it produced in you, *what* [a]clearing *of yourselves, what*
indignation, *what* fear, *what* vehement desire,
what zeal, *what* vindication! In all *things* you
proved yourselves to be [b]clear in this matter.
12 Therefore, although I wrote to you, *I did*
not *do it* for the sake of him who had done the
wrong, nor for the sake of him who suffered
wrong, [a]but that our care for you in the sight of
God might appear to you.

The Joy of Titus

13 Therefore we have been comforted in your
comfort. And we rejoiced exceedingly more for
the joy of Titus, because his spirit [a]has been refreshed by you all.
14 For if in anything I have boasted to him
about you, I am not ashamed. But as we spoke
all things to you in truth, even so our boasting to
Titus was found true.
15 And his affections are greater for you as

KJV

dant toward you, whilst he remembereth [a]the obedience of you all, how with fear and trembling ye received him.

16 I rejoice therefore that [a]I have confidence in you in all *things*.

Excel in Giving

8 Moreover, brethren, we do you to wit of the grace of God bestowed on the churches of Macedonia;

2 How that in a great trial of affliction the abundance of their joy and [a]their deep poverty abounded unto the riches of their liberality.

3 For to *their* power, I bear record, yea, and beyond *their* power *they were* willing of themselves;

4 Praying us with much intreaty that we would receive the gift, and *take upon us* [a]the fellowship of the ministering to the saints.

5 And *this they did*, not as we hoped, but first [a]gave their own selves to the Lord, and unto us by the [b]will of God.

6 Insomuch that [a]we desired Titus, that as he had begun, so he would also finish in you the same grace also.

7 Therefore, as [a]ye abound in every *thing*, *in* faith, and utterance, and knowledge, and *in* all diligence, and *in* your love to us, *see* [b]that ye abound in this grace also.

Christ Our Pattern

8 [a]I speak not by commandment, but by occasion of the forwardness of others, and to prove the sincerity of your love.

9 For ye know the grace of our Lord Jesus Christ, [a]that, though he was rich, yet for your sakes he became poor, that ye through his poverty might be [b]rich.

10 And herein [a]I give *my* advice: for [b]this is expedient for you, who have begun before, not only to do, but also to be [c]forward a year ago.

11 Now therefore perform the doing *of it;* that as *there was* a readiness to will, so *there may be* a performance also out of that which ye have.

12 For [a]if there be first a willing mind, *it is* accepted according to that a man hath, *and* not according to that he hath not.

13 For *I mean* not that other men be eased, and ye burdened:

14 But by an equality, *that* now at this time your abundance *may be a supply* for their want, that their abundance also may be *a supply* for your want: that there may be equality:

15 As it is written, [a]HE THAT *HAD GATHERED* MUCH HAD NOTHING OVER; AND HE THAT *HAD GATHERED* LITTLE HAD NO LACK.

Collection for the Judean Saints

16 But thanks *be* to God, which put the same earnest care into the heart of Titus for you.

17 For indeed he accepted the exhortation; but being more forward, of his own accord he went unto you.

18 And we have sent with him [a]the brother, whose praise *is* in the gospel throughout all the churches;

19 And not *that* only, but who was also [a]chosen of the churches to travel with us with this grace, which is administered by us [b]to the glory of the same Lord, and *declaration of* your ready mind:

20 Avoiding this, that no man should blame us in this abundance which is administered by us:

21 [a]Providing for honest things, not only in the sight of the Lord, but also in the sight of men.

22 And we have sent with them our brother, whom we have oftentimes proved diligent in many things, but now much more diligent, upon the great confidence which *I have* in you.

23 Whether *any do enquire* of [a]Titus, *he is* my partner and fellowhelper concerning you: or

---

15 [a]2 Cor. 2:9; Phil. 2:12
16 [a]2 Cor. 2:3; 8:22; 2 Thess. 3:4; Philem. 8, 21

CHAPTER 8

2 [a]Mark 12:44
4 [a]Acts 11:29; 24:17; Rom. 15:25, 26; 1 Cor. 16:1, 3, 4; 2 Cor. 9:1
5 [a][Rom. 12:1, 2] [b][Eph. 6:6]
6 [a]2 Cor. 8:17; 12:18
7 [a][1 Cor. 1:5; 12:13] [b]2 Cor. 9:8
8 [a]1 Cor. 7:6
9 [a]Matt. 8:20; Luke 9:58; Phil. 2:6, 7 [b]Rom. 9:23; [Eph. 1:7; Rev. 3:18]
10 [a]1 Cor. 7:25, 40 [b][Prov. 19:17; Matt. 10:42; 1 Tim. 6:18, 19; Heb. 13:16] [c]1 Cor. 16:2; 2 Cor. 9:2
12 [a]Mark 12:43, 44; Luke 21:3, 4; 2 Cor. 9:7
15 [a]Ex. 16:18
18 [a]1 Cor. 16:3; 2 Cor. 12:18
19 [a]Acts 14:23; 1 Cor. 16:3, 4 [b]2 Cor. 4:15
21 [a]Rom. 12:17; Phil. 4:8; 1 Pet. 2:12
23 [a]2 Cor. 7:13, 14

*

8:4 NU, M omit *that we would receive*, thus changing text to *urgency for the favor and fellowship*
8:16 NU has *put*

NKJV

he remembers [a]the obedience of you all, how with fear and trembling you received him.

16 Therefore I rejoice that [a]I have confidence in you in everything.

Excel in Giving

8 Moreover, brethren, we make known to you the grace of God bestowed on the churches of Macedonia:

2 that in a great trial of affliction the abundance of their joy and [a]their deep poverty abounded in the riches of their liberality.

3 For I bear witness that according to *their* ability, yes, and beyond *their* ability, *they were* freely willing,

4 imploring us with much urgency *that we would receive the gift and [a]the fellowship of the ministering to the saints.

5 And not *only* as we had hoped, but they first [a]gave themselves to the Lord, and *then* to us by the [b]will of God.

6 So [a]we urged Titus, that as he had begun, so he would also complete this grace in you as well.

7 But as [a]you abound in everything—in faith, in speech, in knowledge, in all diligence, and in your love for us—*see* [b]that you abound in this grace also.

Christ Our Pattern

8 [a]I speak not by commandment, but I am testing the sincerity of your love by the diligence of others.

9 For you know the grace of our Lord Jesus Christ, [a]that though He was rich, yet for your sakes He became poor, that you through His poverty might become [b]rich.

10 And in this [a]I give advice: [b]It is to your advantage not only to be doing what you began and [c]were desiring to do a year ago;

11 but now you also must complete the doing *of it;* that as *there was* a readiness to desire *it*, so *there* also *may be* a completion out of what you have.

12 For [a]if there is first a willing mind, *it is* accepted according to what one has, *and* not according to what he does not have.

13 For *I do* not *mean* that others should be eased and you burdened;

14 but by an equality, *that* now at this time your abundance *may supply* their lack, that their abundance also may supply your lack—that there may be equality.

15 As it is written, [a]*"He who gathered much had nothing left over, and he who gathered little had no lack."*

Collection for the Judean Saints

16 But thanks *be* to God who *puts the same earnest care for you into the heart of Titus.

17 For he not only accepted the exhortation, but being more diligent, he went to you of his own accord.

18 And we have sent with him [a]the brother whose praise *is* in the gospel throughout all the churches,

19 and not only *that*, but who was also [a]chosen by the churches to travel with us with this gift, which is administered by us [b]to the glory of the Lord Himself and *to show* your ready mind,

20 avoiding this: that anyone should blame us in this lavish gift which is administered by us—

21 [a]providing honorable things, not only in the sight of the Lord, but also in the sight of men.

22 And we have sent with them our brother whom we have often proved diligent in many things, but now much more diligent, because of the great confidence which *we have* in you.

23 If *anyone inquires* about [a]Titus, *he is* my partner and fellow worker concerning you. Or if

KJV

our brethren *be enquired of, they are* [b]the messengers of the churches, *and* the glory of Christ.

24 Wherefore shew ye to them, and before the churches, the proof of your love, and of our [a]boasting on your behalf.

Administering the Gift

9 For as touching [a]the ministering to the saints, it is superfluous for me to write to you:

2 For I know the forwardness of your mind, for which I boast of you to them of Macedonia, that Achaia was ready a [a]year ago; and your zeal hath provoked very many.

3 [a]Yet have I sent the brethren, lest our boasting of you should be in vain in this behalf; that, as I said, ye may be ready:

4 Lest haply if they of Macedonia come with me, and find you unprepared, we (that we say not, ye) should be ashamed in this same confident boasting.

5 Therefore I thought it necessary to exhort the brethren, that they would go before unto you, and make up beforehand your bounty, whereof ye had notice before, that the same might be ready, as *a matter of* bounty, and not as *of* covetousness.

The Cheerful Giver

6 [a]But this *I say,* He which soweth sparingly shall reap also sparingly; and he which soweth bountifully shall reap also bountifully.

7 Every man according as he purposeth in his heart, *so let him give;* [a]not grudgingly, or of necessity: for [b]God loveth a cheerful giver.

8 [a]And God *is* able to make all grace abound toward you; that ye, always having all sufficiency in all *things,* may abound to every good work:

9 (As it is written, [a]HE HATH DISPERSED ABROAD; HE HATH GIVEN TO THE POOR: HIS RIGHTEOUSNESS REMAINETH FOR EVER.

10 Now he that [a]ministereth seed to the sower both minister bread for *your* food, and multiply your seed sown, and increase the fruits of your [b]righteousness;)

11 Being enriched in every thing to all bountifulness, [a]which causeth through us thanksgiving to God.

12 For the administration of this service not only [a]supplieth the want of the saints, but is abundant also by many thanksgivings unto God;

13 Whiles by the experiment of this ministration they [a]glorify God for your professed subjection unto the gospel of Christ, and for *your* liberal [b]distribution unto them, and unto all *men;*

14 And by their prayer for you, which long after you for the exceeding [a]grace of God in you.

15 Thanks *be* unto God [a]for his unspeakable gift.

The Spiritual War

10 Now [a]I Paul myself beseech you by the meekness and gentleness of Christ, [b]who in presence *am* base among you, but being absent am bold toward you:

2 But I beseech *you,* [a]that I may not be bold when I am present with that confidence, wherewith I think to be bold against some, which think of us as if we walked according to the flesh.

3 For though we walk in the flesh, we do not war after the flesh:

4 ([a]For the weapons [b]of our warfare *are* not carnal, but [c]mighty through God [d]to the pulling down of strong holds;)

5 [a]Casting down imaginations, and every high thing that exalteth itself against the knowledge of God, and bringing into captivity every thought to the obedience of Christ;

---

23 [b][John 13:16]; Phil. 2:25
24 [a]2 Cor. 7:4, 14; 9:2

CHAPTER 9

1 [a]Acts 11:29; Rom. 15:26; 1 Cor. 16:1; 2 Cor. 8:4; Gal. 2:10
2 [a]2 Cor. 8:10
3 [a]2 Cor. 8:6, 17
6 [a]Prov. 11:24; 22:9; Gal. 6:7, 9
7 [a]Deut. 15:7 [b]Deut. 15:10; 1 Chr. 29:17; [Prov. 11:25]; Rom. 12:8; [2 Cor. 8:12]
8 [a][Prov. 11:24]
9 [a]Ps. 112:9
10 [a]Is. 55:10 [b]Hos. 10:12
11 [a]2 Cor. 1:11
12 [a]2 Cor. 8:14
13 [a][Matt. 5:16] [b][Heb. 13:16]
14 [a]2 Cor. 8:1
15 [a][John 3:16; 4:10; Rom. 6:23; 8:32; Eph. 2:8; James 1:17]

CHAPTER 10

1 [a]Rom. 12:1 [b]1 Thess. 2:7
2 [a]1 Cor. 4:21; 2 Cor. 13:2, 10
4 [a]Eph. 6:13 [b]1 Cor. 9:7; [2 Cor. 6:7]; 1 Tim. 1:18 [c]Acts 7:22 [d]Jer. 1:10; [2 Cor. 10:8; 13:10]
5 [a]1 Cor. 1:19

*
8:24 NU, M omit *and*
9:4 NU *confidence.*
9:10 NU *will supply*

NKJV

our brethren *are inquired about, they are* [b]messengers of the churches, the glory of Christ.

24 Therefore show to them, *and before the churches the proof of your love and of our [a]boasting on your behalf.

Administering the Gift

9 Now concerning [a]the ministering to the saints, it is superfluous for me to write to you;

2 for I know your willingness, about which I boast of you to the Macedonians, that Achaia was ready a [a]year ago; and your zeal has stirred up the majority.

3 [a]Yet I have sent the brethren, lest our boasting of you should be in vain in this respect, that, as I said, you may be ready;

4 lest if *some* Macedonians come with me and find you unprepared, we (not to mention you!) should be ashamed of this *confident boasting.

5 Therefore I thought it necessary to exhort the brethren to go to you ahead of time, and prepare your generous gift beforehand, which *you had* previously promised, that it may be ready as *a matter of* generosity and not as a grudging obligation.

The Cheerful Giver

6 [a]But this *I say:* He who sows sparingly will also reap sparingly, and he who sows bountifully will also reap bountifully.

7 *So let* each one *give* as he purposes in his heart, [a]not grudgingly or of necessity; for [b]God loves a cheerful giver.

8 [a]And God *is* able to make all grace abound toward you, that you, always having all sufficiency in all *things,* may have an abundance for every good work.

9 As it is written:

[a]*"He has dispersed abroad,*
He has given to the poor;
His righteousness endures forever."

10 Now may He who [a]supplies seed to the sower, and bread for food, *supply and multiply the seed you have *sown* and increase the fruits of your [b]righteousness,

11 while *you are* enriched in everything for all liberality, [a]which causes thanksgiving through us to God.

12 For the administration of this service not only [a]supplies the needs of the saints, but also is abounding through many thanksgivings to God,

13 while, through the proof of this ministry, they [a]glorify God for the obedience of your confession to the gospel of Christ, and for *your* liberal [b]sharing with them and all *men,*

14 and by their prayer for you, who long for you because of the exceeding [a]grace of God in you.

15 Thanks *be* to God [a]for His indescribable gift!

The Spiritual War

10 Now [a]I, Paul, myself am pleading with you by the meekness and gentleness of Christ—[b]who in presence *am* lowly among you, but being absent am bold toward you.

2 But I beg *you* [a]that when I am present I may not be bold with that confidence by which I intend to be bold against some, who think of us as if we walked according to the flesh.

3 For though we walk in the flesh, we do not war according to the flesh.

4 [a]For the weapons [b]of our warfare *are* not carnal but [c]mighty in God [d]for pulling down strongholds,

5 [a]casting down arguments and every high thing that exalts itself against the knowledge of God, bringing every thought into captivity to the obedience of Christ,

KJV

6 [a]And having in a readiness to revenge all disobedience, when [b]your obedience is fulfilled.

Reality of Paul's Authority

7 [a]Do ye look on things after the outward appearance? [b]If any man trust to himself that he is Christ's, let him of himself think this again, that, as he *is* Christ's, even so *are* [c]we Christ's.

8 For though I should boast somewhat more [a]of our authority, which the Lord hath given us for edification, and not for your destruction, [b]I should not be ashamed:

9 That I may not seem as if I would terrify you by letters.

10 For *his* letters, say they, *are* weighty and powerful; but [a]*his* bodily presence *is* weak, and *his* [b]speech contemptible.

11 Let such an one think this, that, such as we are in word by letters when we are absent, such *will we be* also in deed when we are present.

Limits of Paul's Authority

12 [a]For we dare not make ourselves of the number, or compare ourselves with some that commend themselves: but they measuring themselves by themselves, and comparing themselves among themselves, are not wise.

13 [a]But we will not boast of things without *our* measure, but according to the measure of the rule which God hath distributed to us, a measure to reach even unto you.

14 For we stretch not ourselves beyond *our measure*, as though we reached not unto you: [a]for we are come as far as to you also in *preaching* the gospel of Christ:

15 Not boasting of things without *our* measure, *that is*, [a]of other men's labours; but having hope, when your faith is increased, that we shall be enlarged by you according to our rule abundantly,

16 To preach the gospel in the *regions* beyond you, *and* not to boast in another man's line of things made ready to our hand.

17 [a]But HE THAT GLORIETH, LET HIM GLORY IN THE LORD.

18 For [a]not he that commendeth himself is approved, but [b]whom the Lord commendeth.

Concern for Their Faithfulness

11 Would to God ye could bear with me a little in [a]*my* folly: and indeed bear with me.

2 For I am [a]jealous over you with godly jealousy: for [b]I have espoused you to one husband, [c]that I may present *you* [d]*as* a chaste virgin to Christ.

3 But I fear, lest by any means, as [a]the serpent beguiled Eve through his subtilty, so your minds [b]should be corrupted from the simplicity that is in Christ.

4 For if he that cometh preacheth another Jesus, whom we have not preached, or *if* ye receive another spirit, which ye have not received, or [a]another gospel, which ye have not accepted, ye might well bear with *him*.

Paul and False Apostles

5 For I suppose [a]I was not a whit behind the very chiefest apostles.

6 But though [a]*I be* rude in speech, yet not [b]in knowledge; but [c]we have been throughly made manifest among you in all things.

7 Have I committed an offence in abasing myself that ye might be exalted, because I have preached to you the gospel of God [a]freely?

8 I robbed other churches, taking wages *of them*, to do you service.

9 And when I was present with you, and wanted, [a]I was chargeable to no man: for that which was lacking to me [b]the brethren which came from Macedonia supplied: and in all *things* I have kept myself from being burdensome unto you, and *so* will I keep *myself*.

---

6 [a]2 Cor. 13:2, 10 [b]2 Cor. 7:15
7 [a][John 7:24]; 2 Cor. 5:12 [b]1 Cor. 1:12; 14:37 [c][Rom. 14:8]; 1 Cor. 3:23
8 [a]2 Cor. 13:10 [b]2 Cor. 7:14
10 [a]1 Cor. 2:3, 4; 2 Cor. 12:7; Gal. 4:13 [b][1 Cor. 1:17]; 2 Cor. 11:6
12 [a]2 Cor. 5:12
13 [a]2 Cor. 10:15
14 [a]1 Cor. 3:5, 6
15 [a]Rom. 15:20
17 [a]Is. 65:16; Jer. 9:24; 1 Cor. 1:31
18 [a]Prov. 27:2 [b]Rom. 2:29; [1 Cor. 4:5]

CHAPTER 11

1 [a]Matt. 17:17; 2 Cor. 11:4, 16, 19
2 [a]Gal. 4:17 [b]Hos. 2:19; [Eph. 5:26] [c]Col. 1:28 [d]Lev. 21:13
3 [a]Gen. 3:4, 13; John 8:44; 1 Thess. 3:5; 1 Tim. 2:14; [Rev. 12:9, 15] [b]Eph. 6:24
4 [a]Gal. 1:6–8
5 [a][1 Cor. 15:10]; 2 Cor. 12:11; Gal. 2:6
6 [a][1 Cor. 1:17] [b][1 Cor. 12:8; Eph. 3:4] [c][2 Cor. 12:12]
7 [a]Acts 18:3; 1 Cor. 9:18; 2 Cor. 12:13
9 [a]Acts 20:33 [b]Phil. 4:10

*

10:7 NU *as we are.*
10:8 NU omits *us*
11:3 NU adds *and purity*
11:6 NU omits *been*

NKJV

6 [a]and being ready to punish all disobedience when [b]your obedience is fulfilled.

Reality of Paul's Authority

7 [a]Do you look at things according to the outward appearance? [b]If anyone is convinced in himself that he is Christ's, let him again consider this in himself, that just as he *is* Christ's, even *so [c]we *are* Christ's.

8 For even if I should boast somewhat more [a]about our authority, which the Lord gave *us for edification and not for your destruction, [b]I shall not be ashamed—

9 lest I seem to terrify you by letters.

10 "For *his* letters," they say, "*are* weighty and powerful, but [a]*his* bodily presence *is* weak, and *his* [b]speech contemptible."

11 Let such a person consider this, that what we are in word by letters when we are absent, such *we will* also *be* in deed when we are present.

Limits of Paul's Authority

12 [a]For we dare not class ourselves or compare ourselves with those who commend themselves. But they, measuring themselves by themselves, and comparing themselves among themselves, are not wise.

13 [a]We, however, will not boast beyond measure, but within the limits of the sphere which God appointed us—a sphere which especially includes you.

14 For we are not overextending ourselves (as though *our authority* did not extend to you), [a]for it was to you that we came with the gospel of Christ;

15 not boasting of things beyond measure, *that is*, [a]in other men's labors, but having hope, *that* as your faith is increased, we shall be greatly enlarged by you in our sphere,

16 to preach the gospel in the *regions* beyond you, *and* not to boast in another man's sphere of accomplishment.

17 But [a]*"he who glories, let him glory in the* LORD."

18 For [a]not he who commends himself is approved, but [b]whom the Lord commends.

Concern for Their Faithfulness

11 Oh, that you would bear with me in a little [a]folly—and indeed you do bear with me.

2 For I am [a]jealous for you with godly jealousy. For [b]I have betrothed you to one husband, [c]that I may present *you* [d]*as* a chaste virgin to Christ.

3 But I fear, lest somehow, as [a]the serpent deceived Eve by his craftiness, so your minds [b]may be corrupted from the *simplicity that is in Christ.

4 For if he who comes preaches another Jesus whom we have not preached, or *if* you receive a different spirit which you have not received, or a [a]different gospel which you have not accepted—you may well put up with it!

Paul and False Apostles

5 For I consider that [a]I am not at all inferior to the most eminent apostles.

6 Even though [a]*I am* untrained in speech, yet *I am* not [b]in knowledge. But [c]we have *been thoroughly manifested among you in all things.

7 Did I commit sin in humbling myself that you might be exalted, because I preached the gospel of God to you [a]free of charge?

8 I robbed other churches, taking wages *from them* to minister to you.

9 And when I was present with you, and in need, [a]I was a burden to no one, for what I lacked [b]the brethren who came from Macedonia supplied. And in everything I kept myself from being burdensome to you, and so I will keep *myself*.

KJV

10 [a]As the truth of Christ is in me, [b]no man
shall stop me of this boasting in the regions of
Achaia.
11 Wherefore? [a]because I love you not? God
knoweth.
12 But what I do, that I will do, [a]that I may
cut off occasion from them which desire occasion;
that wherein they glory, they may be found even
as we.
13 For such [a]*are* false apostles, [b]deceitful
workers, transforming themselves into the apostles of Christ.
14 And no marvel; for Satan himself is transformed into [a]an angel of light.
15 Therefore *it is* no great thing if his ministers also be transformed as the ministers of righteousness; [a]whose end shall be according to their
works.

Reluctant Boasting

16 I say again, Let no man think me a fool;
if otherwise, yet as a fool receive me, that I may
boast myself a little.
17 That which I speak, [a]I speak *it* not after
the Lord, but as it were foolishly, in this confidence of boasting.
18 Seeing that many glory after the flesh, I
will glory also.
19 For ye suffer fools gladly, [a]seeing ye *yourselves* are wise.
20 For ye suffer, [a]if a man bring you into
bondage, if a man devour *you*, if a man take *of
you*, if a man exalt himself, if a man smite you
on the face.
21 I speak as concerning reproach, [a]as
though we had been weak. Howbeit [b]whereinso-
ever any is bold, (I speak foolishly,) I am bold also.

Suffering for Christ

22 Are they [a]Hebrews? so *am* I. Are they Israelites? so *am* I. Are they the seed of Abraham?
so *am* I.
23 Are they ministers of Christ? (I speak as
a fool) I *am* more; [a]in labours more abundant,
[b]in stripes above measure, in prisons more frequent, [c]in deaths oft.
24 Of the Jews five times received I [a]forty
[b]*stripes* save one.
25 Thrice was I [a]beaten with rods, [b]once was
I stoned, thrice I [c]suffered shipwreck, a night and
a day I have been in the deep;
26 *In* journeyings often, *in* perils of waters,
in perils of robbers, [a]*in* perils by *mine own* countrymen, [b]*in* perils by the heathen, *in* perils in the
city, *in* perils in the wilderness, *in* perils in the
sea, *in* perils among false brethren;
27 In weariness and painfulness, [a]in watchings often, [b]in hunger and thirst, in [c]fastings often, in cold and nakedness.
28 Beside those things that are without, that
which cometh upon me daily, [a]the care of all the
churches.
29 [a]Who is weak, and I am not weak? who
is offended, and I burn not?
30 If I must needs glory, [a]I will glory of the
things which concern mine infirmities.
31 [a]The God and Father of our Lord Jesus
Christ, [b]which is blessed for evermore, knoweth
that I lie not.
32 [a]In Damascus the governor under Aretas
the king kept the city of the Damascenes with a
garrison, desirous to apprehend me:
33 And through a window in a basket was I
let down by the wall, and escaped his hands.

The Vision of Paradise

12 It is not expedient for me doubtless to glory.
I will come to [a]visions and [b]revelations of
the Lord.

---

10 [a]Rom. 1:9;
9:1; 2 Cor.
1:23; [Gal.
2:20] [b]1 Cor.
9:15
11 [a]2 Cor.
6:11; 12:15
12 [a]1 Cor.
9:12
13 [a]Acts
15:24; Rom.
16:18; Gal.
1:7; Phil. 1:15;
2 Pet. 2:1; Rev.
2:2 [b]Phil. 3:2;
Titus 1:10
14 [a]Gal. 1:8
15 [a][Phil.
3:19]
17 [a]1 Cor. 7:6
19 [a]1 Cor.
4:10
20 [a]2 Cor.
1:24; [Gal. 2:4;
4:3, 9; 5:1]
21 [a]2 Cor.
10:10 [b]Phil.
3:4
22 [a]Acts 22:3;
Rom. 11:1;
Phil. 3:4–6
23 [a]1 Cor.
15:10 [b]Acts
9:16 [c]1 Cor.
15:30
24 [a]Deut. 25:3
[b]2 Cor. 6:5
25 [a]Acts
16:22, 23;
21:32 [b]Acts
14:5, 19 [c]Acts
27:1–44
26 [a]Acts 9:23,
24; 13:45, 50;
17:5, 13;
1 Thess. 2:15
[b]Acts 14:5,
19; 19:23;
27:42
27 [a]Acts
20:31 [b]1 Cor.
4:11; Phil. 4:12
[c]Acts 9:9;
13:2, 3; 14:23
28 [a]Acts
20:18; [Rom.
1:14]; 2 Cor.
7:12; 12:20;
Gal. 4:11;
1 Thess. 3:10
29 [a][1 Cor.
8:9, 13; 9:22]
30 [a][2 Cor.
12:5, 9, 10]
31 [a]Rom. 1:9;
Gal. 1:20;
1 Thess. 2:5
[b]Rom. 9:5
32 [a]Acts
9:19–25

CHAPTER 12
1 [a]Acts 16:9;
18:9; 22:17, 18;
23:11; 26:13–
15; 27:23
[b]Acts 9:3–6;
1 Cor. 14:6;
2 Cor. 12:7;
[Gal. 1:12; 2:2;
Eph. 3:3–6]

*

12:1 NU *necessary,
though not
profitable, to
boast*

NKJV

10 [a]As the truth of Christ is in me, [b]no one
shall stop me from this boasting in the regions
of Achaia.
11 Why? [a]Because I do not love you? God
knows!
12 But what I do, I will also continue to do,
[a]that I may cut off the opportunity from those who
desire an opportunity to be regarded just as we
are in the things of which they boast.
13 For such [a]*are* false apostles, [b]deceitful
workers, transforming themselves into apostles of
Christ.
14 And no wonder! For Satan himself trans-
forms himself into [a]an angel of light.
15 Therefore *it is* no great thing if his ministers also transform themselves into ministers of
righteousness, [a]whose end will be according to
their works.

Reluctant Boasting

16 I say again, let no one think me a fool. If
otherwise, at least receive me as a fool, that I also
may boast a little.
17 What I speak, [a]I speak not according to
the Lord, but as it were, foolishly, in this confidence of boasting.
18 Seeing that many boast according to the
flesh, I also will boast.
19 For you put up with fools gladly, [a]since
you *yourselves* are wise!
20 For you put up with it [a]if one brings you
into bondage, if one devours *you*, if one takes *from
you*, if one exalts himself, if one strikes you on
the face.
21 To *our* shame [a]I say that we were too
weak for that! But [b]in whatever anyone is bold—
I speak foolishly—I am bold also.

Suffering for Christ

22 Are they [a]Hebrews? So *am* I. Are they Israelites? So *am* I. Are they the seed of Abraham?
So *am* I.
23 Are they ministers of Christ?—I speak as
a fool—I *am* more: [a]in labors more abundant, [b]in
stripes above measure, in prisons more fre-
quently, [c]in deaths often.
24 From the Jews five times I received [a]forty
[b]*stripes* minus one.
25 Three times I was [a]beaten with rods;
[b]once I was stoned; three times I [c]was ship-
wrecked; a night and a day I have been in the
deep;
26 *in* journeys often, *in* perils of waters, *in*
perils of robbers, [a]*in* perils of *my own* countrymen, [b]*in* perils of the Gentiles, *in* perils in the city,
in perils in the wilderness, *in* perils in the sea, *in*
perils among false brethren;
27 in weariness and toil, [a]in sleeplessness often, [b]in hunger and thirst, in [c]fastings often, in
cold and nakedness—
28 besides the other things, what comes
upon me daily: [a]my deep concern for all the
churches.
29 [a]Who is weak, and I am not weak? Who
is made to stumble, and I do not burn *with
indignation*?
30 If I must boast, [a]I will boast in the things
which concern my infirmity.
31 [a]The God and Father of our Lord Jesus
Christ, [b]who is blessed forever, knows that I am
not lying.
32 [a]In Damascus the governor, under Aretas
the king, was guarding the city of the Damascenes
with a garrison, desiring to arrest me;
33 but I was let down in a basket through
a window in the wall, and escaped from his
hands.

The Vision of Paradise

12 It is *doubtless not profitable for me to
boast. I will come to [a]visions and [b]revela-
tions of the Lord:

KJV

2 I knew a man [a]in Christ above fourteen
years ago, (whether in the body, I cannot tell; or
whether out of the body, I cannot tell: God knoweth;) such an one [b]caught up to the third heaven.
3 And I knew such a man, (whether in the
body, or out of the body, I cannot tell: God
knoweth;)
4 How that he was caught up into [a]paradise,
and heard unspeakable words, which it is not lawful for a man to utter.
5 Of such an one will I glory: yet of myself
I will not [a]glory, but in mine infirmities.
6 For though I would desire to glory, I shall
not be a fool; for I will say the truth: but *now* I
forbear, lest any man should think of me above
that which he seeth me *to be,* or *that* he heareth
of me.

The Thorn in the Flesh

7 And lest I should be exalted above measure through the abundance of the revelations,
there was given to me a [a]thorn in the flesh, [b]the
messenger of Satan to buffet me, lest I should be
exalted above measure.
8 [a]For this thing I besought the Lord thrice,
that it might depart from me.
9 And he said unto me, My grace is sufficient for thee: for my strength is made perfect in
weakness. Most gladly therefore [a]will I rather
glory in my infirmities, [b]that the power of Christ
may rest upon me.
10 Therefore [a]I take pleasure in infirmities,
in reproaches, in necessities, in persecutions, in
distresses for Christ's sake: [b]for when I am weak,
then am I strong.

Signs of an Apostle

11 I am become [a]a fool in glorying; ye have
compelled me: for I ought to have been commended of you: for [b]in nothing am I behind the
very chiefest apostles, though [c]I be nothing.
12 [a]Truly the signs of an apostle were
wrought among you in all patience, in signs, and
[b]wonders, and mighty [c]deeds.
13 For what is it wherein ye were inferior to
other churches, except *it be* that I myself was not
burdensome to you? forgive me this wrong.

Love for the Church

14 [a]Behold, the third time I am ready to come
to you; and I will not be burdensome to you: for
[b]I seek not your's, but you: [c]for the children ought
not to lay up for the parents, but the parents for
the children.
15 And I will very gladly spend and be spent
[a]for you; though [b]the more abundantly I love you,
the less I be loved.
16 But be it so, [a]I did not burden you: nevertheless, being crafty, I caught you with guile.
17 Did I make a gain of you by any of them
whom I sent unto you?
18 I desired Titus, and with *him* I sent a
[a]brother. Did Titus make a gain of you? walked
we not in the same spirit? *walked we* not in the
same steps?
19 [a]Again, think ye that we excuse ourselves
unto you? [b]we speak before God in Christ: [c]but
we do all things, dearly beloved, for your edifying.
20 For I fear, lest, when I come, I shall not
find you such as I would, and *that* [a]I shall be
found unto you such as ye would not: lest *there*
be debates, envyings, wraths, strifes, backbitings,
whisperings, swellings, tumults:
21 *And* lest, when I come again, my God [a]will
humble me among you, and *that* I shall bewail
many [b]which have sinned already, and have not
repented of the uncleanness and [c]fornication and
lasciviousness which they have committed.

NKJV

2 I know a man [a]in Christ who fourteen
years ago—whether in the body I do not know,
or whether out of the body I do not know, God
knows—such a one [b]was caught up to the third
heaven.
3 And I know such a man—whether in the
body or out of the body I do not know, God
knows—
4 how he was caught up into [a]Paradise and
heard inexpressible words, which it is not lawful
for a man to utter.
5 Of such a one I will boast; yet of myself I
will not [a]boast, except in my infirmities.
6 For though I might desire to boast, I will
not be a fool; for I will speak the truth. But I refrain, lest anyone should think of me above what
he sees me *to be* or hears from me.

The Thorn in the Flesh

7 And lest I should be exalted above measure by the abundance of the revelations, a [a]thorn
in the flesh was given to me, [b]a messenger of
Satan to buffet me, lest I be exalted above
measure.
8 [a]Concerning this thing I pleaded with
the Lord three times that it might depart from
me.
9 And He said to me, "My grace is sufficient
for you, for My strength is made perfect in weakness." Therefore most gladly [a]I will rather boast
in my infirmities, [b]that the power of Christ may
rest upon me.
10 Therefore [a]I take pleasure in infirmities,
in reproaches, in needs, in persecutions, in distresses, for Christ's sake. [b]For when I am weak,
then I am strong.

Signs of an Apostle

11 I have become [a]a fool *in boasting; you
have compelled me. For I ought to have been commended by you; for [b]in nothing was I behind the
most eminent apostles, though [c]I am nothing.
12 [a]Truly the signs of an apostle were accomplished among you with all perseverance, in signs
and [b]wonders and mighty [c]deeds.
13 For what is it in which you were inferior
to other churches, except that I myself was not
burdensome to you? Forgive me this wrong!

Love for the Church

14 [a]Now *for* the third time I am ready to come
to you. And I will not be burdensome to you; for
[b]I do not seek yours, but you. [c]For the children
ought not to lay up for the parents, but the parents
for the children.
15 And I will very gladly spend and be spent
[a]for your souls; though [b]the more abundantly I
love you, the less I am loved.
16 But be that *as it may,* [a]I did not burden
you. Nevertheless, being crafty, I caught you by
cunning!
17 Did I take advantage of you by any of
those whom I sent to you?
18 I urged Titus, and sent our [a]brother with
him. Did Titus take advantage of you? Did we not
walk in the same spirit? Did *we* not *walk* in the
same steps?
19 [a]Again,* do you think that we excuse ourselves to you? [b]We speak before God in Christ.
[c]But *we do* all things, beloved, for your edification.
20 For I fear lest, when I come, I shall not
find you such as I wish, and *that* [a]I shall be found
by you such as you do not wish; lest *there be*
contentions, jealousies, outbursts of wrath, selfish
ambitions, backbitings, whisperings, conceits,
tumults;
21 lest, when I come again, my God [a]will
humble me among you, and I shall mourn for
many [b]who have sinned before and have not repented of the uncleanness, [c]fornication, and lewdness which they have practiced.

2 [a]Rom. 16:7; Gal. 1:22 [b]Acts 22:17 **4** [a]Luke 23:43; [Rev. 2:7] **5** [a]2 Cor. 11:30 **7** [a]Num. 33:55; Ezek. 28:24; Hos. 2:6; Gal. 4:13, 14 [b]Job 2:7; Matt. 4:10; Luke 13:16; [1 Cor. 5:5] **8** [a]Deut. 3:23; Matt. 26:44 **9** [a]2 Cor. 11:30 [b][1 Pet. 4:14] **10** [a][Rom. 5:3; 8:35] [b]2 Cor. 13:4 **11** [a]2 Cor. 5:13; 11:1, 16; 12:6 [b]1 Cor. 15:10; 2 Cor. 11:5 [c]1 Cor. 3:7; 13:2; 15:9 **12** [a]Acts 14:3; Rom. 15:18 [b]Acts 15:12 [c]Acts 14:8–10; 16:16–18; 19:11, 12; 20:6–12; 28:1–10 **14** [a]2 Cor. 1:15; 13:1, 2 [b]Acts 20:33; [1 Cor. 10:24–33] [c]1 Cor. 4:14; Gal. 4:19 **15** [a]John 10:11; Rom. 9:3; 2 Cor. 1:6; Phil. 2:17; Col. 1:24; 1 Thess. 2:8; [2 Tim. 2:10] [b]2 Cor. 6:12, 13 **16** [a]2 Cor. 11:9 **18** [a]2 Cor. 8:18 **19** [a]2 Cor. 5:12 [b][Rom. 9:1, 2]; 2 Cor. 11:31 [c]1 Cor. 10:33 **20** [a]1 Cor. 4:21; 2 Cor. 13:2, 10 **21** [a]2 Cor. 2:1, 4 [b]2 Cor. 13:2 [c]1 Cor. 5:1

12:11 NU omits *in boasting*
12:19 NU *You have been thinking for a long time that we*

KJV

Coming with Authority

13 This *is* [a]the third *time* I am coming to you.
[b]IN THE MOUTH OF TWO OR THREE WITNESSES
SHALL EVERY WORD BE ESTABLISHED.
2 [a]I told you before, and foretell you, as if
I were present, the second time; and being absent
now I write to them [b]which heretofore have
sinned, and to all other, that, if I come again, [c]I
will not spare:
3 Since ye seek a proof of Christ [a]speaking
in me, which to youward is not weak, but is
mighty [b]in you.
4 [a]For though he was crucified through
weakness, yet [b]he liveth by the power of God.
For [c]we also are weak in him, but we shall live
with him by the power of God toward you.
5 Examine yourselves, whether ye be in the
faith; prove your own selves. Know ye not your
own selves, [a]how that Jesus Christ is in you, except ye be [b]reprobates?
6 But I trust that ye shall know that we are
not reprobates.

Paul Prefers Gentleness

7 Now I pray to God that ye do no evil; not
that we should appear approved, but that ye
should do that which is honest, though [a]we be
as reprobates.
8 For we can do nothing against the truth,
but for the truth.
9 For we are glad, [a]when we are weak, and
ye are strong: and this also we wish, [b]*even* your
perfection.
10 [a]Therefore I write these things being absent, lest being present I should use sharpness,
according to the [b]power which the Lord hath
given me to edification, and not to destruction.

Greetings and Benediction

11 Finally, brethren, farewell. Be perfect, [a]be
of good comfort, be of one mind, live in peace;
and the God of love [b]and peace shall be with you.
12 [a]Greet one another with an holy kiss.
13 All the saints salute you.
14 [a]The grace of the Lord Jesus Christ, and
the love of God, and [b]the communion of the Holy
Ghost, *be* with you all. Amen.

CHAPTER 13
1 [a]2 Cor. 12:14 [b]Num. 35:30; Deut. 17:6; 19:15; Matt. 18:16; John 8:17; Heb. 10:28
2 [a]2 Cor. 10:2 [b]2 Cor. 12:21 [c]2 Cor. 1:23; 10:11
3 [a]Matt. 10:20; [1 Cor. 5:4; 7:40] [b][1 Cor. 9:2]
4 [a]Phil. 2:7, 8; [1 Pet. 3:18] [b][Rom. 1:4; 6:4; 1 Cor. 6:14] [c][2 Cor. 10:3, 4]
5 [a]Rom. 8:10; [Gal. 4:19] [b]1 Cor. 9:27
7 [a]2 Cor. 6:9
9 [a]1 Cor. 4:10 [b]1 Cor. 1:10; 2 Cor. 13:11; Eph. 4:12; [1 Thess. 3:10]
10 [a]1 Cor. 4:21 [b]1 Cor. 5:4; 2 Cor. 10:8
11 [a]Rom. 12:16, 18 [b]Rom. 15:33; Eph. 6:23
12 [a]Rom. 16:16
14 [a]Rom. 16:24 [b]Phil. 2:1

*

13:2 NU omits *I write*
13:7 NU *we*

NKJV

Coming with Authority

13 This *will be* [a]the third *time* I am coming
to you. [b]*"By the mouth of two or three witnesses every word shall be established."*
2 [a]I have told you before, and foretell as if
I were present the second time, and now being
absent *I write to those [b]who have sinned before,
and to all the rest, that if I come again [c]I will not
spare—
3 since you seek a proof of Christ [a]speaking
in me, who is not weak toward you, but mighty
[b]in you.
4 [a]For though He was crucified in weakness, yet [b]He lives by the power of God. For [c]we
also are weak in Him, but we shall live with Him
by the power of God toward you.
5 Examine yourselves *as to* whether you are
in the faith. Test yourselves. Do you not know
yourselves, [a]that Jesus Christ is in you?—unless
indeed you are [b]disqualified.
6 But I trust that you will know that we are
not disqualified.

Paul Prefers Gentleness

7 Now *I pray to God that you do no evil,
not that we should appear approved, but that you
should do what is honorable, though [a]we may
seem disqualified.
8 For we can do nothing against the truth,
but for the truth.
9 For we are glad [a]when we are weak and
you are strong. And this also we pray, [b]that you
may be made complete.
10 [a]Therefore I write these things being absent, lest being present I should use sharpness,
according to the [b]authority which the Lord has
given me for edification and not for destruction.

Greetings and Benediction

11 Finally, brethren, farewell. Become complete. [a]Be of good comfort, be of one mind, live
in peace; and the God of love [b]and peace will be
with you.
12 [a]Greet one another with a holy kiss.
13 All the saints greet you.
14 [a]The grace of the Lord Jesus Christ, and
the love of God, and [b]the communion of the Holy
Spirit *be* with you all. Amen.

KJV

THE EPISTLE OF PAUL THE APOSTLE TO THE GALATIANS

Greeting

1 Paul, an apostle, (not of men, neither by man,
but [a]by Jesus Christ, and God the Father,
[b]who raised him from the dead;)
2 And all the brethren which are with me,
unto the churches of Galatia:
3 Grace *be* to you and peace from God the
Father, and *from* our Lord Jesus Christ,
4 [a]Who gave himself for our sins, that he
might deliver us [b]from this present evil world, according to the will of God and our Father:
5 To whom *be* glory for ever and ever.
Amen.

Only One Gospel

6 I marvel that ye are so soon removed
[a]from him that called you into the grace of Christ
unto another gospel:
7 [a]Which is not another; but there be some
[b]that trouble you, and would [c]pervert the gospel
of Christ.
8 But though [a]we, or an angel from heaven,
preach any other gospel unto you than that which
we have preached unto you, let him be accursed.
9 As we said before, so say I now again, If
any *man* preach any other gospel unto you [a]than
that ye have received, let him be accursed.
10 For [a]do I now [b]persuade men, or God?
or [c]do I seek to please men? for if I yet pleased
men, I should not be the servant of Christ.

Call to Apostleship
(cf. Acts 9:1–25)

11 [a]But I certify you, brethren, that the gospel which was preached of me is not after man.
12 For [a]I neither received it of man, neither
was I taught *it,* but [b]by the revelation of Jesus
Christ.
13 For ye have heard of my conversation in
time past in the Jews' religion, how that [a]beyond
measure I persecuted the church of God, and
[b]wasted it:
14 And profited in the Jews' religion above
many my equals in mine own nation, [a]being more
exceedingly zealous [b]of the traditions of my
fathers.
15 But when it pleased God, [a]who separated
me from my mother's womb, and called *me* by
his grace,
16 [a]To reveal his Son in me, that [b]I might
preach him among the heathen; immediately I
conferred not with [c]flesh and blood:
17 Neither went I up to Jerusalem to them
which were apostles before me; but I went into
Arabia, and returned again unto Damascus.

Contacts at Jerusalem
(cf. Acts 9:26–31)

18 Then after three years [a]I went up to Jerusalem to see Peter, and abode with him fifteen
days.
19 But [a]other of the apostles saw I none, save
[b]James the Lord's brother.

CHAPTER 1
1 [a]Acts 9:6 [b]Acts 2:24
4 [a][Matt. 20:28] [b]Heb. 2:5
6 [a][Rom. 8:28]; Gal. 1:15; 5:8
7 [a]2 Cor. 11:4 [b]Acts 15:1; Gal. 5:10, 12 [c]2 Cor. 2:17
8 [a]1 Cor. 16:22
9 [a]Deut. 4:2
10 [a][1 Cor. 10:33]; 1 Thess. 2:4 [b]1 Sam. 24:7 [c]1 Thess. 2:4
11 [a][Rom. 2:16]; 1 Cor. 15:1
12 [a]1 Cor. 15:1 [b][Eph. 3:3–5]
13 [a]Acts 9:1 [b]Acts 8:3; 22:4, 5
14 [a]Acts 26:9; Phil. 3:6 [b]Jer. 9:14; Matt. 15:2; Mark 7:3; [Col. 2:8]
15 [a]Is. 49:1, 5; Jer. 1:5; Acts 9:15; Rom. 1:1; Gal. 1:6
16 [a][2 Cor. 4:5–7] [b]Acts 9:15; Gal. 2:9 [c]Matt. 16:17
18 [a]Acts 9:26
19 [a]1 Cor. 9:5 [b]Matt. 13:55

***1:18** NU *Cephas*

NKJV

THE EPISTLE OF PAUL THE APOSTLE TO THE GALATIANS

Greeting

1 Paul, an apostle (not from men nor through
man, but [a]through Jesus Christ and God the
Father [b]who raised Him from the dead),
2 and all the brethren who are with me,
To the churches of Galatia:
3 Grace to you and peace from God the Father and our Lord Jesus Christ,
4 [a]who gave Himself for our sins, that He
might deliver us [b]from this present evil age, according to the will of our God and Father,
5 to whom *be* glory forever and ever. Amen.

Only One Gospel

6 I marvel that you are turning away so
soon [a]from Him who called you in the grace of
Christ, to a different gospel,
7 [a]which is not another; but there are some
[b]who trouble you and want to [c]pervert the gospel
of Christ.
8 But even if [a]we, or an angel from heaven,
preach any other gospel to you than what we have
preached to you, let him be accursed.
9 As we have said before, so now I say
again, if anyone preaches any other gospel to you
[a]than what you have received, let him be
accursed.
10 For [a]do I now [b]persuade men, or God?
Or [c]do I seek to please men? For if I still pleased
men, I would not be a bondservant of Christ.

Call to Apostleship
(cf. Acts 9:1–25)

11 [a]But I make known to you, brethren, that
the gospel which was preached by me is not according to man.
12 For [a]I neither received it from man, nor
was I taught *it,* but *it came* [b]through the revelation of Jesus Christ.
13 For you have heard of my former conduct
in Judaism, how [a]I persecuted the church of God
beyond measure and [b]*tried to* destroy it.
14 And I advanced in Judaism beyond many
of my contemporaries in my own nation, [a]being
more exceedingly zealous [b]for the traditions of
my fathers.
15 But when it pleased God, [a]who separated
me from my mother's womb and called *me*
through His grace,
16 [a]to reveal His Son in me, that [b]I might
preach Him among the Gentiles, I did not immediately confer with [c]flesh and blood,
17 nor did I go up to Jerusalem to those *who*
were apostles before me; but I went to Arabia,
and returned again to Damascus.

Contacts at Jerusalem
(cf. Acts 9:26–31)

18 Then after three years [a]I went up to Jerusalem to see *Peter, and remained with him fifteen
days.
19 But [a]I saw none of the other apostles except [b]James, the Lord's brother.

KJV

20 Now the things which I write unto you, behold, before God, I lie not.

21 [a]Afterwards I came into the regions of Syria and Cilicia;

22 And was unknown by face unto the churches of Judaea which [a]were in Christ:

23 But they had [a]heard only, That he which [b]persecuted us in times past now preacheth the faith which once he destroyed.

24 And they [a]glorified God in me.

Defending the Gospel
(*cf. Acts 15:1–21*)

2 Then fourteen years after [a]I went up again to Jerusalem with Barnabas, and took Titus with *me* also.

2 And I went up by revelation, and communicated unto them that gospel which I preach among the Gentiles, but [a]privately to them which were of reputation, lest by any means [b]I should run, or had run, in vain.

3 But neither Titus, who was with me, being a Greek, was compelled to be circumcised:

4 And that because of [a]false brethren unawares brought in, who came in privily to spy out our [b]liberty which we have in Christ Jesus, [c]that they might bring us into bondage:

5 To whom we gave place by subjection, no, not for an hour; that [a]the truth of the gospel might continue with you.

6 But of these [a]who seemed to be somewhat, (whatsoever they were, it maketh no matter to me: [b]God accepteth no man's person:) for they who seemed *to be somewhat* [c]in conference added nothing to me:

7 But contrariwise, [a]when they saw that the gospel of the uncircumcision [b]was committed unto me, as *the gospel* of the circumcision *was* unto Peter;

8 (For he that wrought effectually in Peter to the apostleship of the [a]circumcision, [b]the same was [c]mighty in me toward the Gentiles:)

9 And when James, Cephas, and John, who seemed to be [a]pillars, perceived [b]the grace that was given unto me, they gave to me and Barnabas the right hands of fellowship; [c]that we *should go* unto the heathen, and they unto the circumcision.

10 Only *they would* that we should remember the poor; [a]the same which I also was forward to do.

No Return to the Law

11 [a]But when Peter was come to Antioch, I withstood him to the face, because he was to be blamed.

12 For before that certain came from James, [a]he did eat with the Gentiles: but when they were come, he withdrew and separated himself, fearing them which were of the circumcision.

13 And the other Jews dissembled likewise with him; insomuch that Barnabas also was carried away with their dissimulation.

14 But when I saw that they walked not uprightly according to [a]the truth of the gospel, I said unto Peter [b]before *them* all, [c]If thou, being a Jew, livest after the manner of Gentiles, and not as do the Jews, why compellest thou the Gentiles to live as do the Jews?

15 [a]We *who are* Jews by nature, and not [b]sinners of the Gentiles,

16 [a]Knowing that a man is not justified by the works of the law, but [b]by the faith of Jesus Christ, even we have believed in Jesus Christ, that we might be justified by the faith of Christ, and not by the works of the law: for [c]by the works of the law shall no flesh be justified.

17 But if, while we seek to be justified by Christ, we ourselves also are found [a]sinners, *is* therefore Christ the minister of sin? God forbid.

18 For if I build again the things which I destroyed, I make myself a transgressor.

21 [a]Acts 9:30 **22** [a]Rom. 16:7 **23** [a]Acts 9:20, 21 [b]Acts 8:3 **24** [a]Acts 11:18

CHAPTER 2

1 [a]Acts 15:2 **2** [a]Acts 15:1–4 [b][Rom. 9:16; 1 Cor. 9:24]; Gal. 5:7; Phil. 2:16; 1 Thess. 3:5; 2 Tim. 4:7; Heb. 12:1 **4** [a]Acts 15:1, 24; 2 Cor. 11:13, 26; Gal. 1:7 [b]Gal. 3:25; 5:1, 13; [James 1:25] [c]Gal. 4:3, 9 **5** [a][Gal. 1:6; 2:14; 3:1]; Col. 1:5 **6** [a]Gal. 2:9; 6:3 [b]Acts 10:34; Rom. 2:11 [c]2 Cor. 11:5; 12:11 **7** [a]Acts 9:15; 13:46; 22:21; Rom. 11:13 [b]1 Cor. 9:17; 1 Thess. 2:4; 1 Tim. 1:11 **8** [a]1 Pet. 1:1 [b]Acts 9:15 [c][Gal. 3:5] **9** [a]Matt. 16:18 [b]Rom. 1:5 [c]Acts 13:3 **10** [a]Acts 11:30 **11** [a]Acts 15:35 **12** [a][Acts 10:28; 11:2, 3] **14** [a]Gal. 1:6; 2:5; Col. 1:5 [b]1 Tim. 5:20 [c][Acts 10:28]; Gal. 2:12 **15** [a][Acts 15:10] [b]Matt. 9:11 **16** [a]Acts 13:38, 39; Gal. 3:11 [b]Rom. 1:17 [c]Ps. 143:2; Rom. 3:20 **17** [a][1 John 3:8]

*

2:11 NU *Cephas* **2:14** NU *how can you* • Some interpreters stop the quotation here.

NKJV

20 (Now *concerning* the things which I write to you, indeed, before God, I do not lie.)

21 [a]Afterward I went into the regions of Syria and Cilicia.

22 And I was unknown by face to the churches of Judea which [a]*were* in Christ.

23 But they were [a]hearing only, "He who formerly [b]persecuted us now preaches the faith which he once *tried to* destroy."

24 And they [a]glorified God in me.

Defending the Gospel
(*cf. Acts 15:1–21*)

2 Then after fourteen years [a]I went up again to Jerusalem with Barnabas, and also took Titus with *me*.

2 And I went up by revelation, and communicated to them that gospel which I preach among the Gentiles, but [a]privately to those who were of reputation, lest by any means [b]I might run, or had run, in vain.

3 Yet not even Titus who *was* with me, being a Greek, was compelled to be circumcised.

4 And *this occurred* because of [a]false brethren secretly brought in (who came in by stealth to spy out our [b]liberty which we have in Christ Jesus, [c]that they might bring us into bondage),

5 to whom we did not yield submission even for an hour, that [a]the truth of the gospel might continue with you.

6 But from those [a]who seemed to be something—whatever they were, it makes no difference to me; [b]God shows personal favoritism to no man—for those who seemed *to be something* [c]added nothing to me.

7 But on the contrary, [a]when they saw that the gospel for the uncircumcised [b]had been committed to me, as *the gospel* for the circumcised *was* to Peter

8 (for He who worked effectively in Peter for the apostleship to the [a]circumcised [b]also [c]worked effectively in me toward the Gentiles),

9 and when James, Cephas, and John, who seemed to be [a]pillars, perceived [b]the grace that had been given to me, they gave me and Barnabas the right hand of fellowship, [c]that we *should go* to the Gentiles and they to the circumcised.

10 *They desired* only that we should remember the poor, [a]the very thing which I also was eager to do.

No Return to the Law

11 [a]Now when *Peter had come to Antioch, I withstood him to his face, because he was to be blamed;

12 for before certain men came from James, [a]he would eat with the Gentiles; but when they came, he withdrew and separated himself, fearing those who were of the circumcision.

13 And the rest of the Jews also played the hypocrite with him, so that even Barnabas was carried away with their hypocrisy.

14 But when I saw that they were not straightforward about [a]the truth of the gospel, I said to Peter [b]before *them* all, [c]"If you, being a Jew, live in the manner of Gentiles and not as the Jews, *why do you compel Gentiles to live as *Jews?

15 [a]"We *who are* Jews by nature, and not [b]sinners of the Gentiles,

16 [a]"knowing that a man is not justified by the works of the law but [b]by faith in Jesus Christ, even we have believed in Christ Jesus, that we might be justified by faith in Christ and not [c]by the works of the law; for by the works of the law no flesh shall be justified.

17 "But if, while we seek to be justified by Christ, we ourselves also are found [a]sinners, *is* Christ therefore a minister of sin? Certainly not!

18 "For if I build again those things which I destroyed, I make myself a transgressor.

KJV

19 For I [a]through the law [b]am dead to the
law, that I might [c]live unto God.
20 I am [a]crucified with Christ: nevertheless
I live; yet not I, but Christ liveth in me: and the
life which I now live in the flesh [b]I live by the
faith of the Son of God, [c]who loved me, and gave
himself for me.
21 I do not frustrate the grace of God: for
[a]if righteousness *come* by the law, then Christ is
dead in vain.

Justification by Faith
(cf. Rom. 4:1–25)

3 O foolish Galatians, who hath bewitched you,
that ye should not obey the truth, before
whose eyes Jesus Christ hath been evidently set
forth, crucified among you?
2 This only would I learn of you, Received
ye the Spirit by the works of the law, [a]or by the
hearing of faith?
3 Are ye so foolish? [a]having begun in the
Spirit, are ye now made perfect by [b]the flesh?
4 [a]Have ye suffered so many things in vain?
if *it be* yet in vain.
5 He therefore that ministereth to you in the
Spirit, and worketh miracles among you, *doeth*
he it by the works of the law, or by the hearing
of faith?
6 Even as [a]Abraham BELIEVED GOD, AND IT
WAS ACCOUNTED TO HIM FOR RIGHTEOUSNESS.
7 Know ye therefore that [a]they which are
of faith, the same are the children of Abraham.
8 And [a]the scripture, foreseeing that God
would justify the heathen through faith, preached
before the gospel unto Abraham, *saying,* [b]IN THEE
SHALL ALL NATIONS BE BLESSED.
9 So then they which be of faith are blessed
with faithful Abraham.

The Law Brings a Curse

10 For as many as are of the works of the
law are under the curse: for it is written, [a]CURSED
IS EVERY ONE THAT CONTINUETH NOT IN ALL THINGS
WHICH ARE WRITTEN IN THE BOOK OF THE LAW TO DO
THEM.
11 But that no man is justified by the law in
the sight of God, *it is* evident: for, [a]THE JUST SHALL
LIVE BY FAITH.
12 And [a]the law is not of faith: but, [b]THE MAN
THAT DOETH THEM SHALL LIVE IN THEM.
13 [a]Christ hath redeemed us from the curse
of the law, being made a curse for us: for it is
written, [b]CURSED *IS* EVERY ONE THAT HANGETH ON A
TREE:
14 [a]That the blessing of Abraham might
come on the [b]Gentiles through Jesus Christ; that
we might receive [c]the promise of the Spirit
through faith.

The Changeless Promise
(cf. Gen. 12:1–3)

15 Brethren, I speak after the manner of men;
[a]Though *it be* but a man's covenant, yet *if it be*
confirmed, no man disannulleth, or addeth
thereto.
16 Now to Abraham and his seed were the
promises made. He saith not, And to seeds, as of
many; but as of [a]one, [b]AND TO THY SEED, which
is [c]Christ.
17 And this I say, *that* the covenant, that was
confirmed before of God in Christ, the law, [a]which
was four hundred and thirty years after, cannot
disannul, [b]that it should make the promise of none
effect.
18 For if [a]the inheritance *be* of the law, [b]*it*
is no more of promise: but God gave *it* to Abraham by promise.

Purpose of the Law

19 Wherefore then *serveth* the law? [a]It was
added because of transgressions, till the [b]seed
should come to whom the promise was made; *and*

---

19 [a]Rom. 8:2 [b][Rom. 6:2, 14; 7:4]; 1 Cor. 9:20 [c][Rom. 6:11]
20 [a][Rom. 6:6; Gal. 5:24; 6:14] [b]Rom. 6:8–11; 2 Cor. 5:15; [Eph. 2:4–6; Col. 3:1–4] [c]Is. 53:12; Eph. 5:2
21 [a]Heb. 7:11

CHAPTER 3

2 [a]Rom. 10:16, 17
3 [a][Gal. 4:9] [b]Heb. 7:16
4 [a]Heb. 10:35
6 [a]Gen. 15:6
7 [a]John 8:39
8 [a]Rom. 9:17 [b]Gen. 12:3; 18:18; 22:18; 26:4; 28:14
10 [a]Deut. 27:26
11 [a]Hab. 2:4; Rom. 1:17; Heb. 10:38
12 [a]Rom. 4:4, 5 [b]Lev. 18:5; Rom. 10:5
13 [a][Rom. 8:3] [b]Deut. 21:23
14 [a][Rom. 4:1–5, 9, 16; Gal. 3:28] [b]Is. 42:1, 6; 49:6; Luke 2:32; Rom. 3:29, 30 [c]Is. 32:15
15 [a]Heb. 9:17
16 [a]Gen. 22:18 [b]Gen. 12:3, 7; 13:15; 24:7 [c][1 Cor. 12:12]
17 [a]Gen. 15:13; Ex. 12:40; Acts 7:6 [b][Rom. 4:13]
18 [a][Rom. 8:17] [b]Rom. 4:14
19 [a]John 15:22 [b]Gal. 4:4

*______

3:1 NU omits *that you should not obey the truth* • NU omits *among you*
3:17 NU omits *in Christ*

NKJV

19 "For I [a]through the law [b]died to the law
that I might [c]live to God.
20 "I have been [a]crucified with Christ; it is
no longer I who live, but Christ lives in me; and
the *life* which I now live in the flesh [b]I live by
faith in the Son of God, [c]who loved me and gave
Himself for me.
21 "I do not set aside the grace of God; for
[a]if righteousness *comes* through the law, then
Christ died in vain."

Justification by Faith
(cf. Rom. 4:1–25)

3 O foolish Galatians! Who has bewitched you
*that you should not obey the truth, before
whose eyes Jesus Christ was clearly portrayed
*among you as crucified?
2 This only I want to learn from you: Did
you receive the Spirit by the works of the law,
[a]or by the hearing of faith?
3 Are you so foolish? [a]Having begun in the
Spirit, are you now being made perfect by [b]the
flesh?
4 [a]Have you suffered so many things in
vain—if indeed *it was* in vain?
5 Therefore He who supplies the Spirit to
you and works miracles among you, *does He do*
it by the works of the law, or by the hearing of
faith?—
6 just as Abraham [a]*"believed God, and it*
was accounted to him for righteousness."
7 Therefore know that *only* [a]those who are
of faith are sons of Abraham.
8 And [a]the Scripture, foreseeing that God
would justify the Gentiles by faith, preached the
gospel to Abraham beforehand, *saying,* [b]*"In you*
all the nations shall be blessed."
9 So then those who *are* of faith are blessed
with believing Abraham.

The Law Brings a Curse

10 For as many as are of the works of the
law are under the curse; for it is written, [a]*"Cursed*
is everyone who does not continue in all things
which are written in the book of the law, to do
them."
11 But that no one is justified by the law in
the sight of God *is* evident, for [a]*"the just shall*
live by faith."
12 Yet [a]the law is not of faith, but [b]*"the man*
who does them shall live by them."
13 [a]Christ has redeemed us from the curse
of the law, having become a curse for us (for it
is written, [b]*"Cursed is everyone who hangs on a*
tree"),
14 [a]that the blessing of Abraham might come
upon the [b]Gentiles in Christ Jesus, that we might
receive [c]the promise of the Spirit through faith.

The Changeless Promise
(cf. Gen. 12:1–3)

15 Brethren, I speak in the manner of men:
[a]Though *it is* only a man's covenant, yet *if it is*
confirmed, no one annuls or adds to it.
16 Now to Abraham and his Seed were the
promises made. He does not say, "And to seeds,"
as of many, but as of [a]one, [b]*"And to your Seed,"*
who is [c]Christ.
17 And this I say, *that* the law, [a]which was
four hundred and thirty years later, cannot annul
the covenant that was confirmed before by God
*in Christ, [b]that it should make the promise of
no effect.
18 For if [a]the inheritance *is* of the law, [b]*it is*
no longer of promise; but God gave *it* to Abraham
by promise.

Purpose of the Law

19 What purpose then *does* the law *serve*?
[a]It was added because of transgressions, till the
[b]Seed should come to whom the promise was

KJV

it was [c]ordained by angels in the hand [d]of a mediator.

20 Now a mediator is not *a mediator* of one, [a]but God is one.

21 *Is* the law then against the promises of God? God forbid: for if there had been a law given which could have given life, verily righteousness should have been by the law.

22 But the scripture hath concluded [a]all under sin, [b]that the promise by faith of Jesus Christ might be given to them that believe.

23 But before faith came, we were kept under the law, shut up unto the faith which should afterwards be revealed.

24 Wherefore [a]the law was our schoolmaster *to bring us* unto Christ, [b]that we might be justified by faith.

25 But after that faith is come, we are no longer under a schoolmaster.

Sons and Heirs

26 For ye [a]are all the children of God by faith in Christ Jesus.

27 For [a]as many of you as have been baptized into Christ [b]have put on Christ.

28 [a]There is neither Jew nor Greek, [b]there is neither bond nor free, there is neither male nor female: for ye are all [c]one in Christ Jesus.

29 And [a]if ye *be* Christ's, then are ye Abraham's [b]seed, and [c]heirs according to the promise.

4 Now I say, *That* the heir, as long as he is a child, differeth nothing from a servant, though he be lord of all;

2 But is under tutors and governors until the time appointed of the father.

3 Even so we, when we were children, [a]were in bondage under the elements of the world:

4 But [a]when the fulness of the time was come, God sent forth his Son, [b]made [c]of a woman, [d]made under the law,

5 [a]To redeem them that were under the law, [b]that we might receive the adoption of sons.

6 And because ye are sons, God hath sent forth [a]the Spirit of his Son into your hearts, crying, Abba, Father.

7 Wherefore thou art no more a servant, but a son; [a]and if a son, then an heir of God through Christ.

Fears for the Church

8 Howbeit then, [a]when ye knew not God, [b]ye did service unto them which by nature are no gods.

9 But now, [a]after that ye have known God, or rather are known of God, [b]how turn ye again to [c]the weak and beggarly elements, whereunto ye desire again to be in bondage?

10 [a]Ye observe days, and months, and times, and years.

11 I am afraid of you, [a]lest I have bestowed upon you labour in vain.

12 Brethren, I beseech you, be as I *am;* for I *am* as ye *are:* [a]ye have not injured me at all.

13 Ye know how [a]through infirmity of the flesh I preached the gospel unto you at the first.

14 And my temptation which was in my flesh ye despised not, nor rejected; but received me [a]as an angel of God, [b]*even* as Christ Jesus.

15 Where is then the blessedness ye spake of? for I bear you record, that, if *it had been* possible, ye would have plucked out your own eyes, and have given them to me.

16 Am I therefore become your enemy, because I tell you the truth?

17 They [a]zealously affect you, *but* not well; yea, they would exclude you, that ye might affect them.

18 But *it is* good to be zealously affected always in *a* good *thing,* and not only when I am present with you.

---

19 [c]Acts 7:53 [d]Ex. 20:19; Deut. 5:5
20 [a][Rom. 3:29]
22 [a]Rom. 11:32 [b]Rom. 4:11
24 [a]Rom. 10:4 [b]Acts 13:39
26 [a]John 1:12
27 [a]Matt. 28:19; [Rom. 6:3]; 1 Cor. 10:2 [b]Rom. 10:12; 13:14
28 [a][John 10:16]; Rom. 3:22; 10:12; [Eph. 2:14]; Col. 3:11 [b][1 Cor. 12:13] [c]John 17:11; [1 Cor. 12:13; Eph. 2:15, 16]
29 [a]Gen. 21:10; Heb. 11:18 [b]Rom. 4:11; Gal. 3:7 [c]Gen. 12:3; 18:18; Rom. 8:17

CHAPTER 4

3 [a]Gal. 4:9; Col. 2:8, 20; Heb. 5:12; 9:10
4 [a][Gen. 49:10] [b][John 1:14]; Rom. 1:3; 8:3; [Phil. 2:7] [c]Gen. 3:15; [Is. 7:14; Matt. 1:25] [d][Matt. 5:17]; Luke 2:21, 27
5 [a][Matt. 20:28; Gal. 3:13] [b][John 1:12]
6 [a][Acts 16:7; Rom. 5:5; 8:9, 15, 16; 2 Cor. 3:17]
7 [a][Rom. 8:16, 17]
8 [a]1 Cor. 1:21; Eph. 2:12; 1 Thess. 4:5; 2 Thess. 1:8 [b]Rom. 1:25
9 [a][1 Cor. 8:3] [b]Gal. 3:1–3; Col. 2:20 [c]Heb. 7:18
10 [a]Rom. 14:5; Col. 2:16
11 [a]1 Thess. 3:5
12 [a]2 Cor. 2:5
13 [a]1 Cor. 2:3
14 [a]Mal. 2:7 [b][Luke 10:16]
17 [a]Rom. 10:2

*

4:4 Or *made*
4:7 NU *through God* • NU omits *through Christ*
4:15 NU *Where*

NKJV

made; *and it was* [c]appointed through angels by the hand [d]of a mediator.

20 Now a mediator does not *mediate* for one *only,* [a]but God is one.

21 *Is* the law then against the promises of God? Certainly not! For if there had been a law given which could have given life, truly righteousness would have been by the law.

22 But the Scripture has confined [a]all under sin, [b]that the promise by faith in Jesus Christ might be given to those who believe.

23 But before faith came, we were kept under guard by the law, kept for the faith which would afterward be revealed.

24 Therefore [a]the law was our tutor *to bring us* to Christ, [b]that we might be justified by faith.

25 But after faith has come, we are no longer under a tutor.

Sons and Heirs

26 For you [a]are all sons of God through faith in Christ Jesus.

27 For [a]as many of you as were baptized into Christ [b]have put on Christ.

28 [a]There is neither Jew nor Greek, [b]there is neither slave nor free, there is neither male nor female; for you are all [c]one in Christ Jesus.

29 And [a]if you *are* Christ's, then you are Abraham's [b]seed, and [c]heirs according to the promise.

4 Now I say *that* the heir, as long as he is a child, does not differ at all from a slave, though he is master of all,

2 but is under guardians and stewards until the time appointed by the father.

3 Even so we, when we were children, [a]were in bondage under the elements of the world.

4 But [a]when the fullness of the time had come, God sent forth His Son, [b]born* [c]of a woman, [d]born under the law,

5 [a]to redeem those who were under the law, [b]that we might receive the adoption as sons.

6 And because you are sons, God has sent forth [a]the Spirit of His Son into your hearts, crying out, "Abba, Father!"

7 Therefore you are no longer a slave but a son, [a]and if a son, then an heir *of God *through Christ.

Fears for the Church

8 But then, indeed, [a]when you did not know God, [b]you served those which by nature are not gods.

9 But now [a]after you have known God, or rather are known by God, [b]how *is it that* you turn again to [c]the weak and beggarly elements, to which you desire again to be in bondage?

10 [a]You observe days and months and seasons and years.

11 I am afraid for you, [a]lest I have labored for you in vain.

12 Brethren, I urge you to become like me, for I *became* like you. [a]You have not injured me at all.

13 You know that [a]because of physical infirmity I preached the gospel to you at the first.

14 And my trial which was in my flesh you did not despise or reject, but you received me [a]as an angel of God, [b]*even* as Christ Jesus.

15 *What then was the blessing you *enjoyed?* For I bear you witness that, if possible, you would have plucked out your own eyes and given them to me.

16 Have I therefore become your enemy because I tell you the truth?

17 They [a]zealously court you, *but* for no good; yes, they want to exclude you, that you may be zealous for them.

18 But it is good to be zealous in a good thing always, and not only when I am present with you.

KJV

19 [a]My little children, of whom I travail in birth again until Christ be formed in you,

20 I desire to be present with you now, and to change my voice; for I stand in doubt of you.

Two Covenants
(*Gen. 21:8–21; Is. 54:1*)

21 Tell me, ye that desire to be under the law, do ye not hear the law?

22 For it is written, that Abraham had two sons, [a]the one by a bondmaid, [b]the other by a freewoman.

23 But he *who was* of the bondwoman [a]was born after the flesh; [b]but he of the freewoman *was* by promise.

24 Which things are an allegory: for these are the two covenants; the one from the mount [a]Sinai, which gendereth to bondage, which is Agar.

25 For this Agar is mount Sinai in Arabia, and answereth to Jerusalem which now is, and is in bondage with her children.

26 But [a]Jerusalem which is above is free, which is the mother of us all.

27 For it is written, [a]REJOICE, *THOU* BARREN THAT BEAREST NOT; BREAK FORTH AND CRY, THOU THAT TRAVAILEST NOT: FOR THE DESOLATE HATH MANY MORE CHILDREN THAN SHE WHICH HATH AN HUSBAND.

28 Now [a]we, brethren, as Isaac was, are [b]the children of promise.

29 But as then [a]he that was born after the flesh persecuted him *that was born* after the Spirit, [b]even so *it is* now.

30 Nevertheless what saith [a]the scripture? [b]CAST OUT THE BONDWOMAN AND HER SON: FOR [c]THE SON OF THE BONDWOMAN SHALL NOT BE HEIR WITH THE SON OF THE FREEWOMAN.

31 So then, brethren, we are not children of the bondwoman, but of the free.

Christian Liberty

5 Stand[a] fast therefore in the liberty wherewith Christ hath made us free, and be not entangled again with the [b]yoke of bondage.

2 Behold, I Paul say unto you, that [a]if ye be circumcised, Christ shall profit you nothing.

3 For I testify again to every man that is circumcised, [a]that he is a debtor to do the whole law.

4 [a]Christ is become of no effect unto you, whosoever of you are justified by the law; [b]ye are fallen from grace.

5 For we through the Spirit [a]wait for the hope of righteousness by faith.

6 For [a]in Jesus Christ neither circumcision availeth any thing, nor uncircumcision; but [b]faith which worketh by love.

Love Fulfills the Law

7 Ye [a]did run well; who did hinder you that ye should not obey the truth?

8 This persuasion *cometh* not of him that calleth you.

9 [a]A little leaven leaveneth the whole lump.

10 I have confidence in you through the Lord, that ye will be none otherwise minded: but he that troubleth you shall bear his judgment, whosoever he be.

11 And I, brethren, if I yet preach circumcision, [a]why do I yet suffer persecution? then is [b]the offence of the cross ceased.

12 [a]I would they were even cut off [b]which trouble you.

13 For, brethren, ye have been called unto liberty; only [a]*use* not liberty for an [b]occasion to the flesh, but [c]by love serve one another.

14 For [a]all the law is fulfilled in one word,

---

19 [a]1 Cor. 4:15
22 [a]Gen. 16:15 [b]Gen. 21:2
23 [a]Rom. 9:7, 8; Gal. 4:29 [b]Gen. 16:15; 17:15–19; 18:10; 21:1; Gal. 4:28; Heb. 11:11
24 [a]Ex. 24:6–8; Deut. 33:2
26 [a][Is. 2:2]
27 [a]Is. 54:1
28 [a]Rom. 9:7, 8; Gal. 3:29 [b]Acts 3:25
29 [a]Gen. 21:9 [b]Gal. 5:11
30 [a][Gal. 3:8, 22] [b]Gen. 21:10, 12 [c][John 8:35]

CHAPTER 5

1 [a]Phil. 4:1 [b]Acts 15:10; Gal. 2:4
2 [a]Acts 15:1; Gal. 5:3, 6, 11
3 [a][Deut. 27:26; Rom. 2:25; Gal. 3:10]
4 [a][Rom. 9:31] [b]Heb. 12:15; 2 Pet. 3:17
5 [a]Rom. 8:24
6 [a][1 Cor. 7:19; Gal. 6:15; Col. 3:11] [b]Col. 1:4; 1 Thess. 1:3; [James 2:18, 20, 22]
7 [a]1 Cor. 9:24
9 [a]1 Cor. 5:6
11 [a]1 Cor. 15:30 [b]Rom. 9:33; [1 Cor. 1:23]
12 [a]Josh. 7:25 [b]Acts 15:1, 2
13 [a][Rom. 8:2]; 1 Cor. 8:9; Gal. 5:1 [b]Rom. 6:1; 1 Pet. 2:16 [c]1 Cor. 9:19; Eph. 5:21
14 [a]Matt. 7:12; 22:40; Rom. 13:8, 10; Gal. 6:2

*______

4:24 NU, M omit *the*
5:1 NU *For freedom Christ has made us free; stand fast therefore, and*

NKJV

19 [a]My little children, for whom I labor in birth again until Christ is formed in you,

20 I would like to be present with you now and to change my tone; for I have doubts about you.

Two Covenants
(*Gen. 21:8–21; Is. 54:1*)

21 Tell me, you who desire to be under the law, do you not hear the law?

22 For it is written that Abraham had two sons: [a]the one by a bondwoman, [b]the other by a freewoman.

23 But he *who was* of the bond woman [a]was born according to the flesh, [b]and he of the freewoman through promise,

24 which things are symbolic. For these are *the two covenants: the one from Mount [a]Sinai which gives birth to bondage, which is Hagar—

25 for this Hagar is Mount Sinai in Arabia, and corresponds to Jerusalem which now is, and is in bondage with her children—

26 but the [a]Jerusalem above is free, which is the mother of us all.

27 For it is written:

[a]*"Rejoice, O barren,*
You who do not bear!
Break forth and shout,
You who are not in labor!
For the desolate has many more children
Than she who has a husband."

28 Now [a]we, brethren, as Isaac *was*, are [b]children of promise.

29 But, as [a]he who was born according to the flesh then persecuted him *who was born* according to the Spirit, [b]even so *it is* now.

30 Nevertheless what does [a]the Scripture say? [b]*"Cast out the bondwoman and her son, for* [c]*the son of the bondwoman shall not be heir with the son of the freewoman."*

31 So then, brethren, we are not children of the bondwoman but of the free.

Christian Liberty

5 [a]Stand* fast therefore in the liberty by which Christ has made us free, and do not be entangled again with a [b]yoke of bondage.

2 Indeed I, Paul, say to you that [a]if you become circumcised, Christ will profit you nothing.

3 And I testify again to every man who becomes circumcised [a]that he is a debtor to keep the whole law.

4 [a]You have become estranged from Christ, you who *attempt to* be justified by law; [b]you have fallen from grace.

5 For we through the Spirit eagerly [a]wait for the hope of righteousness by faith.

6 For [a]in Christ Jesus neither circumcision nor uncircumcision avails anything, but [b]faith working through love.

Love Fulfills the Law

7 You [a]ran well. Who hindered you from obeying the truth?

8 This persuasion does not *come* from Him who calls you.

9 [a]A little leaven leavens the whole lump.

10 I have confidence in you, in the Lord, that you will have no other mind; but he who troubles you shall bear his judgment, whoever he is.

11 And I, brethren, if I still preach circumcision, [a]why do I still suffer persecution? Then [b]the offense of the cross has ceased.

12 [a]I could wish that those [b]who trouble you would even cut themselves off!

13 For you, brethren, have been called to liberty; only [a]do not *use* liberty as an [b]opportunity for the flesh, but [c]through love serve one another.

14 For [a]all the law is fulfilled in one word,

KJV

even in this; [b]THOU SHALT LOVE THY NEIGHBOUR AS
THYSELF.
15 But if ye bite and devour one another, take
heed that ye be not consumed one of another.

Walking in the Spirit

16 *This* I say then, [a]Walk in the Spirit, and
ye shall not fulfil the lust of the flesh.
17 For [a]the flesh lusteth against the Spirit,
and the Spirit against the flesh: and these are contrary the one to the other: [b]so that ye cannot do
the things that ye would.
18 But [a]if ye be led of the Spirit, ye are not
under the law.
19 Now [a]the works of the flesh are manifest,
which are *these;* Adultery, fornication, uncleanness, lasciviousness,
20 Idolatry, witchcraft, hatred, variance, em-
ulations, wrath, strife, seditions, heresies,
21 Envyings, murders, drunkenness, revellings, and such like: of the which I tell you before,
as I have also told *you* in time past, that [a]they
which do such things shall not inherit the kingdom of God.
22 But [a]the fruit of the Spirit is [b]love, joy,
peace, longsuffering, gentleness, [c]goodness,
[d]faith,
23 Meekness, temperance: [a]against such
there is no law.
24 And they that are Christ's [a]have crucified
the flesh with the affections and lusts.
25 [a]If we live in the Spirit, let us also walk
in the Spirit.
26 [a]Let us not be desirous of vain glory, provoking one another, envying one another.

Bear and Share the Burdens

6 Brethren, if a man be overtaken in a fault, ye
which are spiritual, restore such an one in the
spirit of [a]meekness; considering thyself, lest thou
also be tempted.
2 [a]Bear ye one another's burdens, and so
fulfil [b]the law of Christ.
3 For [a]if a man think himself to be something, when [b]he is nothing, he deceiveth himself.
4 But [a]let every man prove his own work,
and then shall he have rejoicing in himself alone,
and [b]not in another.
5 For [a]every man shall bear his own burden.

Be Generous and Do Good

6 [a]Let him that is taught in the word communicate unto him that teacheth in all good
things.
7 Be not deceived; God is not mocked: for
[a]whatsoever a man soweth, that shall he also
reap.
8 For he that soweth to his flesh shall of
the flesh reap corruption; but he that soweth to
the Spirit shall of the Spirit reap [a]life everlasting.
9 And [a]let us not be weary in well doing:
for in due season we shall reap, [b]if we faint not.
10 [a]As we have therefore opportunity, [b]let
us do good unto all *men,* [c]especially unto them
who are of the household of faith.

Glory Only in the Cross

11 Ye see how large a letter I have written
unto you with mine own hand.
12 As many as desire to make a fair shew
in the flesh, they constrain you to be circumcised;
[a]only lest they should suffer persecution for the
cross of Christ.
13 For neither they themselves who are circumcised keep the law; but desire to have you
circumcised, that they may glory in your flesh.
14 But God forbid that I should glory, save
in the [a]cross of our Lord Jesus Christ, by whom
the world is crucified unto me, and [b]I unto the
world.
15 For [a]in Christ Jesus neither circumcision

14 [b]Lev. 19:18; Matt. 22:39; Rom. 13:9
16 [a]Rom. 6:12
17 [a]Rom. 7:18, 22, 23; 8:5 [b]Rom. 7:15
18 [a][Rom. 6:14; 7:4; 8:14; 1 Tim. 1:9]
19 [a]Rom. 1:26–31; Eph. 5:3, 11; 2 Tim. 3:2–4
21 [a]1 Cor. 6:9, 10
22 [a][John 15:2] [b][Rom. 5:1–5; 1 Cor. 13:4; Col. 3:12–15] [c]Rom. 15:14 [d]1 Cor. 13:7
23 [a]1 Tim. 1:9
24 [a]Rom. 6:6; [Gal. 2:20; 6:14]
25 [a][Rom. 8:4, 5]
26 [a]Phil. 2:3

CHAPTER 6

1 [a]Eph. 4:2
2 [a]Acts 20:35; Rom. 15:1; 1 Thess. 5:14 [b][James 2:8]
3 [a]Rom. 12:3 [b][2 Cor. 3:5; James 1:22]
4 [a]1 Cor. 11:28 [b]Luke 18:11
5 [a][Rom. 2:6]
6 [a]1 Cor. 9:11, 14
7 [a][Rom. 2:6]
8 [a][Rom. 6:8]
9 [a]1 Cor. 15:58; 2 Cor. 4:1; 2 Thess. 3:13 [b][Matt. 24:13]; Heb. 12:3, 5; [James 5:7, 8]
10 [a]Prov. 3:27; [John 9:4; 12:35] [b]Titus 3:8 [c]Rom. 12:13
12 [a]Gal. 5:11; Phil. 3:8
14 [a][1 Cor. 1:18] [b][Gal. 2:20]; Col. 2:20
15 [a][Rom. 2:26, 28]; 1 Cor. 7:19; [Gal. 5:6]

*

5:19 NU omits *adultery*
5:21 NU omits *murders*
6:14 Or *which,* the cross

NKJV

even in this: [b]*"You shall love your neighbor as*
yourself."
15 But if you bite and devour one another,
beware lest you be consumed by one another!

Walking in the Spirit

16 I say then: [a]Walk in the Spirit, and you
shall not fulfill the lust of the flesh.
17 For [a]the flesh lusts against the Spirit, and
the Spirit against the flesh; and these are contrary
to one another, [b]so that you do not do the things
that you wish.
18 But [a]if you are led by the Spirit, you are
not under the law.
19 Now [a]the works of the flesh are evident,
which are: *adultery, fornication, uncleanness,
lewdness,
20 idolatry, sorcery, hatred, contentions, jealousies, outbursts of wrath, selfish ambitions, dissensions, heresies,
21 envy, *murders, drunkenness, revelries,
and the like; of which I tell you beforehand, just
as I also told *you* in time past, that [a]those who
practice such things will not inherit the kingdom
of God.
22 But [a]the fruit of the Spirit is [b]love, joy,
peace, longsuffering, kindness, [c]goodness, [d]faith-
fulness,
23 gentleness, self-control. [a]Against such
there is no law.
24 And those *who are* Christ's [a]have crucified the flesh with its passions and desires.
25 [a]If we live in the Spirit, let us also walk
in the Spirit.
26 [a]Let us not become conceited, provoking
one another, envying one another.

Bear and Share the Burdens

6 Brethren, if a man is overtaken in any trespass, you who *are* spiritual restore such a one
in a spirit of [a]gentleness, considering yourself lest
you also be tempted.
2 [a]Bear one another's burdens, and so fulfill
[b]the law of Christ.
3 For [a]if anyone thinks himself to be something, when [b]he is nothing, he deceives himself.
4 But [a]let each one examine his own work,
and then he will have rejoicing in himself alone,
and [b]not in another.
5 For [a]each one shall bear his own load.

Be Generous and Do Good

6 [a]Let him who is taught the word share in
all good things with him who teaches.
7 Do not be deceived, God is not mocked;
for [a]whatever a man sows, that he will also reap.
8 For he who sows to his flesh will of the
flesh reap corruption, but he who sows to the
Spirit will of the Spirit reap [a]everlasting life.
9 And [a]let us not grow weary while doing
good, for in due season we shall reap [b]if we do
not lose heart.
10 [a]Therefore, as we have opportunity, [b]let
us do good to all, [c]especially to those who are of
the household of faith.

Glory Only in the Cross

11 See with what large letters I have written
to you with my own hand!
12 As many as desire to make a good showing in the flesh, these *would* compel you to be
circumcised, [a]only that they may not suffer persecution for the cross of Christ.
13 For not even those who are circumcised
keep the law, but they desire to have you circumcised that they may boast in your flesh.
14 But God forbid that I should boast except
in the [a]cross of our Lord Jesus Christ, by *whom
the world has been crucified to me, and [b]I to the
world.
15 For [a]in Christ Jesus neither circumcision

KJV

availeth any thing, nor uncircumcision, but a new
creature.

Blessing and a Plea

16 And as many as walk according to this
rule, peace *be* on them, and mercy, and upon the
Israel of God.
17 From henceforth let no man trouble me:
for I bear in my body the marks of the Lord Jesus.
18 Brethren, the grace of our Lord Jesus
Christ *be* with your spirit. Amen.

NKJV

nor uncircumcision avails anything, but a new
creation.

Blessing and a Plea

16 And as many as walk according to this
rule, peace and mercy *be* upon them, and upon
the Israel of God.
17 From now on let no one trouble me, for I
bear in my body the marks of the Lord Jesus.
18 Brethren, the grace of our Lord Jesus
Christ *be* with your spirit. Amen.

KJV

THE EPISTLE OF PAUL THE APOSTLE TO THE

EPHESIANS

Greeting

1 Paul, an apostle of Jesus Christ by the will of God, to the saints which are at Ephesus, and to the faithful in Christ Jesus:

2 Grace *be* to you, and peace, from God our Father, and *from* the Lord Jesus Christ.

Redemption in Christ

3 [a]Blessed *be* the God and Father of our Lord Jesus Christ, who hath blessed us with all spiritual blessings in heavenly *places* in Christ:

4 According as [a]he hath chosen us in him [b]before the foundation of the world, that we should [c]be holy and without blame before him in love:

5 [a]Having predestinated us unto [b]the adoption of children by Jesus Christ to himself, [c]according to the good pleasure of his will,

6 To the praise of the glory of his grace, [a]wherein he hath made us accepted in [b]the beloved.

7 [a]In whom we have redemption through his blood, the forgiveness of sins, according to [b]the riches of his grace;

8 Wherein he hath abounded toward us in all wisdom and prudence;

9 [a]Having made known unto us the mystery of his will, according to his good pleasure [b]which he hath purposed in himself:

10 That in the dispensation of [a]the fulness of times [b]he might gather together in one [c]all things in Christ, both which are in heaven, and which are on earth; *even* in him:

11 [a]In whom also we have obtained an inheritance, being predestinated according to [b]the purpose of him who worketh all things after the counsel of his own will:

12 [a]That we should be to the praise of his glory, [b]who first trusted in Christ.

13 In whom ye also *trusted,* after that ye heard [a]the word of truth, the gospel of your salvation: in whom also after that ye believed, [b]ye were sealed with that holy Spirit of promise,

14 [a]Which is the earnest of our inheritance [b]until the redemption of [c]the purchased possession, [d]unto the praise of his glory.

Prayer for Spiritual Wisdom

15 Wherefore I also, [a]after I heard of your faith in the Lord Jesus, and love unto all the saints,

16 [a]Cease not to give thanks for you, making mention of you in my prayers;

17 That [a]the God of our Lord Jesus Christ, the Father of glory, [b]may give unto you the spirit of wisdom and revelation in the knowledge of him:

18 [a]The eyes of your understanding being enlightened; that ye may know what is [b]the hope of his calling, and what the riches of the glory of his inheritance in the saints,

19 And what *is* the exceeding greatness of his power to usward who believe, [a]according to the working of his mighty power,

CHAPTER 1

3 [a]2 Cor. 1:3
4 [a]Rom. 8:28 [b]1 Pet. 1:2 [c]Luke 1:75
5 [a]Acts 13:48; [Rom. 8:29] [b]John 1:12 [c][1 Cor. 1:21]
6 [a][Rom. 3:24] [b]Matt. 3:17
7 [a][Heb. 9:12] [b][Rom. 3:24, 25]
9 [a][Rom. 16:25] [b][2 Tim. 1:9]
10 [a]Gal. 4:4 [b]1 Cor. 3:22 [c]Eph. 3:15; [Phil. 2:9; Col. 1:16, 20]
11 [a]Rom. 8:17 [b]Is. 46:10
12 [a]2 Thess. 2:13 [b]James 1:18
13 [a]John 1:17 [b][2 Cor. 1:22]
14 [a]2 Cor. 5:5 [b]Rom. 8:23 [c][Acts 20:28] [d]1 Pet. 2:9
15 [a]Col. 1:4; Philem. 5
16 [a]Rom. 1:9
17 [a]John 20:17; Rom. 15:6 [b]Is. 11:2; Col. 1:9
18 [a]Acts 26:18; 2 Cor. 4:6; Heb. 6:4 [b]Eph. 2:12
19 [a]Col. 2:12

*________

1:10 NU, M omit *both*
1:14 NU *which*
1:18 NU, M *hearts*

NKJV

THE EPISTLE OF PAUL THE APOSTLE TO THE

EPHESIANS

Greeting

1 Paul, an apostle of Jesus Christ by the will of God,

To the saints who are in Ephesus, and faithful in Christ Jesus:

2 Grace to you and peace from God our Father and the Lord Jesus Christ.

Redemption in Christ

3 [a]Blessed *be* the God and Father of our Lord Jesus Christ, who has blessed us with every spiritual blessing in the heavenly *places* in Christ,

4 just as [a]He chose us in Him [b]before the foundation of the world, that we should [c]be holy and without blame before Him in love,

5 [a]having predestined us to [b]adoption as sons by Jesus Christ to Himself, [c]according to the good pleasure of His will,

6 to the praise of the glory of His grace, [a]by which He made us accepted in [b]the Beloved.

7 [a]In Him we have redemption through His blood, the forgiveness of sins, according to [b]the riches of His grace

8 which He made to abound toward us in all wisdom and prudence,

9 [a]having made known to us the mystery of His will, according to His good pleasure [b]which He purposed in Himself,

10 that in the dispensation of [a]the fullness of the times [b]He might gather together in one [c]all things in Christ, *both which are in heaven and which are on earth—in Him.

11 [a]In Him also we have obtained an inheritance, being predestined according to [b]the purpose of Him who works all things according to the counsel of His will,

12 [a]that we [b]who first trusted in Christ should be to the praise of His glory.

13 In Him you also *trusted,* after you heard [a]the word of truth, the gospel of your salvation; in whom also, having believed, [b]you were sealed with the Holy Spirit of promise,

14 [a]who* is the guarantee of our inheritance [b]until the redemption of [c]the purchased possession, [d]to the praise of His glory.

Prayer for Spiritual Wisdom

15 Therefore I also, [a]after I heard of your faith in the Lord Jesus and your love for all the saints,

16 [a]do not cease to give thanks for you, making mention of you in my prayers:

17 that [a]the God of our Lord Jesus Christ, the Father of glory, [b]may give to you the spirit of wisdom and revelation in the knowledge of Him,

18 [a]the eyes of your *understanding being enlightened; that you may know what is [b]the hope of His calling, what are the riches of the glory of His inheritance in the saints,

19 and what *is* the exceeding greatness of His power toward us who believe, [a]according to the working of His mighty power

KJV

20 Which he wrought in Christ, when [a]he raised him from the dead, and [b]set *him* at his own right hand in the heavenly *places*,

21 [a]Far above all [b]principality, and power, and might, and dominion, and every name that is named, not only in this world, but also in that which is to come:

22 And [a]hath put all *things* under his feet, and gave him [b]*to be* the head over all *things* to the church,

23 [a]Which is his body, [b]the fulness of him [c]that filleth all in all.

By Grace Through Faith

2 And [a]you *hath he quickened,* [b]who were dead in trespasses and sins;

2 [a]Wherein in time past ye walked according to the course of this world, according to [b]the prince of the power of the air, the spirit that now worketh in [c]the children of disobedience:

3 [a]Among whom also we all had our conversation in times past in [b]the lusts of our flesh, fulfilling the desires of the flesh and of the mind; and [c]were by nature the children of wrath, even as others.

4 But God, [a]who is rich in mercy, for his [b]great love wherewith he loved us,

5 [a]Even when we were dead in sins, hath [b]quickened us together with Christ, (by grace ye are saved;)

6 And hath raised *us* up together, and made *us* sit together [a]in heavenly *places* in Christ Jesus:

7 That in the ages to come he might shew the exceeding riches of his grace in [a]*his* kindness toward us through Christ Jesus.

8 [a]For by grace are ye saved [b]through faith; and that not of yourselves: [c]*it is* the gift of God:

9 Not of [a]works, lest any man should [b]boast.

10 For we are [a]his workmanship, created in Christ Jesus unto good works, which God hath before ordained that we should walk in them.

Brought Near by His Blood

11 Wherefore remember, that ye *being* in time past Gentiles in the flesh, who are called Uncircumcision by that which is called [a]the Circumcision in the flesh made by hands;

12 That at that time ye were without Christ, being aliens from the commonwealth of Israel, and strangers from the covenants of promise, having no hope, and without God in the world:

13 But now in Christ Jesus ye who sometimes were far off are made nigh by the blood of Christ.

Christ Our Peace

14 For he is our peace, who hath made both one, and hath broken down the middle wall of partition *between us;*

15 Having abolished in his flesh the enmity, *even* the law of commandments *contained* in ordinances; for to make in himself of twain one [a]new man, *so* making peace;

16 And that he might [a]reconcile both unto God in one body by the cross, [b]having slain the enmity thereby:

17 And came and preached peace to you which were afar off, and to them that were nigh.

18 For [a]through him we both have access [b]by one Spirit unto the Father.

Christ Our Cornerstone

19 Now therefore ye are no more strangers and foreigners, but fellowcitizens with the saints, and of the household of God;

20 And are [a]built [b]upon the foundation of the [c]apostles and prophets, Jesus Christ himself being [d]the chief corner *stone;*

21 In whom all the building fitly framed together groweth unto [a]an holy temple in the Lord:

---

20 [a]Acts 2:24 [b]Ps. 110:1 **21** [a]Is. 9:6, 7; Luke 1:32, 33; Phil. 2:9, 10; Rev. 19:12 [b][Rom. 8:38, 39] **22** [a]Ps. 8:6; 110:1; Matt. 28:18; 1 Cor. 15:27 [b]Heb. 2:7 **23** [a]Rom. 12:5 [b]Col. 2:9 [c][1 Cor. 12:6]

CHAPTER 2

1 [a]Eph. 2:5; Col. 2:13 [b]Eph. 4:18 **2** [a]Col. 1:21 [b][John 12:31]; Eph. 6:12 [c]Col. 3:6 **3** [a]1 Pet. 4:3 [b]Gal. 5:16 [c][Ps. 51:5] **4** [a]Ps. 103:8–11; Rom. 10:12 [b]John 3:16; 1 John 4:9, 10 **5** [a]Rom. 5:6, 8 [b][Rom. 6:4, 5] **6** [a]Eph. 1:20 **7** [a]Titus 3:4 **8** [a][2 Tim. 1:9] [b]Rom. 4:16 [c][John 1:12, 13] **9** [a]Rom. 4:4, 5; 11:6 [b]Rom. 3:27 **10** [a]Is. 19:25 **11** [a][Rom. 2:28; Col. 2:11] **15** [a]Gal. 6:15 **16** [a]2 Cor. 5:18; [Col. 1:20–22] [b][Rom. 6:6] **18** [a]John 10:9 [b]1 Cor. 12:13; Eph. 4:4 **20** [a]1 Pet. 2:4 [b]Matt. 16:18; 1 Cor. 3:10, 11; Rev. 21:14 [c]1 Cor. 12:28; Eph. 3:5 [d]Ps. 118:22; Luke 20:17 **21** [a]1 Cor. 3:16, 17

NKJV

20 which He worked in Christ when [a]He raised Him from the dead and [b]seated *Him* at His right hand in the heavenly *places,*

21 [a]far above all [b]principality and power and might and dominion, and every name that is named, not only in this age but also in that which is to come.

22 And [a]He put all *things* under His feet, and gave Him [b]*to be* head over all *things* to the church,

23 [a]which is His body, [b]the fullness of Him [c]who fills all in all.

By Grace Through Faith

2 And [a]you *He made alive,* [b]who were dead in trespasses and sins,

2 [a]in which you once walked according to the course of this world, according to [b]the prince of the power of the air, the spirit who now works in [c]the sons of disobedience,

3 [a]among whom also we all once conducted ourselves in [b]the lusts of our flesh, fulfilling the desires of the flesh and of the mind, and [c]were by nature children of wrath, just as the others.

4 But God, [a]who is rich in mercy, because of His [b]great love with which He loved us,

5 [a]even when we were dead in trespasses, [b]made us alive together with Christ (by grace you have been saved),

6 and raised *us* up together, and made *us* sit together [a]in the heavenly *places* in Christ Jesus,

7 that in the ages to come He might show the exceeding riches of His grace in [a]*His* kindness toward us in Christ Jesus.

8 [a]For by grace you have been saved [b]through faith, and that not of yourselves; [c]*it is* the gift of God,

9 not of [a]works, lest anyone should [b]boast.

10 For we are [a]His workmanship, created in Christ Jesus for good works, which God prepared beforehand that we should walk in them.

Brought Near by His Blood

11 Therefore remember that you, once Gentiles in the flesh—who are called Uncircumcision by what is called [a]the Circumcision made in the flesh by hands—

12 that at that time you were without Christ, being aliens from the commonwealth of Israel and strangers from the covenants of promise, having no hope and without God in the world.

13 But now in Christ Jesus you who once were far off have been brought near by the blood of Christ.

Christ Our Peace

14 For He Himself is our peace, who has made both one, and has broken down the middle wall of separation,

15 having abolished in His flesh the enmity, *that is,* the law of commandments *contained* in ordinances, so as to create in Himself one [a]new man *from* the two, *thus* making peace,

16 and that He might [a]reconcile them both to God in one body through the cross, thereby [b]putting to death the enmity.

17 And He came and preached peace to you who were afar off and to those who were near.

18 For [a]through Him we both have access [b]by one Spirit to the Father.

Christ Our Cornerstone

19 Now, therefore, you are no longer strangers and foreigners, but fellow citizens with the saints and members of the household of God,

20 having been [a]built [b]on the foundation of the [c]apostles and prophets, Jesus Christ Himself being [d]the chief corner*stone,*

21 in whom the whole building, being fitted together, grows into [a]a holy temple in the Lord,

KJV

22 [a]In whom ye also are builded together for an [b]habitation of God through the Spirit.

The Mystery Revealed

3 For this cause I Paul, the prisoner of Jesus Christ for you Gentiles,

2 If ye have heard of the dispensation of the grace of God [a]which is given me to you-ward:

3 [a]How that by revelation [b]he made known unto me the mystery; (as I wrote afore in few words,

4 Whereby, when ye read, ye may understand my knowledge in the mystery of Christ)

5 Which in other ages was not made known unto the sons of men, as it is now revealed unto his holy apostles and prophets by the Spirit;

6 That the Gentiles [a]should be fellowheirs, and of the same body, and partakers of his promise in Christ by the gospel:

7 [a]Whereof I was made a minister, [b]according to the gift of the grace of God given unto me by [c]the effectual working of his power.

Purpose of the Mystery

8 Unto me, [a]who am less than the least of all saints, is this grace given, that I should preach among the Gentiles [b]the unsearchable riches of Christ;

9 And to make all *men* see what *is* the fellowship of the mystery, which from the beginning of the world hath been hid in God, who [a]created all things by Jesus Christ:

10 [a]To the intent that now [c]unto the principalities and powers in heavenly *places* [b]might be known by the church the manifold wisdom of God,

11 [a]According to the eternal purpose which he purposed in Christ Jesus our Lord:

12 In whom we have boldness and access [a]with confidence by the faith of him.

13 [a]Wherefore I desire that ye faint not at my tribulations for you, [b]which is your glory.

Appreciation of the Mystery

14 For this cause I bow my knees unto the [a]Father of our Lord Jesus Christ,

15 Of whom the whole family in heaven and earth is named,

16 That he would grant you, [a]according to the riches of his glory, [b]to be strengthened with might by his Spirit in [c]the inner man;

17 [a]That Christ may dwell in your hearts by faith; that ye, [b]being rooted and grounded in love,

18 [a]May be able to comprehend with all saints [b]what *is* the breadth, and length, and depth, and height;

19 And to know the love of Christ, which passeth knowledge, that ye might be filled [a]with all the fulness of God.

20 Now [a]unto him that is able to do exceeding abundantly [b]above all that we ask or think, [c]according to the power that worketh in us,

21 [a]Unto him *be* glory in the church by Christ Jesus throughout all ages, world without end. Amen.

Walk in Unity

4 I therefore, the prisoner of the Lord, beseech you that ye [a]walk worthy of the vocation wherewith ye are called,

2 With all lowliness and meekness, with longsuffering, forbearing one another in love;

3 Endeavouring to keep the unity of the Spirit [a]in the bond of peace.

4 [a]*There is* one body, and one Spirit, even as ye are called in one hope of your calling;

5 [a]One Lord, [b]one faith, [c]one baptism,

6 [a]One God and Father of all, who *is* above all, and [b]through all, and in you all.

---

22 [a]1 Pet. 2:5 [b]John 17:23

CHAPTER 3

2 [a]Acts 9:15
3 [a]Acts 22:17, 21; 26:16 [b][Rom. 11:25; 16:25; Eph. 3:4, 9; 6:19]; Col. 1:26; 4:3
6 [a]Gal. 3:28, 29
7 [a]Rom. 15:16 [b]Rom. 1:5 [c]Rom. 15:18
8 [a][1 Cor. 15:9] [b][Col. 1:27; 2:2, 3]
9 [a]John 1:3; Col. 1:16; Heb. 1:2
10 [a]1 Pet. 1:12 [b][1 Tim. 3:16] [c]Eph. 1:21; 6:12; Col. 1:16; 2:10, 15
11 [a][Eph. 1:4, 11]
12 [a]2 Cor. 3:4; Heb. 4:16; 10:19, 35; [1 John 2:28; 3:21]
13 [a]Phil. 1:14 [b]2 Cor. 1:6
14 [a]Eph. 1:3
16 [a][Eph. 1:7; 2:4; Phil. 4:19] [b]1 Cor. 16:13; Phil. 4:13; Col. 1:11 [c]Rom. 7:22
17 [a]John 14:23; Rom. 8:9; 2 Cor. 13:5; [Eph. 2:22] [b]Col. 1:23
18 [a]Eph. 1:18 [b]Rom. 8:39
19 [a]Eph. 1:23
20 [a]Rom. 16:25 [b]1 Cor. 2:9 [c]Col. 1:29
21 [a]Rom. 11:36

CHAPTER 4

1 [a]Eph. 2:10; [Col. 1:10; 2:6]; 1 Thess. 2:12
3 [a]Col. 3:14
4 [a]Rom. 12:5
5 [a]1 Cor. 1:13 [b][1 Cor. 15:1–8]; Jude 3 [c]1 Cor. 12:12, 13; [Heb. 6:6]
6 [a]Mal. 2:10; 1 Cor. 8:6; 12:6 [b]Rom. 11:36

*———

3:9 NU, M *stewardship (dispensation)* • NU omits *through Jesus Christ*
3:14 NU omits *of our Lord Jesus Christ*
4:6 NU omits *you;* M *us*

NKJV

22 [a]in whom you also are being built together for a [b]dwelling place of God in the Spirit.

The Mystery Revealed

3 For this reason I, Paul, the prisoner of Christ Jesus for you Gentiles—

2 if indeed you have heard of the dispensation of the grace of God [a]which was given to me for you,

3 [a]how that by revelation [b]He made known to me the mystery (as I have briefly written already,

4 by which, when you read, you may understand my knowledge in the mystery of Christ),

5 which in other ages was not made known to the sons of men, as it has now been revealed by the Spirit to His holy apostles and prophets:

6 that the Gentiles [a]should be fellow heirs, of the same body, and partakers of His promise in Christ through the gospel,

7 [a]of which I became a minister [b]according to the gift of the grace of God given to me by [c]the effective working of His power.

Purpose of the Mystery

8 To me, [a]who am less than the least of all the saints, this grace was given, that I should preach among the Gentiles [b]the unsearchable riches of Christ,

9 and to make all see what *is* the *fellowship of the mystery, which from the beginning of the ages has been hidden in God who [a]created all things *through Jesus Christ;

10 [a]to the intent that now [b]the manifold wisdom of God might be made known by the church [c]to the principalities and powers in the heavenly *places,*

11 [a]according to the eternal purpose which He accomplished in Christ Jesus our Lord,

12 in whom we have boldness and access [a]with confidence through faith in Him.

13 [a]Therefore I ask that you do not lose heart at my tribulations for you, [b]which is your glory.

Appreciation of the Mystery

14 For this reason I bow my knees to the [a]Father *of our Lord Jesus Christ,

15 from whom the whole family in heaven and earth is named,

16 that He would grant you, [a]according to the riches of His glory, [b]to be strengthened with might through His Spirit in [c]the inner man,

17 [a]that Christ may dwell in your hearts through faith; that you, [b]being rooted and grounded in love,

18 [a]may be able to comprehend with all the saints [b]what *is* the width and length and depth and height—

19 to know the love of Christ which passes knowledge; that you may be filled [a]with all the fullness of God.

20 Now [a]to Him who is able to do exceedingly abundantly [b]above all that we ask or think, [c]according to the power that works in us,

21 [a]to Him *be* glory in the church by Christ Jesus to all generations, forever and ever. Amen.

Walk in Unity

4 I, therefore, the prisoner of the Lord, beseech you to [a]walk worthy of the calling with which you were called,

2 with all lowliness and gentleness, with longsuffering, bearing with one another in love,

3 endeavoring to keep the unity of the Spirit [a]in the bond of peace.

4 [a]*There is* one body and one Spirit, just as you were called in one hope of your calling;

5 [a]one Lord, [b]one faith, [c]one baptism;

6 [a]one God and Father of all, who *is* above all, and [b]through all, and in *you all.

KJV

Spiritual Gifts

7 But [a]unto every one of us is given grace
according to the measure of the gift of Christ.
8 Wherefore he saith, [a]WHEN HE ASCENDED
UP ON HIGH, HE LED CAPTIVITY CAPTIVE, AND GAVE
GIFTS UNTO MEN.
9 [a](Now that he ascended, what is it but that
he also descended first into the lower parts of the
earth?
10 He that descended is the same also [a]that
ascended up far above all heavens, [b]that he might
fill all things.)
11 And he gave some, apostles; and some,
prophets; and some, evangelists; and some, pastors and teachers;
12 For the perfecting of the saints, for the
work of the ministry, [a]for the edifying of [b]the
body of Christ:
13 Till we all come in the unity of the faith,
[a]and of the knowledge of the Son of God, unto
[b]a perfect man, unto the measure of the stature
of the fulness of Christ:
14 That we *henceforth* be no more [a]children,
tossed to and fro, and carried about with every
wind of doctrine, by the sleight of men, *and* cunning craftiness, [b]whereby they lie in wait to
deceive;
15 But speaking the truth in love, may grow
up into him in all things, which is the [a]head, *even*
Christ:
16 [a]From whom the whole body fitly joined
together and compacted by that which every joint
supplieth, according to the effectual working in
the measure of every part, maketh increase of the
body unto the edifying of itself in love.

The New Man

17 This I say therefore, and testify in the
Lord, that ye henceforth [a]walk not as other Gentiles walk, in the vanity of their mind,
18 Having the understanding darkened, being alienated from the life of God through the ignorance that is in them, because of the [a]blindness
of their heart:
19 [a]Who being past feeling [b]have given
themselves over unto lasciviousness, to work all
uncleanness with greediness.
20 But ye have not so learned Christ;
21 If so be that ye have heard him, and have
been taught by him, as the truth is in Jesus:
22 That ye [a]put off concerning the former
conversation the old man, which is corrupt according to the deceitful lusts;
23 And [a]be renewed in the spirit of your
mind;
24 And that ye [a]put on the new man, which
after God is created in righteousness and true holiness.

Do Not Grieve the Spirit

25 Wherefore putting away lying, [a]SPEAK
EVERY MAN TRUTH WITH HIS NEIGHBOUR: for [b]we are
members one of another.
26 [a]BE YE ANGRY, AND SIN NOT: let not the sun
go down upon your wrath:
27 [a]Neither give place to the devil.
28 Let him that stole steal no more: but rather
[a]let him labour, working with *his* hands the thing
which is good, that he may have to give [b]to him
that needeth.
29 [a]Let no corrupt communication proceed
out of your mouth, but [b]that which is good to the
use of edifying, [c]that it may minister grace unto
the hearers.
30 And [a]grieve not the holy Spirit of God,
whereby ye are sealed unto the day of redemption.
31 [a]Let all bitterness, and wrath, and anger,
and clamour, and [b]evil speaking, be put away
from you, [c]with all malice:

7 [a][1 Cor. 12:7, 11]
8 [a]Ps. 68:18; [Col. 2:15]
9 [a]Luke 23:43; John 3:13; 20:17; [1 Pet. 3:19, 20]
10 [a]Acts 1:9 [b][Acts 2:33; Eph. 1:23]
12 [a]1 Cor. 14:26 [b]Col. 1:24
13 [a]Col. 2:2 [b]1 Cor. 14:20; Col. 1:28; Heb. 5:14
14 [a]1 Cor. 14:20 [b]Rom. 16:18
15 [a]Eph. 1:22
16 [a][Rom. 12:4]; Col. 2:19
17 [a]Eph. 2:2; 4:22
18 [a]Rom. 1:21
19 [a]1 Tim. 4:2 [b]1 Pet. 4:3
22 [a]Col. 3:8
23 [a][Rom. 12:2; Col. 3:10]
24 [a][Rom. 6:4; 7:6; 12:2; 2 Cor. 5:17; Col. 3:10]
25 [a]Zech. 8:16; Eph. 4:15; Col. 3:9 [b]Rom. 12:5
26 [a]Ps. 4:4; 37:8
27 [a][Rom. 12:19; James 4:7]; 1 Pet. 5:9
28 [a]Acts 20:35; 1 Cor. 4:12; Gal. 6:10 [b]Luke 3:11; 1 Thess. 4:12
29 [a]Matt. 12:34; Eph. 5:4; Col. 3:8 [b]1 Thess. 5:11 [c]Col. 3:16
30 [a]Is. 7:13
31 [a]Rom. 3:14; Col. 3:8, 19 [b]James 4:11 [c]Titus 3:3

*———

4:9 NU omits *first*
4:17 NU omits *the rest of*

NKJV

Spiritual Gifts

7 But [a]to each one of us grace was given
according to the measure of Christ's gift.
8 Therefore He says:

[a]*"When He ascended on high,*
He led captivity captive,
And gave gifts to men."

9 [a](Now this, *"He ascended"*—what does it
mean but that He also *first descended into the
lower parts of the earth?
10 He who descended is also the One [a]who
ascended far above all the heavens, [b]that He
might fill all things.)
11 And He Himself gave some *to be* apostles,
some prophets, some evangelists, and some pastors and teachers,
12 for the equipping of the saints for the
work of ministry, [a]for the edifying of [b]the body
of Christ,
13 till we all come to the unity of the faith
[a]and of the knowledge of the Son of God, to [b]a
perfect man, to the measure of the stature of the
fullness of Christ;
14 that we should no longer be [a]children,
tossed to and fro and carried about with every
wind of doctrine, by the trickery of men, in the
cunning craftiness of [b]deceitful plotting,
15 but, speaking the truth in love, may grow
up in all things into Him who is the [a]head—
Christ—
16 [a]from whom the whole body, joined and
knit together by what every joint supplies, according to the effective working by which every part
does its share, causes growth of the body for the
edifying of itself in love.

The New Man

17 This I say, therefore, and testify in the
Lord, that you should [a]no longer walk as *the rest
of the Gentiles walk, in the futility of their mind,
18 having their understanding darkened, being alienated from the life of God, because of the
ignorance that is in them, because of the [a]blind-
ness of their heart;
19 [a]who, being past feeling, [b]have given
themselves over to lewdness, to work all uncleanness with greediness.
20 But you have not so learned Christ,
21 if indeed you have heard Him and have
been taught by Him, as the truth is in Jesus:
22 that you [a]put off, concerning your former
conduct, the old man which grows corrupt according to the deceitful lusts,
23 and [a]be renewed in the spirit of your
mind,
24 and that you [a]put on the new man which
was created according to God, in true righteousness and holiness.

Do Not Grieve the Spirit

25 Therefore, putting away lying, [a]*"Let each
one of you speak truth with his neighbor,"* for
[b]we are members of one another.
26 [a]*"Be angry, and do not sin"*: do not let
the sun go down on your wrath,
27 [a]nor give place to the devil.
28 Let him who stole steal no longer, but
rather [a]let him labor, working with *his* hands
what is good, that he may have something [b]to
give him who has need.
29 [a]Let no corrupt word proceed out of your
mouth, but [b]what is good for necessary edification, [c]that it may impart grace to the hearers.
30 And [a]do not grieve the Holy Spirit of God,
by whom you were sealed for the day of
redemption.
31 [a]Let all bitterness, wrath, anger, clamor,
and [b]evil speaking be put away from you, [c]with
all malice.

KJV

32 And [a]be ye kind one to another, tenderhearted, [b]forgiving one another, even as God for
Christ's sake hath forgiven you.

Walk in Love

5 Be [a]ye therefore followers of God, as dear
[b]children;
2 And [a]walk in love, [b]as Christ also hath
loved us, and hath given himself for us an offering
and a sacrifice to God [c]for a sweetsmelling
savour.
3 But fornication, and all [a]uncleanness, or
[b]covetousness, let it not be once named among
you, as becometh saints;
4 [a]Neither filthiness, nor [b]foolish talking,
nor jesting, [c]which are not convenient: but rather
[d]giving of thanks.
5 For this ye know, that no whoremonger,
nor unclean person, nor covetous man, who is an
idolater, hath any [a]inheritance in the kingdom of
Christ and of God.
6 Let no man deceive you with vain words:
for because of these things cometh the wrath of
God upon the children of disobedience.
7 Be not ye therefore [a]partakers with them.

Walk in Light

8 For ye were sometimes darkness, but
now *are ye* [a]light in the Lord: walk as children of
light:
9 (For [a]the fruit of the Spirit *is* in all goodness and righteousness and truth;)
10 [a]Proving what is acceptable unto the
Lord.
11 And have [a]no fellowship with the unfruitful works of darkness, but rather reprove *them.*
12 [a]For it is a shame even to speak of those
things which are done of them in secret.
13 But [a]all things that are reproved are made
manifest by the light: for whatsoever doth make
manifest is light.
14 Wherefore he saith, [a]Awake thou that
sleepest, and arise from the dead, and Christ shall
give thee light.

Walk in Wisdom

15 [a]See then that ye walk circumspectly, not
as fools, but as wise,
16 [a]Redeeming the time, [b]because the days
are evil.
17 [a]Wherefore be ye not unwise, but [b]under-
standing [c]what the will of the Lord *is.*
18 And [a]be not drunk with wine, wherein is
excess; but be filled with the Spirit;
19 Speaking to yourselves [a]in psalms and
hymns and spiritual songs, singing and making
[b]melody in your heart to the Lord;
20 [a]Giving thanks always for all things unto
God and the Father [b]in the name of our Lord Jesus Christ;
21 [a]Submitting yourselves one to another in
the fear of God.

Marriage—Christ and the Church
(cf. Col. 3:18, 19)

22 Wives, [a]submit yourselves unto your own
husbands, as unto the Lord.
23 For [a]the husband is the head of the wife,
even as [b]Christ is the head of the church: and he
is the saviour of the body.
24 Therefore as the church is subject unto
Christ, so *let* the wives *be* to their own husbands
[a]in every thing.
25 [a]Husbands, love your wives, even as
Christ also loved the church, and [b]gave himself
for it;
26 That he might sanctify and cleanse it
[a]with the washing of water [b]by the word,
27 [a]That he might present it to himself a glorious church, [b]not having spot, or wrinkle, or any
such thing; but that it should be holy and without
blemish.

---

32 [a]2 Cor. 6:10 [b][Mark 11:25]

CHAPTER 5

1 [a]Luke 6:36 [b]1 Pet. 1:14–16
2 [a]1 Thess. 4:9 [b]Gal. 1:4 [c]2 Cor. 2:14, 15
3 [a]Col. 3:5–7 [b][Luke 12:15]
4 [a]Matt. 12:34, 35 [b]Titus 3:9 [c]Rom. 1:28 [d]Phil. 4:6
5 [a]1 Cor. 6:9, 10
7 [a]1 Tim. 5:22
8 [a]1 Thess. 5:5
9 [a]Gal. 5:22
10 [a][Rom. 12:1, 2]
11 [a]2 Cor. 6:14
12 [a]Rom. 1:24
13 [a][John 3:20, 21]
14 [a][Is. 26:19; 60:1]
15 [a]Col. 4:5
16 [a]Col. 4:5 [b]Eccl. 11:2
17 [a]Col. 4:5 [b][Rom. 12:2] [c]1 Thess. 4:3
18 [a]Prov. 20:1; 23:31
19 [a]Acts 16:25 [b]James 5:13
20 [a]Ps. 34:1 [b][1 Pet. 2:5]
21 [a][Phil. 2:3]
22 [a]Col. 3:18–4:1
23 [a][1 Cor. 11:3] [b]Col. 1:18
24 [a]Titus 2:4, 5
25 [a]Col. 3:19 [b]Acts 20:28
26 [a]John 3:5 [b][John 15:3; 17:17]
27 [a]Col. 1:22 [b]Song 4:7

*

5:5 NU *know this*
5:9 NU *light*
5:21 NU *Christ*

NKJV

32 And [a]be kind to one another, tenderhearted, [b]forgiving one another, even as God in
Christ forgave you.

Walk in Love

5 Therefore[a] be imitators of God as dear
[b]children.
2 And [a]walk in love, [b]as Christ also has
loved us and given Himself for us, an offering and
a sacrifice to God [c]for a sweet-smelling aroma.
3 But fornication and all [a]uncleanness or
[b]covetousness, let it not even be named among
you, as is fitting for saints;
4 [a]neither filthiness, nor [b]foolish talking,
nor coarse jesting, [c]which are not fitting, but
rather [d]giving of thanks.
5 For *this you know, that no fornicator, unclean person, nor covetous man, who is an idolater, has any [a]inheritance in the kingdom of Christ
and God.
6 Let no one deceive you with empty words,
for because of these things the wrath of God
comes upon the sons of disobedience.
7 Therefore do not be [a]partakers with them.

Walk in Light

8 For you were once darkness, but now *you*
are [a]light in the Lord. Walk as children of light
9 (for [a]the fruit of the *Spirit *is* in all goodness, righteousness, and truth),
10 [a]finding out what is acceptable to the
Lord.
11 And have [a]no fellowship with the unfruitful works of darkness, but rather expose *them.*
12 [a]For it is shameful even to speak of those
things which are done by them in secret.
13 But [a]all things that are exposed are made
manifest by the light, for whatever makes manifest is light.
14 Therefore He says:

[a]"Awake, you who sleep,
Arise from the dead,
And Christ will give you light."

Walk in Wisdom

15 [a]See then that you walk circumspectly,
not as fools but as wise,
16 [a]redeeming the time, [b]because the days
are evil.
17 [a]Therefore do not be unwise, but [b]under-
stand [c]what the will of the Lord *is.*
18 And [a]do not be drunk with wine, in which
is dissipation; but be filled with the Spirit,
19 speaking to one another [a]in psalms and
hymns and spiritual songs, singing and making
[b]melody in your heart to the Lord,
20 [a]giving thanks always for all things to
God the Father [b]in the name of our Lord Jesus
Christ,
21 [a]submitting to one another in the fear of
*God.

Marriage—Christ and the Church
(cf. Col. 3:18, 19)

22 Wives, [a]submit to your own husbands, as
to the Lord.
23 For [a]the husband is head of the wife, as
also [b]Christ is head of the church; and He is the
Savior of the body.
24 Therefore, just as the church is subject to
Christ, so *let* the wives *be* to their own husbands
[a]in everything.
25 [a]Husbands, love your wives, just as Christ
also loved the church and [b]gave Himself for her,
26 that He might sanctify and cleanse her
[a]with the washing of water [b]by the word,
27 [a]that He might present her to Himself a
glorious church, [b]not having spot or wrinkle or
any such thing, but that she should be holy and
without blemish.

KJV

28 So ought men to love their wives as their own bodies. He that loveth his wife loveth himself.

29 For no man ever yet hated his own flesh; but nourisheth and cherisheth it, even as the Lord the church:

30 For [a]we are members of his body, of his flesh, and of his bones.

31 [a]FOR THIS CAUSE SHALL A MAN LEAVE HIS FATHER AND MOTHER, AND SHALL BE JOINED UNTO HIS WIFE, AND THEY [b]TWO SHALL BE ONE FLESH.

32 This is a great mystery: but I speak concerning Christ and the church.

33 Nevertheless [a]let every one of you in particular so love his wife even as himself; and the wife *see* that she [b]reverence *her* husband.

Children and Parents
(Ex. 20:12; Deut. 5:16)

6 Children, [a]obey your parents in the Lord: for this is right.

2 [a]HONOUR THY FATHER AND MOTHER; which is the first commandment with promise;

3 THAT IT MAY BE WELL WITH THEE, AND THOU MAYEST LIVE LONG ON THE EARTH.

4 And, [a]ye fathers, provoke not your children to wrath: but [b]bring them up in the nurture and admonition of the Lord.

Bondservants and Masters

5 [a]Servants, be obedient to them that are *your* masters according to the flesh, [b]with fear and trembling, [c]in singleness of your heart, as unto Christ;

6 [a]Not with eyeservice, as menpleasers; but as the servants of Christ, doing the will of God from the heart;

7 With good will doing service, as to the Lord, and not to men:

8 [a]Knowing that whatsoever good thing any man doeth, the same shall he receive of the Lord, whether *he be* bond or free.

9 And, ye masters, do the same things unto them, forbearing threatening: knowing that your [a]Master also is in heaven; [b]neither is there respect of persons with him.

The Whole Armor of God

10 Finally, my brethren, be strong in the Lord, and in the power of his might.

11 [a]Put on the whole armour of God, that ye may be able to stand against the wiles of the devil.

12 For we wrestle not against flesh and blood, but against [a]principalities, against powers, against [b]the rulers of the darkness of this world, against spiritual wickedness in high *places*.

13 [a]Wherefore take unto you the whole armour of God, that ye may be able to withstand [b]in the evil day, and having done all, to stand.

14 Stand therefore, [a]having your loins girt about with truth, and [b]having on the breastplate of righteousness;

15 [a]And your feet shod with the preparation of the gospel of peace;

16 Above all, taking [a]the shield of faith, wherewith ye shall be able to quench all the fiery darts of the wicked.

17 And [a]take the helmet of salvation, and [b]the sword of the Spirit, which is the word of God:

18 [a]Praying always with all prayer and supplication in the Spirit, and [b]watching thereunto with all perseverance and [c]supplication for all saints;

19 And for me, that utterance may be given unto me, [a]that I may open my mouth boldly, to make known the mystery of the gospel,

20 For which [a]I am an ambassador in bonds: that therein I may speak boldly, as I ought to speak.

---

30 [a]Gen. 2:23
31 [a]Gen. 2:24; Matt. 19:5; Mark 10:7 [b][1 Cor. 6:16]
33 [a]Col. 3:19 [b]1 Pet. 3:1, 6

CHAPTER 6

1 [a]Prov. 6:20; 23:22; Col. 3:20
2 [a]Ex. 20:12; Deut. 5:16
4 [a]Col. 3:21 [b]Gen. 18:19; Deut. 6:7; 11:19; Ps. 78:4; Prov. 22:6; 2 Tim. 3:15
5 [a]Col. 3:22; [1 Tim. 6:1]; Titus 2:9; 1 Pet. 2:18 [b]2 Cor. 7:15 [c]1 Chr. 29:17
6 [a]Col. 3:22
8 [a]Rom. 2:6
9 [a]Job 31:13; John 13:13; Col. 4:1 [b]Deut. 10:17; Acts 10:34; Rom. 2:11; Col. 3:25
11 [a][2 Cor. 6:7]
12 [a]Rom. 8:38 [b]Luke 22:53
13 [a][2 Cor. 10:4] [b]Eph. 5:16
14 [a]Is. 11:5; Luke 12:35; 1 Pet. 1:13 [b]Is. 59:17; Rom. 13:12; Eph. 6:13; 1 Thess. 5:8
15 [a]Is. 52:7; Rom. 10:15
16 [a]1 John 5:4
17 [a]1 Thess. 5:8 [b]Is. 49:2; Hos. 6:5; [Heb. 4:12]
18 [a]Luke 18:1; Col. 1:3; 4:2; 1 Thess. 5:17 [b][Matt. 26:41] [c]Phil. 1:4
19 [a]Acts 4:29; Col. 4:3
20 [a]2 Cor. 5:20; Philem. 9

*

5:30 NU omits the rest of v. 30.
6:9 NU *He who is both their Master and yours is*
6:12 NU *this darkness,*

NKJV

28 So husbands ought to love their own wives as their own bodies; he who loves his wife loves himself.

29 For no one ever hated his own flesh, but nourishes and cherishes it, just as the Lord *does* the church.

30 For [a]we are members of His body, *of His flesh and of His bones.

31 [a]*"For this reason a man shall leave his father and mother and be joined to his wife, and the [b]two shall become one flesh."*

32 This is a great mystery, but I speak concerning Christ and the church.

33 Nevertheless [a]let each one of you in particular so love his own wife as himself, and let the wife *see* that she [b]respects *her* husband.

Children and Parents
(Ex. 20:12; Deut. 5:16)

6 Children, [a]obey your parents in the Lord, for this is right.

2 [a]*"Honor your father and mother,"* which is the first commandment with promise:

3 *"that it may be well with you and you may live long on the earth."*

4 And [a]you, fathers, do not provoke your children to wrath, but [b]bring them up in the training and admonition of the Lord.

Bondservants and Masters

5 [a]Bondservants, be obedient to those who are your masters according to the flesh, [b]with fear and trembling, [c]in sincerity of heart, as to Christ;

6 [a]not with eyeservice, as men-pleasers, but as bondservants of Christ, doing the will of God from the heart,

7 with goodwill doing service, as to the Lord, and not to men,

8 [a]knowing that whatever good anyone does, he will receive the same from the Lord, whether *he is* a slave or free.

9 And you, masters, do the same things to them, giving up threatening, knowing that *your own [a]Master also is in heaven, and [b]there is no partiality with Him.

The Whole Armor of God

10 Finally, my brethren, be strong in the Lord and in the power of His might.

11 [a]Put on the whole armor of God, that you may be able to stand against the wiles of the devil.

12 For we do not wrestle against flesh and blood, but against [a]principalities, against powers, against [b]the rulers of *the darkness of this age, against spiritual *hosts* of wickedness in the heavenly *places*.

13 [a]Therefore take up the whole armor of God, that you may be able to withstand [b]in the evil day, and having done all, to stand.

14 Stand therefore, [a]having girded your waist with truth, [b]having put on the breastplate of righteousness,

15 [a]and having shod your feet with the preparation of the gospel of peace;

16 above all, taking [a]the shield of faith with which you will be able to quench all the fiery darts of the wicked one.

17 And [a]take the helmet of salvation, and [b]the sword of the Spirit, which is the word of God;

18 [a]praying always with all prayer and supplication in the Spirit, [b]being watchful to this end with all perseverance and [c]supplication for all the saints—

19 and for me, that utterance may be given to me, [a]that I may open my mouth boldly to make known the mystery of the gospel,

20 for which [a]I am an ambassador in chains; that in it I may speak boldly, as I ought to speak.

KJV

A Gracious Greeting

21 But that ye also may know my affairs, *and*
how I do, [a]Tychicus, a beloved brother and [b]faith-
ful minister in the Lord, shall make known to you
all things:
22 [a]Whom I have sent unto you for the same
purpose, that ye might know our affairs, and *that*
he might [b]comfort your hearts.
23 Peace *be* to the brethren, and love with
faith, from God the Father and the Lord Jesus
Christ.
24 Grace *be* with all them that love our Lord
Jesus Christ in sincerity. Amen.

21 [a]Acts 20:4; 2 Tim. 4:12; Titus 3:12 [b]1 Cor. 4:1, 2
22 [a]Col. 4:8 [b]2 Cor. 1:6

NKJV

A Gracious Greeting

21 But that you also may know my affairs
and how I am doing, [a]Tychicus, a beloved brother
and [b]faithful minister in the Lord, will make all
things known to you;
22 [a]whom I have sent to you for this very
purpose, that you may know our affairs, and *that*
he may [b]comfort your hearts.
23 Peace to the brethren, and love with faith,
from God the Father and the Lord Jesus Christ.
24 Grace *be* with all those who love our Lord
Jesus Christ in sincerity. Amen.

KJV

THE EPISTLE OF PAUL THE APOSTLE TO THE

PHILIPPIANS

Greeting

1 Paul and Timotheus, the servants of Jesus
Christ, to all the saints in Christ Jesus which
are at Philippi, with the bishops and [a]deacons:
2 Grace *be* unto you, and peace, from God
our Father, and *from* the Lord Jesus Christ.

Thankfulness and Prayer

3 [a]I thank my God upon every remembrance of you,
4 Always in [a]every prayer of mine for you
all making request with joy,
5 [a]For your fellowship in the gospel from
the first day until now;
6 Being confident of this very thing, that he
which hath begun [a]a good work in you will perform *it* until the day of Jesus Christ:
7 Even as it is meet for me to think this of
you all, because I have you in my heart; inasmuch
as both in my bonds, and in the defence and confirmation of the gospel, ye all are partakers of
my grace.
8 For God is my record, how greatly I long
after you all in the bowels of Jesus Christ.
9 And this I pray, that your love may
abound yet more and more in knowledge and *in*
all judgment;
10 That ye may approve things that are excellent; that ye may be sincere and without offence till the day of Christ;
11 Being filled with the fruits of righteousness, [a]which are by Jesus Christ, [b]unto the glory
and praise of God.

Christ Is Preached

12 But I would ye should understand, brethren, that the things *which happened* unto me have
fallen out rather unto the furtherance of the
gospel;
13 So that my bonds in Christ are manifest
[a]in all the palace, and in all other *places;*
14 And many of the brethren in the Lord,
waxing confident by my bonds, are much more
bold to speak the word without fear.
15 Some indeed preach Christ even of envy
and strife; and some also of good will:
16 The one preach Christ of contention, not
sincerely, supposing to add affliction to my bonds:
17 But the other of love, knowing that I am
set for the defence of the gospel.
18 What then? notwithstanding, every way,
whether in pretence, or in truth, Christ is
preached; and I therein do rejoice, yea, and will
rejoice.

To Live Is Christ

19 For I know that [a]this shall turn to my salvation through your prayer, and the supply of the
Spirit of Jesus Christ,
20 According to my earnest expectation and

CHAPTER 1
1 [a][1 Tim. 3:8–13]
3 [a]1 Cor. 1:4
4 [a]Eph. 1:16; 1 Thess. 1:2
5 [a][Rom. 12:13]
6 [a][John 6:29]
11 [a][Eph. 2:10]; Col. 1:6 [b]John 15:8
13 [a]Phil. 4:22
19 [a]Job 13:16, LXX

*

1:1 Lit. *overseers*
1:16 NU reverses vv. 16 and 17.

NKJV

THE EPISTLE OF PAUL THE APOSTLE TO THE

PHILIPPIANS

Greeting

1 Paul and Timothy, bondservants of Jesus
Christ,

To all the saints in Christ Jesus who are
in Philippi, with the *bishops and [a]deacons:

2 Grace to you and peace from God our Father and the Lord Jesus Christ.

Thankfulness and Prayer

3 [a]I thank my God upon every remembrance of you,
4 always in [a]every prayer of mine making
request for you all with joy,
5 [a]for your fellowship in the gospel from the
first day until now,
6 being confident of this very thing, that He
who has begun [a]a good work in you will complete
it until the day of Jesus Christ;
7 just as it is right for me to think this of
you all, because I have you in my heart, inasmuch
as both in my chains and in the defense and confirmation of the gospel, you all are partakers with
me of grace.
8 For God is my witness, how greatly I long
for you all with the affection of Jesus Christ.
9 And this I pray, that your love may
abound still more and more in knowledge and all
discernment,
10 that you may approve the things that are
excellent, that you may be sincere and without
offense till the day of Christ,
11 being filled with the fruits of righteousness [a]which *are* by Jesus Christ, [b]to the glory and
praise of God.

Christ Is Preached

12 But I want you to know, brethren, that the
things *which happened* to me have actually turned
out for the furtherance of the gospel,
13 so that it has become evident [a]to the whole
palace guard, and to all the rest, that my chains
are in Christ;
14 and most of the brethren in the Lord, having become confident by my chains, are much
more bold to speak the word without fear.
15 Some indeed preach Christ even
from envy and strife, and some also from goodwill:
16 *The former preach Christ from selfish
ambition, not sincerely, supposing to add affliction to my chains;
17 but the latter out of love, knowing that I
am appointed for the defense of the gospel.
18 What then? Only *that* in every way,
whether in pretense or in truth, Christ is
preached; and in this I rejoice, yes, and will rejoice.

To Live Is Christ

19 For I know that [a]this will turn out for my
deliverance through your prayer and the supply
of the Spirit of Jesus Christ,
20 according to my earnest expectation and

KJV

my hope, that in nothing I shall be ashamed, but *that* [a]with all boldness, as always, *so* now also Christ shall be magnified in my body, whether *it be* by life, [b]or by death.

21 For to me to live *is* Christ, and to die *is* gain.

22 But if I live in the flesh, this *is* the fruit of my labour: yet what I shall choose I wot not.

23 For I am in a strait betwixt two, having a [a]desire to depart, and to be with Christ; which is [b]far better:

24 Nevertheless to abide in the flesh *is* more needful for you.

25 And having this confidence, I know that I shall abide and continue with you all for your furtherance and joy of faith;

26 That [a]your rejoicing may be more abundant in Jesus Christ for me by my coming to you again.

Striving and Suffering for Christ

27 Only [a]let your conversation be as it becometh the gospel of Christ: that whether I come and see you, or else be absent, I may hear of your affairs, that ye stand fast in one spirit, [b]with one mind [c]striving together for the faith of the gospel;

28 And in nothing terrified by your adversaries: which is to them an evident token of perdition, but to you of salvation, and that of God.

29 For unto you [a]it is given in the behalf of Christ, [b]not only to believe on him, but also to [c]suffer for his sake;

30 [a]Having the same conflict [b]which ye saw in me, and now hear *to be* in me.

Unity Through Humility

2 If *there be* therefore any consolation in Christ, if any comfort of love, if any fellowship of the Spirit, if any [a]bowels and mercies,

2 [a]Fulfil ye my joy, [b]that ye be likeminded, having the same love, *being* of [c]one accord, of one mind.

3 [a]*Let* nothing *be done* through strife or vainglory; but [b]in lowliness of mind let each esteem other better than themselves.

4 [a]Look not every man on his own things, but every man also on the things of [b]others.

The Humbled and Exalted Christ

5 [a]Let this mind be in you, which was also in Christ Jesus:

6 Who, [a]being in the form of God, thought it not robbery to be equal with God:

7 [a]But made himself of no reputation, and took upon him the form [b]of a servant, and [c]was made in the likeness of men:

8 And being found in fashion as a man, he humbled himself, and [a]became [b]obedient unto death, even the death of the cross.

9 [a]Wherefore God also [b]hath highly exalted him, and [c]given him a name which is above every name:

10 [a]That at the name of Jesus every knee should bow, of *things* in heaven, and *things* in earth, and *things* under the earth;

11 And [a]*that* every tongue should confess that Jesus Christ *is* Lord, to the glory of God the Father.

Light Bearers

12 Wherefore, my beloved, [a]as ye have always obeyed, not as in my presence only, but now much more in my absence, [b]work out your own salvation with [c]fear and trembling.

13 For [a]it is God which worketh in you both to will and to do [b]of *his* good pleasure.

14 Do all things [a]without murmurings and [b]disputings:

15 That ye may be blameless and harmless, the sons of God, without rebuke, in the midst of

---

20 [a]Eph. 6:19, 20 [b][Rom. 14:8]
23 [a][2 Cor. 5:2, 8]; 2 Tim. 4:6 [b][Ps. 16:11]
26 [a]2 Cor. 1:14
27 [a]Eph. 4:1; 1 Thess. 2:12 [b]1 Cor. 1:10; Eph. 4:3 [c]Jude 3
29 [a][Matt. 5:11, 12; Acts 5:41; Rom. 5:3] [b]Eph. 2:8 [c][2 Tim. 3:12]
30 [a]Col. 1:29; 2:1; 1 Thess. 2:2; 1 Tim. 6:12; 2 Tim. 4:7; Heb. 10:32; 12:1 [b]Acts 16:19–40; Phil. 1:13; 1 Thess. 2:2

CHAPTER 2
1 [a]Col. 3:12
2 [a]John 3:29 [b]Rom. 12:16 [c]Phil. 4:2
3 [a]Gal. 5:26; James 3:14 [b]Rom. 12:10; Eph. 5:21
4 [a]1 Cor. 13:5 [b]Rom. 15:1, 2
5 [a][Matt. 11:29]; Rom. 15:3
6 [a]2 Cor. 4:4
7 [a]Ps. 22:6 [b]Is. 42:1 [c][John 1:14]; Rom. 8:3; Gal. 4:4; [Heb. 2:17]
8 [a]Ps. 40:6–8; Matt. 26:39; John 10:18; [Rom. 5:19] [b]Heb. 5:8
9 [a][Matt. 28:18]; Heb. 2:9 [b]Ps. 68:18; 110:1; Is. 52:13; Acts 2:33 [c]Is. 9:6; Luke 1:32; Eph. 1:21
10 [a]Is. 45:23; Rom. 14:11; Rev. 5:13
11 [a]John 13:13; [Rom. 10:9; 14:9]
12 [a]Phil. 1:5, 6; 4:15 [b]John 6:27, 29; 2 Pet. 1:10 [c]Eph. 6:5
13 [a]Rom. 12:3; 1 Cor. 12:6; 15:10; 2 Cor. 3:5; Heb. 13:20, 21 [b]Eph. 1:5
14 [a]1 Cor. 10:10; 1 Pet. 4:9 [b]Rom. 14:1

*
1:23 NU, M *But*
1:28 NU *of your salvation*

NKJV

hope that in nothing I shall be ashamed, but [a]with all boldness, as always, so now also Christ will be magnified in my body, whether by life [b]or by death.

21 For to me, to live *is* Christ, and to die *is* gain.

22 But if *I* live on in the flesh, this *will mean* fruit from *my* labor; yet what I shall choose I cannot tell.

23 *For I am hard-pressed between the two, having a [a]desire to depart and be with Christ, *which is* [b]far better.

24 Nevertheless to remain in the flesh *is* more needful for you.

25 And being confident of this, I know that I shall remain and continue with you all for your progress and joy of faith,

26 that [a]your rejoicing for me may be more abundant in Jesus Christ by my coming to you again.

Striving and Suffering for Christ

27 Only [a]let your conduct be worthy of the gospel of Christ, so that whether I come and see you or am absent, I may hear of your affairs, that you stand fast in one spirit, [b]with one mind [c]striving together for the faith of the gospel,

28 and not in any way terrified by your adversaries, which is to them a proof of perdition, but *to you of salvation, and that from God.

29 For to you [a]it has been granted on behalf of Christ, [b]not only to believe in Him, but also to [c]suffer for His sake,

30 [a]having the same conflict [b]which you saw in me and now hear *is* in me.

Unity Through Humility

2 Therefore if *there is* any consolation in Christ, if any comfort of love, if any fellowship of the Spirit, if any [a]affection and mercy,

2 [a]fulfill my joy [b]by being like-minded, having the same love, *being* of [c]one accord, of one mind.

3 [a]*Let* nothing *be done* through selfish ambition or conceit, but [b]in lowliness of mind let each esteem others better than himself.

4 [a]Let each of you look out not only for his own interests, but also for the interests of [b]others.

The Humbled and Exalted Christ

5 [a]Let this mind be in you which was also in Christ Jesus,

6 who, [a]being in the form of God, did not consider it robbery to be equal with God,

7 [a]but made Himself of no reputation, taking the form [b]of a bondservant, *and* [c]coming in the likeness of men.

8 And being found in appearance as a man, He humbled Himself and [a]became [b]obedient to *the point of* death, even the death of the cross.

9 [a]Therefore God also [b]has highly exalted Him and [c]given Him the name which is above every name,

10 [a]that at the name of Jesus every knee should bow, of those in heaven, and of those on earth, and of those under the earth,

11 and [a]*that* every tongue should confess that Jesus Christ *is* Lord, to the glory of God the Father.

Light Bearers

12 Therefore, my beloved, [a]as you have always obeyed, not as in my presence only, but now much more in my absence, [b]work out your own salvation with [c]fear and trembling;

13 for [a]it is God who works in you both to will and to do [b]for *His* good pleasure.

14 Do all things [a]without complaining and [b]disputing,

15 that you may become blameless and harmless, children of God without fault in the

KJV

a crooked and perverse nation, among whom ye shine as [a]lights in the world;

16 Holding forth the word of life; that [a]I may rejoice in the day of Christ, that [b]I have not run in vain, neither laboured in [c]vain.

17 Yea, and if [a]I be offered upon the sacrifice [b]and service of your faith, [c]I joy, and rejoice with you all.

18 For the same cause also do ye joy, and rejoice with me.

Timothy Commended

19 But I trust in the Lord Jesus to send [a]Timotheus shortly unto you, that I also may be of good comfort, when I know your state.

20 For I have no man [a]likeminded, who will naturally care for your state.

21 For all seek their own, not the things which are Jesus Christ's.

22 But ye know the proof of him, [a]that, as a son with the father, he hath served with me in the gospel.

23 Him therefore I hope to send presently, so soon as I shall see how it will go with me.

24 But I trust in the Lord that I also myself shall come shortly.

Epaphroditus Praised

25 Yet I supposed it necessary to send to you [a]Epaphroditus, my brother, and companion in labour, and [b]fellowsoldier, [c]but your messenger, and [d]he that ministered to my wants.

26 [a]For he longed after you all, and was full of heaviness, because that ye had heard that he had been sick.

27 For indeed he was sick nigh unto death: but God had mercy on him; and not on him only, but on me also, lest I should have sorrow upon sorrow.

28 I sent him therefore the more carefully, that, when ye see him again, ye may rejoice, and that I may be the less sorrowful.

29 Receive him therefore in the Lord with all gladness; and hold such in reputation:

30 Because for the work of Christ he was nigh unto death, not regarding his life, [a]to supply your lack of service toward me.

All for Christ

3 Finally, my brethren, [a]rejoice in the Lord. To write the same things to you, to me indeed *is* not grievous, but for you *it is* safe.

2 [a]Beware of dogs, beware of [b]evil workers, [c]beware of the concision.

3 For we are [a]the circumcision, [b]which worship God in the spirit, and rejoice in Christ Jesus, and have no confidence in the flesh.

4 Though [a]I might also have confidence in the flesh. If any other man thinketh that he hath whereof he might trust in the flesh, I [b]more:

5 Circumcised the eighth day, of the stock of Israel, [a]*of* the tribe of Benjamin, [b]an Hebrew of the Hebrews; as touching the law, [c]a Pharisee;

6 Concerning zeal, [a]persecuting the church; touching the righteousness which is in the law, blameless.

7 But [a]what things were gain to me, those I counted loss for Christ.

8 Yea doubtless, and I count all things *but* loss [a]for the excellency of the knowledge of Christ Jesus my Lord: for whom I have suffered the loss of all things, and do count them *but* dung, that I may win Christ,

9 And be found in him, not having [a]mine own righteousness, which is of the law, but [b]that which is through the faith of Christ, the righteousness which is of God by faith:

10 That I may know him, and the [a]power of his resurrection, and [b]the fellowship of his sufferings, being made conformable unto his death;

11 If by any means I might [a]attain unto the resurrection of the dead.

---

15 [a]Matt. 5:15, 16
16 [a]2 Cor. 1:14 [b]Gal. 2:2 [c]Is. 49:4; Gal. 4:11; 1 Thess. 3:5
17 [a]2 Cor. 12:15; 2 Tim. 4:6 [b]Num. 28:6, 7; Rom. 15:16 [c]2 Cor. 7:4
19 [a]Rom. 16:21
20 [a]1 Cor. 16:10; 2 Tim. 3:10
22 [a]1 Cor. 4:17
25 [a]Phil. 4:18 [b]Philem. 2 [c]John 13:16; 2 Cor. 8:23 [d]2 Cor. 11:9
26 [a]Phil. 1:8
30 [a]1 Cor. 16:17; Phil. 4:10

CHAPTER 3

1 [a]1 Thess. 5:16
2 [a]Ps. 22:16, 20; Gal. 5:15; Rev. 22:15 [b]Ps. 119:115 [c]Rom. 2:28
3 [a]Deut. 30:6; Rom. 2:28, 29; 9:6; [Gal. 6:15] [b]John 4:24; Rom. 7:6
4 [a]2 Cor. 5:16; 11:18 [b]2 Cor. 11:22, 23
5 [a]Rom. 11:1 [b]2 Cor. 11:22 [c]Acts 23:6
6 [a]Acts 8:3; 22:4, 5; 26:9–11
7 [a]Matt. 13:44
8 [a]Is. 53:11; Jer. 9:23; John 17:3; 1 Cor. 2:2; [Eph. 4:13]
9 [a]Rom. 10:3 [b]Rom. 1:17
10 [a]Eph. 1:19, 20 [b][Rom. 6:3–5]; 2 Cor. 1:5; 1 Pet. 4:13
11 [a]Acts 26:6–8; [1 Cor. 15:23; Rev. 20:5]

---

*

3:3 NU, M *in the Spirit of God*

NKJV

midst of a crooked and perverse generation, among whom you shine as [a]lights in the world,

16 holding fast the word of life, so that [a]I may rejoice in the day of Christ that [b]I have not run in vain or labored in [c]vain.

17 Yes, and if [a]I am being poured out *as a drink offering* on the sacrifice [b]and service of your faith, [c]I am glad and rejoice with you all.

18 For the same reason you also be glad and rejoice with me.

Timothy Commended

19 But I trust in the Lord Jesus to send [a]Timothy to you shortly, that I also may be encouraged when I know your state.

20 For I have no one [a]like-minded, who will sincerely care for your state.

21 For all seek their own, not the things which are of Christ Jesus.

22 But you know his proven character, [a]that as a son with *his* father he served with me in the gospel.

23 Therefore I hope to send him at once, as soon as I see how it goes with me.

24 But I trust in the Lord that I myself shall also come shortly.

Epaphroditus Praised

25 Yet I considered it necessary to send to you [a]Epaphroditus, my brother, fellow worker, and [b]fellow soldier, [c]but your messenger and [d]the one who ministered to my need;

26 [a]since he was longing for you all, and was distressed because you had heard that he was sick.

27 For indeed he was sick almost unto death; but God had mercy on him, and not only on him but on me also, lest I should have sorrow upon sorrow.

28 Therefore I sent him the more eagerly, that when you see him again you may rejoice, and I may be less sorrowful.

29 Receive him therefore in the Lord with all gladness, and hold such men in esteem;

30 because for the work of Christ he came close to death, not regarding his life, [a]to supply what was lacking in your service toward me.

All for Christ

3 Finally, my brethren, [a]rejoice in the Lord. For me to write the same things to you *is* not tedious, but for you *it is* safe.

2 [a]Beware of dogs, beware of [b]evil workers, [c]beware of the mutilation!

3 For we are [a]the circumcision, [b]who worship *God in the Spirit, rejoice in Christ Jesus, and have no confidence in the flesh,

4 though [a]I also might have confidence in the flesh. If anyone else thinks he may have confidence in the flesh, I [b]more so:

5 circumcised the eighth day, of the stock of Israel, [a]*of* the tribe of Benjamin, [b]a Hebrew of the Hebrews; concerning the law, [c]a Pharisee;

6 concerning zeal, [a]persecuting the church; concerning the righteousness which is in the law, blameless.

7 But [a]what things were gain to me, these I have counted loss for Christ.

8 Yet indeed I also count all things loss [a]for the excellence of the knowledge of Christ Jesus my Lord, for whom I have suffered the loss of all things, and count them as rubbish, that I may gain Christ

9 and be found in Him, not having [a]my own righteousness, which *is* from the law, but [b]that which *is* through faith in Christ, the righteousness which is from God by faith;

10 that I may know Him and the [a]power of His resurrection, and [b]the fellowship of His sufferings, being conformed to His death,

11 if, by any means, I may [a]attain to the resurrection from the dead.

KJV

Pressing Toward the Goal

12 Not as though I had already [a]attained, either were already [b]perfect: but I follow after, if
that I may apprehend that for which also I am
apprehended of Christ Jesus.
13 Brethren, I count not myself to have apprehended: but *this* one thing *I do,* [a]forgetting
those things which are behind, and [b]reaching
forth unto those things which are before,
14 [a]I press toward the mark for the prize of
[b]the high calling of God in Christ Jesus.
15 Let us therefore, as many as be [a]perfect,
[b]be thus minded: and if in any thing ye be otherwise minded, [c]God shall reveal even this unto you.
16 Nevertheless, whereto we have already attained, [a]let us walk [b]by the same rule, let us mind
the same thing.

Our Citizenship in Heaven

17 Brethren, [a]be followers together of me,
and mark them which walk so as [b]ye have us for
an ensample.
18 (For many walk, of whom I have told you
often, and now tell you even weeping, *that they
are* [a]the enemies of the cross of Christ:
19 [a]Whose end *is* destruction, [b]whose God
is their belly, and [c]*whose* glory *is* in their shame,
[d]who mind earthly things.)
20 For [a]our conversation is in heaven; [b]from
whence also we [c]look for the Saviour, the Lord
Jesus Christ:
21 [a]Who shall change our vile body, that it
may be fashioned [b]like unto his glorious body,
[c]according to the working whereby he is able
even to [d]subdue all things unto himself.

4 Therefore, my brethren dearly beloved and
[a]longed for, [b]my joy and crown, so [c]stand fast
in the Lord, *my* dearly beloved.

Be United, Joyful, and in Prayer

2 I beseech Euodias, and beseech Syntyche,
[a]that they be of the same mind in the Lord.
3 And I intreat thee also, true yokefellow,
help those women which [a]laboured with me in
the gospel, with Clement also, and *with* other my
fellowlabourers, whose names *are* in [b]the book
of life.
4 [a]Rejoice in the Lord alway: *and* again I
say, Rejoice.
5 Let your moderation be known unto all
men. [a]The Lord *is* at hand.
6 [a]Be careful for nothing; but in every thing
by prayer and supplication with [b]thanksgiving let
your requests be made known unto God.
7 And [a]the peace of God, which passeth all
understanding, shall keep your hearts and minds
through Christ Jesus.

Meditate on These Things

8 Finally, brethren, whatsoever things are
[a]true, whatsoever things *are* [b]honest, whatsoever
things *are* [c]just, [d]whatsoever things *are* pure,
whatsoever things *are* [e]lovely, whatsoever things
are of good report; if *there be* any virtue, and if
there be any praise, think on these things.
9 Those things, which ye have both learned,
and received, and heard, and seen in me, do: and
[a]the God of peace shall be with you.

Philippian Generosity

10 But I rejoiced in the Lord greatly, that
now at the last [a]your care of me hath flourished
again; wherein ye were also careful, but ye lacked
opportunity.
11 Not that I speak in respect of want: for I
have learned, in whatsoever state I am, [a]*therewith* to be content.
12 [a]I know both how to be abased, and I
know how to abound: every where and in all
things I am instructed both to be full and to be
hungry, both to abound and to suffer need.

NKJV

Pressing Toward the Goal

12 Not that I have already [a]attained, or am
already [b]perfected; but I press on, that I may lay
hold of that for which Christ Jesus has also laid
hold of me.
13 Brethren, I do not count myself to have
apprehended; but one thing *I do,* [a]forgetting those
things which are behind and [b]reaching forward
to those things which are ahead,
14 [a]I press toward the goal for the prize of
[b]the upward call of God in Christ Jesus.
15 Therefore let us, as many as are [a]mature,
[b]have this mind; and if in anything you think
otherwise, [c]God will reveal even this to you.
16 Nevertheless, to *the degree* that we have
already attained, [a]let us walk [b]by the same *rule,
let us be of the same mind.

Our Citizenship in Heaven

17 Brethren, [a]join in following my example,
and note those who so walk, as [b]you have us for
a pattern.
18 For many walk, of whom I have told you
often, and now tell you even weeping, *that they
are* [a]the enemies of the cross of Christ:
19 [a]whose end *is* destruction, [b]whose god *is
their* belly, and [c]*whose* glory *is* in their shame—
[d]who set their mind on earthly things.
20 For [a]our citizenship is in heaven, [b]from
which we also [c]eagerly wait for the Savior, the
Lord Jesus Christ,
21 [a]who will transform our lowly body that
it may be [b]conformed to His glorious body, [c]ac-
cording to the working by which He is able even
to [d]subdue all things to Himself.

4 Therefore, my beloved and [a]longed-for brethren, [b]my joy and crown, so [c]stand fast in the
Lord, beloved.

Be United, Joyful, and in Prayer

2 I implore Euodia and I implore Syntyche
[a]to be of the same mind in the Lord.
3 *And I urge you also, true companion,
help these women who [a]labored with me in the
gospel, with Clement also, and the rest of my fellow workers, whose names *are* in [b]the Book of
Life.
4 [a]Rejoice in the Lord always. Again I will
say, rejoice!
5 Let your gentleness be known to all men.
[a]The Lord *is* at hand.
6 [a]Be anxious for nothing, but in everything
by prayer and supplication, with [b]thanksgiving,
let your requests be made known to God;
7 and [a]the peace of God, which surpasses
all understanding, will guard your hearts and
minds through Christ Jesus.

Meditate on These Things

8 Finally, brethren, whatever things are
[a]true, whatever things *are* [b]noble, whatever
things *are* [c]just, [d]whatever things *are* pure, whatever things *are* [e]lovely, whatever things *are* of
good report, if *there is* any virtue and if *there is*
anything praiseworthy—meditate on these things.
9 The things which you learned and received and heard and saw in me, these do, and
[a]the God of peace will be with you.

Philippian Generosity

10 But I rejoiced in the Lord greatly that now
at last [a]your care for me has flourished again;
though you surely did care, but you lacked
opportunity.
11 Not that I speak in regard to need, for I
have learned in whatever state I am, [a]to be
content:
12 [a]I know how to be abased, and I know
how to abound. Everywhere and in all things I
have learned both to be full and to be hungry,
both to abound and to suffer need.

---

12 [a]1 Cor. 9:24; [1 Tim. 6:12, 19] [b]Heb. 12:23
13 [a]Luke 9:62 [b]Heb. 6:1
14 [a]2 Tim. 4:7 [b]Heb. 3:1
15 [a]Matt. 5:48; 1 Cor. 2:6 [b]Gal. 5:10 [c]Hos. 6:3; James 1:5
16 [a]Gal. 6:16 [b]Rom. 12:16; 15:5
17 [a][1 Cor. 4:16; 11:1]; Phil. 4:9 [b]Titus 2:7, 8; 1 Pet. 5:3
18 [a]Gal. 1:7
19 [a]2 Cor. 11:15 [b]1 Tim. 6:5 [c]Hos. 4:7 [d]Rom. 8:5; Col. 3:2
20 [a]Eph. 2:6, 19; Phil. 1:27; [Col. 3:1; Heb. 12:22] [b]Acts 1:11 [c]1 Cor. 1:7
21 [a][1 Cor. 15:43–53] [b]1 John 3:2 [c]Eph. 1:19 [d][1 Cor. 15:28]

CHAPTER 4

1 [a]Phil. 1:8 [b]2 Cor. 1:14 [c]1 Cor. 16:13; Phil. 1:27
2 [a]Phil. 2:2; 3:16
3 [a]Rom. 16:3 [b]Ex. 32:32; Luke 10:20
4 [a]Rom. 12:12
5 [a]1 Cor. 16:22; Heb. 10:25, 37; [James 5:7–9]; Rev. 22:7, 20
6 [a]Ps. 55:22; Matt. 6:25; 1 Pet. 5:7 [b][1 Thess. 5:17, 18]
7 [a][Is. 26:3; John 14:27]; Phil. 4:9; Col. 3:15
8 [a]Eph. 4:25 [b]2 Cor. 8:21 [c]Deut. 16:20 [d]1 Thess. 5:22; James 3:17 [e]1 Cor. 13:4–7
9 [a]Rom. 15:33; Heb. 13:20
10 [a]2 Cor. 11:9; Phil. 2:30
11 [a]2 Cor. 9:8; 1 Tim. 6:6, 8; Heb. 13:5
12 [a]1 Cor. 4:11

*

3:16 NU omits *rule* and the rest of v. 16.
4:3 NU, M *Yes*

KJV

13 I can do all things [a]through Christ which
strengtheneth me.
14 Notwithstanding ye have well done, that
[a]ye did communicate with my affliction.
15 Now ye Philippians know also, that in the
beginning of the gospel, when I departed from
Macedonia, [a]no church communicated with me
as concerning giving and receiving, but ye only.
16 For even in Thessalonica ye sent once and
again unto my necessity.
17 Not because I desire a gift: but I desire
[a]fruit that may abound to your account.
18 But I have all, and abound: I am full, having received of [a]Epaphroditus the things *which
were sent* from you, [b]an odour of a sweet smell,
[c]a sacrifice acceptable, wellpleasing to God.
19 But my God [a]shall supply all your need
according to his riches in glory by Christ Jesus.
20 [a]Now unto God and our Father *be* glory
for ever and ever. Amen.

Greeting and Blessing

21 Salute every saint in Christ Jesus. The
brethren [a]which are with me greet you.
22 All the saints salute you, chiefly they that
are of Caesar's household.
23 The grace of our Lord Jesus Christ *be* with
you all. Amen.

13 [a]John 15:5
14 [a]Phil. 1:7
15 [a]2 Cor. 11:8, 9
17 [a]Titus 3:14
18 [a]Phil. 2:25 [b]Heb. 13:16 [c]Rom. 12:1; 2 Cor. 9:12
19 [a]Ps. 23:1; 2 Cor. 9:8
20 [a]Rom. 16:27
21 [a]Gal. 1:2

*

4:13 NU *Him who*
4:23 NU *your spirit*

NKJV

13 I can do all things [a]through *Christ who
strengthens me.
14 Nevertheless you have done well that
[a]you shared in my distress.
15 Now you Philippians know also that in the
beginning of the gospel, when I departed from
Macedonia, [a]no church shared with me concerning giving and receiving but you only.
16 For even in Thessalonica you sent *aid*
once and again for my necessities.
17 Not that I seek the gift, but I seek [a]the
fruit that abounds to your account.
18 Indeed I have all and abound. I am full,
having received from [a]Epaphroditus the things
sent from you, [b]a sweet-smelling aroma, [c]an acceptable sacrifice, well pleasing to God.
19 And my God [a]shall supply all your need
according to His riches in glory by Christ Jesus.
20 [a]Now to our God and Father *be* glory forever and ever. Amen.

Greeting and Blessing

21 Greet every saint in Christ Jesus. The
brethren [a]who are with me greet you.
22 All the saints greet you, but especially
those who are of Caesar's household.
23 The grace of our Lord Jesus Christ be with
*you all. Amen.

KJV

THE EPISTLE OF PAUL THE APOSTLE TO THE

COLOSSIANS

Greeting

1 Paul, [a]an apostle of Jesus Christ by the will
of God, and Timotheus *our* brother,
2 To the saints [a]and faithful brethren in
Christ which are at Colosse: [b]Grace *be* unto you,
and peace, from God our Father and the Lord Jesus Christ.

Their Faith in Christ

3 [a]We give thanks to God and the Father
of our Lord Jesus Christ, praying always for you,
4 [a]Since we heard of your faith in Christ
Jesus, and of [b]the love *which ye have* to all the
saints,
5 For the hope [a]which is laid up for you in
heaven, whereof ye heard before in the word of
the truth of the gospel;
6 Which is come unto you, [a]as *it is* in all
the world; and [b]bringeth forth fruit, as *it doth*
also in you, since the day ye heard *of it,* and knew
[c]the grace of God in truth:
7 As ye also learned of [a]Epaphras our dear
fellowservant, who is for you [b]a faithful minister
of Christ;
8 Who also declared unto us your [a]love in
the Spirit.

Preeminence of Christ

9 [a]For this cause we also, since the day we
heard *it,* do not cease to pray for you, and to desire [b]that ye might be filled with [c]the knowledge
of his will [d]in all wisdom and spiritual understanding;
10 [a]That ye might walk worthy of the Lord
[b]unto all pleasing, [c]being fruitful in every good
work, and increasing in the [d]knowledge of God;
11 [a]Strengthened with all might, according
to his glorious power, [b]unto all patience and longsuffering [c]with joyfulness;
12 [a]Giving thanks unto the Father, which
hath made us meet to be partakers of [b]the inheritance of the saints in light:
13 Who hath delivered us from [a]the power
of darkness, [b]and hath translated *us* into the kingdom of his dear Son:
14 [a]In whom we have redemption through
his blood, *even* the forgiveness of sins:
15 Who is [a]the image of the invisible God,
[b]the firstborn of every creature:
16 For [a]by him were all things created, that
are in heaven, and that are in earth, visible and
invisible, whether *they be* thrones, or [b]dominions,
or principalities, or powers: all things were created [c]by him, and for him:
17 [a]And he is before all things, and by him
[b]all things consist.
18 And [a]he is the head of the body, the
church: who is the beginning, [b]the firstborn from
the dead; that in all *things* he might have the preeminence.

Reconciled in Christ

19 For it pleased *the Father* that [a]in him
should all fulness dwell;

CHAPTER 1
1 [a]Eph. 1:1
2 [a]1 Cor. 4:17 [b]Gal. 1:3
3 [a]1 Cor. 1:4; Eph. 1:16; Phil. 1:3
4 [a]Eph. 1:15 [b][Heb. 6:10]
5 [a][1 Pet. 1:4]
6 [a]Matt. 24:14 [b]John 15:16 [c]Eph. 3:2
7 [a]Col. 4:12; Philem. 23 [b]1 Cor. 4:1, 2; 2 Cor. 11:23
8 [a]Rom. 15:30
9 [a]Eph. 1:15–17 [b]1 Cor. 1:5 [c][Rom. 12:2]; Eph. 5:17 [d]Eph. 1:8
10 [a]Eph. 4:1; Phil. 1:27; 1 Thess. 2:12 [b]1 Thess. 4:1 [c]Heb. 13:21 [d]2 Pet. 3:18
11 [a][Eph. 3:16; 6:10] [b]Eph. 4:2 [c][Acts 5:41]; 2 Cor. 8:2; [Heb. 10:34]
12 [a][Eph. 5:20] [b]Eph. 1:11
13 [a]Eph. 6:12 [b]2 Pet. 1:11
14 [a]Eph. 1:7
15 [a]2 Cor. 4:4; Heb. 1:3 [b]Ps. 89:27; Rev. 3:14
16 [a]John 1:3; Heb. 1:2, 3 [b][Eph. 1:20, 21; Col. 2:15] [c]John 1:3; Rom. 11:36; 1 Cor. 8:6; Heb. 2:10
17 [a][John 17:5] [b]Heb. 1:3
18 [a]1 Cor. 11:3; Eph. 1:22 [b]Rev. 1:5
19 [a]John 1:16

*

1:2 NU omits *and the Lord Jesus Christ*
1:6 NU, M add *and growing*
1:14 NU, M omit *through His blood*

NKJV

THE EPISTLE OF PAUL THE APOSTLE TO THE

COLOSSIANS

Greeting

1 Paul, [a]an apostle of Jesus Christ by the will
of God, and Timothy our brother,

2 To the saints [a]and faithful brethren in
Christ *who are* in Colosse:

[b]Grace to you and peace from God our
Father *and the Lord Jesus Christ.

Their Faith in Christ

3 [a]We give thanks to the God and Father
of our Lord Jesus Christ, praying always for you,
4 [a]since we heard of your faith in Christ Jesus and of [b]your love for all the saints;
5 because of the hope [a]which is laid up for
you in heaven, of which you heard before in the
word of the truth of the gospel,
6 which has come to you, [a]as *it has* also in
all the world, and [b]is bringing forth *fruit, as *it
is* also among you since the day you heard and
knew [c]the grace of God in truth;
7 as you also learned from [a]Epaphras, our
dear fellow servant, who is [b]a faithful minister
of Christ on your behalf,
8 who also declared to us your [a]love in the
Spirit.

Preeminence of Christ

9 [a]For this reason we also, since the day we
heard it, do not cease to pray for you, and to ask
[b]that you may be filled with [c]the knowledge of
His will [d]in all wisdom and spiritual understanding;
10 [a]that you may walk worthy of the Lord,
[b]fully pleasing *Him,* [c]being fruitful in every good
work and increasing in the [d]knowledge of God;
11 [a]strengthened with all might, according to
His glorious power, [b]for all patience and longsuffering [c]with joy;
12 [a]giving thanks to the Father who has qualified us to be partakers of [b]the inheritance of the
saints in the light.
13 He has delivered us from [a]the power of
darkness [b]and conveyed *us* into the kingdom of
the Son of His love,
14 [a]in whom we have redemption *through
His blood, the forgiveness of sins.
15 He is [a]the image of the invisible God, [b]the
firstborn over all creation.
16 For [a]by Him all things were created that
are in heaven and that are on earth, visible and
invisible, whether thrones or [b]dominions or principalities or powers. All things were created
[c]through Him and for Him.
17 [a]And He is before all things, and in Him
[b]all things consist.
18 And [a]He is the head of the body, the
church, who is the beginning, [b]the firstborn from
the dead, that in all things He may have the preeminence.

Reconciled in Christ

19 For it pleased *the Father that* [a]in Him all
the fullness should dwell,

KJV

20 And, [c]having made peace through the blood of his cross, [a]by him to reconcile [b]all things unto himself; by him, *I say*, whether *they be* things in earth, or things in heaven.

21 And you, [a]that were sometime alienated and enemies in *your* mind [b]by wicked works, yet now hath he [c]reconciled

22 [a]In the body of his flesh through death, [b]to present you holy and unblameable and unreproveable in his sight:

23 If ye continue [a]in the faith grounded and settled, and *be* [b]not moved away from the hope of the gospel, which ye have heard, [c]*and* which was preached to every creature which is under heaven; [d]whereof I Paul am made a minister;

Sacrificial Service for Christ

24 [a]Who now rejoice in my sufferings [b]for you, and fill up [c]that which is behind of the afflictions of Christ in my flesh for [d]his body's sake, which is the church:

25 Whereof I am made a minister, according to [a]the dispensation of God which is given to me for you, to fulfil the word of God;

26 *Even* [a]the mystery which hath been hid from ages and from generations, [b]but now is made manifest to his saints:

27 [a]To whom God would make known what *is* [b]the riches of the glory of this mystery among the Gentiles; which is [c]Christ in you, [d]the hope of glory:

28 Whom we preach, [a]warning every man, and teaching every man in all wisdom; [b]that we may present every man perfect in Christ Jesus:

29 Whereunto I also labour, striving according to his working, which worketh in me [a]mightily.

Not Philosophy but Christ

2 For I would that ye knew what great [a]conflict I have for you, and *for* them at Laodicea, and *for* as many as have not seen my face in the flesh;

2 That their hearts might be comforted, being knit together in love, and unto all riches of the full assurance of understanding, to the acknowledgement of the mystery of God, and of the Father, and of Christ;

3 [a]In whom are hid all the treasures of wisdom and knowledge.

4 And this I say, [a]lest any man should beguile you with enticing words.

5 For [a]though I be absent in the flesh, yet am I with you in the spirit, joying and beholding [b]your order, and the [c]stedfastness of your faith in Christ.

6 [a]As ye have therefore received Christ Jesus the Lord, *so* walk ye in him:

7 [a]Rooted and built up in him, and stablished in the faith, as ye have been taught, abounding therein with thanksgiving.

8 Beware lest any man spoil you through philosophy and vain deceit, after [a]the tradition of men, after the [b]rudiments of the world, and not after Christ.

9 For [a]in him dwelleth all the fulness of the Godhead bodily.

10 And ye are complete in him, which is the [a]head of all principality and power:

Not Legalism but Christ

11 In whom also ye are [a]circumcised with the circumcision made without hands, in [b]putting off the body of the sins of the flesh by the circumcision of Christ:

12 [a]Buried with him in baptism, wherein also ye are risen with *him* through [b]the faith of the operation of God, [c]who hath raised him from the dead.

13 And you, being dead in your sins and the uncircumcision of your flesh, hath he quickened together with him, having forgiven you all trespasses;

---

20 [a]Rom. 5:1; Eph. 2:14 [b]2 Cor. 5:18 [c]Eph. 1:10
21 [a][Eph. 2:1] [b]Titus 1:15 [c]2 Cor. 5:18, 19
22 [a]2 Cor. 5:18; [Eph. 2:14–16] [b][Eph. 5:27]; Col. 1:28
23 [a]Eph. 3:17; Col. 2:7 [b][John 15:6]; 1 Cor. 15:58 [c]Mark 16:15; Acts 2:5; Rom. 10:18; Col. 1:6 [d]Acts 1:17; Eph. 3:7; Col. 1:25
24 [a]2 Cor. 7:4 [b]Eph. 3:1, 13 [c][Rom. 8:17; 2 Cor. 1:5; 12:15]; Phil. 2:17 [d]Eph. 1:23
25 [a]Gal. 2:7
26 [a][1 Cor. 2:7] [b][2 Tim. 1:10]
27 [a]2 Cor. 2:14 [b]Rom. 9:23 [c][Rom. 8:10, 11] [d]1 Tim. 1:1
28 [a]Acts 20:20 [b]Eph. 5:27
29 [a]Eph. 3:7

CHAPTER 2
1 [a]Phil. 1:30; Col. 1:29; 4:12; 1 Thess. 2:2
3 [a]1 Cor. 1:24, 30
4 [a]Rom. 16:18; 2 Cor. 11:13; Eph. 4:14; 5:6
5 [a]1 Thess. 2:17 [b]1 Cor. 14:40 [c]1 Pet. 5:9
6 [a]1 Thess. 4:1
7 [a]Eph. 2:21
8 [a]Gal. 1:14 [b]Gal. 4:3, 9, 10; Col. 2:20
9 [a][John 1:14]; Col. 1:19
10 [a][Eph. 1:20, 21; 1 Pet. 3:22]
11 [a]Deut. 10:16 [b]Rom. 6:6; 7:24; Gal. 5:24; Col. 3:5
12 [a]Rom. 6:4 [b]Eph. 1:19, 20 [c]Acts 2:24

*

1:27 M *who*
2:2 NU omits *both of the Father and*
2:7 NU omits *in it*
2:11 NU omits *of the sins*

NKJV

20 and [a]by Him to reconcile [b]all things to Himself, by Him, whether things on earth or things in heaven, [c]having made peace through the blood of His cross.

21 And you, [a]who once were alienated and enemies in your mind [b]by wicked works, yet now He has [c]reconciled

22 [a]in the body of His flesh through death, [b]to present you holy, and blameless, and above reproach in His sight—

23 if indeed you continue [a]in the faith, grounded and steadfast, and are [b]not moved away from the hope of the gospel which you heard, [c]which was preached to every creature under heaven, [d]of which I, Paul, became a minister.

Sacrificial Service for Christ

24 [a]I now rejoice in my sufferings [b]for you, and fill up in my flesh [c]what is lacking in the afflictions of Christ, for [d]the sake of His body, which is the church,

25 of which I became a minister according to [a]the stewardship from God which was given to me for you, to fulfill the word of God,

26 [a]the mystery which has been hidden from ages and from generations, [b]but now has been revealed to His saints.

27 [a]To them God willed to make known what are [b]the riches of the glory of this mystery among the Gentiles: *which is [c]Christ in you, [d]the hope of glory.

28 Him we preach, [a]warning every man and teaching every man in all wisdom, [b]that we may present every man perfect in Christ Jesus.

29 To this *end* I also labor, striving according to His working which works in me [a]mightily.

Not Philosophy but Christ

2 For I want you to know what a great [a]conflict I have for you and those in Laodicea, and *for* as many as have not seen my face in the flesh,

2 that their hearts may be encouraged, being knit together in love, and *attaining* to all riches of the full assurance of understanding, to the knowledge of the mystery of God, *both of the Father and of Christ,

3 [a]in whom are hidden all the treasures of wisdom and knowledge.

4 Now this I say [a]lest anyone should deceive you with persuasive words.

5 For [a]though I am absent in the flesh, yet I am with you in spirit, rejoicing to see [b]your *good* order and the [c]steadfastness of your faith in Christ.

6 [a]As you therefore have received Christ Jesus the Lord, so walk in Him,

7 [a]rooted and built up in Him and established in the faith, as you have been taught, abounding *in it with thanksgiving.

8 Beware lest anyone cheat you through philosophy and empty deceit, according to [a]the tradition of men, according to the [b]basic principles of the world, and not according to Christ.

9 For [a]in Him dwells all the fullness of the Godhead bodily;

10 and you are complete in Him, who is the [a]head of all principality and power.

Not Legalism but Christ

11 In Him you were also [a]circumcised with the circumcision made without hands, by [b]putting off the body *of the sins of the flesh, by the circumcision of Christ,

12 [a]buried with Him in baptism, in which you also were raised with *Him* through [b]faith in the working of God, [c]who raised Him from the dead.

13 And you, being dead in your trespasses and the uncircumcision of your flesh, He has made alive together with Him, having forgiven you all trespasses,

KJV

14 [a]Blotting out the handwriting of ordinances that was against us, which was contrary to us, and took it out of the way, nailing it to his cross;
15 *And* [a]having spoiled [b]principalities and powers, he made a shew of them openly, triumphing over them in it.
16 Let no man therefore [a]judge you in meat, or in drink, or in respect of an holyday, or of the new moon, or of the sabbath *days:*
17 [a]Which are a shadow of things to come; but the body *is* of Christ.
18 Let no man beguile you of your reward in a voluntary humility and worshipping of angels, intruding into those things which he hath not seen, vainly puffed up by his fleshly mind,
19 And not holding [a]the Head, from which all the body by joints and bands having nourishment ministered, and knit together, [b]increaseth with the increase of God.
20 Wherefore if ye be [a]dead with Christ from the rudiments of the world, [b]why, as though living in the world, are ye subject to ordinances,
21 ([a]Touch not; taste not; handle not;
22 Which all are to perish with the using;) [a]after the commandments and doctrines of men?
23 [a]Which things have indeed a shew of wisdom in will worship, and humility, and neglecting of the body; not in any honour to the satisfying of the flesh.

14 [a][Eph. 2:15, 16]
15 [a][Is. 53:12] [b]Eph. 6:12
16 [a]Rom. 14:3
17 [a]Heb. 8:5; 10:1
19 [a]Eph. 4:15 [b]Eph. 1:23; 4:16
20 [a]Rom. 6:2–5 [b]Gal. 4:3, 9
21 [a]1 Tim. 4:3
22 [a]Titus 1:14
23 [a]1 Tim. 4:8

NKJV

14 [a]having wiped out the handwriting of requirements that was against us, which was contrary to us. And He has taken it out of the way, having nailed it to the cross.
15 [a]Having disarmed [b]principalities and powers, He made a public spectacle of them, triumphing over them in it.
16 So let no one [a]judge you in food or in drink, or regarding a festival or a new moon or sabbaths,
17 [a]which are a shadow of things to come, but the substance is of Christ.
18 Let no one cheat you of your reward, taking delight in *false* humility and worship of angels, intruding into those things which he has *not seen, vainly puffed up by his fleshly mind,
19 and not holding fast to [a]the Head, from whom all the body, nourished and knit together by joints and ligaments, [b]grows with the increase *that is* from God.
20 *Therefore, if you [a]died with Christ from the basic principles of the world, [b]why, as *though* living in the world, do you subject yourselves to regulations—
21 [a]"Do not touch, do not taste, do not handle,"
22 which all concern things which perish with the using—[a]according to the commandments and doctrines of men?
23 [a]These things indeed have an appearance of wisdom in self-imposed religion, *false* humility, and neglect of the body, *but are* of no value against the indulgence of the flesh.

KJV

Not Carnality but Christ

3 If ye then be [a]risen with Christ, seek those things which are above, where [b]Christ sitteth on the right hand of God.
2 Set your affection on things above, not on things on the [a]earth.
3 [a]For ye are dead, [b]and your life is hid with Christ in God.
4 [a]When Christ, *who is* [b]our life, shall appear, then shall ye also appear with him [c]in glory.
5 [a]Mortify therefore [b]your members which are upon the earth; [c]fornication, uncleanness, inordinate affection, evil concupiscence, and covetousness, [d]which is idolatry:
6 [a]For which things' sake the wrath of God cometh on [b]the children of disobedience:
7 [a]In the which ye also walked some time, when ye lived in them.
8 [a]But now ye also put off all these; anger, wrath, malice, blasphemy, filthy communication out of your mouth.
9 Lie not one to another, seeing that ye have put off the old man with his deeds;
10 And have put on the new *man,* which [a]is renewed in knowledge [b]after the image of him that [c]created him:
11 Where there is neither [a]Greek nor Jew, circumcision nor uncircumcision, Barbarian, Scythian, bond *nor* free: [b]but Christ *is* all, and in all.

Character of the New Man

12 Put on therefore, [a]as the elect of God, holy and beloved, [b]bowels of mercies, kindness, humbleness of mind, meekness, longsuffering;
13 [a]Forbearing one another, and forgiving one another, if any man have a quarrel against any: even as Christ forgave you, so also *do* ye.
14 [a]And above all these things [b]*put on* charity, which is the [c]bond of perfectness.
15 And let [a]the peace of God rule in your hearts, [b]to the which also ye are called [c]in one body; and [d]be ye thankful.
16 Let the word of Christ dwell in you richly in all wisdom; teaching and admonishing one another [a]in psalms and hymns and spiritual songs, singing with grace in your hearts to the Lord.

CHAPTER 3

1 [a]Col. 2:12 [b]Eph. 1:20
2 [a][Matt. 6:19–21]
3 [a][Rom. 6:2] [b][2 Cor. 5:7]
4 [a][1 John 3:2] [b]John 14:6 [c]1 Cor. 15:43
5 [a][Rom. 8:13] [b][Rom. 6:13] [c]Eph. 5:3 [d]Eph. 4:19; 5:3, 5
6 [a]Rom. 1:18 [b][Eph. 2:2]
7 [a]1 Cor. 6:11
8 [a]Eph. 4:22
10 [a]Rom. 12:2 [b][Rom. 8:9] [c][Eph. 2:10]
11 [a]Gal. 3:27, 28 [b]Eph. 1:23
12 [a][1 Pet. 1:2] [b]1 John 3:17
13 [a][Mark 11:25]
14 [a]1 Pet. 4:8 [b][1 Cor. 13] [c]Eph. 4:3
15 [a][John 14:27] [b]1 Cor. 7:15 [c]Eph. 4:4 [d][1 Thess. 5:18]
16 [a]Eph. 5:19

NKJV

Not Carnality but Christ

3 If then you were [a]raised with Christ, seek those things which are above, [b]where Christ is, sitting at the right hand of God.
2 Set your mind on things above, not on things on the [a]earth.
3 [a]For you died, [b]and your life is hidden with Christ in God.
4 [a]When Christ *who is* [b]our life appears, then you also will appear with Him in [c]glory.
5 [a]Therefore put to death [b]your members which are on the earth: [c]fornication, uncleanness, passion, evil desire, and covetousness, [d]which is idolatry.
6 [a]Because of these things the wrath of God is coming upon [b]the sons of disobedience,
7 [a]in which you yourselves once walked when you lived in them.
8 [a]But now you yourselves are to put off all these: anger, wrath, malice, blasphemy, filthy language out of your mouth.
9 Do not lie to one another, since you have put off the old man with his deeds,
10 and have put on the new *man* who [a]is renewed in knowledge [b]according to the image of Him who [c]created him,
11 where there is neither [a]Greek nor Jew, circumcised nor uncircumcised, barbarian, Scythian, slave *nor* free, [b]but Christ *is* all and in all.

Character of the New Man

12 Therefore, [a]as *the* elect of God, holy and beloved, [b]put on tender mercies, kindness, humility, meekness, longsuffering;
13 [a]bearing with one another, and forgiving one another, if anyone has a complaint against another; even as Christ forgave you, so you also *must do.*
14 [a]But above all these things [b]put on love, which is the [c]bond of perfection.
15 And let [a]the peace of God rule in your hearts, [b]to which also you were called [c]in one body; and [d]be thankful.
16 Let the word of Christ dwell in you richly in all wisdom, teaching and admonishing one another [a]in psalms and hymns and spiritual songs, singing with grace in your hearts to the Lord.

2:18 NU omits *not*
2:20 NU, M omit *Therefore*

KJV

17 And [a]whatsoever ye do in word or deed,
do all in the name of the Lord Jesus, giving thanks
to God and the Father by him.

The Christian Home
(cf. Eph. 5;21—6:9)

18 [a]Wives, submit yourselves unto your own
husbands, [b]as it is fit in the Lord.
19 [a]Husbands, love *your* wives, and be not
[b]bitter against them.
20 [a]Children, obey *your* parents [b]in all
things: for this is well pleasing unto the Lord.
21 [a]Fathers, provoke not your children *to an-*
ger, lest they be discouraged.
22 [a]Servants, obey in all things *your* masters
according to the flesh; not with eyeservice, as
menpleasers; but in singleness of heart, fearing
God:
23 [a]And whatsoever ye do, do *it* heartily, as
to the Lord, and not unto men;
24 [a]Knowing that of the Lord ye shall receive
the reward of the inheritance: [b]for ye serve the
Lord Christ.
25 But he that doeth wrong shall receive for
the wrong which he hath done: and [a]there is no
respect of persons.

4 Masters,[a] give unto *your* servants that which
is just and equal; knowing that ye also have
a Master in heaven.

Christian Graces

2 [a]Continue in prayer, and watch in the
same [b]with thanksgiving;
3 [a]Withal praying also for us, that God
would [b]open unto us a door of utterance, to speak
[c]the mystery of Christ, [d]for which I am also in
bonds:
4 That I may make it manifest, as I ought
to speak.
5 [a]Walk in [b]wisdom toward them that are
without, [c]redeeming the time.
6 Let your speech *be* alway [a]with grace,
[b]seasoned with salt, [c]that ye may know how ye
ought to answer every man.

Final Greetings
(cf. Eph. 6:21, 22)

7 All my state shall [a]Tychicus declare unto
you, *who is* a beloved brother, and a faithful minister and fellowservant in the Lord:
8 [a]Whom I have sent unto you for the same
purpose, that he might know your estate, and
comfort your hearts;
9 With [a]Onesimus, a faithful and beloved
brother, who is *one* of you. They shall make
known unto you all things which *are done*
here.
10 [a]Aristarchus my fellowprisoner saluteth
you, and [b]Marcus, sister's son to Barnabas,
(touching whom ye received commandments: if
he come unto you, receive him;)
11 And Jesus, which is called Justus, who are
of the circumcision. These only *are my* fellow
workers unto the kingdom of God, which have
been a comfort unto me.
12 [a]Epaphras, who is *one* of you, a servant
of Christ, saluteth you, always [b]labouring fervently for you in prayers, that ye may stand [c]per-
fect and complete in all the will of God.
13 For I bear him record, that he hath a great
zeal for you, and them *that are* in Laodicea, and
them in Hierapolis.
14 [a]Luke, the beloved physician, and [b]De-
mas, greet you.
15 Salute the brethren which are in Laodicea,
and Nymphas, and [a]the church which is in his
house.

Closing Exhortations and Blessing

16 And when [a]this epistle is read among you,
cause that it be read also in the church of the

---

17 [a]1 Cor. 10:31
18 [a]1 Pet. 3:1 [b][Col. 3:18—4:1; Eph. 5:22—6:9]
19 [a][Eph. 5:25; 1 Pet. 3:7] [b]Eph. 4:31
20 [a]Eph. 6:1 [b]Eph. 5:24
21 [a]Eph. 6:4
22 [a]Eph. 6:5; [1 Tim. 6:1]; Titus 2:9; 1 Pet. 2:18
23 [a][Eccl. 9:10]
24 [a]Eph. 6:8 [b]1 Cor. 7:22
25 [a]Rom. 2:11

CHAPTER 4

1 [a]Eph. 6:9
2 [a]Luke 18:1 [b]Col. 2:7
3 [a]Eph. 6:19 [b]1 Cor. 16:9 [c]Eph. 3:3, 4; 6:19 [d]Eph. 6:20
5 [a]Eph. 5:15 [b][Matt. 10:16] [c]Eph. 5:16
6 [a]Eccl. 10:12 [b]Mark 9:50 [c]1 Pet. 3:15
7 [a]Acts 20:4; Eph. 6:21; 2 Tim. 4:12; Titus 3:12
8 [a]Eph. 6:22
9 [a]Philem. 10
10 [a]Acts 19:29; 20:4; 27:2; Philem. 24 [b]Acts 15:37; 2 Tim. 4:11
12 [a]Col. 1:7; Philem. 23 [b]Rom. 15:30 [c]Matt. 5:48; 1 Cor. 2:6
14 [a]2 Tim. 4:11; Philem. 24 [b]2 Tim. 4:10
15 [a]Rom. 16:5; 1 Cor. 16:19
16 [a]1 Thess. 5:27; 2 Thess. 3:14

3:24 NU omits *for*
4:8 NU *you may know our circumstances and he may comfort*
4:12 NU *fully assured*
4:13 NU *concern*
4:15 NU *Nympha* • NU *her*

NKJV

17 And [a]*whatever* you do in word or deed,
do all in the name of the Lord Jesus, giving thanks
to God the Father through Him.

The Christian Home
(cf. Eph. 5:21—6:9)

18 [a]Wives, submit to your own husbands, [b]as
is fitting in the Lord.
19 [a]Husbands, love your wives and do not
be [b]bitter toward them.
20 [a]Children, obey your parents [b]in all
things, for this is well pleasing to the Lord.
21 [a]Fathers, do not provoke your children,
lest they become discouraged.
22 [a]Bondservants, obey in all things your
masters according to the flesh, not with eyeservice, as men-pleasers, but in sincerity of heart,
fearing God.
23 [a]And whatever you do, do it heartily, as
to the Lord and not to men,
24 [a]knowing that from the Lord you will receive the reward of the inheritance; [b]for* you
serve the Lord Christ.
25 But he who does wrong will be repaid for
what he has done, and [a]there is no partiality.

4 Masters,[a] give your bondservants what is just
and fair, knowing that you also have a Master
in heaven.

Christian Graces

2 [a]Continue earnestly in prayer, being vigilant in it [b]with thanksgiving;
3 [a]meanwhile praying also for us, that God
would [b]open to us a door for the word, to speak
[c]the mystery of Christ, [d]for which I am also in
chains,
4 that I may make it manifest, as I ought
to speak.
5 [a]Walk in [b]wisdom toward those *who are*
outside, [c]redeeming the time.
6 *Let* your speech always *be* [a]with grace,
[b]seasoned with salt, [c]that you may know how you
ought to answer each one.

Final Greetings
(cf. Eph. 6:21, 22)

7 [a]Tychicus, a beloved brother, faithful minister, and fellow servant in the Lord, will tell you
all the news about me.
8 [a]I am sending him to you for this very purpose, that *he may know your circumstances and
comfort your hearts,
9 with [a]Onesimus, a faithful and beloved
brother, who is *one* of you. They will make known
to you all things which *are happening* here.
10 [a]Aristarchus my fellow prisoner greets
you, with [b]Mark the cousin of Barnabas (about
whom you received instructions: if he comes to
you, welcome him),
11 and Jesus who is called Justus. These *are*
my only fellow workers for the kingdom of God
who are of the circumcision; they have proved
to be a comfort to me.
12 [a]Epaphras, who is *one* of you, a bondservant of Christ, greets you, always [b]laboring
fervently for you in prayers, that you may stand
[c]perfect and *complete in all the will of God.
13 For I bear him witness that he has a great
*zeal for you, and those who are in Laodicea, and
those in Hierapolis.
14 [a]Luke the beloved physician and [b]Demas
greet you.
15 Greet the brethren who are in Laodicea,
and *Nymphas and [a]the church that *is* in *his
house.

Closing Exhortations and Blessing

16 Now when [a]this epistle is read among you,
see that it is read also in the church of the

KJV

Laodiceans; and that ye likewise read the *epistle* from Laodicea.
17 And say to [a]Archippus, Take heed to [b]the ministry which thou hast received in the Lord, that thou fulfil it.
18 [a]The salutation by the hand of me Paul. [b]Remember my bonds. Grace *be* with you. Amen.

17 [a]Philem. 2 [b]1 Tim. 4:6; 2 Tim. 4:5 **18** [a]1 Cor. 16:21; 2 Thess. 3:17 [b]Heb. 13:3

NKJV

Laodiceans, and that you likewise read the epistle from Laodicea.
17 And say to [a]Archippus, "Take heed to [b]the ministry which you have received in the Lord, that you may fulfill it."
18 [a]This salutation by my own hand—Paul. [b]Remember my chains. Grace *be* with you. Amen.

KJV

THE FIRST EPISTLE OF PAUL THE APOSTLE TO THE

THESSALONIANS

Greeting

1 Paul, and [a]Silvanus, and Timotheus, unto the
church of the [b]Thessalonians *which is* in God
the Father and *in* the Lord Jesus Christ: Grace
be unto you, and peace, from God our Father, and
the Lord Jesus Christ.

Their Good Example

2 [a]We give thanks to God always for you
all, making mention of you in our prayers;
3 Remembering without ceasing [a]your
work of faith, [b]and labour of love, and patience
of hope in our Lord Jesus Christ, in the sight of
God and our Father;
4 Knowing, brethren beloved, [a]your election of God.
5 For [a]our gospel came not unto you in word
only, but also in power, and [b]in the Holy Ghost,
[c]and in much assurance; as ye know what manner
of men we were among you for your sake.
6 And [a]ye became followers of us, and of
the Lord, having received the word in much affliction, [b]with joy of the Holy Ghost:
7 So that we were ensamples to all that believe in Macedonia and Achaia.
8 For from you [a]sounded out the word of
the Lord not only in Macedonia and Achaia, but
also [b]in every place your faith to Godward is
spread abroad; so that we need not to speak any
thing.
9 For they themselves shew of us [a]what
manner of entering in we had unto you, [b]and how
ye turned to God from idols to serve the living
and true God;
10 And [a]to wait for his Son from heaven,
whom he raised from the dead, *even* Jesus, which
delivered us [b]from the wrath to come.

Paul's Conduct
(cf. Acts 17:1–9)

2 For yourselves, brethren, know our entrance
in unto you, that it was not in vain:
2 But even after that we had suffered before,
and were shamefully entreated, as ye know, at
[a]Philippi, we were [b]bold in our God to speak unto
you the gospel of God with much contention.
3 [a]For our exhortation *was* not of deceit, nor
of uncleanness, nor in guile:
4 But as [a]we were allowed of God [b]to be
put in trust with the gospel, even so we speak;
[c]not as pleasing men, but God, [d]which trieth our
hearts.
5 For [a]neither at any time used we flattering
words, as ye know, nor a cloke of covetousness;
[b]God *is* witness:
6 [a]Nor of men sought we glory, neither of
you, nor *yet* of others, when [b]we might have been
[c]burdensome, [d]as the apostles of Christ.
7 But [a]we were gentle among you, even as
a nurse cherisheth her children:
8 So being affectionately desirous of you,
we were willing [a]to have imparted unto you, not

CHAPTER 1

1 [a]1 Pet. 5:12
[b]Acts 17:1–9
2 [a]Rom. 1:8;
2 Thess. 1:3
3 [a]John 6:29
[b]Rom. 16:6
4 [a]Col. 3:12
5 [a]Mark 16:20
[b]2 Cor. 6:6
[c]Heb. 2:3
6 [a]1 Cor. 4:16;
11:1 [b]Acts
5:41; 13:52;
2 Cor. 6:10;
Gal. 5:22
8 [a]Rom. 10:18
[b]Rom. 1:8;
16:19; 2 Cor.
2:14; 2 Thess.
1:4
9 [a]1 Thess.
2:1 [b]1 Cor.
12:2
10 [a][Rom.
2:7] [b]Matt.
3:7; Rom. 5:9

CHAPTER 2

2 [a]Acts 14:5;
16:19–24; Phil.
1:30 [b]Acts
17:1–9
3 [a]2 Cor. 7:2
4 [a]1 Cor. 7:25
[b]Titus 1:3
[c]Gal. 1:10
[d]Prov. 17:3
5 [a]2 Cor. 2:17
[b]Rom. 1:9;
1 Thess. 2:10
6 [a]1 Tim. 5:17
[b]1 Cor. 9:4
[c]2 Cor. 11:9
[d]1 Cor. 9:1
7 [a]1 Cor. 2:3
8 [a]Rom. 1:11

*

1:1 NU omits *from God our Father and the Lord Jesus Christ*
2:2 NU, M omit *even*

NKJV

THE FIRST EPISTLE OF PAUL THE APOSTLE TO THE

THESSALONIANS

Greeting

1 Paul, [a]Silvanus, and Timothy,

To the church of the [b]Thessalonians in
God the Father and the Lord Jesus Christ:

Grace to you and peace *from God our
Father and the Lord Jesus Christ.

Their Good Example

2 [a]We give thanks to God always for you
all, making mention of you in our prayers,
3 remembering without ceasing [a]your work
of faith, [b]labor of love, and patience of hope in
our Lord Jesus Christ in the sight of our God and
Father,
4 knowing, beloved brethren, [a]your election
by God.
5 For [a]our gospel did not come to you in
word only, but also in power, [b]and in the Holy
Spirit [c]and in much assurance, as you know what
kind of men we were among you for your sake.
6 And [a]you became followers of us and of
the Lord, having received the word in much affliction, [b]with joy of the Holy Spirit,
7 so that you became examples to all in
Macedonia and Achaia who believe.
8 For from you the word of the Lord [a]has
sounded forth, not only in Macedonia and Achaia,
but also [b]in every place. Your faith toward God
has gone out, so that we do not need to say
anything.
9 For they themselves declare concerning us
[a]what manner of entry we had to you, [b]and how
you turned to God from idols to serve the living
and true God,
10 and [a]to wait for His Son from heaven,
whom He raised from the dead, *even* Jesus who
delivers us [b]from the wrath to come.

Paul's Conduct
(cf. Acts 17:1–9)

2 For you yourselves know, brethren, that our
coming to you was not in vain.
2 But *even after we had suffered before and
were spitefully treated at [a]Philippi, as you know,
we were [b]bold in our God to speak to you the
gospel of God in much conflict.
3 [a]For our exhortation *did* not *come* from
error or uncleanness, nor *was it* in deceit.
4 But as [a]we have been approved by God
[b]to be entrusted with the gospel, even so we
speak, [c]not as pleasing men, but God [d]who tests
our hearts.
5 For [a]neither at any time did we use flattering words, as you know, nor a cloak for covetousness—[b]God *is* witness.
6 [a]Nor did we seek glory from men, either
from you or from others, when [b]we might have
[c]made demands [d]as apostles of Christ.
7 But [a]we were gentle among you, just as
a nursing *mother* cherishes her own children.
8 So, affectionately longing for you, we
were well pleased [a]to impart to you not only the

KJV

the gospel of God only, but also [b]our own souls, because ye were dear unto us.

9 For ye remember, brethren, our [a]labour and travail: for labouring night and day, [b]because we would not be chargeable unto any of you, we preached unto you the gospel of God.

10 [a]Ye *are* witnesses, and God *also*, [b]how holily and justly and unblameably we behaved ourselves among you that believe:

11 As ye know how we exhorted and comforted and charged every one of you, as a father *doth* his children,

12 [a]That ye would walk worthy of God, [b]who hath called you unto his kingdom and glory.

Their Conversion

13 For this cause also thank we God [a]without ceasing, because, when ye [b]received the word of God which ye heard of us, ye received *it* [c]not *as* the word of men, but as it is in truth, the word of God, which effectually [d]worketh also in you that believe.

14 For ye, brethren, became followers [a]of the churches of God which in Judaea are in Christ Jesus: for [b]ye also have suffered like things of your own countrymen, even as they *have* of the Jews:

15 [a]Who both killed the Lord Jesus, and [b]their own prophets, and have persecuted us; and they please not God, [c]and are contrary to all men:

16 [a]Forbidding us to speak to the Gentiles that they might be saved, [b]to fill up their sins alway: [c]for the wrath is come upon them to the uttermost.

Longing to See Them

17 But we, brethren, being taken from you for a short time [a]in presence, not in heart, endeavoured the more abundantly to see your face with great desire.

18 Wherefore we would have come unto you, even I Paul, once and again; but [a]Satan hindered us.

19 For [a]what *is* our hope, or joy, or [b]crown of rejoicing? *Are* not even ye in the [c]presence of our Lord Jesus Christ [d]at his coming?

20 For ye are our glory and joy.

Concern for Their Faith

3 Wherefore when we could no longer forbear, we thought it good to be left at Athens alone;

2 And sent [a]Timotheus, our brother, and minister of God, and our fellowlabourer in the gospel of Christ, to establish you, and to comfort you concerning your faith:

3 [a]That no man should be moved by these afflictions: for yourselves know that [b]we are appointed thereunto.

4 [a]For verily, when we were with you, we told you before that we should suffer tribulation; even as it came to pass, and ye know.

5 For this cause, when I could no longer forbear, I sent to know your faith, [a]lest by some means the tempter have tempted you, and [b]our labour be in vain.

Encouraged by Timothy

6 [a]But now when Timotheus came from you unto us, and brought us good tidings of your faith and charity, and that ye have good remembrance of us always, desiring greatly to see us, [b]as we also *to see* you:

7 Therefore, brethren, [a]we were comforted over you in all our affliction and distress by your faith:

8 For now we live, if ye [a]stand fast in the Lord.

9 For what thanks can we render to God again for you, for all the joy wherewith we joy for your sakes before our God;

10 Night and day praying exceedingly that

---

8 [b]2 Cor. 12:15; 1 John 3:16
9 [a]Acts 18:3; 20:34, 35; 1 Cor. 4:12; 2 Thess. 3:7, 8 [b]2 Cor. 12:13
10 [a]2 Cor. 1:12; 1 Thess. 1:5 [b]2 Cor. 7:2
12 [a]Eph. 4:1; Col. 1:10 [b]Rom. 8:28; 1 Cor. 1:9; 1 Thess. 5:24; 2 Thess. 2:14; [2 Tim. 1:9]
13 [a]Rom. 1:8; 1 Thess. 1:2, 3 [b]Mark 4:20 [c][Matt. 10:20; Gal. 4:14] [d][1 Pet. 1:23]
14 [a]Gal. 1:22 [b]Acts 17:5; 1 Thess. 3:4; 2 Thess. 1:4
15 [a]Luke 24:20; Acts 2:23 [b]Jer. 2:30; Matt. 5:12; 23:34, 35; Acts 7:52 [c]Esth. 3:8
16 [a]Luke 11:52 [b]Gen. 15:16; Dan. 8:23; Matt. 23:32 [c]Matt. 24:6
17 [a]1 Cor. 5:3
18 [a]Rom. 1:13; 15:22
19 [a]2 Cor. 1:14 [b]Prov. 16:31 [c]Jude 24 [d]1 Cor. 15:23

CHAPTER 3

2 [a]Rom. 16:21
3 [a]Eph. 3:13 [b]John 16:2; Acts 9:16; 14:22; 1 Cor. 4:9; 2 Tim. 3:12; 1 Pet. 2:21
4 [a]Acts 20:24
5 [a]1 Cor. 7:5 [b]Gal. 2:2
6 [a]Acts 18:5 [b]Phil. 1:8
7 [a]2 Cor. 1:4
8 [a][Eph. 6:13, 14]; Phil. 4:1

NKJV

gospel of God, but also [b]our own lives, because you had become dear to us.

9 For you remember, brethren, our [a]labor and toil; for laboring night and day, [b]that we might not be a burden to any of you, we preached to you the gospel of God.

10 [a]You *are* witnesses, and God *also*, [b]how devoutly and justly and blamelessly we behaved ourselves among you who believe;

11 as you know how we exhorted, and comforted, and *charged every one of you, as a father *does* his own children,

12 [a]that you would walk worthy of God [b]who calls you into His own kingdom and glory.

Their Conversion

13 For this reason we also thank God [a]without ceasing, because when you [b]received the word of God which you heard from us, you welcomed *it* [c]not *as* the word of men, but as it is in truth, the word of God, which also effectively [d]works in you who believe.

14 For you, brethren, became imitators [a]of the churches of God which are in Judea in Christ Jesus. For [b]you also suffered the same things from your own countrymen, just as they *did* from the Judeans,

15 [a]who killed both the Lord Jesus and [b]their own prophets, and have persecuted us; and they do not please God [c]and are contrary to all men,

16 [a]forbidding us to speak to the Gentiles that they may be saved, so as always [b]to fill up *the measure of* their sins; [c]but wrath has come upon them to the uttermost.

Longing to See Them

17 But we, brethren, having been taken away from you for a short time [a]in presence, not in heart, endeavored more eagerly to see your face with great desire.

18 Therefore we wanted to come to you—even I, Paul, time and again—but [a]Satan hindered us.

19 For [a]what *is* our hope, or joy, or [b]crown of rejoicing? *Is it* not even you in the [c]presence of our Lord Jesus Christ [d]at His coming?

20 For you are our glory and joy.

Concern for Their Faith

3 Therefore, when we could no longer endure it, we thought it good to be left in Athens alone,

2 and sent [a]Timothy, our brother and minister of God, and our fellow laborer in the gospel of Christ, to establish you and encourage you concerning your faith,

3 [a]that no one should be shaken by these afflictions; for you yourselves know that [b]we are appointed to this.

4 [a]For, in fact, we told you before when we were with you that we would suffer tribulation, just as it happened, and you know.

5 For this reason, when I could no longer endure it, I sent to know your faith, [a]lest by some means the tempter had tempted you, and [b]our labor might be in vain.

Encouraged by Timothy

6 [a]But now that Timothy has come to us from you, and brought us good news of your faith and love, and that you always have good remembrance of us, greatly desiring to see us, [b]as we also *to see* you—

7 therefore, brethren, in all our affliction and distress [a]we were comforted concerning you by your faith.

8 For now we live, if you [a]stand fast in the Lord.

9 For what thanks can we render to God for you, for all the joy with which we rejoice for your sake before our God,

10 night and day praying exceedingly that

---

*2:11 NU, M *implored*

KJV

we might see your face, [a]and might perfect that
which is lacking in your faith?

Prayer for the Church

11 Now God himself and our Father, and our
Lord Jesus Christ, [a]direct our way unto you.
12 And the Lord make you to increase and
[a]abound in love one toward another, and toward
all *men*, even as we *do* toward you:
13 To the end he may stablish [a]your hearts
unblameable in holiness before God, even our Father, at the coming of our Lord Jesus Christ with
all his saints.

Plea for Purity

4 Furthermore then we beseech you, brethren,
and exhort *you* by the Lord Jesus, [b]that as
ye have received of us how ye ought to walk and
to please God, *so* ye would [a]abound more and
more.
2 For ye know what commandments we
gave you by the Lord Jesus.
3 For this is [a]the will of God, *even* [b]your
sanctification, [c]that ye should abstain from fornication:
4 [a]That every one of you should know how
to possess his vessel in sanctification and honour;
5 [a]Not in the lust of concupiscence, [b]even
as the Gentiles [c]which know not God:
6 That no *man* go beyond and defraud his
brother in *any* matter: because that the Lord [a]*is*
the avenger of all such, as we also have fore-
warned you and testified.
7 For God hath not called us unto uncleanness, [a]but unto holiness.
8 [a]He therefore that despiseth, despiseth
not man, but God, [b]who hath also given unto us
his holy Spirit.

A Brotherly and Orderly Life

9 But as touching brotherly love ye need not
that I write unto you: for [a]ye yourselves are taught
of God [b]to love one another.
10 And indeed ye do it toward all the brethren which are in all Macedonia: but we beseech
you, brethren, [a]that ye increase more and
more;
11 And that ye study to be quiet, and [a]to do
your own business, and [b]to work with your own
hands, as we commanded you;
12 [a]That ye may walk honestly toward them
that are without, and *that* ye may have lack of
nothing.

The Comfort of Christ's Coming

13 But I would not have you to be ignorant,
brethren, concerning them which are asleep, that
ye sorrow not, [a]even as others [b]which have no
hope.
14 For [a]if we believe that Jesus died and rose
again, even so [b]them also which sleep in Jesus
will God bring with him.
15 For this we say unto you [a]by the word of
the Lord, that [b]we which are alive *and* remain
unto the coming of the Lord shall not prevent
them which are asleep.
16 For [a]the Lord himself shall descend from
heaven with a shout, with the voice of the archangel, and with [b]the trump of God: [c]and the dead
in Christ shall rise first:
17 [a]Then we which are alive *and* remain shall
be caught up together with them [b]in the clouds,
to meet the Lord in the air: and so [c]shall we ever
be with the Lord.
18 [a]Wherefore comfort one another with
these words.

The Day of the Lord

5 But of [a]the times and the seasons, brethren,
ye have no need that I write unto you.

10 [a]2 Cor. 13:9; Col. 4:12
11 [a]Mark 1:3
12 [a]Phil. 1:9; 1 Thess. 4:1, 10; 2 Thess. 1:3
13 [a]2 Thess. 2:17

CHAPTER 4

1 [a]1 Cor. 15:58 [b]Phil. 1:27; Col. 1:10
3 [a][Rom. 12:2] [b]Eph. 5:27 [c][1 Cor. 6:15–20; Col. 3:5]
4 [a]Rom. 6:19
5 [a]Col. 3:5 [b]Eph. 4:17, 18 [c]1 Cor. 15:34
6 [a]2 Thess. 1:8
7 [a]Lev. 11:44; [Heb. 12:14]; 1 Pet. 1:14–16
8 [a]Luke 10:16 [b]1 Cor. 2:10
9 [a][Jer. 31:33, 34]; John 6:45; 15:12, 17; [1 John 2:27] [b]Matt. 22:39
10 [a]1 Thess. 3:12
11 [a]2 Thess. 3:11; 1 Pet. 4:15 [b]Acts 20:35
12 [a]Rom. 13:13; Col. 4:5; [1 Pet. 2:12]
13 [a]Lev. 19:28 [b][Eph. 2:12]
14 [a]1 Cor. 15:13 [b]1 Cor. 15:20, 23
15 [a]1 Kin. 13:17; 20:35; 2 Cor. 12:1; Gal. 1:12 [b]1 Cor. 15:51, 52; 1 Thess. 5:10
16 [a][Matt. 24:30, 31] [b][1 Cor. 15:52] [c][1 Cor. 15:23]; 2 Thess. 2:1; Rev. 14:13; 20:6
17 [a][1 Cor. 15:51–53]; 1 Thess. 5:10 [b]Dan. 7:13; Acts 1:9; Rev. 11:12 [c]John 14:3; 17:24
18 [a]1 Thess. 5:11

CHAPTER 5

1 [a]Matt. 24:3

*

4:8 NU *who also gives*
4:14 Or *through Jesus sleep*

NKJV

we may see your face [a]and perfect what is lacking
in your faith?

Prayer for the Church

11 Now may our God and Father Himself,
and our Lord Jesus Christ, [a]direct our way to
you.
12 And may the Lord make you increase and
[a]abound in love to one another and to all, just as
we *do* to you,
13 so that He may establish [a]your hearts
blameless in holiness before our God and Father
at the coming of our Lord Jesus Christ with all
His saints.

Plea for Purity

4 Finally then, brethren, we urge and exhort in
the Lord Jesus [a]that you should abound more
and more, [b]just as you received from us how you
ought to walk and to please God;
2 for you know what commandments we
gave you through the Lord Jesus.
3 For this is [a]the will of God, [b]your sanctification: [c]that you should abstain from sexual
immorality;
4 [a]that each of you should know how to possess his own vessel in sanctification and honor,
5 [a]not in passion of lust, [b]like the Gentiles
[c]who do not know God;
6 that no one should take advantage of and
defraud his brother in this matter, because the
Lord [a]*is* the avenger of all such, as we also fore-
warned you and testified.
7 For God did not call us to uncleanness,
[a]but in holiness.
8 [a]Therefore he who rejects *this* does not
reject man, but God, [b]who* has also given us His
Holy Spirit.

A Brotherly and Orderly Life

9 But concerning brotherly love you have
no need that I should write to you, for [a]you yourselves are taught by God [b]to love one another;
10 and indeed you do so toward all the brethren who are in all Macedonia. But we urge you,
brethren, [a]that you increase more and more;
11 that you also aspire to lead a quiet life,
[a]to mind your own business, and [b]to work with
your own hands, as we commanded you,
12 [a]that you may walk properly toward those
who are outside, and *that* you may lack nothing.

The Comfort of Christ's Coming

13 But I do not want you to be ignorant,
brethren, concerning those who have fallen
asleep, lest you sorrow [a]as others [b]who have no
hope.
14 For [a]if we believe that Jesus died and rose
again, even so God will bring with Him [b]those
who *sleep in Jesus.
15 For this we say to you [a]by the word of
the Lord, that [b]we who are alive *and* remain until
the coming of the Lord will by no means precede
those who are asleep.
16 For [a]the Lord Himself will descend from
heaven with a shout, with the voice of an archangel, and with [b]the trumpet of God. [c]And the
dead in Christ will rise first.
17 [a]Then we who are alive *and* remain shall
be caught up together with them [b]in the clouds
to meet the Lord in the air. And thus [c]we shall
always be with the Lord.
18 [a]Therefore comfort one another with
these words.

The Day of the Lord

5 But concerning [a]the times and the seasons,
brethren, you have no need that I should write
to you.

KJV

2 For yourselves know perfectly that [a]the
day of the Lord so cometh as a thief in the night.
3 For when they shall say, Peace and safety;
then [a]sudden destruction cometh upon them, [b]as
travail upon a woman with child; and they shall
not escape.
4 [a]But ye, brethren, are not in darkness, that
that day should overtake you as a thief.
5 Ye are all [a]the children of light, and the
children of the day: we are not of the night, nor
of darkness.
6 [a]Therefore let us not sleep, as *do* others;
but [b]let us watch and be sober.
7 For [a]they that sleep sleep in the night; and
they that be drunken [b]are drunken in the night.
8 But let us, who are of the day, be sober,
[a]putting on the breastplate of faith and love; and
for an helmet, the hope of salvation.
9 For [a]God hath not appointed us to wrath,
[b]but to obtain salvation by our Lord Jesus Christ,
10 [a]Who died for us, that, whether we wake
or sleep, we should live together with him.
11 Wherefore comfort yourselves together,
and edify one another, even as also ye do.

Various Exhortations

12 And we beseech you, brethren, [a]to know
them which labour among you, and are over you
in the Lord, and admonish you;
13 And to esteem them very highly in love
for their work's sake. [a]*And* be at peace among
yourselves.
14 Now we exhort you, brethren, [a]warn them
that are unruly, [b]comfort the feebleminded, [c]sup-
port the weak, [d]be patient toward all *men.*
15 [a]See that none render evil for evil unto
any *man;* but ever [b]follow that which is good, both
among yourselves, and to all *men.*
16 [a]Rejoice evermore.
17 [a]Pray without ceasing.
18 In every thing give thanks: for this is the
will of God in Christ Jesus concerning you.
19 [a]Quench not the Spirit.
20 [a]Despise not prophesyings.
21 [a]Prove all things; [b]hold fast that which is
good.
22 Abstain from all appearance of evil.

Blessing and Admonition

23 And [a]the very God of peace [b]sanctify you
wholly; and *I pray God* your whole spirit and soul
and body [c]be preserved blameless unto the coming of our Lord Jesus Christ.
24 [a]Faithful *is* he that calleth you, who also
will [b]do *it.*
25 Brethren, pray for us.
26 Greet all the brethren with an holy kiss.
27 I charge you by the Lord that this epistle
be read unto all the holy brethren.
28 The grace of our Lord Jesus Christ *be* with
you. Amen.

2 [a]Luke 21:34; 1 Thess. 5:4; [2 Pet. 3:10]; Rev. 3:3; 16:15
3 [a]Is. 13:6–9 [b]Hos. 13:13
4 [a][Acts 26:18]; Rom. 13:12; Eph. 5:8; 1 John 2:8
5 [a]Eph. 5:8
6 [a]Matt. 25:5 [b]Matt. 25:13; Mark 13:35; [1 Pet. 5:8]
7 [a][Luke 21:34] [b]Acts 2:15; 2 Pet. 2:13
8 [a]Is. 59:17; Eph. 6:14
9 [a]Rom. 9:22 [b][2 Thess. 2:13]
10 [a]2 Cor. 5:15
12 [a]1 Cor. 16:18; 1 Tim. 5:17; Heb. 13:7, 17
13 [a]Mark 9:50
14 [a]2 Thess. 3:6, 7, 11 [b]Heb. 12:12 [c]Rom. 14:1; 15:1; 1 Cor. 8:7 [d]Gal. 5:22
15 [a]Lev. 19:18 [b]Rom. 12:9; Gal. 6:10; 1 Thess. 5:21
16 [a][2 Cor. 6:10]
17 [a]Eph. 6:18
19 [a]Eph. 4:30
20 [a]Acts 13:1; 1 Cor. 14:1, 31
21 [a]1 Cor. 14:29; 1 John 4:1 [b]Phil. 4:8
23 [a]Phil. 4:9 [b]1 Thess. 3:13 [c]1 Cor. 1:8, 9
24 [a][1 Cor. 10:13]; 2 Thess. 3:3 [b]Phil. 1:6

NKJV

2 For you yourselves know perfectly that
[a]the day of the Lord so comes as a thief in the
night.
3 For when they say, "Peace and safety!"
then [a]sudden destruction comes upon them, [b]as
labor pains upon a pregnant woman. And they
shall not escape.
4 [a]But you, brethren, are not in darkness,
so that this Day should overtake you as a thief.
5 You are all [a]sons of light and sons of the
day. We are not of the night nor of darkness.
6 [a]Therefore let us not sleep, as others *do,*
but [b]let us watch and be sober.
7 For [a]those who sleep, sleep at night, and
those who get drunk [b]are drunk at night.
8 But let us who are of the day be sober,
[a]putting on the breastplate of faith and love, and
as a helmet the hope of salvation.
9 For [a]God did not appoint us to wrath, [b]but
to obtain salvation through our Lord Jesus Christ,
10 [a]who died for us, that whether we wake
or sleep, we should live together with Him.
11 Therefore comfort each other and edify
one another, just as you also are doing.

Various Exhortations

12 And we urge you, brethren, [a]to recognize
those who labor among you, and are over you in
the Lord and admonish you,
13 and to esteem them very highly in love
for their work's sake. [a]Be at peace among yourselves.
14 Now we exhort you, brethren, [a]warn
those who are unruly, [b]comfort the fainthearted,
[c]uphold the weak, [d]be patient with all.
15 [a]See that no one renders evil for evil to
anyone, but always [b]pursue what is good both
for yourselves and for all.
16 [a]Rejoice always,
17 [a]pray without ceasing,
18 in everything give thanks; for this is the
will of God in Christ Jesus for you.
19 [a]Do not quench the Spirit.
20 [a]Do not despise prophecies.
21 [a]Test all things; [b]hold fast what is good.
22 Abstain from every form of evil.

Blessing and Admonition

23 Now may [a]the God of peace Himself
[b]sanctify you completely; and may your whole
spirit, soul, and body [c]be preserved blameless at
the coming of our Lord Jesus Christ.
24 He who calls you *is* [a]faithful, who also will
[b]do *it.*
25 Brethren, pray for us.
26 Greet all the brethren with a holy kiss.
27 I charge you by the Lord that this epistle
be read to all the *holy brethren.
28 The grace of our Lord Jesus Christ *be* with
you. Amen.

*

5:27 NU omits *holy*

KJV

THE SECOND EPISTLE OF PAUL THE APOSTLE TO THE

THESSALONIANS

Greeting

1 Paul, and Silvanus, and Timotheus, unto the
church of the Thessalonians in God our Father
and the Lord Jesus Christ:
2 [a]Grace unto you, and peace, from God our
Father and the Lord Jesus Christ.

God's Final Judgment and Glory

3 We are bound to thank God always for
you, brethren, as it is meet, because that your faith
groweth exceedingly, and the charity of every one
of you all toward each other aboundeth;
4 So that [a]we ourselves glory in you in the
churches of God [b]for your patience and faith [c]in
all your persecutions and tribulations that ye
endure:
5 *Which is* [a]a manifest token of the righteous judgment of God, that ye may be counted
worthy of the kingdom of God, [b]for which ye also
suffer:
6 [a]Seeing *it is* a righteous thing with God
to recompense tribulation to them that trouble
you;
7 And to you who are troubled [a]rest with
us, when [b]the Lord Jesus shall be revealed from
heaven with his mighty angels,
8 In flaming fire taking vengeance on them
that know not God, and that obey not the gospel
of our Lord Jesus Christ:
9 [a]Who shall be punished with everlasting
destruction from the presence of the Lord, and
[b]from the glory of his power;
10 When he shall come [a]to be [b]glorified in
his saints, and to be admired in all them that believe (because our testimony among you was
believed) in that day.
11 Wherefore also we pray always for you,
that our God would [a]count you worthy of *this* calling, and fulfil all the good pleasure of *his* goodness, and [b]the work of faith with power:
12 [a]That the name of our Lord Jesus Christ
may be glorified in you, and ye in him, according to the grace of our God and the Lord Jesus
Christ.

The Great Apostasy

2 Now we beseech you, brethren, [a]by the coming of our Lord Jesus Christ, [b]and *by* our gathering together unto him,
2 [a]That ye be not soon shaken in mind, or
be troubled, neither by spirit, nor by word, nor
by letter as from us, as that the day of Christ is
at hand.
3 Let no man deceive you by any means:
for *that day shall not come,* [a]except there come
a falling away first, and [b]that man of sin be revealed, [c]the son of perdition;
4 Who opposeth and [a]exalteth himself
[b]above all that is called God, or that is worshipped; so that he as God sitteth in the temple of
God, shewing himself that he is God.
5 Remember ye not, that, when I was yet
with you, I told you these things?

CHAPTER 1

2 [a]1 Cor. 1:3
4 [a]2 Cor. 7:4; [1 Thess. 2:19] [b]1 Thess. 1:3 [c]1 Thess. 2:14
5 [a]Phil. 1:28 [b]1 Thess. 2:14
6 [a]Rev. 6:10
7 [a]Rev. 14:13 [b][1 Thess. 4:16]; Jude 14
9 [a]Phil. 3:19; 1 Thess. 5:3 [b]Deut. 33:2
10 [a]Matt. 25:31 [b]Is. 49:3; John 17:10; 1 Thess. 2:12
11 [a]Col. 1:12 [b]1 Thess. 1:3
12 [a][Col. 3:17]

CHAPTER 2

1 [a]Mark 13:26; [1 Thess. 4:15–17] [b]Matt. 24:31
2 [a]Matt. 24:4
3 [a]1 Tim. 4:1 [b]Dan. 7:25; 8:25; 11:36; 2 Thess. 2:8; Rev. 13:5 [c]John 17:12
4 [a]Is. 14:13, 14; Ezek. 28:2 [b]1 Cor. 8:5

*

1:10 NU, M *have believed*
2:2 NU *the Lord*
2:3 NU *lawlessness*
2:4 NU omits *as God*

NKJV

THE SECOND EPISTLE OF PAUL THE APOSTLE TO THE

THESSALONIANS

Greeting

1 Paul, Silvanus, and Timothy,

To the church of the Thessalonians in God
our Father and the Lord Jesus Christ:

2 [a]Grace to you and peace from God our
Father and the Lord Jesus Christ.

God's Final Judgment and Glory

3 We are bound to thank God always for
you, brethren, as it is fitting, because your faith
grows exceedingly, and the love of every one of
you all abounds toward each other,
4 so that [a]we ourselves boast of you among
the churches of God [b]for your patience and faith
[c]in all your persecutions and tribulations that you
endure,
5 *which is* [a]manifest evidence of the righteous judgment of God, that you may be counted
worthy of the kingdom of God, [b]for which you
also suffer;
6 [a]since *it is* a righteous thing with God to
repay with tribulation those who trouble you,
7 and to *give* you who are troubled [a]rest
with us when [b]the Lord Jesus is revealed from
heaven with His mighty angels,
8 in flaming fire taking vengeance on those
who do not know God, and on those who do not
obey the gospel of our Lord Jesus Christ.
9 [a]These shall be punished with everlasting
destruction from the presence of the Lord and
[b]from the glory of His power,
10 when He comes, in that Day, [a]to be [b]glori-
fied in His saints and to be admired among all
those who *believe, because our testimony among
you was believed.
11 Therefore we also pray always for you
that our God would [a]count you worthy of *this* calling, and fulfill all the good pleasure of *His* goodness and [b]the work of faith with power,
12 [a]that the name of our Lord Jesus Christ
may be glorified in you, and you in Him, according to the grace of our God and the Lord Jesus
Christ.

The Great Apostasy

2 Now, brethren, [a]concerning the coming of our
Lord Jesus Christ [b]and our gathering together
to Him, we ask you,
2 [a]not to be soon shaken in mind or troubled, either by spirit or by word or by letter, as
if from us, as though the day of *Christ had
come.
3 Let no one deceive you by any means; for
that Day will not come [a]unless the falling away
comes first, and [b]the man of *sin is revealed, [c]the
son of perdition,
4 who opposes and [a]exalts himself [b]above
all that is called God or that is worshiped, so that
he sits *as God in the temple of God, showing
himself that he is God.
5 Do you not remember that when I was still
with you I told you these things?

KJV

6 And now ye know what withholdeth that
he might be revealed in his time.
7 For [a]the mystery of iniquity doth already
work: only he who now letteth *will let,* until he
be taken out of the way.
8 And then shall that Wicked be revealed,
[a]whom the Lord shall consume [b]with the spirit
of his mouth, and shall destroy [c]with the brightness of his coming:
9 *Even him,* whose coming is [a]after the
working of Satan with all power and [b]signs and
lying wonders,
10 And with all deceivableness of unrighteousness in [a]them that perish; because they received not [b]the love of the truth, that they might
be saved.
11 And [a]for this cause God shall send them
strong delusion, [b]that they should believe a lie:
12 That they all might be damned who believed not the truth, but [a]had pleasure in unrighteousness.

Stand Fast

13 But we are bound to give thanks alway
to God for you, brethren beloved of the Lord, because God hath [a]from the beginning [b]chosen you
to salvation [c]through sanctification of the Spirit
and belief of the truth:
14 Whereunto he called you by our gospel,
to [a]the obtaining of the glory of our Lord Jesus
Christ.
15 Therefore, brethren, [a]stand fast, and hold
[b]the traditions which ye have been taught,
whether by word, or our epistle.
16 Now our Lord Jesus Christ himself, and
God, even our Father, [a]which hath loved us, and
hath given *us* everlasting consolation and [b]good
hope through grace,
17 Comfort your hearts, [a]and stablish you in
every good word and work.

Pray for Us

3 Finally, brethren, [a]pray for us, that the word
of the Lord may have *free* course, and be
glorified, even as *it is* with you:
2 And [a]that we may be delivered from unreasonable and wicked men: [b]for all *men* have
not faith.
3 But [a]the Lord is faithful, who shall stablish you, and [b]keep *you* from evil.
4 And [a]we have confidence in the Lord
touching you, that ye both do and will do the
things which we command you.
5 And [a]the Lord direct your hearts into the
love of God, and into the patient waiting for
Christ.

Warning Against Idleness

6 Now we command you, brethren, in the
name of our Lord Jesus Christ, [a]that ye withdraw
yourselves [b]from every brother that walketh
[c]disorderly, and not after the tradition which he
received of us.
7 For yourselves know how ye ought to follow us: for we behaved not ourselves disorderly
among you;
8 Neither did we eat any man's bread for
nought; but wrought with [a]labour and travail
night and day, that we might not be chargeable
to any of you:
9 Not because we have not [a]power, but to
make ourselves an ensample unto you to follow
us.
10 For even when we were with you, this we
commanded you, that if any would not work, neither should he eat.
11 For we hear that there are some which
walk among you disorderly, working not at all,
but are [a]busybodies.
12 Now them that are such we command and
exhort by our Lord Jesus Christ, [a]that with quietness they work, and eat their own bread.

7 [a]1 John 2:18
8 [a]Dan. 7:10
[b]Is. 11:4; Rev.
2:16; 19:15
[c]Heb. 10:27
9 [a]John 8:41
[b]Deut. 13:1
10 [a]2 Cor.
2:15 [b]1 Cor.
16:22
11 [a]Rom. 1:28
[b]1 Tim. 4:1
12 [a]Rom.
1:32; 1 Cor.
13:6
13 [a]Eph. 1:4
[b]1 Thess. 1:4
[c]1 Thess. 4:7;
[1 Pet. 1:2]
14 [a]1 Pet. 5:10
15 [a]1 Cor.
16:13 [b]Rom.
6:17; 1 Cor.
11:2; 2 Thess.
3:6; Jude 3
16 [a][Rev. 1:5]
[b]Titus 3:7;
1 Pet. 1:3
17 [a]1 Cor. 1:8

CHAPTER 3

1 [a]Eph. 6:19
2 [a]Rom. 15:31
[b]Acts 28:24
3 [a]1 Cor. 1:9;
1 Thess. 5:24
[b]John 17:15
4 [a]2 Cor. 7:16
5 [a]1 Chr.
29:18
6 [a]Rom. 16:17
[b]1 Cor. 5:1
[c]1 Thess. 4:11
8 [a]1 Thess.
2:9
9 [a]1 Cor. 9:4,
6–14
11 [a]1 Tim.
5:13; 1 Pet.
4:15
12 [a]Eph. 4:28;
1 Thess. 4:11,
12

NKJV

6 And now you know what is restraining,
that he may be revealed in his own time.
7 For [a]the mystery of lawlessness is already
at work; only *He who now restrains *will do so*
until *He is taken out of the way.
8 And then the lawless one will be revealed,
[a]whom the Lord will consume [b]with the breath
of His mouth and destroy [c]with the brightness of
His coming.
9 The coming of the *lawless one* is [a]accord-
ing to the working of Satan, with all power,
[b]signs, and lying wonders,
10 and with all unrighteous deception among
[a]those who perish, because they did not receive
[b]the love of the truth, that they might be saved.
11 And [a]for this reason God will send them
strong delusion, [b]that they should believe the lie,
12 that they all may be condemned who did
not believe the truth but [a]had pleasure in unrighteousness.

Stand Fast

13 But we are bound to give thanks to God
always for you, brethren beloved by the Lord, because God [a]from the beginning [b]chose you for
salvation [c]through sanctification by the Spirit and
belief in the truth,
14 to which He called you by our gospel, for
[a]the obtaining of the glory of our Lord Jesus
Christ.
15 Therefore, brethren, [a]stand fast and hold
[b]the traditions which you were taught, whether
by word or our epistle.
16 Now may our Lord Jesus Christ Himself,
and our God and Father, [a]who has loved us and
given *us* everlasting consolation and [b]good hope
by grace,
17 comfort your hearts [a]and establish you in
every good word and work.

Pray for Us

3 Finally, brethren, [a]pray for us, that the word
of the Lord may run *swiftly* and be glorified,
just as *it is* with you,
2 and [a]that we may be delivered from unreasonable and wicked men; [b]for not all have
faith.
3 But [a]the Lord is faithful, who will establish you and [b]guard *you* from the evil one.
4 And [a]we have confidence in the Lord concerning you, both that you do and will do the
things we command you.
5 Now may [a]the Lord direct your hearts into
the love of God and into the patience of Christ.

Warning Against Idleness

6 But we command you, brethren, in the
name of our Lord Jesus Christ, [a]that you withdraw [b]from every brother who walks [c]disorderly
and not according to the tradition which *he received from us.
7 For you yourselves know how you ought
to follow us, for we were not disorderly among
you;
8 nor did we eat anyone's bread free of
charge, but worked with [a]labor and toil night and
day, that we might not be a burden to any of you,
9 not because we do not have [a]authority,
but to make ourselves an example of how you
should follow us.
10 For even when we were with you, we commanded you this: If anyone will not work, neither
shall he eat.
11 For we hear that there are some who walk
among you in a disorderly manner, not working
at all, but are [a]busybodies.
12 Now those who are such we command and
exhort through our Lord Jesus Christ [a]that they
work in quietness and eat their own bread.

*______

2:7 Or *he* • Or *he*
3:6 NU, M *they*

KJV

13 But ye, brethren, [a]be not weary in well
doing.
14 And if any man obey not our word by this
epistle, note that man, and [a]have no company
with him, that he may be ashamed.
15 [a]Yet count *him* not as an enemy, [b]but admonish *him* as a brother.

Benediction

16 Now [a]the Lord of peace himself give you
peace always by all means. The Lord *be* with you
all.
17 [a]The salutation of Paul with mine own
hand, which is the token in every epistle: so I
write.
18 [a]The grace of our Lord Jesus Christ *be*
with you all. Amen.

13 [a]2 Cor. 4:1; Gal. 6:9
14 [a]Matt. 18:17
15 [a]Lev. 19:17 [b]Titus 3:10
16 [a]John 14:27; Rom. 15:33; Phil. 4:9
17 [a]1 Cor. 16:21
18 [a]Rom. 16:20, 24; 1 Thess. 5:28

NKJV

13 But *as for* you, brethren, [a]do not grow
weary *in* doing good.
14 And if anyone does not obey our word in
this epistle, note that person and [a]do not keep
company with him, that he may be ashamed.
15 [a]Yet do not count *him* as an enemy, [b]but
admonish *him* as a brother.

Benediction

16 Now may [a]the Lord of peace Himself give
you peace always in every way. The Lord *be* with
you all.
17 [a]The salutation of Paul with my own
hand, which is a sign in every epistle; so I write.
18 [a]The grace of our Lord Jesus Christ *be*
with you all. Amen.

KJV

THE FIRST EPISTLE OF PAUL THE APOSTLE TO

TIMOTHY

Greeting

1 Paul, an apostle of Jesus Christ by the commandment of God our Saviour, and Lord Jesus Christ, *which is* our hope;

2 Unto Timothy, [a]*my* own son in the faith: [b]Grace, mercy, *and* peace, from God our Father and Jesus Christ our Lord.

No Other Doctrine

3 As I besought thee to abide still at Ephesus, [a]when I went into Macedonia, that thou mightest charge some [b]that they teach no other doctrine,

4 [a]Neither give heed to fables and endless genealogies, which minister questions, rather than godly edifying which is in faith: *so do.*

5 Now [a]the end of the commandment is charity [b]out of a pure heart, and *of* a good conscience, and *of* faith unfeigned:

6 From which some having swerved have turned aside unto [a]vain jangling;

7 Desiring to be teachers of the law; understanding neither what they say, nor whereof they affirm.

8 But we know that the law *is* [a]good, if a man use it lawfully;

9 Knowing this, that the law is not made for a righteous man, but for the lawless and disobedient, for the ungodly and for sinners, for unholy and profane, for murderers of fathers and murderers of mothers, for manslayers,

10 For whoremongers, for them that defile themselves with mankind, for menstealers, for liars, for perjured persons, and if there be any other thing that is contrary to sound doctrine;

11 According to the glorious gospel of the [a]blessed God, which was [b]committed to my trust.

Glory to God for His Grace
(cf. Acts 8:1–3; 9:1–19)

12 And I thank Christ Jesus our Lord, who hath [a]enabled me, [b]for that he counted me faithful, [c]putting me into the ministry;

13 [a]Who was before a blasphemer, and a persecutor, and injurious: but I obtained mercy, because [b]I did *it* ignorantly in unbelief.

14 [a]And the grace of our Lord was exceeding abundant [b]with faith and love which is in Christ Jesus.

15 [a]This *is* a faithful saying, and worthy of all acceptation, that [b]Christ Jesus came into the world to save sinners; of whom I am chief.

16 Howbeit for this cause I obtained mercy, that in me first Jesus Christ might shew forth all longsuffering, for a pattern to them which should hereafter believe on him to life everlasting.

17 Now unto [a]the King eternal, [b]immortal, [c]invisible, [d]the only wise God, [e]*be* honour and glory for ever and ever. Amen.

Fight the Good Fight

18 This charge I commit unto thee, son Timothy, according to the prophecies which went before on thee, that thou by them mightest war a good warfare;

NKJV

THE FIRST EPISTLE OF PAUL THE APOSTLE TO

TIMOTHY

Greeting

1 Paul, an apostle of Jesus Christ, by the commandment of God our Savior and the Lord Jesus Christ, our hope,

2 To Timothy, a [a]true son in the faith:

[b]Grace, mercy, *and* peace from God our Father and Jesus Christ our Lord.

No Other Doctrine

3 As I urged you [a]when I went into Macedonia—remain in Ephesus that you may charge some [b]that they teach no other doctrine,

4 [a]nor give heed to fables and endless genealogies, which cause disputes rather than godly edification which is in faith.

5 Now [a]the purpose of the commandment is love [b]from a pure heart, *from* a good conscience, and *from* sincere faith,

6 from which some, having strayed, have turned aside to [a]idle talk,

7 desiring to be teachers of the law, understanding neither what they say nor the things which they affirm.

8 But we know that the law *is* [a]good if one uses it lawfully,

9 knowing this: that the law is not made for a righteous person, but for *the* lawless and insubordinate, for *the* ungodly and for sinners, for *the* unholy and profane, for murderers of fathers and murderers of mothers, for manslayers,

10 for fornicators, for sodomites, for kidnappers, for liars, for perjurers, and if there is any other thing that is contrary to sound doctrine,

11 according to the glorious gospel of the [a]blessed God which was [b]committed to my trust.

Glory to God for His Grace
(cf. Acts 8:1–3; 9:1–19)

12 And I thank Christ Jesus our Lord who has [a]enabled me, [b]because He counted me faithful, [c]putting *me* into the ministry,

13 although [a]I was formerly a blasphemer, a persecutor, and an insolent man; but I obtained mercy because [b]I did *it* ignorantly in unbelief.

14 [a]And the grace of our Lord was exceedingly abundant, [b]with faith and love which are in Christ Jesus.

15 [a]This *is* a faithful saying and worthy of all acceptance, that [b]Christ Jesus came into the world to save sinners, of whom I am chief.

16 However, for this reason I obtained mercy, that in me first Jesus Christ might show all longsuffering, as a pattern to those who are going to believe on Him for everlasting life.

17 Now to [a]the King eternal, [b]immortal, [c]invisible, to *God [d]who alone is wise, [e]*be* honor and glory forever and ever. Amen.

Fight the Good Fight

18 This charge I commit to you, son Timothy, according to the prophecies previously made concerning you, that by them you may wage the good warfare,

CHAPTER 1

2 [a]Acts 16:1, 2; Rom. 1:7; 2 Tim. 1:2; Titus 1:4 [b]Gal. 1:3
3 [a]Acts 20:1, 3 [b]Rom. 16:17; 2 Cor. 11:4; Gal. 1:6, 7; 1 Tim. 6:3
4 [a]1 Tim. 6:3, 4, 20; Titus 1:14
5 [a]Rom. 13:8–10; Gal. 5:14 [b]Eph. 6:24
6 [a]1 Tim. 6:4, 20
8 [a]Rom. 7:12, 16
11 [a]1 Tim. 6:15 [b]1 Cor. 9:17
12 [a]1 Cor. 15:10 [b]1 Cor. 7:25 [c]Col. 1:25
13 [a]Acts 8:3; 1 Cor. 15:9 [b]John 4:21
14 [a]Rom. 5:20; 1 Cor. 3:10; 2 Cor. 4:15; Gal. 1:13–16 [b]1 Thess. 1:3; 1 Tim. 2:15; 4:12; 6:11; 2 Tim. 1:13; 2:22; Titus 2:2
15 [a]1 Tim. 3:1; 4:9; 2 Tim. 2:11; Titus 3:8 [b]Is. 53:5; 61:1; Hos. 6:1–3; Matt. 1:21; 9:13
17 [a]Ps. 10:16 [b]Rom. 1:23 [c]Heb. 11:27 [d]Rom. 16:27 [e]1 Chr. 29:11

*

1:17 NU *the only God,*

KJV

19 Holding faith, and a good conscience;
which some having put away concerning faith
have made shipwreck:
20 Of whom is [a]Hymenaeus and [b]Alexander;
whom I have delivered unto Satan, that they may
learn not to [c]blaspheme.

Pray for All Men

2 I exhort therefore, that, first of all, supplications, prayers, intercessions, *and* giving of
thanks, be made for all men;
2 [a]For kings, and [b]*for* all that are in authority; that we may lead a quiet and peaceable life
in all godliness and honesty.
3 For this *is* [a]good and acceptable in the
sight [b]of God our Saviour;
4 [a]Who will have all men to be saved, [b]and
to come unto the knowledge of the truth.
5 [a]For *there is* one God, and [b]one mediator
between God and men, the man Christ Jesus;
6 [a]Who gave himself a ransom for all, to
be testified in due time.
7 [a]Whereunto I am ordained a preacher,
and an apostle, (I speak the truth in Christ, *and*
lie not;) [b]a teacher of the Gentiles in faith and
verity.

Men and Women in the Church

8 I will therefore that men pray [a]every
where, [b]lifting up holy hands, without wrath and
doubting.
9 In like manner also, that [a]women adorn
themselves in modest apparel, with shamefaced-
ness and sobriety; not with broided hair, or gold,
or pearls, or costly array;
10 [a]But (which becometh women professing
godliness) with good works.
11 Let the woman learn in silence with all
subjection.
12 But [a]I suffer not a woman to teach, nor
to usurp authority over the man, but to be in
silence.
13 For Adam was first formed, then Eve.
14 And Adam was not deceived, but the
woman being deceived was in the transgression.
15 Notwithstanding she shall be saved in
childbearing, if they continue in faith and charity
and holiness with sobriety.

Qualifications of Overseers

3 This *is* a true saying, If a man desire the office
of a bishop, he desireth a good work.
2 A bishop then must be blameless, the husband of one wife, vigilant, sober, of good behaviour, given to hospitality, apt to teach;
3 Not given to wine, no striker, not greedy
of filthy lucre; but patient, not a brawler, not
covetous;
4 One that ruleth well his own house, having his children in subjection with all gravity;
5 (For if a man know not how to rule his
own house, how shall he take care of the church
of God?)
6 Not a novice, lest being lifted up with
pride he fall into the condemnation of the devil.
7 Moreover he must have a good report of
them which are without; lest he fall into reproach
and the [a]snare of the devil.

Qualifications of Deacons

8 Likewise *must* the deacons *be* grave, not
doubletongued, [a]not given to much wine, not
greedy of filthy lucre;
9 Holding the mystery of the faith in a pure
conscience.
10 And let these also first be proved; then
let them use the office of a deacon, being *found*
blameless.
11 Even so *must their* wives *be* grave, not
slanderers, sober, faithful in all things.

---

20 [a]2 Tim. 2:17, 18
[b]2 Tim. 4:14
[c]Acts 13:45

CHAPTER 2

2 [a]Ezra 6:10
[b][Rom. 13:1]
3 [a]Rom. 12:2
[b]2 Tim. 1:9
4 [a]Ezek. 18:23, 32; John 3:17; 1 Tim. 4:10; Titus 2:11; 2 Pet. 3:9
[b][John 17:3]
5 [a]1 Cor. 8:6; Gal. 3:20
[b][Heb. 9:15]
6 [a]Mark 10:45
7 [a]Eph. 3:7, 8; 1 Tim. 1:11; 2 Tim. 1:11
[b][Gal. 1:15, 16]
8 [a]Luke 23:34
[b]Ps. 134:2
9 [a]1 Pet. 3:3
10 [a]1 Pet. 3:4
12 [a]1 Cor. 14:34; Titus 2:5

CHAPTER 3

7 [a]1 Tim. 6:9; 2 Tim. 2:26
8 [a]Ezek. 44:21

*

2:7 NU omits *in Christ*
3:1 Lit. *overseer*
3:3 NU omits *not greedy for money*

NKJV

19 having faith and a good conscience, which
some having rejected, concerning the faith have
suffered shipwreck,
20 of whom are [a]Hymenaeus and [b]Alexan-
der, whom I delivered to Satan that they may learn
not to [c]blaspheme.

Pray for All Men

2 Therefore I exhort first of all that supplications, prayers, intercessions, *and* giving of
thanks be made for all men,
2 [a]for kings and [b]all who are in authority,
that we may lead a quiet and peaceable life in
all godliness and reverence.
3 For this *is* [a]good and acceptable in the
sight [b]of God our Savior,
4 [a]who desires all men to be saved [b]and to
come to the knowledge of the truth.
5 [a]For *there is* one God and [b]one Mediator
between God and men, *the* Man Christ Jesus,
6 [a]who gave Himself a ransom for all, to
be testified in due time,
7 [a]for which I was appointed a preacher and
an apostle—I am speaking the truth *in Christ *and*
not lying—[b]a teacher of the Gentiles in faith and
truth.

Men and Women in the Church

8 I desire therefore that the men pray
[a]everywhere, [b]lifting up holy hands, without
wrath and doubting;
9 in like manner also, that the [a]women
adorn themselves in modest apparel, with pro-
priety and moderation, not with braided hair or
gold or pearls or costly clothing,
10 [a]but, which is proper for women professing godliness, with good works.
11 Let a woman learn in silence with all
submission.
12 And [a]I do not permit a woman to teach
or to have authority over a man, but to be in
silence.
13 For Adam was formed first, then Eve.
14 And Adam was not deceived, but the
woman being deceived, fell into transgression.
15 Nevertheless she will be saved in childbearing if they continue in faith, love, and holiness, with self-control.

Qualifications of Overseers

3 This *is* a faithful saying: If a man desires
the position of a *bishop, he desires a good
work.
2 A bishop then must be blameless, the husband of one wife, temperate, sober-minded, of
good behavior, hospitable, able to teach;
3 not given to wine, not violent, *not greedy
for money, but gentle, not quarrelsome, not
covetous;
4 one who rules his own house well, having
his children in submission with all reverence
5 (for if a man does not know how to rule
his own house, how will he take care of the church
of God?);
6 not a novice, lest being puffed up with
pride he fall into the *same* condemnation as the
devil.
7 Moreover he must have a good testimony
among those who are outside, lest he fall into reproach and the [a]snare of the devil.

Qualifications of Deacons

8 Likewise deacons *must be* reverent, not
double-tongued, [a]not given to much wine, not
greedy for money,
9 holding the mystery of the faith with a
pure conscience.
10 But let these also first be tested; then let
them serve as deacons, being *found* blameless.
11 Likewise, *their* wives *must be* reverent,
not slanderers, temperate, faithful in all things.

KJV

12 Let the deacons be the husbands of one wife, ruling their children and their own houses well.

13 For they that have used the office of a deacon [a]well purchase to themselves a good degree, and great boldness in the faith which is in Christ Jesus.

The Great Mystery

14 These things write I unto thee, hoping to come unto thee shortly:

15 But if I tarry long, that thou mayest know how thou oughtest to behave thyself in the house of God, which is the church of the living God, the pillar and ground of the truth.

16 And without controversy great is the mystery of godliness: [a]God was manifest in the flesh, [b]justified in the Spirit, [c]seen of angels, [d]preached unto the Gentiles, [e]believed on in the world, [f]received up into glory.

The Great Apostasy

4 Now the Spirit speaketh expressly, that in the latter times some shall depart from the faith, giving heed [a]to seducing spirits, and doctrines of devils;

2 [a]Speaking lies in hypocrisy; having their conscience [b]seared with a hot iron;

3 Forbidding to marry, *and commanding* to abstain from meats, which God hath created to be received with thanksgiving of them which believe and know the truth.

4 For every creature of God *is* good, and nothing to be refused, if it be received with thanksgiving:

5 For it is sanctified by the word of God and prayer.

A Good Servant of Jesus Christ

6 If thou put the brethren in remembrance of these things, thou shalt be a good minister of Jesus Christ, [a]nourished up in the words of faith and of good doctrine, whereunto thou hast attained.

7 But [a]refuse profane and old wives' fables, and [b]exercise thyself *rather* unto godliness.

8 For [a]bodily exercise profiteth little: but godliness is profitable unto all things, [b]having promise of the life that now is, and of that which is to come.

9 This *is* a faithful saying and worthy of all acceptation.

10 For therefore we both labour and suffer reproach, because we trust in the living God, [a]who is the Saviour of all men, specially of those that believe.

11 These things command and teach.

Take Heed to Your Ministry

12 Let no man despise thy youth; but be thou an [a]example of the believers, in word, in conversation, in charity, in spirit, in faith, in purity.

13 Till I come, give attendance to reading, to exhortation, to doctrine.

14 [a]Neglect not the gift that is in thee, which was given thee by prophecy, [b]with the laying on of the hands of the presbytery.

15 Meditate upon these things; give thyself wholly to them; that thy profiting may appear to all.

16 Take heed unto thyself, and unto the doctrine; continue in them: for in doing this thou shalt both save thyself, and them that hear thee.

Treatment of Church Members

5 Rebuke not an elder, but intreat *him* as a father; *and* the younger men as brethren;

2 The elder women as mothers; the younger as sisters, with all purity.

---

13 [a]Matt. 25:21
16 [a][John 1:14; 1 Pet. 1:20; 1 John 1:2; 3:5, 8] [b][Matt. 3:16; Rom. 1:4] [c]Matt. 28:2 [d]Acts 10:34; Rom. 10:18 [e]Rom. 16:26; 2 Cor. 1:19; Col. 1:6, 23 [f]Luke 24:51

CHAPTER 4

1 [a]2 Tim. 3:13; Rev. 16:14
2 [a]Matt. 7:15 [b]Eph. 4:19
6 [a]2 Tim. 3:14
7 [a]2 Tim. 2:16; Titus 1:14 [b]Heb. 5:14
8 [a]1 Cor. 8:8 [b]Ps. 37:9
10 [a]Ps. 36:6
12 [a]Phil. 3:17; Titus 2:7; 1 Pet. 5:3
14 [a]2 Tim. 1:6 [b]Acts 6:6; 1 Tim. 5:22

*

3:16 NU *Who*
4:10 NU *we labor and strive,*
4:12 NU omits *in spirit*

NKJV

12 Let deacons be the husbands of one wife, ruling *their* children and their own houses well.

13 For those who have served well as deacons [a]obtain for themselves a good standing and great boldness in the faith which is in Christ Jesus.

The Great Mystery

14 These things I write to you, though I hope to come to you shortly;

15 but if I am delayed, *I write* so that you may know how you ought to conduct yourself in the house of God, which is the church of the living God, the pillar and ground of the truth.

16 And without controversy great is the mystery of godliness:

[a]God* was manifested in the flesh,
[b]Justified in the Spirit,
[c]Seen by angels,
[d]Preached among the Gentiles,
[e]Believed on in the world,
[f]Received up in glory.

The Great Apostasy

4 Now the Spirit expressly says that in latter times some will depart from the faith, giving heed [a]to deceiving spirits and doctrines of demons,

2 [a]speaking lies in hypocrisy, having their own conscience [b]seared with a hot iron,

3 forbidding to marry, *and commanding* to abstain from foods which God created to be received with thanksgiving by those who believe and know the truth.

4 For every creature of God *is* good, and nothing is to be refused if it is received with thanksgiving;

5 for it is sanctified by the word of God and prayer.

A Good Servant of Jesus Christ

6 If you instruct the brethren in these things, you will be a good minister of Jesus Christ, [a]nourished in the words of faith and of the good doctrine which you have carefully followed.

7 But [a]reject profane and old wives' fables, and [b]exercise yourself toward godliness.

8 For [a]bodily exercise profits a little, but godliness is profitable for all things, [b]having promise of the life that now is and of that which is to come.

9 This *is* a faithful saying and worthy of all acceptance.

10 For to this *end* *we both labor and suffer reproach, because we trust in the living God, [a]who is *the* Savior of all men, especially of those who believe.

11 These things command and teach.

Take Heed to Your Ministry

12 Let no one despise your youth, but be an [a]example to the believers in word, in conduct, in love, *in spirit, in faith, in purity.

13 Till I come, give attention to reading, to exhortation, to doctrine.

14 [a]Do not neglect the gift that is in you, which was given to you by prophecy [b]with the laying on of the hands of the eldership.

15 Meditate on these things; give yourself entirely to them, that your progress may be evident to all.

16 Take heed to yourself and to the doctrine. Continue in them, for in doing this you will save both yourself and those who hear you.

Treatment of Church Members

5 Do not rebuke an older man, but exhort *him* as a father, younger men as brothers,

2 older women as mothers, younger women as sisters, with all purity.

KJV

Honor True Widows

3 Honour widows that are widows indeed.

4 But if any widow have children or nephews, let them learn first to shew piety at home, and [a]to requite their parents: for that is good and acceptable before God.

5 Now she that is a widow indeed, and desolate, trusteth in God, and continueth in supplications and prayers [a]night and day.

6 But she that liveth in pleasure is dead while she liveth.

7 And these things give in charge, that they may be blameless.

8 But if any provide not for his own, [a]and specially for those of his own house, [b]he hath denied the faith, [c]and is worse than an infidel.

9 Let not a widow be taken into the number under threescore years old, having been the wife of one man,

10 Well reported of for good works; if she have brought up children, if she have lodged strangers, if she have washed the saints' feet, if she have relieved the afflicted, if she have diligently followed every good work.

11 But the younger widows refuse: for when they have begun to wax wanton against Christ, they will marry;

12 Having damnation, because they have cast off their first faith.

13 And withal they learn *to be* idle, wandering about from house to house; and not only idle, but tattlers also and busybodies, speaking things which they ought not.

14 I will therefore that the younger women marry, bear children, guide the house, give none occasion to the adversary to speak reproachfully.

15 For some are already turned aside after Satan.

16 If any man or woman that believeth have widows, let them relieve them, and let not the church be charged; that it may relieve them that are widows indeed.

Honor the Elders

17 Let the elders that rule well be counted worthy of double honour, especially they who labour in the word and doctrine.

18 For the scripture saith, [a]THOU SHALT NOT MUZZLE THE OX THAT TREADETH OUT THE CORN. And, [b]The labourer *is* worthy of his reward.

19 Against an elder receive not an accusation, but [a]before two or three witnesses.

20 Them that sin rebuke before all, that others also may fear.

21 I charge *thee* before God, and the Lord Jesus Christ, and the elect angels, that thou observe these things without preferring [a]one before another, doing nothing by partiality.

22 Lay hands suddenly on no man, neither be [a]partaker of other men's sins: keep thyself pure.

23 Drink no longer water, but use a little wine for thy stomach's sake and thine often infirmities.

24 Some men's sins are [a]open beforehand, going before to judgment; and some *men* they follow after.

25 Likewise also the good works *of some* are manifest beforehand; and they that are otherwise cannot be hid.

Honor Masters

6 Let as many [a]servants as are under the yoke count their own masters worthy of all honour, that the name of God and *his* doctrine be not blasphemed.

2 And they that have believing masters, let them not despise *them*, because they are brethren; but rather do *them* service, because they are faith-

CHAPTER 5

4 [a]Gen. 45:10
5 [a]Acts 26:7
8 [a]Is. 58:7; 2 Cor. 12:14 [b]2 Tim. 3:5 [c]Matt. 18:17
18 [a]Deut. 25:4; 1 Cor. 9:7–9 [b]Lev. 19:13; Deut. 24:15; Matt. 10:10; Luke 10:7; 1 Cor. 9:14
19 [a]Deut. 17:6; 19:15; Matt. 18:16
21 [a]Deut. 1:17
22 [a]Eph. 5:6, 7; 2 John 11
24 [a]Gal. 5:19–21

CHAPTER 6

1 [a]Eph. 6:5; Titus 2:9; 1 Pet. 2:18

*

5:4 NU, M omit *good and*
5:16 NU omits *man or*

NKJV

Honor True Widows

3 Honor widows who are really widows.

4 But if any widow has children or grandchildren, let them first learn to show piety at home and [a]to repay their parents; for this is *good and acceptable before God.

5 Now she who is really a widow, and left alone, trusts in God and continues in supplications and prayers [a]night and day.

6 But she who lives in pleasure is dead while she lives.

7 And these things command, that they may be blameless.

8 But if anyone does not provide for his own, [a]and especially for those of his household, [b]he has denied the faith [c]and is worse than an unbeliever.

9 Do not let a widow under sixty years old be taken into the number, *and not unless* she has been the wife of one man,

10 well reported for good works: if she has brought up children, if she has lodged strangers, if she has washed the saints' feet, if she has relieved the afflicted, if she has diligently followed every good work.

11 But refuse *the* younger widows; for when they have begun to grow wanton against Christ, they desire to marry,

12 having condemnation because they have cast off their first faith.

13 And besides they learn *to be* idle, wandering about from house to house, and not only idle but also gossips and busybodies, saying things which they ought not.

14 Therefore I desire that *the* younger *widows* marry, bear children, manage the house, give no opportunity to the adversary to speak reproachfully.

15 For some have already turned aside after Satan.

16 If any believing *man or woman has widows, let them relieve them, and do not let the church be burdened, that it may relieve those who are really widows.

Honor the Elders

17 Let the elders who rule well be counted worthy of double honor, especially those who labor in the word and doctrine.

18 For the Scripture says, [a]*"You shall not muzzle an ox while it treads out the grain,"* and, [b]"The laborer *is* worthy of his wages."

19 Do not receive an accusation against an elder except [a]from two or three witnesses.

20 Those who are sinning rebuke in the presence of all, that the rest also may fear.

21 I charge *you* before God and the Lord Jesus Christ and the elect angels that you observe these things without [a]prejudice, doing nothing with partiality.

22 Do not lay hands on anyone hastily, nor [a]share in other people's sins; keep yourself pure.

23 No longer drink only water, but use a little wine for your stomach's sake and your frequent infirmities.

24 Some men's sins are [a]clearly evident, preceding *them* to judgment, but those of some *men* follow later.

25 Likewise, the good works *of some* are clearly evident, and those that are otherwise cannot be hidden.

Honor Masters

6 Let as many [a]bondservants as are under the yoke count their own masters worthy of all honor, so that the name of God and *His* doctrine may not be blasphemed.

2 And those who have believing masters, let them not despise *them* because they are brethren, but rather serve *them* because those who are ben-

KJV

ful and beloved, partakers of the benefit. These things teach and exhort.

Error and Greed

3 If any man teach otherwise, and consent not to [a]wholesome words, *even* the words of our Lord Jesus Christ, [b]and to the doctrine which is according to godliness;

4 He is proud, knowing nothing, but doting about questions and strifes of words, whereof cometh envy, strife, railings, evil surmisings,

5 Perverse disputings of men of corrupt minds, and destitute of the truth, supposing that gain is godliness: from [a]such withdraw thyself.

6 But godliness with [a]contentment is great gain.

7 For we brought nothing into *this* world, *and it is* [a]certain we can carry nothing out.

8 And having food and raiment let us be therewith [a]content.

9 But they that will be rich fall into temptation and a snare, and *into* many foolish and hurtful lusts, which drown men in destruction and perdition.

10 For the love of money is the root of all evil: which while some coveted after, they have erred from the faith, and pierced themselves through with many sorrows.

The Good Confession

11 But thou, O man of God, flee these things; and follow after righteousness, godliness, faith, love, patience, meekness.

12 Fight the good fight of faith, lay hold on eternal life, whereunto thou art also called, and hast professed a good profession before many witnesses.

13 I give thee charge in the sight of God, who quickeneth all things, and *before* Christ Jesus, [a]who before Pontius Pilate witnessed a good confession;

14 That thou keep *this* commandment without spot, unrebukeable, until the appearing of our Lord Jesus Christ:

15 Which in his times he shall shew, *who is* the blessed and only Potentate, the King of kings, and Lord of lords;

16 Who only hath immortality, dwelling in the [a]light which no man can approach unto; [b]whom no man hath seen, nor can see: to whom *be* honour and power everlasting. Amen.

Instructions to the Rich

17 Charge them that are rich in this world, that they be not highminded, nor trust in uncertain [a]riches, but in the living God, who giveth us richly all things [b]to enjoy;

18 That they do good, that they be rich in good works, ready to distribute, willing to communicate;

19 [a]Laying up in store for themselves a good foundation against the time to come, that they may lay hold on eternal life.

Guard the Faith

20 O Timothy, [a]keep that which is committed to thy trust, [b]avoiding profane *and* vain babblings, and oppositions of science falsely so called:

21 Which some professing have erred concerning the faith. Grace *be* with thee. Amen.

3 [a]2 Tim. 1:13 [b]Titus 1:1
5 [a]2 Tim. 3:5
6 [a]Phil. 4:11; Heb. 13:5
7 [a]Job 1:21; Ps. 49:17; Eccl. 5:15
8 [a]Prov. 30:8, 9
13 [a]Matt. 27:2; John 18:36, 37
16 [a]Dan. 2:22 [b]John 6:46
17 [a]Jer. 9:23; 48:7 [b]Eccl. 5:18, 19
19 [a][Matt. 6:20, 21; 19:21]
20 [a][2 Tim. 1:12, 14] [b]Titus 1:14

NKJV

efited are believers and beloved. Teach and exhort these things.

Error and Greed

3 If anyone teaches otherwise and does not consent to [a]wholesome words, *even* the words of our Lord Jesus Christ, [b]and to the doctrine which accords with godliness,

4 he is proud, knowing nothing, but is obsessed with disputes and arguments over words, from which come envy, strife, reviling, evil suspicions,

5 *useless wranglings of men of corrupt minds and destitute of the truth, who suppose that godliness is a *means of* gain. *From [a]such withdraw yourself.

6 Now godliness with [a]contentment is great gain.

7 For we brought nothing into *this* world, **and it is* [a]certain we can carry nothing out.

8 And having food and clothing, with these we shall be [a]content.

9 But those who desire to be rich fall into temptation and a snare, and *into* many foolish and harmful lusts which drown men in destruction and perdition.

10 For the love of money is a root of all *kinds of* evil, for which some have strayed from the faith in their greediness, and pierced themselves through with many sorrows.

The Good Confession

11 But you, O man of God, flee these things and pursue righteousness, godliness, faith, love, patience, gentleness.

12 Fight the good fight of faith, lay hold on eternal life, to which you were also called and have confessed the good confession in the presence of many witnesses.

13 I urge you in the sight of God who gives life to all things, and *before* Christ Jesus [a]who witnessed the good confession before Pontius Pilate,

14 that you keep *this* commandment without spot, blameless until our Lord Jesus Christ's appearing,

15 which He will manifest in His own time, *He who is* the blessed and only Potentate, the King of kings and Lord of lords,

16 who alone has immortality, dwelling in [a]unapproachable light, [b]whom no man has seen or can see, to whom *be* honor and everlasting power. Amen.

Instructions to the Rich

17 Command those who are rich in this present age not to be haughty, nor to trust in uncertain [a]riches but in the living God, who gives us richly all things [b]to enjoy.

18 *Let them* do good, that they be rich in good works, ready to give, willing to share,

19 [a]storing up for themselves a good foundation for the time to come, that they may lay hold on eternal life.

Guard the Faith

20 O Timothy! [a]Guard what was committed to your trust, [b]avoiding the profane *and* idle babblings and contradictions of what is falsely called knowledge—

21 by professing it some have strayed concerning the faith. Grace *be* with you. Amen.

*———

6:5 NU, M *constant friction* • NU omits the rest of v. 5.
6:7 NU omits *and it is certain*

KJV

THE SECOND EPISTLE OF PAUL THE APOSTLE TO

TIMOTHY

Greeting

1 Paul, an apostle of Jesus Christ by the will
of God, according to the [a]promise of life
which is in Christ Jesus,
2 To Timothy, *my* dearly [a]beloved son:
Grace, mercy, *and* peace, from God the Father
and Christ Jesus our Lord.

Timothy's Faith and Heritage

3 I thank God, whom I serve from *my* [a]fore-
fathers with pure conscience, that without ceasing
I have remembrance of thee in my prayers night
and day;
4 Greatly desiring to see thee, being mindful
of thy tears, that I may be filled with joy;
5 When I call to remembrance [a]the unfeigned faith that is in thee, which dwelt first in
thy grandmother Lois, and [b]thy mother Eunice;
and I am persuaded that in thee also.
6 Wherefore I put thee in remembrance
[a]that thou stir up the gift of God, which is in thee
by the putting on of my hands.
7 For [a]God hath not given us the spirit of
fear; [b]but of power, and of love, and of a sound
mind.

Not Ashamed of the Gospel

8 [a]Be not thou therefore ashamed of [b]the
testimony of our Lord, nor of me [c]his prisoner:
but be thou partaker of the afflictions of the gospel
according to the power of God;
9 Who hath saved us, and called *us* with an
holy calling, [a]not according to our works, but [b]ac-
cording to his own purpose and grace, which
was given us in Christ Jesus [c]before the world
began,
10 But [a]is now made manifest by the appearing of our Saviour Jesus Christ, who hath abolished death, and hath brought life and immortality
to light through the gospel:
11 [a]Whereunto I am appointed a preacher,
and an apostle, and a teacher of the Gentiles.
12 For the which cause I also suffer these
things: nevertheless I am not ashamed: [a]for I
know whom I have believed, and am persuaded
that he is able to keep that which I have committed unto him against that day.

Be Loyal to the Faith

13 [a]Hold fast [b]the form of [c]sound words,
which thou hast heard of me, in faith and love
which is in Christ Jesus.
14 That good thing which was committed
unto thee keep by the Holy Ghost which dwelleth
in us.
15 This thou knowest, that all they which are
in Asia be turned away from me; of whom are
Phygellus and Hermogenes.
16 The Lord give mercy unto the [a]house of
Onesiphorus; for he oft refreshed me, and was
not ashamed of my chain:
17 But, when he was in Rome, he sought me
out very diligently, and found *me.*
18 The Lord [a]grant unto him that he may
find mercy of the Lord [b]in that day: and in how

CHAPTER 1
1 [a]Titus 1:2
2 [a]1 Tim. 1:2; 2 Tim. 2:1; Titus 1:4
3 [a]Acts 24:14
5 [a]1 Tim. 1:5; 4:6 [b]Acts 16:1
6 [a]1 Tim. 4:14
7 [a]John 14:27; Rom. 8:15; 1 John 4:18 [b][Acts 1:8]
8 [a][Mark 8:38; Luke 9:26; Rom. 1:16]; 2 Tim. 1:12, 16 [b]1 Tim. 2:6 [c]Eph. 3:1; 2 Tim. 1:16
9 [a][Rom. 3:20]; Eph. 2:8, 9 [b]Rom. 8:28 [c]Rom. 16:25; Eph. 1:4; Titus 1:2
10 [a]Eph. 1:9
11 [a]Acts 9:15
12 [a]1 Pet. 4:19
13 [a]2 Tim. 3:14; Titus 1:9 [b]Rom. 2:20; 6:17 [c]1 Tim. 6:3
16 [a]2 Tim. 4:19
18 [a]Matt. 6:4; Mark 9:41 [b]2 Thess. 1:10

*

1:1 NU, M *Christ Jesus*
1:11 NU omits *of the Gentiles*

NKJV

THE SECOND EPISTLE OF PAUL THE APOSTLE TO

TIMOTHY

Greeting

1 Paul, an apostle of *Jesus Christ by the will
of God, according to the [a]promise of life
which is in Christ Jesus,

2 To Timothy, a [a]beloved son:

Grace, mercy, *and* peace from God the Father and Christ Jesus our Lord.

Timothy's Faith and Heritage

3 I thank God, whom I serve with a pure
conscience, as *my* [a]forefathers *did,* as without
ceasing I remember you in my prayers night and
day,
4 greatly desiring to see you, being mindful
of your tears, that I may be filled with joy,
5 when I call to remembrance [a]the genuine
faith that is in you, which dwelt first in your
grandmother Lois and [b]your mother Eunice, and
I am persuaded is in you also.
6 Therefore I remind you [a]to stir up the gift
of God which is in you through the laying on of
my hands.
7 For [a]God has not given us a spirit of fear,
[b]but of power and of love and of a sound mind.

Not Ashamed of the Gospel

8 [a]Therefore do not be ashamed of [b]the testimony of our Lord, nor of me [c]His prisoner, but
share with me in the sufferings for the gospel according to the power of God,
9 who has saved us and called *us* with a
holy calling, [a]not according to our works, but [b]ac-
cording to His own purpose and grace which was
given to us in Christ Jesus [c]before time began,
10 but [a]has now been revealed by the appearing of our Savior Jesus Christ, *who* has abolished
death and brought life and immortality to light
through the gospel,
11 [a]to which I was appointed a preacher, an
apostle, and a teacher *of the Gentiles.
12 For this reason I also suffer these things;
nevertheless I am not ashamed, [a]for I know whom
I have believed and am persuaded that He is able
to keep what I have committed to Him until that
Day.

Be Loyal to the Faith

13 [a]Hold fast [b]the pattern of [c]sound words
which you have heard from me, in faith and love
which are in Christ Jesus.
14 That good thing which was committed to
you, keep by the Holy Spirit who dwells in us.
15 This you know, that all those in Asia have
turned away from me, among whom are Phygellus and Hermogenes.
16 The Lord grant mercy to the [a]household
of Onesiphorus, for he often refreshed me, and
was not ashamed of my chain;
17 but when he arrived in Rome, he sought
me out very zealously and found *me.*
18 The Lord [a]grant to him that he may find
mercy from the Lord [b]in that Day—and you know

KJV

many things he [c]ministered unto me at Ephesus,
thou knowest very well.

Be Strong in Grace

2 Thou therefore, [a]my son, [b]be strong in the
grace that is in Christ Jesus.
2 And the things that thou hast heard of me
among many witnesses, the same commit thou
to faithful men, who shall be able to teach others
also.
3 Thou therefore [a]endure hardness, [b]as a
good soldier of Jesus Christ.
4 [a]No man that warreth entangleth himself
with the affairs of *this* life; that he may please
him who hath chosen him to be a soldier.
5 And [a]if a man also strive for masteries,
yet is he not crowned, except he strive lawfully.
6 The husbandman that laboureth must be
first partaker of the fruits.
7 Consider what I say; and the Lord [a]give
thee understanding in all things.
8 Remember that Jesus Christ [a]of the seed
of David [b]was raised from the dead [c]according
to my gospel:
9 [a]Wherein I suffer trouble, as an evil doer,
[b]*even* unto bonds; [c]but the word of God is not
bound.
10 Therefore [a]I endure all things for the
elect's sakes, [b]that they may also obtain the salvation which is in Christ Jesus with eternal glory.
11 *It is* a faithful saying: For [a]if we be dead
with *him,* we shall also live with *him:*
12 [a]If we suffer, we shall also reign with *him:*
[b]if we deny *him,* he also will deny us:
13 If we believe not, *yet* he abideth faithful:
he [a]cannot deny himself.

Approved and Disapproved Workers

14 Of these things put *them* in remembrance,
[a]charging *them* before the Lord that they strive
not about words to no profit, *but* to the subverting
of the hearers.
15 [a]Study to shew thyself approved unto
God, a workman that needeth not to be ashamed,
rightly dividing the word of truth.
16 But shun profane *and* vain babblings: for
they will increase unto more ungodliness.
17 And their word will eat as doth a canker:
of whom is [a]Hymenaeus and Philetus;
18 Who concerning the truth have erred,
[a]saying that the resurrection is past already; and
overthrow the faith of some.
19 Nevertheless [a]the foundation of God
standeth sure, having this seal, The Lord [b]know-
eth them that are his. And, Let every one that
nameth the name of Christ depart from iniquity.
20 But in a great house there are not only
[a]vessels of gold and of silver, but also of wood
and of earth; and some to honour, and some to
dishonour.
21 If a man therefore purge himself from
these, he shall be a vessel unto honour, sanctified,
and meet for the master's use, *and* [a]prepared unto
every good work.
22 [a]Flee also youthful lusts: but follow righteousness, faith, charity, peace, with them that
call on the Lord out of a pure heart.
23 But foolish and unlearned questions
avoid, knowing that they do gender strifes.
24 And [a]the servant of the Lord must not
strive; but be gentle unto all *men,* [b]apt to teach,
[c]patient,
25 [a]In meekness instructing those that oppose themselves; [b]if God peradventure will give
them repentance [c]to the acknowledging of the
truth;
26 And *that* they may recover themselves
[a]out of the snare of the devil, who are taken captive by him at his will.

18 [c]Heb. 6:10

CHAPTER 2

1 [a]1 Tim. 1:2 [b]Eph. 6:10
3 [a]2 Tim. 4:5 [b]1 Cor. 9:7; 1 Tim. 1:18
4 [a][2 Pet. 2:20]
5 [a][1 Cor. 9:25]
7 [a]Prov. 2:6
8 [a]Rom. 1:3, 4 [b]1 Cor. 15:4 [c]Rom. 2:16
9 [a]Acts 9:16 [b]Eph. 3:1 [c]Acts 28:31; [2 Tim. 4:17]
10 [a]Eph. 3:13 [b]2 Cor. 1:6; 1 Thess. 5:9
11 [a]Rom. 6:5, 8; 1 Thess. 5:10
12 [a][Matt. 19:28]; Luke 22:29; [Rom. 5:17; 8:17] [b]Matt. 10:33; Luke 12:9; 1 Tim. 5:8
13 [a]Num. 23:19; Titus 1:2
14 [a]1 Tim. 5:21; 6:4; 2 Tim. 2:23; Titus 3:9
15 [a]1 Tim. 4:13; 2 Pet. 1:10
17 [a]1 Tim. 1:20
18 [a]1 Cor. 15:12
19 [a]Matt. 24:24; [1 Cor. 3:11] [b]Num. 16:5; [Nah. 1:7]; John 10:14, 27
20 [a]Rom. 9:21
21 [a]2 Cor. 9:8; [Eph. 2:10]; 2 Tim. 3:17
22 [a]1 Tim. 6:11
24 [a]Titus 3:2 [b]Titus 1:9 [c]1 Tim. 3:3; Titus 1:7
25 [a]Gal. 6:1; Titus 3:2; 1 Pet. 3:15 [b]Acts 8:22 [c]1 Tim. 2:4
26 [a]1 Tim. 3:7

NKJV

very well how many ways he [c]ministered **to me*
at Ephesus.

Be Strong in Grace

2 You therefore, [a]my son, [b]be strong in the
grace that is in Christ Jesus.
2 And the things that you have heard from
me among many witnesses, commit these to faithful men who will be able to teach others also.
3 You therefore must [a]endure* hardship [b]as
a good soldier of Jesus Christ.
4 [a]No one engaged in warfare entangles
himself with the affairs of *this* life, that he may
please him who enlisted him as a soldier.
5 And also [a]if anyone competes in athletics,
he is not crowned unless he competes according
to the rules.
6 The hardworking farmer must be first to
partake of the crops.
7 Consider what I say, and *may the Lord
[a]give you understanding in all things.
8 Remember that Jesus Christ, [a]of the seed
of David, [b]was raised from the dead [c]according
to my gospel,
9 [a]for which I suffer trouble as an evildoer,
[b]*even* to the point of chains; [c]but the word of God
is not chained.
10 Therefore [a]I endure all things for the sake
of the elect, [b]that they also may obtain the salvation which is in Christ Jesus with eternal glory.
11 *This is* a faithful saying:

For [a]if we died with *Him,*
We shall also live with *Him.*
12 [a]If we endure,
We shall also reign with *Him.*
[b]If we deny *Him,*
He also will deny us.
13 If we are faithless,
He remains faithful;
He [a]cannot deny Himself.

Approved and Disapproved Workers

14 Remind *them* of these things, [a]charging
them before the Lord not to strive about words
to no profit, to the ruin of the hearers.
15 [a]Be diligent to present yourself approved
to God, a worker who does not need to be
ashamed, rightly dividing the word of truth.
16 But shun profane *and* idle babblings, for
they will increase to more ungodliness.
17 And their message will spread like cancer.
[a]Hymenaeus and Philetus are of this sort,
18 who have strayed concerning the truth,
[a]saying that the resurrection is already past; and
they overthrow the faith of some.
19 Nevertheless [a]the solid foundation of God
stands, having this seal: "The Lord [b]knows those
who are His," and, "Let everyone who names the
name of *Christ depart from iniquity."
20 But in a great house there are not
only [a]vessels of gold and silver, but also of
wood and clay, some for honor and some for
dishonor.
21 Therefore if anyone cleanses himself from
the latter, he will be a vessel for honor, sanctified
and useful for the Master, [a]prepared for every
good work.
22 [a]Flee also youthful lusts; but pursue righteousness, faith, love, peace with those who call
on the Lord out of a pure heart.
23 But avoid foolish and ignorant disputes,
knowing that they generate strife.
24 And [a]a servant of the Lord must not
quarrel but be gentle to all, [b]able to teach,
[c]patient,
25 [a]in humility correcting those who are in
opposition, [b]if God perhaps will grant them repentance, [c]so that they may know the truth,
26 and *that* they may come to their senses
and [a]*escape* the snare of the devil, having been
taken captive by him to *do* his will.

*

1:18 *to me* from Vg., a few Gr. mss.
2:3 NU *You must share*
2:7 NU *the Lord will give you*
2:19 NU, M *the Lord*

KJV

Perilous Times and Perilous Men

3 This know also, that [a]in the last days perilous times shall come.

2 For men shall be lovers of their own selves, covetous, boasters, proud, blasphemers, disobedient to parents, unthankful, unholy,

3 Without natural affection, trucebreakers, false accusers, incontinent, fierce, despisers of those that are good,

4 [a]Traitors, heady, highminded, lovers of pleasures more than lovers of God;

5 [a]Having a form of godliness, but [b]denying the power thereof: [c]from such turn away.

6 For [a]of this sort are they which creep into houses, and lead captive silly women laden with sins, led away with divers lusts,

7 Ever learning, and never able [a]to come to the knowledge of the truth.

8 [a]Now as Jannes and Jambres withstood Moses, so do these also resist the truth: [b]men of corrupt minds, [c]reprobate concerning the faith.

9 But they shall proceed no further: for their folly shall be manifest unto all *men*, [a]as their's also was.

The Man of God and the Word of God

10 [a]But thou hast fully known my doctrine, manner of life, purpose, faith, longsuffering, charity, patience,

11 Persecutions, afflictions, which came unto me [a]at Antioch, [b]at Iconium, [c]at Lystra; what persecutions I endured: but [d]out of *them* all the Lord delivered me.

12 Yea, and [a]all that will live godly in Christ Jesus shall suffer persecution.

13 [a]But evil men and seducers shall wax worse and worse, deceiving, and being deceived.

14 But [a]continue thou in the things which thou hast learned and hast been assured of, knowing of whom thou hast learned *them;*

15 And that from a child thou hast known [a]the holy scriptures, which are able to make thee wise unto salvation through faith which is in Christ Jesus.

16 [a]All scripture *is* given by inspiration of God, [b]and *is* profitable for doctrine, for reproof, for correction, for instruction in righteousness:

17 [a]That the man of God may be perfect, [b]throughly furnished unto all good works.

Preach the Word

4 I [a]charge *thee* therefore before God, and the Lord Jesus Christ, [b]who shall judge the quick and the dead at his appearing and his kingdom;

2 Preach the word; be instant in season, out of season; [a]reprove, [b]rebuke, [c]exhort with all longsuffering and doctrine.

3 [a]For the time will come when they will not endure [b]sound doctrine; [c]but after their own lusts shall they heap to themselves teachers, having itching ears;

4 And they shall turn away *their* ears from the truth, and [a]shall be turned unto fables.

5 But watch thou in all things, [a]endure afflictions, do the work of [b]an evangelist, make full proof of thy ministry.

Paul's Valedictory

6 For [a]I am now ready to be offered, and the time of [b]my departure is at hand.

7 [a]I have fought a good fight, I have finished *my* course, I have kept the faith:

8 Henceforth there is laid up for me [a]a crown of righteousness, which the Lord, the righteous [b]judge, shall give me [c]at that day: and not to me only, but unto all them also that love his appearing.

The Abandoned Apostle

9 Do thy diligence to come shortly unto me:

10 For [a]Demas hath forsaken me, [b]having

CHAPTER 3

1 [a]1 Tim. 4:1; 2 Pet. 3:3; 1 John 2:18; Jude 17, 18
4 [a]2 Pet. 2:10
5 [a]Titus 1:16 [b]1 Tim. 5:8 [c]Matt. 23:3; 2 Thess. 3:6; 1 Tim. 6:5
6 [a]Matt. 23:14; Titus 1:11
7 [a]1 Tim. 2:4
8 [a]Ex. 7:11, 12, 22; 8:7; 9:11 [b]1 Tim. 6:5 [c]Rom. 1:28
9 [a]Ex. 7:11, 12; 8:18; 9:11
10 [a]Phil. 2:20, 22; 1 Tim. 4:6
11 [a]Acts 13:44–52 [b]Acts 14:1–6, 19 [c]Acts 14:8–20 [d]Ps. 34:19
12 [a][Ps. 34:19]
13 [a]2 Thess. 2:11
14 [a]2 Tim. 1:13; Titus 1:9
15 [a]Ps. 119:97–104; John 5:39
16 [a][2 Pet. 1:20] [b]Rom. 4:23; 15:4
17 [a]1 Tim. 6:11 [b]2 Tim. 2:21; Heb. 13:21

CHAPTER 4

1 [a]1 Tim. 5:21; 2 Tim. 4:1 [b]Acts 10:42
2 [a]Titus 2:15 [b]1 Tim. 5:20; Titus 1:13; 2:15 [c]1 Tim. 4:13
3 [a]2 Tim. 3:1 [b]1 Tim. 1:10; 2 Tim. 1:13 [c]Is. 30:9–11; Jer. 5:30, 31; 2 Tim. 3:6
4 [a]1 Tim. 1:4
5 [a]2 Tim. 1:8 [b]Acts 21:8
6 [a]Phil. 2:17 [b][Phil. 1:23]; 2 Pet. 1:14
7 [a]1 Cor. 9:24–27; Phil. 3:13, 14
8 [a][1 Cor. 9:25; 2 Tim. 2:5]; James 1:12 [b]John 5:22 [c]2 Tim. 1:12
10 [a]Col. 4:14; Philem. 24 [b]1 John 2:15

*________

4:1 NU omits *therefore* • NU *and by*

NKJV

Perilous Times and Perilous Men

3 But know this, that [a]in the last days perilous times will come:

2 For men will be lovers of themselves, lovers of money, boasters, proud, blasphemers, disobedient to parents, unthankful, unholy,

3 unloving, unforgiving, slanderers, without self-control, brutal, despisers of good,

4 [a]traitors, headstrong, haughty, lovers of pleasure rather than lovers of God,

5 [a]having a form of godliness but [b]denying its power. And [c]from such people turn away!

6 For [a]of this sort are those who creep into households and make captives of gullible women loaded down with sins, led away by various lusts,

7 always learning and never able [a]to come to the knowledge of the truth.

8 [a]Now as Jannes and Jambres resisted Moses, so do these also resist the truth: [b]men of corrupt minds, [c]disapproved concerning the faith;

9 but they will progress no further, for their folly will be manifest to all, [a]as theirs also was.

The Man of God and the Word of God

10 [a]But you have carefully followed my doctrine, manner of life, purpose, faith, longsuffering, love, perseverance,

11 persecutions, afflictions, which happened to me [a]at Antioch, [b]at Iconium, [c]at Lystra—what persecutions I endured. And [d]out of *them* all the Lord delivered me.

12 Yes, and [a]all who desire to live godly in Christ Jesus will suffer persecution.

13 [a]But evil men and impostors will grow worse and worse, deceiving and being deceived.

14 But you must [a]continue in the things which you have learned and been assured of, knowing from whom you have learned *them,*

15 and that from childhood you have known [a]the Holy Scriptures, which are able to make you wise for salvation through faith which is in Christ Jesus.

16 [a]All Scripture *is* given by inspiration of God, [b]and *is* profitable for doctrine, for reproof, for correction, for instruction in righteousness,

17 [a]that the man of God may be complete, [b]thoroughly equipped for every good work.

Preach the Word

4 I [a]charge *you* *therefore before God and the Lord Jesus Christ, [b]who will judge the living and the dead *at His appearing and His kingdom:

2 Preach the word! Be ready in season *and* out of season. [a]Convince, [b]rebuke, [c]exhort, with all longsuffering and teaching.

3 [a]For the time will come when they will not endure [b]sound doctrine, [c]but according to their own desires, *because* they have itching ears, they will heap up for themselves teachers;

4 and they will turn *their* ears away from the truth, and [a]be turned aside to fables.

5 But you be watchful in all things, [a]endure afflictions, do the work of [b]an evangelist, fulfill your ministry.

Paul's Valedictory

6 For [a]I am already being poured out as a drink offering, and the time of [b]my departure is at hand.

7 [a]I have fought the good fight, I have finished the race, I have kept the faith.

8 Finally, there is laid up for me [a]the crown of righteousness, which the Lord, the righteous [b]Judge, will give to me [c]on that Day, and not to me only but also to all who have loved His appearing.

The Abandoned Apostle

9 Be diligent to come to me quickly;

10 for [a]Demas has forsaken me, [b]having

KJV

loved this present world, and is departed unto Thessalonica; Crescens to Galatia, Titus unto Dalmatia.

11 Only Luke is with me. Take [a]Mark, and bring him with thee: for he is profitable to me for the ministry.

12 And [a]Tychicus have I sent to Ephesus.

13 The cloke that I left at Troas with Carpus, when thou comest, bring *with thee*, and the books, *but* especially the parchments.

14 [a]Alexander the coppersmith did me much evil: the Lord reward him according to his works:

15 Of whom be thou ware also; for he hath greatly withstood our words.

16 At my first answer no man stood with me, but all *men* forsook me: [a]*I pray God* that it may not be laid to their charge.

The Lord Is Faithful

17 [a]Notwithstanding the Lord stood with me, and strengthened me; [b]that by me the preaching might be fully known, and *that* all the Gentiles might hear: and I was delivered [c]out of the mouth of the lion.

18 [a]And the Lord shall deliver me from every evil work, and will preserve *me* unto his heavenly kingdom: [b]to whom *be* glory for ever and ever. Amen.

Come Before Winter

19 Salute [a]Prisca and Aquila, and the household of [b]Onesiphorus.

20 [a]Erastus abode at Corinth: but [b]Trophimus have I left at Miletum sick.

21 Do thy diligence to come before winter. Eubulus greeteth thee, and Pudens, and Linus, and Claudia, and all the brethren.

Farewell

22 The Lord Jesus Christ *be* with thy spirit. Grace *be* with you. Amen.

11 [a]Acts 12:12, 25; 15:37–39; Col. 4:10
12 [a]Acts 20:4; Eph. 6:21, 22; Col. 4:7; Titus 3:12
14 [a]Acts 19:33; 1 Tim. 1:20
16 [a]Acts 7:60; [1 Cor. 13:5]
17 [a]Deut. 31:6; Acts 23:11 [b]Acts 9:15; Phil. 1:12 [c]1 Sam. 17:37; Ps. 22:21
18 [a]Ps. 121:7; [2 Pet. 2:9] [b]Rom. 11:36; Gal. 1:5; Heb. 13:21; 2 Pet. 3:18
19 [a]Acts 18:2; Rom. 16:3 [b]2 Tim. 1:16
20 [a]Acts 19:22; Rom. 16:23 [b]Acts 20:4; 21:29

*
4:22 NU omits *Jesus Christ*

NKJV

loved this present world, and has departed for Thessalonica—Crescens for Galatia, Titus for Dalmatia.

11 Only Luke is with me. Get [a]Mark and bring him with you, for he is useful to me for ministry.

12 And [a]Tychicus I have sent to Ephesus.

13 Bring the cloak that I left with Carpus at Troas when you come—and the books, especially the parchments.

14 [a]Alexander the coppersmith did me much harm. May the Lord repay him according to his works.

15 You also must beware of him, for he has greatly resisted our words.

16 At my first defense no one stood with me, but all forsook me. [a]May it not be charged against them.

The Lord Is Faithful

17 [a]But the Lord stood with me and strengthened me, [b]so that the message might be preached fully through me, and *that* all the Gentiles might hear. Also I was delivered [c]out of the mouth of the lion.

18 [a]And the Lord will deliver me from every evil work and preserve *me* for His heavenly kingdom. [b]To Him *be* glory forever and ever. Amen!

Come Before Winter

19 Greet [a]Prisca and Aquila, and the household of [b]Onesiphorus.

20 [a]Erastus stayed in Corinth, but [b]Trophimus I have left in Miletus sick.

21 Do your utmost to come before winter. Eubulus greets you, as well as Pudens, Linus, Claudia, and all the brethren.

Farewell

22 The Lord *Jesus Christ be with your spirit. Grace be with you. Amen.

KJV

THE EPISTLE OF PAUL THE APOSTLE TO

TITUS

Greeting

1 Paul a servant of God, and an apostle of Jesus Christ, according to the faith of God's elect, and [a]the cknowledging of the truth [b]which is after godliness;

2 In hope of eternal life, which God, that [a]cannot lie, promised before the world began;

3 But hath in due times manifested his word through preaching, which is committed unto me according to the commandment of God our Saviour;

4 To [a]Titus, *mine* own son after the common faith: Grace, mercy, *and* peace, from God the Father and the Lord Jesus Christ our Saviour.

Qualified Elders

5 For this cause left I thee in Crete, that thou shouldest [a]set in order the things that are wanting, and ordain elders in every city, as I had appointed thee:

6 If any be blameless, the husband of one wife, [a]having faithful children not accused of riot or unruly.

7 For a bishop must be blameless, as the steward of God; not selfwilled, not soon angry, [a]not given to wine, no striker, not given to filthy lucre;

8 But a lover of hospitality, a lover of good men, sober, just, holy, temperate;

9 Holding fast the faithful word as he hath been taught, that he may be able by sound doctrine both to exhort and to convince the gainsayers.

The Elders' Task

10 For there are many unruly and vain [a]talkers and deceivers, specially they of the circumcision:

11 Whose mouths must be stopped, who subvert whole houses, teaching things which they ought not, [a]for filthy lucre's sake.

12 [a]One of themselves, *even* a prophet of their own, said, The Cretians *are* alway liars, evil beasts, slow bellies.

13 This witness is true. [a]Wherefore rebuke them sharply, that they may be sound in the faith;

14 Not giving heed to Jewish fables, and [a]commandments of men, that turn from the truth.

15 [a]Unto the pure all things *are* pure: but unto them that are defiled and unbelieving *is* nothing pure; but even their mind and conscience is defiled.

16 They profess that they [a]know God; but [b]in works they deny *him*, being abominable, and disobedient, [c]and unto every good work reprobate.

Qualities of a Sound Church

2 But speak thou the things which become sound doctrine:

2 That the aged men be sober, grave, temperate, sound in faith, in charity, in patience.

3 The aged women likewise, that *they be*

CHAPTER 1

1 [a]2 Tim. 2:25 [b][1 Tim. 3:16]
2 [a]Num. 23:19
4 [a]2 Cor. 2:13; 8:23; Gal. 2:3; 2 Tim. 4:10
5 [a]1 Cor. 11:34
6 [a]1 Tim. 3:2–4; Titus 1:6–8
7 [a]Lev. 10:9
10 [a]James 1:26
11 [a]1 Tim. 6:5
12 [a]Acts 17:28
13 [a]2 Cor. 13:10; 2 Tim. 4:2
14 [a]Is. 29:13
15 [a]Luke 11:41; Rom. 14:14, 20; 1 Cor. 6:12
16 [a]Matt. 7:20–23; 25:12; 1 John 2:4 [b][2 Tim. 3:5, 7] [c]Rom. 1:28

*

1:4 NU *Christ Jesus*
1:7 Lit. *overseer*

NKJV

THE EPISTLE OF PAUL THE APOSTLE TO

TITUS

Greeting

1 Paul, a bondservant of God and an apostle of Jesus Christ, according to the faith of God's elect and [a]the acknowledgment of the truth [b]which accords with godliness,

2 in hope of eternal life which God, who [a]cannot lie, promised before time began,

3 but has in due time manifested His word through preaching, which was committed to me according to the commandment of God our Savior;

4 To [a]Titus, a true son in *our* common faith:

Grace, mercy, *and* peace from God the Father and *the Lord Jesus Christ our Savior.

Qualified Elders

5 For this reason I left you in Crete, that you should [a]set in order the things that are lacking, and appoint elders in every city as I commanded you—

6 if a man is blameless, the husband of one wife, [a]having faithful children not accused of dissipation or insubordination.

7 For a *bishop must be blameless, as a steward of God, not self-willed, not quick-tempered, [a]not given to wine, not violent, not greedy for money,

8 but hospitable, a lover of what is good, sober-minded, just, holy, self-controlled,

9 holding fast the faithful word as he has been taught, that he may be able, by sound doctrine, both to exhort and convict those who contradict.

The Elders' Task

10 For there are many insubordinate, both idle [a]talkers and deceivers, especially those of the circumcision,

11 whose mouths must be stopped, who subvert whole households, teaching things which they ought not, [a]for the sake of dishonest gain.

12 [a]One of them, a prophet of their own, said, "Cretans *are* always liars, evil beasts, lazy gluttons."

13 This testimony is true. [a]Therefore rebuke them sharply, that they may be sound in the faith,

14 not giving heed to Jewish fables and [a]commandments of men who turn from the truth.

15 [a]To the pure all things are pure, but to those who are defiled and unbelieving nothing is pure; but even their mind and conscience are defiled.

16 They profess to [a]know God, but [b]in works they deny Him, being abominable, disobedient, [c]and disqualified for every good work.

Qualities of a Sound Church

2 But as for you, speak the things which are proper for sound doctrine:

2 that the older men be sober, reverent, temperate, sound in faith, in love, in patience;

3 the older women likewise, that they be

KJV

in behaviour as becometh holiness, not false accusers, not given to much wine, teachers of good
things;
4 That they may teach the young women
to be sober, to love their husbands, to love their
children,
5 *To be* discreet, chaste, keepers at [a]home,
good, [b]obedient to their own husbands, [c]that the
word of God be not blasphemed.
6 Young men likewise exhort to be sober
minded.
7 In all things shewing thyself a [a]pattern of
good works: in doctrine *shewing* uncorruptness,
gravity, [b]sincerity,
8 Sound speech, that cannot be condemned;
that he that is of the contrary part may be
ashamed, having no evil thing to say of you.
9 *Exhort* [a]servants to be obedient unto their
own masters, *and* to please *them* well in all *things;*
not answering again;
10 Not purloining, but shewing all good fidelity; that they may adorn the doctrine of God our
Saviour in all things.

Trained by Saving Grace

11 For [a]the grace of God that bringeth salvation hath appeared to all men,
12 Teaching us that, denying ungodliness
and worldly lusts, we should live soberly, righteously, and godly, in this present world;
13 [a]Looking for that blessed [b]hope, and the
glorious appearing of the great God and our Saviour Jesus Christ;
14 [a]Who gave himself for us, that he might
redeem us from all iniquity, [b]and purify unto himself [c]a peculiar people, zealous of good works.
15 These things speak, and [a]exhort, and
rebuke with all authority. Let no man despise
thee.

Graces of the Heirs of Grace

3 Put them in mind [a]to be subject to principalities and powers, to obey magistrates, [b]to be
ready to every good work,
2 To speak evil of no man, to be no brawl-
ers, *but* gentle, shewing all meekness unto all
men.
3 For [a]we ourselves also were sometimes
foolish, disobedient, deceived, serving divers lusts
and pleasures, living in malice and envy, hateful,
and hating one another.
4 But after that [a]the kindness and love of
[b]God our Saviour toward man appeared,
5 [a]Not by works of righteousness which we
have done, but according to his mercy he saved
us, by [b]the washing of regeneration, and renewing of the Holy Ghost;
6 [a]Which he shed on us abundantly through
Jesus Christ our Saviour;
7 That being justified by his grace, [a]we
should be made heirs according to the hope of
eternal life.
8 [a]*This is* a faithful saying, and these things
I will that thou affirm constantly, that they which
have believed in God might be careful to maintain
good works. These things are good and profitable
unto men.

Avoid Dissension

9 But [a]avoid foolish questions, and genealogies, and contentions, and strivings about the law;
for they are unprofitable and vain.
10 A man that is an heretick after the first
and second admonition [a]reject;
11 Knowing that he that is such is subverted,
and sinneth, being condemned of himself.

Final Messages

12 When I shall send Artemas unto thee, or
[a]Tychicus, be diligent to come unto me to Nicopolis: for I have determined there to winter.
13 Bring Zenas the lawyer and [a]Apollos on

CHAPTER 2
5 [a]1 Tim. 5:14 [b]1 Cor. 14:34; 1 Tim. 2:11 [c]Rom. 2:24
7 [a]Phil. 3:17; 1 Tim. 4:12 [b]Eph. 6:24
9 [a]Eph. 6:5; 1 Tim. 6:1
11 [a][Rom. 5:15]
13 [a]1 Cor. 1:7 [b][Col. 3:4]
14 [a]Is. 53:12; Gal. 1:4 [b]Ezek. 37:23; [Heb. 1:3; 9:14; 1 John 1:7] [c]Ex. 15:16
15 [a]1 Tim. 4:13; 5:20; 2 Tim. 4:2

CHAPTER 3
1 [a][Rom. 13:1]; 1 Pet. 2:13 [b]Col. 1:10
3 [a]1 Cor. 6:11; 1 Pet. 4:3
4 [a]Titus 2:11 [b]1 Tim. 2:3
5 [a][Rom. 3:20]; Eph. 2:4–9 [b]John 3:3
6 [a]Ezek. 36:25
7 [a][Matt. 25:34]; Mark 10:17; [Rom. 8:17, 23, 24; Titus 1:2]
8 [a]1 Tim. 1:15
9 [a]1 Tim. 1:4; 2 Tim. 2:23
10 [a]Matt. 18:17
12 [a]Acts 20:4; Eph. 6:21; Col. 4:7; 2 Tim. 4:12
13 [a]Acts 18:24; 1 Cor. 16:12

*
2:7 NU omits *incorruptibility*
2:8 NU, M *us*

NKJV

reverent in behavior, not slanderers, not given to
much wine, teachers of good things—
4 that they admonish the young women to
love their husbands, to love their children,
5 to be discreet, chaste, [a]homemakers,
good, [b]obedient to their own husbands, [c]that the
word of God may not be blasphemed.
6 Likewise, exhort the young men to be
sober-minded,
7 in all things showing yourself *to be* [a]a pattern of good works; in doctrine *showing* integrity,
reverence, [b]incorruptibility,*
8 sound speech that cannot be condemned,
that one who is an opponent may be ashamed,
having nothing evil to say of *you.
9 *Exhort* [a]bondservants to be obedient to
their own masters, to be well pleasing in all
things, not answering back,
10 not pilfering, but showing all good fidelity,
that they may adorn the doctrine of God our Savior in all things.

Trained by Saving Grace

11 For [a]the grace of God that brings salvation
has appeared to all men,
12 teaching us that, denying ungodliness and
worldly lusts, we should live soberly, righteously,
and godly in the present age,
13 [a]looking for the blessed [b]hope and glorious appearing of our great God and Savior Jesus
Christ,
14 [a]who gave Himself for us, that He might
redeem us from every lawless deed [b]and purify
for Himself [c]*His* own special people, zealous for
good works.
15 Speak these things, [a]exhort, and rebuke
with all authority. Let no one despise you.

Graces of the Heirs of Grace

3 Remind them [a]to be subject to rulers and authorities, to obey, [b]to be ready for every good
work,
2 to speak evil of no one, to be peaceable,
gentle, showing all humility to all men.
3 For [a]we ourselves were also once foolish,
disobedient, deceived, serving various lusts and
pleasures, living in malice and envy, hateful and
hating one another.
4 But when [a]the kindness and the love of
[b]God our Savior toward man appeared,
5 [a]not by works of righteousness which we
have done, but according to His mercy He saved
us, through [b]the washing of regeneration and renewing of the Holy Spirit,
6 [a]whom He poured out on us abundantly
through Jesus Christ our Savior,
7 that having been justified by His grace
[a]we should become heirs according to the hope
of eternal life.
8 [a]This is a faithful saying, and these things
I want you to affirm constantly, that those who
have believed in God should be careful to maintain good works. These things are good and profitable to men.

Avoid Dissension

9 But [a]avoid foolish disputes, genealogies,
contentions, and strivings about the law; for they
are unprofitable and useless.
10 [a]Reject a divisive man after the first and
second admonition,
11 knowing that such a person is warped and
sinning, being self-condemned.

Final Messages

12 When I send Artemas to you, or [a]Tychi-
cus, be diligent to come to me at Nicopolis, for I
have decided to spend the winter there.
13 Send Zenas the lawyer and [a]Apollos on

KJV

their journey diligently, that nothing be wanting unto them.
14 And let our's also learn to maintain good works for necessary uses, that they be not unfruitful.

Farewell

15 All that are with me salute thee. Greet them that love us in the faith. Grace *be* with you all. Amen.

NKJV

their journey with haste, that they may lack nothing.
14 And let our *people* also learn to maintain good works, to *meet* urgent needs, that they may not be unfruitful.

Farewell

15 All who *are* with me greet you. Greet those who love us in the faith. Grace *be* with you all. Amen.

KJV

THE EPISTLE OF PAUL THE APOSTLE TO

PHILEMON

Greeting

Paul, a [a]prisoner of Jesus Christ, and Timothy *our* brother, unto Philemon our dearly beloved, and fellowlabourer,

2 And to *our* beloved Apphia, and [a]Archippus our fellowsoldier, and to the church in thy house:

3 Grace to you, and peace, from God our Father and the Lord Jesus Christ.

Philemon's Love and Faith

4 [a]I thank my God, making mention of thee always in my prayers,

5 [a]Hearing of thy love and faith, which thou hast toward the Lord Jesus, and toward all saints;

6 That the communication of thy faith may become effectual [a]by the acknowledging of [b]every good thing which is in you in Christ Jesus.

7 For we have great joy and consolation in thy love, because the bowels of the saints are refreshed by thee, brother.

The Plea for Onesimus

8 Wherefore, though I might be much bold in Christ to enjoin thee that which is convenient,

9 Yet for love's sake I rather beseech *thee*, being such an one as Paul the aged, and now also a prisoner of Jesus Christ.

10 I beseech thee for my son [a]Onesimus, whom I have begotten in my bonds:

11 Which in time past was to thee unprofitable, but now profitable to thee and to me:

12 Whom I have sent again: thou therefore receive him, that is, mine own bowels:

13 Whom I would have retained with me, that in thy stead he might have ministered unto me in the bonds of the gospel:

14 But without thy mind would I do nothing; [a]that thy benefit should not be as it were of necessity, but willingly.

15 For perhaps he therefore departed for a season, that thou shouldest receive him for ever;

16 Not now as a servant, but above a servant, a brother beloved, specially to me, but how much more unto thee, both in the [a]flesh, and in the Lord?

Philemon's Obedience Encouraged

17 If thou count me therefore a partner, receive him as myself.

18 If he hath wronged thee, or oweth *thee* ought, put that on mine account;

19 I Paul have written *it* with mine own [a]hand, I will repay *it*: albeit I do not say to thee how thou owest unto me even thine own self besides.

20 Yea, brother, let me have joy of thee in the Lord: refresh my bowels in the Lord.

21 [a]Having confidence in thy obedience I wrote unto thee, knowing that thou wilt also do more than I say.

22 But withal prepare me also a lodging: for [a]I trust that [b]through your prayers I shall be given unto you.

1 [a]Eph. 3:1
2 [a]Col. 4:17
4 [a]Eph. 1:16; 1 Thess. 1:2; 2 Thess. 1:3
5 [a]Eph. 1:15; Col. 1:4; 1 Thess. 3:6
6 [a]Phil. 1:9; [Col. 1:9; 3:10; James 2:14–17] [b][1 Thess. 5:18]
10 [a]Col. 4:9
14 [a]2 Cor. 9:7; 1 Pet. 5:2
16 [a]Eph. 6:5; Col. 3:22
19 [a]1 Cor. 16:21; Gal. 6:11; 2 Thess. 3:17
21 [a]2 Cor. 7:16
22 [a]Phil. 1:25; 2:24 [b]2 Cor. 1:11

*

2 NU *our sister Apphia*
6 NU, M *us*
7 NU *had* • M *thanksgiving*
12 NU *back to you in person, that is, my own heart,*

NKJV

THE EPISTLE OF PAUL THE APOSTLE TO

PHILEMON

Greeting

Paul, a [a]prisoner of Christ Jesus, and Timothy *our* brother,

To Philemon our beloved *friend* and fellow laborer,

2 to *the beloved Apphia, [a]Archippus our fellow soldier, and to the church in your house:

3 Grace to you and peace from God our Father and the Lord Jesus Christ.

Philemon's Love and Faith

4 [a]I thank my God, making mention of you always in my prayers,

5 [a]hearing of your love and faith which you have toward the Lord Jesus and toward all the saints,

6 that the sharing of your faith may become effective [a]by the acknowledgment of [b]every good thing which is in *you in Christ Jesus.

7 For we *have great *joy and consolation in your love, because the hearts of the saints have been refreshed by you, brother.

The Plea for Onesimus

8 Therefore, though I might be very bold in Christ to command you what is fitting,

9 *yet* for love's sake I rather appeal *to you*—being such a one as Paul, the aged, and now also a prisoner of Jesus Christ—

10 I appeal to you for my son [a]Onesimus, whom I have begotten *while* in my chains,

11 who once was unprofitable to you, but now is profitable to you and to me.

12 I am sending him *back. You therefore receive him, that is, my own heart,

13 whom I wished to keep with me, that on your behalf he might minister to me in my chains for the gospel.

14 But without your consent I wanted to do nothing, [a]that your good deed might not be by compulsion, as it were, but voluntary.

15 For perhaps he departed for a while for this *purpose*, that you might receive him forever,

16 no longer as a slave but more than a slave—a beloved brother, especially to me but how much more to you, both in the [a]flesh and in the Lord.

Philemon's Obedience Encouraged

17 If then you count me as a partner, receive him as *you would* me.

18 But if he has wronged you or owes anything, put that on my account.

19 I, Paul, am writing with my own [a]hand. I will repay—not to mention to you that you owe me even your own self besides.

20 Yes, brother, let me have joy from you in the Lord; refresh my heart in the Lord.

21 [a]Having confidence in your obedience, I write to you, knowing that you will do even more than I say.

22 But, meanwhile, also prepare a guest room for me, for [a]I trust that [b]through your prayers I shall be granted to you.

KJV

Farewell

23 There salute thee [a]Epaphras, my fellowprisoner in Christ Jesus;
24 [a]Marcus, [b]Aristarchus, [c]Demas, [d]Lucas,
my fellowlabourers.
25 [a]The grace of our Lord Jesus Christ *be*
with your spirit. Amen.

23 [a]Col. 1:7; 4:12 **24** [a]Acts 12:12, 25; 15:37–39 [b]Acts 19:29; 27:2 [c]Col. 4:14 [d]2 Tim. 4:11 **25** [a]2 Tim. 4:22

NKJV

Farewell

23 [a]Epaphras, my fellow prisoner in Christ
Jesus, greets you,
24 *as do* [a]Mark, [b]Aristarchus, [c]Demas,
[d]Luke, my fellow laborers.
25 [a]The grace of our Lord Jesus Christ *be*
with your spirit. Amen.

KJV

THE EPISTLE TO THE

HEBREWS

God's Supreme Revelation
(cf. John 1:1–4)

1 God, who at sundry times and [a]in divers
manners spake in time past unto the fathers
by the prophets,
2 Hath in these last days spoken unto us by
his Son, whom he hath appointed heir of all
things, by whom also he made the worlds;
3 [a]Who being the brightness of *his* glory,
and the express [b]image of his person, and [c]up-
holding all things by the word of his power, [d]when
he had by himself purged our sins, [e]sat down on
the right hand of the Majesty on high;
4 Being made so much better than the angels, as [a]he hath by inheritance obtained a more
excellent name than they.

The Son Exalted Above Angels

5 For unto which of the angels said he at
any time, [a]THOU ART MY SON, THIS DAY HAVE I
BEGOTTEN THEE? And again, [b]I WILL BE TO HIM A
FATHER, AND HE SHALL BE TO ME A SON?
6 And again, when he bringeth in [a]the first-
begotten into the world, he saith, [b]AND LET ALL
THE ANGELS OF GOD WORSHIP HIM.
7 And of the angels he saith, [a]WHO MAKETH
HIS ANGELS SPIRITS, AND HIS MINISTERS A FLAME OF
FIRE.
8 But unto the Son *he saith,* [a]THY THRONE,
O GOD, *IS* FOR EVER AND EVER: A SCEPTRE OF RIGH-
TEOUSNESS *IS* THE SCEPTRE OF THY KINGDOM.
9 THOU HAST LOVED RIGHTEOUSNESS, AND
HATED INIQUITY; THEREFORE GOD, *EVEN* THY GOD,
[a]HATH ANOINTED THEE WITH THE OIL OF GLADNESS
ABOVE THY FELLOWS.
10 And, [a]THOU, LORD, IN THE BEGINNING HAST
LAID THE FOUNDATION OF THE EARTH; AND THE HEAV-
ENS ARE THE WORKS OF THINE HANDS:
11 [a]THEY SHALL PERISH; BUT THOU REMAINEST;
AND [b]THEY ALL SHALL WAX OLD AS DOTH A GARMENT;
12 AND AS A VESTURE SHALT THOU FOLD THEM
UP, AND THEY SHALL BE CHANGED: BUT THOU ART THE
[a]SAME, AND THY YEARS SHALL NOT FAIL.

CHAPTER 1
1 [a]Num. 12:6, 8; Joel 2:28
3 [a]John 1:14 [b]2 Cor. 4:4; Col. 1:15 [c]Col. 1:17 [d][Heb. 7:27] [e]Ps. 110:1
4 [a]Is. 9:6, 7; Luke 1:32, 33; [Phil. 2:9, 10]
5 [a]Ps. 2:7; Acts 13:33; Heb. 5:5 [b]2 Sam. 7:14
6 [a]Ps. 89:27; [Rom. 8:29] [b]Deut. 32:43, LXX, DSS; Ps. 97:7; 1 Pet. 3:22; Rev. 5:11–13
7 [a]Ps. 104:4
8 [a]Ps. 45:6, 7
9 [a]Is. 61:1, 3
10 [a]Ps. 102:25–27
11 [a][Is. 34:4] [b]Is. 50:9; 51:6; Heb. 8:13
12 [a]Heb. 13:8

*

1:3 NU omits *by Himself* • NU omits *our*

NKJV

THE EPISTLE TO THE

HEBREWS

God's Supreme Revelation
(cf. John 1:1–4)

1 God, who at various times and [a]in various
ways spoke in time past to the fathers by the
prophets,
2 has in these last days spoken to us by *His*
Son, whom He has appointed heir of all things,
through whom also He made the worlds;
3 [a]who being the brightness of *His* glory
and the express [b]image of His person, and [c]up-
holding all things by the word of His power, [d]when
He had *by Himself purged *our sins, [e]sat down
at the right hand of the Majesty on high,
4 having become so much better than the
angels, as [a]He has by inheritance obtained a more
excellent name than they.

The Son Exalted Above Angels

5 For to which of the angels did He ever
say:

[a]*"You are My Son,*
Today I have begotten You"?

And again:

[b]*"I will be to Him a Father,*
And He shall be to Me a Son"?

6 But when He again brings [a]the firstborn
into the world, He says:

[b]*"Let all the angels of God worship Him."*

7 And of the angels He says:

[a]*"Who makes His angels spirits*
And His ministers a flame of fire."

8 But to the Son *He says:*

[a]*"Your throne, O God, is forever and ever;*
A scepter of righteousness is the scepter of Your kingdom.
9 *You have loved righteousness and hated lawlessness;*
Therefore God, Your God, [a]*has anointed You*
With the oil of gladness more than Your companions."

10 And:

[a]*"You, LORD, in the beginning laid the foundation of the earth,*
And the heavens are the work of Your hands.
11 [a]*They will perish, but You remain;*
And [b]*they will all grow old like a garment;*
12 *Like a cloak You will fold them up,*
And they will be changed.
But You are the [a]*same,*
And Your years will not fail."

KJV

13 But to which of the angels said he at any
time, [a]SIT ON MY RIGHT HAND, UNTIL I MAKE THINE
ENEMIES THY FOOTSTOOL?
14 [a]Are they not all ministering spirits, sent
forth to minister for them who shall be [b]heirs of
salvation?

Do Not Neglect Salvation

2 Therefore we ought to give the more earnest
heed to the things which we have heard, lest
at any time we should let *them* slip.
2 For if the word [a]spoken by angels was
stedfast, and [b]every transgression and disobedience received a just recompence of reward;
3 [a]How shall we escape, if we neglect so
great salvation; [b]which at the first began to be
spoken by the Lord, and was [c]confirmed unto us
by them that heard *him;*
4 [a]God also bearing *them* witness, [b]both
with signs and wonders, and with divers miracles,
and [c]gifts of the Holy Ghost, [d]according to his
own will?

The Son Made Lower than Angels
(cf. Ps. 8:1–9)

5 For unto the angels hath he not put in subjection [a]the world to come, whereof we speak.
6 But one in a certain place testified, saying,
[a]WHAT IS MAN, THAT THOU ART MINDFUL OF HIM? OR
THE SON OF MAN, THAT THOU VISITEST HIM?
7 THOU MADEST HIM A LITTLE LOWER THAN
THE ANGELS; THOU CROWNEDST HIM WITH GLORY
AND HONOUR, AND DIDST SET HIM OVER THE WORKS
OF THY HANDS:
8 [a]THOU HAST PUT ALL THINGS IN SUBJECTION
UNDER HIS FEET. For in that he put all in subjection
under him, he left nothing *that is* not put under
him. But now [b]we see not yet all things put under
him.
9 But we see Jesus, [a]who was made a little
lower than the angels for the suffering of death,
[b]crowned with glory and honour; that he by the
grace of God should taste death [c]for every man.

Bringing Many Sons to Glory

10 For it became him, [a]for whom *are* all
things, and by whom *are* all things, in bringing
many sons unto glory, to make the captain of their
salvation [b]perfect through sufferings.
11 For [a]both he that sanctifieth and they who
are sanctified [b]*are* all of one: for which cause [c]he
is not ashamed to call them brethren,
12 Saying, [a]I WILL DECLARE THY NAME UNTO
MY BRETHREN, IN THE MIDST OF THE CHURCH WILL I
SING PRAISE UNTO THEE.
13 And again, [a]I WILL PUT MY TRUST IN HIM.
And again, [b]BEHOLD I AND THE CHILDREN WHICH
GOD HATH GIVEN ME.
14 Forasmuch then as the children are partakers of flesh and blood, he [a]also himself likewise took part of the same; [b]that through death
he might destroy him that had the power of
[c]death, that is, the devil;
15 And deliver them who [a]through fear of

13 [a]Ps. 110:1; Matt. 22:44; Heb. 1:3
14 [a]Ps. 103:20; Dan. 7:10 [b]Rom. 8:17

CHAPTER 2

2 [a]Deut. 33:2; Acts 7:53; Gal. 3:19 [b]Num. 15:30
3 [a]Heb. 10:28 [b]Matt. 4:17 [c]Mark 16:20; Luke 1:2; 1 John 1:1
4 [a]Mark 16:20 [b]Acts 2:22, 43; 2 Cor. 12:2 [c]1 Cor. 12:4, 7, 11; Eph. 4:7 [d]Eph. 1:5, 9
5 [a][2 Pet. 3:13]
6 [a]Job 7:17; Ps. 8:4–6
8 [a]Matt. 28:18 [b]Ps. 8:6; 1 Cor. 15:25, 27
9 [a]Phil. 2:7–9; Heb. 1:9 [b]Acts 2:33; 3:13; 1 Pet. 1:21 [c]Is. 53:12; [John 3:16]
10 [a]Col. 1:16 [b]Heb. 5:8, 9; 7:28
11 [a]Heb. 10:10 [b]Acts 17:26 [c]Matt. 28:10
12 [a]Ps. 22:22
13 [a]2 Sam. 22:3; Is. 8:17 [b]Is. 8:18
14 [a]John 1:14 [b]Col. 2:15 [c][1 Cor. 15:54–57]; 2 Tim. 1:10
15 [a]Ps. 68:18; Is. 42:7; 45:13; 49:9; 61:1; [Luke 1:74]

*

2:7 NU, M omit the rest of v. 7.

NKJV

13 But to which of the angels has He ever
said:

[a]*"Sit at My right hand,*
Till I make Your enemies Your
footstool"?

14 [a]Are they not all ministering spirits sent
forth to minister for those who will [b]inherit salvation?

Do Not Neglect Salvation

2 Therefore we must give the more earnest heed
to the things we have heard, lest we drift
away.
2 For if the word [a]spoken through angels
proved steadfast, and [b]every transgression and
disobedience received a just reward,
3 [a]how shall we escape if we neglect so
great a salvation, [b]which at the first began to be
spoken by the Lord, and was [c]confirmed to us
by those who heard *Him,*
4 [a]God also bearing witness [b]both with
signs and wonders, with various miracles, and
[c]gifts of the Holy Spirit, [d]according to His own
will?

The Son Made Lower than Angels
(cf. Ps. 8:1–9)

5 For He has not put [a]the world to come,
of which we speak, in subjection to angels.
6 But one testified in a certain place, saying:

[a]*"What is man that You are mindful of him,*
Or the son of man that You take care of
him?
7 *You have made him a little lower than the*
angels;
You have crowned him with glory and
honor,
**And set him over the works of Your*
hands.
8 [a]*You have put all things in subjection*
under his feet."

For in that He put all in subjection under him,
He left nothing *that is* not put under him. But
now [b]we do not yet see all things put under him.
9 But we see Jesus, [a]who was made a little
lower than the angels, for the suffering of death
[b]crowned with glory and honor, that He, by the
grace of God, might taste death [c]for everyone.

Bringing Many Sons to Glory

10 For it was fitting for Him, [a]for whom *are*
all things and by whom *are* all things, in bringing
many sons to glory, to make the captain of their
salvation [b]perfect through sufferings.
11 For [a]both He who sanctifies and those
who are being sanctified [b]*are* all of one, for which
reason [c]He is not ashamed to call them brethren,
12 saying:

[a]*"I will declare Your name to My brethren;*
In the midst of the assembly I will sing
praise to You."

13 And again:

[a]*"I will put My trust in Him."*

And again:

[b]*"Here am I and the children whom God has*
given Me."

14 Inasmuch then as the children have par-
taken of flesh and blood, He [a]Himself likewise
shared in the same, [b]that through death He might
destroy him who had the power of [c]death, that
is, the devil,
15 and release those who [a]through fear of

KJV

death were all their lifetime subject to bondage.
16 For verily he took not on *him the nature*
of angels; but he took on *him* the seed of
Abraham.
17 Wherefore in all things it behoved him [a]to
be made like unto *his* brethren, that he might be
[b]a merciful and faithful high priest in things *per-*
taining to God, to make reconciliation for the sins
of the people.
18 [a]For in that he himself hath suffered being
tempted, he is able to succour them that are
tempted.

The Son Was Faithful

3 Wherefore, holy brethren, partakers of the
heavenly calling, consider the Apostle and
High Priest of our profession, Christ Jesus;
2 Who was faithful to him that appointed
him, as also [a]Moses *was faithful* in all his house.
3 For this *man* was counted worthy of more
glory than Moses, inasmuch as [a]he who hath
builded the house hath more honour than the
house.
4 For every house is builded by some *man;*
but [a]he that built all things *is* God.
5 [a]And Moses verily *was* faithful in all his
house, as [b]a servant, [c]for a testimony of those
things which were to be spoken after;
6 But Christ as [a]a son over his own house;
[b]whose house are we, [c]if we hold fast the confidence and the rejoicing of the hope firm unto the
end.

Be Faithful
(Ps. 95:7–11)

7 Wherefore (as [a]the Holy Ghost saith, [b]TO
DAY IF YE WILL HEAR HIS VOICE,
8 HARDEN NOT YOUR HEARTS, AS IN THE
PROVOCATION, IN THE DAY OF TEMPTATION IN THE
WILDERNESS:
9 WHEN YOUR FATHERS TEMPTED ME, PROVED
ME, AND SAW MY WORKS FORTY YEARS.
10 WHEREFORE I WAS GRIEVED WITH THAT GEN-
ERATION, AND SAID, THEY DO ALWAY ERR IN *THEIR*
HEART; AND THEY HAVE NOT KNOWN MY WAYS.
11 SO I SWARE IN MY WRATH, THEY SHALL NOT
ENTER INTO MY REST.)
12 Take heed, brethren, lest there be in any
of you an evil heart of unbelief, in departing from
the living God.
13 But exhort one another daily, while it is
called To day; lest any of you be hardened
through the deceitfulness of sin.
14 For we are made partakers of Christ, if
we hold the beginning of our confidence stedfast
unto the end;
15 While it is said, [a]TO DAY IF YE WILL HEAR
HIS VOICE, HARDEN NOT YOUR HEARTS, AS IN THE
PROVOCATION.

Failure of the Wilderness Wanderers

16 [a]For some, when they had heard, did provoke: howbeit not all that came out of Egypt by
Moses.
17 But with whom was he grieved forty
years? *was it* not with them that had sinned,
[a]whose carcases fell in the wilderness?
18 And [a]to whom sware he that they should
not enter into his rest, but to them that believed
not?
19 So we see that they could not enter in because of [a]unbelief.

The Promise of Rest

4 Let [a]us therefore fear, lest, a promise being
left *us* of entering into his rest, any of you
should seem to come short of it.

17 [a]Phil. 2:7; Heb. 2:14 [b][Heb. 4:15; 5:1–10]
18 [a][Heb. 4:15, 16]

CHAPTER 3

2 [a]Ps. 110:4; Ex. 40:16; Num. 12:7; Heb. 3:5
3 [a]Zech. 6:12, 13
4 [a][Eph. 2:10]
5 [a]Ex. 40:16; Num. 12:7; Heb. 3:2 [b]Ps. 2:7; Ex. 14:31; Num. 12:7 [c]Deut. 18:15, 18, 19
6 [a]Ps. 110:4; Heb. 1:2 [b][1 Cor. 3:16]; 1 Tim. 3:15 [c][Matt. 10:22]
7 [a]Acts 1:16 [b]Ps. 95:7–11; Heb. 3:15; 4:7
15 [a]Ps. 95:7, 8
16 [a]Num. 14:2, 11, 30; Deut. 1:35, 36, 38
17 [a]Num. 14:22, 23
18 [a]Num. 14:30
19 [a]Num. 14:1–39; 1 Cor. 10:11, 12

CHAPTER 4

1 [a]2 Cor. 6:1; [Gal. 5:4]; Heb. 12:15

*———
3:6 NU omits *firm to the end*

NKJV

death were all their lifetime subject to bondage.
16 For indeed He does not give aid to angels,
but He does give aid to the seed of Abraham.
17 Therefore, in all things He had [a]to be
made like *His* brethren, that He might be [b]a merciful and faithful High Priest in things *pertaining*
to God, to make propitiation for the sins of the
people.
18 [a]For in that He Himself has suffered, being
tempted, He is able to aid those who are tempted.

The Son Was Faithful

3 Therefore, holy brethren, partakers of the
heavenly calling, consider the Apostle and
High Priest of our confession, Christ Jesus,
2 who was faithful to Him who appointed
Him, as [a]Moses also *was faithful* in all His house.
3 For this One has been counted worthy of
more glory than Moses, inasmuch as [a]He who
built the house has more honor than the house.
4 For every house is built by someone, but
[a]He who built all things *is* God.
5 [a]And Moses indeed *was* faithful in all His
house as [b]a servant, [c]for a testimony of those
things which would be spoken *afterward,*
6 but Christ as [a]a Son over His own house,
[b]whose house we are [c]if we hold fast the confidence and the rejoicing of the hope *firm to the
end.

Be Faithful
(Ps. 95:7–11)

7 Therefore, as [a]the Holy Spirit says:

[b]*"Today, if you will hear His voice,*
8 *Do not harden your hearts as in the*
rebellion,
In the day of trial in the wilderness,
9 *Where your fathers tested Me, tried Me,*
And saw My works forty years.
10 *Therefore I was angry with that*
generation,
And said, 'They always go astray in their
heart,
And they have not known My ways.'
11 *So I swore in My wrath,*
'They shall not enter My rest.' "

12 Beware, brethren, lest there be in any of
you an evil heart of unbelief in departing from
the living God;
13 but exhort one another daily, while it is
called *"Today,"* lest any of you be hardened
through the deceitfulness of sin.
14 For we have become partakers of Christ
if we hold the beginning of our confidence steadfast to the end,
15 while it is said:

[a]*"Today, if you will hear His voice,*
Do not harden your hearts as in the
rebellion."

Failure of the Wilderness Wanderers

16 [a]For who, having heard, rebelled? Indeed,
was it not all who came out of Egypt, *led* by
Moses?
17 Now with whom was He angry forty
years? *Was it* not with those who sinned, [a]whose
corpses fell in the wilderness?
18 And [a]to whom did He swear that they
would not enter His rest, but to those who did
not obey?
19 So we see that they could not enter in because of [a]unbelief.

The Promise of Rest

4 Therefore, since a promise remains of entering His rest, [a]let us fear lest any of you seem
to have come short of it.

KJV

2 For unto us was the gospel preached, as well as unto them: but the word preached did not profit them, not being mixed with faith in them that heard *it*.

3 For we which have believed do enter into rest, as he said, [a]AS I HAVE SWORN IN MY WRATH, IF THEY SHALL ENTER INTO MY REST: although the works were finished from the foundation of the world.

4 For he spake in a certain place of the seventh *day* on this wise, [a]AND GOD DID REST THE SEVENTH DAY FROM ALL HIS WORKS.

5 And in this *place* again, [a]IF THEY SHALL ENTER INTO MY REST.

6 Seeing therefore it remaineth that some must enter therein, and they to whom it was first preached entered not in because of unbelief:

7 Again, he limiteth a certain day, saying in David, To day, after so long a time; as it is said, [a]TO DAY IF YE WILL HEAR HIS VOICE, HARDEN NOT YOUR HEARTS.

8 For if Jesus had [a]given them rest, then would he not afterward have spoken of another day.

9 There remaineth therefore a rest to the people of God.

10 For he that is entered into his rest, he also hath ceased from his own works, as God *did* from his.

The Word Discovers Our Condition

11 [a]Let us labour therefore to enter into that rest, lest any man fall after the same example of unbelief.

12 For the word of God *is* [a]quick, and powerful, and [b]sharper than any [c]twoedged sword, piercing even to the dividing asunder of soul and spirit, and of the joints and marrow, and *is* [d]a discerner of the thoughts and intents of the heart.

13 [a]Neither is there any creature that is not manifest in his sight: but all things *are* [b]naked and opened unto the eyes of him with whom we have to do.

Our Compassionate High Priest

14 Seeing then that we have a great [a]high priest, that is passed into the heavens, Jesus the Son of God, [b]let us hold fast *our* profession.

15 For [a]we have not an high priest which cannot be touched with the feeling of our infirmities; but [b]was in all points tempted like as *we are*, [c]*yet* without sin.

16 [a]Let us therefore come boldly unto the throne of grace, that we may obtain mercy, and find grace to help in time of need.

Qualifications for High Priesthood

5 For every high priest taken from among men [a]is ordained for men in things *pertaining* to God, that he may offer both gifts and sacrifices for sins:

2 Who can have compassion on the ignorant, and on them that are out of the way; for that he himself also is compassed with [a]infirmity.

3 And by reason hereof he ought, as for the people, so also for [a]himself, to offer for sins.

4 And no man taketh this honour unto himself, but he that is called of God, as [a]*was* Aaron.

A Priest Forever

5 [a]So also Christ glorified not himself to be made an high priest; but he that said unto him, [b]THOU ART MY SON, TO DAY HAVE I BEGOTTEN THEE.

---

3 [a]Ps. 95:11; Heb. 3:11
4 [a]Gen. 2:2; Ex. 20:11; 31:17
5 [a]Ps. 95:11
7 [a]Ps. 95:7, 8
8 [a]Josh. 22:4
11 [a]2 Pet. 1:10
12 [a]Ps. 147:15 [b]Is. 49:2 [c]Eph. 6:17; Rev. 2:12 [d][John 12:48]; 1 Cor. 14:24, 25
13 [a]2 Chr. 16:9; Ps. 33:13–15; 90:8 [b]Job 26:6; Prov. 15:11
14 [a]Heb. 2:17; 7:26 [b]Heb. 10:23
15 [a]Is. 53:3–5 [b]Luke 22:28 [c]2 Cor. 5:21; Heb. 7:26
16 [a][Eph. 2:18; Heb. 10:19, 22]

CHAPTER 5

1 [a]Heb. 2:17; 8:3
2 [a]Heb. 7:28
3 [a]Lev. 9:7; 16:6; [Heb. 7:27; 9:7]
4 [a]Ex. 28:1; Num. 16:40; 1 Chr. 23:13
5 [a]John 8:54 [b]Ps. 2:7

***4:2** NU, M *since they were not united by faith with those who heeded it*

NKJV

2 For indeed the gospel was preached to us as well as to them; but the word which they heard did not profit them, *not being mixed with faith in those who heard *it*.

3 For we who have believed do enter that rest, as He has said:

> [a]*"So I swore in My wrath,*
> *'They shall not enter My rest,' "*

although the works were finished from the foundation of the world.

4 For He has spoken in a certain place of the seventh *day* in this way: [a]*"And God rested on the seventh day from all His works"*;

5 and again in this *place:* [a]*"They shall not enter My rest."*

6 Since therefore it remains that some *must* enter it, and those to whom it was first preached did not enter because of disobedience,

7 again He designates a certain day, saying in David, *"Today,"* after such a long time, as it has been said:

> [a]*"Today, if you will hear His voice,*
> *Do not harden your hearts."*

8 For if Joshua had [a]given them rest, then He would not afterward have spoken of another day.

9 There remains therefore a rest for the people of God.

10 For he who has entered His rest has himself also ceased from his works as God *did* from His.

The Word Discovers Our Condition

11 [a]Let us therefore be diligent to enter that rest, lest anyone fall according to the same example of disobedience.

12 For the word of God *is* [a]living and powerful, and [b]sharper than any [c]two-edged sword, piercing even to the division of soul and spirit, and of joints and marrow, and is [d]a discerner of the thoughts and intents of the heart.

13 [a]And there is no creature hidden from His sight, but all things *are* [b]naked and open to the eyes of Him to whom we *must give* account.

Our Compassionate High Priest

14 Seeing then that we have a great [a]High Priest who has passed through the heavens, Jesus the Son of God, [b]let us hold fast *our* confession.

15 For [a]we do not have a High Priest who cannot sympathize with our weaknesses, but [b]was in all *points* tempted as *we are,* [c]*yet* without sin.

16 [a]Let us therefore come boldly to the throne of grace, that we may obtain mercy and find grace to help in time of need.

Qualifications for High Priesthood

5 For every high priest taken from among men [a]is appointed for men in things *pertaining* to God, that he may offer both gifts and sacrifices for sins.

2 He can have compassion on those who are ignorant and going astray, since he himself is also subject to [a]weakness.

3 Because of this he is required as for the people, so also for [a]himself, to offer *sacrifices* for sins.

4 And no man takes this honor to himself, but he who is called by God, just as [a]Aaron *was.*

A Priest Forever

5 [a]So also Christ did not glorify Himself to become High Priest, *but it* was He who said to Him:

> [b]*"You are My Son,*
> *Today I have begotten You."*

KJV

6 As he saith also in another *place*, [a]THOU ART A PRIEST FOR EVER AFTER THE ORDER OF MELCHISEDEC.

7 Who in the days of his flesh, when he had [a]offered up prayers and supplications [b]with strong crying and tears unto him [c]that was able to save him from death, and was heard [d]in that he feared;

8 Though he were a Son, yet learned he [a]obedience by the things which he suffered;

9 And [a]being made perfect, he became the author of eternal salvation unto all them that obey him;

10 Called of God an high priest [a]AFTER THE ORDER OF MELCHISEDEC.

11 Of whom [a]we have many things to say, and hard to be uttered, seeing ye are [b]dull of hearing.

Spiritual Immaturity

12 For when for the time ye ought to be teachers, ye have need that one teach you again which *be* the first principles of the oracles of God; and are become such as have need of [a]milk, and not of strong meat.

13 For every one that useth milk *is* unskilful in the word of righteousness: for he is [a]a babe.

14 But strong meat belongeth to them that are of full age, *even* those who by reason of use have their senses exercised [a]to discern both good and evil.

The Peril of Not Progressing

6 Therefore [a]leaving the principles of the doctrine of Christ, let us go on unto perfection; not laying again the foundation of repentance from [b]dead works, and of faith toward God,

2 [a]Of the doctrine of baptisms, [b]and of laying on of hands, [c]and of resurrection of the dead, [d]and of eternal judgment.

3 And this will we do, if God permit.

4 For *it is* impossible for those who were once enlightened, and have tasted of [a]the heavenly gift, and [b]were made partakers of the Holy Ghost,

5 And have tasted the good word of God, and the powers of the world to come,

6 If they shall fall away, to renew them again unto repentance; [a]seeing they crucify to themselves the Son of God afresh, and put *him* to an open shame.

7 For the earth which drinketh in the rain that cometh oft upon it, and bringeth forth herbs meet for them by whom it is dressed, [a]receiveth blessing from God:

8 [a]But that which beareth thorns and briers *is* rejected, and *is* nigh unto cursing; whose end *is* to be burned.

A Better Estimate

9 But, beloved, we are persuaded better things of you, and things that accompany salvation, though we thus speak.

10 For [a]God *is* not unrighteous to forget [b]your work and labour of love, which ye have shewed toward his name, in that ye have [c]ministered to the saints, and do minister.

11 And we desire that every one of you do shew the same diligence [a]to the full assurance of hope unto the end:

12 That ye be not slothful, but followers of them who through faith and patience [a]inherit the promises.

God's Infallible Purpose in Christ
(cf. Gen. 12:1–3)

13 For when God made promise to Abraham, because he could swear by no greater, [a]he sware by himself,

---

6 [a]Ps. 110:4; Heb. 7:17
7 [a]Matt. 26:39, 42, 44; Mark 14:36, 39; Luke 22:41, 44 [b]Ps. 22:1 [c]Matt. 26:53 [d]Matt. 26:37
8 [a]Phil. 2:8
9 [a]Heb. 2:10
10 [a]Ps. 110:4
11 [a][John 16:12]; Heb. 7:1–22 [b][Matt. 13:15]
12 [a]1 Cor. 3:1–3; 1 Pet. 2:2
13 [a]Eph. 4:14
14 [a]Is. 7:15; Phil. 1:9

CHAPTER 6

1 [a]Heb. 5:12 [b][Heb. 9:14]
2 [a]John 3:25; Acts 19:3–5 [b][Acts 8:17] [c]Acts 17:31 [d]Acts 24:25
4 [a][John 4:10]; Eph. 2:8 [b][Gal. 3:2, 5]; Heb. 2:4
6 [a]Heb. 10:29
7 [a]Ps. 65:10
8 [a]Is. 5:6
10 [a]Rom. 3:4 [b]1 Thess. 1:3 [c]Rom. 15:25; Heb. 10:32–34
11 [a]Col. 2:2
12 [a]Heb. 10:36
13 [a]Gen. 22:16, 17; Luke 1:73

NKJV

6 As *He* also *says* in another *place:*

[a]*"You are a priest forever*
According to the order of Melchizedek";

7 who, in the days of His flesh, when He had [a]offered up prayers and supplications, [b]with vehement cries and tears to Him [c]who was able to save Him from death, and was heard [d]because of His godly fear,

8 though He was a Son, *yet* He learned [a]obedience by the things which He suffered.

9 And [a]having been perfected, He became the author of eternal salvation to all who obey Him,

10 called by God as High Priest [a]*"according to the order of Melchizedek,"*

11 of whom [a]we have much to say, and hard to explain, since you have become [b]dull of hearing.

Spiritual Immaturity

12 For though by this time you ought to be teachers, you need *someone* to teach you again the first principles of the oracles of God; and you have come to need [a]milk and not solid food.

13 For everyone who partakes *only* of milk *is* unskilled in the word of righteousness, for he is [a]a babe.

14 But solid food belongs to those who are of full age, *that is,* those who by reason of use have their senses exercised [a]to discern both good and evil.

The Peril of Not Progressing

6 Therefore, [a]leaving the discussion of the elementary *principles* of Christ, let us go on to perfection, not laying again the foundation of repentance from [b]dead works and of faith toward God,

2 [a]of the doctrine of baptisms, [b]of laying on of hands, [c]of resurrection of the dead, [d]and of eternal judgment.

3 And this *we will do if God permits.

4 For *it is* impossible for those who were once enlightened, and have tasted [a]the heavenly gift, and [b]have become partakers of the Holy Spirit,

5 and have tasted the good word of God and the powers of the age to come,

6 *if they fall away, to renew them again to repentance, [a]since they crucify again for themselves the Son of God, and put *Him* to an open shame.

7 For the earth which drinks in the rain that often comes upon it, and bears herbs useful for those by whom it is cultivated, [a]receives blessing from God;

8 [a]but if it bears thorns and briers, *it is* rejected and near to being cursed, whose end *is* to be burned.

A Better Estimate

9 But, beloved, we are confident of better things concerning you, yes, things that accompany salvation, though we speak in this manner.

10 For [a]God *is* not unjust to forget [b]your work and *labor of love which you have shown toward His name, *in that* you have [c]ministered to the saints, and do minister.

11 And we desire that each one of you show the same diligence [a]to the full assurance of hope until the end,

12 that you do not become sluggish, but imitate those who through faith and patience [a]inherit the promises.

God's Infallible Purpose in Christ
(cf. Gen. 12:1–3)

13 For when God made a promise to Abraham, because He could swear by no one greater, [a]He swore by Himself,

---

*

6:3 M *let us do*
6:6 Or *and have fallen away*
6:10 NU omits *labor of*

KJV

14 Saying, [a]SURELY BLESSING I WILL BLESS THEE, AND MULTIPLYING I WILL MULTIPLY THEE.

15 And so, after he had patiently endured, he obtained the [a]promise.

16 For men verily swear by the greater: and [a]an oath for confirmation *is* to them an end of all strife.

17 Wherein God, willing more abundantly to shew unto [a]the heirs of promise [b]the immutability of his counsel, confirmed *it* by an oath:

18 That by two immutable things, in which *it was* impossible for God to [a]lie, we might have a strong consolation, who have fled for refuge to lay hold upon the hope [b]set before us:

19 Which *hope* we have as an anchor of the soul, both sure and stedfast, [a]and which entereth into that within the veil;

20 [a]Whither the forerunner is for us entered, *even* Jesus, [b]made an high priest for ever after the order of Melchisedec.

The King of Righteousness
(Gen. 14:17–20)

7 For this [a]Melchisedec, king of Salem, priest of the most high God, who met Abraham returning from the slaughter of the kings, and blessed him;

2 To whom also Abraham gave a tenth part of all; first being by interpretation King of righteousness, and after that also King of Salem, which is, King of peace;

3 Without father, without mother, without descent, having neither beginning of days, nor end of life; but made like unto the Son of God; abideth a priest continually.

4 Now consider how great this man *was,* unto whom even the patriarch Abraham gave the tenth of the spoils.

5 And verily [a]they that are of the sons of Levi, who receive the office of the priesthood, have a commandment to take tithes of the people according to the law, that is, of their brethren, though they come out of the loins of Abraham:

6 But he whose descent is not counted from them received tithes of Abraham, [a]and blessed [b]him that had the promises.

7 And without all contradiction the less is blessed of the better.

8 And here men that die receive tithes; but there he *receiveth them,* [a]of whom it is witnessed that he liveth.

9 And as I may so say, Levi also, who receiveth tithes, payed tithes in Abraham.

10 For he was yet in the loins of his father, when Melchisedec met him.

Need for a New Priesthood
(Ps. 110:4)

11 [a]If therefore perfection were by the Levitical priesthood, (for under it the people received the law,) what further need *was there* that another priest should rise after the order of Melchisedec, and not be called after the order of Aaron?

12 For the priesthood being changed, there is made of necessity a change also of the law.

13 For he of whom these things are spoken pertaineth to another tribe, of which no man gave attendance at the altar.

14 For *it is* evident that [a]our Lord sprang out of [b]Juda; of which tribe Moses spake nothing concerning priesthood.

15 And it is yet far more evident: for that after the similitude of Melchisedec there ariseth another priest,

16 Who is made, not after the law of a carnal commandment, but after the power of an endless life.

14 [a]Gen. 22:16, 17
15 [a]Gen. 12:4; 21:5
16 [a]Ex. 22:11
17 [a]Rom. 8:17; Heb. 11:9 [b]Rom. 11:29
18 [a]Num. 23:19; 1 Sam. 15:29; Titus 1:2 [b][Col. 1:5]; Heb. 3:6; 7:19; 12:1
19 [a]Lev. 16:2, 15; Heb. 9:3, 7
20 [a][John 14:2; Heb. 4:14] [b]Gen. 14:17–19; Ps. 110:4; Heb. 3:1; 5:10, 11

CHAPTER 7

1 [a]Gen. 14:18–20; Heb. 7:6
5 [a]Num. 18:21–26; 2 Chr. 31:4
6 [a]Gen. 14:19, 20 [b][Rom. 4:13]
8 [a]Heb. 5:6; 6:20; [Rev. 1:18]
11 [a][Rom. 7:7–14]; Gal. 2:21; Heb. 7:18; 8:7
14 [a]Gen. 49:8–10; Num. 24:17; Is. 1:1; Mic. 5:2; Matt. 1:3; 2:6; Rev. 5:5 [b]Matt. 1:2

*———

6:18 M omits *might*
7:14 NU *priests*

NKJV

14 saying, [a]*"Surely blessing I will bless you, and multiplying I will multiply you."*

15 And so, after he had patiently endured, he obtained the [a]promise.

16 For men indeed swear by the greater, and [a]an oath for confirmation *is* for them an end of all dispute.

17 Thus God, determining to show more abundantly to [a]the heirs of promise [b]the immutability of His counsel, confirmed *it* by an oath,

18 that by two immutable things, in which it *is* impossible for God to [a]lie, we *might have strong consolation, who have fled for refuge to lay hold of the hope [b]set before *us.*

19 This *hope* we have as an anchor of the soul, both sure and steadfast, [a]and which enters the Presence *behind* the veil,

20 [a]where the forerunner has entered for us, *even* Jesus, [b]having become High Priest forever according to the order of Melchizedek.

The King of Righteousness
(Gen. 14:17–20)

7 For this [a]Melchizedek, king of Salem, priest of the Most High God, who met Abraham returning from the slaughter of the kings and blessed him,

2 to whom also Abraham gave a tenth part of all, first being translated "king of righteousness," and then also king of Salem, meaning "king of peace,"

3 without father, without mother, without genealogy, having neither beginning of days nor end of life, but made like the Son of God, remains a priest continually.

4 Now consider how great this man *was,* to whom even the patriarch Abraham gave a tenth of the spoils.

5 And indeed [a]those who are of the sons of Levi, who receive the priesthood, have a commandment to receive tithes from the people according to the law, that is, from their brethren, though they have come from the loins of Abraham;

6 but he whose genealogy is not derived from them received tithes from Abraham [a]and blessed [b]him who had the promises.

7 Now beyond all contradiction the lesser is blessed by the better.

8 Here mortal men receive tithes, but there he *receives them,* [a]of whom it is witnessed that he lives.

9 Even Levi, who receives tithes, paid tithes through Abraham, so to speak,

10 for he was still in the loins of his father when Melchizedek met him.

Need for a New Priesthood
(Ps. 110:4)

11 [a]Therefore, if perfection were through the Levitical priesthood (for under it the people received the law), what further need *was there* that another priest should rise according to the order of Melchizedek, and not be called according to the order of Aaron?

12 For the priesthood being changed, of necessity there is also a change of the law.

13 For He of whom these things are spoken belongs to another tribe, from which no man has officiated at the altar.

14 For *it is* evident that [a]our Lord arose from [b]Judah, of which tribe Moses spoke nothing concerning *priesthood.

15 And it is yet far more evident if, in the likeness of Melchizedek, there arises another priest

16 who has come, not according to the law of a fleshly commandment, but according to the power of an endless life.

KJV

17 For he testifieth, [a]THOU *ART* A PRIEST FOR EVER AFTER THE ORDER OF MELCHISEDEC.

18 For there is verily a disannulling of the commandment going before for [a]the weakness and unprofitableness thereof.

19 For [a]the law made nothing perfect, but the bringing in of [b]a better hope *did;* by the which [c]we draw nigh unto God.

Greatness of the New Priest

20 And inasmuch as not without an oath *he was made priest:*

21 (For those priests were made without an oath; but this with an oath by him that said unto him, [a]THE LORD SWARE AND WILL NOT REPENT, THOU *ART* A PRIEST FOR EVER AFTER THE ORDER OF MELCHISEDEC:)

22 By so much was Jesus made a surety of a [a]better testament.

23 And they truly were many priests, because they were not suffered to continue by reason of death:

24 But this *man,* because he continueth ever, hath an unchangeable priesthood.

25 Wherefore he is [a]able also to save them to the uttermost that come unto God by him, seeing he ever liveth [b]to make intercession for them.

26 For such an high priest became us, [a]*who is* holy, harmless, undefiled, separate from sinners, [b]and made higher than the heavens;

27 Who needeth not daily, as those high priests, to offer up sacrifice, first for his [a]own sins, and then for the people's: for this he did once, when he offered up himself.

28 For the law maketh men high priests which have infirmity; but the word of the oath, which was since the law, *maketh* the Son, who is consecrated for evermore.

The New Priestly Service

8 Now of the things which we have spoken *this is* the sum: We have such an high priest, [a]who is set on the right hand of the throne of the Majesty in the heavens;

2 A minister of [a]the sanctuary, and of [b]the true tabernacle, which the Lord pitched, and not man.

3 For [a]every high priest is ordained to offer gifts and sacrifices: wherefore [b]*it is* of necessity that this man have somewhat also to offer.

4 For if he were on earth, he should not be a priest, seeing that there are priests that offer gifts according to the law:

5 Who serve unto the [a]example and [b]shadow of heavenly things, as Moses was admonished of God when he was about to make the tabernacle: [c]for, SEE, saith he, *THAT* THOU MAKE ALL THINGS ACCORDING TO THE PATTERN SHEWED TO THEE IN THE MOUNT.

6 But now [a]hath he obtained a more excellent ministry, by how much also he is the mediator of a [b]better covenant, which was established upon better promises.

A New Covenant
(Jer. 31:31–34)

7 For if that [a]first *covenant* had been faultless, then should no place have been sought for the second.

8 For finding fault with them, he saith, [a]BEHOLD, THE DAYS COME, SAITH THE LORD, WHEN I WILL MAKE A NEW COVENANT WITH THE HOUSE OF ISRAEL AND WITH THE HOUSE OF JUDAH:

17 [a]Ps. 110:4; Heb. 5:6; 6:20; 7:21
18 [a][Rom. 8:3]; Gal. 3:21; Heb. 7:11
19 [a][Acts 13:39]; Rom. 3:20; 7:7; Gal. 2:16; 3:21; Heb. 9:9; 10:1 [b]Heb. 6:18, 19 [c]Lam. 3:57; Rom. 5:2; [Eph. 2:18]; Heb. 4:16; James 4:8
21 [a]Ps. 110:4; Heb. 5:6; 7:17
22 [a]Heb. 8:6
25 [a]Jude 24 [b]Rom. 8:34; 1 Tim. 2:5; Heb. 9:24; 1 John 2:1
26 [a][2 Cor. 5:21]; Heb. 4:15 [b]Eph. 1:20
27 [a]Lev. 9:7; 16:6; Heb. 5:3

CHAPTER 8

1 [a]Ps. 68:18; 110:1; Eph. 1:20; Col. 3:1; Heb. 2:17; 3:1; 10:12
2 [a]Heb. 9:8, 12 [b]Heb. 9:11, 24
3 [a][Rom. 4:25; 5:6, 8; Gal. 2:20; Eph. 5:2]; Heb. 5:1; 8:4 [b][Eph. 5:2; Heb. 9:14]
5 [a]Heb. 9:23, 24 [b]Col. 2:17; Heb. 10:1 [c]Ex. 25:40
6 [a][2 Cor. 3:6–8] [b][Luke 22:20]; Heb. 7:22
7 [a]Ex. 3:8; 19:5
8 [a]Jer. 31: 31–34

*______

7:17 NU *it is testified*
7:21 NU ends the quotation after *forever.*

NKJV

17 For *He testifies:

[a]"*You are a priest forever*
According to the order of Melchizedek."

18 For on the one hand there is an annulling of the former commandment because of [a]its weakness and unprofitableness,

19 for [a]the law made nothing perfect; on the other hand, *there is the* bringing in of [b]a better hope, through which [c]we draw near to God.

Greatness of the New Priest

20 And inasmuch as *He was* not *made priest* without an oath

21 (for they have become priests without an oath, but He with an oath by Him who said to Him:

[a]"*The* LORD *has sworn*
And will not relent,
'*You are a priest *forever*
According to the order of
Melchizedek' "),

22 by so much more Jesus has become a surety of a [a]better covenant.

23 Also there were many priests, because they were prevented by death from continuing.

24 But He, because He continues forever, has an unchangeable priesthood.

25 Therefore He is also [a]able to save to the uttermost those who come to God through Him, since He always lives [b]to make intercession for them.

26 For such a High Priest was fitting for us, [a]*who is* holy, harmless, undefiled, separate from sinners, [b]and has become higher than the heavens;

27 who does not need daily, as those high priests, to offer up sacrifices, first for His [a]own sins and then for the people's, for this He did once for all when He offered up Himself.

28 For the law appoints as high priests men who have weakness, but the word of the oath, which came after the law, *appoints* the Son who has been perfected forever.

The New Priestly Service

8 Now *this is* the main point of the things we are saying: We have such a High Priest, [a]who is seated at the right hand of the throne of the Majesty in the heavens,

2 a Minister of [a]the sanctuary and of [b]the true tabernacle which the Lord erected, and not man.

3 For [a]every high priest is appointed to offer both gifts and sacrifices. Therefore [b]*it is* necessary that this One also have something to offer.

4 For if He were on earth, He would not be a priest, since there are priests who offer the gifts according to the law;

5 who serve [a]the copy and [b]shadow of the heavenly things, as Moses was divinely instructed when he was about to make the tabernacle. For He said, [c]"*See that you make all things according to the pattern shown you on the mountain.*"

6 But now [a]He has obtained a more excellent ministry, inasmuch as He is also Mediator of a [b]better covenant, which was established on better promises.

A New Covenant
(Jer. 31:31–34)

7 For if that [a]first *covenant* had been faultless, then no place would have been sought for a second.

8 Because finding fault with them, He says: [a]"*Behold, the days are coming, says the* LORD, *when I will make a new covenant with the house of Israel and with the house of Judah—*

KJV

9 Not according to the covenant that I made with their fathers in the day when I took them by the hand to lead them out of the land of Egypt; because they continued not in my covenant, and I regarded them not, saith the Lord.

10 For this *is* the covenant that I will make with the house of Israel after those days, saith the [a]Lord; I will put my laws into their mind, and write them in their hearts: and [b]I will be to them a God, and they shall be to me a people:

11 And [a]they shall not teach every man his neighbour, and every man his brother, saying, Know the [b]Lord: for all shall know me, from the least to the greatest.

12 For I will be merciful to their unrighteousness, [a]and their sins and their iniquities will I remember no more.

13 [a]In that he saith, A new *covenant*, he hath made the first old. Now that which decayeth and waxeth old *is* ready to vanish away.

The Earthly Sanctuary
(*cf.* Ex. 25:10–40)

9 Then verily the first *covenant* had also ordinances of divine service, and [a]a worldly sanctuary.

2 For there was a tabernacle made; the first, wherein *was* the candlestick, and the table, and the shewbread; which is called the sanctuary.

3 [a]And after the second veil, the tabernacle which is called the Holiest of all;

4 Which had the [a]golden censer, and [b]the ark of the covenant overlaid round about with gold, wherein *was* [c]the golden pot that had manna, and [d]Aaron's rod that budded, and [e]the tables of the covenant;

5 And [a]over it the cherubims of glory shadowing the mercyseat; of which we cannot now speak particularly.

Limitations of the Earthly Service

6 Now when these things were thus ordained, [a]the priests went always into the first tabernacle, accomplishing the service *of God.*

7 But into the second *went* the high priest alone [a]once every year, not without blood, which he offered for [b]himself, and *for* the errors of the people:

8 The Holy Ghost this signifying, that [a]the way into the holiest of all was not yet made manifest, while as the first tabernacle was yet standing:

9 Which *was* a figure for the time then present, in which were offered both gifts and sacrifices, [a]that could not make him that did the service perfect, as pertaining to the conscience;

10 *Which stood* only in [a]meats and drinks, and [b]divers washings, [c]and carnal ordinances, imposed *on them* until the time of reformation.

The Heavenly Sanctuary

11 But Christ being come an high priest of [a]good things to come, by a greater and more perfect tabernacle, not made with hands, that is to say, not of this building;

12 Neither [a]by the blood of goats and calves, but [b]by his own blood he entered in [c]once into the holy place, [d]having obtained eternal redemption *for us.*

13 For if [a]the blood of bulls and of goats, and [b]the ashes of an heifer sprinkling the unclean, sanctifieth to the purifying of the flesh:

14 How much more shall the blood of Christ, who through the eternal Spirit offered himself without spot to God, [a]purge your conscience from [b]dead works [c]to serve the living God?

15 And for this cause [a]he is the mediator of the new testament, that by means of death, for the redemption of the transgressions *that were* under the first testament, [b]they which are called might receive the promise of eternal inheritance.

10 [a]Jer. 31:33; Rom. 11:27; Heb. 10:16 [b]Zech. 8:8
11 [a]Is. 54:13; John 6:45; [1 John 2:27] [b]Jer. 31:34
12 [a]Rom. 11:27
13 [a][2 Cor. 5:17]; Heb. 1:11

CHAPTER 9

1 [a]Ex. 25:8; [Heb. 8:2; 9:11, 24]
3 [a]Ex. 26:31–35; 40:3
4 [a]Lev. 16:12 [b]Ex. 25:10 [c]Ex. 16:33 [d]Num. 17:1–10 [e]Ex. 25:16; 34:29; Deut. 10:2–5
5 [a]Ex. 25:17, 20; Lev. 16:2; 1 Kin. 8:7
6 [a]Num. 18:2–6; 28:3
7 [a]Ex. 30:10; Lev. 16:34; Heb. 10:3 [b]Heb. 5:3
8 [a][John 14:6; Heb. 10:20]
9 [a][Gal. 3:21]; Heb. 7:19
10 [a]Lev. 11:2; Col. 2:16 [b]Num. 19:7 [c]Eph. 2:15
11 [a][Eph. 1:3–11]; Heb. 10:1
12 [a]Heb. 10:4 [b]Is. 53:12; Eph. 1:7 [c]Zech. 3:9 [d][Dan. 9:24]
13 [a]Lev. 16:14, 15; Heb. 9:19; 10:4 [b]Num. 19:2
14 [a]1 John 1:7 [b]Heb. 6:1 [c]Luke 1:74
15 [a]Rom. 3:25 [b]Heb. 3:1

*

8:12 NU omits *and their lawless deeds*
9:11 NU *that have come*

NKJV

9 *"not according to the covenant that I made with their fathers in the day when I took them by the hand to lead them out of the land of Egypt; because they did not continue in My covenant, and I disregarded them, says the* Lord.

10 *"For this is the covenant that I will make with the house of Israel after those days, says the* [a]*Lord: I will put My laws in their mind and write them on their hearts; and* [b]*I will be their God, and they shall be My people.*

11 [a]*"None of them shall teach his neighbor, and none his brother, saying, 'Know the* [b]*Lord,' for all shall know Me, from the least of them to the greatest of them.*

12 *"For I will be merciful to their unrighteousness,* [a]*and their sins *and their lawless deeds I will remember no more."*

13 [a]In that He says, *"A new covenant,"* He has made the first obsolete. Now what is becoming obsolete and growing old is ready to vanish away.

The Earthly Sanctuary
(*cf.* Ex. 25:10–40)

9 Then indeed, even the first *covenant* had ordinances of divine service and [a]the earthly sanctuary.

2 For a tabernacle was prepared: the first *part,* in which *was* the lampstand, the table, and the showbread, which is called the sanctuary;

3 [a]and behind the second veil, the part of the tabernacle which is called the Holiest of All,

4 which had the [a]golden censer and [b]the ark of the covenant overlaid on all sides with gold, in which *were* [c]the golden pot that had the manna, [d]Aaron's rod that budded, and [e]the tablets of the covenant;

5 and [a]above it were the cherubim of glory overshadowing the mercy seat. Of these things we cannot now speak in detail.

Limitations of the Earthly Service

6 Now when these things had been thus prepared, [a]the priests always went into the first part of the tabernacle, performing *the services.*

7 But into the second part the high priest *went* alone [a]once a year, not without blood, which he offered for [b]himself and *for* the people's sins *committed* in ignorance;

8 the Holy Spirit indicating this, that [a]the way into the Holiest of All was not yet made manifest while the first tabernacle was still standing.

9 It *was* symbolic for the present time in which both gifts and sacrifices are offered [a]which cannot make him who performed the service perfect in regard to the conscience—

10 *concerned* only with [a]foods and drinks, [b]various washings, [c]and fleshly ordinances imposed until the time of reformation.

The Heavenly Sanctuary

11 But Christ came *as* High Priest of [a]the good things *to come, with the greater and more perfect tabernacle not made with hands, that is, not of this creation.

12 Not [a]with the blood of goats and calves, but [b]with His own blood He entered the Most Holy Place [c]once for all, [d]having obtained eternal redemption.

13 For if [a]the blood of bulls and goats and [b]the ashes of a heifer, sprinkling the unclean, sanctifies for the purifying of the flesh,

14 how much more shall the blood of Christ, who through the eternal Spirit offered Himself without spot to God, [a]cleanse your conscience from [b]dead works [c]to serve the living God?

15 And for this reason [a]He is the Mediator of the new covenant, by means of death, for the redemption of the transgressions under the first covenant, that [b]those who are called may receive the promise of the eternal inheritance.

KJV

The Mediator's Death Necessary

16 For where a testament *is,* there must also
of necessity be the death of the testator.
17 For [a]a testament *is* of force after men are
dead: otherwise it is of no strength at all while
the testator liveth.
18 [a]Whereupon neither the first *testament*
was dedicated without blood.
19 For when Moses had spoken every precept to all the people according to the law, [a]he
took the blood of calves and of goats, [b]with water,
and scarlet wool, and hyssop, and sprinkled both
the book, and all the people,
20 Saying, [a]THIS *IS* THE [b]BLOOD OF THE TESTA-
MENT WHICH GOD HATH ENJOINED UNTO YOU.
21 Moreover [a]he sprinkled with blood both
the tabernacle, and all the vessels of the ministry.
22 And almost all things are by the law
purged with blood; and [a]without shedding of
blood is no remission.

Greatness of Christ's Sacrifice

23 *It was* therefore necessary that [a]the patterns of things in the heavens should be purified
with these; but the heavenly things themselves
with better sacrifices than these.
24 For [a]Christ is not entered into the holy
places made with hands, *which are* the figures of
[b]the true; but into heaven itself, now [c]to appear
in the presence of God for us:
25 Nor yet that he should offer himself often,
as [a]the high priest entereth into the holy place
every year with blood of others;
26 For then must he often have suffered since
the foundation of the world: but now once in the
end of the world hath he appeared to put away
sin by the sacrifice of himself.
27 [a]And as it is appointed unto men once to
die, [b]but after this the judgment:
28 So [a]Christ was once [b]offered to bear the
sins [c]of many; and unto them that [d]look for him
shall he appear the second time without sin unto
salvation.

Animal Sacrifices Insufficient

10 For the law having a [a]shadow of good
things to come, *and* not the very image of
the things, [b]can never with those sacrifices which
they offered year by year continually make the
comers thereunto perfect.
2 For then would they not have ceased to
be offered? because that the worshippers once
purged should have had no more conscience of
sins.
3 But in those *sacrifices there is* a remembrance again *made* of sins every year.
4 For [a]*it is* not possible that the blood of
bulls and of goats should take away sins.

Christ's Death Fulfills God's Will
(cf. Ps. 40:6–8)

5 Wherefore when he cometh into the
world, he saith, [a]SACRIFICE AND OFFERING THOU
WOULDEST NOT, BUT A BODY HAST THOU PREPARED
ME:
6 IN BURNT OFFERINGS AND *SACRIFICES* FOR SIN
THOU HAST HAD NO PLEASURE.
7 THEN SAID I, LO, I COME (IN THE VOLUME OF
THE BOOK IT IS WRITTEN OF ME,) TO DO THY WILL, O
GOD.
8 Above when he said, SACRIFICE AND OFFER-
ING AND BURNT OFFERINGS AND *OFFERING* FOR SIN
THOU WOULDEST NOT, NEITHER HADST PLEASURE
THEREIN; which are offered by the law;
9 Then said he, LO, I COME TO DO THY WILL,
O GOD. He taketh away the first, that he may es-
tablish the second.
10 [a]By the which will we are sanctified

17 [a]Gal. 3:15
18 [a]Ex. 24:6
19 [a]Ex. 24:5, 6 [b]Lev. 14:4, 7; Num. 19:6, 18
20 [a][Matt. 26:28] [b]Ex. 24:3–8
21 [a]Ex. 29:12, 36
22 [a]Lev. 17:11
23 [a]Heb. 8:5
24 [a]Heb. 6:20 [b]Heb. 8:2 [c]Rom. 8:34
25 [a]Heb. 9:7
27 [a]Gen. 3:19; Eccl. 3:20 [b][2 Cor. 5:10]; 1 John 4:17
28 [a]Rom. 6:10 [b]Is. 53:12; 1 Pet. 2:24 [c]Matt. 26:28 [d]1 Cor. 1:7; Titus 2:13

CHAPTER 10
1 [a]Heb. 8:5 [b]Heb. 7:19; 9:9
4 [a]Mic. 6:6, 7
5 [a]Ps. 40:6–8
10 [a]John 17:19; [Eph. 5:26; Heb. 2:11; 10:14, 29; 13:12]

*———
10:9 NU, M omit *O God*

NKJV

The Mediator's Death Necessary

16 For where there *is* a testament, there must
also of necessity be the death of the testator.
17 For [a]a testament *is* in force after men are
dead, since it has no power at all while the testator
lives.
18 [a]Therefore not even the first *covenant*
was dedicated without blood.
19 For when Moses had spoken every precept to all the people according to the law, [a]he
took the blood of calves and goats, [b]with water,
scarlet wool, and hyssop, and sprinkled both the
book itself and all the people,
20 saying, [a]*"This is the [b]blood of the covenant which God has commanded you."*
21 Then likewise [a]he sprinkled with blood
both the tabernacle and all the vessels of the
ministry.
22 And according to the law almost all things
are purified with blood, and [a]without shedding
of blood there is no remission.

Greatness of Christ's Sacrifice

23 Therefore *it was* necessary that [a]the copies of the things in the heavens should be purified
with these, but the heavenly things themselves
with better sacrifices than these.
24 For [a]Christ has not entered the holy places
made with hands, *which are* copies of [b]the true,
but into heaven itself, now [c]to appear in the presence of God for us;
25 not that He should offer Himself often, as
[a]the high priest enters the Most Holy Place every
year with blood of another—
26 He then would have had to suffer often
since the foundation of the world; but now, once
at the end of the ages, He has appeared to put
away sin by the sacrifice of Himself.
27 [a]And as it is appointed for men to die
once, [b]but after this the judgment,
28 so [a]Christ was [b]offered once to bear the
sins [c]of many. To those who [d]eagerly wait for
Him He will appear a second time, apart from
sin, for salvation.

Animal Sacrifices Insufficient

10 For the law, having a [a]shadow of the good
things to come, *and* not the very image of
the things, [b]can never with these same sacrifices,
which they offer continually year by year, make
those who approach perfect.
2 For then would they not have ceased to
be offered? For the worshipers, once purified,
would have had no more consciousness of sins.
3 But in those *sacrifices there is* a reminder
of sins every year.
4 For [a]*it is* not possible that the blood of
bulls and goats could take away sins.

Christ's Death Fulfills God's Will
(cf. Ps. 40:6–8)

5 Therefore, when He came into the world,
He said:

[a]*"Sacrifice and offering You did not desire,*
But a body You have prepared for Me.
6 *In burnt offerings and sacrifices for sin*
You had no pleasure.
7 *Then I said, 'Behold, I have come—*
In the volume of the book it is written of
Me—
To do Your will, O God.' "

8 Previously saying, *"Sacrifice and offering,
burnt offerings, and offerings for sin You did not
desire, nor had pleasure in them"* (which are offered according to the law),
9 then He said, *"Behold, I have come to do
Your will, *O God."* He takes away the first that
He may establish the second.
10 [a]By that will we have been sanctified

KJV

[b]through the offering of the body of Jesus Christ once *for all.*

Christ's Death Perfects the Sanctified

11 And every priest standeth [a]daily ministering and offering oftentimes the same sacrifices, which can never take away sins:

12 [a]But this man, after he had offered one sacrifice for sins for ever, sat down [b]on the right hand of God;

13 From henceforth expecting [a]till his enemies be made his footstool.

14 For by one offering he hath perfected for ever them that are sanctified.

15 *Whereof* the Holy Ghost also is a witness to us: for after that he had said before,

16 This *is* the covenant that I will make with them after those days, saith the [a]Lord, I will put my laws into their hearts, and in their minds will I write them;

17 [a]And their sins and iniquities will I remember no more.

18 Now where remission of these *is, there is* no more offering for sin.

Hold Fast Your Confession

19 Having therefore, brethren, [a]boldness to enter [b]into the holiest by the blood of Jesus,

20 By a new and [a]living way, which he hath consecrated for us, through the veil, that is to say, his flesh;

21 And *having* an high priest over the house of God;

22 Let us [a]draw near with a true heart [b]in full assurance of faith, having our hearts sprinkled from an evil conscience, and our bodies washed with pure water.

23 Let us hold fast the profession of *our* faith without wavering; (for [a]he *is* faithful that promised;)

24 And let us consider one another to provoke unto love and to good works:

25 [a]Not forsaking the assembling of ourselves together, as the manner of some *is;* but exhorting *one another:* and [b]so much the more, as ye see [c]the day approaching.

The Just Live by Faith

26 For [a]if we sin wilfully [b]after that we have received the knowledge of the truth, there remaineth [c]no more sacrifice for sins,

27 But a certain fearful looking for of judgment and [a]fiery indignation, which shall devour the adversaries.

28 He that despised Moses' law died without mercy under two or three [a]witnesses:

29 [a]Of how much sorer punishment, suppose ye, shall he be thought worthy, who hath trodden under foot the Son of God, and [b]hath counted the blood of the covenant, wherewith he was sanctified, an unholy thing, [c]and hath done despite unto the Spirit of grace?

30 For we know him that hath said, [a]Vengeance *belongeth* unto me, I will recompense, saith the Lord. And again, [b]The Lord shall judge his people.

31 [a]*It is* a fearful thing to fall into the hands of the living God.

32 But [a]call to remembrance the former days, in which, after ye were illuminated, ye endured a great fight of afflictions;

33 Partly, whilst ye were made [a]a gazingstock both by reproaches and afflictions; and partly, whilst [b]ye became companions of them that were so used.

34 For ye had compassion of me [a]in my bonds, and [b]took joyfully the spoiling of your goods, knowing in yourselves that [c]ye have in heaven a better and an enduring substance.

35 Cast not away therefore your confidence, [a]which hath great recompence of reward.

36 [a]For ye have need of patience, that, after

---

10 [b][Heb. 9:12]
11 [a]Num. 28:3
12 [a]Col. 3:1; Heb. 1:3 [b]Ps. 110:1
13 [a]Ps. 110:1; Heb. 1:13
16 [a]Jer. 31:33, 34; Heb. 8:10
17 [a]Jer. 31:34
19 [a][Eph. 2:18]; Heb. 4:16 [b]Heb. 9:8, 12
20 [a]John 14:6; [Heb. 7:24, 25]
22 [a]Heb. 7:19; 10:1 [b]Eph. 3:12
23 [a]1 Cor. 1:9; 10:13; 1 Thess. 5:24; Heb. 11:11
25 [a]Acts 2:42 [b]Rom. 13:11 [c]Phil. 4:5
26 [a]Num. 15:30 [b]2 Pet. 2:20 [c]Heb. 6:6
27 [a]Zeph. 1:18
28 [a]Deut. 17:2–6; 19:15; Matt. 18:16; Heb. 2:2
29 [a][Heb. 2:3] [b]1 Cor. 11:29 [c][Matt. 12:31]
30 [a]Deut. 32:35; Rom. 12:19 [b]Deut. 32:36
31 [a][Luke 12:5]
32 [a]Gal. 3:4; Heb. 6:9, 10
33 [a]1 Cor. 4:9; Heb. 12:4 [b]Phil. 1:7
34 [a]2 Tim. 1:16 [b]Matt. 5:12 [c]Matt. 6:20
35 [a]Matt. 5:12
36 [a]Luke 21:19; Heb. 12:1

NKJV

[b]through the offering of the body of Jesus Christ once *for all.*

Christ's Death Perfects the Sanctified

11 And every priest stands [a]ministering daily and offering repeatedly the same sacrifices, which can never take away sins.

12 [a]But this Man, after He had offered one sacrifice for sins forever, sat down [b]at the right hand of God,

13 from that time waiting [a]till His enemies are made His footstool.

14 For by one offering He has perfected forever those who are being sanctified.

15 But the Holy Spirit also witnesses to us; for after He had said before,

16 [a]*"This is the covenant that I will make with them after those days, says the Lord: I will put My laws into their hearts, and in their minds I will write them,"*

17 *then He adds,* [a]*"Their sins and their lawless deeds I will remember no more."*

18 Now where there is remission of these, *there is* no longer an offering for sin.

Hold Fast Your Confession

19 Therefore, brethren, having [a]boldness to enter [b]the Holiest by the blood of Jesus,

20 by a new and [a]living way which He consecrated for us, through the veil, that is, His flesh,

21 and *having* a High Priest over the house of God,

22 let us [a]draw near with a true heart [b]in full assurance of faith, having our hearts sprinkled from an evil conscience and our bodies washed with pure water.

23 Let us hold fast the confession of *our* hope without wavering, for [a]He who promised *is* faithful.

24 And let us consider one another in order to stir up love and good works,

25 [a]not forsaking the assembling of ourselves together, as *is* the manner of some, but exhorting *one another,* and [b]so much the more as you see [c]the Day approaching.

The Just Live by Faith

26 For [a]if we sin willfully [b]after we have received the knowledge of the truth, there [c]no longer remains a sacrifice for sins,

27 but a certain fearful expectation of judgment, and [a]fiery indignation which will devour the adversaries.

28 Anyone who has rejected Moses' law dies without mercy on the testimony of two or three [a]witnesses.

29 [a]Of how much worse punishment, do you suppose, will he be thought worthy who has trampled the Son of God underfoot, [b]counted the blood of the covenant by which he was sanctified a common thing, [c]and insulted the Spirit of grace?

30 For we know Him who said, [a]*"Vengeance is Mine, I will repay,"* *says the Lord. And again, [b]*"The Lord will judge His people."*

31 [a]It is a fearful thing to fall into the hands of the living God.

32 But [a]recall the former days in which, after you were illuminated, you endured a great struggle with sufferings:

33 partly while you were made [a]a spectacle both by reproaches and tribulations, and partly while [b]you became companions of those who were so treated;

34 for you had compassion on *me [a]in my chains, and [b]joyfully accepted the plundering of your goods, knowing that [c]you have a better and an enduring possession for yourselves *in heaven.

35 Therefore do not cast away your confidence, [a]which has great reward.

36 [a]For you have need of endurance, so that

---

*

10:30 NU omits *says the Lord*
10:34 NU *the prisoners* instead of *me in my chains* • NU omits *in heaven*

KJV

ye have done the will of God, [b]ye might receive
the promise.
37 FOR [a]YET A LITTLE WHILE, AND [b]HE THAT
SHALL COME WILL COME, AND WILL NOT TARRY.
38 NOW [a]THE JUST SHALL LIVE BY FAITH: BUT IF
ANY MAN DRAW BACK, MY SOUL SHALL HAVE NO PLEA-
SURE IN HIM.
39 But we are not of them [a]who draw back
unto perdition; but of them that [b]believe to the
saving of the soul.

By Faith We Understand

11 Now faith is the substance of things hoped
for, the evidence [a]of things not seen.
2 For by it the elders obtained a good report.
3 Through faith we understand that [a]the
worlds were framed by the word of God, so that
things which are seen were not made of things
which do appear.

Faith at the Dawn of History
(Gen. 4:1–16; 5:18–24; 6:5—8:22)

4 By faith [a]Abel offered unto God a more
excellent sacrifice than Cain, by which he obtained witness that he was righteous, God testifying of his gifts: and by it he being dead yet
[b]speaketh.
5 By faith [a]Enoch was translated that he
should not see death; AND WAS NOT FOUND, BECAUSE
GOD HAD TRANSLATED HIM: for before his translation he had this testimony, that he pleased God.
6 But without faith *it is* impossible to please
him: for he that cometh to God must believe that
he is, and *that* he is a rewarder of them that diligently seek him.
7 By faith [a]Noah, being warned of God of
things not seen as yet, moved with fear, [b]prepared
an ark to the saving of his house; by the which
he condemned the world, and became heir of [c]the
righteousness which is by faith.

Faithful Abraham
(Gen. 15:1–6; 21:1–7)

8 By faith [a]Abraham, when he was called
to go out into a place which he should after receive for an inheritance, obeyed; and he went out,
not knowing whither he went.
9 By faith he sojourned in the land of promise, as *in* a strange country, [a]dwelling in tabernacles with Isaac and Jacob, [b]the heirs with him of
the same promise:
10 For he looked for [a]a city which hath foundations, [b]whose builder and maker *is* God.
11 Through faith also [a]Sara herself received
strength to conceive seed, and [b]was delivered of
a child when she was past age, because she judged
him [c]faithful who had promised.
12 Therefore sprang there even of one, and
him as good as [a]dead, *so many* as the [b]stars of
the sky in multitude, and as the sand which is
by the sea shore innumerable.

The Heavenly Hope

13 These all died in faith, [a]not having received the [b]promises, but [c]having seen them afar
off, and were persuaded of *them,* and embraced
them, and [d]confessed that they were strangers
and pilgrims on the earth.
14 For they that say such things [a]declare
plainly that they seek a country.
15 And truly, if they had been mindful of
[a]that *country* from whence they came out, they
might have had opportunity to have returned.
16 But now they desire a better *country,* that
is, an heavenly: wherefore God is not ashamed
[a]to be called their God: for he hath [b]prepared for
them a city.

NKJV

after you have done the will of God, [b]you may
receive the promise:

37 *"For [a]yet a little while,*
And [b]He who is coming will come and*
will not tarry.
38 *Now [a]the* just shall live by faith;*
But if anyone draws back,
My soul has no pleasure in him."

39 But we are not of those [a]who draw back
to perdition, but of those who [b]believe to the saving of the soul.

By Faith We Understand

11 Now faith is the substance of things hoped
for, the evidence [a]of things not seen.
2 For by it the elders obtained a *good* testimony.
3 By faith we understand that [a]the worlds
were framed by the word of God, so that the
things which are seen were not made of things
which are visible.

Faith at the Dawn of History
(Gen. 4:1–16; 5:18–24; 6:5—8:22)

4 By faith [a]Abel offered to God a more excellent sacrifice than Cain, through which he obtained witness that he was righteous, God testifying of his gifts; and through it he being dead still
[b]speaks.
5 By faith Enoch was taken away so that
he did not see death, [a]*"and was not found, because God had taken him"*; for before he was
taken he had this testimony, that he pleased
God.
6 But without faith *it is* impossible to please
Him, for he who comes to God must believe that
He is, and *that* He is a rewarder of those who
diligently seek Him.
7 By faith [a]Noah, being divinely warned of
things not yet seen, moved with godly fear, [b]pre-
pared an ark for the saving of his household, by
which he condemned the world and became heir
of [c]the righteousness which is according to faith.

Faithful Abraham
(Gen. 15:1–6; 21:1–7)

8 By faith [a]Abraham obeyed when he was
called to go out to the place which he would receive as an inheritance. And he went out, not
knowing where he was going.
9 By faith he dwelt in the land of promise
as *in* a foreign country, [a]dwelling in tents with
Isaac and Jacob, [b]the heirs with him of the same
promise;
10 for he waited for [a]the city which has foundations, [b]whose builder and maker *is* God.
11 By faith [a]Sarah herself also received
strength to conceive seed, and [b]she* bore a child
when she was past the age, because she judged
Him [c]faithful who had promised.
12 Therefore from one man, and him as good
as [a]dead, were born *as many* as the [b]stars of the
sky in multitude—innumerable as the sand which
is by the seashore.

The Heavenly Hope

13 These all died in faith, [a]not having received the [b]promises, but [c]having seen them afar
off *were assured of them, embraced *them* and
[d]confessed that they were strangers and pilgrims
on the earth.
14 For those who say such things [a]declare
plainly that they seek a homeland.
15 And truly if they had called to mind [a]that
country from which they had come out, they
would have had opportunity to return.
16 But now they desire a better, that is, a
heavenly *country.* Therefore God is not ashamed
[a]to be called their God, for He has [b]prepared a
city for them.

36 [b][Col. 3:24] **37** [a]Luke 18:8 [b]Hab. 2:3, 4; Heb. 10:25; Rev. 22:20 **38** [a]Hab. 2:3, 4; Rom. 1:17; Gal. 3:11 **39** [a]2 Pet. 2:20 [b]Acts 16:31

CHAPTER 11

1 [a]Rom. 8:24; [2 Cor. 4:18; 5:7]; Heb. 11:7, 27 **3** [a]Gen. 1:1; Ps. 33:6; [John 1:3]; 2 Pet. 3:5 **4** [a]Gen. 4:3–5; Matt. 23:35; 1 John 3:12 [b]Gen. 4:8–10; Heb. 12:24 **5** [a]Gen. 5:21–24 **7** [a]Gen. 6:13–22 [b]1 Pet. 3:20 [c]Rom. 3:22 **8** [a]Gen. 12:1–4; Acts 7:2–4 **9** [a]Gen. 12:8; 13:3, 18; 18:1, 9 [b]Heb. 6:17 **10** [a][Heb. 12:22; 13:14] [b][Rev. 21:10] **11** [a]Gen. 17:19; 18:11–14; 21:1, 2 [b]Luke 1:36 [c]Heb. 10:23 **12** [a]Rom. 4:19 [b]Gen. 15:5; 22:17; 32:12 **13** [a]Heb. 11:39 [b]Gen. 12:7 [c]John 8:56; Heb. 11:27 [d]Gen. 23:4; 47:9; 1 Chr. 29:15; Ps. 39:12; Eph. 2:19; 1 Pet. 1:17; 2:11 **14** [a]Heb. 13:14 **15** [a]Gen. 11:31 **16** [a]Gen. 26:24; 28:13; Ex. 3:6, 15; 4:5 [b][John 14:2]; Heb. 11:10; [Rev. 21:2]

*

10:37 Or *that which*
10:38 NU *my just one*
11:11 NU omits *she bore a child*
11:13 NU, M omit *were assured of them*

KJV

The Faith of the Patriarchs
(Gen. 22:1–14; 48:8–16; 50:22–25)

17 By faith Abraham, [a]when he was tried,
offered up Isaac: and he that had received the
promises offered up his only begotten *son,*
18 Of whom it was said, [a]That IN ISAAC SHALL
THY SEED BE CALLED:
19 Accounting that God [a]*was* able to raise
him up, even from the dead; from whence also
he received him in a figure.
20 By faith [a]Isaac blessed Jacob and Esau
concerning things to come.
21 By faith Jacob, when he was a dying,
[a]blessed both the sons of Joseph; and worshipped,
leaning upon the top of his staff.
22 By faith [a]Joseph, when he died, made
mention of the departing of the children of Israel;
and gave commandment concerning his bones.

The Faith of Moses
(Ex. 2:1–10; 12:31–51)

23 By faith [a]Moses, when he was born, was
hid three months of his parents, because they saw
he was a proper child; and they were not afraid
of the king's [b]commandment.
24 By faith [a]Moses, when he was come to
years, refused to be called the son of Pharaoh's
daughter;
25 Choosing rather to suffer affliction with
the people of God, than to enjoy the pleasures of
sin for a season;
26 Esteeming [a]the reproach of Christ greater
riches than the treasures in Egypt: for he had respect unto the [b]recompence of the reward.
27 By faith [a]he forsook Egypt, not fearing the
wrath of the king: for he endured, as seeing him
who is invisible.
28 Through faith [a]he kept the passover, and
the sprinkling of blood, lest he that destroyed the
firstborn should touch them.
29 By faith [a]they passed through the Red sea
as by dry *land:* which the Egyptians assaying to
do were drowned.

By Faith They Overcame

30 By faith [a]the walls of Jericho fell down,
after they were compassed about seven days.
31 By faith [a]the harlot Rahab perished not
with them that believed not, when [b]she had received the spies with peace.
32 And what shall I more say? for the time
would fail me to tell of [a]Gedeon, and *of* [b]Barak,
and *of* [c]Samson, and *of* [d]Jephthae; *of* [e]David also,
and [f]Samuel, and *of* the prophets:
33 Who through faith subdued kingdoms,
wrought righteousness, obtained promises,
[a]stopped the mouths of lions,
34 [a]Quenched the violence of fire, escaped
the edge of the sword, out of weakness were made
strong, waxed valiant in fight, turned to flight the
armies of the aliens.
35 [a]Women received their dead raised to life
again: and others were [b]tortured, not accepting
deliverance; that they might obtain a better
resurrection:
36 And others had trial of *cruel* mockings
and scourgings, yea, moreover [a]of bonds and
imprisonment:
37 [a]They were stoned, they were sawn asunder, were tempted, were slain with the sword:
[b]they wandered about [c]in sheepskins and goat-
skins; being destitute, afflicted, tormented;
38 (Of whom the world was not worthy:) they
wandered in deserts, and *in* mountains, and [a]*in*
dens and caves of the earth.
39 And these all, [a]having obtained a good report through faith, received not the promise:
40 God having provided some better thing for

17 [a]Gen. 22:1–14; James 2:21
18 [a]Gen. 21:12; Rom. 9:7
19 [a]Rom. 4:17
20 [a]Gen. 27:26–40
21 [a]Gen. 48:1, 5, 16, 20
22 [a]Gen. 50:24, 25; Ex. 13:19
23 [a]Ex. 2:1–3 [b]Ex. 1:16, 22
24 [a]Ex. 2:11–15
26 [a]Heb. 13:13 [b]Rom. 8:18; 2 Cor. 4:17
27 [a]Ex. 10:28
28 [a]Ex. 12:21
29 [a]Ex. 14:22–29; Jude 5
30 [a]Josh. 6:20
31 [a]Josh. 2:9; 6:23; James 2:25 [b]Josh. 2:1
32 [a]Judg. 6:11; 7:1–25 [b]Judg. 4:6–24 [c]Judg. 13:24—16:31 [d]Judg. 11:1–29; 12:1–7 [e]1 Sam. 16; 17 [f]1 Sam. 7:9–14
33 [a]Judg. 14:6; 1 Sam. 17:34; Dan. 6:22
34 [a]Dan. 3:23–28
35 [a]1 Kin. 17:22; 2 Kin. 4:35–37 [b]Acts 22:25
36 [a]Gen. 39:20; 1 Kin. 22:27; 2 Chr. 18:26; Jer. 20:2; 37:15
37 [a]1 Kin. 21:13; 2 Chr. 24:21; Acts 7:58 [b]2 Kin. 1:8; Matt. 3:4 [c]1 Kin. 19:13, 19; 2 Kin. 2:8, 13; Zech. 13:4
38 [a]1 Kin. 18:4, 13; 19:9
39 [a]Heb. 11:2, 13

*———

11:26 NU, M *of*
11:37 NU omits *were tempted*

NKJV

The Faith of the Patriarchs
(Gen. 22:1–14; 48:8–16; 50:22–25)

17 By faith Abraham, [a]when he was tested,
offered up Isaac, and he who had received the
promises offered up his only begotten *son,*
18 of whom it was said, [a]*"In Isaac your seed
shall be called,"*
19 concluding that God [a]*was* able to raise
him up, even from the dead, from which he also
received him in a figurative sense.
20 By faith [a]Isaac blessed Jacob and Esau
concerning things to come.
21 By faith Jacob, when he was dying,
[a]blessed each of the sons of Joseph, and worshiped, *leaning* on the top of his staff.
22 By faith [a]Joseph, when he was dying,
made mention of the departure of the children of
Israel, and gave instructions concerning his
bones.

The Faith of Moses
(Ex. 2:1–10; 12:31–51)

23 By faith [a]Moses, when he was born, was
hidden three months by his parents, because they
saw *he was* a beautiful child; and they were not
afraid of the king's [b]command.
24 By faith [a]Moses, when he became of age,
refused to be called the son of Pharaoh's
daughter,
25 choosing rather to suffer affliction with
the people of God than to enjoy the passing pleasures of sin,
26 esteeming [a]the reproach of Christ greater
riches than the treasures *in Egypt; for he looked
to the [b]reward.
27 By faith [a]he forsook Egypt, not fearing the
wrath of the king; for he endured as seeing Him
who is invisible.
28 By faith [a]he kept the Passover and the
sprinkling of blood, lest he who destroyed the
firstborn should touch them.
29 By faith [a]they passed through the Red Sea
as by dry *land, whereas* the Egyptians, attempting
to do so, were drowned.

By Faith They Overcame

30 By faith [a]the walls of Jericho fell down
after they were encircled for seven days.
31 By faith [a]the harlot Rahab did not perish
with those who did not believe, when [b]she had
received the spies with peace.
32 And what more shall I say? For the time
would fail me to tell of [a]Gideon and [b]Barak and
[c]Samson and [d]Jephthah, also *of* [e]David and
[f]Samuel and the prophets:
33 who through faith subdued kingdoms,
worked righteousness, obtained promises,
[a]stopped the mouths of lions,
34 [a]quenched the violence of fire, escaped
the edge of the sword, out of weakness were made
strong, became valiant in battle, turned to flight
the armies of the aliens.
35 [a]Women received their dead raised to life
again. Others were [b]tortured, not accepting deliverance, that they might obtain a better resurrection.
36 Still others had trial of mockings and
scourgings, yes, and [a]of chains and imprisonment.
37 [a]They were stoned, they were sawn in
two, *were tempted, were slain with the sword.
[b]They wandered about [c]in sheepskins and goat-
skins, being destitute, afflicted, tormented—
38 of whom the world was not worthy. They
wandered in deserts and mountains, [a]*in* dens and
caves of the earth.
39 And all these, [a]having obtained a good
testimony through faith, did not receive the
promise,
40 God having provided something better for

KJV

us, that they without us should not be [a]made perfect.

The Race of Faith

12 Wherefore seeing we also are compassed about with so great a cloud of witnesses, [a]let us lay aside every weight, and the sin which doth so easily beset *us,* and [b]let us run [c]with patience the race that is set before us,

2 Looking unto Jesus the author and finisher of *our* faith; [a]who for the joy that was set before him [b]endured the cross, despising the shame, and [c]is set down at the right hand of the throne of God.

The Discipline of God
(Prov. 3:11, 12)

3 [a]For consider him that endured such contradiction of sinners against himself, [b]lest ye be wearied and faint in your minds.

4 [a]Ye have not yet resisted unto blood, striving against sin.

5 And ye have forgotten the exhortation which speaketh unto you as unto children, [a]MY SON, DESPISE NOT THOU THE CHASTENING OF THE LORD, NOR FAINT WHEN THOU ART REBUKED OF HIM:

6 FOR [a]WHOM THE LORD LOVETH HE CHASTENETH, AND SCOURGETH EVERY SON WHOM HE RECEIVETH.

7 [a]If ye endure chastening, God dealeth with you as with sons; for what [b]son is he whom the father chasteneth not?

8 But if ye be without chastisement, [a]whereof all are partakers, then are ye bastards, and not sons.

9 Furthermore we have had fathers of our flesh which corrected *us,* and we gave *them* reverence: shall we not much rather be in subjection unto [a]the Father of spirits, and live?

10 For they verily for a few days chastened *us* after their own pleasure; but he for *our* profit, [a]that *we* might be partakers of his holiness.

11 Now no chastening for the present seemeth to be joyous, but grievous: nevertheless afterward it yieldeth [a]the peaceable fruit of righteousness unto them which are exercised thereby.

Renew Your Spiritual Vitality
(Gen. 25:29–34; 27:30–40)

12 Wherefore [a]lift up the hands which hang down, and the feeble knees;

13 And make straight paths for your feet, lest that which is lame be turned out of the way; but let it rather be healed.

14 [a]Follow peace with all *men,* and holiness, [b]without which no man shall see the Lord:

15 Looking diligently lest any man [a]fail of the grace of God; lest any [b]root of bitterness springing up trouble *you,* and thereby many be defiled;

16 Lest there *be* any [a]fornicator, or profane person, as Esau, [b]who for one morsel of meat sold his birthright.

17 For ye know how that afterward, when he would have inherited the blessing, he was [a]rejected: for he found no place of repentance, though he sought it carefully with tears.

The Glorious Company

18 For ye are not come unto [a]the mount that might be touched, and that burned with fire, nor unto blackness, and darkness, and tempest,

19 And the sound of a trumpet, and the voice of words; which *voice* they that heard [a]intreated that the word should not be spoken to them any more:

20 (For they could not endure that which was commanded, [a]AND IF SO MUCH AS A BEAST TOUCH

---

40 [a]Heb. 5:9

CHAPTER 12

1 [a]Col. 3:8 [b]1 Cor. 9:24; Gal. 2:2; Heb. 10:39 [c]Rom. 12:12; Heb. 10:36
2 [a]Luke 24:26 [b]Ps. 69:7, 19; Phil. 2:8; [Heb. 2:9] [c]Ps. 110:1
3 [a]Matt. 10:24 [b]Gal. 6:9; Heb. 12:5
4 [a][1 Cor. 10:13]
5 [a]Job 5:17; Prov. 3:11, 12
6 [a]Ps. 94:12; Rev. 3:19
7 [a]Deut. 8:5; 2 Sam. 7:14 [b]Prov. 13:24; 19:18; 23:13
8 [a]1 Pet. 5:9
9 [a][Job 12:10]
10 [a]Lev. 11:44
11 [a]Is. 32:17; 2 Tim. 4:8; James 3:17, 18
12 [a]Is. 35:3
14 [a]Ps. 34:14 [b]Matt. 5:8; [Heb. 9:28]
15 [a]2 Cor. 6:1; Gal. 5:4; Heb. 4:1 [b]Deut. 29:18
16 [a][1 Cor. 6:13–18] [b]Gen. 25:33
17 [a]Gen. 27:30–40
18 [a]Ex. 19:12, 16; 20:18; Deut. 4:11; 5:22
19 [a]Ex. 20:18–26; Deut. 5:25; 18:16
20 [a]Ex. 19:12, 13

NKJV

us, that they should not be [a]made perfect apart from us.

The Race of Faith

12 Therefore we also, since we are surrounded by so great a cloud of witnesses, [a]let us lay aside every weight, and the sin which so easily ensnares *us,* and [b]let us run [c]with endurance the race that is set before us,

2 looking unto Jesus, the author and finisher of *our* faith, [a]who for the joy that was set before Him [b]endured the cross, despising the shame, and [c]has sat down at the right hand of the throne of God.

The Discipline of God
(Prov. 3:11, 12)

3 [a]For consider Him who endured such hostility from sinners against Himself, [b]lest you become weary and discouraged in your souls.

4 [a]You have not yet resisted to bloodshed, striving against sin.

5 And you have forgotten the exhortation which speaks to you as to sons:

> [a]*"My son, do not despise the chastening of the LORD,*
> *Nor be discouraged when you are rebuked by Him;*

6 *For [a]whom the LORD loves He chastens,*
> *And scourges every son whom He receives."*

7 [a]If* you endure chastening, God deals with you as with sons; for what [b]son is there whom a father does not chasten?

8 But if you are without chastening, [a]of which all have become partakers, then you are illegitimate and not sons.

9 Furthermore, we have had human fathers who corrected *us,* and we paid *them* respect. Shall we not much more readily be in subjection to [a]the Father of spirits and live?

10 For they indeed for a few days chastened *us* as seemed *best* to them, but He for *our* profit, [a]that *we* may be partakers of His holiness.

11 Now no chastening seems to be joyful for the present, but painful; nevertheless, afterward it yields [a]the peaceable fruit of righteousness to those who have been trained by it.

Renew Your Spiritual Vitality
(Gen. 25:29–34; 27:30–40)

12 Therefore [a]strengthen the hands which hang down, and the feeble knees,

13 and make straight paths for your feet, so that what is lame may not be *dislocated,* but rather be healed.

14 [a]Pursue peace with all *people,* and holiness, [b]without which no one will see the Lord:

15 looking carefully lest anyone [a]fall short of the grace of God; lest any [b]root of bitterness springing up cause trouble, and by this many become defiled;

16 lest there *be* any [a]fornicator or profane person like Esau, [b]who for one morsel of food sold his birthright.

17 For you know that afterward, when he wanted to inherit the blessing, he was [a]rejected, for he found no place for repentance, though he sought it diligently with tears.

The Glorious Company

18 For you have not come *to [a]the mountain that may be touched and that burned with fire, and to blackness and *darkness and tempest,

19 and the sound of a trumpet and the voice of words, so that those who heard *it* [a]begged that the word should not be spoken to them anymore.

20 (For they could not endure what was commanded: [a]*"And if so much as a beast touches the*

---

*

12:7 NU, M *It is for discipline that you endure; God*
12:18 NU *to that which* • NU *gloom*

KJV

THE MOUNTAIN, IT SHALL BE STONED, OR THRUST
THROUGH WITH A DART:
21 And so terrible was the sight, *that* Moses
said, [a]I EXCEEDINGLY FEAR AND QUAKE:)
22 But ye are come unto mount Sion, and
unto the city of the living God, the heavenly Jerusalem, and to an innumerable company of angels,
23 To the general assembly and church of
[a]the firstborn, [b]which are written in heaven, and
to God [c]the Judge of all, and to the spirits of just
men [d]made perfect,
24 And to Jesus [a]the mediator of the new
covenant, and to [b]the blood of sprinkling, that
speaketh better things [c]than *that of* Abel.

Hear the Heavenly Voice

25 See that ye refuse not him that speaketh.
For [a]if they escaped not who refused him that
spake on earth, much more *shall not* we *escape*,
if we turn away from him that *speaketh* from
heaven:
26 Whose voice then shook the earth: but
now he hath promised, saying, [a]YET ONCE MORE I
SHAKE NOT THE EARTH ONLY, BUT ALSO HEAVEN.
27 And this *word*, Yet once more, signifieth
the [a]removing of those things that are shaken,
as of things that are made, that those things which
cannot be shaken may remain.
28 Wherefore we receiving a kingdom which
cannot be moved, let us have grace, whereby we
may [a]serve God acceptably with reverence and
godly fear:
29 For [a]our God *is* a consuming fire.

Concluding Moral Directions

13 Let [a]brotherly love continue.
2 [a]Be not forgetful to entertain strangers:
for thereby [b]some have entertained angels
unawares.
3 [a]Remember them that are in bonds, as
bound with them; *and* them which suffer adversity, as being yourselves also in the body.
4 [a]Marriage *is* honourable in all, and the
bed undefiled: [b]but whoremongers and adulterers
God will judge.
5 *Let your* conversation *be* without covetousness; *and be* content with such things as ye
have: for he hath said, [a]I WILL NEVER LEAVE THEE,
NOR FORSAKE THEE.
6 So that we may boldly say, [a]THE LORD *IS*
MY HELPER, AND I WILL NOT FEAR WHAT MAN SHALL
DO UNTO ME.

Concluding Religious Directions

7 Remember them which have the rule over
you, who have spoken unto you the word of God:
whose faith follow, considering the end of *their*
conversation.
8 Jesus Christ [a]the same yesterday, and to
day, and for ever.
9 Be not carried about with divers and
strange doctrines. For *it is* a good thing that the
heart be established with grace; not with meats,
which have not profited them that have been occupied therein.
10 We have an altar, whereof they have no
right to eat which serve the tabernacle.
11 For the bodies of those beasts, whose
blood is brought into the sanctuary by the high
priest for sin, are burned without the camp.
12 Wherefore Jesus also, that he might sanctify the people with his own blood, suffered without the gate.
13 Let us go forth therefore unto him without
the camp, bearing [a]his reproach.
14 For here have we no continuing city, but
we seek one to come.
15 [a]By him therefore let us offer [b]the sacrifice of praise to God continually, that is, [c]the fruit
of *our* lips giving thanks to his name.

21 [a]Deut. 9:19
23 [a][James 1:18] [b]Luke 10:20 [c]Gen. 18:25; Ps. 50:6; 94:2 [d][Phil. 3:12]
24 [a]1 Tim. 2:5; Heb. 8:6; 9:15 [b]Ex. 24:8 [c]Gen. 4:10; Heb. 11:4
25 [a]Heb. 2:2, 3
26 [a]Hag. 2:6
27 [a][Is. 34:4; 54:10; 65:17; Rom. 8:19, 21]; 1 Cor. 7:31; Heb. 1:10
28 [a]Heb. 13:15, 21
29 [a]Ex. 24:17

CHAPTER 13

1 [a]Rom. 12:10
2 [a]Matt. 25:35; Rom. 12:13 [b]Gen. 18:1–22; 19:1
3 [a]Matt. 25:36; Heb. 10:34
4 [a]Prov. 5:18, 19 [b]1 Cor. 6:9; Gal. 5:19, 21; 1 Thess. 4:6
5 [a]Gen. 28:15; Deut. 31:6, 8; Josh. 1:5
6 [a]Ps. 27:1; 118:6
8 [a][John 8:58]; 2 Cor. 1:19; Heb. 1:12
13 [a]1 Pet. 4:14
15 [a]Eph. 5:20 [b]Lev. 7:12 [c]Is. 57:19; Hos. 14:2

*
12:20 NU, M omit the rest of v. 20.
12:26 NU *will shake*
12:28 M omits *may*
13:9 NU, M *away*

NKJV

mountain, it shall be stoned *or shot with an
arrow."*
21 And so terrifying was the sight *that* Moses
said, [a]*"I am exceedingly afraid* and trembling.")
22 But you have come to Mount Zion and to
the city of the living God, the heavenly Jerusalem,
to an innumerable company of angels,
23 to the general assembly and church of
[a]the firstborn [b]*who are* registered in heaven, to
God [c]the Judge of all, to the spirits of just men
[d]made perfect,
24 to Jesus [a]the Mediator of the new covenant, and to [b]the blood of sprinkling that speaks
better things [c]than *that of* Abel.

Hear the Heavenly Voice

25 See that you do not refuse Him who
speaks. For [a]if they did not escape who refused
Him who spoke on earth, much more *shall we
not escape* if we turn away from Him who *speaks*
from heaven,
26 whose voice then shook the earth; but now
He has promised, saying, [a]*"Yet once more I
shake not only the earth, but also heaven."
27 Now this, *"Yet once more,"* indicates the
[a]removal of those things that are being shaken,
as of things that are made, that the things which
cannot be shaken may remain.
28 Therefore, since we are receiving a kingdom which cannot be shaken, let us have grace,
by which we *may [a]serve God acceptably with
reverence and godly fear.
29 For [a]our God *is* a consuming fire.

Concluding Moral Directions

13 Let [a]brotherly love continue.
2 [a]Do not forget to entertain strangers,
for by so *doing* [b]some have unwittingly entertained angels.
3 [a]Remember the prisoners as if chained
with them—those who are mistreated—since you
yourselves are in the body also.
4 [a]Marriage *is* honorable among all, and the
bed undefiled; [b]but fornicators and adulterers
God will judge.
5 *Let your* conduct *be* without covetousness; *be* content with such things as you have.
For He Himself has said, [a]*"I will never leave you
nor forsake you."*
6 So we may boldly say:

[a]*"The LORD is my helper;*
I will not fear.
What can man do to me?"

Concluding Religious Directions

7 Remember those who rule over you, who
have spoken the word of God to you, whose faith
follow, considering the outcome of *their* conduct.
8 Jesus Christ *is* [a]the same yesterday, today,
and forever.
9 Do not be carried *about with various and
strange doctrines. For *it is* good that the heart
be established by grace, not with foods which
have not profited those who have been occupied
with them.
10 We have an altar from which those who
serve the tabernacle have no right to eat.
11 For the bodies of those animals, whose
blood is brought into the sanctuary by the high
priest for sin, are burned outside the camp.
12 Therefore Jesus also, that He might sanctify the people with His own blood, suffered outside the gate.
13 Therefore let us go forth to Him, outside
the camp, bearing [a]His reproach.
14 For here we have no continuing city, but
we seek the one to come.
15 [a]Therefore by Him let us continually offer
[b]the sacrifice of praise to God, that is, [c]the fruit
of *our* lips, giving thanks to His name.

KJV

16 [a]But to do good and to communicate forget not: for [b]with such sacrifices God is well pleased.

17 [a]Obey them that have the rule over you, and submit yourselves: for [b]they watch for your souls, as they that must give account, that they may do it with joy, and not with grief: for that *is* unprofitable for you.

Prayer Requested

18 [a]Pray for us: for we trust we have [b]a good conscience, in all things willing to live honestly.

19 But I beseech *you* the rather to do this, that I may be restored to you the sooner.

Benediction, Final Exhortation, Farewell

20 Now [a]the God of peace, [b]that brought again from the dead our Lord Jesus, [c]that great shepherd of the sheep, [d]through the blood of the everlasting covenant,

21 Make you perfect in every good work to do his will, [a]working in you that which is wellpleasing in his sight, through Jesus Christ; to whom *be* glory for ever and ever. Amen.

22 And I beseech you, brethren, suffer the word of exhortation: for I have written a letter unto you in few words.

23 Know ye that *our* brother Timothy is set at liberty; with whom, if he come shortly, I will see you.

24 Salute all them that have the rule over you, and all the saints. They of Italy salute you.

25 Grace *be* with you all. Amen.

16 [a]Rom. 12:13 [b]2 Cor. 9:12; Phil. 4:18
17 [a]Phil. 2:29 [b]Is. 62:6; Ezek. 3:17; Acts 20:28
18 [a]Eph. 6:19 [b]Acts 23:1
20 [a]Rom. 5:1, 2, 10; 15:33 [b]Ps. 16:10, 11; Hos. 6:2; Rom. 4:24 [c]Ps. 23:1; Is. 40:11; 63:11; John 10:11; 1 Pet. 2:25; 5:4 [d]Zech. 9:11; Heb. 10:29
21 [a]Phil. 2:13

NKJV

16 [a]But do not forget to do good and to share, for [b]with such sacrifices God is well pleased.

17 [a]Obey those who rule over you, and be submissive, for [b]they watch out for your souls, as those who must give account. Let them do so with joy and not with grief, for that would be unprofitable for you.

Prayer Requested

18 [a]Pray for us; for we are confident that we have [b]a good conscience, in all things desiring to live honorably.

19 But I especially urge *you* to do this, that I may be restored to you the sooner.

Benediction, Final Exhortation, Farewell

20 Now may [a]the God of peace [b]who brought up our Lord Jesus from the dead, [c]that great Shepherd of the sheep, [d]through the blood of the everlasting covenant,

21 make you complete in every good work to do His will, [a]working in *you what is well pleasing in His sight, through Jesus Christ, to whom *be* glory forever and ever. Amen.

22 And I appeal to you, brethren, bear with the word of exhortation, for I have written to you in few words.

23 Know that *our* brother Timothy has been set free, with whom I shall see you if he comes shortly.

24 Greet all those who rule over you, and all the saints. Those from Italy greet you.

25 Grace *be* with you all. Amen.

*
13:21 NU, M *us*

KJV

THE EPISTLE OF

JAMES

Greeting to the Twelve Tribes

1 James, [a]a servant of God and of the Lord
Jesus Christ, to the twelve tribes which are
scattered abroad, greeting.

Profiting from Trials

2 My brethren, [a]count it all joy [b]when ye
fall into divers temptations;
3 [a]Knowing *this,* that the trying of your
faith worketh patience.
4 But let patience have *her* perfect work,
that ye may be perfect and entire, wanting
nothing.
5 [a]If any of you lack wisdom, [b]let him ask
of God, that giveth to all *men* liberally, and up-
braideth not; and [c]it shall be given him.
6 [a]But let him ask in faith, nothing wavering. For he that wavereth is like a wave of the
sea driven with the wind and tossed.
7 For let not that man think that he shall
receive any thing of the Lord.
8 [a]A double minded man *is* unstable in all
his ways.

The Perspective of Rich and Poor

9 Let the brother of low degree rejoice in
that he is exalted:
10 But the rich, in that he is made low: because [a]as the flower of the grass he shall pass
away.
11 For the sun is no sooner risen with a burning heat, but it withereth the grass, and the flower
thereof falleth, and the grace of the fashion of it
perisheth: so also shall the rich man fade away
in his ways.

Loving God Under Trials

12 [a]Blessed *is* the man that endureth temptation: for when he is tried, he shall receive [b]the
crown of life, [c]which the Lord hath promised to
them that love him.
13 Let no man say when he is tempted, I am
tempted of God: for God cannot be tempted with
evil, neither tempteth he any man:
14 But every man is tempted, when he is
drawn away of his own lust, and enticed.
15 Then [a]when lust hath conceived, it
bringeth forth sin: and sin, when it is finished,
[b]bringeth forth death.
16 Do not err, my beloved brethren.
17 [a]Every good gift and every perfect gift is
from above, and cometh down from the Father
of lights, [b]with whom is no variableness, neither
shadow of turning.
18 [a]Of his own will begat he us with the
[b]word of truth, [c]that we should be a kind of firstfruits of his creatures.

Qualities Needed in Trials

19 Wherefore, my beloved brethren, let every
man be swift to hear, [a]slow to speak, [b]slow to
wrath:
20 For the wrath of man worketh not the
righteousness of God.

CHAPTER 1
1 [a]Acts 12:17
2 [a]Acts 5:41 [b]2 Pet. 1:6
3 [a]Rom. 5:3–5
5 [a]1 Kin. 3:9; James 3:17 [b]Prov. 2:3–6; Matt. 7:7 [c]Jer. 29:12
6 [a][Mark 11:23, 24]; Acts 10:20
8 [a]James 4:8
10 [a]Job 14:2
12 [a]Job 5:17; Luke 6:22; Heb. 10:36; James 5:11; [1 Pet. 3:14; 4:14] [b][1 Cor. 9:25] [c]Matt. 10:22
15 [a]Job 15:35; Ps. 7:14; Is. 59:4 [b][Rom. 5:12; 6:23]
17 [a]John 3:27 [b]Num. 23:19
18 [a]John 1:13 [b]2 Cor. 6:7; 1 Thess. 2:13; 2 Tim. 2:15; [1 Pet. 1:3, 23] [c][Eph. 1:12, 13]; Heb. 12:23; Rev. 14:4
19 [a]Prov. 10:19; 17:27 [b]Prov. 14:17; 16:32; Eccl. 7:9

NKJV

THE EPISTLE OF

JAMES

Greeting to the Twelve Tribes

1 James, [a]a bondservant of God and of the
Lord Jesus Christ,

To the twelve tribes which are scattered
abroad:

Greetings.

Profiting from Trials

2 My brethren, [a]count it all joy [b]when you
fall into various trials,
3 [a]knowing that the testing of your faith
produces patience.
4 But let patience have *its* perfect work, that
you may be perfect and complete, lacking
nothing.
5 [a]If any of you lacks wisdom, [b]let him ask
of God, who gives to all liberally and without reproach, and [c]it will be given to him.
6 [a]But let him ask in faith, with no doubting,
for he who doubts is like a wave of the sea driven
and tossed by the wind.
7 For let not that man suppose that he will
receive anything from the Lord;
8 *he is* [a]a double-minded man, unstable in
all his ways.

The Perspective of Rich and Poor

9 Let the lowly brother glory in his exaltation,
10 but the rich in his humiliation, because [a]as
a flower of the field he will pass away.
11 For no sooner has the sun risen with a
burning heat than it withers the grass; its flower
falls, and its beautiful appearance perishes. So the
rich man also will fade away in his pursuits.

Loving God Under Trials

12 [a]Blessed *is* the man who endures temptation; for when he has been approved, he will receive [b]the crown of life [c]which the Lord has promised to those who love Him.
13 Let no one say when he is tempted, "I am
tempted by God"; for God cannot be tempted by
evil, nor does He Himself tempt anyone.
14 But each one is tempted when he is drawn
away by his own desires and enticed.
15 Then, [a]when desire has conceived, it gives
birth to sin; and sin, when it is full-grown, [b]brings
forth death.
16 Do not be deceived, my beloved brethren.
17 [a]Every good gift and every perfect gift is
from above, and comes down from the Father of
lights, [b]with whom there is no variation or
shadow of turning.
18 [a]Of His own will He brought us forth by
the [b]word of truth, [c]that we might be a kind of
firstfruits of His creatures.

Qualities Needed in Trials

19 *So then, my beloved brethren, let every
man be swift to hear, [a]slow to speak, [b]slow to
wrath;
20 for the wrath of man does not produce the
righteousness of God.

*———

1:19 NU *Know this* or *This you know*

KJV

Doers—Not Hearers Only

21 Wherefore [a]lay apart all filthiness and superfluity of naughtiness, and receive with meekness the engrafted word, [b]which is able to save your souls.

22 But [a]be ye doers of the word, and not hearers only, deceiving your own selves.

23 For [a]if any be a hearer of the word, and not a doer, he is like unto a man beholding his natural face in a glass:

24 For he beholdeth himself, and goeth his way, and straightway forgetteth what manner of man he was.

25 But [a]whoso looketh into the perfect law of liberty, and continueth *therein,* he being not a forgetful hearer, but a doer of the work, [b]this man shall be blessed in his deed.

26 If any man among you seem to be religious, and [a]bridleth not his tongue, but deceiveth his own heart, this man's religion *is* vain.

27 [a]Pure religion and undefiled before God and the Father is this, [b]To visit the fatherless and widows in their affliction, [c]*and* to keep himself unspotted from the world.

Beware of Personal Favoritism

2 My brethren, have not the faith of our Lord Jesus Christ, [a]*the Lord* of glory, with [b]respect of persons.

2 For if there come unto your assembly a man with a gold ring, in goodly apparel, and there come in also a poor man in vile raiment;

3 And ye have respect to him that weareth the gay clothing, and say unto him, Sit thou here in a good place; and say to the poor, Stand thou there, or sit here under my footstool:

4 Are ye not then partial in yourselves, and are become judges of evil thoughts?

5 Hearken, my beloved brethren, [a]Hath not God chosen the poor of this world [b]rich in faith, and heirs of the kingdom [c]which he hath promised to them that love him?

6 But [a]ye have despised the poor. Do not rich men oppress you, [b]and draw you before the judgment seats?

7 Do not they blaspheme that worthy name by the which ye are [a]called?

8 If ye fulfil the royal law according to the scripture, [a]THOU SHALT LOVE THY NEIGHBOUR AS THYSELF, ye do well:

9 But if ye have respect to persons, ye commit sin, and are convinced of the law as [a]transgressors.

10 For whosoever shall keep the whole law, and yet [a]offend in one *point,* [b]he is guilty of all.

11 For he that said, [a]DO NOT COMMIT ADULTERY, said also, [b]DO NOT KILL. Now if thou commit no adultery, yet if thou kill, thou art become a transgressor of the law.

12 So speak ye, and so do, as they that shall be judged by [a]the law of liberty.

13 For [a]he shall have judgment without mercy, that hath shewed [b]no [c]mercy; and [d]mercy rejoiceth against judgment.

Faith Without Works Is Dead
(cf. Gen. 22; Josh. 2)

14 [a]What *doth it* profit, my brethren, though a man say he hath faith, and have not works? can faith save him?

15 [a]If a brother or sister be naked, and destitute of daily food,

16 And [a]one of you say unto them, Depart in peace, be *ye* warmed and filled; notwithstanding ye give them not those things which are needful to the body; what *doth it* profit?

17 Even so faith, if it hath not works, is dead, being alone.

18 Yea, a man may say, Thou hast faith, and

21 [a]Col. 3:8 [b]Acts 13:26
22 [a]Matt. 7:21–28; Luke 6:46–49; [Rom. 2:13; James 1:22–25; 2:14–20]
23 [a]Luke 6:47
25 [a][John 8:32; Rom. 8:2; 2 Cor. 3:17]; Gal. 2:4; 6:2; James 2:12; 1 Pet. 2:16 [b]John 13:17
26 [a]Ps. 34:13
27 [a]Matt. 25:34–36 [b]Is. 1:17 [c][Rom. 12:2]

CHAPTER 2

1 [a]Acts 7:2; 1 Cor. 2:8 [b]Lev. 19:15
5 [a]Job 34:19; John 7:48; 1 Cor. 1:27 [b]Luke 12:21; 1 Tim. 6:18; Rev. 2:9 [c]Ex. 20:6
6 [a]1 Cor. 11:22 [b]Acts 13:50
7 [a]Acts 11:26; 1 Pet. 4:16
8 [a]Lev. 19:18
9 [a]Lev. 19:15; Deut. 1:17
10 [a]Gal. 3:10 [b]Deut. 27:26
11 [a]Ex. 20:14; Deut. 5:18 [b]Ex. 20:13; Deut. 5:17
12 [a]James 1:25
13 [a]Job 22:6 [b]Prov. 21:13; Matt. 18:32–35; [Luke 6:37] [c]Mic. 7:18; [Matt. 5:7] [d]Rom. 12:8
14 [a]Matt. 7:21–23, 26; 21:28–32
15 [a]Matt. 25:35; Luke 3:11
16 [a][1 John 3:17, 18]

NKJV

Doers—Not Hearers Only

21 Therefore [a]lay aside all filthiness and overflow of wickedness, and receive with meekness the implanted word, [b]which is able to save your souls.

22 But [a]be doers of the word, and not hearers only, deceiving yourselves.

23 For [a]if anyone is a hearer of the word and not a doer, he is like a man observing his natural face in a mirror;

24 for he observes himself, goes away, and immediately forgets what kind of man he was.

25 But [a]he who looks into the perfect law of liberty and continues *in it,* and is not a forgetful hearer but a doer of the work, [b]this one will be blessed in what he does.

26 If anyone *among you thinks he is religious, and [a]does not bridle his tongue but deceives his own heart, this one's religion *is* useless.

27 [a]Pure and undefiled religion before God and the Father is this: [b]to visit orphans and widows in their trouble, [c]*and* to keep oneself unspotted from the world.

Beware of Personal Favoritism

2 My brethren, do not hold the faith of our Lord Jesus Christ, [a]*the Lord* of glory, with [b]partiality.

2 For if there should come into your assembly a man with gold rings, in fine apparel, and there should also come in a poor man in filthy clothes,

3 and you pay attention to the one wearing the fine clothes and say to him, "You sit here in a good place," and say to the poor man, "You stand there," or, "Sit here at my footstool,"

4 have you not shown partiality among yourselves, and become judges with evil thoughts?

5 Listen, my beloved brethren: [a]Has God not chosen the poor of this world *to be* [b]rich in faith and heirs of the kingdom [c]which He promised to those who love Him?

6 But [a]you have dishonored the poor man. Do not the rich oppress you [b]and drag you into the courts?

7 Do they not blaspheme that noble name by which you are [a]called?

8 If you really fulfill *the* royal law according to the Scripture, [a]*"You shall love your neighbor as yourself,"* you do well;

9 but if you show partiality, you commit sin, and are convicted by the law as [a]transgressors.

10 For whoever shall keep the whole law, and yet [a]stumble in one *point,* [b]he is guilty of all.

11 For He who said, [a]*"Do not commit adultery,"* also said, [b]*"Do not murder."* Now if you do not commit adultery, but you do murder, you have become a transgressor of the law.

12 So speak and so do as those who will be judged by [a]the law of liberty.

13 For [a]judgment is without mercy to the one who has shown [b]no [c]mercy. [d]Mercy triumphs over judgment.

Faith Without Works Is Dead
(cf. Gen. 22; Josh. 2)

14 [a]What *does it* profit, my brethren, if someone says he has faith but does not have works? Can faith save him?

15 [a]If a brother or sister is naked and destitute of daily food,

16 and [a]one of you says to them, "Depart in peace, be warmed and filled," but you do not give them the things which are needed for the body, what *does it* profit?

17 Thus also faith by itself, if it does not have works, is dead.

18 But someone will say, "You have faith,

*

1:26 NU omits *among you*

KJV

I have works: [a]shew me thy faith without thy works, [b]and I will shew thee my faith by my works.

19 Thou believest that there is one God; thou doest well: the devils also believe, and tremble.

20 But wilt thou know, O vain man, that faith without works is dead?

21 Was not Abraham our father justified by works, [a]when he had offered Isaac his son upon the altar?

22 Seest thou [a]how faith wrought with his works, and by [b]works was faith made perfect?

23 And the scripture was fulfilled which saith, [a]ABRAHAM BELIEVED GOD, AND IT WAS IMPUTED UNTO HIM FOR RIGHTEOUSNESS: and he was called [b]the Friend of God.

24 Ye see then how that by works a man is justified, and not by faith only.

25 Likewise also [a]was not Rahab the harlot justified by works, when she had received the messengers, and had sent *them* out another way?

26 For as the body without the spirit is dead, so faith without works is dead also.

The Untamable Tongue

3 My brethren, [a]be not many masters, [b]knowing that we shall receive the greater condemnation.

2 For [a]in many things we offend all. [b]If any man offend not in word, [c]the same *is* a perfect man, *and* able also to bridle the whole body.

3 Behold, [a]we put bits in the horses' mouths, that they may obey us; and we turn about their whole body.

4 Behold also the ships, which though *they be* so great, and *are* driven of fierce winds, yet are they turned about with a very small helm, whithersoever the governor listeth.

5 Even so [a]the tongue is a little member, and [b]boasteth great things. Behold, how great a matter a little fire kindleth!

6 And [a]the tongue *is* a fire, a world of iniquity: so is the tongue among our members, that it [b]defileth the whole body, and setteth on fire the course of nature; and it is set on fire of hell.

7 For every kind of beasts, and of birds, and of serpents, and of things in the sea, is tamed, and hath been tamed of mankind:

8 But the tongue can no man tame; *it is* an unruly evil, [a]full of deadly poison.

9 Therewith bless we God, even the Father; and therewith curse we men, which are made [a]after the similitude of God.

10 Out of the same mouth proceedeth blessing and cursing. My brethren, these things ought not so to be.

11 Doth a fountain send forth at the same place sweet *water* and bitter?

12 Can the [a]fig tree, my brethren, bear olive berries? either a vine, figs? so *can* no fountain both yield salt water and fresh.

Heavenly Versus Demonic Wisdom

13 [a]Who *is* a wise man and endued with knowledge among you? let him shew out of a good conversation his works with meekness of wisdom.

14 But if ye have [a]bitter envying and strife in your hearts, [b]glory not, and lie not against the truth.

15 [a]This wisdom descendeth not from above, but *is* earthly, sensual, devilish.

16 For [a]where envying and strife *is*, there *is* confusion and every evil work.

17 But [a]the wisdom that is from above is first pure, then peaceable, gentle, *and* easy to be intreated, full of mercy and good fruits, [b]without partiality, [c]and without hypocrisy.

18 [a]And the fruit of righteousness is sown in peace of them that make peace.

---

18 [a]Col. 1:6; 1 Thess. 1:3; Heb. 6:10 [b][Gal. 5:6]; James 3:13
21 [a]Gen. 22:9, 10, 12, 16–18
22 [a][John 6:29]; Heb. 11:17 [b]John 8:39
23 [a]Gen. 15:6; Rom. 4:3 [b]2 Chr. 20:7; Is. 41:8
25 [a]Heb. 11:31

CHAPTER 3

1 [a][Matt. 23:8]; Rom. 2:21; 1 Tim. 1:7 [b]Luke 6:37
2 [a]1 Kin. 8:46 [b]Ps. 34:13 [c][Matt. 12:34–37; James 3:2–12]
3 [a]Ps. 32:9
5 [a]Prov. 12:18; 15:2; James 1:26 [b]Ps. 12:3; 73:8
6 [a]Ps. 120:2, 3; Prov. 16:27 [b][Matt. 12:36; 15:11, 18]
8 [a]Ps. 140:3; Eccl. 10:11; Rom. 3:13
9 [a]Gen. 1:26; 5:1; 9:6; 1 Cor. 11:7
12 [a]Matt. 7:16–20
13 [a]Gal. 6:4
14 [a]Rom. 13:13 [b]Rom. 2:17
15 [a]Phil. 3:19
16 [a]1 Cor. 3:3
17 [a]1 Cor. 2:6, 7 [b]James 2:1 [c]Rom. 12:9; 2 Cor. 6:6; 1 Pet. 1:22
18 [a]Prov. 11:18; Is. 32:17; Hos. 10:12; Amos 6:12; [Gal. 6:8; Phil. 1:11]

*

2:18 NU omits *your* • NU omits *my*
2:20 NU *useless*
3:3 NU *Now if*
3:12 NU *Neither can a salty spring produce fresh water.*

NKJV

and I have works." [a]Show me your faith without *your works, [b]and I will show you my faith by *my works.

19 You believe that there is one God. You do well. Even the demons believe—and tremble!

20 But do you want to know, O foolish man, that faith without works is *dead?

21 Was not Abraham our father justified by works [a]when he offered Isaac his son on the altar?

22 Do you see [a]that faith was working together with his works, and by [b]works faith was made perfect?

23 And the Scripture was fulfilled which says, [a]*"Abraham believed God, and it was accounted to him for righteousness."* And he was called [b]the friend of God.

24 You see then that a man is justified by works, and not by faith only.

25 Likewise, [a]was not Rahab the harlot also justified by works when she received the messengers and sent *them* out another way?

26 For as the body without the spirit is dead, so faith without works is dead also.

The Untamable Tongue

3 My brethren, [a]let not many of you become teachers, [b]knowing that we shall receive a stricter judgment.

2 For [a]we all stumble in many things. [b]If anyone does not stumble in word, [c]he *is* a perfect man, able also to bridle the whole body.

3 *Indeed, [a]we put bits in horses' mouths that they may obey us, and we turn their whole body.

4 Look also at ships: although they are so large and are driven by fierce winds, they are turned by a very small rudder wherever the pilot desires.

5 Even so [a]the tongue is a little member and [b]boasts great things. See how great a forest a little fire kindles!

6 And [a]the tongue *is* a fire, a world of iniquity. The tongue is so set among our members that it [b]defiles the whole body, and sets on fire the course of nature; and it is set on fire by hell.

7 For every kind of beast and bird, of reptile and creature of the sea, is tamed and has been tamed by mankind.

8 But no man can tame the tongue. *It is* an unruly evil, [a]full of deadly poison.

9 With it we bless our God and Father, and with it we curse men, who have been made [a]in the similitude of God.

10 Out of the same mouth proceed blessing and cursing. My brethren, these things ought not to be so.

11 Does a spring send forth fresh *water* and bitter from the same opening?

12 Can a [a]fig tree, my brethren, bear olives, or a grapevine bear figs? *Thus no spring yields both salt water and fresh.

Heavenly Versus Demonic Wisdom

13 [a]Who *is* wise and understanding among you? Let him show by good conduct *that* his works *are done* in the meekness of wisdom.

14 But if you have [a]bitter envy and self-seeking in your hearts, [b]do not boast and lie against the truth.

15 [a]This wisdom does not descend from above, but *is* earthly, sensual, demonic.

16 For [a]where envy and self-seeking *exist*, confusion and every evil thing *are* there.

17 But [a]the wisdom that is from above is first pure, then peaceable, gentle, willing to yield, full of mercy and good fruits, [b]without partiality [c]and without hypocrisy.

18 [a]Now the fruit of righteousness is sown in peace by those who make peace.

KJV

Pride Promotes Strife

4 From whence *come* wars and fightings among you? *come they* not hence, *even* of your lusts [a]that war in your members?

2 Ye lust, and have not: ye kill, and desire to have, and cannot obtain: ye fight and war, yet ye have not, because ye ask not.

3 [a]Ye ask, and receive not, [b]because ye ask amiss, that ye may consume *it* upon your lusts.

4 Ye adulterers and adulteresses, know ye not that the [a]friendship of the world is enmity with God? [b]whosoever therefore will be a friend of the world is the enemy of God.

5 Do ye think that the scripture saith in vain, [a]The spirit that dwelleth in us lusteth to envy?

6 But he giveth more grace. Wherefore he saith, [a]GOD RESISTETH THE PROUD, BUT GIVETH GRACE UNTO THE HUMBLE.

Humility Cures Worldliness

7 Submit yourselves therefore to God. [a]Resist the devil, and he will flee from you.

8 [a]Draw nigh to God, and he will draw nigh to you. [b]Cleanse *your* hands, *ye* sinners; and [c]purify *your* hearts, *ye* double minded.

9 [a]Be afflicted, and mourn, and weep: let your laughter be turned to mourning, and *your* joy to heaviness.

10 [a]Humble yourselves in the sight of the Lord, and he shall lift you up.

Do Not Judge a Brother

11 [a]Speak not evil one of another, brethren. He that speaketh evil of *his* brother, [b]and judgeth his brother, speaketh evil of the law, and judgeth the law: but if thou judge the law, thou art not a doer of the law, but a judge.

12 There is one lawgiver, [a]who is able to save and to destroy: [b]who art thou that judgest another?

Do Not Boast About Tomorrow

13 Go to now, ye that say, To day or to morrow we will go into such a city, and continue there a year, and buy and sell, and get gain:

14 Whereas ye know not what *shall be* on the morrow. For what *is* your life? [a]It is even a vapour, that appeareth for a little time, and then vanisheth away.

15 For that ye *ought* to say, [a]If the Lord will, we shall live, and do this, or that.

16 But now ye rejoice in your boastings: [a]all such rejoicing is evil.

17 Therefore [a]to him that knoweth to do good, and doeth *it* not, to him it is sin.

Rich Oppressors Will Be Judged

5 Go to now, *ye* [a]rich men, weep and howl for your miseries that shall come upon *you.*

2 Your [a]riches are corrupted, and [b]your garments are motheaten.

3 Your gold and silver is cankered; and the rust of them shall be a witness against you, and shall eat your flesh as it were fire. [a]Ye have heaped treasure together for the last days.

4 Behold, [a]the hire of the labourers who have reaped down your fields, which is of you kept back by fraud, crieth: and [b]the cries of them which have reaped are entered into the ears of the Lord of sabaoth.

5 Ye have lived in pleasure on the earth, and been wanton; ye have nourished your hearts, as in a day of slaughter.

6 Ye have condemned *and* killed the just; *and* he doth not resist you.

CHAPTER 4

1 [a]Rom. 7:23; [Gal. 5:17]; 1 Pet. 2:11
3 [a]Job 27:8, 9 [b][Ps. 66:18]
4 [a]Rom. 8:7; 1 John 2:15 [b]Gal. 1:4
5 [a]Gen. 6:5
6 [a]Job 22:29; Ps. 138:6; Prov. 3:34; Matt. 23:12; 1 Pet. 5:5
7 [a][Eph. 4:27; 6:11]; 1 Pet. 5:8
8 [a]2 Chr. 15:2; Zech. 1:3; Mal. 3:7; Heb. 7:19 [b]Job 17:9; Is. 1:16; 1 Tim. 2:8 [c]Jer. 4:14; James 3:17; 1 Pet. 1:22; 1 John 3:3
9 [a]Matt. 5:4
10 [a]Job 22:29; Luke 14:11; 18:14; 1 Pet. 5:6
11 [a]2 Cor. 12:20; Eph. 4:31; James 5:9; 1 Pet. 2:1–3 [b][Matt. 7:1–5]; Rom. 14:4
12 [a][Matt. 10:28] [b]Rom. 14:4
14 [a]Job 7:7; Ps. 102:3; 1 Pet. 1:24
15 [a]Acts 18:21; 1 Cor. 4:19
16 [a]1 Cor. 5:6
17 [a][Luke 12:47]; John 9:41; 2 Pet. 2:21

CHAPTER 5

1 [a]Prov. 11:28; [Luke 6:24; 1 Tim. 6:9]
2 [a]Jer. 17:11; Matt. 6:19 [b]Job 13:28
3 [a]Rom. 2:5
4 [a]Lev. 19:13; Job 24:10; Jer. 22:13; Mal. 3:5 [b]Ex. 2:23; Deut. 24:15; Job 31:38

*

4:2 NU, M omit *Yet*
4:4 NU omits *Adulterers and*
4:12 NU adds *and Judge* • NU, M *But who* • NU *a neighbor*
4:13 M *let us*
5:4 Lit., in Heb., *Hosts*
5:5 NU omits *as*

NKJV

Pride Promotes Strife

4 Where do wars and fights *come* from among you? Do *they* not *come* from your *desires for* pleasure [a]that war in your members?

2 You lust and do not have. You murder and covet and cannot obtain. You fight and war. *Yet you do not have because you do not ask.

3 [a]You ask and do not receive, [b]because you ask amiss, that you may spend *it* on your pleasures.

4 *Adulterers and adulteresses! Do you not know that [a]friendship with the world is enmity with God? [b]Whoever therefore wants to be a friend of the world makes himself an enemy of God.

5 Or do you think that the Scripture says in vain, [a]"The Spirit who dwells in us yearns jealously"?

6 But He gives more grace. Therefore He says:

[a]*"God resists the proud,*
But gives grace to the humble."

Humility Cures Worldliness

7 Therefore submit to God. [a]Resist the devil and he will flee from you.

8 [a]Draw near to God and He will draw near to you. [b]Cleanse *your* hands, *you* sinners; and [c]purify *your* hearts, *you* double-minded.

9 [a]Lament and mourn and weep! Let your laughter be turned to mourning and *your* joy to gloom.

10 [a]Humble yourselves in the sight of the Lord, and He will lift you up.

Do Not Judge a Brother

11 [a]Do not speak evil of one another, brethren. He who speaks evil of a brother [b]and judges his brother, speaks evil of the law and judges the law. But if you judge the law, you are not a doer of the law but a judge.

12 There is one *Lawgiver, [a]who is able to save and to destroy. [b]Who* are you to judge *another?

Do Not Boast About Tomorrow

13 Come now, you who say, "Today or tomorrow *we will go to such and such a city, spend a year there, buy and sell, and make a profit";

14 whereas you do not know what *will happen* tomorrow. For what *is* your life? [a]It is even a vapor that appears for a little time and then vanishes away.

15 Instead you *ought* to say, [a]"If the Lord wills, we shall live and do this or that."

16 But now you boast in your arrogance. [a]All such boasting is evil.

17 Therefore, [a]to him who knows to do good and does not do *it*, to him it is sin.

Rich Oppressors Will Be Judged

5 Come now, *you* [a]rich, weep and howl for your miseries that are coming upon *you!*

2 Your [a]riches are corrupted, and [b]your garments are moth-eaten.

3 Your gold and silver are corroded, and their corrosion will be a witness against you and will eat your flesh like fire. [a]You have heaped up treasure in the last days.

4 Indeed [a]the wages of the laborers who mowed your fields, which you kept back by fraud, cry out; and [b]the cries of the reapers have reached the ears of the Lord of *Sabaoth.

5 You have lived on the earth in pleasure and luxury; you have fattened your hearts *as in a day of slaughter.

6 You have condemned, you have murdered the just; he does not resist you.

KJV

Be Patient and Persevering

7 Be patient therefore, brethren, unto the coming of the Lord. Behold, the husbandman waiteth for the precious fruit of the earth, and hath long patience for it, until he receive the early and latter rain.

8 Be ye also patient; stablish your hearts: for the coming of the Lord draweth nigh.

9 Grudge not one against another, brethren, lest ye be condemned: behold, the judge standeth before the door.

10 [a]Take, my brethren, the prophets, who have spoken in the name of the Lord, for an example of suffering affliction, and of [b]patience.

11 Behold, [a]we count them happy which [b]endure. Ye have heard of [c]the patience of Job, and have seen [d]the end of the Lord; that [e]the Lord is very pitiful, and of tender mercy.

12 But above all things, my brethren, [a]swear not, neither by heaven, neither by the earth, neither by any other oath: but let your yea be yea; and *your* nay, nay; lest ye fall into condemnation.

Meeting Specific Needs
(*cf. 1 Kin. 18:41–46*)

13 Is any among you afflicted? let him [a]pray. Is any merry? [b]let him sing psalms.

14 Is any sick among you? let him call for the elders of the church; and let them pray over him, [a]anointing him with oil in the name of the Lord:

15 And the prayer of faith shall save the sick, and the Lord shall raise him up; [a]and if he have committed sins, they shall be forgiven him.

16 Confess *your* faults one to another, and pray one for another, that ye may be healed. [a]The effectual fervent prayer of a righteous man availeth much.

17 Elias was a man [a]subject to like passions as we are, and [b]he prayed earnestly that it might not rain: and it rained not on the earth by the space of three years and six months.

18 And he prayed [a]again, and the heaven gave rain, and the earth brought forth her fruit.

Bring Back the Erring One

19 Brethren, if any of you do err from the truth, and one [a]convert him;

20 Let him know, that he which converteth the sinner from the error of his way [a]shall save a soul from death, and [b]shall hide a multitude of sins.

10 [a]Matt. 5:12 [b]Heb. 10:36
11 [a][Ps. 94:12; Matt. 5:10]; James 1:2 [b][James 1:12] [c]Job 1:21, 22; 2:10 [d]Job 42:10 [e]Num. 14:18
12 [a]Matt. 5:34–37
13 [a]Ps. 50:14, 15 [b]Eph. 5:19
14 [a]Mark 6:13; 16:18
15 [a]Is. 33:24
16 [a]Num. 11:2
17 [a]Acts 14:15 [b]1 Kin. 17:1; 18:1
18 [a]1 Kin. 18:1, 42
19 [a]Matt. 18:15; Gal. 6:1
20 [a]Rom. 11:14; 1 Cor. 1:21; James 1:21 [b]Prov. 10:12; [1 Pet. 4:8]

NKJV

Be Patient and Persevering

7 Therefore be patient, brethren, until the coming of the Lord. See *how* the farmer waits for the precious fruit of the earth, waiting patiently for it until it receives the early and latter rain.

8 You also be patient. Establish your hearts, for the coming of the Lord is at hand.

9 Do not grumble against one another, brethren, lest you be *condemned. Behold, the Judge is standing at the door!

10 [a]My brethren, take the prophets, who spoke in the name of the Lord, as an example of suffering and [b]patience.

11 Indeed [a]we count them blessed who [b]endure. You have heard of [c]the perseverance of Job and seen [d]the end *intended by* the Lord—that [e]the Lord is very compassionate and merciful.

12 But above all, my brethren, [a]do not swear, either by heaven or by earth or with any other oath. But let your "Yes" be "Yes," and *your* "No," "No," lest you fall into *judgment.

Meeting Specific Needs
(*cf. 1 Kin. 18:41–46*)

13 Is anyone among you suffering? Let him [a]pray. Is anyone cheerful? [b]Let him sing psalms.

14 Is anyone among you sick? Let him call for the elders of the church, and let them pray over him, [a]anointing him with oil in the name of the Lord.

15 And the prayer of faith will save the sick, and the Lord will raise him up. [a]And if he has committed sins, he will be forgiven.

16 *Confess *your* trespasses to one another, and pray for one another, that you may be healed. [a]The effective, fervent prayer of a righteous man avails much.

17 Elijah was a man [a]with a nature like ours, and [b]he prayed earnestly that it would not rain; and it did not rain on the land for three years and six months.

18 And he prayed [a]again, and the heaven gave rain, and the earth produced its fruit.

Bring Back the Erring One

19 Brethren, if anyone among you wanders from the truth, and someone [a]turns him back,

20 let him know that he who turns a sinner from the error of his way [a]will save *a soul from death and [b]cover a multitude of sins.

*
5:9 NU, M *judged*
5:12 M *hypocrisy*
5:16 NU *Therefore confess your sins*
5:20 NU *his soul*

KJV

THE FIRST EPISTLE OF

PETER

Greeting to the Elect Pilgrims

1 Peter, an apostle of Jesus Christ, to the strangers [a]scattered throughout Pontus, Galatia, Cappadocia, Asia, and Bithynia,

2 [a]Elect [b]according to the foreknowledge of God the Father, [c]through sanctification of the Spirit, unto [d]obedience and [e]sprinkling of the blood of Jesus Christ: [f]Grace unto you, and peace, be multiplied.

A Heavenly Inheritance

3 [a]Blessed *be* the God and Father of our Lord Jesus Christ, which [b]according to his abundant mercy [c]hath begotten us again unto a lively hope [d]by the resurrection of Jesus Christ from the dead,

4 To an inheritance incorruptible, and undefiled, and that fadeth not away, [a]reserved in heaven for you,

5 [a]Who are kept by the power of God through faith unto salvation ready to be revealed in the last time.

6 [a]Wherein ye greatly rejoice, though now [b]for a season, if need be, [c]ye are in heaviness through manifold temptations:

7 That [a]the trial of your faith, being much more precious than of gold that perisheth, though [b]it be tried with fire, [c]might be found unto praise and honour and glory at the appearing of Jesus Christ:

8 [a]Whom having not seen, ye love; [b]in whom, though now ye see *him* not, yet believing, ye rejoice with joy unspeakable and full of glory:

9 Receiving the end of your faith, *even* the salvation of *your* souls.

10 Of which salvation the prophets have enquired and searched diligently, who prophesied of the grace *that should come* unto you:

11 Searching what, or what manner of time [a]the Spirit of Christ which was in them did signify, when it testified beforehand the sufferings of Christ, and the glory that should follow.

12 Unto whom it was revealed, that not unto themselves, but unto us they did minister the things, which are now reported unto you by them that have preached the gospel unto you with the Holy Ghost sent down from heaven; which things the [a]angels desire to look into.

Living Before God Our Father

13 Wherefore gird up the loins of your mind, be sober, and hope to the end for the grace that is to be brought unto you at the revelation of Jesus Christ;

14 As obedient children, not [a]fashioning yourselves according to the former lusts in your ignorance:

15 [a]But as he which hath called you is holy, so be ye holy in all manner of conversation;

16 Because it is written, [a]BE YE HOLY; FOR I AM HOLY.

17 And if ye call on the Father, who [a]without respect of persons judgeth according to every

CHAPTER 1

1 [a]John 7:35; James 1:1
2 [a]Eph. 1:4 [b][Rom. 8:29]; 1 Pet. 1:20 [c]2 Thess. 2:13 [d]Rom. 1:5 [e]Is. 52:15; Heb. 10:22; 12:24 [f]Rom. 1:7
3 [a]Eph. 1:3 [b]Gal. 6:16; Titus 3:5 [c][John 3:3, 5] [d]1 Cor. 15:20; 1 Pet. 3:21
4 [a]Col. 1:5
5 [a]John 10:28; [Phil. 4:7]
6 [a]Matt. 5:12 [b]2 Cor. 4:17 [c]James 1:2; 1 Pet. 4:12
7 [a]James 1:3 [b]Job 23:10 [c][Rom. 2:7]
8 [a]1 John 4:20 [b]John 20:29
11 [a]2 Pet. 1:21
12 [a]Eph. 3:10
14 [a][Rom. 12:2]; 1 Pet. 4:2
15 [a][2 Cor. 7:1]
16 [a]Lev. 11:44, 45; 19:2; 20:7
17 [a]Acts 10:34

*______

1:8 M *known*
1:12 NU, M *you*

NKJV

THE FIRST EPISTLE OF

PETER

Greeting to the Elect Pilgrims

1 Peter, an apostle of Jesus Christ,

To the pilgrims [a]of the Dispersion in Pontus, Galatia, Cappadocia, Asia, and Bithynia,

2 [a]elect [b]according to the foreknowledge of God the Father, [c]in sanctification of the Spirit, for [d]obedience and [e]sprinkling of the blood of Jesus Christ:

[f]Grace to you and peace be multiplied.

A Heavenly Inheritance

3 [a]Blessed *be* the God and Father of our Lord Jesus Christ, who [b]according to His abundant mercy [c]has begotten us again to a living hope [d]through the resurrection of Jesus Christ from the dead,

4 to an inheritance incorruptible and undefiled and that does not fade away, [a]reserved in heaven for you,

5 [a]who are kept by the power of God through faith for salvation ready to be revealed in the last time.

6 [a]In this you greatly rejoice, though now [b]for a little while, if need be, [c]you have been grieved by various trials,

7 that [a]the genuineness of your faith, *being* much more precious than gold that perishes, though [b]it is tested by fire, [c]may be found to praise, honor, and glory at the revelation of Jesus Christ,

8 [a]whom having not *seen you love. [b]Though now you do not see *Him*, yet believing, you rejoice with joy inexpressible and full of glory,

9 receiving the end of your faith—the salvation of *your* souls.

10 Of this salvation the prophets have inquired and searched carefully, who prophesied of the grace *that would come* to you,

11 searching what, or what manner of time, [a]the Spirit of Christ who was in them was indicating when He testified beforehand the sufferings of Christ and the glories that would follow.

12 To them it was revealed that, not to themselves, but to *us they were ministering the things which now have been reported to you through those who have preached the gospel to you by the Holy Spirit sent from heaven—things which [a]angels desire to look into.

Living Before God Our Father

13 Therefore gird up the loins of your mind, be sober, and rest *your* hope fully upon the grace that is to be brought to you at the revelation of Jesus Christ;

14 as obedient children, not [a]conforming yourselves to the former lusts, *as* in your ignorance;

15 [a]but as He who called you *is* holy, you also be holy in all *your* conduct,

16 because it is written, [a]*"Be holy, for I am holy."*

17 And if you call on the Father, who [a]without partiality judges according to each one's

KJV

man's work, pass the time of your sojourning *here*
in fear:
18 Forasmuch as ye know that ye were not
redeemed with corruptible things, *as* silver and
gold, from your vain conversation *received* by tradition from your fathers;
19 But [a]with the precious blood of Christ, [b]as
of a lamb without blemish and without spot:
20 [a]Who verily was foreordained before the
foundation of the world, but was manifest [b]in
these last times for you,
21 Who by him do believe in God, [a]that
raised him up from the dead, and [b]gave him glory;
that your faith and hope might be in God.

The Enduring Word

22 Seeing ye [a]have purified your souls in
obeying the truth through the Spirit unto unfeigned [b]love of the brethren, *see that ye* love one
another with a pure heart fervently:
23 [a]Being born again, not of corruptible seed,
but of incorruptible, [b]by the word of God, which
liveth and abideth for ever.
24 For [a]ALL FLESH *IS* AS GRASS, AND ALL THE
GLORY OF MAN AS THE FLOWER OF GRASS. THE GRASS
WITHERETH, AND THE FLOWER THEREOF FALLETH
AWAY:
25 [a]BUT THE WORD OF THE LORD ENDURETH
FOR EVER. [b]And this is the word which by the
gospel is preached unto you.

2 Wherefore [a]laying aside all malice, and all
guile, and hypocrisies, and envies, and all evil
speakings,
2 [a]As newborn babes, desire the sincere
[b]milk of the word, that ye may grow thereby:
3 If so be ye have [a]tasted that the Lord *is*
gracious.

The Chosen Stone and His Chosen People
(Ps. 118:22; Is. 28:16)

4 To whom coming, *as unto* a living stone,
[a]disallowed indeed of men, but chosen of God,
and precious,
5 Ye also, as lively stones, are built up a
spiritual house, an holy priesthood, to offer up
spiritual sacrifices, acceptable to God by Jesus
Christ.
6 Wherefore also it is contained in the scripture, [a]BEHOLD, I LAY IN SION A CHIEF CORNER STONE,
ELECT, PRECIOUS: AND HE THAT BELIEVETH ON HIM
SHALL NOT BE CONFOUNDED.
7 Unto you therefore which believe *he is*
precious: but unto them which be disobedient,
[a]THE STONE WHICH THE BUILDERS DISALLOWED, THE
SAME IS MADE THE HEAD OF THE CORNER,
8 [a]AND A STONE OF STUMBLING, AND A ROCK
OF OFFENCE, [b]*even to them* which stumble at the
word, being disobedient: [c]whereunto also they
were appointed.
9 But ye *are* a chosen generation, a royal
priesthood, an holy nation, a peculiar people; that
ye should shew forth the praises of him who hath
called you out of [a]darkness into his marvellous
light:
10 [a]Which in time past *were* not a people,
but *are* now the people of God: which had not
obtained mercy, but now have obtained mercy.

19 [a]Acts 20:28; 1 Pet. 1:2 [b]Is. 53:7; Ex. 12:5
20 [a]Rom. 3:25 [b]Gal. 4:4
21 [a]Acts 2:24 [b]Acts 2:33
22 [a]Acts 15:9 [b]John 13:34; Rom. 12:10; Heb. 13:1; 1 Pet. 2:17; 3:8
23 [a]John 1:13 [b]1 Thess. 2:13; James 1:18
24 [a]Is. 40:6–8; James 1:10
25 [a]Is. 40:8 [b][John 1:1]

CHAPTER 2

1 [a]Heb. 12:1
2 [a][Matt. 18:3; 19:14; Mark 10:15; Luke 18:17]; 1 Cor. 14:20 [b]1 Cor. 3:2
3 [a]Ps. 34:8; Titus 3:4; Heb. 6:5
4 [a]Ps. 118:22
6 [a]Is. 28:16; Rom. 9:32, 33; 10:11; 1 Pet. 2:8
7 [a]Ps. 118:22; Matt. 21:42; Luke 2:34
8 [a]Is. 8:14 [b]1 Cor. 1:23; Gal. 5:11 [c]Rom. 9:22
9 [a]Is. 9:2; 42:16; [Acts 26:18; 2 Cor. 4:6]
10 [a]Hos. 1:9, 10; 2:23; Rom. 9:25; 10:19

*

1:22 NU omits *through the Spirit*
1:23 NU omits *forever*
1:24 NU *its glory as*
2:2 NU adds *up to salvation*
2:7 NU *disbelieve*

NKJV

work, conduct yourselves throughout the time of
your stay *here* in fear;
18 knowing that you were not redeemed with
corruptible things, *like* silver or gold, from your
aimless conduct *received* by tradition from your
fathers,
19 but [a]with the precious blood of Christ, [b]as
of a lamb without blemish and without spot.
20 [a]He indeed was foreordained before the
foundation of the world, but was manifest [b]in
these last times for you
21 who through Him believe in God, [a]who
raised Him from the dead and [b]gave Him glory,
so that your faith and hope are in God.

The Enduring Word

22 Since you [a]have purified your souls in
obeying the truth *through the Spirit in sincere
[b]love of the brethren, love one another fervently
with a pure heart,
23 [a]having been born again, not of corruptible seed but incorruptible, [b]through the word of
God which lives and abides *forever,
24 because

[a]*"All flesh is as grass,*
*And all *the glory of man as the flower*
of the grass.
The grass withers,
And its flower falls away,
25 [a]*But the word of the* LORD *endures*
forever."

[b]Now this is the word which by the gospel was
preached to you.

2 Therefore, [a]laying aside all malice, all deceit,
hypocrisy, envy, and all evil speaking,
2 [a]as newborn babes, desire the pure [b]milk
of the word, that you may grow *thereby,
3 if indeed you have [a]tasted that the Lord
is gracious.

The Chosen Stone and His Chosen People
(Ps. 118:22; Is. 28:16)

4 Coming to Him *as to* a living stone, [a]re-
jected indeed by men, but chosen by God *and*
precious,
5 you also, as living stones, are being built
up a spiritual house, a holy priesthood, to offer
up spiritual sacrifices acceptable to God through
Jesus Christ.
6 Therefore it is also contained in the
Scripture,

[a]*"Behold, I lay in Zion*
A chief cornerstone, elect, precious,
And he who believes on Him will by no
means be put to shame."

7 Therefore, to you who believe, *He is* precious; but to those who *are disobedient,

[a]*"The stone which the builders rejected*
Has become the chief cornerstone,"

8 and

[a]*"A stone of stumbling*
And a rock of offense."

[b]They stumble, being disobedient to the word, [c]to
which they also were appointed.
9 But you *are* a chosen generation, a royal
priesthood, a holy nation, His own special people,
that you may proclaim the praises of Him who
called you out of [a]darkness into His marvelous
light;
10 [a]who once *were* not a people but *are* now
the people of God, who had not obtained mercy
but now have obtained mercy.

KJV

Living Before the World

11 Dearly beloved, I beseech *you* as strangers and pilgrims, abstain from fleshly lusts, [a]which war against the soul;

12 [a]Having your conversation honest among the Gentiles: that, whereas they speak against you as evildoers, [b]they may by *your* good works, which they shall behold, glorify God in the day of visitation.

Submission to Government
(cf. Rom. 13:1–5)

13 [a]Submit yourselves to every ordinance of man for the Lord's sake: whether it be to the king, as supreme;

14 Or unto governors, as unto them that are sent by him for the punishment of evildoers, and for the praise of them that do well.

15 For so is the will of God, that with well doing ye may put to silence the ignorance of foolish men:

16 [a]As free, and not [b]using *your* liberty for a cloke of maliciousness, but as the servants of God.

17 Honour all *men*. Love the brotherhood. Fear [a]God. Honour the king.

Submission to Masters
(Is. 53:7–9)

18 [a]Servants, *be* subject to *your* masters with all fear; not only to the good and gentle, but also to the froward.

19 For this *is* [a]thankworthy, if a man for conscience toward God endure grief, suffering wrongfully.

20 For [a]what glory *is it*, if, when ye be buffeted for your faults, ye shall take it patiently? but if, when ye do well, and suffer *for it*, ye take it patiently, this *is* acceptable with God.

21 For [a]even hereunto were ye called: because Christ also suffered for us, [b]leaving us an example, that ye should follow his steps:

22 [a]WHO DID NO SIN, NEITHER WAS GUILE FOUND IN HIS MOUTH:

23 [a]Who, when he was reviled, reviled not again; when he suffered, he threatened not; but [b]committed *himself* to him that judgeth righteously:

24 [a]Who his own self bare our sins in his own body on the tree, [b]that we, being dead to sins, should live unto righteousness: [c]by whose stripes ye were healed.

25 For [a]ye were as sheep going astray; but are now returned [b]unto the Shepherd and Bishop of your souls.

Submission to Husbands

3 Likewise, ye wives, *be* in [a]subjection to your own husbands; that, if any obey not the word, [b]they also may without the word [c]be won by the conversation of the wives;

2 [a]While they behold your chaste conversation *coupled* with fear.

3 [a]Whose adorning let it not be that outward *adorning* of plaiting the hair, and of wearing of gold, or of putting on of apparel;

4 But *let it be* [a]the hidden man of the heart, in that which is not corruptible, *even the ornament* of a meek and quiet spirit, which is in the sight of God of great price.

5 For after this manner in the old time the holy women also, who trusted in God, adorned themselves, being in subjection unto their own husbands:

6 Even as Sara obeyed Abraham, [a]calling him lord: whose daughters ye are, as long as ye do well, and are not afraid with any amazement.

A Word to Husbands

7 [a]Likewise, ye husbands, dwell with *them* according to knowledge, giving honour unto the

---

11 [a][Rom. 8:13]; Gal. 5:17; James 4:1
12 [a]2 Cor. 8:21; Phil. 2:15; Titus 2:8; 1 Pet. 2:15; 3:16 [b]Matt. 5:16; 9:8; John 13:31; 1 Pet. 4:11, 16
13 [a]Matt. 22:21
16 [a]Rom. 6:14, 20, 22; 1 Cor. 7:22; [Gal. 5:1] [b]Gal. 5:13
17 [a]Prov. 24:21
18 [a]Eph. 6:5–8
19 [a]Matt. 5:10
20 [a]Luke 6:32–34
21 [a]Matt. 16:24; 1 Thess. 3:3, 4 [b][1 John 2:6]
22 [a]Is. 53:9; 2 Cor. 5:21
23 [a]Is. 53:7; Heb. 12:3; 1 Pet. 3:9 [b]Luke 23:46
24 [a]Is. 53:4, 11; 1 Cor. 15:3; [Heb. 9:28] [b]Rom. 7:6 [c]Is. 53:5
25 [a]Is. 53:5, 6 [b]Is. 40:11; [Ezek. 34:23]; Zech. 13:7

CHAPTER 3

1 [a]Gen. 3:16; 1 Cor. 14:34; Eph. 5:22; Col. 3:18 [b]1 Cor. 7:16 [c]Matt. 18:15
2 [a]1 Pet. 2:12; 3:6
3 [a]Is. 3:18; 1 Tim. 2:9
4 [a]Rom. 2:29
6 [a]Gen. 18:12
7 [a]1 Cor. 7:3; [Eph. 5:25]; Col. 3:19

*

2:21 NU *you* • NU, M *you*
2:25 Gr. *Episkopos*

NKJV

Living Before the World

11 Beloved, I beg *you* as sojourners and pilgrims, abstain from fleshly lusts [a]which war against the soul,

12 [a]having your conduct honorable among the Gentiles, that when they speak against you as evildoers, [b]they may, by *your* good works which they observe, glorify God in the day of visitation.

Submission to Government
(cf. Rom. 13:1–5)

13 [a]Therefore submit yourselves to every ordinance of man for the Lord's sake, whether to the king as supreme,

14 or to governors, as to those who are sent by him for the punishment of evildoers and *for the* praise of those who do good.

15 For this is the will of God, that by doing good you may put to silence the ignorance of foolish men—

16 [a]as free, yet not [b]using liberty as a cloak for vice, but as bondservants of God.

17 Honor all *people*. Love the brotherhood. Fear [a]God. Honor the king.

Submission to Masters
(Is. 53:7–9)

18 [a]Servants, *be* submissive to *your* masters with all fear, not only to the good and gentle, but also to the harsh.

19 For this *is* [a]commendable, if because of conscience toward God one endures grief, suffering wrongfully.

20 For [a]what credit *is it* if, when you are beaten for your faults, you take it patiently? But when you do good and suffer, if you take it patiently, this *is* commendable before God.

21 For [a]to this you were called, because Christ also suffered for *us, [b]leaving *us an example, that you should follow His steps:

22 *"Who[a] committed no sin,*
Nor was deceit found in His mouth";

23 [a]who, when He was reviled, did not revile in return; when He suffered, He did not threaten, but [b]committed *Himself* to Him who judges righteously;

24 [a]who Himself bore our sins in His own body on the tree, [b]that we, having died to sins, might live for righteousness—[c]by whose stripes you were healed.

25 For [a]you were like sheep going astray, but have now returned [b]to the Shepherd and *Overseer of your souls.

Submission to Husbands

3 Wives, likewise, *be* [a]submissive to your own husbands, that even if some do not obey the word, [b]they, without a word, may [c]be won by the conduct of their wives,

2 [a]when they observe your chaste conduct *accompanied* by fear.

3 [a]Do not let your adornment be *merely* outward—arranging the hair, wearing gold, or putting on *fine* apparel—

4 rather *let it be* [a]the hidden person of the heart, with the incorruptible *beauty* of a gentle and quiet spirit, which is very precious in the sight of God.

5 For in this manner, in former times, the holy women who trusted in God also adorned themselves, being submissive to their own husbands,

6 as Sarah obeyed Abraham, [a]calling him lord, whose daughters you are if you do good and are not afraid with any terror.

A Word to Husbands

7 [a]Husbands, likewise, dwell with *them* with understanding, giving honor to the wife,

KJV

wife, [b]as unto the weaker vessel, and as being
heirs together of the grace of life; [c]that your prayers be not hindered.

Called to Blessing

8 Finally, *be ye* all of one mind, having compassion one of another, love as brethren, *be* pitiful, *be* courteous:
9 [a]Not rendering evil for evil, or railing for
railing: but contrariwise [b]blessing; knowing that
ye are thereunto called, [c]that ye should inherit a
blessing.
10 For [a]HE THAT WILL LOVE LIFE, AND SEE GOOD
DAYS, [b]LET HIM REFRAIN HIS TONGUE FROM EVIL, AND
HIS LIPS THAT THEY SPEAK NO GUILE:
11 LET HIM [a]ESCHEW EVIL, AND DO GOOD; [b]LET
HIM SEEK PEACE, AND ENSUE IT.
12 FOR THE EYES OF THE LORD *ARE* OVER THE
RIGHTEOUS, [a]AND HIS EARS *ARE OPEN* UNTO THEIR
PRAYERS: BUT THE FACE OF THE LORD *IS* AGAINST
THEM THAT DO EVIL.

Suffering for Right and Wrong

13 [a]And who *is* he that will harm you, if ye
be followers of that which is good?
14 [a]But and if ye suffer for righteousness'
sake, happy *are ye*: [b]AND BE NOT AFRAID OF THEIR
TERROR, NEITHER BE TROUBLED;
15 But sanctify the Lord God in your hearts:
and [a]*be* ready always to *give* an answer to every
man that asketh you a reason of the [b]hope that
is in you with meekness and fear:
16 [a]Having a good conscience; that, whereas
they speak evil of you, as of evildoers, they may
be ashamed that falsely accuse your good conversation in Christ.
17 For *it is* better, if the will of God be so,
that ye suffer for well doing, than for evil doing.

Christ's Suffering and Ours

18 For Christ also hath once suffered for sins,
the just for the unjust, that he might bring us to
God, being put to death in the flesh, but quickened
by the Spirit:
19 By which also he went and preached unto
the spirits in prison;
20 Which sometime were disobedient, when
once the longsuffering of God waited in the days
of Noah, while the ark was a preparing, wherein
few, that is, eight souls were saved by water.
21 [a]The like figure whereunto *even* baptism
doth also now save us [b](not the putting away of
the filth of the flesh, [c]but the answer of a good
conscience toward God,) by the resurrection of
Jesus Christ:
22 Who is gone into heaven, and [a]is on the
right hand of God; [b]angels and authorities and
powers being made subject unto him.

4 Forasmuch then as Christ hath suffered for
us in the flesh, arm yourselves likewise with
the same mind: for he that hath suffered in the
flesh hath ceased from sin;
2 That he no longer should live the rest of
his time in the flesh to the lusts of men, [a]but to
the will of God.
3 For the time past of *our* life may suffice
us to have wrought the will of the Gentiles, when
we walked in lasciviousness, lusts, excess of wine,
revellings, banquetings, and abominable idolatries:
4 Wherein they think it strange that ye run
not with *them* to the same excess of riot, speaking
evil of *you*:
5 Who shall give account to him that is
ready [a]to judge the quick and the dead.
6 For for this cause [a]was the gospel
preached also to them that are dead, that they

7 [b]1 Cor. 12:23 [c]Job 42:8
9 [a][Prov. 17:13] [b]Matt. 5:44 [c]Matt. 25:34
10 [a]Ps. 34:12–16 [b]James 1:26
11 [a]Ps. 37:27 [b]Rom. 12:18
12 [a]John 9:31
13 [a]Prov. 16:7
14 [a]James 1:12 [b]Is. 8:12
15 [a]Ps. 119:46 [b][Titus 3:7]
16 [a]1 Tim. 1:5; Heb. 13:18; 1 Pet. 3:21
21 [a]Acts 16:33; Eph. 5:26 [b][Titus 3:5] [c][Rom. 10:10]
22 [a]Ps. 110:1 [b]Rom. 8:38; Heb. 1:6

CHAPTER 4

2 [a]John 1:13
5 [a]Acts 10:42; Rom. 14:9; 2 Tim. 4:1
6 [a]1 Pet. 1:12; 3:19

*———

3:8 NU *humble*
3:15 NU *Christ as Lord*
3:18 NU, M *you*
3:20 NU, M *when the longsuffering of God waited patiently*
4:1 NU omits *for us*
4:3 NU *time*

NKJV

[b]as to the weaker vessel, and as *being* heirs together of the grace of life, [c]that your prayers may
not be hindered.

Called to Blessing

8 Finally, all *of you be* of one mind, having
compassion for one another; love as brothers, *be*
tenderhearted, *be* *courteous;
9 [a]not returning evil for evil or reviling for
reviling, but on the contrary [b]blessing, knowing
that you were called to this, [c]that you may inherit
a blessing.
10 For

[a]*"He who would love life*
And see good days,
[b]*Let him refrain his tongue from evil,*
And his lips from speaking deceit.
11 *Let him* [a]*turn away from evil and do good;*
[b]*Let him seek peace and pursue it.*
12 *For the eyes of the* LORD *are on the*
righteous,
[a]*And His ears are open to their prayers;*
But the face of the LORD *is against those*
who do evil."

Suffering for Right and Wrong

13 [a]And who *is* he who will harm you if you
become followers of what is good?
14 [a]But even if you should suffer for righteousness' sake, *you are* blessed. [b]*"And do not*
be afraid of their threats, nor be troubled."
15 But sanctify *the Lord God in your hearts,
and always [a]*be* ready to *give* a defense to everyone who asks you a reason for the [b]hope that is
in you, with meekness and fear;
16 [a]having a good conscience, that when
they defame you as evildoers, those who revile
your good conduct in Christ may be ashamed.
17 For *it is* better, if it is the will of God, to
suffer for doing good than for doing evil.

Christ's Suffering and Ours

18 For Christ also suffered once for sins, the
just for the unjust, that He might bring *us to God,
being put to death in the flesh but made alive by
the Spirit,
19 by whom also He went and preached to
the spirits in prison,
20 who formerly were disobedient, *when
once the Divine longsuffering waited in the days
of Noah, while *the* ark was being prepared, in
which a few, that is, eight souls, were saved
through water.
21 [a]There is also an antitype which now
saves us—baptism [b](not the removal of the filth
of the flesh, [c]but the answer of a good conscience
toward God), through the resurrection of Jesus
Christ,
22 who has gone into heaven and [a]is at the
right hand of God, [b]angels and authorities and
powers having been made subject to Him.

4 Therefore, since Christ suffered *for us in the
flesh, arm yourselves also with the same
mind, for he who has suffered in the flesh has
ceased from sin,
2 that he no longer should live the rest of
his time in the flesh for the lusts of men, [a]but for
the will of God.
3 For we *have spent* enough of our past
*lifetime in doing the will of the Gentiles—when
we walked in lewdness, lusts, drunkenness, revelries, drinking parties, and abominable idolatries.
4 In regard to these, they think it strange
that you do not run with *them* in the same flood
of dissipation, speaking evil of *you*.
5 They will give an account to Him who is
ready [a]to judge the living and the dead.
6 For this reason [a]the gospel was preached
also to those who are dead, that they might be

KJV

might be judged according to men in the flesh, but [b]live according to God in the spirit.

Serving for God's Glory

7 But [a]the end of all things is at hand: be ye therefore sober, and watch unto prayer.

8 And above all things have fervent charity among yourselves: for [a]CHARITY SHALL COVER THE MULTITUDE OF SINS.

9 [a]Use hospitality one to another [b]without grudging.

10 [a]As every man hath received the gift, *even so* minister the same one to another, [b]as good stewards of [c]the manifold grace of God.

11 [a]If any man speak, *let him speak* as the oracles of God; if any man minister, *let him do it* as of the ability which God giveth: that [b]God in all things may be glorified through Jesus Christ, to whom be praise and dominion for ever and ever. Amen.

Suffering for God's Glory

12 Beloved, think it not strange concerning the fiery trial which is to try you, as though some strange thing happened unto you:

13 But rejoice, [a]inasmuch as ye are partakers of Christ's sufferings; that, [b]when his glory shall be revealed, ye may be glad also with exceeding joy.

14 If ye be reproached for the name of Christ, [a]happy *are ye;* for the spirit of glory and of God resteth upon you: on their part he is evil spoken of, [b]but on your part he is glorified.

15 But let none of you suffer as a murderer, or *as* a thief, or *as* an evildoer, or as a busybody in other men's matters.

16 Yet if *any man suffer* as a Christian, let him not be ashamed; but let him glorify God on this behalf.

17 For the time *is come* [a]that judgment must begin at the house of God: and if *it* first *begin* at us, [b]what shall the end *be* of them that obey not the gospel of God?

18 And [a]IF THE RIGHTEOUS SCARCELY BE SAVED, WHERE SHALL THE UNGODLY AND THE SINNER APPEAR?

19 Wherefore let them that suffer according to the will of God [a]commit the keeping of their souls *to him* in well doing, as unto a faithful Creator.

Shepherd the Flock

5 The elders which are among you I exhort, who am also an elder, and a [a]witness of the sufferings of Christ, and also a partaker of the [b]glory that shall be revealed:

2 [a]Feed the flock of God which is among you, taking the oversight *thereof,* [b]not by constraint, but willingly; [c]not for filthy lucre, but of a ready mind;

3 Neither as [a]being lords over [b]*God's* heritage, but [c]being ensamples to the flock.

4 And when [a]the chief Shepherd shall appear, ye shall receive [b]a crown of glory that fadeth not away.

Submit to God, Resist the Devil

5 Likewise, ye younger, submit yourselves unto the elder. Yea, [a]all *of you* be subject one to another, and be clothed with humility: for [b]GOD RESISTETH THE PROUD, AND [c]GIVETH GRACE TO THE HUMBLE.

6 Humble yourselves therefore under the mighty hand of God, that he may exalt you in due time:

7 Casting all your care upon him; for he careth for you.

8 Be sober, be vigilant; because your adver-

---

6 [b][Rom. 8:9, 13]; Gal. 5:25
7 [a]Rom. 13:11; Heb. 9:26; James 5:8, 9; 1 John 2:18
8 [a][Prov. 10:12]; 1 Cor. 13:4; James 5:20
9 [a]1 Tim. 3:2; Heb. 13:2 [b]2 Cor. 9:7
10 [a]Rom. 12:6–8 [b]Matt. 24:45; 1 Cor. 4:1, 2 [c][1 Cor. 12:4]
11 [a]Eph. 4:29 [b][1 Cor. 10:31]; Eph. 5:20
13 [a]James 1:2 [b]2 Tim. 2:12
14 [a]Matt. 5:11; Luke 6:22; Acts 5:41 [b]Matt. 5:16
17 [a]Is. 10:12 [b]Luke 10:12
18 [a]Prov. 11:31
19 [a]Ps. 37:5–7; 2 Tim. 1:12

CHAPTER 5

1 [a]Matt. 26:37 [b]Rom. 8:17, 18
2 [a]John 21:16; Acts 20:28 [b]1 Cor. 9:17 [c]1 Tim. 3:3
3 [a]Ezek. 34:4; Matt. 20:25 [b]Ps. 33:12 [c]John 13:15; Phil. 3:17; 1 Thess. 1:7; 2 Thess. 3:9; 1 Tim. 4:12; Titus 2:7
4 [a]Is. 40:11; Zech. 13:7; Heb. 13:20; 1 Pet. 2:25 [b]2 Tim. 4:8
5 [a]Rom. 12:10; Eph. 5:21 [b]Prov. 3:34; James 4:6 [c]Is. 57:15

*

4:14 NU omits the rest of v. 14.
4:16 NU *name*
5:2 NU adds *according to God*
5:8 NU, M omit *because*

NKJV

judged according to men in the flesh, but [b]live according to God in the spirit.

Serving for God's Glory

7 But [a]the end of all things is at hand; therefore be serious and watchful in your prayers.

8 And above all things have fervent love for one another, for [a]*"love will cover a multitude of sins."*

9 [a]*Be* hospitable to one another [b]without grumbling.

10 [a]As each one has received a gift, minister it to one another, [b]as good stewards of [c]the manifold grace of God.

11 [a]If anyone speaks, *let him speak* as the oracles of God. If anyone ministers, *let him do it* as with the ability which God supplies, that [b]in all things God may be glorified through Jesus Christ, to whom belong the glory and the dominion forever and ever. Amen.

Suffering for God's Glory

12 Beloved, do not think it strange concerning the fiery trial which is to try you, as though some strange thing happened to you;

13 but rejoice [a]to the extent that you partake of Christ's sufferings, that [b]when His glory is revealed, you may also be glad with exceeding joy.

14 If you are reproached for the name of Christ, [a]blessed *are you,* for the Spirit of glory and of God rests upon you. *On their part He is blasphemed, [b]but on your part He is glorified.

15 But let none of you suffer as a murderer, a thief, an evildoer, or as a busybody in other people's matters.

16 Yet if *anyone suffers* as a Christian, let him not be ashamed, but let him glorify God in this *matter.

17 For the time *has come* [a]for judgment to begin at the house of God; and if *it begins* with us first, [b]what will *be* the end of those who do not obey the gospel of God?

18 Now

[a]*"If the righteous one is scarcely saved,*
Where will the ungodly and the sinner
appear?"

19 Therefore let those who suffer according to the will of God [a]commit their souls *to Him* in doing good, as to a faithful Creator.

Shepherd the Flock

5 The elders who are among you I exhort, I who am a fellow elder and a [a]witness of the sufferings of Christ, and also a partaker of the [b]glory that will be revealed:

2 [a]Shepherd the flock of God which is among you, serving as overseers, [b]not by compulsion but *willingly, [c]not for dishonest gain but eagerly;

3 nor as [a]being lords over [b]those entrusted to you, but [c]being examples to the flock;

4 and when [a]the Chief Shepherd appears, you will receive [b]the crown of glory that does not fade away.

Submit to God, Resist the Devil

5 Likewise you younger people, submit yourselves to *your* elders. Yes, [a]all *of you* be submissive to one another, and be clothed with humility, for

[b]*"God resists the proud,*
But [c]*gives grace to the humble."*

6 Therefore humble yourselves under the mighty hand of God, that He may exalt you in due time,

7 casting all your care upon Him, for He cares for you.

8 Be sober, be vigilant; *because your ad-

KJV

sary the devil, as a roaring lion, walketh about,
seeking whom he may devour:
9 Whom resist stedfast in the faith, knowing
that the same afflictions are accomplished in your
brethren that are in the world.
10 But the God of all grace, [a]who hath called
us unto his eternal glory by Christ Jesus, after
that ye have suffered a while, make you perfect,
stablish, strengthen, settle *you*.
11 [a]To him *be* glory and dominion for ever
and ever. Amen.

Farewell and Peace

12 By [a]Silvanus, a faithful brother unto you,
as I suppose, I have written briefly, exhorting,
and testifying [b]that this is the true grace of God
wherein ye stand.
13 The *church that is* at Babylon, elected together with *you,* saluteth you; and *so doth* [a]Mar-
cus my son.
14 Greet ye one another with a kiss of charity. Peace *be* with you all that are in Christ Jesus.
Amen.

10 [a]1 Cor. 1:9; 1 Thess. 2:12
11 [a]Rev. 1:6
12 [a]2 Cor. 1:19; 1 Thess. 1:1; 2 Thess. 1:1 [b]Acts 20:24
13 [a]Acts 12:12, 25; 15:37, 39; Col. 4:10; Philem. 24

*
5:10 NU *the God of all grace,* • NU, M *you* • NU *will perfect*

NKJV

versary the devil walks about like a roaring lion,
seeking whom he may devour.
9 Resist him, steadfast in the faith, knowing
that the same sufferings are experienced by your
brotherhood in the world.
10 But *may the God of all grace, [a]who called
*us to His eternal glory by Christ Jesus, after you
have suffered a while, *perfect, establish,
strengthen, and settle *you.*
11 [a]To Him *be* the glory and the dominion
forever and ever. Amen.

Farewell and Peace

12 By [a]Silvanus, our faithful brother as I consider him, I have written to you briefly, exhorting
and testifying [b]that this is the true grace of God
in which you stand.
13 She who is in Babylon, elect together with
you, greets you; and *so does* [a]Mark my son.
14 Greet one another with a kiss of love.
Peace to you all who are in Christ Jesus. Amen.

KJV

THE SECOND EPISTLE OF

PETER

Greeting the Faithful

1 Simon Peter, a servant and an [a]apostle of Jesus Christ, to them that have obtained [b]like precious faith with us through the righteousness of God and our Saviour Jesus Christ:

2 [a]Grace and peace be multiplied unto you through the knowledge of God, and of Jesus our Lord,

3 According as his [a]divine power hath given unto us all things that *pertain* unto life and godliness, through the knowledge of him [b]that hath called us to glory and virtue:

4 [a]Whereby are given unto us exceeding great and precious promises: that by these ye might be [b]partakers of the divine nature, having escaped the corruption that is in the world through lust.

Fruitful Growth in the Faith

5 And beside this, [a]giving all diligence, add to your faith virtue; and to virtue [b]knowledge;

6 And to knowledge temperance; and to temperance patience; and to patience godliness;

7 And to godliness brotherly kindness; and [a]to brotherly kindness charity.

8 For if these things be in you, and abound, they make *you that ye shall* neither *be* barren [a]nor unfruitful in the knowledge of our Lord Jesus Christ.

9 But he that lacketh these things is [a]blind, and cannot see afar off, and hath forgotten that he was purged from his old sins.

10 Wherefore the rather, brethren, give diligence [a]to make your calling and election sure: for if ye do these things, ye shall never fall:

11 For so an entrance shall be ministered unto you abundantly into the everlasting kingdom of our Lord and Saviour Jesus Christ.

Peter's Approaching Death

12 Wherefore [a]I will not be negligent to put you always in remembrance of these things, [b]though ye know *them,* and be established in the present truth.

13 Yea, I think it meet, [a]as long as I am in this tabernacle, [b]to stir you up by putting *you* in remembrance;

14 [a]Knowing that shortly I must put off *this* my tabernacle, even as [b]our Lord Jesus Christ hath shewed me.

15 Moreover I will endeavour that ye may be able after my decease to have these things always in remembrance.

The Trustworthy Prophetic Word
(Matt. 17:5; Mark 9:7; Luke 9:35)

16 For we have not followed [a]cunningly devised fables, when we made known unto you the [b]power and [c]coming of our Lord Jesus Christ, but were [d]eyewitnesses of his majesty.

17 For he received from God the Father honour and glory, when there came such a voice to him from the excellent glory, [a]This is my beloved Son, in whom I am well pleased.

18 And this voice which came from heaven

CHAPTER 1

1 [a]Gal. 2:8 [b]Eph. 4:5
2 [a]Dan. 4:1
3 [a]1 Pet. 1:5 [b]1 Thess. 2:12; 2 Thess. 2:14; 1 Pet. 5:10
4 [a]2 Cor. 1:20; 7:1 [b][2 Cor. 3:18]
5 [a]2 Pet. 3:18 [b]1 Pet. 3:7
7 [a]Gal. 6:10
8 [a][John 15:2]
9 [a]1 John 2:9–11
10 [a]2 Cor. 13:5; 1 John 3:19
12 [a]Phil. 3:1; 1 John 2:21; Jude 5 [b]1 Pet. 5:12
13 [a][2 Cor. 5:1, 4]; 2 Pet. 1:14 [b]2 Pet. 3:1
14 [a][2 Cor. 5:1; 2 Tim. 4:6] [b]John 13:36; 21:18, 19
16 [a]1 Cor. 1:17 [b][Matt. 28:18; Eph. 1:19–22] [c][1 Pet. 5:4] [d]Matt. 17:1–5; Luke 1:2
17 [a]Ps. 2:7; Is. 42:1; Matt. 17:5; Mark 9:7; Luke 1:35; 9:35

NKJV

THE SECOND EPISTLE OF

PETER

Greeting the Faithful

1 Simon Peter, a bondservant and [a]apostle of Jesus Christ,

To those who have obtained [b]like precious faith with us by the righteousness of our God and Savior Jesus Christ:

2 [a]Grace and peace be multiplied to you in the knowledge of God and of Jesus our Lord,

3 as His [a]divine power has given to us all things that *pertain* to life and godliness, through the knowledge of Him [b]who called us by glory and virtue,

4 [a]by which have been given to us exceedingly great and precious promises, that through these you may be [b]partakers of the divine nature, having escaped the corruption *that is* in the world through lust.

Fruitful Growth in the Faith

5 But also for this very reason, [a]giving all diligence, add to your faith virtue, to virtue [b]knowledge,

6 to knowledge self-control, to self-control perseverance, to perseverance godliness,

7 to godliness brotherly kindness, and [a]to brotherly kindness love.

8 For if these things are yours and abound, *you will be* neither barren [a]nor unfruitful in the knowledge of our Lord Jesus Christ.

9 For he who lacks these things is [a]shortsighted, even to blindness, and has forgotten that he was cleansed from his old sins.

10 Therefore, brethren, be even more diligent [a]to make your call and election sure, for if you do these things you will never stumble;

11 for so an entrance will be supplied to you abundantly into the everlasting kingdom of our Lord and Savior Jesus Christ.

Peter's Approaching Death

12 For this reason [a]I will not be negligent to remind you always of these things, [b]though you know and are established in the present truth.

13 Yes, I think it is right, [a]as long as I am in this tent, [b]to stir you up by reminding *you,*

14 [a]knowing that shortly I *must* put off my tent, just as [b]our Lord Jesus Christ showed me.

15 Moreover I will be careful to ensure that you always have a reminder of these things after my decease.

The Trustworthy Prophetic Word
(Matt. 17:5; Mark 9:7; Luke 9:35)

16 For we did not follow [a]cunningly devised fables when we made known to you the [b]power and [c]coming of our Lord Jesus Christ, but were [d]eyewitnesses of His majesty.

17 For He received from God the Father honor and glory when such a voice came to Him from the Excellent Glory: [a]"This is My beloved Son, in whom I am well pleased."

18 And we heard this voice which came from

KJV

we heard, when we were with him in [a]the holy mount.

19 We have also a more sure word of prophecy; whereunto ye do well that ye take heed, as unto a [a]light that shineth in a dark place, [b]until the day dawn, and [c]the day star arise in your [d]hearts:

20 Knowing this first, that [a]no prophecy of the scripture is of any private interpretation.

21 For [a]the prophecy came not in old time by the will of man: [b]but holy men of God spake *as they were* moved by the Holy Ghost.

Destructive Doctrines

2 But there were false prophets also among the people, even as there shall be [a]false teachers among you, who privily shall bring in damnable heresies, even denying the Lord that bought them, and bring upon themselves swift destruction.

2 And many shall follow their pernicious ways; by reason of whom the way of truth shall be evil spoken of.

3 And through covetousness shall they with feigned words make merchandise of you: whose judgment now of a long time lingereth not, and their damnation slumbereth not.

Doom of False Teachers

4 For if God spared not the angels that sinned, but cast *them* down to hell, and delivered *them* into chains of darkness, to be reserved unto judgment;

5 And spared not the old world, but saved Noah the eighth *person,* a preacher of righteousness, bringing in the flood upon the world of the ungodly;

6 And turning the cities of [a]Sodom and Gomorrha into ashes condemned *them* with an overthrow, making *them* an ensample unto those that after should live ungodly;

7 And [a]delivered just Lot, vexed with the filthy conversation of the wicked:

8 (For that righteous man dwelling among them, [a]in seeing and hearing, vexed *his* righteous soul from day to day with *their* unlawful deeds;)

9 [a]The Lord knoweth how to deliver the godly out of temptations, and to reserve the unjust unto the day of judgment to be punished:

10 But chiefly [a]them that walk after the flesh in the lust of uncleanness, and despise government. [b]Presumptuous *are they,* selfwilled, they are not afraid to speak evil of dignities.

11 Whereas [a]angels, which are greater in power and might, bring not railing accusation against them before the Lord.

Depravity of False Teachers

12 But these, [a]as natural brute beasts, made to be taken and destroyed, speak evil of the things that they understand not; and shall utterly perish in their own corruption;

13 [a]And shall receive the reward of unrighteousness, *as* they that count it pleasure [b]to riot in the day time. [c]Spots *they are* and blemishes, sporting themselves with their own deceivings while [d]they feast with you;

14 Having eyes full of adultery, and that cannot cease from sin; beguiling unstable souls: [a]an heart they have exercised with covetous practices; cursed children:

15 Which have forsaken the right way, and are gone astray, following the way of [a]Balaam *the son* of Bosor, who loved the wages of unrighteousness;

16 But was rebuked for his iniquity: the dumb ass speaking with man's voice forbad the madness of the prophet.

17 [a]These are wells without water, clouds that are carried with a tempest; to whom the mist of darkness is reserved for ever.

---

18 [a]Matt. 17:1
19 [a][John 1:4, 5, 9] [b]Prov. 4:18 [c]Rev. 2:28; 22:16 [d][2 Cor. 4:5–7]
20 [a][Rom. 12:6]
21 [a]Jer. 23:26; [2 Tim. 3:16] [b]2 Sam. 23:2; Luke 1:70; Acts 1:16; 3:18; 1 Pet. 1:11

CHAPTER 2

1 [a]Matt. 24:5, 24; 1 Tim. 4:1, 2
6 [a]Gen. 19:1–26; Jude 7
7 [a]Gen. 19:16, 29
8 [a]Ps. 119:139
9 [a]Ps. 34:15–19; 1 Cor. 10:13; Rev. 3:10
10 [a]Jude 4, 7, 8 [b]Ex. 22:28; Jude 8
11 [a]Jude 9
12 [a]Jude 10
13 [a]Phil. 3:19 [b]Rom. 13:13 [c]Jude 12 [d]1 Cor. 11:20, 21
14 [a]Jude 11
15 [a]Num. 22:5, 7; Deut. 23:4; Neh. 13:2; Jude 11; Rev. 2:14
17 [a]Jude 12, 13

*

1:19 Or *We also have the more sure prophetic word*
1:20 Or *origin*
1:21 NU *men spoke from God*
2:3 M *will not*
2:17 NU *and mists* • NU omits *forever*

NKJV

heaven when we were with Him on [a]the holy mountain.

19 *And so we have the prophetic word confirmed, which you do well to heed as a [a]light that shines in a dark place, [b]until [c]the day dawns and the morning star rises in your [d]hearts;

20 knowing this first, that [a]no prophecy of Scripture is of any private *interpretation,

21 for [a]prophecy never came by the will of man, [b]but *holy men of God spoke *as they were* moved by the Holy Spirit.

Destructive Doctrines

2 But there were also false prophets among the people, even as there will be [a]false teachers among you, who will secretly bring in destructive heresies, even denying the Lord who bought them, *and* bring on themselves swift destruction.

2 And many will follow their destructive ways, because of whom the way of truth will be blasphemed.

3 By covetousness they will exploit you with deceptive words; for a long time their judgment has not been idle, and their destruction *does not slumber.

Doom of False Teachers

4 For if God did not spare the angels who sinned, but cast *them* down to hell and delivered *them* into chains of darkness, to be reserved for judgment;

5 and did not spare the ancient world, but saved Noah, *one of* eight *people,* a preacher of righteousness, bringing in the flood on the world of the ungodly;

6 and turning the cities of [a]Sodom and Gomorrah into ashes, condemned *them* to destruction, making *them* an example to those who afterward would live ungodly;

7 and [a]delivered righteous Lot, *who was* oppressed by the filthy conduct of the wicked

8 (for that righteous man, dwelling among them, [a]tormented *his* righteous soul from day to day by seeing and hearing *their* lawless deeds)—

9 *then* [a]the Lord knows how to deliver the godly out of temptations and to reserve the unjust under punishment for the day of judgment,

10 and especially [a]those who walk according to the flesh in the lust of uncleanness and despise authority. [b]*They are* presumptuous, self-willed. They are not afraid to speak evil of dignitaries,

11 whereas [a]angels, who are greater in power and might, do not bring a reviling accusation against them before the Lord.

Depravity of False Teachers

12 But these, [a]like natural brute beasts made to be caught and destroyed, speak evil of the things they do not understand, and will utterly perish in their own corruption,

13 [a]*and* will receive the wages of unrighteousness, *as* those who count it pleasure [b]to carouse in the daytime. [c]*They are* spots and blemishes, carousing in their own deceptions while [d]they feast with you,

14 having eyes full of adultery and that cannot cease from sin, enticing unstable souls. [a]*They have* a heart trained in covetous practices, *and are* accursed children.

15 They have forsaken the right way and gone astray, following the way of [a]Balaam the *son* of Beor, who loved the wages of unrighteousness;

16 but he was rebuked for his iniquity: a dumb donkey speaking with a man's voice restrained the madness of the prophet.

17 [a]These are wells without water, *clouds carried by a tempest, for whom is reserved the blackness of darkness *forever.

KJV

Deceptions of False Teachers

18 For when they speak great swelling *words*
of vanity, they allure through the lusts of the
flesh, *through much* wantonness, those that were
clean escaped from them who live in error.
19 While they promise them liberty, they
themselves are the servants of corruption: [a]for of
whom a man is overcome, of the same is he
brought in bondage.
20 For if after they [a]have escaped the pollutions of the world through the knowledge of the
Lord and Saviour Jesus Christ, they are [b]again
entangled therein, and overcome, the latter end
is worse with them than the beginning.
21 For [a]it had been better for them not to
have known the way of righteousness, than, after
they have known *it*, to turn from the holy commandment delivered unto them.
22 But it is happened unto them according
to the true proverb, [a]THE DOG *IS* TURNED TO HIS
OWN VOMIT AGAIN; and the sow that was washed to
her wallowing in the mire.

God's Promise Is Not Slack
(Gen. 6:5—8:22)

3 This second epistle, beloved, I now write unto
you; in *both* which [a]I stir up your pure minds
by way of remembrance:
2 That ye may be mindful of the words
[a]which were spoken before by the holy prophets,
[b]and of the commandment of us the apostles of
the Lord and Saviour:
3 Knowing this first, that there shall come
in the last days scoffers, [a]walking after their own
lusts,
4 And saying, Where is the promise of his
coming? for since the fathers fell asleep, all things
continue as *they were* from the beginning of the
[a]creation.
5 For this they willingly are ignorant of, that
[a]by the word of God the heavens were of old, and
the earth [b]standing out of the water and in the
water:
6 [a]Whereby the world that then was, being
overflowed with water, perished:
7 But [a]the heavens and the earth, which are
now, by the same word are kept in store, reserved
unto [b]fire against the day of judgment and perdition of ungodly men.
8 But, beloved, be not ignorant of this one
thing, that one day *is* with the Lord as a thousand
years, and [a]a thousand years as one day.
9 [a]The Lord is not slack concerning his
promise, as some men count slackness; but [b]is
longsuffering to us-ward, [c]not willing that any
should perish, but [d]that all should come to
repentance.

The Day of the Lord

10 But [a]the day of the Lord will come as a
thief in the night; in the which [b]the heavens shall
pass away with a great noise, and the elements
shall melt with fervent heat, the earth also and
the works that are therein shall be burned up.
11 *Seeing* then *that* all these things shall be
dissolved, what manner *of persons* ought ye to
be [a]in *all* holy conversation and godliness,
12 [a]Looking for and hasting unto the coming
of the day of God, wherein the heavens being on
fire shall [b]be dissolved, and the elements shall
[c]melt with fervent heat?
13 Nevertheless we, according to his promise, look for [a]new heavens and a [b]new earth,
wherein dwelleth righteousness.

Be Steadfast

14 Wherefore, beloved, seeing that ye look
for such things, be diligent [a]that ye may be found
of him in peace, without spot, and blameless.
15 And account *that* [a]the longsuffering of
our Lord *is* salvation; even as our beloved brother

19 [a]John 8:34; Rom. 6:16
20 [a]Matt. 12:45 [b]Luke 11:26; [Heb. 6:4–6]
21 [a]Luke 12:47
22 [a]Prov. 26:11

CHAPTER 3

1 [a]2 Pet. 1:13
2 [a]2 Pet. 1:21 [b]Jude 17
3 [a]2 Pet. 2:10
4 [a]Gen. 6:1–7
5 [a]Gen. 1:6, 9; Heb. 11:3 [b]Ps. 24:2; 136:6
6 [a]Gen. 7:11, 12, 21–23; Matt. 24:37–39; Luke 17:26, 27; 2 Pet. 2:5
7 [a]2 Pet. 3:10, 12 [b]Matt. 25:41; [2 Thess. 1:8]
8 [a]Ps. 90:4
9 [a]Hab. 2:3; Rom. 13:11; Heb. 10:37 [b]Ps. 86:15; Is. 30:18 [c]Ezek. 33:11 [d]Matt. 20:28; [Rom. 2:4]
10 [a]Matt. 24:42, 43; Luke 12:39; 1 Thess. 5:2; Rev. 3:3; 16:15 [b]Gen. 1:6–8; Ps. 102:25, 26; Is. 51:6; Rev. 20:11
11 [a]1 Pet. 1:15
12 [a]1 Cor. 1:7, 8; Titus 2:13– 15 [b]Ps. 50:3 [c]Is. 24:19; 34:4; Mic. 1:4
13 [a]Is. 65:17; 66:22 [b][Rom. 8:21]; Rev. 21:1
14 [a]1 Cor. 1:8; 15:58; [1 Thess. 3:12, 13; 5:23]
15 [a]Ps. 86:15; Rom. 2:4; 1 Pet. 3:20

*

2:18 NU *are barely escaping*
3:2 NU, M *the apostles of your Lord and Savior* or *your apostles of the Lord and Savior*
3:9 NU *you*
3:10 NU *laid bare*, lit. *found*

NKJV

Deceptions of False Teachers

18 For when they speak great swelling *words*
of emptiness, they allure through the lusts of the
flesh, through lewdness, the ones who *have actually escaped from those who live in error.
19 While they promise them liberty, they
themselves are slaves of corruption; [a]for by whom
a person is overcome, by him also he is brought
into bondage.
20 For if, after they [a]have escaped the pollutions of the world through the knowledge of the
Lord and Savior Jesus Christ, they are [b]again entangled in them and overcome, the latter end is
worse for them than the beginning.
21 For [a]it would have been better for them
not to have known the way of righteousness, than
having known *it*, to turn from the holy commandment delivered to them.
22 But it has happened to them according to
the true proverb: [a]*"A dog returns to his own
vomit,"* and, "a sow, having washed, to her wallowing in the mire."

God's Promise Is Not Slack
(Gen. 6:5—8:22)

3 Beloved, I now write to you this second epistle
(in *both of* which [a]I stir up your pure minds
by way of reminder),
2 that you may be mindful of the words
[a]which were spoken before by the holy prophets,
[b]and of the commandment of *us, the apostles of
the Lord and Savior,
3 knowing this first: that scoffers will come
in the last days, [a]walking according to their own
lusts,
4 and saying, "Where is the promise of His
coming? For since the fathers fell asleep, all things
continue as *they were* from the beginning of
[a]creation."
5 For this they willfully forget: that [a]by the
word of God the heavens were of old, and the
earth [b]standing out of water and in the water,
6 [a]by which the world *that* then existed perished, being flooded with water.
7 But [a]the heavens and the earth *which* are
now preserved by the same word, are reserved
for [b]fire until the day of judgment and perdition
of ungodly men.
8 But, beloved, do not forget this one thing,
that with the Lord one day *is* as a thousand years,
and [a]a thousand years as one day.
9 [a]The Lord is not slack concerning *His*
promise, as some count slackness, but [b]is longsuffering toward *us, [c]not willing that any should
perish but [d]that all should come to repentance.

The Day of the Lord

10 But [a]the day of the Lord will come as a
thief in the night, in which [b]the heavens will pass
away with a great noise, and the elements will
melt with fervent heat; both the earth and the
works that are in it will be *burned up.
11 Therefore, since all these things will be
dissolved, what manner *of persons* ought you to
be [a]in holy conduct and godliness,
12 [a]looking for and hastening the coming of
the day of God, because of which the heavens will
[b]be dissolved, being on fire, and the elements will
[c]melt with fervent heat?
13 Nevertheless we, according to His promise, look for [a]new heavens and a [b]new earth in
which righteousness dwells.

Be Steadfast

14 Therefore, beloved, looking forward to
these things, be diligent [a]to be found by Him in
peace, without spot and blameless;
15 and consider *that* [a]the longsuffering of
our Lord *is* salvation—as also our beloved brother

KJV

Paul also according to the wisdom given unto him hath written unto you;
16 As also in all *his* [a]epistles, speaking in them of these things; in which are some things hard to be understood, which they that are unlearned and unstable wrest, as *they do* also the [b]other scriptures, unto their own destruction.
17 Ye therefore, beloved, [a]seeing ye know *these things* before, [b]beware lest ye also, being led away with the error of the wicked, fall from your own stedfastness.
18 [a]But grow in grace, and *in* the knowledge of our Lord and Saviour Jesus Christ. [b]To him *be* glory both now and for ever. Amen.

16 [a]Rom. 8:19; 1 Cor. 15:24; 1 Thess. 4:15; 2 Thess. 1:10 [b]2 Tim. 3:16
17 [a]Mark 13:23 [b]Eph. 4:14
18 [a]Eph. 4:15 [b]Rom. 11:36; 2 Tim. 4:18; Rev. 1:6

NKJV

Paul, according to the wisdom given to him, has written to you,
16 as also in all his [a]epistles, speaking in them of these things, in which are some things hard to understand, which untaught and unstable *people* twist to their own destruction, as *they do* also the [b]rest of the Scriptures.
17 You therefore, beloved, [a]since you know *this* beforehand, [b]beware lest you also fall from your own steadfastness, being led away with the error of the wicked;
18 [a]but grow in the grace and knowledge of our Lord and Savior Jesus Christ. [b]To Him *be* the glory both now and forever. Amen.

KJV

THE FIRST EPISTLE OF

JOHN

What Was Heard, Seen, and Touched
(John 1:1–5)

1 That [a]which was from the beginning, which
we have heard, which we have [b]seen with our
eyes, [c]which we have looked upon, and [d]our
hands have handled, of the [e]Word of life;
2 (For [a]the life [b]was manifested, and we
have seen *it,* [c]and bear witness, and shew unto
you that eternal life, which was [d]with the Father,
and was manifested unto us;)
3 That which we have seen and heard declare we unto you, that ye also may have fellowship with us: and truly our fellowship *is* [a]with the
Father, and with his Son Jesus Christ.
4 And these things write we unto you, [a]that
your joy may be full.

Fellowship with Him and One Another

5 [a]This then is the message which we have
heard of him, and declare unto you, that [b]God is
light, and in him is no darkness at all.
6 [a]If we say that we have fellowship with
him, and walk in darkness, we lie, and do not
the truth:
7 But if we [a]walk in the light, as he is in
the light, we have fellowship one with another,
and [b]the blood of Jesus Christ his Son cleanseth
us from all sin.
8 If we say that we have no sin, we deceive
ourselves, and the truth is not in us.
9 If we [a]confess our sins, he is [b]faithful and
just to forgive us *our* sins, and to [c]cleanse us from
all unrighteousness.
10 If we say that we have not sinned, we
[a]make him a liar, and his word is not in us.

2 My little children, these things write I unto
you, that ye sin not. And if any man sin, [a]we
have an advocate with the Father, Jesus Christ
the righteous:
2 And [a]he is the propitiation for our sins:
and not for our's only, but [b]also for *the sins of*
the whole world.

The Test of Knowing Him

3 And hereby we do know that we know
him, if we keep his commandments.
4 He that saith, I know him, and keepeth
not his commandments, is a [a]liar, and the truth
is not in him.
5 But [a]whoso keepeth his word, [b]in him verily is the love of God perfected: hereby know we
that we are in him.
6 [a]He that saith he abideth in him [b]ought
himself also so to walk, even as he walked.
7 Brethren, I write no new commandment
unto you, but an old commandment which ye had
[a]from the beginning. The old commandment is
the word which ye have heard from the beginning.
8 Again, [a]a new commandment I write unto
you, which thing is true in him and in you: [b]be-
cause the darkness is past, and [c]the true light now
shineth.
9 [a]He that saith he is in the light, and hateth
his brother, is in darkness even until now.

CHAPTER 1

1 [a][John 1:1] [b]John 1:14 [c]2 Pet. 1:16 [d]Luke 24:39 [e][John 1:1, 4, 14]
2 [a]John 1:4 [b]Rom. 16:26 [c]John 21:24 [d][John 1:1, 18; 16:28]
3 [a]1 Cor. 1:9
4 [a]John 15:11; 16:24
5 [a]1 John 3:11 [b][1 Tim. 6:16]
6 [a][1 John 2:9–11]
7 [a]Is. 2:5 [b][1 Cor. 6:11]
9 [a]Prov. 28:13 [b][Rom. 3:24–26] [c]Ps. 51:2
10 [a]1 John 5:10

CHAPTER 2

1 [a]Heb. 7:25; 9:24
2 [a][Rom. 3:25] [b]John 1:29
4 [a]Rom. 3:4
5 [a]John 14:21, 23 [b][1 John 4:12]
6 [a]John 15:4 [b]1 Pet. 2:21
7 [a]1 John 3:11, 23; 4:21
8 [a]John 13:34; 15:12 [b]Rom. 13:12 [c][John 1:9; 8:12; 12:35]
9 [a][1 Cor. 13:2]

*

1:4 NU, M *our*
2:7 NU *Beloved* • NU omits *from the beginning*

NKJV

THE FIRST EPISTLE OF

JOHN

What Was Heard, Seen, and Touched
(John 1:1–5)

1 That [a]which was from the beginning, which
we have heard, which we have [b]seen with our
eyes, [c]which we have looked upon, and [d]our
hands have handled, concerning the [e]Word of
life—
2 [a]the life [b]was manifested, and we have
seen, [c]and bear witness, and declare to you that
eternal life which was [d]with the Father and was
manifested to us—
3 that which we have seen and heard we
declare to you, that you also may have fellowship
with us; and truly our fellowship *is* [a]with the Father and with His Son Jesus Christ.
4 And these things we write to you [a]that
*your joy may be full.

Fellowship with Him and One Another

5 [a]This is the message which we have heard
from Him and declare to you, that [b]God is light
and in Him is no darkness at all.
6 [a]If we say that we have fellowship with
Him, and walk in darkness, we lie and do not
practice the truth.
7 But if we [a]walk in the light as He is in
the light, we have fellowship with one another,
and [b]the blood of Jesus Christ His Son cleanses
us from all sin.
8 If we say that we have no sin, we deceive
ourselves, and the truth is not in us.
9 If we [a]confess our sins, He is [b]faithful and
just to forgive us *our* sins and to [c]cleanse us from
all unrighteousness.
10 If we say that we have not sinned, we
[a]make Him a liar, and His word is not in us.

2 My little children, these things I write to you,
so that you may not sin. And if anyone sins,
[a]we have an Advocate with the Father, Jesus
Christ the righteous.
2 And [a]He Himself is the propitiation for
our sins, and not for ours only but [b]also for the
whole world.

The Test of Knowing Him

3 Now by this we know that we know Him,
if we keep His commandments.
4 He who says, "I know Him," and does not
keep His commandments, is a [a]liar, and the truth
is not in him.
5 But [a]whoever keeps His word, truly the
love of God is perfected [b]in him. By this we know
that we are in Him.
6 [a]He who says he abides in Him [b]ought
himself also to walk just as He walked.
7 *Brethren, I write no new commandment
to you, but an old commandment which you have
had [a]from the beginning. The old commandment
is the word which you heard *from the beginning.
8 Again, [a]a new commandment I write to
you, which thing is true in Him and in you, [b]be-
cause the darkness is passing away, and [c]the true
light is already shining.
9 [a]He who says he is in the light, and hates
his brother, is in darkness until now.

KJV

10 [a]He that loveth his brother abideth in the
light, and [b]there is none occasion of stumbling
in him.
11 But he that [a]hateth his brother is in darkness, and [b]walketh in darkness, and knoweth not
whither he goeth, because that darkness hath
blinded his eyes.

Their Spiritual State

12 I write unto you, little children, because
[a]your sins are forgiven you for his name's sake.
13 I write unto you, fathers, because ye have
known him *that is* [a]from the beginning. I write
unto you, young men, because ye have overcome
the wicked one. I write unto you, little children,
because ye have [b]known the Father.
14 I have written unto you, fathers, because
ye have known him *that is* from the beginning. I
have written unto you, young men, because [a]ye
are strong, and the word of God abideth in you,
and ye have overcome the wicked one.

Do Not Love the World

15 [a]Love not the world, neither the things
that are in the world. [b]If any man love the world,
the love of the Father is not in him.
16 For all that *is* in the world, the lust of the
flesh, [a]and the lust of the eyes, and the pride of
life, is not of the Father, but is of the world.
17 And [a]the world passeth away, and the lust
thereof: but he that doeth the will of God abideth
for ever.

Deceptions of the Last Hour

18 [a]Little children, [b]it is the last time: and
as ye have heard that [c]antichrist shall come, [d]even
now are there many antichrists; whereby we
know [e]that it is the last time.
19 [a]They went out from us, but they were
not of us; for [b]if they had been of us, they would
no doubt have continued with us: but *they went
out*, [c]that they might be made manifest that they
were not all of us.
20 But [a]ye have an unction [b]from the Holy
One, and [c]ye know all things.
21 I have not written unto you because ye
know not the truth, but because ye know it, and
that no lie is of the truth.
22 [a]Who is a liar but he that denieth that
[b]Jesus is the Christ? He is antichrist, that denieth the Father and the Son.
23 [a]Whosoever denieth the Son, the same
hath not the [b]Father: [*but*] [c]*he that acknowl-
edgeth the Son hath the Father also.*

Let Truth Abide in You

24 Let that therefore abide in you, [a]which ye
have heard from the beginning. If that which ye
have heard from the beginning shall remain in
you, [b]ye also shall continue in the Son, and in
the Father.
25 [a]And this is the promise that he hath
promised us, *even* eternal life.
26 These *things* have I written unto you concerning them that seduce you.
27 But the [a]anointing which ye have received
of him abideth in you, and [b]ye need not that any
man teach you: but as the same anointing
[c]teacheth you of all things, and is truth, and is
no lie, and even as it hath taught you, ye shall
abide in him.

The Children of God

28 And now, little children, abide in him;
that, when he shall appear, we may have [a]confi-
dence, and not be ashamed before him at his
coming.
29 [a]If ye know that he is righteous, ye know

10 [a][1 John 3:14] [b]2 Pet. 1:10
11 [a][1 John 2:9; 3:15; 4:20] [b]John 12:35; 1 John 1:6
12 [a][1 Cor. 6:11]
13 [a]John 1:1; Rev. 22:13 [b][Rom. 8:15–17; Gal. 4:6]
14 [a]Eph. 6:10
15 [a][Rom. 12:2]; Gal. 1:4; James 1:27 [b]Matt. 6:24; James 4:4
16 [a][Eccl. 5:10, 11]
17 [a]1 Cor. 7:31; 1 Pet. 1:24
18 [a]John 21:5 [b]Rom. 13:11; 1 Tim. 4:1; Heb. 1:2; 1 Pet. 4:7 [c]2 Thess. 2:3 [d]Matt. 24:5, 24; 1 John 2:22; 4:3; 2 John 7 [e]1 Tim. 4:1
19 [a]Deut. 13:13 [b]Matt. 24:24 [c]1 Cor. 11:19
20 [a]2 Cor. 1:21; Heb. 1:9; 1 John 2:27 [b]Acts 3:14 [c]Prov. 28:5; [John 16:13]; 1 Cor. 2:15, 16
22 [a]2 John 7 [b]1 John 4:3
23 [a]John 15:23 [b]John 5:23 [c]1 John 4:15; 5:1; 2 John 9
24 [a]2 John 6, 7 [b]John 14:23; 1 John 1:3; 2 John 9
25 [a]John 3:14–16; 6:40; 17:2, 3; 1 John 1:2
27 [a][John 14:16; 16:13]; 1 John 2:20 [b][Jer. 31:33] [c][John 14:16; 1 Cor. 2:12]; 1 Thess. 4:9
28 [a]Eph. 3:12; 1 John 3:21; 4:17; 5:14
29 [a]Acts 22:14

NKJV

10 [a]He who loves his brother abides in the
light, and [b]there is no cause for stumbling in
him.
11 But he who [a]hates his brother is in darkness and [b]walks in darkness, and does not know
where he is going, because the darkness has
blinded his eyes.

Their Spiritual State

12 I write to you, little children,
Because [a]your sins are forgiven you for
His name's sake.
13 I write to you, fathers,
Because you have known Him *who is*
[a]from the beginning.
I write to you, young men,
Because you have overcome the wicked
one.
I write to you, little children,
Because you have [b]known the Father.
14 I have written to you, fathers,
Because you have known Him *who is*
from the beginning.
I have written to you, young men,
Because [a]you are strong, and the word
of God abides in you,
And you have overcome the wicked one.

Do Not Love the World

15 [a]Do not love the world or the things in
the world. [b]If anyone loves the world, the love
of the Father is not in him.
16 For all that *is* in the world—the lust of the
flesh, [a]the lust of the eyes, and the pride of life—
is not of the Father but is of the world.
17 And [a]the world is passing away, and the
lust of it; but he who does the will of God abides
forever.

Deceptions of the Last Hour

18 [a]Little children, [b]it is the last hour; and
as you have heard that [c]the* Antichrist is coming,
[d]even now many antichrists have come, by which
we know [e]that it is the last hour.
19 [a]They went out from us, but they were
not of us; for [b]if they had been of us, they would
have continued with us; but *they went out* [c]that
they might be made manifest, that none of them
were of us.
20 But [a]you have an anointing [b]from the
Holy One, and [c]you* know all things.
21 I have not written to you because you do
not know the truth, but because you know it, and
that no lie is of the truth.
22 [a]Who is a liar but he who denies that
[b]Jesus is the Christ? He is antichrist who denies
the Father and the Son.
23 [a]Whoever denies the Son does not have
the [b]Father either; [c]he who acknowledges the Son
has the Father also.

Let Truth Abide in You

24 Therefore let that abide in you [a]which you
heard from the beginning. If what you heard from
the beginning abides in you, [b]you also will abide
in the Son and in the Father.
25 [a]And this is the promise that He has promised us—eternal life.
26 These things I have written to you concerning those who *try to* deceive you.
27 But the [a]anointing which you have received from Him abides in you, and [b]you do not
need that anyone teach you; but as the same
anointing [c]teaches you concerning all things, and
is true, and is not a lie, and just as it has taught
you, you *will abide in Him.

The Children of God

28 And now, little children, abide in Him, that
*when He appears, we may have [a]confidence and
not be ashamed before Him at His coming.
29 [a]If you know that He is righteous, you

***2:18** NU omits *the*
2:20 NU *you all know.*
2:27 NU omits *will*
2:28 NU *if*

KJV

that [b]every one that doeth righteousness is born
of him.

3 Behold, [a]what manner of love the Father hath
bestowed upon us, that [b]we should be called
the sons of God: therefore the world knoweth us
not, [c]because it knew him not.
2 Beloved, [a]now are we the sons of God,
and [b]it doth not yet appear what we shall be: but
we know that, when he shall appear, [c]we shall
be like him; for [d]we shall see him as he is.
3 [a]And every man that hath this hope in him
purifieth himself, even as he is pure.

Sin and the Child of God

4 Whosoever committeth sin transgresseth
also the law: for [a]sin is the transgression of the
law.
5 And ye know [a]that he was manifested [b]to
take away our sins; and [c]in him is no sin.
6 Whosoever abideth in him sinneth not:
whosoever sinneth hath not seen him, neither
known him.
7 Little children, let no man deceive you:
he that doeth righteousness is righteous, even as
he is righteous.
8 [a]He that committeth sin is of the devil;
for the devil sinneth from the beginning. For this
purpose the Son of God was manifested, [b]that he
might destroy the works of the devil.
9 Whosoever is [a]born of God doth not commit sin; for [b]his seed remaineth in him: and he
cannot sin, because he is born of God.

The Imperative of Love
(*Matt. 22:39*)

10 In this the children of God are manifest,
and the children of the devil: whosoever doeth
not righteousness is not of God, neither he that
loveth not his brother.
11 For this is the message that ye heard from
the beginning, [a]that we should love one another.
12 Not as [a]Cain, *who* was of that wicked one,
and slew his brother. And wherefore slew he
him? Because his own works were evil, and his
brother's righteous.
13 Marvel not, my brethren, if [a]the world
hate you.
14 We know that we have passed from death
unto life, because we love the brethren. He that
loveth not *his* brother abideth in death.
15 [a]Whosoever hateth his brother is a murderer: and ye know that [b]no murderer hath eternal life abiding in him.

The Outworking of Love

16 [a]Hereby perceive we the love *of God*, [b]be-
cause he laid down his life for us: and we ought
to lay down *our* lives for the brethren.
17 But [a]whoso hath this world's good, and
seeth his brother have need, and shutteth up his
bowels *of compassion* from him, how dwelleth the
love of God in him?
18 My little children, [a]let us not love in word,
neither in tongue; but in deed and in truth.
19 And hereby we know [a]that we are of the
truth, and shall assure our hearts before him.
20 [a]For if our heart condemn us, God is
greater than our heart, and knoweth all things.
21 Beloved, if our heart condemn us not,
[a]*then* have we confidence toward God.
22 And [a]whatsoever we ask, we receive of
him, because we keep his commandments, [b]and
do those things that are pleasing in his sight.
23 And this is his commandment, That we
should believe on the name of his Son Jesus
Christ, [a]and love one another, as he gave us
commandment.

NKJV

know that [b]everyone who practices righteousness
is born of Him.

3 Behold [a]what manner of love the Father has
bestowed on us, that [b]we should be called children of *God! Therefore the world does not know
*us, [c]because it did not know Him.
2 Beloved, [a]now we are children of God;
and [b]it has not yet been revealed what we shall
be, but we know that when He is revealed, [c]we
shall be like Him, for [d]we shall see Him as He
is.
3 [a]And everyone who has this hope in Him
purifies himself, just as He is pure.

Sin and the Child of God

4 Whoever commits sin also commits lawlessness, and [a]sin is lawlessness.
5 And you know [a]that He was manifested
[b]to take away our sins, and [c]in Him there is no
sin.
6 Whoever abides in Him does not sin.
Whoever sins has neither seen Him nor known
Him.
7 Little children, let no one deceive you. He
who practices righteousness is righteous, just as
He is righteous.
8 [a]He who sins is of the devil, for the devil
has sinned from the beginning. For this purpose
the Son of God was manifested, [b]that He might
destroy the works of the devil.
9 Whoever has been [a]born of God does not
sin, for [b]His seed remains in him; and he cannot
sin, because he has been born of God.

The Imperative of Love
(*Matt. 22:39*)

10 In this the children of God and the children of the devil are manifest: Whoever does not
practice righteousness is not of God, nor *is* he who
does not love his brother.
11 For this is the message that you heard
from the beginning, [a]that we should love one
another,
12 not as [a]Cain *who* was of the wicked one
and murdered his brother. And why did he murder him? Because his works were evil and his
brother's righteous.
13 Do not marvel, my brethren, if [a]the world
hates you.
14 We know that we have passed from death
to life, because we love the brethren. He who does
not love **his* brother abides in death.
15 [a]Whoever hates his brother is a murderer,
and you know that [b]no murderer has eternal life
abiding in him.

The Outworking of Love

16 [a]By this we know love, [b]because He laid
down His life for us. And we also ought to lay
down *our* lives for the brethren.
17 But [a]whoever has this world's goods, and
sees his brother in need, and shuts up his heart
from him, how does the love of God abide in
him?
18 My little children, [a]let us not love in word
or in tongue, but in deed and in truth.
19 And by this we *know [a]that we are of
the truth, and shall assure our hearts before
Him.
20 [a]For if our heart condemns us, God is
greater than our heart, and knows all things.
21 Beloved, if our heart does not condemn
us, [a]we have confidence toward God.
22 And [a]whatever we ask we receive from
Him, because we keep His commandments [b]and
do those things that are pleasing in His sight.
23 And this is His commandment: that we
should believe on the name of His Son Jesus
Christ [a]and love one another, as He gave *us
commandment.

---

29 [b]John 7:18; 1 John 3:7, 10

CHAPTER 3

1 [a][John 3:16; Eph. 2:4–7; 1 John 4:10] [b][John 1:12] [c]John 15:18, 21; 16:3
2 [a][Is. 56:5; Rom. 8:15, 16] [b][Rom. 8:18, 19, 23] [c]Rom. 8:29; 2 Pet. 1:4 [d][Ps. 16:11]
3 [a]1 John 4:17
4 [a]Rom. 4:15; 1 John 5:17
5 [a]1 John 1:2; 3:8 [b][Is. 53:5, 6]; John 1:29; [2 Cor. 5:21; Heb. 9:26] [c][2 Cor. 5:21]; 1 John 2:29
8 [a]Matt. 13:38; John 8:44; 1 John 3:10 [b]Luke 10:18; [Heb. 2:14]
9 [a]John 1:3; 3:3; [1 John 2:29; 4:7; 5:1, 4, 18]; 3 John 11 [b]1 Pet. 1:23
11 [a][John 13:34; 15:12]; 1 John 4:7, 11, 21; 2 John 5
12 [a]Gen. 4:4, 8
13 [a][John 15:18; 17:14]
15 [a]Matt. 5:21; John 8:44 [b][Gal. 5:20, 21; Rev. 21:8]
16 [a][John 3:16] [b]John 10:11; 15:13; Gal. 2:20
17 [a]Deut. 15:7
18 [a]Ezek. 33:31
19 [a]John 18:37
20 [a][1 Cor. 4:4, 5]
21 [a][Heb. 10:22; 1 John 2:28; 5:14]
22 [a]Ps. 34:15; [John 15:7]; 1 John 5:14, 15 [b]John 8:29; Heb. 13:21
23 [a]Matt. 22:39

3:1 NU adds *And we are.* • M *you*
3:14 NU omits *his brother*
3:19 NU *shall know*
3:23 M omits *us*

KJV

The Spirit of Truth and the Spirit of Error

24 And [a]he that keepeth his commandments
[b]dwelleth in him, and he in him. And [c]hereby we
know that he abideth in us, by the Spirit which
he hath given us.

4 Beloved, believe not every spirit, but [a]try the
spirits whether they are of God: because
[b]many false prophets are gone out into the world.
2 Hereby know ye the Spirit of God: [a]Every
spirit that confesseth that Jesus Christ is come
in the flesh is of God:
3 And every spirit that confesseth not that
Jesus Christ is come in the flesh is not of God:
and this is that *spirit* of antichrist, whereof ye
have heard that it should come; and even now
already is it in the world.
4 Ye are of God, little children, and have
overcome them: because greater is he that is in
you, than [a]he that is in the world.
5 [a]They are of the world: therefore speak
they of the world, and [b]the world heareth them.
6 We are of God: he that knoweth God heareth us; he that is not of God heareth not us.
[a]Hereby know we the spirit of truth, and the spirit
of error.

Knowing God Through Love
(cf. John 3:16)

7 [a]Beloved, let us love one another: for love
is of God; and every one that [b]loveth is born of
God, and knoweth God.
8 He that loveth not knoweth not God; for
God is love.
9 [a]In this was manifested the love of God
toward us, because that God sent his only begotten [b]Son into the world, that we might live
through him.
10 Herein is love, [a]not that we loved God,
but that he loved us, and sent his Son [b]*to be* the
propitiation for our sins.
11 Beloved, [a]if God so loved us, we ought
also to love one another.

Seeing God Through Love

12 [a]No man hath seen God at any time. If
we love one another, God dwelleth in us, and his
love is perfected in us.
13 [a]Hereby know we that we dwell in him,
and he in us, because he hath given us of his
Spirit.
14 And [a]we have seen and do testify that [b]the
Father sent the Son *to be* the Saviour of the world.
15 [a]Whosoever shall confess that Jesus is the
Son of God, God dwelleth in him, and he in God.
16 And we have known and believed the love
that God hath to us. God is love; and [a]he that
dwelleth in love dwelleth in God, and God [b]in him.

The Consummation of Love

17 Herein is our love made perfect, that [a]we
may have boldness in the day of judgment: because as he is, so are we in this world.
18 There is no fear in love; but perfect love
casteth out fear: because fear hath torment. He
that feareth is not made perfect in love.
19 [a]We love him, because he first loved us.

Obedience by Faith

20 [a]If a man say, I love God, and hateth his
brother, he is a liar: for he that loveth not his
brother whom he hath seen, how can he love God
[b]whom he hath not seen?
21 And [a]this commandment have we from
him, That he who loveth God love his brother also.

5 Whosoever believeth that [a]Jesus is the Christ
is [b]born of God: and every one that loveth

24 [a]John 14:23 [b]John 14:21; 17:21 [c]John 14:17; Rom. 8:9, 14, 16; 1 Thess. 4:8; 1 John 4:13

CHAPTER 4

1 [a]1 Cor. 14:29 [b]Matt. 24:5
2 [a][Rom. 10:8–10]; 1 Cor. 12:3; 1 John 5:1
4 [a]John 14:30; 16:11
5 [a]John 3:31 [b]John 15:19; 17:14
6 [a][1 Cor. 2:12–16]
7 [a]1 John 3:10, 11, 23 [b]1 Thess. 4:9; [1 John 3:14]
9 [a]Rom. 5:8 [b]Is. 9:6, 7; John 3:16
10 [a]Titus 3:5 [b]1 John 2:2
11 [a]Matt. 18:33
12 [a]John 1:18; 1 Tim. 6:16; 1 John 4:20
13 [a]John 14:20
14 [a]John 1:14 [b]John 3:17; 4:42; 1 John 2:2
15 [a][Rom. 10:9]; 1 John 3:23; 4:2; 5:1, 5
16 [a][1 John 3:24] [b][John 14:23]
17 [a][James 2:13]; 1 John 2:28
19 [a]1 John 4:10
20 [a][1 John 2:4] [b]1 Pet. 1:8; 1 John 4:12
21 [a]Lev. 19:18; [Matt. 5:43, 44; 22:37]; John 13:34

CHAPTER 5

1 [a]1 John 2:22; 4:2, 15 [b]John 1:13

*

4:3 NU omits *that* • NU omits *Christ has come in the flesh*
4:19 NU omits *Him*
4:20 NU *he cannot*

NKJV

The Spirit of Truth and the Spirit of Error

24 Now [a]he who keeps His commandments
[b]abides in Him, and He in him. And [c]by this we
know that He abides in us, by the Spirit whom
He has given us.

4 Beloved, do not believe every spirit, but [a]test
the spirits, whether they are of God; because
[b]many false prophets have gone out into the
world.
2 By this you know the Spirit of God: [a]Every
spirit that confesses that Jesus Christ has come
in the flesh is of God,
3 and every spirit that does not confess *that
Jesus *Christ has come in the flesh is not of God.
And this is the *spirit* of the Antichrist, which you
have heard was coming, and is now already in
the world.
4 You are of God, little children, and have
overcome them, because He who is in you is
greater than [a]he who is in the world.
5 [a]They are of the world. Therefore they
speak *as* of the world, and [b]the world hears
them.
6 We are of God. He who knows God hears
us; he who is not of God does not hear us. [a]By
this we know the spirit of truth and the spirit of
error.

Knowing God Through Love
(cf. John 3:16)

7 [a]Beloved, let us love one another, for love
is of God; and everyone who [b]loves is born of
God and knows God.
8 He who does not love does not know God,
for God is love.
9 [a]In this the love of God was manifested
toward us, that God has sent His only begotten
[b]Son into the world, that we might live through
Him.
10 In this is love, [a]not that we loved God,
but that He loved us and sent His Son [b]*to be* the
propitiation for our sins.
11 Beloved, [a]if God so loved us, we also
ought to love one another.

Seeing God Through Love

12 [a]No one has seen God at any time. If we
love one another, God abides in us, and His love
has been perfected in us.
13 [a]By this we know that we abide in Him,
and He in us, because He has given us of His
Spirit.
14 And [a]we have seen and testify that [b]the
Father has sent the Son *as* Savior of the world.
15 [a]Whoever confesses that Jesus is the Son
of God, God abides in him, and he in God.
16 And we have known and believed the love
that God has for us. God is love, and [a]he who
abides in love abides in God, and God [b]in him.

The Consummation of Love

17 Love has been perfected among us in this:
that [a]we may have boldness in the day of judgment; because as He is, so are we in this world.
18 There is no fear in love; but perfect love
casts out fear, because fear involves torment. But
he who fears has not been made perfect in love.
19 [a]We love *Him because He first loved us.

Obedience by Faith

20 [a]If someone says, "I love God," and hates
his brother, he is a liar; for he who does not love
his brother whom he has seen, *how can he love
God [b]whom he has not seen?
21 And [a]this commandment we have from
Him: that he who loves God *must* love his brother
also.

5 Whoever believes that [a]Jesus is the Christ is
[b]born of God, and everyone who loves Him

KJV

him that begat loveth him also that is begotten of him.

2 By this we know that we love the children of God, when we love God, and [a]keep his commandments.

3 [a]For this is the love of God, that we keep his commandments: and [b]his commandments are not grievous.

4 For [a]whatsoever is born of God overcometh the world: and this is the victory that [b]overcometh the world, *even* our faith.

5 Who is he that overcometh the world, but [a]he that believeth that Jesus is the Son of God?

The Certainty of God's Witness

6 This is he that came [a]by water and blood, *even* Jesus Christ; not by water only, but by water and blood. [b]And it is the Spirit that beareth witness, because the Spirit is truth.

7 For there are three that bear record in heaven, the Father, [a]the Word, and the Holy Ghost: [b]and these three are one.

8 And there are three that bear witness in earth, [a]the spirit, and the water, and the blood: and these three agree in one.

9 If we receive [a]the witness of men, the witness of God is greater: [b]for this is the witness of God which he hath testified of his Son.

10 He that believeth on the Son of God [a]hath the witness in himself: he that believeth not God [b]hath made him a liar; because he believeth not the record that God gave of his Son.

11 And this is the record, that God hath given to us eternal life, and this life is in his Son.

12 [a]He that hath the Son hath life; *and* he that hath not the Son of God hath not life.

13 These things have I written unto you that believe on the name of the Son of God; that ye may know that ye have eternal life, and that ye may believe on the name of the Son of God.

Confidence and Compassion in Prayer

14 And this is the confidence that we have in him, that, [a]if we ask any thing according to his will, he heareth us:

15 And if we know that he hear us, whatsoever we ask, we know that we have the petitions that we desired of him.

16 If any man see his brother sin a sin *which is* not unto death, he shall ask, and [a]he shall give him life for them that sin not unto death. [b]There is a sin unto death: [c]I do not say that he shall pray for it.

17 [a]All unrighteousness is sin: and there is a sin not unto death.

Knowing the True—Rejecting the False

18 We know that [a]whosoever is born of God sinneth not; but he that is begotten of God [b]keepeth himself, and that wicked one toucheth him not.

19 *And* we know that we are of God, and [a]the whole world lieth in wickedness.

20 And we know that the [a]Son of God is come, and [b]hath given us an understanding, [c]that we may know him that is true, and we are in him that is true, *even* in his Son Jesus Christ. [d]This is the true God, [e]and eternal life.

21 Little children, keep yourselves from idols. Amen.

2 [a]John 15:10; 2 John 6 **3** [a]John 14:15; 2 John 6 [b]Mic. 6:8; Matt. 11:30; 23:4 **4** [a]John 16:33 [b]1 John 2:13; 4:4 **5** [a]1 Cor. 15:57 **6** [a]John 1:31–34; [Eph. 5:26, 27] [b][John 14:17] **7** [a][John 1:1] [b]John 10:30 **8** [a]John 15:26 **9** [a]John 5:34, 37; 8:17, 18 [b][Matt. 3:16, 17]; John 5:32, 37 **10** [a][Rom. 8:16]; Gal. 4:6; Rev. 12:17 [b]John 3:18, 33; 1 John 1:10 **12** [a][John 3:15, 36; 6:47; 17:2, 3] **14** [a][1 John 2:28; 3:21, 22] **16** [a]Job 42:8 [b][Matt. 12:31] [c]Jer. 7:16; 14:11 **17** [a]1 John 3:4 **18** [a][1 Pet. 1:23]; 1 John 3:9 [b]James 1:27 **19** [a]John 12:31; 17:15; Gal. 1:4 **20** [a]1 John 4:2 [b]Luke 24:45 [c]John 17:3; Rev. 3:7 [d]Is. 9:6 [e]1 John 5:11, 12

NKJV

who begot also loves him who is begotten of Him.

2 By this we know that we love the children of God, when we love God and [a]keep His commandments.

3 [a]For this is the love of God, that we keep His commandments. And [b]His commandments are not burdensome.

4 For [a]whatever is born of God overcomes the world. And this is the victory that [b]has overcome the world—*our faith.

5 Who is he who overcomes the world, but [a]he who believes that Jesus is the Son of God?

The Certainty of God's Witness

6 This is He who came [a]by water and blood—Jesus Christ; not only by water, but by water and blood. [b]And it is the Spirit who bears witness, because the Spirit is truth.

7 For there are three that bear witness *in heaven: the Father, [a]the Word, and the Holy Spirit; [b]and these three are one.

8 And there are three that bear witness on earth: [a]the Spirit, the water, and the blood; and these three agree as one.

9 If we receive [a]the witness of men, the witness of God is greater; [b]for this is the witness of *God which He has testified of His Son.

10 He who believes in the Son of God [a]has the witness in himself; he who does not believe God [b]has made Him a liar, because he has not believed the testimony that God has given of His Son.

11 And this is the testimony: that God has given us eternal life, and this life is in His Son.

12 [a]He who has the Son has life; he who does not have the Son of God does not have life.

13 These things I have written to you who believe in the name of the Son of God, that you may know that you have eternal life, *and that you may *continue to* believe in the name of the Son of God.

Confidence and Compassion in Prayer

14 Now this is the confidence that we have in Him, that [a]if we ask anything according to His will, He hears us.

15 And if we know that He hears us, whatever we ask, we know that we have the petitions that we have asked of Him.

16 If anyone sees his brother sinning a sin *which does* not *lead* to death, he will ask, and [a]He will give him life for those who commit sin not *leading* to death. [b]There is sin *leading* to death. [c]I do not say that he should pray about that.

17 [a]All unrighteousness is sin, and there is sin not *leading* to death.

Knowing the True—Rejecting the False

18 We know that [a]whoever is born of God does not sin; but he who has been born of God [b]keeps *himself, and the wicked one does not touch him.

19 We know that we are of God, and [a]the whole world lies *under the sway of* the wicked one.

20 And we know that the [a]Son of God has come and [b]has given us an understanding, [c]that we may know Him who is true; and we are in Him who is true, in His Son Jesus Christ. [d]This is the true God [e]and eternal life.

21 Little children, keep yourselves from idols. Amen.

---

*

5:4 M *your* **5:7** NU, M omit the words from *in heaven* (v. 7) through *on earth* (v. 8). Only 4 or 5 very late mss. contain these words in Greek. **5:9** NU *God, that* **5:13** NU omits the rest of v. 13. **5:18** NU *him*

KJV

THE SECOND EPISTLE OF

JOHN

Greeting the Elect Lady

The elder unto the elect lady and her children, whom I love in the truth; and not I only, but also all they that have known [a]the truth;

2 For the truth's sake, which dwelleth in us, and shall be with us for ever.

3 [a]Grace be with you, mercy, *and* peace, from God the Father, and from the Lord Jesus Christ, the Son of the Father, in truth and love.

Walk in Christ's Commandments

4 I [a]rejoiced greatly that I found of thy children walking in truth, as we have received a commandment from the Father.

5 And now I beseech thee, lady, not as though I wrote a new commandment unto thee, but that which we had from the beginning, [a]that we love one another.

6 And [a]this is love, that we walk after his commandments. This is the commandment, That, [b]as ye have heard from the beginning, ye should walk in it.

Beware of Antichrist Deceivers

7 For [a]many deceivers are entered into the world, [b]who confess not that Jesus Christ is come in the flesh. [c]This is a deceiver and an antichrist.

8 [a]Look to yourselves, [b]that we lose not those things which we have wrought, but that we receive a full reward.

9 [a]Whosoever transgresseth, and abideth not in the doctrine of Christ, hath not God. He that abideth in the doctrine of Christ, he hath both the Father and the Son.

10 If there come any unto you, and bring [a]not this doctrine, receive him not into *your* house, neither bid him God speed:

11 For he that biddeth him God speed is partaker of his evil deeds.

John's Farewell Greeting

12 [a]Having many things to write unto you, I would not *write* with paper and ink: but I trust to come unto you, and speak face to face, [b]that our joy may be full.

13 [a]The children of thy elect sister greet thee. Amen.

1 [a]Col. 1:5
3 [a]Rom. 1:7; 1 Tim. 1:2
4 [a]1 Thess. 2:19, 20; 3 John 3, 4
5 [a][John 13:34, 35; 15:12, 17]; 1 John 3:11; 4:7, 11
6 [a]John 14:15; 1 John 2:5; 5:3
[b]1 John 2:24
7 [a]1 John 2:19; 4:1
[b]1 John 4:2
[c]1 John 2:22
8 [a]Mark 13:9
[b]Gal. 3:4
9 [a]John 7:16; 8:31; 1 John 2:19, 23, 24
10 [a]1 Kin. 13:16; Rom. 16:17; 2 Thess. 3:6, 14; Titus 3:10
12 [a]3 John 13, 14 [b]John 17:13
13 [a]1 Pet. 5:13

NKJV

THE SECOND EPISTLE OF

JOHN

Greeting the Elect Lady

The Elder,

To the elect lady and her children, whom I love in truth, and not only I, but also all those who have known [a]the truth,

2 because of the truth which abides in us and will be with us forever:

3 [a]Grace, mercy, *and* peace will be with *you from God the Father and from the Lord Jesus Christ, the Son of the Father, in truth and love.

Walk in Christ's Commandments

4 I [a]rejoiced greatly that I have found *some* of your children walking in truth, as we received commandment from the Father.

5 And now I plead with you, lady, not as though I wrote a new commandment to you, but that which we have had from the beginning: [a]that we love one another.

6 [a]This is love, that we walk according to His commandments. This is the commandment, that [b]as you have heard from the beginning, you should walk in it.

Beware of Antichrist Deceivers

7 For [a]many deceivers have gone out into the world [b]who do not confess Jesus Christ *as* coming in the flesh. [c]This is a deceiver and an antichrist.

8 [a]Look to yourselves, [b]that *we do not lose those things we worked for, but *that* *we may receive a full reward.

9 [a]Whoever *transgresses and does not abide in the doctrine of Christ does not have God. He who abides in the doctrine of Christ has both the Father and the Son.

10 If anyone comes to you and [a]does not bring this doctrine, do not receive him into your house nor greet him;

11 for he who greets him shares in his evil deeds.

John's Farewell Greeting

12 [a]Having many things to write to you, I did not wish *to do so* with paper and ink; but I hope to come to you and speak face to face, [b]that our joy may be full.

13 [a]The children of your elect sister greet you. Amen.

*
3 NU, M *us*
8 NU *you*
• NU *you*
9 NU *goes ahead*

KJV

THE THIRD EPISTLE OF

JOHN

Greeting to Gaius

The elder unto the wellbeloved Gaius, [a]whom I love in the truth.

2 Beloved, I wish above all things that thou mayest prosper and be in health, even as thy soul prospereth.

3 For I [a]rejoiced greatly, when the brethren came and testified of the truth that is in thee, even as thou walkest in the truth.

4 I have no greater [a]joy than to hear that [b]my children walk in truth.

Gaius Commended for Generosity

5 Beloved, thou doest faithfully whatsoever thou doest to the brethren, and to strangers;

6 Which have borne witness of thy charity before the church: whom if thou bring forward on their journey after a godly sort, thou shalt do well:

7 Because that for his name's sake they went forth, [a]taking nothing of the Gentiles.

8 We therefore ought to [a]receive such, that we might be fellowhelpers to the truth.

Diotrephes and Demetrius

9 I wrote unto the church: but Diotrephes, who loveth to have the preeminence among them, receiveth us not.

10 Wherefore, if I come, I will remember his deeds which he doeth, [a]prating against us with malicious words: and not content therewith, neither doth he himself receive the brethren, and forbiddeth them that would, and casteth *them* out of the church.

11 Beloved, [a]follow not that which is evil, but that which is good. [b]He that doeth good is of God: but he that doeth evil hath not seen [c]God.

12 Demetrius [a]hath good report of all *men*, and of the truth itself: yea, and we *also* bear record; [b]and ye know that our record is true.

Farewell Greeting

13 [a]I had many things to write, but I will not with ink and pen write unto thee:

14 But I trust I shall shortly see thee, and we shall speak face to face. Peace *be* to thee. *Our* friends salute thee. Greet the friends by name.

1 [a]2 John 1
3 [a]2 John 4
4 [a]1 Thess. 2:19, 20; 2 John 4 [b][1 Cor. 4:15]
7 [a]1 Cor. 9:12, 15
8 [a]Matt. 10:40; Rom. 12:13; Heb. 13:2; 1 Pet. 4:9
10 [a]Prov. 10:8, 10
11 [a]Ps. 34:14; 37:27; Rom. 14:19; 1 Thess. 5:15; 1 Tim. 6:11; 2 Tim. 2:22 [b][1 John 2:29; 3:10] [c][1 John 3:10]
12 [a]Acts 6:3; 1 Tim. 3:7 [b]John 19:35; 21:24
13 [a]2 John 12

NKJV

THE THIRD EPISTLE OF

JOHN

Greeting to Gaius

The Elder,

To the beloved Gaius, [a]whom I love in truth:

2 Beloved, I pray that you may prosper in all things and be in health, just as your soul prospers.

3 For I [a]rejoiced greatly when brethren came and testified of the truth *that is* in you, just as you walk in the truth.

4 I have no greater [a]joy than to hear that [b]my children walk in *truth.

Gaius Commended for Generosity

5 Beloved, you do faithfully whatever you do for the brethren *and for strangers,

6 who have borne witness of your love before the church. *If* you send them forward on their journey in a manner worthy of God, you will do well,

7 because they went forth for His name's sake, [a]taking nothing from the Gentiles.

8 We therefore ought to [a]receive* such, that we may become fellow workers for the truth.

Diotrephes and Demetrius

9 I wrote to the church, but Diotrephes, who loves to have the preeminence among them, does not receive us.

10 Therefore, if I come, I will call to mind his deeds which he does, [a]prating against us with malicious words. And not content with that, he himself does not receive the brethren, and forbids those who wish to, putting *them* out of the church.

11 Beloved, [a]do not imitate what is evil, but what is good. [b]He who does good is of God, *but he who does evil has not seen [c]God.

12 Demetrius [a]has a *good* testimony from all, and from the truth itself. And we also bear witness, [b]and you know that our testimony is true.

Farewell Greeting

13 [a]I had many things to write, but I do not wish to write to you with pen and ink;

14 but I hope to see you shortly, and we shall speak face to face. Peace to you. Our friends greet you. Greet the friends by name.

---

4 NU *the truth*
5 NU *and especially for*
8 NU *support*
11 NU, M omit *but*

KJV

THE EPISTLE OF

JUDE

Greeting to the Called

Jude, the servant of Jesus Christ, and [a]brother of James, to them that are sanctified by God the Father, and [c]preserved in Jesus Christ, *and* [b]called:

2 Mercy unto you, and [a]peace, and love, be multiplied.

Contend for the Faith

3 Beloved, when I gave all diligence to write unto you [a]of the common salvation, it was needful for me to write unto you, and exhort *you* that [b]ye should earnestly contend for the faith which was once delivered unto the saints.

4 For there are certain men crept in unawares, who were before of old ordained to this condemnation, ungodly men, turning the grace of our God into lasciviousness, and denying the only Lord God, and our Lord Jesus Christ.

Old and New Apostates

5 I will therefore put you in remembrance, though ye once knew this, how that [a]the Lord, having saved the people out of the land of Egypt, afterward destroyed them that believed not.

6 And the angels which kept not their first estate, but left their own habitation, he hath reserved in everlasting chains under darkness unto the judgment of the great day.

7 Even as [a]Sodom and Gomorrha, and the cities about them in like manner, giving themselves over to fornication, and going after strange flesh, are set forth for an example, suffering the vengeance of eternal fire.

8 [a]Likewise also these *filthy* dreamers defile the flesh, despise dominion, and [b]speak evil of dignities.

9 Yet Michael the archangel, when contending with the devil he disputed about the body of Moses, durst not bring against him a railing accusation, but said, [a]The Lord rebuke thee.

10 [a]But these speak evil of those things which they know not: but what they know naturally, as brute beasts, in those things they corrupt themselves.

11 Woe unto them! for they have gone in the way [a]of Cain, and [b]ran greedily after the error of Balaam for reward, and perished [c]in the gainsaying of Core.

Apostates Depraved and Doomed

12 These are spots in your feasts of charity, when they feast with you, feeding themselves without fear: clouds *they are* without water, carried about of winds; trees whose fruit withereth, without fruit, twice dead, plucked up by the roots;

13 [a]Raging waves of the sea, [b]foaming out their own shame; wandering stars, [c]to whom is reserved the blackness of darkness for ever.

14 And Enoch also, the seventh from Adam, prophesied of these, saying, Behold, the Lord cometh with ten thousands of his saints,

1 [a]Acts 1:13 [b]Rom. 1:7 [c]John 17:1
2 [a]1 Pet. 1:2; 2 Pet. 1:2
3 [a]Titus 1:4 [b]Phil. 1:27
5 [a]Ex. 12:51; 1 Cor. 10:5–10; Heb. 3:16
7 [a]Gen. 19:24; 2 Pet. 2:6
8 [a]2 Pet. 2:10 [b]Ex. 22:28
9 [a]Zech. 3:2
10 [a]2 Pet. 2:12
11 [a]Gen. 4:3–8; Heb. 11:4; 1 John 3:12 [b]Num. 31:16; 2 Pet. 2:15; Rev. 2:14 [c]Num. 16:1–3, 31–35
13 [a]Is. 57:20 [b][Phil. 3:19] [c]2 Pet. 2:17; Jude 6

*
1 NU *beloved*
4 NU omits *God*
12 NU, M *along*

NKJV

THE EPISTLE OF

JUDE

Greeting to the Called

Jude, a bondservant of Jesus Christ, and [a]brother of James,

To those who are [b]called, *sanctified by God the Father, and [c]preserved in Jesus Christ:

2 Mercy, [a]peace, and love be multiplied to you.

Contend for the Faith

3 Beloved, while I was very diligent to write to you [a]concerning our common salvation, I found it necessary to write to you exhorting [b]you to contend earnestly for the faith which was once for all delivered to the saints.

4 For certain men have crept in unnoticed, who long ago were marked out for this condemnation, ungodly men, who turn the grace of our God into lewdness and deny the only Lord *God and our Lord Jesus Christ.

Old and New Apostates

5 But I want to remind you, though you once knew this, that [a]the Lord, having saved the people out of the land of Egypt, afterward destroyed those who did not believe.

6 And the angels who did not keep their proper domain, but left their own abode, He has reserved in everlasting chains under darkness for the judgment of the great day;

7 as [a]Sodom and Gomorrah, and the cities around them in a similar manner to these, having given themselves over to sexual immorality and gone after strange flesh, are set forth as an example, suffering the vengeance of eternal fire.

8 [a]Likewise also these dreamers defile the flesh, reject authority, and [b]speak evil of dignitaries.

9 Yet Michael the archangel, in contending with the devil, when he disputed about the body of Moses, dared not bring against him a reviling accusation, but said, [a]"The Lord rebuke you!"

10 [a]But these speak evil of whatever they do not know; and whatever they know naturally, like brute beasts, in these things they corrupt themselves.

11 Woe to them! For they have gone in the way [a]of Cain, [b]have run greedily in the error of Balaam for profit, and perished [c]in the rebellion of Korah.

Apostates Depraved and Doomed

12 These are spots in your love feasts, while they feast with you without fear, serving *only* themselves. *They are* clouds without water, carried *about by the winds; late autumn trees without fruit, twice dead, pulled up by the roots;

13 [a]raging waves of the sea, [b]foaming up their own shame; wandering stars [c]for whom is reserved the blackness of darkness forever.

14 Now Enoch, the seventh from Adam, prophesied about these men also, saying, "Behold, the Lord comes with ten thousands of His saints,

KJV

15 To execute judgment upon all, and to convince all that are ungodly among them of all their ungodly deeds which they have ungodly committed, and of all their [a]hard *speeches* which ungodly sinners have spoken against him.

Apostates Predicted

16 These are murmurers, complainers, walking after their own lusts; and their [a]mouth speaketh great swelling *words,* [b]having men's persons in admiration because of advantage.
17 [a]But, beloved, remember ye the words which were spoken before of the apostles of our Lord Jesus Christ;
18 How that they told you [a]there should be mockers in the last time, who should walk after their own ungodly lusts.
19 These be they who separate themselves, sensual, having not the Spirit.

Maintain Your Life with God

20 But ye, beloved, [a]building up yourselves on your most holy faith, [b]praying in the Holy Ghost,
21 Keep yourselves in the love of God, [a]looking for the mercy of our Lord Jesus Christ unto eternal life.
22 And of some have compassion, making a difference:
23 And others [a]save with fear, [b]pulling *them* out of the fire; hating even [c]the garment spotted by the flesh.

Glory to God

24 [a]Now unto him that is able to keep you from falling, and [b]to present *you* faultless before the presence of his glory with exceeding joy,
25 To the only wise God our Saviour, *be* glory and majesty, dominion and power, both now and ever. Amen.

15 [a]1 Sam. 2:3
16 [a]2 Pet. 2:18 [b]Prov. 28:21
17 [a]2 Pet. 3:2
18 [a]Acts 20:29; [1 Tim. 4:1]; 2 Tim. 3:1; 4:3; 2 Pet. 3:3
20 [a]Col. 2:7; 1 Thess. 5:11 [b][Rom. 8:26]
21 [a]Titus 2:13; Heb. 9:28; 2 Pet. 3:12
23 [a]Rom. 11:14 [b]Amos 4:11; Zech. 3:2; 1 Cor. 3:15 [c][Zech. 3:4, 5]; Rev. 3:4
24 [a][Eph. 3:20] [b]Col. 1:22

*________

22 NU *who are doubting* (or *making distinctions*)
23 NU omits *with fear* • NU adds *and on some have mercy with fear*
24 M *them*
25 NU *the only God our* • NU *Through Jesus Christ our Lord, Be glory* • NU adds *Before all time,*

NKJV

15 "to execute judgment on all, to convict all who are ungodly among them of all their ungodly deeds which they have committed in an ungodly way, and of all the [a]harsh things which ungodly sinners have spoken against Him."

Apostates Predicted

16 These are grumblers, complainers, walking according to their own lusts; and they [a]mouth great swelling *words,* [b]flattering people to gain advantage.
17 [a]But you, beloved, remember the words which were spoken before by the apostles of our Lord Jesus Christ:
18 how they told you that [a]there would be mockers in the last time who would walk according to their own ungodly lusts.
19 These are sensual persons, who cause divisions, not having the Spirit.

Maintain Your Life with God

20 But you, beloved, [a]building yourselves up on your most holy faith, [b]praying in the Holy Spirit,
21 keep yourselves in the love of God, [a]looking for the mercy of our Lord Jesus Christ unto eternal life.
22 And on some have compassion, *making a distinction;
23 but [a]others save *with fear, [b]pulling *them* out of the *fire, hating even [c]the garment defiled by the flesh.

Glory to God

24 [a]Now to Him who is able to keep *you from stumbling,
And [b]to present *you* faultless
Before the presence of His glory with exceeding joy,
25 To *God our Savior,
*Who alone is wise,
Be glory and majesty,
Dominion and *power,
Both now and forever.
Amen.

KJV

THE REVELATION

OF JESUS CHRIST

Introduction and Benediction

1 The Revelation of Jesus Christ, [a]which God
gave unto him, to shew unto his servants
things which must shortly come to pass; and [b]he
sent and signified *it* by his angel unto his servant
John:
2 [a]Who bare record of the word of God, and
of the testimony of Jesus Christ, and of all things
[b]that he saw.
3 [a]Blessed *is* he that readeth, and they that
hear the words of this prophecy, and keep those
things which are written therein: for [b]the time *is*
at hand.

Greeting the Seven Churches

4 John to the seven churches which are in
Asia: Grace *be* unto you, and peace, from him
[a]which is, and [b]which was, and which is to come;
[c]and from the seven Spirits which are before his
throne;
5 And from Jesus Christ, [a]*who is* the faithful
[b]witness, *and* the [c]first begotten of the dead, and
[d]the prince of the kings of the earth. Unto him
[e]that loved us, [f]and washed us from our sins in
his own blood,
6 And hath [a]made us kings and priests unto
God and his Father; [b]to him *be* glory and dominion for ever and ever. Amen.
7 Behold, he cometh with [a]clouds; and
every eye shall see him, and [b]they *also* which
pierced him: and all kindreds of the earth shall
wail because of him. Even so, Amen.
8 [a]I am Alpha and Omega, the beginning
and the ending, saith the Lord, [b]which is, and
which was, and which is to come, the [c]Almighty.

Vision of the Son of Man

9 I John, who also am your brother, and
[a]companion in tribulation, and [b]in the kingdom
and patience of Jesus Christ, was in the isle that
is called Patmos, for the word of God, and for
the testimony of Jesus Christ.
10 [a]I was in the Spirit on [b]the Lord's day,
and heard behind me [c]a great voice, as of a
trumpet,
11 Saying, I am Alpha and Omega, the first
and the last: and, What thou seest, write in a book,
and send *it* unto the seven churches which are
in Asia; unto Ephesus, and unto Smyrna, and unto
Pergamos, and unto Thyatira, and unto Sardis,
and unto Philadelphia, and unto Laodicea.
12 And I turned to see the voice that spake
with me. And being turned, [a]I saw seven golden
candlesticks;
13 [a]And in the midst of the seven candlesticks [b]*one* like unto the Son of man, [c]clothed with
a garment down to the foot, and [d]girt about the
paps with a golden girdle.
14 His head and [a]*his* hairs *were* white like
wool, as white as snow; and [b]his eyes *were* as a
flame of fire;

CHAPTER 1

1 [a]John 3:32 [b]Rev. 22:6
2 [a]1 Cor. 1:6 [b]1 John 1:1
3 [a]Luke 11:28 [b]James 5:8
4 [a]Ex. 3:14 [b]John 1:1 [c][Is. 11:2]
5 [a]John 8:14 [b]Is. 55:4 [c][Col. 1:18] [d]Rev. 17:14 [e]John 13:34 [f]Heb. 9:14
6 [a]1 Pet. 2:5, 9 [b]1 Tim. 6:16
7 [a]Matt. 24:30 [b]Zech. 12:10–14
8 [a]Is. 41:4 [b]Rev. 4:8; 11:17 [c]Is. 9:6
9 [a]Phil. 1:7 [b][2 Tim. 2:12]
10 [a]Acts 10:10 [b]Acts 20:7 [c]Rev. 4:1
12 [a]Ex. 25:37
13 [a]Rev. 2:1 [b]Ezek. 1:26 [c]Dan. 10:5 [d]Rev. 15:6
14 [a]Dan. 7:9 [b]Dan. 10:6

*________

1:5 NU *loves us and freed;* M *loves us and washed*
1:6 NU, M *a kingdom*
1:8 NU, M omit *the Beginning and the End* • NU, M *Lord God*
1:9 NU, M omit *both*
1:11 NU, M omit *"I am the Alpha and the Omega, the First and the Last," and,* • NU, M omit *which are in Asia*

NKJV

THE REVELATION

OF JESUS CHRIST

Introduction and Benediction

1 The Revelation of Jesus Christ, [a]which God
gave Him to show His servants—things which
must shortly take place. And [b]He sent and signified *it* by His angel to His servant John,
2 [a]who bore witness to the word of God,
and to the testimony of Jesus Christ, to all things
[b]that he saw.
3 [a]Blessed *is* he who reads and those who
hear the words of this prophecy, and keep those
things which are written in it; for [b]the time *is* near.

Greeting the Seven Churches

4 John, to the seven churches which are in
Asia:

Grace to you and peace from Him [a]who
is and [b]who was and who is to come, [c]and from
the seven Spirits who are before His throne,
5 and from Jesus Christ, [a]the faithful [b]wit-
ness, the [c]firstborn from the dead, and [d]the ruler
over the kings of the earth. To Him [e]who *loved
us [f]and washed us from our sins in His own blood,
6 and has [a]made us *kings and priests to
His God and Father, [b]to Him *be* glory and dominion forever and ever. Amen.
7 Behold, He is coming with [a]clouds, and
every eye will see Him, even [b]they who pierced
Him. And all the tribes of the earth will mourn
because of Him. Even so, Amen.
8 [a]"I am the Alpha and the Omega, **the* Beginning and *the* End," says the *Lord, [b]"who is
and who was and who is to come, the [c]Almighty."

Vision of the Son of Man

9 I, John, *both your brother and [a]compan-
ion in the tribulation and [b]kingdom and patience
of Jesus Christ, was on the island that is called
Patmos for the word of God and for the testimony
of Jesus Christ.
10 [a]I was in the Spirit on [b]the Lord's Day,
and I heard behind me [c]a loud voice, as of a
trumpet,
11 saying, *"I am the Alpha and the Omega,
the First and the Last," and, "What you see, write
in a book and send *it* to the seven churches *which
are in Asia: to Ephesus, to Smyrna, to Pergamos,
to Thyatira, to Sardis, to Philadelphia, and to
Laodicea."
12 Then I turned to see the voice that spoke
with me. And having turned [a]I saw seven golden
lampstands,
13 [a]and in the midst of the seven lampstands
[b]*One* like the Son of Man, [c]clothed with a garment
down to the feet and [d]girded about the chest with
a golden band.
14 His head and [a]hair *were* white like wool,
as white as snow, and [b]His eyes like a flame of
fire;

KJV

15 [a]And his feet like unto fine brass, as if
they burned in a furnace; and [b]his voice as the
sound of many waters.
16 [a]And he had in his right hand seven stars:
and [b]out of his mouth went a sharp twoedged
sword: [c]and his countenance *was* as the sun shineth in his strength.
17 And [a]when I saw him, I fell at his feet as
dead. And [b]he laid his right hand upon me, saying
unto me, Fear not; [c]I am the first and the last:
18 [a]*I am* he that liveth, and was dead; and,
behold, [b]I am alive for evermore, Amen; and
[c]have the keys of hell and of death.
19 Write the things which thou hast [a]seen,
[b]and the things which are, [c]and the things which
shall be hereafter;
20 The mystery of the seven stars which thou
sawest in my right hand, and the seven golden
candlesticks. The seven stars are [a]the angels of
the seven churches: and [b]the seven candlesticks
which thou sawest are the seven churches.

The Loveless Church

2 Unto the angel of the church of Ephesus write;
These things saith [a]he that holdeth the seven
stars in his right hand, [b]who walketh in the midst
of the seven golden candlesticks;
2 [a]I know thy works, and thy labour, and
thy patience, and how thou canst not bear them
which are evil: and [b]thou hast tried them [c]which
say they are apostles, and are not, and hast found
them liars:
3 And hast borne, and hast patience, and
for my name's sake hast laboured, and hast [a]not
fainted.
4 Nevertheless I have *somewhat* against
thee, because thou hast left thy first love.
5 Remember therefore from whence thou
art fallen, and repent, and do the first works; [a]or
else I will come unto thee quickly, and will remove
thy candlestick out of his place, except thou
repent.
6 But this thou hast, that thou hatest the
deeds of the Nicolaitanes, which I also hate.
7 [a]He that hath an ear, let him hear what
the Spirit saith unto the churches; To him that
overcometh will I give [b]to eat of [c]the tree of life,
which is in the midst of the paradise of God.

The Persecuted Church

8 And unto the angel of the church in
Smyrna write; These things saith [a]the first and
the last, which was dead, and is alive;
9 I know thy works, and tribulation, and
poverty, (but thou art [a]rich) and *I know* the blasphemy of [b]them which say they are Jews, and
are not, [c]but *are* the synagogue of Satan.
10 [a]Fear none of those things which thou
shalt suffer: behold, the devil shall cast *some* of
you into prison, that ye may be tried; and ye shall
have tribulation ten days: [b]be thou faithful unto
death, and I will give thee [c]a crown of life.
11 [a]He that hath an ear, let him hear what
the Spirit saith unto the churches; He that overcometh shall not be hurt of [b]the second death.

The Compromising Church

12 And to the angel of the church in Pergamos write; These things saith [a]he which hath the
sharp sword with two edges;
13 I know thy works, and where thou dwellest, *even* where Satan's seat *is*: and thou holdest
fast my name, and hast not denied my faith, even
in those days wherein Antipas *was* my faithful
martyr, who was slain among you, where Satan
dwelleth.
14 But I have a few things against thee, because thou hast there them that hold the doctrine
of [a]Balaam, who taught Balac to cast a stumbling-

15 [a]Ezek. 1:7 [b]Ezek. 1:24; 43:2
16 [a]Rev. 1:20; 2:1; 3:1 [b]Is. 49:2 [c]Matt. 17:2
17 [a]Ezek. 1:28 [b]Dan. 8:18; 10:10, 12 [c]Is. 41:4; 44:6; 48:12
18 [a]Rom. 6:9 [b]Rev. 4:9 [c]Ps. 68:20
19 [a]Rev. 1:9–18 [b]Rev. 2:1 [c]Rev. 4:1
20 [a]Rev. 2:1 [b]Zech. 4:2

CHAPTER 2
1 [a]Rev. 1:16 [b]Rev. 1:13
2 [a]Ps. 1:6 [b]1 John 4:1 [c]2 Cor. 11:13
3 [a]Gal. 6:9
5 [a]Matt. 21:41
7 [a]Matt. 11:15 [b][Rev. 22:2, 14] [c][Gen. 2:9; 3:22]
8 [a]Rev. 1:8, 17, 18
9 [a]Luke 12:21 [b]Rom. 2:17 [c]Rev. 3:9
10 [a]Matt. 10:22 [b]Matt. 24:13 [c]James 1:12
11 [a]Rev. 13:9 [b][Rev. 20:6, 14; 21:8]
12 [a]Rev. 1:16; 2:16
14 [a]Num. 31:16

NKJV

15 [a]His feet *were* like fine brass, as if refined
in a furnace, and [b]His voice as the sound of many
waters;
16 [a]He had in His right hand seven stars, [b]out
of His mouth went a sharp two-edged sword, [c]and
His countenance *was* like the sun shining in its
strength.
17 And [a]when I saw Him, I fell at His feet
as dead. But [b]He laid His right hand on me, saying
*to me, "Do not be afraid; [c]I am the First and
the Last.
18 [a]"I *am* He who lives, and was dead, and
behold, [b]I am alive forevermore. Amen. And [c]I
have the keys of Hades and of Death.
19 *"Write the things which you have [a]seen,
[b]and the things which are, [c]and the things which
will take place after this.
20 "The mystery of the seven stars which you
saw in My right hand, and the seven golden lampstands: The seven stars are [a]the angels of the
seven churches, and [b]the seven lampstands
*which you saw are the seven churches.

The Loveless Church

2 "To the angel of the church of Ephesus write,
'These things says [a]He who holds the seven
stars in His right hand, [b]who walks in the midst
of the seven golden lampstands:
2 [a]"I know your works, your labor, your patience, and that you cannot bear those who are
evil. And [b]you have tested those [c]who say they
are apostles and are not, and have found them
liars;
3 "and you have persevered and have patience, and have labored for My name's sake and
have [a]not become weary.
4 "Nevertheless I have *this* against you, that
you have left your first love.
5 "Remember therefore from where you
have fallen; repent and do the first works, [a]or else
I will come to you quickly and remove your lampstand from its place—unless you repent.
6 "But this you have, that you hate the deeds
of the Nicolaitans, which I also hate.
7 [a]"He who has an ear, let him hear what
the Spirit says to the churches. To him who overcomes I will give [b]to eat from [c]the tree of
life, which is in the midst of the Paradise of
God." '

The Persecuted Church

8 "And to the angel of the church in Smyrna
write,
'These things says [a]the First and the Last,
who was dead, and came to life:
9 "I know your works, tribulation, and poverty (but you are [a]rich); and *I know* the blasphemy
of [b]those who say they are Jews and are not, [c]but
are a synagogue of Satan.
10 [a]"Do not fear any of those things which
you are about to suffer. Indeed, the devil is about
to throw *some* of you into prison, that you may
be tested, and you will have tribulation ten days.
[b]Be faithful until death, and I will give you [c]the
crown of life.
11 [a]"He who has an ear, let him hear what
the Spirit says to the churches. He who overcomes
shall not be hurt by [b]the second death." '

The Compromising Church

12 "And to the angel of the church in Pergamos write,
'These things says [a]He who has the sharp
two-edged sword:
13 "I know your works, and where you dwell,
where Satan's throne *is*. And you hold fast to My
name, and did not deny My faith even in the days
in which Antipas *was* My faithful martyr, who
was killed among you, where Satan dwells.
14 "But I have a few things against you, because you have there those who hold the doctrine
of [a]Balaam, who taught Balak to put a stumbling

1:17 NU, M omit *to me*
1:19 NU, M *Therefore, write*
1:20 NU, M omit *which you saw*

KJV

block before the children of Israel, [b]to eat things
sacrificed unto idols, [c]and to commit fornication.
15 So hast thou also them that hold the doctrine of the Nicolaitanes, which thing I hate.
16 Repent; or else I will come unto thee
quickly, and [a]will fight against them with the
sword of my mouth.
17 He that hath an ear, let him hear what
the Spirit saith unto the churches; To him that
overcometh will I give to eat of the hidden
[a]manna, and will give him a white stone, and
in the stone [b]a new name written, which no man
knoweth saving he that receiveth *it*.

The Corrupt Church

18 And unto the angel of the church in Thyatira write; These things saith the Son of God, [a]who
hath his eyes like unto a flame of fire, and his
feet *are* like fine brass;
19 [a]I know thy works, and charity, and service, and faith, and thy patience, and thy works;
and the last *to be* more than the first.
20 Notwithstanding I have a few things
against thee, because thou sufferest that woman
[a]Jezebel, which calleth herself a prophetess, to
teach and to seduce my servants [b]to commit fornication, and to eat things sacrificed unto idols.
21 And I gave her space [a]to repent of her
fornication; and she repented not.
22 Behold, I will cast her into a bed, and them
that commit adultery with her into great tribulation, except they repent of their deeds.
23 And I will kill her children with death; and
all the churches shall know that I am he which
[a]searcheth the reins and hearts: and I will give
unto every one of you according to your works.
24 But unto you I say, and unto the rest in
Thyatira, as many as have not this doctrine, and
which have not known the [a]depths of Satan, as
they speak; [b]I will put upon you none other
burden.
25 But [a]that which ye have *already* hold fast
till I come.
26 And he that overcometh, and keepeth [a]my
works unto the end, [b]to him will I give power over
the nations:
27 [a]And HE SHALL RULE THEM WITH A ROD OF
IRON; AS THE VESSELS OF A POTTER SHALL THEY BE
BROKEN TO SHIVERS: even as I received of my
Father.
28 And I will give him [a]the morning star.
29 He that hath an ear, let him hear what
the Spirit saith unto the churches.

The Dead Church

3 And unto the angel of the church in Sardis
write; These things saith he that [a]hath the
seven Spirits of God, and the seven stars; I know
thy works, that thou hast a name that thou livest,
and art dead.
2 Be watchful, and strengthen the things
which remain, that are ready to die: for I have
not found thy works perfect before God.
3 [a]Remember therefore how thou hast received and heard, and hold fast, and [b]repent. [c]If
therefore thou shalt not watch, I will come on thee
[d]as a thief, and thou shalt not know what hour I
will come upon thee.
4 Thou hast [a]a few names even in Sardis
which have not [b]defiled their garments; and they
shall walk with me [c]in white: for they are worthy.
5 He that overcometh, [a]the same shall be
clothed in white raiment; and I will not [b]blot out
his name out of the [c]book of life, but [d]I will confess his name before my Father, and before his
angels.
6 [a]He that hath an ear, let him hear what
the Spirit saith unto the churches.

NKJV

block before the children of Israel, [b]to eat things
sacrificed to idols, [c]and to commit sexual
immorality.
15 "Thus you also have those who hold the
doctrine of the Nicolaitans, *which thing I hate.
16 "Repent, or else I will come to you quickly
and [a]will fight against them with the sword of
My mouth.
17 "He who has an ear, let him hear what
the Spirit says to the churches. To him who overcomes I will give some of the hidden [a]manna to
eat. And I will give him a white stone, and on
the stone [b]a new name written which no one
knows except him who receives *it*." '

The Corrupt Church

18 "And to the angel of the church in Thyatira write,
'These things says the Son of God, [a]who
has eyes like a flame of fire, and His feet like
fine brass:
19 [a]"I know your works, love, *service, faith,
and your patience; and *as* for your works, the last
are more than the first.
20 "Nevertheless I have *a few things against
you, because you allow *that woman [a]Jezebel,
who calls herself a prophetess, *to teach and seduce My servants [b]to commit sexual immorality
and eat things sacrificed to idols.
21 "And I gave her time [a]to *repent of her
sexual immorality, and she did not repent.
22 "Indeed I will cast her into a sickbed, and
those who commit adultery with her into great
tribulation, unless they repent of *their deeds.
23 "I will kill her children with death, and
all the churches shall know that I am He who
[a]searches the minds and hearts. And I will give
to each one of you according to your works.
24 "Now to you I say, *and to the rest in
Thyatira, as many as do not have this doctrine,
who have not known the [a]depths of Satan, as they
say, [b]I *will put on you no other burden.
25 "But hold fast [a]what you have till I come.
26 "And he who overcomes, and keeps [a]My
works until the end, [b]to him I will give power
over the nations—

27 *'He[a] shall rule them with a rod of iron;*
They shall be dashed to pieces like the
potter's vessels'—

as I also have received from My Father;
28 "and I will give him [a]the morning star.
29 "He who has an ear, let him hear what
the Spirit says to the churches." '

The Dead Church

3 "And to the angel of the church in Sardis
write,
'These things says He who [a]has the seven
Spirits of God and the seven stars: "I know your
works, that you have a name that you are alive,
but you are dead.
2 "Be watchful, and strengthen the things
which remain, that are ready to die, for I have
not found your works perfect before *God.
3 [a]"Remember therefore how you have received and heard; hold fast and [b]repent. [c]There-
fore if you will not watch, I will come upon you
[d]as a thief, and you will not know what hour I
will come upon you.
4 *"You have [a]a few names *even in Sardis
who have not [b]defiled their garments; and
they shall walk with Me [c]in white, for they are
worthy.
5 "He who overcomes [a]shall be clothed
in white garments, and I will not [b]blot out his
name from the [c]Book of Life; but [d]I will confess
his name before My Father and before His
angels.
6 [a]"He who has an ear, let him hear what
the Spirit says to the churches." '

---

14 [b]Acts 15:29 [c]1 Cor. 6:13
16 [a]2 Thess. 2:8
17 [a]Ex. 16:33, 34 [b]Rev. 3:12
18 [a]Rev. 1:14, 15
19 [a]Rev. 2:2
20 [a]1 Kin. 16:31; 21:25 [b]Ex. 34:15
21 [a]Rev. 9:20; 16:9, 11
23 [a]Jer. 11:20; 17:10
24 [a]2 Tim. 3:1–9 [b]Acts 15:28
25 [a]Rev. 3:11
26 [a][John 6:29] [b][Matt. 19:28]
27 [a]Ps. 2:8, 9
28 [a]2 Pet. 1:19

CHAPTER 3

1 [a]Rev. 1:4, 16
3 [a]1 Tim. 6:20 [b]Rev. 3:19 [c]Matt. 24:42, 43 [d][Rev. 16:15]
4 [a]Acts 1:15 [b][Jude 23] [c]Rev. 4:4; 6:11
5 [a][Rev. 19:8] [b]Ex. 32:32 [c]Phil. 4:3 [d]Luke 12:8
6 [a]Rev. 2:7

*

2:15 NU, M *likewise.*
2:19 NU, M *faith, service*
2:20 NU, M *against you that you tolerate* • M *your wife Jezebel* • NU, M *and teaches and seduces*
2:21 NU, M *repent, and she does not want to repent of her sexual immorality.*
2:22 NU, M *her*
2:24 NU, M omit *and* • NU, M omit *will*
3:2 NU, M *My God*
3:4 NU, M *Nevertheless you* • NU, M omit *even*

KJV

The Faithful Church

7 And to the angel of the church in Philadelphia write; These things saith [a]he that is holy, [b]he that is true, [c]HE THAT HATH THE KEY OF DAVID, [d]HE THAT OPENETH, AND NO MAN SHUTTETH; AND [e]SHUTTETH, AND NO MAN OPENETH;

8 [a]I know thy works: behold, I have set before thee [b]an open door, and no man can shut it: for thou hast a little strength, and hast kept my word, and hast not denied my name.

9 Behold, I will make [a]them of the synagogue of Satan, which say they are Jews, and are not, but do lie; behold, [b]I will make them to come and worship before thy feet, and to know that I have loved thee.

10 Because thou hast kept the word of my patience, [a]I also will keep thee from the hour of temptation, which shall come upon [b]all the world, to try them that dwell [c]upon the earth.

11 Behold, [a]I come quickly: [b]hold that fast which thou hast, that no man take [c]thy crown.

12 Him that overcometh will I make [a]a pillar in the temple of my God, and he shall [b]go no more out: and [c]I will write upon him the name of my God, and the name of the city of my God, *which is* [d]new Jerusalem, which [e]cometh down out of heaven from my God: [f]and *I will write upon him* my new name.

13 [a]He that hath an ear, let him hear what the Spirit saith unto the churches.

The Lukewarm Church

14 And unto the angel of the church of the Laodiceans write; [a]These things saith the Amen, [b]the faithful and true witness, [c]the beginning of the creation of God;

15 [a]I know thy works, that thou art neither cold nor hot: I would thou wert cold or hot.

16 So then because thou art lukewarm, and neither cold nor hot, I will spue thee out of my mouth.

17 Because thou sayest, [a]I am rich, and increased with goods, and have need of nothing; and knowest not that thou art wretched, and miserable, and poor, and blind, and naked:

18 I counsel thee [a]to buy of me gold tried in the fire, that thou mayest be rich; and [b]white raiment, that thou mayest be clothed, and *that* the shame of thy nakedness do not appear; and anoint thine eyes with eyesalve, that thou mayest see.

19 [a]As many as I love, I rebuke and [b]chasten: be zealous therefore, and repent.

20 Behold, [a]I stand at the door, and knock: [b]if any man hear my voice, and open the door, [c]I will come in to him, and will sup with him, and he with me.

21 To him that overcometh [a]will I grant to sit with me in my throne, even as I also overcame, and am set down with my Father in his throne.

22 [a]He that hath an ear, let him hear what the Spirit saith unto the churches.

The Throne Room of Heaven
(Is. 6:1–3)

4 After this I looked, and, behold, a door *was* [a]opened in heaven: and the first voice which I heard *was* as it were of a [b]trumpet talking with me; which said, Come up hither, and I will shew thee things which must be hereafter.

2 And immediately [a]I was in the spirit: and, behold, [b]a throne was set in heaven, and *one* sat on the throne.

3 And he that sat was to look upon [a]like a jasper and a sardine stone: [b]and *there was* a rainbow round about the throne, in sight like unto an emerald.

4 [a]And round about the throne *were* four

---

7 [a]Acts 3:14 [b]1 John 5:20 [c]Is. 9:7; 22:22 [d][Matt. 16:19] [e]Job 12:14
8 [a]Rev. 3:1 [b]1 Cor. 16:9
9 [a]Rev. 2:9 [b]Is. 45:14; 49:23; 60:14
10 [a]2 Pet. 2:9 [b]Luke 2:1 [c]Is. 24:17
11 [a]Phil. 4:5 [b]Rev. 2:25 [c][Rev. 2:10]
12 [a]1 Kin. 7:21 [b]Ps. 23:6 [c][Rev. 14:1; 22:4] [d][Heb. 12:22] [e]Rev. 21:2 [f][Rev. 2:17; 22:4]
13 [a]Rev. 2:7
14 [a]2 Cor. 1:20 [b]Rev. 1:5; 3:7; 19:11 [c][Col. 1:15]
15 [a]Rev. 3:1
17 [a]Hos. 12:8
18 [a]Is. 55:1 [b]2 Cor. 5:3
19 [a]Job 5:17 [b]Heb. 12:6
20 [a]Song 5:2 [b]Luke 12:36, 37 [c][John 14:23]
21 [a]Matt. 19:28
22 [a]Rev. 2:7

CHAPTER 4
1 [a]Ezek. 1:1 [b]Rev. 1:10
2 [a]Rev. 1:10 [b]Is. 6:1
3 [a]Rev. 21:11 [b]Ezek. 1:28
4 [a]Rev. 11:16

*———
3:8 NU, M *which no one can shut*
3:11 NU, M omit *Behold*
3:14 NU, M *in Laodicea*
3:16 NU, M *hot nor cold*
4:3 M omits *And He who sat there was*, making the following a description of the throne.

NKJV

The Faithful Church

7 "And to the angel of the church in Philadelphia write,

'These things says [a]He who is holy, [b]He who is true, [c]*"He who has the key of David,* [d]*He who opens and no one shuts, and* [e]*shuts and no one opens"*:

8 [a]"I know your works. See, I have set before you [b]an open door, *and no one can shut it; for you have a little strength, have kept My word, and have not denied My name.

9 "Indeed I will make [a]*those* of the synagogue of Satan, who say they are Jews and are not, but lie—indeed [b]I will make them come and worship before your feet, and to know that I have loved you.

10 "Because you have kept My command to persevere, [a]I also will keep you from the hour of trial which shall come upon [b]the whole world, to test those who dwell [c]on the earth.

11 *"Behold, [a]I am coming quickly! [b]Hold fast what you have, that no one may take [c]your crown.

12 "He who overcomes, I will make him [a]a pillar in the temple of My God, and he shall [b]go out no more. [c]I will write on him the name of My God and the name of the city of My God, the [d]New Jerusalem, which [e]comes down out of heaven from My God. [f]And *I will write on him* My new name.

13 [a]"He who has an ear, let him hear what the Spirit says to the churches." '

The Lukewarm Church

14 "And to the angel of the church *of the Laodiceans write,

[a]'These things says the Amen, [b]the Faithful and True Witness, [c]the Beginning of the creation of God:

15 [a]"I know your works, that you are neither cold nor hot. I could wish you were cold or hot.

16 "So then, because you are lukewarm, and neither *cold nor hot, I will vomit you out of My mouth.

17 "Because you say, [a]'I am rich, have become wealthy, and have need of nothing'—and do not know that you are wretched, miserable, poor, blind, and naked—

18 "I counsel you [a]to buy from Me gold refined in the fire, that you may be rich; and [b]white garments, that you may be clothed, *that* the shame of your nakedness may not be revealed; and anoint your eyes with eye salve, that you may see.

19 [a]"As many as I love, I rebuke and [b]chasten. Therefore be zealous and repent.

20 "Behold, [a]I stand at the door and knock. [b]If anyone hears My voice and opens the door, [c]I will come in to him and dine with him, and he with Me.

21 "To him who overcomes [a]I will grant to sit with Me on My throne, as I also overcame and sat down with My Father on His throne.

22 [a]"He who has an ear, let him hear what the Spirit says to the churches." ' "

The Throne Room of Heaven
(Is. 6:1–3)

4 After these things I looked, and behold, a door *standing* [a]open in heaven. And the first voice which I heard *was* like a [b]trumpet speaking with me, saying, "Come up here, and I will show you things which must take place after this."

2 Immediately [a]I was in the Spirit; and behold, [b]a throne set in heaven, and *One* sat on the throne.

3 *And He who sat there was [a]like a jasper and a sardius stone in appearance; [b]and *there was* a rainbow around the throne, in appearance like an emerald.

4 [a]Around the throne *were* twenty-four

KJV

and twenty seats: and upon the seats I saw four
and twenty elders sitting, [b]clothed in white raiment; and they had on their heads crowns of gold.
5 And out of the throne proceeded [a]light-
nings and thunderings and voices: [b]and *there
were* seven lamps of fire burning before the
throne, which are [c]the seven Spirits of God.
6 And before the throne *there was* [a]a sea
of glass like unto crystal: [b]and in the midst of
the throne, and round about the throne, *were* four
beasts full of eyes before and behind.
7 [a]And the first beast *was* like a lion, and
the second beast like a calf, and the third beast
had a face as a man, and the fourth beast *was*
like a flying eagle.
8 And the four beasts had each of them [a]six
wings about *him;* and *they were* full of eyes
within: and they rest not day and night, saying,
[b]Holy, holy, holy, [c]Lord God Almighty, [d]which
was, and is, and is to come.
9 And when those beasts give glory and
honour and thanks to him that sat on the throne,
[a]who liveth for ever and ever,
10 [a]The four and twenty elders fall down before him that sat on the throne, and worship him
that liveth for ever and ever, and cast their crowns
before the throne, saying,
11 [a]Thou art worthy, O Lord, to receive glory
and honour and power: [b]for thou hast created all
things, and for [c]thy pleasure they are and were
created.

The Lamb Takes the Scroll

5 And I saw in the right hand of him that sat
on the throne [a]a book written within and on
the backside, [b]sealed with seven seals.
2 And I saw a strong angel proclaiming with
a loud voice, [a]Who is worthy to open the book,
and to loose the seals thereof?
3 And no man in heaven, nor in earth, neither under the earth, was able to open the book,
neither to look thereon.
4 And I wept much, because no man was
found worthy to open and to read the book, neither to look thereon.
5 And one of the elders saith unto me, Weep
not: behold, [a]the Lion of the tribe of [b]Juda, [c]the
Root of David, hath [d]prevailed to open the book,
[e]and to loose the seven seals thereof.
6 And I beheld, and, lo, in the midst of the
throne and of the four beasts, and in the midst
of the elders, stood [a]a Lamb as it had been slain,
having seven horns and [b]seven eyes, which are
[c]the seven Spirits of God sent forth into all the
earth.
7 And he came and took the book out of
the right hand [a]of him that sat upon the throne.

Worthy Is the Lamb

8 And when he had taken the book, [a]the
four beasts and four *and* twenty elders fell down
before the Lamb, having every one of them harps,
and golden vials full of odours, which are the
[b]prayers of saints.
9 And [a]they sung a new song, saying, [b]Thou
art worthy to take the book, and to open the seals
thereof: for thou wast slain, and [c]hast redeemed
us to God [d]by thy blood out of every kindred, and
tongue, and people, and nation;
10 And hast made us unto our God [a]kings
and [b]priests: and we shall reign on the earth.

4 [b]Rev. 3:4, 5
5 [a]Rev. 8:5; 11:19; 16:18 [b]Ex. 37:23 [c][Rev. 1:4]
6 [a]Rev. 15:2 [b]Ezek. 1:5
7 [a]Ezek. 1:10; 10:14
8 [a]Is. 6:2 [b]Is. 6:3 [c]Rev. 1:8 [d]Rev. 1:4
9 [a]Rev. 1:18
10 [a]Rev. 5:8, 14; 7:11; 11:16; 19:4
11 [a]Rev. 1:6; 5:12 [b]Gen. 1:1 [c]Col. 1:16

CHAPTER 5

1 [a]Ezek. 2:9, 10 [b]Is. 29:11
2 [a]Rev. 4:11; 5:9
5 [a]Gen. 49:9 [b]Heb. 7:14 [c]Is. 11:1, 10 [d]Rev. 3:21 [e]Rev. 6:1
6 [a][John 1:29] [b]Zech. 3:9; 4:10 [c]Rev. 1:4; 3:1; 4:5
7 [a]Rev. 4:2
8 [a]Rev. 4:8–10; 19:4 [b]Rev. 8:3
9 [a]Rev. 14:3 [b]Rev. 4:11 [c]John 1:29 [d][Heb. 9:12]
10 [a]Ex. 19:6 [b]Is. 61:6

*

4:4 NU, M *robes, with crowns*
4:5 NU, M *voices, and thunderings.* • M omits *the*
4:6 NU, M add *something like*
4:8 M has *holy* nine times.
4:11 NU, M *our Lord and God* • NU, M *existed*
5:4 NU, M omit *and read*
5:5 NU, M omit *to loose*
5:6 NU, M *I saw in the midst . . . a Lamb standing*
5:10 NU, M *them* • NU *a kingdom* • NU, M *they*

NKJV

thrones, and on the thrones I saw twenty-four elders sitting, [b]clothed in white *robes; and they
had crowns of gold on their heads.
5 And from the throne proceeded [a]light-
nings, *thunderings, and voices. [b]Seven lamps of
fire *were* burning before the throne, which are
[c]the* seven Spirits of God.
6 Before the throne *there* **was* [a]a sea of
glass, like crystal. [b]And in the midst of the throne,
and around the throne, *were* four living creatures
full of eyes in front and in back.
7 [a]The first living creature *was* like a lion,
the second living creature like a calf, the third
living creature had a face like a man, and the
fourth living creature *was* like a flying eagle.
8 *The* four living creatures, each having [a]six
wings, were full of eyes around and within. And
they do not rest day or night, saying:

[b]"Holy,* holy, holy,
[c]Lord God Almighty,
[d]Who was and is and is to come!"

9 Whenever the living creatures give glory
and honor and thanks to Him who sits on the
throne, [a]who lives forever and ever,
10 [a]the twenty-four elders fall down before
Him who sits on the throne and worship Him who
lives forever and ever, and cast their crowns before the throne, saying:

11 "You[a] are worthy, *O Lord,
To receive glory and honor and power;
[b]For You created all things,
And by [c]Your will they *exist and were
created."

The Lamb Takes the Scroll

5 And I saw in the right *hand* of Him who sat
on the throne [a]a scroll written inside and on
the back, [b]sealed with seven seals.
2 Then I saw a strong angel proclaiming
with a loud voice, [a]"Who is worthy to open the
scroll and to loose its seals?"
3 And no one in heaven or on the earth or
under the earth was able to open the scroll, or to
look at it.
4 So I wept much, because no one was
found worthy to open *and read the scroll, or to
look at it.
5 But one of the elders said to me, "Do not
weep. Behold, [a]the Lion of the tribe of [b]Judah,
[c]the Root of David, has [d]prevailed to open the
scroll [e]and *to loose its seven seals."
6 And I looked, *and behold, in the midst
of the throne and of the four living creatures, and
in the midst of the elders, stood [a]a Lamb as
though it had been slain, having seven horns and
[b]seven eyes, which are [c]the seven Spirits of God
sent out into all the earth.
7 Then He came and took the scroll out of
the right hand [a]of Him who sat on the throne.

Worthy Is the Lamb

8 Now when He had taken the scroll, [a]the
four living creatures and the twenty-four elders
fell down before the Lamb, each having a harp,
and golden bowls full of incense, which are the
[b]prayers of the saints.
9 And [a]they sang a new song, saying:

[b]"You are worthy to take the scroll,
And to open its seals;
For You were slain,
And [c]have redeemed us to God [d]by Your
blood
Out of every tribe and tongue and people
and nation,
10 And have made *us [a]kings* and [b]priests
to our God;
And *we shall reign on the earth."

KJV

11 And I beheld, and I heard the voice of many angels round about the throne and the beasts and the elders: and the number of them was ten thousand times ten thousand, and thousands of thousands;

12 Saying with a loud voice, Worthy is the Lamb that was slain to receive power, and riches, and wisdom, and strength, and honour, and glory, and blessing.

13 And [a]every creature which is in heaven, and on the earth, and under the earth, and such as are in the sea, and all that are in them, heard I saying, [b]Blessing, and honour, and glory, and power, *be* unto him [c]that sitteth upon the throne, and unto the Lamb for ever and ever.

14 And the four beasts said, Amen. And the four *and* twenty elders fell down and worshipped him that liveth for ever and ever.

First Seal: The Conqueror

6 And [a]I saw when the Lamb opened one of the seals, and I heard, as it were the noise of thunder, [b]one of the four beasts saying, Come and see.

2 And I saw, and behold [a]a white horse: [b]and he that sat on him had a bow; [c]and a crown was given unto him: and he went forth [d]conquering, and to conquer.

Second Seal: Conflict on Earth

3 And when he had opened the second seal, [a]I heard the second beast say, Come and see.

4 [a]And there went out another horse *that was* red: and *power* was given to him that sat thereon to [b]take peace from the earth, and that they should kill one another: and there was given unto him a great sword.

Third Seal: Scarcity on Earth

5 And when he had opened the third seal, [a]I heard the third beast say, Come and see. And I beheld, and lo [b]a black horse; and he that sat on him had a pair of [c]balances in his hand.

6 And I heard a voice in the midst of the four beasts say, A measure of wheat for a penny, and three measures of barley for a penny; and [a]*see* thou hurt not the oil and the wine.

Fourth Seal: Widespread Death on Earth

7 And when he had opened the fourth seal, [a]I heard the voice of the fourth beast say, Come and see.

8 [a]And I looked, and behold a pale horse: and his name that sat on him was Death, and Hell followed with him. And power was given unto them over the fourth part of the earth, [b]to kill with sword, and with hunger, and with death, [c]and with the beasts of the earth.

Fifth Seal: The Cry of the Martyrs

9 And when he had opened the fifth seal, I saw under [a]the altar [b]the souls of them that were slain [c]for the word of God, and for [d]the testimony which they held:

10 And they cried with a loud voice, saying, [a]How long, O Lord, [b]holy and true, [c]dost thou not judge and avenge our blood on them that dwell on the earth?

11 And [a]white robes were given unto every one of them; and it was said unto them, [b]that they should rest yet for a little season, until their fellowservants also and their brethren, that should be killed as they *were*, should be fulfilled.

13 [a]Phil. 2:10; Rev. 5:3 [b]1 Chr. 29:11; Rom. 9:5; 1 Tim. 6:16; 1 Pet. 4:11 [c]Rev. 4:2, 3; 6:16; 20:11

CHAPTER 6

1 [a]Is. 53:7; [John 1:29; Rev. 5:5–7, 12; 13:8] [b]Rev. 4:7 **2** [a]Zech. 1:8; 6:3 [b]Ps. 45:4, 5, LXX [c]Zech. 6:11; Rev. 9:7; 14:14; 19:12 [d]Matt. 24:5; Rev. 3:21 **3** [a]Rev. 4:7 **4** [a]Zech. 1:8; 6:2 [b]Matt. 24:6, 7 **5** [a]Rev. 4:7 [b]Zech. 6:2, 6 [c]Matt. 24:7 **6** [a]Rev. 7:3; 9:4 **7** [a]Rev. 4:7 **8** [a]Zech. 6:3 [b]Jer. 14:12; 15:2; 24:10; 29:17; Ezek. 5:12, 17; 14:21; 29:5; Matt. 24:9 [c]Lev. 26:22 **9** [a]Rev. 8:3 [b][Rev. 20:4] [c]Rev. 1:2, 9 [d]2 Tim. 1:8 **10** [a]Ps. 13:1–6; Zech. 1:12 [b]Rev. 3:7 [c]Rev. 11:18 **11** [a]Rev. 3:4, 5; 7:9 [b]Heb. 11:40

*———

5:13 M adds *Amen*
5:14 NU, M omit *twenty-four* • NU, M omit *Him who lives forever and ever*
6:1 NU, M *seven seals*
6:3 NU, M omit *and see*
6:6 Gr. *choinix,* about 1 quart • About 1 day's wage for a worker

NKJV

11 Then I looked, and I heard the voice of many angels around the throne, the living creatures, and the elders; and the number of them was ten thousand times ten thousand, and thousands of thousands,

12 saying with a loud voice:

"Worthy is the Lamb who was slain
To receive power and riches and wisdom,
And strength and honor and glory and
blessing!"

13 And [a]every creature which is in heaven and on the earth and under the earth and such as are in the sea, and all that are in them, I heard saying:

[b]"Blessing and honor and glory and power
Be to Him [c]who sits on the throne,
And to the Lamb, forever and *ever!"

14 Then the four living creatures said, "Amen!" And the *twenty-four elders fell down and worshiped *Him who lives forever and ever.

First Seal: The Conqueror

6 Now [a]I saw when the Lamb opened one of the *seals; and I heard [b]one of the four living creatures saying with a voice like thunder, "Come and see."

2 And I looked, and behold, [a]a white horse. [b]He who sat on it had a bow; [c]and a crown was given to him, and he went out [d]conquering and to conquer.

Second Seal: Conflict on Earth

3 When He opened the second seal, [a]I heard the second living creature saying, "Come *and see."

4 [a]Another horse, fiery red, went out. And it was granted to the one who sat on it to [b]take peace from the earth, and that *people* should kill one another; and there was given to him a great sword.

Third Seal: Scarcity on Earth

5 When He opened the third seal, [a]I heard the third living creature say, "Come and see." So I looked, and behold, [b]a black horse, and he who sat on it had a pair of [c]scales in his hand.

6 And I heard a voice in the midst of the four living creatures saying, "A *quart of wheat for a *denarius, and three quarts of barley for a denarius; and [a]do not harm the oil and the wine."

Fourth Seal: Widespread Death on Earth

7 When He opened the fourth seal, [a]I heard the voice of the fourth living creature saying, "Come and see."

8 [a]So I looked, and behold, a pale horse. And the name of him who sat on it was Death, and Hades followed with him. And power was given to them over a fourth of the earth, [b]to kill with sword, with hunger, with death, [c]and by the beasts of the earth.

Fifth Seal: The Cry of the Martyrs

9 When He opened the fifth seal, I saw under [a]the altar [b]the souls of those who had been slain [c]for the word of God and for [d]the testimony which they held.

10 And they cried with a loud voice, saying, [a]"How long, O Lord, [b]holy and true, [c]until You judge and avenge our blood on those who dwell on the earth?"

11 Then a [a]white robe was given to each of them; and it was said to them [b]that they should rest a little while longer, until both *the number of* their fellow servants and their brethren, who would be killed as they *were,* was completed.

KJV

Sixth Seal: Cosmic Disturbances

12 And I beheld when he had opened the sixth seal, [a]and, lo, there was a great earthquake; and [b]the sun became black as sackcloth of hair, and the moon became as blood;

13 [a]And the stars of heaven fell unto the earth, even as a fig tree casteth her untimely figs, when she is shaken of a mighty wind.

14 [a]And the heaven departed as a scroll when it is rolled together; and [b]every mountain and island were moved out of their places.

15 And the [a]kings of the earth, and the great men, and the rich men, and the chief captains, and the mighty men, and every bondman, and every free man, [b]hid themselves in the dens and in the rocks of the mountains;

16 [a]And said to the mountains and rocks, Fall on us, and hide us from the face of him that [b]sitteth on the throne, and from the wrath of the Lamb:

17 For the great day of his wrath is come; [a]and who shall be able to stand?

The Sealed of Israel

7 And after these things I saw four angels standing on the four corners of the earth, [a]holding the four winds of the earth, [b]that the wind should not blow on the earth, nor on the sea, nor on any tree.

2 And I saw another angel ascending from the east, having the seal of the living God: and he cried with a loud voice to the four angels, to whom it was given to hurt the earth and the sea,

3 Saying, [a]Hurt not the earth, neither the sea, nor the trees, till we have sealed the servants of our God [b]in their foreheads.

4 [a]And I heard the number of them which were sealed: *and there were* sealed [b]an hundred *and* forty *and* four thousand [c]of all the tribes of the children of Israel.

5 Of the tribe of Juda *were* sealed twelve thousand. Of the tribe of Reuben *were* sealed twelve thousand. Of the tribe of Gad *were* sealed twelve thousand.

6 Of the tribe of Aser *were* sealed twelve thousand. Of the tribe of Nepthalim *were* sealed twelve thousand. Of the tribe of Manasses *were* sealed twelve thousand.

7 Of the tribe of Simeon *were* sealed twelve thousand. Of the tribe of Levi *were* sealed twelve thousand. Of the tribe of Issachar *were* sealed twelve thousand.

8 Of the tribe of Zabulon *were* sealed twelve thousand. Of the tribe of Joseph *were* sealed twelve thousand. Of the tribe of Benjamin *were* sealed twelve thousand.

A Multitude from the Great Tribulation

9 After this I beheld, and, lo, [a]a great multitude, which no man could number, [b]of all nations, and kindreds, and people, and tongues, stood before the throne, and before the Lamb, [c]clothed with white robes, and palms in their hands;

10 And cried with a loud voice, saying, [a]Salvation to our God [b]which sitteth upon the throne, and unto the Lamb.

11 [a]And all the angels stood round about the throne, and *about* the elders and the four beasts, and fell before the throne on their faces, and [b]worshipped God,

12 [a]Saying, Amen: Blessing, and glory, and

12 [a]Matt. 24:7; Rev. 8:5; 11:13; 16:18 [b]Is. 13:10; Joel 2:10, 31; 3:15; Matt. 24:29; Mark 13:24
13 [a]Matt. 24:29; Mark 13:25; Rev. 8:10; 9:1
14 [a]Ps. 102:26; Is. 34:4; [2 Pet. 3:10]; Rev. 20:11; 21:1 [b]Jer. 3:23; Rev. 16:20
15 [a]Ps. 2:2–4 [b]Is. 2:10, 19, 21; 24:21; Rev. 19:18
16 [a]Hos. 10:8; Luke 23:29, 30; Rev. 9:6 [b]Rev. 20:11
17 [a]Is. 63:4; Jer. 30:7; Joel 1:15; 2:1, 11, 31; Zeph. 1:14; Rev. 16:14

CHAPTER 7

1 [a]Jer. 49:36; Dan. 7:2; Zech. 6:5; Matt. 24:31 [b]Rev. 7:3; 8:7; 9:4
3 [a]Rev. 6:6 [b]Ezek. 9:4, 6; Rev. 22:4
4 [a]Rev. 9:16 [b]Rev. 14:1, 3 [c]Gen. 49:1–27
9 [a]Is. 60:1–5; Rom. 11:25 [b]Rev. 5:9 [c]Rev. 3:5, 18; 4:4; 6:11
10 [a]Ps. 3:8; Is. 43:11; Jer. 3:23; Hos. 13:4; Rev. 19:1 [b]Rev. 5:13
11 [a]Rev. 4:6 [b]Rev. 4:11; 5:9, 12, 14; 11:16
12 [a]Rev. 5:13, 14

*

6:12 NU, M omit *behold* • NU, M *whole moon*
6:15 NU, M *the commanders, the rich men,*
7:5 NU, M omit *sealed* in vv. 5b–8b.

NKJV

Sixth Seal: Cosmic Disturbances

12 I looked when He opened the sixth seal, [a]and *behold, there was a great earthquake; and [b]the sun became black as sackcloth of hair, and the *moon became like blood.

13 [a]And the stars of heaven fell to the earth, as a fig tree drops its late figs when it is shaken by a mighty wind.

14 [a]Then the sky receded as a scroll when it is rolled up, and [b]every mountain and island was moved out of its place.

15 And the [a]kings of the earth, the great men, *the rich men, the commanders, the mighty men, every slave and every free man, [b]hid themselves in the caves and in the rocks of the mountains,

16 [a]and said to the mountains and rocks, "Fall on us and hide us from the face of Him who [b]sits on the throne and from the wrath of the Lamb!

17 "For the great day of His wrath has come, [a]and who is able to stand?"

The Sealed of Israel

7 After these things I saw four angels standing at the four corners of the earth, [a]holding the four winds of the earth, [b]that the wind should not blow on the earth, on the sea, or on any tree.

2 Then I saw another angel ascending from the east, having the seal of the living God. And he cried with a loud voice to the four angels to whom it was granted to harm the earth and the sea,

3 saying, [a]"Do not harm the earth, the sea, or the trees till we have sealed the servants of our God [b]on their foreheads."

4 [a]And I heard the number of those who were sealed. [b]One hundred *and* forty-four thousand [c]of all the tribes of the children of Israel *were* sealed:

5 of the tribe of Judah
twelve thousand *were* sealed;
of the tribe of Reuben
twelve thousand *were* *sealed;
of the tribe of Gad
twelve thousand *were* sealed;
6 of the tribe of Asher
twelve thousand *were* sealed;
of the tribe of Naphtali
twelve thousand *were* sealed;
of the tribe of Manasseh
twelve thousand *were* sealed;
7 of the tribe of Simeon
twelve thousand *were* sealed;
of the tribe of Levi
twelve thousand *were* sealed;
of the tribe of Issachar
twelve thousand *were* sealed;
8 of the tribe of Zebulun
twelve thousand *were* sealed;
of the tribe of Joseph
twelve thousand *were* sealed;
of the tribe of Benjamin
twelve thousand *were* sealed.

A Multitude from the Great Tribulation

9 After these things I looked, and behold, [a]a great multitude which no one could number, [b]of all nations, tribes, peoples, and tongues, standing before the throne and before the Lamb, [c]clothed with white robes, with palm branches in their hands,

10 and crying out with a loud voice, saying, [a]"Salvation *belongs* to our God [b]who sits on the throne, and to the Lamb!"

11 [a]All the angels stood around the throne and the elders and the four living creatures, and fell on their faces before the throne and [b]worshiped God,

12 [a]saying:

KJV

wisdom, and thanksgiving, and honour, and power, and might, *be* unto our God for ever and ever. Amen.

13 And one of the elders answered, saying unto me, What are these which are arrayed in [a]white robes? and whence came they?

14 And I said unto him, Sir, thou knowest. And he said to me, [a]These are they which came out of great tribulation, and have [b]washed their robes, and made them white in the blood of the Lamb.

15 Therefore are they before the throne of God, and serve him day and night in his temple: and he that sitteth on the throne shall [a]dwell among them.

16 [a]They shall hunger no more, neither thirst any more; [b]neither shall the sun light on them, nor any heat.

17 For the Lamb which is in the midst of the throne [a]shall feed them, and shall lead them unto living fountains of waters: [b]and God shall wipe away all tears from their eyes.

Seventh Seal: Prelude to the Seven Trumpets

8 And [a]when he had opened the seventh seal, there was silence in heaven about the space of half an hour.

2 [a]And I saw the seven angels which stood before God; [b]and to them were given seven trumpets.

3 And another angel came and stood at the altar, having a golden censer; and there was given unto him much incense, that he should offer *it* with [a]the prayers of all saints upon [b]the golden altar which was before the throne.

4 And [a]the smoke of the incense, *which came* with the prayers of the saints, ascended up before God out of the angel's hand.

5 And the angel took the censer, and filled it with fire of the altar, and cast *it* into the earth: and [a]there were voices, and thunderings, [b]and lightnings, [c]and an earthquake.

6 And the seven angels which had the seven trumpets prepared themselves to sound.

First Trumpet: Vegetation Struck

7 The first angel sounded, [a]and there followed hail and fire mingled with blood, and they were cast [b]upon the earth: and the third part [c]of trees was burnt up, and all green grass was burnt up.

Second Trumpet: The Seas Struck

8 And the second angel sounded, [a]and as it were a great mountain burning with fire was cast into the sea: [b]and the third part of the sea [c]became blood;

9 [a]And the third part of the creatures which were in the sea, and had life, died; and the third part of the ships were destroyed.

Third Trumpet: The Waters Struck

10 And the third angel sounded, [a]and there fell a great star from heaven, burning as it were a lamp, [b]and it fell upon the third part of the rivers, and upon the fountains of waters;

11 [a]And the name of the star is called Wormwood: [b]and the third part of the waters became wormwood; and many men died of the waters, because they were made bitter.

Fourth Trumpet: The Heavens Struck

12 [a]And the fourth angel sounded, and the third part of the sun was smitten, and the third part of the moon, and the third part of the stars; so as the third part of them was darkened, and the day shone not for a third part of it, and the night likewise.

13 And I beheld, [a]and heard an angel flying

13 [a]Rev. 7:9
14 [a]Rev. 6:9 [b]Is. 1:18; Zech. 3:3–5; [Heb. 9:14]
15 [a]Is. 4:5, 6; Rev. 21:3
16 [a]Ps. 121:5; Is. 49:10 [b]Ps. 121:6; Rev. 21:4
17 [a]Ps. 23:1; Matt. 2:6; [John 10:11, 14] [b]Is. 25:8; Matt. 5:4; Rev. 21:4

CHAPTER 8
1 [a]Rev. 6:1
2 [a][Matt. 18:10]; Luke 1:19 [b]2 Chr. 29:25–28
3 [a]Rev. 5:8 [b]Ex. 30:1; Rev. 8:3
4 [a]Ps. 141:2; Luke 1:10
5 [a]Ex. 19:16; Rev. 11:19; 16:18 [b]Rev. 4:5 [c]2 Sam. 22:8; 1 Kin. 19:11; Acts 4:31
7 [a]Ex. 9:23; Is. 28:2; Ezek. 38:22; Joel 2:30 [b]Rev. 16:2 [c]Is. 2:13; Rev. 9:4, 15–18
8 [a]Jer. 51:25; Amos 7:4 [b]Ex. 7:17; Rev. 11:6; 16:3 [c]Ezek. 14:19
9 [a]Rev. 16:3
10 [a]Is. 14:12; Rev. 6:13; 9:1 [b]Rev. 14:7; 16:4
11 [a]Ruth 1:20 [b]Ex. 15:23
12 [a]Is. 13:10; Joel 2:31; Amos 8:9; Matt. 24:29; Rev. 6:12
13 [a]Rev. 14:6; 19:17

*

7:14 NU, M *My lord*
7:17 NU, M *fountains of the waters of life*
8:7 NU, M add *and a third of the earth was burned up*
8:13 NU, M *eagle*

NKJV

"Amen! Blessing and glory and wisdom,
Thanksgiving and honor and power and might,
Be to our God forever and ever.
Amen."

13 Then one of the elders answered, saying to me, "Who are these arrayed in [a]white robes, and where did they come from?"

14 And I said to him, *"Sir, you know." So he said to me, [a]"These are the ones who come out of the great tribulation, and [b]washed their robes and made them white in the blood of the Lamb.

15 "Therefore they are before the throne of God, and serve Him day and night in His temple. And He who sits on the throne will [a]dwell among them.

16 [a]"They shall neither hunger anymore nor thirst anymore; [b]the sun shall not strike them, nor any heat;

17 "for the Lamb who is in the midst of the throne [a]will shepherd them and lead them to *living fountains of waters. [b]And God will wipe away every tear from their eyes."

Seventh Seal: Prelude to the Seven Trumpets

8 When[a] He opened the seventh seal, there was silence in heaven for about half an hour.

2 [a]And I saw the seven angels who stand before God, [b]and to them were given seven trumpets.

3 Then another angel, having a golden censer, came and stood at the altar. He was given much incense, that he should offer *it* with [a]the prayers of all the saints upon [b]the golden altar which was before the throne.

4 And [a]the smoke of the incense, with the prayers of the saints, ascended before God from the angel's hand.

5 Then the angel took the censer, filled it with fire from the altar, and threw *it* to the earth. And [a]there were noises, thunderings, [b]lightnings, [c]and an earthquake.

6 So the seven angels who had the seven trumpets prepared themselves to sound.

First Trumpet: Vegetation Struck

7 The first angel sounded: [a]And hail and fire followed, mingled with blood, and they were thrown [b]to the *earth. And a third [c]of the trees were burned up, and all green grass was burned up.

Second Trumpet: The Seas Struck

8 Then the second angel sounded: [a]And *something* like a great mountain burning with fire was thrown into the sea, [b]and a third of the sea [c]became blood.

9 [a]And a third of the living creatures in the sea died, and a third of the ships were destroyed.

Third Trumpet: The Waters Struck

10 Then the third angel sounded: [a]And a great star fell from heaven, burning like a torch, [b]and it fell on a third of the rivers and on the springs of water.

11 [a]The name of the star is Wormwood. [b]A third of the waters became wormwood, and many men died from the water, because it was made bitter.

Fourth Trumpet: The Heavens Struck

12 [a]Then the fourth angel sounded: And a third of the sun was struck, a third of the moon, and a third of the stars, so that a third of them were darkened. A third of the day did not shine, and likewise the night.

13 And I looked, [a]and I heard an *angel fly-

KJV

through the midst of heaven, saying with a loud voice, [b]Woe, woe, woe, to the inhabiters of the earth by reason of the other voices of the trumpet of the three angels, which are yet to sound!

Fifth Trumpet: The Locusts from the Bottomless Pit

9 And the fifth angel sounded, [a]and I saw a star fall from heaven unto the earth: and to him was given the key of [b]the bottomless pit.

2 And he opened the bottomless pit; and there arose a smoke out of the pit, as the smoke of a great furnace; and the [a]sun and the air were darkened by reason of the smoke of the pit.

3 And there came out of the smoke locusts upon the earth: and unto them was given power, [a]as the scorpions of the earth have power.

4 And it was commanded them [a]that they should not hurt [b]the grass of the earth, neither any green thing, neither any tree; but only those men which have not [c]the seal of God in their foreheads.

5 And to them it was given that they should not kill them, [a]but that they should be tormented five months: and their torment *was* as the torment of a scorpion, when he striketh a man.

6 And in those days [a]shall men seek death, and shall not find it; and shall desire to die, and death shall flee from them.

7 And [a]the shapes of the locusts *were* like unto horses prepared unto battle; [b]and on their heads *were* as it were crowns like gold, [c]and their faces *were* as the faces of men.

8 And they had hair as the hair of women, and [a]their teeth were as *the teeth* of lions.

9 And they had breastplates, as it were breastplates of iron; and the sound of their wings *was* [a]as the sound of chariots of many horses running to battle.

10 And they had tails like unto scorpions, and there were stings in their tails: and their power *was* to hurt men five months.

11 And they had a king over them, *which is* [a]the angel of the bottomless pit, whose name in the Hebrew tongue *is* Abaddon, but in the Greek tongue hath *his* name Apollyon.

12 [a]One woe is past; *and*, behold, there come two woes more hereafter.

Sixth Trumpet: The Angels from the Euphrates

13 And the sixth angel sounded, and I heard a voice from the four horns of the [a]golden altar which is before God,

14 Saying to the sixth angel which had the trumpet, Loose the four angels which are bound [a]in the great river Euphrates.

15 And the four angels were loosed, which were prepared for an hour, and a day, and a month, and a year, for to slay the [a]third part of men.

16 And [a]the number of the army [b]of the horsemen *were* two hundred thousand thousand: [c]and I heard the number of them.

17 And thus I saw the horses in the vision, and them that sat on them, having breastplates of fire, and of jacinth, and brimstone: [a]and the heads of the horses *were* as the heads of lions; and out of their mouths issued fire and smoke and brimstone.

18 By these three was the third part of men killed, by the fire, and by the smoke, and by the brimstone, which issued out of their mouths.

19 For their power is in their mouth, and in their tails: [a]for their tails *were* like unto serpents, and had heads, and with them they do hurt.

20 And the rest of the men which were not killed by these plagues [a]yet repented not of the works of their hands, that they should not worship [b]devils, [c]and idols of gold, and silver, and brass, and stone, and of wood: which neither can see, nor hear, nor walk:

13 [b]Rev. 9:12; 11:14; 12:12

CHAPTER 9

1 [a]Luke 10:18; Rev. 8:10 [b]Luke 8:31; Rev. 9:2, 11; 17:8
2 [a]Joel 2:2, 10
3 [a]Ex. 10:4; Judg. 7:12
4 [a]Rev. 6:6 [b]Rev. 8:7 [c]Ex. 12:23; Ezek. 9:4; Rev. 7:2, 3
5 [a][Rev. 9:10; 11:7]
6 [a]Job 3:21; 7:15; Is. 2:19; Jer. 8:3; Rev. 6:16
7 [a]Joel 2:4 [b]Nah. 3:17 [c]Dan. 7:8
8 [a]Joel 1:6
9 [a]Jer. 47:3; Joel 2:5–7
11 [a]Eph. 2:2
12 [a]Rev. 8:13; 11:14
13 [a]Rev. 8:3
14 [a]Gen. 15:18; Deut. 1:7; Josh. 1:4; Rev. 16:12
15 [a]Rev. 8:7–9; 9:18
16 [a]Ps. 68:17; Dan. 7:10 [b]Ezek. 38:4 [c]Rev. 7:4
17 [a]1 Chr. 12:8; Is. 5:28, 29
19 [a]Is. 9:15
20 [a]Deut. 31:29 [b]Lev. 17:7; Deut. 32:17; Ps. 106:37; 1 Cor. 10:20 [c]Ps. 115:4–7; 135:15–17; Dan. 5:23

*———

9:19 NU, M *the power of the horses*

NKJV

ing through the midst of heaven, saying with a loud voice, [b]"Woe, woe, woe to the inhabitants of the earth, because of the remaining blasts of the trumpet of the three angels who are about to sound!"

Fifth Trumpet: The Locusts from the Bottomless Pit

9 Then the fifth angel sounded: [a]And I saw a star fallen from heaven to the earth. To him was given the key to [b]the bottomless pit.

2 And he opened the bottomless pit, and smoke arose out of the pit like the smoke of a great furnace. So the [a]sun and the air were darkened because of the smoke of the pit.

3 Then out of the smoke locusts came upon the earth. And to them was given power, [a]as the scorpions of the earth have power.

4 They were commanded [a]not to harm [b]the grass of the earth, or any green thing, or any tree, but only those men who do not have [c]the seal of God on their foreheads.

5 And they were not given *authority* to kill them, [a]but to torment them *for* five months. Their torment *was* like the torment of a scorpion when it strikes a man.

6 In those days [a]men will seek death and will not find it; they will desire to die, and death will flee from them.

7 [a]The shape of the locusts was like horses prepared for battle. [b]On their heads were crowns of something like gold, [c]and their faces *were* like the faces of men.

8 They had hair like women's hair, and [a]their teeth were like lions' *teeth*.

9 And they had breastplates like breastplates of iron, and the sound of their wings *was* [a]like the sound of chariots with many horses running into battle.

10 They had tails like scorpions, and there were stings in their tails. Their power *was* to hurt men five months.

11 And they had as king over them [a]the angel of the bottomless pit, whose name in Hebrew *is* Abaddon, but in Greek he has the name Apollyon.

12 [a]One woe is past. Behold, still two more woes are coming after these things.

Sixth Trumpet: The Angels from the Euphrates

13 Then the sixth angel sounded: And I heard a voice from the four horns of the [a]golden altar which is before God,

14 saying to the sixth angel who had the trumpet, "Release the four angels who are bound [a]at the great river Euphrates."

15 So the four angels, who had been prepared for the hour and day and month and year, were released to kill a [a]third of mankind.

16 Now [a]the number of the army [b]of the horsemen *was* two hundred million; [c]I heard the number of them.

17 And thus I saw the horses in the vision: those who sat on them had breastplates of fiery red, hyacinth blue, and sulfur yellow; [a]and the heads of the horses *were* like the heads of lions; and out of their mouths came fire, smoke, and brimstone.

18 By these three *plagues* a third of mankind was killed—by the fire and the smoke and the brimstone which came out of their mouths.

19 For *their power is in their mouth and in their tails; [a]for their tails *are* like serpents, having heads; and with them they do harm.

20 But the rest of mankind, who were not killed by these plagues, [a]did not repent of the works of their hands, that they should not worship [b]demons, [c]and idols of gold, silver, brass, stone, and wood, which can neither see nor hear nor walk.

KJV

21 Neither repented they of their murders, [a]nor of their sorceries, nor of their fornication, nor of their thefts.

The Mighty Angel with the Little Book

10 And I saw another mighty angel come down from heaven, clothed with a cloud: [a]and a rainbow *was* upon [b]his head, and his face *was* as it were the sun, and [c]his feet as pillars of fire:

2 And he had in his hand a little book open: [a]and he set his right foot upon the sea, and *his* left *foot* on the earth,

3 And cried with a loud voice, as *when* a lion roareth: and when he had cried, [a]seven thunders uttered their voices.

4 And when the seven thunders had uttered their voices, I was about to write: and I heard a voice from heaven saying unto me, [a]Seal up those things which the seven thunders uttered, and write them not.

5 And the angel which I saw stand upon the sea and upon the earth [a]lifted up his hand to heaven,

6 And sware by him that liveth for ever and ever, [a]who created heaven, and the things that therein are, and the earth, and the things that therein are, and the sea, and the things which are therein, [b]that there should be time no longer:

7 But [a]in the days of the voice of the seventh angel, when he shall begin to sound, the mystery of God should be finished, as he hath declared to his servants the prophets.

John Eats the Little Book

8 And the voice which I heard from heaven spake unto me again, and said, Go *and* take the little book which is open in the hand of the angel which standeth upon the sea and upon the earth.

9 And I went unto the angel, and said unto him, Give me the little book. And he said unto me, [a]Take *it*, and eat it up; and it shall make thy belly bitter, but it shall be in thy mouth sweet as honey.

10 And I took the little book out of the angel's hand, and ate it up; [a]and it was in my mouth sweet as honey: and as soon as I had eaten it, [b]my belly was bitter.

11 And he said unto me, Thou must prophesy again before many peoples, and nations, and tongues, and kings.

The Two Witnesses

11 And there was given me [a]a reed like unto a rod: and the angel stood, saying, [b]Rise, and measure the temple of God, and the altar, and them that worship therein.

2 But [a]the court which is without the temple leave out, and measure it not; [b]for it is given unto the Gentiles: and the holy city shall they [c]tread under foot [d]forty *and* two months.

3 And I will give *power* unto my two [a]witnesses, [b]and they shall prophesy [c]a thousand two hundred *and* threescore days, clothed in sackcloth.

4 These are the [a]two olive trees, and the two candlesticks standing before the God of the earth.

5 And if any man will hurt them, [a]fire proceedeth out of their mouth, and devoureth their enemies: [b]and if any man will hurt them, he must in this manner be killed.

6 These [a]have power to shut heaven, that it rain not in the days of their prophecy: and have power over waters to turn them to blood, and to smite the earth with all plagues, as often as they will.

The Witnesses Killed

7 And when they [a]shall have finished their testimony, [b]the beast that ascendeth [c]out of the bottomless pit [d]shall make war against them, and shall overcome them, and kill them.

---

21 [a]Rev. 21:8; 22:15

CHAPTER 10

1 [a]Ezek. 1:26–28; Rev. 4:3 [b]Matt. 17:2; Rev. 1:16 [c]Rev. 1:15
2 [a]Ps. 95:5; Matt. 28:18
3 [a]Ps. 29:3–9; Rev. 4:5; 8:5
4 [a]Dan. 8:26; 12:4, 9; Rev. 22:10
5 [a]Ex. 6:8; Deut. 32:40; Dan. 12:7
6 [a]Gen. 1:1; Ex. 20:11; Neh. 9:6; Rev. 4:11 [b]Dan. 12:7; Rev. 16:17
7 [a]Rev. 11:15
9 [a]Jer. 15:16; Ezek. 2:8; 3:1–3
10 [a]Ezek. 3:3 [b]Ezek. 2:10

CHAPTER 11

1 [a]Ezek. 40:3—42:20; Zech. 2:1; Rev. 21:15 [b]Num. 23:18
2 [a]Ezek. 40:17, 20 [b]Ps. 79:1; Luke 21:24 [c]Dan. 8:10 [d]Dan. 7:25; 12:7; Rev. 12:6; 13:5
3 [a]Deut. 17:6; Rev. 20:4 [b]Rev. 19:10 [c]Rev. 12:6
4 [a]Ps. 52:8; Jer. 11:16; Zech. 4:2, 3, 11, 14
5 [a]2 Kin. 1:10–12; Jer. 1:10; 5:14; Ezek. 43:3; Hos. 6:5; Rev. 9:17 [b]Num. 16:29
6 [a]1 Kin. 17:1; Luke 4:25; [James 5:16, 17]
7 [a]Luke 13:32 [b]Rev. 13:1, 11; 17:8 [c]Rev. 9:1, 2 [d]Dan. 7:21; Rev. 13:7

*

9:21 NU, M *drugs*
10:4 NU, M *sounded,* • NU, M omit *to me*
10:5 NU, M *right hand*
10:11 NU, M *they*
11:1 NU, M omit *And the angel stood*
11:4 NU, M *Lord*

NKJV

21 And they did not repent of their murders [a]or their *sorceries or their sexual immorality or their thefts.

The Mighty Angel with the Little Book

10 I saw still another mighty angel coming down from heaven, clothed with a cloud. [a]And a rainbow *was* on [b]his head, his face *was* like the sun, and [c]his feet like pillars of fire.

2 He had a little book open in his hand. [a]And he set his right foot on the sea and *his* left *foot* on the land,

3 and cried with a loud voice, as *when* a lion roars. When he cried out, [a]seven thunders uttered their voices.

4 Now when the seven thunders *uttered their voices, I was about to write; but I heard a voice from heaven saying *to me, [a]"Seal up the things which the seven thunders uttered, and do not write them."

5 The angel whom I saw standing on the sea and on the land [a]raised up his *hand to heaven

6 and swore by Him who lives forever and ever, [a]who created heaven and the things that are in it, the earth and the things that are in it, and the sea and the things that are in it, [b]that there should be delay no longer,

7 but [a]in the days of the sounding of the seventh angel, when he is about to sound, the mystery of God would be finished, as He declared to His servants the prophets.

John Eats the Little Book

8 Then the voice which I heard from heaven spoke to me again and said, "Go, take the little book which is open in the hand of the angel who stands on the sea and on the earth."

9 So I went to the angel and said to him, "Give me the little book." And he said to me, [a]"Take and eat it; and it will make your stomach bitter, but it will be as sweet as honey in your mouth."

10 Then I took the little book out of the angel's hand and ate it, [a]and it was as sweet as honey in my mouth. But when I had eaten it, [b]my stomach became bitter.

11 And *he said to me, "You must prophesy again about many peoples, nations, tongues, and kings."

The Two Witnesses

11 Then I was given [a]a reed like a measuring rod. *And the angel stood, saying, [b]"Rise and measure the temple of God, the altar, and those who worship there.

2 "But leave out [a]the court which is outside the temple, and do not measure it, [b]for it has been given to the Gentiles. And they will [c]tread the holy city underfoot *for* [d]forty-two months.

3 "And I will give *power* to my two [a]witnesses, [b]and they will prophesy [c]one thousand two hundred and sixty days, clothed in sackcloth."

4 These are the [a]two olive trees and the two lampstands standing before the *God of the earth.

5 And if anyone wants to harm them, [a]fire proceeds from their mouth and devours their enemies. [b]And if anyone wants to harm them, he must be killed in this manner.

6 These [a]have power to shut heaven, so that no rain falls in the days of their prophecy; and they have power over waters to turn them to blood, and to strike the earth with all plagues, as often as they desire.

The Witnesses Killed

7 When they [a]finish their testimony, [b]the beast that ascends [c]out of the bottomless pit [d]will make war against them, overcome them, and kill them.

KJV

8 And their dead bodies *shall lie* in the street of [a]the great city, which spiritually is called Sodom and Egypt, [b]where also our Lord was crucified.

9 [a]And they of the people and kindreds and tongues and nations shall see their dead bodies three days and an half, [b]and shall not suffer their dead bodies to be put in graves.

10 [a]And they that dwell upon the earth shall rejoice over them, and make merry, [b]and shall send gifts one to another; [c]because these two prophets tormented them that dwelt on the earth.

The Witnesses Resurrected

11 [a]And after three days and an half [b]the Spirit of life from God entered into them, and they stood upon their feet; and great fear fell upon them which saw them.

12 And they heard a great voice from heaven saying unto them, Come up hither. [a]And they ascended up to heaven [b]in a cloud; [c]and their enemies beheld them.

13 And the same hour [a]was there a great earthquake, [b]and the tenth part of the city fell, and in the earthquake were slain of men seven thousand: and the remnant were affrighted, [c]and gave glory to the God of heaven.

14 [a]The second woe is past; *and,* behold, the third woe cometh quickly.

Seventh Trumpet: The Kingdom Proclaimed

15 And [a]the seventh angel sounded; [b]and there were great voices in heaven, saying, [c]The kingdoms of this world are become *the kingdoms* of our Lord, and of his Christ; [d]and he shall reign for ever and ever.

16 And [a]the four and twenty elders, which sat before God on their seats, fell upon their faces, and [b]worshipped God,

17 Saying, We give thee thanks, O Lord God Almighty, [a]which art, and wast, and art to come; because thou hast taken to thee thy great power, [b]and hast reigned.

18 And the nations were [a]angry, and thy wrath is come, and the time of the [b]dead, that they should be judged, and that thou shouldest give reward unto thy servants the prophets, and to the saints, and them that fear thy name, small and great; and shouldest destroy them which destroy the earth.

19 And [a]the temple of God was opened in heaven, and there was seen in his temple the ark of his testament: and [b]there were lightnings, and voices, and thunderings, and an earthquake, [c]and great hail.

The Woman, the Child, and the Dragon

12 And there appeared a great wonder in heaven; a woman clothed with the sun, and the moon under her feet, and upon her head a crown of twelve stars:

2 And she being with child cried, [a]travailing in birth, and pained to be delivered.

3 And there appeared another wonder in heaven; and behold [a]a great red dragon, having seven heads and ten horns, and seven crowns upon his heads.

4 And [a]his tail drew the third part [b]of the stars of heaven, [c]and did cast them to the earth: and the dragon stood [d]before the woman which was ready to be delivered, [e]for to devour her child as soon as it was born.

5 And she brought forth a man child, [a]who was to rule all nations with a rod of iron: and her child was [b]caught up unto God, and *to* his throne.

8 [a]Rev. 14:8 [b]Heb. 13:12
9 [a]Rev. 17:15 [b]1 Kin. 13:22; Ps. 79:2, 3
10 [a]Rev. 12:12 [b]Neh. 8:10, 12; Esth. 9:19, 22 [c]Rev. 16:10
11 [a]Rev. 11:9 [b]Ezek. 37:5, 9, 10
12 [a]Is. 14:13 [b]Is. 60:8; Acts 1:9 [c]2 Kin. 2:1
13 [a]Rev. 6:12; 8:5; 11:19; 16:18 [b]Rev. 16:19 [c]Josh. 7:19; John 9:24; Rev. 14:7; 16:9; 19:7
14 [a]Rev. 8:13; 9:12
15 [a]Rev. 8:2; 10:7 [b]Is. 27:13 [c]Rev. 12:10 [d]Ex. 15:18; Dan. 2:44; 7:14, 27; Luke 1:33
16 [a]Matt. 19:28; Rev. 4:4 [b]Rev. 4:11; 5:9, 12, 14; 7:11
17 [a]Rev. 16:5 [b]Rev. 19:6
18 [a]Ps. 2:1 [b]Dan. 7:10; [Rev. 20:12, 13]
19 [a]Rev. 4:1; 15:5, 8 [b]Rev. 8:5 [c]Rev. 16:21

CHAPTER 12

2 [a]Is. 26:17; 66:6–9; Mic. 4:9; Gal. 4:19
3 [a]Rev. 13:1; 17:3, 7, 9
4 [a]Rev. 9:10, 19 [b]Rev. 8:7, 12 [c]Dan. 8:10 [d]Rev. 12:2 [e]Ex. 1:16; Matt. 2:16
5 [a]Ps. 2:9; Is. 7:14; 9:6; Rev. 2:27; 19:15 [b]Luke 24:51; Acts 1:9–11

*

11:8 NU, M *their*
11:9 NU, M *see . . . and will not allow*
11:12 M *I*
11:15 NU, M *kingdom . . . has become the kingdom*
11:17 NU, M omit *and who is to come*
11:19 M *the covenant of the Lord*

NKJV

8 And their dead bodies *will lie* in the street of [a]the great city which spiritually is called Sodom and Egypt, [b]where also *our Lord was crucified.

9 [a]Then *those* from the peoples, tribes, tongues, and nations *will see their dead bodies three-and-a-half days, [b]and not allow their dead bodies to be put into graves.

10 [a]And those who dwell on the earth will rejoice over them, make merry, [b]and send gifts to one another, [c]because these two prophets tormented those who dwell on the earth.

The Witnesses Resurrected

11 [a]Now after the three-and-a-half days [b]the breath of life from God entered them, and they stood on their feet, and great fear fell on those who saw them.

12 And *they heard a loud voice from heaven saying to them, "Come up here." [a]And they ascended to heaven [b]in a cloud, [c]and their enemies saw them.

13 In the same hour [a]there was a great earthquake, [b]and a tenth of the city fell. In the earthquake seven thousand people were killed, and the rest were afraid [c]and gave glory to the God of heaven.

14 [a]The second woe is past. Behold, the third woe is coming quickly.

Seventh Trumpet: The Kingdom Proclaimed

15 Then [a]the seventh angel sounded: [b]And there were loud voices in heaven, saying, [c]"The *kingdoms of this world have become *the kingdoms* of our Lord and of His Christ, [d]and He shall reign forever and ever!"

16 And [a]the twenty-four elders who sat before God on their thrones fell on their faces and [b]worshiped God,

17 saying:

"We give You thanks, O Lord God
Almighty,
The One [a]who is and who was *and who
is to come,
Because You have taken Your great
power [b]and reigned.

18 The nations were [a]angry, and Your wrath
has come,
And the time of the [b]dead, that they
should be judged,
And that You should reward Your
servants the prophets and the saints,
And those who fear Your name, small and
great,
And should destroy those who destroy the
earth."

19 Then [a]the temple of God was opened in heaven, and the ark of *His covenant was seen in His temple. And [b]there were lightnings, noises, thunderings, an earthquake, [c]and great hail.

The Woman, the Child, and the Dragon

12 Now a great sign appeared in heaven: a woman clothed with the sun, with the moon under her feet, and on her head a garland of twelve stars.

2 Then being with child, she cried out [a]in labor and in pain to give birth.

3 And another sign appeared in heaven: behold, [a]a great, fiery red dragon having seven heads and ten horns, and seven diadems on his heads.

4 [a]His tail drew a third [b]of the stars of heaven [c]and threw them to the earth. And the dragon stood [d]before the woman who was ready to give birth, [e]to devour her Child as soon as it was born.

5 She bore a male Child [a]who was to rule all nations with a rod of iron. And her Child was [b]caught up to God and His throne.

KJV

6 And [a]the woman fled into the wilderness,
where she hath a place prepared of God, that they
should feed her there [b]a thousand two hundred
and threescore days.

Satan Thrown Out of Heaven

7 And there was war in heaven: [a]Michael
and his angels fought [b]against the dragon; and
the dragon fought and his angels,
8 And prevailed not; neither was their place
found any more in heaven.
9 And [a]the great dragon was cast out, [b]that
old serpent, called the Devil, and Satan, [c]which
deceiveth the whole world: [d]he was cast out into
the earth, and his angels were cast out with him.
10 And I heard a loud voice saying in heaven,
[a]Now is come salvation, and strength, and the
kingdom of our God, and the power of his Christ:
for the accuser of our brethren is cast down,
[b]which accused them before our God day and
night.
11 And [a]they overcame him by the blood of
the Lamb, and by the word of their testimony;
[b]and they loved not their lives unto the death.
12 Therefore [a]rejoice, *ye* heavens, and ye
that dwell in them. [b]Woe to the inhabiters of the
earth and of the sea! for the devil is come down
unto you, having great wrath, [c]because he knoweth that he hath but a short time.

The Woman Persecuted

13 And when the dragon saw that he was cast
unto the earth, he persecuted [a]the woman which
brought forth the man *child*.
14 [a]And to the woman were given two wings
of a great eagle, [b]that she might fly [c]into the wilderness, into her place, where she is nourished
[d]for a time, and times, and half a time, from the
face of the serpent.
15 And the serpent [a]cast out of his mouth
water as a flood after the woman, that he might
cause her to be carried away of the flood.
16 And the earth helped the woman, and the
earth opened her mouth, and swallowed up the
flood which the dragon cast out of his mouth.
17 And the dragon was wroth with the
woman, and went to make war with the remnant
of her seed, which keep the commandments of
God, and have the testimony of Jesus Christ.

The Beast from the Sea

13 And I stood upon the sand of the sea, and
saw [a]a beast rise up out of the sea, [b]having
seven heads and ten horns, and upon his horns
ten crowns, and upon his heads the [c]name of
blasphemy.
2 And the beast which I saw was like unto
a leopard, and his feet were as *the feet* of a bear,
and his mouth as the mouth of a lion: and the
[a]dragon gave him his power, and his seat, and
great authority.
3 And I saw one of his heads [a]as it were
wounded to death; and his deadly wound was
healed: and [b]all the world wondered after the
beast.
4 And they worshipped the dragon which
gave power unto the beast: and they worshipped
the beast, saying, [a]Who *is* like unto the beast?
who is able to make war with him?
5 And there was given unto him [a]a mouth
speaking great things and blasphemies; and
power was given unto him to continue [b]forty *and*
two months.
6 And he opened his mouth in blasphemy
against God, to blaspheme his name, [a]and his tabernacle, and them that dwell in heaven.
7 And it was given unto him [a]to make war
with the saints, and to overcome them: [b]and
power was given him over all kindreds, and
tongues, and nations.
8 And all that dwell upon the earth shall

6 [a]Rev. 12:4, 14 [b]Rev. 11:3; 13:5
7 [a]Dan. 10:13, 21; 12:1; Jude 9 [b]Rev. 20:2
9 [a]Luke 10:18; John 12:31 [b]Gen. 3:1, 4; 2 Cor. 11:3; Rev. 12:15; 20:2 [c]Rev. 20:3 [d]Rev. 9:1
10 [a]Rev. 11:15 [b]Job 1:9, 11; 2:5; Zech. 3:1
11 [a]Rom. 16:20 [b]Luke 14:26; [Rev. 2:10]
12 [a]Ps. 96:11; Is. 44:23; Rev. 18:20 [b]Rev. 8:13 [c]Rev. 10:6
13 [a]Rev. 12:5
14 [a]Ex. 19:4; Deut. 32:11; Is. 40:31 [b]Rev. 12:6 [c]Rev. 17:3 [d]Dan. 7:25; 12:7
15 [a]Is. 59:19

CHAPTER 13
1 [a]Dan. 7:2, 7 [b]Rev. 12:3 [c]Dan. 7:8; 11:36; Rev. 17:3
2 [a]Rev. 12:3, 9; 13:4, 12
3 [a]Rev. 13:12, 14 [b]Rev. 17:8
4 [a]Ex. 15:11; Is. 46:5; Rev. 18:18
5 [a]Dan. 7:8, 11, 20, 25; 11:36; 2 Thess. 2:3 [b]Rev. 11:2
6 [a][John 1:14; Col. 2:9]
7 [a]Dan. 7:21; Rev. 11:7 [b]Rev. 11:18

*
12:8 M *him*
12:17 NU, M omit *Christ*
13:1 NU *he* • NU, M *ten horns and seven heads*
13:5 M *make war*
13:7 NU, M add *and people*

NKJV

6 Then [a]the woman fled into the wilderness,
where she has a place prepared by God, that they
should feed her there [b]one thousand two hundred
and sixty days.

Satan Thrown Out of Heaven

7 And war broke out in heaven: [a]Michael
and his angels fought [b]with the dragon; and the
dragon and his angels fought,
8 but they did not prevail, nor was a place
found for *them in heaven any longer.
9 So [a]the great dragon was cast out, [b]that
serpent of old, called the Devil and Satan, [c]who
deceives the whole world; [d]he was cast to the
earth, and his angels were cast out with him.
10 Then I heard a loud voice saying in
heaven, [a]"Now salvation, and strength, and the
kingdom of our God, and the power of His Christ
have come, for the accuser of our brethren, [b]who
accused them before our God day and night, has
been cast down.
11 "And [a]they overcame him by the blood
of the Lamb and by the word of their testimony,
[b]and they did not love their lives to the death.
12 "Therefore [a]rejoice, O heavens, and you
who dwell in them! [b]Woe to the inhabitants of
the earth and the sea! For the devil has come down
to you, having great wrath, [c]because he knows
that he has a short time."

The Woman Persecuted

13 Now when the dragon saw that he had
been cast to the earth, he persecuted [a]the woman
who gave birth to the male *Child*.
14 [a]But the woman was given two wings of
a great eagle, [b]that she might fly [c]into the wilderness to her place, where she is nourished [d]for a
time and times and half a time, from the presence
of the serpent.
15 So the serpent [a]spewed water out of his
mouth like a flood after the woman, that he might
cause her to be carried away by the flood.
16 But the earth helped the woman, and the
earth opened its mouth and swallowed up the
flood which the dragon had spewed out of his
mouth.
17 And the dragon was enraged with the
woman, and he went to make war with the rest
of her offspring, who keep the commandments
of God and have the testimony of Jesus *Christ.

The Beast from the Sea

13 Then *I stood on the sand of the sea. And
I saw [a]a beast rising up out of the sea, [b]hav-
ing *seven heads and ten horns, and on his horns
ten crowns, and on his heads a [c]blasphemous
name.
2 Now the beast which I saw was like a leopard, his feet were like *the feet of* a bear, and his
mouth like the mouth of a lion. The [a]dragon gave
him his power, his throne, and great authority.
3 And *I saw* one of his heads [a]as if it had
been mortally wounded, and his deadly wound
was healed. And [b]all the world marveled and followed the beast.
4 So they worshiped the dragon who gave
authority to the beast; and they worshiped the
beast, saying, [a]"Who *is* like the beast? Who is
able to make war with him?"
5 And he was given [a]a mouth speaking
great things and blasphemies, and he was given
authority to *continue for [b]forty-two months.
6 Then he opened his mouth in blasphemy
against God, to blaspheme His name, [a]His tabernacle, and those who dwell in heaven.
7 It was granted to him [a]to make war with
the saints and to overcome them. And [b]authority
was given him over every *tribe, tongue, and
nation.
8 All who dwell on the earth will worship

KJV

worship him, [a]whose names are not written in
the book of life of the Lamb slain [b]from the foundation of the world.
9 [a]If any man have an ear, let him hear.
10 [a]He that leadeth into captivity shall go
into captivity: [b]he that killeth with the sword must
be killed with the sword. [c]Here is the patience
and the faith of the saints.

The Beast from the Earth

11 And I beheld another beast [a]coming up
out of the earth; and he had two horns like a lamb,
and he spake as a dragon.
12 And he exerciseth all the power of the first
beast before him, and causeth the earth and them
which dwell therein to worship the first beast,
[a]whose deadly wound was healed.
13 And [a]he doeth great wonders, [b]so that he
maketh fire come down from heaven on the earth
in the sight of men,
14 [a]And deceiveth them that dwell on the
earth [b]by *the means of* those miracles which he
had power to do in the sight of the beast; saying
to them that dwell on the earth, that they should
make an image to the beast, which had the wound
by a sword, [c]and did live.
15 And he had power to give life unto the
image of the beast, that the image of the beast
should both speak, [a]and cause that as many as
would not worship the image of the beast should
be killed.
16 And he causeth all, both small and great,
rich and poor, free and bond, [a]to receive a mark
in their right hand, or in their foreheads:
17 And that no man might buy or sell, save
he that had the mark, or [a]the name of the beast,
[b]or the number of his name.
18 [a]Here is wisdom. Let him that hath [b]un-
derstanding count [c]the number of the beast: [d]for
it is the number of a man; and his number *is* Six
hundred threescore *and* six.

The Lamb and the 144,000

14 And I looked, and, lo, a [a]Lamb stood on
the mount Sion, and with him an [b]hundred
forty *and* four thousand, having his Father's name
[c]written in their foreheads.
2 And I heard a voice from heaven, [a]as the
voice of many waters, and as the voice of a great
thunder: and I heard the voice of [b]harpers harping
with their harps:
3 And they sung as it were a new song before the throne, and before the four beasts, and
the elders: and no man could learn that song [a]but
the hundred *and* forty *and* four thousand, which
were redeemed from the earth.
4 These are they which were not defiled
with women; [a]for they are virgins. These are they
[b]which follow the Lamb whithersoever he goeth.
These [c]were redeemed from among men, [d]*being*
the firstfruits unto God and to the Lamb.
5 And [a]in their mouth was found no guile:
for [b]they are without fault before the throne of
God.

The Proclamations of Three Angels

6 And I saw another angel [a]fly in the midst
of heaven, [b]having the everlasting gospel to
preach unto them that dwell on the earth, [c]and
to every nation, and kindred, and tongue, and
people,
7 Saying with a loud voice, [a]Fear God, and
give glory to him; for the hour of his judgment
is come: [b]and worship him that made heaven,
and earth, and the sea, and the fountains of
waters.
8 And there followed another angel, saying,
[a]Babylon is fallen, is fallen, that great city, because [b]she made all nations drink of the wine of
the wrath of her fornication.
9 And the third angel followed them, saying
with a loud voice, [a]If any man worship the beast

NKJV

him, [a]whose names have not been written in the
Book of Life of the Lamb slain [b]from the foundation of the world.
9 [a]If anyone has an ear, let him hear.
10 [a]He who leads into captivity shall go into
captivity; [b]he who kills with the sword must be
killed with the sword. [c]Here is the patience and
the faith of the saints.

The Beast from the Earth

11 Then I saw another beast [a]coming up out
of the earth, and he had two horns like a lamb
and spoke like a dragon.
12 And he exercises all the authority of the
first beast in his presence, and causes the earth
and those who dwell in it to worship the first
beast, [a]whose deadly wound was healed.
13 [a]He performs great signs, [b]so that he even
makes fire come down from heaven on the earth
in the sight of men.
14 [a]And he deceives *those who dwell on the
earth [b]by those signs which he was granted to
do in the sight of the beast, telling those who dwell
on the earth to make an image to the beast who
was wounded by the sword [c]and lived.
15 He was granted *power* to give breath to
the image of the beast, that the image of the beast
should both speak [a]and cause as many as would
not worship the image of the beast to be killed.
16 He causes all, both small and great, rich
and poor, free and slave, [a]to receive a mark on
their right hand or on their foreheads,
17 and that no one may buy or sell except
one who has *the mark or [a]the name of the beast,
[b]or the number of his name.
18 [a]Here is wisdom. Let him who has [b]under-
standing calculate [c]the number of the beast, [d]for
it is the number of a man: His number *is* 666.

The Lamb and the 144,000

14 Then I looked, and behold, *a [a]Lamb standing on Mount Zion, and with Him [b]one hundred *and* forty-four thousand, *having His Father's name [c]written on their foreheads.
2 And I heard a voice from heaven, [a]like
the voice of many waters, and like the voice of
loud thunder. And I heard the sound of [b]harpists
playing their harps.
3 They sang as it were a new song before
the throne, before the four living creatures, and
the elders; and no one could learn that song [a]ex-
cept the hundred *and* forty-four thousand who
were redeemed from the earth.
4 These are the ones who were not defiled
with women, [a]for they are virgins. These are the
ones [b]who follow the Lamb wherever He goes.
These [c]were *redeemed from *among* men, [d]*being*
firstfruits to God and to the Lamb.
5 And [a]in their mouth was found no *deceit,
for [b]they are without fault *before the throne of
God.

The Proclamations of Three Angels

6 Then I saw another angel [a]flying in the
midst of heaven, [b]having the everlasting gospel
to preach to those who dwell on the earth—[c]to
every nation, tribe, tongue, and people—
7 saying with a loud voice, [a]"Fear God and
give glory to Him, for the hour of His judgment
has come; [b]and worship Him who made heaven
and earth, the sea and springs of water."
8 And another angel followed, saying,
[a]"Babylon* is fallen, is fallen, that great city, because [b]she has made all nations drink of the wine
of the wrath of her fornication."
9 Then a third angel followed them, saying
with a loud voice, [a]"If anyone worships the beast

---

8 [a]Ex. 32:32 [b]Rev. 17:8
9 [a]Rev. 2:7
10 [a]Is. 33:1 [b]Gen. 9:6 [c]Rev. 14:12
11 [a]Rev. 11:7
12 [a]Rev. 13:3, 4
13 [a]Matt. 24:24 [b]1 Kin. 18:38
14 [a]Rev. 12:9 [b]2 Thess. 2:9 [c]2 Kin. 20:7
15 [a]Rev. 16:2
16 [a]Rev. 7:3; 14:9; 20:4
17 [a]Rev. 14:9–11 [b]Rev. 15:2
18 [a]Rev. 17:9 [b][1 Cor. 2:14] [c]Rev. 15:2 [d]Rev. 21:17

CHAPTER 14

1 [a]Rev. 5:6 [b]Rev. 7:4; 14:3 [c]Rev. 7:3; 22:4
2 [a]Rev. 1:15; 19:6 [b]Rev. 5:8
3 [a]Rev. 5:9
4 [a][2 Cor. 11:2] [b]Rev. 3:4; 7:17 [c]Rev. 5:9 [d]James 1:18
5 [a]Ps. 32:2 [b]Eph. 5:27
6 [a]Rev. 8:13 [b]Eph. 3:9 [c]Rev. 13:7
7 [a]Rev. 11:18 [b]Neh. 9:6
8 [a]Is. 21:9 [b]Jer. 51:7
9 [a]Rev. 13:14, 15; 14:11

*

13:14 M *my own people*
13:17 NU, M *the mark, the name*
14:1 NU, M *the* • NU, M add *His name and*
14:4 M adds *by Jesus*
14:5 NU, M *falsehood* • NU, M omit the rest of v. 5.
14:8 NU *Babylon the great is fallen, is fallen, which has made;* M *Babylon the great is fallen. She has made*

KJV

and his image, and receive *his* [b]mark in his forehead, or in his hand,

10 The same [a]shall drink of the wine of the wrath of God, which is [b]poured out without mixture into [c]the cup of his indignation; and [d]he shall be tormented with [e]fire and brimstone in the presence of the holy angels, and in the presence of the Lamb:

11 And [a]the smoke of their torment ascendeth up for ever and ever: and they have no rest day nor night, who worship the beast and his image, and whosoever receiveth the mark of his name.

12 [a]Here is the patience of the saints: [b]here *are* they that keep the commandments of God, and the faith of Jesus.

13 And I heard a voice from heaven saying unto me, Write, [a]Blessed *are* the dead [b]which die in the Lord from henceforth: Yea, saith the Spirit, [c]that they may rest from their labours; and their works do follow [d]them.

Reaping the Earth's Harvest

14 And I looked, and behold a white cloud, and upon the cloud *one* sat like unto the Son of man, having on his head a golden crown, and in his hand a sharp sickle.

15 And another angel [a]came out of the temple, crying with a loud voice to him that sat on the cloud, [b]Thrust in thy sickle, and reap: for the time is come for thee to reap; for the harvest [c]of the earth is ripe.

16 And he that sat on the cloud thrust in his sickle on the earth; and the earth was reaped.

Reaping the Grapes of Wrath

17 And another angel came out of the temple which is in heaven, he also having a sharp sickle.

18 And another angel came out from the altar, [a]which had power over fire; and cried with a loud cry to him that had the sharp sickle, saying, [b]Thrust in thy sharp sickle, and gather the clusters of the vine of the earth; for her grapes are fully ripe.

19 And the angel thrust in his sickle into the earth, and gathered the vine of the earth, and cast *it* into [a]the great winepress of the wrath of God.

20 And [a]the winepress was trodden [b]without the city, and blood came out of the winepress, [c]even unto the horse bridles, by the space of a thousand *and* six hundred furlongs.

Prelude to the Bowl Judgments

15 And [a]I saw another sign in heaven, great and marvellous, [b]seven angels having the seven last plagues; [c]for in them is filled up the wrath of God.

2 And I saw as it were [a]a sea of glass [b]mingled with fire: and them that had gotten the victory over the beast, [c]and over his image, and over his mark, *and* over the [d]number of his name, stand on the sea of glass, [e]having the harps of God.

3 And they sing [a]the song of Moses the servant of God, and the song of the [b]Lamb, saying, [c]Great and marvellous *are* thy works, Lord God Almighty; [d]just and true *are* thy ways, thou King of saints.

4 [a]Who shall not fear thee, O Lord, and glorify thy name? For *thou* only *art* [b]holy: for [c]all nations shall come and worship before thee; for thy judgments are made manifest.

5 And after that I looked, and, behold, [a]the temple of the tabernacle of the testimony in heaven was opened:

6 And the seven angels came out of the temple, having the seven plagues, [a]clothed in pure

---

9 [b]Rev. 13:16
10 [a]Ps. 75:8 [b]Rev. 18:6 [c]Rev. 16:19 [d]Rev. 20:10 [e]2 Thess. 1:7
11 [a]Is. 34:8–10
12 [a]Rev. 13:10 [b]Rev. 12:17
13 [a]Eccl. 4:1, 2 [b]1 Cor. 15:18 [c]Heb. 4:9, 10 [d][1 Cor. 3:11–15; 15:58]
15 [a]Rev. 16:17 [b]Joel 3:13 [c]Jer. 51:33
18 [a]Rev. 16:8 [b]Joel 3:13
19 [a]Rev. 19:15
20 [a]Is. 63:3 [b]Heb. 13:12 [c]Is. 34:3

CHAPTER 15

1 [a]Rev. 12:1, 3 [b]Rev. 21:9 [c]Rev. 14:10
2 [a]Rev. 4:6 [b][Matt. 3:11] [c]Rev. 13:14, 15 [d]Rev. 13:17 [e]Rev. 5:8
3 [a]Ex. 15:1–21 [b]Rev. 15:3 [c]Deut. 32:3, 4 [d]Ps. 145:17
4 [a]Ex. 15:14 [b]Lev. 11:44 [c]Is. 66:23
5 [a]Num. 1:50
6 [a]Ex. 28:6

*

14:12 NU, M omit *here are those*
14:13 NU, M omit *to me*
14:15 NU, M omit *for You*
15:2 NU, M omit *over his mark*
15:3 NU, M *nations*
15:5 NU, M omit *behold*

NKJV

and his image, and receives *his* [b]mark on his forehead or on his hand,

10 "he himself [a]shall also drink of the wine of the wrath of God, which is [b]poured out full strength into [c]the cup of His indignation. [d]He shall be tormented with [e]fire and brimstone in the presence of the holy angels and in the presence of the Lamb.

11 "And [a]the smoke of their torment ascends forever and ever; and they have no rest day or night, who worship the beast and his image, and whoever receives the mark of his name."

12 [a]Here is the patience of the saints; [b]here* *are* those who keep the commandments of God and the faith of Jesus.

13 Then I heard a voice from heaven saying *to me, "Write: [a]'Blessed *are* the dead [b]who die in the Lord from now on.' " "Yes," says the Spirit, [c]"that they may rest from their labors, and their works follow [d]them."

Reaping the Earth's Harvest

14 Then I looked, and behold, a white cloud, and on the cloud sat *One* like the Son of Man, having on His head a golden crown, and in His hand a sharp sickle.

15 And another angel [a]came out of the temple, crying with a loud voice to Him who sat on the cloud, [b]"Thrust in Your sickle and reap, for the time has come *for You to reap, for the harvest [c]of the earth is ripe."

16 So He who sat on the cloud thrust in His sickle on the earth, and the earth was reaped.

Reaping the Grapes of Wrath

17 Then another angel came out of the temple which is in heaven, he also having a sharp sickle.

18 And another angel came out from the altar, [a]who had power over fire, and he cried with a loud cry to him who had the sharp sickle, saying, [b]"Thrust in your sharp sickle and gather the clusters of the vine of the earth, for her grapes are fully ripe."

19 So the angel thrust his sickle into the earth and gathered the vine of the earth, and threw *it* into [a]the great winepress of the wrath of God.

20 And [a]the winepress was trampled [b]outside the city, and blood came out of the winepress, [c]up to the horses' bridles, for one thousand six hundred furlongs.

Prelude to the Bowl Judgments

15 Then [a]I saw another sign in heaven, great and marvelous: [b]seven angels having the seven last plagues, [c]for in them the wrath of God is complete.

2 And I saw *something* like [a]a sea of glass [b]mingled with fire, and those who have the victory over the beast, [c]over his image and *over his mark *and* over the [d]number of his name, standing on the sea of glass, [e]having harps of God.

3 They sing [a]the song of Moses, the servant of God, and the song of the [b]Lamb, saying:

> [c]"Great and marvelous *are* Your works,
> Lord God Almighty!
> [d]Just and true *are* Your ways,
> O King of the *saints!

4 [a]Who shall not fear You, O Lord, and
> glorify Your name?
> For *You* alone *are* [b]holy.
> For [c]all nations shall come and worship
> before You,
> For Your judgments have been
> manifested."

5 After these things I looked, and *behold, [a]the temple of the tabernacle of the testimony in heaven was opened.

6 And out of the temple came the seven angels having the seven plagues, [a]clothed in pure

KJV

and white linen, and having their breasts girded
with golden girdles.
7 [a]And one of the four beasts gave unto the
seven angels seven golden vials full of the wrath
of God, [b]who liveth for ever and ever.
8 And [a]the temple was filled with smoke
[b]from the glory of God, and from his power; and
no man was able to enter into the temple, till the
seven plagues of the seven angels were fulfilled.

16 And I heard a great voice out of the temple
saying [a]to the seven angels, Go your ways,
and pour out the vials [b]of the wrath of God upon
the earth.

First Bowl: Loathsome Sores

2 And the first went, and poured out his vial
[a]upon the earth; and [b]there fell a noisome and
grievous sore upon the men [c]which had the mark
of the beast, and *upon* them [d]which worshipped
his image.

Second Bowl: The Sea Turns to Blood

3 And the second angel poured out his vial
[a]upon the sea; and [b]it became as the blood of a
dead *man:* [c]and every living soul died in the sea.

Third Bowl: The Waters Turn to Blood

4 And the third angel poured out his vial
[a]upon the rivers and fountains of waters; [b]and
they became blood.
5 And I heard the angel of the waters say,
[a]Thou art righteous, O Lord, [b]which art, and wast,
and shalt be, because thou hast judged thus.
6 For [a]they have shed the blood [b]of saints
and prophets, [c]and thou hast given them blood
to drink; for they are worthy.
7 And I heard another out of the altar say,
Even so, [a]Lord God Almighty, [b]true and righteous
are thy judgments.

Fourth Bowl: Men Are Scorched

8 And the fourth angel poured out his vial
[a]upon the sun; [b]and power was given unto him
to scorch men with fire.
9 And men were scorched with great heat,
and [a]blasphemed the name of God, which hath
power over these plagues: [b]and they repented not
[c]to give him glory.

Fifth Bowl: Darkness and Pain

10 And the fifth angel poured out his vial
[a]upon the seat of the beast; [b]and his kingdom was
full of darkness; [c]and they gnawed their tongues
for pain,
11 And blasphemed the God of heaven because of their pains and their sores, and repented
not of their deeds.

Sixth Bowl: Euphrates Dried Up

12 And the sixth angel poured out his vial
[a]upon the great river Euphrates; [b]and the water
thereof was dried up, [c]that the way of the kings
of the east might be prepared.
13 And I saw three unclean [a]spirits like frogs
come out of the mouth of [b]the dragon, and out
of the mouth of the beast, and out of the mouth
of [c]the false prophet.
14 For they are the spirits of devils, [a]working
miracles, *which* go forth unto the kings of the
earth [b]and of the whole world, to gather them to
[c]the battle of that great day of God Almighty.
15 [a]Behold, I come as a thief. Blessed *is* he
that watcheth, and keepeth his garments, [b]lest he
walk naked, and they see his shame.
16 [a]And he gathered them together into a
place called in the Hebrew tongue Armageddon.

7 [a]Rev. 4:6 [b]1 Thess. 1:9
8 [a]Ex. 19:18; 40:34; Lev. 16:2; 1 Kin. 8:10; 2 Chr. 5:13; Is. 6:4 [b]2 Thess. 1:9

CHAPTER 16

1 [a]Rev. 15:1 [b]Rev. 14:10
2 [a]Rev. 8:7 [b]Ex. 9:9–11; Deut. 28:35; Rev. 16:11 [c]Rev. 13:15–17; 14:9 [d]Rev. 13:14
3 [a]Rev. 8:8; 11:6 [b]Ex. 7:17–21 [c]Rev. 8:9
4 [a]Rev. 8:10 [b]Ex. 7:17–20; Ps. 78:44; Rev. 11:6
5 [a]Rev. 15:3, 4 [b]Rev. 1:4, 8
6 [a]Matt. 23:34 [b]Rev. 11:18 [c]Is. 49:26; Luke 11:49–51
7 [a]Rev. 15:3 [b]Rev. 13:10; 19:2
8 [a]Rev. 8:12 [b]Rev. 9:17, 18
9 [a]Rev. 16:11 [b]Dan. 5:22 [c]Rev. 11:13
10 [a]Rev. 13:2 [b]Ex. 10:21; Is. 8:22; Rev. 8:12; 9:2 [c]Rev. 11:10
12 [a]Rev. 9:14 [b]Jer. 50:38 [c]Is. 41:2, 25; 46:11
13 [a]1 John 4:1 [b]Rev. 12:3, 9 [c]Rev. 13:11, 14; 19:20; 20:10
14 [a]2 Thess. 2:9 [b]Luke 2:1 [c]1 Kin. 22:21–23; Rev. 17:14; 19:19; 20:8
15 [a]Matt. 24:43; Luke 12:39; Rev. 3:3, 11 [b]2 Cor. 5:3
16 [a]Rev. 19:19

NKJV

bright linen, and having their chests girded with
golden bands.
7 [a]Then one of the four living creatures
gave to the seven angels seven golden bowls full
of the wrath of God [b]who lives forever and ever.
8 [a]The temple was filled with smoke [b]from
the glory of God and from His power, and no one
was able to enter the temple till the seven plagues
of the seven angels were completed.

16 Then I heard a loud voice from the temple
saying [a]to the seven angels, "Go and pour
out the *bowls [b]of the wrath of God on the earth."

First Bowl: Loathsome Sores

2 So the first went and poured out his bowl
[a]upon the earth, and a foul and [b]loathsome sore
came upon the men [c]who had the mark of the
beast and those [d]who worshiped his image.

Second Bowl: The Sea Turns to Blood

3 Then the second angel poured out his
bowl [a]on the sea, and [b]it became blood as of a
dead *man;* [c]and every living creature in the sea
died.

Third Bowl: The Waters Turn to Blood

4 Then the third angel poured out his bowl
[a]on the rivers and springs of water, [b]and they
became blood.
5 And I heard the angel of the waters saying:

[a]"You are righteous, *O Lord,
The One [b]who is and who *was and who
is to be,
Because You have judged these things.
6 For [a]they have shed the blood [b]of saints
and prophets,
[c]And You have given them blood to drink.
*For it is their just due."

7 And I heard *another from the altar saying, "Even so, [a]Lord God Almighty, [b]true and
righteous *are* Your judgments."

Fourth Bowl: Men Are Scorched

8 Then the fourth angel poured out his bowl
[a]on the sun, [b]and power was given to him to
scorch men with fire.
9 And men were scorched with great heat,
and they [a]blasphemed the name of God who has
power over these plagues; [b]and they did not repent [c]and give Him glory.

Fifth Bowl: Darkness and Pain

10 Then the fifth angel poured out his bowl
[a]on the throne of the beast, [b]and his kingdom became full of darkness; [c]and they gnawed their
tongues because of the pain.
11 They blasphemed the God of heaven because of their pains and their sores, and did not
repent of their deeds.

Sixth Bowl: Euphrates Dried Up

12 Then the sixth angel poured out his bowl
[a]on the great river Euphrates, [b]and its water was
dried up, [c]so that the way of the kings from the
east might be prepared.
13 And I saw three unclean [a]spirits like frogs
coming out of the mouth of [b]the dragon, out of
the mouth of the beast, and out of the mouth of
[c]the false prophet.
14 For they are spirits of demons, [a]perform-
ing signs, *which* go out to the kings *of the earth
and of [b]the whole world, to gather them to [c]the
battle of that great day of God Almighty.
15 [a]"Behold, I am coming as a thief. Blessed
is he who watches, and keeps his garments, [b]lest
he walk naked and they see his shame."
16 [a]And they gathered them together to the
place called in Hebrew, *Armageddon.

* 16:1 NU, M *seven bowls*
16:5 NU, M omit *O Lord* • NU, M *was, the Holy One*
16:6 NU, M omit *For*
16:7 NU, M omit *another from*
16:14 NU, M omit *of the earth and*
16:16 Lit. *Mount Megiddo;* M *Megiddo*

KJV

Seventh Bowl: The Earth Utterly Shaken

17 And the seventh angel poured out his vial into the air; and there came a great voice out of the temple of heaven, from the throne, saying, [a]It is done.

18 And [a]there were voices, and thunders, and lightnings; [b]and there was a great earthquake, [c]such as was not since men were upon the earth, so mighty an earthquake, *and* so great.

19 And [a]the great city was divided into three parts, and the cities of the nations fell: and [b]great Babylon [c]came in remembrance before God, [d]to give unto her the cup of the wine of the fierceness of his wrath.

20 And [a]every island fled away, and the mountains were not found.

21 And there fell upon men a great hail out of heaven, *every stone* about the weight of a talent: and men blasphemed God because of the plague of the hail; for the plague thereof was exceeding great.

The Scarlet Woman and the Scarlet Beast

17 And there came [a]one of the seven angels which had the seven vials, and talked with me, saying unto me, Come hither; [b]I will shew unto thee the judgment of [c]the great whore [d]that sitteth upon many waters:

2 [a]With whom the kings of the earth have committed fornication, and [b]the inhabitants of the earth have been made drunk with the wine of her fornication.

3 So he carried me away in the spirit [a]into the wilderness: and I saw a woman sit [b]upon a scarlet coloured beast, full of [c]names of blasphemy, having seven heads and ten horns.

4 And the woman [a]was arrayed in purple and scarlet colour, [b]and decked with gold and precious stones and pearls, [c]having a golden cup in her hand [d]full of abominations and filthiness of her fornication:

5 And upon her forehead *was* a name written, [a]MYSTERY, BABYLON THE GREAT, THE MOTHER OF HARLOTS AND ABOMINATIONS OF THE EARTH.

6 And I saw [a]the woman drunken [b]with the blood of the saints, and with the blood of [c]the martyrs of Jesus: and when I saw her, I wondered with great admiration.

The Meaning of the Woman and the Beast

7 And the angel said unto me, Wherefore didst thou marvel? I will tell thee the mystery of the woman, and of the beast that carrieth her, which hath the seven heads and ten horns.

8 The beast that thou sawest was, and is not; and [a]shall ascend out of the bottomless pit, and [b]go into perdition: and they that [c]dwell on the earth [d]shall wonder, [e]whose names were not written in the book of life from the foundation of the world, when they behold the beast that was, and is not, and yet is.

9 And [a]here *is* the mind which hath wisdom. [b]The seven heads are seven mountains, on which the woman sitteth.

10 And there are seven kings: five are fallen, and one is, *and* the other is not yet come; and when he cometh, he must [a]continue a short space.

11 And the [a]beast that was, and is not, even he is the eighth, and is of the seven, and goeth into perdition.

12 And [a]the ten horns which thou sawest are ten kings, which have received no kingdom as yet; but receive power as kings one hour with the beast.

13 These have one mind, and shall give their power and strength unto the beast.

14 [a]These shall make war with the Lamb, and the Lamb shall [b]overcome them: [c]for he is Lord of lords, and King of kings: [d]and they that are with him *are* called, and chosen, and faithful.

17 [a]Rev. 10:6; 21:6
18 [a]Rev. 4:5 [b]Rev. 11:13 [c]Dan. 12:1; Matt. 24:21
19 [a]Rev. 14:8 [b]Rev. 17:5, 18 [c]Rev. 14:8; 18:5 [d]Is. 51:17; Rev. 14:10
20 [a]Rev. 6:14; 20:11

CHAPTER 17

1 [a]Rev. 1:1; 21:9 [b]Rev. 16:19 [c]Is. 1:21; Jer. 2:20; Nah. 3:4; Rev. 17:5, 15; 19:2 [d]Jer. 51:13; Rev. 17:15
2 [a]Rev. 2:22; 18:3, 9 [b]Jer. 51:7; Rev. 14:8
3 [a]Rev. 12:6, 14; 21:10 [b]Rev. 12:3 [c]Rev. 13:1
4 [a]Ezek. 28:13; Rev. 18:12, 16 [b]Dan. 11:38 [c]Jer. 51:7; Rev. 18:6 [d]Rev. 14:8
5 [a]2 Thess. 2:7; Rev. 1:20; 17:7
6 [a]Rev. 18:24 [b]Rev. 13:15 [c]Rev. 6:9, 10
8 [a]Rev. 11:7 [b]Rev. 13:10; 17:11 [c]Rev. 3:10 [d]Rev. 13:3 [e]Matt. 25:34; Rev. 13:8
9 [a]Rev. 13:18 [b]Rev. 13:1
10 [a]Rev. 13:5
11 [a]Rev. 13:3, 12, 14; 17:8
12 [a]Dan. 7:20
14 [a]Rev. 16:14; 19:19 [b]Rev. 19:20 [c]Deut. 10:17; 1 Tim. 6:15; Rev. 19:16 [d]Jer. 50:44

NKJV

Seventh Bowl: The Earth Utterly Shaken

17 Then the seventh angel poured out his bowl into the air, and a loud voice came out of the temple of heaven, from the throne, saying, [a]"It is done!"

18 And [a]there were noises and thunderings and lightnings; [b]and there was a great earthquake, such a mighty and great earthquake [c]as had not occurred since men were on the earth.

19 Now [a]the great city was divided into three parts, and the cities of the nations fell. And [b]great Babylon [c]was remembered before God, [d]to give her the cup of the wine of the fierceness of His wrath.

20 Then [a]every island fled away, and the mountains were not found.

21 And great hail from heaven fell upon men, *each hailstone* about the weight of a talent. Men blasphemed God because of the plague of the hail, since that plague was exceedingly great.

The Scarlet Woman and the Scarlet Beast

17 Then [a]one of the seven angels who had the seven bowls came and talked with me, saying *to me, "Come, [b]I will show you the judgment of [c]the great harlot [d]who sits on many waters,

2 [a]"with whom the kings of the earth committed fornication, and [b]the inhabitants of the earth were made drunk with the wine of her fornication."

3 So he carried me away in the Spirit [a]into the wilderness. And I saw a woman sitting [b]on a scarlet beast *which was* full of [c]names of blasphemy, having seven heads and ten horns.

4 The woman [a]was arrayed in purple and scarlet, [b]and adorned with gold and precious stones and pearls, [c]having in her hand a golden cup [d]full of abominations and the filthiness of *her fornication.

5 And on her forehead a name *was* written:

[a]MYSTERY, BABYLON THE GREAT, THE MOTHER OF HARLOTS AND OF THE ABOMINATIONS OF THE EARTH.

6 I saw [a]the woman, drunk [b]with the blood of the saints and with the blood of [c]the martyrs of Jesus. And when I saw her, I marveled with great amazement.

The Meaning of the Woman and the Beast

7 But the angel said to me, "Why did you marvel? I will tell you the mystery of the woman and of the beast that carries her, which has the seven heads and the ten horns.

8 "The beast that you saw was, and is not, and [a]will ascend out of the bottomless pit and [b]go to perdition. And those who [c]dwell on the earth [d]will marvel, [e]whose names are not written in the Book of Life from the foundation of the world, when they see the beast that was, and is not, and *yet is.

9 [a]"Here *is* the mind which has wisdom: [b]The seven heads are seven mountains on which the woman sits.

10 "There are also seven kings. Five have fallen, one is, *and* the other has not yet come. And when he comes, he must [a]continue a short time.

11 "The [a]beast that was, and is not, is himself also the eighth, and is of the seven, and is going to perdition.

12 [a]"The ten horns which you saw are ten kings who have received no kingdom as yet, but they receive authority for one hour as kings with the beast.

13 "These are of one mind, and they will give their power and authority to the beast.

14 [a]"These will make war with the Lamb, and the Lamb will [b]overcome them, [c]for He is Lord of lords and King of kings; [d]and those *who are* with Him *are* called, chosen, and faithful."

17:1 NU, M omit *to me*
17:4 M *the fornication of the earth*
17:8 NU, M *shall be present*

KJV

15 And he saith unto me, [a]The waters which thou sawest, where the whore sitteth, [b]are peoples, and multitudes, and nations, and tongues.

16 And the ten horns which thou sawest upon the beast, [a]these shall hate the whore, and shall make her [b]desolate [c]and naked, and shall eat her flesh, and [d]burn her with fire.

17 [a]For God hath put in their hearts to fulfil his will, and to agree, and give their kingdom unto the beast, [b]until the words of God shall be fulfilled.

18 And the woman which thou sawest [a]is that great city, [b]which reigneth over the kings of the earth.

The Fall of Babylon the Great

18 And [a]after these things I saw another angel come down from heaven, having great power; [b]and the earth was lightened with his glory.

2 And he cried mightily with a strong voice, saying, [a]Babylon the great is fallen, is fallen, and [b]is become the habitation of devils, and the hold of every foul spirit, and [c]a cage of every unclean and hateful bird.

3 For all nations [a]have drunk of the wine of the wrath of her fornication, and the kings of the earth have committed fornication with her, [b]and the merchants of the earth are waxed rich through the abundance of her delicacies.

4 And I heard another voice from heaven, saying, [a]Come out of her, my people, that ye be not partakers of her sins, and that ye receive not of her plagues.

5 [a]For her sins have reached unto heaven, and [b]God hath remembered her iniquities.

6 [a]Reward her even as she rewarded you, and double unto her double according to her works: [b]in the cup which she hath filled [c]fill to her double.

7 [a]How much she hath glorified herself, and lived deliciously, so much torment and sorrow give her: for she saith in her heart, I sit a [b]queen, and am no widow, and shall see no sorrow.

8 Therefore shall her plagues come [a]in one day, death, and mourning, and famine; and [b]she shall be utterly burned with fire: [c]for strong *is* the Lord God who judgeth her.

The World Mourns Babylon's Fall

9 And [a]the kings of the earth, who have committed fornication and lived deliciously with her, [b]shall bewail her, and lament for her, [c]when they shall see the smoke of her burning,

10 Standing afar off for the fear of her torment, saying, [a]Alas, alas that great city Babylon, that mighty city! [b]for in one hour is thy judgment come.

11 And [a]the merchants of the earth shall weep and mourn over her; for no man buyeth their merchandise any more:

12 [a]The merchandise of gold, and silver, and precious stones, and of pearls, and fine linen, and purple, and silk, and scarlet, and all thyine wood, and all manner vessels of ivory, and all manner vessels of most precious wood, and of brass, and iron, and marble,

13 And cinnamon, and odours, and ointments, and frankincense, and wine, and oil, and fine flour, and wheat, and beasts, and sheep, and horses, and chariots, and slaves, and [a]souls of men.

14 And the fruits that thy soul lusted after are departed from thee, and all things which were dainty and goodly are departed from thee, and thou shalt find them no more at all.

15 The merchants of these things, which were made rich by her, shall stand afar off for the fear of her torment, weeping and wailing,

16 And saying, Alas, alas [a]that great city, [b]that was clothed in fine linen, and purple, and

---

15 [a]Is. 8:7; Jer. 47:2; Rev. 17:1 [b]Rev. 13:7
16 [a]Jer. 50:41 [b]Rev. 18:17, 19 [c]Ezek. 16:37, 39 [d]Rev. 18:8
17 [a]2 Thess. 2:11 [b]Rev. 10:7
18 [a]Rev. 11:8; 16:19 [b]Rev. 12:4

CHAPTER 18

1 [a]Rev. 17:1, 7 [b]Ezek. 43:2
2 [a]Is. 13:19; 21:9; Jer. 51:8; Rev. 14:8 [b]Is. 13:21; 34:11, 13–15; Jer. 50:39; 51:37; Zeph. 2:14 [c]Is. 14:23
3 [a]Jer. 51:7; Rev. 14:8 [b]Is. 47:15
4 [a]Is. 48:20
5 [a]Gen. 18:20 [b]Rev. 16:19
6 [a]Ps. 137:8; Jer. 50:15, 29 [b]Rev. 14:10 [c]Rev. 16:19
7 [a]Ezek. 28:2–8 [b]Is. 47:7, 8; Zeph. 2:15
8 [a]Is. 47:9; Jer. 50:31; Rev. 18:10 [b]Rev. 17:16 [c]Jer. 50:34; Heb. 10:31; Rev. 11:17
9 [a]Ezek. 26:16; 27:35 [b]Jer. 50:46; Rev. 17:2; 18:3 [c]Rev. 19:3
10 [a]Is. 21:9 [b]Rev. 18:17, 19
11 [a]Ezek. 27:27–34
12 [a]Ezek. 27:12–22; Rev. 17:4
13 [a]1 Chr. 5:21; Ezek. 27:13
16 [a]Rev. 17:18 [b]Rev. 17:4

*

17:16 NU, M *saw, and the beast*
18:2 NU, M omit *mightily*
18:5 NU, M *have been heaped up*
18:6 NU, M omit *to you*
18:8 NU, M *has judged*
18:14 NU, M *been lost to you*

NKJV

15 Then he said to me, [a]"The waters which you saw, where the harlot sits, [b]are peoples, multitudes, nations, and tongues.

16 "And the ten horns which you *saw on the beast, [a]these will hate the harlot, make her [b]desolate [c]and naked, eat her flesh and [d]burn her with fire.

17 [a]"For God has put it into their hearts to fulfill His purpose, to be of one mind, and to give their kingdom to the beast, [b]until the words of God are fulfilled.

18 "And the woman whom you saw [a]is that great city [b]which reigns over the kings of the earth."

The Fall of Babylon the Great

18 After[a] these things I saw another angel coming down from heaven, having great authority, [b]and the earth was illuminated with his glory.

2 And he cried *mightily with a loud voice, saying, [a]"Babylon the great is fallen, is fallen, and [b]has become a dwelling place of demons, a prison for every foul spirit, and [c]a cage for every unclean and hated bird!

3 "For all the nations [a]have drunk of the wine of the wrath of her fornication, the kings of the earth have committed fornication with her, [b]and the merchants of the earth have become rich through the abundance of her luxury."

4 And I heard another voice from heaven saying, [a]"Come out of her, my people, lest you share in her sins, and lest you receive of her plagues.

5 [a]"For her sins *have reached to heaven, and [b]God has remembered her iniquities.

6 [a]"Render to her just as she rendered *to you, and repay her double according to her works; [b]in the cup which she has mixed, [c]mix double for her.

7 [a]"In the measure that she glorified herself and lived luxuriously, in the same measure give her torment and sorrow; for she says in her heart, 'I sit *as* [b]queen, and am no widow, and will not see sorrow.'

8 "Therefore her plagues will come [a]in one day—death and mourning and famine. And [b]she will be utterly burned with fire, [c]for strong *is* the Lord God who *judges her.

The World Mourns Babylon's Fall

9 [a]"The kings of the earth who committed fornication and lived luxuriously with her [b]will weep and lament for her, [c]when they see the smoke of her burning,

10 "standing at a distance for fear of her torment, saying, [a]'Alas, alas, that great city Babylon, that mighty city! [b]For in one hour your judgment has come.'

11 "And [a]the merchants of the earth will weep and mourn over her, for no one buys their merchandise anymore:

12 [a]"merchandise of gold and silver, precious stones and pearls, fine linen and purple, silk and scarlet, every kind of citron wood, every kind of object of ivory, every kind of object of most precious wood, bronze, iron, and marble;

13 "and cinnamon and incense, fragrant oil and frankincense, wine and oil, fine flour and wheat, cattle and sheep, horses and chariots, and bodies and [a]souls of men.

14 "The fruit that your soul longed for has gone from you, and all the things which are rich and splendid have *gone from you, and you shall find them no more at all.

15 "The merchants of these things, who became rich by her, will stand at a distance for fear of her torment, weeping and wailing,

16 "and saying, 'Alas, alas, [a]that great city [b]that was clothed in fine linen, purple, and scarlet,

KJV

scarlet, and decked with gold, and precious stones, and pearls!

17 [a]For in one hour so great riches is come to nought. And [b]every shipmaster, and all the company in ships, and sailors, and as many as trade by sea, stood afar off,

18 [a]And cried when they saw the smoke of her burning, saying, [b]What *city is* like unto this great city!

19 And [a]they cast dust on their heads, and cried, weeping and wailing, saying, Alas, alas that great city, wherein were made rich all that had ships in the sea by reason of her costliness! [b]for in one hour is she made desolate.

20 [a]Rejoice over her, *thou* heaven, and *ye* holy apostles and prophets; for [b]God hath avenged you on her.

Finality of Babylon's Fall

21 And a mighty angel took up a stone like a great millstone, and cast *it* into the sea, saying, [a]Thus with violence shall that great city Babylon be thrown down, and [b]shall be found no more at all.

22 [a]And the voice of harpers, and musicians, and of pipers, and trumpeters, shall be heard no more at all in thee; and no craftsman, of whatsoever craft *he be,* shall be found any more in thee; and the sound of a millstone shall be heard no more at all in thee;

23 [a]And the light of a candle shall shine no more at all in thee; [b]and the voice of the bridegroom and of the bride shall be heard no more at all in thee: for [c]thy merchants were the great men of the earth; [d]for by thy sorceries were all nations deceived.

24 And [a]in her was found the blood of prophets, and of saints, and of all that [b]were slain upon the earth.

Heaven Exults over Babylon

19 And after these things [a]I heard a great voice of much people in heaven, saying, Alleluia; [b]Salvation, and glory, and honour, and power, unto the Lord our God:

2 For [a]true and righteous *are* his judgments: for he hath judged the great whore, which did corrupt the earth with her fornication, and [b]hath avenged the blood of his servants at her hand.

3 And again they said, Alleluia. [a]And her smoke rose up for ever and ever.

4 And [a]the four and twenty elders and the four beasts fell down and worshipped God that sat on the throne, saying, [b]Amen; Alleluia.

5 And a voice came out of the throne, saying, [a]Praise our God, all ye his servants, and ye that fear him, [b]both small and great.

6 [a]And I heard as it were the voice of a great multitude, and as the voice of many waters, and as the voice of mighty thunderings, saying, Alleluia: for [b]the Lord God omnipotent reigneth.

7 Let us be glad and rejoice, and give honour to him: for [a]the marriage of the Lamb is come, and his wife hath made herself ready.

8 And [a]to her was granted that she should be arrayed in fine linen, clean and white: [b]for the fine linen is the righteousness of saints.

9 And he saith unto me, Write, [a]Blessed *are* they which are called unto the marriage supper of the Lamb. And he saith unto me, [b]These are the true sayings of God.

10 And [a]I fell at his feet to worship him. And he said unto me, [b]See *thou do it* not: I am thy [c]fellowservant, and of thy brethren [d]that have the testimony of Jesus: worship God: for the [e]testimony of Jesus is the spirit of prophecy.

Christ on a White Horse

11 [a]And I saw heaven opened, and behold [b]a white horse; and he that sat upon him *was*

---

17 [a]Rev. 18:10 [b]Is. 23:14
18 [a]Ezek. 27:30 [b]Rev. 13:4
19 [a]Josh. 7:6 [b]Rev. 18:8
20 [a]Jer. 51:48 [b]Luke 11:49
21 [a]Jer. 51:63, 64 [b]Rev. 12:8; 16:20
22 [a]Jer. 7:34; 16:9; 25:10
23 [a]Jer. 25:10 [b]Jer. 7:34; 16:9 [c]Is. 23:8 [d]2 Kin. 9:22
24 [a]Rev. 16:6; 17:6 [b]Jer. 51:49

CHAPTER 19

1 [a]Rev. 11:15; 19:6 [b]Rev. 4:11
2 [a]Rev. 15:3; 16:7 [b]Deut. 32:43
3 [a]Is. 34:10
4 [a]Rev. 4:4, 6, 10 [b]1 Chr. 16:36
5 [a]Ps. 134:1 [b]Rev. 11:18
6 [a]Ezek. 1:24 [b]Rev. 11:15
7 [a][Matt. 22:2; 25:10]
8 [a]Ezek. 16:10 [b]Ps. 132:9
9 [a]Luke 14:15 [b]Rev. 22:6
10 [a]Rev. 22:8 [b]Acts 10:26 [c][Heb. 1:14] [d]1 John 5:10 [e]Luke 24:27
11 [a]Rev. 15:5 [b]Rev. 6:2; 19:19, 21

NKJV

and adorned with gold and precious stones and pearls!

17 [a]'For in one hour such great riches came to nothing.' [b]Every shipmaster, all who travel by ship, sailors, and as many as trade on the sea, stood at a distance

18 [a]"and cried out when they saw the smoke of her burning, saying, [b]'What *is* like this great city?'

19 [a]"They threw dust on their heads and cried out, weeping and wailing, and saying, 'Alas, alas, that great city, in which all who had ships on the sea became rich by her wealth! [b]For in one hour she is made desolate.'

20 [a]"Rejoice over her, O heaven, and *you* *holy apostles and prophets, for [b]God has avenged you on her!"

Finality of Babylon's Fall

21 Then a mighty angel took up a stone like a great millstone and threw *it* into the sea, saying, [a]"Thus with violence the great city Babylon shall be thrown down, and [b]shall not be found anymore.

22 [a]"The sound of harpists, musicians, flutists, and trumpeters shall not be heard in you anymore. No craftsman of any craft shall be found in you anymore, and the sound of a millstone shall not be heard in you anymore.

23 [a]"The light of a lamp shall not shine in you anymore, [b]and the voice of bridegroom and bride shall not be heard in you anymore. For [c]your merchants were the great men of the earth, [d]for by your sorcery all the nations were deceived.

24 "And [a]in her was found the blood of prophets and saints, and of all who [b]were slain on the earth."

Heaven Exults over Babylon

19 After these things [a]I *heard a loud voice of a great multitude in heaven, saying, "Alleluia! [b]Salvation and glory and honor and power *belong* to *the Lord our God!

2 "For [a]true and righteous *are* His judgments, because He has judged the great harlot who corrupted the earth with her fornication; and He [b]has avenged on her the blood of His servants *shed* by her."

3 Again they said, "Alleluia! [a]Her smoke rises up forever and ever!"

4 And [a]the twenty-four elders and the four living creatures fell down and worshiped God who sat on the throne, saying, [b]"Amen! Alleluia!"

5 Then a voice came from the throne, saying, [a]"Praise our God, all you His servants and those who fear Him, [b]both* small and great!"

6 [a]And I heard, as it were, the voice of a great multitude, as the sound of many waters and as the sound of mighty thunderings, saying, "Alleluia! For [b]the* Lord God Omnipotent reigns!

7 "Let us be glad and rejoice and give Him glory, for [a]the marriage of the Lamb has come, and His wife has made herself ready."

8 And [a]to her it was granted to be arrayed in fine linen, clean and bright, [b]for the fine linen is the righteous acts of the saints.

9 Then he said to me, "Write: [a]'Blessed *are* those who are called to the marriage supper of the Lamb!'" And he said to me, [b]"These are the true sayings of God."

10 And [a]I fell at his feet to worship him. But he said to me, [b]"See *that you do* not *do that!* I am your [c]fellow servant, and of your brethren [d]who have the testimony of Jesus. Worship God! For the [e]testimony of Jesus is the spirit of prophecy."

Christ on a White Horse

11 [a]Now I saw heaven opened, and behold, [b]a white horse. And He who sat on him *was* called

---

*

18:20 NU, M *saints and apostles*
19:1 NU, M add *something like*
• NU, M omit *the Lord*
19:5 NU, M omit *both*
19:6 NU, M *our*

KJV

called [c]Faithful and True, and [d]in righteousness he doth judge and make war.

12 [a]His eyes *were* as a flame of fire, and on his head *were* many crowns; [b]and he had a name written, that no man knew, but he himself.

13 [a]And he *was* clothed with a vesture dipped in blood: and his name is called [b]The Word of God.

14 [a]And the armies *which were* in heaven followed him upon white horses, [b]clothed in fine linen, white and clean.

15 And [a]out of his mouth goeth a sharp sword, that with it he should smite the nations: and [b]he shall rule them with a rod of iron: and [c]he treadeth the winepress of the fierceness and wrath of Almighty God.

16 And [a]he hath on *his* vesture and on his thigh a name written, [b]KING OF KINGS, AND LORD OF LORDS.

The Beast and His Armies Defeated

17 And I saw an angel standing in the sun; and he cried with a loud voice, saying to all the fowls that fly in the midst of heaven, [a]Come and gather yourselves together unto the supper of the great God;

18 [a]That ye may eat the flesh of kings, and the flesh of captains, and the flesh of mighty men, and the flesh of horses, and of them that sit on them, and the flesh of all *men, both* free and bond, both small and great.

19 [a]And I saw the beast, and the kings of the earth, and their armies, gathered together to make war against him that sat on the horse, and against his army.

20 [a]And the beast was taken, and with him the false prophet that wrought miracles before him, with which he deceived them that had received the mark of the beast, and [b]them that worshipped his image. [c]These both were cast alive into a lake of fire [d]burning with brimstone.

21 And the remnant [a]were slain with the sword of him that sat upon the horse, which *sword* proceeded out of his mouth: [b]and all the fowls [c]were filled with their flesh.

Satan Bound 1000 Years

20 And I saw an angel come down from heaven, [a]having the key of the bottomless pit and a great chain in his hand.

2 And he laid hold on [a]the dragon, that old serpent, which is the Devil, and Satan, and bound him a thousand years,

3 And cast him into the bottomless pit, and shut him up, and [a]set a seal upon him, [b]that he should deceive the nations no more, till the thousand years should be fulfilled: and after that he must be loosed a little season.

The Saints Reign with Christ 1000 Years

4 And I saw [a]thrones, and they sat upon them, and [b]judgment was given unto them: and *I saw* [c]the souls of them that were beheaded for the witness of Jesus, and for the word of God, and [d]which had not worshipped the beast, [e]neither his image, neither had received *his* mark upon their foreheads, or in their hands; and they [f]lived and [g]reigned with Christ a thousand years.

5 But the rest of the dead lived not again until the thousand years were finished. This *is* the first resurrection.

6 Blessed and holy *is* he that hath part in the first resurrection: on such [a]the second death hath no power, but they shall be [b]priests of God and of Christ, [c]and shall reign with him a thousand years.

Satanic Rebellion Crushed
(cf. Ezek. 38; 39)

7 And when the thousand years are expired, Satan shall be loosed out of his prison,

8 And shall go out [a]to deceive the nations

11 [c]Rev. 3:7, 14 [d]Is. 11:4
12 [a]Rev. 1:14 [b]Rev. 2:17; 19:16
13 [a]Is. 63:2, 3 [b][John 1:1, 14]
14 [a]Rev. 14:20 [b]Matt. 28:3
15 [a]Is. 11:4 [b]Ps. 2:8, 9 [c]Is. 63:3–6
16 [a]Rev. 2:17; 19:12 [b]Dan. 2:47
17 [a]Ezek. 39:17
18 [a]Ezek. 39:18–20
19 [a]Rev. 16:13–16
20 [a]Rev. 16:13 [b]Rev. 13:8, 12, 13 [c]Dan. 7:11 [d]Rev. 14:10
21 [a]Rev. 19:15 [b]Rev. 19:17, 18 [c]Rev. 17:16

CHAPTER 20

1 [a]Rev. 1:18; 9:1
2 [a]2 Pet. 2:4
3 [a]Dan. 6:17 [b]Rev. 12:9; 20:8, 10
4 [a]Dan. 7:9 [b][1 Cor. 6:2, 3] [c]Rev. 6:9 [d]Rev. 13:12 [e]Rev. 13:15 [f]John 14:19 [g]Rom. 8:17
6 [a][Rev. 2:11; 20:14] [b]Is. 61:6 [c]Rev. 20:4
8 [a]Rev. 12:9; 20:3, 10

*

19:12 M adds *names written, and*
19:14 NU, M *pure white linen*
19:15 M *sharp two-edged*
19:17 NU, M *great supper of God*
19:18 NU, M *both free*
20:4 M *the*

NKJV

[c]Faithful and True, and [d]in righteousness He judges and makes war.

12 [a]His eyes *were* like a flame of fire, and on His head *were* many crowns. [b]He *had a name written that no one knew except Himself.

13 [a]He *was* clothed with a robe dipped in blood, and His name is called [b]The Word of God.

14 [a]And the armies in heaven, [b]clothed in *fine linen, white and clean, followed Him on white horses.

15 Now [a]out of His mouth goes a *sharp sword, that with it He should strike the nations. And [b]He Himself will rule them with a rod of iron. [c]He Himself treads the winepress of the fierceness and wrath of Almighty God.

16 And [a]He has on *His* robe and on His thigh a name written:

[b]KING OF KINGS AND LORD OF LORDS.

The Beast and His Armies Defeated

17 Then I saw an angel standing in the sun; and he cried with a loud voice, saying to all the birds that fly in the midst of heaven, [a]"Come and gather together for the *supper of the great God,

18 [a]"that you may eat the flesh of kings, the flesh of captains, the flesh of mighty men, the flesh of horses and of those who sit on them, and the flesh of all *people*, *free and slave, both small and great."

19 [a]And I saw the beast, the kings of the earth, and their armies, gathered together to make war against Him who sat on the horse and against His army.

20 [a]Then the beast was captured, and with him the false prophet who worked signs in his presence, by which he deceived those who received the mark of the beast and [b]those who worshiped his image. [c]These two were cast alive into the lake of fire [d]burning with brimstone.

21 And the rest [a]were killed with the sword which proceeded from the mouth of Him who sat on the horse. [b]And all the birds [c]were filled with their flesh.

Satan Bound 1000 Years

20 Then I saw an angel coming down from heaven, [a]having the key to the bottomless pit and a great chain in his hand.

2 He laid hold of [a]the dragon, that serpent of old, who is *the* Devil and Satan, and bound him for a thousand years;

3 and he cast him into the bottomless pit, and shut him up, and [a]set a seal on him, [b]so that he should deceive the nations no more till the thousand years were finished. But after these things he must be released for a little while.

The Saints Reign with Christ 1000 Years

4 And I saw [a]thrones, and they sat on them, and [b]judgment was committed to them. Then *I saw* [c]the souls of those who had been beheaded for their witness to Jesus and for the word of God, [d]who had not worshiped the beast [e]or his image, and had not received *his* mark on their foreheads or on their hands. And they [f]lived and [g]reigned with Christ for *a thousand years.

5 But the rest of the dead did not live again until the thousand years were finished. This *is* the first resurrection.

6 Blessed and holy *is* he who has part in the first resurrection. Over such [a]the second death has no power, but they shall be [b]priests of God and of Christ, [c]and shall reign with Him a thousand years.

Satanic Rebellion Crushed
(cf. Ezek. 38; 39)

7 Now when the thousand years have expired, Satan will be released from his prison

8 and will go out [a]to deceive the nations

KJV

which are in the four quarters of the earth, [b]Gog and Magog, [c]to gather them together to battle: the number of whom *is* as the sand of the sea.

9 [a]And they went up on the breadth of the earth, and compassed the camp of the saints about, and the beloved city: and fire came down from God out of heaven, and devoured them.

10 And the devil that deceived them was cast into the lake of fire and brimstone, [a]where the beast and the false prophet *are*, and [b]shall be tormented day and night for ever and ever.

The Great White Throne Judgment

11 And I saw a great white throne, and him that sat on it, from whose face [a]the earth and the heaven fled away; [b]and there was found no place for them.

12 And I saw the dead, [a]small and great, stand before God; [b]and the books were opened: and another [c]book was opened, which is *the book* of life: and the dead were judged out of those things which were written in the books, [d]according to their works.

13 And the sea gave up the dead which were in it; [a]and death and hell delivered up the dead which were in them: [b]and they were judged every man according to their works.

14 And [a]death and hell were cast into the lake of fire. [b]This is the second death.

15 And whosoever was not found written in the book of life [a]was cast into the lake of fire.

All Things Made New

21 And [a]I saw a new heaven and a new earth: [b]for the first heaven and the first earth were passed away; and there was no more sea.

2 And I John saw [a]the holy city, new Jerusalem, coming down from God out of heaven, prepared [b]as a bride adorned for her husband.

3 And I heard a great voice out of heaven saying, Behold, [a]the tabernacle of God *is* with men, and he will dwell with them, and they shall be his people, and God himself shall be with them, *and be* their God.

4 [a]And God shall wipe away all tears from their eyes; and [b]there shall be no more death, [c]neither sorrow, nor crying, neither shall there be any more pain: for the former things are passed away.

5 And [a]he that sat upon the throne said, [b]Behold, I make all things new. And he said unto me, Write: for [c]these words are true and faithful.

6 And he said unto me, [a]It is done. [b]I am Alpha and Omega, the beginning and the end. [c]I will give unto him that is athirst of the fountain of the water of life freely.

7 He that overcometh shall inherit all things; and [a]I will be his God, and he shall be my son.

8 [a]But the fearful, and unbelieving, and the abominable, and murderers, and whoremongers, and sorcerers, and idolaters, and all liars, shall have their part in [b]the lake which burneth with fire and brimstone: which is the second death.

The New Jerusalem
(cf. Ezek. 48:30–35)

9 And there came unto me one of [a]the seven angels which had the seven vials full of the seven last plagues, and talked with me, saying, Come hither, I will shew thee [b]the bride, the Lamb's wife.

10 And he carried me away [a]in the spirit to a great and high mountain, and shewed me [b]that great city, the holy Jerusalem, descending out of heaven from God,

11 [a]Having the glory of God: and her light *was* like unto a stone most precious, even like a jasper stone, clear as crystal;

12 And had a wall great and high, *and* had [a]twelve gates, and at the gates twelve angels, and

---

8 [b]Ezek. 38:2; 39:1, 6 [c]Rev. 16:14
9 [a]Ezek. 38:9, 16
10 [a]Rev. 19:20; 20:14, 15 [b]Rev. 14:10
11 [a]2 Pet. 3:7 [b]Dan. 2:35
12 [a]Rev. 19:5 [b]Dan. 7:10 [c]Ps. 69:28 [d]Matt. 16:27
13 [a]Rev. 1:18; 6:8; 21:4 [b]Rev. 2:23; 20:12
14 [a]1 Cor. 15:26 [b]Rev. 21:8
15 [a]Rev. 19:20

CHAPTER 21

1 [a][2 Pet. 3:13] [b]Rev. 20:11
2 [a]Is. 52:1 [b]2 Cor. 11:2
3 [a]Lev. 26:11
4 [a]Is. 25:8 [b]1 Cor. 15:26 [c]Is. 35:10; 51:11; 65:19
5 [a]Rev. 4:2, 9; 20:11 [b]Is. 43:19 [c]Rev. 19:9; 22:6
6 [a]Rev. 10:6; 16:17 [b]Rev. 1:8; 22:13 [c]John 4:10
7 [a]Zech. 8:8
8 [a]1 Cor. 6:9 [b]Rev. 20:14
9 [a]Rev. 15:1 [b]Rev. 19:7; 21:2
10 [a]Rev. 1:10 [b]Ezek. 48
11 [a]Rev. 15:8; 21:23; 22:5
12 [a]Ezek. 48:31–34

*

20:10 NU, M *where also*
20:12 NU, M *the throne*
20:14 NU, M *death, the lake of fire.*
21:2 NU, M omit *John*
21:5 NU, M omit *to me*
21:6 M omits *It is done*
21:7 M *I shall give him these things*
21:8 M adds *and sinners,*
21:9 NU, M omit *to me* • M *woman, the Lamb's bride*
21:10 NU, M omit *great* • NU, M *holy city, Jerusalem*

NKJV

which are in the four corners of the earth, [b]Gog and Magog, [c]to gather them together to battle, whose number *is* as the sand of the sea.

9 [a]They went up on the breadth of the earth and surrounded the camp of the saints and the beloved city. And fire came down from God out of heaven and devoured them.

10 The devil, who deceived them, was cast into the lake of fire and brimstone [a]where* the beast and the false prophet *are*. And they [b]will be tormented day and night forever and ever.

The Great White Throne Judgment

11 Then I saw a great white throne and Him who sat on it, from whose face [a]the earth and the heaven fled away. [b]And there was found no place for them.

12 And I saw the dead, [a]small and great, standing before *God, [b]and books were opened. And another [c]book was opened, which is *the* Book of Life. And the dead were judged [d]according to their works, by the things which were written in the books.

13 The sea gave up the dead who were in it, [a]and Death and Hades delivered up the dead who were in them. [b]And they were judged, each one according to his works.

14 Then [a]Death and Hades were cast into the lake of fire. [b]This is the second *death.

15 And anyone not found written in the Book of Life [a]was cast into the lake of fire.

All Things Made New

21 Now [a]I saw a new heaven and a new earth, [b]for the first heaven and the first earth had passed away. Also there was no more sea.

2 Then I, *John, saw [a]the holy city, New Jerusalem, coming down out of heaven from God, prepared [b]as a bride adorned for her husband.

3 And I heard a loud voice from heaven saying, "Behold, [a]the tabernacle of God *is* with men, and He will dwell with them, and they shall be His people. God Himself will be with them *and be* their God.

4 [a]"And God will wipe away every tear from their eyes; [b]there shall be no more death, [c]nor sorrow, nor crying. There shall be no more pain, for the former things have passed away."

5 Then [a]He who sat on the throne said, [b]"Behold, I make all things new." And He said *to me, "Write, for [c]these words are true and faithful."

6 And He said to me, [a]"It* is done! [b]I am the Alpha and the Omega, the Beginning and the End. [c]I will give of the fountain of the water of life freely to him who thirsts.

7 "He who overcomes *shall inherit all things, and [a]I will be his God and he shall be My son.

8 [a]"But the cowardly, *unbelieving, abominable, murderers, sexually immoral, sorcerers, idolaters, and all liars shall have their part in [b]the lake which burns with fire and brimstone, which is the second death."

The New Jerusalem
(cf. Ezek. 48:30–35)

9 Then one of [a]the seven angels who had the seven bowls filled with the seven last plagues came *to me and talked with me, saying, "Come, I will show you [b]the *bride, the Lamb's wife."

10 And he carried me away [a]in the Spirit to a great and high mountain, and showed me [b]the *great city, the *holy Jerusalem, descending out of heaven from God,

11 [a]having the glory of God. Her light *was* like a most precious stone, like a jasper stone, clear as crystal.

12 Also she had a great and high wall with [a]twelve gates, and twelve angels at the gates, and

KJV

names written thereon, which are *the names* of
the twelve tribes of the children of Israel:
13 [a]On the east three gates; on the north
three gates; on the south three gates; and on the
west three gates.
14 And the wall of the city had twelve foundations, and [a]in them the names of the twelve
apostles of the Lamb.
15 And he that talked with me [a]had a golden
reed to measure the city, and the gates thereof,
and the wall thereof.
16 And the city lieth foursquare, and the
length is as large as the breadth: and he measured
the city with the reed, twelve thousand furlongs.
The length and the breadth and the height of it
are equal.
17 And he measured the wall thereof, an hundred *and* forty *and* four cubits, *according to* the
measure of a man, that is, of the angel.
18 And the building of the wall of it was *of*
jasper: and the city *was* pure gold, like unto clear
glass.
19 [a]And the foundations of the wall of the
city *were* garnished with all manner of precious
stones. The first foundation *was* jasper; the second, sapphire; the third, a chalcedony; the fourth,
an emerald;
20 The fifth, sardonyx; the sixth, sardius; the
seventh, chrysolyte; the eighth, beryl; the ninth,
a topaz; the tenth, a chrysoprasus; the eleventh,
a jacinth; the twelfth, an amethyst.
21 And the twelve gates *were* twelve [a]pearls;
every several gate was of one pearl: [b]and the
street of the city *was* pure gold, as it were transparent glass.

The Glory of the New Jerusalem

22 [a]And I saw no temple therein: for the Lord
God Almighty and the Lamb are the temple of it.
23 [a]And the city had no need of the sun, neither of the moon, to shine in it: for the glory of
God did lighten it, and the Lamb *is* the light
thereof.
24 [a]And the nations of them which are saved
shall walk in the light of it: and the kings of the
earth do bring their glory and honour into it.
25 [a]And the gates of it shall not be shut at
all by day: for [b]there shall be no night there.
26 [a]And they shall bring the glory and honour of the nations into it.
27 And [a]there shall in no wise enter into it
any thing that defileth, neither *whatsoever* worketh abomination, or *maketh* a lie: but they which
are written in the Lamb's [b]book of life.

The River of Life

22 And he shewed me [a]a pure river of water
of life, clear as crystal, proceeding out of
the throne of God and of the Lamb.
2 [a]In the midst of the street of it, and on
either side of the river, *was there* [b]the tree of life,
which bare twelve *manner of* fruits, *and* yielded
her fruit every month: and the leaves of the tree
were [c]for the healing of the nations.
3 And [a]there shall be no more curse: [b]but
the throne of God and of the Lamb shall be in it;
and his [c]servants shall serve him:
4 And [a]they shall see his face; and [b]his
name *shall be* in their foreheads.
5 [a]And there shall be no night there; and
they need no candle, neither [b]light of the sun; for
[c]the Lord God giveth them light: [d]and they shall
reign for ever and ever.

The Time Is Near

6 And he said unto me, [a]These sayings *are*
faithful and true: and the Lord God of the holy
prophets [b]sent his angel to shew unto his servants
the things which must [c]shortly be done.
7 [a]Behold, I come quickly: [b]blessed *is* he
that keepeth the sayings of the prophecy of this
book.

NKJV

names written on them, which are *the names* of
the twelve tribes of the children of Israel:
13 [a]three gates on the east, three gates on
the north, three gates on the south, and three
gates on the west.
14 Now the wall of the city had twelve foundations, and [a]on them were the *names of the
twelve apostles of the Lamb.
15 And he who talked with me [a]had a gold
reed to measure the city, its gates, and its wall.
16 The city is laid out as a square; its length
is as great as its breadth. And he measured the
city with the reed: twelve thousand furlongs. Its
length, breadth, and height are equal.
17 Then he measured its wall: one hundred
and forty-four cubits, *according* to the measure
of a man, that is, of an angel.
18 The construction of its wall was *of* jasper;
and the city *was* pure gold, like clear glass.
19 [a]The foundations of the wall of the city
were adorned with all kinds of precious stones:
the first foundation *was* jasper, the second sapphire, the third chalcedony, the fourth emerald,
20 the fifth sardonyx, the sixth sardius, the
seventh chrysolite, the eighth beryl, the ninth topaz, the tenth chrysoprase, the eleventh jacinth,
and the twelfth amethyst.
21 The twelve gates *were* twelve [a]pearls:
each individual gate was of one pearl. [b]And the
street of the city *was* pure gold, like transparent
glass.

The Glory of the New Jerusalem

22 [a]But I saw no temple in it, for the Lord
God Almighty and the Lamb are its temple.
23 [a]The city had no need of the sun or of
the moon to shine *in it, for the *glory of God
illuminated it. The Lamb *is* its light.
24 [a]And the nations *of those who are saved
shall walk in its light, and the kings of the earth
bring their glory and honor *into it.
25 [a]Its gates shall not be shut at all by day
[b](there shall be no night there).
26 [a]And they shall bring the glory and the
honor of the nations into *it.
27 But [a]there shall by no means enter it anything *that defiles, or causes an abomination or
a lie, but only those who are written in the Lamb's
[b]Book of Life.

The River of Life

22 And he showed me [a]a *pure river of water
of life, clear as crystal, proceeding from the
throne of God and of the Lamb.
2 [a]In the middle of its street, and on either
side of the river, *was* [b]the tree of life, which bore
twelve fruits, each *tree* yielding its fruit every
month. The leaves of the tree *were* [c]for the healing
of the nations.
3 And [a]there shall be no more curse, [b]but
the throne of God and of the Lamb shall be in it,
and His [c]servants shall serve Him.
4 [a]They shall see His face, and [b]His name
shall be on their foreheads.
5 [a]There shall be no night there: They need
no lamp nor [b]light of the sun, for [c]the Lord God
gives them light. [d]And they shall reign forever
and ever.

The Time Is Near

6 Then he said to me, [a]"These words *are*
faithful and true." And the Lord God of the *holy
prophets [b]sent His angel to show His servants the
things which must [c]shortly take place.
7 [a]"Behold, I am coming quickly! [b]Blessed
is he who keeps the words of the prophecy of this
book."

---

13 [a]Ezek. 48:31–34
14 [a]Eph. 2:20
15 [a]Ezek. 40:3
19 [a]Is. 54:11
21 [a]Matt. 13:45, 46 [b]Rev. 22:2
22 [a]John 4:21, 23
23 [a]Is. 24:23; 60:19, 20
24 [a]Is. 60:3, 5; 66:12
25 [a]Is. 60:11 [b]Is. 60:20
26 [a]Rev. 21:24
27 [a]Joel 3:17 [b]Phil. 4:3

CHAPTER 22
1 [a]Ezek. 47:1
2 [a]Ezek. 47:12 [b]Gen. 2:9 [c]Rev. 21:24
3 [a]Zech. 14:11 [b]Ezek. 48:35 [c]Rev. 7:15
4 [a][Matt. 5:8] [b]Rev. 14:1
5 [a]Rev. 21:23 [b]Rev. 7:15 [c]Ps. 36:9 [d]Dan. 7:18, 27
6 [a]Rev. 19:9 [b]Rev. 1:1 [c]Heb. 10:37
7 [a][Rev. 3:11] [b]Rev. 1:3

*

21:14 NU, M *twelve names*
21:23 NU, M omit *in it* • M *very glory*
21:24 NU, M omit *of those who are saved* • M *of the nations to Him*
21:26 M adds *that they may enter in.*
21:27 NU, M *profane, nor one who causes*
22:1 NU, M omit *pure*
22:6 NU, M *spirits of the prophets*

KJV

8 And I John saw these things, and heard
them. And when I had heard and seen, [a]I fell
down to worship before the feet of the angel
which shewed me these things.
9 Then saith he unto me, [a]See *thou do it*
not: for I am thy fellowservant, and of thy brethren the prophets, and of them which keep the sayings of this book: worship God.
10 [a]And he saith unto me, Seal not the sayings of the prophecy of this book: [b]for the time
is at hand.
11 He that is unjust, let him be unjust still:
and he which is filthy, let him be filthy still: and
he that is righteous, let him be righteous still: and
he that is holy, let him be holy still.

Jesus Testifies to the Churches

12 And, behold, I come quickly; and [a]my reward *is* with me, [b]to give every man according
as his work shall be.
13 [a]I am Alpha and Omega, the beginning
and the end, the first and the last.
14 [a]Blessed *are* they that do his commandments, that they may have right [b]to the tree of
life, [c]and may enter in through the gates into the
city.
15 For [a]without *are* [b]dogs, and sorcerers, and
whoremongers, and murderers, and idolaters, and
whosoever loveth and maketh a lie.
16 [a]I Jesus have sent mine angel to testify
unto you these things in the churches. [b]I am the
root and the offspring of David, *and* [c]the bright
and morning star.
17 And the Spirit and [a]the bride say, Come.
And let him that heareth say, Come. [b]And let him
that is athirst come. And whosoever will, let him
take the water of life freely.

A Warning

18 For I testify unto every man that heareth
the words of the prophecy of this book, [a]If any
man shall add unto these things, God shall add
unto him the plagues that are written in this book:
19 And if any man shall take away from the
words of the book of this prophecy, [a]God shall
take away his part out of the book of life, and
out of the holy city, and *from* the things which
are written in this book.

I Am Coming Quickly

20 He which testifieth these things saith,
Surely I come quickly. Amen. Even so, come, Lord
Jesus.
21 The grace of our Lord Jesus Christ *be* with
you all. Amen.

8 [a]Rev. 19:10
9 [a]Rev. 19:10
10 [a]Dan. 8:26 [b]Rev. 1:3
12 [a]Is. 40:10; 62:11 [b]Rev. 20:12
13 [a]Is. 41:4
14 [a]Dan. 12:12 [b][Prov. 11:30] [c]Rev. 21:27
15 [a]1 Cor. 6:9 [b]Phil. 3:2
16 [a]Rev. 1:1 [b]Rev. 5:5 [c]Num. 24:17
17 [a][Rev. 21:2, 9] [b]Is. 55:1
18 [a]Deut. 4:2; 12:32
19 [a]Ex. 32:33

*

22:8 NU, M *am the one who heard and saw*
22:9 NU, M omit *For*
22:11 NU, M *do right*
22:13 NU, M *First and the Last, the Beginning and the End.*
22:14 NU *wash their robes,*
22:15 NU, M omit *But*
22:18 NU, M omit *For* • M *may God add*
22:19 M *may God take away* • NU, M *tree of life*
22:21 NU *with all;* M *with all the saints*

NKJV

8 Now I, John, *saw and heard these things.
And when I heard and saw, [a]I fell down to worship before the feet of the angel who showed me
these things.
9 Then he said to me, [a]"See *that you do*
not *do that.* *For I am your fellow servant, and
of your brethren the prophets, and of those who
keep the words of this book. Worship God."
10 [a]And he said to me, "Do not seal the
words of the prophecy of this book, [b]for the time
is at hand.
11 "He who is unjust, let him be unjust still;
he who is filthy, let him be filthy still; he who is
righteous, let him *be righteous still; he who is
holy, let him be holy still."

Jesus Testifies to the Churches

12 "And behold, I am coming quickly, and
[a]My reward *is* with Me, [b]to give to every one according to his work.
13 [a]"I am the Alpha and the Omega, *the* *Beginning and *the* End, the First and the Last."
14 [a]Blessed *are* those who *do His commandments, that they may have the right [b]to the tree
of life, [c]and may enter through the gates into the
city.
15 *But [a]outside *are* [b]dogs and sorcerers and
sexually immoral and murderers and idolaters,
and whoever loves and practices a lie.
16 [a]"I, Jesus, have sent My angel to testify
to you these things in the churches. [b]I am the Root
and the Offspring of David, [c]the Bright and Morning Star."
17 And the Spirit and [a]the bride say,
"Come!" And let him who hears say, "Come!"
[b]And let him who thirsts come. Whoever desires,
let him take the water of life freely.

A Warning

18 *For I testify to everyone who hears the
words of the prophecy of this book: [a]If anyone
adds to these things, *God will add to him the
plagues that are written in this book;
19 and if anyone takes away from the words
of the book of this prophecy, [a]God* shall take
away his part from the *Book of Life, from the
holy city, and *from* the things which are written
in this book.

I Am Coming Quickly

20 He who testifies to these things says,
"Surely I am coming quickly." Amen. Even so,
come, Lord Jesus!
21 The grace of our Lord Jesus Christ *be*
*with you all. Amen.